The Garland Encyclopedia of World Music

Volume 10

The World's Music: General Perspectives and Reference Tools

THE GARLAND ENCYCLOPEDIA OF WORLD MUSIC

Volume 1
AFRICA
edited by Ruth M. Stone

Volume 2
SOUTH AMERICA, MEXICO,
CENTRAL AMERICA, AND THE CARIBBEAN
edited by Dale A. Olsen and Daniel E. Sheehy

Volume 3
THE UNITED STATES AND CANADA
edited by Ellen Koskoff

Volume 4
SOUTHEAST ASIA
edited by Terry E. Miller and Sean Williams

Volume 5
SOUTH ASIA: THE INDIAN SUBCONTINENT
edited by Alison Arnold

Volume 6
THE MIDDLE EAST
edited by Virginia Danielson, Scott Marcus, and Dwight Reynolds

Volume 7
EAST ASIA: CHINA, JAPAN, AND KOREA
edited by Robert C. Provine, Yosihiko Tokumaru, and J. Lawrence Witzleben

Volume 8
EUROPE
edited by Timothy Rice, James Porter, and Chris Goertzen

Volume 9
AUSTRALIA AND THE PACIFIC ISLANDS
edited by Adrienne L. Kaeppler and J. Wainwright Love

Volume 10
THE WORLD'S MUSIC: GENERAL PERSPECTIVES AND REFERENCE TOOLS
edited by Ruth M. Stone

Advisory Editors
Bruno Nettl and Ruth M. Stone

Founding Editors
James Porter and Timothy Rice

The Garland Encyclopedia of World Music
Volume 10

The World's Music: General Perspectives and Reference Tools

Ruth M. Stone
Editor

ROUTLEDGE
New York and London
2002

The initial planning of *The Garland Encyclopedia of World Music* was assisted by a grant from the National Endowment for the Humanities.

Published by
Routledge
29 West 35th Street
New York, NY 10001

Published in Great Britain by
Routledge
11 New Fetter Lane
London EC4P 4EE

Routledge is an imprint of the Taylor & Francis Group.

Project Editor: Susan Gamer
Director of Production: Dennis Teston
Copyeditor: Usha Sanyal
Indexer: Marilyn Bliss
Cover design: Jennifer Crisp
Publishing Director: Sylvia K. Miller
Vice President and Publisher: Linda Hollick

Library of Congress Cataloging-in-Publication Data
The Garland encyclopedia of world music / [advisory editors, Bruno Nettl and Ruth M. Stone; founding editors, James Porter and Timothy Rice].
    p. cm.
    Includes bibliographical references, discographies, and indexes.
    Contents: v. 10. The World's Music: General Perspectives and Reference Tools / Ruth M. Stone, editor
    ISBN 0-8153-1084-6 (alk. Paper)
    Music—Encyclopedias.   2. Folk music—Encyclopedias.   3. Popular music—Encyclopedias.
    I. Nettl, Bruno, 1930–   II. Stone, Ruth M.   III. Porter, James, 1937–   IV. Rice, Timothy, 1945–
    ML100.G16   2002
    780′.9—dc21   97-9671
                                                                               CIP
                                                                               MN

Cover illustration: Drums, photo by Jack Vartoogian; mandolin, Photodisc; sitar, Photodisc; sleigh bells, Corel; moroccas, Corel; *t'aep'yŏngso*, Keith Howard.
Photo researcher: Jennifer Crisp

Printed on acid-free, 250-year-life paper
Manufactured in the United States of America

Contents

About *The Garland Encyclopedia of World Music*   vii
Preface   ix
Contributing Authors   xiii

Part 1
Ethnomusicologists at Work   1

South Asia and East Asia   *Bonnie C. Wade*   3
East Asia and North America   *Bell Yung*   17
Africa and East Asia   *Kenichi Tsukada*   27
Southeast Asia   *R. Anderson Sutton*   41
Africa and the Middle East   *Ruth M. Stone*   55
Africa, the Middle East, and North America
    Kay Kaufman Shelemay   67
Latin America and North America (I)   *Daniel Sheehy*   77
Latin America and North America (II)   *Brenda Romero*   87
Latin America and East Asia   *Dale A. Olsen*   97
Africa, Latin America, and North America   *Gerhard Kubik*   109
North America and the Middle East   *Ellen Koskoff*   127
Africa and North America   *Jacqueline Cogdell DjeDje*   137
Europe and North America   *Philip V. Bohlman*   157

Part 2
Resources and Research Tools   169

General Glossary   171

Africa   331
Publications on African Music   333
Recordings of African Music   339
Films and Videos of African Music   343

South America, Mexico, Central America, and the Caribbean   345
Publications on South American, Mexican, Central American, and
    Caribbean Music   347
Recordings of South American, Mexican, Central American, and
    Caribbean Music   357
Films and Videos of South American, Mexican, Central American, and
    Caribbean Music   363

The United States and Canada   365
Publications on the Music of the United States and Canada   367
Recordings of the Music of the United States and Canada   383
Films and Videos of the Music of the United States and Canada   387

Southeast Asia   389
Publications on Southeast Asian Music   391
Recordings of Southeast Asian Music   409
Films and Videos of Southeast Asian Music   415

South Asia: The Indian Subcontinent   419
Publications on South Asian Music   421
Recordings of South Asian Music   433
Films and Videos of South Asian Music   441

The Middle East   443
Publications on Middle Eastern Music   445
Recordings of Middle Eastern Music   475
Films and Videos of Middle Eastern Music   485

East Asia: China, Japan, Korea, and Inner Asia   487
Publications on East Asian Music   489
Recordings of East Asian Music   517
Films and Videos of East Asian Music   527

Europe   531
Publications on European Music   533
Recordings of European Traditional Music   537
Films and Videos of European Traditional Music   543

Australia and the Pacific Islands   545
Publications on the Music of Oceania   547
Recordings of Oceanic Music   553
Films and Videos of Oceanic Performing Arts   561

General Index   569

About *The Garland Encyclopedia of World Music*

Scholars have created many kinds of encyclopedias devoted to preserving and transmitting knowledge about the world. The study of music has itself been the subject of numerous encyclopedias in many languages. Yet until now the term *music encyclopedia* has been synonymous with surveys of the history, theory, and performance practice of European-based traditions.

In July 1988, the editors of *The Garland Encyclopedia of World Music* gathered for a meeting to determine the nature and scope of a massive new undertaking. For this, the first encyclopedia devoted to the music of all the world's peoples, the editors decided against the traditional alphabetic approach to compartmentalizing knowledge from A to Z. Instead, they chose a geographic approach, with each volume devoted to a single region and coverage assigned to the world's experts on specific music cultures.

For several decades, ethnomusicologists (following the practice of previous generations of comparative musicologists) have been documenting the music of the world through fieldwork, recording, and analysis. Now, for the first time, they have created an encyclopedia that summarizes in one place the major findings that have resulted from the explosion in such documentation since the 1960s. The volumes in the series comprise contributions from all those specialists who have from the start defined the field of ethnomusicology: anthropologists, linguists, dance ethnologists, cultural historians, and performers. This multidisciplinary approach continues to enrich the field, and future generations of students and scholars will find *The Garland Encyclopedia of World Music* to be an invaluable resource that contributes to knowledge in all its varieties.

Each volume (with the exception of the tenth and final volume) has a similar design and organization: large sections that cover the major topics of a region from broad general issues to specific music practices. Each section consists of articles written by leading researchers, and extensive glossaries and indexes give the reader easy access to terms, names, and places of interest.

Part 1: Introduction to the region, its culture, and its music, as well as a survey of previous music scholarship and research.
Part 2: Major issues and processes that link the musics of the region.
Part 3: Detailed accounts of individual music cultures. In Volume 7, East Asia, more than one part serves this function (Part 3, China; Part 4, Japan; Part 5, Korea; and Part 6, Inner Asia).

The editors of each volume have determined how this format is to be constructed and applied, depending on the nature of their regions of interest. The concepts covered in Part 2 will therefore differ from volume to volume; likewise, the articles in Part 3 might be about the music of nations, ethnic groups, islands, or subregions. The picture of music presented in each volume is thus comprehensive yet remains focused on critical ideas and issues.

Complementing the texts of the encyclopedia's articles are numerous illustrations: photographs, drawings, maps, charts, song texts, and musical examples. At the end of each volume is a useful set of study and research tools, including a glossary of terms, lists of audio and visual resources, and an extensive bibliography. An audio compact disk will be found inside the back cover of each volume (except Volume 10), with sound examples that are linked (with a ⏺ in the margin) to discussions in the text.

The Garland Encyclopedia of World Music represents the work of hundreds of specialists guided by a team of distinguished editors. With a sense of pride, the publisher offers this new series to readers everywhere.

Preface: Closing the Circle

After fifteen years of planning, writing, and editing, the *Garland Encyclopedia of World Music* has come full circle with the completion of the ten volumes that make up its first edition. As I observed in the preface to Volume 1, *Africa* (1998:*xi*), "a circle of learning implies connections and relations from one area of knowledge to another, but not an exhaustive knowledge." Beginning with that initial volume, hundreds of scholars have come together to provide the first reference work of this scope for the discipline of ethnomusicology, and a true circle of knowledge has resulted from their extensive and sustained effort to provide connections and relationships for music performance around the world. It is an elastic circle that will be continually refined as research is incorporated and modifies our current views. Subsequent editions will build on the foundation of this first edition.

The ideas and analyses presented in these volumes result from original field research conducted by many of the authors and represent the latest knowledge in a wide range of topics, much of which is being presented for the first time.

The work of the authors has been orchestrated by the dedicated editors who took on the management of the individual volumes. In some cases they have been joined by associate editors and consulting editors. As well, numerous graduate students have assisted with virtually every phase of the project. Such assistance has been particularly critical for Volume 10, *The World's Music*, for which a team of students spent the summer of 2001 preparing the general glossary and the various guides to publications, recordings, and films and videos. The volume editors and their support staff have been assisted and supported in turn by the publisher's production editors. All this has, of course, taken time: the individual volumes have each involved involved an effort lasting from perhaps five to eight years.

Ethnomusicology is young, as disciplines are measured. It was born in the optimism following World War II and grew from its predecessor discipline, comparative musicology (*vergleichende Musikwissenschaft*). The first reference work was a single volume published in 1950 by the Dutch scholar Jaap Kunst—*Musicologica: A Study of the Nature of Ethno-Musicology, Its Problems, Method, and Representative Personalities*. The hyphenated term *ethno-musicology* in Kunst's title was significant: its adoption marked a pivotal moment.

Some fifty years later, *ethnomusicology* is a single, unhyphenated word, and the discipline of ethnomusicology is widely known. It is an area in which students can major, and the term is used to designate departments and programs all over the world. With *The Garland Encyclopedia of World Music*, we now have ten volumes devoted to this discipline.

Ethnomusicologists are by no means a unified group with a closely shared, tightly defined set of research practices. They do, however, share a strong commitment to exploring their topics through ethnography or fieldwork. That is, they obtain data through face-to-face research with the people and the musical practices that they seek to understand. They travel to the parts of the world that are their focus and spend extended periods of residence conducting painstaking research into musical life in those regions. They may also conduct the same kind of research within their local communities and thus include, say, the United States and Europe as areas of research interest, not simply confining their work to a study of the exotic "other."

When this encyclopedia project started in the late 1980s, a major topic of discussion at an organizational meeting in Los Angeles, funded by the National Endowment for the Humanities, focused on how the material should be divided. Some scholars felt that we should organize the knowledge country by country in order to provide coverage of specific geographic areas, particularly those for which no material then existed in print—in the Pacific, for instance, there were islands whose musical performance practices had never been described. While such an organization provided handy labels and fairly easily identifiable units, it also presented some problems. In many cases, political units and boundaries did not necessarily coincide with areas of indigenous musical styles. The Dan of Côte d'Ivoire (Ivory Coast), for example, were a people who shared musical practices and even a spoken language with the Gio people of Liberia, but those similarities might be lost in a country-by-country division of topics.

Other scholars argued for a thematic approach that would treat issues and processes such as migration, protest, notation, technology, and rural-urban interchange. These topics would involve crossing recognized political boundaries to treat the issues and would therefore reveal new sorts of knowledge that would not necessarily be treated in regional case studies.

The discussion centered on more than just the technicalities of organizing an encyclopedia. It revealed much about how ethnomusicologists viewed the topics they study, and how their views were changing. An ethnography of that meeting in Los Angeles would have provided a good sense of the dominant ethnomusicological approaches to studying music throughout the world. For many years, work in the field had emphasized studies centered on geographically bounded units. But a shift to topics that transcended political and geographic boundaries was beginning in the late 1980s, and this new tendency has increased since then. This shift in topics acknowledged the movement of people and ideas across space—a movement that has occurred for centuries, even millennia, but is now accelerated by automobiles and the Internet.

Ultimately, the editors who had gathered at the meeting decided to accommodate both approaches to studying music around the world. Therefore, each of the regional volumes was organized so as to include articles that address issues and processes as well as regional case studies.

If you read the various tables of contents, you will notice that in some volumes the section on issues and processes is much more expanded than it is in other volumes, where the case studies are more prominent. The plan has been elastic, then, and it illustrates two important approaches to research in ethnomusicology. Today, these two approaches coexist. In the future, the focus on issues and processes will, I predict, become more dominant; indeed, that has been the tendency in some of the volumes since the project began.

The integration of *The Garland Encyclopedia of World Music* was greatly aided by several subsequent meetings held in Washington, D.C., and during the annual meetings of the Society for Ethnomusicology each fall over the course of the project. On these occasions, the editors were able to share their plans and discuss how they were handling various issues. The project thus moved from a group of isolated volumes to a connected, coordinated multivolume work. Furthermore, the bonds that formed in the course of these discussions have served to create a better final product and a deeper understanding among the editors about research in the various areas of the world. The volumes also provide important surveys of each major region, giving us a bird's-eye view of musical practices. In many cases, the surveys of music scholarship provide an extended intellectual history of music research in a region, often making this history available for the first time in the discipline of ethnomusicology.

Another important issue at the first planning meeting in Los Angeles was where to allocate certain topics. For instance, which volume should have an article on "music in Islam"? Should this appear in the volume on the Middle East, the volume on Africa, or both volumes? In this regard, the ethnomusicologists at the meeting decided that some topics should be treated in more than one volume. Such topics warranted this treatment because they were not confined to a single geographic region, although the volumes were labeled that way.

During the time when the encyclopedia was taking shape, national and international developments showed that even political boundaries were somewhat fluid. In several cases, changes in governments and in the names of countries necessitated adjustments as the project unfolded. Just as the volume on Africa went to press, for instance, Zaïre had a change in government and became the Democratic Republic of the Congo. It was too late to change every mention of Zaïre, and so we inserted an explanatory line below the map of Central Africa (Volume 1:648).

A project like this one is a testament to scholars' perseverance, and to their willingness to tackle projects that reach beyond their own work. It also points to a new level of maturity for ethnomusicology, which can now present a more comprehensive view of music in the world than has ever been available in the past.

HOW THIS VOLUME IS ORGANIZED

Volume 10, the final volume of *The Garland Encyclopedia of World Music*, is a comprehensive compilation of the reference sections of Volumes 1 through 9. It also offers a glimpse of the fabric and work of conducting the research presented in those volumes. Part 1 presents a select group of ethnomusicologists who describe in their own words how they entered the profession and how they have carried out their research, teaching, and publication. Part 2 provides an integrated glossary for all ten volumes, and then a comprehensive guide to publications, recordings, and films and videos for all the geographic areas. The glossary gives readers a way to find where terms related to concepts, instruments, and so on occur in different volumes.

Ethnomusicologists at work

Each profile by an ethnomusicologist is a unique perspective; together, the profiles give considerable detail about how researchers build their careers and what choices they make along the way. These essays will serve to acquaint readers both within and outside ethnomusicology with the concrete ways ethnomusicologists conduct research and fit that work into their larger careers. Many things which those in the discipline simply take for granted as part of their lives are described in these accounts, as scholars turn from their subject itself to a critical examination of their professional practices of work.

The thirteen ethnomusicologists have done research in many places. Scholars such as Brenda Romero and Ellen Koskoff have conducted their research within North America. Others have worked in more than one major area—examples are Kenichi Tsukada's work in Africa and Japan, Dale Olsen's work in Latin America and Japan, and Bonnie Wade's work in Japan and India. Gerhard Kubik and Jacqueline DjeDje have both worked on African and African-American music at some point in their careers. Bell Yung has had multiple academic locations, splitting his time between the United States and East Asia; this has affected his career in ways that he analyzes in his essay.

These ethnomusicologists, at various points in their careers, have been trained in various approaches to the field, and they represent a range of ethnic backgrounds. They include people living in the United States and in several other countries around the world. While most work in academia, some—such as Daniel Sheehy—work almost entirely in the public sector.

Their profiles reveal that the one practice uniting the entire group is fieldwork. All these ethnomusicologists have conducted extensive fieldwork as part of completing a doctorate, and most have continued fieldwork throughout their careers. Sometimes this fieldwork has been observational; at other times it has extended to participation, particularly playing instruments and performing local music.

Part 1, therefore, provides a behind-the-scenes look at how the work in ethnomusicology is accomplished. These practitioners look at their own lives in an effort to convey a better understanding of their field. Their essays make the craft of ethnomusicology more transparent and clarifiy the structure underlying the articles in the other volumes.

Comprehensive glossary

The task of providing a single comprehensive glossary for the ten volumes has been complex, given the various special symbols and variations in terminology from place to place. With this glossary, readers have a source for many concepts and terms that they will encounter in the other volumes and in other sources; they can also see how certain terms are used in, and are relevant to, multiple places in the world. Volume numbers are provided for the terms so that readers who want to pursue an idea in more depth can turn to the appropriate volume.

Guide to publications, recordings, films, and videos

The extensive guides to reference sources for each of the regions show how research and documentation have proliferated in recent years. Many of the sources listed have been created in the past two decades. While the sources provided are only a part of what is available, they provide a good starting point for scholars and students interested in particular topics.

ACKNOWLEDGMENTS

I am indebted to a number of people and institutions who have helped make Volume 10 possible. First, I am very grateful to the College of Arts and Sciences at Indiana University for providing funds to support graduate student assistants throughout the years I've worked on this project. Second, I'm deeply appreciative of the work of Susan Oehler, who coordinated the development of the comprehensive resources, supervising the work of other graduate students. Third, I want to thank Jessica Anderson Turner, who took over as coordinator in the fall of 2001. These two coordinators were assisted by Patrick Feaster, Christopher Geyer, Sally McSpadden, Mark Miyake, Rhonda Sewald, Mellissa Suarez, Steve Turner, and Richard Walter. Fourth, a special acknowledgment to Marilyn Bliss, who was the indexer for the entire encyclopedia and has now prepared the general index that is such an important feature of Volume 10. Finally, to the people at Garland and Routledge who worked on this volume, beginning with Leo Balk, Gary Kuris, Richard Wallis, Soo Mee Kwon, and Gillian Rodger and ending with Susan Gamer and Sylvia Miller, I want to express my support for your constant willingness to do whatever was necessary to bring this massive project to fruition.

—Ruth M. Stone

Contributing Authors

Philip V. Bohlman
University of Chicago
Illinois, United States

Jacqueline Cogdell DjeDje
University of California, Los Angeles
California, United States

Ellen Koskoff
Eastman School of Music
University of Rochester
New York, United States

Gerhard Kubik
Institut für Musikwissenschaft
University of Vienna
Austria

Dale Olsen
Florida State University
Tallahassee, Florida, United States

Brenda Romero
University of Colorado at Boulder
United States

Daniel Sheehy
Smithsonian Institution
Center for Folklife and Cultural
  Heritage
Washington, D.C., United States

Kay Kaufman Shelemay
Harvard University
Cambridge, Massachusetts, United
  States

Ruth M. Stone
Indiana University
Bloomington, Indiana, United States

R. Anderson Sutton
University of Wisconsin, Madison
United States

Kenichi Tsukada
Hiroshima City University
Japan

Bonnie C. Wade
University of California, Berkeley
United States

Bell Yung
University of Pittsburgh
Pennsylvania, United States

The Garland Encyclopedia of World Music

Volume 10

The World's Music: General Perspectives and Reference Tools

Part 1
Ethnomusicologists at Work

In Part 1, ethnomusicologists provide insight into their work and their careers. These essays offer access to their research practices. Fieldwork is the link that unites them as they pursue knowledge about music making around the world.

Meithei women playing small drums, cymbals, and gongs at a temple festival. Impal, India, 1994. Photo © Lindsay Hebberd/Corbis.

South Asia and East Asia
Bonnie C. Wade

When I am asked, as one frequently is, just how I became an ethnomusicologist, my answer can be quick and sure: an epiphany and people. The epiphany: As I stood at the edge of an Andean cliff at Machu Picchu (Peru) in 1962, a haunting flute melody floated up from the chasm below. Because its melodic mode had little to do with any I had experienced in my youthful life, devoted to intensive study of Western classical music, this melody struck me like a thunderbolt. It was *different*. Why had no one mentioned to me that there was *other* music out there? Even worse, why had I never noticed other music?

From the moment I recognized my selective hearing, my life was changed. When I returned to Boston University to complete the bachelor of music program with a major in history (Western classical music, of course), my epiphany could have faded into memory or been authoritatively squashed had not the right teacher been there at the right time. (Take note: Teaching is important!) Professor Emerita Pauline Alderman (University of Southern California) had come to Boston as a replacement for the musicologist Karl Geiringer. As someone who had watched the birth of the Institute for Ethnomusicology at neighboring University of California, Los Angeles (UCLA), she was sympathetic to diverse musics. "Prove to me that you can find sources and document writing properly," she said, "and you may write your honors thesis on whatever music you wish to study." Thus was an ethnomusicologist "born."

A bachelor of music degree (in Western classical music) has limited utility for preparing one to become an ethnomusicologist. By the time I graduated, I yearned for what I knew I needed: a liberal arts education. Fortunately, I had two good college friends who were determined to see the world, and off we went. To make a long saga very short, we spent two and a half years traveling, dragging along few clothes but many books and maps about the places we went; catching freighters, trains, buses, and a few planes; stopping to work when we ran short of money. That was my liberal arts education; that was the response to the epiphany.

First long stop: Japan (December 1963 to November 1964). Another supportive person came along: Professor William Malm (University of Michigan). I had written my senior honors thesis on Japanese music, basing it on whatever I could learn from the few sources I could find in English—Malm's pioneering book on Japanese music was one of them—and on conversations with Japanese whom I found living in Boston. Malm's response to a letter of inquiry I had written to him from Boston was welcoming: "I'll be in Japan when you get there; look me up." Malm introduced me to Professor Shigeo Kishibe, an eminent musicologist, who introduced me to his wife, Yori, an eminent *koto* performer in the Yamada *ryû*, who became my *koto* and *syamisen* teacher. I taught the English language to earn my way, and of course I studied the Japanese language; more important, I studied *koto* intensively and went to every concert of traditional music I could find. This is from my diary:

> One tremendously important day came—my *koto* and *syamisen* recital (figures 1 and 2). Calmly taking everything in my stride, I spent the morning in the bathroom and the evening wishing I were in the bathroom. At the recital, at about 2:30, Nihon-teki, my invited friends, . . . Dr. Nakajima and family, Matsuzawa Hito, Mini, Hiro, Midori, and Midori's mother . . . were there. I played OK, though shaking, and Midori charmingly presented me with a huge bouquet of purple flowers. Already at home were red carnations from a friend, and on my

FIGURE 1 The author performing on *syamisen*. Recital, Tôkyô, Japan, 5 July 1964. Photos are from the author.

FIGURE 2 The author and her teacher: Kishibe-sensei to the rescue. Recital, 5 July 1964.

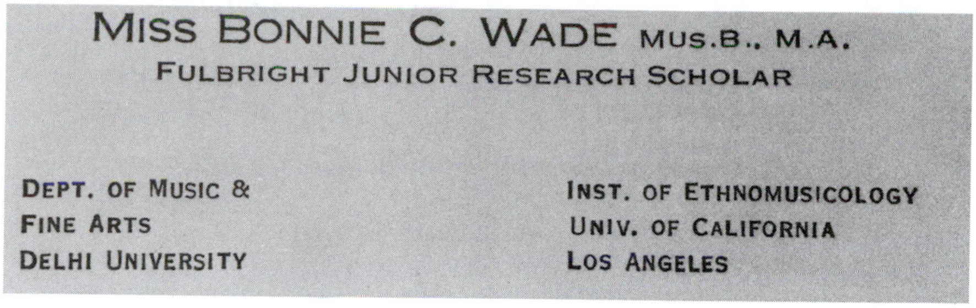

FIGURE 3 Calling card for research, a necessity in the field.

> ### MISS BONNIE C. WADE MUS.B., M.A.
> #### FULBRIGHT JUNIOR RESEARCH SCHOLAR
>
> DEPT. OF MUSIC &   INST. OF ETHNOMUSICOLOGY
> FINE ARTS   UNIV. OF CALIFORNIA
> DELHI UNIVERSITY   LOS ANGELES

shoulder to match my dress was a gardenia carefully snitched from a neighborhood garden. I shall press three flowers and have the tape recording to remember the day by. For me it was special, celebrating the accomplishment of my goal here in Japan.

The next longish stop in a circuitous journey from Australia to Southeast Asia and beyond came in India (six weeks meandering about on third-class trains) and Pakistan (three months, teaching fifth grade in the American school in Karachi, studying *sitar*). Though we also explored Africa and the Middle East before we returned to the United States in early 1966, my decision was easy: an M.A. focused on Japan, a Ph.D. focused on north India.

Four years later, as I studied Hindustani singing at Delhi University as a Fulbright Junior Scholar (1968–1969; figure 3), I noted in my journal the value of my earlier performance study in Asia:

> Singing class will be a challenge musically, I'm happy to say. It began casually—thirty minutes late because Mrs. M. was having tea with someone. There are eight students, counting me. We are accompanied by a *tabla* player and a *sāraṅgī* player and led by Mrs. M. We're learning a song in *Rag Sarang*. The singing began with an exercise, *sthāī* to *antarā* in traditional fashion, Mrs. M. singing and we repeating, doubling the speed as we progressed. Then I worked on a song in Hindi which the class had learned (by rote) last Monday. Their memories must be well trained! I cannot learn from rote so easily—and if it were not for my previous music study in Asia, I would be at a sheer loss now!

Needless to say, I asked permission to tape-record the lessons, although it meant trekking up a steep hill from my apartment to the university, carrying about thirty-five pounds of Nagra and batteries.

Once I had undertaken graduate study (exhilarating years at UCLA's Institute for Ethnomusicology in the department of music, under the guidance of Klaus Wachsmann, Charles Seeger, and Mantle Hood), which also included work in anthropology and folklore and the study of Hindi-Urdu and some Sanskrit, and returned to the field for dissertation research, I gained a new perspective on my earlier education through travel.

Lesson 1

- Experiencing "the field," even beginning to study in the field independently, is invaluable for professional development. However, it is not to be confused with field research with a focus informed by thoughtful guidance and systematic planning.

I was determined to carry out a dissertation project, the like of which no one else in Indian studies (from the music side of ethnomusicology) seemed to be doing—folk music. I wanted to work with women, and with a woman's genre of music; weddings were the only female sphere of life I could find written up with sufficient mention of music to guide me at all. Villages were the practical location for studying women's

Field research requires flexibility in ways and to degrees one can hardly imagine in the planning stages.

wedding songs. Where should I situate myself to have access to village life? In order to collect enough songs by attending enough ceremonies, I would have to work in several villages. Having traveled widely in India previously, I knew that I did not want to live in a village.

Lesson 2

- Even an exuberant, adaptable ethnomusicologist who can adjust to whatever comes along needs to be realistic about the living conditions necessary for personal and professional well-being while doing research.

I had learned that I am an urban person, and the possibility of warm showers in the cold north Indian winter was something I considered necessary for good health. In addition, urban life means both individual privacy (there is none in a village) and the potential for relatively easy mobility (travel to many villages). Mobility from one village, particularly for a woman, was difficult. Besides, if the batteries I had brought to India were to last for the precious recordings, they had to be stored in a refrigerator. (In the 1960s batteries purchased in India had very short life.) That required electricity, which was not to be assumed in village India at the time. Fortunately, the Fulbright organization in Delhi kept apartments for grantees, and I enjoyed relatively ideal living conditions.

Lesson 3

In the process of carrying out my folk music project, I learned lesson 3:

- Field research requires flexibility in ways and to degrees one can hardly imagine in the planning stages.

How do I tell this in a short space? The pacing of one's work is all-important. Weddings happen seasonally—all at once everywhere. I had read about that, but the implications did not become real until I was there. I wrote in a report to Professor Mantle Hood at UCLA in October 1968:

> The wedding season will run mostly in November, some in December, then again in March. I shall have time to pursue other things, in both folk and classical music. . . . There are also future projects to plan for while I am here.

In Ramlila season (September) I snatched the opportunity to pursue an early love of music in the theater by recording performances of various sorts—a professional traveling folk troupe in Uttar Pradesh state and a local amateur troupe in Haryana state, for instance, not to mention the most fantastic of all Ramlila festivities, the royal pageant at Ramnagar, across the river from Benares (Varanasi). The last experience made me one of those visitors to India with a maharajah story, for I worked with Balwant Gargi, a historian of theater, who was doing a book on the Ramnagar Ramlila, as a guest of the maharajah himself. I quote here from my field notes about that great adventure:

At the Indian Airlines office in Benares, I looked up "Maharajah" in the phone book, knowing no other way to find Balwant Gargi, who did not expect me at that late date. Sure enough, there was a listing under "Maharajah," and I spoke briefly to the house manager of the palace in Benares where guests stay. . . .

Balwant wanted to go to the fort at Ramnagar where the maharajah lives to make arrangements to use the archive and work with the pandits who read and interpret the Tulsidas Ramayana for him. . . . At 1:00 we were admitted to the fort and told to wait in the drawing room of the fort guest house, the first building on the right as one enters the enclosure. Once inside the portals I was shocked. The fort is in decay, in need of paint everywhere, with grass growing irregularly, looking generally deserted. My heart really ached for this young maharajah whom I had never met. How he could afford to maintain it at all I cannot understand. Balwant explained that the maharajah preferred to spend his money on other things, like sponsoring editions of Purana translations (to English), donating land to colleges, continuing the Ramlila tradition—and his elephants, which are significantly symbolic of his former status. He has seven of them.

Tea was set up for us on the balcony of the guest house, overlooking the entrance courtyard. As we sat sipping, peasants began to file into the courtyard, then through it into a second courtyard opposite, through a gate guarded by one of the gorgeously austere guards bearing arms. The number of peasants grew and grew until there was a veritable stream, interspersed with sadhus and beggars in all states of dress and undress, including one man covered with ash and wearing only a loincloth of chain that merely encircled his hips. Just as it began to dawn on me that the maharajah was due to make an appearance before all those people, there was a distant blare of trumpets and everyone rose. I hopped up, acting like a schoolgirl on a holiday, grabbed the camera, and waited impatiently for His Highness to appear in the courtyard in procession to the gate where his horse-drawn carriage was waiting to take him to the Ramlila performance, which begins at 7:00. There he came . . . in formal Indian dress, white covered by a very thin pink outer coat, utterly delicate golden brocaded shoes, a circular cap. Servants held the royal umbrella over him as he walked. His ministers preceded and followed him, as did his soldiers. He looked up and folded his hands in greeting as he passed beneath our balcony.

With much haste we piled into Balwant's car and followed the procession to the performance ground. . . . When we arrived there, the maharajah had already mounted his seventeen-foot-high elephant, and the first scene of the night's episode of the Ramlila began.

In Ramnagar there had been plots of land in various locations donated by the maharajah's family over the centuries for the performing arena of Ramlila. Tonight's performance was at Lanka, Ceylon; the plot called Ayodhya was at some distance; the last scene of the night was where Rama was in exile in the forest, and it was a mile from Lanka. . . . When the scene changed, the acting arena changed, with the actors walking, the elephants preceding with the royal chanters (Ramayani) following, and the audience all around, walking to the next location. We were riding on an elephant with the minister of elephants. One really got the feeling of the logistics of the story. . . .

No microphones or electric lights are used, though distances are far and performances continue until after dark. There is a dramatic arrangement of narration of the story. On the night of the twenty-third there were close to 20,000 spectators at the performance. They sat facing the grove where Sita was, straining to catch the chantlike speeches of the actors. . . . At the completion of each episode-speech complex, the narration was repeated exactly by the Ramayani, who sat in a circle on the ground just in front of the maharajah's elephant at the very back edge of the crowd, a good eighth of a mile from the grove. I was up and down off that elephant several times [it was quite a production to have the elephant kneel so that I could descend], recording the chanting of the Ramayani and dialogue both from a distance and close up. All was over by 8:30 or 9:00.

The next day there was an audience with His Highness.

I soon learned of another challenge to my dissertation project on wedding songs of village women: rituals happen simultaneously in the groom's village and the bride's village, but I could be in only one place at one time. Furthermore, like most humanities scholars, I had assumed that I would work alone. Alas, the study of women's wedding songs in any depth requires a team. I needed to situate myself with singers while a kinship specialist identified the persons who took roles in the event and a ritual specialist filmed the action for later study and correlation with the recordings. This was not only an ideal but a necessity, as a field note for a groom's *ban* (ritual bath) demonstrates:

After we got to the village, we sat and watched the plowing and fertilizing and seeding for a long while, talking about India in general. I finally asked if there really was to be a *ban* ceremony that morning. . . .

By the time I got to the house the women were singing already, and I heard familiar strains as I entered. I got three songs, the first sung by young and old together, eleven women singing. . . . When the groom joined us, they moved into the inner room. I could tape through the window again; the ceremony conveniently took place in the corner of the inner room just by my window. It's a good thing that I remained in the outer room, because at the end old women sang out with me while the ceremony went on within (figure 4).

There was great gaiety. I just let the tape run to capture the mood and noise. The boy sat down on a low wooden stool . . . under which was a large bowl of grain that I didn't see until it was used in the ceremony. Two girls (his sisters?) stood directly in front of him, each holding a large, heavy pounding stick, the sticks of different lengths, one about a foot and a half shorter. They mock-pounded onto grain in a tray which had been brought to the scene of the ceremony, moving the sticks from front to back, alternating in the motion—one front, the other back, etc.—on either side of an orange string which had been tied across the tray. . . . Four times they dished out the grain. Then all of it was poured out into the towel by one girl, only to be put back into the pan. . . .

FIGURE 4   Recording layout, *ban* ceremony, Singhola village, 23 November 1968.

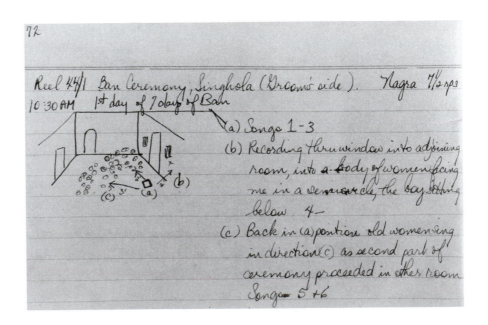

FIGURE 5   The author in the field.

> [After the ceremonial bath] the singing continued as the women returned to the outer room. The groom dried himself, with only a few women left in the room. Old women begin to sing. They continued to sing as the ceremony suddenly continued in the other room. (Singhola village, 23 November 1968)

Finally I had to commit the ultimate act of flexibility and face the fact that I had come to India to accomplish a goal that, as I had planned it, was not attainable. The months in the field, staying with anthropology colleagues in various villages while attending, filming, and recording innumerable wedding ceremonies, folk music, folk theater performances, and rural and urban festivals, were invaluable for me later in my teaching and also in several scholarly articles (figure 5). But I had made a commitment to change the focus of my research, a focus that was more compatible with the possibility of achieving a definable goal and also with urban life.

With trepidation I switched gears completely and decided to tackle the topic of *khyāl,* the foremost vocal genre of Hindustani classical music. Fortunately, as an affiliate at Delhi University, I had begun vocal lessons immediately upon arrival, and I could simply intensify that focus. As I wrote to Professor Hood, who had to approve the new dissertation topic: "My mind is awhirl over my study of *khyāl.* I'm having daily questioning sessions at the university, daily singing and *tabla* lessons to drum in as much as possible. I listen, listen, listen, transcribe, and record until it seems my earphones will get stuck on" (figure 6).

When I began studying vocal music privately, I experienced a variant of lesson 2:

• One must decide who one is in a context, and conduct oneself accordingly.

In ethnomusicology this lesson frequently emerges in the form of insider-outsider status. While there was no question that I was a total outsider to the Indian musical tradition, the relationship one structures with one's teachers determines relative degrees of being an outsider. Because I was totally taken with the music of one of the instructors at the university, Pandit Pran Nath, I asked him to teach me privately. My mentors at the university predicted that this would be difficult for reasons having to do with the voice, but (as they no doubt knew but did not say) it proved to be difficult in other ways, since he was an old-fashioned *guru.* My journal heard my remarks:

> He is demanding. . . . If he doesn't like something in his view, he makes me move it; I must open the door for him to make a grand exit. Once he asked me to massage his back, but I refused, saying I wouldn't do that for anyone—not even

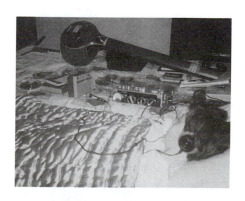

FIGURE 6   Fieldwork is rough.

my father when he drew that comparison. He likes my coat and has asked me more than once to give it to him. According to the rule, I should. But I tell him he has plenty of shawls but I have only one coat. It has turned into a fairly constant struggle in my mind as to just what role I should play. I cannot really enter into the *guru-śisya* relationship the way he patterns it. I am too objective and too Western, besides just being by nature conservative that way.

Most significantly, had I become a formal disciple of any singer, it would have been very difficult for me to have written the dissertation (and later the book) on *khyāl* that I really wanted to write. That is to say, I wanted to consider the improvised genre as performed by vocalists in several of the traditional groups (*gharānā*). Had I become a disciple in Pran Nath's Kirana *gharānā*, I am certain that I would have felt considerably constrained in my perspective. (After my book *Khyal: Creativity within North India's Classical Music Tradition* was published, by Cambridge University Press in 1984, I sent a copy to Pran Nath, who was then teaching at Mills College in Oakland, California, at the behest of the composer Terry Riley. Through a student we had in common, Pran Nath sent back word concerning my discussion of Kirana *gharānā*, and his own style: "It is all correct." We could now be at peace. Pran Nath was a truly great artist of Hindustani vocal music.) The almost daily lessons taught me to hear, and I am grateful to my teachers, Pran Nath and Sumati Mutatkar, and also the *tabla* player Sita Ram, for what they taught me.

For an ethnomusicologist, as for any scholar, the process of turning a thesis into a book—albeit a book totally different from the dissertation—offers an opportunity to grow. For instance, as a musician I am almost totally attuned to melody, but in order to "hear" Indian classical music, one has to be attuned to rhythm as well. The only cure for my musical condition was to continue studying *tabla*. Fortunately, a fantastic teacher, Sharda Sahai (figure 7), was a visiting artist at Wesleyan University, close to Brown University, where I began my teaching career. I continued *tabla* lessons with him for the entire time I was at Brown (1971–1975). At the same time, however, I continued to teach the *koto* and to perform on it, as I had been doing throughout graduate school and would continue to do at Berkeley.

Also while teaching at Brown University, I realized that ethnomusicologists rarely had the time—nor was it part of their mind-set—to produce textbooks. So busy were we developing new courses, having to teach about almost all the world's musics, and

FIGURE 7   The author with Sharda Sahai at his home, Benares, India, May 1978.

writing monographs in our specialities, that the idea of a textbook was not a priority. I decided, however, that I needed one on Indian music, so I melded my fieldwork, research, performance, and teaching goals to write *Music in India: The Classical Traditions* (1979, 1999), reprinted several times and now in a second edition. Today, textbooks are fairly common in our discipline, but at the time it was rare for anyone to write a textbook in ethnomusicology.

I also realized that I had completed a book on *khyāl* but still knew nothing of its history. Returning to India in 1978 for more field research to complete the drastically revised *khyāl* project, I was inspired by Shahab Sarmadee, a historian of the Mughal period who was a professor at Aligarh Muslim University. And I reached two conclusions that led to my next major research thrust. Visiting sites of the Mughal period and viewing exhibitions of Mughal-period paintings in India's major museums confirmed that I am a "visual person" (figure 8).

I also decided that some projects just need doing in order to further an entire field of research or push it in a different direction. A study of the Mughal period, when Hindustani music came much closer to what it is today, appeared to me to be such a project, and visual sources leaped out as a rich resource lode for it. It required of me retooling in the history and art history of the Mughal period, but, after all, multidisciplinary work is at the heart of ethnomusicology. So is historical study (that is, a diachronic perspective). Ethnomusicologists working in non-Asian cultures tend to start with contemporary music and work backward in order to elucidate the present; it is mostly in Asian studies that one would be just as likely to work from the past to the present. I intended to focus entirely on the past, however, unlike other American scholars working in India who were focusing almost entirely on the present. This led me to lesson 4, something I had learned in a graduate course in field methods but now remembered anew.

Lesson 4

- Archival and library research—especially when it takes you into new fields of endeavor and unfamiliar places—is a form of field research.

I now had an opportunity to experience the thrill of studying a sixteenth-century illustrated manuscript and the fairly ritualized process of doing so under the watchful eye of a mistrustful curator deep in the vault of a museum. I had to face a consequence of colonialism as I gradually realized that most of the art of Mughal India is owned outside India. Even in the museums I experienced subtle hints of disapproval in some quarters for focusing on a Muslim heritage in contemporary Hindu times. I could contextualize far more meaningfully the maharajah of Ramnagar I had met in 1968, whose fostering of pandits and traditional festivals continued a pattern of patronage I was "seeing" in the miniature paintings and reading about in the writings of the time.

Mention of the historical project that resulted in *Imaging Sound: An Ethnomusicological Study of Music, Art, and Culture in Mughal India* (1998) provides an excuse to enunciate lesson 5, which concerns less my research than my professional modus operandi.

Lesson 5

- A single ethnomusicologist may be the sole representative of the field on an academic faculty. It is often left to us to reach out to colleagues and students in other spheres of music study. Common interests are good avenues for doing that—performing and historical study being just two.

In fact, connecting with people is inherent in the ethnomusicological way of life; this is a "people" field. I have enjoyed cultivating that aspect of ethnomusicology in the academic environment, as a teacher, of course, and also as an administrator (chair, department of music; and dean of the college of letters and science). An administrator needs to organize projects involving and affecting people, needs to know how to listen as well as to investigate, needs to see the forest as well as the trees (that is, contextualize). Ethnomusicologists are also required to learn about multiple cultures; for an administrator, "cultures" may be multiple academic departments, for example, but we're ready to learn about them and work within that breadth of perspective. And ethnomusicologists cultivate and foster working relationships with scholars and performers in their fieldwork, their research, and their teaching.

Some ethnomusicologists—myself among them—conduct research in more than one culture. In 1988, with *Imaging Sound* well under way, I made the momentous decision that I would prepare myself to do research in Japan, build on musical connections fostered through the years, return to learning from people as primary sources, and focus on contemporary musical life (figure 9). Twenty-five years had passed since

FIGURE 9   Minoru Miki and the author at Miki's home, Tôkyô, Japan, February 1999.

I had first ventured into foreign fields, so this was not a step to be taken lightly. I took a sabbatical leave in 1990, after just one and a half years of Japanese language study among the Berkeley undergraduates, to weigh the decision. When one is young and inexperienced, one is likely to be welcomed in a foreign culture as a student. When one is an established scholar, the situation can be quite different. This reinforced lesson 6, which I had learned some years earlier.

Lesson 6

- Ethnomusicological research potentially puts one in the social position of student throughout one's professional life.

The following entry from my journal, describing an initial visit with a distinguished Japanese ethnomusicologist, Osamu Yamaguti, demonstrates one manner in which this can be managed later in life. Although my first book had been about a major genre of Japanese music (*Tegotomono: Music for the Japanese Koto*, 1976), it had been published a long time ago, and he knew me now as a scholar of Indian music.

Osamu Yamaguti greeted me skeptically, although cordially. He really wanted to know why I was there. So I told him my autobiographical story—about my first trip to Japan, playing *koto*, traveling, UCLA, India as my specialty, the departmental chairmanship as a demarcation point in my professional life, and then cancer. I have embarked on a new life. After that he wanted to know why Ôsaka, so I explained that too—I had friends here; I had lived in Tôkyô; I wanted a different experience of Japan, Kansai (as opposed to the Kanto area); I was interested in cultural history. He responded that it is good that I came, and he became a friendly person. How could he help, he asked. I responded by asking if he could recommend a basic book in Japanese on Japanese music. He pulled one off the shelf—about *koto* music—and presented it to me with his compliments. He then arranged with Otsuka Haiko, his Ph.D. student (a professional *syamisen nagauta* player) to work with me, once a week. We agreed that I would begin with the table of contents, and she made an enlarged photocopy of it. (Tough stuff it turned out to be! Two dense pages of new *kanzi*!) In return, I offered to help with the Symposium of the International Musicological Society (SIMS) [to be held the following summer]—which offer was taken up. It seems that Riley Lee (a *syakuhati* player who had been their help) had left. I think we struck a fair trade. I check the English in abstracts, at this point.

Between 19 and 26 January, when I went a second time, I *slaved* over that T of C. But what an accomplishment! I finished it only yesterday (the twenty-ninth). Haikosan went over every word with me. Clearly, I passed with good marks on the assignment! Osamu Yamaguti presented me with a copy of their publication—on orality and written work in music. We worked on two SIMS abstracts together and seem to be on the same track, intellectually. That is gratifying to learn. For Friday next, I will read (or begin . . .) a chapter in that book on the history of *ziuta*. But it is a very basic book, and they are thinking of what to do with me next (figure 10).

Now, several years later, my project is blossoming. It can be generally described as a study of the indigenization of Western music in Japan (figure 11). I returned to India and Japan many times throughout the 1970s, 1980s, and 1990s, and I now am making annual trips to Japan to continue research on my new topic, which is essentially urban ethnographic research, testing new theories and new methodologies. In 1991 I went back to Tôkyô and stayed with Keiko Nosaka while I did research for my article about her, Minoru Miki, and the invention of the twenty-stringed *koto*. After several shorter trips, I spent my sabbatical in 1999 in Tôkyô, doing concerted research on

FIGURE 10   Doing research: the author with the ethnomusicologist Osamu Yamaguti, foreground, toasting a visiting Korean performer and composer, Hwang Byung-ki, January 1990, near Ôsaka University, Japan.

FIGURE 11   The author at home, with her research assistant, Tokiko Inoue, Tôkyô, May 1999.

contemporary music in Japan, not simply so-called Western or Japanese "classical" music but all kinds of music (figure 12).

Some things have changed in the decades I have been doing fieldwork and practicing ethnomusicology: I no longer lug around two tape recorders, tons of batteries, movie camera, slide camera, other cameras, and additional heavy equipment; I have replaced them with a single lightweight minidigital camera, combination slide and photo camera, and digital recorder. Other things remain the same: journals, diaries, recordings, interviews, attending performances, making sketches, working with research assistants.

When I stop to think about it, there is a sort of continuous flow from my early experiences to the present time. I enjoy pursuing multiple interests and seeing the big picture. I like teaching undergraduates, both majors and nonmajors, and graduate students. And I alternate periods when I pursue primarily professional activities with periods when I add administrative work to the mix. My first work was in Japanese music doing genre-based study; then I shifted for a long time to north Indian (Hindustani) musics; then I pursued new directions in ethnomusicological research, push-

FIGURE 12   The author with the *nô* performing artist Akira Matsui, the *nô* specialist Richard Emmert, the *gagaku* scholar Steven Nelson, and the *kyômono* musician Akira Mark Oshima, at Emmert's home, Tôkyô, Japan, June 1999.

ing out disciplinary boundaries by working on a multidisciplinary project involving new methodologies and theories; and now I have returned to Japanese music, this time focusing on contemporary Japanese musical culture. As it is put so nicely in Indic culture: The end is my beginning . . .

REFERENCES

Wade, Bonnie Claire. 1971. "Khyal: A Study in Hindustani Classical Vocal Music." Vol. 1, "Text"; Vol. 2, "Musical Transcriptions." Ph.D. dissertation, University of California, Los Angeles.

———. 1976. *Tegotomono: Music for the Japanese Koto*. Westport, Conn.: Greenwood.

———. 1984. *Khyal: Creativity within North India's Classical Music Tradition*. Cambridge: Cambridge University Press.

———. 1998. *Imaging Sound: An Ethnomusicological Study of Music, Art, and Culture in Mughal India*. Chicago: University of Chicago Press.

———. 1999 [1979]. *Music in India: The Classical Traditions*, 2nd ed. New Delhi: Manohar.

East Asia and North America
Bell Yung

Teachers
Research
Research on Chinese Music in China and the West

I am very much an in-between kind of person. Although my formative years were spent largely in China and Hong Kong, my college and graduate training and most of my professional years were spent in the United States. I am also an in-between person in the sense that I feel simultaneously at home and a visitor, whether I am in China or in the United States.

My musical life began with piano lessons when I was a toddler—in Shanghai, where I was born. The lessons continued through my childhood and adolescence in Hong Kong, and later during my days as a graduate student in Cambridge, Massachusetts. Thus, my initial musical exposure was, paradoxically, mainly Western but in a largely Chinese cultural environment: I was introduced to Beethoven before I knew about the great tradition of the Chinese *qin* (a seven-stringed zither), and I fell in love with Wagner before I was aware of Tang Xianzu or Mei Lanfang. It was only many years later, after a detour into physics, that I started reading about Chinese music and learning to play the *qin* in the mid-1970s. Ironically, it was in a largely Western cultural environment that I discovered China and Chinese musical culture. Since then, my professional activities have been almost exclusively in the realm of Chinese music, although the Western classical repertoire is still closest to my heart. Thus I feel myself to be an in-between person in terms of my musical background and involvement as well.

Most of my postsecondary education was in science; I earned a B.Sc. degree in engineering physics from the University of California at Berkeley and a Ph.D. in physics from the Massachusetts Institute of Technology. Immediately upon leaving M.I.T., I entered the graduate program in music at Harvard University, earning a Ph.D. there. Despite my many years of teaching and writing about music after I received the music degree, my scientific training has left an indelible mark on how I think and continues to affect my musicological work. Thus I am also an in-between person in terms of my intellectual orientation and thought processes.

Currently, moreover, I am an in-between person literally as well as figuratively in the sense that I hold joint appointments at the University of Pittsburgh and the University of Hong Kong, shuttling between two continents, two cities, two cultures, two universities, two music departments, and two sets of colleagues and students.

Being in between can occasionally be confusing, but by and large the experience has been stimulating and rewarding. After all, the intellectual core of ethnomusicology is interdisciplinary—in orientation, outlook, and research methodology. To be in between is to enjoy a wide range of possibilities, increased flexibility, and an extra potential for growth. I feel blessed that I eventually found my way to ethnomusicology, because the field seems to match my life experience.

TEACHERS

In my long, convoluted intellectual and professional journey, I have been helped by many cherished teachers. Among those who introduced me to music making were the pianists Caroline Braga and Harry Ore in my early years, and later and for the longest period, Betty Drown, all of Hong Kong. Much later, during my years at M.I.T. in the mid-1960s, I studied with Kyriana Siloti of the Juilliard School in New York, who came to teach one day a week at the Longy School of Music in Cambridge.

As part of my research on Cantonese opera in the early 1970s in Hong Kong, I took lessons from Guo Lun, focusing on the *yangqin* (a hammered dulcimer), but also dabbled in the *erhu* (a two-stringed bowed lute) and the *sanxian* (a three-stringed plucked lute). In mid-1970, I began lessons in the *qin*. My first *qin* teacher—for only a few lessons, however—was the late Cheung Sai-bung, who was then a visiting scholar at Harvard. I began my serious study in 1978 with Tsar Teh-yun of Hong Kong and, in 1980, the late Yao Bingyan of Shanghai. In 1977, I studied the *gendèr* (metallophone) of the Javanese gamelan with John Pemberton at Cornell University; a few years later, I spent a summer in Yogyakarta and took more lessons on the *gendèr* with Pak Djokowaluya. Among these teachers, the most important and influential ones were no doubt Tsar *laoshi* and Yao *laoshi*—*laoshi* being an honorific for one's teacher.

My most intense period of study with Tsar *laoshi* was from 1978 to early 1981, a period when I was teaching at the Chinese University of Hong Kong and when she was already in her mid-seventies. She laid a solid foundation for me. At that time, metal strings were being widely used and a newer style of playing was sweeping across the mainland, but nevertheless Tsar *laoshi* quietly insisted on the traditional silk strings and on the style of playing that she had learned from her own teacher, Shen Caonong.

Tsar Teh-yun's playing is seemingly paradoxical: in appearance, she is almost motionless, delicate, and inwardly focused—the classic posture and disposition of a *qin* player—yet the resulting sound soars with astonishing strength and rhythmic suppleness. In teaching, she applies the method of playing in unison with her students, and this has proved to be the only way for us to grasp her musicality. The reason is that her rhythmic interpretation of a piece almost never follows a simple metrical pattern; the rhythm appears to be always shifting and to be quite inimitable. Certainly, some aspects of her rhythm could never be captured in musical notation. Even multiple listenings to a recording do not reveal the secret of particularly elusive passages. But by repeatedly playing with her in unison, patient and perceptive students could eventually capture the rhythmic nuances, without even realizing how they did it.

After moving to the University of Pittsburgh in 1981, I visited Hong Kong regularly at least once a year. No matter how brief the trip was, I always dropped in to pay my respects to Tsar *laoshi* and to play in unison with her. During trips that lasted a month or more, I would learn new pieces. For example, I learned one of my favorite pieces, *Longxiang* 'Soaring Dragon', during a visit in the early 1990s. At the end of the 1990s, Tsar *laoshi* cut down on her playing because of a constantly aching shoulder; but she still plays occasionally, her ear and mind are as sharp as ever, and her memory for music—and for anything else—is still formidable. Most of the time now, she asks a student to play by himself or herself, and, if we are lucky, she may say

FIGURE I   Tsar Teh-yun playing the *qin* at her home in Hong Kong, 2000. Photo by Poon Tak-lun.

a few words about our playing. Ninety-six years old in 2001, Tsar *laoshi* continues to inspire me with her music, her conversation, and her friendship (figure 1).

I studied with Yao *laoshi* for a much shorter time. In three consecutive summers beginning in 1980, I visited him in Shanghai for two days, two weeks, and almost two months respectively. His kindness and generosity were such that I could spend as much time with him as I liked during those short visits. In a volume of *qin* music based on his performance, I wrote:

> In the most extensive period of study in 1982, I met with him every other day for seven weeks. My lessons usually began at shortly after 9 A.M. when I arrived at his apartment. The morning would be filled with music and conversation until noon, when Yao *shimu* (an honorific form of address for the wife of one's teacher) would have an exquisite lunch prepared for us. Our conversation would continue over wine and food for a leisurely two hours, in which we were occasionally joined by Yao *shimu*. Only after that would I leave and Yao *laoshi* would take his afternoon nap. I shall always remember those mornings with deep gratitude for his generosity and friendship, and for her warm and quiet hospitality. (1997:viii)

Like Tsar *laoshi*, Yao *laoshi* adhered to the older tradition that he had learned from his teacher, who was Xu Yuanbai. Nevertheless, his musical style was quite different from Tsar's: he played with a steady sense of pulse and clearly projected the large architectonic form of a composition. The dignity and elegance of his playing were unmatched among his peers. He was known particularly for his research into compositions that are preserved in the instrument's unique tablature notation, some of them centuries old but forgotten in the living repertoire. He would study the programmatic content of a piece based on bibliographic research, the meaning of antiquated notational symbols, and the finger techniques; he would reconstruct the music by providing an original rhythmic interpretation—a process known as *dapu* (Yung 1985). In this way, he resurrected many pieces for modern ears. Yao Bingyan died in the spring of 1983, at age sixty-three.

Both Tsar and Yao fit the image (perhaps a stereotype) of the scholar-musician—almost nonexistent in China by the late twentieth century—that one reads about in essays and memoirs from the past. They shared certain notable traits, such as a determined refusal to perform in public despite repeated, even urgent, requests; great erudition in the Chinese classics; and high accomplishment in the arts of poetry and calligraphy. Both also overcame enormous obstacles to follow their literary and artistic calling. Tsar, despite a privileged upbringing and an elite education in cosmopolitan Shanghai, had to overcome a deep-rooted bias in patriarchal Chinese culture against women who aspired to intellectual and professional independence. Yao had to overcome obstacles of a different kind: he was the son of a blind fortune-teller–musician and thus suffered from a low social status, although he had inherited his father's rich musical talent. Mainly through self-education, Yao became recognized as an accomplished calligrapher and *qin* player and was accepted in the literary and artistic circles of Shanghai. In both of these teachers, I caught a glimpse of the true amateur scholar-musician in traditional Chinese culture, one who, while keeping completely aloof from the commercial aspects of music and having no expectations from society, devotes a lifetime simply and purely to artistry. As their student, I learned not merely music but a philosophy of life.

While making music warms my heart, thinking, talking, and writing about music enrich my mind. My approach to these activities has been shaped by several important mentors to whom I owe my intellectual and professional development. My formal academic training in music began when I first enrolled in my second doctorate program. Although I knew from the start that my interest would be in musicology, I could not resist the many rich pickings among the courses being offered at Harvard. During my first year there, 1969, I took composition with the young David Del Tredici, a seminar in harpsichord literature with the august Gustave Leonhard, and piano tutoring from the brilliant Louise Vosgerchien.

My serious training began, however, with John Ward's musicology seminar for first-year graduate students. I still vividly remember our research projects on the minor sixteenth-century English composer Philip Van Wilder, and on Stravinsky and *Le sacre du printemps*. Through this seminar and others of Ward's, I began to understand the ideology and methodology of musicological research: to learn to think and write as clearly as possible about the infinitely complex subject of music and society. It was in his course "Music of the Oral Tradition" that I was first introduced to the writings of Charles Seeger. In serving as Ward's teaching assistant for the courses "Music and Ritual" and "Music and Narrative," which he designed and taught with Rulan Chao Pian, I became acquainted with a wide variety of musical material, from the morris dance to Navaho culture, and learned the art and science of designing and teaching undergraduate courses. Last but not least, he kindly served on my dissertation committee and, to my eternal gratitude, was never sparing in his criticism.

If Ward laid the foundation of my training, Charles Seeger inspired me to pursue originality and creativity in musicological ideas. I was fortunate to be at Harvard in 1972, when Seeger was a visiting professor and offered a seminar. Between then and the time of his death, I had several opportunities to meet with him and discuss his writings. These included a visit to his home in Connecticut in 1973, the inauguration of the Seeger Room in the Music Department at Harvard in 1976, a visit which he made to Cornell in 1977 and which I organized (I was a Mellon Fellow there), and the Seeger Celebration in Berkeley in 1977 (figure 2). Even though these meetings were brief, our conversations were always intense, and their impact on me was profound and long-lasting. I found these personal contacts with Seeger mesmerizing, and they induced me to read all of his publications that I could lay my hands on. Because his intellectual slant was philosophical, he noted fundamental questions of a sort seldom raised by other musicologists; he took nothing for granted, and he pondered and queried the meaning of every word he used. He was also a poet at heart; not only did he derive great enjoyment from playing with language for its own sake, but his love of language in turn inspired his musicological thought. These two halves of Seeger—the philosopher and the poet—made his writing not merely musicology but something at an even higher intellectual level, unceasingly intriguing and exhilarating.

If Seeger stimulated my mind with exciting new ideas, Rulan Chao Pian opened my heart to the joy of musicology. I first met Pian in 1967, when I was at M.I.T. and was the accompanist and later the conductor of the Chinese Intercollegiate Choral Society, a group consisting mainly of students from Taiwan and Hong Kong. Once I got to know Rulan Chao Pian, she became my main reason for reentering graduate school in music, for choosing Harvard as the place to do so, for focusing on musicology, and for doing research and writing on Chinese music. Through the years, her works on Chinese music history, on Peking opera, and on oral literature and the performing arts in general have set a standard for me to try to reach. As regards methodology, I learned from her to be absolutely meticulous in the handling of source material, never to be too cautious in interpretation, and never to take the readers' undivided attention for granted. I learned how a modest demeanor can hide a brilliant intellect, and how a gentle disposition can conceal unbending principles of scholarly excellence. Most important, I learned to be generous and kind to others, particularly to my students, as she has been to hers. She allowed me free use of her personal library, let me stay at her house whenever I needed to, and made me feel like a member of the family. Indeed, from Pian I learned not only scholarship but a lesson on how to live compassionately and joyously, and that is perhaps the most precious lesson anyone

FIGURE 2   Charles Seeger listening to Bell Yung, at a party after the inauguration of the Charles Seeger Room at Harvard University, 1976. Behind them is Robert Provine. Photo by Rulan Chao Pian.

can learn from a teacher (figure 3). Upon her retirement from Harvard, I was honored to be able to coedit her *Festschrift* (1994) with Joseph Lam, another former student of hers.

RESEARCH

My research has centered mainly on the music of China. With every new project, I find myself venturing into different worlds within China's rich tradition, using different approaches and research methods and discovering new musicological issues that inform not only Chinese music but musicality in general. Let me outline some of these projects.

My first project, on the music of Cantonese opera, was inspired largely by Rulan Chao Pian's work on Peking opera. I was particularly interested in the complex creative process behind a production of Cantonese opera, which lasts for four hours and may involve no fewer than twenty singer-actors and musicians, and in which there is no musical notation, no conductor, and often no rehearsal. In attempting to explain how that is possible, I probed into several issues touching on the basic nature of music making and how singers create tunes. One of those issues concerns tune identity, a question inspired both by Pian and by Charles Seeger's work, and one that has intrigued me ever since. My fieldwork took me into the inner world of Cantonese opera in Hong Kong, a world both familiar and alien. With my fluent but slightly Shanghai-accented Cantonese, I was treated by singers and musicians as both an insider and an outsider, and I came face to face with the complicated but fascinating issue of the relationship between the scholar and his "teacher-informant."

My work on the *qin* introduced me to historical research. Even though my primary interest was in present-day *qin* musicians and their playing, I was naturally led to study the long history of the instrument and the vast amount of historical material relating to it. I came to recognize the close relationship between my work and that of historical musicologists of Western music, and I began to question the term *ethnomusicology* and the territorial and methodological self-ghettoization of the discipline within musicology as a whole that results in part from the adoption of this word. Working in mainland China also led me to recognize the powerful but not entirely healthy influence of ethnomusicology on Chinese scholarship. Many people have written perceptively and sensitively on the ideological imperialism of the West, which is linked to political and economic power, but few offer real solutions to the problem.

FIGURE 3   Rulan Chao Pian and Bell Yung at a party during the annual meeting of SEM in Pittsburgh, 1997. Photo by Ted Pian.

In *qin* music, I also came to recognize a kind of tradition that is not normally written about in ethnomusicology. *Qin* musicians are deliberate in the cultivation of their craft, are very self-reflective about their creative process, and are highly conscious of their aesthetic value system; the philosophy and practice of this tradition have been relatively unbroken for about two millennia, and the tradition has been preserved in copious volumes of both words and musical notation. In this respect, the *qin* culture of China parallels that of European art music. Yet in other respects it is obviously quite different, for, being of great antiquity, and one of the most conservative of musical traditions, it embodies the essence of Chinese philosophy, particularly Confucianism and Daoism. My journey into the world of *qin* has been at the same time a journey of self-discovery and an investigation of my roots and cultural heritage.

My scholarly interest in *qin* also returned me to serious study of music performance. *Qin* music is of course quite different from piano music, despite the fact that both have a long tradition, a vast repertoire, and an infinite variety of structures and styles. The *qin* is mostly quiet, always subtle, and highly introspective, like a little brook, deep in the mountains, without a care in the world; the piano is assertive, often brilliant, and always reaching out to the audience, like a torrential river, sweeping bystanders along emotionally. The *qin* repertoire does include a few compositions, such as *Guanglingsan* 'Assassination of the King of Han', that are dramatic and dazzling, and the piano repertoire includes many quiet, contemplative pieces. Nevertheless, these instruments contrast greatly in performance practice, aesthetic ideals, and social context. Even the fact that the playing method of the *qin* requires the musician to have long fingernails whereas the piano cannot tolerate long nails poses a dilemma for anyone who plays both instruments. I feel fortunate to have had the chance to know both instruments and their music. It makes me think that serious music lovers should be involved in at least two contrasting musical idioms, to increase their appreciation of each.

That teaching and research nourish one another and that the teacher learns as much from his students as the other way around are truisms in our profession. My interest in Charles Seeger, which started in my days as a graduate student, illustrates this point. From my very first encounter with his writings, particularly those on the philosophy of music, I became fascinated and inspired by his originality, his insights, and, for lack of a better word, the sheer joy that he exudes in his intellectual explorations. While some others have found his writing dense and his sentence structure awkward, I have always felt that I could discern the reasons why he wrote the way he did—reasons having to do with the fact that he combined a logician's mind and a poet's heart. I set out on a systematic program of reading, interpreting, and developing the ideas contained in his hundred-odd articles, including many from his early years that are seldom cited.

When I started teaching at the University of Pittsburgh, I began to offer a graduate seminar on Seeger, for I wanted the students to share my excitement and fascination, and to be inspired by his words as much as I had been. The seminars also gave me an excuse to reread his articles every few years, and an opportunity to try out on new groups of students the thoughts that I had developed from Seeger's. Each seminar generated a number of high-quality term projects, some of which were read at annual meetings of the Society for Ethnomusicology. A volume of essays (1999) that I coedited with Helen Rees is the fruition of those seminars and, I hope, the first of a series. I shall always be grateful to the participants in the seminars, without whom I probably would not have been able to sustain my active interest in and writing on Seeger, and from whom I learned much.

One of my most treasured experiences has been my collaborative work with two colleagues at the University of Pittsburgh. In the early 1990s, the social historian Evelyn Rawski was working on a book-length project on the Qing imperial household, in which ritual had a major role in all public and private activities. The cultural anthropologist Rubie Watson, a specialist in southern China, was studying material on bridal laments that she had collected some years before. I myself had a long-standing interest in ritual and ritual music, ever since I served as a teaching assistant for the course "Music and Ritual" at Harvard. The three of us found our common ground in the recognition that ritual and ritual music form a nexus around which different disciplines can converge effectively and through which social behaviors can be fruitfully interpreted. We also recognized that within Chinese studies, music was possibly the last frontier, the only area in which there was still little cross-disciplinary work. Few if any musicologists working on China have fellow sinologists in mind when they do their research and writing; conversely, with few exceptions, humanists and social scientists pay scant attention to music as a valuable supplementary resource for their research on China.

After many informal meetings, we devised a two-stage plan for collaborative research. The first stage consisted of three sections: (1) jointly teaching a graduate seminar on ritual and ritual music of China; (2) conducting a research workshop with presentations by invited specialists from several disciplines; (3) publication of a volume of essays based on the workshop, which would serve as a theoretical framework for our fieldwork. Our seminar in 1991 attracted graduate students from several departments. The reading list was compiled by the three of us, and all three were present at every session. Two years later, we held a week-long workshop, supported by a grant from the National Endowment for the Humanities, to which scholars from ethnomusicology, history, anthropology, and religious studies were invited. The four invited discussants were David McAllester, Victor Mair, Rulan Chao Pian, and Anthony Seeger. The papers were eventually published in a collection edited by the three of us (Yung, Rawski, and Watson 1996). This first stage, designed to encourage each of us to learn from the others about our respective disciplines, was intended as a preparation for the second stage, when we would go into the field as a team. Unfortunately, stage two was indefinitely postponed, in part because of my Guggenheim Fellowship and an unexpected opportunity to teach at the University of Hong Kong in 1996.

Nevertheless, the experience was unforgettable and inspiring. It also underscored the almost impossible challenge facing ethnomusicologists. Not only are many of us expected to be bilingual, bicultural, and bimusical; we are also expected to be—among other things—musicologists, historians, anthropologists, sociologists, folklorists, and cognitive psychologists. Since we consider interdisciplinarity the core of our field, we demand interdisciplinary training, an interdisciplinary outlook, and interdisciplinary output. Are we setting an impossible task for ourselves? My collaborative experience with colleagues shows that it doesn't have to be this way. By reaching out across disciplines, we can tap into the intellectual resources of others and work together as a team, both in teaching and in research. In the process, moreover, the attention paid to our specialty—music—need not be compromised.

One's research is also inevitably related to other professional activities. Because of my work on Cantonese opera and on Cantonese narrative songs, I became intensely involved with an organization called the Conference on Chinese Oral and Performing Literature, serving as its president and the editor of its journal in the mid-1990s. In 1986, I founded the Association for Chinese Music Research (ACMR); I served as its president and edited its journal until 1997, when Joseph Lam took over both responsibilities. An affiliate of the Society for Ethnomusicology, ACMR meets annually in conjunction with its parent organization and serves as a forum where Chinese music researchers can meet and talk.

Since I started teaching at the University of Hong Kong in 1996, my research directions and professional interests have been slowly evolving. In a largely Chinese environment, I have become more aware of the social responsibility of the ethnomusicologist and have devoted more attention to what might be called "applied" research. For example, in 1998, in collaboration with the University Museum and Art Gallery of the University of Hong Kong, I curated an exhibition, "Gems of Ancient Chinese Zithers," that displayed some sixty instruments, the earliest dating from the tenth century. I edited the exhibition catalog (1998a), organized a concert of *qin* music played on some of the instruments on display, and produced a compact disk (1998b) in conjunction with the exhibition and concert. As of this writing, I am curating "The Musical Arts of Ancient China," in collaboration with the same museum, which will (from September 2001 to January 2002) display more than 100 musical instruments, as well as samplings of books and scores, most on loan from the Music Research Institute of Beijing. In 1998 I established the Center for Cultural Policy Research at the University of Hong Kong. With workshops, lectures, and forums, some in collaboration with other local organizations, this center aims to serve Hong Kong by helping it develop a vision and chart a course in cultural matters at this transitional period of its history. I have undertaken these and other endeavors because I feel there is a need for community outreach, and the financial resources that are available for such work in Hong Kong allow me to do so.

RESEARCH ON CHINESE MUSIC IN CHINA AND THE WEST

Because I was trained in the United States, my intellectual and professional activities centered mostly on academic institutions and professional organizations in the West, even though I was keenly aware of musical research in China and had visited many institutions and attended professional conferences there. Through living and working in a Chinese environment in recent years, and through closer and more frequent contacts with music scholars from the mainland, I began to shift the center of my activities from the United States to China and develop a different perspective on musical scholarship. Accordingly, some of my professional activities have also changed. For example, in the summer of 2000 I organized the Second National Conference on Melody Studies at the University of Hong Kong, with thirty scholars from the mainland and ten from overseas. (The National Society of Melody Studies was established in 1998 in China and held its first conference in Hohhot, Inner Mongolia, that summer.) This was the first China-centered conference I organized; Putonghua Chinese was the official language. Essays from the conference were compiled as a volume (forthcoming in 2002) coedited by me and Zhao Songguang of the Xinhai Conservatory of Guangzhou. In June 2001, I organized a conference, again at the University of Hong Kong and cosponsored by the Leisure and Culture Services Department of the Hong Kong government, entitled "What Is Chinese Opera? The Tradition and Innovation of Artistic Expressions." Again, the official language was Putonghua Chinese.

Accompanying this shift in my attention is my growing awareness of the relationship—or nonrelationship—between Chinese music research studies produced in English and research studies from mainland China produced in Chinese. How are they similar or different? What should their relationship be? These are questions that all Chinese music scholars will face sooner or later because Chinese music research—probably more than any other geocultural area of musical study in the West—has a significant counterpart of scholarship in its "home" country, a parallel universe if you will, that cannot be ignored and indeed must be embraced.

Chinese music research overseas developed as an integral part of Western ethnomusicology, adopting its ideology and methodology. Music research in China, on the other hand, follows the long tradition of Chinese scholarship in general. Even more important, Chinese music in the West is regarded as one among many "world" music cultures to be studied in the global context in order to gain a broader comprehension of what music and musical culture are. But in China, Chinese music is considered within its own historical and cultural contexts. For example, some types are considered "fine" or "art" and thus deserving of study, while others are considered less so. China's study of its own music has much to do with national pride in artistic accomplishments and with a broader context of national development. The goal is to promote, improve, and disseminate as much as to do research and to understand. The method is—in Seeger's terminology—critical as much as scientific. In that respect, the approach and methodology are somewhat closer to the study of Western music by Westerners. Ultimately, the fundamental factors that shape the ideology, methodology, and goals of research are the scholar's sense of cultural and national identity and the relation of that identity to the music being studied. In contrast, the heart of the discipline of Western "ethnomusicology" is, ideally, the absence of any such sense of identity; the founding philosophy of Western ethnomusicology was laid down to a great extent by scholars engaged in the objective and scientific study of "other" people's music.

That scholars in China have a strong sense of cultural and national identity with Chinese music is unquestionable; by contrast, the sense of identity felt by scholars abroad ranges over a wide spectrum, from some who identify nearly completely with China to those who identify hardly at all. How such a sense of identity develops depends to a considerable degree, of course, on one's ethnicity, cultural heritage, and upbringing; on where one grew up; on where one has been or is living and working; and on other factors that might be very personal. Last but not least, the fact that scholars may be trained in the West within the discipline of ethnomusicology or may currently work in the profession naturally also influences their position along the spectrum.

The issue of insider versus outsider is of major interest to Western ethnomusicologists. Whether one is an insider, an outsider, or somewhere in between, one can discuss the issue on a theoretical level and at a safe distance. But one's particular position along the insider-outsider spectrum is quite personal and inseparable from one's sense of self, being deeply emotional and developed subliminally, often beyond one's conscious control. Regardless of one's theoretical understanding of the issue, one's sense of identity inevitably influences the purpose, research questions, approach, methodology, scope, and ultimate aim of one's research. Wu Ben's master's thesis, written under my supervision at the University of Pittsburgh some years ago and later published (1998), compares research on Tibetan music by Western scholars as a group and that by Chinese—mostly Han—scholars as a group. His conclusions illuminate the issue at hand, however debatable it may be how much and in what way Han scholars identify with Tibetan culture.

The issue here is not whether one approach is better or preferable. Rather, we need to recognize the differences, understand the unspoken forces behind each approach, and try to view each with eyes both critical and compassionate. For those of us who feel that we are in between—perhaps most of us, regardless of ethnicity or cultural heritage—the forces that are constantly tugging us from either side can be at times painful and confusing. However, it is my sense that such forces need not be destructive or divisive, but rather can prove to be invigorating and inspiring if we learn to deal with them successfully. Indeed, I strongly believe (and Joseph Lam and I have talked about this often) that those ethnomusicologists who work on China in the West have much to contribute to the field of musicology and ethnomusicology in the West on the one hand, and to musicological research in China on the other, because of our privileged position of being in between and thus of being able to draw ideas from both sides.

REFERENCES

Wu, Ben. 1998. "Music Scholarship, West and East: Tibetan Music as a Case Study." *Asian Music* 29(2):31–56.

Yung, Bell. 1985. "*Da Pu*: The Recreative Process for the Music of the Seven-String Zither." In *Music and Context: Essays in Honor of John Ward*, ed. Anne Dhu Shapiro, 370–384. Cambridge: Music Department, Harvard University.

———. 1997. *Celestial Airs of Antiquity: Music of the Seven-String Zither of China*. Madison, Wisc.: A-R Editions.

———, ed. 1998a. *Exhibition Catalogue: Gems of Ancient Chinese Zithers*. Hong Kong: University Museum and Art Gallery, University of Hong Kong.

———. 1998b. *Qin Music on Antique Instruments*. Hong Kong: Music Department, University of Hong Kong. Compact disk.

Yung, Bell, and Joseph Lam, eds. 1994. *Themes and Variations: Writings on Music in Honor of Rulan Chao Pian*. Cambridge and Hong Kong: Music Department, Harvard University and Institute for Chinese Studies, Chinese University of Hong Kong.

Yung, Bell, Evelyn Rawski, and Rubie S. Watson, eds. 1996. *Harmony and Counterpoint: Ritual Music in Chinese Context*. Stanford, Calif.: Stanford University Press.

Yung, Bell, and Helen Rees, eds. 1999. *Understanding Charles Seeger, Pioneer in American Musicology*. Urbana: University of Illinois Press.

Zhao, Songguang, and Bell Yung, eds. 2002 (forthcoming). *Xuanlü yanjiu lunji* (Essays on the Study of Melody), Vol. 2. Beijing: Wenhua Yishu Chubanshe.

Africa and East Asia
Kenichi Tsukada

Working as an Ethnomusicologist
My Place in Ethnomusicology
Appendix: Song Texts

My background was modern Western music, with little knowledge of Japanese musical traditions. As an undergraduate student of musicology at Tôkyô University of Fine Arts and Music (Tôkyô Geijutsu Daigaku), I was particularly interested in the philosophy and aesthetics of music under the strong influence of German traditions. After I completed my B.A. thesis, "Existieren in der Musik," in German, I switched from Western music to ethnomusicology for my postgraduate studies. This shift of subject cannot be explained without mentioning one Japanese name: Fumio Koizumi, whose influence changed the course of my life. Koizumi, then a professor at Tôkyô University of Fine Arts and Music, was without doubt the founder of ethnomusicology in Japan, though he was little known to the Western world except among scholars in Japanese studies. Japan had a relatively long tradition of academic research on its own music and that of the rest of Asia and Oceania (for example, Iida 1936; Kishibe 1937; Tanabe 1925), but the study of ethnomusicology in the contemporary sense has been comparatively recent.

Koizumi (1927–1983) started his career as specialist in Japanese music (Koizumi 1958). After studying in India for about two years in the late 1950s, he conducted extensive field research in Asia and also in some parts of North and South America, Africa, and Europe. His course in ethnomusicology at the university was extremely appealing, since it included vivid descriptions, based on his own fieldwork, of various musical cultures. He was also very influential among the general public as an educator. Through diverse media, he conveyed the fascination of "world music" and made ethnomusicology known to the public. What I learned from this charismatic figure was the importance of an empirical rather than a speculative approach to music, and the significance, for the study of music, of a researcher's own experience in the field and in performance.

My shift in academic subjects changed my life dramatically. Partly because of Koizumi's ideological influence, I began to study both the theory and the practice of Japanese music. As a Japanese, I felt it irrational to be ignorant of my own musical traditions, especially because I considered myself an ethnomusicologist. I took lessons every week in *syakuhati* (a bamboo flute), *syamisen* (a three-stringed lute) of *nagauta*, *sho* (a mouth organ) of *gagaku*, and *utai* (singing) of *nô* drama, with leading performers in each genre, such as Reibo Aoki (who is now a "national asset" of *syakuhati*

Detailed analysis of *Fetu Afahye* could be expected to shed light on several important aspects of Fanti society, because the festival involves chieftancy, military organizations, and other significant institutions. It would also be an opportunity to explore ethnic identity.

performance). The *syakuhati* and the *syamisen* meant to me, as an ethnomusicologist, what the piano meant to John Blacking. I developed a passion for the *syakuhati* in particular; later, I would perform a contemporary *syakuhati* piece by a Japanese composer with the Indiana University Orchestra, and I was invited to Iceland as a *syakuhati* player, to perform with the Icelandic Orchestra in Reykjavik.

Despite this change in my musical life, my academic interests were still biased by my earlier training in Western music. As a new ethnomusicologist who was shifting away from Western music, I was fascinated by the question of how harmonic structures, specifically triads, developed in some "traditional" cultures, independently of Western influence. This rather classic question of comparative musicology, however outdated it may seem now, did stimulate my ethnomusicological interest. In order to reexamine previous theories, I conducted my first fieldwork among the Bunun, Taiwanese Aborigines. Earlier work by Japanese scholars, such as Kurosawa (1952), had indicated that the Bunun would provide a good illustration of the issue. Detailed analyses of the tonal structures of their music, and spectrographic data, demonstrated a clear connection between vocal harmonic structures and natural harmonics produced on the Jew's harp (Tsukada 1980). I followed this research by conducting fieldwork in the Sepik Valley of Papua New Guinea, examining the same topic in a different geographical region. This fieldwork (Tsukada 1983, 1998a) had a crucial impact on my academic career. In the field, I was made aware of my lack of anthropological training, which I felt was indispensable for ethnomusicological research. Therefore, I decided to study at Indiana University, where Alan Merriam was teaching.

In the United States, I was impressed by the way ethnomusicology was taught at universities. I appreciated the systematic ethnomusicology program at Indiana University, whose leading faculty members in this subject were then Alan Merriam, Frank Gillis, Ronald Smith, and Ruth Stone. Merriam and Stone introduced me to contemporary trends in American ethnomusicology, and I also absorbed the theoretical rigor of social studies from an anthropologist, Ivan Karp. At that time, I had it in mind to study the Bororo in Mato Grosso, in Brazil, with reference to my previous studies. However, while I was a student at Indiana University, two things happened that changed my mind.

First, I became close to several African and African-American students. I felt sympathetic to their social history as an oppressed people; and as a Japanese, I also felt myself sharing, somewhat, their sense of problems related to the Western domination of the world. At the same time, I was impressed by what African-Americans had achieved in many fields in their society. Overall, this experience gradually directed my interest toward Africa. Second, John Blacking and Gerhard Kubik were invited to Indiana University, at different times, to lecture. Blacking's creative ideas and his deep passion for African cultures stimulated me greatly, and Kubik's lecture had a decisive effect on my academic life. My determination to study the Bororo began to waver, and my interest eventually turned from South America to Africa. Thus I decided to become an Africanist.

Merriam's sudden death in 1980 also changed the course of my life. Afterward, I moved to Belfast to study with John Blacking, having completed my master's degree in anthropology. Blacking was always inspiring. His ideas were flexible, and he had deep insights not only into music and culture but also into daily life. The important lessons I learned from him were his humanistic attitude toward the people in the field and his open-mindedness about local beliefs, such as possession and witchcraft.

Listening to African music, particularly the *Sound of Africa Series* produced by Hugh Tracey (1973), was a major impetus in my selection of a geographical area for my doctoral research. I found the music of the Bemba in the Northern Province of Zambia most interesting, especially with regard to my early focus on harmonic structures. However, during my pilot fieldwork I consulted with Mwesa I. Mapoma, a Zambian ethnomusicologist who specialized in Bemba music; and he advised me to select another ethnic group with a similar musical style, the Luvale in the Northwestern Province, reasoning that it would not be good for the country if researchers concentrated on one ethnic group while others were left unexplored. My pilot research among the Luvale convinced me that their *mukanda*, initiation rites for boys, represented and reflected many essential features of their culture and music. Consequently, I chose the *mukanda* for my dissertation, analyzing the epistemological discrepancies between discourse and practice and musical performance in these rites (Tsukada 1988, 1998b).

Toward the end of my long period of fieldwork in Zambia, I developed an unidentified illness, and it took me a year to recover my health in Britain and Japan. I did not resume my field research in Africa until five years after I had completed my Ph.D. By this time, I was beginning to think about the possibility of a comparative study of African culture and my own Japanese culture. My central concern became the "oral mnemonics" in African drumming, with reference to sound symbolism, because this was also a cultural practice among traditional Japanese musicians. I chose Ghana for this topic because of its advanced level of studies of African drumming. After some discussions with Kwabena Nketia at the University of Ghana, I decided to specialize in the music culture of the Fanti in the Central Region. I learned drumming and the "nonsense syllables" of *fɔntɔmfrɔm* (the royal drum ensemble) and *asafo* (the military drum ensemble) from royal musicians in Cape Coast. I also investigated Fanti sound symbolism by conducting experiments person by person and applying statistical analysis to the data (Tsukada 1995, 2001a). I used a similar method to explore Luvale oral mnemonics and sound symbolism in Zambia, as a comparison (Tsukada 1997).

WORKING AS AN ETHNOMUSICOLOGIST

Although I have conducted fieldwork among the Fanti intermittently since 1993, my interest in Fanti society has changed over time. Topics such as oral mnemonics and sound symbolism were obviously not comprehensive enough to cover many aspects of this culture. My field diary in 1997 reveals my frustration over my lack of knowledge about Fanti society in general—a frustration that intensified when I attended *Panafesta*, the festival of African performing arts held biennially in Cape Coast:

> The Fanti chiefdom is huge. Many chiefs were brought in palanquins to the festival. But how much do I know about them? My topic is too narrow to encompass Fanti society and culture. The ethnic complex in Cape Coast displayed at the festival inspired me with an idea that the ethnic identity expressed by various groups in their performing arts would be a good topic for my future research. (30 August 1997)

Although I wavered in my thinking the next day, when I was deeply moved by the music and dance at an interdenominational church service, I finally made up my mind toward the end of the festival. It was essential for me to choose a topic that would give me opportunities to deal with various aspects of Fanti society and would hold a promise of future development. I thought that *Fetu Afahye*, the annual Fanti festival in Cape Coast—with particular reference to the identity of participants of different ethnic backgrounds—was the most appropriate subject.

Fetu Afahye is a series of traditional celebrations held each year from the end of July to early September. For the Fanti, its main purpose is to renew their allegiance to the paramount chief and to express their thanks for the year's harvest, but other ethnic groups in Cape Coast, such as the Ashanti, Ewe, Hausa, and Mole-Dagbani (the Mamprusi, Mossi, and others), also participate in this festival. Detailed analysis of *Fetu Afahye* could be expected to shed light on several important aspects of Fanti society, because the festival involved chieftaincy, military organizations, and other significant institutions. It would also be an opportunity to explore the construction of ethnic identity of different groups through their performing arts.

During my fieldwork in 1997, I was able to record the *Fetu Afahye* on cassette and videotape, take plenty of photos, and conduct interviews about various facets of the ceremonies. Almost all the interviews were recorded on tape. Later, when I played the videotapes of the ceremonies in my room, I interviewed my research assistant, Kweku Sheburah, about what these tapes showed. (Kweku Sheburah, a middle-aged drummer who is a well-known master of the royal drum ensemble for the paramount chief of Cape Coast and is very knowledgeable about Fanti traditions, has worked with me since I began my field studies in 1993.)

Toward the end of this fieldwork, I was also able to conduct preliminary interviews with eleven people of different ethnic backgrounds—two Ewe, two Hausa, and seven Fanti. I asked them about their commitment to *Fetu Afahye*, and several points emerged from these interviews that became guidelines for my future studies. First, the Ewe and Hausa tended to associate themselves with their own ethnic festivals (such as *Eteza* for the Ewe in the Volta Region) rather than with *Fetu Afahye*; thus their commitment to the latter was limited. Second, with regard to *Fetu Afahye* there were different levels of ethnic consciousness among the Fanti. Educated Fanti (such as university graduates) tended to understand and articulate the significance of the festival for their ethnicity better than less educated Fanti. Among the less educated Fanti, the sense of ethnic identity seemed to be so deeply embedded in everyday life that I found it difficult to make them "problematize" it. Third, a certain difficulty arose with regard to the interviews, partly because I had not been sufficiently prepared, methodologically, for this new project. For instance, when an Ewe girl responded, "I took a part in the festival, but I did not sing and dance" (interview tape GF97-11A), how was I to interpret this? Did she really mean that she had not sung or danced, or had she perhaps responded in this way because I, a foreign researcher, was forcing her to explain her commitment to a Fanti festival? (Non-Fanti women do in fact sometimes sing and dance at *Fetu Afahye*.) In my diary, I confessed several times that I was finding it hard to get close to the core of the issue of ethnicity. In the end, I left Ghana with a strong impression that this problem must be first tackled by investigating the migration history of various ethnic groups in Cape Coast.

Fieldwork: An unexpected development

When I returned to Ghana the following year, 1998, my research took an unexpected direction. I began by consulting two specialists on Fanti society at the University of Ghana: George Hagan, a Fanti sociologist at the Institute of African Studies; and John Fynn, a Fanti historian in the department of history. They offered me rather different perspectives for my research. Hagan maintained that Cape Coast had originally been a settlement of various groups whose different cultures mingled over a long period of time, becoming so intertwined that the important issue was not so much ethnicity as the process by which these diverse cultural factors had fused to create the "culture of Cape

Coast." Fynn explained how such a settlement had occurred after the Europeans began to fortify the coastal regions in the fifteenth century and how the settlers and their descendants became culturally and ethnically assimilated into the dominant Fanti.

In order to verify these views, with particular reference to Cape Coast, I searched for publications about Cape Coast history at libraries—but in vain, except for James Graham Jr. (1994), although there were some general historical accounts of the coastal regions (Boahen 1965a; Fynn 1971). I then began to interview the Fanti about their historical constructions of Cape Coast and *Fetu Afahye*. After interviewing three Fanti elders, however, I stopped, greatly disappointed: "I have been stranded in my investigation of the oral history of Cape Coast" (field diary, 15 August 1998). The reason was that some parts of their historical accounts conflicted so sharply with the objective facts that the reliability of their discourse was questionable, and their history of *Fetu Afahye* was not very informative. Obviously, something had gone wrong with my approach, but I had no idea how to deal with the problem. Several days passed with no progress, and I was beginning to despair. But a new prospect appeared three days later (18 August), when I interviewed a divisional chief, Nana Kwamina Nimfa IX, in Antem village.

Nimfa IX explained many aspects of Fanti society, and what struck me most was his remark that an important objective of the *Fetu Afahye* festival was harmony and unity among individuals, military organizations, and ethnic groups. This was consistent with the appeal for peace made by the paramount chief at the festival, such as the one published in the journal *Oguaa Fetu Afahye*: "I hope that all citizens will cooperate to bring about peace, harmony, unity, and love in our various homes" (Afahye Planning Committee 1995:3). This idea, differently phrased but with the same implications, appeared in almost every issue of the journal. King-Gaisie, head of the administrative office of the Traditional Council of Cape Coast, also made the same point when I interviewed him. I asked what such a persistent emphasis on social unity implied; I had a strong impression that there might be something behind this statement, and I suspected that it might signify an opposite element in Fanti society—diversity. In retrospect, the interview with Nimfa IX played a crucial role in the later development of my research.

Sources on the history of Ghana (Boahen 1965b; Buah 1980; Claridge 1915; Graham 1994; Okyere 1997) later verified my idea; these sources revealed that the Fanti chiefdoms had experienced numerous riots and inter- and intrastate wars over the past several hundred years. Particularly noteworthy were the very frequent conflicts between military organizations called *asafo* companies. An *asafo* company is a military institution, originally intended to defend the state in interstate wars. The Fanti of Cape Coast have had seven *asafo* companies, distinguished by name, number, color, and emblem (figure 1). Historical accounts by some authors, such as Johnston (1963), and my own interviews with several Fanti made it clear that clashes between *asafo* companies were a cause of social disorder, even though these companies also fought as allies against their common enemies.

On 20 August, an interview with my assistant, Sheburah, about his *ebusua* (clan) drew my attention to one fascinating aspect of the Fanti social system. The Fanti have seven clans, and their descent is matrilineal; but *asafo* membership is based on patrilineal descent. Every member of the society, whether male or female, belongs to one *asafo* company in the paternal line and one *ebusua* in the maternal line. Thus the two lines of descent intersect. An important implication is that members of rival *asafo* companies can be relatives in the maternal line. Figure 2 shows an example: Fanti A and Fanti B are brothers by the same mother, of the Twidan clan, but by different fathers, one from Bentsir company and the other from Anaafo. These two brothers may become enemies if their companies clash. I had a feeling that this system of double descent is of tremendous significance for understanding Fanti society. Around

FIGURE 1 A Nkum *asafo* company in procession. (Photos are by the author.)

FIGURE 2 Intersection of the *ebusua* maternal line and the *asafo* paternal line.

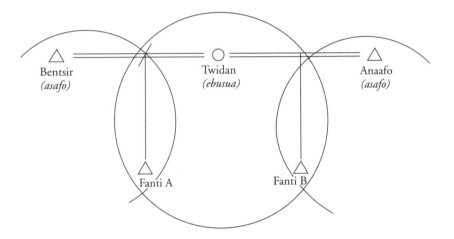

Bentsir
(*asafo*)

Twidan
(*ebusua*)

Anaafo
(*asafo*)

Fanti A

Fanti B

the same time, I uncovered another clue. Kobia Minnah, captain of the Akrampa *asafo* company, commented in an interview that music has an important role in *asafo* activities and that *asafo* music includes many songs with warlike texts. I had an impression that the present anthropological issue might become an important ethnomusicological issue.

By this time, my main interest had already shifted from the original topic—*Fetu Afahye* and ethnic identity—to a new one. I was beginning to formulate the issue as two opposing forces in Fanti society: schism and unity.

Inquiry: Opposing social forces

Now that I had decided to focus on this issue in my research, the next step was to collect supporting data. First, I tried to gather evidence for the social tendency toward schism. I went to the Central Regional Archives Office in Cape Coast to examine historical records of conflicts between *asafo* companies in this region over the past hundred years. The archives had numerous valuable official documents dating from the British colonial period. I was fascinated by this raw material, which conveyed direct information about what had happened in Cape Coast. A mass of documents grouped under "Cape Coast Native Affairs," in particular, were of tremendous help to me.

One sheaf of papers, for instance, included an official letter by the commissioner of Central Province to the district commissioner of Cape Coast dated 5 March 1942 (Archival Record, ADM 23/l/932). This letter took up the question of disbanding *asafo* companies in the colony; the reason was that the governor was seriously concerned about several riots and other disturbances set off by members of the companies. Particularly in the coastal regions, the commissioner wrote, "these riots have frequently resulted in the loss of life, the number killed on one occasion being as high as 92." This was taken as clear evidence of a social tendency toward disunity, though it is likely that the colonial government tried to take advantage of the disturbances to get rid of a possible military threat to its rule. Another frequent problem documented in "Cape Coast Native Affairs" was "chieftaincy disputes." I found one example in a file on the "destoolment" of the paramount chief Francis Sinbad Bilson on 2 November 1916 (Archival Record, ADM 23/l/280). This file described the incident from its inception to the development of an intense feud between two factions of the royal family: Bilson was "destooled" by the assembly of chiefs for his "repeated misconduct," but the case was taken into the provincial court at Cape Coast Castle by Bilson's faction. Although the colonial government approved of his destoolment, the vacant chieftaincy became a focus of dispute between the two branches of the royal family, Kwonna and Efikessim.

Almost all the material I came across contained evidence of what I have called the social forces of schism in Fanti society. I spent several days at the Archives Office and made copies of hundreds of letters and papers. (Later, I visited the National Archives of Ghana in Accra and the Public Record Office in London, both of which also provided material that was as useful for my inquiry.) Several writings, such as Graham (1994) and Johnston (1963), also described clashes between *asafo* companies. The best-known is a battle between the Nkum company and six other companies in 1856, which destroyed almost the whole town of Cape Coast. Much evidence of chieftaincy disputes came from the people. A recent case involved Kwesi Atta, a new paramount chief who succeeded Kodwo Mbra V in 1998; that case was taken to court by the opposing faction and was still pending at the time of this writing.

On the other hand, the *Fetu Afahye* festival seemed to contribute in two ways to the social forces of unity. First, it gave the paramount chief an occasion on which he could, in his address at the ceremony, appeal officially to the public for peace and unity; this appeal, as we have seen, also appeared in the journal *Oguaa Fetu Afahye*. Second, certain details of the festival make such an appeal effective. Toward the end of the festival, the paramount chief and other chiefs are carried in procession in their palanquins (figure 3), cheered by thousands of people. This creates an image of the Fanti as socially united under one paramount chief.

The system of double descent also contributes to unity. Sheburah explained in a later interview that the matrilineal *ebusua* operated to deter conflicts between *asafo* companies: "Kobina Spio and I are both members of Twidan clan in the maternal line. We are relatives. But he belongs to Bentsir company and I belong to Intsin. So, when the two companies clashed, we would become enemies. But I would not fight with him. I would give him a sign to leave the place to avoid fighting" (interview tape GF98-5B). Interestingly, however, when I returned to Accra and read *Double Descent among the Fanti* by James Christensen (1954) at the University of Ghana, I was surprised to see that Christensen ignored this deterrent effect of the matrilineal clan.

Fieldwork: Further developments

At this stage, my greatest concern was how music making was related to these social forces. To me, it seemed obvious that there was a close relationship, because *asafo* companies had their own military bands and music was important in *Fetu Afahye*. I assumed that the *asafo* military drum ensemble would be related to the forces of schism

FIGURE 3   A chief in procession on his palanquin, cheered by the crowd.

and the royal drum ensemble *fɔntɔmfrɔm* to the forces of unity. I reasoned that *asafo* was a musical genre inseparable from the (often conflicting) companies, whereas *fɔntɔmfrɔm* was an important musical genre for the royal festival (figure 4), which promoted peace and unity; still, I needed to verify this. First of all, I ruled out the possibility of a relationship between sound structures and social forces. I had already learned *asafo* and *fɔntɔmfrɔm* drumming, but I could not find any perspective from which I would be able to explore connections between musical genres and social forces in terms of sound structure. Kobina Minnah's earlier comment suggested to me that the connection should be sought in the song texts; the result, however, was a great disappointment. Analysis of *fɔntɔmfrɔm* song texts disclosed that they were mostly designed for entertainment and had no implications for social unity. I was deeply puzzled. I had no idea how to relate music making to the issue at hand.

A crucial moment came a week later (2 September), when I interviewed Sheburah once again about the song texts. I had already collected a number of texts for *asafo*

FIGURE 4   *Fɔntɔmfrɔm* performance by royal musicians.

and *fɔntɔmfrɔm* music, and what emerged from his interpretation of these texts was a contrast between the two genres. *Asafo* texts dealt with conflicts between *asafo* companies and related historical events, in order to raise morale. Some texts were highly provocative to other companies. The same was true of messages conveyed by a talking drum, the *asafo-kyen.* In contrast, *fɔntɔmfrɔm* texts created a different picture of Fanti society, describing life as full of joy and joking; the varied topics of these songs included *Fetu Afahye*, drummers, love affairs, praise of chiefdoms, and jokes about musicians. (A few texts are given in the appendix at the end of this article.) The important point—which I had missed earlier—was that although *fɔntɔmfrɔm* texts often dealt with jokes and "trivial" matters, such topics could provide entertainment at the festival and thus contribute to social unity by bringing people of different factions together. Sheburah put it as follows (interview tape GFM98-2B): "*Asafo* songs are *ako ndwom* 'war songs' and *hū* 'dangerous', whereas *fɔntɔmfrɔm* songs are *enyigye ndwom* 'entertainment songs' and *dew* 'sweet'." Now it was clear that the two genres, *asafo* and *fɔntɔmfrɔm*, did correspond, respectively, to the social forces of schism and unity.

I was fascinated by this beautiful correlation between social forces and music in Fanti culture. But the story did not stop there. Toward the end of my fieldwork, the final ceremony of *Fetu Afahye*, the state durbar, took place, and I watched chiefs and *asafo* companies march in procession. What I observed then was quite different from what I have just described: *asafo* companies acted friendly to each other rather than being hostile. There was nothing that suggested tension or conflict. The traditional warlike *asafo* songs were rarely performed. What the *asafo* groups sang in procession were mostly church songs and "highlife" songs. Some members of the Bentsir company joined the procession of the Intsin company, wearing Intsin costumes and playing music with them (figure 5).

What had happened? Was my analysis altogether wrong? Or did my conclusion require some revisions? When I conducted feedback interviews with Sheburah, while watching the video recordings of the ceremony, the following facts were revealed: clashes between *asafo* companies had decreased significantly in the 1960s, and the long history of the *asafo* feuds ended in the mid-1970s. With the end of the conflicts, various new music and dance groups were formed within the companies.

These groups sing entertaining songs, such as church and "highlife" songs, when the companies appear at *Fetu Afahye*. Although the traditional ensembles remain, the

FIGURE 5   A Nkum *asafo* company performing in procession.

new *asafo* groups are increasing in number. I see this social phenomenon as reflecting postcolonial changes. It seems that in recent years, the social forces of schism exist only in the chieftaincy disputes and no longer exist among *asafo* companies. This may indicate that Fanti society has been shifting toward unity as part of the general social change which followed independence. This shift has also involved changes in the traditional roles of the military organizations and the incorporation of new musical genres into their repertoire. I found this new idea very attractive; it suggested post-colonial themes for future research.

My field diary dated 9 September 1998, two days before I left Cape Coast, reads roughly as follows:

> Two opposing social forces have operated in the Fanti society of Ghana over the past few hundred years: one force tends to split the society into several factions and the other to deter schism and to unite various factions. The former force is found in the continual disputes over chieftaincy and the long-standing feuds between *asafo* companies. On the other hand, the latter force operates at the annual festival *Fetu Afahye* and in the matrilineal *ebusua*, in that the festival emphasizes the importance of peace and unity and the *ebusua* lessens the tensions between *asafo* companies by making members of the patrilineal companies matri-lineally related to each other. These social forces find cultural expression in two important genres of music: the military drum ensemble *asafo* and the royal drum ensemble *fontomfrom*. Analysis of song texts reveals a contrast between the two genres. *Asafo* song texts generally deal with conflicts between companies, whereas *fontomfrom* song texts are mainly designed for entertainment and contribute to uniting different factions by entertaining them together on festive occasions. In recent years, however, a new development has been observed as a result of social change after independence. As the conflicts between *asafo* companies have ended and the society has been shifting toward unity, new music and dance groups have been formed within the companies to perform the genres of music more asso-ciated with social unity. The end of *asafo* conflicts and the subsequent rise of "new" genres of music provide another illustration of close connections between social factors and music making in Fanti society.

MY PLACE IN ETHNOMUSICOLOGY

During my field research, I was aware that schism and unity, though phrased differently by different authors, were one of the classic anthropological topics in African studies. Evans-Pritchard (1940) and Victor Turner (1957) in earlier years, and Eugene Men-donsa (1979) and Frederick Quinn (1980) more recently—to mention only a few—all inquired into this aspect of African societies. Mendonsa, for instance, shows in his analysis of Sisala society in Ghana that the fission of their patrilineage does not mean a negation of kinship; rather, the new group is incorporated into a more inclusive higher level of the segmentary lineage system. What can be viewed as a split actually indicates unity at a higher level in this social system. But what I do not find in these African studies is the link between such social structures and music making. My own ethnomusicological study will, I hope, help to bridge this gap (figure 6).

An attempt similar to mine can be found in another geographical area: this is Thomas Turino's work (1989, 1993) on the Aymara in Peru. In his ethnography, Turino demonstrates the significance of what he describes as the "coherence" of social and musical styles. The Aymara social pattern is marked by a "solidarity/factionalism para-dox." The Aymara have a strong sense of group solidarity on the one hand, but on the other hand they show a tendency toward internal factionalism. Turino shows that these contrasting aspects of Aymara society find parallel expression in their music making.

FIGURE 6   The author with John B. Crayner, cultural organizer and *fɔntɔmfrɔm* player, in Mankessim, Central Region, August 2000.

Turino's analysis of Aymara society coincides with my analysis of the Fanti in two significant ways. First, in both societies there are two inherent contradictory tendencies—toward schism ("factionalism") and unity ("solidarity"). Second, in both societies these tendencies are expressed in music making. There is, however, a considerable difference between the two societies. Whereas Turino's analysis shows that the contradictory tendencies reflect and are reflected in the process of music making at a sonic, structural level, my research found a relationship between social practice and music making only at the semantic level. That is, Fanti society illustrates this coherence only with reference to song texts that reveal the contrasting aspects and sentiments of the culture (Tsukada 2001b).

APPENDIX: SONG TEXTS

Asafo songs

Example 1

Mbofra nketseketse.	A small group of children!
Mpanyin nketseketse.	A small group of elders!
Akyem bi resan me.	Some birds are disturbing me.
Na mennyi nan na matu.	I have no legs. I cannot chase the birds.
Ɔyaa, Ɔyaa. Ɔdom nkɔsua a. Ɔyaa.	A crowd should carry him.
Yie a, yie a.	Okay, okay.

In this first song, a person named Ɔyaa calls upon elders and children and complains, "The birds are noisy. I want to chase them. But I cannot because I have no legs." Another person hears this and says to the elders and children, "Carry him, then." Here, Ɔyaa is described as a handicapped man who would not be able to fight in a war. When members of one *asafo* company sing this song to another company, the latter will understand that they are being compared to Ɔyaa. Thus the song is provocative.

Example 2

Abura, hɛnko edaano.	Abura people! Our fight the other day.
Yɛko. Yɛnsuro.	We fight. We do not fear.

| *Bisa opanyi.* | Ask your elders (if you should fight). |
| *Yɛ ko. Yɛnsuro.* | We fight. We do not fear. |

This song is based on a historical battle between the Nkum company of Cape Coast and a company of Abura. The members of the Nkum company sing this song to provoke the Abura people, saying that the Abura should ask their elders whether they should fight such a strong company as Nkum.

Fɔntɔmfrɔm songs

Example 1

Afahye aba o.	Afahye has come.
Oguaaman Aye yi.	The state of Cape Coast is fine.
Yaa, Yaa. Kwesi da. Kese da.	Yes, yes. Kwesi's day! A great day!
Yaa, Yaa, Ako o. Yaa, Yaa.	Yes, yes. Repeat! Yes, yes.

This is one of a few songs whose association with unity may be explicit. It is a well-known song performed at the *Fetu Afahye* festival. "Kwesi" is a man noted for the contributions he made to the development of Cape Coast long ago. The general implication of the song is as follows: The festival has begun. Many people have arrived from afar to attend it. Our country is now in perfect shape. This is a great day, the day of the great man—Kwesi.

Example 2

Fa mpaboa bahyia me.	Put on your shoes and meet me.
I am a boy, yie.	I am a boy, yes.
Fa mpaboa bahyia me.	Put on your shoes and meet me.
Na nyinara ye mbosabo.	Many stones on the ground.

In recent years, "highlife," a style of Ghanaian popular music, has been introduced into the *fɔntɔmfrɔm* ensemble. This song is one example. In it, a boy asks his girlfriend to join him in a "highlife" dance: "Put on your shoes and meet me"—that is, dance with me. "There are a lot of stones on the ground."

REFERENCES

Afahye Planning Committee. 1995. *Oguaa Fetu Afahye 1995.* Cape Coast: Africa Best Enterprise.

Archival Records. n.d. ADM 23/l/932 and ADM 23/1/280. Central Regional Archives Office, Cape Coast.

Boahen, A. Adu. 1965a. "Asante and Fante A.D. 1000–1800." In *A Thousand Years of West African History*, ed. J. F. Ade Ajaya and Ian Espie, 165–190. Ibadan: Ibadan University Press.

———. 1965b. "Asante, Fante, and the British, 1800–1880." In *A Thousand Years of West African History*, ed. J. F. Ade Ajaya and Ian Espie, 346–363. Ibadan: Ibadan University Press.

Buah, F. K. 1980. *A History of Ghana.* London: Macmillan Educational.

Christensen, James. 1954. *Double Descent among the Fanti.* New Haven: Human Relations Area Files.

Claridge, Walton. 1915. *A History of the Gold Coast and Ashanti.* 2 vols. London: John Murray.

Evans-Pritchard, E. E. 1940. *The Nuer: A Description of the Modes of Livelihood and Political Institutions of a Nilotic People.* Oxford: Oxford University Press.

Fynn, John. 1971. *Asante and Its Neighbours c. 1700–1807.* London: Longmans.

Graham, James E., Jr. 1994. *Cape Coast in History.* Cape Coast: Anglican Printing Press.

Iida Tadasumi. 1936. "Chusei Arabiajin no Onga-kukan (The Arabic Philosophy of Music in the Medieval Period)." *Toyo Ongaku Kenkyu* (Journal of the Society for Research in Asiatic Music) 1st series:91–110.

Johnston, Kwesi. 1963. "The Asafu in Cape Coast History." Unpublished paper.

Kishibe Shigeo. 1937. "Saiko no Indo Ongaku-sho ni tsuite (The Oldest Book on Music in India)." *Toyo Ongaku Kenkyu* (Journal of the Society for Research in Asiatic Music) 2nd series:62–76.

Koizumi Fumio. 1958. *Nihon Dento Ongaku no Kenkyu (A Study of Japanese Traditional Music).* Tôkyô: Ongaku no Tomosha.

Kurosawa Takatomo. 1952. "Takasago Bunun-zoku no Kyukin to Godan Onkai Hassei no Shisa (The Origin of Pentatonic Scale and the Musical Bow among the Bunun of Taiwan)." *Toyo Ongaku Kenkyu* (Journal of the Society for Research in Asiatic Music) 10–11:18–32.

Mendonsa, Eugene. 1979. "Economic, Residential, and Ritual Fission of Sisala Domestic Groups, Ghana." *Africa* 49(4):388–407.

Okyere, Vincent N. 1997. *Ghana: A Historical Survey.* Cape Coast: Catholic Mission Press.

Quinn, Frederick. 1980. "Beti Society in the Nineteenth Century." *Africa* 50(3):293–304.

Tanabe Hisao. 1925. *Nihon Ongaku no Kenkyu (A Study of Japanese Music).* Tôkyô: Kyobunsha.

Tracey, Hugh. 1973. *Catalogue: The Sound of Africa Series. 210 LP Records of Music and Songs from Central, Eastern, and Southern Africa.* 2 vols. Roodepoort, South Africa: International Library of African Music.

Tsukada Kenichi. 1980. "Taiwan Sanchi Bununzoku no Kokin to Waonshoho no Kigen (The Jew's Harp and the Origin of Triadic Harmony among the Bunun of Taiwan)." *Toyo Ongaku Kenkyu* (Journal of the Society for Research in Asiatic Music) 45:1–44.

———. 1983. "Bamboo Flutes and Iatmul Musical Heterogeneity." *Bikmaus* 4:85–92.

———. 1988. "Luvale Perceptions of Mukanda in Discourse and Music." Ph.D.dissertation, Queen's University of Belfast. Ann Arbor: University Microfilms International. (DA8917245)

———. 1995. "Fanti Drumming from a 'Phon-aesthetic' Perspective." Paper presented at the Thirty-Third World Conference of the International Council for Traditional Music, 5–11 January, Canberra.

———. 1997. "Drumming, Onomatopoeia, and Sound Symbolism among the Luvale of Zambia." In *Cultures sonores d'Afrique*, ed. J. Kawada, 349–393. Tôkyô: Recherches sur les Langues et Cultures d'Asie et d'Afrique.

———. 1998a. "Music and Education: Iatmul." In *The Garland Encyclopedia of World Music*. Vol. 9, *Australia and the Pacific Islands*, ed. Adrienne Kaeppler and Jacob Love, 257–258. New York: Garland.

———. 1998b. "Harmony in Luvale Music of Zambia." In *The Garland Encyclopedia of World Music*. Vol. 1, *Africa*, ed. Ruth M. Stone, 722–743. New York: Garland.

———. 2001a. "Japanese Drums Meet African Drums: A Cross-Cultural Study of 'Phonaesthetic' Aspects of Japanese and Fanti Music Cultures." In *Intercultural Music*, Vol. 3, ed. Cynthia Tse Kimberlin and Akin Euba, 149–168. Richmond, Va.: MRI.

———. 2001b. "Asafo and Fontomfrom: Conflict and Unity in Fante Society of Ghana." In *Cultures sonores d'Afrique*, 2: *Aspects dynamiques*, ed. Junzo Kawada and Kenichi Tsukada, 31–59. Hiroshima: Hiroshima City University.

Turino, Thomas. 1989. "The Coherence of Social Style and Musical Creation among the Aymara in Southern Peru." *Ethnomusicology* 33(1):1–30.

———. 1993. *Moving Away from Silence: Music of the Peruvian Altiplano and the Experience of Urban Migration*. Chicago, Ill.: University of Chicago Press.

Turner, Victor. 1957. *Schism and Continuity in an African Society*. Manchester: Manchester University Press.

Southeast Asia

R. Anderson Sutton

Working as an Ethnomusicologist
Recording and Record Keeping
Informants, Teachers, Friends
My Scholarship in Ethnomusicology

My musical interests—like those of many other Americans growing up in the 1960s—developed in several directions. I heard not only a great amount of Western art music, top-forty rock and roll, Anglo-American folk music, and Broadway show tunes, but also early recordings of West African music (78-rpm disks made by Richard Waterman) and my grandfather singing Blackfoot songs he had learned during his many visits to the Blackfoot reservation in Montana. (A Philadelphia lawyer of British and Scandinavian background, he provided *pro bono* legal service for the Blackfoot and, he told us, had been made an "honorary" member of the Blackfoot nation.) My early formal training in music had been in choral music and classical piano. During my teenage years I abandoned the study of classical piano to learn folk guitar and, soon after, rock guitar and organ; but I returned to classical study as a music major at Wesleyan University, where, unsuspecting, I was to be hit full-force by the marvel of the world's musical diversity.

My formal training in ethnomusicology began unexpectedly, as it probably has begun for many. In 1968, I was among the eighty or so undergraduates at Wesleyan enrolled in the introductory course in music history, during which the march of Western music history through the periods was suddenly interrupted for two intensive weeks devoted to South Indian classical music, under the inspired instruction of the late Jon Higgins. The music program at Wesleyan was so committed to what the faculty called "world music" (a term denoting an inventory of the world's musical traditions, not the hybrid combinations of today's "world music" or "world beat"), that even this standard course on Western music history took a radical detour to Madras to study *raga* and *tala*, *vina* (*vīṇai*) and *mridangam*, *kriti* and *varṇam*, and their cultural contexts. These two exhilarating weeks redefined my interests in music. Already intending to major in music, I determined at this point to explore "world music"—or "world musics"—including South Indian, in greater depth.

At Wesleyan I took academic courses in Indian civilization and North and South Indian music theory, and two years of lessons in *vina* from Kalyanakrishna Bhagavatar, a master musician from Madras. My music curriculum also included piano lessons and courses in counterpoint, piano literature, Schenkerian analysis, and electronic music (John Cage was in residence then); the world music survey (with Robert E. Brown and numerous visiting artists from around the world); and, during my senior

The work that many ethnomusicologists do involves imposing oneself as politely and congenially as possible in a hitherto unfamiliar musical situation, speaking with the musicians, reading what is available, learning through musical participation, making recordings for transcription and analysis, and writing up one's findings.

year, beginning Javanese *gamelan* performance (with the late Prawotosaputro). I had heard this music periodically since my freshman year but had at first found it both confusing and rather uncompelling.

Choosing graduate study in ethnomusicology over law school, I was offered a teaching assistantship at the University of Hawaii in 1971 and, at age twenty-one, found myself moving a quarter of the way around the globe and leading discussion sections with undergraduates of many diverse Asian and Pacific backgrounds, often on the music of their heritage. It was at the University of Hawaii—under the guidance of Barbara Smith, the founder of the program there; and two relatively new hires, Ricardo Trimillos and Hardja Susilo—that I cut my teeth as an ethnomusicologist. Along with training in how to teach undergraduates about unfamiliar musics, I had seminars in ethnomusicological theory, field methodology, and particular traditions (Javanese *gamelan*, Japanese theater music); courses in performance (Hawaiian chant and *hula*, Okinawan *uta sansin*, Javanese *gamelan*); and, along with all the graduate students in the ethnomusicology program, courses in languages and area studies. Despite my earlier interest in Indian music, the presence of Hardja Susilo and the rare opportunity to study Javanese language (offered as a course there for the first time that year) propelled me toward a specialization in the music of Java, an interest that has sustained me now for thirty years. I also took Dutch in order to be able to read historical sources on Indonesia.

The proseminar in ethnomusicology, taught by Barbara Smith, had all eight of the new ethnomusicology graduate students reading Bruno Nettl's *Theory and Method in Ethnomusicology* (1964), Alan Merriam's *The Anthropology of Music* (1964), and Mantle Hood's new work *The Ethnomusicologist* (1971). Each of us conducted a semester-long field project in the community, writing up results in a lengthy paper and presenting a distillation or portion in a formal conference at the end of the semester. I joined an Okinawan music study group, attended rehearsals and a recital ("music party"), made recordings, took photographs, and conducted interviews.

This model, modified and expanded, remains "the work" that I, and many of my colleagues, continue to do. It involves imposing oneself as politely and congenially as possible in a hitherto unfamiliar musical situation, speaking with the musicians, reading what is available, learning through musical participation, making recordings for transcription and analysis, and writing up one's findings within the frame of theoretical issues of interest to (1) the scholarly world of ethnomusicologists, (2) scholars of the area or "culture" studied, and (3) the musicians of the area or "culture" in question.

Like many of my fellow students, I was fortunate in being able to conduct research over an extended period (ten months in central Java) before writing my master's thesis at the University of Hawaii. My entry into the musical world of central Java was smoothed by two major factors. First, I had studied one year of Javanese language and two years of Indonesian beforehand and could carry on conversations fairly easily in the latter. Second, unlike many first-time researchers, I was part of a large study group, led by Hardja Susilo and Ricardo Trimillos, and thus was among more than twenty fellow students as we all made adjustments to living and studying in Java for ten weeks during the summer of 1973. I returned to central Java without the large group six months later to complete my master's research, having already established the contacts and made many of the musical acquaintances I needed for the project—on the Javanese *gambang* (xylophone) and its music. I worked closely with three musicians of different aesthetic orientations and wound up basing most of my thesis on the playing and explications by Suhardi, a fine all-around *gamelan* musician who went on to become the director of the *gamelan* musicians at the national radio station in Yogyakarta. As advised by the faculty at Hawaii, in my thesis I aimed at description first, with theory "growing out of the data." (The intellectual world of anthropology and ethnomusicology has since raised doubts about this sort of approach, based as it is on a presumed but elusive objectivity.) Thus, I aimed at answering questions about Javanese music and testing Javanese musical theories by analyzing performances I had recorded and transcribed.

Following the completion of my thesis (Sutton 1974), I taught music courses as a lecturer in 1975–1976 at the University of Hawaii and at Windward Community College in Kaneohe, including "Music in World Cultures" (a survey), "Music in Modern America," and "Introduction to Western Music History," as well as Javanese *gamelan* performance. In the summer of 1976 I participated in an eight-week workshop on Okinawan music at the University of Hawaii, with four visiting artists from Okinawa (this resulted in an article on Okinawan drumming published in 1980).

Pursuing my doctorate at the University of Michigan in 1976, I was to have my intellectual horizons widened and my assumptions challenged first and foremost by my adviser, Judith Becker, and by the linguist Alton Becker, not only through exposure to their own interpretive and linguistic approaches but also through their guidance in reading works of interpretive cultural anthropology (especially by Clifford Geertz and others) and oral tradition (especially by Albert Lord and Walter Ong), and works by Javanese theorists (especially Martopangrawit and Sindusawarno) and other scholars who focused on Indonesia (especially Benedict Anderson and James Peacock). I continued to study Indonesian and Javanese and took an intensive year of Dutch aimed specifically at reading scholarly Dutch. As I worked my way through various courses in Western music history and theory in preparation for doctoral preliminary exams, I also prepared for a more theoretical dissertation. Again I chose to conduct my research in Yogyakarta, working primarily with the same musicians I had studied with earlier. The result was a dissertation (1982) that explored and theorized about the nature of variation in Javanese *gamelan* music, which I interpreted (perhaps too easily) as an aesthetic manifestation of certain deep-seated cultural values: steadiness, limited adventurousness, and group harmony over individual virtuosic display. In retrospect, although these values and their connections to the music were often suggested, indirectly or even explicitly, by musicians and other Javanese, they indicate a cultural essentialism that recent thinking has found highly problematic—simplistic and potentially dangerous in its sense of Javanese "otherness."

Of the many teachers with whom I was privileged to study, I identify six who were especially influential with regard to my professional development: Barbara Smith, who stressed ethics and hard work from the very beginning; Ricardo Trimillos, who helped me to understand the personal dynamics of cross-cultural research; Hardja Susilo, whose long experience in the United States made him an ideal intermediary and who not only taught me much about Javanese music and dance but smoothed the path for my study and residence in his native Java; Alton Becker and Judith Becker, whose insightful interpretations of Javanese arts and aesthetics inspired much of my own research, beginning in 1978 with my first published article, on variation in Javanese *gendèr* (metallophone), and continuing through my dissertation and many subsequent articles; and Suhardi, a musician of consummate skill not only as a performer but as a creative thinker and explicator of Javanese *gamelan* performance as it evolved from the 1960s through the 1990s.

WORKING AS AN ETHNOMUSICOLOGIST

After my first field research working with Okinawan musicians in Honolulu in 1971, nearly all of my ethnomusicological work has involved extensive fieldwork, and nearly all of that has been in Indonesia. During most of 1974 I lived in a small house in the heart of Yogyakarta and set up a weekly schedule of activities. On Mondays and Wednesdays I spent a good part of the day at Suhardi's home, where I took lessons in *gambang* and *gendèr* and talked about *gamelan* music theory and his experiences as a musician. His wife, an accomplished *pesindhèn* (female singer), occasionally sang during my lessons and also provided us with a meal. On Mondays I would arrive in the afternoon and stay through dinner, after which we would ride our bicycles to the "Uyon-uyon Mana Suka," a weekly *gamelan* concert broadcast live by the Yogyakarta branch of the national radio station (RRI), in which Suhardi performed. Once or twice a week, I also participated in rehearsals and occasional RRI broadcasts of *gamelan* music with two amateur groups led by Suhardi: Ngudyo Wiromo and Hudyana Widya Mardawa. These rehearsals and broadcasts gave me an opportunity to play the *gendèr* and *gambang* parts I had been learning from Suhardi (figure 1). On Tuesdays and Thursdays I took lessons in drumming and *gambang* at the home of Prajasudirja, a former RRI musician who also taught *gamelan* music at several performing arts high schools. These lessons lasted from one to two hours. On Fridays I took lessons on *bonang* (a gong-chime) at the home of Sastrapustaka, who lived down a small alley just across the street from my house (figure 2). He was in his sixties, a kind and gentle person who knew much about Yogyakarta palace culture, often borrowing books from the palace library (where he was an official court servant) and helping me learn to interpret them. I had lessons in the morning and would usually return on Friday evenings, from about 8:30 to 11:30, for a weekly rehearsal that Sastrapustaka held in his living room, a modest space filled almost entirely with his *sléndro* (five-tone) *gamelan*. In an effort to gain fluency in Javanese, I took private lessons in conversational Javanese twice a week (on Saturday and Tuesday afternoons) and insisted on speaking Javanese as much as possible during my lessons and other encounters with Javanese.

When I returned for doctoral research in 1979, I took the same approach—private music lessons, participation in several amateur groups, lessons in Javanese language,

FIGURE 1   The author playing *gendèr* at the national radio station (RRI) in Yogyakarta, August 1974, with members of the music group Ngudyo Wiromo (Narimo and Sukadji), directed by his teacher Suhardi (not shown). Photo by Sukardi.

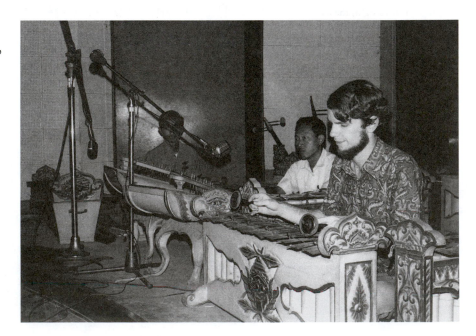

and attendance at performances and rehearsals (figure 3). The relationships I had established in 1974 and had maintained through correspondence, particularly with Suhardi and Sastrapustaka, were very solid. Although I recorded and studied with others as well, my return to work with these same teachers was a strong indication of my commitment to them as instructors and to the serious study of Javanese *gamelan* (figure 4). For my doctoral research, however, I traveled more widely, beginning to explore different regional styles of *gamelan* music (which, after further research in the 1980s, became the subject of my first book). I also interviewed local scholars in related fields: literature, anthropology, and history. And in order to gain a historical perspective on the tradition I was examining, I spent some of my time in libraries, reading, transcribing, and photocopying manuscripts, treatises, books of notation, and other works by Javanese and Dutch scholars.

FIGURE 2   One of the author's *gamelan* teachers, Sastrapustaka, demonstrating *bonang* technique in his living room, Panembahan, Yogyakarta, June 1974. Photo by the author.

FIGURE 3   Left to right, the author, Brian Dumaine (his brother-in-law), Peggy Choy (his wife), Hartono and Nugroho (his children), and Suhardi, September 1979. Photo by Caroline Sutton Dumaine.

FIGURE 4   Suhardi; his wife and children, Istinah, Jumadi, Rusmi; and the author, departing after fifteen months of fieldwork, at Adisutjipto airport, Yogyakarta, May 1980. Photo by Peggy Choy.

On subsequent trips to Java in 1983, 1984, 1986, 1989, and 1991, I stayed for shorter periods (one to three months) and focused on a specific research topic each time. I continued to consult my former teachers but now spent most of my time traveling to different locales in central and eastern Java, observing performances, and interviewing musicians (and not taking lessons). During my longer stays in the 1970s I had made occasional use of local libraries but had devoted most of my time to direct observation, conversations, and lessons. On the subsequent trips I spent more time in libraries, seeking contemporary and historical sources related to Javanese music and its contexts of performance. Some of the sources were in Javanese script, handwritten and printed, others in Indonesian or in Dutch.

In 1993, my interests in Indonesia's cultural plurality and my awareness of a lack of scholarship on performance outside the Javanese-Balinese-Sundanese mainstream led me to shift my main research site to the Makassar region of South Sulawesi. I arrived with little knowledge of local musical practice and with the names of only two contacts. Through these first two individuals (Mukhlis Paeni and A. Halilintar Lathief), I was able to meet many local musicians and dancers, attend numerous rehearsals and performances, and be accepted formally as a student of Abdul Muin Daeng Mile, one of the area's top drummers. Yet from the beginning this was a kind of fieldwork very different from the research I had conducted in Java, particularly on my two long trips in the 1970s. Each year in the 1990s, I was able to stay only for one to three months at a time and was busy every day with many activities, especially interviews. Although I studied drum in long sessions, interspersed with wide-ranging conversation and often a meal, I was not trying to attain a professional level of performance in preparation for teaching Makassarese drum ensemble music (with *shawm*, gong, and slit gong) in the United States. I took language lessons in Makassarese but devoted much of the lesson time to working on translations of song texts and discussing local performing arts terminology, rather than attaining conversational fluency. Here I expanded my inquiry beyond my initial interests in distinctive local traditions to observe and interview pop musicians, owners and technicians of local recording companies, and radio and television staff members. I was concerned primarily with the cultural politics of this area—how local musicians and dancers position themselves relative to others in the province of South Sulawesi and relative to the larger world of Javanese-dominated Indonesia and the international community.

In 1998, I initiated research on musical arts on Indonesian television, particularly popular music (live shows and video clips), from MTV to regional music in Java and South Sulawesi. A day of research now finds me at television studios, in executive offices, reading television tabloids, chatting with people about their television viewing habits, and (of course) watching and dubbing music television shows.

In addition to my research in Indonesia, I spent several short periods of research in Honolulu, resulting in publications on Okinawan drumming (the article mentioned earlier), the history of Okinawan music in Hawaii, and Korean music in Hawaii. These were based on lessons and interviews with musicians (and dancers) who lived in Hawaii and on my archival research in Honolulu.

RECORDING AND RECORD KEEPING

At many of my lessons in Java and South Sulawesi, I used a small Sony cassette recorder to record individual parts and some conversation, but most of my verbal documentation has been in the form of note-taking. I entered all my jottings from lessons, performances, interviews, and subsequent reflections in chronological order in a field journal *cum* personal diary. I tended not to write long personal entries, other than reflections on my research, though I tried to force myself to write at least something every day and to keep at least a cursory record of my activities other than research. These I supplemented in Java with several books in which I compiled notation of the main melody (*balungan*) for Javanese pieces, organized by tuning system and by *pathet* classification. These books were essential for participation in the study groups I attended. In thin books of graph paper, I made transcriptions of parts I had recorded at lessons, though these were for analysis and private practice and were not used in performance or group rehearsals. In addition, I kept a separate notebook for language study, consisting mostly of word and phrase lists in Javanese or Makassarese with definitions in a mixture of Indonesian and English.

The following excerpts from my field notebooks offer a taste of my approaches to writing in the field. The first three excerpts are from my first full year of *gamelan* study in Yogyakarta. The last is from a hectic day in Jakarta, which I spent telephoning and interviewing people to discuss music television there. I have added some explanations and translations in brackets.

1. Lesson on *gendèr* with Suhardi (4 March 1974):
Damping is a problem. My left hand is too eager to stop the keys. Mas Hardi [Suhardi] lets one ring until he has hit several others in fast playing, then remembers he has not damped it and does so. This makes the part more audible. He said the hands must not constantly rest on the keys but be above so that there is more sound when the keys are struck. He warned me that people whose wrists bend a lot are not such good *gendèr* players. The wrists must be loose, but don't damp too soon. Staccato should be only where it is specific to the pattern.

2. Before a *bonang* lesson, Sastrapustaka talks about the music for the sacred *Bedhaya Semang* dance (17 March 1974):
Pak Sas [Sastrapustaka] told me of *Gendhing Semang*, which he just made a copy of after a *sajèn* [offering] was performed. The *gérong* [choral vocal part] tells of Ratu Kidul's love affair with Sultan Agung, and as such is a sacred piece. It lasts three hours and is forty-three pages (three books!) in transcription. The old *niagas* [gamelan players] were afraid to rehearse it at first but after two times with no ill effects they were no longer afraid. The old *dalangs* [puppeteers] who air *wayang* [shadow puppets] were startled and were all talking about it. Pak Sas said the book containing the notation was old and covered with dust, and he scarcely dared open it even after asking the head *gamelan* musician. Another *sajèn* was

performed after Pak Sas's transnotation was completed. It has been rehearsed now six times.

3. Two brief reflections on *rasa* 'feeling' and *gambang* (a xylophone) by Suhardi (8 April 1974) and Prajasudirja (16 April 1974):

First, for Mas Hardi there is a difference between happy (*gembira*) pieces and classic pieces, even for *gambang*. For instance:

$$\dot{2}\ \dot{2}\ \dot{2}\ 5\ 3\ \dot{2}\ 1\ 6\ 55\text{-}5\text{-}\ 5\ 6\ 5\ 6\ 5\ 1 \qquad \text{for happy pieces}$$
$$2\ 2\ 2\ 5\ 3\ 2\ 1\ 6\ 5\ 5\ 2\ 5\ 6\ 1\ 2\ 1\ \text{-}$$

$$\dot{2}\ \dot{2}\ \dot{2}\ 5\ 3\ \dot{2}\ 1\ 6\ 5\ 5\ 6\ 5\ 6\ 1\ 5\ 6\ 1 \qquad \text{for classic pieces}$$
$$2\ 2\ 2\ 5\ 3\ 2\ 1\ 6\ 5\ 5\ 6\ 5\ 6\ 1\ 5\ 6\ 1$$

But in essence, [these are] the same pattern. It is the similarity in Javanese music which leads to the importance of small differences, such as this.

Second, according to Pak Praja [Prajasudirja], the *gambangan* [part played by the *gambang*] is the same for classic and happy pieces: *gambang biasa* [normal *gambang*] except for the use of fewer variations. Feeling comes from the piece itself, not *gambangan*. This is contrary to Mas Hardi's view! Is it old versus young? [Prajasudirja is in his sixties, Suhardi in his thirties.] Yogya versus Solo? [These are two rival court traditions of Yogyakarta and Surakarta.]

4. An afternoon in Jakarta (11 August 1999):

I call Djaduk on a hand phone. [Djaduk Ferianto is a popular composer and performer of experimental music using mostly indigenous instruments; like many young stars and businesspeople, he carries a cell phone, in Indonesia called hand phone.] He is in Yogya but heading back to Jakarta for RCTI's [private television station's] HUT [Hari Ulang Tahun—anniversary] and *Dua Warna* [*Two Colors*— the name of a television show featuring a mixture of Djaduk's music with pop music by various stars]. I mention Suhardi [my *gamelan* teacher] and MSPI [Masyarakat Seni Pertunjukan Indonesia—the Indonesian Performing Arts Society, whose scholarly meeting I am planning to attend the following month, in Bali], and he becomes very apologetic and defensive. [He tells me that] he is not a purist, not an "art for art" guy but interested in art for *masyarakat* [society, the people]; he wants to *merubah iklim pergaulan dalam kesenian* [change the atmosphere for interaction in the arts]. His Kua Etnika [As if Ethnic—the name of his music group] will perform at a percussion festival at TMII [Taman Mini Indonesia Indah—a cultural park on the outskirts of Jakarta] on 16–17 September. He seems sure that MSPI members are against his commercial and experimental approach to music. He also mentions Harry Roesli [a politically active experimental musician based in Bandung] as a big influence on him.

The connection is cut off, and I am late for my appointment with D. Tumiwa, so I head there (Gedung Perfilman Indonesia, Lantai III). I interview Danny [Tumiwa] at [the Indonesian offices of] MTV at 3:00 P.M.—he is very gracious and articulate. It has been a great year for MTV—the staff has many ideas for expansion, and MTV still has one and a half years of contract with AN [ANteve, the private television station that carries terrestrial broadcasts of MTV Southeast Asia daily]. He eventually wants a twenty-four-hour channel for MTV Indonesia. Here are notes from my conversation with him: Sony launches a new label for *dangdut* [a form of lowbrow Indonesian popular music]. Warner Music already has a *dangdut* album by Cici Paramida (album—*Wulan Merindu* or *Wulan Asmara*?). UI seminar [on *dangdut*] at Fakultas ISIP [University of Indonesia seminar at the Sociology and Political Science Faculty], 250 attendants,

Elvy Sukaesih sang a few songs. "MTV *tidak pernah* subtitle" [MTV never sub-titles]. Sarah [Sechan] and Jamie [Aditya] announcers for MTV *Salam Dangdut* [new MTV Southeast Asia show devoted to *dangdut*, formerly eschewed by MTV as too unsophisticated]. MTV Asia split to MTV Southeast Asia and MTV Korea as of 1 January 1999. Leads to much faster decision making.

Obviously, research on the media industry and popular culture yields a different kind of field notes or, more accurately, a different feel. My relatively short periods of research on television (three to four weeks at a time) have been compensated for by my determination to fill every day with as much activity as possible, resulting in a disinclination to write much in the way of reflection in my field notebook. Yet I still try to document what I have learned in interviews, describing performances. And the notebook continues to be, in my estimation, the single most valuable item at the end of any field trip.

Most of the audio recordings I have made, in Java and South Sulawesi, have been for study rather than for commercial release. Primarily, this has meant recording my teachers at lessons or sometimes assembling a small group to perform pieces I wished to have for future study. In Java in 1974, after my first month of attendance at the weekly RRI broadcasts, I received permission from the musicians and the radio per-sonnel to record these sessions with my monaural Sony casette recorder. I usually sat near the *gambang* or *gendèr* and was thereby able to record these "soft" instruments relatively clearly within the thick texture of the overall ensemble. I seldom attempted to make more balanced recordings of whole ensembles in concert in Java, although I brought a Uher stereo recorder with two fine Sennheiser cardioid microphones in the 1970s and a Sony Walkman Pro and Marantz PMD 430 with Sony electret condensor microphones in the 1980s and 1990s. The commercial cassette industry was booming from the 1970s into the early 1990s in Java, with what seemed like a new release almost every week of *gamelan* pieces by top groups and of the many varieties of theater accompanied by *gamelan* (*wayang kulit*, *kethoprak*, *wayang orang*, and so on).

In South Sulawesi, where the local recording companies have concentrated on popular music with Western scales and harmonies, I recorded more widely, either at sessions I arranged, or, with permission, at rehearsals and performances. I also used a Sony Handycam Hi-8 video camcorder to record performances and rehearsals of local music and dance. A compact disk to be packaged with my forthcoming book on South Sulawesi contains a number of the sessions I recorded, along with selections of local popular music from commercial cassettes.

INFORMANTS, TEACHERS, FRIENDS

The basis of my fieldwork has been personal interactions beyond those of interviewer and interviewee or student and teacher. The long hours I spent with Suhardi—formal "lesson" time, eating, and attending weekly broadcasts—enabled me to establish a very close relationship, which continued until his death (in August 2000) and was in a sense ambiguous, involving both the distance between student and teacher and a deep friendship. I would not claim this kind of friendship with any other of the musicians I have known, though my drum teacher in South Sulawesi, Daeng Mile, and I have shared a lot (figure 5). From my first extended period of interaction with Suhardi in 1974, I was aware of the structural imbalance in a relationship between myself, a comparatively well-funded foreign researcher seeking an advanced degree, and a poorly paid older musician (Suhardi was ten years my senior). Add to this our different postcolonial experiences as a white from the West and a Javanese in the Netherlands' most famous former colony. To some extent we navigated through these contrasts by means of humor, self-effacement, and an evolving familiarity and concern for each other's families. (My wife also studied *rebab* and singing with Suhardi in the 1970s,

FIGURE 5   The author taking notes at a drum
lesson with the master musician Abdul Muis
Daeng Mile, at the latter's home in the village of
Kalaserena, Gowa, South Sulawesi, August
1996. Photo by Daeng Bombong.

before we were married and later when she accompanied me to Java while I was doing
my doctoral research.) However complicated my relationship with Suhardi was, we
came, through extended interaction, to know each other deeply, learning much from
one another that went far beyond music. We spent hours talking about matters of
health, particularly after he was diagnosed with diabetes in the late 1980s. Earlier, we
often talked about sports and leisure time. For example, we shared a passion for fishing,
although we come from radically different fishing traditions. I did my best to explain
to him the practice and philosophy of fly fishing; he took me several times to nearby
rivers where, with bait, we caught small local fish for dinner. He taught me serious
badminton, which we played (and at which I almost always lost) after nearly every
lesson during 1979–1980.

As I began to work in other parts of Java, in South Sulawesi, and most recently
among television technicians and popular musicians in Jakarta and elsewhere, I continued to visit Suhardi on every trip to Indonesia, take part in his Sunday rehearsal,
and add a little to my knowledge of Javanese *gamelan* music. He told me frankly that
I could learn much more, but he seemed to understand that the nature of my research
compelled me to go beyond Javanese *gamelan* as he knew and practiced it.

The other teachers I worked with in Yogyakarta—Sastrapustaka and Prajasudirja—were both much older than I. Our interactions were mostly limited to music,
with me listening and watching, then imitating; we would then discuss aspects of
performance practice and theory. With Sastrapustaka, though, discussion sometimes
roamed more widely, often including historical and literary sources.

A second Javanese musician with whom I felt rapport from our first meeting, in
1983, is Rasito, who is almost exactly my age (less than a year younger) and has
contributed greatly to my knowledge of *gamelan* practice in the Banyumas region.
Despite a grueling schedule of teaching at the local high school of performing arts
(SMKI Banyumas) and drumming for the region's most popular and most active
shadow puppeteer (Ki Sugino), Rasito found time not merely to answer my questions
but to do his best to bring me into his musical world. Now, fifteen years after my
research with him, we write and occasionally talk on the telephone; and twice during
the 1990s he was able to come to the United States to teach, once for eight months
with me at the University of Wisconsin-Madison. (I had suggested that Suhardi be
invited as a visiting artist at the University of Michigan during my doctoral study

there, but he declined the offer, citing his extreme apprehension about traveling even in Indonesia, let alone about living abroad for a semester or a year in a place where the temperature might dip below 18 degrees Celsius.)

My decision to take on an extended research project in South Sulawesi in the 1990s has no doubt struck the Javanese with whom I worked and studied as a curious development. With so much more to learn about Javanese music, *gamelan* and other genres, why my sudden focus on Makassarese music? These musical genres, though admittedly "Indonesian," seem quite strange to many Javanese, particularly those most devoted to *gamelan* music. And to some extent, I sense that performers I have come to know in South Sulawesi may be wary of my extended earlier study of (and thus my devotion to) Javanese music and my continued involvement with it as a teacher and writer. Yet my encounters with Daeng Mile in South Sulawesi have been unencumbered, it would seem, as he has worked with me on the difficult repertoire of drum music for Makassarese ritual and dance (*pakarena* and *salonreng*). Although I have made no pretense of starting a study group or of performing Makassarese music in public in the United Staes, he has consistently tried to help me understand the complexities of his music, commenting politely on my progress without pretending that my level of proficiency merits public display. Although my comings and goings constitute rather unusual behavior for a student, he has always been willing to pick up where we left off the previous year and to push me as far along as our period of lessons allows. Like Suhardi, Daeng Mile is formally my teacher, and I am formally his student. We are almost the same age (he is one year my senior), but again the difference in status is vast, in terms of formal education and wealth. We have conversed extensively about a range of matters beyond music, from personal family concerns to local and global politics.

MY SCHOLARSHIP IN ETHNOMUSICOLOGY

When I began research on Javanese music, I did so in part because ethnomusicologists seemed to have emphasized other regions. Kunst's study of Java had taken place mostly in the 1920s, though the English-language version of his monumental *Music in Java* did not appear until 1949. Hood's book *The Nuclear Theme as a Determinant of Patet in Javanese Music* (1954) had appeared five years later. There had not been a major study of Javanese music in nearly twenty years, although Judith Becker's dissertation (1972) was under way and appeared during my graduate studies. My own early work, for my master's thesis and for my dissertation, involved close scrutiny of current musical practice, situated in the social and aesthetic world articulated by the Javanese. My first article dealt with the aesthetics of variation in *gendèr* playing (1978), using a structuralist grammatical paradigm directly inspired by Alton and Judith Becker's soon-to-be published grammar of Srepegan (1979 [1983]). In 1979, in an article that was a revised chapter of my master's thesis, I discussed two notions of underlying melody in Javanese *gamelan* playing: the *lagu* 'melody', a concept I had learned from Suhardi; and the *lagu batin* 'inner melody', described by Sumarsam in an article (1975) and in his subsequent master's thesis (1976, 1984).

Most of my publications in the 1980s related either to variation in central Javanese *gamelan* music or to Javanese regional *gamelan* traditions. The former included articles derived from my dissertation, on variation and composition (1987) and on individual variation (1988a). These issues can also be found in Kunst (1949 [1973]) and Becker (1972 [1980]). My regional focus resulted in articles on *gamelan* music in Yogyakarta (1984), in three regions peripheral to the mainstream court-derived traditions (Banyumas, Semarang, and East Java; 1985a), in the Banyumas region (1986a, 1986b), and as represented in the cassette industry (1985b). With these and a working paper on East Java (1988b), I laid the groundwork for my book *Traditions of Gamelan Music in Java* (1991). The articles and the book were intended to draw attention to the

FIGURE 6   The author giving a talk on popular music and politics in Indonesia, at a conference, "Performativity in Contemporary Indonesia," at the University of California at Riverside, 21 May 1999. Photo by Steve Walag/UCR Photographic Services.

plurality of Java's regional traditions, largely ignored in what was by then becoming a substantial body of scholarship on Javanese music. Beyond detailing divergent traditions in central and eastern Java, I explored the educational and media institutions that reflected and perpetuated some differences but effaced others. Other scholars, drawn by active performance experience in *gamelan* study groups in the United States, Europe, and Australia, as well as Javanese musician-scholars (especially Sumarsam, Sri Hastanto, and Rahayu Supanggah), greatly expanded the scholarly discourse on Javanese music in the 1980s and 1990s. The scholars whose work is most closely related to my own focus on performance practice and variation, going well beyond my dissertation, are Brinner (1995) and Perlman (1993); their studies in turn helped shape my article on Javanese improvisation (1998).

My decision to conduct research on South Sulawesi was a next step in moving my focus away from the center and eventually away from Indonesia's national center altogether. An explosion of literature in anthropology and ethnomusicology on hegemony, nationalism, and identity politics made South Sulawesi an especially attractive site from which to observe the politics of culture in Indonesia and the role of the performing arts (music and dance) in local transformations. The issues include a "festivalization" of culture, a secularization of the performing arts, attempts to reclaim the spirituality of these arts, the use of officially sanctioned frameworks (such as the national independence day) for performances by the opposition, the persistence of aesthetic power in local forms, and the role of local and national commercial media (recording and broadcasting) in shaping local arts, including pop music. With very little available in anything other than Indonesian language on the arts of this region, it has been necessary to provide some basic description, but the emphasis of my study has not been to reveal unique local musical practice in detail. Thus my approach has differed from that of two ethnomusicologists who have contributed greatly to knowledge of Indonesia outside Java and Bali in recent years: Margaret Kartomi (who has written many journal and encyclopedia articles and issued recordings) and Philip Yampolsky (primarily through his twenty-volume set of extensively documented compact disks, Smithsonian Folkways 1991–1999). I chose instead to concentrate on one area (the Makassarese region of South Sulawesi) and to situate the music and dance of this area in the contentious world of power hierarchies, as local artists vie for international, national, and local recognition. Though not specifically modeled on or inspired by

FIGURE 7   The author with masked dance (*topeng*) students and villagers, in Glagah Dowo, Tumpang, Malang District, East Java, July 1986. Photo by Mohamed Soleh Adipramono.

any particular earlier work in ethnomusicology, my study of South Sulawesi has drawn inspiration from Timothy Rice's *May It Fill Your Soul* (1994), Thomas Turino's *Moving Away from Silence* (1993), Mark Slobin's *Subcultural Sounds* (1992), and Peter Manuel's *Cassette Cultures* (1993), as well as from writings by Veit Erlmann, Jocelyne Guilbault, and Christopher Waterman.

My newest research focuses more on the media industry and investigates cultural flows between the global, national, and local levels. I am among a rapidly growing number of ethnomusicologists, not to mention anthropologists and cultural studies scholars from various other disciplines, who are interpreting the electronic media—content, production, and reception—within and across social and political boundaries (figure 6). When I look back to what drew me to ethnomusicology and to my formal training at Wesleyan, the University of Hawaii, and the University of Michigan, I would hardly have predicted that I would spend my research time interviewing television producers, technicians, and pop stars. Nevertheless, my grounding in technical knowledge of musical styles and in ethnographic method continues to serve as the basis for my research.

REFERENCES

Becker, Alton, and Judith Becker. 1979. "A Grammar of the Musical Genre Srepegan." *Journal of Music Theory* 23:1–43. (Reprint: 1983. *Asian Music* 14(1):30–72.)

Becker, Judith. 1972. "Traditional Music in Modern Java." Ph.D. dissertation, University of Michigan.

———. 1980. *Traditional Music in Modern Java: Gamelan in a Changing Society.* Honolulu: University of Hawaii Press.

Brinner, Ben. 1995. *Knowing Music, Making Music: Javanese Gamelan and the Theory of Musical Competence and Interaction.* Chicago: University of Chicago Press.

Hood, Mantle. 1954. *The Nuclear Theme as a Determinant of Patet in Javanese Music.* Groningen: J. B. Wolters.

———. 1971. *The Ethnomusicologist.* New York: McGraw-Hill.

Kunst, Jaap. 1949. *Music in Java: Its History, Its Theory, and Its Technique,* 2nd rev. ed. The Hague: Martinus Nijhoff. See also 3rd rev. enlarged ed. (1973).

Manuel, Peter. 1993. *Cassette Cultures: Popular Music and Technology in North India.* Chicago: University of Chicago Press.

Merriam, Alan P. 1964. *The Anthropology of Music.* Evanston, Ill.: Northwestern University Press.

Nettl, Bruno. 1964. *Theory and Method in Ethnomusicology.* New York: Free Press.

Perlman, Marc. 1993. "Unplayed Melodies: Music Theory in Postcolonial Java." Ph.D. dissertation, Wesleyan University.

Rice, Timothy. 1994. *May It Fill Your Soul: Experiencing Bulgarian Folk Music.* Chicago: University of Chicago Press.

Slobin, Mark. 1992. *Subcultural Sounds: Micromusics of the West.* Middletown, Conn.: Wesleyan University Press.

Sumarsam. 1975. "Inner Melody in Javanese Gamelan Music." *Asian Music* 7(1):3–13.

———. 1976. "Inner Melody in Javanese Gamelan Music." M.A. thesis, Wesleyan University. (Published in: 1984. *Karawitan: Source Readings in Javanese Gamelan and Vocal Music* 1:245-304. Ann Arbor: Center for South and Southeast Asian Studies, University of Michigan.)

Sutton, R. Anderson. 1974. "The Javanese Gambang and Its Music." M.A. thesis, University of Hawaii.

———. 1978. "Notes toward a Grammar of Variation in Javanese Gendèr Playing." *Ethnomusicology* 22(May):275–296.

———. 1979. "Concept and Treatment in Javanese Gamelan Music, with Reference to the Gambang." *Asian Music* 11(fall):59–79.

———. 1980. "Drumming in Okinawan Classical Music: A Catalogue of Gestures." *Dance Research Journal* 13(fall):17–28.

———. 1982. "Variation in Javanese Gamelan Music: Dynamics of a Steady State." Ph.D. dissertation, University of Michigan.

———. 1984. "Change and Ambiguity: Gamelan Music and Regional Identity in Yogyakarta." In *Aesthetic Tradition and Cultural Transition in Java and Bali,* ed. Stephanie Morgan and Laurie J. Sears, 221–245. Madison, Wisc.: Center for Southeast Asian Studies.

———. 1985a. "Musical Pluralism in Java: Three Local Traditions." *Ethnomusicology* 29 (winter):56–85.

———. 1985b. "Commercial Cassette Recordings of Traditional Music in Java: Implications for Performers and Scholars." *World of Music* 27(3):23–45. (Reprint: 1992. *Cassette Mythos,* ed. Robin James, 26–35. New York: Autonomedia.)

———. 1986a. "The Crystallization of a Marginal Tradition: Music in Banyumas, West Central Java." *Yearbook for Traditional Music* 18:115–132.

———. 1986b. "New Theory for Traditional Music in Banyumas, West Central Java." *Pacific Review of Ethnomusicology* 3:79–101.

———. 1987. "Variation and Composition in Java." *Yearbook for Traditional Music* 19:65–95.

———. 1988a. "Individual Variation in Javanese Gamelan Performance." *Journal of Musicology* 6(2):169–197.

———. 1988b. *East Javanese Gamelan Tradition.* Alumni Working Papers Series. Honolulu: East-West Center.

———. 1991. *Traditions of Gamelan Music in Java: Musical Pluralism and Regional Identity.* Cambridge: Cambridge University Press.

———. 1993. *Variation in Central Javanese Gamelan Music: Dynamics of a Steady State.* DeKalb: Northern Illinois University, Center for Southeast Asian Studies.

———. 1998. "Do Javanese Musicians Really Improvise?" In *In the Course of Performance: Studies in the World of Improvisation,* ed. Bruno Nettl, 69–92. Chicago: University of Chicago Press.

———. 2002. *Calling Back the Spirit: Music, Dance, and Cultural Politics in Lowland South Sulawesi.* New York: Oxford University Press.

Turino, Thomas. 1993. *Moving Away from Silence: Music of the Peruvian Altiplano and the Experience of Urban Migration.* Chicago: University of Chicago Press.

Yampolsky, Philip. 1991–1999. *Music of Indonesia.* Smithsonian Folkways. 20 compact disks, each with liner notes.

Africa and the Middle East
Ruth M. Stone

Beginnings
Fieldwork Trips
The Nature of Field Research
Teaching and Research
The Trajectory of a Career
Within the Field of Ethnomusicology

Today, at a time when we are poised on the edge of a digital revolution in computer technology, changes that enhance and challenge our work as ethnomusicologists engage our attention. They are new, but they are not totally unlike the changes that took place when I was doing my doctoral research twenty-five years ago: then, we felt excited about being able to take black-and-white video recordings on a reel-to-reel device. We are also involved in shifts in disciplinary boundaries that tantalize us with new possibilities. This moment provides an opportunity to ponder and characterize the styles and themes that have become part of our work. Differences abound among those who call themselves ethnomusicologists, but certain common threads bind us together.

BEGINNINGS

My introduction to a career in ethnomusicology began long before my formal education at a university. This engagement started inconspicuously—in fact, I was not aware of it at the time—when I was enculturated into Kpelle life in Liberia, West Africa. As a young girl, I walked the forest paths to the rice farms, sat with other young girls at the edge of town when they graduated from the Sande "secret society," watched the music and dance performances, and absorbed the pulse of everyday life and, on occasion, ritual life. These experiences took place on weekdays after I had finished my Western home schooling in the village of Yanekwele, where my father headed a language training and translation center for the Lutheran Church in Liberia. From about 10:30 A.M. onward, I lived in the Kpelle world—speaking, eating, and always attempting to imitate the life. For I wanted to be part of the Kpelle world, in part because I knew no English-speaking children of my own age except my brother and sister. I learned to speak the Kpelle language without consciously realizing that I had done so.

When I was an adolescent, my parents, quite wisely, realized that I also needed to be socialized into the Western world and sent me to live with relatives in the United States so that I could attend high school, there being no American or international school in Liberia at the time. During my high school and college years, I learned to appreciate and perform Western art music. I sang in Mozart's operas, Handel's *Messiah*, and Orff's *Carmina Burana*. Several years later, I moved to New York to further my training in voice; there, I learned—through a newspaper ad—of an ethnomusicology course that was being offered by Rose Brandel at Hunter College. Though I knew nothing about the field, I was intrigued.

My first course in ethnomusicology brought my interest in Africa together with my engagement in music. I knew quite soon that I had found a focus for my life, and I began to study for a master's degree with Professor Brandel, a protégé of the comparative musicologist Curt Sachs. I also enrolled in graduate courses in anthropology and linguistics. This was a heady period of discovery, as I also found a compatible group of fellow students with whom I have had many years of friendship and collaboration: Ronald Smith, with whom I later taught at Indiana University for nearly twenty years; Roberta Singer, who has worked with City Lore in New York for many years; Caroline Card Wendt, who taught at the University of Indianapolis until recently; and Patricia Matusky Yamaguchi, who taught in Malaysia and sent students to Indiana University for further training.

Our training with Rose Brandel focused on intensive sound analysis, ranging from Bulgarian dance music to Central African ritual performance. We learned to apply a Western sound grid to these wide-ranging musics.

By the second semester I had developed a plan to write my thesis on the music of the Kpelle people, and I conceived of it as a survey because no previous studies had appeared in the literature. I needed to carry out fieldwork in Liberia. So in the summer of 1970, my husband and I boarded a Pan American flight to travel to the site of my first fieldwork. In some ways, this trip to Liberia was a return home—I contacted many of the people I had known. But I also plunged into a whole world that I had never known before. The specialized knowledge and vocabulary of music were new. Verlon, my husband, was a partner in all this, as he was responsible for making the recordings and photographs. As I reentered that space and tried to sort out and assimilate a world that was both familiar and strange, I actually dreamed in Kpelle at night. Twelve years of absence had to be bridged; but after six weeks of absorbing life in central Bong County, I was once more familiar with my childhood home and was, as well, developing an entirely new perspective.

I completed my M.A. at Hunter College and, following the lead of my classmate Ronald Smith, applied to Indiana University to study for a Ph.D. Roberta Singer and Caroline Card Wendt followed in short order. To these fellow students were added new colleagues, including Carolina Robertson and Steven Feld. When I began my study in 1972, my horizons expanded yet again. For there were three ethnomusicologists with whom to study, representing somewhat different perspectives: Alan P. Merriam emphasized the anthropological approach; George List favored sound analysis, taking a special interest in transcription, but grounded in fieldwork; Charles Boilés brought linguistic models to the study.

During my first semester as a student at Indiana University, Merriam's course "Arts in Anthropology" opened to me the world of social scientific interpretations of the arts. We also became enthusiastic about approaches we picked up from other academics at Indiana University, such as semiotic-cybernetic communication theory and symbolic interaction. Paradigmatic structuralism was the buzz of academic meetings. We bonded during the *rite de passage,* otherwise known as George List's course "Transcription and Analysis," and to this day I remember the now legendary examples, such as "Streets of Laredo," that we attempted to represent on paper. Charles Boilés's course "Paradigms in Ethnomusicology," which might better have been called "Linguistic Paradigms in Ethnomusicology," taught us how to create generative grammars and branching tree diagrams for music performances. Our classroom discussions spilled over into weekends, evenings, and parties. Well-known scholars gave lectures, and we were able to query Bruno Nettl, David Ames, John Carrington, Francis Bebey, and Mantle Hood directly.

By 1975 I returned to Liberia for extended dissertation research supported by a joint Fulbright-Hays and Social Science Research Council grant. I arrived with a minor in African studies and with intermediate-level competence in Bambara, the trade language of Liberia and other parts of West Africa. My dissertation research proved to be a life-changing period that lasted a year and a half. I moved ever deeper into Kpelle music and culture as I listened, watched, and often just sat and talked with people. I had proposed a research project that would focus on indigenous ideas of cuing within a musical event. I had a great deal to learn, because this project demanded an extraordinary understanding of indigenous ideas about performance. A number of the members of my dissertation committee back in Indiana were a bit skeptical about how much I could elicit on Kpelle concepts about performance.

The world I inhabited by day was for the most part Kpelle. At dusk, as we ate supper, Verlon and I spoke English and reflected on our separate schedules of the day. Then in the evening we reentered the Kpelle world, as we attended and recorded performances. My husband commented that my bargaining skills, gestures, and gaze patterns changed when I shifted into the Kpelle world.

When I returned to Indiana University to write my dissertation, several events had intervened to change my anticipated future. George List, faced with health problems, wrote to tell me that he was retiring. Thus I worked with Alan P. Merriam as my primary ethnomusicology adviser for the final writing. The premature birth of my daughter, Angela, meant that a year was devoted to her health problems; and medical bills threatened to derail the completion of my dissertation. But in the summer of 1978, with my mother and mother-in-law taking over child care, I was finally able to spend twelve weeks writing and revising the first draft. My work reflected the broad range of ideas I had experienced, from the Sachs-Brandel heritage to the Herskovits-Merriam, McLeod-Boilés, and Herzog-List lineage.

FIELDWORK TRIPS

Since my first two field trips to Liberia in 1970 and 1975–1976, I have returned on a research trip in 1982–1983 sponsored by the National Endowment for the Humanities, and for a period of postdoctoral research in 1988–1989 (figure 1) supported by a Fulbright fellowship. The extended civil war that broke out several months after I last departed has largely disrupted normal life.

FIGURE I   The Kpelle choir of St. Peter's Lutheran Church, Monrovia, Liberia, led by the vocal soloist Feme Neni-kole (front). Photo by Verlon L. Stone, 1988.

FIGURE 2   Ruth M. Stone (right) after
performing with an ensemble at a madrigal
dinner as part of her study of expatriate life.
Photo by Michael Pape, 1999.

FIGURE 2   Ruth M. Stone (right) after
performing with an ensemble at a madrigal
dinner as part of her study of expatriate life.
Photo by Michael Pape, 1999.

I found new opportunities for research in the 1980s and 1990s. When my husband went to work in the Middle East from 1982 to 1986 and later from 1991 to 2001, I began spending summers and the month of December there. I realized early on that the musical practices of expatriates living and working in this region offered an opportunity for fruitful research and study on performance (figure 2). I was also able to turn from studying only the "other" to, in a sense, studying "ourselves." Thus I embarked on a project to understand how people—particularly Americans and Europeans living in the community—created notions of home through musical performance. I expanded my research time with semester-long leaves in 1986, 1992, and 1996. This research provided me with a population very different from that of my earlier work and has been a nice balance to my research in Africa. I was also able to connect to the earlier African work when I discovered a strong African influence in the Arabian Gulf region.

This formal research has taken place against a backdrop of travel to Malawi, Zimbabwe, South Africa, Madagascar, Ghana, Bahrain, and Oman. In Zimbabwe, I worked to help establish a diploma program in ethnomusicology at the Zimbabwe College of Music. Lectures, classes, and workshops in Zimbabwe and these various countries enlarged my understanding of performance in African settings—performance that had some commonalities with Liberia, where I had worked most extensively, but also differed sharply in certain ways.

THE NATURE OF FIELD RESEARCH

Event as object

Throughout my career, I have focused my research on the musical event. Here I have found a conceptual place where sound and behavior are created, appreciated, and critically evaluated. There is great scope for study within this focus. In my first book, *Let the Inside Be Sweet* (in which I revised my dissertation research), I described the approach as follows:

> While the study object is the event, the locus of the interest in this event is the participants' interaction. In focusing on the interaction with all its idiosyncrasies and incongruities, we are looking at musical meaning as "world producing" rather than as simply a product of the nature of things (Berger and Luckmann 1966:89). Such recognition is profoundly important for it acknowledges the centrality of meaning created in interaction.

The participants in music events include both the individuals producing music and the people experiencing the music performance as listeners or audience, and the auditors' meanings and interpretations are just as significant as those of the performers. (Stone 1982:4)

In studying musical events, I soon discovered that many structural details were obscured during the course of a performance. Only when an event broke down for some reason did the construction become transparent. I thus looked for these opportunities—points at which things went wrong—to reveal what was otherwise nearly impossible to perceive. When things became problematic, people often discussed what was needed to repair the situation and, in the process, unconsciously instructed me.

Temporal dimensions

For my second book, *Dried Millet Breaking* (1988a), I developed ideas that I had discovered in the course of my earlier work and focused on the multiple temporal layers of a complex epic event among the Kpelle. As I explained in the preface:

In this book I propose to follow the facets of timing as found in the *woi-meni-pele*, an epic that centers on the hero Woi. I am concerned not only with the rhythms of music sound and the placement of music text, but also with the larger event flow and ultimately the movement of time for both the individual and the family, rhythms that impinge on those of musical performance. (vii)

Focusing my fieldwork on temporal aspects led me to consider these patterns within the larger African and theoretical context of ethnomusicology in several settings (Stone 1985, 1986, 2001). I find that the focus on time constitutes an abiding and evolving interest.

Feedback interview

I have also used what I call a feedback interview (Stone and Stone 1981). The feedback interview is, to my mind, a powerful tool because it allows me to present data to people without overly structuring those data in a text. A video of a musical event can be played for people, and they can then comment on it.

I have used video recordings for feedback interviews since 1975, when I worked with black-and-white reel-to-reel recordings. At that time, knowledge of how Africans might respond was limited and concepts were often naive. I remember being queried in an interview for a Social Science Research Council fellowship about whether I thought people would be able to understand video images. What I found was that the Kpelle people were indeed capable of decoding and interpreting video images very quickly.

In studying communication processes such as dance, music, and dramatic events, the advantages of being able to record and store continuous iconic images of sound and motion for later playback and interviewing are obvious and overwhelming. Such advantages facilitate processual analysis.

Videotape recording of an event collects and records visual and audio information very rapidly, but while it provides retrievable images, which *appear* to be realistic, the recorder encodes and alters information just as certainly as written notes. For example, three-dimensional objects and events are encoded into electronic impulses which when retrieved and displayed are only two-dimensional. (Stone 1982:52)

I have also used high-quality sound recordings for feedback interviews; samples have been released on Folkways Records (Stone and Stone 1972). And I have used photographs of instruments to stimulate feedback and discussion, showing them to people and eliciting their commentary.

Recording the responses to feedback interviews and then transcribing them is a good way to store important data for later retrieval. Although my transcripts may

The details of how musical events develop, change, and disappear can be documented only over months and years of careful observation and study.

contain some irrelevant talk, unique insights almost always emerge from them. It was this tool, in fact, that revealed an all-important distinction between ritual and entertainment events.

> Structural segmentation in Kpelle events is an important concept and music events show varying degrees of segmentation. On one hand, segmentation is highly valued in the performance of entertainment music but, on the other hand, it is obscured in certain respects in the performance of ritual and religious music. While entertainment events, for example, emphasize segmented dance movements, in the quasi-ritual *koli-gong-song-pele,* these segments are deliberately obscured. This is somewhat analogous to the contrast in segmentation between *meni-pele* (chant fable) and *woi-meni-pele* (epic). (Stone 1982:120)

Field notes

Of all the tools I use, field notes are the most basic and are indispensable. To record observations, recollections, and questions, I need no more than a notebook and a pen or pencil. I also keep a daily journal, not just when I travel abroad but wherever I am. I started this habit years ago, after I observed John Blacking writing in his daily journal at a board meeting of the Society for Ethnomusicology. I have told my fieldwork classes that for an ethnomusicologist, the most critical skill is to learn how to take field notes.

I started creating notes in the 1970s by typing an original and multiple copies, using carbon paper and a manual typewriter. More recently, I have typed my notes on a laptop computer. In the journal that comprises my field notes is a daily log of what I have done, no matter how mundane, ranging from daily housekeeping chores to events recorded and trips made. I also include musings, ideas, and questions—most often partly unformed and not yet fully coherent. These ideas help me trace the process of my analysis, and I return to them when I begin to form some conclusions.

Most surprising to me has been the amount of time I spend writing notes. Initially, I was not prepared for the time—several hours a day—required to use this tool effectively. But field notes have become a disciplined activity each day, helping me to capture the ebb and flow of daily life.

Typically, ethnomusicologists share with their colleagues, and with the larger public, only a very small portion of their field notes—a tip of the iceberg. In a recent CD-ROM publication (2000) I did something quite different: I included whole sections of my notes as a kind of ethnomusicological sketchbook. In the project *Five Windows on Africa,* I worked with a team of scholars, programmers, instructional developers, and graduate student assistants. One day I brought in some of these notes to help them better understand my conclusions and the themes of the project as I envisioned it. The team members found the notes very revealing and encouraged me to include them in the final product. Since space was not the issue that it is in conventional typesetting by a compositor, I was free to add them. These notes provided a background for my conclusions, revealing some of the structural details that are normally obscured in the work of ethnomusicologists and thus also revealing more of the ethnomusicologist's craft.

Textual transcriptions and translations

I have devoted a great deal of effort to transcribing and translating the songs, interviews, and events I record. Transcription and translation reveal rich uses of language to express affect, communicate protest, and pass on moral mandates. But even as a fluent speaker of Kpelle, I have found that this work can be rough going at times. Ideally, I try to work initially with a research assistant to write down the text. Then we review the text, if at all possible, with the performers, correcting mishearings. Finally, the very difficult translation process begins, and we discover, for example, rapid shifts of tense and many archaic words, particularly in rituals and children's performances. Consider that a singer often alerts the audience to upcoming nuggets of richness: *Ka ká woli ké ndoo wule mâ, nga ke doôi, nge maa yorong bo* 'Listen to my singing song; as I sing it, I open its net'. Then the singer presents rich allusions, such as *Kú baraa kpèla-pelee, nga ńgei té ngelei su, ńga nyèng. Ngei-ya è pù gata-gata yê gbài-kpàng-sú-gbài* 'Our fellow young women, I raised my eyes to the sky, I lowered them. My tears fell *gata-gata* like corn from an old corn farm'.

Apprenticeship

I have also made use of apprenticeship as a way of obtaining data about how people conceptualize music. During my dissertation research, I took lessons on the *konîng* (a triangular-frame zither) with Bena Long. Those lessons provided important data about spirit tutelaries that I might not have obtained without this kind of involvement: "He discussed the special and sometimes dangerous power entailed in being a performer. He discussed how others would regard this role and revealed how being a musician had affected his life. While some musicians had alluded to such knowledge, it was not until I actually entered the role myself that I began to obtain rich detail" (Stone 1982:55).

When I began intensive research among expatriates in West Asia, I joined three vocal groups in order to study the nuances of interaction. Many details were shared with me that might not have been apparent if I had simply remained a listener and onlooker.

My research tools have sustained my longtime interest in an in-depth understanding of any ethnographic situation. I have carried out fieldwork in relatively few locations, but I have been able to take a longitudinal perspective by continuing a study over time. Such work is important if we are to have more than a snapshot of life in a particular area. The details of how musical events develop, change, and disappear can be documented only over months and years of careful observation and study.

Relationships in fieldwork

In my fieldwork, human relationships have lasted long beyond any single project, and the nature of these relationships has evolved over the years that I have been an ethnomusicologist. During the project *Five Windows on Africa*, I had a rare opportunity to involve one of the central participants of the event in helping to shape the presentation of data. The funeral that formed the central event had become a moment for political protest against the repressive regime of President Samuel Doe. Bishop Ronald Diggs of the Lutheran Church in Liberia had agreed that the church could be a major participant in the funeral after James Gbarbea was denied a state funeral, and Bishop Diggs denounced the actions of the government in his sermon at the funeral.

As we were finishing our work on the CD-ROM, some ten years after the event, I learned that Bishop Diggs was in the United States and was not able to return to Liberia for fear of reprisals by the government that had been installed after the ensuing civil war. I was able to bring him to Indiana University and show him the footage we were planning to use. I was also able to record and include his interpretation of the event ten years after it had occurred, with the war as a backdrop for his discussion. This unique opportunity allowed another voice—another layer—in the analysis of the event and the assessment of its significance. The occasion also gave the entire team a chance to meet this charismatic leader and to deepen their understanding of what they were creating. The line between the field and the laboratory was blurred as we conducted a lengthy interview in the recording studio at the university.

TEACHING AND RESEARCH

Teaching and research have been closely related in my work. Teaching is a crucible for ideas and offers an opportunity to think through ideas with students.

On a number of occasions, I have taught classes on topics closely related to my research. I offered a seminar in African studies, "Performance in Africa Today," which—as its title indicates—was related to the performance event. Over the course of the semester, invited speakers from a range of disciplines shared their ideas about performance. After the class had ended, we held a conference to give all the participants a chance to discuss their approaches face-to-face and to receive critiques of their papers. Finally, a publication of selected papers offered these ideas to the wider scholarly world (Stone 1988b).

While I was working through some of my research on temporal dimensions, I taught a course called "African Dimensions of Time" in order to gain a better perspective on the topic. This teaching enhanced my own view and gave my students a glimpse of my research activity.

Ethnomusicologists usually write in solitude. *Five Windows on Africa* proved to be the closest project I have had to the kind of team effort represented by a scientist working with a laboratory team. The graduate assistants in ethnomusicology had an opportunity to work directly on the project, and I learned and benefited from their insights. Furthermore, we all learned from working with the programmers and instructional developers. Learning, research, and analysis took place on all sides. Where new technology was concerned, I was a learner. Where field research was concerned, I taught my perspective on the data to the team. They tried, in turn, to find the most effective means of presenting these ideas in the new medium of interactive computer programs. We always tried to make sure that our tools would illuminate the aesthetic style of Kpelle performers.

On several occasions I have also had an opportunity to visit a student who was conducting fieldwork on location. When Jak Njoku, originally from Nigeria, was studying the indigenization of the Catholic mass in Zimbabwe among the Shona people, the chance to see the performance, share his field notes, and watch him at work proved mutually beneficial. I learned as much as I advised.

THE TRAJECTORY OF A CAREER

Institutionalization

Throughout my career, I have worked at a university that had an established program in ethnomusicology. Therefore, I began very early on to teach courses in ethnomusicology and to direct M.A. and Ph.D. theses and dissertations. The institutionalization of ethnomusicology at Indiana University was precarious in the early 1980s, in part because of its marginal position relative to better-established disciplines. Although courses in ethnomusicology were offered from the time George Herzog arrived in 1948, it was not until my second year as a faculty member—1980—that an official graduate Ph.D. minor was established. At that time an interdepartmental program was officially set up. Twenty years later, many of the faculty members who teach in this area moved to the newly named Department of Folklore and Ethnomusicology, and an Ethnomusicology Institute was established to balance the Folklore Institute

FIGURE 3   A class of *marimba* students led by Sheasby Matiure, teacher. Indiana University, Ethnomusicology Program, 1999.

within that department. With the revision of a core curriculum that emphasizes training in theory and methods of ethnomusicology, years of work have been institutionalized for the future (figure 3).

I have been vitally involved with this long process by working in administration over the years, first as director of the Ethnomusicology Program, later as director of the Archives of Traditional Music, and more recently as director of the newly created Ethnomusicology Institute. While I have sometimes had misgivings about the time I needed to devote to this area of my career, in balance I think it has been crucial to the future of ethnomusicology at Indiana University.

Since ethnomusicology has been placed primarily in the Folklore Department at Indiana University, I have also benefited from interaction with colleagues studying related phenomena, and I took my turn as chair of the department for four years. Such service acknowledged the reality of existence within a larger institution.

I have also been involved with ethnomusicology from the perspective of a learned society. Over the years I have served in multiple capacities with the Society for Ethnomusicology, culminating in a term as president several years ago. Such work, I believe, contributes to securing a future for ethnomusicology.

Complexities of a career

Students sometimes ask me how an ethnomusicologist can have a family life and simultaneously succeed in the field. My own answer has always been to search for creative, and not necessarily conventional, solutions. When I began my career, my husband, who also had a Ph.D., developed a career in the business world. Over the years the locations of this work have often entailed a commuting marriage. First, we traveled between Bloomington and Chicago. For fourteen years, we have commuted between Bloomington and the Middle East. While I am tempted to enumerate the disadvantages of this setup, I will focus on the positive aspects. First, in the longer of the two commutes we had longer periods of time together. I have spent summers and every December in the Middle East. When I was alone, I could concentrate on my own work. When I was in the Middle East, I lived in a rich field site, removed far enough from home to be able to work intensively. Our daughter, Angela, who split her time between the two sites, grew closer to her father during the time they lived together.

When my daughter was in college, her autumn break week typically fell around the time of the meetings of the Society for Ethnomusicology. The year we met in Los

Angeles, I brought her out with me for a weekend together before the conference started. The year we hosted the meeting in Bloomington, I engaged her to help with the conference. She was able to gain valuable work experience, touch base with people she knew, and share time with me in the evening after the last event was over.

When I was alone in Bloomington, I benefited from the assistance of my parents, who could take care of Angela when I traveled, for they had retired to be near us. As with the extended family that became familiar to us in Africa, they are an active part of our life.

Commuting became even more complicated when I first entered administration in 1988. I was still able to work from the Middle East, using Federal Express, United Parcel Service, telephone, fax, and increasingly the computer during the summer months.

I am so attuned to living in two worlds at once that when I'm in the Middle East, I'm always conscious that at four o'clock in the afternoon it is eight o'clock in the morning in Bloomington—the time when my E-mail of the day will be read. I have a regular schedule for telephone conferences, and these are now done, very economically, through computer links. Weekends in the two worlds do not coincide: on Wednesday, the last workday in the Middle East, the momentum of work in Bloomington is at its height. In order not to miss Thursday's and Friday's messages—these days are the weekend in the Middle East—I must get up early in the morning and check and answer messages. With E-mail attachments, I'm able to read and edit dissertations, manuscripts, and a variety of publications. When I arrive back in Bloomington, a great deal has been accomplished through computers and Internet technology.

WITHIN THE FIELD OF ETHNOMUSICOLOGY

A dominant theme of my work has always been to take, as far as possible, a perspective that honors the view of the participants in music performance. To achieve this emphasis I have conducted sustained and in-depth research in each of my primary sites over a period of nearly twenty years for the Middle East and more than thirty years for the Kpelle region of Liberia, West Africa. I could have conducted less intensive research in some of the other African countries where I have traveled, but I feel that without competence in the languages of these countries, I could not achieve the goals that have been most important in my work.

Another theme in my work is a close integration of music with related genres of performance in the sonic, visual, and kinetic arts. In this regard I have benefited from colleagues in folklore and African studies who have nourished this approach, and from performers such as the Kpelle of Liberia who insist on this way of viewing performance. Team-teaching a course such as "The Aesthetics of African Music and Cloth" with my colleague Patrick McNaughton in fine arts has been most stimulating.

Among the aspects of performance that I have most enjoyed studying is the temporal dimension—that is, time—not only in music but in everyday life, particularly as everyday life impinges on a performance. This has led me to extensive reading in philosophy and psychology and to membership and participation in the International Society for the Study of Time.

Finally, I have always been interested in and concerned with broad theoretical issues in ethnomusicology. For this reason, I have often included theoretical discussions in my publications. As I see it, theory is created by scholars as well as performers—by those studying as well as those being studied.

I also began early in my career to teach the course "Paradigms in Ethnomusicology." After more than twenty years of teaching, I have completed the first draft of a manuscript for a book on this topic, which I have shared with a recent class and am now in the process of revising (Stone 2001).

The future seems to hold ever more possibilities for exploring the themes that have been most important to me in the course of my career. Working as an ethnomusicologist holds even more excitement for me today than it did when I began my work more than twenty years ago. The technological developments in computers and the Internet are a fascinating frontier, which we are just beginning to glimpse.

REFERENCES

Berger, Peter L., and A. Luckmann. 1966. *The Social Construction of Reality.* New York: Anchor.

Stone, Ruth M. 1979. "Communication and Interaction Processes in Music Events among the Kpelle of Liberia." Ph.D. dissertation, Indiana University.

———. 1982. *Let the Inside Be Sweet: The Interpretation of Music Event among the Kpelle of Liberia.* Bloomington: Indiana University Press.

———. 1985. "In Search of Time in African Music." *Music Theory Spectrum* 7:139–148.

———. 1986. "Commentary: The Value of Local Ideas in Understanding West African Rhythm." *Ethnomusicology* 30:54–57.

———. 1988a. *Dried Millet Breaking: Time, Words, and Song in the Woi Epic of the Kpelle.* Bloomington: Indiana University Press.

———, ed. 1988b. *Performance in Contemporary African Arts.* Introduction by Ruth M. Stone. Bloomington: African Studies and Journal of Folklore Research. See also: *Journal of Folklore Research* 25(1–2, double issue).

———. 2000. *Five Windows on Africa: Traveling Home—Music, Politics, and the Commemoration of a Life.* Bloomington: Indiana University Press.

———. 2001. *Theory in Ethnomusicology Today.* Unpublished manuscript.

Stone, Ruth M., and Verlon L. Stone. 1972. *Music of the Kpelle of Liberia.* New York: Folkways Record Corporation, FE 4385.

Stone, Ruth M., and Verlon L. Stone. 1981. "Event, Feedback, and Analysis: Research Media in the Study of Music Events." *Ethnomusicology* 25:215–225.

Africa, the Middle East, and North America
Kay Kaufman Shelemay

Thoughts on Musical Ethnography
Ethnomusicology in the Real World
Teaching Ethnomusicology
Toward a New Agenda

Ethnomusicological work, it seems to me, has its own social history, in a sense its own life cycle. Similarly, an individual ethnomusicologist's career path can be viewed in terms of changes that occur not just in research and scholarly agendas over time, but also in terms of the impact of real-world concerns. In this essay, I will map my own experience of that process.

My involvement as an ethnomusicologist grew out of a deep love of music and a fascination with people; later, a preoccupation with travel and cross-cultural differences joined and transformed these interests. The moment when music, people, and difference came into alignment occurred during my first semester in graduate school, while I was beginning musicology studies in what was conventionally termed twentieth-century music. At that point, I was intrigued with what seemed to me at the time a still living tradition in a distant place (early-twentieth-century Vienna) and a musical revolution (the dissolution of Western tonality) that had challenged the conventions of the European past. But during my first semester in graduate school, as part of a course exploring the music of medieval and Renaissance Europe, the professor brought in for the sake of comparison a recording of the liturgical music of an Ethiopian people then called the Falasha or Beta Israel. I decided to investigate the subject further for a semester paper and learned that there was an ongoing debate concerning the history and religious identity of Beta Israel. Why, I remember thinking, had no one studied its music and liturgy? How could scholars debate a people's religious identity for more than a century while ignoring the very materials most likely to hold an answer? So that is the long and the short of how I became an ethnomusicologist. I was drawn to a problem for which materials from a musical domain promised a solution, and for which musical ethnography provided the only viable method or approach.

In stepping back from this transformative moment, I realize that my move into ethnomusicology had its roots in, first, lateral intellectual stimulation and, second, recognition of a problem demanding a solution. This type of chance encounter with a compelling issue or problem has over the years led me to explore new intellectual directions. I would venture to say that in a field like ethnomusicology, which values interdisciplinarity, serendipitous encounters provide a stimulus for many new directions.

As I look back nearly thirty years later, my early period as a student of Ethiopian musics seems distant indeed. This is because life intervened in the form of the Ethiopian revolution, separating me from my first "field" for seventeen years, a period during which I necessarily moved on to new areas. Since I've documented my Ethiopian research in books (Shelemay 1986 [1989], Shelemay and Jeffery 1994–1997) and a memoir (Shelemay 1991)—the memoir tracking my experience and working methods—here I'd like to move forward in time. In some ways, my subsequent ethnomusicological career has been a reaction to that first, rather classical field experience abroad. When I left "for the field" as a graduate student in 1973, it seemed natural to me, given the thinking of the time, that I should go to rural Ethiopia and that I would seek to gather data which might provide original historical and cultural insights. In the intervening years, it has been a challenge to honor my commitment to fully explore and publish the Ethiopian materials I gathered while moving forward in terms of my own changing interests and those of our field. I suspect that many ethnomusicologists confront such quandaries as the years go by, and for this reason many doctoral dissertations never come to publication.

Over the years, my interests have moved to a deeper concern with method and theory. And now my idea of a proper place to work is just about anywhere, but especially close to home. While the greatest intellectual continuity can be seen in my abiding interest in solving problems and issues, especially those that involve exploring ambiguous musical and cultural boundaries, there is no doubt that over time my work has become more focused on methodological, political, and pedagogical matters. In terms of methodological shifts, I have moved from a single-minded focus on independent fieldwork to conceiving and directing team initiatives. The practical and political came into focus as I pursued interests that speak more directly to the "real world" of musical transmission and performance all around us. Finally, years of combining research with teaching have raised concerns about bringing pedagogical approaches into line with the increasingly sophisticated research perspectives and goals of ethnomusicology. Having traveled this road well into midcareer in the ethnomusicological life cycle, I find that the process never ends. As I write this essay, I am once again at work defining a new chapter of my research agenda. In the following sections, I will move through the three areas of interest just sketched: the methodological concerns that have led me to advocate team fieldwork, the pros and cons of engaging with the "real world," and the vicissitudes of teaching ethnomusicology. I will end with some brief musings on future directions.

THOUGHTS ON MUSICAL ETHNOGRAPHY

While I found that my Ethiopian fieldwork projects were a great challenge and have mined them over the years for publications, I have derived an equally full measure of insights and gratification from research nearer home in North America. Perhaps it is not coincidental that my move to "the field at home"—primarily urban musical studies in the United States—brought with it a change of method to team pursuits. Ethnomusicology, like anthropology, is about "people studying people" (Georges and Jones 1980). Yet just as many of us have found that our research associates in the field are much more than our informants, quickly becoming friends and collaborators, so may we wish to pursue projects planned from the outset with a research team (Shelemay 1988). Indeed, David Damrosch (1995) has suggested that much work in the humanities, like that of the social sciences and sciences, might be usefully and creatively undertaken as collaborative ventures. In the field at home there are almost always colleagues and students with whom one might wish to share a research experience. There is no doubt, too, that the notion of the team works equally well in classical sites abroad, especially if one incorporates local colleagues and students into the venture, sharing resources and expertise.

When and where might one conduct team research? Just about anytime and anywhere. Virtually any project can gain from a collaborative process. With more than one fieldworker, one can draw on complementary linguistic, technological, and personal expertise. And it's not as if ethnomusicologists are inexperienced in collaborating: many have acknowledged the presence of supportive partners in the field, providing an extra pair of hands, additional skills, and an entrée into new domains, depending on their gender, their age, or both. Indeed, some spouses, such as Veronica Doubleday ([1988] 1990), have worked on their own projects and written their own books about the field experience. Still, although a number of well-known couples have collaborated in the field or on publication projects in anthropology, such partners have not tended to carry out fieldwork together in ethnomusicology.

My own team fieldwork has been undertaken primarily with students at the universities at which I have taught, including graduate students in music at New York University and a broad-based team of undergraduate and graduate students in music and other fields at Harvard. The New York project documented a traditional hymn repertoire, the *pizmonim*, among a religious-ethnic community, Jews of Syrian descent living in Brooklyn. The Boston project focused on an affinity community, musicians involved in so-called early music, working with several small professional music ensembles active in that world. Both projects engaged teams of student researchers studying many musicians; the Boston early music study also involved close collaboration and team teaching with two of my colleagues on the faculty at Harvard, Thomas Kelly and Carol Babiracki. In both cases, the team fieldwork had a pedagogical edge: students were enrolled for credit in seminars that featured fieldwork as their central activity, although if the truth be told, the courses took far more time than was commensurate with the credit given.

Team research pays dividends, offering multiple perspectives and providing opportunities to discuss events as they unfold. There is always a possibility that someone else will catch a vital observation that you missed because you were looking the other way, or will share a special insight that would never have occurred to you. Team research also provides more openings for midcourse corrections, since continual dialogue about the research process can lead to recognition of problems before they jeopardize the work. Of course, the growing technological challenges of fieldwork, as one seeks to document musical events and interviews in various media, are immeasurably eased by the presence of several team members who can share such tasks.

Collaboration, among fieldworkers and with those transmitting the musical tradition, is the biggest payoff of a team venture. One challenge of the team process is the eventual disposition of the research materials, in terms of preservation and publication. Both team projects in which I was involved gathered enormous amounts of data, which we spent considerable time documenting and analyzing. We shared interview tapes and transcripts with the interviewees throughout the course of the fieldwork and deposited copies of all materials in community and university archives. In both projects there was a critical mass of participants to undertake and complete expeditiously the onerous field tasks of transcribing interviews, writing thank-you notes, and chasing down ancillary materials.

However, if there is a downside to team research, it is the fact that collective responsibility for the research process does not always translate into enough momentum to publish the results. In the case of the project on Syrian music in New York, the one individual who drew on the team's data for a dissertation and subsequent publications was not a member of the team but a graduate student who consulted the materials after the completion of the project in conjunction with his own original research (Kligman 1997). I did seven years of subsequent independent research on Syrian Jewish music, extending my fieldwork to Mexico and Jerusalem, and eventually published articles and a book on this subject (Shelemay 1996, 1998). But by the time

FIGURE 1   Students recordings *pizmonim* in the Sephardic Community Center, Brooklyn, New York. Photos are from the author.

my book appeared, several individuals who had participated in the original study more than a decade earlier had died, and I would guess that others had secretly suspected that the publication would never appear at all. It can be complicated to explain to individuals outside the academy that publication processes in the scholarly world are painfully slow at best. But when you are working with a community that has strong interests in perpetuating a tradition it has shared with you, publication is not just a hope but an expectation.

The Boston project on early music was conceived as the first stage of an ongoing ethnographic venture, which we have so far been unable to find the time to continue. As in the New York project on Syrian music (Shelemay 1988), I published an article discussing the research of the early music team (2001a) and included some general materials as part of a Boston ethnography in *Soundscapes* (2001b). There is no question that collaborating with musicians in the field raises expectations for publication, as does the existence of a large team of investigators. It is probably a good idea to begin a team project with some sort of specific publication goal in mind; for instance, early on we published a recording (figures 1 and 2) in collaboration with the Syrian Jewish community (Shelemay and Weiss, 1985). At many points during the years between the end of the team research and the publication of my book, the recording constituted a tangible memento of our collaboration. Indeed, when I traveled to Mexico and Israel to work with Syrian Jews there, a number of them showed me their copies of the recording, which had circulated internationally on cassette among members of the community.

The process of doing fieldwork "at home" brought the research process into focus as part of both my academic and my personal experience. Fieldwork was no longer something I did only abroad; rather, it had become an integral part of my daily life. As we worked together in a research process, my students and I developed deeper relationships. Our strengths and weaknesses emerged, and learning became a collaborative experience. Any number of very practical issues also came to the fore as fieldwork became much more than a methodology for research. It forced us to think through practical issues, such as how to fit interviews and music sessions into our own busy schedules and those of the musicians with whom we worked. Music making had to be approached and appreciated as part of life, as the practicalities and human dimensions of our work took center stage. Politics, too, emerged as paramount to the communities with which we were engaged, and the broader concerns of carrying out

FIGURE 2   Cover of *pizmon* recording.

an informed and ethical research process assumed signal importance. In the case of the Syrian music project, we had to negotiate with some challenging personalities and in an atmosphere of community tensions. In the early music project, we had to be cautious about intragroup competition and had to protect confidentiality with regard to the musicians' economic concerns. Carrying out team fieldwork takes one to many "places" not envisioned in the original research design, including the "real world" of music.

ETHNOMUSICOLOGY IN THE REAL WORLD

When I became an ethnomusicologist in the early 1970s, the field was still a bracketed space where one went to carry out research, more often than not spatially separated from one's own home and past. Given these assumptions and models, it was perhaps predictable that I would choose to work in a place as remote as Ethiopia. My field site within Ethiopia was yet more isolated, in villages requiring hours of travel on foot or horseback beyond the nearest road, miles from the nearest small town. Yet even in "distant" Ethiopia, I quickly learned, the field and home could become one. Within a short time, I had married a permanent resident and experienced the Ethiopian revolution as an insider. The transformation was completed when I returned to the United States after nearly four years abroad. By early 1977, when I moved to New York City as a new Ph.D. to begin teaching at Columbia University, I was startled to find that thousands of Ethiopians had settled on the Upper West Side of Manhattan, where I lived. One of my closest friends and research associates from Addis Ababa, a venerable Eritrean monk and priest, moved to New York City the same month I did and found a home one block away from my apartment. We were closer neighbors in New York City than we had been in Addis Ababa.

All this brought home to me in a visceral way that boundaries, geographical and intellectual, are porous. The field had moved with me and became part of my life almost imperceptibly. It felt right to be involved as an ethnomusicologist in the real world around me. Early in the fall of 1977, I sought out my first local fieldwork project at home in New York and began to sing with David Hykes's Harmonic Choir, which was then in residence at the Cathedral of Saint John the Divine on nearby 110th Street. I conceptualized that project as participant-observation in New York's "new music scene," but I secretly reveled in learning the basics of *khöömei* 'throat' singing and Tibetan chant in the same environment in which I had long performed in opera and musical theater.

During this period, there were several people who helped shape my changing ethnomusicological worldview in important ways. A significant influence during my early years in New York City was Adelaida Reyes, who was at that time a visiting professor at Columbia. Her then recently completed dissertation (1975) about music and musicians in Harlem provided a splendid model for local research; her clearly articulated interest in fieldwork methodology provided a map for moving in that direction. I had been very fortunate during my graduate years at the University of Michigan to have supportive and stimulating mentors—William P. Malm and Judith Becker. But at Columbia, in the formative years of my academic career, my peers also influenced me deeply. In retrospect, I have come to believe that one is particularly receptive and open to new ideas during the period just following doctoral studies, when the pressure of the dissertation has been lifted. In addition to Adelaida Reyes, I was fortunate to be a colleague of Carolina Robertson from 1977 to 1979. From her I gained additional exposure to anthropological theories I had earlier acquired in the classroom as well as an appreciation of how musical ethnography must cross boundaries into other social and cultural domains. A third, unexpectedly strong influence on my professional and personal development was Ellen Harris, a historical musicologist who also started her teaching career at Columbia in 1977. While many of us

What can an ethnomusicologist do in and for the real world of music? The options are many, almost unlimited.

assume that we will find mentors among our teachers, sometimes our peers and colleagues, with whom intellectual agendas can be more freely vented and shared, emerge as the most powerful influence. For Ellen Harris and myself, peer mentoring across boundaries within broader musicology became a rewarding collaborative venture, one that has continued over the years as we encounter new professional opportunities and challenges.

Once life and ethnomusicology occupied the same locale and were more fully intertwined in my world, it was but a small step to begin to think of music and musical scholarship as part of a broader realm of artistic expression and social action. New York City was for me a very formative influence in this regard, since a step outside the front door brings one into immediate contact with the widest range of sounds and performance strategies. New York City is truly a complete world of music in and of itself.

In New York City, too, there are an unusually large number of active colleagues working in public and nonprofit institutions. Their creativity and drive have led to the founding of organizations that support and sponsor community music making across the five boroughs, including (among others) the Center for Traditional Music and Dance, and presenters of diverse musical traditions such as the World Music Institute. In the 1980s, the founding of City Lore brought front and center an organization committed to cultural activism and a participatory cultural life. All these nonprofit organizations fought to establish themselves and continue to struggle to perpetuate their musical and cultural agendas. It was exhilarating to witness and sometimes participate in the important work being carried out on behalf of diverse musical traditions and a broader community.

A transformative experience during my years in New York was a summer spent as part of a "faculty in residence" at CBS (soon to become Sony) Records in 1986. Four academics had been invited into the corporation to bring concerns and ideas from the university to the business world. Here I had my first in-depth contact with the real world of popular music and corporate music culture. The impact of new technologies on the transmission and performance of music became startlingly clear, and I began research in this area. In terms of economic realities and long-term goals, the contrast between this world and the university or the public sector was striking.

What can an ethnomusicologist do in and for the real world of music? The options are many, almost unlimited. Supporting and collaborating with nonprofit organizations is one route. Another is carrying out ethnomusicological research projects that aid communities of descent or affinity in their efforts to document and perpetuate their own traditions. For instance, our team project with Syrian Jews in Brooklyn began as a collaborative effort to document a repertoire of songs of great historical importance and ongoing significance to the community. Syrian Jews were interested in recording songs to ensure that they would be transmitted to the younger generation; as ethnomusicologists, we provided the necessary equipment and expertise. An unexpected outcome of this study was that the interest and activity of a group of ethnomusicologists, which because of our number was perceived as a community in itself, aroused interest among Syrian Jews who carried the musical tradition. Within the Brooklyn community, singing *pizmonim* acquired enhanced value—additional cultural capital—in part because of the interest of outsiders. The real-world result was that there was a resurgence of interest in learning and singing *pizmonim*.

Ethnomusicologists can also work to reinforce vulnerable musical institutions and cultivate resources that support worthy ventures through grants. Anthony Seeger (1986) has written eloquently about the importance of preserving our field recordings and other ethnographic materials in archives. Beyond depositing our own materials, we can take as part of our real-world responsibilities the task of building archives and finding resources to support them. The longer one works in ethnomusicology, the more fleeting both musical traditions and individual careers appear to be, and the more important it becomes to institutionalize resources for the future. In recent years, I have become increasingly active in these domains, working with colleagues to build an archive of world music at Harvard, where resources can be marshaled to preserve ephemeral materials that will otherwise be lost. A most important aspect of my real-world activities in recent years has been on behalf of the American Folklife Center at the Library of Congress. This national repository for the American musical heritage was founded as recently as 1976 and received permanent authorization from the United States Congress even more recently, in 1998. The fragility of our national commitment to vernacular culture and music has, for me, constituted a call to action. Each of us may select different domains or causes to which we choose to devote time and energy—including efforts to transform the very institutions within which we work—but such activities move us beyond the traditional goals of the academy or the boundaries of a single musical organization. Once one has entered the real world of music, it is impossible to retreat.

TEACHING ETHNOMUSICOLOGY

It has been said that individuals teach in order to replicate themselves. My own belief is that we should train students not to replicate ourselves but to move beyond our own intellectual comfort zones, and most certainly to make different mistakes. Michael Tomasello (1999) has argued that cultural transmission is a unique aspect of the human cognitive process and that it is conveyed by three types of social learning: imitative, instructed, and collaborative. If this is indeed the case and social learning is at the heart of what makes us human, we may want to rethink the low priority we give to pedagogy in our field. Just as ethnomusicologists study processes of social learning at the core of musical transmission, equally important social learning processes are set in motion when we teach students at all levels.

Pedagogy has become a top priority for me in recent years. Ironically, I did not start out to have a career in teaching; I began in a challenging administrative position at the University of Michigan, working for a performing arts organization deeply involved in community musical life. But an academic offer from Columbia University, and the siren sound (mythologically speaking, of course) of New York City proved irresistible. Working in academia ensures one's ongoing education, and the university is an institution worth a substantial investment of personal time and effort. I have continued on this career path in part because it permits me to pursue an ambitious research agenda and also gives me the freedom to pursue real-world activities. Over the last decade, however, pedagogy has emerged as an increasingly important third axis of my professional activities and concerns.

An aspect of my own academic career that has undoubtedly affected my concern with pedagogy has been the fact that I have moved several times and have taught, either as a regular faculty member or as a visitor, at some six institutions. Each place had its own culture and different expectations for everything from course content to educational standards. Over the years, I have spent many more hours than I could have anticipated recasting courses. I have also worked regularly to conceive new offerings when what I had been doing all along didn't "feel right" in a new locale. Someone (I can't remember who) once said that we each teach only one course, over and over again; but I believe, or fervently hope, that this is not the case.

I have been particularly struck by the ways in which pedagogical approaches in ethnomusicology lag behind the research perspectives of a given moment, particularly in the separation in ethnomusicological teaching between communicating musical materials and conveying a broader intellectual framework. Today ethnomusicologists increasingly feel a need to theorize meaningfully about fast-changing traditions. Yet, at the same time, most still transmit "world music" to their students by taking a descriptive approach, surveying foreign cultures. After working for years with heterogeneous student populations, primarily in major urban centers, I have felt obligated to recast my own pedagogical approaches. Many of the musics I was teaching were already well established in the locality in which I lived, allowing for on-site exploration of subjects ranging from musical style to global connections.

While most ethnomusicologists actively theorize about their graduate-level pedagogy, they appear to give much less attention to conceptualizing undergraduate teaching. Except for a handful of hardworking colleagues who specialize in "music education," virtually none have devoted attention to primary and secondary education (K–12). Just as ethnomusicology has brought the field home and has begun to acknowledge the collaborative nature of research projects and ethnographic process, it is time to attempt pedagogy at all levels that will be congruent with these new realities. My own solution has been to develop a locally grounded ethnographic approach, which I adapt to students' different levels of expertise and to the situation at hand. But it is clear that a diverse musical world necessitates multiple, flexible approaches; this means that each of us constantly needs to be alert for ways to improve musical pedagogy and to ensure that it reaches a broader constituency.

TOWARD A NEW AGENDA

I am writing this essay during a stay at a research center in Italy. In this quiet corner of rural Umbria, it is possible to step back from my own real world, push away distractions, and reflect on where my intellectual agenda may take me from here. I brought along with me a great deal of lateral reading, in fields that appear to present challenges ethnomusicologists have not yet fully explored. I am now looking at a borderland where cultural and cognitive studies meet, although from my exposure so far I would observe that, today, ideas from the domains of cultural and cognitive studies more often collide than inform each other.

Some of these interests emerge from my earlier work on the Syrian Jewish *pizmonim*, which led me deep into concerns about memory. This subject, allied to studies of history and the past, is one with which ethnomusicological scholarship has not generally concerned itself. Through a wonderful lateral connection, I participated during the last five years at Harvard in an initiative that brought together scholars from across the disciplines, from neuroscience to literature, under the rubric "mind, brain, and behavior." After working for some time on memory, I moved on to explore with a group of like-minded colleagues from different fields the manner in which pain is expressed, mediated, and mitigated through expressive culture. Part of my work now is editing a book of essays on that subject.

But where to go with this subject in the future? If scholars such as Tomasello (1999:54) are correct that human cultural processes take fundamental cognitive skills in new and surprising directions, it may be possible for cross-cultural ethnographic work to make real contributions to cognitive studies and move it beyond the limitations of the laboratory. This research might also have real-world significance if we can draw on it to convince others that music is—or musics are—much more than bells and whistles and that music can make important contributions to our understanding of the world around us. Is there a new ethnomusicological subfield in the borderland between cultural and cognitive studies? Is there any realistic prospect of linking the cultural questions we ask as ethnomusicologists to the questions pursued by neuroscientists, psychologists, and others exploring cognition? I cannot yet offer an answer to these questions, but the challenge of a frontier to which ethnomusicology stands to make a contribution is incentive enough for continuing exploration. And I am confident that just over the horizon there are many new agendas for ethnomusicologists. The social history of our discipline demonstrates that ethnomusicology, like any field of study, is at its best when it moves beyond current assumptions to test future possibilities. In any case, this exploration is certain to be continued.

REFERENCES

Damrosch, David. 1995. *We Scholars: Changing the Culture of the University*. Cambridge, Mass.: Harvard University Press.

Doubleday, Veronica. [1988] 1990. *Three Women of Herat*. Austin: University of Texas Press.

Georges, Robert A., and Michael O. Jones. 1980. *People Studying People: The Human Element in Fieldwork*. Berkeley: University of California Press.

Kligman, Mark Loren. 1997. "Modes of Prayer: Arabic Maqamat in the Sabbath Morning Liturgical Music of the Syrian Jews in Brooklyn." Ph.D, dissertation, New York University.

Reyes Schramm, Adelaida. 1975. "The Role of Music in the Interaction of Black Americans and Hispanos in New York City's East Harlem." Ph.D. dissertation, Columbia University.

Seeger, Anthony. 1986. "The Role of Sound Archives in Ethnomusicology." *Ethnomusicology* 30:261–276.

Shelemay, Kay Kaufman. 1986 [1989]. *Music, Ritual, and Falasha History*. Lansing: Michigan State University Press.

———. 1988. "Together in the Field: Team Research among Syrian Jews in Brooklyn, New York." *Ethnomusicology* 32:369–384.

———. 1991. *A Song of Longing: An Ethiopian Journey*. Urbana: University of Illinois Press.

———. 1996. "The Ethnomusicologist and the Transmission of Tradition." *Journal of Musicology*. 14:35–51.

———. 1998. *Let Jasmine Rain Down: Song and Remembrance among Syrian Jews*. Chicago: University of Chicago Press.

———. 2001a. "Toward an Ethnomusicology of the Early Music Movement: Thoughts on Bridging Disciplines and Musical Worlds." *Ethnomusicology* 45(1):1–29.

———. 2001b. *Soundscapes: Exploring Music in a Changing World*. New York: Norton.

Shelemay, Kay Kaufman, and Peter Jeffery. 1994–1997. *Ethiopian Christian Liturgical Chant: An Anthology*. 3 vols. Madison, Wisc.: A-R Editions. (With compact disk.)

Shelemay, Kay Kaufman, and Sarah Weiss. 1985. *Pizmon: Syrian Jewish Religious and Social Song*. Ho-Ho-Kus, N.J.

Tomasello, Michael. 1999. *The Cultural Origins of Cultural Cognition*. Cambridge, Mass.: Harvard University Press.

Latin America and North America (I)

Daniel Sheehy

Becoming an Ethnomusicologist
Working as an Ethnomusicologist in the Public Sector

BECOMING AN ETHNOMUSICOLOGIST

"How would you define ethnomusicology?" was the opening question in Professor Nazir Jairazbhoy's graduate seminar at the University of California, Los Angeles (UCLA), in the mid-1970s. "The study of all the world's music," said one student. "The study of music in its cultural context," said another. "No, it's the study of culture *through* music," rejoined another, and so on. On short notice, all of the definitional terrain lying between the two major philosophical placeholders of the day—the ethnomusicologist Mantle Hood and the anthropologist of music Alan Merriam—had been claimed by my fellow students, and I was the only one still left to answer the question. I had no idea that what I was about to say would be a personal epiphany in which a loose collection of past experiences would crystallize into a philosophical point of view and would prepare me to take a number of "nontraditional" career paths later on. I had grown bored and impatient with the unending and often acrimonious debate around whether ethnomusicology should be the study of music or the study of culture through music, as though there were a single universal truth governing the approach to ethnomusicology. (Later, Groucho Marx's purported comment, "The contrary is also true," would bolster my outlook in this regard.) Frankly, I was also feeling increasingly alienated from the limitations of the most prominent products and goals of academic life—writing papers and articles on highly specialized topics for academic peer groups and defining one's professional success mainly in terms of "publish or perish." So, without thinking, I blurted out, "Ethnomusicology is . . . ethnomusicology is what you make it!"

Without realizing it, I had found the professional "direction" I needed. My answer gave me greater confidence to forge my own career rather than limit myself to the received knowledge of student life that pushed me toward a career as a college professor. The irony of this statement, though, is that I honestly have never felt that I forged my career; rather, I feel that a series of career opportunities forged me. Allow me to explain.

In the late 1960s, I was an undergraduate at UCLA studying to be a high school band director. I had been successful in music during my high school years in Bakersfield, California, playing trumpet in the marching and concert bands, the community

For the public-sector ethnomusicologist, training never ends, and one is always in a state of becoming.

symphony, a semiprofessional musical theater group, and the local musicians' union concert band. Learning the professional skills to run a high school music program was a natural next step in my education. But my plan was knocked off center by a series of opportunities. I joined an African-American rhythm and blues band called the Thunder Brothers that played in a modest nightclub called Jefty's in the predominantly black neighborhood of Compton. Three nights a week for two years, I found myself immersed in an all-black club scene playing the music of James Brown, Otis Redding, Aretha Franklin, and Marvin Gaye. The music's synchrony, sentiment, and drive transformed my appreciation of music, and—along with the thrill I felt at the extraordinary skill of so many of the dancers—raised questions in my mind about what had been missing in my own musical life. During that time, I met the Ashanti drummer Kwasi Badu, who had come from Ghana to teach performance in the ethnomusicology program at UCLA. We became friends, and I began playing *adowa* and *kete* (dance musics) in his student music group. I soon realized that this music was far more rhythmically complex than any I had known previously. I also came to see musical and cultural stylistic connections between what Kwasi taught me and the music and ambience at Jefty's. When the rhythm-and-blues band War recruited the Thunder Brothers' guitar player Howard Scott (who went on to write the hit song "The Cisco Kid"), the group came to an end. A student friend asked me to join the UCLA *mariachi* performance group, taught by the Mexican violinist Jesús Sánchez, which at the time needed a trumpet player, and I accepted. The rhythmic and melodic nuances of the *sones* and the *música ranchera* that we played and the lively social ethos that infused the music were mind-expanding and exciting.

My career plans were shattered. I could never be content as a high school band director. There was too much irresistible music to be discovered. I also had discovered that there were social hierarchies governing musical life, and I found them both objectionable and intellectually engaging. Why had not the music of James Brown, Kwasi Badu, and Jesús Sánchez been part of my musical education? Why weren't their biographies in the music history textbooks? Who had decided what I would learn and why? Why were certain styles of music favored over others? Why were entire "worlds" of music—even those that could be found in my own country and my own hometown—excluded from the music education curriculum? I was not happy about what I had discovered, and I developed a countercultural passion (it was the 1960s, after all) that increased my desire to learn more about music and the circumstances affecting it. In 1970 I entered UCLA's graduate program in ethnomusicology, where I would remain as a graduate student until 1977.

At the time of this writing, 2001, after more than two decades working in government institutions outside the academy, I find it interesting to think about which aspects of my academic training served me best in my professional career, and about what gaps there were. In general, I cannot remember a single graduate course to which I have not referred in some way during my professional career. Mantle Hood's expansive approach to the analysis of musical sound and style certainly helped me to spot important stylistic traits and place them in a larger musical and cultural matrix. In Peter Crossley-Holland's seminar, students were forced to write in various formats and styles, although four art forms—the memorandum, the grant application, the budget justification, and the press release—were not among them. General world music courses and in-depth courses on specific music cultures would all serve me as I was confronted with a wide range of cultural styles and traditions in the public sector.

Only one seminar (but one was more than the norm in those days) contained any explicit applied ethnomusicology. Mantle Hood asked us to develop a plan to "infect" a community of our choice with a music of our choice. I liked this idea. In hindsight, I realize that there was little methodical questioning of *why* we would be attempting this musical contagion within the target community. Our project did not go much beyond strategies and tactics; we did not examine broader ethical, political, or philosophical issues. As I have suggested above, in my case the *why* of action was already relatively clear, and it was easy for me to feel confident about taking action. I was excited by the idea of including radio and television stations, record production and distribution networks, public schools and training programs, and concerts as we considered how we would apply and develop our skills. I developed a plan to infect my hometown, Bakersfield, with Mexican regional music through radio, concerts, and performance classes. (Little did I know that ten years later, the Radio Bilingüe radio network and the movement of *mariachi* festivals and training programs spreading through the Southwest would begin to do precisely what I had in mind.)

While most of my ethnomusicological graduate training has proved useful in my work outside the academy, virtually none of it was conceived to address extra-academic professional needs. Only incidentally or accidentally did it address the orientation and the set of skills that I would later value. For example, my training in fieldwork methods and techniques was a good start toward appreciating the technological tools of documentation, such as tape recorders, microphones, and cameras. The next logical step, however, the dissemination of that documentation through technology, was not taken. How to produce and promote a radio program, a film or video for television, a commercially available recording, a curriculum package, or a festival is fundamental to many public-sector ethnomusicologists. The requirement of actual fieldwork was important, but there was no approach to fieldwork that assumed a programmatic outlet for the results other than scholarly writings or lectures. From the perspective of the public sector, the ultimate application of any specific fieldwork should "frontload" its purpose, plan, priorities, and direction.

To take another example, the notion of bimusicality was a philosophical cornerstone of UCLA's program, equipping students with the "unspeakables" of musical style and the meaning of musical cultures—the *musical* knowledge that is most clearly communicated through music making, not through speaking or writing. For me, however, the one-on-one study of Ashanti (Asante) drumming with Kwasi Badu, Persian *santūr* (a zither) with Manoochehr Sadeghi, *mariachi* music with Jesús Sánchez, and Japanese *gagaku* (court music and dance) with Suenobu Togi offered another, unstated opportunity. Spending so much time with musicians deepened my admiration for my teachers as people and improved my skill at communicating across cultural barriers of language, style, and custom. The sense of connection and commitment to musicians of different cultural backgrounds that emerged from my study—in short, accountability to the artist—would direct my actions for the rest of my career.

Perhaps the most severe gap in my graduate training was the nearly total absence of professional role models other than college professors. How many students would pursue careers as environmentalists, oncologists, or business administrators if they had never heard of these people? Why were the extra-academic activities of ethnomusicologists such as Alan Lomax and Charles Seeger not put forward as valid, vital directions for students to consider? As a graduate student, I had no notion of career

FIGURE 1   During fieldwork in Boca del Río, Veracruz, Mexico, Daniel Sheehy (bottom left) poses with the *jarocho* musicians Daniel Ramos (bottom right), Isidoro Gutiérrez (the principal fieldwork consultant, top left), and Luis Zamudio (top right). Photo by Daniel Sheehy, 1978.

opportunities outside the university setting that would require my ethnomusicological skills. It took another unexpected turn of events to change that.

As I was completing my master's thesis on the *son jarocho* (a Mestizo musical tradition) of Veracruz in the early 1970s, I received a call from Bess Lomax Hawes, a professor of folklore and anthropology at California State University, Northridge, who was the daughter of the pioneering American folklorist John Lomax and the sister of Alan Lomax. (Pete Seeger once described Alan Lomax as the individual who had done the most to bring folk music to broad American audiences in the twentieth century.) Bess invited me to teach one of her courses while she was on leave to the Smithsonian Institution in Washington, D.C. There, she would direct the "Regional America" component of the mammoth twelve-week Bicentennial Smithsonian Festival of American Folklife that was held on the National Mall in Washington in 1976. I agreed, and not long after Bess had become familiar with my work and my interests, she contracted me as a fieldworker to suggest and locate Mexican immigrant musicians, groups, and styles to be part of the representation of folklife in California at the festival. What I had stumbled into was to be close to a dream come true.

I spent many days and many more nights learning about the hangouts, networks, and settings of musicians performing different styles of Mexican music (figure 1). I was being paid to go to bars, dance halls, and homes to meet musicians whom I much admired playing music that I loved. To top it off, some of them would be paid to travel to Washington, D.C., and perform for adoring audiences there. At the same time, Bess led extraordinarily stimulating, complex, and practical intellectual discussions about the strategy, cultural politics, aesthetics, public impact, and financial realities of the festival. For me, this consciousness-expanding experience included learning about the applied activities of other fields such as folklore and anthropology, and about institutions such as the Smithsonian. The close connection with musicians, the work on their behalf, the engagement with a broad public, and the sense of purpose and intellectual seriousness of the cultural workers were irresistable. I would in some way work for the annual Smithsonian Folklife Festival (as it is now called) nearly every year since then, as well as on countless other festivals, tours, recordings, and educational publications.

Another important mentorship in 1973 offered lessons that would undergird my later professional views and skills. Dr. Robert Stevenson, the preeminent historian of Latin American music, recommended me as an exchange scholar to spend six months with the University of Chile, teaching and doing fieldwork. My principal contact was the veteran Chilean folklorist Manuel Dannemann. Manuel was a highly energetic academic, constantly engaged in fieldwork throughout Chile and extraordinarily dedicated to the people and the expressive traditions he studied. In two months' time, we undertook four fieldwork excursions to four communities scattered thousands of miles apart in that long, thin nation, including a several-day trip in a Red Cross ambulance to the high Andean town of Pachama, near the Bolivian border, where the celebration of a patron saint was being held. With a Nagra tape recorder and a 35-mm single-lens reflex camera in hand, we recorded, photographed, and wrote about the rituals and music central to the celebration. Manuel's labors went far beyond those of documentarian. He constantly inquired into the needs of the people of the community: Did they need musical instruments? Was the adobe church in need of restoration? Did they need help with government paperwork? When he was not carrying out fieldwork, he would promote marketing opportunities for Chilean craftsworkers or organize public presentations of rural musicians in the capital city of Santiago, honoring them and making them and their communities more visible in the Chilean body politic. In that regard, to this day Manuel Dannemann remains close to my ideal of the academic culturologist—equally devoted to the teaching and scholarly endeavors of his university career and to the people whose expressions he studies. This model of scholarly behavior was an overarching lesson of my experience in Chile. Another was a greater appreciation for the view of folklorists who approached music as an integral aspect of a larger cultural *Gestalt*. Yet another was the often brutal connection between politics and culture: in September of 1973, the Chilean armed forces killed President Salvador Allende, along with tens of thousands of others, and outlawed certain forms of music associated with left-leaning population groups. Radical, though less lethal, politics would later come to bear on my work.

I seem to have gotten ahead of myself, and the section that follows indicates several pithy abiding opinions concerning training that I have acquired during my process of becoming an ethnomusicologist working in the public sector: (1) Public-sector work usually entails greater public accountability than academic work. (2) Field-work which engenders appreciation and awareness of the dynamics of music in community life, and which leads to an informed sense of accountability to the people one serves, is paramount in becoming a public-sector ethnomusicologist. (3) Intern-ships outside the academic setting that introduce journeymen ethnomusicologists to extra-academic role models, professional lifestyles, and required skills not taught in the academy are invaluable forms of training and the most effective means of profes-sional "networking." (4) If university programs in ethnomusicology are to address the needs of the student and society more effectively, they must offer better training of relevance to extra-academic professional life. (5) Mentorship—working in a practical setting under the close tutelage of a more experienced professional—is the ideal form of advanced training. (6) For the public-sector ethnomusicologist, training never ends, and one is always in a state of becoming, as the challenges of responding to public needs and working effectively in public institutions continuously evolve.

WORKING AS AN ETHNOMUSICOLOGIST IN THE PUBLIC SECTOR

My early stages of becoming an ethnomusicologist necessarily involved working as one, but for the sake of this article "Working as an Ethnomusicologist" begins in 1978, when I joined the National Endowment for the Arts, a federal agency in Wash-ington, D.C. At this juncture, my experience departed radically from that of my academic colleagues. My title was arts specialist; I spent hours each day on the tele-phone with grant applicants; I rarely lectured on musical topics; and there was no institutional incentive for me to do scholarly research or writing. There was little time or opportunity during official government work hours to do the things I had cherished most during my years of becoming—fieldwork, study, producing public programs, and teaching. Nevertheless, this was one of the most intellectually and professionally exciting and expansive stages of my career. It was also one of the most humbling.

Bess Lomax Hawes had been appointed director of the NEA's Folk Arts initiative in 1977 and by 1978 had successfully argued for placing the folk arts on a bureaucratic footing with other arts disciplines. The Folk Arts Program was given a grant budget of slightly less than two million dollars; and, in addition to Bess, an administrator, a secretary, a folklorist, and an ethnomusicologist were hired to run the grant program. The challenges we faced were significant. The NEA legislation required that we give matching grants to federally sanctioned nonprofit organizations in the United States and its territories (Guam, American Samoa, the Northern Marianas, Puerto Rico, and the U.S. Virgin Islands). In the culture of the NEA, the fine arts critical approach to evaluating and supporting art had a privileged position; this approach focused on the art object in relative isolation from its context. The NEA was created in large part as a result of pressure from influential fine arts professionals and devotees, and the his-torical prominence of orchestral music, modern and classical dance, theater, contem-porary painting, and other "high" arts had contributed to an accepted canon of artistic expression often referred to as Culture with a capital C. Furthermore, much of the NEA's orientation and success since its founding in 1965 had resulted from its role in creating and nurturing nonprofit organizations devoted exclusively to the arts, in most cases to a single discipline.

The expressions we at the NEA called folk arts, in contrast, were rarely allied with nonprofit organizations; still more rarely did these arts organize themselves into formal groups with boards, bylaws, federal certification of nonprofit status, and grant writers. Professionally staffed nonprofit organizations for the folk arts, such as the National Council for the Traditional Arts (in the Washington, D.C., area), the Center for Traditional Music and Dance (then called the Balkan Arts Center, in New York City), and the Center for Southern Folklore (in Memphis, Tennessee) were extremely few. In our more anthropological approach to the folk arts, cultural context and process were seen as inextricably related to the appreciation and support of the artistic expressions themselves. Organizations and individuals representing the folk arts had played no significant role in the NEA's genesis and formative stages and had little political status. Consequently, the chairmanship of the NEA and the membership of the National Council on the Arts, which oversaw NEA's activities—in both cases appointed by the president of the United States—included little significant representation of the folk arts. (Later, major exceptions would be the council member Robert Garfias, an ethnomusicologist; and the chairman, Bill Ivey, a folklorist.) The folk arts, including an array of expressions such as old-time Appalachian fiddle music, African-American quilts, Samoan tattoos, New Mexican Hispanic folk drama, Filipino *rondalla* music, and Native American moccasins, were usually outside—sometimes far outside—inherited notions of the fine arts. These inconsistencies with the NEA's normal way of doing business, along with the sheer size and diversity of our field and its physical and psychological distance from Washington, presented major challenges.

Our assets included our belief in the beauty, integrity, and inherent value of the arts, artists, and communities we served; the formidable personality, stature, and strategic acumen of our director, Bess Lomax Hawes; the public's recognition (despite ambiguity as to its exact definition) of the term *folk* in American popular culture; and, to no small extent, our underdog, counterculture status within the agency and among the arts. Also, Bess's work with the Smithsonian had strengthened ties between literally hundreds of cultural experts scattered throughout the United States and the budding efforts at cultural conservation and public representation in Washington, providing a brain trust to inform our work.

Endless discussions among those of us on the staff, folklore experts whom we would convene to evaluate grant applications, and others in our field yielded several important strategies for carrying out our mission. To remedy the lack of nonprofit institutions in our field, Bess favored courting the fifty-six governmental state and territorial arts agencies as host organizations for professional folklorists to act as field-worker liaisons at a more local level, in effect amplifying our ability to identify and address the needs of our folk arts constituents. By the 1990s, fifty states or territories would have statewide folk arts coordinators, as we called them, though many of them ended up being based in other types of organizations. In the early 1980s, we launched a program of support for apprenticeships to encourage one-on-one extended mentor-disciple relationships that were essential to passing on the knowledge, meaning, and skills of the folk arts. This effort evolved into a program of support for state-based apprenticeship programs that numbered forty at its peak and by the mid-1990s had supported more than 2,500 master-apprentice relationships. In 1982, the National Heritage Fellowship program was launched, annually recognizing numerous outstanding folk artists through national press releases, an awards ceremony in Washington, and a fellowship grant (which grew from an initial $5,000 to $10,000). By its twentieth year, in 2001, more than 250 individuals and groups had been honored in ceremonies in Congress or in the White House, and the award itself had achieved

FIGURE 2 Daniel Sheehy hands Hillary Clinton (then the first lady) a National Heritage Fellowship certificate for Liz Carroll of Chicago, an Irish-American fiddler. The occasion was an award ceremony in Washington, D.C., in the Caucus Room of the Russell Senate office building. At the rear, presiding, is Jane Alexander, chairman of the National Endowment for the Arts. Photo by Nick Spitzer, 1994.

national prominence, elevating the status of the folk arts overall in arts and governmental circles (figure 2).

I have long found it difficult to put into words the exact nature of my work at the NEA and how I relied on my ethnomusicological training to do it. A broad knowledge of the cultural panorama of the United States was fundamental, and acquiring and maintaining this knowledge was an unending task, as new immigrants constantly arrived and more cultural communities became connected to the network of institutional support. Offering technical assistance to our growing field was a major part of our work, and the more training I had in particular musical styles, the more effective I could be in giving advice and evaluating project proposals. Knowledge of the available expertise—of folklorists and ethnomusicologists in particular—was critical to our ability to evaluate activities in the field and adjudicate grant applications. One of my earliest memories of my work at the NEA illustrates the relevance of these issues. I received a telephone call from an individual who wanted to organize a *kantele* festival in the Washington, D.C., area and was looking for both financial support and connections to others who had organized similar events. My attempt to seem knowledgeable was futile. Given the limitations of my ethnomusicological emphases, I had no idea what culture the *kantele* was from (it is Finnish), let alone what it was (a psaltery—often called Finland's national instrument) or what other *kantele*-related events might already exist. Through the network of my ethnomusicological colleagues, I found the answers to all my and the caller's questions and suggested that my caller contact more experienced *kantele* festival organizers in Michigan. At that point, I was able to help the caller put together a grant application that would have some hope of success. The experience of being confronted with unknown cultural terrain was unending over the twenty-two years I spent at the NEA and had a wonderfully humbling effect. It taught me that knowing what I didn't know—that is, appreciating the vastness and and complexity of my field—was a first step in knowing how to proceed.

Fieldwork has been essential to me, even though it could not possibly be my major activity while I was at the NEA. Except for field research that I conducted on my own, the fieldwork I conducted for the NEA mainly took the form of brief trips to advise cultural organizers from local communities or nonprofit groups and to evaluate local efforts. Time limitations required an economy of effort and an insistence on relevance, so that our inquiries would yield the best information possible, both to assist grant applicants in formulating their plans and requests and to enable us to evaluate them in the framework of the competition for grants. This essential contact with our constituents was brief, and far from ideal, though approaching it with the intellectual and intuitive tools learned through more in-depth fieldwork helped greatly in planning, carrying out, and assessing our efforts. In addition, plans for fieldwork were built into many of the project proposals that came to us, and the ability to critique them came from training and experience. In the "on the ground" activities of public-sector cultural workers that our program funded, fieldwork was the essential foundation of practically any form of programming.

Communication skills were paramount in my work. It was extraordinarily challenging to explain the culturally diverse, nonprofessional, noninstitutionalized, community-based character of the folk arts—among other complexities—to arts administrators and others unfamiliar with these arts. Yet such explanations were essential in justifying the need for support of activities (fieldwork, for example) that were atypical of arts administration. Convincing agency policymakers of the importance of grants to organizations that did not specialize in the arts was critical to our efforts. Grants such as those given to a fire station in rural Virginia for a fiddle-making workshop and to an urban Jewish welfare group for a Cambodian dance workshop series raised eyebrows and required explanation. We had to tailor our language about our field for in-house agency meetings, memoranda, talks to general audiences, and the like; and we had to explain grant application procedures to novice grant writers.

Communication and a sense of bureaucratic strategy were never more important than during the time of the radical budget cutbacks and restructuring that resulted in 1995 from the attacks on the NEA by politically conservative individuals and organizations. I had become director of folk and traditional arts after Bess's retirement in 1992, and the many idiosyncrasies of our field were challenged as the staff and the grant budget were both reduced nearly by half. Uniform guidelines and procedures for grants were mandated, and our ability to give grants to state arts agencies, to nonprofit groups other than arts organizations, to recently organized groups, and to individuals was threatened.

The solutions to this major problem took two principal forms: (1) integrating our most useful grant strategies into a uniform approach and (2) arguing for set-aside exceptions. In accomplishing this, some triage was to be expected. The goals were to save the most important elements, and, if possible, find new opportunities in the shifting organizational terrain. Defining apprenticeship programs as "tradition-based learning" and positioning them as central to our field's priorities in the areas of education and heritage, two of the new high-priority rubrics for grants, helped to ensure continued support for them. The paucity of dollars in the overall budget, however, contributed to the demise of many of these statewide programs. The creation of the principal NEA grant category called "Heritage/Preservation," based on a concept akin to the "Folk and Traditional Arts," was a great benefit, as the number of NEA grant categories was reduced from more than a hundred (including several in folk and traditional arts) to four. With the support of Jane Alexander as chairman, our partnership efforts with state arts agencies in some ways were strengthened through the creation of the "Folk and Traditional Arts Infrastructure Initiative," a singular exception to the agency's restructuring, designed to expand statewide support for our field. A heightened focus on our field's underinstitutionalization made it possible to create a new "fast-track" source of technical assistance, called the "Traditional Arts Growth" (TAG) fund. Fellowship grants to individuals were under severe attack from certain elements in Congress, based mainly on inaccurate perceptions that they were the root cause of alleged obscene or otherwise controversial art. Both honorific fellowship categories were saved—by allying the National Heritage Fellowships with the NEA's Jazz

FIGURE 3 Daniel Sheehy at his desk in the offices of Smithsonian Folkways Recordings, Washington, D.C. Photo by Terence Liu.

Masters fellowship program, underscoring their character as "heritage preservation," and by the individuals in our field who enlisted the support of Senator Jeff Bingaman, a Democrat from New Mexico.

After I left the National Endowment for the Arts in 2000 to become the director and curator of Smithsonian Folkways Recordings (figure 3), a division of the Smithsonian Institution's Center for Folklife and Cultural Heritage, the change of perspective helped me see more clearly what had *not* been accomplished while I was at the NEA. Although many more ethnomusicologists had been invited into public-sector activities, I saw little progress in changing the culture of ethnomusicology to include applied activities per se among its central concerns. More publications, more forums for discussion and student involvement, and a broader vision of professional possibilities are needed for this to occur. I had managed to publish a couple of articles on the topic (1992a; 1992b), but the corpus of literature on applied issues aimed at ethnomusicologists had not grown much. A notable exception was an issue of *Ethnomusicology* (fall 1992) called "Special Issue: Music and the Public Interest," conceived of by the journal's editor, Jeff Todd Titon. Relevant publications by folklorists are more plentiful; one example is *Public Folklore*, edited by Robert Baron and Nicholas R. Spitzer (1992), though ethnomusicologists seem to have taken little notice. The current emergence of an applied ethnomusicology special interest section, spearheaded by Martha Davis, Doris Dyen, and others within the Society for Ethnomusicology, is encouraging. Infusing the spirit of "ethnomusicology is what you make it" into our daily discourse can only lead to a livelier intellectual ambience and to more societal esteem for the ethnomusicologist's skills.

REFERENCES

Baron, Robert, and Nicholas R. Spitzer, eds. 1992. *Public Folklore*. Washington, D.C.: Smithsonian Institution Press.

Sheehy, Daniel. 1992a. "A Few Notions about Philosophy and Strategy in Applied Ethnomusicology." *Ethnomusicology* 36(3):323–336.

———. 1992b. "Crossover Dreams: The Folklorist and the Folk Arrival." In *Public Folklore*, eds. Robert Baron and Nicholas R. Spitzer. Washington, D.C.: Smithsonian Institution Press.

Latin America and North America (II)

Brenda Romero

Becoming an Ethnomusicologist
Working as an Ethnomusicologist
My Place in the Field of Ethnomusicology

BECOMING AN ETHNOMUSICOLOGIST

I have always been fascinated by different cultures. Consequently, in high school I studied (with one other student in a group of our own) a number of foreign languages, including French, German, Russian, and Arabic (both colloquial and literary). Of these, I became most proficient in German, but I have only maintained French. I am a native speaker of Spanish and have studied Spanish at the university, as well as traveled or conducted research (or both) in Spain, Ecuador, and most recently Mexico. While I was in high school, my language teachers, Paul Haines and the late Alan Wilson, were my most important influences. Wilson was a polyglot with a wide repertoire of anecdotes and humorous multilingual puns. Haines taught only French but was also an avant-garde poet. At that time he was writing the lyrics to Carla Bley's avant-garde jazz opera *Escalator Over the Hill*. I baby-sat for Haines and his wife, Jo, in Paris and London, when they were on their way to teach at the American School in New Delhi after leaving New Mexico. I was with them in Paris in 1968 when the student demonstrations there signaled the start of a new era. I still remember the manifestos on the walls of the school of medicine—and the Haineses' incessant references to music in everything they did. As I got to know them better, I began to listen differently.

Music was a regular aspect of my life while I was growing up, as my uncles and brothers all played some instrument and my mother and sisters sang. At age two, I begin to imitate church and popular singers on the radio, sometimes learning songs in English, although I didn't speak the language. I joined choirs in middle school and high school, and at age thirteen I taught myself to play the ukulele with the help of books, and especially with the help of two girlfriends who played it. At seventeen I again used books to begin learning the classical guitar, using a guitar that a friend had bought for me in Spain. I began formal instruction in classical guitar with a Cuban teacher, Hector García, during my freshman year at the University of New Mexico (UNM).

I took my first ethnomusicology course (in Indian music, with a visiting professor, Henry Powers) at the University of California at Berkeley in 1970, but I left the university to start a family. I lived for three years in Brisbane, Australia, in the early 1970s, and there I studied voice at the Brisbane Conservatory and Japanese at the

University of Queensland. When I returned from Australia, I again studied at the University of New Mexico, spending five months in Quito, Ecuador. There I took courses in Latin American anthropology, history, and literature and Spanish phonology at the Centro Andino, a joint venture (now discontinued) between UNM and Northwestern University.

I returned to UNM in Albuquerque and became a music major. I eventually received a bachelor's degree and a master's degree in music theory and composition, having also studied voice and classical guitar. At UNM I was chagrined to learn that there were no courses on the musics of local Hispano or Native cultures, although a rather sizable collection of recordings was housed in the John Donald Robb Archives of Southwestern Music. In my third and final year in the master's program, I received special funding from the graduate school to work with the Robb collection and develop teaching materials for a course I taught in the spring semester of 1986. The course culminated in a public concert that I directed with the students in the class.

This led to my pursuing a doctorate in ethnomusicology, although I also felt (rightly or wrongly) that the study of composition at the doctoral level would undermine the emotional dimensions of music and would be entirely Western-focused. Additionally, I was particularly interested in the possibility that ethnomusicology could attract members of minority groups to the university, where they could presumably learn to teach about their own cultural musics. I completed my doctorate at the University of California, Los Angeles (UCLA), in 1993.

My composition teachers at the university, William Wood and Scott Wilkinson, were influential because they recognized my talent in writing music and helped me develop my skills. The direction and expertise of a number of scholars at UCLA were crucial to my development in ethnomusicology. Elaine Barkin offered diverse approaches to composition that took into account non-Western musical cultures. Steven Loza, Charlotte Heth, Jihad Racy, Jacque DjeDje, and Amy Catlin, each in one way or another, inspired me and nurtured my academic development at UCLA and after I left to take a job at the University of Colorado in Boulder in 1988.

My early fieldwork on the Matachines dance in New Mexico paralleled that of the anthropologist Sylvia Rodriguez, and we often ran into each other in the field and compared notes. Most recently, the literary folklorist Enrique Lamadrid and the anthropologist Charles L. Briggs (the grandson of John Donald Robb) have been critical to the direction that my work on New Mexico and Mexico is taking. I recently completed a nine-month Fulbright scholarship in Mexico. I am indebted to Professor Jesús Jáuregui of the Instituto Nacional de Antropología e Historia and his students for the thorough and methodical ethnographic work they have done on *danza* in Mexico, providing contexts for the ethnomusicological research I am conducting there. In the area of performance, Steven Loza, Jihad Racy, and the Mexican ethnomusicologists Guillermo Contreras Arias and Gonzalo Camacho have been particularly helpful and inspiring.

WORKING AS AN ETHNOMUSICOLOGIST

I have conducted field studies among Hispano and Native peoples in California, New Mexico, Colorado, and Mexico. I conducted part of the research for my dissertation in a variety of libraries in Spain, and familiarity with Spanish musical customs has proved useful to my understanding of the music traditions of Latin America and the Southwestern United States. Although I also recorded flamenco singers at a number of public fiestas in Spain and southern France, I did not pursue ethnographic field or library research on this subject.

My work among the Cahuilla of southern California began as a collaborative video project when I was in graduate school, studying field methodology with Amy Catlin at UCLA. I continued to follow the Birdsong Festival for two years after I moved to Colorado. In the mid-1990s I conducted fieldwork on the Ute Bear Dance at Ute Mountain in Toyoac, Colorado. I was allowed to play with the musicians in the early part of the day, before people arrived—a unique experience. The work at Ute Mountain involved returning copies of my video and audio documentation in a very formal legal manner.

I began conducting field research on the Matachines dance of New Mexico in 1987. I worked in two Pueblo Indian locations (the Pueblo of Jemez and San Juan Pueblo) and one Hispano location (Alcalde). In 1989, although still something of a novice, I became the violin player for the dance in Jemez in order to prevent the tradition from declining or disappearing for lack of a fiddler. I completed my dissertation and doctoral degree in 1993 but devoted another five years to playing in Jemez, assisting three local players in learning the Matachines repertoire. The Pueblo continued to invite me year after year; but when I was satisfied that one of the local players could perform all the pieces well enough, I stopped going and he was allowed to play. He is the grandson of the fiddler who preceded me. Before playing the violin, at age seventeen he had accompanied me on the guitar following the Pueblo guitarist's death in 1994. The violin repertoire is demanding enough that none of the local folk players had been able to take my place, and I had coached my replacement on the technique required for one fast piece in particular.

My acting in such a practical capacity at Jemez was a result of my graduate training at UCLA under Charlotte Heth, who had stressed the importance of community-based field research for Native America. As one of the musicians for the Matachines dance ceremony, I was able to return something to the Pueblo at the same time as I was conducting field research. Since then, community-based research has become a developing aspect of my work wherever I am; thus, my initial contact with a community entails a commitment to return something, eventually, if at all possible.

Having received permission to conduct my fieldwork in Jemez when I first went there, and since the Pueblo continued to invite me to play, I failed to realize that it was necessary to ask permission of the Pueblo governors who took office at the beginning of subsequent years. Further, when I submitted my dissertation to the then governor, I was informed that it could take a year for the spiritual leaders to approve the content. I could accept this condition, or I could delete all the ethnographical materials I had collected about Jemez. Since the dissertation did not depend entirely on the material from Jemez, and since it would not be professionally advantageous for me to prolong completion of my doctoral degree, I omitted that material. I plan to obtain permission to include selected unproblematic portions in a study focusing on the Matachines on both sides of the border.

The problems with my dissertation arose in part from an earlier controversial dissertation focusing on Jemez. This work, written by a member of the clergy who had not asked permission, had violated Pueblo rules that prohibit the writing of Towa, the Jemez native language.

I continue to be greeted with "Welcome home" each time I visit the Pueblo. I have provided the Pueblo with video copies of my final performance with the Jemez, a rare presentation outside the Pueblo that took place in a public conciliatory quincentennial performance at a festival produced by Enrique Lamadrid in September 1998 at the University of New Mexico. This festival celebrated the little-recognized but centuries-long bridge between Indio and Hispano in New Mexico through customs like those practiced by the Matachines, customs that are neither well known nor well understood by outsiders.

In Mexico I have not only collected as much literature about the Matachines *danza* as possible but also conducted field research in a number of states (figure 1). My initial study has focused on identifying regional styles and variants, as well as getting a general sense of the musical and cultural forces and values that affect the

FIGURE 1   Brenda M. Romero with members of the local Matachines *danza* in Trancoso, Zacatecas, Mexico, for the Feast of Our Lady of Guadalupe, celebrated not in December but on 12 February 2001. Photo from the author.

danza from region to region and place to place. As with my focus on the *danza* in New Mexico and Colorado, in Mexico I have concentrated on Indigenous-Mestizo (in New Mexico I call it Pueblo-Hispano) cultural interaction, although the situation in Mexico is considerably more complicated. My recent stay in Mexico gave me a better understanding of Mexican societies and cultures, greatly improved my Spanish, and allowed me to gain a general idea of what the *danza* looks and sounds like throughout Mexico. I am now planning specific site studies in Chihuahua, Zacatecas, and possibly a third state, which will focus on the semiotic interconnections among the various aspects of the *danza*, including music and cultural change. This includes finding entire musical repertoires, which are rapidly declining as Mexico becomes a technological society. Some of these repertoires take several days to perform and are now rarely heard in ceremonial contexts, even when a fiesta lasts for a week or more. Louder musical groups like the *banda* (a large, popular wind band similar to the old swing bands) and amplified rock bands are encroaching on what was once sacred ground.

In all these settings, either I am introduced or, if I have no host, I strike up informal conversations with the musicians and *danzantes*. After introducing myself and my project, I obtain permission to conduct interviews and make videos and tape recordings. The most difficult part of this is conforming to the requirements of the Human Resource Committee at my university, because it is not always feasible or desirable to have everyone sign a consent form. I offer copies of important materials to individuals, or to cultural centers to which many of these individuals might have access. Delivering the materials gives me an opportunity to gather culturally informed documentation to add to my own field and recording notes as I view a video with selected individuals. This is something that I am adapting from the field methods of Amy Catlin and Nazir Jairazbhoy, as well as from Amie Maciszewski's work in India. I am also teaching members of some regional cultural institutions to log and document their own recordings so that these recordings will have archival value. Again, this applied focus is a result of UCLA's emphasis on community-based research.

In New Mexico I could not even carry a notebook while conducting fieldwork in the Pueblos; once, in San Ildefonso, I saw someone else's small notebook confiscated. I could take photographs in San Juan Pueblo during certain years, when photographing the Matachines was allowed for a fee. In Jemez I was allowed to tape-record my own performances in the central ceremonial plaza, but nothing else. I took some photographs outside the plaza, but never of the ceremonies. In San Juan it was not unusual to see members of the culture taking pictures of their loved ones during sacred public ceremonies, but this was rare in Jemez except outside the plaza. My usual practice in the Pueblos of New Mexico (a practice I learned from Sylvia Rodriguez) has been to dictate my impressions to a tape recorder while they are fresh, usually while I am driving from the Pueblo to my mother's home in New Mexico or to my own home in Colorado. This process is very effective, although transcribing the cassettes later is extremely time-consuming.

Such restrictions on field research are rare in Hispano settings throughout New Mexico and Mexico. There, it is not unusual for me to make videos and tape recordings simultaneously, and perhaps shoot a few rolls of film when I am not video-recording. Although I always ask permission, I often see others recording without permission. I typically develop two sets of prints and send one set to key people. I recently acquired a digital camera, and this will facilitate giving away enlargements or edited photos. I always carry a notebook, but my experience in the Pueblo has left me with a sense that I do not want people to feel "studied," so I try not to write when they can see me, except to make quick notes and take down the names and addresses of those to whom I am promising materials. In Mexico, I tried writing my field notes when I returned from the field, as part of the process of logging and documenting my field

FIGURE 2   In Aguacatitlán, Guerrero, 24 July 1999. Left to right: Rubén Luéngas Pérez and Patricia García López (ethnomusicology students and performers at UNAM), Juan Carranza Soriano (director of the Casa de Cultura in Chilpancingo, Guerrero), Brenda M. Romero, Guillermo Contreras Arias (ethnomusicologist and performer at UNAM and CENIDIM), and Edgar Serralde Mayer (ethnomusicology student and performer at UNAM). Photo by Pablo Pérez Márquez.

recordings. As a result, there is a symbiotic relationship between my field notes and tape logs (see below).

I consider doing solitary fieldwork the most limiting aspect of field research, and I deplore the fact that the United States has no equivalent of France's Centre National de Recherche Scientifique, whose interdisciplinary teams of researchers go into the field together for extended periods of time. A team minimizes the individual researcher's limitations, which result from our typical life in highly specialized academic contexts.

In Mexico, collaboration in the field was possible in only a few instances and primarily involved taking ethnomusicology students along (figure 2). Here is an excerpt from my field notes, followed by a tape log of one collaborative field trip that included the Mexican ethnomusicologist Guillermo Contreras Arias and two students, Rubén Luéngas Perez and Pablo Márquez. The occasion was a vigil for the feast day of Nuestra Señora de Guadalupe, the patron saint of Mexico, on the night of 11–12 December 2000. As you can see, the students contributed humorous musings.

> Everywhere people were lying on thick blankets, waiting for the dawn—*el amanecer*—when the majority would fulfill their pilgrimage by dancing for the Virgen. G spotted a group of Matlachines [a common Mexican variant of the name] from their tall five-color feathered *penachos*. Since we had two small portable stools, we pushed in front of the crowd and sat, I videotaping and G taking notes. Rubén audiotaped, and Pablo took pictures. This was the Matlachines Internacionales de Aguascalientes. The fringe over the face was layered horizontally, rather than vertically, over the eyes. The overall look was Toltec to me (I had seen the Voladores many times while growing up in Gallup, New Mexico, when they came to the August Gallup Ceremonials) rather than Matachines in the far northern contexts. The fringe was sequined and flashy, as is usual for Matachines in Mexico. The design reminded me of the way I imagine the descriptions I have read of how the fringe was used to resemble a hand to prevent *mal de ojo* among the Moors. I need to try to find drawings or photos of that Moorish custom.

> I videotaped against large lights set up on two sides; and I eventually moved to the other side, where there was less glare, although there was another pair of lights at the opposite end. The worst of it was that inside the Basílica there was

The Matachines tradition is binational and has the potential to bring better intercultural understanding to people on both sides of the border.

an official "show" going on, with every famous singer singing praises to the Virgen. The sound was transmitted at a very high volume to the crowd outside the Basílica, with a huge television screen (made up of at least nine sections) at the top of the front entrance to the Basílica. The Matlachines and a Danza Azteca group behind us (closer to the entrance to the square) were the only ones who tried to keep on dancing as midnight approached. As the "show" got quiet—or at least quieter—the Matlachines would pick up. The *danzantes* struggled to concentrate on their steps as the transmitted blare became overwhelmingly loud at times. Furthermore, I was struck by the contrast between the "legitimacy" of the cultivated people, featured in the "show" inside, and the poor pilgrims who had sacrificed to come to Mexico City to play and dance for the Virgen, to make supplications for healing and blessings. Rubén, Pablo, and I discussed this at length later. They suggested that I launch a campaign to marry the president (Fox) [who was unmarried at the time], and then to inculcate some learning about and sensitivity to such problems [which are rapidly becoming more common throughout Mexico].

Compare this description with the forty-minute SVHSC tape log:

Velación para Nuesta Sra. de Guadalupe, before midnight
Tape 2/4
    0:00
    0:37. I am now situated in front of the crowd. I am facing a bright light and am distant enough from the drum that my microphone picks up, equally with the drum, the music that is being transmitted from the loudspeakers—the spectacle that is going on inside the Basílica—and being broadcast internationally.
    2:17. Loss of focus.
    2:33. Focused; *danzantes* stand in place; one makes adjustments to his *penacho* [headdress].
    4:35. Drum begins to sound and *danzantes* begin to dance again, with occasional yells at particular points in the choreography.
    10:18. The *danzantes* pause again. A drumbeat in the background is from another dance group behind us. One hears the broadcast inside the Basílica.
    13:20. Camera goes to the big screen, where the attention of much of the public is focused during this brief *descanso* [rest] for the *danzantes*.
    13:55. *Danza* begins again; the broadcast is especially piercing and is in marked contrast to the *danza*.
    17:20. Lots of yells (yelps).
    19:34. *Danzantes* pause again; drumbeat in the background.
    20:40. *Danzantes* continue.
    25:00. Drumbeat in the background like heartbeat; shortly thereafter, the church music becomes "indigenous," accompanying a dance that Guillermo says is from Guerrero; the *danzantes* continue.

28:49. I changed positions during the pause that took place and am now shooting from the opposite end, a little closer to the drum. Much of the drum performance involves adjusting its rhythm to that of the events taking place inside the Basílica.

29:40. Close-up of the drum, with the group's name: "Matlachines Internacionales de Aguascalientes."

33:10. Pause; it's midnight and *Las Mañanitas* [a ceremonial greeting song] is broadcast. Instead of singing, the crowd listens and watches the big screen where the *mariachi* is playing. I am aghast with disappointment, having expected to hear the 10,000 voices outside singing it all together.

34:47. I promise to deliver or send a copy of the video and note the address and telephone number.

36:20. During the applause, the helper tells me that they have traveled to Cuba, Jamaica, Costa Rica, and Venezuela. He says he is also a *danzante*, but he has hurt his back, so he helps. He has been with the group forty-one years, and he has been coming to the *velación* for forty-one years.

37:05. The *danza* resumes while another version of *Las Mañanitas* continues to be broadcast.

39:50. *Danza* ends; *danzantes* depart.

When I was accompanied, my research was broader in scope, as my coworkers asked their own questions and we followed up on leads together. A comprehensive write-up of the accounts above is pending, after we view a copy of the field tape together and compile each individual's contributions. This is identical to the process of returning to a community to view and discuss log footage together. These notes will be incomplete until I have viewed the tape with the musicians and *danza* leaders and recorded their comments.

Collaborative fieldwork can be a challenge for those who are used to being in charge or who may not have the social skills necessary to work in an egalitarian atmosphere. It requires a great deal of trust among coworkers, and this trust is not necessarily easily come by, because of the competitive mind-set typical of Western capitalist societies. Collaborative field research is particularly difficult in situations involving men and women who come from countries with sharply differing attitudes toward gender roles.

In Mexico City, I taught a seminar for the ethnomusicology students at the Universidad Nacional Autónoma de México. Half of the time, I focused on speaking about the music of New Mexico, providing cultural analyses of Hispano and Pueblo musics, including Matachines music. Proceeding in a southerly direction, I used Matachines music and *danza* as a frame of reference for understanding how indigenous and *mestizo* cultural elements can be read. My presentations were based on my version of fundamental ethnomusicological theory, and the students were able to see how some of the ideas they had been reading about and discussing can be applied in a field study. They were also happy to learn more about a tradition that has great importance in the northern part of the republic but is almost unknown in Mexico City and farther south. Here are some notes I used in class to establish the questions basic to my study of the Matachines in Mexico:

A. *Los hechos hasta ahora* [what I have done so far].
My study of the *danza* from 1987 to the present.
Reflexivity, studying my own culture.
Cultural interaction in New Mexico.
Etc.

Extending to Mexico: trying to see a larger picture from the continuities and discontinuities across and within borders. What does it mean to see so many different versions of the Matachines? What distinguishes the Matachines from similar *danzas* with different names? How significant are the differences? Do similar *danzas* have similar meanings? How do regional styles differ? What accounts for the differences in regional styles? Cultural differences? Economical status? Are there some aspects that are always the same? If so, what are they?

How is the study ethnomusicological as opposed to dance-ethnographical? Focus at the beginning would be the same for both; has to begin by defining the social and physical contexts of the music and dance.

Is the event a *fiesta patronal*? Festival? Political function? Are the dancers or musicians complying with a *manda* or *promesa*? Are the Matachines there on a contractual arrangement? If so, how much are they paid? Does this include the cost of the musicians? Where does the *danza* take place? Does it occupy different locations? If so, what are they? Do the locations have spiritual or social significance? Is a special status accorded to some locations but not others?

At some point this study has to switch from a focus on choreography and gestures to a focus on the musical culture and the music itself. Without the music there is no *danza*. What is the nature of the music? Is it old or is it newly composed? Are there any beliefs associated with the music? Are there specific repertoires, genres, or both? What are the names of the pieces played? Why are they called by these names? How many songs make up the sequence of the *danza*? What instruments are used? What are the names of the instruments and their parts? What materials are they made of? Where did the performers get them, or who made them? Are any special accessories needed for the instruments? Are some instruments more or less essential to the *danza*? Do the instruments have significance beyond producing sound? If so, what is that significance? Who are the musicians? Are they paid? If so, who pays them? How much? Is anyone allowed to play? What is the social organization of the musicians? Does the tradition stay within families? Where did the musicians learn the particular songs or repertoire? What is the role of the musicians with regard to the dance and the *danza*?

What is the relationship between the music and the dance? Do the dancers provide musical elements? If so, how? Does the dance determine the form of the music in any way? If so, how?

The students found much of interest in the tradition and were amazed by the virtuosity required of the Matachines musicians and dancers in some regions. I illustrated the materials on Mexico with my field videotapes, and the students were also able to see how I interview people and how I establish a rapport with interviewees. The female students were particularly inspired; and, as my hair is cut short, my Mexican colleagues teased me, saying that some of the young women had also cut their hair short, in my honor. I was very pleased to help the students discover something of their own cultural heritage, about which they knew very little; this is a tradition that continues across the border into the southwestern United States and links us despite political barriers.

This underscores one of the reasons that I continue to focus on this tradition: it is binational and has the potential to bring better intercultural understanding to people on both sides of the border. People in the small towns of New Mexico often believe that the Matachines represent a strictly local tradition. Perhaps with time they will develop an interest in seeing how groups in Mexico perform the *danza*. Toward this end, I am collaborating with Dr. Norma Cantú of the University of Texas at San Antonio to facilitate a binational gathering of Matachines groups and researchers. We hope to publish the proceedings in both Spanish and English.

In the Southwest and elsewhere in the United States, I have often given classroom and public presentations on the Matachines *danza* and played recorded selections of Matachines tunes from both sides of the border. Audiences find it very interesting to hear aspects of the Mexican tunes in the New Mexican ones, and vice versa. It is also fascinating, for many people, to see such a seemingly indigenous ceremony among the Hispanos of New Mexico. This helps to dispel stereotypes and arouses interest in the history of Pueblo-Hispano intercultural relationships in the Southwest and in the cultural relationships we share with people in Mexico.

MY PLACE IN THE FIELD OF ETHNOMUSICOLOGY

Until relatively recently, I concentrated on the modern concept of worldviews and cultural systems. Today, although I still find this focus, and historical research, useful in the early stages of a study, I am seeking more effective investigative approaches. That the Matachines *danza* is found on both sides of the border between the United States and Mexico has led me to current discussions about borderlands in the writings of Latino literary scholars and in the work of Charles L. Briggs, who has also done considerable work in performance anthropology. Victor Turner's theory of "liminality" continues to be current in this area. The multiple variants and sites of the Matachines have also led me to the anthropologist George Marcus's ideas about a world system and its implications for multisited ethnography. At the same time, I am uncomfortable about abandoning the idea of specificity, and so I am attempting to identify larger "fractal" cultural patterning to account for the range of variation. The ideas of Mexican scholars who have been working with the anthropologist Jesús Jáuregui have led me to join them in a search for creation narratives and metanarratives that continue to inform the *danza* in all its variations.

I have long been interested in the relationship between cultural interaction, music, and spirituality. The tradition of the Matachines brings ephemeral rewards, hard to capture for the ethnographical document. The emphasis on semiotics in my work arises from a search for meaning in the ephemeral and nonverbal aspects of music. It is a challenge to create a discourse for mystical experiences, such as apparitions of the Virgen de Guadalupe, that inform the intent of the *danza*. Finally, I am eager to highlight local musicians, following a tradition established by ethnomusicologists such as David MacAllester.

An innovative dimension of my work has been an emphasis on social change and applied ethnomusicology. Influenced early on by Baha'i religious teachings, I have long been convinced that the world is facing a spiritual crisis and have taken to heart the Baha'i injunction that it is my obligation to find myself in the company of people from different cultures. In New Mexico I focused not so much on conflict as on junctures where Pueblo and Hispano cultures have found something in common through music. I tried to exemplify this through my relationship with the people I worked with in the Pueblos. I have tried to focus on the contributions of the so-called subaltern, and this has been particularly easy in Mexico, where so much of the cultural fabric has been shaped consciously or subconsciously by the descendants of the great indigenous societies that preceded the European conquest. I have sought to make the musicians of different cultures more visible and to bring their voices to the forefront by devising strategies to include more of their commentary and emphases in my field documentation. I have tried to be not just an ethnographer but a friend of the people with whom I work, and I have tried to return something of my work to the communities where I have conducted field research. In these aspects of my work, I have been inspired by Charlotte Heth, Amy Catlin, John Schechter, and many others.

I also find myself spending more and more time organizing field notes, tape logs, and visual documentation like digital photographs and field videos in computer formats. This is crucial to the process of returning materials to the people in a timely way and maximizes the utility of the field document while preparing it to be deposited in an archive.

REFERENCES

Briggs, Charles L., and Richard Bauman. 1992. "Genre, Intertextuality, and Social Power." *Journal of Linguistic Anthropology* 2(2):131–172.

Comaroff, John L. 1987. "Of Totemism and Ethnicity: Consciousness, Practice, and the Signs of Inequality." *Ethnos* 52:301–323.

Guyette, Susan. 1983. *Community-Based Research: A Handbook for Native Americans*. Los Angeles: Regents of the University of California.

Jáuregui, Jesús, and Carlo Bonfiglioli, eds. 1992. *Las danzas de conquista en el México contemporá-neo*. México: Consejo Nacional Papa la Cultura y las Artes—Fondo de Cultura Económica.

Lamadrid, Enrique. 1997. "El Sentimiento Trágico de la Vida: Notes on Regional Style in Nuevo Mexicano Ballads." *Aztlán* 22 (1, spring):1–21.

———. 2000. *Nuevo México Profundo: Rituals of an Indo-Hispano Homeland*. With Miguel Gandert, Ramón Gutiérrez, Lucy Lippard, and Chris Wilson. Santa Fe: Museum of New Mexico Press.

Marcus, George E. 1995. "Ethnography in/of the World System: The Emergence of Multi-Sited Ethnography." *Annual Review of Anthropology* 24:95–117.

Nájera-Ramirez, Olga. 1997. *La Fiesta de los Tastaones: Critical Encounters in Mexican Festival Performance*. Albuquerque: University of New Mexico Press.

Rodriguez, Sylvia. 1996. *The Matachines Dance: Ritual Symbolism and Interethnic Relations in the Rio Grande Valley*. Albuquerque: University of New Mexico Press.

Latin America and East Asia
Dale A. Olsen

Background, Topics, and Preparations
Fieldwork
Laboratory Work
Dissemination

"Ah, such beautiful music!" said the jaguar.
"Now you must not eat me," replied the monkey.
"Certainly not," said the jaguar,
"because you are a musician." (Olsen 1996:110)

I collected that wonderful narrative from one of my Warao teachers in 1972, and it was one of the reasons that encouraged me to define ethnomusicology as follows: "Ethnomusicology is the study of a culture's music undertaken to learn something about how that culture thinks about itself and the world it lives in. . . . An important question the ethnomusicologist must ask is, what can music tell us about a civilization, a nation, a tribe, a village, a person, that nothing else can tell us?" (1996:xxv). The narrative about the jaguar and the monkey tells me that among the Warao, music has aesthetic qualities and magical powers, musical performance is essential, and performers are valued.

Mantle Hood, my teacher and mentor at the University of California, Los Angeles (UCLA), explained, "Ethnomusicology is an approach to the study of *any* music" (1969:298). As an approach, ethnomusicology can be applied to many musical situations; the most common are living communities or individuals with whom the ethnomusicologist can personally interact. (I prefer to call the people with whom I interact my teachers or friends, although others may use the term *informants* or *consultants*.) Additionally, as an approach, ethnomusicology can be applied to music history, music iconography, "organology," dance, or any number of other disciplines. For example, besides researching the ethnomusicology of living people such as the Warao, the *nikkei* communities, and many others in many parts of the world, I have also conducted ethnomusicological research in archaeology. For this type of investigation I have coined the term *ethnoarchaeomusicology*—a combination of ethnomusicology, ethnoarchaeology, and archaeomusicology, by which I mean the cultural and interpretative study of music from archaeological sources (Olsen 2002:8).

When I am asked to lecture about ethnomusicology as a discipline, I usually begin by writing "e t h n o M U S I C o l o g y" on the blackboard, emphasizing that music is at the center of the word. I do this because of my particular interest in and approaches to the discipline, which are greatly influenced by music as sound and music as performance. I continue to explain how sound and the performance that produces sound can tell us something about the people who make music. I then explain that there are three primary aspects of ethnomusicology: fieldwork, laboratory work, and dissemination.

In this essay about an ethnomusicologist at work, I will discuss how I prepare for the field, the philosophical and practical foundations of what I do in the field and why, my approaches to laboratory analysis, and the outcomes of my research.

BACKGROUND, TOPICS, AND PREPARATIONS

Before beginning any type of original ethnomusicological work for which fieldwork is important (and I cannot think of any time when fieldwork is not integral to original ethnomusicological research), one has to spend many months thinking about research design and learning about the people among whom and the regions in which the work will take place. This time must also be spent seeking funding for the research and making contacts with many people.

Warao

I spent approximately one year studying about the Warao of Venezuela before traveling to the Orinoco River delta. I was fortunate to be at UCLA and to be involved with Johannes Wilbert and the Latin American Center—the study of the Warao is one area of specialization there, and the UCLA libraries probably own everything ever published about the Warao. Through Wilbert's course on South American Indians I became very interested in music and shamanism. One day, after he played a Warao rainmaking song in class, I offered to transcribe it for him. When he saw the results, he was apparently impressed because he suggested that I do research among the Warao for my Ph.D. dissertation in ethnomusicology. It was his excitement about the possible contributions I could make with the Warao, a culture he had devoted a lifetime to studying, that encouraged me to follow his advice.

During that time I also sought funding and submitted a proposal for the Clifton Webb Award. The dean of fine arts at UCLA liked my proposal and invited me to his office to discuss how he could financially assist me. I asked him to call Dr. Wilbert, then director of the Latin American Center, and encourage him to match the funds from the fine arts department. (I suggested that he say, "I will give Olsen x dollars if you will match it.") Professor Wilbert did, and I was ready to begin my travel preparations.

Because of the interest at UCLA in the Warao, I was able to discuss very specific details about the logistics of Warao research with anthropology students who had just returned from the Orinoco delta. Dr. Wilbert also made arrangements for me to use his personal guide to transport me by canoe to the village where I would live (figure 1). There was still much for me to do on my own, of course, but such logistical details are vitally important before a trip to a rain forest, or any other locations far from urban centers.

Additional research trips to the Orinoco River delta were funded by UCLA and grants from Florida State University (FSU), where I was hired upon graduation in 1973. I have been fortunate to obtain grants quite easily, partially because of luck, but I think also because of the uniqueness of the regions in South America where I have chosen to do fieldwork. My experiences as a Peace Corps volunteer for nearly three years in Chile were of tremendous help in developing an understanding of South America, and, of course, I became quite fluent in Spanish (and also in Portuguese). The entire process of winning grants is what I call the mushroom effect: the more grants you receive, the more you will continue to receive, as long as you are successful and productive—meaning that you must publish.

FIGURE 1   Cesáreo Soto, a Warao river pilot and boat captain, guides his motorized canoe through one of the many rivers of the Orinoco delta to transport the author from the Venezuelan village of Barrancas on the Orinoco River to the Warao village of Yaruaro Akoho on the Winikina River—a two-day journey in 1973. The sheets of plastic protect the luggage and equipment from the rain. Photo by Dale A. Olsen.

Nikkei: Japanese immigrant communities

When I went to UCLA for my Ph.D. I put my flute skills (B.A. and M.A. in flute performance and historical musicology) to work by studying the Japanese *syakuhati* with Mitsuru Yuge, a master player of the Kinko *ryû* 'school'. When I was hired by Florida State University, I was given a small sum of money to buy ten *syakuhati* in Japan, where I spent part of the summer of 1972. The school of music wanted me to develop a Japanese music ensemble, and teaching *syakuhati* was to be a part of this plan. After several years I heard about a company in Jacksonville called Denny's Payless Grocery and Salvage Mart that had ten Japanese *koto* for sale for $50 each. The dean of the school of music gave me a check for $500, and I drove to Jacksonville to buy them. Suddenly, Florida State University had ten *syakuhati*, a *syakuhati* teacher, ten *koto*, and no *koto* teacher. Therefore, I applied to the Japan Foundation for a grant and proposed that FSU should be funded to hire a *koto* teacher. I was awarded the grant for two years, during which time we had five artists-in-residence to teach *koto* and *syamisen* (in English, samisen), two each academic year and one additional person during the summers. Besides teaching the Japanese instruments, we formed an ensemble and traveled throughout the United States presenting concerts of traditional music for Japanese artistic, business, and political functions. This story is leading up to what has become another major research area for me—music in the lives of Japanese immigrant (*nikkei*) societies in South America.

I was awarded a Fulbright grant in 1979 to teach ethnomusicology and conduct research in Lima, Peru, where I gave *syakuhati* lessons to several *nikkei* men and performed several concerts with two *nikkei* women. In 1981 I was awarded a grant to conduct similar research with *nikkei* in Brazil. One of the first things I did in São Paulo was to visit the Japanese consul, and when we first met he said, "I have heard about you." He had learned about me through the Japan Foundation and the numerous concerts I had performed with Florida State University's artists-in-residence from 1979 through early 1981. I have often been amazed at the networking that becomes possible when one performs music, interacts with music makers and listeners, and studies and writes about music. Through the consul's introductions I met many *nikkei* musicians in Brazil, gave several concerts, and was eventually awarded a *natori* (a teaching diploma and professional name) in *syakuhati* from an *iemoto* (master) who had immigrated to Brazil in 1957 (figure 2).

In 1993 I received a sabbatical and research grant to expand my studies of the South American *nikkei*. Through an Argentinean visiting professor at FSU, I made arrangements to perform Japanese music in Buenos Aires and La Plata. One of my graduate students had grown up in Paraguay, and through him I made contacts that I needed for living in Asunción and Ciudad del Este. *Nikkei* networks between editors of Japanese-language newspapers in Buenos Aires and Asunción enabled me to give a concert in Asunción. Then I traveled to the interior of Brazil, again contacting people whose names had been given to me by new friends and teachers in Paraguay. I also returned to São Paulo to work more with my *syakuhati* teacher, and then went back to Buenos Aires to perform another concert. On my way back to the United States I stopped off in Santa Cruz, Bolivia, where I met more *nikkei* musicians. An invitation to present a *syakuhati* recital at a Latin American flute festival in Lima in 1996 brought me back to Peru, where I performed five concerts during July. Thus, through a combination of contacts made in advance and contacts made by chance, I conducted fieldwork among the *nikkei* of South America, and my performances on *syakuhati* were crucial to my research.

Ethnoarchaeomusicology

My background interests and experiences with the musical instruments of ancient South America began when my wife, Diane, and I were Peace Corps volunteers in the

FIGURE 2   The *syakuhati iemoto* 'master' Tsuna Iwami and the author—his student—playing at Iwami's house in São Paulo, Brazil. Coincidentally, our instruments were both made by Nôtomi Judô, one of the greatest *syakuhati* masters, who was a Japanese "living treasure" until his death in the 1970s. Photo by Dale A. Olsen.

FIGURE 3   Eduardo Calderón, a north coastal Peruvian *curandero* 'shaman', demontrates an ancient Moche globular flute in his pottery workshop at his home in Las Delicias, Moche (near Trujillo), Peru. He used this instrument to call the spirits of the mountain and the ocean to assist him during his curing rituals (1979). Photo by Dale A. Olsen.

late 1960s. In the Peace Corps, I performed for two seasons as principal flutist with the Philharmonic Orchestra of Chile. As a sideline I developed a fascination with the traditional flutes of the Andes. My first exposure to South American pre-Columbian flutes and pottery in general was at a small museum in San Pedro de Atacama, in the Chilean province of Antofagasta. But it was the collection in the National Museum of Anthropology and Archaeology in Lima, Peru, which we visited in 1968, that inspired me to study pre-Columbian musical instruments and ancient music making through depictions (iconography) etched into, painted on, or modeled as pottery vessels.

In 1974, a grant from the National Endowment for the Humanities took me to Bogotá, Colombia, where I began my first systematic study of more than 400 ceramic globular and tubular flutes from the Sinú, Tairona, and other ancient Colombian cultures. I also traveled again to Peru, where I photographed more ancient musical instruments and related artifacts, working primarily with César Bolaños in the National Museum of Anthropology and Archaeology in Lima. I also traveled to Trujillo on the north coast, where I spent several weeks working with Eduardo Calderón, a shaman who performed on pre-Columbian musical instruments during his curing rituals (figure 3). I received an award from FSU in 1982 to conduct research at the Field Museum of Natural History in Chicago, where I worked exclusively with John Alden Mason's original field notes, documentation, and musical instruments that he had collected in the 1940s in northern Colombia. During the summer of 1983 I worked with the collection of pre-Columbian musical instruments in the Metropolitan Museum of Art in New York. I also spent several weeks studying pottery making, primarily attempting to make ceramic globular flutes with duct mouthpieces and four finger holes. In 1991, out of a collection of more than 125,000 photographs of Moche artifacts in the UCLA Moche Archive, I studied all that pertained to music and dance. In 1996 I returned to Trujillo, Peru, where I again spent several days with Calderón, reading to him chapters from my completed manuscript that pertained to the Moche culture.

While all these activities are types of fieldwork, archaeological excavation has not been a part of my research, and I do not consider myself an archaeologist in any sense of the word. My approach has been through performance, description, and interpretation of ancient artifacts, both as musical instruments and as objects of art that can be interpreted musically, iconographically, and symbolically.

FIELDWORK

I define the field in ethnomusicology as the place where the people under study are actively or passively making music within a context where they would normally do so. While this definition is probably similar to those given by other ethnomusicologists, perhaps the difference is that I consider passive music making equal in importance to active music making.

What is passive music making? It is listening to music and enjoying the groove—that is, becoming involved in the music. Why is passive music making as important as active music making? The answer has to do with the listener's personal involvement in the music. Music pervades the airwaves in most places of the world, and it invades the minds of humans everywhere. Music is one of the things that characterize the human species. Therefore, passive music making is just as prevalent in a person's life as active music making—in fact, for most people it is more prevalent. The ethnomusicological study of passive music making opens up a vast new world to the ethnomusicologist and offers many challenges. Ponder, if you will, these thoughts about and from one of my friends in Paraguay (from field notes based on an interview in 1993):

> José Mitsui is a college-educated agronomist and owner of the only hotel in La Colmena (Hotel Fujimi). He was born in 1947 in Paraguay and has lived almost all his life in La Colmena except for three years spent in Japan. He recalled many things about his childhood, especially his grandmother's love for Japanese *min'yô* and *enka*. Music was extremely important to his grandmother, who lived in La Colmena until she died at age eighty-five. She listened to *min'yô* (folk songs) and *enka* (a popular genre) every day on 78-rpm Victrola recordings. As José Mitsui explained: "Music had great value for her. Unfortunately for us children, however, the music had its greatest value because of the song texts. We children sang along because we liked it, but we didn't know what the words meant. For us, we liked the music, but 85 percent of us didn't understand it. We liked the rhythm, and some of it sounded sad."

José cannot play a note of music. Nevertheless, his interest in Japanese music as a passive music maker explains much about his ethnic identity as a Japanese-Paraguayan.

I often explain to my students that fieldwork in ethnomusicology is indeed work. At other times, I explain that fieldwork is also play. It is, of course, a combination of the two, and when work and play are properly balanced or in sync, fieldwork can be one of the most enjoyable experiences of the ethnomusicologist.

The *work* aspect of fieldwork has many facets, as has been explained in great detail by several ethnomusicologists (Barz and Cooley 1997; Herndon and McLeod 1983; Hood 1982; Merriam 1964; Myers 1992; Nettl 1964, 1983). I was first influenced by the fieldwork perspectives of Bruno Nettl (whose book *Theory and Method in Ethnomusicology* I read on a thirty-six-hour bus ride from Santiago to La Tirana, Chile, in 1967) and Mantle Hood (whose book *The Ethnomusicologist* was one of my formative sacred texts in ethnomusicology), among others. Any anecdotes, suggestions, or details by successful people about fieldwork, however, are just that: anecdotes, suggestions, or details. Each person's fieldwork experience is unique, and while you can prepare for fieldwork, you have to take each day as it comes and handle it yourself, using your own common sense.

What I call *play* in fieldwork is the daily participation with the people under study. It is living in proximity with them, playing their music for and with them, dancing their dances with them, and also playing your music for them. All these activities are what a musician does at home, when not in the field; therefore, they should also be what a musician does away from home, in the field (figure 4).

What are the objectives of fieldwork? They could include problem solving and working with specific hypotheses; they could include learning musical instruments, songs, or dances for personal reasons; they could include collecting instruments, music, and related information for teaching, making films, television broadcasting, or composition; in fact, they could include about as many objectives as there are people who conduct fieldwork. Ethnomusicologists, however, primarily engage in fieldwork to solve problems and prove or disprove hypotheses.

One type of problem solving was suggested by Mantle Hood (1969) when he wrote that ethnomusicology is "the study of all varieties of music found in one locale or region . . . ; in other words, all music being used by the people of a given area." When I worked with the Warao during my first field trip in 1972, one of my objectives was to study all the music within Yaruara Akoho, a Warao village on the Winikina River. After several months I began to focus on music in shamanism and other practices involving power. I did not really have a hypothesis other than "Music is power," which is a very broad statement. I think I proved that music is power among the Warao, but

FIGURE 4   Kyôko Yumoto on *koto* and the author on *syakuhati*, during the latter's final concert (to receive a diploma as a *natori*, or licensed teacher) at the University of São Paulo in 1981. Mrs. Yumoto is a *natori* of the Sei-ha school (a branch of Ikuta *ryû*) in Tôkyô. She developed a Sei-ha branch *koto* school in São Paulo in 1979, where she lived for three years. Photo by Diane Olsen.

The researcher who becomes involved as an observer and participant has an effect on the process and outcome of an event and becomes as much a part of the event as the subjects of the research.

one can ask further, "What is power?" There is supernatural power, there is political power, there is physical strength, and there are many other ramifications of that rather overused word. Nevertheless, many years after my dissertation, I finished a book on the Warao that followed Seeger's idea, on a much smaller scale, and also tackled my original hypothesis and others that developed as I worked with my material. Often, hypotheses appear after initial fieldwork has been completed, and unless follow-up fieldwork is possible, they may never be proved or even tested. Thankfully, I had collected so much material during my three field trips to the Orinoco delta that I was able to complete a thorough study of Warao music.

Another broad objective that I have followed in my research is the study of how music functions as identity among *nikkei* in South America. This was a logical outcome of my two subjects of specialization at UCLA—music of South America and music of Japan—although I happened upon the topic quite by accident in 1979 while living in Lima, Peru, as a Fulbright scholar. On one of my walks in the San Isidro district, I came, by chance, to the Peruvian-Japanese Cultural Center. I entered the building and introduced myself to a visiting Japanese dignitary and several *nikkei* who were about to begin a meeting in preparation for the eightieth anniversary of Japanese immigration to Peru. When I told them that I played Kinko-*ryû syakuhati*, one of the men produced a plastic instrument from a cabinet. Even before I had blown a sound, the Japanese man asked me if I could play a well-known song, "El Cóndor Pasa." I improvised a version for him and also played some Japanese folk songs; all this piqued their interest and led to an invitation to give a concert. This was the beginning of more than twenty years of research among people of Japanese heritage in Argentina, Bolivia, Brazil, Paraguay, and Peru. I have endeavored to learn about the breadth and depth of music in their lives, both passively and actively, and to understand how music functions as identity across three generations of South American *nikkei*.

My fieldwork methodology often includes my performances on particular flute-type instruments, depending on the nature of my research. While researching the music of the Warao of Venezuela in the 1970s, for example, I often played a small plastic recorder for my Warao friends in the Orinoco delta. The children, especially, responded with enthusiasm when I played a variety of tunes, including some of their own dance songs and those from neighboring villages. This proved to be a very effective way to build rapport with the Warao, and it inspired them, in return, to express their own musicality to me—to "be musical" for me. Our performances for each other became a common, almost a daily, event.

As I have studied music making among the *nikkei* in South America, the Japanese *syakuhati* has been a principal factor in my research. I have given more than twenty-five concerts in five countries, many of which have included my explanations of the music I perform. I have also rehearsed and jammed with numerous *nikkei* and other musicians, playing *min'yô*, *honkyoku* (Buddhist music), *sôkyoku* (music with *koto*), *sankyoku* (music for three instruments), jazz, and folk music from the various countries where I have conducted research. As with the Warao, but to a much greater degree, I was able to create rapport that broke down many barriers and led to lasting friendships.

My ethnoarchaeomusicological research has also included my own playing of more than 500 pre-Columbian flutelike instruments. My reason for playing them and recording the results of my carefully thought out performances is that I believe the scales of these instruments can tell us something about the cultures which made them. This approach is related to the so-called new archaeology, which is based on the premise that through archaeology it is possible to learn about the social organization and religious beliefs of ancient peoples (Renfrew 1987:80).

After establishing rapport with living musicians and other people, I generally use a variety of methods for gathering information. When I conduct research in urban areas, I include archives, bookstores, libraries, newspaper offices, museums, and other repositories. While researching *nikkei* music in South America, for example, I read, took notes on, and photocopied many newspaper and magazine accounts of past and present *nikkei* musical events, other cultural events, experiences, critiques, and thoughts. I also found many invaluable memoirs written by immigrants and their children. In both rural and urban situations, I always conduct numerous interviews with musicians and other people. In certain situations (depending on my research objectives) I use questionnaires.

Another method that is certainly applied by all ethnomusicologists, as well as tourists and the general public, is nonparticipant observation, such as attendance at concerts, festivals, parades, celebrations, rituals, and so forth. Perhaps sitting in a concert hall or watching a parade is considered participant observation by some scholars, but such participation is passive rather than active. I consider participant observation to be more active than just being in attendance at an event; it would include participating in an event as a member of a family or club, perhaps interacting (clapping, laughing, dancing, meditating) or perhaps just listening. Indeed, observation (whether nonparticipant or participant) should be thought of as a continuum from the general to the specific, known as a G-S line (Hood 1982). To accommodate my experiences as a participant in music I use what I call bimusical participatory reflection; I have used this extensively with my research on the *nikkei*. Basically, bimusical participatory reflection is my documentation and interpretation of phenomena relative to my own performances on *syakuhati* with and for *nikkei*. I write about many of my musical impressions of the various *nikkei* subcultures, and about my musical experiences among them, in the form of brief narratives; they are my subjective impressions about the musical events in which I participate as a musician *with* and often *for* the people who are the subjects of my research. These narratives originate as field notes, as diaries (journals), or as letters to my wife, written after my *syakuhati* concerts, rehearsals, and other musical interactions with the South American *nikkei*. Here is a sample from my field notes, written during research in Peru in 1996:

> Another inspiring experience—two *syakuhati* concerts in one day, the first for the elderly Japanese and the second for the *nikkei* youth and others. The first concert was held in the auditorium of the Centro Cultural Peruano Japonés, the same stage where I performed seventeen years earlier. . . . Because of this, I felt that I knew the stage somewhat. Actually, though, I had remembered very little about it, except that it is very high and much removed from the audience. I had thought all week that I would come down to the floor level and walk among the people, sort of like a modern *komusô* (a wandering monk musician)—strolling. But I decided to keep it formal because of the didactic nature of the performance and the fact that I had to speak into a microphone. I felt a closeness with the people, in any case, because of the reserved enthusiasm of a crowd of mostly octogenarians. But it was very important for me that they were Japanese, and

that this was their music. Maybe the distance between the stage and the audience also convinced some that I, too, was Japanese—depending on their eyesight. In the United States, when I am dressed in *kimono* and *hakama*, some people would think I was Japanese (even with a name like Olsen).

What can this method of bimusical participatory reflection tell us about a culture or a the music of a culture? In my case, among the South American *nikkei*, bimusical participatory reflection revealed some of their attitudes toward Japanese classical and folk music, as the following field notes, made after the performance in 1996, suggest:

> The stage itself was stark—no *byôbu* screens, no plants, just a curtain about twenty feet behind me. But no matter—the audience was Japanese, and I felt good. The best ambience for Japanese music is a Japanese audience. Ambience is more than a physical phenomenon—it is also spiritual, or perhaps more accurately philosophical. What is the correct word? I am neither Buddhist nor Shinto, but then, most of the *issei* (the first generation, that is, immigrants) in Lima are also Christian, having converted years ago. Still, there is a metaphysical closeness, a familiar ambience, when I play Japanese music for the Japanese. I had similar feelings of a familiar ambience, or a type of metaphysical communication, when I played alone in Buddhist graveyards in Nara, Japan. I definitely felt surrounded by a friendly and appreciative ambience.

> The concert began about 3:15 P.M. and ended about 4:30. I began with *Kimi Gayo*, the Japanese national anthem, but I hadn't realized that everybody would stand and sing along. My intention was to make them happy by playing music they would remember—this certainly was the right piece for that! My second purpose was to demonstrate the *yôsempo* scale (a pentatonic scale without half steps). I continued with *Haru Kaze* 'Spring Wind', which was actually composed by Stephen Foster and is known in the United States as "Massa's in the Cold, Cold Ground." This was another sing-along piece (I feel like a human karaoke machine), and I related to them my experience in Londrina, Brazil, at the main Sunday service at the Japanese Evangelical Holiness Church, when the congregation also sang along—the tune is also a Christian hymn, which was in their Methodist hymnal as "Jesus, Our Friend." Another goal I had here in Lima was to show how many of the common Japanese songs are borrowed from other cultures or are also known in other countries. I also played *Hotaru no Hikari*, which has the same tune as "Auld Lang Syne." I remember that long ago a Japanese friend or acquaintance (I cannot remember who) told me that "Auld Lang Syne" was actually written by a Japanese composer. This little demonstration of scales ended with *Sôran Bushi*, a *min'yô* from Hokkaido. Once again, everybody sang along. Next, I demonstrated the *insempo* scale (a pentatonic scale with semitones) and played more popular tunes, such as *Kojo no Tsuki* and *Kuroda Bushi*—more singing.

My feelings about my own musical performances, rehearsals, learning experiences, and observations often tell me something that nothing else can tell me about *nikkei* individuals and even groups. Why is this? It is because the researcher who becomes involved as an observer and participant has an effect on the process and outcome of an event and becomes as much a part of the event as the subjects of the resesarch. What is told? The reflections of the researcher (both participatory and nonparticipatory) are important to the nature of any study, whether it is bibliographic, ethnographic, or psychological, because the researcher's bias must be revealed. A researcher cannot (usually) describe his or her bias, but reflection will often reveal it. Bias enters into all research, because the researcher always has to decide what to include and what to leave out. Even when searching for information about musical events from old newspapers, the researcher decides what is important and what is not. Reflection may help to explain why such choices are made.

Andrew Killick (in a paper for the SEM conference in 1999) has advocated "writing down, writing up" as a way to conduct research. While he advocates the use of computers in the field, I have always preferred to use inexpensive notebooks intended for schoolchildren, because I like to write anytime, anywhere, and everywhere—in parks, restaurants, and coffee shops as well as hotel rooms. To begin, I usually buy half a dozen notebooks of the same size (6 by 7 inches, about 15 by 17 centimeters), designating one as a photographic and recording log, another as a journal (for my diary or field notes), another for translations of materials, and others for writing prose, including outline development and individual chapters. I always write in blue ink with a ballpoint pen because I find that blue ink lasts longest and doesn't bleed through the pages. I write prose on alternate lines; this allows me to add words, make other changes, and insert comments.

LABORATORY WORK

Laboratory work in ethnomusicology has several facets, of which, for my work, the most important are the transcription and analysis of interviews and music, and the analysis of photographs. I call these *textual laboratory work*, *musical laboratory work*, and *photographic laboratory work*. Depending on the research design of a project, other types of laboratory work may also be important, such as the analysis of films, videos, and dances as well as "organological" and iconographic analysis.

Textual laboratory work

During my field trips to the Orinoco delta to study the Warao, I carried an expensive Nagra III reel-to-reel tape recorder for maximum fidelity of musical materials, and a cheap cassette tape recorder for backup of the music and interviews and for playback in the field. For music, I made recordings simultaneously with both machines, attaching both microphones in one shock mount. I used the cassette machine only for playback (the batteries were very heavy and could not, of course, be bought in the rain forest). My methodology included transliterating the Warao song texts with the singer, either immediately after they were sung or as soon afterward as possible. Because Warao orthography is very similar to Spanish, it soon became fairly easy for me to transliterate the songs from listening to the cassette recordings. Then I would read my transliterations to the singer, and he would translate them line by line (figure 5). This is a form of textual laboratory work accomplished in the field, and it has at least one obvious benefit: the translations can be followed by interpretive interviews. In several situations, however, because the original singer was from another village and was not available, I had to rely on another Warao man to translate some of the shamanic texts. Unfortunately, my ad hoc translator did not understand the archaic texts, although he claimed that he did; he deceived me by inventing meanings. I did not discover this deception until I had returned to Los Angeles, and several months later I had to make another field trip to the Orinoco delta to retranslate many of the shamanic texts.

All my Warao interviews are in Spanish; I translated them in the laboratory setting of my homes, either in the delta or in the United States. Other interviews (among the *nikkei*, for example) are in either Spanish or Portuguese. To play back these materials I use a Dictaphone, which is a secretary's machine with a foot pedal for stopping or rewinding the tape. The pedal enables me to keep my hands constantly on the computer keyboard and enter translations into a word processing program.

These techniques, of course, are very common in ethnomusicology. Because I never include Spanish or Portuguese transcripts of my interviews in my publications, transliteration problems do not occur (as they can, for example, when one works with broken or pidgin English).

FIGURE 5   Cesáreo Soto, who is bilingual in Spanish and Warao, assists the author with translations of Warao shamanic song texts. During my fieldwork among the Warao in 1973, I retranslated all my shamanic song texts with Mr. Soto's help. Photo by Dale A. Olsen.

Musical laboratory work

The nature and extent of musical laboratory work depend on the research design of a project. No analysis of music should be done just for its own sake, and no transcription should be included in a publication just to take up space. Likewise, no musical transcription should be included in a publication with a statement such as "Here is a transcription of the song" or "The following transcription will give you an idea of the music." Every musical transcription must be included for a purpose other than mere description, unless the description leads up to some type of problem solving. In other words, musical analysis for the sake of analysis and musical transcription for the sake of transcription are not acceptable, unless they are part of a seminar on transcription and analysis.

When I was working on my dissertation, it was necessary to make transcriptions of all my Warao shamanistic musical materials, because I was seeking verification of my hypothesis that Warao shamans used a variety of melodic patterns to delineate functional sections in the music (calling on helpful spirits, naming, inflicting, removing evil essences, and so forth). This analysis was based solely on intervallic relationships, and I found that cipher notation worked perfectly. I had learned how to transcribe in cipher notation by working with Javanese *rebab* recordings for Mantle Hood, and I got so good at it that I could type out corresponding numbers on my typewriter while listening to the shaman's songs at half speed. Although I have not published them anywhere else, I did include these notations in my dissertation—they were vital to my research design, and I was able to prove my hypothesis.

For such musical transcription, a reel-to-reel tape recorder is required. It is also essential for transcribing with regular Western staff notation. Today, I make field recordings with a DAT machine, but I always transfer the examples I want to transcribe onto a reel-to-reel machine at 15 inches per second (ips). From that I make a dubbing onto a cassette (playing the original back at 15 ips, 7½ ips, and 3¾ ips), and transcribe the music using the same Dictaphone that I use for textual transcriptions.

Photographic laboratory work

I like to follow John and Malcolm Collier's photographic guidelines, discussed in their book *Visual Anthropology: Photography as a Research Method* (1986). There have been many times, for example, when I have made visual inventories at the homes of my teachers or have made photograph documentations of instrument building (Olsen 1996). I also consider visual landscape documentation very important. Ideally, I use two cameras, one for black-and-white and the other for color transparencies. Recently, I have carried a digital camera into the field as well, because I find JPEG files very useful for Internet design.

For many years I did my own black-and-white printing of proof sheets and 5- by 7-inch prints for publication (I set up a darkroom in one of my bathrooms). Then one summer I developed a bronchial irritation from the chemical fumes and was forced to stop. I miss not having the flexibility of doing my own printing, because there is so much I can do in the darkroom to make my photographs outstanding for publication (and having my own darkroom is much less expensive than using a commercial service).

I use slides for teaching to a great extent, and it is now very easy to scan slides, edit them as JPEG files, and use them in Powerpoint presentations or on Internet pages. I have developed an entire Internet-based distance-learning course, "Music Cultures of the World," in which I use more than 100 JPEG files made from my slides, digital pictures on a floppy disk, or individual frames from a Hi-8 video recorder. Such dissemination of ethnomusicological materials and knowledge is one of the most important aspects of our field.

DISSEMINATION

I believe that one of the most important concerns of ethnomusicology today should be the dissemination of knowledge. All ethnomusicologists should ask themselves this question: How can we disseminate what we know about music, what we want to know about music, and what we want others to know about music? All ethnomusicologists should think of themselves as advocates for cross-cultural understanding. We need to think constantly about how we can communicate musically to every living thing and, in turn, be musically inspired (inspiration is a form of communication) by every living thing.

Publication, of course, is probably the easiest way to disseminate knowledge. The audiences reached in this way are often very small, however, if scholarly journals or books are the only type of publication being considered. Textbooks may reach a larger audience, and the Internet is capable of a tremendous outreach. I have published in all these formats, and I would say that while articles and books are very important for a career in academia, textbooks and Internet pages are in some ways even more important because through them a scholar's work can reach a large number of people. In 2000 I developed and published an Internet site, "Ethnomusicology as Advocacy," in which I express my concern about how many of the people with whom I have conducted research are suffering the onslaught of oil exploration, narcotics trafficking, and other evils of postcolonialism.

Ethnomusicology is indeed a remarkable field because it deals with human beings through our music, which is perhaps our most personal form of expression. If we can learn to appreciate and understand the music of a culture, then perhaps we can learn to appreciate its members as human beings and respect them as individuals—and they can learn to appreciate and respect us. I firmly believe that this should be the most important goal of ethnomusicology.

REFERENCES

Barz, Gregory F., and Timothy J. Cooley, eds. 1997. *Shadows in the Field: New Perspectives for Fieldwork in Ethnomusicology.* New York: Oxford University Press.

Collier, John Jr., and Malcolm Collier. 1986. *Visual Anthropology: Photography as a Research Method*, 2nd ed. Albuquerque: University of New Mexico Press.

Herndon, Marcia, and Norma McLeod. 1983. *Field Manual for Ethnomusicology.* Norwood, Pa.: Norwood Editions.

Hood, Mantle. 1969. "Ethnomusicology." *Harvard Dictionary of Music*, 2nd ed. Cambridge, Mass.: Harvard University Press.

———. 1982. *The Ethnomusicologist*, 2nd ed. Kent, Ohio: Kent State University Press.

Killick, Andrew. 1999. "Writing Down, Writing Up." Unpublished paper presented at the Annual Meeting of the Society for Ethnomusicology, Austin, Texas.

Merriam, Alan P. 1964. *The Anthropology of Music.* Evanston, Ill.: Northwestern University Press.

Myers, Helen, ed. 1992. *Ethnomusicology: An Introduction.* New York: Norton.

Nettl, Bruno. 1964. *Theory and Method in Ethnomusicology.* London: Free Press of Glencoe, Collier-Macmillan. .

———. 1983. *The Study of Ethnomusicology: Twenty-Nine Issues and Concepts.* Urbana: University of Illinois Press.

Olsen, Dale A. 1996. *Music of the Warao of Venezuela: Song People of the Rain Forest.* Gainesville: University Press of Florida.

———. 2000. *Ethnomusicology as Advocacy.* Internet site: http://otto.cmr.fsu.edu/~muh2052/students/warao_indians_venezuela/

———. 2002. *Music of El Dorado: The Ethnomusicology of Ancient South American Cultures.* Gainesville: University Press of Florida.

Renfrew, Colin. 1987. "What's New in Archaeology?" In *Anthropology: Contemporary Perspectives*, 5th ed., ed. Phillip Whitten and David E. K. Hunter, 78–81. Boston: Little, Brown.

Africa, Latin America, and North America
Gerhard Kubik

Learning to Gather Data

Learning to Write

The Idea of Chronicles and a Diary

Hitchhiking as a Technique of Anthropological Fieldwork

Transculturation and the "Writing Culture"

O Fim do Mundo

Chance Patterns and Dead Ends

The Place of Individual Researchers in History

Avenues for Scientific Discovery

Human endeavor is not easily analyzed. Its background can be assessed only by studying the histories of individual lives.

What motivates a person to do scientific research? Is it a philanthropic undertaking, so that future generations may benefit from one's findings, or is it ultimately a self-serving exercise? Does the person who tries to decode the genetic instructions of a virus or make sense of the odd behavior of neutrinos in particle physics follow an abstract purpose, or perhaps only obey the dictates of a personal neurosis?

To discover is "to find something that already existed but was not known about before" (Longman 1990:290). Obviously some of us are driven by an urge to find out about existing facts, connections, relationships, and causes, and thereby to learn something about the workings of the human mind and the structure of the universe. Eventually, our findings can benefit others in *their* search, but it would be difficult to postulate a built-in program of benevolence in biological organisms.

Many people never discover anything, and the idea that they could does not even occur to them. But some of us venture into situations where we are bound to bump into something unknown. In an article entitled "Why Go to Mars?" the science writer Glenn Zorpette (2000:22) has given the following assessment of Christopher Columbus and the Apollo astronauts: "Although their missions blended commercial and political-military imperatives, the explorers involved all accomplished some significant science simply by going where no scientists had gone before." Sigmund Freud in his journeys through the depths of the human mind was doing the same. He analyzed dreams, parapraxis, and other strange phenomena with the gaze of an intelligent child penetrating terrain no one had probed before.

A discovery can come about through various avenues, but when it happens—especially if it is a scientific insight—there is always an element of amazement. This is also true of an invention: the finding of something that did not exist before, such as a new technical device or the creation of a work of art. Discoveries and inventions both tend to occur to the individual in a flash, as a sudden insight, although they are usually brought about only by long and painstaking work. Coming to terms with a discovery, the individual then passes through a stage of beginning to "appropriate" it, to integrate this new element into his or her own personality.

In Africa, more nascent musical styles die than
survive, and this is true not only of inventions in
remote rural areas with poor communications.
Traditions have a life span.

But what if all new insights result from some form of external inspiration? What
if they are implanted in the brain in a fraction of a moment by an external power,
with the pinprick sealed immediately? Split personalities sometimes claim that they
hear "voices," but they are quickly referred to a psychiatric ward.

LEARNING TO GATHER DATA

I cannot easily reconstruct the moments when I began to ask scientific questions. But
it seems that this inclination began when I was about nine years old. During the hot
summer of 1943, in Vienna, my city of birth, I started to gather data about events
that seemed inexorable: I began a chronological documentation of the Allied air raids
on Vienna and its surroundings. We were living in constant fear of the next day; but
I was the foremost pupil in my classroom, and expressing fear was not appropriate.
Perhaps my diary of these events was a magical device for taming them—it gave me
the illusion of being able to control what would happen. By undertaking this sacrificial
exercise, I might avert a direct hit on our house.

My air-raid diary opened with the first Allied air raid on Wiener Neustadt, a
small town south of Vienna, on 13 August 1943. Thereafter I documented all the air
raids that occurred, and I even reconstructed the dates of earlier raids, going back to
1942. Every week I made entries in my notebook. I would begin an entry by writing
down the call of the sirens—in red for daylight attacks, in blue when the sirens howled
at night. I noted how long the alert lasted, which districts and places were bombed
or targeted by area bombardment, at what time (down to the minute) the all-clear
signal was given, and—if I had access to the information—how many casualties
resulted.

I completed my diary of World War II on 15 April 1945. In contrast to Anne
Frank's famous diary, mine was almost impersonal, not reflecting my intense feelings.
It is probably my first scientific work, and my drawings in colored pencil of the sound
of the sirens are my first "musical" notation. Scientific conclusions always depend on
a reliable database; without empirical data, there can be no insights. One can, of course,
make chance discoveries by pondering chaotic events, but such discoveries will remain
ancillary as long as one is unable to put them into a broader context—a difficult task.
In a sense, my air-raid notebook was a start on that path.

LEARNING TO WRITE

I took my next step toward becoming a scientist and a writer when I was at secondary
school, Realgymnasium Wien 17, Geblergasse. In 1947, during holidays for the children of war victims in a place called Würmla (west of Vienna), I had some upsetting
experiences; and, trying to come to terms with them, I wrote a novel re-creating the
events—how I had been terrorized by a gang of thirteen-year-olds and how I had
finally escaped from the hostel. The novel is a mixture of fact and fiction. It is fictitious
in that the roles are reversed: the winners and losers in the conflict have been ex-

changed, so that I would always emerge unscathed, not because of cowardice but because of moral superiority.

I called my novel *Im Schloss* 'In the Castle' (1948). The similarity of the title to Franz Kafka's famous book is coincidental; I had not heard yet of Kafka. I wanted to get my novel printed (it never was, however), and so I also painted a self-portrait for the cover. I made this portrait standing in front of our big mirror, which, significantly, was called "Psyche." The mirror had been with me from my early childhood, and it still is. I was thirteen at the time and had read a lot of so-called trash literature, the adventure stories available in the postwar market, such as Tom Shark. They encouraged me to try my own versions.

A year later I began to write a second novel. I worked on it for days at a time, in seclusion, for more than a year. Its setting was a place I have never been—China— and in contrast to my earlier novel, this one was not written in the first person. I reached page 127, but gradually I lost my zeal and my momentum. My cursive writing also slowed down, as if I had crossed the event horizon of a black hole. Predictably, I never finished this second novel.

At that time, when I was about fourteen, I often used to pester my mother to allow me to emigrate to Alaska once I finished high school. I also developed musical interests. We were living in the American occupation zone, and from 1946 on I had become acquainted with American jazz through the U.S. Air Force radio, dance clubs, and cinema, such as the film *Sun Valley Serenade*, which featured Glenn Miller's music. My love of jazz, especially swing and bebop, would continue through secondary school, and this, if anything, paved the way for my later involvement in ethnomusicology. At age sixteen I took clarinet lessons. But at that time I had other interests to which I gave about the same weight: I studied Sigmund Freud, and Ludwig Klages's system of graphology; I read the poetry of Rimbaud and Verlaine (in French); and French symbolism became a major interest when I was about seventeen. Later, the roster of my favorite authors included Franz Kafka, Georg Trakl, Stefan Zweig, Arthur Schopenhauer, and George Orwell. I resumed writing poetry and short stories from my late teens into my twenties, and some of it got published, though much later (Andika and Kubik n.d.). I also played jazz; my ensemble won first prize at the Vienna jazz festival in 1959.

By then I was already a university student. I majored in comparative musicology and *Afrikanistik* (African studies). This choice was inspired by literature I had read. Pursuing the African roots of jazz, I read Rudi Blesh, Richard A. Waterman, and Alan P. Merriam; and I became interested in African music, collecting the records published by Gilbert Rouget at the Musée de l'Homme in Paris and the records by Hugh Tracey. In 1957 I became a member of the African Music Society, South Africa. I read A. M. Jones (1949) but (interestingly) I did not yet understand his discovery of a "multiple main beat" in *ngwayi* drumming among the Bemba of Zambia. Possibly because I was a jazz musician, I was unable to imagine that performers in a group would *not* all refer their phrases to a common ground beat. I had to rediscover Jones's findings later, in Uganda, when studying *akadinda* xylophone music.

THE IDEA OF CHRONICLES AND A DIARY

From 1954 on I had intimate contact with the art scene in Vienna because I played jazz at the Vienna Art Club near Kärntnerstrasse. I made the acquaintance of painters who were on the verge of becoming famous, such as Fritz Hundertwasser (later Friedensreich Hundertwasser), Ernst Fuchs, Anton Lehmden, Buddy (now Padhi) Frieberger, and Ernst Steiner; writers; jazz musicians, such as Ossi (Oswald) Wiener and Walter Terharen; and others. No doubt they all exerted some influence on my intellectual development.

My friend Buddy Frieberger used to create books by patching together "artifacts" of contemporary events in the manner of a collage. He called such a book *Chronik* 'Chronicle'. Like the dadaists of Zürich in 1916 and the surrealists in France around 1925 (André Breton and others), he glued into these books all sorts of material objects—mainly paper, but also flowers, hair, and pieces of fabric—in chronological order of the events they memorialized. He collected drawings by friends, railroad and streetcar tickets, cinema programs, and the like. He also modified newspaper clippings by exchanging some letters to construct a different message. Buddy was a self-centered personality who did not tolerate opposition. He wanted to change the world, and he vehemently attacked the consumer society, the "common fool" in the streets, and all academics, artists, and musicians. In a state of uncertainty about myself, I was an easy target for Buddy; and, through transference, I was easily molded by his libidinal and aggressive tendencies. Under his influence I began to start my own patchwork *Chronik*. But this brought me back to data gathering; somewhere in the back of my mind was my own childhood chronicle of the air raids of 1943–1945. . . .

In 1955 I became acquainted with another painter, Ernst Steiner, and together we founded our own jazz band, in which Buddy also played. Ernst was from Switzerland. At first, his company was a great relief from Buddy's outbursts and fits of anger; but Ernst soon revealed a similar, though more covert, potential for aggression—he was capable of the most elaborate devices to hurt his friends. Ernst, like Buddy, expected absolute loyalty: his friends had to love precisely what he loved in art and music—the same writers, artists, and philosophers—and if they did not, they would be dismissed as "tasteless" and "repulsive." It was under Ernst's influence that I eventually started a real diary. That happened during a lonely trip to Finland in 1958. Ernst had said that it was important for a poet to keep a diary, and I was a poet at that time, or wanted to become one. My first diary entry was written in a forest in central Finland, near Äkäslompolo (Suomi), on 20 July 1958.

HITCHHIKING AS A TECHNIQUE OF ANTHROPOLOGICAL FIELDWORK

During the years 1955 to 1958 I traveled extensively through Europe with a rucksack, sometimes standing for hours at a roadside waiting for a lift. I traveled through France, England, Spain, Portugal, and Italy. I played jazz with Mike Peters in London in 1955. In Spain I crossed the semidesert of Los Monegros on foot, and in Scandinavia I walked through the tundra of Lapland. This hardened me physically, and in a sense it was a preparation for my later field trips in Africa.

Although I was then enrolled at the University of Vienna, I was rarely seen there. The knowledge I was trying to accumulate came almost exclusively from literature. In ethnomusicology I read Jones, Tracey, Rycroft, Waterman, Rouget, Merriam, Nketia, and others. And from the analysis of jazz records and recordings of African music I tentatively formed some ideas. My first public lecture, on jazz and African music, was given at Club Bel Étage in Zürich, in 1955, in the presence of Else Leuzinger of the Rietberg Museum.

My relationship with Ernst gradually deteriorated; it reached a low point in early 1959, just when our jazz band had reached the height of its success. The consequent breakup of the band left a psychological scar and would be a major impetus in my decision to take off for Africa. I had a vague hope that in Africa I might find musicians with whom to play, if not jazz, then something else.

I set out from Vienna on 7 October, hitchhiking all the way to Uganda. All my equipment was packed in one rucksack: tent, sleeping bag, recording machine, camera, water bottle, flashlight, and some personal belongings. The small battery-driven tape recorder, a Stuzzi Magnette, had been kindly placed at my disposal by Dr. Walter Graf, then director of the Phonogrammarchiv Vienna. My funds for one year—from the estate of my Aunt Herma, who had died in June 1959—consisted of eighty pounds sterling in travelers' checks.

As in my European travels, I did not have a preconceived program but relied on chance as my guide. Before my departure, I had read nothing about the African countries that I would visit; I said that reading would only make me prejudiced. So I placed myself at the mercy of the unpredictable. But I did have one basic concern, to learn to perform with musicians in Africa; and, logically, I said to myself that I would first have to find a teacher.

In 1959, I did not anticipate that this idea constituted a violation of colonial taboos. In Kampala and elsewhere (except months later, in Nigeria) my first experience would be the raised eyebrows of colonial administrators and the disbelief of local people who had long internalized the colonizers' viewpoint. However, when I eventually found a teacher for the *amadinda* (xylophone) in Evaristo Muyinda—a former musician of the *kabaka* (king), it was more than good luck.

My first three African trips were in 1959–1960, through twelve countries; in 1961–1963 (figure 1) in East Africa, Nyasaland, Mozambique, South Africa, and Sudan; and in 1963–1964, from Oshogbo in Nigeria across northern Nigeria, Cameroon, and the Central African Republic with a Solex autocycle. During these trips, I developed a certain routine of field interaction—for example, in making first contacts. This routine was much in the style of my earlier travels as a hitchhiker in Europe. At dusk I was normally stranded somewhere: a driver had dropped me at a crossroad or, exhausted, I had stopped cycling or walking. I would look for a place to sleep; it never took me long to find one, and that was often the start of contacts and sometimes of miraculous recordings. This was a consciously devised research method.

There were exceptions to this approach, but it is important to outline the general pattern, because my early work in the field proceeded very much along these lines. The technique could be described as floating like a raft in a sea of events, although with a built-in autopilot that kept the raft away from dangerous waters. The exceptions occurred when someone had given me a letter recommending a particular place. For instance, my acquaintance with the blind musicians at Salama, south of Mukono (Lake Victoria, Uganda) resulted from contacts originally provided by the Catholic mission at Namagunga. My contact with Evaristo Muyinda took place the same way; Father Ortner from the south Tirol, who worked at the mission, took me on his motorbike

FIGURE I   The author waiting for a lift at a roadside in Rhodesia (Zimbabwe) while hitchhiking through southern Africa in 1962. Photos are by Gerhard Kubik.

to Kampala and to the Uganda Museum, where Mr. Muyinda was working. Similarly, my three-month stay with the family of Duro Ladipo from August to October 1960 in Oshogbo, Nigeria—and thereby all my studies of *àló* Yoruba stories—came about because Professor Ulli Beier of the University of Ibadan introduced me to him; I had contacted Ulli earlier by letter. However, the fact that I ended up studying *àló* and not something else was the result of a chance event (Kubik 1989a). I had started to study two other Yoruba genres, *apala* and *sakara* music, but my tape recorder broke down, and *àló* turned out to be a subject I thought I could manage with just notebook ethnography. So I learned the songs; and, drawing on my expertise as a jazz musician, I was able to write down quickly on paper, from the mouths of singers, the most complex offbeat phrasings of melodic accents (Richard A. Waterman's term). My study of *àló* was inseparable from my integration into Duro Ladipo's household and my friendship with members of his family, notably his brother Gboyega Ladipo and his twin sisters Taye and Kehinde. The help which the family gave me was paid back in kind. Money I did not have, so I helped Duro to write down in somewhat modified staff notation his Christmas cantatas and the beginnings of what would become his famous Yoruba operas, such as *Oba koso*. I do not know whether any of the manuscripts are still extant in Duro's estate. His wife, Abiodun, does not mention them in her relatively recent article (Duro-Ladipo and Kolawole 1998).

My friends in many countries often shared my hardships. Once, in southwestern Tanganyika in 1960, Basilius Saprapason and I walked down the steep mountains of the Livingstone massif to Lake Nyasa, a two-day walk from Madunda to Makonde, and we got lost in the forest under the glaring eyes of a *chui* (leopard). We lit a fire in front of our tent and kept it burning all night. . . .

I recorded any kind of music—lamellophones, guitars, anything I found (figures 2 and 3). I became interested in oral literature, notably storytelling, and I photographed landscapes, villages, people, musicians, instruments, material culture, and technologies.

During my early trips I soon formed personal relationships that would be lifelong, such as my friendship with the blind *kadongo* (lamellophone) troubadour Waiswa Lubogo, whom Helmut Hillegeist and I had first met at the Agricultural Training

FIGURE 2   The author recording the *kihoda* girls' dance among the Wakisi at Makonda, southwestern Tanzania. February 1962.

FIGURE 3 The xylophone player Mrs. Muhua, with her children. Northern Mozambique. October 1962.

Center for the Blind in Salama (Uganda) in 1962. When Moya A. Malamusi and I revisited Uganda in January and February 2000 on a project financed by De Ijsbreker, Amsterdam, we found Waiswa still living in Bumanya, his home, with his music unchanged. This was one of the most gratifying moments I have experienced recently.

TRANSCULTURATION AND THE "WRITING CULTURE"

My early scientific discoveries in Uganda and elsewhere had to do mostly with audiopsychology and were thus relevant to the branch we now call cognitive ethnomusicology (Wegner 1993). These discoveries included illusion effects as compositional devices (Kubik 1960, 1989b, 2000). To express some of my findings, I modified the Western notational system and also developed alternative notations, such as a cipher or number system that I devised jointly with Evaristo Muyinda (Kubik 1994b, 2000; figure 4).

FIGURE 4 The author's transcription of *mangolongondo* xylophone players' strokes, illustrating a finding reached through field research and video analysis. The interlocking parts of the three performers organize movement in a "total motional pattern" that includes musically significant but inaudible air strokes.

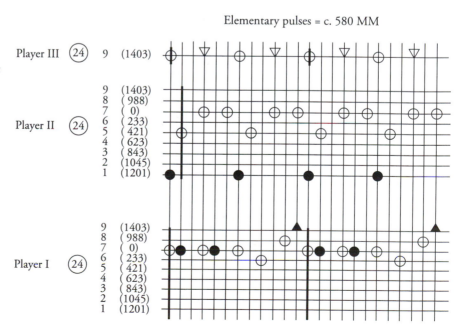

In retrospect, I realize that Evaristo taught me infinitely more than music. For one thing, using simple but effective methods, he reinforced my overall awareness of conceptual relativity. For example, when in December 1959 he realized that in *amadinda* (xylophone) performance—this music consists of two interlocking tone rows—I regularly missed the entry point for my interlocking part because I was proceeding from a common ground beat (as in jazz) and "syncopating," he stopped and said that I should start again with my tone row alone. When I did that, of course, it was impossible for me to syncopate, because there was nothing to syncopate against. So I played my part, the *okwawula*, just the way I had played the basic part (*okunaga*) before; and Evaristo fell in between my strokes with his tone row. Through this nonverbal teaching trick, he got me to understand that there was no ground beat to be shared by the two of us, but that we were operating within a relativistic universe, interlocking the two tone rows like cogwheels, each from his own gravitational standpoint. Dancers would reshuffle the structure in yet another way. Their internalized ground beat would always combine three pulses of our tone bank. In *akadinda* music, constructed on triple interlocking, there was a similar relativity. At last I understood A. M. Jones's findings on Bemba drumming.

It is probably accurate to say that I was the first ethnomusicologist from outside Africa to come there and actually learn a genre of African music from a competent African musician. My objective was not to retrieve folk music for use in composed music, nor was it to exhibit myself and the stolen music in a pop group. Having gained access to something that existed but that in this case *I* had not known before, I reacted with admiration and respect, and with a feeling that I wanted to contribute to preserving some of these court compositions for Buganda; so I wrote down 102 of them. A year later Andrew Tracey followed a similar path in Zimbabwe (then Rhodesia) when he put himself under the tutorship of Jege A Tapera (Tracey 1961). In those days there was as yet no campus culture anywhere in Africa, in the sense that foreigners would flock to African universities to study African drumming. This may sound presumptuous, but it is likely that through my reports and articles I inadvertently triggered some of these later developments.

In the early 1960s and later I also worked on other subjects, notably the psychology of cultural contact, projection and transference, and racial and ethnic stereotypes. I analyzed these phenomena from various theoretical standpoints (1971, 1994a, and so on).

Initially, I kept my personal diaries separate from my ethnographic field notes. A decade later, that would change, when I realized that my personal experiences were inseparable from my scientific observations. Thereafter I kept only one diary for everything, recording all events and observations in chronological order. Most of my diary notes are written in shorthand (figure 5). This is an unusual practice, and I had not used it in Finland; but I discovered that it could serve as a cryptographic device to prevent curious friends from spying on my notes, and only when I wrote in shorthand did I feel relaxed enough to make honest and personal entries. Increasingly, I began to use my diary as an interlocutor, as a virtual consultant to talk to about unsolved questions and problems. Sometimes, answers and solutions—including solutions to scientific problems—emerged from the pages.

My use of shorthand in the field has proved invaluable. Many informants will not speak freely if confronted with a microphone, let alone a laptop computer; and writing in longhand can disturb the flow of a conversation because the researcher, who simply cannot write as fast as an informant is speaking, has to break in frequently with questions. Scribbling in shorthand can be done at the speed of conversation and is minimally invasive; it attracts little attention because the researcher can maintain eye contact with speaker while at the same time recording the conversation almost flawlessly.

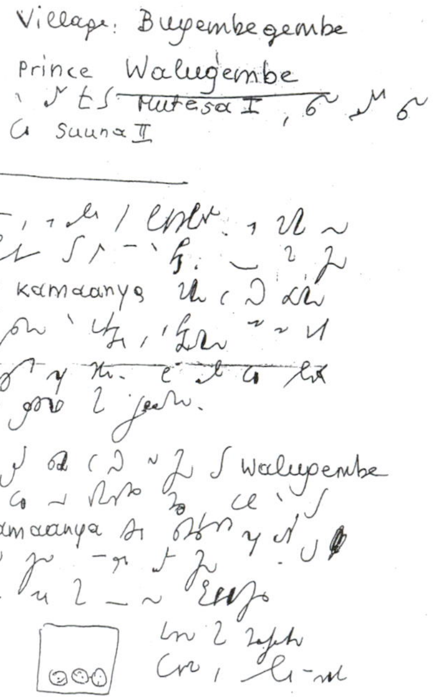

FIGURE 5   Diary entry from the author's most recent fieldwork in the kingdom of Buganda, made during a visit to the royal shrine of Prince Walugembe at Bugembegembe village northwest of Kampala. 9 February 2000.

O FIM DO MUNDO

FIGURE 6   *Kalelwa* mask from the Kwitu River area, southeastern Angola. 1965.

After three long research trips, from 1959 to 1964, I had a chance to do research in Angola, upon the recommendation of the Portuguese anthropologists António Jorge and Margot Dias. My work in southeastern Angola from July to December 1965 (figure 6) was a turning point in my life, bringing about significant changes in my approach, interests, and methods. I had spent the previous years surveying many countries of Africa (these years included the memorable trip on a Solex autocycle from Nigeria to the Central African Republic, mentioned earlier), but I had begun to feel that I was overspecializing in one scientific realm and that ethnomusicology had to be given a role within broader scientific inquiry. So I chose to work on something else, in a place that the Portuguese would call *o fim do mundo* 'the end of the world'.

I did not fall off the edge. But I was once again walking. During six months of anthropological fieldwork among Mbwela-Nkhangala-speaking people, I walked from settlement to settlement within a radius of some 80 kilometers from the administration posts of Cuito-Cuanavale and Longa. Most of these places could not be reached even by a Land Rover, so I was safe from intruders. This time, I started my research in a new way—not with the music but with the language. I began to learn Mbwela, one variant of a cluster of languages summarized by Malcolm Guthrie (1948) as group 10 within his zone K of the Bantu languages. I soon discovered that a knowledge of Mbwela-Nkhangala would open up for me a vast region extending into northwestern Zambia. In fact, I continued this research in Zambia in 1971, immediately after I had earned my Ph.D. in cultural anthropology. The Mbwela language is positioned somewhere between Lucazi and Mbunda, and it is also related to Cokwe and Luvale.

I had to learn the language from scratch, because no linguistic studies existed. I learned mainly in the company of children and adolescents, who were freer than adults to walk around with me, and so I was drawn into their subculture. Mbwela-Nkhangala society has an age-group system in which each stage is associated with a corresponding educational stage. Acquisition of knowledge—and thus progression from one age group to the next—is regulated separately for males and females. The earliest initiation procedures are *mukanda* (a circumcision school) for males and *cikula* (an initiation with no operation) for females. *Mukanda* initiation includes instruction in the tradition of masked performances, *makisi* (singular, *likisi*).

I realized that from the viewpoint of Mbwela society I was pretty much uneducated. So I opted for a more comprehensive form of participant ethnography than I had practiced earlier in Uganda, Nigeria, the Central African Republic, and elsewhere by learning to play musical instruments. I decided to undergo Mbwela initiation rites. It was clear that this would have effects on my own personality, and I am glad to have passed through these experiences (see also Nurse 1996). What resulted from my work in Mbwela-Nkhangala- and Lucazi-speaking communities in Angola, and across the border in Zambia, was a comprehensive documentation of these cultures, from 1965 to the late 1970s, on film, on tape, and in field notes, and an in-depth analysis of the *mukanda* initiation rites, their taboos, and defense mechanisms from the viewpoint of psychoanalytic theory. Here, the analysis of song texts helped me considerably, and this is where my ethnomusicological expertise began to merge with different branches of scientific inquiry. It also included a study of the performing arts: masked dancing, pantomime, and the historiographic meanings of masks.

What happens if one wears a mask? Anthropomorphic masks may represent prominent ancestors; zoomorphic masks may represent fantastic creatures of the bush. While in seclusion, each initiate is nominally devoted to a *mpumpu* mask that is made for him personally. It is always an effigy of Mwene Nyumbu, the mythical founder of the *mukanda* rites. However, the initiate is never allowed—even in later life—to wear this mask. Rather, the personal mask functions as a remote parental symbol watching over the candidate's psychological transformation into an adult; it is a powerful superego image to be internalized. Later, in adulthood, nothing particularly mysterious happens when one wears any other mask (Kubik 1993).

In this society, wearing a mask must not be confused with spirit possession. The latter belongs to the realm of the *mahamba* (dissatisfied spirits) ceremonies, in which a medium functions as a channel through which a spirit can express complaints. *Makisi* masked performance is different. The dancer does not fall into a trance. Only nominally does he "become" a spirit, and then only in relation to the noninitiates in the audience, not to his peers. An initiate can approach a masquerader during a performance, briefly stop him, and whisper something to him. The performer is not in any special state. Different information about the meaning of masks is given to graduates of *mukanda* and to noninitiates among the general public.

CHANCE PATTERNS AND DEAD ENDS

It is not my purpose in this essay to write my memoirs. Rather, I am using details from my personal history to highlight developmental situations and interactions between researcher and research subjects in the field, and to trace and explain changes in my individual approach and methodology.

From a wider perspective, this suggests the extent to which history really is a result of chance sequences—how unpredictable it is and how chance effects accumulate. Discoveries and inventions take place within this context. In the history of cultures, mutations and innovations abound, though most do not survive; most innovative trends, perhaps astonishingly, tend to disappear quickly. In Africa, for instance, more nascent musical styles die than survive, and this is true not only of inventions in remote rural areas with poor communications. I learned this from a comparative study of lamellophones collected by the thousands for museums between the mid-nineteenth and mid-twentieth centuries; what I found was that many ingenious devices were not pursued further after having been invented (1998, 1999a). Sometimes an invention becomes current for a short period, only to disappear later, leaving scarcely a trace. Traditions, then, have a life span (Kubik, Malamusi, et al. 1987). In Africa, this is particularly evident with regard to technology: someone invents a new technique of manufacture or a new performance technique on an instrument (such as the *kwela* flute embouchure invented by a youngster in South Africa), but if it is not taken up vigorously and continued by subsequent generations, the inventor and his or her peers will carry it to their graves. There are many such blind alleys. One example is the achievements of Daniel Kachamba (1947–1987), a Malawi guitarist and composer: much of what he came up with in the mid-1980s, including his "metric style" and his ingenious technique of playing the electric guitar with only the left hand, disappeared after his death.

The death of any individual can end an extraordinary development. Mwenda Jean Bosco, also known as Mwenda wa Bayeke, Congo's most famous early guitarist (he was first recorded in Jadotville, Likasi, on 3 February 1952 by Hugh Tracey), died in a car accident in 1991 at the height of his second career. Alan P. Merriam died in a plane crash in Poland; and my own life, and my life's work, nearly ended on Friday 22 October 1976 in an accident caused by a drunken driver in the mountains of Upangwa, southwestern Tanzania.

My brush with death was traumatic both physically and psychologically, and it led to an important decision—I have never again traveled anywhere by hitchhiking. What had been a practical and even an enjoyable method in the 1950s and 1960s had, I decided, outlived its usefulness. Interestingly, in the introductory text to a compact disk featuring some of his own field recordings in southeastern Africa, Moya Aliya Malamusi (1999) reports a similar change in his means of travel in Malawi during the early 1990s.

FIGURE 7   The Kachamba brothers' band, near Chileka, Malawi. Left to right: Moya Aliya Malamusi with rattle, Daniel Kachamba playing a bottle-neck guitar in *hauyani* style, Donald Kachamba playing a one-stringed bass, and Bulandisoni Kapirikitsa holding a pennywhistle. June 1967. (A 16-mm movie with synchronized sound is privately owned and unpublished.)

FIGURE 8   Lidiya Malamusi-Kubik, the oral literature researcher, playing the *nkangala*, a mouth-resonated musical bow. August 1985.

There are always nodes in an individual life. In 1967 Maurice Djenda, an anthropologist from the Central African Republic, and I were offered a chance to do a countrywide survey of musical traditions in Tanzania. For reasons that were never clarified, the project was suddenly canceled a few weeks before it was to start. However, the government of a neighboring country, Malawi, stepped in and told us that we would be welcome there. We changed territory and embarked on a nine-month survey of Malawi musical traditions that resulted in the most comprehensive ethnomusicological documentation ever carried out in a single African country (see the archival collections Djenda-Kubik in the Ethnographic Museum, Berlin; and the Learning Resources Center of the Chancellor College Library, University of Malawi).

One evening in Blantyre, on 25 February 1967, I was tired of working at my desk and said to my companion that I would go out for an hour's walk. As I walked through the streets I became attracted by the sound of a *kwela* band playing at a street corner near the market. It was the band of the Kachamba brothers (figure 7), and the rest of the story is well known. If I had never met them, my life and subsequent research would certainly have taken a different turn. I would never have become a clarinet player in their band; I would not have traveled to Brazil with the young Donald Kachamba; I might never have known Lidiya Malamusi (figure 8), whom I married fifteen years later; and Lidiya might not have died on 26 November 1989. Even if I had met the Kachambas later, under different circumstances, a different sequence of events would probably have resulted; but unfortunately we cannot download and compare all the possible alternative scenarios from the cyberspace of another universe.

THE PLACE OF INDIVIDUAL RESEARCHERS IN HISTORY

Only later generations can define and redefine an individual's place in the history of a discipline. When I delivered the John Blacking Memorial lecture at the ESEM meeting in London on 15 November 1999, I felt the presence of several ancestral spirits in the hall of the School of Oriental and African Studies: apart from Blacking, there were A. M. Jones, Klaus Wachsmann, David Rycroft, and others. They seemed to have assembled in silence, listening critically to what I had to say. The last thing I wanted to do was to disappoint them. So I tried hard to show that I had made some progress since 28 March 1963, when those illustrious people had decided that an undergraduate student should give a lecture at the Royal Anthropological Institute of Great Britain and Ireland about his findings in Uganda. Klaus Wachsmann had introduced me to the audience, and A. M. Jones had participated in the discussions.

A. M. Jones has had a considerable intellectual influence upon me through his various discoveries, including the relative beat in some Bemba drumming and his analysis of asymmetric time-line patterns (1949). Although I have added new findings to his research and, in the process, modified some of his concepts (Kubik 1989a, b; 1994b; 1999b), I feel no need to criticize him or, for that matter, to probe the alleged mistakes of past generations. The paleontologist Stephen Gould has warned us against perceiving too many dichotomies and becoming arrogant: "Since we have a lamentable tendency to view our own age as best, these divisions often saddle the past with pejorative names while designating successively more modern epochs with words of light and progress" (1996:39). Gould was referring to the "dark ages." Certainly, knowledge is increasing, but the human intellect has remained essentially the same—at least, I see no improvement in it. Sometimes the same problems recur cyclically and the same mistakes reappear, though worded differently.

Klaus Wachsmann's work was also an inspiration to me from the moment (in the late 1970s) when I first grasped his ideas. His interest in the historical dimension of African music guided me in reconstructing aspects of the musical history of East, Central, and West Africa (Kubik 1994b, 1998, 1999a). Wachsmann's fascinating reconstruction of the history of African harps (1964) and the migratory pathways of instruments in the interlacustrine area of East Africa (1971) are milestones on a route opened up by earlier researchers such as Bernhard Ankermann, Erich Moritz von Hornbostel, and Fritz Graebner.

Another place where spirits still speak to me is South Africa. Hugh Tracey never tired of encouraging me in my early work; he wrote many letters to me while I was on my early trips, and I am not sure that I actually deserved so much attention. Our personal encounters are unforgettable—as is my association with the Portuguese anthropologists António Jorge Dias and Margot Dias, without whom I would not have become, in 1965, the first (and it now seems the last) cultural anthropologist and ethnomusicologist to work among the rural population of southeastern Angola.

AVENUES FOR SCIENTIFIC DISCOVERY

Ultimately, the human mind is a closed system. One does not have to consult Arthur Schopenhauer to realize this. Essentially, there is no way out of its circuit. Some societies have seen a possibility of divine inspiration, that is, extrasystemic origins of ideas; thus it is sometimes said that in states of trance, such as those researched by Gilbert Rouget (1980), an external power called a spirit, *orisa* or *vodu*, breaks into the circuit. But as soon as the possessed person returns to a normal state, the experience appears to be wiped away and the channel seems to be sealed off again. Multiple mind wiring—temporary connections between the brains of different individuals, human to human or human to animal—may be undertaken in this century, and the experiments may yield surprising findings about what constitutes consciousness. As it stands now, however, each human being has accumulated (since birth and shortly before) his or her own memory traces, which have condensed into what we experience as personal consciousness. We can no more explain exactly what it is that makes us aware of ourselves—that makes us say, "This is I"—than we can explain the perception of color to a person who is color-blind, and only by inference do we conclude that other persons are also conscious; there is no way of directly experiencing the consciousness of another individual.

But I can imagine how the phenomenon of consciousness arises. Self-awareness and consciousness are phenomenologically related to the fact that all mental activity is encased in a circuit. That is the *conditio qua non* of consciousness. A sort of centripetal process comparable to a gestalt effect then results from the interaction of the memory traces stored in the brain, forming units, clusters, and connected complexes. Essentially, therefore, consciousness is a phenomenon simply arising from the interconnectedness, the merry-go-round of all our memory traces, including continuous perceptual input. As a closed circuit in which the neurological pathways are constantly energized, the system must crystallize into an all-permeating identity. It begins to experience itself. This may seem to be an enigma, but it really is not.

From this discovery many others might follow. One is that the mind of animals is not in principle different from the human mind; animals may also be conscious and self-aware, although they cannot think verbally about their self-awareness or communicate it to us, and so we tend to deny that they are conscious. Similarly, since consciousness arises from closed mental circuits or energized neurological superhighways, we might predict that advanced computers or robots which move around and accumulate data through sensors will also develop consciousness and self-awareness, if each is designed as a closed system of circuits.

The realization that discoveries and inventions are not necessarily made only by people of special talent or abilities conforms to some of these insights. Rather, such discoveries tend to be made by individuals who have been in exceptionally sensitizing circumstances that have triggered unusual developments. This comment is not to be misunderstood as a preference for nurture over nature, but we can reasonably think of the human genome as what it is: a huge set of possibilities.

There are many pathways for extraordinary scientific discoveries by individuals, depending on training, personal outlook, and experience. Problem-oriented research projects, for example, easily yield what they are designed for: routine solutions to specifically stated problems. But even with a measure of good luck, the researcher had better be prepared to keep more than one problem in reserve. In some instances, problem-oriented research proposals lead nowhere, except to a grant. Research questions may be phantoms arising merely from a juggling of contrived or poorly defined categories. In such cases the solution to the problem is an empty set.

There is no recipe for making a significant discovery. There are useful guidelines for research, but no blueprints. And yet certain avenues besides the strict pursuit of a specific scientific question are worth exploring.

Sometimes one can cultivate a mental state in which one is simply tinkering with ideas against the background of a set of data. A much neglected but important problem-solving activity is dreaming. A dreamer is both agent and observer. Animals also dream, but only human beings, beginning with the anonymous prehistoric cave painters (as at Lascaux and Tassili n'Ajjer) have felt a need to project their dreams outward. Since dreams are predominantly visual sequences, early artists produced pictures, both representational and abstract. The latter can be inspired by phosphenes, luminous endogenous patterns experienced when the eyes are closed (McDougall 1977:392). Even the aura of a migraine attack, if it occurs during sleep, can actually be seen by the dreamer. Eventually, dream imagery was transferred into auditory expression; it crystallized into sequences of sounds, phonetic sequences, and words and could be communicated in this form to others. Long before writing was invented, humans had begun to compose stories analogous to dream sequences.

The mental activity responsible for our dreams can be tapped: mathematicians have occasionally found solutions to puzzling number problems in their dreams, and composers have found new ideas. However, it is the combination of rational thought, the tireless pursuit of a specific issue, and the ability to turn on an autopilot and let free association proceed within its own laws that often leads to discoveries. A sudden insight can then be formalized and regulated by the intellect.

Unfortunately, we have not yet devised any way to tap dreams during REM sleep, although it is possible to imagine digitalizing a dreamer's brain activity and displaying the visual content of the dream on, say, a television screen—indeed, that might also come in this century. My thirteen-year old nephew Yohane (figure 9), who was with us in Namibia in 1991–1993 (Kubik 2000:11), told me recently that he was working on this, and I have given him the year 2011 as a deadline.

Chains of associations, as in dreams, daydreams, and psychoanalysis, with minimal interference by the intellect, are paralleled by a mental state that could be called perceptual floating: an almost playful, nonselective form of observing combined with a low level of alertness. Alexander Fleming (1881–1955) probably discovered penicillin in this manner. In 1928, while working with staphylococcus bacteria, he suddenly noticed a bacteria-free circle around a mold growth near his culture; he investigated the mold (spores of *Penicillium notatum*) and discovered a substance in it that prevented bacterial growth, even when it was diluted 800 times. What if he had remained indifferent and paid no attention to the mold? That is the crux of the matter: his discovery took place because, as a researcher, he had developed a continual state of "mild" alertness.

Something similar may have happened when I finally succeeded in decoding the geometrical puzzle of *tusona* ideographs drawn by Angolan elders in the sand (1987),

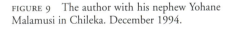

FIGURE 9   The author with his nephew Yohane Malamusi in Chileka. December 1994.

and perhaps also in 1962, when it dawned on me that there might be a common abstract principle behind several African multipart singing styles. As I was tinkering with thoughts about Pangwa and Gogo singing styles and their different tonal systems, something suddenly happened: an insight took me by surprise. I have called my discovery a "skipping" process. This term designated a structural principle regulating the functional interrelationship between several African tonal systems and their associated multipart patterns, both vocal and instrumental. The principle (which is interregional and does not depend on the nature of the tonal system itself) is that in homophonic multipart styles, particularly in East and Central Africa, a second singer usually constructs his or her melodic line (in harmony with the line of the first singer) by skipping one note of their common scale. The simultaneous sounds arising from this process are predictable; they are a logical consequence of the structure of the underlying tonal system (whether heptatonic, equiheptatonic, pentatonic, tetratonic, derived from natural partials or not, and so on) when the skipping process is applied (1994b, 1999b).

More recently, I developed a theory of the African genealogy of the so-called blue notes permeating African-American musical traditions in North America (1999b). How I condensed this from my West African database and decoded the logic of the system is something I cannot now reconstruct. I am a passionate walker, and on long walks my thoughts turn to problems without forcing premature solutions; all of a sudden, a solution simply occurs.

Another avenue for making a discovery is to place oneself in extraordinary situations. For instance, a successful Mars probe is bound to find something surprising; another example would be tracking a computer virus to its source. Setting out in an arbitrary direction, experimentally, increases the likelihood of an unusual encounter. It may be annoying, but may also be delightful. A blindfolded walker who stumbles over a root may have found the beginning or the end of a tunnel.

Was there anything unusual about my circumstances when I set out for Africa in 1959? Plenty: my mode of travel, my despair, my readiness to accept any hardship, my determination to carry a self-imposed program to its end, my philosophy of associating with my hosts, and my specific intellectual background—Freud (the unconscious), Schopenhauer (the relativity of all values), Kafka (the strangeness of our existence), and my conviction that free will is an illusion. So I learned to switch on the autopilot.

Extraordinary situations can also lie at our doorstep. What then emerges depends on the individual's courage, intellectual curiosity, and ability to recognize possibilities. One can explore a new path that has suddenly opened up, ignore it, or react with indifference, reluctance, or even fear. How one reacts to new situations is determined by early childhood experiences. Healthy curiosity in a child can be encouraged or inhibited by the attitude of parents, who might punish or ridicule or simply neglect it. Society also puts considerable pressure on individuals. It expects a youngster to act in certain ways: "like an adult" (abandoning "childish" behavior), "like a girl" (internalizing gender identity), "like a Fulbe and *not* a Kutin," "like a Serb and *not* an Albanian," "like a white person," "like a black person." Oppressive commandments about identity are extremely damaging; they stunt intellectual growth. And once such commandments have been internalized and have become unconscious, a cure—liberation from socially imposed stereotypes—is difficult. Neither alcohol nor drugs can help; but sometimes controlled free association, a kind of mental free jazz, can be effective.

One day I discovered that I had acquired a strange habit while telephoning. I do not mean that I was indulging in lascivious or libelous talk; this was something totally different—without being conscious of it, I was composing abstract graphs. This habit seems to have begun in the early 1980s and has continued ever since. During a stimulating conversation with a colleague or an acquaintance—preferably an overseas call (if it is not on my telephone bill)—my hand almost automatically takes a ballpoint pen (black, red, blue, or sometimes green) and draws figures, mostly abstract, on any paper within reach. At first I was unaware of this habit, until I discovered the results lying around near the phone. I then began to collect these drawings. Of course, I soon realized that consciousness of my action, the mere fact that I had begun to observe what I was doing, affected the quality of the drawings. And this took place not at Werner Heisenberg's quantum level but in the macro world. At the moment when I began to think of my telephone drawings as art, they tended to lose their spontaneity. The activity became purposeful, as if I were preparing for an exhibition. Fortunately, however, I regularly forget about my habit, especially in the excitement of a lively conversation, and then the drawings become automatic again. Studying my "telephone art," I find that the act of drawing is a sort of visual daydreaming, and in their abstract design the drawings are in a sense analogous to musical improvisation. I can easily remember which ones are authentic—that is, drawn almost unconsciously—and which are not.

Yet another avenue for making discoveries can open up when an individual is under intense pressure. Hard-pressed by a problem, whatever it may be (such as a serious personal situation), without a discernable way out, one may react in various ways. Some people commit suicide; but the psyche also explores ways to heal itself, normally by transference of the problem to an analogous relationship with another person. Initially this provides some relief, but it postpones the solution. Some people project the problem outward by composing figures, sound patterns, or intrinsically ordered symbols like the *mandala* studied by Carl Gustav Jung (1950). An individual who still has surplus energy may develop a systematic program to search for a way out. Most long-term research ultimately symbolizes disguised psychological problems. That is not despicable—after all, the fuel must come from somewhere. And this is how "thriving on a riff" (in Charlie Parker's words) eventually crystallizes into anthropology.

REFERENCES

Andika, Helmut, and Gerhard Kubik. n.d. *Zeichnungen und Aquarelle/Gedichte und Prosa*. Wien: Verlag

———. c. 1965. *Junge Generation*. N.p.

Djenda, Maurice. 1994a. "De la croyance religieuse des Mpyɛmɔ. Précis d'une analyse en ethnologie de la religion." In *For Gerhard Kubik: Festschrift on the Occasion of His Sixtieth Birthday*, eds. August Schmidhofer and Dietrih Schüller, with foreword by David Rycroft, 73–82. Frankfurt/Main: Peter Lang.

———. 1994b. "Die neuere Ethnologie im Lichte de des Völker- und Selbstverständnisses. Analysen eines afrikanischen Stammesangelhörigen." In *For Gerhard Kubik. Festschrift on the Occasion of His Sixtieth Birthday*, eds. August Schmidhofer and Dietrih Schüller, with foreword by David Rycroft, 503–516. Frankfurt/Main: Peter Lang.

Duro-Ladipo, Abiodun, and Gbowega Kolawole. 1998. "Opera in Nigeria: The Case of Duro Ladipo's 'Oba Koso,'" *Black Music Research Journal* 17(1, spring):101–129.

Gould, Stephen Jay. 1996. *Dinosaur in a Haystack: Reflections in Natural History*. London: Cape.

Guthrie, Malcolm. 1948. *The Classification of the Bantu Languages*. London: Oxford University Press.

Jones, Arthur M. 1949. *African Music in Northern Rhodesia and Some Other Places*. Occasional Papers of the Rhodes Livingstone Museum, 4. Manchester: Manchester University Press

Jung, Carl Gustav. 1950. *Gestaltungen des Unbewßten*. Psychologische Abhandlungen 7. Zürich: Rascher Verlag.

Kubik, Gerhard. 1945. *Notizbuch über Luftalarme in Weltkrieg 1939–1945*. Completed 15 April at Wien 17. Bz. Haslingergasse 68/2. Private archive of G. Kubik. Unpublished, original title.

———. 1948. *Im Schloss* (In the Castle). Unpublished manuscript of a short novel.

———. 1960. "The Structure of Kiganda Xylophone Music." *African Music* 2(3):6–30. Corrigenda in 1970. *African Music* 4(4):136–137.

———. 1971. "Zur inneren Kritik ethnographischer Feldberichte aus der kolonialen Periode." *Weiner Ethnohistorische Blätter* 2:31–41.

———. 1987. *Tusona-Luchazi Ideographs: A Graphic Tradition Practiced by a People of West Central Africa*. Föhrenau-Wien: E. Stiglmayr.

———. 1989a. "Àló—Yoruba Chantefables: An Integrated Approach towards West African Music and Oral Literature." In *African Musicology: Current Trends. A Festschrift Presented to J. H. Kwabena Nketia*, Vol. 1, ed. Jacqueline Cogdell DjeDje and Willim G. Carter, 129–182. Los Angeles: UCLA African Studies Center and African Arts Magazine.

———. 1989b. "Die Mukanda-Erfahrung: Zur Psychologie der Initiation der Jungen im Ost-Angola-Kulturraum." In *Kinder: Ethnologische Forschungen in fünf Kontinenten*, ed. Marié-José van de Loo and Margarete Reinhart, 308–347. München: Trickster.

———. 1989c. "Subjective Patterns in African Music." *Cross Rhythms: Papers in African Folklore/Music* 3:129–154.

———. 1993. *Makisi-Nyau-Mapiko: Maskentraditionen im Bantusprachigen Afrika*. München: Trickster.

———. 1994a. "Ethnicity, Cultural Identity, and the Psychology of Culture Contact." In *Music and Black Ethnicity: The Caribbean and South*

America, ed. Gerard H. Béhague, 17–46. New Brunswick and London: Transaction.

———. 1994b. *Theory of African Music*, Vol. 1. Wilhelmshaven: Noetzel.

———. 1998. "Intra-African Streams of Influences." In *The Garland Encyclopedia of World Music*, Vol. 1, *Africa*, ed. Ruth M. Stone, 651–680. New York and London: Garland.

———. 1999a. "African and African American Lamellophones: History, Typology, Nomenclature, Performers, and Intracultural Concepts." In *Turn Up the Volume! A Celebration of African Music*, ed. Jacqueline Cogdell DjeDje, 20–57. Los Angeles: UCLA Fowler Museum of Cultural History.

———. 1999b. *Africa and the Blues*. Jackson: University Press of Mississippi.

———. 2000. "Interconnectedness in Ethnomusicological Research." *Ethnomusicology* 44(1, winter):1–14

Kubik, Gerhard, Moya A. Malamusi, Lidiya Malamusi, and Donald Kachamba. 1987. *Malawian Music—A Framework for Analysis*. Zomba: Center for Social Research and Department of Fine and Performing Arts, University of Malawi.

Longman Group UK Limited. 1990. *Dictionary of Contemporary English*. Harlow: Longman House.

Malamusi, Moya Aliya. 1999. *From Lake Malawi to the Zambezi: Aspects of Music and Oral Literature in Southeast Africa in the 1990s*. Frankfurt am Main: Popular African Music, Pamap 602. Compact disk and pamphlet.

McDougall, Lorna. 1977. "Symbols and Somatic Structures." In *The Anthropology of the Body*, ed. John Blacking, 391–406. London: Academic.

Nurse, George T. 1996. "Masked Men Dancing and the Lordship Over Land: A Review Essay." *African Music* 7(3):96–102.

Rouget, Gilbert. 1980. *La musique et la trance: Esquisse d'une théorie générale des relations de la musique et de la possession*. Paris: Éditions Gallimard.

Tracey, Andrew. 1961. "Mbira Music of Jege A Tapera." *African Music* 2(4):44–63.

Wachsmann, Klaus Peter. 1964. "Human Migration and African Harps." *Journal of the International Folk Music Council* 16:84–88.

———. 1971. "Musical Instruments in the Kiganda Tradition and Their Place in the East African Scene." In *Essays on Music and History in Africa*, ed. Klaus P. Wachsmann, 93–134, Evanston, Ill.: Northwestern University Press.

Wegner, Ulrich. 1993. "Cognitive Aspects of *Amadinda* Xylophone Music from Buganda: Inherent Patterns Reconsidered." *Ethnomusicology* 37(2):201–241.

Zorpette, Glenn. 2000."Why Go to Mars?" *Scientific American* 282(3, March):22–25.

North America and the
Middle East
Ellen Koskoff

Prologue
Stumbling into the Field
Fieldwork
Life after the Dissertation
An Ethnomusicologist at Eastman
Coming Full Circle

PROLOGUE

In 1948, when I was four years old, a small group of Lubavitcher Hasidim (ultra-orthodox Jews) moved into my neighborhood—Squirrel Hill in Pittsburgh, Pennsylvania—and, taking over the house at my corner for a religious school, immediately caused an uproar on Hobart Street. (For a more detailed version of this story, see Koskoff 2000.) Most of the people there were like my family: upwardly mobile, middle-class, "secular" Jewish families, mainly living there because in the 1930s and 1940s, when many of them had moved to Pittsburgh, Jews could not easily buy houses in other parts of the city. Having Hasidim around, though, reminded them of all they and their parents had left when they immigrated to the United States in the late nineteenth and early twentieth centuries.

As I grew up I frequently passed the Lubavitcher yeshiva on my way to elementary school or to the neighborhood drugstore. Sometimes in the evenings I would hear the most wonderful singing filtering out of the open windows. As I peered in through the new fence surrounding the building, I would see the faces and bodies of the men and boys inside transformed by the music. They seemed so alive, immediate, and intense.

I recognized that feeling. Having been a musical child, I had started studying the piano when I was five. I had often experienced the feeling myself, especially when playing Bach or Mozart—a feeling of freedom, of being transported out of one's body, of losing the consciousness of playing the music and actually merging with it. But I also knew that I could not communicate this to my parents or to my neighborhood friends, who, I sensed, would not have understood my feeling even if I had been able to articulate it at the time.

Thus, I came to believe that the Lubavitchers and I shared a great secret: if you gave all of yourself to performing music, you could actually *become the music itself*. No longer just an ordinary person going through an everyday routine, you could transform yourself into sound. This, for me, had nothing to do with a religious belief or a ritual; rather, it had to do with personal knowledge of the transformative power of music, and I somehow knew that these strange, otherworldly people living in my neighborhood also understood it.

My parents, however, had a different opinion. For many like my father, a well-known and highly respected doctor, being raised in the United States had been a blessing. Although part of the "quota system" at Yale (an unacknowledged and now abandoned policy of allowing only a certain number of Jews to enter the college in any given year), my father had earned both a Ph.D. and an M.D. Moving to Pittsburgh and joining the staff of the Jewish hospital, Montefiore, had secured for him a place in the medical community. My mother, descended on her mother's side from the Lithuanian Hasidic Kalisher family, had grown up in Cambridge, Massachusetts, as the daughter of the composer Henry F. Gilbert (1868–1928). An early bohemian with a talent for writing and painting, my mother grew up as part of a left-wing intellectual community that eschewed all religious beliefs and practices and had no special Jewish cultural identity.

My parents' relationship to the Jewish community in Pittsburgh was thus ambivalent from the start: although openly acknowledging their Jewishness, they constructed it as a cultural, ethnic identity, not a religious one. We never went to the synagogue, and we saw all religious holidays simply as an excuse for a good family meal. The Hasidim in the neighborhood challenged this construction. "They're too Jewish," my parents said. "Better stay away." Although I did not recognize it at the time, my first encounters with Lubavitchers and my parents' reaction to them marked the beginning of my life as an ethnomusicologist.

STUMBLING INTO THE FIELD

I have spent much of my academic life studying a variety of musics and social contexts that focus on the relationship between people, their ideas, and their music. I began by examining the relationship between a socioreligious philosophical system and its realization through musical performance. Working with Lubavitcher Hasidim over many years—in Pittsburgh, Pennsylvania; Crown Heights, Brooklyn, New York; and St. Paul, Minnesota—I have concentrated in many of my publications on the ways in which music and its performance mediate relationships between Lubavitchers themselves, between Lubavitchers and God, and between Lubavitchers and the largely secular world of late-twentieth-century America. Along the way I have also become interested in and have contributed to other areas that have intersected with ethnomusicology: feminist and gender studies, cognitive psychology, and psychological anthropology. And rather recently I have fallen in love with Balinese music and hope to study *gamelan angklung*, the Balinese village ensemble used primarily for Hindu cremation ceremonies.

One of the most important things I have learned doing this work is that life is full of surprises. Paying attention to them can be both frightening and liberating. Like the joyful surprise of recognizing an emotional connection between my four-year-old musical self and a group of pious orthodox Jews, other surprises, both good and bad, have come my way, making my life as an ethnomusicologist interesting and rewarding.

My formal training in ethnomusicology was haphazard, yet there were a few teachers along the way whose special personalities or insightful work opened up unimagined possibilities for me. In 1971, I entered the doctoral musicology program at the University of Pittsburgh, hoping to study the keyboard works of Bach. By then, I had a bachelor of music degree from the Boston University School of Fine Arts (1965) and a master of arts in music education from Columbia University in New York (1968), and I was teaching music to children while pursuing a performing career as a harpsichordist. I had pretty much forgotten about Lubavitchers. At the same time, I was growing more political, marching against the Vietnam War and reading the burgeoning literature of the feminist movement. Performing and teaching Western classical music began to seem hollow to me, part of an elitist enterprise that I felt uncomfortable participating in.

When I decided to go back to school for a Ph.D. in musicology, I was unaware that ethnomusicology existed. There were no ethnomusicologists at the University of

Pittsburgh in 1971, and I was happy enough, at least at the beginning, to concentrate on early music, a subfield of musicology that was also developing at the time. I began taking courses in early chant and transcription, which I greatly enjoyed. They seemed marginal enough to the mainstream work of historical musicology—the German master composers—which I found oppressive. Eventually, I became interested in the fifteenth-century composer Gilles Binchois (c. 1400–1460) and contemplated doing my dissertation on his vocal music.

At the beginning of my studies, when I was a young scholar, two special men inspired and greatly helped me. One was Robert Snow, a musicologist interested in sixteenth-century chant, who was so infectiously enthusiastic and buoyant about his work and about sharing it with students that I developed from the beginning the notion of scholarship as fun, perhaps the intellectual equivalent of a wondrous treasure hunt. Dr. Snow was one of the first teachers I had with a sense of self-depreciating humor, one who truly loved what he did and who loved us. The other professor I especially cherished at that time was Donald Beikman, who was the first person to treat me with true professional dignity—not as a student but as a colleague. At the beginning of my studies in musicology, I was unsure if I had chosen a viable career path. The discipline of musicology seemed—especially then—to be the primary force validating and perpetuating the elitist values of Western classical music and the hierarchies that supported them. Did I really want to be associated with this, even as an early music scholar? Dr. Beikman sensed my discomfort early on and took me under his wing. He helped me with my writing, took me to musicology conferences, and generally saw me as a junior colleague. While Dr. Snow introduced me to the fun, the excitement, and even the humor of scholarship, Dr. Beikman helped me to see that scholarship and an academic life were within my grasp.

However, it wasn't until 1973, when I was completely finished with my musicology course work and qualifying exams, that the surprise of ethnomusicology fell into my lap. The person whose work catapulted me into the field was Alan Merriam, a man whom I have never met but whose ideas I cherish to this day as the catalyst for my "conversion." One day while working on my dissertation proposal on Binchois in the music library, I was wandering down the aisles looking for some obscure source when I saw a bright-yellow book standing out somewhat from its fellows on the shelf. As I reached up to push it back so that it would be flush with its neighbors, I saw its title, *The Anthropology of Music* (1964). I took the book home and read it, much as I would a have read a love story or a mystery—from start to finish in one swoop—and from that moment on I knew that I wanted to be an ethnomusicologist, to work with living people who could share their feelings with me directly, through their own words in face-to-face dialogue.

Thus my entrance into ethnomusicology came as a complete surprise to me—a true "aha!" experience. I was not attracted by any one music, any one instrument, any one culture, or even any of the places I had visited that were "foreign" to me; rather, I was attracted by the radical idea (radical to me, in 1973) that music was not only something one could read, play, or study but also a process of social interaction through which shared values could be expressed. It was precisely at that moment that I remembered the Lubavitchers. Now would be the time to discover the nature of the relationship between Lubavitchers and their music and between Lubavitchers and me. I would have to change my dissertation topic.

Of course, my switch to ethnomusicology came as a complete surprise to my advisers, too. There were still no ethnomusicologists at Pitt. If I left and went to another school, I would lose all the credits I had built up (and possibly have to go through my Ph.D. qualifying exams again). So I began to hunt for people in the anthropology department who could help me; I also began reading other works, especially those of Mantle Hood (1971), Hugo Zemp (1971), and John Blacking (1974),

One of the surprises of fieldwork is that it becomes a time for learning not only about the people and music you have "chosen" but also about yourself, because as you address the other, your ideas about yourself begin to change.

which were extremely helpful. Oddly enough, my professors did not stop me. Although they were largely as unaware of the discipline of ethnomusicology as I was, they encouraged me to make my first forays into the Pittsburgh Lubavitcher community, and I began to do fieldwork there, gradually moving on to Crown Heights.

Carol Robertson-DeCarbo (now Carolina Robertson) arrived in Pittsburgh two years later, just as I was becoming overwhelmed with data gathered in the communities of Pittsburgh and Crown Heights. A student of Alan Merriam's at Indiana University, Carol was invaluable as an adviser and friend. If I could not actually study with Alan Merriam, Carol would be the next best thing. Having had little formal training in ethnomusicology, cultural anthropology, or Jewish studies, though, I needed help with the organization, theoretical context, and interpretation of my data, and—even more important—I needed to understand how my work fit within the intersecting disciplines of ethnomusicology, American ethnicity, Jewish music, and the anthropology of religion, all of which my dissertation topic touched on. Carol was my link to these bodies of knowledge and, with tremendous insight and patience, guided me through the maze to a completed dissertation, "The Concept of *Nigun* among Lubavitcher Hasidim in the United States" (1976). After I received my Ph.D. in 1976, I remained in Pittsburgh for the next four years to continue my "training" in ethnomusicology, sitting in on classes with Carol and later with Robert Kaufmann, an Africanist, who succeeded her at the university.

One finds teachers and major influences, however, not only in the classroom or library. During fieldwork, especially work conducted over a period of twenty years or more, various individuals emerge as teachers, colleagues, and friends. Perhaps my best and most cherished Lubavitcher teachers were Rabbi Ephraim Rosenblum and his wife, Miriam Rosenblum, of Pittsburgh, who took me into their home and taught me much about Hasidic life, music, and Lubavitcher gender arrangements, and who also made it possible for me to travel and live in Brooklyn. Others, such as Eli Lipsker, Rus Dvorah Shatkin, Moshe Teleshevski, and Hersh Gansbourg, whom I interviewed and recorded many times, were invaluable as teachers and sources of information on Lubavitcher musical practices throughout the years.

FIELDWORK

Fieldwork is the hallmark of ethnomusicology, the process that separates it from all other musical disciplines and links it inextricably to anthropology and other ethnographic scholarship. One of the surprises of fieldwork, however, is that it becomes a time for learning not only about the people and music you have "chosen" but also about yourself, because as you address the other, your ideas about yourself begin to change. Of course, this is not a surprise to anyone trained in the field today. Issues of representation and voice, now well documented in the postmodern anthropological and cultural studies of the 1980s and 1990s, have helped us understand the relativity and intersubjectivity of selves and others, of peripheries and centers, and of ethical issues in scholarship; but in 1973, when I entered the field, it was all new to me.

Two unexpected situations arose during fieldwork that profoundly affected this experience and continued long past my dissertation to shape my work. The first proved to be the more difficult to deal with. Unlike most people in ethnomusicology in the mid-1970s, who went off to faraway places like Indonesia, Ghana, or India, I was conducting fieldwork in "exotic" Brooklyn, a place I thought I knew fairly well, where everyone I worked with spoke English and was (I imagined) not much different from me. Furthermore, I could easily travel back and forth, and often did, sometimes daily or weekly, between my "field site" and my "home site," a process that actually heightened the discomfort of "culture shock" (because I was always in it). What caused a major problem for me was my social and ethical position vis à vis the orthodox Lubavitcher communities with which I worked and later with the largely nonreligious audiences for my work.

On the one hand, being at least nominally Jewish allowed me easy access to various Lubavitcher families both within and outside Crown Heights. Also, being a musician counted for something among Lubavitchers, so I was welcomed as a person who "did music"; and at first I found it fairly easy to come and go, conduct interviews, record *nigunim* and other songs, take photographs, and attend *farbrengen* 'gatherings', weddings, and various other social events. As I stayed longer and longer in the community, however, a certain tension began to develop and grow. The Lubavitchers wanted me to become more religiously observant; they wanted me to become "more Jewish."

Lubavitchers regard any Jew who is not a *hasid* as having fallen away from the divine source. Returning such a person to a more religious life is regarded as a *mitzvah* 'blessing'. Proselytization, a practice generally avoided by most other Jews, is encouraged within Lubavitcher culture (although Lubavitchers bristle at this term, preferring to speak of outreach). As a result of major efforts over the past decades, most Lubavitchers living in Crown Heights today were born in the United States and entered the community as adults, where they are known as *ba'alei teshuvah* 'masters of repentance', an honorific that acknowledges all they have given up.

Thus I began to be seen less as a scholar interested in music and more as a possible recruit. Why else would I be spending so much time in Crown Heights? I slowly came to understand that Lubavitchers saw my fieldwork and their outreach efforts as a fair exchange: information about music for me and a newly returned Jewish soul for them. During conversations about music, its performance contexts, or just about any other subject, especially with newcomers to the community, the topic would inevitably turn to my Jewishness and questions would be asked about my religious beliefs, my religious education, or why I seemed so resistant to making a commitment to orthodoxy. Usually, I was able to deal successfully with this, but there were occasions when I would become uncomfortable, defensive, or argumentative, completely losing my desire for objectivity.

The second special situation I encountered during fieldwork actually helped me to transform my work and to become politically active in the new discipline of feminist ethnomusicology. During fieldwork, being female was both a source of frustration and an opportunity. On the one hand, my growing feminism often made me wary of (even angry at) Lubavitcher essentialist arguments for maintaining rigid gender arrangements. Some of my early interviews, for example, are marred by my interest in "raising women's consciousness" (that is, their consciousness of their *true*, secondary status). Lubavitcher women simply laughed at me, dismissing my naive attempts to liberate them as evidence that I still did not understand the essence of the Jewish worldview: women are more holy than men because they can have children, and, like God, create something from nothing. It is the men who need prayer and music to help them catch up! But believing women to be spiritually (and "naturally") superior to men, although certainly a reversal of the values that seemed to prevail in secular society, still seemed inherently sexist to me.

On the other hand, being a woman, I often lived with other women or with young married couples, most of whom were *ba'alei teshuvah*. Many of these women were not so different from me: most had been raised in secular Jewish homes, many had been to college, some had graduate degrees, others worked as doctors or teachers, and many were musicians. In the 1970s very little had been written about the differences between Jewish men's and women's music, between performance contexts, practices, and reception, or, more specifically, about the Orthodox Jewish laws of *kol isha*, the precepts that prohibit observant Jewish men from hearing women sing.

This presented an opportunity I had not expected. Living with other women, especially women who had been involved in music in their secular lives, gave me a picture of Hasidic culture that had not been previously represented in the literature. But it was difficult, especially at the beginning, to take a position in my own writing that I could defend. On the one hand I could do what Jewish feminists wanted—dismiss the Lubavitcher woman's voice, seeing it as a cultural rationalization for a debased position within Jewish law. On the other hand, I could do what Lubavitchers wanted—undermine my own personal feminist voice by accepting the Lubavitcher position as "true."

It took me a while to sort this out and to determine what I wanted, which was neither of these. First, I wanted a dialogue between the two positions that could allow for each simply to understand the other, not necessarily to embrace but to tolerate differences. Second, I wanted to deconstruct and destabilize male hegemony in my own world, the world of music scholarship and of the academy more generally. Perhaps I could not have much of an effect on Lubavitcher gender arrangements, but I could document women's traditions—such documentation was sorely needed in the ethnomusicological literature—and thereby contribute not only to a more holistic view of Lubavitcher musical culture but also to the growing understanding of gender hierarchies outside the Lubavitcher world.

Distinguishing between these two issues was one of the main tasks of many of my publications (1987, 1991, 1993). The entrance of many more women into the academy and other public positions of power since the 1960s has undoubtedly changed the larger society; and as theoretical work in ethnomusicology and other disciplines dealing with gender and with varying cultural perspectives has grown in recent decades, we have all come to see that ethnographic truth lies not in one voice but in interactions and negotiation between and among multiple voices. Again, though, in the 1970s and early 1980s this had the feel and excitement of new and uncharted terrain.

LIFE AFTER THE DISSERTATION

In 1976, after I had completed my dissertation, something about its writing began to nag at me: in constructing and refining my themes and theories, I was leaving much of my data out of the picture. Points that were interesting but perhaps peripheral to a central discussion, an interview that didn't quite "fit in," a connection made by a person that hadn't made sense at the time, and many other bits of data seem to have "fallen onto the cutting-room floor." What would happen if, instead of writing about groups of people, I wrote about one person as a sort of ideo-music-culture, a society of one, where salient pieces of information gathered could somehow be shown graphically, as in a snapshot? This might not reveal much about society as a system, but it might come closer to the way one person conceptualized music. This naturally led me into cognitive psychology and psychological anthropology, especially toward work dealing with memory and with the internal structures of knowledge; the eventual result was a textbook, *The Musical Self* (1980), written for the University of Pittsburgh, and three articles (1982, 1984, 1988).

Although I was finding my intellectual life quite stimulating at this time, I was having problems on another front: I couldn't find a permanent job teaching ethnomusicology. My work seemed too "out there," perhaps not on the main track of ethnomusicology or Jewish music studies, and, frankly, jobs in ethnomusicology were pretty scarce in the late 1970s. So, for the four years following the completion of my dissertation, I worked as a visiting assistant professor in the music department at the University of Pittsburgh, as an instructor in the External Studies Program there, as a vocal instructor at Allegheny College, as the music director at a local Jewish day school, and at any other job that would help support me while I continued writing.

AN ETHNOMUSICOLOGIST AT EASTMAN

In 1980 I moved to Rochester, New York, to begin teaching part time in the musicology department at the University of Rochester's Eastman School of Music. Being the only ethnomusicologist in a large, prestigious school of music devoted to Western classical and jazz traditions has been, over the years, both frustrating and energizing: frustrating because the school has been slow to acknowledge other musics, and yet energizing in that along the way there have been exciting moments of opportunity and change where real progress toward musical (and social) acceptance has been made.

During the first few years, while I was teaching in the musicology and anthropology departments, and as a visiting professor at Syracuse University, New York University, and the University of California, Los Angeles, I became aware of a central problem many ethnomusicologists face when they are first employed in the academy: they often find themselves in places where their work or their field is not well understood. On the one hand, music colleagues often see ethnomusicologists, as well as the subjects they teach (and the people they "represent") as "other"; and although institutions may be motivated by good intentions—to broaden the canon, or to allow space for new musics—it often takes many years for most ethnomusicologists to feel completely integrated and comfortable within this environment. On the other hand, anthropology colleagues, although they tend to understand the issues surrounding fieldwork and representations of the other, are generally unable to deal adequately with music. So ethnomusicologists often find themselves "in the cracks," challenging both sides of their academic families, and are generally seen at best as enhancements to a program or at worst as nuisances.

Thus, in the 1980s, in addition to research, writing, teaching courses in world music, and teaching occasional topical courses in my various specialties (including one on "MTV-Land"), I decided that one of my main jobs would be to familiarize my colleagues with ethnomusicology and with what ethnomusicologists do. When I first arrived at Eastman, there were a few people who were familiar with and even knowledgeable about some non-Western musical traditions, but the discipline of ethnomusicology—especially the anthropologically oriented discipline it had become during the 1960s and 1970s—was largely unknown. So I began a sort of outreach program of my own, trying to make connections with other colleagues and departments with like interests.

In that first year I gave a set of public lectures called "What Is Ethnomusicology?" to which I invited the faculty, administrators, and students. These lectures served as a forum for ideas and questions about the field and—at least at the beginning—piqued the community's curiosity. Soon afterward, I established a yearly World Music Concert Series, which continues to this day to bring in some of the world's finest musicians and to open the school to new audiences. Later, I created a short spot on Rochester's local NPR radio affiliate, called "What in the World Is Music?" (a title that had been suggested to me long ago by Robert Kaufman) to help generate more of an audience for new activities at the school and elsewhere in Rochester. In 1984, I wrote an article in which I interviewed a number of Eastman's faculty members concerning universals in music. I wanted to get to know them, and I wanted them to get to know me and what I did; fieldwork, which is at the heart of my discipline—and is a process I truly

FIGURE I   Ellen Koskoff at an outing after the SEM conference, in the wine country of western New York state. Photo by Martha Ellen Davis.

enjoy—seemed the best way to do that. But I suppose the biggest event for me during this time was hosting the annual meeting of the Society for Ethnomusicology at the school in 1986 (figure 1). A member of the city council declared the days of the meeting "Ethnomusicology Week in Rochester," and the Seeger Lecture was delivered by Professor Barbara B. Smith, the first graduate of the Eastman School to become an ethnomusicologist.

There was often a sense of trial and error in my interactions with other colleagues. I was never sure which of my "ethno-ideas" would take hold and which would seem too odd or too strange, but it was important to me that I simply continue trying to negotiate, to open up ways in which I could help promote what I perceived to be the core values of the field. All these efforts were moderately successful, so that by the end of the 1980s they had opened the door to a growing understanding of the field not only as the study and performance of "non-Western" musics but more generally as an approach to all music—including Western classical music—that integrated social, cultural, and musical meanings.

I became a full-time member of the musicology department in 1989 and earned tenure five years later. By this time new faculty members with some training in or exposure to non-Western musics and ethnomusicology had joined the school. A small but growing community of like-minded people, such as the school's director, Robert Freeman, and his successor, James Undercoffler, who wished to revitalize the school's mission and curriculum, began to develop.

In the twenty years since I have been at Eastman, my efforts, and those of many of my colleagues, have begun to take hold; and the school, although it still has no ethnomusicology department, has developed what I call an "ethnomusicology spirit," that is, a willingness to see and teach a variety of musics as social process, as well as sound structure and history; to value excellent performance, no matter what the tradition; and to interact in new ways with the larger community. We have recently, for example, developed a new curriculum with courses such as the Eastman Colloquium, a required course that all freshmen take in their first semester and that exposes them to a variety of musics outside the Western classical canon. And our Balinese *gamelan angklung*, Lila Muni 'Beautiful Sound'—the first non-Western music ensemble for which students receive credit—has unexpectedly become an important context, an intersection of my values and the values of the school.

COMING FULL CIRCLE

We purchased our *gamelan* in 1991 from Bowling Green State University, and this began a process that, much to my delight, has brought me full circle—back to the transfixed child I was when I first discovered the power of music and the sheer fun of performing. My performing life, long passed, had been limited to Western classical music. Aside from my visit to UCLA in 1986, during which I had sat in on rehearsals of the Javanese *gamelan*, I had no experience either directing or playing in a *gamelan*. I sought help from ethnomusicology colleagues and found, much to my surprise, that many Balinese *gamelan* existed in North America, and that outstanding musicians from Indonesia regularly came here to teach. During our first few years, we shared teachers with the University of Montreal, inviting some of the finest performers and composers from Bali to teach at Eastman; these included Wayan Suweca, one of the founders of the first Balinese *gamelan* in the United States, Sekar Jaya. Then, with the help of the Gamelan List-Serve, we found Nyoman Suadin, who for the past four years has become a permanent fixture at Eastman and whose wonderful teaching and bubbling personality have inspired many of my students to travel to Bali, both to learn and to perform.

So it was, somewhat unexpectedly, that I reentered the world of performance, and in a way, reentered the field of ethnomusicology, by taking a more traditional route than I had done the first time around—through the music itself. One of the considerable benefits of working at the Eastman School is that I am surrounded by extraordinary musicians who love to perform. It has been a wonderful experience for me at this time of my life to sit on the floor surrounded by students, faculty colleagues, members of the Rochester community, and superb Balinese musicians and simply play music again. The Balinese process of learning and performing has provided a wonderfully safe, healthy environment for me and my students to experience an other, different kind of music.

In a way, it seems odd to write about myself as an ethnomusicologist, because I cannot really separate the ethnomusicologist from the rest of me. What I do is what I am. Being an ethnomusicologist has enabled me to live in a way that has been meaningful to me precisely because in doing such work I have been able to integrate my musical, intellectual, and political passions and beliefs into a satisfying whole—and for that I am grateful, to my colleagues, my students, and to my ethnomusicological forebears.

REFERENCES

Blacking, John. 1974. *How Musical Is Man?* Seattle: University of Washington Press.

Hood, Mantle. 1971. *The Ethnomusicologist.* New York: McGraw-Hill.

Koskoff, Ellen. 1976. "The Concept of *Nigun* among Lubavitcher Hasidim in the United States." Ph.D. dissertation, University of Pittsburgh.

———. 1980. *The Musical Self.* Pittsburgh: University of Pittsburgh, External Studies Program.

———. 1982. "The Music-Network: A Model for the Organization of Music Concepts." *Ethnomusicology* 25(3):353–370.

———. 1984. "Thoughts on Universals in Music." *World of Music* (2):66–87.

———. 1986. *Women and Music in Cross-Cultural Perspective.* Westport, Conn.:

Greenwood. Reprint: 1987. University of Illinois Press.

———. 1987. "The Sound of a Woman's Voice: Gender and Music in an American Hasidic Community." In *Women and Music in Cross-Cultural Perspective*, Ellen Koskoff, ed. Westport, Conn.: Greenwood.

———. 1988. "Cognitive Strategies in Rehearsal: A Case Study of a Western Classical Percussion Ensemble." *Selected Reports in Ethnomusicology: Issues in the Conceptualization of Music*, James Porter and Ali Jihad Racy, eds. 7:59–69. Los Angeles: University of California.

———. 1989. "Both In and Between: Women's Musical Roles in Ritual Life." *Concilium* 222: 97–110.

———. 1991. "Gender, Power, and Music." In *The Musical Woman: An International Perspective*,

Judith Laing Zaimont, ed. Westport, Conn.: Greenwood.

———. 1993. "Miriam Sings Her Song: The Self and Other in Anthropological Discourse." In *Musicology and Difference*, Ruth Solie, ed. Berkeley: University of California Press.

———. 2000. *Music in Lubavitcher Life.* Champaign-Urbana: University of Illinois Press.

Merriam, Alan. 1964. *The Anthropology of Music.* Evanston, Ill.: Northwestern University Press.

Zemp, Hugo. 1971. *Musique Dan: La musique dans la pensée et la vie sociale d'une société africaine.* Paris and The Hague: Mouton.

Africa and North America
Jacqueline Cogdell DjeDje

Becoming an Ethnomusicologist

Life as a Researcher

Issues That Have Affected My Research: Ownership of Cultural Products and
    Local Politics

The Role of Research in Professional Life

The Place of My Work in Ethnomusicology

Over my twenty-year career as a professor of ethnomusicology at the University of California, Los Angeles (UCLA), I have read hundreds of applications from individuals who are interested in ethnomusicology as a future profession. Two factors seem to be common to many people as well as myself: (1) the decision to become an ethnomusicologist, not surprisingly, occurs when individuals reach adulthood instead of in their teens or earlier and (2) the decision sometimes becomes a life-changing experience. Because ethnomusicologists have had similar encounters, my narrative serves as one case study that may not be very different from others.

BECOMING AN ETHNOMUSICOLOGIST

I entered the field of ethnomusicology from a background in Western music performance and musicology. Although Fisk University, where I attended college, was a historically black university, founded in 1866 in Nashville, Tennessee, primarily to educate and uplift former slaves and their children, the music curriculum at Fisk was very similar to that of Oberlin Conservatory (of music) and Indiana University, the institutions where most of my teachers had received their graduate training. In fact, I chose Fisk for my higher education because it was considered one of the premier universities for the study of European art music that welcomed African-Americans. To understand the significance of Fisk and the role it played in shaping my future as an ethnomusicologist, some background information is necessary.

Early formative years

When I was five years old, my paternal grandmother, Ellen Cogdell, bought a piano for me and encouraged my parents (Leslie and Georgia Cogdell) to make arrangements for me to take lessons. As I took private piano lessons throughout elementary and junior high school in Jesup, Georgia (the town where I was born and raised), my teachers began to tell my parents that I had talent. Susanne McDaniel, my piano teacher, was impressed that I was able to learn quickly and perform relatively well all the pieces in the graded piano method books compiled by John M. Williams, Shaylor Turner, and John Thompson. When she organized her annual community piano recitals, I was considered the star pupil and played the most difficult pieces.

I performed African-American sacred music in my church for Sunday school and worship services: for example, hymns, spirituals, and gospel songs from *Gospel Pearls* (1921) and *The Baptist Standard Hymnal* (Townsend 1961); music by gospel composers such as Thomas Dorsey, Lucie Campbell, Kenneth Morris, Doris Akers, and J. Earle Hines; and popular music of the times ("Lonely Teardrops," recorded by Jackie Wilson; "It's Just a Matter of Time," recorded by Brook Benton; "Hello Stranger," recorded by Barbara Lewis; "Please, Mr. Sun," recorded by Tommy Edwards; "Silhouettes," recorded by the Rays; "Georgia on My Mind," recorded by Ray Charles; "Moon River," written by Henry Mancini). However, African-American music was *not* the performance tradition that *I* respected, nor was this the music that my teachers and members of my community used to measure my musical competence. It was the "classics" (music by Bach, Beethoven, Haydn, and Liszt) that placed me on a pedestal and made me different from my family, friends, and peers. My music teachers urged my parents to send me to a college preparatory school where my musical talent could be properly nurtured, and I could be challenged academically.

When I reached tenth grade, my parents sent me to Boggs Academy, a Presbyterian-run college preparatory high school in Keysville, Georgia, about 125 miles from Jesup. My teachers and parents were correct; Boggs was both motivating and enriching. It was at Boggs that my piano teacher, Celeste Gadsden, introduced me to more challenging piano literature. More important, she instilled in all her students a sense of pride and worth, emphasizing that we could achieve whatever we wanted if we only tried. As a result of her teaching and with the support of the school, I began to travel to other parts of the southeast United States to enter regional and state piano competitions. Although Boggs did not have a band, it had an outstanding choir director, Charles W. Francis, who was committed to the performance not only of African-American spirituals but also of European choral music (such as works by Palestrina, Bach, Handel, Mozart, and twentieth-century composers) and Broadway musicals. Finally, it was at Boggs that I learned about Fisk and what it had to offer. Instead of attending one of the historically black state-supported colleges in Georgia, I was encouraged to apply to Fisk.

When I arrived at Fisk in fall 1966, the social climate of the United States was beginning to change rapidly. Students at various universities had begun to be mobilized by the speeches and calls to action of Stokely Carmichael's Student Nonviolent Coordinating Committee (SNCC) and other civil rights organizations. During my freshman year, Carmichael spoke at Fisk, and this was another important juncture in my life. His message and his energy were both controversial and exhilarating. As I became caught up in the momentum of the times, I found that my personal background (cultural and musical) and my training at Fisk (which glorified European art music) were beginning to clash with my new values. I began to question my aspirations and to ask myself why I was attending Fisk. Still, although I was not happy or satisfied, I continued to pursue my studies, including piano, to the best of my ability. For example, while most students gave only a senior recital, my teacher, Anne Gamble Kennedy, who had had a professional career as a concert pianist, persuaded me to give both a junior and a senior recital.

In spite of my achievements, I began to realize that I no longer wanted to be a concert pianist. Questions were forming in my mind: What contribution could I make to my community and my culture by becoming a concert pianist? As a black woman, would I be able to get the right opportunities to excel? What kind of life would I have? How would I survive? Although I had black role models (Natalie Hinderas at Temple University and my own teacher, Anne Gamble Kennedy), performing or teaching European art music no longer appealed to me. Nor did an opportunity to study piano performance at Yale University entice me. But while I knew that I did not want to be a performer, I still had no idea what I wanted to do with my life after leaving Fisk.

The answers to these questions came during my senior year (1969–1970) at Fisk, as a result of several encounters. First, Darius Thieme, an ethnomusicologist who specialized in African music, was offered a teaching position. In fall 1969, I took one of his courses, "Cross-Currents in African and African-American Music." Not only did Thieme include material on Africa; he also presented information on the African diaspora. In addition, I remember being introduced to the works of Alan Merriam, Bruno Nettl, Erich M. von Hornbostel, Richard Waterman, A. M. Jones, and W. E. Ward. The fact that this course was offered is significant. To my knowledge, it was the first course on African or African-American music ever taught at Fisk, and Fisk may have been one of very few institutions in the country to include such a course in the music curriculum.

Second, in the spring of my senior year I took a course in conducting and decided to do a project on black composers of choral music. Because there was little information on this subject in the sources available to me at Fisk, I wrote to scholars of black music and and to black composers (they included Dominique de Lerma, George Walker, David Baker, and T. J. Anderson) and asked for assistance. Many of them answered my letters and made suggestions. So this undertaking helped me to become familiar with important people in the field and also taught me much about research methods.

Third, at Fisk's Forty-First Annual Arts Festival in April 1970, several guests made presentations on various aspects of the African-American experience. Pearl Williams-Jones, a noted scholar and performer of gospel music, and Natalie Hinderas were among the lecturers. In addition, Fisk organized a symposium, "The Influence of Jazz in the Musical World," which included well-known people in the field: David N. Baker, Arthur Cunnningham, and Nathaniel Williams. For a young woman who had grown up in a small town in southeast Georgia, seeing black intellectuals in this setting was enlightening and stimulating.

The fourth and most memorable encounter was a lecture-demonstration on gospel music that Pearl Williams-Jones presented in one of our classes. A black woman giving an academic lecture on the music that I had lived and breathed all my life—this too was exhilarating. I was pleasantly surprised that this type of music was being presented in a college setting, although I also wondered why the scholarly study of African-American music was not better integrated into the curriculum at Fisk and other black institutions.

When I think back on my senior year at Fisk, I realize that my interest in ethnomusicology must have occurred immediately, not only because of the social and personal changes I was experiencing but also because of Thieme's enthusiasm for the subject and the encouragement he gave me. Although I applied to several universities for graduate study, Thieme believed that UCLA would be best for ethnomusicology. So there was no question in my mind: UCLA was the place for me. Mantle Hood's philosophy of bimusicality fitted well with my background in performance and musicology. Also, at UCLA I could become more knowledgeable about scholarship in African-American music and nurture my growing interest in African music.

Student days at UCLA

When I arrived at UCLA in fall 1970, I felt inadequate and insecure because I had had only a brief introduction to ethnomusicology and my knowledge of African-American music was based primarily on personal experience. I rarely made comments in class, not because I did not understand but because I was intimidated by the breadth, insight, and discourse of my peers and felt that my own interpretation of the material was not as brilliant as theirs. I believe that much of my insecurity had to do with the fact that I had graduated from a historically black college, which most people, including myself, considered inferior to predominantly white institutions. Not only was I just beginning to come to terms with my own identity as a black person; I was in the process of discovering and accepting the fact that I had a history and a culture worthy of study. Perhaps this is why many of the projects that I did for my classes concerned African-American music and, to a lesser degree, African music.

Yet as I began to meet the other students, I learned that their backgrounds, skills, and abilities were no different from mine. Also, I was encouraged by the fact that some professors seemed to be interested in my work. Most of my courses in the theory and method of ethnomusicology were given by Peter Crossley-Holland, Jozef Pacholczyk, and David Morton. Crossley-Holland also taught a three-quarter series of courses on musical cultures of the world, which I took during my first year. My training in area studies was acquired from J. H. Kwabena Nketia (African music), Rodney Vlasak (African music and the blues), William G. Carter (African-American music), and Manocheer Sadeghi (Persian music). In addition to a performance course on the music and dance of Ghana, taught by the Asante master drummer Kwasi Badu, Sadeghi gave me private lessons in the Persian *santūr* (a zither).

All students specializing in ethnomusicology at UCLA were expected to take or audit the main seminar in ethnomusicology (Music 280). Mantle Hood usually taught this course, but others (such as Charles Seeger) led discussions. Thus, the three hours from three to six o'clock Wednesday afternoons were a sacred time. Even if the same professor taught Music 280 each quarter, the focus of the seminar changed. What I remember most was the stimulating but loosely structured discourse that took place. A democratic process was used to decide on the subject matter. If my memory serves me correctly, the theme of the course during my first year was "mode." When I took the course for credit in fall 1971 and Crossley-Holland was one of the professors, a different topic was chosen. To document what was discussed, a student was assigned to take minutes and distribute copies to everyone the following week. Here are the minutes taken by Linda O'Brien (1971) during the first class meeting:

> After discussion in which various members of the group presented problems for possible consideration, we arrived at three questions . . . : (1) What are the determinants of style in music and of the musical styles found in different cultures? (2) What is the relationship between music as value and music as fact (a) in different cultures and (b) in principle? (3) Does music reflect the distinctive attitudes of a society, and if so, in what ways?
>
> Professor Pacholczyk suggested that a practical approach to these problems be adopted and that we move in the areas of our expertise. Perhaps this could be accomplished by use of the comparative method.
>
> It was agreed to form committees which would consider the sources, primary and secondary, each in its chosen area.

My primary goal during my early period at UCLA was to complete my M.A. and teach in a community college. I had no desire for a Ph.D. It was not until the latter part of my first year that David Morton, my main adviser, who would eventually be the chair of my M.A. thesis, encouraged me to think about pursuing a Ph.D. In fact, he assumed that this was my plan all along. One day he remarked, "Now, *when* you get your Ph.D. . . . ," giving me the impression that my entering the doctoral program was understood—and also giving me confidence, for he was implying that I had the "stuff" to earn a Ph.D. at a major research institution.

At that time, ethnomusicologists at UCLA took a two-pronged approach: (1) music in itself and (2) music in its cultural context. Although we were expected to include some cultural information in class projects, more emphasis was placed on transcription and musical analysis. Many students also spent a lot of time analyzing scales and modes. Whenever possible, we were encouraged to use the melograph as a tool to obtain a deeper understanding of sound.

During my first year, Jozef Pacholczyk was a great inspiration to me. A project that I began with him in winter 1971 in Music 190B (a proseminar in ethnomusicology) became the basis for my M.A. thesis (1972). Its focus was African-American religious music—a comparative analysis of spirituals and gospel songs. Angeline Butler, a graduate of Fisk who was also taking courses in the graduate program at UCLA, agreed to record several songs. Both the spirituals and the gospel music were recorded a cappella because the objective was to use the melograph for a timbral and spectral analysis. When I entered the field in the 1970s, there was still considerable discussion about the disadvantages of a comparative approach, particularly for non-Western and Western traditions, yet comparisons fascinated me. Perhaps this was because of the work I had done with Thieme at Fisk, or perhaps I had been inspired by Pearl Williams-Jones, who used a comparative method to discuss African-American religious music (1970). In any case, it is significant that I chose for my research a methodology which was out of fashion or out of step with the discourse in the rest of the field. Although I did not realize it at the time, I was gaining confidence in myself. Instead of pursuing a topic or a methodology that was in vogue, I decided to use the theories and methods that would inform my study in the manner that I thought best.

As I neared the completion of my M.A. degree, I began to wonder what I might do with my life. I could teach at a college—this was why I had wanted to pursue graduate studies—or I could become more deeply involved in African music. While my primary interest at the M.A. level was African-American music, I also took courses in West African music and history. I believed that knowing more about Africa would help me to understand African-American culture better. One of my most enjoyable experiences was participating in the Ghanaian music ensemble and working with Kwasi Badu. The students in the ensemble were a cohesive group, and the performances at public schools, community colleges, festivals, and other events in southern California were highlights that made the learning experience even more exciting. During that time we all followed the African tradition. While most of the men played the drums, women danced, sang, and played the bell. Because Badu was Akan, most of the pieces—*adowa* (a type of funeral music) and *kete* (a court music tradition)—were from his culture. My own interest in and commitment to Africa began to grow even greater, and I decided to apply for the University of California's Education Abroad Program (EAP) so that I could spend a year studying in Ghana.

I often tell my friends and colleagues that if I used an elaborate multicourse meal as a metaphor for life, my encounters in Africa, particularly those in the early 1970s, could be regarded as dessert. In addition to my visits and residence in various regions of Ghana, I obtained a large part of my training in Africa from my experiences at the University of Ghana, in Legon. I was able to observe and learn about Africa both informally and formally. Taking performance courses in Akan, Ewe, and Dagbamba music at the University of Ghana allowed me to get inside the culture in a way that would not have been possible if I had spent all my time in a village.

LIFE AS A RESEARCHER

Throughout my career, the African world has been my arena. I am fascinated by the variety of creative expressions that have developed from African and African-derived cultures, and by the factors that gave rise to these creations. I constantly remind myself as well as my students that African music is not monolithic. While unity exists, there is also much diversity. Partly for this reason, I have not devoted my attention to one area or tradition; instead, I have examined several musical forms in different parts of the world.

African music is not monolithic. While unity exists, there is also much diversity.

Research projects

1. Spirituals and gospel songs—southeast Georgia, summer 1971
2. Fiddle music in West Africa—Ghana (team research), Burkina Faso, Niger, Nigeria, The Gambia, Senegal, 1972–1974, 1990, 1994, 1995
3. Bete dance festivals—Côte d'Ivoire, 1972–1973
4. Gospel music in the Catholic church—Los Angeles, 1981–1983
5. Urban music—Abidjan, Côte d'Ivoire, Summer 1983
6. Maroon music—Jamaica (team research), 1985–1986
7. Fiddle music in African-American culture—United States (Florida, Georgia, Kentucky, Louisiana, Michigan, New York, North Carolina, Tennessee, Virginia), 1987–1988
8. California gospel—Los Angeles, San Francisco Bay area, San Diego, Chicago, 1987–1998 (team research took place in 1992–1993)

Deciding on a research topic

Of the eight research projects for which I conducted fieldwork, I initiated half—projects 1, 3, 5, and 7. Two projects (2 and 8) were suggested by other researchers, and two (4 and 6) were proposed by culture bearers. Personal factors drew me to the projects that I initiated. For example, my interest in the African-American fiddle tradition (project 7) came about because my daughter, who decided to take violin lessons when she was a youngster, had a difficult time adjusting socially to the instrument because she had few role models. Few individuals within her world knew about fiddling in Africa, and even those who knew something about it did not realize that blacks had been the major performers of the violin in the United States during the eighteenth and nineteenth centuries.

My interest in the West African fiddle (project 2) began at UCLA in a class on African music taught by J. H. Kwabena Nketia in spring 1971. As my final project for this class, I wrote an essay on the fiddle music of the Luo of Kenya. Considering that I had been taking a performance course in Asante music and dance of Ghana, I am not sure why I chose East Africa or the violin as the focus for my class project. By the time I completed my M.A., I had decided to conduct research on *adowa* (1992:151). But this decision changed after my arrival in Ghana. An entry in my diary, which gives more information about my change in plans, indicates that I was quite surprised by this turn of events:

University of Ghana, Legon
Tuesday, 10 October 1972
Professor Nketia gave me the biggest surprise of my life; he really expects me to do research for my Ph.D. He has already planned my course work, the area I should work in, the instrument I should study, and the title of my dissertation. He was talking so fast that all I could do was nod my head and agree with

everything he said. In the long run, this work might be useful one day. The outline is as follows:

> Area—northern Ghana, Dagbani [*sic*] people
>
> Instrument—One-string fiddle (*gonge* [*sic*] or *gonje*)
>
> Ph.D. title—Comparative study of how the instrument is used in various musical types in the Dagbani culture.
>
> Informants—present in Legon (three persons) [Salisu Mahama, M. D. Sulley, and M. Iddi]. One would take me north to do fieldwork. One also would teach the instrument technique to me. I could go on and on about this plan. I'm going to do my best.

After I met the people who would be involved in the project with me, I became excited and felt more confident about pursuing research on the fiddle. In my diary, I wrote:

> University of Ghana, Legon
>
> Monday, 16 October 972
>
> On Wednesday [11 October 1972], I went to the Institute of African Studies [IAS] and met all of my professors. All of them seemed to be nice and friendly. . . . They seemed very enthusiastic about my doing research in northern Ghana. They have agreed to help me in all my endeavors, make an instrument for me, act as informants, and even take me up to northern Ghana for research into the area.
>
> Sulley, the informant who speaks English, took me to the Institute library and showed me where I could find readings about Dagbani music. Sulley and Iddi have written several, or rather many, articles on the music. I think that the research should not be too difficult.
>
> The first article I read was perfect. All of the information concerning the origin of the *goondze* [term for the violin in Dagbani] was compiled historically and chronologically.

Three of my research projects (2, 6, and 8) were conducted as part of a team. In Ghana, I worked with two culture bearers. As representatives of the IAS, Sulley (the linguist) and Mahama (the fiddler) were responsible for collecting material for the University of Ghana in addition to assisting me. Since the project was important to them personally and to the history of Dagbon, my study gave them the impetus as well as the political and economic means to conduct the research. The power relations between the three of us were different from what I had ever experienced. Throughout the project, they controlled my accessibility to primary cultural material. Therefore, they directly influenced my concepts of the culture and its artifacts. While I had my own ideas about what I wanted to accomplish, much of this depended on their willingness to help me. I will admit that there were moments when we were not in complete agreement, because of cultural differences and individual preferences. However, on the whole we worked splendidly together.

Although the team that conducted the research project in Jamaica consisted of non-culture bearers from UCLA (Carol Merrill-Mirsky, a graduate student who was considering Maroon music as a dissertation topic; Jeff Richmond, a staff person with expertise in videotaping; and myself), the project was introduced to us by Jamaicans. As in the Ghana project, the culture bearers were in control of what the team was able to accomplish during the fieldwork because they defined the goals and parameters of the project before we went into the field—the objective was to produce a video of the January Sixth celebration that could be used for publicity and education by members of their community (DjeDje and Merrill-Mirsky 1987). While we donated our technical expertise and research experience, they provided unpublished written sources as well as access to individuals and the performance event.

I became interested in gospel music in California (project 4) in the early 1980s because a culture bearer (Charles Johnson, a gospel musician who was director of the gospel choir at Saint Brigid Catholic Church in Los Angeles) believed that changes occurring in the black Catholic community were so dramatic that some type of documentation needed to take place. After visiting several churches, I decided to do a comparative analysis of the role of music in worship in different churches (1983b, 1986), for I believed that this was the only way to demonstrate the complexity of the subject matter and explain how the situation in Los Angeles was distinct from what was occurring in other parts of the United States. My research on the general history of gospel music in Los Angeles (project 8) began in 1987 when Samuel Floyd, director of the Center for Black Music Research (CBMR) in Chicago, invited me to participate in a conference he planned to organize in Los Angeles that would highlight the musical experiences of blacks in California. Therefore, I began collecting data in the late 1980s—starting in Los Angeles in 1987 and continuing in the San Francisco Bay Area in 1989 and 1990 and San Diego in early 1992. Although the conference did not materialize, two of CBMR's publications, which included two of my articles (1988, 1989), focused on black music in California.

The team research in 1992–1993 (project 8) was initiated by Bernice Johnson Reagon, founder and director of the internationally known a cappella female singing group Sweet Honey in the Rock. She had been invited by the organizers of the Los Angeles Festival, with support from AT&T, to curate a concert for the festival in 1993. In addition, she intended to use the material as part of her radio series *Wade in the Water: Black Sacred Music in the United States* that was to be aired in 1994. This team research differed from the other projects in several ways. Instead of going into the field as a group, the team (Ray Funk, a researcher and avid collector of audio and visual data on quartet music; Lee Hildebrand, a journalist from the San Francisco Bay Area who had written numerous articles on contemporary gospel music; Reagon; and myself) worked as a committee: we suggested individuals to be interviewed, shared data (audio and video recordings as well as written material), and advised each other on various aspects of the project. Then, we individually pursued the research on our own. Since each person had much knowledge about the tradition and was not dependent on others for information, we had autonomy and were free to pursue some of our own interests. The culture bearers (gospel musicians in California) did not play an active role in collecting the data, but they were in control of the presentation of their culture in the public arena because Reagon relied on their expertise in organizing the concerts for the Los Angeles Festival.

Fieldwork

My most enjoyable and rewarding experiences as an ethnomusicologist have occurred during fieldwork. Trying to understand and make sense of the behavior of individuals and the impact of my role can be overwhelming, exasperating, and exhilarating. Yet this is one of the activities that distinguish ethnomusicologists from other music researchers. The way I conduct fieldwork varies and depends on my knowledge of the tradition, my relationship with the culture bearers, my length of time in the field, and the goals of the projects. Fieldwork normally involves a variety of simultaneous activities: identifying, reviewing, and collecting sources (written, sound, and visual) on the subject; learning to read or speak the language (or both); learning to perform a musical tradition; identifying and establishing rapport with individuals who are willing to share information; and so on. Here, I will present three research projects that demonstrate some of the strategies for collecting data. In each narrative, I explain how I entered the community, the methods I used to collect the information, how I established rapport, and how I learned to perform the music. I include material from my diary (a detailed record of personal activities, reflections, and feelings) and my log (a brief accounting of daily activities), which were the most useful tools for documenting my experiences.

Southeast Georgia: Spirituals and gospel songs

My first fieldwork experience began with a study of spirituals and gospel songs from southeast Georgia. When I entered the field, several collections of spirituals (such as Johnson and Johnson 1969 [1925]; Work 1940) had been published; most included transcriptions of the songs with a discussion of musical characteristics and a short history of African-American music; also, much work had been done on the social implications of the spiritual. However, only a few articles and dissertations had been written on gospel music; and although George Robinson Ricks and Horace Clarence Boyer had done extensive social and musical analyses of gospel and had begun to identify important figures (for example, Thomas Dorsey and Sallie Martin), no comparative musical analysis of spirituals and gospels had been published. Also, most writers discussed this topic generally, without mentioning local traditions.

When I conducted fieldwork, I used only an audiotape recorder, because my focus was on sound. Although I participated in performance events and observed the behavior of the people involved, I did not keep a log or diary; I did not conduct lengthy interviews; and I did not take many photographs of individuals. Several reasons account for the methods I used. First, I was working in a context (southeast Georgia, where I had been born and raised) with which I was familiar and with people whom I knew intimately. Second, my work reflected my interests and early training in ethnomusicology. In the models that I followed for my work during the 1970s, while the human element was important in the research, the culture bearer's voice was almost nonexistent in the final results of the study and in public discourse. Once the culture bearer gave information to the researcher, it was the latter who became the authority; this explained why the voice or image of the culture bearer need not be included in the discourse. In fact, photographs of individuals or lengthy quotations from culture bearers were the exception rather than the norm. In the monograph and recording based on my research in southeast Georgia, I do include brief quotations from culture bearers (1978b, 1983a). However, such quoting is minimal compared with the representations of culture bearers in some of my more recent work (1998a, b; 1999a, b).

West Africa: Fiddle music

During my fieldwork in Ghana, I used a variety of methods to document the fiddle tradition. My equipment included a 35-mm camera (for still photography) and an audiotape recorder. It was not until 1994 that I began to use a videotape recorder. In addition to keeping a diary and a log in which I drew sketches of performance spaces and instruments, I attended, observed, and participated in performance events and conducted interviews. Everyone involved in the project (the culture bearers, Nketia, and myself) thought it was important that I learn how to perform on the *goondze*. Therefore, during my first year in Ghana, I spent anywhere from one to three hours working with Mahama each day. Not only did he give me lessons in the fiddle; he taught me the song texts for the fiddle melodies and explained their meaning. Also, he began to teach me basic terms in the Dagbani language, the history of the instrument, and information about Dagbamba culture.

While I was taking fiddle lessons, I also conducted a literature review on Dagbamba history and culture in the library and took seminars in African studies (anthropology, religion, and music) offered at IAS. Mahama and Sulley felt that I should not do fieldwork in northern Ghana until January 1973. By that time, they believed, I would have become more familiar with the music and culture. Also, attending the Tsimsi Tsugu Festival, scheduled to take place in January, would give me an opportunity to observe the fiddle and other instruments in a formal musical context. Entries in my log provide evidence of how I progressed. After almost three weeks of working with Mahama, I wrote:

> University of Ghana, Legon
> Monday, 30 October 1972
> My research work is developing or rather taking some shape at this point. I've been trying to compile a bibliography that would be helpful. But this is hard because so many books are not available in the library here. I have begun preparing an outline of my research proposal; however, it is not complete. I believe that I am progressing very well on the *goondze*. Salisu Mahama, my teacher, seems to be pleased. He even talks about having us perform on TV or before a public audience, but I don't know about this because I am still shy of audiences.

Since I had never played a violin, I had to find some way to remember the bowing and fingering and relate this to the melody. So I invented a notation system. After Mahama wrote the song texts for me in Dagbani, I rewrote them in my own handwriting and notated the music using my own system. My log provides an insight into what I learned:

> 20 November 1972, *goondze* lesson, 2:00 P.M.
> Lesson went along better than I expected. I remembered a few of the pieces. The second piece gives me a lot of trouble and Salisu becomes impatient, but he doesn't pressure me or become angry with me. After several intervals, we stopped around 3:30 P.M.

> 21 November 1972, *goondze* lesson, 10:30 A.M.
> Two or three drumming classes were going on [at IAS]. . . . So this lesson was very short, although I did learn a few techniques with the third song. The second song is still bad but a little better in tone quality. We ended at 11:30 A.M.
>
> [Later in the day] I talked with Sulley today about translations of song texts. He was helpful but he didn't know many things himself—[he] said these were exclusive sayings by the musicians themselves. Therefore, I need to get together with Salisu for translations the next time.
>
> Also, [he said I should] get Salisu to play repertoire examples of *goondze* music for certain occasions—[Friday] morning [homage at the king's palace], naming ceremony, wedding, puberty, and so on.

> 22 November 1972, 9:45 A.M.
> New song—*Yun Taa Jili Ma* (figure 1)
> Salisu came late this morning; he was sick and had been to the doctor. He was not in the best condition to teach. He said I was the "professor" this morning because I told him what to do. However, he did begin teaching a new song, the fourth now. I seem to learn faster now, since I've developed some means for recording the songs.

FIGURE I   *Yun Taa Jili Ma.* (Proverb: He who respects you is better than he who gives you gold.) The notation I created to learn the fingering and bowing for the Dagbamba *goondze* is shown at the top. The numbers represent fingers on the hand: 1 (thumb), 2 (index finger), 3 (middle finger), 5 (small finger). The arrows indicate the direction in which the bow should be moved. The Western staff notation for this musical excerpt is given underneath. (For text and musical transcription of the entire song, see DjeDje 1978a:740, 1183–1194.)

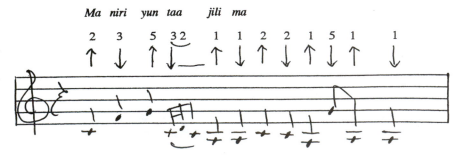

Salisu saw two of the books that I had on Dagomba history and migrations. He wanted to use them for his personal satisfaction, so he went with me to check them out of the library. I was in a better mood this morning.

28 November 1972

We went over the three songs. Number 1 was performed best. Some improvement was made on number 2 and number 3. He began teaching me a new song today.

He looked through my workbook and saw the article concerning the history of the *goondze*. He was very pleased and recognized the name Yantsibli. He said Yantsibli is his grandfather from about 500 years ago. Naa Sigli was the *yaa naa* [Dagbani term for king] for one of his grandfathers.

Mahama seemed upset when I told him where I had gotten this information from. He says Sulley's notes are not correct and he wanted to see the book. I took him to the library and he checked the book out.

4 December 1972, *goondze* lesson

Today's lesson was spent in an interview session with Salisu and Sulley as the interpreter. We started the session around 2:30 P.M. Surprisingly, everything went extremely well. Salisu cooperated in answering all the questions. Sulley was equally important in interpreting, although I believe he interjected some of his own ideas and beliefs into the interpretation.

Much, much information was gained from this session. I shall use this information for Aning's paper [Ben Aning was one of my professors at IAS] and as the term paper for Nketia.

The session lasted until around 4:15 P.M. . . . The entire afternoon was very rewarding socially and academically. Much was accomplished. In some cases my questions were not understood and I obtained the wrong answers. It was pointed out by both of them that they would not give this information to everyone— I'm special.

5 December 1972, *goondze* lesson, 10:30 A.M.

I did not play too well today, because I hadn't practiced. We went through the three songs—the second song was the worst. I don't know why I can't play that song any better than I do. When Salisu began playing the third song, one of the Dagomba drummers passed by humming and dancing to the tune, so I asked him to show me the dance to the song. He did and it was very nice.

I began learning my new song today along with the text. It is hard to remember the fingering and rhythm. I need to record the song so that I can listen to the tune at home.

Salisu wants to teach me the dance with the music. He wants to record and then teach the dance. . . . At the end of the session, he taught me the days of the week in Dagbani.

7 December 1972, 10:30 A.M.

The lesson on Thursday morning was a good one. Salisu was in the process of making or constructing some *goondze* instruments. The gourd calabash body had been cut and two holes at the top on each side had been made. Now he was supporting the gourd body by placing a stick that extended from either side and was bound with string.

When I arrived he stopped his work to teach me. I played well today for some reason. He was very pleased. He even began teaching me song number 5. . . . He was inspired enough to tell me the meaning of the song. I asked one of his coworkers to translate from Twi exactly what Salisu was trying to say.

After the lesson, I began making *goondze* instruments. He taught me how to bind and tie the string onto the gourd calabash. Class ended around 12:30 P.M.

I use a variety of techniques to establish rapport. First, I allow the people with whom I am working to set the agenda, and I participate with them in everyday activities (for instance, visiting friends, eating, shopping, and attending social and recreational events). In northern Ghana, Sulley and Mahama were my guides. Of course, I understood that their relationship with me gave them a special status within their community, and this may have affected their decisions about where we went.

Second, I try to learn as much as possible about the social organization of the community and the musical tradition. Who is the community leader, and what is his or her relationship with the musicians? Are the performers attached to or identified with a political, religious, or social institution? If so, I make every effort to meet the leaders of these institutions before proceeding with the research, so that I can be sure they are aware of my project and have no objections. I normally choose a person from the community who is well known and respected to make the introductions.

In northern Ghana, it was critical that I meet the *yaa naa*, the king of Dagbon, for fiddlers are part of his royal court and are expected to attend to his needs before involving themselves with other community activities. Because *goondze* musicians are organized within a family structure with an installed chief (called the *yamba naa*), it was important that I meet this chief as well. Also, the situation in northern Ghana was politically sensitive because the "enskinment" of the reigning *yaa naa* was being contested by a rival faction. Interestingly, Mahama and Sulley supported different leaders, so this became a point of contention between them. To resolve some of the problems, it was decided that I should meet both leaders. Yet they agreed that I would meet the reigning *yaa naa* (Mohamudu Abudulai IV) and his court musicians first, before being introduced to the rival faction. It is noteworthy that neither of them was present when I met the rival candidate. For example, when I went to the *yaa naa's* palace, Mahama suddenly became ill and could not join us. When I visited the leader of the rival faction (Yakubu Andani, who won the suit and became the reigning *yaa naa* in 1974) during a Muslim celebration, Sulley never arrived, though he had promised to attend. My diary provides details about my visit to the *yaa naa* Abudulai's palace.

> Tuesday, 16 January, Yendi, Ghana
> We did not arrive at our appointment with the *yaa naa* until 4:15 P.M. Upon entering the *yaa naa's* palace, [we see that] many elders are seated there, relaxing; there are horses in front of the palace eating grass. I marveled at the way the horses had been painted—half . . . [of the horse's] legs were painted orange, and long orange streaks [were painted] over the back. (I look at a photo of this.)
>
> The *yaa naa* is a young, handsome man [about thirty years old]. He appears to be very humble and agreeable toward his subjects, which is good. The customary procedure for entering the palace is:
>
> Remove shoes upon entrance to the palace.
> Bow to any elders before entering, as a form of greeting. (During any greeting, the inferior subject bows to his superior.)
> Upon entrance to the *yaa naa's* room, subjects are to remain bowing at all times.
> Whenever praises are given to the chief, subjects clap their hands or pop their fingers (two hands—fourth and fifth fingers).
>
> The *yaa naa* was dressed in green *kente* cloth. He was sitting on a rising that was covered with several pillows—there was nothing ornate . . . about the appearance of his dress or the room. Two men sat in front of him on the floor as he spoke to us. Other elders were also seated on the floor. I was a special

case—the only person to sit in a chair. We paid the chief homage by giving him two *cedis* [Ghanaian money]. He seemed surprised by the gesture. This particular *yaa naa* has been enskinned for the past three years; however, there is still dispute over the rightful owner of the skins. This particular *yaa naa* was the son of the late *yaa naa*.

One of the best ways to establish rapport is to participate actively in a performance event; culture bearers seem to appreciate the effort that a stranger makes to join in. My opportunity to participate in an event came when I interviewed one of the leaders of the *yamba naa*'s family. After the interview, we went to a wedding where fiddlers were performing.

> Sunday, 21 January 1973, began as usual. I woke up at 5:45 A.M. to wash and prepare for my interview with Sulemana Goondze at 8:00 A.M. After finishing breakfast around 8:15 A.M., we finally arrived at Sulemana's house around 8:45 A.M. He was not present, but someone immediately sent for him and he came within two minutes. He had been attending a customary marriage function next door to his house. The *goondze* (at least four of them) were playing for this function. We began the interview about 9:00 A.M. and finished between 10:45 and 11:00 A.M. It was quite interesting, and I obtained more bits of information. Sulemana joked about going to the United States. He wants a small tape recorder from the United States. I took his name and address and said I would inform Salisu if getting a tape recorder was possible, but I mentioned that it was difficult to obtain one.
>
> When we completed the interview, Sulley and I joined Sulemana at the marriage function. The attendants consisted almost entirely of about thirty to forty women—the only males were the four *goondze* men and Sulemana (figure 2). It seems that the marriage ceremony had taken place a week ago, but celebrations had continued daily after the actual ceremony. This particular celebration was mainly for women, who danced individually in a circle as the *goondze* played. Sulemana began to dance, and people gave him money—almost two *cedis* in change. Then someone invited me—at least, Sulemana invited me—to dance with him. I was somewhat embarrassed, but I danced (figure 3). Women began dropping coins into my hands and at my feet and placed them on my forehead. Sulley took a photo as Sulemana and I danced. After the dance, I gave all the change to the *goondze* players (figure 4).

California: Gospel music

In urban areas, various sources that do not exist in nonurban settings (such as audio, visual, and print media) are available to researchers. However, problems often arise when researchers attempt to use the same methods in both contexts. When I conducted research in California in 1987–1992, I had to modify the way I collected data in different cities because each had its own personality, which also affected the gospel community. There was no one person who had the power or authority to give me access to everyone and everything I needed. In Los Angeles, not only is the African-American community extremely heterogeneous, but the social organization of the gospel music community is complex as well. Gospel artists can be identified by the style of music they emphasize in performance (traditional, contemporary, quartet); the church they attend (African Methodist Episcopal, Baptist, Catholic, Methodist, Pentecostal, and so on); the size of the church (storefront, large church, or megachurch); the generation they belong to (young, young adult, senior); the type of choir they perform with (church or mass—that is, community—choir); and the location of their church, home, or performing group, which may all be different.

FIGURE 2   Sulemana Iddrisu Goondze dancing at a Dagbamba wedding celebration in Yendi, Ghana, 21 January 1973. Photos are from the author.

FIGURE 3   Sulemana Iddrisu Goondze and Jacqueline Cogdell DjeDje dancing at a Dagbamba wedding celebration in Yendi, Ghana, 21 January 1973.

FIGURE 4   *Goondze* (fiddlers) and *zaabia* (rattlers) performing at a Dagbamba wedding celebration in Yendi, Ghana, 21 January 1973.

I entered the Los Angeles gospel community in 1987 by contacting individuals I knew—Ineze Caston, a musician in my home church; and Charles Johnson, who had first suggested that I do research in Los Angeles. When I interviewed them, I asked each to suggest names of others I could contact for information about the history and development of gospel music in Los Angeles. It is noteworthy that although these two gave me about ten to fifteen names each, only one or two names appeared on both lists. More important, gospel musicians who had brought fame to the city—for example, James Cleveland (who was still alive when I began my research), Andraé Crouch, and some whom people residing outside Los Angeles would probably identify with the city—were not on either list. The exclusion of these artists left several unanswered questions in my mind. Did it mean that, because of their wider fame, Cleveland and Crouch were not considered Los Angeles musicians? Or were they excluded because my two contacts believed that I would not be able to obtain access to them? Or were Crouch and Cleveland simply not part of my contacts' network or circle of friends?

In terms of equipment, I relied primarily on an audiotape recorder for interviews, which were conducted in homes and churches. One person visited UCLA for the interview because she worked in the area. Although I often took my 35-mm camera with me, most people did not allow me to take pictures; they preferred that I use professional photographs which had already been taken of them. Probably, they were reluctant to be photographed because most were elderly and believed that their physical appearance had changed dramatically since the time when they considered themselves stars. If a photograph had to be taken, they wanted it done in a formal context, when they were properly dressed. Therefore, many of the photos I took were at concerts, banquets, or church services. Because I had so little success with still photography, I did not even attempt to videotape. In some cases, though, I invited gospel musicians to UCLA for lecture-demonstrations and did videotape these presentations.

While conducting interviews, I also reviewed local newspapers, which became my primary source for documenting social, political, and cultural changes; also, information from newspapers helped to support and stimulate discussion in interviews. Whenever I talked with people, I always asked for sheet music, photographs, and recordings (made either commercially or by their churches), concert and church programs, souvenir booklets, and so on.

After identifying the data, I decided to limit my study to developments that had occurred before 1970. There were several reasons for this. First, I wanted to avoid the local politics between traditional and contemporary gospel musicians. Also, I found that contemporary gospel musicians were less accessible. Seniors felt honored by my interest in their work; they were extremely supportive, and most looked forward to our meetings, which gave them an opportunity to stay active and reminisce about the old days. For my part, I liked talking with them because traditional gospel music was more familiar to me—this was the music I had performed at home, at my church in southeast Georgia.

I also limited the study by focusing on four or five churches that were regarded as major centers for gospel because of the prominence of their choirs, the pastor's innovations, or the use of media (radio, television, or both) to capture the community's attention. Many of the noted gospel artists who migrated to the city joined one of these churches. Because these churches had been prominent in gospel music when the African-American community in Los Angeles was more cohesive, choosing them allowed me to limit my study spatially to a five- or ten-block area instead of a fifteen- to twenty-mile (about 30-kilometer) radius.

ISSUES THAT HAVE AFFECTED MY RESEARCH:
OWNERSHIP OF CULTURAL PRODUCTS AND LOCAL POLITICS

Because some researchers are sensitive to "ownership" of cultural products, formal agreements with culture bearers have become more common. My research among the Jamaican Maroons is noteworthy because Accompong political leaders wanted to use the expertise of the UCLA research team to help them develop a product with which to disseminate information about their culture. When the issue of ownership and profit from cultural products arose, some sensitive negotiations had to take place before an agreement could be made between the two parties: the Kojo Council and the Regents of the University of California. But when agreements are made with outsiders, who within the culture actually owns or has rights to the products? Even though representatives from the Accompong government invited us to document Kojo Day, the rivals of Colonel Harris N. Cawley (the leader of Accompong) did not approve of the Kojo Council's entering into the agreement. A conversation I had with one person who was disgruntled about the project sheds light on the controversy and how I handled the situation:

> Wednesday, 1 January 1986
> We went to the colonel's house for lunch and to wait for the Christmas marching to take place. Jeff went to set up near the monument.
>
> The march began around 2:30 P.M. at Mrs. Wright's house. The procession stopped briefly at the colonel's house to gather more marchers before continuing through town.
>
> Carol and Jeff documented this through the town. As Jeff was leaving, a man approached him, asking how Accompong would profit from the making of the video.
>
> When Jeff left, the man expressed his feelings to me—he was not in agreement that we should be here. Also, he indicated that he was the opposition to Colonel Cawley. Some members of the community were concerned that previous groups had come to Accompong and made millions, but the people of Accompong had received no profit.
>
> I indicated that an agreement, which had been signed, had been drawn up by the Kojo Council. He wanted me to give or show him a copy of the agreement. I declined, indicating that it was not my place to interfere with politics. He responded by threatening to disrupt our work here. Mann O. Rowe [the former deputy colonel of the Kojo Council] was present during the discussion.
>
> When the other man left, Mr. Rowe . . . asked me for my address and he gave me his. He also made some brief remarks about Maroon history and culture.

In many classes in field research methods, students are advised to be aware of national and international affairs because such political issues may have an impact on research in a particular area. But in my situation, *local* politics affected what I was able to accomplish. In northern Ghana, rival factions were involved in the Yendi "skin crisis." In Accompong, an individual was opposed to the agenda of the elected leaders. In Los Angeles, there was tension between traditional and contemporary gospel musicians, between performers of gospels and spirituals, between rival musicians, and between cities (such as Los Angeles and San Diego). Also, being aware of a political climate is one thing; learning how to maneuver through political strife so that it does not impair your work is another thing—and not always easy to resolve.

THE ROLE OF RESEARCH IN PROFESSIONAL LIFE

Throughout my career, it has been important for me to make my material accessible to the community that was its source. In Africa, this has not always been possible to the degree that I would like, but in the United States I have been fairly successful.

The way I write and the topics I choose reflect my effort to make my material interesting to culture bearers as well as to academics.

I have also integrated my research with other institutions to make it accessible to a larger community. Working in partnership with three museums in Los Angeles on exhibitions (called "The Heritage of African Music") that celebrate the contributions of African and African-derived cultures has given my work and that of others much more visibility than I could have imagined. I served as one of the curators for an exhibit at the Fowler Museum at UCLA ("Music in the Life of Africa") and was the editor of the book that accompanied the exhibitions (1999a). To complement the public programming at the museums, I organized a number of activities in the department of ethnomusicology that allowed students to learn and gain experience with other ways of communicating and sharing knowledge. The theme of these activities was "The Globalization of African Music," but the department of ethnomusicology referred to 1999–2000 as the "Year of African Music." Not only did we have symposia, lectures, concerts, performances, and courses by visiting lecturers who came directly from Africa; the department also produced compact disks and videos of the music and performances of the visiting artists with students.

My research in California has had a dramatic impact on my teaching. I have developed two courses. One, "Urbanism and Music," deals with the theoretical literature, but the students also use Los Angeles as a laboratory to test their theories about the music of the city. The second course, "African-American Music in California," examines how the different personalities and cultural dynamics of various urban areas in the state affect musical creativity. So far, I have been the chair (of thesis and dissertation committees) for ten student projects that have focused on diverse topics (popular music, jazz, religious music, African music) related to African and African-derived music in California.

THE PLACE OF MY WORK IN ETHNOMUSICOLOGY

Because some of my research has been regional, I have conducted investigations in a variety of areas. My projects have also been diverse in terms of context, types of music, and ideology. I have worked in villages (in northern Ghana and The Gambia), small towns (in the southeast United States), and urban settings (in Ghana, Nigeria, Côte d'Ivoire, Senegal, and the United States). I have been interested in both the sacred (African-American spiritual and gospel songs, Hausa *Bori*) and the secular (popular Ivoirian music). I have worked with traditions associated with royalty (Dagbamba fiddle) and with commoners (Hausa fiddle music as well as Bete and Maroon festivals). Although most of my projects focus on traditions dominated by men, women are the primary performers of some musical forms (gospel and Maroon singing), and I have highlighted this in my studies (1985a; 1993; 1998a, b). For me, the individual is important, as are the ways musicians organize sound and interact with their patrons (1982, 1984b, 1993).

While I do not regard the people or traditions that I have studied as exotic, some researchers may feel differently. What seems to be common to all these traditions is that the creators and their creations tend to be marginalized within the larger culture. Perhaps my choice of topics relates in some ways to myself as an individual. Although I do not want to draw attention to myself in public, I also do not want my contributions to be slighted or ignored. In a room full of people, probably no one would know I was there. Yet I believe that my presence is just as important as anyone else's, because it adds something to the experience of the group. Although some of my topics may seem esoteric, they should be included in the discourse, because they help us understand the layers, branches, and streams that make up African world music.

In addition, I believe it is important for people of color to write narratives from their own perspective. When I entered the field, very little information was available

Much can be gained from including both insiders'
and outsiders' perspectives: a multivoice discourse
leads to more interesting interpretations and a fuller
understanding of a tradition.

on the music of African and African-derived cultures, and much of it had not been
written by blacks. As in other ethnomusicological studies before the 1960s and 1970s,
the voice of the person being studied was not heard; few researchers felt it necessary
or even useful to include that voice. Many Westerners have problems with the subject
as the object of study, particularly in regard to non-Western art music; when Europeans
study their own art music, they are rarely worried about objectivity, bias, or the reliability of the findings. But we now know that much can be gained from including
both insiders' and outsiders' perspectives: a multivoice discourse leads to more interesting interpretations and a fuller understanding of a tradition. Also, when the voice
of the society under study is absent, the resulting scholarly environment can be un-
healthy for all. It implies that culture bearers are unqualified to discuss or report on
their own music, and that their interpretations or theories are therefore uninteresting
and unimportant to the general discussion.

Some people would probably regard me as an insider simply because I am an
African-American and my research has focused on African or African-derived musics;
but this is a simplistic conclusion that disregards the enormous diversity of the African
world. Also, the insider's position is relative. For example, while I performed gospel
during my formative years, my setting was a small town, quite different from the
church settings where I observed music making in urban California. Thus in California
gospel circles, I do not regard myself as an insider. Still, because the roots and performance aesthetics of the music are similar, I do feel a bond or kinship with these
circles.

I have been interested in many theoretical issues and concepts. Instead of abstrac-
tions, I prefer to write narratives and to discuss individuals and local traditions that
shed light on what might be more universal. Much of my work has focused on processes: the history of gospel music in California, change and differentiation in Catholic
churches in Los Angeles as a result of the adoption of gospel music, the levels of
urbanization that take place when a musical genre moves from a city in the Midwest
to one on the West Coast. Most of my studies would have to be regarded as musical
ethnographies because they include "both detailed descriptions and general statements
about music based on personal experience and fieldwork" (Seeger 1992:89). Much of
my research has been comparative, for I believe we can learn more about one tradition
by comparing it with another. For example, if I had focused all my attention on the
fiddle in Ghana and not included Nigeria, my findings would have misrepresented
fiddling in West Africa; I have discovered that Dagbamba is almost unique, for few
societies use the fiddle as a court instrument (1978a).

More recently, diaspora studies have interested me. In addition to examining the
movement of people across continents, I have begun to look at diasporas within smaller
areas (such as the Fulbe diaspora in Sudanic Africa) as well as at interculturalism in
Africa. Cross-cultural studies between African and African-American music have been
commonplace; but in such studies, researchers tend to be interested in Africa only as
a point of origin, and this is not very different from the perspective of early comparative

musicologists who looked at origins in order to conclude that European music was more advanced than African music. When I focus on cross-cultural issues, I prefer to give equal importance to each tradition. Just as we continue to investigate transformations within the Americas, I believe that changes occurring in Africa need to be documented. That is what I have done in my work on urban music in Abidjan and am now doing in my research on fiddling in West African and African-American cultures.

REFERENCES

DjeDje, Jacqueline Cogdell. 1972. "An Analytical Study of the Similarities and Differences in the American Black Spiritual and Gospel Song from the Southeast Region of Georgia." M.A. thesis, UCLA.

————. 1978a. "The One String Fiddle in West Africa: A Comparison of Hausa and Dagomba Traditions." Ph.D. dissertation, UCLA.

————. 1978b. *American Black Spiritual and Gospel Songs from Southeast Georgia: A Comparative Study.* Los Angeles: UCLA Center for Afro-American Studies Monograph Series, No. 7.

————. 1982. "The Concept of Patronage: An Examination of Hausa and Dagomba One String Fiddle Music." *Journal of African Studies* 9(3):116–127.

————. 1983a. *Black American Religious Music from Southeast Georgia.* Folkways Records FS 34010.

————. 1983b. "An Expression of Black Identity: The Use of Gospel Music in a Los Angeles Catholic Church." *Western Journal of Black Studies* 7(3):148–160.

————. 1984a. "Song Type and Performance Practice in Hausa and Dagomba Possession (*Bori*) Music." *Black Perspective in Music* 12(2):166–182.

————. 1984b. "The Interplay of Melodic Phrases: An Analysis of Hausa and Dagomba One String Fiddle Music." In *Selected Reports in Ethnomusicology*, Vol. 5, ed. J. H. Kwabena Nketia and Jacqueline Cogdell DjeDje, 81–118. Los Angeles: UCLA Program in Ethnomusicology, Department of Music.

————. 1985a. "Women and Music in Sudanic Africa." In *More Than Drumming: Essays on African and Afro-Latin American Music and Musicians*, ed. Irene V. Jackson, 67–89. Westport, Conn.: Greenwood.

————. 1985b. "The Role of the Mass Media in the Development of Urban African Popular Music: A Case Study in Abidjan, Ivory Coast."

In *Occasional Papers: Proceedings of the African Studies Conference (Post-Independence Africa: Its Problems and Prospects)*, ed. Skyne Uku-Wertimer, 150–163. Long Beach: California State University Press.

————. 1986. "Change and Differentiation: The Adoption of Black American Gospel Music in the Catholic Church." *Ethnomusicology* 30(2):223–252.

————. 1988. "A Historical Overview of Black Gospel Music in Los Angeles." *Black Music Research Bulletin* 10(1):1–5.

————. 1989. "Gospel Music in the Los Angeles Black Community: A Historical Overview." *Black Music Research Journal* 9(1, spring):35–79.

————. 1992. "Music and History: An Analysis of Hausa and Dagbamba Fiddle Traditions." In *African Musicology: Current Trends. A Festschrift Presented to J. H. Kwabena Nketia*, ed. Jacqueline Cogdell DjeDje, 151–179. Los Angeles and Atlanta: UCLA International Studies and Overseas Program and the James S. Coleman African Studies Center/Crossroads Press and African Studies Association.

————. 1993. "Los Angeles Composers of African American Gospel Music: The First Generations." *American Music* 11(4, winter):412–457.

————. 1998a. "The California Black Gospel Music Tradition: A Confluence of Musical Styles and Cultures." In *California Soul: Music of African Americans in the West*, ed. Jacqueline Cogdell DjeDje and Eddie S. Meadows, 124–175. Berkeley: University of California Press.

————. 1998b. "Remembering Kojo: History, Music, and Gender in the January Sixth Celebration of the Jamaican Accompong Maroons." *Black Music Research Journal* 18(1/2, spring/fall):67–120.

————, ed. 1999a. *Turn Up the Volume! A Celebration of African Music.* Los Angeles: UCLA Fowler Museum of Cultural History.

————. 1999b. "The Fulbe Fiddle in The Gambia: A Symbol of Ethnic Identity." In *Turn Up the Volume! A Celebration of African Music*, ed. Jacqueline Cogdell DjeDje, 98–113. Los Angeles: UCLA Fowler Museum of Cultural History.

DjeDje, Jacqueline Cogdell, and Carol Merrill-Mirsky. 1987. *Remembering Kojo: A Celebration of the Maroon People of Accompong, Jamaica.* Los Angeles: UCLA Department of Music. Videotape.

Gospel Pearls. 1921. Nashville: Sunday School Publishing Board, National Baptist Convention, U.S.A.

Johnson, James Weldon, and J. Rosamond Johnson. 1969 [1925 1926, 1953, 1954]. *The Books of American Negro Spirituals, Including the Book of American Negro Spirituals and the Second Book of Negro Spirituals.* New York: Viking.

O'Brien, Linda. 1971. "Minutes of the Seminar in Ethnomusicology, Fall 1971." First meeting, 6 October 1971, Schoenberg Hall, UCLA, Room B424.

Seeger, Anthony. 1992. "Ethnography of Music." In *Ethnomusicology: An Introduction*, ed. Helen Myers, 88–109. New York: Norton.

Townsend, Mrs. A. M., ed. 1961. *The Baptist Standard Hymnal with Responsive Readings: A New Book for All Services.* Nashville, Tenn.: Sunday School Publishing Board, National Baptist Convention.

Williams-Jones, Pearl. 1970. "Afro-American Gospel Music: A Brief Historical and Analytical Survey." In *Development of Materials for a One-Year Course in African Music for the General Undergraduate Student*, ed. Vada E. Butcher, 199–219. Washington, D.C.: U.S. Department of Health, Education, and Welfare.

Work, John W., ed. 1940. *American Negro Songs and Spirituals: A Comprehensive Collection of 230 Folk Songs, Religious and Secular, with a Foreword by John W. Work.* New York: Bonanza.

Europe and North America
Philip V. Bohlman

Prologue: The Ordinary Work of an American Ethnomusicologist
Self-Profile in Brief
Journeys of an Ethnomusicologist at Work
Representation
Epilogue: The Ordinary Knows No Boundaries

PROLOGUE: THE ORDINARY WORK OF AN AMERICAN ETHNOMUSICOLOGIST

If difference has traditionally served as one of the most powerful motivations for ethnomusicology, it was a degree of difference barely perceptible as difference that first arrested my attention and drew me into ethnomusicology. I daresay there is nothing extraordinary about my path to ethnomusicology. On the contrary, it was in every way quite ordinary. The early experiences of my life, spent entirely in a small Midwestern town, were ordinary in every way, and I should be the first to say that there is no real point in attempting to identify one aspect of this ordinary world that was auspicious for my future. The ordinary, however, may be no less significant than the extraordinary in the making of many ethnomusicologists. The ordinary, the everyday, the quotidian—all conditions of the traditional—also constitute the work ethnomusicologists do. In the work done by ethnomusicologists, difference that does not reveal itself as difference may be the most extraordinary because of its ordinariness.

There is no reason not to dispense quickly with the broad outlines of my youth. I was born in 1952 and grew up in Boscobel, Wisconsin, where my father was a pharmacist, my mother a painter (and later town historian), my maternal grandmother a country schoolteacher, and my grandfather a farmer. My hometown gave free rein to my interests but supplied little that might really have spurred them on. While I was in grade school, I had the opportunity to work on my grandfather's dairy farm, in my father's drugstore, and at various odd jobs on which the well-being of a small town depends. In the course of my youth I was thus able to save enough to allow me to attend public schools and later the public universities where I took all my degrees. I also functioned as a de facto town musician, playing and singing in school and civic ensembles, accompanying on the piano all my schoolmates when they performed at every conceivable event, and playing (organ when in good repair, piano when in tune) at two churches every Sunday morning.

That was it. These are the broad outlines, such as they are—all very ordinary. Virtually none of this had anything to do with making me an ethnomusicologist; virtually all of it had everything to do with making me an ethnomusicologist.

The work we do as ethnomusicologists is not about the ordinary per se, but rather about the ways in which music makes it extraordinary. As ethnomusicologists, we participate in this transformation and the forms of representation that set it in motion.

Through these forms of representation we seek a type of truth—call it truth in representation—which in turn depends on honesty and a sense of ethical engagement. Such truth is at its most demanding when the differences are most difficult to perceive, when the task of representation is at its greatest. I preface this essay with these remarks because I wonder whether the entirely unremarkable character of my youth was not crucial for the passionate engagement with representing the ordinary that has motivated me as a teacher and scholar, as a student of the everyday, as an ethnomusicologist who has chosen the ordinary as the gateway to the extraordinary.

SELF-PROFILE IN BRIEF

The ordinariness of my approach to ethnomusicology notwithstanding, there is much about my profile as an ethnomusicologist that is distinctive, and before I trace the more nuanced stages of my work as an ethnomusicologist, it might be helpful to sketch a self-profile with rather broad strokes. At the outset, I should like to observe that I am quite well aware that many ethnomusicologists and historical musicologists regard my approach to ethnomusicology as, to put it politely, atypical. My work lies somewhere between the strictly ethnographic and the clearly historical. I am able to speak to musical scholars of all stripes. Whereas I do not—and, of course, I could not—object to this assessment of professional in-betweenness as inaccurate or unfair, I want to state rather unequivocally that my intellectual and academic affinity and alignment are to ethnomusicology. More to the point, if I in fact do take approaches that are not universally regarded as typical, I do so because of the intellectual breadth of ethnomusicology. Recognition of this intellectual breadth might well be, I believe, one of the most critical lessons we learn as we examine how ethnomusicologists work.

As I have already noted, I do not deny the claim that my thinking is historical. It would be almost inconceivable for me not to bring perspectives from the past to bear on the present. Ethnographic moments constitute history—indeed, must constitute history the moment we record and represent them. Still, it is not my intent to give history a privileged position relative to ethnography, and it surely has never been my intent to write music history with no ethnographic context. Even the most historical of my current projects (Bohlman forthcoming), a translation and assessment of Johann Gottfried Herder's studies on music and nationalism, was motivated by a challenge to my contemporaries to rethink fundamental tracts on music and the nation-state during our own era of sharply intensifying nationalism.

Another way in which many consider my profile as an ethnomusicologist atypical is that I neither specialize nor work extensively in a specialized area connected to the study of "selfness." I cannot deny these assessments; again, however, there may be latitude for interpreting them. There is, I argue with some frequency, a center to my work, to which I return time and again, and that center, of course, is Jewish music. That I am not Jewish and that scholars of Jewish music overwhelmingly are Jewish would seem at first glance to confirm my uncharacteristic relation both to specialties and to the study of selfness. Yet again, however, I should argue that ethnomusicology affords me the intellectual freedom to belie any claims that ethnomusicology begins with the study of self before progressing to the study of others.

One observation about my profile that I surely do not wish to refute is that I am intensively—some would say, excessively—concerned with problems, forms, and media of representation. There can be no question that I fuss a great deal about how I write, not just about what I write. I choose prose styles very carefully, and I find myself constantly in a position of negotiating about which language or which style of presentation will serve my representational goals most effectively. And I mean effectively, not efficiently, for, as often as I write in languages other than my mother tongue, especially German, I do so embracing the struggle that this involves. The representational challenge of ethnomusicology extends no less to the music, and for this reason

FIGURE I   The author playing the Austrian button-box accordion. Photo by Roland Mahr—his accordion teacher, his student at the University of Vienna, and a longtime colleague in fieldwork.

I have taken up the challenge of exploring new ways to realize music through transcriptions and critical editions that allow us to explore the music itself, thus "problematizing" the selfness of music. The most obvious forum for exploring the representation of music has been the series "Recent Researches in the Oral Traditions of Music," for which I have served as general editor since its establishment in the late 1980s.

I would be remiss not to dispel a final myth about my profile as an ethnomusicologist. I have always been a musician (figure 1), and I have never turned from participant-observation as an essential component of fieldwork. Most recently, I have brought works from Central and East European Jewish cabaret to life on the stage, and this has allowed me to expand the ways I examine the presence of music in Jewish modernism. The first performances of the ensemble for which I serve as artistic director, the New Budapest Orpheum Society, took place in 1998 at the University of Chicago, but within a few years the ensemble's performances had been extended beyond academic settings. If uncharacteristic, my penchant for performance grows directly from the ethnomusicological recognition of the many ways the scholar-musician acknowledges the barriers between ourselves and those we seek to understand, also as musicians.

In the end, I wonder whether the self-profile I have just sketched really is atypical or uncharacteristic. Are such descriptions really necessary or even meaningful in assessing the work we do as ethnomusicologists? At its best, so my self-profile or so the self-profiles of every reader might reveal, ethnomusicology empowers us to transcend the typical and the characteristic.

JOURNEYS OF AN ETHNOMUSICOLOGIST AT WORK

There is a story that accompanies, or metaphorically represents, the making of every ethnomusicologist. The decisions we make about where and what to study, about how to enter and maintain community, and about how to embark on collaborations with colleagues in the field and in the classroom are responsible for the ways in which the chapters of our stories take shape. The metaphors that provide frameworks for the chapters may also be, when we are fortunate, the metaphors by which we live.

The work I do as an ethnomusicologist follows the metaphorical path of a journey, during which I have sojourned at certain stations, mapping out the territories on which I am about to embark. The metaphorical stages and stations have increasingly provided the rhetorical stuff for the stories about my work as an ethnomusicologist since the early 1990s, when I began studying the relation of music and pilgrimage (Bohlman 1996). By no means do I wish to arrogate the path of the ethnomusicologist as a sacred journey. It is the everyday, not the sacred, that provides the real substance of the journey and the narrative power that accrues to it.

In most ways, the metaphorical journey of an ethnomusicologist at work may be entirely lacking in distinctiveness, if it is to be truly quotidian in every sense. The distinctiveness of the pilgrim's journey, nonetheless, lies in its steady momentum and its movement into challenging, ever-changing landscapes. The path through the ordinary leads ceaselessly toward the extraordinary. In my own case ethnomusicology has provided me with the cartographic tools to make this journey. The stations along the path of the journey also provide crucial moments of narrative reflection and ethnographic "reflexivity." Reflection takes the form of reading, writing, and returning to previous stations. Reflexivity encourages us to reach out to join fellow travelers, those with whom we share the journey and its many stations.

In the sections that follow I call attention to those moments which were most formative in the journey that made me an ethnomusicologist. In some ways my own journey as an ethnomusicologist has been typical of my generation, which came of age in an era of academic liberalness but immediately encountered an era of

In certain ways, the challenge of fieldwork is something the ethnomusicologist never fully overcomes. Fieldwork allows us to ask questions and to pose solutions, but it does not provide answers.

professional conservatism. Still, I hesitate to suggest that there is anything special, beyond the ordinary, about the path I have followed, for again I find myself most convinced of ethnomusicology's capacity to accommodate many different paths in the making of ethnomusicologists. I especially sense the camaraderie of that generation as I reach the first station.

Station one: Discovering the ordinary

The first moment that revealed the journey of ethnomusicology to me occurred when I learned to hear and listen to folk music. The experience of folk music was for me overwhelming, all the more so because I did not have that experience until the beginning of my graduate studies at the University of Illinois. It was because I had not heard folk music for so many years that the initial experiences were so profound and that I have never been able to shake them. The encounter with folk music was, moreover, one of listening and hearing, and thus of reconfiguring the body for the experience with music that is so crucial in Islam in the aesthetic concept of *samā'*. Before graduate school, my formative years in the rural Midwest notwithstanding, I had simply failed to hear folk music, and this failure, once I recognized it, was deeply troubling, for it brought about a crisis of musical faith, which in turn led me directly to ethnomusicology.

Why folk music? There are two simple answers to this question. First, there was no folk music, in any form, language, or social context, that I could count as my own. The very ordinariness of its difference drew me to it, not on a path of discovering something that I had lost or that had once belonged to my ancestors, but on a path of wonderment at the transcendent qualities of folk music. Second, the teachers from whom I learned what I know about folk music used the ordinary to reveal extraordinarily complex lessons. The teacher who first encouraged me to listen to folk music, Bruno Nettl, remains a mentor to this day. Charlie Bannen, the first musician with whom I conducted intensive fieldwork, worked miracles as I listened to him perform a repertoire of Irish and American songs and ballads that seemed almost boundless (Bohlman 1980a). It is, in fact, the boundless and boundaryless qualities of folk music that situate it at the core of ethnomusicology as I continue to explore it and follow the many paths it opens. In graduate school, folk music shaped my master's thesis, a study of German-American traditions in northern Wisconsin (1980b). The first monograph of my academic years examined folk music research as a field of study (1988). My most recent book, a critical edition, is also a study of music long identified as folk song (Bohlman and Holzapfel 2001), and at the time of this writing I have a book in press that is a discursive history of Jewish folk music. None of these folk musics, however, is my own, and it is for that reason that they all challenge me to listen harder than I might if my encounter with them were determined by familiarity.

Station two: In the field

Fieldwork challenges the ethnomusicological complacency that can, and to some extent should, accompany the familiarity we have with musics we come to understand as our own. In certain ways, the challenge of fieldwork is something the ethnomusicologist never fully overcomes. Fieldwork consists of methodologies, but it is not itself a methodology. It allows us to ask questions and to pose solutions, but it does not provide answers. For these reasons fieldwork is not simply a set of procedures that we accomplish early in a project or career, but rather a lifelong process whereby we learn from our encounters with others and change in response to these lessons. As one measure of our lives as ethnomusicologists, fieldwork must be highly personal, despite the fact that it is carried out under the most public of conditions.

I seldom reflect more on the personal practices and meanings of ethnomusicology than at the stations determined by fieldwork. However long the ethnographic sojourn at a station, I depart recognizing that I have been completely transformed, from the moment of arrival. Fieldwork, therefore, was the catalyst for the transformation from my student years to my early years as a teacher and academic, not just because it provided the empirical data for a dissertation but because it powerfully connected my life as an ethnomusicologist to those whose lives I was trying to represent.

The two years (1980–1982) that I spent in Israel remain one of the most transformative stations along my path toward becoming an ethnomusicologist. At the time I hardly recognized that I was embarking on an ethnographic project that few would approach through fieldwork. The historical components of the project—studying the music culture of an immigrant and ethnic community from Central Europe—were so obvious that they did not seem at odds with the anthropological components. I quickly took my position as a participant-observer, playing chamber music in a culture that accorded tremendous symbolic value to making music in small groups. I documented rituals and fleshed out the genealogies of musicians. I collected oral histories and folk songs alike, and I traveled to various sites in the complex landscape of the diaspora. I also spent long hours in archives, and I unearthed documents that served as written records of the past (Bohlman 1992). In the field I was fully aware of fulfilling as many desiderata of thorough ethnography as possible, and these never seemed at odds with history. The products of my fieldwork in Israel, however, would conform to few models or paradigms (1989). They would, unquestionably, be products of ethnomusicology shaped by fieldwork. They established, moreover, the foundations of a life in ethnomusicology shaped by fieldwork.

Station three: Survival

The professional path along which ethnomusicologists must travel is never easy, and we often reach a station along that path after an enormous struggle. How often, I sometimes wonder, do we really reflect on the true nature of these struggles, or even on the reasons ethnomusicologists must endure more than their fair share of such struggles? I should like to pause briefly at this symbolic station to reflect on the difficulties ethnomusicologists face as they attempt to establish themselves professionally and academically. I do this not only because I, like many who read these essays, had to overcome hurdles to ensure my professional survival, but also because the questions raised by professional survival necessarily shape our place in the academic world. The struggle we face, be it acquiring a position, securing tenure, or receiving a fair level of funding, is part of who we are, not as individuals but rather as ethnomusicologists whose presence challenges the status quo and destabilizes the institutions maintaining it.

In the 1990s there was extensive discussion about the relations between traditional and nontraditional disciplines. On the traditional side, disciplines sequestered themselves behind bastions—the institutions that had long served their best interests. On the other side, nontraditional disciplines demanded, vociferously more often than not, their right to support from the dominant institutions, even while launching forays against those institutions. If this was a matter of canon-building and canon-bashing, the disputes between academic disciplines were largely being waged with the same rules. Within the traditional arenas of musical research, the lines were drawn very clearly, for example between "old musicology" and "new musicology."

What is also striking about these battles is that ethnomusicology, by and large, did not participate in them, even though it might have seemed obvious that ethnomusicologists would weigh in on the side of the nontraditional disciplines. "Tradition," in this sense, was determined according to institutional criteria, which is to say according to an internal tension that was ultimately meant to sustain the institution. Ethnomusicology was spared this institutionalization of tradition, but its position in the institution remained insecure. I suspect that such an explanation of ethnomusicology's position outside academic and professional institutions will offer little solace to students and younger scholars. Perhaps, however, there are important lessons to be learned from our perspective on the outside looking in. We might ask ourselves what we achieve by winning one more place at the institutional table, or what we accomplish by playing according to the rules that maintain the hegemony of an intellectual tradition which we may want to dismantle. For ethnomusicology, the stakes are different, but they are also higher.

Station four: At the borders

It has always been reassuring and challenging to me that ethnomusicology does not demand conformity to orthodoxies. Unlike many other fields and disciplines, moreover, ethnomusicology does not require that one become a specialist in any single area or that one circumscribe a specialty with some form of ownership (for instance, with rubrics such as "my culture" or "my period"). This does not mean that I have ever been especially comfortable as a nonspecialist. Ethnomusicology does not, in fact, ask one to eschew specialties; rather, it asks one to reconceptualize specialties so that they will allow us to map our journeys as ethnographers and teachers in different, I daresay distinctive and innovative, ways. In my case, there are several "centers" to my research—especially folk music, Jewish music, and religion and music—to which I return with some frequency as I consider the ways I shall move away from them to push beyond the periphery. The longer journey, thus, contains continual alternation between center and periphery, with the former providing a stable station and the latter providing temporary way stations along new borders as I travel into uncharted territories.

As an ethnographer, I welcome the opportunity to find myself at way stations along the borders. The new ethnographic journeys I have undertaken have always benefited from crossing those borders, and each time I enter a new ethnographic "field" I am greeted by the excitement and recognition that I have been able to enter it because I am an ethnomusicologist. To illustrate this point, I might turn for a moment to my most recent European ethnographic journeys. In a literally geographic sense, my researches have undergone a shift from Europe's center to its periphery over the course of the past decade. Throughout the 1980s I was concerned largely with understanding the convergence of music histories that had engendered the centeredness of Central Europe. A new centrifugal force was set in motion in the 1990s, as the "old Europe" maintained at the center gave way to the fragmentation of the "new Europe." In order to engage ethnographically with the dramatic decentralization that followed, I undertook a new set of journeys, varying them as much as possible. I found myself joining pilgrims as they crossed political and religious borders (figure 2). I followed the course along which the "festivalization" of folk and popular music was passing. I attempted to identify traces of Jewish music in the borderlands of Eastern Europe (figure 3) and on Europe's Mediterranean littoral. All this pushed me far beyond the limits of my ethnographic experiences. At the beginning of the twenty-first century, I have not lost sight of the centers that fields other than ethnomusicology might call specialties, but

FIGURE 2 The author at work at transcription during research on pilgrimage. Photo by Christine Wilkie Bohlman, Mariazell, Austria, January 1996.

FIGURE 3   The author with a local folklorist, Dr. Adalbert Putz, in the border town of Deutschkreuz, a Jewish-Hungarian-Croatian-Austrian village. This picture illustrates themes of border crossings and political activism at the time of the fall of the iron curtain and the velvet revolutions in Eastern Europe. Photo by Professor Rudolf Pietsch, Institute for Folk Music Research, Vienna, 1989.

I find myself more eager than ever to journey to the next set of way stations that form along the next set of borders that need to be crossed.

Station five: Activism and political engagement

What we do as ethnomusicologists is very important, and I should like to pause at the fifth station to reflect on this basic fact. Ethnomusicologists give voice to the voiceless. We examine the phenomena that accompany oppression and injustice. We intervene at moments when human beings and cultures are at risk. The peoples and musics we study have often been denied histories of their own, and we take it as our responsibility to restore that history. We do all this and more not because it is exceptional but because it is a part of the everyday work of an ethnomusicologist. At base, it provides the reason that many of us become ethnomusicologists in the first place.

We should not lose sight of the fact that many view ethnomusicology's political engagement and activist stance with a fair degree of trepidation. Be it the absolute qualities of music or the putative withholding of judgment in any scientific endeavor, the criticism of ethnomusicology's political engagement takes many forms. In 1993 I published what amounted to a frontal attack on the politics of musicology's denial of politics, for which I was either praised or chastised. Remarkably, I have even heard, with some frequency, the question, Does ethnomusicology *have* to be concerned with all those oppressed peoples and musics? The answer to that question, of course, is obvious.

I first became acutely aware of ethnomusicology's activist calling when studying the ways music might help us understand the unfathomable tragedy of the Holocaust. It currently motivates my activist intervention in the complicated impact of nationalism on the transformations of the "new Europe." As I explore the aesthetics of representing the everyday, I increasingly realize that I am actually confronting the politics of representation. The moment when we examine the ways music represents identity and race is also the moment when it is impossible to deny the politics of race. These are the issues that make the everyday so compelling for ethnomusicology and that charge us with the responsibility of activism.

Station six: Teaching, mentoring, and learning

We have the great good fortune in ethnomusicology of never reaching a point at which learning is not crucial. We are endowed with an extraordinarily reflexive mentoring system; by this, I mean the ways in which we serve as mentors to students and they to us. During my years as student and teacher, I have been blessed with extraordinary teachers and students, and they—perhaps more than any single factor—have collectively shaped the work I do as an ethnomusicologist. I reach these mentors and students at the final station of this reflective essay because it is with them that beginnings and endings dovetail, creating ethnomusicological moments when teaching and learning converge.

What constitutes the process of learning for an ethnomusicologist? This is hardly a question that one can answer in a few brief sentences. Still, it is a question that I do not choose to avoid just because my answers might be too brief. Fundamental to the ways in which I learn as an ethnomusicologist is listening: listening as a process of perceiving the music making of others; listening as a means of absorbing the stories people tell about their most meaningful experiences; listening as half of the discursive equation we call discussion; listening as a means of allowing others to teach; and listening as a means of reflecting on how best to teach others.

I have also come to believe that teaching in ethnomusicology is at its most effective when it opens spaces in which diverse kinds of learning can take place. Orthodoxies and institutionally bound schools of ethnomusicology would impose restrictions and mute the voices that call for change. They are surely anathema to what the field does best. The pedagogical openness so central to ethnomusicology was the earliest lesson I learned from my first mentor, Bruno Nettl. There can be no question that one measure of Bruno as a pedagogue is that his students bear so little resemblance to him and have themselves followed such divergent pedagogical routes. Bruno Nettl's openness as a mentor is abundantly evident in the *Festschrift* for his sixtieth birthday (Blum, Neuman, and Bohlman 1991). Again and again, Bruno's students continue to turn to him as a mentor.

FIGURE 4 The author during fieldwork with a Jewish farmer in the central Carpathians, on the Romanian side of the border with Ukraine. Photo by Professor Rudolf Pietsch, February 1996.

As I myself followed the paths toward and through various research projects, mentoring and learning continued to converge as I benefited from collegial relationships with so many along the way. As I explored the folk music landscapes of Central and Eastern Europe, Otto Holzapfel and Rudolf Pietsch made it possible for me to learn about traditions that were distant from my own experiences (figure 4). In more recent collaborations with Tullia Magrini, Ronald Radano, and Martin Stokes I again realized that I had much to learn but wonderful colleagues to help me learn. Finally, there is that legion of colleagues, my student-mentors at the University of Chicago, who teach me every day, assuring me that learning in ethnomusicology is an everyday experience. It is because of the mentor-student web that the final station in the present essay represents both a fulfillment of the intellectual journey and a stimulus to push on toward yet another station.

REPRESENTATION

If, at the end of the twentieth century, I had made a singular, even perhaps influential, contribution that cut across the field of ethnomusicology, it grew from my active pursuit of new possibilities for disseminating ethnomusicological research—in other words, for publishing. Two substantive concerns motivated my attempts to establish and develop new publishing programs for the field; additionally, there was one more aesthetic, if also personal, motivation. First, at the time I made the transition from student to teacher in the early and middle 1980s, I was struck by the fact that ethnomusicologists had few options in their own field for publishing their monographs. To the extent that there were ethnomusicology series labeled as such—the series John Blacking had been editing at Cambridge University Press, for instance—they survived rather precariously. For the most part, ethnomusicologists had to look beyond the borders of ethnomusicology to find presses with special strengths in an area of study or to find acquisitions editors with a special sympathy for ethnomusicology, such as Judith McCulloch at the University of Illinois Press. All too often, ethnomusicologists in search of a publisher were asked to make compromises and to alter their manuscripts to suit a publication series that included few if any other books in ethnomusicology. Ethnomusicology, one heard rather often, did not produce best-sellers. It was with this practical concern in mind that I began discussions in 1987 with Gabriele Dotto, then responsible for music publications at the University of Chicago Press. In 1992, Gabe Dotto became an editor and publisher at Ricordi in Milan. His successor at the University of Chicago Press, Kathleen Hansell, while not directly responsible for books in ethnomusicology, works closely with many aspects of acquisitions and production. "Chicago Studies in Ethnomusicology"—a series coedited by Bruno Nettl and stewarded at the University of Chicago Press since 1992 by T. David Brent—grew out of those discussions. At the time of this writing, forty volumes have appeared in "Chicago Studies in Ethnomusicology," with numerous other volumes, directly or less directly related to ethnomusicology, also appearing at the University of Chicago Press.

My second substantive concern was that ethnomusicologists were often excluded from some of the most common genres of music publishing, for example, critical editions of music. Various criticisms were used to justify such exclusion. From ethnomusicological and publishing camps alike came the allegation that editions of music were possible only for written traditions and hence should be restricted almost exclusively to Western art music. Other criticisms combined the practical and the substantive. Should the notation one uses for a transcription, for example, be descriptive or prescriptive? To what extent would it be necessary to invent new notations for each repertoire transmitted orally? Could such notation convey meaning other than the most basic aspects of sound? There were plenty of reasons not to pursue the possibilities any further, but I determined, instead, to take those reasons as a challenge. Again, I turned to a well-established and distinguished publisher, A-R Editions of Madison, Wisconsin, to find solutions. As I worked closely with editors at A-R Editions—first with Steven Moore Whiting and in recent years with Paul Ranzini—"Recent Researches in the Oral Traditions of Music" took shape.

It is not my purpose in this essay to assess the successes and failures of such attempts to take new directions in ethnomusicological publishing. Few, however, would deny that the options available for disseminating high-quality and innovative work in ethnomusicology have greatly expanded over the past fifteen years. The expansion has spread to several other publishers, which have opened their lists to monographs because of their excellence in ethnomusicology itself. One of the most direct results of this expansion has been the growth of a new readership both within and outside ethnomusicology. Books in ethnomusicology are much more common fare in historical musicology, in anthropology, and in a wide variety of less closely related disciplines. A complex array of factors accounts for the expansion of ethnomusicology during the past fifteen years, of course, and the increased dissemination of our work is only one of those factors. As a factor, however, ethnomusicological publishing is particularly responsible for the visibility of the field, and it is, moreover, crucial in the sweeping transformation of ethnomusicological discourse.

The larger question that arises has to do with discourse and representation. Ethnomusicologists have long had a particularly tortured struggle with the dilemmas of representation. That struggle has taken on the dimensions of a crisis of conscience: If one represents the music and culture of others, does one necessarily do violence to them? Does any form of representing music—with words or with notes—ultimately "essentialize" music? The expansion in ethnomusicological publishing has not, I should argue, provided convenient answers to these pressing questions, but it has repeatedly raised and reformulated such questions, intensifying our need to respond effectively.

At the outset of this section I mentioned a third reason for my interest in encouraging new areas of ethnomusicological publication, a reason that has aesthetic and personal dimensions. In fact, I like to write, and I regard writing as one professional activity that is intensely personal. Writing draws me into the passion of representation in the many forms and genres that ethnomusicology makes possible. With its multiple forms of representation, ethnomusicology allows us to be intensely personal and to draw our readers closer to the intensely personal worlds in which music making takes place. It is ethnomusicology, indeed, that engenders ever greater possibilities for those acts of representation which draw us closer to the distinctiveness of the human experience. This is indeed something well worth sharing with others.

EPILOGUE: THE ORDINARY KNOWS NO BOUNDARIES

Ethnomusicologists had much to celebrate at the end of the twentieth century. Their employment picture had brightened. Some of their old battles were finally subsiding, with ethnomusicology winning the day. The research of the field had greater visibility, within and outside academia, not least because of the growing amount and diversity of literature by and about ethnomusicologists. There was a greater general awareness of what ethnomusicologists had to say, and there was growing evidence of the very real impact of the field on several domains of cultural politics.

If we take stock of these achievements and learn from them, however, I wonder whether this moment—or any moment, for that matter—really calls for prolonged celebration. In a certain sense, returning to the field is too important to allow us to rest on our laurels. Ultimately, this field, in the more literal ethnographic sense and in the more figurative discursive sense, remains unstable, changing, and fragile. It is a field that is in many ways ordinary—constitutive of the very ordinariness that makes human music making so extraordinary. Would we really want to stake out the boundaries of that field and claim that they preserve several decades of disciplinary triumphs? I, personally and professionally, should not; rather, I prefer to think of ethnomusicology as a field that knows no boundaries, that compels us to make and remake our field and ourselves.

REFERENCES

Blum, Stephen, Daniel M. Neuman, and Philip V. Bohlman, eds. 1991. *Ethnomusicology and Modern Music History*. Urbana: University of Illinois Press.

Bohlman, Philip V. 1980a. "The Folk Songs of Charles Bannen: The Interaction of Music and History in Wisconsin." *Transactions of the Wisconsin Academy of Sciences, Arts, and Letters* 68:167–187.

———. 1980b. "Music in the Culture of German-Americans in North-Central Wisconsin." Master's thesis, University of Illinois at Urbana-Champaign.

———. 1988. *The Study of Folk Music in the Modern World*. Bloomington: Indiana University Press.

———. 1989. "*The Land Where Two Streams Flow*": Music in the German-Jewish Community of Israel. Urbana: University of Illinois Press.

———. 1992. *The World Centre for Jewish Music in Palestine 1936–1940: Jewish Musical Life on the Eve of World War II*. Oxford: Oxford University Press.

———. 1993. "Musicology as a Political Act." *Journal of Musicology* 11(4):411–436.

———. 1996. "Pilgrimage, Politics, and the Musical Remapping of the New Europe." *Ethnomusicology* 40(3):375–412.

———. In press. *"Jüdische Volksmusik"—Eine mitteleuropäische Geistesgeschichte*. Vienna: Böhlau Verlag.

———. Forthcoming. *Herder on Music and Nationalism*. Berkeley: University of California Press.

Bohlman, Philip V., and Otto Holzapfel. 2001. *The Folk Songs of Ashkenaz*. Middleton, Wisc.: A-R Editions.

Part 2
Resources and Research Tools

Part 2
Resources and Research Tools

Research in ethnomusicology has grown exponentially in the past twenty-five years. Scholars work in a multiplicity of languages and cultures, and they present their analyses in written, audio, and visual forms. These presentations, such as the many listed in Part 2, enrich our knowledge of local performance around the world.

Part 2 begins with a general glossary that brings together the terminology in all the volumes. This glossary not only provides a basic set of terms and definitions associated with the music of the world but also can serve as a keyword summary of what is contained in the *Garland Encyclopedia of World Music*.

A Dayak man of the Bunaq people plays gongs in a village near the Mahakan River. Borneo, Indonesia, 1991. Photo © Charles and Josette Lenars/ Corbis.

Glossary

General Glossary

Note: Numbers in **boldface** following entries are volume numbers.

aak 'Elegant music', Korean Confucian ritual music. (**7**)

Aaksŏ Office of Ritual Music, Korean *Chosŏn* period. (**7**)

Aaktae Korean court music department, under Japanese colonial rule. (**7**)

aalakan Tausug deep-rimmed bossed gong. (**4**)

abajeños 'From lower lands', Purépecha instrumental mestizo music for *zapateados*. (**2**)

Abaluhya Subgroup of the Luhya cluster of peoples living in Kenya. (**1**)

abanderado Chilean conductor of a *baile* or *cofradía* dancing group. (**2**)

abangan Syncretic Javanese Muslims. (**4**)

abangarang (Also *abaŋgaraŋ*.) Berta song-accompanying lyre. (**1**)

abaphakathi South African popular performers whose competence and versatility secured a free existence for them. (**1**)

abaqhafi "Street cowboys" who wandered through South African cities and played Zulu guitar songs. (**1**)

abbaddata Southern Corsican term for a dance around a corpse; *see ballata*. (**8**)

abbaṅga Posture used in *odissi* dance. (**5**)

abbinaya Portrayal of emotions or expression through gestures, postures, and facial expression. (**5**)

abbisbēka Ritual bathing of a deity's statue in various sacred substances. (**5**)

abchodnyja pieśni Belarusan festive "walkabout" songs, sung while villagers make the rounds of their neighbors' homesteads in spring. (**8**)

abeimahani Unaccompanied Garifuna women's song, a category of *úyanu*. (**2**)

abelagudahani 'Bringing-in' song performed at the beginning of the Garifuna *dügü* ritual to escort fishermen to and from the sea. (**2**)

abeng Jamaican cow-horn trumpet. (**2**)

abhang (Also *abhaṅg, abhango*.) Devotional songs of Maharashtra and Gujarat. (**5**)

ābhog Fourth section of *dirrupad* composition. (**5**)

abi Zaghawi old women's song praising camel men. (**1**)

aboakyere Festival of the Brong and Effutu of Ghana, in which local residents may criticize the chief. (**1**)

abofoo Dance performed by Akan hunters to cleanse the hunter who killed the animal. (**1**)

aboio Brazilian *cantoria* cowboy cattle-herding song genre featuring the imitation of cattle. (**2**)

abyāt Vocal introduction to the *nūba* in Tunisian traditional music. (**6**)

ācārya (Also *paṇḍit*.) Learned individual qualified to serve as a guru. (**5**)

ACCESS Arab Community Center for Economic and Social Services, an institution providing support for Arab music and musicians in Detroit, among other services. (**6**)

accordeon (Dutch.) Accordion of the Low Countries. (**8**)

accordéon (French.) Accordion of the Low Countries. (**8**)

accordéon jurassien Musette-tuned accordion of Jura, Switzerland. (**8**)

accordion Portable wind instrument with a keyboard. (**3**)

acculturation Assimilation of traits from one culture to another; changes that occur when members of different cultures come into continuous contact, involving complex relationships of cultural, economic, and political dominance. (**1, 2**)

Acemaşiran Common Turkish *makam* resembling the Western major scale. (**6**)

achangur Abkhazian four-stringed plucked lute. (**8**)

achari (Also *devi ke gīt*.) Songs in the Bundeli dialect in praise of the Mother Goddess. (**5**)

acharpan Abkhazian whistle flute, made from mountain grass. (**8**)

achetringele Clapper bell of Laupen, Bern, Switzerland. (**8**)

Achimota School Prestigious institution in Ghana where Ephraim Amu taught indigenous music. (**1**)

Acholi A people living in Uganda. (**1**)

acid house Subcategory of house music repertoire that media often associate with drugs, especially Ecstasy (or "E"). (**3**)

açiş (Also *ayak*.) Prelude in free rhythm to the Turkish instrumental *uzun hava*. (**6**)

acordeon Accordion of Romania. (**8**)

acordeón 'Accordion', in many regions of Spanish-speaking America, a multiple single-reed-concussion aerophone with bellows, either with buttons or keyboard for melody, and buttons for bass notes. (**2**)

acoustic rules Constraints on the quality of sound produced by a voice or an instrument. (**1**)

'açrī 'Contemporary', genre of Algerian popular music drawing on Western dance music. (**6**)

adaha Style of highlife that grew out of colonial military-band music. (**1**)

adaha ademi hidi Yekuana garden song festival. (**2**)

adakem Struck box idiophone of West Africa. (**1**)

adalo Colo kudu or waterbuck horn with lateral mouth hole and calabash bell. (**1**)

àdàmǫ Yoruba pressure drum. (**1**)

adaul Abkhazian double-headed drum. (**8**)

aḍavu Dance steps used in *mōhini āttam*. (**5**)

adawo Jamaican machete played as an idiophone struck with a piece of metal. (**2**)

adbbuta 'Wondrous', one of the eight emotional states (*rasa*) codified in the *Nātyaśāstra*. (**5**)

ademi Yekuana large group song. (**2**)

adhān (Also *azan, ezan*.) Islamic call to prayer, performed five times per day by a solo vocalist from the mosque. (**1, 4, 6**)

adhān shar'ī Syllabic rendition of the *adhān* (call to prayer), alternating between two notes a step apart. (**6**)

adho nāc Malwa dance with vocal and instrumental accompaniment. (**5**)

Volume Key: **1**, Africa; **2**, South America, Mexico, etc.; **3**, United States and Canada; **4**, Southeast Asia; **5**, South Asia; **6**, Middle East; **7**, East Asia; **8**, Europe; **9**, Australia and the Pacific Islands; **10**, The World's Music.

ādhunik gān 'Modern song', popular urban entertainment music produced largely by Bengali recording and film companies in Calcutta, early 1930s. (5)

ādhunik gīt Modern song. (5)

adī tāḷa (Also *ādi tālam.*) Eight-beat metrical cycle in Karnatak music. (5)

ading Kalinga solo peacemaking song. (4)

adivāsī 'Original inhibitions'; replaced the British colonial term "scheduled tribe," referring to tribal peoples. (5)

adok Minangkabau frame drum. (4)

adonai malakh One of the two most common Ashkenazic Jewish modes (*shtayger*); *see ahavah rabbah.* (8)

adowa Dance of the Gā of Ghana that involves stamped bamboo tubes and a bell or rattle, utilizing a timeline; also, funeral music. (1, 10)

Adradžeńnie 'Belarusan Renaissance': movement toward cultural and national assertion, reflected in urban music. (8)

adufe (1) Portuguese square frame drum; (2) Spanish tambourine; (3) Guatemalan quadrangular double-skinned frame drum, with or without a rattle inside the body. (2, 8)

âdurâ (Also *kaṭṭāḍiya, yakâdurā.*) Term for a drummer-priest of the old religion in Sri Lanka. (5)

adxoky-pondur Chechen and Ingush three-stringed bowed lute. (8)

adzida Kind of dance performance in Ghana. (1)

aeag-ashva Abkhazian harvest songs, performed during traditional feasts; *see arash-vara-ashva.* (8)

Aegukka Korean national anthem. (7)

aembo-aembo Sama onomatopoeic play song. (4)

aerg Abkhazian hunting songs, performed during traditional feasts; *see azhveipshaar-ashva.* (8)

aerophone 'Air sounder', musical instrument (such as a flute) whose sound is produced by vibrating air, often a column of air, enclosed within it or immediately surrounding it. (1, 2, 3, 5, 9)

aewŏnsŏng 'Sorrowful voice', Korean vocal timbre in *p'ansori.* (7)

afã Anlo-Ewe cult. (1)

Afa Ewe god of divination. (1)

afãᴠu Music of the *afã* cult of the Anlo-Ewe. (1)

Afghani *rabāb* Short-necked, unfretted, plucked lure in Afghanistan, northwestern Pakistan, and Kashmir. (5)

Afikpo A people living in Nigeria. (1)

afirkhatsar-ashva Abkhazian heroic songs, performed during traditional feasts. (8)

afoxé Contemporary Afro-Brazilian carnival music. (2)

African Fiesta Brass-heavy big band that became publicly acclaimed in Congo and Zaïre in the 1950s and 1960s. (1)

African Jazz Joseph Kabasele's band, which defined and popularized Congo-Zaïre rumba. (1)

African Music Research Transcription Library Collection of African music begun in South Africa by Hugh Tracey. (1)

African Music Society Newsletter Publication begun in South Africa by Hugh Tracey and later transformed into an academic journal. (1)

African Musicology Journal founded at the University of Nairobi in the 1980s. (1)

African Studies Institute at the University of Ife Creative-arts center that encouraged research in African music. (1)

Afrikaans Language spoke by the Afrikaner people of South Africa. (1)

afrobeat Yoruba musical genre deriving in the late 1960s from highlife, jazz, and soul, and influential in *jùjú* and *fújì.* (1)

afrodisco Disco-based style of African music, influenced in the 1980s by Angelique Kidjo. (1)

afrojazz Style of jazz popular in Africa in the mid-1990s. (1)

afroma Style of jazz popular in Africa in the mid-1990s. (1)

agachi ngere Suyá day songs in rainy season. (2)

agadan iish Chechen women's lullaby. (8)

agar Bontok women's funeral song. (4)

agbadza Dance in Ghana identified with the Anlo-Ewe people in rural and urban areas. (1)

agbegijo Masquerade of the Yoruba people of Nigeria. (1)

agbekor Energetic dance of the Anlo-Ewe of Ghana, involving intricate steps. (1)

age uta (Japan.) (1) Segment of *nô* chanting in a high register; (2) *heikyoku* melodic pattern. (7)

aggu (Plural, *aggutan.*) Tuareg *griot* of the artisanal caste, who performs music professionally. (1)

aghānī 'Songs', as in titles of early Arabic song collections, for example *Kitāb al-aghānī*; singular, *ughniya.* See also *ughniyya.* (6)

aghānī al-ghaws 'Diving songs', local term for pearl divers' songs in the Gulf region; also *nahma* 'animal sound' or 'voice of the whale'. (6)

aghānī dīniyya 'Religious songs'. In Islamic hymnody in Egypt, songs combining the urban Arab music tradition with poetry containing Islamic themes. Popular singers

may perform or record such songs for religious occasions. (6)

aghānī shabābiyya (Also *aghānī al-jīl* 'new generation songs'.) 'Youth songs', popular musical tradition of the Mashriq characterized by brief songs with a Western-influenced, heavily synthesized accompaniment. (6)

āghāz Initial tone of a *gūshe* in Iranian music. (6)

agida Lowest-pitched drum of the battery of Maroon ritual drums in Surinam. (2)

agidìgbo (1) Large box-resonated Yoruba lamellophone resembling a Cuban lamellophone. (2) Yoruba version of *konkoma* music, brought to Lagos by Ewe and Fanti migrant workers. (1)

ağıt Turkish funeral dirge. (6)

ağız 'Dialect' (Turkish), referring to the specific regional character of Turkish folk melodies; in urban areas, also *tavır.* (6)

agnicayana Vedic ritual involving construction of a large fire altar. (5)

agogô Brazilian double or triple cone-shaped bell played with metal stick. (2)

agogo 'Iron bell', struck clapperless bell of the Yoruba of Nigeria that plays the timeline. (1)

Agona An Akan-speaking people of Ghana. (1)

Agra *gharānā* Stylistic school of singing whose exponents originally came from the city of Agra. (5)

âgu (Japan.) Generic term for traditional secular songs of the Miyako Islands with poetic texts based on legends or praises. (7)

agua 'e nieve (Also *agüenieve.*) Afro-Peruvian male competition dance. (2)

agua larga Colombian *currulao* rhythm. (2)

aguang Large vertical gong of Sumatra. (4)

agudu amaro 'Those who have been away', emancipated Africans from Brazil and Cuba living in West Africa. (1)

aguinaldo Strophic song genre throughout Hispanic America that is usually sung around Christmas and that involves a gift of coins, candy, food, or drink in exchange for music; it takes its name from this small offering, which is called *aguinaldo.* Also, a Spanish Christmas song. (2, 3, 8)

agung Suspended bossed gong of Sumatra and the Philippines. (4)

agung a bentong Maguindanao bamboo slit drum. (4)

agwāl (Also *aqwāl.*) Small clay goblet-shaped drum used by the Moroccan Berbers. (6)

agwisŏng (Also *agusŏng.*) 'Jaw voice', vocal technique in Korean *p'ansori.* (7)

ahá Yoruba idiophone made from a gourd cut in half. (1)

ahal Courtship gathering that features love songs, poetical recitations, jokes, and games of wit. (**1**)

āhang 'Tune' or 'melody type', Persian term adapted into Arabic as *hank* (plural, *hunūk*). (**6**)

ahavah rabbah One of the two most common Ashkenazic Jewish modes (*shtayger*); *see adonai malakh.* (**8**)

ahelli Nocturnal festival dance of Gourara, Algeria. (**1**)

ahellil (Also *ahellel.*) Song of praise by Moroccan Berbers for seasonal or life-cycle events. (**6**)

ahidus (Also *ahidous, haidous.*) (1) Berber dance of the middle and eastern High Atlas. (2) Term used in the Tamazight region of Berber Morocco for a gathering of villagers, their participation in songs and dances, and the songs and dances themselves, accompanied by the beating or clapping of the feet or hands. (**1, 6**)

Ahuso ryû (Japan.) School of Okinawan classical music. (**7**)

ahuu Hanging bronze gongs of Ambon. (**4**)

ahwash Berber dance of the western High Atlas. (**1**)

ahwash Moroccan collective dance accompanied by drums; in Berber Morocco, may also refer to the gathering of villagers, their participation in songs and dances, and the songs and dances themselves. (**6**)

ahwash n'timgharin 'Women's *ahwash*', women's version of the Moroccan Berber *ahwash* involving poetic contests and dancing. (**6**)

AIATSIS Australian Institute of Aboriginal and Torres Strait Islander Studies. (**9**)

aijuma Abkhazian fourteen-stringed harp. (**8**)

aikata (Japan.) (1) Instrumental interludes in *nagauta* (*syamisen* song); (2) *syamisen* instrumental music performed by the *kabuki* offstage ensemble. (**7**)

ainkjaga Abkhazian rattle. (**8**)

ainoyama busi (Japan.) Folk song quoted in *gidayû busi* (narrative *syamisen* music). (**7**)

Ainu (Japan.) Indigenous people of Hokkaidô Prefecture. (**7**)

Aïr Subgroup of the Tuareg, nomadic peoples of the Sahara and Sahel regions of Africa. (**1**)

aires nacionales 'National songs', traditional Mexican and other Latin American melodies arranged for piano. (**2**)

aitake (Japan.) Five- or six-note clusters played on the *syô* (mouth organ). (**7**)

aitys Kazakh music and poetry contest, usually taking the form of a competitive dialogue between two or more performers. (**6**)

aiyāi Ethical-meditative song genre of Algeria, performed by *gawwāl* 'singer-poets'. (**6**)

Aizo A people living in Benin. (**1**)

ajabeba Spanish transverse flute. (**8**)

ajaeng Korean bowed zither with seven to nine strings and movable bridges. (**7**)

'ajam One of the primary Arab *maqāmāt.* (**6**)

ajewwaq Traditional Berber flute (plural, *tajewwaqt*). (**6**)

ajísáàrì Yoruba music customarily performed before dawn during Ramadan by young men associated with neighborhood mosques. (**1**)

ajköki Bribri songs that tell of birth or death, or are for circumcision rites, the first menstrual period, and weddings. (**2**)

ak Sino-Korean term for music. (**7**)

akadinda Xylophone of the Buganda in Uganda, having seventeen to twenty-two notes, played by several players, and associated with the court. (**1, 10**)

ākam (Also *akam.*) Domestic or home performance. (**5**)

Akan A people speaking the Akan language in Ghana, West Africa. (**1**)

akapkap Abkhazian rattle. (**8**)

akaryna Belarusan clay ovoid ocarina, with eight to ten holes for fingering. (**8**)

akchang Classical Korean songs. (**7**)

akcho Korean mode and scale. (**7**)

Akha Tibeto-Burman-speaking people living in northern Thailand, Burma, and China. (**4**)

Akhak kwebŏm 'Guide to the Study of Music', Korean treatise of 1493. (**7**)

Akhak togam Office of Music Study, Korean Chosŏn period. (**7**)

akhal-teke Performance style of southern Turkmenistan. (**6**)

akhārā Social and artistic lineages found in some Bhojpuri folk music communities; (2) centers for training and rehearsal of folk performing genres. (**5**)

akhbār 'Accounts', in Arabic titles on the lives of musicians, such as *Akhbār al-mughannīn.* (Singular, *khabar.*) (**6**)

akhima Abkhazian twenty-four-stringed zither. (**8**)

ākhyān Legend or tale in Gujarat. (**5**)

akia Suyá individual shout songs. (**2**)

Akim An Akan-speaking people of Ghana. (**1**)

akin Kyrgyz epic singer. (**6**)

akpewu Music of the Ewe, dominated by the clapping of hands or wooden clappers. (**1**)

akritika Cypriot songs about the guards of the Byzantine Empire. (**8**)

aksak 'Limping', 'staggering'. (1) In Turkish music, term for asymmetrical rhythmic patterns (*usûl*). (2) Any of numerous asymmetrical, additive, unequal-part meters in Turkish and Eastern European music, also found in some Spanish forms. (**6, 8**)

aksara Beat, in a Karnatak tala cycle. (**5**)

āksiptikā (1) Metrical song demonstrating the properties of a raga; (2) 'tossing outward', the first statement of the Karnatak *ālāpana.* (**5**)

Aksumite Empire (Or Axum.) Political structure centered in territory that has become the modern state of Ethiopia. (**1**)

àkúbà Yoruba conga, based on Latin American prototypes. (**1**)

akulavye Mpyεmɔ girls' secret society. (**1**)

Akwamu An Akan-speaking people of Ghana. (**1**)

Akwapim An Akan-speaking people of Ghana. (**1**)

āla (Musical) instrument. In Morocco, also refers to the classical Andalusian *nūba* repertoire. (Plural, *ālāt.*) (**6**)

alaarinjo 'One who dances as he walks', a theatrical troupe that emerged from the *egungun* tradition. (**1**)

alabado (Also *albao, alavado.*) 'Praised'. (1) In Colombia and many other Spanish-speaking regions, a folk adaptation of a Catholic hymn. (2) Announcement played by the *clarinero* in Peru. (3) Form of free-meter religious folk song developed in late-nineteenth- and early-twentieth-century New Mexico, typically sung unaccompanied and in unison by a group of worshipers; occasionally a *pito* or small flute accompanies the singers. (**2, 3**)

alabanza 'Praise'. (1) Unaccompanied religious praise song in Argentina and elsewhere in Spanish-speaking America in two, three, or four voices. (2) Responsorial Christian hymn in praise of the eucharist. (3) New Mexican Hispano hymn type that is distinguished from the very distinctive *alabados* ; the most common and frequent contemporary arena for the performance of these hymns is the Catholic Church. (**2, 3**)

alabês Afro-Brazilian drummers in Candomblé. (**2**)

Alacaluf (Also Halakwalup.) Extinct native American culture of Tierra del Fuego. (**2**)

aladura 'Owners of prayer', indigenous Yoruba syncretic religious movement. (**1**)

alafranga Turkish term for European aesthetic ideals, espoused in the Tanzimat period of the Ottoman Empire; cf. *alaturka.* (**6**)

āla hawā'iyya 'Wind instrument', Arabic term for aerophones. (**6**)

āla iqā'iyya 'Rhythmic instrument', Arabic term for membranophones and idiophones. (**6**)

āla jildiyya (Also *ālā dhāt al-jild.*) Specific Arabic term for membranophones. (**6**)

alamāri Wandering performing group in Karnataka. (**5**)

'ālam-i mithāl World of analogies, between the world that can be sensed and the world of ideas; a way of musical understanding in the Islamic world. (**6**)

āla mūsīqiyya 'Musical instrument'. Most widespread term for musical instrument in the Arab world. (Plural, *ālāt mūsīqiyya*.) **(6)**

alaṅkāra (1) Embellishment, beauty. (2) Exercises; pieces for students by Purandara Dasa. **(5)**

ālāp (Also *alap*.) Nonmetric exposition of a raga; introductory section of a raga performance; improvisation within a Hindustani composition. **(4, 5)**

ālāpana Nonmetric improvisation on a raga. **(5)**

alap-jor-jhala Sequence of musical sections at the beginning of a Hindustani instrumental performance. **(3)**

alārippu Invocatory dance that begins a *bharata nātyam* performance by a solo dancer. **(5)**

ālātī Instrumentalist (plural, *ālātiyya*). **(6)**

alaturka (Also *à la Turka*.) 'In Turkish style'. (1) Style of singing used by Sephardic Jewish men in Bosnia-Hercegovina for religious songs. (2) Turkish term referring to native Turkish aesthetic sensibilities, considered outmoded in the Ottoman *Tanzimat* period; cf. *alafranga*. (3) Turkish style of music played at Armenian community events. **(3, 6, 8)**

āla watariyya 'Instrument with strings', Arabic term for chordophones. **(6)**

albazo Ecuadorian national folk music genre. **(2)**

alboka Basque double-pipe aerophone, each pipe having a single reed and a horn at each end, one acting as a bell and the other as a mouthpiece. **(8)**

alborada (1) Spanish music-and-dance genre of central and eastern Castile-León and Extremadura. (2) Municipal band music for patronal festivals. **(2, 8)**

alcahuete (Also *adulón*.) Drums other than *palo mayor* used in the *palos*. **(2)**

alcatraz Afro-Peruvian novelty couple dance. **(2)**

a-lce lha-mo Traditional Tibetan musical theater. **(5)**

alé liwon Introduction to the St. Lucian *débòt* dance performed in a circle. **(2)**

aleke Percussive genre of the Maroons of Surinam. **(2)**

Alevī 'Follower of Ali', Sufi-related Shi'ite religious group of Anatolia, encompassing Turks, Kurds, and Zazas, doctrinally related to the Bektaşī *tarikat*. **(6)**

alfandoques Ecuadorian tubular rattles. **(2)**

alférez (Also *alferéz, alferece*.) Administrative director, conductor, or main sponsor of a *baile* or *cofradía* dancing group in Chile. **(2)**

algaita (Also *algeita*.) Oboe of the Hausa and other peoples in North Africa. **(1)**

alghoza (Also *algojā, alghozā, alghozah, donal, giraw*.) Double duct flute in northwestern India and Pakistan. **(5)**

Ālhā Sung epic poem in North and Central India. **(5)**

'al-hawá Type of Palestinian wedding song. **(6)**

Ali People living in Chad and the Central African Republic. **(1)**

āligum Sidhi tribal dance in Karnataka. **(5)**

'ālima (Also *'alma*.) 'Learned woman' (plural, *'awālīm*), professional female musician or dancer who performs for a female audience. **(6)**

aliwen Nuptial song performed by women in the Ahaggar and Tassili-n-Ajjer regions of Algeria. **(1)**

aliyot Hebrew term for Jewish immigrants who settled in Palestine. **(6)**

All-Eastern Nigeria Music Festival Event organized in 1951 for participation of the best choirs in Eastern Nigeria. **(1)**

Alleluia Proper section of the mass, derived from a joyous exclamation (Hebrew *hallelujah* 'praise Yahweh'), grafted onto a chant. **(8)**

allemande Country dance popular in Luxembourg. **(8)**

allspelslåtar Standardized repertoire of Swedish tunes that all fiddlers are expected to know. **(8)**

allun Large frame drum of the Atlas Mountains in Morocco; *see bandīr*. **(6)**

almschroa Austrian solo dairymaid's yodel. **(8)**

àló Yoruba stories. **(10)**

aloha A prime Hawaiian cultural value, often conveyed in greeting, farewell, and lyrics, emphasizing sharing, cooperation, respect for self and others, responsibility, and industriousness. **(9)**

"Aloha 'Oe" Hawaiian song that in 1878 Princess (later Queen) Lili'uokalani textually composed and musically adapted from part of Charles Crozat Converse's hymn "The Rock Beside the Sea." **(9)**

alpa Relatively weak tone in a raga. **(5)**

alpatva 'Weakness'; weak pitches in a Hindustani raga. **(5)**

alphorn Usually long wooden trumpet. **(8)**

alphorn-fa Sharp intonation of the eleventh partial (F in a C scale) as played by Swiss alphorns, a tone also found in traditional Swiss singing. **(8)**

al revés In the Chilean *tonada*, term used when a quatrain starts with the retrograde of the previous one. **(2)**

alsi Malay song genre using fixed texts. **(4)**

alta Red liquid applied to the palms, fingertips, and soles of the feet by female *odissi* dancers. **(5)**

altiplano 'High plain', the cold, high central plain of southern Peru and Bolivia. (This term is also used for the region around Bogotá, Colombia.) **(2)**

alti-yarim makom 'Six and a half *maqāmlar*', referring to the Khorezm (Khiva) *maqām* tradition of Uzbekistan. **(6)**

alu Pestle used for pounding rice in Borneo. **(4)**

aluan Large frame drums on Ternate and Tidore. **(4)**

al-'ūd Arab lute, used in recent times in Sudan. *See also 'ūd*. **(1)**

Aluk To Dolo Torajan animist religion. **(4)**

Aluku Maroon people who live on the Maroni River in French Guiana and Surinam. **(2)**

alun-alun Town square in Java. **(4)**

Alur A people of Uganda. **(1)**

alus 'Refined, subtle', term applied to Javanese style or to character in Balinese dance. **(4)**

alusan Refined male character type in Javanese dance. **(4)**

alvorada Portuguese religious festival announced by a civil wind band or a bagpipe-and-drum ensemble. **(8)**

'ama In Tzotzil language, a Guatemalan highland Maya cane flute. **(2)**

amadare byôsi (Japan.) Metric structure in *syômyô, nô*, and *gidayû busi*. **(7)**

amadikh Tuareg panegyric poetry sung in praise of the prophet Muhammad. **(1)**

amadinda Twelve-key log xylophone of the Ganda style in Uganda; two players sit on each side of it. **(1, 10)**

amakondere (Also *amakondeere*.) Royal trumpet ensemble of the Buganda in Uganda. **(1)**

'amal (Also *'aml*.) (1) 'Work', 'craft', the practical art (of music), in contrast to theory (*'ilm*); refers more specifically to the *ma'lūf* when performed in Sufi contexts. (2) Song type within the Andalusian *nūba*. **(6)**

ámalihani Complex dance of the Garifuna *dügü* ritual in Belize, characterized by movement in a circular pattern and reversals of direction. **(2)**

Amami sansin (Japan.) *Sansin* (Okinawan three-stringed lute) used in the Amami Islands, which has relatively thin strings and is plucked with a flexible bamboo pick. **(7)**

amane (Plural, *amanedes*.) Improvisatory vocal pieces in free rhythm that originated in Greek enclaves in Asia Minor. **(3)**

amanedhes Greek improvised poetry punctuated by the exclamation *aman!* 'alas!'. **(8)**

amarantina See *viola*. **(8)**

amarrao 'Tied', Puerto Rican dance choreography. **(2)**

ambā Fishermen's work songs. **(5)**

ambalavāsi Female temple dancers in Kerala. **(5)**

Ambassadeurs Twelve-piece band established by Salif Keita in Mali for combining modern urban pop with indigenous African instruments and Islamic vocals. (**1**)

Ambassadeurs Internationales Name of Les Ambassadeurs after 1978, when it moved to the capital of Côte d'Ivoire. (**1**)

ambush Jamaican *salo* song type. (**2**)

amdyaz Male musicians of Morocco. (Plural, *imdyazn*.) (**6**)

ame utiwa (Japan.) Instrument of the *kabuki* offstage ensemble. (**7**)

Amhara Peoples who speak the Amharic language of Ethiopia. (**1**)

'amidab 'Standing'. In the Yemenite Jewish liturgy, prayer said while standing, consisting of a series of blessings. It forms the third part of the weekday morning service in the Yemenite Jewish liturgy. (**6**)

amirzakan Abkhazian accordion. (**8**)

amkbllf Sung poetry contest in the women's *ahwash* of Berber Morocco. (**6**)

'āmme Ordinary musicians in Persia under Nasr al-Dīn Shāh who performed light music. (**6**)

ammessad Berber singer-poert who performs for *ahidus* and *ahwash*. (**1**)

amor fino Afro-Peruvian competitive song form. (**2**)

amoureuse Country dance popular in Luxembourg. (**8**)

amssad Type of Berber *ahidus* among the Ayt Yahya involving singing and dancing by young men; cf. *hayfa*. (**6**)

amto ngere Suyá mouse ceremony. (**2**)

amyrga Tuvan hunting horn, used to imitate the mating call of a stag. (**6**)

än Kazakh term for melody. (**6**)

ana 'Mother', Turkish term for basic or fundamental meters. (**6**)

añafil Spanish long, straight trumpet. (**8**)

anak becing Buginese-Makassarese metal percussion bars. (**4**)

an dro Breton line or circle dance performed as part of a three-part suite. (**8**)

analytical records Recordings in which each performer plays separately so that parts can be more easily transcribed. (**1**)

anamisi 'One and a half': a tune type of the Cypriot *tsiattista* genre; the name refers to the number of distichs fitted to the melody. (**8**)

anamongu Bronze or iron gongs from Sumba. (**4**)

ānandalaharī Plucked stringed instrument in which the string is attached on one end to a membrane-covered resonator and on the other to a small membrane-covered pot. (**5**)

an'anevi 'Traditional' (Turkish). (**6**)

anastenaria Macedonian fire-walking healing rituals, performed on 21 May. (**8**)

anata Bolivian wooden duct flute, another term for *tarka*. (**2**)

anatolitika Anatolian (Turkish) style of Greek *rebetika*. (**8**)

anba tonèl 'Under the arbor', descriptive term for traditional rural music in Haiti. (**2**)

Andalusia (Also al-Andalus.) Geographical term for the medieval Islamic civilization in Spain. (**6**)

Andalusian North African branch of urban art music, thought to have originated in the Moorish Islamic courts of medieval Spain. (**6**)

andartika Greek patriotic songs of the left-wing partisan resistance of the 1940s. (**8**)

andhong Javanese female singer-dancer. (**4**)

andung Maranao old style of playing. (**4**)

ang (Also *anga*.) (1) Style of music; (2) complex hand gestures combined to form tala structures. (**5**)

angara Afro-Peruvian calabash idiophone with one side opened. (**2**)

angaroha Conch trumpet used during the ceremony of the bath of the royal relics in Madagascar. (**1**)

angelitos 'Little angels', songs and instrumental music for deceased infants and children. (**2**)

angkalung Shaken bamboo idiophone of Thailand, played in pitched sets. (**4**)

angklung Tuned, shaken bamboo rattles from Indonesia. (**4**)

Angkor Vat Temple complex in Cambodia, center of ancient Khmer civilization. (**4**)

angkosi Dance with cross-gender responsorial quatrain singing in Tanimbar. (**4**)

angkuoch Khmer Jew's harp of bamboo or iron. (**4**)

anglaise 'English' (French), country dance of the Low Countries. (**8**)

anglas Swedish contra dance, especially in southern and eastern Sweden. (**8**)

anglois Country dance popular in Friesland. (**8**)

angrezi baind 'English band', brass band that plays processional music in North India. (**5**)

angroti ngere Suyá wild pig ceremony. (**2**)

angsel Dramatic rhythmic break in Balinese music. (**4**)

angu'á Paraguayan double-headed membranophone. (**2**)

anhemitonic Inventory of pitches with no semitones (minor seconds). (**1**)

anibaddh 'Unbound', Hindustani ragas rendered without meter (tala). (**5**)

ánimas Spanish songs about the sufferings of souls in purgatory. (**8**)

animism Religion that personifies natural elements. (**4**)

aniri Dialogue or narrative portions of Korean *p'ansori*. (**7**)

ānjanēya vēṣa Monkey-costume dance in Karnataka. (**5**)

anju pan Seated repertoire of Korean *samul nori*. (**7**)

Anlo-Ewe Subgroup of the Ewe-speaking people of the southeast coast of Ghana. (**1**)

anninnia Cradle songs, part of the Sardinian *a tenore* repertoire. (**8**)

anonan Maranao upper gongs of the *kulintang*. (**4**)

'anqā' Medieval zither or dulcimer. (**6**)

änshi (Also *sal, seri.*) Kazakh lyric singer. (**6**)

änshilik Term for Kazakh folk song. (**6**)

ant'aek kut Korean shaman ritual for household tranquillity. (**7**)

antan Pestle used for pounding rice in Borneo. (**4**)

antara (Also *andara.*) Quechua term for single-unit panpipe in Peru, played by one person. (**2**)

antarā Second section of a Hindustani composition emphasizing the upper octave tonic. (**5**)

anthem Bahamian religious song genre closely related to the spiritual of slaves and other blacks from the southern United States. (**2**)

anthropomorphization Attribution of human form or character, frequently to musical instruments. (**1**)

antuni Genre of peasant songs reflecting the life of homeless Armenians expelled from their land by foreign invaders. (**6**)

anubandham Coda. (**5**)

anudātta Accent in Vedic recitation that normally precedes the *udātta* accent. (**5**)

anulōma Diminution in Karnatak music, by which a theme is repeated twice at double speed and four times at quadruple speed. (**5**)

anulōma-pratilōma Diminution and augmentation in Karnatak music. (**5**)

anun Maguindanao modern *binalig* rhythmic mode. (**4**)

anupallavi Second section of a Karnatak composition, following the *pallavi*. (**5**)

anuvādi (Also *anuvādī.*) Subordinate tone in raga. (**5**)

anyeiñ Burmese entertainment theater of music, women vocalists, and clowns. (**4**)

anzad (Also *anzhad; imzad.*) Tuareg one-stringed fiddle. (**1**)

Aotearoa Māori, 'Long White Cloud'. Indigenous name of the South Pacific islands that Europeans colonized and named New Zealand. (**9**)

apagado 'Stopped', guitar-strumming technique. (**2**)

àpàlà (Also *apala*.) Yoruba musical genre that originated in the Ijebu area, probably in the early 1940s. **(1, 10)**

apandur Abkhazian three-stringed plucked lute. **(8)**

apdziedāšanās Latvian antiphonal, humorous, competitive singing at weddings, with texts largely improvised. **(8)**

apesin Single-membrane cylindrical drum of the Yoruba of Nigeria. **(1)**

apidan 'One who performs magic', a theatrical troupe that emerged from the *egungun* tradition. **(1)**

apinti Maroon goblet-shaped drum derived from the *apentemma* of the Ashanti in Ghana. **(2)**

apkhertsa Abkhazian two-stringed bowed lute. **(8)**

apocope Loss of a sound or sounds at the end of a word; whispering or omitting the last syllable of a song in northern Poland. **(8)**

apoo Festival of the Brong and Effutu of Ghana, in which participants may criticize the chief. **(1)**

apsara Khmer heavenly maiden. **(4)**

aqausiq Arctic song composed by a relative at the birth of a child, consecrating a lifelong link between the two people. **(3)**

aqqayn Term for sung lyrics among Moroccan Berbers; also refers to seeds and certain nuts. **(6)**

aquaquam Ecstatic liturgical dance performed in the Monophysite Christian Church of highland Ethiopia. **(1)**

aqyn Kazakh poet-improviser with shamanistic qualities who takes part in music and poetry contests. **(6)**

aqyndyq Kazakh term for improvised composition, derived from *aqyn* 'poet-improviser'. **(6)**

arabesk (1) Form of Turkish popular music favored among "guest workers" in Germany and Roma in Kosova (Kosovo). (2) Syncretic urban popular genre, usually dated from 1969, and popular in Turkey throughout the 1970s and 1980s. **(6, 8)**

arabi Genre of Algerian popular music. **(1)**

arabies Greek dance of Asia Minor, as performed in Cyprus. **(8)**

ārādhana Celebration of the anniversary of a saint's death. **(5)**

arakk Khmer ceremony for worshiping spirits. **(4)**

arangērram (Also *arangētram*.) Debut performance. **(5)**

arap tarzı 'Arab style' (Turkish), connoting an Arab, non-Turkish tradition in twentieth-century Turkish musical discourse. **(6)**

arashvara-ashva Abkhazian harvest songs, performed during traditional feasts; *see aeag-ashva*. **(8)**

aras napat Miskitu horse-jawbone idiophone rasped or struck with a deer horn or large nail, like the *quijada*. **(2)**

ārati (1) Devotional form of collective singing; (2) clockwise, vertical circling of a flame before an image of a deity. **(5)**

Arbeterring 'Workmen's Circle', a fraternal, socialist-leaning organization among East European Jewish immigrants. **(3)**

arca (Also *arka*.) 'Follower'; in Aymara, one of the halves (female) of the *siku* and several other double-unit panpipes in the central Andes; counterpart of *ira* half, 'leader'. **(2)**

arched harp Harp of Indian antiquity with a boat-shaped resonator and curved neck. **(5)**

archéologie sonore 'Sonorous archaeology' (French), music archaeology. **(8)**

'arda (Also *'ardah*.) Warrior song and dance of the bedouin of the Arabian Peninsula. **(6)**

'arda bahriyya Dance performed by pearl fishers of the Gulf region when their ships are ready to return to shore. **(6)**

ardin Mauritanian ten- to twelve-stringed harp, traditionally played by women. **(6)**

areito (Also *areyto*.) Pre-Columbian celebratory event of the Taino Indians of the Caribbean, with music and dance. **(2)**

arèk East Javanese heartland. **(4)**

arghūl Type of double clarinet used in the Mashriq and Maghrib, often with tubes of unequal length, one of which serves as a drone. **(6)**

argismo (Also *argia*.) Sardinian spider-poisoning ritual resembling the Italian *tarantismo*. **(8)**

argul Double clarinet of southern Turkey; cf. *arghūl*. **(6)**

aria In European art music of the Baroque and later, an elaborate type of accompanied solo vocal composition, often with a memorable melody; used in opera in alternation with recitative. **(8)**

ariccantiran nāṭakam Tamil folk drama about the mythological figure Harishchandra. **(5)**

arija Melody to which rhymed couplets are set in Slavonia, Croatia. **(8)**

arinarin Basque chain dance. **(8)**

'arioi Eighteenth-century professional traveling entertainers of the Society Islands. **(9)**

Arirang One of Korea's most popular folk songs, with regional varieties. **(7)**

arisiki Tarahumara bottle gourd rattle. **(2)**

arja Balinese operetta about romance and comedy. **(4)**

arkiestry Orchestras in western Belarus. **(8)**

armailli Herdsmen in Haute-Gruyère, Switzerland, who call their cattle with melodious calls (*ayóber*). **(8)**

armonías 'Harmonies', brass-band saxhorns. **(2)**

armshell Shell cut into a ring, often decorated with suspended smaller shells and worn on the upper arm. **(9)**

Aro-Chuku oracle Final arbiter for intertribal strife among the Igbo of Nigeria. **(1)**

āroh (Also *arēhaṇa*.) Ascent of scale pitches in a raga. **(5)**

arokas Tuareg dance performed in the Agadez area of Niger. **(1)**

arpa 'Harp', diatonic harp without pedals, found in many regions of Central and South America, especially Chile, Ecuador, Mexico, Paraguay, Peru, and Venezuela; there are many regional variants. **(2, 3)**

arraial Secular Portuguese celebration beginning immediately after a religious procession and ending in the late evening; it includes performances of music and dance. **(8)**

arrasta-pé Dance music genre of northeast Brazil. **(2)**

arruada (Also *peditório, recolha de andores*.) Portuguese religious festival in which a band performs marches in front of each house in a village. **(8)**

arrullo (1) Colombian religious folk song; (2) children's game song and lullaby. **(2)**

'arruz Poetic meters that influence rhythmic patterns in Uygur (Uighur) music. **(6)**

ärsary Performance style of eastern Turkmenistan. **(6)**

ars musica 'Musical art' (Latin), music theory in the Middle Ages. **(8)**

ars nova 'New art' (Latin). In European music history, the period of the early 1300s, when complex polyphonic innovations arose, especially in France. **(8)**

ars subtilior 'Subtler art' (Latin), late-fourteenth-century complex polyphonic music. **(8)**

art Any cultural process or product that uses words, sounds, movements, materials, scents, or spaces to formalize the nonformal, much as poetry intensifies the formalization of language. **(9)**

art-composed music Often called classical music; in Nigeria, school music and church music. **(1)**

'arūbī Improvisatory vocal genre originating in the rural area around Algiers, and stemming from Andalusian repertoires. Also, a common folk song genre among Moroccan Jews. **(6)**

aruchicos Ecuadorian forceful dances. **(2)**

ārudi (Also *aruti*.) Arrival point in a Karnatak composition. **(5)**

aruding Palawan Jew's harp. **(4)**

arumba Bamboo xylophone ensemble of Sunda. **(4)**

'aruz (Also *'arūt.*) Quantitative poetic meters in Turkish, classical Arabic, and Persian poetry. **(6)**

Arya Samaj Hindu social-reform organization founded by Swami Dayananda in the early twentieth century; now powerful among the Indian diaspora populations of Trinidad and Mauritius. **(5)**

asafo Military drum ensemble in Ghana. **(10)**

asafo-kyen Talking drum in Ghana. **(10)**

asafu Dance of the Fanti of Ghana that may be performed only by men belonging to the warrior company. **(1)**

Asahi kai (Japan.) School of *tikuzen biwa* founded by Tatibanak Kyokuô (1848–1919) in 1909. **(7)**

Asakusa opera (Japan.) Operas and operettas presented in popularized, simplified form with Japanese translation in Asakusa (a downtown leisure quarter in Tôkyô) during the 1920s. **(7)**

āśān 'Preceptor' in Kerala. **(5)**

Asante *See* Ashanti.

Asantehene Paramount ruler of a confederation of provincial chiefs in Ghana. **(1)**

asāre Music for the rice-transplanting season in Nepal. **(5)**

a sa seria (Also *boghe'e notte.*) Songs in slow tempo based on serious themes in Sardinian *a tenore* singing. **(8)**

a să văji Judgment of how well two *strigături* go together in Maramureş, Romania. **(8)**

Asen An Akan-speaking people of Ghana. **(1)**

asæzaghu (Also *asɔso*) Berta calabash rattle. **(1)**

āsh Early-morning gathering of men for food and music at Central Asian weddings, a typical site for the performance of *maqām.* **(6)**

aṣḥāb al-ghinā' al-'arabī 'Advocates of Arab music', in ninth-century discussions with (*aṣḥāb al-mūsīqī*) 'advocates of Greek music theory'. **(6)**

aṣḥāb al-mūsīqī 'Advocates of Greek music theory'; cf. *aṣḥāb al-ghinā' al-'arabī.* **(6)**

Ashanti (Also *Asante.*) An Akan-speaking people of Ghana. **(1)**

'āsheq (Also *ashiq, 'ashiq, aşık, aşıq.*) 'Lover', bard or minstrel who performs folk poetry and narrative song, found in many parts of Turkey and elsewhere. **(6)**

Ashkenazim Israeli Jews of European heritage. **(6)**

asht prahar Special sessions of *kīrtan* singing in Orissa, sometimes lasting twenty-four hours. **(5)**

ashugh Professional musician of Armenia, replacing the traditional *gusan.* The *ashugh* has the same social role and professional character as the *gusan,* but the form and content

of the music and some features of the performance differ. **(6)**

Ashura Shi'ite ceremony commemorating the martyrdom of the saints Hasan and Husayn in 680 C.E., observed in most Shi'ite communities. **(6)**

aşık *See* '*āsheq.* **(6)**

aşikò Yoruba dance-drumming style of early *jùjú,* performed mainly by Christian boys' clubs. **(1)**

aṣīl 'Authentic', 'pure', 'unmixed', 'possessing roots' (*rīshe*); a central term, for example, in Persian discourse on *sonnati* 'traditional' music. **(6)**

aşıq *See* '*āsheq.* **(6)**

aşıq havası Short lyric love poem of Iranian Azerbaijan. **(6)**

asirai (Japan.) Fluid playing style without defined rhythmic correlations between instruments or between instruments and voice. **(7)**

asirai huki (Japan.) Playing the flute in *asirai* style. **(7)**

asirai uti (Japan.) Beating an instrument in *asirai* style. **(7)**

āsirvādam (Also *asi.*) 'Blessings', 'good wishes', or 'prosperity', in Tamil; also, contemporary term for Pentecostal or evangelical theology promising rewards in heaven for those who are saved. **(5)**

asli langgam Modern Malay song genre with *biola* (violin). **(4)**

ason Haitian gourd rattle covered with beads. **(2)**

asonko Percussion logs played to accompany recreational music by the Akan of Ghana. **(1)**

asoso Handheld Sudanese rattle. **(1)**

assakalabu (Also *aghalabo.*) Tuareg gourd upturned in a basin of water and struck with sticks. **(1)**

assergig 'Trembling', dance movement in the *ahidus* of the Ayt Brahim (Moroccan Berbers). **(6)**

ass-pipe Car-exhaust tube of the Virgin Islands played like a tuba, often used as a bass instrument. **(2)**

astāī (Also *sthāī.*) 'Stable', the first line or section of a composition. **(5)**

astalske pesme 'Table songs', café songs in Vojvodina, Serbia. **(8)**

aṣṭapadī (Also *aṣṭapadi.*) Eight-stanza song form used by Jayadeva in the *Gīta Govinda.* **(5)**

astara-n-ighariwn 'Shoulder walk', women's dance interpolated into the Moroccan Berber warrior dance *taskiwin.* **(6)**

astūti Music played at shrines in Nepal. **(5)**

'aṭābā Popular folk song genre of the Mashriq, similar to the *mawwāl.* In Palestinian wedding celebrations, it is a semi-

improvisatory genre for sung poetic contests. **(6)**

'aṭābā al-nashid Type of *'aṭābā* featuring song duels. **(6)**

'ataba and mijana Improvised sung folk poetry, with alternation of metric and nonmetric sections. **(3)**

atabales (1) Large Nicaraguan and Guatemalan drums the size and shape of standard snare drums but made of wood; (2) longdrum music and instruments associated with saints' festivals; (3) single- or double-headed kettledrums. **(2)**

atabaque Brazilian and Uruguayan conical single-headed drum. **(2)**

atanatra Xylophone in Madagascar that consists of planks of wood resting on one of the players' thighs. **(1)**

ātata Category of single-headed drums, as well as drums played with the hand, in the Buddhist *pañcatūrya nāda* system. **(5)**

ātatavitata Category of stringed drums; also, drums played with both hands and sticks, in the *pañcatūrya nāda* system. **(5)**

atatsaagara-ashva Abkhazian wedding songs, performed during traditional feasts. **(8)**

aṭavu Dance steps in Tamil Nadu. **(5)**

Atengenoba Summer ritual celebrated in the mountain districts of eastern Georgia with the sacrifice of sheep and the performance of circle dances. **(8)**

a tenore A secular polyphonic singing style of Sardinia. **(8)**

atenteben Bamboo flute played by Akan peoples of Ghana. **(1)**

Atharvaveda Collection of magical formulas and spells; one of the four religious and cultural texts (Vedas) of the Vedic Aryans. **(5)**

athuṇ (Also *attan.*) National Pakhtun dance. **(5)**

atışma Song dueling by Turkish minstrels. **(6)**

ātin āyi 'Teacher-mother', female carrier of religious and spiritual traditions in Uzbekistan and Tajikistan; the term *ātin-bibi* 'teacher-grandmother' is also found. **(6)**

atitish Berta dried-fruit leg-tied rattle. **(1)**

atlarchopa Abkhazian healing songs, performed during traditional feasts. **(8)**

Atman World Soul. **(5)**

ato biki (Japan.) Instrumental postlude of a song. **(7)**

ato za (Japan.) Rear section of the main stage of *nô,* for instrumentalists. **(7)**

atonalism Musical style in which no single tonality is dominant and each tone receives equal weight. **(1)**

Atoni Predominant ethnic group in West Timor. **(4)**

ator Bontok men's sleeping and meeting place. **(4)**

at-raban Handheld frame drum in Sri Lanka. (5)

atsiagbekɔ Genre of dancing performed in Ghana. (1)

attan Pashtun dance considered a national expression of Afghanistan. (5)

åttondelspolskor Swedish *polska*, in eighth-note rhythms. (8)

atumpan Asante single-headed barrel drums played in pairs tuned a perfect fourth apart. (1)

aukan' e 'Helloning', Russian solo lament, sung by women to birds in the forest. (8)

aulos Ancient Greek conical double-reed aerophone, typically played in pairs by one player. (8)

aural perception Listening that allows into the conscious mind only a useful fraction of signals. (1)

auroras Spanish songs to call people to the rosary. (8)

Austroasiatic Language family including Khmer, Vietnamese, and Senoi. (4)

Austropop Term applied since the 1960s to dialect-sung Austrian pop music. (8)

auto Early religious musical drama and allegorical or religious play throughout the colonial Americas, used by priests for teaching about Christianity. (2)

autoharp String instrument similar to a zither, used as accompaniment in folk and country and western music. (3)

autos sacramentales Short Spanish religious dramas typically performed on religious feast days and including music and dance. (3)

avanaddha vādya Musical-instrument category in the *Nāṭyaśāstra* referring to membranophones. (5)

avanaddha varga Drum ensemble associated with performances of Sanskrit drama. (5)

avaroh (Also *avarōhaṇa*.) Descent of scale pitches in a raga. (5)

āvartan (Also *āvarta*.) One complete cycle of a tala. (5)

avaz Near Eastern term used in Albania and Montenegro to name performances. (8)

āvāz Melody, mode; singing governed by the quantitative poetic meters of classical Persian poetry; an instrumental solo based on appropriate sections of the Persian *radīf*; one of five or more secondary systems in Persian art music. (6)

avkoritiki 'From Avkorou village', tune type within the Cypriot *tsiattista* genre. (8)

avtorskie pesni 'Authored songs', popular Russian songs distributed as self-published cassette tapes. (8)

awai Waiãpi ankle shaker. (2)

'awālim 'Learned women'. Women's wedding party. (Singular, *'ālima*.) (6)

awedeng Bontok Jew's harp. (4)

āwīhā Palestinian wedding song, performed by a woman and responded to with ululation by other guests. (6)

awit Metrical romances of Christians and Muslims, recited on melodic formulas. (4)

awitan Solo section of *subli* performance in Philippines. (4)

'awj (Also *awdj*, *'awdj*.) 'Apogee', point of culmination in a musical phrase. Also refers to one of the major notes of the Arab fundamental scale. (6)

awlād il-kār 'People of the trade', term used by the performers of Muḥammad 'Alī Street in Cairo to describe themselves. (6)

axatsevu Ewe music dominated by rattles. (1)

axé Brazilian popular music genre; (2) Yoruba word for the vital spiritual force of Candomblé. (2)

ayacachtli Náhuatl name for a gourd or gourd-shaped rattle, made from clay or gold. (2)

ayai Cambodian repartee singing accompanied by a small ensemble, sometimes performed by Cambodians in the United States. (3)

ayak Turkish term for mode; cf. *makam*. (6)

ayaq 'Foot, knee, leg' (Turkic), cadence or return to the initial register of an Azerbaijani *muğam*; the lowest note in a tetrachord. (6)

ayarachi Peruvian panpipe tradition subdivided into three different groups of instruments tuned to the octave. (2)

ayaye Cambodian village vocal repartee with instrumental ensemble. (4)

ayidewoh Performer who dances at Igede funerals in Nigeria while singing in ways likened to a bird. (1)

āyīn (Also *mukabbele*.) Ritual of a *tarikat*, performed at set times and on set days, often accompanied by music. The Mevlevī *āyīn* had the most elaborate musical compositions of all the Ottoman *tarikatlar*. (6)

ayīnhān Chanter of the Mevlevī *āyīn*. (6)

āyīn-i cem' 'Ritual of unity' of the Alevi and Bektaşi religious groups. (6)

ayô (Japan.) Folk songs in the Yaeyama Islands that pray for a fruitful year, a safe voyage, or rain; primarily sung at festivals. (7)

ayóber Melodious cattle calls, sung by herdsmen in Haute-Gruyère, Switzerland. (8)

ayotl Náhuatl name for a tortoiseshell idiophone struck with antlers. (2)

ayudantes 'Helpers', backup singers for Yuma social dance music. (2)

Ayuthaya Capital of Siam from 1350 to 1767. (4)

'ayyāla Official tribal dance of the Emirates. (6)

ayyeng Bontok men's ritual antiphonal song. (4)

azan (Also *adzan*, *adhān*.) Muslim call to prayer. (1, 4, 6)

Azande (1) A people living in the Central African Republic and Zaïre; (2) a people of southern Sudan, living south of the Bonga. (1)

azar Abkhazian funeral songs, performed during traditional feasts. (8)

azel (Plural, *izlan*.) Tuareg air composed for performance on the *anzad*. (1)

azhveipshaar-ashva Abkhazian hunting songs, performed during traditional feasts; *see aerg*. (8)

'āzī Omani song of praise. (6)

azri Genre of modern Moroccan popular music. (1)

azuma asobi Japanese genre of court music and dance of indigenous origin. (7)

azuma ryû (Japan.) Two-stringed (*nigen*) *kin*; two-stringed zither and its music created by Tôsya Rosen (1830–1889). (7)

'Azūziyya Tunisian Sufi brotherhood. (6)

B-52 Drum made from a 55-gallon oil drum. (2)

baakisimba National dance of the Baganda, most commonly performed for feasts. (1)

ba'al tokeah 'Master of blowing' (Hebrew), community specialist who plays the shofar. (8)

baa wéhai Yaqui idiophone made with a large gourd placed closed side up in a container of water and struck with a stick. (2)

baayii Hausa term for slaves. (1)

baba One-stringed struck bamboo idiochord of Flores. (4)

babalaô Brazilian 'diviner' of initiation rite. (2)

babalorixá Female temple leader in Brazilian Candomblé. (2)

babandil (1) Maguindanao medium-size bossed gong; (2) Subanen suspended gong. (4)

babarang Street performance in Cirebon. (4)

BaBenzele A Pygmy people of Central Africa. (1)

baboula Antillean membranophone constructed from a tree trunk or barrel. (2)

bắc One of two modal systems in Vietnam. (4)

bacha Traditional Central Asian boy dancer who dresses in women's garb, banned under Soviet rule. (6)

bacha naghma Muslim folk-dance theatricals of Kashmir. (5)

backbeat Emphasis placed on beats 2 and 4, usually by the snare drum. (3)

bād Notebooks in which Vaishnav singers keep their songs. (5)

bada mingqu (China.) The "eight great famous pieces" in *Jiangnan sizhu*. (7)

badéde Functional sung poetry from Lombok and Sumbawa. **(4)**

badhan 'Jester' who entertains with rhymes and songs at Jewish weddings. **(6)**

badhanim Jewish musical professionals (each a combination of trickster, acrobat, and jester), who often performed at weddings. **(8)**

badiw Ibaloy antiphonal singing. **(4)**

bagad Breton *biniou* and *bombarde* band, modeled after Scottish pipe bands. **(8)**

bagdaduri Georgian dance accompanied by Middle Eastern instruments, such as the *zurna*, the *duduki*, and the *doli*. **(8)**

baghalbīn Bagpipe played by the Qalandar in Punjab, Pakistan. **(5)**

bağlama Long-necked, fretted Turkish folk lute; *see saz*. Also, plucked lute of the Turkish *saz* family, used in Greek *rebetika*; *see bakllama*. **(6, 8)**

bago Maranao new style of playing. **(4)**

baggy See *bakhshī*. **(6)**

baguala Argentine song with or without allusive texts. **(2)**

baha (1) Grenadian aerophone, a 1.5-meter-long cardboard tube; (2) St. Lucian tubular trumpet made from wood or plastic. **(2)**

bahanarotu 'Owner of *bahana*', Warao shaman in charge of the eastern cosmic realm. **(2)**

baho Bass voice in the Philippines. **(4)**

bahr-e osul Term for rhythmic modes in Iranian classical music. **(6)**

Bahurūpi 'One with many disguises', professional male entertainer of Maharashtra. **(5)**

bahutva 'Strength'; strong tones in a Hindustani raga. **(5)**

bāī Professional female singer. **(5)**

bai (1) In Japan, category of Buddhist chant (*syômyô*) for purifying and ornamenting a hall. (2) Spectacular Palauan structure, profusely decorated with carved and painted interior beams and gables illustrating events and symbolizing wealth. **(7, 9)**

baian (1) Russian version of the Ukrainian accordion; (2) Russian and Belarusan fully chromatic button accordion. **(8)**

baião Brazilian social dance music from Northeast Brazil typically played by trios of accordion, triangle, and *zabumba* drum. **(2)**

baiduska Greek Thracian dance in 5/8 or 6/8 time. **(8)**

bailā (Also *bayala*.) Popular Sinhalese music and dance genre in Sri Lanka incorporating Portuguese rhythms. **(5)**

baìla Jamaican spirit possession and recreational songs. **(2)**

bailadeira Portuguese Goan term for *devadāsī*. **(5)**

bailaderos Colombian entertainment businesses established in private homes. **(2)**

bailados Afro-Brazilian country dramatic dances. **(2)**

bailanta (Also *bailable*.) Argentine large dance hall. **(2)**

baile (Spanish.) 'Dance', 'dancing', 'ball', ballet'. In the Hispanic Americas, term referring to dozens of costumed folkloric events. **(2, 8)**

baile de venado Deer dance performed by the Yaqui Indians during the Easter season. **(3)**

Baisākhī Punjabi harvest festival featuring the *bhangra* dance. **(5)**

bai si Spirit ritual common to Thailand, Laos, and Burma. **(4)**

bāj Playing style or lineage in Hindustani instrumental music and drumming. **(5)**

bāja (1) Instrumental music in Uttar Pradesh. (2) Musical instrument, ensemble, or music in Nepal. **(5)**

Bajan (1) Form of expressive communication combining African grammar and English; (2) term used locally for a person from Barbados. **(2)**

bajé Tumtum double-headed drum accompanying dance. **(1)**

bajista *Bajo sexto* or *bajo quinto* player. **(3)**

bajo 'Bass'. (1) Bolivian baritone horn; (2) *bajo de caja*, one-stringed harp similar to the washtub bass; (3) *bajo sexto*, large twelve-stringed Mexican guitar. **(2)**

bajo de uñas (1) Fretted, flat-backed lute with four strings that are either plucked or struck with a mallet; similar to the orchestral string bass in shape and function. (2) In the Philippines, bass guitar. **(3, 4)**

bajón 'Big bass', (1) Bolivian multiple-tubed trumpet; (2) Purépecha bassoon; (3) *bajones*, 'big basses', large rafted trumpets of the Moxo. **(2)**

bajo quinto *Bajo sexto* without the sixth (E/e) string pair. **(3)**

Bajram Muslim calendric feast, celebrated in Macedonia and Albania. **(8)**

bajo sexto Guitar with six double courses of steel strings, used in Texas-Mexican *conjunto* music. **(3)**

bajs Double bass of northwestern Croatia. **(8)**

baka aapa 'Cane harp', Yaqui mouth bow. **(2)**

baka-baka Double-headed drum of the Ternate *kulintang* ensemble. **(4)**

bakánawi Tarahumara curing ceremony. **(2)**

bakashot Night vigils held during the winter by Sephardi Jews; also refers to sacred poems sung before morning prayers by Moroccan and Spanish Jews before 1492. **(6)**

bakhshī (Also, in Turkmen, *baggy*.) In Iranian Khorasan and Turkmenistan, a bard who performs a traditional repertoire and, in some cases, original songs, accompanying himself or herself on the *dūtār*. **(6)**

bakllama Near Eastern long-necked plucked lute, played in Albania during the Ottoman period. **(8)**

bakohi Warao trumpet made of bamboo, cow horn, or both, used as a substitute for a conch-shell trumpet. **(2)**

bal (1) Berta one-pitched bamboo flute without fingerholes; (2) Ingassana nuptial and harvest-festival music. **(1)**

bal folk Folk-dance nights in the Low Countries. **(8)**

bal granmoun Martinique old-time evening balls. **(2)**

bala Mande xylophone with wooden keys fastened to a frame of gourd resonators. **(1)**

balabaika (Eastern Ukrainian.) *Balalaika*. **(8)**

bālābān (Also *düdük, mey*.) Aerophone with a cylindrical bore and a large double reed. It accompanies the *aşiq* in northwest Iran. **(6)**

bālah Yemeni dance involving poetic competition. **(6)**

balabolo Basic Mandinka xylophone pattern. **(1)**

balada Commercially called Latin pop, can be considered the continuation of a long-standing pan-Hispanic tradition of guitar-based romantic song. **(2)**

balade Romanian epic ballads that flourished between the sixteenth and nineteenth centuries; also known as *cîntece bătrînești* 'old-time songs'. **(8)**

baladī 'Folk', 'of the folk'; common 8-beat rhythmic pattern in Arab folk music; also known as *maşmūdī şaghīr*. Also refers to an Egyptian musical genre evocative of rural life. **(6)**

balafo (*Balaphon*.) African xylophone. **(3)**

balafon See *bala*. **(1)**

balakadri From the French *bal à quadrilles*, in Martinique, fashion on which *zouk* was based. **(2)**

balalaika Russian-Balkan plucked fretted lute with a triangle-shaped resonator; Russian three-stringed lute with a triangular sound box, also found in Ukraine. **(3, 8)**

balangi Manding xylophone with fifteen to nineteen keys. **(1)**

balawas Samawan sung poetry. **(4)**

bali (1) (Also *baali*.) Berta percussion sticks, carried over the right shoulder and struck with a cow horn. (2) Name of an important cluster of rituals associated with Sri Lanka's old religion. **(1, 5)**

balikata Tiruray parables. **(4)**

balingbing Kalinga bamboo buzzer. **(4)**

balitaw Cebu poetic song debate. **(4)**

ballad Narrative song in oral tradition, but, with the spread of literacy, also transmitted in printed form. **(8)**

Volume Key: **6**, Middle East; **7**, East Asia; **8**, Europe; **9**, Australia and the Pacific Islands; **10**, The World's Music.

ballad meter English poetic meter, consisting of eight-syllable lines in four-line stanzas; also, long common meter. **(8)**

ballad opera Originating in eighteenth-century England, a comic play with songs in which new texts are set to familiar tunes. **(3)**

ballada 'Ballads', a type of Hungarian folk song. **(8)**

ballade French fixed verse form, usually consisting of three stanzas with recurrent rhymes, an envoi, and an identical refrain for each part; also, a musical composition in this form. **(8)**

ballarella Variant of the saltarello. **(8)**

ballata Corsican dance once performed around a corpse; known in southern Corsica as *abbaddata*. **(8)**

ballet (1) Theatrical art form combining conventional movements, costumes, scenery, and music usually to narrate a story or convey a theme; (2) 'ballad', a broadside in Ireland. **(8)**

ballet folklórico 'Folkloric ballet', often a Latin American country's professional troupe that performs nationalistic or ideological reinterpretions of rural music and dance. **(2)**

ballets de cour Lavish commemorative spectacles hosted by monarchs and aristocrats during the French Renaissance, with elaborate scenery, costumes, music, poetry, and dance. **(8)**

balletti (Singular, *balletto*.) Social dances presented in Italian Renaissance courts. **(8)**

balletto polacco A name of the mazurka outside Poland. **(8)**

balon (Also *balun*.) Dance of the northern Adriatic zone of Croatia. **(8)**

ballos Venetian-influenced dance of the Aegean Islands, Greece. **(8)**

ballu Sardinian line dance; when performed in a circle, it is known as *ballu tundu*. **(8)**

bal naggaro 'Flute drum', Berta flute-and-drum ensemble and its music. **(1)**

bals Breton figure dances. **(8)**

balsería Friendly week-long, all-male competition between two Guaymí communities. **(2)**

balungan (Java.) Main melody. **(10)**

bam 'Above' (Persian). On an *'ud* or another lute, the string or course of strings that lies closest to the player's head and produces the lowest pitches. **(6)**

Bamana (Also Bambara.) A northern Mande-speaking people of Mali. **(1)**

bamba (1) Masakin double-headed drum accompanying dance; (2) stamped tubes of Bonaire that accompany the feasts of saints John and Peter; (3) large, single-headed standing drum of Sumba. **(1, 2, 4)**

Bambara Trade language of Senegal, developed from the Mande subfamily of the Niger-Congo family. **(1)**

bambaro (Also *bamboro*.) Hausa and Songhai lamellophone. **(1)**

bambòch Haitian informal party. **(2)**

bamboo band Band of guitars and tuned lengths of bamboo, whose open ends players strike with a rubber thong or thongs in patterns evoking a boogie-woogie bass. **(9)**

bamboula Extinct or reconstructed tradition of African-style dance, drumming, and song associated with St. Thomas. **(2)**

bambuco (1) Colombian "national" song and pursuit couple dance genre in compound duple (6/8 + 3/4) meter, musically characterized by syncopation and performed most often on the *tiple* as the main instrument. (2) Mexican romantic, slow, often melancholic vocal genre. (3) Ecuadorian pursuit dance, most common of the *currulao* genre. **(2)**

bambúes Set of bamboo tubes played in interlocking fashion. **(2)**

bambu gila Men's trance dance with bamboo poles on Ambon. **(4)**

bambulá (Also *bamboulá*.) Pan-Caribbean *velación* dance. **(2)**

bambulia Songs performed collectively by devotees in Madhya Pradesh. **(5)**

BaMbuti A Pygmy people living in the Ituri forest of Zaïre. **(1)**

bambūtiyya (From English *bumboat*.) Dance of the Suez Canal Zone, possibly of Western origin, accompanied by the *simsimiyya*, *riqq*, and *darabukka*. **(6)**

ban (1) Small Mandinka kettledrum played with one stick. (2) Chinese hollow wood block instrument; wooden clappers. (3) (China.) Beat, tempo, or meter. (4) (Japan.) Set of short *tikuzen biwa* interludes. (5) (India.) Ritual bath. **(1, 3, 10)**

bānam Bowed string instrument of Orissa with a coconut resonator and a bamboo neck. **(5)**

banatske gajde Large three-voiced bagpipe of Vojvodina, Serbia. **(8)**

banbou *See vaksin.* **(2)**

banci Bidayuh large-mouth flute. **(4)**

Banda Culture group in the Central African Republic. **(1)**

banda (1) 'Band', usually either a brass band, a large ensemble of mixed European-derived wind instruments, or any ensemble of aerophones and percussion instruments. **(2)**

banda (1) Brass band, wind band. (2) In Mexico, particular regional musical styles and repertoires; and, in the 1990s, a highly popular commercial music based on regional *bandas*. (3) Brass band of Ticino, in Italian-speaking Switzerland. **(2, 3, 8)**

banda communale Italian municipal wind band. **(8)**

banda de música Spanish municipal wind band. **(8)**

banda-orquesta Synonymous terms for Tejano dance bands similar in instrumentation to Anglo-American swing bands. **(3)**

banda sinaloense Performing style from the state of Sinaloa in Mexico. **(3)**

banda típica Early-twentieth-century Texas-Mexican string band. **(3)**

bandanā Song of entreaty addressed to a specific deity in Uttar Pradesh. **(5)**

bande (Also *goslarije*.) Slovenian band of two to four violins, one or two violas, one or two clarinets, a bass, and a cimbalon. **(8)**

bandella Small *banda* of Ticino, in Italian-speaking Switzerland. **(8)**

bānde pāther 'Musician's theater', folk theatricals of Kashmir. **(5)**

bandiirii Hausa set of drums including a single-headed circular frame drum and a bowl-shaped drum. **(1)**

bandīr (Also *bendīr*.) Large circular Maghribi frame drum with snares. **(6)**

bandiś 'Composition' in Hindustani music. **(5)**

bandola (1) Relative of the mandolin and direct descendant of the Spanish *bandurria*; (2) in Colombia, a teardrop-shaped or round lute with sixteen metal strings in four courses of three strings and two courses of two strings; (3) four-stringed pear-shaped lute chordophone; (4) in Chile, an hourglass-shaped lute with four courses of four strings each. **(2)**

bandolim (From Italian *mandolino*.) Small double-course Brazilian chordophone. **(2)**

bandolín Small five-stringed, triple-course plucked lute of Ecuador. **(2)**

bandoneón Argentine button accordion used in tango music, invented in Germany by Heinrich Band in 1854 and brought to Buenos Aires about 1890; particularly popular in the revival of Argentine tango music in the late twentieth century. **(2, 3)**

bandura (Also *kobza*.) Ukrainian multistringed lute-zither. **(8)**

bandurria (1) Guatemalan twelve-stringed lute. (2) Sixteen- to twenty-stringed chordophone shaped like a mandolin. (3) (Also *bandurría*.) Fretted, flat-backed plucked lute with fourteen strings in six courses used for soprano and alto voices in the *rondalla*, found in Spain and Latin America. (4) European pear-shaped plucked lute, found in the Philippines. **(2, 3, 4)**

bang Islamic call to prayer, Philippines. **(4)**

bangdi (China.) High-pitch bamboo flute that is a fourth higher than the *qudi*. **(7)**

banggi Iloilo song debate on love. **(4)**

bangibang Ifugao wooden percussion bars. **(4)**

BaNgombe A Mongo people of Zaïre. **(1)**

bangqiang (China.) 'Group melody'; refers to melodies sung by a soloist and a chorus. **(7)**

bangsawan Theater shows of the Malay nobility, derived from Persia. (4)

bangsi End-blown bamboo flute of Sumatra. (4)

bangu Type of Chinese drum. (3)

bangwe Equiheptatonically tuned Sena zither. (1)

banhu (China.) Wooden-faced spiked bowed lute popularized in the northwest regions. (7)

bāni Stylistic performance traits unique to an individual artist. (5)

bani 'Bass', the lowest part in Georgian three-part singing, the only part traditionally sung by a group. (8)

banja Name for calypso before the 1930s. (2)

banjo Fretted, plucked-lute chordophone with circular membranophone resonator, of African origin, with four or five strings on a neck attached to a drumlike body; depending on the number of strings, played with a plectrum or finger picks. (2, 3)

Bankalawa A plains Jawara people of northern Nigeria. (1)

Bänkelsänger German semiprofessional ballad-eers. (8)

bāṅkiā Brass trumpet played in Rajasthan. (5)

banku-raban Large frame drum of Sri Lanka. (5)

bano Ankle bracelets with metal jingles, worn in West Timor. (4)

banqiang (China.) Vocal melody regulated by a variety of rhythm and meter or clapper patterns. (7)

banqiangti (China.) System for setting texts in which the music functions as an element subsidiary to the text. (7)

banshi bianzou (China.) Beat variation. (7)

bansiki (Japan.) (1) Note corresponding to the pitch B; (2) mode in *nô* instrumental music. (7)

bansiki tyô (Japan.) *Gagaku* scale built on the note *bansiki* (B). (7)

bånsuller Norwegian lullabies. (8)

bānsurī (Also *bānsī*.) North Indian bamboo flute. (5)

Bantous Brass-heavy big band that became publicly acclaimed in Congo and Zaïre in the 1950s and 1960s. (1)

Bantu Group of more than 500 languages in central and southern Africa. (1)

banzipu (China.) Half character notation. (7)

banzjó Banjo of the Netherland Antilles. (2)

Baoulé An Akan-speaking people of Ghana. (1)

bapa Narratives and genealogies in ritual language of Roti. (4)

bapang Ostinato pattern accompanying animal dances in Bali. (4)

bapla 'Marriage', Santal marriage songs. (5)

bappe Senegalese five-stringed plucked lute. (1)

baquetas Guatemalan marimba mallets. (2)

baquiné (Also *baquiní*.) Ecuadorian, Dominican, and Puerto Rican festive wake, celebrated at the death of an infant or young child. (2)

bar mitzvah 'Son of the law' (Hebrew), a Jewish boy who reaches his thirteenth birthday; a celebration, with music, recognizing a boy as a bar mitzvah. (8)

bara (1) Large Miskitu flutes related to the *bratara*; (2) two- to four-holed Sumu bamboo flutes with mouthpieces formed from beeswax. (2)

bar'a (Also *bara'*.) 'To surpass oneself', 'excellence', 'bravery'; men's warrior dance of the high plateaus of Yemen. (6)

baraban Large two-headed Polish drum; Ukrainian field drum. (8)

baraban z talerkami Belarusan cylindrical double-headed drum with a brass cymbal attached to the frame. (8)

barabanče Macedonian snare drum. (8)

bārahamāsā Twelvemonth song of Uttar Pradesh; the primary theme is a husband's separation from his wife. (5)

baṛā khyāl Hindustani *khyāl* performance at a slow or medium speed. (5)

barang Javanese pitch name. (4)

baranung Lowland Chăm single-headed drum. (4)

barapan kebo Sumbawan dance based on water buffalos' movements. (4)

barbāṭ (Plural, *barābit*.) Ancient Greek term for a lyre, an early precursor of the *'ūd*. (6)

barbiton (Also *barbitos*.) Ancient Greek large lyre, used to accompany erotic songs. (8)

barcarole Venetian gondoliers' song, usually in 6/8 or 12/8 time. (8)

bard Poet-singer of heroes and their feats; applied in Eastern Europe to any of numerous modern urban singer-songwriters. (8)

bardo Recitation during the first nine days of mourning to help the deceased separate himself or herself from the earthly world. (2)

bargham (Also *barghum*.) Cow horn used in Omani tribal traditions. (6)

barikata Maguindanao modern style of playing. (4)

bārike Barrel-shaped, skin-covered instrument in the *caudike* tradition of Karnataka. (5)

baris Men's temple dance of Bali. (4)

barmasa (Also *choumasa*.) Songs describing the rainy season in Madhya Pradesh. (5)

barongan Trance dance, prelude to *kuda kepang*. (4)

Baroque In European music history, the period from about 1600 to 1750. (8)

baroud (Also *berzana*.) North African men's dance with guns, climaxed by synchronized shooting toward the earth. (1)

barrio 'Suburb' (Spanish.) (2)

Barundi Kirundi-speaking people of Burundi. (1)

barva-lur Extant Iron Age animal-horn instrument of Sweden. (8)

barwal (Plural, *brāwal*, *barāwīl*.) One of the canonical rhythms of the *ma'lūf*, commonly used by the 'Īsāwiyya; also refers to a Maghribi vocal genre using this rhythm. (6)

barwal nūba Shorter version of the Libyan *nūba*. (6)

Barzanji Biographical and praise songs about Muhammad. (4)

bas (Also *tanbourin*.) Haitian frame drum of low pitch. (2)

bas (1) 'Bass', the lowest voice in Slovene three-part singing. (2) Ukrainian usually three-stringed bass, about the size and shape of a violoncello. (3) Short for *na bas*, a singing style of the Dinaric Alps and Pannonia. (2, 8)

basakk Khmer village theater genre of Chinese origin. (4)

basal Palawan gong ensemble. (4)

bāsān-kōb (Also *basamkub*.) Five-stringed lyre of the Hadendowa of eastern Sudan. (1)

Basant Spring festival in North India and Pakistan. (5)

basarake Titled Nyamalthu men of the former Bauchi State in Nigeria. (1)

basavāṭa gangettinavaru (Also *kolē basava*.) Street performance involving a cow and a musician, in Karnataka. (5)

basavi (Also *dēvadāsi*.) Female temple dancer in Karnataka and Tamil Nadu. (5)

basetla Belarusan bass fiddle. (8)

bashraf 'Prelude', 'to go before' (from Persian *pīsh-row*); introductory instrumental form, of Turkish origin, found in various Arab suite forms and characterized by a long, complex rhythmic cycle. (6)

basiranje (Also *na ariju*, *na bas*.) 'Bassing', Serbian singing style in which the lower voice sings in parallel thirds with the melody and forms a perfect fifth at the cadence. (8)

basīṭ 'Simple', section of light music in the classical *nūba* repertoire. (6)

basoi Maloh obsolete musical bow with resonator. (4)

bass Large double-headed cylindrical drum played in Trinidad with *tāssā* drums. (5)

Bassa A people of south-central Liberia. (1)

bassa Lowest voice in Corsican *paghjelle* that implies tonal harmony. (8)

Volume Key: **6**, Middle East; **7**, East Asia; **8**, Europe; **9**, Australia and the Pacific Islands; **10**, The World's Music.

bassgeige Bass violin in ensembles of Italian southern Tyrol until World War I.   (8)

basso continuo In European art music of the Baroque period, one or more instruments that within an ensemble furnish a partially improvised accompaniment to voices or other instruments; also known simply as continuo.   (8)

basta (Also *bista*.) Traditional Iraqi strophic song, often used in Iraqi *maqām*.   (6)

bastau Introductory section of a Kazakh epic tale.   (6)

bastel (Also *seoe*.) Water drum made from half of a large gourd placed open side down in a water-filled tub and played with the hands.   (2)

bàtá Yoruba ensemble of conical, double-headed drums, associated with the thunder god Şango.   (1)

batel Repetitive pattern accompanying fight scenes in Bali.   (4)

bātere Kiribati short song with interpretive movements, adapted from the Tokelauan *fātele*.   (9)

bati (Japan.) Plectrum.   (7)

batidorcitos 'Little noisemakers', ratchets.   (2)

batik Patterned, waxed, and dyed cloth from Indonesia.   (4)

batil Malay overturned brass bowl hit with sticks.   (4)

batimen (Japan.) Broad strip of leather that protects the *biwa* soundboard from the plectrum.   (7)

bātin 'Internal', 'hidden', 'esoteric'.   (6)

batlejka Belarusan folk puppet theater, having elements of *skamarochi* (minstrel) singing.   (8)

batonebo Two- and three-part curing song for whooping cough and the measles, sung by women in western Georgia; cf. *iavnana*.   (8)

battaglia (Also *battalia*.) German Baroque programmatic battle pieces.   (8)

batu Second dance number in an *oḍissi* performance.   (5)

batucada (1) Brazilian percussion ensemble and percussive dance music; (2) drumming session or performance of a samba percussion ensemble.   (2)

ba tum-tum Gumuz women's vocal ensemble accompanied with beating on gourds and clapping.   (1)

Batuque (From Portuguese *bater* 'to hit'.) (1) Afro-Brazilian religion and dance in Pará, São Paulo, and Rio Grande do Sul states; (2) *batuque*, Afro-Brazilian round dance of Angolese or Congolese origin; (3) Argentine variant of Afro-Brazilian religion.   (2)

batyrlar zhyry Kazakh epic tales about heroes, the performance of which may be accompanied by narrative songs and instrumental genres.   (6)

Bāul Mystical sect of Bengal, noted for its unique religious and musical practices.   (5)

baut-baut Epic songs sung in processions of boats on Kait.   (4)

Bavanīlu Telugu narrative singers; in performance, they usually play the *jamikiḷi*.   (5)

bavugu !Kung bamboo stamping tubes.   (1)

baxši Turkmen or Karakalpak epic singer; cf. *bakhshī*.   (6)

baya Mandinka entertainment song that advises against deception or going behind another's back.   (1)

bāyak Musician who plays the *mridang* and cymbal and accompanies the presentation of *pala*, in Orissa.   (5)

bayamonés Style of *seis* from Bayamón, Puerto Rico.   (2)

bāyaṅ (Also *ḍagga*.) Larger, lower-pitched left drum of the tabla pair.   (5)

Bayete Internationally acclaimed South African pan-African-playing group of the mid-1990s.   (1)

bayin (China.) Eight-tones instrument classification system.   (7)

bayok Maguindanao syllabic style of singing.   (4)

bayram (Turkish.) Muslim celebration.   (8)

bayt (1) (Also *beyt*.) Line of poetry; in Kurdistan, sung narrative in rhymed verse. (2) 'Rhymed couplets' (Arabic); *see bejte*.   (6, 8)

bayt al-ḥikma 'House of Wisdom', scholarly institution founded by Caliph al-Ma'mum (r. 813–833) in Baghdaa, which translated numerous Greek treatises into Arabic.   (6)

bayyātī (Also, in Turkish, *beyati*.) One of the primary Arab *maqāmāt*.   (6)

bāz (Also *ṭabl bāz* or *bāza*.) 'Falcon', small copper kettledrums used by Sufi and other religious orders in Iraq, Egypt, and Libya.   (6)

bāzi-hā-ye nemāyeshī Women's domestic theater tradition in Iran.   (6)

bazm In Iran, private musical social events; evening entertainments involving music.   (3, 6)

bāzum Social gathering in the home for dancing, in the Northern Areas of Pakistan.   (5)

bazuna Long wooden trumpet of Pomerania, Poland.   (8)

Bear Dance Ute ceremony usually (but not always) conducted in the spring; characterized by women's choice couple dancing and the use of a large rasp that accompanies the singing.   (3)

beat box (Also drum machine.) (1) Electronic percussion characteristic of hip-hop music from the 1980s; (2) orally produced percussion sound imitating an electronic beat box or drum machine; (3) to produce hip-hop oral percussion, usually to accompany an MC.   (3)

beboka BaAka singing, dancing, and drumming.   (1)

bebonangan Processional ensemble of Bali.   (4)

bećarac 'Bachelor's song', Bosnia-Hercegovinian polyphonic singing in which two voices sing in parallel thirds and cadence on a fifth.   (8)

bećarci Serbian male youths gathered in cafés to sing and carouse.   (8)

bêche de mer (Also *trepang*.) Large sea cucumbers, boiled, dried, and used mostly by Chinese for making soup.   (9)

Beda Ladakhi folk musician, player of oboe or kettledrum.   (5)

bedana Muslim-influenced songs and dances in Sumatra.   (4)

bedhaya Refined women's court dance of Java.   (4)

bedhaya semang Sacred dance.   (10)

bedhug Large double-headed cylindrical drum of Java.   (4)

bedug (1) Ritual drum, sounded for the traditional and daily Islamic call to prayer in Guyana. (2) Large double-headed barrel drum of Cirebon and Lombok.   (2, 4)

begena (Also *begana*.) Amhara lyre with a box resonator.   (1)

begenggong Jew's harp of the Talang Mamak, Sumatra.   (4)

begenna Ethiopian lyre.   (6)

begii iish Ingush humorous songs.   (8)

beguine Social dance of Martinique, popular in Italy.   (8)

begum Respectable woman; lady.   (5)

Behulā Sung epic poem in Mithila.   (5)

bei Polyphonic singing of Tuscany.   (8)

beipai (China.) Northern style.   (7)

beiqu (China.) Northern tunes in the theatrical genres of the Yuan and Ming dynasty.   (7)

bejte Rhymed couplets exchanged by Albanian men during social gatherings.   (8)

bekace Short Polish clarinet.   (8)

beklog Subanen wedding ceremony.   (4)

beko fui Five-stringed bamboo idiochord tube zither of Flores.   (4)

Bektaşi Major Sufi *tarikat* of Turkey, doctrinally related to the Alevi group.   (6)

Belau Alternative spelling of *Palau*.   (9)

bel canto Italian opera style of the eighteenth and early nineteenth centuries that emphasizes beautiful vocal tone and lyrical phrasing.   (3)

bélè (1) Cylindrical single-headed membranophone of Martinique; (2) dance style performed since colonial times in the French Caribbean; (3) St. Lucian category of song-dances accompanied by drumming; (4) another name for the *ka* drum; (5) Trinidad and Tobago song-dances originating in the

French Windwards; (6) *bélé*, Dominican song-dances accompanied by a drum of the same name. **(2)**

bele, belair (1) Grenadian song-dance; (2) Creole precursor of *calypso*. **(2)**

belembaotuyan From *berimbau*, a Brazilian chordophone, possibly derived from an Angolan gourd-resonated musical bow. Introduced musical bow of the Mariana Islands that has become an icon of Chamorro cultural identity. **(9)**

Belu Collective term for peoples of East Timor. **(4)**

beluria In Belize, all-night Garifuna ritual in commemoration of a recently deceased relative, often concluding with communitywide participation in singing, drumming, and dancing. **(2)**

bem Javanese pitch name. **(4)**

bʌm From Persian *bam* 'above'. Triple course of strings on the Azerbaijani *saz* that is tuned to the lowest pitch and provides a drone. **(6)**

Bemba A people living in Zambia. **(1)**

bembe (1) (Also Bembe.) Afro-Cuban religious music celebration. (2) Second drum of the Orisa ensemble. (3) Yoruba double-headed drum incorporated into *aladura* churches. **(1, 2, 3)**

bemol Flat (Turkish). **(6)**

bemu nggri-nggo One-stringed struck bamboo idiochord of Flores. **(4)**

bènaden Stylized Guadeloupe arm wrestling accompanied by drumming and singing. **(2)**

bendêr Term for a wooden circular frame drum in Kurdistan; cf. *bandîr*. **(6)**

bendiban (China.) Local troupes. **(7)**

bendir Tunisian single-headed frame drum, used with *mizwid* to accompany canticles of praise. **(1)**

bendu Single-headed standing drum of Sumba. **(4)**

benebene (Also *beriberi*.) Masakin five-stringed lyre of the Sudan. **(1)**

Benesh notation (Also Benesh movement notation.) System of notation on five-line staffs running left to right developed between 1947 and 1955 by Rudolf Benesh (1916–1975) and Joan Benesh (b. 1920) to transcribe human movements; cf. *Labanotation*. **(9)**

benga Definitive popular music of Kenya, developed by the Luo of western Kenya. **(1)**

bengo Long songs to accompany stone dragging in Sumba. **(4)**

beni (1) Competitive associations in East Africa that used European instruments and stressed precision of movement; (2) interethnic style of playing kazoos and moving associated with British marching bands from the Great War (1914–1918); (3) synthesis of dance and competitive modes, influenced by colonial brass-band music in East Africa. **(1)**

bènjo Keyed zither common among the Baloch in Karachi and southern Balochistan. **(5)**

benna Early calypso type of Antigua. **(2)**

bensi (Also *bengsi*.) Sumatran end-blown flute. **(4)**

bensiranay Iloilo song debate on love. **(4)**

benta (1) Mouth-resonated bow from Curaçao, made from a local hardwood and strung with coconut fiber; (2) plucked idiophone among Surinam Maroons, similar to the African *mbira*. **(2)**

bentere Gourd drums adopted by the Akan of Ghana from their northern neighbors. **(1)**

bepha Collective visits by youthful performers sent by one chief to another among the Venda and Tsonga. **(1)**

berampakan Samawan thanksgiving dance after a harvest. **(4)**

berançe Macedonian dance in 12/8 time. **(8)**

berasi Vocal duet from East Flores. **(4)**

berceuses French lullabies, usually in 6/8 time. **(8)**

berda In the Slovene *tamburica* ensemble, a lute that plays the bass part. **(8)**

bərdaşt 'Introduction' (Azerbaijani, from Persian), an introductory passage, moving from a higher to a lower register, in the *maye* of an Azerbaijani *muqam*. **(6)**

berestiankka Belarusan horn. **(8)**

bèri Cirebonese round metal rattles. **(4)**

berikaoba Masqueraders' performances at *kvelieri* in rural Georgia. **(8)**

berimbak Jew's harp in the Aru islands. **(4)**

berimbao Used to accompany the Brazilian *capoeira* dance, a musical bow with gourd resonator held against the chest and struck on its metal string with a small stick. **(3)**

berimbau (1) Brazilian chordophone, possibly derived from the *mbulumbumba*, an Angolan gourd-resonated bow. (2) Struck musical bow with a calabash resonator common to Bahia, Brazil, and derived from Angola. (3) *Berimbau de Angola*, another, more complete name for the *berimbau*. (4) *Berimbau de barriga*, 'berimbau of the belly', another name for the Afro-Brazilian musical bow, so called because the calabash resonator is stopped by pressing it against the player's stomach. (5) Brazilian musical bow, now used in Swedish folk music. **(1, 2, 8)**

Bernerstil 'Bern style' (German), musical style of Bern, Switzerland, that uses a chromatic accordion and a clarinet to mimic Bernese yodeling. **(8)**

berokan Monster play of Cirebon. **(4)**

Berta A people living south of Ed Damazin in southernmost Blue Nile Province, Sudan. **(1)**

bertsu Improvisation of new verses for an existing Basque tune. **(8)**

bertsulari Basque versifiers who improvise new texts in competitions. **(8)**

berunsai Bajau song and dance form. **(4)**

berusu In Belize, Garifuna musical form for solo voice and guitar for general entertainment, often played at wakes. **(2)**

Beruva Sinhala caste of drummers in Sri Lanka. **(5)**

beshik zhirla 'Cradle song', Balkar and Karachaevi lullaby. **(8)**

besi tiga hoek European triangle in Ternate. **(4)**

beste Major Turkish song genre using a wide variety of rhythmic cycles (*usûl*) and lengthy melodic lines, a primary constituent of the *fasıl*. **(6)**

beta zuke (Japan.) Essentially unison style of arrangement for an additional instrumental part. **(7)**

betbut Maltese whistle. **(8)**

Bété A people of Côte d'Ivoire. **(1)**

betel Kernel of the seed of the areca palm, chewed with the leaves, stems, or catkins of betel pepper, slaked lime, and flavorings. **(9)**

Beth-Gazô 'Thesaurus', 'treasury'; in the Syrian Christian church, a collection of nonbiblical liturgical chants in the form of sung hymns and melodies, in which only the initial poetic meter is indicated. Also refers to a compendium of model strophes for Syriac poetry. **(6)**

betruf Swiss "Alpine blessing," having the range of a fifth and important as a national icon. **(8)**

bettô (Japan.) Second highest of four ranks in the *tôdô* (a guild for blind artisans): from lower to higher, the ranks are *zatô*, *kôtô*, *bettô*, and *kengyô*. **(7)**

beyābānī 'Pertaining to the desert' (Persian), a vocal genre of southern Khorasan, sung in open, uninhabited spaces. **(6)**

bey choan Long rhythmic cycle, "third level" in Khmer music. **(4)**

beytbij Semiprofessional singer in Kurdistan. **(6)**

bhadaiya bhajan Bhajan sung only on the day celebrated as Krishna's birthday. **(5)**

bhāgavata mēlā (Also *bhāgavata mēlam*.) Form of classical dance drama in South India; enacted before temple idols by all-male troupes. **(5)**

Bhāgavata Purāṇa Sanskrit text containing stories of Krishna. **(5)**

Bhāgavatar (1) Tamil Vaishnava devotional music leader. (2) *Harikathā* performer. (3) Director and conductor of a *yakṣagāna* drama. **(5)**

bhajan (1) Hymns of devotion and praise sung at Hindu religious services in Trinidad. (2) (Also *bhajana, bhajane*.) Devotional hymn;

Hindu devotional song genre. (3) (Also *bhajanai.*) Hindu devotional songs performed by the laity. **(2, 3, 4, 5)**

bhajan kavvali Hindu devotional song genre of the Fiji Indian community. **(5)**

bhajan maṇḍal Male or female devotee singing groups in Gujarat. **(5)**

bhajanik Bhajan singer. **(5)**

bhakti Hindu tradition of devotion and love directed toward a personal god, encompassing religious practices, literature, and philosophy. **(5)**

bhakti gīt (Also *bhaktigāna.*) Devotional songs, mostly in vernacular languages. **(5)**

bhakti yoga Path of devotion. **(5)**

bhamakalapam Female temple dance of Andhra Pradesh. **(5)**

bhāṇd (Also *bhagat.*) Male professionals who perform *bānde pāther* in Kashmir. **(5)**

bhand-jashna Folk drama of Kashmir. **(5)**

bhangi Cannabis, often smoked by performers of regional music, in Karnataka. **(5)**

bhangra (1) Popular Indian-derived dance-song. (2) Lively folk music and dance style of the Punjab; adapted as a popular syncretic style. (3) Popular dance music of Punjabi immigrants in England. **(4, 5, 8)**

bhapang Plucked chordophone with a single metal string and a hollow cylindrical base, in Rajasthan. **(5)**

bharata nat Theater of the *ādivāsī* tribal populations in the Mastar region of Madhya Pradesh. **(5)**

bharata nāṭyam South Indian classical dance form. **(5)**

bharud Hymn of praise in Maharashtra. **(5)**

bharyā 'Daughter-in-law', a category of the *parivār* classification system dividing ragas into family groups consisting of one male raga, five or six wives (*rāgiṇī*), sons (*putra*), and daughters-in-law. **(5)**

bhātiāli Bengali boatmen's songs. **(5)**

bhāva Emotion; passion. **(5)**

bhavāī Dramatic performance involving music and dance in Gujarat and Rajasthan. **(5)**

bhavana Religious drama of Assam. **(5)**

bhavāyā Performer of *bhavāī.* **(5)**

bhāvgīt 'Songs of the emotions', popular, topical songs of Maharashtra. **(5)**

bhayānaka 'Terrible', one of the eight emotional states (*rasa*) codified in the *Nāṭyaśāstra.* **(5)**

bheṇt Hindi devotional songs to the Mother Goddess. **(5)**

bher Large, stick-played folk kettledrum. **(5)**

bherī Double-headed drum of medieval India played with one hand and a stick. **(5)**

bhīmul pandum Dance and music festival of Madhya Pradesh; takes place before the monsoon. **(5)**

bhogum (Also *kalavantulu, sani.*) Female temple dancers in Andhra Pradesh. **(5)**

bhoom Successful Guyfesta rhythmic experiment to establish a Guyanese beat. **(2)**

bhopā (1) Folk priest or medium in Rajasthan who provides curing and other ritual services; (2) professional ballad singers in Rajasthan. **(5)**

bhuchyāh Cymbals in Nepal. **(5)**

bhūta kōla Traditional worship in Tulunad in which family deities and local caste heroes, both called *bhūta*, are honored with songs and through spirit possession. **(5)**

bianwen (China.) Buddhist-inspired stories performed by professional storytellers during the Tang dynasty. **(7)**

bianzhong (China.) Arrangement of clapperless bronze bells in a set. **(7)**

bianzou (China.) Variations. **(7)**

bianzouti (China.) Variation form. **(7)**

biarozka Belarusan dance performed in *žanićba Ciareśki.* **(8)**

biasiednyja pieśni Belarusan table songs. **(8)**

bibaw Welsh mouth harp, made of wood or metal, held between the teeth, and struck with the finger, popular until the early 1900s; *see sturmant.* **(8)**

Bibayak A Pygmy people of Gabon. **(1)**

biculë (Also *cylëdyjare.*) Short, double-bore duct flute played by herdsmen in Labëri, Albania. **(8)**

bhūtam (Also *teyyam.*) 'Spirits' in Kerala. **(5)**

bidāī gīt 'Departure song' performed in North India when a woman leaves her natal home after marriage. **(5)**

bidesia Folk drama of Bihar. **(5)**

big-band music Popular orchestral music of the 1930s and 1940s, often played for dancing. **(9)**

bigin (Japan.) Genre of *biwa* (lute) music created by Yamazaki Kyokusui (b. 1906) and consisting of the recitation of Chinese poems (*sigin*) accompanied by *tikuzen biwa* interludes. **(7)**

bigin bélè Martinique Creole term for 'drum biguine' type. **(2)**

biguine Social dance music genre in Martinique. **(2)**

bijambò Maltese mouth harp. **(8)**

Bijja Pandum Gond festival, which takes place in the spring. **(5)**

bijol Four-stringed fretless plucked lute of West Timor. **(4)**

bijuela Musical bow found in New Mexican Hispano communities. **(3)**

bikàkla Bribri master of ceremonies. **(2)**

biksha Mendicant or beggar. **(5)**

bilbil Duct flute played by northern Albanian herdsmen. **(8)**

bili (China.) Double-reed cylindrical pipe of the Sui and Tang dynasties, similar to the modern-day *guanzi.* **(7)**

bilûlê asin (Also *şimşal.*) End-blown flute made of iron pipe, common in Kurdish areas of western Iran. **(6)**

bilwari Men's songs accompanying agricultural work. **(5)**

bimūl Flat (pitch). **(6)**

bimusical environment Social context in which two traditions of music are present. **(1)**

bīn (1) (Also *rudra vīṇā.*) Plucked stick zither with gourds attached to each end. (2) (Also *murlī, puṅgī.*) Single-reed horn pipe popularly associated with snake charmers in South Asia. **(5)**

binalig Maguindanao rhythmic mode. **(4)**

bīṇ bājā Arched harp of present-day central India. **(5)**

binbir halka Large tambourine played in some dervish rituals in Bosnia-Hercegovina. **(8)**

biṅdī (Also *tilak.*) Red dot worn on the forehead of a *bharata nāṭyam* dancer; also worn as a sign that one is a Hindu. **(5)**

bines Acehnese female song and dance form. **(4)**

bini Rotinese ritual language form using parallelisms. **(4)**

biniou Bagpipe of Brittany (France). **(8)**

biniou bihan 'Little bagpipe' (Breton). **(8)**

biniou bras In Brittany, the Scottish Highland bagpipes. **(8)**

biniou koz 'Old bagpipe' (Breton), mouth-blown bagpipe with one drone, pitched an octave above the Scottish Highland bagpipes. **(8)**

binjak (Also *pelqesë*). 'Twin', double-bore duct flute, played by Albanians in Macedonia and Kosova. **(8)**

binṣir Ring finger; the fret played by this finger. **(6)**

biola (1) European violin. (2) Low-pitched violin in Sumbawa. **(4)**

bira Shona spirit-possession ceremony in which participants seek assistance from their deceased ancestors. **(1)**

birahā (1) Bhojpuri men's folk song genre; (2) songs of separation in Punjab; (3) rhyming poem sung by Guyanese Indian livestock herders. **(5)**

birbyné Lithuanian single-reed pipe. **(8)**

bird of paradise Any of numerous brilliantly colored birds of the family Paradiseidae native to New Guinea and important for their plumage, often used in costumes. **(9)**

birimbao (Also *birimbau.*) (1) Argentine criollo jaw's harp; (2) Venezuelan jaw's harp. **(2)**

birleşik 'Compound', Turkish term for additive types of meters. **(6)**

bisernica High-pitched lutes in the Slovene *tamburica* ensemble. **(8)**

bishnicë Albanian bagpipe. **(8)**

Bislama English *beach-la-mar*, from French *bêche de mer*. Common pidgin of Vanuatu. **(9)**

Bismarck Mountains Papua New Guinean mountain chain defining the border of Madang and the Highlands provinces, south of the Ramu River. **(9)**

bitsitsi Reed instrument played by the Zuni Indians. **(3)**

biwa Japanese pear-shaped plucked lute with a bent neck, usually having four or five strings and played with a large plectrum. **(3, 7)**

biwa hôsi (Japan.) Blind *biwa* (lute) players. **(7)**

Biwa syo tyôsi bon (Japan.) 'Collection of Tuning Pieces for *Biwa*'; short collection of notations transmitted by the Chinese lute master Lian Cheng-wu to Huziwara no Sada-tosi (897–867). **(7)**

bix rxin nawal Songs of the ancestors in Guatemala. **(2)**

biyānu al-sharqī 'Oriental piano', term for the modified Western piano introduced into Egypt in the nineteenth century. **(6)**

bizen gagaku (Japan.) *Gagaku* as practiced by Shinto (Sintô) priests of the Bizen area (in present-day Okayama Prefecture) since the seventeenth century. **(7)**

bîzoi Drone pipe of the Romanian bagpipe. **(8)**

blackface Practice common in American minstrelsy, in which African-Americans are portrayed by performers whose faces have been blackened by burnt cork. **(3)**

blazeveer Bowed pseudo-bass of the Low Countries. **(8)**

Blechbesetzung Swiss instrumental ensemble of brass instruments. **(8)**

Blechmusik 'Brass-band musik' (German). **(8)**

bleh-muzika (Also *bleh-orkestri*.) Serbian rural brass bands; from German *Blechmusik*. **(8)**

bloco afro Contemporary Afro-Brazilian carnival music. **(2)**

blokviool Plucked dulcimer of the Low Countries. **(8)**

blòtjé St. Lucian pelvis-thrusting dance movement. **(2)**

blow harmony Technique used by singers to blow vocables into a microphone for sound effects. **(3)**

blowon Tiboli bossed gongs. **(4)**

bluegrass Hybrid of Appalachian "old-time" (hillbilly) music developed by Bill Munroe in 1938 in Kentucky; usually performed by four to seven people singing and accompanying themselves on acoustic chordophones including guitar, mandolin, fiddle, five-stringed banjo, and bass. **(3)**

blue note In blues and blues-influenced music (for example, jazz, rock and roll), a note that falls between two adjacent notes in the modern Western division of the octave (twelve equal intervals), expressed variously as a neutral pitch, an upward slur within a semi-tone range, a wavering of pitch, or a simultaneous sounding of flat and natural pitches. **(3)**

blues scale Scale incorporating one or more blue notes. **(3)**

blūr (Also *bulūl*, *belwēr*.) End-blown wooden flute in Kurdistan. **(6)**

bo Chinese small cymbals mainly used in theatres and on ceremonial occasions. **(3, 7)**

Bobbili Yuddha Katha Telugu epic dating from the mid-eighteenth century. **(5)**

boben Slovene drum. **(8)**

bobi End-blown bamboo flute of West Timor. **(4)**

bobine (Also *ulké*.) Hourglass drum played on Réunion Island. **(5)**

bobre Musical bow played on Réunion Island. **(5)**

bocete 'Laments' in Romanian burial rituals. **(8)**

bocina 'Horn'. (1) Ecuadorian straight or curved trumpet; (2) *bocinas*, colonial Spanish term for 'horns' sounded by natives in Paraguay before an attack. **(2)**

Bocondo Vai term for Muslim observance of Id al-Fitr. **(1)**

bodhrán Traditional Irish handheld frame drum. **(3)**

bodhrán Irish single-headed goatskin frame drum, played with a short stick; also imported into Wales. **(8)**

boeng mang kawk Thai set of seven tuned drums, of Mon origin. **(4)**

boerenschots "Scottish" square dance of the West-Friesland area. **(8)**

boghe'e notte Songs in slow tempo based on serious themes in Sardinian *a tenore* singing; also called *a sa seria*. **(8)**

boi 'Bull' in Portuguese. (1) Afro-Brazilian bull character; (2) *boi de orquestra*, Afro-Brazilian *aboio* brass-band style; (3) *boi de zabumba*, Afro-Brazilian *aboio* style. **(2)**

bokkai gaku (Japan.) Musics from somewhere in Manchuria, introduced to Japan during the Nara period (from 710 to 794). **(7)**

bol Word or syllable representing a drum stroke; the drum stroke itself. **(5)**

bola'bola' Sama wooden castanets. **(4)**

bolālāp In Hindustani vocal music, melodic improvisation on a text. **(5)**

bol banāo In Hindustani vocal music, variation and elaboration of a text. **(5)**

bol bānṭ In Hindustani vocal music, rhythm-oriented improvisation on a text. **(5)**

bolero (1) Cuban-derived song genre for listening and dancing, attributed to José "Pepe" Sánchez. (2) Spanish dance in triple meter, originating in the late eighteenth century and frequently performed by a pair of dancers with castanets. (3) Cuban duple-meter dance and song form characterized by distinctive, interlocking rhythmic patterns. (4) Romantic song of Mexican origin with a slow rumba beat. **(2, 3)**

bolero-son Cuban genre that combines elements of the *bolero* and the *son*. **(2)**

bolgarski rospev 'Bulgarian manner of singing' (Bulgarian), identified in the notation of certain seventeenth- and eighteenth-century manuscripts. **(8)**

bolī Punjabi folk songs. (Plural, *boliyāṅ*.) **(5)**

boḷkoṭ Koḍagu circle dance around a lamp, accompanied by song and sometimes drumming. **(5)**

bolo gbili Mandinka songs of praise whose musical and verbal allusions convey history and important myths. **(1)**

bolo Berta one-pitched flute without finger-holes. **(1)**

bolo shuru Berta music played by a *bolo* flute ensemble. **(1)**

bolon Manding and Fulɓe large three- or four-stringed arched harp, associated with war. **(1)**

boltān In Hindustani vocal music, fast melodic figure sung to a text. **(5)**

bomba (1) Afro-Puerto Rican drum and music-dance genre. (2) 'Praise' interjections by men and women during songs and dances. (3) Ecuadorian circle dance (often performed around a cross) and its music. (4) Genre of Afro-Puerto Rican music and dance centered on the *bomba* drums. **(2, 3)**

bombarde Double-reed shawm of Brittany and the Low Countries. **(8)**

bombardon Dance-band wind instrument of the Low Countries. **(8)**

bomber Drum made by stretching a goatskin over one end of a washing-machine barrel. **(2)**

bombo (1) European-derived cylindrical double-headed bass drum membranophone, played with sticks. (2) For *candombe*, African-derived double-headed conical membranophone. (3) Large bass drum of the Philippines. (4) Portuguese bass drum. **(2, 4, 8)**

bomboro Fulani lamellophone. **(1)**

bomma (Also *singerman*.) Jamaican leader of agricultural labor call-and-response songs. **(2)**

bon dance (Japan.) Folk dance performed at a summer festival called *bon*; it also entered into popular entertainment in the 1930s. **(7)**

bon **festival** (Japan.) Summer festival to welcome and console dead relatives and friends. **(7)**

bon odori Dance performed to celebrate O-Bon. **(7, 9)**

bonang Gong-chime, found throughout Java. **(4, 10)**

bonang barung Larger of two gong-chimes in Java. **(4)**

bonang panerus Smaller of two gong-chimes in Java. **(4)**

bonbai (Japan.) Another name for *syômyô*. **(7)**

bongai Malay repartee singing for weddings, circumcisions, and so on. **(4)**

Bongo A people of southern Sudan, living north of the Azande. **(1)**

bongo At a Trinidadian wake, music and dance to placate ancestors. **(2)**

bongo drums (Also *bongos*.) (1) Pair of small hand-played conical single-headed Afro-Cuban drums from which different pitches and percussive qualities may be produced. (2) Cuban and Puerto Rican membranophone consisting of two small drums joined by a piece of wood. **(2, 3)**

Bongu Papua New Guinean village near the western end of the Rai Coast. **(9)**

bonn chaul chhnaim Khmer new year festival. **(4)**

bonn cheat Khmer festival honoring the nation. **(4)**

bonn kathinn Khmer festival of offerings to Buddhist monks. **(4)**

bonn phka Khmer flower festival to raise money. **(4)**

bonn omm touk Khmer water festival with boat races. **(4)**

bonnon (Japan.) Category of Buddhist chant (*syômyô*) for purifying and ornamenting a hall. **(7)**

boo Kpelle flute. **(1)**

boogie-woogie Style of playing blues on the piano, characterized by a fast, steady rhythmic bass, often outlining triads. **(9)**

boogie-woogie bass line Rhythmic pattern that outlines chord structures on the first, third, fifth, sixth, and eighth degrees of the scale in a series of eighth notes; played by the left hand on the piano or a bass guitar in a combo against a syncopated pattern in the right hand. **(3)**

bôoku no koe (Japan.) *Nô* vocalization intended to convey compassion. **(7)**

boompipe Antiguan musical horn made from a plumbing joint. **(2)**

borbangnadyr Type of Tuvan *khöömei* involving a rhythmic treatment of harmonics suggesting rapid movement, for example of water, wind, or a horse. **(6)**

bordi Maltese contrabass used in small ensembles for ambulatory street music, weddings, parties, and picnics. **(8)**

bordón Ostinato bass phrase with slight variation. **(2)**

bordonúa Puerto Rican low-pitched, plucked lute chordophone with six double courses of strings. **(2)**

boria Theatrical genre from Penang area. **(4)**

borii (Also *bori*.) Hausa groups organized around possession-trance performances. **(1)**

borije Montenegrin folk trumpet, mentioned in literary sources and folk songs. **(8)**

bormliza Improvised or partly improvised Maltese *ghana*, regarded as having originated in North Africa. **(8)**

Borobudur Buddhist temple in Central Java. **(4)**

borona 'Harrow', Russian ritual cacophony, produced as women simultaneously sing calendric songs from all the seasons, to ward off evil spirits. **(8)**

boru (Turkish.) Trumpet. **(6)**

bosanski mekam 'Bosnian *maqam*', style used by Sephardic Jewish men in Bosnia-Hercegovina to sing religious songs. **(8)**

boselis Stringed instrument from Lithuania with an air- and pea-filled bladder as a bridge. **(8)**

bossed gong Tuned gong with a raised center for striking. **(4)**

botija Cuban aerophone made from earthen jugs with small hole in the side, through which the performer blows. **(2)**

botta u rispota Maltese improvised witty repartee. **(8)**

boudha caryagīt Buddhist devotional songs of the tenth to twelfth centuries in Orissa. *See also caryā gīt.* **(5)**

boula (1) (Also *tanbou dibas*.) In Guadeloupe, a large tambourine used in *quadrille*. (2) Grenadian open-bottomed membranophone of the big drum ceremony. (3) Small, high-pitched Haitian drum played with two sticks or the two hands. **(2)**

bouladjèl Guadeloupe rhythmic sounds produced by the throat. **(2)**

boum boum Dominican lip-concussion aerophone used to produce low percussive sounds, similar to the *vaksin*. **(2)**

bouñci Large, double-headed barrel drum of Burma. **(4)**

Bourbon Codex Nahua early colonial codex describing the Aztec world. **(2)**

bourdon Drone played on violin, hurdy-gurdy, and bagpipes to accompany a solo instrumental melody. **(8)**

bouzouki Greek long-necked, multistringed plucked lute, the principal instrument of *rebetika*. Since the late 1970s it has been incorporated into Irish traditional music. **(3, 8)**

bouzoukia Establishments where Greek urban popular music was performed; *see skiladhika*. **(8)**

Bowu Vai male masquerader in Liberia. **(1)**

box drum Box-shaped wooden drum, open at both ends, sometimes played at North Alaskan feasts. **(3)**

box fiddle In the Eastern Arctic, a three-stringed box-shaped fiddle, presumably inspired by the fiddles observed in the hands of the early whalers. **(3)**

Boxing Day Day after Christmas, official beginning of carnival in Montserrat. **(2)**

bozik Macedonian boys' house-to-house caroling at Christmas and the new year. **(8)**

bozlak 'Song of anguish', form of Turkish *uzun hava* found throughout central-southern Anatolia and the Taurus Mountains. **(6)**

bozuk Long-necked Turkish lute; Turkish name of the Albanian *buzuq*. **(6, 8)**

brač Lute in the Slovene *tamburica* ensemble that improvises countermelodies. **(8)**

braced bow Musical bow in which a thread (sometimes called a tuning noose) links the string to the bow, making the string vibrate in two sections. **(1)**

braci Viola that supplies rhythmic-harmonic accompaniment in Romanian and Hungarian music in parts of Transylvania. **(8)**

bragir Melodies of Icelandic *rímur*; *see stemmur*. **(8)**

braguesa *See viola.* **(8)**

braguinha Madeiran name of the Portuguese *cavaquinho*. **(8)**

Brahman Hindu god of creation. **(4)**

Brahmasaṅgīt Songs in praise of Brahma; prayer songs of the Brahma Samāj religious sect, founded in Calcutta in 1828. **(5)**

Brahmin (Also *Brāhmaṇ*.) Traditionally, the highest group or class (*varṇa*) of Hindu society, many of whom served as priests. **(5)**

brai (1) Cirebonese large frame drum without jingles. (2) Muslim ensemble. **(4)**

Braj Bhasha Western Hindi language used in devotional poetry and song texts. **(5)**

bra-tara Large bamboo Sumu flute up to 2 meters long, played only by the shaman. **(2)**

brana (Also *cimprekelj, male cimbale, oprekelj, pretl*.) Slovene trapezoidal struck zither. **(8)**

branle French courtly dance popular from the sixteenth to the late nineteenth centuries. **(8)**

brão Brazilian enigmatic musical genre performed during *mutirões*. **(2)**

brass band Musical ensemble popular during the nineteenth century, normally consisting of brass and percussion instruments, but sometimes joined by other aerophones and percussion. (3, 9)

Brauchtumslieder German customary songs. (8)

brazhotki Belarusan rattles. (8)

brazo 'Arm', referring to the neck of lute chordophones from Puerto Rico. (2)

break Section of a popular rhythm and blues (R&B), disco, or funk song of the 1970s and early 1980s in which harmonic instruments drop out and percussion (that is, congas, bongos, cowbells, and timbales) is featured; considered by disk jockeys and dancers to be the most rhythmically exciting section. (3)

bridge (1) Mechanical device made of wood, metal, bone, or some combination of these, located at or near the center of the body of a chordophone and over which the strings pass, causing the body of the instrument to resonate the vibrations produced by the strings; (2) term used to describe melodic structure in popular music, the bridge being the second or B part of a two-part A, B melody or a contrasting instrumental section in songs. (3)

brindisi Italian song type preserved in Corsica. (8)

briolage French singing to oxen while plowing. (8)

briolées French farmers' cries urging on a team of horses. (8)

brnica (Also *drumlica, drumelca.*) Slovene mouth harp. (8)

brnkač (Also *zingulca.*) Slovene noisemaker (made from a piece of wood or bone attached to a string) that produces a whirring sound when spun. (8)

broadside Song sheet containing ballad texts, printed for sale in England between the sixteenth and late nineteenth centuries. (8)

broadside ballad Songs published cheaply on large pieces of newspaper (broadsides) that present stories in a straightforward manner, accompanied by blocky, often undistinguished tunes that may be reused. (3)

broancă Double bass that provides rhythmic-harmonic accompaniment in Romanian and Hungarian music in parts of Transylvania. (8)

brolga Australian crane that performs elaborate movements, possibly as part of a courtship display, often the subject of singing and dancing by Aboriginal Australians. (9)

Bruckins Jamaican annual celebration of emancipation from slavery. (2)

brukdown (1) Type of dance and song reflecting usual and unusual events in the life of the common Belizean; (2) specific rhythmic organization in Belize. (2)

brungan Komi zither. (8)

brunkula (Also *bunkula, ta-velika citira.*) Basset—a small three-stringed bass—played in Resia, Slovenia, to accompany violins. (8)

btāyḥī Vocal genre within the Maghribi *nūba*; also refers to a rhythmic cycle used in this genre. (6)

bua Tausug and Sama large hanging gong. (4)

bua loi Thai ensemble for boxing and theater, same as *klawng khaek.* (4)

bubanj Cylindrical drum played by Vlahs in Serbia and Bosnia-Hercegovina. (8)

bubaran Formal arrangement of a Javanese gamelan piece. (4)

bubblegum South African synthesized dance music, originating in the 1980s. (1)

buben z brazhotkami Belarusan tambourine with jingles. (8)

bubon Ukrainian single-headed frame drum played with a small wooden mallet. (8)

bubundir Maranao medium-size bossed gong. (4)

buccina Romanian trumpet or horn. (8)

bucerata (Also *buceru, voceru.*) Corsican lament for a violent death. (8)

büchel Small Swiss alphorn in a coiled shape; *see* *grada büchel.* (8)

bucium Romanian alphorn. (8)

bucoliasme Cattle tenders' work songs of French-speaking Switzerland. (8)

budaixi (China.) Hand-puppet theater. (7)

budeļi Masked, singing Christmas revelers in Kurzeme and western Zemgale, Latvia. (8)

budindang Lampung free-meter song form. (4)

budongo Basoga box-resonated lamellophone in southern Uganda. (1)

budyung Hanunoo shell trumpet. (4)

būga (Also *mu'asti.*) Metallic tubular drum used on national, social, and personal occasions in Yemen. (6)

bugaku (Japan.) Instrumental court music with dance, of foreign origin. (7)

bugalú Blend of Latin rhythms and African-American rhythm and blues. (3)

bugarija Long-necked lute in Croatian and Slovenian *tamburica* ensembles. (8)

bughya Unmeasured instrumental prelude in the Maghribi *nūba.* (6)

bugīr (Also *buguri.*) Kota end-blown bamboo trumpet; same as Toda *puxury.* (5)

bugle Military trumpet developed around 1880 that has side holes operated by keys. (3)

bugutá Guaymí dance performed by both men and women. (2)

buhahay Subanen bamboo dibbling pole. (4)

buhai Romanian friction drum. (8)

buka panggung Ritual opening for shadow theater, in Malaysia and Cirebon. (4)

bukhsa (1) Nuba gourd pot, struck with a thin stick for dancing; (2) Nuba set of small gourd trumpets. (1)

buki Georgian large trumpet popular at court in celebratory contexts and in military contexts. (8)

bukkehorn Norwegian buck horn, with or without holes for fingering. (8)

bul (1) Colo long conical drum; (2) Colo young people's festival dance to the beat of drums. (1)

bulerías Spanish *cante chico* based on a 12-beat structure. (8)

bullérengue Colombian and Afro-Panamanian responsorial song and dance genre. (2)

bullroarer (Also *bull roarer.*) Friction aerophone, or wind instrument, typically constructed as a trapezoid-shaped wooden slab tied to a string or leather thong and whirled in the air to produce a buzzing sound, found in the Arctic and elsewhere in the world. In Denmark, an instrument consisting of a hollow tile or a small oblong wooden plate with a hole, tied to the end of a string and swung in circles to produce a whirring sound. (3, 8)

bulsique Cabécar dance similar to the Bribri *sörbö.* (2)

buluŋ Berta cow horn, used to strike percussion sticks. (1)

bumba meu boi (Also *bumba-meu-boi.*) (1) 'Bull celebration,' dramatic genre brought to Africa by Brazilians and Cubans. (2) Afro-Brazilian dance that is the last dramatic dance of the *reisado* cycle. (1, 2)

bummâḍiya Sri Lankan pot drum with clay body, short flaring neck, and iguana-skin drumhead. (5)

bunde (1) African-derived dance of Colombia and Panama; (2) currently a Colombian funerary song. (2)

bundu Mask of eastern Sierra Leone. (1)

bungo busi (Japan.) Genre of narrative *syamisen* music established by Miyakozi Bungo no zyô (d. 1740). (7)

bungo kei zyôruri (Japan.) Offshoots of *bungo busi* (a narrative *syamisen* genre). (7)

bunka hu (Japan.) *Syamisen* notation developed in the early 1920s. (7)

bunraku (Japan.) Puppet theater accompanied by *gidayû busi.* (7)

bunsiti (Japan.) Head of a *bunraku* puppet used for the role of a virtuous middle-aged warrior. (7)

bun'ya (Also *bun'ya busi.*) Genre of early Japanese narrative *syamisen* music (*ko zyôruri*) begun by Okamoto Bun'ya (1633–1694). (7)

būq Horn or trumpet. (6)

būq zamri Horn. (6)

burämusig 'Farmer's music', old term for the Swiss *ländlerkapelle.* (8)

burczybas Friction drum used in carnival masquerades in Pomerania, Poland. (8)

burdah Arabic hymn singing with *rebana*. (4)

burłackija pieśni Belarusan nonritual barge haulers' songs. (8)

burmiyya (From *barama* 'to twist'.) Simple, quasi-stationary dance of the Siwa oasis of Egypt, involving a shuffling, hip-swinging action. (6)

burra katha Popular style of Telugu narrative singing derived from a folk model. (5)

burro Venezuelan single-headed log drum. (2)

burroquite 'Little donkey' of Trinidadian carnival, derived from the Hindu goddess Durga. (2)

buru (1) Jamaican masquerade celebration; (2) set of drums in Jamaica. (2)

būs Type of clarinet used in Saudi Arabia, played by shepherds and amateurs. (6)

bušen (Also *rikalo*.) Bark trumpet more than 3 meters long, played by Vlah men of Serbia for festivities on St. George's day. (8)

busi (Japan.) Suffix form of *husi*, a generic term for melody. (7)

business dances Jamaican Maroon religious dances named after particular ethnic groups. (2)

busking Performing for money on streets or in subways. (8)

busô (Japan.) Category of Buddhist chant (*syômyô*) for invoking or sending off Buddha or other deities, such as guardian deities. (7)

buta (1) (Also *buuta*.) Hausa gourd rattle. (2) Ogre character in Javanese dance. (1, 4)

butcher-bird Any of several Australian and New Guinean shrikes of the genus *Cracticus*, so called because they impale their prey (including small birds) on spikes or thorns, or wedge it in the forks of trees. (9)

button accordion Musical instrument having two hexagonal headboards connected by a folding bellows and eliciting sounds from free-beating metal tongues set into vibration by the actions of buttons; cf. *piano accordion*. (9)

butumyô (Japan.) Category of Buddhist chant (*syômyô*) for worshiping various buddhas and bodhisattvas. (7)

buusa Hausa term for blowing, including a musical instrument. (1)

buyei Garifuna shaman in Belize. (2)

buyūt 'Houses', term used by al-Ḥaṣkafī in describing scalar degrees. (Singular, *bayt*.) (6)

Buzan ha (Japan.) One of three branches of the Singon school of Buddhist chant (*syômyô*). (7)

buzika (Also *garmon*.) Georgian accordion. (8)

buzuk Near Eastern long-necked plucked lute, played in Albania during the Ottoman period. (8)

buzuq Long-necked lute of the eastern Arab world. (6)

buzyô (Japan.) Category of Buddhist chant (*syômyô*) for invoking or sending off deities and purifying and ornamenting a hall. (7)

bwa Guadeloupe hardwood sticks that are struck against drum or each other. (2)

bwa pòyé St. Lucian banjo. (2)

bwola Achola musical ensemble. (1)

byāh ke gīt Bhojpuri wedding song. (5)

byau' Burmese wooden block struck with a stick. (4)

bygde Indigenous dances of Norway. (8)

bygdelag Community life and traditional activities of Norwegian settlers; in the United States these practices fell into decline in the early twentieth century. (3)

byliny Russian epic songs; *see stariny*. (8)

byńk Belarusan dance performed in *žanićba Ciareški*. (8)

byò Pair of large, stick-beaten drums from Burma. (4)

byôsi (Japan.) Suffix form of *hyôsi*, a generic term for rhythm and meter. (7)

bywoners White tenant farmers in South Africa who introduced the concertina, guitar, and violin. (1)

byz Udmurt bagpipe. (8)

byzaanchy Type of upright Tuvan fiddle. (6)

bzhami Adighian ritual whistle flute. (8)

bzhe Adighian women's funeral songs. (8)

C-natural Nigerian guitar-fingering pattern. (1)

cabildo (1) Secret society in Cuba and other Hispanic-Caribbean areas; (2) place for religious conversion by Catholic missionaries in Colombia, Peru, and elsewhere in Spanish-speaking South America; (3) Bolivian community authority who may sponsor fiestas; (4) Chilean male or female hierarchical organization for patronal festivals. (2)

cabildos Cuban term for social brotherhoods of slaves. (1)

caboclinho (Also *terno de caboclos*.) Brazilian children's dramatic dance; same as *caiapó*. (2)

caboclo Brazilian *mestizo* of Native American and Portuguese heritages, especially in the northeast. (2)

cabreta Bellows-blown bagpipe of Auvergne, France. (8)

cabrette Bagpipe of Limousin and Auvergne, France. (8)

cācā Newār Buddhist hymn repertoire in Nepal. (5)

čäčän Tatar epic singer. (6)

cachimbo Northern Chilean dance. (2)

cacho (1) Peruvian circular valveless trumpet made of connected bull-horn sections; (2) *cachos*, Venezuelan ductless deerskull flutes played in pairs. (2)

cachu Cow-horn trumpet of the Netherlands Antilles. (2)

cadacada Mapuche shell rasps. (2)

cadence Resolution of a harmonic progression. (4)

cadence-lypso Fusion of Haitian *konpa* or *kadans* with Trinidadian calypso. (2)

cadi Welsh ritual in May, in which a man wearing women's clothing and wielding a broom, accompanied by dancers in blackface, performs to celebrate the coming of spring. (8)

cadir Ritual dance form of Tamil Nadu that evolved into modern-day *bharata nāṭyam*. (5)

café aman (1) Coffeehouse tradition of music, conversation, and refreshment in American Middle Eastern communities. (2) Greek musical cafés where *amanedhes* were sung. (3, 8)

café cantante 'Singing café' (Spanish), pubs featuring flamenco, especially in Madrid and Seville. (8)

café chantant 'Singing café' (French), nineteenth-century pub in the Low Countries. (8)

çağana Turkish military cymbals. (6)

cagüeño Puerto Rican *seis* from Caguas. (2)

ca huế Vocal chamber music of central Vietnam and Huế area. (4)

caiapó (Also *terno de caiapós*.) Brazilian dramatic dance group that combines Native American, African, and Portuguese elements. (2)

cai luong Genre of popular southern Vietnamese theater that developed around 1920. (4)

caitī Love song genre of Uttar Pradesh. (5)

caiti ghoṛa nāc Dance form associated with the Hindu Shakta cult in Orissa; ritual dummy-horse dance of the fishing community of Orissa. (5)

caixa Portuguese snare drum. (8)

caj (From Spanish *caja* 'box'.) Snare drum among the Quiché Maya. (2)

caja 'Box', small membranophone in many Spanish-speaking countries, either single-headed or double-headed, often with a snare. (2)

caja chayera Atacameño double-headed, frame snare drum adopted from the Spanish. (2)

cajita 'Little box', coastal Afro-Peruvian idiophone made from a small wooden box with a hinged lid, played by shutting the lid in rhythm and striking the box with a stick. (2)

cajita musical 'Small musical box', mounted on a stand and played with two sticks as part of the Afro-Cuban rumba ensemble. **(3)**

cajón (Plural, *cajones*.) 'Big box', (1) Afro-Peruvian and *criollo* idiophone made from a wooden box with a sound hole in the back; (2) *cajón de tapeo*, wooden Mixtec box struck with the hands, similar to the *cajón* of Peru; (3) *cajones harmónicos*, Guatemalan wooden-box marimba resonators; (4) boxes played like drums in Afro-Cuban music. **(3)**

cajuavé Small mouth-resonated bow among the Chaco of Paraguay. **(2)**

cakalele (1) Vigorous male dances on Ternate and Tidore; (2) centuries-old dance drama on the Banda islands; (3) martial dance accompanied by drums and gong on Ambon. **(4)**

cakapung Male vocal imitation of Balinese gamelan. **(4)**

cakkardār Type of *paran* (*pakhāvaj* composition) played three times. **(5)**

ca kịch hué Recent theatrical genre of Huế area in Vietnam. **(4)**

cākyār Temple performance genre for solo actor-storyteller in Kerala. **(5)**

cākyār kūttu Dramatic performance by the Cākyār community of Kerala. **(5)**

ēalan (Also *gat-qā'ida*.) Tabla composition. **(5)**

čalgadžii Rom musicians in Macedonia. **(8)**

čalgija (Also *çalgi*.) Macedonian, Albanian, and Serbian Rom urban professional ensemble. **(8)**

calinda African dance performed in the French West Indies and Louisiana. **(3)**

call and response (Also *call-response*.) (1) Structural form in which phrases performed by a soloist alternate with phrases performed by a choir or ensemble. (2) Style of antiphonal singing between leader and chorus; major musical characteristic of African-American music, especially work songs and blues. **(1, 3)**

caller Person who calls out the choreography to the dancers during a performance of social square dance. **(3)**

calonarang Nineteenth-century Balinese theatrical form. **(4)**

calul (Also *caiuṭi*.) 'Hobby horses', Romanian winter festival with masked dancing in north-central Moldavia and Bucovina. **(8)**

calung Struck bamboo xylophone ensemble of Java and Sunda. **(4)**

căluṣ Romanian healing ritual performed by male dancers to the accompaniment of instrumental music. **(8)**

căluṣari Romanian male dancers who perform a healing ritual. **(8)**

căluṣul 'Little horse', Romanian young men's ritual dance to bring fecundity or to heal or prevent illness, in Oltenia, Muntenia, and parts of Dobruja. **(8)**

calypso (1) Caribbean song form attributed to Trinidad, characterized by humorous language, rhyme, and the improvisational treatment of text and music which are often satirical. (2) Trinidadian rhythmical instrumental genre associated with steelbands and carnival. (3) West Indian topical-song genre in duple meter with usually satirical lyrics, typically sung at carnival and popular in Britain. **(2, 8)**

camil Adighian whistle flute. **(8)**

campana 'Bell', (1) used in Roman Catholic religious processions; (2) *campanilla*, little Afro-Peruvian handbell, used in the dances of the *hatajo de negritos*. **(2)**

campanti Tamil marriage songs in which the groom's and bride's families make fun of each other. **(5)**

čampareta Small cymbals of Bosnia-Hercegovina. **(8)**

Can Con regulations Regulations introduced by the Canadian Radio and Telecommunications Commission in 1970 requiring Canadian radio stations to play a certain quota of Canadian music. **(3)**

caña (1) Bolivian long cane trumpet; (2) Paraguayan 'cane' alcohol in bottles securely balanced on heads of *galoperas*; (3) Q'ero vertical, notched, six-note edge aerophone made of reed or plastic pipe; (4) long, valveless wooden or cane trumpet. **(2)**

cana Portuguese split-cane tube about 60 centimeters long used as a percussion instrument. **(8)**

caña de millo Colombian idioglottal transverse clarinet made from cane; *see also pito*. **(2)**

canang (1) Pair of small knobbed gongs in rack in Malaysia; (2) Sumatran gong-chime and ensemble. **(4)**

canção de intervenção 'Song of intervention' (Portuguese), used for political protest. **(8)**

canchis sipas Q'ero panpipes with a double set of seven reed tubes. **(2)**

canción (Plural, *canciones*.) (1) Popular Mexican song genre; (2) topical song. **(3)**

canción de protesta 'Protest song', any Latin American protest song, often influenced by the Cuban revolution. **(2)**

canción ranchera (1) Mexican song type linked to the rise of the popular media and to the popularity of folk-derived ensembles such as the modern *mariachi*. (2) Mexican country song, encompassing a variety of formal structures, meters, and tempos, evocative of rural life or themes. (3) Folk and popular song genre throughout the Pacific coast of Nicaragua. **(2, 3)**

canción romántica (1) Mexican tradition of the nineteenth-century romantic song; (2) romantic popular song tradition sustained at the annual Gastón music festival in Managua, Nicaragua. **(2)**

canción trovadoresca Cuban genre created by singer-composers of Santiago de Cuba. **(2)**

canções praieiras Afro-Brazilian fisherman's or beach songs. **(2)**

cancioneros Spanish literary anthologies of poetic texts, with or without music, first published in the 1200s. **(8)**

candombe (1) Afro-Uruguayan dances and dance locales. (2) (Also *charanda*, *ramba*.) Argentine entertainment dance. **(2)**

Candomblé (1) Afro-Brazilian religion in Bahia; (2) Argentine variant of Afro-Brazilian religion observed in place of Batuque; (3) Candomblé de Caboclo, Afro-Brazilian religion in Sergipe. **(2)**

candrasārang North Indian bowed, fretless lute invented by Alauddin Khan. **(5)**

canens "Performing" the verse in Finnish *runon-laulu*. **(8)**

canget Lampung Buddhist-Hindu dance. **(4)**

Cankam literature Thologies of Tamil poetry dating from about the first to fourth centuries C.E. **(5)**

canned music (1) Prerecorded music, as opposed to live performance; (2) expression used by musicians to refer derogatorily to recorded music. **(3)**

Cannon Stars Band of Bangui, Central African Republic, popular in the early 1980s. **(1)**

cannacione Italian countrified version of the medieval *colascione*, derived from Turkish, Arabic, and Greek long-necked lutes. **(8)**

canntaireachd Scottish vocable system for the teaching of the classical piping tradition (*piobaireachd*). **(8)**

cantaduras (Also *cantadurs*.) Historic singing societies from the Romansh-speaking area of Switzerland. **(8)**

cantalante Lead singer in Panamanian women's chorus. **(2)**

cantaor (Also *cantador*.) Person who memorizes Puerto Rican *décimas* in order to sing them. **(2)**

cantares de ayuda 'Aid-songs', Spanish songs for the gathering of alms. **(8)**

cantares ao desafio Portuguese improvised vocal genre. **(8)**

cântaro Portuguese large clay pot whose opening is hit with a straw or leather fan. **(8)**

cántaro Large jug tuned with water and used for low-pitched accompaniment in El Salvador. **(2)**

cantastorie 'Song-storytellers', Italian itinerants, often blind professional bards; *see torototéla*. **(8)**

cantautori Italian singer-songwriters of the 1970s and later. **(8)**

cante (Spanish.) A song. **(8)**

cante chico 'Small song', any of three types of Spanish flamenco singing, with a rhythmic structure less complex than that of the *cante jondo*. **(8)**

cante intermedio 'Intermediate song', any of three types of Spanish flamenco singing, a hybrid of *cante jondo* and forms from Spanish folk and popular music styles, especially the fandango. **(8)**

cante jondo 'Deep song', any of the three types of throaty, impassioned improvised flamenco song, considered the oldest and most serious. **(3, 8)**

canti all'altalena Swinging songs of Basilicata, southern Italy. **(8)**

canti alla boara Type of Italian lyric song. **(8)**

canti carnascialeschi Italian carnival songs of Renaissance Florence. **(8)**

canti epico-lirici Italian ballads, found mostly in the north. **(8)**

canti lirico-monostrofici Italian lyric songs, common south of the Apennines. **(3, 8)**

canti alla longa Type of Italian lyric song. **(8)**

canti a pera Type of Italian lyric song. **(8)**

canti di questua Italian begging songs used in seasonal celebrations. **(8)**

canti alla stesa Type of Italian lyric song. **(8)**

canti a vatoccu 'Songs in the manner of a bell clapper', Italian narrow-interval, two-voiced songs. **(8)**

cantiga (1) Monophonic song in the Luso-Galician troubadour tradition dating back to the thirteenth century. (2) 'Song' (Portuguese), a metered strophic song. **(8)**

cantimbanchi Italian semiprofessional ballad-eers. **(8)**

cantiques (1) French hymnody surviving on Carriacou. (2) French religious ballads. **(2, 8)**

canto 'Song' (Spanish), (1) *canto nuevo*, 'new song', clandestine successor to *nueva canción* ('new song') in Chile after the coup of 1973; (2) *cantos de ángeles* Chilean 'songs of angels'; (3) *cantos de nana*, Mexican coddling songs. **(2)**

canto a chiterra Sardinian guitar-accompanied song. **(8)**

canto a dispetto 'Song of the despised', Italian polyphonic form akin to *canti a vatoccu*. **(8)**

canto della passione (Also *orologio della passione* 'clock of the passion'.) Central Italian begging song, performed the week before Easter. **(8)**

canto popular uruguayo 'Popular Uruguayan song' featuring texts that express desire for social and political change. **(2)**

cantor Singer of sacred music hired by a Jewish congregation to act as messenger of their prayers; more recently, a member of the staff clergy. **(3)**

cantoria (1) Brazilian secular music of the northeast performed by singer-bards; (2)

Brazilian folk singing usually involving an improvised duel, also known as *desafío*. **(2)**

cantrik Disciple character type in Javanese dance. **(4)**

cantus Song (Middle Ages). **(8)**

cantus super librum 'Song above a book' (Latin), improvisation of one or more parts over a chant notated in a liturgical book. **(8)**

canu gyda'r tannau 'Singing with the strings', style of Welsh singing in which the singer improvises the vocal parts to suit the harmonic accompaniment of a harp. **(8)**

canu penillion 'Singing verses', style of Welsh singing in which the singer improvises the vocal parts to suit the harmonic accompaniment of a harp. **(8)**

canu'r pwnc 'Singing the text', form of Welsh folk declamation connected with reciting biblical scriptures at catechismal festivals. **(8)**

canzone italiana Twentieth-century styles of Italian song. **(8)**

canzoni a ballo Italian lyric songs intended for dancing; *see maitinade, polesane*. **(8)**

canzune Sicilian lyric song type. **(8)**

caoine Irish lament for the dead. **(8)**

caoineadh (Also *caoineadh na marbh*.) Irish death lament, anglicized as *keening*. **(8)**

Cape Coon Carnival Minstrel parades on New Year's Day in Cape Town, accompanied by jazz musicians. **(1)**

caper In English morris dances, section in which the instrumentalist is required to play at a slower tempo or at half-speed with note values doubled, while the dancers perform high leaps. **(8)**

capitán (1) Nahua chief; (2) Nahua dancer of Corpus Christi; (3) guitar leader of Salva-doran dance of the little devils. **(2)**

capoeira (1) Afro-Brazilian game-fight dance. (2) *Capoeira Angola*, Afro-Brazilian traditional dance of possibly Angolan origin. (3) *Capoeira regional*, Afro-Brazilian innovative form developed by Mestre Bimba. (4) Brazilian tradition of dance of a martial arts character, with accompanying music played on the *berimbao* musical bow. **(2, 3)**

capoeiristas Afro-Brazilian couples of (usually) male dancer-fighters in *capoeira*. **(2)**

caporal Chilean artistic director of a patronal dance. **(2)**

capra 'Goat', Romanian winter festival with masked dancing in Transylvania, Maramureş, Bucovina, Moldavia, and Muntenia. **(8)**

caquiliztli Náhuatl word for sound or noise. **(2)**

carabiné Dominican Republic imitation dance of nineteenth-century occupying Haitian soldiers. **(2)**

ca ra bộ Southern Vietnamese chamber music performed with gestures. **(4)**

carachacha (Also *carraca, quijada*.) Idiophone, scraped or struck, made from the lower jawbone of an ass, a mule, or a horse. **(2)**

caracol Conch-shell trumpet. **(2)**

caramba (Also *zambumbia*.) (1) Honduran long music bow (onomatopoetically, *bumbum*); (2) Salvadoran musical bow with gourd resonator possibly descended from the African hunting bow. **(2)**

caranam "Foot" or verse of a song in Karnatak music. **(5)**

caramusa Corsican goatskin bagpipe. **(8)**

carángano Large Afro-Colombian idiochord bamboo tube zither. **(2)**

carangueijo Brazilian circular social dance with many variants, especially popular along border areas of Uruguay. **(2)**

čardáš Slovak couple dance with set and impro-vised steps. **(8)**

caretta 'Fancy dance', Brazilian contredanse that influenced dancing in Yoruba *jùjú*. **(1)**

çargâh Common melodic mode (*makam*) in Turkish folk music. **(6)**

cargo During patronal festivals, the musician's role of service to the community to placate the gods and ensure the well-being of the people. **(2)**

caribeño Colombian fusion of *zouk* and *salsa*. **(2)**

Carifesta Guyanese festival held since 1972. **(2)**

carillo Tagalog shadow play. **(4)**

carimbó Afro-Brazilian popular dance from Pará. **(2)**

carnaval 'Carnival', (1) secular celebration before Lent in Brazil and throughout most of Hispanic America; (2) Atacameño *mestizo* agrarian fertility rite in Chile. **(2)**

carnevale Italian carnival celebration. **(8)**

carnival Nual historic, national, theatrical secular celebration before Lent in Trinidad and Tobago and elsewhere in the English-speaking Caribbean. **(2)**

carnyx Celtic horn of the La Tène period, emerging during the first millennium B.C.E.; it has been defined as an animal-headed trumpet and a war trumpet. **(8)**

čarojičarske pjesme Songs for masked ritual processions in Bosnia-Hercegovina. **(8)**

carole French dance tradition that emerged from medieval ring dances and chain dances. **(8)**

čarotki Belarusan reed aerophones. **(8)**

carraca Wooden rattle of Arab origin. **(2)**

carrasca (Also *raspador*.) (1) Scraper in Honduras; (2) scraped idiophone of Colombia. **(2)**

carrizo (1) Kogi cane used to make instruments; (2) Venezuelan panpipe. **(2)**

cartas anuas Nual reports made by each Jesuit province to the Jesuit general in Rome. **(2)**

caryā gīt (Also *boudha caryāgīt*.) Principal song genre in Bengal from the ninth through twelfth centuries, with Buddhist texts. **(5)**

casa de baile Dance house of the Aymara region associated with patronal festivals. **(2)**

casadh 'The turn', second of two sections within an Irish dance tune. **(8)**

cascabeles Spanish and Argentine metal bell jingles. **(2, 8)**

cascola Corsican children's game accompanied by verses. **(8)**

cashua taki Inca line dance. **(2)**

cassella Corsican kettledrum; large Corsican frame drum played with a pair of sticks. **(8)**

cassuto Scrapers, particularly among Kumbundu-speakers of Angola. **(1)**

cassowary Any of several large birds of genus *Casuarius*, closely related to the emu and symbolically important in many highland New Guinean cultures. **(9)**

castañuelas (1) 'Castanets', from the Spanish word for chestnuts. (2) Panamanian struck hardwood idiophones. **(2, 8)**

caste Rigid social class, one of which is designated for musicians in parts of West Africa. **(1)**

castillos Ecuadorian fruit-bearing poles along Corpus procession route. **(2)**

častuški Belarusan rhymed poems on humorous themes. **(8)**

catá (1) Stick used to hit the body of the long-drum in the Dominican Republic. (2) Cuban idiophone made from a hollowed-out log and struck with two sticks. **(2)**

catabaucalise (Also *nunnie*.) Children's nurses' work songs from French-speaking Switzerland. **(8)**

cateretê (Also *catiretê*.) Brazilian social dance genre found in rural areas. **(2)**

ca trù Northern Vietnamese chamber music. **(4)**

catta Jamaican sticks beaten on the side of the *kbandu* drum. **(2)**

caudike Single-stringed, barrel-shaped drone instrument in Karnataka; also, a type of *katha*. **(5)**

caupadi Love songs performed at village gatherings in Orissa. **(5)**

cautāl (Also *chowtal*, *fāg*.) Men's festive songs of the springtime Holī season in Trinidad, Guyana, and Fiji. **(5)**

cautārā Drone lute played by devotional singers in Rajasthan. **(5)**

caval Romanian duct flute played by shepherds. **(8)**

cavalaria Afro-Brazilian rhythmic pattern. **(2)**

cavaquinho (1) Small Portuguese guitar with four courses of strings; it diffused to Hawai'i (where it is called *'ukelele*) and Indonesia (where it is called *kroncong*). (2) Four-stringed treble guitar used throughout Brazil. **(2, 3)**

cavittunāṭakam Foot-stamping drama performed by the Latin Christians of Kerala. **(5)**

caxixi Afro-Brazilian basket rattle, played by the same musician who plays the *berimbau*. **(2)**

cayaar Major class of Somali performance that includes dance-songs, often with topical subjects. **(1)**

caza de la tortuga 'Turtle hunt' festival among the Maleku, for ritual purification to emphasize aspects of reciprocity between humans and nature. **(2)**

céilí (1) Irish domestic evening entertainment and visiting where friends and neighbors gather to drink, sing, dance, tell stories, and play music. (2) Evening gathering, in Australia usually held monthly by people of Irish ancestry and often involving social dances (including the waltz), solo or group displays, and vocal solos. **(8, 9)**

céili band Large Irish dance band with fiddles, flutes, accordions, piano, and drum. **(8)**

ceilidh Scottish evening entertainments, gatherings where people sing, dance, drink, and play music. **(8)**

ček (Also *wau*.) Colo poet-composer-singer. **(1)**

cēkanti Bronze gong tied to the waist and played with a stick in Tamil Nadu. **(5)**

celempong Riau gong-chime and ensemble. **(4)**

celempung Four-legged metal-stringed box zither of Java. **(4)**

Celvetī Sufi *tarikat*, offshoot of the Halvetīye. **(6)**

cem (Also *ayin*, *āyīn*.) Term for closed religious musical services by the Turkish Alveī sect. **(6)**

cembalo Italian trapezoidal struck zither. **(8)**

cempala Wooden knocker used by *dhalang* in Javanese *wayang kulit*. **(4)**

cencerro (1) Cuban metallic idiophone, similiar to a bell with no clapper; (2) Bolivian bronze llama bells; (3) Ecuadorian cowbells. **(2)**

çeng Classical Turkish harp. **(6)**

ceng-ceng Small hand cymbals of Bali and Lombok. **(4)**

çengī Female professional dancers of Ottoman Turkey. **(6)**

cèngkok Formulas for variation and improvisation in Javanese music. **(4)**

cenoi Temiar term for rays of light said to bear spiritual substances throughout the universe. **(4)**

ceṅṅala Small handheld gong of Kerala. **(5)**

cent One one-hundredth of an equal-tempered semitone, a unit of measurement introduced by Alexander J. Ellis (1814–1890) and based on the division of the octave into 1,200 equal parts; a semitone spans a hundred cents. Cents are used to measure intervals. **(1, 6, 9)**

cenṭa Double-headed cylindrical drum of Kerala, played with two curved sticks. **(5)**

cenṭa mēḷam Ritual music ensemble of Kerala. **(5)**

centonization Process that establishes the melody and poetic meter of hymns and melodies using set formulas. **(6)**

cepung Men's choral and dance form of Lombok. **(4)**

ceòl beag 'Little music', Scottish songs, marches, and dance tunes. **(8)**

ceòl mór 'Great music', a theme-and-variation form of Scottish piping that tests a piper's mastery. **(8)**

cerca Corsican dances. **(8)**

cerdd dant 'The craft of the string' (Welsh). **(8)**

cerek Malay pairs of wood or bamboo sticks struck together. **(4)**

Cerrāhī Subdivision of the Halvetīye sect. **(6)**

cetera Corsican and Sardinian pear-shaped plucked lute with a flat-bottomed sound box. **(8)**

četrpāru dancis Latvian dance for four couples. **(8)**

cēvai palakai Tambourine with a lizard-skin head in Tamil Nadu. **(5)**

çeyrek Quarter tone (Turkish). **(6)**

cēyvaiyāttam Dance performed by Kampalattar Nāyakars in Tamil Nadu. **(5)**

cha Cymbals used in Afro-Cuban music. **(3)**

chaba Female Algerian singer of *rai*, a North African music popular in France. **(8)**

chāb rai 'Rai of the young', form of Algerian *rai* that developed in the 1980s and featured Western electrophones such as the synthesizer and drum machine. **(6)**

chabreta Bellows-blown bagpipe of Limousin, France. **(8)**

chacarera Argentine social dance performed during *jineteada*. **(2)**

cha-cha-cha (Also *cha-cha-chá*.) Cuban dance style and genre created by Enrique Jorrin during the 1950s. **(2, 3)**

chac-chac In Grenada and Trinidad and Tobago, gourd-constructed rattle. **(2)**

chacha Guadeloupe large hollowed-out calabash filled with seeds. **(2)**

chaein Korean male performers. *See kwangdae*. **(7)**

chaein ch'ŏng Korean performers' associations. **(7)**

chaguan (China.) Teahouse. **(7)**

chagŭn kut Small Korean shaman ritual. **(7)**

chagŭn mudang Korean minor shaman. **(7)**

chahārbeiti Persian-language folk song form of four-line verses, western Afghanistan. **(5)**

chahār maqām 'Four *maqāmlar*', term for the Ferghana-Tashkent *maqām* tradition, consisting of the four independent suites *bayāt*, *chargāh*, *dugāh-husayni*, and *gulyār-shahnāz*. **(6)**

chahār meżrāb 'Four strokes' (Persian), a composition emphasizing instrumental virtuosity. **(6)**

chairígoas (Also Yaqui *teneboim*.) Guarijio rattles made from the cocoons of the giant silk moth and wrapped around the dancers' legs from ankle to knee. **(2)**

chajinmori Korean rhythmic pattern (*changdan*), fast 12/8 meter. **(7)**

chakchak (1) Dominican calabash idiophone filled with beads or small pebbles and mounted on a stick; (2) St. Lucian small calabash idiophone filled with seeds and mounted on a stick. **(2)**

chakpŏp Korean Buddhist ritual dance. **(7)**

chakri Vocal genre of Kashmir. **(5)**

chalandamarz Celebration in March in Graubünden, Switzerland, with songs that praise the coming spring. **(8)**

chalangalang (Also *changalang*.) Hawaiian manner of strumming *'ukulele* and guitar, sometimes called twangy. **(9)**

Chalcedon, Council of Christian church council in 451 that condemned Monophysitism; the Maronite church evolved out of the Chalcedonian group, which believed in two natures of Christ within a single person. **(6)**

Chaldean Church Christian sect espousing the Eastern Syro-Antiochene rite, united with the Roman See from the seventeenth century. **(6)**

chālghī al-baghdādī (Also *jālghī al-baghdādī*.) (1) 'Baghdadi ensemble', traditional ensemble for the performance of Iraqi *maqām*, consisting of two chordophones (*santūr*, *jōza*) and two or three membranophones (*daff*, *dumbuk*, *naqqāra*). (2) Characteristically Iraqi compound form or suite. **(6)**

chālīsā Common Hindu prayer form. **(5)**

challa Men's amorous songs of Madhya Pradesh. **(5)**

'cham Tibetan ritual ballet, performed in monastery courtyards. **(5)**

chamamé Argentine polka-derived social dance performed during a *jineteada*. **(2)**

chamblai (Also *raj nplaim*.) Hmong free-reed side-blown pipe with a high falling tone, short low tone, and glottalized ending pattern. **(3)**

champa de Song tale of Madhya Pradesh, blending prose, verse, and recitation. **(5)**

Chamorro (Also Chamoru.) The indigenous people and language of the Mariana Islands. **(9)**

chamrieng 'Vocals', Cambodian singing featured in the *pinnpeat* ensemble. **(3)**

chanántskua Purépecha collective performance game-dance. **(2)**

chand (Also *gīt*.) Extended poetic verse, in Gujarat. **(5)**

chanda Section of Oriya oral epic tale sung by professional balladeers in Orissa. **(5)**

chan dio Shortest of three rhythmic cycles in Thai music. **(4)**

chanfa (China.) In Buddhism, a confession. **(7)**

chang (1) Mouth harp played in Afghanistan. (1) In Xinjiang-Uygur, a trapezoidal dulcimer with metal strings which has replaced the older *kalun* or *kanun*; also refers to a Central Asian struck zither. (2) Medieval Persian harp; cf. *jank*. **(5, 6, 8)**

chāṅg Large shallow-rimmed frame drum of Rajasthan. **(5)**

Changagwŏn Music Supervisory Institute, Korean Chosŏn period. **(7)**

Changakkwa Music Management Bureau, late Korean Chosŏn period. **(7)**

ch'angbu Character in a Korean village ritual play, often a monk of dubious morality. **(7)**

changdan 'Long-short', traditional Korean rhythmic patterns. **(7)**

changduan (China.) Sung portions of the storytelling interespersed in passages of narration in *Suzhou tanci*. **(7)**

changgo (Also *changgu* and, in Japan, *changko*.) Korean double-headed hourglass drum. **(7)**

changgoch'um (Also *changgo nori*.) Korean folk dance with hourglass-shaped drum. **(7)**

ch'anggŭk Korean musical drama with *p'ansori*-style singing. **(7)**

ch'angjak ŭmak Contemporary Korean creative music. **(7)**

changi Six-stringed harp of Svaneti, Georgia. **(8)**

chang-kobuz Metal Jew's harp of Central Asia. **(6)**

changmian Peking opera music ensemble. **(3)**

changpian (China.) Full-length stories in *Suzhou tanci*. **(7)**

changqiang (China.) Sung melody. **(7)**

ch'angu Korean folk entertainer. **(7)**

changüi Cuban genre belonging to the *son* family. **(2)**

chan karak 'Fine melody', rhythmic ornamentation added to Korean *chandan*. **(7)**

chanson 'Song' (French), a locally produced popular song. **(8)**

chanson d'aventure (French), Welsh folk love song. **(8)**

chanson de bord French heterophonic responsorial sea chantey. **(8)**

chanson de danse (Also *chanson en laisse*.) French strophic song, consisting of one or more isosyllabic lines of from six to sixteen syllables. **(8)**

chanson à danser French term for Breton *kan da gorell*. **(8)**

chanson de geste French and Breton stichic heroic song of the 1100s and earlier. **(8)**

chanson de métier French work song. **(8)**

chanson à repondre (Also *chanson doubleé*.) 'Response style', in which everyone participates by singing refrain lines, repeating the verse line, or both. **(3)**

chanson à repouner French heterophonic responsorial dance song. **(8)**

chanson de travail French work song. **(8)**

chansonnier (1) Urban French musical style that uses the accordion; (2) singer in a style of urban French popular music, especially a cabaret singer. **(8)**

chant (1) Musical recitation of a sacred text. (2) In European music, any of various forms of monophonic music used in Jewish rituals and especially Christian liturgies; *see Gregorian chant*. (3) Recitational singing, often on one or two tones, with rhythms deriving from those of the words. **(4, 8, 9)**

chanté 'Sung' (French), (1) *chanté abwè*, St. Lucian 'songs to drink', the songs or their performance during Christmas season; (2) *chanté kont*, St. Lucian 'song-drama' often enacted in pantomime and usually performed at wakes; (3) *chanté mas*, Dominican masquerade songs based on call and response; (4) *chanté siay*, St. Lucian work songs to accompany wood sawing; (5) *chants-charrue*, songs of farmers in Guadeloupe. **(2)**

chantwèl (1) Dominican song leader; (2) St. Lucian song leader, typically of the La Rose and La Marguerite societies. **(2)**

chantwell (Also *chantrel*.) Song leader in Caribbean creole cultures. **(2)**

chap Medium-size Thai cymbals connected by a cord, flatter and thinner than the *ching*. **(4)**

chapbooks Pocket-sized books printed with texts of ballads. **(8)**

chập chòa In Vietnam, pair of medium-size cymbals. **(4)**

chapei (Also *chapey*, *chapey dang veng*.) Cambodian long-necked lute with two to four strings. The *chapei dang veng* is used in Khmer wedding and epic singing ensembles. **(3, 4)**

chapetones Biting satire dance of colonial Spanish manners. **(2)**

chapka (Also *chwach'ang*.) 'Miscellaneous song', professional vocal genre of Korea. **(7)**

chap kuk In Iranian music, tuning for the female vocal range. **(6)**

chappar Wooden clappers. **(5)**

chaprī Rectangular wooden clappers. **(5)**

chapsaek 'Motley crew', Korean costumed actors associated with agricultural entertainment. **(7)**

chapsaek nori Korean farmers' percussion band sideshow performances. **(7)**

chapuli (Also *raj pus lim.*) Hmong fipple flute with low- to mid-level tone, short low tone, and glottalized ending pattern. **(3)**

chaqui-capitán Ecuadorian foot-captain. **(2)**

charaki Chromatic pitches and microtones in Uighur (Uygur) music. **(6)**

charanga (1) Afro-Cuban dance band style originating in the 1950s. (2) (Also *charanga típica, charanga francesa.*) Cuban ensemble combining piano, violin, and flute with percussion. (3) *Charanga-vallenato*, Colombian *vallenato* style. **(2, 3)**

charango (1) In the Andes of Argentina, Bolivia, and southern Peru, a small guitar made of wood or an armadillo shell with eight to fifteen metal or nylon strings tuned in five courses; (2) Bolivian small plucked lute with four or five double courses; (3) Ecuadorian small six-stringed plucked lute with double courses. **(2)**

chārbeitī (Also *dobeitī, dobeytī* 'couplet'.) 'Quatrian' (Persian), genre of sung poetry consisting of couplets (that is, four half-lines) normally sung in succession, with or without instrumental accompaniment. **(6)**

charcheta Three-valve tenor horn used to play offbeats in the Sinaloan *banda* ensemble. **(3)**

chareos Mixtec dance related to Saint James. **(2)**

charieng chapay Narrative genre from Cambodia. **(4)**

charivari Noisy mock serenade to newlyweds. **(8)**

charm Brazilian popular music form of the 1990s. **(2)**

charrango Chilean board zither. **(2)**

charrasca Venezuelan ridged idiophone scraped with a stick. **(2)**

chārzarb 'Four strokes', form of rhythmic chanting in four beats of one of the names of God, forming the basis of Central Asian Sufi *zikr*. **(6)**

chasa gīt 'Cultivator's songs' of agricultural laborers in Orissa. **(5)**

Chasidic pop Style of Israeli popular music appealing to Zionist religious groups in Israel, developed in the 1970s. **(6)**

chastushka 'Short ditty', Russian instrumental-vocal genre in short, single-stanza couplets accompanied by an accordion or a balalaika. **(8)**

chatagan Tuvan zither. **(6)**

chatni (Also *chutney.*) 'Hot and spicy', popular music genre of the Indo-Guyanese. **(5)**

chattīs Mystical and didactic songs performed by folk singers and village elders in Orissa. **(5)**

chāu Dance form of eastern India, performed by men during spring festivals. **(5)**

chàu văn Vietnamese spirit possession ritual. **(4)**

che Style, system, or school (of Korean *p'ansori* performance). **(7)**

cheb Male Algerian singer of *rai*, a North African music popular in France. **(8)**

chediao Chinese melodic mode. **(7)**

chegança (1) Brazilian dance drama and procession depicting the Christians battling the Moors; (2) a sensuous Afro-Brazilian dance. **(3)**

chegbe Struck idiophone made of a bottle or kerosene can and played to accompany palm-wine guitar music. **(1)**

cheironomy Hand and finger gestures used in directing music. **(8)**

Cheju minyo Korean folk songs from Cheju Island. **(7)**

che koetie (Also *chichothi*.) Old Sri Lankan term probably referring to a performance tradition involving word dueling and verbal competition. **(5)**

chelā Pupil, student. **(5)**

chenci (China.) Decorative phrases or words. **(7)**

chenepri Anyi drums, taller and slimmer than *atumpan* and played with L-shaped sticks. **(1)**

chenzi (China.) Padding syllables. **(7)**

chèo Traditional theater of northern Vietnam. **(4)**

chequeré Cuban idiophone of African origin. **(2)**

cheshui ge (China.) Water lifters. **(7)**

chesslete Winter parade in Solothurn, Switzerland, with homemade noisemakers. **(8)**

Chewa Culture group of Malawi. **(1)**

chhap Medium Khmer cymbals, thinner than *chhing*. **(4)**

chhing Cambodian pair of small, thick metal cymbals connected by a cord; played as part of the *pinnpeat* ensemble, in which it serves as the timekeeper. **(3, 4)**

chi Korean transverse wooden flute. **(7)**

chiam' e rispondi 'Call and response', Corsican poetic contests between rival singers. **(8)**

chianuri (Also *chuniri.*) Georgian three-stringed bowed lute, often played at funerals in Achara and Tusheti. **(8)**

chiboni (Also *chimoni.*) Bagpipe of Achara, Georgia. **(8)**

chica Neo-African social dance practiced by Afro-Haitians in nineteenth-century New Orleans. **(3)**

chicha (1) Argentine popular alcoholic drink made from *algarrobo* tree. (2) Corn or maize beer in the Andes. (3) (Also *cumbia andina.*) Distinctly Peruvian variant of *cumbia* that creolized the Colombian *cumbia* rhythms with highland *huayno* melodies. **(2)**

chicheros 'Chicha drinkers', Nicaraguan musicians who perform in *bandas de chicheros* or *bandas filarmónicas* for funerary masses and processions. **(2)**

Chichewa Language spoken in Malawi, Zambia, and parts of northern Mozambique. **(1)**

chichodromos Locales for *chicha* events in Peru. **(2)**

chicote Kogi circle dance. **(2)**

chifonie French medieval hurdy-gurdy. **(8)**

chift kavali Pair of *kavals* that play melody-and-drone duets in southwestern Pirin, Bulgaria. **(8)**

chigualo (1) Introductory percussive music of Ecuador; (2) Colombian religious wake song. **(2)**

chikap ne (Japan.) 'Bird dance', a genre of Ainu dance imitating the flight of cranes and swallows. **(7)**

chikappo reki (Japan.) 'Bird song', a genre of Ainu songs. **(7)**

chihumba Ovambo eight-stringed multiple-bow lute. **(1)**

chilamate Ensemble of chordophones that accompanies the Salvadoran dance of the Herods. **(2)**

chilchil (1) Ecuadorian fruit-capsule rattle; (2) small Nicaraguan bells. **(2)**

Child ballads (1) Oldest substantial body of oral-tradition sung English-language poetry, often concerning love. (2) Repertoire first systematically collected by Sir Francis James Child (1825–1896) in Great Britain and North America. (3) Any of a repertoire of popular English, Irish, and Scottish ballads with short, usually four-phrase melodies. **(3, 8)**

chilena (1) Chilean couple dance, with Afro-Hispanic rhythms and Spanish stanzas, related to the *zamacueca* and the *cueca* of the coast of Peru and Chile; (2) Mexican regional style of the Costa Chica, along the Pacific coast of Oaxaca and Guerrero states. **(2)**

chili-gari-ai 'Juniper and goat', purifying ritual theater of the Northern Areas of Pakistan. **(5)**

chillador 'Screamer' (Spanish), in the Andes (especially northern Chile) a small guitar (like a *charango* but smaller) of five or six courses made of wood or armadillo shell. **(2)**

chilopa 'Blood sacrifice' among the Tumbuka of Malawi. **(1)**

ch'ima Traditional Korean skirt. (7)

chimarrita Brazilian folk dance popular along border areas of Uruguay. (2)

chimbangueles Set of four to seven Afro-Venezuelan conical drums whose single skins are tightened by hoops and wooden wedges. (2)

chimoni (Also *chiboni*.) Bagpipe of Achara, Georgia. (8)

chimta (Also *cimṭā*.) Metal tongs with brass disks attached. (5)

chimurenga 'Songs of liberation', *mbira*-derived songs related to the uprising in Zimbabwe, or to modern Shona political processes in Zimbabwe. (1)

Chin Ethnic group from Burma. (4)

chinchir Cymbals played in Balochistan. (5)

chindli jodel Songs of Appenzell, Switzerland, that mainly function as lullabies. (8)

chindzembeltti zardjite 'Songs to accompany the bride', Ossetian best-man's songs. (8)

ching (1) Pair of small Thai cymbals connected by a cord. (2) Large Korean gong. (4, 7)

chin'go Largest Korean barrel drum, used for Confucian rituals or court music. (7)

chino 'Humble servant'. In Quechua, Chilean dancers who honor the Virgin and are the oldest type of dancing group, consisting of miners in Chilean patronal festivals. (2)

chinogut Korean shaman ritual for the dead. (7)

chin-ujo Majestic Korean melodic mode. (7)

chinŭl mandŭlda (Also *chinŭl p'unda* or *p'ulda*.) Formation in a Korean farmers' band, transforming straight lines to tight circles. (7)

chinyang (Also *chinyangjo*.) Korean rhythmic pattern (*changdan*), very slow 18/8 meter. (7)

chipch'e yesul (Also *chip ch'e ch'angjak*.) 'Collective art', 'collective creation'; North Korean ideology. (7)

chipendani Shona mouth-resonated braced bow with a thick handle carved onto the center of the bow. (1)

chiphonie Hurdy-gurdy of the Low Countries. (8)

chip kut Shaman household ritual in Korea. (7)

chipsa Organizer, a character in a Korean village ritual play. (7)

chiquit Bolivian special dances at initiation and marriage ceremonies. (2)

chiriguano (1) Large panpipes of Huancané, Peru. (2) (Also *chiriwanu*.) Bolivian tradition of panpipes subdivided into three different groups tuned to the octave. (3) (Also Chiriwano.) In the Andes and Paraguay, the name for an Indian culture. (2)

chirimía (1) In Bolivia, Guatemala, Mexico (among the Purépecha, Maya, and Nahua especially), and parts of Peru, an oboe-type instrument of early Spanish colonial importation played by native Americans or *mestizos*; (2) Colombian musical ensemble or band originating in the Chocó region and consisting of brass instruments, *bombo*, *cununo*, and cymbals. (2)

chirisuya Type of oboe played in highlands of the Peruvian departments of Lima, Huancavelica, and Ayacucho. (2)

chironuup rimse (Japan.) 'Fox dance', genre of Ainu festival dance songs. (7)

chirula Three-holed flute played with a *ttunttun* in the Basque country and Gascony, France. (8)

chischiles Current name for small bells sewn onto Nicaraguan folk dancers' shoes. (2)

chishapshina Adighian two-stringed long-necked plucked lute that accompanies epic songs and two-part vocal polyphony. (8)

ch'isŏng 'Teeth voice', vocal timbre in Korea *p'ansori*. (7)

chissori Long chant of Korean Buddhist *pŏmp'ae*. (7)

chisungu Nubility rite for Bemba girls in which scenes of grinding maize and collecting potatoes are enacted. (1)

chitara 'Guitar' (Romanian). (8)

chitarra battente 'Beaten guitar' (Italian), central and southern Italian guitar, played with a plectrum to accompany singing. (8)

chitrāli sitār Long-necked lute popular throughout the North West Frontier Province. (5)

chivoti Flute of the coastal Bantu peoples of Kenya. (1)

chläuse Carnival characters of Switzerland. (8)

chlause Clapper bell of Kaltbrunn, St. Gallen, Switzerland. (8)

chlausjage Jingle bells on a harness in Hallwil, Aargau, Switzerland. (8)

chlepfe Swiss whip-cracking. (8)

cho Mode or melodic type in Korean music, often implying a mood or sentiment. (7)

chocalho Brazilian idiophone shaker. (2)

Choctaw social dance songs Set of songs originally associated with the Ballgame cycle performed among American Indians of the Eastern Woodlands and Great Lakes but now performed in secular contexts such as festivals. (3)

chodzony Walking dance in Polish folk music. (8)

chogān Ritual spiritual music and dance of the Zikris of Pakistan. (5)

chŏgori Traditional Korean jacket. (7)

chŏk Korean vertical bamboo flute. (7)

chŏlgo Large Korean barrel drum, used for Confucian rituals or court music. (7)

chŏl kollip Korean fund-raising performance on behalf of Buddhist temples. (7)

Ch'ŏllima undong Korean "galloping horse" movement.

chŏllip Korean felt-domed hat with rotating plume. (7)

ch'ŏlsŏng 'Iron voice', 'metallic voice'; vocal timbre in Korean *p'ansori*. (7)

chona Songs performed during the Georgian ritual of *chonaoba*. (8)

chonaoba Georgian ritual held on Palm Sunday, when maskers go through a village singing a ritual song (*chona*) and begging for food and red eggs, then hold a ritual feast. (8)

chong Korean term for bell, including huge Buddhist bells. (7)

ch'ŏng Central tone of Korean melodic modes. (7)

chŏngak 'Proper music', court music of Korea. (7)

Chŏngaksŏ Office for Ritual Music, Korean Koryŏ dynasty. (7)

chŏngga 'Proper song', vocal repertoire of Korean *chŏngak*. See *kagok*, *kasa*, *sijo*. (7)

chŏngganbo Korean mensural notation. (7)

Chŏnggwajŏng Korean song of the Koryŏ dynasty, prototype of *kagok*. (7)

chŏngjaron 'Seed theory', Korean ideology. (7)

Chong nagma 'Great music', term for the first and most essential section of the Uygur *muqam*, in which various instruments enter successively; it follows a short instrumental prelude. (6)

chŏngsa 'Proper history', authentic Korean historical documents. *See yasa.* (7)

chonguri Georgian unfretted medium-sized long-necked four-stringed lute, played primarily by Samegrelo and Guria women to accompany singing and dancing. (8)

ch'ŏn'gusŏng 'Gifted voice', vocal timbre in Korean *p'ansori*. (7)

ch'ŏnmin Korean caste of outcasts, including certain musicians and shamans. (7)

ch'ŏnsŏng Korean melodic ornamentation, "rolling." (7)

chonta Ecuadorian palm tree used to make marimba keys. (2)

Chonyi Migikenda culture group of Kenya. (1)

Chopi Culture group of southern Africa. (1)

chopí Paraguayan folk couple dance. (2)

chopāni Pastoral shepherd song of northern Afghanistan. (5)

chorale (1) Hymn tune of the German Protestant Church. (2) In European music, a hymn of the Lutheran church, typically monophonic in its original (usually sixteenth-century) form, but subsequently used in polyphonic settings. (3, 8)

chordophone 'String sounder'. Musical instrument such as a violin or guitar, whose principal sound is produced by one or more stretched, vibrating strings. (**1, 2, 3, 4, 5, 9**)

chorea polonica Name of the mazurka outside Poland. (**8**)

chorijung Character in a Korean village ritual play who checks the altar offerings. (**7**)

chorimori Pre-Encounter Atacameño rattle of metal bells without clappers. (**2**)

choro (1) Brazilian dance music ensemble; (2) Afro-Brazilian musical genre based on polka-*maxixe* rhythm. (**2**)

chorões 'Weepers', Brazilian strolling street musician-serenaders. (**2**)

chorovod Czech and Slovak line and round dances, particularly by young women. (**8**)

chorumbal Transverse flute of the Fulɓe of The Gambia. (**1**)

Chosŏn chŏngak chŏnsŭpso Korean Court Music Study Institute, established in 1911. (**7**)

Chosŏn dynasty Or Yi dynasty, Korean, 1392–1910. (**7**)

Chosŏn kamu yŏn'guhoe Korean Music and Dance Society. (**7**)

Chosŏn minsokhakhoe Korean Folklore Society. (**7**)

Chosŏn sŏngak yŏn'guhoe Korean Vocal Music Association. (**7**)

Chosŏn ŭmak hyŏphoe Korean Music Society, established in 1941. (**7**)

Chosŏn ŭmnyul hyŏphoe Korean performance troupe. (**7**)

Chosŏn wangjo sillok 'Annals of the Chosŏn Dynasty', Korean historical document. (**7**)

ch'osudaeyŏp Slow initial piece in a Korean *kagok* song cycle performed by a male. *See isudaeyŏp.* (**7**)

choṭā gīt 'Small songs', men's songs derived from women's repertoire, performed by the Langās and Manganihārs in Rajasthan. (**5**)

choṭā khyāl Hindustani vocal music genre in a medium or fast tempo. (**5**)

chotis *Waila* dance form whose name is derived from the German *schottisch*, originally brought to Madrid from Scotland; later became popular in Latin America. (**3**)

choṭī sāraṅgī Small bowed lute of Punjab, Pakistan. (**5**)

chŏttae (Also *taegŭm.*) Large Korean transverse bamboo flute. (**7**)

chou (China.) Actor of comic roles. (**7**)

chowtal In Indo-Caribbean culture, a vigorous responsorial male song genre performed during the springtime *phagwa* festival. (**3**)

Choyang kurakpu Korean Choyang Club (music institute), established in 1908. (**7**)

chrieng chapei (1) (Also *chireng chapey.*) Khmer narrative accompanied by long-necked lute

(*chapey*). (2) Cambodian epic singing in which a vocalist accompanies himself on a long-necked lute; has not survived within the Cambodian community in the United States. (**3, 4**)

chromatic In Western music, pertaining to a scale or passage that contains only half steps. (**3**)

chronos protos Greek term meaning the shortest perceivable duration, used as the unit of measurement. It was the cornerstone of Arabic medieval rhythmic theories. (**6**)

chuanqi (China.) 'Tales of the marvelous'; refers to a new genre of tales written in literary language during the sixteenth century. (**7**)

chucho Colombian cylindrical rattle. (**2**)

chuch'ŏnmok (Also *pan'gyŏngdŭrŭm.*) Cheerful, buoyant melodic mode, used in Korean *p'ansori.* (**7**)

chuḍke Popular dance and instrumental piece in Nepal. (**5**)

chuida Outdoor ensemble from China. (**4**)

chuidayue (China.) Music for winds and percussion. (**7**)

chuige (China.) Songs for winds. (**7**)

ch'imsae Vocal interjections by the drummer, the audience, or both in Korean folk music and *p'ansori.* (**7**)

ch'uk Korean instrument in the form of a boxlike wooden mortar struck with a thick pestle. (**7**)

chula (1) Brazilian song texts of *samba de viola.* (2) Portuguese couple dance in duple meter. (**2, 8**)

chulp'ungnyu Korean "string music." (**7**)

chumba (1) Guatemalan erotic dance; (2) in Belize, old dance performed by a soloist in a highly individualized manner. (**2**)

chunan Mapuche shell rattles. (**2**)

chungangsŏng (Also *t'ongsŏng.*) Principal vocal technique in Korean *p'ansori.* (**7**)

ch'unchu Bolivian caricature dance. (**2**)

Chungdaeyŏp 'Moderately large piece', prototype of Korean *kagok.* (**7**)

chunggoje Central school of the Korean *p'ansori* tradition. (**7**)

Chungguk 'Central country', Korean name for China. (**7**)

chunggŭm Korean medium-sized bamboo flute, now obsolete. (**7**)

chungin Korean middle class. (**7**)

chungjungmori Korean rhythmic pattern (*changdan*), dancelike 12/8 meter. (**7**)

chungmori Korean rhythmic pattern (*changdan*), moderate 12-beat meter, 12/4. (**7**)

chungsa Medium-sized Korean rites. (**7**)

chuning (From English *tuning.*) Shona concept of pitch-based tuning that includes timbre and loudness. (**1**)

chuniri (Also *chianuri.*) Svanetian or Georgian two- or three-stringed bowed lute, often played at funerals. (**8**)

chunyu (China.) Percussion instrument of the Zhou period, made of a copper barrel and a pair of beaters. (**7**)

chuqila (1) Bolivian ritual vicuña-hunt dance; (2) Bolivian vertical end-blown notched flute. (**2**)

churu (1) Conch-shell trumpet in Amazonas; (2) Ecuadorian conch-shell trumpet. (**2**)

churwassay Bontok honorary funeral song. (**4**)

ch'usŏk Korean autumn holiday. (**7**)

chutney (Also Indian *soca, soca chutney.*) Hot, spicy songs in traditional Bhojpuri culture; lively, sexy dance songs in Trinidad. (**5**)

chutti Curved white frame used in *kathakaḷi* face makeup. (**5**)

Chuuk Main island complex, and a state, of the Federated States of Micronesia. (**9**)

chuyūkh (Also *chaykāt, shuyūkh, shaykāt.*) 'Masters' or 'mistresses' of Algerian *rai.* (**6**)

chwach'ang 'Sitting songs', long Korean folks songs, often performed by professionals. (**7**)

chwado nongak 'Left', regional style of Korean farmers' band music. (**7**)

chwago Large Korean seated drum. (**7**)

ch'wit'a (Also *t'aech'wit'a.*) 'Blowing and beating', Korean military and royal processional music. (**7**)

ci Chinese sung poetry. (**7**)

cialambella (Also *cialambedda, cialamedda, cialemella.*) Corsican single-reed aerophone with a slightly conical wooden body, a bell, and six holes for fingering; see *ciaramella.* (**8**)

ciałušačka Belarusan genre that musically depicts the emotions of losing and finding a herd animal. (**8**)

ciaramella Italian single-reed aerophone (oboe) played in sets of two or three; see *cialembella.* (**3, 8**)

cifra Argentine traditional *pampa* musical form performed during *jineteada.* (**2**)

çifte Turkish double clarinet with a box-shaped body. (**6**)

čiftečelli The 4/4 rhythm of Romanian *manea.* (**8**)

çifteli (Also *çiteli.*) Albanian fretted long-necked plucked lute. (**8**)

çifte-na're Small Turkish kettledrums. (**6**)

čift kavali Pair of Macedonian bevel-edged, rim-blown flutes that play melody and drone. (**8**)

čigāni Type of Latvian masquerader (*budeļi*) meant to evoke the image of Gypsies (Roma). (**8**)

ciganski kjuček The 9/8 variant of the Bulgarian Rom *kjuček.* (**8**) *cikāra* (Also *cakārā*.) Short-necked and spike fiddles played in Madhya Pradesh, Rajasthan, and Kashmir. **(5)**

cikārī Drone strings on many North Indian plucked string instruments. **(5)**

Cilappatikāram 'The Tale of the Anklet', first great Tamil epic. **(5)**

cilokaq Wind, string, and drum ensemble of Lombok. **(4)**

cimarrona Small traditional Costa Rican ensemble of woodwinds, brass, and percussion. **(2)**

cimbál Czech and Slovak trapezoidal struck zither. **(8)**

cimbalom Trapezoidal struck dulcimer, central to Hungarian Gypsy string orchestras. **(8)**

cimbalová muzika Eastern Moravian and Slovakian dulcimer band with violins, violas, clarinets, a string bass, and a trapezoidal struck zither (*cimbál*). **(8)**

cimpoi Romanian bagpipe. **(8)**

cimprekelj (Also *brana, male cimbale, oprekelj, pretl.*) Slovene trapezoidal struck zither. **(8)**

cimţā (Also *chimta.*) Two flat iron bars joined at one end with metal platelets attached, used in folk and devotional music of northern regions. **(5)**

cinco 'Five', (1) Venezuelan small guitar with five strings; (2) *cinco de seis cuerdas,* Venezuelan small guitar with six strings; (3) *cinco y medio,* Venezuelan small guitar with 'five and a half' strings. **(2)**

cine pāṭṭu South Indian film songs. **(5)**

cingonë (Also *curle, surle, zurle.*) Albanian conical-bore double-reed aerophone. **(8)**

cinna kaţci 'Small faction' of devotees at a Tyagaraja festival. **(5)**

cinna mēlam 'Small ensemble' of musicians with a dancer. **(5)**

cinquillo Five-beat "throb" cast in duple meter; also a feature of Cuban *contradanzas*, most likely via the French *contradanse.* **(3)**

cîntec Romanian strophic song. **(8)**

cîntece bătrîneşti 'Old-time songs', songs performed by professional musicians (*lăutari*) at wedding banquets and other occasions in southern Romania; *see balade.* **(8)**

cîntece ceremoniale 'Ceremonial songs', Romanian burial laments, performed by professional lamenters. **(8)**

cîntece de leagăn Romanian lullabies. **(8)**

cîntece de mahala 'Songs of the neighborhood', urban Romanian Rom songs. **(8)**

cîntece de stea 'Star songs', Romanian children's winter repertoire, with texts inspired by biblical scriptures. **(8)**

cintu Strophic song with a short melody and many verses, in Tamil Nadu. **(5)**

Cinyanji Language spoken in Malawi, Zambia, and parts of northern Mozambique. **(1)**

ciplā Pair of wooden clappers with metal jingles, in South India. **(5)**

ciplyā Clappers, wooden strips with inserted metal rings, used for rhythm in the devotional music of Maharashtra. **(5)**

cipu (China.) Song registers that contain texts, rhyme schemes, phrase structures, and musical information. **(7)**

ciranda Brazilian children's game-song genre. **(2)**

circle of fifths Schematic representation depicting the major keys most closely related to one another within the Western tonal system, located a fifth apart. **(3)**

cire perdue Technology of lost-wax casting, used by ancient Scandinavian and Irish craftsmen to manufacture musical instruments such as the *lur* and the bronze horn. **(8)**

cisanji Small board-shaped lamellophones in the Shiluba area of Zaïre. **(1)**

çiteli (Also *çifteli.*) Albanian fretted long-necked plucked lute. **(8)**

ciţike Wooden clapper used in Karnataka to keep time in *tatva* singing. **(5)**

cítira Violin of Resia, Slovenia. **(8)**

citra Slovene zither. **(8)**

citrāvīṇā (Also *citrā vīṇā.*) 'Artful *vīṇā* stopped with a sliding stick; seven-stringed arched harp of Indian antiquity. **(5)**

citta svara Composed *svara* passages occasionally included in Karnatak *kriti* and *varṇam.* **(5)**

cittern (1) Long-necked, multistringed instrument used to play Irish traditional music. (2) Guitarlike Renaissance stringed instrument with a flat pear-shaped body. **(3, 8)**

ciwaiñ Burmese set of twenty-one graduated bossed gongs mounted horizontally in a circle. **(4)**

cīz Vocal composition, in Hindustani music. **(5)**

claca Romanian work parties involving song, instrumental music, and dance. **(8)**

cláirseach Irish harp; *see cruit.* **(8)**

clansong Song owned by a clan (546); in Aboriginal Australia, a song said to be created by totemic ancestral spirits and performed publicly to celebrate the spirits' activities. **(9)**

clapsticks In Aboriginal Australia, a concussed pair of sticks or boomerangs. **(9)**

clarín (1) In Cajamarca, Peru, a long cane side-blown tranverse trumpet; (2) a long valveless, transverse wooden or cane trumpet in Peru; (3) in Chile, a pre-Encounter Atacameño 2-meter transverse trumpet without resonator made of a cane bound with colored wool. **(2)**

clarine French cowbell. **(8)**

clarinet-shawm In Denmark, a reed instrument made of pine wood, split and hollowed out, and bound or wedged together. **(8)**

clàrsach Harp played by bards in early Scotland and later revived. **(8)**

Classical In European music history, the period from approximately 1750 to the death of Beethoven (1827). **(8)**

clausula (Plural, *clausulae.*) 'Close, conclusion, cadence' (Latin), style of twelfth- and thirteenth-century note-againste-note Parisian liturgical polyphony. **(8)**

clave (1) 'Key', Cuban rhythm consisting of 3 + 2 or (reverse *clave*) 2 + 3. (2) *Claves,* in Cuba and other Latin American regions, two hardwood dowels struck together to mark the *clave* or basic meter. (3) One of a pair of sticks used to play a rhythm that serves as the rhythmic base of Afro-Cuban music. **(2, 3)**

cling-a-ching Tiguan triangle. **(2)**

cliquen Swiss fife-and-drum band. **(8)**

clopote (Also *zurgălăi.*) Romanian bells used in New Year's ceremonies and weddings and hung around the necks of cattle and sheep as signal devices. **(8)**

čobanske pjesme Shepherds' songs of Croatia, Montenegro, and Bosnia-Hercegovina. **(8)**

cobla Catalonian ensemble that accompanies the *sardana.* **(8)**

cobza Romanian plucked short-necked lute. **(8)**

čoček Dance of south Serbian and Macedonian Gypsies. **(8)**

côco (1) Afro-Brazilian coconut dance; (2) *côco-de-décima,* Afro-Brazilian dance based on a ten-line stanza song structure; (3) *côco-de-embolada,* Afro-Brazilian dance based on a tongue-twisting song form; (4) *côco-de-ganzá,* Afro-Brazilian shaker dance. **(2)**

cofradía 'Confraternity', (1) Roman Catholic religious brotherhood founded for African slaves and their descendants; (2) Afro-Peruvian church-sponsored confraternity or sodality devoted to a patron saint; (3) Guatemalan Indian prayer house. **(2)**

çöğür Long-necked plucked Turkish folk lute with movable frets. **(6)**

colascione Medieval Italian long-necked lute; *see cannacione.* **(8)**

colindatori Romanian carolers. **(8)**

colinde Good-luck visits with singing at the new year in Romania. **(8)**

coliseos Open theaters that were venues of Peruvian music in the 1970s in Lima. **(2)**

colonne "English" longways dance (Frence), country dance popular in the Low Countries in the eighteenth and nineteenth centuries. **(8)**

colotomic structure Organization of music by periodic punctuation. **(4)**

columbia Cuban music and dance genre belonging to the *rumba* family. **(2)**

Columbia Major recording label, which by the 1930s was distributing its products across Africa. **(1)**

combo Cuban name given to musical ensembles toward the end of the 1950s. **(2)**

comedia Full-length Spanish drama, lasting up to three hours, in several (usually three) acts and typically incorporating song, dance, and instrumental music. **(3)**

comenzi Romanian calls, often integrated into a polyrhythmic texture. **(8)**

comparsa (1) Form of percussive Afro-Cuban processional music used in *carnaval* and other festive settings. (2) Ensemble of musicians playing *comparsa* music. (3) Cuban characteristic dance in *carnaval*. (4) (Also *comparza*.) Plucked-string ensemble from the lowland Philippines. **(2, 3, 4)**

compás Complex counterrhythms in flamenco. **(8)**

compas direct (Also *konpa*.) Modified *merengue* danced at a leisurely tempo, which became popular among Haitians and Haitian-Americans in the 1950s and 1960s. **(3)**

compitu Consican lament, especially for the dead; *see lamentu.* **(8)**

complainte (1) French term for Breton *gwerz*. (2) Song text in French-speaking Switzerland that deals with religious folk themes or political satire. **(8)**

complessi Italian modern soft-rock groups. **(8)**

composo Visayas heroic-political ballad. **(4)**

comuncha Ayacucho guitar tuning pattern (E–B–G–D–B–G) used primarily to play peasant *huaynos* in E minor. **(2)**

conca Italian dances preserved in Corsica. **(8)**

concertina (1) Small button accordion in hexagonal shape. (2) Small reed instrument in the accordion family. (3) Free-reed aerophone with bellows that produces different pitches on a given button, depending on whether air is pushed or pulled through the reeds. **(2, 3, 8)**

conchero Nahua dance accompanied by an armadillo-shell guitar, called by the same name. **(2)**

concerto In European art music of the eighteenth century and later, instrumental composition in which passages for one or more soloists alternate and combine with passages for a larger ensemble. **(8)**

conch band Musical ensemble formed of conch trumpets, with one performer and one note per instrument, invented around 1925 in Morobe, New Guinea, by the Lutheran missionary Heinrich Zahn (1880–1944). **(9)**

conch trumpet Trumpet made from the empty shell of a conch of the genus *Cassis, Fusus,* *Strombus,* or *Triton;* possibly the most widespread indigenous instrument of Oceania. **(9)**

concurso Spanish competition, especially in flamenco. **(8)**

concussive idiophone Idiophone made to sound by the action of one part against another, as with clapsticks, paired stones, and castanets; cf. *percussive idiophone.* **(9)**

conductus 'Led together' (Latin), style of twelfth- and thirteenth-century note-against-note Parisian liturgical polyphony. **(8)**

confraternite Sardinian religious brotherhoods, some of which preserve and teach polyphonic singing. **(8)**

Confucius (China.) One of the most influential scholars and philosophers of the Warring States period (475–221 B.C.E.). **(7)**

conga drum (Also, plural, *congas*.) Afro-Cuban narrow barrel-shaped or tapering drum, now also used in Swedish folk music. **(3, 5, 8)**

congo (1) (Also *congada*.) Brazilian dramatic dance group that combines African and Iberian influences. (2) Afro-Panamanian music, dance, and theater tradition. (3) Song genre of Sango bands in Trinidadian carnival. (4) *Congos,* ensemble music of the Brotherhood of the Holy Spirit of Villa Mella. **(2)**

Congo Success Brass-heavy big band that became publicly acclaimed in Congo and Zaïre in the 1950s and 1960s. **(1)**

conguero Player of the conga drum. **(3)**

conjunto 'Combo', 'ensemble'. (1) Throughout the Spanish-speaking Americas, a musical ensemble that performs folk music. (2) Contemporary salsa brass and percussion-based ensemble. (3) Term used to describe many regional Latin musical ensembles; in Texas, synonymous with *conjunto tejano,* the accordion-driven Texas-Mexican ensemble. **(2, 3)**

conjunto norteño Mexican term for *conjunto.* **(3)**

conkā Folk rhythm instrument of Maharashtra that produces variable-pitch sounds, similar to the *khamak.* **(5)**

consonance In European art music, one of certain musical intervals, including octaves, fifths, and (after the Middle Ages) thirds, conventionally regarded as pleasant or sonorous. **(8)**

container rattle Rattle containing seeds or other small objects that when shaken produce sound. **(3)**

content analysis Principles that make a language grammatically functional. **(1)**

conterdans (Also *contredans* and *contredanse*.) Country dance evolved from the minuet in the late eighteenth century in the Low Countries. **(8)**

contra Chilean alto-register *sikuri.* **(2)**

contră (Also *săcunda*.) Second violin, which supplies rhythmic-harmonic accompaniment in Romanian and Hungarian music in parts of Transylvania. **(8)**

contra dance *See country dance.* **(8)**

contradanza (1) Cuban genre with French origins, belonging to the *danzón* family. (2) Guarijio song-dance in duple meter with a triple subdivision (6/8). (3) Iberian and Hispanic-American dance derived from the English country dance; in Cuba, a variant of the French creole *contradanse.* **(2, 3)**

contrapunto Chilean competitive dialogue singing, often with improvised quatrains. **(2)**

contrato High voice part of the Venezuelan *tonos* ensemble. **(2)**

contredanse (1) Type of French Creole figure dance practiced in Louisiana by French and Haitian immigrants. (2) Set or figure dance most popular in France in the late 1700s, an ancestor of the quadrille. **(3, 8)**

Cool Stars Band from Bangui, Central African Republic, of the early 1980s. **(1)**

coordinate monophony Simultaneous performance of two or more melodies, unrelated or related only through a common tone, as in Angan choral singing, or meter, as in Yupno *njaguo konggap* and among the Isirawa. **(9)**

coordinate polyphony Simultaneous performance of two or more independent phrases, as in the Bellonese *suahongi* and the Tongan *me'etu'upaki.* **(9)**

copla 'Couplet', 'couple' (Spanish). (1) Spanish-derived narrative musical genre from Chile, Colombia, and other Hispanic-American countries. (2) Popular improvised Spanish verse form. (3) *Copla de carnaval,* Chilean 'carnival couplet', main musical genre of the Atacameño carnival. (4) Wake song addressed to dead child and its parents. (4) Poem or song in quatrains of octosyllabic lines, with consonant or assonant rhymes in even-numbered lines. (5) Competitive male pole dance of Spain, involving mock combat. **(2, 8)**

copla de seguidilla (Also *cuarteta*.) Spanish metric-song form. **(8)**

coplas (1) Spanish term for couplets typically performed in sets as four-line stanzas with lines two and four ending in rhyme and operating either as independent songs or as part of longer forms such as the romance or *villancico.* (2) Judeo-Spanish strophic songs on Jewish topics, sung by Moroccan Jews. **(3, 6)**

copra Dried coconut meat, exported from many Pacific islands for processing into palm oil. **(9)**

coraula Dance-song of French-speaking Switzerland in which two choruses sing antiphonally. **(8)**

cordyline Relating to *ti* plants. **(9)**

corn buellin Semicircular Welsh bugle horn. **(8)**

corn songs Songs improvised at or associated with seasonal harvest celebrations called corn shuckings. **(3)**

cornamusa Corsican panpipes. **(8)**

cornemuse French bagpipes. **(8)**

cornicyll Welsh concealed-reed instrument similar to *pibgorn* hornpipes, with a mouthpiece that screwed on and off. **(8)**

cornet Soprano brass instrument similar to the trumpet, but with a conical rather than cylindrical bore producing a more mellow timbre; popular in military bands in the nineteenth and early twentieth centuries and in jazz. **(3)**

corneta 'Cornet', Andean animal-horn lip-concussion aerophone. **(2)**

cornu (Also *cornu marinu, culombu.*) Corsican conch-shell trumpet associated with the struggle for independence. **(8)**

cornua Romanian trumpet or horn. **(8)**

coro Horn of the Mbeere people of Mount Kenya. **(1)**

corpophone 'Body sounder', the body used as a musical instrument by striking or popping a body part (or parts), such as a hand clap or thigh slap. **(2)**

corps de ballet Group of dancers, often exclusively female, who dance together as a type of chorus. **(8)**

Corpus Christi (Also *corpus.*) Annual Catholic festival and liturgical holiday in honor of the eucharist, 15 June. **(2)**

corredinho Portuguese song genre of Goa based on Western tonal harmony. **(5)**

corridinho Fast virtuosic duple-meter couple dance of Faro, Portugal. **(8)**

corrido (1) Song form descended from the Spanish *romance* with lyrics structured in the format of the *copla* ballad. (2) Narrative song genre of Chile and Mexico. (3) Mexican balladic musical genre, derived from the Spanish *romance*, with texts usually concerning local, historical, or legendary events, set in stanzas of eight-syllable lines. (4) Mexican folk ballad and strophic song stemming from the romance tradition, featuring sets of *coplas* with eight-syllable lines. (5) Story about Christians and Muslims, recited on melodic formulas. **(2, 3, 4, 9)**

corroboree Aboriginal Australian nocturnal festivity with singing and dancing. **(9)**

cortesía (Also *reverencia.*) Act of demonstrating respect for the *son* dance. **(2)**

cottiljon Swedish contra dance, especially in southern and eastern Sweden. **(8)**

country dance (1) (Also drum dance, goatskin dance.) Five-part Montserrat dance performed by four male-female couples. (2) (Also contra dance.) Any of various English dances, developed in the 1600s and 1700s and taken to the continent, in which partners face each other, usually in rows. **(2, 8)**

country dancing English mixed social dancing. **(8)**

courante Dance of Italian origin featuring rapid running steps. **(8)**

counterpoint Simultaneous multiple lines of music with different rhythms. **(4)**

cover record (1) Remake of an old recording; (2) imitative recordings of black music by white artists. **(3)**

cowboy genre (Also country and western.) Later hybrid of hillbilly music developed in western North America in the 1930s and 1940s by film stars such as Gene Autry and Roy Rogers. **(3)**

cow horn Horn of a cow, used as a trumpet, often to give signals, sometimes with holes for fingering, and fixed with a duct to serve as a horn-flute. **(8)**

coyole Belt rattle used among the O'odham Indians. **(3)**

coyolli Náhuatl name for idiophone rattle made of clay, copper, dried fruit, gold, and nutshells. **(2)**

crâmignon Open-air *farandole*, danced in and around the town of Liège in the Dutch province of Limburg. **(8)**

Creative Nation Australian federal policy implemented in 1994 to further "cultural industry," tourism, and artistic technology, and to assist emerging artists. **(9)**

creole Language deriving from two or more languages and serving as its speakers' native language; cf. *pidgin.* **(9)**

creole musics Musics practiced by French and Caribbean settlers in the U.S. gulf states, characterized by syncopated rhythms. **(3)**

crin-crin French fiddle, played at balls and weddings. **(8)**

criniki Bowed pseudo-bass of the Low Countries. **(8)**

criolismo 'Creolism', (1) mixing of African and European cultural traits; (2) term referring to Europeans' descendants born in the New World. **(2)**

criolla 'Creole', (1) Cuban urban genre with rural themes belonging to the *canción* family; (2) *criollas*, Uruguayan societies whose principal objective is the preservation of traditional rural festivals. **(2)**

criollo 'Creole', (1) originally, a black person born in the New World, as opposed to an African brought from Africa; (2) later, term applied to anyone born in the colonies; (3) more recently, term applied to a person, a behavior, a music, a style, or some other element that displays or promotes the distinctive traditions, sentiments, and customs of the culture of coastal Peru; (4) *criollos*, whites, Spanish-Americans. **(2)**

criolloismo Afro-Peruvian philosophy and attitude that reflects nationalistic pride. **(2)**

cronistas 'Chroniclers', early Spanish writers. **(2)**

crooning songs (1) Songs or intoned formulas that include loving crooning sounds of a mother for her child; (2) popular singing style of the 1930s. **(3)**

crop over Originally a celebration held to mark the end of the sugarcane harvest in Barbados. **(2)**

crossover Originally the process by which a recording released in a secondary market achieves hit status in the mainstream or pop market. **(3)**

crossrhythms Rhythms of two or more voices that create distinctively different and opposing patterns. **(1)**

cruit Small, triangular handheld harp or lyre in Ireland and Scotland; see *cláirseach.* **(8)**

cruz de mayo Venezuelan 'May cross' *velorio.* **(2)**

crwth Welsh rectangular bowed lyre with three to six strings, used to accompany bardic declamation as early as the first century B.C.E. **(8)**

csárdás Lively 2/4 rhythmic type of Hungarian *nóta*; closed circle dances of Hungarians and Slovaks in Croatia. **(8)**

cuadrilla (1) 'Quadrille', square dance. (2) In New Mexico, a dance similar to the American square dance in that it is danced in groups of two or more couples, but without the use of a caller. **(2, 3)**

cuadro Team of dancers, singers, and guitarist in flamenco. **(8)**

cuando Hispanic narrative song, marked by the inclusion of the term *cuando* 'when' in the text, usually at the beginning. **(3)**

cuarteada Argentine couple dance named after the carried hindquarters of a sacrificed animal. **(2)**

cuarteta (1) 'Couplet', four-line Puerto Rican poem. (2) (Also *copla de seguidilla.*) Spanish metric-song form. **(2, 8)**

cuarteto (1) Pop music from Córdoba, Argentina; (2) *cuarteto-cuarteto*, musical style based on early *cuarteto* music. **(2)**

cuatra Derived from the Venezuelan *cuatro*, a four-stringed guitar of the Netherlands Antilles. **(2)**

cuatrillo Polyrhythm of four against three. **(2)**

cuatro 'Four' (Spanish). (1) Four-stringed small guitar originally from Venezuela and diffused to Colombia, Grenada, Trinidad, and other regions close to Venezuela. (2) Puerto Rican ten-stringed guitar with double courses. (3) *Cuatro y medio*, Venezuelan small guitar with 'four and a half' strings. (4) Puerto Rican creole lead guitar with five steel-stringed double courses (originally four gut single strings), central to *música jíbara*. (**2, 3, 9**)

cue system Rubric under which to classify the signal systems used in musical communication: aural, tactile, gestural, and visual (notation). (**8**)

cueca (1) (Also *cueca chilena, cueca chilenera, cueca porteña*.) Chilean folk-urban *criollo* song and genre of couple dance (male pursuit of female) that is considered a national symbol (also found in Bolivia), characterized by composite 6/8 and 3/4 *sesquiáltera*-hemiola meter and song texts that sometimes reveal nationalistic, historical, or social commentary. (2) Chilean dance in alternating 3/4 and 6/8 meter, usually with text set in quatrains of eight-syllable lines and melody sung in parallel thirds on tonic and dominant triads accompanied by hand claps and guitars. (**2, 9**)

cuíca Single-headed Brazilian friction membranophone used in the samba, sounded by rubbing a short stick attached to and protruding from the bottom of the drum skin into the wooden or metal body. (**2**)

cuica tlamatiliztli Nahua singing. (**2**)

cuicalli Aztec formal schools that included music education. (**2**)

cuisle Irish pipelike or flutelike instrument. (**8**)

culeado Guatemalan women's *punta* dance. (**2**)

culebrillando Single-file serpentine dance of Ecuador. (**2**)

culjke Swinging songs for St. George's Day in Montenegro. (**8**)

culombu (Also *cornu, cornu marinu*.) Corsican conch-shell trumpet associated with the struggle for independence. (**8**)

čumackija pieśni Belarusan Chumak nonritual male sociolyrical epic poetry and song. (**8**)

cumaco Large African-derived drum of Venezuela. (**2**)

cumanana Afro-Peruvian song form, often competitive, accompanied by guitar. (**2**)

cumbanchero Popular music dance ensemble from the Philippines. (**4**)

cumbia (1) Colombian genre of Caribbean music, existing in both rural and urban forms, the latter popular throughout Latin America's Pacific rim regions from Chile to Central America and Mexico as a salsa genre. (2) Panamanian group circle dance. (3) Lively dance music in duple meter, with origins in Panama and Colombia, now popular in many communities of Latin America and the United States. (**2, 3**)

cumbiamberos Colombian fusion of *cumbia* and *songo*. (**2**)

cümbüş Banjo-like Turkish lute. (**6**)

cumparsa Plucked-string ensemble of the Philippines. (**4**)

cuna 'Cradle,' referring to a figure in the form of a baby's cradle that Hispano dancers create by interweaving their arms during the course of a dance. (**3**)

cunculcahue Argentine musical bow. (**2**)

cuñeros Spanish cradle songs or lullabies. (**8**)

cungo 'Let's go', Belizean creole style of popular music that emerged in the 1980s. (**2**)

cununa 'Wreath', traditional feast at the end of the harvest in Transylvania, Romania. (**8**)

cununia 'Church ceremony', part of the Romanian wedding ritual, accompanied by specific songs or instrumental tunes. (**8**)

cununo Colombian and Ecuadorian conical single-headed drum from the Pacific coast, used in the *currulao* ensemble. (**2**)

cuplé flamenco Spanish sentimental songs from *operismos*. (**8**)

cura Small Turkish lute. (**6**)

curandero 'Curer', native ritual healer. (**2**)

curbata In the Venezuelan longdrum ensemble, the short drum that is paired with the *mina*. (**2**)

curijurijanporetec Love songs of the Maleku. (**2**)

curle (Also *cingonë, surle, zurle*.) Albanian conical-bore double-reed aerophone. (**8**)

currente Corsican improvised poem accompanied by a violin, normally played by the singer. (**8**)

currulao Colombian and Ecuadorian couple pursuit dance or marimba dance. (**2**)

cururu Musical or dance style in Brazil. (**2**)

cuyacas All-female dancing group of Aymara region. (**2**)

cuzao (China.) Coarse. (**7**)

cwène Pastoral horn flute of the Low Countries. (**8**)

cyas Jamaican Kumina ceremonial drum. (**2**)

cykace (Also *grajcary*.) Polish frame drum with jingles. (**8**)

cylëdyjare (Also *biculë*.) Short, double-bore duct flute, played by herdsmen in Labëri, Albania. (**8**)

cymbály Czech hammered dulcimer. (**3**)

cymbały (1) Belarusan hammered dulcimer. (2) Polish trapezoidal struck zither. (**8**)

cynghanedd Welsh verbal embroidery, including alliteration and internal rhyme, used in *plygain* or carols. (**8**)

cyweirdant Welsh harper's chord, in various combinations with a second chord (*tyniad*), made up twenty-four different patterns. (**8**)

czardas Hungarian dance in duple meter in which dancers start slowly and finish in vivacious whirls; cf. *csárdás*. (**8**)

czarny kozioł doślubny 'Black he-goat of the wedding', bagpipe of western Poland, played at weddings. (**8**)

ɗaa (Vai) Islamic fortieth-day death feast. (**1**)

ɗaabo kulε 'Arabic voice', Vai stylistic designation for Qur'ānic recitation. (**1**)

dabakan Goblet drum of the Philippines. (**4**)

dabi-dabi Cymbals in Ternate. (**4**)

dabka (Also *dabkah, dabkeh, dabkih*.) (1) 'Stamping the feet', popular folk dance of the Mashriq. (2) Common folk dance rhythm, adopted in Hebrew song and Israeli dance. (3) In Arabic music, a folk line dance and the accompanying song or music. (**3, 6**)

daboih Acehnese Sufi ritual of self-mortification. (**4**)

dabu-dabu Maranaon large religious drum. (**4**)

dabus (1) Sufi ritual of self-mortification; (2) Sufi-derived dance with iron awl. (**4**)

dada Small and medium hanging gongs on Kai. (**4**)

dadaiko (Japan.) Largest drum used in *gagaku*. (**7**)

ḍaḍañ Double-headed drum of the Northern Areas of Pakistan. (**5**)

dadara bagandang Women's harvest dance of Sumbawa. (**4**)

dadara nesek Samawan women's weaving dance. (**4**)

dadariya Important Gond music and dance form of Madhya Pradesh. (**5**)

dādrā Light classical vocal form, in Hindustani music. (**5**)

dadεwε 'Bush spirit' or nature divinity of the Vai Poro society. (**1**)

daf (Also *daff, daph, duff, duph*.) (1) Moroccan frame drum. (2) Frame drum with wood or metal frame. (3) Arabic squarish frame drum. (4) In the Arab world, generic term for a frame drum or tambourine, sometimes containing snares; cf. *riqq*. (**1, 5, 6, 8**)

daff zinjārī Iraqi tambourine with five pairs of small cymbals. (**6**)

Dagbamba Culture group of northern Ghana. (**1**)

dagg al-ḥabb Yemeni folk song accompanying the milling of grain. (**6**)

ḍagga (Also *bāyāṇ*.) Left-hand kettledrum of the *tabla* pair. (**5**)

dagomba Kru guitar style influenced by early highlife music of Ghana. (**1**)

dahalira Mbojo women's martial arts dance. (**4**)

dahechang (China.) Grand vocal cycles; large-scale chorus music accompanied by an instrumental ensemble. (**7**)

---

dāhinā (Also *dāya, tabla.*) Smaller, higher-pitched right-hand drum of the *tabla* pair. (5)

daigon Cebu Christmas songs. (4)

đại hồng chung Large bell for Buddhist ceremonies in Vietnam. (4)

daiko Japanese drum; same word as *taiko*, but *t* changes to *d* when it used in a compound word. (3)

daimyô (Japan.) Feudal lord. (7)

daina Basic form of a Latvian folk-song text, a short self-contained quatrain of two nonrhyming couplets. (8)

dainas Lithuanian strophic songs in long single lines and two-line strophes. (8)

đại nhạc Oboe-dominated ritual ensemble of Vietnam's court. (4)

dai nihon katei ongaku kai siki (Japan.) Modern notation for *koto* and *syamisen*. (7)

Dai Nihon siryô (Japan.) 'Great Collection of Historical Sources of Japan', arranged chronologically from 887 to 1867. (7)

dāira Arabic roundish frame drum. (8)

dā'irā (Also *dāireh, daf.*) Frame drum with jingles. (5)

dā'ira (Also *daire*, Turkish; *dāyra, dāire.*) (1) Generic term for round frame drum. (2) Short prelude in free rhythm in the Maghribi *nūba*. (6)

daira Georgian frame drum with jingles; *see daf, dāira, daphi, tof.* (8)

dairea Romanian single-headed frame drum. (8)

dāire-zangī Frame drum with attached metal rings. (6)

daizyô e (Japan.) Court ritual to celebrate the emperor's coronation. (7)

daisyû (Japan.) *See sikisyû.* (7)

Dajo Sudanese people of the Nuba Mountains. (1)

dajre (Also *daire.*) Albanian, Macedonian, and Bulgarian single-headed frame drum. (8)

dajre def Albanian frame drum ensemble consisting of two female frame drummers, who sing and dance. (8)

dāk Kota percussion rhythm pattern. (5)

dakke Hourglass-shaped pressure drum used to accompany *dakke bali.* (5)

dakke bali (Also *nāga mandala.*) Form of cobra (*nāga*) worship with circular dancing, singing, and drumming. (5)

dakkinī Trumpet of Indian antiquity. (5)

dako Community unit in Kru settlements, with territorial, dialect, and social identity. (1)

dakoho Warao dance or entertainment song. (2)

dakṣiṇā Gift to a *guru* from his student in place of payment for lessons. (5)

dala-fandir Ossetian plucked long-necked fretted lute, played to accompany solo singing. (8)

dalagu (China.) Hourglass-shaped drum imported from Central Asia during the sixth century. (7)

dalair Feast dances performed in the Aru islands. (4)

dalang (1) Person usually of Javanese descent in Surinam who leads the *wayang* puppet theater. (2) (Also *dhalang.*) Puppeteer in shadow-puppet theater. (3) Puppeteer. (2, 4, 10)

daldala Hanging gong in the Aru islands. (4)

dalit Praise song for the Virgin Mary. (4)

Dalit 'Broken', 'oppressed', communities formerly called untouchables or Harijans. (5)

dalkhai (Also *rasarkeli.*) Songs of Orissa describing incidents in Krishna's life. (5)

dalūka Sudanese single-headed cup-shaped clay drum. (1)

dal'ūna (Also *dal'ōna.*) Folk song accompanying a line dance, or *dabkah*, among eastern Mediterranean rural communities. (6)

daluo Large Chinese gong. (3)

daluogu Percussion ensemble from China. (4)

dalupal Yakan bamboo clapper. (4)

dam Breath (spirit) that brings an effect. (6)

d'am In Armenian music, the tonic drone tone, usually provided by one of two *duduk* players. (6)

damāhā Large kettledrum played in Nepal. (5)

ḍāmal Kettledrum pair of the Northern Areas of Pakistan. (5)

daman Tibetan kettledrum pair. (5)

damana Performance style of southwestern Turkmenistan. (6)

ḍamaru (Also *ḍamrū.*) Small hourglass-shaped drum with knotted strings that strike the heads when the drum is rotated. (5)

dambatimbu Simplified versions of *mbira* songs used in learning. (1)

damburā (Also *damburo, dambura, danburo, dhambura.*) Long-necked, unfretted, plucked lutes of Pakistan and Afghanistan. (5)

dambūrag Long-necked unfretted lute of Balochistan, used as a rhythm-keeping instrument, mostly with the *suroz* and *nal.* (5)

damḍi Small tambourine of Karnataka, with iguana-skin head. (5)

d'amkash Musician who provides the drone pitch in Armenian music. (6)

dammām Polygonal frame drum used in Iraq. (6)

Dan Southern Mande culture group in eastern Liberia (Gio) and western Côte d'Ivoire (Yacouba). (1)

dan (1) Nyamalthu dance of the brave in the former Bauchi State in Nigeria. (2) Female role in opera (China). (3) Generic term for a section of music and theatricals (Japan). (1, 7)

dān Omani women's ensemble. (6)

danaj Duple-meter Moravian couple dance with a hesitation step. (8)

dan awase (Japan.) Ensemble technique that involves playing two *dan* sections of a piece simultaneously. (7)

đàn bầu Monochord with box resonator from Vietnam. (4)

dân ca Modernized Vietnamese folk song. (4)

dance Specially marked or elaborated and culturally specific system of movement resulting from creative processes that manipulate human bodies in time and space to formalize and intensify movement, much as poetry intensifies and formalizes language. (9)

dance hall (Also dancehall.) (1) Style of music from Jamaica, West Indies, and New York City; (2) hip-hop and reggae-influenced genre, delivered in Jamaican patois, directly linked to earlier "toasting" Jamaican disk jockeys who rhymed over prerecorded music at public dances (dance halls) in the 1950s and 1960s. (3)

dance ring Circular space defined by the placement of audience and dancers. (1)

dance des sept sauts 'Dance of the seven leaps' (French), dance-song of the Low Countries; *see zevensprong.* (8)

Dances of Universal Peace Body of spiritual practices that integrate breath, movement, and music, originating in California in the mid-1960s and now found worldwide. (3)

dancis 'Dance', Latvian bagpipe dance tunes. (8)

đàn cò Vietnamese two-stringed fiddle with narrow, waisted body. (4)

danda jatra Songs sung to accompany the *patna jatra* dance in Orissa. (5)

dandanata gīt Dance songs of Orissa in question-and-answer form. (5)

daṇḍa tāl Iron bar struck rhythmically with an iron rod in Fiji; *see also ḍhantāl.* (5)

đàn đáy Vietnamese long-necked, trapezoidal lute with three strings. (4)

dandi Stick- and hand-beaten drum in an *mbira* ensemble, which plays improvisations. (1)

ḍāṇḍiā rās (Also *rās.*) Stick dance of Gujarat. (5)

đàn độc huyền Vietnamese monochord with box resonator. (4)

dāng (Persian.) Tetrachord, in Persian music theory; equivalent to Arabic *zolarba'* or *dhū'larba'.* (6)

đàn gáo Vietnamese two-stringed fiddle with coconut-shell body. (4)

dangdut (1) Popular music influenced by Hindi films, common to Malaysia and Indonesia. (2) Lowbrow popular music in Indonesia. (**4, 10**)

dangdut Sasak *Dangdut* sung in Sasak. (**4**)

dàn ghi-ta Modified Spanish guitar, found in Vietnam. (**4**)

dan gire (Japan.) (1) Last section of each *dan* (act) of a *kabuki* play; (2) cadential *syamisen* melodic patterns at the end of a piece. (**7**)

dan giri (Japan.) Last section of each *dan* (act) of a *gidayû busi* play. (**7**)

dangiri no senritu (Japan.) *Gidayû busi* melodic pattern used in the last section of each *dan* (act). (**7**)

dango (1) Kalinga solo peacemaking song; (2) Bontok long solo song. (**4**)

dan mono (Japan.) Sectional instrumental pieces for *koto*. (**7**)

dan mono awase (Japan.) Ensemble technique that involves playing two different *dan mono* pieces simultaneously. (**7**)

dàn nguyột (Also *dàn kìm*.) Vietnamese long-necked, moon-shaped lute. (**4**)

dāni Category of tunes accompanied by *surnāī* or transverse flute, in the Northern Areas of Pakistan. (**5**)

danka mawari (Japan.) Buddhist priests' visits to the houses affiliated with their temples to perform religious rites. (**7**)

dàn nhị Vietnamese two-stringed fiddle with a narrow, waisted body. (**4**)

dans plinn Breton line or circle dance, performed as part of a three-part suite. (**8**)

dansaq Scissors dance in Ayacucho, Peru. (**2**)

danse des pélerins Pilgrims' sword dance of Marbissoux, province of Brabant, Low Countries. (**8**)

danse polonaise 'Polish dance' (French), a name of the mazurka outside Poland. (**8**)

danshus Swedish dancing house, dedicated to preserving dance music and modeled on the Hungarian *táncház*. (**8**)

dansi Non-Islamic popular music that developed in East Africa by the 1940s. (**1**)

dánta Irish lullaby; an Irish religious song performed at Easter. (**8**)

dantal In Indo-Caribbean culture and Bhojpuri-region North India, a metal rod struck rhythmically with a U-shaped clapper. (**3**)

dàn tam Vietnamese long-necked, snakeskin-covered lute, from the Chinese *sanxian*. (**4**)

dàn tam thập lục Vietnamese hammered zither with thirty-six strings, of Chinese origin. (**4**)

dan tranh Vietnamese zither. (**7**)

dàn tranh (Also *dàn thập lục*.) Vietnamese semi-tubular board zither with sixteen or seventeen strings. (**4**)

dàn tỳ-bà Vietnamese pear-shaped lute, from Chinese *pipa*. (**4**)

dàn xến Vietnamese lute with a petal-shaped body. (**4**)

danza 'Dance' (Spanish). (1) (Also *danzón*.) Nineteenth-century Hispanic-Caribbean creole urban dance genre of the French Creole *contradanse*; Cuban variant of French Creole *contradanse*. (2) Romantic vocal music genre with Afro-Caribbean roots. (3) Cuban genre belonging to the *danzón* family, part of the evolution of the *contradanza*. (4) Sardinian virtuosic couple dance. (5) Habanera-derived music and dance of the Philippines. (6) Couple dance, usually without sung text, in duple meter and sectional form, often involving an initial promenade (*paseo*). (**2, 3, 4, 8, 9**)

danzón (1) Cuban instrumental dance genre created by Miguel Failde in 1879; the national dance of Cuba. (**2**)

danzonete Cuban genre belonging to the *danzón* family. (**2**)

daoban (China.) Interjected aria that exaggerates the rubato of *sanban*. (**7**)

daouli Large, double-headed drum, often played with *zournadhes* by Macedonian Gypsies in Greece. (**8**)

daoulia Ensembles of two *zournadhes* and one *daouli* in Greek Macedonia. (**8**)

dap Single-headed frame drum of Xinkiang-Uygur. (**6**)

dapchang (Also *chang*.) Mouth harp, one of the most common musical instruments of the Baloch. (**5**)

dāphā Hymn-singing tradition of the Newārs in Nepal. (**5**)

daphalā Frame drum of Uttar Pradesh. (**5**)

daphdaphi Georgian large double-headed drum, played with an accordion to accompany dancing; more commonly called *doli*. (**8**)

daphi Georgian frame drum with jingles, played by a female dancer in Kartli, Kakheti, Racha, Samegrelo, and Tusheti; *see daf, dāira, daira, tof*. (**8**)

ḍappu (Also *dappu*.) Frame drum of Andhra Pradesh and Karnataka. (**5**)

dapu Process of reconstructing music by providing an original rhythmic interpretation. (**10**)

daqing (China.) Large bronze bell attached to a wooden handle. (**7**)

daqqa (Plural, *daqqāt*.) 'Beat', 'thrust', general term for rhythmic periods. (**6**)

daqu (China.) Multimovement works of music and dance from the Tang dynasty. (**7**)

dara Romanian one-headed frame drum, played in Oltenia and Muntenia. (**8**)

darabana Romanian snare drum. (**8**)

darabuka Vase-shaped single-headed drum, played by Roma in the Balkans. (**8**)

darabukka Arabic single-headed ceramic cylindrical drum. (**3**)

daraja (Plural, *darajāt*.) Scale degree, pitch, note, or sound. (**6**)

darāmad 'Coming out' (Persian), one of the initial *gushe-hā* in a *dastgāh*. In the Central Asian *shash maqām*, also refers to an introductory section in a low tessitura in the melodic development of a *shu'be*. (**6**)

ḍarb (Plural, *ḍurūb*.) 'Beat', 'tap', 'pulse', general term for rhythmic modes or periods. (**6**)

darbār (Also *rāj darbār*.) Royal court. (**5**)

darbouka Goblet-shaped Algerian drum, played by immigrants in France. (**8**)

darbuka (Also *darabuka, darabukka*.) Near Eastern vase-shaped drum, played in Swedish folk music. (**8**)

darbūka (Also *darabuka, darbeka, darabukka, daraduka, darbakkeh, darbukka*.) Goblet-shaped single-headed drum found throughout the Arab world. (**5, 6**)

dargāh Muslim mausoleum housing a saint or another important personage. (**5**)

darśan Visual contact with a god, the embodiment of a god, or a highly respected personage. (**5**)

dasa Traditional Yemeni dance for two performers. (**6**)

das'a, greater Rhythmic period in Yemenite music (*darb, daqqa, īqā*) with internal structure of $2 + 3 + 3 + 3$. (**6**)

das'a, lesser Rhythmic period in Yemenite music with internal structure of $3 + 2 + 2$. (**6**)

Dāsari Oral narrative singers in Andhra Pradesh, devotees of Vishnu. (**5**)

dasi āṭṭam (Also *sadir kacheri*.) Obsolete term referring to the *bharata nāṭyam* dance. (**5**)

daskathia (Also *ramkathi*.) Popular type of *chanda* song performed by balladeers in Orissa. (**5**)

dāstān (1) Ballads or stories performed by a ballad singer (*dāstāngoh*) in Punjab, Pakistan. (2) (Also *destan*.) Sung poetic narrative of Turkey and Central Asia, performed by an *'āsheq* or *bakhshī*. (**5, 6**)

dastānag Short love songs of eastern Balochistan, accompanied by a single-reed pipe. (**5**)

daste In Iran, a group of men who meet to perform *nowhe sīne-zanī* and *nowhe zanjīr-zanī*, poetic laments for martyrs. (**6**)

dastgāh (Also *dastgah*.) 'System', 'apparatus' (Persian; Azerbaijani *dәstgah*). One of the seven canonical systems (*shūr, segāh, chāhargāh, māhūr, homāyūn, navā, rāst panjgāh*) that constitute the *radif*, or modal system, of Persian music; a Persian musical mode. (**6, 8**) *datu* Muslim patriarchal leader. (4)

daulbas Double-headed drum of Turkish origin, once played in Montenegro. (8)

daule (Also *daula*, *sabaragamuwa* drum.) Double-headed barrel drum in the *hēvisi* Buddhist ensemble of Sri Lanka. (5)

daulle (Also *lodër*, *lodërti*, *tupan*.) Albanian two-headed bass drum. (8)

Daura Hausa state. (1)

davluri Georgian mixed-couple dance with instrumental accompaniment. (8)

davul Large double-headed Turkish drum, generally appearing with the *zurna*. (6)

dawnsio ha' Welsh May-dancing. (8)

dawr (Also *dōr*.) Vocal composition, especially popular in nineteenth-century and early-twentieth-century Egyptian music, involving a degree of vocal improvisation; performed by a vocal soloist accompanied by a chorus and *takht*. (Plural, *adwār*.) (6)

dāya (Also *dāhinā*, *tabla*.) Right-hand conical wooden drum of the *tabla* pair. (5)

dayegon (Also *daygon*.) Cebu Christmas songs. (4)

dayin (China.) Playing technique for a wind instrument in which a finger "hits" the hole to produce a grace note. (7)

dayirigaba Dance of Nyamalthu or Terawa youths in the former Bauchi State in Nigeria. (1)

dāyra See *dā'ira*. (6)

dayuray Bukidnon one-stringed fiddle. (4)

dazoo Head of Poro activities in Vai communities. (1)

dažynačnya pieśni Belarusan end-of-harvest songs. (8)

dbu-mdzad Tibetan precentor. (5)

dbyangs Type of solemn chanting in Tibetan Buddhist rituals. (5)

ddikr (Plural, *ladkar*.) Song of praise of God and the Prophet, sung by Moroccan Berbers (the Chleuh or Shleuh people) for seasonal or life-cycle events. (6)

ddrst 'Row', 'chain'; type of *ahwash* dance of the Ida Ouzddout, referring to the arrangement of dancers in a long line. (6)

debate *bailā* Word dueling and verbal repartee in Sri Lanka. (5)

de bayasi (Japan.) *Kabuki* instrumental ensemble and its music played onstage. (7)

de bef jagen In the Dutch-speaking areas of the Low Countries, the extinct custom of making noise on instruments and utensils outside the house of newlyweds; *see charivari*. (8)

deblek Single-headed Turkish hourglass drum; cf. *darbuka*. (6)

débòt St. Lucian song-dance accompanied by drumming. (2)

dechik-pondur Chechen and Ingush three-stringed long-necked plucked lute. (8)

dechovka muzika Czech and Slovak brass band. (8)

decibel Logarithmic unit, abbreviated dB, for expressing relative power levels. The sound-pressure level of 0 dB is ordinarily referred to as a pressure level of 20 micropascals, the approximate threshold of human hearing. The average threshold of pain is about 130 dB. (9)

décima 'Tenth' (Spanish). (1) Spanish and Hispanic-American song containing ten-line stanzas, eight syllables per stanza, and a particular rhythm scheme. (2) Sung genre for courtship or expression of religious and social commentary. (3) Most learned poetic form of New Mexican Hispano music that flourished in fifteenth-century Spain and was subsequently spread throughout the New World; *décima* texts feature a rather intricate formal scheme: four ten-line stanzas, introduced by a four-line quatrain. (4) (Also *décima espinela*.) Spanish poetic form having ten eight-syllable lines rhyming *abba:accddc*, the colon denoting a pause. (2, 3, 9)

decimilla 'Little *décima*', same as *décima* but with six syllables per line. (2)

decknni Goan music and dance genre, performed by Christians. (5)

de coleo Chilean *tonada* quatrain starting with the last line of the previous one. (2)

deculturation Loss of a culture without the implication of its replacement by another. (2)

dede Alevī holy man who supervises rituals and religious instruction. (6)

dedegungan Gamelan-based *kacapi-suling* pieces of Sunda. (4)

de dragoste 'Of love', newer type of *doina*, popular in southern Romania. (8)

deep house Subcategory of house music, known as soulful house in the United Kingdom, and characterized by a gospel-influenced vocal track, a minimalist instrumental arrangement, or both. (3)

def (1) Frame drum with or without jingles; cf. *daff*. (2) Frame drum played in the Balkans. (6, 8)

dɔf Azerbaijani frame frum; cf. *def*. (6)

dé fas Guadeloupe double-headed, barrel-shaped membranophone. (2)

deff Square double-headed frame drum; cf. *daff*. (6)

defi Greek frame drum. (8)

degung Sundanese gong-chime. (4)

degung kawih Gamelan *degung* with vocals, from Sunda. (4)

deha (Japan.) *Nô* instrumental piece for the entrance of a god. (7)

dēhī (Also *līko*, *zabīrok*.) Songs of separation, travel, and work popular in eastern Balochistan. (5)

dehol Double-headed cylindrical drum in Kurdistan, played by professional musicians, *mitirp*; cf. Turkish *davul*, Arabic *tabla*. (6)

Dei People living in Liberia. (1)

dek rap Thai rap music. (4)

Delaware Big House song Song performed as part of the annual harvest rituals of the Delaware Indians. (3)

deliro Small hand drum of Sumba. (4)

delrubā Bowed lute of western Afghanistan. (5)

deme Songs of mystical love, performed in Alevī ceremonies. (6)

dendang (1) West Sumatra songs with *saluang*; (2) Bengkulu songs with *biola* and *redap*. (4)

dende Venda braced gourd-resonated bow. (1)

dengaku (Japan.) Genre of medieval performing art originally related to the rice crop; a precursor of *nô*. (7)

denkmal 'Monument' (German), term for an authoritatively edited musical score. (8)

dep Bengkulu heavy frame drum. (4)

dera 'Clay pot with covered mouth', a scraped membranophone of Maharashtra. (5)

derbiderissa Greek "free" women who participated in the *rebetika* subculture. (8)

derbuka North African single-headed goblet-shaped drum. (1)

dere Single-headed stranding drum of Savu. (4)

dergāh Sufi lodge or *tekke*, especially one with an attached tomb. (6)

dervish (1) Follower of a spiritual way in Islam. (2) Religious mendicant. (5, 6)

desafio Iberian song duel; *see cantoria*. (2)

deseterac Ten-syllable poetic line of Serbian-Croatian epic songs. (8)

desgarrada Portuguese improvised vocal genre. (8)

de shot and rattle Jamaican calabash spike rattle filled with stones and fitted with a handle. (2)

desī (1) Regional musics of the medieval period. (2) Relatively unrefined regional traditions and practices. (5)

desi karam Solo male dance of western Orissa. (5)

Dēśingurāju Katha Popular Telugu oral narrative song. (5)

desī sitār Folk sitar of Gujarat. (5)

desī tala Regional rhythmic pattern in cyclic form. (5)

despique Portuguese improvised vocal genre. (8)

dessan (From Persian *dāstān*.) Long narrative epic of Turkmenistan. (6)

dessanchy bagshy (Also *dessançy baggy*.) Singer of *dessan* in Turkmenistan. (6)

deutsche Harmonika See *Handäoline.* (8)

devadāsī (Also *dēvadāsi.*) Hereditary female temple and court dancers. (5)

dēvālē Shrine for Hindu guardian deities in Sri Lanka. (5)

devatā Minor divinity; term used to refer to ragas. (5)

devī (1) Local or regional goddess. (2) Lady; respectable woman. (5)

Devr 'God', annual festival of the Kotas. (5)

devr-i kebīr Complex Turkish rhythmic cycle in 28/4, characterizing the *peşrev* genre. (6)

devr koḷ Special "god melodies" played at the annual Devr festival of Kota worship. (5)

deyiş 'Poem' (Turkish), genre of mystical poetry. (6)

dəyişmə 'Exchange' (Azerbaijani), contest of sung poetry in which two *aşıqlar* exchange strophes. (6)

dhadha Javanese pitch name. (4)

ḍhāk Mina hourglass pressure drum of Rajasthan. (5)

ḍhāḷ Melody in Gujarat; particularly, one adaptable to several different texts. (5)

dhalang (Also *dalang.*) Puppeteer in shadow puppet theater. (4)

dhalo Goan music and dance of Hindu origin performed by women. (5)

dhamāl (1) Drum rhythm often associated with Sufi shrines; (2) dance associated with Holī, in Rajasthan. (5)

dhamal Mystic dervish dance of Sindh. (5)

dhamār Hindustani vocal genre similar to *dhrupad.* (5)

dhāmi Nepali term for shaman. (5)

Dhammayut Sect of Buddhism founded in the 1830s. (4)

dhamsa Large kettledrum. (5)

dhangari ovya Song and dance genre of the Dhangars of Maharashtra. (5)

ḍhantāl Meter-long iron rod struck rhythmically to accompany Indian songs in Trinidad and Guyana. See also *daṇḍa tāl.* (5)

dhāp Locally made bass "boom" drum of the Indo-Guyanese. (5)

Ḍhaṛhī Lower-class Muslim minstrel in North India. (5)

dharma Predestined spiritual duty. (5)

dhavale Marriage songs performed by women in Maharashtra. (5)

dhikr (Also *zikr, zekar.*) 'Remembrance', from the verb *dhakara* 'to remember'. (1) In its general sense, this term refers to the remembrance of Allah by any means. More specifically, it refers to a portion of the Sufi liturgy: the regular chanting of a name of Allah, usually accompanied by regular body movements. (2) Ecstatic ritual of the Sufi Islamic sect. (1, 3, 6)

dhimay Cylindrical drum of Nepal. (5)

dhimaybājā Music and musical ensemble of Nepal. (5)

dhimotika Greek folk songs. (8)

dhog-dhog Single-headed drum of Java. (4)

dhol Large double-headed cylindrical drum played by hand or stick, widespread in northern regions of South Asia. (5)

dhol (Also *dholki.*) Punjabi double-sided membranophone used in *bhangra,* a hybrid genre popular in Britain. (8)

dholā Sung epic poem in North India. (5)

dholak (1) Guyanese drum for popular music. (2) Double-headed barrel drum common in Indian and Indo-Caribbean music. (2, 3)

ḍholak (Also *ḍholakī.*) Double-headed barrel drum played with sticks or hands, widespread throughout the northern regions of South Asia. (5)

ḍholī Player of the *ḍhol;* a class of ritual musicians including drummers. (5)

ḍholkī Smaller version of the *ḍhol.* (5)

dhromi Greek melodic modes. (8)

dhrupad Preeminent Hindustani court vocal and instrumental music genre of the premodern era. (5)

dhruvapada (1) Repeated refrain in a *bhajan* or *dhrupad;* (2) 'song on God'; ancient musical style believed to be the precursor of Hindustani *dhrupad.* (5)

dhudak (Also *dahanki.*) Hourglass drum of the Kahars in Madhya Pradesh. (5)

dhūmsa Double-headed drum of Rajasthan. (5)

dhun Light classical genre in Hindustani music. (5)

dhunmuniyā kajalī Form of Bhojpuri *kajalī* in which performers dance while they sing. (5)

dhyāṅgro Double-headed frame drum used by Nepali shamans. (5)

di (China.) Side-blown flute that was usually made of bamboo. (7)

diablada (Also *diabladas.*) 'Deviled', Bolivian carnival and patronal festival devil dance and dancers. (2)

diablicos sucios 'Dirty devils', Panamanian devil dance tradition. (2)

diablos 'Devils', costumed dancers in Hispanic-American folkloric events. (2)

diadizha iish Ingush women's lullaby. (8)

dialekt-rock Norwegian term for rock performed in the linguistic and musical dialects of specific localities. (8)

diana mbajá Dawn trumpet signal to begin patronal feast days in Paraguay. (2)

diao (China.) Key and mode. (7)

diaoshi (China.) Inclusive term for tonal aspects and overall attributes and properties of a melody. (7)

diaoxing bianzou (China.) Modal variation. (7)

diassare Senegalese five-stringed plucked lute. (1)

dideba 'Glory', Georgian women's circle dance, performed to antiphonal music at the celebration of the Christian saint White George, the central summer ritual. (8)

didgeridu (Also *didjeridu.*) (1) Australian Aborigine drone instrument whose distinctive sound has become a staple of world beat recordings. (2) Wooden trumpet, about 1 to 1.5 meters long, played mainly by Aborigines of northern Australia. (3, 9)

didi Generic term for songs in the Aru islands. (4)

dīdišana Ritual swinging and rocking of a baby by all participants at Latvian christenings in southwestern Kurzeme, accompanied by special songs. (8)

didong Acehnese women's dance with *pantun.* (4)

die (China.) To repeat. (7)

điệu Vietnamese system of modes. (4)

dievturīc Latvian neopagan movement that occurred between the world wars and developed a special choral style. (8)

diez Sharp (Turkish). (6)

difference tone Sound of frequency $f_1 - f_2$ or $f_2 - f_1$, generated when pure sounds of frequency f_1 and f_2 are fed simultaneously into a nonlinear system. (9)

ḍigaṛī Small kettledrum of Mithila. (5)

digital sampler Computer program that allows any recorded sound to be translated into digital code and thereby combined with other sounds to create novel compositions. (3)

Digo Mijikena people of Kenya. (1)

dikil (Also *dikir.*) Poetic songs about the prophet Muhammad. (4)

dikir barat Malay men's choral singing of secular texts. (4)

dilliara Songhai clarinet. (1)

dilrubā North Indian bowed, unfretted, long-necked lute similar to the *isrāj.* (5)

dinagyang Ilongo religious festival. (4)

dinaladay Maguindanao lute mode. (4)

dingboku BaAka dance performed by a line of women related by residential camp or clan. (1)

Dīpāvali (Also **Dīvālī.**) Hindu "festival of lights," celebrated in October–November. (5)

diple 'Double pipe'. Croatian, Montenegrin, Hercegovinan, and Slovene pipes, played with a wooden mouthpiece or as a bagpipe. (8)

diple s mijehom (Also *mješnice.*) 'Double pipe with bag', Croatian bagpipe. (8)

diple z mehom 'Double pipe with bag', Slovene bagpipe. (8)

diplipito Georgian set of two or occasionally three to five skin-covered clay pots struck with small sticks, each sounding a unique pitch; see *gosha-nagara, nagara*. (8)

direct transcription Writing down music notation during live performances or from memory. (1)

discante Alternative Venezuelan name for *cuatro*, a four-stringed small guitar. (2)

discantus 'Descant' (Latin), style of twelfth- and thirteenth-century note-against-note Parisian liturgical polyphony. (8)

disco Category of 1970s dance music, derived from the abbreviation of *discothèque*, its main venue. (3)

disco blending (Also mixing.) Construction of an uninterrupted flow of music inside a *discothèque*, by a disk jockey using two or more turntables and an audio mixer. (3)

dishkant (Also *golosnik*.) Soloist who sings an anhemitonic tune with text in the vocal music of the Cossacks in southern Russia. (8)

diskaner Breton countersinger of *kan has diskan* who repeats the phrase sung by the *kaner*. (8)

dissonance In European art music, one of certain musical intervals, including sevenths, seconds, and tritones, that are conventionally regarded as unpleasant or unharmonious. (8)

distal In "organology," the portion of a musical instrument farthest from the mouthpiece. (2)

distanzton (Japan.) Nonnuclear tone in a theory of scales formulated by Sibata Minao (1916–1996). (7)

dīv Powerful demon in Iranian mythology. (6)

divālī ke gīt Men's seasonal songs of Madhya Pradesh. (5)

divān Musical genre of Turkish coffeehouses based on urbanized versions of Anatolian songs and urban *şarkı* and *türkü*; it typically begins a Turkish song duel. (6)

dīvāni ghazal (Also *ragām, rubāyi*.) Poetic form, either recited or sung in the North West Frontier Province. (5)

divisions Figurations of a melody, especially the variations on English dance tunes characteristic of the Northumbrian smallpipes repertoire. (8)

divyanāma sankīrtana Divine names and praises in Tamil Nadu, often sung while devotees circumambulate a sacred oil lamp. (5)

Divya Prabandham 'The Sacred Collection', 4,000 Tamil verses by the Vaishnava Āḷvārs. (5)

dīwān Algerian ritual involving dance, music, poetry, and song; cf. *gnāwa, stambūlī*. (6)

diyār thaqāfa 'Houses of Culture' in modern Tunisia hosting a network of music clubs for the cultivation of *ma'lūf*. (6)

diyāz Sharp (pitch). (6)

diždancis Solemn Latvian couple dance, performed at the beginning of a wedding feast, characteristically involving walking. (8)

dizhi (China.) The twelve "earthly branches" used with the "heavenly items" to generate years, months, days, and hours. (7)

dizi (China.) Six-hole bamboo flute whose tone is characterized by the buzzing of the membrane situated between the first hole and the embouchure hole. (3, 7)

djalkmi Clansong style of Central Arnhem Land. (9)

djatpangarri (Also *djedbangari*.) In writing, often called fun songs. Didjeridu-accompanied songs with formulaic, mainly "nonsense" texts, sung by young unmarried men, especially in northeastern Arnhem Land. (9)

djeguako Adighian performer of historical songs. (8)

djembe Wassoulou goblet-shaped drum. (1)

djouba (Also *juba*.) Creole rural dances from colonial times in the French-speaking Caribbean. (2)

dlisung Subanen slit drum. (4)

doàn văn công Vietnamese traveling performance troupes. (4)

doba Romanian drum. (8)

dōbeitī Poetic form of Kashmir. (5)

dobeitī See *chārbeitī*. (6)

doble 'Double', (1) Argentine dance; (2) combination of a smaller and a larger Chiapan marimba. (2)

dobro Six-stringed guitar with a metal resonator beneath the bridge and a raised nut, noted (or fretted) with a steel bar and plucked with finger picks. (3)

do byôsi (Japan.) Type of cymbal. (7)

dodāta Theater tradition of north Karnataka. (5)

dodecaphony Twelve-tone or serial composition technique, in which the composer assigns equal musical significance to each note. (1)

dodekachordon Modal system developed by the Swiss theorist Glareanus and announced in a book published in 1547. (8)

dodo Hausa masked dancer in northern Nigeria. (1)

dodoitu (Japan.) Style of popular song in the mid-nineteenth century. (7)

dodola Summer rain-begging ritual in Serbia. (8)

doedelzak (German *Dudelsack* 'bagpipe'.) Bagpipe of the Low Countries; cf. *moezel, moezelzak*. (8)

Dogon Speakers of a Gur language in the Boundiagara region of Mali. (1)

dôgu gaesi (Japan.) Melodic pattern in *gidayû busi*. (7)

dohol (1) Cylindrical double-headed drum, usually played with a switch and a stick; cf. *dehol*. (2) Double-headed drum of Afghanistan. (5, 6)

doholak (Also *dholak, drokkol*.) Double-headed cylindrical drum of Baluchistan, played with the hands; cf. *dehol*. (6)

dohori gīt Song duel; competition song in Nepal. (5)

doina Romanian improvised lyrical song genre; see *hora lunga*. (8)

dokra Drum pair; Hindustani *tabla* imported into Kashmir from India. (5)

dokugin (Japan.) *Nô* performance by a solo chanter without dancing and instrumentalists. (7)

doli Georgian large double-headed drum; see *daphdaphi*. (8)

doli gīt 'Swing songs' performed by girls in Orissa. (5)

ḍolu Popular double-headed folk drum of Karnataka. (5)

ḍom Various professional musician groups in the northern region. (5)

ḍomb Musicians and singers of the Ludi caste in eastern Balochistan. (5)

dombira Short-necked lute of Kyrgyzstan. (6)

dombra Plucked two-stringed long-necked lute of Central Asia. (6)

domingacha Small Peruvian diatonic harp with pear-shaped sound box. (2)

dom kultury 'House of culture' (Belarusan), home to regional performance groups. (8)

domra (1) Russian-Balkan plucked fretted lute with a bowl-shaped resonator. (2) Ukrainian folk plucked chordophone. (3, 8)

dɔŋ 'Song' (Vai). (1)

donal (Also *alghoza, giraw*.) Double flute of southern Balochistan. (5)

dondang sayang Improvised-text song genre from Melaka. (4)

donelī Baluchi double duct-flute, played with circular breathing. (6)

đồng dao Children's songs of Vietnam. (4)

Đông Son Early period in Southeast Asian history, characterized by bronze drum casting, spreading as far as the Philippines and Borneo. (4)

dongxiao Chinese end-blown bamboo flute. (7)

donkilila la Singing often interspersed with words of praise in performance of the Mandinka of Sierra Leone. (1)

donno Hourglass drum adopted by the Akan from their northern neighbors. (1)

doodo Songhai double-headed hourglass tension drum. **(1)**

doo-wop groups Vocal harmony groups that emphasize the rhythmic delivery of a phrase consisting of vocables such as "doo-wop-doo-wop" or "doo-doo-doo" in the song arrangement. **(3)**

'doption Trinidadian song style and possession rite of the Spiritual Baptists. **(2)**

DOR Abbreviation for dance-oriented rock. **(3)**

dorakadarsane Annual Buddhist ceremony in Sri Lanka celebrating the arrival of the Siam ordination lineage from Thailand in 1753. **(5)**

dordolec (Also *peperona*.) Rain-begging ritual performed by Albanian children in the late spring or early summer of a dry year; a child dressed in greenery for the ritual. **(8)**

dôsi (Japan.) Head monk leading a Buddhist ceremony. **(7)**

dosvitky Ukrainian social gatherings for unmarried girls to sew, embroider, sing, and dance. **(8)**

dôtaku (Japan.) Bronze bells. **(7)**

dōtār Short-necked lute of Kyrgyzstan; cf. *dūtār*. **(6)**

dotārā Unfretted lute of Bengal played by the Bāuls. **(5)**

dotāro String drone instrument of western India resembling the *ektār*. **(5)**

dottagialin iish Chechen and Ingush table songs. **(8)**

do'u da Manggarai xylophone connected with string. **(4)**

doumbeleki Greek hourglass-shaped hand drum. **(3)**

doùpá Burmese small double-headed barrel drum. **(4)**

douz edmi Early twentieth-century Haitian dance costing twelve and a half centimes. **(2)**

down the coast Area south and east of Liberia, including Fernando Po and other West African countries. **(1)**

doxology Coptic hymn of praise for the Virgin Mary, saints, or angels. **(6)**

draailier (Also *lier*.) Hurdy-gurdy of the Low Countries. **(8)**

drăgaica Harvest ritual on 24 June in Muntenia, Romania. **(8)**

draj (Plural, *adrāj*.) Lively vocal genre in the Maghribi *nūba*. **(6)**

draznilki 'Taunting ditties', genre of wedding song in Russia. **(8)**

drdra Slovene noisemaker made from nutshells. **(8)**

Dreaming Realm of Aboriginal Australians' ancestral and totemic spirits, accessible in dreams. **(9)**

dream songs In Subarctic regions, songs that emanate from a person's dreams or visions and that signal the confirmation of a relationship with one's spirit helpers. **(3)**

'dre-dkar Tibetan itinerant musician who recites auspicious songs at the Tibetan new year. **(5)**

dredl (Also *dreidl, dreidel*.) Toy top spun during Hanukkah to sung accompaniment. **(8)**

dril-bu Tibetan handbell used in Buddhist rituals. **(5)**

drîmba Romanian mouth harp. **(8)**

drin drin French custom of tinkling knives against glasses. **(8)**

driven musical instrument Instrument whose vibrating system is driven by continuous stimulation with a sustained tone. **(1)**

drmeš Northwestern Croatian couple dance with shaking. **(8)**

drone (1) Sustained musical tone or pattern of tones, against which one part or several parts may move. (2) Continuous sound. (3) Tone or interval that continues throughout a piece to help sustain a melodic line, especially in Indian music. **(3, 4, 9)**

Druckvorlage (German.) Printer's copy of a score. **(8)**

drum recorder Machine invented by A. M. Jones to produce in real time a schematic representation of rhythm. **(1)**

drumelca (Also *drumlica, brnica*.) Slovene mouth harp. **(8)**

drut Fast tempo in Hindustani music. **(5)**

drutam Hand gesture comprising a clap and a wave (two beats) in Karnatak music. **(5)**

drymba Ukrainian mouth harp. **(8)**

duadastanon-fandir Ossetian harp having ten to twelve diatonically tuned strings. **(8)**

duan Scottish narrative song. **(8)**

duanpian (China.) Short stories in *Suzhou tanci*. **(7)**

duanwen (China.) Fine cracks and patterns that develop in the lacquer of a *qin*. **(7)**

duaya Pangasinan lullaby. **(4)**

dub Jamaican modern popular music. **(2)**

dubakan Goblet-shaped drum of Philippines. **(4)**

dūbayt 'Two-line' (Persian), form of Arab vocal music sung to paired lines of poetry. **(6)**

dube Romanian double-headed drum, played in Arad, Banat, Bihor, and Hundeora. **(8)**

duda (Plural, *dudy*.) Common name of the bagpipe in Central and Eastern Europe and the Balkans. **(8)**

dudakdeğmez 'Lips don't touch'; form of Turkish song dueling in which the *aşık* must avoid the pronunciation of certain consonants, and is compelled to do so by placing a pin between the upper and lower palate. **(6)**

dude Slovene bagpipe. **(8)**

Dudey German small shawm with a reed cap. **(8)**

duḍi Hourglass-shaped drum of the Koḍagu and Tulu in Karnataka. **(5)**

dudka (1) Bagpipe (*duda*) of Hutsul'shchyna, Ukraine. (2) (Also *sopel* or *pizhatka*.) Eastern Slavic aerophone: Russian duct flute with five or six holes for fingering. (3) Belarusan duct flute. (4) Small wooden duct flute of Polissia, Ukraine. **(8)**

dudka jazyćkovaia Belarusan reed horn. **(8)**

duduk (1) (Also *düdük, bālābān, mey*.) Double-reed aerophone with a cylindrical bore, used mostly in ensembles. It has a warm and slightly nasal timbre and is very popular among folk and professional musicians. (2) Georgian urban reed aerophone. (3) Bulgarian and Macedonian short end-blown whistle-flute with six holes for fingering. (4) large duct flute of Serbian Vlahs. (5) Rim-blown flute played by Montenegrin shepherds. **(6, 8)**

duduki Middle Eastern fipple flute, used to accompany Georgian *bagdaduri* and *kintouri*. **(8)**

dudurejš Pair of stopped tubes, played by Serbian Vlah women for magical charms and ritual pieces. **(8)**

duende Transcendent emotion, often involved in Spanish flamenco. **(8)**

dueto bambuquero Typical Andean folk music duet in Colombia. **(2)**

duff (1) Arabic tambourine. (2) North African frame drum, the ancestor of the *adufe*. (3) (Also *ḍaf, duph*.) Large shallow-rimmed frame drum. **(3, 5, 8)**

dugački glas 'Long voice', Serbian songs with melismatic sections. **(8)**

duge pjesme 'Long songs', narrative women's ballads of Bosnia-Hercegovina. **(8)**

ḍuggī (Also *ḍugi, ḍukkar, khurḍak*.) One or a pair of small hand-played kettledrums in North India. **(5)**

dugi napjevi 'Long melodies'. In Bosnia-Hercegovina, songs having texts subordinate to melodies. **(8)**

dügü (Also *adügürühani*.) Garifuna feasting for the dead, the last of the postmortem rituals. **(2)**

ḍuhl Any of various double-headed barrel drums, played mostly for festive occasions in Balochistan by a Ludi drummer (*ḍuhlī*). **(5)**

duho (Also *dohāro*.) Poetic couplet in Gujarat. **(5)**

duizixi (China.) 'Paired drama', centered on a male and a female character. **(7)**

dūkā One of the major notes of the Arab fundamental scale. **(6)**

dukduk In New Britain and the Duke of York Islands, male (in Nissan, female) masks with heavy pandanus-leaf skirts, worn by men who perform gyrating movements before seated drummers; complementary to *tubuan* (*tumbuan*). (**9**)

dukhūl Short instrumental prelude in the Maghribi *nūba*. (**6**)

dukkur Double-headed barrel drum of Balochistan. (**5**)

dukun Male or female shaman of Javanese descent in Surinam who performs love-controlling magic and curing rituals. (**2**)

dūlāb (Also *dulab*.) Precomposed instrumental piece that opens various Arab suite forms (*fāsil, nūba, wasla*). (**6**)

dulbas Kettledrum of Bosnia-Hercegovina. (**8**)

dulcimer (1) Name for two types of folk zither: the Appalachian lap dulcimer, a slender strummed instrument with three or four strings, and the much rarer hammered dulcimer, a trapezoidal instrument with several dozen pairs of strings, descended from the Persian-Indian *santour* or Hungarian *cimbalom*. (2) (Often *hammer dulcimer*.) Trapezoidal chordophone played with light, handheld hammers. (**3, 9**)

duldang-duldang Sama song-dance debate. (**4**)

Dul Muluk South Sumatran heroic theater. (**4**)

dulpod Goan music and dance genre performed by Christians. (**5**)

duma Gumuz small clay kettledrum. (**1**)

dumbah (Also *dumbak*.) Arabic goblet drum, used in *taarab* orchestras of Zanzibar in the 1950s. (**1**)

dumbak (1) Bidayuh, Iban small double-headed drums. (2) (Also *dumbuk, dumbuq*.) Goblet-shaped single-headed drum. (**4, 6**)

dumbuli Georgian membranophone in medieval court ensembles. (**8**)

dumduma (Also *tungura*.) Small, deep kettledrum of the Tihāma made of clay or other appropriate materials, surrounded with straps and having a double skin. (**6**)

düm, tek (Also *dumm, tak*.) Terms used for high and low drum pitches in Turkish and other Middle Eastern musical metrics. (**6**)

dumy Ukrainian epic songs. (**8**)

dunasr Third section in the melodic development of a *shu'be*, an octave above the opening *darāmad*. (**6**)

dūnāy Reed pipe with two tubes. (**6**)

dunde Central Sulawesi bar zither. (**4**)

dundhukī Folk rhythm instrument of Orissa with variable-pitch sounds; similar to the *khamak*. (**5**)

dùndún Yoruba double-headed hourglass-shaped pressure drum, which can produce glides of speech; a symbol of pan-Yoruba identity. (**1**)

dunekpoe Anlo-Ewe musical ensemble. (**1**)

dung-dkar End-blown conch-shell trumpet of Tibet, known elsewhere in South Asia as *śankh*. (**5**)

dungga roro One-stringed fiddle of Sumba. (**4**)

dunya 'World universe', term used at the ends of phrases in Maninka singing of praises. (**1**)

duplo Poetic game of wit, played in Philippines. (**4**)

dupree (Also *dolkay, tabla*.) Drum pair. (**5**)

durak (1) Type of Turkish meter. (2) Musical genre associated with Sufi liturgy. (**6**)

durbakkih Palestinian term for *darbūka*, or goblet-shaped drum. (**6**)

duri dana Nias bamboo-tube buzzers. (**4**)

duru Yoruba two-stringed plucked lute. (**1**)

duru-duru Sardinian infant-dandling songs. (**8**)

duruitoare Romanian ratchet-type rattle, whirled on a handle for masked dances at the new year and to scare birds away. (**8**)

Dusun Ethnic group from Kalimantan. (**4**)

dutār Long-necked fretted plucked lute of Afghanistan. (**5**)

dūtār (Also *dotār, bam, zīr*.) 'Two strings' (Persian), long-necked plucked lute. (**6**)

dutra Chechen and Ingush shepherds' whistle flute. (**8**)

dűvő Regular rhythm with slurred, offbeat accentuation that often accompanies slow Hungarian dances. (**8**)

duvački orkestri Macedonian brass bands. (**8**)

Duwa Mandinka song praising warriors. (**1**)

duwagey Manobo one-stringed fiddle. (**4**)

duwahan Tausug and Sama pair of hanging gongs. (**4**)

duwan From Persian *diwana*, 'mendicant', 'holy fool', 'possessed one'; term for itinerant dervishes in Kyrgyzstan. (**6**)

duyug Maguindanao rhythmic mode. (**4**)

dûzele (Also *dödük, zimare*.) 'Of two reeds' (Kurdish), a double clariner of Kurdistan. (**6**)

düzen Tuning (Turkish). (**6**)

dviina fleita Ukrainian double flute with two pipes leading from one mouthpiece, each pipe with a separate fingering system. (**8**)

dvojanka Macedonian double duct flute with a melody and drone pipe. (**8**)

dvojice (Also *dvojnice*.) 'Pair', Croatian and Serbian double duct flutes with three holes in one pipe and four in the other. (**8**)

dyeli (Also French *griot*.) Professional musician among the Manding of Mali, often belonging to a specific caste. (**1**)

dyo Bambara concept of a state of stability and immutability. (**1**)

dyrevisene Norwegian humorous animal songs, often with a moral message. (**8**)

Dyula (1) Northern Mande-speaking people of Côte d'Ivoire. (2) Trade language in West Africa. (**1**)

dzeoba Georgian birth ritual. (**8**)

džez 'Jazz', drum set used in Albanian *čalgija* ensembles. (**8**)

dzhaz 'Jazz', Ukrainian drum-cymbal combination. (**8**)

dziavočnik (Also *na viankach, subornaja subota*.) Belarusan bridal fair the day before the wedding, when girls gather, accompanied by ritual songs. (**8**)

dziedāt 'To sing' (Old Latvian), label for vocal music. (**8**)

dziesmas (Also *dziedamās*.) Solo Latvian songs with ornamentation, short vocalizations, and refrains. (**8**)

džumbuš Long-necked skin-faced plucked lute, originally from the Middle East; still played in the Balkans. (**8**)

ebani Obsolete Georgian harp, mentioned in medieval literary sources. (**8**)

ebenza Stick zither in the area of Nanga-Eboko in Cameroon. (**1**)

ebugyô (Also *egyôzi*.) In Japan, Buddhist monk directing a ritual without performing Buddhist music. (**7**)

echoi The eight Byzantine modes, still used in traditional Cypriot music. (**8**)

edel Tagakaolu log drum. (**4**)

Edi festival Observance that commemorates a heroine of Ife who saved the town. (**1**)

ediski Tuvan single-reed aerophone imitating the sound of a female musk deer. (**6**)

Edo (1) Culture group that includes the Bini and other related peoples of Nigeria. (2) (Japan.) Period from 1600 to 1867. (**1, 7**)

edo hauta (Japan.) See *hauta*. (**7**)

edo kouta (Japan.) See *kouta*. (**7**)

edo nagauta (Japan.) See *nagauta*. (**7**)

edo zyôruri (Japan.) Generic term for narrative *syamisen* music (*zyôruri*) established in Edo (present-day Tôkyô). (**7**)

eduppu Point in a Karnatak *tala* cycle where the song text begins. (**5**)

e'ea Roti circle dance with antiphonal singing. (**4**)

Efik An Ibibio-speaking people of Nigeria. (**1**)

efterklangsviser Danish ballads, grouped according to content as spiritual, secular, and historical. (**8**)

eglīte Latvian fir-tree top decorated with colored feathers and hanging bells and jingles, played mostly by women, formerly used to accompany the singing of *godu balss* in wedding or winter-solstice rituals. (**8**)

egungun Formal theatrical association for masquerades that reincarnates deceased ancestors in Nigeria. **(1)**

egyôzi (Japan.) *See ebugyô.* **(7)**

ehti Zaghawi double-headed drum, one head struck with a stick and the other by hand. **(1)**

ehuru Warao double-headed drum with skins of howler monkeys and a snare on one end, played with one stick. **(2)**

ei (Japan.) Equivalent of the Western sharp. **(7)**

eisâ (Japan.) Okinawan folk dance that originated as a *bon* dance performed to commemorate the souls of ancestors, but mainly developed as a popular genre emphasizing drumming by young men. **(7)**

eisteddfod 'Session', Welsh competitive festival of poetry and singing. **(8)**

əkänzam (Plural, *iəkänzaman.*) Tuareg shallow frame drum. **(1)**

ekine Mask of Calabar, Nigeria. **(1)**

Ekiti One of the seven principal Yoruba peoples of Nigeria. **(1)**

ekô (Japan.) Category of Buddhist chant (*syômyô*) for sharing religious effects. **(7)**

ekphonetics Signs giving phonetic and rhythmic indications. **(6)**

ektār (Also *ekanādā, ēktāri, iktār.*) Single-stringed, plucked drone lute. **(5)**

ektārā (Also *gopīyantra.*) Single-stringed, plucked drum. **(5)**

ekun iyawo Yoruba nuptial song, performed by brides the day before the wedding. **(1)**

ekwe Igbo struck log idiophone. **(1)**

elafra Greek light popular music played in urban nightclubs. **(8)**

elafrolaika Greek "light" *laika.* **(8)**

electric band Common Oceanic name for an electrically amplified musical ensemble. **(9)**

electrophone 'Electronic sounder', musical instrument whose sound is produced by a vibration or action made by electronic means. **(2)**

elektrobağlama Electronically amplified Turkish *bağlama.* **(6)**

elerun Yoruba mask. **(1)**

el grupo Tejano ensemble consisting of keyboards, guitar, bass, and drums. **(3)**

El Güegüence Earliest-known Latin American folk drama with partial Náhuatl text that is still performed in the Diriamba area of Nicaragua. **(2)**

Eliaoba Georgian rain-begging ritual, performed by girls and young women who carry a female figure and sing. **(8)**

élive Weavers' work songs of French-speaking Switzerland. **(8)**

Ellice Islands Former name of Tuvalu. **(9)**

elliniko rok Greek rock music. **(8)**

el pilón Venezuelan large mortar and pestle used during grain pounding songs. **(2)**

elüwún Mapuche funeral rite. **(2)**

embaire Log xylophone of Uganda using fourteen slats with three players. **(1)**

embirekó 'Wife', smaller bow of the Paraguayan *guyrapa* double musical bow. **(2)**

embolada Brazilian 'tongue-twister' song genre performed by dueling singers accompanying themselves on *pandeiro* or *ganzá.* **(2)**

emibala Drummed texts that accompany special songs addressed to specific spirits in turn. **(1)**

emic (From *phonemic.*) Of sounds, perceivable as distinctive according to the subjective sense they make to participants in the cultures that generate or value them; cf. *etic.* **(9)**

empa-empal Large drum to accompany ceremonies in Tanimbar. **(4)**

emusi rimese (Japan.) 'Sword dance', genre of Ainu festival dance song (*rimse*) performed by men. **(7)**

enbai (Japan.) Gliding-pitch technique used with the *hitiriki* (a double-reed oboe in *gagaku*). **(7)**

encio Bidayuh small mouth flute. **(4)**

encomienda System by which land and peasants were governed by Spanish landlords. **(2)**

endere Flute used in Uganda. **(1)**

enfloramiento Aymara livestock marking ritual. **(2)**

engalabi Long drum used in Uganda. **(1)**

engoma Drum used in Uganda. **(1)**

engkeratung Maloh obsolete harp zither. **(4)**

engkeromung Iban gong-chime of *gendang panjai.* **(4)**

engkuk-kemong Pair of kettle gongs in *sléndro* tuning, Java. **(4)**

engwara Kazoos made from narrow conical sections of dried gourds and played for *enswezi* cult performance. **(1)**

enka (Japan.) Genre of popular music that appeared in the 1880s; originally street songs with political content but later transformed to mostly sentimental love songs with distinctly Japanese musical characteristics. **(7)**

enkana Lusoga lyre with a bowl-shaped calabash resonator. **(1)**

enkaya (Also *enkasi.*) In Japan, term of the Taisyô period (1912–1926) referring to professional performers of *enka,* a popular song genre. **(7)**

enkyoku (Japan.) *See sôga.* **(7)**

ennen (Japan.) Genre performed for pleasure after a Buddhist ritual. **(7)**

ensasi Rattle used in Uganda. **(1)**

ensuling Bamboo ring-stop flute of Borneo. **(4)**

enswezi Cult in southern Uganda whose music is marked by the use of four drums interlocking in fast triple rhythm. **(1)**

entenga Buganda drum chime. **(1)**

entongoli Lyre used in Uganda. **(1)**

entrées 'Entries, entrances' (French), series of dances in late-seventeenth-century *opéra-ballet.* **(8)**

entriega (From the Spanish *entregar* 'to send forth'.) Musical sending forth of a group or social entity into the community or into a ritual function; the term is used primarily in Hispanic wedding contexts. **(3)**

entriega de novios In times when Roman Catholic priests were very rare in New Mexican society, the *entriega de novios* actually substituted for the church wedding ceremony. **(3)**

Enugu Jazz Club Nigerian ensemble in which Okechukwu Ndubuisi performed and which met at the British Embassy. **(1)**

Enugu Musical Society Choral group in Nigeria. **(1)**

Enugu Operatic Society Nigerian group founded in 1960 to perform excerpts and occasionally full-scale operas and musicals. **(1)**

enumerative songs In France, songs that are recapitulative, augmenting the strophe progressively. **(8)**

epena (Also *ebena, yopo.*) Yanomamö hallucinogenic snuff. **(2)**

Ephesus, Council of Christian church council in 431 that condemned the Nestorian heresy, which proposed that Christ had two distinct natures and persons, one human and one divine. **(6)**

épiaulie (Also *hymée.*) Millers' work songs of French-speaking Switzerland. **(8)**

epic Long narrative poem recounting the feats of a historical or legendary hero and usually sung in formal settings. **(8)**

Epic of Palnādu (Also *Palnāṭi Vīrula Katha.*) Extended Telugu oral epic with roots in the twelfth century. **(5)**

epinet (Also *épinette, pinet.*) Plucked dulcimer of the Low Countries. **(8)**

épinette des Vosges 'Spinet of the Vosges', French plucked dulcimer. **(8)**

Epirotika Greek songs from or in the style of Epirus. **(8)**

epí trapézios 'At the table', genre of male singing in Greece. **(8)**

equal-tempered tuning Tuning based on harmonic overtone series. **(4)**

equidistant heptatonic scale Seven-note pitch inventory in which all intervals are of equal size. **(1)**

equipentatonic Pitch inventory with five equally spaced pitches to the octave. **(1)**

erebane Term for a circular wooden frame drum in Kurdistan; cf. *bendêr, def.* **(6)**

Volume Key: **6**, Middle East; **7**, East Asia; **8**, Europe; **9**, Australia and the Pacific Islands; **10**, The World's Music.

ereki bûmu (Japan.) 'Elec boom', craze of the 1960s among young Japanese people, focused on the electric guitar. (7)

erets Yisrael 'Land of Israel', Hebrew, biblical term for the land settled in Palestine between 1880 and 1948 by Jews of the diaspora. (6)

erhu (Also *er hu*.) (1) Low-pitched two-stringed fiddle from China. (2) (China.) Two-stringed bowed spike lute whose sound box is covered with snakeskin. (3, 4, 7, 10)

erhuang (China.) Important type of aria in Peking opera. *Erhuang* melodies stress the second and the lower fifth degrees of the scale. This music is considered suitable for serious and heroic stories. (7)

erke (1) Bolivian animal-horn single-reed-concussion aerophone; (2) small trumpet made from a single cow or bull horn; (3) *erque*, Argentine very long lip-concussion aerophone made from cane. (2)

erkencho (Also *erquencho*.) Argentine single-reed-concussion aerophone without finger holes. (2)

ērrap pāṭṭu Tamil work song (now rarely performed) to accompany the hoisting of water buckets from a well. (5)

ersipu (China.) 'Two four notation', simplified form of an ancient numeric notation used in Chaozhou music. (7)

ērtabaṭk Kota kettle drum, Tamil Nadu. (5)

er xian Two-stringed fiddle of southeastern China. (3)

esālat 'Authenticity' (Persian). In Iran, term of praise for music of quality and taste that invokes rapture, or *ḥāl; see also aṣīl.* (6)

esampe uwante (Japan.) Ainu dance game or contest. (7)

escapularios Profane musical performance given by blacks during religious festivities in colonial Mexico. (2)

escobillada Afro-Peruvian dance step in which the foot is brushed along the floor or ground. (2)

escobillero Acrobatic dancer in Argentine *candombe*. (2)

escola de samba Brazilian 'samba school', urban samba group for carnival. (2)

eshāre Ornament alluding to the next melodic tone in Persian music. (6)

esharsh Chechen and Ingush solo songs with instrumental accompaniment. (8)

esime Intensified rhythmic section in BaAka performance. (1)

espagnol Zambian guitar tuning, D–a–d–f-sharp–a–c-sharp. (1)

espinela Ten-line structure of *décima*. (2)

esquinazo Chilean *tonada* performed as a serenade. (2)

estilo 'Style', Argentine traditional *pampa* musical form used during a *jineteada*. (2)

estrada Russian term for regional traditional popular music (as in Kazakhstan). (6)

estradna muzika Bulgarian popular music. (8)

estradnaja muzyka 'Staged music' of Belarus, often sung in Russian. (8)

estribillo 'Refrain' in the Spanish poetic tradition. (8)

estudiantina 'Student ensemble', (1) group of musicians playing instrumental music with Spanish-derived instruments, especially common in Colombia and Peru, and in late-nineteenth-century Cuba; *see also lira, rondalla, tuna*. (2) Ensemble in Puno that includes guitars, *charangos*, mandolins, and accordion. (3) Students' plucked string ensemble, found in the Philippines. (2, 4)

esz-tam Hungarian term used onomatopoeically to denote downbeat-offbeat rhythmic patterns in Croatian-Hungarian borderlands. (8)

etenraku utaimono (Japan.) *Gagaku* piece *Etenraku* sung with lyrics. (7)

ethnocentrism Valuing a particular culture over others. (4)

ethnomusicology Study of music as culture, integrating the analysis of sound and behavior. (1)

etic (From *phonetic*.) Of sounds, perceivable as present and actual acoustic events according to an assumed objective measurement or description; cf. *emic*. (9)

ǝttebel Large ceremonial kettledrum, symbol of Tuareg chieftainship. (1)

Ettu Jamaican African-based cult. (2)

ettugaḍa svara 'Deceiving' melodic passages in Karnatak genres such as *varṇam*; type of *citta svara*. (5)

Eurocentrism Interpretation of events and situations with European assumptions and principles. (1)

Ewe A Kwa-speaking people of Ghana and Togo. (1)

exogamy Marriage outside one's own group, especially as required by custom or law. (9)

expandable moment Segment of performance conceived as a unit and subject to layering of sound. (1)

exvoto (Latin *ex voto* 'out of the vow'.) Spanish song of thanks for a miraculous cure or a providential intercession. (8)

Eyuphoro Mozambican band that became internationally popular in the 1980s. (1)

ezan Call to prayer (Turkish); *see adhān*. (6)

ezenggileer Strictly mimetic type of Tuvan *khöömei*. (6)

ezhy 'Everybody', bass part in Adighian, Balkar, and Karachaevi polyphony. (8)

ezpata dantza Basque sword dance. (3)

ǝzziker (From Arabic *dhikr*.) Tuareg ritual music sung recollecting Allah in mosques and improvised places of worship. (1)

fa'ataupati Sāmoan dance with slapping, usually done by men. (9)

facture French instrument making; *see lutherie*. (8)

fado Portuguese urban genre of song accompanied by one to four guitarists. (8)

fado Melancholy Portuguese solo song type generally accompanied by the *guitarra* (ten- or twelve-stringed Portuguese guitar) or the *violao* (Spanish guitar); features aspects of the Portuguese ballad tradition (*modhinha*), including rhyming quatrains (*coplas*) and dance rhythms; popular in grassroots Portuguese communities. (3)

fado canção 'Sung *fado*' (Portuguese). (8)

fado castiço 'Authentic *fado*' (Portuguese). (8)

fãg (Also *cautāl*.) Song genre of Fiji Indians performed during the Holī festival. (5)

faglung Bilaan two-stringed lute. (4)

falak Folk genre of a melancholic nature from Badakhshan. (5)

Falasha Jewish cultural group of Ethiopia. (1)

falawatus (Also *falawitas*.) Andean cane or wooden transverse flute with six finger holes. (2)

falliwes Bontok dance music with sticks. (4)

falsa High voice part of Venezuelan *tonos* ensemble. (2)

falsafat al-laḥn 'Philosophy of the melody', referring to stable forms from which a Yemeni *'ūd* player develops variations. (6)

falsetas Spanish flamenco guitar style that involves plucking the melodic phrases. (8)

falsetto Timbre, usually with high pitch, resulting from forced limitations of the larynx. (9)

fam (Also *skamóra, puzyr', álonka*.) Mordovinian bagpipe. (8)

famifami Yoruba short wooden trumpet, borrowed from the Hausa *famfami*. (1)

famo Wild, risqué version of *marabi* that appeared among Basotho migrants. (1)

famuge (China.) Woodcutters' songs. (7)

fanbei (1) Chants used specifically to praise buddhas and bodhisattvas (China). (2) Chinese reading of the Chinese characters for *bonbai*, Buddhist chant (Japan). (7)

fandang Trinidadian secular dance used in conjunction with *veiquoix*. (2)

fandango (1) Colombian place where festivities occur, or musical dance style. (2) Venezuelan predecessor of the *joropo*. (3) Brazilian generic term for a dance event. (4) Rapid, triple-meter Spanish dance. (5) Basque, Portuguese, and Spanish dance in 6/8 time. (2, 4, 8)

fanfa Haitian municipal, school, or military fanfare by wind orchestra. (2)

fanfares mixtes Instrumental ensembles of brass instruments, from the French-speaking area of Switzerland. (8)

Fang A neo-Bantu-speaking people of Gabon. **(1)**

fangpaige (China.) Raft workers' songs. **(7)**

fangshi (China.) Man of magical techniques. **(7)**

fangxiang (China.) Suspended metal plates. **(7)**

fann 'Art'. (Plural, *funun.*) **(6)**

fantaziya 'Fantasy', Maghrib spectacle involving choreographed movements by horses and men, accompanied by drums. **(1)**

Fanti A Twi-speaking (Akan) people of Ghana and other West African coastal areas. **(1)**

fanxian (China.) To transpose a fourth up the scale without a conceptual shift of the tonic note in the original key. **(7)**

fao Gã rattles strung with nets of beads. **(1)**

faqi (China.) Ritual instruments. **(7)**

faqīr (Plural, *fuqārā*.) 'A poor person'. Dervish, *malang*, or *qalandar*; religious mendicant; devotee. **(5, 6)**

farandole French open chain dance. **(8)**

farara Free-reed rice-stalk pipe of Madagascar; it produces a strong, piercing sound. **(1)**

far'awi Musical genre used in dancing at Palestinian wedding celebrations. **(6)**

Farfisa Single-manual electronic organ produced by the Italian company Farfisa, with electronic oscillators instead of reeds; the portability and distinctive timbre of the Farfisa organ made it a natural choice for popular musicians of the 1960s as well as such conservatory-trained composer-performers as David Borden, Philip Glass, and Steve Reich. **(3)**

farīsa 'Hobby horse dance', women's dance of the Gulf region in which a performer wearing a cardboard horse costume dances in the midst of a circle of women playing tambourines. **(6)**

fariseos 'Pharisees', Tarahumara dancers during Lenten celebrations accompanied by pipe-and-tabor musicians. **(2)**

farmaisī Complex form of *cakkardār* composition for North Indian *pakhāaj*. **(5)**

fartash 'Search'; Yemeni instrumental genre with variations on a short melodic motive. **(6)**

faryādī 'Crying out' (Persian), vocal genre of southern Khorasan, sung in open, uninhabited spaces. **(6)**

fāṣil Syrian suite form, similar to the *nūba* or *waṣla*, consisting largely of *muwashshaḥāt* in gradually livelier meters; cf. *fasıl.* **(6)**

fasıl Turkish suite form originating in the Ottoman court, beginning with a *peşrev* and containing *taksim*, a *saz semai*, and various song genres. **(6)**

fasıla (Plural, *faṣā'il.*) Families into which theorists group various *maqāmāt.* **(6)**

fasıl-i hanende Specifically vocal performance cycle in Ottoman Turkish music. **(6)**

fasıl-i sazende Specifically instrumental performance cycle in Ottoman Turkish music. **(6)**

Fasnacht Carnival festivities in Germany. **(8)**

fātele Tokelauan short song with interpretive movements, adapted in Kiribati as the *bātere*. **(9)**

fatt 'Fact', 'true story'; ballad, the oldest documented traditional Maltese song form. **(8)**

favelas Brazilian hillside slums. **(2)**

fawātīh Invocation of several individuals or groups, followed by the recitation of *Sūrat al-fātiḥa*, the opening chapter of the Qur'ān, as a benediction. A sequence of call-response *fawātīh* usually opens and closes the Sufi *ḥaḍra.* **(6)**

fawn Various kinds of northern Thai dance, such as *fawn thian.* **(4)**

feadán Irish whistle. **(8)**

fedefede Tumtum Nuba five-stringed lyre of the Sudan. **(1)**

fedel Danish stringed instrument of the violin family. **(8)**

feko Transverse flute of Flores. **(4)**

feko genda Flute and drum ensemble of Flores. **(4)**

feku Wooden ocarina of West Timor. **(4)**

felak 'Fate' (Persian, from Arabic). Afghan and Tajik equivalent of the Iranian genre *gharībī.* **(6)**

félibres Provençal poets and intellectuals dedicated to the revival of their regional dialects. **(8)**

fell Musical genre performed by Christians in Goa. **(5)**

Fellani (Also Fellata.) *See* Fulɓe. **(1)**

felu-ko-felu 'Iron-against-iron', two pieces of iron that are hit together by Surinam Maroons. **(2)**

fengci ge (China.) Satirical songs. **(7)**

fengsu ge (China.) Songs related to folk customs. **(7)**

ferrinhos Portuguese triangle. **(8)**

festa (1) Maltese and Portuguese religious festival with music. (2) Italian feast day, typically including a procession with music. **(3, 8)**

festejo Afro-Peruvian form often interrupted at phrase endings by a sudden pause or long, held pitch. **(2)**

festivales de folklore Argentine 'folkloric festivals', annual revivalistic competitions and exhibitions of song and dance. **(2)**

fest noz 'Night festival', Breton event featuring songs, dances, and, more recently, contests. **(8)**

Festspiel German form of folk theater. **(8)**

fet patwonal Haitian patron's day festivals. **(2)**

feuilles olantes 'Flying sheets', French broadsides. **(8)**

fidao Vai ceremony of redemption held for the deceased. **(1)**

fiddle Alternative name for the violin; typically describes a violin used to perform vernacular (as opposed to concert) music. **(3)**

Fidel Vielle used to accompany singing in Germany in the Middle Ages. **(8)**

fidiog Ossetian bull or wild goat horn with four or five holes and a mouthpiece, associated with hunting. **(8)**

fiðla (1) Ancient Norwegian lyre or harp; *see harpa*. (2) Icelandic trapezoidal bowed zither. **(8)**

field drum Side drum. **(8)**

field music Military musicians performing on drums, fifes, bagpipes, trumpets, or bugles, who beat or sound the camp duty calls that regulate military life. **(3)**

field recordings Recordings made by ethnomusicologists on location as people perform in various events. **(1)**

field-rerecording technique Simha Arom's analytical method, based on musicians' reconstructions of a song through referential parts. **(1)**

fieldwork Observation of musical performance, usually with recording, interviewing, and transcribing for later analysis. **(1, 10)**

fiesta 'Feast', 'festival' (Spanish). (1) Holy day, party, or celebration. (2) Celebration of the feast of the patron saint of a town, according to the Catholic calendar. (3) Occasion for communal sharing of foods, drinking, dancing, music making, and merriment. **(2, 8)**

fifa Single-pitched notched flute, played in Oltenia, Romania, by women who alter its note with yodel-like singing. **(8)**

fi fa gun Vocal slides, which usually appear at the beginning or end of Yoruba phrases. **(1)**

fife Traditionally, a one-piece cylindrical transverse wooden flute with mouth and six finger holes, commonly pitched in B-flat but transposing to D, primarily used with drum accompaniment in military and military-styled civilian marching bands. **(3)**

fifra Maltese fife played with a bass drum for public announcements. **(8)**

fifre (Also *fijfel*, *fijfer*.) Side-blown flute of the Low Countries. **(8)**

figure-ground Image with background; in visual illusions, viewers may reverse the figure and ground. **(1)**

figurines Individual Chilean dancers in a patronal festival. **(2)**

Fiji kaali Secular narrative songs of Fiji Indians. **(5)**

fijīrī (Also *fijiri*, *fijrī*, *fijīrī*.) 'Until dawn', popular song tradition of pearl fishermen in the Gulf region. (6)

filastrocche Corsican children's songs performed by linking rows of verses, often with nonlexical words. (8)

filmi (1) Popular song from Indian films. (2) Music of Hindi films, also performed live, popular among Indian immigrants in Britain. (4, 8)

filmī gīt 'Film song', composed and recorded for commercial Indian films. (5)

filutu Bamboo duct flute on Ternate and Tidore. (4)

Finisterre Range Papua New Guinean mountains running inland of the Rai Coast, between the coast and the border with Morobe. (9)

fireman Guitar-fingering pattern associated with Kru styles. (1)

firlinfeu Italian panpipes. (8)

firozkhānī gat Fast-tempo Hindustani instrumental composition. (5)

firqa (Plural, *firaq*.) 'Group', 'troupe', 'ensemble'; the term generally refers to a larger group than the chamber ensemble or *takht*. (6)

firqah Egyptian kind of orchestra, whose style led to that of modern Egyptian film music. (1)

firqat al-dān Women's ensemble in Oman, which may also include male drummers. (6)

firqat al-qurba Omani bagpipe ensemble. (6)

firqat al-razḥa Omani group practicing the arts of the sword, rituals involving sung poetry, dancing, and duels with swordplay; known generically as *al-razīf*; cf. *'arḍa*. (6)

fisarmonica (1) Italian chromatic piano accordion. (2) Sardinian large chromatic accordion. (3, 8)

fisarmonica a nümar 'Figure-accordion', diatonic accordion of Italian-speaking Switzerland. (8)

fischju (Also *pirula*.) Corsican long, thin, reed flute having three to six holes for fingering. (8)

fission of the fundamental Separation of the fundamental pitch from the rest of the harmonic frequencies. (1)

fixed-pitch instruments Instruments, such as xylophones and gong circles, whose pitch cannot be changed during performance. (4)

flamenco (1) Song, dance, and guitar style developed in Andalucia in the south of Spain blending elements of local practice with that from Morocco, Egypt, India, Pakistan, Greece, and other parts of the Near and Far East. (2) Style of Gypsy music with guitar, song, and hand clapping, of southern Spanish origin but diffused throughout the Americas and beyond. (3) Spanish musical genre gener-

ally associated with *gitanos*, Spanish Gypsies. (3, 8)

flamenco arabe 'Arab flamenco' (Spanish), fusion of flamenco with Arabic music. (8)

flatfele 'Flat violin', Norwegian name of the standard violin (*vanleg fele*). (8)

flatterzunge Flutter tonguing (Norwegian). (8)

flauta 'Flute', common Spanish term for a cane or bamboo transverse flute, usually with six finger holes. (2)

flautón 'Big flute', Chilean *chino* dancer's single-tubed ductless flute (like a single tube of a panpipe) played in sets. (2)

flawta Bolivian duct flute. (2)

fleadh Competitive festival of Irish music. (8)

flejguta Maltese shepherd's reed pipe, used in outdoor music. (8)

flexible melody Notion describing the melodic content of the Iranian *radīf*, in which a given melodic contour may be rhythmically elaborated in different ways according to the meter of the poetry. (6)

flisak Genre from the Lubelskie region of Poland, often sung by raftsmen. (8)

flor de nube 'Cloud flower', Mixtec song with string accompaniment. (2)

Florentine Codex Nahua early colonial codex by Fray Bernardino Sahagún. (2)

flores 'Flowers', Mixtec dance genre accompanied by string music. (2)

flores de Mayo May rite with flowers and song, in the Philippines. (4)

floyera Greek end-blown bevel-edged flute played by shepherds. (8)

fluier Romanian six-holed duct flute. (8)

FM Tango Argentine radio station in the 1990s, dedicated exclusively to tango. (2)

foekepot Friction drum of the Low Countries. (8)

fofa Dance found in Brazil and Portugal. (8)

fogli olanti 'Flying leaves', Italian broadsides. (8)

foi doa Ngada double flute. (4)

foi dogo Ngada triple flute. (4)

foi mere (Also *foi pai*.) Ngada indirectly blown bass flute. (4)

fola Mandinka words of praise, often interspersed with instrumental playing. (1)

folia Brazilian ensemble that goes from house to house, singing, playing instruments, and collecting donations for popular Catholic festivals, such as the *folia de reis*, 'festival of kings' (Magi) around Christmas. (2)

folklig musik Swedish term for folk music (*gammeldans*) and other forms of popular music since the 1970s. (8)

folklore (After German *Volkskunde*.) Traditional customs, tales, songs, dances, and other art forms. (8)

folklorismo 'Folklorism'. In Spain, self-conscious re-creation of older folk styles. (8)

folkmusik Orally transmitted music of the rural classes in old Swedish peasant society. (8)

folknici Czech and Slovak musical genre that combined music of popular folk singers (*písničkaři*) and rock musicians in the late 1960s. (8)

folkparker Outdoor Swedish amusement parks that became important venues for dance music of the modern and old types after 1900. (8)

follay Songhai religious music. (1)

fololtsy Panpipes made from flexible reeds and played by children guarding cattle in Madagascar. (1)

Fon A people of the Republic of Benin. (1)

fones Traditional tune types used by Cypriot singers to create songs with new texts. (8)

fonn 'The tune'. In Irish dance tunes, the first section, which consists of two four-measure phrases. (8)

fontomfrom (Also *fɔntɔmfrɔm*.) Genre of Akan music characterized by slow, dignified movements and played by royal orchestras. (1, 10)

foqu (China.) Vocal pieces composed to fit the texts of Buddhist scriptures. (7)

formant Any of several frequency bands comprising groups of prominent overtones of a complex tone, in the human voice determining the phonetic identity of vowels. (9)

formes fixes French poetic and song forms of the fourteenth and fifteenth centuries, chiefly the *ballade*, the *rondeau*, and the *irelai*. (8)

formula, melodic Tone or series of tones (some variously optional or alternative), whose rhythmic realization depends mostly on the words that give breath. (9)

forró (1) Brazilian social dance music; (2) *caboclo* dance party of Brazil; (3) accordion-based dance music of northeast Brazil derived from *baião*. (2)

forty-niners (49ers.) Social song genre that incorporates English lyrics with American Indian vocables, found in Puerto Rico and elsewhere. (3)

forūd 'Descent' (Persian), gradual return to and cadence in the initial low register, in a performance of Persian classical music. (6)

fotuto Archaic Colombian gourd, shell, or wooden trumpet. (2)

Foulah. *See* Fulɓe. (1)

Fourier analysis Mathematical procedure, automated in signal-analysis equipment, that decomposes a complex waveform into sine waves (fundamental and overtones) of well-defined frequencies. (9)

Fouta Toro Region along the Senegal River; an important Muslim state in the 1700s and 1800s. (1)

frajtonarica Slovene diatonic accordion with buttons. **(8)**

frame drum (1) Most typical in Arctic and Subarctic regions, a drum consisting of a single (rarely double) membrane stretched over a variably sized bent wood or bone round frame and tied with lacing around the frame or in the back; in the Arctic, the handheld frame drum features a handle. (2) Shallow single-headed drum often having jingles attached to the frame, usually played by being struck, especially with fingers, knuckles, fists, and knees and sometimes with sticks. **(3, 8)**

Fränzli music Eighteenth-century Swiss instrumental style. **(8)**

free-reed pipe Aerophone with a freestanding reed. **(4)**

frequency Number of repetitions of a periodic process in a unit of time; in the analysis of sound, usually measured in hertz. **(9)**

fret (1) Thin metal bar inlaid across the fingerboard on the neck of a chordophone, beneath the strings, which protrudes above the surface, enabling the player to press a string or strings behind it and thus shorten the vibrating portion of the string to change the pitch; (2) to change the pitch of a string or strings on a chordophone. **(3)**

frevo Brass-band carnival march and dance music from Recife, Pernambuco, and electrified version of this music in Salvador, Bahia. **(2)**

fricote Brazilian carnival dance music. **(2)**

friction bow Instrument in which scraping a stick across notches carved into the bow indirectly vibrates the string. **(1)**

frigate bird Any of several rapacious seabirds of the family Fregatidae; a dance or mimetically performed motif or set of motifs of Kiribati, Nauru, and other islands; cf. *tropic bird.* **(9)**

frula Croatian and Serbian duct flute. **(8)**

FSM Federated States of Micronesia, comprising Chuuk, Kosrae, Pohnpei, and Yap. **(9)**

fuga 'Flight'. (1) Type of faster coda in Andean music; (2) Afro-Peruvian musical appendage used as a lively closing section; (3) Colombian Christmas song; (4) Colombian *currulao* rhythm; (5) in Andean music, a contrasting theme in a faster tempo, usually a *huayno* following a *yaraví.* **(2)**

fugddi Goan women's music and dance genre of Hindu origin. **(5)**

fujara Two-meter-long Slovak duct flute with three holes for fingering, supplemented by a short blowing tube. **(8)**

fujarka End-blown. ductless, holeless shepherd's flute of the Carpathian area of Poland. **(8)**

fújì The most popular Yoruba musical genre of the early 1990s, using a lead singer, a chorus, and drummers, a development from *ajísáàrì.* **(1)**

fuká Surinam Maroon *sêkêti* song of hardship. **(2)**

fukuinkai Japanese-American Christian gospel society. **(3)**

Fulɓe (Also Fula, Fulani.) Pastoral people scattered throughout the western Sudan region. **(1)**

Fulɓeni Hausa term for Fulɓe, used in the Central Sudanic and Voltaic clusters. **(1)**

fulia Drum-accompanied Venezuelan responsorial song genre. **(2)**

fulklūr 'Folklore', Lebanese urban repertoire embracing music, dance, and drama, dating from the 1950s. **(6)**

fulu Upland Thai (Lisu) mouth organ with bamboo pipes and gourd wind chest. **(4)**

fulyrka Six- or seven-holed duct flute of the Carpathian area of Poland. **(8)**

fundamental Component of a musical sound which has the lowest frequency and on which a series of overtones may be based. **(9)**

fundeh Jamaican single-headed membranophone played with the hands. **(2)**

funk Syncopated, eclectic form of rhythm and blues (R&B), beginning in the late 1960s. **(3)**

funk groove Polyrhythmic foundation built on a syncopated bass line that locks with the bass drum pattern and is accentuated by a heavy backbeat. **(3)**

Fur A Sudanese people. **(1)**

furāward Concluding section in the melodic development of a *shu'be.* **(6)**

furiant Triple-meter Bohemian dance with alternating duple and triple accentual patterns. **(8)**

furruco Single-headed Venezuelan friction membranophone sounded by rubbing a long stick attached to and protruding from the top of the drum skin. **(2)**

fusion of the fundamental Joining of the fundamental to the rest of the harmonic frequencies. **(1)**

fuṣūl (Singular, *fāṣil.*) Cycles in which individual *maqāmāt* may be ordered in the Iraqi *maqām.* **(6)**

fyell Albanian shepherd's flute. **(8)**

fyelldrejti Duct flute played by northern Albanian herdsmen. **(8)**

Gã A people of southeastern Ghana. **(1)**

gabay Somali poetry that deals with politics, war, peace, and social debate, and functions like editorials. **(1)**

gabbang Bamboo xylophone, common to Borneo and the Philippines. **(4)**

gabu (Japan.) Head of the *bunraku* puppet used in special situations in which a character suddenly changes into a demon. **(7)**

gabusi Plucked lute of the Comoro Islands. **(1)**

gaekwad (Also *maharaja.*) 'Great ruler'. **(5)**

Gaelic song Vocal music in the Scottish Gaelic or Irish Gaelic language. **(3)**

gafieiras Brazilian large dance halls patronized by the urban popular classes. **(2)**

gagá Haitian-derived ensemble in the Dominican Republic. **(2)**

gagah 'Strong, robust' (Javanese). **(4)**

gagahan Male strong character type in Javanese dance. **(4)**

gagaku (Japan.) Music and dance of the court; also performed at Buddhist temples and Shinto (Sintô) shrines. **(7, 10)**

gagaku biwa (Japan.) *Biwa* lute used in *gagaku.* **(7)**

Gagaku ryô (Also *Utamai no tukasa.*) In Japan, first official department established in 701 for teaching and performing *gagaku.* **(7)**

gagaku syakuhati (Japan.) See *syôsôin syakuhati.* **(7)**

gagalo Three-meter stilts used by dancers at a Yoruba harvest festival in Nigeria in honor of the town's protector. **(1)**

gagashi Long, end-blown trumpet of the Fulɓe in Togo. **(1)**

gagliarda 'Galliard', Corsican dance piece. **(8)**

gagong pon Subanen heavy gong. **(4)**

gāh Ways of progressing through various *maqāmāt* (Persian). **(6)**

gagra Higi dance that tests men's bravery. **(1)**

gahu Genre of dancing in Ghana. **(1)**

gaida Thracian bagpipe. **(8)**

gaikyoku (Japan.) Repertoire borrowed from other instruments or genres, used particularly with *syakuhati* and *kokyû.* **(7)**

gaita (Probably from Arabic *algaita.*) (1) Colombian vertical duct flute. (2) Basque double-reed aerophone of Arabic origin with eight holes for fingering; the variant in Soule is called *txanbela.* (3) Bagpipe of Northern Spain. **(2, 8)**

gaita-de-foles Portuguese bagpipe, played especially in the north. **(8)**

gajda Bulgarian and Macedonian bagpipe. **(8)**

gajdaši Player of a Serbian bagpipe. **(8)**

gajde Albanian and Serbian bagpipe. **(8)**

gajdy Czech, Polish, and Slovak bagpipe. **(8)**

Gakka roku (Japan.) 'Records of Musician Families'; *gagaku* compendium completed in 1690 by Abe Suehisa (1622–1708). **(7)**

gakki (Japan.) Generic term for musical instruments. **(7)**

gaku (Japan.) (1) *Nô* dance performed as *bugaku* (court dance); (2) dance modeled after the *gaku.* **(7)**

gaku biwa (Japan.) See *gagaku biwa.* **(7)**

gaku daiko (Japan.) *See turi daiko.* (7)

Gaku dokoro (Japan.) *See Gakuso.* (7)

Gakunin bunin (Japan.) 'Record of Appointments of Musicians', chronological record from 107 to 1262, mentioning 280 musicians by name. (7)

Gakuso (Also *Gakusyo, Gaku dokoro.*) In Japan, institute established by the tenth century for teaching and performing foreign-derived *gagaku* music. (7)

gakusô (Japan.) Thirteen-stringed long plucked zither used in *gagaku.* (7)

Gakuso bunin (Japan.) *See Gakunin bunin.* (7)

Gakusyo (Japan.) *See Gakuso.* (7)

Gakusyo yôroku (Japan.) Chinese theoretical treatises on music brought to Japan in 735. (7)

Galambawa A people of northern Nigeria. (1)

galant style Late Baroque style that favored regular phrasing, ornamented melodies, and simple harmonies. (8)

galdur 'Incantation', form of Icelandic musical performance. (8)

galerón Venezuelan dance music genre. (2)

gālī Insult song performed during weddings and on other occasions in North India. (5)

galombang West Sumatra circular dance form. (4)

galop Lively couple dance in duple meter. (8)

galopa 'Gallop', Paraguayan outdoor fast dance consisting of two contrasting musical sections: a polka and a syncopated section. (2)

galoperas 'Dancers', Paraguayan women who dance to fulfill religious vows. (2)

galopp Swiss regional dance. (8)

galoubet Three-holed flute played with a *tambourin* in Provence. (8)

gamaka Musical ornament. (5)

gamat West Sumatra male-male couple dance. (4)

gambang (Also *gambang kayu.*) Eighteen-key wooden xylophone of Java. (4, 10)

gambang kromong Chinese-oriented Indonesian music. (4)

gambaré Soninke four-stringed plucked lute. (1)

gambo Eight-stringed plucked lute of Sumbawa. (4)

gambuh Theatrical genre of Bali. (4)

gambus Plucked, pear-shaped lute, related to the *'ūd*, common to Malaysia and Indonesia. (4)

gambus Arab Lampung Arabic song with violin and *rebana.* (4)

gambyak Double-headed East Javanese drum. (4)

gambyong Javanese nonnarrative women's dance. (4)

gamelan (1) Indonesian orchestra consisting mostly of struck idiophones, performed by people of Javanese heritage in Surinam. (2) Indonesian stratified gong-chime ensemble. (3) Multitimbre melodic percussion ensemble from Indonesia similar to other "gong-chime" ensembles of Southeast Asia; most *gamelan* have a low gongs to punctuate melodic phrases, metallophones or other keyed instruments to play a trunk melody, a variety of instruments that elaborate on the melodic structure, and drums that lead changes in tempo. (2, 3, 4, 10)

gamelan angklung Four-tone village ensemble of Bali and Lombok. (4, 10)

gamelan arja Balinese *suling* and percussion ensemble. (4)

gamelan balé bandung Cirebonese court ensemble similar to *gamelan rénténg.* (4)

gamelan baleganjur Processional ensemble of Bali and Lombok. (4)

gamelan baris Gong-chime ensemble of Lombok. (4)

gamelan barong tengkok Wedding ensemble of Lombok. (4)

gamelan cara balèn Ceremonial historical ensemble of Java. (4)

gamelan degung Sundanese *pélog* gong-chime ensemble. (4)

gamelan denggung Oldest court ensemble of Cirebon. (4)

gamelan gadhon Small, soft-sounding ensemble of Java. (4)

gamelan gambang Sacred xylophone and metallophone ensemble of Bali. (4)

gamelan gambuh *Suling, rebab,* and percussion ensemble of Bali. (4)

gamelan gendang beleq Main traditional Sasak ensemble. (4)

gamelan gong Large, older ceremonial ensemble of Bali. (4)

gamelan gong kebyar Balinese dynamic modern *gamelan* style. (4)

gamelan gong kuna Main ceremonial ensemble of Lombok. (4)

gamelan gong Sasak Modern Sasak ensemble. (4)

gamelan grantang Rare ensemble accompanying social dance in Lombok. (4)

gamelan jegog West Bali bamboo xylophone ensemble. (4)

gamelan jerujeng Sacred ensemble of Boda people. (4)

gamelan klenèngan Small, soft-sounding ensemble in Java. (4)

gamelan klentang Interlocking *klentang* processional ensemble in Lombok. (4)

gamelan kodhok ngorèk Ceremonial historical ensemble in Java. (4)

gamelan luang Balinese sacred xylophone and metallophone ensemble. (4)

gamelan Maulid Lombok sacred ensemble played during Maulid. (4)

gamelan munggang Ceremonial three-toned historical ensemble of Java. (4)

gamelan pelégongan Balinese ensemble accompanying *legong.* (4)

gamelan pélog *Pélog* ensemble used to accompany *tayuban* dance in Cirebon. (4)

gamelan prawa *Sléndro* ensemble used to accompany *wayang topèng* in Cirebon. (4)

gamelan rebana Drums tuned to *gamelan* pitches in Lombok. (4)

gamelan saléndro Sundanese *saléndro* gong-chime ensemble. (4)

gamelan sekati Ceremonial historical ensemble of Java and Cirebon. (4)

gamelan selundeng Sacred iron-bar metallophone ensemble of Bali. (4)

gamelan Semar pegulingan Small, soft-sounding court ensemble of Bali. (4)

gamelan tambur Drum and gong ensemble for dance in Lombok. (4)

gamelan wayang Sasak Ensemble to accompany wayang puppetry in Lombok. (4)

gamkivani 'Like the cock's sound', version of *modzakhili*, the second voice of Georgian three-part singing. (8)

gamlestev 'Old stanza' (Norwegian), poetic form with medieval roots. (8)

gamma suid Kuna paired bamboo, single-tubed, end-blown flutes played by puberty chanters. (2)

gammaldansane 'Old dances', dances such as polkas and waltzes, which went to Norway in the 1800s. (8)

gammaldansmusik Scandinavian old-time dance music. (8)

gammeldans 'Old-time dance-music', music that developed as Swedish urban folklore in the 1920s. (8)

gammel vals 'Old-fashioned waltz', a Danish waltz. (8)

gammu burui Kuna bamboo panpipes played in pairs. (2)

gāna (1) Incidental music, in early Indian theater; (2) popular music genre in Tamil Nadu. (5)

gānā Singing or song, vocal music in Uttar Pradesh. (5)

ganasaṅgīt 'People's songs' with heroic sentiments upholding the socialist cause, composed and sung by Indian Communist Party activists. (5)

Ganda (Also Baganda.) Cultural group in Uganda. (1)

gaṇḍā bandhan (Also *gaṇḍā bandhan.*) Initiation ceremony by which a *śisya* becomes a disciple. (5)

gandang (1) Sumatran two-headed drum; (2) Samawan topical sung poetry; (3) Tausug two-headed drum; (4) Yakan cracked bamboo instrument. (4)

gandang lasuang West Sumatra rice-stamping trough. (4)

gāndharva Ritual music for the early Indian theater. (5)

gandingan (1) Maguindanao bossed gong; (2) Subanen sacred medium-size gong. (4)

gandrung (1) Java female singer-dancer; (2) Banyuwangi percussion ensemble. (4)

ganga Rural polyphonic vocal genre of Bosnia and Hercegovina. (8)

ganga (Plural, *gangatan*.) (1) Tuareg drum; (2) double-headed cylindrical drum played in Niger to herald the beginning and end of Ramadan; (3) northern Nigerian double-headed cylindrical drums with a snare string. (1)

gangan Cylindrical drum of the Fur people. (1)

gángan Yoruba "talking drum." (1)

gangar One of three Norwegian dances characterized by a fairly slow gait in 2/4 or 6/8 meter; *see halling, rull.* (8)

gangettinavaru *See basavāṭa gangettinavaru.* (5)

gangha Ifugao flat gongs. (4)

gangsa (1) Generic term in the Cordillera (upland Luzon, Philippines) for flat gongs played in ensembles and struck either with mallets or with the hands using hocket techniques. (2) Kalinga and Bontok flat gongs. (3) Metallophone of Bali and Lombok. (3, 4)

gangsaran Balinese up-tempo piece. (4)

ganika Dancing girl or courtesan. (5)

gano Traditional BaAka legends in which Komba, the creator god, is a friend and caretaker. (1)

ganrang Buginese-Makassarese two-headed cylindrical drums. (4)

ganzá Brazilian shaken metal tube filled with beans, seeds, shells or other material. (2)

gaohu (1) High-pitched two-stringed fiddle used in Cantonese opera or music. (2) (China.) High-pitched bowed spiked fiddle. (3, 7)

gaojia (China.) Operatic tradition in Fujian Province. (7)

gao qiang (China.) 'High pitch', melismatic high-pitched singing style characterized by its declamatory qualities. (7)

gar Tibetan dance form. (5)

garabato 1940s African-derived musical style in Colombia. (2)

garabī Type of *garbo* text, and alternative type of *garbo*, in Gujarat. (5)

garage British term for American club music of the late 1980s and early 1990s, referring to

the most influential underground dance venue of the time, Paradise Garage in New York City. (3)

garamut Any hollowed log idiophone of Papua New Guinea. (9)

garantung Toba Batak wooden xylophone. (4)

garaón (Also *garawung*.) (1) Garífuna single-headed, conical drum in Guatemala; (2) *garaón primera*, the smaller drum of the set; (3) *garaón segunda*, the larger drum of the set. (2)

garapan Formulas for variation and improvisation in Javanese music. (4)

gara poetica Sardinian poets' sung duels. (8)

garavón Garífuna single-headed, conical drum in Nicaragua, in a set with the distinctions *primera* (smaller) and *segunda* (larger). (2)

garawoun Garifuna single-headed, cylindrical drum in Belize, in a set with the distinctions *primero* (smaller) and *segunda* (larger). (2)

garaya (Also *gàraayàa*.) Hausa two-stringed lute. (1)

garba Malwa dance form with vocal and instrumental accompaniment. (5)

garbī Alternative form of *garbo* dedicated to Krishna or sung from a male point of view. (5)

garbo (Plural, *garbā*, also *garbī*.) Gujarati devotional song and dance, usually dedicated to mother goddesses. (5)

gardagi Praise, satirical, or censorious Baggāra song. (1)

gardon Hungarian stringed instrument, roughly the shape and size of a violoncello (cello), played as a percussion instrument by beating the strings with a wooden stick and plucking them with fingers. (8)

garey Bontok men's funeral song. (4)

gargy tibydilk Long end-blown Turkmen flute. (6)

Garip 'Strange'. (1) Turkish romance about the minstrel Garip. (2) Specific Turkish instrumental melody in free rhythm. (6)

garip ayağı Common melodic mode (*makam*) in Turkish folk music. (6)

garmon (Also *buzika*.) Georgian accordion. (8)

garmon' (Also *garmonika, garmoshka*.) Russian diatonic button accordion. (8)

garokot Maranao bamboo scraper. (4)

gasba (Also *qasaba, shbēb, shabbāba*.) Term for the *nāy*, or flute, in North Africa. (Plural, *gasbāt*.) (6)

Gassenhauer German popular street songs. (8)

Gastarbeiter 'Guest workers', foreign workers in Germany, of whom a million arrived from Turkey after 1961. (8)

gat (1) Hindustani instrumental composition; (2) compositional genre in the *tabla* repertoire. (5)

gâṭa bera (Also *gata bera*, up-country drum, Kandyan drum.) Double-headed barrel drum used in the Buddhist *hēvisi pūjā* ensemble in Sri Lanka. (4, 5)

gatački pesni Macedonian short, recitative-like songs. (8)

gaṭibhēda Subdivision of the basic pulse into 3, 5, 7, or 9 in Karnatak music. (5)

gato 'Cat'. (1) Argentine social dance performed during a *jineteada*; (2) *gato polceado*, fusion of German polka and Argentine *gato*; (3) *gato salvaje* 'wild cat', Yuma song-dance cycle that begins at sunset, with songs about the first stars. (2)

gat-qā'ida *Tabla* composition. (5)

gātra vīnā 'Body instrument'; singer, in the *Nāṭyaśāstra*. (5)

gaucho Rural-dwelling nativist, traditionalist, or cowboy of the *pampa* region of Argentina; also found in Uruguay and in the southern state of Rio Grande do Sul, Brazil. (2)

gaulan Devotional song genre of Maharashtra with texts on Krishna's pranks and his teasing of the milkmaids in Gokul. (5)

gauri kalyāṇam 'Marriage of the goddess Gauri', an auspicious song. (5)

gaval Chechen and Ingush double-headed drum; *see vota*. (8)

gavayyā Male and female singers in the North Indian classical tradition. (5)

gavilēt 'To cheer, exhault, shout, howl' (Old Latvian), loud outdoor solo song, including characteristic cheering or howling formulas. (8)

gavotte Breton line or circle dance, performed as part of a three-part suite. (8)

gawe Mouth harp of the Low Countries. (8)

gawi Ceremonial circle dance of Flores. (4)

gawwāl Singer-poet of Algeria; cf. *qawwāl*. (6)

gaya 'Song', Gumuz responsorial genre, performed for deaths, epidemics, wars, and other special occasions. (1)

gāyak Main singer who presents *pala* ballads and leads a chorus (*palia*). (5)

gāyakī aṅg 'Singing style', the imitation of vocal styles in Hindustani instrumental music. (5)

gāyan (Also *samāj-gāyan*.) 'Singing'; in Maharashtra, a wide spectrum of vocal expression; devotional song form. (5)

gāyansālā North Indian vocal music school. (5)

Gay Gaieties Zimbabwean all-female jazz band. (1)

gayumba Central African-derived earth bow in the Dominican Republic. (2)

gaz Horsehair bow used for playing the *sārindā*, in North West Frontier Province. (5)

gazanjyk Performance style of western Turkmenistan. (6)

Volume Key: **6**, Middle East; **7**, East Asia; **8**, Europe; **9**, Australia and the Pacific Islands; **10**, The World's Music.

gazel Major lyric form in Ottoman-Turkish poetry; free-rhythm improvised singing of such lyric texts, corresponding to the instrumental *taksīm*. (6)

gazino (Also *fasıl*.) Turkish nightclub music, dominated by Gypsy performers and styles. (6)

gazoku (Japan.) Principle of culture versus vulgarity. (7)

Gbaya A people of the Central African Republic. (1)

gbee-kee Kpelle single-stringed bow-lute. (1)

gbegbetêle Kpelle multiple bow-lute. (1)

gbèlee Kpelle lamellophone. (1)

gbo Dan funeral lament. (1)

ge (1) Song (China). (2) Buddhist chant (*syômyô*) for lecturing about or discussing Buddha or other Buddhist topics (Japan). (3) Lowest principal note in *nô* chanting (Japan). (7)

geçki Turkish term for modulation between two *makamlar*. (6)

geduk Malay double-headed barrel drum hit with a stick. (4)

gedumbak Malay single-headed goblet-shaped drum. (4)

geeraar Somali poetical genre distinguished from other genres by scansion, melody, topic, and function. (1)

geerewal Fulɓe ceremonial dance in which anklets add rhythmic sounds to performers' rapid hops. (1)

ge'e tambio O'odham Indian term for big drum. (3)

gegaboran Balinese ostinato pattern accompanying women's dance. (4)

gehui (Also *gejie*.) In China, festival of songs. (7)

geilwad Welsh plowboy whose job was to walk backward facing the oxen and sing oxen-songs to keep them calm. (8)

geissler Swiss whip-crackers. (8)

geitlokkar Norwegian ornamented goat-calls. (8)

geki (Also *geki busi*.) In Japan, genre of early narrative *syamisen* music (*ko zyôruri*). (7)

gekkin Japanese name for the Chinese round-shaped lute *yue qin*. (7)

geko Ende xylophone. (4)

geliri Term for Kurdish folk music. (6)

gém St. Lucian games accompanied by singing and drumming. (2)

gema (Also *gemanash*.) Chechen and Ingush rattle made of split wood and played during traditional dances. (8)

gembyung Cirebonese large frame drum without jingles. (4)

geming gequ (China.) Revolutionary songs. (7)

genda Frame drum of Flores. (4)

gendai hôgaku (Japan.) Generic term for contemporary (generally post-World War II) compositions for traditional Japanese instruments; broadly, including *sin nihon ongaku*, a new genre of Western-influenced Japanese music that appeared during the Taisyô period (1912–1926). (7)

genda Mbojo Mbojo court ensemble. (4)

gendang Large double-headed drum from Malaysia and Indonesia. (4)

gendang beleq Lombok dance with two drummers. (4)

gendang panjai Iban gong-chime ensemble. (4)

gendang raya Iban gong ensemble. (4)

gendang sarunei Karo Batak drum and gong ensemble. (4)

gender Social construction of male and female sexuality, involving expectations about behavior and attributions of intent. (9)

gendèr Indonesian metallophone with tube-resonated keys. (4, 10)

genderang Pakpak Batak drum and gong ensemble. (4)

gendèr barung Javanese lower-pitched metallophone with tube-resonated keys. (4)

gendèr panerus Javanese higher-pitched metallophone with tube-resonated keys. (4)

gendèr slenthem Javanese deepest metallophone with tube-resonated keys. (4)

gendèr wayang Balinese metallophone quartet for *wayang kulit*. (4)

gendhing *Gamelan*-based musical composition of Java. (4)

gendhing bonang Formal arrangement of a Javanese *gamelan* piece. (4)

gendhing lampah Theatrical pieces used in Javanese *wayang*. (4)

gending *Gamelan*-based musical composition of Bali. (4)

geng (qeej) Hmong (Vietnamese) six-tube free-reed mouth organ. (3)

genggong Balinese Jew's harp. (4)

genjring (1) Cirebonese frame drum with jingles; (2) Cirebonese ensemble. (4)

ge no tyû (Japan.) Lowered *tyû* (middle principal note in *nô* chanting). (7)

genta Buddhist-Hindu bronze ankle bells, worn in Sumatra. (4)

genus durum 'Hard kind' (Latin), the major mode as named by Johannes Kepler in 1619. (8)

genus molle 'Soft kind' (Latin), the minor mode as named by Johannes Kepler in 1619. (8)

Genzi monogatari (Japan.) 'The Tale of Genzi', masterpiece by Murasaki Sikibu (c. 973–1014). (7)

geon (Japan.) (1) Low pitch area in Buddhist chant; (2) common melodic patterns used in the *geon* pitch area. (7)

gérong (1) Javanese male chorus accompanied by *gamelan*. (2) Choral vocal part. (4, 10)

geruding Jew's harp of Borneo. (4)

Gesangbuch Mennonite songbook. (3)

Ge-sar King and hero of a Tibetan epic. (5)

geshi (China.) Song master. (7)

gęsle Polish bowed stringed instrument found at eleventh- and thirteenth-century archaeological sites. (8)

gesó-gesó Buginese-Makassarese two-stringed spike fiddle. (4)

gesok-gesok Torajan one-stringed fiddle. (4)

getai Contemporary Singaporean stage performance of Chinese origin. (4)

geundrang Acehnese two-headed cylindrical drum. (4)

gewel (Plural, *awlu'be*.) Name for a musician among the Wolof and Fulɓe of The Gambia and Senegal. (1)

Ge'z Liturgical language of the Christian church in Ethiopia. (1)

gezaixi (China.) Folk opera originating in Fujian Province and popularized in Taiwan and Singapore. (7)

gezan (China.) Melodious, melismatic Buddhist chanting. (7)

geza ongaku (Japan.) *Kabuki* music performed by the offstage ensemble. (7)

geza uta (Japan.) Songs performed by the *kabuki* offstage ensemble, mostly with *syamisen* accompaniment. (7)

gezinti In Turkish *uzun hava*, instrumental preludes and interludes performed with vocal and instrumental melodies in strict meter. (6)

ghada Clay 'pitcher drum' of Kashmir. (5)

ghadyal-tipru Metal disk struck with a mallet, in performances by a Nandiwāla. (5)

ghaita (1) Moroccan oboe. (2) Category of idiophones in the *Nātyaśāstra* and the Buddhist *pañcatūrya nāda* systems. (3) (Also *ghayta, gaida*.) Term for a shawm or double-reed pipe in North Africa. (4) 'Song', traditional Maltese music form. (1, 5, 6, 8)

Ghana Music Society Organization formed in 1958 for research, programming broadcasts on radio, and publishing results of music studies. (1)

ghana rāga pañcaratna Five songs in medium tempo composed by Tyagaraja in the five *ghana* ragas. See *pañcaratna*. (5)

ghana ragas 'Weighty' ragas; set of five specific ragas in Karnatak music. (5)

ghana ta' spirtu pront 'Quick-witted song', Maltese genre of dialogue singing. (8)

ghana vādya Musical instrument category in the *Nātyaśāstra* designating idiophones. (5)

ghannej Singer of *ghana*. (8)

gharānā Musical lineage; stylistic school of musical practice in Hindustani music. (5, 10)

gharībī 'Condition of a stranger' (Persian); one type of Persian *chārbeitī*, with verses that refer to the singer's sense of isolation. (6)

gharnāṭī (Also *ghurnāṭī*.) 'Granadan', regional term for Andalusian music in North Africa. (6)

ghaṭam Clay pot percussion instrument, in Karnatak music. (5)

ghā̃ṭu Guruṅg dance drama in Nepal. (5)

ghawāzī Local Egyptian dance entertainers. (6)

ghazal (1) Genre of Malaysian folk music derived from India and the Middle East. (2) Urdu poetic genre; light classical vocal genre with Urdu text. (3) (Also *gazel, ghazel*.) 'Flirtation', 'love'; principal genre of classical poetry in Persian, Azerbaijani, and Turkish, dominating vocal performance of classical music in Iran and Azerbaijan; typically has five to seventeen lines. (4) South Asian vocal genre, performed by immigrants in Britain. (4, 5, 6, 8)

ghāziyya (Plural, *ghawāzī*.) Female musician-dancer in Egypt. (6)

ghichak West Asian bowed lute. (5)

ghīchak (Also *ghijak, kemanche*.) Persian spike fiddle used in medieval Indo-Persian courts and still found in Afghanistan. (5)

ghijak (Also *ghichek, ghidjak*.) Spike fiddle. (6)

ghinā' 'Music', 'song'. (6)

ghinā' al-maqām 'Singing the *maqām*', since the 1930s, term for performance of the Iraqi *maqām*. (6)

ghinā' al-Ṣan'ānī 'Song of Ṣan'ā', term for the oldest urban tradition of classical vocal and instrumental music in Yemen. (6)

ghinā' mulhī 'Entertaining music', term used by Ibn Ḥazm. (6)

ghinā' mutqan 'Perfect singing'. (1) Term for art music in the medieval Middle East. (2) Modern, professional musical performances. (6)

ghinnāwa Repertoire of Egyptian bedouin song. (6)

ghirbāl Early Arabic term, possibly referring to a round frame drum. (6)

ghironda Hurdy-gurdy of Piedmont, Lombardy, and Emilia. (8)

ghol 'Small bell' of Maharashtra. (5)

ghora nāc gīt Song form associated with the Hindu Shakta cult in Orissa. (5)

Ghorwane Large Mozambican band, with a lineup of three guitars, trumpet, sax, and percussion. (1)

Ghost Dance Native revivalist movement that sprang up among the Paiute people in the 1880s, spreading rapidly, particularly across the Great Plains, in which believers received songs while in trancelike states induced by a rapidly accelerating dance; it was believed that participation in Ghost Dance activities would bring back the world as it had been befor the invasion by whites, and that the whites would disappear. (3)

Ghrība 'Lonely one', 'stranger', synagogue on the outskirts of Ḥāra Ṣghīra on the island of Djerba, a pilgrimage site for Jews and Muslims. (6)

ghūmar Popular circle dance that has become the state symbol of Rajasthan. (5)

ghuṅghrū Small metal bells played or worn as ankle bells by dancers. (5)

gidayû busi (Also *gidayû*.) Genre of Japanese narrative *syamisen* music founded in 1684 by Takemoto Gidayû (1651–1714). (7)

gidayû syamisen (Japan.) *Syamisen* used in *gidayû busi*; large-size *syamisen* (*huto zao*). (7)

giddhā Punjabi women's folk dance. (5)

gievrie South Saami frame drum, used by shamans. (8)

gigaku (Japan.) Masked dance drama transmitted in 612 by Mimasi, a musician from the ancient Korean kingdom Paekche. (7)

gigante Nicaraguan folk drama. (2)

gigantona Primarily verbal performance and the principal folk expression of León, Nicaragua. (2)

gīgī Song form in Karnataka with "*gī ya gī ya*" as the refrain text. (5)

gigue (1) Lively dance in triple time, popular in France in the early eighteenth century, featuring complex, rhythmical footwork; still danced in Québec. (2) (Also *jig*.) Lively English, Scottish, and Irish dance in 6/8 time. (3, 8)

gilak Balinese ostinato pattern for men's strong dances. (4)

Gilbert Islands Archipelago formerly part of the Gilbert and Ellice Islands Colony and now part of the Republic of Kiribati. (9)

gilo lukah West Sumatra men's fish-trap dance. (4)

Gilyak (Japan.) *See* Nivkhi. (7)

gimbal Palawan cylindrical drum. (4)

gimbrī (Also *gunbrī, ginbrī, gumbrī, jumbrī, hajiy*.) Long-necked lute of North Africa with two or three strings. (6)

gime Poems on religious themes and secular topics composed in Fulfulde. (1)

gin (Japan.) Term in *gidayû busi* notation indicating pitch or manner of singing. (7)

ginān Chanted religious compositions in the Northern Areas of Pakistan. (5)

ginga Brazilian swaying motion. (2)

ginggong (Also *ginggung*.) Sumatran Jew's harp. (4)

gingiru Dogon four-stringed lute, made only by physicians and used to provide rhythm for the spirit to heal. (1)

gini Small cymbals of Orissa. (5)

gion bayasi (Japan.) *Hayasi* instrumental ensemble and its music associated with the Gion Shrine festival in Kyôto. (7)

Giorgoba Georgian celebration of St. George, performed in November with ritual feasts and circle dances. (8)

giraw (Also *alghoza, donal*.) Double flute in northern Balochistan. (5)

Giriama A Mijikenda people of Kenya. (1)

Gisi gakki zu (Japan.) 'Charts of Mr. Wei's Instruments', printed in 1780; describes a set of instruments that belonged to the Wei (Japanese name Ôga) family, of Chinese descent, who introduced a form of Ming dynasty music and dance (*min gaku*) to Japan in the seventeenth century. (7)

Gisi gakuhu (Japan.) 'Mr. Wei's Scores'; scores of a form of Ming dynasty music (*min gaku*) by Wei Hao (Japanese name Ôga Minbu, d. 1774) printed in 1768. (7)

gīt (Also *gīta*.) (1) 'Song', nonclassical song in a regional language; (2) poetic versification in the context of bardic poetry. (5)

Gīta Govinda Twelfth-century love poems by Jayadeva. (5)

gītam Song passed down in the *prabandha* tradition; some examples are simple songs created for teaching purposes. (5)

gitanos 'Gypsies', Chilean patronal festival dance group. (2)

gitara Six-stringed guitar of the Philippines. (4)

gitgit Hanunoo three-stringed fiddle. (4)

gīti Song text, or song text and music. (5)

gīti nāṭak Modern, sophisticated genre of sung narrative poems in Nepal. (5)

giusto 'Just' (Italian), term used especially by Hungarian scholars to denote a singing style executed strictly according to a metric framework. (8)

giying Balinese metallophone used in *gong kebyar*. (4)

gjâmë Elegy for dead males, sung in the northern Albanian highlands by male lament specialists. (8)

glagoljaška pjevanje 'Glagolitic singing', liturgical and paraliturgical form surviving on the northern Dalmatian coast and Kvarner Gulf in Croatia. (8)

glamer zither Swiss board zither, played mainly by women. (8)

glas (Also *kajda* in some areas.) 'Voice' (Slavic). In Bulgarian music, any sung part; a system of eight melodic modes, used in Russian chant until the 1600s; a Serbian concept of a melodic type, distinguished by social occasion, musical form, textual content, and ethnic or geographic designation. (8)

glas na oj ubava Serbian song with the refrain *o ubava*. **(8)**

glasoečki pesni (Also *vozeni, ikoečki pesni*.) Macedonian songs with elaborate melodies. **(8)**

glee Unaccompanied choral work in three or more parts for male voices. **(3)**

glee singing Eighteenth-century English form of amateur singing in three or more unaccompanied parts. **(8)**

glendi Greek social gathering or party featuring the singing and playing of *mandinades*. **(3)**

glendia Greek summer celebrations with singing on some Greek islands. **(8)**

gling-bu Bamboo duct flute of Tibet. **(5)**

glorias Argentine unaccompanied religious songs. **(2)**

glosa 'Gloss', Spanish term for four-stanza *décima*. **(2)**

glosador Colombian and Ecuadorian male lead singer. **(2)**

glottal stop During vocalization, the interruption of the breath by closure of the glottis (the space between the vocal cords); also, a typographical sign for this action. **(9)**

glottochronology (Also *lexicostatistics*.) Method of measuring the history of related languages by quantifying the degree to which they share cognate words. **(9)**

glu Tibetan folk song genre. **(5)**

gnāwa (1) Moroccan ritual involving dance, music, poetry, and song; cf. *dīwān, stambūlī*. (2) Moroccan musical genre performed by immigrants in France. **(6, 8)**

gnelé Among the Guaymí of Costa Rica, friction idiophone made of turtleshell covered with beeswax. **(2)**

gô (Japan.) Set of short *tikuzen biwa* interludes. **(7)**

gobato Three-stringed bamboo idiochord tube zither of Flores. **(4)**

gobdas North Saami kettledrum with a reindeer-skin head. **(8)**

godu balss 'Family celebration tune', Latvian melodic formula. **(8)**

goebe Friction drum of the Low Countries. **(8)**

goeika (Japan.) Nonliturgical Buddhist songs sung by the populace. **(7)**

gogeru Fulani one-stringed bowed lute. **(1)**

go-go Style of music popular in Washington, D.C., and parts of the South that prominently features live percussion (congas, *timbales*, cowbells). **(3)**

gogyô (Japan.) Chinese concept of the five elements: wood, fire, soil, metal, and water. **(7)**

gɔh Temiar tube stampers, used in healing rituals. **(4)**

goigs Catalan medieval songs that recount the Virgin Mary's seven joys; known in Spanish as *gozos*; cf. *gosos*. **(8)**

goin (Japan.) *See gosei.* **(7)**

goin hakase (Also *goin bakase*.) In Japan, neume-like notation system for Buddhist chant. **(7)**

goje (Also *goge, gòjé*). (1) Hausa one-stringed bowed lute with resonating hole on the membrane, not the body. (2) Yoruba single-stringed bowed lute, made of a calabash and covered with skin. **(1)**

goke Kuna bamboo panpipes played in sets of three. **(2)**

gol 'Weeping', textually unfixed, partly sung, partly sobbing expression of grief that followed the Irish *caoineadh na marbh*. **(8)**

Gola A people of western Liberia. **(1)**

Gold Coast Colonial name of the present nation Ghana. **(1)**

Gold Coast Review Academic journal that provided a forum for literary and scientific contributions, including music. **(1)**

Golla Suddulu Narrative singers of the Telugu herding caste. **(5)**

gollu Balkar and Karachaevi circle dance featuring triplets in 2/4 and 4/4 meters. **(8)**

golosnik (1) (Also *diskant*.) Soloist who sings a texted anhemitonic tune in Cossack vocal music of southern Russia. (2) Second voice in polyphonic vocal music of central and southern Russia. **(8)**

golpe 'Hit', (1) rhythmic accompaniment performed by hand slaps on a diatonic harp sound box by an assistant (*golpeador*) in Ecuador; (2) Venezuelan dance music genre; (3) *golpes*, Brazilian *capoeira* dance figures. **(2)**

golpeador In Ecuador, a person who beats on the box of the harp as a percussion instrument while a harpist plucks the strings. **(2)**

goma Men's dance with slow, precise movements, using European accoutrements, including dark glasses. **(1)**

goma hu (Also *goma ten*.) Vocal notation used in Japanese *nô* and *bunraku*. **(7)**

gomboy Dogon hourglass-shaped tension drum. **(1)**

gome (Also *gombay*.) Earliest popular music of West Africa, believed to have developed in Freetown, Sierra Leone. **(1)**

gondang Toba Batak tuned drum ensemble. **(4)**

gondhal Ritual theater form of Maharashtra. **(5)**

gondolieri 'People who propel gondolas' (Italian), medieval Italian epic reciters, who adopted and developed written literature and notated music. **(8)**

gong ageng Large hanging gong of Indonesia. **(4)**

gongchepu (Also *gongche, gongche pu*.) (1) Chinese music notation. (2) Traditional notational system used in common-practice Chinese music. (3) (China.) Notation using the pitch names *shang, che, gong fan, liu, wu*, and *yi* and with rhythm indicated by marks. **(3, 4, 7)**

gong gedé Rare largest ceremonial *gamelan* gong in Bali. **(4)**

gong genang Samawan ensemble to accompany *pencak*. **(4)**

gong kebyar Balinese dynamic modern *gamelan* style. **(4)**

gong kodeq Small hanging gong of Lombok. **(4)**

gong lanang Smaller "male" hanging gong of Lombok. **(4)**

gong sabet Medium-sized gong of Cirebon. **(4)**

gong suling *Suling* used to replicate *gamelan* in Bali. **(4)**

gong tondu Five-stringed bamboo idiochord tube zither in Flores. **(4)**

gong wadon Larger "female" hanging gong in Lombok. **(4)**

Gonja A cultural group of Ghana. **(1)**

Gonjaoba Georgian rain-begging ritual performed by girls and young women, who carry a female figure and sing. **(8)**

gonje Ghanaian one-stringed bowed lute. **(1)**

gonrang Simalungun Batak drum ensemble. **(4)**

goombay (1) Term for calypso in the Bahamas, primarily sung dance music; (2) Bahamian onomatopoeic term for a single-headed frame drum. **(2)**

Goombeh African-based Jamaican cult. **(2)**

goombeh Jamaican square goatskin frame drum played with the fingers, considered male. **(2)**

goon (Japan.) *See gosei.* **(7)**

goondze Dagbani violin. **(10)**

goong Jarai bamboo tube zither of Vietnam. **(4)**

go'ong Large hanging gong of Sunda. **(4)**

goong teng leng Beaten bamboo tubes of upland Vietnam. **(4)**

gopī Milkmaid. **(5)**

Gopīcand Sung epic poem of North India used in *nauṭankī* folk drama. **(5)**

gopīyantra (Also *ektārā, gopīyantro*.) Plucked string drone; the string is attached at one end to a membrane-covered resonator, at the other to the instrument's forked bamboo frame. **(5)**

gora Southern African musical bow in which the musician vibrates the string by blowing onto a feather attached to the bow. **(1)**

góralski 'Highlanders' dance', couple dance in the Carpathian area of Poland. **(8)**

gordang (1) Large bass drum in Toba Batak *gondang*; (2) Mandailing Batak drum and gong ensemble. **(4)**

gordang sembilan Mandailing Batak nine-drum ensemble. **(4)**

gordună Cello that provides rhythmic-harmonic accompaniment in Romanian and Hungarian music in parts of Transylvania. **(8)**

gorgholi Epic songs in Badakhshan and other Central Asian regions. **(5)**

gorodao Accordion in Madagascar that requires specific techniques by musicians to obtain desired tones. **(1)**

gosan (Japan.) Category of Buddhist chant (*syômyô*), hymn chant that follows the chanting of a sutra. **(7)**

gosei (Also *goin, goon*.) Japanese and ancient Chinese pentatonic scale. **(7)**

goseti no mai (Japan.) Indigenous genre of court dance performed by five unmarried girls at the coronation of a new emperor (*daizyô e*). **(7)**

gosha-nagara (Also *diplipito*.) Azerbaijani set of skin-covered clay pots. **(8)**

goslarije (Also *bande*.) Slovenian band of two to four violins, one or two violas, one or two clarinets, a bass, and a cimbalom. **(8)**

gosos Sardinian religious hymns, part of the Sardinian *a tenore* repertoire; cf. *goigs, gozos*. **(8)**

gospel Style of vernacular religious music originally associated with evangelistic revival meetings. **(3)**

Gospin plač 'The Madonna's Lament', song cycle performed by pilgrims during Holy Week in Dalmatia, Croatia. **(8)**

gostevye Guests' songs in Udmurt, Mari, Chuvash, and Tatar-Kriashen folklore. **(8)**

gosyôrei (Japan.) Category of Buddhist chant (*syômyô*) for worship. **(7)**

gotipua Young male temple dancers in Orissa. **(5)**

gottuvādyam (Also *citravīṇā*.) Unfretted *vina* played as a slide lute. **(5)**

goujiao (China.) Small vertical gong. **(7)**

gourd bow Musical bow that has as its resonator a gourd fastened to or held against the bow. **(1)**

govend Kurdish dance. **(6)**

goweto One-stringed struck bamboo idiochord of Flores. **(4)**

goygoy Pejorative term for cetain "Arab" vocal practices in twentieth-century Turkish musical discourse. **(6)**

goze (Japan.) Blind female performers who were wandering minstrels. **(7)**

gozen hù (Japan.) Category of Okinawan classical music associated with royal ceremonies. **(7)**

gozos (1) Argentine 'praises' or unaccompanied religious songs. (2) Spanish medieval songs that recount the Virgin Mary's seven joys; known in Catalan as *goigs*; cf. *gosos*. **(2, 8)**

Graceland Long-playing album released in 1986 featuring Paul Simon's crossover collaboration with South African musicians. **(1)**

grada büchel Long Swiss straight alphorn with a curved bell, carved from a fir-tree trunk and wrapped in birch bark; *see büchel*. **(8)**

gradski pesni Bulgarian city songs. **(3)**

grajcary (Also *cykake*.) Polish frame drum with jingles. **(8)**

grāma (Also *grama*.) Scale. **(5)**

grammaticality System of rules governing a particular language. **(1)**

gran diablos 'Great devils', Panamanian devil-dance tradition. **(2)**

grandy Jamaican membranophone similar to the *prenting*, considered female. **(2)**

graphic notation System of musical notation that uses a grid of horizontal and vertical lines. **(1)**

Great War European military conflict of 1914–1918, retrospectively called World War I. **(9)**

Grebo A Kru-speaking people of southeastern Liberia. **(1)**

Gregorian chant Rhythmically free unison chant of the medieval Roman Catholic Church in Western Europe, formalized and promulgated around 800 C.E. and continuing in use. **(8, 9)**

grelot French sheep bell. **(8)**

griot (French.) West African musical specialist, usually a custodian of important historical and cultural knowledge. **(1, 8)**

griot-**model society** Socially despised professional musicians who work within a highly stratified social fabric. **(1)**

griteria 'Shouting', 7 December Nicaraguan nighttime tradition of singing one or more *purísimas* at different homes for sweets. **(2)**

gritos Shouts of emotional expression during musical and dance performances. **(2)**

grotto Open-air tavern of Ticino, a public place for singing in Italian-speaking Switzerland. **(8)**

group bow Musical bow played by three individuals and known as *kambulumbumba*. **(1)**

gruppo folk 'Folk group', any of numerous Sardinian folk-music groups. **(8)**

gu (China.) (1) Generic term for drum. (2) 'Bone', term used by *nanguan* musicians for the skeleton melody played by the *pipa* and *sanxian*. **(7)**

guabina (1) Humorous, lively, and sometimes melancholy romantic vocal-folk-music genre of Colombia; (2) *guabina veleña*, an impro-

vised and noncommercialized type of *guabina* from Vélez, Santander, Colombia. **(2)**

guacharaca Colombian stick rasp. **(2)**

guadúa Bamboo resonator or trumpet bell of Ecuador. **(2)**

guaguancó (1) Cuban couple-dance genre belonging to the *rumba* family. (2) Popular form of Afro-Cuban rumba music that also has been incorporated into popular salsa music. **(2, 3)**

guaiá Brazilian rattle. **(2)**

guajira 'Rural peasant', 'country girl' (Spanish). (1) Cuban genre belonging to the *canción cubana* family. (2) *Guajira-son*, Cuban genre that combines elements of the *guajira* and the *son*. (3) Term referring to the music of the Cuban countryside. **(2, 3)**

guajolote 'Turkey', Mixtec nuptial dance in which the dancers carry a live turkey and other wedding-banquet foods. **(2)**

gualambau Guaraní term for a musical bow similar to the Brazilian *berimbau*. **(2)**

Guam Southern and largest of the Mariana Islands, governmentally separate from the Northern Marianas. **(9)**

guamo Conch-shell lip-concussion aerophone used by the pre-Columbian inhabitants of Cuba and Puerto Rico. **(2)**

Guangdong yinyue 'Cantonese music', instrumental ensemble music popular in the Pearl River Delta in the southern part of Guangdong Province of China. **(3)**

guanmen (China.) Term for scale, key, and modality in *nanguan* music. **(7)**

guaracha (1) Cuban genre belonging to the *son* family. (2) Cuban mimetic dance form that incorporates the Spanish and African vocal practice of solo verses and regular chorus refrains. (3) Medium-fast strophic song-dance of Cuban origin, in duple meter and stanza-refrain form. **(2, 3, 9)**

guaránia National song genre tradition of Paraguay, created in 1925 by José Asunción Flores. **(2)**

guarura Venezuelan conch-shell trumpet. **(2)**

guasá (Also *guacho*.) Colombian and Ecuadorian bamboo or metal rattles played by women. **(2)**

guataca Hoe blade that is used to keep the rhythmic timeline in Afro-Cuban music. **(3)**

guaya Handheld Nicaraguan shaker. **(2)**

guayo 'Grater', Cuban metal rasp like the gourd *güiro*, played with a metal scraper. **(2)**

gubgubī Double-headed scraped membranophone played by a Nandiwālā in performance. **(5)**

gubo Men's gourd-resonated bow of Zulu origin. **(1)**

guchui (China.) Dumming and blowing. **(7)**

guci (Also *gunci*.) 'Fiddlers', ensemble of violins and bass of northwestern Croatia. **(8)**

güçlü Dominant note in a Turkish *makam*. **(6)**

gudalo Slovene friction drum made of a clay pot covered by a pig's bladder, with a reed or string inserted through the skin. **(8)**

gudastviri Georgian bagpipe of Racha and Kartli. **(8)**

gude Albanian name of the one-stringed bowed fiddle (*gusle*) in Montenegro. **(8)**

gudi (China.) Bone flute. **(7)**

gudiao (China.) Traditional tunes. **(7)**

gudok (Also *guduk*.) Russian three-stringed, pear-shaped, bowed lute made of one piece of wood. **(8)**

guduki Chordophone of the nomadic Kela tribe. **(5)**

gŭdulka Bulgarian pear-shaped bowed lute with three or four metal playing strings and about eight sympathetic strings. **(8)**

guedra (1) Moroccan pottery drum; (2) pottery-drum-accompanied dance performed in southern Morocco. **(1)**

guffal Women's song of the Gulf region, performed to greet returning pearl fishers. **(6)**

guganyin (China.) Skeleton melody. **(7)**

guggemusig Swiss carnival music of Stans, Unterwalden, performed during carnival at Basel. **(8)**

gugu Azande struck hollow-log idiophone. **(1)**

guía 'Guide', lead singer of Venezuelan *tonos* ensemble. **(2)**

guimbard Jew's harp. **(3)**

guimbarde (French), mouth harp of the Low Countries. **(8)**

güiro 'Gourd', 'bottle gourd' (Spanish). (1) Perhaps of native or Afro-Cuban or Puerto Rican origin, scraped gourd idiophone with inscribed grooves or notches, found throughout the Caribbean, Central America, and parts of Mexico. (2) Mainly Caribbean scraped gourd idiophone, used in German folk music after the revival of the 1960s. (3) Gourd (sometimes in Hawai'i, metal) scraper, of Amerindian origin, providing usually stressed downbeats and rhythms varied according to the dance accompanied. **(2, 8, 9)**

guitarillo High-pitched Spanish guitar. **(8)**

guitarra 'Guitar' (Spanish). (1) Corsican guitar. (2) (Also *guitarra Portuguesa*.) Portuguese guitar with a pear-shaped soundboard and six double courses of metal strings. (3) Term often used in Hispanic America to refer to the electric guitar. (4) Spanish term for six-stringed (usually nylon, but also metal in some rural areas of Latin America) plucked or strummed lute chordophone with an hour-glass shape (*violão* in Brazil); numerous variants exist with the same name. **(2, 3, 8)**

guitarrilla (Also *tiple*.) 'Little guitar'. (1) Guatemalan rare five-stringed guitar with gourd as resonator; (2) Bolivian deep-bodied guitar tuned in five courses; (3) four-metal-stringed guitar placed on the treble side of the Nicaraguan marimba; (4) 'little guitar' of El Salvador with four strings; (5) hourglass-shaped chordophone with five double courses of strings and a slightly rounded back. **(2)**

guitarrón 'Large guitar'. (1) Low-pitched Spanish guitar. (2) Chilean hourglass-shaped plucked chordophone with twenty-five strings in five courses. (3) Mexican bass lute with rounded back, used in *mariachi*. (4) Mexican six-stringed bass. **(2, 3, 8)**

gujarātan sāraṅgī Small bowed unfretted lute played by the Laṅgā musicians of Rajasthan. **(5)**

gukania Yells in the calendric songs of southwestern Russia. **(8)**

gula gending Ensemble of tin sugar containers in Lombok. **(4)**

gule wa mukulu Chewa musical genre. **(1)**

guli Kuna bamboo panpipes played in six parts. **(2)**

gulintangan Gong-chime ensemble of Brunei. **(4)**

gullu Kasena-Nankani cylindrical double-headed drums, played in sets of four. **(1)**

gulu Javanese pitch name. **(4)**

gulyaniia Russian outdoor parties. **(8)**

gumaṭe Double-headed pot or brass drum with variable pitch, in Karnataka. **(5)**

gumatt Goan clay pot drum. **(5)**

gumbeh Boom drum, a double-headed membranophone in Belize. **(2)**

gumbri Gnawa three-stringed lute. **(1)**

gummeṭa Jug-shaped drum played by Telugu oral narrative singers. **(5)**

Gumuz A western Ethiopian people living in Sudan east of the Blue Nile. **(1)**

gunci (Also *guci*.) 'Fiddlers', ensemble of violins and bass of northwestern Croatia. **(8)**

gung Large vertical gong of Sumatra. **(4)**

gunggele Cowbell of Muotatal, Switzerland; *see* *trychle*. **(8)**

gungonga Kasena-Nankani hourglass-shaped pressure drum, playable with flutes. **(1)**

gunjci (Also *gunci*, *violine*, *muzika*.) Instrumental ensemble of Istria, Croatia. **(8)**

gunka (Japan.) Soldiers' songs. **(7)**

gunmen (China.) Classification of songs; each *gunmen* contains several tunes, and each tune can be used in different songs. **(7)**

Gunsyo ruizyū (Japan.) 'Anthology of Myriad Books', including a significant number of source materials related to music, compiled by Hanawa Hokiiti (1724–1821). **(7)**

guntang Balinese one-stringed bamboo tube zither. **(4)**

gúnydals 'Mocking songs', Hungarian songs performed in the marketplace. **(8)**

gunyei Guatemalan courting songs. **(2)**

guochangqu (China.) "Crossing the stage" tunes. **(7)**

guoyue (China.) 'National music'; refers to twentieth-century concert hall music. **(7)**

guoyuehui (China.) National music societies. **(7)**

guozhiqu (China.) Transitional songs in *nanguan* used as a bridge between one song and the next. **(7)**

gurbānī Sikh devotional songs. **(5)**

gurdwara Sikh place of worship. **(5)**

guritan South Sumatra long narrative form. **(4)**

gurmi Hausa two-stringed plucked lute with a hemispherical calabash resonator. **(1)**

gurr Conch shell played during festive dances in Balochistan. **(5)**

guru Indian music teacher and master; spiritual guide. **(4, 5, 10)**

guru dakṣinā Student-teacher relationship in which the student does not live in the teacher's home (*gurukul*) but pays a form of tuition (*dakṣinā*). **(5)**

gurudeva Honorific, a respectful term of address to one's *guru*. **(5)**

gurudvāra Guru's residence. **(5)**

gurukul Household of the *guru*; student-teacher relationship in which the student lives with the teacher. **(5)**

Gurupañcāśikā 'Fifty Verses of Guru Devotion', poem from the first century B.C.E. describing the *guru*-student relationship. **(5)**

gurûpu saunzu (Japan.) 'Group sounds', Japanese popular music of the 1960s, performed by four to seven long-haired male singers wearing identical clothing and playing electric guitars and drums. **(7)**

gurupūrṇimā Day on which pupils honor their *guru*, celebrated on the day of the full moon in the Hindu month of Asāṛh. **(5)**

guru-śiṣya (1) 'Master-disciple', relationship with a Hindu teacher; (2) *guru-śiṣya paramparā*, master-disciple tradition. *See also* *ustād-śagird*. **(5, 10)**

gusan (1) Professional Armenian musician, who is at once a storyteller, singer, instrumentalist, dancer, comedian, and tragic actor. (2) Armenian colloquial song genre. **(6)**

gūshe 'Corner' (Persian), one section of the *radif* of Persian music, either a relatively fixed short composition or a melody type allowing for more or less elaborate realization in performance. **(6)**

gusla (Also *kemene*.) Macedonian three-stringed, pear-shaped bowed lute. **(8)**

guslari (In Serbian and Croatian, also *guslači*.) (1) Epic singers, derived from the name of the bowed lute (*gusle*) with which they accompany themselves. (2) Blind Macedonian itinerant beggars, who sang and played the *gusla* for money. **(8)**

guslarske junačke pjesme In Montenegro, a *gusle*-accompanied heroic song. **(8)**

gusle One-stringed bowed lute typical of the central Dinaric Mountains of Serbia, Montenegro, and Bosnia-Hercegovina. **(8)**

gusli Northwestern Russian plucked zither. **(8)**

guslya Chuvash zither. **(8)**

gutbucket Chordophone consisting of a string stretched across a board inserted into a washtub or large empty can. **(9)**

guwel Acehnese frame drum; basis of all Gayo dances. **(4)**

guyanda Female professional mourner in Central Asia. **(6)**

Guyfesta Guyanese British-style music festival. **(2)**

guyrambau (Also *lambau, mbarimbau*.) Large mouth bow found among the Mbyá. **(2)**

guyrapa-i Double musical bow in use among various Guaraní groups of Paraguay. **(2)**

guyusa Garifuna predominantly female ritual singers in Belize. **(2)**

güzellemə *Qoşma* on themes of love and nature. **(6)**

gwaj (Also *syak*.) Dominican and St. Lucian shaken and scraped tin cylinder idiophone pierced with nail holes and filled with pebbles or seeds. **(2)**

Gwalior *gharānā* Hindustani vocal style and lineage whose exponents were originally from the city of Gwalior. **(5)**

Gwashinda Upper-caste male singers in Balochistan. **(5)**

gwāt (Also *parī, jinn, bād*.) (1) 'Wind' (Baluchi), spirit thought to be responsible for certain illnesses. (2) The adjectival form, *gwātī*, may refer to the patient or to a musician involved in the healing ceremony, in which trance is induced through music. **(6)**

gwātī Person possessed by an evil spirit known as *gwāt* 'wind', who is treated with music, singing, and animal sacrifices and liberated from the *gwāt* by a healer (*gwātī-ē māt*) when both enter a state of trance. **(5)**

gwerz Breton ballads or narrative songs that recount historical, legendary, or dramatic events; *see complainte*. **(8)**

gwoka (1) Guadeloupe drum music; (2) membranophone playing the basic rhythms at the *léwòz* festival in St. Lucia. **(2)**

Gŵyl Fair y Canhwyllau Welsh festival celebrating the arrival of spring. **(8)**

gŵyl mabsant Boisterous Welsh patron-saint festival, eventually condemned by religious enthusiasts partly because of the use of the harp to accompany singing and dancing. **(8)**

gyile Xylophone used in Ghana. **(1)**

gyilgo Gonja lamellophone. **(1)**

gyô (Japan.) Calligraphic style of Chinese characters in between a printed style (*sin*) and a cursive, elegant style (*sô*); this concept has been applied to various arts. **(7)**

gyoyû (Japan.) Chamber concerts held at the Heian court among nobles of high rank. **(7)**

gzhas Tibetan folk song genre usually accompanied by dance. **(5)**

Ha Cultural group of Rwanda and Burundi. **(1)**

ha (Japan.) Development or exposition; middle part of the tripartite principle of *zyo ha kyû*. **(7)**

haaggeri Whip-crackers of Richterswil, Zurich. **(8)**

haba (Japan.) Opening scene of each act (*dan*) of *bunraku* (puppet theater) except the fifth act and the *mitiyuki* scene. **(7)**

habanera 'From Havana'. (1) Nineteenth-century Cuban song and dance form featuring a slow to moderate duple meter and a characteristic dotted eighth sixteenth rhythm followed by two even eighth notes; its name reflects its origins in Havana, from where it spread to Spain, Europe, and throughout Latin America. (2) Cuban dance of Spanish origin in slow 2/4 time featuring the rhythm of a dotted eighth, a sixteenth, and two eighths, used in Italian popular music. (3) Cuban genre belonging to the *canción cubana* family. (4) Brazilian dance form featuring dotted rhythm. **(2, 3, 4, 8)**

habi-sanuka Small Warao container rattle of calabash with wooden spiked handle. **(2)**

hablado Quasi-spoken lines in the *sarswela* of Philippines. **(4)**

habɔbo Voluntary association of the Anlo-Ewe in urban centers where music is a central part of the interaction. **(1)**

habrban One of the oldest genres of Armenian peasant song. **(6)**

hackbrett (1) Swiss and northern Italian trapezoidal, struck zither, mainly of Appenzell and the Goms Valley, Upper Valais. (2) Hammered dulcimer often used in Russian (Volga) German wedding bands. **(3, 8)**

haddarat Moroccan female singer-instrumentalists. **(1)**

hade gumi (Japan.) Set of moderately hard pieces in the *syamisen* song cycle (*kumiuta*). **(7)**

hadharī (Also *ḥadarī, wahrāni* 'from Oran'.) Urban popular music style of Algeria, especially of Oran. **(6)**

hadis Tausug songs about death. **(4)**

ḥadīth 'Sayings' of the Prophet Muḥammad, a source of Islamic law. **(5, 6)**

hadj Pilgrimage to Mecca that devout Muslims are encouraged to make. **(1)**

ḥaḍra (Also *hadra, hadrah*.) 'Presence'. (1) Primary corporate Sufi ritual, having as its goal a mystical experience of the divine presence; typically, it includes *fawātiḥ, ḥizb, dhikr*, and *inshād*. Religious sermons and Qur'ānic recitations may also be included; food, beverages, and perfumes are often presented to each participant. (2) Arabic praise songs about Muhammad. (3) Malaysian theatrical genre derived from Islamic singing. (4) Single-headed frame drum of Arabic origin. **(4, 6)**

ḥadrāt Women's musical ensemble of Tunisia. **(6)**

hadrat nabi Islamic praise songs on Ternate and Tidore. **(4)**

haegŭm Korean two-stringed spike fiddle. **(7)**

ḥāfiz (1) 'Guardian', 'memorizer' (of the Qur'ān). (2) General term for a musician who has committed a body of music to memory. (3) Solo singer of devotional music in Central Asian Sufi *zikr*. (4) Professional chanter of the Qur'ān in Turkey. **(6)**

ḥāfiza Professional female dancers of the eighteenth and nineteenth centuries in Kashmir. **(5)**

ḥafla Musical performance, concert. **(6)**

ḥaflah Arab-American party with music, food, drink, and dance. **(3)**

ḥaflat al-zaffāf Arab wedding party or procession; a Saudi women's wedding party. **(6)**

hagelung Tiboli two-stringed lute. **(4)**

ḥāgir Large cylindrical drum of the Hadramawt, tensed by cords. **(6)**

hagwŏn Korean private music institutes. **(7)**

haidi (China.) Small double-reed shawm or *suona* mostly used at weddings. **(7)**

haik Palm-leaf resonator for the *sasandu*. **(4)**

haiku (Japan.) Seventeen-syllable poem. **(7)**

haïvky Ukrainian musical game played by people of all ages and both sexes. **(8)**

ḥajar Large double-headed cylindrical drum of the Arabian Peninsula. **(6)**

hajat Ritual feast or celebration in Sunda. **(4)**

hajji Muslim who has been to Mecca. **(4)**

hakamma Baggāra female poets and bards. **(1)**

hakāmma In the Darfur area of Sudan, a woman who sings to encourage warriors in battle. **(6)**

hakase (Japan.) Notation system for Buddhist chant. **(7)**

hakayat (Also *drokōstran*.) Sung narrative in Kurdistan alternating spoken and sung prose. **(6)**

hakkebord Trapezoidal struck zither of the Low Countries. **(8)**

haksaeng sonyŏn kungjŏng North Korean children's music palaces. **(7)**

Hakuga no hue hu (Japan.) 'Flute Score of Hakuga', collection of music notation for the transverse flute of *gagaku* compiled in 966 by Minamoto no Hiromasa (918?–980). (**7**)

hakusindô siki (Japan.) Modern tablature notation system for the *koto*. (**7**)

hal Anlo-Ewe competitive musical performances, which often escalated into insults and, consequently, disruptive behavior. (**1**)

ḥāl Internal state, emotion, aesthetic or mystical rapture. (**6**)

halaʔ (Also, as called by the Temiar, *halaaʔ*.) Semang shaman. (**4**)

hāḷadū Lullabies, in Gujarat. (**5**)

halage Generic term for membranophones in Karnataka. (**5**)

halakhah Jewish religious law, which addresses aesthetic and ethical questions concerning music. (**6, 8**)

hałašeńni Belarusan laments. (**8**)

hałasnoha śpievu 'Open-air singing' (Belarusan). *See na voli.* (**8**)

hālau Hawaiian school of *hula*, requiring long apprenticeship and the study of customs. (**9**)

halay Turkish folk dance genre performed in central and eastern Anatolia. (**6**)

halbstarke 'Half-naked' (German). Austrian youth subculture of the 1960s, with its own popular music. (**8**)

halel In Syriac, acclamations of God based on the syllables that together make up God's name, *Elohim Aloho*, which is so sacred that speaking it is forbidden. (**6**)

hali' Gourd rattle which is the only traditional musical instrument used by the Guarijio. (**2**)

halia gīt Songs of bullock-cart drivers and farmers in Orissa. (**5**)

halile Drum pair used in Mevlevī ceremonies. (**6**)

halk 'Folk music', 'people's music'; usually refers to rural Anatolian music. (**6**)

Halk Eğitim Merkezleri 'People's Educational Centers', institutions that carried on the work of the *Halk Evleri* 'People's Houses' after c. 1960 in promoting Turkish folk music and culture. (**6**)

Halk Evleri 'People's Houses', from the 1930s to c. 1960, Turkish institutions that promoted the collection, preservation, teaching, and performance of folk music. (**6**)

halk hikayecileri 'Popular storytellers' of the Adana plain in Turkey. (**6**)

hallel In Yemenite Jewish liturgy, the recitation of Psalms 113–118, preceded and followed by short blessings, for festivals and on the first day of each month. (**6**)

Hallelujah Guyanese syncretic religion of some native Americans living in the savannah. (**2**)

hallgató Slow, rhythmically free type of *nóta*. (**8**)

halling (1) Men's athletic dance of Norway. (2) Rural Norwegian folk dance performed for an audience. (**3, 8**)

halmi (Also *halmi kwangdae*.) Ugly wife, character in a Korean village ritual play. (**7**)

hālo (Also *lāḍo*.) Wedding and circumcision songs of Balochistan. (**5**)

ḥāl o ḥavā 'Condition', 'atmosphere', 'ambience'. In discourse about Persian music, refers to the situation of a musician or listener, or to an epoch. (**6**)

ḥalqat al-lewa Omani ensemble consisting of twenty to forty male singers and dancers (descendants of slaves), who perform several types of circle dances. (**6**)

ḥalqat al-mālid Omani men's ensemble performing poetry, song, and dance in honor of the birth and life of the Prophet. (**6**)

ḥalqat al-pākit Omani men's ensemble performing a type of musical theater at weddings. (**6**)

halsingod Welsh metrical psalm in the vernacular, born of the religious turbulence in south Wales during the 1600s. (**8**)

halszither Swiss long-necked lute-zither. (**8**)

Halvetī Turkish Sufi *tarikat* that entered Anatolia from Azerbaijan in the fifteenth century and spread throughout the Ottoman Empire. (**6**)

Ham (Also Jaba.) A people of northern Nigeria. (**1**)

Hamadsha Brotherhood in North Africa whose members seek healing through a dance. (**1**)

hamarreko Basque dance-song type with five-couplet stanzas. (**8**)

hambo Modernized, nonimprovised version of the Swedish *polska*. (**3, 8**)

hame mono Music played by an instrumental ensemble (*hayasi*) to accompany *rakugo* (comic monologue) in the Kansai area. (**7**)

han (1) Idiophone used in Buddhist music; a suspended flat wooden plate struck with a mallet (Japan). (2) Sentiment—deep-rooted, profound sadness (Korea). (**7**)

Hanacpachap Cussicuinin Four-part polyphonic piece published in Quechua by the Franciscan Juan Pérez Bocanegra in Lima, 1631. (**2**)

hanawkwa Yekuana conch-shell trumpet. (**2**)

hanbok Korean traditional costume. (**7**)

hand Drum pattern in Trinidad. (**5**)

Handäoline (Also *deutsche Harmonika*.) Later name of the *Mundäoline*, an accordion invented in Berlin in 1821 by F. Buschmann and now known as the concertina. (**8**)

hāne Major subdivision of the seventeenth- and eighteenth-century *peşrev*. (**6**)

hangar Ifugao ritual clapper. (**4**)

hangonda Gond priest in charge of funeral rites. (**5**)

Han'guk chŏngsin munhwa yŏn'guwŏn Academy of Korean Studies. (**7**)

Han'guk kugak hakhoe Korean Musicological Society. (**7**)

Han'guk kugak yesul hakkyo Korean Traditional Music Arts School. (**7**)

Han'guk munhwa yesul chinhŭngwŏn Korean Culture and Arts Foundation. (**7**)

Han'guk ŭmak Korean music. (**7**)

haniwa (Japan.) Terra-cotta figures. (**7**)

Hannibal Small independent British recording label. (**1**)

hanske knap Clapper of the Low Countries, in the form of a wolf's or bear's head. (**8**)

hanter dro Breton line or circle dance, performed as part of a three-part suite. (**8**)

hantes In the Armenian-American community, all-day church picnic with music; sometimes held indoors. (**3**)

hanyami Malawi musical style. (**10**)

haozi (China.) Work songs. (**7**)

hapa haole Hawaiian term, from *hapa* 'half' (from English *half*) and *haole* 'foreign'. Of part-European ancestry or origin, especially Hawaiian-European. (**9**)

hapchabo 'Combined character notation', Korean tablature system. (**7**)

hap changdan Initial downbeat of a Korean rhythmic pattern. (**7**)

harana Serenade in the Philippines. (**4**)

Harapu Gond festival that takes place in the spring. (**5**)

harawi (Also *haraui*.) Pre-Columbian Incan nostalgic monophonic love song from which the Peruvian *yaraví* may be derived. (**2**)

harawiq Group of Andean elder women who sing *harawi* in high-pitched, nasal voices. (**2**)

ḥarba 'Arrowhead', refrain in the performance of a *qaṣīda*, containing the poetic form, theme of the poem, and basic melody. (**6**)

hardingfele 'Hardanger fiddle'. (1) Norwegian modified form of the violin, having four sympathetic strings. (2) Type of violin originating in western Norway, with a flatter fingerboard and bridge and a shorter neck than the European concert violin; played by Norwegian immigrants at both weddings and informal gatherings. (**3, 8**)

harikathā 'The Story of the Lord', narrated and sung stories of Lord Vishnu, which may include drama and dance. (**5**)

harikīrtan Repetitious devotional hymn. (**5**)

harīm Chorus. (**6**)

harīp In the Northern Areas of Pakistan, (1) music, instrumental music, or tune; (2) music of the Burusho double-reed and drum ensemble. (**5**)

harmoníai Tunings in ancient Greek musical theory. (8)

harmonic Overtone whose vibrational frequency is an exact integer multiple of that of the fundamental; the component with frequency n times that of the fundamental is the nth harmonic. (9)

harmonica (Also *monika*, mouth organ.) Small box with free reeds set into slots and sounded by exhaling and inhaling. (8)

harmoniebesetzung 'Harmonious composition' (German), Swiss brass ensemble that incorporates woodwinds. (8)

harmoniemusik Musical wind ensemble, usually five to eight instruments, consisting of pairs of oboes or clarinets (or both), horns, and one or two bassoons, without drums; popular during the eighteenth century. (3)

harmoniia Ukrainian free-reed button accordion; *see baian*. (8)

harmonik Belarusan accordion. (8)

harmonika Slovenian and Croatian diatonic accordion. (8)

harmonium (1) Hand-pumped keyboard instrument, commonly used to accompany Indian and Indo-Caribbean music, which has recently become popular in the United States and Canada, in part because of its popularization by the late Nusrat Fatah Ali Khan, one of the greatest stars of world music–world beat. (2) Portable hand-pumped organ widely used for devotional and light classical music. (3, 5)

harp (1) Chordophone with plucked strings perpendicular to the soundboard. (2) In Ireland, medieval chordophone known as *cláirseach* and *cruit*. (8)

harp, shelved type Harp found in a small area of Gabon and in the southernmost Central African Republic. (1)

harp, spoon-in-the-cup type Baganda *ennanga*, found in the Great Lakes region of Africa. (1)

harp, tanged type Azande *kundi*. (1)

harpa Norwegian instrument most frequently mentioned in ancient literary sources: either a lyre or a harp. (8)

harppu Finnish harp. (8)

harpsichord Western European keyboard instrument having strings plucked by plectra (traditionally quills), engaged by the action of the keys. (8)

haru (Japan.) Term in *gidayû busi* notation indicating pitch or manner of singing. (7)

haru husi (Japan.) *Gidayû busi* melodic pattern. (7)

harvest home Feast at the close of harvest, often featuring singing. (8)

hasa Refined men's dance in Ternate, accompanied by a *tifa*. (4)

hasa bunga Men's martial dance in Ternate. (4)

hasapikos *Rebetika* dance rhythm in moderate 4/4 time. (8)

ha-shir ha-Yisraeli (Also *ha-zemer ha-'ivri* 'Hebrew song'.) 'Israeli song', denoting the canonical Israel folk song repertoire developed by the Zionist movement. (6)

Ḥasidim Mystical sect of orthodox Ashkenazi Judaism. (6)

hasi gakari (Japan.) Entranceway to the main *nô* stage. (7)

hasiri mai (Japan.) Energetic court dances of foreign origin. (7)

hasuha-a Fast responsorial singing on Buru. (4)

hāsya 'Comic', one of the eight emotional states (*rasa*) codified in the *Nātyaśāstra*. (5)

hát 'Singing'. Vietnamese term, prefix for theater genres. (4)

hát à dào Alternative name for *ca trù* chamber song in Vietnam. (4)

Hatano *ryû* (Japan.) School of *heike biwa*. (7)

hát bài chòi Traditional theater of central Vietnam. (4)

hát bá trạo Vietnamese "paddle dance" folk theater of central Vietnam. (4)

hát bội Central Vietnamese theater. (4)

hát chầu văn Spirit possession ceremony in Vietnam. (4)

hát chèo tầu Ancient folk drama of Gối near Hanoi. (4)

hatigatu odori (Japan.) 'August dance', a major folk genre in the Amami Islands. (7)

Hatikvah 'The Hope' (Hebrew), Israeli national anthem. (6)

Hatizyô kaden syo (Japan.) 'Writings on the Transmission of the Flower', books on *nô* published c. 596–1624. (7)

hatizyû gen sô (Japan.) Eighty-stringed *koto* invented in 1929 by Miyagi Mitio (1894–1965). (7)

hát sắc bùa Vietnamese wishing songs for the new year (Tết). (4)

hatu (Japan.) Idiophone used in Buddhist music; cymbals struck or rubbed together. (7)

hăulit Yodel of the Gorj zone of Oltenia, Romania. (8)

haur kantu txapelketa Basque annual championship of children's singing. (8)

Hausa A people of northern Nigeria and Ghana; their language is a trade language of the region. (1)

Hausmusik 'Domestic music' (German-Yiddish), European domestic music tradition brought to Palestine by Central European Jews during the Nazi era. (6)

hauta (Japan.) (1) (Also *edo hauta*.) Genre of short *syamisen* songs of Edo (present-day Tôkyô). (2) (Also *kamigata hauta*.) *Ziuta* (*syamisen* music) repertoire of short compositions emphasizing vocal melody. (7)

hautboys (Also *hautbois*.) (1) Literally, the oboe, a double-reed musical instrument; (2) musical wind ensemble usually consisting of three oboes and a bass oboe or bassoon, with snare drums, popular in military units from the end of the seventeenth to the middle of the eighteenth century. (3)

hạuy cầm Hawaiian steel guitar, found in Vietnam. (4)

havā 'Air' (Persian and Turkic, from Arabic *hawā*). Turkic term for a tune or melody type; refers to any melody used by an *aşiq*. (6)

havan Vedic ceremony performed at dawn, noon, and dusk; still found in Trinidad. (5)

havelī 'Mansion', house of worship. (5)

havelī saṅgīt Music performed as part of worship in a Vallabhacharya *havelī*. (5)

havelī saṅgītkār Musician of the Vallabhacharya religious tradition. (5)

Hawaiian guitar Electric guitar played with a slide. (5)

hawaiienne 'Hawaiian' (French), tuning used by Masengo guitarists. (1)

hawfī Women's genre of Algerian urban folk music, related closely to *hawzī*. (6)

hăwiawan Yanomamö priest-shaman. (2)

hawzi (Also *hawzī*.) (1) Musical genre popular in the Tell region of Algeria. (2) Semipopular song style of Algeria, resembling the Andalusian *zajal* with respect to poetic form and generally having lyrics pertaining to love. (1, 6)

Haya Cultural group of Tanzania. (1)

haya byôsi (Japan.) Four-beat rhythmic cycle in *gagaku*. (7)

haya gaki (Japan.) Basic plucking pattern of the *gakusô* (zither used in *gagaku*). (7)

haya hue (Japan.) *Nô* instrumental piece for the introduction of demons. (7)

haya mai (Japan.) *Nô* dance performed by the ghost of a nobleman. (7)

hayama kouta (Japan.) *See kouta*. (7)

hayari uta (Japan.) Generic term for popular songs; used especially in the Edo period (1600–1867) to refer to new popular song, usually accompanied by *syamisen* and associated with the pleasure quarters or the theater. (7)

hayasi (Japan.) (1) Generic term for instrumental ensembles (generally excluding the *syamisen*), the performers, and the music itself in various forms of theatricals, *nagauta* (*syamisen* music), and folk music; (2) abbreviation of *hayasi kotoba*; (3) abbreviation of *hayasi kata*. (7)

hayasi kata (Japan.) Generic term for instrumentalists in *hayasi* ensembles. (7)

Volume Key: **6**, Middle East; **7**, East Asia; **8**, Europe; **9**, Australia and the Pacific Islands; **10**, The World's Music.

hayasi kotoba (Japan.) Nonlexical syllables or words of encouragement inserted in folk song to motivate the singer, or for musical effects, or both. (7)

hayasi mono (Japan.) Style of medieval street entertainment in the Kyôto region, in which a man wearing an elaborate costume would act or dance, accompanied by an instrumental ensemble. (7)

haya tada byôsi (Japan.) 2 + 4-beat rhythmic cycle in *gagaku*. (7)

haya yo hyôsi (Japan.) Rhythmic cycle in *gagaku* comprising four 4-beat measures. (7)

Haydar Alevī composition for voice and *bağlama*, using twentieth-century Bektaşī poetry by the radio and recording artist Ali Ekber Çiçek. (6)

hayfa (Also *taghzzaft*.) Berber *aḥidus* among the Ayt Yahya involving singing and dancing by mature men; cf. *amssad*. (6)

haylli Call-and-response harvest song in ancient Peru. (2)

hazaj Light style appropriate for love songs. (6)

ḥazanim Turkish term for Jewish cantors in major urban centers. (6)

ḥazanut (1) Cantorial art of Eastern European Jews. (2) Composed religious music similar in social function to Western "art" music. (6)

ḥazzan (Plural, *ḥazzanim*.) 'Cantor', 'the one serving'. (Hebrew). (3, 8)

heavy-lift songs Kru mariners' songs for unloading ships and handling other hard jobs. (1)

hebu Warao ancestor spirit that can cause illness. (2)

hebu mataro Large Warao container rattle made from a calabash with a wooden spiked handle. (2)

heello Youth-controlled Somali poetry, often treating political themes. (1)

hees Somali songs accompanying work, differentiated mainly by function and the performers' sex. (1)

Hehe Cultural group of Tanzania. (1)

Heian (Japan.) Period from 794 to 1192. (7)

heike biwa (Also *heikyoku*.) In Japan, form of *biwa* (lute) and its music consisting of the recitation of the tale of the Heike accompanied by this instrument. (7)

Heike mabusi (Japan.) 'The Correct Tunes of Heike', detailed score for *heike biwa* created in 1776. (7)

Heike monogatari (Japan.) 'The Tale of the Heike', military chronicle of the war of 1180–1185 war between the Heike and Genzi clans; the theme of *heike biwa*. (7)

heikyoku (Japan.) See *heike biwa*. (7)

heilagvisene Norwegian pre-Christian and Christian sacred songs. (8)

Heimatlieder For German-Americans, songs about the European homeland. (3)

Heiva Principal festival of French Polynesia, held in Tahiti each July. (9)

ḥekāye (Also *hikâye*.) Narrative alternating prose and verse, performed by an *'āsheq* or *bakhshī*. (6)

hekido Four-holed bamboo ring-stop flute of Savu. (4)

hekunukabe Warao ductless vertical flute made from a plant stalk. (2)

hekura (Also *híkola*.) Yanomamö spirit or spirit helper said to cause illness. (2)

heliaki In Tongan verbal expression, indirectness or veiled meaning. (9)

Helmholtz resonator After Hermann von Helmholtz (1821–1894). Any sound-making object partly enclosing an air-filled cavity, whose pitch is set by the size or sizes—not the position—of the opening or openings, as with hollowed log idiophones and vessel flutes. (9)

Helong Inhabitants of the island of Semau. (4)

hemiola Ratio of 3 to 2; musically, the substitution of 3 beats for 2 or 2 beats for 3, conventionally notated as the alternation of 3/4 and 6/8 time or 3/2 and 6/4 time. (8)

hen (Japan.) Equivalent of the Western flat. (7)

hennon (Japan.) Modulation in Buddhist chant. (7)

hennon kyoku (Japan.) Buddhist chant of the Singon sect. (7)

heo Viola in Timor. (4)

heptatonic equitonal scale Pitch inventory with seven pitches equally spaced within the octave. (1)

heränneet Finnish Lutheran folk revivalists who embellish their performances of psalms. (8)

heresemoi Warao conch-shell end-blown lip-concussion aerophone. (2)

hermandades Chilean brotherhoods of patronal festivals honoring the Virgin Mary. (2)

hermaphrodite pig (Also intersex pig.) Pig with male and female genitalia, highly valued in Vanuatu for use in grade-taking rituals. (9)

herranza Marking of animals in the Andes, a context for ritual music making. (2)

hertz Abbreviated Hz. Number of oscillations per second produced by a vibrating body or a sound wave. (9)

heterometer (Adjective, heterometric.) Use of more than one metric scheme in a piece of music. (8)

heterophony Musical texture deriving from the simultaneous performance of many variations of a musical line. (3)

hēvisi (Also *hēvisi pūjā*.) Buddhist kettledrum-and-oboe ceremonial ensemble in Sri Lanka. (5)

hey'at In Iran, a group of men who meet for religious exercises of various kinds. (6)

hicaz Common Turkish *makam*; cf. *ḥijāz*. (6)

ḥida' (1) Folk song of the ancient Middle East, associated with camel-driving. (2) In Palestine, a popular genre of improvised sung poetry. (6)

hiden (Japan.) To secretly transmit certain techniques and pieces to selected individuals; also, the techniques and pieces transmitted. (7)

hidžaz makam Turkish mode used in singing love songs (*sevdalinka*) of Bosnia-Hercegovina. (8)

higasi hû (Japan.) (1) *Gidayû busi* style established by Toyotake Wakatayû (1681–1764). (2) *Gidayû busi* pieces premiered at the Toyotake *za* theater. (7)

Highland bagpipe Scottish bagpipe with a blowpipe, a double-reed chanter, and a single reed in each of three drone pipes. (8)

highland dancing Formal, balletlike, athletic, and frequently competitive type of dancing that developed in Scotland and is usually performed to bagpipe music. (3)

highland fling Antiguan carnival dance derived from Scottish folk dance. (2)

highlife Popular West African musical genre that originated in Ghana in the early 1900s and became part of European world music and world beat. Highlife combines international pop with traditional rhythms and textures and features clarinets, trumpets, cornets, baritones, trombones, tuba, and parade drums. (1, 3, 8)

Higi A people of northern Nigeria. (1)

higo biwa (Japan.) *Biwa* (lute) tradition developed by blind players in the Higo region of central Kyûsyû. (7)

hiiukannel Estonian three- or four-stringed bowed lyre; see *rootsikannel*. (8)

hijaz Turkish melodic mode, used in Macedonia. (8)

ḥijāz (Also *hicaz*, Turkish.) One of the primary Arab *maqāmāt*. (6)

hijikirini From *hij kirin* 'to make love', term for Kurdish love song, indistinguishable in form and structure from heroic songs. (6)

hikayat Sasak Islamic writings on palm leaf. (4)

Hikmat 'Wisdom' of Hoja Ahmad Yassawi; mystical poetry often sung in the *zikr* of the Yassawi Sufi order of Uzbekistan-Kazakhstan. (6)

hilulah (Plural, *hilulot*.) Jewish celebration on the anniversary of the death of a saintly person. (6)

him 'Power, strength'; aesthetic basis of vitality in Korean music. (7)

Hima Pastoralists of western Uganda. **(1)**

himene (Also *hīmene*, Society Islands, Manihiki; *hīmeni*, Hawai'i; *īmene*, Pukapuka; *'īmene*, southern Cook Islands.) From French *hymne* or English *hymn*. East Polynesian choral singing, originally combining indigenous musical textures with European harmonies and now perceived as an original cultural expression. **(9)**

Hindustani music Classical music of North India. **(5)**

hi-NRG (Also high energy.) (1) Category of dance music of the 1980s geared toward a mainly white, gay audience. (2) Term used to describe dance music not derived from rhythm and blues (R&B), often by European, especially British, artists and producers. *See also disco.* **(3)**

hip-hop Beginning in the early 1970s, a primarily black and Latino street culture that comprised rap music, break dancing, and graffiti art. **(3)**

hip house House music featuring rap rhymes. **(3)**

hira-gasy Improvisatory theatrical form most representative of the Malagasy highlands. **(1)**

hira mai (Japan.) Calm court dances of foreign origin. **(7)**

hira nori (Japan.) Rhythmic style of *nô* chanting. **(7)**

hira zyôsi (Japan.) Basic *koto* tuning system devised by Yatuhasi *kengyô* (1614–1685). **(7)**

hiri Trading network of the Motu people of southern New Guinea. **(9)**

Hiri Motu (Also *Police Motu*.) Pidgin commonly spoken in Papua New Guinea, especially in the Papuan Region. **(9)**

hirmologion Byzantine compendium of model strophes within an eight-mode system. **(6)**

hirmos Byzantine model strophe. **(6)**

hiroi (Japan.) Term in *gidayû busi* notation indicating a narrative technique. **(7)**

hirð skáld Oral art of Icelandic court poets. **(8)**

hisigi (Japan.) Piercing highest sound of the *nô* flute. **(7)**

His Master's Voice (HMV.) London-based recording label, which by the 1930s was distributing its products across Africa. **(1)**

hitiriki (Japan.) Double-read oboe used in *gagaku*. **(7)**

hito (Also *wíchu, fhidyu*.) Yekuana long-tubed vertical duct flute with closed distal end. **(2)**

hitoyogiti (Also *hitoyogiti syakuhati*.) Shorter precursor of the contemporary Japanese *syakuhati*. **(7)**

hiva kakala Tongan popular song. **(9)**

ḥizb Fixed group prayer, assembled by a Sufi *shaykh* from religious texts. A collection of

ḥizb is associated with each Sufi order; one of these is typically recited during the *ḥaḍra*. **(6)**

hjīnī Early form of bedouin sung poetry in the Arabian Peninsula. **(6)**

Hmong Sino-Tibetan upland group living in Laos, Thailand, Vietnam, and China. **(4)**

hnè Burmese conical aerophone with six-piece reed and detached bell. **(4)**

hnyìn Extinct Burmese free-reed mouth organ. **(4)**

hò Vietnamese work songs in rice fields and on rivers. **(4)**

hoa Warao prayerful song for curing illnesses. **(2)**

hoaetpul ssaum Korean farmers' band formation in which opposing forces strive to push each other back. **(7)**

hoarotu 'Owner of *hoa*', Warao shaman in charge of the western cosmic realm. **(2)**

hô bài chòi Vietnamese songs associated with playing cards. **(4)**

hocket (1) Distribution of a melody among several voices so that each voice performs only intermittent notes. (2) Borrowed European term meaning interlocking parts, often referring to the alternating manner of playing panpipe halves in the Andes or *vaksin* trumpets in Haiti. (3) Ensemble performance technique that produces a single composite melody from a number of interlocking rhythmic ostinatos; akin to Euro-American bell ringing. (4) Texture in which two or more voices rapidly alternate melodic notes or groups of notes, one part resting while the other sounds. **(1, 2, 3, 9)**

hoddu Fulbe three- to five-stringed lute. **(1)**

hodo (Japan.) Tone produced on the *ko tuzumi*. **(7)**

hôe (Japan.) Generic term for Buddhist ceremonies. **(7)**

hoesimgok 'Song of Release', Korean Buddhist folk song. **(7)**

hogalikke 'To praise the name and deeds of deities'; Kannada variant of the Tulu *pāḍḍana*. **(5)**

hôgô (Japan.) Buddhist chant (*syômyô*) for reciting the name of Buddha or a bodhisattva. **(7)**

hoho Nias solo and choral singing. **(4)**

hòi Vietnamese ornamentation specific to a mode. **(4)**

hoiku syôka (Japan.) Educational songs for kindergarten children composed in the early Meizi era (1868–1912), mostly between 1877 and 1880. **(7)**

hòi quảng Cantonese tune adopted by Vietnamese musicians. **(4)**

hokh Adighian wishes for prosperity in magical song. **(8)**

hôki (Japan.) Generic term for religious tools. **(7)**

hokke Berta harvest-festival songs and dances. **(1)**

Holī North Indian Hindu festival celebrating the defeat of the mythical ruler Hiranyaka-sipu by the man-lion incarnation of Vishnu. **(5)**

ḥomaynī Style of lyrical poetry, or *ghazal*, influenced by colloquial Yemeni Arabic. **(6)**

hommel Plucked dulcimer of the Low Countries. **(8)**

hômonka (Japan.) Buddhist popular songs. **(7)**

homotony Measurement of the number of syllables in a poetic line according to their accented stresses. **(6)**

homrong Thai ceremonial suites and overtures in classical music. **(4)**

hon bakase (Japan.) *Hakase* Buddhist chant notation. **(7)**

hon busi (Japan.) *Gidayû busi* melodic pattern. **(7)**

honkyoku (Japan.) (1) Original pieces for a certain instrument, particularly *kokyû* or *syakuhati*. (2) (Also *koten honkyoku*.) *Syakuhati* repertoire developed by Buddhist monks of the Huke sect (*komusô*). **(7, 10)**

honte (Japan.) Original melody line of an ensemble piece. **(7)**

hon tesuri (Japan.) Rail on a contemporary *bunraku* (puppet theater) stage that serves as a boundary between indoor and other scenery. **(7)**

hon tyôsi (Japan.) Basic tuning of the *syamisen* and the *sansin* (Okinawan three-stringed lute). **(7)**

hon zi (Japan.) Unit of 8 beats per poetic line in *nô* chanting. **(7)**

hook lines Short repetitive phrases of text, set to sing-along-type melodies. **(3)**

hora (1) Popular Israeli dance, extolled by some Israeli composers (such as Mark Lavri) as a token of the national spirit. (2) (Japan.) Conch shell trumpet. (3) Circle dance of Romania and Israel; *see horo, oro.* **(6, 7, 8)**

hora lăutarescă (Also *hora tsigăneasca, hora tsigănwasca*.) Romanian Rom improvised dance. **(8)**

hora lunga 'Long song', a name of the Romanian *doina*. **(8)**

horanâva Quadruple-reed conical bore aerophone of Sri Lanka, used in the lay-Buddhist musical *hēvisi* ensemble and in diverse secular contexts. **(5)**

horde Fulani hemispherical gourd calabash held against the chest and struck with finger rings. **(1)**

hornada 'Batch', 'ovenful'; medley of Venezuelan *revueltas* or *pasajes*. **(2)**

hornpipe (1) Wooden or bone pipe having a single reed and holes for fingering. (2) Lively English and Irish dance in 4/4 time, originally accompanied by a hornpipe. (**3, 8**)

horo Generic term for Bulgarian dance, usually an open or closed circle of dancers holding hands; see *hora, oro*. (**8**)

horo na pesen Bulgarian dance accompanied by singing. (**8**)

horon Turkish folk dance genre performed in the Black Sea region, characterized by 7/16 meter. (**6**)

horovel One of the most important genres of Armenian peasant work songs. The term derives from *ho* (an exclamation) and *arhavel* (meaning unplowed ground between two furrows). (**6**)

horse head (Also *buru.*) Jamaican slave celebration for the Christmas holiday. (**2**)

hos Hymn of praise in the Coptic liturgy. (**6**)

Hosay Jamaican Muslim celebration brought by indentured workers from India. (**2**)

hosha'not In Yemenite Jewish liturgy, procession around the pulpit during the festival of Tabernacles. (**6**)

hosho Shona seed-filled gourd rattle that accompanies singing, *mbira dzavadzimu* ensembles, and panpipes. (**1**)

hosi (Japan.) Section of *mikagura*, Shinto music and dance performed at the imperial court. (**7**)

hossori Simple chant of Korean Buddhist *pŏmp'ae*. (**7**)

Hôsyô ryû (Japan.) School of *nô* specializing in *site kata* and *waki kata*. (**7**)

Hotado Maramma In Karnataka, icon of the popular goddess Maramma in a basket. (**5**)

hotchin sori 'Simple voice', 'one-layered voice', vocal timbre in Korean *p'ansori*. (**7**)

hotṛ Chief Ṛgveda priest in Vedic rituals. (**5**)

Hottentots Old European name for pastoral peoples around the Cape of Good Hope, now known as Khoi and living in South Africa and Namibia. (**1**)

houguan (1) Double-reed wind instrument. (2) (China.) Double-reed pipe. (**3, 7**)

house Style of dance music originating at gay black clubs in Chicago in the early 1980s; its musical elements reflect the heritage of disco while incorporating production techniques characteristic of the emerging home studio industry that helped disk jockeys become producers and artists. (**3**)

hoyo Preburial dirges sung by women in Sumba. (**4**)

hozon kai (Japan.) Societies for preserving regional traditions. (**7**)

hsaìnwaìn Burmese classical ensemble. (**4**)

huaben (China.) Scripts used by professional storytellers during the Song dynasty. (**7**)

huada Mapuche calabash rattle. (**2**)

hua'er (China.) Folk song in northwest China. (**7**)

hua'erhui (China.) *Hua'er* song competition held annually in Gansu and Qinghai provinces. (**7**)

huaguxi (China.) Flower-drum song-and-dance skit. (**7**)

huahua Mixtec danced game. (**2**)

huancar Inca drum. (**2**)

huang (China.) 'Reed', ancient term for the modern-day jaw's harp (Jew's harp) *kouhuang* or *kouxian*. (**7**)

huangse (China.) 'Yellow'; implies vulgarity or pornography. (**7**)

huapango (1) Mexican variety of the *son*. (2) *Huapango arribeño* 'highland *huapango*'. (3) *Huapango huasteco*, played by a string trio at a fast tempo. (4) Genre of folk music and dance rooted in the rural *mestizo* cultures of several east Mexican states. (5) Popular Mexican musical form with a distinctive rhythm and frequent falsetto vocal embellishments. (**2, 3**)

huapanguera (Also *guitarra quinta*.) Deep-bodied Mexican guitar with eight strings in five single and double courses. (**2**)

huarumu Long, straight tubular trumpet of Ecuador. (**2**)

huaylas Harvest ritual song genre of the central Andes of Peru. (**2**)

huayno (Also *huayño, wayno*.) (1) Central Andean dance in fast duple meter with free choreography consisting of two musical phrases in periodic form (*aabb*). (2) Native American–derived (Quechua) Peruvian fast duple-meter song and dance form featuring long-short-short rhythmical pattern. (3) Most popular highland Peruvian song form, used to transmit narrative texts. (4) *Huayño* is Bolivian (Aymara) orthography for dance in duple meter. (**2**)

hubbān Line dance of Kuwait and the Emirates performed by Iranian immigrant communities, named after its signature instrument, the *hubbān* 'bagpipe'. (**6**)

huchage 'Calling', French shepherds' singing over long distances or for herding flocks. (**8**)

hudhud Ifugao epic. (**4**)

hudka Hourglass pressure drum played by Fiji Indians. (**5**)

hudki (Also *huruk, hudukka*.) Hourglass pressure drum of the western Himalayas. (**5**)

huduk apa Kayan pest-dispersal ceremony. (**4**)

hue (Japan.) Generic term for flutes. (**7**)

huéhuetl Nahua large, single-headed, cylindrical, hollowed-out log drum, also used by the Maya. (**2**)

hui (China.) Inlays or studs on the surface of a seven-stringed plucked zither *qin*. (**7**)

huibe Bowed pseudo bass of the Low Countries. (**8**)

huíbiju Kogi ceramic globular aerophone. (**2**)

huilacapiztli Nahua ceramic globular aerophone. (**2**)

huju (China.) Shanghai opera. (**7**)

Huke (Japan.) Zen Buddhist sect using the *syakuhati* as a religious instrument. (**7**)

huke syakuhati (Japan.) (1) End-blown bamboo flute played by Buddhist monks of the Huke; (2) *syakuhati* music played by the Huke sect. (**7**)

hukura (Japan.) Lower register of the *ryûrteki* (transverse flute used in *gagaku*), produced by blowing softly. (**7**)

Hukuô ryû (Japan.) School of *nô* specializing in *waki kata*. (**7**)

hula Polynesian-Hawaiian dance. (**9, 10**)

hula'auana 'Modern *hula*' (Hawaiian). *Hula* style incorporating newer movements, with harmonized sung text accompanied by plucked chordophones of Western origin. (**9**)

hula kahiko 'Ancient *hula*' (Hawaiian). *Hula* style incorporating older movements, with monophonically recited text accompanied by indigenous instruments. (**9**)

huli vēṣa Tiger-costume dance in Karnataka. (**5**)

huluna Tagalog lullaby. (**4**)

humenta Palm Sunday procession in the Philippines. (**4**)

humisyagi (Japan.) Important types of *ayô* (a genre of Yaeyama folk songs) performed at a rice harvest festival called *pûri*. (**7**)

hummel Swedish plucked dulcimer. (**8**)

humpe nene (Japan.) 'Whale dance', Ainu dramatic dance. (**7**)

humppa Style of Finnish music for dance that mixes jazz, fox-trot, polka, *rekilaulu*, and Russian romances. (**8**)

hun (1) Northeast Thai Jew's harp. (2) Korean ceramic globular ocarina. (**4, 7**)

hunazoko (Japan.) Low floor behind the rails of a contemporary *bunraku* (puppet theater) stage; the puppeteers' legs are hidden from the knees down. (**7**)

hŭng Korean sentiment—elation or heightened emotion. (**7**)

hüngühüngü In Belize, popular Garifuna dance in triple meter with unison singing frequently performed at holidays, processionals, and other festive occasions. (**2**)

hün krabawk Classical-based rod puppet theater of Thailand. (**4**)

hunt supper English social event, often a context for music and song. (**8**)

huowu (China.) Playing technique in *Chaozhou xianshiyue*, which involves applying wide vibrato to the second pitch of the scale to create modal ambiguity. (7)

huqin (China.) Imported bowed spike lute, the predecessor of the modern *erhu*. (7)

hurtkampaniya (Also *kapela, muzyki, skamarochi, viasielnyja muzyki*.) Belarusan traditional folk instrumental ensemble. (8)

huryû (Japan.) Street entertainment including dancing with fancy costumes and instrumental and vocal music. (7)

huryû odori (Japan.) Dance performed in *huryû*. (7)

husa (Japan.) Genre of folk songs in the Miyako Islands, performed only by women with religious status. (7)

husapi Lute from Borneo and Sumatra. (4)

ḥusaynī (Also *hüseyni*, Turkish.) (1) One of the notes of the Arab fundamental scale. (2) One of the *maqāmāt*. (6)

Husayni-xāna Shi'a prayer houses in pre-Soviet Bukhara, hosting laments for Imam Husayn as well as *taziyah*, religious theater. (6)

husi (Japan.) (1) Generic term for melody; (2) node. (7)

husi oti (Japan.) Cadential melodic pattern of *gidayû busi*. (7)

husi zuke (Japan.) Composing the vocal part of a piece. (7)

hûsya (Japan.) *Kabuki* offstage instruments used for sound effects. (7)

huto zao (Japan.) Large *syamisen*. (7)

hutsul'ka Dance of the Hutsul'shchyna region of Ukraine. (8)

hutsul'ka do spivi 'Hutsul'ka for singing', regional melodies played on the *dudka* in market squares and village bazaars. (8)

Hutterites Group in the Anabaptist tradition that practices communal living. (3)

huuwai (1) Yekuana shaman; (2) malevolent spirit. (2)

huving Norwegian elaborated shouts; *see laling*. (8)

huzām One of the primary Arab *maqāmāt*. (6)

Huzita ryû (Japan.) School of *nô* flute (*nôkan*). (7)

huzoku (Japan.) Generic term for ancient indigenous music and dance. (7)

hvēsegasse Danish whirring disk: button or a round plate of cardboard spun and sounded by rhythmically tightening or slackening a string noose threaded through two holes in the middle of the button or plate. (8)

hwach'ŏng Korean Buddhist chant in the vernacular. (7)

hwarang (1) Elite youth corps of Korean entertainers; (2) colloquial term for shaman musicians. (7)

hwimori Korean rhythmic pattern (*changdan*), rapid 4/4 meter with duple subdivision. (7)

hwin krã Suyá strung rattle with *piqui* pits or deer or wild pig hooves. (2)

hwyl Declamatory technique used by Welsh preachers in the 1800s and early 1900s to heighten religious fervor. (8)

hyangak Korean court music of indigenous origin; *see tangak*. (7)

hyang pip'a Korean five-stringed plucked lute. (7)

hyang p'iri Korean cylindrical double-reed bamboo oboe. (7)

hymée (Also *épiaulie*.) Millers' work songs of French-speaking Switzerland. (8)

hymn Musical composition praising God or articulating religious faith. (1)

hymnody (1) Hymn singing; (2) hymn writing; (3) hymns of a time, place, or church; (4) study of hymn singing practices. (3)

hyôbaku (Japan.) Buddhist offertory chant (*syômyô*) with Japanese texts. (7)

hyôgu (*busi*) (Japan.) *Gidayû busi* melodic pattern quoted from *hyôguya busi*, a genre of early narrative *syamisen* music (*ko zyôruri*). (7)

hyŏmnyulsa Korean touring variety troupes. (7)

Hyŏnak Yŏngsan hoesang Korean suite *Yŏngsan hoesang* in a version for string ensemble. (7)

hyŏngsŏng 'Formation', gradual development of Korean music. (7)

hyôsi (Japan.) Generic term for rhythm or meter. (7)

hyôsi ai (Japan.) Metered sections in *nô* music. (7)

hyôsi awazu (Japan.) Sections in free rhythm in *nô* music. (7)

hyôsigi (Japan.) Wooden clappers. (7)

hyôzyô (Japan.) (1) Note corresponding to E; (2) *gagaku* scale built on it. (7)

hyperinstrument Specially modified acoustic instrument whose performance involves computer technology; the additional computer hardware and software allows the performer to play music that exceeds the normal limitations of the instrument or to send triggers to other digital music instruments. Hyperinstruments were pioneered by the American composer Tod Machover (b. 1953). (3)

iablochko 'Beautiful apple' (Russian), style of Gypsy song. (8)

ialorixá Brazilian female temple leader in Candomblé. (2)

iamuricuma Ceremony in the Xingú region of Brazil. (2)

iancunú Garifuna masked dance genre related to Caribbean *junkanoo*. (2)

iaren Recitative-like speech form used in Suyá ceremonies. (2)

iavnana Two- and three-part song for curing whooping cough and measles, performed by men in eastern Georgia; cf. *batonebo*. (8)

Iban Ethnic group from Borneo. (4)

Ibibio A people of Nigeria. (1)

Ibo Cultural group of southern Nigeria. *See also Igbo*. (1)

ibtihāl Supplications to God; these prayers are commonly performed as solo nonmetric *inshād*, especially before the dawn prayer and during Ramadan. (6)

icai nātakam (Also special *nātakam*.) Music drama; form of Tamil drama employing performers who do not rehearse together. (5)

iconography Visual representation of a subject. (4)

iḍakku (also *itaykka*) Variable-pitch hourglass drum of Kerala. (5)

ideograph Graphic depiction of meaning, as in Chinese characters. (4)

'idda General Arabic term indicating specific groupings of musical instruments connected with specific musical arts. (6)

'iddat al-lewa 'Tools of *lewa*', term for an instrumental ensemble in the Gulf states, which accompanies the Afro-Arab *lewa* tradition of song and dance. (6)

'Īd-ĕ-azḥā Muslim holiday commemorating Abraham's sacrifice of Isaac. (5)

idiophone 'Self-sounder', musical instrument (such as a rattle or chime) whose principal sound is the vibration not of a membrane, a string, or the air but of the material or primary material of the instrument itself. (1, 2, 3, 4, 5, 9)

idol kayô (Japan.) *Kayôkyoku*, a major genre of Japanese popular songs. (7)

iduffu Haya large, circular frame drum used in a Muslim ritual dance, *kuzikiri*. (1)

'Īdu'l-fiṭr Muslim holiday celebrating the end of Ramadan. (5)

iekai (Japan.) Ainu responsorial singing in which a group repeats a phrase sung by a leader. (7)

iemoto (Japan.) Master of a school of art. (7, 10)

iertările 'Forgiveness', part of the Romanian wedding ritual, accompanied by specific songs or instrumental tunes. (8)

iet rotaḷās Latvian pastime among youths, including playing games, usually circle dances with singing. (8)

Ifaluk Former spelling of Ifalik, an atoll in Yap State. (9)

Ife Music Editions Publisher of selected works of famous educated and trained composers in Nigeria. (1)

igala Kuna 'language', 'path', or 'way', characteristic of the systematic nature of instrumental music and chanting traditions. (2)

igba Igbo membranophone. (1)

igbá Yoruba gourd held in both hands and struck with ringed fingers. (1)

Igbo Cultural group of southern Nigeria. *See also Ibo.* (1)

igil Upright horsehead fiddle of Tuva, played so as to emphasize harmonic pitches. (6)

igra 'Game' (from the Bulgarian verb *igrae* 'to dance'). Bulgarian term for games and dances, specifically children's musical games. (8)

igranke Spontaneous dance parties in Croatia. (8)

igrovoi khorovad Russian dance game with pantomiming soloists inside a circle of singers. (8)

ihumke (Japan.) Ainu lullaby. (7)

ijala Yoruba hunters' poetry that is sung and may also reproduce aspects of speech tone. (1)

ijala are ode Yoruba hunters' entertainment music. (1)

Ijebu One of the seven principal subgroups of Yoruba peoples. (1)

ijexá (1) Afro-Bahian culture associated with Candomblé; (2) rhythm, style, and dance in Brazilian *afoxé* music. (2)

Ijo Culture group of Nigeria. (1)

ikembe Plucked lamellophone of Burundi. (1)

iki (Japan.) Chic, stylish elegance. (7)

I-Kiribati People of Kiribati. (9)

ikko (Japan.) Hourglass-shaped drum formerly used in *gagaku*. (7)

ikoečki pesni (Also *glasoečki, vozeni.*) Macedonian songs with elaborate melodies. (8)

ikoyeniaka Greek 'family songs,' unaccompanied table songs of Skyros. (8)

Ikuta ryû (Japan.) School of *koto* founded in 1695 by Ikuta *kengyô* (1655–1715). (7)

ilāhī Hymn or song of praise. (6)

ilahije Muslim paraliturgical hymns, also adopted into the religious musical practice of Sephardic Jews in Bosnia-Hercegovina. (8)

ilê Yoruba 'house' or 'temple' in Cuban Santería. (2)

Ile-Ife Religious center of the Yoruba peoples. (1)

ilhamli ashik 'God-inspired poet', Turkish *aşık* thought to have received divine inspiration. (6)

il kosu, i myŏngch'ang 'First the drummer, second the singer'; Korean proverb. (7)

illacu Guatemalan shell rattles strung around the calves of dancers. (2)

illalah Poem or song in Alevī ceremonies, incorporating the *tahlīl* formula, meant to create an atmosphere of *zikr*. (6)

illi Chechen and Ingush historical songs. (8)

'ilm 'Science' (of music), in contrast to practical art, *'amal*. (6)

'ilm al-tajwīd Art of Qur'ānic cantillation. (6)

'ilm-i mūsīqī 'Science of music', referring to the systematization of melodic intervals and scales. (6)

ilo 'Joy', alternative name for the Finnish *kantele*. (8)

il p'ae First grade of Korean *kisaeng*, associated with government offices. (7)

iltama Finnish-American community festival featuring musical performance, poetry, plays, and social dancing. (3)

iltamat Finnish public entertainment that concluded with a one-hour dance. (8)

ilugan (Also *ilujan, ilaguan.*) Tuareg spectacle involving choreographed movements of camels and men. (1)

il verticale Mechanical piano of Italian-speaking Switzerland. (8)

Imahuzi (Japan.) School of *nagauta* (a lyrical *syamisen* genre). (7)

imam (Also *imām.*) (1) Islamic teacher, doctor, scribe, musical leader, religious leader, and interpreter of the Qur'ān. (2) Title for a Shia religious leader. (1, 4, 6)

imāmbārā Building in which Shia services are held to commemorate the martyrdom of Husain and his family. (5)

imayô (Japan.) Ancient popular song genre. (7)

imazighen (Singular, *amazigh.*) 'Free men', indigenous term by which Berber populations of Morocco and Algeria identify themselves. (6)

Imbaya Ifugao harvest festival. (4)

îmbrăcatul 'Dressing of the bride', part of the Romanian wedding ritual, accompanied by specific songs or instrumental tunes. (8)

imbutu Kumbu horn used as a chiefly emblem and considered the most sacred possession of the chiefdom. (1)

imdyazn Professional musicians native to the eastern regions of Morocco. (1)

imeddahen (Also *imdyazen.*) Professional Berber poets who travel from village to village, offering sung commentary on recent social and political affairs. (6)

iména 'Husband', larger half of the Paraguayan *guyrapa* double musical bow. (2)

impact notation Cinematographic technique that measures time between strikes on a drum. (1)

impulsive instrument Plucked or struck instrument; after each impulse the sound rings and dies out. (1)

imzad (1) (Also *anzad.*) Tuareg bowed lute, played by women. (2) Circular monochord

fiddle of the Saharan regions of Algeria and Libya. (1, 6)

imyôn Understanding of the deep meaning and sentiments of Korean *p'ansori* texts. (7)

in (Japan.) Pentatonic scale with a semitone. (7)

inaka uta (Japan.) 'Rural song', term used for folk song before the term *min'yo* 'folk song' was introduced. (7)

inām Gift or reward given to a musician during a performance. (5)

inang Genre of folk dance in Malaysia. (4)

inanga Burundi trough zither with eight to twelve strings. (1)

inanga chuchotée 'Whispered zither', Burundi musical genre in which the *inanga* is used. (1)

inanka Miskitu laments sung by women at wakes. (2)

inarem Ilocos song debate. (4)

indang In West Sumatra, (1) religious-political performance; (2) frame drum. (4)

Indian *rabāb* (Also *dhrupad rabāb.*) Long-necked plucked unfretted lute with skin-covered body and gut strings (obsolete). (5)

indiki Zulu spirits in southern Africa. (1)

indita Narrative song form very similar to the *corrido*, but found in a particular locality within New Mexico; further distinguished by influences from Southwestern Native American music, especially in its rhythms. (3)

Indorock Genre of Dutch rock and roll played by *Indos*, people of mixed Indonesian and European origin. (8)

indunduma Zulu piano-vamp style of *marabi* in South Africa. (1)

infantiles Spanish children's play songs. (8)

ingá Afro-Peruvian novelty circle dance. (2)

ingaku (Japan.) Licentious music. (7)

in'gan munhwajae 'Human treasure', holder of a Korean cultural asset. (7)

Ingassana Arabic name for ethnic groups inhabiting the Tabi Hills of Sudan. (1)

ingermatura Corsican children's game accompanied by verses. (8)

ingetu (Japan.) Resonance hole of the *biwa* (lute) hidden under the string holder. (7)

inharmonicity Quality (for example in instruments excited percussively, such as bells and gongs) arising when the overtones in a complex musical sound are not harmonics of the fundamental. (9)

inherent rhythms Rhythms that may be heard by a listener but are not played as such by any of the performers. (1)

inila-ud Kalinga-Tinggian ensemble of three gongs. (4)

inkin (Japan.) Idiophone used in Buddhist music, a small bowl-shaped bronze instrument with a handle, struck with a mallet. (7)

inner tempo Number of rhythmic impulses per minute, regardless of their periodicity or regularity of occurrence, the distribution of accents, and the presence of a meter. **(9)**

inori (Japan.) *Nô* dance accompanying a confrontation between a priest and the specter of a woman. **(7)**

insempo (Japanese.) Pentatonic scale with semitones. **(10)**

inshād dīnī 'Islamic hymnody'. Melodic vocal recitation of poetry, performed as worship. Principal themes are supplications to and praise of Allah, and praise of the Prophet Muhammad. **(6)**

inshād ṭab' al-naghma Vocal prelude in the Moroccan *nūba*. **(6)**

insi Maranao ring-stop flute. **(4)**

inside-outside Distinction often made in describing social order or musical performance in West Africa. **(1)**

inṣirāf (1) Vocal genre in the Maghribi *nūba*. (2) Specific Maghribi rhythmic mode with a 5/8 or 10/8 cycle. **(6)**

Institute of African Studies Institute in Ghana whose Music and Related Arts section was developed by J. H. Kwabena Nketia. **(1)**

insuba (Also *simbaika*.) Miskitu handleless rattle made from a dry gourd filled with small stones or hard seeds. **(2)**

intermedi Lavish commemorative spectacles hosted by monarchs and aristocrats during the Italian Renaissance, with elaborate scenery, costumes, music, poetry, and dance. **(8)**

International Folk Music Council International society of professional ethnomusicologists. **(1)**

International Library of African Music Series of recordings of African music founded by Hugh Tracey in South Africa. **(1)**

intifāda Palestinian revolt against Israeli rule, from 1987 on. **(6)**

intonatsiia 'Intonation', musicological concept developed by Boleslav Yavorsky and Boris Asaf'ev. **(8)**

iomante (Japan.) Ainu bear cult. **(7)**

i p'ae Second grade of Korean *kisaeng*, employed in entertainment houses. **(7)**

ipála Bolivian special wedding feast song. **(2)**

ipch'ang 'Standing songs', long Korean folk songs, often performed by professionals. **(7)**

þróttir Essential accomplishments of a well-educated Icelandic gentleman, which included rhyming and harping. **(8)**

īqā' (Plural, *īqā'āt*.) 'Falling', 'causing to fall', general Arabic term for rhythmic periods or modes. This term is represented in the titles of early Arabic music theoretical works such as *Kitāb al-īqā'*. **(6)**

iqamat Arabic isorhythmic musical patterns. **(1)**

'iqd (Plural, *'uqūd*.) Tonal unit within each mode of a *nūba* defined by a characteristic succession of intervals. **(6)**

ira 'Leader' in Aymara, one of the halves (male) of the *siku* and several other double-unit panpipes in the central Andes (counterpart of the female half *arca* 'follower'). **(2)**

irak Wayana ceremony that is part of the *marake* initiation ritual. **(2)**

irama Tempo and subdivision levels in Javanese music. **(4)**

'irāq Name of a melodic mode or *maqām*, first mentioned in the late fifth century A.H., eleventh century C.E. **(6)**

Irigwe A people of Nigeria. **(1)**

irizi (1) Drummed rhythm of the Moroccan Berbers. (2) Type of dance tune in the Berber *aḥwash* of the Anti-Atlas Mountains. **(6)**

irki Bolivian animal-horn single-reed-concussion aerophone. **(2)**

ırlayış Popular Turkish musical form. **(6)**

iro (Japan.) (1) Vocal or instrumental ornamentation; (2) section of *gidayû busi* narrated in a style in between melody (*zi* or *zi ai*) and speech (*kotoba*). **(7)**

iro dome (Japan.) Short *gidayû busi syamisen* pattern used as a transition between *zi* (melodic) and *kotoba* (dramatic dialogue) sections. **(7)**

iron-kandzal-fandir Ossetian accordion, a woman's instrument. **(8)**

Iroquois Social Dance song Music performed in association with the longhouse tradition. **(3)**

irpu pandum Madia sacred harvest celebration in Madhya Pradesh. **(5)**

iru (Japan.) Term in *gidayû busi* notation indicating a narrative technique. **(7)**

Iśai Vēḷḷāḷar South Indian upper-middle caste of musicians, dancers, and dance teachers. **(5)**

isal Metric structure of Mappila (Muslim) songs of Kerala. **(5)**

'Isāwiyya Tunisian Sufi brotherhood. **(6)**

iṣbahān Name of a mode, first mentioned by Ibn Sīnā. **(6)**

iscathamiya Secular male a cappella performance tradition from South Africa that became popular worldwide through the rock star Paul Simon's famous collaboration with Ladysmith Black Mambazo. **(3)**

ishia 'Straight', tune type of the Cypriot *tsiattista* genre. **(8)**

'ishqi Love song of Northern Afghanistan. **(5)**

isicathamiya (Also *isicatamiya*.) Step dancing of choirs that blended ragtime and indigenous part singing in South Africa. **(1)**

Isii ryû (Japan.) School of *nô* specializing in *ô tuzumi*. **(7)**

isikunzi Amateur variety shows in South Africa. **(1)**

isimoi Sacred Warao heteroglottal single-reed-concussion aerophone without finger holes. **(2)**

isin densin (Japan.) Wordless or telepathic communication. **(7)**

isingni 'Soul', (1) Miskitu deceased; (2) manifestation of person's soul in a firefly; (3) *isingni ulan*, 'soul mounted', day-long Miskitu curative ritual by shaman to remove a dead person's soul from a seriously ill patient. **(2)**

isinyago Makua masks. **(1)**

iskelmä Finnish term for locally produced popular songs. **(8)**

iskoki Hausa term for spirits. **(1)**

islamei Adighian fast virtuoso solo dance. **(8)**

Island Records Company whose Mango label signed Salif Keita, launching his international career. **(1)**

iso Albanian term for a drone. **(8)**

isometer (Adjective, isometric.) Use of the same metric scheme throughout a piece of music. **(8)**

ison (Greek.) Fixed, wordless drone. **(8)**

ispratnica Festivities held in Serbia when a man departs for military service. **(8)**

isqī al-'iṭāsh 'Give water to the thirsty'. Originally religious chant (*inshād*) sung in Aleppo during droughts and involving elaborate music and dance. **(6)**

isrāj (Also *esraj*.) Bowed long-necked fretted lute combining features of the sitar and the *sāraṅgī*. **(5)**

iss Rest. **(6)**

issei (1) In Japanese music, *nô* instrumental piece for the entrance of a madwoman or a ghost and (2) *kyôgen* instrumental piece for the entrance of a character, a simplified version of *issei*. (3) First-generation Japanese immigrant, especially to the United States. **(7, 10)**

Issô ryû (Japan.) School of *nô* flute (*nôkan*). **(7)**

ist Tone that occurs at the end of a cadence in a Persian *gūshe*. **(6)**

istiftāḥ Maghribi instrumental or vocal prelude in free rhythm. **(6)**

istihlāl Medieval Arabic vocal prelude in free rhythm. **(6)**

istikhbār Improvised prelude in the Algerian and Libyan *nūba*. **(6)**

isudaeyŏp Slow second piece in a Korean *kagok* song cycle, performed by a female; see *ch'osudaeyŏp*. **(7)**

iṭaykka (Also *iḍakka*.) Small hourglass drum of Kerala. **(5)**

Itelmen (Japan.) Minority ethnic group in the Kamchatk peninsula in eastern Siberia. **(7)**

iti age (Japan.) Tuning of the *sansin* (Okinawan three-stringed lute). **(7)**

itigen kin (Also *suma goto*.) One-stringed long Japanese zither. **(7)**

itikotu tyô (Japan.) *Gagaku* scale built on the note *itikotu*. **(7)**

itku 'Cry, weep', term for the lament, one of the oldest Finnish song genres. **(8)**

ito (Japan.) Extinct genre of work songs in the Amami Islands. **(7)**

ittyô (Japan.) *Nô* performance by one singer and one drummer. **(7)**

ittyû busi (Japan.) Genre of narrative *syamisen* music. **(7)**

Ituri Forest Large tropical forest in central Africa. **(1)**

iúna Afro-Brazilian rhythmic pattern. **(2)**

ivy leaf Reportedly used in Ireland as an aerophone that vibrated against the upper lip to make a variably high-pitched sound. **(8)**

iwi Yoruba genre associated with ancestors and often sung in a nasal falsetto. **(1)**

iyal Literature of Tamil Nadu. **(5)**

iyá'lù (Also *iya ilu*.) Yoruba 'mother drum', principal instrument in a Yoruba drum ensemble. **(1)**

iyohay ochis (Japan.) Ainu lyric songs (*sinotcha*) about sad memories. **(7)**

izglasa (Also *izvika*.) 'Out loud', male vocal genre of Montenegro, characterized by a tense vocal technique. **(8)**

izibongo Poetry of praise associated with chieftainship in groups of Ngoni descendants. **(1)**

izli (Plural, *izlan*.) (1) Berber songs performed for *ahidus* and *ahwash*. (2) Light, amorous musical genre performed by the *imdyazn* (Moroccan Berber troupe). **(1, 6)**

Izumi ryû (Japan.) School of *nô* specializing in *kyôgen kata*. **(7)**

izumo goto (Japan.) Former name of *yakumo goto*. **(7)**

izvika (Also *izglasa*.) 'Called out', male vocal genre of Montenegro, characterized by a tense vocal technique. **(8)**

izvorna muzika 'Music of the source or spring', music played on Macedonian radio by a folk orchestra. **(8)**

izvorni 'Original', term used for Croatian songs and dances assumed to be ancient, native, and free of foreign influences. **(8)**

izwirrign Moroccan wedding song. **(6)**

jabadao Breton figure dance. **(8)**

jabd 'Captivation', ecstatic state of a Sufi devotee. **(6)**

jab-jab Trinidadian carnival band characterized by devil costumes. **(2)**

Jabo Subgroup of the Kru-speaking peoples of Liberia. **(1)**

jabo Heavy brass rings given by Tuareg women to daughters and worn on the thighs until the daughter gives birth to a child. **(1)**

jadīd 'The new', term for newer, Western-influenced Egyptian repertoires from the 1930s and 1940s. **(6)**

jafra Type of Palestinian wedding song. **(6)**

jāgaran (1) All-night event of singing and dancing, usually devoted to a deity or ancestor. (2) *Gondhal* ritual theater in Maharashtra. **(5)**

jahala (Also *jahla*.) Clay pot used as an idiophone by pearl fishermen of the Gulf region. **(6)**

jahārka (Also *jahārkāh*.) One of the major notes of the Arab fundamental scale. **(6)**

Jaiminīya School of Sāmavedic chanting. **(5)**

jaipongan Sundanese indigenous popular dance form. **(4)**

jairo Mandinka general praise. **(1)**

jajmān (Also *jajmānī, yajmān*.) Patron, one who conducts or sponsors a ritual. **(5)**

jajmānī (Also *jajmān*.) Hereditary patron-client relationship. **(5)**

ja-khe Thai three-stringed floor zither in the shape of a crocodile. **(4)**

jalacomapacuaper Sung or recited Maleku prayers for protection against human wrongdoing or evil spirits. **(2)**

jalajala Colombian bunch rattle. **(2)**

jalāla Rhythmic chanting of poetry of praise, accompanied by drums, in Omani wedding ceremonies and performed by a *ḥalqat almālid*. **(6)**

jalanpong Bronze gong-chime ensemble in Tidore. **(4)**

jaleo Encouraging and admiring shouts of the audience in a Spanish flamenco performance. **(8)**

jali (Plural, *jalolu*.) Professional musicians among the Maninka of Guinea and Mandinka of Gambia. **(1)**

jalikumolu Miscellaneous commentary of the Mandinka. **(1)**

jaliya-type ensembles Groups featuring a *jali* or professional singer. **(1)**

jālra Small, flat cymbals of Tamil Nadu and Kerala. **(5)**

jaltarangam (Also *jaltarang*.) Set of porcelain bowls filled with different levels of water, played by striking the edges with bamboo sticks. **(5)**

jalwih Palestinian song and dance for the bride's wedding eve celebration, usually conducted by an older woman from the village. **(6)**

jam' 'Collection', 'group'. (1) Sufi assembly. (2) Joining of tetrachords to create different *maqāmāt*. **(6)**

jamiluddin Yakan wedding song. **(4)**

jamikili (Also *jamiḍiki*.) Drum played by plucking a string attached to the head. **(5)**

Jamoan Jamaican-Sāmoan reggae, cultivated by the I Don't Know Band, a musical ensemble based in Saipan. **(9)**

jamundiro Patronymic Mandinka praise that contains references to the past. **(1)**

jan Santal charm song believed to have curative powers. **(5)**

janaka (Also *mēḷa*.) Seven-tone scale capable of generating ragas. **(5)**

janānā 'To inform', solo devotional songs performed by Hindu devotees in Orissa. **(5)**

janapada gēyālu People's songs; folk songs in Andhra Pradesh. **(5)**

janapada sāhityam People's literature; folk literature in Andhra Pradesh. **(5)**

jangam Devotee of Shiva and performer of Shaivite narrative songs. **(5)**

jangama 'One who moves', mendicant. **(5)**

jangar (Also *jaṇar*.) Ingassana lyre. **(1)**

jangī 'Warrior'. In Baluchistan, warrior or bard who sings epic tales. **(6)**

Jāṇi Latvian celebration of the midsummer solstice. **(8)**

jank Andalusian harp. **(6)**

jank al-miṣrī (Also *jank misrī*.) 'Egyptian harp', described in the anonymous *Kashf al-humūm*. **(6)**

jantar Stick zither of northwest India related to the North Indian *bīn*. **(5)**

jantarka Bolivian two-tone pipe played by women during carnival. **(2)**

janya Karnatak raga derived from the *janaka* scale. **(5)**

jarabe Mexican *son* intended especially for dancing. **(2)**

jarana (1) Nahua five-stringed hourglass-shaped chordophone, often with double courses. (2) (Also *guitarra de golpe*.) Mexican folk guitar in a variety of shapes, sizes, courses, strings, and regional types, played primarily as a harmonic or metrical accompaniment to singing or melody instruments. (3) Mexican couple dance found in the state of Yucatan and resembling the Spanish *jota* in choreography and meter. (4) Afro-Peruvian competitive song form. (5) Early twentieth-century private party in lower-class neighborhoods of Peru. **(2, 3)**

jaravyja pieśni Belarusan songs performed during the harvest of the spring sowing. **(8)**

Jarawa A people of northern Nigeria. **(1)**

jārī (Also *jhāl*.) Hand cymbals. **(5)**

jāriya (Plural, *jawārī*.) General term for a slave girl who was a musical entertainer at early Arab courts; cf. *qayna*. **(6)**

jarocho (1) *Mestizo* culture of Veracruz, Mexico. (2) Dance style originally from the Mexican state of Veracruz and especially popular among Mexican *folklorico* dance groups in Los Angeles. **(2, 3)**

jas Compositions sung in praise of the Mother Goddess in Madhya Pradesh. **(5)**

jataka Story of a past life of the Buddha. **(4)**

jatā-jatin 'Boy-girl', folk operetta sung by women in Mithila. **(5)**

jata pandum Gond festival that takes place in autumn. **(5)**

jati South Indian dance master's spoken syllables. **(5)**

jāti (1) Ancient mode class. (2) Class of rhythms in Karnatak music. (3) (Also *jāt.*) Caste or species. **(5)**

jatisvaram Second part of the *mōhini āṭṭam* dance. **(5)**

jātrā (1) Bengali folk theater; (2) fairs and festivals connected with deities in Nepal. **(5)**

jātra Village fair in Karnataka. **(5)**

jatsi 'Jazz' (Finnish). **(8)**

jatung utang Kenyah wooden xylophone. **(4)**

jauje Hausa double-headed hourglass-shaped tension drum, reserved for royalty. **(1)**

javā Triangular coconut-shell plectrum used with the *sarod* and other instruments. **(5)**

javāb-e āvāz In Persian classical music, an immediate instrumental response to a phrase sung by the vocalist. **(6)**

jāvaḷi (1) Light vocal genre used to accompany South Indian dance performances. (2) Sung Karnatak performances. **(5)**

jawābī 'Respondents', chorus of a singing group in Balochistan. **(5)**

Jawaiian Hawaiian adaptation of reggae, most popular in the 1980s. **(9)**

jaway Ecuadorian agricultural harvest song. **(2)**

jawbone Jamaican *salo* song type. **(2)**

jawq Small chamber ensemble that has traditionally performed *nūbāt* in Algeria. **(6)**

jawza (Also *jawz, jōza, jōz'e.*) Four-stringed spike fiddle used in Iraqi musical traditions, similar to the Persian *kamanche.* **(6)**

jayamaṅgala gâta Sinhala blessing songs. **(5)**

Jazīrat al-Maghrib 'Island of the West', early Arab term for North Africa. **(6)**

jazz balett (1) Swedish ballet accompanied by live jazz. (2) Gymnastic movement for young people and adults, accompanied by jazz or jazz-derived recordings. **(8)**

jazz bands Street bands in Kinshasha playing music unlike American jazz. **(1)**

jednojke Single-pipe duct flute of Bosnia-Hercegovina. **(8)**

jehio Guaymí dance that begins in a single file and ends in a circle. **(2)**

jejy Singly or multiply stringed bowed lute of Madagascar. **(1)**

jeke Vai basket rattle. **(1)**

jeli Man who specializes in singing praises, often playing the harp-lute as accompaniment. **(1)**

jeliklu Mandinka men who sing praises. **(1)**

jelimuso Mandinka women who sing praises. **(1)**

jemblung Vocal performance of Banyumas *gamelan.* **(4)**

jènbe Conical drum with a single stretched-skin drumhead. **(1)**

jenge BaNgombe Pygmies' men's society, featuring masking. **(1)**

jenglong (1) Cirebonese low-pitch horizontal kettle gongs; (2) Sundanese set of six hanging gongs. **(4)**

jengsi Sisaala seventeen-keyed xylophones, normally played in pairs. **(1)**

jēn-paduna Songs performed by Jēnu Kurumba tribal people while gathering honey. **(5)**

jhāl (1) Brass cymbals played in Trinidad with *tāssā* and bass drums. (2) Locally made variant of traditional Indian cymbals played by Hindu musicians and singers in Guyana. **(5)**

jhālā Fast, virtuosic improvisatory section with rhythmic pulse following *joṛ* in Hindustani instrumental music. **(5)**

jhāñjh (1) Pair of cymbals. (2) Idiophone consisting of four wooden frames with small cymbals, two held in each hand. (3) Trinidadian cymbals in the *tassa* ensemble. **(2, 5)**

jharpat Gond music and dance form of Madhya Pradesh. **(5)**

jhelā Responsorial singers in *samāj-gāyan* devotional singing. **(5)**

jhika *Sistrum* played by Fiji Indians. **(5)**

jhora gīt Magar women's songs performed at the Tij festival in Nepal. **(5)**

jhūmar Gond music and dance form of Madhya Pradesh. **(5)**

jhyāli Cymbals in Nepal. **(5)**

jhyāure (1) Popular dance piece in Nepal; (2) 6/8 and 12/8 meters in Nepal. **(5)**

jiahua (China.) 'Adding flowers'; term for the technique of embellishing the main skeleton melody. **(7)**

jiajian sheng (China.) Keyed *sheng* with chromatic capability. **(7)**

jiangjing (China.) Buddhist sermon. **(7)**

Jiangnan siznu (Also *Jiang nan si zhu.*) (1) 'Silk', music performed on string and bamboo instruments from south of the Yangzi (Yangtze) River. (2) 'Music from South of the Yangzi River', chamber ensemble popularized in eastern central China and around the city of Shanghai. **(3, 7)**

jianzipu (China.) Abbreviated ideogram tablature used in *qin* music, in which characters are condensed into symbols. **(7)**

jiaose (China.) Role types. **(7)**

jíbaros 'Country folk' of Puerto Rico. **(2)**

jibendiao (China.) Fundamental melody in *Suzhou tanci.* **(7)**

jidur Large barrel drum of Indonesia. **(4)**

Jie A Karamojong people of Uganda. **(1)**

jiegu (China.) Cylindrical drum with cord-bracing struck by beaters, popularized during the Sui and Tang dynasties. **(7)**

jiezi (China.) Borrowed notes. **(7)**

jig (Also *gigue.*) Lively English, Scottish, and Irish dance in 6/8 time. **(8)**

jihad (Arabic.) Holy war; several such wars were fought in Africa in the past. **(1)**

jikay Comic theatrical genre of Malaysia and southern Thailand. **(4)**

jikong yinyue (China.) Music for the worship of Confucius. **(7)**

jíkuri Peyote used by the Tarahumara. **(2)**

jīm Conch trumpet. **(6)**

jindua Song genre of the Punjab in solo-chorus style. **(5)**

jineteada (Also *jineteada y doma.*) Argentine spectacle organized by traditionalist societies, local municipal authorities, or merchants, featuring traditional music and dance. **(2)**

jing (China.) Actor of painted-face roles. **(7)**

jingbai (China.) One of the two dramatic speeches in Peking opera, which is basically in Peking dialect. **(7)**

jinghu (China.) (1) Instrument similar to the *erhu* but smaller and with body and neck made of bamboo rather than wood. (2) Leading high-pitched two-stringed fiddle used in Peking opera. **(3, 7)**

jingju (China.) Peking opera. **(7)**

jinn Ambivalent spirit that may cause harm to humans. **(6)**

jins (Plural, *ajnās.*) From Greek *genus*, term referring to a tetrachord or pentachord from which a modal scale may be constructed. **(6)**

jirba (Also *gurba, habban.*) Term for bagpipes in the Gulf states. **(6)**

jitarrón Flat-backed *charango*-like instrument played during the rainy season in southern Peru and northern Bolivia. **(2)**

jiti Popular music in Zimbabwe, combining African drumming and European harmonies in responsorial form. **(1)**

jitterbug Jazz variation of the two-step, in which mixed couples vigorously swing and twirl in quick, often jerky, movements. **(9)**

jiuge (China.) Drinking songs. **(7)**

joaldunak Basque masked carnival characters. **(8)**

joc Closed circle dances of Romanians in the Pannonian zone of Serbia. **(8)**

Volume Key: **6**, Middle East; **7**, East Asia; **8**, Europe; **9**, Australia and the Pacific Islands; **10**, The World's Music.

jocho Popular music in Zimbabwe in the 1970s that showed little European influence. **(1)**

jocul de pomana 'Alms dance', performed in Banat, Romania, for those who die young. **(8)**

jodel 'Yodel' (German), Swiss singing technique involving rapid shifting between chest voice and head voice. **(8)**

jodellied Swiss verse songs that incorporate yodels as choruses. **(8)**

jōdippaṭṭu Vocal duet in Karnatak music. **(5)**

jodler Austrian yodels. **(8)**

joge bungin Samawan women's dance for palace events. **(4)**

joged (Also *jogett.*) Genre of popular social dance, common to Malaysia and Indonesia. **(4)**

joget gamelan Dance-drama of Terengganu, accompanied by *gamelan.* **(4)**

Jogī Caste of hereditary mendicant musicians in Uttar Pradesh. **(5)**

jogīā sāraṅgī Bowed, unfretted, two-stringed lute played by Jogīs to accompany their balled singing. **(5)**

Johannesburg International Arts Alive Festival Music festival established in 1992 to encourage experimental interchanges between international and local artists. **(1)**

John Frum movement Religious-political movement ("cargo cult") that originated in Tanna in the 1940s. **(9)**

Johnny Walker Guitar-fingering pattern used in Nigeria. **(1)**

joi Northern Thai courtship singing. **(4)**

joik Saami vocal genre. **(8)**

jokulatori Czech and Slovak medieval professional musicians and singers. **(8)**

Jola (Diola) Cultural group of the Cassamance region of Senegal. **(1)**

jolting Playing technique for log-idiophones, in which the player hits the instrument with the end of a thick stick or a bundle of sticks; cf. *striking.* **(9)**

jondo Panamanian single-headed drum played with the hands. **(2)**

jongleresses Twelfth-century French female traveling musicians who performed for harvest gatherings and for the amusement of the aristocratic elite. **(8)**

jongleur Medieval French minstrel who sang heroic chants. **(8)**

jongo (1) Kasena-Nankani stamping dance. (2) Afro-Brazilian social dance. **(1, 2)**

Jonkunnu Jamaican slave celebration for the Christmas holiday. **(2)**

joobai Vai male masquerader. **(1)**

Jopará Widespread language mixture of Guaraní and Spanish in Paraguay. **(2)**

jōqa Troupe of singer-poets, dancers, and musicians in the Arabian Peninsula. **(6)**

joṛ Solo instrumental section with a recurring pulse in the introductory *ālāp* of a Hindustani raga performance. **(5)**

joṛā 'Pair', the two main playing strings on a *chitrāli sitār* of the North West Frontier Province. **(5)**

Jordanites Members of an African-, Catholic-, and Protestant-derived syncretic religion of Guyana. **(2)**

joṛi Pair of cane duct flutes connected to one mouthpiece. **(5)**

joropo European-derived "national" couple dance, music genre, and event of Venezuela. **(2)**

jōruri (Also *zyôruri.*) Traditional Japanese narrative ballad originally accompanied by the *biwa* and later by the *syamisen* 'samisen'; combined with puppet theater to develop a musical drama of high artistic quality called *bunraku.* **(3, 7)**

jota (1) Spanish folk dance and song in triple meter, developed from ancient poetic forms. (2) Spanish song and dance form using compound duple meter and hemiola or *sesquiáltera* (6/8 + 3/4), from which the *cueca* and other American forms may have developed. (3) Basque chain dance. (4) Aragonese couple dance in quick triple time, accompanied by castanets. (5) Triple-time Spanish-derived dance. **(2, 3, 4, 8)**

jouhikko Finnish bowed lyre. **(8)**

Journée Internationale du Créole 'International Creole Day', annual celebration founded in the 1980s and held on 28 October in Martinique. **(2)**

jovem guarda Term derived from a television program (*Jovem Guarda*, 1965–1969) in São Paulo; later came to refer generically to *iê-iê-iê* (from the Beatles' "Yeah! Yeah! Yeah!"), early Brazilian rock and roll. **(2)**

jōze Iraqi spike fiddle. **(6)**

J-pops (Japan.) Generic term for contemporary Japanese popular songs, excluding *enka.* **(7)**

jrāna Tunisian term for the violin; *see kamanja.* **(6)**

juba Neo-African social dance featuring a two-player drum, practiced by Afro-Haitians in nineteenth-century New Orleans. **(3)**

juche (Also *juche sasang.*) North Korean ideology of self-reliance. **(7)**

juco Small friction drum once found in the Masaya area of Nicaragua. **(2)**

juergas Spanish *gitano* jam sessions, one of the earliest contexts for flamenco. **(8)**

juey Puerto Rican 'crab' dance choreography. **(2)**

jugalbandī (1) Pair of Hindustani soloists who play instruments of contrasting timbre. (2) South Indian concert combining Hindustani and Karnatak instruments. **(5)**

jùjú (Also *juju.*) (1) Yoruba tambourine. (2) Yoruba musical genre originating in Lagos around 1932 featuring a singer-banjoist, a *ṣẹ̀kẹ̀rẹ́*, and a *jùjú.* (3) Yoruba musical genre exported from Nigeria and popular in European "world music" and world beat. **(1, 3, 8)**

julajula Large panpipes of La Paz and northern Potosí departments, Bolivia. **(2)**

juljul Musical bell. **(6)**

Juluka South African musical duo formed by Johnny Clegg and Sipho Mchunu; it disbanded in 1985. **(1)**

jumbie (1) Montserrat drum identical to the *babala*, but approximately 76 centimeters in diameter. (2) Religious dance and music, identical to the country dance. (3) Spirit that can be summoned from the grave by music. **(2)**

jumpa Swedish two-step, a local variation of ballroom dancing. **(8)**

jump-in dance (Also jumping dance.) In the Bahamas, a solo dance in which the current dancer selects the next dancer to "jump in." **(2)**

Jump-Up Day New Year's Day emancipation celebration in Montserrat. **(2)**

junačke pesme 'Heroic songs', Serbo-Croatian epics, accompanied by a lute. **(8)**

jungga Two-stringed lute of Sumba. **(4)**

jungle music (Also drum 'n' bass.) Mostly instrumental dance style of music emanating from black communities in Britain. **(3)**

junkafunk Innovation of the Bahamian musical group Bahamen, involving using junkanoo rhythms on modern electronic instruments. **(2)**

junkanoo In the Bahama Islands, traditional *goombay* music performed by acoustic instruments in the context of junkanoo parades during the Christmas season. **(2)**

juoigan Fjeld Saami term for *joiking.* **(8)**

juoi'gat joik Saami genre thought to heighten relationships of copresence among ancestors, kinfolk, neighbors, animals, trees, and other features of the landscape or other inanimate objects. **(8)**

juoigos Saami songs that refer to various subjects to master an inhospitable environment. **(8)**

Jurjeŭskija Belarusan St. George's Day. **(8)**

jüüz (Also *jüüzli.*) Swiss natural yodeling of Muotatal. **(8)**

juwwāk (Also *shabāba.*) End-blown flute of North Africa. **(6)**

juzhong (China.) Types of drama that differ from one another mainly in dialect. **(7)**

jwé St. Lucian play activities often accompanied by singing and drumming. **(2)**

ka St. Lucian barrel-shaped, single-headed membranophone played with the bare hands. **(2)**

ka (Japan.) *See tonkori.* **(7)**

kàakàakii (Also *kakaki*.) Hausa long trumpet, made of thin brass or metal from a kerosene tin. **(1)**

kaba (1) Malay storytelling accompanied by *biola* (violin). (2) West Sumatra narratives with two-stringed fiddles. (3) Near Eastern term sometimes used by Albanian flute players to name performances. **(4, 8)**

kaba gajda Large, low-pitched bagpipe of the Rhodope Mountains of Bulgaria. **(8)**

kabak kemane Turkish bowed spike lute. **(6)**

kabardinka Ossetian couple dance; see *khonga-kaft*. **(8)**

kabaya Close-fitting, long-sleeved women's blouse of Sunda. **(4)**

kabbāde Heavy rattle with metal disks attached to the links of a chain; it is lifted and shaken by athletes in the Iranian *zūr-khāne*. **(6)**

kabita Popular Tuluva women's field-song genre; sung during the rice-planting season. **(5)**

kabosa (Also *kabosy*.) Plucked lute of Madagascar that is identical to the *qubuz*, played in Arabia from c. 500 to 1500 C.E. **(1)**

Kabu hinmoku (Japan.) 'Items of Song and Dance', ten-volume dictionary of *gagaku* by Ogawa Morinaka (1760–1823). **(7)**

kabuki Highly stylized traditional Japanese play with singing, instrumental music, and dancing; an important music-dance theatrical form established in the Edo period (1600–1867). **(3, 7)**

kabuki odori (Japan.) Musical dance drama first performed by a female troupe led by a woman named Izumo no Okuni at the beginning of the Edo period (c. 1600), which became the foundation of *kabuki*. **(7)**

kabupaten Regency, administrative district in Sunda and Cirebon. **(4)**

kaca-kaca Sundanese structure symbolizing the center of the universe. **(4)**

kacapi (1) Large eighteen-stringed zither from Sunda; (2) Malay tube zither played solo; (3) Makassarese boat-shaped two-stringed lute. **(4)**

kacapian Modern *kacapi*-accompanied vocal music. **(4)**

kacaping Buginese boat-shaped two-stringed lute. **(4)**

kacapi-suling Instrumental version of *tembang Sunda*. **(4)**

kaccēri Concert of Karnatak music. **(5)**

kachacha Dance that involves a set of single-headed goblet-shaped drums and sometimes a two-note xylophone. **(1)**

kachi-kachi Japanese-Hawaiian plantation term for the scratching of a *güiro*; in Hawai'i,

generic term for Puerto Rican dance-music. **(9)**

kada (Japan.) Buddhist chant (*syômyô*) for praising buddhas, bodhisattvas, and other symbols of Buddhism. **(7)**

kaḍaga Silver bracelets worn by *sōma* dancer in Karnataka. **(5)**

kadambaka 'Series, collection'; early name for *rāgamālikā*. **(5)**

kadamjāi (Also *ziyarātgāx*.) Holy place of pilgrimage or worship. **(6)**

kadans (Also *kadans-ranpa* 'cadence'.) (1) *Konpa*-like genre developed in Haiti by Wébert Sicot; (2) Haitian-derived musical genre of Martinique. **(2)**

kadavu Poetic verse; text providing the principal structure for *mān bhaṭṭ ākhyān*. **(5)**

kadeg Ossetian epic song performed by a soloist (*kadeganag*) who provides his own instrumental accompaniment. **(8)**

kaḍime Irula clay barrel drum. **(5)**

Kadīrī Major Sufi *tarikat* of the Muslim world, which entered the Ottoman Empire in the fifteenth century. **(6)**

kado barai (Japan.) *See kôzin kyô.* **(7)**

Kadono ryû (Japan.) School of *nô* specializing in *ô tuzumi*. **(7)**

kadril Dutch quadrille that usually consisted of four or five figures having different tunes in 2/4 or 6/8 time. **(8)**

kadrilj Swedish contra dance, especially in southern and eastern Sweden. **(8)**

kaede (Also *kaete*.) In Japan, second melody line played with the original melody line (*honte*) of a piece. **(7)**

kaede siki (Japan.) '*Kaede* style', contrapuntal arrangement for an additional instrumental part. **(7)**

kaeryang akki Modern Korean modified instruments. **(7)**

kaete (Japan.) *See kaede.* **(7)**

kafa Adighian competitive dance. **(8)**

kafana (1) Macedonian café that features the performance of music. (2) 'Café', musical classification used by Vojvodinan Serbs describing where music takes place. **(8)**

kaff Social dance of Upper Egypt in which one or more veiled women parade, pivot, advance, and retreat before a row of men. **(6)**

kaff al-'arab Common bedouin dance involving one or more female dancers interacting with a row of male singers. **(6)**

kaffeehaus 'Coffeehouse'. In nineteenth-century Germany and Austria, a place for listening to popular arrangements of music. **(8)**

kaffriñgnā Dance and music genre associated with African-Portuguese performance traditions in Sri Lanka. **(5)**

kāfi Mystical poetry of the Punjab and Sindh. **(5)**

kagaek Korean professional singer. **(7)**

kagami ita (Japan.) Back wall of the *nô* stage, painted with a pine tree. **(7)**

kagami no ma (Japan.) Room at the end of the entranceway of the *nô* stage where actors put on their masks and instrumentalists tune and warm up. **(7)**

kage bayasi (Japan.) Another term for *geza ongaku*. **(7)**

kageki (Japan.) Genre of Okinawan music drama, created in the late nineteenth century, combining court and folk traditions. **(7)**

kagok Long narrative song cycles of Korea. **(7)**

kagoksŏng-ujo Korean melodic mode with long melismatic phrases and wide vibrato. **(7)**

kagong Bataan curing ritual. **(4)**

kagul (1) Maguindanao scraper-type instrument; (2) Tiruray suspended percussion beams. **(4)**

kagura (Japan.) (1) Generic term for Shinto (Sintô) music and dance; (2) *nô* dance performed by a goddess or shrine maiden. **(7)**

kagura bue (Also *yamato bue*.) In Japan, flute for *mikagura* (Shinto music and dance at the imperial court). **(7)**

kahale Indigenous brass instruments of Karnataka. **(5)**

kahco (Japan.) Single-headed frame drum used by Ainu female shamans. **(7)**

k'aho Hausa horn. **(1)**

kahran kaság ngere Suyá big turtle songs for the dry season. **(2)**

kahua Main celebratory ritual on Seram. **(4)**

kaiga Mordvinian zither. **(8)**

kaikkottikkali Clap dance; village dance form in Tamil Nadu. **(5)**

kailao 'Uvean and Tongan men's dance performed with clubs. **(9)**

kain Length of batik worn as a skirt in Sunda. **(4)**

kaipian (China.) Musical prelude sung before the storytelling proper in *Suzhou tanci*. **(7)**

kaiso (1) Hausa word suggested as one of the origins of the word *calypso*; (2) staged calypso in Trinidad. **(2)**

kājal Charcoal used by women as eye makeup. **(5)**

kajalī (Also *kajarī*.) (1) 'Dark eyes', romantic songs for the rainy season in North India; also sung in Trinidad. (2) Tambourine played by Fiji Indians. **(5)**

kajar Horizontal kettle gong of Lombok. **(4)**

kajda (Also *glas*.) 'Note', Serbian concept of a melodic type, distinguished by social occasion, musical form, textual content, and ethnic or geographic designation. **(8)**

kakalaku Ceremonial ululation of women in Sumba. **(4)**

Volume Key: **6**, Middle East; **7**, East Asia; **8**, Europe; **9**, Australia and the Pacific Islands; **10**, The World's Music.

kakeai (Japan.) (1) Style of alternate playing by multiple performers; (2) segment of a *nô* play and its performance style, in which two or more characters chant a dialogue in an unfixed rhythm; (3) ensemble technique involving alternate performances of a piece by different *syamisen* schools or in different genres. (7)

kakegoe (Japan.) Nonsemantic vocal calls or signals by instrumental players or folk singers. (7)

kakeri (Japan.) *Nô* dance expressing the restless mood of a madwoman or the ghost of a warrior. (7)

kake zume (Japan.) Fixed *koto* pattern occurring at the beginning of each phrase of *kumi uta* (song cycle). (7)

kaki te (Japan.) *Koto* technique involving plucking two strings simultaneously. (7)

kakko (Japan.) (1) Stick-struck double-headed cylindrical drum of Chinese origin used in *gagaku*; (2) *nô* dance derived from popular music of the Muromati period (1334–1573). (7)

kakolintang Maranao art of playing the *kulintang*. (4)

kakoxa Two-stringed bowed lute inspired by seventeenth- or eighteenth-century Iberian stringed instruments. (1)

kaksi (Also *ch'önyö.*) Young maiden, a character in a Korean village ritual play. (7)

kaku (Japan.) Third note in the scale *gosei*. (7)

kaku zume (Japan.) Square *koto* picks. (7)

Kakyô (Japan.) 'Mirror of the flower', *nô* treatise by Zeami Motokiyo (c. 1363–1443). (7)

kakyoku (Japan.) Generic term for (1) short vocal pieces or (2) short solo vocal pieces in the style of Western art music, including those by Japanese composers. (7)

kaladki Belarusan carols of the winter song cycle. (8)

kalai Art. (5)

kalakiya Sudanese entertainment song, performed by men while drinking date wine. (1)

kālakṣēpam Musical epic storytelling and preaching genre, performed by a lead singer or preacher playing wooden clappers and accompanied by a small orchestra. (5)

kalaleng Bontok nose flute of the *te-er* ritual. (4)

kalamatiano Dance of the Greek mainland, important in Cyprus. (8)

kalangan Sama strophic fishing song. (4)

kalangan magsangkalia Sama shark-fishing song. (4)

kalangan taebba Sama shallow-reef-fishing song. (4)

kalangu Hausa double-headed hourglass-shaped tension drum, associated with butchers and recreation. (1)

kalatong (Also *kalutang.*) Bamboo or wooden percussion sticks of the Philippines. (4)

Kalāvant Professional, highly skilled singer or instrumentalist in the Hindustani tradition. (5)

kalavantulu (Also *bhogum, sani.*) Female temple dancers in Andhra Pradesh. (5)

ka law Southern Thai Buddhist ritual ensemble. (4)

kalektyŭnaje halašeńnie Collective wailing during World War II for Soviet soldiers, partisans, and inhabitants of burned villages. (8)

kalektyvy Belarusan amateur rural ensembles. (8)

kalela Zambian name of the genre *beni*. (1)

kalenda (Also *calenda.*) (1) Ancient African song-dance, precursor of calypso. (2) Caribbean variations on a West African stick fight-dance with musical accompaniment. (3) Trinidadian martial sport-dance accompanied by drumming and song. (4) Neo-African social dance practiced by Afro-Haitians in nineteenth-century New Orleans. (2, 3)

kalenderi Common melodic mode in Turkish folk music; cf. *qalandar*. (6)

kalenge Kasena-Nankani metal pails or large tins. (1)

Kalevala Finno-Karelian epic, whose text was sung at all social occasions. (8)

kālgūc āṭ Kota dance performed at the beginning of any set of dances. (5)

kalimusta (1) Kalinga love song. (2) Bontok long solo song. (4)

kalindo Northeast Sulawesi bar zither. (4)

kalon'ny fahiny Operas in which Malagasy artists drew from legends on patriotic themes, or on daily life. (1)

kalpanā saṅgīta Improvised music. (5)

kalpana svara (Also *svara kalpana.*) Improvised solfège passages in Karnatak music that return to a main theme. (5)

kalpita (Also *kalpita saṅgīta.*) 'Already conceived'; composed music. (5)

kalusschellen Clapper bell of canton Glarus, Switzerland. (8)

kalyāṇam Marriage. (5)

kamaicā (Also *kamāychā.*) Bowed unfretted lute played by the Manganihārs of Rajasthan. (5)

Kamakura (Japan.) Period from 1192 to 1333. (7)

kamān (Also *kamānja, kamānche.*) Generic term for unfretted spike fiddle in the Arab world. It is also often used to describe the Western violin, which has come into widespread use. (6)

k'aman Long rectangular three- or four-stringed fiddle of Armenia. (6)

k'amanch'a Long Armenian spike fiddle with three or four strings and a round, skin-covered, often beautifully decorated body. (6)

kamanche (Also *kemanche.*) Persian spike fiddle. (5)

kamanja (1) North African bowed lute, held vertically on the knee. (2) Adapted Arabic violin. (1, 3)

kamānja kabīra European viola, used in Algerian ensembles by the late nineteenth century. (6)

Kāmasūtra Medieval Indian manual of love and courtesan life. (5)

kambala Miri dance of initiation. (1)

kambori Torajan song performed by men to greet the day. (4)

Kamehameha Day Hawaiian state holiday honoring King Kamehameha I (1758?–1819), the monarch who first united the islands. (9)

kamele ngoni Wassoulou six-stringed harp. (1)

kami agari (Japan.) Closing section of *mikagura* (Shinto music and dance performed at the imperial court), to send off the gods. (7)

kami asobi (Japan.) Middle section of *mikagura* (Shinto music and dance performed at the imperial court), to entertain the gods. (7)

kami gakari (Japan.) Kanze and Hôsyô schools of *nô*, specializing in the main role (*site*) and the attendant role (*ture*). (7)

kamigata (Japan.) Kyôto-Ôsaka area. (7)

kamigata nagauta (Japan.) *Ziuta* repertoire (*syamisen* music) consisting of through-composed verses of a single poem. (7)

kami mai (Japan.) Fastest *nô* dance, associated with the role of a young god. (7)

kami mukae (Japan.) Section of *yakumo goto* performed as festival music for the Ômoto sect of Shinto, to welcome the gods. (7)

kami nô (Also *waki nô.*) Japanese *nô* plays in which the main character is a god or a messenger of a god. (7)

kami okuri (Japan.) Section of a Shinto ceremony in which the gods are sent off. (7)

kami orosi (Japan.) Beginning section of *mikagura* (Shinto music and dance performed at the imperial court), to summon the gods. (7)

kampfrichter 'Fight judges', Swiss officials who judge yodels in competitive festivals. (8)

kampita Ornamental shake. (5)

kamsāḷe (1) *Katha* tradition in Karnataka. (2) Medium-size cymbal. (5)

Kamulaan Mindanao highlands festival. (4)

kamuychikap omante (Japan.) Ainu owl cult. (7)

kamuy yukar (Japan.) 'Mythic epic', oldest Ainu narrative repertoire. (7)

kan (Japan.) Tone produced on the *ô tuzumi* and *ko tuzumi*. (7)

kana Japanese alphabets. (7)

Kanak Name the indigenous people of New Caledonia use for themselves. (9)

Kanaky Name the indigenous people of New Caledonia use for their country. (9)

kànàngó Yoruba small hourglass-shaped drum, used singly or in sets of two or three to accompany *fújì*. (1)

kancha karuvi Tamil musical instrument category referring to idiophones. (5)

kanci Hand cymbals in Karnataka. (5)

kan da gorell Breton songs for dancing; *see chanson à danser*. (8)

kandang rayah Iban gong ensemble. (4)

kandeleh Karelian plucked zither. (8)

kandla Livonian plucked zither resembling the Finnish *kantele*. (8)

kan dokoro (Japan.) *Syamisen* fingering points. (7)

kane (Japan.) Generic germ for (1) bells or (2) gongs. (7)

kaneka Contemporary indigenous music of Kanaky. (9)

kane mukkuri (Japan.) Ainu iron Jew's harp (*mukkuri*). (7)

kaner Breton singer of *kan has diskan* who begins each phrase and trades off with the *diskaner*. (8)

kang Colo small metal trumpet. (1)

kanga Dajo trumpet, played in sets of four to six sizes and lengths. (1)

kângë kreshnikësh 'Long heroic songs', genre of Albanian narrative songs. (8)

kângë majekrahi (Also *kângë malësorçe*.) 'Song of the peak of the arm', performance in which Albanian men place a finger in one ear or cup their ear, raise their elbow above eye level, and sing out at full volume. (8)

kangen (Japan.) Instrumental court music of foreign origin, without dance. (7)

Kangen ongi (Japan.) 'Interpretation of Mode and Tuning in *Gagaku*', treatise written in 1303. (7)

kângë të çobaneshave 'Shepherdesses' songs', performed by pairs of Albanian girls. (8)

kangsinmu Spirit possession in Korea. (7)

kan has diskan Unaccompanied responsorial singing for dance in western Brittany. (8)

kanhi Lowland Chăm fiddle with a turtle-shell body. (4)

kanja Mbojo women's martial arts dance. (4)

kâñjanī (1) Frame drum of Orissa; (2) *kâñjanī bhajan*, popular devotional song form for group expression in Orissa. (5)

kâñjanī ke bhajan (Also *naradi bhajan*.) Nirguṇ songs; those not in praise of a particular incarnation of a deity. (5)

kañjarī (Also *kañcira, kañjīrā, khanjarī, khanjira, khanjiri*.) Frame drum, often with small cymbals attached. (5)

kankala Medieval one-stringed plucked instrument of Indian origin with a gourd-shaped box. (6)

kankara sansin (Japan.) Okinawan three-stringed lute (*sansin*) made of discarded cans. (7)

kanklès (Also *kankles*.) Lithuanian plucked zither, often used to accompany singing, played by ensembles mainly of young people. (3, 8)

kannel Estonian plucked zither. (8)

kannöl Votian plucked zither resembling the Finnish *kantele*. (8)

Kano Chronicle Nineteenth-century manuscript. (1)

k'anon Armenian trapezoidal zither with twenty-four courses and seventy-two total strings; *see qānūn*. (6)

kanonaki Greek plucked zither. (8)

kant Russian three-part singing style with top voices in parallel thirds and an independent third voice. (8)

kānṭ Balochi horn, usually an ox horn. (5)

kantadhes Greek romantic popular serenades of the Ionian islands. (8)

kantaduri Croatian singers who perform the extended melismatic lament of *Gospin plač*. (8)

kantan chamorrita Chamorro songs distinguished by metaphors and other allusions. (9)

kanta zaharak 'Old songs', Basque songs that require two voices. (8)

kantele Finnish and Karelian plucked zither (psaltery). (3, 8, 10)

kantig Breton religious hymns; *see cantique*. (8)

kantikamò Guadeloupe canticles for the dead. (2)

kantor Slovakian schoolmaster, responsible for the musical aspect of religious and public city life in churches and schools. (8)

kantrüm Khmer village ensemble in northeast Thailand. (4)

kantún Mapuche improvised songs. (2)

kantus Double-unit panpipe tradition of Charazani, Bolivia. (2)

kanun (1) Originally a Middle Eastern plucked zither, still played in the Balkans. (2) Georgian urban chordophone played from the 1600s to the 1800s. (3) Greek plucked zither. (4) (Also *qānūn*.) Arab plucked zither. (3, 6, 8)

Kanz al-Tuḥaf 'Treasure of Rarities' (anonymous fourteenth-century Persian treatise). (6)

Kanze ryû (Japan.) School of *nô* specializing in *site kata, ko tuzumi*, and *ô tuzumi*. (7)

kanzi (Japan.) Chinese characters. (7, 10)

kanzin (Japan.) (1) Solicitation of alms for pious purposes; (2) public performances for the benefit of the players. (7)

kanzin hiziri (Japan.) Buddhist mendicant priests. (7)

kanzin sarugaku (Japan.) *Sarugaku* performance for the purpose of promoting the players. (7)

kanziri (Japan.) Bottom end of the *syakuhati*. (7)

kanzunetta 'Popular song', Maltese genre bridging folk and popular music. (8)

kanzyô (Japan.) Buddhist chant (*syômyô*) for invoking or sending off Buddha or other deities, such as guardian deities. (7)

kaona (Hawaiian.) Veiled or layered verbal meaning. (9)

kapalik Oral epic performance genre of Madhya Pradesh. (5)

kapamelo-malong Maranao song about traditional dress. (4)

kapanirong Maranao serenade ensemble. (4)

kapela (Also *hurtkampaniya, muzyki, skamarochi, viasielnyja muzyki*.) Belarusan traditional folk instrumental ensemble. (8)

kapika Four-holed bamboo ring-stop flute of Sumba. (4)

kapobalo 'Head of the dance', leader in Croatian dances of the northern Adriatic zone. (8)

kapohina 'To strike' (idiophones), term used to describe instrumental playing in Madagascar. (1)

kappleikar (1) Finnish-American fiddle competition held until the outbreak of World War II. (2) Norwegian fiddle competitions (started in 1888), which have become important manifestations of national cultural heritage. (3, 8)

kapurala Lay Buddhist ritual specialist in the old religion of Sri Lanka. (5)

kar Khmer wedding ceremony. (4)

kār Major Turkish song genre, a primary constituent of the *fasıl*. (6)

karabe Bagpipes played by the Vlahs of Serbia. (8)

karaḍi vēṣa Bear-costume dance in Karnataka. (5)

karadjuzen Long-necked plucked lute of northern and central Bosnia. (8)

karagatan Poetic game, played in the Philippines. (4)

karahody Belarusan spring and summer round dances. (8)

karakam (1) Clay vessel. (2) South Indian ritual folk dance with clay vessels balanced on the dancers' heads. (5)

karākīb (Also, in Morocco, *karkabūs*; in Libya, *shikshakāt*.) Pair of medium-sized circular cymbals connected by a clasp, used in the Afro-Arab traditions of North Africa. (6)

Karakoyun 'Black sheep', name of a specific instrumental melody in the Turkish *uzun hava* in free rhythm. (6)

karakukua Costa Rican five-holed cane flute played by guests at a funeral. (2)

karam Tribal dance-song form of central and eastern India. (5)

Karamojong Cultural group of Uganda. (1)

karamoutza Greek double-reed shawm. (8)

Karanga Shona subgroup of Zimbabwe. (1)

Karangu People of Zimbabwe. (1)

karansa Cavite outdoor working song. (4)

karaoke 'Empty orchestra'. (1) Japanese recorded pop and folk music minus the singer, a type of sing-along to cassette tapes and videos, introduced by Japanese immigrants and popular in South America. (2) Any amateur singing to prerecorded accompaniment. (2, 4, 7)

kara pandum Gond festival that takes place in autumn. (5)

karar ses 'Resting tone' (Turkish), tonic note of a melody. (6)

karavaj Round wedding bread prepared during Belarusan weddings, accompanied by ritual songs. (8)

karawitan Javanese *gamelan*-based court music. (4)

karcığar Common melodic mode in Turkish music. (6)

kardi majalu Ensemble of northern Karnataka. (5)

kareku kandei Rice pounder and mortar music of Sumbawa. (4)

Karen Upland ethnic group from northern Thailand and Burma. (4)

kargish inar Balkar and Karachaevi improvisatory antiphonal song competition. (8)

kargyraa Type of Tuvan *khöömei* characterized by low-pitched, raspy vocal production. (6)

kari (Japan.) (1) *Syukahati* technique of raising a pitch by moving one's head up; (2) basic note produced by a specific finger position on the *hitiriki*. (7)

kari bakase (Japan.) *Hakase* Buddhist chant notation. (7)

karicka Eastern Slovakian women's circle dance having complex heel-stamping patterns. (8)

karifu Japanese neumatic notation, set in vertical columns read from left to right. (8)

karimba Small *mbira*, often serving as a novice's instrument. (1)

karing'aringa Motor-engine flywheel that accompanies performance in the central highlands of Kenya. (1)

karinyan Cylindrical iron bell suspended by a string from a finger of one hand and struck by an iron beater. (1)

karjapasun Estonian wooden herding trumpet. (8)

karkhā Narrative songs of the Gāines. (5)

Karlovačko pojanje 'Karlovo singing', Serbian liturgical chant. (8)

karma 'Mixed', referring to meters in Turkish music. (6)

karnāl Natural trumpet in Nepal. (5)

karnata Cylindrical shawm used by Turkmen populations in Iraq. (6)

Karnatak music Classical music of South India. (5)

Kärntnerlied Austrian love song of Carinthia, performed by choruses in four-part harmony. (8)

Karoo Festival Afrikaans-language musical festival, which in the mid-1990s gained mass public appeal. (1)

kars Balkar and Karachaevi rattle. (8)

karshkuli Ingush ritual intended to control the weather, dedicated to Sela, goddess of thunder and lightning. (8)

karsilama (Also *karşılama*, *karsilamas*.) Dance in 9/8 meter (originally from coastal Asia Minor) of the Macedonian Rom, of Turkey (where it is a dance genre performed mostly in Thrace), and of Greece (6, 8)

karşilaşma 'To encounter', 'to meet'; Turkish term for song dueling. (6)

kartāl (1) (Also *kartāḷa*.) Pair of wooden or iron clappers, sometimes with metal disks attached, played with one hand in folk and devotional musics. (2) Clappers consisting of four iron rods, two held in each hand, used in the *birahā* genre of Uttar Pradesh. (3) (Also *khartāl*.) Cymbals. (5)

kartinniki 'Picture drawers', Russian genre in which performers draw pictures suggested by song texts and throw them into the audience. (8)

kartsganag Ossetian wooden castanets, played to accompany dancing. (8)

kartuli Georgian mixed-couple dance with instrumental accompaniment. (8)

kartzilamades Cypriot dance, consisting of two sequences of five movements for men and women, who stand face to face. (8)

karu (Japan.) (1) Raising a pitch on the *syukahati* by moving one's head up; (2) playing the basic note produced by a specific finger position on the *hitiriki*. (7)

karuna 'Compassionate', one of the eight emotional states (*rasa*) codified in the *Nātyaśāstra*. (5)

karunashtak Devotional songs consisting of eight stanzas, performed by a soloist or in a group in Maharashtra. (5)

karuvi General term for musical instrument in Tamil. (5)

kārvai Any group of unarticulated pulses; gaps between three statements of a Karnatak *mōrā* cadence. (5)

kās Sudanese handheld cymbals, played for *nōba*. (1)

kasa Long narrative Korean song cycle. (7)

kasai bayasi (Japan.) *Hayasi* instrumental ensemble and its music, originating in a festival in Edo (present-day Tôkyô). (7)

kasala Luba songs of mourning. (1)

kasamintu Bolivian special tuning. (2)

kasapsko oro 'Butcher's dance' in Macedonia. (8)

kasar (1) 'Crude, rough', Javanese term. (2) Medium-size double-headed drum played in Afro-Arab ceremonies in Iraq. (4, 6)

kase' (Also *kase*.) 'Break', radical change in the Haitian master drum's pattern to induce spirit possession in Vodou ceremonies. (2, 3)

kāse Dance performed for the male deity Virabhadra in Karnataka. (5)

kaseko (Also *casser le corps* 'break the body'.) (1) Creole dance accompanied by drum and song found in French Guiana and Surinam. (2) Pop genre that merges many Caribbean and African styles, often blending Caribbean calypso, reggae, and *zouk* with West African *soukous* and Surinam Maroon Djuka drumming. (2)

Kasena-Nankani Cultural group of northern Ghana. (1)

Kashmiri *setār* Small sitar closely resembling the Iranian *setār*. (5)

kashwa (Also *cachiua*.) Cheerful song and circle dance genre of pre-Columbian Andean origins, performed by young, single men and women and usually associated with nocturnal harvest rituals. (2)

kasidah (Also *qasidah*.) Muslim devotional songs in Arabic. (4)

kaside (1) Turkish term for vocal *taksīm* performed in Sufi rituals. (2) Muslim paraliturgical hymns sung in Bosnia-Hercegovina. (6, 8)

kasīde Panegyric poem; any *ilāhī* poem sung in free rhythm during the· *zikr*. See also *qaṣīda*. (6)

kāsījoda Pair of handheld cymbals slightly heavier than the *mañjīrā*. (5)

kaşik In Turkey, two spoons played like castanets, often accompanying dance. (6)

kasiko dokoro (Japan.) Shrine of the goddess Amaterasu in the imperial palace. (7)

kasinoman Ritual party for youth in Cirebon. (4)

kasīr Small double-headed drum of Oman. (6)

kasira (Japan.) (1) Tone produced on the *ô tuzumi* and the *ko tuzumi*. (2) Wooden head of a *bunraku* puppet. (7)

kaskawilla Chilean bell rattle. (2)

kassatu (Japan.) Buddhist chant (*syômyô*) for reciting the name of Buddha or a bodhisattva. (7)

kastom (Pidgin, from English *custom*.) Indigenous attitudes, beliefs, concepts, and behavior, especially in New Guinea and Melanesia. (9)

kata (1) Grenadian open-bottomed, principal membranophone of the big drum ceremony. (2) Time pattern beat on the wooden part of the drum that is played during Afro-Haitian *juba* dancing. (3) (Japan.) Generic term for standard movements, forms, and styles in various arts. (2, 3, 7)

katai pāṭṭu Tamil story-song. (5)

katajjaq Women's game played in the Eastern Arctic, using extremely varied vocal sound patterns. (3)

kata-kata Yakan and Sama epic poems. (4)

Katamaraju Hero of *Kāṭamarāju Katha*, an extended Telugu oral epic with roots in the thirteenth century. (5)

katarai (Japan.) (1) Rolling pattern played on the *kakko* drum with one stick. (2) Narrative segment of a *nô* play. (7)

katav Prosodic form used for descriptive and didactic songs with quick tempos and simple tunes, in Maharashtra. (5)

kata zi (Japan.) Unit of 6 beats per poetic line in *nô* chanting. (7)

katei siki (Japan.) Abbreviation for *dai nihon katei ongaku kai siki* notation. (7)

kateobak Mentawei single-headed cylindrical drum. (4)

kathā (Also *katha, kathālu*.) Story; sung narrative. (5)

kathak Classical dance of North India. (5)

kathakaḷi Dance drama of Kerala. (5)

katikubi Vernacular Mixtec *son* with non-Western structure and improvised texts. (2)

katimbok Tagakaolu paired-string zither. (4)

katô busi (Japan.) Genre of narrative *syamisen* music founded by Masumi Katô (1684–1725). (7)

katta ashula 'Great song'. Unmetered, declamatory setting of spiritual poetry in a high tessitura, widely performed in the Ferghana valley of Uzbekistan. (6)

kaṭṭadiya Drummer who controls communication with spirits of the old religion in Sri Lanka. See also *âdurā, yakâdurā*. (5)

kaṭṭaikkūttu Tamil dance drama based on stories from Hindu epics. (5)

kaṭṭ pāṭukiratu Manner of shouting or singing with great forcefulness in Tamil folk music. (5)

katuba Maltese bass drum, played with a fife for public announcements. (8)

katyâsî (Japan.) Okinawan improvised free dance performed spontaneously with a fast-tempo *sansin* accompaniment as an expression of delight at the end of a festivity. (7)

kaul (Sundanese.) Casual participation in a musical event. (4)

ka'um Islamic religious leader of Javanese descent in Surinam. (2)

Kauthuma School of Sāmavedic chanting. (5)

kava *Piper methysticum* or an infusion of its roots and stems pulverized or (formerly) masticated, serving as a beverage often consumed with formalities encoding important elements of social structure. (9)

kaval (1) End-blown Turkish flute. (2) Bulgarian and Macedonian end-blown, rim-blown flute. (6, 8)

kavall Eight-holed rim-blown flutes with chromatic fingering, played in pairs by Albanian herdsmen in western Macedonia. (8)

kāvaṭi (1) Bow-shaped burden carried on the shoulders in honor of the Tamil deity Murugan, especially during the *kāvaṭiyāṭṭam* dance. (2) Tamil dance associated with the god Murugan, in which a possessed dancer carries a *kāvaṭi* on the shoulders. (5)

kāvaṭi cintu Tamil musical poetic genre sung or played to accompany the *kāvaṭiyāṭṭam* dance associated with the god Murugan. (5)

kavikāra maḍuva Group of lay Buddhist singers who perform in secret at the Daladā Māligawa, the Buddhism Temple of the Tooth in Sri Lanka. (5)

kawadi dejë Yekuana small end-blown ductless flute (made of a deer's tibia), with an internal wax diaphragm. (2)

kawāla (Also *kawwala*.) Reed flute resembling the *nāy*, but shorter and lacking the thumb hole. In Egypt, the *kawāla* is typically used to accompany Sufi *inshād* of the public *ḥaḍra*. (6)

kawayawaya Central African friction bow. (1)

kawih Fixed-meter songs of Sunda. (4)

kawina Oldest creole musical form of Surinam. (2)

kawoking Teasing courtship songs of Sumba. (4)

kayagŭm Korean twelve-stringed zither with movable bridges, related to the Japanese *koto*. (7)

kayagŭm pyŏngch'ang Songs from Korean *p'ansori* in which the singer accompanies himself or herself on a zither. (7)

kayagŭm sanjo Solo genre for Korean *kayagŭm*. (7)

kayaka Ceremonial men's cries of Sumba. (4)

kayamb (Also *kayamm, caimbe*.) Raft-shaped cane rattle played by Indians on Réunion Island. (5)

kayamba Rectangular reed box, filled with stones or seeds and played in coastal communities of Kenya. (1)

kayaq Lombok theater with melancholic songs. (4)

kayari Section of the *pamanhikan* in the Philippines. (4)

kayôkyoku (Japan.) Genre of Japanese popular songs combining modified vernacular expressions and adapted European and American idioms. (7)

kazandik Miri five-stringed lyre of the Sudan. (1)

kāzu balss 'Wedding tune', Latvian melodic formula for singing *apdziedāšanās*. See *godu balss*. (8)

kazura nô (Japan.) *Nô* plays in which the main character is the ghost of a beautiful woman or the spirit of a plant appearing as a woman. (7)

kbach Khmer system of dance gestures. (4)

kbandu Jamaican single-headed, cylindrical membranophone played with the hands during Kumina ritual. (2)

kbolo Two largest *sene* gongs of West Timor. (4)

kcim Albanian solo women's dance, featuring graceful arm movements. (8)

kebele Dogon *sistrum*. (1)

kebluk Large kettle gong of Cirebon. (4)

kebudayaan pasisir Coastal culture of north Java. (4)

kecak Balinese male chorus representing a monkey army. (4)

kecimol Wind, string, and drum ensemble of Lombok. (4)

kecrèk Javanese and Sundanese idiophone made of hanging metal plates. (4)

ke'e Mixtec log idiophone, similar to the Nahua *teponaztli*. (2)

keen To wail, lament. (3)

keening Lament for the dead, especially in Ireland. (8)

keenoba Masqueraders' performances at *kvelieri* in urban areas of Georgia. (8)

keer (Also *kitiar*.) Ecuadorian bowed-lute chordophone. (2)

kef (Also *kefi*.) Term used in Greece and the Balkans for a heightened experience created by music and other forms of social interaction. (8)

kef-time In the Armenian-American community, weekend-long music retreat featuring multiple bands. (3)

kehillah Term designating different forms of Jewish culture and music. (8)

kei (Japan.) Idiophone used in Buddhist music, a suspended flat bronze plate struck with a mallet. (2) *Gidayû busi syamisen* pattern. (7)

keiko (Japan.) Lessons in and practices of an art, including performing and martial arts. (7)

keizi (Japan.) (1) Section of puppet theater and *gidayû busi* (narrative *syamisen* music) that emphasizes lyrical and musical expression rather than narrative. (2) *Bunraku* (puppet theater) repertoire of one-act dance dramas. (7)

kekawin Sung poetry in Old Javanese. (4)

kekhat-pondur Chechen and Ingush accordion, played by women; *see komuk, komuz*. (8)

keleŋ Vai struck log idiophone. (1)

kélé St. Lucian religious tradition particular to the *djiné*. (2)

keledi Kajang mouth organ. (4)

kéleng Kpelle struck log idiophone. (1)

kelenongan Gong-chime and ensemble of Sumatra. (4)

kelîme-i tevhîd 'There is no god but God'; formula of unity. (6)

kelintang (Also *kelitang, kelittang*.) Gong-chime and ensemble of Sumatra. (4)

keluni Songs of the Kela tribe of Orissa. (5)

keluri Kenyah mouth organ. (4)

keman Turkish fiddle; *see kamān*. (6)

kemanak Banana-shaped metal idiophone of Java and Cirebon. (4)

kemancha Georgian urban chordophone, played from the 1600s to the 1800s. (8)

kemanche (Also *ghīchak, kamanche*.) Persian spike fiddle of the medieval Indo-Persian courts; still found in Afghanistan. (5)

kemane Turkish instrument resembling the Greek lyre. (6)

kembe Lamellophone of the Mpyɛmɔ̃ (Nola District, Central African Republic). (1)

kemençe (1) Turkish pear-shaped fiddle. (2) Albanian pear-shaped bowed lute; *see lyra*. (6, 8)

kəmənçe Azerbaijani spike fiddle; cf. *kamān*. (6)

kemençe rûmî Small Turkish three-stringed fiddle. (6)

kemenche (Also *kemençe, riçek*.) Spike fiddle played by professional musicians, *mitirp*, in Kurdistan; *see kamān*. (6)

kemene (Also *gusla*.) Macedonian three-stringed pear-shaped bowed lute; *see lyra*. (8)

kemenje Pontic Greek three-stringed bowed lute; *see lyra*. (8)

kèmès Haitian early evening dance. (2)

kemidi rudat Popular theatrical form in Lombok. (4)

kemong Balinese small hanging gong. (4)

kempli Balinese horizontally mounted gong. (4)

kempul Small hanging gong of Indonesia. (4)

kempur (1) South Sumatra large horizontal gong. (2) Small hanging gong of Bali. (4)

kempurvísur Danish heroic songs of the Faroe Islands, sung by line dancers. (8)

kempyang Javanese small kettle gong, *pélog* tuning only. (4)

kemyang High-pitched gong-chime of Cirebon. (4)

ken (1) Free-reed mouth organ in raft form, found in Cambodia, Laos, and Thailand. (2) (Japan.) Clay vessel flute. (4, 7)

kèn Family of double-reed aerophones of Vietnam. (4)

kena (Spanish orthography, *quena*.) Central Andean end-blown notched flute of Aymara origin with five to eight finger holes; *see also quena, qina*. (2)

kenat Horizontal kettle gong of Lombok. (4)

kendai (Japan.) Music stand. (7)

kendang (1) Double-headed membranophone of Indonesian origin played in *gamelan* ensembles in Surinam. (2) Double-headed drum from Indonesia. (2, 4)

kendang penca Percussive ensemble used for *penca silat*. (4)

kendara Bowed chordophone of Orissa. (5)

kendhang Double-headed drum of Java. (4)

kendhang ciblon Medium double-headed barrel drum of Java. (4)

kendhang gendhing Large double-headed barrel drum of Java. (4)

kendhang ketipung Small double–headed barrel drum of Java. (4)

keneo Enggano conch shell. (4)

kengai Vai women who supervise Sande musical activities; expert Vai dancers and singers. (1)

këngë 'Songs' (Albanian). (8)

kêngë me të marrje me të prerje (Also *këngë me iso, këngë me të rënkuar, këngë me të zier*.) 'Songs with taking and cutting' (Albanian), Tosk polyphonic singing. (8)

këngë me të rënkuar (Also *këngë me të marrje me të prerje, këngë me iso, këngë me të zier*.) 'Songs with groaning' (Albanian), Tosk polyphonic singing. (8)

këngi Purépecha elderly native authority of celebrations and responsorial singer. (2)

kengyô (Japan.) Highest rank in the *tôdô* (a guild for blind artisans). (7)

kenong (1) South Sumatra large horizontal gong. (2) Large, deep-rimmed kettle gong of Indonesia. (4)

kenrā Bowed instrument of Bihar, with a coconut resonator and bamboo neck. (5)

kente Cloth worn by royalty in Ghana. (1)

kenten (Japan.) In Buddhist chant (*syômyô*), dot indicating the intonations of each Chinese character in the text. (7)

kenthongan Javanese wooden slit gong. (4)

k'epa Inca trumpet. (2)

keprak Javanese wooden box used to accompany dance. (4)

kepu Conch-shell trumpet in the Andes. (2)

kerân-non-koning Kpelle harp-lute. (1)

keras 'Strong, coarse'; term applied to characters in Balinese dance. (4)

Kerem (Also *kerem*.) Name of a minstrel. (1) In the Turkish *uzun hava*, a specific instrumental melody in free rhythm. (2) The fundamental mode, related to *hüseyni*, of Turkish folk music. (6)

kereshme Rhythmic realization of a *gūshe* in Persian music involving hemiola patterns. (6)

kerla esharsh Chechen and Ingush new songs for traditional feasts. (8)

keromongan Sumatran gong-chime and ensemble. (4)

kerona Fulɓe two- to nine-stringed plucked lute. (1)

keroncong Portuguese-derived folk music from Melakka. (4)

kertok kelapa Series of slabs over coconut resonators, found in Malaysia. (4)

keruncung Bidayuh bamboo tubes. (4)

keserves 'Bitter song', Hungarian lament songs with improvised lines. (8)

kesi Malaysian pair of small cymbals. (4)

kesong (China.) Daily services in Buddhist ritual. (7)

kesuling Bamboo ring-stop flute of Borneo. (4)

kesut Kajang bamboo pole stamping. (4)

keśyā Bawdy songs performed on a variety of occasions in Rajasthan. (5)

ketadu Two-stringed boat lute of Savu. (4)

ketadu haba Eight-stringed tube zither with resonator, from Savu. (4)

ketadu mara Nine-keyed wooden trough xylophone of Savu. (4)

ketawang Formal arrangement of a Javanese *gamelan* piece. (4)

kete (1) Asante master drum. (2) Yoruba globular cylindrical drum. (3) Ghanaian dance music. (4) Ghanaian court music tradition. (1, 10)

keteng-keteng Karo Batak tube zither. (4)

kethoprak Javanese spoken historical theater with music. (4)

kethuk Javanese small kettle gong. (4)

ketipung Cirebonese small double-headed barrel drum. (4)

ketobung Riau two-headed drums. (4)

kĕtruyên Narratives of poetry and prose of Vietnam. (4)

kēṭṭi mēḷam 'Loud, robust ensemble'; rapid, loud playing of all instruments in a South Indian ensemble (usually *tavil* and *nāgasvaram*) used to draw attention to an important moment and drown out inauspicious sounds. **(5)**

ketuk Small kettle gong of Cirebon. **(4)**

ketuk telu Small village ensemble of Cirebon. **(4)**

ketuk tilu Sundanese small coastal village ensemble. **(4)**

keyed bugle (Also *Royal Kent bugle*.) Soprano brass instrument similar to the trumpet, but with a conical rather than cylindrical bore, to which five to seven woodwind-like keys have been attached to make the instrument chromatic. **(3)**

khaen Free-reed mouth organ from northeast Thailand and Laos. **(4)**

'khafif Light, quick. **(6)**

khafif (Plural, *khfāyif*.) Vocal genre within the Maghribi *nūba*. **(6)**

khālī Hand gesture (wave) signifying an unstressed, "empty" subdivision of a Hindustani tala. **(5)**

khalīfa (From Arabic *khalifa* 'caliph'.) (1) Female wedding entertainer in Khorezm, Central Asia. (2) Spiritual head of an Omani *ḥalqat almālid*, assisted by a *shawūsh*. **(6)**

khalīfe (1) Officiant within a group of dervishes, perhaps the singer. (2) Shaman or *ostā* in the *gwātī* ritual. **(6)**

khalkhar Chechen and Ingush dance melodies. **(8)**

khalkharan iish Chechen instrumental music accompanying dances, processions, and horse races. **(8)**

khamak Folk rhythm instrument of Bengal consisting of a small drum with a string attached that produces variable-pitch sounds when plucked. **(5)**

khan (China.) Tribal leader of the Mongols. **(7)**

khānaqāh (Also, in Iran, *khāneqāh*.) Sufi dwelling. **(6)**

khanaqah (Also *khāneqāh, tekke*.) Sufi fraternity house. **(5)**

khāṇḍana Rice-pounding or swing songs performed during more general rites by girls of south Gujarat, to secure good husbands. **(5)**

khānh Chimes of stone or bronze, found in Vietnam. **(4)**

khanjani Small cymbals. **(5)**

khanjarī (Also *kañjarī, kañjīrā, khanjiri*.) Small frame drum with jingles. **(5)**

khao Northern Thai narrative genre, sometimes accompanied. **(4)**

khap (Also *khǎp*.) Vocal genres common to northeast Thailand and central and northern Laos. **(4)**

khap ngeum Repartee song genre of the Vientiane area. **(4)**

khap phuan Repartee song genre of the Phuan minority, northern Laos. **(4)**

khap sam neua Repartee song genre of Houaphanh province. **(4)**

khap thai dam Vocal genre of the Thai Dam minority, northern Laos. **(4)**

khap thum Repartee song genre of Luang Phrabang. **(4)**

kharābāt Folk genre of Baghlan derived from Persian mystical poetry. **(5)**

kharja Procession of a Sufi *ṭarīqa*, involving chanting and the playing of instruments. **(6)**

kharsha (Plural, *kharashāt*.) 'Decoration', improvised variation on sections of a basic melody in Yemeni tradition. **(6)**

khartāl (Also *kartāl*.) Cymbals. **(5)**

kha:s Braced mouth-resonated bow played by Khoikhoi women. **(1)**

khashba (Also *khashaba*.) 'Piece of wood', small single-headed Mesopotamian drum; cf. *ṭabla*. **(6)**

khāṣṣe 'Musicians of the elite' in Persia under Naṣr al-Dīn Shāh. **(6)**

khatim (Also *khatm*; plural, *akhtām*.) Concluding, lively vocal section within the Andalusian-Tunisian *nūba*. **(6)**

khawal Egyptian male dancer. **(6)**

khaw law Original name of *pong lang* in northeast Thailand. **(4)**

khawng Single, bossed gongs of Thailand. **(4)**

khawng khu Southern Thai pair of bossed gongs. **(4)**

khawng mawn Thai vertical, U-shaped set of bossed gongs. **(4)**

khawng wong lek Smaller circle of eighteen bossed gongs from Thailand. **(4)**

khawng wong yai Larger circle of sixteen bossed gongs from Thailand. **(4)**

khayāl Devotional songs of Madhya Pradesh. **(5)**

khazer Armenian neumatic notation invented in the ninth century. **(6)**

khelimaski djili Vlach Rom duple-meter songs with sung imitations of musical instruments. **(8)**

khelovantmtavari 'Head of the arts', Georgian professional composers who worked in Georgian churches from the eighth to the eleventh centuries. **(8)**

khene (In Thailand, also *khaen*.) Lao free-reed mouth organ. **(4)**

khī Newār drum in Nepal. **(5)**

khim Small hammered zither of Chaozhou, Chinese origin. **(4)**

khimm (1) 'Hammered dulcimer', Cambodian string instrument played in contemporary versions of the *pinnpeat* ensemble. (2) Hammered zither of Chinese origin. **(3, 4)**

khinṣir Little finger, or the fret played by this finger. **(6)**

khirkhṣha (In Sudan, also *atetash*.) Rattle usually intended for children, but used in selected musical traditions in Sudan, Libya, and elsewhere. (Plural, *khirkhashāt*.) **(6)**

khirlee In Tuva, a thin piece of wood that imitates the sound of wind when spun like a propeller on a tensed, twisted string. **(6)**

khitm Concluding section within Sufi performance of *ma'lūf*; cf. *khatim*. **(6)**

khloy 'Duct flute', Cambodian wind instrument played in contemporary versions of the *pinnpeat* ensemble, sometimes replaced by the Western flute or recorder. **(3)**

khloy Khmer end-blown duct flute of bamboo. **(4)**

khlui Thai bamboo or wood fipple flutes, in three sizes. **(4)**

Khmer Mainstream culture of Cambodia. **(4)**

Khmer Rouge Communist political organization of Cambodia. **(4)**

khodovoi khorovod (Also *kjodiachii, zmeika*.) 'Walking *khorovod*', Russian dance in which all participants walk in a circle or in a serpentine movement down a street. **(8)**

khögzbüm 'Music', Mongolian term for music, implying the use of musical instruments. **(6)**

khoiisar-fandir Ossetian two- or three-stringed bowed lute, used to accompany epics; see *kisin-fandir*. **(8)**

Khoisan (1) "Click" languages of southern Africa. (2) Speakers of any of these languages. **(1)**

khol Double-headed clay barrel drum of northeastern India. **(5)**

khomba Tsonga "turning" dance to make women fertile. **(1)**

khomus Jew's harp. **(6)**

khon Classical masked theater, based on the *Ramayana* ; found in Thailand and Laos. **(4)**

khonga-kaft Ossetian couple dance; see *kabardinka*. **(8)**

khong vong Lao series of bossed gongs on circular rattan frame. **(4)**

khöömei 'Throat', 'pharynx'; Mongolian term for biphonic throat-singing in Tuva. **(6, 8, 10)**

khöömeizhi Performer of Tuvan *khöömei*. **(6)**

khorovod (Also *tanok, krugi*.) Russian collective circle and figure dances. **(8)**

khorumi Acharian and Gurian military dance in 5/4 meter. **(8)**

khromka 'Chromatic', the chromatic Russian accordion. **(8)**

khru Thai teacher. **(4)**

khrüang sai Thai court entertainment ensemble of strings and flute. **(4)**

khse muoy Half-gourd resonated monochord from Cambodia. **(4)**

khui Lao bamboo fipple flute. (4)

khumāsī Pentatonic *maqām* used in Nubian traditions. (6)

khurdak (Also *ḍuggī*, *ḍukkaṛ*.) Small hand-played kettledrum pair of North India. (5)

khushnī (Plural, *khashānā*.) 'Nonentertainer', 'intruder'; pejorative term for a new musician on Muḥammad 'Alī Street in Cairo. (6)

khwan Spirit essence of a human being. (4)

khyal (Also *khyāl*.) Since the late eighteenth century, the preeminent Hindustani vocal genre. (3, 5, 10)

khyāli 4/4 and 2/2 meters in Nepal. (5)

kibbutz (Plural, *kibbutzim*.) Israeli communal settlement combining ideals of European socialism with a Jewish revolt against religious orthodoxy. (6)

kibi asobi (Japan.) Collective name for the *gagaku*-based songs composed by Kisimoto Yosihide (1821–1890), the founder of *kibigaku*, after his composition of the so-called *kibikyoku* in the 1870s. (7)

kibigaku (Japan.) Genre of *gagaku*-based music and dance founded by Kisimoto Yosihide (1821–1890) during the Meizi era, used as festival music of the Kurozumi and Konkô sects of Shinto (Sintô). (7)

kibikyoku (Japan.) Collective name for the eleven song pieces with *gagaku* instrumental accompaniment composed in the 1870s by Kisimoto Yosihide (1821–1890), the founder of *kibigaku*. (7)

kịch nói Western-inspired spoken theater of Vietnam. (4)

kiɗa Hausa term for drumming. (1)

kidiu Kenyah bullroarer. (4)

kidung Type of metered sung poetry in Bali and Lombok. (4)

kigan (Japan.) Buddhist chant (*syômyô*) for praying for national or personal blessings. (7)

Kiganda Language of the Baganda, a people of Uganda. (1)

kikkake tyô (Japan.) *See tuke tyô*. (7)

Kikuyu People of Kenya. (1)

kilagi-turra Folk drama form of Madhya Pradesh featuring competitive poetry singing. (5)

kilassiki muzika 'Classical music', term referring to the *muqam* tradition of Uygur-Xinjiang. (6)

kili Comb and tissue kazoo from West Timor. (4)

kiliwāli Popular music in Afghanistan. (5)

kil-kobuz Balkar and Karachaevi plucked lute. (8)

k'illpa Bolivian animal fertility ritual. (2)

kilumi Akamba dance. (1)

kin (1) Large, four-stringed Chiapas bass guitar. (2) (Japan.) Generic term for zithers. (3)

(Japan.) Idiophone used in Buddhist music, a bowl-shaped vessel struck with a mallet. (2, 7)

kina (Tok Pisin.) Large mother-of-pearl, traditionally used for trade in the Papua New Guinea highlands; since 1975, the basic unit of Papua New Guinea currency, divided into 100 *toea*. (9)

kinanda Accordion, as known in the central highlands of Kenya. (1)

kinang Lowland Chăm two-headed drum. (4)

kineme Minimal unit of movement recognized as contrastive by people of a given dance tradition. (9)

kinesphere Space within reach around an individual. (1)

Kineya (Japan.) School of *nagauta* (a lyrical *syamisen* genre). (7)

king (1) Stick zither of Jammu and Kashmir, related to the North Indian *bīn* and the medieval *vīnā*. (2) Plucked lute of Punjab, Pakistan. (5)

kingi Competitive association in East Africa that emphasized precision of movement and European instruments. (1)

kingiri Bowed chordophone with a coconut shell resonator, in Madhya Pradesh. (5)

kingir-kobuz Balkar and Karachaevi harp. (8)

kingotoner Danish tunes in a hymnbook compiled by Bishop Thomas Kingo (1634–1703); used in the Faroe Islands as the basis for extensive improvisation in informal worship at home. (8)

kinh Mainstream, lowland Vietnamese population. (4)

kinilisong Subanen gong ensemble. (4)

kinka Anlo-Ewe genre of music and musical ensemble. (1)

Kinka hu (Japan.) 'Notations of Songs for Zither', tenth-century manuscript on the ancient vocal music *ŏuta*. (7)

Kinko ryû (Japan.) *Syakuhati* school derived from a tradition established by Kurosawa Kinko (1701–1771). (7)

kinnāra (Plural, *kinnārāt*.) Early Arabic term for a lyre. (6)

kinnarī vīnā Stick zither described in medieval musicological texts. (5)

kinsei hôgaku (Japan.) Generic term for the Japanese music established in the Edo period (1600–1867), referring mainly to *koto* and *syamisen* music. (7)

Kinsin ryû (Japan.) School of *satuma biwa* (lute) founded in 1915 by Nagata Kinsin (1885–1927). (7)

kintouri Georgian dance accompanied by Middle Eastern instruments such as the *doli*, *duduki*, and *zurna*. (8)

kinuta mono (Japan.) Music, especially for *ziuta* and *koto*, that imitates the sound of beating cloth on wooden blocks. (7)

kipango Board zither in the Iranga District of Tanzania, with six strings and a gourd resonator at one end. (1)

kip'ŭnmat 'Rich flavor', 'full flavor'; vocal aesthetic in Korean *p'ansori*. (7)

kirang (1) Nuba conical drum. (2) Nuba stamping dance. (1)

kirdān One of the major notes of the Arab fundamental scale. (6)

kiri (Japan.) Last section of the tripartite division of an act in *bunraku* (puppet theater). (7)

kiriba (Japan.) Closing scene of each *dan* (act) of *bunraku* (puppet theater), except the fifth act and the *nitiyuki* scene. (7)

kiridžijske pjesme Caravan songs, performed by merchants in Bosnia-Hercegovina. (8)

kirikaṭṭi (Also *kuṇṭalam*.) Pair of conical drums tied around the player's waist and played with curved sticks, in Tamil Nadu. (5)

kırık hava 'Broken melody', category of Turkish folk music with melodies in strict meter. (6)

kirikiri Name for Zaïrean rumba. (1)

kiringoringo Kenyan boys' and girls' dance, accompanied by vocal and instrumental music. (1)

kiringua Purépecha slit-drum idiophone played with two sticks. (2)

kiri nô (Japan.) *Nô* plays in which the main character is a supernatural being, such as a demon. (7)

kirmaš Belarusan rural marketplace, often dramatized in government-sponsored staged folklore. (8)

kīrtan (1) (Also *kīrtana*.) Devotional praise song. (2) (Also *sankīrtan*.) Congregational dancing and chanting of a holy name, often that of Krishna. (5)

kīrtankār Performer of *kīrtan*. (5)

Kirundi Language spoken by the Barundi, a people of Burundi. (1)

kisaeng Korean female entertainers. (7)

kishavi Taita dance. (1)

Kisii Cultural group of Kenya. (1)

kisin-fandir Ossetian two- or three-stringed bowed lute, played to accompany epics; *see khoiisar-fandir*. (8)

kisir (Also *kisr*.) Type of lyre played by Nubians and Egyptian bedouin on the Red Sea coast. (1, 6)

Kitāb al-aghānī 'Book of Songs' by al-Iṣfahānī (d. 967), one of the most important medieval sources for Arab music. (6)

kitar (From English *guitar*.) Rustically manufactured plucked wooden lute in Guatemala. (2)

kitarlawana (Also *tiun*.) '*Kitar* song', Guatemalan songs composed by men, in which the lyric content centers on a woman. (2)

kitarra biss Maltese genre of songless guitar music, performed by an ensemble of lead guitar (*prejjem*) and one or two chord-playing guitars. (**8**)

Kita ryû (Japan.) School of *nô* specializing in *site kata*. (**7**)

kithara (1) Greek term for guitar (possibly via Arabic *qitara*) that appears in European texts from the thirteenth century. (2) Seven- or eight-stringed plucked lyre of ancient Greece, played by professional musicians accompanying choruses. (**1, 8**)

kitka 'Bouquet' (Bulgarian), arrangment of well-known folk and urban popular songs for bands or a cappella choirs. (**8**)

Kituxe e os Acompanhantes Angolan band that performs a mix of *merengue*, rumba, and rural Angolan styles. (**1**)

kiwul Small gong of Cirebon. (**4**)

kiyomoto (Also *kiyomoto busi*.) In Japan, genre of narrative *syamisen* music founded by Kiyomoto Enzyu dayû (1777–1825). (**7**)

kjempevisene Norwegian heroic songs. (**8**)

kjuček Bulgarian Rom instrumental genre in 2/4 or 9/8 time. (**8**)

kjyy Balkar and Karachaevi women's lyrical song genre. (**8**)

kkaebôsŭn sori 'Naked voice', vocal timbre in Korean *p'ansori*. (**7**)

kkoktu kaksi norŭm Korean marionette show. (**7**)

kkwaenggwari (Also *kkwaengmaegu*.) Small Korean gong. (**7**)

klang chhnakk Khmer ensemble used for funerals. (**4**)

klapa 'Club, group of friends'; songs and a singing style in four-part harmony performed by men in urban areas along the Dalmatian coast of Croatia and Montenegro. (**8**)

klapsarika Greek nonmetrical, weeping melodies. (**8**)

klarino Greek clarinet having the Albert system of keying. (**8**)

klāsik (Also *musiqī-ye klāsik*.) Classical music in Afghanistan. (**5**)

klasik müziği 'Classical music' of Ottoman Turkey. (**6**)

klâsik Türk müziği (Also *klâsik Türk musikisi*.) 'Turkish classical music' performed by elite instrumentalists and singers and supported institutionally. (**6**)

klausjagen Swiss whip-crackers of Küssnacht am Rhein, canton Schwyz. (**8**)

klavirka 'Piano accordion' (Slovenian). (**8**)

klawng ae Long Northern Thai single-headed drum. (**4**)

klawng khaek (1) Thai two-headed barrel drums; (2) ensemble for boxing and theater. (**4**)

klawng that Pair of Thai large barrel drums played with sticks. (**4**)

klawng yao Long Central Thai single-headed drum. (**4**)

kleftika Heroic songs of mainland Greece, imported to Cyprus. (**8**)

klènang Pair of small kettle gongs from Cirebon. (**4**)

klenèngan Social events accompanying ceremonies in Java. (**4**)

Klenotnice 'Treasury', Czechoslovakian program to support traditional folk music activity and collecting. (**8**)

klentang Single key fixed on wooden box, from Lombok. (**4**)

klentong Balinese small hanging gong. (**4**)

klezmer music (1) Ensemble music of Eastern European Jewish origin. (2) Important music revival in the United States. (3) (Plural, *klezmorim*.) Jewish professional instrumental musician who appeared most commonly at celebrations, particularly weddings. (4) Traditional instrumental music of Ashkenazi Jews. (**3, 6, 8**)

kliningan Sundanese vocal music in *gamelan saléndro*. (**4**)

klisang Miskitu mirliton made from a piece of cane and a membrane from a bat's wing, a cow's gut, or thin paper and used to sanctify water for curative rituals. (**2**)

klong-klong Three-stringed bamboo idiochord tube zither from Flores. (**4**)

klông pút Vietnamese group of seven sounding bamboo tubes, activated by clapping. (**4**)

knari Obsolete Georgian harp, mentioned in medieval literary sources. (**8**)

k'ni Bowed monochord stick zither of the Jarai, Vietnam. (**4**)

knizhnye pesni 'Book songs', suburban Russian songs, drawn from eighteenth- and nineteenth-century literary sources. (**8**)

knobe besi Metal jaw harp from West Timor. (**4**)

knobe kbetas Musical bow from West Timor. (**4**)

knobe oh Wooden jaw harp from West Timor. (**4**)

koa Rhythmic song spoken to musical accompaniment, from West Timor. (**4**)

koangtac Sedang hydraulic bamboo xylophone, Vietnam. (**4**)

kob Kota curved brass horn. (**5**)

kobusi (Japan.) Melismatic melodic formulas. (**7**)

kobza (1) (Also *lira, rela*.) Belarusan hurdy-gurdy. (2) (Also *bandura*.) Ukrainian plucked bowl lute. (**8**)

kobzari Ukrainian blind peasant minstrels who played the *kobza*. See *lirnyky*. (**8**)

köçek (Also *tavşan*.) Dancing boys at Ottoman imperial festivals, or more recently at Turkish weddings. (**6**)

koch'wi 'Hitting and blowing', Korean military music of the Silla dynasty. (**7**)

Kodak Hula Show Hawaiian music-and-dance show, founded in 1937 by Louise Akeo and the Royal Hawaiian Girls' Glee Club and still presented outdoors, once a week or more often, at Waikīkī. (**9**)

kodedo Yekuana turtleshell rubbed or friction idiophone. (**2**)

koenkelpot Friction drum of the Low Countries. (**8**)

Koguryŏ Korean dynastic period, 37 B.C.E. to 668 C.E. (**7**)

kohomba kankāriya Important ritual to bring about peace, a bountiful harvest, and the general welfare, in Sinhala Sri Lanka's upcountry. (**5**)

Kohun (Japan.) Prehistoric period of Japan, c. 270–710 C.E. (**7**)

k'ojom Guatemalan cylindrical, double-headed drum. (**2**)

kôkin (Japan.) Jew's harp. (**7**)

kokin gumi (Japan.) Collective name for five compositions for *koto* by Yosizawa *kengyô* (c. 1808–1872): *Haru no kyoku, Natu no kyoku, Aki no kyoku, Huyu no kyoku,* and *Tidori no kyoku,* which are based on a tuning called *kokin zyôsi* invented by Yosizawa. (**7**)

kokin zyôsi (Japan.) *Koto* tuning invented by Yosizawa *kengyô* (c. 1808–1872). (**7**)

kokkara Metal scraper of Kerala, used in sorcery. (**5**)

kokles Latvian plucked zither, carved from a wooden plank and having five to twelve strings. (**8**)

kokugaku (Japan.) 'National music', concept proposed by politicians during the Meizi era (1868–1912), with the intention of symbolizing national community within a modern monarchy by blending Japanese and Western musics. (**7**)

kokuhû kabu (Japan.) Indigenous court music and dance. (**7**)

kokyoku (Japan.) 'Old music'; term referring to the four genres of narrative *syamisen* music: *ittyû busi, miyazono busi, katô busi,* and *ogie busi*. (**7**)

kokyū (Also *kokyû*.) In Japan, long-necked bowed lute. (2) Bowed samisen-type lute played by people of Japanese ancestry in South America. (**2, 7**)

koḷ Kota double-reed aerophone with conical bore. (**5**)

kola (1) Miri ceremonial earthen-pot drum; (2) Miri rainmaking festival. (**1**)

kōlai cintu Songs popular in the late nineteenth and early twentieth centuries in Tamil Nadu, recounting tales of famous murders. (**5**) *kolam* Sinhala masked theater of southern and southwestern Sri Lanka. (5)

kołatki (Also *terkotki*.) Clappers used in annual church ceremonies in Poland. (8)

kōlāṭṭam South Indian stick dance, accompanied by song. (5)

kōle basava Performing cow, in the Karnataka *basavāṭa gangettinavaru* street performance. (5)

koleda Bulgarian and Serbian caroling ritual for the winter solstice, Christmas, or the new year. (8)

koledari Bulgarian performers of *koleda*. (8)

koledarske pjesme Christmas carols of Montenegro. (8)

kolednice Carols sung door-to-door in Slovenia between Christmas and Epiphany. (8)

koledniki Slovene carolers who perform from door to door between Christmas and Epiphany. (8)

koledovanje Door-to-door caroling in Slovenia between Christmas and Epiphany. (8)

kolendarë Albanian children who caroled from door-to-door on Christmas and St. Lazarus's Day. (8)

koliada Russian caroling ritual at Christmas and on St. Vasil's Day. (8)

koliadky Ukrainian Christmas carols. (8)

kolinje (Also *svinjokolje*.) Slavonian communal hog-butchering parties, held in the late fall with singing, dancing, and merrymaking, (8)

kolintang Minahasan xylophone. (4)

kolitong Kalinga polychordal zither. (4)

kōlkkaḷi Stick dance in Kerala. (5)

Kolla Suyu Mapuche Southern Kingdom of the Inca empire. (2)

kŏllip 'Grain begging', Korean fund-raising performance by folk bands. (7)

kŏllipp'ae Korean Buddhist entertainer; *see chŏl kŏllip*. (7)

kolo Serbo-Croatian line or circle dance, or the music for it. (3, 8)

kologo Internal-spike lute of Ghana. (1)

kolokie Volcano-calming ceremony on Ternate. (4)

kolokua Ensemble of the Fur people (two drums, end-blown flute, two side-blown antelope horns) that plays at harvesting and circumcision festivities. (1)

Kɔlɔpɔɔ Vai male masquerader. (1)

kolo u šest (Also *kolo*.) Serbian circle dance in six steps. (8)

kol̤var Instruments central to a Kota ensemble: *koḷ*, *par*, and *tabaṭk*. (5)

komabue (Japan.) Transverse flute of Korean origin used in *gagaku*. (7)

komad s pevanjem 'Dramatic play with singing', Serbian variant of the Central European singspiel. (8)

komagaku (Japan.) Court music and dance of Korean origin. (7)

komal 'Flatted', as a flatted note. (5)

koma sesler (Turkish.) Microtonal pitches. (6)

Komba BaAka creator god. (1)

kombu (Also *kompā*.) Animal horn; curved brass horn. (5)

kombu kahaḷe Bugles; ensemble of animal and brass horns. (5)

kome (1) Gumuz end-blown flute; (2) Gumuz ensemble for light recreation involving singing and dancing. (1)

komedi stambul Dutch-influenced stage theater in Sumatra. (4)

komintang Tagalog courtship song. (4)

kommu Crescent-shaped brass horn used particularly by singers of the Telugu herding caste. (5)

komo Maninka secret society that uses wind instruments. (1)

komosô (Japan.) 'Straw mat monks' of the early Edo period. (7)

kompā (Also *kombu*, *śṛṅga*.) Semicircular trumpet of South India. (5)

kompang Malay single-headed frame drum of Arab origin. (4)

komuk Chechen and Ingush accordion, played by women; *see kekhat-pondur*. (8)

kŏmun'go Korean six-stringed plucked zither with fixed bridges. (7)

komusô (Japan.) 'Monks of emptiness' in the middle Edo period. (7, 10)

komuz Plucked fretless lute in Kyrgyzstan. (6)

kòn-kpàla Kpelle musical bow. (1)

konakkoḷ Gurgling syllables recited to rhythmic patterns in Karnatak music. (5)

konbit Haitian collective labor association that uses music to accompany work. (2)

koncovka Slovak flute without holes for fingering. (8)

kondi Azande and Moro lamellophone. (1)

kondyslies (Also, in western and central Crete, *mantinadhes*.) Greek genre of improvised, rhyming couplets of eastern Crete. (8)

kongch'ŏk (Chinese, *gongche*.) Rarely used Korean letter notation borrowed from China. (7)

konggap (Yupno, 'ghost voice'.) Any short tune uniquely identified with an individual Yupno, of Madang Province, Papua New Guinea. (9)

kŏn'go Large Korean barrel-shaped drum. (7)

koŋgoma Large lamellophone with three or four metal tongues and a box resonator. (1)

Kongô ryû (Japan.) School of *nô* specializing in *site kata*. (7)

koni Maninka four-stringed lute. (1)

konîng Kpelle triangular frame zither. (1, 10)

konkoba Mandinka songs praising farmers. (1)

kónkoma Kpelle lamellophone. (1)

konmandè (1) Guadeloupe call-and-response song leader; (2) person who calls quadrille steps. (2)

kóno Kpelle handheld struck log idiophone. (1)

konpa-dirèk Haitian popular dance modeled on the Dominican *merengue*. (2)

Konparu ryû (Japan.) School of *nô* specializing in *site kata* and *taiko* (stick drum). (7)

Konsonanzton (Japan.) Nuclear tone in a theory of scales formulated by Sibata Minao (1916–1996). (7)

kont (1) Dominican storytelling with short, fixed, recurrent song theme. (2) St. Lucian unaccompanied songs performed at wakes. (2)

konting Five-string plucked lute of the Mandinka of The Gambia. (1)

kontra 'Rhythmic-harmonic support', part played by one musician in a Hungarian folk violin duo. (8)

kootsoo (Also *kotsoo*.) Fulani or Hausa single-headed hourglass-shaped tension drum. (1)

kopak-kopak Long bamboo pole to disperse birds in the Philippines. (4)

kopuz Turkish folk lute. (6)

kora (1) Manding harp-lute with nineteen or twenty-one strings that traditionally accompanies singing of praises and historical songs but has been incorporated into international styles. (2) One of many non-Western traditional instruments used frequently in world beat recording projects. (3) West African harp-lute played by immigrants in France. (1, 3, 8)

koraippu Section of a Karnatak drum solo involving more than one drummer. (5)

Koran *See* Qur'ān. (6)

Koranko Northern Mande-speaking people of northern Sierra Leone. (1)

koravanji Women tattoo artists and singers in Karnataka villages; *see also kuravanji*. (5)

kôrei sai (Japan.) Court ritual intended to comfort the spirits of imperial ancestors, performed at the vernal and autumnal equinoxes; a performance context for *azuma asobi*. (7)

kori Kasena-Nankani gourd drums, played in sets of two. (1)

kŏri Portion of a larger Korean shaman ritual. (7)

korima Tarahumara harvest ceremony. (2)

korizne goblice Slovenian homemade fiddle, made by rubbing two corn stalks together. (8)

korneto Greek brass horn. **(8)**

korng mong Khmer single, suspended bossed gong. **(4)**

korng vung 'Circular frame of gongs', Cambodian percussion instrument played as part of the *pinnpeat* ensemble; Khmer gong circle. **(3, 4)**

korng vung tauch Khmer higher-pitched gong circle, with sixteen to eighteen gongs. **(4)**

korng vung thomm Khmer lower-pitched gong circle, with sixteen gongs. **(4)**

Köroğlu 'The Blind Man's Son', epic of Central Asian origin. **(6)**

koron Symbol for a half-flat in notation of Persian music. **(6)**

korro Dogon struck log idiophone. **(1)**

korta pandum Gond festival during the rainy season. **(5)**

kortsili Georgian wedding in which all songs are polyphonic. **(8)**

kŏrvai Intricate rhythmic composition in a Karnatak drum solo. **(5)**

Koryŏ Korean dynastic period, 918–1392. **(7)**

Koryŏsa 'History of Koryŏ Dynasty', Korean historical document of 1451. **(7)**

Kô ryû (Japan.) School of *nô* specializing in *ko tuzumi*. **(7)**

kös Large Turkish kettledrums. **(6)**

kosa In Korea, offering of a sacrifice to spirits. **(7)**

kosačke pjesme Grass-cutting songs of Bosnia-Hercegovina. **(8)**

ko saibari (Japan.) Section of *mikagura* (Shinto music and dance performed at the imperial court). **(7)**

Kôsei ryû (Japan.) School of *nô* specializing in *ko tuzumi*. **(7)**

kósi Maroon *sêkêti* song of cursing in Surinam. **(2)**

kôsiki (Japan.) Chant (*syômyô*) for lecturing on or discussing Buddha or other Buddhist topics. **(7)**

koşma (Also *qoşma*.) Common form of Turkish and Azerbaijani lyric verse with eleven- or eight-syllable lines, favored by minstrels. **(6)**

kosok kancing Samawan life-cycle dance for the nobility. **(4)**

Kosrae Island and state of the Federated States of Micronesia. **(9)**

kosu Korean drummer accompanying a *p'ansori* performance. **(7)**

Kotafon Cultural group of Benin. **(1)**

kōtānki Small, hourglass-shaped pressure drum in Tamil Nadu. **(5)**

kotekan Rapid, interlocking figuration characteristic of Balinese music. **(4)**

koten Okinawan classical music, performed by musicians of Okinawan heritage in Argentina, Brazil, and Peru. **(2)**

koten honkyoku (Japan.) *See honkyoku.* **(7)**

koto (Also, in romanized Okinawan orthography, *kutu*.) (1) Japanese board zither having thirteen silk strings set on movable bridges and played with ivory picks. (2) (Japan.) Generic term for plucked zithers. (3) Thirteen-stringed Japanese zither played by musicians of Japanese heritage in Argentina, Brazil, and Peru. **(2, 3, 7, 9, 10)**

koto kumiuta (Japan.) *Koto*-accompanied song cycles, earliest chamber music for *koto*. **(7)**

kôtô (Japan.) Second lowest of four ranks in the *tôdô* (guild for blind artisans). From lower to higher, the ranks are: *zatô*, *kôtô*, *bettô*, and *kengyô*. **(7)**

kotoba (Japan.) Nonmelodic dramatic speech section of *gidayû busi* narratives. **(7)**

kotodama sinkô (Japan.) Faith in the spirit in words. **(7)**

kotsaki Greek genre of improvised, rhyming couplets of Crete. **(8)**

kotsari Pontic Greek dance. **(8)**

kōṭṭi (Sanskrit *gōṣṭhi*). Tamil party of *bhajan* singers. **(5)**

kottippāṭisseva 'Drumming-and-singing offering', temple music genre of Kerala. **(5)**

ko tuzumi (Japan.) Hourglass-shaped drum held on the shoulder. **(7)**

kotyapi Maranao two-stringed plucked lute. **(4)**

koudyay Carnival-like Haitian celebration, not necessarily at carnival time. **(2)**

koumpania Greek ensemble of instrumentalists and vocalists that performed *rebetika* before the 1930s. **(8)**

kouta (Also *edo kouta, hayama kouta*.) In Japan, genre of short *syamisen* songs developed from *edo hauta*. **(7)**

koutalia Greek spoons, used percussively in *rehetika*. **(8)**

koutoumba St. Lucian wake ceremony or a song-dance performed by the *djiné*. **(2)**

kovur pancaratnam (Also *pañcaratna*.) Five songs composed by Tyagaraja on the deity Sundaresvara, who presides at the main temple at Kovur, near Madras. **(5)**

koza Bagpipe of Podhale, Poland. **(8)**

kozak Ukrainian dance form. **(8)**

Koziki (Japan.) 'Record of Ancient Matters', oldest extant historical work in Japan. **(7)**

kôzin kyô (Japan.) 'Sutra of the hearth', purification ritual performed by blind priests. **(7)**

kozioł Polish bagpipes. **(8)**

kozioł biały 'White he-goat', bagpipe of western Poland. **(8)**

ko zyôruri (Japan.) Generic term for narrative *syamisen* music for puppet theater established before *gidayû busi*. **(7)**

kpáníngbá (Also *kpaningbo, kpäningbä*.) Azande log xylophone, usually with twelve or fourteen keys. **(1)**

kpanlogo Fast dance of Ghana. **(1)**

Kpelle Southern Mande people of central Liberia and Guinea. **(1)**

kpom kpom kpom Igbo verbalization of the sound of knocking, used by Ndubuisi in a composition. **(1)**

kponingbo Twelve- or thirteen-keyed log xylophone, accompanied by a struck hollow-log idiophone (*guru*) and a double-headed drum. **(1)**

krajappi Central Thai long-necked lute with four strings. **(4)**

krakowiak Popular duple-meter dance in Poland. **(8)**

krakowiak Polish regional dance. **(3)**

krap Several kinds of Thai concussion idiophones. **(4)**

krapeu (1) Three-stringed floor zither of Cambodia. (2) Cambodian stringed instrument played in contemporary versions of the *pinnpeat* ensemble. **(3, 4)**

krapp Khmer pair of bamboo or wood clappers. **(4)**

krar Regional type of Ethiopian lyre. **(6)**

kratki glas 'Short voice', Serbian songs with syllabic text settings. **(8)**

kratki napjevi 'Short melodies', Bosnia-Hercegovinan songs having a melody subordinate to a text and often consisting of one short melodic pattern. **(8)**

kraton One of the Central Javanese courts. **(4)**

kraw Thai slit-bamboo signaling device. **(4)**

kreasi baru (Pan-Indonesian term.) New musical composition. **(4)**

kreuzpolka Swiss regional dance. **(8)**

krez' Udmurt zither, song, or melody. **(8)**

krienser halszither Swiss long-necked lute-zither resembling a guitar. **(8)**

krik-krac Martinique oral tradition of tales told at wakes. **(2)**

krimanchuli 'Distorted falsetto, distorted jaw'; the yodeling part in three-part singing of western Georgia. **(8)**

kris Fine laminated dagger, made in Java. **(4)**

Krismis (From English *Christmas*.) (1) Miskitu term for December. (2) Miskitu calendrical festival dance in a circle. **(2)**

krita Miskitu scraper. **(2)**

kriti Karnatak classical vocal genre derived from the *kīrtan* devotional tradition. **(5, 10)**

kriuk 'Hook', earliest neumatic notation of Russian church music. **(8)**

kriyā Hand movements that mark subdivisions of Karnatak talas. (**5**)

kroeung damm Khmer classification term for percussion instruments. (**4**)

kroeung khse Khmer classification term for stringed instruments. (**4**)

kroeung phlomm Khmer classification term for wind instruments. (**4**)

kromanti (1) Maroon warrior gods, ancestral spirits in Surinam; (2) Maroon play or dance in Jamaica; (3) Jamaican principal ritual for summoning Maroon ancestral spirits. (**2**)

kromong (Also *kromongan*.) Sumatran gong-chime and ensemble. (**4**)

kroncong (1) Eurasian colonial-based popular music of Indonesia. (2) Indonesian name of the *cavaquinho*. (**4, 8**)

kroncong asli 'Original' *kroncong* music. (**4**)

krong Large slit-bamboo signaling device from Thailand. (**4**)

Kṛṣṇa Janmāṣṭāmī North Indian festival celebrating the birthday of Krishna. (**5**)

kṛṣṇa līlā Theatrical enactment of Krishna's pastimes with the milkmaids, performed by boys in Bangladesh. (**5**)

Kṛṣṇalīlātaraṅginī Seventeenth-century Sanskrit musical poem by Narayanatirtha on the Krishna theme. (**5**)

kṛṣṇāṭṭam Ritual temple dance drama of Kerala. (**5**)

krsteno Macedonian dance in 12/8 time. (**8**)

Kru Liberian speakers of Kru or Krao, a language of the Kwa group, who worked on ships up and down the West African coast. (**1**)

krugi (Also *khorovod, tanok*.) 'Circles', Russian collective circle and figure dances. (**8**)

Krusbass Yoruba two-finger guitar style in which all right-hand passages were played with the thumb and index fingers. (**1**)

krusta dancis Latvian dancing and jumping over crossed poles or swords. (**8**)

krywá Cane tube, open on both ends, into which the player hums, played exclusively by women among the Aché-Guayakí of Paraguay. (**2**)

ksenitias Greek songs of exile. (**8**)

Kshatriya (Also *Kṣatriya*.) Traditionally the second-highest group or class (*varṇā*) in Hindu society, whose members served as rulers and fighters. (**5**)

k'shots Armenian cult instrument made of silver plates with jingles. (**6**)

k'tsurt Form of Armenian sacred music. (**6**)

kuaiban (China.) (1) Fast tempo or animated aria in Peking opera. (2) Genre of storytelling that uses a pair of clappers as the primary accompaniment. (**7**)

kūbah 'Drinking glass', early Arabic term for single-headed goblet drum. (**6**)

kubing Mindanao Jew's harp. (**4**)

kücek 'Belly-dance hip movement' (Turkish), the source of *čoček*, a dance of Serbian Gypsies. (**8**)

kuchipuḍi Classical dance form originating in Andhra Pradesh. (**5**)

kuda kepang Malay hobby-horse trance dance, preceded by *barongan*. (**4**)

kuḍam Struck brass pot on which the *villu* bow rests. (**5**)

kudara gaku (Japan.) Music imported from the Korean kingdom of Paekche. (**7**)

kuden (Japan.) Verbal transmission, consisting mostly of suggestions for adding interest or color to a performance; usually, this transmission takes place at an advanced level of study of specific pieces. (**7**)

kudlung Hanunoo paired-string zither. (**4**)

kudoki (Japan.) (1) Genre of long quasi-narrative folk songs, often used as dance songs or performed by itinerants; (2) segment of lamentation in a *nô* play; (3) *heikyoku* vocal melody pattern (*kyokusetu*) in narrative style; (4) section of *gidayû busi* in which a character reveals feelings; (5) two-line poetic form of the Ryûkyû Islands, derived from mainland Japan, with a syllable pattern of 7 + 5 or 7 + 7; (6) category of Okinawan classical narrative song using the *kudoki* poetic form, which accompanies *nisai odori* 'young man's dance'; (7) category of Okinawan narrative folk song. (**7**)

kudum Small kettledrum, played in some dervish rituals in Bosnia-Hercegovina. (**8**)

kudüm Small pair of drums used in Mevlevī ceremonies. (**6**)

kuduti (Japan.) *Kudoki* (poetic form or musical genre) in Okinawan dialect. (**7**)

kudya Bontok love song, antiphonal song. (**4**)

kudyapi (Also *kudyapiq*.) Maguindanao two-stringed lute. (**4**)

kue (Also *kui*.) Kenyah rice-planting ceremony. (**4**)

kuêna (Also *umui*.) Okinawan religious songs performed by women to pray for a good harvest, fishing, or hunting, or a safe voyage. (**7**)

kugak Korean traditional music. (**7**)

Kugak hakhoe Original name of the Korean Musicological Society; today *Han'guk Kugak Hakhoe*. (**7**)

Kugak hyŏphoe Korean Traditional Music Society. (**7**)

Kugak kwanhyŏn aktan Traditional Music Orchestra of the Korea Broadcasting System. (**7**)

Kugaksa yangsŏngso Korean music school, established in 1954. (**7**)

kugikly (Also *kuvikly*.) Archaic Russian panpipes. (**8**)

kugiran Guitar-dominated popular song genre of Malaysia. (**4**)

Kühreihen (Also *kuhreigen*.) Melismatic Swiss cattle call; *see ranz des vaches*. (**8**)

kuísi (Also *kuizi*.) Kogi vertical cane duct flute with a mouthpiece shaped like a hatchet (made of pitch and ash with a quill for a duct), often played in pairs, one male (*kuísi sigi* or *kuísi macho*) and the other female (*kuísi bunzi* or *kuísi hembra*). (**2**)

kuityâ âgu (Japan.) Subgenre of *âgu* (a folk song genre of the Miyako Islands) performed in unison or antiphonally by two groups of men and women; used to accompany a circle dance. (**7**)

kujawiak Polish folk dance. (**8**)

kuji Nyamlthu chief in the former Bauchi State in Nigeria. (**1**)

Kukche op'erasa Korean International Opera Company. (**7**)

kukeri (Also *startsi*.) Bulgarian masked characters who make good-luck visits with music before Lent. (**8**)

kukerski igri Dances of the Bulgarian *kukeri*. (**8**)

kuki Female figure carried during Lazeroba, the Georgian rain-begging ritual. (**8**)

Kukka misul chakp'um simŭi wiwŏnhoe North Korean National Arts Council. (**7**)

kuku Albanian lament or stylized form of crying, whose name derives from a sorrowful exclamation. (**8**)

kukuma Hausa small one-stringed bowed lute. (**1**)

kula Extensive trading network of southeast New Guinea. (**9**)

kulaing Yakan Jew's harp. (**4**)

kulal Small South Indian double-reed pipe or bamboo flute. (**5**)

kulè 'To speak out or shout', work songs or chants sung by Bribri men. (**2**)

kulɛ nyia (Vai) 'Fine voice'. (**1**)

kulimbet Ibaloy drum and flat gong ensemble. (**4**)

kulintang (1) Gong chime melodic instrument; (2) gong ensemble that features this melodic instrument from the southern Philippines. (**3**)

kulintang (Also *kulintangan*.) Horizontal bronze gong-chime and ensemble of Indonesia and the Philippines. (**4**)

kulitang Horizontal bronze gong-chime and ensemble of Sumatra. (**4**)

kullkull Mapuche cow-horn lip-concussion aerophone. (**2**)

k'ullu charango Small Bolivian *charango* associated with the dry season. (**2**)

kulning Swedish cattle calls. (**8**)

kulokkar Norweigian ornamented cow calls. (**8**)

kultrún Mapuche single-headed, kettle-shaped membranophone played with one stick by the *machi* shaman. (**2**)

kulturno-umetnička društva Cultural-artistic ensembles in the former Yugoslavia. (**8**)

kuluk-kuluk Rattle made of coconut and bamboo from the Philippines. (**4**)

kŭm (Chinese, *qin*.) Korean seven-stringed zither (**7**)

kuma San raft zither. (**1**)

kumārapūrṇimā gīt Songs performed by girls in Orissa at the Kumārapūrṇimā festival. (**5**)

Kŭm bapchabo 'Tablature Notation for *Kŏmun'go*' (1572), first Korean tablature book. (**7**)

kumbing Subanen Jew's harp. (**4**)

kumemai (Japan.) Genre of indigenous court dance performed at the coronation of an emperor (*daizyô e*). (**7**)

kumeuta (Japan.) Indigenous genre of court songs accompanying the *kumemai* dance. (**7**)

kumidya Spanish-influenced stage play from the Philippines. (**4**)

Kumina (1) Jamaican religion practiced by the descendants of postemancipation indentured laborers from Central Africa; (2) call-and-response song type signaling the start of every ritual ceremony. (**2**)

kuminjaré Five-stringed Mbyá shamanic guitar of Paraguay. (**2**)

kumintang Philippine song and dance depicting love. (**4**)

kumi odori (Japan.) Okinawan genre combining music, dance, recitation of poems, and acting; first introduced in 1719 by Tamagusuku Tyôkun (1684–1734), the official director of Ryûkyû court music and dance. (**7**)

kumi udui (Japan.) *Kumi odori* (Okinawan music dance drama) in Okinawan dialect. (**7**)

kumiuta (Japan.) Song cycles for *koto* and *syamisen*. (**7**)

kummi Tamil women's circle dance. (**5**)

kummiyaṭi Hand clapping in *kummi* songs of Tamil Nadu. (**5**)

kumoi zyôsi (Japan.) *Koto* tuning system devised by Yatuhasi *kengyô* (1614–1685). (**7**)

kumú Tukano religious practitioner, said to cure illnesses caused by the supernatural intrusion of pathogenic agents (stones, splinters, thorns) into the patient's body. (**2**)

Kumulipo Long, versified genealogical narrative honoring Lono-i-ka-Makahiki, an ancestor of King Kalākaua of Hawai'i. (**9**)

Kunaityô gakubu (Japan.) Department of music in the imperial household agency. (**7**)

kunak Korean military music of the Koryŏ dynasty. (**7**)

kundi (1) Bongo anthropomorphically carved harp, probably adopted from the Azande; (2) tanged harp in the region of the Central African Republic. (**1**)

kundiman Filipino genre of composed and published love songs, stylistically related to romantic European light classical forms. (**3**)

kundiman (1) Lyrical love song of the Philippines. (2) Lowland Filipino song, composed in an art-song style with piano accompaniment. (**4, 9**)

kundongan Maranao lower-pitched gongs of the *kulintang*. (**4**)

Kundu Network service of the National Broadcasting Commission of Papua New Guinea. (**9**)

kundu Papua New Guinean hourglass-shaped drum, held with one hand and struck with the other, mostly by men. (**9**)

kung (1) Onomatopoeic Korean term for slapping a drum with an open hand; (2) "central tone" of Korean modes. (**7**)

!Kung Subgroup of the San, living in southern Africa. (**1**)

kungbi Large Miskitu double-headed cylindrical drum played with the hands. (**2**)

kunggul ch'ae (Also *kung ch'ae*.) Korean hammer-shaped drumstick. (**7**)

kungjung ŭmak (Also *kungjungak*.) Korean court music. (**7**)

kungkuvak North Borneo reed pipe. (**4**)

Kungnip ch'anggŭk tan Korean Traditional Opera Troupe. (**7**)

Kungnip kugagwŏn National Center for Traditional Korean Performing Arts. (**7**)

Kungnip kugak kodŭng hakkyo Korean National Traditional Music High School. (**7**)

Kungnip kŭkchang Korean National Theater. (**7**)

Kungnip muyong tan Korean Dance Troupe. (**7**)

kuṇita Generic term for dance in Karnataka. (**5**)

kunkunsî (Japan.) Notation system for *sansin* (Okinawan three-stringed lute). (**7**)

k'ŭn kut Large Korean shaman ritual. (**7**)

k'ŭn mudang Korean senior shaman who conducts rituals with singing and dancing. (**7**)

kunnbi Dance associated with agricultural work performed by Goan Christians. (**5**)

kunqu (China.) Opera style originating in the Kunshan area in Jiangsu Province. (**7**)

kunshanqiang (Also *kunqu*.) In China, style popularized by a singer, Gu Jian, around the mid-fourteenth century; (**7**)

kuṇṭalam (Also *kirikaṭṭi*.) Pair of conical drums tied around the waist and played with curved sticks in Tamil Nadu. (**5**)

kuntigi Hausa one-stringed plucked lute. (**1**)

kuntiji Songhai one-stringed bowed lute. (**1**)

kŭnŭl 'Shadow', 'shade'; aesthetic quality in Korean *p'ansori*. (**7**)

kŭnzag Earthen water pot used as a rhythm-producing instrument; played by a *kŭnzagī*. (**5**)

kuomboka Lozi ceremony marked yearly by a procession of boats as the people migrate ceremonially to dry land. (**1**)

Kupalle Belarusan summer-solstice ritual. (**8**)

kupalskie pesni Summer-solstice songs performed in western Russia on midsummer day. (**8**)

kupalskija pieśni Belarusan summer-song cycle. (**8**)

kuplés Hungarian cabaret songs popularized in the 1930s. (**8**)

kupuna (Plural, *kūpuna*.) Hawaiian-speaking elder, revered as a living repository of indigenous culture. (**9**)

kurai Bashkir and Tatar rim-blown flute. (**8**)

kuranji South Indian raga name; often used in Tamil swinging songs. (**5**)

kuraqkuna Bolivian community authority who may sponsor fiestas. (**2**)

kuravai (1) Tamil song form associated with agriculture. (2) Type of ululation performed by women at important moments in rituals. (**5**)

kuravanji Dramatic form about Gypsies, in Tanjavur. See also *koravanji*. (**5**)

kuravan-kuratti Dance and song in the form of playful, erotic banter between a Gypsy man and woman, in Tamil Nadu. (**5**)

kurban bairam (Also *kurban xayit*, *xayit*; Arabic, *id al-adkha*, *'id al-aḍḥā*.) Feast of the Sacrifice, the most important religious holiday in Central Asia. (**6**)

kurbi (Also *al-bakurbo*.) Five-stringed harp of the Baggāra of Darfur. (**1**)

kurei Parrot associated with Waiãpi edge aerophones. (**2**)

kuri (Japan.) (1) Introductory recitative segment in a *nô* play; (2) note in the scales for *nô* chanting. (**7**)

Kuria Cultural group of Kenya. (**1**)

kuri-kuri Yuma song cycles performed during holidays. (**2**)

kuriri Tausug and Yakan single-part piece. (**4**)

kurnetta Maltese shawm. (**8**)

kuromisu (Japan.) Small room to the right of the *kabuki* stage that is partitioned off by a reed screen and used by the offstage ensemble. (**7**)

kuromisu music (Japan.) Another term for *geza ongaku*. (**7**)

kursī Short, quick instrumental introduction in the Andalusian-Algerian *nūba*. (**6**) *kuru* (Japan.) Term in *gidayû busi* notation indicating a narrative technique. (7)

kuse (Japan.) Narrative song segment in a *nô* play. (7)

kusemai (Japan.) Medieval genre of narrative song chanted rhythmically with dance. (7)

kushaura Leading *mbira* part, which plays melodic and higher notes. (1)

kust 'Bush', Belarusan songs for Pentecost, when a girl clothed in greenery is taken around the village. (8)

kuswa taya Miskitu tortoiseshell idiophone that produces two tones when struck on the free ends of its ventral side with a deer's horn, wooden stick, or large nail. (2)

kusyapiq Palawan two-stringed lute. (4)

kut Korean shaman ritual. (7)

kutahiri Circumcision celebrations in rural coastal areas of Kenya. (1)

kutam Musical bow of Kerala. (5)

kutapa Melodic ensemble associated with Sanskrit drama, consisting of a singer, players of hand cymbals marking the meter and tempo, and string and flute players. (5)

kut chŏng Korean purifying ritual to ward off evil spirits. (7)

kutet Subanen one-stringed fiddle. (4)

kuti (Japan.) First section of the tripartite division of an act in *bunraku* (puppet theater). (7)

Kutin Culture group of Cameroon. (1)

kutirai 'Horse dance', processional dance performed in village festivals in Tamil Nadu. (5)

kutiridingo Conical drum from The Gambia, played with one stick and one hand. (1)

kuti syôga (Japan.) *See syôga.* (7)

kuti utusi (Japan.) Method of oral transmission emphasizing the student's faithful imitation of the teacher's model. (7)

kūṭiyāṭṭam Sanskrit dance drama of Kerala. (5)

kutkŏri Korean rhythmic pattern (*changdan*), swaying 6/8 or 12/8 meter. (7)

kutok 'Corner', section of a Ukrainian village that shared an aesthetic and musical knowledge. (8)

kut p'an Dance repertoire of Korean *samul nori*. (7)

kutsinhira Following part on the *mbira* that emphasizes root movements of harmonic patterns. (1)

kūttambalam 'Drama hall', room in a temple in which dance dramas are staged. (5)

kūttu (Also *terukkūttu.*) Popular street dance and drama in Tamil Nadu. (5)

kutu (1) Japanese *koto* (long zither) in Okinawan dialect. (2) Okinawan zither. (7, 9)

kutyapiq Maguindanao two-stringed plucked lute. (4)

kûtyô (Japan.) *Kokyû* (long-necked bowed lute) in Okinawan dialect. (7)

kuŭm 'Mouth sounds'. (1) Vocal imitation of an instrumental sound. (2) *Kuŭm akpo*, an early Korean notational system. (7)

kuŭm sinawi Korean improvised instrumental genre including the singing of meaningless syllables. (7)

kuvara Of a disease, to mature, among the Tumbuka. (1)

kuvikly (Also *kugikly.*) Archaic Russian panpipes. (8)

kuvina nthenda Tumbuka term used when both patient and healer "dance their disease." (1)

kuwai Wayana shaker attached to the legs of a dancer or stick, often used by shamans. (2)

Ku wanggung aakpu Old Emperor's Palace Music Office of Korea, ancestor of today's *Kungnip Kugagwŏn*. (7)

kuyabilo Ila-Tonga musical genre. (1)

Kuyate Originally the name of Manding families of professional musicians in Mali. (1)

kuyômon (Japan.) Buddhist chant (*syômyô*) for worshiping the "three treasures," Buddha, *dharma*, and Sangha. (7)

kuzure (Japan.) (1) Blind priests' *biwa* ballads of heroes fallen in battle; (2) *satuma biwa* narrative and instrumental interludes used for battle scenes. (7)

kvæðamaður Icelandic chanter renowned for special abilities. (8)

kvæði (Singular, *kvæðir.*) (1) Chanting of *rímur* in Iceland. (2) Lengthy heroic ballads of the Faroe Islands, dramatized by singers performing a line dance. (8)

kvelieri Main Georgian ritual complex, the last week of carnival, marking the beginning of the agricultural year. (8)

kveða (Also *kveðir, kvað, kveðið.*) In Iceland, to compose, write poetry, narrate, and chant. (8)

kveðandi 'Recitation', considered a form of Icelandic musical performance. (8)

kviria Georgian song of Svaneti, connected to the fertility deity. (8)

kvirostviri 'Loud-shouting *stviri*', Georgian metallic military instrument. (8)

kvöldvaka 'Evening watch', winter vigils once held in Iceland, when performers (*kvæðamaður*) would recite *rímur*. (8)

kwadril 'Quadrille', St. Lucian social dance of European origin. (2)

kwadwom Akan genre of musical poetry in Ghana. (1)

Kwahu Akan-speaking people of Ghana. (1)

kwakwa Maroon squat wooden bench or stool beaten with two sticks in Surinam. (2)

kwal taya Miskitu shaman's wake for the deceased. (2)

Kwanak Yŏngsan hoesang Korean suite *Yŏngsan hoesang* in a version for wind ensemble. (7)

Kwanangoma College Institution founded in Bulawayo, Zimbabwe, in 1961 to foster African musical scholarship. (1)

kwangdae Korean entertainer or singer of *p'ansori*. (7)

Kwangdaega 'Song of the *P'ansori* Singer', a famous Korean poem. (7)

Kwansŭp togam Office of Customs, Korean Chosŏn period. (7)

kwasa kwasa Name for the Zaïrean rumba. (1)

kwat Length of bamboo beaten with two sticks among Jamaican Maroons. (2)

kwaya 'Choir', term used in southern Africa. (1)

kwela Style of street jazz that sprang up in southern Africa in the 1940s and 1950s and featured pennywhistles, the precursor of *mbaqanga*. (1, 10)

kwintangan Yakan set of bossed gongs. (4)

kwintangan kayu Yakan hanging log beams. (4)

kwītra Short-necked lute of Morocco and Algeria. (6)

kwŏnbŏn Korean training house for *kisaeng*. (7)

kwv txhiaj Hmong courtship game songs. (4)

kwv txhiaj plees Hmong sung poetry; amatory songs. (4)

kyemyŏnjo (Also *sŏrŭmjo.*) Sorrowful Korean melodic mode. (7)

kyô (Japan.) Chant (*syômyô*) for lecturing on or discussing Buddha or other Buddhist topics. (7)

kyobanggo Short suspended Korean barrel-shaped drum. (7)

kyôbû tegotomono (Japan.) *See kyôryû tegotomono.* (7)

kyogaku (Japan.) Theatrical pieces created by Kisimoto Yositake, a son of the founder of *kibigaku*, Kisimoto Yosihide (1821–1890). (7)

kyôgen (Japan.) Genre of classical comedy consisting mainly of dialogue and pantomime. (7)

kyôgen kata (Japan.) Performers of both *kyôgen* and *nô*. (7)

Kyôgoku ryû (Japan.) School of *koto* founded in 1901 by Suziki Koson (1875–1931). (7)

kyôke (Japan.) Buddhist chant (*syômyô*) for enlightenment. (7)

Kyôkun syô (Japan.) 'A Selection of Instructions', oldest book on music in Japan, compiled in 1233 by Koma no Tikazane (1177–1242), dealing with *gagaku*. (7)

Volume Key: **1**, Africa; **2**, South America, Mexico, etc.; **3**, United States and Canada; **4**, Southeast Asia; **5**, South Asia

kyokusetu (Japan.) Set of *heikyoku* vocal melody patterns consisting of combinations of fixed, smaller melodic formulas. (7)

kyômono (Japan.) Abbreviation for *kyôhû* or *kyôryû tegotomono*. (7)

kyŏngdŭrŭm (Also *kyŏngjo*.) Cheerful melodic mode from the central region of Korea. (7)

kyŏnggi minyo Korean folk songs in the regional style of Seoul and Kyŏnggi Province. (7)

kyŏnggi nongak Seoul and Kyŏnggi Province style of Korean farmers' band music. (7)

kyŏngje sijo Short lyric songs from Seoul and Kyŏnggi Province, Korea. (7)

kyŏngnaech'wi (Also *chorach'i*.) Korean Buddhist outdoor band. (7)

kyŏngsŏ t'ori Song style from northwestern Korea. (7)

kyôryû tegotomono (Also *kyôhû tegotomono*, *kyômono*.) In Japan, *tegoto mono* compositions (*syamisen* music) with a part (*kaede*) by the *koto*; typically, they involve alternate playing (*kakeai*) between the *syamisen* and the *koto*. (7)

kyoslë Chuvash zither. (8)

kyôsyaku (Japan.) Chant (*syômyô*) for lecturing on or discussing Buddha or other Buddhist topics. (7)

kyosyô (Japan.) One of four intonations (*sisyô*) used to pronounce a Chinese character in Buddhist chant (*syômyô*) texts. (7)

kyû (Japan.) (1) First note in the Japanese scale *gosei* ; (2) rushing to the end or denouement, the last part of the tripartite principle of *zyo ha kyû*. (7)

kyuchek Solo dance of the Bulgarian Roma. (8)

kyui (Also *kui*.) 'Frame of mind', 'mood'. In Central Asia, an independent instrumental piece, played on lutes such as the *dombra* and *dutâr*, that seeks to narrate a story. (6)

kyuiler Kazakh instrumental music. (6)

kyuslë Mari box zither. (8)

la'ba Yemeni dance performed by male couples, accompanied by the *mizmâr*. (6)

laba dera Single-headed squat hand drum of Flores. (4)

laba go Drum and gong ensemble of Flores. (4)

labanoru dùda Lithuanian bagpipe with a blowpipe, a melody pipe, and a drone pipe. (8)

Labanotation (also *kinetography Laban*.) System of notation running from bottom to top developed in the 1920s by Rudolf von Laban (1879–1958) to transcribe human movements; cf. *Benesh notation*. (9)

la batalla 'The battle', Venezuelan stick dance. (2)

laba toda High, narrow standing drum of Flores. (4)

laba wai Single-headed standing drum of Flores. (4)

labu Single-headed standing drum of Roti. (4)

lachārī Saucy women's songs for weddings and childbirth celebrations, sung in Trinidad and Bhojpur. (5)

La condanna della vecchiaccia 'The condemnation of the crone', Italian mid-Lenten ceremony in Umbria. (8)

ladainhas 'Litanies', *capoeira* song repertoire in Brazil. (2)

Ladinos (1) Guatemalan urbanites whose primary language is Spanish; (2) sixteenth-century Spanish-speaking Christians of African descent brought from Spain to the Dominican Republic. (2)

ladkana Monophonic narrow-range wedding melodies of lowland western Ukraine. (8)

ladrang Formal arrangement of a Javanese *gamelan* piece. (4)

ladugiju iish 'Melodies for listening', Chechen instrumental music. (8)

laduvane Bulgarian fortune-telling ritual for boys and girls performed with songs in some areas at the new year. (8)

Ladysmith Black Mambazo South African band that achieved major international renown partly as a result of Paul Simon's album *Graceland*. (1)

laendler (Also *ländler*.) Austrian-Swiss dance in triple meter. (3)

lagatoi Trading vessels of the Motu people of New Guinea. (9)

Lag ba-'Omer Largest of the Jewish *hilulot*, festivals on the anniversary of the death of a saintly person, taking place on the thirty-third day after Passover; it is observed by Jews and Muslims alike on the island of Djerba. (6)

laggī Short, fast-tempo Hindustani *tabla* composition. (5)

la grande coquille de Gruyère 'The big shell of Gruyère', communal dance of French-speaking Gruyère, Switzerland. (8)

lagu (1) Musical piece from Cirebon and Sunda. (2) 'Melody', concept in Javanese *gamelan* playing. (4, 10)

lagu batin 'Inner melody', concept in Javanese gamelan playing. (10)

lagu cengeng 'Weepy song' from Indonesia. (4)

lagu dolanan Javanese light, humorous pieces. (4)

lagu dua Sumatran dance songs in triple meter. (4)

lagu-lagu rakyat Pan-Malaysian contemporary songs. (4)

laḥn (Plural, *alḥān*.) (1) 'Song', 'tune'. (2) Model strophe in Arabic poetry. (6)

lahutë One-stringed fiddle played to accompany Albanian narrative songs. (8)

lahw (Also *lahu*.) 'Entertainment', 'idle pleasure', pejorative term for music in Islamic *samā'* literature. (6)

lai Modal system used for performance on the Thai *khaen*. (4)

laika Greek popular urban songs. (8)

lajerkosten Large Slovene hurdy-gurdy on legs. (8)

lajna Slovene hurdy-gurdy. (8)

lakalaka (1) Formal Tongan dance developed from the *me'elaufola* in the 1800s. (2) Generic term for dance in the Banks Islands, Vanuatu. (9)

lakhon (Also *lakhawn*.) Various types of Thai dance-drama. (4)

lakodalmas 'Wedding rock' in Hungary. (8)

lakonmèt Sole closed-couple dance said to have originated in St. Lucia. (2)

lakṣaṇa Characteristic feature. (5)

Lakṣmi kalyāṇam 'The Wedding of Lakshmi', song played during Tamil weddings. (5)

lala *Sistrum* with small pieces of round circular gourds threaded on a stick. (1)

lalai Lullaby of northern Afghanistan. (5)

lāl al-'ūd 'Great shout', Omani dance consisting of antiphonal calls and slow, even-metered singing and dancing. (6)

lale devri 'Tulip time', cultural renaissance in eighteenth-century Turkey. (6)

lāli Lilting tune in *kuranji* raga, sung during the swinging ceremony at Tamil weddings. (5)

lalim uadindz Ossetian bagpipe. (8)

laling Norwegian elaborated shouts and hollers; see *huving*. (8)

lam Vocal performance common to northeast Thailand. (4)

la marsiliana Corsican dance imported from France. (8)

lamba Single-headed standing drum of Sumba. (4)

lambada Brazilian adaptation of the *carimbó* popular dance form. (2)

lam ban xok Repartee song genre of central-southern Laos. (4)

lāmbā vīrkāvyo Long poems about bravery, in Gujarat. (5)

Lambeg drums Large, two-headed drums that accompany the keyless fife in Ulster. (8)

lamellophone Musical instrument whose sound is the vibration of a tonguelike projection. (9, 10)

lamenti di banditi Corsican autobiographical songs of famous bandits. (8)

lamentu (Also *ballata*, *compitu*, *voceru*.) Corsican lament, especially for the dead. (8)

lam khon savan Repartee song genre of Savannakhet area, central-south Laos. (4)

Volume Key: **6**, Middle East; **7**, East Asia; **8**, Europe; **9**, Australia and the Pacific Islands; **10**, The World's Music.

lam klawn Northeast Thai repartee song with *khaen*. (4)

lam mahaxay Repartee song genre of central-southern Laos. (4)

lam mu Theatrical genre in northeast Thailand. (4)

lam phanya yoi Regional type of repartee song with *khaen* in northeast Thailand. (4)

lam phi fa Northeast Thai spirit-healing ceremony. (4)

lam phlün Local theater of northeast Thailand. (4)

lam phün Northeast Thai narrative song accompanied by *khaen*. (4)

lam phu thai Vocal genre of the Phu Thai minority of southern Laos. (4)

lam ploen Theatrical genre in northeast Thailand. (4)

lam rueang Adaptation of northeast Thai theater. (4)

lam salavane Vocal genre of Salavane province, Laos. (4)

lam sing Modern form of *lam* in northeast Thailand. (4)

lam sithandone Repartee vocal genre from the Champassak area. (4)

lam som Nearly extinct vocal genre of southern Laos. (4)

lam tang vay Repartee song genre of central-southern Laos. (4)

l'amt Yearly gathering of drummers among the Shleuh group of Moroccan Berbers, in which playing and improvisation are learned. (6)

lanat Laotian suspended horizontal xylophone. (4)

lanbi Haitian conch-shell trumpet. (2)

lanca In Bima, fighting style using the knees. (4)

lancang kuning Malay royal barge rowing competition. (4)

lancaran Formal arrangement of a Javanese *gamelan* piece. (4)

lancers English social dance derived from the quadrille. (2)

landay (Also *tappa*.) Two-line verse form in the southeastern Pashtun areas of Afghanistan and Pakistan. (5)

ländler (1) Austrian waltzlike dance in slow 3/4 time, popular in western Europe. (2) In Switzerland, last dance of a common cycle (*räschtli*), often performed fast. (8)

ländlerkappelle (1) Swiss-German instrumental ensemble, consisting of a clarinet, accordions, and a double bass; (2) corresponding style of dancing and its accompanying music; see *burämusig*. (8)

landó Afro-Peruvian song and dance form with a syncopated accompaniment and an underlying (4 + 2)/4 time, said to have come from the Brazilian *lundú*. (2)

landsgemeinde Swiss open-air parliaments, accompanied by drums in Graubünden and Appenzell Ausserrhoden. (8)

landskappleik Fiddlers' festival in Norway. (8)

Landsknechttrommel Medieval German mercenary's drum, revived in the 1920s by German youth groups. (8)

Laṅgā Caste of hereditary musicians in Rajasthan. (5)

langan bataq-bataq Tausug lullaby. (4)

langeleik Norwegian plucked zither. (8)

langen driyan Javanese women's dance-drama with sung dialogue. (4)

langen mandra wanara Javanese men's dance-drama with sung dialogue. (4)

langgam jawa *Kroncong* music specific to Java. (4)

langgam kroncong *Kroncong* music from Indonesia. (4)

langkit Tausug ballad. (4)

langko Samawan competitive sung poetry. (4)

langspil Icelandic bowed zither with two to six strings. (8)

lanigi garawoun 'Heart drum' among the Garifuna in Belize. (2)

lansaran Murut headhunting song and dance form. (4)

lantoy Manobo chip-on-ledge flute. (4)

lanza Short for *la cuadrilla de lanceros* 'lancers' quadrille', popular among semiurban middle classes of Honduras in the early 1880s. (2)

laodan (China.) Role of an old woman in opera. (7)

laodong ge (China.) Work songs. (7)

laoidh Scottish lay (narrative song). (8)

laoi Fiannaiochta Old Irish genre, known as the Fenian or Ossianic heroic lay. (8)

laouto Greek long-necked fretted plucked lute. (3, 8)

lapinka (In Oman, also *yim, buk*.) Marine shell horn of the Gulf region. (6)

Lapita cultural complex Archaeologically documented tradition of earthenware ceramics from the Bismarck Archipelago, the coast of New Guinea, Melanesia, and West Polynesia. (9)

lapo kabwit 'Goatskin', generic Dominican term for drums. (2)

larakaraka Acholi ensembles of struck calabashes. (1)

laras Tuning, scale, in Javanese. (4)

larchemi 'Cane', Samegrelian panpipe; see *soinari* and *sastsrapo*. (8)

laremuna wadaguman Work-accompanying songs for Garifuna men in Belize. (2)

laridé Breton line or circle dance, performed as part of a three-part suite; see *ridée*. (8)

lasowe 'Of the forest', genre of open-air song of the Zywiecke region of Poland. (8)

lassú Slow section of the Hungarian Szék dance cycle, intended for listening. (8)

lāsya Feminine aspects of dance; one of the main principles of dance in the twelfth-century treatise *Abhinaya Chandrika*. See also *taṇḍava*. (5)

la tarascona Corsican dance imported from France. (8)

laterna Greek mechanical music box on legs. (8)

latihan Sundanese public jam session or rehearsal. (4)

latinos Latin American people, so named because they speak Spanish, a Latin-derived romance language. (2)

laud (1) Spanish fretted, flat-backed plucked lute with fourteen strings in six courses, used for tenor and baritone voices in the *rondalla* and sounding an octave lower than the *bandurria*. (2) Pear-shaped plucked lute from the Philippines. (3, 4)

laúd 'Lute', Cuban Spanish-derived (*la'ud*) twelve-stringed chordophone. (2)

laude (Singular, *lauda*.) Italian religious strophic songs, in Latin or the vernacular. (8)

laulaa 'To sing' (Finnish), originally 'to enchant'. (8)

laulu 'Song' (Finnish). (8)

launeddas Sardinian aerophone with three single-reed pipes played by one person. (8)

laures (Also *palos*.) Venezuelan sticks beaten on the side of the wooden-bodied *mina* drum. (2)

lausavísur 'Loose stanzas', single stanzas or epigrams in Iceland. (8)

lauta Fretted plucked lute, a Middle Eastern instrument, played in *čalgija* ensembles of Macedonia. (8)

lăutari Professional Romanian musicians, many of whom are Gypsies. (8)

lavitti Love songs using informal verse in Sumba. (4)

lāvṇi (1) Song form with improvised text, in Karnataka. (2) Tamil form, of Marathi origin, in which two parties engage in a musical debate on philosophical or mythological themes. (5)

lavta Turkish lute. (6)

lavwa Dominican chorus that responds to the *chantwèl*. (2)

lawatu Bolivian duct flute. (2)

lawentuchen 'Small therapies', Mapuche medical ritual. (2)

'lawi Algerian Saharan dance performed by men striking sticks or batons. (1)

lawik Term in northern Iraq and western Iran for one genre of lyrical song. (6)

lay Simple narrative poem and its music, especially as developed in northern France in the thirteenth century, best known in the works of Marie de France and Guillaume de Machaut and preserved in folk repertoires of various peoples. **(8)**

láy Patterned ornamentation characteristic of *tuồng* theater, Vietnam. **(4)**

laya (Also *lay.*) Tempo or rhythm. **(5)**

layālī 'Nights', section of vocal improvisation, analagous to instrumental *taqsīm*, and using the words *yā layl* 'O night' or *yā 'aynī* 'O my eye'. **(6)**

laykārī Complex rhythmic play in Hindustani music. **(5)**

layla (Plural, *layālī.*) 'Night', Egyptian Sufi musical concert, performed at night on religious and social occasions. **(6)**

laylat al-ḥinna (Also *lailat al-hanna.*) 'Henna night', festivity preceding a wedding, during which the bride's and sometimes the groom's hands and feet are dyed with henna as a prophylactic against the evil eye. **(6)**

lazarica House-to-house caroling by young children before Easter in Macedonia. **(8)**

lazarice Serbian girls who sing Lazarus's songs. **(8)**

lazaričke pesme 'Lazarus's songs', performed in Serbia, Bosnia-Hercegovina, and Montenegro by girls on St. Lazarus's Saturday to mark the beginning of the agricultural work cycle. **(8)**

lazaroba Georgian rain-begging ritual, performed by girls and young women, who carry a female figure and sing the song *Lazare. See Eliaobu, Gonjaoba.* **(8)**

lazarovden 'Lazar's Day', Bulgarian spring fertility ritual with singing and dancing, performed by women and girls. **(8)**

lāzima Instrumental interlude; in Yemeni tradition, a short coda played at the end of a song which underlines the basic rhythm and characteristic pitches of the mode. **(6)**

lê Afro-Brazilian smallest *atabaque* drum. **(2)**

lea-lea Buginese-Makassarese bamboo tube zither. **(4)**

le'b (Also *lēb.*) 'Play' in Arabic, Baluchi term for the *gwātī* ritual of possession or exorcism. **(6)**

lebad Yakan musical unit in instrumental music. **(4)**

Lebaran Feast held after Ramadan. **(4)**

lèdèk Female religious dancer of Javanese descent in Surinam. **(2)**

Leexo Composed Somali poem played on radio and credited with influencing political change. **(1)**

lego Circular men's or women's song and dance of Buru. **(4)**

lego-lego Women's court dance with vocals on Ternate. **(4)**

légong Girls' narrative dances of Bali. **(4)**

lehakot tsva'iyot Troupes or ensembles for the entertainment of the Israeli Defense Forces; to the 1970s, their music combined "native" elements with international popular styles. **(6)**

lehrā Sindhi folk composition believed to drive evil spirits from the body of a possessed woman. **(5)**

lehut In Montenegro, the Albanian name of the one-stringed bowed fiddle. **(8)**

Leikarring movement Revival of "song dancing"—dancers singing without accompaniment—in the Norwegian-American community during the 1920s and 1930s. **(3)**

leku Four-stringed fretless plucked lute from West Timor. **(4)**

lekupa Kenyah-Badang songs and dances. **(4)**

lela ma sorek 'Children of the gourd', Miri slim tubular gourd trumpet ensemble. **(1)**

lelambatan Slow, stately piece of Balinese music. **(4)**

le'le' Tausug humorous song. **(4)**

lelekanje (Also, in Albanian, *thirrje vaji.*) Montenegrin men's lament. **(8)**

leleng (1) (Also *lekŋ.*) Colo small kettledrum. (2) Tausug and Sama love repartee. **(1, 4)**

lellang Sama spirit possession piece. **(4)**

lemambang Iban bard. **(4)**

lemesidi Guatemalan Christian songs for liturgical use at Mass or prayer services. **(2)**

leng Dinka small drum. **(1)**

lènggèr Javanese female singer-dancer. **(4)**

lenggo Mbojo nonnarrative welcoming dance. **(4)**

lenjengo Recreational dance from The Gambia. **(1)**

leremuna égi Work songs of Garifuna women. **(2)**

lergøg (Also clay cuckoo.) Version of the Danish vessel flute or clay pipe. **(8)**

lesavyja pieśni Belarusan forest songs. **(8)**

lesiba Southern Sotho musical bow played by blowing air past a feather to vibrate the string. **(1)**

leśna (Plural, *leśne.*) 'Of the forest'. Genre of slow melismatic songs, performed in open woods and fields, of the Kurpie region of Poland. **(8)**

lesno oro (Also *pravo oro.*) (1) Macedonian line dance in a metric pattern of 3 + 2 + 2. (2) 'Easy dance', common Macedonian dance in 2/4 and 7/8 time. **(3, 8)**

lesung Rice-pounding block from Java and Borneo. **(4)**

leteuve yered Adighian song for a child's first independent step. **(8)**

letor Sikku and Lio xylophone. **(4)**

letter notation Musical notation that uses the letters of the alphabet to designate pitches. **(3)**

letzim Jewish musical professionals, especially instrumentalists. **(8)**

levantada (1) Second section of a Yuma song characterized by melodic devices and transposition. (2) *Levantada de muertos* 'raising of the dead', Mixtec custom in which people in disguise roam around a town accompanied by music. **(2)**

lev'dd Primary music genre of the Skolts, a Saami people of eastern Finland. **(8)**

lewa (Also *līwa.*) Afro-Arab performance tradition in the Gulf states involving song and dance, accompanied by an instrumental ensemble featuring percussion instruments and the *ṣurnāy*, or oboe. **(6)**

lēwā Festive dance common among fishermen along the Baloch coast; also performed by coastal Baloch living in Karachi. **(5)**

léwòz 'La rose' in French Creole (Kwéyòl). In Guadeloupe and St. Lucia, a musical genre, the evening of its performance, and its basic rhythm. **(2)**

lexicostatistics (Also glottochronology.) Method of measuring the history of related languages by quantifying the degree to which they share cognate words. **(9)**

lezginka Ossetian couple dance; *see timbil-kaft.* **(8)**

liaopai (China.) Term for meter in *nanguan* music. **(7)**

liban Sumu globular flute with three finger holes made from a crab's claw and beeswax. **(2)**

libres Free African-American people of Colombia. **(2)**

libretto 'Little book', text of a work, particularly an opera, for musical theater. **(3)**

lichiwayu (Also *lechewayo, lichiguayo.*) (1) Bolivian notched end-blown flute. (2) *Lichiguayo*, thick Chilean *kena* bound with llama tendons. **(2)**

lidovky Czech and Slovak folk music presented in a popular format. **(8)**

Lieder (Singular, *Lied.*) German, 'song'. **(3)**

Lieder der Bewegung German songs of the Nazi movement. **(8)**

Liederschulen German song schools in Berlin, Leipzig, and Swabia. **(8)**

Liederspiele 'Song plays', folkloric German musical theater with alternating spoken parts and song. **(8)**

Liedertafel German military male choir. **(8)**

Liedmessen German sung masses. **(8)**

lier (Also *draailier.*) Hurdy-gurdy of the Low Countries. **(8)**

ligawka Long wooden trumpet of Mazovia, Poland. **(8)**

light music (Also *mel iśai*.) Popular style of Tamil music, often combining Western harmony on guitar or keyboard with Indian melody, Indian folk or dance rhythms, and film-style vocals. (**5**)

ligombo Hehe narrow three-stringed trough zither with a gourd resonator at one end. (**1**)

līgotnes Latvian vocal genre connected with *Jāņi*, the midsummer-solstice celebration. (**8**)

lijerica Croatian three-stringed, pear-shaped bowed lute. (**8**)

Liji (Also *Li ji*.) 'Records on Rites', book of music theory dating from the seventh-century Chinese court. One section, *Yueji* 'Annotations on Music', has documentary sources of early Japanese music history. (**7**)

li-ke Thai urban street theater. (**4**)

lī-keḷi Sinhala stick dance now performed in Buddhist temple processions (*perahēra*). (**5**)

likembe (Also *mbira*.) East African lamellophone, performed by ensembles of up to fifteen players. (**1**)

līko (Also *ḍēhī, zahīrok*.) Songs of separation, travel, and work, popular in northern Balochistan. (**5**)

likū Baluchi form of melismatic singing. (**6**)

liku Chilean soprano-register *siku*. (**2**)

līlā Religious drama of North India. *See also kṛṣhṇa līlā, rās līlā*. (**5**)

lilandi Composite trumpet made of seven to fourteen gourds, used in nuptial rituals in Tanzania. (**1**)

lile Song of Svaneti, Georgia, connected with the cult of the sun. (**8**)

līlo Cradle songs and lullabies in Balochistan. (**5**)

lima Javanese pitch name. (**4**)

Limba Cultural group closely related to the Temne of Sierra Leone. (**1**)

limena glazba Brass band of Istria, Croatia. (**8**)

lindo Dance of the Dalmatia region of Croatia and Hercegovina. (**8**)

line dance Popular social form in which dancers in long lines execute identical steps. (**3**)

ling Chinese small bell. (**8**)

linga (Also *lingam*.) Phallic symbol of Shiva's creative power. (**5**)

Lingala Dominant language of Congo-Zaïre. (**1**)

ling dzo Chinese gong. (**8**)

lingigui garavon 'Main drum' or 'drum of the heart' of the Nicaraguan Garífuna *garavon* drum ensemble. (**2**)

lingkung seni Performing arts group in Sunda. (**4**)

linguistic rule Any elemental constraint determined by, or having its origin in, the language of a text. (**1**)

lini (Also *tsintsila*.) Georgian pair of copper plates, found in archaeological excavations of fourth-century sites. (**8**)

lining out Style of singing religious songs in which a leader sings a phrase to remind the congregation of its contour; the congregation then repeats the phrase much more slowly. (**3**)

linnet Subgenre of Pame religious song in which two singers, or groups of singers, compete and show off their memory skills. (**2**)

lion dance Movements made by a lionlike effigy worked from inside, usually by members of martial-arts organizations; an important marker of Chinese identity on celebratory occasions. (**9**)

lira (1) (Also *rela, kobza*.) Belarusan and Ukrainian hurdy-gurdy. (2) (Also *lirica, lyra*.) Three-stringed bowed lute of the Balkans, especially the central Dinaric Mountains, and of Calabria. (3) In Colombia, group playing instrumental music with Spanish-derived instruments; *see also estudiantina, rondalla, tuna*. (**2, 8**)

lirica (Also *lira*.) Three-stringed bowed lute of Bosnia-Hercegovina. (**8**)

lirihan Javanese soft-playing ensemble. (**4**)

lirnici (Also *lirnyky, kobzari*.) Ukrainian professional, often blind minstrels who played the *lira*. (**8**)

liscio Northern Italian songs to accompany rural dances. (**8**)

listwa St. Lucian storytelling, usually including a short song. (**2**)

Lisu Tibeto-Burman-speaking people living in Thailand, Burma, and China. (**4**)

literátska bratrstva Czech and Slovak literary fraternities of the Hussite era (1400s and 1500s), which formed male choirs. (**8**)

lithophone (1) Musical instrument comprising separate pieces of stone that sound successive scale pitches when struck. (2) Stone xylophone. (**4, 5**)

litungu East African eight-stringed lyre. (**1**)

liturgy Rite prescribed for religious worship, often associated with particular types of music. (**8**)

lituus Etruscan and Roman horn that emerged during the first millennium B.C.E. (**8**)

lituus alpinus 'Alpine *lituus*', Latin name of the Swiss alphorn. (**8**)

lityerse Reapers' work songs of French-speaking Switzerland. (**8**)

liupai (China.) School, lineage, or style. (**7**)

liushuiban (China.) One beat per measure without subdivisions. (**7**)

liuxing gequ (China.) Popular songs; the term was invented by the communist government

to differentiate this music from the discredited Shanghai popular songs of the 1930s. (**7**)

live band (Tok Pisin *laiv ben*.) New Guinean name for an electrically amplified musical ensemble. (**9**)

livret de colportage Small French chapbooks of song texts. (**8**)

lkhaon Khmer generic term referring primarily to theater or play. (**4**)

lkhaon basakk Cambodian theater of Chinese origin sometimes performed in the United States. (**3**)

lkhaon khaol Elaborate masked play practiced in Cambodia by men only; rarely, staged by Cambodian immigrants in the United States. (**3**)

lkhaon khaol Masked play of the Khmer court. (**4**)

lkhaon sbek Rarely performed Cambodian shadow play featuring a set of large leather puppets. (**3**)

lkhaon yike Cambodian folk theater of Muslim origin, sometimes performed in the United States. (**3**)

lkmnža Moroccan alto fiddle. (**1**)

llakichina 'To make sad', Ecuadorian women's songs intended to cause love. (**2**)

llamada *Clarín* call in northern Peru that tells the workers at a *mita* to begin working. (**2**)

llamado Guatemalan rhythm-establishing introduction. (**2**)

llamador 'Caller'. (1) Panamanian single-headed drum; (2) *llamador del tigre*, 'caller of the jaguar', friction drum made from a large hollow gourd across which goatskin is stretched, to which a stick is attached and rubbed. (**2**)

llameras All-female dancing group of Aymara region. (**2**)

llanero Adjective referring to the plains (*llanos*) of Colombia and Venezuela. (**2**)

llanto Panamanian *torrente* used to sing sad or love *décimas*. (**2**)

llautë Albanian large pear-shaped fretted plucked lute. (**8**)

llofft-stabal 'Stable loft', informal entertainment of Welsh farmhands quartered in stables. (**8**)

llungur Long valveless, transverse, wooden or cane trumpet in the central Andes. (**2**)

lmsaq Singing contest among Moroccan Berbers. (**6**)

lnovyja Belarusan songs performed during the flax harvest. (**8**)

Lobi Cultural group of northeastern Côte d'Ivoire. (**1**)

lóbi Maroon *sêkêti* song of love in Surinam. (**2**)

lobsh 'Crowning hymn', Coptic nonbiblical text on a biblical theme, usually recited rather than chanted. (**6**)

locations Black residential areas attached to towns in South Africa. (**1**)

löckler Swiss melismatic, nonmetrical solo calls. (**8**)

lockrop Swedish melismatic herding calls. (**8**)

LoDagaa Subgroup of the Dagari-speaking people of Ghana. (**1**)

lodër (Also *lodërti, daulle, tupan.*) Albanian two-headed bass drum. (**8**)

lodo paghili Work songs of Sumba. (**4**)

log drum Musical instrument constructed from a log of wood that is beaten with a stick; although called a drum, it is really an idiophone. (**3**)

log idiophone Hollowed log, branch, or other piece of timber, played by being struck or jolted, often in ensemble. (**9**)

lokarina Bulgarian clay globular flute with eight finger holes and two thumb holes. (**8**)

lok gīt 'Folk song' in Nepal. (**5**)

loki djili Vlach Rom slow songs. (**8**)

lolling (Also *sulling, tralling, tulling.*) Vocal imitation of the *hardanger* violin in Norway. (**8**)

lolote Ossetian monophonic women's lullaby. (**8**)

loncomeo (Also *lonkomeo.*) (1) Mapuche rhea imitation dance by young boys; (2) Mapuche 'moving the head' virtuosic solo dance. (**2**)

London Missionary Society (LMS.) British interdenominational Christian organization that began sending missionaries to Oceania in 1797. (**9**)

longa (1) Ottoman light classical genre, played by Rom musicians in Macedonia. (2) 'Club', 'clubhouse', Turkish term for a Turko-Arab instrumental genre with a fixed rhythmic pattern, often appearing at the conclusion of a suite. (**6, 8**)

long meter English quatrain of eight-syllable (or four-stress) lines, of which the second and fourth lines often rhyme. (**8**)

longo Central African portable, gourd-resonated xylophone. (**1**)

longtom Any of various elongate Australian marine and estuarine fishes of the family Belonidae. (**9**)

longzhou (China.) 'Dragon boat', Cantonese narrative song accompanied by a small gong and drum. (**7**)

lontar Palm-leaf manuscripts used in some areas of Indonesia to record literary and religious works and music notation. (**4**)

lontará Buginese palm-leaf manuscripts. (**4**)

loor Dinka large drum. (**1**)

lopi Guyfesta rhythmic experiment to establish a Guyanese beat. (**2**)

lorik Sung epic poem in North India. (**5**)

lōtār Circular long-necked lute of the Moroccan Berbers. (**6**)

lotusbird Northern and eastern Australian jacana, a bird of the genus *Jacana* able to run on floating vegetation. (**9**)

lowland bagpipe Bellows-blown bagpipe of the Scottish Lowlands with a chanter and three drones. (**8**)

Lozi Dominant cultural group of the Barotse kingdom of Zambia. (**1**)

lü (China.) Temperament or a justly tuned cycle of twelve pitches. (**7**)

luanchui (China.) 'Confused strokes', combining triple and duple beats and used to signify the confused state of mind of a character. (**7**)

lu'b 'Play', term sometimes applied to dance; *see also le'b.* (**6**)

lubak-lubak Tausug dance piece. (**4**)

lubok 'Chapbook', book of Russian folk songs. (**8**)

Lucazi (Also Luchazi.) Cultural group of eastern Angola and northwestern Zambia. (**1**)

lục huyền cầm Modified Spanish guitar found in Vietnam. (**4**)

luck visit Good-luck visit, seasonal ritual in which singers, sometimes masked, visit houses and sing songs of well-wishing in exchange for small gifts. (**8**)

ludag Isneg large conical drum. (**4**)

ludruk Javanese contemporary or local theater. (**4**)

lué (1) Wayana generic term for aerophones; (2) specific flute made from a large armadillo's nail; (3) *lué kôriró*, Wayana end-blown flute with four finger holes. (**2**)

Lugbara Cultural group of eastern Angola and northwestern Zambia. (**1**)

luguh Formula of Qur'ānic recitation. (**4**)

łuhovyja pieśni Belarusan meadow songs. (**8**)

Luhya Cultural group of Kenya. (**1**)

luk krung Big band jazz from Thailand. (**4**)

luk mot Coda affixed to a Thai classical composition. (**4**)

luk thung Thai popular music genre. (**4**)

lulling (Also *sulling, tralling, tulling.*) Norwegian vocal genre that uses mnemonic syllables for singing fiddle pieces. (**8**)

lülü Chinese letter notation. (**7**)

lulya New year ritual fertility dances in the Babar islands. (**4**)

luma Reed pipes popular among Ituri Forest Pygmies of central Africa. (**1**)

lumalú Colombian traditional funerary music. (**2**)

lumpovanje 'Carousing'; drinking, talking, and singing by prosperous young men in Serbian cafés. (**8**)

lundu (1) Early Brazilian song type derived from Afro-Brazilian folk dance. (2) (Also *lundum.*) Afro-Brazilian song and dance of Angolan origin brought to Brazil by Bantu slaves; the song and couple dance featured sensuous exchange partners that later gave rise to many contemporary song forms including the Portuguese *fado.* (3) Brazilian dance and vocal genre of African origin taken to Portugal. (**2, 3, 8**)

lunfardo Dialect used by the social classes among which the Argentine tango originated. (**2**)

luñku (Also *lungku.*) Sumu musical bow that uses the mouth as a resonator, usually played by women. (**2**)

luntang Maguindanao and Timray suspended xylophone. (**4**)

luogujing (China.) Musical shorthand used in memorizing percussion music. (**7**)

luohou (China.) Backward. (**7**)

luohti North Saami *joik.* (**8**)

lur Instrument mentioned in ancient Nordic literature (*lúð ur* in Old Norse); the term is now used to denote long trumpets, especially a Swedish bronze horn. (**8**)

luruvan garavón 'Third drum' or 'helping drum' of the Nicaraguan Garífuna *garavon* or drum ensemble. (**2**)

lus rov Hmong vocal genre with disguised text. (**4**)

lute (1) Plucked chordophone having a usually pear-shaped body, a fretted fingerboard, and a head with tuning pegs, often angled backward from the neck. *See also bouzouki, lira, tamburica.* (2) (Also stick zither.) Chordophone whose strings are stretched over a broad neck that extends from a resonant body. (**8, 9**)

lutherie French instrument making; *see facture.* (**8**)

lu'ui Sama lament to relieve bereavement. (**4**)

lwa (Also *loa.*) Haitian Vodou spirit. (**2**)

Lwa (Also *mistè, zany.*) Deities of the Afro-Haitian religion Vodou. (**3**)

ly Class of Vietnamese folk song comparing human actions to nature. (**4**)

lydarslåttar Norwegian pieces for listening, played in early evenings, when *sæter* women did their weaving and embroidering. (**8**)

lyóba por la rindja 'Calling-song for the descent', song performed by herdsmen bringing their cattle down from alpine pastures in Haute-Gruyère, Switzerland. (**8**)

lyra Pear-shaped three-stringed bowed lute common in Greece and Crete; *see kemenje.* (**8**)

lyre Ancient Greek chordophone having a soundbox made of a tortoiseshell or a shaped wooden frame and covered by ox hide. (**8**)

lyric songs Songs suitable for performance with lyre: generally nonnarrative songs, often expressing emotions or describing the ritual action they accompany. (**8**)

łyżki Belarusan spoons. (**8**)

ma (Japan.) (1) Space, pause, or interval. (2) *Uma* (a bamboo bridge of the *sansin* lute) in Okinawan dialect. (**7**)

maa Chechen and Ingush horn. (**8**)

ma'allim (Also *mu'allim, bāshā kyatrī.*) Leader of the classical *nūba* ensemble in North Africa, who plays the *kwītra*. (**6**)

maalmii Hausa Qur'ānic scholar-teacher. (**1**)

ma'ani Spiritual meanings. (**6**)

Maasai People of Kenya and Tanzania. (**1**)

maazo Head of women's secret society, Sande, among the Vai. (**1**)

mabo Hunting-related dance, one of the most popular BaAka dances of the late 1980s. (**1**)

macakkaippāṭṭu Morning-sickness song for newly pregnant Tamil women. (**5**)

macamaca Afro-Peruvian watermelon harvest festivities. (**2**)

macapat Metered sung poetry of Java. (**4**)

machetero 'Swordsman dance' performed during Moxo festivals. (**2**)

machi Mapuche shaman. (**2**)

machilwün Mapuche shaman initiation rite. (**2**)

machitún Mapuche shamanic ceremony involving treatment for physical and spiritual illnesses. (**2**)

maclotte 'Sailor's dance', in 2/4 or 6/8 time, of Liège and Luxembourg; see *madlot, matelotte*. (**8**)

macron Long mark, written above a vowel to show that in pronunciation the vowel takes more time than typical unmarked vowels. (**9**)

Macuilxochitl 'Five Flowers', Aztec god of dance and sports. (**2**)

maculelê Afro-Brazilian fighting dance. (**2**)

Macumba Afro-Brazilian syncretic religion in Rio de Janeiro. (**2**)

madad 'Help', assistance that God, through the saints, may provide to the sincere Muslim seeker. A Sufi *munshid* typically requests *madad* from various saints during his performance. (**6**)

madā'iḥ w-adhkār Sufi songs of praise or remembrance. (**6**)

madaka Yekuana shaman's container rattle. (**2**)

mādal Large double-headed cylindrical drum of Nepal. (**5**)

madang nori Korean village-square play. (**7**)

madb Social performance of funeral laments, common in the eastern Mediterranean. (**6**)

maddāḥ (Also *qissakhān.*) Sufi religious story-teller. (**6**)

maddāḥa Algerian female musician. (**6**)

maddaḷam South Indian double-headed barrel drum. (**5**)

maddale Double-headed drum. (**5**)

madhya (1) (Also *madhyama.*) (1) Medium or middle, as in medium tempo or middle register. (2) (Also *madhyam.*) Intermediate level of college education in North India. (**5**)

madiaba Popular music in Kinshasa from 1988, based on a variant of the rumba. (**1**)

madīh 'Praise'. (1) Sudanese hymn praising Allah and the prophet Muhammad. (2) Any poem of praise, especially an encomium for the Prophet Muhammad. Such poems are frequently performed as *inshād*, especially in Sufi contexts. (**1, 6**)

madimba Central African gourd-resonated xylophones, probably deriving from southeast African models. (**1**)

madlot 'Sailor's dance', in 6/8 time, of Friesland; see *maclotte, matelotte*. (**8**)

madrigal In European art music, any of several types of usually unaccompanied vocal polyphony used especially in the Renaissance and most often set to secular Italian poetry. (**8**)

madrigali Italian songs preserved in Corsica, sung in three parts with the leading voice (*secunda*) in the middle. (**8**)

madrūf Yemeni edge-blown open transverse flute with five fingerholes. (**6**)

Maeda *ryû* (Japan.) School of *heike biwa*. (**7**)

mãe de santo Female temple leader in Brazilian Candomblé. (**2**)

maegut Korean village cleansing ritual. (**7**)

maestro del coro Guatemalan *maestro cantor* or sacristan specialist in ritual music. (**2**)

maestros cantores Men who fulfill musical duties of an office established by Franciscan missionaries in colonial times. (**2**)

magadis Ancient Greek harp, commonly played by women. (**8**)

magagung Kadazan music in which gongs are beaten in interlocking rhythms. (**4**)

magavhu Large gourd rattles worn on dancers' legs in Zimbabwe. (**1**)

magbinua Sama song about a dream world. (**4**)

maggi a serenata Love songs in Italian *maggio drammatico*. (**8**)

maggio May ritual. (**8**)

maggio drammatico 'Dramatic May', drama staged during the Italian *maggio* that treats the life of a saint or a historic hero. (**8**)

Māgha Hindu month (January–February). (**5**)

maghna (Also *ṭarab*; among conservative musicians, *al-qadīm* 'the old'.) Turkish-influenced urban repertorie popular in Egypt from the mid-nineteenth to the early twentieth century. (**6**)

Maghrib Geographical term for the western, North African part of the Arab world, including Morocco, Algeria, and Tunisia. (**6**)

magigal jin Sama dance of possession. (**4**)

magnitizadi Russian term for cassette tapes. (**8**)

magrūna (Also *majrūna.*) Double clarinet of the Maghrib. In Tunisia, it appears with cow horn bells; cf. *tormāy, suggarat*. (**6**)

magu'da Woman specializing in celebratory ululation in West Africa. (**1**)

Maguzawa People of northern Nigeria. (**1**)

magyar nóta 'Hungarian song', any of numerous songs composed by nineteenth-century Hungarian urban middle-class amateurs, but also known by peasants. (**8**)

Mahabharata One of the great ancient Indian Hindu epics, consisting of 100,000 verses. (**4, 5**)

mahadjiri-ashva Abkhazian nostalgic migrant songs, performed during traditional feasts. (**8**)

Maha Gitá Printed anthology of Burmese classical songs. (**4**)

mahali (Also *musiqī-ye mahali.*) (1) Folk music. (2) Local or regional styles in Afghanistan. (**5**)

maḥallī 'Regional', with reference to rural or folkloric music in Iran. (**6**)

maḥall-i ẓubūr Site of epiphany in a Sufi ceremony. (**6**)

Mahanikai Older, typical sect of Buddhism. (**4**)

Mahā-Parinibbāna-Sutta Pali Buddhist text describing lay-Buddhist instrumental musical offerings. (**5**)

maharaja (Also *gaekwad.*) 'Great ruler'. (**5**)

mahāri Female temple dancers in Orissa. (**5**)

Mahayana Buddhist sect from China. (**4**)

maḥmūl 'Carried', early Arabic name for a mode, widely used in the East and in Muslim Spain before the seventh century A.H., thirteenth century C.E. (**6**)

mahobelo Choral singing of the Sotho peoples of southern Africa. (**1**)

Mahodi Vai term for the Muslim observance of Mawlid. (**1**)

maholi String and flute classical ensemble in Vientiane. (**4**)

mahon'era (Also *mahonyera.*) Zimbabwean bass-like singing, primarily on roots of bichords, with yodeling. (**1**)

mahorathük Bronze "drum" idiophone in Thailand. (**4**)

mahori Court ensemble blending idiophones and chordophones. (**4**)

Mahotella Queens Female *mbaqanga* chorus, an internationally celebrated South African group of the 1990s. **(1)**

mahrajan (Also *mahrajān*.) In the Arab-American community, outdoor weekend-long festival or picnic with music. **(3, 6)**

maḥṣūr Early Arabic mode name, cf. *maḥmūl*. **(6)**

maḥūn (Also *milḥūn*.) (1) Colloquial North African language, used in popular genres like *'arūbī* and *ḥawzī*. (2) Sung poetry tradition of Morocco. **(6)**

mahurī (Also *mohurī*.) Double-reed aerophone of Orissa. **(5)**

mai (Japan.) Generic term for dance. **(7)**

mai bayasi (Japan.) *Nô* performance with dancing by an actor who wears neither a costume nor a mask. **(7)**

mai busa Performer on an aerophone in West Africa. **(1)**

mai kyôgen (Japan.) *Kyôgen* plays constructed according to the dramaturgy of *nô* with chorus and instrumental accompaniment. **(7)**

Maimuna Festival originally among Moroccan Jews occurring on the last day of Passover; it is widely observed in modern Israel. **(6)**

ma'inang (1) Sumatran fast-meter dance songs; (2) Bengkulu *pantun* singing. **(4)**

main caci Competitive whip dueling in Flores. **(4)**

mainline Guitar-fingering pattern associated with Kru sailor styles. **(1)**

main pulau Type of song performed by Malaysian women weeding dry rice fields. **(4)**

main puteri Malay healing ceremony. **(4)**

maipuli (1) Wayana host and participants of the *okoma* ceremony; (2) genre of Wayana dance. **(2)**

maitinade Italian song typical of Trent, composed of quatrains or six-line stanzas of eleven-syllable lines, part of the *canzoni a ballo* genre; see *polesane*. **(8)**

maje krahi 'Of the ear', Albanian men's musical genre of Montenegro. **(8)**

majika Indigenous Mozambican rhythm that is the basis of *marrabenta*. **(1)**

majles (Also *majlis*.) Term for a social gathering in Iran and Central Asia which may include poetry and music. **(6)**

majlis (Also *majilis*.) Shiite mourning session, usually during Muharram. **(5)**

majò jon Haitian male baton twirler and dancer in *rara* bands. **(2)**

makab Large, low-pitched cylindrical drum tensed by cords in Bayt al-Faqīh-Tihāma. **(6)**

maka'di Generic term for players of membranophones, chordophones, and idiophones. **(1)**

makahiki Three-month precontact Hawaiian festival in which competitive games and sports were played under the eye of Lono, god of peace and agriculture. **(9)**

makam (Also *maqam*, *mugam*.) (1) Turkish musical mode (plural, *makamlar*.) The term can also refer to a song or tune. (2) Ottoman Turkish melodic mode still used in parts of the Balkans and North Caucasia. **(6, 8)**

makawa Chilean double-headed membranophone. **(2)**

Makembe Band from Bangui, Central African Republic, popular in the early 1980s. **(1)**

makhdara Enclosed room (or other place) in which a bride awaits the arrival of the groom. **(6)**

makhololo Venda rulers, as distinguished from common people. **(1)**

maki (Japan.) Generic term for a section of literature and theatricals. **(7)**

makich Ecuadorian fruit-capsule ankle rattle. **(2)**

makie (Japan.) Lacquering. **(7)**

makisi (Singular, *likisi*.) Masked performances in Angola. **(10)**

makkjetta 'Comic sketch', Maltese genre bridging folk and popular music. **(8)**

makkŏlli Korean rice wine. **(7)**

Makonde People of Mozambique. **(1)**

makossa Cameroonian popular urban musical genre, also popular in France. **(1, 8)**

makot Chant style of Dhammayut-sect Buddhist temples. **(4)**

maktab In Central Asia, a school affiliated with a mosque, Sufi house, or shrine, in which Qur'ānic recitation is studied. **(6)**

makura (Japan.) Opening section of each scene but the very first in *bunraku* (puppet theater). **(7)**

makuṭam 'Crown', concluding melodic or rhythmic passages involving repetitions. **(5)**

makwaya Music whose name is derived from the word *choir*, featuring songs, marching routines, and special costumes. **(1)**

makyè (1) Guadeloupe drummer who "marks" the choreography of the *léwòz* dancer; (2) membranophone used in the *léwòz* dance. **(2)**

mak'-ye-ups Songs invented by Scottish Lowland Travellers. **(8)**

mak yong Dance-drama of Kelantan province, Malaysia. **(4)**

mak yong laut Malay theater from southern Thailand, similar to *jikay*. **(4)**

mál Icelandic concept of speech, which in ancient times included forms of musical performance. **(8)**

malae (Also *mala'e*, Tongan; *marä'e*, Rotuma; *marae*, East Polynesian.) Sāmoan formal communal grounds, in East Polynesia serving as a sacred space usually marked with imposing stone or wooden structures. **(9)**

malaga Ceremonial Sāmoan visit, often marked by formalities including orations and *kava* and celebrated with singing and dancing. **(9)**

malahiya Tagalog fishing song. **(4)**

malaila Genre performed in Zambia to honor a dead warrior. **(1)**

mālai mārrira pāṭṭu Garland-exchange song of Tamil Nadu. **(5)**

malang Term in eastern Iran and Pakistan for dervishes who are particularly inclined toward ecstatic trance; applied to a *gwātī* after several years of therapy. **(6)**

malanggan Dramatic commemorative rites of northern New Ireland, involving masked performers who often voice their messages through the sounds of musical instruments. **(9)**

malá selcká muzika Czech band consisting of a violin, a clarinet, and a bagpipe. **(8)**

Malayo-Polynesian Language family including Malay, Chăm, and Jarai. **(4)**

Malbar drum (Also *tapou*.) Frame drum of Réunion Island. **(5)**

male Hawaiian poetic text and its vocalization: *mele hula*, singing with dancing; *mele oli*, singing without dancing. **(9)**

male cimbale (Also *brana*, *cimprekelj*, *oprekelj*, *pretl*.) Slovene trapezoidal struck zither. **(8)**

malembe 'Softly', 'slowly', 'take it easy'; a Venezuelan rhythm and song. **(2)**

malhão Portuguese duple-meter circle dance of the western coast from the north to central Portugal. **(8)**

mālid Omani ritual involving poetry, song, and body movements, in honor of the Prophet. **(6)**

mālid Ritual dance of Balochistan performed on various occasions, accompanied by tambourines (*samā*). **(5)**

malimba Sena equiheptatonically tuned lamellophone. **(1)**

Malinke Group of northern Mande-speakers of Mali, Guinea, and Côte d'Ivoire. **(1)**

malipenga Malawian name of the genre *beni*. **(1)**

malka kuñin (Also *malaka kuñini*, *malaka kuñkana*.) Single-tone Sumu flute made from the femur of a deer, a tapir, or another large animal and used as a hunting lure. **(2)**

mallāri Repertoire of compositions without texts, performed by *nāgasvaram* or *tavil* players. **(5)**

mal orkestar 'Little orchestra', ensemble for Macedonian radio, consisting of clarinet, accordion, and other manufactured instruments. **(8)**

maloya Popular musical genre on Réunion Island encompassing several styles. **(5)**

ma'lūf Term for Andalusian (art) music of the Maghrib. Varieties include *ma'lūf al-hazl* 'frivolous' or 'profane', *ma'lūf al-jadd* 'serious' or 'sacred', and *ma'lūf al-khām* 'raw' or 'unrefined', a practice associated with Sufi brotherhoods characterized by unison singing accompanied by hand clapping or by percussion instruments. **(6)**

mama jaliya Mandinka genealogical recitation. **(1)**

Mamanchí Guaymí syncretic religious movement combining Catholicism with indigenous religious and musical elements. **(2)**

mámarakka Torajan funeral music for bamboo flutes and female vocalist. **(4)**

mambo Cuban ballroom dance genre of the 1940s and 1950s belonging to the *danzón* family and created by Orestes López. **(2, 3)**

mamokhorong One-stringed Basotho violin, developed in South Africa. **(1)**

mamongu (1) Bronze or iron gong. (2) Anaka-langu language. **(4)**

mampulorios Alternative Venezuelan name for children's wakes (*velorios de angelito*). **(2)**

mān (Also *gāgar.*) Large globular metal pot of Gujarat. **(5)**

mana (From Polynesian.) Supernatural power and authority. **(9)**

manahelo Roti chanter fluent in poetic language. **(4)**

mañanitas 'Early morning'. Nearly synonymous with *serenata*, it includes a range of songs that vary greatly according to local custom in Mexico. **(2)**

Manas Kyrgyz heroic epic, a primary symbol of nationhood. **(6)**

manascı (Also *semeteycı, manaschi.*) Kyrgyz epic singer. **(6)**

ma'nāwī Spiritual. **(6)**

manban (China.) Slow tempo. **(7)**

mān bhaṭṭ ākhyān Religious stories told by a *mān bhaṭṭ.* **(5)**

mān bhaṭṭ kīrtan Singer who accompanies himself on the *mān*, in Gujarat. **(5)**

manbo Haitian Vodou priestess. **(2)**

manch Musical theater in Madhya Pradesh. **(5)**

manch ke nāc Malwa dance form with vocal and instrumental accompaniment. **(5)**

mānd Rajasthani folk song. **(5)**

manda Musical promise to God, a saint, the Virgin Mary, or some other religious figure throughout Catholic America. **(2)**

Mandaeyŏp 'Slow large piece', prototype of Korean *kagok.* **(7)**

mandala Geometrical sacred figure. **(6)**

maṇḍala sthāna Dance position in *kathakaḷi.* **(5)**

Manden (Also Manding.) Speakers of northern Mande languages. **(1)**

mandinade Greek song composed of improvised couplets with texts about recent events or issues. **(3)**

Mandingoes Group of northern Mande-speakers of Liberia. **(1)**

Mandinka People including the Manding, Malinke, Mandingo, and Maninka. **(1)**

mandjindji Bongo large, wooden, anthropo-morphically carved trumpet. **(1)**

mandó Goan Christian song and dance genre. **(5)**

mandole Combination of lute and mandolin, said to have been invented in Italy, which has been used in Algerian *sha'bī*, or popular, music since the 1930s. **(6)**

mandolin Lute-shaped fretted chordophone of Italian origin with eight strings in double courses, tuned like a violin and played with a plectrum. **(3)**

mandolina 'Mandolin', flat-backed Latin or round-backed West Asian plucked chordophone of the lute family, found throughout Spanish-speaking America. **(2)**

mane Free-rhythmic improvisation in Macedonian music. **(8)**

manea Highly ornamented dance and musical form of urban Romanian Rom. **(8)**

māngāi (Also *gaṛāi.*) Clay water pot idiophone. **(5)**

maṅgal (Also *maṅgaḷa.*) Auspicious song. **(5)**

maṅgalācaraṇ Slow invocatory dance including *pushpāñjali* and *raṅgbhūmi pranām*; the first dance in an *oḍissi* performance. **(5)**

maṅgala gān Medieval Bengali narrative songs in praise of power-cult goddesses such as Manasa and Candi and gods such as Dharma. **(5)**

mangalam Short ending piece of a Karnatak concert; auspicious concluding song. **(5)**

mangala vādyam 'Auspicious musical instruments', ensemble including *nāgasvaram* and *tavil* common in South Indian temples, rituals, and processions. **(5)**

Manganihār Professional musician caste in Rajasthan. **(5)**

Mangbetu Speakers of a Central Sudanic language in northeastern Zaïre. **(1)**

mangologondo Makua loose-log xylophone with nine keys. **(1)**

mangulina Dance of the southwest Dominican Republic. **(2)**

mang'wanda Belt worn around the waist of Tumbuka dancers, whose movements make it produce a distinctive timbre. **(1)**

mani Common type of Turkish folk verse with seven- or eight-syllable lines, thought to have been the domain of women. **(6)**

manikarka Lithuanian one-stringed cello, used in church. **(8)**

mani khavesi Turkish cafés where music was performed. **(8)**

maniler Turkish songs about love of Macedonia. **(8)**

Maninka Group of northern Mande-speakers in Guinea and Liberia. **(1)**

Manipa Tibetan itinerant musician whose repertoire includes the mantra *Om mani padme hum* and religious songs. **(5)**

mani-rimdu Sherpa Buddhist folk dance drama of Nepal. **(5)**

manje-manje *See simanjemanje.* **(1)**

mañjīrā Small cup-shaped handheld cymbals used in North Indian and diaspora dance and devotional music accompaniment. **(5)**

manjūr Jingle girdle made of animal hooves sewn onto a piece of cloth, used in the Afro-Arab *nuban* ritual. **(6)**

Mān Kutūhal Early sixteenth-century music treatise. **(5)**

manman Large drum played by a Haitian master drummer. **(2)**

manodharma Improvised material in a Karnatak raga. **(5)**

manolin Instrument similar to the European mandolin, found in Bali and Lombok. **(4)**

manora Type of southern Thai theater named for the leading character, also performed in Malaysia. **(4)**

manpa St. Lucian dance in duple rhythm. **(2)**

mansalingo Mandinka proverb. **(1)**

mansin Shaman from northern Korea. **(7)**

mantinadhes Greek genre of improvised, rhyming couplets, from Crete and other Greek islands. **(8)**

mantra Sacred word or phrase with magical powers. **(5)**

manyanga Generic Swahili name for an array of shaken seed-filled rattles, mostly calabashes or coconuts. **(1)**

Manza People of Central African Republic. **(1)**

manza Zande pentatonically tuned xylophone associated with royalty. **(1)**

marghul Instrumental elaborations of the *dastan* within the Uygur *mugam.* **(6)**

Māori Term used by Polynesians of Aotearoa and the Cook Islands to refer to themselves. **(9)**

mapag Sri Cirebonese welcoming ceremony for the goddess Sri. **(4)**

mapag tamba Cirebonese post-planting ceremony. **(4)**

mapalé African-derived carnival genre of Colombia. **(2)**

mapfuwe Dance of the Shona of Zimbabwe, used in making rain. **(1)**

maqām (Also *makam, mugam.*) (1) Generic term for melodic mode in the Arab world (plural, *maqāmāt*). (2) In Central Asia, a classical tradition of art song. (3) Melodic mode or melody type; also a collection of instrumental pieces and songs for performance in a specific melodic mode in Kashmir. (3) Arabic modes that influenced some Spanish music. (5, 6, 8)

al-maqām al-ʿirāqī Term evoking a primary urban vocal repertoire in Iraq involving a vocal soloist and a small instrumental ensemble. (6)

maqāmāt al-aṣliyya Term designating the primary *maqāmāt*. (6)

maqsūm Common 8-beat rhythmic pattern. (6)

marabi South African hybrid of indigenous and urban music, dance, and context. (1)

marabout Itinerant Muslim cleric who possesses special powers. (1)

maraca Gourd or calabash container rattle in Cuba, Mexico, Puerto Rico, Venezuela, and many regions of the Americas; usually played in pairs (*maracas*). (2)

maraka (Also *marari.*) Container rattle played by Waiãpi shamans. (2)

marake Wayana cycle of ceremonies constituting the initiation ritual for boys. (2)

maram Cylindrical hand drum of Kerala. (5)

Marapu Sumbanese indigenous belief system. (4)

Marari People of Malawi. (1)

march (1) Musical composition usually in duple time with a strongly stressed beat suitable for marching. (2) Irish dance in 2/4 time, adopted from abroad. (8)

Marche dans le Feu 'Firewalk', annual ceremony on Réunion Island celebrating the virginity of the goddess Pandyale. (5)

marcia 'March', Corsican dance. (8)

mardala Drum (Sanskrit); cognates throughout India refer to a variety of drums. (5)

mare-hoa Warao prayerful song sung by a man to entice a woman. (2)

mareicãe Wayana women's songs sung by men to attract women. (2)

maremare 'Happy-happy', panpipe played by Venezuelan creoles. (2)

mārga (1) Ancient classical music. (2) Culture of a high or refined "way" or "path" usually associated with social elites at important cultural centers. (3) Governed by rules of raga and tala. (4) Telugu classical literature. (5)

mārgam 'Path', ideal suite for dance concerts as codified c. 1800. (5)

margamkali 'The Play of the Way', performed by the Christians of Kerala. (5)

Margi People of northern Nigeria. (1)

mariachi (1) Mexican-style musical ensemble typically consisting of *guitarrón* (bass guitar), *vihuela* (five-stringed guitarlike instrument), violins, trumpets, and singers; the most nationally prominent folk-derived Mexican musical ensemble since the 1930s. (2) Individual *mariachi* musician. (2, 3, 10)

Mariamoba Georgian celebration of the death of Saint Mary, performed in August and centered on the theme of motherhood. (8)

Marian antiphon Antiphonal song in praise of the Virgin Mary. (2)

Mari Lwyd 'Gray Mare', Welsh seasonal festival. (8)

marimba (1) African-derived term for a xylophone found in Central America, Colombia, Mexico, and Venezuela. (2) African-derived lamellophone in the Dominican Republic. (3) Box-resonated xylophone played in the islands of Zanzibar and Pemba and on the nearby mainland. (4) In Mexican and Central American traditions, a xylophone played by several musicians. *See also marímbola.* (1, 2, 3)

marímbola (Also *marímbula.*) African-derived lamellophone consisting of a large wooden box with tuned metal strips or tongues that are plucked; at present from Cuba, Dominican Republic, and Puerto Rico, and (rarely) in other Caribbean islands, Colombia, and Venezuela. (2)

marinera Peruvian dance and song genre in composite 6/8 and 3/4 *sesquiáltera*-hemiola meter, related to the *cueca* and given its name in honor of seamen who died in the War of the Pacific (1879–1883). *See also zamacueca.* (2)

maringa (1) Variant of the palm-wine-guitar style, using more strumming and incorporating West Indian rhythms. (2) Intertribal social dance, popular on the west coast of Africa from Sierra Leone to Zaïre. (1)

Mārkali Tamil month (mid-December to mid-January). (5)

marka pandum Sacred Madia festival held to solemnize the pounding of the first corn in April. (5)

marko band Slovenian vocal-instrumental ensemble. (8)

Marley, Robert Nesta (Bob Marley, 1945–1981.) Jamaican reggae musician who toured parts of Oceania in 1979. (9)

maro dandorā Telugu folk drum-music genre. (5)

marokaa (Also *maroka.*) Nigerian Hausa singers of praises. (1)

marok'i (Female, *marok'iya.*) West African professional singer of praises. (1)

maroma Mixtec acrobatic performance, accompanied by violin, flute, and guitar with singing and dancing atop boards placed on crates. (2)

maromeros Mixtec acrobats who do stunts associated with the flier's dance (*baile del volador*). (2)

Maronite church Eastern Antiochene church that uses the Syriac language. (6)

Maroon 'Runaway'. (1) Descendant of African slaves living in the interior of Surinam, French Guiana, Guyana, and Jamaica. (2) Jamaican creole culture and cult mixing Arawak, Spanish, and predominantly African elements. (2)

marrabenta Mozambican topical music, performed on three guitars and danced in a sexually suggestive style. (1)

marranzanu Sicilian mouth harp; *see scacciapensieri.* (8)

marsīyā (Also *marsiya, marṣiya, marsiyah.*) Elegy chanted or sung by Shiite Muslims. (5)

martellu Corsican wooden scraper. (8)

Martinshorn German automobile horn, adapted and used in wind bands during the Weimar Republic. (8)

marujada Dramatic Afro-Brazilian dance. (2)

maru zume (Japan.) Round *koto* picks. (7)

marwaha *See mirwaha.* (6)

marwas Small, two-headed drums of Ternate and Tidore. (4)

maryna In Great Poland, a bowed instrument played as a percussion instrument by striking its leg against the floor. (8)

mas' In Grenada and Trinidad, short for masquerade. (2)

MASA (Marché des Arts et Spectacles Africains.) Important musical trade fair held in Abidjan on alternate years. (1)

masabe Tonga dance. (1)

maśak Bagpipe played by the *bhopā* community of Rajasthan. (5)

Masakin Sudanese people of the Nuba Mountains. (1)

masa mare 'Grand feast', part of the Romanian wedding ritual, accompanied by specific songs or instrumental tunes. (8)

mascaritas 'Little masks', Mixtec graceful dances imitating quadrilles of the 1800s. (2)

maseukat Acehnese men's percussive dance form. (4)

mashaira Swahili love poetry accompanied by *taarab* music. (1)

mashave Foreign spirits said to possess and afflict the Tonga of Zambia and the Shona of Zimbabwe. (1)

mashramani Celebration in Guyana held after a successful harvest featuring steelbands. (2)

mashrap Derived from the name of the Uighur (Uygur) poet Mashrap (1641–1711), term for the final section of the Uighur *muqam*, involving dance and dominated by the kettledrum. (6)

Mashriq Eastern Arab world, usually including Egypt, Jordan, Lebanon, Iraq, Syria, and Palestine. **(6)**

masi Sumu conch trumpet that serves as a signaling device across distances. **(2)**

masibusi (Japan.) Notation of melodic contour combined with the *goma hu* vocal notation. **(7)**

masītkẖānī gat Slow-tempo Hindustani instrumental composition said to have been created by Masit Khan in the eighteenth century. **(5)**

masjid Building designated for Islamic gatherings. **(4)**

Maślenicnyja pieśni Belarusan spring song cycle performed the day after Ash Wednesday, mainly on swings. **(8)**

maslenitsa Shrovetide songs, sung at carnival in Russia. **(8)**

maṣmūdī ṣaghīr (Also *baladī.*) Common 8-beat rhythmic pattern. **(6)**

masnavī Classical Persian poetic form consisting of rhymed couplets. **(6)**

masque Short allegorical drama, enacted by masked actors, often with music and dance, especially in the 1500s and 1600s. **(8)**

masquerade band Costumed Caribbean group in a carnival celebration. **(2)**

masquerade jig Paid entertainment of the Virgin Islands that combines theater, oratory, and music. **(2)**

masqueraders Costumed Montserrat dance groups. **(2)**

mäsräp (1) Major section of the Uighur (Uygur) *muqam*, characterized by a quick, accelerating rhythm. (2) Festive gathering among the Dolan people involving music. **(6)**

masri Genre of Malay dance. **(4)**

mass (1) Liturgy of holy communion (eucharist), the essential rite of the Roman Catholic church and other apostolic churches. (2) In European art music, a composition whose text is that of the "ordinary," the invariant portion of the service. **(8, 9)**

Mass Games Annual Korean-style mixture of fine arts held during February in Guyana. **(2)**

mast Intoxicated, drunk; mad; excited. **(5)**

mastī 'Drunkenness', referring to the trance induced by the Baluchi *gwātī* ritual. **(6)**

mastušij rožok Belarusan horn. **(8)**

mat 'Opinion'; attribution of raga family groupings to a particular author or theoretician. **(5)**

matachines (Also *awíeme*, Matachines *danza.*) Sacred ceremonial dances in northern Mexico and adjacent areas in the southwestern United States, featuring Native American and Ibero-European elements. **(2, 3, 10)**

mataco Tukano double-duct flute. **(2)**

mātam Self-flagellation, usually beating oneself on the breast with the hands, practiced by Shias in Pakistan. **(5)**

matelotte 'Sailor's dance'. French dance, introduced into the Low Countries in the late 1700s; see *maclotte, madlot.* **(8)**

matenik 'Muddle' (Czech), couple dance of Central Europe, alternating duple and triple meter. **(8)**

matihû (Japan.) *Satuma biwa* playing style reflecting townspeople's elegant aesthetics. **(7)**

maṭkī kā nāc Malwa dance with vocal and instrumental accompaniment. **(5)**

mātrā (1) Beat; duration of 2 beats. (2) Pulse groups in Karnatak tala beats. **(5)**

matraca (1) Argentine *criollo* gourd rattle; (2) Bolivian cog ratchet; (3) Brazilian rattle; (4) in El Salvador, Guatemala, and Honduras, a long-handled wooden ratchet of Arab origin that is swung above the head. **(2)**

matrilineal Tracing descent through the female line; cf. *patrilineal.* **(9)**

matrimonial Thin plank with four or more sets of copper or tin disks nailed loosely to it. **(2)**

matruz Song tradition of Maghribi Jews, treating religious and secular topics and combining Hebrew with Judeo-Arabic or Judeo-Spanish. **(6)**

mattaḷam Tamil double-headed ceramic barrel drum. **(5)**

matumusi (Japan.) Small gongs used offstage in *kabuki.* **(7)**

maturi bayasi (Japan.) (1) Instrumental ensembles (*hayasi*) and their music for shrine festivities; (2) various performing arts offered for the gods at shrine festivals. **(7)**

Maulid Prophet's birthday, in Sumbawa. **(4)**

maŭl kut Korean shaman village ritual. **(7)**

maulūd Sindhi men's song genre honoring the Prophet Muhammad, especially on his birthday. **(5)**

mā'ulu'ulu Sāmoan and Tongan sung speech with choreographic movements. **(9)**

maùṅ Hanging, bossed gong of Burma. **(4)**

maùṅsaìṅ Burmese set of eighteen or nineteen bossed gongs on wooden frames in five rows. **(4)**

Mavlud (Also *mavlud al-nabi.*) (1) Birthday of the Prophet Muhammad, widely observed in Central Asia. (2) Songs recounting the life and deeds of Muhammad, sung on this holiday. **(6)**

mavrigikhān Male singer-dancer of Central Asia, typically a descendant of Bukharan Iranis or Farsis. **(6)**

mawak'i West African professional male singer, composer, or both. **(1)**

mawlam Singer of northeast Thailand. **(4)**

mawwāl (Also *muwal, muwwal.*) 'Causing to bend', 'repeatedly bending'. (1) Form of Arabic colloquial poetry featuring clever wordplay. (2) Solo singing of Arabic poetry, nonmetric though sometimes with metric accompaniment, in the *maqām* modal system; often improvised. **(6)**

mawwāl ḥalabī Aleppan version of *mawwāl.* **(6)**

maxixe (Also *maxixi.*) Brazilian fast syncopated dance music from the late nineteenth century until today. **(2)**

maya (Also *varsaġı, hoyrat.*) Northeastern Turkish term for the *uzun hava* repertoire. **(6)**

māye In Persian music, two tetrachords that constitute the basis of a *dastgāh* or an important *gūshe*, along with characteristic melodic gestures; the "essence" of a mode. **(6)**

mayohuacán Wooden slit drum in the ancient Caribbean. **(2)**

mayolè Guadeloupe stylized stick fighting accompanied by drumming and singing. **(2)**

ma'yong (1) Malaysian theater; (2) Riau masked theater. **(4)**

mayordomo Individual steward or sponsor of patronal festivals in the southern Americas. **(2)**

maypole Most widely known traditional dance of Nicaragua. **(2)**

mayura Bolivian minor fiesta sponsor. **(2)**

mazamba Skin or cloth skirt, cut into many thin strips, that patients wear in northern Malawi. **(1)**

mazanki Small figure-eight-shaped fiddle of western Poland. **(8)**

mazar Saint's tomb. **(6)**

mazhar (1) Arab tambourine. (2) (Also *miżhar.*) Skin-bellied lute of the medieval Middle East. (3) (Also *miżhar.*) Early type of frame drum. **(3, 6)**

mazmūm Early Arabic mode name, cf. *mahmūl.* **(6)**

mazurek 'Mazurka', Polish folk dance. **(8)**

mazurka (1) Polish-origin dance or tune in 2/4 time resembling the polka. (2) Polish dance in moderate triple meter. (3) Popular nineteenth-century European couple dance in moderate 3/4 or 3/8 time. (4) Triple-meter music and associated dance introduced into Nicaragua by Central European immigrants in the latter half of the 1800s. (5) *Mazurka segoviana* 'Segovian mazurka', music-and-dance complex in northern Nicaragua. **(2, 3, 8, 9)**

mba'e pu ovava'é Cylindrical drum of the Paraguayan Mbyá used by shamans and to accompany a hunter's propitiatory songs to the animals he has killed. **(2)**

mbalax (Wolof, 'percussion-based music'). Senegalese popular music, mixing Cuban rhythms with *kora*-based traditional melodies, sung in a high-pitched style. **(1)**

mbaqanga (1) South African jazz idiom that took its name from a stiff corn porridge. (2) South African popular music that has been successful in world music and world beat. **(1, 3)**

mbaraká (1) Guaraní large spiked shamanic rattle with stones or seeds inside. (2) Guaraní name for a guitar of standard European design. **(2)**

Mbem People of Cameroon. **(1)**

mbila Chopi word for a xylophone key; the term is closely related to *mbira*, which designates a lamellophone. **(1)**

mbila dzamadeza Venda twenty-seven-keyed lamellophone. **(1)**

mbila mutondo Venda twenty-one-keyed xylophone. **(1)**

mbira Shona plucked lamellophone, played singly or in ensembles. **(1)**

mbira dzavadzimu 'Mbira of the ancestral spirits', Zimbabwean lamellophone with twenty-two or more wide keys. **(1)**

mbombing South African choirs with high-pitched yells imitating falling bombs as seen in newsreels of World War II. **(1)**

mbongo Central Cameroonian Tikar raffia lamellophone. **(1)**

mborahéi pukú 'Long song', Guaraní song-dance genre. **(2)**

mbube Style of Zulu male singing in South Africa. **(1)**

mbulumbumba (Also, in Brazil, *berimbau*.) Angolan gourd-resonated bow. **(1)**

m'buôt Free-reed mouth organ with gourd wind chest, found in the Truòng Son Ranges. **(4)**

Mbyá (Also Mbïá.) Native American culture of Misiones Province, Argentina, and parts of Paraguay (Mbïá is Argentine orthography; Mbyá is Paraguayan orthography). **(2)**

m'dinga Gumuz large barrel drum. **(1)**

me bati (Japan.) 'Female stroke', weak stroke played by the left hand on the double-headed barrel-shaped *taiko* in *gagaku*. **(7)**

məclis 'Gathering', Azerbaijani spelling of Persian *majles*, from Arabic. **(6)**

Mediterranean music Term coined by the Israeli composer Alexander Boscovitch (1907–1964) to describe a style that rejected European, Romantic tendencies in favor of expression of the collective will, geography, and culture of Palestine. **(6)**

medium Tranced ritualist who is said to be possessed by visiting spirits. **(4)**

me'elaufola Tongan dance observed during Cook's third voyage; prototype of the *lakalaka*. **(9)**

me'etu'upaki Tongan dance in which standing men manipulate paddles. **(9)**

megapode Bird that lays its eggs in mounds of debris, where heat from composting vegetable matter incubates them. **(9)**

megayep Subanen healing gong ensemble. **(4)**

megiddo Traditional lyre of Palestine. **(6)**

me gisht në fyt 'With finger on the throat', Albanian girls' singing style, in which each singer vibrates her larynx with her right thumb to alter vocal timbre. **(8)**

meglebulebu seputangan Yakan song debate. **(4)**

mehfil Assembly, congregation. **(5)**

mehter Turkish janissary band. **(6)**

mehterhana Turkish military ensembles, influential in Balkan music. **(8)**

mehter-i birün 'Unoffical *mehter*', principal outdoor ensemble of Ottoman Turkey. **(6)**

Meistersinger songs Songs written by a guild of fifteenth- and sixteenth-century German musicians. **(3)**

Meizi (Also Meiji.) In Japan, the period from 1868 to 1912. **(7)**

Meizi restoration (Japan.) (1) Coup d'état of 1868 that overthrew the Tokugawa shogunate and began the Meizi era; (2) the westernization, modernization, and industrialization of Japan during the Meizi era. **(7)**

Meizi sentei hu (Japan.) 'Notation edited in the Meizi period', standard *gagaku* score compiled in 1876 and 1888. **(7)**

meizi sinkyoku (Japan.) *Koto* compositions of the Meizi period (1868–1912). **(7)**

mejorana Panamanian term denoting a particular song form, dance, scale, and musical instrument. **(2)**

mek Berta chief. **(1)**

mek mulung Traditional theater of Kedah state, Malaysia. **(4)**

meko Bronze or iron gong of Roti. **(4)**

meko ai Nine-keyed trough xylophone. **(4)**

mel Unit of measurement of pitch: if a sound of frequency 1000 Hz is arbitrarily taken to have a pitch of 1000 mels, people trying to set a pitch half as high (500 mels) choose a sound of about 400 Hz, and people trying to set a pitch twice as high (2000 mels) choose a pitch of about 3000 Hz. **(9)**

mēḷa (1) (Also *janaka*.) Seven-tone scale capable of generating Karnatak ragas. (2) (Also *mēḷam*.) Ensemble. **(5)**

mēḷā Festival (Tamil). **(5)**

mēḷam (1) Ensemble of instruments. (2) Frets on a *vina*. **(5)**

melanda Wayana genre of love songs performed by adult men. **(2)**

melê Afro-Brazilian friction rattle in the southern region. **(2)**

melekket System of musical notation invented by Ethiopian clerics in the mid-1500s. **(1)**

mel iśai 'Soft music' (Tamil), light music. **(5)**

melisma (Adjective, melismatic.) Use of more than one note of music per syllable of vocal text. **(3, 8)**

mellī 'National', with reference to music of the Iranian nation; cf. *mahallī* 'regional'. **(6)**

melodeon Button accordion introduced especially in English and Irish music in the mid-nineteenth century. **(8)**

melodic downdrift Basic melodic movement from high to low, characteristic of much African music. **(1)**

melody regions Scales, ragas; this term was proposed by the Sinhala musicologist C. de S. Kulatillake. **(5)**

melorhythmic codes Elements of musical sound, as defined by Lazarus Ekwueme. **(1)**

membranophone 'Skin sounder'. Any musical instrument (such as a drum) whose sound or principal sound is the vibration of a stretched skin (membrane). **(1, 2, 3, 5, 9)**

membrillo Guatemalan branch hoop around which skin is wrapped for drums. **(2)**

menarche First menstrual period. **(9)**

menari t'ŏri (Also *menarijo*.) Song style and melodic mode from eastern Korea. **(7)**

Mende People of western Liberia and eastern Sierra Leone. **(1)**

mendzaŋ Central African xylophone. **(1)**

menhdī Muslim and Hindu wedding ritual in northern regions, in which henna is applied to the hands of the bride. **(5)**

mento (1) Jamaican indigenous song-instrumental-dance style and ensemble, popular until the 1940s. (2) Most common folk musical form of Nicaragua, with a basic structure of alternating responsorial solo verse and chorus. **(2)**

meraklis Performer of *mantinadhes* in ritual celebrations on some Greek islands. **(8)**

mereng (Also *méringue*.) (1) Haitian dance-song tradition related to the Dominican *merengue*. (2) (Also *mereng kanaval*.) *Mereng koudyay*, a very fast Haitian carnival composition. (3) *Mereng-lant*, a slow Haitian elite parlor dance. (4) *Mereng-Vodou*, big-band instrumentation with a Vodou temple percussion section. **(2)**

merengue (1) Dominican Republic music and dance genre that has become a symbol of national identity. (2) *Merengue redondo* 'round merengue', based on circular movements of the dancing couple. (3) Haitian and Dominican ballroom dance, popular in Africa as a result of dissemination on gramophone records. (4) Fast-paced duple-meter form of Dominican music and dance played by small, regional, accordion-driven ensembles as well as by contemporary *salsa* dance orchestras. **(1, 2, 3)**

merengue cibaeño Regional form of *merengue* from the Dominican region of Cibao, popular far beyond that region. **(3)**

meri (Verb, *meru*.) In Japan, (1) *syukahati* technique of lowering a pitch by moving one's head down; (2) lower note or notes produced by a specific finger position on the *hitiriki*. **(7)**

merrywang Jamaican fiddle. **(2)**

mersiye Laments for Imam Husayn, performed in Alevi ceremonies. **(6)**

meru *See meri.* **(7)**

mesa 'Table', Spanish term in Peru for a shaman's altar on which ritual objects are placed, including musical instruments. **(2)**

mesa de ruidos 'Table of noises'; *see tamborete, tormento.* **(2)**

meşk 'Lesson', 'model' (Turkish), traditional pedagogical system for training vocalists in Turkey. **(6)**

mēslu talka Latvian ritual of spreading manure on fields, often accompanied by the playing of goat horns. **(8)**

mesnevī Narrative poem in couplets; usually the famous *mesnevī-i ma'nevī* of Cellālüddin Rūmī (1207–1273). **(6)**

meṣrā' Hemistich within a line of *ghazal*. **(6)**

mestisaje (Also *mestizaje*, Spanish.) 'Miscegenation', term for the process of mixing of race and culture, usually assumed between Native American and Spanish or Portuguese. **(2)**

mestizo (Spanish.) Individual of Iberian and Native American cultural heritage. **(2)**

mestre capoeira Brazilian 'capoeira master'. **(2)**

mestvire Georgian performer of *stviri*. **(8)**

metabole Transmigration of pitches allowing modal modulation. **(4)**

metallophone Metal xylophone. **(4)**

metaphor Figure of speech by which a stated denotation (vehicle) delivers an unstated message (tenor). **(9)**

metelytsia Ukrainian dance. **(8)**

me të qarë 'With crying', Albanian lament or stylized form of crying. **(8)**

meter Underlying pattern of strong and weak stresses per musical measure; cf. *rhythm, tempo.* **(9)**

métissage Martinique intercultural marriages mainly with the French and later with the Tamils. **(2)**

metsaka Tarahumara reference to the Virgin Mary. **(2)**

meṭṭu (Tamil.) (1) Melody. (2) Fingerboard of the vina. **(5)**

Mevlevī (Also *Mevlevi*.) Religious sect in Sufi Islam, known popularly as whirling dervishes. **(6)**

mevlīd-i şerīf (Also *mevlit*.) (1) Birthday of the Prophet Muhammed. (2) Poem describing the birth of the Prophet. **(6)**

Mevlut (Also *Mevlit*.) Epic of the life of the Prophet in the Turkish *mesnevi* poetic style, composed by Süleyman Çelebi. **(6)**

mexhelis Albanian men's gatherings; *see muabet*. **(8)**

mexicanos de este lado Mexican-Americans. **(3)**

mexicanos del otro lado Mexican nationals. **(3)**

mey (Also *ney*.) Turkish term for *bālābān* or *düdük*, a cylindrical double-reed aerophone. **(6)**

meyan Third line of a four-line Turkish vocal composition, set apart by modulation or other means. **(6)**

meyasu Japanese neumatic notation, set in vertical columns read from left to right. **(8)**

meydan sazı Large Turkish lute. **(6)**

mezrāb (1) Stroke. (2) Plectrum or nail of index finger used in playing a string instrument. (3) Plucking technique. **(6)**

mganda Tanzanian name of the genre *beni*. **(1)**

mgur Tibetan song form on a religious theme. **(5)**

mhito Shona small, stick-beaten drum that maintains a basic rhythm in an *mbira* ensemble. **(1)**

mhorabih Palestinian improvisatory song for wedding processions. **(6)**

microtone Interval less than a semitone (100 cents); interval smaller than a minor second. **(1, 4)**

midare (Japan.) *Nô* dance performed by a drunken sea spirit. **(7)**

Middle Ages In European history, the period from the end of the Western Roman Empire (476 C.E.) to the start of the Renaissance (early fifteenth century). **(8)**

MIDI (Musical Instrument Digital Interface.) Hardware and software system developed in the early 1980s by several electronic instrument manufacturers to allow their products to communicate with each other; allows for compatibility of analog and digital instruments, such as sequencers, computers, synthesizers, and drum machines; became standard in recording studios by the mid-1980s. **(3, 9)**

midwinterhoorn Long Dutch traditional trumpet, used for seasonal customs. **(8)**

mie (Japan.) Stylized poses of *kabuki* actors. **(7)**

mihbash (Also *mihba*.) Bedouin mortar or pounder, pounded in particular rhythms and symbolizing social hospitality. **(6)**

mihkuhika First change in Nahua dance. **(2)**

mihtutilo Change in Nahua dance. **(2)**

mijānā Popular genre of Mashriqī music. **(6)**

mi jaùn Mon crocodile-shaped floor zither. **(4)**

Mijikenda Cultural group of Kenya. **(1)**

mijwiz (Also *mizwij*.) Single-reed double clarinet. **(6)**

mikagura (Japan.) Shinto (Sintô) music and dance at the imperial court. **(7)**

mikagura no gi (Japan.) Court ritual performed in mid-December to entertain gods; a performance context for *mikagura*. **(7)**

miko Transpositional technique in playing Baganda xylophones. **(1)**

mikrasiatika Songs of Asia Minor, imported to Cyprus. **(8)**

mīlād (Also *milad, milād*.) 'Birth', especially the birthday of the Prophet Muhammad. **(5)**

Milaji Vai term for the Muslim observance of Miraj. **(1)**

milāvu Oversize pot drum of Kerala. **(5)**

milḥūn *See malḥūn.* **(6)**

milli musiki 'National' style of music in the late Ottoman Empire, cultivated to appeal to Western tastes. **(6)**

milo BaAka term for non-Pygmy dark-skinned Africans, whom the BaAka see as separate and distinct from themselves. **(1)**

milonga (1) Argentine song. (2) Uruguayan musical form used in the *payada*. **(2)**

mimby Generic Guaraní term for flute. **(2)**

mime-dances Performances that imitate phenomena, sometimes symbolizing the relationship between people and their environment. **(1)**

Mimuna *See Maimuna.* **(6)**

mina (1) Venezuelan (Barlovento region) set of two single-headed drums; (2) the longer drum of the set paired with the shorter *curbata*; the *mina* is the membranophone that plays improvisations. **(2)**

Minangkabau Ethnic group of Sumatra. **(4)**

mīnḍ Glide between two or more tones, in Hindustani instrumental music. **(5)**

min gaku (Japan.) Form of Ming dynasty dance and music transmitted in the seventeenth century by a Chinese trader in Nagasaki Prefecture, Wei Zhuyan (Japanese surname Ōga; 1613–1690). **(7)**

min'ge (China.) Folk song. **(7)**

mini-djaz (Also *minidjaz*.) Haitian *konpa* ensemble influenced by rock and roll; these ensembles originated in Haiti in the 1960s and later formed in North American cities with Haitian communities. **(2, 3)**

minimalism Musical style that emerged in America in the mid-1960s, in which repeating patterns of diatonic or modal music in a regular (usually fast) pulse are developed. **(3)**

MiniMoog Compact portable version of the professional studio electronic music synthesizer developed by Robert Moog in the late 1960s; oscillators generate audio signals that are modified by means of voltage-controlled devices which allow the user to shape attacks, decays, timbre, and so on. **(3)**

minjayra Lebanese end-blown flute. **(6)**

Minjok akki kaeryang saŏpkwa People's Instrument Improvement Collective of North Korea. **(7)**

minjok kagŭk North Korean national opera. **(7)**

minjok kiak hakpu North Korean instrumental music school. **(7)**

Minjok ŭmak yŏn'gusil People's Music Study Institute of North Korea. **(7)**

minjung 'The people', Korean populist movement. **(7)**

minjung munhwa 'The people's culture', Korean popular arts and culture. **(7)**

Minnesängerharfe Hand harp used to accompany singing in Germany in the Middle Ages. **(8)**

minsin gaku (Japan.) Generic term for the music of the Chinese Ming and Qing dynasties introduced into Japan (*min gaku* and *sin gaku*); (2) the *sin gaku* that absorbed part of the *min gaku* repertoire, which became very popular throughout Japan during the Meizi period (1868–1912). **(7)**

minsok ŭmak (Also *minsogak.*) Korean folk music. **(7)**

minstrel show Full-length theatrical entertainment featuring players in blackface who perform songs, dances, and comic skits based on parodies and stereotypes of African-American life and manners. **(3)**

minuet Graceful, mainly eighteenth-century dance in slow 3/4 time, in which performers bow, point their toes, and move to describe S- or Z-shaped floor patterns; music for or in the style of such a dance. **(8)**

minuete Instrumental genre practiced by the Chichimec and the Pame and unrelated to the European minuet. **(2)**

minuetto 'Minuet', Corsican dance piece. **(8)**

minuna Maguindanao old *kulintang* playing style. **(4)**

minyao (China.) Folk ballad or rhyme. **(7)**

minyō (Also *minyo, min'yô.*) (1) Japanese folk song, popular among people of Japanese ancestry in South America. (2) Japanese genre of rural song. (3) Generic term for Japanese folk songs. (4) Korean folk songs. **(2, 7, 9, 10)**

min'yô tetrachord (Japan.) Three pitches outlining the interval of a fourth with an intermediate pitch dividing the fourth into a minor third and a major second from low to high (for instance, D-F-G); one of the four tetrachords proposed by the ethnomusicologist Koizumi Fumio (1927–1983). **(7)**

minyue Music for Chinese instruments. **(3)**

minzoku geinô (Japan.) Generic term for folk performing arts. **(7)**

minzu (China.) Nationalities, the officially recognized ethnic categories. **(7)**

miraciye Turkish poem commemorating the Prophet's ascension to heaven; musical composition for such a poem, the most famous of which was composed by the Mevlevī Osman Dede (1652–1730). **(6)**

miraçlama Song about Muhammad's ascension to heaven, performed in Alevi ceremonies. **(6)**

mīrāse farhangī (Persian, from Arabic *mīrāth.*) 'Cultural heritage', concept applied after the Iranian revolution of 1979 to certain musical repertoires, such as those of the *'āsheq* and the *bakhshī*. **(6)**

Mīrāsī Caste of hereditary musicians in North India and Pakistan. **(5)**

mirfa' (Pplural, *marāfi'.*) Shallow pot- or pan-shaped kettledrum, with the head tensed by a turning ring, used particularly in the Yemeni highlands. **(6)**

Miri Sudanese people of the Nuba Mountains, living near Kadugli. **(1)**

mirliton Object or membrane made to sound by the indirect action of the vibration of an instrument to which it is attached; its sound is often described as a buzz. **(1, 2)**

miroloyia Greek laments for the dead, either instrumental or sung by women. **(8)**

mirwaḥa (Also *marwaḥa.*) Idiophone with silver jingles attached to a circular silver disk, used in the Syrian, Maronite, Coptic, and Armenian Christian churches; the sound is thought to symbolize the murmuring of angels. **(6)**

mirwās Small double-headed drum, used throughout southern Iraq and the Arabian Peninsula. **(6)**

mishāliyya Instrumental prelude in free rhythm in the Moroccan *nūba*. **(6)**

mishnicë Albanian bagpipe. **(8)**

mıskal Archaic Turkish pan flute, displaced by the *ney* in Ottoman Turkish ensembles. **(6)**

misket Common melodic mode (*makam*) in Turkish folk music. **(6)**

mišnice Croatian aerophone with two single-reed pipes. **(8)**

missa 'Mass' (Latin), Portuguese sung mass, in church. **(8)**

mistakbbār al-ṣan'a (Also, in Tlemcen, *mishāliyya.*) Term for an instrumental prelude in the *nūba* practice of Algiers. **(6)**

mita (Also *minka, minga.*) Communal work in the Andes, often accompanied by music. **(2)**

mitatru karuvi 'Throat instrument' (Tamil), referring to a vocalist. **(5)**

mitirp (From Arabic *muṭrib.*) Professional musicians in Kurdistan, understood to be "Gypsies" or a minority. **(6)**

mitiyuki (Japan.) 'Walking the way'. (1) Generic term for a depiction a journey in music, literature, theatricals, dance, and so on; or music accompanying a procession or an entrance. (2) Section of *nô, kyôgen, kabuki,* puppet theater, or narrative *syamisen* music (*zyôruri*), expressing a journey. (3) Section of *kabuki* actors' entrance along the *hanamiti* (raised passage from the back of the theater to the stage). (4) Entrance music in court dances (*bugaku*). **(7)**

mitote (1) Pre-Hispanic Pame cane flute with four finger holes and one hole near the proximal end covered with matted cobweb that acts as a mirliton. (2) Pame dance accompanied by the *mitote* flute. (3) Communal song-dances of the pre-Columbian Chorotega used for sacrificial and agricultural harvest rites. **(2)**

mituzi (Japan.) Drum pattern in *nô*. **(7)**

miyagi hu (Also *katei siki.*) Japanese *koto* notation popularized by Miyagi Mitio (1894–1956). **(7)**

miyagi kokyû (Japan.) Bowed lute invented in the 1920s by Miyagi Mitio (1894–1956). **(7)**

miyako busi tetrachord (Japan.) Three pitches outlining the interval of a fourth with an intermediate pitch dividing the fourth into a minor second and a major third from low to high (for instance, E-F-A); one of four tetrachords proposed by the ethnomusicologist Koizumi Fumio (1927–1983). **(7)**

miyān 'Middle', middle section of a musical composition which usually modulates. **(6)**

miyānkbāna Second melodic section in the melodic development of a *shu'be*. **(6)**

miyazono busi (Also *sonohati busi.*) In Japan, genre of narrative *syamisen* music founded by Miyakozi Sonohati (1716–1736). **(7)**

mi'zaf (Also *mi'zafa.*) Archaic term for lyre (plural, *ma'āzif*). **(6)**

mīzān General term for rhythm or rhythmic periods, especially in North African music (plural, *mawāzīn*). **(6)**

miẓhar (Also *maẓhar.*) (1) Skin-bellied lute of the medieval Middle East. (2) Early type of frame drum. **(6)**

mizik angaje 'Engaged music', Haitian protest music (or politically or socially concerned music) developed within the *kilti libete* movement. **(2, 3)**

mizik rasin 'Roots music', Haitian movement that arose in the 1980s, devoted to fusing popular commercial dance music with traditional music of Vodou and *rara*; it gained prominence in the United States in the early 1990s. **(3)**

mizik vidé (Also *mizik a mas.*) Guadeloupe carnival music. **(2)**

mizimu Tumbuka ancestral spirits. **(1)**

mizmār (Also, in Egypt, *mizmār baladī, sibsaba.*) General term for a double-reed aerophone in the Arab world. **(6)**

---

mizmār al-jarāb Bagpipe. (6)

mizmār wa-ṭābl baladī Egyptian ensemble of three *mizmār* players and two drummers. (6)

mizrāb Wire plectrum worn on the forefinger, used to play the *sitar* and other stringed instruments. (5)

Mizrahim 'Eastern' or 'Oriental' Jews of Asian and African heritage. (6)

mizwed (Also *mizwid*.) North African bagpipe with a double clarinet attached to the bag; cf. *mizwij*. (6)

mizwid Tunisian bagpipe, used with *bendir* to accompany canticles of praise. (1)

mjarrad Five-beat rhythm associated with the 'Īsāwiyya of Tunis. (6)

mješnice (Also *diple s mijehom*.) Croatian bagpipe. (8)

mnemonic Syllables that indicate relative pitch, rhythm, and timbre of rhythmic phrases. (1)

mo (China.) Actor of subsidiary male roles. (7)

mō Vietnamese wooden slit drum in fish shape for Buddhist rituals. (4)

mọbeke Aka whistle of the Central African Republic. (1)

moçambique Brazilian dramatic dance ensemble similar to the *congada*. (2)

moda (1) 'Fashion' (Portuguese), metered unaccompanied polyphonic strophic song sung by either sex in any of various contexts. (2) Generic term for a secular song genre in Brazil and Portugal. (2, 8)

moda-de-viola 'Manner of the *viola*', traditional song form of rural south-central Brazil, sung as a duet to the accompaniment of two *violas*. (2)

mode (1) Set of pitches used hierarchically in a musical structure. (2) Set of pitches and a grammar for their use, often written graphically as a scale. (3) Way of generating a piece of music, given a set of pitches. (4) In Western music, scales codified by the early Roman Catholic church. (5) Fundamental guidelines for composition and improvisation. (6) In European music, a category of musical compositions defined principally by scale and final note; Gregorian chant and Renaissance polyphony used eight modes, a number reduced to two—major and minor—in later, tonal music. (3, 4, 8)

moderna 'Modern', movement in Slovak music of the 1930s, in which composers used folk songs in their compositions. (8)

modern dance Styles and techniques of theatrical dancing that developed during the early twentieth century as an alternative to the strict discipline of classical ballet. (9)

moderno Rock- and jazz-based *cuarteto* style in Argentina. (2)

modinha (1) Brazilian sentimental song genre, originating in the late colonial period. (2) Genre of Portuguese and Brazilian salon art song popular from the mid-1700s to the mid-1800s. (2, 8)

modzakhili 'Follower', high second voice of Georgian three-part singing. (8)

moezelzak (Also *moezel*.) Bagpipe of the Low Countries. (8)

mohan vīṇā Modified slide guitar developed by Vishwa Mohan Bhatt. (5)

mōhini āṭṭam 'Solo dance of the divine temptress', semiclassical dance of Kerala dedicated to the goddess Mohini. (5)

mohlam Lao singer from northeast Thailand. (4)

mohori Khmer court ensemble for entertainment music. (4)

mohrā Brief melodic fragment ending an improvisation, in Hindustani music. (5)

mohurī (Also *mahurī*, *mohorī*.) Double-reed folk aerophone. (5)

moiety One of two basic complementary subdivisions of a group of people. (9)

mojos Magical spells or charms of African origin, later associated with African-American Vodou. (3)

moko jumby (1) Trinidadian carnival stilt dancer of African provenance; (2) Moko Jumbie, Caribbean stilt dancer of carnival. (2)

mokondi General BaAka name for dances involving spirits. (1)

mokṣa Spiritual liberation from the Hindu cycle of reincarnation. (5)

mokṣa nata Fast-tempo dance, the concluding item in *oḍissi* dance performance. (5)

mokt'ak Buddhist wooden slit gong of Korea. (7)

mokugyo (Japan.) Wooden idiophone used in Buddhist music. (7)

molam Traditional singer of Laos. (4)

molimo BaMbuti death ceremonies, which emphasize cooperation among surviving mortals. (1)

mɔli Sande Muslim version of a women's secret society among the Vai. (1)

moll Short vocal oscillation, in Goa. (5)

molo Senegalese one-stringed plucked lute. (1)

móló Yoruba three-stringed lute, commonly used in *sákárà* ensembles during the 1920s and 1930s. (1)

molon Double-headed cylindrical drum on Réunion Island. (5)

Moluche Mapuche warriors and hunters of former times from the pampas. (2)

momačko kolo Showy young men's dance of the Bunjevci minority in Vojvodina, Serbia. (8)

momong Acehnese medium horizontal gong. (4)

Mon Ladakhi folk musician, player of oboe and kettledrum. (5)

mondharp (Also *mondtrom*.) Mouth harp of the Low Countries. (8)

mondô (Japan.) Dialogue segment of a *nô* play.

monferina Italian dance preserved in Corsica; cf. *monferrina*, *monfrina*. (8)

monferrina Italian dance once popular in northeastern Italy and Piedmont; cf. *monferina*, *monfrina*. (8)

monfrina Dance in 6/8 time of Ticino, Switzerland, originally of Monferrato in the Italian province of Piedmont; cf. *monferina*, *monferrina*. (8)

mongmong Small gongs of Mandailing Batak ensembles. (4)

monkey Jamaican cylindrical membranophone of the Maroons. (2)

monochord (1) Chordophone with one string. (2) Single-stringed instrument used to match pitches of instruments and determine tunings. (1, 4)

monody Monophonic vocal piece; in folk singing performance style, always unaccompanied. (8)

Monophysitism Early Christian doctrine that Christ had a single nature, both human and divine; this doctrine was condemned by the Council of Chalcedon in 451. (6)

montuno Final section of a Cuban *son*. (2)

moonshine dahlins Jamaican yard entertainment and recreation on moonlit nights. (2)

mora In a given language, the duration of a typical short syllable; temporal duration of a short vowel in poetry. (1, 9)

mōrā Karnatak rhythmic cadential structure. (5)

morache Rasp instrument used by the Utes in the Bear Dance ceremony. (3)

moraic rhythm Rhythm created by the difference in length of short vowels and long vowels. (1)

morākab khāni (Also *morākab navāzi*.) Modulation between one *dastgāh* and another in Persian music. (6)

moráo Bolivian ten-tubed panpipe of the lowland Moré. (2)

morchang Wrought-iron mouth harp played by Langās in Rajasthan. (5)

morenada Bolivian carnival dance of black slaves. (2)

morenos Dancing group of *mestizo* people from the Aymara region of Bolivia. (2)

moriones Mindoro masked celebration in Holy Week. (4)

Morita ryû (Japan.) School of *nô* flute (*nôkan*). (7)

moro Guarijío 'manager' of the *pascola*. (2)

moro-moro Christian-Muslim folk drama. (4)

mororai (Japan.) Rolling pattern played on the *kakko* drum with two sticks. (**7**)

moros y cristianos 'Moors and Christians', dance reenactment of Moorish and Spanish battles, popular throughout Hispanic America. (**2**)

morphokine Smallest unit that has meaning as movement in the structure of a movement system. (**9**)

morris dance (1) Vigorous dance of central and southern England, performed by costumed men wearing bells. (2) Folk dance once common throughout England, featuring men (very rarely, women) who perform vigorous, intricate choreography in three or four couples, accompanied by folk instruments such as the pipe and tabor, melodeon, or fiddle, in streets or garden spaces in the manner of street theater. (**3, 8**)

morrocoyo Kogi rubbed turtleshell idiophone. (**2**)

morshed (Also *murshid*, Arabic.) (1) Spiritual guide, in a Sufi order. (2) Man whose singing and drumming direct the exercises in an Iranian *zūr-khāne*. (**6**)

morsing (Also *murcing*.) South Indian mouth harp played as a percussion instrument. (**5**)

moshembe da Gumuz exorcism dance. (**1**)

môsô (Japan.) Blind priests. (**7**)

môsô biwa (Japan.) Form of *biwa* (lute) and its music associated with blind priests. (**7**)

mosque Building designated for Islamic gatherings. (**4**)

most 'Bridge', Bulgarian game similar to "London Bridge Is Falling Down." (**8**)

mŏt (From *mat* 'taste'.) Korean aesthetic concept. (**7**)

motā gīt 'Big songs'. Sophisticated, refined songs performed by the Laṅgās and Manganihārs in Rajasthan. (**5**)

motaqayyer (Also *motaghayyer*.) 'Changing tone', tone within a Persian *gūshe* that changes depending on whether the melodic line ascends or descends. (**6**)

motengene Hip-swiveling, rib-rotating dance traditional among the Mbati Pygmies. (**1**)

motet In European art music, any of several distinct types of polyphonic composition: a variety of sacred or secular medieval works, in which multiple voices simultaneously sing different verbal texts; a sacred work of the Renaissance and later, with several voices that sing a single text not drawn from the ordinary of the mass. (**8**)

motif In dance analysis, a culturally grammatical sequence of movement combining kinemes and morphokines in a characteristic way and verbalized and recognized by people indigenous to the culture. (**9**)

motive Short melodic phrase. (**4**)

mōṭk Baluchi lament for the dead. (**6**)

motk Elegies of Balochistan. (**5**)

moṭlaq (Also *muṭlaq*.) Open string. (**6**)

moto byôsi (Japan.) Main singer of the *moto kata* section of *mikagura* musicians. (**7**)

moto kata (Japan.) One of the two sections of *mikagura* musicians. (**7**)

moto uta (Japan.) First of two verses of a *mikagura* song; the solo part is performed by the *moto byôsi*, the main singer of the *moto kata* section. (**7**)

Motown Slang for Motor Town (Detroit), where Motown Records, a highly successful black-owned record company, was founded. (**3**)

moṭreb In Iran, one member of a duo or small troupe that performs urban popular music; considered socially undersirable by religious leaders and others; cf. *muṭrib*. (**6**)

mouran (1) Guyanese Indian women's songs performed after birth. (2) Head-shaving ceremony for an infant. (**5**)

mousikē Greek term for the arts presided over by the Muses, including music, poetry, and dance. (**8**)

mouth harp Small, U-shaped metal brace with a single vibrating metal tongue, whose overtones are resonated in the buccal cavity; commonly but inexplicably known as a Jew's harp. (**8**)

mouth organ Blown free-reed instrument that produces different pitches on a given key or hole, depending on whether air is pushed or pulled past the reeds; known as the French fiddle in Ireland and the harmonica in the United States. (**8**)

movement signature Element of movement that consistently marks a dance. (**1**)

mphepo Spirit wind among the Tumbuka people of northern Malawi. (**1**)

mpintín Puerto Rican rhythmic pattern derived from the Ghanaian Akan. (**2**)

mṛdang (Also *pakhāvaj*.) North Indian barrel drum. (**5**)

mridang Barrel-shaped double-headed classical and folk drum of South Asia. (**5**)

mridanga Barrel-shaped drum from India. (**4**)

mridangam 'Clay unit', double-headed barrel drum, nowadays of wood, played in Karnatak music. (**5, 10**)

mṣaddar (Plural, *mṣadrāt*.) Introductory vocal genre with instrumental overture within the Maghribi *nūba*. (**6**)

mṣaddar nūba Longer and more significant form of the Andalusian-Libyan *nūba*. (**6**)

msamaʿ (Plural, *msamaʿāt*.) Traditional women's ensemble of Algeria. (**6**)

msamʿat Algerian urban female professional singer-dancers. (**1**)

mshāgblāt Vocal genre in the Andalusian-Tunisian *nūba* derived from popular songs. (**6**)

mshālya (Also, in Algiers, *mustakhbar al-ṣanʿa*.) Instrumental introduction to the Algerian *nūba*. (**6**)

msondo Cylindrical drum with pegged or tacked-on head, played along the coast of Tanzania. (**1**)

mtiuluri Eastern Georgian mountain dance. (**8**)

mtskobri Georgian military ensemble of *bukis*. (**8**)

múa bá trạo Vietnamese oar dance, associated with rituals of the sacred whale. (**4**)

muabet Albanian men's gatherings; *see mexhelis*. (**8**)

múa dâng bông Vietnamese "flower dance," associated with religious occasions. (**4**)

mu'adhdbin (Also *muezzin, mu'adhdhin*.) Performer of the *adhān*, or Islamic call to prayer. (**4, 5, 6**)

muakuke Cabécar 'game of the drums'. (**2**)

múa rối nước Water-puppet theater in northern Vietnam. (**4**)

mucapata Lamellophone with a bell-type resonator that is probably of Cokwe or Cokwe-Mbangala invention. (**1**)

muchafou (Also *muchosa*.) Bagpipe of the Low Countries. (**8**)

muchongolo Tsonga dance representing warriors' actions in battle and featuring asymmetrical rhythms. (**1**)

muchungwa Kikuyu dance in which idiophones are attached to the dancers' legs. (**1**)

mŭdal 'Art song', vocal music composed mainly by nineteenth-century Hungarian urban middle-class amateurs. (**8**)

mudang Korean shaman. (**7**)

muḍivu In a Karnatak tala, the starting point of the first half of a *pallavi* theme. (**5**)

mudong Korean dancing children dressed as shamans. (**7**)

mudrā Hand gesture used by Vedic reciters and chanters. (**5**)

mudra (1) 'Stamp', 'insignia', or signature of the composer, integrated in the text of a song. (2) Name of the song's raga, tala, other musical features, or a deity integrated into the song text. (**5**)

mudzimu Ancestral spirits of the Shona of Zimbabwe. (**1**)

muezzin (Also *mu'adhdbin, mu'adhdhin*.) Performer of *azan*, the Islamic call to prayer. (**4, 5, 6**)

mugam Middle Eastern modal concept in North Caucasia; cf. *makam, maqam*. (**8**)

muğam (Also *mugam, mogam, mugham*.) Azerbaijani term for *maqām*. (**6**)

muge (China.) Herders' songs. (**7**)

mugen nô (Japan.) *Nô* plays in which the main characteris are spirits. (**7**) *mughannī* 'Singer', a singer or musician; more recent term for a soloist in the Iraqi *maqām*. (6)

mugulmānī Large single-headed cylindrical tripod drum played on festive occasions and for ritual dances in coastal Balochistan and among the Baloch in Karachi. (5)

muḥarrak (Plural, *muḥarrakāt*.) Type of song in the Andalusian *nūba*. (6)

Muharram (1) Muslim festival that is also celebrated by Hindus in Surinam. (2) Muslim month; also a holiday of special importance to Shiites memorializing members of the Prophet Muhammad's family who died defending Islam on the battlefields of Karbala, Iraq, in 680 C.E. (2, 5)

muḥarrikāt (Also *muḥarrakāt*.) 'Moving', 'emotionally moved'; section in the performance of the classical *nūba*. (6)

muḥāsaba Instrumental responses that enter into dialogue with the vocal part in the Iraqi *maqām*. (6)

muḥayyar *Maqām* similar to *maqām bayyātī*. (6)

muḥayyer Turkish melodic mode similar to *hüseyni*. (6)

muhurtam Auspicious hour-and-a-half period during which the central ritual of a Hindu wedding must be performed. (5)

muhusemoi Warao deer-bone vertical flute with slightly notched mouthpiece and three finger holes. (2)

Muhyŏng munhwajae Korean Intangible Cultural Asset. (7)

mujarrad-i khiyāl Independent images in Islamic metaphysics. (6)

mujawwad (Also *tartīl*, *tajwīd*.) 'Improved', 'beautified'; melodically elaborate, intense style of Qur'ānic recitation. (6)

mukabelle Mevlevī evening ceremony of *semā*; this term is sometimes applied to the *zikr* ceremony of other *tarikatlar*. (6)

mukanda (1) Boys' age-grade circumcision schools established outside villages in central Africa. (2) Initiation rites. (1, 10)

mukasi busi (Japan.) Okinawan classical music characterized by highly melismatic singing at a very slow tempo. (7)

mukhammas Classical Arabic poetic form often used in Central Asian *maqām* traditions. (6)

mukhannath (Plural, *mukhannathūn*.) Male musician who dressed as a woman in medieval Medina and Mecca. (6)

mukhavīṇā Small South Indian double-reed instrument. (5)

mukhiyā Lead devotional singer in North Indian *samāj-gāyan*. (5)

mukhliṣ Final vocal piece within the Andalusian-Algerian *nūba*. (6)

mukhṛa Opening section of Hindustani instrumental composition, serving to emphasize the first beat of a tala cycle. (5)

mukhtai svara Solfège passage sometimes performed following the *anupallavi* in some Karnatak *varṇam*; a type of *citta svara*. (5)

mukkuri (Japan.) Ainu Jew's harp. (7)

mukululu (Also *mullu*.) End-blown notched flute with four finger holes from the department of La Paz, Bolivia. (2)

mukupela Drum played only at a royal death or installation in central Africa. (1)

mulatshagos Vlach Rom drinking and singing celebrations. (8)

mulatteru Corsican mule driver, who sang with a long-drawn-out call-like quality. (8)

mülāzime Major subdivision of the seventeenth- and eighteenth-century *peşrev*. (6)

mūlid (Plural, *mawālid*.) Saint's day celebration. (6)

mu muraso 'In the blood'. A musician in Burundi used this phrase to describe extraordinary ability for performance. (1)

Mundäoline Accordion invented in Berlin by F. Buschmann in 1821, later called the concertina. (8)

mundharp Norwegian mouth harp. (8)

munfaṣil 'Disjunct', type of tetrachordal joining. (6)

mungiga Swedish mouth harp. (8)

Munhwajae kwalliguk Korean Office of Cultural Assets. (7)

Munhwajae pohobŏp Korean Cultural Assets Preservation Law. (7)

munshid (Plural, *munshidīn*.) General term for a singer or vocalist, especially in a Sufi context. (6)

mūnūlūj 'Monologue', through-composed song with great emotional intensity popular in twentieth-century Egypt. (6)

muoy choan 'First level', Khmer short rhythmic cycle. (4)

muqaddam Muslim leader of a sect. (1)

muqaddima Instrumental introduction; in the Iraqi *maqām*, either *muqaddima* or *taqsīm* (instrumental improvisation) is required in performance. (6)

muqam (1) In Uighur (Uygur) music, term for a modal, monodic suite using varying rhythmic cycles as well as unmeasured rhythms. (2) (China.) Variously spelled. Modal system of the Uighurs in Xinjiang Province, similar to the Middle Eastern *maqam* or *makam*. (6, 7)

murabba (1) Uighur (Uygur) poem with four-verse stanzas. (2) Major Turkish vocal genre setting poetry in a nonmetered, improvisatory style. (6)

murādā Women's dance of Qatar and Bahrain, in which the rhythm is created by foot stamping. (6)

murāghī 'Recurring', 'repeating'; 'additional', 'supplementary', in Yemen. (6)

murakkaz Vocal genre within the Andalusian-Libyan *nūba*. (6)

murattal (Also *tartīl*, *tajwīd*.) Unembellished style of Qur'ānic recitation; cf. *mujawwad*. (6)

mūrccanā Process of creating new Karnatak ragas by shifting the tonic to a different scale tone. (5)

murga (1) Musical-theatrical carnival group in Uruguay; (2) informal street festival music ensemble in Uruguay; (3) urban carnival song genre in Argentina. (2)

murkvamoba-kviriaoba Svanetian fertility ceremony that retains elements of an ancient phallic cult. (8)

murlī (Also *bīn*, *puṅgī*.) Double clarinet with a gourd wind chamber. (5)

Muromati (Japan.) Period from 1334 to 1573. (7)

murŭp changdan Korean rhythmic patterns tapped out on the knees. (7)

musaf Special service in the Jewish liturgy for the sabbath, festivals, high holidays, and every first day of the Jewish month. (6)

musakalunga 'Shiver dance' of the Handa people of southwestern Angola. (1)

musawwitāt al-watariyya 'Chordophones', translation of the Greek term in the title of a book by al-Kindī. (6)

musette French bagpipe. (8)

mushāira Urdu poetry reading. (5)

mushqilāt Instrumental section of a suite in the Bukharan tradition of *shash maqām*. (6)

música caipira Brazilian 'country music'. (2)

música champeta Colombian pejorative reference to African-derived music. (2)

música criolla 'Creole music'. (1) In Venezuela, music of Venezuelan peasants of mixed ancestry. (2) Catholic-Spanish, Arab-Andalusian, and Chilean foundations of Chilean musical-poetic practice. (3) Coastal Peruvian music showing Afro-Peruvian influences. (2)

música cuartetera (Also *música de cuarteto*.) Popular Argentine dance music genre from Córdoba. (2)

música de golpe 'Strike music', group with violin accompanied by double-headed membranophones such as snare and bass drum. (2)

música jíbara Multifaceted tradition of music associated with rural communities of Puerto Rico, in which stringed instruments dominate and improvised texts are common. (3)

musica lăutarească Urban Rom music of southern Romania. (8)

musica leggera 'Light music' (Italian), locally produced Italian popular songs.   (8)

música nacional 'National music', usually referring to folk music.   (2)

música de proyección folklórica Argentine style based on urbanization of traditional rural repertoires.   (2)

música ranchera Mexican country music associated particularly with the *mariachi* ensemble. (3, 10)

música regional 'Regional music'.   (2)

música terapía Colombian therapy music or "feel-good"; the term refers to African-derived music.   (2)

música típica In Costa Rica, 'typical music', music of known authors that uses traditional song-dance styles and forms.   (2)

música tropical 'Tropical music', Afro-Caribbean dance-musics, particularly *salsa*, *cumbia*, and *merengue*, popular throughout the Americans.   (2)

música vallenata Accordion-driven dance music of coastal Colombia.   (3)

musical area Concept that societies sharing musical traits can be said to constitute a single musical area; the term is borrowed from anthropologists' *culture area*.   (3)

musical bow Instrument having a string fastened with tension at each end of a curved stick, which can be plucked or struck.   (1)

musical theater Popular form of theatrical entertainment incorporating drama, music, and dance in various combinations and proportions.   (3)

musickers Montserrat musicians.   (2)

musiikki Finnish term for music beginning in the early twentieth century.   (8)

musiikkiopisto Finnish music college.   (8)

Musiki Band from Bangui, Central African Republic, of the early 1980s.   (1)

musikong bumbong Bamboo instrument ensemble of Philippines.   (4)

musiñu (Also *mohoceño*.) Bolivian vertical (small one) and transverse (large one) duct flute. (2)

mūsīqā (Also *musiqa*.) Arabic, 'music'. (1) Music as distinct from chant. (2) General term for music, usually implying the presence of melodic instruments. It can also refer to the theory of music, as opposed to practice (*ghinā*).   (4, 6)

al-mūsīqā al-qadīma Term referring to traditional Egyptian classical music involving improvisation; cf. *al-turāth*.   (6)

mūsīqī Music (Urdu).   (5)

musique à bouche French mouth music, played on the harmonica.   (8)

musique concrète Form of electronic music that first appeared in 1948 in Paris; it involves recording naturally occurring sounds (such as the human voice or breaking glass) and then using electronic devices (such as a tape recorder or filters that attenuate certain frequencies) to modify the sounds, sometimes beyond recognition.   (3)

musique de collectage French field recordings. (8)

musique ethnographique French traditional music.   (8)

musique métissée 'Half-caste music' (French), acculturated, pop-folk music.   (8)

musique moderne zaïroise Guitar-based music that emerged after the 1940s in the Brazzaville and Kinshasa area.   (1)

musique résidu 'Residual music' (French), "remnant" music, surviving from earlier times.   (8)

musique savante 'Learned music' (French), classical music.   (8)

musiqueada Long Paraguayan *serenata*.   (2)

muška 'Male', term distinguishing men's singing styles in genres sung by men and women in Bosnia-Hercegovina.   (8)

mussoll Musical genre associated with a Christian martial dance, in Goa.   (5)

mustaftīh In the Sufi *dhikr*, the leader who regulates the tempo, movement, and chanting.   (6)

musta-guduchg Chechen ritual intended to control the weather, dedicated to Sela, the goddess of thunder and lightning.   (8)

mustazād Classical poetic form often used in Central Asian *maqām* traditions.   (6)

musu Spell or curse invoked with words alone or in combination with ritual acts among the Ga.   (1)

musume (Japan.) Head of the *bunraku* puppet often used for the role of a sweet teenage girl. (7)

musume gidayû (Japan.) *Gidayû busi* (narrative *syamisen* music) performed by girls.   (7)

mutadākbil Overlapping type of tetrachordal joining.   (6)

mutawwal 'Stretched', Yemeni fixed composition with an unmeasured form.   (6)

mutawwala Slow, binary variant of the Yemeni *wastā* rhythm.   (6)

mutettu (Also *mutu*.) Poetic form, usually about love, in the Sardinian *a tenore* repertoire.   (8)

mutirães Brazilian voluntary work parties.   (2)

mutlaq Early Arabic mode name; cf. *maḥmūl*. (6)

mutrib l mutriba (1) Highly talented performer who is thought to evoke *ṭarab*, or musical ecstasy. (2) Vocal soloist in a *takht* ensemble. (3) Lead songstress in a women's *firqa*.   (6)

muttaṣil 'Joined', conjunct type of tetrachordal joining.   (6)

mutumba Shona low-pitched, waist-high drum that plays a limited amount of variation.   (1)

muwashshah (Also *muwashshah*.) (1) Form of popular strophic Arab poetry that originated in Andalusian Spain as an alternative to the older *qaṣīda* ; a fixed vocal composition based on this poetic form. (2) Vocal genre of Muslim Andalucía. (3) Form of Arabic (or Andalucian) strophic poetry set to song, especially cultivated in southern Spain and Morocco. (4) North African court poetry, developed in Spain and having strophic texts with instrumental refrains.   (1, 3, 6, 8)

muyu (China.) Wood block in the shape of a fish, used mostly in religious chanting.   (7)

mùyu (Also *mukíyu*.) 'Wooden fish song', important narrative tradition in South China. (3)

muzica orientala Late-twentieth-century genre popular among Romanian Rom.   (8)

muzik klasik (Also *muzik seriosa*.) Western classical music in Malaysia.   (4)

muzika (Also *gunci, gunjci, violine*.) Instrumental ensemble of Istria, Croatia.   (8)

muzika mizraḥit 'Oriental music', 'Mediterranean music'; genre of Israeli popular music that developed in the 1970s and 1980s, mixing traditional Arab idioms and instruments with Western-influenced Israeli song. (6)

muzyka (1) (Accent on *u*.) Ukrainian term for music. (2) (Accent on *y*.) Ukrainian village term for a trio.   (8)

muzyki (Also *burtkampaniya, kapela, skamarochi, viasielnyja muzyki*.) Belarusan traditional folk instrumental ensemble.   (8)

mvet (1) Stick zither with idiochord strings lifted from the raffia. (2) Genre of oral literature in the central African region.   (1)

Mwai (Also Mai.) Iatmul men's ceremony involving masks.   (9)

mwai (Also *mai*.) Iatmul paired, end-blown, bamboo voice modifiers used during the Mwai ceremony.   (9)

mwanzele Rabai dance in which brief rhythmic patterns regulate performances.   (1)

mwinjiro Mbeere dance in which brief rhythmic patterns regulate performances.   (1)

Myanmar Current official name of Burma.   (4)

myaso yakukuwa Lucazi or Luvale songs performed at night during circumcision ceremonies, accompanied by concussion sticks. (1)

Myôan honkyoku (Japan.) Classical pieces (*honkyoku*) for *syakuhati* transmitted at the Myôanzi temple in Kyôto.   (7)

myŏngch'ang Master singers of Korean *p'ansori*. (7)

myŏngdu Korean shaman.   (7)

mzayyan Saudi dance involving poetic competition.   (6)

mzayyin In Yemen, term for a professional musician of low social status, as a descendant of former slaves. **(6)**

na' Burmese spirit. **(4)**

na ariju (Also *basiranje, na bas.*) 'On a melody', Serbian melodic style in which the lower voice sings in parallel thirds with the melody and forms a perfect fifth at the cadence. **(8)**

na'ash (Also *tanawush*; in Yemen, *nuwwāsh, rishi.*) Women's dance movement of the Arabian Peninsula; the dancer holds her right hand lightly on the upper chest while swinging her head and loose tresses. **(6)**

na'at (Also *na't.*) Muslim devotional song of praise. **(6)**

na'at-i şerîf Precomposed rubato form opening the Mevlevi *āyīn* ceremony. **(6)**

nabal (Also *nap'al.*) Korean brass trumpet. **(7)**

nabar panas pela Blood-drinking ceremony in Tanimbar. **(4)**

na bas (Also *bas, basiranje, bećarac, na ariju.*) 'On a bass', singing style of the Dinaric Alps and Pannonian regions of Croatia and Serbia. **(8)**

nabaṭī Cantillated bedouin poetry of the Arabian Peninsula. **(6)**

nabich'um 'Butterfly dance', Korean Buddhist dance. **(7)**

nabiki (Japan.) Vibrato in *nô* chanting. **(7)**

nabona Kasena-Nankani side-blown ivory trumpets, usually played in sets of six or seven. **(1)**

nacchere (1) (Also *cassella, paghjolu.*) Corsican kettledrum used in the Good Friday procession in Erbalunga, on Cape Corse. (2) Large frame drum played with a pair of sticks and used to accompany certain dances like the *tarasco* (*tarascona*). **(8)**

nachttrichjer Clapper bell of Fiesch, Valais, Switzerland. **(8)**

naḍ (Also *nal.*) Flute, in Balochistan; usually a shepherd's instrument. **(5)**

nāda Primordial sound; musical sound. **(5)**

Nāda-Brahman Cosmic primordial sound, in yoga and music. **(5)**

nādagama (Also *nadagam, nadhagam.*) Nineteenth-century Sinhala theatrical genre. **(5)**

nāda yoga Spiritual path of devotion to musical sound. **(5)**

nadṛ Omani ceremony for the well-being of a newborn, involving poetry, hymns, and rhythmic body movements. **(6)**

nadran Cirebonese ceremony honoring Allah, the sea, and fish. **(4)**

naduri Four-part harvest songs of Guria and Achara, Georgia. **(8)**

nafali Vai male masquerader. **(1)**

na filek Bulgarian songs for games played during Lent. **(8)**

nafir North African metallic trumpet, played during Ramadan and for street processions during weddings. **(6)**

nafiri Straight trumpet of a *nobat* ensemble in Malaysia. **(4)**

naga Mythological serpent. **(4)**

naga âgu (Japan.) Nonmetric *âgu*, a folk song genre of the Miyako Islands. **(7)**

nagak Korean conch horn. **(7)**

nagara (1) Gumuz clay kettledrum, both *duma* and *sarma*. (2) Armenian set of skin-covered clay pots; *see diplipito*. **(1, 8)**

nagārā (1) Double-headed cylindrical folk drum of Guyana, 2 meters or more in height and played by one or two men with thick rounded sticks. (2) Performing drummer group and Ahīr singer-dancers of Guyana. **(5)**

nagāṛā (Also *nagare, naqqārā.*) Pair of clay or metal kettledrums played with two curved beaters, used in folk, popular, and temple contexts. **(5)**

nagarāt (Also *nagharāt, naqarāt.*) Pair of differently tuned drums used in North Africa. **(6)**

nagare (Japan.) Extinct religious folk song genre of the Amami Islands, similar to Okinawan *umui*. **(7)**

nagarit Kettledrums of the emperor of Ethiopia; forty-four pairs played in his processions. **(1)**

nāgasankīrtan Processional singing of devotional songs. **(5)**

nāgasvaram Large South Indian double-reed aerophone with a conical bore, played in temples, rituals, and processions. **(5)**

nāgasvaramu Gourd wind instrument played by snake charmers in Andhra Pradesh. **(5)**

nagauta (1) Japanese long epic song or ballad chanted to the accompaniment of *syamisen* 'samisen', often with drums and flutes added, for dances performed in *kabuki* theater. (2) (Japan.) Genre of lyrical *syamisen* music. **(3, 7, 10)**

nagauta syamisen (Japan.) *Syamisen* used in *nagauta*; a slender *syamisen* (*hoso zao*). **(7)**

naga zi (Japan.) Melodic pattern in *gidayû busi*. **(7)**

naggaro Berta drum. **(1)**

nagham (1) Mode or melody, interchangeable with *maqām*. (2) 'Tones', a discipline of early Arabic music theory represented in book titles such as *Kitāb al-nagham*. **(6)**

naghāra Kettledrums in Central Asia. **(6)**

naghma-ye kashāl Afghan instrumental form. **(5)**

naghme 'Tune' in Iranian classical music, or subsidiary modal system derived from a *dastgāh*; similar to *āvāz*. **(6)**

nagla 'Passing', 'transition' between two melodies in a Yemeni suite, *qawma*. **(6)**

na glas Serbian singing style with two-part polyphony in which the interval of a second predominates. **(8)**

nağme Melody (Turkish). **(6)**

Nago (1) African-based Jamaican cult. (2) Variety of Brazilian Candomblé. **(2)**

nahana Yakan song about a famous person. **(4)**

nahanamu Warao harvest festival. **(2)**

nahāwand One of the primary Arab *maqāmāt*. **(6)**

nahenahe A prime Hawaiian cultural value, emphasizing gentleness, calmness, and laid-back ease, often used to differentiate Hawaiian musical styles from others. **(9)**

naḥḥām Professional singer of pearl divers' music of the Gulf. **(6)**

nahma 'Animal sound', 'voice of the whale'; local term for pearl divers' songs in the Gulf region. **(6)**

nai Obliquely blown flute of Zanzibar. **(1)**

nai Romanian panpipe. **(8)**

nā'ī West Asian horizontal flute. **(5)**

naigrýt 'Dance until you drop' (Russian), instrumental ostinato dance tunes used to accompany *pliasky*. **(8)**

NAISDA National Aboriginal Islander Skills Development Association. **(9)**

naiyadi Kandyan dance form of Sri Lanka. **(5)**

naiyānṭi mēḷam Tamil folk instrumental ensemble consisting of drums and double reeds. **(5)**

naj (Also *ncas, nja.*) Hmong *guimbard* or Jew's harp, made of a flat piece of metal with a vibrating tongue. **(3)**

naka (1) Mbojo men's dance with daggers. (2) (Japan.) Middle section of the tripartite division of an act in *bunraku* (pupper theater). (3) (Japan.) Term in *gidayû busi* notation indicating pitch or manner of singing. **(4, 7)**

naka bû (Japan.) Poetic form of the Ryûkyû Islands consisting of four or five lines; the first half is set in Japanese style, the second half in Okinawan style. **(7)**

naki busi (Japan.) Sobbing tune that characterizes *bun'ya busi*, an early narrative music for *syamisen*. **(7)**

nakkaraxāna Term for an emir's military orchestra in traditional Bukhara. **(6)**

nakkare Kettledrums (Turkish); cf. *naqqāra*. **(6)**

nâkunî (Japan.) Genre of Okinawan narrative songs with specific tunes, to which young people often improvised poems to tell of their love. **(7)**

nal Flute, in Balochistan. **(5)**

nāl Folk barrel drum played by Gujaratis in the United States. **(5)**

nalunku Tamil wedding ritual in which the bride and groom apply paint to one another's feet, joke with one another, and sing. **(5)**

nam One of two Vietnamese modal systems. **(4)**

namangngu Bronze or iron gong of Savu. **(4)**

nāmasiddhanta Recitation of holy names as a path to enlightenment in South India. **(5)**

namaskāram (Also *namaste*.) (1) Putting the hands together as in prayer or prostrating the body, as a greeting or obeisance. (2) Traditional verbal greeting. **(5)**

Nambudiri Brahmin caste in Kerala that practices ancient forms of Vedic recitation and chant. **(5)**

namdo minyo Korean folk songs in the southern regional style. **(7)**

nām-kīrtan Singing the names of God, in North India. **(5)**

nana Georgian ritual lullaby sung by the mother a few days after a birth, to protect her infant. **(8)**

ñanappāṭṭu European (particularly German) hymns translated into Tamil and sung primarily by Lutherans in Tamil Nadu. **(5)**

nanarismata Greek lullabies. **(8)**

nande baeth Unaccompanied songs performed throughout the Valley of Kashmir during the planting, cleaning, and harvesting of rice. **(5)**

nande chakri Song genre similar in style to *nande baeth*, but performed in homes with instrumental accompaniment. **(5)**

Nandiwālā Specialist performer who gives animal-training shows in the villages of Maharashtra. **(5)**

Nangayivuza Individual for whom a healing cult in northern Burundi was named. **(1)**

nang pra mo thai Northeast Thai shadow-puppet theater. **(4)**

nang talung Southern Thai shadow-puppet theater, also found in Malaysia. **(4)**

nanguan (1) (Also *nan guan*.) South Fukien music of the Tang dynasty. (2) (China.) 'Southern pipes', a vocal and instrumental chamber ensemble popularized in Fujian Province and Taiwan. **(4, 7)**

Nangû biwa hu (Japan.) 'Biwa score of the Southern Prince', short collection of *biwa* notations compiled in 921 by Prince Sadayasu (870–924). **(7)**

nang yai Large-shadow-puppet theater of Thailand. **(4)**

naniwa-bushi Popular narrative style of Japanese singing that combines storytelling with singing accompanied by *syamisen* 'samisen'. **(3)**

nanori (Japan.) Segment of a *nô* play in which the characters introduce themselves. **(7)**

nanori bue (Japan.) *Nô* flute solo played for the entrance of the *waki* (a secondary role). **(7)**

nanpai (China.) Southern style. **(7)**

nanqu (China.) Southern tunes in the theatrical genres of the Yuan and Ming dynasties. **(7)**

nanyin (China.) 'Southern sound', a category of Cantonese narrative songs. **(7)**

Nanzan *sin ryû* (Japan.) One of three branches of the Singon school of Buddhist chant (*syômyô*). **(7)**

napevky Czech and Slovak brief melodic and rhythmic fragments, repeated to create a kind of musical mosaic. **(8)**

naphat Classical music genre from Thailand. **(4)**

naprej 'Forward', middle-range leading voice in Slovene three-part singing. **(8)**

napurete 'Song', Maleku term. **(2)**

na pŭt 'On the road', Bulgarian term for music sung while walking from a village to the fields and back. **(8)**

na'pwè Spirit propitiation rite of Burma. **(4)**

naqqāl In Iran, a man who sings verses from Ferdowsī's epic *Shāh-nāme* in teahouses and other settings, perhaps adding prose narration of the stories. **(6)**

naqqālī Popular Persian tradition of prose story-telling and poetic recitation. **(6)**

naqqāra (1) Sudanese paired small kettledrums, played for *nōba*. (2) (Plural, *naqqārāt*.) Small kettledrum, usually played in pairs. (3) (Also *naqqārā, nagārā, naqqāre, nagare*.) Pair of kettledrums, found in various sizes, played with sticks. **(1, 5, 6)**

naqrazān Small kettledrums, sometimes suspended from the player's neck. **(6)**

naqsh Vocal form in Arab music involving a prelude-like treatment of various *ghazal* tunes. **(6)**

naqus (Also *nāqūs*.) Antiphonal singing of the Moroccan Atlas mountains, accompanied by idiophones made from found objects. **(6)**

nāqūs General term describing metallic idiophones, including bells and cymbals. **(6)**

nāṛ Obliquely held end-blown folk flute of Sindh and Rajasthan. **(5)**

Nara (Japan.) Period from 710 to 794. **(7)**

naradi bhajan (Also *kañjanī ke bhajan*.) *Nirguṇ* songs, those not in praise of a particular incarnation of a deity. **(5)**

Nāradīyaśikṣā Treatise providing practical instruction for the chanting of Sāmavedic hymns, compiled in the fifth or sixth century. **(5)**

narampu karuvi Tamil musical category referring to chordophones. **(5)**

Nara *syômyô* (Japan.) Generic term for schools of Buddhist chant (*syômyô*) performed in temples established during the Nara period (710–794). **(7)**

naricanje Slovene laments. **(8)**

narimono (Japan.) (1) Generic term for musical instruments; (2) synonym for *hayasi* (instrumental ensembles), usually excluding the *syamisen*; (3) music performed by the *hayasi* (instrumental ensemble) excluding the *syamisen*. **(7)**

narinik (1) Term for lullabies in central Kurdistan. (2) Certain wedding songs. **(6)**

naroden orkestar 'Folk orchestra', Macedonian village instrumental ensemble that plays for radio. **(8)**

narodna muzika 'Folk music', 'national music', 'popular music'. Broad generic term in Slavic-speaking Balkan countries. **(8)**

narodna orchestra Modern folk orchestra of Serbia. **(8)**

narodna umotvorina 'Folk creation', 'folklore' (Serbo-Croatian). **(8)**

narodni muzychny instrumenty Ukrainian folk music instruments of the Soviet period. **(8)**

narodni orkestar Folk orchestra of Bosnia-Hercegovina. **(8)**

narodni orkestri Bulgarian orchestras of folk instruments. **(8)**

narodni pesni 'Folk songs' in Macedonia. **(8)**

narodnjaci Players of newly composed folk music in Serbia. **(8)**

narodnosť 'Nationality', 'peopleness', 'national identity'. Concept used in the mid-1960s by young Russian composers who turned to Russian folk music for inspiration. **(8)**

narodno-zabavni ansambli Slovene folk-popular bands. **(8)**

narsinga Long curved natural horn of Nepal. **(5)**

narslon Oboe of the *nāgasvaram* family on Réunion Island. **(5)**

nart Any of several North Caucasian epic heroes. **(8)**

narton simd '*Simd* of Nart', Ossetian dance in two sections. **(8)**

Nart-Orkurst 'Nart of Evil Forces', Chechen and Ingush epic genre. **(8)**

narye Annual rite of exorcism established by the Korean Silla dynasty. **(7)**

nash'at kār Smaller Aleppan variant of the *'ūd*. **(6)**

nashīd (1) Medieval Arabic vocal prelude in free rhythm. (2) General term for song. **(6)**

nashshād (1) 'Singer of *nashīd*', performer of the Yemeni vocal suite or *tawshīḥ*. (2) Yemeni religious hymnody. **(6)**

nasis Calabash rattle of the Kuna. **(2)**

nasr Vocal section within a suite in the Bukharan *shash maqām* tradition. **(6)**

na štrtko Five-part Slovene singing. **(8)**

nasyon *Lwa* Vodou spirit family, usually associated with a West African ethnic group. **(2)**

na't (1) Religious music honoring the Prophet Muhammad and his offspring. (2) Turkish poem praising the Prophet. (3) Musical genre stylistically related to the *durak*; cf. *na'at*. (**5, 6**)

nathap Thai cycle of drum strokes. (**4**)

nathap propkai Thai longer set of three drum-cycle patterns. (**4**)

nathap sawngmai Thai shorter set of three drum-cycle patterns. (**4**)

näther Optional solo song following the *shakl* in a Kashmiri *maqām* performance. (**5**)

National Academy of Music Institution in Winneba, southern Ghana, founded to train teachers of music. (**1**)

National Dance Company Resident troupe at the Institute of African Studies in Ghana. (**1**)

nations Term used in Brazil for slaves' social brotherhoods. (**1**)

native airs Africanized hymns that came out of separatist African churches. (**1**)

native blues Guitar-playing idiom practiced in interior villages. (**1**)

native drama Dramatic tradition that grew out of the African-church movement in Nigeria. (**1**)

natori (Japan.) (1) Acquisition of part of an *iemoto*'s name by pupils as proof of their accomplishment. (2) Pupils who have acquired part of an *iemoto*'s name. (**7**)

na trapeza 'At the table', Bulgarian nonmetrical songs, originally sung around a table while people are eating and drinking. (**8**)

na tretro Slovenian four-part singing. (**8**)

naṭṭupuram 'Countryside', 'folk' (Tamil). (**5**)

naṭṭuvanār Dance master, especially of *bharata nāṭyam*. (**5**)

naturjodel 'Natural yodel' (German), natural sharpening of the eleventh partial in the overtone series of open tubes. (**8**)

nāṭya Drama, acting, and a combination of dance and drama, from which come both pure dance (*nṛtta*) and that which displays sentiment (*nṛtya*) through expression (*abhinaya*). (**5**)

nāṭya kaccēri Dance concert honoring a deity as part of a village festival in Tamil Nadu. (**5**)

nāṭya saṅgīt Marathi musical drama. (**5**)

Nāṭyaśāstra Celebrated Sanskrit treatise on drama, music, and dance by Bharata, dated c. 200 B.C.E. to 200 C.E. (**5**)

naubat Outdoor court ensemble of trumpets, drums, cymbals, and double-reed instruments in medieval North India. (**5**)

naubat khānā (1) Ensemble of kettledrums, sometimes including double-reed instruments with conical bores. (2) Building where such an ensemble plays. (**5**)

naudi gīt Dance songs of Orissa telling of Krishna and his exploits. (**5**)

nauḥah Lament sung by Shiites during Muharram, often accompanied by self-flagellation (*mātam*). (**5**)

Naukācaritram Telugu musical story by Tyagaraja, consisting of verses and announcements woven around Krishna songs. (**5**)

naumati bājā Damāi ensemble of nine instruments in Nepal. (**5**)

nauṭaṅkī North Indian folk musical drama. (**5**)

navagraha kriti Songs on the nine houses, or planets, in their deified form; the best-known set of such Karnatak compositions is by Muttusvami Dikshitar (1775–1835). (**5**)

navel (Also *nevel*.) Biblical instrument cited in various texts written over a period of some 700 years, but no specimen exists. (**8**)

na viankach (Also *dziavočnik*, *subornaja subota*.) Belarusan bridal fair the day before a wedding, when girls gather accompanied by ritual songs. (**8**)

ñavi maillai Traditional wedding ritual of Ecuador. (**2**)

na vole 'With freedom', 'without walls', Russian style of singing with an open, loud sound. (**8**)

na voli 'Singing freely' (Belarusan); *see haɫasnoha śpievu*. (**8**)

Navrātrī 'Nine nights', Hindu festival of North and South India. (**5**)

naw Upland Thai (Lahu) gourd mouth organ. (**4**)

nawā One of the major notes of the Arab fundamental scale. (**6**)

nawa-wakal Single-tone Sumu flute made from jaguar bone and used in the *sikro* funerary ceremony. (**2**)

nawāzenda Musician or instrumentalist; formerly, the term meant professional performers only. (**5**)

nawba (1) Early Andalusian musical-poetic tradition developed in colonial times. (2) Sung or instrumental suite in classical Arab music; *see nūba*. (**2, 6**)

nawbah Arabic source of the Albanian *nibet*. (**8**)

nawḥ Lament. (**6**)

nay (Also *nāy*, *ney*, *nai*.) (1) Reed flute, rarely heard at first in the United States, but heard more and more as professional immigrants from the Arab world came there to perform. (2) (Plural, *nāyāt*.) End-blown flute or reed pipe found throughout the Arab world, having six finger holes plus one thumbhole. (3) Flutes of the recorder family. (4) In Badakhshan, a conical end-blown fipple flute. (**3, 5, 6**)

nāyaka nāyikā 'Hero-heroine' theme of women in love, found in South Asian literature. (**5**)

nāyanam South Indian double-reed instrument, slightly shorter than the *nāgasvaram*. (**5**)

nāykhī Barrel drum of Nepal. (**5**)

nāzenk (1) Baluchi wedding song genre. (2) Praise songs for male relatives in Balochistan. (**5**)

nazira Music created by a student in imitation of a master, a central idea in the transmission of Central Asian *maqām*. (**6**)

nazm Chechen and Ingush funeral prayers; *see zikr*. (**8**)

ncas Hmong Jew's harp made of metal. (**4**)

nchimi Tumbuka diviner-healer. (**1**)

ncomane Tsonga tambourine, played for exorcism-related rituals. (**1**)

Ndebele Cultural group of southern Africa. (**1**)

ndere Senegalese five-stringed lute. (**1**)

Ndogo A people of southern Sudan. (**1**)

Ndubuisi bass Arpeggiated bass rhythmic pattern used pervasively by the Nigerian composer Ndubuisi. (**1**)

né Mandinka bells in The Gambia. (**1**)

nefes Mystical hymn performed in Alevi ceremonies. (**6**)

nefir Turkish trumpet; cf. *nafîr*. (**6**)

negre jardin Trinidadian disguise of nineteenth-century aristocrats imitating agricultural servants. (**2**)

negritos (Also *hatajo de negritos*.) (1) Afro-Peruvian young men who perform in front of *nacimiento* dressed as Magi. (2) Purépecha dancers wearing masks of black men. (**2**)

Negro jig African dance adapted by Europeans in eighteenth-century Virginia and Carolina. (**3**)

Negro spiritual Nineteenth-century sacred folk song of African-American origin. (**3**)

nehara Kettledrum of the *nobat* ensemble, Malaysia. (**4**)

ñe'icuda Term used for song makers among the O'odham Indians. (**3**)

neifu (China.) Qing dynasty palace bureau of music and theater responsible for arranging music and training musicians. (**7**)

neikurrewén Mapuche shamanic initiation rite. (**2**)

nekara Bronze Đông Son drum of Kai Kecil. (**4**)

nem Javanese pitch name. (**4**)

ñembo'é kaagüy Guaraní fertility-related prayer dance. (**2**)

ñemongaraí Argentine Mbyá annual ceremony related to the ripening of fruits. (**2**)

nenbutu (Japan.) Buddhist chant (*syômyô*) for reciting the name of Buddha or a bodhisattva. (**7**)

nenbutu odori (Japan.) Genre of Buddhist folk music and dance. (**7**)

nenet Bengkulu women's ceremonial dances. (**4**)

nengge shanwu (China.) Good at singing and dancing. **(7)**

neodhimotika Greek new popular versions of folk songs. **(8)**

neo-*klezmer* **music** Music of North American bands that reinterprets and revitalizes the *klezmer* tradition, beginning in the mid-1970s. **(3)**

neo-Melanesian Any local pidgin spoken in Melanesia. **(9)**

népies műdal 'Folklike art song', music composed mainly by nineteenth-century Hungarian urban middle-class amateurs. **(8)**

nestinarstvo Bulgarian fire-walking ritual, accompanied by *gajda* and *tŭpan*. **(8)**

Nestorian heresy Belief, condemned by the Council of Ephesus in 431, that Christ had two distinct natures and persons. **(6)**

netori (Japan.) Short nonmetric preludes of *gagaku* instrumental pieces without dance (*kangen*). **(7)**

netotiliztli Nahua dancing. **(2)**

neutral third Interval of a third that is larger than a minor third but smaller than a major third. **(1)**

nevbet 'Striking the watch', music played by the janissary *mehter* ensemble in the early morning at the Ottoman court. **(6)**

nevestinsko oro 'Bride's dance', Macedonian women's dance. **(8)**

New Hebrides Former name of Vanuatu. **(9)**

new music (Japan). Popular music of the 1970s created by singer-songwriters, derived from contemporary Japanese "folk" songs of the 1960s—which in turn were modeled on the American folk revival—and from rock of the early 1970s. **(7)**

newsong verse (For Yolngu *yuta manikay* 'new song'.) Newly composed song of northeastern Arnhem Land. **(9)**

ney (1) End-blown rim flute, indigenous to Iran; (2) Turkish flute; cf. *nāy*. **(6)**

nfir Moroccan trumpet. **(1)**

ngā Frame drum of the Guruṅg shaman. **(5)**

ngajat Iban men's war-entertainment dance. **(4)**

nganga Musical bow of Fipa women, who live southeast of Lake Tanganyika. **(1)**

ngarkana Clansong style of Central Arnhem Land. **(9)**

ngayau Kajang ancient headhunting ceremony. **(4)**

Ngbaka-Manza A people of the Central African Republic. **(1)**

ngel-ngel Melismatic free-meter ceremonial songs on Kai. **(4)**

ngere (1) Suyá 'ceremony', 'song-dance'. (2) Specific genre of singing in unison. **(2)**

nggo Ende-Lio gong. **(4)**

nggri-nggo Five-stringed bamboo idiochord tube zither of Flores. **(4)**

nggunggi Bamboo jaw harp of Sumba. **(4)**

ngodo Chopi dance cycles accompanied by large ensembles of xylophones. **(1)**

Ngoma Greek-owned recording studio in Kinshasa that began operating in the 1940s. **(1)**

ngoma (Also *ng'oma, ng'oma*.) (1) East African performances that feature dancing with an emphasis on circular movements of the hips. (2) East African term for drums and performances. (3) 'Drum', a membranophone; a healing complex of central, southern, and parts of equatorial Africa. **(1)**

ngombi (1) Faŋ term for the harp. (2) Stick zither outside the Bulu-Beti-Faŋ cluster. **(1)**

ngongi Double bells, which can be used only by royal ensembles of the Lozi and Nkoya of southern Africa. **(1)**

Ngoni Cultural group of Malawi and Zambia. **(1)**

ngorda Dance of the nobility of the former Bauchi State in Nigeria. **(1)**

ngororombe Shona panpipes played in ensemble in hocket style for entertainment. **(1)**

ngoyo Bongo satirical song. **(1)**

ngrémo Nonnarrative men's dance of Java. **(4)**

Ng Sheung Chi *Muyu* 'fish song' singer from South China. **(3)**

nguchu Mbeere dance in which the performers wear bells tied to their legs. **(1)**

ngufa-ngufa Main performers of *dabus* on Ternate and Tidore. **(4)**

ngulei-sîyge-nuu 'Song-raising-person', Kpelle solo singer. **(1)**

Nguni Cultural group of South Africa and Namibia. **(1)**

ngunjung Cirebonese thanksgiving ceremony. **(4)**

nguri Samawan slow women's reception dance. **(4)**

ngwayi **drumming** Type of performance by the Bemba of Zambia. **(10)**

nhac cải cách Form of Vietnamese popular music from the late 1930s. **(4)**

nhạc dân tộc cải biên Modernized "traditional" Vietnamese music mixing lowland and upland genres. **(4)**

nhạc huyền Nguyễn-dynasty court ensemble. **(4)**

nhạc lễ Ritual ensemble of southern Vietnam. **(4)**

nhạc mới Modern popular songs of Vietnam. **(4)**

nhạc tài tử Vocal-instrumental chamber music of southern Vietnam. **(4)**

nhạc tiên chiến Romantic Vietnamese songs of the 1940s, inspired by German *Lieder*. **(4)**

nha nhac (Japan.) Vietnamese court music. **(7)**

nhimia Generic Waiãpi name for aerophones. **(2)**

nhip Metrical organization of rhythm in Vietnamese music. **(4)**

niaga *Gamelan* player. **(10)**

ni agari (Japan.) *Syamisen* tuning. **(7)**

ni age (Japan.) (1) Tuning of the *sansin* (Okinawan three-stringed lute) equivalent to the *ni agari* tuning of the *syamisen*; (2) Okinawan classical songs in the *ni age* tuning with themes of ardent love, pessimistic love, or lamentation; (3) Okinawan popular tunes in the *ni age* tuning. **(7)**

niansong (China.) Recitation of Buddhist chants using the same note. **(7)**

nibaddh 'Bound', Hindustani ragas rendered with meter (tala). **(5)**

nibet In Albania, a sequence of musical genres that includes nonmetric improvisations, song tunes, and instrumental pieces. **(8)**

nigen kin (Japan.) *See* yakumo goto. **(7)**

Nigerian Broadcasting Corporation Governmental agency that sponsors choirs of Nigerian-trained musicians. **(1)**

Nigerian Institute of Music Institution founded at Onitsha in 1949 with the primary objective of promoting Nigerian music. **(1)**

niggun Textless song genre with vocables that first appeared among Hasidic Jews in Poland and Ukraine during the 1700s. **(8)**

nign From Hebrew *nigun*, 'melody'; term used among Hasidic Jews to refer to spiritually powerful tunes. **(3)**

nigunei Meron 'Meron tunes' based on Arab, Turkish, Greek, and Druze tunes, performed in the *klezmer* repertoire for Jewish *hilulah* festivals. **(6)**

nigunim (Singular, *nigun*.) (1) Vocal songs and improvisations performed during the Hasidic *tish*. (2) Lubavitcher songs. **(6, 10)**

nihal de Song tale of Madhya Pradesh, blending prose, verse, and recitation. **(5)**

nihas (From Arabic *nahās* 'copper'.) Baggāra copper kettledrums, symbols of tribal power and sovereignty. **(1)**

nihavent Common Turkish *makam* resembling the Western minor scale. **(6)**

Nihon syoki (Also *Nihon gi*.) 'Chronicles of Japan', the first official Japanese history compiled by the state. **(7)**

nikriz Type of Turkish melodic mode, or *makam*. **(6)**

Nilotes Peoples of the northeast Sudan. **(1)**

nimaj k'ojom Guatemalan large cylindrical double-headed drum. **(2)**

nīmakai Passionate song of North West Frontier Province. **(5)**

nimra (Also *nimar.*) (1) Entertainment act. (2) Shorthand term for entertainers. **(6)**

ninai daiko (Japan.) Double-headed barrel-shape *gagaku* drum; used in processions, carried on the shoulders of the two people; a musician beats it. **(7)**

ninai syôko (Japan.) *Gagaku* gong used in processions. **(7)**

nine night That part of a Jamaican wake when the spirit of the dead person is said to return to be entertained. **(2)**

ninna-nanna Corsican lullabies sung in a lamentlike mood and style. **(8)**

Niño Alcalde Argentine 'Child Mayor', theatrical veneration of the infant Jesus. **(2)**

ni no tesuri (Japan.) Rail on a contemporary *bunraku* (puppet theater) stage to mark off outdoor scenery. **(7)**

ninulla Albanian lullabies. **(8)**

ninzyô (Japan.) Leader of the *mikagura* ceremony (Shinto music and dance at the imperial court). **(7)**

nipjiiht Pame end-blown cane flute played during religious rites and processions. **(2)**

nipuṇ Supplementary or final level of college education in North India. **(5)**

niraval (Also *neraval, sāhitya prastāra.*) Improvisation in Karnatak music that retains the text of the original composition but changes the melody. **(5)**

nirgun Bhakti tradition describing God in ineffable form. *See kañjanī ke bhajan.* **(5)**

nirguṇ gīt Songs of Orissa that present theological riddles in question-and-answer format. **(5)**

nîri (Japan.) Genre of folk song in the Miyako Islands; paeans to the ancestor-gods sung by men in call-and-response fashion. **(7)**

nirvāhaṇa Entrance of the first character in *kūṭiyāṭṭam* dance drama. **(5)**

nisai odori (Japan.) 'Young man's dance', Okinawan classical dance with movements based on *karate*, an art of self-defense. **(7)**

nisi hû (Japan.) (1) *Gidayû busi* style established by Takemoto Masatayû (1691–1744). (2) *Gidayû busi* pieces premiered at the Takemoto *za* theater. **(7)**

nisiki biwa (Japan.) (1) School of *satuma biwa* founded by Suitô Kinzyô (1911–1973); (2) five-stringed *biwa* invented by Suitô. **(7)**

nisiotika Songs of the Greek islands. **(8)**

nīti cintu Tamil morality songs. **(5)**

Nitiren syû (Japan.) Sect of Hokke Buddhism. **(7)**

Ni-Vanuatu People of Vanuatu. **(9)**

Nivkhi (Also *Gilyak.*) People in Sakhalin. **(7)**

nizam Formerly, Muslim ruler of Hyderabad State (now Andhra Pradesh). **(5)**

nizyû (Japan.) (1) Second lowest octave in a piece; (2) second lowest pitch level in

Buddhist chants; (3) common melodic patterns used in the *nizyû* pitch area. **(7)**

nizyû gen sô (Japan.) Twenty-stringed *koto.* **(7)**

njuga Swahili term for a string of small iron bells that dancers wear around their ankles. **(1)**

nkangala Women's mouth-resonated bow, of Zulu origin. **(1)**

nkharamu Spirit of the lion among the Tumbuka people of northern Malawi. **(1)**

nkoni Bambara six- to nine-stringed harp-lute played by members of the hunters' society. **(1)**

n'lapa Single-headed drums of Madagascar, one of which resembles certain West African drums. **(1)**

nnawunta Ghanaian double bells. **(1)**

nô (Also *nō, noh.*) Traditional classic Japanese music-dance theater, developed in the fourteenth century from religious sources and folk myths, characterized by highly stylized acting, unique vocalizations, wooden masks, elaborate costumes, and symbolism presented in a minimalist setting and performance style. **(3, 7, 10)**

noaidi Saami shaman who uses *joik* to induce a trance state in himself. **(8)**

nōba (Also *nawba.*) Sudanese ceremonies of the Qādirīya brotherhood. **(1)**

nobān Possession ritual of the Gulf region. **(6)**

nobat Malay-based Muslim drum and oboe ensemble. **(4)**

nobe byôsi (Japan.) 8-beat rhythmic cycle in *gagaku.* **(7)**

nobe tada byôsi (Japan.) 4 + 8-beat rhythmic cycle in *gagaku.* **(7)**

nodas (Also *pikkiadas.*) Thematic formulas in a Sardinian *sonata.* **(8)**

node Vibration-free point. **(4)**

nodo (1) Small tube inserted in a *nô* flute, *nôkan* (Japan). (2) Korean four-headed pellet drum. **(7)**

noëls French Christmas carols. **(8)**

nôgaku (Japan.) Korean farmers' music and dance; *nongak* or *p'ungmul* in Korean. **(7)**

Nogawa ryû (Japan.) Style of *syamisen kumiuta* (song cycle). **(7)**

noggaara Sudanese cylindrical drum. **(1)**

nogo Korean four-headed drum. **(7)**

nói lói Metrically free introductory phrases for Vietnamese songs. **(4)**

Noisy Boys Vanuatu band. **(9)**

nôkan (Japan.) Transverse flute used in *nô* and elsewhere. **(7)**

nolkín Mapuche hollow-stemmed lip-concussion aerophone played by inhaling. **(2)**

nomos aulodikos Solo instrumental piece for the *aulos.* **(8)**

nomos kitharodikos Solo instrumental piece for the *kithara.* **(8)**

nom-tom ālāp Improvised *ālāp* section with rhythmic pulse in Hindustani vocal music. **(5)**

Nomura kunkunsî (Japan.) Standard collection of scores for *sansin* (Okinawan three-stringed lute) edited in 1869 by Nomura Antyô (1805–1871) and his assistant Matamura Sinsin (1831–1898). **(7)**

Nomura ryû (Japan.) School of Okinawan classical music. **(7)**

nongak, p'ungmul Korean farmers' percussion music. **(7)**

nong geng ge (China.) Songs that accompany planting and agricultural activities. **(7)**

nonggi Korean banner used in folk band processions. **(7)**

nonlinearity Situation in which increasing input energy (or force) increases the loudness of the output and changes its timbre, as with sustained-tone instruments, whose sound-generating mechanism makes the overtones exact harmonics, and with electronic sound systems, whose nonlinearity produces harmonic distortion. **(9)**

nono Gã clapperless iron bell. **(1)**

no-no language Any of several southeast Australian Aboriginal languages whose names consist of the repeated local word for *no.* **(9)**

nonstrophic songs Songs in which text and music lack the formal conventions of strophic songs. **(8)**

noṇti cintu Song form associated with *noṇti nāṭakam*, the one-man musical-dramatic genre of Tamil Nadu. **(5)**

noṇti nāṭakam One-man musical-dramatic genre in Tamil Nadu. **(5)**

noordse balk Plucked dulcimer of the Low Countries. **(8)**

nora Alternative name for *manora* theater in Thailand. **(4)**

noraebang Commercial place where customers can sing in a small room equipped with a video monitor, speakers, and microphones, popular in Korea. **(3)**

norangmok 'Yellow voice', vocal timbre forbidden in Korean *p'ansori.* **(7)**

nori madang Korean outdoor performance space. **(7)**

normal score Melody found by quantitative inference from transcriptions of sampled performances. **(9)**

norteno Northern Mexican style distinguished by use of the accordion. **(3)**

norteño-fronterizo "Near the United States border," popular Yuma genre heard on the radio. **(2)**

Northumbrian small-pipes Bellows-blown bagpipe of northern England. **(8)**

nose flute Small, soft-sounding flute activated by air from the player's nostrils. **(4)**

nóta Hungarian popular art song, disseminated largely by Gypsies. **(8)**

notation Any system of written signs. **(1, 8)**

note Tone occurring as part of a musical piece; transcriptive sign of such a tone or any other musically significant sound. **(9)**

nouvel jenerasyon 'New generation', Haitian cosmopolitan pop music of the late 1980s and 1990s for international markets. **(2, 3)**

novena Brazilian Catholic religious ritual in honor of a saint or religious figure. **(2)**

novenaria (Also *última novena*, 'novenary'.) (1) Nine *tercios* or nine-day period of prayer, a Roman Catholic ritual; (2) Colombian and Guatemalan wake for an adult; (3) *novenario de difuntos*, Puerto Rican nine-day period of prayer for the dead. **(2)**

noviny Soviet-period genre of new songs celebrating Soviet life. **(8)**

novokomponirane narodne pjesme 'Newly composed folk songs' of Croatia and Bosnia-Hercegovina. **(8)**

novokomponovana narodna muzika 'Newly composed folk music' of the former Yugoslavia. **(8)**

nowbe Suite or cycle of compositions in the system of Persian *radīf*; cf. *nūba*. **(6)**

nowḥe Poetic laments for the martyred Shi'a imams and members of their families; often performed responsorially with *sīne-zanī* or *zanjīr-zanī*. **(6)**

no-with language Any of several southeast Australian Aboriginal languages whose names consist of local words for *no* and *with*. **(9)**

Nowrūz (Also *nawruz*.) Iranian new year, coinciding with the vernal equinox, widely celebrated by Persians, Kurds, Afghans, Tajiks, and other Iranian peoples. **(6)**

nozheh Medieval Persian dulcimer. **(6)**

nquillatún (Also *ŋillipún*, *nguillatún*.) Mapuche annual fertility-harvest rite, a seasonal ritual during which the *trutruka* is played. **(2)**

nṛtta (1) (Also *nritta*.) Nonrepresentational or "pure" dance. (2) (Also *nritya*, *nṛtta*.) Representational dance. **(5)**

nṛtya (Also *nurti*.) Sinhala popular music based on Marathi and Parsi theater music of the late nineteenth and early twentieth centuries. **(5)**

nṛtya-nāṭya Dance drama in Bangladesh. **(5)**

nsambi Central African multiple-bow lute. **(1)**

Nsenga Subgroup of the Maravi peoples of Malawi. **(1)**

nsogwe Dance of the Nsenga and the Southern Chewa after the birth of a woman's first child. **(1)**

ntahera Set of five or seven ivory trumpets associated with Akan royalty. **(1)**

nthenda ya uchimi 'Disease of the prophets', said to change ordinary Tumbuka into diviner-healers. **(1)**

nua Song tradition of spontaneously trading verses in Sumbawa. **(4)**

nuba North African suite of songs: (1) Moroccan, in five movements, each in one of five rhythmic modes and performed in a fixed order; (2) Algerian, in nine alternating instrumental and vocal movements; (3) Tunisian, in ten movements. **(1)**

nūba (Also *nawba*.) 'Suite' in Andalusian music, comprising a common stock of vocal and instrumental genres, each representing a different *īqā'* and performed in a given sequence. (Plural, *nūbāt*.) **(6)**

nuban Afro-Arab possession and healing ritual involving sung poetry and dancing. **(6)**

nūbat al-inqilābāt Folklike, simpler form of the Maghribi *nūba*. **(6)**

nūbat neqlāb *Nūba* of more recent origin and modest dimensions in the Algerian repertoire; seven of these join the twelve traditional *nūbat*. **(6)**

nūbat tūshiyya Originally instrumental overture within the Moroccan *nūba*, to which words were later adapted. **(6)**

Nubians (Also *Barabra*.) Cultural group of the Nubian desert in northeast Africa. **(1)**

Nuestra Señora del Rosario 'Our Lady of the Rosary', one of the oldest religious festivals in *mestizo* Spanish-speaking America. **(2)**

nueva canción 'New song'. (1) (Also *nueva canción chilena*.) Generic name for pan-Latin American neofolk-protest music that began in Chile in the 1960s and spread throughout the Americas. (2) Dominican Republic counterpart of the Cuban *nueva trova*. (3) *Nueva canción latinoamericana*, 'new Latin American song', movement of the 1970s that influenced politically conscious university students. (4) Stream of urban song and its accompanying music, often drawing from South American folk elements and representing some form of social protest. **(2, 3)**

nueva canción andaluza 'New Andalusian song', popular music of southern Spain. **(8)**

nueva trova 'New song', name given in 1972 to the *canción protesta* 'protest song' created in 1967, which began in Cuba. **(2)**

nuevo flamenco 'New flamenco', fusion of flamenco with other styles of music since the 1960s. **(8)**

nukana-rendana pandum Madia sacred autumn festivities. **(5)**

num Among the !Kung of southern Africa, source of spiritual energy. **(1)**

nunalca Slovene children's whistle made of thick reeds. **(8)**

nung-subaldá Large Kogi calabash trumpet. **(2)**

nünichlingler Clapper bell of Ziefen, Baselland, Switzerland. **(8)**

nunnie (Also *catabaucalise*.) Children's nurses' work songs of French-speaking Switzerland. **(8)**

nuqta Monetary tip. **(6)**

nurá-mëe 'Horsefly', free-swinging whirled-plaque aerophone (bullroarer) among the Desana. **(2)**

nusah Ashkenazic Jewish sung prayer. **(8)**

nusaḥ erets Yisrael 'Tradition of the land of Israel', musical style developed by the synagogues of the Ashkenazi national-religious sector. **(6)**

nüssler Traditional Swiss maskers in winter festivals before carnival. **(8)**

nūt Struck clay pot idiophone of Kashmir, similar to the South Indian *ghaṭam*. **(5)**

nuta 'Note', harmonic structure central to the music of Podhale, Poland. **(8)**

nuwwah Women's tradition of mourning songs among Moroccan Jews. **(6)**

nyama Kind of power of the Mandinka peoples of West Africa. **(1)**

Nyamwezi Cultural group of Tanzania. **(1)**

nyanga Nyungwe reed-pipe dances with one instrumental tune, within which singers improvise their parts. **(1)**

nyanyuru Fulɓe and Tukulor one-stringed bowed lute. **(1)**

nyavikali Central African trumpets. **(1)**

nyckelharpa Swedish keyed, bowed fiddle. **(8)**

nyisi Metal idiophones tied around the waist and ankles for Tumbuka healing dances. **(1)**

nyô (Japan.) Idiophone used in Buddhist music, a gong struck with a mallet. **(7)**

nystev 'New stanza', Norwegian musical genre in which each of four lines consists of four stressed syllables, and an end rhyme links the first two and the last two lines; *see stev*. **(8)**

nzapa Sango term for the Christian God in central Africa. **(1)**

nzumari Double-reed aerophone of the coastal Bantu peoples of Kenya. **(1)**

ŏ Korean wooden tiger-shaped scraper. **(7)**

oba Edo king in Benin and Nigeria. **(1)**

Ôbaku syû (Japan.) Sect of Zyôdo Buddhism introduced from Ming China by a Chinese monk, Ingen. **(7)**

o bati (Japan.) 'Male stroke', strong stroke played by the right hand on the double-headed barrel-shaped *taiko* in *gagaku*. **(7)**

oberek Dance music in the "new style" in central and eastern Poland. **(8)**

oberek Polish dance in fast triple meter, with two against three cross-rhythms and energetic leaping and stomping. **(3)**

ôbesi (Japan.) *Nô* instrumental piece to introduce demons. **(7)**

obkrocák Duple-meter Bohemian couple dance. **(8)**

O-Bon Japanese Buddhist commemoration of deceased friends and relatives. **(9)**

obuk nori Korean folk dance with five barrel-shaped drums. **(7)**

ôc Conch shell trumpet of Vietnam. **(4)**

ocarina Usually earthenware duct flute, with an oval body and holes for fingering. **(8)**

OCORA (Office de Coopration Radiophonique.) Organization that produced recordings of African music. **(1)**

octave Musical interval encompassing eight diatonic degrees; the interval between a referential sound and a sound of twice or half its frequency; people trying to set tones an octave apart typically stretch this interval by about 1 percent. **(9)**

octavina Guitar-shaped plucked lute of the Philippines. **(4)**

octo echos (Also *oktōēchos.*) Byzantine system of melodic modes. **(6)**

ô daiko (Japan.) (1) Generic term for large drums; (2) large barrel-shaped tacked drum used in *kabuki*, religious music, folk music, and so on. **(7)**

Odeon Major recording label, which by the 1930s was distributing its products across Africa. **(1)**

odissi Major classical dance form of India, with roots in temple dance of Orissa. **(5)**

odonso Guitar-playing idiom practiced in West African villages. **(1)**

odurugya Notched flute made of cane husk and played at the Asantehene's court. **(1)**

Oduvar Hereditary temple singers of the *tiruppugal* hymns in South India. **(5)**

ogan Haitian iron idiophone struck with a stick. **(2)**

Ogboni Yoruba secret society. **(1)**

ogede Edo mask in Nigeria. **(1)**

oggu Small hourglass-shaped drum of Shiva in Andhra Pradesh. **(5)**

ògìdo Yoruba bass conga, based on Latin American prototypes. **(1)**

ogu kut Korean shaman ritual for the dead. **(7)**

ogung Large vertical gong of Sumatra. **(4)**

Ôhara ryû (Japan.) One of two branches of the Tendai school of Buddhist chant (*syômyô*). **(7)**

ohonji (Also *onkhonji.*) Nkhumbi or Luhanda term for a hunting bow or mouth-resonated musical bow, braced in the center, which is played with the end pressed against the inside of the cheek. **(1)**

ohugua Guitar-playing idiom practiced in West African villages. **(1)**

ohun orisa 'Voices of the deities', Yoruba stylized traditional singing. **(1)**

oiwake (Japan.) Style of Japanese folk songs characterized by free rhythm and melismatic setting of texts. **(7)**

ojapali Religious drama form of Assam. **(5)**

ojkanje 'Singing with *oj*', Bosnia-Hercegovinan and Croatian vocal techinque in which singers perform an emphatic exclammatory section on the syllable *oj*. **(8)**

okarina Eastern European and Balkan ocarina. **(8)**

Okayasu (Japan.) School of *nagauta* (lyrical *syamisen* genre). **(7)**

okès bastreng Haitian urban, French-influenced string and wind bands. **(2)**

Okina (Japan.) Repertoire of *nô* derived from *sarugaku* in the Kamakura period (1192–1333). **(7)**

okinawa tetrachord (Also *ryûkyû* tetrachord.) In Japan, three pitches outlining the interval of a fourth with an intermediate pitch dividing the fourth into a major third and a minor second from low to high (for instance, C-E-F); one of the four tetrachords proposed by the ethnomusicologist Koizumi Fumio (1927–1983). **(7)**

OK Jazz Zaïrean band, internationally renowned in the 1960s. **(1)**

OK Success Brass-heavy big band, acclaimed in Congo and Zaïre in the 1950s and 1960s. **(1)**

okoma Large Wayana ceremony that is part of the *marake* initiation ritual for boys. **(2)**

oksh (Also *mangour.*) Belt rattle of goat hooves; **(6)**

oktavina Fretted flat-backed plucked waisted lute with fourteen strings in six courses in the tenor range typically used for countermelodies. **(3)**

okunaga Basic part in *amadinda* performance (Uganda). **(10)**

Ôkura ryû (Japan.) (1) School of *nô* specializing in *kyôgen kata*; (2) school of *nô* specializing in *ô tuzumi* and *ko tuzumi*. **(7)**

ôkurauro (Japan.) *Syakuhati* with flute-like key mechanisms invented by Ôkura Kisitirô (1882–1963). **(7)**

okuri (Japan.) Opening melodic pattern in *gidayû busi*. **(7)**

okuri zi (Japan.) Unit of 2 beats per poetic line in *nô* chanting. **(7)**

okwaula Part in *amadinda* performance (Uganda). **(10)**

ôl Mapuche precomposed style of ceremonial song. **(2)**

old religion One of the two primary religions of the Sinhala in Sri Lanka; includes worship of localized spirit entities, popular Hinduism, and astrology. **(5)**

old-time genre (Also known as hillbilly music.) Folk music originating in the Appalachian Mountains of the United States more than 100 years ago, mainly involving fiddle, guitar, and banjo. **(3)**

olimong Kalinga whistle flute. **(4)**

olimpiady Soviet-era Ukrainian musical Olympics, at which ensembles competed in a highly virtuosic style. **(8)**

ollin aragiid Clapping-accompanied dancing in Halfa areas of Sudan and Kenuzi Nubian areas of Egypt. **(1)**

Olodumare (Also Olorun.) Supreme being of the Yoruba people of Nigeria. **(1)**

ol-tnalan Set of bells worn on elaborate leather bands by the Maasai Moran. **(1)**

omans St. Lucian triple-meter dance resembling the waltz. **(2)**

ōmayn Sound of all instruments playing simultaneously in a Kota ensemble. **(5)**

omele Smallest membranophone in the *orisa* drum ensemble in Trinidad. **(2)**

omele Yoruba 'supporting drums', which play ostinatos designed to interlock rhythmically. **(1)**

omichicahuaztli Náhuatl name for rasp made from the bone of a deer or deerlike animal. **(2)**

ommegang Pageant with music of Dendermonde, Oost-Vlaanderen Province, Low Countries. **(8)**

omolu Three pot drums and two pegged cylindrical wooden drums used to worship Omolu. **(1)**

Omolu Yoruba god of water and fertility. **(1)**

Omoluaiya festival Event designed to protect people from smallpox by invoking the deity Sopona. **(1)**

omori (Japan.) Extinct religious song genre of the Amami Islands, similar to the Okinawan *umui*. **(7)**

omote gumi (Japan.) Set of basic pieces of a *syamisen* song cycle (*kumiuta*). **(7)**

omote ma (Japan.) Front beat of a pair of beats. **(7)**

omulanga Harpist for the ruler of Buganda in the area of Lake Victoria. **(1)**

omvok Note in the center of the xylophone where tuning begins, considered head of the family. **(1)**

onai Ossetian women's polyphonic song that accompanied the making of traditional clothing. **(8)**

ônaobiuta (Japan.) (1) Indigenous genre of short court songs. (2) Purification song in the *tinkon sai* rite. **(7)**

ondo (Japan.) (1) Form of folk songs; (2) folk songs in *ondo* form; (3) generic term for various types of folk songs. **(7)**

Ondo One of the seven principal Yoruba peoples of Nigeria. **(1)**

Ongaku zassi (Japan.) 'Music Magazine', the first music periodical in Japan, published in 1900. **(7)**

ongnyugŭm North Korean harp-zither. **(7)**

Ongyoku kuden syo (Japan.) 'A Book of Oral Transmission about Music', on *zyôruri* by Takemoto Harima no syôzyô (later Takemoto Gidayû II, 1961–1744). **(7)**

onidan 'One who has tricks', theatrical troupe that came out of the *egungun* tradition. **(1)**

on ikki 'Twelve', term for classical *muqam*. (*maqām*) practice in Uighur (Uyghur) Xinkiang, referring more to a sequence of pieces in twelve *muqam* than to a modal category. **(6)**

oniya-niya Maranao reed instrument. **(4)**

onjènikon Haitian song specialist. **(2)**

ŏnmori Korean rhythmic pattern (*changdan*) in 10/8 meter. **(7)**

onna gata (Japan.) *Kabuki* actors who take female roles. **(7)**

onna odori (Japan.) 'Women's dance', category of Okinawan classical dance. **(7)**

ô no koe (Japan.) Deep, strong, sturdy voice in *nô* chanting. **(7)**

onomatopoeic vocalization Drummed or sung syllables that represent the rhythm and timbre of sounds depicted. **(1)**

onor Maranao *bayok* singer. **(4)**

ô nori (Japan.) Rhythmic style in *nô* chanting. **(7)**

ónwehani Among the Garifuna of Belize, spiritual possession said to occur frequently as female participants dance during the *dügü* ritual. **(2)**

on zukai (Japan.) Technique of vocalization in *gidayû busi*. **(7)**

oorlams Popular working-class musicians who were "coloured" or "black" Africans and served as cultural brokers in South Africa. **(1)**

ô otosi (Japan.) Melodic pattern in *gidayû busi*. **(7)**

open-en-toe Accordion of the Low Countries. **(8)**

opera In European art music since the Baroque, compositional genre consisting of a lengthy dramatic text (often in verse) mainly or entirely sung with orchestral accompaniment, usually in large theaters with elaborate costumes, staging, and action, including dance. **(8)**

opéra-ballet Genre introduced in France at the end of the seventeenth century that told dramatic stories in a series of dances. **(8)**

opéra-comique French operatic genre on light or sentimental subjects, with happy endings and usually (until the mid-1800s) spoken dialogue. **(8)**

operismo Spanish flamenco opera. **(8)**

opim Guitar-playing idiom practiced in West African villages. **(1)**

oplakvane Bulgarian lamenting. **(8)**

opowe Long cry indicating the end of a vocal or instrumental Waiãpi tune. **(2)**

oppana Popular dance of the Mappilas (Muslims) of Kerala. **(5)**

oppāri Tamil lament. **(5)**

oprekelj (Also *brana, cimprekelj, male cimbale, pretl*.) Slovene trapezoidal struck zither. **(8)**

orang Alifuru Aboriginal inhabitants of Ambon, Buru, and environs. **(4)**

Orang Asli Upland peoples of peninsular Malaysia. **(4)**

orasyo (Japan.) Equivalent to *oratio* in Latin; prayer songs introduced to Japan with Christianity in the sixteenth century, secretly transmitted by "hidden" Christians when Christianity was prohibited during the Edo period (1600–1867); these songs are still maintained on remote islands in present-day Nagasaki Prefecture. **(7)**

orati 'One beat' (Tamil). **(5)**

oratorio Profane musical performance given by blacks during religious festivities in colonial Mexico. **(2)**

Orchestra Ethiopia Ethiopian ensemble founded in 1963 for the modern presentation of traditional music. **(1)**

Orchestra Makassy Tanzanian band joined by Remmy Ongala in 1964. **(1)**

Orchestra Matimila Tanzanian band joined by Remmy Ongala in 1981, after Orchestra Makassy had disbanded. **(1)**

Orchestra Super Matimila Tanzanian band formed by Remmy Ongala in the 1990s. **(1)**

orchestral *biguine* Urban *biguine* of Martinique, showing a strong French influence and sung in Creole. **(2)**

orchestre champêtre Orchestra featuring an accordion of the French-speaking area of Switzerland. **(8)**

organ Wind instrument equipped with one or more keyboards that control one or more sets of pipes, each having a distinctive pitch and timbre; used principally in churches for the performance of sacred polyphony. **(8)**

organetto Italian small diatonic button accordion. **(3, 8)**

organology Study of musical instruments. **(4)**

organum (Plural, *organa*.) Liturgical vocal polyphony used in Western Europe during the central Middle Ages, roughly 900 to 1300 C.E. **(8)**

orgni Maltese term for the harmonica, concertina, portable harmonium, and hurdy-gurdy. **(8)**

original appenzeller striichmusig 'Original Appenzell string band', Swiss band with two violins, a cello, a dulcimer, and a bowed double bass. **(8)**

oriki Yoruba poetry praising an individual, a deity, a town, or even an inanimate object. **(1)**

orile Yoruba poetry praising lineages, royal families, and ancient kingdoms. **(1)**

orisa (1) 'Deity' in Yoruba (Trinidadian spelling). (2) Orisa, religion that celebrates Yoruba deities in Trinidad. (3) Drum ensemble. **(2)**

orisa pipe Yoruba sung or semisung praises of any deity. **(1)**

orisha (1) 'Deity' in Yoruba (Cuban spelling), in Cuban Santería. (2) (Also *orisa*.) Yoruba intermediate deities below the high god, Olodumare. **(1, 2)**

orixá 'Deity' in Yoruba (Brazilian spelling), in Brazilian Candomblé. **(2)**

orkes bea Torajan conch and flute ensemble. **(4)**

orkes gambus South Sumatra Arab-influenced music. **(4)**

orkes Lampung Lampung wind, string, and drum ensemble. **(4)**

orkes Melayu Malay songs with stringed instruments. **(4)**

orkes sinandung timur Acehnese Malay-based string ensemble. **(4)**

orlo Purépecha double-reed, capped, tubular aerophone (similar to the European krummhorn) introduced by colonial missionaries. **(2)**

oro (1) Yoruba secret society of night hunters, symbolized by the playing of a bullroarer. (2) Macedonian, Montenegrin, and Serbian circle dance. **(1, 8)**

orocoveño Puerto Rican *seis* from Orocovis. **(2)**

orologio della passione (Also *canto della passione*.) Begging song of central Italy performed the week before Easter. **(8)**

orovela Georgian solo male songs of plowing, threshing, and winnowing. **(8)**

orquesta de toros Ecuadorian ensemble of transverse flute, *caja*, and *bombo*. **(2)**

orquesta típica 'Typical orchestra,' (1) Argentine tango ensemble of 1920s; (2) ensemble in the central Peruvian highlands consisting of saxophones, clarinets, violins, and harp; (3) Mexican ensemble in which musicians clad in folkloric garb played regional melodies on a conglomeration of (primarily stringed) instruments; (4) instrumental ensemble characteristic of Cuban music. **(2)**

oru Afro-Cuban song in praise of one of more deities of the Yoruba-derived *lucumí* religious tradition. **(3)**

orugôru (Japan.) Set of small gongs used offstage in *kabuki*. **(7)**

orum Supernatural world in Yoruba cosmology. (**2**)

oru olai 'One cooking pot'; as used by the liberation theologian Theophilus Appavoo, the pooling together by poor people of Tamil Nadu of their financial and labor resources to fight social oppression and perform daily worship. (**5**)

orutu Luo one-stringed lute-fiddle. (**1**)

orvuolle South Saami *joik*. (**8**)

osikasane (Japan.) *Nagauta* melodic pattern quoted from *ôzatuma busi*, an early narrative genre of *syamisen* music. (**7**)

ôsiki (Japan.) (1) Note corresponding to the pitch A; (2) mode of *nô* instrumental music. (**7**)

ôsiki tyô (Japan.) *Ritu* scale built on the note *ôsiki* (A); one of the six modes used in *gagaku*. (**7**)

oss Hobbyhorse that dances to the accompaniment of melodeons and drums at Padstow in Cornwall, England. (**8**)

ostā 'Master' (Baluchi), officiant in the *gwātī* ritual; synonymous with *khalīfe*. (**6**)

ostād 'Master' (Persian), honorific bestowed on those who have fully mastered musical and other arts. (**6**)

ostinato Continuously repeated pattern. (**4**)

ô syôko (Japan.) Largest gong in *gagaku*. (**7**)

Os Zimbos *See Zimbos, Os.* (**1**)

OTAC Office Territorial d'Action Culturelle, based in Pape'ete, Tahiti. (**9**)

ōṭam Boat songs in Tamil Nadu. (**5**)

ōtchungmori Korean rhythmic pattern (*changdan*) of irregular *chungmori*, 6/4 meter. (**7**)

ote Medium-size *sene* gongs of West Timor. (**4**)

ôteki (Japan.) *See ryûteki.* (**7**)

oticonte Nahua friction idiophone made from half a calabash covered with a skin to which a stick is attached and then rubbed. (**2**)

otoko mai (Japan.) (1) *Nô* dance performed by a warrior character; (2) dance performed at festivals of the Kurozumi sect of Shinto (Sintô). (**7**)

otoko yaku (Japan.) Actresses who take male roles. (**7**)

otosi (Japan.) (1) Cadential melodic patterns for *syamisen*, used at transitions; (2) melodic pattern in *gidayû busi*; (3) left-hand technique for *syamisen*; (4) right-hand technique for *koto*. (**7**)

oṭṭan (Also *paṛayan, sīthangan.*) One of three kinds of popular dance drama (*tuḷḷal*) in Kerala. (**5**)

ottava rima 'Eighth rhyme' (Italian), stanza of eight lines rhyming abababcc. (**8**)

ottu South Indian double-reed drone pipe. (**5**)

otu (Japan.) Tone produced on the *ko tuzumi*. (**7**)

ô tuzumi (Japan.) Hourglass-shape drum held at the hip. (**7**)

oud (Also *'ūd.*) (1) North African plucked lute with pear-shaped resonator; a short-necked plucked lute of Zanzibar. (2) Plucked Arab lute found throughout the Middle East. (**1, 6**)

oulé (Also *houlé, ouleur, roulé, rouleur.*) Large cylindrical drum on Réunion Island. (**5**)

oŭm yakpo Korean five-tone simplified notation. (**7**)

oungan Haitian Vodou priest. (**2**)

ounsi Haitian Vodou initiate. (**2**)

ôuta (Japan.) Indigenous genre of court songs accompanying the court dance *goseti no mai*. (**7**)

Ôuta dokoro (Japan.) Institute established in the Heian period (794–1192) for teaching and performing indigenous *gagaku* music. (**7**)

outi Greek bent-necked, unfretted plucked lute. (**3, 8**)

óuu Mixtec single-headed, deep-bodied wooden membranophone resembling the Nahua *huéhuetl*. (**2**)

Ouvéa French name of the island sometimes called West 'Uvea. (**9**)

overtone Any of the high, quiet sounds produced with a fundamental and joining with that fundamental in constituting a tone. (**9**)

ovi (1) Women's songs of Maharashtra. (2) Unaccompanied devotional song genre of central India with a loosely structured form allowing singers freedom for extemporaneous composition. (**5**)

ovsenki Refrain of a *koliada*, sung during winter rituals in Russia. (**8**)

owirúame Tarahumara curer. (**2**)

owj 'Climax', 'summit' (Persian). (1) Highest register attained during a performance; cf. *'awj*. (2) Name of a *gūshe* in the *dastgāh* of *shūr* and the *āvāzāt* of *dashtī* and *bayāt-e esfahān*. (**6**)

oxen songs Welsh songs that plowboys sing to oxen to keep them calm. (**8**)

oxote Basque choral music with eight male voices singing a cappella. (**8**)

Ox Tum Modern-day Guatemalan version of *Baile del Tun*. (**2**)

oyilāṭṭam (Also *oyirkummi.*) Tamil men's line dance with athletic movements and call-and-response vocals. (**5**)

oyne 'Weeping', long mourning ceremony for a Tukano leader or elder. (**2**)

Oyo Yoruba kingdom, the most powerful coastal state that rose to prominence before 1500. (**1**)

oyun havalar Turkish dance tune; the term implies instrumental performance. (**6**)

oyun havası 'Dance tune' in Turkey, generic term. (**6**)

ozan Archaic term for a minstrel or poet in Iran, Turkey, and Azerbaijan; *see aşıq*. (**6**)

ozasiki nagauta (Japan.) *Nagauta* (*syamisen* music) performed as chamber music outside theater. (**7**)

ôzatuma busi (Also *ôzatuma.*) Genre of Japanese narrative *syamisen* music. (**7**)

özgün müziği 'Alternative' music with didactic, leftist tendencies, embraced by some Turkish Alevi. (**6**)

òzi Long, single-headed goblet-shaped drum of Burma. (**4**)

ožragis Lithuanian goat horn with four or five holes for fingering. (**8**)

ozyn-kyi Tatar long-drawn-out lyric songs. (**8**)

päämies Lead singer in Finnish *runonlaulu*. (**8**)

pábarrung Torajan sugar-palm leaf horn. (**4**)

pabasa Chanting of Christ's Passion in the Philippines. (**4**)

pacarā (Also *mātā māī kī gīt.*) Mother goddess songs, performed by women in Uttar Pradesh. (**5**)

pachallampe Chilean Aymara potato-sowing ritual. (**2**)

Pachamama 'Mother earth' in the ancient Andes. (**2**)

pachanga Cuban dance made famous in Africa by Aragon and Johnny Pacheco. (**1**)

pachavalnyja hałaseńni Belarusan funeral laments. (**8**)

pach-pi Breton figure dance; cf. *passepied*. (**8**)

pachvāṅ 'Western', style of *tabla* playing in North India. (**5**)

Pacific Festival of Arts Quadrennial international cultural festival featuring the nations of Oceania, first held in 1972. (**9**)

pad Maharashtran song. (**5**)

pada (1) In the early period, a word or line of a poem referring to the verbal element of music or song (the current term in South India is *matu*). (2) Song text. (3) Various song types, in Karnataka. (**5**)

padam South Indian dance and song form; a song to the Divine Lover. (**5**)

padāvali kīrtan Refined Bengali devotional music. (**5**)

pada varṇam Major South Indian dance genre. (**5**)

pāddana Tulu genre of sung narratives associated with an indigenous Tuluva category of deities called *bhūta*. (**5**)

padhati Received tradition or rules for performing a particular piece or genre. (**5**)

padoa Savunese circle dance with ankle baskets. (**4**)

padyam (Also *viruttam.*) Style of singing poetry without a pulse. **(5)**

Paekche Korean dynastic period, 18 B.C.E. to 660 C.E. **(7)**

pagan Kenyan lyre with a box resonator. **(1)**

pagar mandas (Also *promesas, ofrendas.*) Throughout the Spanish- and Portuguese-speaking Americas, the fulfilling of religious vows, promises, or offerings for divine intervention. **(2)**

paggabbang Tausug secular singing style. **(4)**

paghiling Sung by serenaders in the *harana* ritual, the Philippines. **(4)**

paghjella Corsican polyphonic form sung in church with sacred texts and on social occasions with secular texts. **(8)**

paghjolu (Also *cassella, nacchere.*) Corsican kettledrum used in the Good Friday procession in Erbalunga, on Cape Corse; large frame drum played with a pair of sticks to accompany certain dances, including the *tarasco (tarascona).* **(8)**

pagode Variety of Brazilian samba song form in the 1980s, with racial and political overtones. **(2)**

pagtumbok Sung by serenaders in the *harana* ritual, the Philippines. **(4)**

pahiyas Tagalog harvest festival. **(4)**

pahko Religious fiesta among the Yaqui. **(2)**

pahlawān 'Champion', Baluchi performer of narrative songs that combine recitative, instrumental ritornello, and melismatic sections. **(6)**

Pahlawān Male singer of *shēr* in Balochistan, accompanied by stringed instruments. **(5)**

pahu East Polynesian hand-struck footed drum having a shark- or ray-skin head and a body usually carved from coconut or breadfruit wood, ranging from 22 to 114 centimeters high. **(9)**

pai (China.) Rhythm. **(7)**

pa'i Mbyá religious leader. **(2)**

paiban (China.) Wooden clappers. **(7)**

paichochi Bolivian seed pod rattles worn on the ankles. **(2)**

pai de santo Brazilian male temple leader in Candomblé. **(2)**

Pai he Cantonese opera music ensemble. **(3)**

pailas Cuban paired membranophones with cylindrical metal bodies. **(2)**

paired phrasing Simple repetition of a musical phrase, including words and melody, as a stylistic identifier. **(3)**

paisade Quadrille dance movement that imitates the construction of wattle-and-daub homes in Carriacou. **(2)**

paisanazgo (Also *guancasco.*) Honduran celebrations with a variety of music and dance, often revolving around the physical meeting of images of the patron saints of each community. **(2)**

pajaga Buginese court dance accompanied by *ganrang* and gong. **(4)**

pajé Term for a shaman in many native South American cultures. **(2)**

Pajelança Brazilian religion in the Amazon region. **(2)**

pajupill (Also *vilepill.*) Estonian willow flute with duct but without holes for fingering. **(8)**

pak Korean clappers, used to begin and end a court ensemble piece. **(7)**

pakaṛ Identifying phrase or catchphrase of a Hindustani raga. **(5)**

pakarena Makassarese court dance performed by girls; Makassarese ritual. **(4, 10)**

pakhavaj Drum from India. **(4)**

pakhāvaj (Also *mṛdang.*) North Indian double-headed barrel drum. **(5)**

paki Ecuadorian male lead singer. **(2)**

pakkung Ibaloy bamboo buzzer. **(4)**

pala (1) (Also *mano.*) Puerto Rican pegbox. (2) Popular type of ballad in Orissa, associated with the worship of Satyapir. **(2, 5)**

palabunibunyan Maguindanao traditional ensemble. **(4)**

palais Simple tentlike structure in which Orisa feasts are held in Trinidad. **(2)**

palavyja piesni Belarusan field songs. **(8)**

Palchasqa (Also *Palcha.*) O'ero alpaca fertility ritual in February or March. **(2)**

p'alchin Korean farmers' band formation that involves marching in parallel lines. **(7)**

paldong Kalinga notched flute. **(4)**

palendag Maguindanao notched flute. **(4)**

p'algwanhoe Annual Korean court festival for national peace. **(7)**

Pali Sacred language of Theravada Buddhism. **(4)**

palia Group of five to seven singers led by a main singer (*gāyak*), presenting *pala* ballads. **(5)**

palipal Ifugao ritual clapper. **(4)**

pallavi First section of a Karnatak composition; improvisational section, with text and tala. **(5)**

pallim Gestures and physical actions in Korean *p'ansori.* **(7)**

palmas Claps used for rhythmic accompaniment in flamenco. **(8)**

palmetas Colombian wooden spatulas that are struck together. **(2)**

palm-wine guitar style (Also *sea-breeze music.*) Music played with a guitar and a bottle or hollowed-log idiophone. **(1)**

Palnāṭi Vīrula Katha (Also *Epic of Palnāḍu.*) Extended Telugu oral epic with roots in the twelfth century. **(5)**

palo 'Stick', 'log'. (1) Long drum and its music, associated with saints' festivals in the Dominican Republic. (2) *Palos*, Venezuelan stick idiophone played on the side of wooden-bodied drums. **(2)**

palo seco Stick used for rhythmic accompaniment in flamenco. **(8)**

palos 'Forms', the three main types of song for flamenco: *cante chico, cante intermedio,* and *cante jondo.* **(8)**

palos siguiriyas *Cante jondo* based on a complex 12-beat rhythmic structure; *see soleá.* **(8)**

p'al ŭm Korean term for Chinese eight-part instrument classification system. **(7)**

palwei Bamboo end-blown fipple flute of Burma. **(4)**

pāmalai American and British hymns translated into Tamil, sung primarily in the Church of South India and former British and American missions in Tamil Nadu. **(5)**

pamamaalam Serenade at the end of the *harana* ritual in the Philippines. **(4)**

pamanhikan Tradition followed during a marriage proposal in the Philippines. **(4)**

pambajōḍu Pair of double-headed drums used in Telugu epic performances. **(5)**

pampa corneta In Huancavelica, Peru, vertical wooden trumpet 3 to 4 meters long. **(2)**

pampai South Indian double cylindrical drum. **(5)**

pamploi Gā bamboo tubes. **(1)**

pan Single instrument from the steelband tradition of the Caribbean, made from a steel oil drum. **(2)**

paṇ Ancient melody of Tamil Nadu described in early texts on Tamil music and believed to be the precursor of all South Indian ragas. **(5)**

p'an (Also *p'an'gut.*) (1) Korean village meeting place where *p'ansori* was traditionally performed; (2) type of festive Korean band performance. **(7)**

panalivio (Also *penalivio.*) Afro-Peruvian sarcastic song of lament about slavery. **(2)**

panambih Fixed-meter portion of *tembang Sunda.* **(4)**

pananapat Practice of itinerant chanters in Rizal province, the Philippines. **(4)**

pananapatan (1) First songs of the *harana* ritual in the Philippines. (2) (Also *pananawagan.*) Tagalog outdoor Christmas drama. **(4)**

pāncai bājā (Also *pañcai bājā.*) 'Five instruments', Damāi ensemble of Nepal equivalent to the *naubat khānā.* **(5)**

pancāla Worshipers of the male deity Virabhadra. **(5)**

pañcaratna 'Five jewels', set of compositions by Tyagaraja. **(5)**

pañcatūrya nāda Buddhist fivefold system of instrument classification, in Sri Lanka. **(5)**

pañcavādyam South Indian ritual percussion and wind ensemble. (5)

pancer Transitional tone within *patokan* in Sundanese music. (4)

pancharzyna (Also *sierszeńki, siesieńki*.) Bagpipe for beginners in western Poland. (8)

pandanggo Batangas song-dance. (4)

pandeiro (1) (Also *pandeireta*.) Portuguese round frame drum with metal jingles. (2) Brazilian frame drum like a tambourine with jingles. (2, 8)

pandereta In Puerto Rico, round frame drum grouped in several sizes, playing in multilayered interlocking rhythms and used to accompany the *plena*. (3)

pandero (1) Basque, Spanish, and Bosnian Sephardic frame drum. (2) Puerto Rican and Dominican round frame drum, like a tambourine but without jingles. (2, 8)

paṇḍit Hindu teacher's honorific. (5)

p'andukht'i Genre of Armenian peasant songs reflecting the life of a *p'andukht*, one who is forced to live and work abroad. (6)

panduri Georgian medium-sized long-necked three-stringed fretted lute. (8)

panerus Low-pitched metallophone of Sunda. (4)

pangangaluluwa Songs performed from house to house in the Philippines. (4)

panghyang Korean set of sixteen suspended iron slabs. (7)

panghyang tolgi Korean farmers' band formation that involves creating circles. (7)

pangongka'an Sama gong ensemble. (4)

pangpagaq Kenyah concussion idiophones. (4)

pāṇi 'Palm of the hand', drum patterns played on the *timila* to summon the gods to a ritual. (5)

paniyiri Greek saint's day celebration. (8)

pano' Temiar ceremonial genre in which spirits are contacted. (4)

panpipe (Also panpipes.) Set of differently pitched tubular flutes, usually bound in a bundle or row. (9)

p'ansori Korean musical storytelling; narrative folk music. (7)

P'ansori hakhoe Korean *p'ansori* association. (7)

p'ansu Blind Korean fortune-teller. (7)

pantañ (Also *panatañ*.) Upright hourglass Sumu drum, hollowed from a solid block of mahogany or cedar. (2)

pantheru Kandyan dance form of Sri Lanka. (5)

pantun (1) Malay form of four-line poetry verses. (2) Rhymed couplets, pan-Indonesian. (3) Buginese-Makassarese sung quatrains, also found in Maluku. (4) Sundanese narrative epic performances with *kacapi*. (4)

pantun saut Cross-gender responsorial singing on Ternate and Tidore. (4)

pañuelo 'Handkerchief', Puerto Rican dance choreography that includes swinging a handkerchief. (2)

panunuluyan Outdoor Christmas drama in the Philippines. (4)

paparuda 'Rain-caller', Romanian rain-begging ritual. (8)

par Kota cylindrical drum in Tamil Nadu. (5)

para (Also *chabara*.) Korean paired cymbals. (7)

parabién 'Best wishes'. (1) Chilean genre similar to the *tonada*, performed as a marriage greeting and congratulatory song for a bride. (2) Wake for a dead child. (2)

paracá Guarijio harp. (2)

para ch'um Korean Buddhist dance with cymbals. (7)

paradiddle Onomatopoeic word used by percussionists to designate a quick succession of beats, alternating left- and right-hand strokes typically in the pattern L-R-L-L, R-L-R-R. (8)

parai (Also *pirai*.) Tamil frame drum played by hand or with two thin sticks; the traditional occupation of the Paṟaiyar caste. (5)

parakata uarakua 'Butterfly dance' of Purépecha temple priestesses. (2)

paralimnitiki 'Of Paralimni village', tune type of the Cypriot *tsiattista* genre. (8)

paramparā Tradition, as in *guru-śiṣya paramparā*. (5)

paran Hindustani *pakhāvaj* drum composition. (5)

paranda (From Spanish *parranda*.) In Belize, a Garifuna genre resembling a serenade and serving as a vehicle of social criticism, usually composed by men. (2)

parang In Grenada and Trinidad and Tobago, a Venezuelan-inspired Christmas caroling tradition accompanied by a *cuatro* guitar; the term is a corruption of *parranda*. (2)

parani gi Sinhalese classical music style. (5)

pararayki (Japan.) Three- to five-stringed zither used by the Kuril Ainu. (7)

paṟayan (Also *oṭṭan, sīthanga*.) One of three kinds of popular dance drama (*tuḷḷal*) in Kerala. (5)

parda Frets consisting of plastic thread wrapped around the neck of a *chitrāli sitār*. (5)

parda-dārī (Also *parda-gū ī*.) Solo performance genre in which a man recites and sings narratives in Persian while displaying a canvas painting of the story. (6)

parde (Also *pördö*, Azerbaijani.) 'Curtain', 'membrane' (Persian), one fret on a *dutār*, *sāz*, *tār*, or another chordophone; modal entity associated with a particular fret. (6)

pardeh Frets on the Afghani *dutār*. (5)

pardon Breton annual religious festival. (8)

parea In a Greek chain dance, a group of friends who have requested the dance and paid the musicians for it. (8)

pareado Chilean two-line stanza of seven and five syllables. (2)

pareja In Imbabura, Ecuador, dance music for a child's wake performed on harp with *golpeador*, characterized by a fast 2/4 or 6/8 meter. (2)

parī Invisible creature; colorful, winged, rather feminine angel of ambivalent nature in Iranian mythology. (6)

paricamuṭṭukaḷi Dance with swords and shields performed by the Christians and Muslims of Kerala. (5)

pariji (Also *kuŭm*.) Korean vocal melody with meaningless syllables. (7)

parīkhān One who exorcises a *parī*. (6)

parise (1) Mock battle dance between men in Sumbawa. (2) Florinese whip dueling. (4)

parivār 'Family' system of raga classification that grouped each of the six primary ragas with five or six wives (*rāgiṇī*) and could be extended to include sons (*putra*) and daughters-in-law (*bharyā*). (5)

parlando rubato 'Robbed speaking', singing style with a speechlike, variable beat. (8)

párosító 'Pairing songs', type of Hungarian folk song. (8)

parranda (Also *sarabanda*.) (1) Christmas caroling tradition in Spanish-speaking America. (2) Guatemalan music used for celebrating in the streets. (2)

parrilladas Steakhouses that feature Paraguayan folk music. (2)

partial Upper partial tone; overtone. (9)

particello Score showing only the most important voices. (8)

partido-alto Afro-Brazilian folklike dance of primarily black connoisseurs. (2)

paruntsi Ecuadorian musical bow. (2)

parwa Balinese human theater derived from *wayang wong*. (4)

pas de deux 'Step for two' (French). In classical ballet, a dance for two performers, usually a male and a female. (8)

pasacalle Ecuadorian national folk music genre. (2)

pasada See zapateo criollo. (2)

pasaje Venezuelan dance music genre. (2)

pasam Passion hymns; corpus of Sinhala Christian religious songs ascribed to Jacome Gonsalvez, a Goan priest (1767–1842). (5)

pasante Bolivian festival ritual sponsor. (2)

pasasalamat Songs performed during the *harana* ritual in the Philippines. (4)

paşbend 'After the verse', Kurdish song in a relatively straightforward musical meter, performed after a vocal genre that avoids a recurring meter or rhythmic pattern. **(6)**

paśbiśča pieśni Belarusan pasture songs. **(8)**

pascola Guarijio comic dance; ritual host and dancer of the *pahko*. **(2)**

pascolas Sacred dance of the Yaqui Indians featuring dancers wearing masks and ankle rattles, accompanied by a fiddle and harp. **(3)**

pasillo (1) Colombian and Ecuadorian folk music genre that is an adaptation of the Austrian waltz; (2) *pasillo instrumental*, fast, sectional instrumental genre of Colombia, characterized by alternation of duple and triple meters; (3) *pasillo lento*, waltzlike vocal folk music genre of Colombia and Ecuador, known for its nostalgic and romantic texts and melancholic melodies. **(2)**

pasindén Female vocalist for *gamelan saléndro*, Sunda. **(4)**

pasodoble March in double time. **(4)**

pasola Marapu ritual jousting match. **(4)**

passe-pied Lively dance in quick 3/8 or 6/8 time, especially popular in the early 1700s; a country dance popular in Luxembourg; cf. *pach-pi*. **(8)**

pass-play Children's game songs of Carriacou and Trinidad and Tobago. **(2)**

passu torrau Form of the Sardinian *danza*, based on a six-note rhythmic pattern. **(8)**

pastorale Basque play accompanied by songs and dances, supposedly a descendant of late medieval mystery plays dating from the 1500s. **(8)**

pastorelas (Also *pastores*.) Based on the birth of Christ, these musical dramas performed in Hispanic communities depict the journey of the shepherds to the nativity manger. **(3)**

pastores Christmas songs in the Philippines. **(4)**

pastourelles Pastoral songs of French-speaking Switzerland. **(8)**

pasu In Sri Lanka, masked folk drama that is a Roman Catholic passion play. **(5)**

pasyon Vernacular text about Christ's Passion, sung in the Philippines. **(4)**

patacoré Rapid, complex *currulao* rhythm of Colombia. **(2)**

Patagon (Also *Tehuelche*.) Extinct Native American culture of Tierra del Fuego. **(2)**

pāṭal Song (Tamil). **(5)**

pa'talà Burmese suspended bamboo xylophone with twenty-four keys. **(4)**

patang-ug Kalinga quill-shaped bamboo percussion tubes. **(4)**

Pathé-Marconi Major recording label, which by the 1930s was distributing its products across Africa. **(1)**

pathet Javanese modal classification system. **(4, 10)**

pāthya Recitation. **(5)**

patinadha Genre of improvised rhyming couplets of Chios, Greece. **(8)**

patna jatra Festival dance performed at temples in Orissa. **(5)**

patokan Structural outline of a piece of Sundanese music. **(4)**

patrilineal Tracing descent through the male line; cf. *matrilineal*. **(9)**

patronal festivals Saint's-day celebrations. **(2)**

paṭṭābiṣēkam 'Coronation' of Rama as king in the *rāma nāṭakam* drama. **(5)**

patting juba (Also pattin' *juba*.) African-American style of drumming in which beats are played on parts of the body; derived from drumming accompanying the Afro-Haitian *juba* dance. **(3)**

pattiyam Wedding ritual in Tamil Nadu, in which the bride sings of her wishes and desires. **(5)**

pattong Kalinga wooden sticks for striking gongs. **(4)**

pāṭū 'Song' (Kodagu) in Karnataka. **(5)**

patut Cirebonese modal classification system. **(4)**

patutan Balinese modal classification system. **(4)**

pāwā (Also *satāra*.) Paired flute of Rajasthan with one pipe used as a drone, played by the Laṅgās. **(5)**

pa'waïñ Burmese circle of twenty-one tuned drums in a wood frame. **(4)**

paya Chilean audience-proposed theme developed as an octosyllabic line. **(2)**

payada Uruguayan musical duel or competition. **(2)**

payador (1) Uruguayan singer who improvises poetic texts to a given musical form. (2) (Usually plural, *payadores*.) Argentine challenge singers and vocal ensembles. **(2)**

payé Powerful Tukano shaman who presides over life-cycle ceremonies and is said to cure illnesses and to function as the communicator between Tukano hunters and the supernatural masters of the animals. **(2)**

pāye Rhythmic motive in Persian music. **(6)**

payola (Also pay for play.) Industry term for money, or other forms of compensation, given in order to have a composition played in public. **(3)**

paytan Singer of Hebrew *piyyutim*, religious poems. **(6)**

pečalbarski pesni 'Songs of workers abroad', mourning Macedonian village men who work in cities or other countries. **(8)**

Peda People of Benin. **(1)**

pedagogy Methods of teaching. **(4)**

peditório (Also *arruada, recolha de andores*.) Portuguese religious festival in which a band performs marches in front of each house in a village. **(8)**

pee 'Play', generic term for Aluku ceremonies. **(2)**

pegbox Part of a stringed instrument that holds the tuning keys or pegs. **(3)**

pehlivan In Albania, a Turkish-style wrestling match, accompanied by music. **(8)**

peiyin (China.) Accompanying notes. **(7)**

pejogedan bumbung Xylophone ensemble for the *joged* dance in Bali. **(4)**

peking Sundanese high-pitched metallophone. **(4)**

Peking opera (Also Beijing opera, *jingju*.) Popular theater of China that developed in the nineteenth century. **(7)**

pele Performance of the Kpelle of Liberia that features singing, dancing, playing instruments, and speaking. **(1)**

pellet drum Hourglass drum struck by two pellets attached to the ends of strings tied to the drum's narrow middle section. Twirling the drum back and forth activates the striking action. **(5)**

pellet rattle Small, generally spherical clay rattle, with a hollow center containing a few pellets that cause the instrument to sound when shaken. **(5)**

pélog Gapped-scale pentatonic tuning system, found throughout Indonesia. **(4)**

pelota tatá Activity of the Paraguayan *fiesta de San Juan* in which a ball of rags soaked in tar and kerosene is set afire and kicked through the crowd. **(2)**

pelqesë (Also *binjak*.) Double-bore duct flute of Albanians in Macedonia and Kosova. **(8)**

pemptos Fifth movement of the Cypriot *kartzilamades* dance cycle, performed in 2/4, 3/4, or 7/8 time. **(8)**

pena Bowed string instrument of Manipur with a coconut resonator and bamboo neck. **(5)**

peña (1) Folk music nightclub of South American origin. (2) Private gathering place or touristic nightclub where folk musicians perform in certain Andean cities where tourism is common. (3) In Argentina, a regionally oriented meeting place for dance and food celebrations. (4) *Peña folklórica*, restaurant featuring neofolkloric music. (5) Small Spanish flamenco club. **(2, 3, 8)**

penanggisa-an Maranao deep-rimmed bossed gong. **(4)**

penca (Also *pencak silat*.) Indonesian martial arts performance. **(4)**

pendhapa Large pavilions at Javanese courts. **(4)**

pengawak "Body" section of fixed-meter piece of Balinese music. **(4)**

penja duriyang Northern Thai ensemble of free reeds and strings. **(4)**

penna Plectrum for the Corsican *cetera*. (8)

pennywhistle Metal whistle with several holes for fingering, usually cheaply manufactured and sold. (1)

pennywhistle jive Alternative name for *kwela*. (1)

pentatonic Having a pitch inventory of five tones to the octave. (1)

pentozali (Also *pidhiktos*.) Acrobatic dance of Crete. (8)

penunggul Javanese pitch name. (4)

peperona (Also *dordolec*.) Rain-begging ritual, performed by Albanian children in the late spring or early summer of a dry year. (8)

peperuda 'Butterfly', Bulgarian rain-begging ritual, performed as needed during spring and summer droughts. (8)

perahēra Buddhist temple processions in Sri Lanka. (5)

percussive idiophone Idiophone made to sound by the action of a beater, as with log idiophones, wooden plaques, and xylophones; cf. *concussive idiophone*. (9)

perepelka Ukrainian musical game, played only on the day after Easter by girls of a given *kutok*. (8)

périco ripiao Nickname of small *merengue típico* 'typical *merengue*' dance music group in the Dominican Republic, from the name of a brothel in the 1930s. (2)

perico ripiao Regional folk *merengue* music and couples dance form, promoted by the former dictator Rafael Trujillo as a symbol of Dominican national identity. (3)

perde Fret on a Turkmen *dutar*. (6)

pərdələr Frets on an Azerbaijani *saz*. (6)

peristil Large area of a Haitian temple where dancing takes place. (2)

periya kaṭci 'Large faction', devotee group at a Tyagaraja festival. (5)

periya mēlam (Also *mangaḷa vādyam*.) Large ensemble of *nāgasvaram* and *tavil* players who perform for auspicious occasions in South India. (5)

perkhisa Georgian suite of line dances in which some dancers may stand on others' shoulders. (8)

perkhuli Circle dance considered the most archaic Georgian dance. (8)

pero Slovene leaf whistles. (8)

peroveta anedia 'Prophet song', twentieth-century New Guinean musical genre whose melodic, rhythmic, harmonic, and textural style, and originally language, were brought by Polynesian LMS (London Missionary Society) missionaries. (9)

Persian *rabāb* Persian unfretted plucked lute; used at medieval Indian courts. (5)

peruncung Bidayuh bamboo tubes. (4)

pesenniki Published Russian songbooks. (8)

pesennost' 'Songness', Russian musicological concept developed by Boris Asaf'ev. (8)

pesindhèn Female Javanese vocalist accompanied by a *gamelan*. (4, 10)

pesnopojki Chapbooks of urban songs published outside Bulgaria during the mid-1800s. (8)

peşrev Ottoman light-classical genre, played by Rom musicians in Macedonia. (8)

peşrev (Also *peshrev*; in Arabic, *bashraf*.) Prelude in Turkish instrumental music with a fixed rhythmic pattern. (6)

peste Rhythmic popular song that concludes the Iraqi *maqām* in secular contexts; cf. *bastah*, *tawshīḥ*. (6)

petición de lluvia Mixtec petition for rain on Saint Mark's Day. (2)

Petro Creole deities of Vodou in Haiti, possibly with some Taino influence. (2)

peṭṭi (Also *śruti* box, *śruti peṭṭi*.) 'Box'; bellows-driven reed organ in South India. (5)

petuk Timekeeping horizontal kettle gong of Lombok. (4)

pevačka društva Serbian singing societies. (8)

pewutún Diagnostic Mapuche medical ritual. (2)

pey-aw Khmer cylindrical double-reed aerophone. (4)

peyote song Song associated with the Native American Church. (3)

pey pork Khmer free-reed pipe with finger holes. (4)

pey prabauh Khmer cylindrical double-reed aerophone. (4)

peyú vári (Also *goo*.) 'Turtle to scratch', large tortoiseshell idiophone covered with beeswax and rubbed with the musician's hand, producing a low-pitched hum. (2)

phách Piece of wood or bamboo struck by two beaters in Vietnam. (4)

Phāguā Holī Springtime festival in Trinidad. (5)

phaguā Songs of the Holī season in Uttar Pradesh. (5)

phāgu gīt Men's seasonal songs of Madhya Pradesh. (5)

phalahuita Transverse flute of Peru. (2)

phanya Courtship poetry in northeast Thailand. (4)

phata-phata Urban popular dance-song genre drawing from South African choral music. (1)

phin Plucked lute of northeast Thailand. (4)

phin hai Northeast Thai ceramic jars with plucked rubber bands. (4)

phin nam tao Chest-resonated stick zither of northern Thailand. (4)

phin phia Multistringed stick zither of northern Thailand. (4)

phleng dio Solo instrumental classical Thai compositions. (4)

phleng hang khrüang Short coda pieces attached to longer compositions in Thailand. (4)

phleng kar Cambodian village wedding song. (4)

phleng khorat Repartee songs of Nakhon Ratchasima (Khorat) city, Thailand. (4)

phleng kret Classification term for miscellaneous compositions in Thai music. (4)

phleng la Thai compositions for ending a concert. (4)

phleng laim Class of Khmer court compositions for dance. (4)

phleng lamtat Repartee village song of central Thailand. (4)

phleng luk krung Thai popular song accompanied by Western instruments. (4)

phleng luk thung Popular music genre of Thailand. (4)

phleng naphat Thai instrumental compositions for ceremonies and theater. (4)

phleng phua chiwit Thai popular music incorporating social criticism. (4)

phleng phuang malai Thai village song genre performed in a circle. (4)

phleng phün ban Village folk song genres of Thailand. (4)

phleng phün muang Agricultural song of Thailand. (4)

phleng rüa Antiphonal songs for men and women, sung on boats in Thailand. (4)

phleng rüang Ceremonial suites and overtures in Thai classical music. (4)

phleng samai Modern Cambodian music. (4)

phleng skor Category of classical compositions for Khmer drumming. (4)

phleng tap Short suites of melodious compositions in Thailand. (4)

phleng thai düm Classical repertoire of Thailand. (4)

phleng thai sakon Thai popular music genre. (4)

phleng thao Thai composition in three *chan* tempo levels. (4)

phleng yai Long, texturally complex classical Thai compositions. (4)

phoneme Minimal unit of distinctive linguistic sound. (9)

phram Leader of a spirit ritual in Thailand, Laos, or Burma. (4)

phutu wankara Bolivian long double-headed cylindrical drum. (2)

pi Thai family of double or quadruple reeds of various shapes. (4)

pia manadi In Belize, processional play resembling English mumming plays, involving the death and resurrection of one of the characters. **(2)**

piano European keyboard instrument with wire strings that sound when struck by small, felt-covered hammers attached to the keys; popular since the late eighteenth century. **(8)**

piano accordion Musical instrument having two rectangular headboards connected by a folding bellows and eliciting sounds from free-beating metal tongues set into vibration by the actions of keys on a pianolike keyboard on the right side and buttons on the left; cf. *button accordion*. **(9)**

piaofang (China.) Peking opera clubs organized by performers for whom this music is an avocation. **(3, 7)**

piaoyou (China.) Friend of the *piaofang*. **(7)**

pi aw Thai short, cylindrical quadruple reed; rare. **(4)**

pibau Welsh pipes, a main traditional instrument of medieval and renaissance Wales. **(8)**

pibau cod Welsh bagpipes popular from the 1600s to the early 1800s. **(8)**

pibgorn Welsh single-reed hornpipe with a cow-horn bell and wood or bone barrels pierced by seven holes for fingering. **(8)**

pibroch English for Scottish *piobaireachd*. **(8)**

Piccukaguntlu Telugu narrative singers who sing primarily for certain agricultural and herding castes. **(5)**

pi chanai Double-reed aerophone from Thailand. **(4)**

pi chawa Thai conical wooden quadruple reed, of Javanese origin. **(4)**

pichel Local name of the alphorn in Uri, Switzerland. **(8)**

pi choan 'Second level', Khmer medium rhythmic cycle. **(4)**

pi chum Northern Thai free-reed pipes with finger holes. **(4)**

picó Powerful, elaborately decorated mobile sound system in Colombia for the playing of pop music by disk jockeys. **(2)**

picong Verbal duels or "wars" between calypsonians in Trinidad and Tobago. **(2)**

picotage In France, constant alternation of a low note with a melody by a solo instrumentalist to produce a drone effect. **(8)**

pidgin Simplified speech serving for communication among peoples having different native languages; cf. *creole*. **(9)**

pidhiktos (Also *pentozali*.) Acrobatic dance of Crete. **(8)**

pidkiavali Cypriot single-reed cylindrical cane aerophone, played by shepherds. **(8)**

pie forzado 'Forced foot', style of *décima* in which the tenth line is always the same. **(2)**

pieles rojas 'Red skins', Chilean patronal festival dance group that imitates American Indians

with dances and costumes derived from North American movies. **(2)**

Pierrot Grenade Carnival characterization of an effete, shabbily dressed patois-speaker in Grenada and Trinidad and Tobago. **(2)**

piezas sagradas 'Sacred pieces'. **(2)**

pífano (Also *pifano*.) (1) Northeastern Brazilian *caboclo* transverse flute made of cane, plastic, or metal. (2) Bolivian cane transverse flute with six finger holes. (3) Ecuadorian duct flute with six finger holes. **(2)**

piffero Italian double-reed aerophone, played in sets of two or three. **(8)**

pifülka (Also *pifilka*.) Mapuche single- and double-tubed ductless flute (panpipe type), usually made from wood but sometimes made from cane. **(2)**

pignatu Corsican friction drum. **(8)**

pihuangqiang (China.) Amalgamation of two systems of tunes called *xipi* and *erhuang*. **(7)**

Pijin Pidgin commonly spoken in the Solomon Islands. **(9)**

pijpersfluit (Also *pijperfluit*.) Side-blown flute of the Low Countries. **(8)**

pijpzak Bagpipe of the Low Countries. **(8)**

pi kaeo Quadruple reed with a bulbous body, from Laos. **(4)**

piké Idiophone of bamboo mounted in an iron frame, on Réunion Island. **(5)**

pikkiadas (Also *nodas*.) Thematic formulas in a Sardinian *sonata*. **(8)**

pilākkaṇam Tamil lament. **(5)**

Pilates System of physical rehabilitation developed by Joseph Pilates; studied by many dancers to help develop strength and flexibility. **(3)**

Pilipaŭskija piesni Belarusan ancient epic and lyrical songs performed during Advent. **(8)**

piḷḷari gīta 'Ganapati songs'; Karnatak beginners' pieces honoring Ganesha, Lord of Beginnings. **(5)**

pilli Finnish single-reed pipe. **(8)**

piloilo Chilean two- to five-tubed panpipe made of stone, clay, cane, or wood. **(2)**

pilu (Taken into French as *pilou*.) Presentational Kanak dancing, often by numerous ensembles. **(9)**

pi mawn Large conical quadruple reed of the Mon ensemble. **(4)**

pina (Also *penah*.) Gumuz gourd aerophone. **(1)**

pi nai Double-reed aerophone from Thailand. **(4)**

pinalaiyan Kalinga-Tinggian gong and drum ensemble. **(4)**

pinghou (Also *pihng hauh* in Cantonese opera.) In China, low-pitched male voice type. **(7)**

pinghua (China.) Unornamented speech. **(7)**

pingqiang (China.) Narrative singing style commonly used in descriptive passages. **(7)**

ping-ze (China.) Even-oblique tone system used in poetry and storytelling. **(7)**

pinkster Midyear celebration originated by the Dutch, later associated with African-Americans. **(3)**

pinkui Ecuadorian transverse flute with one blowhole and two finger holes. **(2)**

pinkullu (Also *pincollo, pinculu, pincullo, pincullu, pingollo, pinkillo, pinkuyllo, pinquillo*.) (1) Central Andean end-blown duct flute of Quechua origin with three to eight finger holes. (2) Chilean cane duct flute (*pinquillo*) played alone or accompanied by *bandola*. (3) Ecuadorian end-blown duct flute (*pingullo*), played in pipe-and-tabor fashion. (4) Q'ero vertical, notched, six-note edge aerophone (*pinculu*). **(2)**

pinkullwe Mapuche cane vertical flute. **(2)**

pinn Extinct angular harp shown in Angkor carvings. **(4)**

pinna Maltese guitar pick. **(8)**

pinnal kōlāṭṭam Stick dance in Tamil Nadu, in which dancers hold colorful ribbons tied to a central pole. **(5)**

pinnpeat (Also *pinn peat*.) Khmer classical court ensemble. **(4)**

pin pāṭṭu Vocal support parts in Tamil drama. **(5)**

piobaireachd Classical Scottish piping tradition; see also *pibroch*. **(8)**

píopaí Early Irish bagpipes. **(8)**

pipa (China.) Pear-shaped short-necked plucked lute originating in Persia and imported into China from India in the fourth century. **(3, 4, 7)**

P'i pada kagŭk tan Sea of Blood Opera Company of North Korea. **(7)**

pipahī (1) Double-reed aerophone. (2) Ensemble accompanied by kettledrums. **(5)**

pipe band Musical ensemble formed of bagpipes and usually a battery of side and bass drums. **(9)**

pipes Abbreviated term for the Irish bellows-blown *uilleann* pipes. **(8)**

pipezë Albanian single-reed cane pipe. **(8)**

piphat Classical ensemble of Thailand. **(4)**

piphat mai khaeng Thai *piphat* ensemble with hard mallets. **(4)**

piphat mai nuam Thai *piphat* ensemble with padded mallets. **(4)**

piphat mawn Ensemble of Mon origin for funerals. **(4)**

pipimemyra End-blown Waiāpi edge aerophone. **(2)**

piping Playing the bagpipes. **(3)**

pipiza Greek double-reed shawm. **(8)**

pipsac Bagpipe of the Low Countries. **(8)**

pīr (1) Muslim holy man or saint. (2) Sufi saint. (3) Turkish spiritual elder; founder of a *tarikat*. (**5, 6**)

pirekua (1) Purépecha singing genres influenced by the waltz. (2) (Also *pirekua-abajeño*.) Purépecha song variant of *abajeño* featuring hemiola. (**2**)

p'iri Korean double-reed bamboo pipe. (**7**)

pirit Buddhist chant in Sri Lanka. (**5**)

pirkansa Ceremonial communal construction music in the Peruvian Andes. (**2**)

pirula (Also *fischju*.) Corsican long, thin reed flute having three to six holes for fingering. (**8**)

piščyki Belarusan reed aerophones. (**8**)

pishchik (Also *zhaleika*.) Russian single-reed aerophone with one or two pipes with a horn bell. (**8**)

pīsh darāmad Instrumental composition played by a melodic instrument and drum or by a small ensemble before the initial *gūshe-hā* of a Persian *dastgāh*. (**6**)

pisheh Medieval Persian flute. (**6**)

pisirk In the Eastern Arctic, song that expresses personal emotions or relates anecdotes. (**3**)

pismatiko Improvised rhyming couplets of Rhodes, Greece. (**8**)

pismice (Also *pjesmice*.) 'Small songs', song type common in Slavonia. (**8**)

písničkáři Czech and Slovak popular folk singers. (**8**)

pisŏng 'Nasal voice', vocal timbre forbidden in Korean *p'ansori*. (**7**)

pissenlit Trinidadian transvestite band during carnival, before 1884. (**2**)

pisteros (Also *fiesteros*, Spanish.) Tarahumara feast sponsors. (**2**)

pištik Belarusan reed pipe. (**8**)

pisu Four-stringed fretless plucked lute of West Timor. (**4**)

piszczałka Duct flute with a double pipe of the Carpathian area of Poland. (**8**)

pitch Perceived height or "location" of sound, measurable in mels; cf. *frequency, note, tone*. (**9**)

pito (Also *pitu*.) 'Pipe' (Spanish). (1) Central Andean cane, metal, wooden, or plastic end-blown duct flute of Spanish or indigenous origin with two to six finger holes, often used with a small tambor to accompany *mestizo* dances. (2) Cane or wooden transverse flute with six finger holes in southern Peru and Panama. (3) Another name for the Atlantic coastal Colombian *caña de millo*, an idioglottal transverse clarinet of cane or millet with four finger holes, used in traditional *cumbia*. (4) *Pito y tambor* 'pipe and tabor', *mestizo* one-person ensemble of flute and drum to accompany saint's-day dances. (5) Small vertical Mexican flute. (**2, 3**)

pitos Finger snaps used for rhythmic accompaniment in Spanish flamenco. (**8**)

piṭṭa katha Digression from the main story, in a Telugu oral narrative performance. (**5**)

pitucahue Mapuche stone panpipes. (**2**)

piva Northern Italian and Italian-Swiss bagpipe. (**8**)

pivačka tambura 'Singer's tambura', long-necked two-stringed plucked lute. (**8**)

pivana Corsican cow- or goat-horn duct flute with six holes for fingering. (**8**)

pive Double-chanter bagpipe played by the Italian minority in Istria, Croatia. (**8**)

piv-i-røv-hest Danish vessel flute or clay pipe in the shape of a horse. (**8**)

pi-wang Small Tibetan spike fiddle, used to accompany songs in most Himalayan areas. (**5**)

piyuṭ (Plural, *piyuṭim*.) Jewish festal song, setting Hebrew rhymed poetry. (**6**)

piyyutim Nonliturgical sacred Jewish hymns. (**8**)

pizhatka (Also *dudka, sopel*.) Russian duct flute with five or six holes for fingering. (**8**)

pizmon (Plural, *pizmonin*.) (1) Jewish song genre in which preexisting texts, particularly those for important holidays, are provided with variant musical settings. (2) Hymn sung by Sephardic Jews. (3) Paraliturgical hymn. (4) Hebrew songs stressing urban, individualistic experiences instead of collective, agricultural topics, popular from the 1970s. (**3, 6, 8, 10**)

pjesme u kolu Songs performed while dancing the *kolo* in Bosnia-Hercegovina. (**8**)

pjesmice (Also *pismice*.) 'Small songs', common in Slavonia. (**8**)

pjevanje uz bešiku 'Singing beside the cradle' in Bosnia-Hercegovina. (**8**)

pkhachich Adighian rattle, used to accompany dance. (**8**)

plastinky 'Phonograph records' (Russian). (**8**)

platillos Colombian cymbals. (**2**)

playback singer Vocalist who records songs for Indian commercial film productions. (**5**)

plectrum Pick. (**8**)

plena (1) Twentieth-century Puerto Rican dance-music genre featuring commentary about work and events. (2) Strophic song genre with percussion accompaniment rooted in African-derived communities of coastal Puerto Rico. (3) Fast song-dance genre, of African–Puerto Rican origin, in duple meter and sometimes improvised stanza-refrain form. (**2, 3, 9**)

pliasky Russian solo dances. (**8**)

pliasovoi khorovod Russian dance with solo dancers inside a circle of singers who step lightly in place. (**8**)

plonarca Two-row diatonic accordion of western Slovenia. (**8**)

plosa Structure of Tagalog poetry. (**4**)

plow-whistles Rare category of Irish traditional songs with mostly descending melodies. (**8**)

plugarul (Also *plugușorul*.) 'Plowman', Romanian festival with music to honor the first farmer to plow his fields. (**8**)

pluriarc Multiple-bow lute. (**1**)

plygain Welsh carols associated with the winter solstice. (**8**)

Pocomía Syncretic religion incorporating traditional African and Protestant beliefs and practices in Costa Rica. (**2**)

podbliudnye pesni 'Fortune-telling songs', Russian songs performed during winter rituals. (**8**)

pod draku 'At a fight', western Russian subgenre of *chastushki*, sung as men engage in fisticuffs. (**8**)

pod iazyk 'Under the tongue', how Russian singers perform instrumental accompaniments without actual instruments. (**8**)

podkorak 'Lined with the step', Bosnia-Hercegovinian vocal style in which the rhythm of songs is based on the rhythm of body movement. (**8**)

podruznik Genre of the Lubelskie region of Poland, often played to accompany a wedding procession. (**8**)

podvodka Central Russian polyphonic vocal music, with a lower voice and an improvised descant. (**8**)

poetas populares Chilean 'popular poets', singer-composers of the *verso*. (**2**)

poeti a braccio Italian performers of lyric songs, such as *stornelli*, who improvise song texts. (**8**)

poetics Examination of the poetry of songs by studying aesthetic systems and compositional procedures. (**1**)

poghi Nose flute of Sumba. (**4**)

pohaci Sundanese spirit. (**4**)

Pohnpei Main island, and a state, of the Federated States of Micronesia. (**9**)

poietarides Professional Cypriot poet-singers. (**8**)

poietarikes Melodic type for poems of the Cypriot *poietarides*. (**8**)

poiushchii poet 'Singing poet', Russian singer-songwriter. (**8**)

pokok Central melody and basis for figuration in Balinese music. (**4**)

pokos (Also *senokos*.) 'Haymaking' (Russian). (**8**)

polanowe 'Of the mountain pastureland', genre of open-air song of the Beskidy Mountain region of Poland. (**8**)

pol-beat Politically-oriented Hungarian music of the 1960s. (**8**) *polca* (1) (Spanish, from *polka*.) European-derived social dance. (2) Dance similar to the European-derived dance form except in the Paraguayan tradition, in which it is a triple-metered genre particularly favored by harpists. **(2, 3)**

polesane Type of Italian song for dancing; *see maitinade*. **(8)**

põliannez (Also *põlian'ias*.) Komi panpipe. **(8)**

polka Vivacious nineteenth-century European couple dance of Bohemian or Polish origin, in 2/4 meter. **(3, 8)**

polli gīt Bengali folk songs. **(5)**

polne 'Of the fields', genre of open-air song of the Sandomierz region of Poland. **(8)**

polnischer Tanz Name of the mazurka outside Poland. **(8)**

polonaise Stately Polish processional dance popular in the 1800s. **(8)**

polonez 'Polonaise', slowest dance in Polish folk music. **(8)**

polska (1) Swedish improvisatory dance in 3/4 time. (2) Danish dance. (3) Finnish vocal genre based on instrumental dance rhythms. **(8)**

polykinetic Having multiple movements, as a dance in which individuals or groups perform movements that differ from those of other individuals or groups, or in which movements of some of an individual's body parts differ from those of the same individual's other body parts as they move together. **(9)**

polyrhythm Simultaneous use of different rhythms. **(1)**

pombeiros African-Portuguese traders. **(1)**

pŏmp'ae Korean Buddhist solemn ritual chant, performed by specialists. **(7)**

pompang Torajan ensemble of bamboo flutes. **(4)**

Ponape The entity now known as Pohnpei. **(9)**

pong lang Northeast Thai vertical xylophone of logs. **(4)**

pont-neufs French songs associated with the Pont-Neuf, a marketplace in Paris. **(8)**

pop bhajan Popular devotional songs (*bhajan*) influenced by the Urdu pop *ghazal*. **(5)**

pop Indonesia Western-influenced popular music of Indonesia. **(4)**

pop Melayu Western pop band with solo singer in Sumatra. **(4)**

pop Sunda Indigenous popular music of Sunda. **(4)**

popevki Short melodic turns, motifs, and models for traditional Russian melodies. **(8)**

pŏpkuch'um 'Ritual drum dance', Korean Buddhist dance. **(7)**

pŏpku nori Korean dance in which the performers play small drums while twirling ribbons attached to domed hats. **(7)**

Popol Vuh 'Book of Counsel', manuscript of shortly after the Spanish Encounter, from the Quiché region of central Guatemala. **(2)**

populärmusik Swedish term for modern urban music. **(8)**

popygua'i Guaraní idiophone made of two wooden sticks struck together. **(2)**

pore Iruḷa clay barrel drum in Tamil Nadu. **(5)**

porfia Brazilian musical duel. **(2)**

pork knockers Guyanese colloquial name for gold diggers. **(2)**

poro General term for men's secret societies of West Africa. **(1)**

porro Fast rhythmical Atlantic coastal Colombian musical style for the ensemble of *gaitas* that developed from the *cumbia*. **(2)**

port-a-beul 'Mouth music', Scottish vocal dance music, originally sung when instrumental music was outlawed. **(8)**

portaireacht 'Lilt', singing instrumental Irish dance tunes to nonlexical syllables. **(8)**

portamento Melodic slide between two pitches. **(4)**

porteños Argentine 'people of the port', residents of Buenos Aires. **(2)**

posad (Also *sloboda*.) Russian surburban zone, with its own styles of music. **(8)**

posadas (1) Guatemalan pre-Christmas singing, mainly a Ladino custom. (2) Mexican musical reenactment of Mary and Joseph's journey to Bethlehem. (3) Play or plays about Mary and Joseph seeking lodging on the night of Christ's birth. (4) Mexican outdoor Christmas drama, found in the Philippines. **(2, 3, 4)**

posal Korean diviner. **(7)**

Posaunenchöre German trombone ensembles. **(8)**

posidelki Social gatherings in Russian houses where lyric songs are performed. **(8)**

poskočica 'Leaping dance', dance cycle of the Dalmatia region of Croatia and Montenegro. **(8)**

po-skomorosh'i 'Like a minstrel', western Russian style of playing the violin. **(8)**

postranica Slovene duct flute. **(8)**

post-zouk Martinique continuation of *zouk* using richer harmonies and orchestral diversity. **(2)**

p'osu Hunter, a character in a Korean village ritual play. **(7)**

poṭi vēśa Warrior-costume dance in Karnataka. **(5)**

potresanje 'Shaking', singing technique in Bosnia-Hercegovina. **(8)**

powada Heroic ballad genre of Maharashtra. **(5)**

power band (Tok Pisin *pawa ben*.) New Guinean name for an electrically amplified musical ensemble. **(9)**

powiślak 'Over the Vistula', 'along the Vistula'; genre of the Lubelskie region of Poland, often sung by groups of women in a bride's home. **(8)**

powwow American Indian intertribal context for music and dance performance. **(3)**

poy Free-reed mouth organ of upland Cambodia. **(4)**

poy kāl kutirai Tamil dummy-horse dance. **(5)**

poyuja Holder of a Korean Cultural Asset. **(7)**

poyuja hubo Future holder of a Korean Cultural Asset. **(7)**

prabandha (Also *prabandham*.) Medieval song form. **(5)**

pracaya Accentless syllables in Vedic chant that often follow the sounded accent (*svarita*). **(5)**

pragmatic research Study aimed at rediscovering one's musical culture for immediate practical use. **(1)**

praise-proverb mode In epic performance, style with heightened melodic and rhythmic tension. **(1)**

prajuritan Javanese soldier's music. **(4)**

Prambanan Hindu temple in Central Java. **(4)**

prapołačnyja pieśni Belarusan weeding songs. **(8)**

prasaja 'Forthright, austere' (Javanese). **(4)**

praśasti Songs of praise; Sinhala vocal genre sometimes characterized as Kandyan court music. **(5)**

pratham Initial or primary level of college education in North India. **(5)**

prātī Mithila devotional songs. **(5)**

pratnja 'Accompanied by instrumentalists', adjunct to *lumpovanje*, carousing by prosperous young men in Serbian cafés. **(8)**

prato-e-faca Brazilian 'plate-and-knife' idiophone. **(2)**

pravo horo 'Straight dance', most typical Bulgarian circle dance, in 2/4 time. **(8)**

pravo oro (Also *lesno oro*.) 'Straight dance', common Macedonian dance, in 2/4 and 7/8 time. **(8)**

prawa Cirebonese five-tone tuning system. **(4)**

prayōga Melodic phrase of a Karnatak raga. **(5)**

praznyk Annual celebration held on the feast day of the saint to which a church is dedicated. **(3)**

pre-Columbian Before Columbus, referring to the ancient Americas. **(2)**

precordillera Lower elevations or foothills of the Andes. **(2)**

pregón Peruvian street vendor's call or song. **(2)**

prelo In Croatia, gatherings of women to spin and sew, often accompanied by music and dancing. (8)

prempresiwa Large lamellophone with three or four metal tongues and a box resonator. (1)

premtāl Folk rhythm instrument of northern India consisting of a small drum with a string attached that produces variable-pitch sounds when plucked; similar to the *khamak*. (5)

prenting Jamaican long cylindrical membranophone. (2)

preret Wooden double-reed aerophone of Bali and Lombok. (4)

prescriptive transcription Notation that indicates to performers how to create specific musical sounds. (1)

preson Lamaholot xylophone. (4)

pretl (Also *brana, cimprekelj, male cimbale, oprekelj*.) Slovene trapezoidal struck zither. (8)

prichitaniia Russian lament that resembles epic and liturgical narrative singing. (8)

Prince Alexander Mountains Papua New Guinean mountains in East Sepik, an extension of the Torricelli Range. (9)

principle of harmonic equivalence Feature of Venda music in which notes of the same harmonic series are substituted. (1)

pripevki Bulgarian dancelike songs sung at a *sedyanka* by girls to tease one another about boyfriends. (8)

pritrkavanje z zvonovi Slovenian bell ringing on festive occasions. (8)

priveghi Romanian wakes, involving humorous games and, in some areas, masked dancers. (8)

procissão In Portugal, procession that moves solemnly through a village to the rhythm of marches performed by a band: the high point of religious festivities. (8)

programas folklóricos 'Folk programs' on several commercial radio stations in Lima, Peru. (2)

programmatic music In European art music since the eighteenth century, a composition intended to represent or depict a narrative or a particular thing, person, or other extramusical object. (8)

promeseros Paraguayan festival pilgrims, both children and adults, often dressed as the patron saint. (2)

protiazhnaia pesnia (Also *protiazhniie*.) 'Drawn-out song', Russian nonmeterical song. (8)

Proto-Polynesian Hypothesized language held to be an ancestor of the Polynesian languages. (9)

proximal In organology, the portion of the musical instrument closest to the mouthpiece. (2)

prporuše Rain-invocation ritual songs of Montenegro. (8)

przyśpiewka Popular Polish folk song with a two-line text, often containing improvised malicious remarks. (8)

przytrampywane 'Songs with foot-tapping', local classification of songs performed with dancelike movements in the Kurpie region of northeastern Poland. (8)

psalis (Also *madaya*, Arabic.) Psalms in the Coptic church. (6)

psalmodikon Swedish bowed monochord, invented in Denmark in the 1840s and intended to support psalm singing in homes. (8)

psalmodiyya Choral service sung daily in the Coptic church. (6)

psalmody The singing of psalms; became the basis in the early eighteenth century for learning to read music. (3)

psal'my Christian songs, the main part of the *kobzari* and *lirnyky* repertoire. (8)

psalterion Harp of ancient Greece, commonly played by women. (8)

psaltis Greek ecclesiastical chanter. (8)

pshine Adighian accordion. (8)

psikhere Adighian ritual melody played on the *bzhami*. (8)

psuqei d'zimrah First part of the weekday morning service in the Yemenite Jewish liturgy. (6)

pu (1) (China.) Music score. (2) (China.) Instrumental suites in *nanguan*. (3) Large Korean ceramic pot, struck with a split bamboo stick. (7)

puaka North Sumatra invocational healing songs. (4)

pueblos Spanish rural towns. (8)

puel purrún Mapuche 'dance to the east', social dance. (8)

puerca Gourd-and-membrane friction drum. (2)

puesia Corsican song using improvised texts with existing tunes. (8)

Pugutan Open-air drama, climax of the *moriones* festival in the Philippines. (4)

pūjā Worship ritual; any of many different ritual ceremonies honoring deities. (5)

pujador 'Pusher', Panamanian drum used in *conjuntos*. (2)

pujārī Priest who has direct contact with both an image of a deity and offerings to the deity. (5)

puk Korean barrel-shaped drum. (7)

puk ch'um Korean folk dance with barrel-shaped drum. (7)

Pukkumina (Also *Pukko*.) Jamaican revival tradition. (2)

pulakan Tausug-Sama deep-rimmed bossed gong. (4)

pulang Kota simple idioglottal clarinet with down-cut reed, made of bamboo. (5)

pulao Sama bamboo ring-stop flute. (4)

pulilitu Bolivian animal-horn trumpet. (2)

pulipuli Notched end-blown flute in the central Andes. (2)

pullavān kudam Plucked chordophone with a pot resonator, in Kerala. (5)

pullavān vīnā Small folk fiddle of Kerala. (5)

pulley In Montserrat, an accordion, concertina, or melodion. (2)

Pullo (Also Pulo.) *See Fulɓe*. (1)

p'ulp'iri Korean grass oboe. (7)

pululu Bolivian gourd trumpet. (2)

pumalsan Maranao deep-rimmed gong, one of the pair of *agung*. (4)

pump Membranophone made from a hollow tree trunk with goatskin or sheepskin on either end. (2)

punakawan Clown-servant character type in Javanese dance. (4)

punch'ang 'Divided singing', Korean *p'ansori* narratives performed with several singers taking the roles of different characters. (7)

punctus contra punctum 'Note against note' (Latin), vertical organization of pitches among clerical singers in the Middle Ages. (8)

punebre Funeral march music in the Philippines. (4)

pung Hand-played barrel drum of Manipur. (5)

puṅgī (Also *bīn, murli*.) Snake charmer's instrument consisting of a wind pipe inserted into the top of a gourd air chamber, and two single-reed pipes extending from the bottom, which sound the melody and a drone. (5)

p'ungjang Korean band to accompany or bless fishing expeditions. (7)

p'ungmul, nongak Outdoor Korean farmers' band music. (7)

p'ungnyu 'Wind and stream', Korean scholarly term for music; *see Yŏngsan hosesang*. (7)

p'ungwŏl 'Wind and moon', Korean scholarly term for poetry. (7)

punta (1) Social-commentary song-and-dance form, the most popular and best-liked Garifuna genre; (2) *punta* rock, Guatemalan fusion of traditional *punta* and rock rhythms. (2)

punteado Spanish term for a picking technique on guitar and other lute-type stringed instruments. (2)

punto (1) Elegant, stately Panamanian couple dance. (2) Cuban instrumental accompaniment related to the *punto campesino*. (3) Standard melodic formula in the Philippines. (2, 4)

punto campesino (Also *punto guajiro*.) Cuban song genre associated with the rural population, usually based on the *décima* and its many variants. **(2)**

punto guajiro Spanish-derived musical form associated with rural Cuban populations, marked by improvised song texts and accompanied by an ensemble consisting mainly of stringed instruments. **(3)**

purab 'Eastern', style of *tabla* playing in North India. **(5)**

purahéi asy 'Mournful polka', song on the subject of the Passion. **(2)**

pūram (Also *puṛam.*) Public performances, as opposed to performances in a domestic context. **(5)**

Purana Hindu sacred texts containing ancient historical and cosmic stories; *see Bhāgavata Purāṇa.* **(5)**

puṛappāṭu First part of a *kūṭiyāṭṭam* dance drama, during which the dancer performs movements behind a curtain. **(5)**

pûri (Japan.) Rice harvest festival in the Yaeyama Islands. **(7)**

Purimshpil (Also *Purimspil.*) (1) Traditional folk drama staged among European Jews for the springtime holiday of Purim. (2) Jewish Purim play of the Book of Esther, which recounts a narrative of persecution and freedom. **(3, 8)**

purísimas Songs of the Nicaraguan Pacific Coast praising the Virgin Mary; the term refers to the Immaculate Conception. **(2)**

puro Ecuadorian gourd aerophone. **(2)**

purrum Argentine *nquillatún* song of supplication by women. **(2)**

purusha Male ragas, in the classification of raga families. **(5)**

purvaṅga First part of a *pallavi* theme in Karnatak music; precedes the *uttaraṅga.* **(5)**

pūrvaraṅga Ritual prelude to a play. **(5)**

pushpāñjali 'Offering of flowers', part of the *mangalācaraṇ* in *oḍissi* dance. *See also mangalācaraṇ, raṅgbhūmi pranām.* **(5)**

puškaitis Latvian wooden stick decorated with colored feathers, strips of cloth, and bells, used to accompany singing of *godu balss* in wedding or winter solstice rituals. **(8)**

pušteno oro Macedonian dance in 12/8 time. **(8)**

putipù Italian friction drum. **(8)**

putničke Traveling songs in Croatia and Bosnia-Hercegovina. **(8)**

putong Celebratory wreath or crown in the Philippines. **(4)**

putra 'Sons', category of the *parivār* classification system dividing ragas into family groups of one male raga, five or six wives (*rāgiṇī*), sons, and daughters-in-law (*bharyā*). **(5)**

putri Female character type in Javanese dance. **(4)**

pūttari pāṭu Koḍagu 'new rice ceremony' in Karnataka. **(5)**

pututu Small Andean valveless trumpet made from a single cow horn, conch shell, or piece of tin. **(2)**

puukko Knife with a birch handle and curved sheath used by Finnish woodsman as a tool and weapon; "knifemen" figured in Finnish-American ballads of the nineteenth and early twentieth centuries. **(3)**

pūvaṭi cintu 'Flower-feet' song, about the Prophet Muhammad; sung by Tamil converts to Islam. **(5)**

puwasa Islamic month of fasting in the Philippines. **(4)**

puwelke Mapuche cane flute. **(2)**

puwí-puwí Buginese-Makassarese reed pipe. **(4)**

puxury Toda end-blown bamboo trumpet; same as the Kota *būgir.* **(5)**

puya Fast, rhythmically complex style in Colombia. **(2)**

puzyŕ' (Also *fam, skamóra, válonka.*) Mordvinian bagpipe. **(8)**

pyâsi (Japan.) Folk song genre of the Miyako Islands, analogous to *humisyagi* in the Yaeyama Islands. **(7)**

pyŏlsin kut Korean shaman ritual for the prosperity of a village. **(7)**

p'yŏngjo Peaceful Korean melodic mode. **(7)**

P'yŏngyang minjok ŭmak tan P'yŏngyang People's Music Ensemble of North Korea. **(7)**

P'yŏngyang muyong p'yogibŏp yŏn'gusil P'yŏngyang Dance Notational Study Institute of North Korea. **(7)**

p'yŏn'gyŏng Korean set of sixteen hanging stone slabs. **(7)**

p'yŏnjong Korean set of sixteen hanging bronze bells. **(7)**

qadd (Plural, *qudūd.*) Strophic song in colloquial Arabic, associated with Aleppo. **(6)**

Qaddiriyya Islamic brotherhood that traces its roots to Sufi sects of North Africa. **(1)**

qaḍīb Wand or stick. **(6)**

qādriyya (Plural, *qādriyyāt.*) Women's musical genre of Algeria, setting multiple stanzas of love poetry. **(6)**

qafl Rapid concluding song within a cycle of Andalusian-Moroccan *nūba.* **(6)**

qafla (Plural, *qaflāt.*) Melodic or poetic cadence. **(6)**

qā'ida 'Basis', 'law', 'custom', 'pattern', referring to the basic melodic and rhythmic structure of a song that must be reproduced in performance. **(6)**

qā'ida Hindustani theme-and-variations composition for *tabla.* **(5)**

qaiyrma 'Turn', conclusion of a Kazakh epic tale involving the performance of textless vocables. **(6)**

qalam Curved wooden mallets used to strike the *santūr* while playing. **(5)**

qalandar (1) Wandering mystic; one who has abandoned family, friends, and possessions. (2) Dervish inclined to the state of ecstasy; the adjective *qalandarī* may refer to music in Baluchi *gwātī* rituals. **(5, 6)**

qāleb In Persian music, a matrix, mold, model, or melodic structure that makes creative performance possible. **(6)**

qanbūṣ (Also *bagus, 'ūd ṣan'ānī, turbi.*) Yemeni short-necked lute. **(6)**

qanṭara Relatively fast song within a cycle of the Andalusian-Moroccan *nūba.* **(6)**

qanun (Also *qānūn, kanun, kanoon.*) (1) Plucked zither with approximately seventy-two strings in triple courses that are fine-tuned during performance with a series of small levers that are moved up and down. (2) Persian box zither, played at the medieval Indo-Persian courts of North India. (3) (Plural, *qawānīn.*) Trapezoidal plucked zither or psaltery found throughout the Arab world. **(3, 5, 6)**

qara öleng 'Simple song', lyrical songs sung by Kazakh women in various contexts. **(6)**

qarār (Also *asās.*) Tonic pitch of a *maqām.* **(6)**

qāri (1) (Also *qāri'*; in Central Asia, *hafiz.*) Reciter of the Qur'ān. (2) Solo male performer in the Iraqi *maqām.* **(5, 6)**

qarqabu (Also *qarqaba.*) North African instrument consisting of two pairs of iron castanets joined by a connecting bar, one pair held in each hand. **(1)**

qarrādī Genre of Palestinian improvised sung poetry. **(6)**

qasaba (Also *qaṣaba.*) (1) Open, edge-blown transverse flute with six finger holes. (2) Arab flute played by Tuareg herders in Algeria and Niger. **(1, 6)**

qaṣīd (Also *hudjeinī, hjīnī.*) Solo bedouin heroic vocal repertoire, accompanied by the *rabāba.* **(6)**

qasida (Also *qaṣīda.*) (1) North African solo vocal improvisation deriving from West Asian traditions. (2) Long ode with rhyming couplets related to the *ghazal,* often in praise of the Prophet Muhammad's family. (3) (Plural, *qaṣā'id.*) Poem in classical Arabic usually having a single rhyme scheme and meter throughout, following one of the sixteen poetic meters (*buhūr*); or a musical composition setting such a poem. **(1, 5, 6)**

qasidah (Also *kasidah.*) Type of Islamic-based popular music. **(4)**

qasidah rebana Arabic solo praise song. **(4)**

qaṣṣafiyya Lively Omani dance with weapons. **(6)**

qaul Speech, word, or saying. **(5)**

Volume Key: **6**, Middle East; **7**, East Asia; **8**, Europe; **9**, Australia and the Pacific Islands; **10**, The World's Music.

qāvāl Azerbaijani frame drum (tambourine), 40–50 centimeters in diameter, with attached metal rings; accompanies performance of an *aşıq* in northwest Iran. **(6)**

qawachan In Peru, contrasting theme in a faster tempo. **(2)**

qawma Term for a suite of pieces in Yemeni tradition, related to the Andalusian *nūba*, containing three melodies of different rhythmic cycles and tempi. **(6)**

qawwāl (1) Singer or reciter of the Qur'ān. (2) More generally, a poet or singer. (3) Singer of *qawwali*. **(5, 6)**

qawwali (1) (Singular, *qawwal*.) Body of Pakistani ecstatic devotional songs and the hereditary group of singers and instrumentalists who perform them; originated in thirteenth-century India. (2) (Also *kavvali*.) Solo-chorus Sufi devotional song form. **(3, 5)**

qaycı Epic reciter in the Altai culture. **(6)**

q'ayma 'Insipid', referring to old Bolivian carnival melodies. **(2)**

qayna (Plural, *qaynāt, qiyān*.) Singing-girl or songstress; possibly a slave in the home of a noble family. **(6)**

qāyim wa-rasf Vocal cycle within the Moroccan *nūba*. **(6)**

qeej Hmong free-reed mouth organ with bamboo pipes and elongated wind chest. **(4)**

qeej (Lao, *khaen*.) Hmong multiple free-reed pipe. **(9)**

qene Ethiopian Christian religious poetry chanted in Ge'ez. **(1)**

qi (China.) Configured energy. **(7)**

qia 'Leader' in the *julajula* Bolivian double-unit panpipe tradition. **(2)**

qiang (China.) Melody. **(7)**

qin (China.) Seven-stringed plucked zither. **(7, 10)**

qina (Also *qina-qina, kena, quena*.) Aymara end-blown notched flute. **(2)**

qing (China.) Stone chime. **(7)**

qing luoguyue (China.) Percussion music performed without strings or winds. **(7)**

qingsan zhongliu (China.) Modal designation in *Chaozhou xianshiyue*; it indicates lowering the sixth note and raising the third note. **(7)**

qing'ge (China.) Love songs. **(7)**

qinīn Ancient Ethiopian lyre. **(6)**

qinqin Chinese two-stringed plucked lute with frets. **(3)**

qirā'a 'Reading', the correct reading of the Qur'ān. **(6)**

qirā'āt Scholarly discipline presenting and explaining authoritative interpretations of the Qur'ān. **(6)**

qirā'at al-maqām 'Reciting the *maqām*', traditional term for singing the Iraqi *maqām*. **(6)**

qir'at Highly elaborated style of Qur'ānic recitation cultivated in Egypt. **(5)**

qiṣas dīniyya 'Religious stories', religious or moralistic stories performed as a genre of *inshād* by a solo *munshid* using a variety of literary and musical styles, with *takht* accompaniment. **(6)**

qit'a General term for a musical piece. **(6)**

qitara 'Guitar' (Arabic). **(1)**

qitāra Circular five-stringed lyre found in upper Egypt and used in secular repertoires. **(6)**

qobız Horsehair fiddle. **(6)**

qobuz (Also *qobyz, qyl-qobyz*.) Concave bowed lute of Central Asia; cf. *qubūz*. **(6)**

qoshnay End-blown double-pipe aerophone of Central Asia with single reeds. **(6)**

qoş-nağara 'Pair of kettledrums' (Azerbaijani). **(6)**

qrāqab Heavy Moroccan cymbals. **(6)**

qu (China.) (1) Melody or song. (2) Short songs. (3) One of the three main categories of songs in *nanguan*. **(7)**

quadriglia 'Quadrille', Corsican dance. **(8)**

quadrilha Brazilian social dance or square dance generally associated with festivals in honor of Saint John during the June celebrations in the northeast. **(2)**

quadrille (Also set dance.) (1) Afro-Caribbean interpretation of nineteenth-century European set dance. (2) The five parts of the country and jumbie dances. (3) *Quadrille au commandement*, Guadeloupe quadrille in which the *konmandè* calls the dancers' steps. (4) Square dance for four couples in a set of five or six figures, mainly in 2/4 and 6/8 time. (5) Type of French Creole figure dance among French and Haitian immigrants in Louisiana. **(2, 3, 8)**

quadrivium Of the seven medieval liberal arts, those that dealt with arithmetic, astronomy, geometry, and music; cf. *trivium*. **(8)**

quan họ Northern Vietnamese antiphonal song performed in boats. **(4)**

quantitative time Time based on clocks, metronomes, or other forms of chronometry. **(1)**

quddām Rapid vocal movement within the Moroccan *nūba*. **(6)**

qudi (China.) Medium-range bamboo flute usually tuned to the key of D. **(7)**

quebrado 'Broken' or 'turned' motion in Nahua dance. **(2)**

quelbeys Topical songs of local origin in the Virgin Islands. **(2)**

quena Spanish orthography of an Aymara name for a notched, end-blown edge aerophone of the central Andes. *See also kena, qina.* **(2)**

quenacane Open-ended notch-flute associated with the South American Andean region. **(3)**

que-que Guyanese action song-dance performed at weddings and wakes. **(2)**

quijada (Also *charrasga*.) African-derived scraped or struck idiophone made from the defleshed, dried jawbone of an ass, mule, or horse. **(2)**

quijongo Nicaraguan and Costa Rican musical-bow monochord of African origin, made from a long wooden bow with a single metal string and one or two gourd resonators. **(2)**

quinceañera Girl's fifteenth-birthday celebration in Paraguay, a time for music making. **(2)**

quinceaños 'Fifteen years old', debutante parties in Costa Rica. **(2)**

quinjengue Afro-Brazilian drum. **(2)**

quinquerche (Also *quinquercahue*.) Mapuche musical bow. **(2)**

quintillas Five-line *copla*. **(2)**

quinto (1) Smallest and highest-pitched of the Cuban *tumbadora* membranophones. (2) Small drum of the *tumbadora* type that often plays a lead role in rumba music. **(2, 3)**

quioscos Bandstands set up in town plazas across Mexico in the late 1800s. **(2)**

quipa (Also *qquepa*.) Conch-shell trumpet in Ecuador and Peru. **(2)**

quirquincho (Also *charango*.) 'Armadillo', small guitar made from the shell of an armadillo. **(2)**

quitiplás Venezuelan bamboo stamping tubes. **(2)**

qupai (China.) Precomposed labeled melody. **(7)**

qupaiti (China.) Type of Chinese opera using the fixed tunes called *qupai*. **(7)**

Qur'ān (Also Koran.) Primary sacred text of Islam, the Islamic canon of Muhammad's teachings. **(4, 6)**

qūshme (Possibly derived from Turkic *qoş-ney* 'pair of reeds'.) Double clarinet played in Iranian Khorasan, made of two equal lengths of bird bone. **(6)**

quyi (China.) Vocal arts that include mostly art songs and narrative songs. **(7)**

quxiang pipa (China.) Curved-neck *pipa*. **(7)**

ra'anga Generic Waiãpi category for edge and reed-concussion aerophones. **(2)**

R&B Rhythm and blues, black popular music that combined elements of jazz and the blues beginning in the late 1940s. **(3)**

rabab (Also *rabāb, rabāba, rababah, rababah, rbeb, rebab, rebāb, ribāb, rribab, rubab, rubāb*.) (1) (Plural, *rababāt*.) Generic term for unfretted bowed chordophones of various shapes and with varied numbers of strings. (2) Arab fiddle. (3) North African two-stringed fiddle. (4) Short-necked lute with

---

five playing strings and thirteen to fifteen sympathetic strings. (6) Six-stringed unfretted plucked lute, from which the Indian *sarod* developed. (6) Sudanese lyre.   (**1, 5, 6, 8, 10**)

rabābī Muslim professional singer in the Indian Punjab.   (**5**)

rababu Bowed spike lute of Ternate and Tidore.   (**4**)

rabāna Frame drum of Sri Lanka.   (**5**)

rabbimman Women's genre of religious song, especially in the Ferghana valley of Uzbekistan.   (**6**)

rabbit dance Male-female partner dances performed in the context of a Native American powwow.   (**3**)

rabeca Brazilian three- or four-stringed bowed lute.   (**2**)

rabel (1) Spanish fiddle similar to the Arab *rabab*. (2) (Also *violín*.) European-derived stringed instrument originating in the Renaissance period, usually with three strings, played with a bow like a violin.   (**2, 8**)

rabga Double-headed conical drum played with sticks, in Bihar.   (**5**)

rabi al-'awwal Third month of the Islamic Hijra calendar.   (**1**)

Rabinal Achí 'Hero of Rabinal', modern-day version of the Guatemalan *Baile del Tun*.   (**2**)

Rabindra saṅgīt Songs of the Bengali poet and musician Rabindranath Tagore.   (**5**)

rada Trinidadian songs of the Arada immigrants from the Dahomean city of Allada.   (**2**)

Radá White deities of Vodou in Haiti.   (**2**)

rada-ason *See tchatcha*.   (**2**)

radīf 'Row' (Persian). (1) Canonical repertoire of melody-types and modes, organized in the personal style of a great master. (2) Word that follows the rhyming syllable or syllables in each line of a poem.   (**6**)

Radio Congo Belge First government-controlled station in Kinshasa, which opened in 1940.   (**1**)

Radio Congo Belge pour les Indigènes Governmental station that opened in 1948.   (**1**)

Radio Congolia Privately owned radio station in Kinshasa, which began broadcasting in 1939.   (**1**)

Radio Fantástica Argentine FM radio station dedicated exclusively to *música tropical*.   (**2**)

Radio-Léo Jesuit-owned radio station in Kinshasa, which broadcast 1937–1948.   (**1**)

Radio Tropical Argentine FM radio station dedicated exclusively to *música tropical*.   (**2**)

radzilnyja pieśni Belarusan birth songs, addressed to the midwife and the parents of the newborn.   (**8**)

Raffele German Alpine zither.   (**8**)

raffle (Also *rärri* and *rüffle*.) Swiss wooden ratchet, a noisemaker.   (**8**)

raga (Also *rāga, rag, rāg*.) (1) Modal system used in India. (2) System governing melody; melodic mode; melodic resource for composition and improvisation.   (**4, 5, 10**)

rāga gamaka Microtonal ornamentation of raga pitches; *see also gamaka*.   (**5**)

rāgamālikā (Also *rāgmālā*.) Karnatak non-metered improvisation on different ragas; presentation of several ragas in sequence, used in various Karnatak genres.   (**5**)

rāgam-tānam-pallavi Karnatak genre consisting of improvisation on a raga followed by variations on a texted theme (*pallavi*); requires the highest level of musicianship.   (**5**)

ragana Corsican scraper, a mechanized wooden rasp.   (**8**)

raganelle Italian cog rattles.   (**8**)

ragas Lithuanian single-pitched wooden trumpet.   (**8**)

rāga tāla mālikā Karnatak melody in a series of ragas and talas.   (**5**)

rāgdāri Classical singing in North Indian style in Punjab, Pakistan.   (**5**)

rāgdhyāna (Also *dhyāna*.) Written raga visualizations.   (**5**)

rag-dung (Also *dung-chen*.) Long metal trumpet, used in Tibetan Buddhist rituals in South Asia.   (**5**)

ragga Jamaican music similar to reggae but played entirely (or mostly) with digital instrumentation.   (**3**)

raggī Musician in the Indian Punjab who performs devotional music.   (**5**)

ragi (1) 'One who brings color', a second "character" who joins the main singer in oral epic performances in Madhya Pradesh. (2) Latvian horns or hornpipes, associated with herding.   (**5, 8**)

rāginī Female ragas; the "wives" of the main (male) ragas in the *parivār* classification system of raga families.   (**5**)

raglja Slovene children's rattle used at Easter.   (**8**)

rāgmālā (1) 'Garland of ragas', iconographic and poetic personification of ragas. (2) (Also *rāgamālikā*.) In Hindustani music, improvisation on different ragas in sequence.   (**5**)

rāg pradhān gān Bengali songs in Hindustani classical style, particularly *khyāl*, by composers working for gramophone companies in Calcutta during the 1930s.   (**5**)

ragtime Style of music, popular at the turn of the twentieth century, characterized by a syncopated melody placed against a steady bass line.   (**3**)

rāhber 'Leader' (Persian), singer who assumes the leader's role in a ritual performance.   (**6**)

raḥmānī Large double-headed drum of Oman.   (**6**)

rai (1) North African Arabic style of cabaret music, also performed in France. (2) 'Opinion', 'destiny', energetic form of Algerian popular music that gained prominence in the 1980s, influenced by local Algerian and Western popular styles, and has found an audience among American and Canadian world beat enthusiasts. (3) (Japan.) *Kakko* drum stroke.   (**1, 3, 6, 7, 8**)

Rai Coast Papua New Guinean coast of Madang Province, extending from the town of Madang eastward to the Morobe border.   (**9**)

raibutu (Also *raisan*.) In Japan, Buddhist chant (*syômyô*) for worshiping various buddhas and bodhisattvas;.   (**7**)

Rail Band Guitar-based band that flourished in Mali in the late twentieth century.   (**1**)

ra'īs Leader of an ensemble.   (**6**)

raisya (Japan.) Instrument for sound effects in *kabuki*.   (**7**)

rājā Ruler.   (**5**)

rājadāsi Performers for kings at the royal courts of Tamil Nadu. *See also dēvadāsi*.   (**5**)

rajaleña Improvisational street festival *bambuco*-related song genre of Colombia, characterized by African-derived traits such as cross rhythms and responsorial singing, often to insulting, critical, and sexually oriented texts.   (**2**)

rājasik 'Passionate', 'greedy', 'vain'; antiheroic character type in *kathakaḷi* dance drama.   (**5**)

rāj darbār (Also *darbār*.) Royal audience hall, court.   (**5**)

raj nplaim Hmong free-reed pipe with finger holes.   (**4**)

raj pus li Hmong fipple flute.   (**4**)

rake 'n' scrape (1) Music historically used to accompany quadrille dances in the Bahamas; (2) term of the 1990s derived from the characteristic idiophones used to perform this rhythmic music (carpenter's saw or ridged bottle).   (**2**)

rakugo (Japan.) Comic monologue.   (**7**)

rama Advent tradition in Mexico that involves groups of adults, children, or both going from home to home asking for gifts.   (**2**)

Rama Character from the Indian epic *Ramayana*.   (**4**)

ramada (1) Rustic dwelling. (2) Mapuche song and dance feast.   (**2**)

Ramadan Ninth month of the Islamic lunar calendar, during which the Qur'ān was first revealed to the Prophet Muhammad. During Ramadan, Muslims fast from dawn to sunset. *Inshād dīnī* is frequently performed during this month.   (**1, 2, 4, 5, 6**)

Ramakian Thai version of the Indian *Ramayana* epic.   (**4**)

rāma nāṭakam Tamil dance drama based on stories of the god Rama.   (**5**)

rāmanāṭṭam Dance drama on the life of Rama; temple dance of Kerala. **(5)**

Rāmaṇṇa Style of Sāmavedic chanting. **(5)**

Ramayana Indian epic of Lord Rama, his wife Sita, and the demon king Ravana. **(4, 5)**

rambutan Red, podlike fruit with a "hairy" appearance, native to the Malay peninsula. **(4)**

ramkie Lute with three or four strings, played by southern Africans in Cape Town. **(1)**

rāmlīlā Devotional dance drama of Uttar Pradesh depicting events from Rama's life. **(5)**

rammana Thai wooden frame drum with single head. **(4)**

ramoncelle Bowed pseudo-bass of the Low Countries. **(8)**

ramonika Three-row diatonic accordion in Istria, Croatia. **(8)**

ramos Spanish songs for autumn processions in which people carry boughs and narrate the lives of saints and Jesus Christ. **(8)**

rampak kendang *Gamelan saléndro* with drummers as soloists. **(4)**

ramsatta *Kīrtan* danced by youths in Madhya Pradesh. **(5)**

ramwong Western-influenced social dance from Thailand. **(4)**

ranat Thai xylophones. **(4)**

ranat ek Lead xylophone in a Thai classical ensemble. **(4)**

ranat ek lek (Also *ranat thawng.*) Thai higher-pitched metallophone, with twenty-one keys. **(4)**

ranat kaeo Thai crystallophone (struck idiophone with glass keys). **(4)**

ranat thum Thai lower-pitched xylophone, with seventeen or eighteen keys. **(4)**

ranat thum lek Thai lower-pitched metallophone, with sixteen to eighteen keys. **(4)**

Rāṇāyanīya School of Sāmavedic chanting. **(5)**

ran byôsi (Japan.) Section in *nô.* **(7)**

ranchera (1) Popular Mexican song resembling American country and western. (2) Argentine social dance performed during a *jineteada.* (3) Uruguayan name for the European *mazurca* dance. (4) Chilean dance following religious festivals and communal work. **(2, 3)**

rancherías (1) Hamlets of several families, each occupying a one- or two-room house, in the Sierra Madre of Mexico; (2) slums in Venezuela. **(2)**

rancheros de pastorela Purépecha Christmas shepherds and farmers. **(2)**

rancho foclórico Formally organized Portuguese music-and-dance revival group. **(8)**

randai (1) Type of Minangkabau theater including self-defense (*pencak silat*). (2) West Sumatra danced theatrical form. (3) South Sumatra welcoming dance. **(4)**

randu kentir Folk dance of Indramayu. **(4)**

rangbhūmi pranām 'Obeisance to the earth', part of the *magṅgalācaraṇ* in *oḍissi* dance. **(5)**

rangle Norwegian rattle, made of large and small iron rings. **(8)**

rantak kudo West Sumatra ceremonial hobby-horse dance. **(4)**

rantamplan Onomatopoeic imitation of musical instruments in ring dances of the French-speaking area of Switzerland; *see roupioupiou, turlututu.* **(8)**

rantok Rice-stamping tube and trough in Lombok and Sumbawa. **(4)**

ranz des vaches Swiss cowherds' song; *see kühreihen.* **(8)**

rao Introductory unmetered improvisation in Vietnamese music. **(4)**

rap Form of primarily African-American spoken-word music, originally one element of hip-hop culture. **(3)**

rap consciência Afro-Brazilian 'consciousness rap', an alternative to hip-hop. **(2)**

rapá Hunting bow that the Aché-Guayakí use as a musical instrument by placing it over a resonating container. **(2)**

rapa'i Acehnese frame drum. **(4)**

rappresentazioni Fifteenth- and sixteenth-century Italian songs preserved in the songs of the *maggio* celebration. **(8)**

rapsodi 'Rhapsodies', northern Albanian narrative songs performed by epic singers. **(8)**

raqd Syriac lamentation dance. **(6)**

raqs (Also *raqṣ, raks.*) (1) Dance or dance music in Northern Afghanistan. (2) Dance or dancing in Pakistan. (3) Dance in the Middle East. **(5, 6)**

raqṣ bil-'aṣā 'Stick dance', sometimes accompanying the martial *taḥṭīb* dance of Egypt. **(6)**

raqṣ iskandarānī 'Alexandrian dance', acrobatic martial dance performed with various types of weapons in Lower Egypt. **(6)**

raqṣ al-khayl 'Horse dancing', Egyptian traditional dance in which a horse performs a variety of exercises to instrumental accompaniment; the rider may also dance standing on the horse's back. **(6)**

raqṣ al-shamʿīdān Form of *raqṣ sharqī,* known in the West as a belly dance, in which the performer balances a weighty candelabrum on her head. **(6)**

raqṣ sharqī 'Oriental dance', characterized by articulated pelvic movements, common in Egypt; known in the West as belly dance. **(6)**

rara (1) Speechlike singing initially associated with Esu, trickster deity of the Yoruba. (2) Widespread and popular processional ritual in Haiti that takes place over the Lenten season and culminates on Easter weekend; *rara*

ensembles have been organized in recent years in Haitian communities of North America, and *rara* music was a major influence in the *mizik rasin* movement. (2) Religious societies of the sugarcane plantations of Haiti and the Dominican republic. **(1, 2, 3)**

rärri (Also *raffle, rüffle.*) Swiss wooden ratchet, a noisemaker. **(8)**

rās (Also *dāṇḍiā rās.*) Stick dance and its music in northwest India. **(5)**

rasa 'Essence', 'emotion', 'feeling', in Indonesia. **(5, 10)**

rāsa (1) Temple music played by Damāis in Nepal. (2) (Also *rāso, rāsaka.*) Epic poem recounting the battles and exploits of Gujarat's kings and generals. **(5)**

räschtli Dance cycle of central Switzerland, consisting of a *schottisch,* a waltz, a polka, a mazurka, and a *ländler.* **(8)**

rās garbā Folk dance music of northwest India that has evolved into a popular style. **(5)**

rasgueado 'Strummed' (Spanish). (1) Term for chordal strumming with fingernails on guitar and lute-type stringed instruments. (2) Characteristic strumming style of flamenco guitar playing. **(2, 8)**

rasguido doble Argentine polka-derived social dance. **(2)**

Rashīdiyya Institute Institute founded in Tunis in 1934 with the aim of preserving traditional Tunisian music. **(6)**

rasika Connoisseur of aesthetic bliss. **(5)**

rasiyā Vulgar folk song of the Braj region of North India. **(5)**

rās līlā Devotional dance drama portraying Krishna and the milkmaids, performed by boys in Uttar Pradesh. **(5)**

rāso (Also *rāsa, rāsaka.*) Epic poem recounting the battles and exploits of Gujarat's kings and generals. **(5)**

rasp Percussive instrument consisting of a notched stick or gourd scraped with another object. **(3)**

raspev Russian long-drawn-out secular songs. **(8)**

raspevshchiki Russian singers of long-drawn-out songs and liturgical music. **(8)**

raspu Gourd rasp of the Netherlands Antilles. **(2)**

rāst (Also *rast.*) (1) Name of the principal mode of traditional Arab art and court music, first alluded to by Ibn Sīnā. (2) Name given to the open strings of the lute in Ibn Kurr's description of the tonal system. (3) One of the primary notes of the Arab fundamental scale. **(6)**

Rastafarianism Afro-Jamaican religion based on peace, love, self-expression, self-reliance, and black dignity, musically important for the origins of reggae. **(2)**

rāst kūk In Iranian music, tuning for the male vocal range. **(6)**

rāṣṭrīya gīt National song. **(5)**

raṭa yakuma Sri Lankan ceremony performed to ensure the safety of a child or fetus. **(5)**

ratok West Sumatra lament. **(4)**

rattle drum Drum made from the sapling of a tree with metal objects inserted. **(3)**

raudra 'Furious', one of the eight emotional states (*rasa*) codified in the *Nāṭyaśāstra*. **(5)**

rāvanhatta (Also *rāvaṇahatthā*.) Long-necked, two-stringed bowed lute made from a long bamboo stick inserted in a half coconut shell covered with membrane; played by the Bhopā singers of Rajasthan. **(5)**

rave Legal or illegal dance party, originally held outdoors to accommodate thousands of dancers; features European and especially British forms of house and techno music, supplied by several disk jockeys playing on separate stages or taking turns on one set. **(3)**

ravé Mbyá descendant of the *rabel*, a three-stringed bowed chordophone. **(2)**

rawa Mbojo Music for female singer and *biola* in Sumbawa. **(4)**

rawap Ancient Uygur bowl-shaped lute; cf. *dūtār*. **(6)**

rāwī Bard or poet-singer. **(6)**

raysat Female singer-dancers of Morocco who perform in urban *rways* troupes. **(6)**

razākhānī gat Fast-tempo Hindustani instrumental composition allegedly created by Ghulam Raza Khan in the nineteenth century. **(5)**

razha Omani men's warrior dance; cf. *'arḍa*. **(6)**

ražki Belarusan reed aerophones. **(8)**

reaho Yanomamö feast that often celebrates the dead. **(2)**

Reamker Cambodian version of the Indian *Ramayana*. **(4)**

rebab (Also *rebāb*.) (1) Two-stringed bowed spike lute found throughout Southeast Asia. (2) Malay three-stringed, long-necked fiddle. (3) Short-necked plucked stringed instrument of Kashmir. (4) Georgian urban chordophone popular from the 1600s to the 1800s. *See also rabab*. **(4, 5, 6, 8)**

rebana (1) Malay single-headed round frame drum, sometimes with spokes. (2) Frame and bowl-shaped drums of Indonesia. **(4)**

rebana besar Islamic vocal performance with *rebana ubi* drums. **(4)**

rebana rea Samawan drums to accompany Arabic song. **(4)**

rebana ubi Large, single-headed wooden conical drum of Malaysia. **(4)**

rebetika (1) (Also *rembetika*.) Urban music genre, derived from Asia Minor, that devel-

oped in the 1920s in Greek port cities. (2) Urban popular music developed by Greeks expelled from Turkey in the 1920s and popularized internationally in the 1960s. **(3, 8)**

recitative In European art music since the Baroque, a style of usually accompanied singing whose melodic and rhythmic inflections are intended to resemble those of ordinary speech; used for dialogue in operas and narration in oratorios and cantatas, in alternation with arias. **(8, 9)**

recolha de andores (Also *arruada*, *peditório*.) Portuguese religious festival in which a band performs marches in front of each house in a village. **(8)**

recomposition Seamless interaction of creativity and presentation. **(8)**

rêco-rêco Brazilian percussive gourd, metal, or door-spring scraper used in a wide variety of musical traditions. **(2)**

recreos Sunday morning concerts following the church mass in Costa Rica. **(2)**

redada Abkhazian wedding songs. **(8)**

redap Bengkulu frame drum. **(4)**

redeb Two-stringed bowed spike lute of Lombok. **(4)**

redoblante (1) Uruguayan snare drum. (2) Venezuelan side drum. **(2)**

redondo (1) Venezuelan double-headed drum with an internal hourglass shape. (2) Fast Mexican-Spanish waltz. **(2, 3)**

redowa (1) Dance or tune in 3/4 or 2/4 meter of Bohemian origin resembling the mazurka. (2) Couple dance of the Low Countries. **(3, 8)**

reducciones 'Reductions', mission towns established by the Jesuits in Paraguay that were important for music teaching and performance by native Americans. **(2)**

reel (1) Lively Scottish Highland dance in 4/4 time, characteristic of the British Isles. (2) Couples dance from Scotland, accompanied by brisk duple-time binary melodies, disseminated in North America and now flourishing in folk fiddling. (3) (Also reel dance.) Family ritual of Tobago accompanied by Scottish violin reels. **(2, 3, 8)**

reggae (1) Internationally popular Jamaican music derived from *mento* with Rastafarian influences, combining native styles with elements of rock and soul and characterized by an accent on the offbeat; adopted by the West Indian population in Britain as a source of cultural pride. (2) *Reggae resistência*, Brazilian 'resistance' synthesis in reggae form. **(2, 3, 4, 8)**

reggaespañol Colombian hip-hop or dance-hall reggae with Spanish lyrics. **(2)**

regivärss Ancient Estonian 'runic' melodies; *see runo*. **(8)**

rei (Japan.) Copper bell sounded by an interior tongue; used in Buddhist music. **(7)**

reibo (Japan.) Group of *syakuhati* pieces whose titles include the term *reibo* as a suffix, a category of *syakuhati honkyoku* (original pieces) developed by the Huke sect of Buddhist monks (*komusô*). **(7)**

rei kin (Japan.) Bowed lute invented in the 1920s by Tanabe Hisao (1883–1984). **(7)**

reigaku (Japan.) Principle of manners and music. **(7)**

reinschrift Conductor's copy of a score for the first performance. **(8)**

reisado Brazilian cycle of dramatic dances typically featuring the appearance of a bull. **(2)**

rejang Balinese women's temple dance. **(4)**

reki Finnish meter with seven feet per line and a variable number of unstressed syllables per foot. **(8)**

rekilaulu Finnish round-dance song. **(8)**

rekukkara (Japan.) Ainu throat-singing game. **(7)**

rela (Also *kobza*, *lira*.) Belarusan hurdy-gurdy. **(8)**

relā (1) Hindustani theme-and-variations composition for *tabla*. (2) Similar composition for *pakhāvaj* barrel drum. **(5)**

relinchidos 'Whinnies', high-trilling vocal cries in Spanish music. **(8)**

rembetika See rebetika. **(8)**

Renaissance In European music history, the period from the early fifteenth century to about 1600. **(8)**

rendai Bengkulu acrobatic round dance. **(4)**

reṇḍaṭi 'Two beats' (Tamil). **(5)**

reng Persian or Azerbaijani composition associated with dancing. Each *dastgāh* concludes with one or more *reng-hā*. **(6)**

renggong Common musical form in Cirebon. **(4)**

réong Gong-chime with several players in Bali and Lombok. **(4)**

repartee Sung debate pitting men against women; often a courtship ritual. **(4)**

repeater Shorter version of the Jamaican *fundeh*. **(2)**

repicador (1) Panamanian single-headed drum. (2) Puerto Rican first *bomba* drum. **(2)**

repique Brazilian high-pitched snare drum. **(2)**

répondè Guadeloupe choir that answers the song leader in call-and-response songs. **(2)**

reque reque Portuguese wood scraper. **(8)**

requinteo Melodic ornamentation in Costa Rica. **(2)**

requinto (1) High-pitched Spanish guitar. (2) Small acoustic lead-guitar type of El Salvador and Paraguay. (3) Four-stringed, narrow-bodied Mexican guitar, plucked with a plectrum fashioned from cow horn or a plastic comb. (3) Small Colombian ten- or twelve-stringed *tiple*. (4) Small six-stringed guitar, found in the central and northwestern parts of Honduras. (**2, 8**)

requinto jarocho Thin-bodied four-stringed guitar used to play melody in the *son jarocho*, folk music of southern coastal Veracruz in Mexico. (**3**)

rere Torajan bamboo ensemble. (**4**)

resbalosa Amorous Peruvian song and dance with syncopated rhythm and choreography based on *escobillada*. (**2**)

res facta 'A done thing' (Latin), composition in writing, executed from a score. (**8**)

respodadoras (Also *respondedoras*.) Responsorial chorus of women in Colombia and Ecuador. (**2**)

responsa 'Answers' to public queries by Jewish rabbis. (**6**)

responsero Singer of funeral music in Peru. (**2**)

retirada Final part of *murga* theatrical presentations in Uruguay. (**2**)

retreta Sunday performances by municipal, paramilitary, or military bands in Costa Rica, the Dominican Republic, and Uruguay. (**2**)

réveillez French customary begging for eggs and other gifts while singing religious songs at Easter. (**8**)

Revival Principal Jamaican Afro-Christian cult. (**2**)

revuelta Alternative name for Venezuelan *joropo* music. (**2**)

rewe Mapuche altar. (**2**)

reyes (Also *reis*, Poruguese.) 'Kings' in Spanish. Christmas music tradition throughout Latin America, having to do with the Magi or Three Kings. (**2**)

réyog Processional dance genre of Ponorogo. (**4**)

rezadores Folk priests in the Dominican Republic. (**2**)

rezos 'Prayers' in Spanish; meetings in Costa Rica at which the rosary is recited. (**2**)

rezwār-shāir Official poet of a tribe in Balochistan, who would record all important events in verse and teach them to the tribal minstrel; the minstrel then sang them at public gatherings and tribal assemblies. (**5**)

RFO Radiodiffusion Télévision Française pour Outre-Mer, the French overseas television broadcasting system. (**9**)

Ṛgveda Oldest religious and cultural text (*veda*) of the Vedic Aryans, consisting of hymns addressed to their gods. (**5**)

rgya-gling Tibetan oboe used in Buddhist rituals, played with the circular breathing technique. (**5**)

rhapsodic Extravagantly emotional; in France, said of improvisation using motifs of variable length, rather than measured phrases. (**8**)

rhyming spiritual Unaccompanied song genre derived from the Bahamian anthem. (**2**)

rhythm Pattern of strong and weak elements in a flow of sound, musically often recurring or grouping at several levels of organization; cf. *meter, tempo*. (**9**)

ribeba 'Rebab', Italian regional name of the mouth harp. (**8**)

riberbula (Also *riebula, rivergula*.) Corsican mouth harp. (**8**)

riçak In Kurdistan, a spike fiddle. (**6**)

riddarvisene Norwegian songs about knights. (**8**)

ridée Breton line or circle dance, performed as part of a three-part suite; *see laridé*. (**8**)

ridu Ngada xylophone. (**4**)

riebula (Also *riberbula, rivergula*.) Corsican mouth harp. (**8**)

riff In blues and related African-American musics, a repeated short melodic rhythmic phrase. (**3**)

rigaudon 'Rigadoon', lively seventeenth- and eighteenth-century dance, still popular in France. (**8**)

rigodón Opening dance in the Philippines. (**4**)

rib Curved conical wooden horn of the Hutsul'shchyna and neighboring Carpathian regions of Ukraine, used to accompany *koliadky*. (**8**)

riha Svanetian ritual Christmas song. (**8**)

rika Tambourine of Zanzibar. (**1**)

rikalo (Also *bušen*.) Bark trumpet played by Serbian Vlachs. (**8**)

rimba Xylophone of the coastal Bantu people of Kenya. (**1**)

rímnaflokkur Cycle of Icelandic rhymed verse, sometimes consisting of thousands of stanzas. (**8**)

rímnakveðskapur Icelandic genre involving repetitions of a short melody. (**8**)

rimse (Japan.) Genre of Ainu festival songs performed with dance. (**7**)

rímur Icelandic ballads, sometimes having up to 100 stanzas. (**8**)

rīna Baiga women's dance of Madhya Pradesh. (**5**)

rincik (1) Sundanese small fifteen-stringed zither. (2) High-pitched gong-chime of Sunda. (3) Balinese small set of upturned cymbals. (**4**)

Rindentrompete German trumpet made of a bark scroll. (**8**)

rindja 'Descent', annual descent from alpine pastures, when herdsmen of Haute-Gruyère, Switzerland, performed *lyóba* and *tchira*. (**8**)

ring (Also *sehal, ṭāsa*.) In Oman, medium-size cymbals that accompany the singing and dancing of professional groups. (**6**)

ring dance In Jamaica, African-derived solo dance performed in the center of a ring made by the other dancers. (**2**)

ring games Jamaican song-games played by children and adults at wakes and moonshine *dahlins*. (**2**)

ring-play African-derived children's play in Jamaica that is heavily influenced by European children's games and related to the jump-in dance. (**2**)

rin'yû gaku (Japan.) Music of present-day Vietnam or India introduced to Japan during the Nara period (714–794). (**7**)

Rinzai syû (Japan.) Sect of Zyôdo Buddhism introduced from Song China by Eisai (1141–1215). (**7**)

riondâ French-speaking Swiss dialect word for singing and dancing. (**8**)

riqq (1) (Also *daff*.) Arabic tambourine with heavy brass jingles. (2) Arab tambourine used in Egypt and in Sudanese ceremonies of the Qādirīya brotherhood. (3) (Also, in Yemen, *duff*.) Small frame drum or tambourine, usually with five small cymbals inserted into the frame. (**1, 3, 6**)

rīshe 'Roots'; in Iran, term referring to the bases, age, depth, and origin of music. (**6**)

rīshqālā Model strophe in Syro-Maronite chant. (**6**)

rispetti Type of Italian lyric song. (**8**)

risyukyô (Japan.) Buddhist chant (*syômyô*) for a *sutra*. (**7**)

risyu zanmai (Japan.) Esoteric Buddhist ceremonies; the basic ceremony of the Singon sect of Buddhism. (**7**)

riti Wolof bowed lute with a holed gourd resonator. (**1**)

ritu (Japan.) (1) Pitches; (2) type of scale; (3) type of Buddhist chant; (4) one of two halves of *gyoyû* chamber concerts at the Heian court. (**7**)

ritu kaku (Japan.) Third note (*kaku*) in the *ritu* scale. (**7**)

ritu kyoku (Japan.) Buddhist chants based on the *ritu* scale. (**7**)

ritu tetrachord (Japan.) Three pitches outlining the interval of a fourth with an intermediate pitch dividing the fourth into a major second and a minor third from low to high (for instance, C-D-F); one of four tetrachords proposed by the ethnomusicologist Koizumi Fumio (1927–1983). (**7**)

Ritugen hakki (Japan.) 'Demonstration of the Origins of Measurements' (1692), treatise on music pitch theory by Nakane Genki (d. 1733) published in the 1690s. (**7**)

rivergula (Also *riberbula, riebula*.) Corsican mouth harp. (**8**)

riyaz (Also *riāz, riyāz*.) Dedicated and regular music practice. (**5**)

rizitika Unaccompanied table songs of the White Mountains of western Crete. (**8**)

rkang-gling Tibetan trumpet, originally made from a human femur. (**5**) *rnga* Large double-headed frame drum of Tibet. (5)

road march Trinidadian music for street dancing. (2)

roam vung Khmer popular social dance in circular form. (4)

robā'i Quatrain, classical Persian poetic form. (6)

robaim kbach buran Traditional Cambodian court dance performed by females only. (3)

robaim prapeyney Cambodian folk dance sometimes performed by Cambodian-Americans. (3)

rock en español Rock sung in Spanish. (2)

rock steady Short-lived music and dance fad in Jamaica in the late 1960s. (2)

rockandroll Music of art-punk musicians in Hungary. (8)

rodat (1) Malaysian theatrical genre of Islamic origin. (2) South Sumatra secularized *zikir* performance. (4)

rôei (Japan.) Genre of court vocal music, of both indigenous and foreign origin. (7)

rog Bosnia-Hercegovinian animal horn with a single idioglot reed. (8)

rogalj 'Street corners', gatherings of young people in Vojvodina, Serbia, to sing. (8)

rogativa Spanish prayer song to a local patron saint, asking for the protection of crops from drought and disease. (8)

rog-kaft Ossetian virtuoso solo dance. (8)

rogovi Slovene horns made of animal horn. (8)

roh Belarusan horns made of animal horn, wood, or metal. (8)

rôi nuóc Water-puppet theater in northern Vietnam. (4)

roitschäggätä Swiss late-winter masking festival in Lötschental, Valais. (8)

rojão (Also *baião de viola*.) Brazilian syncopated instrumental pattern performed on the *viola* during a *desafio*. (2)

rōkati pātalu Songs performed while working with a mortar and pestle in Andhra Pradesh. (5)

rok'on fada Hausa state ceremonial music. (1)

roƙoo Term for begging among the Hausa of Nigeria. (1)

roku tyôsi (Japan.) Six modes used in *gagaku*. (7)

Rolantskvœði Faroe epic songs (*kvœði*) dealing with the exploits of Charlemagne, his uncle, and his daughter. (8)

rolli Swiss small closed bells containing little rocks, used on harnesses and worn by women in winter festivals. (8)

rol-mo (Also *sbug-chal*.) Brass cymbals of Tibet. (5)

Rom Ceremony performed by Aboriginal Australians of Arnhem Land as a mark of friendship, with singing and dancing. (9)

romance (1) Spanish and Portuguese ballad, also sung by Sephardic Jews in Bosnia-Hercegovina. (2) Sephardic songs based on medieval Spanish balladry. (3) Narrative song in the ballad tradition with a poetic text typically set as a series of sixteen-syllable strophes and concerning topics associated with historic or legendary persons. (4) Spanish colonial narrative song form or ballad, usually sung solo or with guitar accompaniment. (5) In Chile, old-style narrative song with an indeterminate number of quatrains recited or sung in one musical sentence. (2, 3, 8)

romanceiro Portuguese ballad. (8)

romancero Sephardic Jewish secular narrative ballad. (8)

romanse Song genre popular in Croatia between the world wars. (8)

romansot sfaradiyot Judeo-Spanish songs that became popular in Israel from the 1960s. (6)

Romantic In European music history, a period corresponding roughly to the nineteenth century; its name and certain aesthetic principles derive from the Romantic movement in European art and literature of the late eighteenth and early nineteenth centuries. (8)

romantica 'Romantic', popular style of *salsa* in the 1980s. (3)

romarias 'Pilgrimages', Portuguese religious pilgrimages with music. (8)

romerías 'Pilgrimages', Spanish sacred and secular songs to accompany autumn pilgrimages to local shrines. (8)

rommelpot (1) Friction drum of the Low Countries; cf. *rumlepotte*. (2) European term for a Khoikhoi drum made by placing skins over a pot. (1, 8)

roncadora 'Snorer', cane or wooden duct flute played in pipe-and-tabor fashion in Ancash Department, Peru. (2)

ronda (1) Circular children's game of Mexico; (2) Chilean children's game-song derivative of the *romance*; (3) *rondas infantiles*, children's game or ring songs. (2)

rondador 'One who makes the rounds', single-unit panpipe from Ecuador with up to thirty tubes, so named because it was once used by night watchmen who made the rounds in Quito, playing their panpipes. (2)

rondadorcillos Small eight-tubed single-unit panpipe from Ecuador. (2)

rondalla (1) Spanish guitar-based band that accompanies *rondas*. (2) Filipino string band, consisting of mandolinlike melodic instruments (*bandurria* and *laud*), guitars, and a bass. (3) Plucked-string band, ubiquitous throughout the Lowland Philippines, appropriated from Iberian *cumparsa* and

estudiantina ensembles. (3) In Colombia, a group of musicians playing instrumental music with Spanish-derived instruments; *see also* estudiantina, lira, tuna. (2, 3, 4, 8, 9)

rondas 'Rounds'. In Spain, songs usually performed by groups. (8)

ronde French and French-Swiss closed ring dance, sung and danced by the dancers, often in 3/4 time. (8)

rondeau French medieval verse form and the music for it. (8)

rondes enfantines French children's songs in Corsica. (8)

rondo Musical form based on a recurring phrase. (4)

roneat (1) Khmer xylophone. (2) 'Xylophone', 'metallophone'; Cambodian percussion instrument played as part of the *pinnpeat* ensemble. (3, 4)

roneat dek Khmer higher-pitched metallophone, with twenty-one keys. (4)

roneat ek (1) 'High-pitched xylophone', Cambodian percussion instrument played as part of the *pinnpeat* ensemble. (2) Khmer higher-pitched xylophone with twenty-one keys. (3, 4)

roneat thong Khmer lower-pitched metallophone with sixteen keys, now obsolete. (4)

roneat thung Khmer lower-pitched xylophone with sixteen keys. (4)

ronggeng (1) Professional female singer-dancer of Indonesia. (2) Genre of popular social dance in Malaysia. (3) Couple dancing and singing. (4)

rongi (Japan.) Chant (*syômyô*) for lecturing on or discussing Buddha or other Buddhist topics. (7)

rongo (1) Ndogo log xylophone with long gourd resonators. (2) Dance of Sudanese origin accompanied by the *ringu*, or xylophone. (1, 6)

rônin (Japan.) Masterless *samurai*. (7)

rook jaw In Barbados, scraped idiophone consisting of two jagged sticks that are rubbed together. (2)

roopill Estonian reed pipe with four to six holes for fingering. (8)

rootsikannel Estonian bowed lyre with three or four strings; *see* hiiukannel. (8)

rosario 'Rosary'. (1) *Rosario a la Santa Cruz*, Puerto Rican sung rosary to the Holy Cross. (2) (Also *rosario cantao*.) *Rosario cantado*, sung version of the rosary. (3) *Rosario de promesas*, Puerto Rican sung 'rosary of promises'. (4) *Rosario para los muertos*, Puerto Rican sung rosary ritual for 'good living' or 'dying'. (2)

Rosh Hashanah Jewish new year. (8)

rospev Russian religious chants. (8)

rotāšana Latvian custom between Easter Monday and Whitsunday, when girls gathered on hillsides and sang. (8)

rou (China.) 'Flesh'; term used by *nanguan* musicians to refer to the elaborated melody played by the *dongxiao* and *erxian*. (7)

roupioupiou (Also *rantamplan, turlututu.*) Onomatopoeic imitation of musical instruments used in ring dances of the French-speaking area of Switzerland. (8)

rowże-khân In Iran and elsewhere, a performer of narratives about the martyrdom of Imam Hosein, other Shi'a imams, or members of their families. (6)

Royal College of Music School in London where many African musicians, including Ephraim Amu, studied. (1)

rozenhoed 'Hat of roses', dance in the Dutch-language area of the Low Countries. (8)

roženice Double-reed oboes played in Istria, Croatia. (8)

rozhok Russian wooden trumpet with five finger holes and one thumb hole. (8)

rozigaku (Japan.) Chinese outdoor music introduced to the Ryûkyû Islands (present-day Okinawa). (7)

rôzin odori (Japan.) 'Old man's dance', category of Okinawan classical dance. (7)

ru Class of Vietnamese lullaby songs. (4)

ruan (1) Chinese moon-shaped lute. (2) (China.) Four-stringed lute. (4, 7)

rubāb (1) Short-necked plucked lute of western Afghanistan. (2) Long-necked lute of medieval Persia and Central Asia. *See also rabab.* (5, 6)

rubaī (1) (Also *rubā'i.*) Poetic genre, often in quatrain form. (2) Classical poetic form often used in Central Asian *maqām* traditions. (5, 6)

rǔchenitsa Bulgarian solo dance with improvised steps in 7/8 time. (8)

rudat Performance held inside mosques in Cirebon. (4)

ruding Jew's harp of Borneo. (4)

rudra vīṇā (Also *bīn.*) North Indian plucked stick zither. (5)

rudzu balss Latvian tune sung in rye fields. (8)

ruedas Spanish circle dances. (8)

rūf (1) Secular vocal genre in Kashmir related to *chakri.* (2) Religious song and dance genre in Kashmir performed by women during Ramadan. (5)

rüffle (Also *raffle, rärri.*) Swiss wooden ratchet, a noisemaker. (8)

rūḥ Spirit. (6)

rū-howzī Iranian comic improvised theater, involving solo dancing. (6)

ruika (Japan.) Indigenous genre of court songs performed only at an emperor's funeral; lament and eulogy for the dead. (7)

rujih Cymbals of Sumatra. (4)

rukhsat In Pakistan, departure of the bride from her parents' home. (5)

rull One of three Norwegian dances, characterized by a slow gait in 2/4 or 6/8 time; *see gangar, halling.* (8)

rum Largest Brazilian *atabaque* drum. (2)

rum shop Montserrat bar and provision store hosting storytelling, music, song, and dance performers. (2)

rumanea Khmer frame drum with single head. (4)

rumba (1) Ballroom dance of Cuban origin in 2/4 or 4/4 time with emphatic hip movements. (2) Nineteenth-century suburban Cuban musical genre at popular secular festivals. (3) Cuban-derived couple-dance genre. (4) (Also *rhumba.*) Short repetitive, syncopated rhythmic pattern of Afro-Cuban origin defined by a quarter note followed by an eighth rest, an eighth note tied to a quarter note, and a quarter note; dance featuring this rhythmic pattern. (2, 3, 8)

rumba catalán Type of Spanish popular music. (8)

rumlepotte In Denmark, a friction drum made of a pot sealed with the skin of a pig's bladder and having a goose quill or a piece of reed attached to the middle; cf. *rommelpot.* (8)

rumpi Middle-size Brazilian *atabaque* drum. (2)

runo Ancient Finnish-Estonian song genre, in which the *Kalevala* was sung. (8)

runonlaulu In Finland, the singing of old poems by a leader and a supporting singer. (8)

runqiang (China.) Melodic variations or embellished melodies. (7)

rusalka 'Mermaid', dramatization in Belarusan calendrical celebrations at the beginning of summer. (8)

rusalnyna pieśni 'Water-nymph songs', any of several Belarusan *valačobnyja pieśni.* (8)

rushin' Form of marching or dancing with shuffling steps in the Bahamas. (2)

russkogo 'Of Russians', style of Gypsy song in Russia. (8)

ruwatan Type of protective *wayang* ceremony in Java and Cirebon. (4)

ruzûbun (Japan.) Concluding part of a Buddhist *sutra.* (7)

rways (1) Itinerant musicians of southern Morocco who perform Arab-Andalusian, European, Arab popular, and West African acculturated styles. (2) Sung poetry tradition among Moroccan Berbers of the Tashlhiyt region. (1, 6)

ryo (Japan.) (1) Type of scale; (2) type of Buddhist chant; (3) one of two halves of the *gyoyû* chamber concerts at the Heian court. (7)

ryo kyoku (Japan.) Buddhist chants based on the *ryo* scale. (7)

ryôka (Japan.) Boarding-school songs. (7)

ryu "Schools" associated with particular Korean musicians. (7)

ryû (Also *ryûha.*) In Japan, generic term for schools of an art. (7, 10)

ryûka (Japan.) Short poetic form of the Ryûkyû Islands, consisting of four lines with a syllable pattern of 8 + 8 + 8 + 6. (7)

ryûkôka (Japan.) Generic term for popular songs; in the narrow sense, a synonym for *kayôkyoku.* (7)

ryûkyû scale (Japan.) Scale used predominantly in the music of the Ryûkyû Islands; C-(D)-E-F-G-B-C (with D sometimes appearing in descending melodies). (7)

ryûkyû tetrachord (Japan.) *See okinawa tetrachord.* (7)

ryûteki (Also *ôteki.*) Transverse flute of Chinese origin used in Japanese *gagaku.* (7)

sa (Chinese, *ci.*) Korean sung poetry. (7)

ṣabā One of the primary Arab *maqāmāt.* (6)

sababa Six-holed end-blown flute of Madagascar, similar to the Arabic *shabab.* (1)

sabalan Chanted game of wit, played in the Philippines. (4)

Sabanga People of the Central African Republic. (1)

śabdam Dance item in *bharata nātyam.* (5)

śabda pūja Offerings of sound in Buddhist temple worship, in Sri Lanka. (5)

sabda vidya (Japan.) Sanskrit term for studies of language; the term was translated into Chinese as *sheng-ming* (read in Japanese as *syômyô*) to refer to Buddhist chant. (7)

sabhā (Also *sangit sabhā.*) Music society; organization that arranges music, dance, and drama performances for public entertainment. (5)

sabi (Japan.) Aesthetic principle; used to describe a deep, seasoned voice. (7)

sabii zegakiye Adighian song to make a child walk. (8)

sacabuche (Also *zambomba.*) In El Salvador and Honduras, friction membranophone, constructed from a large gourd, cut and covered at one end with a skin into which a stick is inserted and rubbed. (2)

säckpipa Swedish bagpipe revived in the 1980s. (8)

săcunda (Also *contră.*) Second violin, which supplies rhythmic-harmonic accompaniment, played in Romanian and Hungarian music in parts of Transylvania. (8)

sadam Lampung ring-stop flute music. (4)

sadangp'ae (Also *namsadang, kŏsa p'ae.*) Korean (male) itinerant musical group. (7)

sadasnje pjesme 'Present-day songs' in Gabela, Hercegovina. (8)

sa'dawi Tunisian dance usually performed by women featuring hip movements and gestures with a handheld scarf. **(1)**

SADC Music Festival (Southern African Development Community Music Festival.) Regionally cooperative festival, first held in October 1995. **(1)**

sāddhanā Self-realization; in religious disciplines such as fasting and worship, music is a path to this goal. **(5)**

sādhakan 'Practice', technical exercise for drum students in Kerala. **(5)**

sadiah West Sumatra slow, sad songs. **(4)**

sadir kacheri (Also *dasi āṭṭam*.) Obsolete term for the *bharata nāṭyam* dance. **(5)**

Saemaǔl undong Korean "new village" movement. **(7)**

saenghwang Korean free-reed mouth organ. **(7)**

sæter Norwegian summer farm for highland pasturing, where the *lur* was traditionally played. **(8)**

saf Dance song performed by women of the Saharan Atlas for religious feasts. **(6)**

safail Type of rattle used in Central Asian *zikr* ceremonies. **(6)**

safe Lute from Borneo and Sumatra. **(4)**

ṣaff Line of men acting as a chorus in Palestinian wedding celebrations. **(6)**

saffāqatān Archaic term for cymbals or castanets. **(6)**

safina (Plural, *safā'in*.) 'Vessel,' manuscript or printed collection of poetic texts. **(6)**

saga Icelandic prose narrative, considered a form of musical performance. **(8)**

sagat tūra (Also *ṣājāt*.) Large finger cymbals. **(6)**

sagayan Maguindanao spirit communication dance. **(4)**

sage uta (Japan.) Segment of *nô* chanting in the lower register. **(7)**

saggeypo Kalinga set of five pipes. **(4)**

śāgird Student. **(5)**

Sahel Dry borderland region between the savanna and the Sahara Desert. **(1)**

ṣahfa Shallow vessel drum of the north Tihāma, made of clay with an open bottom, two antipodal handles, and a turning ring for tightening the head. **(6)**

sāhitya (Also *sāhityam*.) Song text. **(5)**

sāhitya prastāra (Also *niraval*.) In Karnatak music, improvisation that retains the text of the original composition but changes the melody. **(5)**

ṣahn Gong-shaped flat dish made of thin metal, used as a percussion instrument. **(6)**

śahnāī (Also *ṣanai, sannāyi, surnāī, surnāīe*.) North Indian double-reed aerophone used in concert, popular, and folk musics. **(5)**

ṣaḥn nuḥāsī Flat circular copper tray used as a struck idiophone in Yemen. **(6)**

saibara (Japan.) Genre of court vocal music of both indigenous and foreign origin. **(7)**

ṣa'īdī Common 8-beat rhythmic pattern, named after the Ṣa'īd region of Upper Egypt. **(6)**

Saidor Papua New Guinean town on the Rai Coast, immediately east of Serieng. **(9)**

saih Tuning, scale in Balinese music. **(4)**

saih angklung Tuning system for Balinese *gamelan angklung*. **(4)**

saih gendèr wayang Five-tone tuning system in Balinese music. **(4)**

saih gong Tuning system for Balinese *gamelan gong*. **(4)**

saih pitu Seven-tone tuning system in Balinese music. **(4)**

saila Baiga men's martial dance of Madhya Pradesh. **(5)**

saimon (Japan.) (1) Offertory Buddhist chant (*syômyô*); (2) genre of Buddhist folk music. **(7)**

saing Khmer conch shell trumpet. **(4)**

Saipan Capital island of the Commonwealth of the Northern Mariana Islands. **(9)**

ṣa'ir (Also *lawjebij* 'sayer of songs'.) 'Poet', term for a performer of heroic songs in Kurdistan. **(6)**

saire ke gīt Men's seasonal songs of Madhya Pradesh. **(5)**

säistäjä (Also *puoltaja*.) Supporting singer in Finnish *runonlaulu*. **(8)**

saj' (1) Ancient rhymed prose. (2) Quick, march-like Yemeni rhythmic pattern. **(6)**

sajani Gond music and dance form of Madhya Pradesh. **(5)**

sājāt (Also *sagat*.) Small brass finger cymbals. **(6)**

sajèn Offering, in Indonesia. **(10)**

sajin sori 'Photographic singing', derogatory term for exact repetition of a teacher's singing style in Korean *p'ansori*. **(7)**

sákàrà (1) Yoruba single-membrane clay-bodied frame drum. (2) Yoruba musical genre for dancing and praising, performed and patronized mostly by Muslims. **(1, 10)**

sakau (Pohnpeian.) Kava. **(9)**

sakeco Samawan topical and humorous sung poetry. **(4)**

saketa Samawan spontaneous antiphonal work songs. **(4)**

Saktaeyŏp 'Fast large piece', prototype of Korean *kagok*. **(7)**

śāktapadasaṅgīt Literary song genre of West Bengal and Bangladesh devoted to power-cult gods and goddesses and using music of various styles including *dhrupad, khyāl, ṭappā*, and even *kīrtan*. **(5)**

sakti Single-headed drum of Réunion Island. **(5)**

śakti (Also *satti*.) 'Power' (Sanskrit), especially that of a goddess. **(5)**

saku mono (Japan.) *Ziuta* repertoire (*syamisen* music) with humorous lyrics. **(7)**

Sakuramento teiyô (Japan.) 'Manual of Sacraments', published in 1605 in Nagasaki; it included nineteen Gregorian chants with notation. **(7)**

salai jin Healing rituals in Ternate and Tidore. **(4)**

salām 'Greeting', musical salutation consisting of a popular song. **(6)**

salamuri Wooden cane flute of eastern Georgia. **(8)**

salaw Northern Thai bowed lute with two or three strings. **(4)**

salawek dulang West Sumatra vocal and brass-tray music. **(4)**

salaysay Style of chanting the Passion in the Philippines. **(4)**

saléndro Nearly equidistant pentatonic tuning system in Sundanese music. **(4)**

saleone Jamaican *salo* song type. **(2)**

salidommay Bontok popular group songs. **(4)**

saliman Cylindrical membranophone of the Jamaican Maroons. **(2)**

šaljive pjesme Comic or joking songs in Bosnia-Hercegovina. **(8)**

salo Jamaican secular song. **(2)**

saloma Panamanian vocal melody or recited chant with words or vocables. **(2)**

salonreng Makassarese dance. **(10)**

salsa 'Sauce'. (1) Latin American musical fusion of rhythm and blues, jazz, and rock, popular in Africa as a result of dissemination on gramophone records. (2) Afro-Hispanic Caribbean song and dance form rooted in the Cuban *son* that is today an internationalized form no longer associated with any one country. **(1, 2, 3)**

salsódromos Nightclubs for dancing salsa in Peru. **(2)**

salṭana Ecstatic state thought to arise from hearing or performing the *maqām*. **(6)**

saltarello (Also *ballarella, saltarella, savaterelle, stuzzichetto*.) Italian Renaissance court dance featuring a hop at the start of each measure; preserved in Italy and Corsica as a courting dance, sometimes with gentle, slow movements. **(8)**

saluang West Sumatra end-blown bamboo flute. **(4)**

salubong Staged meeting between the Virgin Mary and Christ, in the Philippines. **(4)**

salve (1) Unaccompanied song with religious texts diffused by missionaries since colonial times, sung at *velorios*; (2) *salve con versos*, in the Dominican Republic a *salve* with added text in an Africanized musical style; (3) *Salve regina* 'Hail, Holy Queen', Spanish translation of a Marian antiphon. (**2**)

salyr-saryk Performance style of southeastern Turkmenistan. (**6**)

sam (Also *sama*.) First beat of a tala cycle. (**5**)

samā' (1) 'Hearing', 'listening', 'spiritual concert', especially in a Sufi context. (2) Synonym for music, a concert, or a recital. (**5, 6**)

samā Tambourine without jingles, played for ritual dances by a *samāī*. (**5**)

samabhaṅga Posture in *oḍissi* dance. (**5**)

samādhi Holy person's death that occurs during meditation; the place where it occurs. (**5**)

samāḥ Aleppan sacred dance, possibly related to the Turkish Alevi *sema* dance. (**6**)

samā'ī Common Arab instrumental overture, formally related to the Turkish *bashraf* or *peşrev*. (**6**)

samaia Georgian women's dance with instrumental accompaniment. (**8**)

samāj-gāyan Vaishnav devotional singing of Braj, northern India. (**5**)

saman Acehnese men's percussive religious dance. (**4**)

sāman Hymn of the Sāmaveda. (**5**)

Sāmaveda Musical *veda*, a religious and cultural text of the Vedic Aryans consisting of notated melodies set mostly to *Ṛgveda* texts. (**5**)

Samawa West Sumbawan culture area. (**4**)

samba (1) Brazilian generic term for a wide variety of secular musical and dance styles of African origin. (2) Form of popular Brazilian music and dance with prominent percussion accompaniment and group song, especially important during carnival. (3) Brazilian dance with syncopated rhythms in 2/4 meter. (**1, 2, 3, 9**)

sámbà (Also *samba*.) (1) Quadrangular wooden frame drum introduced by Brazilian returnees to African churches. (2) Yoruba square drum, derived from Latin American or Caribbean models and associated with immigrant black Christians. (**1**)

samba caporal Chilean *bailes de salto* of Brazilian-Bolivian origin. (**2**)

sambay Guatemalan erotic dance. (**2**)

sam chan Longest of three rhythmic cycles in Thai music. (**4**)

Samguk sagi 'History of the Three Kingdoms', Korean document with musical information. (**7**)

Samguk yusa 'Memorabilia of the Three Kingdoms', Korean historical document. (**7**)

samhúda Yekuana cylindrical double-headed drum. (**2**)

samica 'By itself', Croatian plucked lute played solo. (**8**)

sāmirī Poetic genre of the Arabian Peninsula performed with music and dance. (**6**)

samizdat 'Self-published' (Russian). (**8**)

sam p'ae Third grade of Korean *kisaeng*, often employed as prostitutes. (**7**)

sam pa sabie 'Free of restrictions', Belarusan term for improvisational mastery of instrumental folk tunes. (**8**)

sampho (1) Khmer horizontal barrel drum with two heads. (2) Small double-headed barrel drum, Cambodian percussion instrument played as part of the *pinnpeat* ensemble. (**3, 4**)

sampi' (Also *sampeq*.) Kenyah-Kayan plucked lute. (**4**)

sampradāya (1) Tradition passed on through a teacher-student lineage of Karnatak music, similar to the Hindustani *guru-śisya paramparā*. (2) Genre of women's life-cycle songs in Karnataka. (**5**)

samrī (1) Bedouin communal dance performed with antiphonal singing in the Mashriq. (2) Love songs of sedentary bedouin of the Arabian Peninsula. (**6**)

samskara (Also *saṅskār*.) 'Mental impression', imprint left on the subconscious that shapes and colors life; therefore, a ritual that seeks to make a beneficial impression on the life of an individual or community. (**5**)

samudraghōsha In Sri Lanka, popular meter of most Sinhala thematic songs such as carters' songs and boatmen's songs. (**5**)

samul nori Seated Korean percussion quartet. (**7**)

samvādi (Also *samvādī*.) Second most important tone in a raga. (**5**)

San People of southern Africa. (**1**)

san (Japan.) Chant (*syômyô*) for praising buddhas, bodhisattvas, or other symbols of Buddhism. (**7**)

ṣan'a 'Art', the traditional Arab-Andalusian repertoire of the Maghrib. (**6**)

sanang Palawan pair of suspended gongs. (**4**)

sanat 'Art' (German *Kunst*) music, usually referring to urban Turkish genres of the nineteenth and twentieth centuries. (**6**)

sanat musikisi 'Art music', Turkish classical music. (**6**)

sanba (1) Haitian poet-composer; (2) soloist in call-and-response singing of the *konbit*. (**2**)

sanban (China.) Declamatory aria sung with considerable rubato. (**7**)

San Blás Saint Blaise, patron saint of Paraguay, whose feast is celebrated on 3 February. (**2**)

sanbun son'eki (Japan.) Chinese system for mathematically calculating the twelve pitches, roughly equivalent to the twelve Western semitones. (**7**)

sañcārī Third section of a Hindustani *dhrupad* composition. (**5**)

sañcāri gita Teaching song illustrating the characteristics of a raga. (**5**)

sandaehŭi (Also *sandae nori*.) 'Stage play', early Korean court entertainment. (**7**)

sandan (Japan.) Chant (*syômyô*) for praising buddhas, bodhisattvas, and other symbols of Buddhism. (**7**)

sandan no mai (Japan.) *Kyôgen* dance. (**7**)

sandara (1) Solo song. (2) Song accompanied by music in North West Frontier Province. (**5**)

Sandawe Cultural group of Tanzania. (**1**)

sande Generic term for women's secret societies in West Africa. (**1**)

sānde Melancholy song recited by women during tragic events in North West Frontier Province. (**5**)

sàndeyà Old Burmese term now applied to the piano. (**4**)

sandhyā Ancient Vedic ceremony centered on a sacrificial fire, still practiced in Trinidad. (**5**)

sandouri Greek trapezoidal struck zither. (**8**)

sanfen sunyi (China.) Three-part–addition–subtraction; algorithm used to generate twelve pitches. (**7**)

sang Conch shell horn of Thailand. (**4**)

sangam 'Meeting', 'conference', 'congress', 'organization'. (**5**)

sangati Melodic variation, often in a progressive series. (**5**)

saŋba Vai conical single-headed drum. (**1**)

sange (Japan.) Buddhist chant (*syômyô*) for purifying and ornamenting a hall and confessing and making vows to Buddha. (**7**)

sangel Maguindanao lullaby. (**4**)

sangen (Japan.) Another name for the *syamisen* used in *ziuta*. (**7**)

Sängerbunde German singing league. (**3**)

sangere Suyá invocations to influence the body. (**2**)

Sängerfeste German singing festival. (**3**)

sanghiyang Cavite curing ritual. (**4**)

sanghyang Trance dance of Bali. (**4**)

saṅgīta (Also *sangīt*.) 'Music' (Sanskrit); includes vocal and instrumental music as well as dance. (**5**)

saṅgītācārya One who has vast knowledge of music. (**5**)

Saṅgītaratnākara Thirteenth-century music treatise by Sarngadeva. (**5**)

sangita sabhā (Also *sabhā*.) Music society. (**5**)

sangīta sandarśanaya All-night popular music shows in Sri Lanka. (**5**)

saṅgīt nāṭak Marathi music drama genre. (**5**)

Sango African-derived syncretic religion of Trinidad and Tobago; *see also Shango*. (**2**)

sangoma Nguni healers. (**1**)

Sango yôroku (Japan.) Tablatures for *biwa* compiled by Huziwara no Moronaga (1138–1392). (**7**)

sangsoe (Also *sangmo*.) Korean folk band leader; (**7**)

sangui North Borneo nose flute. (**4**)

Sanguozhi (China.) 'Romance of the Three Kingdoms'. (**7**)

sangwe Gumuz five-stringed lyre. (**1**)

sang yok Chant style of Mahanikai Buddhist temples. (**4**)

sanha Chilean tenor-register *siku*. (**2**)

sani (Also *bhogum, kalavantulu*.) Female temple dancers in Andhra Pradesh. (**5**)

ṣanj (1) Generic term for cymbals. (2) Type of early harp. (3) Possibly, a medieval Chinese gong. (**6**)

sanjo 'Scattered melodies', extended Korean instrumental solo music. (**7**)

sanjuán (1) Popular *mestizo* dance form in Ecuador. (2) In Imbabura, Ecuador, dance music for a child's wake performed on harp with *golpeador*, characterized by its simple duple meter and melodic repetition. (**2**)

San Juan Saint John, patron saint throughout the southern Americas, whose feast is celebrated on 24 June. (**2**)

sanjuanero Southern Colombian festive *bambuco*. (**2**)

sanjuanito 'Little *sanjuán*', term used by *mestizo* and Afro-Ecuadorian musicians to denote an expanded form of *sanjuán* that may have detailed narrative song texts. (**2**)

sankan gaku (Japan.) Music of the three ancient Korean kingdoms—Silla, Paekche, and Koguryo—brought to Japan in 683; later unified as *komagaku* (music of Korean origin) in the court (*gagaku*) repertoire. (**7**)

sankeys St. Lucian gospel hymns named after the evangelist Ira David Sankey. (**2**)

śaṅkh (Also *śaṅkha, śaṅku*.) Conch shell trumpet played mostly in rituals. (**5**)

sankīn samāʿi Common 6/8 rhythmic pattern. (**6**)

sankīrtan Devotional music genre emphasizing collectivity, iteration of God's name, and dancing. (**5**)

sankyoku (Also *sankyoku gassô*.) Traditional Japanese chamber music, featuring *koto, syamisen*, and *syakuhati* or *kokyû*, a bowed lute. (**3, 7, 10**)

sannāyi (Also *śahnāī*.) Double-reed instrument used in classical and folk music in Andhra Pradesh. (**5**)

sanni yakku Dance form in Sri Lanka believed to be curative. (**5**)

san no tuzumi (Japan.) Stick-struck hourglass-shaped drum of Korean origin used in *gagaku*. (**7**)

sänntumsschölle Swiss cowbell, worn by male singers in winter festivals. (**8**)

sanoe (Also *sanae*.) Religious folk music of Korea's Silla kingdom. (**7**)

sanrai (Japan.) Buddhist chant (*syômyô*) for worshiping the "three treasures," Buddha, *dharma*, and Sangha. (**7**)

san sagari (Japan.) *Syamisen* tuning.

san sage (Japan.) Tuning for *sansin* (Okinawan three-stringed lute). (**7**)

sansei Third-generation Japanese-American, the second generation to be born on American soil. (**3**)

sanshin Three-stringed plucked Okinawan lute, similar to the *syamisen* but covered with snakeskin, played also by people of Okinawan heritage in Argentina, Brazil, Paraguay, and Peru. (**2, 7**)

Sanskrit Classical language of India. (**4**)

santacrusan Christian Maytime processions in the Philippines. (**4**)

Santa Cruz Feast of the Holy Cross. (**2**)

Santa Maria Afro-Brazilian rhythmic pattern. (**2**)

śānti muhurtam Tamil ritual associated with a married couple's first night together. (**5**)

santo Six-stringed bamboo idiochord tube zither of Flores. (**4**)

santoer Trapezoidal struck zither of the Low Countries. (**8**)

santouri Greek trapezoidal struck zither. (**3, 8**)

santri Orthodox Javanese Muslims. (**4**)

santur (Also *santūr, santŭr*.) (1) Mallet-hammered dulcimer or zither of North Africa and West Asia. (2) Iranian trapezoidal zither struck with hammers. (3) Trapezoidal zither struck with two mallets, today played largely in Iraq. (4) Box zither played with two light wooden hammers; used as a Hindustani concert instrument as well as in regional music of Kashmir. (5) Georgian urban chordophone of the 1600s to the 1800s. (**1, 3, 5, 6, 8**)

sanu Northeast Thai musical bow attached to a kite. (**4**)

sanxian (China.) Three-stringed long-necked plucked lute related to the Japanese *syamisen* 'samisen'. (**3, 7, 10**)

sanyāsin One who has renounced the world. (**5**)

sanzitou (China.) Three-syllable unit. (**7**)

sanzyû (Japan.) (1) Third lowest octave in a piece; (2) third lowest pitch level in Buddhist chants; (3) common melodic partterns used in the *sanzyû* pitch area; (4) *heikyoku* vocal melody pattern (*kyokusetu*) in *arioso* style; (5) opening melodic pattern in *gidayû busi*. (**7**)

sanzyû gen sô (Japan.) Thirty-stringed *koto*. (**7**)

sáo Horizontal bamboo flute without membrane. (**4**)

São Bento grande Brazilian *berimbau* rhythmic pattern in *capoeira*. (**2**)

São Bento pequeno Brazilian *berimbau* rhythmic pattern in *capoeira*. (**2**)

sapeh (Also *sapiʾ*.) Kenyah-Kayan plucked lute. (**4**)

sapeur Member of the Society of Ambienceurs and Persons of Elegance. (**1**)

sappôsi (Japan.) Chinese ambassador to the Ryûkyû kingdom. (**7**)

saqfa suwaysī 'Suez clapping', complex syncopated clapping performed during wedding celebrations in the Suez. (**6**)

šara 'Ornament, iridescence'; small rhythmic shakes that characterize Pannonian dances in Croatia and Serbia. (**8**)

sarabande Stately (originally wild) seventeenth- and eighteenth-century dance in slow (originally fast) triple time with an accent on the second beat. (**8**)

saragi Vertical gong of the Ternate *kulintang* ensemble. (**4**)

sarakhbār Somber, meditative genre of Central Asian *maqām*. (**6**)

sarala gī 'Straight' or 'simple' song; twentieth-century genre of Sinhala light classical music. (**5**)

sarambo *Velación* genre based on the *zapateo* in the Dominican Republic. (**2**)

saranai Lowland Chăm double-reed aerophone. (**4**)

śaranaru Devotees of Shiva in Karnataka. (**5**)

sarāṅg (Also *sarān, sārindā, surindā, sarangi, sāraṅgī, sāraṅg*.) (1) Any of various bowed chordophones of southern Afghanistan, Pakistan, and North India. (2) Bowed chordophone with a short neck, a waisted, skin-covered body, and metal strings; used as both a solo and an accompanying instrument in Hindustani classical and folk music. (3) Bowed lute of Indian origin, used as a melodic instrument in Surinam, Guyana, Trinidad, and elsewhere by people of Indian heritage. (**2, 5, 10**)

saransara Maguzawa feast with dancing in northern Nigeria. (**1**)

saraos Evening parties with dancing and music in Costa Rica. (**2**)

saraphan Tuneful Buddhist chant for laypeople. (**4**)

sarasvatī pūjā Worship of Sarasvati, the goddess of learning and music, on the ninth day of Navrātrī. (**5**)

sarasvatī vīṇā Plucked stringed instrument associated with Sarasvati, in Karnatak music. (**5**)

saratoga Australian freshwater fish of the genus *Scleropages*. (**9**)

Volume Key: **6**, Middle East; **7**, East Asia; **8**, Europe; **9**, Australia and the Pacific Islands; **10**, The World's Music.

saravane Type of Cambodian rhythm, often used by Cambodian rock bands playing popular songs with Western instruments. (**3**)

sardana Catalonian urban-rural circle dance. (**8**)

sarewa Hausa four-holed flute, made of a reed or metal tube. (**1**)

sargam (Also *svara* syllables.) Indian sol-fa syllables. (**5**)

šargija Long-necked plucked four- to six-stringed lute of northern and central Bosnia. (**8**)

sāri' Quicker variant of the Yemeni *wasṭā* rhythm. (**6**)

sārindā (Also *sarān, sarāng, surindā.*) Bowed folk chordophone with a distinctive deeply waisted double body and a deep, arched back. (**5**)

şarki Ottoman light classical genre, played by Rom musicians in Macedonia. (**8**)

şarkı Urban form of the *türkü* folk song, first developed in the seventeenth century and still current. (**6**)

šarkuny Belarusan jingle bells. (**8**)

sarma Gumuz large clay kettledrum. (**1**)

sarnai (Also *shapar.*) Chuvash begpipe. (**8**)

sarocla 'Little mule', game-dance in Costa Rica. (**2**)

sarod Short unfretted plucked lute with a deep-waisted, skin-covered body that narrows into a metal-plated neck; one of the premier concert instruments of Hindustani music. (**5**)

sarogān Leader of a singing group in Balochistan. (**5**)

saron Indonesian metallophone with trough resonator. (**4**)

saron barung Javanese medium metallophone with trough resonator. (**4**)

saron demung Javanese large metallophone with trough resonator. (**4**)

saron peking Javanese small metallophone with trough resonator. (**4**)

sarronca Northwestern Portuguese friction drum, a clay pot with a narrow opening, covered with a skin that vibrates through the movement of a friction stick. (**8**)

sarswela Spanish-derived music-drama of the Philippines. (**4**)

sarugaka (Japan.) Popular theatrical entertainment established in the Heian period, a predecessor of *nô* and *kyôgen.* (**7**)

sarunay Miniature version of a *kulintang* in the Philippines. (**4**)

sarune (Also *sarunei.*) Reed aerophone of Sumatra. (**4**)

sarurun rimse (Japan.) 'Crane dance', genre of Ainu festival dance songs. (**7**)

sāruvayya Mendicant fortune-teller. (**5**)

Saruwaged Range Papua New Guinean mountains in Morobe, between the Markham River and the border with Madang. (**9**)

sasaa Vai gourd rattle. (**1**)

sasa biwa (Japan.) Another term for *môsô biwa.* (**7**)

sasando biola Diatonic *sasandu* used for hymns and folk songs. (**4**)

sasandu Multistringed tube zither with resonator from Roti. (**4**)

sasa-ture Dance for chaotic social situations in the former Bauchi state, Nigeria. (**1**)

sasi (Japan.) Recitative segment of a *nô* play, chanted in an unfixed rhythm with instrumental accompaniment. (**7**)

sasi zyô on (Japan.) Lowered *zyô* (the highest principal note in *nô* chanting) used at the beginning of the *sasi* segment of a *nô* play. (**7**)

sasŏl sijo Korean long narrative poems used as *sijo* song texts. (**7**)

śāstra Treatise, field of study. (**5**)

śāstriya Based on a rule or treatise. (**5**)

sastsrapo 'Urgent', Gurian panpipe; *see larchemi, soinari.* (**8**)

satandiro Mandinka extemporized vocal lines. (**1**)

satāra (Also *pāwā.*) Paired flute of Rajasthan with one pipe used as a drone, played by Laṅgās. (**5**)

sato Central Asian bowed lute; in Uygur Xinkiang, pear-shaped fiddle with three bowed strings and twelve sympathetic strings; related to *ghidjak.* (**6**)

sato kagura (Japan.) Local Shinto shrine music and dance. (**7**)

satong Kajang bamboo tube zither. (**4**)

satti (Also *śakti.*) 'Power' (Tamil), especially of a goddess. (**5**)

Satuma band (Japan.) First Japanese military ensemble formed by the clansmen of Simazu Hisamitu (1817–1887), lord of the Satuma clan (in present-day Kagosima Prefecture); modeled after an English military band in Yokohama led by John William Fenton (b. 1828). (**7**)

satuma biwa (Japan.) Form of the *biwa* (lute) and its music in southern Kyûsyû, a region called Satuma. (**7**)

satuma môsô biwa (Japan.) Blind priests' *biwa* (lute) tradition developed in southern Kyûsyû (Satuma). (**7**)

satvik 'Divine', 'noble', 'heroic', 'generous', 'refined'; character type in *kathakali* dance. (**5**)

sau 'Ground', Sumu funerary ritual held for the death of a woman. (**2**)

sauelokkar Norwegian ornamented hog-calls. (**8**)

saùn Arched harp of Burma (the last surviving harp in Southeast Asia), with a tradition that continues today. (**4, 5**)

savāl javāb Rhythmic question-and-answer exchange between instrumental soloist and accompanist in a Hindustani performance. (**5**)

savarngil Bamboo flute on Kai. (**4**)

savatarelle Variant of the *saltarello.* (**8**)

Savuka South African duo formed by Johnny Clegg after 1985. (**1**)

saw Northern Thai repartee song accompanied by *pi chum* ensemble. (**4**)

sawaere Wayana body of children's songs learned from the Saramaca Maroons in French Guiana. (**2**)

sawagoro Vanuatu genre of popular song. (**9**)

sawākāt Vocal genre in the Andalusian-Tunisian *nūba* derived from popular songs. (**6**)

sawari (Japan.) (1) Device on the neck of a *syamisen* to produce a special sound; (2) the sound this device produces. (**7**)

saw bang Northeastern Thai bowed tube zither. (**4**)

saw duang Two-stringed fiddle from Thailand. (**4**)

saw lakhawn Northern Thai theater. (**4**)

saw pip Northeast Thai bowed lute with metal can body. (**4**)

saw sam sai Thai three-stringed spike fiddle with coconut body. (**4**)

saw sam sai (Japan.) Thai three-stringed bowed lute. (**7**)

saw u Thai two-stringed fiddle with coconut body. (**4**)

sawng chan Medium-length rhythmic cycle in Thai music. (**4**)

sawng na Two-headed cylindrical drum of Thailand. (**4**)

ṣawt 'Voice', 'sound'. (1) Term for a classical Arab vocal repertoire. (2) Highly stylized song cycle of the Gulf region, often performed in prosperous homes. (3) Genre of popular music in the Gulf region. (**6**)

ṣawt al-tays Solo falsetto vocalist in a Tunisian ensemble. (**6**)

saya Afro-Bolivian tropical syncretic music style, formerly a praise song. (**2**)

say diev Half-gourd chest-resonated monochord of Cambodia. (**4**)

sayr 'Path', model for the unfolding of a *maqām* presented in theoretical or pedagogical contexts. (**6**)

sāz (1) Classical music or melody, in northern Pakistan; (2) music or musical instrument. (**5**)

saz (Also *s'az, sāz.*) (1) Fretted long-necked lute of Turkey, imported into the Balkans and Georgia during the Ottoman period and still played by Muslim minorities in some areas. (2) Armenian lute with a long pear-shaped body and long neck, usually with six to eight metal strings and ten to thirteen frets. (3) (Also *sornā*.) Long-necked fretted plucked Turkish and Azerbaijani folk lute. (4) One tube of a double aerophone (as in Persian *dosāz* 'two tubes'). (5) Any musical instrument; harmony, concord. (**6, 8**)

sāzanda Female wedding entertainer in Bukhara and Samarkand, Uzbekistan; cf. *khalfa*. (**6**)

sazandari Small Georgian ensembles of Middle Eastern musical instruments. (**8**)

sāzdohol Shawm and drum pair, in western Afghanistan. (**5**)

saze Albanian professional instrumental ensemble, generally of Roma. (**8**)

sāz-e-kashmīrī Spike fiddle, a relative of the Persian *kamanche*. (**5**)

sāzī Musicians; instrumentalists, in Balochistan. (**5**)

sāzinda Musicians; instrumentalists or instrument makers in Punjab, Pakistan. (**5**)

saz payı Instrumental interludes in Turkish vocal music. (**6**)

saz semai (Also *saz semaisi*.) Primary composed instrumental form in Turkish music. (**6**)

sbek tauch Khmer small-size shadow-puppet theater. (**4**)

sbek thomm Khmer large-shadow-puppet theater. (**4**)

scacciamarzo 'March-chaser', Italian spring celebration that includes the singing of *canti di questua*. (**8**)

scacciapensieri 'Care-chaser', northern Italian mouth harp; *see marranzanu*. (**8**)

ščadroŭki Belarusan songs for the winter solstice and Christmas. (**8**)

scallamanu Corsican children's game, accompanied by verses. (**8**)

scaloian Romanian rain-begging ritual, held in spring and summer and involving a mock funeral lament for a doll. (**8**)

scharminkelen Noisemaking on instruments and household utensils in the Dutch Low Countries. (**8**)

Scheitholt Medieval German name of the stringed instrument from which the Slovene drone zither evolved. (**8**)

Scheitholz German zither revived in the folk movement of the 1960s. (**8**)

schellenschötte 'Bell-shaking', Swiss technique of ringing bells in regular rhythm to accompany the singing of a *zäuerli*. (**8**)

Schlager Austrian and German popular musical hits. (**8**)

schlottere (Also *bääle, solo-doppeliere*.) Competitive heelwork in dances of Appenzell, Switzerland. (**8**)

Schnadahupfl (Also *Schnaderhüpfl*.) Song genre associated with Bavaria and Austria; consists of improvised texts alternating with a refrain. (**3**)

schnelzer Swiss accelerating yodels of Appenzell. (**8**)

schnitzelbänke Swiss derisive songs that critique political and social events of the past year. (**8**)

schnulze Austrian crooning song that expresses loneliness, farewell, and homesickness. (**8**)

Schnurpflockspannung (German.) Cord-and-peg tension for fastening single-headed drums. (**1**)

schola Latina 'Latin school', any of several schools founded in Romania during the Renaissance. (**8**)

schots (Also *schotz*.) 'Scottish', square dance of the Low Countries. (**8**)

schottische (Also *schottisch*.) (1) European couple dance in 2/4 time. (2) Dance or tune in 2/4 time similar to the polka, but somewhat slower. (**3, 8**)

Schrammel Nineteenth-century Viennese restaurant music. (**8**)

Schuhplattler Men's presentational dance of Austria and Germany, with elaborate foot and thigh slapping. (**8**)

schuppel Group of Swiss singers in winter festivals. (**8**)

schützenfest German annual interregional civil-militia celebration that uses tenor drums in its parades. (**8**)

Schwegel German fife. (**8**)

schwegepfyfli Swiss piccolo-like side-blown flute. (**8**)

Schwirrholz German bullroarer or thunderstick. (**8**)

schwyzerörgeli Swiss small diatonic accordion of Schwyz. (**8**)

schwyzerörgeli quartetten Swiss button accordion quartets. (**8**)

schwyzerpfyf Swiss solider's side-blown flute. (**8**)

schwyzerstil Musical style of central Switzerland that incorporates a B-flat clarinet, a *schwyzerörgeli*, a piano, and a double bass. (**8**)

schwyzer zither Swiss board zither, played mainly by women. (**8**)

sciotiscia 'Schottisch', Corsican dance. (**8**)

scordatura Any nonstandard tuning of stringed instruments. (**8**)

scotchi Competitive associations in East Africa that used bagpipes or locally made representations. (**1**)

scratch To produce percussive sounds from a vinyl recording by manually moving a selected part of a song rhythmically back and forth under a phonograph needle; common technique of hip-hop disk jockeys. (**3**)

scratch bands (Also *fungi* bands.) Ensembles identified with a movement to maintain native cultural traditions of the Virgin Islands; they perform at social dances, festivals, fairs, and private parties. (**2**)

scrubbers Small band of strolling musicians hoping for a reward from householders during the Christmas season in Barbados. (**2**)

se (China.) Ancient twenty-five-stringed zither, usually paired with the seven-stringed zither *qin*. (**7**)

seanchas Old Irish lore. (**8**)

sean-nós 'Old manner', style of singing with melodic ornamentation, especially prominent in the Irish-speaking areas of Munster and Connaught. (**8**)

sean-nós song 'Old style' song, unaccompanied solo song performed in Irish or English. (**3**)

Şeb-i'Arūs Melvlevī celebration on the anniversary of Jalûluddin Rûmî. (**6**)

sebiba Choreographed spectacle held at the oasis of Djanet, in southeastern Algeria. (**1**)

sechseläuten March performed during Sechseläuten, a Swiss festival, every April. (**8**)

seco Panamanian single-headed drum. (**2**)

sedláčká 'Peasant dance', Moravian couple dance with an uneven, offbeat-accented rhythm. (**8**)

sedyanka 'Sitting bee', Bulgarian autumnal social gatherings for spinning or embroidery, accompanied by singing. (**8**)

sefala (Also *sefela*.) Long, musical poetic narratives developed by Sotho veteran migrants on their travels to South African mines. (**1**)

sega Popular musical genre of Réunion Island. (**5**)

Sega la vecchia 'Saw the witch', Italian mid-Lenten ceremony with music. (**8**)

segon Haitian drum of medium size and pitch that "talks" with the *manman*. (**2**)

seguidilla (1) Cuban genre belonging to the *punto campesino* family. (2) Chilean genre with seven-line *cueca* stanzas of five and seven syllables with fourth line repeated. (3) Southern Spanish couple dance in moderately fast triple time, especially associated with Castile. (**2, 8**)

seguidillas (1) Song form with strophes of four or seven lines, each between five and seven syllables, frequently set to music in 6/8 meter; (2) one of the most popular Spanish dance types. (**3**)

segunda 'Second' (supporting) drum of the Garifuna in Belize. (**2**)

Segye samul nori kyŏrugi World *Samul nori* Contest. (**7**)

Şehnaz Common Turkish *makam* featuring augmented-second intervals. (**6**)

sei (Japan.) Solid, strong stroke on the *kakko* drum. (**7**)

Volume Key: **6**, Middle East; **7**, East Asia; **8**, Europe; **9**, Australia and the Pacific Islands; **10**, The World's Music.

seigan (Japan.) Chant (*syômyô*) for confessing and making vows to Buddha. (**7**)

sei ha (Japan.) 'Orthodox school' of *satuma biwa* preceding the founding of the Kinsin school in 1915. (**7**)

seihu (Japan.) Prescriptive notation developed by Hirano Kenji (b. 1929). (**7**)

Seikyoku ruisan (Japan.) 'Anthology of Pieces for Voice', six-volume historical study of genres of *zyôruri* published in the mid-nineteenth century by Saitô Gessin (1804–1878). (**7**)

seis 'Six' (Spanish). (1) Puerto Rican lively genre for dancing. (2) Puerto Rican slow genre for singing. (3) Small Venezuelan guitar with six strings. (4) Medium-fast duple strophic song-dance, set to the poetic form of a *décima*. (**2, 9**)

seisúns Irish traditional instrumental music sessions. (**3**)

seiza (Japan.) Kneeling position with the back held erect. (**7**)

Sejong sillok Korean 'Annals of King Sejong'. (**7**)

seka Communal music-making group in Bali and Lombok. (**4**)

sèkèrè (Also *sekere*.) Yoruba bottle-gourd rattle. (**1**)

sekeseke Warao rustic violin played for entertainment. (**2**)

sêkêti Often cryptic Surinam Maroon songs and dances that are a major form of social commentary. (**2**)

sekkyô (Japan.) Buddhist preaching. (**7**)

sekkyô busi (Japan.) Genre of Buddhistic folk music; also used in puppet drama. (**7**)

selâm (Also *selãm*.) Section within the Mevlevi *âyîn* ceremony. (**6**)

selampit Malay narrative genre accompanied by *rebab*. (**4**)

selengut (Also *selingut*.) North Borneo nose flute. (**4**)

sèlí (Also *pèrèsèkè*.) Yoruba tin cymbals with jingles, used to accompany *wáka*. (**1**)

selisir Tuning system for Balinese *gamelan pelégongan*. (**4**)

seljačko 'Of the village', narrow-interval singing style of the Croatian Dinaric Alps. (**8**)

seljefløyte Norwegian duct flute without holes for fingering. (**8**)

şelpe Style of playing the Turkish *bağlama* with the fingertips, derived from Central Asian practice. (**6**)

semā' Medieval Sufi musical ritual, term inherited by the Mevlevî sect, later also applied to the *zikr* of the Sunnî *tarikatlar* and to the *âyîn-i cem'* of the Alevî and Bektaşî sects. (**6**)

sema Ritual dance performed in Alevî ceremonies by couples. (**6**)

semach'i Korean rhythmic mode (*changdan*), moderate 9/8 meter. (**7**)

semagi Tiboli set of melody gongs. (**4**)

Semana Santa Holy Week. (**2**)

semaneros 'Workers by the week', Purépecha organized by Friar Juan de San Miguel for the study of European organ and choral practice. (**2**)

semangat 'Soul', 'enthusiasm' (Indonesia). (**4**)

semantic coherence Textual unity in both plot and diction. (**1**)

Semba Tropical Angolan national orchestra, founded after 1975 by the ministry of culture. (**1**)

seme (Japan.) (1) Higher register of the *ryûteki* (transverse flute in *gagaku*), produced by blowing strongly; (2) *tikuzen biwa* narrative and instrumental playing used for battle scenes. (**7**)

semenovna 'Simeon's daughter' (Russian), style of Gypsy song. (**8**)

semivocale Partial vowel sound, like /n/, as the basis for singing; cf. *vocale*. (**8**)

semma (Arabic *sama*.) Audition, listening, or concert among the Sufis. (**3**)

sempelong Riau flute for love magic. (**4**)

senaculo Outdoor Passion play. (**4**)

señalada Mapuche annual animal-branding gathering. (**2**)

senasawim Rattle with a wooden handle and metal disks, like a *sistrum*, among the Yaqui. (**2**)

senasum Guarijio *sistrum*. (**2**)

sencilla Chiapas marimba. (**2**)

sendratari Modern Indonesian dance-drama with music, created in the mid-twentieth century. (**4**)

sene Gong of West Timor. (**4**)

Senegambians People living west of the Mandinka in West Africa. (**1**)

sene hauh Trough xylophone of West Timor. (**4**)

sene kaka Six-stringed bamboo idiochord of West Timor. (**4**)

sene tufu Gong and drum ensemble of West Timor. (**4**)

seŋ feŋ Vai term for instrumental performance. (**1**)

senhor de bomfim 'Lord of good fire', genre brought to Africa by Brazilians and Cubans. (**1**)

senna 'Quarrel', Icelandic form of musical performance. (**8**)

senokos (Also *pokos*.) 'Haymaking' (Russian). (**8**)

senritu kei (Japan.) Generic term for melodic patterns. (**7**)

Sensacional Maringa da Angola Angolan fifteen-piece band that mixes *merengue*, *rumba*, and rural Angolan styles. (**1**)

Senufo Gur-speaking cultural group of north-central Côte d'Ivoire. (**1**)

senzu manzai (Japan.) Genre of medieval folk performance. (**7**)

seperewa (Also *sanku*.) Harp-lute of the Guinea Coast. (**1**)

sepha Thai narrative genre accompanied by a pair of *krap*. (**4**)

Sephardic Jews 'Spanish Jews', today referring to non-Ashkenazi Jews in Israel. (**6**)

sēpi Patron-client relationship in Punjab, Pakistan, that corresponds to the *jajmānī* system. (**5**)

se p'iri Small Korean double-reed bamboo oboe. (**7**)

sep noi (Also *maholi* in Vientiane.) Laotian string and flute ensemble of Luang Phrabang. (**4**)

sep nyai (Also *piphat* in Vientiane.) Laotian classical ensemble of Luang Phrabang. (**4**)

şer (Also *merxoş*.) Kurdish heroic sung narrative. (**6**)

serampang duabelas Malay twelve-step dance. (**4**)

serdam South Sumatra end-blown ring flute. (**4**)

sere Mbojo noble men's warrior dance. (**4**)

seremoni In Haiti, Vodoun service that includes song, dance, and drumming. (**2**)

serenata 'Serenade'. (1) Song genre frequently performed at Paraguayan *quinceañeras*; a courting, congratulatory, or devotional serenade. (2) *Serenatas*, the early hours, when *serenata* performances traditionally occur. (3) Among professional *mariachi* musicians, a short performance of several songs. (**2, 3**)

Serer Cultural group of north-central Côte d'Ivoire. (**1**)

serga Guruṅ funeral dance of Nepal. (**5**)

Serieng Papua New Guinean village in the center of the Rai Coast, immediately west of Saidor. (**9**)

serkalla Miri stamping dance. (**1**)

serndu Transverse flute of The Gambia. (**1**)

serone Single-reed clarinet of East Sumbawa. (**4**)

serpent (1) English undulating wooden lip-driven low-pitched aerophone with six holes for fingering. (2) Lip-vibrated wind instrument in serpentine form with six finger holes used as a bass instrument in military and church bands in the seventeenth and eighteenth centuries. (**3, 8**)

serra Pontic Greek dance. (**8**)

serraba Short introductory song in a quick meter, performed as part of *malhûn*. (**6**) *serragia* Sardinian bowed, one-stringed stick zither with a pig-bladder resonator. **(8)**

seruling (1) Malay whistle flute. (2) Bamboo ring-stop flute of Indonesia. **(4)**

serunai Malay multiple-reed wooden aerophone. **(4)**

serune (1) Sumatran reed aerophone; (2) Lombok single-rice-stalk aerophone, also a double-reed aerophone; (3) single-reed clarinet of West Sumbawa. **(4)**

şeşbendi Term for wedding songs in central Kurdistan, performed by close relatives of the bride and groom. **(6)**

sèsè Aesthetic quality of buzzing added to musical sounds by the Mandinka of Sierra Leone. **(1)**

sesŏng 'Fine voice', head voice with narrow vibrato used by Korean *kagok* singers. **(7)**

sesquiáltera (1) 'Hemiola' (Spanish), alternation between 3/4 and 6/8 times. (2) Spanish-derived dual meter consisting of superimposed 3/4 and 6/8, often with alternation or hemiola. **(2, 8)**

sesŭmmu Korean hereditary shaman. **(7)**

sesyû (Japan.) Hereditary transmission. **(7)**

setar (Also *setār, sehtar.*) (1) Iranian plucked lute. (2) 'Three strings' (Persian), long-necked lute with four strings, plucked with the nail of the index finger. (3) Long-necked fretted lute of the Persian music tradition. **(3, 5, 6)**

set dances European-derived Jamaican dances. **(2)**

seti Guatemalan square dance. **(2)**

settyû (Japan.) Fusion, blend. **(7)**

set-up Jamaican wake activities on the night of death. **(2)**

seudati Acehnese men's martial group dance. **(4)**

seung pong fai Laotian responsorial singing in the streets during the rocket festival. **(4)**

sevdalinke 'Love songs' of urban Muslim culture in Bosnia-Hercegovina; known as *turčije* 'Turkish-like' songs before the late 1800s. **(8)**

sewaa Competitive singing on Seram after a feast. **(4)**

sewa mono (Japan.) *Kabuki* plays and narrative *syamisen* music (*zyôruri*) dealing with the life of common people in the Edo period. **(7)**

sewei Sacred Warao strung rattle. **(2)**

sextilla Six-line *copla*. **(2)**

sextondelspolskor Form of Swedish *polska* in sixteenth-note rhythms predominant in southern and eastern Sweden. **(8)**

seyir Basic melody capturing the essentials of a Turkish *makam* for students. **(6)**

sez See *zorne.* **(6)**

sezarb Form of religious song in the Central Asian *zikr*, involving rhythmic refrains containing one of the names of God. **(6)**

sezatoarea Romanian social evenings, involving song, music, and dance. **(8)**

sgra-snyan Long-necked lute of Tibet and the entire Himalayan region. **(5)**

sgrung-mkhan Tibetan bard whose repertoire is centered on the hero Ge-sar. **(5)**

shabbāba End-blown cane flute. **(6)**

shabd kīrtan (Also *shabad.*) Sikh song form. **(5)**

sha'bi (Also *sha'bī.*) (1) Genre of Maghrib popular music. (2) Urban popular style of North Africa, developed in the 1930s and influenced by Western jazz and popular music. (3) Generic term for "folk" music in the Mashriq. **(1, 6)**

shabih See *ta'zīye.* **(6)**

shabori (Also *sablí, sapuli, saboli, shapori, shaboliwa.*) Yanomamö shaman. **(2)**

shadd (Plural, *shudūd.*) Name for a mode in the school of al-Urmawī. **(6)**

Shādhiliyya One of the oldest and most prominent North African Sufi brotherhoods. **(6)**

shagird Apprentice or student to a master musician (*ustaz*) in Central Asia. **(6)**

shahānā Punjabi songs for weddings. **(5)**

shāhed 'Witness tone', tonal center of a *gūshe* in Persian music. **(6)**

shāh gūshe 'King *gūshe*', primary *gūshe* in Persian music, forming the basic modal sections of the *dastgāh* structure. **(6)**

Shāh-nāme (Also *Shāhnāma.*) Epic poem in Persian composed by Ferdowsī in the tenth century C.E., fourth century A.H., formerly recited in teahouses by *naqqāl-hā.* **(6)**

shāhrūd Type of medieval box zither. **(6)**

shāir Poet in Balochistan. **(5)**

shā'ir (Plural, *shu'ara'.*) Professional poet-epic singer. **(6)**

shairi Georgian folk-poetry competitions. **(8)**

shakap Ecuadorian fruit-capsule waist rattle. **(2)**

shakl Solo instrumental prelude to a *maqām* performance in Kashmir. **(5)**

shakkas Jamaican maracas. **(2)**

shak-shak (1) Onomatopoeic name for an idiophone rattle made of mahogany or poinciana tree pod with its seeds inside (respectively, in the Bahamas and Barbados). (2) Common maracas in Guyana. **(2)**

shakuhachi (Also *syakuhati.*) Japanese notched vertical bamboo flute with four finger holes and one thumb hole (played also by some people of Japanese descent in Brazil), whose sound has become familiar to Western audiences through "new age," world beat, and other popular genres. **(2, 3, 4, 7, 9)**

shaman Animistic medium who enters a trance state and is said to communicate and deal with spirits. **(4)**

shambar Instrumental form in Algerian classical music, of Turkish origin. **(6)**

sham'dān 'Candelabra', dance with candelabra. **(6)**

shamisen (Also *syamisen.*) 'Samisen'. Japanese box-shaped three-stringed long-necked fretless lute, played with a plectrum; also found among people of Japanese heritage in Brazil and Peru. **(3, 7, 9)**

shanbaal Carved wooden handheld clappers played in southern Somalia. **(1)**

shanbar Instrumental overture within the Andalusian-Tunisian *nūba.* **(6)**

shangdiao (China.) Pentatonic structure (re-mi-sol-la-do) that emphasizes the pitches re and la. **(7)**

shan'ge (China.) Mountain songs. **(7)**

shangju (China.) Upper or first textual line. **(7)**

Shango (Also Xangô, in Brazil; Changó, in Cuba and Miami; Şango.) (1) Yoruba god of thunder. (2) Yoruba 'power', music devoted to the *orisa* deity of fire. *See also* Sango. **(1, 2)**

shang-qobyz Kazakh term for a Jew's harp played mainly by women. **(6)**

shangshou (China.) 'Upper hand'; refers to the main storyteller in *Suzhou tanci.* **(7)**

shanshui (China.) Mountain and water. **(7)**

shantu Hausa women's percussion tube. **(1)**

shaoshu minzu (China.) National minorities. **(7)**

shapar (Also *sarnai.*) Chuvash bagpipe. **(8)**

shape-note notation Type of notation in which the shape of the note head indicates the solmization syllable of the note. **(3)**

shaptāgi Baluchi vocal genre, performed for six days following the birth of a child. **(6)**

sharakan Canonical hymns sung in the Armenian divine office. **(6)**

sharaknots Collection of *sharakan* hymns. **(6)**

shareero Coastal Somali six-stringed lyre. **(1)**

sharh Popular couples dance of southern Yemen. **(6)**

sharia 'The path to follow', Islamic law. **(5)**

sharki Albanian large long-necked plucked lute, popular in Kosova. **(8)**

sharmanka Russian street barrel organ. **(8)**

sharqī 'Eastern', term for Egyptian styles that became popular in twentieth-century Algeria along with jazz and European dance music. **(6)**

shashmaqam Central Asian melodic modes linked to Polish folk music. **(8)**

shash maqām (Also *shashmakom, shashmaqom.*) 'Six *maqāmāt*', repertoire of Uzbek and Tajik classical art song native to Bukhara and Samarkand. **(6)**

shatam Sudanese small single-headed cup-shaped clay drum. (1)

shāyarī kajalī Professional or semiprofessional form of the Bhojpuri folk music genre *kajalī*. (5)

shaykh Traditional honorary title bestowed on (1) an elder; (2) a tribal leader; (3) a religious scholar; (4) a Sufi spiritual leader; (5) a religious singer (*munshid*). (6)

shebeen Unlicensed bar, often a private home, where patrons gather to drink and perform music. (1)

shedag Chechen and Ingush double reed with a straight pipe. (8)

shekeres Beaded gourd rattle used in Afro-Cuban music. (3)

shekī Performance (*lēb*) including music, singing, sacrifice, and trance, by a *shek* (spiritual guide) or *gwātī-ē māt* (spiritual healer). (5)

shemba Subanen term for short songs. (4)

shenai Conical double-reed aerophone from India. (4)

sheng (1) Chinese free-reed mouth organ, similar to the Japanese *sho* (*syô*). (2) Mature male role in Chinese opera. (3, 4, 7)

sheng-ming (Japan.) Chinese terms for *syômyô* (Buddhist chant). (7)

shengqiang (China.) Systems of tunes; this term also implies general modal characteristics and vocal ornaments. (7)

shenqu (China.) Shanghai musical pieces. (7)

shēparjā In Balochistan, ritual dance performed with drum accompaniment. (5)

shēr (1) In Balochistan, long verse narrative without refrain, sung by minstrels with string accompaniment or recited by common people without musical accompaniment. (2) Baluchi epic or courtly poem, sung with simple, measured refrains. (5, 6)

shertpe 'Plucking', 'flicking', 'fingering'; type of Kazakh *kyui* (instrumental music) involving the plucking of strings by individual fingers. (6)

shetani Spirits believed to possess and afflict Swahili-speaking people of East Africa. (1)

shiapshe yeredkher Adighian healing songs. (8)

shibāba Shepherd's flute; see *shabbaba*. (6)

shible ydj Adighian circle dance honoring the god of thunder. (8)

shidaiqu (China.) Contemporary songs. (7)

shifan luogu (China.) Drum and percussion style of Zhejiang Province that is musically related to *Jiangnan sizhu*. (7)

shifu Teacher, within the context of Cantonese music societies. (3)

shigin Japanese recited poetry. (9)

shigin Melodies set to Chinese poems. (3)

shigongxian (China.) One of the fourth modes in Cantonese music (la-do-re-mi-sol), also known as the la-mi mode. (7)

shikh (Plural, *shikhāt*.) Professional musician of Berber Morocco. (6)

shimolo Set of bells that Chagga male dancers of Tanzania wear on their backs. (1)

Shinto See *Sintô*. (7)

shi'r Poetry. (6)

shirah betsibur 'Communal singing', Israeli institution in which an audience gathers to sing songs whose texts are projected on a screen or distributed on paper. (6)

Shirati Jazz Band founded by D. O. Misiani to play *benga*. (1)

shirei erets Yisrael 'Songs of the land of Israel', specific repertoire of folk songs in modern Hebrew canonized by the political establishment. (6)

shīrīn navāzī 'Sweetened style' of the Persian *radīf* demanded by the new bourgeois society of twentieth-century Iran. (6)

shiriri Luhyia one-stringed lute-fiddle. (1)

Shiva Hindu deity. (4)

sho (Also *syô*.) Japanese mouth organ. (7, 10)

sho'be Modal branch in Persian music. (6)

shofar Ram's-horn military and religious trumpet of the ancient Hebrews, now blown on Jewish high holidays and in synagogues during certain important services. (6, 8)

Shona People of Zimbabwe. (1)

shouling (China.) Handheld bell used mostly for religious purposes. (7)

shpelāi Duct flute of the North West Frontier Province. (5)

shtayger 'Climber' (Yiddish), any of several modes of Ashkenazic Jewish music. (8)

shuangling (China.) Double bell. (7)

shūbāsh Precomposed congratulatory song performed at a Palestinian wedding for the entry of the groom after he has gotten dressed. (6)

shu'be 'Branch', referring to a subdivision of pieces within the Bukharan *shash maqām*. (6)

shuchang (China.) Recital halls for storytelling. (7)

Shudra (*Śūdra*) Group or class (*varṇa*) in Hindu society, traditionally the artisans and laborers. (5)

shuffle In country and bluegrass fiddle music, a term used to describe bowing techniques that produce rhythmic two-note chord patterns. (3)

shuffle rhythm Triplet pattern characterized by a quarter-note triplet followed by an eighth note triplet. (3)

shughl Vocal form in the Mashriq, similar to the *muwashshah*. (6)

shukonghou (China.) Vertical angular harp that was imported from western Asia during the Han dynasty. (7)

shukster Chordophone made with guitar string stretched from end to end on the side of a wooden house in Barbados. (2)

shuochang (China.) 'Speaking and singing'; refers to all oral performing arts, such as narrative songs and storytelling. (7)

shūr Most fundamental and characteristic mode in the Iranian musical system. (6)

shūrī One of the primary Arab *maqāmāt*. (6)

shuvyr Mari bagpipe. (8)

sì Pair of small, bell-shaped cymbals from Burma. (4)

sia Nocturnal mimetic dance that originated in the Siasi Islands and spread to become a cultural icon of the Mamose Region of Papua New Guinea. (9)

Siamese Former name for peoples of Thailand. (4)

siang tok Melodic pitch simultaneous with final drum cycle stroke in Thai music. (4)

siasid Tiruray parables. (4)

sibai uta (Japan.) *Ziuta* repertoire (*syamisen* music) derived from *kabuki*. (7)

sibi ch'a, sibi ch'ae 'Twelve sequences' or 'twelve bears'; rhythms used by Korean folk bands. (7)

sibi kasa 'Twelve *kasa*', long Korean vocal narrative song cycle. (7)

sibizgi Balkar and Karachaevi shepherd's whistle flute. (8)

si byôsi (Japan.) Four instruments used in *nô*: *nô-kan*, *ko tuzumi*, *ô tuzumi*, and *taiko*. (7)

sichyāh Cymbals, in Nepal. (5)

sidai (Japan.) (1) Introductory section of *nô* drama; (2) *nô* instrumental piece for the entrance of a living person or a reincarnated character; (3) *kyôgen* instrumental piece for the entrance of a character. (7)

sidapurna Acrobatic performance of Cirebon. (4)

side drum Snare drum. (8)

sidekah bumi Earth blessing ceremony of Cirebon. (4)

sienakosnyja pieśni Belarusan haying songs. (8)

sierszeńki (Also *siesieńki*, *pancharzyna*.) Bagpipe for beginners in western Poland. (8)

sifang (China.) Four quarters or directions (north, south, east, west). (7)

sife Side-blown flute of the Low Countries. (8)

sigimsae 'Refined vocal techniques', aesthetic quality in Korean vocal music. (7)

sigin (Japan.) Recitation of Chinese poems. (7)

Sigmundarkvœði Faroe Island epic songs (*kvœði*) that contain a verse recounting the original settlement of the islands. (8)

sihu (China.) Four-stringed spiked bowed lute of the northeast, used to accompany ballads and narratives. (7)

sihû (Japan.) Traditional *samurai* style of playing the *satuma biwa*. (7)

sijo Short lyric songs of Korea. (7)

sijo ch'ang 'Sijo singing', performance of Korean *sijo*. (7)

sijŏlga Literary form of Korean *sijo* poems. (7)

sīkā One of the major notes of the Arab fundamental scale. (6)

sikisyû (Also called *daisyû*.) In Japan, Buddhist monks, except for the head monk who leads a ceremony. (7)

sikkim kut Korean shaman ritual for the dead. (7)

sikô (Japan.) Finger hole. (7)

sikro (Also *sikru* 'world'.) Sumu and Miskitu funerary ritual held for the death of a man. (2)

śikṣā Phonetic manual. (5)

siku (Also *sico*; plural, *sikuri*, in Bolivia.) Double-unit panpipe consisting of six to eight (or more, seventeen tubes in Bolivia) closed cane tubes per half, requiring two people to play one instrument by interlocking the music; *see also arca, ira*. (2)

sikuai (China.) Percussion instrument used in *nanguan*, made of four pieces of wood. (7)

sikuri (1) Sets or groups of *siku* or *siku* performers; (2) type of music played by particular *siku* groups in Peru. (2)

silat Malaysian dance derived from the martial arts, with drum accompaniment. (4)

Silla Korean dynastic period, 57 B.C.E. to 668 C.E. (7)

sillok Korean dynastic annals. (7)

silsila Dervishes of the Qādiri order in Kashmir. (5)

silsile Chain of initiates or genealogy reaching back to the Prophet. (6)

silu Double-reed aerophone of Sumbawa. (4)

silung Maguindanao form of modern *binalig*. (4)

silväschtertrösche Swiss threshing in rhythmic patterns. (8)

silvesterchläuse Clapper bell of Wald, Zurich, Switzerland. (8)

silvesterklüuse Jingle bells on a harness in Oberschau, St. Gallen, Switzerland. (8)

simai (Japan.) *Nô* dancing. (7)

simaku Transverse flute of West Timor. (4)

simanjemanje (1) Urban dance-song, drawing from South African choral music. (2) Soft female chorus that backs up a male "groaner" in South African *mbaqanga*. (1)

sima uta (Japan.) Okinawan or Amami entertainment songs accompanied by the *sansin* (three-stringed lute); in the Amami Islands, the Amami *sansin* may be used for accompaniment. (7)

simbang (1) Archaic Korean term for a shaman; (2) shaman from Cheju Island in Korea. (7)

simbanggok Shaman-based music of Korea. *See sinawi*. (7)

simbing Manding six- or seven-stringed arched harp that is smaller than the *bolon*. (1)

simbolo Frame drum played by the Italian minority in Istria, Croatia. (8)

Simchas Torah 'Rejoicing of the Torah', Jewish autumn religious holiday with processions and ecstatic dances. (8)

simd Most popular Ossetian dance. (8)

sime daiko (Japan.) Drum with leather heads attached by cords to a cylindrical body. (7)

simo gakari (Japan.) Konparu, Kongô, and Kita schools of *nô* specializing in the main role (*site*) and the attendant role (*ture*). (7)

sīmorgh Mythical bird in Iranian mythology, symbolizing the celestial soul, the spiritual guide and physician, the object of the quest; the most important piece of music in the Baluchi *gwātī* ceremony, with numerous variants. (6)

simpa Japanese new school theater. (7)

simsimyya Small lyre with bowl-shaped body and five strings, used primarily in Egypt and Yemen. (6)

sin (1) (Also *xian*, in pinyin romanization.) Cantonese word for mode (China). (2) Printed calligraphic style of Chinese characters, a concept applied to various arts (Japan). (7)

sinād Genre of highly ornamented songs sung to classical Arabic poetry, typical of women's music of the medieval Arabian Peninsula. (6)

sinaguna Maguindanao modern *kulintang* playing. (4)

sinandung North Sumatra women's wistful dance-song. (4)

siŋar Ingassana gourd trumpet. (1)

sinawi Accompanying music for a Korean shaman's dance, now performed as an independent ensemble genre. (7)

sinch'ŏng Korean shaman associations. (7)

sindhī sāraṅgī Small bowed unfretted lute played by Laṅgā musicians or Rajasthan. (5)

sindil Maguindanaon love songs. (4)

sindīrana Mythic male doll representing a son of Kali; the dance in which the doll is carried. (5)

sīne be sīne 'Chest to chest' or, by extension, 'memory to memory' (Persian); oral transmission. (6)

sinebui Garifuna shaman in Belize. (2)

sineta (Also *adjá*.) Small bronze bell in Uruguay. (2)

sīne-zanī 'Breast-beating' (Persian), responsorial singing of *nowḥe* by Shī'a men who strike their shoulders with small, light chains as they move in rhythm. (6)

sing Pair of Lao small cymbals connected with cord. (4)

sin gaku (Japan.) Folk music of the Chinese Qing dynasty introduced to Japan in the 1820s and 1830s. (7)

sing'anga Tumbuka local herbalist. (1)

singapop Singaporean popular songs of the 1980s and 1990s. (4)

singing pubs English alehouses or pubs where customers sing for enjoyment. (8)

Singon (Japan.) Buddhist sect founded by Kûkai (774–835) during the Heian period. (7)

singon (Japan.) Mantra, a category of Buddhist chant (*syômyô*). (7)

Singon syômyô (Japan.) *Syômyô* (Buddhist chant) school of the Singon sect, founded by Kûkai (774–835) in the Heian period. (7)

singsing In Papua New Guinea, performance of a song or songs, especially in public, with dancing by decorated performers. (9)

sin gyô sô (Japan.) Three calligraphic styles of Chinese characters, a concept applied to various arts. (7)

sinh tiền Vietnamese scraped wooden clapper with jingling coins. (4)

sinkinī In the Gulf region, dance performed to mournful poetry while pearl divers' vessels were readied for sea. (6)

sin minyo Newly composed Korean folk songs. (7)

sinnai busi (Also *sinnai*.) Genre of Japanese narrative *syamisen* music begun by Turuga Sinnai (d. 1810). (7)

sinnai nagasi (Japan.) Street performance of *sinnai busi* (*syamisen* music) by pairs of players; also, the performers. (7)

sin nihon ongaku (Japan.) New movement in Japanese music during the Taisyô period (1912–1926), led by Miyagi Mitio (1894–1956); also, the Western-influenced music for Japanese instruments that was born from this movement. (7)

sin no zyo no mai (Japan.) Slowest *nô* dance, performed by an old god. (7)

sinobue (Japan.) *See take bue*. (7)

sinŏmŏni 'Spiritual mother', initiating shaman in Korea. (7)

sinotcha (Japan.) Ainu lyric songs expressing the emotions of everyday life. (7)

Sino-Tibetan Language family including Burmese, Hmong, and Yao. (4)

sinrili Buginese-Makassarese epics and traditional stories. (4)

Sin sarugaku ki (Japan.) Essay of c. 1050 that describes performing arts and entertainments of the time. (7)

Sinsen gakudô ruizyû taizen (Japan.) 'Newly Edited Anthology on the Way of Music', thirty-volume historical and theoretical work on *gagaku* by Oka Masana (1681–1759). (7)

sinsiru Bolivian bronze llama bells. (2)

Sintô (Japan.) Indigenous religion of Japan; in English, Shinto. (7)

sintren Ensemble of stamping tubes and pots in Cirebon. (4)

sinug Tausug two-part *kulintang* piece. (4)

sinulug Maguindanao rhythmic mode. (4)

sin ŭmak Korean newly composed music. (7)

Sin Yatuhasi ryû (Japan.) School of *koto* derived from the Ikuta *ryû*. (7)

Siomucha (Also *Zialonyja śviatki*.) Belarusan Pentecost. (8)

sipatt Prayer and praise songs sung on the birth of a child, in Balochistan. (5)

sipsi Small Turkish reed or bamboo clarinet. (6)

sîra (Plural, *siyar*.) Traditional genre of Arabic versified heroic narratives. (6)

sirabe o (Japan.) Cords attaching two pieces of leather to the body of the *taiko* and *tuzumi* drums used in *nô*. (7)

sira byôsi (Japan.) Dance by women in male attire, popular in the twelfth century; also, the professional women who performed it. (7)

siragi gaku (Japan.) Music imported from the Korean kingdom of Silla. (7)

siragoe (Also *sirakoe*.) In Japan, *heikyoku* vocal melody pattern (*kyokusetu*) in declamatory style. (7)

Sîrat Banî Hilâl Lengthy epic of the Banî Halâl bedouin tribe (Egypt), one of the last epics to survive in oral tradition. (6)

siratò Hungarian funeral lament. (8)

sîrba Romanian line dance. (8)

sirijna Balkar and Karachaevi double reed with a flared bell. (8)

sirinata a i sposi 'Serenade for the couple', Corsican *currente* sung at a wedding. (8)

sirinato Italian song type preserved in Corsica; some examples are locally composed and sung to *lamentu* or *puesia* tunes. (8)

sirínus 'Sirens', Andean supernatural beings, often carved into the necks of *charangos* and harps. (2)

sirongaganding Maranao tube zither. (4)

sirventes French satiric troubadour songs. (8)

sisheng (Japan.) Chinese reading of *sisyô*. (7)

sisi (Japan.) *Nô* dance portraying a lion spirit living in a holy mountain. (7)

sisi odori (Japan.) Folk song quoted in *gidayû busi*. (7)

sisira Container rattle of the main Garifuna shaman in Belize (also *magara*) and Guatemala (also *chichira*). (2)

Sisters Trung Two celebrated Vietnamese sisters who led a rebellion against the Chinese about 40 C.E. (4)

sistrum Shaken idiophone consisting of rattles attached to a stick or frame. (1)

sisya Disciple; music student. (5)

sisyô (Japan.) Four kinds of intonation used for each Chinese character of texts in Buddhist chant (*syômyô*). (7)

Sita Female leading character from the Indian epic *Ramayana*. (4)

sita mori (Japan.) *Syamisen* pattern in *gidayû busi*. (7)

sitar (Also *sitār*.) (1) Long-necked plucked lute of North India. (2) Hindustani long-necked, fretted, plucked lute; one of the premier concert instruments of Hindustani music. (3, 4, 5)

sit-down dance Torres Strait Islanders' adaptation of Sāmoan singing and dancing. (9)

site (Japan.) Principal actor in *nô* theater. (7)

site kata (Japan.) *Nô* actors who play the main character (*site*) and the attendant role (*ture*). (7)

siter Small Javanese board zither. (4)

sīthangan (Also *oṭṭan*, *paṛayan*.) One of three kinds of popular dance drama (*tuḷḷal*) in Kerala. (5)

Sitiku syosin syû (Japan.) 'Beginners' Pieces for String and Bamboo Instruments' (1664), instruction manual for amateur *koto*, *syamisen*, and *syakuhati* players. (7)

sitisei (Japan.) Japanese and ancient Chinese heptatonic scale. (7)

sito Large, double-headed "royal" drum of Burma. (4)

siṭṭhnī Songs of insult in the Indian Punjab. (5)

śivēli Temple procession ritual in Kerala. (5)

sivpada Quatrain with lines of equal length; popular framework for prosody in the Kotte period. (5)

siwo Yekuana bark trumpet. (2)

sīyāh-bāzī Iranian comic improvised theater involving dance. (6)

siyāhī Circle of black paste placed on the heads of Hindustani drums to aid tuning and resonance. (5)

siyem Medium hanging gong of Java. (4)

Siyong hyangakpo 'Collection of Current Korean Music', Korean historical document, including folk music, c. 1500. (7)

sizhu Indoor ensemble from China. (4)

sizu gaki (Japan.) Basic plucking pattern of the *gakusô* (zither used in *gagaku*). (7)

sjŏ̄ Bronze bell of the Guruṅg shaman in Nepal. (5)

Sjurdarkvœði Faroe epic songs (*kvœði*) dealing with Germanic legends about Sigurd the Dragonslayer. (8)

ska Jamaican dance music that began in the early 1960s, performed by a small rock-style band and especially popular in Britain. (2, 8)

skald Ancient Icelandic and Norwegian poet-singer. (8)

skamarochi (Also *hurtkam-paniya*, *kapela*, *muzyki*, *viasielnyja muzyki*.) 'Minstrels', Belarusan traditional folk instrumental ensemble. (8)

skamóra (Also *fam*, *puzyŕ*, *válonka*.) Mordvinian bagpipe. (8)

skiffle Music played on folk instruments and on "found" instrumentation such as jugs, washboards, and so on; popular among African-Americans in the 1920s; experienced a revival in England and Ireland in the 1950s and 1960s. (3)

skiladhika 'Dogs' dens', working-class establishments where Greek urban popular music was performed; *see bouzoukia*. (8)

skillingtryck Swedish broadside ballads. (8)

skiparar Leader of line dancing in the Faroe Islands. (8)

skipping process Uniquely African way of producing harmony by singing a note and the next one after skipping one. (1)

skomorokhi Russian secular minstrels. (8)

skor arakk Khmer single-headed goblet-shaped drum of clay or wood. (4)

skor chey Khmer two-headed cylindrical drum. (4)

skor chhaiyaim Long, vase-shaped single-headed Khmer drum. (4)

skor khek Pair of long drums from Cambodia. (4)

skor klang khek Khmer long, cylindrical, two-headed drums. (4)

skor thomm (1) Large double-headed barreled drum, Cambodian percussion instrument played as part of the *pinnpeat* ensemble. (2) Pair of large barrel drums from Cambodia. (3, 4)

skor yike Large frame drum in *yike* theater of Cambodia. (4)

Skotse fjoar 'Scottish four', square dance of Terschelling Island. (8)

Skotse trije 'Scottish three', national dance of Friesland in the late nineteenth century. (8)

skripka 'To squeak', Russian violin made of glued pieces of wood with three strings. (8)

skroud St. Lucian homemade local banjo. (2)

skrypka Belarusan and Ukrainian fiddle or violin. (8)

skrzypce 'Violin' (Polish). (8)

skrzypce podwiązane 'Bound-up violin', referring to the Polish practice of binding the neck of factory-made violins to tune them to the bagpipe. **(8)**

skudutis Lithuanian panpipes, played in ensembles of three to seven. **(8)**

skur-orgel Barker's stick, made of building materials and used to accompany the singing of Danish builders as they waited in the workmen's shack for the weather to clear so that they could resume work. **(8)**

sláciková muzika Eastern Moravian and Slovakian string band of two to four stringed instruments. **(8)**

slack-key tuning (Hawaiian *kī hōalu.*) Hawaiian-developed method of playing acoustic guitar by which the player loosens the strings to alter the tuning. **(9)**

šlageri 'Hits', Croatian songs popularized in operettas and films. **(8)**

slametan Indonesian ritual that affirms the unity of the Javanese community in Surinam. **(2)**

slått Norwegian *hardingfele* piece. **(8)**

slava (1) Serbo-Croatian celebration in honor of a family's or a church's patron saint, for which musicians may be hired. **(2)** Saint's-day celebration in Macedonia and Serbia, an important occasion for dancing. **(3, 8)**

slavianofily 'Slavophiles', advocates of vernacular Russian traditions. **(8)**

slavonsko kolo 'Slavonian kolo', circle dance of Slavonia. **(8)**

slekk Tree-leaf mirliton of Cambodia. **(4)**

sléndro (Also *saléndro* in Sunda.) Nearly equidistant tuning system, found throughout Indonesia. **(4)**

slédro gamelan Five-tone *gamelan*. **(10)**

sléttubönd Elaborate Icelandic verse form using palindromic rhymes to deliver coded messages. **(8)**

slide Irish jig in 12/8 time. **(8)**

slip jig Irish jig in 9/8 time; Irish traditional dance tune and dance step in 9/8 rhythm. **(3, 8)**

sloboda (Also *posad.*) Russian suburban zone, with its own styles of music. **(8)**

śloka (1) Metrical couplet; verse; (2) ancient prosodic meter used for devotional and didactic texts, usually recited in a highly stylized manner. **(5)**

slomprèt Double-reed aerophone. **(4)**

slow air (Also lament.) Type of Irish traditional instrumental tune. **(3)**

sluday Bilaan polychordal tube zither. **(4)**

smørbon Norwegian butter-making song. **(8)**

smṛti Tradition. **(5)**

smyrneika Greek songs of Smyrna. **(8)**

snare drum Small cylindrical wooden-shelled two-headed drum with snares stretched over the lower head; cf. *tenor drum*. **(8)**

snehet-snehet Songs of advice on Kai. **(4)**

sneng Khmer animal horn with free reed. **(4)**

snitra Algerian term (diminutive of *sanṭūr*) for the Western mandolin, introduced in the eighteenth century. **(6)**

so Korean panpipes. **(7)**

sô (Japan.) (1) Synonym for *koto*; (2) cursive, elegant style of Chinese characters, a concept applied to various arts. **(7)**

sôbāna Wedding songs performed by women in Karnataka. **(5)**

sobor Fair with music and dancing in Macedonia. **(8)**

soborski pesni 'Fair songs', urban-influenced Macedonian songs. **(8)**

soca Modern, danceable Trinidadian calypso form, short for soul calypso. **(2)**

socabón (Also *socavón.*) Simple Peruvian guitar accompaniment to the *décima*. **(2)**

Society for Ethnomusicology Professional society with headquarters in the United States but open to interested persons worldwide. **(1)**

Society of Ambienceurs and Persons of Elegance Trend set by the Zaïrean musician Papa Wemba, who in the 1970s cultivated a style of dress reminiscent of Parisian fashion of the 1950s and eighteenth-century dandyism. **(1)**

sŏdo minyo Korean folk songs in the western style. **(7)**

sofračke pjesme Table songs in Bosnia-Hercegovina. **(8)**

sôga (Also *enkyoku.*) Extinct vocal form, popular with Japanese priests and the military classes in the fourteenth and fifteenth centuries. **(7)**

sogak Korean music. **(7)**

sogo (Also *pŏpku.*) Small Korean hand drums. **(7)**

sogonghu Korean thirteen-stringed harp, now obsolete. **(7)**

sogŭm Small Korean transverse flute. **(7)**

sohar Songs performed at the birth of an Indian baby, in Trinidad and Guyana. **(5)**

so i Lao two-stringed fiddle with cylindrical body. **(4)**

soinari 'Hollow', Gurian panpipe; see *larchemi, sastsrapo*. **(8)**

soitto Improvisation on the Finnish *kantele*. **(8)**

soittokunta Finnish brass bands that developed in the United States in the late nineteenth and early twentieth centuries, sponsored by temperance societies and socialist organizations. **(3)**

sŏk Portion of a larger Korean shaman ritual. **(7)**

sokačke pesme Songs performed by young people on street corners in Vojvodina, Serbia. **(8)**

sokak 'Street', 'lane'; musical classification used by Vojvodina Serbs describing where people sing street songs. **(8)**

sokari Folk play of the up-country Sinhala people of Sri Lanka. **(5)**

Sŏkchŏn 'Sacrifice to Confucius', Korean ritual performance. **(7)**

sokch'ŏng 'Inner voice', head voice with narrow vibrato used by Korean *kagok* singers. **(7)**

sôke (Japan.) Master of an artistic clan. **(7)**

sô kengyô (Japan.) Highest position within the *kengyô*, the highest rank in the *tôdô* (guild for blind artisans). **(7)**

sŏkhwaje Cheerful, peaceful Korean melodic mode, used in *p'ansori*. **(7)**

sokusarv Estonian buckhorn trumpet, often with holes for fingering. **(8)**

sôkyoku (Japan.) *Koto* music. **(7, 10)**

Soldatenlieder German songs about soldiers and war. **(3)**

soldatskie pesni 'Soldiers' song', any of numerous Russian city songs with fanfare-like melodies. **(8)**

soleá Type of Spanish *cante jondo* based on a complex 12-beat rhythmic structure; see *palos siguiriyas*. **(8)**

solfège (Also *solfeggio*, Italian; Wilhem method.) French name of the fixed-do system of sol-fa syllables in which vocables signify absolute pitches. **(8)**

śolkaṭṭu Spoken rhythms derived from drum sounds in Karnatak music. **(5)**

sŏllongje Exclamatory Korean melodic mode, used in *p'ansori*: (1) (Also *kwŏnmasŏngje.*) 'Loud call style'. (2) *Hogŏclche* 'heroic style'. **(7)**

solmization System of sol-fa syllables that represent interval relationships within the tonal scheme and can be placed at any pitch level. **(8)**

sōma Mask dance of Karnataka. **(5)**

someak Inuit-Eskimo single-headed frame drum with a short handle of wood, ivory, or bone on the lower side of the instrument. **(3)**

son Breton-language songs; see *chanson*. **(8)**

son (Plural, *sones*; diminutive, *sonecito*; possibly from *sonar* 'to sound'.) (1) Mexican genre at the core of most regional musical styles oriented toward accompanying social dance, with vigorous, marked rhythm and fast tempo. (2) Cuban song tradition forming a type of *son* complex of genres. (3) Cuban strophic song with interludes of instrumental improvisation and fixed *clave*. (4) Traditional musical genre of Cuba, popular in Africa as a result of dissemination on gramophone records. (5) In Mexico, a *mestizo* musical genre marked by regional traditions, usually with vigorous rhythm, simple harmony, and strophic form. (**1, 2, 3, 10**)

son jarocho Variety of *son* associated with the *jarocho* regional culture of southern coastal Veracruz in Mexico. (**3, 10**)

son montuno Slow-medium song-dance of Cuban origin, in duple meter and stanza-refrain form, followed by an African-influenced improvised responsorial section. (**9**)

sonador Second Puerto Rican *bomba* drum. (**2**)

sonae (Japan.) *Syamisen* pattern in *gidayû busi* played at the beginning of an act. (**7**)

sonagram Graphic printout of an electronically analyzed segment of sound. (**9**)

sonaja 'Timbrel' (Spanish). (1) Container idiophone of various forms. (2) In Honduras and Guatemala, spiked vessel rattle made from a gourd or calabash and filled with tiny stones or dried seeds. (3) Nicaraguan handheld semicircular wooden tambourine with metal jingles but no membrane. (**2**)

sonajas de azófar Spanish metal castanets. (**8**)

sŏnang (Also *sŏnang kut*.) Korean shaman ritual for the prosperity of a village. (**7**)

sona rupa de Song tale of Madhya Pradesh blending prose, verse, and recitation. (**5**)

sonata Sardinian *launeddas* composition consisting of a series of thematic formulas corresponding to the figures of the dance. (**8**)

sonata In European art music since the Baroque, a genre of composition for one or several instruments, usually consisting of several distinct sections (movements), each of which may be several minutes to about a quarter hour long. (**8**)

sonata form In European art music since the late eighteenth century, a plan (form) applied usually in the first movements of sonatas, concertos, symphonies, and other compositions, incorporating sections called exposition, development, and recapitulation. (**8**)

sonbrer 'Combination of two *piké*', played on Réunion Island. (**5**)

sonerion Breton duet of *biniou koz* or *biniou bihan* and *bombarde*. See *sonneurs de couple*. (**8**)

sonettu Sardinian small diatonic accordion. (**8**)

Songhai People of West Africa. (**1**)

song lang Vietnamese foot-operated wooden drum with clapper attached. (**4**)

songline Term popularized by Bruce Chatwin to denote the geographical path evoked or taken by a series of related Aboriginal Australian ceremonial songs. (**9**)

song mode Lyrical section of epic-style performance with decreased melodic and rhythm tension. (**1**)

songmok (Also *hamsŏng*.) 'Inhibited voice', vocal timbre forbidden in Korean *p'ansori*. (**7**)

Songo Rotinese indigenous belief system. (**4**)

song plugging Music industry designation for the promotional work done by a publisher on behalf of its compositions. (**3**)

söngur Icelandic song. (**8**)

sonics Study of the pure sound of utterances. (**9**)

sonim (Also *sones*.) Melodies among the Yaqui. (**2**)

Soninke Group of Mande-speakers of northern Mali. (**1**)

sonnatī 'Traditional' (Persian, from Arabic); term applied to numerous phenomena, including several types of music, following the Iranian revolution. (**6**)

sonner 'To ring', a playing stroke on Swiss church bells. (**8**)

sonneurs de couple French term for the Breton *sonerion*. (**8**)

sonohati busi (Japan.) See *miyazono busi*. (**7**)

sŏnsori 'Standing song', professional vocal genre of Korea. (**7**)

sontárusi (Also Spanish, *soldados*.) 'Soldiers' who take part in Tarahumara feast activities. (**2**)

soñu zaharak 'Old melodies', Basque dance tunes with a variable number of bars to each phrase. (**8**)

so'o kangwera Small deer-bone edge aerophone among the Waiãpi. (**2**)

soot Ceremonial vessel stick rattle among the Lacandón Maya. (**2**)

so ou Lao two-stringed fiddle with coconut body. (**4**)

sōpāna 'Stone steps', praise songs of Kerala, performed on the steps leading to the image of a deity. (**5**)

sopel (Also *dudka*, *pizhatka*.) Russian duct flute with five or six holes for fingering. (**8**)

sopile Double-reed oboes played in pairs on the island of Krk in the northern Adriatic region of Croatia. (**8**)

sopilka Ukrainian end-blown flute played especially by boys while pasturing cattle and in other nonritual settings. (**8**)

sŏp'yŏnje Western school of the Korean *p'ansori* tradition. (**7**)

sôrai (Japan.) Buddhist chant (*syômyô*) for worshiping the "three treasures," Buddha, *dharma*, and Sangha. (**7**)

soran Loud-playing ensemble of Java. (**4**)

sorath Song tale of Madhya Pradesh blending prose, verse, and recitation. (**5**)

sorathī Guruñg dance drama in Nepal. (**5**)

sörbö Circle dance to commemorate the creation of the Bribri world and to depict animals of the rain forest. (**2**)

sorek Dance performed during the ritual harvest-festivals of the Miri of the Nuba Mountains in Sudan. (**1**)

sori (1) Vocal ornamentation in Buddhist chant, *syômyô* (Japan). (2) Sound; human voice; music (Korea). (**7**)

sorī Symbol for a half-sharp in notation of Persian music. (**6**)

sornā (1) Aerophone with conical bore, found in Iran. (2) Shawm; double-reed wind instrument of Afghanistan, played in the open air. (**5**)

sornāī Double-reed aerophone in the North West Frontier Province. (**5**)

sorog Gapped scale pentatonic tuning system in Sundanese music. (**4**)

soron Maninka harp-lute with nineteen or twenty-one strings. (**1**)

sorry songs (Also mourning songs.) In western Subarctic regions, songs expressive of sadness at the memory of a deceased friend or relative. (**3**)

sorūd (Also *soroz*, *qeychek*.) Baluchi waisted fiddle with four strings and sympathetic strings. (**6**)

sôsi enka (Japan.) Earliest form of the popular song genre *enka*, which appeared in the 1880s; street songs with political content sung by the activists known as *sôsi* 'men of high purpose'. (**7**)

sot Short love songs performed on Balochi festive occasions by Sotī singers. (**5**)

Sotī Lower-caste male or female singer of *sot* and wedding songs. (**5**)

Sôtô syû (Japan.) Sect of Zen Buddhism introduced from Song China by Dôgen (1200–1253). (**7**)

soukous (1) Name for Zaïrean rumba, featuring three guitar parts and a solo singer. (2) Congolese dance music, popular in the Caribbean. (3) Highly danceable Latin-influenced popular music style from Zaire that has met with some success in world music and world beat. (4) Blend of Central African and Cuban *rumba* styles, popular in France. (**1, 2, 3, 8**)

Soul Caking Traditional play at Antrobus in Cheshire, England. (**8**)

Sŏul sirip kugak kwanhyŏn aktan Seoul City Traditional Music Orchestra. (**7**)

sound instrument Object that makes a sound, not necessarily used within a musical context. (**3**)

sousa Traditional Cypriot swinging-game songs. (**8**)

sousedská Bohemian couple round dance in moderate triple meter. (**8**)

sousou Shaman of the pre-Islamic *salai jin* healing ceremony. (**4**) *sousta* Dance of the Greek islands, also important in Cyprus. (**8**)

Southern African Development Community Cooperative forum that economically and culturally links twelve countries of southern Africa. (**1**)

Southern Cross Constellation visible in the southern hemisphere, often seen as a Christian symbol. (**9**)

sovèyan Guadeloupe stylized hand-to-hand fighting accompanied by drumming and singing. (**2**)

sowe-ey Bontok ritual song for wedding feasts. (**4**)

sowito One-stringed struck bamboo idiochord of Flores. (**4**)

sŏyang ŭmak (Also *yangak*.) Korean term for Western music. (**7**)

soz Shia lament. (**5**)

sözlü ezgiler Turkish vocal melodies, such as the sung poetry of minstrels. (**6**)

sözlü oyun havalar Turkish dance songs. (**6**)

sôzyô (Japan.) (1) Note corresponding to the pitch G.; (2) *gagaku* scale built on this note. (**7**)

spailpini (Also tattie-howkers.) Irish migrant workers, important disseminators of song and music in Ireland and between Ireland and Scotland. (**8**)

spasovskaya Local variety of Russian *chastushki*, named after the locality where it is sung. *See also chastushka*. (**8**)

special *nāṭakam* (Also *icai nāṭakam*.) 'Special drama' in Tamil Nadu. (**5**)

spectrogram Graphic representation of aspects of sound including pitch, rhythm, dynamics, and timbre. (**1**)

speech surrogate Use of musical performance, often by instruments, to reproduce pitch and rhythm of speech. (**1**)

spèktak (Also *gala*.) 'Spectacle', elaborate concert of Haitian urban music featuring a variety of entertainment, often including dance bands, folkloric troupes, comedians, and singers. (**2, 3**)

spelemann Norwegian instrumentalist. (**8**)

spēlmanis 'Player', Latvian term for a violinist or a fiddler. (**8**)

spelmanslag Swedish fiddlers' ensemble. (**8**)

spelmansstämma Swedish musical festival. (**8**)

spelmansstämmor Informal gatherings of Swedish fiddlers. (**8**)

spelpipa Swedish duct flute. (**8**)

Spielleute German traveling musicians, organized into regional brotherhoods. (**8**)

spilendz-churi 'Copper barrel', Georgian metal percussion, mentioned in medieval literary sources. (**8**)

spouge Particular rhythm underlying *spouge* music in Barbados, played on the cowbell, bass guitar, trap set, and other rhythm and electronic instruments. (**2**)

Sprechgesänge German recitative songs. (**8**)

springar Norwegian couple dance. (**8**)

spuntini Sardinian weekend picnics, occasions for song dueling. (**8**)

square dance Social dance in which sets of four couples form squares and execute a series of patterns shouted out by a caller. (**3**)

squash Hollow open-ended gourd idiophone of the Virgin Islands with notched grooves carved into one side and scratched with a multipronged metal scraper, used in scratch bands. (**2**)

sralai Khmer multiple-reed aerophone with a bulging shape. (**4**)

sralai 'Shawm', Cambodian quadruple-reed wind instrument played as part of the *pinn-peat* ensemble, in the court, and at funerals. (**3**)

sralai klang khek Khmer small wood or ivory double reed with flared bell. (**4**)

Śrī Jayantī South Indian celebration of the birth of Krishna. (**5**)

srimpi Refined women's court dance of Java. (**4**)

srnaj Term for a shawm in the Gulf region. (**6**)

śṛngāra (Also *śṛngāra*.) 'Erotic', one of eight emotional states (*rasa*) codified in the *Nāṭyaśāstra*. (**5**)

sronèn Madurese percussion ensemble. (**4**)

sroteš Couple dance of northwestern Croatia. (**8**)

śruti (Also *sruti*.) (1) Microtone; drone; intonation. (2) 'That which has been heard', knowledge received orally, referring to the learning of the sages transmitted through the Vedas. (**5**)

śruti box (Also *peṭṭi*, *śruti peṭṭi*.) Small bellows-driven reed organ that provides the drone pitch. *See also surpeṭī*. (**5**)

stabules Latvian wooden flutes with six or seven finger holes or reeds, associated with herding. (**8**)

Stadtmusikanten Musicians' guilds in medieval Germany. (**8**)

Stadtpfeifer German professional town musicians who performed music for civic festivities and functions. (**8**)

staff notation Notation using the lines and spaces common to the representation of Western art music. (**1**)

stalki Belarusan triangles. (**8**)

stambul Theatrical form based in Jakarta. (**4**)

stambūlī Tunisian ritual involving dance, music, poetry, and song; cf. *gnāwa*, *dīwān*. (**6**)

Standard Bank Grahamstown Arts Festival Largest and most securely established musical festival in South Africa. (**1**)

standard harmonic pattern Harmonic cycle for playing *mbira* that involves a succession of fifths. (**1**)

stanza Division of a poem, consisting of verses sometimes arranged in a recurring patterns, as of meter, rhyme, or syntax. (**9**)

stanzl Jewish song genre based on Purim texts and found in rural areas of the former Hapsburg Empire. (**8**)

starchykhy Ukrainian women's group of vocalists who wandered village roads and performed in regional markets and bazaars. (**8**)

starets Ukrainian blind traveling singer. (**8**)

starina (Also *starinki*.) 'Old song', Russian folk term for a sung epic. (Plural, *stariny*.) *See byliny*. (**8**)

starinki (Also *stariny*.) 'Old tales', Russian genre known to scholars since the 1830s as *bylina*. *See byliny*. (**8**)

starinshchik Specialized performer of the Russian *stariny* or *starinski*. (**8**)

starinske pjesme Ancient songs in Gabela, Hercegovina (Bosnia). (**8**)

starodávny 'Old-rime dance' of eastern Moravia. (**8**)

starogradske pjesme (Also *starogradske pesme*.) (1) Late-nineteenth-century city songs from Croatia and Serbia. (2) 'Old-city songs', Macedonian urban songs. (**3, 8**)

starosevetská 'Old-world dance' of southeastern Moravia. (**8**)

startsi Ukrainian group of male vocalists who wandered village roads and performed in regional markets and bazaars; alternative term for Bulgarian *kukeri*. (**8**)

stavan Eulogy. (**5**)

steagul 'Flag', part of the Romanian wedding ritual, accompanied by specific songs or instrumental tunes. (**8**)

steelband (Also pan.) Trinidadian ensemble of tuned idiophones formed from metal oil drums, also found in Guyana and elsewhere in the English-speaking Caribbean. (**2**)

steel guitar (Hawaiian *kīkā kila*.) Hawaiian-developed style of playing the guitar by sliding a steel bar along the strings to make microtonal slides, harmonics, and timbral variations. (**9**)

Steirisch Austrian trapezoidal struck zither of Styria. (**8**)

stemmur Melodies of Icelandic *rímur*. *See bragir*. (**8**)

step dance (1) Solo dance in hard-soled shoes, executed with quick, rhythmical footwork close to the ground; still performed in the Maritimes and Québec, where step dance competitions are popular. (2) Scottish and Irish virtuosic and competitive solo dancing with elaborate footwork. **(3, 8)**

Sterns Small independent British recording label. **(1)**

stev (1) Singing consisting of short one-strophe poems set to formulaic melodies, practiced by Norwegian immigrants in the nineteenth century. (2) Norwegian four-line rhymed stanza. **(3, 8)**

sthāī (Also *sthāya*.) First melodic phrase or section of a Hindustani composition; first section of a Hindustani composition emphasizing the lower tetrachord of the octave. **(5, 10)**

sthāvara 'Settled in one location', as opposed to wandering. **(5)**

stichic Characteristic of songs whose performance repeats a single musical phrase corresponding to a single line of verse. **(8)**

Stierische (1) Austrian multipart dance of Styria. (2) Button accordion which plays that genre. **(8)**

stili Ossetian double clarinet with a five-holed melody pipe and a single-holed drone pipe. **(8)**

stilyagi Russian youth subculture with its own popular music. **(8)**

stock and horn Scottish name of the hornpipe. **(8)**

Stomp Dance Songs performed among the Creek Indians in the summer. **(3)**

stools Trinidadian altars commemorating various gods. **(2)**

stornelli Type of Italian lyric song. **(8)**

stornello Genre of sung Sicilian poetry. **(3)**

stotra Large combinations of chants. **(5)**

stradaniia 'Sufferings', 'cruel romances'; subgenre of *chastushki* and soldiers' songs. **(8)**

strambotti Type of Italian lyric song. **(8)**

stranotti Type of Italian lyric song. **(8)**

stranščice Slovene duct flutes. **(8)**

strathspey Grenadian slow waltz. **(2)**

strī Female ragas. **(5)**

strigături 'Extemporized verses' shouted during dancing in the Romanian wedding ritual. **(8)**

striichmusig 'Bowed music', Swiss band consisting of a violin, a dulcimer, a bowed double bass, and a chromatic accordion or a piano, in Appenzell and Toggenburg, St. Gallen. **(8)**

striking Log-idiophone-playing technique by which the player hits the instrument with the side of a stick or two short sticks, one in each hand; cf. *jolting*. **(9)**

string Thai rock and roll music. **(4)**

string band (1) In the late 1980s, Montserrat youth band of guitars, banjos, ukuleles, and accordions. (2) (Tok Pisin *stringben*.) Musical ensemble formed mainly of chordophones, usually guitars, sometimes incorporating ukuleles and rarely banjos. **(2, 9)**

string figure Loop of string manipulated into a pattern or patterns perceived as meaningful and often accompanied by or interpreting a sung text. **(9)**

string quartet In European art music since the eighteenth century, an ensemble consisting of two violins, one viola, and one violoncello (cello); a composition for such an ensemble, usually in several movements, like a sonata. **(8)**

strophic Designation for a poem consisting of two or more lines whose rhythmic pattern repeats as a unit, or a song in which each stanza of the lyrics is sung to the same music. **(9)**

strophic songs Songs in which the same music is repeated for each new stanza (strophe) of music. **(8)**

stsóköl Funerary singer among the Bribri and Cabécar who performs during a *sulàr* ceremony. **(2)**

stsóköl sini'pa Assistants of the *stsóköl*. **(2)**

Stubenmusi Bavarian bar music. **(8)**

sturmant Welsh mouth harp, made of wood or metal, held between the teeth, and struck with a finger, popular until the early 1900s; see *bibaw*. **(8)**

stuzzichetto Variant of the *saltarello*. **(8)**

stviri Georgian wooden aerophones. **(8)**

suara Kuna single external-duct bamboo end-blown edge aerophones that are played in pairs. **(2)**

suat Ordinary style of chanting Buddhist texts. **(4)**

subaŋ Character, reputation, social face as defined by the Gã people of Ghana. **(1)**

subli Devotional practice in the Philippines. **(4)**

subornaja subota (Also *dziavočnik, na viankach*.) Belarusan bridal fair the day before a wedding, when girls gather, accompanied by ritual songs. **(8)**

subü Lisu three-stringed fretted lute. **(4)**

su concordu Sardinian three-person chorus that accompanies *gana poetica*, poets' sung duels. **(8)**

sudmaliņas 'Mill', third of four or more sections of the Latvian *četrpāru dancis*, sometimes considered a separate dance. **(8)**

suduchu Yekuana five-tubed panpipe. **(2)**

sue byôsi (Japan.) Main singer of the *sue kata* section of *mikagura* musicians. **(7)**

sue kata (Japan.) One of the two sections of *mikagura* musicians. **(7)**

sue te (Japan.) Ending melodic pattern in *gidayû busi*. **(7)**

sue uta (Japan.) Second of the two verses of a *mikagura* song in which the solo part is performed by the *sue byôsi*, the main singer of the *sue kata* section. **(7)**

ṣuffārā (Also *suffāra, salamiyya*.) Small Egyptian flute. **(6)**

Sufi (1) Mystic cult of Islam; also, an adherent of this cult. (2) Mystical dimension of Islam, comprising social, doctrinal, and ritual aspects; considered by Sufis to constitute the essence of Islam. **(5, 6)**

ṣūfyāna (Also *ṣūfyāna kālam, ṣūfyāna mūsīqī*.) 'Sufi music', classical music of the urban elite in Kashmir, with roots in Persian music. **(5)**

sugagaki huri (Japan.) Section of *yakumo goto* performed as festival music for the Ômoto sect of Shinto, to send off the gods. **(7)**

sugam saṅgīt Carefully rehearsed unison choral presentations of religious song. **(5)**

suggarāt Double clarinet with cow horn bells used in Algeria; cf. *tormāy, magrūna*. **(6)**

sugonghu Korean twenty-one-stringed vertical harp, now obsolete. **(7)**

sugu (Japan.) Unornamented melody types in Buddhist chant. **(7)**

suḥbat 'Company'; spiritual conversation in Sufism. **(5)**

suila jut'as Bolivian heavy metal spurs attached to wooden sandals. **(2)**

suisin Small, three-stringed fretless lute with a skin-covered body, used in Morocco. **(6)**

suizen (Japan.) Playing of *syakuhati* as Zen meditation. **(7)**

suizi (China.) Semi-improvised ostinato phrases stressing pivotal notes. **(7)**

sujiang (China.) Secular Buddhist sermon. **(7)**

suka 'Bitch', vertically played bowed fiddle of Poland. **(8)**

sukhwan Spirit ritual common to Thailand, Laos, and Burma. **(4)**

sukia (1) Nicaraguan Garífuna shaman; (2) traditional Miskitu shaman. **(2)**

sukiyaki Dinner accompanied by Laotian classical music. **(4)**

suku-ba Vai professional Qur'ānic reciter. **(1)**

suku sisipan Ethnically distinct marginal groups of Cirebon. **(4)**

sŭl (Chinese, *se*.) Twenty-five-stringed Korean zither with movable bridges. **(7)**

sūlādi Karnatak compositional form. **(5)**

sulàr 'Music for our people', one of the main funerary ceremonies of the Bribri and Cabécar. **(2)**

sulibao Ibaloy conical drum and ensemble. **(4)**

suling End-blown bamboo ring-stop flute, found throughout Indonesia and the Philippines. **(4)**

suling bambu Bamboo flutes used in Catholic services on Kai. (4)

suling lembang Torajan bamboo flute with carved buffalo-horn flare. (4)

suling miring Transverse bamboo flute with membrane in Java. (4)

sulling (Also *lulling, tralling, tulling.*) Norwegian vocal genre that uses mnemonic syllables for singing fiddle pieces. (8)

sulukan Mood song performed by *dhalang* in Java. (4)

sulyāq Medieval term, probably denoting a lyre. (6)

suma goto (Japan.) *See itigen kin.* (7)

sum and difference frequencies Frequencies of $f_1 + f_2$ (sum frequency) and $f_1 - f_2$ (difference frequency), generated when pure pitches of frequency f_1 and f_2 are fed into a nonlinear system; the most prominent members of a set of nonlinearly generated pitches of frequency $nf_1 \pm mf_2$, where n and m are integers. (9)

sunan chuida (China.) Wind and percussion music of the southern Jiangsu region. (7)

Sunburst Tanzanian jazz band that included native Tanzanians, African-Americans, and a Jamaican. (1)

sundatang Two- or three-stringed plucked lute of Borneo. (4)

sunet Albanian circumcision ceremony with music. (8)

süng Northern Thai plucked lute. (4)

Sŭngmu Korean Buddhist drum dance. (7)

Sunjata Historic warrior revered in song by Mande peoples of West Africa. (1)

suntang Torajan bar zither.

suntu Central Sulawesi bar zither. (4)

ṣunūj Cymbals or castanets. (6)

ṣunūj al-aṣābi' (Also Egypt, *sajāt*; Iraq, *chumparāt*; Morocco, *nuiqsāt*; Libya, *zel.*) Finger cymbals. (6)

suona (China.) Double-reed conical pipe (shawm) introduced from Central Asia during the third to fifth centuries; Chinese oboe. (3, 4, 7)

supe Kuna single external-duct bamboo end-blown edge aerophones played in pairs. (2)

šupelka Macedonian shepherds' flute, a short tube open at both ends with six holes for fingering. (8)

supra Georgian traditional feasts with singing. (8)

sur (1) Pitch, tone; melody or melodic modes. (2) Baluchi circumcision song. (5, 6)

surbahār Large sitar invented to imitate the sound and repertoire of the Hindustani *bīn*. (5)

surdo Double-headed drum used in many genres of Brazilian music, especially *samba* and its derivatives. (2)

surdulina Italian bagpipe. (8)

surindā (Also *sarā, sarāng, sārindā.*) Any of various bowed chordophones of southern Afghanistan, Pakistan, and North India. (5)

surisŏng 'Husky voice', vocal timbre in Korean *p'ansori*. (7)

suri zume (Japan.) *Koto* technique in which the picks scrape the strings. (7)

surjaran In the Armenian-American community, coffeehouse tradition of music, conversation, and refreshment. (3)

surle (Also *cingonë, curle, zurle.*) Albanian conical-bore double-reed aerophone. (8)

surnā Double-reed oboe played to the accompaniment of drums by lower-caste musicians. (5)

surnāī (Also *śahnāī.*) Double-reed aerophone. (5)

surnāy Double-reed aerophone of Kashmir; instrumental ensemble accompanying folk theatricals (*bānde pāther*) in Kashmir. (5)

surnāy (1) Type of oboe used in the Afro-Arab music of the Gulf region. (2) Archaic term for flute or oboe. (6)

suroz Spike fiddle, the only bowed stringed instrument in Balochistan used for multiple purposes; national instrument of the Baloch, similar to the Iranian *ghīchak*. (5)

surpetī Hand-pumped drone aerophone of Gujarat. *See also śruti peṭi.* (5)

sursiṅgār Modification of the *dhrupad rabāb*, with a wooden face and metal strings (obsolete). (5)

suruídey Sounding device, or vibrating reed, of the Yekuana bamboo clarinet (*tekeyë*). (2)

susap (Tok Pisin, from English *Jew's harp.*) Mainly Papua New Guinean lamellophone, usually played for private entertainment by males. (9)

suṣira Category of aerophones in the Buddhist *pañcatūrya nāda* system. (5)

suṣira vādya Aerophone (instrument category), in the *Nāṭyaśāstra*. (5)

susŏng karak (Also *susŏngjil.*) Korean technique of instrumental accompaniment following the vocal line. (7)

suspension rattle (Also jingle rattle, jingle rattles.) Rattle made by suspending objects from a stick or other device so that when shaken the objects strike one another and produce sound. (3)

sutartinė Traditional polyphonic vocal music of southeast Lithuania. (8)

sutartines Archaic Lithuanian song genre that features contrapuntal singing and is usually performed by two to four people. (3)

sūtra Saying, maxim, aphoristic verse. (5)

sūtradhāra 'Chief musician', 'narrator' of a dance drama, who keeps the beat with a pair of cymbals, recites dance syllables, and may join in the dancing. (5)

sūtra gomeyāṭa String-puppet play, in Karnataka. (5)

su utai (Japan.) *Nô* performance in which the entire text is chanted without instrumentalists. (7)

suvāra Sufi-related song cycle of Khwarezm (Khorezm), Uzbekistan-Kazakhstan, setting spiritual poetry to music. (6)

suvvi Refrain used in songs in Karnataka. (5)

Suzhou tanci (China.) Sung storytelling in Suzhou dialect. (7)

suzipu (China.) Vulgar character notation. (7)

suzu (Japan.) Generic term for bells. (7)

su zyôruri (Japan.) Narrative music (*zyôruri*) for *syamisen* performed independently of puppet theater or *kabuki*. (7)

svadbene pjesme Montenegrin wedding songs. (8)

svara (1) Scale degree; pitch in general. (2) (Also *dhatu.*) Melodic aspect of music. (5)

svara exercises Musical passages of increasing complexity based on *svara* syllables, as exercises for beginning music students. (5)

svarajāti (1) Didactic form, in Karnatak music. (2) Composition based on a *svara* syllable form and given a meaningful text. (5)

svara kalpana Karnatak melodic improvisation (*manodharma*) using sol-fa syllables. (5)

svarākṣara Punning use of *svara* names in a Karnatak song text. (5)

svara pallavi Section following the *batu* in an *odissi* dance performance. (5)

svaraprastāra Raga development in Karnatak music. (5)

svara sthānam (Also *svara-sthān.*) Pitch location, within the system of twelve *svara* to the octave. (5)

svara syllables (Also *sargam.*) Indian sol-fa syllables sa, ri, ga, ma, pa, dha, ni, used as text material in musical composition and improvisation. (5)

svarāvali Melodic exercise pieces for students of Karnatak music. (5)

svarita Transitional sounded accent, in Vedic recitation; often follows the *udātta* accent. (5)

svarlipi Indian music notation. (5)

svarmaṇḍal Box zither, strummed and plucked as background filler for a Hindustani vocal performance. (5)

svatba Bulgarian wedding, which requires specific songs and music for each stage of the festivities. (8)

svatovske pjesme Wedding songs in Bosnia-Hercegovina. (8)

svilpes Latvian bark or clay whistles, associated with herding. (8)

svingbruse In Denmark, instrument consisting of a hollow tile or a small oblong wooden plate with a hole, tied to the end of a string and swung in circles to produce a whirring sound. (8)

svinjokolje (Also *kolinje*.) Slavonian communal hog-butchering parties, held in late fall with singing, dancing, and merrymaking. (8)

svirač Serbian term for a musician. (8)

svirale Serbo-Croatian term for wind instruments, commonly used to denote duct flutes. (8)

svirka Bulgarian short end-blown ductless flute with six finger holes and perhaps a thumb hole. (8)

svirni Bulgarian nonmetrical instrumental tunes. (8)

svrljiške gajde Three-voiced bagpipe of southeast Serbia. (8)

swadeśī gān Patriotic songs. (5)

Swahili (1) East African cultural group. (2) Trade language that draws on the structures and vocabularies of Bantu languages and Arabic. (1)

sware Haitian late-night dance. (2)

swidden Agricultural practice in which steep hillside fields are cleared and burned. (4)

swing Musical genre developed in North America in the 1920s and popularized in the 1930s to accompany jazz dancing in moderate tempo with smooth syncopation. (9)

swung slat Simple, but often sacred, aerophone consisting of a thin lens- or rhomboid-shaped wooden slat attached to a string and made to hum by being whirled through the air. (9)

syak Guadeloupe scraper made from a bamboo log ridged with transverse notches and rubbed by thin sticks. (2)

syaku byôsi (Japan.) Pair of wooden clappers used in *mikagura*. (7)

syakuhati (Also *shakuhachi*.) Japanese end-blown bamboo flute. (7, 10)

syakuzyô (Japan.) (1) Buddhist chant (*syômyô*) for purifying and ornamenting a hall; (2) rattle used in Buddhist music. (7)

syamisen (Also *shamisen*.) 'Samisen', Japanese three-stringed plucked lute. (7, 10)

syamisen kumiuta (Japan.) Song cycles accompanied by *syamisen*, the earliest chamber music for this instrument. (7)

sybysghy Elongated open flute, played by Kazakh shepherds. (6)

sybyzyk Short single-reed pipe made of cane, found in Central Asia. (6)

sygyt 'Whistle', type of Tuvan *khöömei* involving high, clear, piercing harmonics. (6)

syllabic Style of vocalizing the text of a song in which there is one syllable of text to one note of music. (3)

symphony In European art music since the Classical period, a genre of composition formally resembling a sonata, but composed for an orchestra. (8)

syncopation In Western music, the displacement or shifting of an accent so that it falls on a weak metric beat. (3)

syncretism Combination of two or more different cultural systems of belief or practice. (9)

syô (1) (Also *sho*.) Chinese-derived Japanese mouth organ used in *gagaku*. (2) Second note in the Japanese scale *gosei*. (7, 10)

syôga (Japan.) (1) Method of memorizing and transmitting melodic lines, rhythmic patterns, playing techniques, and tone color by reciting Japanese syllables. (2) Written forms of this method. (7)

syôgaku syôka (Japan.) Educational songs for children in primary school, compiled during the Meizi era (1868–1912). (7)

syôka (Japan.) Educational songs taught at schools. (7)

syôko (Japan.) (1) Small gongs in *gagaku*. (2) Classicism or devotion to things classical. (7)

syômyô (Also *bonbai*.) In Japan, generic term for Buddhist chant. (7)

Syômyô syû (Japan.) Collection of scores for Buddhist chant printed in 1472. (7)

syôrei (Japan.) Buddhist chant (*syômyô*) for worshiping various buddhas and bodhisattvas. (7)

syosa goto (Japan.) Dance part of *kabuki*. (7)

syosei busi (Japan.) *Enka* (popular song) performed in the streets by college students during the Meizi period (1868–1912). (7)

Syôsôin (Japan.) Repository (storehouse) of the imperial treasury at Nara. (7)

syôsôin syakuhati (Also *gagaku syakuhati*.) Eight specimens of the six-hole end-blown flutes used in Japanese *gagaku* (court music) that are preserved in the Syôsôin. (7)

Syôwa (Japan.) Period from 1926 to 1989. (7)

syozyû (Japan.) (1) Lowest octave in a piece; (2) lowest pitch level in Buddhist chant; (3) common melodic patterns in the *syozyû* pitch area. (7)

syôzyûbun (Japan.) Main part of a Buddhist *sutra*. (7)

Syriac Semitic language, derived from Aramaic, once spoken by the inhabitants of historical Syria. (6)

syrinx Ancient Greek panpipes. (8)

syrmatika Narrative songs of the Greek island of Karpathos. (8)

Syro-Catholic church Christian church espousing the Western Syro-Antiochene rite, united with the Roman See since the eighteenth century. (6)

Syro-Orthodox church Christian church espousing the Western Syro-Antiochene rite. (6)

syrtos Common Greek line dance. (8)

syû (Japan.) Generic term for a sect. (7)

syu (Japan.) Tablature notation for the *syamisen* part in *gidayû busi*. (7)

syugan (Japan.) Chant (*syômyô*) for confessing and making vowa to Buddha. (7)

syûgen no koe (Japan.) *Nô* vocalization to emphasize happiness and joy. (7)

syûmei (Japan.) To succeed to a teacher's name. (7)

syu no koe (Japan.) Thin, soft, sentimental voice in *nô* chanting. (7)

syura nô (Japan.) *Nô* plays in which the main character is the ghost of a warrior of the Heike or Genzi clan. (7)

syusi (Japan.) Prayers of esoteric Buddhism. (7)

syusi sarugaku (Japan.) Ancient performing art, the origin of *nô*. (7)

szopka Polish Christmas puppet story resembling the Belarusan *batlejka* and the Ukrainian *vertep*. (8)

taar Northern Sudanese frame drum. (1)

taarab (Arabic 'joy', 'pleasure', 'delight'.) Popular coastal East African music that traditionally accompanied Swahili love-related poetry, often played at weddings. (1)

ta asobi (Japan.) Folk ritual of prayer for abundant crops. (7)

ṭabʿ (Plural, *ṭubūʿ*.) (1) Generic term for musical mode. (2) Nature, stamp, or character of a *nūba*. (6)

tabaṭk Kota frame drum of Tamil Nadu. (5)

tabi (Japan.) Epic song of the Miyako Islands celebrating the ancestor-gods. (7)

tabil (Also *davul*.) Large Turkish drum. (6)

ṭabl (Plural, *ṭubūl*.) Generic term for various types of drums in the Arab world. (5, 6)

ṭabl baladī Double-headed bass drum. (6)

ṭabl bôga In Yemen, a large, low-pitched cylindrical drum tensed by cords. (6)

ṭabl al-lewa Tubular drum used in Yemeni possession ceremonies. (6)

ṭabl marad In Zabīd-Tihāma, Yemen, a large, low-pitched cylindrical drum tensed by cords. (6)

ṭabl muʾasṭā In the Tihāma, Yemen, a large, high-pitched cylindrical drum tensed by cords, played in ensembles accompanying dance. (6)

ṭabl sāgh In Bayt al-Faqīh-Tihāma, a large, high-pitched cylindrical drum tensed by cords; see *ṭabl muʾasṭā*. (6)

ṭabl al-ṣaghīr (Also *ṭabl ṣaghīr*.) Small double-headed drum played by women on festive occasions in Yemen. (6)

ṭabla (Plural, *ṭablāt*.) (1) Generic term for drum; cf. *ṭabl*. (2) (Also *darbūka*; in Algeria, *gelal*;

in Libya, *galal*.) More specifically, a single-headed portable drum used throughout the Arab world. **(6)**

tabla (1) Sudanese small drum. (2) North Indian small drums played as a pair. (2) Pair of hand-played tuned drums used for Hindustani classical, semiclassical, and film musics. (3) (Also *dāhinā*, *dāya*.) Right-hand drum of the Indian *tabla* pair. **(1, 3, 5, 10)**

tabla charango Bolivian flat-backed *charango* played during the rainy season. **(2)**

tablados Uruguayan street stages for carnival musical competitions. **(2)**

tablak Small version of the Georgian *diplipito*. **(8)**

tablaos Spanish nightclubs where flamenco is performed. **(8)**

tablātarang Pitched row of tuned *dāhinā* (right-hand *tabla* drums). **(5)**

tablature Notational system that places numbers or letters on a diagram resembling the strings or keys of an instrument. **(1)**

tabor Small handheld drum that accompanies a pipe or fife, played by the same person in a combination known generally as pipe and tabor and in England as whittle and dub; *see tambourinaire*. **(8)**

tabor pipe Duct flute with two finger holes and a thumb hole. **(8)**

tabot Bengkulu religious theatrical work. **(4)**

tabu (Also *taboo, tapu, kapu*.) Interdictions and protocols serving to protect *mana* and keep the sacred separate from the secular. **(9)**

tabuh Individual composition in Balinese music. **(4)**

tabuhan Gong-chime and ensemble of Sumatra. **(4)**

tabut West Sumatra religious theatrical work. **(4)**

tabwrdd Drum known only from early Welsh historical sources. **(8)**

tāca Tamil version of the *tāshā* drum. **(5)**

taccule Corsican wooden scraper. **(8)**

tactus 'Beat' (Latin). In medieval Europe, the silent waving of the conductor's arm alternately downward and upward to signal the beat. **(8)**

taeak (Also, *chŏngak*.) 'Great music', royal court music of Korea. **(7)**

Taeaksŏ Office for Great Music of the Korean Koryŏ dynasty. **(7)**

taeborŭm Korean village cleansing ritual. **(7)**

taegŭk 'Great absolute', onomatopoeic Korean term for simultaneously hitting both heads of a drum. **(7)**

taegŭm Large Korean transverse bamboo flute. **(7)**

Taehan kugagwŏn Korean Traditional Music Institute. **(7)**

taehyŏng mandŭlgi Korean farmers' band formation, a line with the leader in front. **(7)**

taejaeng Fifteen-stringed Korean zither, now obsolete. **(7)**

taemadi taejangdan Basic, unornamented rhythmic patterns used in Korean drumming and singing. **(7)**

taep'ungnyu Korean "bamboo music". **(7)**

t'aep'yŏngso (Also *nallari, hojŏk, soenap*.) Korean conical shawm. **(7)**

taesa Korean great rites. **(7)**

tættir Satirical ballads of the Faroe Islands, dealing with topical events and sung by dancers in a line dance. **(8)**

taganing (1) Acehnese bamboo zither and ensemble. (2) Toba Batak graded drums. **(4)**

tagunggo (1) Rhythmic mode in the Philippines. (2) Yakan *kulintang* ensemble. (3) Kalagan set of heavy suspended gongs. **(4)**

tagutok Maranao scraper. **(4)**

tahardent (1) Tuareg three-stringed lute, resembling the Mauritanian *tidinit*. (2) Tuareg musical genre that has become popular in Niger. **(1)**

tahareta Meaningless syllables used by Santals to teach melodies that can accompany different texts. **(5)**

taha-taha Subanen bamboo dibbling pole. **(4)**

Tahir Classical mode, or *makam*, in Turkish folk music. **(6)**

táhle 'Protracted, drawn-out', term describing eastern Moravian nondance music in parlando rubato style. **(8)**

taḥmila Short, fixed instrumental composition involving call-and-response by various solo instruments, common in the Egyptian *takht* repertoire. **(6)**

taḥrīr (Also *badwa*.) Opening section of melismatic vocalization within the Iraqi *maqām*. **(6)**

taḥtīb Egyptian martial dance in which the participants wield large bamboo or wooden staves. **(6)**

Tai Language family common to mainland Southeast Asia. **(4)**

taibobo (Also *taibubu*.) So-called Kiwai dance, a genre of singing and dancing adapted from Rotuman genres and performed by Torres Strait Islanders and coastal peoples of Western Province, Papua New Guinea. **(9)**

taieira Dramatic Afro-Brazilian dance. **(2)**

Tai-Kadai Language family including Thai, Lao, and Shan. **(4)**

taiko (1) Japanese large barrel-shaped two-headed drum, whose skins are usually tacked. (2) Generic term for Japanese and non-Japanese drums. (3) Generic term for Japanese stick-struck barrel drums. (4) *Taiko* drumming, contemporary ensemble based on

Japanese drumming genres and sometimes including flutes, gongs, or stringed instruments. **(3, 7, 9)**

taisiki tyô (Japan.) *Ryo* scale built on the note *taisiki* (E) used in *gagaku*. **(7)**

taisô (Japan.) Court ritual for an emperor's funeral; a performance context for *ruika*. **(7)**

Taisyô (Japan.) (1) Period from 1912 to 1926. (2) Taisyô democracy, liberal democratic spirit and policies of the Taisyô period. **(7)**

taisyô goto (Also *taisyô kin*.) Two-stringed instrument with typewriter-like keys, invented at the beginning of the Japanese Taisyô period (c. 1912). **(7)**

taita Lead male singer for Moxo *machetero* dance. **(2)**

tajwīd (1) Qur'ānic recitation. (2) Rules governing its proper performance. (3) A more melodically elaborate style of Qur'ānic recitation. **(6)**

tak (Also *takk*.) High-pitched drum stroke; cf. *dumm*. **(6)**

Takayasu ryû (Japan.) School of *nô* specializing in *waki kata* and *ô tuzumi*. **(7)**

takbīr Qur'ānic recitation in Central Asian Sufi ceremonies. **(6)**

take Nyamalthu praise-name performance in the former Bauchi State in Nigeria. **(1)**

take bue (Also *takebue, sinobue*.) Japanese transverse bamboo flute. **(3, 7)**

takomba New Tuareg genre in which seated listeners respond to rhythms with undulating movements of the torso. **(1)**

Takenoko syû (Japan.) 'A Collection of *Zyôruri*' by Uzi Kaga no zyô (1635–1711). **(7)**

takhmîr 'Leavening', 'fermentation'; term for the trance or ecstasy of a Sufi devotee. **(6)**

takht (Also *takht alsharqī, takht sharqī*.) Small chamber ensemble of three to five or more musicians, common in the nineteenth and twentieth-century Mashriq. **(6)**

takik Bontok men's dance. **(4)**

takipayanaku Bolivian insult songs sung by in-laws at weddings. **(2)**

taklempong Malay ensemble for *randai*, consisting of three gong chimes. **(4)**

tako'ah Biblical word for trumpet. **(8)**

taksim Nonmetric improvisation in Turkish and Arabic classical music, played also in the Balkans. **(8)**

taksīm Solo instrumental improvisation (Turkish); see *taqsīm*. **(6)**

taku (Japan.) Wooden clapper in Buddhist music. **(7)**

takuapú Indigenous Paraguayan bamboo stamping tube that may have strings of rattles attached, played by women. **(2)**

takumbo Mandaya paired-string zither. **(4)**

tāl (1) Large cymbal pair of Rajasthan and Uttar Pradesh. (2) Steel plate with a wooden handle, played with two sticks in Balochistan. (5)

tala (1) Bronze or iron gong, Weyewa language. (2) 'Talk', 'tale'; considered a form of Icelandic musical performance. (4, 8)

tala (Also *tāl, tāḷa.*) (1) Organization of time, rhythm, and meter in Indian music; a metric cycle. (1) Rhythmic modal system used in Indian classical performance. (2) Indian rhythmic cycle. (4, 5, 7, 10)

tāla (Also *tāl, tāḷam, talam.*) Pair of small metal hand cymbals used to mark metrical patterns and indicate tempo. (2) Small Indian cymbals. (4, 5)

talalay Batangas working song. (4)

tāḷamālikā 'Garland of talas'; rhythmic or melodic piece performed in a series of talas. (5)

talambas Kettledrum of Bosnia-Hercegovina and Montenegro. (8)

tālampoṭa Pair of large cymbals used in the Buddhist *hēvisi pūjā* ensemble of Sri Lanka. (5)

tālāṭṭu Tamil lullaby. (5)

talátur Chilean water-praising invocation for irrigation. (2)

talava Principal Rom musical genre in Kosovo, Serbia. (8)

talawat Moroccan flute. (1)

talawi Three-part Muslim song of the Philippines. (4)

t'alch'um Korean masked dance drama. (7)

talèdhèk Javanese female singer-dancer. (4)

taleli Four-holed bamboo ring-stop flute of Sumba. (4)

talempong (Also *tilempong.*) West and North Sumatra gong-chime and ensemble. (4)

talerschwingen Swiss tradition of rolling a five-franc piece around the inside of an earthenware bowl to produce a sound that accompanies local yodeling. (8)

taletenga Idioglot reed pipe of the Akan of Ghana. (1)

tālī Clapping gesture signifying a stressed subdivision of a Hindustáni tala. (5)

tali Palm-beaten cylindrical wooden membranophone. (2)

talibun Bengkulu vocal genre similar to *pantun.* (4)

ta'līf 'Composition', a discipline of early Arabic music theory, represented in book titles such as *Ta'līf al-alḥān.* (6)

tālīm Training; musical training or lessons. (5)

talk-men Kru sailors who served as interpreters because of their fluency in pidgin English. (1)

talku balss Latvian tune sung during communal fieldwork. (8)

Tallensi People of Ghana. (1)

tallunt Drum of the Moroccan Berbers. (6)

tāl-maddale (Also *tāla maddaḷe.*) 'Cymbal and double-headed barrel drum', narrative drama of Karnataka believed to be the precursor of *yakṣagāna.* (5)

taločnyja pieśni Belarusan spring, summer, and autumn team songs, performed by groups gathered to help fellow farmers. (8)

talqin Devotional songs in Sufi *zikr* or *dhikr,* transmitted through lineages of musical specialists, *talqinchi.* (6)

talwīn Modulation from one mode, or *maqām,* to another. (6)

tal'wwatt Moroccan Berber flute. (6)

talyanka 'Italian accordion', title of a Russian collection of *chastushka* texts. (8)

tama (1) Double-headed hourglass-shaped tension drum of the Western Sudanic cluster. (2) (Japan.) Additional virtuosic *syamisen* part in the *nagauta.* (1, 7)

tamada Georgian toastmaster who leads the complex structure of toasts with songs at a banquet. (8)

tamagoto (Japan.) Former name of *yakumo goto.* (7)

tamagusi (Japan.) Shinto sacred branch. (7)

tamai (Japan.) Indigenous genre of court ceremonial music and dance that originated among farmers. (7)

tamāśā Folk drama of Maharashtra. (5)

tamāshā Dance ceremony; public entertainment in the Northern Areas of Pakistan. (5)

tāmasik 'Evil', 'cruel'; vicious character type in *kathakaḷi* dance. (5)

tamaṭe Large tambourine played with sticks in Karnataka. (5)

ṭambal Romanian trapezoidal struck zither. (8)

tambaran (Tok Pisin.) In Papua New Guinea, a spirit or its representation in sight (as by carved wood) or sound (as by a flute). (9)

tambari Hausa large kettledrum with a resonator of wood, symbolizing royalty. (1)

tambilaw Palawan harvest ceremony. (4)

tambing Fulɓe transverse flute. (1)

tambito Local song-dance of Guanacaste, Costa Rica, attributed to the Talolingas ensemble. (2)

tamble (Also *chamba, dar, darjal.*) Frame drum popular among Pakhtun women of the North West Frontier Province. (5)

Tambo Jamaican African-based cult. (2)

tamboo-bamboo (1) Grenada bamboo stamping tubes; (2) early twentieth-century Trinidadian carnival music played on lengths of bamboo. (2)

tambor (1) Generic Spanish masculine term for a membranophone that exists in a variety of forms, either single- or double-headed, the latter often with a snare. (2) Spanish drum that accompanies flute playing. (2, 8)

tambora (1) Generic Spanish feminine term for membranophone. (2) In the Dominican Republic, small drum used especially to accompany the *merengue* with prominent percussion accompaniment and group song, especially important during carnival. (3) Long, tubular Afro-Venezuelan membranophone made from a log with two skin heads, played with one stick while held between the knees. (4) Cuyo Christmas song. (5) Drum of the Philippines. (2, 3, 4)

tamborazos zacatecanos Zacatecas-style Mexican pop bands. (2)

tamborero In Peru, a person who beats on the box of the harp as a percussion instrument while a harpist plucks the strings. (2)

tambores Ensemble music of the Brotherhood of San Juan Bautista of Baní, Dominican Republic. (2)

tamborete Peruvian version of the Chilean *tormento.* (2)

tamboril (1) Ecuadorian double-headed drum, varying in size. (2) Uruguayan small drum. (3) Small Basque drum, typically played with the right hand while the left hand plays a three-holed flute; see *tabor, txistu.* (4) Drum played in northeast Portugal. (2, 3, 8)

tamborim Brazilian membranophone consisting of a small metal or plastic frame covered with a tight skin, played with a stick. (2)

tamborita Small double-headed drum of Mexico, played on the head and rim with two drumsticks. (2)

tamborito 'Little drum', national couple dance of Panama, featuring drum accompaniment. (2)

tamboula African drum associated with La Calinda. (3)

tambour Drum. (8)

tambourin Snare-drum played with *galoubet* in Provence, France. (8)

tambourinaire French pipe-and-tabor player. (8)

tambourine Small drum, especially a frame drum with metallic jingles loosely attached to the frame. (8)

tambú (Also *barí.*) (1) Music-and-dance complex of Curaçao. (2) Membranophone, the most important African-derived instrument in the Dutch islands of the Leeward Antilles. (3) (Also *tambu.*) Brazilian large conical single-headed membranophone. (4) (Also *tambu.*) Jamaican *salo* song. (2)

tambul (1) Sama long bronze cylindrical drum. (2) Kalinga-Tinggian cylindrical drum. (4)

tambur Metal-bodied Muslim frame drum. (4)

tambūr (Also *tambura, tanbur, tambūrā.*) Long-necked, unfretted, plucked drone lute; see *tambūri, tānpūrā.* (2) Long-necked fretted lute of Iran and elsewhere in the Middle East, popular at medieval Indo-Persian courts of

India. (3) Middle Eastern fretted long-necked lute, imported into the Balkans during the Ottoman period.   (5, 6, 8)

ṭambūra (Also *ṭambra, ṭanbūra, ṭanbūrah.*) Lyre.   (6)

tambura (1) Sudanese usually six-stringed lyre. (2) Sudanese ritual organized by women, involving music-induced possession by spirits; (3) Sudanese large drum.   (1)

tambūrā bhajan Solo song genre of the Fiji Indians.   (5)

tamburaši Players of the *tambura*.   (8)

tamburaški orkestar *Tamburica* orchestra.   (8)

tamburello Italian small frame drum used in *trantella*.   (8)

tambūrī Small *tambūrā* carried by devotees of the poet-saint Tukaram, in Maharashtra.   (5)

tamburica (1) Related and variously sized long-necked fretted lutes. (2) (Also *tamburaški orkestar.*) Ensemble of plucked chordophones (*tambure*).   (8)

tamburini Italian tambourines.   (8)

tamburitza Fretted long-necked lute plucked with a flat plectrum, found in South Slavic areas of the Balkans.   (3)

tamdyazt Moral or political type of song performed by the Moroccan Berber *imdyazn* troupe.   (6)

tamghra Berber dance performed for or by a bride and her attendants.   (1)

Tamil Iśai 'Tamil Music', movement of the 1940s.   (5)

tamil isai valipāṭṭu 'Tamil music liturgy', seven Tamil musical liturgies, including one in folk style, in use at the Tamil Nadu Theological Seminary.   (5)

tamlang agung Maguindanao small bamboo half-tubes.   (4)

tammâṭṭa (Also *tamukku.*) Kettledrum pair used in the Buddhist *hēvisi* ensemble of Sri Lanka.   (5)

tammorra (Also *tammurro.*) Italian tambourine.   (8)

tammuriata Italian couple dance performed to syllabic *strambotti*.   (8)

tampiang Small frame drum on Ternate.   (4)

tampoutsia Cypriot frame drum used in the *vkiolarides* ensemble.   (8)

tamssust (1) Dance song of the Moroccan Berbers. (2) The act of knocking down fruit from trees.   (6)

tamuk Sama large hanging gong.   (4)

tamunangue Venezuelan suite of dances and music.   (2)

tāmūrē Popular term for *'ori tahiti*, Tahitian couple dancing, associated with joy and pleasure.   (9)

tan (1) Dan dance-song. (2) (China.) Religious altar.   (1, 7)

tān Improvisatory melodic phrase, often in fast tempo, in Hindustani vocal and instrumental music; sometimes used synonymously with *vistār*.   (5)

tan singing Form of Indo-Caribbean neotraditional music performed by semiprofessional specialists.   (3)

tanak Rare Samawan dance for happy occasions.   (4)

tanaka (Also *pato.*) Large jerrycan for oil or fat, used as an idiophone by Afro-Arab populations in the Gulf states in the *lewa* musical tradition.   (6)

tānam Unmetered, pulsed improvisation on a Karnatak raga.   (5)

tanbīre (1) (Also *tanburag, setār.*) Long-necked lute that provides a drone in Baluchi music. (2) Lyre of the Gulf region used in *nobān* ceremonies; cf. *ṭunbūr*.   (6)

tanbou Membranophone in French or French-influenced locales.   (2)

tanbur Maltese tambourine played with a *zavzava* to accompany a *zaqq*.   (8)

tanbur (Also *tanbūr.*) Long-necked fretted plucked lute with oval body, in northern regions.   (5)

ṭanbūr (Also *ṭanbūra.*) Sudanese-Arabic lyre.   (1)

ṭanbūra (Also *nuban,* a term related to its Nubian roots.) Song and dance tradition of the Gulf region, held as a weekly social event or on special occasions to treat maladies associated with spirit possession. The ritual is named for the lyre commonly used in the ceremony; cf. *ṭambūra*.   (6)

táncdalok 'Dance songs', general Hungarian designation for pop music.   (8)

táncház 'Dance house', any of numerous revival dance meetings organized by university students in Budapest, Hungary.   (8)

tanci (China.) Lyrics sung to instrumental accompaniment.   (7)

tandak geroh Sung couplets with *suling*, Lombok.   (4)

tandana tāna (Also *tana tandana.*) Refrain of a song in Karnataka.   (5)

tāṅḍava Masculine aspects of dance; one of the main principles of dance in the twelfth-century *Abhinaya Chandrika. See also lāsya.*   (5)

tandhak Javanese female singer-dancer.   (4)

tanduro Unfretted plucked lute used to provide a drone in Rajasthan.   (5)

tang Tiboli lowest-sounding gong.   (4)

tan'ga 'Short song', introductory song of a Korean *p'ansori* performance.   (7)

tangak Korean court music of Chinese origin; see *hyangak*.   (7)

tangará Mbyá ritual dance-song.   (2)

tangbut Kayan struck bamboo tubes.   (4)

tanggol Shaman from southern Korea.   (7)

tangje Korean shaman ritual for a bounteous harvest.   (7)

tangkel Four-stringed tube zither of the Philippines.   (4)

tangkol Bukidnon polychordal zither.   (4)

tang kut Korean shaman ritual for the prosperity of a village.   (7)

tango (1) Argentine nostalgic, melancholy music and dance that originated in and is centered on Buenos Aires. (2) *Tango canción,* Argentine sung *tango* genre. (3) *Tango característico,* Argentine characteristic sung *tango* genre. (4) *Tango romanza,* Argentine instrumental *tango* genre. (5) Argentine dance in 2/4 meter. (6) Ballroom dance of Argentine origin in 4/4 time featuring stylized bodily postures.   (2, 3, 4, 8)

tang pip'a Korean four-stringed plucked lute.   (7)

tang p'iri Korean conical double-reed bamboo oboe for Chinese-derived music.   (7)

tangsan kut Korean shaman ritual for village prosperity.   (7)

tanguería 'Tango place'; in Argentina and Uruguay, a recent Argentine name for a dance club or locale where live *tango* performers can be seen.   (2)

tani Kogi calabash container rattle.   (2)

tani āvartanam Extended percussion solo in a Karnatak concert.   (5)

tanjidor Brass bands in Sumatra.   (4)

tanka (Japan.) Thirty-one-syllable poem.   (7)

tanmori Korean rhythmic pattern (*changdan*), extremely fast 4/4 meter.   (7)

tanna Lowest-pitched of the three small cylindrical drums in the drum ensembles of Shiḥr (southern Hadramawt), generally known as *mirwās*.   (6)

tân nhạc Modern popular songs of Vietnam.   (4)

tanok (Also *khorovod, krugi.*) Russian collective circle and figure dances.   (8)

tanpura (Also *tānpūrā, tambūrā, tambura.*) (1) Long-necked, unfretted, plucked drone lute. (2) Among East Indian communities in Guyana, Surinam, Trinidad, and elsewhere, a plucked lute that provides a drone.   (2, 5)

tān saṅgīt Form of Indo-Guyanese classical music.   (5)

tanso Small Korean notched bamboo vertical flute.   (7)

Tantric Referring to an esoteric cult within Hinduism and Buddhism.   (5)

Tanzimat Period of reform in the nineteenth-century Ottoman empire, emphasizing the principle of westernization in society, culture, and aesthetics.   (6)

taoqu (China.) Suite of related pieces.   (7)

taozhong (China.) Clapperless pottery bell.   (7)

tapa Cloth made from pounded bark, usually of the paper mulberry. (**9**)

tapan (Also *tŭpan.*) Balkan cylindrical double-headed drum. (**8**)

tapatan Chanted game of wit, played in the Philippines. (**4**)

taphon Thai asymmetrical two-headed barrel drum mounted horizontally. (**4**)

tapkar (Japan.) 'Stamping dance', Ainu dance performed by men. (**7**)

ṭap-khyāl Mixed form of *ṭappā* and *khyāl* popular among Bengali urban composers in the nineteenth century and the first half of the twentieth century. (**5**)

tapou (Also Malbar drum.) Frame drum of Martinique and Réunion Island. (**5**)

ṭappā Vocal form based on Punjabi song. (**5**)

ṭappaṭṭai Frame drum of Tamil Nadu. (**5**)

ṭappū Locally made frame drum played with a bamboo stick, in Guyanese Tamil music. (**5**)

tapujeados Dance performed in El Salvador by men who disguise themselves with masks and eccentric clothing. (**2**)

tapur Conch trumpet in the Aru islands. (**4**)

taqbil Maltese art of rhyming, used in *ghana ta' spirtu pront.* (**8**)

taqlīd 'Imitation' (Arabic); routine imitation, necessary in the early stages of musical apprenticeship but devalued in religious and artistic traditions. (**6**)

taqsīm (Also *taqāsīm;* Turkish, *taksim.*) Introductory instrumental section of music involving free improvisation. In performance of the Iraqi *maqām,* either *taqsīm* or *muqaddima* (instrumental introduction) is required. (**6**)

taqtuqa Maltese castanets, used in small ensembles for ambulatory street music, weddings, parties, and picnics. (**8**)

ṭaqṭūqa Short strophic song, popular in early-twentieth-century Egypt. (**6**)

taquirari Bolivian tropical syncretic song style from the lowlands. (**2**)

tar (1) North African frame drum with attached cymbals. (2) (Also *ṭār.*) Sudanese frame drum, played for *nōba.* (3) (Also *dāff.*) Single-membrane frame drum, widespread in the Near East. (4) (Also *ṭār.*) Small round frame drum with small metal cymbals (tambourine), used in the Maghrib and Mashriq; or a larger type of frame drum. (4) Frame drum with jingles, from Lombok. (**1, 3, 4, 6**)

tar (1) Iranian plucked lute. (2) (Also *t'ar.*) Long-necked Armenian lute with a body in the shape of a figure-eight, a skin soundboard, and five to nine, eleven, or fourteen strings. (3) (Also *ṭār.*) Persian, 'string'; long-necked lute with three double courses of strings, found in Iran and Central Asia. (4)

Tār śahnāī, North Indian bowed long-necked fretted lute related to the *isrāj.* (**3, 5, 6**)

tara Bolivian broad flute timbre dense with harmonics. (**2**)

ṭarab Acute joy, enthusiasm, or grief; also, artistry. (**6**)

ṭarab (Also *qanbūs.*) Traditional Yemeni lute covered in goatskin. (**6**)

tarabuka Goblet-shaped drum, used in Gypsy bands in Serbia. (**8**)

tarabuka (Also *darabuka.*) Middle Eastern goblet-shaped drum played in the Balkans. (**8**)

taraf Romanian instrumental ensemble. (**8**)

taragot Romanian single-reed keyed wooden aerophone with a conical bore. (**8**)

taralala (Rightly *tarālalā,* probably from English *tra-la-la.*) Fijian mixed couples' dance in duple meter and lively tempo, with cheerful text and music deriving from European popular styles of the 1800s. (**9**)

tarānā Rhythm-focused Hindustani vocal genre using vocables. (**5**)

tarāne Traditional Baluchi song for weddings and celebrations, derived from Indo-Pakistani light music. (**6**)

tarantella Italian and Corsican dance in vivacious 6/8 time that derives its name from a dance-therapy ritual prescribed for a person supposedly bitten by a tarantula. (**3, 8**)

tarantismo Name of the *tarantella* in the area of Apulia. (**8**)

tarāwīd Light songs sung at henna parties preceding Palestinian weddings. (**6**)

ṭarda Egyptian combat game of presumed bedouin origin, involving the mutual pursuit of armed horsemen. (**6**)

tardeada Hispanic afternoon dance. (**3**)

tarek Palawan dance of young women. (**4**)

tarfi' Medium-pitched drum of three small cylindrical drums in ensembles of Shiḥr (southern Hadramawt), generally known as *mirwās.* (**6**)

tarh Coptic hymn paraphrasing a biblical text. (**6**)

tari Dance (pan-Indonesian term). (**4**)

tari asyek Court-derived dance and dance-drama of Malaysia. (**4**)

tari inai Northern Malay dance genre. (**4**)

tari kibas Fan dance on Kai. (**4**)

tari kursus Refined social dance of Sunda. (**4**)

tari lala Mixed-couple dancing on Ternate and Tidore. (**4**)

tari lilin Dance with candles on a plate, from Sumbawa. (**4**)

tari rebana Men's dance-drumming form of Sumbawa. (**4**)

tari sasoi Special dance on Kai to honor the raja. (**4**)

tari tidi Torajan dance with swords. (**4**)

t'arija Small single-headed vase drum, typical in performance of Moroccan *malḥūn.* (**6**)

tarikat (Plural, *tarikatlar.*) Turkish Sufi order; cf. *ṭarīqa.* (**6**)

tarima Wooden platform for foot-stamping (*zapateado*) dances among the Mixtec. (**2**)

ṭarīqa (Plural, *ṭuruq.*) Sufi order. (**6**)

tariray Sama women's dance. (**4**)

ta'riya Moroccan clay cylindrical drum. (**1**)

tarjama 'Translation', ornamented variation of a vocalist's melody by the instrumentalists of a *takht.* (**6**)

tarjī' Technique in which text repetitions are sung to new, improvised melodies. (**6**)

tarka In Bolivia, Chile, and Peru, a square or slightly hexagonal-shaped (cross-section) wooden duct flute with a hoarse sound. (**2**)

tarkeada Music played by a *tarka* ensemble. (**2**)

tarling Guitar-and-flute-based popular music of Cirebon. (**4**)

tárogató Hungarian single-reed keyed wooden aerophone with a conical bore. (**8**)

tarol Brazilian thin snare drum. (**2**)

tarola Spanish term for snare drum. (**2**)

tarompet (1) Western cornet played in *ngoma* performances. (2) Double-reed oboe from Sunda and Java. (**1, 4**)

tarpe Aerophone with two gourd resonators, in Maharashtra. (**5**)

tār śahnāī North Indian bowed long-necked fretted lute related to the *isrāj.* (**5**)

tarsila Historical record of genealogies in the Philippines. (**4**)

tartīl (1) Qur'ānic recitation; (2) the less melodically elaborate style of Qur'ānic recitation; cf. *tajwīd.* (**6**)

tartys-kyui 'Contest piece' performed on the Kazakh *dombra.* (**6**)

tāṣ Folk kettledrum of North India, played with sticks. (**5**)

ṭāsa (1) Shallow dish-shaped kettledrum with head tensed by a turning ring, in modern practice using screws attached to the head assembly; widespread throughout Yemen, particularly in the highlands. (2) Copper bowl struck with sticks, played in the 'Isāwa Sufi ritual of Morocco. (**6**)

tasabia (Arabic.) String of prayer beads. (**1**)

taṣdīra First, relatively slow song within a Andalusian-Moroccan *nūba* cycle. (**6**)

tasfiq Hand clapping. (**6**)

tāshā Shallow bowl-shaped drum in Pakistan. (**5**)

taskiwin 'Powderhorns', warrior dances performed in the Moroccan Berber *aḥwash* by men in a circle. (**6**)

taslīm Concluding or refrain section, for example in the Iraqi *maqām*. (**6**)

tasnewa Paya ritual that marks both birth and death. (**2**)

tasnīf Vocal composition with a poetic text in Persian or Azeri, included at specified points in performances of classical music and representing a simplification of the *radīf* system. (**6**)

tassa Drum and drum ensemble, found at weddings, Muslim Moharrum commemorations (in Trinidad Hosay), and other events. (**3**)

tassa (Also *tāssā*.) (1) Earthenware kettledrum with laced goatskin head, in Trinidad and Guyana. (2) Kettle-type drum played with a stick at Muslim festivals and weddings in Guyana and Trinidad and Tobago. (**2, 5**)

tasŭrŭm Introductory instrumental portion of a Korean piece. (**7**)

tatabuang Set of small gongs in Central Maluku. (**4**)

tatabuhan kayu Wooden xylophones of Ambon. (**4**)

tataki (Japan.) Folk song quoted in *gidayû busi*. (**7**)

tatarizo Scraped bamboo idiophone of southern Tanzania. (**1**)

tata vādya Chordophone (instrument category), in the *Nāṭyaśāstra*. (**5**)

tate (Japan.) Leader of an instrumental or vocal section. (**7**)

ta'thīr Effect, ethos. (**6**)

Tatibana *kai* (Japan.) School of *tikuzen biwa* founded by in 1920 by Tatibana Kyokusô (d. 1967). (**7**)

tati kata (Japan.) Generic term for *nô* actors. (**7**)

tātū Small bridge of horny bone on the Afghani *rabāb*. (**5**)

tatŭm Double bell in the border area of the Central African Republic and the Congo. (**1**)

tatva Abstract philosophical song genre in Karnataka. (**5**)

tatyan Genre of eastern Turkish vocal music. (**6**)

taualuga Finale of a Sāmoan performance of singing and dancing, featuring a distinguished woman (*tāupou*) and attendants (*'aiuli*). (**9**)

tau'olunga Tongan dance performed by women. (**9**)

taures Latvian wooden and birch-bark trumpets with a mouthpiece or a single reed, associated with herding. (**8**)

tāus Bowed, long-necked, fretted lute shaped like a peacock (obsolete). (**5**)

tau-tau Torajan funeral effigy. (**4**)

tavājud Ecstasy; trance; forced ecstasy; psychic and unconscious conditioning in order to reach ecstasy. (**6**)

ta-velika citira (Also *brunkula, bunkula*.) Basset, a small three-stringed bass, played in Resia, Slovenia, to accompany violins. (**8**)

tavil (1) Double-headed drum played in South Indian temples, rituals, and processions. (2) Drum from India. (**4, 5**)

tavṣan 'Rabbit', male dancer in Ottoman Turkish traditions; cf. *köçek*. (**6**)

tawag (Also *tawak*.) Large, deep-rimmed gongs of Borneo. (**4**)

tawāif Courtesan singer and dancer. (**5**)

tawak-tawak Medium-size suspended gong of Sumatra. (**4**)

tawāshī (Plural, *tūshiya*.) Internal musical segments embellishing the framework of an Andalusian *nūba*. (**6**)

tawashīḥ dīniyya Genre of *inshād dīnī* performed by a solo *munshid* supported by a small chorus (*biṭāna*). (**6**)

tawḥīd Islamic creed, *Lā illāha illa Allāh* 'There is no God but God'. (**6**)

tawshīḥ (1) Rhythmic song; may conclude a performance of the Iraqi *maqām* in ritual contexts; cf. *peste*. (2) (Also *tathlīth* 'tripling', referring to its threefold structure.) Type of vocal suite in Yemeni tradition, related to the *qawma*. (**6**)

taxim Greek nonmetrical instrumental modal improvisation preceding rhythmic dance-songs. (**8**)

tāyampaka Temple performance in Kerala. (**5**)

tayil (1) Mapuche women's song of ritual, healing, and lineage. (2) Tausug slow singing style. (**2, 4**)

tayò Violin-shaped Mon fiddle, obsolete. (**4**)

tayû (Japan.) Vocalists in narrative *syamisen* music. (**7**)

tayuban Musical party with singer-dancers, common in Indonesia and Malaysia. (**4**)

taẓammart (Also *tasansagh, tasensigh*.) Tuareg four-holed flute, made of a reed or metal tube. (**1**)

tazâwat Medium-sized kettledrum, played by women in the Azawagh region of Niger. (**1**)

tazengherit Tuareg ecstatic music and dance, performed especially at Tazruk and Hirafok oases, Ahaggar. (**1**)

ta'zīye (Also *shabih* 'likeness' in Iranian Khorasan.) Dramatic representation of events surrounding the martyrdom of Imam Husayn or another Shī'a imam, in which imams and their supporters sing lines of verse while their opponents recite in an unmelodious manner. (**6**)

tazrrart (1) (Plural, *tizrrarin*.) Responsorial song of Morocco; in some forms, men and women in separate rooms respond to one another. (2)

"Limping" rhythm used in Moroccan Berber *ahwash*. (**6**)

tazu ma sorek 'Songs of the gourd', Miri men's bawdy songs in hocket style. (**1**)

tbel Moroccan kettledrum. (**1**)

tchatcha Gourd rattle filled with pellets for use during Haitian Petro rites, analogous to *rada ason*. (**2**)

tchiattisma Improvised rhyming couplets of Cyprus. (**8**)

tchira 'Cry', less melodious version of the *lyóba por la rindja*, sung by herdsmen bringing their cattle down from alpine pastures in Haute-Gruyère, Switzerland. (**8**)

teatro callejero Traditional Uruguayan theatrical form. (**2**)

teatro de revistas Type of light comic theater in Montevideo, Uruguay. (**2**)

tebe Wooden jaw harp of Savu. (**4**)

te byôsi (Japan.) Hand clapping. (**7**)

techno Category of fast electronic dance music of the 1980s. (**3**)

techno-lindo Contemporary Croatian popular music that sets traditional Dalmatian dance music on electronic instruments. (**8**)

tecolote 'Owl', whose hoot at dawn signals the end of Yuma social dance. (**2**)

tecvīt Qur'ānic recitation (Turkish); cf. *tajwīd*. (**6**)

te-ed Yakan introductory instrumental piece. (**4**)

te-er Bontok ritual of abstinence from work. (**4**)

tegennewt Algerian kettledrum, made from a wooden or enameled metal bowl and occasionally played by the Tuareg. (**1**)

tegerek-tepsey Balkar and Karachaevi circle dance in 2/4 and 4/4 time. (**8**)

tegoto (Japan.) Extended instrumental interludes in *syamisen* or *koto* music. (**7**)

tegoto mono (Japan.) *Ziuta* repertoire (*syamisen* music) with extended instrumental interludes (*tegoto*) framed by songs. (**7**)

te gumi (Japan.) Set of 8-beat drum patterns in *nô*. (**7**)

tehemmet Tuareg dance of Tassili-n-Ajjer, accompanied by songs, clapping, and one or more drums. (**1**)

tehigelt Tuareg dance of Ahaggar, accompanied by songs, clapping, and one or more drums. (**1**)

tehyan Two-stringed bowed lute from Indonesia. (**4**)

teicamās dziesmas Latvian songs recited in traditional contexts and celebrations, such as weddings, lullabies, field labor, and breeding cattle. (**8**)

Tejano music Popular music from the border regions of Texas and Mexico. (**3**)

tejón 'Badger', dance among the Mixtec. (2)

teké Greek hashish den, the center of *rebetika* activity. (8)

tekerő Hungarian hurdy-gurdy. (8)

tekeyë (Also *tekeya, wanna.*) Yekuana ritual bamboo idioglottal clarinet with internal reed (*suruídey*), played in pairs, one male and the other female. (2)

tekke (1) Dervish lodge; place of meeting or residence for members of a *tarikat*. (2) (Also *khanaqah.*) Sufi fraternity house in Kashmir. (5, 6)

têku (Japan.) *Taiko* (drums) in Okinawan dialect. (7)

Telemark *springar* Any of the principal Norwegian dances, with an accented second beat in each measure. (8)

telenn Breton small Celtic harp, revived in the 1950s. (8)

telwan Nuptial songs of the Fiji Indians. (5)

telyn Welsh harp; symbolically the most important Welsh musical instrument. (8)

tembaga Tiboli heaviest bossed gongs. (4)

tembang Type of metered vocal performance in Indonesia. (4)

tembang Sasak Sasak metered sung poetry. (4)

tembang Sunda Aristocratic sung poetry of Sunda. (4)

temcîd Night prayer sung in the mosque during the month of fasting (Turkish), associated with the Sufi liturgy. (6)

Temiar Subgroup of the Senoi people of upland Malaysia. (4)

temïmbi-púku Argentine vertical flute among the Chiriguano-Chané. (2)

temimby ie piasá Transverse flute among the Chriwano of Paraguay. (2)

temja Algerian six-holed wooden flute. (1)

temmāngu pāṭṭu Tamil song form in which two performers (sometimes representing lovers) take alternate lines. (5)

Temne Cultural group of Sierra Leone. (1)

temple 'Tuning'. (1) *Temple arpa*, Peruvian guitar tuning pattern (E–B–F-sharp–D–A–F-sharp), used to play a *huayno* or *carnaval* in B minor. (2) *Temple diable*, Peruvian guitar tuning pattern (E–C–G–D–B-flat–G), used to play a *yaraví* in G minor. (2)

tempo Perceived speed of a musical performance; cf. *meter, rhythm.* (9)

Tendai (Japan.) Buddhist sect founded by Saityô (767–822) in the Heian period. (7)

Tendai syômyô (Japan.) *Syômyô* (Buddhist chant) school of the Tendai sect founded by Ennin (a disciple of Saityô, the founder of the sect) in the Heian period (794–1192). (7)

tende (Also *tindi.*) Tuareg single-headed mortar drum. (1)

tende n-ɔmnas Events at which the mortar drum is played and which feature personalized references to camels. (1)

tendrena 'To play', Malagasy verb used to denote playing chordophones and keyboard instruments. (1)

teneboim (Also *chairígoas.*) Guarijío leg rattles made of moth cocoons filled with seeds. (2)

tengai (Japan.) Straw hat worn by mendicant monks of the Huke sect of Buddhism (*komusô*). (7)

Tengger Ethnic group from Java. (4)

Tengrianism Ancient trinitarian religion of Kazakh nomads, aspects of which many Kazakhs blend with Islamic beliefs. (6)

teng thing Northern Thai barrel drum, similar to *taphon.* (4)

tengu (Japan.) Offertory Buddhist chant (*syômyô*). (7)

tenor (Also *tenorete.*) Low voice part in Venezuelan *tonos* ensemble. (2)

tenor drum Wooden-shelled snareless drum larger than a snare drum. (8)

tenpuku (Japan.) *Syakuhati* used in Kagosima Prefecture. (7)

Tenpyô biwa hu (Japan.) '*Biwa* Score of the Tenpyô Era', fragment of the *gagaku biwa* notation of 742 C.E.; the oldest documented lute tablature in the world, and the oldest extant Japanese instrumental tablature. (7)

te oh Ankle bracelets with leaf baskets, from West Timor. (4)

tep Chechen and Ingush frame drum; see *zhirga.* (8)

tepežnicw Spanking songs, sung in Slovenia on 28 December to bring fertility. (8)

teponahuastle (Also *tepunahuaste.*) In Mexico, the present-day Nahua *teponaztle* 'log idiophone' used in Christian ceremonies; *see also teponaztli, tun, tunkul.* (2)

teponaztli (Also *teponaztle.*) In Mexico, a Nahua hollowed-out log slit drum or gong with an H-shaped incision on its top. (2)

tepsi Large, round copper tray, used by Albanian women to provide a resonator for their singing. (8)

tepsija Copper pan, used by Kosovo Serbs to provide a resonator for their singing. (8)

tepuzquiquiztli Náhuatl name for a wooden or metal trumpet. (2)

të qarë (Also *vajtim.*) 'Cried', Albanian flute melodies that draw on women's vocal laments. (8)

të qarë me zë 'Cried with the voice', Albanian lament or stylized form of crying. (8)

tequina Taino responsorial song leader. (2)

terbana Large bowl-shaped drum of Bali and Lombok. (4)

terbang Indonesian single-headed Muslim frame drum. (4)

tercets proverbes Corsican form of *chiam'e rispondi*, in which a traditional proverb sung by one singer had to be answered with a suitable proverb by another singer. (8)

terkîb Subdivision of the *mülâzime* and *hâne* in the Turkish *peşrev*, consisting of two or more cycles (*devr*) of the *usûl*; used in a modular fashion in the early Ottoman *peşrev*. (6)

terkotki (Also *kosatki.*) Clappers used in annual church ceremonies in Poland. (8)

terme 'Threading', term for a variety of short narrative songs that surround the performance of the Kazakh epic tale. (6)

terno Brazilian generic term for dramatic dance groups that perform during patron saints' festivals. (2)

terokará Board zither with five to seven strings played by the Aché-Guayakí of Paraguay. (2)

terreiro 'Temple' in Afro-Brazilian syncretic religious worship in Brazil, Paraguay, and Uruguay. (2)

terrimaxka Maltese barrel organ on wheels with clockwork dancing figures, played for amusement and dancing on Sundays and at feasts, often accompanied by a monkey's antics. (8)

terukkūttu (Also *terrukkūttu pāṭṭu.*) 'Street drama', 'street dance', 'street music' (Tamil); popular dramatic narrative form in Tamil Nadu. (5)

tesbîh Morning prayer sung in the mosque during the month of fasting (Turkish). (6)

tesiwit Pastoral Tuareg strophic poems performed solo to formulaic melodies or motifs. (1)

teško oro 'Heavy dance', Macedonian men's dance. (8)

teslim Refrain with a Turkish musical form; cf. *taslīm.* (6)

tessitura Most comfortable or general range of a voice or instrument. (3)

testamenti Italian song genre. (8)

tetartos Fourth movement of the Cypriot *kartzilamades* dance cycle, performed in 9/8 time. (8)

tetawak (1) Single hanging bossed gong of Malaysia; (2) hanging gong of Sumatra. (4)

tètèt Double-reed aerophone of Java. (4)

tetrachord (Japan.) Unit of the fourth in Japanese scales proposed by Koizumi Fumio (1927–1983). (7)

te tuke (Japan.) Composing an instrumental part. (7)

tetun Smallest *sene* gongs of West Timor. (4)

tēvāram (Also *tevāram.*) 'Garland of the Divine', collection of Tamil hymns to Shiva, composed by Tamil Shaivite saints from the seventh to ninth centuries. (5)

tēvārāṭṭam Dance genre performed by Kampalattar Nāyakars in Tamil Nadu. (5)

tevşîh Metrical hymn performed on the birthday of the Prophet or another holiday; cf. *tawshîh, tawashîh diniyya*. (6)

text envelope Area of knowledge to be drawn on that is larger than any single text. (1)

teyyam Gods, in Kerala; ritual form of worship of folk and tribal gods, goddesses, and benevolent or malevolent spirits (*bhūtam*). (5)

t'gah In Armenian music, a sung poem, lyrical, dramatic, or solemnly laudatory. There are secular and religious *tagher*. (6)

thālī (Also *thāl*.) Metal plate struck with a stick. (5)

thambobok Subanen paired-string zither. (4)

tham khwan Thai ceremony to restore a person's spiritual essence. (4)

thandahar Dance of the Bastar tribe of Madhya Pradesh. (5)

thang (1) Thai melodic idiom of a particular instrument. (2) Thai style of a teacher or "school." (3) Thai pitch level of a composition; mode. (4)

thanggunggu Subanen gong ensemble. (4)

thañ hmañ Tonic pitch based on lowest note of *hnè*, Burma. (4)

thaqīl 'Heavy', slow in tempo. (6)

thāṭ Parent scale in Hindustani music theory. (5)

thaun Goblet-shaped drum with single head, Cambodia. (4)

thefteros Second movement of the Cypriot *kartzilamades* dance cycle, performed in 7/8 time. (8)

thekā Drum pattern representing a Hindustani tala. (5)

theotokia Hymns in honor of the Virgin Mary, sung in the Coptic church. (6)

Theravada (Also Theravada Buddhism.) Doctrine of the Elders; considered the most orthodox form of Buddhism, thought to have begun in Sri Lanka c. 250 B.C.E. and spread to Southeast Asia around the eleventh century. (4, 5)

thet Thai Buddhist preaching, in Pali or the vernacular. (4)

thet mahachat Thai preaching-chanting of the story of Prince Wetsandon, the Buddha-to-be. (4)

thirrje vaji (Also known *lelekanje*, Serbo-Croatian.) 'Provocation of cry', Albanian men's lament in Montenegro. (8)

thōb nashal Long traditional dancing dress of the Arabian peninsula. (6)

thobo Bamboo stamping tubes of Flores. (4)

thon Thai wood or clay single-headed goblet-shaped drum. (4)

Three Kingdoms Korean dynastic periods including Koguryŏ, Paekche, and Silla. (7)

thumrī Light classical Hindustani vocal form and style; associated with dance and dramatic gesture. (5)

thunderstick (Also *Schwirrholz*, German.) Bull-roarer. (8)

thuộng Upland minority population of Vietnam. (4)

ti Any of several Oceanic shrubs of the genus *Cordyline*, of the lily family. (9)

ti (Japan.) Fourth note in the Japanese scale *gosei*. (7)

tian'ge (China.) Field songs. (7)

tiaoge (China.) Dance of northwestern minorities, with instrumental accompaniment but without singing. (7)

tiaoxian (China.) Tuning the strings. (7)

tiba Swiss term for the alphorn in Bundner Oberland. (8)

tibag Reenactment, in the Philippines, of the search for the Holy Cross. (4)

tibia Romanian trumpet or horn. (8)

tibiae pares 'Paired pipes' (Latin), flutes taken as far north as the border settlement of Noviomagus (now Nijmegen, Netherlands) during the first century. (8)

tibwa Martinique rhythm sticks. (2)

tickey draai Dance accompanied by the guitar and popular until the 1940s in South Africa. (1)

tidinit (1) Mauritanian lute. (2) Long-necked lute used in classical music by Arab tribes of Mauritania. (1, 6)

tidtu Maguindanao rhythmic mode. (4)

tienbasser Accordion of the Low Countries. (8)

tietäjä 'Knower', 'soothsayer', Finnish singer with above-average knowledge. (8)

tiêu End-blown notch flute of Vietnam. (4)

tiêu nhạc Vietnam's court ensemble of strings. (4)

tifa Ubiquitous pan-Maluku drum. (4)

tifa gila Long drum in Ternate used to accompany the *hasa* dance. (4)

tifa podo Vase-shaped short drums of the Ternate *kulintang* ensemble. (4)

tifa tui Bamboo idiochord zither on Ternate and Tidore. (4)

tigul (Nissan.) Also *tsigul* (Banoni, Buka.) Nocturnal session of dancing, drumming, and singing; the genres performed at such sessions. (9)

tihāī Hindustani cadential pattern consisting of a musical phrase repeated three times, ending at the *mukhṛā* or *sam*. (5)

ti'ilangga Traditional palm-leaf hat of Roti. (4)

tiir Italian polyphonic singing style in Primana, Lombardy. (8)

ţiituri 'Rhythmic formulas', patterns played on the Romanian *cobza*. (8)

Tijaniyya Islamic brotherhood that traces its roots to Sufi sects of North Africa. (1)

tik Pontic Greek dance. (8)

tiki Polynesian stone or wooden image of a supernatural power. (9)

Tikuho ryû (Japan.) *Syakuhati* school founded in 1917 by Sakai Tikuho I (1892–1984). (7)

tikuzen biwa (Japan.) Form of the *biwa* (lute) and its music—sometimes called *tikuzen môsô biwa*—developed from the blind priests' *biwa* tradition of northern Kyûsyû, a region known as Tikuzen. (7)

tilak (Also *biṅdī*.) Red dot worn on the forehead of a *yakṣagāna* dance or a *bharata nātyam* dancer, also worn as a sign that one is a Hindu. (5)

tilinca (Also *tininca*.) Northern Romanian end-blown, rim-blown shepherd's flute, with no duct and no holes for fingering. (8)

tillāna Lively, fast-paced song form that is the last piece of a *bharata nātyam* dance concert. (5)

tīm Toda women's work-song genre in Tamil Nadu. (5)

timang Iban ritual chanting. (4)

timbalada Afro-Bahian popular genre featuring the timbre of the *timbal*. (2)

timbales (1) Cuban membranophones constructed from metal semispherical closed containers. (2) Metal-shelled single-headed drums popular in Cuban dance styles. (2, 3)

timbila South African Chopi xylophones played in large ensembles. (1)

timbil-kaft Ossetian couple dance; see *lezginka*. (8)

timbre (1) Quality of a musical sound, an interval, or an ensemble that distinguishes it from another. (2) Quality of sound that makes one voice or instrument sound different from another while producing identical pitches. (3) Perceived quality of a sound, defined by the presence and intensities of overtones. (1, 3, 4, 8, 9)

timbre (French.) Borrowed tune or its title applied to a text. (8)

timbrh Raffia lamellophone of the Vute of central Cameroon. (1)

ţîmbuk Small barrel drum (*ḍuhl*) played as rhythmic accompaniment. (5)

timeline Any of several repeating rhythmic patterns underlying much West African ensemble music and usually played by a high-pitched struck idiophone, such as a double clapperless bell. (1)

timila Elongated double-headed hourglass drum of Kerala. (5)

Volume Key: **6**, Middle East; **7**, East Asia; **8**, Europe; **9**, Australia and the Pacific Islands; **10**, The World's Music.

timple High-pitched Spanish guitar. (**8**)

tina (From Spanish 'washtub'.) Miskitu chordo-phone consisting of a single string made from vegetable fiber and fixed between the protruding end of a meter-long wooden pole and the bottom of an upturned tin washtub. (**2**)

tinding One-stringed struck bamboo idiochord of Flores. (**4**)

tingkat Unofficial caste system of Bali. (**4**)

tingklik Bamboo xylophone of Bali. (**4**)

tingo Salvadoran log idiophone, related to the ancient *tepunahuaste*, personifying Saint Tingo. (**2**)

tingting Dominican triangle. (**2**)

tingtung Cirebonese stamping tubes used in *sintren*. (**4**)

tinka Carnival celebration in Peru in which a llama is sacrificed and ritual offerings are buried for the deities. (**2**)

tinkon (Japan.) Ritual songs to appease the spirits of the dead. (**7**)

tinkon sai (Japan.) Court ritual held on 22 November to energize and uplift the soul of the emperor; a performance context for *ônaobiuta*. (**7**)

tinku 'Encounter'. (1) Annual community rivalry ritual of Ecuador. (2) Bolivian ritual fighting. (**2**)

tiñni Sumu drumstick. (**2**)

Tin Pan Alley (1) Nickname given to a neigh-borhood in New York City where many music publishers were located in the early twentieth century; the name is credited to a newspaperman who thought that so many pianos in one locale sounded like tin pans being banged together. (2) Style of music that originated in New York in the 1890s and became popular from about 1912. (3) Neigh-borhood or area where many composers and music publishers work. (**3, 9**)

tinquy Q'ero intercommunity popular social dance. (**2**)

tintenelle French sheep bell. (**8**)

tinter 'To ring softly', playing stroke on Swiss church bells. (**8**)

tin whistle Six-holed whistle flute of England and Ireland. (**8**)

tinya Small Quechua handheld double-skin frame drum in Peru. (**2**)

tiompán (Also *timpan*, Old Irish.) Irish plucked or bowed chordophone. (**8**)

tīpaṇī Gujarati song and dance form associated with the work of compacting earthen floors. (**5**)

tiple Soprano voice or boy soprano, in the Phil-ippines. (**4**)

tiple 'Treble'. (1) Medium-size twelve-stringed four-course guitar from Colombia. (2) Three-stringed chordophone in Honduras. (3) (Also *tiplillo*.) High-pitched Spanish guitar. (**2, 4, 8**)

tiplero (Also *requintador*, 'one who plays treble'.) Player who improvises contrapuntal melodies on *marimba* in Ecuador. (**2**)

tiqrqqawin Metal castanets used by Moroccan Berbers. (**6**)

tirade (1) Borrowed Greek term referring to a verse form in which an indefinite number of lines are joined by a single rhyme pattern; it is used to describe an ancient form of Kazakh epic composition. (2) Epic tunes of the Lake Onega region of Russia, with stanzas of varying lengths. (**6, 8**)

tirana Brazilian folk dance popular along border areas of Uruguay. (**2**)

tirasi (Japan.) Conventional practice in the Ryûkyû Islands of programming a lighter piece after a large-scale piece in a slow tempo. (**7**)

tirmechy bagshy (Also *tirmeçy bagsy*.) 'Collector', Turkmen singer of poems. (**6**)

tırnak kemençe Fiddle played with the finger-nails, native to nomads of southwestern Turkey. (**6**)

tirtha Balinese holy water. (**4**)

tirtir Chadian circular dance performed by the Zaghawa and characterized by solemn hopping. (**1**)

tiruppāvai Vashnavite devotional genre of Tamil Nadu. (**5**)

tiruppugal Tamil devotional songs to the deity Murugan, from the fifteenth and sixteenth centuries. (**5**)

tiruvarutpā Nineteenth-century hymns to the deity Murugan. (**5**)

tiruvempāvai Shaivite devotional genre in Tamil Nadu. (**5**)

tish Hasidic sabbath meal, involving singing (of *nigunim*) and dancing. (**6**)

tishbibt Metal flute, Egypt. (**6**)

tis kunias Greek courtship songs, performed while boys swing girls on swings. (**8**)

tis tavas (Also *tou trapeziou*.) Greek table song, performed by men and women sitting at a table with friends and relatives. (**8**)

tisse di tch'va Hurdy-gurdy of the Low Coun-tries. (**8**)

titik jin Sama dance of possession. (**4**)

titik tagunggu Sama piece in the *kulintang* repertoire. (**4**)

titil High-pitched metallophone of Cirebon. (**4**)

titiru (Also *tiroro*.) Wayana wooden lip-concus-sion aerophone used in rituals. (**2**)

titti Goatskin bagpipe drone used in Telugu epic performance. (**5**)

tiun 'Song', 'tune'; Miskitu young person's song. (**2**)

tīvra 'Sharped', as a sharped note. (**5**)

tiwa nam *Ronggeng*-like fan dance performed by adolescent girls on Kai. (**4**)

tiyoo Mixtec tortoiseshell struck with a deer antler, similar to the Nahua *ayotl*. (**2**)

Tizan ha (Japan.) One of three branches of the Singon school of Buddhist chant (*syômyô*). (**7**)

tjuz tepsey Balkar and Karachaevi couple dance featuring triplets in 2/4 and 4/4 time. (**8**)

tlapitzalli Náhuatl name for an end-blown clay or bone tubular duct flute with four holes. (**2**)

tlatlazcaliztli Nahua sound of trumpets. (**2**)

tlŭka Bulgarian autumnal social gatherings for communal work, accompanied by singing. (**8**)

t'nabar Ceremonial dances of Tanimbar. (**4**)

t'nabar mpuk-ulu War dance to display a captured head in Tanimbar. (**4**)

toá Bolivian beeswax friction idiophone. (**2**)

toaca Romanian wooden plank or metal plate struck with one or two wooden hammers, played in monasteries and by children. (**8**)

toada Brazilian generic term for song, often associated with popular Catholicism; analo-gous to Spanish *tonada*. (**2**)

toá-toré 'Cavity', Tukano log idiophone and the sound it makes. (**2**)

toba mare Bass drum played in Romania. (**8**)

tobarâma (Japan.) Lyrical folk song in the Yaeyama Islands. (**7**)

tobol Small drum played for the *sebiba*. (**1**)

toch'ang Narrator in Korean *punch'ang* and *ch'anggŭk*. (**7**)

toda Bamboo slit drum of Flores. (**4**)

todagu Bamboo slit drum and drum ensemble of Flores. (**4**)

toddy Fermented coconut-palm sap. (**9**)

tôdô (Japan.) Government-authorized guild for blind artisans established in the fourteenth century. (**7**)

Todos Santos 'All Saints' or All Souls celebra-tion in the Americas. (**2**)

toduksum 'Stolen breath', short breath taken in the middle of an extended note in Korean music. (**7**)

toeira (Also *amarantina*, *braguesa*, *viola*.) Portu-guese term for guitar, usually with five double or triple courses of metal strings, that provides harmonic and rhythmic accompani-ment for *fado*. (**8**)

t'oesŏng Korean melodic ornamentation, sliding down. (**7**)

tof Hebrew squarish frame drum. (**8**)

togalu bombē Puppets made from hide in Karnataka. (**5**)

tôgaku (Japan.) Court music and dance of Chinese origin. (**7**) *tôgani* (Japan.) Musical genre of the Miyako Islands. (7)

toggenburger halszither Swiss long-necked lute-zither with a flat body, shaped like half a pear. (8)

toghorā Funeral piece played by the Burusho people, Northern Areas of Pakistan. (5)

togo Tiruray polychordal zither. (4)

togunggak (Also *togunggu*.) Murut interlocking bamboo tubes. (4)

toi Festive celebration involving hospitality and musical performance, common in Central Asia; *see also toy*. (6)

toja Musical play based on legends in Sumbawa. (4)

tokara Folk rhythm instrument of Assam, consisting of a small drum with a string attached that produces variable-pitch sounds when plucked; similar to the *khamak*. (5)

tokiwazu busi (Also *tokiwazu*.) Genre of Japanese narrative *syamisen* music founded by Tokiwazu Mozi dayû (1709–1781). (7)

Tôkô kinpu (Japan.) 'Notations of *Qin* by Tôkô Zenzi', by the Ming priest Tôkô Zenzi (Chinese name Xin Yue), who brought music for *qin* to Japan in the seventeenth century. (7)

tôkpe 'Stream', 'flow', type of *kyui* (instrumental music) common in western Kazakhstan, consisting of sweeping movements of the right hand resulting in a drone-like texture. (6)

Tok Pisin (English *talk pidgin*.) Pidgin commonly spoken in Papua New Guinea. (9)

tôkyoku (Japan.) *Gagaku* music to accompany the main part of *bugaku* (foreign-origin dance) pieces. (7)

tole karuvi Membranophones (Tamil instrument category). (5)

tolochnye pesni Collective-help songs, sung during the harvest in Russia. (8)

tololoche Mexican-style string bass, often with three strings rather than the four strings typical of the symphonic string bass. (3)

tom (1) Shilluk lyre. (2) Colo rain dance. (1)

to mábadong Torajan male funeral dancer. (4)

t'omak sori 'Cut singing', 'short singing'; single episode or song from a Korean *p'ansori* tale. (7)

tombak (Also *zarb*.) Goblet drum named for the two basic sounds *dom* (struck in the center, lower in pitch, resonant) and *tak* (struck on the rim, brighter in timbre, dry). (6)

tɔmbɔ Vai word for dance. (1)

tɔmbɔ kɛ bɔɔniɛ-nu Vai troupe of Sande society young initiate dancers. (1)

tomimoto busi (Also *tomimoto*.) Genre of Japanese narrative *syamisen* music founded by Tomimoto Buzen dayû (1716–1764). (7)

tonada 'Tune' (Spanish). (1) Originally any intoned melody. (2) Chilean song of the 1990s performed by one or two singers in parallel thirds in nasal style. (3) Characteristic Cuban melody in the *punto guajiro*. (4) *Tonada de toros* 'song of the bulls', improvisatory verbal genre associated with ritualized alms collection in the Dominican Republic. (2)

tonadilla escénica (1) Late sixteenth-century Spanish short comic opera that used folk and popular melodies. (2) In Mexico, short, simple drama, replete with new *sones* and other local melodies. (2, 8)

tonal center In any melody, the tone that serves as a typical structural goal or point of repose. (9)

tonality In European music, a system of tonal organization characteristic of compositions of the seventeenth through nineteenth centuries (applied in popular and some concert music through the twentieth century), characterized by certain technical features, notably the use of a single key as the basis of each composition; the keys, also tonalities, are understood by reference to a final note and a mode, e.g., C major and a minor. (8)

tonbak Iranian wooden single-headed drum. (3)

tôndáxin Mixtec rattle. (2)

tondero Amorous dance and song of northern coastal Peru, related to *marinera* and *zamacueca*. (2)

tone Pitch of definite frequency; a pitch or range of pitches treated within a musical system as a sonic identity, analyzable as a scalar unit; cf. *frequency, note, pitch*. (9)

tone cluster Group of pitches contiguous either diatonically or chromatically, played together; pioneered by the American composer Henry Cowell (1897–1965). (3)

tong Kajang Jew's harp. (4)

tongatong Kalinga stamping tubes. (4)

tongbo (China.) Bronze cymbals. (7)

tongbu minyo Korean folk songs in the eastern regional style. (7)

tonggu (China.) Bronze drum. (7)

tonggyo Korean children's songs. (7)

tongkungon Sabah bamboo tube zither. (4)

Tongnip mun Korean Independence Gate. (7)

tongp'yŏnje Eastern school of the Korean *p'ansori* tradition. (7)

t'ongsok Korean "widespread" folk songs, known in various regions. (7)

t'ongsŏng (Also *chungangsŏng*.) 'Straight voice', principal vocal timbre in Korean *p'ansori*. (7)

tongsu gequ (China.) 'Popular songs'; term invented by the communist government. (7)

tonic sol-fa (Also *solfège*.) Verbal syllables that represent relative pitches. (1)

toŋ ito Two double iron bells of the Central African flange-welded type, with a bow grip. (1)

tonkori (Also *ka*.) Five-stringed wooden zither of the Ainu. (7)

tonkori ramatohu '*Tonkori* spirit', one or two small beads inserted in the soundboard of the *tonkori* (Ainu zither), which are believed to bring the instrument to life. (7)

tonkori sapa Head part of the *tonkori* (Ainu zither). (7)

tonkori tapera Shoulder part of the *tonkori* (Ainu zither). (7)

Tonle Sap 'Great Lake' in western Cambodia. (4)

tonnosť 'Toneness', Russian musicological concept developed by Boris Asaf'ev. (8)

tono 'Tune', 'tone'. (1) European-derived polyphonic song of Venezuela. (2) *Tono de sikuri*, Chilean pentatonic *sikuri* music for processions. (3) *Tono y rueda* 'tone and round', principal genre of the Chilean Aymara carnival festival. (2)

tonos Mode of ancient Greek music and music theory. (8)

tŏnŭm Personal styles and compositions in Korean *p'ansori*. (7)

toombah Eighteenth- to nineteenth-century Antiguan drum fixed with tin jingles and shells. (2)

topamiento de comadres Argentine female funeral dramatization ceremony of carnival. (2)

topayya Kalinga gong ensemble of six men. (4)

topeng Indonesian mask or masked dance performance. (4)

topeng banjet Modern village music of Java. (4)

top mukkuri Ainu Jew's harp (*mukkuri*) made of bamboo. (7)

toppi madalam 'Barrel drum and vina'; obsolete ensemble once used to accompany *mōhini āṭṭam*. (5)

toque (1) 'Hit' (Spanish and Portuguese). Brazilian rhythmic pattern played on *berimbau* and other struck instruments in Latin America. (2) 'Touch', 'beat'; Spanish guitar playing. (2, 8)

tora gaku (Japan.) Music of present-day Vietnam or Cheju, Korea, introduced to Japan during the Nara period (710–794). (7)

toré Among some native South Americans, a single-reed concussion aerophone, or clarinet type. (2)

torimono (Japan.) *Mikagura* songs danced with certain objects called *torimono*. (7)

torito 'Little bull'. (1) Purépecha musical form for carnival. (2) Artifact for dance-games. (3) *Torito kiringua*, slit drum idiophone. **(2)**

tori zi (Japan.) Unit of 4 beats per poetic line in *nô* chanting. **(7)**

tormāy Egyptian double clarinet (*mizmār*) with cow horn bells; cf. *magrūna*, *suggarat*. **(6)**

tormento 'Storm', Peruvian and Chilean idiophone made from a sheet of wood on four legs with bottle caps and wood chips placed or partially nailed on top. **(2)**

toro 'Bull'. (1) *Toro candil*, costume in Paraguay in which one or two men play the part of a fighting bull; (2) *toro huaco*, annual saint's day performance in Diriamba, Nicaragua; (3) *toro que brinca*, among the Mixtec, dance of the 'bull that jumps'; (4) *toros*, masked youths of Ecuador. **(2)**

torotótela (Also *cantastorie*.) Local term for story-singers in Italian-speaking Switzerland. **(8)**

torototela Northeast Italian one-stringed bowed fiddle. **(8)**

torra Corsican children's game, accompanied by verses. **(8)**

torrente Panamanian musical concept similar to scale. **(2)**

Torricelli Mountains Papua New Guinean coastal mountains at the border of East and West Sepik, an extension of the Prince Alexander Range. **(9)**

tortuga 'Turtle'. (1) In Guatemala and elsewhere, a tortoiseshell gong struck on its ventral side with a bone, stick, or antler; (2) Mixtec turtle dance. **(2)**

torupill Estonian bagpipe single-reed melody pipe and drone pipes that sound the tonic and the dominant. **(8)**

tŏrŭrŭ Onomatopoeic Korean term for gently rolling a drumstick. **(7)**

torvi Finnish trumpet made of cow or ox horn or birch or alder bark. **(8)**

t'osin Korean shaman ritual for household prosperity. **(7)**

t'osok "Local" Korean folk songs, known within limited geographical areas. **(7)**

totem Object, as a plant or an animal, or a depiction of an object serving as the sign of a family or a clan. **(9)**

totobuang (1) Double-row gong-chimes of Ambon. (2) Set of large and small gongs on Buru. **(4)**

totobuan kawat Idiochord bamboo zither of Buru. **(4)**

totuma Fruit of a calabash tree, used to make rattles, trumpets, and other implements among the Kogi, Warao, and other northern South American cultures. **(2)**

toubeleki Greek vase-shaped drum. **(8)**

touta Swiss term for the alphorn in Anniviers. **(8)**

tou trapeziou (Also *tis tavas*.) Greek table song, performed by men and women sitting at a table with friends and relatives. **(8)**

touxian (1) Chinese two-stringed fiddle of Chaozhou province. (2) (Also known as *erxian*.) In China, leading bowed stringed instrument in *Chaozhou xianshiyue*. **(4, 7)**

tovil Nexus of rituals in Sinhala Sri Lanka performed for the control or expulsion of a variety of malignant influences. **(5)**

towo Wards of Anlo-Ewe towns in Ghana. **(1)**

toy 'Banquet' (Turkic). Festive celebration of a birth, circumcision, wedding, or the like; the major occasion for performances by an *'āsheq* or *bakhshī*; cf. *toi*. **(6)**

Tozan ryû (Japan.) *Syakuhati* school founded in 1896 by Nakao Tozan (1876–1956). **(7)**

't patertje Kissing dance of the Dutch-language area of the Low Countries. **(8)**

trabajo 'Work'. In northern Peru, the working period signified by the music of a *clarín*. **(2)**

traccule Corsican scraper with small wooden slabs, played like castanets. **(8)**

traceform Shape of the pathways traced by an individual's limbs as they move through space. **(9)**

trachten-gruppen Folk-costume groups', traditional performers in Germany. **(8)**

tradition Continual creation and re-creation of culture by the manipulation of symbolic elements and the reordering and refocusing of inherited cultural constructs to reflect present-day needs and desires. **(9)**

tradizioni popolari 'Popular traditions'. Italian folklore. **(8)**

trae Various kinds of Thai trumpets. **(4)**

trallalero Florid six-part polyphonic male singing in and around the port of Genoa, Italy. **(8)**

traliing (Also *lolling, sulling, tulling*.) Vocal imitation of the *hardanger* violin in Norway. **(8)**

trallning Swedish vocalizations imitating fiddle sounds with onomatopoeic syllables like *tidadi* and *dili-diliadi*. **(8)**

tratto marzo Italian spring celebration that includes the singing of *canti di questua*. **(8)**

trawantel Sword dance of Westerlo, Antwerp Province, Belgium. **(8)**

trebang Frame drum of Cirebon. **(4)**

trebang randu kentir Drumming ensemble of Indramayu. **(4)**

trekbuul (Also *trekorgel, trekzak*.) Accordion of the Low Countries. **(8)**

trekkspil Norwegian accordion. **(8)**

trembita (1) Silesian long wooden trumpet. (2) Ukrainian long cylindrical wooden trumpet, used to signal danger or villagers' deaths and to perform ceremonial music at funerals. **(8)**

tremolo Right-hand plectrum technique, used on the mandolin especially but also on other chordophones played with the plectrum, in which the plectrum is moved rapidly back and forth over one or more strings to produce a sustained sound consisting of thirty-second or sixty-fourth notes. **(3)**

trepang (Also *bêche de mer*.) Large sea cucumbers, boiled, dried, and used mostly by Chinese for making soup. **(9)**

treq 'Path', Judeo-Spanish tradition of compound musical compositions resembling the Andalusian *nūba*, performed at life-cycle and communal celebrations. **(6)**

tres (1) Cuban guitarlike instrument. (2) Cuban six-stringed, double-coursed chordophone of the guitar family. **(2, 3)**

tresche French dance tradition that emerged out of medieval ring and chain dances. **(8)**

tres-dos Cuban medium-sized *tumbadora* membranophone. **(2)**

tresillo Three-note rhythmic ostinato in Cuban popular music. **(3)**

treskanje 'Shaking', Croatian singing style. **(8)**

treskavice Croatian vocal genre whose name derives from the word *treskanje*. **(8)**

treujenn gaol 'Cabbage stump', Breton clarinet with four or five keys, often made of boxwood. **(8)**

triad Any chord of three tones, usually a root and its third and fifth, forming the harmonic basis of tonal music. **(9)**

trianto Metal triangle used in Coptic chant. **(6)**

tribbiera Italian and Corsican free-metered threshing song, performed in a strained timbre by farmers as they drive oxen around a threshing floor. **(8)**

tribhanga 'Three bends', posture in the *oḍissi* dance. **(5)**

triccaballacche Italian wooden clapper. **(3)**

tricchéballacche Neapolitan rattle having three or five mallets set in a wooden frame. **(8)**

trīdeksnis Latvian wooden stick with hanging bells and jingles, used to accompany singing of *godu balss* in wedding or winter solstice rituals. **(8)**

trigona Pontic Greek dance. **(8)**

trigonon Harp of ancient Greece, commonly played by women. **(8)**

trikititxa Basque ensemble consisting of a diatonic accordion, a drum, and singing. **(8)**

trimitis Lithuanian wooden trumpet, capable of producing a natural scale through overblowing. **(8)**

trío 'Group of three'. (1) In Ibero-American countries, three (usually) male musicians who sing while they accompany themselves on stringed instruments (guitar and guitar types) and possibly percussion (maracas, depending on the country). (2) *Trio elétrico*, Brazilian electric guitar trio accompanied by a small percussion group typical of Bahian carnival. (3) *Trío romántico*, Mexican-derived ensemble of three male musicians who sing sad, nostalgic, and romantic songs while accompanying themselves on guitars. **(2)**

triolpolskor Form of Swedish *polska* in triplet rhythms, predominant in western Sweden. **(8)**

triplo High-pitched Spanish guitar. **(8)**

triste Term in Bolivia and Chile for a nostalgic song musically analogous to the Peruvian *yaraví.* **(2)**

tritone Tonal interval of an augmented fourth or diminished fifth. **(9)**

tritos Third movement of the Cypriot *kartzilamades* dance cycle, performed in 2/4 time. **(8)**

trivium Of the seven medieval liberal arts, those that dealt with grammar, logic, and rhetoric; cf. *quadrivium.* **(8)**

trochus shell Conical shell produced by a mollusk of the genus *Trochus.* **(9)**

troet Accordion of the Low Countries. **(8)**

Troicskija Belarusan Trinity holiday. **(8)**

troïsta muzyka Ukrainian trio ensembles, a term used by researchers; see *muzyka.* **(8)**

troitskie 'Whitsunday', the seventh Sunday after Easter. **(8)**

trollvisene Ancient indigenous Norwegian songs about the supernatural. **(8)**

tromba Corsican idioglot clarinet. **(8)**

tromba degli zingari 'Trumpet of the Gypsies', a name of the Italian mouth harp. **(8)**

trompa (1) Venezuelan jaw's harp (Jew's harp), a plucked lamellophone. (2) Uruguayan chronicler's term for a trumpet type. **(2)**

trompe (1) Mapuche jaw's harp. (2) (Also *tromp.*) Mouth harp of the Low Countries. **(8)**

trompeta de caracol Spanish term for conch-shell trumpet. **(2)**

trompong Balinese gong-chime played by a soloist. **(4)**

trønderrock Norwegian rock music; see *dialekt-rock.* **(8)**

trống Generic term for Vietnamese drums, most with one or more nailed heads. **(4)**

trống chầu In *tuồng* theater of Vietnam, a large drum played by an audience member offering praise or criticism. **(4)**

trống com Vietnamese two-headed drum with rice paste on the heads. **(4)**

trống đồng Bronze drum idiophone of Vietnam. **(4)**

trống quân One-stringed zither played over a hole in the ground, Vietnam. **(4)**

tropa 'Troop', Andean group of musicians who play a single type of instrument, such as a *tropa de sikuri.* **(2)**

tropical 'Tropical'. (1) Caribbean-based *cuarteto* style; (2) *tropicália*, Brazilian avant-garde music movement; (3) *tropicalismo*, vanguard popular music movement of the late 1960s in Brazil. **(2)**

tropic bird Any of several web-footed birds of the genus *Phaethon*, often seen far from land; in some cultures, a dance so named; cf. *frigate bird.* **(9)**

tror (1) Generic Khmer term for bowed lutes. (2) 'Two-stringed fiddle', Cambodian instrument played in contemporary versions of the *pinnpeat* ensemble. **(3, 4)**

tror chhe Khmer two-stringed cylindrical fiddle, tuned D–A. **(4)**

tror Khmer Khmer three-stringed spike fiddle with a coconut body. **(4)**

tror ou Khmer two-stringed fiddle with a coconut resonator. **(4)**

tror so tauch Khmer two-stringed cylindrical fiidle, tuned G–D. **(4)**

tror so thomm Khmer lower-pitched two-stringed fiddle, tuned D–A. **(4)**

trote 'Trot', term used in Chile for the Andean *huayno*. See *wayno, huayño.* **(2)**

trova 'Tune', any song of the late nineteenth-century to the present, performed by Cuban singers called *trovadores.* **(2)**

trovadore Composer-songmakers who were an important part of traditional New Mexican Hispano society. **(3)**

trovo In Hispano culture, song duel in which two or more performers sing alternative verses. **(3)**

trstene orglice Slovene panpipes. **(8)**

trstenke Slovene reed pipes. **(8)**

truba (1) Trumpet used in Macedonian *čalgija* ensembles. (2) Belarusan shepherds' conical trumpet made of wood wrapped in birch bark or of hammered metal. (3) Ukrainian conical wooden trumpet of Polissia and Volyn'. (3) Serbian trumpet, named in *Zlatna Truba* ('Golden Horn'), a west Serbian festival. **(8)**

Truk The entity now known as Chuuk. **(9)**

trumba Gumuz trumpet of animal horn or aluminum. **(1)**

trump Scottish name of the mouth harp. **(8)**

trunfa 'Trump'. regional name of the Italian mouth harp. **(8)**

t'rung Upland Vietnamese vertical bamboo xylophone. **(4)**

Truòng Son Ranges Mountain range running through southern Vietnam. **(4)**

trutruka Mapuche long end-blast cane trumpet with oblique mouthpiece and attached cow-horn bell. **(2)**

trychle Swiss cowbell of Muotatal; see *gunggele.* **(8)**

trychlen (Also *übersitz.*) Swiss whip-crackers of Meiringen, Bern. **(8)**

tsaba-tsaba Urban popular dance-song genre, drawing from South African choral music. **(1)**

tsakismata Verbal interjections in Greek singing. **(8)**

tsambouna Bagpipe of the Greek islands. **(8)**

tsamiko Dance of the Greek mainland, also important in Cyprus. **(8)**

tsan 'Song', singing by herdsmen in Haute-Gruyère, Switzerland. **(8)**

tsayantur Ecuadorian musical bow. **(2)**

tschäggätä 'Dappled ones', Swiss masked men in the festival of *roitschäggäta.* **(8)**

tshikona Venda music produced by an ensemble of one-pitch pipes played in hocket style. **(1)**

tshizambi Venda friction bow, obtained from the Tsonga. **(1)**

tsiattista Cypriot genre of improvised couplets set to traditional tune types. **(8)**

tsifte teli Greek belly dance of Turkish origin. **(8)**

tsikatray Frame rattle constructed from a square frame of wood covered by rushes and filled with seeds. **(1)**

tsimbalo Greek trapezoidal struck zither. **(8)**

tsintsila (Also *lini.*) Georgian pair of copper plates, found in archaeological excavations of the fourth century. **(8)**

tsofina 'To blow' (aerophones), Malagasy term denoting the playing of musical instrumentals. **(1)**

tsopai Ossetian circle dance, connected to the cult of thunder and lightning. **(8)**

tsuzam Chechen and Ingush children's instrument made of a goose feather or a stalk of grass. **(8)**

tswawo Small gourd rattles worn on dancers' legs in Zimbabwe. **(1)**

tsyganochka 'Beautiful Gypsy girl' (Russian), style of Gypsy song. **(8)**

tsymbaly (1) Ukrainian hammered dulcimer. (2) Trapezoidal struck zither of Ukraine, Poland, and Belarus. **(3, 8)**

ttiki 'Small lines', Basque poetic form divided into 7- and 6-syllable hemistichs in the *zortziko* dance-song type. **(8)**

ttŏk Onomatopoeic Korean term for hitting a drum once with a drumstick. **(7)**

ttŏngmok 'Tough voice', vocal timbre in Korean *p'ansori.* **(7)**

ttunttun Basque struck zither with six strings hit with a wooden stick. **(8)**

tu (China.) Chart or picture. **(7)**

Tuareg Nomadic people of Algeria, Mali, and Niger. **(1)**

tuata Conical metal trumpet used in Iraqi Shi'ite centers during the ceremony of mourning for Husayn. (6)

TUBS Time Unit Box System of notation, developed in 1962 for teaching African drumming. (1)

tubuan (Also *tumbuan*.) (1) Southern New Ireland commemorative rites involving masked dancers. (2) In New Britain and the Duke of York Islands, female (in Nissan, male) masks with heavy pandanus-leaf skirts, worn by men who perform gyrating movements before seated drummers; complementary to *dukduk*. (9)

tuburada Solemn ritual of the Guarijio, a subsection of the *túmari* ceremony. (2)

tudukkan (Also *tudukkat*.) Mentawai slit drum ensemble. (4)

tufu Single-headed standing drum of West Timor. (4)

tugai mai (Japan.) In *gagaku*, the custom of pairing *bugaku* (foreign-origin) dance pieces with similar movement types (*hasiri mai* or *hira mai*) from the two different sections (right and left) of the *bugaku* repertoire. (7)

Tugaru Ikuta ryû (Japan.) School of *koto* derived from the Ikuta school. (7)

tugaru zyamisen (Japan.) Folk *syamisen* music of the Tugaru area of Aomori Prefecture. (7)

tŭgŭm 'Accomplished sound', mastery of Korean *p'ansori* singing techniques. (7)

Tuguyama ryû (Japan.) School of *koto* derived from the Ikuta school. (7)

tuilage French singing technique in which two voices alternate, overlapping slightly. (8)

tuitin (Japan.) Wooden clapper in Buddhist music. (7)

tuk **band** Barbados ensemble featuring bass drummer, snare drummer, flute player, and triangle featuring a fusion of African and British elements. (2)

tuke (Japan.) See *tukegi*. (7)

tuke dokoro (Japan.) In *gagaku*, the point at which (1) each instrument joins in after the flute solo or (2) the chorus and instrumentalists join in after solo singing. (7)

tukegi (Also *tuke*.) Pair of wooden clappers beaten against a board; used for sound effects in Japanese *kabuki*. (7)

tuke tyô (Also *kikkake tyô*.) Cue books for the Japanese *kabuki hayasi* (an instrumental ensemble). (7)

tukimug Maranao poetic segment in music. (4)

tukṛā *Tabla* composition based on a *pakhāvaj* barrel drum *paran*. (5)

tuku Single-headed wooden goblet drum that accompanied music of the Kru of Liberia. (1)

tukusi goto (Japan.) *Koto*-accompanied song cycles that appeared in the mid-sixteenth century in the Tukusi district of northern Kyûsyû. (7)

tuḷai karuvi Aerophones (Tamil instrument category). (5)

tulali Torajan flute. (4)

tulé Wayana single-reed aerophone played in ensembles. (2)

tuḷḷal 'Jumping', dance drama of Kerala based on Hindu epics. (5)

tulling (Also *lolling, sulling, tralling*.) Vocal imitation of the *hardanger* violin in Norway. (8)

tulon bololu 'Play songs' of the Mandinka of northern Sierra Leone. (1)

tulu lulu (Also *tulululu*.) Traditional Nicaraguan song-dance in which dancers pass one at a time under a couple's extended arms while onlookers sing out their names in the song's lyrics. (2)

tulum (1) Turkish bagpipe. (2) (Also *chimoni*.) Georgian bagpipe of Meshketi. (6, 8)

tumank Ecuadorian musical bow that uses the mouth as resonator. (2)

tumao Cylindrical single-headed log drum of Surinam Maroons. (2)

ṭūmār Teacher's scroll outlining the narrative of a Persian epic, copied by the student. (6)

túmari (Also *túguri, tuwúri*.) Guarijio celebration for thanksgiving, benediction, propitiation, fertilization, or curing; sometimes related to the agricultural cycle. (2)

tumba (1) Most popular dance and rhythm of the mid-twentieth century in all the Netherlands Antilles; (2) *tumba dominicana*, a *velación* of the northern part of the Dominican Republic; (3) *tumba francesa*, former ballroom dance of Santiago de Cuba, now performed only by national troupes. (2)

tumbadora (1) Cuban membranophone (basically a *conga* drum) that originated in the context of the *rumba*. (2) Single-headed, elongated, barrel-shaped drum, commonly called *conga*, used particularly in Afro-Cuban *rumba* music. (2, 3)

tumbaknari Open-ended goblet drum similar to the West Asian *dombek*. (5)

tumbao Ostinato pattern resulting from interlocking rhythms played by the bass and conga, found in *son*. (3)

ṭumbara Yemeni lyre; cf. *ṭambūra*. (6)

tumbas *Conga* drums. (2)

ṭūmbī Single-stringed short-necked plucked lute, in the Indian Punjab. (5)

tumble Bowl-shaped drum of the Fur people. (1)

tumbu Drone pipe of the Sardinian *launeddas*. (8)

tumbuizo Genre of songs performed (in Swahili) by women in Kenya. (1)

Tumbuka Language spoken by people of northern Malawi. (1)

tumbuk kalang Malaysian folk performance derived from rice-pounding songs. (4)

tume (Japan.) Picks for zithers. (7)

Tumtum Sudanese people of the Nuba Mountains. (1)

tum-tum In Barbados, double-headed log membranophone played by two men. (2)

tun (1) In Guatemala, a Quiché Maya hollowed-out log slit drum or gong with H-shaped incision on its top; see *teponaztli, tunkul*. (2) (Also *tum* 'cylinder'.) Long Guatemalan wooden or metal valveless trumpet. (2)

tuna (1) Group of musicians playing instrumental music with Spanish-derived instruments, especially common in Colombia and Peru; see also *estudiantina, lira, rondalla*. (2) Panamanian street parade of musicians, singers, and townspeople. (2)

tunagi (Japan.) *Syamisen* pattern in *gidayû busi*. (7)

tunas Portuguese ensembles formed of families of stringed instruments, including different kinds of *cavaquinho*, mandolin, *viola*, and *viola baixo*. (8)

ṭunbūr (Also *ṭanbūr, tanbur, tanbūr*.) (1) Fretted long-necked lute played with a plectrum. (Plural, *ṭanābīr*.) (2) Rare early Arabic designation for lyre. (6)

tundito Pipe-and-tabor duet among the Otopame, each performer simultaneously playing both a flute and a drum. (2)

tune family Group of related melodies descended from a common ancestor and sharing melodic contours and important structural pitches; most often applied to groups of Child ballads. (3)

tunga-tunga Accompaniment pattern of Argentine *cuarteto* music. (2)

tunggalan Tausug large *agung*. (4)

t'ungso Korean large notched vertical flute with mirliton. (7)

tung-tung Tausug rhythmic ostinato in *kulintangan*. (4)

ṭungura (Also *dumduma*.) Small, deep kettledrum of the Tihāma made of clay or other appropriate materials, surrounded with straps and having a double skin. (6)

tuning (Tok Pisin *ki* 'key'.) In Oceania, array of tones to which the strings of a chordophone are set. (9)

tunkul In Guatemala, a Yucatec Mayan hollowed-out log slit drum or gong with H-shaped incision on its top; see *teponaztli, tun*. (2)

tunrung ganrang Makassarese processional drum music for sailors. (4)

tuntina (Also *tuntune*.) Marathi plucked drum. (5)

tuntui (Also *tunduy*.) Ecuadorian large slit drum. (**2**)

tuntungan (1) Tausug upper *kulintang* gong. (2) Yakan log drum. (**4**)

tuồng Vietnamese theater genre. (**4**)

tuoqiang (China.) Instrumental accompaniment in narrative and opera. (**7**)

tŭpan Bulgarian cylindrical two-headed drum, played with a thick stick and a thin wand. (**8**)

tupan (Also *daulle*, *lodër*, *lodërti*.) Albanian two-headed bass drum. (**8**)

ṭūra Medium-sized Egyptian cymbals, played in religious contexts. (**6**)

turali North Borneo nose flute. (**4**)

turas Venezuelan vertical male-female flute. (**2**)

turāth 'Heritage'. (1) Generic term for classical Arab music. (2) More specifically, Egyptian style of classical music that emerged in the 1950s. (**6**)

turba Pangasinan song debate. (**4**)

turčije Turkish song style in Montenegro and Bosnia-Hercegovina, known as *sevdalinke* since the late 1800s. (**8**)

ture (1) (Also *tule*, *turé*, *tore*.) Large bamboo single-reed aerophone used throughout the Amazon. (2) (Japan.) Attendant role in *nô* theater. (**2, 7**)

ture kut Korean farmers' band accompanying weeding activities; this term is interchangeable with *p'ungmul*. (**7**)

turélo Guarijio chanter. (**2**)

turi bati (Japan.) Technique for the *satuma biwa* (lute) introduced by Turuta Kinsi (1912–1995), in which the plectrum glides horizontally over the strings to produce a highly expressive sound. (**7**)

turi daiko (Japan.) Suspended drum in *gagaku*. (**7**)

turi syōko (Japan.) Small suspended drum in *gagaku*. (**7**)

Türk halk müzıği 'Turkish folk music culture', promoted under the leadership of Mustafa Kemal Atatürk. (**6**)

türkü Turkish folk song. (**6**)

turku Urban songs played by Rom musicians in Macedonia. (**8**)

turlututu Onomatopoeic imitation of musical instruments used in ring dances of the French-speaking of Switzerland; *see rantamplan*, *roupioupiou*. (**8**)

turning Montserrat possession dance. (**2**)

turno Street fair in Costa Rica. (**2**)

turntable Phonograph; an essential component of a hip-hop disk jockey's equipment. (**3**)

turopolski drmeš Couple dance, with shaking, of Turopolje, Croatia. (**8**)

Turski kjuček Duple-meter variant of the Bulgarian Rom *kjuček*. (**8**)

turu Daura dance, for which singers praise the royal ancesters. (**1**)

turú Guaraní generic and onomatopoeic name for trumpet. (**2**)

túru Kpelle side-blown horn. (**1**)

Turuta ryû (Japan.) School of *satuma biwa* (lute) established in the 1990s by Turuta Kinsi (1912–1995). (**7**)

turu-turu Miskitu mirliton made with a bat's wing stretched between two small pieces of reed held together by beeswax. (**2**)

tūrya 'Musical instrument'. (**5**)

tūryaugha Ensemble of musical instruments. (**5**)

tūshiyat al-kamāl Concluding instrumental piece within the Andalusian-Algerian *nūba*. (**6**)

tūshiya zīdān Classical instrumental overture of Algeria, found in varying forms in Tlemcen, Constantine, and Algiers. (**6**)

tusona Graphic configurations of dots circumscribed by lines of the Luchazi culture of Angola and Zambia. (**1**)

tutari High-pitched horn of Bhutan. (**5**)

tūtī Double-reed folk aerophone of North India. (**5**)

tutohato Slow responsorial singing to honor someone on Buru. (**4**)

Tutsi Cultural group of Rwanda and Burundi. (**1**)

tutuguri Entire Tarahumara pre-Columbian ceremony complex. (**2**)

Tuvan throat singing Striking vocal tradition from the steppes of Mongolia that has been successful internationally in world music. (**3, 6, 7**)

tuxi (China.) Indigenous opera. (**7**)

tuyogin (Japan.) (1) Basic *nô* vocalization with wide vibrato using a strong breath. (2) Dynamic mode of *nô* chanting. (**7**)

tužbalica Serbo-Croatian lament, performed by women. (**8**)

tuzumi (Japan.) Generic term for hourglass-shaped hand drums. (**7**)

tvísöngur 'Two-singing', Icelandic vocal form and technique of accompanying another voice in parallel fifths. (**8**)

Twi Language family spoken by Akan peoples in Ghana and Côte d'Ivoire. (**1**)

twip'uri Epilogue or last song in Korean *p'ansori*. (**7**)

twmpath Mound where Welsh musicians traditionally stood to play for dancing. (**8**)

twoubadou Haitian groups that perform guitar-based music influenced by Cuban *son* groups. (**2**)

txalaparta Basque idiophone, consisting of one or more wooden planks beaten by two players to create different rhythmic patterns. (**8**)

txirula Small Basque wooden flute. (**8**)

txistu Basque three-holed duct flute, typically played by the left hand while the right hand plays a drum. (**3, 8**)

txistulari Basque musicians who accompany dances by fingering a *txistu* with one hand and beating a drum with the other. (**8**)

tyāmko Small kettledrum of Nepal. (**5**)

ty bā lệnh Nguyễn-dynasty ritual court ensemble. (**4**)

tyi wara Bambara mask that comes from a narrative about a farmer of that name. (**1**)

tympanon Trapezoidal struck zither of the Low Countries. (**8**)

tyniad Welsh harper's chord, which, in various combinations with a second chord (*cyweirdant*), made up twenty-four patterns. (**8**)

tyônin (Japan.) Merchant class. (**7**)

tyû (Japan.) Middle principal note in *nô* chanting. (**7**)

tyû kyoku (Japan.) Buddhist chants with mixed scales. (**7**)

tyû no mai (Japan.) *Nô* dance performed by various characters in a moderate tempo. (**7**)

tyû nori (Japan.) Rhythmic style in *nô* chanting. (**7**)

tyûon (Japan.) (1) Middle pitch area in Buddhist chant; (2) common melodic patterns in the *tyûon* pitch area. (**7**)

tyûseigaku (Japan.) Ceremonial music of the Konkô sect of Shinto, combining *gagaku* and *kibigaku*. (**7**)

tyû zao (Japan.) Medium-size *syamisen*. (**7**)

tzas 'Drum' (Macedonian, Vlach). (**8**)

tzazi Macedonian brass band with a *klarino*. (**8**)

tzijolah Among the Guatemalan highland Maya, a three-holed flute that utilizes the harmonic series by a system of overblowing. (**2**)

u (Japan.) Fifth note in the scale *gosei*. (**7**)

uadindz Ossetian ancient whistle flute, sometimes now made of a gun barrel. (**8**)

uaitúge From 'bell', Tukano external strung rattles of dried seeds worn on dancers' ankles, upper arms, or both. (**2**)

ua neeb Hmong shaman ceremony accompanied by gong, *sistrum*, and rattle. (**4**)

uaricza araui Pre-Columbian antiphonal dance of men and women sung by the Inca and a choir of young virgins. (**2**)

uatapú Guaraní trumpet used to attract fish. (**2**)

übersitz (Also *trychlen*.) Swiss whip-crackers of Meiringen, Bern. (**8**)

u contrastu Corsican improvised poetic dialogue, sung by two lovers or a married couple. (**8**)

ud (Also *'ud, 'ūd, 'ud, oud, ood*.) (1) Plucked Arab lute found throughout the Middle East. (Plural, *a'wād, 'īdān*.) (2) Fretless pear-shaped lute with a round belly, bent neck, and eleven strings, ten of which are in double courses. (3) North African four-stringed lute. (4) Plucked short-necked fretless lute, originally of the Middle East, still played in the Balkans and known in Georgia. (**1, 3, 6, 8**)

'ūd 'arbī (Also *'ūd tūnisī, 'ūd maghribī*.) Fretless short-necked Algerian lute with four pairs of strings. (**6**)

'ūd sharqī 'Eastern lute' of the Mashriq, with six pairs of strings. (**6**)

udakkai (Also *udakki, uḍukkai, uḍḍukā*.) South Indian hourglass pressure drum with a snare. (**5**)

udātta Principal, raised accent in Vedic recitation. (**5**)

udekki Kandyan dance form of Sri Lanka. (**5**)

'udi Swahili plucked lute of East Africa. (**1**)

udj Adighian collective circle dance, performed in ritual processions. (**8**)

udo nongak 'Right' regional style of Korean farmers' band music. (**7**)

uḍukkai pāṭṭu Sung narrative, in the Konku region of Tamil Nadu. (**5**)

Ueda ryû (Japan.) *Syakuhati* school founded in 1917 by Ueda Hôdô (1892–1974). (**7**)

ufār Dancelike genre in Central Asian *maqām*. (**6**)

ufisha tayil Mapuche sheep lineage soul chant. (**2**)

Uganda Museum Site of major research and teaching program in ethnomusicology directed by Klaus Wachsmann. (**1**)

ughniyya (Also *ughnīya*.) 'Song', 'tune'; twentieth-century genre of long sectionalized colloquial song. (Plural, *ughniyyāt, aghānī*.) (**6**)

ugod Bontok epic. (**4**)

ugubhu Zulu unbraced gourd-resonated musical bow more than a meter long. (**1**)

uhzūja (Plural, *ahāzīj*.) 'Swift song', piece concluding the performance of the classical *nūba*, synonymous with *ṭaqṭūqa*, a light, popular genre. (**6**)

ŭigwe Korean manuals (of music). (**7**)

uilleann pipes Traditional Irish bellows-blown bagpipe. (**3, 8**)

ujamaa Villages that served as resettlement habitats under President Nyerere's regime in Tanzania. (**1**)

ujo Korean melodic mode. (**7**)

új stílusú népdal 'New-style folk song', term used by scholars for nineteenth-century new song compositions among Hungarian peasants. (**8**)

uki (Japan.) Passing auxiliary notes used in *nô* chanting. (**7**)

ukoninumchari upopo (Japan.) 'Scattering walnuts song', genre of Ainu festival song to purify the site of a cult ceremony and expel evil spirits. (**7**)

ukouku (Japan.) Ainu style of polyphonic singing. (**7**)

uku (Japan.) Term in *gidayû busi* notation indicating pitch or manner of singing. (**7**)

ukuku Q'ero costumed representation of a bear during Corpus Christi. (**2**)

'ukulele Hawaiian name given during the 1880s to the Madeiran *braguinha*, a small four-stringed Portuguese musical instrument of the guitar family (a kind of *cavaquinho*). (**8, 9**)

ulimba Makonde-Mwera lamellophone with broad iron tongues and no bridge. (**1**)

ulké (Also *bobine*.) Hourglass drum played on Réunion Island. (**5**)

ulla Korean gong chimes. (**7**)

ullagoner Irish Traveller woman called on to keen or lament at funerals. (**8**)

ullalim (1) Kalinga epic song. (2) Bontok long solo song. (**4**)

ülutún 'Small therapies', Mapuche medical ritual. (**2**)

uma (Japan.) Bamboo bridge of the *sansin* (Okinawan three-stringed lute). (**7**)

ŭmak Korean term for music, often referring to Western-style music. (**7**)

umakhweyana Zulu gourd-resonated musical bow braced near the center. (**1**)

uma lopo Atoni beehive-shaped traditional dwelling. (**4**)

umattāta Dance performed by Kodagu women in Karnataka. (**5**)

Umbanda Twentieth-century Afro-Brazilian syncretic religion that borrows from aspects of Candomblé, Macumba, and spiritism. (**2**)

umbigada 'Navel', choreographic stomach bump of many Afro-Brazilian circle dances. (**2**)

umkiki Baggāra one-stringed fiddle, played to accompany *gardagi*. (**1**)

umngqokolo Form of overtone singing performed by Xhosa women and girls in southern Africa. (**1**)

umrhubhe Bow played by scraping a string with a stick in southern Africa. (**1**)

Ŭmsŏngsŏ Korean Court Music Office of the Unified Silla period. (**7**)

umui (Also *kuêna*.) Okinawan religious songs performed by women to pray for a good harvest, good fishing, good hunting, or a safe voyage. (**7**)

umva Miri double-headed drum accompanying dance. (**1**)

ŭm, yang (Chinese *yin, yang*.) Korean concept of cosmic dual forces. (**7**)

una Short fife used in funerary celebrations among the Sumu. (**2**)

uñcal Tamil swing song in a slow tempo, performed at weddings. (**5**)

uncavritti (Also *uñcavritti bhajana*.) Procession with singing at a Tyagaraja festival. (**5**)

ungá See *ingá*. (**2**)

uniphons Discrete pitches in a scalar system. (**8**)

unison Concept or performance of musical parts on the same tone or (loosely) at the octave; consonant simultaneous sounding of multiple instruments, as of kundus beaten together in precise rhythm. (**9**)

University of Ibadan Unit of music research established in 1962 under the direction of Fela Sowande. (**1**)

University of Nigeria (Nsukka) Department of music for teaching degree-qualifying courses in ethnomusicology. (**1**)

uñjal 'Swing songs' of Tamil Nadu. (**5**)

uopk (Japan.) Ainu style of unison singing. (**7**)

upanayana Elaborate initiation ceremony that students undergo before they can begin study with a *guru*. (**5**)

upla pruan bara Miskitu wake. (**2**)

upopo (Japan.) Genre of Ainu festival songs performed by seated women. (**7**)

uraccal tōrram Songs to urge the onset of possession in *teyyam* in Kerala. (**5**)

ura gumi (Japan.) Set *syamisen* song cycle (*kumiuta*) pieces classified as difficult. (**7**)

ural Tuluva plowing songs of Karnataka. (**5**)

ura ma (Japan.) Back beat of a pair of beats. (**7**)

urar (Also *ural*.) Berber ritual verses, sung usually by women at weddings and circumcision ceremonies. (**1**)

urārile Traditional musical-poetic greetings spoken rhythmically or sung on simple melodies by Romanian children at Christmas and the new year. (**8**)

uravan 'Plain', singing style in Bosnia-Hercegovina in which the rhythm of songs is based on the rhythm of the words. (**8**)

urghanīn Byzantine organ. (**6**)

urjūza Poem in the *rajaz* meter, used for didactic purposes. (**6**)

urkestr 'Orchestra', English term adapted in the Mashriq. (**6**)

urlar 'Floor, ground'; term used for the return to the original theme in Scottish *ceòl mór*. (**8**)

urlatori 'Shouters', generation of Italian singers influenced by American rock and roll and rhythm and blues. (**8**)

'urs (Also *urs*.) Death anniversary of a Sufi saint. (**5**)

urschrift First full score. (**8**)

ursul 'Bear', Romanian winter festival with masked dancing, found in north-central Moldavia and Bucovina. (**8**)

urtext Original text; authoritative edition of a composer's authentic work. **(8)**

urtyn dun Mongolian long-song. **(7, 8)**

urucu Red dye used in body painting and for the Waiãpi shaman. **(2)**

urume Double-headed drum played with sticks in Karnataka. **(5)**

uṟumi Hourglass-shaped rubbed membranophone of Tamil Nadu. **(5)**

usali Men's daytime war dance of Seram. **(4)**

úsêköl High priest among the Bribri. **(2)**

USO United Service Organization, a morale-building entity serving the U.S. military. **(9)**

uspavanke Croatian lullabies. **(8)**

uşşak Common melodic mode (*makam*) in Turkish music. **(6)**

ustā (Plural, *ustāwāt*.) Chief of a group of performers. **(6)**

ustad (Also *ustād*.) Master musician; honorific for a Muslim teacher. **(5)**

ustādh Teacher; see also *ostād*. **(6)**

ustād-sagird (Also *guru-śisya*.) Master-student; relationship with a Muslim teacher. **(5)**

ustaz Master musician in Central Asia. **(6)**

ustne harmonike (Also *ustne orglic*.) Slovene mouth organ. **(8)**

usudêku (Japan.) Most important type of Okinawan folk music performed by women. **(7)**

usul (Also *usūl*.) (1) Turkish term for rhythmic cycles. (2) Turkish rhythmic mode, adapted in the Balkans. (3) Rhythmic patterns in Uighur (Uygur) music. (4) Repeating metric cycle in the Bukharan *shash maqām*. **(6, 8)**

ut Short-necked fretless plucked lute, a Middle Eastern instrument played in *čalgija* ensembles of Macedonia. **(8)**

uta (Japan.) Generic term for song. **(7)**

uta asobi (Japan.) 'Singing game', folk song in the Amami Islands involving antiphonal singing (*uta kake*) in which singers or groups of singers vie with each other in the witty selection of poetic texts and in improvisation. **(7)**

uta kake (Japan.) Antiphonal style in the folk song of the Ryûkyû Islands. **(7)**

uta sansin (Japan.) Major genre of Okinawan classical music in which a singer accompanies himself or herself on the *sansin* (Okinawan three-stringed lute); the accompaniment may include other instruments as well. **(7, 10)**

uta sya (Japan.) Master performers of Amami entertainment songs, *sima uta*. **(7)**

uta zaimon (Japan.) Genre of Buddhist folk music. **(7)**

utaguti (Japan.) Blowing edge of a wind instrument. **(7)**

utai (1) Chanting of Japanese *nô* texts. (2) Vocalization of *nō* chanting sometimes performed outside the theater by amateurs. **(3, 7, 10)**

utai bon (Japan.) Librettos or scores of *nô*. **(7)**

utai mono (Japan.) (1) Generic term for *gagaku* vocal pieces; (2) *ziuta* repertoire (*syamisen* music) derived from *nô* plays. **(7)**

Utamaduni Tanzanian National Dance Troupe, founded in 1964 to amalgamate music styles in Tanzania. **(1)**

Utamai no tukasa (Japan.) *See Gagaku ryô*. **(7)**

utazawa (Japan.) Genre of short *syamisen* songs developed from *hauta*. **(7)**

ut dun Protracted lyrical songs of the Kalmyks of southeastern European Russia. **(8)**

utidesi (Japan.) (1) System of transmitting an art in which a student lives in the house of the teacher and learns the art over a period of years while sharing the teacher's daily life. (2) Students in this system. **(7)**

u timpanu Corsican triangle. **(8)**

utsava-sampradāya-kīrtana 'Song form used in the tradition of festivity'. Songs that accompany the various daily rituals in the worship of a deity. **(5)**

uttaraṅga Second part of a *pallavi* theme, in Karnataka music; follows the *purvaṅga*. **(5)**

uṭukkai pāṭṭu Tamil folk drum music. **(5)**

uwa mori (Japan.) *Syamisen* pattern in *gidayû busi*. **(7)**

uwa zyôsi (Japan.) (1) High-register additional melody line in a *syamisen* ensemble performance; (2) *syamisen* tuned to a higher register to play the *uwa zyôsi* part, and its performer. **(7)**

úyanu In Belize, Garifuna unaccompanied, semisacred, usually mournful gesture-accompanying songs in irregular meter. **(2)**

uyon-uyon Social events accompanying ceremonies in Java. **(4)**

uzliau Throat singing of the Bashkirs of Russia. **(8)**

uzsaukums 'Call, air'; slow-tempo versions of Latvian bagpipe tunes. **(8)**

uzun hava 'Long melody', quasi-improvisational category of Turkish folk music. **(6)**

uzun yry 'Long song', melismatic style of Tuvan *khöömei*, using poetic analogies to link the external world with human feelings. **(6, 7)**

uzyn sonar 'Long hunt', central section of recitative in a Kazakh epic, based on a recurring rhythmic motive. **(6)**

vacación In Imbabura, Ecuador, music for a child's wake performed on harp, characterized by its steady tempo and gradually descending melody, meant to drive away the demon from beneath the platform supporting the dead child. **(2)**

vādi (Also *vādī*.) Most important tone of a raga in Hindustani and Karnatak systems. **(5)**

vādya Musical instrument (Sanskrit); instrumental music. **(5)**

vāggeyakāra 'Word-song-maker', composer. **(5)**

Vai (Also *Vey*.) Northern Mande-speakers of northwest Liberia. **(1)**

vaidika Vedic. **(5)**

Vaishya (Also *Vaiśya*.) Traditionally the third-highest group or class (*varṇa*) in Hindu society, consisting of merchants and traders. **(5)**

vaj Albanian lament or stylized form of crying, whose name derives from a sorrowful exclamation. **(8)**

vajdudule House-to-house caroling in Macedonia during a drought. **(8)**

vajtim (Also *të qarë*.) 'Cried', Albanian flute melodies that draw on women's vocal laments. **(8)**

vakarēšana In Latvia, a gathering of women on autumn and winter evenings to do needlework and handicrafts while singing. **(8)**

vāḳēšana Latvian prefuneral wake, nowadays observed only in Latgale. **(8)**

vaksin (Also *banbou, vaccine*.) Haitian single-note lip-concussion aerophone made of bamboo, PVC pipe, or metal and played in groups in interlocking fashion. **(2)**

vāḳu rotaḷas Latvian games with recited narrow-range melodies, performed beside a corpse the night before its funeral in western Kurzeme. **(8)**

valačobnyja pieśni Belarusan 'wandering' spring songs. **(8)**

valaiyal cintu Tamil song performed by bangle sellers in Tamil Nadu on special ritual occasions. **(5)**

valaṇ Verse summarizing the preceding story section, in *māṇ bhaṭṭ ākhyān*. **(5)**

valiha Wire-stringed tube zither, the best-known instrument of Madagascar, also played in Tanzania. **(1)**

valiha vero Malagasy raft zither that consists of ten bamboo tubes arranged progressively by length. **(1)**

valimba Sena xylophone in south-central Africa. **(1)**

valimba (Also *ulimba*.) Gourd-resonated large xylophone of southern Malawi. **(1)**

valinaṭai cintu Tamil song performed by pilgrims or travelers to pass the time on a long journey. **(5)**

vallehorn Traditional horn blown for seasonal customs and related to no-longer-extant ancient horns. **(8)**

vallenato (1) Rural musical and dance genre from northern Colombia, featuring accordion, drum, and scraper; (2) urban musical and dance genre derived from its rural counterpart of northern Colombia, adding bass, guitar, *conga*, and cowbell to the rural accordion, drum, and scraper. **(2)**

valona *Décima*-based genre in several parts found in the *tierra caliente* (hotlands), the western part of the state of Michoacán, Mexico. **(2)**

válonka (Also *fam, puzyŕ, skamóra*.) Mordvinian bagpipe. **(8)**

vals 'Waltz'. (1) Romantic vocal music genre in triple meter found throughout Spanish-speaking America; (2) Argentine social dance performed during *jineteada*; (3) *vals criollo*, 'creole waltz', most popular national music form in coastal Peru, with origins in the mid-eighteenth-century Viennese waltz. **(2)**

valse (1) 'Waltz' (French). (2) European-influenced waltz. **(4, 8)**

valseao (Also *valseado*.) 'Waltzed' choreography. **(2)**

valsu 'Waltz' (Corsican). **(8)**

vamzdis Lithuanian wooden flute with few holes for fingering. **(8)**

vaṅsī (Also *baṅsī, vaṃsa*.) Transverse bamboo folk flute in northern regions. **(5)**

Vapostori Separatist church in Zimbabwe that forbids the use of African drums. **(1)**

vaquería Colombian genre, sung by herders to quiet cattle and communicate among themselves. **(2)**

vaquita 'Dance of the cow' in Managua, Nicaragua. **(2)**

variable-pitch instruments Instruments, such as fiddles and flutes, whose pitch is infinitely controllable during performance. **(4)**

variaciones 'Variations', instrumental introduction to a Spanish *jota*. **(8)**

varialaika Greek 'heavy' *laika*. **(8)**

variété Blend of African and international styles with Western popular instrumentation in the former French colonies of Africa. **(8)**

varṇa Group or class; one of the four major divisions of Hindu society: Brahmin, Kshatriya, Vaishya, and Shudra. **(5)**

varṇam Karnatak composition, performed at the beginning of Karnatak concerts. **(5, 10)**

varsağī Popular Turkish musical form. **(6)**

vasietnija pieśni Belarusan autumn songs. **(8)**

vāsudev gīt Melodic solo songs of Maharashtra performed by an itinerant male singer-dancer. **(5)**

vatoccu 'Bell clapper', polyphonic singing style of central Italy, with links to medieval descant. **(8)**

vaṭṭakali Mullu Kurumba chant-song and circle dance around a sacred lamp in Tamil Nadu. **(5)**

vaudeville (1) (Also *voix-de-ville*.) French urban popular song of the sixteenth to eighteenth centuries. (2) Theatrical form consisting of a variety of unrelated performing acts, including actors, singers, dancers, acrobats, comedians, magicians, and trained animals. **(3, 8)**

vè Class of satirical songs of Vietnam. **(4)**

Veda (Also *veda*.) Any one of four compilations of the religious and cultural texts of the Vedic Aryans; the earliest Hindu sacred writings. **(5)**

vedamati Oral epic performance genre of Madhya Pradesh, performed in a sitting posture. **(5)**

veillée Major context for French recreative singing not associated with meals, rarely practiced in contemporary French culture; cf. *viellée*. **(8)**

veiquoix Trinidadian Spanish-language songs. **(2)**

vejiga Struck air-filled idiophone made from the bladder of an animal in Panama. **(2)**

velación (1) Individually sponsored annual saint's celebration in the Dominican Republic. (2) Mixtec wake that lasts all night, accompanied by music. **(2)**

veladas (1) Evening performances among some members of the African-descended population in the Dominican Republic; (2) *veladas escolares*, public performances at schools in Costa Rica. **(2)**

velezina 'To beat', 'to give life to' (membrane drums); Malagasy term to denote instrumental playing. **(1)**

velike cimbale Hungarian pedal cimbalom played in Slovenia, mostly by Gypsies in Prekmurje and Porabje. **(8)**

velké muzika Czech large ensemble, consisting of two violins, two clarinets, two bagpipes, and a string bass. **(8)**

velorio (1) Nightlong celebration or night watch to honor a saint or the Holy Cross in many Spanish-speaking countries. (2) Nightlong wake for the dead in many Spanish-speaking countries. (3) (Also *wawa velorio*, in Venezuela, *mampulorio*.) *Velorio de angelito*, Ecuadorian festive wake for an infant or young child. (4) *Velorio de angelito*, Paraguayan wake for a young child. (5) *Velorio de cruz* 'wake of the Cross' in Venezuela. **(2)**

velvele Subdivision of beats in the performance of Turkish rhythmic patterns (*usûl*). **(6)**

vemmalvärss Form of Estonian rhyming folk song that appeared in the nineteenth century and superseded the runic *regivärss* songs. **(8)**

vénérés Eleventh night after a death in Guadeloupe. **(2)**

vēṇu Karnatak bamboo flute. **(5)**

veó-páme 'Cane parallel objects', panpipe of the Desana subfamily of Tukano, played antiphonally in male-female pairs. **(2)**

verbunk Duple-meter Moravian and Slovak recruit's dance in which singing alternates with improvised dance steps. **(8)**

verbunkos Hungarian military-recruitment dance. **(8)**

verd In Iran, a Sufi litany. **(6)**

verse Line of text. **(9)**

verso 'Verse'. (1) Sung poetry accompanied by guitar or *guitarrón* in Chile. (2) Ritual song genre in the Dominican Republic for saints in folk Catholicism. **(2)**

verşuri Songs based on the literate tradition and composed for burial services in parts of Transylvania, Romania. **(8)**

vertep Ukrainian Nativity play. **(8)**

ves Kandyan dance form of Sri Lanka. **(5)**

vēṣa Costumed performance in Karnataka. **(5)**

veśa Short play, part of a *bhavāī* performance, in Gujarat. **(5)**

vǝsǝt 'Middle' course of strings on the Azerbaijani *saz*, used as part of the drone. **(6)**

vesnianky Ukrainian spring songs, performed by groups of two or more girls in open or cleared spaces in or near a village. **(8)**

vessel flute Instrument in the form of a vessel with one or more finger holes on the circumference. **(5)**

veuze Breton single-drone bagpipe of southeastern Brittany and northern Vendée, played alone or with an accordion or a fiddle. **(8)**

vevlira Swedish hurdy-gurdy. **(8)**

vèyé boukousou Guadeloupe wake celebrations. **(2)**

viasielnyja halaśeńni Belarusan wedding laments. **(8)**

viasielnyja muzyki (Also *kapela, hurkampaniya, muzyki, skamarochi*.) 'Wedding musicians', Belarusan traditional folk-instrumental ensembles. **(8)**

vībhatsa 'Disgusting', one of the eight emotional states (*rasa*) codified in the *Nātyaśāstra*. **(5)**

vibrato Tremulous quality given to a musical tone by rapid variations in its pitch or intensity. **(9)**

vicitra vīṇā Hindustani stick zither constructed like an unfretted *bīn*, played by sliding a glass ball over the strings and stroking them with wire plectra. **(5)**

vidé Spontaneous Martinique street parade. **(2)**

vidhināṭak Religious drama of Andhra Pradesh. **(5)**

vidūṣaka Buffoon character common in South Indian regional dance forms. **(5)**

vidvān Mature, accomplished Karnatak performer. **(5)**

viejitos Purépecha dancers who wear old-man masks. **(2)**

vièle (Also *vielle*.) French generic name of a bowed lute. **(8)**

vielle à roue Hurdy-gurdy in France and the Low Countries. **(8)**

viellée French evening gathering where people socialized, drank, sang, and danced; cf. *veillée*. **(8)**

Vierzeiler Four-line song of Upper Austria. **(8)**

viggianesi Italian itinerant ensembles from the town of Viggiano that disseminated operatic tunes across Italy, Europe, and Turkey during the nineteenth century. **(8)**

vihó Tukano mind-altering snuff inhaled through the nose by the *payé*. **(2)**

vihuela (1) European-derived five-stringed hour-glass-shaped plucked chordophone. (2) Five-stringed Mexican guitar with a convex back. (3) Six-course sixteenth-century Spanish guitar. (4) *Vihuela de mano* 'of the hand', Purépecha six-stringed hourglass-shaped plucked and strummed chordophone. (5) *Vihuela de arco* 'of the bow', Purépecha bowed chordophone introduced by colonial missionaries. (6) Five-stringed Mexican guitar with spined, convex back, used in the *mariachi* ensemble and in the *conjunto de arpa grande* ensemble. (7) High-pitched Spanish guitar. **(2, 3, 8)**

vikivaka kvœði Refrain sung by dancers in Icelandic *vikivakalag* songs. **(8)**

vikivakalag Icelandic strophic dance-song with refrains performed responsorially by the dancers. **(8)**

vikram samvat Hindu calendar. **(5)**

vilambit (Also *vilamba*.) Slow tempo. **(5)**

vilepill (Also *pajupill*.) Estonian willow duct flute without holes for fingering. **(8)**

villādi vādyam Musical bow (about 2.5 meters long) of Tamil Nadu. **(5)**

villancico 'Rustic song'. (1) Popular Christmas song genre in Spanish-speaking America. (2) Peruvian religious genre sung in Spanish and sometimes in Quechua. (3) Chilean *tonada* performed as a Christmas carol. (4) Exclusively religious Nicaraguan songs that show a remarkable retention of their (originally Spanish) melodic and lyrical form and content. (5) *Villancico navideño*, Nicaraguan song genre praising the Virgin Mary and the Infant Jesus, sung during the Christmas season. (6) Spanish-derived polyphonic religious composition, found in the Philippines. (7) Luso-Hispanic song genre whose form and character changed over its long history; today the term refers to a Christmas carol or a popular song with verses and a refrain. (8) Spanish Christmas carol. **(2, 3, 4, 8)**

villotte Type of Italian lyric song. **(8)**

villuppāṭṭu 'Bow song'; Tamil ritual storytelling form named for the musical bow featured in its performance. **(5)**

vilōma anulōma (Also *pratilōma*.) Augmentation, a variation technique in Karnatak music in which the theme or the meter is made twice and then four times as slow. **(5)**

vimbuza Tumbuka spirits. **(1)**

vīṇā Plucked lute from India. **(4)**

vina (Also *vīṇai*.) (1) Lute or struck zither with seven strings (four melody strings, three drone strings) of Indian classical music. (2) South Indian fretted plucked lute. **(3, 5, 10)**

vioara Romanian name of the violin. **(8)**

viol Three-stringed bowed chordophone of Buru. **(4)**

viola (1) (Also *amarantina, braguesa, toeira*.) Portuguese guitar, usually with five double or triple courses of metal strings, that provides harmonic and rhythmic accompaniment for *fado*. (2) Brazilian plucked and strummed chordophone of Iberian origin (from *viola de mão* 'of the hand'), with five double courses of ten or twelve metal strings. **(2, 8)**

viola baixo Large bass guitar that plays the bass line in a performance of Portuguese *fado*. **(8)**

viola da gamba In European art music, a fretted most often six-stringed bowed lute having a range approximating that of the cello; used during the Renaissance and Baroque periods for sacred and secular polyphony and revived in the twentieth century. **(8)**

violão 'Guitar' (Portuguese). (1) The common Iberian six-stringed guitar. (2) Portuguese (Brazilian) guitar. **(2, 3)**

violas de arames Portuguese and Brazilian guitar-like instruments whose strings vary in number (five, seven, eight, ten, twelve, fourteen) according to the region of origin. **(3)**

violin Western stringed instrument adopted as a solo and accompanying instrument in South Asia, with some alteration as to playing position, tuning, and playing technique. **(5)**

violín 'Violin' (Spanish). (1) Common European violin, introduced by colonial missionaries and disseminated throughout the Americas. (2) *Violín de talalate*, northern Nicaraguan violin named for the soft, white *talalate* wood. **(2)**

violine (Also *gunci, gunjci, muzika*.) Instrumental ensemble of Istria, Croatia. **(8)**

violon Breton fiddle. **(8)**

vipañci vīṇā Arched harp of Indian antiquity, played with a plectrum. **(5)**

vipasan Armenian storyteller and poet of the Middle Ages. **(6)**

vipattu cintu Tamil song form recounting accidents. **(5)**

vīra 'Heroic', one of the eight emotional states (*rasa*) codified in the *Nāṭyaśāstra*. **(5)**

vira One of the oldest Portuguese couple dances, in 6/8 meter and most common in northwest Portugal. **(8)**

vīragāse Dance of Karnataka venerating the male deity Virabhadra. **(5)**

virágének 'Flower songs', type of Hungarian lyric song. **(8)**

virah gīt Songs of separation of Uttar Pradesh. **(5)**

virani Devotional songs of Maharashtra on the separation of the beloved (devotee) from the lover (deity). **(5)**

Viraviyavantulu Traditional singers of the *Epic of Palnāḍu*, in Andhra Pradesh. **(5)**

virelai French medieval verse and song form. **(8)**

virgen 'Virgin'. (1) Roman Catholic icon symbolizing the Virgin Mary, but under different names, the object of devotion in many patronal festivals in the Americas; (2) Virgen de Guadalupe, religious festivity for all the Mixtec; (3) Virgen de La Candelaria, 'Virgin of the Candles', ancient Chilean Catholic festivity; (4) Virgen de La Tirana, 'Virgin of the Tyrant', largest expression of religious syncretism in northern Chile; (5) Virgen de Las Peñas, 'Virgin of the Rocks', oldest patronal festival among the Chilean Aymara; (6) Virgen de Punta Corral, Argentine procession attracting the largest number of the faithful in the province of Jujuy. **(2)**

virsi (Also *itku*.) In modern Finnish, a Lutheran psalm. **(8)**

viruttam (Also *padyam*.) Karnatak style of singing poetry without a pulse. **(5)**

viśārad Advanced level of college education in North India. **(5)**

Vishnu Hindu deity. **(4)**

vishnupad Vaishnav songs in *dhrupad* style. **(5)**

visitas 'Visiting centers', (1) places where friars introduced European Christian music to Purépecha culture; (2) small, nearby suburbs of a mission in northwest Mexico. **(2)**

vistār 'Expansion', variations or improvisations following the composition in Hindustani instrumental music; in melodic improvisation, sometimes used synonymously with *tān*. **(5)**

vitata Category of double-headed drums played with sticks, in the Buddhist *pañcatūrya nāda* system. **(5)**

vīthinātaka Street-theater form of Andhra Pradesh. **(5)**

viuda Ecuadorian widow figure of the new year celebration. **(2)**

viula di orbi 'Blind man's viola', hurdy-gurdy of Italian-speaking Switzerland. **(8)**

viulinu Corsican violin. **(8)**

viulu Finnish violin. **(8)**

viunishnye pesni 'Newlywed songs', performed by carolers at newlyweds' houses on the first Sunday after Easter in the Kostroma region near the Volga River in Russia. **(8)**

viyolonsel 'Cello' (Turkish.) **(6)**

vkiolarides Typical ensemble for dance-music in Cyprus, consisting of a violin playing the melody, a *laouto* playing accompaniment, and a *tampoutsia* keeping the rhythm. **(8)**

vlačiljske pjesme Wool-combing songs of Bosnia-Hercegovina. **(8)**

vlier Plucked dulcimer of the Low Countries. **(8)**

vlöggelen Chain dance of Ootmarsum, performed on Easter Sunday and Monday by more than a thousand men, accompanied by religious songs. **(8)**

vocable (1) Syllable that is consistent with the phonemes of a language but carries no referential meaning; used to vocalize music, as in "fa-la-la"; often carries emotional meaning. (2) Spoken or sung wordlike sound having no lexical meaning. **(3, 9)**

vocale Full vowel sound, like /a/, as the basis for singing; cf. *semivocale*. **(8)**

voceru (Also *buceru, bucerata*.) Corsican lament for a violent death. **(8)**

Vodou (Also Anglicized as *voodoo*.) Afro-Haitian religious system and Fon term for spirit in Haiti. **(2)**

vodoun (Also *vodun*.) Deities of the people of Dahomey. **(1)**

vodu (Also *papagadu*.) Maroon ritual to the snake god in Surinam. **(2)**

vodú Ceremony of African heritage in the Dominican Republic, characterized by spirit possession. **(2)**

voeyesi Swiss dance-song performed around fountains during the burning of the fields in the French-language areas. **(8)**

voggevise 'Rocking song', Norwegian work song to lull a baby. **(8)**

voiced speech Speech marked by a periodic wave of a fundamental and partials. **(1)**

volcanto 'Volcano song', Nicaraguan genre of *nueva canción* associated with the Sandinista Revolution. **(2)**

volksbal Folk-dance nights in the Low Countries. **(8)**

Volkshochschulen German public colleges that often have courses in folk music. **(8)**

volkslied 'Folk song', term coined in the early 1770s by Johann Gottfried von Herder. **(8)**

volksmusik Folk music, especially popularized forms in German-speaking areas of Central Europe. **(8)**

volksthümliches Lied Term for folklike song in German-speaking areas of Central Europe. **(8)**

volkstümlichemusik Austrian commercialized folk music, played by brass- or accordion-based ensembles. **(8)**

volochebnye pesni 'Trudging songs', Russian songs performed at Easter when animals are led to summer pasture. **(8)**

volynka Russian bagpipe. **(8)**

vóng cổ Expandable song structure used in *cả luong* theater, Vietnam. **(4)**

vopli Russian lament. **(8)**

vorgeige (Also *primgeige*.) Lead violin in ensembles of Italian southern Tyrol. **(8)**

Vorsanger Mennonite lead singer of hymns. **(3)**

vorzäurer Soloist in the *zäuerle* style of yodeling of Urnasch, Switzerland. **(8)**

vota Chechen and Ingush double-headed drum; see *gaval*. **(8)**

vozeni pesni (Also *glasoečki, ikoečki pesni*.) Macedonian songs with elaborate melodies. **(8)**

vrličcko kolo '*Kolo* of Vrlika', Croatina *kolo* in which the only sounds heard are dancers' footfalls and the coin jewelry bouncing on women's costumes. **(8)**

vučarske pjesme 'Wolf songs', Bosnia-Hercegovinian, sung after hunting wolves in winter. **(8)**

ɗufofo 'Drumming', Anlo-Ewe performance, including drumming, singing, dancing, and costuming. **(1)**

ɗumegãwo 'Big men or women of the drum', persons who lead the hierarchy of urban Anlo-Ewe performing ensembles. **(1)**

vung phleng pey keo Khmer court ensemble for worship of ancestors. **(4)**

vuvă Romanian one-headed frame drum, played in Oltenia and Muntenia. **(8)**

vuyɔyɔ Anlo-Ewe genre of performance that draws on rural musical practice. **(1)**

vyanusi Tumbuka dance in which the spirit of the Ngoni comes out and transforms people. **(1)**

wa (1) Kajang sung narrative form. (2) (Japan.) Harmony. **(4, 7)**

wà Small clapper of split bamboo, from Burma. **(4)**

wada Mapuche gourd rattle. **(2)**

Wādankusa-ratnamāla 'Science of Music'; eighteenth-century Sinhala chronicle containing theory of drum music. **(5)**

Wagogo People of central Tanzania. **(1)**

wagon (Japan.) Zither used in *gagaku*. **(7)**

wagonghu Korean thirteen-stringed horizontal harp, now obsolete. **(7)**

waḥda Common 8-beat rhythm in modern Arab vocal music. **(6)**

wahhābiyya Omani dance with weapons, similar to the *qaṣṣafiyya*. **(6)**

waī Sindhi lyrical poems sung by a chorus. **(5)**

waijianghan (China.) Outside troupes. **(7)**

waika (Also *guaika*.) 'To kill a man or animal already dying from a wound', an outsider term for some subgroups of the Yanomamö native Americans in southern Venezuela. **(2)**

wai khru Thai ritual ceremony to honor one's teacher. **(4)**

waila Social dance music, sometimes called "chicken scratch," of the Tohono O'odham people featuring accordion, bass, guitar, drums, and saxophone (fiddles in the old style). **(3)**

wa'iz Public sermon delivered by a Sufi. **(6)**

wajd 'Ecstasy', mystical rapture that may result from proper performance of Sufi rituals, especially from *dhikr* and *inshād*. **(6)**

waka (1) Guadeloupe music accompanied only by throat sounds, hand clapping, and foot stomping. (2) Segment of a Japanese *nô* play. (3) Generic term for indigenous poetic forms of the Japanese Nara period (710–794), of which only the *tanka* (a thirty-one-syllable poem) still survives. **(2, 7)**

wákà Yoruba musical genre, adopted from the Hausa and usually performed by women. **(1)**

waka pinkillu Bolivian 'bull flute', three-holed duct flute played in pipe-and-tabor fashion. **(2)**

waka tokori Bolivian dance that caricatures a Spanish bullfight. **(2)**

waki (Japan.) (1) Secondary role in *nô*; subleader of an instrumental or vocal section who sits beside the leader (*tate*). **(7)**

waki kata (Japan.) *Nô* actors who play a secondary role called *waki*. **(7)**

waki nô (Japan.) See *kami nô*. **(7)**

wak'rapuku (Also *wakrapuku*.) Quechua Peruvian circular or spiral valveless trumpet made of cattle-horn sections or pieces of tin, often played in pairs of *primera* and *segunda*. **(2)**

Waktu Lima Orthodox Muslims in Lombok. **(4)**

Waktu Telu Nominal Muslims in Lombok. **(4)**

wala (Vai.) Wooden boards on which Qur'ānic inscriptions are written. **(1)**

walagallo Curative ritual of the Nicaraguan Garífuna. **(2)**

wale'hkou' From Burma, large clappers of slit bamboo section. **(4)**

wali Cirebonese term for Islamic saint. **(4)**

walina Fixed song genre exclusively associated with the ceremonial cleaning of irrigation channels in Peru. **(2)**

wals 'Waltz' (Dutch). **(8)**

waltz (1) Pan-European dance in triple time that became popular in North America early in the nineteenth century and became the dominant basis for popular song at the turn of the twentieth century; survives today both in the ballroom and in folk fiddling. (2) Popular European couple dance in 3/4 time. (3) Ballroom dance in moderate triple time. **(3, 8, 9)**

waná Tubes used in Yekuana clarinet construction. (2)

wanaragua (Also John Canoe.) Old song-and-dance genre, composed and performed solely by men in Belize. (2)

wanawun Women's song genre in Kashmir. (5)

Wancay Bolivian mythical singer who has the mouth of a toad. (2)

wanch'ang 'Complete singing', performance of an entire Korean *p'ansori* tale. (7)

Wandervogel German outdoor clubs with their own repertoire of folk songs. (8)

wandindi Originally single-stringed Kikuyu lute-fiddle; later received an extra string, which usually sounds a fourth below the other and functions as a drone. (1)

wandora Warao *cuatro*, small, four-stringed chordophone. (2)

wangga Northwestern Australian Aboriginal songs, usually said to be received from spirits in dreams. (9)

wanka (Also *uanca*.) Bolivian love song. (2)

wankara (1) Bolivian small handheld single-headed cylindrical drum with snare. (2) Bolivian large cylindrical double-headed drum. (2)

Wanyamwezi Cultural group of Tanzania. (1)

warahan Lampung theatrical stories of Sumatra. (4)

warime Ceremony among the Venezuelan Pairoa. (2)

wárini Masked dance that is a prelude to *wanaragua* among the Garifuna of Belize. (2)

wari zume (Japan.) *Koto* technique, plucking two strings simultaneously. (7)

Wasa An Akan-speaking people of Ghana. (1)

wasaha Yekuana pole or staff rattle. (2)

wasan (Japan.) Buddhist chant (*syômyô*) with Japanese texts. (7)

wasan bòorii Spirit-possession dance that occurs in many Hausa communities. (1)

wasan maharba Dance in which performers reenact personal experiences of going on hunts. (1)

waṣla 'Stretch', 'connection'; traditional vocal suite of the Mashriq, comparable to the Andalusian *nūba*. (6)

wassailing English carol-singing custom combining house visits with the performance of specific songs. (8)

wasṭa Rhythmic period in Yemenite music with internal structure of 3 + 3 + 2. (6)

wasṭā al-kawkabāniyya 'The Kawkabān *wasṭā*', triplet variant of the Yemeni *wasṭā* rhythm. (6)

wat Buddhist temple complex in Thailand. (4)

water drum American Indian drum that is partially filled with water. (3)

wau (Also *ɔek*.) Colo poet-composer-singer. (1)

waulking 'Wool shrinking', occasion for songs in Scotland. (8)

wawallo Ecuadorian festive wake for an infant or a young child. (2)

wayang (1) Javanese puppet theater, performed by people of Javanese descent in Surinam to the accompaniment of a *gamelan*. (2) Shadow puppetry of Indonesia. (2, 4)

wayang gedek Malay shadow-puppet theater in Thai style (*nang talung*). (4)

wayang gedhog East Javanese wayang based on *Panji* stories. (4)

wayang golek (1) Puppet theater using rod puppets with wooden heads, torso, and arms, particularly popular in West Java (Sunda) but also found in Central Java. (2) (Also *wayang golèk*.) Three-dimensional rod puppetry in Java, Cirebon, and Sunda. (3, 4)

wayang klithik Javanese flat wooden puppetry. (4)

wayang kulit (1) General term for leather shadow-puppet theater, throughout Indonesia and Malaysia. (2) Shadow puppet theater using perforated leather puppets against an illuminated cloth screen, often accompanied by *gamelan* music; in Java the performance sometimes lasts up to nine hours and audiences view both sides of the screen; in Bali a performance may last three to four hours with the audience mostly on the shadow side; the stories most often dramatized are from the Hindu epics *Mahabharata* and *Ramayana*, with local characters and topics added. (3, 4)

wayang kulit Jawa Indonesian *wayang purwa* in Malaysia. (4)

wayang melayu Nearly extinct, formerly royal shadow puppet theater of Malaysia. (4)

wayang potèhi Chinese puppetry accompanied by Chinese music, found in Java. (4)

wayang purwa Shadow puppetry based on Hindu epics, found in Java and Sumatra. (4)

wayang Sasak Shadow puppetry about Amir Hamza, found in Lombok. (4)

wayang Siam Indigenous shadow-puppet theater in northern Malaysia. (4)

wayang topèng Masked dance based on *Panji* stories, Java. (4)

wayang wong Masked human theater of Bali and Java. (4)

wayno (Also *huayno* in Quechua; *huayño* in Aymara.) Central Andean fast dance in duple meter, featuring a long-short-short rhythmic pattern. (2)

wayô gassô (Japan.) Mixture of Japanese and European instrumental arrangements. (7)

waza (1) Berta conical trumpet. (2) Berta music played by a *waza* ensemble. (1)

wazn (Plural, *awzān*.) Rhythmic mode; cf. *ʿīqā*. (6)

wedge-and-ring-tension drum Drum with a wedge-tensioned girdle attached to leather lacings around its body. (1)

wenchang luo Civil gong, large size, used in Chinese music. (3)

wenhuaju (China.) Bureau of culture. (7)

Wenxian tongkao Chinese historical document. (7)

wenzhangdiao (China.) Early reciting styles of *Suzhou tanci*. (7)

wenzipu (China.) Music notation relying on characters rather than symbols. (7)

wepasuni Guarijio goat stew served at the end of the *túmari* ceremony. (2)

werkbegriff Musical product as a finite, conceptual entity. (8)

West African Cultural Society Organization for preserving and promoting African culture, with branches in several countries. (1)

west gallery music English church music between 1750 and 1850 that has survived in oral tradition and involves elaborate fuguing tunes. (8)

Western Sāmoa Until July 1997, the administrative and national name of the western and most populous part of Sāmoa, mainly Savai'i and 'Upolu islands. (9)

whisper Speech in which the vocal cords are loose and caught in the blast of air from the lungs, creating turbulent noise. (1)

whittle and dub In England, a term for the combination of a three-holed pipe and a tabor, played by a one-man band. (8)

wibòt Evening during which the St. Lucian *chanté abwè* are performed. (2)

widyadhari Nymphlike goddess of Bali. (4)

Wiegenlieder Christmas manger songs of Germany in 6/8 or 3/4 time. (8)

wiejska Village-style Polish band. (3)

Wienerlied Austrian genre from Vienna. (8)

wierzchowe 'Of the peaks', genre of open-air song of the Tatra Highlands, Poland. (8)

wilet Density referent of a piece of Sundanese music. (4)

Wilhelm, Mount Papua New Guinean mountain at the intersection of Chimbu, Madang, and Western Highlands. (9)

Wilhem method (Also *solfège, solfeggio*.) Fixed-do system of sol-fa syllables in which vocables singnify absolute pitches. (8)

wird Sufi religious litany. (6)

wiri Rasp made from an elongated piece of steel serrated and scraped with a metal rod. (2)

wiriki (Also *widiki*.) Yekuana quartz pebbles used in container rattles. (2)

wisiratu 'Owner of pains', Warao priest-shaman in charge of the upper cosmic realm. (2)

wiskanie Women's calls in Poland. **(8)**

witakultruntufe 'Women carrying the drum', Mapuche female healers. **(2)**

wiwat Dance tunes in duple or triple time, popular in Great Poland. **(8)**

wokonghou (China.) Ancient harp. **(7)**

woleko Ceremony of thanksgiving in Sumba. **(4)**

Wolf Dance In the Western Arctic, a dance named according to the animal honored in the song text. **(3)**

wŏlgŭm 'Moon instrument', Korean plucked lute with round body. **(7)**

Wolof Cultural group of Senegal. **(1)**

WOMAD World of Music Arts and Dance, festival conceived by the British rock musician Peter Gabriel in 1980. **(1)**

wŏnbak Basic beat of a Korean rhythmic pattern. **(7)**

woowoo (Also French reel.) *Jumbie* drum of Montserrat. **(2)**

wo paheli Savunese cymbals. **(4)**

word painting Use of melody to depict a visual effect, a technique sometimes used by Ndubuisi. **(1)**

world beat (Also worldbeat.) Term used to describe hybrid music that combines traditional and non-Western musical elements with contemporary pop styles and production values; often the result of cross-cultural collaboration between producers and musicians. **(3)**

World Circuit Small independent British recording label. **(1)**

world music Term used in marketing folk, classical, and popular musics from outside the Anglo-American mainstream to Western audiences. **(3)**

wot Circular bamboo panpipes of northeast Thailand. **(4)**

wowipits (Asmat.) Any man skilled at carving wood. **(9)**

woyaya Pygmy dance accompanied by a 24-pulse-unit pattern played on a percussion beam. **(1)**

wua Kasena-Nankani two- or three-holed vertical flute, the most common melody-producing instrument of Ghana. **(1)**

wuchang luo Small military gong used in Chinese music. **(3)**

wule Term for song among the Kpelle of Liberia; songs can be of various proportions. **(1)**

wusheng (China.) Five notes: *gong, shang, jue (jiao), zhi, yu.* **(7)**

wushi (China.) Shaman and spirit-medium. **(7)**

wustā Middle finger; the fret played by this finger. **(6)**

wuxian pipa (China.) Five-stringed *pipa.* **(7)**

wuxing (China.) The five elements (metal, wood, water, fire, earth) that were believed to have made the physical universe. **(7)**

xácara Brazilian ballad of Iberian origin. **(2)**

xalam (Also *halam, khalam.*) Wolof five-stringed plucked lute. **(1)**

xälq naxsisi Term for popular songs in Uighur (Uygur) Xinjiang. **(6)**

xānakāi 'Performed in the *khānāqa* ', vocal genre related to Sufi chanting, especially in Uzbekistan. **(6)**

xancaa Dance of pre-Hispanic origin among the Otopame. **(2)**

Xangô Portuguese orthography of Shango, a religion in Pernambuco, Brazil. **(2)**

xaxado Men's line dance of northeast Brazil. **(2)**

xayácatl (1) *Xayácatl de alastik,* Nahua dance of the flat disguise; (2) *xayácatl pasultik,* Nahua dance of the curled disguise. **(2)**

Xhosa Cultural group of South Africa. **(1)**

xiaju (China.) Lower or second textual line. **(7)**

xiang (China.) Four fret-ledges located near the neck of a modern *pipa.* **(7)**

xiangsheng (China.) Comic piece performed by one or two singers. **(7)**

xiangzhan (China.) Small horizontal gong. **(7)**

xianpu (China.) Tunes featuring stringed instruments. **(7)**

xianshiyue (China.) 'String and poetry'; refers to the string ensemble style of the Chaozhou region in Guangdong Province. **(7)**

xiao (China.) Vertical bamboo flute with five finger holes and one thumb hole that is similar to the Japanese *syukahiti.* **(7)**

xiaodiao (China.) Type of tune or melody popularized in cities and small towns and performed by semiprofessional or professional musicians. **(7)**

xiaoluo Small gong. **(3)**

xiaoqu (China.) Popular songs. **(7)**

xiaosheng (China.) Young male role in opera. **(7)**

xiashou (China.) 'Lower hand'; refers to the supporting storytellers in *Suzhou tanci.* **(7)**

xingqiang (China.) 'Performance' melody; refers to a singer's diction and delivery. **(7)**

xinyao Contemporary Singaporean songs in Mandarin Chinese. **(4)**

xipi (China.) One category of arias in Peking opera. *Xipi* melodies stress the third and sixth degrees of the scale and are considered suitable for lively, cheerful stories. **(7)**

xiqu (1) Generic term for Chinese opera. (2) General term for about 350 distinct types of music-drama in contemporary China. **(3, 7)**

xique (Also *xike, sique.*) Most popular and widely dispersed *mestizo* dance of Honduras. **(2)**

xi xov Hmong two-stringed fiddle. **(4)**

Xocotl Huetzi 'When the fruits fall down', ancient Aztec calendrical month celebration. **(2)**

xote Northeastern Brazilian slow *caboclo* dance genre based on the *schottisch.* **(2)**

xuân phả Ancient genre of masked plays from Thanh Hóa province. **(4)**

xudjiko (Also *xudjiku.*) Tukano long bark trumpets. **(2)**

xuetang yuege (China.) School songs. **(7)**

xul (1) Guatemalan vertical duct flute, open at the distal end. (2) Maya transverse cane flute with beeswax diaphragm and membrane mirliton. **(2)**

xun (1) Clay ocarina (Japan). (2) Chinese pronunciation of *ken.* **(7)**

xunhuanti (China.) Cyclic form. **(7)**

yaawn tashee Predawn Ramadan procession during which musicians perform. **(1)**

yabon sarakai Hausa court-praise music. **(1)**

yagi busi (Japan.) Style of Japanese folk songs characterized by metered rhythm and syllabic setting of texts. **(7)**

ya hyōsi (Japan.) 8-beat unit in *gagaku.* **(7)**

yaigho All-night singing ceremony in Sumba. **(4)**

yajé Banisteriopsis caapi, source of a mind-altering drink used by the Tukano *payé.* **(2)**

yajmān (Also *jajmān, jajmānī.*) One who conducts or sponsors a ritual. **(5)**

yajmānī Patronage. **(5)**

Yajurveda Collection of sacrificial verses and prose formulas used in Vedic sacrifices; one of the four religious and cultural texts (Vedas) of the Vedic Aryans. **(5)**

yak Korean vertical bamboo flute. **(7)**

Yakabi kunkunsî (Japan.) Oldest extant Okinawan scores, compiled by Yakabi Tyôki (1716–1775), containing 117 pieces of music for *sansin* (three-stringed lute). **(7)**

yakâdurā Drummer of the old religion in Sri Lanka who controls communication with spirits; *see also âdurā, kaṭṭādiya.* **(5)**

yak bera (Also *devol bera,* low-country drum.) Double-headed cylindrical drum of Sri Lanka. **(5)**

yakkaxāni (Also, in Uzbek, *yakkaxānlik.*) 'Individual song' (Tajik term), performed during breaks in the Central Asian Sufi *zikr.* **(6)**

yakṣagāna (Also *yakṣagāna bayalata.*) Elaborate masked and costumed temple dance drama of Karnataka. **(5)**

yaktāro One- or two-stringed plucked lute, used by Sindhi *faqir* for a rhythmic drone. **(5)**

yakumo goto (Also *nigen kin*.) Japanese two-stringed long zither. **(7)**

yakwìñ Pair of Burmese large cymbals. **(4)**

yalla (Aso *lapar*.) Women's repertoire of strophic dance songs in the Ferghana valley in Uzbekistan. **(6)**

Yalunka Cultural group of Guinea and Sierra Leone. **(1)**

Yamada *ryû* (Japan.) *Koto* school founded by Yamada *kengyô* (1757–1817). **(7)**

yamato bue (Japan.) *See kagura bue.* **(7)**

yamato gaku (Japan.) Genre of *syamisen* music begun in 1933. **(7)**

yamato mai (Japan.) Indigenous genre of court dance. **(7)**

yamatouta (Japan.) Indigenous genre of short court songs, performed in the *tinkon sai* rite. **(7)**

Yanagawa *ryû* (Japan.) Style of playing in *syamisen kumiuta* (song cycle). **(7)**

Yanagawa-style *ziuta syamisen* (Japan.) Relatively thin-necked *syamisen* used in *ziuta* in Kyôto. **(7)**

yang Chinese principle of the positive; cf. *yin*. **(7)**

yangban (1) Korean aristocrat; (2) one who plays an aristocrat in a village ritual play. **(7)**

yangbanxi (China.) Model opera. **(7)**

yanggŭm Korean hammered dulcimer. **(7)**

yangqin (China.) Hammered dulcimer imported during the sixteenth century from Central Asia. **(3, 7, 10)**

yangsŏng 'Bright voice', vocal timbre in Korean *p'ansori*. **(7)**

yangsuch'ok Gypsy-like émigrés who moved south into Korea during the Three Hans period. **(7)**

yangyun (China.) Chants praising the virtues and power of the gods. **(7)**

yanık 'Burned', 'consumed by love'; term for a Turkish solo repertoire for the *bağlama*. **(6)**

yankunu Probably from John Canoe, Guatemalan masked warrior dance. **(2)**

Yao (1) Cultural group of Tanzania. (2) Upland Sino-Tibetan group living in Thailand, Vietnam, and Laos. **(2, 4)**

yao (China.) Ballad or rhyme. **(7)**

yaoban (China.) Dramatic aria in Peking opera. **(7)**

Yap Main island complex, and a state, of the Federated States of Micronesia. **(9)**

yaponsa (From the Ghanaian song "*Yaa Amponsah*.") Guitar-fingering pattern of Nigeria. **(1)**

yaqona Kava (Fijian.) **(9)**

yará'a Medieval flute. **(6)**

ya-rakma Limbu dance performed at corn threshing in Nepal. **(5)**

yaravi From Quechua *hawari*, in Peru a slow, lyrical, often emotional section of a song. **(2)**

yarghūl Shepherd's flute of Palestine, similar to the *mijwiz* but with one melody and one drone pipe. *See also arghūl.* **(6)**

yarraba African-derived Yoruba songs for secular dances in Trinidad and Tobago. **(2)**

yasa "Unauthentic" Korean historical documents (diaries and essays); *see chǒngsa.* **(7)**

yataibayashi Musical ensemble seated on a float used in processions for traditional Japanese festivals. **(3)**

yatara byôsi (Japan.) 2 + 3-beat rhythmic cycle in *gagaku*. **(7)**

yatga Mongolian zither. **(7)**

yati Rhythmic shape of text phrases in Karnatak music. **(5)**

yatu byôsi (Japan.) Standard 8-beat rhythmic cycle in *nô*. **(7)**

Yatuhasi *ryû*. (Japan.) School of *koto*. **(7)**

yavi Vai male masquerader in Liberia. **(1)**

yawera Violin among the Guarijio in northern Mexico. **(2)**

yaya Yakan lullaby. **(4)**

yaykatekara (Japan.) Ainu love songs, a type of lyric songs (*sinotcha*). **(7)**

yaylı tanbur Long-necked bowed Turkish urban lute. **(6)**

Yayoi (Japan.) Prehistoric period, c. 200 B.C.E. to 250 C.E. **(7)**

yaysama (Japan.) Ainu lyric songs (*sinotcha*) generally dealing with ordinary emotions of everyday life. **(7)**

yayue (1) Chinese court music. (2) Confucian ritual music. **(7)**

Yazdaxum 'Eleventh', Sufi group in Bukhara that celebrated *zikr* on the eleventh day of each month. **(6)**

yazheng (China.) Half-tube bridged zither bowed with a small bamboo stick. **(7)**

Yebu Board of Rites of the Korean Unified Silla period. **(7)**

yechumadi Yekuana solo song. **(2)**

yehu (China.) Two-stringed spiked bowed lute with a body made of coconut shell, popularized in Cantonese and Chaozhou music. **(7)**

Yellow Blues Zimbabwean all-female jazz band. **(1)**

yeniçeri Turkish janissary band. **(6)**

yeshivot Hebrew religious schools. **(6)**

Yesul üi chǒndang Seoul (Korea) Arts Center. **(7)**

Yewe Ewe god of thunder and lightning. **(1)**

yeye Haitian rock music of the early 1960s, from the Beatles' "Yeah! Yeah! Yeah!" **(2)**

yifan Cantonese mode in which the intervals fa and ti are prominent. **(3)**

yifanxian (China.) Mode in Cantonese music, produced by changing the second and fifth note of the *zhengxian* scale (sol-ti-do-re-fa). **(7)**

Yiftos Greek word for Roma, synonymous with musician. **(8)**

yikay Shan (Burma) dance drama. **(4)**

yike Village theater genre of Chăm origin. **(4)**

yin Chinese principle of the negative; cf. *yang*. **(7)**

yishuv 'Settlement', term for the Jewish community of Palestine before 1948. **(6)**

Yiwangjik aakpu Korean court music institute, under Japanese colonial rule. **(7)**

yiyangqiang (China.) One of several localized *shenqiang*, systems of tunes. **(7)**

yô (Japan.) Pentatonic scale without semitone. **(7)**

yodel (Also yodeling.) (1) Rapid shifting between a singer's upper and lower registers. (2) Singing technique, and in some cases a song genre, involving the rapid alternation of full or chest voice with falsetto or head voice; *see jodel.* **(1, 8, 9)**

yô gaku (Japan.) Generic term for Western music. **(7)**

yogi gīt Songs performed by itinerant followers of the Nāth cult in Orissa. **(5)**

yo hyôsi (Japan.) 4-beat unit in *gagaku*. **(7)**

yol 'Road', 'wandering', 'direction'; Turkmen term referring to performance style, song, *dessan* or its narration, or a *bagshy* (*bagxy*) performance. **(6)**

yŏl ch'ae Korean thin whiplike drumstick. **(7)**

yŏltu pal sangmo Korean dance in which an acrobat twirls a hat with a long plume. **(7)**

yŏmbul Korean Buddhist invocation chants. **(7)**

yomiuri (Japan.) Balladeers of the Edo period (1600–1867) who walked the streets singing the news and vending booklets of the lyrics. **(7)**

Yom Kippur Jewish Day of Atonement. **(8)**

yomut-gökleng Performance style of northern Turkmenistan. **(6)**

yonbòt St. Lucian song-dance accompanied by the *ka*. **(2)**

yŏnch'ang Consecutive singing of Korean *p'ansori* episodes by different performers. **(7)**

yon fas Single-headed, barrel-shaped drum in Guadeloupe. **(2)**

yŏngdŭnghoe Ancient Korean court rite, appealing for Buddhist blessings. **(7)**

yŏnggi Korean triangular flags used in folk band processions. **(7)**

yonggo 'Dragon drum', Korean barrel drum used in royal processional music. **(7)**

Yŏngsan hoesang Long Korean chamber suite. **(7)**

yonika Bulgarian synthesizer. (8)

yonsei Fourth-generation Japanese-American; third generation to be born on American soil. (3)

yŏnŭmp'yo Korean notational system of simple neumes. (7)

Yoruba Dominant cultural group of southwest Nigeria. (1)

yŏsadang (Also *sŭptang.*) Korean female itinerant troupes. (7)

yose (Japan.) Vaudeville theater. (7)

yose bayasi (Japan.) Instrumental ensemble (*hayasi*) and its music in *yose*. (7)

yosempo In Japanese music, pentatonic scale without half steps. (10)

yŏsŏng kukkŭk tan All-female Korean *ch'anggŭk* opera troupe. (7)

yotuma (Japan.) *Syamisen* pattern in *gidayû busi*. (7)

yoùdayà Burmese genre of classical songs said to be derived from the Siamese at Ayuthaya. (4)

yŏŭm 'Aftertone', reverberation created when a Korean stringed instrument is plucked. (7)

yowagin (Japan.) Basic *nô* vocalization with melodious lines using a soft breath; melodic mode of *nô* chanting. (7)

yuanshi (China.) Primitive. (7)

yubiana (Japan.) Finger hole. (7)

yudiao Chinese melodic mode. (7)

yueju (Also *yuht kehk.*) Cantonese opera; major southern Chinese operatic genre from the Pearl River delta, as well as Hong Kong. (3, 7)

yue'ou (China.) 'Cantonese song', relatively short Cantonese song that consists of ten or more lines of unequal lengths. (7)

yue qin Chinese moon-shaped lute. (4)

yueqin (Also *yue qin*; in Japanese, *yue qui.*) (1) Moon-shaped four-stringed Chinese plucked lute. (2) (China.) Short-necked lute with a round body. (3, 4, 7)

yuequ (China.) Cantonese opera song. (7)

yue she Chinese music clubs, found in Vietnam. (4)

Yueshu yaolu (Japan.) 'Essentials of Books on Music', ten-volume theoretical work of the seventh-century Chinese court, brought to Japan in 735 as *Gakusyo yôroku*. (7)

yuhaengga Korean popular songs, based on the Japanese *enka* style. (7)

yuka (1) Older style of *rumba*. (2) (Japan.) Platform at the right of the *bunraku* (puppet theater) stage where the narrator and the *syamisen* player sit. (3, 7)

yuka hon (Japan.) Scripts of *gidayû busi* used onstage. (7)

yukchabaegi Korean folk songs in the southwestern regional style. (7)

yukpo Korean mnemonic notational system. (7)

yuksŏng 'Natural voice', chest voice with wide, slow vibrato used by Korean *kagok* singers. (7)

yulchabo (Also Chinese, *lu-lu.*) Korean letter notation borrowed from China. (7)

yule Woolworkers' work songs of French-speaking Switzerland. (8)

yúmari Traditional Tarahumara dance performed in a circle within the larger *tutuguri* ceremony. (2)

yunbai (China.) Kind of artificial speech resembling Hubei or Anhui dialect. (7)

yunluo (China.) Set of eight to fourteen small gongs suspended on a rack. (7)

yunqiang (China.) Daoist chant sung as a solo, in unison, or antiphonally by two or more priests. (7)

yunta (Japan.) Major style of folk songs in the Yaeyama Islands, accompanying work or for amusement. (7)

yuri (Japan.) Vocal or instrumental technique in which the sound is ornamented by waving or shaking. (7)

yurupari (1) Tukano ceremonial complex; (2) huge duct flutes, the most powerful Tukano aerophones, played in male-female pairs. (2)

yusap Sumu mouth-resonated jaw's harp or plucked idiophone. (2)

ywok Colo funeral and memorial dance. (1)

zabarii iish Chechen humorous songs. (8)

zabavna muzika Serbo-Croatian pop or rock songs. (8)

ẓābir Apparent, manifest. (6)

zabiya Professional female singer in West Africa. (1)

zabumba (1) Brazilian large, double-headed bass drum; (2) name for *banda de pífanos*. (2)

zaffa March or procession, often seen in weddings. (6)

zaffih Palestinian song for the shaving of the groom. (6)

zafina Early Arabic term for dance. (6)

zafindraona 'Popular religious song', genre of the rural Betsileo area of Madagascar. (1)

zafn Type of dance that produces no sound and consists of moving the shoulders, eyebrows, head, and so on. (6)

zafra Colombian field song of farmers, sung for their own entertainment. (2)

zagaku (Japan.) Chinese court chamber music introduced to the Ryûkyû Islands (present-day Okinawa). (7)

zagara Tunisian dance performed by paired men brandishing swords. (1)

zagharît (Singular, *zaghrûta*.) Cries of joy; ululation. (6)

Zaghawa A camel-breeding people of Darfur. (1)

zahīrok Baluchi instrumental genre, equivalent to the vocal *līkū*. (6)

zahīrok (Also *ḍēhī, līko*.) Songs of separation, travel, and work; most popular in southern Balochistan. (5)

zā'id (Also *zā'id*.) 'Extra' (Arabic), an additional fret, not named for a finger. (6)

Zaiko Langa Langa Congo-Zaïre *rumba* band that in the 1970s popularized *soukous*. (1)

zajal (Plural, *azjāl*.) (1) Popular North African court poetry, developed in Spain and having strophic texts with instrumental refrains. (2) Form of colloquial, popular Arabic poetry, first appearing in medieval Islamic Spain. (3) Musical setting of this poetry. (1, 6)

zakir (Also *güvende, sazende, aşık.*) Musician who performs in Alevi ceremonies. (6)

zaklikatnie viasny Belarusan songs invoking the spring season. (8)

žalejka Belarusan reed pipe. (8)

zamacueca (Also *zambacueca*.) Amorous pantomime dance of courtship in nineteenth-century Peru, a predecessor of the *marinera*. (2)

zambomba (Also *zambudia*.) (1) Salvadoran friction drum with fixed sticks attached to a single head; (2) Guatemalan small friction drum; (3) single-headed clay friction drum of Ecuador. (2)

zambra Moorish festival of song and dance. (6)

zammar Moroccan double clarinet. (1)

zammār Central figure in the Omani *ḥalqat allewa*, who plays a double-reed instrument or *mizmār*. (6)

zampogna (1) Italian bagpipe. (2) (Also *zanfoña, zumpogna*.) 'Symphony'; in Italy and Corsica, any instrument that produces a drone and a melodic line, including bagpipes, hurdy-gurdies, and mouth harps. (3, 8)

zampoña (1) Spanish term principally used in Chile for the panpipe, especially the double-unit panpipe or *siku* played in northern Chile; see *siku*. (2) Cane panpipes, often played in complementary pairs, associated with the Andean region of South America. (2, 3)

zampoñero Bolivian large stone statue of panpipe player of c. 1000 C.E. (2)

zamr (Also *zammr*.) Early designation for a wind instrument; today refers to a Maghribi double clarinet. (6)

zamzamāt Women's musical ensemble in Libya. (6)

Zanahary Malagasy creator god, who gave human beings instruments to entertain themselves. (1)

zanfona Spanish five-stringed hurdy-gurdy, characteristic of Galicia. (8)

žanićba Ciareški Belarusan calendrical ritual game in which a symbolic mother and father, chosen from older members of a community, pair young unmarried men and women and 'marry' them to each other. **(8)**

zanj (Plural, *zunūj*.) Cymbal. **(6)**

zanjīr-zanī 'Chain-striking' (Persian), responsorial singing of *nowḥe* by Shī'a men who strike their shoulders with small, light chains as they move in rhythm. **(6)**

zaowzaya Mauritanian four-holed flute, made of acacia root or bark. **(1)**

zapadniki 'Westernizers', Russian advocates of Western musical models. **(8)**

zapateado Dance patterns involving the stamping of the feet characteristic of an array of Spanish and Hispanic American dances. **(3)**

zapateo (Also *zapateado*, from Spanish 'foot stamping'.) (1) Dance technique involving rhythmic striking of heels and toes against the floor or each other. (2) Bolivian energetic stamping dance. (3) Rural Cuban dance associated with the *punto campesino*. (4) *Zapateo criollo*, Peruvian dance genre based on foot stamping. (5) Dancer's footwork in Spanish flamenco. **(2, 8)**

zapev Solo introduction to a choral song in Russian polyphonic singing. **(8)**

zapevanje Serbian lament for the dead. **(8)**

zapin West Asian-derived songs and dances of Malaysia and Sumatra. **(4)**

za'pwè Burmese classical theater accompanied by *hsaiṅ*. **(4)**

zaqq 'Belly', Maltese bagpipe, usually accompanied by a tambourine and a friction drum. **(8)**

zār (1) Ceremony in Kashmir that accompanies a boy's first haircut. (2) Evil spirit; by extension, a possession ritual of African origin widespread on the Red Sea and Gulf coasts. (3) Northeast African curing ceremony involving singing, dancing, and drumming. **(1, 5, 6)**

zarabanda (1) Seventeenth-century Spanish dance in triple meter; (2) popular music in highland Guatemala. **(2)**

żarb Iranian goblet drum of walnut, clay, or plastic; sometimes called *tombak*, with the exception of the large *żarb* played in the *zūr-khāne*. **(6)**

żarbī Particular rhythmic realization of a *gushe* in Persian music. **(6)**

zari Gurian polyphonic funeral songs having structures based on liturgical forms. **(8)**

ẓarīf al-ṭūl Palestinian wedding song. **(6)**

zarzuela (1) Spanish court-based musical play with sung choruses and *coplas* alternating with spoken lines. (2) Distinctively Spanish musical theatrical genre with origins dating back to sixteenth-century court entertainment and today sharing features with opera and operetta. (3) Spanish-derived light opera, especially popular in Argentina and Uruguay. (4) Spanish-language play with music and dance. **(2, 3, 4, 8)**

zatô (Japan.) (1) Blind *biwa* (lute) players not affiliated with the priesthood; (2) lowest rank in the *tôdô* (guild for blind artisans). **(7)**

zatu nô (Japan.) *Nô* plays with miscellaneous subjects. **(7)**

zäuerle (Also *zäuerli*.) Style of Swiss yodel. **(8)**

zavzava Maltese friction drum played with a tambourine to accompany a bagpipe. **(8)**

zāwiya (Plural, *zāwāyā*.) Sufi lodge or shrine, typically built around the tomb of a saint. **(6)**

zbójnicki 'Robbers' dance', men's dance in the Carpathian area of Poland. **(8)**

zdravice Songs of salutation in Bosnia-Hercegovina. **(8)**

zeibekiko Greek solo dance in 9/4 time, originally of coastal Asia Minor; the principal dance of *rebetika*. **(8)**

zejel Chilean Andalusian musical-poetic tradition, developed in colonial times. **(2)**

zekete-zekete Popular music from 1977 to 1987 in Kinshasa, based on a variant of the *rumba*. **(1)**

zekr (Also *ẕekr*.) 'Remembrance' (of God); Persian, from Arabic *dhikr*. Sufi method of verbal recall in the form of a litany; cf. *dhik*, *zikir*. **(6)**

zelenyj kúsek Bohemian dance in which duple and triple meters alternate. **(8)**

zēmā Ethiopian Christian chant liturgy. **(1)**

Zen (Japan.) Sect of Buddhism. **(7)**

zendani Genre of Maghrib popular music, played and sung by urban female professionals at family festivals. **(1)**

Zenpô zatudan (Japan.) Book (c. 1513) of sayings of Konparu Zenpô (1454–c. 1532). **(7)**

zensan (Japan.) Hymnlike Buddhist chant (*syômyô*) preceding the chanting of a *sutra*. **(7)**

ženska 'Female', used to distinguish women's singing styles in genres sung by men and women in Bosnia-Hercegovina. **(8)**

zensyôrei (Japan.) Buddhist chant (*syômyô*) preceding worship. **(7)**

zerizaykheizh yeredkher Adighian songs of acquittal that try to persuade the community of a singer's innocence of a crime. **(8)**

žetelačke pjesme Bosnia-Hercegovinian harvest songs. **(8)**

žetvarski glas 'Harvest voice', style in which Serbian harvest songs are performed. **(8)**

zevensprong (Also French, *danse des sept sauts*.) 'Seven jumps' (Dutch), jump-dance song of seven steps of the Low Countries; **(8)**

zevu Anlo-Ewe pot drum, adapted from pot drums of Nigeria. **(1)**

zeybek Turkish folk dance genre performed in the Aegean region. **(6)**

zeze Generic Tanzanian term for bar zithers, bows, and lutes. **(1)**

zhaleika (Also *piṣhchik*.) Russian single-reed aerophone with one or two pipes with a horn bell. **(8)**

zhāng Bells tied in a string, in Balochistan. **(5)**

zheng (1) Sixteen- or twenty-one-stringed Chinese zither. (2) (China.) Half-tube bridged zither with seventeen to twenty-one strings, related to the Japanese *koto*. **3, 4, 7)**

zhengtong (China.) Continuous genealogy of rulership. **(7)**

zhengxian (China.) Authentic mode (sol-la-do-re-mi) in Cantonese music, with the first note starting on the pitch G. **(7)**

zhi (China.) Song suites, one of the three main categories of songs in *nanguan*. **(7)**

zhil-kobuz Balkar and Karachaevi bowed lute. **(8)**

zhir baschi 'Head of song', Balkar and Karachaevi term for melody. **(8)**

zhirga Chechen and Ingush frame drum; *see tep*. **(8)**

zhita Higi boys' inititiation ritual in northern Nigeria. **(1)**

zhiyin (China.) Someone who truly knows the music. **(7)**

zhong (China.) (1) Clapperless bronze bell. (2) Chinese term for *kane* (Japanese Buddhist bells). **(7)**

zhongban (China.) Moderate tempo. **(7)**

zhongpian (China.) Medium-length stories in *Suzhou tanci*. **(7)**

zhongsan qingliu (China.) Modal designation in Chaozhou *xianshiyue*; it indicates raising the sixth note and lowering the third note. **(7)**

zhongsan zhongliu (China.) Modal designation in Chaozhou *xianshiyue*; it indicates raising the sixth note and the third note. **(7)**

zhu (China.) Stick zither of the Zhou dynasty. **(7)**

zhuanye (China.) Professional. **(7)**

zhuyin (China.) Root tone or main note. **(7)**

zhyr Kazakh term for epic or epic poetry. **(6)**

zhyrau Kazakh epic singer. **(6)**

zi (Japan.) (1) Abbreviation for *zi tyôsi*; the original melody line of a *syamisen* piece played by an ensemble. (2) Short melodic figure repeated in an ensemble performance. (3) (Also *zi ai*.) Melodic part of the *gidyû busi* narratives. (4) Bridge of a *koto*. (5) Smooth coating on the inner bore of a *syakuhati*. **(7)**

Zialonyja śviatki (Also *Siomucha*.) Belarusan Pentecost. **(8)**

zidai mono (Japan.) *Kabuki* plays and narrative *syamisen* music (*zyôruri*) dealing with political events before the Edo period. **(7)**

Ziehharmonika Vernacular German for accordion. **(8)**

zigarella 'Tape', name of an hour-long Maltese *spirtu pront*, performed at gatherings in bars. **(8)**

zihou (Also *ji hauh* in Cantonese opera.) In Chinese music, female falsetto voice. **(7)**

zi iro (Japan.) Section of *gidayû busi* narrated in an intermediate style, more speechlike than *zi ai* (or *zi*) but more melodic than *iro*. **(7)**

zikir (Also *zikr, dhikr, dikir*.) (1) Chanting of Islamic verse, usually accompanied by drumming. (2) 'Remembrance of God'; ritual formula for Shia worship. (3) (Turkish.) Invocation of God's name. **(1, 4, 5, 6)**

zikr Chechen and Ingush funeral prayers; *see nazm*. **(8)**

zikr jaxri (Also *zikr jari, jaxriyya*.) 'Loud' *zikr*, Central Asian term; this involves singing, reciting poetry, and dancing. **(6)**

zikr khafi (Also *zikr khufi*.) 'Silent' *zikr*, Central Asian term; the name of Allah and sacred formulas are pronounced silently. **(6)**

zikrzamman Women's choral music of Lombok. **(4)**

zil (1) Cymbals, Turkish. (2) From Persian *zir* 'below'. Triple course of strings on the Azerbaijani *saz*, tuned to the highest pitch and used for the melody. **(6)**

zili Small metal finger-cymbals of Turkish origin, played in the Balkans. **(8)**

zilia Metal finger-cymbals, used in Greek *rebetika*. **(8)**

zilli maşa 'Fire tongs with bells', type of Turkish idiophone. **(6)**

Zimbos, Os Angolan band that performs a mix of *merengue, rumba*, and rural Angolan styles. **(1)**

Zimon ryû (Japan.) One of two branches of the Tendai school of Buddhist chant (*syômyô*). **(7)**

zi nasi syakuhati (Japan.) *Syakuhati* without a smooth coating over the inner bore (*zi*). **(7)**

zinbun (Japan.) Buddhist chant (*syômyô*), (1) offertory or (2) invoking or sending off Buddha or other deities, such as guardian deities. **(7)**

zin'ges Latvian popular songs of the 1700s and 1800s. **(8)**

zingulca (Also *brnakač*.) Slovene noisemaker, made of a piece of wood or bone attached to a string, which produces a whirring sound when spun. **(8)**

Zinti yôyoku (Japan.) Tablatures for the *sô* (thirteen-stringed long zither) compiled by Huziwara no Moronaga (1138–1392). **(7)**

zi nuri syakuhati (Japan.) *Syakuhati* with a smooth coating over the inner bore (*zi*). **(7)**

Zion Part of Jamaican Revival tradition. **(2)**

Zionists Separatist church in Zimbabwe that used African drums in its rituals. **(1)**

zīr 'Below' (Persian); on an *'ud, dutār*, or *sāz*, the string or course of strings that lies farthest from the player's head and produces the highest pitches. **(6)**

zıraw (Also *aqın*.) Epic reciter in Kazakhstan. **(6)**

zirbaghali Goblet-shaped single-headed pottery drum of Northern Afghanistan played with two hands. **(5)**

zisin kyô (Japan.) 'Sutra of the earth spirit', major rite of Buddhist temples of blind priests. **(7)**

Zi syû (Japan.) Sect of Zyôdo Buddhism. **(7)**

zither (1) Chordophone with parallel strings. (2) Stringed instrument with a shallow horizontal soundboard, played with pick and fingers. **(3, 4)**

ziuta (Japan.) Genre of lyrical *syamisen* music, generally performed by an ensemble including a *koto*. **(7)**

zi utai (Japan.) *Nô* chanting in unison. **(7)**

ziutai kata (Japan.) Performers of unison *nô* chanting. **(7)**

ziuta mai (Japan.) Dance accompanied by *ziuta*. **(7)**

ziuta sôkyoku (Japan.) *Ziuta* pieces performed with *koto*. **(7)**

złóbcoki Small, rebec-like fiddle of Polish highlanders of the Tatra Mountains. **(8)**

zlöö 'Praise song', musical genre of the Dan of West Africa. **(1)**

ziutai za (Japan.) Right section of the main stage in *nô*, for the chorus. **(7)**

zmeika (Also *kjodiachii, khodovoi khorovod*.) 'Snake', Russian dance in which all participants walk in a circle or a serpentine pattern down a street. **(8)**

znamenny rospev 'Chanting by signs', Russian notational system for long-drawn-out songs. **(8)**

žniŭnyja pieśni Belarusan harvest songs. **(8)**

zo St. Lucian idiophonic pair of bones or hardwood sticks struck against one another. **(2)**

zokela Urban dance music based in the Central African Republic city of Bangui. **(1)**

zokkyoku (Japan.) 'Vulgar music'. (1) Generic term for popular *syamisen* songs performed as entertainment at banquets or in vaudeville theaters (*yose*). (2) Term for folk songs, used before the term *min'yo* was introduced. **(7)**

Zokugaku senritu kô (Japan.) 'On the Melodies of Japanese Vernacular Music' (1895), book by Uehara Rokusirô (1848–1913). **(7)**

Zoku gunsyo ruizyû (Japan.) 'Continuation of *Gunsyo Ruizyû*', second series of *Gunsyo ruizyû*. **(7)**

zokyuô (Japan.) 'Vulgar folk songs', local songs with instrumental accompaniment. **(7)**

zolarbā' Arabic term for tetrachord. **(6)**

zonaradhiko Greek Thracian belt dance in 6/8 meter. **(8)**

zongora In Romania, the guitar of Maramureş. **(8)**

zooba Sande masked dancer who impersonates a male ancestor water-dwelling spirit. **(1)**

zô odori (Japan.) Genre of Okinawan dance depicting the life and feelings of the common people, created in the late nineteenth century. **(7)**

zorne (From Turkish *zurna*, Arabic *mizmār*.) Double-reed aerophone used in Kurdistan; cf. *sez, zūrnā*. **(6)**

zortiko Dance song in a rapid 5/8 meter, generally divided into units of 3 and 2 beats. **(3)**

zortziko 'Made of eights', most popular Basque dance-song type, in asymmetric rhythm and consisting of eight steps. **(8)**

zouchang Singaporean narrative tradition of Chinese origin. **(4)**

zô udui (Japan.) *Zô odori* (Okinawan dance genre) in Okinawan dialect. **(7)**

zouk (1) Martinique dance party; (2) popular music genre of the French Antilles, developed in the 1980s and also popular in France. **(2, 8)**

zournadhes (Also *zourna*.) Pair of conical double-reed shawms, played by Macedonian Gypsies in Greece. **(8)**

zowq 'Taste', 'passion' (Persian). **(6)**

zrokha kudi 'Cow's tail', Georgian small metal military instrument, mentioned in medieval literary sources. **(8)**

zubac Guatemalan bone flute. **(2)**

zūkra Double-reed aerophone of North Africa. **(6)**

zukra Tunisian bagpipe, used to accompany a scarf dance. **(1)**

Zulu Cultural group of South Africa. **(1)**

zumare Albanian and Montenegrin single-reed double-pipe aerophone. **(8)**

zumbador Mixtec membrane mirliton placed over a hole in the central part of the calabash trumpet. **(2)**

zummār Oboes. **(6)**

zurgălăi (Also *clopote*.) Romanian bells, used in ceremonies for the new year and weddings and hung around the necks of cattle and sheep as signal devices. **(8)**

zūr-khāne 'House of strength' (Persian); gymnasium in which men's athletic exercises are coordinated with the singing and drumming of a *morshed*. **(6)**

Volume Key: **1**, Africa; **2**, South America, Mexico, etc.; **3**, United States and Canada; **4**, Southeast Asia; **5**, South Asia

zurla (Also *zurna*.) Middle Eastern double-reed, conical-bore shawm, imported into the Balkans and Georgia during the Ottoman period; *see zurle*. (**8**)

zurle (Also *cingonë, curle, surle*.) Albanian conical-bore double-reed aerophone; *see zurla*. (**8**)

zurna Generic term for double-reed aerophone in the eastern Arab world; cf. *sornā*. (**6**)

z'urna Armenian bell-mouth wind instrument made from wood or metal; because of its very strong sound, it is used mostly as an outdoor instrument. (**6**)

zvanočak Belarusan two-clappered hand bells of metal and wood. (**8**)

žvegla Slovene duct flute. (**8**)

zvon Belarusan bronze clappered bells. (**8**)

zvončari Croatian bell carriers. (**8**)

žvrgolci Bird- or horse-shaped one-to-three-holed clay whistles, played by children in Prekmurje and Lower Carniola, Slovenia. (**8**)

Zwiefache 'Two-timers', Bavarian couple dance that shifts between 2/4 and 3/4 time. (**8**)

zyô (Japan.) Highest principal note in *nô* chanting. (**7**)

zyo (Japan.) Introduction, first part of the tripartite principle of *zyo ha kyû*. (**7**)

zyobun (Japan.) Introductory part of a Buddhist *sutra*. (**7**)

zyôdai kabu (Japan.) Generic term for ancient indigenous music and dance. (**7**)

Zyôdo Sin syû (Japan.) Sect of Zyôdo Buddhism. (**7**)

Zyôdo syû (Japan.) Sect of Zyôdo Buddhism. (**7**)

zyo ha kyû (Japan.) Basic tripartite aesthetic principle in Japanese music. (**7**)

Zyômon (Japan.) Prehistoric period, c. 11,000–200 B.C.E. (**7**)

zyo no mai (Japan.) Section of slow-tempo dance in *nô*. (**7**)

zyôon (Japan.) (1) Upper pitch area in Buddhist chant; (2) common melodic patterns in this pitch area. (**7**)

zyôruri (Also *jōruri*.) Generic term for Japanese narrative *syamisen* music. (**7**)

zyôruri mono (Japan.) *Ziuta* repertoire (*syamisen* music) imitating narrative *syamisen* genres (*zyôruri*). (**7**)

zyoryû (Japan.) 'In the women's style', word added to female performances of theatrical music outside the theater. (**7**)

zyôzi (Japan.) Young Buddhist monks assisting the *ebugyô* monk who directs a ritual. (**7**)

zyun hôgaku (Japan.) Classical as opposed to popular or contemporary music. (**7**)

zyun pati gyaku roku (Japan.) System of mathematically calculating the twelve pitches, roughly equivalent to the twelve Western semitones. (**7**)

zyûsiti gen sô (Japan.) Seventeen-stringed *koto* invented in 1921 by Miyago Mitio (1894–1956). (**7**)

Volume Key: **6**, Middle East; **7**, East Asia; **8**, Europe; **9**, Australia and the Pacific Islands; **10**, The World's Music.

Africa

Publications on African Music

REFERENCE WORKS

Aning, Ben Akosa. 1967. *An Annotated Bibliography of Music and Dance in English Speaking Africa*. Legon: Institute of African Studies.

Gaskin, Lionel John Palmer. 1965. *Select Bibliography of African Music*. London: International African Institute.

Gray, John. 1991. *African Music: A Bibliographical Guide to the Traditional, Popular, Arts, and Liturgical Musics of Sub-Saharan Africa*. New York and Westport, Conn.: Greenwood.

Greenberg, Joseph H. 1966. *The Languages of Africa*. Bloomington, Ind.: Research Center for the Language Sciences.

Guthrie, Malcolm. 1948. *The Classification of Bantu Languages*. London: International African Institute.

Merriam, Alan P. 1970. *African Music on LP*. Evanston, Ill.: Northwestern University Press.

Murdock, George Peter. 1967. *Ethnographic Atlas*. Pittsburgh, Pa.: University of Pittsburgh Press.

Murray, Jocelyn, ed. 1981. *Cultural Atlas of Africa*. Oxford: Elsevier.

Stone, Ruth M., and Frank J. Gillis. 1976. *African Music and Oral Data: A Catalog of Field Recordings, 1902–1975*. Bloomington and London: Indiana University Press.

Thieme, Darius L. 1964. *African Music: A Brief Annotated Bibliography*. Washington, D.C.: Library of Congress.

Tracey, Hugh. 1973. *Catalogue of the Sound of Africa Recordings*. Roodepoort, South Africa: International Library of African Music.

Varley, Douglas H. 1936. *African Native Music: An Annotated Bibliography*. London: Royal Empire Society.

GENERAL

Anderson, Lois Ann. 1971. "The Interrelation of African and Arab Musics: Some Preliminary Considerations." In *Essays in Music and History in Africa,* ed. Klaus P. Wachsmann, 143–169. Evanston, Ill.: Northwestern University Press.

Ankermann, Bernhard. 1901. "Die afrikanischen Musikinstrumente." *Ethnologisches Notizblatt* 3:1–X, 1–32.

Arom, Simha. 1976. "The Use of Play-Back Techniques in the Study of Oral Polyphonies." *Ethnomusicology* 20(3):483–519.

———. 1991. *African Polyphony and Polyrhythm,* trans. Martin Thom et al. Cambridge and Paris: Cambridge University Press and Éditions de la Maison des Sciences de l'Homme.

———. 1992. "A Synthesizer in the Central African Bush: A Method of Interactive Exploration of Musical Scales." In *Für Gyorgy Ligeti: Die Referate des Ligeti-Kongresses Hamburg 1988,* ed. Peter Petersen, 163–178. Hamburger Jahrbuch für Musikwissenschaft, 11. Hamburg: Laaber-Verlag.

Ballanta, Nicholas George Julius. 1926. "Gathering Folk Tunes in the African Country." *Musical America* 44(23):3–11.

Bebey, Francis. 1975. *African Music: A People's Art,* trans. Josephine Bennett. Westport, Conn.: Lawrence Hill.

Blacking, John. 1955. "Some Notes on a Theory of African Rhythm Advanced by Erich von Hombostel." *African Music* 1(2):12–20.

Bowdich, Edward T. 1821. *An Essay on the Superstitions, Customs, and Art Common to the Ancient Egyptians, Abyssinians, and Ashantees*. Paris: J. Smith.

Carrington, John. 1949. *Talking Drums of Africa*. London: Carey Kingsgate.

Collins, John. 1985. *African Pop Roots*. London: W. Foulsham.

Curtin, Philip. 1964. *The Image of Africa: British Ideas and Action, 1780–1850*. Madison: University of Wisconsin Press.

Danielson, Virginia. 1988. "The Arab Middle East." In *Popular Musics of the Non-Western World,* by Peter Manuel, 141–160. New York: Oxford University Press.

Davidson, Basil. 1966. *African Kingdoms*. New York: Time-Life Books.

Erlmann, Veit. 1981. *Populäre Musik in Afrika*. Berlin: Staatliche Museen Preussischer Kulturbesitz. Veröffentlichungen des Museums für Völkerkunde Berlin, Neue Folge 53, Abteilung Musikethnologie 8.

Faruqi, Lois I. al. 1986. "Handasah al Sawt or the Art of Sound." In *The Cultural Atlas of Islam,* ed. Isma'il al Faruqi and Lois Lamya' al Faruqi, 441– 479. New York: Macmillan.

———. 1986. "The Mawlid." *World of Music* 28(3):79–89.

Finnegan, Ruth. 1970. *Oral Literature in Africa*. Nairobi: Oxford University Press.

Gibb, H. A. R. 1929. *Ibn Battuta, Travels in Asia and Africa*. London: Darf.

Hampton, Barbara. 1980. "A Revised Analytical Approach to Musical Processes in Urban Africa." *African Urban Studies* 6:1–16.

Herzog, George. 1934. "Speech-Melody and Primitive Music." *Musical Quarterly* 20(4):452–466.

Hornbostel, Erich M. von. 1928. "African Negro Music." *Africa* 1:30–62.

———. 1933. "The Ethnology of African Sound Instruments." *Africa* 6:129–154, 277–311.

Jones, Arthur M. 1971 [1959]. *Studies in African Music*. 2 vols. London: Oxford University Press.

———. 1964. *Africa and Indonesia: The Evidence of the Xylophone and Other Musical and Cultural Factors,* 2nd ed. Leiden: Brill.

———. 1976. *African Hymnody in Christian Worship: A Contribution to the History of Its Development*. Gwelo, Zimbabwe: Mambo.

Kauffman, Robert. 1980. "African Rhythm: A Reassessment." *Ethnomusicology* 24:393–415.

Kubik, Gerhard. 1962. "The Phenomenon of Inherent Rhythms in East and Central African Instrumental Music." *African Music* 1:33–42.

———. 1965. "Transcription of Mangwilo Xylophone Music from Film Strips." *African Music* 3(4):35–41.

———. 1972. "Transcription of African Music from Silent Film: Theory and Methods." *African Music* 5(1):28–39.

———. 1977. "Patterns of Body Movement in the Music of Boys' Initiation in South-East

Angola." In *The Anthropology of the Body*, ed. John Blacking, 253–274. London: Academic.

———. 1985. "African Tone Systems: A Reassessment." *Yearbook for Traditional Music* 17:31–63.

———. 1986. "Stability and Change in African Musical Traditions." *World of Music* 27:44–69.

Livingstone, David. 1857. *A Narrative of Dr. Livingstone's Discoveries in South-Central Africa*. London: Routledge.

Manuel, Peter. 1988. *Popular Musics of the Non-Western World*. New York: Oxford University Press.

Merriam, Alan P. 1959. "African Music." In *Continuity and Change in African Cultures*, ed. William R. Bascom and Melville J. Herskovits, 49–86. Chicago: University of Chicago Press.

———. 1964. *The Anthropology of Music*. Evanston, Ill.: Northwestern University Press.

———. 1972. *The Arts and Humanities in African Studies*. Bloomington: African Studies Program, Indiana University.

———. 1981. "African Musical Rhythm and Concepts of Time-Reckoning." In *Music East and West: Essays in Honor of Walter Kaufmann*, ed. Thomas Noblitt, 123–142. New York: Pendragon.

———. 1982. *African Music in Perspective*. New York: Garland.

Mudimbe, V. Y. 1988. *The Invention of Africa: Gnosis, Philosophy, and the Order of Knowledge*. Bloomington: Indiana University Press.

Mukuna, Kazadi wa. 1992. "The Genesis of Urban Music." *African Music* 7(2):72–74.

Murdock, George P. 1959. *Africa: Its People and Their Culture History*. New York: McGraw-Hill.

Nketia, J. H. Kwabena. 1962a. "The Hocket Technique in African Music." *Journal of the International Folk Music Council* 14:44–55.

———. 1962b. "The Problem of Meaning in African Music." *Ethnomusicology* 6(l):1–7.

———. 1974. *The Music of Africa*. New York: Norton.

———. 1982. "On the Historicity of Music in African Cultures." *Journal of African Studies* 9(3):1–9.

Nketia, J. H. Kwabena, and Jacqueline C. DjeDje. 1984. "Trends in African Musicology." In *Selected Reports in Ethnomusicology*. 5, *Studies in African Music*, ix–xx. Los Angeles: UCLA.

Omibiyi, Mosunmola. 1973–1974. "A Model for the Study of African Music." *African Music* 5(3):6–11.

Rouget, Gilbert. 1985. *Music and Trance: A Theory of the Relations between Music and Possession*, trans. Brunhilde Biebuyck. Chicago: University of Chicago Press.

Serwadda, Moses, and Hewitt Pantaleoni. 1968, "A Possible Notation for African Dance Drumming." *African Music* 4(2):47–52.

Simon, Artur, ed. 1983. *Musik in Afrika*. Berlin: Museum für Völkerkunde.

Stapleton, Chris, and Chris May. 1990. *African Rock: The Pop Music of a Continent*. New York: Dutton.

Stone, Ruth M. 1985. "In Search of Time in African Music." *Music Theory Spectrum* 7:139–158.

Stone, Ruth M., and Verlon Stone. 1981. "Event, Feedback, and Analysis: Research Media in the Study of Music Events." *Ethnomusicology* 25(2):215–225.

Thompson, Robert Farris. 1974. *African Art in Motion*. Berkeley and Los Angeles: University of California Press.

Vansina, Jan. 1969. "The Bells of Kings." *Journal of African History* 10(2):187–197.

Wachsmann, Klaus R. 1964a. "Human Migration and African Harps." *Journal of the International Folk Music Council* 16:84–88.

———. 1964b. "Problems of Musical Stratigraphy in Africa." In *Colloques de Wégimont* 3:19–22.

———. 1966. "The Trend of Musicology in Africa." *Selected Reports in Ethnomusicology* (UCLA) 1(1):61–65.

———. 1970. "Ethnomusicology in Africa." In *African Experience*, ed. John N. Paden and Edward W. Soja, 128–151. Evanston, Ill.: Northwestern University Press.

———, ed. 1971. *Essays on Music and History in Africa*. Evanston, Ill.: Northwestern University Press.

Wallaschek, Richard. 1893. *Primitive Music: An Inquiry into the Origin and Development of Music, Songs, Instruments, Dances, and Pantomimes of Savage Races*. London: Longmans, Green.

Waterman, Richard A. 1952. "African Influence on the Music of the Americas." In *Acculturation in the Americas*, Vol. 2, ed. Sol Tax, 207–218. Chicago: University of Chicago Press.

Wegner, Ulrich. 1984. *Afrikanische Saiteninstrumente*. Berlin: Staadliche Museen Preussischer Kulturbesitz. Museum für Völkerkunde Berlin, Abteilung Musikethnologie, New Series, 41.

WEST AFRICA

Agawu, Kofi. 1986. "'Gi Dunu,' 'Nyekpadudo,' and the Study of West African Rhythm." *Ethnomusicology* 30(l):64–83.

———. 1987. "The Rhythmic Structure of West African Music." *Journal of Musicology* 5(3):400–418.

———. 1990. "Variation Procedures in Northern Ewe Song." *Ethnomusicology* 34(2):221–243.

Akpabot, Samuel. 1972. "Theories on African Rhythm." *African Arts* (Los Angeles) 6(l):59–62, 88.

Ames, David W. 1973. "A Sociocultural View of Hausa Musical Activity." In *The Traditional Artist in African Societies*, ed. Warren d'Azevedo, 128–161. Bloomington: Indiana University Press.

Ames, David W., and Anthony V. King. 1971. *Glossary of Hausa Music in Its Social Contexts*. Evanston, Ill.: Northwestern University Press.

Amu, Ephraim. 1933. *Twenty-Five African Songs*. London: Sheldon.

Anyidoho, Kofi. 1982. "Death and Burial of the Dead: Ewe Funeral Folklore." M.A. thesis, Indiana University.

Arntson, Laura. 1992. "The Play of Ambiguity in Praise-Song Performance: A Definition of the Genre through an Examination of Its Practice in Northern Sierra Leone." Ph.D. dissertation, Indiana University.

Avorgbedor, Daniel Kodzo. 1986. "Modes of Musical Continuity among the Anlo-Ewe of Accra: A Study in Urban Ethnomusicology." Ph.D. dissertation, Indiana University.

———. 1992. "The Impact of Rural-Urban Migration on a Village Music Culture: Some Implications for Applied Ethnomusicology." *African Music* 7(2):45–57.

Besmer, Fremont. 1972. *Hausa Court Music in Kano, Nigeria*. Ann Arbor, Mich.: University Microfilms.

———. 1974. *Kídàn Dàràn Sállà: Music for the Muslim Festivals of Id al-Fitr and Id al-Kabir in Kano, Nigeria*. Bloomington: African Studies Program, Indiana University. Indiana University Monographs.

———. 1983. *Horses, Musicians, and Gods: The Hausa Cult of Possession-Trance*. South Hadley, Mass.: Bergin and Garvey.

Bird, Charles S., and Martha B. Kendall. 1980. "The Mande Hero." In *Explorations in African Systems of Thought*, ed. Ivan Karp and Charles S. Bird, 13–26. Bloomington: Indiana University Press.

Bird, Charles S., Mamadou Koita, and Bourama Soumaoro. 1974. *The Songs of Seydou Camara*, Vol. 1: *Kambili*. Bloomington: African Studies Center, Indiana University.

Bosman, William. 1967 [1705]. *A New and Accurate Description of the Coast of Guinea*. London: Frank Cass. (Facsimile of the 1705 English edition.)

Burton, Sir Richard Francis. 1966 [1893]. *A Mission to Gelele, King of Dahome*. London: Routledge and Kegan Paul.

Chernoff, John M. 1979. *African Rhythm and African Sensibility: Aesthetics and Social Action in African Musical Idioms*. Chicago: University of Chicago Press.

Collins, E. John. 1977. "Post-War Popular Band Music in West Africa." *African Arts* 10(3):53–60.

———. 1985. *Musicmakers of West Africa*. Washington: Three Continents.

————. 1986. *E. T. Mensah, King of Highlife.* London: Off the Record.

————. 1987. "Jazz Feedback to Africa." *American Music* 5(2):176–193.

————. 1989. "The Early History of West African Highlife Music." *Popular Music* 8(3): 221–230.

Collins, E. John, and Paul Richards. 1982. "Popular Music in West Africa." In *Popular Music Perspectives*, ed. David Horn and Philip Tagg, 111–141. Göteborg, Exeter: International Association for the Study of Popular Music.

DjeDje, Jacqueline Cogdell. 1980. *Distribution of the One String Fiddle in West Africa.* Los Angeles: UCLA Program in Ethnomusicology, Department of Music.

————. 1982. "The Concept of Patronage: An Examination of Hausa and Dagomba One-String Fiddle Traditions." *Journal of African Studies* 9(3): 116–127.

Duran, Lucy, et al. 1987. "On Music in Contemporary West Africa: Jaliya and the Role of the Jali in Present Day Manding Society." *African Affairs: Journal of the Royal African Society* 86(343):233–236.

Ekwueme, Lazarus. 1975–1976. "Structural Levels of Rhythm and Form in African Music with Particular Reference to the West Coast." *African Music* 5(4):105–129.

Euba, Akin. 1970. "New Idioms of Music-Drama among the Yoruba: An Introductory Study." *Yearbook of the International Folk Music Council* 92–107.

————. 1971. "Islamic Musical Culture among the Yoruba: A Preliminary Survey." In *Essays on Music and History in Africa,* ed. Klaus P. Wachsmann, 171–184. Evanston, Ill.: Northwestern University Press.

————. 1977. "An Introduction to Music in Nigeria." In *Nigerian Music Review*, No. 1, ed. Akin Euba, 1–38. Ife: Department of Music, University of Ife.

————. 1990. *Yoruba Drumming: The Dùndún Tradition.* Bayreuth African Studies, 21–22. Germany: Bayreuth University.

Fiagbedzi, Nissio. 1976. "The Music of the Anlo: Its Historical Background, Cultural Matrix, and Style." Ph.D. dissertation, University of California, Los Angeles.

Gourlay, Kenneth A. 1982. "Long Trumpets of Northern Nigeria—In History and Today." *African Music* 6(2):48–72.

Hampton, Barbara L. 1992. "Music and Gender in Gã Society: Aclaawe Song Poetry" In *African Musicology: Current Trends*, Vol. 2, ed. Jacqueline Cogdell DjeDje, 135–149. Los Angeles: University of California Press.

Harper, Peggy. 1970. "A Festival of Nigerian Dances." *African Arts* 3(2):48–53.

Herzog, George. 1945. "Drum-Signaling in a West African Tribe." *Word: Journal of the Linguistic Circle of New York* 1(3):217–238.

Keil, Charles. 1979. *Tiv Song.* Chicago: University of Chicago Press.

Kinney, Esi Sylvia. 1970. "Urban West African Music and Dance." *African Urban Notes* 5(4):3–10.

Knight, Roderic. 1972. "Towards a Notation and Tablature for the Kora." *African Music* 1(5):23–35.

————. 1974. "Mandinka Drumming." *African Arts* 7(4):25–35.

————. 1984a. "Music in Africa: The Manding Contexts." In *Performance Practice: Ethnomusicological Perspectives,* ed. Gerard Béhague, 53–90. Contributions in Intercultural and Comparative Studies, 12. Westport, Conn.: Greenwood.

————. 1984b. "The Style of Mandinka Music: A Study in Extracting Theory from Practice." In *Selected Reports in Ethnomusicology*, 5: *Studies in African Music*, ed. J. H. Kwabena Nketia and Jacqueline Cogdell DjeDje, 3–66. Los Angeles: University of California.

Koetting, James. 1970. "Analysis and Notation of West African Drum Ensemble Music." *Selected Reports in Ethnomusicology*, ed. J. H. Kwabena Nketia and Jacqueline Cogdell DjeDje, 1(3):115–146. Los Angeles: Institute of Ethnomusicology, University of California.

————. 1984. "Hocket Concept and Structure in Kasena Flute Ensemble Music." In *Selected Reports in Ethnomusicology*, 5: *Studies in African Music*, ed. J. H. Kwabena Nketia and Jacqueline Cogdell DjeDje, 161–172. Los Angeles: University of California.

Ladzekpo, S. Kobla. 1971. "The Social Mechanics of Good Music: A Description of Dance Clubs among the Anlo Ewe-Speaking People of Ghana." *African Music* 5(1):6–22.

Little, Kenneth. 1965. *West African Urbanization: A Study of Voluntary Associations in Social Change.* Cambridge: Cambridge University Press.

Locke, David. 1982. "Principles of Offbeat Timing and Cross-Rhythm in Southern Eye Dance Drumming." *Ethnomusicology* 26(2):217–246.

————. 1987. *Drum Gahu.* Crown Point, Ind.: White-Cliffs Media.

Locke, David, and Godwin K. Agbeli. 1980. "A Study of the Drum Language in Adzogbo." *African Music* 6(1):32–51.

Mensah, Atta Annan. 1958. "Professionalism in the Musical Practice of Ghana." *Music in Ghana* l(l):28–35.

Monts, Lester P. 1982. "Music Clusteral Relationships in a Liberian-Sierra Leonean Region: A Preliminary Analysis." *Journal of African Studies* 9(3):101–115.

Nketia, J. H. Kwabena. 1962. "The Problem of Meaning in African Music." *Ethnomusicology* 6: 1–7.

————. 1963. *Drumming in Akan Communities of Ghana.* London: University of Ghana and Thomas Nelson.

————. 1973. "The Musician in Akan Society." In *The Traditional Artist in African Societies,* ed. Warren d'Azevedo, 79–100. Bloomington: Indiana University Press.

Nzewi, Meki. 1974. "Melo-Rhythmic Essence and Hot Rhythm in Nigerian Folk Music." *Black Perspective in Music* 2(l):23–28.

Omibiyi, M. A. 1981. "Popular Music in Nigeria." *Jazzforschung* 13:51–168.

Parkin, David. 1969. "Urban Voluntary Associations as Institutions of Adaptation." *Man* 1(1): 90–95.

Peil, Margaret. 1972. *The Ghanaian Factory Worker Industrial Man in Africa.* Cambridge: Cambridge University Press.

Phillips, Ekundayo. 1953. *Yoruba Music.* Johannesburg: African Music Society.

Phillips, Ruth B. 1978. "Masking in Mande Sande Society Initiation Rituals." *Africa* 48:265–277.

Robertson, Claire. 1984. *Sharing in the Same Bowl: A Socioeconomic History of Women and Class in Accra.* Bloomington: Indiana University Press.

Smith, M. G. 1957. "The Social Functions and Meaning of Hausa Praise Singing." *Africa* 27:26–45.

————. 1959. "The Hausa System of Social Status." *Africa* 29:239–252.

Stone, Ruth. 1982. *Let the Inside Be Sweet: The Interpretation of Music Event among the Kpelle of Liberia.* Bloomington: Indiana University Press.

————. 1988. *Dried Millet Breaking: Time, Words, and Song in the Woi Epic of the Kpelle.* Bloomington: Indiana University Press.

Thieme, Darius. 1967. "A Descriptive Catalog of Yoruba Musical Instruments." Ph.D. dissertation, Catholic University of America.

Thompson, Robert F. 1966. "An Aesthetic of the Cool: West African Dance." *African Forum* 2(2): 85–102.

————. 1974. *African Art in Motion: Icon and Act in the Collection of Katherine Coryton White.* Los Angeles: University of California Press.

Turay, A. K. 1966. "A Vocabulary of Temne Musical Instruments." *Sierra Leone Language Review* (Freetown) 5:27–33.

Ward, William Ernest. 1927. "Music in the Gold Coast." *Gold Coast Review* 3(2):199–223.

Waterman, Christopher A. 1990. *Jùjú: A Social History and Ethnography of an African Popular Music.* Chicago: University of Chicago Press.

Yankah, Kwesi. 1983. "To Praise or Not to Praise the King: The Akan *Akpae* in the Context of Referential Poetry." *Research in African Literatures* 14(3):381–400.

————. 1985. "Voicing and Drumming the Poetry of Praise: The Case for Aural Literature." In *Interdisciplinary Dimensions of African Literature,* ed. Kofi Anyidoho et al., 137–153. Washington, D.C.: Three Continents.

Zemp, Hugo. 1967. *Musique Dan.* Paris: Mouton.

NORTH AFRICA

Carlisle, Roxane. 1975. "Women Singers in Darfur, Sudan Republic." *Black Perspective in Music* 3(3):253–268.

Daw, Ali al-, and Abd-Alla Muhammad. 1985. *Traditional Musical Instruments in Sudan.* Khartoum: Institute of African and Asian Studies, University of Khartoum.

———. 1988. *Al-mūsīqa al-taqlīdīya fī maǧtamaʿa al-Berta* (Traditional Music in al-Berta Society). Khartoum: Institute of African and Asian Studies, University of Khartoum.

Deng, Francis Mading. 1973. *The Dinka and Their Songs.* Oxford: Oxford University Press.

Erlmann, Veit. 1974. "Some Sources on Music in Western Sudan from 1300–1700." *African Music* 5(3):34–39.

Farmer, Henry George. 1924. "The Arab Influence on Music of the Western Soudan." *Musical Standard* 24:158–159.

———. 1939. "Early References to Music in the Western Sūdān." *Journal of the Royal Asiatic Society of Great Britain and Ireland*, Part 4 (October):569–579.

Ismail, Mahi. 1970. "Musical Traditions in the Sudan." *Revue Musicale* 288–289:87–93.

Saada, Nadia Mécheri. 1986. "La musique de l'Ahaggar." Ph.D. dissertation, University of Paris.

Schmidt-Wrenger, Barbara. 1979. *Rituelle Frauengesänge der Tshokwe: Untersuchungen zu einem Säkularisierungsprozess in Angola und Zaire.* 3 vols. Tervuren: Musée Royal de l'Afrique Centrale.

Simon, Artur. 1989a. "Musical Traditions, Islam, and Cultural Identity in the Sudan." In *Perspectives on African Music,* ed. Wolfgang Bender, 25–41. Bayreuth: Bayreuth African Studies, Series 9.

———. 1989b. "Trumpet and Flute Ensembles of the Berta People in the Sudan." In *African Musicology: Current Trends,* ed. Jacqueline C. DjeDje and William G. Carter, 1:183–217. Los Angeles: Crossroad; Festschrift J. H. K. Nketia.

———. 1991. "Sudan City Music." In *Populäre Musik in Afrika,* ed. Veit Erlmann, 165–180. Berlin: Museum für Völkerkunde.

Tucker, A. N. 1932. "Music in South Sudan." *Man* 32:18–19.

———. 1933a. "Children's Games and Songs in the Southern Sudan." *Journal of the Royal Anthropological Institute of Great Britain and Ireland* 63: 165–187.

———. 1933b. *Tribal Music and Dancing in the Southern Sudan (Africa) at Social and Ceremonial Gatherings.* London: W. Reeves.

Wendt, Caroline Card. 1994. "Regional Style in Tuareg *Anzad* Music." In *To the Four Corners,* ed. Ellen Leichtman. Warren, Mich.: Harmonie Park.

EAST AFRICA

Abokor, Ahmed Ali. 1990. "Somali Pastoral Work Songs: The Poetic Voice of the Politically Powerless." M.A. thesis, Indiana University.

Anderson, Lois. 1967. "The African Xylophone." *African Arts/Arts d'Afrique* 1:46–49.

———. 1977. "The Entenga Tuned-Drum Ensemble." In *Essays for a Humanist: An Offering to Klaus Wachsmann,* 1–57. New York: Town House.

Campbell, C. A., and C. M. Eastman. 1984. "Ngoma: Swahili Adult Song Performance in Context." *Ethnomusicology* 28(3):467–494.

Cooke, Peter. 1970. "Ganda Xylophone Music: Another Approach." *African Music* 4(4).

———. 1990. "Report on Pitch Perception Carried Out in Buganda and Busoga (Uganda) August 1990." *ICTM Study Group* 33:2–6.

Cooke, Peter, and Martin Doornbos. 1982. "Rwenzururu Protest Songs." *Africa* 52(1):37–60.

DeVale, Sue Carole. 1984. "Prolegomena to a Study of Harp and Voice Sounds in Uganda: A Graphic System for the Notation of Texture." In *Selected Reports in Ethnomusicology*, Vol. 5, ed. J. H. Kwabena Nketia and Jacqueline Cogdell DjeDje, 284–315. Los Angeles: University of California.

Giannattasio, Francesco. 1983. "Somalia: La Terapia Coreutico-Musicali del Mingis." *Culture Musicali* 2(3):93–119.

———. 1988a. "Strumenti Musicali." In *Aspetti dell' Espressione Artistica in Somalia,* ed. Annarita Puglielli, 73–89. Rome: University of Rome.

———. 1988b. "The Study of Somali Music: Present State." In *Proceedings of the Third International Congress of Somali Studies,* ed. Annarita Puglielli, 158–167. Rome: Il Pensiero Scientifico Editore.

Gnielinski, Anneliese von. 1985. *Traditional Music Instruments of Tanzania in the National Museum.* Occasional Paper 6. Dar es Salaam: National Museums.

Gourlay. Kenneth A. 1972. *The Making of Karimojong Cattle Songs.* Discussion Paper 18. Nairobi: Institute of African Studies, University of Nairobi.

Hartwig, Gerald W. 1969. "The Historical and Social Role of Kerebe Music." *Tanzania Notes and Records* 70:41–56.

Kavyu, Paul. 1978. "The Development of Guitar Music in Kenya." *Jazzforschung* 10:111–119.

Kimberlin, Cynthia. 1978. "The Baganna of Ethiopia." *Ethiopianist Notes* 2(2).

Kubik, Gerhard. 1967. "The Traditional Music of Tanzania." *Afrika* 8(2):29–32.

———. 1981. "Popular Music in East Africa since 1945." *Popular Music* 1:83–104.

Low, John. 1982a. "A History of Kenyan Guitar Music: 1945–1980." *African Music* 6(2):17–36.

———. 1982b. *Shaba Diary: A Trip to Rediscover the 'Katanga' Guitar Styles and Songs of the 1950s and 1960s.* Acta Ethnologica et Linguistica, 54. Vienna: Fohrenau.

Martin, Stephen H. 1991a. "Brass Bands and the Beni Phenomenon in Urban East Africa." *African Music* 8 (1):72–81.

———. 1991b. "Popular Music in Urban East Africa." *Black Music Research Journal* 11(1):39–53.

Omondi, Washington A. 1984. "The Tuning of the Thum, the Luo Lyre: A Systematic Analysis." In *Selected Reports in Ethnomusicology,* 5: *Studies in African Music,* 263–281. Los Angeles: UCLA.

Ranger, T. O. 1975. *Dance and Society in Eastern Africa.* Berkeley and Los Angeles: University of California Press.

Roberts, J. S. 1968. "Popular Music in Kenya." *African Music* 4(2):53–55.

Shelemay, Kay Kaufman. 1983. "A New System of Musical Notation in Ethiopia." In *Ethiopian Studies Dedicated to Wolf Leslau,* ed. Stanislav Segert and Andras J. E. Bodrogligeti, 571–582. Wiesbaden: Otto Harrassowitz.

———. 1989 [1986]. *Music, Ritual, and Falasha History.* East Lansing: Michigan State University Press.

Wachsmann, Klaus P. 1971. "Musical Instruments in Kiganda Tradition and Their Place in the East African Scene." In *Essays on Music and History in Africa,* ed. Klaus P. Wachsmann, 93–134. Evanston, Ill.: Northwestern University Press.

CENTRAL AFRICA

Arom, Simha. 1967. "Instruments de musique particuliers à certaines ethnies de la République Centrafricaine." *Journal of the International Folk Music Council* 19:104–108.

Blakely, Pamela A. 1993. "Performing Dangerous Thoughts: Women's Song-Dance Performance Events in a Hemba Funeral Ritual (Republic of Zaïre)." Ph.D. dissertation, Indiana University.

Brandel, Rose. 1961. *The Music of Central Africa.* The Hague: Martinus Nijhoff.

Carrington, John E. 1949. *A Comparative Study of Some Central African Gong-Languages*. Brussels: Institut Royal Colonial Belge.

Dehoux, Vincent, and Frédéric Voisin. 1992. "Analytic Procedures with Scales in Central African Xylophone Music." In *European Studies in Ethnomusicology: Historical Developments and Recent Trends,* ed. Max Peter Baumann et al., 174–188. Intercultural Music Studies, 4. Wilhelmshaven: Florian Noetzel.

———. 1993. "An Interactive Experimental Method for the Determination of Musical Scales in Oral Cultures: Application to the Xylophone Music of Central Africa." *Contemporary Music Review* 9:13–19.

Gansemans, Jos. 1978. *La musique et son rôle dans la vie sociale et rituelle Luba*. Sciences Humaines, 95. Tervuren, Belgium: Musée Royal de l'Afrique Centrale.

———. 1980. *Les instruments de musique Luba*. Sciences Humaines, 103. Tervuren, Belgium: Musée Royal de l'Afrique Centrale.

Gansemans, Jos, and Barbara Schmidt-Wrenger. 1986. *Zentralafrika*. Musikgeschichte in Bildern, 1, part 12. Leipzig: Deutscher Verlag für Musik.

Kubik, Gerhard. 1964. "Harp Music of the Azande and Related Peoples in the Central African Republic." *African Music* 3(3):37–76.

Laurenty, Jean Sébastien. 1960. *Les cordophones du Congo Belge et du Ruanda-Urundi*. Tervuren: Musée Royale de l'Afrique Centrale.

———. 1962. *Les sanza du Congo Belge*. Tervuren, Belgium: Musée Royale de l'Afrique Centrale.

———. 1968. *Les tambours à fente de l'Afrique centrale*. Tervuren, Belgium: Musée Royale de l'Afrique Centrale.

———. 1974. *La systematique des aérophones de l'Afrique centrale*. Tervuren: Musée Royale de l'Afrique Centrale.

Merriam, Alan P. 1973. "The Bala Musician." In *The Traditional Artist in African Societies,* ed.

Warren d'Azevedo, 23–81. Bloomington: Indiana University Press.

Mukuna, Kazadi wa. 1973. "Trends of Nineteenth- and Twentieth-Century Music in the Congo-Zaïre." In *Musikkulturen Asiens, Afrikas und Ozeanien im 19. Jahrhundert,* ed. Robert Günther, 267–284. Regensburg: Gustav Bosse.

———. 1980. "The Origin of Zaïrean Modern Music: A Socioeconomic Aspect." *African Urban Studies* 6:77–78.

Schweinfurth, Georg A. 1873. *In the Heart of Africa: Three Years' Travels and Adventures in the Unexplored Regions of Central Africa from 1868–1871*. London: S. Low, Marsten, Low, and Searle.

Voisin, Frédéric. 1994. "Musical Scales in Central Africa and Java: Modeling by Synthesis." *Leonardo Music Journal* 4:85–90.

SOUTHERN AFRICA

Adams, Charles R. 1974. "Ethnography of Basotho: Evaluative Expression in the Cognitive Domain Lipapali (Games)." Ph.D. dissertation, Indiana University.

Brown, Ernest Douglas. 1984. "Drums of Life: Royal Music and Social Life in Western Zambia." Ph.D. dissertation, University of Washington.

Berliner, Paul. 1978. *The Soul of Mbira: Music and Traditions of the Shona People of Zimbabwe*. Berkeley and Los Angeles: University of California Press.

Blacking, John. 1967. *Venda Children's Songs*. Johannesburg: Witwatersrand University Press.

———. 1985. "Movement, Dance, Music, and the Venda Girls' Initiation Cycle." In *Society and the Dance: The Social Anthropology of Process and Performance,* ed. Paul Spencer, 64–91. Cambridge: Cambridge University Press.

Colson, Elizabeth. 1969. "Spirit-Possession among the Tonga of Zambia." In *Spirit Mediumship in Society in Africa,* ed. John Beattie and John Middleton, 69–103. London: Routledge and Kegan Paul.

Coplan, David B. 1985. In *Township Tonight! South Africa's Black City Music and Theatre*. London: Longman.

———. 1988. "Musical Understanding: The Ethnoaesthetics of Migrant Workers' Poetic Song in Lesotho." *Ethnomusicology* 32:337–368.

Erlmann, Veit. 1991. *African Stars: Studies in Black South African Performance*. Chicago: University of Chicago Press.

Johnston, Thomas. 1970. "Xizambi Friction-Bow Music of the Shangana-Tsonga." *African Music* 4(4):81–95.

———. 1971. "Shangana-Tsonga Drum and Bow Rhythms." *African Music* 5(1):59–72.

———. 1972. "Possession Music of the Shangana-Tsonga." *African Music* 5(2):10–22.

———. 1987. "Children's Music of the Shangana-Tsonga." *African Music* 6(4):126–143.

Joseph, Rosemary. 1983. "Zulu Women's Music." *African Music* 6(3):53–89.

Kauffman, Robert. 1969. "Some Aspects of Aesthetics in Shona Music of Rhodesia." *Ethnomusicology* 13(3):507–511.

———. 1972. "Shona Urban Music and the Problem of Acculturation." *IFMC Yearbook* 4:47–56.

Kirby, Percival R. 1937 [1967]. "The Musical Practices of the Native Races of South Africa." In *Western Civilization and the Natives of South Africa,* ed. Isaac Schapera, 131–140. New York: Humanities.

———. 1965. *The Musical Instruments of the Native Races of South Africa,* 2nd ed. Johannesburg: Witwatersrand University Press.

Kubik, Gerhard. 1964. "Harp Music of the Azande and Related Peoples in the Central African Republic." *African Music* 3(3):37–76.

———. 1971. "Carl Mauch's Mbira Musical Transcriptions of 1872." *Review of Ethnology* 3(10):73–80.

———. 1988. "Nsenga/Shona Harmonic Patterns and the San Heritage in Southern Africa." *Ethnomusicology* 32(2):39–76 (211–248).

———. 1989. "The Southern African Periphery: Banjo Traditions in Zambia and Malaŵi." *World of Music* 31:3–29.

Kubik, Gerhard, Maya Aliya Malamusi, Lidiya Malamusi, and Donald Kachamba. 1987. *Malaŵian Music: A Framework for Analysis*. Zomba: University of Malaŵi, Department of Fine and Performing Arts.

Malamusi, Moya Aliya. 1984. "The Zambian Popular Music Scene." *Jazzforschung* 16:189–195.

Marshall, Loma. 1969. "The Medicine Dance of the !Kung Bushmen." *Africa* 39(4):347–381.

McLeod, Norma. 1977. "Musical Instruments and History in Madagascar." In *Essays for a Humanist: An Offering to Klaus Wachsmann*. New York: Town House.

Mthethwa, Bongani. 1980. "Zulu Children's Songs." In *Papers Presented at the Symposium on Ethnomusicology: Rhodes University, Grahamstown, October 10–11, 1980,* ed. Andrew Tracey, 23–35. Grahamstown: Rhodes University.

Rycroft, David. 1961. "The Guitar Improvisations of Mwenda Jean Bosco." *African Music* 2(4):81–98.

———. 1962. "The Guitar Improvisations of Mwenda Jean Bosco (Part II)." *African Music* 3(1):86–102.

———. 1971. "Stylistic Evidence in Nguni Song." In *Essays on Music and History in Africa,* ed. Klaus P. Wachsmann, 213–241. Evanston, Ill.: Northwestern University Press.

Tracey, Andrew. 1971. "The Nyanga Panpipe Dance." *African Music* 5(1):73–89.

Tracey, Hugh. 1970. *Chopi Musicians: Their Music, Poetry, and Instruments*. London and New York: International African Institute, Oxford University Press.

Tsukada, Kenichi. 1988. "Luvale Perceptions of Mukanda in Discourse and Music." Ph.D. dissertation, Queen's University of Belfast.

———. 1990. "*Kukuwa* and *Kachacha*: Classification and Rhythm in the Music of the Luvale of Central Africa." In *People and Rhythm,* ed. Tetsuo Sakurai, 229–276. Tôkyô: Tôkyô Shoseki. (In Japanese.)

———. 1991a. *"Mukanda* Rites and Music: A Study of Initiation Rites in Central Africa." In *Ritual and Music*, Vol. 2, ed. Tomoaki Fujii, 177–228. Tôkyô: Tôkyô Shoseki. (In Japanese.)

———. 1991b. "*Kalindula* in *Mukanda:* The Incorporation of Westernized Music into the Boys' Initiation Rites of the Luvale of Zambia." In *Tradition and Its Future in Music,* ed. Yosihiko Tokumaru et al., 547–551. Tôkyô: Mita.

Turner, Victor. 1968. *The Drums of Affliction: A Study of Religious Processes among the Ndembu of Zambia*. Oxford: International African Institute.

Westphal, E. O. J. 1978. "Observations on Current Bushmen and Hottentot Musical Practices." *Review of Ethnology* 5(2–3):9–15.

Zenkovsky, S. 1950. "Zar and Tambura as Practiced by the Women of Omdurman." *Sudan Notes and Records* 31:65–85.

Recordings of African Music

CATALOGS AND AUDIOGRAPHIES

Catalogue of Zonophone West African Records by Native Artists. 1929. Hayes, Middix.: British Zonophone.

Merriam, Alan P. 1970. *African Music on LP: An Annotated Discography.* Evanston, Ill.: Northwestern University Press.

Tracey, Hugh. 1973. *Catalogue: The Sound of Africa Series.* Roodepoort, South Africa: International Library of African Music.

GENERAL

Africa Dances. 1980. Authentic Records, ARM 601C Authentic. Audiocassette.

Courlander, Harold, and Alan P. Merriam. 1957. *Africa South of the Sahara.* Folkways Records FE 4503. 2 LP disks.

Discover a Whole New World of Music. 1991. Newton, N.J.: Shanachie Records 9101, CD 124. Compact disk.

Hood, Mantle. 1969. *Africa East and West.* Los Angeles: Institute of Ethnomusicology, University of California. IER 6571.

Kronos Quartet and Judith Sherman. 1992. *Pieces of Africa.* Elektra/Nonesuch 979275-2. Compact disk.

Tracey, Hugh. 1953. *The Guitars of Africa.* Music of Africa, 5. London LB-829. LP disk.

WEST AFRICA

Adé, Sunny. 1976. *Synchro System Movement.* African Songs AS26. LP disk.

———. 1982. *Juju Music.* Island Records CID 9712. Compact disk.

Aingo, George Williams. 1992. *Roots of High-life—1927.* Heritage HT CD 17. Compact disk.

Ames, David. 1964. *The Music of Nigeria, Hausa Music*, Vol. 1. Bärenreiter-Musicaphon Records BM 30 SL 2306. LP disk.

———. c. 1976. *Nigeria, 3: Igbo Music.* Bärenreiter-Musicaphon Records BM 30 SL 2311. LP disk.

Amoaku, W. K. 1978. *African Songs and Rhythms for Children.* Folkways Records FC 7844. LP disk.

Arom, Simha. 1975. *The Music of the Peuls.* EMI Odeon. LP disk.

Bebey, Francis. 1978. *Francis Bebey: Ballades africaines—Guitare.* Paris: Ozileka 3306. LP disk.

———. 1984. Akwaaba. Tivoli, N.Y.: Original Music OMCD 005. Compact disk.

Camara, Ladji. 1993. *Les ballets africains de Papa Ladji Camara.* Lyrichord. LP disk.

Dairo, I. K., and His Blue Spots. 1962. *Elele Ture.* Decca NWA 5079.

Dieterlen, Germaine. 1957. *Musique Dogon Mali.* Ocora OCR 33. LP disk.

———. 1966. *Musique Maure Mauritania.* OCR 28. LP disk.

Diamonds, Black. c. 1971. *Songs and Rhythms from Sierra Leone.* New Rochelle, N.Y.: Afro Request SRLP 5 03 1. LP disk.

Duran, Lucy. 1985. *Jaliya! Malamini Jobarteh and Dembo Konte.* London: Stern's Africa. LP disk.

———. 1990. *Boubacar Traoré: Mariama.* London: Stern's Africa 1032. LP disk.

Forster, Till. 1987. *Musik der Senufo, Elfenbeinkuste.* Berlin: Musikethnologische Abteilung, Museum für Völkerkunde MC 4. 2 LP disks.

Freire, João. 1992. *Travadinha: The Violin of Cape Verde.* Buda Records 92556-2. Compact disk.

Iṣọla, Haruna. 1959. *Hogan Bassey.* Decca WA 3120. 78-rpm 10-inch disk.

Jenkins, Jean. 1985. *Sierra Leone: Musiques traditionnelles.* Paris: OCORA 558–549. LP disk.

Johnson, Kathleen. 1983. *Rhythms of the Grasslands: Music of Upper Volta*, Vol. 2. Los Angeles: Elektra/Asylum/Nonesuch 72090. 2. LP disk.

Kouyate, Tata Bambo. 1989. *Tata Bambo Kouyate.* London: Globestyle ORB 042. LP disk.

Kroo Young Stars Rhythm Group. 1953. *O Gi Te Bi.* Decca DKWA 1335. LP disk.

Leigh, Stuart. 1981. *Music of Sierra Leone: Kono Mende Farmer's Songs.* Folkways Records FE 4330. LP disk.

Maal, Baaba. 1991. *Baayo.* New York: Island Records, Mango Records 162 539907-2. Compact disk.

Rouget, Gilbert. 1971. *Musique Malinke, Guinée.* Paris: Vogue LDM 30 113. LP disk.

———. 1981. *Sénégal: Musique des Bassari.* Paris: Chant du Monde LDX 74 753. LP disk.

Okie, Packard, ed. 1955. *Folk Music of Liberia.* Folkways Records FE 4465.

Weka-Yamo, Aladji, and Ayivi Go Togbassa. 1992. *Togo: Music from West Africa.* Rounder CD 5004. Compact disk.

Stone, Ruth M., and Verlon L. Stone. 1972. *Music of the Kpelle of Liberia.* Folkways FE 4385. LP disk.

Zemp, Hugo. 1971. *Musique Guère: Côte d'Ivoire.* Paris: Vogue LD 764. LP disk.

NORTH AFRICA

Atiya, Aziz S. 1960. *Coptic Music.* Folkways Records. LP disk.

Deng, Francis M. 1976. *Music of the Sudan: The Role of Song and Dance in Dinka Society.* Folkways Records FE 4301-03. 3 LP disks.

Duvelle, Charles. 1966. *Musique maure.* Paris: OCORA OCR 28. LP disk.

Gottlieb, Robert. N.d. *Sudan 1: Music of the Blue Nile Province—The Gumuz Tribe.* Cassel: Bärenreiter Musicaphon BM 30L 2312. LP disk.

———. N.d. *Sudan 2: The Ingessana and Berta Tribes.* Cassel: Bärenreiter Musicaphon BM 30L 2313. LP disk.

Guignard, Michel. 1975. *Mauritanie: Musique traditionnelle des griots maures.* SELAF/ORSTOM

(Collection Tradition Orale) CETO 752-3. 2 LP disks.

Laade, Wolfgang. 1962. *Tunisia*, Vol. 2, "Religious Songs and Cantillations." Folkways Records FW 8862. LP disk.

Lortat-Jacob, Bernard, and H. Jouad. 1979. *Berbères du Maroc: Ahwach.* Collection du Centre National de la Recherche Scientifique du Musée de l'Homme LDX 74705. LP disk.

Lortat-Jacob, Bernard, and Gilbert Rouget. 1971. *Musique berbère du haut Atlas.* Paris: Disques Vogue LD 786. LP disk.

Musiciens du Nil. 1988. Paris: OCORA D559006. Compact disk.

Pacholczyk, Jozef M. 1976. *Andalusian Music of Morocco.* Tucson, Ariz.: Ethnodisc ER 45154. LP disk.

Schuyler, Philip. N.d. *The Music of Islam and Sufism in Morocco.* Bärenreiter-Musicaphon BM 30 SL 2027. LP disk.

———. 1977. *Morocco: Arabic Tradition in Moroccan Music.* UNESCO Collection. EMI Odeon 3C 064-18264.

Simon, Artur. 1980a. *Musik der Nubier/Nordsudan (Music of the Nubians/Northern Sudan).* Berlin: Musikethnologische Abteilung, Museum für Völkerkunde MC 9. 2 LP disks.

———. 1980b. *Dikr und Madih, Gesänge und Zeremonien: Islamisches Brauchtunt im Sudan.* Berlin: Museum Collection MC 10.

Yassin, H. M., and Amel Benhassine. 1986. *Sounds of Sudan*, Vol. 3: *Mohamed Gubara.* London: Record World Circuit, WCB 005. LP disk.

Yurchenco, Henrietta. 1983. *Ballads, Wedding Songs, and Piyyutim of the Sephardic Jews of Tetuan and Tangier, Morocco.* 1983. Folkways Records FE 4208. LP disk.

EAST AFRICA

Abana Ba Nasery. 1992. *Nursery Boys Go Ahead! The Guitar and Bottle Kids of Kenya.* Green Linnet GLCD 4002. Compact disk.

African Acoustic. 1988. Tivoli, N.Y.: Original Music OMA 110C. Audiocassette.

Boyd, Alan. 1985. *Music of the Waswahili of Lamu, Kenya.* Folkways Records, FE 4093–4095. 3 LP disks.

Burundi Drums: Batimbo—Musiques et Chants. 1992. Auvidis, Playa Sound PS 65089. Audiocassette.

Graebner, Werner. 1989. *Nyota: Black Star and Lucky Star Musical Clubs.* Globestyle CDORBD 044. Compact disk.

———. 1990. *Zein Musical Party: Mtindo Was Mombasa/The Style of Mombasa.* Globestyle CDORBD 066. Compact disk.

Kenya: Musiques du Nyanza. 1993. Paris: OCORA C 560022/23. 2 compact discs.

Mandelson, Ben, and Werner Graebner. 1990. *Mombasa Wedding Special—Maulidi and Musical Party.* Global Style CDORBD 058. Compact disk.

The Nairobi Sound. 1982. Brooklyn, N.Y.: Original Music OMA 101C. Audiocassette.

Nzomo, David. 1976. *Gospel Songs from Kenya: Kikamha Hymns.* Folkways FR 8911. LP disk.

Roberts, John Storm. 1988? *The Kampala Sound: 1960s Ugandan Dance Music.* Tivoli, N.Y.: OMA 109C. Audiocassette.

Songs the Swahili Sing—Classics from the Kenya Coast. 1980. Brooklyn, N.Y.: Original Music OMA 103C. Audiocassette.

Ssalongo, Christopher Kizza, and Peter Cooke, art. and ed. 1988. *The Budongo of Uganda.* Edinburgh: K and C Productions KAC 100 1. Audiocassette.

The Tanzania Sound. 1980s. Tivoli, N.Y.: Original Music OMA 106C. Audiocassette.

Tanzania Yetu. 1985. Terra 101. London: Triple Earth Records. LP disk.

CENTRAL AFRICA

Arom, Simha. 1965. *Ba-Benzélé.* UNESCO Collection. Bärenreiter Musicaphon BM 30 L 2303. LP disk.

———. 1980. *Anthologie de la musique des Pygmées Aka.* Paris: OCORA 558.526.27.28. 3 LP disks and notes.

———. 1992. *République Centrafricaine: Banda Polyphony.* UNESCO/Auvidis D 8043. Compact disk.

Arom, Simha, and G. Dournon-Taurelle. 1971. *Musiques Banda: République Centrafricaine.* Disques RA 558.526–528. LP disk.

Bourgine, Caroline. 1991. *Congo: Cérémonie du Bobé.* OCORA W 560010.

Dehoux, Vincent. 1992. *Centrafiique: Musique Gbáyá—Chants à penser* Paris: OCORA C 580008.

Fernandez, James W. 1973. *Music from an Equatorial Microcosm: Fang Bwiti Music from Gabon Republic, Africa, with Mbira Selections.* Folkways Records FE 4214. LP disk.

Gabon: Pygmées bibayak et chantres des bapounou et des fang. 1980. Paris: OCORA 4.504.515. Audiocassette.

Gansmans, Jos. 1981. *Zaïre: Musique des Salampasu.* Paris: OCORA 558.597. LP disk.

Jangoux, Jacques. 1973? *Music of Zaïre: Peoples of the Ngiri River.* Folkways Records FE 4241–4242. 2 LP disks.

Kisliuk, Michelle. 1992. *Mbuti Pygmies of the Ituri Rain Forest.* Recordings by Colin Turnbull and Frances S. Chapman. Smithsonian/Folkways CDSF 40401. Compact disk.

Papa Wemba: Le voyageur. 1992. Filament Music Publishers/WOMAD, Real World CD RW 20. Compact disk.

Roots of O.K. Jazz: Zaïre Classics 1955–56. 1993. Cramworld Crammed Discs Craw 7. Compact disk.

Sallée, Pierre. c. 1968. *Gabon: Musiques des Mitsogho et des Batéké.* Paris. OCORA 84. LP disk.

Zaïre: Musiques urbaines à Kinshasa. 1987. Paris: OCORA 559.007. LP disk.

Zaïre: La musique des Nande. 1991. Geneva: VDE-Ge Gallo CD-652. Compact disk.

SOUTHERN AFRICA

Barkaak, Odd Are, and Pearson Likukela. *Knomboka Music [Zambia].* Nayuma Museum. Audiocassette.

Chimurenga Songs: Music of the Revolutionary People's War in Zimbabwe. 1988. Harare, Zimbabwe: Gramma Records L4VZ5. Audiocassette.

Chiweshe, Stella. 1990. *Stella Chiweshe: Ambuya?* Newton, N.J.: Shanachie 65006. Compact disk.

D'Gary. *Malagasy Guitar Music from Madagascar.* 1992. Newton, N.J.: Shanachie 65009. Compact disk.

Dube, William (William Dube Jairos Jiri Sunrise Kwela Band). 1980. *Take Cover.* Bulawayo, Zimbabwe: Teal Record Company ZIM 32. LP disk.

Erlmann, Veit. 1986. *Zulu Songs of South Africa.* Lyrichord LLST 7401. LP disk.

———. 1988. *Mbube Roots: Zulu Choral Music from South Africa, 1930s–1960s.* Rounder CD5025. Compact disk.

Gesthuisen, Birger, and Henry Kaiser. 1992. *A World Out of Time: Henry Kaiser and David Lindley in Madagascar.* Shanachie 64041. Compact disk.

Hanna, Marilyn, ed. 1985. *Ephat Mujuru: Master of Mbira from Zimbabwe*. Lyrichord LLST 7398. LP disk.

Hallis, Ron, and Ophera Hallis. 1980. *Music from Mozambique*. Folkways Records FE 4310. LP disk.

Homeland 2: A Collection of Black South African Music. 1990. Rounder CD 5028. Compact disk.

Kachamba, Donald, Moya Aliya Malamusi, Gerhard Kubik, and Stuwadi Mpotalinga. *Malawi: Concert Kwela*. Chant du Monde CDM LDX 274972. Compact disk.

Kivnick, Helen, and Gary Gardner. 1987. *Let Their Voices Be Heard*. Rounder Records 5024. LP disk.

Kubik, Gerhard. 1981. *Mukanda na makisi— Circumcision School and Masks*. Berlin: Museum für Völkerkunde MC 11. LP disk and notes.

Kubik, Gerhard, and Moya Aliya Malamusi. 1989. *Opeka nyimbo: Musician-Composers from Southern Malaŵi*. Museum für Völkerkunde, Musikethnologische Abteilung. Museum Collection MC 15. 2 LP disks and notes.

Laade, Wolfgang. 1991. *Zimbabwe: The Ndebele People*. Westbury, N.Y: Koch International, Jecklin-Disco JD 654-2. LP disk.

Mapoma, Isaiah Mwesa. 1971. *Inyimbo: Songs of the Bemba People of Zambia*. Tucson, Ariz.: Ethnodisc ER 12103. LP disk.

Mazai Mbira Group. c. 1989. Harare, Zimbabwe: Gramma Records L4AML. Audiocassette.

Mujuru, Ephat. c. 1980. *Rhythms of Life*. Lyrichord LLCT 7407. Audiocassette.

Project Grassworks. 1990. *Sounds Sung by South African Children*. Athlone: Grassroots Education Trust. Audiocassette.

Randafison, Sylvestre, and Jean-Baptiste Rama-ronandrasana. 1989. *Madagascar: Le valiha*. Harmonia Mundi Playa Sound PS 65046. Compact disk.

Tchiumba, Lilly. 1975. *Angola: Songs of My People*. Monitor Records MFS 767.

Tracey, Hugh. 1956. *International Library of African Music*. Roodepoort, South Africa.

Tracey, Hugh, and John Storm Roberts. 1989a. *Siya Hamba!* Tivoli, N.Y.: Original Music OMCD 003. LP disk.

———. 1989b. *From the Copperbelt: Zambian Miners' Songs*. Tivoli, N.Y.: Original Music OMCD 004. Compact disk.

Wood, Bill. 1976. *Music of Lesotho*. Folkways Records FE 4224. LP disk.

Films and Videos of African Music

GENERAL

Katsumori, Ichikawa, prod. 1990. *JVC Video Anthology of World Music and Dance*. Tôkyô: JVC, Victor Company of Japan. Vols. 17, 18, and 19. Videocassettes.

WEST AFRICA

Chevallier, Laurent, and Nicole Jouve. 1991. *Djembefola*. New York: Interama. 16mm.

Cohen, Hervé. 1991. *Sikambano: The Sons of the Sacred Wood*. Paris: Films du Village. Videocassette.

Haas, Philip. c. 1990. *Seni's Children*. New York: Milestone Film and Video. Videocassette.

Hale, Thomas A. 1990. *Griottes of the Sahel: Female Keepers of the Songhay Oral Tradition in Niger*. University Park: Pennsylvania State University. Videocassette.

Holender, Jacques. 1991. *Juju Music!* New York: Rhapsody.

Knight, Roderic. 1992a. *Jali Nyama Suso: Kora Player of the Gambia*. Tivoli, N.Y.: Original Music. Videocassette.

———. 1992b. *Music of the Mande*. Tivoli, N.Y.: Original Music. Videocassette.

Locke, David. 1990. *A Performance of Kpegisu by the Wodome-Akatsi Kpegisu Habobo*. Tempe, Ariz.: White Cliffs Media. Videocassette.

Marre, Jeremy. 1983. *Konkombe: Nigerian Pop Music Scene*. Newton, N.J.: Shanachie Records. Videocassette.

Rossellini, Jim. 1983. *Dance of the Bella*. Venice, Calif: African Family Films. Videocassette.

NORTH AFRICA

Guindi, Fadwa El. 1990. *El Moulid-Egyptian Religious Festival*. Los Angeles: El Nil Research. Videocassette, 16mm.

Llewellyn-Davies, Melissa, and Elizabeth Fernea. 1978. *Saints and Spirits*. Chicago: Films Incorporated Video. Videocassette.

Marre, Jeremy. 1991 [1983]. *The Romany Trail: Part 1: Gypsy Music into Africa*. Newton, N.J.: Shanachie Records.

Mendizza, Michael, and Philip D. Schuyler. 1983. *The Master Musicians of Jabjouka*. New York: Alegrías.

Wickett, Elizabeth. 1990. *For Those Who Sail to Heaven*. New York: Icarus. Videocassette, 16mm.

EAST AFRICA

Hawkins, Richard, and Suzette Heald. 1988. *Imbalu: Ritual of Manhood of the Bagisu of Uganda*. London: Royal Anthropological Institute, University of Manchester, Media Support and Development Centre.

Woodhead, Leslie. 1991. *The Mursi: Nitha*. New York: Granada Television. Videocassette.

CENTRAL AFRICA

Villers, Violaine de. 1992. *Mizike Mama*. New York: Interama. 16mm.

SOUTHERN AFRICA

Gavshon, Harriet. 1992. *A Stranger in a Strange Land—Paul Simon in South Africa*. Johannesburg: Free Film-Makers. Videocassette.

Hallis, Ron, and Ophera Hallis. 1989. *Music of the Spirits*. El Cerrito, Calif.: Flower. Videocassette.

———. 1992. *Chopi Music of Mozambique and Banguza*. El Cerrito, Calif.: Flower. Videocassette, 16mm.

Marshall, John, Robert Gardner, and Lorna Marshall. 1989. *The Hunters*. Chicago: Films Incorporated Video. Videocassette.

Morell, Karen, and Steven Friedson. *Prophet Healers of Northern Malawi*. 1990. Seattle, Wash.: African Encounters PC-45. Videocassette.

May, Deborah. 1991. *We Jive Like This*. New York: Filmakers Library. Videocassette.

Poschl, Rupert, and Ulrike Poschl. 1990. *Vimbuza-Chilopa: A Spirit Possession Cult among the Tumbuka of Malawi*. University Park: Pennsylvania State University, Audio-Visual Services. Videocassette.

South America, Mexico, Central America, and the Caribbean

Publications on South American, Mexican, Central American, and Caribbean Music

REFERENCE WORKS

Beaudet, Jean-Michel. 1982. "Musiques d'Amérique tropicale: Discographie analytique et critique des Amérindiens des basses terres." *Journal de la Société des Américanistes* 68:149–203. Paris: Musée de l'Homme.

Béhague, Gérard. 1975. "Latin American Music: An Annotated Bibliography of Recent Publications." *Yearbook for Inter-American Musical Research* 11:190–218.

———. 1993. "Latin America." In *Ethnomusicology: Historical and Regional Studies*, ed. Helen Myers, 472–494. New York: Norton.

Black Music Research Journal. Chicago: Columbia College.

Chase, Gilbert. 1972 [1962]. *A Guide to the Music of Latin America*, 2nd ed. Washington, D.C.: Pan American Union.

Ethnomusicology (Journal of the Society for Ethnomusicology). "Americas": "Current Bibliography," "Discography," and "Filmography." (3 issues per year.)

Fairley, Jan. 1985. "Annotated Bibliography of Latin-American Popular Music with Particular Reference to Chile and to *Nueva Canción.*" In *Popular Music*, Vol. 5, *Continuity and Change*, 305–356. Cambridge: Cambridge University Press.

Figueroa, Rafael, comp. 1992. *Salsa and Related Genres: A Bibliographical Guide.* Westport, Conn.: Greenwood.

Lotis, Howard, comp. 1981. *Latin American Music Materials Available at the University of Pitts-burgh and at Carnegie Library of Pittsburgh.* Pittsburgh: Center for Latin American Studies.

Kuss, Malena. 1984. "Current State of Bibliographic Research in Latin American Music." *Fontes Artis Musicae* 31(4):206–228.

Latin American Music Review. Austin: University of Texas Press.

Myers, Helen. 1993. "The West Indies." In *Ethnomusicology: Historical and Regional Studies*, ed. Helen Myers, 461–471. New York: Norton.

Nava, Teresa. 1994. "Dance Research in Mexico." *Dance Research Journal* 26(2):73–78.

The New Grove Dictionary of Music and Musicians, ed. Stanley Sadie. 20 vols. London: Macmillan.

Rodríguez, David J., et al. 1993. *Puerto Rico: Recordings in the Archive of Folk Culture.* Washington, D.C.: Archive of Folk Culture, American Folklife Center.

Schaeffer, Nancy. 1995. "Directory of Latin American Films and Videos: Music, Dance, Mask, and Ritual." *Latin American Music Review* 16(2):221–241.

Schechter, John M. 1987a. "A Selected Bibliography on Latin American Urban Popular Music." In *Latin American Masses and Minorities: Their Images and Realities*, Vol. 2, ed. Dan C. Hazen, 679–682. Madison: Seminar on the Acquisition of Latin American Library Materials (SALALM), Memorial Library, University of Wisconsin.

———. 1987b. "Doctoral Dissertations in Latin American Ethnomusicology: 1965–1984." In *Latin American Masses and Minorities: Their Images and Realities*, Vol. 2, ed. Dan C. Hazen, 673–678. Madison: Seminar on the Acquisition of Latin American Library Materials (SALALM), Memorial Library, University of Wisconsin.

———. 1987c. "Selected Bibliographic Sources in Latin American Ethnomusicology." In *Latin American Masses and Minorities: Their Images and Realities*, Vol. 2, ed. Dan C. Hazen, 664–672. Madison: Seminar on the Acquisition of Latin American Library Materials (SALALM), Memorial Library, University of Wisconsin.

Smith, Ronald R. 1972. "Latin American Ethnomusicology: A Discussion of Central America and Northern South America." *Latin American Music Review* 3(1):8–14.

Stevenson, Robert. 1975. *A Guide to Caribbean Music History.* Lima: Ediciones Cultura.

Steward, Julian H., ed. 1949. *Handbook of South American Indians.* 5 vols. New York: Cooper Square.

Thomas, Jeffrey Ross. 1992. *Forty Years of Steel: An Annotated Discography of Steel Band and Pan Recordings, 1951–1991.* Westport, Conn.: Greenwood.

Thompson, Donald. 1982. *Music Research in Puerto Rico.* San Juan: Office of the Governor of Puerto Rico, La Fortaleza, Office of Cultural Affairs.

Thompson, Donald, and Annie F. Thompson. 1991. *Music and Dance in Puerto Rico from the Age of Columbus to Modern Times: An Annotated Bibliography.* Metuchen, N.J.: Scarecrow.

GENERAL

Aretz, Isabel. 1977. *América latina en su música.* México, D.F.: Siglo XXI.

———. 1991. *Historia de la etnomusicología en América latina: Desde la época precolombina hasta nuestros días.* Caracas: Ediciones Fundef-Conac-Oea.

Aretz, Isabel, Gérard Béhague, and Robert Stevenson. 1980. "Latin America." In *The New Grove Dictionary of Music and Musicians*, ed. Stanley Sadie. London: Macmillan.

Béhague, Gérard. 1973. "Latin American Folk Music." In *Folk and Traditional Music of the Western Continents*, ed. Bruno Nettl, 2nd ed., 179–206. Englewood Cliffs, N.J.: Prentice Hall.

———. 1979. *Music in Latin America: An Introduction.* Englewood Cliffs, N.J.: Prentice Hall.

———, ed. 1994. *Music and Black Ethnicity: The Caribbean and South America.* Miami: University of Miami North-South Center.

Béhague, Gérard, and Bruno Nettl. "Afro-American Folk Music in North and Latin America." In *Folk and Traditional Music of the Western Continents*, ed. Bruno Nettl, 2nd ed., 207–234. Englewood Cliffs, N.J.: Prentice Hall.

Bergman, Billy. 1985. *Hot Sauces: Latin and Caribbean Pop.* New York: Quarto.

Bevilacqua, Norberto A. 1996. *El tango afrocubano, el tango andaluz, el tango criollo.* Buenos Aires: Lilah Ediciones.

Boiles, Charles Lafayette. 1978. *Man, Magic, and Musical Occasions.* Columbus: Collegiate.

Card, Caroline, et al. 1978. *Discourse in Ethnomusicology: Essays in Honor of George List.* Bloomington: Indiana University Archives of Traditional Music (Ethnomusicology Publications Group).

Courlander, Harold. 1976. *A Treasury of Afro-American Folklore.* New York: Crown.

Díaz Roig, Mercedes. 1990. *Romancero tradicional de América.* Serie Estudios de lingüística y literatura, 19. México, D.F.: Colegio de México.

Escobar, Luís Antonio. 1985. *La música precolombina.* Bogotá: Universidad Central.

Figueroa, Frank M. 1994. *Encyclopedia of Latin American Music in New York.* St. Petersburg, Fla.: Pillar.

Garofalo, Reebee. 1992. *Rockin' the Boat: Mass Music and Mass Movements.* Boston: South End.

Greenberg, Joseph. 1987. *Language in the Americas.* Stanford, Calif.: Stanford University Press.

Hernández, Clara, ed. 1982. *Ensayos de música latinoamericana.* Havana: Casa de las Americas.

Heth, Charlotte, ed. 1992. *Native American Dance: Ceremonies and Social Traditions.* Washington, D.C.: National Museum of the American Indian.

Jackson, Irene V., ed. 1985. *More Than Drumming: Essays on African and Afro-Latin Music and Musicians.* Contributions in Afro-American and African Studies, 80. Westport, Conn.: Greenwood. (Prepared under the auspices of the Center for Ethnic Music, Howard University.)

List, George, and Juan Orrego-Salas, eds. 1967. *Music in the Americas.* Inter-American Music Monograph Series, Vol. 1. Bloomington: Indiana University Research Center in Anthropology, Folklore, and Linguistics.

Loukotka, Cestmír. 1968. *Classification of South American Indian Languages.* Reference Series, Vol. 7. Los Angeles: Latin American Center, University of California, Los Angeles.

Manuel, Peter. 1988. *Popular Musics of the Non-Western World: An Introductory Survey.* New York: Oxford University Press.

Marre, Jeremy, and Hannah Charlton. 1985. *Beats of the Heart: Popular Music of the World.* New York: Pantheon.

Moreno Fraginals, Manuel, ed. 1984 [1977]. *Africa in Latin America: Essays on History, Culture, and Socialization,* trans. Leonor Blum. New York: Holms and Meier.

Mukuna, Kazadi wa. 1990–1991. "The Study of African Musical Contributions to Latin America and the Caribbean: A Methodological Guideline." *Bulletin of the International Committee on Urgent Anthropological Research* 32–33:47–49.

Murphy, Joseph M. 1994. *Working the Spirit: Ceremonies of the African Diaspora.* Boston: Beacon.

Olsen, Dale A., Daniel E. Sheehy, and Charles A. Perrone, eds. 1987. "Music of Latin America: Mexico, Ecuador, Brazil." In *Sounds of the World.* Washington, D.C.: Music Educators National Conference. (3 audiocassettes and study guide.)

Olsen, Dale A., and Selwyn Ahyoung. 1995 [1989]. "Latin America and the Caribbean." In *Multicultural Perspectives in Music Education,* ed. William M. Anderson and Patricia Shehan Campbell, 2nd ed., 124–177. Reston, Va.: Music Educators National Conference.

den Otter, Elisabeth. 1994. *Pre-Colombian Musical Instruments: Silenced Sounds in the Tropenmuseum Collection.* Amsterdam: KIT/Tropenmuseum.

Pineda de Valle, César, comp. 1994. *Antologia de la marimba en América.* Guatemala: Librería Artemis-Edinter.

Primera Conferencia Interamericana de Etnomusicología. Unión Panamericana, Washington, D.C., February 1963.

Roberts, John Storm. 1979. *The Latin Tinge: The Impact of Latin American Music on the United States.* New York and Oxford: Oxford University Press.

———. 1998. *Black Music of Two Worlds,* 2nd ed. New York: Schirmer.

Robertson, Carol E., ed. 1992. *Musical Repercussions of 1492: Encounters in Text and Performance.* Washington, D.C., and London: Smithsonian Institution Press.

Schechter, John M. 1996. "Latin America/Ecuador." In *Worlds of Music: An Introduction to the Music of the World's Peoples,* ed. Jeff Todd Titon, 3rd ed., 428–494. New York: Schirmer.

———. 1999. *Music in Latin American Culture: Regional Traditions.* New York: Schirmer.

Slonimsky, Nicholas. 1945. *Music of Latin America.* New York: Crowell.

Stevenson, Robert. 1968a. *Music in Aztec and Inca Territory.* Berkeley: University of California Press.

———. 1968b. "The African Legacy to 1800." *Musical Quarterly* 54(4):475–502.

———. 1991. "Latin American Music Bibliography." In *Libraries, History, Diplomacy, and the Performing Arts: Essays in Honor of Carleton Sprague Smith,* ed. I. J. Katz, 85–99. Stuyvesant, N.Y.: Pendragon.

Turino, Thomas. 1992. "Music in Latin America." In *Excursions in World Music,* ed. Bruno Nettl, 232–259. Englewood Cliffs, N.J.: Prentice Hall.

Whitten, Norman E., Jr., and John F. Szwed, eds. 1970. *Afro-American Anthropology: Contemporary Perspectives.* New York: Free Press.

SOUTH AMERICA

Abadía Morales, Guillermo. 1973. *La música folklórica colombiana.* Bogotá: Universidad Nacional de Colombia.

———. 1991. *Instrumentos musicales: Folklore colombiano.* Bogotá: Banco Popular.

Alencar, Edigar de. 1965. *O carnaval carioca através da música.* 2 vols. Rio de Janeiro: Livraria Freitas Bastos.

———. 1968. *Nosso Sinhô do samba.* Rio de Janeiro: Civilização Brasileira Editora.

Almeida, Bira (Mestre Acordeon). 1986. *Capoeira—A Brazilian Art Form: History, Philosophy, and Practice.* Berkeley, Calif.: North Atlantic.

Almeida, Raimundo Cesar Alves de. 1993. *Bibliografia crítica da capoeira.* Brasília: Defer/GDF, Centro de Documentação e Informação Sobre a Capoeira.

Almeida, Renato. 1942. *História da música brasileira,* 2nd ed. Rio de Janeiro: F. Briguiet.

Alvarenga, Oneyda. 1982. *Música popular brasileira,* 2nd ed. São Paulo: Duas Cidades.

Alves, Henrique L. 1968. *Sua excelência o samba.* Palermo, Brazil: A. Palma.

Anaya Arze, Franklin. 1994. *La música en Latinoamérica y en Bolivia.* Cochabamba: Editorial Serrano.

Andrade, Mário de. 1928. *Ensaio sobre a música brasileira.* São Paulo: Martins.

———. 1933. *Compêndio de história da música,* 2nd ed. São Paulo: Miranda.

———. 1963. *Música, doce música,* 2nd ed. São Paulo: Martins.

———. 1975. *Aspectos da música brasileira,* 2nd ed. São Paulo: Martins.

———. 1982. *Danças dramaticas do Brasil,* 2nd ed. 3 vols. Belo Horizonte: Ed. Itatiaia.

———. 1989. *Dicionário musical brasileiro.* São Paulo: Editora da Universidade de São Paulo.

Añez, Jorge. 1968. *Canciones y recuerdos,* rev. ed. Bogotá: Ediciones Mundial.

Appleby, David P. 1983. *The Music of Brazil.* Austin: University of Texas Press.

Araújo, Alceu Maynard. 1964. *Folclore nacional.* 3 vols. São Paulo: Melhoramentos.

Araújo, Mozart de. 1963. *A modinha e o lundu no século XVIII.* São Paulo: Ricordi Brasileira.

Archivo de Música Tradicional Andina. 1995. *Católogo del Archivo de Música Tradicional Andina.* Lima: Pontificia Universidad Católica del Peru, Institute, Riva Agüero.

Aretz, Isabel. 1954. *Costumbres tradicionales argentinas.* Buenos Aires: Huemul.

———. 1967. *Instrumentos musicales de Venezuela.* Cumaná: Editorial Universitaria de Oriente.

———. 1970. *El Tamunangue.* Barquisimeto: Universidad Centro Occidental.

———. 1991. *Música de los Aborígenes de Venezuela.* Caracas: Fundación de Etnomusicología y Folklore.

Aretz-Thiele, Isabel. 1946. *Música tradicional argentina: Tucumán historia y folklore.* Buenos Aires: Universidad Nacional de Tucumán.

Arguedas, José Maria. 1957. *Singing Mountaineers: Songs and Tales of the Quechua People.* Austin: University of Texas Press.

———. 1975. *Formación de una cultura nacional indoamericana.* México: Siglo XXI.

———. 1977. *Nuestra música popular y sus intérpretes*. Lima: Mosca Azul y Horizonte.

———. 1989. *Canto Kechua*, rev. ed. Lima: Horizonte.

Arvelo Ramos, Alberto. 1992. *El cuatro*. Caracas: J. J. Castro Fotografía Infrarroja.

Ayala, María Ignez Novais. 1988. *No arranco do grito: Aspectos da cantoria nordestina*. São Paulo: Atica.

Ayestarán, Lauro. 1953. *La música en el Uruguay*, Vol. 1. Montevideo: Servicio Oficial de Difusión Radioeléctrica.

———. 1967. *El folklore musical uruguayo*. Montevideo: Arca.

———. 1968. *Teoría y práctica del folklore*. Montevideo: Arca.

———. 1994. *Las músicas primitivas en el Uruguay*. Montevideo: Arca.

Aytai, Desiderio. 1985. *O mundo sonoro, Xavante*. Coleção Museu Paulista, Ethnologia, Vol. 5. São Paulo: Universidade de São Paulo.

Bahiana, Ana Maria. 1980. *Nada será como antes: A MPB dos años 70*. São Paulo: Perspectiva.

Barral, P. Basilio María de. 1964. *Los Indios guaraunos y su concionero*. Madrid: Consejo Superior de Investigaciones Científicas, Departamento de Misionología Española.

Basso, Ellen B. 1985. *A Musical View of the Universe*. Philadelphia: University of Pennsylvania Press.

Bastien, Joseph W. 1978. *Mountain of the Condor: Metaphor and Ritual in an Andean Ayllu*. St. Paul: West.

Bastos, Rafael Jose de Menezes. 1978. *A musicológica kamayurá*. Brasília: Fundação Nacional do Indio.

Baumann, Max Peter, ed. 1992. *Cosmología y música en los Andes*. Berlin: IITM.

Bayardo, Nelson. 1996. *Informe sobre el tango*. Montevideo: Ediciones de la Plaza.

Beaudet, Jean-Michel. 1983. "Les orchestres de clarinettes *tule* des Wayãpi du haut Oyapock (Guyane Française)." Ph.D. dissertation, Université de Paris X-Nanterre.

Becerra Casanovas, Rogers. 1990. *Reliquias de Moxos*. La Paz: Proinsa.

Béhague, Gerard. 1971. *The Beginnings of Musical Nationalism in Brazil*. Detroit Monographs in Musicology, 1. Detroit: Information Coordinators, Inc.

———. 1979. *Music in Latin America: An Introduction*. Englewood Cliffs, N.J.: Prentice Hall, Inc.

Bermúdez, Egberto. 1985. *Los instrumentos musicales en Colombia*. Bogotá: Universidad Nacional de Colombia.

Biocca, Ettore. 1966. *Viaggi tra gli indi: Alto Rio Negro–Alto Orinoco. Appunti di un biologo*. 4 vols. Rome: Consiglio Nazionale delle Ricerche.

Blérald-Ndagamo, Monique. 1996. *Musiques et danses créoles au tambour de la Guyane française*. Cayenne: Ibis Roque Editions.

Boettner, Juan Max. n.d. (c. 1956). *Música y músicos del Paraguay*. Asunción: Autores Paraguayos Asociados.

Bolaños, César. 1981. *Música y danza en el antiguo Perú*. Lima: Museo Nacional de Antropología y Arqueología, Instituto Nacional de Cultura.

———. 1988. *Las Antaras Aasca*. Lima: Instituto Andino de Estudios Arqueológicos.

———. 1995. *La música nacional en los medios de comunicación electrónicos de Lima metropolitana*. Lima: Universidad de Lima, Facultad de Ciencias de la Comunicación (Cuadernos Cicosul).

Borges, Bia. 1990. *Música popular do Brasil/Brazilian Popular Music*. São Paulo: B. Borges.

Brandão, Carlos Rodrigues. 1981. *Sacerdotes da viola*. Petrópolis, Brazil: Vozes.

Browning, Barbara. 1995. *Samba: Resistance in Motion*. Bloomington: Indiana University Press.

Bureau du Patrimoine Ethnologique, ed. 1989. *Musiques en Guyane*. Cayenne: Conseil Régional de la Guyane.

Bustillos Vallejo, Freddy. 1982. *Bibliografía boliviana de etnomusicología*. La Paz: Instituto Nacional de Antropologia.

———. 1989. *Instrumentos musicales de Tiwanaku*. La Paz: Museo Nacional de Etnografía y Folklore.

Cabral, Sérgio. 1996. *As escolas de samba do Rio de Janeiro*. Rio de Janeiro: Lumiar Editoria.

Caldas, Waldenyr. 1979. *Acorde na aurora: Música sertaneja e indústria cultural*, 2nd ed. São Paulo: Nacional.

———. 1985. *Introdução à música popular brasileira*. São Paulo: Atica.

Cameu, Helza. 1977. *Introdução ao estudo da música indígena brasileira*. Rio de Janeiro: Conselho Federal de Cultura.

Campos, Augusto de. 1974. *Balanço da bossa e outras bossas*. São Paulo: Perspectiva.

Cardozo Ocampo, Mauricio. *Mundo folklorico paraguayo*. 3 vols. Asunción: Editorial Cuadernos Republicanos.

Carpio Muñoz, Juan. 1976. *El Yaraví arequipeño*. Arequipa: La Colmena.

Carvalho, José Jorge de. 1994. *The Multiplicity of Black Identities in Brazilian Popular Music*. Brasilia: Universidade de Brasilia.

Carvallo-Neto, Pablo de. 1964. *Diccionario del folklore ecuatoriano*. Quito: Editorial Casa de la Cultura Ecuatoriana.

———. 1971. *Estudios afros: Brasil, Paraguay, Uruguay, Ecuador*. Serie de Folklore-Instituto de Antropología e Historia, Universidad Central de Venezuela. Caracas: Instituto de Antropología e Historia, Facultad de Humanidades y Educación, Universidad Central de Venezuela.

Cascudo, Luís da Câmara. 1979. *Dicionário do folclore brasileiro*, 5th ed. São Paulo: Melhoramentos.

Castro, Donald S. 1991. *The Argentine Tango as Social History, 1880–1955: The Soul of the People*. Lewiston: E. Mellen.

Castro, Ruy. 1990. *Chega de saudade: A história e as histórias da bossa nova*. São Paulo: Companhia das Letras.

Céspedes, Gilka Wara. 1993. "*Huayno, Saya, and Chuntunqui*: Bolivian Identity in the Music of 'Los Kjarkas.'" *Latin American Music Review* 14(l):52–101.

Clam, Samuel, et al. 1994. *Chilena o cueca tradicional: De acuerdo con las enseñazas de Fernando González Maraboli*. Santiago: Ediciones Universidad Católica de Chile.

Coba Andrade, Carlos Alberto. 1981. *Instrumentos musicales populares registrados en el Ecuador*. Cultura Popular, Vol. 1. Otavalo, Ecuador: Instituto Otavaleño de Antropología.

———. 1985. *Danzas y bailes en el Ecuador*. Quito: Ediciones Abya-yala.

———. 1992. *Instrumentos musicales populares registrados en el Ecuador*, Vol. 2. Quito: Ediciones del Banco Central del Ecuador, and Instituto Otavaleño de Antropología.

Collier, Simon. 1990. *The Life, Music, and Times of Carlos Gardel*. Pittsburgh: University of Pittsburgh Press.

Collier, Simon, Artemis Cooper, María Susana Azzi, and Richard Martin. 1995. *¡Tango! The Dance, the Song, the Story*. London: Thames and Hudson.

Corrêa, Roberto Nunes. 1989. *Viola caipira*. Brasília: Viola Corrêa.

Costal, Reginaldo de Silveira. 1993. *O caminho do berimbau: Arte, filosofia, e crescimento na capoeira*. Brasília: Thesaurus Editora.

Crook, Larry Norman. 1991. "*Zabumba* Music from Caruaru, Pernambuco: Musical Style, Gender, and the Interpenetration of Rural and Urban Worlds." Ph.D. dissertation, University of Texas.

Dark, Philip. 1970. *Bush Negro Art*. London: Alec Tiranti.

Davidson, Harry C. 1970. *Diccionario folklórico de Colombia: Música, instrumentos, y danzas*. 3 vols. Bogotá: Banco de la República.

Delfino, Jean Paul. 1988. *Brasil bossa nova*. Aix-en-Provence: Édisud.

Díaz Gainza, José. 1962. *Historia musical de Bolivia*. Potosí: Universidad Tomás Frias.

Dicks, Ted, ed. 1976. *Victor Jara: His Life and Songs*. London: Elm Tree.

Dolabela, Marcelo. 1987. *ABZ do rock brasileiro*. São Paulo: Estrela do Sul.

Dolphin, Lynette, comp. 1991. *National Songs of Guyana*. Georgetown, Guyana: Department of Culture.

Domínguez, Luis Arturo. 1992. *Fiestas y danzas folklóricas en Venezuela*, 2nd ed. Caracas: Monte Avila Editores.

Efegê, Jota. 1978/79. *Figuras e coisas da música popular brasileira*. 2 vols. Rio de Janeiro: Funarte.

Fernaud, Alvaro. 1984. *El Golpe larense*. Caracas: Fundación de Etnomusicología y Folklore.

Ferrer, Horacio. 1977. *El libro del tango*. 2 vols. Buenos Aires: Galerna.

Flores, Hilda Agnes Hübner. 1983. *Canção dos imigrantes*. Porto Alegrel: Escola Superior de Teologia São Lourenço de Brindes, Universidade de Caxias do Sul.

Fules, Victor. 1989. "Demonstration of Multiple Relationships between Music and Culture of the Waiãpi Indians of Brazil." Ph.D. dissertation, Indiana University.

Gallardo, Jorge Emilio. 1986. *Presencia africana en la cultura de América latina: Vigencia de los cultos afroamericanos*. Buenos Aires: Fernando García Cambeiro.

Garcilaso de la Vega, El Inca. 1961. *The Royal Commentaries of the Inca*, ed. Alain Gheerbrant. New York: Orion/Avon.

Garrido, Pablo. 1943. *Biografía de la Cueca*. Santiago: Ediciones Ercilla.

Góes, Fred de. 1982. *O país do carnaval elétrico*. São Paulo: Editora Corrupio Comércio.

Goldfeder, Miriam. 1981. *Por trás das ondas da rádio nacional*. São Paulo: Paz e Terra.

González, Juan-Pablo. 1991. "Hegemony and Counter-Hegemony of Music in Latin America: The Chilean Pop." *Popular Music and Society* 15(2):63–78.

González Torres, Dionisio M. 1991. *Folklore del Paraguay*. Asunción: Editora Litocolor.

Gradante, William J. 1991. "'¡Viva el San Pedro en La Plata!': Tradition, Creativity, and Folk Musical Performance in a Southern Colombian Festival." Ph.D. dissertation, University of Texas.

Gruszcynska-Zilókowska, Anna. 1995. *El poder del sonido: El papel de las crónicas españolas en la etnomusicología andina*. Cayambe, Ecuador: Ediciones Abya-Yala.

Grebe, María Ester. 1980. "Generative Models, Symbolic Structures, and Acculturation in the Panpipe Music of the Aimara of Tarapaca, Chile." Ph.D. dissertation, Queen's University of Belfast.

Guardia Crespo, Marcelo. 1994. *Música popular y comunicación en Bolivia: Las interpretaciones y conflictos*. Cochabamba: U.C.B.

Guillermoprieto, Alma. 1990. *Samba*. New York: Knopf.

Guss, David M. 1989. *To Weave and Sing: Art, Symbol, and Narrative in the South American Rain Forest*. Berkeley: University of California Press.

d'Harcourt, Raoul, and M. d'Harcourt. 1925. *La musique des Incas et ses survivances*. Paris: Librairie Orientaliste Paul Geuthner.

d'Harcourt, Raoul, and M. d'Harcourt. 1959. *La musique des Aymaras sur les hauts plateaux boliviens d'après enregistremems sonores de Louis Girault*. Paris: Societé des Americanistes, Musée de l'Homme.

d'Harcourt, Raoul, and Marguerite d'Harcourt. 1990. *La música de los Incas y sus supervivencias*. Lima: Occidental Petroleum Corporation of Peru. (General translation from the French by Roberto Miro Quesada.)

Harrison, Regina. 1989. *Signs, Songs, and Memory in the Andes: Translating Quichua Language and Culture*. Austin: University of Texas Press.

Herskovits, Melville J., and Frances S. Herskovits. 1969 [1936]. *Suriname Folk-Lore*. Columbia Contributions to Anthropology, Vol. 27, Part 3. New York: AMS.

Hickmann, Ellen. 1990. *Musik aus dem Altertum der Neuen Welt: Archäologische Dokumente des Musizierens in präkolumbischen Kulturen Perus, Ekuadors, und Kolumbiens*. Frankfurt am Main: Peter Lang.

Hill, Jonathan D. 1993. *Keepers of the Sacred Chants: The Poetics of Ritual Power in an Amazonian Society*. Tucson: University of Arizona Press.

Holzmann, Rodolfo, and José María Arguedas. 1966. *Panorama de la música tradicional del Perú*. Lima: Ministerio de Educación Pública, Escuela National de Música y Danzas Folklóricas (Servicio Musicológico), y la Casa Mozart.

Holzmann, Rodolfo. 1986. *Q'ero pueblo y música*. Lima: Patronata Popular y Porvenir, Pro Música Clásica.

Hurtado Suárez, Wilfredo. 1995. *Chicha peruana: Música de las nuevos migrantes*. Lima: Eco-Grupo de Investigaciones Económicas.

Godoy Aguirre, Mario. n.d. *Florilegio de la música ecuatoriana: La música popular en el Ecuador*, Vol. 1. Editorial del Pacifico.

Instituto Nacional de Musicología "Carlos Vega." 1988. *Instrumentos musicales etnográficos y folklóricos de la Argentina: Síntesis de los datos obtenidos en investigación de campo (1931–1988)*. Buenos Aires: Instituto Nacional de Musicología "Carlos Vega."

Izikowitz, Karl Gustav. 1970. *Musical and Other Sound Instruments of the South American Indians: A Comparative Ethnographical Study*, rev. ed. East Ardsley, Wakefield, Yorks.: S.R.

Jara, Joan. 1984. *An Unfinished Song: The Life of Victor Jara*. New York: Ticknor and Fields.

Jijón, Inés. 1971. *Museo de Instrumentos Musicales Pedro Pablo Traversari*. Quito: Casa de la Cultura Ecuatoriana.

Jiménez Borja, Arturo. 1951. *Instrumentos musicales del Perú*. Lima: Museo de la Cultura.

Koorn, Dirk. 1977. "Folk Music of the Colombian Andes." Ph.D. dissertation, University of Washington.

Labraña, Luis, and Ana Sebastián. 1992. *Tango: Una historia*. Buenos Aires: Ediciones Corregidor.

Lange, Francisco Curt. 1966. *A organização musical durante o período colonial*. Actas do V Coloquio Internacional de Estudos Luso-Brasileiros, Separata do Vol. 4.

Lewis, J. Lowell. 1992. *Ring of Liberation: Deceptive Discourse in Brazilian Capoeira*. Chicago: University of Chicago Press.

Lisboa, Luiz Américo. Jr. 1990. *A presença da Bahia na música popular brasileira*. Brasília: MusiMed.

Liscano, Juan. 1973. *La fiesta de San Juan El Bautista*. Caracas: Monte Avila Editores.

List, George. 1983. *Music and Poetry in a Colombian Village*. Bloomington: Indiana University Press.

Lopes, Nei. 1992. *O negro no Rio de Janeiro e sua tradição musical: Partido-alto, calango, chula, e outras cantorias*. Rio de Janeiro: Pallas.

Lloréns, José Antonio. 1983. *Música popular en Lima: Criollos y andinos*. Lima: Instituto de Estudios Peruanos.

Mamani P., Mauricio. 1987. *Los instrumentos musicales en los Andes bolivianos*. La Paz: Museo Nacional de Etnografía y Folklore.

Marcondes, Marcos Antonio, ed. 1977. *Enciclopédia da música brasileira: Erudita, folclórica, popular*. São Paulo: Editora Arte.

Margullo Osvaldo-Muñz, Pancho. 1986. *El rock en la Argentina*. Buenos Aires: Galerna.

Mariz, Vasco. 1983. *História da música no Brasil*, 2nd ed. Rio de Janeiro: Civilização Brasileira.

Martín, Miguel Angel. 1991. *Del folclor llanero*, 2nd ed. Sante Fé de Bogotá: Ecoe Ediciones.

Martins, Carlos A. 1986. *Música popular uruguaya 1973–1982: Un fenómeno de comunicación alternativa*. Montevideo: Ediciones de la Banda Oriental.

Máximo, Joao, and Carlos Didier. 1990. *Noel Rosa: Una biografia*. Brasília: Editora Universidade de Brasília.

McGowan, Chris, and Ricardo Pessanha. 1991. *The Brazilian Sound: Samba, Bossa Nova, and the Popular Music of Brazil*. New York: Billboard.

Mendonça, Belkiss S. Carneiro, de. 1981. *A música em Goiás*, 2nd ed. Goiânia: Editora da Universidade Federal de Goiás.

Menezes Bastos, R. J. de. 1978. *A musicológica kamayura: Para uma antropologia da comunicação no alto Xingu*. Brasília: Funai.

Meyer, Augusto. 1958. *Cancioneiro gaúcho*. Porto Alegre: Globo.

Montoya, Rodrigo, Edwin Montoya, and Luís Montoya. 1987. *La sangre de los cerros: Antologia de la poesía quechua que se canta en el Perú*. Lima: Cepes, Mosca Azul Editores y UNMSM.

Moreno Andrade, Segundo Luis. 1923. *La música en la provincia de Imbabura*. Quito: Tipografía y Encuadernación Salesianas.

———. 1949. *Música y danzas autóctonas del Ecuador* (Indigenous Music and Dance of Ecuador). Quito: Editorial Fray Jacobo Ricke.

———. 1972. *Historia de la música en el Ecuador*. Vol. 1: *Prehistoria*. Quito: Editorial Casa de la Cultura Ecuatoriana.

Moura, Roberto M. 1986. *Carnaval: Da redentora a praça do apocalipse*. Rio de Janeiro: Jorge Zahar.

Mukuna, Kazadi wa. 1979. *Contribuição bantu na música popular brasileira*. São Paulo: Global Editora.

Núñez Rebaza, Lucy. 1990. *Los dansaq*. Lima: Instituto Nacional de Cultura, Museo Nacional de la Cultura Peruana.

Nyberg, John L. 1974. "An Examination of Vessel Flutes from Pre-Hispanic Cultures of

Ecuador." Ph.D. dissertation, University of Minnesota.

Oliveira, Valdemar de. 1971. *Frevo, capoeira, e "passo."* Recife: Companhia Editora de Pernambuco.

Oliveira Pinto, Tiago de. 1991. *Capoeira, samba, candomblé: Afro-brasilianische Musik im Recôncavo, Bahio.* Berlin: Museum für Völkerkunde Berlin.

Olsen, Dale A. 1980a. "Folk Music of South Amcrica—A Musical Mosaic." In *Musics of Many Cultures: An Introduction,* ed. Elizabeth May, 386–425. Berkeley: University of California Press.

———. 1980b. "Symbol and Function in South American Indian Music." In *Musics of Many Cultures: An Introduction,* ed. Elizabeth May, 363–385. Berkeley: University of California Press.

———. 1989. "The Magic Flutes of El Dorado: A Model for Research in Archaeomusicology as Applied to the Sinú of Ancient Colombia." In *Early Music Cultures, Selected Papers from the Third International Meeting of the ICTM Study Group on Music Archaeology,* ed. Ellen Hickman and David Hughes, 305–328. Bonn: N.p.

———. 1996. *Music of the Warao of Venezuela: Song People of the Rain Forest.* Gainesville: University Press of Florida. (Book and compact disk.)

———. 2002. *Music of El Dorado: The Ethnomusicology of Ancient South American Cultures.* Gainsville: University Press of Florida.

Ortiz, Alfredo Rolando. 1984 [1979]. *Latin American Harp Music and Techniques for Pedal and Non-Pedal Harpists,* 2nd ed. Corona, Calif: Alfredo Rolando Ortíz.

den Otter, Elisabeth. 1985. *Music and Dance of Indians and Mestizos in an Andean Valley of Peru.* Delft: Eburon.

Pallavicino, María L. 1987. *Umbanda: Religiosidad afro-brasileña en Montevideo.* Montevideo: Pettirossi Hnos.

Pardo Tovar, Andrés. 1966. *La cultura musical en Colombia.* Bogotá: Ediciones Lerner.

———. 1976. *El archivo musical de la catedral de Bogotá.* Bogotá: Publicaciones del Instituto Caro y Cuervo.

Paredes Candia, Antonio. 1980. *Folklore de Potosí.* La Paz: Ediciones Isla.

Parra, Violeta. 1970. *Décimas: Autobiografía en versos chilenos.* Santiago: Ediciones Nueva Universidad, Universidad Católica de Chile.

———. 1979. *Cantos folklóricos chilenos.* Santiago: Editorial Nascimento.

Perdomo Escobar, José Ignacio. 1963. *Historia de la música en Colombia,* 3rd ed. Bogotá: Editorial ABC.

Pereira-Salas, Eugenio. 1941. *Los orígenes del arte musical en Chile.* Santiago: Publicaciones de la Universidad de Chile.

Pérez Bugallo, Rubén. 1993. *Catálogo ilustrado de instrumentos musicales argentinos.* Biblioteca de cultura popular, 19. Buenos Aires: Ediciones de Sol.

Perrone, Charles A. 1989. *Masters of Contemporary Brazilian Song: MPB 1965–1985.* Austin: University of Texas Press.

Pinnell, Richard. 1993. *The Rioplatense Guitar: The Early Guitar and Its Content in Argentina and Uruguay.* Westport, Conn.: Bold Strummer.

Pinto, Tiago de Oliveira, ed. 1986. *Welt Musik: Brazilien.* Mainz: Schott.

———. 1991. *Capoeira, samba, candomblé: Afro-brasilianische Musik im Recôncavo, Bahia.* Berlin: Staatliche Museen Preussischer Kulturbesitz.

Pinto, Tiago de Oliveira, and Dudu Tucci. 1992. *Samba und Sambistas in Brasilien.* Wihelmshaven: F. Noetzel.

Plath, Oreste. 1979. *Folklore chileno.* Santiago: Editorial Nascimento.

Pollak-Eltz, Angelina. 1972. *Cultos afroamericanos.* Caracas: Universidad Católica "Andres Bello."

Pombo Hernández, Gerardo. 1995. *Kumbia, legado, cultura de los indígenas del Caribe colombiano.* Barranquilla: Editorial Antillas.

Portorrico, Emilio Pedro. 1997. *Diccionario biográfica de la música argentina de raíz folklórica.* Florida, Prov. de Buenos Aires: E.P. Portorrico.

Preiss, Jorge Hirt. 1988. *A música nas missões jesuíticas nos séculos XVII e XVIII.* Porto Alegre: Martins Livreiro Editor.

Price, Richard, and Sally Price. 1980. *Afro-American Arts of the Surinam Rain Forest.* Los Angeles: Museum of Cultural History and University of California Press.

———. 1991. *Two Evenings in Saramaka.* Chicago: University of Chicago Press.

Price, Sally. 1984. *Co-Wives and Calabashes.* Ann Arbor: University of Michigan Press.

Primera Conferencia Interamericana de Etnomusicología. 1963. Trabajos Presentados, 131–151. Washington, D.C.: Unión Panamericana, Secretaría General de la OEA.

Puerta Zuluaga, David. 1988. *Los caminos del Tiple.* Bogotá: Damel.

Ramón y Rivera, Luís Felipe. 1953. *El joropo, baile nacional de Venezuela.* Caracas: Ediciones del Ministerio de Educación.

———. 1967. *Música indígena, folklórica, y popular de Venezuela.* Buenos Aires: Ricordi Americana.

———. 1969. *La música folklórica de Venezuela.* Caracas: Monte Avila Editores.

———. 1971. *La música afrovenezolana.* Caracas: Universidad Central de Venezuela.

———. 1992. *La música de la Décima.* Caracas: Fundación de Etnomusicología y Folklore.

Ramón y Rivera, Luís Felipe, and Isabel Aretz. 1996. *La música típica del Táchira: El folklore tachirense.* Caracas: Biblioteca de Autores y Temas Tachirenses.

Real, Katarina. 1990. *O folclore no carnaval do Recife,* 2nd ed. Recife: Editora Massangana (Fundação Joaquim Nabuco).

Rephann, Richard. 1978. *A Catalogue of the Pedro Traversari Collection of Musical Instruments/*

Catálogo de la colección de instrumentos musicales Pedro Traversari. Organization of American States and Yale University Collection of Musical Instruments. Quito: Casa de la Cultura Ecuatoriana.

Rodríguez de Ayestarán, Flor de María. 1994. *La danza popular en el Uruguay: Desde sus orígenes a 1900.* Montevideo: Cal y Canto.

Roel Pineda, Josafáto. 1990. *El wayno del Cusco.* Qosqo, Peru: Municipalidad del Qosqo.

Roel Pineda, Josafáto, et al. 1978. *Mapa de los instrumentos musicales de uso popular en el Perú.* Lima: Instituto Nacional de Cultura, Oficina de Música y Danza.

Romero, Raúl R. 1985. "La música tradicional y popular." In *La música en el Perú,* 215–283. Lima: Patronato Popular y Porvenir Pro Música Clásica.

———. 1993. *Música, danzas, y máscaras en los Andes.* Lima: Pontífica Universidad Católica del Perú.

Roth, Walter E. 1924. "An Introductory Study of the Arts, Crafts, and Customs of the Guiana Indians." In *Thirty-Eighth Annual Report of the Bureau of American Ethnology to the Secretary of the Smithsonian Institution, 1916–1917.* Washington, D.C.: U.S. Government Printing Office.

Salazar, Briseida. 1990. *San Benito: Canta y baila con sus chimbangueleros.* Caracas: Fundación Bigott.

Sant'anna, Affonso Romano de. 1986. *Música popular e moderna poesia brasileira,* 3rd ed. Petrópolis: Vozes.

Santa Cruz, César. 1977. *El waltz y el vals criollo.* Lima: Instituto Nacional de Cultura.

Savigliano, Marta E. 1995. *Tango and the Political Economy of Passion.* Boulder, San Francisco, and Oxford: Westview.

Schechter, John M. 1992. *The Indispensable Harp: Historical Development, Modern Roles, Configurations, and Performance Practices in Ecuador and Latin America.* Kent, Ohio: Kent State University Press.

Schneider, Jens. 1993. "The Nolkin: A Chilean Sucked Trumpet." *Galpin Society Journal* 46:69–82.

Seeger, Anthony 1987. *Why Suyá Sing: A Musical Anthropology of an Amazonian People.* Cambridge: Cambridge University Press. (Book and audiocassette.)

Setti, Kilza. 1985. *Ubatuba nos cantos das praias: Estudo do caiçara paulista e de sua produçåo musical.* São Paulo: Atica.

Sherzer, Joel, and Greg Urban, eds. 1986. *Native South American Discourse.* Berlin: Mouton de Gruyter.

Shreiner, Claus. 1993. *Musica Brasileira: A History of Popular Music and the People of Brazil.* New York: M. Boyars.

Sigueira, Batista. 1979. *Modinhas do passado,* 2nd ed. Rio de Janeiro: Folha Carioca.

Silva Sifuentes, Jorge E. 1978. *Instrumentos musicales pre-colombinos.* Serie Investigaciones, 2. Lima: Universidad Nacional Mayor de San Marcos, Gabinete de Arqueología, Colegio Real.

Smith, Robert J. 1975. *The Art of the Festival*. Publications in Anthropology, 6. Lawrence: University of Kansas Press.

Sodré, Muniz. 1979. *Samba: O dono do corpo*. Rio de Janeiro: Codecri.

Souza, Tárik de, et al. 1988. *Brazil musical*. Rio de Janeiro: Art Bureau Representações e Edições de Arte.

Stevenson, Robert. 1960. *The Music of Peru: Aboriginal and Viceroyal Epochs*. Washington, D.C.: Organization of American States.

Stobart, Henry. 1987. *Primeros datos sobre la música campesina del norte de Potosí*. La Paz: Museo Nacional de Etnografía y Folklore.

———. 1994. "Flourishing Horns and Enchanted Tubers: Music and Potatoes in Highland Bolivia." *British Journal of Ethnomusicology* 3: 35–48.

Suzigan, Geraldo. 1990. *Bossa nova: Música, política, e educação no Brasil*. São Paulo: Clam-Zimbo.

Tayler, Donald. 1972. *The Music of Some Indian Tribes of Colombia*. London: British Institute of Recorded Sound. (Book and 3 LP disks.)

Taylor, Julie. 1998. *Paper Tangos*. Durham, N.C.: Duke University Press.

Tinhorão, José Ramos. 1974. *Pequena história da música popular: Da modinha a cançāo de protesto*. Petrópolis: Vozes.

———. 1981. *Música popular—Do gramofone ao rádio e TV*. São Paulo: Atica.

———. 1986. *Pequena história da música popular: Da modinha ao tropicalismo*, 5th ed. São Paulo: Arte Editora.

———. 1988. *Os sons dos negros no Brasil*. São Paulo: Arte Editora.

———. 1990. *História social do música popular Brasileira*. Lison: Caminho da Música.

———. 1992. *A música popular no romance brasileiro*, Vol. I.: *Século XVIII–século XIX*. Belo Horizonte: Oficina de Livros.

———. 1994. *Fado, dança do Brasil, cantar de Lisboa: O fim de um mito*. Lisboa: Editorial Caminho.

Traversari Salazar, Pedro Pablo, ed. 1961. *Católogo general del Museo de Instrumentos Musicales*. Quito: Editorial Casa de la Cultura Ecuatoriana.

Turino, Thomas. 1993. *Moving Away from Silence: Music of the Peruvian Altiplano and the Experience of Urban Migration*. Chicago: University of Chicago Press.

Ulloa, Alejandro. 1992. *La salsa en Cali*. Cali, Colombia: Ediciones Universidad del Valle.

Valencia Chacón, Américo. 1983. *El siku bipolar altiplánico*. Lima: Artex Editores.

———. 1989. *El siku o zampoña: The Altiplano Bipolar Siku—Study and Projection of Peruvian Panpipe Orchestras*. Lima: Artex Editores.

Vasconcellos, Gilberto. 1977. *Música popular: De olho na fesia*. Rio de Janeiro: Graal.

Vasconcelos, Ary. 1991. *Raízes da música popular Brasileira*, rev. ed. Rio de Janeiro: Rio Fundo Editora.

Vásquez Rodríguez, Rosa Elena. 1982. *La práctica musical de la población negra en el Perú: La danza de negritos de El Carmen*. Havana: Casa de las Américas/Ediciones Vitral.

Vásquez, Rosa Elena, and Abilio Vergara Figueroa. 1988. *¡Chayraq!: Carnaval ayacuchano*. Lima: Centro de Desarrollo Agropecuario.

Vega, Carlos. 1944. *Panorama de la música popular argentina, con un ensayo sobre la ciencia del folklore*. Buenos Aires: Losada.

———. 1946. *Los instrumentos musicales aborígenes y criollos de la Argentina*. Buenos Aires: Ediciones Centurión.

———. 1952. *Las danzas populares argentinas*, 2nd ed. Buenos Aires: Instituto Nacional de Musicología "Carlos Vega."

———. 1953. *La zamacueca (cueca, zamba, chilena, marinera)*. Buenos Aires: Ed. Julio Korn.

———. 1956. *El origen de las danzas folklóricas*. Buenos Aires: Ricordi Americana.

———. 1965. *Las canciones folklóricas de la Argentina*. Buenos Aires: Instituto Nacional de Musicología.

Verger, Pierre, ed. *Fiestas y danzas en el Cuzco y en los Andes*. Buenos Aires: Editorial Sudamericana.

Vianna, Hermanno. 1995. *O mistério do samba*. Rio de Janeiro: Jorge Zahar/UFRJ.

Vilcapoma I., José Carlos. 1995. *Waylarsh: Amor y violencia de carnaval*. Lima: Pakarina Ediciones.

Whitten, Norman E., Jr. 1965. *Class, Kinship, and Power in an Ecuadorian Town: The Negroes of San Lorenzo*. Stanford, Calif.: Stanford University Press.

———. 1974a. *Black Frontiersman: A South American Case*. Cambridge, Mass.: Shenkman.

———. 1974b. *Black Frontiersmen. Afro-Hispanic Culture of Ecuador and Colombia*. Prospect Heights, Ill.: Waveland.

MEXICO AND CENTRAL AMERICA

Acevedo Vargas, Jorge Luís. 1986. *La música en Guanacaste*, 2nd ed. San José: Editorial Universidad de Costa Rica.

———. 1986. *La música en las reservas indígenas de Costa Rica*. San José: Editorial de la Universidad de Costa Rica.

Andrews V., and E. Wyllys. 1972. *Flautas precolombinas procedentes de Quelepa, El Salvador*. San Salvador: Ministerio de Educación, Dirección de Cultura, Dirección de Publicaciones.

Anguiano, Marina, and Guido Munch. 1979. *La danza de Malinche*. Mexico: Culturas Populares, Secretaría de Educación Pública.

Beezley. William H., et al. 1994. *Rituals of Rule, Rituals of Resistance: Public Celebrations and Popular Culture in Mexico*. Wilmington: Scholarly Resources.

Cardenal Argüello, Salvador. 1977. *Nicaragua: Música y canto*. Managua: Banco de América. (Liner notes.)

Cargalv, H. (Héctor C. Gálvez). 1983. *Historia de la música de Honduras y sus símbolos nacionales*. Tegucigalpa: N. p.

Carmona Maya, Sergio Iván. 1989. *La música, un fenomeno cosmogónico en la cultura kuna*. Medellín: Editorial Universidad de Antioquia.

Chamorro, Arturo. 1994. *Sones de la guerra: Rivalidad y emoción en la práctica de la música p'uréipecha*. Zamora: El Colegio de Michoacán.

Chenoweth, Vida. 1964. *Marimbas of Guatemala*. Lexington: University of Kentucky Press.

Cheville, Lila R., and Richard A. Cheville. 1977. *Festivals and Dances of Panama*. Panama: Lila and Richard Cheville.

Crossley-Holland, Peter. 1980. *Musical Artifacts of Pre-Hispanic West Mexico: Towards an Interdisciplinary Approach*. Los Angeles: Program in Ethnomusicology, Department of Music, University of California, Los Angeles.

Cuadra, Pablo Antonio, and Francisco Pérez Estrada. 1978. *Muestrario del folklore nicaragüense*. Managua: Banco de América.

Densmore, Frances. 1926. *Music of the Tule Indians of Panama*. Smithsonian Miscellaneous Collections 77(11):1–39. Publication No. 2864. Washington, D.C.: Smithsonian Institution.

———. 1932. *Yuman and Yaqui Music*. Bulletin 110. Washington, D.C.: Bureau of American Ethnology.

Drolet, Patricia Lund. 1980. "The Congo Ritual of Northeastern Panama: An Afro-American Expressive Structure of Cultural Adaptation."

Ph.D. dissertation, University of Illinois at Urbana-Champaign.

Evers, Laurence J., and Felipe Molina. 1987. *Yaqui Deer Songs/Maso Bwikam: A Native American Poetry*. Tucson: University of Arizona Press.

Flores, Bernal. 1978. *La música en Costa Rica*. San José: Editorial Costa Rica.

Florers y Escalanate, Jesús, and Pablo Dueñas Herrera. 1994. *Cirilo Marmolejo: Historia del mariachi en la Ciudad de México*. México, D.F.: Asociación Mexicana de Estudios Fonográficas.

Franco Arce, Samuel. 1991. *Music of the Maya*. Guatemala: Casa K'ojom.

Garay, Narciso. 1930. *Tradiciones y cantares de Panama, ensayo folklórico*. Brussels: Presses de l'Expansion Belge.

García Escobar, Carlos René. 1996. *Atlas danzario de Guatemala*. Guatemala: Universidad de San Carlos de Guatemala.

García Flores, Raúl. 1993. *¡Pure mitote!: La música, el canto, y la danza entre los chichimecas del noreste*. Monterrey: Fondo Editorial Nuevo León.

González Sol, Rafael. 1940. *Datos históricos sobre el arte de la música en El Salvador*. San Salvador: Imprenta Mercurio.

Hayans, Guillermo. 1963. *Dos cantos shamanísticos de los índios cunas*, trans. Nils M. Holmer and S. Henry Wassen. Göteborg: Etnografiska Museet.

Holmer, Nils M., and S. H. Wassén. 1963. *Dos cantos shamanísticos de los índios cunas*. Etnologiska Studier, 27. Göteborgs Etnografiska Museum. Göteborg: Elanders Boktryckeri Aktiebolag.

Jáuregui, Jesús. 1990. *El mariachi: Símbolo musical de México*. Mexico: Banpaís.

Joly, Luz Graciela. 1981. *The Ritual "Play of the Congos" of North-Central Panama: Its Sociolinguistic Implications*. Sociolinguistic Working Paper No. 85. Austin: Southwest Educational Development Laboratory.

Kaptain, Laurence. 1992. *The Wood That Sings: The Marimba in Chiapas, Mexico*. Everett, Pa.: HoneyRock.

Mace, Carroll E. 1970. *Two Spanish-Quiché Dance Dramas of Rabinal*. Tulane Studies in Romance Languages and Literature, Publication No. 3. New Orleans: Tulane University Press.

Manzanares Aguilar, Rafael. 1960. *Canciones de Honduras/Songs of Honduras*. Washington, D.C.: Secretaría General, Unión Panamericana, Organización de los Estados Americanos.

———. 1972. *La danza folklórica hondureña*. Tegucigalpa: Talleres del Partido Nacional.

Martí, Samuel. 1955. *Instrumentos musicales precortesianos*. México, D.F.: Instituto Nacional de Antropología.

———. 1961. *Canto, danza, y música precortesianos*. México, D.F.: Fondo de Cultura Económica.

———. 1968. *Instrumentos musicales precortesianos*, 1st and 2nd eds. México, D.F.: Instituto Nacional de Antropología e Historia.

Mayer-Serra, Otto. 1941. *Panorama de la música mexicana desde la independencia hasta la actualidad*. México, D.F.: Colegio de México.

McCosker, Sandra Smith. 1974. *The Lullabies of the San Blas Cuna Indians of Panama*. Etnologiska Studier, 33. Göteborgs Etnografiska Museum. Göteborg: Elanders Boktryckeri Aktiebolag.

Mendoza, Vicente T. 1939. *El romance español y el corrido mexicano: Estudio comparativo*. México, D.F.: Ediciones de la Universidad Nacional Autónoma de México.

———. 1984 [1956]. *Panorama de la música tradicional de México*. México, D.F.: Universidad Nacional Autónoma de México, Instituto de Investigaciones Estéticas.

Moreno Rivas, Yolanda. 1989. *Historia de la música popular mexicana*, 2nd ed. México, D.F.: Consejo Nacional para la Cultura y las Artes, Alianza Editorial Mexicana.

Muñoz Tábora, Jesús. 1997 [1988]. *Organología del folklore Hondureño*, new ed. Tegucigalpa: Secretaría del Turismo y Cultura.

Núñez, Evangelina de. 1956. *Costa Rica y su folklore*. San José: Imprenta Nacional.

Peña Hernández, Enrique. 1968. *Folklore de Nicaragua*. Masaya: Editorial Unión, Cardoza y Cia.

Pérez Fernández, Rolando Antonio. 1990. *La música afromestiza mexicana*. Xalapa: Biblioteca Universidad Veracruzana.

Pineda del Valle, César. 1990. *Fogarada: Antología de la marimba*. Tuxtla Gutiérrez: Gobierno del Estado de Chiapas, Instituto Chiapaneco de Cultura.

Prado Quesada, Alcides, ed. 1962. *Costa Rica: Su música típica y sus autores*. San José: Editorial Antonio Lehmann.

Programa de Investigación Cultural. 1997. *Música prehispánica en las culturas y comunidades del estado de México*. Toluca: Universidad Autónoma del Estado de México.

Reuter, Jas. 1992 [1985]. *La música popular de México: Orígen e historia de la música que canta y toca el pueblo mexicano*. México, D.F.: Panorama Editoria.

Rivera y Rivera, Roberto. 1977. *Los instrumentos musicales de los Mayas*. México, D.F.: Instituto Nacional de Antropología e Historia.

Salazar Salvatierra, Rodrigo. 1985. *La música popular afrolimonense*. San José: Organización de los Estados Americanos, Ministerio de Cultura, Juventud, y Deportes.

———. 1988. *La marimba: Empleo, diseño, y construcción*. San José: Editorial Universidad de Costa Rica.

———. 1992. *Instrumentos musicales del folclór costarricense*. Cartago: Editorial Instituto Technológico de Costa Rica.

Saldávar, Gabriel. 1934. *Historia de la música en México: Epocas precortesiana y colonial*. México, D.F.: Editorial "Cultura."

———. 1937. *El jarabe, baile popular mexicano*. Mexico: Talleres Gráficos de la Nación.

Sánchez Hernández, Carlos Alfonso. 1997. *Máscaras y danzas tradicionales*. Toluca: Universidad Autónoma del Estado de México.

Scruggs, T. M. 1998. "Cultural Capital, Appropriate Transformations, and Transfer by Appropriation in Western Nicaragua: *El baile de la marimba*." *Latin American Music Review* 19(l):1–30.

———. 1999a. "'Let's Enjoy as Nicaraguans': The Use of Music in the Construction of a Nicaraguan National Consciousness." *Ethnomusicology* 43(2):297–321.

———. 1999b. "Nicaraguan State Cultural Initiative and 'the Unseen Made Manifest.'" *Yearbook for Traditional Music* 31.

Sheehy, Daniel Edward. 1979. "The 'Son Jarocho': The History, Style, and Repertory of a Changing Mexican Musical Tradition." Ph.D. dissertation, University of California at Los Angeles.

Sherzer, Joel. 1983. *Kuna Ways of Speaking: An Ethnographic Perspective*. Texas Linguistics Series. Austin: University of Texas Press.

Smith, Ronald R. 1985. "They Sing with the Voice of the Drum: Afro-Panamanian Musical Traditions." In *More Than Drumming: Essays on African and Afro-Latin American Music*, ed. Irene Jackson-Brown, 163–198. Westport, Conn.: Greenwood.

Smith, Sandra. 1984. "Panpipes for Power, Panpipes for Play: The Social Management of Cultural Expression in Kuna Society." Ph.D. dissertation, University of California, Berkeley.

Stevenson, Robert. 1952. *Music in Mexico: A Historical Survey*. New York: Crowell.

———. 1968. *Music in Aztec and Inca Territory*. Berkeley: University of California Press.

Suco Campos, Idalberto. 1987. *La música en el complejo cultural del Walagallo en Nicaragua*. La Habana: Casa de las Américas.

Tello Solís, Eduardo. 1993. *Semblanza de la canción yucateca*. Mérida: Universidad Autónoma de Yucatán.

Varela, Leticia. 1986. *La música en la vida de los Yaquis*. Hermosillo: El Gobierno del Estado de Sonora, Secretaría de Fomento Educativo y Cultura.

Zárate, Dora Pérez de. 1971. *Textos del tamborito panameño: Un estudio folklórico-literario de los textos del tamborito en Panamá*. Panamá: Dora Pérez de Zárate.

———. 1996. *Sobre nuestra música típica*. Panama: Editorial Universitaria.

Zárate, Manuel F., and Dora Pérez de Zárate. 1968. *Tambor y socavón: Un estudio comprensivo de dos temas del folklore panameño, y de sus implicaciones históricas y culturales*. Panamá: Ediciones del Ministerio de Educación, Dirección Nacional de Cultura.

CARIBBEAN

Ahye, Molly. 1978. *Golden Heritage: The Dance in Trinidad and Tobago*. Petit Valley: Heritage Cultures.

Alén Rodríguez, Olavo. 1986. *La música de las sociedades de tumba francesa en Cuba*. Havana: Casa de Las Américas.

———. 1994. *De lo afrocubano a la salsa*, 2nd ed. Havana: Artex S. A. Editions.

———. 1995. *Rumba: Dance and Social Change in Contemporary Cuba*. Bloomington: Indiana University Press.

Aparicio, Frances. R. 1998. *Listening to Salsa: Gender, Latin Popular Music, and Puerto Rican Cultures*. Hanover, N.H.: University Press of New England.

Austerlitz, Paul. 1997. *Merengue: Dominican Music and Dominican Identity*. Philadelphia: Temple University Press.

Averill, Gage. 1997. *A Day for the Hunter, a Day for the Prey: Popular Music and Power in Haiti*. Chicago: University of Chicago Press.

Benôit, Édouard. 1990. *Musique populaire de la Guadeloupe: De la biguine au zouk, 1940–1980*. Pointe-à-Pitre: Office Régional du Patrimoine Guadeloupéen.

Bigott, Luís Antonio. 1993. *Historia del bolero cubano, 1883–1950*. Caracas: Ediciones Los Heraldos Negros.

Bilby, Kenneth. 1985. *The Caribbean as a Musical Region*. Washington, D.C.: Woodrow Wilson International Center for Scholars.

Boggs, Vernon W., ed. 1992. *Salsiology: Afro-Cuban Music and the Evolution of Salsa in New York City*. New York: Excelsior Music.

Carpentier, Alejo. 1946. *La música en Cuba*. México, D.F.: Fondo de Cultura Económica.

Chang, Kevin O'Brien, and Wayne Chen. 1998. *Reggae Routes: The Story of Jamaican Music*. Philadelphia: Temple University Press.

Constance, Zeno Obi. 1991. *Tassa, Chutney, and Soca: The East Indian Contribution to the Calypso*. San Fernando, Trinidad and Tobago: Z. O. Constance.

Coopersmith, J. M. 1949. *Music and Musicians of the Dominican Republic*, ed. Charles Seeger. Music Series, No. 15. Washington, D.C.: Pan American Union.

Courlander, Harold. 1973. *The Drum and the Hoe: Life and Lore of the Haitian People*. Berkeley: University of California Press.

Cowley, John. 1996. *Carnival Canboulay and Calypso: Traditions in the Making*. Cambridge: Cambridge University Press.

Daniel, Yvonne. 1995. *Rumba: Dance and Social Change in Contemporary Cuba*. Bloomington: Indiana University Press.

Dauphin, Claude. 1980. *Guide d'organologie haïtienne*. Montréal: Société de Recherche et Diffusion de la Musique Haitienne.

———. *Brit kolobrit: Introduction méthodologique suivie de 30 chansons enfantiles haïtiennes*. Québec: Éditions Naaman de Sherbrooke.

———. 1983. *La chanson haïtienne folklorique et classique*. Montréal: N. p.

———. 1986. *Musique du vaudou: Fonctions, structures, et styles*. de Sherbrooke: Editions Naaman.

Davis, Martha Ellen. 1976. "Afro-Dominican Religious Brotherhoods: Structure, Ritual, and Music." Ph.D. dissertation, University of Illinois at Urbana-Champaign.

———. 1981. *Voces del purgatorio: Estudio de la salve dominicana*. Santo Domingo: Museo del Hombre Dominicano.

Deren, Maya. 1984 [1953]. *Divine Horsemen: The Living Gods of Haiti*. London and New York: Thames and Hudson. New Paltz, N.Y.: McPherson.

Desroches, Monique. 1989. *Les instruments de musique traditionnels à la Martinique*. Fort-de-France: Bureau du Patrimoine, Conseil Régional de la Martinique.

———. 1996. *Tambours des dieux: Musique et sacrifice d'origine tamoule en Martinique*. Montréal: L'Harmattan.

Diaz Ayala, Cristóbal. 1994. *Cuba canta y baila: Discografía de la música cubana*, Vol. 1: *1898–1925*. San Juan, P.R.: Fundación Musicalia.

———. 1998. *Cuando salí de la Habana, 1898–1997: Cien años de música cubana por el mundo*. San Juan, P.R.: Fundación Musicalia.

Dobbin, Jay D. 1986. *The Jombee Dance of Montserrat*. Columbus: Ohio State University Press.

Dumervé, Etienne Constantin Eugène Moïse. 1968. *Histoire de la musique en Haïti*. Port-au-Prince: Imprimerie des Antilles.

Edwards, Charles L. 1942 [1895]. *Bahama Songs and Stories*. New York: G. E. Steckert.

Elder, Jacob D. 1969. *From Congo Drum to Steel Band*. St. Augustine, Trinidad: University of the West Indies.

Evora, Tony. 1997. *Orígenes de la música cubana: Los amores de las cuerdas y el tambor*. Madrid: Alianza Editorial.

Fleurant, Gerdès. 1987. "The Ethnomusicology of Yanvalou: A Study of the Rada Rite of Haiti." Ph.D. dissertation, Tufts University.

———. 1996. *Dancing Spirits: Rhythms and Rituals of Haitian Vodun, the Rada Rite*. Westport, Conn.: Greenwood.

Fouchard, Jean. 1988. *La méringue, danse nationale d'Haïti*. Port-au-Prince: Éditions Henri Deschamps.

Gerard, Charlie, and Marty Sheller. 1989. *Salsa: The Rhythm of Latin Music*. Crown Point, Ind.: White Cliffs Media.

Goddard, George. 1991. *Forty Years in the Steelbands, 1939–1979*. London: Karia.

Guilbault, Jocelyne. 1993. *Zouk: World Music in the West Indies*. Chicago: University of Chicago Press.

Hebdige, Dick. 1987. *Cut 'n' Mix: Culture, Identity, and Caribbean Music*. London: Methuen.

Hedrick, Basil C., and Jeanette E. Stephens. 1976. *In the Days of Yesterday and in the Days of Today: An Overview of Bahamian Folk Music*. Southern Illinois University Museum Studies No. 8. Carbondale: Southern Illinois University Press.

Hernández, Julio Alberto. 1969. *Música tradicional dominicana*. Santo Domingo: Julio D. Postigo.

———. 1992. *Música dominicana*. Santo Domingo: Universidad Autónoma de Santo Domingo.

Herskovits, Melville. 1975 [1937]. *Life in a Haitian Valley*. New York: Octagon.

Herskovits, Melville J., and Francis S. Herskovits. 1964 [1947]. *Trinidad Village*. New York: Octagon.

Hill, Donald R. 1993. *Calypso Calaloo: Early Carnival Music in Trinidad*. Gainesville: University Press of Florida.

Hill, Errol. 1972. *The Trinidad Carnival Mandate for a National Theater*. Austin: University of Texas Press.

Inchdáustegui, Arístides. 1988. *El disco en la República Dominicana*. Santo Domingo: Amigo del Hogar.

Jahn, Brian, and Tom Weber. 1992. *Reggae Island: Jamaican Music in the Digital Age*. Kingston: Kingston Publishers.

Johnson, Howard, and Jim Pines. 1982. *Reggae: Deep Roots Music*. London: Proteus.

Laguerre, Michel S. 1980. *Voodoo Heritage*. Sage Library of Social Research, Vol. 98. Beverly Hills and London: Sage.

La Motta, Bill, and Joyce La Motta. 1990. *Virgin Island Folk Songs*. St. Thomas: Joyce La Motta's Tsukimaro.

Largey, Michael. 1991. "Musical Ethnography in Haiti: A Study of Elite Hegemony and Musical Composition." Ph.D. dissertation, Indiana University.

Lent, John A., ed. 1990. *Caribbean Popular Culture*. Bowling Green, Ohio: Bowling Green State University Popular Press.

Leon, Algeliers. 1984. *Del canto y el tiempo*. Havana: Letras Cubanas Editorial.

Lewin, Olive. 1973. *Forty Folk Songs of Jamaica*. Washington, D.C.: Organization of American States.

Linares, Maria Teresa. *La música y el pueblo*. Havana: Pueblo y Educación Editorial, 1974.

López Cruz, Francisco. 1991 [1967]. *La música folklórica de Puerto Rico*, 9th ed. Sharon, Conn.: Troutman.

Malavet Vega, Pedro. 1992. *Historia de la canción popular en Puerto Rico (1493–1898)*. Ponce: Pedro Malavet Vega.

Manuel, Peter, ed. 1991. *Essays on Cuban Music: North American and Cuban Perspectives*. Lanham, Md.: University Press of America.

———. 1995. *Caribbean Currents*. Philadelphia: Temple University Press.

Mason, Peter. 1998. *Bacchanal: Carnival, Calypso, and the Popular Culture of Trinidad*. Philadelphia: Temple University Press.

McCoy, James A. 1968. "The Bomba and Aguinaldo of Puerto Rico as They Have Evolved from Indigenous, African, and European Cultures." Ph.D. dissertation, Florida State University.

McDaniel, Lorna. 1998. *The Big Drum Ritual of Carriacou: Praisesongs in Rememory of Flight*. Gainesville: University Press of Florida.

Métraux, Alfred. 1972. *Voodoo in Haiti*. New York: Schocken.

Moldes, Rhyna. 1975. *Música folklórica cubana*. Miami: Ediciones Universal.

Moore, Robin D. 1997. *Nationalizing Blackness: Afrocubanismo and Artistic Revolution in Havana, 1920–1940*. Pittsburgh, Pa.: University of Pittsburgh Press.

Myers, Helen. 1998. *Music of Hindu Trinidad: Songs from the Indian Diaspora*. Chicago: University of Chicago Press.

Nolasco, Flérida de. 1939. *La música en Santo Domingo y otros ensayos*. Ciudad Trujillo: Montalvo.

Núñez, María Virtudes, and Ramón Guntín. 1992. *Salsa caribe y otras músicas antillanas*. Madrid: Ediciones Cúbicas.

Ortiz, Fernando. 1954. *Los instrumentos de la música afrocubana*. Havana: Cárdenas y Cia Editorial.

———. 1965. *Africanía de la música en Cuba*, 2nd ed. Havana: N. p.

Ortiz Ramos, Pablo Marcial. 1991. *A tres voces y guitarras: Los tríos en Puerto Rico*. San Juan: N. p.

Paul, Emmanuel. 1962. *Panorama du folklore haïtien: Présence africaine en Haiti*. Port-au-Prince: Imprimerie de l'État.

Potash, Chris, ed. 1997. *Reggae, Rasta, Revolution: Jamaican Music from Ska to Dub*. New York: Schirmer.

Quevedo, Raymond. 1983. *Atilla's Kaiso: A Short History of the Trinidad Calypso*. St. Augustine, Trinidad: University of the West Indies.

Quintero-Rivera, A. G. 1989. *Music, Social Classes, and the National Question of Puerto Rico*. Washington, D.C.: Woodrow Wilson International Center for Scholars.

Rodríguez Demorizi, Emilio. 1971. *Música y baile en Santo Domingo*. Santo Domingo: Librería Hispaniola.

Regis, Louis. 1999. *The Political Calypso: True Opposition in Trinidad and Tobago, 1962–1987*. Gainesville: University Press of Florida.

Rohlehr, Gordon. 1990. *Calypso and Society in Pre-Independence Trinidad*. Port of Spain: G. Rohlehr.

Rosa-Nieves, Cesarro. 1991 [1967]. *Voz folklórica de Puerto Rico*. Sharon, Conn.: Troutman.

Rosemain, Jacqueline. 1986. *La musique dans la société antillaise, 1635–1902: Martinique et Guadeloupe*. Paris: Éditions l'Harmattan.

Sekou, Lasana M., ed. 1992. *Fête: Celebrating St. Martin's Traditional Festive Music*. Philipsburg, St. Martin: House of Nehesi.

Shaw, Lisa. 1999. *The Social History of the Brazilian Samba*. Aldershot: Ashgate.

Simpson, George. 1965. *The Shango Cult in Trinidad*. Río Piedras: Institute of Caribbean Studies, University of Puerto Rico.

Stuempfle, Stephen. 1995. *The Steelband Movement: The Forging of a National Art in Trinidad and Tobago*. Philadelphia: University of Pennsylvania Press.

Uri, Alex, and Françoise Uri. 1991. *Musiques and musiciens de la Guadeloupe: Le chant de Karukéra*. Paris: Con Brio.

Vega Drouet, Héctor. 1979. "Historical and Ethnological Survey on Probable African Origins

of the Puerto Rico Bomba, Including a Description of Santiago Apostol Festivities at Loiza Aldea." Ph.D. dissertation, Wesleyan University.

Verba, Daniel. 1995. *Trinidad: Carnaval, Steelbands, Calypso*. Paris: Éditions Alternatives.

Vianna, Hermano. 1999. *The Mystery of Samba: Popular Music and National Identity in Brazil*, ed. and trans. John Charles Chasteen. Chapel Hill: University of North Carolina Press.

Wallis, Roger, and Krister Malm. 1984. *Big Sounds from Small Peoples: The Music Industry in Small Countries*. London: Constable; New York: Pendragon.

Warner, Keith Q. 1985. *Kaiso! The Trinidad Calypso: A Study of the Calypso as Oral Literature*. Washington, D.C.: Three Continents.

Waters, Anita M. 1989. *Race, Class, and Political Symbols: Rastafari and Reggae in Jamaican Politics*. New Brunswick. N.J.: Transaction.

White, Timothy. 1989. *Catch a Fire: The Life of Bob Marley*. New York: Holt.

Wilcken, Lois. 1992. *The Drums of Vodou*. Tempe, Ariz.: White Cities Media.

Wood, Vivian Nina Michelle. 1995. "Rushin' Hard and Runnin' Hot: Experiencing the Music of the *Junkanoo* Parade in Nassau, Bahamas." Ph.D. dissertation, Indiana University.

Recordings of South American, Mexican, Central American, and Caribbean Music

GENERAL

Música de la tierra: Instrumental and Vocal Music, Vol. 2. 1992. Produced by Bob Haddad. Music of the World CDC-207. Compact disk.

Shaman, Jhankri, and Néle: Music Healers of Indigenous Cultures. 1997. Written and produced by Pat Moffitt Cook. Roslyn, N.Y.: Ellipsis Arts. CD3550. Compact disk and book.

The Spirit Cries: Music from the Rainforests of South America and the Caribbean. 1993. Produced by Mickey Hart and Alan Jabbour. Notes by Kenneth Bilby. Rykodisc RCD 10250. Compact disk.

SOUTH AMERICA

A bailar la bomba, con los Hermanos Congo. 1985. Quito: Famosa-Fadisa, 700211. LP disk.

A bailar la bomba, con los Hermanos Congo, Vol. 2. 1986. Guayaquil: Producciones Maldonado-IFE-SA 339-5881. LP disk.

Aboios/Ceará. 1983. Documentário, Sonoro do Folclore Brasileiro, INF-039. LP disk.

Aconcagua. 1995 [1982]. *Los jaivas* [*Chile*]. Colombia CNIA-2-461823. Compact disk.

Afro-Hispanic Music from Western Colombia and Ecuador. 1967. Recorded and edited by Norman E. Whitten. Ethnic Folkways Library FE 4376. LP disk.

Afro-Peruvian Classics: The Soul of Black Peru. 1995. Compiled by David Byrne and Yale Evelev. Luaka Bop 9 45878-2. Compact disk.

Alma del sur. 1993. Narada Collection Series ND-63908. Compact disk. (Liner essay, "A Celebration of South American Music," by Dale A. Olsen.)

Amazonia: Cult Music of Northern Brazil. N.d. Produced by Morton Marks. New York: Lyrichord LLST 7300. LP disk.

La América de Bolívar canta. N.d. Caracas: Colección INIDEF. V.D. 82-033. LP disk.

Amerindian Songs from Surinam: The Maroni River Caribs. 1975. Produced by Peter Kloos. Amsterdam: Royal Tropical Institute. LP disk.

Amérique du Sud: Musiques hispaniques. 1993. Auvidis-Ethnic B 6782. Compact disk.

Andean Legacy. 1996. Narada Collection Series ND-63927. Compact disk. (Liner essay, "Music of the Central Andes," by Dale A. Olsen.)

Astor Piazzolla: Octeto Buenos Aires. 1995. Astor Piazzolla (Argentina). ANS Records ANS 15276-2. Compact disk.

Banda Cabaçal/Ceará. 1978. Documentário Sonoro do Folclore Brasileiro CDFB-023. LP disk.

Bandoneón Pure: Dances of Uruguay. 1993. René Marino Rivero, *bandoneón*. Recorded by Tiago de Oliveira Pinto. Notes by Maria Dunkel. Smithsonian/Folkways CD SF 40431.

Basta. 1995. Quilapayún. Disco Alerce CDAL 0223. Compact disk.

Baú dos oito baixos: Bucho com bucho. 1982. Sebastiáo Moraes. Som da Gente SDG-011. LP disk.

Berimbau: The Art of Berimbau. N.d. François Kokelaere. Buda 92678-2. Compact disk.

Bolivia: Calendar Music in the Central Valleys. 1992. Recorded by Bruno Flety and Rosalia Martínez. Notes by Rosalia Martínez. Chant du Monde LDX 274938 CM 251. Compact disk.

Bolivia Panpipes/Syrinx de Bolivie. Recorded by Louis Girault. Notes by Xavier Bellenger. UNESCO Collection, AUVIDIS D 8009. Compact disk.

Bororo vive. 1990. Federal University of Mato Grosso and Museu Rondon. Idéia Livre 19 521.404.030. LP disk.

Bossa nova: Sua história, sua gente. 1991. Notes by Aloyso de Oliveira. Philips/Polygram 848 302-2. 2 compact disks.

Brazil: The Bororo World of Sound. 1989. Produced by Ricardo Canzio. UNESCO/AUVDIS D 8201. Compact disk.

Brazil Classics, 3: Forró, etc. 1991. Luaka Bop/Warner Bros. 9 26323-2. Compact disk.

Brésil: Amérindiens d'Amazonie—Asurini et Arara/ Brazil: American Indians of the Amazon—Asurini and Arara. 1995. Jean-Pierre Estival. Ocora C 560084. Compact disk.

Brésil central: Chants et danses des Indiens Kaiapo. 1989. Recorded by René Fuerst, George Love, Pascal Rosseels, and Gustaaf Verswijver. Archives Internationales de Musique Populaire. AIMP and VDE-GALLO CD-554/555. 2 compact disks.

Brésil—Musiques du haut Xingu. 1992. Produced by Pierre Toureille. OCORA Radio France, Harmonia Mundi, C 580022. Compact disk.

Las canciones folklóricas de la Argentina: Antología. 1984. Buenos Aires: Instituto Nacional de Musicología "Carlos Vega." 3 LP disks.

La candela vida. 1993. Totó la Momposina y Sus Tambores. Carol/Real World CD 2337-2. Compact disk.

¡Cantando! 1992. Diomedes Díaz and Nicholas "Colacho" Mendoza (Colombia). GlobeStyle ORB 055. Compact disk.

Cantos costeõs: Folksongs of the Atlantic Coastal Region of Colombia. 1973. Produced by George List with Delia Zapata Olivella, Manuel Zapata Olivella, and Winston Caballero Salguedo. Ethnosound EST 8003. LP disk.

Capoeira Angola from Salvador, Brazil. 1996. Grupo de Capoeira Angola Pelourinho. Smithsonian/Folkways SF CD 40465. Compact disk.

Capoeira: Legendary Music of Brazil. 1998. Guilherme Franco. Lyrichord LYRDC 7441. Compact disk.

Capoeira, Samba, Candomblé, Bahia, Brasil. 1990. Recordings and notes by Tiago de Oliveira Pinto. Berlin: Museum Collection. Compact disk.

Chants et rythmes du Chile: Violeta Parra, Los Calhakis, Isabel et Angel Paria. 1991. Arion ARN 64142. Compact disk.

El Charango. 1988. Ernesto Cavour. La Paz: CIMA. LP disk.

Charango cuzqueño. 1985. Julio Benavente Díaz, *charango*. Recorded by Xavier Bellenger. Notes by Thomas Turino. GREM G 1504.

Chocolate: Peru's Master Percussionist. 1992. Lyrichord LYRCD 7417.

Colombia 92. 1992. Sony CD80804/Globo Records. Compact disk.

Cuando el indio llora: Los Huayanay. 1989. Quito: FAMOSO LDF-1040. LP disk.

Cumbia/Cumbia 2: La epoca dorada de Cumbias Colombias. 1993. Produced by Nick Gold. World Circuit WCD 033. Compact disk.

Dance Music from the Countryside. 1992. Pé de Serra Forró Band, Brazil. Haus der Kulturen der Welt SM 1509-2. LP disk.

Danzas y cantos afrovenezolanos. 1978. Caracas: Oswaldo Lares. LP disk.

Danzas y canciones para los niños. 1981. Caracas: Ediciones Fredy Reyna. LP disk.

The Discoteca Collection: Missão de pesquisas folklóricas. 1997. Rykodisc, RCD 10403. Compact disk.

Documental folklórico de la provincia de La Pampa. 1973. Produced by Ercilia Moreno Chá. Buenos Aires: Instituto Nacional de Antropología–Dirección de Cultura de La Pampa. Qualiton QF 3015/16. 2 LP disks.

Do jeito que a gente gosta. 1984. Elba Ramalho. Barclay 823 030-1. LP disk.

Équateur: Le monde sonore des Shuar/Ecuador: The Shuar World of Sound. 1995. Buda 92638-2. Compact disk.

Flutes and Strings of the Andes: Native Musicians from the Altiplano. 1990. Produced by Bob Haddad. Music of the World CDT-106. Compact disk.

Folklore de mi tieria: Conjunto indígena "Peguche." 1977. Industria Fonográfica Ecuatoriana S.A. (IFESA). Orion 330-0063. Guayaquil, Ecuador: distributed by Emporio Musical S.A., Guayaquil and Psje. Amador, Quito. LP disk.

Folklore de Venezuela, Vols. 1–8. 1971. Caracas: Sonido Laffer. 8 LP disks.

Folklore musical y música folklórica Argentina. 1966. Buenos Aires: Fondo Nacional de las Artes. Qualiton QF 3000/5. 6 LP disks.

From Slavery to Freedom: Music of the Saramaka Maroons of Suriname. 1977. Lyrichord LLST 7354. LP disk.

Fuego. 1993. Joe Arroyo y La Verdad. Sony CDZ 81063. Compact disk.

Los grandes de la bomba, con Fabián Congo y Milton Tadeo. 1989. Ecuador: Novedades, LP323102. LP disk.

Grandes éxitos, Vol. 2. 1993. Joe Arroyo y La Verdad. Vedisco 1017-2. Compact disk.

Hekura: Yanomamö Shamanism from Southern Venezuela. 1980. Recorded by David Toop and Nestor Figueras. Quartz Publications 004. LP disk.

Huaynos and Huaylas: The Real Music of Peru. 1991. Compiled by Ben Mandelson, notes by Lucy Duran. GlobeStyle Records GDORBD 064. Compact disk.

Indian Music of Brazil. Musique indienne Brésil. 1972. Recorded with notes by Simone Dreyfus. Ed. Gilbert Rouget. Collection Musée de l'Homme. Vogue VG 403 LDM 30112. LP disk.

Indiens d'Amazonie. N.d. Recorded by Richard Chapelle. Chant du Monde LDX 74501. LP disk.

Inti-Illimani, 2: La nueva canción chilena. 1991. Monitor MCD 71794.

Jarishimi kichuapi (La voz del hombre en Kichua). 1984. Enrique Males. Teen Internacional LP-41586. Guayaquil: Fediscos. LP disk.

¡¡Jatari!! 4. 1978. Quito: Fábrica de Discos S.A. (FADISA) 710129. LP disk.

Javanese Music from Suriname. 1977. Lyrichord LLST 7317. LP disk.

L.H. Correa de Azevedo: Music of Ceara and Minas Gerais. 1997. Produced by Mickey Hart and Alan Jabbour, Library of Congress/Endangered Music Project Rykodisc RCD 10404. Compact disk.

Lowland Tribes of Ecuador. 1986. Recorded by David Blair Stiffler. Ethnic Folkways Records FE 4375. LP disk.

Los Masis: El corazón del pueblo. 1996. Los Masis. Tumi CD 062. Compact disk.

Marimba Cayapas: Típica marimba esmeraldeña. 1979. Guayaquil: ONIX-Fediscos, LP-50031. LP disk.

Lo mejor de la Cumbia soledeña. 1977. Polydor 2404041. LP disk.

Mountain Music of Peru. 1991 [1964]. Produced by John Cohen. Smithsonian Folkways SF 40020 and 40021. 2 compact disks.

Mushuc huaira huacamujun. 1979. Conjunto Indígena "Peguche." Guayaquil: IFESA, RUNA CAUSAY 339-0651. LP disk.

Music of the Andes. Illapa, Inti-Illimani, Kollahuara, Quilapayun, and Victor Jara. Hemisphere 7243 8 28190 28. Compact disk.

Music of Colombia. 1961. Recorded by A. H. Whiteford. Folkways Records, FW 6804. LP disk.

Music of the Haut Oyopok: Oyampi and Emerillon Indian Tribes, French Guiana, South America. 1981. Recorded with notes by David Blair Stiffler. Ethnic Folkways Records FE 4235.

Music of the Jívaro of Ecuador. 1973. Recorded by Michael J. Harner, Ethnic Folkways FE 4386. LP disk.

Music from Saramaka. 1977. Produced by Richard Price and Sally Price. Ethnic Folkways Records FE 4225. LP disk.

The Music of Some Indian Tribes of Colombia. 1972. Produced by Donald Tayler. London: British Institute of Recorded Sound. 3 LP disks.

Music of the Tukano and Cuna Peoples of Colombia. 1987. Recorded by Brian Moser and Donald Tayler. Rogue Records, FMS/NSA 002. LP disk.

The Music of Venezuela. 1990. Memphis: Memphis State University. High Water Recording Company, LP1013. LP disk.

Music of the Venezuelan Yekuana Indians. 1975. Produced by Walter Coppens and Isaías Rodríguez V. Folkways Records Album FE 4104. LP disk.

Music of the Warao: Song People of the Rain Forest. 1996. Recorded and produced by Dale A. Olsen. Gainesville: University Press of Florida. Book and compact disk.

Música andina de Bolivia: IV festival folklórico Luz Mila Patiño. 1979. Produced by Max Peter Baumann. Cochabamba: Centro Portales y Lauro y Cía. LP disk.

Música andina del Perú. 1987. Produced by Raúl Romero. Lima: Archivo de Música Tradicional, Pontífica Universidad Católica del Perú, Instituto Riva Agüero. LP disk.

Música autóctona del norte de Potosí: VII festival folklórico Luz Mila Patiño. 1991. Produced by Luz María Calvo and Walter Sánchez C. Cochabamba: Centro Portales y Lauro y Cia. LP disk.

Música etnográfica y folklórica del Ecuador. Culturas: Shuar, Chachi, Quichua, Afro, Mestizo. 1990. Recorded by José Peñín, Ronny Velásquez, and Carlos Alberto Coba Andrade. Otavalo: Instituto Otavaleño de Antropología. 2 LP disks.

Música indígena Guahibo. ca. 1978. Caracas: Fundación La Salle/Instituto Interamericano de Etnomusicología e Folklore. LP disk.

Música indígena: Arte vocal dos Suyá. 1982. Recorded and produced by Anthony Seeger. São João del Rei: Tacape 007. LP disk.

Música popular tradicional de Venezuela. 1983. Caracas: Instituto Nacional del Folklore. LP disk.

Música tradicional de Bolivia: VI festival folklórico nacional Luz Mila Patiño. 1984. Produced by Luz María Calvo and Roberto Guzmán. Cochabamba: Centro Portales y Lauro y Cia. LP disk.

Música tradicional de Cajamarca. 1988. Produced by Gisela Canepa Koch and Raul R. Romero. Lima: Archivo de Música Tradicional, Pontífica Universidad Católica del Perú, Instituto Riva-Agüero. AMTA-3. LP disk, cassette (1997).

Música tradicional del Callijón de Huaylas. 1997. Edited by Manuel Ráez Retamozo. Lima: Archivo de Música Tradicional, Pontífica Universidad Católica del Perú, Instituto Riva-Agüero. AMTA-7. Cassette.

Música tradicional del Cusco. 1992. Edited by Raúl R. Romero. Lima: Archivo de Música Tradicional, Pontífica Universidad Católica del Perú, Instituto Riva-Agüero. AMTA-5. LP disk, cassette (1997).

Música tradicional de Lambayeque. 1992. Edited by Raúl R. Romero. Lima: Archivo de Música Tradicional, Pontífica Universidad Católica del Perú, Instituto Riva-Agüero. AMTA-6. LP disk, cassette (1997).

Música tradicional de Piura. 1997. Edited by Manuel Ráez Retamozo and Ana Teresa Lecaros. Lima: Archivo de Música Tradicional, Pontífica Universidad Católica del Perú, Instituto Riva-Agüero. AMTA-9. Cassette.

Música tradional de la Sierra de Lima. 1997. Edited by Manuel Ráez Retamozo and Ana Teresa Lecaros. Lima: Archivo de Música Tradicional, Pontífica Universidad Católica del Perú, Instituto Riva-Agüero. AMTA-8. Cassette.

Música tradicional del Valle de Colca. 1989. Edited by Manuel Ráez Retamozo and Leonidas Casas Roque. Lima: Archivo de Música Tradicional, Pontífica Universidad Católica del Perú, Instituto Riva-Agüero. AMTA-4. LP disk, cassette (1997).

Música tradicional del Valle del Mantaro. 1986. Edited by Raúl R. Romero. Lima: Archivo de

Música Tradicional, Pontífica Universidad Católica del Perú, Instituto Riva-Agüero. AMTA-1.LP disk, cassette (1997).

Música de Venezuela: Cantos y danzas de la costa central. N.d. Caracas: Oswaldo Laress. LP disk.

Música de Venezuela: Indio figueredo (*Homenaje al Indio figueredo*). 1969. Caracas: Oswaldo Lares. LP disk.

Musik im Andenhochland/Bolivien (Music in the Andean Highlands/Bolivia). 1982. Recording and notes by Max Peter Baumann. Edited by Artur Simon. Museum Collection Berlin MC 14. LP disk.

Musique boni et wayana de Guyana. 1968. Produced by Jean-Marcel Hurault. Paris: Collection Musée de l'Homme. Disque Vogue LVLX 290. LP disk.

Musique des Indiens Bora et Witoto d'Amazonie colombienne. 1976. Recorded by Mireille Guyot and Jürg Gasche. Paris: Musée de l'Homme. AEM 01. LP disk.

Musique instrumentale des Wayana du Litani (The Wayana of the Litani River). N.d. Buda 92637-2. Compact disk.

Ñanda mañachi, 1 and 2 (*Préstame el camino*). 1977, 1979. Produced by Jean Chopin Thermes-Ibarra. Guayaquil: Llaquiclla–Ifesa 339-0502. 2 LP disks.

Ñanda mañachi: ¡Churay, Churay! 1983. Guayaquil: Llaquiclla. Onix-Fediscos LP-59003. LP disk.

The Noble Songbook of Colombia. N.d. Produced by Joaquín Piñeros Corpos. Bogotá: Universidad de los Andes, LP 501-03. LP disks.

Ñuca llacta. 1975. *Conjunto los Tucumbes*. Auténtico Conjunto Folklórico interpretando música autóctona de nuestro país. Ritmos indígenas. Quito: Sibelius, S-4256-SIB-12. LP-12501. LP disk.

O bom do carnaval. 1980. Claudionor Germano. RCA/Cadmen 107.0317. LP disk.

O melhor de Luiz Gonzaga. 1989. Luiz Gonzaga. RCA CDM 10032. LP disk.

Paiter Merewá: Cantam os Suruis de Rondônia. 1984. São Paulo: Discos Memoria 803.146. LP disk.

Pelas ruas do Recife. 1979. Banda de Pau e Corda. RCA 103.0319. LP disk.

Percussions d'Amérique latine. 1986. Arion CD64023. Compact disk (tracks 3, 7, 12, 14, 17).

Percussions d'Amérique latine. N.d. Produced by Gérard Krémer. Arion CD64023. LP disk.

Pérou: Huayno, valse créole et marinera. 1994. Playasound PS 65133. Compact disk.

Pérou: Taquile, Île du Ciel—Musique quechua du Lac Titicaca. 1992. Ocora C580 015. Compact disk.

Peru: Ayarachi and Chiriguano. 1983. Xavier Bellenger. UNESCO MTC 1. LP disk.

Perú: Máximo Damián—El violín de Ishua. 1992. A.S.P.I.C. X55514. Compact disk.

Perú: Música negra. 1992. A.S.P.I.C. X55515. Compact disk.

Quechua. Margarita Alvear. 1976. Guayaquil: ONIX. Fediscos, LP-50154. LP disk.

Rebellión. 1992. Joe Arroyo y La Verdad. World Circuit WCD 012. Compact disk.

Reisado do Piauí. 1977. Documentário Sonoto do Folclore Brasileiro CDFB-019. LP disk.

Relevamiento etnomusicolígico de Salta, Argentina. 1984. Selección de textos: Rubén Pérez Bugallo. Buenos Aires: Instituto Nacional de Musicología "Carlos Vega." 2 LP disks.

Repentes e emboladas. 1986. Manoel Batista and Zé Batista. Phonodisc LP 0-34-405-215. LP disk.

Ritmos e danças: Frevo. N.d. Fundáçio Nacional de Arte SCDP-PF-0 I-PE. LP disk.

Ritual Music of the Kayapó-Xikrin, Brazil. 1995. Recorded by Max Peter Baumann. Notes by Lux Boelitz Vidal and Isabelle Vidal Giannini. Smithsonian/Folkways CD SF 40433. Compact disk and booklet.

The Rough Guide to the Music of the Andes. 1996. Produced by Phil Stanton. World Music Network. RGNET 1009. Compact disk.

Selk'nam Chants of Tierra del Fuego, Argentina. 1972. Notes and translations of texts by Anne Chapman. Ethnic Folkways FE 4176. 2 LP disks.

Selk'nam Chants of Tierra del Fuego, Argentina. 1978. Notes and transcriptions by Anne Chapman. Ethnic Folkways Records FE 4179. 2 LP disks.

Songs of Paraguay: Papi Basaldua and Grupo Cantares. 1994. JVC VICG 5341-2. Compact disk.

Soul Vine Shaman. 1979. Produced by Neelon Crawford and Norman E. Whitten, Jr., with Julian Santi Vargas, María Aguinda Marnallacta, and William Belzner. New York: Neelon Crawford. LP disk.

Surinam: Javanese Music. 1977. Produced by Annemarie de Waal Malefijt and Verna Gillis. Lyrichord LLST 7317. LP disk.

Tango: Zero Hour. 1986. Astor Piazzolla and the New Tango Quintet. Produced by Kip Hanrahan. American Clave. MCA Records. PAND-42138. Compact disk.

Todos os sons. 1995. Marlui Miranda. São Paulo, Brazil: Associação IHU, Pró Musica e Arte Indigenas. Pau Brasil Som Imagem e Editora, CGC 65.012l.478/0001-87. Compact disk.

Traditional Music of Peru, 1: Festivals of Cusco. 1995. Smithsonian Folkways SF CD 40466. Compact disk.

Trio elétrico/Carnaval de Bahia. 1990. RGE 3 GLO 121. LP disk.

Tropicalísimo. 1989. Peregoyo y Su Combo Vicana (Colombia). World Circuit WCD 015.

Txai! 1990. Milton Nascimento. Brazil: Discos C.B.S. 177.228/1-464138. Cassette.

Typiquement D.O.M Compilation 89 Antilles-Guyane. 1989. Produced by Dany Play. Cayenne: TDM production. LP disk.

Vallenato dynamos! 1990. Meriño Brothers (Colombia). GlobeStyle ORB 049. Compact disk.

Venezuela y su folklore: A Taste of Venezuela. 1997. Agave Music SDL 27039. Compact disk.

Victor Jara: Canto libre. 1993. Victor Jara (Chile). Monitor MCD 71799.

Violas da minha terra. 1978. Moacir Laurentino and Sebastião da Silva. Chantecler: 2-04-405075. LP disk.

Yanoama: Tecniche vocali sciamanismo. 1979. Recorded by Ettore Biocca. Produced by Diego Carpitella. Suoni CETRA SU 5003. LP disk.

Wayãpi guyane. 1980. Produced by Jean-Michel Beaudet. Paris: Musée de l'Homme, SELAF-ORSTOM CETO 792. LP disk.

Zabumba/SE. 1979. Documentário Sonoro do Folclore Brasileiro CDFB-031(1979). LP disk.

MEXICO AND CENTRAL AMERICA

Amando en tiempo de guerra (Loving in Times of War). 1988. Luis Enrique Mejía Godoy and Mancotal. Redwood Records 8805. LP disk.

Antología del son de México. 1985. Produced by Baruj Lieberman, Eduardo Llerenas, and Enrique Ramírez de Arellano. México, D.F.: Corason. Cambridge, Mass.: Rounder Records, distributor. 3 compact disks.

Berry Wine Days. 1996. Peter's Boom and Chime. Produced by Gina Scott. Stonetree Records. LP disk.

The Black Caribs of Honduras. 1953. Produced by Doris Stone. Folkways FE 4435. LP disk.

Black History/Black Culture. 1991. Soul Vibrations. Aural Tradition ATRCD 118 and Redwood Records. LP disk.

El Caimán: Sones huastecos. 1996. Eduardo Llerenas. Corason CORA 129. Compact disk.

Calypsos of Costa Rica. N.d. Produced by Walter Ferguson. Folkways Records, FTS 31309. LP disk.

Cantos de tierra adentro. 1980. Los Soñadores de Sarawaska. Ocarina MC-004. LP disk.

Chatuye: Heartbeat in the Music. 1992. Produced by G. Simeon Pillich. Arhoolie Productions, CD-383. Compact disk.

Chicken Scratch—Popular Dance Music of the Indians of Southern Arizona. 1972. Canyon C-6085 and C-6162. 2 LP disks.

Cinco siglos de bandas en México, Vols. 2–4. N.d. México, D.F.: Archivo Etnográfico del Instituto Nacional Indigenista FONAPAS. 3 LP disks.

El Conjunto Murrietta Tocando Norteño. 1978. Canyon C-6162. LP disk.

Dabuyabarugu: Inside the Temple—Sacred Music of the Garifuna of Belize. 1982. Produced by Carol Jenkins and Travis Jenkins. Smithsonian Folkways Records, FE 4032. LP disk.

Deer Dancer: Jessita Reyes and Grupo Yaqui. 1991. Talking Taco Records TT 110. Compact disk.

Dinastía hidalguense: Sones huastecos. 1996. Corason CORA 130. Compact disk.

En busca de la música maya: Canción de la Selva Lacandona. 1976. Produced by Yuichi Matsumura and Mabuchi Usaburo. Japan: King Records GXH (k) 5001-3. LP disk.

Fiesta de palo de Mayo. 1986. Dimensión Costeña. ENIGRAC CE-6009. LP disk.

Fiesta tropical. 1991. Banda Blanca. Sonotone Music POW 6017. LP disk.

Flautas indigenas de México. 1995. México, D.F.: Departamento de Etnomusicología del Instituto Nacional Indigenista, serie 7: Organología Indígena, Vol. 1, INI-VII-0. Compact disk.

Guaymi—Térraba: Antología de música indígena costarricense. N.d. Asociación Indígena de Costa Rica, Pablo Presbere. Onda Nueva. LP disk.

Guitarra armada. 1988. Carlos Mejía Godoy and Luis Enrique Mejía Godoy. Rounder Records 4022. Originally released on INDICA, S.A. (Costa Rica) MC-1147, 1979; reissued on ENIGRAC MC-015 and MC 1147, 1980. LP disk.

Harp of Veracruz: Canto de América. 1997. Hoshikawa Kyoji. King/Seven Seas KICC 5218. Compact disk.

Honduras—Música folklórica. N.d. [1988.] Tegucigalpa: Secretaría del Turismo y Cultura. LP disk.

La iguana: Sones jarochos. 1996. Eduardo Llerenas. Corason COCD 127. Compact disk.

Indian Music of Mexico. 1952. Recorded and produced by Henrietta Yurchenco. Folkways FE-4413. LP disk.

Indian Music of Mexico. 1957. Recorded and produced by Laura Boulton. Folkways FW-8851. LP disk.

Indian Music of Northwest Mexico. 1977, 1978. Canyon C-8001. LP disk.

Instrumental Folk Music of Panama. 1994. Danzas Panama. JVC VICG-5338. Compact disk.

Kunda erer ma-ir ranto niuff/Aguilas que no se olvidan. 1996. Grupo Indígena Chichimeca de San Luis de la Paz, Guanajuato. México, D.F.: Departamento de Etnomusicología del Instituto Nacional Indigenista. INI-VI-05. Compact disk.

Lanlaya—Canciones de amor miskito. 1987. Grupo Lardaya (Nicaragua). ENIGRAC CE-021. LP disk.

Malekú—Guatuso: Antología de música indígena costarricense. N.d. Asociación Indígena de Costa Rica, Pablo Presbere. Onda Nueva. LP disk.

Mama Let Me Go. 1989. Dimensión Costeña. ENIGRAC CE-6028. LP disk.

Mariachi coculense "Rodriguez" de Cirilo Marmolejo 1926–1936. 1993. Reissue produced by Chris Strachwitz. Arhoolie/Folklyric CD 7011. Compact disk.

El mariachi Tepalcatepec de Michoacán: El Michoacano. 1994. Discos Dos Coronas DDC 9401. Compact disk.

Mayapax—Música tradicional maya de Tixcacal Guardia, Quintana Roo. 1993. Instituto Nacional Indigenista. México, D.F.: XEPET "La voz de los mayas," INI-RAD 1-1 (XEPET). Compact disk.

Mariachi tapatío de José Marmolejo. 1994. Reissue produced by Chris Strachwitz. Arhoolie/Folklyric CD 7012. Compact disk.

Maya K'ekchi Strings. 1996. Produced by Gina Scott. Stonetree Records. LP disk.

The Mexican Revolution: Corridos about the Heroes and Events, 1910–1920 and Beyond! 1996. Chris Strachwitz. Arhoolie/Folklyric CD 7041-7044. Four compact disks.

Mexico: Fiestas of Chiapas and Oaxaca. 1991. Recorded by David Lewiston. Notes by Walter F. Morris, Jr., and David Lewiston. Elektra/Nonesuch 9 72070-2. Compact disk.

Mexico's Pioneer Mariachis, Vol. 1. 1993. Mariachi Coculense de Cirilo Marmolejo and Cuarteto Coculense. Produced by Chris Strachwitz. El Cerrito, Calif.: Arhoolie-Folklyric CD7011. Compact disk.

Mexico's Pioneer Mariachis, Vol. 3. 1992. Produced by Chris Strachwitz. Mariachi Vargas de Tecalitlán. El Cerrito, Calif.: Arhoolie-Folklyric CD7015. Compact disk.

La misa campesina. N.d. [1980]. Carlos Mejía Godoy and El Taller de Sonido Popular. ENIGRAC NCLP—5012. LP disk.

Mixtecos y triquis en la frontera norte. 1994. México, D.F.: Subdirección de Radio del Institute, Nacional Indigenista and Secretaria de Desarrollo Social, Serie Sonidos del México Profundo, 5, INI-RAD-II-5 (XEQIN). Compact disk.

Modern Maya: The Indian Music of Chiapas, Mexico. 1975. Produced by Richard Anderson. Folkways FE 4377. LP disk.

Music of the Indians of Panama: The Cuna (Tule) and Chocoe (Embera) Tribes. 1983. Recorded and produced by David Blair Stiffler. Folkways Records, FE 4326. LP disk.

Music of Mexico, Vol. 1. 1994. Conjunto Alma Jarocha, "Sones Jarochos" (Veracruz). Produced by Daniel E. Sheehy and Chris Strachwitz. El Cerrito, Calif.: Arhoolie CD354. Compact disk.

Music of Mexico, Vol. 2. 1994. Ignacio Montes de Oca H. Conjunto Alma de Apatzingán, "Arriba Tierra Caliente" (Michoacán). El Cerrito, Calif.: Arhoolie CD426. Compact disk.

Music of Mexico, Vol. 3. 1995. La Huasteca; Huapangos y Sones Huastecos; Los Caimanes (1995) and Los Caporales de Pánuco (1978). Produced by Chris Strachwitz. El Cerrito, Calif.: Arhoolie 431. Compact disk.

Music of the Miskito Indians of Honduras and Nicaragua. 1981. Recorded and produced by

David Blair Stiffler. Smithsonian Folkways Cassette Series 4237. Cassette with liner notes.

Music of the Tarascan Indians of Mexico: Music of Michoacan and Nearby Mestizo Country. 1970. Recorded and produced by Henrietta Yurchenko. New York: Folkways 4217. LP disk.

Music of Veracruz: The Sones Jarochos of Los Pregoneros del Puerto. 1990. Produced by Dan Sheehy and Joe Wilson. Rounder Records CD 5048. Compact disk.

Música afroantillana de Mexico: Combo Ninguno, Traigo Este Son. N.d. Combo Ninguno. Discos Pentagrama PCD-070. Compact disk.

Música y canciones de Honduras. 1975. Produced by Rafael Manzanares. ELIA 0 1—03. 3 LP disks.

Música de la Costa Chica de Guerrero y Oaxaca. 1977. Produced by Thomas Stanford. México, D.F.: Instituto Nacional de Antropología e Historia, Serie de Discos INAH 21. LP disk.

Música indígena de México, Vol. 5—*Música indígena del nordeste.* 1976. Produced by Arturo Warman. México, D.F.: Instituto Nacional de Antropología e Historia. LP disk.

La música en la Mixteca. 1994. México, D.F.: Subdirección de Radio del Instituto Nacional Indigenista and Secretaría de Desarrollo Social, Serie Sonidos del México Profundo, 7, INI-RAD-II-7; XETLA. Compact disk.

La música en la montaña de Guerrero. 1994. México, D.F.: Subdirección de Radio del Instituto Nacional Indigenista and Secretaría de Desarrollo Social; Serie Sonidos del México Profundo, 10, INI-RAD-II-10; XEZV. Compact disk.

Música popular mexicana: Sones huastecos. 1990. Trio Xoxocapa. Discos Pentagrama PCD 117. Compact disk.

Música popular poblana: Homenaje a don Vicente T. Mendoza. 1995. Produced by Garza Marcue and Rosa María. México, D.F.: Fonoteca del Instituto Nacional de Antropología e Historia, INAH 032. LP disk.

Musiques des communautés indigínes du Mexique. a1969–1970. Produced by François Jouffa, Maurice Morea, and Serge Roterdam. Vogue LDM 30103. LP disk.

Nicaragua—Música y canto. 1992 [1977]. Produced by Salvador Cardenal Argüello. Managua: Radio Güegüence (Banco de América LP). 7 compact disks.

¡Nicaragua . . . Presente!—Music from Nicaragua Libre. 1989. Produced by John McCutcheon. Rounder Records 4020/4021. LP disk.

Nicaraguan Folk Music from Masaya: Música Folklírica de Masaya. 1988. Recorded and produced by T. M. Scruggs. Flying Fish FF474. LP disk.

Palo de Mayo. N.d. [1976]. Los Bárbaros del Ritmo. Andino 010. LP disk.

Panamá: Tamboritos y mejoranas. 1987. Produced by Eduardo Llerenas and Enrique Ramírez de Arellano. Música Tradicional MT10. LP disk.

Panamanian Folk Music and Dance. 1971 [1968]. Produced by Lila Cheville. LP disk.

Pure Purepecha: Pirekuas and Abajeños. 1994. Corason COCD 119. Compact disk.

Qué resuene la tarima. 1990. Grupo Tacoteno. Produced by Modesto López and Juan Meléndez. Discos Pentagrama PCD-146. Compact disk.

Quinto Festival de Música y Danza Indígena. 1994. México: Departamento de Etnomusicología del Instituto Nacional Indigenista, serie 8. Archivo Sonoro, Digital de la Música Indígena INI-ETM-VIII-01. Compact disk.

Saumuk Raya—Semilla Nueva. N.d. [1986, Nicaragua.] ENIGRAC 018. LP disk.

Serie de Discos. 1967–1979. Irene Vázquez Valle, general editor. México, D.F.: Instituto Nacional de Antropología. 24 LP disks. (Mexican regional and indigenous music with descriptive notes.)

Sewere. 1996. Scott, Gina, Original Turtle Shell Band. Produced by Gina Scott. Stonetree Records. LP disk.

La Sierra Gorda que canta: A lo divino y a lo humano. 1995. Recorded and produced by María Isabel Flores Solano et al. Guanajuato: Instituto de la Cultura del Estado de Guanajuato, Dirección General de Culturas Populares y Discos Corazón. Compact disk.

Sistema de radiodifusoras culturales indigenistas. 1995. Testimonio Musical del Trabajo Radiofónico. México, D.F.: Subdirección de Radio del Instituto Nacional Indigenista and Secretaría de Desarrollo Social, INI-RAD-I-5. 2 compact disks.

¡Son tus perfumenes mujer! N.d. [mid-1970s.] Los Bisturices Harmónicos. Banco Nicaraguense. LP disk.

Sones from Jalisco. 1994. Mariachi Reyes del Aserradero. Produced by Eduardo Llerenas. Corason COCD 108. Distributed by Rounder Records, Cambridge, Mass. Compact disk.

Songs and Dances of Honduras. 1955. Produced by Doris Stone. Folkways 6834. LP disk.

Songs of the Garifuna. 1994. Produced by Lita Ariran. JVC VICG-5337. Compact disk.

Street Music of Panama. 1985. Produced by Michel Blaise. Original Music, OML 401. LP disk.

Tarahumara Matachin Music/Matachines tarahumaras. 1979. Canyon C-8000.

Tradiciones populares de Costa Rica. N.d. Grupo Curime. San José: Indica S.A., PP-17-83. LP disk.

Traditional Music of the Garifuna (Black Carib) of Belize. 1982. Produced by Carol Jenkins and Travis Jenkins. Smithsonian Folkways Records, FE 4031. LP disk.

El Triunfo: Los Camperos de Valles—Sones de la Huasteca. 1992. Los Camperos de Valles. Produced by Eduardo Llerenas. Música Tradicional MTCD 007. Cassette disk.

The Vanishing Indians: Costa Rica and Panama, Tribes of the Talamanca Division. N.d. Lyrichord Stereo LLST 7378. LP disk.

La voz de la Costa Chica. 1994. Instituto Nacional Indigenista. Subdirección de Radio Difusora XEJAM, "La Voz de la Costa Chica," Jamiltepec, Oaxaca, and Secretaría de Desarrollo Social, INI-RAD-I-3. Compact disk.

La voz de las Huastecas. 1994. Instituto Nacional Indigenista. México, D.F.: Subdirección de Radio Difusora XEANT, "La Voz de las Huastecas," and Secretaría de Desarrollo Social, INI-RAD-I-2. Compact disk.

La voz de la sierra: Segundo aniversario. 1994. Instituto Nacional Indigenista. México, D.F.: Subdirección de Radio Difusora XEGLO "La voz de la Sierra," and Secretaría de Desarrollo Social, INI-RAD-I-4. Compact disk.

Yaqui Dances—The Pascola Music of the Yaqui Indians of Sonora, Mexico. 1957. Produced by Samuel Charters. Folkways FW-957. LP disk.

Yaqui Festive and Ritual Music. 1972. Canyon C-6140. LP disk.

Yaqui Fiesta and Religious Music—Historic Recordings from Old Pascua Village. 1980. Produced by Edward H. Spicer. Canyon CR-7999. LP disk.

Yaqui—Music of the Pascola and Deer Dance. 1976. Canyon C-6099. LP disk.

Yaqui Pascola Music of Arizona. 1980. Canyon CR-7998. LP disk.

Yaqui Ritual and Festive Music. 1976. Produced by Robert Nuss, Canyon C-6140. LP disk.

Ye Stsoke: Breve antología de la música indígena de Talamanca. N.d. Indica S.A., PP-470-A. LP disk.

CARIBBEAN

Afro-Cuba: A Musical Anthology. 1994. Produced by Morton Marks. Rounder CD 1088. Compact disk.

Afro-Cuban Roots, Vols. 1–6. 1998. Max MXD 2061, 2062, 2073, 2074, 2089, 2090. 6 compact disks.

Afro-Dominican Music from San Cristóbal, Dominican Republic. 1983. Produced by Morton Marks. Folkways FE 4285. LP disk.

Aires Tropicales/Tropical Breeze. 1996–1997. Various artists. Sony CD 82363/2-469889. Compact disk.

L'âme nègre en exil au bal antillais: Franco-Creole Biguines from Martinique. 1988. Produced by Chris Strachwitz. Notes by Richard K. Spottswood. Folklyric Records 9050. Compact disk.

Angels in the Mirror: Vodou Music of Haiti. 1997. Ellipsis Arts CD 4120. Compact disk.

Bahamas 1935: Chanteys and Anthems from Andros and Cat Island. 1999. Alan Lomax Collection. Rounder 11661-1822-2. Compact disk.

Boukman Eksperyans: Vodou Adjae. 1991. Notes and translations by Gage Averill. Mango Records 162-539-899-2. Compact disk.

Calypso at Midnight: The 1946 Town Hall Calypso Concert. 1999. Alan Lomax Collection. Rounder 11661-1840-2. Compact disk.

Calypso after Midnight: The 1946 Town Hall Calypso Concert, Part 2. 1999. Alan Lomax Collection. Rounder 11661-1841-2. Compact disk.

Calypso Breakaway, 1927–1941. 1990. Rounder Records. Compact disk.

Calypso Calaloo: Early Carnival Music in Trinidad. 1993. Compiled by Donald R. Hill. Gainesville: University Press of Florida. Book and compact disk.

Calypso Pioneers, 1912–1937. 1989. Produced by Dick Spottswood. Rounder Records 1039. Compact disk.

Calypso Season. 1990. Mango Records. Compact disk.

Cantar Maravilloso: Los Muñequitos de Matanzas. 1990. Compiled by Ben Mandelson. Notes by Lucy Duran. GlobeStyle CDORB 053. Compact disk.

Caribbean Carnivals/Carnavale des Caraïbes. 1991. Seeds Records SRC 119. Compact disk.

Caribbean Island Music: Songs and Dances of Haiti, the Dominican Republic and Jamaica. N.d. Produced by John Storm Roberts. Nonesuch H-72047-2. Compact disk.

Caribbean Revels: Haitian Rara and Dominican Gaga. 1991. Recorded by Verna Gillis. Notes by Gage Averill and Verna Gillis. Smithsonian Folkways CD SF 40402. Compact disk.

Caribbean Voyage: Brown Girl in the Ring. 1997. Alan Lomax Collection. Rounder CD 1716. Compact disk.

Caribbean Voyage: Caribbean Sampler. 1999. Alan Lomax Collection. Rounder 11661-1721-2. Compact disk.

Caribbean Voyage: Carriacou—Calaloo. 1999. Alan Lomax Collection. Rounder 11661-1722-2. Compact disk.

Caribbean Voyage: East Indian Music in the West Indies. 1999. Alan Lomax Collection. Rounder 11661-1723-2. Compact disk.

A Carnival of Cuban Music. 1990. Routes of Rhythm, Vol. 1. Produced by Howard Dratch et al. Rounder CD 5049. Compact disk.

Carnival Jump Up: Steelbands of Trinidad and Tobago. 1989. Delos DE 4014. Compact disk.

Cien por ciento puertoriqueño. c. 1997. Edwin Colón Zayas y su Taller Campesino (Puerto Rico). Disco Hit Productions DHCD-8034.

Con un poco de songo. 1989. Batacumbelé (Puerto Rico). Disco Hit Productions DHLP-008-CD.

Cradle of the New World. 1976. Recorded by Verna Gillis. Folkways FE 4283. LP disk.

Cuban Counterpoint: History of the Son Montuno. 1992. Rounder CD 1078. Compact disk.

Cuban Dance Party. 1990. Routes of Rhythm, Vol. 2. Produced by Howard Dratch et al. Rounder CD 5050. Compact disk.

Dance! Cadence! N.d. GlobeStyle ORB 002. Compact disk.

Dancehall Style: The Best of Reggae Dancehall Music, Vols. 1 and 2. 1990. Profile Records PRO 1271 and 1291.

Dansez . . . chantez. 1992. Ethnikolor. France: Musidisc MU760. Compact disk.

Divine Horsemen: The Voodoo Gods of Haiti. 1980. Recordings by Maya Deren. Produced by Teiji Ito and Cheryl Ito. Lyrichord LLST 7341. LP disk.

Drums of Defiance: Maroon Music from the Earliest Free Black Communities of Jamaica. 1992. Recorded and compiled by Kenneth Bilby. Smithsonian/Folkways CD SF 40412. Compact disk.

En jíbaro y tropical. 1997. Taller Musical Retablo (Puerto Rico). TMR02CD. Compact disk.

La fête antillaise continue . . . , Vol. 2. 1991. Ethnikolor. France: Ethnikolor Productions et Carrère Music CA808. Compact disk.

The Golden Age of Calypso: Dances of the Caribbean Islands. 1996. Compiled by Philippe Zani. EPM Musique 995772. Compact disk.

Guadeloupe: Le Gwoka, Soirée Léwòz, à Cacao. 1992. Ocora C560 031. Compact disk.

Heart of Steel: Featuring Steelbands of Trinidad and Tobago. 1990. Flying Fish. Compact disk.

Heat in de Place: Soca Music from Trinidad. 1990. Rounder Records. Compact disk.

History of Ska: The Golden Years, 1960–1965. N.d. Mango Records.

Hurricane Zouk. N.d. Virgin/Earthworks 7 90882-1. Compact disk.

Intensified! Original Ska, 1962–1966. N.d. Mango Records MLPS 9524. Compact disk.

The Island of Española. 1976. Recorded by Verna Gillis. Folkways FE 4282. LP disk.

The Island of Quisqueya. 1976. Recorded by Verna Gillis. Folkways FE 4281. LP disk.

Jazz and Hot Dance in Martinique, 1929–1950. N.d. Harlequin HQ2018. Produced by Bruce Bastin. Notes by Alain Boulanger. Compact disk.

Jazz Jamaica. N.d. Studio One Sol 1140.

Kali. 1988. Racines. France and Switzerland: Hibiscus Records HR 88020 CS 750. Compact disk.

Kassav' grands succès, Vol. 1. 1987. Productions Georges Debs GDC10501, Sono disc distribution, Martinique and France. Compact disk.

Kassav' Vini Pou. 1987. Holland: CBS CB811. Compact disk.

Konbit: Burning Rhythms of Haiti. 1989. Produced by Jonathan Demme, Fred Paul, and

Gage Averill. Notes by Gage Averill and Jonathan Demme. AandM Records CD 5281. Compact disk.

Kwak a de, vlopé!!! 1994. Jean-Michel Mauriello, ed. France: Hibiscus Records. Compact disk.

Legend: The Legacy of Bob Marley and the Wailers. N.d. Tuff Gong/Island Records. LP disk.

Mario Canonge (et le groupe Kann') retourne aux sources. 1991. S.N.A. 150960, Distribution NATAL, France. Compact disk.

Maroon Music from the Earliest Free Black Communities of Jamaica. 1992. Produced by Kenneth Bilby. Washington, D.C.: Smithsonian/Folkways Recordings CD ST 40412. Compact disk.

Los muñequitos de Matanzas: Vacunao. 1995. Qbadisc QB 9017. Compact disk.

Music from Oriente de Cuba: The Estudiantina Tradition. 1995. Estudiantina Invasora. Nimbus NI 5448. Compact disk.

Music of Haiti, Vols. 1–3: (1) *Folk Music of Haiti;* (2) *Drums of Haiti;* (3) *Songs and Dances of Haiti.* 1952. Recordings and notes by Harold Courlander. Ethnic Folkways FE4403/4407/4432. LP disks.

The Music of Santería: The Oru del Igbodu. 1994. Produced by John Amira. Companion book by John Amira and Steven Cornelius. White Cliffs Media WCM 9346. Compact disk.

Musical Traditions of St. Lucia, West Indies: Dances and Songs from a Caribbean Island. 1993. Compiled by Jocelyne Guilbault and Embert Charles. Smithsonian/Folkways CD SF 40416. Compact disk.

Neville Marcano: The Growling Tiger of Calypso. 1998. Alan Lomax Collection. Rounder CD 1717. Compact disk.

The Original Mambo Kings: An Introduction to Afro-Cubop 1948–1954. 1993. Notes by Max Salazar. Verve 3214-513-876-2. Compact disk.

Orquesta Aragon: The Heart of Havana, Vol. 2. 1993. RCA 3488-2-RL. Compact disk.

Pan Champs, Vols. 1–2. 1990. Blue Rhythm Records. Compact disk.

Pan Jazz 'n' Calypso: Vat 19 Fonclaire Steel Orchestra—Trinidad. 1991. Delos DE 4016. Compact disk.

Panorama: Steelbands of Trinidad and Tobago. 1991. Delos DE 4015. Compact disk.

Pa' que suene el pandero . . . (Plenealo!). c. 1997. (Puerto Rico.) Disco Hit Productions DHCD-8102. Compact disk.

Paracumbé tambó. 1997. Produced by Emanuel Dufrasne González and Nelie Lebón Robles (Puerto Rico). Distributed by Rounder Records. Ashé CD 2005. Compact disk.

Planet Zouk: The World of Antilles Music. 1991. Compiled by Eric Basset. Rhythm Safari CDL 57165. Compact disk.

Los Pleneros de la 21 and Conjunto Melodia Tropical: Puerto Rico, Puerto Rico, mi tierra natal. 1990. Notes by Howard Weiss, Morton Marks, and Ethel Raim. Shanachie SH 65001. Compact disk.

El rey y la reina del merengue. 1996. Johnny Ventura y Milly (Dominican Republic). Sony PROD-7060. Compact disk.

Rhythms of Rapture: Sacred Musics of Haitian Voodou. 1995. Produced by Elizabeth McAlister. Smithsonian/Folkways SF CD 49464. Compact disk.

Roots of Haiti: Voodoo, Vols. 1–6. 1978, 1979. Directed by Jacques Fortère. Produced by Fred Paul. Mini Records MRS 1063-6, 1071, 1073. LP disks.

Sacred Rhythms of Cuban Santería/Ritmos sagrados de la santería cubana. 1995. Centro de Investigación y Desarrollo de la Música Cubana. Smithsonian/Folkways SF CD 40419. Compact disk.

Septetos cubanos: Sones de Cuba. 1990. Produced by Eduardo Llerenas. Música Tradicional MTCD 113/4. Distributed by Rounder. 2 compact disks.

Sing de Chorus: Calypso from Trinidad and Tobago. 1992. Delos DE 4018. Compact disk.

The Skatalites: Scattered Lights. N.d. Alligator Records AL 8309. Compact disk.

Sones cubanos: Sextetos cubanos, Vol. 1, *Sones 1930.* 1991. Produced by Chris Strachwitz and Michael Iván Avalos. Arhoolie CD 7003. Compact disk.

Songs from the North. 1978. Recorded by Verna Gillis. Folkways FE 4284. LP disk.

Spirit Rhythms: Sacred Drumming and Chants from Cuba. N.d. Nueva Generación. Latitudes LT 50603. Compact disk.

The Story of Jamaican Music. 1993. Mango Records 162-539 935-2 (518 399-2). 4 compact disks.

This Is Reggae Music, Vols. 1–5. N.d. Mango Records. Compact disk.

Twenty Reggae Classics, Vols. 1–4. Trojan Records. Compact disk.

Voodoo Trance Music: Ritual Drums of Haiti. 1974. Recordings and notes by Richard Hill and Morton Marks. Lyrichord LLST 7279. LP disk.

West Indies: An Island Carnival. 1991. Produced by Krister Malm. Notes by Daniel Sheehy and Krister Malm. Compact disk.

Where Was Butler? A Calypso Documentary from Trinidad. 1987. Produced by Chris Strachwitz. Notes by Richard K. Spottswood. Folklyric 9048. Compact disk.

Zoop Zoop Zoop: Traditional Music and Folklore of St. Croix, St. Thomas, and St. John. 1993. Notes by Mary Jane Soule. New World Records 80427-2. Compact disk.

Films and Videos of South American, Mexican, Central American, and Caribbean Music

GENERAL

The Americas, 2. 1990. Tomoaki Fujii, ed. Produced by Katsumori Ichikawa. JVC Video Anthology of World Music and Dance, Vol. 28 (VTMV-58). Videocassette.

Central and South America: Mexico, Nicaragua, Peru, Venezuela. 1995. Yuki Okada, director.

JVC/Smithsonian Folkways Video Anthology of World Music and Dance of the Americas, Vol. 6 (VTMV-230). Videocassette.

"Teaching the Music of Hispanic Americans." 1991. Organized by Dale A. Olsen, Linda O'Brien-Rothe, and Daniel E. Sheehy for

Teaching Music with a Multicultural Approach. MENC Preconference Symposium of the Music Educators National Conference Annual Meeting, Washington, D.C., 1990. Reston, Va.: Music Educators National Conference. Videocassette and book.

SOUTH AMERICA

A festa de moça (*The Girl's Celebration*). 1987. Directed by Vincent Carelli. Distributed by Video Data Bank, Chicago, Ill. Videocassette.

An Argentine Journey. 1998. 3-part series: *Songs of the Gauchos*; *Songs of the Argentine Provinces*; *Songs of the Poor*. Princeton, N.J.: Films for the Humanities and Science, distributor. 3 videocassettes.

Apu Condor (*The Condor God*). 1992. Directed by Gianfranco Norelli. Watertown, Mass.: Documentary Educational Resources, distributor. Videocassette.

Bossa Nova: Music and Reminiscences. 1993. Directed by Walter Saslles. Barre, Vt.: Multicultural Media. Videocassette.

Carnival Bahia. 1982. Produced by Carlo Pasini and Peter Fry. Chicago: Films Incorporated Video. Videocassette.

Carnival in Q'eros: Where the Mountains Meet the Jungle. 1990. Written and filmed by John Cohen. Berkeley: University of California Extension Media Center, distributor. Videocassette, 16mm.

Caxiri or Manioc Beer. 1987. Victor Fuks. Bloomington: Indiana University Audio/Visual Center, distributor. Videocassette.

Central and South America: Mexico, Nicaragua, Peru, Venezuela. 1995. Yuki Okada, director. JVC/Smithsonian Folkways Video Anthology of World Music and Dance of the Americas, Vol. 6 (VTMV-230). Videocassette.

El Charanguero: Jaime Torres, the Charango Player. 1996. Produced by Simona and Jeffrey Briggs. Multicultural Media 1007E. Videocassette.

Corpus Christi en Cusco. 1996. Directed by Luis Figueroa. Produced by Juan Ossio. Archive of Traditional Andean Music, Pontífica Universidad Católica del Perú. VAMTA-7. Videocassette. (Festival in Cusco, Peru.)

Las cruces de porcón. 1997. Directed by Gisela Cánepa Koch. Archive of Traditional Andean

Music, Pontífica Universidad Católica del Perú. VAMTA-6. Videocassette. (Festival in Cajamarca, Peru.)

Demonstration of Multiple Relationships between Music and Culture of the Waiãpi. 1989. Victor Fuks. Bloomington: Indiana University Audio/Visual Center, distributor. Videocassette.

Fiesta de la Virgen del Carmen de Paucartambo. 1994. Directed by Gisela Cánepa Koch. Archive of Traditional Andean Music, Pontífica Universidad Católica del Perú. VAMTA-2. Videocassette. (Festival in Paucartambo, Peru.)

Gaiteros: The Music of Northern Colombia. N.d. Produced by Egberto Bermúdez. 3/4-inch videocassette.

Gilberto Gil: Tempo Rei. 1997. Produced and directed by Andrew Weddington et al. Videocassette.

Instrumentos y géneros musicales de Lamayeque. 1994. Directed by Gisela Cánepa Koch. Archive of Traditional Andean Music, Pontífica Universidad Católica del Perú. VAMA-3. Videocassette. (Northern Peru.)

José Carlos and His Spirits: The Ritual Initiation of Zelador Dos Orixas in a Brazilian Umbanda Center. 1989. Produced by Sidney M. Greenfield. Department of Anthropology, University of Wisconsin-Milwaukee. Videocassette.

The Festival of Mamacha Carmen. 1993. Directed by Gisela Cámepa Koch. Archive of Traditional Andean music, Pontífica Universidad Católica del Perú. VAMTA. Videocassette.

La fiesta del agua. 1995. Diected by Gisela Cánepa Koch. Archive of Traditional Andean Music, Pontífica Universidad Católica del Perú. VAMTA-5. Videocassette. (Festival in Huarochirí, Lima, Peru.)

Mamita candelaria. 1996. Directed by Luis Figueroa. Produced by Juan Ossio. Archive of Traditional Andean Music, Pontífica Universidad

Católica del Perú. VAMTA-8. Videocassette. (Festival in Puno, Peru.)

Mountain Music of Peru. 1984. John Cohen. New York: Cinema Guild. Videocassette, 16mm.

Music, Dance, and Festival. 1987. Victor Fuks. Bloomington: Indiana University Audio/Visual Center. Videocassette.

Musical Instruments and Genres of Lambayeque. 1993. Directed by Gisela Cánepa Koch. Archive of Traditional Andean Music, Pontífica Universidad Católica del Perú. VAMTA. Videocassette.

Palenque: Un canto. 1992. Produced and directed by María Raquel Bozzi. Los Angeles, Calif.: María Raquel Bozzi, distributor. Videocasssette. (About San Basilio de Palenque, Colombia.)

Peruvian Weaving: A Continuous Warp. 1980. John Cohen. New York: Cinema Guild. Videocassette, 16mm.

Q'eros: The Shape of Survival. 1979. John Cohen. New York: Cinema Guild. Videocassette, 16mm.

Qoyllur Rit'i: A Woman's Journey. 1999. Produced by Holly Wissler, directed by Gavriela Martínez Escobar. Videocassette.

Shotguns and Accordions: Music of the Marijuana Regions of Colombia. 1983. Beats of the Heart Series. Produced and directed by Jeremy Marre. Shanachie SH-1205. Videocassette.

The Spirit of Samba: Black Music of Brazil. 1983. Beats of the Heart Series. Produced and directed by Jeremy Marre. Shanachie SH-1207. Videocassette.

Survivors of the Rainforest. 1993. Directed by Andy Jillings. London: Channel 4, distributor. Videocassette.

Tinka de Alpaca. 1994. Directed by Gisela Cánepa Koch. Archive of Traditional Andean Music, Pontífica Universidad Católica del Perú. VAMTA-12. Videocassette. (Festival in Arequipa, Peru.)

Toro pucllay: El juego del toro. 1997. Directed by Luis Figueroa. Produced by Juan Ossio. Archive of Traditional Andean Music, Pontífica Universidad Católica del Perú. VAMTA-9. Videocassette. (Festival in Apurímac, Peru.)

Umbanda: The Problem Solver. Produced by Steven Cross and Peter Fry. Chicago: Films Incorporated Video. Videocassette.

Waiampi Instrumental Music. 1987, 1988. Victor Fuks. Bloomington: Indiana University Audio/Visual Center, distributor. Videocassette.

Warao. 1975. Jorge Preloran. University of California, Los Angeles. Videocassette, 16mm.

Wylancha. 1991. Directed by Gisela Cánepa Koch. Archive of Traditional Andean Music, Pontífica Universidad Católica del Perú. VAMTA-4. Videocassette.

Yanomamö. 1975. Napoleon A. Chagnon and Timothy Asch. University of Pennsylvania, distributor. Videocassette, 16mm.

MEXICO AND CENTRAL AMERICA

Central and South America: Mexico, Nicaragua, Peru, Venezuela. 1995. Yuki Okada, director. JVC/Smithsonian Folkways Video Anthology of World Music and Dance of the Americas, Vol. 6 (VTMV-230). Videocassette.

The Devil's Dream. 1992. Mary Ellen Davis. New York: Cinema Guild. 16mm. (About Guatemalan music.)

Enemies of Silence. 1991. Produced by Jeremy Marre. Harcourt Films, London. Videocassette, 16mm. (About two *mariachi* musicians in Mexico.)

Gimme Punta Rock . . . Belizean Music. 1994. Produced by Peter and Suzanne Coonradt. Available from Partners in Video, 3762 Elizabeth Street, Riverside, Calif. 92506. Videocassette.

Huichol Sacred Pilgrimage to Wirikuta. 1991. Produced by Larain Boyll. University of California Extension Center for Media and Independent Learning, Berkeley. Videocassette.

Maya Fiesta. 1988. Produced by Allan F. Burns and Alan Saperstein. Indiantown, Fla.: Corn-Maya. Videocassette. (About the San Miguel festival of Guatemalan migrants in Florida.)

Tex-Mex, Music of the Texas-Mexican Borderlands. Beats of the Heart Series. Produced and directed by Jeremy Matte. Shanachie SH-1206. Videocassette.

CARIBBEAN

Before Reggae Hit the Town. 1992. Produced by Mark Gorney. Berkeley: University of California Extension Center for Media and Independent Learning. Videocassette.

Bob Marley and the Wailers: Time Will Tell. 1991. Commerce, Calif.: Island Visual Arts. Videocassette.

The Bob Marley Story: Caribbean Nights. 1990. Executive Producers: Chris Blackwell and Alan Yentob. Produced by Anthony Walland Nigel Finch. Directed by Jo Mendell and Charles Chabot. Island Records. Videocassette.

Caribbean Crucible. 1984. Directed by Dennis Marks. *Repercussions: A Celebration of African-American Music* (series). Videocassette. (About African background, Dominican Republic, and Jamaica.)

Divine Horsemen: The Living Gods of Haiti. 1985. Filmed by Maya Deren. Mystic Fire M101. Videocassette.

En el país de los Orichas. 1993. Conjunto Folklórico Nacional de Cuba. Brooklyn, N.Y.: Blackmind Book Boutique, distributor. Videocassette.

Haiti: Dreams of Democracy. 1987. Produced and directed by Jonathan Demme and Jo Menell. Clinica Estetico. Videocassette.

The King Does Not Lie: The Initiation of a Shango Priest. 1992. Produced by Judith Gleason and Elisa Mereghette. New York: Filmmakers Library. Videocassette.

Legacy of the Spirits. 1985. Filmed by Karen Kramer. New York: Erzulie Films. 16mm.

Los muñequitos de Matanzas. 1993. Produced by E. Natatcha Estebanez. Boston, Mass.: WGBH Educational Foundation, distributor. Videocassette. (About Cuban music.)

Mas Fever. 1987. Produced by Glen Micallef and Larry Johnson. Filmsound Video, Videocassette.

Oggun. 1993. Conjunto Folklórico Nacional de Cuba. Brooklyn, N.Y.: Blackmind Book Boutique, distributor. Videocassette.

Pan in A Minor and Steel Bands of Trinidad. N.d. Produced by Daniel Verba and Jean-Jacques Mrejen. Villon Films.

Roots Rock Reggae: Jamaican Music. 1988. Beats of the Heart Series. Produced and directed by Jeremy Marre. Shanachie SH-1202. Videocassette.

Routes of Rhythm. c. 1993. Narrated by Harry Belafonte. Distributed by Multicultural Media. 3 videocassettes and study guide. (Cuban music and dance.)

Rumbas y comparsas de Cuba. 1993. Brooklyn, N.Y.: Blackmind Book Boutique, distributor. Videocassette.

Salsa: Latin Pop in the Cities. 1983. Beats of the Heart Series. Produced and directed by Jeremy Marre. Shanachie SH-1201. Videocassette.

Sworn to the Drum: A Tribute to Francisco Aguabella. 1995. Directed by Les Blank. El Cerrito, Calif.: Flower Films, distributor. Videocassette, 16mm.

Voices of the Orishas. 1994. Produced and directed by Alvaro Pérez Betancourt. Berkeley: University of California Extension Center for Media and Independent Learning. Videocassette.

The United States
and Canada

Publications on the Music of the United States and Canada

GENERAL

Abrahams, Roger D. 1992. *Singing the Master: The Emergence of African American Folk Culture in the Plantation South*. New York: Pantheon.

Adjaye, Joseph K., and Adrianne R. Andrews, eds. 1997. *Language, Rhythm and Sound: Black Popular Cultures into the Twenty-First Century*. Pittsburgh: University of Pittsburgh Press.

Adorno, Theodor. 1998. *Introduction to the Sociology of Music*, trans. E. B. Ashton. New York: Continuum.

Ahlquist, Karen. 1997. *Democracy at the Opera: Music, Theater, and Culture in New York City, 1815–1860*. Chicago: University of Illinois Press.

Alba, Richard D. 1990. *Ethnic Identity: The Transformation of White America*. New Haven, Conn.: Yale University Press.

Allen, James Paul. 1988. *We the People: An Atlas of America's Ethnic Diversity*. New York: Macmillan.

Allen, Ray, and Lois Wilcken, eds. 1998. *Island Sounds in the Global City: Caribbean Popular Music and Identity in New York*. New York: Brooklyn College and New York Folklore Society and the Institute for Studies in American Music.

Ammer, Christine. 1980. *Unsung: A History of Women in American Music*. Contributions in Women's Studies 14. Westport, Conn.: Greenwood.

Amoss, Pamela. 1978. *Coast Salish Spirit Dancing: The Survival of an Ancestral Religion*. Seattle: University of Washington Press.

Aparicio, Frances R. 1998. *Listening to Salsa: Gender, Latin Popular Music, and Puerto Rican Cultures*. Middletown, Conn.: Wesleyan University Press.

Arts in America 1990: The Bridge between Creativity and Community. 1990. Washington, D.C.: National Endowment for the Arts.

Attali, Jacques. 1985. *Noise: The Political Economy of Music*, trans. Brian Massumi. Minneapolis: University of Minnesota Press.

Auerbach, Susan. 1994. *Encyclopedia of Multiculturalism*. New York: Marshall Cavendish.

Austin, William W. 1987. *"Susanna," "Jeanie," and "The Old Folks at Home": The Songs of Stephen C. Foster from His Time to Ours*, 2nd ed. Urbana: University of Illinois Press.

Barbeau, Marius. 1946. *Alouette*. Montréal: Thériens.

Barlow, William. 1999. *Voice Over: The Making of Black Radio*. Philadelphia: Temple University Press.

Beckwith, John. 1997. *Music Papers: Articles and Talks by a Canadian Composer 1961–1994*. Ottawa: The Golden Dog Press.

Berland, Jody. 1988. "Locating Listening: Technological Space, Popular Music, Canadian Mediations." *Cultural Studies* 2(3):343–358.

———. 1990. "Radio Space and Industrial Time: Music Formats, Local Narratives and Technological Mediation." *Popular Music* 9(2):179–192.

———. 1994a. "Radio Space and Industrial Time: The Case of Music Formats." In *Canadian Music: Issues of Hegemony and Identity*, ed. Beverley Diamond and Robert Witmer, 173–188. Toronto: Canadian Scholars' Press.

———. 1994b. "Toward a Creative Anachronism: Radio, the State, and Sound Government." In *Radio Rethink: Art, Sound, and Transmission*, ed. D. Augaitis and D. Lander, 33–44. Banff: Walter Phillips Gallery, Banff Centre for the Arts.

———. 1998. "Locating Listening: Technological Space, Popular Music, and Canadian Mediations." In *The Place of Music*, ed. Andrew Leyshon, David Matless, and George Revill, 129–150. New York: Guilford.

Bindas, Kenneth J. 1995. *All of This Music Belongs to the Nation: The WPA's Federal Music Project and American Society, 1935–1939*. Knoxville: University of Tennessee Press.

Birosek, Patti Jean. 1989. *The New Age Music Guide*. New York: Collier.

Boas, Franz. 1966. *Kwakiutl Ethnography*, ed. Helen Codere. Chicago: University of Chicago Press.

Boggs, Vernon, ed. 1992. *Salsiology: Afro-Cuban Music and the Evolution of Salsa in New York City*. New York: Greenwood.

Breton, Raymond. 1980. *Cultural Boundaries and the Cohesion of Canada*. Montréal: Institute for Research on Public Policy.

Broughton, Simon, et al., eds. 1994. *World Music: The Rough Guide*. London: Rough Guides.

Brown, Charles T. 1983. *The Rock and Roll Story: From the Sounds of Rebellion to an American Art Form*. Englewood Cliffs, N.J.: Prentice Hall.

Brown, Royal S. 1994. *Overtones and Undertones: Reading Film Music*. Berkeley: University of California Press.

Broyles, Michael. 1992. *"Music of the Highest Class": Elitism and Populism in Antebellum Boston*. New Haven, Conn.: Yale University Press.

Burnett, Robert. 1996. *The Global Jukebox*. London: Routledge.

Cage, John. 1961. *Silence: Lectures and Writings*. Middletown, Conn.: Wesleyan University Press.

Camus, Raoul François. 1980. "Military Music of Colonial Boston. In *Music in Colonial Massachusetts, 1630–1820*, Vol 1: *Music in Public Places*, 75–103. Boston: Colonial Society of Massachusetts and University Press of Virginia.

Carder, Polly, ed. 1990. *The Eclectic Curriculum in American Music Education*, rev. 2nd ed. Reston, Va.: Music Educators National Conference.

Casey, Betty. 1985. *Dance Across Texas*. Austin: University of Texas Press.

Cateforis, Theo, and Elena Humphreys. 1997. "Constructing Communities and Identities: Riot Grrl New York City." In *Musics of Multicultural America*, ed. Kip Lornell and Anne K. Rasmussen, 317–342. New York: Prentice Hall.

Cavanagh, Beverley (Diamond). 1989. "Writing about Music and Gender in the Sub-Arctic Algonquian Area." In *Women in North American Music: Six Essays*, ed. Richard Keeling, 55–66. Special Series, 6. Bloomington, Ind.: Society for Ethnomusicology.

Chadabe, Joel. 1997. *Electric Sound: The Past and Promise of Electronic Music*. Englewood Cliffs, N.J.: Prentice Hall.

Chase, Gilbert. 1987 [1955]. *America's Music: From the Pilgrims to the Present*. New York: McGraw-Hill.

Child, Francis James. 1882–1898. *The English and Scottish Popular Ballads*. Boston: Houghton Mifflin.

Chiswick, Barry R., ed. 1992. *Immigration, Language, and Ethnicity: Canada and the United States*. Washington, D.C.: AEI.

Choksy, Lois, Robert Abramson, David Woods, and Avon Gillespie. 1986. *Teaching Music in the Twentieth Century*. Englewood Cliffs, N.J.: Prentice Hall.

Clément, Catherine. 1988. *Opera, or the Undoing of Women*, trans. Betsy Wong. Minneapolis: University of Minnesota Press.

Cockrell, Dale. 1997. *Demons of Disorder: Early Blackface Minstrels and Their World*. Cambridge: Cambridge University Press.

Cohen, Norm. 1981. *Long Steel Rail: The Railroad in American Folksong*. Urbana: University of Illinois Press.

Cohen, Selma Jeanne, ed. 1998. *International Encyclopedia of Dance*. New York: Oxford University Press.

Collier, Cliff, and Pierre Guilmette. 1982. *Dance Resources in Canadian Libraries*. Ottawa: National Library of Canada.

Cook, Susan C., and Judy S. Tsou, eds. 1994. *Cecilia Reclaimed: Feminist Perspectives on Gender and Music*. Urbana: University of Illinois Press.

Covach, John, and Graeme M. Boone, eds. 1997. *Understanding Rock: Essays in Musical Analysis*. New York: Oxford University Press.

Crawford, Richard. 1993. *The American Musical Landscape*. Berkeley: University of California Press.

Daniel, Linda J. 1999. "Singing Out! Canadian Women in Country Music." D.Ed. dissertation, Ontario Institute for the Study of Education, University of Toronto.

Daniel, Ralph. 1966. *The Anthem in New England before 1800*. Evanston, Ill.: Northwestern University Press.

Dannen, Frederic. 1990. *Record Men: Power Brokers and Fast Money inside the Music Business*. New York: Times Books.

Davis, Mary B., ed. 1994. *Native America in the Twentieth Century: An Encyclopedia*. New York: Garland.

Denisoff, R. Serge. 1971. *Great Day Coming: Folk Music and the American Left*. Chicago: University of Illinois Press.

Densmore, Frances. 1918. *Teton Sioux Music*. Bureau of American Ethnology Bulletin 61. Washington, D.C.: Smithsonian Institution.

———. 1923. *Mandan and Hidatsa Music*. Bureau of American Ethnology Bulletin 80. Washington, D.C.: Smithsonian Institution.

———. 1939. *Nootka and Quileute Music*. Bureau of American Ethnology Bulletin 124. Washington, D.C.: Smithsonian Institution.

———. 1943. *Music of the Indians of British Columbia*. Bureau of American Ethnology Bulletin 136. Washington, D.C.: Smithsonian Institution.

Desmond, Jane C. 1997. "Embodying Difference: Issues in Dance and Cultural Studies." In *Everynight Life: Culture and Dance in Latino America*, ed. Celeste Frasier Delgado and José Esteban Muñoz, 33–64. Durham, N.C.: Duke University Press.

Diamond, Beverley. 2000. *Gender and Music: Negotiating Shifting Worlds*. Urbana: University of Illinois Press.

Diamond, Beverley, and Robert Witmer, eds. 1994. *Canadian Music: Issues of Hegemony and Identity*. Toronto: Canadian Scholars' Press.

DiMaggio, Paul. 1972. "Country Music: Ballad of the Silent Majority." In *The Sounds of Social Change*, ed. R. Denisoff and R. Peterson, 31–56. Chicago: Rand McNally.

Dorland, Michael. 1996. *The Cultural Industries in Canada: Problems, Policies, and Prospects*. Toronto: James Lorimer.

Driedger, Leo, ed. 1978. *The Canadian Ethnic Mosaic*. Canadian Ethnic Studies Association Series, 6. Toronto: McClelland and Stewart.

Drucker, Philip. 1940. "Kwakiutl Dancing Societies." *Anthropological Records* 2(6):201–230. Berkeley: University of California Press.

———. 1951. *The Northern and Central Nootkan Tribes*. Bureau of American Ethnology Bulletin 144. Washington, D.C.: Smithsonian Institution.

———. 1963. *Indians of the Northwest Coast*. Garden City, N.Y.: Natural History.

———. 1965. *Cultures of the North Pacific Coast*. San Francisco: Chandler.

Dwight, John Sullivan, ed. 1852–1881. *Dwight's Journal of Music*. Boston: Houghton Osgood.

Eisenberg, Evan. 1987. *The Recording Angel: Music, Records, and Culture from Aristotle to Zappa*. New York: McGraw-Hill.

Eisler, Hanns, and Theodor Adorno. 1947. *Composing for the Films*. New York: Oxford University Press.

Epstein, Dena J. 1977. *Sinful Tunes and Spirituals: Black Folk Music to the Civil War*. Urbana: University of Illinois Press.

Escott, Colin, and Martin Hawkins. 1991. *Good Rockin' Tonight: Sun Records and the Birth of Rock 'n' Roll*. New York: St. Martin's.

Ewen, David. 1962. *Popular American Composers, from Revolutionary Times to the Present*. New York: H. W. Wilson.

———. 1977. *All the Years of American Popular Music*. Englewood Cliffs, N.J.: Prentice Hall.

Ewen, David, ed. 1966. *American Popular Songs from the Revolutionary War to the Present*. New York: Random House.

Faris, James C. 1990. *The Nightway: A History and a History of Documentation of a Navajo Ceremonial*. Albuquerque: University of New Mexico Press.

Fiske, Roger. 1973. *English Theater Music in the Eighteenth Century*. London: Oxford University Press.

Fletcher, Alice C., and Francis La Flesche. 1970 [1911]. "The Omaha Tribe." In *Twenty-Seventh Annual Report of the U. S. Bureau of American Ethnology to the Secretary of the Smithsonian Institution, 1905–1906*, 19–672. New York: Johnson Reprint. (Reprint.)

Flinn, Caryl. 1992. *Strains of Utopia: Gender, Nostalgia, and Hollywood Film Music*. Princeton, N.J.: Princeton University Press.

Ford, Clifford. 1982. *Canada's Music: An Historical Survey*. Agincourt, Ont.: GLC.

Friedlander, Paul. 1996. *Rock and Roll: A Social History*. Boulder, Colo.: Westview.

Frisbie, Charlotte J. 1987. *Navajo Medicine Bundles or Jish: Acquisition, Transmission, and Disposition in the Past and Present*. Albuquerque: University of New Mexico Press.

Frith, Simon. 1978. *The Sociology of Rock*. London: Constable.

Frith, Simon, and Andrew Goodwin, eds. 1990. *On Record: Rock, Pop, and the Written Word*. New York: Pantheon.

Gaar, Gillian G. 1992. *She's a Rebel: The History of Women in Rock and Roll*. Seattle: Seal.

Gagnon, Ernest. 1865. *Chansons populaires du Canada*. Québec: Bureau du "Foyer Canadien."

———. 1935 [1865, 1880]. *Chansons populaires du Canada*. Montréal: Beauchemin.

Garofalo, Reebee. 1997. *Rockin' Out: Popular Music in the U.S.A.* Boston: Allyn and Bacon.

Garofalo, Reebee, and Steve Chapple. 1977. *Rock and Roll Is Here to Pay: The History and Politics of the Music Industry*. Chicago: Nelson Hall.

Giglio, Virginia. 1994. *Southern Cheyenne Women's Songs*. Norman: University of Oklahoma Press.

Gillett, Charlie. 1970. *The Sound of The City: The Rise of Rock and Roll*. London: Souvenir Press.

Goldstein, Paul. 1994. *Copyright's Highway: From Gutenberg to the Celestial Jukebox*. New York: Hill and Wang.

Green, J. Paul, and Nancy F. Vogan. 1991. *Music Education in Canada: A Historical Account*. Toronto: University of Toronto Press.

Green, Mildred Denby. 1983. *Black Women Composers: A Genesis*. Boston: Twayne.

Grenier, Line. 1993. "Policing French-Language Music on Canadian Radio: The Twilight of the Popular Record Era?" In *Rock and Popular Music: Politics, Policies, Institutions*, ed. Tony Bennett, Simon Frith, Lawrence Grossberg, John Shepherd, and Graeme Turner, 119–141. London: Routledge.

Guralnick, Peter. 1994. *Last Train to Memphis: The Rise of Elvis Presley*. New York: Little, Brown.

Halpern, Ida. 1968. "Music of the B.C. Northwest Coast Indians." In *Centennial Workshop on Ethnomusicology*, 23–42. Vancouver: University of British Columbia.

Hamm, Charles. 1979. *Yesterdays: Popular Song in America*. New York: Norton.

———. 1983. *Music in the New World*. New York: Norton.

Hampton, Wayne. 1986. *Guerrilla Minstrels*. Knoxville: University of Tennessee Press.

Handy, D. Antoinette. 1981. *Black Women in American Bands and Orchestras*. Metuchen, N.J.: Scarecrow.

Hayward, Victoria. 1922. *Romantic Canada*. Toronto: Macmillan Canada.

Hitchcock, H. Wiley. 1988. *Music in the United States: A Historical Introduction*, 3rd ed. Englewood Cliffs, N.J.: Prentice Hall.

Hitchcock, H. Wiley, and Stanley Sadie, eds. 1986. *The New Grove Dictionary of American Music*. London: Macmillan.

Hood, George. 1846. *History of Music in New England, with Biographical Sketches of Reformers and Psalmists*. Boston: Wilkins, Carter.

Howard, John Tasker. 1931. *Our American Music: Three Hundred Years of It*. New York: Crowell. (Rev. eds.: 1939, 1946, 1965.)

Jackson, George Pullen. 1943. *White and Negro Spirituals*. Locust Valley N.Y.: J. J. Augustin.

Johnston, Thomas F. 1975. "Eskimo Music of the Northern Interior Alaska." *Polar Notes* 14:54–57.

Kallmann, Helmut. 1960. *A History of Music in Canada 1534–1914*. Toronto: University of Toronto Press.

Kallmann, Helmut, Gilles Potvin, and Kenneth Winters, eds. 1992. *Encyclopedia of Music in Canada*, 2nd ed. Toronto: Toronto University Press.

Kassabian, Anahid. 2000. *Hearing Film: Tracking Identifications in Contemporary Hollywood Film Music*. New York: Routledge.

Keeling, Richard, ed. 1989. *Women in North American Indian Music: Six Essays*. Special Series, 6. Bloomington, Ind.: Society for Ethnomusicology.

Keil, Charles, and Steven Feld, eds. 1994. *Music Grooves*. Chicago: University of Chicago Press.

Kingman, Daniel. 1998. *American Music: A Panorama*. New York: Schirmer.

Kivi, K. Linda. 1992. *Canadian Women Making Music*. Toronto: Green Dragon.

Klassen, Doreen Helen. 1989. *Singing Mennonite: Low German Songs among the Mennonites*. Winnipeg: University of Manitoba Press.

Kodish, Debora. 1986. *Good Friends and Bad Enemies: Robert Winslow Gordon and the Study of American Folksong*. Urbana: University of Illinois Press.

Korson, George. 1927. *Songs and Ballads of the Anthracite Miner*. New York: F. H. Hitchcock.

Koskoff, Ellen, ed. 1989. *Women and Music in Cross-Cultural Perspective*. Urbana: University of Illinois Press.

Kostelanetz, Richard, ed. 1996. *Classic Essays on Twentieth-Century Music: A Continuing Symposium*. New York: Schirmer.

Laing, Dave. 1985. *One Chord Wonders: Power and Meaning in Punk Rock*. Philadelphia: Open University Press.

Lambert, Barbara, ed. 1985. *Music in Colonial Massachusetts, 1630–1820*. 2 vols. Boston: Colonial Society of Massachusetts.

Lang, Andrew. 1895. *Border Ballads*. London: Lawrence and Bullen.

Larson, Gary O. 1983. *The Reluctant Patron: The United States Government and the Arts, 1943–1965*. Philadelphia: University of Pennsylvania Press.

Lewis, Lisa A. 1990. *Gender Politics and MTV*. Philadelphia: Temple University Press.

Linn, Karen. 1991. *That Half-Barbaric Twang: The Banjo in American Popular Culture*. Urbana: University of Illinois Press.

Lomax, John. 1910. *Cowboy Songs and Other Frontier Ballads*. New York: Sturgis and Walton.

Lomax, John A., and Alan Lomax. 1934. *American Ballads and Folk Songs*. New York: Macmillan.

Lomax, John A., and Alan Lomax. 1947. *Folk Song U.S.A.* New York: Duell, Sloan, and Pearce.

Lott, Eric. 1993. *Love and Theft: Blackface Minstrelsy, and the American Working Class*. New York: Oxford University Press.

Lull, James, ed. 1987. *Popular Music and Communication*. Newbury Park, Calif.: Sage.

Lum, Casey Man Kong. 1996. *In Search of a Voice: Karaoke and the Construction of Identity in Chinese America*. Mahwah, N.J.: Lawrence Erlbaum.

Magocsi, Paul, ed. 1988. *Encyclopedia of Canada's Peoples*. Toronto: University of Toronto Press.

Malm, Krister, and Roger Wallace. 1992. *Media Policy and Music Activity*. London: Routledge.

Malone, Bill C. 1985. *Country Music U.S.A.*, rev ed. Austin: University of Texas Press.

Manning, Peter. 1993. *Electronic and Computer Music*. Oxford: Clarendon.

Marco, Guy A., ed. 1993. *Encyclopedia of Recorded Sound in the United States*. New York: Garland.

Marcus, Greil. 1975. *Mystery Train: Images of America in Rock 'n' Roll Music*. New York: Dutton.

Mark, Michael L., and Charles L. Gary. 1992. *A History of American Music Education*. New York: Schirmer.

Mason, Lowell. 1839. "Historical Sketches of Sacred and Church Music, from the Earliest Times to the Present." *Boston Musical Gazette* 1:51, 57, 65–66, 83, 97–98, 105, 113, 122, 130, 139.

Mates, Julian. 1985. *America's Musical Stage: Two Hundred Years of Musical Theater*. Westport, Conn.: Greenwood.

Mayer, Margaret M. 1994. *The American Dream: American Popular Music*. Bethesda, Md.: Front Desk.

McClary, Susan. 1991. *Feminine Endings: Music, Gender, Sexuality*. Minneapolis: University of Minnesota Press.

McGee, Timothy J., ed. 1995. *Taking a Stand: Essays in Honour of John Beckwith*. Toronto: University of Toronto Press.

McKay, Ian. 1994. *The Quest of the Folk: Anti-modernism and Cultural Selection in Twentieth-Century Nova Scotia*. Montreal and Kingston: McGill Queen's University Press.

Mellers, Wilfrid. 1964. *Music in a New Found Land: Themes and Developments in the History of American Music*. London: Barrie and Rockcliffe.

Millard, André. 1995. *America on Record: A History of Recorded Sound*. Cambridge: Cambridge University Press.

Mishler, Craig. 1993. *The Crooked Stovepipe: Athapaskan Fiddle Music and Square Dancing in Northeast Alaska and Northwest Canada*. Urbana: University of Illinois Press.

Moffitt, W. O. 1878. *The National Temperance Songster*. Debuque, Iowa: Gay and Schermerhorn.

Moogk, Edward B. 1975. *Roll Back the Years: A History of Canadian Recorded Sound and Its Legacy, Genesis to 1930*. Ottawa: National Library of Canada.

Morris, Robert. 1997. "Milton Babbitt's Electronic Music: The Medium and the Message." *Perspectives of New Music* 35(2):85–99.

Naimpally, Anuradha. 1988. "The Teaching of Bharata Natyam in Canada: Modifications within the Canadian Context." Master's thesis, York University.

Negus, Keith. 1992. *Producing Pop: Culture and Conflict in the Popular Music Industry*. London: Edward Arnold.

Peacock, Kenneth. 1966. *Twenty Ethnic Songs from Western Canada*. Ottawa: National Museum of Canada.

Pegley, Karen. 1998. "Femme Fatale and Lesbian Representation in Alban Berg's Lulu." In *Encrypted Messages in Alban Berg's Music*, ed. Siglind Bruhn, 249–277. New York: Garland.

———. 1999. "An Analysis of the Construction of National, Racial, and Gendered Identities on MuchMusic (Canada) and MTV (U.S.)." Ph.D. dissertation, York University.

Pendle, Karin, ed. 1997. "American Women Composers." *Contemporary Music Review* 16(1–2).

Peretti, Burton W. 1992. *The Creation of Jazz: Music, Race, and Culture in Urban America*. Urbana: University of Illinois Press.

Peterson, Elizabeth. 1996. *The Changing Faces of Tradition: A Report on the Folk and Traditional Arts in the United States*. Washington, D.C.: National Endowment for the Arts.

Porter, Susan L. 1991. *With an Air Debonair: Musical Theater in America, 1785–1815*. Washington, D.C.: Smithsonian Institution Press.

Preston, Katherine K. 1993. *Opera on the Road: Traveling Opera Companies in the United States, 1825–1860*. Urbana: University of Illinois Press.

Proctor, George A. 1980. *Canadian Music of the Twentieth Century*. Toronto: University of Toronto Press.

Qureshi, Regula Burckhardt. 1972. "Ethnomusicological Research among Canadian Communities of Arab and East Indian Origin." *Ethnomusicology* 16(3):381–396.

Radano, Ronald, and Philip V. Bohlman, eds. 2000. *Music and the Racial Imagination*. Chicago Studies in Ethnomusicology. Chicago: University of Chicago Press.

Rapée, Erno. 1978 [1970]. *Encyclopedia of Music for Pictures*. New York: Ayer.

Riis, Thomas L. 1989. *Just before Jazz: Black Musical Theater in New York, 1890–1915*. Washington, D.C.: Smithsonian Institution Press.

Roberts, Helen H. 1936. *Musical Areas in Aboriginal North America*. Publications in Anthropology, 12. New Haven, Conn.: Yale University Press.

Rockwell, John. 1983. *All American Music*. New York: Knopf.

Root, Deane L. 1981. *American Popular Stage Music: 1860–1880*. Ann Arbor, Mich.: UMI Research Press.

Rose, Tricia. 1994. *Black Noise: Rap Music and Black Culture in Contemporary America*. Hanover, N.H.: University Press of New England.

Rosenberg, Neil V., ed. 1993. *Transforming Tradition: Folk Music Revivals Examined*. Chicago: University of Illinois Press.

Ryan, John. 1985. *The Production of Culture in the Music Industry: The ASCAP-BMI Controversy*. Lanham, Md.: University Press of America.

Sakolsky, Ron, and Fred Ho. 1995. *Sounding Off: Music as Subversion/Resistance/Revolution*. New York: Autonomedia.

Sanjek, Russell. 1988. *American Popular Music and Its Business: The First Four Hundred Years*. New York: Oxford University Press.

Sanjek, Russell, and David Sanjek. 1991. *American Popular Music Business in the Twentieth Century*. New York: Oxford University Press.

Schramm, A. Reyes. 1975. "The Role of Music in the Interaction of Black Americans and Hispanos in New York City's East Harlem." Ph.D. dissertation, Columbia University.

Scott, Derek. 1989. *The Singing Bourgeois: Songs of the Victorian Drawing Room and Parlour*. Milton Keynes, Eng.: Open University Press.

Seeger, Charles. 1945. "Music in the Americas: Oral and Written Traditions in the Americas." *Bulletin of the Pan American Union* 79:290–293, 341–344.

Shepherd, John, Phil Virden, Graham Vulliamy, and Trevor Wishart, eds. 1977. *Whose Music? A Sociology of Musical Languages*. New Brunswick, N.J.: Transaction.

Slobin, Mark. 1993. *Subcultural Sounds: Micromusics of the West*. Hanover and London: Wesleyan University Press.

Small, Christopher. 1996. *Music, Society, Education*. Hanover, N.H.: University Press of New England.

Smith, Jeff. 1998. *The Sounds of Commerce: Marketing Popular Film Music*. New York: Columbia University Press.

Sonneck, O. G. 1916 [1913]. *A Survey of Music in America*. Reprinted in O. G. Sonneck, *Suum Cuique: Essays on Music*, 121–124. New York: Schirmer.

Sonneck, Oscar George Theodore. 1983. *Oscar Sonneck and American Music*. Urbana: University of Illinois Press.

Spaeth, Sigmund. 1948. *A History of Popular Music in America*. New York: Random House.

Spencer, Peter. 1992. *World Beat: A Listener's Guide to Contemporary World Music on CD*. Pennington, N.J.: A Capella.

Stevenson, Robert. 1970. *Philosophies of American Music History*. Washington, D.C.: Library of Congress.

Straw, Will. 1996. "Sound Recording." In *The Cultural Industries in Canada: Problems, Policies, and Prospects*, ed. Michael Dorland, 95–117. Toronto: James Lorimer.

Supicí, Ivan. 1987. *Music in Society: A Guide to the Sociology of Music* (*Elementi sociologije muzike*). Stuyvesant, N.Y.: Pendragon.

Swain, Joseph P. 1990. *The Broadway Musical: A Critical and Musical Survey*. New York: Oxford University Press.

Swiss, Thomas, John Sloop, and Andrew Herman, eds. 1997. *Mapping the Beat: Popular Music and Contemporary Theory*. London: Blackwell.

Szatmary, David P. 1996. *A Time to Rock: A Social History of Rock-and-Roll*. New York: Schirmer.

Tawa, Nicholas E. 1980. *Sweet Songs for Gentle Americans: The Parlor Song in America, 1790–1860*. Bowling Green, Ohio: Bowling Green University Popular Press.

———. 1982. *A Sound of Strangers: Musical Culture, Acculturation, and the Post–Civil War Ethnic American*. Metuchen, N.J.: Scarecrow.

———. 1990. *The Way to Tin Pan Alley: American Popular Song*. New York: Schirmer.

Taylor, Timothy D. 1997. *Global Pop: World Music, World Markets*. New York: Routledge.

Théberge, Paul. 1997. *Any Sound You Can Imagine: Making Music/Consuming Technology*. Hanover, N.H.: University Press of New England.

Tick, Judith. 1983. *American Women Composers before 1870*. Rochester, N.Y.: University of Rochester.

Tosches, Nick. 1984. *Unsung Heroes of Rock 'n' Roll*. New York: Scribner.

Van Zile, Judy. 1982. *The Japanese Bon Dance in Hawaii*. Kailua, Hawaii: Press Pacifica.

Vander, Judith. 1988. *Songprints: The Musical Experience of Five Shoshone Women*. Urbana and Chicago: University of Illinois Press.

Ventura, Michael. 1985. "White Boys Dancing." In *Shadow Dancing in the USA*, 42–51. Los Angeles: Tarchor.

Voyer, Simone. 1986. *La danse traditionnelle dans l'est du Canada: Quadrilles et cotillon*. Québec: Presses de l'Université Laval.

Waksman, Steve. 1999. *Instruments of Desire: The Electric Guitar and the Shaping of Musical Experience*. Cambridge: Harvard University Press.

Walser, Robert. 1993. *Running with the Devil: Power, Gender, and Madness in Heavy Metal Music*. Hanover, N.H.: University Press of New England.

Walter, Arnold, ed. 1969. *Aspects of Music in Canada*. Toronto: University of Toronto Press.

Ward, Brian. 1998. *Just My Soul Responding: Rhythm and Blues, Black Consciousness, and Race Relations*. London: University College London Press.

Wilgus, Donald K. 1959. *Anglo-American Folksong Scholarship since 1898*. New Brunswick, N.J.: Rutgers University Press.

Wilson, Pamela. 1998. "Mountains of Contradictions: Gender, Class, and Region in the Star Image of Dolly Parton." In *Reading Country Music*, ed. Cecelia Tichi, 98–120. Durham, N.C.: Duke University Press.

Witmer, Robert, ed. 1990. *Ethnomusicology in Canada: Proceedings of the First Conference on Ethnomusicology in Canada*. Toronto: Institute for Canadian Music.

AMERICAN INDIANS, FIRST NATIONS

Adams, Robert H. 1991 [1977]. *Songs of Our Grandfathers: Music of the Unami Delaware Indians*. Dewey, Okla.: Touching Leaves Indian Crafts.

American Folklife Center. 1984–1990. *The Federal Cylinder Project: A Guide to Field Cylinder Collections in Federal Agencies*. Washington, D.C.: American Folklife Center, Library of Congress.

Amoss, Pamela. 1978. *Coast Salish Spirit Dancing: The Survival of an Ancestral Religion*. Seattle: University of Washington Press.

Asch, Michael. 1988. *Kinship and the Drum Dance in a Northern Dene Community*. Edmonton: Boreal Institute for Northern Studies.

Bahr, Donald M., and Richard J. Haefer. 1974. *Piman Shamanism and Staying Sickness (Ka:cim Mumkidag)*. Tucson: University of Arizona Press.

Bahti, Tom. 1970. *Southwestern Indian Ceremonials*. Flagstaff, Ariz.: KC.

Beaudry, Nicole. 1986. "La danse à tambour des Esquimaux yupik du sud-ouest de l'Alaska: performance et contexte." Ph.D. dissertation, Université de Montréal.

Black Bear, Ben, Sr., and R. D. Theisz. 1976. *Songs and Dances of the Lakota*. Rosebud, S. Dak.: Sinte Gleska College.

Boas, Franz. 1966. *Kwakiutl Ethnography*, ed. Helen Codere. Chicago: University of Chicago Press.

———. 1888. *The Central Eskimo*. Sixth Annual Report of the Bureau of American Ethnology. Washington: Smithsonian Institution.

Brown, Donald N. 1962. *Masks, Mantas, and Moccasins: Dance Costumes of the Pueblo Indians*. Colorado Springs: Taylor Museum.

Browner, Tara Colleen. 1995. "Transposing Cultures: The Appropriation of Native North American Musics, 1890–1990." Ph.D. dissertation, University of Michigan.

Callahan, Alice A. 1990. *The Osage Ceremonial Dance I'n-Lon-Schka*. Norman: University of Oklahoma Press.

Cavanagh, Beverley. 1982. *Music of the Netsilik Eskimo: A Study of Stability and Change*. 2 vols. Mercury Series, 82. Ottawa: National Museum of Man. (Record included. LP disk.)

Cole, Douglas, and Ira Chaikin. 1990. *An Iron Hand upon the People: The Law against the Potlatch on the Northwest Coast*. Seattle: University of Washington Press.

Curtis, Natalie. 1905. *Songs of Ancient America: Three Pueblo Indian Corn-Grinding Songs from Laguna, New Mexico*. New York: Schirmer.

Densmore, Frances. 1910–1913. *Chippewa Music*. 2 vols. Bureau of American Ethnology Bulletin 45, 53. Washington, D.C.: Smithsonian Institution.

———. 1918. *Teton Sioux Music and Culture*. Washington, D.C.: U.S. Government Printing Office. Bureau of American Ethnology, Bulletin 61. Reprint, Lincoln: University of Nebraska Press, 1992.

———. 1921. *Indian Action Songs*. Boston: C. C. Birchard.

———. 1922. *Northern Ute Music*. Bureau of American Ethnology Bulletin 75. Washington, D.C.: Smithsonian Institution.

———. 1923. *Mandan and Hidatsa Music*. Bureau of American Ethnology Bulletin 80. Washington, D.C.: Smithsonian Institution.

———. 1926. *The American Indians and Their Music*. New York: Woman's Press.

———. 1929. *Chippewa Customs*. Bureau of American Ethnology Bulletin 86. Washington, D.C.: Smithsonian Institution.

———. 1929. *Papago Music*. Bureau of American Ethnology Bulletin 90. Washington, D.C.: Smithsonian Institution.

———. 1932. *Menominee Music*. Bureau of American Ethnology Bulletin 102. Washington, D.C.: Smithsonian Institution.

———. 1936. *Cheyenne and Arapaho Music*. Southwest Museum Papers, No. 10. Los Angeles: Southwest Museum.

———. 1939. *Nootka and Quileute Music*. Bureau of American Ethnology Bulletin 124. Washington, D.C.: Smithsonian Institution.

———. 1942. "The Study of Indian Music." From the Annual Report of the Smithsonian Institution for 1941. Publication 3671. Washington, D.C.: U.S. Government Printing Office.

———. 1953. "The Use of Music in the Treatment of the Sick by American Indians." From the Annual Report of the Smithsonian Institution for 1952. Publication 4128. Washington, D.C.: U.S. Government Printing Office.

———. 1957. *Music of Acoma, Isleta, Cochiti, and Zuñi Pueblos*. Bureau of American Ethnology Bulletin 165. Washington, D.C.: Smithsonian Institution.

———. 1958. *Music of the Maidu Indians of California*. Los Angeles: Southwest Museum.

———. 1958. *Seminole Music*. Bureau of American Ethnology Bulletin No. 141. Washington, D.C.: Smithsonian Institution.

———. 1972 [1943]. *Choctaw Music*. New York: Da Capo.

———. 1979. *Chippewa Customs*. Minneapolis: Minnesota Historical Society Press.

Diamond, Beverley, et al. 1994. *Visions of Sound: Musical Instruments of First Nations Communities in Northeastern America*. Chicago: University of Chicago Press; Waterloo: Wilfrid Laurier University Press.

Dyal, Susan. 1985. *Preserving Traditional Arts: A Toolkit for Native American Communities*. Los Angeles: University of California American Indian Studies Center.

Enrico, John, and Wendy Bross Stuart. 1996. *Northern Haida Songs*. Lincoln: University of Nebraska Press.

Evers, Larry, and Felipe S. Molina. 1987. *Yaqui Deer Songs: Maso Bwikan: A Native American Poetry*. Tucson: Sun Tracks, University of Arizona Press.

Fenton, William N. 1940. *Masked Medicine Societies of the Iroquois*. Annual Report of the Smithsonian Institution for 1940. Washington, D.C.: Government Printing Office, 397–429.

———. 1978. *Iroquois Social Dance Songs*. 3 vols. Iroqrafts, Ont.: Ohsweken.

Fletcher, Alice C. 1893. "A Study of Omaha Indian Music." *Archaeological and Ethnological Papers of the Peabody Museum* 1:237–287.

Frisbie, Charlotte J. 1977. *Music and Dance Research of Southwestern United States Indians: Past Trends, Present Activities, and Suggestions for Future Research*. Detroit Studies in Music Bibliography, No. 36. Detroit: Information Coordinators.

———, ed. 1989 [1980]. *Southwest Indian Ritual Drama*. Prospect Heights, Ill.: Waveland.

———. 1993 [1967]. *Kinaldá. A Study of the Navajo Girls' Puberty Ceremony*. Middletown, Conn.: Wesleyan University Press.

Frisbie, Charlotte J., and David P. McAllester. 1978. *Navajo Blessingway Singer: The Autobiography of Frank Mitchell, 1881–1967*. Tucson: University of Arizona Press.

Gibbons, Roy. 1980b. "Ethnomusicology of the Métis in Alberta and Saskatchewan: A Distinct Cultural Display of Anglo-Celtic, French and Native Elements." Audiotape, Video Collection, and Field Report. Canadian Centre for Folk Culture Studies, National Museum of Civilization.

Gifford, Edward. 1955. "Central Miwok Ceremonies." *University of California* (Berkeley) *Anthropological Records* 14(4):261–318.

Giglio, Virginia. 1994. *Southern Cheyenne Women's Songs*. Norman: University of Oklahoma Press.

Goldschmidt, Walter, and Harold Driver. 1940. "The Hupa White Deerskin Dance." *University of California* (Berkeley) *Publications in American Archeology and Ethnology* 35:103–142.

Gombert, Greg. 1994. *A Guide to Native American Music Recordings*. Fort Collins, Colo.: Multi Cultural.

Goodman, Linda J. 1977. *Music and Dance in Northwest Coast Indian Life*. Occasional Papers, Vol. 111, Music and Dance Series, No. 3. Tsaile, Ariz.: Navajo Community College Press.

Gray, John, comp. 1988. *Blacks in Classical Music: A Bibliographical Guide to Composers, Performers, and Ensembles*. Westport, Conn.: Greenwood.

Haefer, J. Richard. 1977. *Papago Music and Dance*. Tsaile, Ariz.: Navajo Community College Press.

Halpern, Abraham M. 1988. "Southeastern Pomo Ceremonials: The Kuksu Cult and Its Successors." *University of California* (Berkeley) *Anthropological Records* 29.

Hawkes, Ernest W. 1914. "The Dance Festivals of the Alaskan Eskimos." *University of Pennsylvania Anthropological Publications* 6(2):1–41.

Herzog, George. 1936. *Research in Primitive and Folk Music in the United States: A Survey*. Washington, D.C.: American Council of Learned Societies.

Hodge, Frederick W., ed. 1913. *The North American Indian,* Vol. 9. Norwood, Mass.: Plimpton.

Hoffman, Walter J. 1885–1886. "The Midéwiwin or 'Grand Medicine' Society of the Ojibwe." *Bureau of American Ethnology Annual Report* 7:143–300.

Howard, James H., and Victoria Lindsay Levine. 1990. *Choctaw Music and Dance*. Norman: University of Oklahoma Press.

Howard, James Henri. 1981. *Shawnee: The Ceremonialism of a Native Indian Tribe and Its Cultural Background*. Athens: Ohio University Press.

———. 1984. *The Canadian Sioux*. Lincoln: University of Nebraska Press.

Institute of Alaska Native Arts. 1987. *Interior Tunes: Athapaskan Old-Time Music*. Fairbanks: Institute of Alaska Native Arts.

Jenness, Diamond. 1935. *The Ojibwa Indians of Parry Sound, Their Social and Religious Life*. Bulletin 78. Ottawa: Department of Mines, National Museum of Canada.

———. 1943. *The Carrier Indians of the Bulkley River: Their Social and Religious Life*. Bureau of Ethnology Paper 25, Bulletin 133. Washington, D.C.: Smithsonian Institution.

———. 1943. *The Sekani Indians of British Columbia*. Bulletin 84, Anthropological Series 20. Ottawa: Department of Mines and Resources.

Jilek, Wolfgang. 1982. *Indian Healing: Shamanic Ceremonialism in the Pacific Northwest Today*. Surrey, B.C.: Hancock House.

Johnston, Basil. 1990. *Ojibwey Ceremonies.* Lincoln: University of Nebraska Press.

Johnston, Thomas F. 1976. *Eskimo Music, a Comparative Circumpolar Study.* Mercury Series, 32. Ottawa: National Museum of Man.

Johnston, Thomas F., et al. 1978. *Koyukan Athapaskan Dance Songs.* Anchorage, Alaska: National Bilingual Materials Development Center.

Keeling, Richard. 1997. *North American Indian Music: A Guide to Published Sources and Selected Recordings (1535–1995).* Garland Library of Music Ethnology, 5. New York: Garland.

Keeling, Richard H. 1992. *Cry for Luck: Sacred Song and Speech among the Yurok, Hupa, and Karok Indians of Northwestern California.* Berkeley: University of California Press.

Koranda, Lorraine. 1972. *Alaskan Eskimo Songs and Stories.* Seattle: University of Washington Press.

Kurath, Gertrude. 1968. *Dance and Song Rituals of Six Nations Reserve.* Bulletin 220. Ottawa: National Museum.

Kurath, Gertrude P., with Antonio Garcia. 1970. *Music and Dance of the Tewa Pueblos.* Museum of New Mexico Records, 8. Santa Fe: Museum of New Mexico Press.

Kurath, Gertrude Prokosch. 1964. *Iroquois Music and Dance: Ceremonial Arts of Two Seneca Longhouses.* Bureau of American Ethnology Bulletin 187. Washington, D.C.: Smithsonian Institution.

———. 1966. *Michigan Indian Festivals.* Ann Arbor, Mich.: Ann Arbor.

———. 1968. *Dance and Song Rituals of Six Nations Reserve, Ontario.* Bulletin of the National Museum of Canada, No. 220; Folklore series, No. 4. Ottawa: Queen's Printer.

———. 1977. *Iroquois Music and Dance: Ceremonial Arts of Two Seneca Longhouses,* St. Clair Shores, Mich.: Scholarly.

———. 1981. *Tutelo Rituals on Six Nations Reserve, Ontario.* Ann Arbor, Mich.: Society for Ethnomusicology.

Lederman, Anne. 1984. "Fiddling in Western Manitoba." Audiotape Collection and Field Report. Canadian Centre for Folk Culture Studies, Canadian Museum of Civilization.

Lee, Dorothy Sara. 1979. *Native North American Music and Oral Data: A Catalogue of Sound Recordings 1893–1976* (at the Archives of Traditional Music, Indiana University). Bloomington: Indiana University Press.

Lowie, Robert. 1915. "Dances and Societies of the Plains Shoshone." *Anthropological Papers of the American Museum of Natural History* 11(1):803–835.

Lutz, Maija. 1982. *Musical Traditions of the Labrador Coast Inuit.* Mercury Series, 79. Ottawa: National Museum of Man.

Mason, Alden F. 1946. *Notes on the Indians of the Great Slave Lake Area.* Publications in Anthropology, 34. New Haven, Conn.: Yale University.

McAllester, David P. 1964. *Peyote Music.* New York: Johnson Reprint.

———. 1973. *Enemy Way Music: A Study of Social and Esthetic Values as Seen in Navaho Music.* Milwood, N.Y.: Kraus Reprint.

———. 1980. *Hogans: Navajo Houses and House Songs,* trans. and arranged by David P. McAllester. Middletown, Conn.: Wesleyan University Press.

McIlwraith, Thomas F. 1948. *The Bella Coola Indians.* 2 vols. Toronto: University of Toronto Press.

Merriam, Alan P. 1967. *Ethnomusicology of the Flathead Indians.* Chicago: Aldine.

Messenger, Phyllis Mauch, ed. 1989. *The Ethics of Collecting Cultural Property: Whose Culture? Whose Property?* Albuquerque: University of New Mexico Press.

Mishler, Craig. 1993. *The Crooked Stovepipe: Athapaskan Fiddle Music and Square Dancing in Northeast Alaska and Northwest Canada.* Urbana: University of Illinois Press.

Mooney, James. 1973 [1896]. *The Ghost Dance Religion and Wounded Knee.* Reprint of the Fourteenth Annual Report (Part 2) of the Bureau of Ethnology to the Smithsonian Institution, 1892–1893: *The Ghost-Dance Religion and the Sioux Outbreak of 1890.* Mineola, N.Y.: Dover.

Morgan, Lewis Henry. 1962 [1851]. *League of the Ho-dé-no-sau-nee or Iroquois.* Secaucus, N.J.: Citadel.

Murdock, George P. 1936. "Rank and Potlatch among the Haida." *Anthropology,* 13. New Haven, Conn.: Yale University Publications.

Nettl, Bruno. 1954. *North American Indian Musical Styles.* Memoirs of the American Folklore Society, Vol. 45. Philadelphia: American Folklore Society.

———. 1979. *An Historical Album of Blackfoot Indian Music.* New York: Folkways Records.

Painter, Muriel Thayer. 1986. *With Good Heart: Yaqui Beliefs and Ceremonies in Pascua Village.* Tucson: University of Arizona Press.

Pelinski, Ramon, et al. 1979. *Inuit Songs from Eskimo Point.* Mercury Series, 60. Ottawa: National Museum of Man. Record included. LP disk.

Peterson, Jacquelin, and J. Brown, eds. 1987. *The New Peoples: Being and Becoming Métis in North America.* Winnipeg: University of Manitoba Press.

Powers, William K. 1977. *Oglala Religion.* Lincoln: University of Nebraska Press.

———. 1982. *Yuwipi: Vision and Experience in Oglala.* Lincoln: University of Nebraska Press.

———. 1987. *Beyond the Vision: Essays on American Indian Culture.* Civilization of the American Indian Series, Vol. 184. Norman: University of Oklahoma Press.

———. 1990a. *Voices from the Spirit World: Lakota Ghost Dance Songs.* Kendall Park, N.J.: Lakota.

———. 1990b. *War Dance: Plains Indian Musical Performance.* Tuscon: University of Arizona Press.

———. 1998. *Lakota Cosmos: Religion and the Reinvention of Culture.* Kendall Park, N.J.: Lakota.

Ridington, Robin. 1978. *Swan People: A Study of the Dunne-Za Prophet Dance.* Mercury Series, 38. Ottawa: National Museum of Man.

Roberts, Helen, and Diamond Jenness. 1925. "Songs of the Copper Eskimos." In *Report of the Canadian Arctic Expedition, 1913–1918,* Vol. 14. Ottawa: F. A. Ackland.

Roberts, Helen H. 1933. *Form in Primitive Music: An Analytical and Comparative Study of the Melodic Form of Some Ancient Southern California Indian Songs.* American Library of Musicology. New York: Norton.

Roberts, Helen H., and Morris Swadesh. 1955. *Songs of the Nootka Indians of Western Vancouver Island.* Philadelphia: American Philosophical Society.

Ross, W. Gillies. 1984. "The Earliest Sound Recordings among the North American Inuit." *Arctic* 37(3):291–292.

Seeger, Anthony, and Louise S. Spear, eds. 1987. *Early Field Recordings: A Catalogue of the Cylinder Collections at the Indiana University Archives of Traditional Music.* Bloomington: Indiana University Press.

Shimkin, Demitri B. 1953. *The Wind River Shoshone Sun Dance.* Bureau of American Ethnology Bulletin 151. Washington, D.C.: Smithsonian Institution, 399–491.

Smyth, Willie, and Esme Ryan, ed. 1999. *Spirit of the First People: Native American Music Traditions of Washington State.* Seattle: University of Washington Press.

Speck, Frank G., and Leonard Broom. 1983. *Cherokee Dance and Drama,* 2nd ed. Norman: University of Oklahoma Press.

Speck, Frank G., and George Herzog. 1942. *The Tutelo Adoption Ceremony: Reclothing the Living in the Name of the Dead.* Harrisburg: Pennsylvania Historical Commission.

Speck, Frank Gouldsmith. 1911. "Ceremonial Songs of the Creek and Yuchi Indians." *University of Pennsylvania, University Museum Anthropological Publications* 50(2):157–245.

Sturtevant, William C., and David Damas, eds. 1984. *Handbook of North American Indians,* Vol. 5: *Arctic.* Washington, D.C.: Smithsonian Institution.

Swanton, John R. 1912. "Haida Songs." *Publications of the American Ethnological Society* 3:1–63.

Sweet, Jill D. 1985. *Dances of the Tewa Pueblo Indians.* Santa Fe: School of American Research.

Underhill, Ruth Murray. 1973 [1938]. *Singing for Power: The Song Magic of the Papago Indians of Southern Arizona.* New York: Ballantine.

Vander, Judith. 1986. *Ghost Dance Songs and Religion of a Wind River Shoshone Woman.* Urbana: University of Illinois Press.

————. 1988. *Songprints: The Musical Experience of Five Shoshone Women*. Urbana and Chicago: University of Illinois Press.

————. 1997. *Shoshone Ghost Dance Religion: Poetry Songs and Great Basin Context*. Urbana: University of Illinois Press.

Vermont, Thomas Jr. 1982. *The Ojibwa Dance Drum: Its History and Construction*. Smithsonian Folklife Studies, 2. Washington, D.C.: Smithsonian Institution Press.

Whiddon, Lynn. 1993. *Métis Songs: Visiting Was the Métis Way*. New York: Gabriel Dumont Institute.

————. 1986. "An Ethnomusicological Study of the Traditional Songs of the Chisasibi Cree." Ph.D. dissertation, Université de Montréal.

Wyman, Leland Clifton. 1970. *Blessingway*. Tucson: University of Arizona Press.

————. 1975. *The Mountainway of the Navajo*. Tucson: University of Arizona Press.

UNITED STATES

Abrahams, Roger D., and George Foss. 1968. *Anglo-American Folksong Style*. Englewood Cliffs, N.J.: Prentice Hall.

Alderfer, E. G. 1985. *The Ephrata Commune: An Early American Counterculture*. Pittsburgh: University of Pittsburgh Press.

Allen, Ray. 1991. *Singing in the Spirit: African American Sacred Quartets in New York City*. Philadelphia: University of Pennsylvania Press.

Allen, Ray, and Lois Wilcken, eds. 1998. *Island Sounds in the Global City: Caribbean Popular Music and Identity in New York*. New York: Brooklyn College and New York Folklore Society and the Institute for Studies in American Music.

Allen, William Francis, Charles Pickard Ware, and Lucy McKim Garrison, comps. 1951 [1867]. *Slave Songs of the United States*. New York: Peter Smith.

Allen, William Francis, Charles Pickard Ware, and Lucy McKim Garrison, eds. 1965 [1867]. *Slave Songs of the United States*. New York: Oak.

Ancelet, Barry Jean. 1989. *Cajun Music: Its Origins and Development*. Lafayette: Center for Louisiana Studies, University of Southwestern Louisiana.

Ancelet, Barry Jean, and Philip Gould. 1992. *Cajun Music and Zydeco*. Baton Rouge: Louisiana State University.

Andrews, Edward Deming. 1962 [1940]. *The Gift to Be Simple: Songs, Dances, and Rituals of the American Shakers*. New York: Dover.

Arapaho Music and Spoken Word Collection. Alice Cunningham Fletcher Collection. Archive of Folk Culture, Library of Congress AFS 20308 and 20324.

Armistead, Samuel. 1992. *The Spanish Tradition in Louisiana*. Vol. 1: *Isleño Folkliterature*, with transcriptions by Israel Katz. Newark, Del.: Juan de la Cuesta.

Arnold, Alison. 1985. "Aspects of Asian Indian Musical Life in North America." *Selected Reports in Ethnomusicology* 6:25–38.

Artis, Bob. 1975. *Bluegrass*. New York: Hawthorne.

Arya, Usharbudh. 1968. *Ritual Songs and Folksongs of the Hindus of Surinam*. Leiden, Netherlands: Brill.

Attali, Jacques. 1985. *Noise: The Political Economy of Music*, trans. Brian Massumi. Minneapolis: University of Minnesota Press.

Austerlitz, Paul. 1996. *Dominican Music and Dominican Identity*. Philadelphia: Temple University Press.

————. 1997. *Merengue: Dominican Music and Dominican Identity*. Philadelphia: Temple University Press.

Averill, Gage. 1997. *A Day for the Hunter, a Day for the Prey: Popular Music and Power in Haiti*. Chicago: University of Chicago Press.

Baker, David. 1985. *How To Play Bebop*. 3 vols. Bloomington, Ind.: Frangipani.

Balys, Jonas, ed. 1958. *Lithuanian Folksongs in America*. A Treasury of Lithuanian Folklore, No. 5. Boston: Lithuanian Encyclopedia.

Bandera, Mark Jaroslav. 1991. *The Tsymbaly Maker and His Craft: The Ukrainian Hammered Dulcimer in Alberta*. Canadian Series in Ukrainian Ethnology, No. 1. Edmonton: Canadian Institute of Ukrainian Studies Press, University of Alberta.

Barlow, William. 1989. *"Looking Up at Down": The Emergence of Blues Culture*. Philadelphia: Temple University Press.

Barrand, Anthony G. 1991. *Six Fools and a Dancer: The Timeless Way of the Morris*. Plainfield, Vt.: Northern Harmony.

Bastin, Bruce. 1986. *Red River Blues: The Blues Tradition in the Southeast*. Urbana: University of Illinois Press.

Bauman, Richard, ed. 1993. *Folklore and Culture on the Texas-Mexican Border*. Austin: Center for Mexican American Studies, University of Texas.

Bayard, Samuel P. 1944. *Hill Country Tunes: Instrumental Folk Music of Southwestern Pennsylvania*. Philadelphia: American Folklore Society.

Beckwith, John. 1997. *Music Papers: Articles and Talks by a Canadian Composer 1961–1994*. Ottawa: Golden Dog.

Behague, Gerard H., ed. 1994. *Music and Black Ethnicity: The Caribbean and South America*. Miami: University of Miami North-South Center.

Benary, Barbara. 1983. "One Perspective on Gamelan in America." *Asian Music* 15(1):82–101.

————. 1993a. *Gamelan Works, Vol 1: The Braid Pieces*. Lebanon, N.H.: American Gamelan Institute.

Berendt, Joachim. 1975. *The Jazz Book: From New Orleans to Rock and Free Jazz*, trans. Dan Morgenstern and Helmut and Barbara Bredigkeit. Westport, Conn.: Lawrence Hill.

Berlin, Edward A. 1980. *Ragtime: A Musical and Cultural History*. Berkeley: University of California Press.

Berliner, Paul F. 1994. *Thinking in Jazz: The Infinite Art of Improvisation*. Chicago: University of Chicago Press.

Bierley, Paul. 1984. *The Works of John Philip Sousa*. Columbus, Ohio: Integrity.

Blegen, Theodore C., and Martin B. Ruud, eds. 1936. *Norwegian Emigrant Songs and Ballads*. London: Oxford University Press.

Blesh, Rudi. 1946. *Shining Trumpets. A History of Jazz*. New York: Knopf.

————. 1985. *Shining Trumpets: A History of Jazz*. 2nd ed. New York: Knopf.

Blesh, Rudi, and Harriet Janis. 1971 [1966]. *They All Played Ragtime*, 4th ed. New York: Oak.

Boggs, Vernon, ed. 1992. *Salsiology: Afro-Cuban Music and the Evolution of Salsa in New York City*. New York: Greenwood.

Bohlman, Philip V. 1988. *The Study of Folk Music in the Modern World*. Bloomington: Indiana University Press.

Bowman, Rob. 1997. *Soulsville U.S.A.: The Story of Stax Records*. New York: Schirmer.

Boyer, Horace. 1995. *How Sweet the Sound: The Golden Age of Gospel*. Washington, D.C.: Elliott Clark.

Boyer, Walter E., Albert F. Buffington, and Don Yoder, eds. 1951. *Songs along the Mahantango: Pennsylvania Dutch Folksongs*. Hatboro, Pa.: Folklore Associates.

Bronson, Bertrand. 1959–1972. *The Traditional Tunes of the Child Ballads*. 4 vols. Princeton, N.J.: Princeton University Press.

————. 1976. *The Singing Tradition of Child's Popular Ballads*. Princeton, N.J.: Princeton University Press.

Bronson, Bertrand H. 1976. *The Singing Tradition of Child's Popular Ballads*. Princeton, N.J.: Princeton University Press. (Abridgment of *The Traditional Tunes of the Child Ballads*. 4 vols., 1959–1972.)

Brown, Rae Linda. 1990. "William Grant Still, Florence Price, and William Dawson: Echoes of the Harlem Renaissance." In *Black Music in the Harlem Renaissance: A Collection of Essays*, ed. Samuel A. Floyd Jr., 71–86. Westport, Conn.: Greenwood.

Broyles, Michael. 1992. *"Music of the Highest Class": Elitism and Populism in Antebellum Boston*. New Haven, Conn.: Yale University Press.

Bryant, Carolyn. 1975. *And the Band Played On, 1776–1976*. Washington, D.C.: Smithsonian Institution Press.

Budds, Michael J. 1990. *Jazz in the Sixties: The Expansion of Musical Resources and Techniques.* Iowa City: University of Iowa.

Buertle, Jack V., and Danny Barker. 1973. *Bourbon Street Black: The New Orleans Black Jazzman.* New York: Oxford University Press.

Buffington, Albert F. 1974. *Pennsylvania German Secular Folksongs.* Publications of the Pennsylvania German Society, Vol. 8. Breinigsville: Pennsylvania German Society.

Bufwack, Mary A., and Robert K. Oermann. 1993. *Finding Her Voice: The Saga of Women in Country Music.* New York: Crown.

Burr, Ramiro. 1999. *The Billboard Guide to Tejano and Regional Mexican Music.* New York: Billboard.

Cage, John. 1961. *Silence: Lectures and Writings.* Middletown, Conn.: Wesleyan University Press.

California's Musical Wealth: Sources for the Study of Music in California, ed. Stephen M. Fry, 55–78. Southern California Chapter, Music Library Association.

Camus, Raoul F. 1976. *Military Music of the American Revolution.* Chapel Hill: University of North Carolina Press.

———. 1992. *American Wind and Percussion Music.* Three Centuries of American Music, Vol. 12. Boston: G. K. Hall.

Cantwell, Bob. 1984. *Bluegrass Breakdown.* Urbana: University of Illinois Press.

Cantwell, Robert. 1996. *When We Were Good: The Folk Revival.* Cambridge: Harvard University Press.

Carter, Madison H. 1986. *An Annotated Catalog of Composers of African Ancestry.* New York: Vantage.

Catlin, Amy, ed. 1992. *Khmer Classical Dance Songbook.* Van Nuys, Calif.: Apsara Media for Intercultural Education.

Cavanagh, Beverley. 1982. *Music of the Net Silik Eskimo: A Study of Stability and Change.* Ottawa: National Museums.

Champe, Flavia Water. 1983. *The Matachines Dance of the Upper Rio Grande: History, Music, and Choreography.* Lincoln: University of Texas Press.

Chapple, Steve, and Reebee Garofalo. 1977. *Rock 'n' Roll Is Here to Pay: The History of Politics in the Music Industry.* Chicago: Nelson-Hall.

Charters, Samuel B. 1959. *The Country Blues.* New York: Rinehart.

Chen, Jack. 1980. *The Chinese of America.* New York: Harper and Row.

Chinn, Thomas W., ed. 1989. *Bridging the Pacific: San Francisco Chinatown and Its People.* San Francisco: Chinese Historical Society of America.

Cipolla, Frank, J., and Donald Hunsberger, eds. 1994. *The Wind Ensemble and Its Repertoire.* Rochester, N.Y.: University of Rochester Press.

Coffin, Tristram P. 1963. *The British Traditional Ballad in North America.* Philadelphia: American Folklore Society.

Colcord, Joanna C. 1938. *Songs of American Sailormen.* New York: Norton.

Cole, Bill. 1993 [1976]. *John Coltrane.* New York: Da Capo.

Collier, James Lincoln. 1978. *The Making of Jazz: A Comprehensive History.* Boston: Houghton Mifflin.

Cornelius, Steven. 1989. "The Convergence of Power: An Investigation into the Music Liturgy of Santeria in New York City." Ph.D. dissertation, University of California, Los Angeles.

Courlander, Harold. 1963. *Negro Folk Music, U.S.A.* New York: Columbia University Press.

Cowell, Henry, ed. 1961 [1933]. *American Composers on American Music: A Symposium.* New York: Frederick Ungar.

Cowell, Sidney Robertson, collector. 1938–1940. "Alberto Mendes, Manuel Lemos, and Mr. Franks Performing Portuguese Songs and Music from the Azores, 1939." In *California Gold: Northern California Folk Music from the Thirties.* WPA California Folk Music Project. Washington, D.C.: American Folklife Center, Library of Congress. Available from website http://lcweb2.loc.gov/ammem/afcchtml/0009.html.

Cowley, John, and Paul Oliver, eds. 1996. *The New Blackwell Guide to Recorded Blues.* Oxford: Blackwell.

Crawford, Richard, ed. 1984. *The Core Repertory of Early American Psalmody.* Recent Researches in American Music, Vols. 11 and 12. Madison, Wisc.: A-R Editions.

Cross, Brian. 1993. *It's Not about a Salary: Rap, Race, and Resistance in Los Angeles.* New York: Verso.

Cuney-Hare, Maud. 1974 [1936]. *Negro Musicians and Their Music.* New York: Da Capo.

Da Silva, Owen F. 1941. *Mission Music in California.* Los Angeles: Warren F. Lewis.

Davis, Angela Y. 1998. *Blues Legacies and Black Feminism: Gertrude "Ma" Rainey, Bessie Smith, and Billie Holiday.* New York: Pantheon.

Davis, Stephen. 1985. *Hammer of the Gods: The Led Zeppelin Saga.* New York: Ballantine.

DeVeaux, Scott. 1997. *The Birth of Bebop: A Social and Musical History.* Berkeley: University of California Press.

Diamond, Beverley. 1991. "Canadian Music Studies in University Curricula." *ACS Newsletter* 12(2).

Diamond, Beverley, M. Sam Cronk, and Franziska von Rosen. 1994. *Visions of Sound: Musical Instruments of First Nations Communities in Northeastern America.* Chicago Studies in Ethnomusicology. Chicago: University of Chicago Press.

Diamond, Beverley, and Robert Witmer, eds. 1994. *Canadian Music: Issues of Hegemony and Identity.* Toronto: Canadian Scholars' Press.

Diamond, Jody. 1992a. "Making Choices: American Gamelan in Composition and Education (From the Java Jive to Eine Kleine Gamelan Music)." In *Essays on Southeast Asian Performing Arts: Local Manifestations and Cross-Cultural Implications,* ed. Kathy Foley. Berkeley, Calif.: Centers for South and Southeast Asian Studies.

Dilling, Margaret Walker. 1994. "Kumdori Born Again in Boston: The Life Cycle of Music by a Korean American." *Korean Culture* 15(3):14–25.

Dixon, Robert M. W., and John Godrich. 1963. *Blues and Gospel Records (1902–1942).* Middlesex, Eng.: Storyville.

DjeDje, Jacqueline Cogdell, and Eddie S. Meadows, eds. 1998. *California Soul: Music of African Americans in the West,* Berkeley: University of California Press.

Dyson, Michael E. 1996. *Between God and Gangsta Rap: Bearing Witness to Black Culture.* New York: Oxford University Press.

Emery; Lynne Fauley. 1972. *Black Dance in the United States from 1619 to 1970.* Palo Alto, Calif.: National Press.

Epstein, Dena J. 1977. *Sinful Tunes and Spirituals: Black Folk Music to the Civil War.* Urbana: University of Illinois Press.

Eskew, Harry, David W. Music, and Paul A. Richardson. 1994. *Singing Baptists: Studies in Baptist Hymnody in America.* Nashville, Tenn.: Church Street.

Estavan, Lawrence. 1991 [1938]. *The Italian Theater in San Francisco.* San Bernardino, Calif.: Borgo.

Ethnic Recordings in America: A Neglected Heritage. 1982. Washington, D.C.: Library of Congress American Folklife Center.

Evans, David. 1982. *Big Road Blues: Tradition and Creativity in the Folk Blues.* Berkeley: University of California Press.

Farrell, Gerry. 1997. *Indian Music and the West.* Oxford: Clarendon.

Feather, Leonard, and Ira Gitler. 1999. *The Biographical Encyclopedia of Jazz.* New York: Oxford University Press.

Feintuch, Burt. 1993. "Musical Revival as Musical Transformation." In *Transforming Tradition: Folk Music Revivals Examined,* ed. Neil V. Rosenberg. Urbana: University of Illinois Press.

Feldman, Walter. 1975. "Middle Eastern Music among Immigrant Communities in New York City." In *Balkan-Arts Traditions,* ed. Martin Koenig, 19–25. New York: Balkan Arts Center.

Fernando, S. H., Jr. 1994. *The New Beats: Exploring the Music, Culture, and Attitudes of Hip-Hop.* New York: Anchor/Doubleday.

Ferris, William, and Mary L. Hart, eds. 1982. *Folk Music and Modern Sound.* Jackson: University Press of Mississippi.

Ferris, William, Jr. 1970. *Blues from the Delta.* London: Studio Vista.

Figueroa, Frank M. 1994. *Encyclopedia of Latin American Music in New York.* St. Petersburg, Fla.: Pillar.

Fikentscher, Kai. 2000. *"You Better Work!" Underground Dance Music in New York City.* Hanover, N.H.: Wesleyan University Press/University Press of New England.

Flaherty, David H., and Frank E. Manning, eds. 1993. *The Beaver Bites Back? American Popular*

Culture in Canada. Montreal and Kingston: McGill Queen's University Press.

Fletcher, Alice C., Francis La Flesche, and John C. Fillmore. 1893. *A Study of Omaha Indian Music*. Peabody Museum Archaeological and Ethnological Papers, Vol. 1, No. 5. Cambridge, Mass.: Peabody Museum of American Archaeology and Ethnology, Harvard University.

Flores, Richard R. 1995. *Los Pastores: History and Performance in the Mexican Shepherds' Play of South Texas*. Washington, D.C.: Smithsonian Institution Press.

Floyd, Samuel, ed. 1990. *Black Music in the Harlem Renaissance: A Collection of Essays*. New York: Greenwood.

Floyd, Samuel A., Jr., and Marsha J. Reisser. 1983. *Black Music in the United States., An Annotated Bibliography of Selected Reference and Research Materials*. Millwood, N.Y.: Kraus International.

Floyd, Samuel A., Jr., and Marsha J. Reisser. 1987. *Black Music Biography: An Annotated Bibliography*. White Plains, N.Y.: Kraus International.

Folb, Edith. 1980. *Runnin' Down Some Lines: The Language and Culture of Black Teenagers*. Cambridge: Harvard University Press.

Fong-Torres, Ben. 1998. *The Hits Just Keep on Coming: The History of Top Forty Radio*. San Francisco: Miller Freeman.

Frey, J. William. 1949. "Amish Hymns as Folk Music." In *Pennsylvania Songs and Legends*, ed. George Korson, 129–162. Philadelphia: University of Pennsylvania Press.

Friedlander, Paul David. 1990. "Rocking the Yangtze: Impressions of Chinese Popular Music and Technology." *Popular Music and Society* 14(1):63–74.

Friend, Robyn, and Neil Siegel. 1986. "Contemporary Contexts for Iranian Professional Musical Performance." In *Cultural Parameters of Iranian Musical Expression*, ed. Margaret Caton and Neil Siegel, 10–17. Redondo Beach, Calif.: Institute of Persian Performing Arts.

Frigyesi, Judit. 1996. "The Aesthetic of the Hungarian Revival Movement." In *Retuning Culture: Musical Changes in Central and Eastern Europe*, ed. Mark Slobin, 54–75. Durham, N.C.: Duke University Press.

Frith, Simon, and Andrew Goodwin, eds. 1990. *On Record: Rock, Pop, and the Written Word*. New York: Pantheon.

Ganam, King. 1957. *Canadian Fiddle Tunes*. Don Mills, Ontario: BMI Canada.

Garofalo, Reebee. 1997. *Rockin' Out: Popular Music in the U.S.A.* Boston: Allyn and Bacon.

Geldard, Alison. 1980. "Music and Musical Performance Among the East Indians in Chicago." Master's thesis, University of Illinois at Urbana-Champaign.

George, Nelson. 1998. *Hip Hop America*. New York: Penguin.

Gillett, Charlie. 1983 [1970]. *The Sound of the City*, rev. and expanded ed. New York: Pantheon.

Gitler, Ira. 1985. *Swing to Bop: An Oral History of the Transition in Jazz in the 1940s*. New York: Oxford University Press.

Goldman, Albert. 1978. *Disco*. New York: Hawthorn.

Gould, Nathaniel D. 1972 [1853]. *Church Music in America, Comprising Its History and Its Peculiarities of Different Periods with Cursory Remarks*. New York: AMS.

Grame, Theodore C. 1976. *America's Ethnic Music*. Tarpon Springs, Fla.: Cultural Maintenance.

Green, Mildred Denby. 1983. *Black Women Composers: A Genesis*. Boston: Twayne.

Greene, Victor. 1992. *A Passion for Polka: Old Time Ethnic Music in America*. Berkeley: University of California Press.

Greenhill, Pauline. 1997. *Undisciplined Women: Tradition and Culture in Canada*. Montréal: McGill Queen's University Press.

Grenet, Emilio. 1939. *Popular Cuban Music: Eighty Revised and Corrected Compositions, Together with an Essay on the Evolution of Music in Cuba*. Havana: Carasa.

Gridley, Mark. 1991. *Jazz Styles: History and Analysis*, 4th ed. Englewood Cliffs, N.J.: Prentice Hall.

Griffiths, John. 1788. *A Collection of the Newest and Most Fashionable Country Dances and Cotillions, The Greater Part by Mr. John Griffiths, Dancing Master, in Providence*. Providence, R.I.

Gronow, Pekka. 1977. *Studies in Scandinavian-American Discography*. Helsinki: Finnish Institute of Recorded Sound.

Groom, Bob. 1971. *The Blues Revival*. London: November Books.

Guralnick, Peter. 1986. *Sweet Soul Music: Rhythm and Blues and the Southern Dream of Freedom*. New York: Harper and Row.

Hadley, Peter. 1993. "New Music for Gamelan by North American Composers." Master's thesis, Wesleyan University. Distributed by the American Gamelan Institute.

Haefer, J. Richard. 1989 [1980]. "O'odharm Celkona: The Papago Skipping Dance." In *Southwest Indian Ritual Drama*, ed. Charlotte J. Frisbie. Prospect Heights, Ill.: Waveland.

Hague, Eleanor. 1917. *Spanish-American Folk-Songs*. Lancaster, Pa.: American Folklore Society.

———. 1922. *Early Spanish-Californian Folk-Songs*. New York: Pantheon.

Hakala, Joyce. 1997. *Memento of Finland: A Musical Legacy*. St. Paul, Minn.: Pikebone Music.

Hall, Leslie. 1982. "Turkish Musical Culture in Toronto." *Canadian Folk Music Journal* 10:48–52.

Hambly. Scott. 1977. "Mandolins in the United States: An Industrial and Sociological History since 1880." Ph.D. dissertation, University of Pennsylvania.

Hamm, Charles. 1979. *Yesterdays: Popular Song in America*. New York: Norton.

———. 1983. *Music in the New World*. New York: Norton.

Handy, D. Antoinette. 1995. *Black Conductors*. Lanham, Md.: Scarecrow.

Haralambos, Michael. 1985 [1974]. *Soul Music: The Birth of a Sound in Black America*. New York: Da Capo.

Hark, J. M. 1972 [1889]. *Chronicon Ephratense: A History of the Community of the Seventh Day Baptists at Ephrata*. New York: Burt Franklin.

Harris, Michael W. 1992. *The Rise of Gospel Blues: The Music of Thomas Andrew Dorsey in the Urban Church*. New York: Oxford University Press.

Hart, Mary L., et al. 1989. *The Blues: A Bibliographical Guide*. New York: Garland.

Haskell, Harry. 1988. *The Early Music Revival: A History*. London: Thames and Hudson.

Hast, Dorothea. 1994. "Music, Dance, and Community: Contra Dance in New England." Ph.D. dissertation, Wesleyan University.

Hatch, James V. 1970. *Black Image on the American Stage: A Bibliography of Plays and Musicals, 1770–1970*. New York: DBS.

Haugen, Einar, and Camilla Cai. 1993. *Ole Bull: Norway's Romantic Musician and Cosmopolitan Patriot*. Madison: University of Wisconsin Press.

Hay, Samuel A, 1994. *African American Theater: A Historical and Critical Analysis*. Cambridge: Cambridge University Press.

Hazen, Margaret Hindle, and Robert M. Hazen. 1987. *The Music Men. An Illustrated History of Brass Bands in America, 1800–1920*. Washington, D.C.: Smithsonian Institution Press.

Heilbut, Anthony. 1971. *The Gospel Sound: Good News and Bad Times*. New York: Simon and Schuster.

Hentoff, Nat. 1961. *The Jazz Life*. New York: Dial.

Hernández, Guillermo. 1978. *Cancionero de la Raza: Songs of the Chicano Experience*. Berkeley, Calif.: El Fuego de Aztlán.

Herrera-Sobek, Maria. 1993. *Northward Bound: The Mexican Emigrant Experience in Ballad and Song*. Bloomington: Indiana University Press.

Herskovits, Melville J. 1958 [1941]. *The Myth of the Negro Past*. Boston: Beacon.

Heskes, Irene. 1977. *The Resource Book of Jewish Music: A Bibliographical and Topical Guide to the Book and Journal Literature and Program Materials*. Westport, Conn.: Greenwood.

Heth, Charlotte, ed. 1992. *Native American Dance: Ceremonies and Social Traditions*. Washington, D.C.: Smithsonian Institution.

Hines, Michele. 1997. *Radio Voices: American Broadcasting, 1922–1952*. Minneapolis: University of Minnesota Press.

Hispano Folk Music of the Past. 1998. Music of New Mexico Series, Vol. 1. Albuquerque, N.M.: Albuquerque Museum.

Hispano Music and Culture of the Northern Rio Grande. 1940. Juan B. Rael Collection. Washington, D.C.: American Folklife Center, Library of Congress. Available from website http://memory.loc.gov/ammem/rghtm/rghome.html.

Hitchcock, H. Wiley, and Stanley Sadie, eds. 1986. *The New Grove Dictionary of American Music*. London: Macmillan.

Hoe, Ban Seng. 1989. *Beyond the Golden Mountain: Chinese Cultural Traditions in Canada*. Canada: Canadian Museum of Civilization.

Hohmann, Rupert K. 1959. "The Church Music of the Old Order Amish of the United States." Ph.D. dissertation, Northwestern University.

Hom, Marlon K. 1987. *Songs of Gold Mountain: Cantonese Rhymes from San Francisco Chinatown*. Berkeley: University of California Press.

Hood, George. 1970 [1846]. *A History of Music in New England: With Biographical Sketches of Reformers and Psalmists*. New York: Johnson Reprint.

Hoogland, Eric, ed. 1987. *Crossing the Waters: Arabic-Speaking Immigrants to the United States before 1940*. Washington, D.C.: Smithsonian Institution Press.

Horn, David. 1977. *The Literature of American Music in Books and Folk Music Collections*. Metuchen, N.J.: Scarecrow.

Houser, George J. 1976. *The Swedish Community at Eriksdale, Manitoba*. Canadian Centre for Folk Culture Studies Paper, No. 14. Ottawa: National Museum of Man Mercury Series.

Hubbard, W. L., ed. 1910. *The American History and Encyclopedia of Music*. Irving Squire.

Intergalactic Gamelan: Gamelan Galak Tika. 1996. Directed by Evan Ziporyn. (Compositions for *gong kebyar* by Evan Ziporyn, I Gede Manik, and Desak Made Suarti Laksmi. Independently produced cassette.)

Ishaya, Arian, and Eden Naby. 1980. "Assyrians." In *Harvard Encyclopedia of American Ethnic Groups*, ed. Stephan Thernstron, 160–163. Cambridge, Mass.: Belknap Press of Harvard University Press.

Jackson, George P. 1933. *White Spirituals in the Southern Uplands*. Chapel Hill: University of North Carolina Press.

———. 1975 [1943]. *White and Negro Spirituals: Their Life-Span and Kinship*. New York: Da Capo.

Jackson, George Pullen. 1965 [1933]. *White Spirituals in the Southern Uplands*. New York: Dover.

Jackson, Irene V., ed. 1985. *More Than Dancing*. Westport, Conn.: Greenwood.

Jairazbhoy, Nazir, and Sue Carole de Vale, eds. 1985. *Asian Music in North America*. Vol. 6 of *Selected Reports in Ethnomusicology*. Los Angeles: University of California Press.

John Biggs Consort. 1974. *California Mission Music*. KSK Recording KSK-75218, University of California, Berkeley. (LP disk.)

Jones, LeRoi (Amiri Baraka). 1963. *Blues People: Negro Music in White America*. New York: Morrow.

Keck, George R., and Sherrill V. Martin, eds. 1988. *Feel the Spirit: Studies in Nineteenth-Century Afro-American Music*. Westport, Conn.: Greenwood.

Keil, Charles, Angeliki Keil, and Dick Blau. 1992. *Polka Happiness*. Philadelphia: Temple University Press.

Keil, Charles, Angeliki Keil, and Dick Blau. 1966. *Urban Blues*. Chicago: University of Chicago Press.

Kelly, Ron, Jonathan Friedlander, and Anita Colby, eds. 1993b. *Irangeles: Iranians in Los Angeles*. Berkeley: University of California Press.

Kenney, William H. 1993. *Chicago Jazz: A Cultural History 1904–1930*. New York: Oxford University Press.

Kernfeld, Barry. 1988. *The New Grove Dictionary of Jazz*. London: Macmillan.

Key Kool and Rhettmatic. 1995. *Behind the Mask*. Toronto: Lasis.

Kingsbury, Paul, ed. 1998. *The Encyclopedia of Country Music*. New York: Oxford University Press.

Kivy, Peter. 1995. *Authenticities: Philosophical Reflections on Music Performance*. Ithaca, N.Y.: Cornell University Press.

Klymasz, Robert B. 1970a. *An Introduction to the Ukrainian-Canadian Immigrant Folksong Cycle*. Bulletin No. 234, Folklore Series No. 8. Ottawa: National Museums of Canada.

———. 1970b. *The Ukrainian Winter Folksong Cycle in Canada*. Bulletin No. 236, Folklore Series No. 9. Ottawa: National Museums of Canada.

———. 1989. *The Ukrainian Folk Ballad in Canada*. Immigrant Communities and Ethnic Minorities in the United States and Canada, No. 65. New York: AMS.

Kmen, Henry A. 1977. *The Roots of Jazz: The Negro and Music in New Orleans 1791–1900*. Urbana: University of Illinois Press.

Kodish, Debora, ed. 1994. *The Giant Never Wins: Lakhon Bassac (Cambodian Folk Opera) in Philadelphia*. Philadelphia: Philadelphia Folklore Project.

Kofsky, Frank. 1970. *Black Nationalism and the Revolution in Music*. New York: Pathfinder.

Kolar, Walter W. 1975. *The Tambura in America*. Vol. 2 of *A History of the Tambura*. Pittsburgh: Duquesne University Tamburitzans Institute of Folk Arts.

Koskoff, Ellen. 2000. *Music in Lubavitcher Life*. Urbana: University of Illinois Press.

Krasnow, Carolyn. 1993. "Fear and Loathing in the Seventies: Race, Sexuality, and Disco." *Stanford Humanities Review* 3(2):37–45.

Kraus, Richard Curt. 1989. *Pianos and Politics in China: Middle-Class Ambitions and the Struggle over Western Music*. New York: Oxford University Press.

Krehbiel, Henry. 1962 [1914]. *Afro-American Folk Songs*. New York: Frederick Ungar.

Kreitner, Kenneth. 1990. *Discoursing Sweet Music: Brass Bands and Community Life in Turn-of-the-Century Pennsylvania*. Urbana: University of Illinois Press.

Krims, Adam. 2000. *Rap Music and the Poetics of Identity*. Cambridge: Cambridge University Press.

"Lady Soul Singing It Like It Is." 1968. *Time* (28 June):62–66.

Lamadrid, Enrique R., Jack Loeffler, and Miguel A. Gandert. 1994. *Tesoros del Espiritu: A Portrait in Sound of Hispanic New Mexico*. Embudo, N.M.: El Norte/Academia.

Larkin, Rochelle. 1970. *Soul Music*. New York: Lancer.

Lawless, Ray M. 1960. *Folksingers and Folksongs in America*. New York: Duell, Sloan, and Pearce.

Laws, George Malcolm. 1950. *Native American Balladry: A Descriptive Study and a Bibliographical Syllabus*. Philadelphia: American Folklore Society.

———. 1957. *American Balladry from British Broadsides: A Guide for Students and Collectors of Traditional Song*. Philadelphia: American Folklore Society.

Leary, James P. 1990. "Minnesota Polka: Polka Music, American Music." Booklet with recording, *Minnesota Polka: Dance Music from Four Traditions*. Minneapolis: Minnesota Historical Society Press.

Lebrecht, Norman. 1997. *Who Killed Classical Music? Maestros, Managers, and Corporate Politics*. Secaucus, N.J.: Birch Lane.

Levine, Lawrence W. 1977. *Black Culture and Black Consciousness: Afro-American Folk Thought from Slavery to Freedom*. New York: Oxford University Press.

Lewis, Samuel L. 1990 [1975]. *Spiritual Dance and Walk: An Introduction*, ed. Neil Douglas-Klotz. Seattle: Peace Works-INDUP.

Li, Guangming. 1994. "Music in the Chinese Community of Los Angeles: An Overview." In *Musical Aesthetics and Multiculturalism in Los Angeles*, ed. Steven Loza, 105–127. Selected Reports in Ethnomusicology, 10. Los Angeles: University of California.

Library of Congress, Music Division. 1942. *Checklist of Recorded Songs in the English Language in the Archive of American Folk Song to July, 1940*. Washington, D.C.: Library of Congress.

Lieb, Sandra R. 1981. *Mother of the Blues: A Study of Ma Rainey*. Amherst: University of Massachusetts Press.

Lipsitz, George. 1994. *Dangerous Crossroads: Popular Music, Postmodernism, and the Poetics of Place*. London: Verso.

Loeffler, Jack, with Katherine Loeffler and Enrique Lamadrid. 1999. *La Música de los Viejitos: Hispanic Folk Music of the Rio Grande del Norte*. Albuquerque: University of New Mexico Press.

Loesser, Arthur. 1954. *Men, Women, and Pianos: A Social History*. New York: Simon and Schuster.

Lomax, Alan. 1960. *The Folk Songs of North America in the English Language*. New York: Doubleday.

———. 1975. *The Folk Songs of North America*. New York: Doubleday/Dolphin.

Longstreet, Stephen. 1965. *Sportin' House: A History of the New Orleans Sinners and the Birth of Jazz*. Los Angeles: Sherbourne.

Lornell, Kip, and Anne K. Rasmussen, eds. 1997. *Musics of Multicultural America: A Study of Twelve Musical Communities*. New York: Schirmer.

Lovell, John, Jr. 1972. *Black Song: The Forge and the Flame*. New York: Macmillan.

Lovoll, Odd Sverre. 1975. *A Folk Epic: The Bygdelag in America*. Boston: Twayne Publishers for the Norwegian American Historical Association.

Lowe, Lisa. 1996. *Immigrant Acts: On Asian American Cultural Politics*. Durham, N.C.: Duke University Press.

Loza, Steven J. 1993. *Barrio Rhythm: Mexican American Music in Los Angeles*. Urbana: University of Illinois Press.

Magocsi, Paul R., ed. 1999. *Encyclopedia of Canada's Peoples*. Toronto: University of Toronto Press.

Malone, Bill C. 1985. *Country Music U.S.A.*, rev. ed. Austin: University of Texas Press.

Malone, Bill, and Judith McCulloh. 1975. *Stars of Country Music*. Urbana: University of Illinois Press.

Manuel, Peter, ed. 1991. *Essays on Cuban Music: North American and Cuban Perspectives*. Lanham, Md.: University Press of America.

Manuel, Peter L. 1988. *Popular Musics of the Non-Western World: An Introductory Survey*. New York: Oxford University Press. (See also 1990 ed.)

Manuel, Peter, with Kenneth Bilby and Michael Largey. 1995. *Caribbean Currents: Caribbean Music from Rumba to Reggae*. Philadelphia: Temple University Press.

Mates, Julian. 1985. *America's Musical Stage: Two Hundred Years of Musical Theater*. Westport, Conn.: Greenwood.

Mattfeld, Julius. 1952. *Variety Musical Cavalcade, 1620–1950: A Chronology of Vocal and Instrumental Music Popular in the United States*. New York: Prentice Hall.

McAllester, David P. 1954. *Enemy Way Music*. Cambridge, Mass.: Peabody Museum of American Archaeology and Ethnology, Harvard University.

McCoy. 1926. *Folk Songs of the Spanish Californians*. San Francisco: Sherman and Clay.

McGowan, Chris, and Ricardo Pessanha. 1998. *The Brazilian Sound*. Philadelphia: Temple University Press.

McKay, Ian. 1994. *The Quest of the Folk: Antimodernism and Cultural Selection in Twentieth-Century Nova Scotia*. Montreal and Kingston: McGill Queen's University Press.

Meadows, Eddie S. 1981. *Jazz Reference and Research Materials: A Bibliography*. New York: Garland.

Mertens, Wim. 1983. *American Minimal Music: La Monte Young, Terry Riley, Steve Reich, Philip Glass*, trans. J. Hautekiet. New York: Alexander Broude.

Miller, Jim, ed. 1980. *The Rolling Stone Illustrated History of Rock and Roll*. New York: Random House/Rolling Stone.

Miller, Mark. 1997. *Such Melodious Racket: The Lost History of Jazz in Canada 1914–1949*. Toronto: Mercury.

Miller, Terry. 1986. *Folk Music in America: A Reference Guide*. New York: Garland.

Monson, Ingrid. 1996. *Saying Something: Jazz Improvisation and Interaction*. Chicago: University of Chicago Press.

Monson, Ingrid. n.d. *Freedom Sounds: Jazz, Civil Rights, and Africa, 1950–1967*. New York: Oxford University Press. (Forthcoming.)

Montell, William Lynwood. 1991. *Singing the Glory Down: Amateur Gospel Music in South Central Kentucky 1900–1990*. Lexington: University Press of Kentucky.

Morrison, Craig. 1996. *Go Cat Go!: Rockabilly and Its Makers*. Urbana: University of Illinois Press.

Myers, Helen. 1993b. "North America." In *Ethnomusicology: Historical and Regional Studies*, ed. Helen Myers, 401–460. New York: Norton.

———. 1998. *Music of Hindu Trinidad Songs from the Indian Diaspora*. Chicago: University of Chicago Press.

Naficy, Hamid. 1993a. *The Making of Exile Cultures: Iranian Television in Los Angeles*. Minneapolis: University of Minnesota Press.

Narváez, Peter, and Martin Laba, eds. 1986. *Media Sense: The Folklore-Popular Culture Continuum*. Bowling Green, Ohio: Bowling Green State University Popular Press.

Negus, Keith. 1992. *Producing Pop: Culture and Conflict in the Popular Music Industry*. London: Edward Arnold.

Nettl, Bruno. 1949. *An Introduction to Folk Music in the United States*. 2nd ed. 1960. 3d ed., rev. and expanded by Helen Myers, 1972, under the title *Folk Music in the United States: An Introduction*. Detroit: Wayne State University Press.

Neuman, Daniel. 1984. "The Ecology of Indian Music in North America." *Bansuri* 1:9–15.

Nguyen, Phong, with Adelaida Reyes Schramm and Patricia Shehan Campbell. 1995. *Searching for a Niche: Vietnamese Music at Home in America*. Kent, Ohio: Viet Music.

Nicholls, David, ed. 1999. *The Cambridge History of American Music*. Cambridge: Cambridge University Press.

O'Leary, Timothy J., and David Levinsohn, eds. *Encyclopedia of World Cultures*, Vol. 1: *North America*. Boston: G. K. Hall.

Oja, Carol. 1990. *Colin McPhee: Composer in Two Worlds*. Washington, D.C.: Smithsonian Institution Press.

Oliver, Paul. 1984. *Songsters and Saints: Vocal Traditions on Race Records*. New York: Cambridge.

———. 1998. *The Story of the Blues*, new ed. Boston: Northeastern University Press.

Olson, Kenneth E. 1981. *Music and Musket: Bands and Bandsmen of the American Civil War*. Westport, Conn.: Greenwood.

Otis, Johnny. 1993. *Upside Your Head! Rhythm and Blues on Central Avenue*. Hanover, N.H.: University Press of New England.

Pacini Hernández, Deborah. 1995. *Bachata: A Social History of a Dominican Popular Music*. Philadelphia: Temple University Press.

Palmer, Robert. 1981. *Deep Blues*. New York: Viking.

Panassié, Hugues. 1970 [1936]. *Hot Jazz: The Guide to Swing Music*. Westport, Conn.: Negro Universities Press.

Paredes, Americo. 1958. *With His Pistol in His Hand*. Austin: University of Texas Press.

———. 1976. *A Texas-Mexican Cancionero: Folksongs of the Lower Border*. Urbana: University of Illinois Press.

Patterson, Beverly Bush. 1995. *The Sound of the Dove: Singing in Appalachian Primitive Baptist Churches*. Urbana: University of Illinois Press.

Patterson, Daniel W. 1979. *The Shaker Spiritual*. Princeton, N.J.: Princeton University Press.

Peacock, Kenneth. 1970. *Songs of the Doukhobors: An Introductory Outline*. Bulletin No. 231, Folklore Series No. 7. Ottawa: National Museums of Canada.

Pearson, Barry Lee. 1984. *Sounds So Good to Me: The Bluesman's Story*. Philadelphia: University of Pennsylvania Press.

Peña, Manuel H. 1985. *The Texas-Mexican Conjunto: History of a Working Class Music*. Austin: University of Texas Press.

Peretti, Burton W. 1992. *The Creation of Jazz: Music, Race, and Culture in Urban America*. Urbana: University of Illinois Press.

Perkins, William Eric, ed. 1996. *Droppin' Science: Critical Essays on Rap Music and Hip Hop Culture*. Philadelphia: Temple University Press.

Perlman, Marc. 1983. "Some Reflections on New American Gamelan Music." *Ear Magazine* 7(4):4–5.

Peterson, Bernard L., Jr. 1993. *A Century of Musicals in Black and White*. Westport, Conn.: Garland.

Peterson, Elizabeth. 1996. *The Changing Faces of Tradition: A Report on the Folk and Traditional Arts in the United States*. Washington, D.C.: National Endowment for the Arts.

Peterson, Richard. 1997. *Creating Country Music: Fabricating Authenticity*. Chicago: University of Chicago Press.

Petkov, Steven, and Leonard Mustazza, eds. 1995. *The Frank Sinatra Reader*. New York: Oxford University Press.

Porter, Lewis, and Michael Ullman. 1993. *Jazz: From Its Origins to the Present*. Englewood Cliffs, N.J.: Prentice Hall.

Porter, Susan L. 1991. *With an Air Debonair: Musical Theater in America, 1785–1815*. Washington, D.C.: Smithsonian Institution Press.

Poschardt, Ulf. 1995. *DJ Culture*. Hamburg, Germany: Rogner and Bernard.

Potter, Keith. 2000. *Four Musical Minimalists: La Monte Young, Terry Riley, Steve Reich, Philip Glass*. New York and Cambridge: Cambridge University Press.

Potter, Russell. 1995. *Spectacular Vernaculars: Hip Hop and the Politics of Postmodernism*. State University of New York Series in Postmodern Culture. Albany: State University of New York Press.

Preston, Katherine K. 1992. *Music for Hire: A Study of Professional Musicians in Washington (1877–1900)*. Stuyvesant, N.Y.: Pendragon.

Pritchett, James. 1993. *The Music of John Cage*. New York and Cambridge: Cambridge University Press.

Pruter, Robert. 1996. *Doowop: The Chicago Scene*. Urbana: University of Illinois Press.

Qureshi, Regula. 1972. "Ethnomusicological Research among Canadian Communities of Arab and East Indian Origin." *Ethnomusicology* 16:381–396.

Racy, Ali Jihad, and Simon Shaheen. 1992. "An Evening in the Orient: The Middle Eastern Nightclub in America." *Asian Music* 23(2):63–88.

Rasmussen, Anne K. 1991. "Individuality and Social Change in the Music of Arab Americans." Ph.D. dissertation, University of California, Los Angeles.

Reagon, Bernice L., ed. 1992. *We'll Understand It Better By and By: Pioneering African American Gospel Composers*. Washington, D.C.: Smithsonian Institution Press.

Redhead, Steve. 1990. *The End-of-the-Century Party: Youth and Pop towards 2000*. Manchester, Eng.: Manchester University Press.

Rehrig, William H. 1991. *The Heritage Encyclopedia of Band Music: Composers and Their Music*, ed. Paul Bierley. 2 vols. Westerville, Ohio: Integrity.

Reich, Steve. 1974. *Writings about Music*. Halifax: Press of Nova Scotia College of Art and Design.

Reyes, Adelaida. 1999. *Songs of the Caged, Songs of the Free: Music and the Vietnamese Refugee Experience*. Philadelphia: Temple University Press.

Reyes, Luis I. 1995. *Made in Paradise: Hollywood's Films of Hawaii and the South Seas*. Honolulu: Mutual.

Reynolds, Simon, and Joy Press. 1995. *The Sex Revolts: Gender, Rebellion and Rock 'n' Roll*. Cambridge: Harvard University Press.

Riddle, Ronald. 1983. *Flying Dragons, Flowing Streams: Music in the Life of San Francisco's Chinese*. Westport, Conn.: Greenwood.

Riis, Thomas L. 1989. *Just before Jazz: Black Musical Theater in New York, 1890–1915*. Washington, D.C.: Smithsonian Institution Press.

Robb, John Donald. 1980. *Hispanic Folk Music of New Mexico and the Southwest: A Self-Portrait of a People*. Norman: University of Oklahoma Press.

Roberts, Helen Heffron. 1970 [1936]. *Musical Areas in Aboriginal North America*. Yale University Publications in Anthropology, No. 12. New Haven, Conn.: Yale University Press.

Roberts, John Storm. 1972. *Black Music of the Americas*. New York: Praeger.

———. 1979. *The Latin Tinge: The Impact of Latin American Music on the United States*. New York: Oxford University Press.

———. 1999. *The Latin Tinge: The Impact of Latin American Music on the United States*, 2nd ed. New York: Oxford University Press.

Robertson, Carol E., ed. 1992. *Musical Repercussions of 1492: Encounters in Text and Performance*. Washington, D.C.: Smithsonian Institution Press.

Rochberg, George. 1984. *The Aesthetics of Survival: A Composer's View of Twentieth-Century Music*. Ann Arbor: University of Michigan Press.

Rose, Tricia. 1994. *Black Noise: Rap Music and Black Culture in Contemporary America*. Hanover, N.H.: University Press of New England.

Rosenberg, Neil V. 1985. *Bluegrass: A History*. Urbana: University of Illinois Press.

Rosenberg, Neil V., ed. 1993. *Transforming Tradition: Folk Music Revivals Examined*. Chicago: University of Illinois Press.

Ross, Andrew, and Tricia Rose, eds. 1994. *Microphone Fiends: Youth Music and Youth Culture*. New York: Routledge.

Rowe, Mike. 1981 [1975]. *Chicago Blues: The City and the Music*. New York: Da Capo.

Russell, Tony. 1970. *Blacks, Whites, and Blues*, ed. Paul Oliver. New York: Stein and Day.

Ruymar, Lorene. 1996. *The Hawaiian Steel Guitar and Its Great Hawaiian Musicians*. Anaheim Hills, Calif.: Centerstream.

Sablosky, Irving L. 1969. *American Music*. Chicago: University of Chicago Press.

Sachse, Johann F. 1903. *The Music of the Ephrata Cloister; also Conrad Beissel's A Preface to the "Turtel Taube" of 1747*. Lancaster: Pennsylvania German Society 12.

Sakolsky, Ron, and Fred Ho. 1995. *Sounding Off: Music as Subversion/Resistance/Revolution*. New York: Autonomedia.

Sam, Sam-Ang, and Patricia Shehan Campbell. 1991. *Silent Temples, Songful Hearts: Traditional Music of Cambodia*. Danbury, Conn.: World Music.

Sargeant, Winthrop. 1975 [1938]. *Jazz, Hot and Hybrid*, 3rd ed. New York: Da Capo.

Sarkissian, Margaret Lynne. 1987. "Armenian Musical Culture in Toronto: Political and Social Divisions in an Immigrant Community." Master's thesis, University of Illinois, Urbana-Champaign.

Sawaie, Mohammed. 1985. *Arabic Speaking Immigrants in the U.S. and Canada: An Annotated Bibliographic Guide*. Lexington, Ky.: Mazda.

Schafer, William J., with Richard B. Allen. 1977. *Brass Bands and New Orleans Jazz*. Baton Rouge: Louisiana State University Press.

Schuller, Gunther. 1968. *Early Jazz: Its Roots and Musical Development*. New York: Oxford University Press.

———. 1989. *The Swing Era: The Development of Jazz 1930–1945*. New York: Oxford University Press.

Sealey, John, and Krister Malm. 1982. *Music in the Caribbean*. Toronto: Hodder and Stoughton.

Seeger, Anthony. 1992. "Ethnomusicology and Music Law." *Ethnomusicology* 36(3):345–359.

Sexton, Adam, ed. 1995. *Rap on Rap: Straight-Up Talk on Hip-Hop Culture*. New York: Delta.

Shanet, Howard. 1975. *Philharmonic: A History of New York's Orchestra*. New York: Doubleday.

Shank, Barry. 1994. *Dissonant Identities: The Rock 'n' Roll Scene in Austin, Texas*. Hanover, N.H.: Wesleyan University Press.

Shannon, Doug. 1982. *Off the Record: The Disco Concept*. Cleveland: Pacesetter.

Sharp, Cecil. 1932. *English Folk Songs from the Southern Appalachians*. London: Oxford University Press.

Singer, Roberta L. 1982. "My Music Is Who I Am and What I Do: Latin Popular Music and Identity in New York City." Ph.D. dissertation, Indiana University.

Slobin, Mark. 1982. *Tenement Songs: The Popular Music of the Jewish Immigrants*. Urbana: University of Illinois Press.

———. 1990a. *Chosen Voices: The Story of the American Cantorate*. Urbana: University of Illinois Press.

———. 1993. *Subcultural Sounds: Micromusics of the West*. Hanover and London: Wesleyan University Press.

———. 2000. *Fiddler on the Move: Exploring the World of Klezmer*. New York: Oxford University Press.

Smith, Barbara B. 1975. "Chinese Music in Hawaii." *Asian Music* 6(1–2):225–230.

Smyth, Willie, ed. 1989. *Songs of Indian Territory: Native American Music Traditions of Oklahoma*. Oklahoma City: Center of the American Indian.

Sonneborn, Daniel Atesh. 1995. *Music and Meaning in American Sufism: The Ritual of Dhikr at Sami Mahal, a Chishtiyya-Derived Sufi Center*. Ann Arbor, Mich.: University Microfilms.

Southern, Eileen. 1983a [1971]. *The Music of Black Americans: A History*, 2nd ed. New York: Norton. (See also 3rd ed., 1997.)

Bibliography of Literature, Collections, and Artworks. Westport, Conn.: Greenwood.

Southern, Eileen, ed. 1983a [1967]. *Readings in Black American Music*, 2nd ed. New York: Norton.

———. 1994. *African-American Theater: Out of Bondage (1876) and Peculiar Sam; or The Underground Railroad (1879)*. Vol. 9 of *Nineteenth-Century American Musical Theater*, ed. Deane Root. New York: Garland.

Southern, Eileen, and Josephine Wright, comps. 1990. *African American Traditions in Song, Sermon, Tale, and Dance, 1600s–1920: An Annotated Bibliography of Literature, Collections, and Artworks*. Westport, Conn.: Greenwood.

Spicer, Edward H. 1985. *The Yaquis: A Cultural History*. Tucson: University of Arizona Press.

Spottswood, Richard K., ed. 1982. *Ethnic Recordings in America: A Neglected Heritage*. Washington, D.C.: American Folklife Center, Library of Congress.

Stark, Richard B. 1969. *Music of the Spanish Folk Plays in New Mexico*. Santa Fe: Museum of New Mexico Press.

Stearns, Marshall. 1970 [1956]. *The Story of Jazz*. New York: Oxford University Press.

Stevenson, Robert M. 1960. *Spanish Music in the Age of Columbus*. The Hague: Martinus Nijhoff.

———. 1988a. "Local Music History Research in Los Angeles Area Libraries: Part I." *Inter-American Music Review* 10(1):19–38.

———. 1988b. "Music in Southern California: A Tale of Two Cities (Los Angeles: The First Biennium and Beyond)." *Inter-American Music Review* 10(1):39–111.

Stowe, David W. 1994. *Swing Changes: Big Band Jazz in New Deal America*. Cambridge: Harvard University Press.

Stuessy, Joe. 1990. *Rock and Roll: Its History and Stylistic Development*. Englewood Cliffs, N.J.: Prentice Hall.

Sturman, Janet. 2000. *Zarzuela: Spanish Operetta, American Stage*. Urbana: University of Illinois Press.

Sudhalter, Richard M. 1999. *Lost Chords: White Musicians and Their Contributions to Jazz, 1915–1945*. New York: Oxford University Press.

Sugarman, Jane Cicely. 1997. *Engendering Song: Singing and Subjectivity at Prespa Albanian Weddings*. Chicago: University of Chicago Press.

Summit, Jeffrey A. 1993. "I'm a Yankee Doodle Dandy?: Identity and Melody at an American *Simhat Torah* Celebration." *Ethnomusicology* 37(1):41–62.

Sung, Betty Lee. 1967. *Mountain of Gold: The Story of the Chinese in America*. New York: Macmillan.

Swan, Howard. 1952. *Music in the Southwest, 1825–1950*. San Marino, Calif.: Huntington Library.

Tallant, Robert. 1983 [1966]. *Voodoo in New Orleans*. New York: Macmillan.

Talley, Thomas V. 1922. *Negro Folk Rhymes: Wise and Otherwise*. New York: Macmillan.

Tawa, Nicholas. 1995. *American Composers and Their Public: A Critical Look*. Metuchen, N.J.: Scarecrow.

Tawa, Nicholas E. 1982. *A Sound of Strangers: Musical Culture, Acculturation, and the Post–Civil War Ethnic-American*. Metuchen, N.J.: Scarecrow.

Thomas, J. C. 1975. *Chasin' the Trane: The Music and Mystique of John Coltrane*. Garden City, N.Y.: Doubleday.

Thompson, Gordon, and Medha Yodh. 1985. "Garba and the Gujaratis of Southern California." *Selected Reports in Ethnomusicology* 6:59–79.

Thomson, Virgil. 1971. *American Music since 1910*. New York: Holt, Rinehart, and Winston.

Tick, Judith. 1997. *Ruth Crawford Seeger: A Composer's Search for American Music*. New York: Oxford University Press.

Tinker, Edward Laroque. 1961. *Corridos and Calaveras*. Austin: University of Texas Press.

Tirro, Frank. 1977. *Jazz: A History*. New York: Norton.

Tischler, Barbara L. 1986. *An American Music: The Search for an American Musical Identity*. New York: Oxford University Press.

Titon, Jeff Todd. 1994 [1977]. *Early Downhome Blues: A Musical and Cultural Analysis*, 2nd ed. Chapel Hill: University of North Carolina Press.

Turner, Frederick. 1994. *Remembering Song: Encounters with the New Orleans Jazz Tradition*. New York: Da Capo.

Tuuletargad (Wind Wizards). 2000. *Estonian Instrumental Folk Music*. Chicago: Innovative Mechanics.

Varzi, Morteza, with Margaret Caton, Robyn C. Friend, and Neil Siegel. 1986. "Performer-Audience Relationships in the *Bazm*." In *Cultural Parameters of Iranian Musical Expression*, ed. Margaret Caton and Neil Siegel, 1–9. Redondo Beach, Calif.: Institute of Persian Performing Arts.

Vecoli, Rudolph J., Judy Galens, Anna Sheets, and Robyn V. Young, eds. 1985. *Gale Encyclopedia of Multicultural America*. Detroit: Gale Research.

Vincent, Rickey. 1996. *Funk: The Music, the People, and the Rhythm of the One*. New York: St. Martin's/Griffin.

Walser, Robert, ed. 1999. *Keeping Time: Readings in Jazz History*. New York: Oxford University Press.

Ward, Brian. 1998. *Just My Soul Responding: Rhythm and Blues, Black Consciousness, and Race Relations*. London: University College London Press.

Warren, Mark. 1990. *Dutch Hops: Colorado Music of the Germans from Russia, 1865–1965*. Evergreen, Colo.: Shadow Canyon Graphics.

Watkins, Glenn. 1988. *Soundings: Music in the Twentieth Century*. New York: Schirmer.

Weinstein, Deena. 1991. *Heavy Metal: A Cultural Sociology*. New York: Lexington.

Whisnant, David. 1983. *All That Is Native and Fine: The Politics of Culture in an American Region*. Chapel Hill: University of North Carolina Press.

White, William C. 1944. *A History of Military Music in America*. New York: Exposition.

Whiteley, Sheila, ed. 1997. *Sexing the Groove: Popular Music and Gender*. New York: Routledge.

Whitfield, Irène Thérèsa. 1981 [1939]. *Louisiana French Folk Songs*, 3rd ed. Eunice, La.: Hebert.

Wilcken, Lois E. 1991. *Music Folklore among Haitians in New York: Staged Representations and the Negotiation of Identity*. Ph.D. dissertation, Columbia University.

Wilcken, Lois, with Frisner Augustin. 1992. *The Drums of Vodou*. Crown Point, Ind.: White Cliffs Media.

Wilgus, Donald K. 1959. *Anglo-American Folksong Scholarship since 1898*. New Brunswick, N.J.: Rutgers University Press.

Williams, Martin. 1970. *The Jazz Tradition*. New York: Oxford University Press.

Witmer, Robert, ed. 1990. *Ethnomusicology in Canada: Proceedings of the First Conference on Ethnomusicology in Canada*. Toronto: Institute for Canadian Music.

Wolfe, Charles K. 1976. *Tennessee Strings: The Story of Country Music in Tennessee*. Knoxville: University of Tennessee Press.

———. 1982. *Kentucky Country*. Lexington: University of Kentucky Press.

———. 1999. *A Good Natured Riot: The Birth of the Grand Ole Opry*. Nashville: Vanderbilt University Press and Country Music Hall of Fame.

Wolfe, Richard J. *Secular Music in America: 1801–1825*. 3 vols. New York: New York Public Library.

Woll, Allen. 1989. *Black Musical Theater: From "Coontown" to "Dreamgirls."* Baton Rouge: Louisiana State University Press.

Wong, Isabel K. F. 1985. "The Many Roles of Peking Opera in San Francisco in the 1980s." In *The Asian Musician in North America,* ed. Nazir Jairazbhoy, 173–188. Selected Reports in Ethnomusicology, 6. Los Angeles: University of California.

Work, John W., III. 1940. *American Negro Songs and Spirituals: A Comprehensive Collection of 230 Folk Songs, Religious and Secular*. New York: Bonanza.

Wright, Robert L. 1965. *Swedish Emigrant Ballads*. Lincoln: University of Nebraska Press.

Zhang, Wei Hua. 1994. "The Musical Activities of the Chinese American Communities in the San Francisco Bay Area: A Social and Cultural Study." Ph.D. dissertation, University of California at Berkeley.

Zheng, Su de San. 1993. "Immigrant Music and Transnational Discourse: Chinese American Music Culture in New York City." Ph.D. dissertation, Wesleyan University.

Zheng, Su. 2001. *Claiming Diaspora: Music, Transnationalism, and Cultural Politics in Asian/Chinese America*. Oxford: Oxford University Press.

CANADA

Amtmann, Willy. 1975. *Music in Canada 1600–1800.* Montréal: Habitex.

Anthologie d'oeuvres musicales canadiennes (Anthology of Canadian Music). 1983–. Ottawa: Canadian Musical Heritage Society. (Collection of 25 volumes of printed Canadian music written before 1950.)

Barbeau, Marius. 1979 [1962]. *Le rossignol y chante.* Ottawa: National Museum of Canada.

Barbeau, Marius, and Jean Beck. 1962. *Jongleur Songs of Old Quebec.* New Brunswick, N.J.: Rutgers University Press.

Barbeau, Marius, and Marguerite d'Harcourt. 1937. *The Romancero du Canada.* Toronto: Macmillan.

Barbeau, Marius, and Edward Sapir. 1925. *Folk Songs of French Canada.* New Haven, Conn.: Yale University Press.

Beaton, Virginia, and Stephen Pederson. 1992. *Maritime Music Greats: Fifty Years of Hits and Heartbreak.* Halifax: Nimbus.

Beckwith, John, ed. 1986. *Hymn Tunes.* The Canadian Musical Heritage, Vol. 5. Ottawa: Canadian Musical Heritage Society.

———. 1987. "On Compiling an Anthology of Canadian Hymn Tunes." In *Sing Out the Glad News: Hymn Tunes in Canada. CanMus Documents* 1:3–32.

Beckwith, John, and Frederick A. Hall, eds. 1988. *Musical Canada: Words and Music Honouring Helmut Kallmann.* Toronto: University of Toronto Press.

Bégin, Carmelle. 1992. *La musique traditionnelle pour violon: Jean Carignan.* Ottawa: National Museum of Canada.

———. 1992. *Opus: The Making of Musical Instruments in Canada.* Hull: Canadian Museum of Civilization.

Béland, Madeleine. 1982. *Chansons de voyageurs, coureurs de bois, et forestiers.* Québec: Presses de l'Université Laval.

Berdugo-Cohen, Yolande, and Joseph Levy. 1987. *Juifs marocains à Montréal.* Montréal: VLB Editeur.

Berg, Wesley. 1985. *From Russia with Love: A Study of the Mennonite Choral Singing Tradition in Canada.* Winnipeg: Hyperion.

Berland, Jody. 1986. "Cultural Re/Percussions: The Social Production of Music Broadcasting in Canada." Ph.D. dissertation, York University.

Bohlman, Philip V. 1988. *The Study of Folk Music in the Modern World.* Bloomington: Indiana University Press.

Bonner, Simon. 1987. *Old Time Music Makers of New York State.* Syracuse, N.Y.: Syracuse University Press.

Brednich, Rolf Wilhelm. 1981. "Beharrung und Wandel im Liedgut der hutterischen Bruder: Ein Beitrag zur empirischen Hymnologie." *Jahrbuch für Volksliedforschung* 26:44–60.

Brydon, Anne, 2000. "Mother to Her Distant Children: The Icelandic *Fjallkona* in Canada." In *Undisciplined Women: Tradition and Culture in Canada,* ed. Pauline Greenhill and Diane Tye, 87–100. Montreal: McGill-Queen's University Press.

Burlin, Natalie Curtis. 1968 [1907]. *The Indians' Book.* New York: Dover.

Cahiers de la Société Québécoise de Recherche en Musique (SQRM). 1983–. Montréal. (Formerly: Association pour l'Avancement de la Recherche en Musique du Québec.)

Calderisi, Maria. 1981. *Music Publishing in the Canadas, 1800–1867.* Ottawa: National Library.

Canada's Year of Asia Pacific Multicultural Bibliography. 1997. Vancouver, B.C.: British Columbia Teacher-Librarians' Association.

The Canadian Musical Heritage/Le patrimoine musical canadien. 1983–1999. Website: http://www.cmhs.carleton.ca. (25 volumes of pre-1950 Canadian notated music, each edition preceded by an essay on the genre concerned.)

Carpenter, Carole Henderson. 1979. *Many Voices: A Study of Folklore Activities in Canada and Their Role in Canadian Culture.* Ottawa: National Museums of Canada.

Carruthers, Glen, and Gordana Lazarevich, eds. 1996. *A Celebration of Canada's Arts 1930–1970.* Toronto: Canadian Scholars'.

Cass-Beggs, Barbara. 1967. *Seven Métis Songs.* Don Mills: BMI Canada.

CBC. 1981. *Culture, Broadcasting, and the Canadian Identity.* S.L.: Canadian Broadcasting Corporation. (Pamphlet.)

Chiasson, Père Anselme. 1942–1979. *Chansons d'Acadie.* Vols. 1–3, Pointe-aux-Trembles, P.Q.: Le Réparation. Vols. 4–5, Moncton: Éditions des Aboiteaux.

Clairmont, D. H., and Magill, Dennis W. 1974. *Africville: The Life and Death of a Canadian Black Community.* Toronto: McClelland and Stewart.

Creighton, Helen. 1961. *Maritime Folk Songs.* Toronto: Ryerson.

———. 1966. *Songs and Ballads from Nova Scotia.* New York: Dover.

———. 1971. *Folksongs from Southern New Brunswick.* Ottawa: National Museum of Civilization.

———. 1988. *La fleur du rosier: Chansons folkloriques d'Acadie,* ed. Ronald Labelle. Ottawa and Sydney: Canadian Museum of Civilization and University College of Cape Breton.

Creighton, Helen, and Calum MacLeod. 1979. *Gaelic Songs in Nova Scotia.* Ottawa: National Museums of Canada.

Creighton, Helen, and Doreen Senior. 1950. *Traditional Songs from Nova Scotia.* Toronto: Ryerson.

Croft, Clary. 1999. *Helen Creighton: Canada's First Lady of Folklore.* Halifax: Nimbus.

Daigle, Jean, ed. 1982. *The Acadians of the Maritimes: Thematic Studies.* Moncton: Centre d'Études Acadiennes.

Davies, Sandra, et al. 1982. *The Chinese People: Music, Instruments, Folklore.* Vancouver, B.C.: Western Education Development Group.

Davies, Sandra, et al. 1986. *Japanese People: Music, Instruments, Arts, Crafts.* Vancouver, B.C.: Western Education Development Group.

Denisoff, R. Serge. 1972. *Sing a Song of Social Significance.* Bowling Green, Ohio: Bowling Green University Popular Press.

Deschenes, Donald. 1982. *C'était la plus jolie des filles: Répertoire des chansons d'Angélina Paradis-Fraser.* Montréal: Éditions Quinze.

Diamond, Beverley, and James Robbins. 1992. "Ethnomusicology." In *Encyclopedia of Music in Canada,* ed. Helmut Kallmann et al., 422–431. Toronto: University of Toronto.

Diamond, Beverley, and Robert Witmer, eds. 1994. *Canadian Music: Issues of Hegemony and Identity.* Toronto: Canadian Scholars'.

Diamond, Beverley, et al. 1994. *Visions of Sound: Musical Instruments of First Nations Communities in Northeastern America.* Chicago: University of Chicago Press; Waterloo: Wilfrid Laurier University Press.

Dibblee, Randall, and Dorothy Dibblee. 1973. *Folksongs from Prince Edward Island.* Summerside: Williams and Crue.

Doherty, Elizabeth A. 1996. "The Paradox of the Periphery: Evolution of the Cape Breton Fiddle Tradition 1928–1995." Ph.D. dissertation, University of Limerick.

Drakich, Janice, Edward Kovarik, and Ramona Lumpkin, eds. 1995. *With a Song in Her Heart: A Celebration of Canadian Women Composers.* Windsor, Ont.: University of Windsor Humanities Research Group.

Driedger, Leo, ed. 1978. *The Canadian Ethnic Mosaic: A Quest for Identity.* Toronto: McClelland and Stewart.

Dunlay, Kate, and David Greenberg. 1996. *Traditional Celtic Violin Music of Cape Breton: The DunGreen Collection.* Mississauga, Ont.: DunGreen Music.

Eagle, John A. 1989. *The Canadian Pacific Railway and the Development of Western Canada, 1896–1914.* Kingston: McGill-Queen's University Press.

Einarsson, Magnús. 1992. *Icelandic-Canadian Memory Lore.* Ottawa: Canadian Museum of Civilization.

Elliott, Robin. 1997. *Counterpoint to a City: The First One Hundred Years of the Women's Musical Club of Toronto.* Toronto: ECW.

Epp, Frank H. 1982. *Mennonites in Canada 1920–1940: A People's Struggle for Survival.* Toronto: Macmillan of Canada.

Farquharson, Dorothy H. 1983. *Oh for a Thousand Tongues to Sing: A History of Singing Schools in Early Canada.* Waterdown, Ont.

Fleming, Lee. 1997. *Rock, Rhythm, and Reels: Canada's East Coast Musicians on Stage.* Charlottetown: Ragweed.

Fowke, Edith. 1965. *Traditional Singers and Songs from Ontario*. Hatboro: Folklore Associates.

———. 1985. *Lumbering Songs from the Northern Woods*. Toronto: NC.

———. 1988. *Canadian Folklore*. Toronto: Oxford University Press.

Fowke, Edith, and Jay Rahn. 1994. *A Family Heritage: LaRena Clark's Story and Songs*. Calgary: University of Calgary Press.

Friesen, Gerald. 1984. *The Canadian Prairies: A History*. Toronto: University of Toronto Press.

Gagnon, F. Ernest A. 1880 [1865–1867]. *Chansons populaires du Canada*. Montréal: Beauchemin.

Gareau, Laurier. 1990. *Le défi de la radio française en Saskatchewan*. Regina: Société Historique de la Saskatchewan.

Gibbons, Roy W. 1982. *As It Comes: Folk Fiddling in Prince George, British Columbia*. Mercury Series, 42. Ottawa: National Museum of Man.

Gibson, John G. 1998. *Traditional Gaelic Bagpiping, 1745–1945*. Montréal: McGill-Queen's University Press.

Giroux, Robert, ed. 1984. *Les aires de la chanson québécoise*. Montréal: Tryptique.

Gledhill, Christopher. 1973. *Folksongs of Prince Edward Island*. Summerside: Williams and Crue.

Green, J. Paul, and Nancy F. Vogan. 1991. *Music Education in Canada: A Historical Account*. Toronto: University of Toronto Press.

Hahn, R. Richard. 1981. *The Role of Radio in the Canadian Music Industry*. Toronto: Canadian Association of Broadcasters. (Prepared for submission to the CRTC.)

d'Harcourt, Marguerite, and Raoul d'Harcourt. 1956. *Chansons folkloriques du Canada*. Québec: Presses de L'Université Laval.

Helm, June, and Nancy Lurie. 1962. *The Dogrib Hand Game*. Ottawa: National Museum of Man.

Henry, Frances. 1975. "Black Music in the Maritimes." *Canadian Folk Music Journal/Revue de Musique Folklorique Canadienne* 3:3–10.

Historical Anthology of Canadian Music. 1996. Ottawa: Canadian Music Heritage Society.

Hoe, Ban Seng. 1979. *Structural Changes of Two Chinese Communities in Alberta, Canada*. Canadian Center for Folk Culture Studies Paper 19. Ottawa: National Museums of Canada.

Ives, Edward D. 1989. *Folksongs of New Brunswick*. Fredericton: Goose Lane Editions.

Jackson, Peter. 1992. "The Politics of the Streets: A Geography of Caribana." *Political Geography* 11(2):130–151.

Kallmann, Helmut. 1960. *A History of Music in Canada, 1534–1914*. Toronto: University of Toronto Press.

Kallmann, Helmut, and Gilles Potvin, eds. 1992. *Encyclopedia of Music in Canada*, 2nd ed. Toronto: University of Toronto Press.

Keeling, Richard, ed. 1992. *Music and Spiritual Power among the Indians of North America*. Special Issue, *World of Music* 92(2).

Keillor, Elaine. 1997. "*Auf Kanadischer Welle:* The Establishment of the Germanic Musical Canon in Canada." In *Kanada-Studien: Music in Canada*, ed. Guido Bimberg, 49–76. Bochum, Germany: Brockmeyer.

Kelly, Wayne. 1991. *Downright Upright: A History of the Canadian Piano Industry*. Toronto: National Heritage/National History.

Klassen, Doreen Helen. 1989. *Singing Mennonite: Low German Songs among the Mennonites*. Winnipeg: University of Manitoba Press.

Klymasz, Robert B. 1972. "'Sounds You Never Before Heard': Ukrainian Country Music in Western Canada." *Ethnomusicology* 16(3):372–380.

———. 1989. *The Ukrainian Folk Ballad in Canada*. New York: AMS. (Transcriptions by Ken Peacock.)

———. 1991. *Art and Ethnicity: The Ukrainian Tradition in Canada*. Hull, P.Q.: Canadian Museum of Civilization.

———. 1992. *Sviéto: Celebrating Ukrainian Canadian Ritual in East Central Alberta through the Generations*. Edmonton: Alberta Culture and Multiculturalism, Historical Resources Division.

Lapointe, Jean-François. 1994. *Portrait de la distribution indépendante de phonogrammes au Québec: Principaux rôles et enjeux*. Montréal: Mémoire de Maîtrise, Université de Montréal.

Lehr, Genevieve. 1985. *Come and I Will Sing You: A Newfoundland Songbook*. Toronto: University of Toronto Press.

Lemieux, Germain. 1974. *Chansonnier franco-ontarien 1*. Sudbury: Centre Franco-Ontarien de Folklore, University of Sudbury.

———. 1975. *Chansonnier franco-ontarien 2*. Sudbury: Centre Franco-Ontarien de Folklore, University of Sudbury.

Levine, Lawrence W. 1988. *Highbrow/Lowbrow: The Emergence of Cultural Hierarchy in America*. Cambridge, Mass.: Harvard University Press.

Lutz, Maija. 1978. *The Effects of Acculturation on Eskimo Music of Cumberland Sound Peninsula*. Mercury Series, 41. Ottawa: National Museum of Man. (Record included.)

———. 1982. *Musical Traditions of the Labrador Coast Inuit*. Ottawa: National Museums.

MacDonell, Margaret. 1982. *The Emigrant Experience: Songs of Highland Emigrants in North America*. Toronto: University of Toronto Press.

MacGillivray, Allister. 1981. *The Cape Breton Fiddler*. Sydney, N.S.: College of Cape Breton Press.

MacMillan, Keith, and John Beckwith, eds. 1975. *Contemporary Canadian Composers*. Toronto: Oxford University Press.

Magocsi, Paul R., ed. 1999. *Encyclopedia of Canada's Peoples*. Toronto: University of Toronto Press.

McGee, Timothy J. 1985. *The Music of Canada*. New York: Norton.

McGuire, Matthew D. 1998. *Music in Nova Scotia: The Oral Tradition*. Halifax: Nova Scotia Museum Curatorial Report No. 84.

McIntosh, Dale. 1989. *History of Music in British Columbia, 1850–1950*. Victoria, B.C.: Sono Nis.

McIntyre, Paul. 1976. *Black Pentecostal Music in Windsor*. Mercury Series, 15. Ottawa: National Museums of Manitoba.

Mercer, Paul. 1979. *Newfoundland Songs and Ballads in Print, 1842–1974: A Title and First Line Index*. St. John's: Memorial University of Newfoundland.

Morey, Carl. 1997. *Music in Canada: A Research and Information Guide*. New York and London: Garland.

Peacock, Kenneth. 1965a. *Songs of the Newfoundland Outports*. 3 vols. Ottawa: National Museums.

———. 1965b. *A Survey of Ethnic Folk Music across Western Canada*. Ottawa: National Museums.

———. 1966. *Twenty Ethnic Songs from Western Canada*. Ottawa: National Museum of Canada.

———. 1970. *Songs of the Doukhobors*. Bulletin 231, Folklore Series 7. Ottawa: National Museum of Man. (Includes 3 LP disks. Flexidiscs TM 3.)

———. 1970. *Songs of the Doukhobors*. Ottawa: National Museums.

———. 1971. *A Garland of Rue: Lithuanian Folksongs of Love and Betrothal*. Ottawa: National Museums of Canada.

Pelinski, Ramon. 1975. "The Music of Canada's Ethnic Minorities." *Canadian Music Book* 10:59–83.

Perkowski, Jan L. 1973–74. *Gusle and Ganga among the Herzegovians of Toronto*. Ann Arbor, Mich.: University Microfilms International.

Proctor, George A. 1980. *Canadian Music of the Twentieth Century*. Toronto: University of Toronto Press.

Quigley, Colin. 1985. *Close to the Floor: Folk Dance in Newfoundland*. St. John's: Memorial University of Newfoundland, Folklore Department.

Qureshi, Regula Burckhardt. 1972. "Ethnomusicological Research among Canadian Communities of Arab and East Indian Origin." *Ethnomusicology* 16(3):381–396.

Rogers, Tim B. 1990. "Country Music Bands in Canada during the 1950s: A Comparative Survey." In *Ethnomusicology in Canada*, ed. Robert Witmer, 226–234. CanMus Documents, 5. Toronto: Institute for Canadian Music.

Ruprecht, Alvina, and Cecilia Taiana, eds. 1995. *The Reordering of Culture: Latin America, the Caribbean, and Canada in the Hood*. Ottawa: Carleton University Press.

Sale, David. 1968. "Toronto's Pre-Confederation Music Societies." Master's thesis, University of Toronto.

Schafer, R. Murray. 1977. *The Tuning of the World*. Toronto: McClelland and Stewart.

Seguin, Robert-Lionel. 1986. *La danse traditionnelle à Québec*. Québec: Presses de l'Université Laval.

Stiles, J. Mark, and Jacques Lachance. 1988. *History and Present Status of Community Radio in Québec*. Ottawa: Stiles Associates. (Ministry of Culture and Communications, Government of Ontario.)

Straw, Will, et al., eds. 1995. *Popular Music: Style and Identity*. Montréal: Center for Research on Canadian Cultural Industries and Institutions.

Sugarman, Jane. 1997. *Embodied Subjectivities: Singing and Subjectivity at Prespa Albanian Weddings*. Chicago: University of Chicago Press.

Thérien, Robert, and Isabelle D'Amours. 1992. *Dictionnaire de la musique populaire au Québec 1955–1992*. Montréal. Institut Québécois de Recherche sur la Culture.

Thomas, Philip J. 1979. *Songs of the Pacific Northwest*. Saanichton, B.C.: Hancock House.

Tippett, Maria. 1990. *Making Culture: English-Canadian Institutions and the Arts before the Massey Commission*. Toronto: University of Toronto Press.

Tremblay, Danielle. 1993. "Le développement historique et le fonctionnement de l'industrie de la chanson québécoise." *Research Report Presented to Québec City Museum of Civilization* (26 March):1–83.

Vennum, Thomas, Jr. 1982. *The Ojibwa Dance Drum: Its History and Construction*. Smithsonian Folklife Studies, 2. Washington, D.C.: Smithsonian Institution Press.

Walter, Arnold, ed. 1969. *Aspects of Music in Canada*. Toronto: University of Toronto Press.

Wilkinson, Kealy, and Associates. 1988. *Community Radio in Ontario*. Toronto: Ministry of Culture and Communications.

Witmer, Robert. 1982. *The Musical Life of the Blood Indians*. Ottawa: National Museums.

Witmer, Robert, ed. 1990. *Ethnomusicology in Canada*. CanMus Documents, 5. Toronto: Institute for Canadian Music.

Woodford, Paul. 1988. *We Love the Place, O Lord: A History of the Written Musical Tradition of Newfoundland and Labrador to 1949*. St. John's: Creative Printers and Publishers.

Wrazen, Louise. 1991. "Traditional Music Performance among *Gorale* in Canada." *Ethnomusicology* 35:173–193.

Young, Russell Scott. 1956. "Vieilles chansons de Nouvelle France." *Archives de Folklore* 7. Québec: Presses de l'Université Laval.

Recordings of the Music of the United States and Canada

GENERAL

After the Ball: A Treasury of Turn-of-the-Century Popular Songs. Elektra-Nonesuch 79148-2. Compact disk.

American Dreamer: Songs of Stephen Foster. 1992. Angel CDC 07777-54621-28. Compact disk.

American Popular Song: Six Decades of Songwriters and Singers. 1984. Smithsonian R031 P7 17983. Compact disk.

Boley, Raymond. 1976. *Gourd Dance Songs of the Kiowa*. Canyon Records C-6148.

Brand, Oscar. 1960. *Election Songs of the United States*. New York: Folkways Records FH5280. LP disk.

Cohen, Norm. 1991. Notes to "Folk Song America: A Twentieth-Century Revival." Notes for *Smithsonian Collection of Recordings* R 046/P6 21489. Compact disk.

Densmore, Frances. 1952. *Songs of the Nootka and Quileute*. Library of Congress AAFS L32. LP disk.

Fenton, William N. 1942. *Songs from the Iroquois Longhouse*. Library of Congress AFS L6. LP disk.

The Great American Composers: Irving Berlin. 1989. CBS C21/2 7929. Compact disk.

The Great American Composers: George and Ira Gershwin. 1989. CBS C21/2 7925. Compact disk.

The Great American Composers: Jerome Kern. 1990. CBS C21/2 7973. Compact disk.

The Great American Composers: Cole Porter. 1989. CBS C21/2 7926. Compact disk.

The Great American Composers: Rodgers and Hart. 1990. CBS C21/2 7971. Compact disk.

Indian Music of the Pacific Northwest Coast. 1967. Collected and recorded by Ida Halpern. Folkways Records FE 4523. LP disk.

Kwakiutl Indian Music of the Pacific Northwest. n.d. Ethnic Folkways Record Library FE 4122. LP disk.

Moore's Irish Melodies. 1984. Nonesuch 79059. LP disk.

Rhodes, Willard. 1950. *Northwest (Puget Sound)*. Library of Congress AFS L34. LP disk.

Simon, Paul. 1986. *Graceland*. Warner Bros. 9 26098-2. Compact disk.

Sing along with Millard Fillmore: The Life Album of Presidential Campaign Songs. Columbia Mono-CL 2260. LP disk.

The Smithsonian Collection of American Musical Theater: Shows, Songs, and Stars. 1989. Smithsonian RD 036 A4 20483. Compact disk.

AMERICAN INDIANS, FIRST NATIONS

Anon. 1970. *Songs of the Muskogee Creek*, Parts 1–2. Indian House IH 3001, IH 3002. LP disk.

———. 1971, 1974. *American Indian Music of the Mississippi Choctaws*, Vols. 1–2. United Sound Recorders USR 3519, USR 7133. LP disk.

———. 1976. *Songs of the Caddo*. Canyon Records C 6146. LP disk.

d'Azevedo, Warren L. 1972. *Washo-Peyote Songs: Songs of the American Indian Native Church-Peyotist*. 12-page reprint of a 1957 study by Alan P. Merriam and Warren L. d'Azevedo. Ethnic Folkways Library Album No. FE 4384. LP disk.

Beaudry, Nicole. 1984. *Inuit Traditional Songs and Games*. Canadian Broadcasting Corporation, Northern Québec Service. SQN 108. LP disk.

Boley, Raymond. 1976. *Gourd Dance Songs of the Kiowa*. Canyon Records C-6148.

Boulton, Laura. 1954. *The Eskimos of Hudson Bay and Alaska*. Folkways Records FE 4444. LP disk.

———. 1992 [1933, 1940/1992]. *Navajo Songs*. Notes by Charlotte J. Frisbie and David P. McAllester. Smithsonian Folkways CD SF 40403. Compact disk.

Bouvette, Reg. c. 1970. *Red River Jig*. Sunshine Records SSB 402. LP disk and cassette.

Haida Indian Music of the Pacific Northwest. 1986, Recorded and annotated by Ida Halpern. Folkways Records. LP disk.

Healing Songs of the American Indians. 1965. Notes by Charles Hofmann. Ethnic Folkways Library FE 425 1. LP disk.

Honor the Earth Powwow: Songs of the Great Lakes Indians. 1991. Thomas Vennum Jr., notes; Mickey Hart, Jens McVoy, and Thomas Vermont Jr., research and recording. Rykodisc RACS 0 199.

Indian Music of the Pacific Northwest Coast. 1967. Collected and recorded by Ida Halpern. Folkways Records FE 4523. LP disk.

Jones, Owen R., Jr. 1972. *Music of the Algonkians: Woodland Indians (Cree, Montagnais, Naskapi)*. Folkways FE 4253. LP disk.

Kwakiutl: Indian Music of the Pacific Northwest. 1981. Collected, recorded, and annotated by Ida Halpern. Folkways Records. LP disk.

Lederman, Anne. 1987a. *Old Native and Métis Fiddling in Manitoba*, Vols. 1 and 2. Falcon Productions FP 187, FP 287. Compact disks.

Le Mouël, J. F., and M. Le Mouël. n.d. *Music of the Inuit. The Copper Eskimo Tradition*. Unesco Collection, Musical Atlas. EMI-Odon 64-240278 1. LP disk.

Meilleur, Marcel. 1984. *Turtle Mountain Music*. Folkways FES 4140. Compact disk.

Mishler, Craig. 1974. *Music of the Alaskan Kutchin Indians*. Folkways FE 4070. LP disk.

Nattiez, Jean-Jacques. 1989. *Jeux vocaux des Inuit (Inuit du Caribou, Netsilik, et Igloolik)*. Ocora. CD HM83.

Ned, Buster. 1976–1977. *Choctaw-Chickasaw Dance Songs*, Vols. 1–2. Mannsville, Okla.: Choctaw-Chickasaw Heritage Committee. LP disk.

Nootka Indian Music of the Pacific Northwest Coast. 1974. Collected, recorded, and annotated by Ida Halpern. Folkways Records FE 4524. LP disk.

Plains Chippewa/Métis Music from Turtle Mountain: Drums, Fiddles, Chansons, and Rock and Roll. 1992. Smithsonian/Folkways SF 40411. Compact disk.

Relocation. Originally Canyon Records C-7121, released in 1977. Since 1990, available on CD and cassette as S.O.A.R. 131 (Sound of America Record).

Rhodes, Willard, ed. 1984. *Music of the American Indian, Great Basin: Paiute, Washo, Ute, Bannock, Shoshone*. Library of Congress Archive of Folk

Culture, Recording Laboratory AFS L38. Cassette.

Rhodes, Willard. n.d. *Delaware, Cherokee, Choctaw, Creek*. Library of Congress AFS L37. LP disk.

Seneca Social Dance Music. 1980. Smithsonian Folkways Recordings FE 4072. Compact disk.

Songs and Dances of the Great Lakes Indians. 1956. Recording and liner notes by Gertrude Prokosch Kurath. Monograph Series of the Ethnic Folkways Library. Smithsonian-Folkways Recordings P 1003. LP disk.

Songs of the Chippewa, Vol. 1: *Game and Social Dance Songs*. 1977. Recording and liner notes by Paul Parthun. Smithsonian-Folkways FE 4392.

Songs of Earth, Water, Fire, and Sky: Music of the American Indians. 1976. New World Records NW 246. LP disk.

Southern Ute Singers. 1974. Canyon Records CR-6113-C.

Sryker, Miriam. 1966. *Eskimo Songs from Alaska*. Record FE 4069 and booklet. New York: Folkways.

Suluk, Donald, and Alice Suluk. n.d. *Inuit Songs and Dances*. Canadian Broadcasting Corporation, Northern Québec Services. Cassette.

Vennum, Thomas, Jr. 1973. *Chippewa Grass Dance Songs: The Kingbird Singers of Ponemah, Minnesota*. Canyon Records C-6106.

Wood That Sings: Indian Fiddle Music of the Americas. 1997. Smithsonian Folkways SF CD 40472. Compact disk.

UNITED STATES

Alpert, Michael. 1993. *Like in a Different World: Leon Schwartz, a Traditional Jewish Klezmer Violinist from Ukraine*. Global Village C 117. Cassette.

American Fiddle Tunes from the Library of Congress, AFS L62. Washington, D.C.: Library of Congress.

American Works for Balinese Gamelan Orchestra. Gamelan Sekar Jaya, Seka Gong Abdi Budaya, and students at STSI Denpasar. 1993. Produced by Evan Ziporyn, Michael Tenzer, and Wayne Vitale. Notes by Marc Perlman. Compositions by Ziporyn, I Nyoman Windha, Tenzer, and Vitale. New World Records 80430-2. Compact disk.

B.A.N.G. (Bay Area New Gamelan). 1986. Directed by Jody Diamond and Daniel Schmidt. Instruments built by Daniel Schmidt. Compositions by Schmidt, Diamond, and Ingram Marshall. Lebanon, N.H.: American Gamelan Institute. AGIO1. Cassette.

Basque Music of Boise Tradizioa Bizirik (The Tradition Lives). 1995. Boise, Idaho: Basque Museum and Cultural Center. Audiocassette.

Batacumbele. 1987. *Afro Caribbean Jazz*. Montieno, Records MLP 525. LP disk.

The Best of the Sufi Choir: A Jubilee Selection. 1993. San Francisco: SIRS Caravan Publications CMM 010. Compact disk.

Big Band and Quartet in Concert. 1963. Columbia C58964. LP disk.

Black 47: Fire of Freedom. 1993. New York: EMI Records. Compact disk.

Blades, Rubén. 1983. *El que la hace la paga*. Fania JM 624. LP disk.

Borderlands: From Conjunto to Chicken Scratch: Music of the Rio Grande Valley of Texas and Southern Arizona. 1993. Smithsonian Folkways SF-40418. Compact disk.

Boston Camerata. 1994. *Nueva España: Close Encounters in the New World 1590–1690*. Cohen, Joel, director. WEA/Atlantic/Erato 45977. Compact disk.

Botkin, Benjamin Albert. 1959 [1942]. Notes to *Negro Work Songs and Calls*. Library of Congress, Division of Music, Recording Laboratory AAFS L8. LP disk.

Caliente = Hot: Puerto Rican and Cuban Musical Expression in New York. 1977. New World Records NW 244. LP disk.

Los Camperos de Nati Cano. 1972. *El super Mariachi los Camperos*. Discos Latin International DLIS 2003. LP disk.

Castel, Nico. 1977. *Sefarad: The Sephardic Tradition in Ladino Song*. New York: Tara Productions. Tambour TR-590. Compact disk.

Chávez, Alex J. 1995 [1965]. *El Testamento*. Albuquerque Museum's Music of New Mexico Series. *Hispano Folk Music of the Past*, Cantante C95-1. Compact disk.

The Clancy Brothers with Tommy Makem: Luck of the Irish. 1992. New York: Columbia/Legacy CK47900. Reissue of classic recording on compact disk.

Coltrane, John. 1968. *Om*. Impulse A-9140. LP disk.

¡Conjunto! Texas-Mexican Border Music. 1988. Vol. 1. Rounder Records ROUN6023. Compact disk.

———. 1988. Vol. 2. Rounder Records ROUN6024. Compact disk.

———. 1990a. Vol. 3. Rounder Records ROUN6030. Compact disk.

———. 1990b. Vol. 4. Rounder Records ROUN6034. Compact disk.

———. 1994a. Vol. 5. Rounder Records ROUN6051. Compact disk.

———. 1994b. Vol. 6. Rounder Records ROUN6052. Compact disk.

Corridos, Part 1: *1930–1934*. 1975. Texas-Mexican Border Music, Vol. 2. Folklyric 9004. LP disk.

Corridos, Part 2: *1929–1936*. 1975. Texas-Mexican Border Music, Vol. 3. Folklyric 9005. LP disk.

Dances of Universal Peace, Vol. 1. 1987 [1975]. Seattle: PeaceWorks INDUP T100. Audiocassette.

Dark and Light in Spanish New Mexico. 1995 [1978]. New World Records 80292-2. Compact disk.

Das Efx. 1992. *Dead Serious*. East West Records America 7 91627-4. Compact disk.

Denny, Martin. 1957. *Exotica*. Liberty Records, LRP-3034. LP disk.

Dr. Dre. 1991. *The Chronic*. Priority Records P257129. Compact disk.

East Coast–West Coast: American Music for Gamelan. Venerable Showers of Beauty/A

Different Song. Directed by Vincent McDermott and Widiyanto S. Putro; Gamelan Son of Lion directed by Barbara Benary. Compositions by McDermott and Benary. Independently produced cassette.

East Side Revue: 40 Hits by East Los Angeles' Most Popular Groups. 1969 [1966]. Rampart; distributed by American Pie as LP 3303. LP disk.

East Side Story, Vols. 1–12. n.d. Trojan LP-2012. LP disk.

El Chicano. 1988. *¡Viva! El Chicano: Their Very Best*. MCA.

El Gran Combo. 1977. *Homenaje a México*. Combo C 1011. LP disk.

Endo, Kenny. *Taiko* Ensemble. 1994. *Eternal Energy*. AsianImprov Records AIR 002 1. Compact disk.

Eternal Voices: Traditional Vietnamese Music in the United States. 1993. New Alliance Records NAR CD 053. Compact disk.

Euzkadil: Songs and Dances of the Basque Juan Onatibia. 1954. Smithsonian-Folkways F-6830. LP disc.

Evans, David. 1978. Notes to *Let's Get Loose: Folk and Popular Blues Styles from the Beginnings to the Early 1940s*. New World Records NW 290. LP disk.

Fania All Stars. 1981. *Perfect Blend*. CBS Records 10453. LP disk.

Flatt, Lester, and Earl Scruggs. 1991. *Flatt & Scruggs, 1948–1959*. Notes by Neil V. Rosenberg. Bear Family BCD 15472. Compact disk.

Golden Treasures, Vol. 1: *West Coast East Side Revue*. 1966. Rampart 3303. LP disk.

Golden Treasures, Vol. 2: *West Coast East Side Revue*. 1969. Rampart 3305. LP disk.

The Hadrat. 1982. Sufi Zikr Series, no. 3. San Francisco: Sufi Islamia/Prophecy Publications SI/P 003. Audiocassette.

Hancock, Herbie. 1983. *Future Shock*. Columbia/Legacy CK 65962. Compact disk.

Heth, Charlotte, ed. 1976. *New World Records*, Vol. 1. New York, N246. LP New World Records.

Hiroshima. 1979. *Hiroshima*. Arista Records AB 4252. LP disk.

———. 1979/1980. *Ongaku*. Arista Records ARCD 8437. Compact disk.

———. 1980. *Odori*. Arista Records AL 9541. LP.

The History of Latino Rock, Vol. 1, *1956–1965: The Eastside Sound*. 1983. Zyanya; distributed by Rhino. LP disk.

Horiuchi, Glenn. 1989a. *Issei Spirit*. AsianImprov Records. LP disk.

Hot Rize. 1990. *Take It Home*. Sugar Hill SH-CD-3784. Compact disk.

James, Willis Laurence. 1970. *Afro-American Music: A Demonstration Recording by Dr. Willis James*. ASCH Records AA702. LP disk.

Journey to the Lord of Beauty. 1982. Sufi Zikr Series, No. 2. San Francisco: Sufi Islamia/ Prophecy Publications SI/P 003. Audiocassette.

Kef Time: Exciting Sounds of the Middle East. 1994 [1986]. Produced by Harold G. Hagopian. With 6-page booklet of notes and song lyrics. Traditional Crossroads CD 4269. Compact disk.

Krauss, Alison. 1990. *I've Got That Old Feeling*. Rounder CD 0275. Compact disk.

Kurath, Gertrude Prokosch. 1956. "Voices of the Waterways." Liner notes for *Songs and Dances of the Great Lakes Indians*. Monograph Series of Ethnic Folkways Library. Smithsonian-Folkways Recordings P 1003. LP disk.

Latin Alliance. n.d. *Latin Alliance*. Virgin Records 91625-4. LP disk.

Lawson, Doyle, and Quicksilver. 1990 [1979]. *Rock My Soul*. Sugar Hill SH-CD-3717. Compact disk.

Leadbitter, Mike, and Neil Slaven. 1987. *Blues Records 1943–1970: A Selective Discography*. London: Record Information Services.

Leadbitter, Mike, et al. 1994. *Blues Records, 1943–1970*, Vol. 2. London: Record Information Services.

Levin, Theodore. 1996. Liner notes for *Mademoiselle, Voulez-Vous Danser? Franco-American Music from the New England Borderlands*. Washington, D.C.: Smithsonian Folkways Recordings. SFW CD 40116. Compact disk.

Liebert, Otto. 1990. *Nouveau Flamenco*. Higher Octave Music. HOMCD 77520. Compact disk.

Lomax, Alan. 1956 [1942]. *Afro-American Spirituals, Work Songs, and Ballads*, record notes. Library of Congress, Division of Music, Recording Laboratory AAFS L3. LP disk.

Lornell, Christopher "Kip." 1978. *Non-Blues Secular Black Music*, record notes. BRI Records BRI 001.

Lou Harrison: Gamelan Music. 1992. Gamelan Si Betty. Directed by Trish Neilsen and Jody Diamond. Instruments by Lou Harrison and William Colvig. Compositions by Lou Harrison. Music Masters 01612-67091-2. Compact disk.

Machito and His Salsa Big Band. 1982. Timeless Records SJF 161. LP disk.

Los Madrugadores. *Los Madrugadores*. 1985. Texas-Mexican Border Music, Vol. 18. Folklyric 9036.

March, Richard. 1998. *Deep Polka: Dance Music from the Midwest*. Washington, D.C.: Smith-

sonian Folkways SF CD 40088. Compact disk and 28-page booklet.

Monroe, Bill. 1989. *Blue Grass 1950–1958*. Notes by Neil V. Rosenberg and Charles K. Wolfe. Bear Family BCD 15423. Compact disk.

Montoya, Carlos. 1999. *Tango Flamenco*. Fine Tune 2227. Compact disk.

More and More Awake: New Music from the Mevlevi Zikr. 1982. Fairfax, Calif.: Mevlevi Order of America. Audiocassette.

Mountain Music Bluegrass Style. 1991 [1959]. Recorded, edited, and with notes by Mike Seeger. Smithsonian/Folkways CD SF 40038. Compact disk.

Murasaki Ensemble. 1994. *Niji*. A Murasaki Production. TME 8994. Compact disk.

The Music of Arab Americans: A Retrospective Collection. Produced by Anne K. Rasmussen. With 20-page booklet of notes, photographs, and song lyrics. Rounder CD 1122. Compact disk.

Music of New Mexico: Hispanic Traditions. 1992. Smithsonian Folkways Recordings SF CD 40409. Compact disk.

Navarro, Fats, and Tadd Dameron. 1968. *Milestone*. M-4704. LP disk.

New Gamelan/New York. 1995. Gamelan Son of Lion. Directed by Barbara Benary. Compositions by Jody Kruskal, Laura Liben, David Demnitz, Mark Steven Brooks, David Simons, Daniel Goode, and Benary. GSOL CD-1. Compact disk.

Omad Poisi (Our Own Guys). 1979. Baltimore: Rukki Records/Sheffeld Recordings.

Orquesta Broadway. 1979. *No Tiene Comparación*. Coco Records CLP 158X. LP disk.

Palace. 1996. Evergreen Club. Directed by Blair Mackay. Artifact Music (Canada) ART-012. Compositions for Sundanese gamelan *degung* and other instruments, by Mark Duggan, Lou Harrison, John Wyre, Jon Siddal, and Alain Thibault. Compact disk.

Palmieri, Eddie, and Friends. 1973. *Live at the University of Puerto Rico*. Coco Records DOLP 107. LP disk.

Puente, Tito. 1984. *Los grandes exitos de Tito Puente*, Vol 2. RCA Records IL 57294. LP disk.

———. 1987. *On Broadway*. Concord Picante Records CJP 207. LP disk.

Puente, Tito, and His Latin Ensemble. 1984. *El rey*. Concord Picante Records CJP 250. LP disk.

Racy, Ali Jihad. 1997. *Mystical Legacies: Ali Jihad Racy Performs Music of the Middle East*. With Ali Jihad Racy (*nay, buzuq, 'ud*, and bowed *tanbur*) and Souhail Kaspar (percussion). Lyrichord LYRCD 7437.

Racy, Ali Jihad, and Simon Shaheen. 1991 [1979]. *Taqasim: The Art of Improvisation in Arab Music*. Ali Jihad Racy, *buzuq*; and Simon Shaheen, *'ud*. With documentary notes by Philip Schuyler. Lyrichord LYRCD 7374.

Ramsey, Frederic. 1960. Notes to *Been Here and Gone*. Folkways Records FA 2659. LP disk.

Reyes, Al. n.d. *California Corazón: Songs from the San Joaquin Valley*. Cuervo Records S-1001. LP disk.

Rhodes, Willard. 1950. *Northwest (Puget Sound)*. Library of Congress AFS L34. LP disk.

———. 1954. *Music of the American Indian from the Archive of Folk Culture: Northwest (Puget Sound)*. Library of Congress AFS L34–43. (Accompanying booklet revised in 1984.)

Rinzler, Ralph. 1957. Notes to *American Banjo Scruggs Style*. Folkways FA 2314. LP disk.

Robb, John D. 1961 [1952]. *Spanish and Mexican Folk Music of New Mexico*. Ethnic Folkways Library FE 4426. LP disk.

Robb, John, collector. 1961. *Spanish Folk Songs of New Mexico*. Folkways FA 2204. LP disk. (Available on special order as cassette or compact disk 02204.)

Rodrigues, Amália. 1996. *The Best of Fado*. Double Gold DBG53026. Compact disk.

Rodríguez, Tito, and Louie Ramirez. n.d. *Algo Nuevo*. TR Records TR 300. LP disk.

Santamaría, Mongo. 1972. *Afro Roots*. Prestige Records 24018. LP disk.

Santana. n.d. *Santana's Greatest Hits*. Columbia PC 33050. LP disk.

Sapoznik, Henry. 1999 [1981]. *Klezmer Music: 1910–42*. Folkways Records FSS34021. Compact disk rerelease.

Seeger, Mike. 1959. Notes to *Mountain Music Bluegrass Style*. Folkways FA 2318. LP disk.

Shaheen, Simon. 1992. *Turath: Simon Shaheen Performs Masterworks of the Middle East*. With 8-page booklet of notes and photographs by Ali Jihad Racy. CMP 3006. Compact disk.

Shelemay, Kay K. 1985. *Pizmon: Syrian-Jewish Religious and Social Song*. Meadowlark/Shanachie Records ML 105. Cassette.

Slobin, Mark, and Barbara Kirshenblatt-Gimblett. 1986. *Folksongs in the East European Jewish Tradition from the Repertoire of Mariam Nirenberg*. Global Village GVM117 and subsequent Global Village solo-singer albums, for example, *Lifshe Schaechter Widman*, C111. Cassette.

Song of the Banyan: Folk Music of Vietnam by Phong Nguyen Ensemble. 1997. Music of the World. WMI Latitudes LAT 50607. Compact disk.

Sonora Matancera con Justo Betancourt. 1981. Barbaro Records B 207. LP disk.

Sounds Like 1996: Music by Asian American Artists. 1996. AsianImprov Records IEL 0002. Compact disk.

Spanish and Mexican Folk Music of New Mexico. 1952 (1961). Folkways Records and Service Corporation LP Ethnic Folkways Library FE 4426.

The Stanley Brothers. 1990 [c. 1964]. *Long Journey Home*. Notes by Bill Vernon. Rebel CD 1110. Compact disk.

Sugar Hill Gang. 1992 [1979]. *"Rapper's Delight," Street Jams: Hip-Hop from the Top*, Part 1. Rhino R2 70577 (Sugar Hill 542). Compact disk.

Surinach, Carlos. *Ritmo Jondo*. 1996. Bronx Arts Ensemble. New World Records 80505-2. Compact disk.

Taquachito Nights: Conjunto Music from South Texas. 1999. Produced by Cynthia Vidaurri and Pete Reiniger, in collaboration with the Narciso Martínez Cultural Arts Center. Smithsonian Folkways Recordings SFW CD 40477. Compact disk.

Texas-Mexican Border Music, Vol. 1, *Una historia de la música de la frontera: An Introduction 1930–1960*. 1974. Folklyric Records 9003. LP disk.

The Texas Mexican Conjunto. 1975. Texas-Mexican Border Music, Vol. 24. Folklyric 9049. LP disk.

Trance Gong. 1994. Gamelan Pacifica. Directed by Jarrad Powell. Iron and brass instruments by Suhirjan (Central Java) and aluminum instruments by Schmidt, Dresher, Devereaux, Powell.

Compositions by Powell, Jeff Morris, John Cage (arr. Powell), and other group members. ¿What Next? Recordings WN0016.

Valens, Ritchie. 1958, 1959. *The Best of Ritchie Valens*. Del-Fi; distributed by Rhino as RNDF 200. LP disk.

Wheels of the World, Vols. 1 and 2. 1997. Newton, N.J.: Shanachie Records. Yazoo 7008 and 7009. Compact disk.

CANADA

AfroCan Routes. 1992. CBC Variety Recordings World Music Series 2, VRCD 10 15. Compact disk.

Aglukark, Susan. 1999. *Unsung Heroes*. EMI Canada. 7243 8 53393 2 5. Compact disk.

Alfred, Jerry. 1998. *Kehlonn*. Caribou Records. CRCD004. Compact disk.

Anthologie de la musique canadienne (Anthology of Canadian Music). 1978–1991. Radio-Canada International. Boxed set of 32 LP disks and 6 compact disks.

Anthology of Canadian Music. 1978–1991. Canadian Broadcasting Corporation and Canadian Music Center. 39 boxed sets. Originally LP disks; rereleased as compact disks.

Arsenault, Eddy. 1993. *Piling on the Bois Sec*. Wellington, PEI: House Party Productions, HPP1 Compact disk.

Bartlett, Wayne. 1992. "She's Gone Boys, She's Gone." SWC Productions. Audiocassette.

Brouhaha. c. 1980s. *Vision*. Brouhaha Music BENT CD 001. Compact disk.

Czerny, Al. *Fiddle Country*. TeeVee Records TA-1019. LP. (Many others available.)

Figgy Duff. 1991. *Weather Out the Storm* (and others). Hypnotic 71356-1000. Compact disk.

Fin de siècle: Nouvelle musique montréalaise. 1994. Ensemble Contemporain de Montréal, dir. Véronique Lacroix. SNE 590. Compact disk.

Folksongs of the Miramichi. 1962. Folkways FM 4053, LP disk.

Four the Moment. 1993. *Four the Moment: Live*. JAM FTM 101. Compact disk.

———. 1996. *In My Soul*. Atlantic. Compact disk.

Freed, Don, and Prince Albert students. 1996. *Singing about the Métis*. Bush League Records BL8. Cassette.

Gasser, Alan. 1996. Notes to *Introduction to Canadian Music*. (Orchestral music, choral music, chamber music, electroacoustic music.) Naxos 8.550171-2. 2 compact disks.

Haida Indian Music of the Pacific Northwest. 1986. Folkways FE 4119. LP disk.

Here and Now/En nos temps et lieux: A Celebration of Canadian Music/Une Célébration de la musique canadienne. 1995. (Music of the first peoples and folk music, classical music, jazz, and world music; artists and styles of historical importance.) Canada Council, produced in partnership with the Canadian Broadcasting Corporation. CDSP 4510, 4511, 4512, 4513. 4 compact disks.

Hibbs, Harry. c. 1970s. *At the Caribou Club* (and others). ARC 794. LP disk.

Huronia Old Time Country Band. c. 1980s. *Old Time Fiddle Music with Marcel, Martin, Eric, and Gerrard*. n.p. MRD 001. Cassette.

Indian Music of the Pacific Northwest Coast. 1967. Collected and recorded by Ida Halpern. Folkways Records FE 4523. LP disk.

Irish Descendants. 1994. "Will They Lie There Evermore?" *Gypsies Lovers*. Warner Music Canada. CD W88. Compact disk.

Joyce, Jim. 1991. "Hard, Hard Times." On *Another Time: The Songs of Newfoundland*, Kelly Russell and Don Walsh, producers. Pigeon Inlet Production CD PIPCD 7326. Compact disk.

Kwakiutl Indian Music of the Pacific Northwest. 1981. Folkways FE 4122. LP disk.

Landry, Ned. c. 1960s. *Saturday Night Breakdown* (and others). RCA Camden CAL 780. LP disk.

L'époque de Julie Papineau. 1997. Musiques du Québec, Vol. 1. Ensemble Nouvelle-France. Lanoraie ORCD41081, Interdisq Distr. Compact disk.

MacIsaac, Ashley. 1995. *Hi™ How Are You Today?* Ancient Music/A and M Records, 31454 0522 2. Compact disk.

———. 1996. *Fine® Thank You Very Much*. Ancient Music/A and M Records. 79602 2002-2. Compact disk.

Made in Canada: Our Rock and Roll History. 1990. BMG Canada KCD1-7156, 7157, 7158, 7159. 4 compact disks.

Maritime Folk Songs. 1962. Folkways FE-4307. LP disk.

Matton, Roger. n.d. *Acadie et Québec: Field Recordings*. Québec: Archives de Folklore. RCA Records CGP-139. LP disk.

Montréal postmoderne. 1994. Centrediscs. Compact disk.

Ne blâmez jamais les bédouins. 1992. Chants Libres, dir. Pauline Vaillancourt. Diffusion i MéDIA IMSO 9202. Compact disk.

Nolan, Faith. 1984. *Africville*. M.W.L.C. Records 11161A. Compact disk.

Nootka Indian Music of the Pacific Northwest Coast. 1974. Collected, recorded, and annotated by Ida Halpern. Folkways Records FE 4524. LP disk.

Oeuvres symphoniques: Patrimoine musical du Canada français. 1990. Orchestre Métropolitain, dir. Gilles Auger and Louis Lavigueur. SRC SMCD 5090. Compact disk.

Oh! What a Feeling: A Vital Collection of Canadian Music, Twenty-Five Years of Juno Award Winners. 1996. Canadian Academy of Recording Arts and Sciences JUNO 251-4. 4 compact disks.

Old Time Couple Dances. Folkways FW 8827. LP.

Ontario Ballads and Folksongs. 1962. Prestige/International INT 25014. LP.

Overlords. 1999. *Overlords Caravan 2000*. Trobiz Records. Compact disk.

Panneton, Isabelle. n.d. *Cantate de la fin du jour*. Fonovox VOX 7824-2. Compact disk.

Party Acadien. 1995. House Party Productions. Compact disk.

Perlman, Ken. 1993. *The Old Time Fiddlers of Prince Edward Island*. Booklet accompanying Marimac Recordings C-6501. Audiocassette.

Prince Edward Island Fiddlers, Vols. 1 and 2. Islander Records SVC-002, SVC-001387.

Puamuna-Montagnais Hunting Songs. 1982. Canadian Broadcasting Corporation, Northern Quebec Service SQN 100. LP disk.

Sealy, Joe. 1996. *Africville Suite*. SEA JAM Records. Compact disk.

Shreyer, Pierre. 1996. *New Canadian Waltz*. New Canadian Records NCCD-9610. Compact disk, cassette.

Songs of the Great Lakes. Folk FM 4018. LP.

Songs of the Newfoundland Outports. 1984. Pigeon Inlet Productions PP-7319. LP disk.

Townsend, Graham. *The Great Canadian Fiddle*. Rounder Records 7002. LP. (Many others available.)

Un concert en Nouvelle-France. 1995. Ensemble Arion, CBC Records SRC-MVCD 1081. Compact disk.

York, Muddy. 1984. *Scatter the Ashes: Music of Old Ontario*. Boot BOS 7244. LP, cassette.

Films and Videos of the Music of the United States and Canada

AMERICAN INDIANS, FIRST NATIONS

Loukinen, Michael. 1992. *Medicine Fiddle*. Marquette, Mich.: Up Front Films.

UNITED STATES

Catlin, Amy. 1997. *Hmong Musicians in America: Interactions with Three Generations of Hmong American Musicians, 1978–1996*. Van Nuys, Calif.: Apsara Media for Intercultural Education. 60-minute videotape.

Mandell, Joan. 1995. *Tales from Arab Detroit*. Detroit and Los Angeles: ACCESS and Olive Branch Productions. Film.

Mullins, Patrick, and Rebecca Miller. *From Shore to Shore: Irish Traditional Music in New York*. 1993. New York: Cherry Lane Productions. Video. Distributed by Cinema Guild, 1697 Broadway, Suite 506, New York, New York 10019-5904 (telephone 800-723-5522).

Okada, Yuki, director. 1995. *The Caribbean*. JVC/Smithsonian Folkways Video Anthology of

Music and Dance of the Americas, Vol. 4. Barre, Vt.: Multicultural Media VTMV-288. Video.

Parsons, Jack, producer. 1993. *La música de la gente* (The Music of the People). Derry, N.H.: Chip Taylor Communications. Videocassette.

CANADA

Boulton, Laura. 1942. *Ukrainian Winter Holidays*. National Film Board of Canada. Film.

MacInnis, Ron, producer. 1971. *The Vanishing Cape Breton Fiddler*. Halifax: CBC. Film.

National Film Board of Canada. 1975. *Seven Shades of Pale*. Documentary film.

Reed-Olsen, Joan, producer and director. 1991. *Mas Camp to Parade*. Hands Over Time series.

(28 minutes.) TV Ontario and Ontario Educational Communications Authority. Video.

Rojas, Lenten P. 1982. *From the Strings of My Guitar*. Ottawa: Cordillera Films.

Southeast Asia

Publications on Southeast Asian Music

GENERAL WORKS ON SOUTHEAST ASIAN MUSIC, DANCE, AND THEATER

Becker, Judith. 1968. "Percussive Patterns in the Music of Mainland Southeast Asia." *Ethnomusicology* 12(2):173–191.

Bernatzik, Hugh Adolf. 1940. "Musikinstrumente der Bergvoelker Hinderindiens." *Atlantis* 12:152–155.

Brandon, James R. 1967. *Theatre in Southeast Asia*. Cambridge, Mass.: Harvard University Press.

Cogniat, Raymond. 1932. *Danses d'Indochine*. Paris: Éditions des Chroniques du Jour.

Emmert, Richard, and Yuki Minegishi. 1980. *Musical Voices of Asia: Report of Asian Traditional Performing Arts*. Tôkyô: Heibonsha.

Ghulam-Sarwar Yousof. 1994. *Dictionary of Traditional South-East Asian Theatre*. Kuala Lumpur: Oxford University Press.

Gironcourt, Georges de. 1943. "Recherches de géographie musicale en Indochine." *Bulletin de la Société des Études Indochinoises* 17:3–174.

Gronow, Pekka. 1981. "The Record Industry Comes to the Orient." *Ethnomusicology* 25(2):251–284.

Heger, F. 1902. *Alte Metalltrommeln aus Südost-Asien* (Old Metal Drums in Southeast Asia). Leipzig: K. von Hiersemann.

Heinze, Ruth-Inge. 1988. *Trance and Healing in Southeast Asia Today*. Bangkok: White Lotus.

Higham, Charles. *The Archaeology of Mainland Southeast Asia*. Cambridge and New York: Cambridge University Press.

Hood, Mantle. 1975. "Improvisation in the Stratified Ensembles of Southeast Asia." *Selected Reports in Ethnomusicology* 2(2):25–34.

Jones, Arthur M. 1971. *Africa and Indonesia: The Evidence of the Xylophone and Other Musical and Cultural Factors*, 2nd ed. Leiden: Brill.

Kartomi, Margaret J. 1995. "'Traditional Music Weeps' and Other Themes in the Discourse on Music, Dance, and Theatre of Indonesia, Malaysia and Thailand." *Journal of Southeast Asian Studies* 26(2):366–400.

Kempers, A. J. Bernet. 1988. "The Kettledrums of Southeast Asia." In *Modern Quaternary Research in Southeast Asia*, Vol. 10. Rotterdam: A. A. Balkema.

Knosp, Gaston. 1907. "La musique indochinoise." *Mercure Musical* 3:889–956.

———. 1909–1910. "Notes sur la musique indochinoise." *Revista Musicale Italiana* 16:821–846; 17:415–432.

———. 1911–1912. "Rapport sur une mission officielle d'étude musicale en Indochine." *International Archiv für Ethnographie* 20:121–151, 165–188, 217–248; 21:1–25, 49–77.

———. 1922. "Histoire de la musique dans l'Indochine." In *Encyclopédie de la musique*, ed. Albert Lavignac, 3100–3146. Paris: Librarie Delagrave.

Koizumi, Fumio, Yoshihiko Tokumaru, and Osamu Yamaguti, eds. 1977. *Asian Musics in an Asian Perspective: Report of [Asian Traditional Performing Arts, 1976]*. Tôkyô: Heibonsha.

Manuel, Peter. 1988. *Popular Musics of the Non-Western World*. New York: Oxford University Press.

May, Elizabeth, ed. 1980. *Musics of Many Cultures*. Berkeley: University of California Press.

Miettinen, Jukka O. 1992. *Classical Dance and Theatre in South-East Asia*. Singapore: Oxford University Press.

Miller, Terry E. 1982. "Free-Reed Instruments in Asia: A Preliminary Classification." In *Music East and West: Essays in Honor of Walter Kaufmann*, ed. Thomas Noblitt, 63–100. New York: Pendragon.

Mohd. Taib Osman, ed. 1974. *Traditional Drama and Music of Southeast Asia*. Kuala Lumpur: Dewan Bahasa dan Pustaka.

Morton, David. 1975. "Instruments and Instrumental Functions in the Ensembles of Southeast Asia: A Cross-Cultural Comparison." *Selected Reports in Ethnomusicology* 2(2):7–16.

The New Grove Dictionary of Music and Musicians. 1980. 20 vols., ed. Stanley Sadie. London: Macmillan. (Articles on Burma, Indonesia, Kampuchea, Laos, Malaysia, the Philippines, Thailand, and Vietnam.)

The New Grove Dictionary of Musical Instruments. 1984. 3 vols, ed. Stanley Sadie. London: Macmillan.

Reid, Anthony. 1988. *The Lands below the Winds*. Southeast Asia in the Age of Commerce, 1450–1680, 1. New Haven, Conn.: Yale University Press.

Ryker, Harrison, ed. 1991. *New Music in the Orient: Essays on Composition in Asia since World War II*. Buren, Netherlands: Frits Knuf.

Scanlon, Phil, Jr. 1985. *Southeast Asia: A Cultural Study through Celebration*. Monograph Series, Special Report 23. De Kalb: Center for Southeast Asian Studies, Northern Illinois University.

Shadow Images of Asia. 1979. Washington, D.C.: American Museum of Natural History.

Smith, R. B., and W. Watson. 1979. *Early South East Asia: Essays in Archaeology, History, and Historical Geography*. New York: Oxford University Press.

Taylor, Eric. 1989. *Musical Instruments of South-East Asia*. Singapore: Oxford University Press.

Zarina, Xenia. 1967. *Classic Dances of the Orient*. New York: Crown.

MAINLAND SOUTHEAST ASIA

Cambodia

Anak Charanyananda. 1989. "Srei Khmauu and Phliang, the Principal Songs in Rwam Mamuad, a Curing Ritual, in Surin, Thailand." M.A. thesis, University of the Philippines.

Brunet, Jacques. 1969. *Nang Sbek: Théâtre d'ombres—Danse du Cambodge*. Berlin: Institut International d'Études Comparatives de la Musique.

———. 1979. "L'orchestre de mariage cambodgien et ses instruments." *Bulletin de l'École Française d'Extrême-Orient* 66:203–247.

Catlin, Amy. 1987. "Apsaras and Other Goddesses in Khmer Music, Dance, and Ritual." In *Apsara: The Feminine in Cambodian Art*, ed. Amy Catlin, 28–36. Los Angeles: Woman's Building.

———. 1992. *Khmer Classical Dance Songbook*. Van Nuys, Calif.: Apsara Media for Intercultural Education.

Cravath, Paul. 1985. "Earth in Flower: An Historical and Descriptive Study of the Classical Dance Drama of Cambodia." Ph.D. dissertation, University of Hawaii.

———. 1986. "The Ritual Origins of the Classical Dance Drama of Cambodia." *Asian Theater Journal* 3(2):179–203.

———. 1992. "Khmer Classical Dance: Performance Rites of the Goddess in the Context of a Feminine Mythology." *Selected Reports in Ethnomusicology* 9:81–92.

Daniélou, Alain. 1957. *La musique du Cambodge et du Laos*. Pondichéry: Publications de l'Institut Français d'Indologie.

de Gironcourt, George. 1941. "Motifs de chants cambodgiens." *Bulletin de la Société des Études Indochinoises* 16(l):51–105.

———. 1944. "Recherches de géographie musicale en Cambodge et à Java." *Bulletin de la Société des Études Indochinoises* 19(3):49–83.

Groslier, Bernard-Philippe. 1965. "Danse et musique sous les rois d'Angkor." In *Felicitation Volumes of Southeast Asian Studies*, 2:283–292. Bangkok: Siam Society.

Groslier, George. 1929. "Le théâtre et la danse au Cambodge." *Journal Asiatique* (January–March):125–143.

Kodish, Debora, ed. 1994. *The Giant Never Wins: Lakhon Bassac (Cambodian Folk Opera) in Philadelphia*. Philadelphia: Philadelphia Folklore Project.

Leclere, Adhemard. 1911. *Le théâtre cambodgien*. Paris: Ernest Leroux.

———. 1912. *Cambodge: Contes, légendes, et jatakas*. Niort: Imprimerie Nouvelle G. Clouzot.

Miller, Terry E., and Sam-Ang Sam. 1995. "The Classical Musics of Cambodia and Thailand: A Study of Distinctions." *Ethnomusicology* 39(2):229–243.

Musique khmère. 1969. Phnom Penh: Imprimerie Sangkum Reastr Niyum.

Phleng phun ban lae ganlalen pun ban jangwat surin (Local Music and Entertainments of Surin Province). 1984. Surin, Thailand: Surin Teachers College.

Pich, Sal. 1970. *Lumnoam Sangkhep ney Phleng Khmer* (A Brief Survey of Khmer Music). Phnom Penh: Éditions de l'Institut Bouddhique.

Prasidh Silapabanleng. 1975. "Thai Music at the Court of Cambodia." *Selected Reports in Ethnomusicology* 2(2):3–6.

Sam, Chan Moly. 1987. *Khmer Court Dance*. Newington, Conn.: Khmer Studies Institute.

———. 1992. "Muni Mekhala: The Magic Moment in Khmer Court Dance." *Selected Reports in Ethnomusicology* 9:93–114.

Sam, Sam-Ang. 1988. "The Pin Peat Ensemble: Its History, Music, and Context." Ph.D. dissertation, Wesleyan University.

———. 1989. *Khmer Court Dance: A Performance Manual*. Newington, Conn.: Khmer Studies Institute.

———. 1992. "The Gloating Maiden in Khmer Shadow Play: Its Text, Context, and Performance." *Selected Reports in Ethnomusicology* 9:115–130.

Sam, Sam-Ang, and Patricia Shehan Campbell. 1991. *Silent Temples, Songful Hearts: Traditional Music of Cambodia*. Danbury, Conn.: World Music.

Sam, Sam-Ang, and Chan Moly Sam. 1987. *Khmer Folk Dance*. Newington, Conn.: Khmer Studies Institute.

Sem, Sara. 1967. "Lakhon Khol au village de Svay Andet, son rôle dans les rites agraires." *Annales de l'Université des Beaux-Arts* 1:157–200.

Sheppard, Dato Haji Mubin. 1968. "The Khmer Shadow Play and Its Links with Ancient India: A Possible Source of the Malay Shadow Play of Kelantan and Trengganu." *Royal Asiatic Society, Malaysian Branch, Journal* 41(l):199–204.

Sisowath. N.d. *Musique du Cambodge*. Phnom Penh: Direction du Tourisme Khmer.

Strickland-Anderson, Lily. 1926. "The Cambodian Ballet." *Musical Quarterly* 12:266–274.

Le théâtre dans la vie khmère. 1973. Phnom Penh: Université des Beaux Arts.

Thierry, Solange. 1963. *Les danses sacrées*. Paris: Sources Orientales.

Thiounn (Saindech Chaufea). 1930. *Danses cambodgiennes*. Phnom Penh: Bibliothèque Royale du Cambodge.

Thailand

(Phya) Anuman Rajadhon. 1961. *Life and Ritual in Old Siam: Three Studies of Thai Life and Customs*, ed. and trans. William J. Gedney. New Haven, Conn.: HRAF.

———. 1968. *Essays on Thai Folklore*. Bangkok: Social Science Association Press of Thailand.

———. 1990. *Thet Maha Chat*, 3rd ed. Thai Culture, New Series, 21. Bangkok: Fine Arts Department.

Becker, Judith. 1964. "Music of the Pwo Karen of Northern Thailand." *Ethnomusicology* 8(2):137–153.

———. 1980. "A Southeast Asian Musical Process: Thai Thaw and Javanese Irama." *Ethnomusicology* 24:453–464.

Bidyalankarana, Prince. 1926. "The Pastime of Rhyme-Making and Singing in Rural Siam." *Journal of the Siam Society* 20:101–127.

———. 1941. "Sebha Recitation and the Story of Khun Chang Khun Phan." *Journal of the Thailand Research Society* 33:1–22.

Bowring, John. 1969 [1857]. *The Kingdom and People of Siam*. 2 vols. Kuala Lumpur: Oxford University Press.

Brereton, Bonnie Pacala. 1995. *Thai Tellings of Phra Malai: Texts and Rituals Concerning a Popular Buddhist Saint*. Tempe: Program for Southeast Asian Studies, Arizona State University.

Broman, Sven. 1996. *Shadows of Life: Nang Talung—Thai Popular Shadow Theatre*. Bangkok: White Orchid.

Chaturong Montrisart. 1961. "The Classical Dance." *Journal of the Music Academy Madras* 32:127–143.

(Phra) Chen Duriyanga. 1990a. *Thai Music*, 6th ed. Thai Culture, New Series, 15. Bangkok: Fine Arts Department.

———. 1990b. *Thai Music in Western Notation*, 4th ed. Thai Culture, New Series, 16. Bangkok: Fine Arts Department.

Coedes, George. 1963. "Origine et evolution des diverses formes du théâtre traditionnel en Thailande." *Bulletin de la Société des Études Indochinoises* 38:489–506.

Cooler, Richard. 1986. "The Use of Karen Bronze Drums in the Royal Courts and Buddhist Temples of Burma and Thailand: A Continuing Mon Tradition?" In *Papers from a Conference on Thai Studies in Honor of William J Gedney*, ed. Robert J. Bickner, Thomas J. Hudak, and Patcharin Peyasantiwong, 107–120. Ann Arbor: Center for South and Southeast Asian Studies, University of Michigan.

His Royal Highness Prince S. A. R. Damrong Rajanubhab. 1928. "L'orchestre siamois." *Extrême Asie-Revue Indochinoise*, New Series 27:132–142.

———. 1931. *Siamese Musical Instruments*, 2nd ed. Bangkok: Royal Institute.

His Highness Prince Dhani Nivat Kromamun Bidyalabh Birdhyakorn. 1947. "Pageantry of the Siamese Stage." *National Geographic Magazine* 91:200–212.

———. 1948. "The Shadow-Play as a Possible Origin of the Masked Play." *Journal of the Siam Society* 37(1):27–33.

———. 1952. "Traditional Dress in the Classic Dance of Siam." *Journal of the Siam Society* 40(2):133–146.

———. 1965. "Hide Figures of the Ramakien at the Ledermuseum in Offenbach, Germany." *Journal of the Siam Society* 53(1):61–66.

———. 1988. *Shadow Play (The Nang)*, 6th ed. Thai Culture, New Series, 3. Bangkok: Fine Arts Department.

Dhanit Yupho. 1952. *Classical Siamese Theatre*, trans. P. S. Sastri. Bangkok: Hatha Dhip.

———. 1963. *The Khon and Lakon*. Bangkok: Fine Arts Department.

———. 1987 [1971]. *Thai Musical Instruments*, 2nd ed., trans. David Morton. Bangkok: Fine Arts Department.

———. 1989a. *The Khon*, 6th ed. Thai Culture, New Series, 6. Bangkok: Fine Arts Department.

———. 1989b. *Khon Masks*, 6th ed. Thai Culture, New Series, 7. Bangkok: Fine Arts Department.

———. 1990a. *The Custom and Rite of Paying Homage to Teachers of Khon, Lakhon, and Piphat*, 5th ed. Thai Culture, New Series, 11. Bangkok: Fine Arts Department.

———. 1990b. *The Preliminary Course of Training in Thai Theatrical Art*, 8th ed. Thai Culture, New Series, 13. Bangkok: Fine Arts Department.

Duangjai Thewtong. 1984. "Village Music in Central Thailand: A Field Study of Mooban Pohuk." M.A. thesis, Kent State University.

Durrenberger, E. P. 1975. "A Soul's Journey: A Lisu Song from Northern Thailand." *Asian Folklore Studies* 34:35–50.

Dyck, Gerald P. 1975a. "Lung Noi Na Kampan Makes a Drumhead for a Northern Thai Long Drum." *Selected Reports in Ethnomusicology* 2(2):183–204.

———. 1975b. "They Also Serve." *Selected Reports in Ethnomusicology* 2(2):205–216.

———. 1975c. "The Vanishing Phia: An Ethnomusicological Photo Story." *Selected Reports in Ethnomusicology* 2(2):217–229.

Ellis, Alexander J. 1885a. "On the Musical Scales of Various Nations." *Journal of the Society of Arts* 33:485–527.

———. 1885b. "Appendix to Mr. Alexander J. Ellis's Paper on 'The Musical Scales of Various Nations' read 25 March 1885." *Journal of the Society of Arts* 33:1102–1111.

Fuller, Paul. 1979. "Review of *The Traditional Music of Thailand*, by David Morton." *Ethnomusicology* 23(2):339–343.

———. 1983. "Thai Music, 1968–1981." *Yearbook for Traditional Music* 1983:152–155.

Gaston, Bruce. 1987. "Thai Court Music: Buddhism and Hinduism in Harmony." In *Music of the Royal Courts,* 15–18. Bangkok: Sound Bank Board.

Gerini, G. E. 2000 [1912]. *Siam and Its Productions, Arts, and Manufactures* (*1911*). Bangkok: White Lotus. (Reprint.)

Gervaise, Nicolas. 1688. *Histoire naturelle et politique du Royaume de Siam*. Paris: Claude Barbin.

Ginsberg, Henry D. 1972. "The Mahohra Dance-Drama: An Introduction." *Journal of the Siam Society* 60:169–181.

Guelden, Marlane. 1995. *Thailand: Into the Spirit World*. Singapore: Times Editions.

Hamilton, Annette. 1993. "Video Crackdown, or the Sacrificial Pirate: Censorship and Cultural Consequences in Thailand." *Public Culture* 5(3):515–531.

Hipkins, A. J. 1945 [1888]. *Musical Instruments Historic, Rare, and Unique*. London: A. and C. Black.

Hornbostel, Erich M. von. 1920. "Formanalysen an siamesischen Orchesterstücken." *Archiv für Musikwissenschaft* 2:306–333.

Kobkul Phutharaporn. 1985. "Country Folk Songs and Thai Society." In *Traditional and Changing Thai World View*. Bangkok: Chulalongkorn University Research Institute and Southeast Asian Studies Programme.

Krebs, Stephanie Laird. 1975. "Nonverbal Communication in Khon Dance-Drama: Thai Society Onstage." Ph.D. dissertation, Harvard University.

Kurosawa, T. 1941. *Investigation of Musical Instruments in Thailand*. Bangkok: Nippon-tai Bunka Kenkyusyo.

La Loubere, Simon de. 1691. *Du Royaume de Siam*. Paris: Jean-Baptiste Coignard.

———. 1969 [1693]. *A New Historical Relation of the Kingdom of Siam*. Kuala Lumpur: Oxford University Press.

Larson, Hans Peter. 1976. "The Instrumental Music of the Lisu in Northern Thailand." In *Lampang Reports*, 225–268. Copenhagen: Scandinavian Institute of Asian Studies.

———. 1984. "The Music of the Lisu of Northern Thailand." *Asian Folklore Studies* 43(l):41–62.

Léonowens, Anna Harriette. 1870. *The English Governess at the Siamese Court*. Boston: Fields, Osgood.

Lewis, Paul, and Elaine Lewis. 1984. *Peoples of the Golden Triangle: Six Tribes in Thailand*. London: Thames and Hudson.

List, George. 1961. "Speech Melody and Song Melody in Central Thailand." *Ethnomusicology* 5:16–32.

Mareschal, Eric. 1976. *La musique des Hmong*. Paris: Musée Guimet.

Marre, Jeremy, and Hannah Charlton. 1985. "Two Faces of Thailand." In *Beats of the Heart: Popular Music of the World*, 198–214. New York: Pantheon.

Marshall, Harry Ignatius. 1932. "The Use of the Bronze Drum in Siam." *Journal of the Burma Research Society* 22:21–22.

Mattani Rutnin, ed. 1975. *The Siamese Theatre: A Collection of Reprints from the Journals of the Siam Society*. Bangkok: Siam Society.

———. 1978. "The Modernization of Thai Dance-Drama, with Special Reference to the Reign of King Chulalongkorn." Ph.D. dissertation, University of London.

Mendenhall, Stanley T. 1975. "Interaction of Linguistic and Musical Tone in Thai Song." *Selected Reports in Ethnomusicology* 2(2):17–24.

Miller, Terry E. 1979. "The Musical Traditions of Northeast Thailand." *Journal of the Siam Society* 67(l):1–16.

———. 1981. "The *Mawlum Pee Fah* Ceremony of Northeastern Thailand." In *Proceedings of the Saint Thyagaraja Music Festivals: Cleveland, Ohio, 1978–1981*, ed. T. Temple Tuttle, 82–93. Cleveland: Greater Cleveland Ethnographic Museum.

———. 1984. "Reconstructing Siamese Musical History from Historical Sources: 1548–1932." *Asian Music* 15(2):32–42.

———. 1985. *Traditional Music of the Lao: Kaen Playing and Mawlum Singing in Northeast Thailand*. Contributions in Intercultural and Comparative Studies, 13. Westport, Conn., and London: Greenwood.

———. 1991. *An Introduction to Playing the Kaen*, rev. ed. Kent, Ohio: Author.

———. 1992a. "Thai Classical Music Comes to America: Cultivating a Rare Species in a Musical Greenhouse." *Journal of the Siam Society* 80(2):143–148.

———. 1992b. "The Theory and Practice of Thai Musical Notations." *Ethnomusicology* 36(2):197–222.

———. 1999. "The Khaen, Northeast Thailand's Free-Reed Mouth Organ in the Age of Modernization." *Free-Reed Journal* 1:43–54.

Miller, Terry E., and Jarernchai Chonpairot. 1979. "Shadow Puppet Theatre in Northeast Thailand." *Theatre Journal* 31(3):293–311.

Miller, Terry E., and Jarernchai Chonpairot. 1981. "The Ranat and Bong-Lang: The Question of Origin of the Thai Xylophones." *Journal of the Siam Society* 69:145–163.

———. 1994. "A History of Siamese Music Reconstructed from Western Documents, 1505–1932." *Crossroads: An Interdisciplinary Journal of Southeast Asian Studies* 8(2):1–192.

Miller, Terry E., and Sam Sam-Ang. 1995. "The Classical Musics of Cambodia and Thailand: A Study of Distinctions." *Ethnomusicology* 39(2):229–243.

Mom Dusdi Paribatra Na Ayuthya. 1962. *The Regional Dances of Thailand*. Bangkok: Foundation for Advancement of Educational Materials.

Moore, Sidney. 1969. "Thai Songs in 7/4 Meter." *Ethnomusicology* 13(2):309–312.

Morton, David. 1968. *The Traditional Music of Thailand: Introduction, Commentary, and Analyses*. Los Angeles: Regents of the University of California.

———. 1974. "Vocal Tones in Traditional Thai Music." *Selected Reports in Ethnomusicology* 2(l):88–101.

———. 1975. "Luang Pradit Phairo." *Selected Reports in Ethnomusicology* 2(2):v–viii.

———. 1976. *The Traditional Music of Thailand*. Berkeley: University of California Press.

The Musical Compositions of His Majesty King Bhumibol Adulyadej of Thailand. Bangkok: Chitralada School, 1996.

Myers-Moro, Pamela. 1986. "'Songs for Life': Leftist Thai Popular Music in the 1970s." *Journal of Popular Culture* 20(3):93–113.

———. 1988. "Names and Civil Service Titles of Siamese Musicians." *Asian Music* 19(2):82–92.

———. 1989. "Thai Music and Attitudes towards the Past." *Journal of American Folklore* 102:190–194.

———. 1990. "Musical Notation in Thailand." *Journal of the Siam Society* 78:101–108.

———. 1991. "Teachers on Tape: Innovation and Experimentation in Teaching Thai Music." *Balungan* 5(l):15–20.

———. 1993. *Thai Music and Musicians in Contemporary Bangkok*. Center for Southeast Asian Studies Monographs, 34. Berkeley: University of California Press.

Nicolas, René. 1924. "Le lakhon nora ou lakhon chatri et les origines du théâtre classique siamois." *Journal of the Siam Society* 18(2):85–110.

———. 1927. "Le théâtre d'ombres au Siam." *Journal of the Siam Society* 21:37–52.

Nitaya Kanchanawan. 1979. "Elvis, Thailand, and I." *Southern Quarterly* 18(l):162–168.

Panya Roongrüang. 1990. *Thai Music in Sound*. Bangkok: Author. (Book and 3 cassettes.)

———, ed. 2000. *Collected Works of the Thai Classical Repertoire* (*The Lost Thai Music Manuscript Restoration Project*). 6 vols. (36 projected). Bangkok: Kasetsat University.

Paritta Chalermpow Koanantakool. 1980. "A Popular Drama in Its Social Context: Nang Tatung, the Shadow Puppet Theatre of South Thailand." Ph.D. dissertation, Cambridge University.

Picken, Lawrence E. R. 1984. "The Sound-Producing Instrumentarium of a Village in Northeast Thailand." In *Musica Asiatica* 4:213–244. Cambridge: Cambridge University Press.

Picken, L. E. R., C. J. Adkins, and T. F. Page. 1984. "The Making of a Khāen: The Free-Reed Mouth-Organ of North-East Thailand." *Musica Asiatica* 4:117–154.

Prasidh Silapabanleng. 1975. "Thai Music at the Court of Cambodia: A Personal Souvenir of Luang Pradit Phairoh's Visit in 1930." *Selected Reports in Ethnomusicology* 2(2):3–5.

Pratuan Charoenchitt, ed. N.d. [c. 1987]. *Folk Music and Traditional Performing Arts of Thailand*. Bangkok: Office of the National Culture Commission, Ministry of Education.

Pringsheim, Klaus. 1944. "Music of Thailand." *Contemporary Japan* 13:745–767.

Schwörer, Gretel. 1982. "Die Mundorgel bei den Lahu in Nord Thailand: Bauweise, Funktion, und Musik." *Beiträge zur Ethnomusikologie* 10.

Seelig, Paul S. 1932. *Siamese Music*. Bandoeng: J. H. Seelig.

Smithies, Michael. 1971. "Likay: A Note on the Origin, Form, and Future of Siamese Folk Opera." *Journal of the Siam Society* 59:33–64.

———. 1972. "Nang Tatung: The Shadow Theatre of Siam." *Journal of the Siam Society* 60:377–387.

Smithies, Michael, and Euayporn Kerdchouay. 1974. "The Wai Khru Ceremony of the Nang Yai." *Journal of the Siam Society* 62(1):143–147.

Stern, Theodore, and Theodore A. Stern. 1971. "'I Pluck My Harp': Musical Acculturation among the Karen of Western Thailand." *Ethnomusicology* 15:186–219.

Stumpf, Carl. 1901. "Tonsystem und Musik der Siamesen." *Beiträge zur Akustik und Musikwissenschaft* 3:69–138.

Sumrongthong, Bussakorn, and Neil Sorrell. 2000. "Melodic Paradoxes in the Music of the Thai Pi-Phat and Javanese Gamelan." *Yearbook for Traditional Music* 32:67–80.

Surapone Virulrak. 1980. "Likay: A Popular Theater in Thailand." Ph.D. dissertation, University of Hawaii.

Tambiah, S. J. 1968. "Literacy in a Buddhist Village in North-East Thailand." In *Literacy in Traditional Societies*, ed. Jack Goody, 86–131. Cambridge: Cambridge University Press.

———. 1970. *Buddhism and the Spirit Cults in North-East Thailand*. Cambridge: Cambridge University Press.

Tanese-Ito, Yoko. 1988a. "The Relationship between Speech-Tones and Vocal Melody in Thai Court Song." *Musica Asiatica* 5:109–139.

———. 1988b. "Taikoku koten kakyoku ni okeru kasi no seichou to uta no senritu tono kankei (The Relationship between Speech Tones and Vocal Melody in Thai Court Song)." D.M. dissertation, Tôkyô National University of Fine Arts and Music.

Terwiel, B. J. 1979. *Monks and Magic: An Analysis of Religious Ceremonies in Central Thailand*, 2nd ed. Bangkok: Curzon.

Thai Classical Music, 2nd ed. 1971. Bangkok: Fine Arts Department.

Ubonrat Siriyuvasak. 1990a. "Commercialising the Sound of the People: *Pleng Luktoong* and the Thai Pop Music Industry." *Popular Music* 9(l):61–77.

———. 1990b. *The Dynamics of Audience Media Activities: An Ethnography of Women Textile Workers*. Bangkok: Women's Studies Program, Chulalongkorn University.

Vajiravudh, Maha. 1967. "Notes on the Siamese Theatre." *Journal of the Siam Society* 55(l):1–30.

Vantanee Moungboon. 1996. *String-Puppets of the Thai Ramayana*. Bangkok: Institute of Drama and Music, Department of Fine Arts. (In Thai and English.)

Verney, Frederick. 1885. *Notes on Siamese Musical Instruments*. London: William Clowes.

Walker, Anthony R. 1983. *Lahu Nyi (Red Lahu) New Year Celebrations in North Thailand: Ethnographic and Textual Materials*. Taipei: Orient Cultural Service.

Wells, Kenneth E. 1975. *Thai Buddhism: Its Rites and Activities*. Bangkok: Suriyabun.

Wong, Deborah Anne. 1990. "Thai Cassettes and Their Covers: Two Case Histories." *Asian Music* 21(l):78–104.

———. 1991. "The Empowered Teacher: Ritual, Performance, and Epistemology in Contemporary Bangkok." Ph.D. dissertation, University of Michigan.

———. 1995. "Thai Cassettes and Their Covers: Two Case Histories." In *Asian Popular Culture*, ed. John Lent, 43–59. Boulder, Colo.: Westview.

Wong, Deborah Anne, and René T. A. Lysloff. 1991. "Threshold of the Sacred: The Overture in Thai and Javanese Ritual Performance." *Ethnomusicology* 35:315–348.

Laos

Archaimbault, Charles. 1991. *Le sacrifice du buffle a S'ieng Khwang (Laos)*. Paris: École Française d'Extrême-Orient.

Bertrain, Yves. 1986. *Kab Ke Pam Tuag: Cov Zaj—Les funerailles: Chants et récitatifs*. Javouhey, Guyana: Hmong Patrimony Series.

———. 1987. *Kab Ke Pam Tuag: Txheej Txheem—Les funerailles: Ordonnance de la cérémonie*. Javouhey, Guyana: Hmong Patrimony Series.

Berval, René de, ed. 1959. *Kingdom of Laos: The Land of the Million Elephants and of the White Parasol*, trans. Mrs. Teissier du Cros et al. Saigon: France-Asie.

Bond, Katherine, and Kingsavanh Pathammavong. 1992. "Contexts of Dontrii Lao Deum: Traditional Lao Music." *Selected Reports in Ethnomusicology* 9:131–148.

Brengues, Jean. 1904. "Les mo lam: La chanson au Laos." *Revue Indochinoise*, New Series 2:588–592.

Catlin, Amy. 1981. *Music of the Hmong: Singing Voices and Talking Reeds*. Providence: Rhode Island College.

———. 1983. *Music of the Hmong: Singing Voices and Talking Reeds*. Providence, R.I.: Center for Hmong Lore, Museum of Natural History.

———. 1985a. "Harmonizing the Generations in Hmong Musical Performance." *Selected Reports in Ethnomusicology* 6:83–98.

———. 1985b. "Speech Surrogate Systems of the Hmong: From Singing Voices to Talking Reeds." In *The Hmong in the West: Observations and Reports*, ed. Bruce Downey and Douglas Olney, 170–197. Minneapolis: University of Minnesota Press.

———. 1986. "The Hmong and Their Music: A Critique of Pure Speech." In *Hmong Art: Tradition and Change*, ed. Joanne Cubbs, 11–18. Sheboygan, Wisc.: Kohler Arts Center.

———. 1992. "Homo Cantens: Why Hmong Sing during Interactive Courtship Rituals." *Selected Reports in Ethnomusicology* 9:43–60.

Chonpairot, Jarernchai. 1990. "Lam Khon Sawan: A Vocal Genre of Southern Laos." Ph.D dissertation, Kent State University.

Compton, Carol. 1975. "Lam Khon Savan: A Traditional Form and a Contemporary Theme." In *A Tai Festschrift for William J Gedney*, ed. Thomas W. Gething, 55–82. Southeast Asian Studies Working Paper 8. Honolulu: University of Hawaii.

———. 1977. "Linguistic and Cultural Aspects of the Lam: The Song of the Lao Mohlam." Ph.D. dissertation, University of Michigan.

———. 1979. *Courting Poetry in Laos: A Textual and Linguistic Analysis*. Special Report 18. De Kalb: Northern Illinois University.

———. 1992. "Traditional Verbal Arts in Laos: Functions, Forms, Continuities, and Changes in Texts, Contexts, and Performances." *Selected Reports in Ethnomusicology* 9:149–160.

Conquergood, Dwight. 1989. *I Am a Shaman: A Hmong Life Story with Ethnographic Commentary*. Minneapolis: SARS Project, University of Minnesota.

Daniélou, Alain. 1957. *La musique du Cambodge et du Laos*. Pondichéry: Publications de l'Institut Français d'Indologie.

Escoffier, Andrés. 1942. *Dans le Laos aux chants des khènes, poèmes*. Hanoi: Imprimerie d'Extrême-Orient.

Gagneux, Mme. Anne Marie. 1971. "Le khène et la musique Lao." *Bulletin des Amis du Royaume Lao* 6:175–181.

Guillemet, Mme. Eugène. 1923. *Les chants du khène laotien.* Hanoi: Imprimerie d'Extrême-Orient.

Hang, Ly. 1962. "Musique de danse laotienne." *Musica* 99(June):13–17.

Hartmann, John F. 1992. "The Context, Text, and Performance of Khap Lue." *Selected Reports in Ethnomusicology* 9:33–42.

Houmphanh Rattanavong. 1992a. "The Lamluang: A Popular Entertainment." *Selected Reports in Ethnomusicology* 9:189–192.

———. 1992b. "Music and Instruments in Laos: Historical Antecedents and the Democratic Revolution." *Selected Reports in Ethnomusicology* 9:193–202.

Humbert-Lavergne, M. 1934. "La musique à travers la vie laotienne." *Zeitschrift für Vergleichende Musikwissenschaft* 2(l):14–19.

Kham-Ouane Ratanavong. 1973. "Learn to Play the Khène/Apprenez le khène." *Bulletin des Amis du Royaume Lao* (Vientiane).

Knosp, Gaston. 1922. *Laotian Songs.* Bangkok.

Lefevre-Pontalis, Pierre. 1896. *Chansons et fêtes du Laos.* Paris: Ernest Leroux.

Lindell, Kristina, et al. 1982. *The Kammu Year: Its Lore and Music.* London: Curzon.

Lundstrom, Hakan. 1984. "A Kammu Song and Its Structure." *Asian Folklore Studies* 43(l):29–39.

Lundstrom, Hakan, and Damrong Tayanin. 1981. "Kammu Gongs and Drums." *Asian Folklore Studies* 40:65–86, 173–189.

Mahoney, Therese Mary. 1995. "The White Parasol and the Red Star: The Laos Classical Music Culture in a Climate of Change." Ph.D. dissertation, University of California at Los Angeles.

Mareschal, Eric. 1976. *La musique des Hmong.* Paris: Author.

Miller, Terry E. 1985. "The Survival of Lao Traditional Music in America." *Selected Reports in Ethnomusicology* 6:99–110.

———. 1992. "A Melody Not Sung: The Performance of Lao Buddhist Texts in Northeast Thailand." *Selected Reports in Ethnomusicology* 9:161–188.

———. 1998. "The Past as Future for the Regional Music of Laos." In *New Laos, New Challenges,* ed. Jacqueline Butler-Diaz, 87–96. Tempe: Arizona State University (Program for Southeast Asian Studies).

Miller, Terry E., and Jarernchai Chonpairot. 1979. "Review-Essay: The Problems of Lao Discography." *Asian Music* 11(1):124–139.

Mottin, Jean. 1979. *Contes et légendes Hmong Blanc.* Bangkok: Don Bosco.

———. 1980a. *55 chants d'amour Hmong Blanc.* Bangkok: Siam Society.

———. 1980b. *Fêtes du nouvel au chez les Hmong Blanc de Thailande.* Bangkok: Siam Society.

———. 1982. *Allons faire le tour du ciel et de la terre: Le chamanisme des Hmong vu dans les textes.* Bangkok: White Lotus.

———. 1984. "A Hmong Shaman's Séance." *Asian Folklore Studies* 43(l):99–108.

Burma (Myanmar)

Becker, Judith. 1967. "The Migration of the Arched Harp from India to Burma." *Galpin Society Journal* 20:17–23, pl. v–vii.

———. 1969. "Anatomy of a Mode." *Ethnomusicology* 13(2):267–279.

Fraser-Lu, Sylvia. 1983. "Frog Drums and Their Importance in Karen Culture." *Arts in Asia* (September–October):50–63.

Frost, Helen, and Lily Strickland. 1927. *Oriental and Character Dances.* New York: Barnes.

Garfias, Robert. 1975a. "A Musical Visit to Burma." *World of Music* 17(l):3–13.

———. 1975b. "Preliminary Thoughts on Burmese Modes." *Asian Music* 7(1):39–49.

———. 1981. "Speech and Melodic Contour Interdependence in Burmese Music." *College Music Symposium* 21(l):33–39.

———. 1985. "The Development of the Modern Burmese Hsaing Ensemble." *Asian Music* 16:1–28.

Guillon, E. 1971. "Sur 21 chansons populaires mon." *Homme* 11:58–108.

Halliday, Robert. 1914. "The Kalok Dance of the Talaings." *Journal of the Burma Research Society* 4:93–101.

Juvenis. 1825. "To the Editor: The Harp of Martaban." *Quarterly Musical Magazine and Review* 7:451–456.

K [U Khin Zaw]. 1981. *Burmese Culture: General and Particular.* Rangoon: Sarpay Beikman.

Khin Zaw, U. 1940. "Burmese Music: A Preliminary Enquiry." *Journal of the Burma Research Society* 30(3):387–460.

———. 1975. "A Folk Song Collector's Letter from Shwebo." *Selected Reports in Ethnomusicology* 2(2):165–170.

Marano, P. A. 1900. "A Note on Burmese Music." In *Burma,* ed. Max Ferrar and Bertha Ferrar, app. C. London: Sampson Low, Marston.

Marshall, Harry Ignatius. 1929. "Karen Bronze Drums." *Journal of the Burma Research Society* 19:1–14.

Obayashi, T. 1966. "The Wooden Slit Drum of the Wa in the Sino-Burmese Border Area." *Beiträge Japan* 3:72–88.

Okell, John. 1964. "Learning Music from a Burmese Master." *Man* 64:183.

———. 1971. "The Burmese Double-Reed Nhai." *Asian Music* 2(l):25–31.

Picken, Lawrence E. R. 1984. "Instruments in an Orchestra from Pyu (Upper Burma) in 802." *Musica Asiatica* 4:245–270.

Rao, H. S. 1928. "Note on a Musical Instrument Common in the Northern Shan States." *Man in India* 8:61–62.

Rodrigue, Yves. 1992. *Nat-Pwe: Burma's Supernatural Sub-Culture.* Kiscadale, Scotland: Paul Strachan.

Sachs, Curt. 1917. *Die Musikinstrumente Birmas und Assams im K. Ethnographischen Museum zu München.* Munich: Verlag der Königlichen Bayerischen Akademie der Wissenschaften.

Shway, Yoe. 1963 [1882]. *The Burman: His Life and Notions.* New York: Norton. (Reprint of 3rd ed., 1909.)

Singer, Noel E. 1992. *Burmese Puppets.* New York: Oxford University Press.

———. 1995. *Burmese Dance and Theatre.* Kuala Lumpur: Oxford University Press.

Stewart, J. A. 1932. "A Mon Song of the Seasons with a Translation and Notes." *Journal of the Burma Research Society* 22:135–150.

———. 1937–1939. "The Song of the Three Mons." *Bulletin of the School of Oriental and African Studies* 9:33–39.

Tekkatho Maung Thu Hlaing. 1993. *Myanmar Traditional Orchestra Instruments.* Rangoon [Yangon]: U Tin Ohn.

Williamson, Muriel. 1968. "The Construction and Decoration of One Burmese Harp." *Selected Reports in Ethnomusicology* 1(2):45–72.

———. 1975a. "Aspects of Traditional Style Maintained in Burma's First Thirteen Kyò Songs." *Selected Reports in Ethnomusicology* 2(2):117–163.

———. 1975b. "A Supplement to the Construction and Decoration of One Burmese Harp." *Selected Reports in Ethnomusicology* 2(2):111–115.

———. 1979a. "The Basic Tune of a Late Eighteenth-Century Burmese Classical Song." *Musica Asiatica* 2:155–195.

———. 1979b. "A Biographical Note on Myáwadi Sá, Burmese Poet and Composer." *Musica Asiatica* 2:151–154.

———. 1981. "The Correlation between Speech-Tones of Text-Syllables and Their Musical Setting in a Burmese Classical Song." *Musica Asiatica* 3:11–28.

Malaysia

Abdullah bin Mohamed (Dato). 1971. "The Ghazal in Arabic Literature and in Malay Music." *Malaya in History* 14(l).

Affan Seljug. 1967. "Some Notes on the Origin and Development of the Naubat." *Journal of the Royal Asiatic Society, Malaysian Branch* 40(1):149–152.

Ahmad Omar. 1984. "Joget Gamelan: The Art of Orchestral Dance." *Performing Arts* 1(1):38–41.

Aishah Ali. 1981. "A Glorious Chapter in the Malay Film Industry." In *New Straits Times Annual,* 36–45. Kuala Lumpur: Straits Times Press.

Balfour, Henry L. 1904. *Report on a Collection of Musical Instruments from the Siamese Malay States and Perak.* Fasciculi Malayanses, Anthropology. London: University Press of Liverpool.

Beamish, Tony. 1954. *The Arts of Malaya.* Singapore: Donald Moore.

Blacking, J. A. R. 1954–1955. "Musical Instruments of the Malayan Aborigines." *Federation Museums Journal* 1(11):35–52.

Brunet, Jacques. 1971. *Wayang Kulit: Schatten-theater aus Malaysia*. Berlin: Internationalen Institut für Vergleichende Musikstudien und Dokumentation.

Chopyak, James. 1986. "Music in Modern Malaysia: A Survey of the Musics Affecting the Development of Malaysian Popular Music." *Asian Music* 18(l):111–138.

———. 1987. "The Role of Music in Mass Media, Public Education, and the Formation of a Malaysian National Culture." *Ethnomusicology* 31(3):431–454.

Couillard, Marie-Andrée, M. Elizabeth Cardosa, and Margaret R. Martinez. 1982. "Jah Hut Musical Culture and Content." *Contributions to Southeast Asian Ethnography* 1:35–55.

D'Cruz, Marion Francena. 1979. "Joget Gamelan, a Study of Its Contemporary Practice." M.A. thesis, Universiti Sains Malaysia.

Cuisinier, Jeanne. 1936. *Danses magiques de Kelantan*. Paris: Gallimard.

———. 1957. *Le théâtre d'ombres à Kelantan*. Paris: Gallimard.

Dobbs, Jack Percival Baker. 1972. "Music in the Multiracial Society of West Malaysia." Ph.D. dissertation, University of London.

Endicott, Kirk. 1979. *Batek Negrito Religion: The World-View and Rituals of a Hunting and Gathering People of Peninsular Malaysia*. Oxford: Clarendon.

Frame, Edward. 1976. "Several Major Musical Forms of Sabah Malaysia." *Journal of the Royal Asiatic Society, Malaysian Branch* 49(2):154–163.

———. 1982. "The Musical Instruments of Sabah, Malaysia." *Ethnomusicology* 26(2):247–274.

Ghulam-Sarwar Yousof. 1976. "The Kelantan Mak Yong Dance Theater, a Study of Performance Structure." Ph.D. dissertation, University of Hawaii.

———. 1982a. "Mak Yong: The Ancient Malay Dance Theatre." *Asian Studies* 20:108–121.

———. 1982b. "Nora Chatri in Kedah: A Preliminary Report." *Journal of the Royal Asiatic Society, Malaysian Branch* 55(1):53–61.

———. 1983. "Feasting of the Spirits: The Berjamu Ritual Performance in the Kelantanese Wayang Siam Shadow Play." *Kajian Malaysia* 1(1):95–115.

———. 1987. "Bangsawan: The Malay Opera." *Tenggara* 20:3–20.

———. 1992. *Pangguiig Semar: Essays on Traditional Malay Theatre*. Kuala Lumpur: Tempo.

Ginsberg, Henry D. 1972. "The Manora Dance-Drama: An Introduction." *Journal of the Siam Society* 60:169–181.

Gorlinski, Virginia. 1988. "Some Insights into the Art of Sape' Playing." *Sarawak Museum Journal* 39(60):77–104.

Hamilton, A. W. 1920. "The Boria." *Journal of the Royal Asiatic Society, Straits Branch* 82:139–144.

———. 1982. *Malay Pantuns*. Singapore: Eastern Universities Press.

Hose, Charles, and McDougall, William. 1912. *The Pagan Tribes of Borneo*. 2 vols. London: Macmillan.

Kloss, C. B. 1906. "Malaysian Musical Instruments." *Journal of the Royal Asiatic Society, Straits Branch* 46:285–287.

Ku Zam Zam, Ku Idris. 1983. "Alat-Alat Muzik Dalam Ensembel Wayang Kulit, Mek Mulung dan Gendang Keling di Kedah Utara (Musical Instruments in the Shadow Play, *Mek Mulung*, and *Gendang Keling* Ensembles of North Kedah)." In *Kajian Budaya dan Masyarakat di Malaysia*, ed. Mohd. Taib Osman and Wan Kadir Yusoff, 1–52. Kuala Lumpur: Dewan Bahasa dan Pustaka.

———. 1993a. "Nobat: Music in the Service of the King—The Symbol of Power and Status in Traditional Malay Society." In *Tinta Kenangan*, ed. Nik Safiah Karim, 175–193. Kuala Lumpur: Jabatan Pengajian Melayu, Universiti Malaya.

———. 1993b. "Tumbuk Kalang: Satu Genre Muzik Ke'a Pertanian Padi (*Tumbuk Kalang*: A Musical Genre Related to the Cultivation of Rice)." In *Segemal Padi Sekunca Budi*, ed. Nik Safiah Karim, 207–222. Kuala Lumpur: Akademi Pengajian Melayu, Universiti Malaya.

Ladderman, Carol. 1991. *Taming the Wind of Desire: Psychology, Medicine, and Aesthetics in Malay Shamanistic Performance*. Los Angeles: University of California Press.

Linehan, W. 1951. "Nobat and the Orang Kalau of Perak." *Journal of the Royal Asiatic Society, Malayan Branch* 24(3):60–68.

Lockard, Craig A. 1991. "Reflections of Change: Sociopolitical Commentary and Criticism in Malaysian Popular Music since 1950." *Crossroads: An Interdisciplinary Journal of Southeast Asian Studies* 6(l):1–106.

Malm, William P. 1969. "Music of the Ma'yong." *Tenggara* 5:114–120.

———. 1971. "Malaysian Ma'yong Theater." *Drama Review* 15(3):108–121.

———. 1974. "Music in Kelantan, Malaysia, and Some of Its Cultural Implications." In *Studies in Malaysian Oral and Musical Traditions*, 1–49. Michigan Papers on South and Southeast Asia, 8. Ann Arbor: University of Michigan.

———. 1979. "Music in Malaysia." *World of Music* 21(3):6–18.

Matusky, Patricia. 1980. "Music in the Malay Shadow Puppet Theater." Ph.D. dissertation, University of Michigan.

———. 1982. "Musical Instruments and Musicians of the Malay Shadow Puppet Theater." *Journal of the American Musical Instrument Society* 8:38–68.

———. 1985. "An Introduction to the Major Instruments and Forms of Traditional Malay Music." *Asian Music* 16(2):121–182.

———. 1986. "Aspects of Musical Style among the Kajang, Kayan, and Kenyah-Badang of the Upper Rejang River [Sarawak]." *Sarawak Museum Journal* 36(57):185–229.

———. 1989. "Alat-Alat dan Bentuk-Bentuk Muzik Tradisi Masyarakat Melayu (Instruments and Forms of Traditional Music in Malay Society). In *Masydrakat Melayu: Struktur, Organisasi, dan Manifestasi*, ed. Mohd. Taib Osman, 248–319. Kuala Lumpur: Dewan Bahasa dan Pustaka.

———. 1990. "Aspects of Musical Style among the Kayan, Kenyah-Badang, and Malay Peoples of the Upper Rejang River [Sarawak]." *Sarawak Museum Journal* 41(62):115–149.

———. 1992. "Musical Instruments of the Indigenous Peoples." In *Sarawak—A Cultural Legacy*, ed. Lucas Chin, 217–230. Kuching: Society Atelier Sarawak.

———. 1993. *Malaysian Shadow Play and Music: Continuity of an Oral Tradition*. Kuala Lumpur: Oxford University Press.

———. 1994. "Music of the Mak Yong Theater of Malaysia: A Fusion of Southeast Asian Malay and Middle Eastern Islamic Elements." In *To the Four Corners*, ed. Ellen Leichtman, 25–53. Warren, Mich.: Harmonie Park.

Mohammad Anis Mohammad Nor. 1986. *Randai Dance of Minangkabau Sumatra, with Labanotation Scores*. Kuala Lumpur: University of Malaysia Press.

———. 1993. *Zapin: Folk Dance of the Malay World*. Singapore: Oxford University Press.

Mohammad Ghouse Nasaruddin. 1979. "The Desa Performing Arts of Malaysia." Ph.D. dissertation, Indiana University.

Mohd. Taib Osman, ed. 1974. *Traditional Drama and Music in Southeast Asia*. Kuala Lumpur: Dewan Bahasa dan Pustaka.

Oesch, Hans. 1973. "Musikalische Kontinuität bei Naturvölkern: Dargestellt an der Musik der Senoi auf Malakka." In *Studien zur Tradition in der Musik: Kurt von Fischer am 60. Geburtstag*, ed. H. H. Eggebrecht and M. Lotolf, 227–246. Munich.

———. 1974a. "Musikalische Gattungen bei Naturvölkern: Untersuchungen am vokalen und instrumentalen Repertoire des Schamanen Terhin und seiner Senoi-Leute von Stammer der Temiar am oberen Nenggiri auf Malakka." In *Festschrift für Arno Volk*, ed. Carl Kahlhaus and Hans Oesch, 7–30. Cologne: Musikverlag Hans Gerig.

———. 1974b. "Oekonomie und Musik: Zur Bedeutung der Produktionsverhältnisse für die Herausbildung einer Musikkultur, dargestellt am Beispiel der Inlandstamme auf Malakka und der Balier." In *Convivium Musicorum: Festschrift Wolfgang Boetticher zum sechzigsten Geburistag am 19 August 1974*, ed. H. Hoschen and D. R Moser, 246–253. Berlin: Verlag Merseburger.

Rahmah Bujang. 1977. "The Boria: A Study of a Malay Theater in Its Sociocultural Context," Ph.D. dissertation, University of Hull.

———. 1987. *Boria, a Form of Malay Theatre*. Singapore: Institute of Southeast Asian Studies.

Roseman, Marina. 1984. "The Social Structuring of Sound: The Temiar of Peninsular Malaysia." *Ethnomusicology* 28(3):411–445.

———. 1989. "Inversion and Conjuncture: Male and Female in Temiar Performance." In *Women and Music in Cross-Cultural Perspective*, ed. Ellen Koskoff, 131–150. Urbana and Chicago: University of Illinois Press.

———. 1990. "Head, Heart, Odor, and Shadow: The Structure of the Self, Ritual Performance, and the Emotional World." *Ethos* 18(3):227–250.

———. 1991. *Healing Sounds from the Malaysian Rainforest*. Berkeley: University of California Press.

———. 1994. "Les chants de rêve: Des frontières mouvantes dans le monde temiar." *Anthropologie et Sociétés* 18(2):121–144.

———. 1996. "'Pure Products Go Crazy': Rainforest Healing in a Nation-State." In *The Performance of Healing*, ed. Carol Laderman and Marina Roseman, 233–269. New York: Routledge.

———. 2000a. "Shifting Landscapes: Musical Mediations of Modernity in the Malaysian Rainforest." *Yearbook for Traditional Music* 32:31–65.

———. 2000b. "The Canned Sardine Spirit Takes the Mic." *World of Music* 42(2):115–136.

Sarkissian, Margaret. 1993a. "Music, Dance, and the Construction of Identity among Portuguese Eurasians in Melaka, Malaysia: A Preliminary Report." *Tirai Panggung: Jurnal Seni Persembahan* 1(1):1–16.

———. 1993b. "Music, Identity, and the Impact of Tourism on the Portuguese Settlement, Melaka, Malaysia." Ph.D. dissertation, University of Illinois at Urbana-Champaign.

———. 1994. "Whose Tradition?—Tourism as a Catalyst in the Creation of a Modern Malaysian 'Tradition.'" *Nhac Việt* 3:31–46.

———. 1995. "'Sinhalese Girl' Meets 'Aunty Annie': Competing Expressions of Ethnic Identity in the Portuguese Settlement, Melaka, Malaysia." *Asian Music* 27(l):37–62.

———. 2000. *D'Albuquerque's Children: Performing Tradition in Malaysia's Portuguese Settlement*. Chicago: University of Chicago Press.

Sheppard, Mubin. 1938. "The Trengganu Rodat." *Journal of the Royal Asiatic Society, Malayan Branch* 16(1):109–114.

———. 1967. "Joget Gamelan Trengganu." *Journal of the Royal Asiatic Society, Malaysian Branch* 40(l):149–152.

———. 1972. *Taman Indera: Malay Decorative Arts and Pastimes*. Kuala Lumpur: Oxford University Press.

———. 1973. "Manora in Kelantan." *Journal of the Royal Asiatic Society, Malaysian Branch* 46(l):161–170.

———. 1975. "Traditional Musical Instruments of Malaysia." *Selected Reports in Ethnomusicology* 2(2):171–182.

———. 1983. *Taman Saujana: Dance, Drama, Music, and Magic in Malaya Long and Not-So-Long Ago*. Petaling Jaya: International Book Service.

Strickland-Anderson, Lily. 1925. "Music in Malaya." *Musical Quarterly* 11:506–514.

Sweeney, Amin. 1972a. *Malay Shadow Puppets: The Wayang Siam of Kelantan*. London: British Museum.

———. 1972b. *Ramayana and the Malay Shadow Play*. Kuala Lumpur: National University of Malaysia Press.

———. 1974. "Professional Malay Story-Telling: Some Questions of Style and Presentation." In *Studies in Malaysian Oral and Musical Traditions*, 47–99. Michigan Papers on South and Southeast Asia, 8. Ann Arbor: University of Michigan.

Tan Sooi Beng. 1988. "The Thai Manora in Malaysia: Adapting to the Penang Chinese Community." *Asian Folklore Studies* 47(1):19–34.

———. 1989a. "From Popular to 'Traditional' Theatre: The Dynamics of Change in Bangsawan of Malaysia." *Ethnomusicology* 33(2):229–274.

———. 1989b. "The Performing Arts in Malaysia: State and Society." *Asian Music* 21(1):137–171.

———. 1989c. "A Social and Stylistic History of Bangsawan, c. 1880–1980: Correspondences between Social-Historical and Musical-Theatrical Change." Ph.D. dissertation, Monash University.

———. 1993. *Bangsawan: A Social and Stylistic History of Popular Malay Opera*. Singapore: Oxford University Press.

———. 1994. "Moving Centre Stage: Women in Malay Opera in Early Twentieth-Century Malaya." *Kajian Malaysia* 12(1–2):96–118.

Teeuw, A., and Wyatt, D. K. 1970. *Hikayat Patani*. The Hague: Martinus Nijhoff.

Thomas, Phillip Lee. 1986. *Like Tigers around a Piece of Meat: The Baba Style of Dondang Sayang*. Singapore: Institute of Southeast Asian Studies.

Tunku Nong Jiwa, Raja Badri Shah, and Haji Mubin Sheppard. 1962. "The Kedah and Perak Nobat." *Malaya in History* 7(2):7–11.

Ulbricht, H. 1970. *Wayang Purwa: Shadows of the Past*. Kuala Lumpur: Oxford University Press.

Wan Kadir Yusoff. 1983. "Pertumbuhan Budaya Popular Masyarakat Melayu Bandaran Sebelum Perang Dunia Kedua (The Establishment of Urban Malay Popular Culture before the Second World War)." In *Kajian Budaya dan Masyarakat di*, ed. Mohd. Taib Osman and Wan Kadir Yusoff, 53–107. Kuala Lumpur: Dewan Bahasa dan Pustaka.

———. 1988. *Budaya Popular Dalam Masyarakat Melayu Bandaran* (Popular Culture in Malay Urban Society). Kuala Lumpur: Dewan Bahasa dan Pustaka.

Werner, R. 1973. "Nose Flute Blowers of the Malayan Aborigines (Orang Asli)." *Anthropos* 68:181–191.

Wilkinson, R. J., and Windstedt, R. O. 1957. *Pantun Melayu*. Singapore: Malaya.

Williamson, Muriel C. 2000. *The Burmese Harp: Its Classical Music, Tunings, and Modes*. DeKalb: Center for Southeast Asian Studies, Northern Illinois University.

Winstedt, R. O. 1929. "The Perak Royal Musical Instruments." *Journal of the Royal Asiatic Society, Malayan Branch* 12:451.

Wright, Barbara Ann Stein. "Wayang Siam: An Ethnographic Study of the Malay Shadow Play of Kelantan." Ph.D. dissertation, Yale University.

Yousof, Ghulam-Sarwar. 1997. *The Malay Shadow Play: An Introduction*. Penang Kuala Lumpur: National Academy of Arts.

Vietnam

Addiss, Stephen. 1971a. "Music of the Cham Peoples." *Asian Music* 2(l):32–38.

———. 1971b. "Theater Music of Vietnam." *Southeast Asia* 1:129–152.

———. 1973. "*Hat A Dao*, the Sung Poetry of North Vietnam." *Journal of the American Oriental Society* 93(1):18–31.

———. 1992. "Text and Context in Vietnamese Sung Poetry: The Art of Hat A Dao." *Selected Reports in Ethnomusicology* 9:203–224.

Arana, Miranda. 1999. *Neotraditional Music in Vietnam*. Kent, Ohio: International Association for Research in Vietnamese Music.

Bamman, Richard Jones. 1991. "The Đàn Tranh and the Lục Huyền Gầm." In *New Perspectives on Vietnamese Music*, ed. Phong T. Nguyễn, 67–78. New Haven, Conn.: Yale Council on Southeast Asia Studies.

Bezacier, L., 1946. "Des découvertes archéologiques au Tonkin (Archaeological Discoveries in Tonkin)." *Revue de l'Académie des Inscriptions* 412–428.

Condominas, George. 1951–1952. "Le lithophone préhistorique de Ngut Lieng Krak." *Bulletin de l'École Française d'Extrême-Orient* 45(2):359–392.

Dong Son Drums in Viet Nam. 1990. Hanoi: Viet Nam Social Science.

Dournes, Jacques. 1965. "La musique chez les Jorai." *Objets et Mondes* 5(4):211–244.

Dumoutier, Georges. 1890. *Les chants et les traditions populaires des annamites* (Songs and Popular Traditions of the Annamites). Paris: Ernest Leroux.

Hoàng Yên. 1919. "La musique à Hué, Donnguyet, et Don-tranh." *Bulletin des Amis du Vieux Hué*: 233–287. (See also translation: 1953. *Music at Hué, Don-Nguyet, and Don-Tranh*, trans. Keith Botsford. New Haven, Conn.: HRAF.)

Hùynh Khắc Dụng. 1970. *Hat Boi: Theatre traditionnel du Viet-Nam*. Saigon: Kim Lai An Qui.

Janse, O. R. T. 1962. "On the Origins of Traditional Vietnamese Music." *Asian Perspectives* 6:145–162.

Le Ba Sinh. N.d. *Marionnettes sur eau/Water Puppetry*. Ho Chi Minh City: History Museum.

Le Bris, E. 1922. "Musique annamite: Airs traditionnels." *Bulletin des Amis du Vieux Hué* 9:255–309.

———. 1927. "Musique annamite: Les musiciens aveugles de Hue-Le Tu-dai-canh." *Bulletin des Amis du Vieux Hué* 14:137–148.

Lê Tuấn Hùng. 1991. *The Dynamics of Change in Hue and Tai Tu Music of Vietnam between c. 1890 and c. 1920*. Working Paper 67. Clayton:

Centre of Southeast Asian Studies, Monash University.

———. 1998. *Dàn Tranh Music of Vietnam: Traditional and Innovations*. Melbourne-Tôkyô: Australia Asia Foundation.

Nguyễn Đình Lai. 1955. "Étude sur la musique Sino-Vietnamienne et les chants populaires du Viet-Nam." *Bulletin de la Société des Études Indochinoises*, New Series, 31(l):1–91.

Nguyễn Huy Hong, and Trần Trung Chính. 1992. *Les marionnettes sur eau traditionnelles du Vietnam*. Hanoi: Éditions en Langues Étrangères.

Nguyen, Phong, with Adelaida Reyes Schramm and Patricia Shehan Campbell. 1995. *Searching for a Niche: Vietnamese Music at Home in America*. Kent, Ohio: Viet Music.

Nguyễn Thuyết Phong. 1982. "La musique bouddhique du Vietnam." Ph.D. dissertation, University of Paris (Sorbonne).

———. 1989. "Restructuring the Fixed Pitches of the Vietnamese Dan Nguyet Lute." *Asian Music* 18(1):56–70.

———, ed. 1990a. *New Perspectives in Vietnamese Music*. New Haven, Conn.: Department of International and Area Studies, Yale University.

———. 1990b. *Textes et chants de la liturgie bouddhique vietnamienne en France*. Kent, Ohio: Association for Research in Vietnamese Music.

Nguyễn Thuyết Phong, and Patricia Shehan Campbell. 1990. *From Rice Paddies and Temple Yards: Traditional Music of Vietnam*. Danbury, Conn.: World Music.

Nguyễn Văn Huyen. 1933. *Les chants alternés des garçons et des filles en Anninn*. Paris: Paul Geuthier.

Norton, Barley. 2000. "Vietnamese Mediumship Rituals: The Musical Construction of the Spirits." *World of Music* 42(2):75–98.

Phạm Duy. 1975. *Musics of Vietnam*, ed. Dale R. Whiteside. Carbondale: Southern Illinois University Press.

Pham Huy Thông. 1990. *Dong Son Drums in Viet Nam*. Hanoi: Viet Nam Social Science.

Reyes, Adelaida. 1999. *Songs of the Caged, Songs of the Free: Music and the Vietnamese Refugee Experience*. Philadelphia: Temple University Press.

Schaeffner, André. 1951. "Le lithophone préhistorique de Ndut Lieng Krak." *Revue de Musicologie* 97–98:1–19.

Song Bân. 1960. *The Vietnamese Theatre*. Hanoi: Foreign Languages.

Trần Văn Khê. 1960. "Instruments de musique revelés par des fouilles archéologiques; au Viet Nam." *Arts Asiatiques* 7(2):141–152.

———. 1961. "Aspects de la cantillation: Techniques du Viet Nam." *Revue de Musicologie* 47:37–53.

———. 1962. *La musique vietnamienne traditionelle*. Paris: Presses Universitaires de France.

———. 1967. *Viet-Nam: Les traditions musicales*. Paris: Buchet-Chastel.

———. 1969. "La musique dans la société vietnamienne actuelle." In *La musique dans la vie*, 2:121–156. Paris: ORTE.

———. 1975. "Vietnamese Music." *Selected Reports in Ethnomusicology* 2(2):35–48.

Varton, Paul. 1908. "Journal d'une chanteuse annamite." *Bulletin Française, Société International de Musique* 4:165–180.

Weiss, Peter. 1970. *Notes on the Cultural Life of the Democratic Republic of Vietnam*. New York: Dell. (Translated from the German edition: 1968. *Notizen zurn Kulturellen Leben in der Demokratischen Republik Viet Nam*.)

Singapore

Kong, Lily. 1995. "Popular Music and a 'Sense of Place' in Singapore." *Crossroads: An Interdisciplinary Journal of Southeast Asian Studies* 9(2):51–77.

Lee Tong Soon. 1999. "Technology and the Production of Islamic Space: The Call to Prayer in Singapore." *Ethnomusicology* 43(1):86–100.

———. 2000. "Professional Chinese Opera Troupes and Street Opera Performance in Singapore." *Asian Music* 31(2):35–69.

Perris, Arnold. 1978. "Chinese Wayang: The Survival of Chinese Opera in the Streets of Singapore." *Ethnomusicology* 22(2):297–306.

ISLAND SOUTHEAST ASIA

Indonesia

Abidin, Andi Zainal. 1974. "The I La Galigo Epic Cycle of South Celebes and Its Diffusion," trans. C. C. Macknight. *Indonesia* 17:161–169.

Adams, Marie Jeanne (Monni). 1981. "Instruments and Songs of Sumba, Indonesia: A Preliminary Survey." *Asian Music* 13:73–83.

Anderson, Benedict. 1965. *Mythology and the Tolerance of the Javanese*. Monograph Series, Modern Indonesia Project. Ithaca, N.Y.: Cornell University Press.

Arjo, Irawati Durban. 1989. "Women's Dance among the Sundanese of West Java, Indonesia." *Asian Theatre Journal* 6(2):168–178.

Arps, Bernard. 1992. *Tembang in Two Traditions: Performance and Interpretation of Javanese Literature*. London: School of Oriental and African Studies.

———, ed. 1993. *Performance in Java and Bali: Studies of Narrative, Theatre, Music, and Dance*. London: School of Oriental and African Studies, University of London.

Baier, Randal E. 1985. "The Angklung Ensemble of West Java: Continuity of an Agricultural Tradition." *Balungan* 2:8–16.

———. 1986. "Si Duriat Keueung: The Sundanese Angklung Ensemble of West Java, Indonesia." M.A. thesis, Wesleyan University.

Bakan, Michael B. 1993. "Balinese Kreasi Baleganjur: An Ethnography of Musical Experience." Ph.D. dissertation, University of California, Los Angeles.

———. 1993–1994. "Lessons from a World: Balinese Applied Music Instruction and the Teaching of Western 'Art' Music." *College Music Symposium* 33–34:1–22.

———. 1997–1998. "From Oxymoron to Reality: Agendas of Gender and the Rise of Balinese Women's Gamelan Beleganjur in Bali, Indonesia." *Asian Music* 29(1):37–85.

———. 1998. "Walking Warriors: Battles of Culture and Ideology in the Balinese Gamelan Beleganjur World." *Ethnomusicology* 42(3):441–484.

———. 1999. *Music of Death and New Creation: Experiences in the World of Balinese Gamelan Beleganjur*. Chicago: University of Chicago Press.

Bandem, I Made. 1980. "Bali: Music." *The New Grove Dictionary of Music and Musicians*, ed. Stanley Sadie. London: Macmillan.

Bandem, I Made, and Fredrik Eugene deBoer. 1981. *Kaja and Kelod: Balinese Dance in Transition*. Selangor, Malaysia: Oxford University Press.

Barraud, Cecile. 1990. "A Turtle Turned on the Sand in the Kei Islands: Society's Shares and Values." *Bijdragen tot de Taal-, Land-, en Volkenkunde* 1:146:35–55.

Basile, Christopher. 1996. "The Troubled Grass and the Bamboo's Cry: The Significance of the Rotinese Sasandu." *Asian Arts Society of Australia Review* 5(1):5.

Becker, A. L. 1979. "Text Building, Epistemology, and Aesthetics in Javanese Shadow Theater." In *The Imagination of Reality: Essays in Southeast Asian Coherence Systems*, ed. A. L. Becker and Aram Yengoyan, 211–243. Norwood, N.J.: Ablex.

Becker, A. L., and Judith Becker. 1981. "A Musical Icon: Power and Meaning in Javanese Gamelan Music." In *The Sign in Music and Literature*, ed. Wendy Steiner, 203–215. Austin: University of Texas Press.

———. 1983 [1979]. "A Grammar of the Musical Genre Srepegan." *Asian Music* 14(1):30–72.

Becker, A. L., and Aram Yengoyan, eds. 1979. *The Imagination of Reality: Essays in Southeast Asian Coherence Systems*. Norwood, N.J.: Ablex.

Becker, Judith. 1975. "Kroncong, Indonesian Popular Music." *Asian Music* 7(1):14–19.

———. 1979a. "Time and Tune in Java." In *The Imagination of Reality: Essays in Southeast Asian Coherence Systems*, ed. A. L. Becker and Aram Yengoyan, 197–210. Norwood, N.J.: Ablex.

———. 1979b. "People Who Sing; People Who Dance." In *What Is Modern Indonesian Culture?*

ed. Gloria Davis, 3–10. Athens: Ohio University Center for International Studies.

———. 1980. *Traditional Music in Modern Java: Gamelan in a Changing Society*. Honolulu: University of Hawaii Press.

———. 1988. "Earth, Fire, Sakti, and the Javanese Gamelan." *Ethnomusicology* 32(3):385–391.

———. 1991. "The Javanese Court Bedhaya Dance as a Tantric Analogy." In *Metaphor: A Musical Dimension*, ed. Jamie C. Kassler, 109–120. Sydney: Currency.

———. 1993. *Gamelan Stories: Tantrism, Islam, and Aesthetics in Central Java*. Monographs in Southeast Asian Studies. Tempe: Arizona State University Press.

Becker, Judith, and Alan Feinstein, eds. 1984, 1987, 1988. *Karawitan: Source Readings in Javanese Gamelan and Vocal Music*. 3 vols. Ann Arbor: Center for South and Southeast Asian Studies, University of Michigan.

Belo, Jane, ed. 1970. *Traditional Balinese Culture*. New York: Columbia University Press.

Bosch, E. D. K. 1951. "Guru, Drietand en Bron." *Bijdragen tot de Taal-, Land-, en Volkenkunde* 107:117–134.

Brakel-Papenhuijzen, Clara. 1992. *The Beahaya Court Dances of Central Java*. Leiden: Brill.

Brandon, James R. 1967. *Theatre in Southeast Asia*. Cambridge, Mass.: Harvard University Press.

———. 1970. *On Thrones of Gold: Three Javanese Shadow Plays*. Cambridge, Mass.: Harvard University Press.

Brandts Buys, J. S. 1921. "Over de ontwikkelingsmogelijkheden van de muziek op Java (On the Developmental Possibilities of Music in Java)." *Djawa* 1, *Praeadvies* 2:1–90.

———. 1926. "Over muziek in het Banjoewangische (On Music in Banyuwangi)." *Djawa* 6:205–228.

———. 1928. "De toonkunst bij de Madoereezen (The Music of the Madurese)." *Djawa* 8:1–290.

———. 1929. "Een en ander over Javaansche muziek (This and That about Javanese Music)." *Programma Van het Vijfde-Congres ter Gelegenheid van het Tienjarig Bestaan van het Java Instituut*, 45–63.

———. 1925. "Oude Klanken (Old Sounds)." *Djawa* 5(1):16–56.

Brandts Buys, J. S., and A. Brandts Buys-van Zijp. 1929. "Inlandsche dans en muziek." *Timboel* 3(2):13–18.

Brinner, Benjamin E. 1989–1990. "At the Border of Sound and Silence: The Use and Function of Pathetan in Javanese Gamelan." *Asian Music* 21(l):1–34.

———. 1992. "Performer Interaction in a New Form of Javanese Wayang." In *Essays on Southeast Asian Performing Arts: Local Manifestations and Cross-Cultural Implications*, ed. Kathy Foley, 96–114. Berkeley: Centers for South and Southeast Asia Studies, University of California.

———. 1993a. "Freedom and Formulaity in the Suling Playing of Bapak Tarnopangrawit." *Asian Music* 24(2):1–37.

———. 1993b. "A Musical Time Capsule from Java." *Journal of the American Musicological Society* 46(2):221–260.

———. 1995a. "Cultural Matrices and the Shaping of Innovation in Central Javanese Performing Arts." *Ethnomusicology* 39(3):433–456.

———. 1995b. *Knowing Music, Making Music: Javanese Gamelan and the Theory of Musical Competence and Interaction*. Chicago: University of Chicago Press.

———. 1999. "Cognitive and Interpersonal Dimensions of Listening in Javanese Gamelan Performance." *World of Music* 41(1):19–36.

Carle, Rainer. 1981, 1982. *Die Opera Batak: Das Wandestheater der Toba-Batak in Nord Sumatra*. 2 vols. Berlin: Dietrich Reimer Verlag.

Choy, Peggy. 1984. "Texts through Time: The Golèk Dance of Java." In *Aesthetic Tradition and Cultural Transition in Java and Bali*, ed. Stephanie Morgan and Laurie Jo Sears, 51–81. Madison: University of Wisconsin Center for Southeast Asian Studies.

Clara van Groenendael, Victoria. 1985. *The Dalang behind the Wayang*. Verhandelingen van de Koninklijk Instituut voor Taal-, Land-, en Volkenkunde, 114. Dordrecht, Netherlands, and Providence, R.I.: Foris.

———. 1987. *Wayang Theatre in Indonesia*. Koninklijk Instituut voor Taal-, Land-, en Volkenkunde, Bibliographical Series 16. Dordrecht, Netherlands, and Providence, R.I.: Foris.

———. 1990. *"Po-té-hi*: The Chinese Glove-Puppet Theatre in East Java." Paper presented at the International Symposium on Indonesian Performing Arts, School of Oriental and African Studies, University of London, July–August 1990.

———. 1993. *"Po-té-hi*: The Chinese Glove Puppet Theatre in East Java." In *Performance in Java and Bali: Studies of Narrative, Theatre, Music, and Dance*, ed. Bernard Arps, 11–33. London: School of Oriental and African Studies, University of London.

Cornets de Groot, A. D. 1852. "Bijdrage tot de kennis van de zeden en gewoonten der Javanen (Contribution to the Knowledge of the Manners and Customs of the Javanese)." *Tijdschrift voor Nederlandsch Indie* 14(2):257–280, 346–367, 393–424.

Covarrubias, Miguel. 1937. *The Island of Bali*. New York: Knopf.

Crawford, Michael. 1980. "Indonesia: East Java." *The New Grove Dictionary of Music and Musicians*, ed. Stanley Sadie. London: Macmillan.

Crystal, Eric, and Catherine Crystal. 1973. *Music of Sulawesi*. Ethnic Folkways FE 4351. (Notes to LP disk.)

DeVale, Sue Carole, and I Wayan Dibia. 1991. "Sekar Anyar: An Exploration of Meaning in Balinese Gamelan." *World of Music* 33(l):5–51.

deBoer, Fredrik E. 1989. "Balinese Sendratari: A Modern Dramatic Dance Genre." *Asian Theatre Journal* 6(2):179–193.

de Zoete, Beryl, and Walter Spies. 1973 [1938]. *Dance and Drama in Bali*. Selangor, Malaysia: Oxford University Press.

Dewantara, Ki Hadjar. 1964. *Serat Sari Swara* (Essence of Sound/Voice), 2nd ed. Jakarta: P. N. Pradnjaparamita.

Ellis, Alexander J. 1884. "Tonometrical Observations on Some Existing Nonharmonic Musical Scales," *Proceedings of the Royal Society* 37:368–385.

Erb, Maribeth. 1988. "Flores: Cosmology, Art, and Ritual." In *Islands and Ancestors: Indigenous Styles of Southeast Asia*, ed. Jean-Paul Barbier and Douglas Newton, 106–119. Munich: Prestel.

Falk, Catherine A. 1982. "The Tarawangsa Tradition in West Java." Ph.D. dissertation, Monash University.

Foley, Kathy, ed. 1992. *Essays on Southeast Asian Performing Arts: Local Manifestations and Cross-Cultural Implications*. Berkeley: Center for South and Southeast Asian Studies, University of California.

Foley, M. Kathleen. 1979. "The Sundanese 'Wayang Golek': The Rod Puppet Theatre of West Java." Ph.D. dissertation, University of Hawaii.

———. 1984. "Of Dalang and Dukun-Spirit and Men: Curing and Performance in the Wayang of West Java." *Asian Theatre Journal* 1(1):52–75.

———. 1985. "The Dancer and the Danced: Trance Dance and Theatrical Performance in West Java." *Asian Theatre Journal* 2(l):28–49.

———. 1986. "At the Graves of the Ancestors: Chronicle Plays in the Wayang Cepak Puppet Theatre of Cirebon, Indonesia." In *Historical Drama*, ed. James Redmond, 31–49. Themes in Drama, 8. Cambridge: Cambridge University Press.

———. 1990. "My Bodies: The Performer in West Java." *Drama Review* 34(2):62–80.

Forrest, Wayne Jeffrey. 1980. "Concepts of Melodic Pattern in Contemporary Solonese Gamelan Music." *Asian Music* 11(2):53–127.

Fox, James J. 1974. "Our Ancestors Spoke in Pairs: Rotinese Views of Language, Dialect, and Code." In *Explorations in the Ethnography of Speaking*, ed. Richard Bauman and Joel Sherzer, 65–85. London: Cambridge University Press.

———. 1977. *Harvest of the Palm: Ecological Change in Eastern Indonesia*. Cambridge, Mass.: Harvard University Press.

———. 1979a. "The Ceremonial System of Savu." In *The Imagination of Reality: Essays in Southeast Asian Coherence Systems*, ed. A. L. Becker and Aram Yengoyan, 145–173. Norwood, N.J.: Ablex.

———. 1979b. "Standing in Time and Place: The Structure of Rotinese Historical Narratives." In *Southeast Asian Perceptions of the Past*, No. 4, ed. A. Reid and D. Marr, 10–25. Kuala Lumpur: Heinemann.

———. 1988. *To Speak in Pairs: Essays on the Ritual Languages of Eastern Indonesia*, ed. James J. Fox, 1–28. Cambridge: Cambridge University Press.

Frederick, William H. 1982. "Rhoma Irama and the Dangdut Style: Aspects of Contemporary Indonesian Popular Culture." *Indonesia* 34:103–130.

Geertz, Clifford. 1960. *The Religion of Java*. New York: Free Press.

Geirnaert, Danielle C. 1989. "The Pogo Nauta Ritual in Laboya (West Sumba): Of Tubers and Mamuli." *Bijdragen tot de Taal-, Land-, en Volkenkunde* 145(4):445–463.

Gieben, Claartje, Renée Heijnen, and Anneke Sapuletej. 1984. *Muziek en dans Spelletjes en Kinderliedjes van de Molukken*. Hoevelaken, Netherlands: Christelijk Pedagogisch Studiecentrum.

Gold, Lisa. 1992. "Musical Expression in the Gender Wayang Repertoire: A Bridge between Narrative and Ritual." In *Balinese Music in Context: A Sixty-Fifth Birthday Tribute to Hans Oesch*, ed. Danker Schaareman, 245–275. Winterthur: Amadeus.

Goldsworthy, David. 1978. "Honey-Collecting Ceremonies on the East Coast of North Sumatra." In *Studies in Indonesian Music*, ed. Margaret J. Kartomi, 1–44. Clayton: Centre of Southeast Asian Studies, Monash University.

———. 1979. "Melayu Music of North Sumatra." Ph.D. dissertation, Monash University.

———. 1986. "The Dancing Fish Trap (*Lukah Menari*): A Spirit Invocation Song and a Spirit-Possession 'Dance' from North Sumatra." *Musicology Australia* 9:12–28.

Groneman, J. 1890. *De Gamelan te Jogjakarta*. Amsterdam: Johannes Müller.

Harnish, David D. 1985. "Musical Traditions of the Lombok Balinese: Antecedents from Bali and Lombok." M.A. thesis, University of Hawai'i.

———. 1986. "Sasak Music in Lombok." *Balungan* 2(3):17–22.

———. 1988. "Religion and Music: Syncretism, Orthodox Islam, and Musical Change in Lombok." *Selected Reports in Ethnomusicology* 7:123–138.

———. 1990. "The Preret of the Lombok Balinese: Transformation and Continuity within a Sacred Tradition." *Selected Reports in Ethnomusicology* 8:201–220.

———. 1991. "Music at the Lingsar Temple Festival: The Encapsulation of Meaning in the Balinese/Sasak Interface in Lombok, Indonesia." Ph.D. dissertation, University of California at Los Angeles.

———. 1992. "The Performance, Context, and Meaning of Balinese Music in Lombok." In *Balinese Music in Context: A Sixty-Fifth Birthday Tribute to Hans Oesch*, ed. Danker Schaareman, 29–58. Winterthur: Amadeus.

———. 1993. "The Future Meets the Past in the Present: Music and Buddhism in Lombok." *Asian Music* 25(1–2):29–50.

———. 1994. "The Future Meets the Past in the Present: Music and Buddhism in Lombok." *Asian Music* 25(2):29–50.

———. 1997. "Music, Myth, and Liturgy at the Lingsar Temple Festival in Lombok, Indonesia." *Yearbook for Traditional Music* 29:80–106.

Harrell, Max Leigh. 1974. "The Music of the Gamelan Degung of West Java." Ph.D. dissertation, University of California at Los Angeles.

———. 1975. "Some Aspects of Sundanese Music." *Selected Reports in Ethnomusicology* 2(2):81–100.

Hastanto, Sri. 1985. "The Concept of Pathet in Javanese Gamelan Music." Ph.D. dissertation, University of Durham.

Hatch, Martin. 1976. "The Song Is Ended: Changes in the Use of Macapat in Central Java." *Asian Music* 7(2):59–71.

———. 1979. "Towards a More Open Approach to the History of Javanese Music." *Indonesia* 27:129–154.

———. 1980. "Lagu, Laras, Layang: Rethinking Melody in Javanese Music." Ph.D. dissertation, Cornell University.

———. 1985. "Popular Music in Indonesia." In *Popular Music Perspectives*, Vol. 2, ed. D. Horn, 210–227. Göteborg: International Association for the Study of Popular Music.

———. 1989. "Popular Music in Indonesia." In *World Music, Politics, and Social Change: Papers from the International Association for the Study of Popular Music*, ed. Simon Frith, 47–67. Manchester: Manchester University Press.

Hatley, Barbara. 1971. "Wayang and Ludruk: Polarities in Java." *Drama Review* 15(3):88–101.

———. 1980. *Ketoprak Theatre and the Wayang Tradition*. Melbourne: Monash University Press.

Hefner, Robert W. 1985. *Hindu Javanese: Tengger Tradition and Islam*. Princeton, N.J.: Princeton University Press.

———. 1987. "The Politics of Popular Art: Tayuban Dance and Culture Change in East Java." *Indonesia* 43:75–94.

Heimarck, Brita Renee. 1999. "Balinese Discourses on Music: Musical Modernization in the Ideas and Practices of Shadow Play Performers from Sukawati and the Indonesian College of the Arts." Ph.D. dissertation, Cornell University.

Heins, Ernst L. 1967. "Music of the Serimpi Anglir Mendung." *Indonesia* 3:135–151.

———. 1969. "Tempo (Irama) in de M.-Javaanse gamelanmuziek." *Kultuurpatronen* 10–11:31–57.

———. 1970. "Cueing the Gamelan in Javanese Wayang Performance." *Indonesia* 9(April):101–127.

———. 1975. "Kroncong and Tanjidor: Two Cases of Urban Folk Music in Jakarta." *Asian Music* 7(l):20–32.

———. 1977. "*Goong Renteng*: Aspects of Orchestral Music in a Sundanese Village." Ph.D. dissertation, University of Amsterdam.

Heins, Ernst L., and G. van Wengen. 1979. "Maluku (Molukken)." In *Musikgeschichte in Bildern: Südostasien*, ed. Paul Collaer, 142–143. Leipzig: VEB Deutschen Verlag.

Heinze, R. von. 1909. "Über Batak-Musik." In *Die Bataklånder*, ed. Wilhelm Volz, 373–381. Nord-Sumatra, 1. Berlin: D. Reimer.

Henschkel, Marina. 1994. "Perceptions of Popular Culture in Contemporary Indonesia: Five Articles from *Tempo*, 1980–1990." *Review of Indonesian and Malaysian Affairs* 28(2):53–71.

Herbst, Edward. 1997. *Voices in Bali: Energies and Perceptions in Vocal Music and Dance Theater*. Hanover and London: Wesleyan University Press.

Hicks, David. 1988. "Art and Religion on Timor." In *Islands and Ancestors: Indigenous Styles of Southeast Asia*, ed. Jean-Paul Barbier and Douglas Newton, 138–151. Munich: Prestel-Verlag.

Hidding, Klaas A. H. 1929. "Nyi Pohatji Sangjang Sri." Ph.D. dissertation, Rijksuniversiteit Leiden.

Hoffman, Stanley B. 1978. "Epistemology and Music: A Javanese Example." *Ethnomusicology* 22(l):69–88.

Holt, Claire. 1939. *Dance Quest in Celebes*. Paris: Archives Internationales de la Danse.

———. 1967. *Art in Indonesia: Continuities and Change*. Ithaca, N.Y.: Cornell University Press.

———. 1971a. "Dances of Sumatra and Nias: Notes." *Indonesia* 11:1–20.

———. 1971b. "Batak Dances: Notes." *Indonesia* 12:65–84.

———. 1972. "Dances of Minangkabau: Notes." *Indonesia* 14:73–96.

Hood, Mantle. 1954. *The Nuclear Theme as a Determinant of Paṭet in Javanese Music*. Groningen: J. B. Wolters.

———. 1963. "The Enduring Tradition: Music and Theatre in Java and Bali." In *Indonesia*, ed. Ruth McVey, 438–471. New Haven, Conn.: Human Relations Area Files.

———. 1966. "Sléndro and Pélog Redefined." *Selected Reports in Ethnomusicology* l(l):28–48.

———. 1970. "The Effect of Medieval Technology on Musical Styles in the Orient." *Selected Reports in Ethnomusicology* 1(3):148–170.

———. 1971. "Aspects of Group Improvisation in the Javanese Gamelan." In *Musics of Asia*. Manila: National Music Council.

———. 1972. "Music of Indonesia." In *Music*, ed. Mantle Hood and José Maceda, 1–27. Leiden and Cologne: Brill.

———. 1975. "Improvisation in the Stratified Ensembles of Southeast Asia." *Selected Reports in Ethnomusicology* 2(2):25–34.

———. 1980. *The Evolution of Javanese Gamelan*, Book 1: *Music of the Roaring Sea*. Wilhelmshaven: Edition Heinrichshofen.

———. 1984. *The Evolution of Javanese Gamelan*, Book 2: *Legacy of the Roaring Sea*. Wilhelmshaven: Edition Heinrichshofen.

———. 1988. *The Evolution of Javanese Gamelan*, Book 3: *Paragon of the Roaring Sea*. Wilhelmshaven: Edition Heinrichshofen.

Hornbostel, Erich M. von. 1908. "Über die Musik der Kubu." In *Die Orang-Kubu auf Sumatra*, ed. B. Hagen, 245–256. Frankfurt: Baer.

Hoskins, Janet. 1988a. "Arts and Cultures of Sumba." In *Islands and Ancestors: Indigenous Styles of Southeast Asia*, ed. Jean Paul Barbier and Douglas Newton, 120–138. Munich: Prestel-Verlag.

———. 1988b. "The Drum Is the Shaman, the Spear Guides His Voice." *Social Sciences Medicine* 27(8):819–828.

———. 1993. *The Play of Time: Kodi Perspectives on Calendars, History, and Exchange*. Berkeley: University of California Press.

Hughes, David. 1988. "Deep Structure and Surface Structure in Javanese Music: A Grammar of *Gendhing Lampah*." *Ethnomusicology* 32(l):23–74.

Hughes-Freeland, Felicia. 1990. "Tayuban: Culture on the Edge." *Indonesia Circle* 52:36–44.

———. 1993. "*Golèk Ménak* and *Tayuban*: Patronage and Professionalism in Spheres of Central Javanese Culture." In *Performance in Java and Bali: Studies of Narrative, Theatre, Music, and Dance*, ed. Bernard Arps, 88–120. London: School of Oriental and African Studies, University of London.

Jacobson, Edward, and J. H. van Hasselt. 1975 [1907]. "The Manufacture of Gongs in Sema-rang," trans. Andrew Toth. *Indonesia* 19:127–152, plates.

Jansen, Arlin D. 1980. "Gonrang Music: Its Structure and Functions in Simalungun Batak Society in Sumatra." Ph.D. dissertation, University of Washington.

Jessup, Helen Ibbitson. 1990. *Court Arts of Indonesia*. New York: Asia Society Galleries Harry N. Abrams.

Joest, W. 1892. "Malayische Lieder und Tänze aus Ambon und den Uliase (Molukken)." *Internationales Archiv für Ethnographie* 5:1–34.

Jones, Arthur M. 1971. *Africa and Indonesia: The Evidence of the Xylophone and Other Musical and Cultural Factors*. Leiden: Brill.

Jordaan, Roy E. 1984. "The Mystery of Nyai Lara Kidul, Goddess of the Southern Ocean." *Archipel* 28:99–116.

———. 1991. "Text, Temple, and Tirtha." In *The Art and Culture of South-East Asia*, ed. Lokesh Chandra, 165–180. New Delhi: International Academy of Indian Culture and Aditya Prakashan.

Kartomi, Karen S. 1986. "Mendu Theatre on the Island of Bunguran, Sumatra." Honors thesis, Monash University.

Kartomi, Margaret J. 1972. "Tiger-Capturing Music in Minangkabau, West Sumatra." *Sumatra Research Bulletin* 2(l):24–41. Reprinted: "Tigers into Kittens." *Hemisphere* 20(5):9–15, 20(6):7–13.

———. 1973a. *Matjapat Songs in Central and West Java*. Canberra: Australian National University Press.

———. 1973b. "Music and Trance in Java." *Ethnomusicology* 17(2):163–208.

———. 1976. "Performance, Music, and Meaning in *Réyog Ponorogo*." *Indonesia* 22:85–130.

———. 1979. "Minangkabau Musical Culture: The Contemporary Scene and Recent Attempts at Its Modernization." In *What Is Modern Indonesian Culture?* ed. G. Davis, 19–36. Athens, Ohio: Ohio University Press.

———. 1980. "Musical Strata in Sumatra, Java, and Bali." In *Musics of Many Cultures*, ed. Elizabeth May, 111–133. Berkeley, Los Angeles, London: University of California Press.

———. 1981a. "Dualism in Unity: The Ceremonial Music of the Mandailing Raja Tradition." *Asian Music* 12(2):74–108.

———. 1981b. "Lovely When Heard from Afar: Mandailing Ideas of Musical Beauty." In *Five Essays on the Indonesian Arts*, ed. Margaret J. Kartomi, 1–16. Clayton: Centre of Southeast Asian Studies, Monash University.

———. 1981c. "Randai Theatre in West Sumatra: Components, Music, Origins, and Recent Change." *Review of Indonesian and Malaysian Affairs* 15(1):1–44.

———. 1981d. "His Skyward Path the Rainbow Is: Funeral Music of the Sa'dan Toraja." *Hemisphere* 25(5):303–309.

———. 1983a. *The Angkola People of Sumatra: An Anthology of Southeast Asian Music*. Bärenreiter Musicaphon BM30 SL2568. (LP disk and liner notes.)

———. 1983b. *The Mandailing People of Sumatra: An Anthology of Southeast Asian Music*. Bärenreiter Musicaphon BM30 SL2567. (LP disk and liner notes.)

———. 1986a. "Kapri: A Synthesis of Malay and Portuguese Music on the West Coast of North Sumatra." In *Cultures and Societies of North Sumatra*, ed. Rainer Carle, 351–393. Berlin and Hamburg: Dietrich Reimer Verlag.

———. 1986b. "Muslim Music in West Sumatran Culture." *World of Music* 3:13–32.

———. 1986c. "Tabut—A Shi'a Ritual Transplanted from India to Sumatra." In *Nineteenth and Twentieth Century Indonesia: Essays in Honour of Professor J. D. Legge*, ed. David P. Chandler and M. C. Ricklefs, 141–162. Monash: Monash University Centre of Southeast Asian Studies.

———. 1988. "Ritual Music and Dance: Contact and Change in the Lowlands of South Sulawesi." In *The Twelfth Festival of Asian Arts*, ed. J. Thompson, 26–35. Hong Kong: Urban Council.

———, ed. 1990a. *On Concepts and Classifications of Musical Instruments*. Chicago Studies in Ethnomusicology. Chicago: University of Chicago Press.

———. 1990b. "Parallels between Social Structure and Ensemble Classification in Mandailing." In *On Concepts and Classifications of Musical Instruments*, 215–224. Chicago: University of Chicago Press.

———. 1990c. "Taxonomical Models of the Instrumentarium and Regional Ensembles in Minangkabau." In *On Concepts and Classifications of Musical Instruments*, 225–234. Chicago: University of Chicago Press.

———. 1991a. "Experience-Near and Experience-Distant Perceptions of the Daboih Ritual in Aceh, Sumatra." In *Von der Vielfalt musikalischer Kultur: Festschrift für Josef Kuckertz, zur Vollendung des 60 Lebensjahres*, ed. Rüdiger Schumacher, 247–260. Berlin: Free University.

———. 1991b. "Dabuih in West Sumatra: A Synthesis of Muslim and Pre-Muslim Ceremony and Musical Style." *Archipel* 41:33–52.

———. 1992. "Appropriation of Music and Dance in Contemporary Ternate and Tidore." *Studies in Music* 26:85–95.

———. 1993a. "The Paradoxical and Nostalgic History of 'Gending Sriwijaya' in South Sumatra." *Archipel* 44:37–50.

———. 1993b. "Revival of Feudal Music, Dance, and Ritual in the Former 'Spice Islands' of Ternate and Tidore." In *Culture and Society in New Order Indonesia*, ed. Virginia Hooker, 185–220. New York, Oxford: Oxford University Press.

———. 1994. "Is Maluku Still Musicological Terra Incognita?—An Overview of the Music Cultures of the Province of Maluku." *Journal of Southeast Asian Studies* 25(1):141–171.

———. 1996. "Contact and Synthesis in the Development of the Music of South Sumatra." In *All Kinds of Music, in Honour of Andrew Mc-Credie*, ed. Graham Strahle and David Swale, 234–253. Wilhelmshaven: Florian Noetzel Verlag.

———. 1997. "The Royal *Nobat* Ensemble of Indragiri in Riau, Sumatra, in Colonial and Post-Colonial Times." *Galpin Society Journal* 50(l):3–15.

———. 1998. "The Pan-East/Southeast Asian and National Indonesian Song 'Bengawan Solo' and Its Javanese Composer." *Yearbook for Traditional Music* 30:85–100.

———. 1998–1999. "The Music-Culture of South-Coast West Sumatra: Backwater of the Minangkabau 'Heartland' or Home of the Sacred Mermaid and the Earth Goddess?" *Asian Music* 30(1):133–181.

Kaudern, Walter A. 1927. *Musical Instruments in Celebes*. Ethnographical Studies in Celebes, 3. Göteborg: Elanders Boktryckeri.

Keeler, Ward. 1975. "Musical Encounter in Java and Bali." *Indonesia* 19:85–126.

———. 1987. *Javanese Shadow Plays, Javanese Selves*. Princeton, N.J.: Princeton University Press.

Kornhauser, Bronia. 1978. "In Defence of Kroncong." In *Studies in Indonesian Music*, 104–183. Monash Papers on Southeast Asia, 7. Clayton: Monash University.

———. 1935. "De rijstgodin op Midden-Celebes, en de Maangodin." *Mensch en Maatschappij* 11(2):109–122.

Kunst, Jaap. 1938. *Music in Nias.* Supplement 38. Leiden: Internationales Archiv für Ethnographie.

———. 1942. *Music in Flores: A Study of the Vocal and Instrumental Music among the Tribes Living in Flores.* Leiden: Brill.

———. 1945. *Een en Ander Over de Muziek en den dans Op de Keieilanden.* Mededeling, 64. Amsterdam: Koninklijke Vereeniging Indisch Instituut.

———. 1950. "Die 2000-jährige Geschichte Süd-Sumatras gespiegelt in ihrer Musik." *Kongress-Bericht Lüneburg,* 160–167.

———. 1960 [1954]. *Cultural Relations between the Balkans and Indonesia,* 2nd ed. Afdeling Culturele en Physische Anthropologie, 47, Mededeling 107. Amsterdam: Koninklijk Instituut voor de Tropen (Royal Tropical Institute).

———. 1968 [1927]. *Hindu-Javanese Musical Instruments.* The Hague: Martinus Nijhoff.

———. 1973 [1934]. *Music in Java: Its History, Its Theory, and Its Technique,* 3rd ed., rev. and enlarged Ernst L. Heins. 2 vols. The Hague: Martinus Nijhoff.

———. 1994. *Indonesian Music and Dance: Traditional Music and Its Interaction with the West: A Compilation of Articles (1934–1952) Originally Published in Dutch, with Biographical Essays by Ernst Heins, Elizabeth den Otter, Feliz van Lantsweerde.* Amsterdam: Ethnomusicology Centre "Jaap Kunst," Royal Tropical Institute and University of Amsterdam.

Kunst, Jaap, and C. J. A. Kunst-Van Wely. 1924. *De Toonkunst van Bali.* Weltevreden: G. Kolff.

Lentz, Donald. 1965. *The Gamelan Music of Java and Bali: An Artistic Anomaly Complementary to Primary Tonal Theoretical Systems.* Lincoln: University of Nebraska Press.

Lindsay, Jennifer. 1985. "Klasik, Kirsch or Contemporary: A Study of the Javanese Performing Arts." Ph.D. dissertation, University of Sydney.

Lockard, Craig A. 1998. *Dance of Life: Popular Music and Politics in Southeast Asia.* Honolulu: University of Hawaii Press.

Lysloff, René T. A. 1986. "The *Bonang Barung* in Contemporary Gamelan Performance Practice." *Balungan* 2(1–2):31–40.

———. 1990a. *"Srikandhi* Dances *Lènggèr:* A Performance of Music and Shadow Theater in Banyumas (West Central Java)." 2 vols. Ph.D. dissertation, University of Michigan.

———. 1990b. "Non-Puppets and Non-Gamelan: Wayang Parody in Banyumas." *Ethnomusicology* 34(l):19–36.

———. 1993. "A Wrinkle in Time: The Shadow Puppet Theatre of Banyumas (West Central Java)." *Asian Theatre Journal* 10(l):49–80.

Lysloff, René T. A., and Deborah Wong. 1991. "Threshold to the Sacred: The Overture in Thai and Javanese Ritual Performance." *Ethnomusicology* 35(3):315–348.

Manuel, Peter, and Randal E. Baier. 1986. "Jaipongan: Indigenous Popular Music of West Java." *Asian Music* 18(l):91–110.

Manik, Liberty. 1973–74. "Eine Studienreise zur Erforschung der rituellen Gondang-Musik der Batak auf Sumatra." *Mitteilungen der Deutschen Gesellschaft für Musik des Orients* 12:134–137.

McDermott, Vincent. 1986. "Gamelans and New Music." *Musical Quarterly* 72(1):16–27.

McDermott, Vincent, and Sumarsam. 1975. "Central Javanese Music: The Paṭet of Laras Sléndro and the Gendèr Barung." *Ethnomusicology* 19:233–244.

McGraw, Andrew C. 1999–2000. "The Development of the Gamelan Semara Dana and the Expansion of the Modal System in Bali." *Asian Music* 31(1):63–93.

McPhee, Colin. 1966. *Music in Bali: A Study in Form and Instrumental Organization in Balinese Orchestral Music.* New Haven, Conn., and London: Yale University Press.

Messner, Gerald Florian. 1989. "Jaap Kunst Revisited: Multipart Singing in Three East Florinese Villages Fifty Years Later—A Preliminary Investigation." *World of Music* 21(2):3–50.

Moore, Lynette M. 1985. "Songs of the Pakpak of North Sumatra." Ph.D. dissertation, Monash University.

Morgan, Stephanie, and Laurie Jo Sears, eds. 1984. *Aesthetic Tradition and Cultural Transition in Java and Bali.* Madison: University of Wisconsin Center for Southeast Asian Studies.

Muller, Karl. 1991. *East of Bali: From Lombok to Timor.* Singapore: Periplus.

Murgiyanto, Sal. 1991. *Dance of Indonesia.* New York: Festival of Indonesia Foundation.

Natapradja, Iwan. 1975. "Sundanese Dances." *Selected Reports in Ethnomusicology* 2(2):103–108.

Nizar, M. 1994. *"Dangdut:* Sebuah Perjalanan *(Dangdut:* A Journey)." *Citra* 221–225. (Five-part series.)

Nooey-Palm, Clémentine H. M. 1988. "The Mamasa and Sa'dan Toraja of Sulawesi." In *Islands and Ancestors: Indigenous Styles of Southeast Asia,* ed. Jean-Paul Barbier and Douglas Newton, 86–105. New York: Metropolitan Museum of Art.

North, Richard. 1988. "An Introduction to the Musical Traditions of Cirebon." *Balungan* 3(3):2–6.

Notosudirdjo, R. Franki S. 1990. "European Music in Colonial Life in Nineteenth-Century Java: A Preliminary Study." M.A. thesis, University of Wisconsin-Madison.

Okazaki, Yoshiko. 1994. "Music Identity and Religious Change among the Toba Batak People of North Sumatra." Ph.D. dissertation, University of California at Los Angeles.

Onghokham. 1972. "The Wayang Topèng World of Malang." *Indonesia* 14:111–124.

Ornstein, Ruby Sue. 1971. "Gamelan Gong Kebjar: The Development of a Balinese Musical Tradition." Ph.D. dissertation, University of California at Los Angeles.

Pacholcyzk, Józef M. 1986. "Music and Islam in Indonesia." *World of Music* 28(3):3–12.

Peacock, James. 1968. *Rites of Modernization: Symbolic and Social Aspects of Indonesian Proletarian Drama.* Chicago: University of Chicago Press.

Pemberton, John. 1987. "Musical Politics in Central Java, or How Not to Listen to a Javanese Gamelan." *Indonesia* 44(October):17–29.

———. 1994. *On the Subject of "Java."* Ithaca, N.Y.: Cornell University Press.

Perlman, Marc. 1983. "Notes on 'A Grammar of the Musical Genre Srepegan.'" *Asian Music* 14(l):17–29.

———. 1993. "Unplayed Melodies: Music Theory in Post-Colonial Java." Ph.D. dissertation, Wesleyan University.

———. 1998. "The Social Meanings of Modal Practices: Status, Gender, History, and Pathet in Central Javanese Music." *Ethnomusicology* 42(1):45–80.

Phillips, Nigel. 1980. *Sijobang.* Cambridge: Cambridge University Press.

Pigeaud, T. 1938. *Javaanse Volksvertoningen: Bijdrage tot de Beschrijving van Land en Volk.* Batavia: Volkslectuur.

Piper, Suzan, and Sawung Jabo. 1987. "Indonesian Music from the 1950s to the 1980s." *Prisma* 43(March):25–37.

Powers, Harold. 1980. "Mode." *The New Grove Dictionary of Music and Musicians,* ed. Stanley Sadie. London: Macmillan.

Probohardjono, R. Ng. S. 1984 [1966]. *Sléndro Songs of the Dhalang,* trans. Susan Pratt Walton. In *Karawitan: Source Readings in Javanese Gamelan and Vocal Music,* ed. Judith Becker and Alan Feinstein, 1:439–523. Ann Arbor: Center for South and Southeast Asian Studies, University of Michigan.

Purba, Mauly. 1997. "Gondang Sabangunan: Functions and Meaning of Performance in Contemporary Protestant Toba Batah Society." Ph.D. dissertation, Monash University.

Raffles, Thomas Stamford. 1978 [1817]. *The History of Java.* 2 vols. Kuala Lumpur: Oxford University Press.

Rai, I. Nyoman. 1996. "Balinese *Gamelan Semar Pegulingan Saih Pitu:* The Modal System." Ph.D. dissertation, University of Maryland, Baltimore County.

Ramseyer, Urs. 1977. *The Art and Culture of Bali.* Singapore: Oxford University Press.

Rasmussen, Anne K. 2001. "The Qur'an in Indonesian Daily Life: The Public Project of Musical Oratory." *Ethnomusicology* 45(1):30–57.

Rassers, W. H. 1959. *Pañji, the Culture Hero.* Koninklijk Instituut voor Taal-, Land-, en Volkenkunde, Translation Series, 3. The Hague: Martinus Nijhoff.

Revel-Macdonald, Nicole. 1988. "The Dayak of Borneo." In *Islands and Ancestors: Indigenous Styles of Southeast Asia,* ed. Jean-Paul Barbier and Douglas Newton, 66–85. Munich: Prestel.

Ricklefs, M. C. 1981. *A History of Modern Indonesia: c. 1300 to the Present.* Bloomington: Indiana University Press.

Rodgers, Susan. 1986. "Batak Tape Cassette Kinship: Constructing Kinship through the Indonesian National Mass Media." *American Ethnologist* 13(l):23–42.

Rogers-Aguiniga, Pamela. 1986. "Topeng Cirebon: The Masked Dance of West Java as Performed in the Village of Slangit." M.A. thesis, University of California at Los Angeles.

Schaareman, Darker, ed. 1992. *Balinese Music in Context: A Sixty-Fifth Birthday Tribute to Hans Oesch*. Winterthur: Amadeus-Verlag.

Schlager, Ernst. 1976. *Rituelle Siebenton-Musik auf Bali*. Bern: Franck.

Schnitger, F. M. 1937. *The Archaeology of Hindoo Sumatra*. Leiden: Brill.

Schumacher, Rüdiger. 1980. *Die Suluk-Gesang des Dalang im Schattenspiel Zentraljavas*. 2 vols. Munich and Salzburg: Musikverlag Emil Katsbichler.

Scott-Maxwell, Aline. 1993. "The Dynamics of the Yogyakarta Gamelan Music Tradition." Ph.D. dissertation, Monash University.

Sears, Laurie Jo. 1984. "Epic Voyages: The Transmission of the Ramayana and Mahabharata from India to Java." In *Aesthetic Tradition and Cultural Transition in Java and Bali*, ed. Stephanie Morgan and Laurie Jo Sears, 1–30. Madison: University of Wisconsin Center for Southeast Asian Studies.

———. 1991. "Javanese *Mahabharata* Stories: Oral Performances and Written Texts." In *Boundaries of the Text*, ed. Joyce B. Flueckiger and Laurie J. Sears, 61–82. Ann Arbor: Center for South and Southeast Asian Studies, University of Michigan.

Sedana, I. Nyoman. 1993. "The Education of a Balinese Dalang." *Asian Theatre Journal* 10(l):81–100.

Seebass, Tilman. 1990. "Theory (English), Lehre (German), versus Teori (Indonesian)." *Report of the Fourteenth International Congress of the International Musicological Society, Held at Bologna, 1987*, 200–211.

———. 1996. "Change in Balinese Musical Life: Kebiar in the 1920s and 1930s." In *Being Modern in Bali: Image and Change*, ed. Adrian Vickers, 71–91. New Haven, Conn.: Yale University Southeast Asian Studies.

Seebass, Tilman, I Gusti Bagus Nyoman Panji, I Nyoman Rembang, and I Poedijono. 1976. *The Music of Lombok: A First Survey*. Bern: Franke.

Siddique, Sharon. 1977. "Relics of the Past: A Sociological Study of the Sultanates of Cirebon, West Java." Ph.D. dissertation, Universität Bielefeld.

Simon, Artur. 1982. "Altreligiöse und soziale Zeremonien der Batak." *Zeitschrift für Ethnologie* 107(2):177–206.

———. 1984. "Functional Changes in Batak Traditional Music and Its Role in Modern Indonesian Society." *Asian Music* 15(2):58–66.

———. 1984–1985. *Gondang Toba/Northern Sumatra*. Museum Collection Berlin (West), 12. (2 LP disks and liner notes.)

———. 1985. "The Terminology of Batak Instrumental Music in Northern Sumatra." *Yearbook for Traditional Music* 113–145.

———. 1987. *Gendang Karo/Northern Sumatra, Indonesia—Trance and Dance Music of the Akro Batak*. Museum Collection, Berlin (West), 13. (LP disk and liner notes.)

———. 1993. "Gondang, Gods, and Ancestors: Religious Implications of Batak Ceremonial Music." *Yearbook for Traditional Music* 25:81–88.

Sindoesawarno, Ki. 1987 [1955]. *The Science of Gamelan*, trans. Martin Hatch. In *Karawitan: Source Readings in Javanese Gamelan and Vocal Music*, ed. Judith Becker and Alan Feinstein, 2:389–407. Ann Arbor: Center for South and Southeast Asian Studies, University of Michigan.

Snelleman, J. F. 1918. "Muziek en Muziekinstrumentum in Nederlandsch Oost-Indië." In *Encyclopedie van Nederlandsch-Indië*, 24–26.

Snouck Hurgronje, C. 1906 [1893–c. l894]. *The Acehnese*, trans. A. W. S. O'Sullivan. 2 vols. Leiden: Brill.

Soedarsono. 1969. "Classical Javanese Dance: History and Characterization." *Ethnomusicology* 13(3):498–506.

———. 1974. *Dances in Indonesia*. Jakarta: Gunung Agung.

———. 1984. *Wayang Wong: The State Ritual Dance Drama in the Court of Yogyakarta*. Yogyakarta: Gadjah Mada University Press.

Sorrell, Neil. 1990. *A Guide to the Gamelan*. London: Faber and Faber.

Spiller, Henry. 1996. "Continuity in Sundanese Dance Drumming: Clues from the 1893 Chicago Exposition." *World of Music* 38(2):23–40.

Suanda Endo. 1981. "The Social Context of Cirebonese Performing Artists." *Asian Music* 13(l):27–42.

———. 1986. "Cirebonese Topeng and Wayang of the Present Day." *Asian Music* 16(2):84–120.

———. 1988. "Dancing in Cirebonese Topeng." *Balungan* 3(3):7–15.

Suharto, Ben. 1990. "Dance Power: The Concept of Mataya in Yogyakarta Dance." M.A. thesis, University of California at Los Angeles.

Sumarsam. 1975a. "Inner Melody in Javanese Gamelan Music." *Asian Music* 7(1):3–13.

———. 1975b. "Gendèr Barung, Its Technique and Function in the Context of Javanese Gamelan." *Indonesia* 20:161–172.

———. 1981. "The Musical Practice of the Gamelan Sekatèn." *Asian Music* 12(2):54–73.

———. 1984a. "Gamelan Music and the Javanese Wayang Kulit." In *Aesthetic Tradition and Cultural Transition in Java and Bali*, ed. Stephanie Morgan and Laurie Jo Sears, 105–116. Madison: University of Wisconsin Center for Southeast Asian Studies.

———. 1984b. "Inner Melody in Javanese Gamelan." M.A. thesis, Wesleyan University. In *Karawitan: Source Readings in Javanese Gamelan and Vocal Music*, ed. Judith Becker and Alan Feinstein, 2:245–304. Ann Arbor: Center for

South and Southeast Asian Studies, University of Michigan.

———. 1987. "Introduction to Ciblon Drumming in Javanese Gamelan." In *Karawitan: Source Readings in Javanese Gamelan and Vocal Music*, ed. Judith Becker and Alan Feinstein, 2:171–203. Ann Arbor: Center for South and Southeast Asian Studies, University of Michigan.

———. 1995. *Gamelan: Cultural Interaction and Musical Development in Central Java*. Chicago: University of Chicago Press.

Supanggah, Rahayu. 1985. "Introduction aux styles d'interpretation dans la musique javanaise." Ph.D. dissertation, University of Paris.

Surjodiningrat, R. M. Wasisto. 1970. *Gamelan, Dance, and Wayang in Jogjakarta*. Yogyakarta: University of Gadjah Mada Press.

Surjodiningrat, R. M. Wasisto, P. J. Sudarjana, and Adhi Susanto. 1972. *Tone Measurements of Outstanding Javanese Gamelans in Jogjakarta and Surakarta*. Yogyakarta: Gadjah Mada University Press.

Suryabrata [Ijzerdraat], Bernard. 1987. *The Island of Music: An Essay in Social Musicology*. Jakarta: Balai Pustaka.

Susilo, Hardja. 1967. "Drumming in the Context of Javanese Gamelan." M.A. thesis, University of California at Los Angeles.

———. 1984. "Wayang Wong Panggung: Its Social Context, Technique, and Music." In *Aesthetic Tradition and Cultural Transition in Java and Bali*, ed. Stephanie Morgan and Laurie Jo Sears, 117–161. Madison: University of Wisconsin Center for Southeast Asian Studies.

———. 1989. "The Logogenesis of Gendhing Lampah." *Progress Reports in Ethnomusicology* 2(5).

Sutton, R. Anderson. 1975. "The Javanese Gambang and Its Music." M.A. thesis, University of Hawaii.

———. 1979. "Concept and Treatment in Javanese Gamelan Music, with Reference to the Gambang." *Asian Music* 9(2):59–79.

———. 1982. "Variation in Javanese Gamelan Music: Dynamics of a Steady State." Ph.D. dissertation, University of Michigan.

———. 1984a. "Who Is the *Pesindhèn*? Notes on the Female Singing Tradition in Java." *Indonesia* 37:118–131.

———. 1984b. "Change and Ambiguity: Gamelan Style and Regional Identity in Yogyakarta." In *Aesthetic Tradition and Cultural Transition in Java and Bali*, ed. Stephanie Morgan and Laurie Jo Sears, 221–245. Madison: University of Wisconsin Center for Southeast Asian Studies.

———. 1985a. "Musical Pluralism in Java: Three Local Traditions." *Ethnomusicology* 29(l):56–85.

———. 1985b. "Commercial Cassette Recordings of Traditional Music in Java: Implications for Performers and Scholars." *World of Music* 27(3):23–45.

———. 1986a. "The Crystallization of a Marginal Tradition: Music in Banyumas, West

Central Java." *Yearbook for Traditional Music* 18:115–132.

———. 1986b. "New Theory for Traditional Music in Banyumas, West Central Java." *Pacific Review of Ethnomusicology* 3:79–101.

———. 1987. "Variation and Composition in Java." *Yearbook for Traditional Music* 19:65–95.

———. 1988. "Individual Variation in Javanese Gamelan Performance." *Journal of Musicology* 6(2):169–197.

———. 1989. "Identity and Individuality in an Ensemble Tradition: The Female Vocalist in Java." In *Women and Music in Cross-Cultural Perspective*, ed. Ellen Koskoff, 111–130. Urbana and Chicago: University of Illinois Press.

———. 1991a. *Traditions of Gamelan Music in Java: Musical Pluralism and Regional Identity.* Cambridge Studies in Ethnomusicology. Cambridge: Cambridge University Press.

———. 1991b. "Music of Indonesia." In *Aspects of Indonesian Culture*, ed. William Frederick. New York: Festival of Indonesia Foundation.

———. 1993a. *Variation in Central Javanese Gamelan Music: Dynamics of a Steady State.* Special Reports, 28. De Kalb: Center for Southeast Asian Studies, Northern Illinois University.

———. 1993b. "Semang and Seblang: Thoughts on Music, Dance, and the Sacred in Central and East Java." In *Performance in Java and Bali: Studies of Narrative, Theatre, Music, and Dance*, ed. Bernard Arps, 121–143. London: School of Oriental and African Studies, University of London.

———. 1996. "Interpreting Electronic Sound Technology in the Contemporary Javanese Soundscape." *Ethnomusicology* 40(2):249–268.

———. 1998. "From Ritual Enactment to Stage Entertainment: Andi Nurhani Sapada and the Aestheticization of South Sulawesi's Music and Dance 1940s–1970s." *Asian Music* 29(2):1–29.

Suyenaga, Joan. 1984. "Patterns in Process: Java through Gamelan." In *Aesthetic Tradition and Cultural Transition in Java and Bali*, ed. Stephanie Morgan and Laurie Jo Sears, 83–104. Madison: University of Wisconsin Center for Southeast Asian Studies.

Taylor, Paul Michael, and Lorraine V. Aragon. 1991. *Beyond the Java Sea: Art of Indonesia's Outer Islands.* Washington, D.C.: National Museum of Natural History.

Tenzer, Michael. 1991. *Balinese Music.* Singapore: Periplus.

———. 1997. "The Life in Gendhing: Approaches to Javanese Gamelan." *Indonesia* 63:169–186.

———. 2000. *Gamelan Gong Kebyar: The Art of Twentieth-Century Balinese Music.* Chicago: University of Chicago Press.

Toth, Andrew F. 1970. "Music of the Gamelan Sekati." B.A. honors thesis, Wesleyan University.

———. 1975. "The Gamelan Luang of Tangkas, Bali." In *Selected Reports in Ethnomusicology* 2(2):65–80.

Tsuchiya, Kenji, and James Siegel. 1990. "Invincible Kitsch or as Tourists in the Age of Des Alwi." *Indonesia* 50:61–76.

Turner, Ashley M. 1982. "Duri-Dana Music and Hoho Songs in South Nias." B.A. thesis, Monash University.

———. 1991. "Belian as a Symbol of Cosmic Reunification." In *Metaphor and Analogy: A Musical Dimension*, ed. Margaret Kartomi, 121–145. Sydney: Currency.

Valentijn, François. 1724–1726. *Oud en Nieuw Oost-Indien, Vervattende een Naauwkeurige en Vitvoerige Verhandelinge van Nederlands Mogentheyd in die Gewesten, Benevens eene Wydlustige Beschryvinge der Moluccos, Amboine, Banda, Timor, en Solor Java, etc.* 5 vols. Dordrecht: Joannes van Braam. Amsterdam: Gerard onder de Linden.

Valeri, Valerio. 1990. "Autonomy and Heteronomy in the Kahua Ritual: A Short Meditation on Huaulu Society." *Bijdragen tot de Taal-, Land-, en Volkenkunde* 1(146):56–73.

van Dijk, Toos, and Nico de Jonge. 1990. "After Sunshine Comes Rain: A Comparative Analysis of Fertility Rituals in Marsela and Luang, South-East Moluccas." *Bijdragen tot de Taal-, Land-, en Volkenkunde* 1(146):3–20.

van Hoandell, G. W. W. C., Baron. 1875. *Ambon en Meer Bepaaldelijk de Oehasers, Geografisch, Ethnographisch, Politisch, en Historisch.* Dordrecht: Joannes van Braam. Amsterdam: Gerard onder de Linden.

van Zanten, Wim. 1984. "The Poetry of Tembang Sunda." *Bijdragen tot de wal, Land-, en Volkenkunde* 140(2/3):289–316.

———. 1985. "Structure in the Panambih Pelog Songs of Tembang Sunda." In *Teken van Leven, Studies in Etnocommunicatie*, ed. Ad Boeren, Fransje Brinkgreve, and Sandy Roels, 187–198. Leiden: Instituut voor Culturele Antropologie en Sociologie der Niet-Westerse Volken.

———. 1986. "The Tone Material of the Kacapi in Tembang Sunda in West Java." *Ethnomusicology* 30(l):84–112.

———. 1989. *Sundanese Music in the Cianjuran Style: Anthropological and Musicological Aspects of Tembang Sunaa.* Providence, R. I. Foris.

———. 1993. "Sung Epic Narrative and Lyrical Songs: Carita Pantun and Tembang Sunda." In *Performance in Java and Bali: Studies of Narrative, Theatre, Music, and Dance*, ed. Bernard Arps, 144–161. London: School of Oriental and African Studies, University of London.

———. 1994a. "Aspects of Baduy Singing." Paper Presented at Workshop "Performing Arts in South-East Asia" at Koninklijk Instituut voor Taal-, Land-, en Volkenkunde, Leiden University, Netherlands.

———. 1994b. "L'esthétique musicale de Sunda (Java-Ouest)." *Cahiers de Musiques Traditionnelles* 7:75–93.

———. 1995. "Aspects of Baduy Music in Its Sociocultural Context, with Special Reference to Singing and Angklung." *Bijdragen tot de Taal-, Land-, en Volkenkunde* 151:516–544.

———. 1997. "Inner and Outer Voices: Listening and Hearing in West-Java." *World of Music* 39(2):41–50.

van Zanten, Wim, and Marjolijn van Roon. 1995. "Notation of Music: Theory and Practice in West Java." *Oideion: The Performing Arts World-Wide* 2:209–233.

Vetter, Roger. 1977. "Formal Aspects of Performance Practice in Central Javanese Gamelan Music." MA. thesis, University of Hawaii.

———. 1981. "Flexibility in the Performance Practice of Central Javanese Music." *Ethnomusicology* 25(2):199–214.

———. 1984. "Poetic, Musical, and Dramatic Structures in a Langen Mandra Wanara Performance." In *Aesthetic Tradition and Cultural Transition in Java and Bali*, ed. Stephanie Morgan and Laurie Jo Sears, 163–208. Madison: University of Wisconsin Center for Southeast Asian Studies.

———. 1986. "Music for 'The Lap of the World': Gamelan Performance, Performers, and Repertoire in the Kraton Yogyakarta." Ph.D. dissertation, University of Wisconsin at Madison.

———. 1989. "A Retrospect on a Century of Gamelan Tone Measurements." *Ethnomusicology* 33(2):217–227.

Vetter, Valerie Mau. 1984. "In Search of Panji." In *Aesthetic Tradition and Cultural Transition in Java and Bali*, ed. Stephanie Morgan and Laurie Jo Sears, 31–50. Madison: University of Wisconsin Center for Southeast Asian Studies.

Vickers, Adrian. 1985. "The Realm of the Senses: Images of the Court Music of Pre-Colonial Bali." *Imago Musicae* 2:43–77.

Vitale, Wayne. 1990. "Kotekan: The Technique of Interlocking Parts in Balinese Music." *Balungan* 4(2):2–15.

Wagner, Frits A. 1959. *Indonesia: The Art of an Island Group.* New York: Crown.

Wallace, Alfred Russel. 1869. *The Malay Archipelago.* London: Macmillan.

Wallis, Richard Herman. 1979. "The Voice as a Mode of Cultural Expression in Bali." Ph.D. dissertation, University of Michigan.

Walton, Susan Pratt. 1987. *Mode in Javanese Music.* Athens: Ohio University Center for International Studies.

Warsadiningrat. 1987 [1972]. *Sacred Knowledge about Gamelan Music*, trans. Susan P. Walton. In *Karawitan: Source Readings in Javanese Gamelan and Vocal Music*, ed. Judith Becker and Alan Feinstein, 2:1–170. Ann Arbor: Center for South and Southeast Asian Studies, University of Michigan.

Weijden, Gera van der. 1981. *Indonesische Reisrituale.* Basler Beitrage zur Ethnologie, 20. Basel: Ethnologisches Seminar der Universitat und Museum für Völkerkunde.

Weintraub, Andrew. 1990. "The Music of Pantun Sunda: An Epic Narrative Tradition of West Java, Indonesia." M.A. thesis, University of Hawaii.

———. 1993. "Theory as Institutionalized Pedagogy and 'Theory in Practice' for Sundanese Gamelan Music." *Ethnomusicology* 37(l):29–40.

———. 1993–1994. "Tune, Text, and the Function of Lagu in Pantun Sunda, a Sundanese Oral Narrative Tradition." *Asian Music* 26(l):175–211.

———. 1997. "Constructing the Popular: Superstars, Performance, and Cultural Authority in Sundanese Wayang Golek Purwa of West Java, Indonesia." Ph.D. dissertation, University of California, Berkeley.

Weiss, Sarah. 1993. "Gender and Gendèr: Gender Ideology and the Female Gendèr Player in Central Java." In *Rediscovering the Muses: Women's Musical Traditions*, ed. Kimberly Marshall, 21–48. Boston: Northeastern University Press.

Wenten, I. Nyoman. 1996. "The Creative World of Ki Wasitodipuro: The Life and Work of a Javanese Composer." Ph.D. dissertation, University of California at Los Angeles.

Wessing, Robert. 1977. "The Position of the Baduy in the Larger West Javanese Society." *Man* 12(2):293–303.

———. 1978. *Cosmology and Social Behavior in a West Javanese Settlement.* Athens: Ohio University Center for International Studies, Southeast Asia Program.

———. 1990. "Sri and Sedana and Sita and Rama: Myths of Fertility and Generation." *Asian Folklore Studies* 49(2):235–257.

Wilken, G. A. 1912. "Het animisme bij de volken van den Indischen Archipel." In *De Verspreide Geschriften van Prof. Dr. G. A. Wilken*, ed. E. D. E. van Ossenbruggen, 3–287. Semarang: G. C. T. van Dorp.

Williams, Sean. 1989. "Current Developments in Sundanese Popular Music." *Asian Music* 21(l):105–136.

———. 1990. "The Urbanization of *Tembang Sunda*, an Aristocratic Musical Genre of West Java, Indonesia." Ph.D. dissertation, University of Washington.

———. 1998. "Constructing Gender in Sundanese Music." *Yearbook for Traditional Music* 30:74–84.

———. 1999. "Competition in the Sundanese Performing Arts of West Java, Indonesia." *Current Musicology* 63:27–45.

———. 2001. *The Sound of the Ancestral Ship: Highland Music of West Java*. New York: Oxford University Press.

Wolbers, Paul Arthur. 1986. "*Gandrung* and *Angklung* from Banyuwangi: Remnants of a Past Shared with Bali." *Asian Music* 18(1):71–90.

———. 1987. "Account of an *Angklung Caruk*, July 28, 1985." *Indonesia* 43:66–74.

———. 1989. "Transvestism, Eroticism, and Religion: In Search of a Contextual Background for the *Gandrung* and *Seblang* Traditions of Banyuwangi, East Java." *Progress Reports in Ethnomusicology* 2(6).

———. 1992. "Maintaining and Using Identity through Musical Performance: *Seblang* and *Gandrung* of Banyuwangi, East Java (Indonesia)." Ph.D. dissertation, University of Illinois at Urbana-Champaign.

Wongsosewojo, R. Abroad. 1930. "Loedroek." *Djawa* 10:204–207.

Wright, Michael R. 1978. "The Music Culture of Cirebon." Ph.D. dissertation, University of California at Los Angeles.

———. 1988. "Tarling: Modern Music from Cirebon." *Balurgan* 3(3):21–25.

Yampolsky, Philip. 1987. *Lokananta: A Discography of the National Recording Company of Indonesia, 1957–1985.* Madison: University of Wisconsin Center for Southeast Asian Studies.

———. 1989. "*Hati Yang Luka*: An Indonesian Hit." *Indonesia* 47:1–17.

———. 1991a. *Music of Indonesia, 2: Indonesian Popular Music.* Washington, D.C.: Smithsonian Folkways SFCD 40056. (Liner notes.)

———. 1991b. *Music of Indonesia, 3: Music from the Outskirts of Jakarta—Gambang Kromong.* Washington, D.C.: Smithsonian/Folkways SFCD 40057. (Liner notes.)

———. 1995a. "Forces for Change in the Regional Performing Arts of Indonesia." *Bijdragen tot de Taal-, Land-, en Volkenkunde* 151(4):700–725.

———. 1995b. *Music of Indonesia, 8: Vocal and Instrumental Music from East and Central Flores.* Washington, D.C.: Smithsonian/Folkways SFCD 40424. (Compact disk and liner notes.)

———. 1995c. *Music of Indonesia, 9: Vocal Music from Central and West Flores.* Washington, D.C.: Smithsonian/Folkways SFCD 40425. (Compact disk and liner notes.)

Yaningsih, Dra. Sri, Urnar Siradz, and I Gusti Bagus Mahartha. 1988. *Peralaian Hiburan dan Kesenian Tadisional Daerah Nusa Tenggard Barat.* Mataram: Departemen Pendidikan dan Kebudayaan.

Borneo

Alman, J. H. 1961. "If You Can't Sing, You Can Beat a Gong." *Journal of the Sabah Society* 1:29–41.

Bastin, J. 1971. "Brass Kettledrums in Sabah." *Bulletin of the School of African and Oriental Studies* 24(l):132.

Brunei Delegation. 1974. "A Short Survey of Brunei Gulintangan Orchestra." In *Traditional Music and Drama of Southeast Asia*, ed. Mohd. Taib Osman, 198–308. Kuala Lumpur: Dewan Bahasa dan Pustaka.

Chong, Julia. 1989. "Towards the Integration of Sarawak Traditional Instruments into Twentieth-Century Malaysian Music." *Sarawak Museum Journal* 40(61):125–130.

Crump, Juliette T. 1991. "Some Features of the Solo Dance That Maintain Its Viability for Tribes in Transition in Sarawak." *Sarawak Museum Journal* 42 (63):159–176.

Davis, G. C. 1960. "Borneo Bisaya Music in Western Ears." *Sarawak Museum Journal* 9(15–16):496–498.

Frame, Edward. 1975. "A Preliminary Survey of Several Major Musical Instruments and Form Types of Sabah, Malaysia." *Borneo Research Bulletin* 7(l):16–24.

———. 1976. "Major Musical Forms in Sabah." *Journal of the Royal Asiatic Society, Malaysian Branch* 49(2):156–163.

———. 1982. "The Musical Instruments of Sabah, Malaysia." *Ethnomusicology* 26(2):247–274.

Galvin, A. Dennis. 1962. "Five Sorts of Sarawak and Kalimantan Kenyah Song." *Sarawak Museum Journal* 10:501–510.

———. 1966. "Some Baram Kenyah Songs." *Sarawak Museum Journal* 14:6–14.

———. 1968. "*Mamat* Chants and Ceremonies, Long Moh." *Sarawak Museum Journal* 33:235–248.

———. 1972. "A *Sebop* Dirge (Sung on the Occasion of the Death of Tama Jangan by Belawing Lupa)." *Brunei Museum Journal* 2(4):1–158.

———. 1975a. "*Suket* (Long Julan)." *Brunei Museum Journal* 3(3):13–19.

———. 1975b. "Two Kenyah Love Songs." *Brunei Museum Journal* 3(3):20–26.

Georgie, E. 1959. "A Dayak (Love) Song." *Sarawak Museum Journal* 9(13–14):21–24.

Gorlinski, Virginia K. 1988. "Some Insights into the Art of Sapé Playing." *Sarawak Museum Journal* 39(60):77–104.

———. 1989a. "*Pangpagaq*: Religious and Social Significance of a Traditional Kenyah Music-Dance Form." *Sarawak Museum Journal* 40, 61, New Series, Part 3:280–301.

———. 1989b. "The Sampéq of East Kalimantan, Indonesia: A Case Study of the Recreational Music Tradition." M.A. thesis, University of Hawaii.

———. 1994 "Gongs among the Kenyah Uma' Jalan: Past and Present Position of an Instrumental Tradition." *Yearbook for Traditional Music* 26:81–99.

———. 1995. "Songs of Honor, Words of Respect: Social Contours of *Kenyah Lepo' Tau* Versification, Sarawak, Malaysia." Ph.D. dissertation, University of Wisconsin.

Harrisson, Tom. 1949. "Singing Prehistory." *Journal of the Royal Asiatic Society, Malayan Branch* 22(l):123–142.

———. 1966. "A Kalimantan Writing Board and the Mamat Festival." *Sarawak Museum Journal* 13:287–295.

Hood, Mantle. 1980. "Outer Islands: Borneo (Kalimantan)." *The New Grove Dictionary of Music and Musicians*, ed. Stanley Sadie. London: Macmillan.

Hudson, Judith M. 1971. "Some Observations on Dance in Kalimantan." *Indonesia* 12:133–150.

Koizumi, Furnio, ed. 1976. *Asian Musics in an Asian Perspective: Report of Asian Traditional Performing Arts.* Tôkyô: Heibonsha.

Leach, Edmund. 1950. *Social Science Research in Sarawak.* London: Her Majesty's Stationery Office.

Liew, Richard. 1962. "Music and Musical Instruments in Sabah." *Journal of the Sabah College Borneo Society* 3:10.

Maceda, José. 1962. "Field-Recording Sea-Dayak Music." *Sarawak Museum Journal* 10(19–20):486–500.

———. 1977. "Report of a Music Workshop in East Kalimantan." *Borneo Research Bulletin* 10(2):83–103.

Masing, James Jemut. 1981. "The Coming of the Gods: A Study of the Invocatory Chant (*Timang Gawai Amat*) of the Iban of the Baleh Region of Sarawak." Ph.D. dissertation, Australian National University.

Matusky, Patricia. 1986. "Aspects of Musical Style among the Kajang, Kayan, and Kenyah-Badang of the Upper Rejang River: A Preliminary Survey." *Sarawak Museum Journal* 36:185–229.

———. 1989. "Ethnomusicology and the Musical Heritage of Sarawak: Implications for the Future." *Sarawak Museum Journal* 40(61):131–149.

———. 1990. "Music Styles among the Kayan, Kenyah-Badang, and Malay Peoples of the Upper Rejang River (Sarawak): A Preliminary Survey." *Sarawak Museum Journal* 41(62):115–149.

———. 1991. "Musical Instruments of the Indigenous Peoples." In *Sarawak Cultural Legacy*, ed. Lucas Chin, 232–246. Kuching, Sarawak: Society Atelier Sarawak.

Maxwell, Allen R. 1989. "A Survey of the Oral Traditions of Sarawak." *Sarawak Museum Journal* 40(61):167–208.

Myers, Charles Samuel. 1913. "A Study of Sarawak Music." *Sammelbände der Internationalen Muzikgesellschaft* 15:296–308.

Ongkili, James P. 1974. "The Traditional Musical Instruments of Sabah." In *Traditional Music and Drama of Southeast Asia*, ed. Mohd. Taib Osman, 327–335. Kuala Lumpur: Dewan Bahasa dan Pustaka.

Revel-Macdonald, Nicole. 1978. "La danse des hudoq (Kalimantan-Timur)." *Objets et Mondes* 18(1–2):31–44.

———. 1981. "Masks in Kalimantan Timur." *World of Music* 23(3):52–56.

Roth, Henry Ling. 1980 [1896]. *The Natives of Sarawak and British North Borneo.* 2 vols. London: Truslove and Hanson; Kuala Lumpur: University of Malaya Press.

Rousseau, Jérôme. 1989a. "The People of Central Borneo." *Sarawak Museum Journal* 40, 61, New Series, Part 3:7–17.

———. 1989b. *Central Borneo: Ethnic Identity and Social Life in a Stratified Society.* London: Oxford University Press.

Rubenstein, Carol. 1973. "Poems of Indigenous Peoples of Sarawak: Some of the Songs and Chants." Special Monograph. *Sarawak Museum Journal* 21(42).

———. 1985. *The Honey Tree Song, Poems and Chants of Sarawak Dayaks.* Athens, Ohio, and London: Ohio University Press.

———. 1989a. "Some Notes and Long Songs of the Dayak Oral Literature." *Sarawak Gazette* 115(1508):21–28.

———. 1989b. "'For Marrying Lian during Durian Season': A Song of the Penan Urun." *Sarawak Gazette* 115(1509):22–30.

———. 1990a. *The Nightbird Sings: Chants and Songs of Sarawak Dayaks.* Dumfriesshire, Scotland: Tynron.

———. 1990b. "'Like Early Mist': Five Songs of the Penan Urun." *Sarawak Museum Journal* 41(62):151–188.

———. 1990c. "'So Unable to Speak Am I . . .': Sarawak Dayaks and Forms of Social Address in Song." *Asian Music* 21(2):1–37.

Sandin, Benedict. 1974. "Iban Music." In *Traditional Music and Drama of Southeast Asia*, ed. Mohd. Taib Osman, 320–326. Kuala Lumpur: Dewan Bahasa dan Pustaka.

Seeler, Joan DeWitt. 1969. "Some Notes on Traditional Dances of Sarawak." *Sarawak Museum Journal* 17:163–201.

———. 1975. "Kenyah Dance, Sarawak, Malaysia: A Description and Analysis." M.A. thesis, University of Hawaii.

———. 1977. "Research on Kenyah Dance: Reason and Method." *Sarawak Museum Journal* 25:165–175.

Skog, Inge. 1993. *North Borneo Gongs and the Javanese Gamelan: Studies in Southeast Asian Gong Traditions.* Studies in Musicology, 2. Stockholm: Stockholms Universitet.

Soedarsono. 1968. *Dances in Indonesia.* Jakarta: P. T. Gunung Agung.

Strickland, S. S. 1988. "Preliminary Notes on a Kejaman-Sekapan Oral Narrative Form." *Sarawak Museum Journal* 39, 60, New Series:67–75.

Wan Ulok, Stephen, and A. Dennis Galvin. 1955. "A Kenyah Song." *Sarawak Museum Journal* 6:287–289.

Williams, Thomas Rhys. 1961. "Form, Function, and Culture History of a Borneo Musical Instrument." *Oceania* 32:178–186.

Philippines

Abubakar, Carmen. 1983. "Islamization of Southern Philippines: An Overview." In *Filipino Muslims: Their Social Institutions and Cultural Achievements*, ed. F. Landa Jocano, 6–13. Diliman: Asian Center, University of the Philippines.

Bañas y Castillo, Raymundo C. 1975. *Filipino Music and Theater.* Quezon City: Manlapaz.

Beyer, Henry Otley. 1948. "Philippine and East Asian Archeology." *National Research Council of the Philippines* 29(December):1–82.

Blair, Emma Helen, and James Alexander Robertson, eds. 1973 [1903]. *The Philippine Islands 1493–1898.* 55 vols. Mandaluyong: Cachos Hermanosted.

Butocan, Aga Mayo. 1987. *Palabunibunyan: A Repertoire of Musical Pieces for the Maguindanaon Kulimangan.* Manila: Philippine Women's University.

Cadar, Usopay Hamdag. 1975. "The Role of Kulintang Music in Maranao Society." *Selected Reports in Ethnomusicology* 2(2):49–62.

———. 1980. "Context and Style in the Vocal Music of the Muranao in Mindanao, Philippines." Ph.D. dissertation, University of Washington.

———. 1996a. "The Role of Kolintang Music in Maranao Society." *Asian Music* 27(2):81–104.

———. 1996b. "Maranao Kolintang Music and Its Journey in America." *Asian Music* 27(2):131–148.

Cadar, Usopay Hamdag, and Robert Garfias. 1974. "Some Principles of Formal Variation in the Kolintang Music of the Maranao." *Ethnomusicology* 18(l):43–55.

———. 1996. "Some Principles of Formal Variation in the Kolintang Music of the Maranao." *Asian Music* 27(2):105–122.

Casiño, Eric. 1976. *The Jama Mapun: A Changing Samal Society in Southern Philippines.* Quezon City: Ateneo de Manila University Press.

Castro y Amadeo, Pedro de. 1790. "Historia de la Provincia de Batangas por Don Pedro Andrés de Castro y Amadeo en sus viajes y contraviajes en toda esta Provincia año de 1790." Madrid: MS Archivo Nacional, Códice 931, 7.

Chung, Lilia Hernandez. 1979. *Jovita Fuentes: A Lifetime of Music.* Manila: Jovita Fuentes Musicultural Society.

de la Concepción, Juan. 1788–1792. *Historia general de las islas Filipinas.* Manila: Agustín de la Rosa y Balagtas.

Conservatory of Music, University of the Philippines: 1916–1960. 1960. Quezon City: University of the Philippines Conservatory of Music.

de León, Felipe Padilla. 1977. "Banda Uno, Banda Dos." *Filipino Heritage: The Making of a Nation*, 8.

Dioquino, Corazón C. 1982. "Musicology in the Philippines." *Acta Musicologica* 54:124–147.

Dulawan, Manuel. 1970s. "Tuwali Oral Folk Literature." University of the Philippines, College of Music, Department of Music Research. Typescript.

Ellis, Henry T. 1856. *Hongkong to Manila and the Lakes of Luzon in the Philippine Islands in the Year 1856.* London: Smith, Elder.

Eugenio, Damiana. 1987. *Awit and Corrido: Philippine Metrical Romances.* Quezon City: University of the Philippines Press.

Fernández, Doreen G. 1978. *The Iloilo Zarzuela 1903–1930.* Quezon City: Ateneo de Manila University Press.

———. 1981 [1905]. "Introduction." In *The Filipino Drama*, ed. Arthur Stanley Riggs. Manila: Ministry of Human Settlements.

Fernando-Amilbangsa, Ligaya. 1983. *Pangalay: Traditional Dances and Related Folk Artistic Expressions.* Los Angeles: Philippine Expressions.

Fox, Robert. 1959. *The Philippines in Pre-Historic Times: A Handbook for the First National Exhibition of Filipino Prehistory and Culture.* Manila:

UNESCO National Commission of the Philippines.

———. 1961. "Social Aspects of the Rice-Wine Complex among the Tagbanwa of Palawan Island, Philippines." Typescript.

———. 1977. "Manunggul Cave." *Filipino Heritage* 1:169–173.

Francisco, Juan R. 1993. "The Ramayana in the Philippines." In *Ang Paglalakbay ni Radya Mangandiri*. (Souvenir program of Philippine Educational Theater Association Kalinangan Ensemble.)

Georsua, Racquel. 1987. "Traditional Practices among the Subanen in Lapuyan, Zamboanga del Sur, with Special Reference to Music." M.A. thesis, University of the Philippines.

Kalundayan, Danongan S. 1996. "Instruments, Instrumentation, and Social Context of Maguindanaon Kulintang Music." *Asian Music* 27(2):3–18.

Kiefer, Thomas. 1970. *Music from the Tausug of Sulu*. Bloomington: Indiana University. (LP disk and liner notes.)

Lambrecht, Francis. 1967. "The Hudhud of Dinulawan and Bugan at Gondahan." *Saint Louis University Journal* 5(3–4):267–713.

Larkin, John. 1978. "The Capampangan Zarzuela: Theatre for a Provincial Elite." In *Southeast Asian Transitions: Approaches through Social History*, ed. Ruth T. McVey, 186–189. New Haven, Conn.: Yale University Press.

Laureola, Asuncion. 1971. "Musical References from Books Published before 1900 in the U.P. Filipiniana Library." M.Mus. thesis, University of the Philippines.

Maceda, José M. 1963. "The Music of the Maguindanao in the Philippines." Ph.D. dissertation, University of California at Los Angeles.

———, ed. 1971. *Musics of Asia*. Manila: National Music Council of the Philippines and UNESCO.

———. 1973. "Music in the Philippines in the Nineteenth Century." In *Musikkulturen Asiens, Afrikas, und Ozeaniens im 19. Jahrhundert*, ed. Robert Gunther, 216–232. Regensburg: Gustave Bosse.

———. 1974. "Drone and Melody in Philippine Musical Instruments." In *Traditional Drama and Music of Southeast Asia*, ed. Mohd. Taib Osman, 246–273. Kuala Lumpur: Kementerian Pelajaran Malaysia.

———. 1984. "A Cure of the Sick Bpagipat in Dulawan, Cotabato (Philippines)." *Acta Musicologica* 56:93–105.

———, ed. 1988. *Kulintang and Kudyapiq: Gong Ensemble and Two-String Lute among the Maguindanaon in Mindanao Philippines*. University of the Philippines. (2 LP disks and liner notes.)

———. 1990. "In Search of a Source of Pentatonic Hemitonic and Anhemitonic Scales in Southeast Asia." *Acta Musicologica* 72(23):192–223.

Maceda, José M., and Alain Martenot. 1976. *Sama de Sitangkai*. Office de la Récherche Scientifique et Technique Outre-Mer (Société de la Récherche Linguistique et Anthropologique de France). (LP disk and liner notes.)

Majul, Cesar Adib. 1974. "The Muslims in the Philippines: An Historical Perspective." In *The Muslim Filipinos: Their History, Society, and Contemporary Problems*, ed. Peter Gowing and Robert McAmis, 1–12. Manila: La Solidaridad.

Mallat, Jean Baptiste. 1846. *Les Philippines: Histoire, géographie, moeurs, agriculture, industrie, et commerce des colonies espagnoles dans l'Oceanie*. 2 vols. Paris: Imprimerie de Madame Veuve Bouchard-Hazard.

Manuel, E. Arsenio. 1958. *The Maiden of the Buhong Sky, a Complete Song from the Bagobo Epic Tuwaang*. Quezon City: University of the Philippines.

———. 1978. "Towards an Inventory of Philippine Musical Instruments." *Asian Studies* 1978:1–72.

Mantaring, Melissa. 1983. "Philippine Musical References from the Lopez Museum 1601–1848." M.Mus. thesis, University of the Philippines.

Maranan, Eduardo, E. Arsenio Manuel, and Jonathan Chua. 1994. "Epic." In *Philippine Literature*, ed. Nicanor G. Tiongson. CCP Encyclopedia of Philippine Art, 9. Manila: Cultural Center of the Philippines.

Martinez de Zúñiga, Joaquín. 1893. *Estadismo de las Islas Filipinas y mis Viajes por este País*. Madrid: Imprenta de la Viuda de M. Minuesa de los Rios.

Mas, Sinibaldo de. 1843. *Informe Sobre el Esiado de las Islas Filipinas en 1842*. Madrid.

McFarland, Curtis D. 1983. *A Linguistic Atlas of the Philippines*. Manila: Linguistic Society of the Philippines.

Mednick, Melvin. 1957. "Some Problems of Moro History and Political Organization." *Philippine Sociological Review* 5(1):39–52.

de la Merced, Aniceto. 1852. *El libro de la vida: Historia sagrado con santas reflexiones y doctrinas morales para la vida cristiana en verso tagalo* (The Book of Life: Sacred History with Pious Reflections and Moral Teachings for the Christian Life Written in Tagalog Verse). Manila: Librería y Papelaría de J. Martínez.

Molina, Antonio J. 1977. "The Sentiments of Kundiman." *Filipino Heritage* 8:2026–2029.

Molina, Exequiel. 1977. "The Philippine Pop Music Scene." *Asian Culture* 15:21–24.

Ness, Sally A. 1995. "When Seeing Is Believing: The Changing Role of Visuality in a Philippine Dance." *Anthropological Quarterly* 68(l):1–13.

Nicolas, Arsenio. 1987. "Ritual Transformations and Musical Parameters: A Study of Selected Headhunting Rites in the Southern Cordillera, Northern Luzon." M.A. thesis, University of the Philippines.

Otto, Steven W. 1985. *The Muranao Kakolintang: An Approach to the Repertoire*. Marawi City: Mindanao State University.

———. 1996. "Repertorial Nomenclature in Muranao Kolintang Music." *Asian Music* 27(2):123–130.

Paterno, Pedro. 1893. *El individuo Tagalo y su arte*. Madrid: Imprenta de los Sucesores de Cuesta.

Patricio, Maria Cristina. 1955. "The Development of the Rondalla in the Philippines." Research paper, University of the Philippines.

Pfeiffer, William. 1976. *Filipino Music: Indigenous, Folk, Modern*. Dumaguete City: Silliman Music Foundation.

Posner, Karen. 1996. "A Preliminary Analysis of Maguindanaon Kulintang Music." *Asian Music* 27(2):19–32.

Prudente, Fe. 1986. "Musical Process in the Gasumbi Epic of the Buwaya Kalinga People of Northern Philippines." Ph.D. dissertation, University of Michigan.

Puya y Ruiz, Adolfo. 1838. *Filipinas: Descripción General de la Provincia de Bulacan*. Manila: R. Mercantil de Diaz Puertas.

Reid, Laurence. 1961. "A Guinaang Wedding Ceremony, Dancing and Music." *Philippine Sociological Review* 9(3–4):1–84.

Revel, Nicole. 1987. *Philippines: Musique des hautes terres Palawan*. CNRS, Chant du Monde LDX 74 865. (LP disk and liner notes.)

Retana, Wenceslao Emilio. 1888. *El Indio Batnagueno*, 3rd ed. Manila: Tipo Litografía de Chofre y Cía.

———. 1895–1905. *Archivo del Bibliófile Filipino. Recopilación de documentos históricos, cientificos, literarios, y politicos, y estudios bibliográficos*. 4 vols. Madrid: Imprenta de la Viuda de M. Minuesa de los Rios.

Ronquillo, Wilfredo. 1987. "The Butuan Archeological Finds: Profound Implications for Philippines and Southeast Asian History." *Man and Culture in Oceania* 3:71–78.

Saint Scholastica's College. 1992. *A Harvest in Sprung Rhythm: St. Scholastica's College School of Music 1907–1992*. Manila. (Anniversary pamphlet.)

Samson, Helen. 1972. "Extant Music in the Zarzuelas of Severino Reyes." M.Mus. thesis, University of the Philippines.

San Nicolás, Fray Andrés de. 1973. "General History of the Discalced Augustinian Fathers." In *The Philippine Islands 1493–1898*, ed. Emma Helen Blair and James Alexander Robertson, 21:111–317. Mandaluyong: Cachos Hermanos.

San Agustín, Gaspar de. 1890. *Conquistas de las Islas Filipinas*. Villadolid: Luis N. de Gavira.

Santos, Ramón R. 1992. "Nationalism in Philippine Music during the Japanese Occupation: Art or Propaganda?" *Panahon ng Hipon* (Japanese Time) 2:93–106.

———. 1994. "The American Colonial and Contemporary Traditions." In *Music*, ed. Corazon C. Dioquino and Ramon P. Santos.

CCP Encyclopedia of Philippine Art, 6. Manila: Cultural Center of the Philippines.

Scholz, Scott. 1996. "The Supportive Instruments of the Maguindanaon Kulintang Ensemble." *Asian Music* 27(2):33–52.

Stewart, A. M. 1831. *A Visit to the South Seas in the U. S. Ship Vincennes, during the Years 1829 and 1830, with Scenes in Brazil, Peru, Manilla, the Cape of Good Hope, and St. Helena*, Vol. 2. New York: John P. Haven.

Stone, Richard L. 1962. "Intergroup Relations among the Tausug, Samal, and Badjaw of Sulu." *Philippine Sociological Review* 10(3–4):107–133.

Terada, Yoshitaka. 1996. "Variational and Improvisational Techniques of Gandingan Playing in the Magindanaon Kulintang Ensemble." *Asian Music* 27(2):53–80.

Tiongson, Nicanor G., ed. 1991. *The Cultural Traditional Media of the Philippines*. Manila: ASEAN and Cultural Center of the Philippines.

————, ed. 1994. *Philippine Literature*. CCP Encyclopedia of Philippine Art, 9. Manila: Cultural Center of the Philippines.

Trimillos, Ricardo D. 1972. "Tradition and Repertory in the Cultivated Music of the Tausug of Sulu, Philippines." Ph.D. dissertation, University of California at Los Angeles.

Walls y Merino, Manuel. 1982. *La musica popular de Filipinas*. Madrid: Libreto de Fernando Fe. (LP disk and liner notes.)

Recordings of Southeast Asian Music

MAINLAND SOUTHEAST ASIA

Collections

Music of Southeast Asia. 1956. Compiled by Harold Courlander; commentary by Henry Cowell. Smithsonian/Folkways 04423. LP disk, cassette.

Cambodia

Apsara: The Feminine in Cambodian Art. 1987. Los Angeles: Woman's Building Gallery. Cassette.

Cambodge. 1976. Recording and commentary by Jacques Brunet. Musiques de l'Asie Traditionnelle, 1. Playasound PS 33501. LP disk.

Cambodge: Musique classique khmère, théâtre d'ombres, et chants de mariage. 1995. Recording and commentary by Loch Chhanchhai and Pierre Bois. Paris: Inédit, Maison des Cultures du Monde W 260002. Compact disk.

Cambodge: Musique instrumentale. 1973. Recording by Jacques Brunet and Hubert de Fraysseix; commentary by Jacques Brunet. Musiques et Traditions du Monde. CBS 65522. LP disk.

Cambodia. 1990. Commentary in French by Catherine Basset, based on remarks by Jacques Brunet; trans. (into English) Jeffrey Grice, (into Italian) Marie-Christine Reverte, and (into German) Brigitte Nelles. Music of the Ramayana, 2. Ocora Radio France C 560015. Compact disk.

Cambodia: Folk and Ceremonial Music. 1996. Musical Atlas. Recording and commentary by Jacques Brunet. Auvidis-Unesco D-8068. Compact disk.

Cambodia: Music of the Exile. 1992. Orchestra of the Khmer Classical Dance Troupe. Recording by Jean-Daniel Bloesch and Khao-I Dang; commentary by Giovanni Giurate with Jean-Daniel Bloesch. VDE-Gallo 698. Compact disk.

Cambodia: Music of the Royal Palace (the 1960s). 1994. Commentary in French by Jacques Brunet; trans. (into English) Peter Lee and (into German) Volker Haller. Ocora Radio France C 560034. Compact disk.

Cambodia: Royal Music. 1971–1989. Recording and commentary by Jacques Brunet. Musics and Musicians of the World. International Music Council. Auvidis/Unesco D 8011. Compact disk.

Cambodian Mohori: Khmer Entertainment Music. 1991. Sam-Ang Sam Ensemble. World Music Institute WMI-015. Cassette.

Cambodian Traditional Music in Minnesota. 1983. World Music Enterprises. Cassette.

Court Dance of Cambodia. 1994. Recording by Teodor Octavio Graca; commentary by Sam-Ang Sam. AVL 95001. Compact disk.

Echoes from the Palace: Court Music of Cambodia—Sam-Ang Sam Ensemble. 1996. Recording and commentary by Sam-Ang Sam. Music of the World CDT-140. Compact disk.

Instrumental and Vocal Pieces. 1978. Recording and commentary by Chinary Ung. Cambodia Traditional Music, 1. Folkways FE 4081. LP disk.

Mohori: Sam Ang Sam Ensemble. 1997. World Music Institute and Music of the World. Latitudes LAT50609.

The Music of Cambodia. c. 1960s. Recording and commentary by Alain Daniélou. Musical Anthology of the Orient. Bärenreiter-Musicaphon BM 30 L 2002. LP disk.

Music of Cambodia. 1989. Sam-Ang Sam Ensemble. The New Americans. World Music Institute WMI-0 007. Cassette.

Musicians of the National Dance Company of Cambodia: Homrong. 1991. Recording by Richard Blair; lyrics transcribed by students of Fine Arts University of Phnom Penh, trans. Sam Phany and Bill Lobban. Real World Records 2-91734. Compact disk.

Musiques du Cambodge des forêts. 1975. Commentary by Bernard Dupaigne. Anthologie de la Musique de Peuples. AMP 2902. LP disk.

Nine Gong Gamelan Recorded inside Angkor Wat. 1993. Recording by David and Kay Parsons; commentary by John Schaefer. The Music of Cambodia, 1. Celestial Harmonies 13074-2. Compact disk.

Royal Court Music Recorded in Phnom Penh. 1992. Recording by David and Kay Parsons; commentary by John Schaefer. The Music of Cambodia, 2. Celestial Harmonies 13075-2. Compact disk.

Solo Instrumental Music Recorded in Phnom Penh. 1994. Recording by David and Kay Parsons; commentary by John Schaefer. The Music of Cambodia, 3. Celestial Harmonies 13076-2. Compact disk.

Silent Temple, Songful Hearts: Traditional Music of Cambodia. 1991. Sam-Ang Sam and Ensemble. World Music Press WMP-008. Cassette.

Traditional Music of Cambodia. 1987. Sam-Ang Sam. Recording and commentary by Sam-Ang Sam. MC-SS-NR001. LP disk.

Tribe Music, Folk Music, and Popular Dances. 1979. Recording and commentary by Chinary Ung. Cambodia Traditional Music, 2. Folkways FE 4082. LP disk.

Thailand

Buddist [sic] *Chants: 1,000 Chants and Dasana Mahachat.* c. 1999. Produced by Ministry of Education and College of Music, Mahidol University. 10 compact disks. (Brief commentary in English, extensive in Thai.)

Ceremonial Music of Thailand: Music for Sacred Rituals and Theatre. 1989. Siamese Music Ensemble. Pacific Music 8.260581. Compact disk.

Chang Saw: Ensemble Si Nuan Thung Pong—Village Music of Northern Thailand. 2000. Recording and commentary by Fred Gales. Pan 2075CD. Compact disk.

Classical Music of Thailand. 1991. World Music Library. King Record KICC 5125. Compact disk.

Dontri Chao Sayam—Traditional Folk Music of Siam. 1993. Produced by Saeng Arun Arts Centre. SAACI CD 001-006. 6 compact disks.

Drums of Thailand. 1974. Compiled by Princess Chumbhot of Nagor Svarga. Folkways FE 4215B. LP disk.

En Thaïlande: La musique traditionnelle des Môn. 1979. Ocora 558.535. LP disk.

The Flower of Isan: Songs and Music from North-East Thailand. 1989. Commentary by Ginny Landgraf. Ace Records CDORBD 051. Compact disk.

Fong Naam: Ancient–Contemporary Music from Thailand. 1995. Produced and with commentary by Bruce Gaston. Celestial Harmonies 14098-2. 2 compact disks.

Fong Naam: Jakajan—Music from New Siam. 1996. Produced and with commentary by Bruce Gaston and Kaiwan Tilokavichai. Nimbus NI 5486. Compact disk.

Instrumental Music of Northeast Thailand. 1991. World Music Library. King Record KICC 5124. Compact disk.

Karenni: Music from the Border Areas of Thailand and Burma. 1994. Recording and commentary by Fred Gales. Paradox Records PAN 2040CD. Compact disk.

Khantoke. 1998. Produced by Phanuthat Aphichanatong and Bringkop Vora-Urai. Kannika Buacheen Production (Chiangmai). Compact disk. (Northern Thai music.)

The La hu nyi of Thailand. c. 1970s. Recording by Gretel Schworer-Kohl and Hans Oesch; commentary by Gretel Schworer-Kohl. Bärenreiter-Musicaphon BM 30 L 2572. LP disk.

Lao Music of the Northeast. 1981. Recording and commentary by Terry E. Miller. Lyrichord LLST 7357. LP disk.

Maan Mongkhon: An Auspicious Piece in the Burmese Style. 1997. Thai Music Circle (London). Pan Records 2049. Compact disk.

The Mahori Orchestra. 1994. Fong Naam. Commentary by Prasarn Wongwirojruk and Bruce Gaston. Siamese Classical Music, 5. HNH International. Marco Polo 8.223493. Compact disk.

Mo Lam Singing of Northeast Thailand. 1991. Chawiwan Damnoen and Thongkham Thaikla. World Music Library. King Record KICC 5123. Compact disk.

Les Môns de Thaïlande. 1976. Hum Rong Krathai Ten. Musiques et Traditions du Monde. CBS 81389. LP disk.

Music of Minorities in the Northwestern Thailand. 1980. Recording and commentary by Ruriko Uchida; trans. Gen'ichi Tsuge. Victor SJ 1010 2. LP disk.

Music of Northeast Thailand. 1992. Chagkachan. Commentary in Japanese by Sentoku Miho; trans. Larry Richards. World Music Library. King Record KICC 5159. Compact disk.

Music of Northern Thailand: Instrumental Music. 1999. Produced by Phanuthat Aphichanatong. Na Khantoke Production (Chiangmai). Compact disk.

Music of Thailand. 1959. Recording and commentary by Howard K. Kaufman. Folkways FE 4463. LP disk.

Music from Thailand: Field Recordings by Master Ethnomusicologist Deben Bhattacharya. 1999 [1973]. Recording and commentary by Deben Bhattacharya. ARC Music EUCD 1557. Compact disk.

Music from Thailand and Laos. 1997. Recordings and commentary in English, German, and French by David Fanshawe. ARC Music EUCD 1425. Compact disk.

Musique des tribus chinoises du Triangle d'Or. 1980. Recording and commentary by François Jouffa. Arion ARN 33535. LP disk.

The Nang Hong Suite: Siamese Funeral Music. 1992. Fong Naam. Commentary by Neil Sorrell and Bruce Gaston. Nimbus Records NI 5332. Compact disk.

The Piphat Ensemble before 1400 A.D. 1990. Fong Naam. Commentary by Bruce Gaston. Siamese Classical Music, 1. HNH International. Marco Polo 8.223197. Compact disk.

The Piphat Ensemble 1351–1767 A.D. (The Afternoon Overture). 1990. Fong Naam. Commentary

by Montri Tramoj. Siamese Classical Music, 2. HNH International. Marco Polo 8.223198. Compact disk.

The Piphat Sepha. 1992. Fong Naam. Commentary by Prasarn Wongwirojruk and Bruce Gaston. Siamese Classical Music, 4. HNH International. Marco Polo 8.223200. Compact disk.

Royal Court Music of Thailand. 1994. Recording and commentary by M. R. Chakrarot Chitrabongs. Smithsonian/Folkways Recordings SF 40413. Compact disk.

Shiva's Drum: Spiritual Music from the Beginning of Time. 1989. Siamese Music Ensemble. Commentary by Bruce Gaston. Pacific Music 8.260582. Compact disk.

Siamese Traditional Music: Songs of Siam by the "Divine Guru" Prince Naris. c. 2000. Produced by Princess Maha Chakri Sirindhorn Anthropology Centre (Bangkok). 3 compact disks.

The Sleeping Angel: Thai Classical Music. 1991. Fong Naam. Commentary by Neil Sorrell and Bruce Gaston. Nimbus Records NI 5319. Compact disk.

The String Ensemble. 1992. Fong Naam. Siamese Classical Music, 3. HNH International. Marco Polo 8.223199. Compact disk.

Thai Classical Music. 1994. Prasit Thawon Ensemble. Commentary by Somsak Ketukaenchan and Donald Mitchell. Nimbus Records. NI 5412. Compact disk.

Thailand: Ceremonial and Court Music from Central Thailand. 1997. Produced by James Upton and Mahidol University. Multicultural Media MCM 3014. Compact disk.

Thailand: Classical Instrumental Traditions. 1993. JVC Musical Industries VICG 5262-2. Compact disk. (Recorded in 1976, JVC World Sounds.)

Thailand: The Music of Chieng Mai. 1988 [1975]. Recording and commentary by Jacques Brunet. Musics and Musicians of the World, International Music Council. Auvidis/Unesco D 8007. Compact disk.

Thaïlande: Danses. 1994 [1979]. Recording and commentary by Gérard Krémer. Arion ARN 64284.

Thaïlande: Musique classique du nord. c. 1980s. Recording and commentary by Jacques Brunet. Musiques de l'Asie Traditionnelle, 17. Playasound PS 33522. LP disk.

Thaïlande: La musique des Môns/The Music of the Môns. 1988 (1976). Recording and commentary by Hubert de Fraysseix. Playasound PS 65019. Compact disk.

The Traditional Music of Siam: Bai-Sri Su-Khwan (Tham Khwan). 1994. Commentary in English and Thai by Sujit Wongthes; produced by College of Music, Mahidol University (Bangkok). Compact disk.

The Traditional Music of Siam: King Rama VII's Centennial. 1994. Commentary in English and Thai by Sujit Wongthes; produced by College of Music, Mahidol University (Bangkok). Compact disk.

The Traditional Music of Siam: Nang Hong, Sip-Song Phasa—The Nang Hong Ensemble. 1994.

Commentary in English and Thai by Sujit Wongthes; produced by College of Music, Mahidol University (Bangkok). Compact disk.

The Traditional Music of Siam: Tham Boon—The Music of Auspiciousness. 1994. Commentary in English and Thai by Sujit Wongthes; produced by College of Music, Mahidol University (Bangkok). 3 compact disks.

The Traditional Music of Siam: Wai Khru. 1994. Commentary in English and Thai by Sujit Wongthes; produced by College of Music, Mahidol University (Bangkok). Compact disk.

Virtuosi of Thai Classical Music. 1991. Benjarong Thanakoset and Chaloem Muangphresis. Commentary by Adul Kananasin. World Music Library. King Record KICC 5158. Compact disk.

Laos

Anthology of World Music: The Music of Laos. 1999 [c. 1960s]. Recordings and commentary by Alain Daniélou; trans. (from French) John Evarts. Rounder 5119. Compact disk. (Replaces earlier 12-inch disk.)

Bamboo on the Mountains: Kmhmu Highlanders from Southeast Asia and the U.S. 1999. Compiled, edited, and annotated by Frank Proschan et al. Smithsonian Folkways SFW 40456.

Bamboo Voices: Folk Music from Laos. 1997. World Music Institute and Music of the World. Latitudes LAT50601.

Boua Xou Mua: The Music of the Hmong People of Laos. 1995. Produced by Alan Govenar for Documentary Arts. Arhoolie CD 446. Compact disk.

Lam lao sut phiset: Phouvieng and Malavanh. 1995. Huntington Beach, Calif.: JKB Productions. Compact disk.

Laos. Recorded by Jacques Brunet. 1989. Ocora C 559 058. Compact disk.

Laos: Musique pour le khène/Lam Saravane. 1989. Recording and commentary by Jacques Brunet; trans. David Stevens. Ocora C 559 058. Compact disk.

Laos: Musiques du nord. 1976. Recording and commentary by Jacques Brunet. Musiques de l'Asie Traditionnelle. Playasound PS 33502. LP disk.

Laos: Traditional Music of the South. 1992 [1973]. Recording and commentary by Jacques Brunet. International Music Council. Musics and Musicians of the World. Auvidis/Unesco D 8042. Compact disk.

Mohlan of Siiphandon/Wannaa Keaopidom. 1997. King Record KICC 5225. Compact disk.

The Music of Laos. c. 1960s. Recording and commentary in French by Alain Daniélou; trans. (into English) John Evarts and (into German) Ingrid Brainard. A Musical Anthology of the Orient. Bärenreiter-Musicaphon BM 30 L 2001. LP disk.

Music from Southern Laos. 1994. Molam Lao. Recording by Robin Broadbank; commentary in French by Jacques Brunet; trans. Atlas Translations, Cambridge, England. Nimbus Records NI 5401. Compact disk.

Music from Thailand and Laos. 1997. Recordings and commentary in English, German, and French by David Fanshawe. ARC Music EUCD 1425. Compact disk.

Musique des Hmong du Laos: Cour d'amour et culte des ancêtres. 1981. Commentary by Eric Mareschal; trans. Marguerite Garling. Anthologie de la Musique des Peuples. AMP 2911. LP disk.

The Songs of the Lao. 1997. Musicians of National Music School, Vientiane. King Record KICC 5226. Compact disk.

Thinking about the Old Village: Traditional Lao Music. 1982. Khamvong Insixiengmai. Minneapolis: Lao Association. Cassette.

Traditional Music of Luang Prabang. 2000. Produced by College of Music, Mahidol University (Bangkok). 2 compact disks. (Commentary in English and Thai.)

Virgins, Orphans, Widows, Bards: Songs of Hmong Women. 1987. Recordings by Amy Catlin. Los Angeles: Woman's Building Gallery. Cassette.

Visions of the Orient: Nouthong Phimvilayphone—Music from Laos. 1995. Amiata Records ARNR 0195. Compact disk.

Burma (Myanmar)

Asian Percussions: Bali, Burma, China, India, Sri Lanka, Thailand. 1988. Commentary by Gérard Krémer. Playasound PS 65026. Compact disk.

Birmanie: Musique d'art. 1989. Recording and commentary by Jacques Brunet; trans. (into English) Derek Yeld. Ocora 559019/20. 2 compact disks.

Birmanie/Myanmar. 1998. Air Mail Music (Auvidis) SA 141026. Compact disk. (Music and singing recorded in Burma by François Jouffa.)

Burmese Folk and Traditional Music. 1953. Commentary by Maung Than Myint. Folkways FE 4436. LP disk.

La harpe birmane. 1980. Commentary by Jacques Brunet. Musiques de l'Asie Traditionnelle, 22. Playasound PS 33528. LP disk.

Harpe birmane/Burmese Harp: Moe Moe Yee. 1994. Commentary by Moe Moe Yee. Playasound PS 65135. Compact disk.

Hsaing Waing of Myanmar. 1992. World Music Library. King Record KICC 5162. Compact disk.

Music of Myanmar. 1988. World Music Library. King Record KICC 5132. Compact disk.

Pat Waing: The Magic Drum Circle of Burma Featuring Kyaw Kyaw Naing. 1998. Produced by Rick Heizman. Shanachie 66005. Compact disk.

Piano birman/Burmese Piano: U Ko Ko. 1995. UM MUS, SRC Radio (Canada) UMM 203. Compact disk.

Sandaya: The Spellbinding Piano of Burma Featuring U Yee Nwe. 1998. Produced by Rick Heizman. Shanachie 66007. Compact disk.

White Elephants and Golden Ducks: Enchanting Musical Treasures from Burma. 1997. Newton, N.J.: Shanachie 64087. Compact disk.

Malaysia

Dream Songs and Healing Sounds in the Rainforests of Malaysia. 1995. Recordings and commentary by Marina Roseman. Smithsonian/Folkways SF CD 40417. Compact disk.

Malaisie. 1975. Recording by Hubert De Fraysseix; commentary by Jacques Brunet. Musiques et Traditions du Monde: Musique Traditionelle. CBS 80934. LP disk.

Malaisie. c. 1980s. Commentary by Guy Saint-Clair. Musiques de l'Asie Traditionnelle, 13. Playasound PS 33517. LP disk.

Malaysia: Traditional Music of West Malaysia. c. 1970s. Recording by Jacques Brunet; commentary by Mubin Sheppard; trans. (into German) Wilfried Sczepan. A Musical Anthology of the Orient. Bärenreiter-Musicaphon BM 30 L 2026. LP disk.

The Negrito of Malacca. 1977 [1963]. Recording and commentary by Hans Oesch; trans. Nancy van Deusen. Anthology of South-East Asian Music. Bärenreiter-Musicaphon BM 30 L 2562. LP disk.

The Protomalayans of Malacca. 1977 [1963]. Recording and commentary by Hans Oesch; trans. Nancy van Deusen. Anthology of South-East Asian Music. Bärenreiter-Musicaphon BM 30 L 2563. LP disk.

The Senoi of Malacca. 1977 [1963]. Recording and commentary by Hans Oesch; trans. L. W. Vyse. Anthology of South-East Asian Music. Bärenreiter-Musicaphon BM 30 L 2561. LP disk.

Temiar Dream Songs from Malaya. 1955. Recording by Malaya Broadcasting System (1941); commentary by E. D. Robertson and H. D. Noone. Smithsonian/Folkways 04460. LP disk, cassette.

Singapore

New Music Compositions. 1993. Second ASEAN Composers Forum on Traditional Music, 1. ASEAN Committee on Culture and Information. Compact disk.

Traditional Music of Singapore. 1993. Second ASEAN Composers Forum on Traditional Music, 2. ASEAN Committee on Culture and Information. Compact disk.

Vietnam

Anthology of World Music: The Music of Vietnam. 1999 [c. 1968]. Recording and commentary by Trân van Khê. Rounder 5140/41. 2 compact disks.

L'art du Khên. 1995. Recording and commentary in English and French by Patrick Kersalé. Arion ARN 60367. Compact disk.

The Art of Kim Sinh. 1992. Kim Sinh; commentary in Japanese by Hoshikawa Kyoji; trans. Larry Richards. World Music Library. King Record KICC 5161. Compact disk.

L'art vièle vietnamienne/The Art of the Vietnamese Fiddle: Nguyên Minh Nhuong. 1998. Commentary in English and French. Arion ARN 60417. Compact disk.

The City of Huê. 1995. Commentary by Sten Sandahl. Music from Vietnam, 2. Caprice Records CAP 21463. Compact disk.

Dân Ca Cô Truyên V. N. 1993. Hohàng Oanh. Hohàng Oanh Music Center HOCD 08. Compact disk.

Escale au Vietnam/A Journey to Vietnam. 1995. Commentary and recording by Gérard Krémer. Playasound PS 66509. Compact disk.

Eternal Voices: Traditional Vietnamese Music in the United States. 1993. Commentary by Phong Nguyen and Terry E. Miller. New Alliance Records NAR CD 053. Compact disk.

Ethnic Minorities. 1995. Commentary by Sten Sandahl. Music from Vietnam, 3. Caprice Records CAP 21479. Compact disk.

Folk Songs of Viet Nam Sung by Pham Duy et al. 1991 [1968]. Smithsonian/Folkways 31303. LP disk, cassette.

From Rice Paddies and Temple Yards: Traditional Music of Vietnam. 1990. Phong Thuyêt Nguyên. Danbury, Conn.: World Music. Cassette. (Companion recording for the book by the same name, published by World Music Press. Book and tape set ISBN 0-937203-34-3.)

Greetings from Vietnam: Twenty Traditional Favorites. 1995. Peter's Music Factory (Netherlands) 91.001-2. Compact disk.

Imperial Court Music Recorded in Huê. 1994. The Music of Vietnam, 2. 13084-2. Celestial Harmonies. Compact disk.

Instrumental Music of Vietnam. 1992. Commentary in Japanese by Hoshikawa Kyoji; trans. Larry Richards. World Music Library. King Record KICC 5160. Compact disk.

Introduction to the Music of Viet Nam. 1991 [1965]. Commentary and recordings by Pham Duy. Smithsonian/Folkways 04352. LP disk, cassette.

Landscape of the Highlands. 1997. Tran Quang Hai. Chapel Hill, N.C.: Music of the World. Latitudes LAT 50612.

Khac Chi Ensemble: Spirit of Vietnam. 1999. Produced by Jon Siddall. Jericho Beach Music JBM 9902. Compact disk.

Mekong River: Traditional Music of Vietnam. 1992. Ngoc Lam and Que Lam; recording by Oliver DiCicco. I L CD. Compact disk.

Music from the Lost Kingdom: Huê, Vietnam. 1998. Recording and commentary by Phong T. Nguyen and Terry E. Miller. Lyrichord LYRCD 7440. Compact disk.

Music from Vietnam. 1991. Commentary by Nguyen Thuy Loan and Sten Sandahl. Caprice Records CAP 21406. Compact disk.

Music from Vietnam, 3: Ethnic Minorities. 1995. Commentary by Sten Sandahl. Caprice CAP 21479. Compact disk.

The Music of Vietnam, Vol. 1.1. 1994. Recording by David and Kay Parsons; commentary by John Schaefer. Celestial Harmonies 13082-2. Compact disk.

The Music of Vietnam, Vol. 1.2. 1994. Recording by David and Kay Parsons; commentary by John

Schaefer. Celestial Harmonies 13083-2. Compact disk.

Nhạc Lễ Ritual Music of Vietnam. 1997. King Record KICC 5224. Compact disk.

Song of the Banyan: Folk Music of Vietnam. 1997. Phong Nguyen Ensemble. World Music Institute and Music of the World. Latitudes LAT 50607. Compact disk.

Stilling Time: Nguồ Ru Thờ Gian. 1994. Recording by Philip Blackburn and Miranda Arana. Innova 112. Compact disk.

String Instruments of Vietnam. 1991. World Music Library. King Record KICC 5121. Compact disk.

Thich Nhat Hanh and Sister Chân Không with the Monks and Nuns of Plum Village [France]: *Drops of Emptiness*. 1997. Sounds True M003D. Compact disk. (Translations of song texts.)

The Traditional Songs of Huế. 1997. King Record KICC 5223. Compact disk.

Viet Nam Ca Trù: Tradition du nord—Ensemble Ca Trù Thái Hà de Hanoi. 1996. Paris: Inédit, Maison des Cultures du Monde W 260070. Compact disk.

Vietnam: Court Theatre Music—Hat-bôi. 1994 [1985]. Recording and commentary in English and French by Trân Van Khê. Auvidis-Unesco D 8085. Compact disk.

Vietnam Hat Cheo: Traditional Folk Theatre. 1989 [1978]. Recording and commentary by Trân Van Khê. Anthology of Traditional Musics. International Music Council. Auvidis/Unesco D 8022. Compact disk.

Viêt-Nam: Instruments et ensembles de musique traditionnelle. 1995 [1984]. Recorded by Maison des Cultures du Monde, Paris. Arion ARN 64603. Compact disk.

Vietnam: Music of the Truong Son Mountains. 1997. Compiled by Dr. Phong Nguyễn and Dr. Terry E. Miller. White Cliffs Media, WCM 9990. Compact disk.

Viêt Nam: Musique bouddhique de Huê/Buddhist Music from Huê. 1998. Recording by Pierre Bois. Commentary in English and French by Trân Van Khê. Inédit W 260082. Compact disk.

Viêt-Nam: Musique funéraire du nord—Nhac dám ma. 1998. Recording and commentary in English and French by Patrick Kersalé, Dàm Quang Minh, and Nguyên van Su. Arion ARN 58456. Compact disk.

Viet-Nam: Musiques et chants des minorités du nord. 1997. Buda 92669-2. Compact disk.

Viet Nam: Musiques de Huê. 1996. Paris: Inédit W 260073. Compact disk.

Vietnam: Musiques des Montagnards. 1997. Recordings by Pribislav Pitoëff, Georges Condominas, and Tô Ngoc Thanh, from the Collection Centre National de la Recherche Scientifique et du Musée de l'Homme; commentary by P. Pitoëff. Harmonia Mundi, CNR 2741085. 2 compact disks.

Viêt-Nam du Nord: Chants de possession. N.d. Recording and commentary by Dàm Quang Minh and Patrick Kersalé. Buda 92657-2. Compact disk.

Viet-Nam: Poésies et chants. 1994. Tran Van Khe and Tran Thi Thuy Ngoc; commentary in French by Professor Tran Van Khe; trans. (into English) Jeffrey Grice and (into German) Volker Haller. Ocora C 560054. Compact disk.

Vietnam: Reviving a Tradition. 1993. Bibliographic references by Tran Van Khe; commentary in French by Bac Thai Hao and Patrick Kersale; trans. (into English) Mary Pardoe. Auvidis Playasound PS 65116. Compact disc.

Viêt-Nam: Théâtre populaire du nord (Hát chèo). 1995. Commentary in English and French by Dàm Quang Minh. Arion ARN 64368. Compact disk.

Viet Nam: Tradition of the South. 1993 [1975]. Recording by Hubert de Fratsseix; commentary by Tran Van Khe. Anthology of Traditional Music. International Music Council. Auvidis/UNESCO D 8070. Compact disk.

Vietnam: Tradition du sud by Nguyên vinh Bao and Trân Van Khê. 1992. Recording and commentary in English, French, and German by Trân Van Khê. Ocora C580043. Compact disk.

Viet Nam: Traditional Music—Ca Tru Quan Ho. 1991 [1978]. Recording and commentary by Trân Van Khê. Auvidis-UNESCO D 8035.

Vietnam: World Sounds—Instrumental Textures/Song of the Native Land Ensemble. 1996. JVC VICG-5454-2. Compact disk.

Vietnamese Folk Theater: Hat Cheo. 1991. World Music Library. King Record KICC 5122. Compact disk.

Vietnamese Traditional Music by Pham Duc Thanh. 1999. Oliver Sudden Productions [Canada] K 10-14CD. Compact disk.

Vietnamese Zither: The Water and the Wind. 1993. Trân Quang Hai; trans. (into English) Mary Pardoe. Auvidis Playasound PS 65103. Compact disk.

ISLAND SOUTHEAST ASIA

Sumatra

The Angkola People of Sumatra: An Anthology of Southeast Asian Music. 1983. Bärenreiter Musicaphon SL 2568. LP disk.

Batak of North Sumatra. 1992. New Albion Records NA 046. Compact disk. Bärenreiter Musicaphon BM 30 SL 2567. LP disk.

Gondang Toba/Northern Sumatra. 1985. Museum Collection Berlin, ISBN 3 88 609 5126. LP disk.

Kartomi, Margaret J. 1979. *The Mandailing People of Sumatra: An Anthology of Southeast Asian Music*. Bärenreiter Musicaphon BM 30 SL 2567. LP disk.

Melayu Music of Sumatra and the Riau Islands: Zapin, Mak Yong, Mendu, Ronggeng. 1996. Music of Indonesia, 11. Smithsonian/Folkways SF 40427. Compact disk.

Music from the Forests of Riau and Mentawai. 1995. Music of Indonesia, 7. Smithsonian Folkways SF 40423. Compact disk.

Music of Nias and North Sumatra: Hoho, Gendang Karo, Gondang Toba. 1992. Music of Indonesia, 4. Smithsonian/Folkways SF 40420. Compact disk.

Nias: Epic Songs and Instrumental Music. 1994. Pan Records PAN 2014CD. Compact disk.

Night Music of West Sumatra: Saluang, Rabab Pariaman, Dendang Pauah. 1994. Music of Indonesia, 6. Smithsonian/Folkways SF 40422. Compact disk.

Simon, Artur. 1984–1985. *Gondang Toba/Northern Sumatra*. Museum Collection Berlin (West), 12. 2 LP disks.

———. 1987. *Gendang Karo/Northern Sumatra, Indonesia—Trance and Dance Music of the Karo Batak*. Museum Collection, Berlin (West), 13. LP disk.

Sumatra: Gongs and Vocal Music. 1996. Music of Indonesia, 12. Smithsonian/Folkways SF 40428. Compact disk.

Java (Including Cirebon, Sunda, and Madura)

Asmat Dream: New Music Indonesia, Vol. 1. 1992. Lyrichord LYRCD 7415. Compact disk.

Bêdhaya Duradasih—Court Music of Kraton Surakarta, 2. 1995. World Music Library KICC-5193. Compact disk.

Betawi and Sundanese Music of the North Coast of Java: Topeng Betawi, Tanjidor, Ajeng. 1994. Music of Indonesia, 5. Smithsonian/Folkways SF 40421. Compact disk.

Chamber Music of Central Java. 1992. World Music Library KICC-5152. Compact disk.

Court Music of Kraton Surakarta. 1992. World Music Library KICC-5151. Compact disk.

Detty Kurnia: Coyor Panon. 1993. Timbuktu Records FLTRCD519. Compact disk.

The Gamelan of Cirebon. 199 . World Music Library KICC-5130. Compact disk.

Gamelan Degung: Classical Music of Sunda, West Java. 1996. Pan Records Pan 2053 CD. Compact disk.

Gamelan Music from Java. 1963. Philips 831209. LP disk.

Indonesia, 1: Java Court Music. 1970s. Bärenreiter Musicaphon BM SL 2031. LP disk.

Indonesian Music: From New Guinea, the Moluccas, Borneo, Bali, and Java. 1954. Columbia SL 210. LP disk.

Indonesian Popular Music: Kroncong, Dangdut, and Langgaam Jawa. 1991. Music of Indonesia,

2. Smithsonian/Folkways SF 40056. Compact disk.

Jaipongan Java: Euis Komariah with Jugala Orchestra. 1990. Globestyle CDORB 057. Compact disk.

The Jasmine Isle: Javanese Gamelan Music. 1969. Nonesuch H-72031. LP disk.

Java: Gamelans from the Sultan's Palace in Jogjakarta. 1973. Music Traditions in Asia Series. Archiv 2723 017. LP disk.

Java: Historic Gamelans. 1972. UNESCO Collection, Musical Sources, Art Music from Southeast Asia Series, 9, 2. Philips 6586 004. LP disk.

Java: "Langen Mandra Wanara," opéra de Danuredjo VII. 1987. Musiques Traditionelles Vivantes, 3. Ocora C559 014/15. Compact disk.

Java: Une nuit de Wayang Aulit; Légende de Wahju Tjakraningrat. 1973. CDS 65.440. Compact disk.

Javanese Court Gamelan from the Pura Paku Alaman, Jogjakarta. 1971. Nonesuch H-72044. LP disk.

Javanese Court Gamelan, Vol. 2: Recorded at the Istana Mangkunegaran, Surakarta. 1977. Nonesuch H-72074. LP disk.

Javanese Court Gamelan, Vol. 3: Recorded at the Kraton, Yogyakarta. 1979. Nonesuch H72083. LP disk.

The Javanese Gamelan. 1987. World Music Library KICC-5129. Compact disk.

Javanese Music from Surinam. 1977. Lyrichord. LLST 7317. LP disk.

Klênêngan Session of Solonese Gamelan, 1. 1994. World Music Library KICC-5185. Compact disk.

Langêndriyan—Music of Mangkunêgaran Solo, 2. 1995. World Music Library KICC-5194. Compact disk.

Lolongkrang: Gamelan Degung Music of West Java. 1994. Sakti Records Sakti 33. Compact disk.

Music from West Java. 1992. Ethnic/Auvidis Series D8041. Compact disk.

The Music of K. R. T. Wasitodiningrat: Performed by Gamelan Sekar Tunjung. 1991. Creative Music Productions CMP CD 3007. Compact disk.

The Music of Madura. 1991. ODE Recording ODE CD 1381. Compact disk.

Music of Mangkunêgaran Solo, 1. 1994. World Music Library KICC-5184. Compact disk.

Music from the Outskirts of Jakarta: Gambang Kromong. 1991. Music of Indonesia, 3. Smithsonian/Folkways SF 40057. Compact disk.

Music of the Venerable Dark Cloud: The Javanese Gamelan Khjai Mandung. 1967. Institute of Ethnomusicology (University of California at Los Angeles) IER-7501. LP disk.

Musiques populaires d'Indonesie: Folk Music from West Java. 1968. Ocora OCR 46. LP disk.

Musiques du Ramayana, Vol. 3: Bali-Sunda. 1990. Ocora C560016. Compact disk.

Nasida Ria: Qasidah Music from Java. 1991. Piranha Music PIR 26-2. Compact disk.

Palais Royal de Yogyakarta, Musique de Concert. 1995. Ocora C560087. Compact disk.

Sangkala. 1985. Icon Records 5501. LP disk.

Songs before Dawn: Gandrung Banyuwangi Music of Indonesia, Vol. 1. 1991. Smithsonian/Folkways SF 40055. Compact disk.

The Sound of Sunda. 1990. Globestyle CDORB 060. Compact disk.

Street Music of Central Java. 1976. Lyrichord LLST 7310. Compact disk.

Street Music of Java. 1989. Original Music OMCD 006. Compact disk.

The Sultan's Pleasure: Javanese Gamelan and Vocal Music. 1994. Music of the World CDT-116. Compact disk.

Sunda: Musique et chants traditionnels. 1985. Ocora 558 502. LP disk.

Sundanese Classical Music. 1991. World Music Library KICC-5131. Compact disk.

Sundanese Music from Java. 1976. Philips 6586 031. LP disk.

Tembang Sunda: Sundanese Classical Songs. 1993. Nimbus Records NI 5378. Compact disk.

Tonggeret. 1987. Electra/Nonesuch 79173-2. Compact disk.

Vocal Art from Java. 1979. Philips 6586 041. Compact disk.

Bali

Baleganjur of Pande and Angklung of Sidan, Bali. 1995. World Music Library KICC-5197. Compact disk.

Bali: Barong—The Dance Drama of Singapadu Village. 1992. JVC World Sounds. JVC VICG 5217. Compact disk.

Bali: The Celebrated Gamelans. 1976. Musical Heritage Society MHS 3505. LP disk.

Bali: Divertissements musicaux et danses de transe. 1973. Ocora OCR 72. LP disk.

Bah: Gamelan and kecak. 1989. Nonesuch 9 79204. LP disk.

Bali: Joged Bumbung. 1987. Ocora 558 501. LP disk.

Bali: Le Gong Gedé de Batur. 1975. Ocora 558 5 10. LP disk.

Bali: Musique de danse. 1976. Playa Sound PS 33503. LP disk.

Bali: Musique et théâtre. 1971. Ocora OCR 60. LP disk.

Bali: Musique pour le Gong Gedé de Batur. 1987. Ocora C559002. Compact disk.

Bali: Musique sacrée. 1972. CBS 65173. LP disk.

Bali: Musiques du nord-ouest. 1992. Ethnic/Auvidis B 6769. Compact disk.

Bali Stage and Dance Music. 1973. Philips 6586 0 15. LP disk.

Barong, drame musical balinais. 1971. Vogue LD 763. LP disk.

Dancers of Bali. 1952. Columbia ML 4618. LP disk.

The Exotic Sounds of Bali. 1963. Columbia ML 5845. LP disk.

Fantastic and Meditative Gamelan: "Tirta Sari"—Semar Pegulingan of Peliatan Village. 1988. JVC Ethnic Sound, 7. JVC VID 25024. Compact disk.

Fantastic Sound Art "Mahabharata" "Wayang Krit"—A Virtuoso Shadow Play in Bali. 1987. JVC Ethnic Sound, 14. JVC VID 25028. Compact disk.

The Gamelan of Bali. 1975. Arion. FARN 91009. LP disk.

Gamelan Batel Wayang Ramayana. 1990. Creative Music Productions CMP CD 3003. Compact disk.

Gamelan Gong Gedé of Batur Temple. 1992. World Music Library KICC-5153. Compact disk.

Gamelan Gong Kelyar of "Eka Cita," Abian Kapas Kaja. 1992. World Music Library. KICC-5154. Compact disk.

Gamelan Joged Bumbung "Suar Agung," Negara. 1994. World Music Library KICC-5181. Compact disk.

Gamelan Music of Bali. 1960s. Lyrichord LLST 7179. LP disk.

The Gamelan Music of Bali. 1991. World Music Library KICC-5126. Compact disk.

Gamelan Selonding "Guna Winangun," Teganan. 1994. World Music Library KICC-5182. Compact disk.

Gamelan Semar Pegulingan of Binoh Village. 1992. World Music Library KICC-5155. Compact disk.

Gamelan Semar Pegulingan: Gamelan of the Love God. 1972. Nonesuch H-72046. LP disk.

Gamelan Semar Pegulingan "Gunung Jati," Br. Teges Kanginan. 1994. World Music Library KICC-5180. Compact disk.

Gamelan Semar Pegulingan Saih Pitu: The Heavenly Orchestra of Bali. 1991. Creative Music Productions CMP CD 3008. Compact disk.

Geguntangan Arja "Arja Bon Bali." 1994. World Music Library KlCC-5183. Compact disk.

Gendèr Wayang of Sukawati Village. 1992. World Music Library KICC-5156. Compact disk.

Golden Rain: Balinese Gamelan Music. 1969. Nonesuch H-72028. LP disk.

Golden Rain/Gong Kebyar of Gunung Sari, Bali. 1995. World Music Library KICC-5195. Compact disk.

Jegog: Dynamic Sound of the Earth—A Percussion Ensemble of Gigantic Bamboo in Sangkar Agung, Bali. 1987. JVC Ethnic Sound, 12. JVC VID 25026. Compact disk.

Jegog of Negara. 1992. World Music Library KICC-5157. Compact disk.

Jegog [2]: "Suar Agung," The Bamboo Ensemble of Sangkar Agung Village. 1992. JVC World Sounds. JVC VICG-5218. Compact disk.

Kecak: A Balinese Music Drama. 1990. Bridge BCD 9019. Compact disk.

Kecak in the Forest of Anima: The Choral Spectacle of Singapadu Village in Bali. 1987. JVC Ethnic Sound, 13. JVC VID 25027. Compact disk.

Kecak and Sanghyang of Bali. 1991. World Music Library KICC-5128. Compact disk.

Music in Bali. 1991. World Music Library KICC5127. Compact disk.

Music for the Balinese Shadow Play: Gendèr Wayang from Teges Kanyinan, Pliatan, Bali. 1970. Nonesuch H-72037. LP disk.

Music for the Gods: The Fahnestock South Sea Expedition—Indonesia. 1994. Rykodisc RCD 10315. Compact disk.

Music from the Morning of the World: The Balinese Gamelan. 1967. Nonesuch H-22015. LP disk.

Musiques du Ramayana, Vol. 3: *Bali-Sunda*. 1990. Ocora C560016. Compact disk.

Panji in Bali, 1. 1972. Bärenreiter Musicaphon BM 30 SL 2565. LP disk.

The Polyphony of South-East Asia: Court Music and Banjar Music. 1971. Philips 6586 008. LP disk.

Saron of Singapadu. 1995. World Music Library KICC-5196. Compact disk.

Scintillating Sounds of Bali. 1976. Lyrichord LLST 7305. LP disk.

Tektekan: The Dance Drama "Calonarang" of Krambitan Village. 1991. JVC World Sounds JVC VICG-5226. Compact disk.

Nusa Tenggara Barat

Cilokaq Music of Lombok. 1994. World Music Library KICC-5178. Compact disk.

The Music of Lombok. 1995. World Music Library KICC-5198. Compact disk.

Panji in Lombok, 1. 1972. Bärenreiter Musicaphon BM 30 SL 2560. LP disk.

Panji in Lombok, 2. 1970s. Bärenreiter Musicaphon BM 30 SL 2564. LP disk.

Nusa Tenggara Timur

Music of Sasandu. 1994. World Music Library KICC-5179. Compact disk.

Vocal and Instrumental Music from East and Central Flores. 1995. Music of Indonesia, 8. Smithsonian/Folkways SF 40424. Compact disk.

Vocal Music from Central and West Flores. 1995. Music of Indonesia, 9. Smithsonian/Folkways SF 40425. Compact disk.

Sulawesi

Indonesia, Toraja: Funerals and Fertility Feasts. 1995. Recordings by Dana Rappoport. Collection du Centre National de la Recherche Scientifique et du Musée de l'Homme, CNR 2741004. Compact disk.

Music of Sulawesi. 1973. Ethnic Folkways FE 4351. LP disk.

Borneo

Borneo: Musiques traditionelles. 1979. Playa P533506. Compact disk.

Dayak Festival and Ritual Music. 1997. Music of Indonesia, 14. Smithsonian/Folkways. Compact disk.

Dayak Lutes. 1997. Music of Indonesia, 13. Smithsonian/Folkways. Compact disk.

Murut Music of North Borneo. 1961. Folkways FE 4459. LP disk.

The Music of the Kenyah and Modang in East Kalimantan, Indonesia. 1979. UNESCO: University of Philippines. LP disk.

Musique Dayak. 1972. Collection Musée de l'Homme. Disques Vogue LDM 30108. LP disk.

A Visit to Borneo. 1961. Capitol T 10271. LP disk.

Philippines

Gifts from the Past: Philippine Music of the Kalinga, Maranao, and Yakan People. 1996. Notes by Ramon Santos. P&C Ode Records CD MANU 1518. Compact disk.

Hanunoo Music from the Philippines. 1956. Folkways FE 4466. LP disk.

Kulintang: Ancient Gong/Drum Music from the Southern Philippines. 1994. World Kulintang Institute WKCD 72551. Compact disk.

Kulintang and Kudyapiq: Gong Ensemble and Two-String Lute among the Maguinanaon in Mindanao Philippines. 1989. College of Music, University of the Philippines UPCM-LP UP. Compact disk.

Muranao Kakolintang: Philippine Gong Music from Lanao, Vol. 1: *The Villages of Romayas and Buribid*. 1978. Lyrichord LLST 7322. LP disk.

Muranao Kakolintang: Philippine Gong Music from Lanao, Vol. 2: *The Villages of Taraka, Molondo, and Bagoaingud*. 1970s. Lyrichord LLST 7326. LP disk.

Music from the Tausug of Sulu. 1970. Ethnosound EST 8000-8001. LP disk.

Revel, Nicole. 1987. *Philippines: Musique des hautes terres Palawan*. CNRS, Chant du Monde LDX 74 865. Compact disk.

Films and Videos of Southeast Asian Music

CAMBODIA

From Angkor to America: The Cambodian Dance and Music Project of Van Nuys, California, 1984–1990. 1991. Directed by Amy Catlin. Video.

Khmer Court Dance. 1992. Produced by Sam-Ang Sam. Khmer Studies Institute. Video.

Samsara. 1990. Directed by Ellen Bruno. Video.

Vietnam and Cambodia. 1988. JVC Video Anthology of World Music and Dance. Southeast Asia 1(6).

The Tenth Dancer. 1992. Directed by Sally Ingleton. Film.

THAILAND

The Diamond Finger. 1957. Film.

Hymn of Praise of Deity: Celestial Drama of Siam. N.d. Bangkok: Arts for Charity Foundation. Video.

Ladyboys. 1992. Produced and directed by Jeremy Marre. Video.

Land of Smiles: Thailand. 1995 [1973]. Produced by Deben Bhattacharya, Video-Forum V 72543. Film, video.

Miao Year. 1971. Produced by William Geddes. Two-part film.

Nang Yai: Thai Shadow Puppet Drama. N.d. Produced by Banhong Kosalawat and Stephanie Krebs. Film.

Rum Thai: Thai Classical Dance. N.d. Bangkok: Foto House Camera and Video. Video.

Sounds of Bamboo. 1976. Produced by the Japan Foundation. Tôkyô: Mitsu Productions, Japan Foundation. Film. (Philippines and Thailand.)

Thailand, Myanmar (Burma). 1988. JVC Video Anthology of World Music and Dance. Southeast Asia 2(7). Video.

Thai Traditional Music and Classical Dance. 1961. Bangkok: Fine Arts Department. Film.

Two Faces of Thailand: A Musical Portrait. 1994. Newton, N.J.: Shanachie Entertainment. SH 1214. Video.

LAOS

Between Two Worlds: The Hmong Shaman in America. 1985. 16mm. Produced by Taggart Siegel and Dwight Conquergood. Evanston, Ill.: Siegel Productions. Film, video.

Blue Collar and Buddha. 1987. Siegel Productions. Video.

Ib Hnub Hauv Hmoob Lub Neej (Daily Life of the Hmong). 1991. CJV Video.

A New Year for the Mien. 1986. Guy Phillips Productions. Video.

BURMA

The Dancers and Musicians of the Burmese National Theatre. N.d. Asia Society. Written and narrated by Beate Gordon; produced and directed by David W. MacLennan at Brooklyn College Television Center. Video.

Dances and Rites at the Dispelling of Death Spirits. 1962. Film.

Myanmar: Buddhist Monks and Nuns. c. 1994. Win Tin Win Presentation. Yangon, Myanmar: Av Media. Video.

Myanmar: Theatrical Dances of Myanmar. c. 1994. Win Tin Win Presentation. Yangon, Myanmar: Av Media. Video.

Myanmar: Traditional Marionette Dances. c. 1994. Thakuma Video Garden. Yangon, Myanmar: Onpa Trading Company. Video.

Myanmar (Burma). 1988. JVC Video Anthology of World Music and Dance. Southeast Asia 2(7). Video.

Tribal Dances of Myanmar. c. 1994. Win Tin Win Presentation. Yangon, Myanmar: Av Media. Video.

MALAYSIA

Borneo Playback: A Sabah Story. 1984. Produced by Carol Kreeger Davidson. Video.

Brides of the Gods. 1986 [1956]. Produced by W. R. Geddes. Video.

Floating in the Air, Followed by the Wind. 1973. Produced by Ronald Simmons. Film.

The Ibans of Sarawak. 1983. Educational Images. 80 slides and audiotape.

Malaysia, Philippines. 1988. JVC Video Anthology of World Music and Dance. Southeast Asia 3(8). Video.

VIETNAM

Ca Dao: The Folk Poetry of Vietnam. 1984. Produced and directed by David Grubin and Columbia University. David Grubin Productions. University Park: Pennsylvania State Audio-Visual Services. Video.

Cultic Dances in a Buddhistic Pagoda near Hue. 1973. Film.

Music of Vietnam. N.d. Filmed and recorded by Robert Garfias and Harold Schutz. Washington Films, Ethnic Music and Dance Series, University of Washington Press. Film. (Trần Van Khe plays the *dan tranh*.)

Vietnam and Cambodia. 1988. JVC Video Anthology of World Music and Dance. Southeast Asia 1(6). Video.

Vietnam Mission: Fifty Years among the Montagnards. 1994. Produced and directed by Douglas W. Smith. Video.

SINGAPORE

Singapore Street Opera. 1985. Atlanta: Super Station WTBS. Video.

INDONESIA

General

Indonesia: A Balinese Gong Orchestra. 1974. Film.

Indonesia: An Angklung Orchestra. 1974. Film.

Indonesia, 1. 1988. JVC Video Anthology of World Music and Dance. Southeast Asia 4(9). Video.

Indonesia, 2. 1988. JVC Video Anthology of World Music and Dance. Southeast Asia 5(10). Video.

Sumatra

Karo-Batak—Erpangir kalau: Fest der Haarwaschung in Sukanalu. 1994. Directed by Franz Simon and Artur Simon. Göttingen: Institut für den Wissenschaftlichen Film.

Karo-Batak—Gendang-Musik "mari-mari" und "patam-patam." 1994. Directed by Artur Simon. Göttingen: Institut für den Wissenschaftlichen Film.

Karo-Batak—Gendang-Musik "mari-mari" mit Röhrenzithern und Flöte. 1994. Directed by Artur Simon. Göttingen: Institut für den Wissenschaftlichen Film.

Karo-Batak—Gendang-Musik "silengguri" mit Röhrenzither und Laute. 1994. Directed by Artur Simon. Göttingen: Institut für den Wissenschaftlichen Film.

Karo-Batak—Tanze anlasslich einer Haarwaschzeremonie in Kata Mbelin. 1994. Directed by Franz Simon and Artur Simon. Göttingen: Institut für den Wissenschaftlichen Film.

Karo-Batak—Die Zeremonie "Njujungi beras piher." 1994. Directed by Franz Simon and Artur Simon. Göttingen: Institut für den Wissenschaftlichen Film.

Pakpak-Batak—Genderang-Musik. 1994. Directed by Artur Simon. Göttingen: Institut für den Wissenschaftlichen Film.

Pakpak-Batak—Spielen auf der Längsflöte "sordam." 1994. Directed by Artur Simon. Göttingen: Institut für den Wissenschaftlichen Film.

Pakpak-Batak—Xylophonmusik "kuku endek-endek" und "tangis-tangis beru ikan." 1994. Directed by Artur Simon. Göttingen: Institut für den Wissenschaftlichen Film.

Simalungun-Batak—Gonrang-Musik "olob-olob" und "sabung-sabung anduhur." 1994. Directed by Artur Simon. Göttingen: Institut für den Wissenschaftlichen Film.

Simalungun-Batak—Gonrang-Musik (sidua-dua) "parahot." 1994. Directed by Artur Simon. Göttingen: Institut für den Wissenschaftlichen Film.

Simalungun-Batak—Spielen auf dem Reishalminstrument "ole-ole." 1994. Directed by Artur Simon. Göttingen: Institut für den Wissenschaftlichen Film.

Toba-Batak—Gondang-Musik "sampur marmeme." 1994. Directed by Artur Simon. Göttingen: Institut für den Wissenschaftlichen Film.

Toba-Batak—Gondang-Musik "somba-somba." 1994. Directed by Artur Simon. Göttingen: Institut für den Wissenschaftlichen Film.

Java

Karya: Video Portraits of Four Indonesian Composers. 1992. Produced by Jody Diamond. American Gamelan Institute. Video.

Gambyong Pangkun: Traditional Javanese Court Dance from Solo. 1993. Resonance Media. Video.

The Prosperity of Wibisana: A Performance of Wayang Kulit. 1995. Resonance Media. Video.

The Prosperity of Wibisana: A Study Guide and Analysis of Javanese Wayang Kulit. 1995. Resonance Media. Video.

Bali

Bali beyond the Postcard. 1991. Produced and directed by Nancy Dine, Peggy Stern, and David Dawkins. New York: Filmmakers Library.

Balinese Children Learn to Dance. N.d. Filmed by Gregory Bateson and Margaret Mead. New York: Filmmakers Library. Video.

Dance and Trance of Balinese Children. N.d. Produced by Madeleine Richeport-Haley and Jay Haley from the film *Learning to Dance in Bali.* Video.

Isle of Temples: Bali. 1995 [1973]. Produced by Deben Bhattacharya. Video Forum V72542. Film, video.

Kembali—To Return. 1991. Produced by Jim Mayer, Lynn Adler, and John Rogers. Berkeley: Center for Media and Independent Learning, University of California Extension. Video.

Learning to Dance in Bali. 1978 [1939]. Gregory Bateson and Margaret Mead. New York: Gregory Bateson and Margaret Mead. Film, video.

Nini Pantun: Rice Cultivation and Rice Rituals in Bali. 1988. Berkeley: Center for Media and Independent Learning, University of California Extension. Video.

Releasing the Spirits: A Village Cremation in Bali. 1981. Directed by Patsy Asch, Linda Connor, et al. Documentary Educational Resources. Video.

Taksu: Music in the Life of Bali. 1991. Jann Pasler. Berkeley: University of California, Extension Media Center. Video.

Trance and Dance in Bali. 1988 [1952]. Gregory Bateson, Jane Belo, and Margaret Mead. Institute for Intercultural Studies. Film, video.

Outer Islands

A Celebration of Origins. 1992. Directed by Timothy Asch. Documentary Educational Recources. Video.

Trance of the Toraja. 1974. Eric Crystal and Lee Rhoads. Color, 21 min. Berkeley: University of California Extension Media Center. Video.

Borneo

Kayan-Dayak—Frauentanz "Karangarum" in Padua. 1990. Directed by Franz Simon and Sonja Balbach. Göttingen: Institut für den Wissenschaftlichen Film. Video.

Kayan-Dayak—Frauentanz "Tinaak Anaak" in Padua. 1990. Directed by Franz Simon and Sonja Balbach. Göttingen: Institut für den Wissenschaftlichen Film. Video.

Kayan-Dayak—Kriegstanz "Hivaar Peyitang" in Padua. 1990. Directed by Franz Simon and Sonja Balbach. Göttingen: Institut für den Wissenschaftlichen Film. Video.

PHILIPPINES

Hanunoo. 1958. Directed by H. C. Conklin. Film.

Ilocano Music and Dance of the Northern Philippines. 1971. Filmed and recorded by Robert Garfias and Harold Schutz. Washington Films, Ethnic Music and Dance Series, University of Washington Press. Film.

Maguindanao Kuliniang Ensembles from Mindanao, the Philippines. 1971. Filmed and recorded by Robert Garfias and Harold Schutz. Washington Films, Ethnic Music and Dance Series, University of Washington Press. Video.

Music and Dance of the Bagobo and Manobo Peoples of Mindanao, the Philippines. 1969. Filmed and recorded by Robert Garfias and Harold Schutz. Washington Films, Ethnic Music and Dance Series, University of Washington Press. Video.

Music and Dance of the Hill People of the Northern Philippines. 1971. Filmed and recorded by Robert Garfias and Harold Schutz. Washington Films, Ethnic Music and Dance Series, University of Washington Press. Two-part film.

Music and Dance of the Ibaloy Group of the Northern Philippines. 1971. Filmed and recorded by Robert Garfias and Harold Schutz. Washington Films, Ethnic Music and Dance Series, University of Washington Press. Film.

Music and Dance of the Maranao People of Mindanao, the Philippines. 1971. Filmed and recorded by Robert Garfias and Harold Schutz. Washington Films, Ethnic Music and Dance Series, University of Washington Press. Film.

Music and Dance from Mindanao, the Philippines. 1971. Filmed and recorded by Robert Garfias and Harold Schutz. Washington Films, Ethnic Music and Dance Series, University of Washington Press. Film.

Music and Dance from the Sulu Islands, the Philippines. 1971. Filmed and recorded by Robert Garfias and Harold Schutz. Washington Films, Ethnic Music and Dance Series, University of Washington Press. Film.

Music and Dance of the Yakan People of Basilan Island, the Philippines. 1971. Filmed and recorded by Robert Garfias and Harold Schutz. Washington Films, Ethnic Music and Dance Series, University of Washington Press. Film.

Samal Dances from Taluksangay. 1971. Filmed and recorded by Robert Garfias and Harold Schutz. Washington Films, Ethnic Music and Dance Series, University of Washington Press. Film.

Sounds of Bamboo. 1976. Produced by the Japan Foundation. Tôkyô: Mitsu Productions, Japan Foundation. Film. (Philippines and Thailand.)

Malaysia, Philippines. 1988. JVC Video Anthology of World Music and Dance. Southeast Asia 3(8). Video.

South Asia:
The Indian Subcontinent

Publications on
South Asian Music

REFERENCE WORKS

Barnett, Elise B. 1970. "Special Bibliography: Art Music of India." *Ethnomusicology* 14:278–312.

———. 1975. *A Discography of the Art Music of India*. Ann Arbor, Mich.: Society for Ethnomusicology.

Bech, Terence R. 1978. *Catalog of the Terence R. Bech Nepal Music Research Collection*. Bloomington: Indiana University Press.

Bhowmik, Swarnakamal, and Mudrika Jani. 1990. *The Heritage of Musical Instruments (A Catalogue of Musical Instruments in the Museums of Gujarat)*. Vadodara: Department of Museums.

Bor, Joep. 1988. "The Rise of Ethnomusicology: Sources on Indian Music c. 1780–c. 1890." *Yearbook for Traditional Music* 20:51–73.

Darnal, R. S. 1997. "Bibliography of Nepali Music." *European Bulletin of Himalayan Research* 12–13:240–251.

Dasgupta, Kalpana, and Bhagwan K. Prasad, comps. 1982. *Mass Communication in India: An Annotated Bibliography*. New Delhi: Indian Institute of Mass Communications.

Helffer, Mireille. 1997. "Bibliography of Himalayan Music." *European Bulletin of Himalayan Research* 12–13:222–239.

Hornbostel, Erich M. von, and Curt Sachs. 1961 [1914]. "Classification of Musical Instruments:

Translated from the Original German by Anthony Baines and Klaus P. Wachsmann." In *The Garland Library of Readings in Ethnomusicology*, ed. Kay K. Shelemay, Vol. 6, 119–145. New York: Garland.

Katz, Jonathan. 1983. "Indian Musicological Literature and Its Context." *Puruṣārtha* 7:57–75.

Kendadamath, G. C. 1986. *Indian Music and Dance: A Select Bibliography*. Varanasi: Indian Bibliographic Centre.

Kinnear, Michael. 1985. *A Discography of Hindustani and Karnatic Music*. Westport, Conn.: Greenwood.

———. 1994. *The Gramophone Company's First Indian Recordings 1899–1908*. Bombay: Popular Prakashan.

Kuppuswamy, Gowri, and M. Hariharan. 1981. *Index of Songs in South Indian Music*. Delhi: B. R. Publishing.

———. 1981. *Indian Dance and Music Literature: A Select Bibliography*. New Delhi: Biblia Impex.

Mehta, R. C., ed. 1993. "Directory of Doctoral Studies in Indian Music." *Journal of the Indian Musicological Society* 24:1–74.

Menon, Raghava R. 1995. *The Penguin Dictionary of Indian Classical Music*. New Delhi and New York: Penguin.

Nijenhuis, Emmie te. 1977. *Musicological Literature*. Wiesbaden: Otto Harrassowitz.

Rajagopalan, N. 1990. *A Garland: A Biographical Dictionary of Carnatic Composers and Musicians*. Bombay: Bharatiya Vidya Bhavan.

Sambamurthy, Pichu. 1952–1971. *A Dictionary of South Indian Music and Musicians*. 3 vols. Madras: Indian Music Publishing House.

———. 1962. *Catalogue of Musical Instruments Exhibited in the Government Museum, Madras*, 3rd ed. Madras: Government of Madras, Controller of Stationery and Printing.

Subbha Rao, B. 1993 [1956–1966]. *Raga Nidhi: A Comparative Study of Hindustani and Carnatic Ragas*. Madras: Music Academy.

Sundaram, B. M., comp. 1987. *Tala Sangraha: Compendium of Talas in Karnatak Music*. Bangalore: Percussive Arts Centre.

Tingey, Carol. 1985. "An Annotated Bibliography and Discography of Nepalese Musics." *Journal of the International Council for Traditional Music (U.K. Chapter)* 11:4–20; 12:35–44.

Who's Who of Indian Musicians. 1968. New Delhi: Sangeet Natak Akademi.

GENERAL

Allen, Matthew. 1998. "Tales Tunes Tell: Deepening the Dialogue between 'Classical' and 'Non-Classical' in the Music of India." *Yearbook for Traditional Music* 30:22–52.

Appadurai, Arjun, Frank J. Korom, and Margaret Mills, eds. 1991. *Gender, Genre, and Power in South Asian Expressive Traditions*. Philadelphia: University of Pennsylvania Press.

Archer, William G. 1974. *The Hill of Flutes*. Pittsburgh: University of Pittsburgh Press.

Arnold, Alison. "Popular Film Song in India: A Case of Mass-Market Musical Eclecticism." *Popular Music* 7(2):177–188.

———. 1991. "Hindi Filmī Gīt: On the History of Commercial Indian Popular Music." Ph.D. dissertation, University of Illinois at Urbana-Champaign.

———. 2001. "India, Film Music." In *The New Grove Dictionary of Music and Musicians,* 7th ed., ed. Stanley Sadie. London: Macmillan.

Ashton, Roger, ed. 1966. *Music East and West*. Bombay: Indian Council for Cultural Relations.

Baily, John, and Paul Oliver. 1988. "South Asia and the West." *Popular Music* 7(2) (entire issue). Published separately as *Popular Music in India*. 1988. New Delhi: Manohar.

Bake, Arnold A. 1970. "Stick Dances." *Yearbook of the International Folk Music Council* 2:56–62.

Banarjee, Jayasri. 1986. "The Methodology of Teaching Indian Classical Music: A Statement on the Problem." *Sangeet Natak* 79:11–48.

Banerji, S. C. 1976. *Fundamentals of Ancient Indian Music and Dance*. Ahmedabad: L. D. Institute of Indology.

Bandyopadhyaya, Shripada. 1980. *Musical Instruments of India (with Forty-Six Rare Illustrations)*. Varanasi and Delhi: Chaukhambha Orientalia.

———. 1985. *Indian Music through the Ages: 2400 B.C. to the Present Era*. Delhi: B. R. Publishing.

Barreto, Lourdino. 1968. "Aesthetic Indian Music as a Bridge between Christian and Indian Religious Music." Ph.D. dissertation, Pontifical Institute of Sacred Music.

Beck, Guy L. 1993. *Sonic Theology: Hinduism and Sacred Sound*. Columbia: University of South Carolina Press.

Bharata. 1926–1964 [second century]. *Nāṭyaśāstra of Bharatamuni, with the Commentary Abhinavabhāratī by Abhinavaguptācārya*, ed. M. Ramakrishna Kavi and J. S. Pade. 4 vols.

Gaeckwad's Oriental Series 36, 68, 124, and 145. Baroda: Oriental Institute.

———. 1951–1961 [second century]. *The Nātyaśāstra*, trans. Manomohan Ghosh. 2 vols. Calcutta: Asiatic Society.

Bhattacharya, Sudhibhushan. 1968. *Ethnomusicology in India*. Calcutta: Indian Publications.

Bhimani, Harish. 1995. *In Search of Lata Mangeshkar*. New Delhi: HarperCollins India.

Blackburn, Stuart. 1988. *Singing of Birth and Death: Texts in Performance*. Philadelphia: University of Pennsylvania Press.

Blackburn, Stuart, Peter Claus, Joyce Flueckiger, and Susan Wadley, eds. 1989. *Oral Epics in India*. Berkeley: University of California Press.

Booth, Gregory D. 1990. "Brass Bands: Tradition, Change, and the Mass Media in Indian Wedding Music." *Ethnomusicology* 34(2):245–262.

———. 1997. "Socio-Musical Mobility among South Asian Clarinet Players." *Ethnomusicology* 41(3):489–516.

Bor, Joep, and Philippe Bruguière. 1992. *Masters of Raga*. Berlin: Haus der Kulturen der Welt.

Bose, Sunil Kumar. c. 1990. *Indian Classical Music: Essence and Emotions*. New Delhi: Vikas.

Chakravarti, Indrani, ed. 1994. *Music: Its Methods and Techniques of Teaching in Higher Education*. New Dehli: Mittal.

Daniélou, Alain. 1959. *Textes des Purāṇa sur la théorie musicale*. Pondicherry: Institut Français d'Indologie.

Dattila. 1988 [second century]. *Dattilam*, rev. ed., trans. and ed. Mukund Lath. New Delhi: Indira Gandhi National Centre for the Arts.

de Tassy, Garcin. 1995. *Music Festivals in India and Other Essays*, trans. and ed. M. Waseem. Delhi: Oxford University Press.

Deva, B. Chaitanya. 1981. *The Music of India: A Scientific Study*. Delhi: Munshiram Manoharlal.

———. 1986. *Indian Music*. New Delhi: India. Council for Cultural Relations.

———. 1993 [1978]. *Musical Instruments of India: Their History and Development*, rev. ed. Delhi: National Book Trust.

Ebeling, Klaus. 1973. *Ragamala Painting*. Basel: Ravi Kumar.

Erdman, Joan, ed. 1992. *Arts Patronage in India: Methods, Motives, and Markets*. New Delhi: Manohar.

Farrell, Gerry. 1997. *Indian Music and the West*. Oxford: Clarendon.

Flora, Reis. 1987. "Miniature Paintings: Important Sources for Music History." *Asian Music* 18(2):196–230.

Gangoly, Ordhendra C. 1989 [1934]. *Ragas and Raginis*. New Delhi: Munishiram Manoharlal.

Gautam, M. R. 1980. *The Musical Heritage of India*. New Delhi: Abhinav.

———. 1989. *Evolution of Raga and Tala in Indian Music*. New Delhi: Munshiram Manoharlal.

Goswami, O. 1957. *The Story of Indian Music: Its Growth and Synthesis*. Bombay: Asia Publications.

Hardgrave, Robert L., Jr., and Stephen M. Slawek. 1997. "Instruments and Music Culture in Eighteenth-Century India: The Solvyns Portraits." *Asian Music* 20(1) (1988–1989):1–92. Reprinted in *Musical Instruments of North India: Eighteenth-Century Portraits by Baliazard Solvyns*. New Delhi: Manohar.

Holoien, Renee A. 1984. "Ancient Indian Dramatic Music and Aspects of Melodic Theory in Bharata's Natyasastra." Ph.D. dissertation, University of Minnesota.

Howard, Wayne. 1977. *Sāmavedic Chant*. New Haven and London: Yale University Press.

———. 1982. "Music and Accentuation in Vedic Literature." *World of Music* 24(3):23–34.

———. 1987. "The Body of the Bodiless *Gāyatra*." *Indo-Iranian Journal* 30:161–173.

Jairazbhoy, Nazir A. 1980. "The South Asian Oboe Reconsidered." *Ethnomusicology* 24(1):147–156.

———. 1988. *A Musical Journey through India 1963–1964*. Los Angeles: UCLA Ethnomusicology Publications. (With 3 cassettes.)

Jackson, K. David. 1990. *Sing without Shame: Oral Traditions in Indo-Portuguese Creole Verse*. Amsterdam and Philadelphia: John Benjamins and Instituto Cultural de Macau.

Joshi, G. N. 1988. "A Concise History of the Phonograph Industry in India." *Popular Music* 7(2):147–156.

Kabir, Nasreen, and Rupert Snell. 1994. "Bollywood Nights: The Voices behind the Stars." *World Music: The Rough Guide*, ed. Simon Broughton et al., 219–222. London: Rough Guides (Penguin).

Kakar, Sudhir. 1982. *Shamans, Mystics, and Doctors: A Psychological Inquiry into India and Its Healing Traditions*. New York: Knopf.

Katz, Jonathan, ed. 1992. *The Traditional Indian Theory and Practice of Music and Dance: Proceedings of the Seventh World Sanskrit Conference, Kern Institute, 1987*. Leiden and New York: Brill.

Kaufmann, Walter. 1968. "Some Reflections on the Notations of Vedic Chant." In *Essays in Musicology: A Birthday Offering for Willi Appel*, ed. Hans Tischler, 1–18. Bloomington: Indiana University School of Music.

Knight, Roderic. 1985. "The Harp in India Today." *Ethnomusicology* 29(1):9–28.

Kothari, Komal S. 1968. *Indian Folk Musical Instruments*. New Delhi: Sangeet Natak Akademi.

Kramrisch, Stella. 1965. *The Art of India: Traditions of Indian Sculpture, Painting, and Architecture*, 3rd ed. London: Phaidon.

Krishna Murthy, K. 1985. *Archaeology of Indian Musical Instruments*. Delhi: Sundeep Prakashan.

Krishnaswamy, S. 1971. *Musical Instruments of India*. Boston: Crescendo.

Kuckertz, Jozef. 1976. "Reception of Classical Indian Music in Western Countries during the Twentieth Century." *Journal of the Indian Musicological Society* 7(4):5–14.

Kuppuswamy, Gowri. 1984. *Royal Patronage to Indian Music*. Delhi: Sundeep Prakashan.

Kuppuswamy, Gowri, and M. Hariharan, eds. 1980. *Indian Music: A Perspective*. Delhi: Sundeep Prakashan.

Kuppuswamy, Gowri, and M. Hariharan, eds. 1982. *Glimpses of Indian Music*. Delhi: Sundeep Prakashan.

Kuppuswamy, Gowri, and M. Hariharan, eds. 1989. *An Anthology of Indian Music*. Delhi: Sundeep Prakashan.

Lath, Mukund. 1978. *A Study of Dattilam: A Treatise on the Sacred Music of Ancient India*. New Delhi: Impex India.

Lutgendorf, Philip. 1991. *The Life of a Text: Performing the Rāmcaritmānas of Tulsidas*. Berkeley: University of California Press.

Manuel, Peter. 1988a. "Popular Music in India: 1901–1986." *Popular Music* 7(2):157–176.

———. 1988b. *Popular Musics of the Non-Western World*. New York: Oxford University Press.

Marre, Jeremy, and Hannah Charlton. 1985. "There'll Always Be Stars in the Sky: The Indian Film Music Phenomenon." In *Beats of the Heart: Popular Music of the World*, 137–154. New York: Pantheon.

Massey, Reginald. 1992. "From Bharata to the Cinema: A Study in Unity and Continuity." *Ariel: A Journal of International English Literature* 23(1):59–71.

Massey, Reginald, and Jamila Massey. 1993. *The Music of India*. London: Kahn and Averill.

Matanga. 1928 [ninth century]. *The Bṛhaddeśī of Mataṅgamuni*, ed. K. Sambasiva Sastri. Trivandrum: Sanskrit Series.

———. 1992–1994 [ninth century]. *Bṛhaddeśī of Śrī Mataṅga Muni*, trans. and ed. Prem Lata Sharma. 2 vols. New Delhi: Indira Gandhi National Centre for the Arts.

Nanyadeva. 1869–1870 [twelfth century]. *Sarasvatīhṛdayālaṁkāra or Bharatabhāṣya*. Govt. MS No. 111. Poona: Bhandarkar Oriental Research Institute Library.

Narada. 1986 [n.d.]. *Nāradīya Śikṣā, with the Commentary of Bhaṭṭa Śobhākara*, trans. and ed. Usha R. Bhise. Poona: Bhandarkar Oriental Research Institute, 1986.

Nijenhuis, Emmie te. 1974. *Indian Music: History and Structure*. Leiden: Brill.

———. 1977. *The Ragas of Somnatha*. Leiden: Brill.

———. 1992. *Saṅgītaśiromaṇi: A Medieval Handbook of Indian Music*. Leiden and New York: Brill.

Neuman, Daniel. 1978. "Journey to the West." *Contributions to Asian Studies* 12:40–53.

Pal, Pratapaditya. 1967. *Rāgmālā Paintings in the Museum of Fine Arts, Boston*. Boston: Museum of Fine Arts.

Pandey, Kanti Chandra. 1963. *Abhinavagupta: An Historical and Philosophical Study*, 2nd rev. ed. Varanasi: Chowkhamba Sanskrit Series.

Parmar, Shyam. 1977. *Folk Music and Mass Media*. New Delhi: Communication Publications.

Parsvadeva. 1925 [thirteenth century]. *The Saṅgī-tasamayasāra of Saṅgītākara Śrī Pārśvadeva*, ed. T. Ganapati Sastri. Trivandrum: Sanskrit Series.

Popley, Herbert. 1950. *The Music of India*. Calcutta: YMCA Publishers.

Post, Jennifer. 1989. "Professional Women in Indian Music: The Death of the Courtesan Tradition." In *Women and Music in Cross-Cultural Perspective*, ed. Ellen Koskoff, 97–109. Urbana: University of Illinois Press.

Powers, Harold. 1965. "Indian Music and the English Language: A Review Essay." *Ethnomusicology* 9:1–12.

———. 1980a. "Illustrated Inventories of Indian Rāgamālā Painting." *Journal of the American Oriental Society* 100(4):473–493.

———. 1980b. "India, Subcontinent of, 1, 2." In *The New Grove Dictionary of Music and Musicians*, ed. Stanley Sadie. London: Macmillan.

Prajnanananda, Swami. 1973 [1960]. *Historical Development of Indian Music*. Calcutta: Mukhopadhyay.

———. 1979. *Music: Its Form, Function, and Value*. New Delhi: Munshiram Marmharlal.

———. 1981 [1965]. *Historical Study of Indian Music*. New Delhi: Munshiram Manoharlal.

Pringle, B. A. 1962 [1894]. *The History of Indian Music*. Delhi: Susil Gupta.

Qureshi, Regula. 1991. "Whose Music? Sources and Contexts in Indic Musicology." In *Comparative Musicology and Anthropology of Music: Essays on the History of Ethnomusicology*, ed. Bruno Nettl and Philip Bohlman, 152–168. Chicago: University of Chicago Press.

Raghavan, V. 1967. *The Number of Rasa-s*. Madras: Adyar Library.

———. 1979 [1966]. *The Great Integrators: The Saint-Singers of India*. New Delhi: Ministry of Information and Broadcasting.

Ramanathan, S. 1979. *Music in Cilappatikaaram*. Madurai: Madurai Kamaraj University.

Ranade, Ashok D. 1992. *Indology and Ethnomusicology: Contours of the Indo-British Relationship*. Springfield, Va.: Nataraj.

Randhawa, M. S. 1971. *Kangra Rāgmālā Paintings*. New Delhi: National Museum.

Rangacharya, Adya. 1986. *Natyasastra*. Bangalore: IBH Prakashana.

Rowell, Lewis. 1977. "Abhinavagupta, Augustine, Time, and Music." *Journal of the Indian Musicological Society* 13(2):18–36.

———. 1992. *Music and Musical Thought in Early India*. Chicago: University of Chicago Press.

Sarngadeva. 1943–1953 [thirteenth century]. *Saṅgītaratnākara of Śārṅgadeva, with Kalāniahi of Kallinātha and Sudhākara of Siṃhabhūpāla*, ed. S. Subrahmanya Sastri. 4 vols. Madras: Adyar Library.

———. 1945 [thirteenth century]. *Saṅgītarat-nākara of Śarnadeva*, trans. C. Kuhnan Raja, Vol. 1, ch. 1. Madras: Adyar Library.

———. 1976 [thirteenth century]. *The Saṃgī-taratnākara of Śārṅgadeva*, trans. K. Kunjunni Raja and Radha Burnier, Vol. 4. Madras: Adyar Library.

———. 1978–1989 [thirteenth century]. *Saṅgī-taratnākara of Śārṅgadeva. Sanskrit Text and English Translation with Comments and Notes*, trans. R. K. Shringy and Prem Lata Sharma. Vol. 1, Delhi: Motilal Banarsidass; Vol. 2, New Delhi: Munshirain Marmharlal.

Santhianathan, Shantsheela. 1996. *Contributions of Saints and Seers to the Music of India*, Vol. 2. New Delhi: Kanishka.

Schubel, James. 1993. *Religious Performance in Contemporary Islam: Shi'ia Devotional Rituals in South Asia*. Columbia: University of South Carolina Press.

Sharma, Amal Das. 1993. *Musicians of India*. Calcutta: Naya Prokash.

Shirali, Vishnudass. 1970. *Sargam: An Introduction to Indian Music*. New Delhi: Abhinav.

Silver, Brian Q. 1996. "Another Musical Universe: The American Recording Industry and Indian Music, 1955–1965." In *Seminar on Indian Music and the West*, ed. Arvind Parekh, 225–236. Bombay: Sangeet Research Academy.

Simon, Robert L. 1984. *Spiritual Aspects of Indian Music*. Delhi: Sundeep Prakashan.

Somesvara. 1925–1961 [1131]. *The Mānasollāsa of King Someśvara*, ed. G. K. Srigondekar. 3 vols. Gaekwad's Oriental Series 28, 84, and 138. Baroda: Oriental Institute.

Staal, J. Fritz. 1961. *Nombudiri Veda Recitation*. The Hague: Mouton.

Stooke, Herbert J., and Karl Khandalavala. 1953. *The Laud Rāgamālā Miniatures: A Study of Indian Painting and Music*. Oxford: Bruno Cassirer.

Sudhakalasa. 1961. *Saṅgītopanishat Sāroddhāra*, ed. U. P. Shah. Gaekwad's Oriental Series. Baroda: Oriental Institute.

Tagore, Sourindro M. 1976 [1875]. *Yantra Kosha or A Treasury of the Musical Instruments of Ancient and of Modern India, and of Various Other Countries*. New York: American Musicological Society.

Tarlekar, G. H., and Nalini Tarlekar. 1972. *Musical Instruments in Indian Sculpture*. Pune: Vidyarthi Griha Prakashan.

Thielemann, Selina. 1996. "Offering, Blessing, Expression of Divine Love: The Role of Music in Several Religious Contexts in India." *Journal of the Indian Musicological Society* 27:1–16.

Vidyarthi, Govind, trans. 1959a. "Melody through the Centuries." *Sangeet Natak Akademi Bulletin* 11–12:13–26. (Trans. of a portion of *Ma'dan-ul-Mūsīqī* 'Mine of Music,' c. 1860.)

———. 1959b. "Effects of Raga and Mannerism in Singing." *Sangeet Natak Akademi Bulletin* 13–14:6–14. (Trans. of a portion of *Ma'dan-ul-Mūsīqī* 'Mine of Music,' c. 1860.)

Wade, Bonnie. 1979. *Music in India: The Classical Traditions*. Englewood Cliffs, N.J.: Prentice Hall. Rev. ed. 1987. New Delhi: Manohar.

Wade, Bonnie C., ed., 1983. *Performing Arts in India: Essays on Music, Dance, and Drama*. Berkeley: University of California Press; Lanham, Md.: University Press of America.

———. 1984. "Performance Practice in Indian Classical Music." In *Performance Practice: Ethnomusicological Perspectives*, ed. Gerard Béhague, 13–52. Westport, Conn. and London: Greenwood.

Wade, Bonnie C., and Ann M. Pescatello. 1979. "The Status of Women in the Performing Arts of India and Iberia: Cross-Cultural Perspectives from Historical Accounts and Field Reports." In *The Performing Arts: Music and Dance*, ed. John Blacking and Joanne W. Kealiinohomoku, 119–137. The Hague: Mouton.

Widdess, D. R. 1980. "The Kuḍumiyāmalai Inscription: A Source of Early Indian Music in Notation." *Musica Asiatica* 2:115–150.

———. 1995. *The Ragas of Early Indian Music: Modes, Melodies, and Musical Notations from the Gupta Period to c. 1250*. Oxford: Clarendon.

———. 1996. "The Oral in Writing: Early Indian Music Notations." *Early Music* 24(3):391–405.

Yule, Paul, and Martin Bemmann. 1988. "Lithophones from Orissa—The Earliest Musical Instruments from India?" *Archaeologia Musicalis* 1(88):46–50. (In German, 41–46.)

MUSIC IN NORTHERN AREAS

Ahmad, Najma Perveen. 1984. *Hindustani Music: A Study of Its Development in the Seventeenth and Eighteenth Centuries*. New Delhi: Manohar.

Alter, Andrew B. 1994. "*Gurus, Shishyas*, and Educators: Adaptive Strategies in Post-Colonial North Indian Music Institutions." In *Music Cultures in Contact: Convergences and Collisions*, ed. Stephen Blum and Margaret J. Kartomi, 158–168. Sydney: Gordon and Breach.

———. 1997a. "Garhwali Bagpipes: Syncretic Processes in a North Indian Regional Musical Tradition." *Asian Music* 29(1):1–16.

———. 1997b. "Key Processes in the Oral Transmission of Hindustani Vocal Music." *Journal of the Musicological Society of Australia* 20:61–83.

Anderson, Robert, and Edna M. Mitchell. 1978. "The Politics of Music in Nepal." *Anthropology Quarterly* 51(4):247–259.

Arnold, Alison. 1991. "Hindi Filmī Gīt: On the History of Commercial Indian Popular Music."

Ph.D. dissertation, University of Illinois at Urbana-Champaign.

———. 1992–1993. "Aspects of Production and Consumption in the Popular Hindi Film Song Industry." *Asian Music* 24(1): 122–136.

Babiracki, Carol. 1991. "Musical and Cultural Interaction in Tribal India: The *Karam* Repertory of the Mundas of Chotanagpur." Ph.D. dissertation, University of Illinois at Urbana-Champaign.

Baily, John. 1976. "Recent Changes in the Dutar of Herat." *Asian Music* 8(1):29–64.

———. 1981. "Cross-Cultural Perspectives in Popular Music: The Case of Afghanistan." *Popular Music* 1:105–122.

———. 1988. *Music of Afghanistan: Professional Musicians in the City of Herat.* Cambridge: Cambridge University Press. (With audiocassette.)

Baloch, N. A. 1973. *Development of Music in Sindh.* Hyderabad: Sindh University Press.

Baloch, Nabi B.K.B. 1975. *Musical Instruments of the Lower Indus Valley of Sindh,* 2nd ed. Hyderabad, Sindh: Zeb Adabi Markaz.

Bandyopadhyay, Sudhansu M. 1976. *Baul Songs of Bengal.* Calcutta: United Writers.

Bech, Terence. 1975. "Nepal: The Gaine Caste of Beggar-Musicians." *World of Music* 17(1):28–35.

Beck, Guy L. 1996. "Vaiṣṇava Music in the Braj Region of North India." *Journal of Vaiṣṇava Studies* 4(2):115–147.

Bernède, Franck. 1997. "Music and Identity among Maharjan Farmers. The Dhimay Senegu of Kathmandu." *European Bulletin of Himalayan Research* 12–13:21–56. (Special double issue, *Himalayan Music: State of the Art,* ed. Franck Bernède.)

Bhatkhande, Vishnu Narayan. 1971. "A Short Historical Survey of the Music of Upper India." *Journal of the Indian Musicological Society* 2:1–43.

———. 1972 [1941]. "A Comparative Study of Some of the Leading Musical Systems of the Fifteenth, Sixteenth, Seventeenth, and Eighteenth Centuries." *Journal of the Indian Musicological Society* 3:1–61. (Also published separately: 1971. Baroda: Indian Musicological Society.)

———. 1981. *Bhātkhaṇḍe Saṅgīt-Śastra: Hiṅdustānī Sagīt-Paddhati,* trans. into Hindi by Sudama Prasad Dube et al. 4 vols. Hathras: Sangeet Karyalaya.

———. 1985. *Hiṅdustānī Saṅgīt-Paddhati: Kramik Pustak-Mālikā,* trans. into Hindi by Vaman N. Bhatt et al. 6 vols. Hathras: Sangeet Karyalaya.

Bhattacharya, Deben. 1969. *The Mirror of the Sky: Songs of the Bāuls from Bengal.* London: Allen and Unwin; New York: Grove.

Bhattacharya, Jotin. 1979. *Ustad Allauddin Khan and His Music.* Ahmedabad: B. S. Shah Prakashan.

Bhimani, Harish. 1995. *In Search of Lata Mangeshkar.* New Delhi: HarperCollins India.

Bor, Joep. 1986–1987. "The Voice of the Sarangi: An Illustrated History of Bowing in India." *National Centre for the Performing Arts Quarterly Journal* 15(3–4)/16(1):1–183.

Bryce, L. Winifred. 1961. *Women's Folk Songs of Rajputana.* New Delhi: Ministry of Information and Broadcasting, Government of India.

Capwell, Charles. 1986a. "Musical Life in Nineteenth Century Calcutta as a Component in the History of a Secondary Urban Center." *Asian Music* 18(1):139–163.

———. 1986b. *Music of the Bauls of Bengal.* Kent, Ohio: Kent State University Press.

———. 1991. "Marginality and Musicology in Nineteenth-Century Calcutta: The Case of Sourindro Mohun Tagore." In *Comparative Musicology and Anthropology of Music,* ed. Bruno Nettl and Philip Bohlman, 228–243. Chicago: University of Chicago Press.

Catlin, Amy R. 1977. "Whither the Manganihars? An Investigation into Change among Professional Musicians in Western Rajasthan." *Bulletin of the Institute of Traditional Cultures, Madras* (January–June):165–178.

Chakrabarty, Ramakanta. 1988. "Vaiṣṇava Kīrtan in Bengal." In *The Music of Bengal: Essays in Contemporary Perspective,* ed. Jayasri Banerjee, 12–30. Bombay and Baroda: Indian Musicological Society. Reprint: 1996. *Journal of Vaiṣṇava Studies* 4(2):179–199.

Chandola, Anoop. 1977. *Folk Drumming in the Himalayas: A Linguistic Approach to Music.* New York: AMS.

Chang, Garma C. C. 1967. "Form and Style in Tibetan Folk Song Melody." *Jahrbuch für Musikalische Volks- und Völkerkunde* 3:9–69, 109–126.

———. 1970a. *The Hundred Thousand Songs of Milarepa.* New York and London: Harper and Row.

———. 1970b. "Rgya-gling Hymns of the Karma-Kagyu: The Rhythmitonal Architecture of Some Instrumental Airs." *Selected Reports in Ethnomusicology* 1(3):79–114.

Chaudhuri, Debu, ed. 1993. *Indian Music and Ustad Mushtaq Ali Khan.* New Delhi: Har-Anand.

Dahmen-Dallapiccola, A. L. 1975. *Ragamala Miniaturen von 1475 bis 1700.* Wiesbaden: Otto Harrassowitz.

Daniélou, Alain. 1980. *The Ragas of North Indian Music.* New Delhi: Munshiram Manoharlal.

Dasasarma, Amala. 1993. *Musicians of India: Past and Present Gharanas of Hindustani Music and Genealogies.* Calcutta: Naya Prokash.

Deodhar, B. R. 1973. "Pandit Vishnu Digambar in His Younger Days." *Journal of the Indian Musicological Society* 4(2):21–51.

———. 1993. *Pillars of Hindustani Music,* trans. Ram Deshmukh. Bombay: Popular Prakashan.

Deshpande, Vamanrao Hari. 1972. *Maharashtra's Contribution to Music.* New Delhi: Maharashtra Information Service.

———. 1987 [1973]. *Indian Musical Traditions: An Aesthetic Study of the Gharanas in Hindustani Music.* Bombay: Popular Prakashan.

Dhar, Sheila. 1995. *Here's Someone I'd Like You to Meet: Tales of Innocents, Musicians, and Bureaucrats.* Delhi: Oxford University Press.

Dhar, Sunita. 1989. *Senia Gharana—Its Contribution to Indian Classical Music.* New Delhi: Reliance.

Dhar Chowdhury, Sisirkona. 1982. "Acharya Allauddin Khansahib." *Journal of the Department of Instrumental Music.* (Calcutta: Rabindra Bharati University.)

Dick, Alastair. 1984. "Sarod." In *The New Grove Dictionary of Musical Instruments,* ed. Stanley Sadie. London: Macmillan.

———. 1984. "Sitar." In *The New Grove Dictionary of Musical Instruments,* ed. Stanley Sadie. London: Macmillan.

Divas, Tulsi. 1977. *Musical Instruments of Nepal.* Kathmandu: Royal Nepal Academy.

Doubleday, Veronica. 1990. *Three Women of Herat.* Austin: University of Texas Press.

Dvivedi, H. 1954. *Mānsimha aur Mānkutūhal.* Gwalior: Vidya Mandir Prakasan. In Hindi.

Ellingson, Terry J. 1979. "The Mandala of Sound: Concepts and Sound Structures in Tibetan Ritual Music." 2 vols. Ph.D. dissertation, University of Wisconsin-Madison.

———. 1980. "Ancient Indian Drum Syllables and Bu Ston's *Sham Pa Ta* Ritual." *Ethnomusicology* 24(3):431–452.

———. 1991. "Nasadya, Newar God of Music: A Photo Essay." *Selected Reports in Ethnomusicology* 8:221–272.

Erdman, Joan L. 1978. "The Maharaja's Musicians: The Organization of Cultural Performance at Jaipur in the Nineteenth Century." In *American Studies in the Anthropology of India,* ed. Sylvia Vatuk, 342–367. New Delhi: Manohar.

———. 1985. *Patrons and Performers in Rajasthan.* Delhi: Chanakya.

Farhana, Faruqi, Ashok Kumar, Anwar Mohyuddin, and Hiromi Lorraine Sakata. 1989. *Musical Survey of Pakistan: Three Pilot Studies.* Islamabad: Lok Virsa Research Centre.

Flora, Reis. 1988. "Music Archaeological Data from the Indus Valley Civilization, c. 2400–1700 B.C." In *The Archaeology of Early Music Cultures, Third International Meeting of the ICTM Study Group on Music Archaeology,* ed. Ellen Hickmann and David Hughes, 207–221. Bonn: Verlag für Systematische Musikwissenschaft.

———. In press. "Music Archaeological Data for Culture Contact between Sumer and the Greater Indus Area, c. 2500–2000 B.C.: An Introductory Study." In *Hearing the Past: Essays in Historical Ethnomusicology and the Archaeology of Sound,* ed. Ann Buckley. Liège: Université de Liège Presse.

Fox-Strangways, Arthur. 1965 [1914]. *The Music of Hindoostan.* Oxford: Clarendon.

Gaston, Anne-Marie. 1994. "Continuity and Tradition in the Music of Nāthdvāra: A Participant Observer's View." In *The Idea of Rajasthan: Explorations in Regional Identity,* ed. Karine Schomer et al., Vol. 1, 238–277. Columbia, Mo.: South Asia.

———. 1997. *Krishna's Musicians: Musicians and Music Making in the Temples* of Nathdvara, Rajasthan. New Delhi: Manohar.

Gautam, M. R. 1980. *The Musical Heritage of India.* New Delhi: Abhinav.

Ghose, Santidev. 1978. *Music and Dance in Rabindranath Tagore's Education Philosophy.* New Delhi: Sahitya Akademi.

Gold, Ann G. 1994. "Sexuality, Fertility, and Erotic Imagination in Rajasthani Women's Songs." In *Listen to the Heron's Words: Reimagining Gender and Kinship in North India,* ed. Gloria G. Raheja and Ann G. Gold, 30–72. Berkeley: University of California Press.

Goswami, Karunamaya. 1990. *Aspects of Nazrul Songs.* Dhaka: Nazrul Institute.

———. 1994. *History of Bengali Music in Sound.* Khulna, Bangladesh: Losauk.

———. 1996. *Music and Dance of Bangladesh.* Dhaka: Silpakala Academy.

Gottlieb, Robert S. 1977. *The Major Traditions of North Indian Tabla Drumming.* 2 vols. Munich: Musikverlag Emil Katzbichler.

———. 1993. *Solo Tabla Drumming of North India: Its Repertoire, Styles, and Performance Practices.* 2 vols. Delhi: Motilal Banarsidass. (With 2 audiocassettes.)

Grandin, Ingemar. 1989. *Music and Media in Local Life: Music Practice in a Newar Neighbourhood in Nepal.* Linköping: Tema.

———. 1994. "Nepalese Urbanism: A Musical Exploration." In *Anthropology of Nepal: People, Problems, and Processes,* ed. Michael Allen, 160–175. Kathmandu: Mandala Book Point.

———. 1997. "Raga Basanta and the Spring Songs of the Kathmandu Valley: A Musical Great Tradition among Himalayan Farmers?" *European Bulletin of Himalayan Research* 12–13:57–80.

Greig, J. Andrew. 1987. "*Tārīkh-i Saṅgīta:* The Foundations of North Indian Music in the Sixteenth Century." Ph.D. dissertation, University of California, Los Angeles.

Gupt, Bharat. 1982. "Origin of Dhruvapada and Krishna Bhakti in Brijabhasha." *Sangeet Natak Akademi Bulletin* 64–65:55–63.

Gurung, Kishor. 1993. "What Is Nepali Music?" *Himal* 6(6):8–11.

———. 1996. *Ghamtu: A Narrative Ritual Music Tradition as Observed by the Gurungs of Nepal.* Kathmandu: United States Information Service.

Hamilton, James Sadler. 1988. *The Sitar Music of Calcutta.* Calgary: University of Calgary Press.

Hardgrave, Robert L., and Stephen M. Slawek. 1988–1989. "Instruments and Music Culture in Eighteenth-Century India: The Solvyns Portraits." *Asian Music* 20(1):1–92. (Enlarged and rev.: 1997. *Musical Instruments of North India: Eighteenth-Century Portraits by Baltazard Solvyns.* Delhi: Manohar.)

Hawley, John S. 1984. *Sūr Dās: Poet, Singer, Saint.* Seattle: University of Washington Press.

Helffer, Mireille. 1977. "Une caste des chanteurs-musiciens: Les gaine du Népal." *Ethnographie* 73:45–75.

———. 1990. "Recherches récentes concernant l'emploi des notations musicales dans la tradition tibetaine." In *Tibet: Civilisation et société,* ed. Fernand Meyer, 59–84. Paris: Foundation Singer-Polignac.

———. 1992. "An Overview of Western Work on Ritual Music of Tibetan Buddhism." In *European Studies in Ethnomusicology: Historical Developments and Recent Trends,* ed. Max P. Baumann, A. Simon, and U. Wegner, 87–101. Wilhelmshaven: Florian Noetzel.

———. 1994. *Mchod-rol, les instruments de la musique tibetaine.* Paris: CNRS Éditions/Éditions de la Maison des Sciences de l'Homme.

———. 1997. "The Drums of Nepalese Mediums." *European Bulletin of Himalayan Research* 12–13:176–196.

Helffer, Mireille, and Alexander W. Macdonald. 1966. "Sur un sarangi de gaine." *Objets et Mondes* 6(2):133–142.

———. 1975. "Remarks on Nepali Song Verse." In *Essays on the Ethnology of Nepal and South Asia,* ed. H. K. Kuloy, 175–265. Kathmandu: Ratna Pustak.

Henderson, David. 1996. "Emotion and Devotion, Lingering and Longing in Some Nepali Songs." *Ethnomusicology* 40(3):440–468.

Henry, Edward O. 1975. "North Indian Wedding Songs." *Journal of South Asian Literature* 11(1, 2):61–93.

———. 1988. *Chant the Names of God: Music and Culture in Bhojpuri-Speaking India.* San Diego, Calif.: San Diego State University Press.

———. 1991. "*Jogis* and *Nirgun Bhajans* in Bhojpuri-Speaking India: Intra-Genre Heterogeneity, Adaptation, and Functional Shift." *Ethnomusicology* 35(2):221–242.

———. 1995. "The Vitality of the *Nirgun Bhajan:* Sampling the Contemporary Tradition." In *Bhakti Religion in North India: Community Identity and Political Action,* ed. David N. Lorenzen, 231–250. Albany: State University of New York Press.

———. 1998. "Maithil Women's Song: Distinctive and Endangered Species." *Ethnomusicology* 42(3):415–440.

Hoerburger, Felix. 1970. "Folk Music in the Caste System of Nepal." *Yearbook of the International Folk Music Council* 2:142–147.

Howard, Wayne. 1986. *Veda Recitation in Vārāṇasī.* Delhi: Motilal Banarsidass.

Huehns, Colin. 1991. "Music of Northern Pakistan." Ph.D. dissertation, Cambridge University.

Hurie, Harriette Cook. 1980. "A Comparative Study of Khyal Style: Pandit Omkarnath Thakur and His Student Pandit B. R. Bhatt." M.A. thesis, Wesleyan University.

Imam, Mohammad Karam. 1959. "'Melody through the Centuries': A Chapter from *Ma'danul Musiqi* (1857)," trans. Govind Vidyarti. *Sangeet Natak Bulletin* 11:13–26, 33.

Jairazbhoy, Nazir A. 1977. "Music in Western Rajasthan: Continuity and Change." *Yearbook of the International Folk Music Council* 9:50–60.

———. 1980. "Embryo of a Classical Music Tradition in Western Rajasthan." In *The Communication of Ideas,* ed. J. S. Yadava and V. Gautam, 99–109. Tenth ICAES Series, No. 3. New Delhi: Concept.

———. 1995. *The Rāgs of North Indian Music: Their Structure and Evolution,* 2nd ed. Bombay: Popular Prakashan. (With audiocassette: Ustad Vilayat Khan, sitar; and Ustad Umrao Bundu Khan, *sāraṅgī* and voice.)

Jairazbhoy, Nazir, and A. W. Stone. 1963. "Intonation in Present-Day North Indian Classical Music." *Bulletin of the School of Oriental and African Studies* 26(1):119–132.

Jamyang Norbu, ed. 1986. *Zlos-gar, Performing Traditions of Tibet.* Dharamsala: Tibetan Institute of Performing Arts.

Karnani, Chetan. 1976. *Listening to Hindustani Music.* Bombay: Orient Longman.

Kaufmann, Walter. 1965. "Rasa, Rāgamālā, and Performance Times in North Indian Rāgas." *Ethnomusicology* 9(3):272–291.

———. 1968. *The Ragas of North India.* Bloomington: Indiana University Press.

Khan, Ali Akbar, ed. 1996. *The Classical Music of North India.* Book 2: *Evening Rags of Asawari That.* Vol. 1: *Rag Darbari Kanra.* Vol. 2: *Rag Chandranandan.* Vol. 3: *Rag Kirwani.* Notation by George Ruckert. Staunton, Va.: East Bay.

———, ed. 1998 [1991]. *The Classical Music of North India.* Book 1: *Introduction to the Classical Music of North India.* Vol. 1: *The First Year's Study.* Staunton, Va.: East Bay.

———, ed. In press. *The Classical Music of North India.* Book 1: *Introduction to the Classical Music of North India.* Vol. 2: *Instrumental Compositions in Morning Ragas.* Notation by George Rucker. Staunton, Va.: East Bay.

Kippen, James. 1988. *The Tabla of Lucknow: A Cultural Analysis of a Musical Tradition.* Cambridge: Cambridge University Press.

———. 1989. "Changes in the Social Status of Tabla Players." *Journal of the Indian Musicological Society* 20(1,2):37–46.

Korvald, Tordis. 1994. "The Dancing Gods of Bhaktapur and Their Audience. Presentation of Navadurgaa Pyaakham: The Drama and the People Involved." In *The Anthropology of Nepal: People, Problems, and Processes,* ed. Michael Allen, 405–415. Kathmandu: Mandala Book Point.

Kothari, Komal. 1972. *Monograph on Langas: A Folk Musician Caste of Rajasthan.* Borunda, Jodhpur: Rajasthan Institute of Folklore.

———. 1977. *Folk Musical Instruments of Rajasthan: A Folio.* Borunda: Rajasthan Institute of Folklore.

Kumar, Nita. 1988. *The Artisans of Banaras: Popular Culture and Identity, 1880–1986.* Princeton, N.J.: Princeton University Press.

Levy, Mark. 1982. *Intonation in North Indian Music: A Select Comparison of Theories with Contemporary Practice.* New Delhi: Biblia Impex.

Lienhard, Siegfried. 1984. *Songs of Nepal: An Anthology of Newar Folksongs and Hymns.* Honolulu: University of Hawaii Press.

Malik, M. Saeed. 1983. *The Musical Heritage of Pakistan*. Islamabad: Idara Saqafat-e-Pakistan.

Mansukhani, Gobind Singh. c. 1982. *Indian Classical Music and Sikh Kirtan*. London: Oxford University Press.

Manuel, Peter L. 1979. "The Light-Classical Urdu Ghazal-Song." M.A. thesis, University of California, Los Angeles.

———. 1988/1989. "A Historical Survey of the Urdu Gazal-Song in India." *Asian Music* 20(1):93–113.

———. 1989. *Ṭhumrī in Historical and Stylistic Perspectives*. Delhi: Motilal Banarsidass.

———. 1993. *Cassette Culture: Popular Music and Technology in North India*. Chicago: University of Chicago Press.

———. 1994. "Syncretism and Adaptation in Rasiya, a Braj Folksong Genre." *Journal of Vaiṣṇava Studies* 3(1):33–60.

Marcus, Scott L. 1989. "The Rise of a Folk Music Genre: Biraha." In *Culture and Power in Banaras: Community, Performance, and Environment, 1800–1980*, ed. Sandra Freitag, 93–113. Berkeley: University of California Press.

———. 1993. "Recycling Indian Film-Songs: Popular Music as a Source of Melodies for North Indian Folk Musicians." *Asian Music* 24(1):101–110.

———. 1995a. "On Cassette Rather Than Live: Religious Music in India Today." In *Media and the Transformation of Religion in South Asia*, ed. Lawrence A. Babb and Susan Wadley, 167–185. Philadelphia: University of Pennsylvania Press.

———. 1995b. "Parody-Generated Texts: The Process of Composition in *Birahā*, a North Indian Folk Music Genre." *Asian Music* 26(1):95–147.

McDaniel, June. 1989. *The Madness of Saints: Ecstatic Religion in Bengal*. Chicago: University of Chicago Press.

McNeil, Adrian. 1992. "The Dynamics of Social and Musical Status in Hindustānī Music: *Sarodiyās, Seniyās*, and the *Mārgī-Deśī* Paradigm." Ph.D. dissertation, Monash University.

Meer, Wim Van Der. 1980. *Hindustani Music in the Twentieth Century*. The Hague: Martinus Nijhoff.

Middlebrook, Joyce. 1991. "Customs and Women's Wedding Songs in Two Northern California Sikh Communities." M.A. thesis, California State University.

Miner, Allyn. 1993. *Sitar and Sarod in the Eighteenth and Nineteenth Centuries*. Wilhelmshaven: Florian Noetzel Verlag. (First Indian ed.: 1997. Delhi: Motilal Banarsidass.)

Misra, Susheela. 1985. *Music Makers of the Bhatkhande College of Hindustani Music*. Calcutta: Sangeet Research Academy.

———. 1990. *Some Immortals of Hindustani Music*. New Delhi: Harman.

———. 1991. *Musical Heritage of Lucknow*. New Delhi: Harman.

Moisala, Pirkko. 1989a. "An Ethnographic Description of the Madal-Drum and Its Making among the Gurungs." *Suomen Antropologi* 4:234–239.

———. 1989b. "Gurung Music and Cultural Identity." *Kailash* 15(3–4):207–222.

———. 1991. *Cultural Cognition in Music. Continuity and Change in the Gurung Music of Nepal*. Jyväskylä: Gummerus.

———. 1994. "Gurung Music in Terms of Gender." *Etnomusikologian Vuosikirja* 6:135–147.

———. 1997. "Gurung Cultural Models in the Ghantu." *European Bulletin of Himalayan Research* 12–13:152–175.

Moutal, Patrick. 1991. *Hindustānī Rāgas Index*. New Delhi: Munshiram Manoharlal.

———. 1991. *A Comparative Survey of Selected Hindustānī Rāgas Based on Contemporary Practice*. New Delhi: Munshirarn Manoharlal.

Nag, Deepali. 1985. *Ustad Faiyaaz Khan*. New Delhi: Sangeet Natak Akademi.

Narayan, Kirin. 1986. "Birds on a Branch: Girlfriends and Wedding Songs in Kangra." *Ethos* 14(1):47–75.

Nayyar, Adam. 1988. *Qawwali*. Islamabad: Lok Virsa Research Centre.

Neuman, Daniel. 1978. "*Gharanas*: The Rise of Musical 'Houses' in Delhi and Neighboring Cities." In *Eight Urban Musical Cultures: Tradition and Change*, ed. Bruno Nettl, 186–222. Urbana: University of Illinois Press.

———. 1980. *The Life of Music in North India: The Organization of an Artistic Tradition*. Detroit: Wayne State University Press. Reprint: 1990. Chicago: University of Chicago Press.

Oldenburg, Veena Talwar. 1990. "Lifestyle as Resistance: The Case of the Courtesans of Lucknow, India." *Feminist Studies* 16(2):259–288.

Ollikkala, Robert. 1997. "Concerning Begurm Akhtar, 'Queen of Ghazal.'" Ph.D. dissertation, University of Illinois at Urbana-Champaign.

Owens, Naomi. 1983. "The Dagar Gharānā: A Case Study of Performing Artists." In *Performing Arts in India. Essays on Music, Dance, and Drama*, ed. Bonnie C. Wade. Lanham, Md.: University Press of America. (Reprint: 1987. *Asian Music* 18(2):158–195.)

Pacholczyk, Józef M. 1978. "Sufyana Kalam, the Classical Music of Kashmir." *Asian Music* 10(1):1–16.

———. 1979. "Traditional Music of Kashmir." *World of Music* 21(3):50–59.

———. 1989. "Musical Determinants of the Maqam in Sufyana Kalam." In *Maqam, Raga Zeilenmelodik: Konzeptionen und Prinzipien der Musikproduktion*, ed. Jürgen Elsner, 248–258. Berlin: International Council for Traditional Music and Sekretariat Internationale Nichtstaatliche Musikorganisationen.

———. 1992. "Towards a Comparative Study of a Suite Tradition in the Islamic Near East and Central Asia: Kashmir and Morocco." In *Regionale Maqām—Traditionen in Geschichte und Gegenwart*, ed. Jürgen Elsner and Gisa Jähnichen, 429–463. Berlin: International Council for Traditional Music.

———. 1996. *Ṣūfyāna Mūsiqī, the Classical Tradition of Kashmir*. Berlin: International Institute for Traditional Music.

Paintal, Ajit Singh. 1971. "The Nature and Place of Music in Sikh Devotional Music and Its Affinity with Hindustani Classical Music." Ph.D. dissertation, University of Delhi.

Pandey, Shyam M. 1979. *Hindi Oral Epic Loriki*. Allahabad: Sahitya Bhawan Private.

———. 1982. *Hindi Oral Epic Canaini*. Allahabad: Sahitya Bhawan Private.

———. 1987. *Hindi Oral Epic Lorikayan*. Allahabad: Sahitya Bhawan Private.

Parmar, Shyam. 1977. *Folk Music and Mass Media*. New Delhi: Communication Publications.

Patel, Madhubhai. 1974. *Folksongs of Southern Gujarat*. Baroda: Indian Musicological Society.

Pereira, José, and Micael Martins. 1981. "Song of Goa, an Anthology of Mandos." In *Boletim do Instituto Menezes de Bragança* 128. Bastora: Tipgrafi Rangel.

Post, Jennifer C. 1982. "Marathi and Konkani Women in Hindustani Music, 1880–1940." Ph.D. dissertation, University of Minnesota.

———. 1992. "Professional Women in Indian Music: The Death of the Courtesan Tradition." In *Women and Music in Cross-Cultural Perspective*, ed. Ellen Koskoff, 97–109. New York: Greenwood.

Powers, Harold. 1980a. "Classical Music, Cultural Roots, and Colonial Rule: An Indic Musicologist Looks at the Muslim World." *Asian Music* 12(1):5–13.

———. 1980b. "Illustrated Inventories of Indian Rāgamālā Painting." *Journal of the American Oriental Society* 100(4):473–493.

———. 1980c. "Kashmir." In *The New Grove Dictionary of Music and Musicians*, ed. Stanley Sadie. London: Macmillan.

Prasad, Onkar. 1985. *Santal Music: A Study in Pattern and Process of Cultural Persistence*. New Delhi: Inter-India Publications.

Qalandar, Qaisar. 1976. "Music in Kashmir, an Introduction." *Journal of the Indian Musicological Society* 7(4):15–22.

Qureshi, Regula B. 1972. "Indo-Muslim Religious Music: An Overview." *Asian Music* 3:15–22.

———. 1981a. "Islamic Music in an Indian Environment: The Shi'a Majlis." *Ethnomusicology* 25:41–71.

———. 1981b. "Music and Culture in Sind: An Ethnomusicological Perspective." In *Sind through the Centuries*, ed. Hamida Khuhro, 237–244. Karachi: Oxford University Press.

———. 1986. *Sufi Music of India and Pakistan: Sound, Context, and Meaning in Qawwali*. Cambridge: Cambridge University Press.

———. 1990. "Musical Gesture and Extra-Musical Meaning: Words and Music in the Urdu

Ghazal." *Journal of the American Musicological Society* 43(3):457–497.

———. 1993. "Text, Tune, and Context: Analyzing the Urdu *Ghazal*." In *Text, Tone, and Tune: Parameters of Music in Multicultural Perspective*, ed. Bonnie C. Wade, 133–158. New Delhi: Oxford and IBH. (With audiocassette.)

———. 1997. "The Indian Sarangi: Sound of Affect, Site of Contest." *Yearbook for Traditional Music* 29:1–38.

Rana, Jagadish. 1990. "Bhaktapur, Nepal's Capital of Music and Dance: A Study of Conservation and Promotion of Traditional Music and Dance." *Kailash* 16(1–2):5–12.

Ranade, Ashok D. 1984. *On Music and Musicians of Hindoostan*. New Delhi: Promilla.

———. 1986. *Stage Music of Maharashtra*. New Delhi: Sangeet Natak Akademi.

———. 1989. *Maharashtra: Art Music*. New Delhi: Maharashtra Information Centre.

———. 1990. *Hindustani Classical Music: Keywords and Concepts*. New Delhi: Promilla.

Ranade, Garesh H. 1960. *Music in Maharashtra*. New Delhi: Maharashtra Information Centre.

———. 1971. *Hindusthani Music: Its Physics and Aesthetics*, 3rd ed. Bombay: Popular Prakashan.

Ray, Sukumar. 1985. *Music of Eastern India*. Calcutta: Firma KLM.

———. 1988. *Folk-Music of Eastern India: With Special Reference to Bengal*. Shimla: Indian Institute of Advanced Study.

Roach, David. 1971. "The Sitar: Its Tradition, Technique, and Compositions." M.A. thesis, Wesleyan University.

———. 1972. "The Benares Bāj—The *Tablā* Tradition of a North Indian City." *Asian Music* 3(2):29–41.

Roche, David. 1996. "Devi Amba's Drum: Mina Miracle Chant and the Ritual Ostinato of Spirit Possession Ritual Performance in Southern Rajasthan." Ph.D. dissertation, University of California, Berkeley.

Row, Peter. 1977. "The Device of Modulation in Hindustani Art Music." *Essays in Arts and Sciences* 6(1):104–20.

Ruckert, George. 1991. *Introduction to the Classical Music of North India*. St. Louis: East Bay—MMB Music.

Sá, Mário Cabral e. 1997. *Wind of Fire: The Music and Musicians of Goa*. New Delhi: Promilla.

Sahai-Achuthan, Nisha. 1987. "Folk Songs of Uttar Pradesh." *Ethnomusicology* 31(3):395–406.

Sakata, Hiromi Lorraine. 1983. *Music in the Mind: The Concepts of Music and Musician in Afghanistan*. Kent, Ohio: Kent State University Press. (With 2 audiocassettes.)

———. 1989. "Hazara Women in Afghanistan: Innovators and Preservers of a Musical Tradition." In *Women and Music in Cross-Cultural Perspective*, ed. Ellen Koskoff, 85–95. Urbana: University of Illinois Press.

———. 1993. *The Sacred and the Profane: The Dual Nature of Qawwali*. Berlin: International Institute of Traditional Music.

———. 1994. "The Sacred and the Profane: Qawwali Represented in Performances of Nusrat Fateh Ali Khan." *World of Music* 36(3):86–99.

Samuel, Geoffrey. 1976. "Songs of Lhasa." *Ethnomusicology* 20(3):407–449.

Sardo, Susana. In progress. "Singing Stories: Goan Catholic Music as a Strategy of Defining Identity." Ph.D. dissertation, Universidade Nova de Lisboa.

Sarmadee, Shabab. 1975. *Musical Genius of Amir Khusrau*. New Delhi: Ministry of Information and Broadcasting, Government of India.

———. 1976. "About Music and Amir Khusrau's Own Writings on Music." In *Life, Times, and Works of Amir Khusrau Dehlavi*, 241–269. New Delhi: Shri Hasnuddin Amad for the National Amir Khusrau Society. (Seventh centenary commemoration volume.)

———. 1984–1985. "*Mankutuhal* and *Rag Darpan*—Reflections of a Great Seventeenth-Century Scholar-Musician." *ISTAR Newsletter* 3–4:15–28.

———, ed. 1978. *Ghunyat-ul-Munya: The Earliest Known Persian Work on Indian Music*. Bombay: Asia Publishing House.

Satpathy, Sunil Kumar. 1990. *Anthology of Santal Songs, Dance, and Music of Orissa*. Bhubaneswar: Indian Academy of Folk and Tribal Art.

Shankar, Ravi. 1968. *My Music, My Life*. New York: Simon and Schuster.

Shepherd, Frances. 1976. "Tabla and the Benares Gharana." Ph.D. dissertation, Wesleyan University.

Silver, Brian. 1976. "On Becoming an Ustad: Six Life Sketches in the Evolution of a Gharana." *Asian Music* 7(2):27–58.

Singh, Khushwant. 1978. *Hymns of Guru Nanak*. Bombay: Sangam.

Slawek, Stephen M. 1986. "Kirtan: A Study of the Sonic Manifestations of the Divine in the Popular Hindu Culture of Banāras." Ph.D. dissertation, University of Illinois at Urbana-Champaign.

———. 1987. *Sitār Technique in Nibaddh Forms*. Delhi: Motilal Banarsidass.

———. 1988. "Popular *Kīrtan* in Benares: Some 'Great' Aspects of a Little Tradition." *Ethnomusicology* 32(2):77–92.

———. 1991. "Ravi Shankar as Mediator between a Traditional Music and Modernity." In *Ethnomusicology and Modern Music History*, ed. Stephen Blum, Philip V. Bohlman, and Daniel M. Neuman, 161–180. Urbana: University of Illinois Press.

———. 1996. "The Definition of Kirtan: An Historical and Geographical Perspective." *Journal of Vaiṣnva Studies* 4(2):57–113.

Slobin, Mark. 1974. "Music in Contemporary Afghan Society." In *Afghanistan in the 1970s*, ed. Louis Dupree and Linette Albert, 239–248. New York: Praeger.

———. 1976. *Music in the Culture of Northern Afghanistan*. Tucson: University of Arizona Press.

Söhnen, Renate. 1993. "Music from Baltistan." In *Contemporary German Contributions to the History and Culture of Pakistan*, ed. Stephanie Zingel-Avé Lallemant and Wolfgang-Peter Zingel, 109–126. Bonn: Deutsch-Pakistanisches Forum e.V.

Solis, Theodore. 1976. "The Sarod." M.A. thesis, University of Hawaii at Manoa.

Sorensen, Per K. 1990. *Divinity Secularized: An Inquiry into the Nature and Form of the Songs Ascribed to the Sixth Dalai Lama*. Vienna: Arbeitskreis für Tibetische und Buddhistische Studien, Universität Wien.

Sorrell, Neil, and Ram Narayan. 1980. *Indian Music in Performance: A Practical Introduction*. Manchester: University of Manchester Press.

Srivastava, Indurama. 1980 [1977]. *Dhrupada: A Study of Its Origin, Historical Development, Structure, and Present State*. Delhi: Motilal Banarsidass.

Stewart, Rebecca M. 1974. "The Tablā in Perspective." Ph.D. dissertation, University of California, Los Angeles.

Tagore, Sourindro Mohun. 1965 [1875]. *Hindu Music from Various Authors*. Varanasi: Chowkhamba Sanskrit Series Office.

Tewari, Laxmi. 1974. "Folk Music of India: Uttar Pradesh." Ph.D. dissertation, Wesleyan University.

———. 1977. "Ceremonial Songs of the Kanyakubja Brahmans." *Essays in Arts and Sciences* 6:30–52.

Thielemann, Selina. 1997. *The Darbhangā Tradition: Dhrupada in the School of Pandit Vidur Mallik*. Varanasi: Indica.

Thompson, Gordon R. 1987. "Music and Values in Gujarati-Speaking Western India." Ph.D. dissertation, University of California, Los Angeles.

———. 1991. "The Cāraṇs of Gujarat: Caste Identity, Music, and Cultural Change." *Ethnomusicology* 35:381–391.

———. 1992–1993. "The Bārots of Gujarati-Speaking Western India: Musicianship and Caste Identity." *Asian Music* 24(1):1–17.

———. 1995a. "Music and Values in Gujarati Western India." *Pacific Review of Ethnomusicology* 7:57–78.

———. 1995b. "What's in a *Ḍhāḷ*? Evidence of *Raga*-Like Approaches in a Gujarati Musical Tradition." *Ethnomusicology* 39(3):417–432.

Tingey, Carol. 1992. "Sacred Kettledrums in the Temples of Central Nepal." *Asian Music* 23(2):97–104.

———. 1994. *Auspicious Music in a Changing Society: The Damāi Musicians of Nepal*. New Delhi: Heritage; London: School of Oriental and African Studies, University of London.

———. 1997. "Music for the Royal Dasai." *European Bulletin of Himalayan Research* 12–13:81–120.

Trewin, Mark. 1990. "Rhythmic Style in Ladakhi Music and Dance." In *Wissenschaft und Gegenwärtige Forschungen in Nordwest-Indien*, ed. L. Icke-Schwalbe and G. Meier, 273–276. Dresden: Staatliches Museum für Völkerkunde Dresden Forschungstelle.

———. 1993. "*Lha-rnga*: A Form of Ladakhi Folk Music and Its Relationship to the Great Tradition of Tibet." In *Anthropology of Tibet and the Himalaya*, ed. Ch. Ramble and M. Brauen, 377–385. Zurich: Ethnological Museum of the University of Zurich.

———. 1995. "On the History and Origin of *Gar*, the Court Ceremonial Music of Tibet." *CHIME Journal* 8:4–31.

———. 1996. "Rhythms of the Gods. The Musical Symbolics of Power and Authority in the Buddhist Kingdom of Ladakh." Ph.D. dissertation, City University, London.

Verma, Vijay. 1987. *The Living Music of Rajasthan*. New Delhi: Office of the Registrar General.

Wade, Bonnie C. 1972. "Songs of Traditional Wedding Ceremonies in North India." *Yearbook of the International Folk Music Council* 4:57–65.

———. 1984a. *Khyal: Creativity within North India's Classical Music Tradition*. Cambridge: Cambridge University Press. (Reprint: 1997. Delhi: Motilal Banarsidass.)

———. 1984b. "Performance Practice in Indian Classical Music." In *Performance Practice: Ethnomusicological Perspectives*, ed. Gerard Béhague, 13–52. Contributions in Intercultural and Comparative Studies No. 12. Westport, Conn., and London: Greenwood.

———. 1990. "The Meeting of Musical Cultures in the Sixteenth-Century Court of the Mughal Akbar." *World of Music* 32(2):3–25.

———. 1996. "Performing the Drone in Hindustani Classical Music: What Mughal Paintings Show Us to Hear." *World of Music* 38(2):41–67.

———. 1998. *Imaging Sound: An Ethnomusicological Study of Music, Art and Culture in Mughal India*. Chicago: University of Chicago Press.

Wadley, Susan S. 1983. "Dhola: A North Indian Folk Genre." *Asian Folklore Studies* 42:3–26.

Waldschmidt, Ernst, and Rose L. Waldschmidt. 1967. *Miniatures of Musical Inspiration in the Collection of the Berlin Museum of Indian Art*. Part 1: *Rāgamālā-Pictures from the Western Himālaya Promontory*. Bombay: Popular Prakashan.

Wegner, Gert-Matthias. 1986. *The Dhimaybaja of Bhaktapur—Studies in Newar Drumming*, 1. Stuttgart: Franz Steiner.

———. 1988. *The Naykhibaja of the Newar Butchers—Studies in Newar Drumming*, 2. Stuttgart: Franz Steiner.

Widdess, Richard. 1981. "Aspects of Form in North Indian *Ālāp* and *Dhrupad*." In *Music and Tradition: Essays on Asian and Other Musics Presented to Lawrence Picken*, ed. D. R. Widdess and R. F. Wolpert, 148–181. Cambridge: Cambridge University Press.

———. 1994. "Festivals of *Dhrupad* in Northern India: New Contexts for an Ancient Art." *British Journal of Ethnomusicology* 3:89–109.

———. 1997. "Carya: The Revival of a Tradition?" *European Bulletin of Himalayan Research* 12–13:12–20.

Wiehler-Schneider, Sigrun, and Hartmut Wiehler. 1980. "A Classification of the Traditional Musical Instruments of the Newars." *Journal of the Nepal Research Centre* 4:67–132.

Yusuf, Zohra, ed. 1988. *Rhythms of the Lower Indus: Perspectives on the Music of Sindh*. Karachi: Department of Culture and Tourism, Government of Sindh.

MUSIC IN SOUTHERN AREAS

Ames, Michael M. 1977. *Tovil, the Ritual Chanting, Dance, and Drumming of Exorcism in Sri Lanka*. New York: Performing Arts Program of the Asia Society.

Ariyaratne, Sunil. 1987. *Karol, Pasam, Kantaru: A Survey of Sinhala Christian Hymns in Sri Lanka*. Colombo: Supersun Educational Services.

———. 1989. *Sindu Vistaraya: An Investigation into the Word "Sindu" in Sinhala Literature and Music*. Colombo: Dayawansa Jayakody.

Atikal, Ilanko. 1993 [fifth century]. *The Cilappatikāram of Ilanko Atikal: An Epic of South India*, trans. R. Parthasarathy. New York: Columbia University Press.

Ayyar, S. Venkita. Subramonia. 1975. *Swati Tirunal and His Music*. Trivandrum: College Book House.

Balakrishnan, Shyamala. N.d. "Folk Music of Cholamandalam." *Kalakshetra Quarterly* 9(4):16–18.

Baskaran, S[undararaj] Theodore. 1981. *The Message Bearers: The Nationalist Politics and the Entertainment Media in South India 1880–1945*. Madras: Cre-A.

Beck, Brenda. 1982. *The Three Twins: The Telling of a South Indian Folk Epic*. Bloomington: Indiana University Press.

Berberich, Frank J., III. 1974. "The Tavil: Construction, Technique, and Context in Present-Day Jaffna." M.A. thesis, University of Hawaii.

Blackburn, Stuart H. 1988. *Songs of Birth and Death: Texts in Performance*. Philadelphia: University of Pennsylvania Press.

Blackburn, Stuart H., and A. K. Ramanujan, eds. 1986. *Another Harmony: New Essays on the Folklore of India*. Berkeley: University of California Press.

Booth, Gregory D. 1996. "The Madras Corporation Band: A Story of Social Change and Indigenization." *Asian Music* 28(1):61–86.

Brown, Robert. 1965. "The Mṛdaṅga: A Study of Drumming in South India." 2 vols. Ph.D. dissertation, University of California, Los Angeles.

Carter, John R. 1983. "Music in the Theravada Buddhist Heritage: In Chant, in Song, in Sri Lanka." In *Sacred Sound: Music in Religious Thought and Practice*, ed. Joyce Irwin, 127–147. Chico, Calif.: Scholars.

Casinader, Rex A. 1981. *Miner's Folk Songs of Sri Lanka*. Göteborg: Göteborgs Ethnografiska Museum.

Catlin, Amy. 1980. "Variability and Change in Three Karṇāṭak Kritis: A Study of South Indian Classical Music." Ph.D. dissertation, Brown University.

———. 1985. "Pallavi and Kriti of Karnatak Music: Evolutionary Processes and Survival Strategies." *National Centre for the Performing Arts Quarterly Journal* 14(1):26–44.

———. 1991. "'Vatapi Ganapatim': Sculptural, Poetic, and Musical Texts in a Hymn to Ganesa." In *Ganesh: Studies of an Asian God*, ed. Robert L. Brown, 141–169. Albany: State University of New York Press.

Cutler, Norman. 1987. *Songs of Experience: The Poetics of Tamil Devotion*. Bloomington: Indiana University Press.

Day, Charles. 1974 [1891]. *The Music and Musical Instruments of Southern India and the Deccan*. Delhi: B. R. Publishing.

Deva, B. Chaitanya. 1989. *Musical Instruments in Sculpture in Karnataka*. Delhi: Motilal Banarsidass.

Dickey, Sara. 1993. *Cinema and the Urban Poor in South India*. New Delhi: Foundation.

Diksitar, Subbarama. 1963–1983 [1904]. *Sangīta Sampradāya Pradarṣiṇi*. Madras: Music Academy.

Francis, Dyanandan, ed. 1988. *Christian Lyrics and Songs of New Life*, rev. ed. Madras: Christian Literature Society.

Gowrie, Kuppuswamy, and M. Hariharan, eds. 1989. *An Anthology of Indian Music*. Delhi: Sundeep Prakashan. (Articles mostly on Karnatak music.)

Greene, Paul D. 1995. "Cassettes in Culture: Emotion, Politics, and Performance in Rural Tamil Nadu." Ph.D. dissertation, University of Pennsylvania.

———. In press. "Sound Engineering in a Tamil Village; Playing Audio Cassettes as Devotional Performance." *Ethnomusicology* 44.

Groesbeck, Rolf. 1995. "Pedagogy and Performance in 'Tayampaka,' a Genre of Temple Instrumental Music in Kerala, India." Ph.D. dissertation, New York University.

———. 1999a. "'Classical Music,' 'Folk Music,' and the Brahmanical Temple in Kerala, India." *Asian Music* 30(20):87–112.

———. 1999b. "Cultural Constructions of Improvisation in *Tāyampaka*, a Genre of Temple

Instrumental Music in Kerala, India." *Ethnomusicology* 43(1):1–30.

Gurumurthi, Prameela. 1989. "The Evolution of Harikatha." *Sruti* 53:37–39.

Hart, George L. 1975. *The Poems of Ancient Tamil: Their Milieu and Their Ancient Counterparts.* Berkeley: University of California Press.

Higgins, Jon. 1976. "From Prince to Populace: Patronage as a Determinant of Change in South Indian (Karnatak) Music." *Asian Music* 7(2):20–26.

Howard, Wayne, ed. 1988. *Mātrālakṣaṇam: Text, Translation, Extracts from the Commentary, and Notes, Including References to Two Oral Traditions of South India.* New Delhi: Indira Gandhi National Centre for the Arts; Delhi: Motilal Banarsidass.

Jackson, William J. 1991. *Tyagaraja: Life and Lyrics.* Madras: Oxford University Press.

————. 1994. *Tyagaraja and the Renewal of Tradition: Translations and Reflections.* Delhi: Motilal Banarsidass.

————, ed. 1994. *The Power of the Sacred Name: V. Raghavan's Studies on Namasiddhanta and Indian Culture.* New Delhi: India Book Centre.

Janaki, S. S., ed. 1989. *Bibliography of [V. Raghavan's] Writings on Music, Dance.* Madras: Kuppuswami Sastri Institute.

Jayalakshmi, Salem S. 1990. "Tamil Music: A Survey." In *Encyclopedia of Tamil Literature,* Vol. 1, 175–186. Madras: Institute of Asian Studies.

Jayaraman, Lalgudi G. 1986. "The Violin in Carnatic Music." *Kalakshetra Quarterly* 8(1–2):28–34.

Kaufmann, Walter. c. 1976. *The Ragas of South India.* Bloomington: Indiana University Press.

Kassebaum, Gayathri R. 1975. "Gamaka in Alapana Performance in Karnatic Music." M.A. thesis, University of Hawaii.

————. 1987. "Improvisation in Alapana Performance: A Comparative View of Raga Shankarabharana." *Yearbook for Traditional Music* 19:45–64.

————. 1994. "Katha: Six Performance Traditions and Preservations of Group Identity in Karnataka, South India." Ph.D. dissertation, University of Washington, Seattle.

Keuneman, Herbert. 1973. "Traditional Drums of Ceylon." *Arts of Asia* 3(2):28–33.

Khokar, Mohan. NA "Bommalattam (Puppetry)." *Kalakshetra Quarterly* 9(4):23.

————. N.d. "Bhagavata Mela Nataka." *Kalakshetra Quarterly* 9(3):23–25.

————. N.d. "Kuravanchi Natakam." *Kalakshetra Quarterly* 9(3):26–27.

Kulatillake, Cyril de Silva. 1974–1975. "Samudraghosha Metre and the Seepada Styles of Singing in Sri Lanka." *Mitteilungen der Deutschen Gesellschaft für Musik des Orients* 13:39–55.

————. 1976. *A Background to Sinhala Traditional Music of Sri Lanka.* Colombo: Department of Cultural Affairs.

————. 1977. "The Gi Metre in Sinhala Music." *Proceedings of the National Symposium on Traditional Rural Culture of Sri Lanka,* 123–133.

————. 1980. *Metre, Melody, and Rhythm in Sinhala Music.* Sinhala Music Research Bulletin 2. Colombo: Sinhala Music Research Unit, Sri Lanka Broadcasting Corporation.

————. 1982a. "Buddhist Chant in Sri Lanka: Its Structure and Musical Elements." *Jahrbuch für musikalische Volks- und Völkerkunde* 10:20–32.

————. 1982b. *The Vannams in Sinhala Traditional Music.* Colombo: Sangita Paryesana Amsaya, Sri Lanka Buvan Viduli Samsthava.

————. 1984–1985. "Raban-Sellama and Its Music." *Journal of the Royal Asiatic Society (Sri Lanka)* 29:19–32.

————. 1991. *Ethnomusicology, Its Content and Growth; and Ethnomusicological Aspects of Sri Lanka.* Colombo: S. Godage.

Kuppuswamy, Gowri, and M. Hariharan, comps. 1981. *Index of Songs in South Indian Music.* Delhi: B. R. Publishing.

Laade, Wolfgang. 1993–1994. "The Influence of Buddhism on the Singhalese Music of Sri Lanka." *Asian Music* 25(1–2):51–68.

L'Armand, Kathleen, and Adrian L'Armand. 1978. "Music in Madras: The Urbanization of a Cultural Tradition." In *Eight Urban Musical Cultures,* ed. Bruno Nettl, 115–145. Urbana: University of Illinois Press.

McGilvray, Dennis B. 1983. "Paraiyar Drummers of Sri Lanka: Consensus and Constraint in an Untouchable Caste." *American Ethnological Society* 10:97–115.

Mohan, Anuradha. 1994. "Ilaiyaraja: Composer as Phenomenon in Tamil Film Culture." M.A. thesis, Wesleyan University.

Nelson, David P. 1991. "*Mrdangam* Mind: The *Tani Āvartanam* in *Karṇāṭak* Music." Ph.D. dissertation, Wesleyan University.

Nijenhuis, Emmie te. 1987. *Sacred Songs of India: Dikshitar's Cycle of Hymns to the Goddess Kamala.* Winterthur, Switzerland: Amadeus.

Palackal, Joseph J. 1995. "Puttan pāna: A Musical Study." M.A. thesis, Hunter College, City University of New York.

————. 2001. "Christian Music." In *The New Grove Dictionary of Music and Musicians,* 7th ed., ed. Stanley Sadie. London: Macmillan.

Parthasarathy, S. V. 1980. "The Teaching of Music (Tamiz)." *Journal of the Music Academy, Madras* 51:140–146.

Parthasarathy, T. S. 1975. "Contemporaries and Disciples of Sri Muthuswami Dikshitar." *Birth Bi-Centenary of Sri Muthuswami Dikshitar.* Special issue of *Journal of the Indian Musicological Society* 6(3):28–32. (Baroda: Indian Musicological Society.)

————. 1982. *Music Composers of India.* Madras: C. F. Ramaswami Aiyar Foundation.

Pattabhi Raman, N. 1994. "Carnatic Music during the Decade: How It Was Ten Years Ago." *Sruti* 125(July):21–37. Excerpt from a 6-part series from *Sruti* 3 (December 1983).

Pesch, Ludwig. 1999. *The Illustrated Companion to South Indian Classical Music.* Delhi: Oxford University Press.

Peterson, Indira V. 1989. *Poems to Siva: The Hymns of the Tamil Saints.* Princeton, N.J.: Princeton University Press.

Premeela, M. N.d. "Harikatha—A Composite Art Form." *Kalakshetra Quarterly* 9(4):24.

Raghavan, A. Srinivasa. N.d. "Rama Nataka Kirtanas." *Kalakshetra Quarterly* 6(2):22–24.

Raghavan, V. 1979. *The Great Integrators: The Singer-Saints of India.* New Delhi: Ministry of Information, Government of India.

————, ed. 1975. *Muttuswami Dikshitar.* Special issue (September) of *National Center for the Performing Arts Quarterly Journal.* (Bombay: National Centre for the Performing Arts.)

Raghavan, V., and C. Ramanujacari. 1981. *The Spiritual Heritage of Tyāgarāja,* Madras: Sri Ramakrishna Math.

Rajagopalan, L. S. 1967. "Thayambaka: Laya Vinyasa." *Journal of the Madras Music Academy* 38:83–102.

————. 1974. "Folk Musical Instruments of Kerala." *Sangeet Natak Academy Journal* 33:40–55.

Rajagopalan, L. S., and Wayne Howard. 1989. "A Report on the Prācheena Kauthuma Sāmaveda of Palghat." *Journal of the Indian Musicological Society* 20(1–2):5–16.

Rajagopalan, N. 1990. *A Garland (Biographical Dictionary of Carnatic Composers and Musicians).* Bombay: Bharatiya Vidya Bhavan.

Ramachandran, Anandhi. 1983. "Oduvars: A Hoary Tradition of Hymn Singing." *Sruti* 2(November):12–13.

Raman, V. P. 1966. "The Music of the Ancient Tamils." *Tamil Culture* 12:203–21. (Reprinted: 1979. In *Readings on Indian Music,* ed. Gowrie Kuppuswamy and M. Hariharan, 80–99. Trivandrum: College Book House.)

Ramanathan, S. 1960. "A Survey of the Traditions of Music, Dance, and Drama in the Madras State." *Bulletin of the Institute of Traditional Cultures, Madras* 2:214–221.

Ramanathan, Subrahmanya. 1974. "Music in Cilappatikaaram." Ph.D. dissertation, Wesleyan University.

Ramanujachari, C., and V. Raghavan. 1981. *The Spiritual Heritage of Tyagaraja,* 3rd ed. Madras: Ramakrishna Matha.

Ramanujan, A. K. 1981. *Hymns for the Drowning.* Princeton, N.J.: Princeton University Press.

Rangaramanuja Ayyangar, R. 1972. *History of South Indian (Carnatic) Music: From Vedic Times to the Present.* Madras: Author.

Ravikiran, Chitravina N. 1997. *Appreciating Carnatic Music.* Madras: Ganesh.

Roberts, Michael. 1990. "Noise as a Cultural Struggle: Tom-Tom Beating, the British, and Communal Disturbances in Sri Lanka, 1880s–1930s." In *Mirrors of Violence: Communities, Riots, and Survivors in South Asia,* ed. Veena Das,

240–285. Delhi and New York: Oxford University Press.

Roghair, Gene H. 1982. *The Epic of Palnāḍu: A Study and Translation of Palnāṭi Vīrula Katha.* Oxford: Clarendon.

Ross, Israel J. 1978. "Cross-Cultural Dynamics in Musical Traditions: The Music of the Jews of Cochin." *Musica Judaica* 2(1):51–72.

———. 1979. "Ritual and Music in South India: Syrian Christian Liturgical Music in Kerala." *Asian Music* 11(1):80–98.

Rothenberg, Jerome, ed. 1968. *Technicians of the Sacred.* New York: Doubleday.

Sambamurthy, Pichu. 1952–1971. *A Dictionary of South Indian Music and Musicians.* 3 vols. Madras: Indian Music.

———. 1962–1970. *Great Composers.* 2 vols. Madras: Indian Music.

———. 1963–1973. *South Indian Music.* 6 vols. Madras: Indian Music.

———. 1967. *The Flute.* Madras: Indian Music.

Sankaran, Trichy. 1975. "The Nagaswaram Tradition Systematised by Ramaswami Dikshitar." In *Birth Bi-Centenary of Sri Muthuswami Dikshitar.* Special issue of *Journal of the Indian Musicological Society* 6(3):16–21. (Baroda: Indian Musicological Society.)

———. 1984. "Bangalore Nagaratnammal: A Devadasi True." *Sruti* 4:14–16.

———. 1989. "Fiddle Govindaswamy Pillai (1879–1931): A Prince among Musicians." *Sruti* 55:19–25.

———. 1994. *The Rhythmic Principles and Practice of South Indian Drumming.* Toronto: Lalith.

Sarma, Harihara. 1969. *The Art of Mridhangam.* Madras: Sri Jaya Ganesh Talavadya Vidyalaya.

Sastri, S. Subrahmanya, ed. 1937. *The Mela-Raga-Malika of Maha Vaidyanatha Sivan* (Iyer). Adyar: Adyar Library.

Seetha, S. 1981. *Tanjore as a Seat of Music during the Seventeenth, Eighteenth, and Nineteenth Centuries.* Madras: University of Madras.

Seneviratna, Anuradha. 1975. "Musical Rituals of the *Dalada Maligawa* Pertaining to the Temple of the Sacred Tooth." *Sangeet Natak* 36:21–42.

———. 1979. "*Pañcatūrya Nāda* and the *Hēwisi Pūjā.*" *Ethnomusicology* 23(1):49–56.

———. 1981. "Some Notes on 'Gaman Hewisi' (March Beats): An Aspect of Sinhala Drum Music of Sri Lanka." *Sangeet Natak* 61–62:5–13.

Shankar, L. 1974. "The Art of Violin Accompaniment in South Indian Classical Music." Ph.D. dissertation, Wesleyan University.

Sheeran, Anne. 1997. "White Noise: European Modernity, Sinhala Musical Nationalism, and the Practice of a Creole Popular Music in Modern Sri Lanka." Ph.D. dissertation, University of Washington, Seattle.

Simpson, Bob. 1985. "Ritual Tradition and Performance: The Berava Caste of Southern Sri Lanka." Ph.D. dissertation, University of Durham.

———. 1997. "Possession, Dispossession, and the Social Distribution of Knowledge among Sri Lankan Ritual Specialists." *Journal of the Royal Anthropological Institute* (N.S.) 3:43–59.

Singer, Milton. 1980 [1972]. "The *Rādhā Krishna Bhajanas* of Madras City." In *When a Great Tradition Modernizes: An Anthropological Approach to Indian Civilization,* 199–249. Chicago: University of Chicago Press; Midway Reprint.

Siromoney, Gift. N.d. "Musical Instruments from Pallava Sculpture." *Kalakshetra Quarterly* 2(4):11–20.

Spector, Johanna. 1972. "Shingli Tunes of the Cochin Jews." *Asian Music* 3(2):23–28.

Srinivas, M. N. 1943–1944. "Some Tamil Folksongs," Parts 1 and 2. *Journal of the University of Bombay* 12(1, 4, July 1943):48–80 and (January 1944): 6–86. (Reprint.)

Srinivasa Iyer, P. S. 1937. *Articles on Indian Music.* Tirupapuliyur: Kamala.

Srinivasa Rao, Sandyavandanam. 1980. "Music Teaching—Under Gurukula System and in Recognised Institutions." *Journal of the Music Academy, Madras* 51:133–139.

Srinivasan, R., ed. *Professor P. Sambamurti Silver Jubilee Commemoration Volume.* Chennai: Prof. P. Sambamurti Silver Jubilee Celebration Committee.

Sruti: South Indian Classical Music and Dance Monthly. Madras: P. N. Sundaresan.

Staal, J. Fritz. 1961. *Nambudiri Veda Recitation.* The Hague: Mouton.

Subramaniam, Karaikudi S. 1985. "An Introduction to the Vina." *Asian Music* 16(2):7–82.

Subramaniam, V. 1990. "Annamalai Reddiar's Kavadichindu: Beautiful Songs for Dance—but Neglected." *Sruti* 67:36–38.

Terada, Yoshitaka. 1992. "Multiple Interpretations of a Charismatic Individual: The Case of the Great *Nagasvaram* Musician T. N. Rajarattinam Pillai." Ph.D. dissertation, Wesleyan University.

Vasantha, Kumara. 1993. *Symphony of the Temple Drums: Buddhist Symbolism through Ritual Art.* Kandy: Vanantha Kumara.

Vedavalli, M. B. 1995. *Ragam Tanam Pallavi: Their Evolution, Structure, and Exposition.* Bangalore: M. R. J.

Venkitasubramonia Iyer, S. 1969. "Some Rare Talas in Kerala Music." *Sangeet Natak* 14:5–11.

———. 1975. *Swati Tirunal and His Music.* Trivandrum: College Book House.

Vidya, S. 1948. *Kritis of Syama Sastri,* Vol. 3. Madras: C. S. Iyer.

Viswanathan, Tanjore. 1975. "*Rāga Ālāpana* in South Indian Music." Ph.D. dissertation, Wesleyan University.

———. 1977. "The Analysis of *Rāga Ālāpana* in South Indian Music." *Asian Music* 9(1):13–71.

Wadley, Susan. 1986. "The Katha of Sakat: Two Tellings." In *Another Harmony: New Essays on the Folklore of India,* ed. Stuart H. Blackburn and A. K. Ramanujan, 195–232. Berkeley: University of California Press.

Walcott, Ronald. 1978. "*Kohomba Kankariya:* An Ethnomusicological Study." Ph.D. dissertation, University of Sri Lanka.

Wolf, Richard. 1997. "Of God and Death: Music in Ritual and Everyday Life. A Musical Ethnography of the Kotas of South India." Ph.D, dissertation, University of Illinois at Urbana-Champaign.

DANCE AND DRAMA

Allen, Matthew. 1997. "Rewriting the Script for South Indian Dance." *TDR (The Drama Review)* 41(13):63–100.

Amunugama, Sarath. 1978. "John de Silva and the Nationalist Theatre." *Ceylon Historical Journal* 25(1–4):285–304.

Arnold, Alison. 1998. "Film Musicals: Bollywood Film Musicals." *The International Encyclopedia of Dance.* Oxford: Oxford University Press.

Arudra. 1986a. "Bhagavata Mela: The Telugu Heritage of Tamil Nadu." *Sruti* 22:18–24.

———. 1986b. "The Resurrection of the Bhagavata Mela." *Sruti* 22:25–28.

———. 1986–1987. "The Transformation of a Traditional Dance." *Sruti* 27–28:17–36.

Ashley, Wayne. 1993. "Recodings: Ritual, Theatre, and Political Display in Kerala State, South India." Ph.D. dissertation, New York University.

Ashton, Martha B., and Bruce Christie. 1977. *Yakshagana: A Dance Drama of India.* New Delhi: Abhinav.

Ashton-Sikora, Martha. Forthcoming. "*Yakṣā-gāna.*" In *South Asian Folklore: An Encyclopedia,* ed. Peter J. Claus and Margaret Mills. New York: Garland.

Bhatt, Haridas. 1983. "Transmission of Yakshagana Art through the Generations." In *Dance and Music in South Asian Drama,* ed. Richard Emmert et al., 180–187. Tôkyô: Japan Foundation.

Bruin, Hanne de. 1994. "*Kaṭṭaikkūttu:* The Flexibility of a South Indian Theatre Tradition." Ph.D. dissertation, University of Leiden.

Caldwell, Sarah. 1995. "Oh Terrifying Mother: The Mudiyettu Ritual Drama of Kerala, South India." Ph.D. dissertation, University of California, Berkeley.

Chandrasekharan, K. N.d. "Kuravanji Dance of Kalakshetra." *Kalakshetra Quarterly* 3(4):7–14.

Dance and Music in South Asian Drama: Chhau, Mahakali Pyakhan, and Yakshagana. 1983. Report of Asian Traditional Performing Arts (ATPA) III, 1981. Tôkyô: Japan Foundation.

Desai, Sudha. 1972. *Bhavai: A Medieval Form of Ancient Indian Dramatic Art (Natya) as Prevalent in Gujarat.* Ahmedabad: Gujarat University Press.

De Zoete, Beryl. 1957. *Dance and Magic Drama in Ceylon.* London: Faber and Faber.

Falk Dances of India. 1956. Publications Division, Ministry of Information and Broadcasting, Government of India.

Frasca, Richard A. 1990. *The Theatre of the Mahābhārata: Terukkūttu Performances in South India.* Honolulu: University of Hawaii Press.

Freeman, John Richardson, Jr. 1991. "Purity and Violence: Sacred Power in the Teyyam Worship of Malabar." Ph.D. dissertation, University of Pennsylvania.

Gaston, Anne-Marie. 1991. "Dance and the Hindu Woman: Bharata Natyam Reritualized." In *Roles and Rituals for Hindu Women,* ed. Julia Leslie, 149–173. London: Pinter.

———. 1996. *Bharata Nāṭam: From Temple to Theatre.* Delhi: Motilal Banarsidass.

Goonatilleka, M. H. 1982. "Drum Dictates the Tune in Kolam of Sri Lanka." *Sangeet Natak* 63:6–14.

———. 1984. *Nadagama, the First Sri Lankan Theatre.* Delhi: Sri Satguru.

Gunawardana, A. J. 1976. *Theatre in Sri Lanka.* Colombo: Department of Cultural Affairs, Government of Sri Lanka.

Hansen, Kathryn. 1992. *Grounds for Play: The Nautanki Theatre of North India.* Berkeley: University of California Press.

Higgins, Jon B. 1993. *The Music of Bharata Nāṭyam.* New Delhi: Oxford and IBH.

Jogan, Shankar. 1990. *Devadasi Cult: A Sociological Analysis.* New Delhi: Ashish.

Jones, Betty True. 1983. "Kathakali Dance-Drama: An Historical Perspective." In *The Performing Arts in India: Essays on Music, Dance, and Drama,* ed. Bonnie Wade, 14–44. Berkeley: University of California Center for South and Southeast Asian Studies.

Jones, Betty True, and Clifford Jones. 1970. *Kathakali: An Introduction to the Dance-Drama of Kerala.* New York and San Francisco: American Society for Eastern Arts.

Jones, Clifford. 1982. "Kālam Ezuttu: Art and Ritual in Kerala." In *Religious Festivals in South India and Sri Lanka,* ed. Guy Welbon and Glenn Yocum, 269–294. New Delhi: Manohar.

Kambar, Chandrasekhar. 1972. "Ritual in Kannada Folk Theatre." *Sangeet Natak* 25:5–22.

Karanth, Shivarama K. 1975. *Yakshagana.* Mysore: University of Mysore Press.

Kersenboom, Saskia. 1995. *Word, Sound, Image: The Life of the Tamil Text.* Oxford: Washington, Berg.

———. 1996 [1987]. *Nityasumangali, Devadasī Tradition in South India,* 2nd ed. Delhi: Motilal Banarsidass.

Khokar, Mohan. 1987. *Dancing for Themselves: Folk, Tribal, and Ritual Dance of India.* New Delhi: Himalayan.

Kliger, George, ed. 1993. *Bharata Natyam in Cultural Perspective.* New Delhi: Manohar/American Institute of Indian Studies.

Kuppuswamy, Gowri, and M. Hariharan. 1982. *Bharatanatya in Indian Music.* New Delhi: Cosmo.

Makulloluwa, W. B. 1976. *Dances of Sri Lanka.* Colombo: Department of Cultural Affairs, Government of Sri Lanka.

Marglin, Frédérique. 1985. *Wives of the God-King: The Rituals of the Devadasis of Puri.* Oxford: Oxford University Press.

Massey, Reginald, and Jamila Massey. 1989. *The Dances of India: A General Survey and Dancers' Guide.* London: Tricolour.

Misra, Susheela. 1989. *Invitation to Indian Dances.* New Delhi: Gulab Vazirani for Arnold (India).

Mukhopadhyay, Durgadas, ed. 1978. *Lesser Known Forms of Performing Arts in India.* New Delhi: Sterling.

Nambiar, Balan. c. 1981. "Gods and Ghosts, *Teyyam* and *Bhūtam* Rituals." *Marg* 34(3):63–75.

Nanda, Serena. 1990. *Neither Man nor Woman: The Hijras of India.* Belmont, Calif.: Wadsworth.

Neff, Deborah. 1995. "Fertility and Power in Kerala Serpent Ritual (India)." Ph.D. dissertation, University of Wisconsin.

Nixon, Michael. 1988. "Nantanār Carattiram in Performance: An Item in the Tamil Musical-Dramatic Repertoire." M.A. thesis, Wesleyan University.

Omchery, Leela. 1969. "The Music of Kerala: A Study." *Sangeet Natak* 14:12–23.

Oster, Akos. 1980. *The Play of the Gods: Locality, Ideology, Structure, and Time in the Festivals of a Bengali Town.* Chicago: University of Chicago Press.

Pani, Jiwan. 1992. *Sonal Mansingh: Contribution to Odissi Dance.* Delhi: Motilal Banarsidass.

Patnaik, D. N. 1971. *Odissi Dance.* Bhubaneswar: Orissa Sangeet Natak Akademi.

Peiris, Edmund. 1974. "The Origin and Development of Simhala Nadagam." *Journal of the Royal Asiatic Society (Sri Lanka)* 18(N.S.):27–40.

Pertold, Otakar. 1973. *The Ceremonial Dances of the Sinhalese: An Inquiry into Sinhalese Folk Religion.* Dehiwala: Tisara Prakasakayo.

Perumal, A. N. 1981. *Tamil Drama: Origin and Development.* Madras: International Institute of Tamil Studies.

Radhakrishnan, N., ed. 1982. *The Beating Drum and the Dancing Feet: An Introduction to Indian Folk Performing Arts.* Kerala: National Centre for Development Education and Performing Arts.

Raghavan, M. D. 1967. *Sinhala Natum: Dances of the Sinhalese.* Colombo: M. D. Gunasena.

Rana, Kironmoy. 1980. *Bengali Theatre.* New Delhi: National Book Trust. (Reprint.)

Raman, Indu. 1995. "Vanishing Traditions: Bhagavatha Mela Natakams of Melattur." *Journal of the Indian Musicological Society* 26:52–64.

Ramasamy, Thulasi. 1987. *Tamil Yakṣagaanas.* Madurai: Vizhikal.

Ramasubramaniam, V. N.d. "Kamban's Epic as Shadow Play." *Kalakshetra Quarterly* 3(4):25–34.

Ranade, Ashok D. 1986. *Stage Music of Maharashtra.* New Delhi: Sangeet Natak Akademi.

Rangacharya, Adya. 1971. *The Indian Theatre.* New Delhi: National Book Trust.

Rao, H. Gopala. 1983. "Rhythm and Drums in Badagatittu Yakshagana Dance-Drama." In *Dance and Music in South Asian Drama,* ed. Richard Emmert et al., 188–204. Tokyo: Japan Foundation.

Reed, Susan. 1991. "The Transformation of Ritual and Dance in Sri Lanka: *Kohomha Kankariya* and the Kandyan Dance." Ph.D. dissertation, Brown University.

Richmond, Farley P., Darius L. Swann, and Phillip B. Zarrilli, eds. 1990. *Indian Theatre: Traditions of Performance.* Honolulu: University of Hawaii Press.

Samson, Leela. 1987. *Rhythm in Joy: Classical Indian Dance Traditions.* New Delhi: Lustre Press Private.

Sarachchandra, E. R. 1966. *The Folk Drama of Ceylon,* 2nd ed. Sri Lanka: Department of Cultural Affairs.

Seneviratna, Anuradha. 1984. *Traditional Dance of Sri Lanka.* Colombo: Central Cultural Fund, Ministry of Cultural Affairs.

Srampickal, Jacob. 1994. *Voice to the Voiceless: The Power of People's Theatre in India.* Delhi: Motilal Banarsidass.

Tarlekar, T. G. 1991. *Studies in the Natyasastra,* 2nd ed. Delhi: Motilal Banarsidass.

Varadpande, M. L. 1983. *Religion and Theatre.* New Delhi: Abhinav.

Vatsyayan, Kapila. 1974. *Indian Classical Dance.* New Delhi: Ministry of Information and Broadcasting.

———. 1980a. "India, 7: Dance." In *The New Grove Dictionary of Music and Musicians,* ed. Stanley Sadie. London: Macmillan.

———. 1980b. *Traditional Indian Theatre: Multiple Streams.* New Delhi: National Book Trust.

———. 1982. *Dance in Indian Painting.* Atlantic Highlands, N.J.: Humanities.

———. 1987 [1976]. "The Deccan, Eastern and Western Ghats." In *Traditions of Indian Folk Dance,* 2nd ed., 303–368. New Delhi: Clarion.

———. 1996. *Bharata, The Nāṭyāśtra.* New Delhi: Sahitya Akademi.

Venu, G., and Nirmala Paniker. 1983. *Mohiniyattam.* Trivandrum: G. Venu.

Zarrilli, Phillip. 1984. *The Kathakali Complex: Actor, Performance, and Structure.* New Delhi: Abhinav.

Zarrilli, Phillip, Farley Richmond, and Darius Swann, eds. 1990. *Indian Theater: Traditions of Performance.* Honolulu: University of Hawaii Press.

SOUTH ASIAN DIASPORA

Arnold, Alison. 1985. "Aspects of Asian Indian Musical Life in North America." *Selected Reports in Ethnomusicology* 6:25–38.

Arya, Usharbudh. 1968. *Ritual Songs and Folksongs of the Hindus of Surinam.* Leiden: Brill.

Baily, John. 1990. "Qawwali in Bradford: Traditional Music in a Muslim Community." In *Black Music in Britain*, ed. Paul Oliver, 153–165. Milton Keynes: Open University Press.

———. 1995. "The Role of Music in Three British Muslim Communities." *Diaspora* 4(1):77–88.

Baily, John, and Paul Oliver, eds. 1988. *Popular Music* 7(2). ("South Asia and the West" issue.)

Bake, Arnold. 1953. "The Impact of Western Music on the Indian Musical System." *Journal of the International Folk Music Council* 5:57–60.

Banerji, Sabita. 1988. "Ghazals to Bhangra in Great Britain." In *Popular Music* 7(2):207–213.

Banerji, Sabita, and Gerd Baumann. 1990. "Bhangra 1984–1988: Fusion and Professionalization in a Genre of South Asian Dance Music." In *Black Music in Britain*, ed. Paul Oliver, 137–152. Milton Keynes: Open University Press.

Baumann, Gerd. 1990. "The Re-Invention of *Bhangra*: Social Change and Aesthetic Shifts in a Punjabi Music in Britain." *World of Music* 32(2):81–97.

Brenneis, Donald. 1983. "The Emerging Soloist: Kavvali in Bhatgaon." *Asian Folklore Studies* 42:67–80.

———. 1985. "Passion and Performance in Fiji Indian Vernacular Song." *Ethnomusicology* 29:397–408.

———. 1987. "Performing Passions: Aesthetics and Politics in an Occasionally Egalitarian Community." *American Ethnologist* 14:236–250.

———. 1991. "Aesthetics, Performance, and the Enactment of Tradition in a Fiji Indian Community." In *Gender, Genre, and Power in South Asian Expressive Traditions*, ed. Arjun Appadurai, Margaret Mills, and Frank Korom, 362–378. Philadelphia: University of Pennsylvania Press.

Brenneis, Donald, and Ram Padarath. 1975. "'About Those Scoundrels I'll Let Everyone Know': Challenge Singing in a Fiji Indian Community." *Journal of American Folklore* 88:283–291.

Chaudenson, Robert, et al. 1981. "Musiques, chansons, et danses." In *Encyclopédie de La Réunion*, Vol. 5, 75–107. St. Denis, La Réunion: Livres Réunion.

Desroches, Monique. 1996. *Tambours des dieux.* Montreal: Harmattan.

Desroches, Monique, and Jean Benoist. 1997. "Musiques, cultes, et société indienne à La Réunion." *Anthropologie et Sociétés* 21(1):39–52.

DesRosiers, Brigitte. 1993. "Analyse de la relation entre les discours sur la musique et les stratégies identitaires à l'île de La Réunion." M.A. thesis, University of Montreal.

———. 1992. "Île de La Réunion: Musiques et identité." *Canadian Folk Music Journal* 20:47–54.

Erdman, Joan. 1985. "Today and the Good Old Days: South Asian Music and Dance Performances in Chicago." *Selected Reports in Ethnomusicology* 6:39–58.

Farrell, Gerry. 1994. *South Asian Music Teaching in Change.* London: David Fulton.

Geldard [Arnold], Alison. 1981. "Music and Musical Performance among the East Indians in Chicago." M.M. thesis, University of Illinois at Urbana-Champaign.

Jackson, Melveen B. 1988. "An Introduction to the History of Music amongst Indian South Africans in Natal, 1860–1948: Towards a Politico-Cultural Understanding." M.Mus. thesis, Natal University, South Africa.

Jairazbhoy, Nazir. 1986. "Asian-American Music, 1: Introduction; 5: South Asian." In *The New Grove Dictionary of American Music*, ed. H. Wiley Hitchcock and Stanley Sadie. London: Macmillan.

Klass, Morton. 1991. *Singing with Sai Baba: The Politics of Revitalization in Trinidad.* Boulder, Colo.: Westview.

Manuel, Peter. 1997. "Music, Identity, and Images of India in the Indo-Caribbean Diaspora." *Asian Music* 29(1):17–35.

Middlebrook, Joyce. 1991. "Customs and Women's Wedding Songs in Two Northern California Sikh Communities." M.A. thesis, California State University, Sacramento.

Myers, Helen. 1980. "Trinidad and Tobago." In *The New Grove Dictionary of Music and Musicians*, ed. Stanley Sadie. London: Macmillan.

———. 1983 [1978]. "The Process of Change in Trinidad East Indian Music." In *Essays in Musicology*, ed. R. C. Mehta. Bombay and Baroda: Indian Musicological Society.

———. 1997. *Music of Hindu Trinidad, Songs from the India Diaspora.* Chicago: University of Chicago Press.

Neuman, Daniel. 1984. "The Ecology of Indian Music in North America." *Bansuri* 1:9–15.

Pillay, Jayendran. 1988. "Teaching South Indian Music Abroad: Case Studies from South Africa and North America." M.A. thesis, Wesleyan University.

———. 1994a. "Music, Ritual, and Identity among Hindu South Africans." Ph.D. dissertation, Wesleyan University.

———. 1994b. "Indian Music in the Indian School in South Africa: The Use of Cultural Forms as a Political Tool." *Ethnomusicology* 38(2):281–301.

Qureshi, Regula. 1972. "Ethnomusicological Research among Canadian Communities of Arab and East Indian Origin." *Ethnomusicology* 16:381–396.

Thompson, Gordon. 1985. "Songs in Circles: Gujaratis in America." In *1985 Festival of American Folklife Program Book.* Washington, D.C.: Smithsonian Institution.

Thompson, Gordon, and Medha Yodh. 1985. "*Garbā* and the Gujaratis of Southern California." *Selected Reports in Ethnomusicology* 6:59–79.

Upadhyaya, Hari S. 1988. *Bhojpuri Folksongs from Ballia.* Atlanta: Indian Enterprises.

Wade, Bonnie C. 1978. "Indian Classical Music in North America: Cultural Give and Take." *Contributions to Asian Studies* 12:29–39.

Recordings of South Asian Music

GENERAL

Encyclopedia of Musical Instruments. N.d. OCD 7037W-E. Distributed by Multicultural Media: http://www.worldmusicstore.com. CD-ROM for Windows only. (Covers Western and world instruments; more than 120 minutes of audio and video performances.)

The Four Vedas. 1969. Recorded by Fritz Staal. Asch Mankind Series AHM 4126. LP disk.

The Language of Rhythm: Drumming from North and South India. N.d. Produced by Bob Haddad; notes by David Nelson. Music of the World MOW 150. 2 compact disks. (Features Bikram Ghosh, tabla; and Trichy Sankaran, mridangam.)

L. Subramaniam and Bismillah Khan—Live in Geneva. 1991. Audiorec ACCD 1020. Compact disk. (Instrumental duet with L. Subramaniam; Karnatak, violin; and Bismillah Khan, Hindustani *shahnai*.)

A Musical Anthology of the Orient: India I. 1965. Recorded by Alain Daniélou. Bärenreiter Musicaphon BM 30 L 2006. LP disk.

A Musical Journey through India 1963–1964. 1988. Recordings by Nazir A. Jairazbhoy. Los Angeles: UCLA Ethnomusicology Publications. 3 audiocassettes and booklet.

Pandit Bhimsen Joshi and Balamurali Krishna Live. 1991. Navras Records NRCD 0022. Compact disk. (Duet with the Hindustani vocalist Bhimsen Joshi and the Karnatak vocalist Balamurali Krishna, and Shashikant Muley, tabla.

Ragas Darbari Kanada, Malkauns/Hindolam, and Bhairavi.)

Rough Guide to the Music of India and Pakistan. N.d. Distributed by Multicultural Media WMNW-1008. Compact disk. (Artists include Ali Akbar Khan, Bismillah Khan, Amjad Ali Khan, Shiv Kumar Sharma, Hariprasad Chaurasia, the Sabri Brothers, Nusrat Fateh Ali Khan, and Purna Das Bard.)

Vintage Music from India: Early Twentieth Century Classical and Light-Classical Music. 1993. Produced by Richard Spottswood, with notes by Peter Manuel. Rounder Records CD 1083. Compact disk.

MUSIC IN NORTHERN AREAS

Afghanistan: On Marco Polo's Road—The Musicians of Kunduz and Faizabad. 1997. Produced by Stephen McArthur. Music of the Earth Series. Multicultural Media MCM 3003. Compact disk.

Afghānistān: Musique instrumentale et chant. 1990. Recorded by Hubert de Fraysseix, notes by George Wen. Sunset-France, Playa Sound PS 65058. Compact disk.

Afghanistan: Ritchak, Zer-Barhali, Toolah, Rabab, Tumbur, Tabla. 1990. Playa Sound PS 65058. Compact disk.

Afghanistan: Rubab et Dutâr. 1995. Performed by Ustad Rahim Khushnawaz, rubab; Gada Mohammad, dutar; and Azim Hassanpur, tabla. Notes by John Baily. Ocora C 560080. Compact disk.

Afghanistan: The Rubāb of Herat—Mohammad Rahim Khushnawaz. 1993. Recorded by John Baily. VDE-Gallo AIMP XXV. Compact disk with accompanying notes.

Alisha: Madonna—Jadoo. 1989. Gramophone Company of India PSLP 5111. Compact disk. ("Indipop" artist.)

Amdo: Tibetan Monastery of Labrang. N.d. Distributed by Multicultural Media C-56101. Compact disk.

Amjad Ali Khan—Touch of Class. 1990. Audiorec ACCD 1009. Compact disk. (Hindustani sarod performance, ragas Desh and Hemavati, and two bhajans, with Sukhvinder Singh, tabla.)

Ananya: Usiad Amir Khan—Navras Nav-Ratna: The Great Masters. N.d. Navras 0091/92. 2 compact disks. (Khyal vocal performance of ragas Yaman, Hansadhwani, Puriya, and Abhogi. Live performance recorded c. 1965.)

Anindo and His Tabla: Anindo Chatterjee. 1992. Audiorec ACCD 1016–1017. Compact disk. (Tabla solos in tintal, dhamar, pancham sawari, and ektal, with Ramesh Mishra, sarangi.)

Anthology of World Music: North Indian Classical Music. N.d. Multicultural Media 5101–5104. 4 compact disks with a 40-page booklet. (Original UNESCO LP recordings digitally transferred to CD.)

Anup Jalota—In Classical Mood. 1995. Navras Records NRCD 0055. Compact disk. (The ghazal singer Anup Jalota performs three bhajans in ragas Yaman, Malkauns, and Gurjari Todi, with tabla, guitar, and santur accompaniment.)

Artistic Sound of Sarod: Ali Akbar Khan. N.d. Chhanda Dhara 3386. Compact disk. (Hindustani sarod performance of raga Basant Mukhari with Jogia.)

Ashit Desai—Songs of Narsinh Mehta, Vols. 1–3. 1996. Navras Records NRCD 0062–0064. 3 compact disks. (Gujarati devotional songs. Song texts and descriptions in Gujarati only.)

Ashit Desai—Jai Jai Srinathji. 1995. Navras Records NRCD 0069. Compact disk. (Gujarati devotional songs performed by Lata Mangeshkar, Jagjit Singh, Anup Jalota, and others.)

Baloutchistan: Musiques d'extase et de guérison/ Baloutchistan: Ecstasy and Healing Musics. 1992. Recorded and with notes by Jean During. Ocora Radio France C 580017/18. 2 compact disks.

Bardes de l'Himalaya: Népal [et] Inde—Épopées et musiques de transe/Bards of the Himalayas: Nepal [and] India—Epics and Trance Music. 1997. Recorded and with notes by Frank Bernède. Chant du Monde CNR 274 1080. Compact disk.

The Best of Shakti. N.d. Moment Records MRCD 1011. Compact disk. (Compilation of pieces from three albums, 1975–1977, by the fusion group Shakti: John McLauglin, Shankar, Zakir Hussain, and T. H. Vinayakram.)

Bhajan Lal Sopori—A World of String and Sound. 1993. Academy of Indian Music AIMCD 003. Compact disk. (Santur performance of ragas Ahir Lalit, Marwa, and Mishra Kafi, with Mohammad Akram Khan, tabla.)

Brilliancy and Oldest Tradition: Tabla Solo and Duet (with Kumar Bose). 1993. Kishan Maharaj. Chhanda Dhara SNCD 70493. Compact disk.

Buddhadev Das Gupta, Sarod: Morning Concert. 1989. Raga Records 206. Compact disk. (Hindustani sarod performance of raga Ahir Bhairav, with Anand Gopal Bandopdhyay, tabla.)

Captivating Melodies of Sitar: Ustad Vilayat Khan. N.d. Raga Mian Ki Todi. Produced by Rangasami Parthasarathy. Oriental Records CD 120. Compact disk.

Chant the Names of God: Village Music of the Bhojpuri-Speaking Area of India. 1981. Recorded by Edward O. Henry. Rounder Records 5008. LP disk.

Chants in Praise of Krishna. 1990. Recorded in Dwarikadhish Temple, Mathura, India. JVC World Sounds JVC VICG 5034. Compact disk.

Classical Music of North India: Sitar and Tabla, 1. N.d. King World Music Library 5111. Compact disk. (Manilal Nag, sitar, performs raga Suha Kanada.)

The Dagar Brothers: Rag Kambhoji. 1989. Produced by Bob Haddad. Music of the World CDT-114. Compact disk. (Vocal dhrupad performance.)

Dagar Brothers: Raga Miyan ki Todi. 1988. Jecklin Disco JD628-2. Compact disk. (Hindustani vocal dhrupad performance.)

The Day, the Night, the Dawn, the Dusk: Nusrat Fateh Ali Khan. N.d. Shanachie 64032. Compact disk. (Qawwali performance.)

Dhrupad: Vocal Art of Hindustan. 1990. Dagar Brothers. JVC World Sounds VICG 5032-2. Compact disk.

The Emperor of Sarod: Live, Vol. 1, *Ali Akbar Khan.* N.d. Chhanda Dhara 71090. Compact disk. (Performance of raga Bageswari Kanada.)

Evergreen Hits from Old Films. 1994. Gramophone Company of India. PMLP 5831. Compact disk. (Songs from Hindi films, 1936–1949.)

Festival of India: A Hindustani Sampler. N.d. Produced by Bob Haddad. Music of the World MOW 121. Compact disk. (Artists include Sultan Khan, *sāraṅgī*; V. G. Jog, violin; G. S. Sachdev, South Indian flute; Purna Das Baul, Bengali folk ensemble; and the Dagar Brothers, dhrupad vocal music.)

Folk Music of Nepal. 1994. World Music Library 74. Seven Seas/King Records KICC-5174. Compact disk. (Includes Gaine musicians, *mādal* drumming, and popular music.)

Folk Music of Uttar Pradesh, India. 1991. Recorded by Laxmi Tewari. International Institute for Comparative Music Studies/Musicaphon BM 55802 ADD. Compact disk.

Flutes of Rajasthan. 1989. Recorded and with notes by Geneviève Dournon; produced by CNRS/Musée de l'Homme. Chant du Monde LDX 274645. Compact disk.

Gangubai Hangal: The Voice of Tradition. N.d. Wergo (Welt Musik) SM 1501. Compact disk. (Hindustani khyal performance of ragas Shuddha Kalyan, Abhogi, and Basanta.)

Gauhar Jan—Malka Jan. 1994. Gramophone Company of India. CMC 882517/18. 2 compact disks. (Historical recordings of Hindustani vocal music by Gauhar Jan and Malka Jan from 1902 to 1907.)

Gavana—Goa: A viagem dos sons/The Journey of Sounds. 1998. Accompanying booklet by Susana Sardo. Tradisom VSO1. Compact disk. (Music of the Goan Catholic community.)

Ghalib—Portrait of a Genius: A Ghalib Centenary Presentation, Ghazal. Begum Akhtar and

Mohammed Rafi. 1968. Gramophone Company of India. ECSD 2404. LP disk.

Ghazals. 1991. Music India CDNF 154. Compact disk. (Begum Akhtar sings ghazals.)

Girija Devi. 1989. Moment Records MRCD 1004. Compact disk. (Live performance of the Hindustani vocalist Girija Devi, with Zakir Hussain, tabla. Khyal in raga Puriya Kalyan, tappa, and thumri.)

Gopal Krishnan: Dhrupad and Khyal. N.d. Multicultural Media C-560078. Compact disk. (Three ragas performed on *vicitra vīṇā.*)

The Greatest Hits. 1997. Sabri Brothers. Shanachie 64090. Compact disk.

Greatest Hits of the 1950s, Vol. 3. 1997. Gramophone Company of India. CDF 130121. Compact disk. (Hindi film songs by the music directors C. Ramchandra, Naushad, O. P. Nayyar, Shankar-Jaikishen, and others.)

Greatest Hits of the 1960s, Vol. 3. 1997. Gramophone Company of India. CDF 130126. Compact disk. (Hindi film songs by the music directors Naushad, Shankar-Jaikishen, S. D. Burman, Lakshmikant-Pyarelal, and others.)

Greatest Hits of the 1970s, Vol. 3. 1997. Gramophone Company of India. CDF 130136. Compact disk. (Hindi film songs by the music directors R. D. Burman, Shankar-Jaikishen, Lakshmikant-Pyarelal, Kalyanji-Anandji, and others.)

Greatest Hits of the 1980s, Vol. 1. 1997. Gramophone Company of India. CDF 130118. Compact disk. (Hindi film songs by the music directors Shiv Hari, Lakshmikant-Pyarelal, R. D. Burman, Khayyam, and others.)

Great Master, Great Music: Ustad Abdul Wahid Khan. 1976. Gramophone Company of India. ECLP 2541. LP disk. (Hindustani khyal performance.)

Great Masters of the Rudra-Veena: Ustad Zia Mohiuddin Dagar. 1988. Auvidis A 6131. Compact disk. (Raga Pancham Kosh.)

G. S. Sachdev—Spirit. 1995. Audiorec ACCD 1029. Compact disk. (Hindustani flute performance in ragas Bihag, Kalavati, and Chandrakauns, with Zakir Hussain, tabla.)

Gundecha Brothers—Raga Darbari. 1997. Audiorec ACCD 1036. Compact disk. (Hindustani vocal dhrupad performance, with Shrikant Mishra, pakhavaj.)

Hirabai Barodekar and Saraswati Rane—Classical Vocal. 1992. Gramophone Company of India. HMV 04B 7434/35. 2 compact disks.

Hypnotic Santur: Shivkumar Sharma. 1988. Produced by Shefali Nag. Chhanda Dhara SP 83088. Compact disk. (Shafaat Ahmed Khan, tabla; Shefali Nag, tambura. Raga Gorack Kalyan and Dogri folklore.)

Immortal R. D. Burman—His Own Voice. 1997. Polygram India. CDF 201. Compact disk. (Hindi film songs composed and sung by R. D. Burman.)

Inde Centrale/Central India: Traditions musicales des Gond/Musical Traditions of the Gond. 1990. Recorded by Jan Van Alphen 1978–1981. AIMP

XX, Archives Internationales de Musique Populaire. VDE/Gallo CD 618. Compact disk.

Inde du Nord: L'art de la vichitra vina. N.d. Ocora/Radio France C 560048/49. 2 compact disks. (Performance of ragas Bairagi and Jog by Gopal Krishan.)

Inde du Nord/North India: Mithila: Chants d'amour de Vidyapati/Love Songs of Vidyapati. 1995. Notes by Georges Luneau. Ocora C 580063. Compact disk.

India Festival. N.d. Magic Software, F-6 Kailash Colony, New Delhi 110048. Available from www.magicsw.com/cd-rom/index.htm. CD-ROM. (Multimedia celebration of India's fairs and festivals.)

India Musica. N.d. Magic Software Pvt. Ltd., F-6 Kailash Colony, New Delhi 110048. Available from www.magicsw.com/cd-rom/index.htm. CD-ROM. (Interactive guide to Hindustani music.)

India Mystica. N.d. Magic Software Pvt. Ltd., F-6 Kailash Colony, New Delhi 110048. Available from www.magicsw.com/cd-rom/index.htm. CD-ROM. (Interactive multimedia encyclopedia of Indian culture, traditions, and beliefs.)

India: Traveling Artists of the Desert—The Vernacular Musical Culture of Rajasthan. 1997. Recorded by Keiji Azami. Multicultural Media MCM 3002. Compact disk.

Indian Folk Music. N.d. Recorded by Alan Lomax. Columbia Records 9102021. LP disk.

Indian Night Live, Stuttgart 1988: Memorable Tabla Duet. 1991. Zakir Hussain and Sultan Khan. Chhanda Dhara SNCD 70891. Compact disk.

Inédit—Shâhjahân Miah—Chants mystiques bâuls du Bangladesh (Mystical Baul songs of Bangladesh). 1992. Notes by Pierre Bois. Maison des Cultures du Monde W 260039. Compact disk.

Instrumental Music of Rajasthan: Langas and Monganiyars. N.d. World Music Library KICC-5118. Compact disk.

Jaffar Hussain Khan—The Voice of the Mystics. 1992. Academy of Indian Music AIMCD 001. Compact disk. (Qawwali ensemble.)

Jagdeep Singh Bedi—Sitar and Surbahar: Soft and True. N.d. Produced by Martha Lorantos and Bob Haddad. Music of the World MOW 108. Compact disk. (Performed with Kailash Chandra Sharma, flute; and Ravi Kumar, tabla.)

The King of Dhrupad: Ram Chatur Mallik in Concert. 1988. Ragas Vinod, Sindura, Paraj. Recorded in Vrindavan in 1982 by Gottfried Düren; produced by Peter Pannke. Wergo Spectrum SM 1076-50. Compact disk.

Kirvani: Tarun Bhattacharya, Santur, and Bikram Ghosh, Tabla. N.d. Produced by Bob Haddad. Music of the World MOW 139. Compact disk.

Kishori Amonkar. 1991. Music Today CD A-91006. Compact disk. (Hindustani khyal performance.)

Kishori Amonkar—Sadhana. 1997. Audiorec ACCD 1035. Compact disk. (Vocal performance of religious bhajans.)

Kohinoor Langa Group: Music from the Desert Nomads. N.d. Multicultural Media WDR-34. Compact disk. (Vocal and instrumental music.)

Ladakh: Musique de monastère et de village/ Ladakh: Monastic and Village Music. 1989. Recorded by Mireille Helffer. Chant du Monde LDX 274662/CM 251. Compact disk with 32-page booklet.

Ladakh: Songs and Dances from the Highlands of Western Tibet. 1971. Recorded by David Lewiston. Nonesuch Explorer H-72075. LP disk.

Lakshmi Shankar—Bhakti Ras. N.d. Navras Records NRCD 0056. Compact disk. (Lakshmi Shankar sings bhajans.)

Lakshmi Shankar—Live in London. 1992. Navras Records NRCD 0006. Compact disk. (The Hindustani vocalist performs khyal in raga Madhukauns, thumri in raga Mishra Kafi, and bhajan, with Shiv Shankar Ray, tabla.)

The Legendary Lineage: Ustad Hafiz Ali Khan, Ustad Amjad Khan, Amaan and Ayaan Ali Bangash. 1996. Navras Records NRCD 0084/85. 2 compact disks. (Three generations of this musical family are presented: Hafiz Ali Khan, c. 1968, performs ragas Bilaskhani Todi, Yaman Kalyan, Desh, and Pilu Jungala; Amjad Ali Khan, 1966, performs raga Darbari Kanada; Amaan and Ayaan Ali Bangash, 1966, perform raga Bhairav.)

Legends: Lata Mangeshkar "The Nightingale." 1997. Gramophone Company of India. CDF 130111/15. 5 compact disks with accompanying 32-page booklet. (Digitally remastered Hindi film songs performed by Lata Mangeshkar between 1949 and 1997.)

Lower Caste Religious Music from India: Monks, Transvestites, Midwives, and Folksingers. N.d. Recorded by Rosina Schlenker. Lyrichord LLST 7344. LP disk.

The Lyrical Tradition of Dhrupad, 6: Uday Bhawalkar. N.d. Makar Records 031. Compact disk. (Hindustani vocal dhrupad performance in raga Gurjari Todi.)

The Lyrical Tradition of Khyal, 1: Ustad Iqbal Ahmad Khan—Delhi Gharana. N.d. Makar Records 003. Compact disk. (Hindustani khyal performance in ragas Komal Rishab Asavari and Mian ki Todi.)

Maestro's Choice: Alla Rakha and Zakir Hussain. 1991. Music Today A19013. Compact disk. (Hindustani tabla.)

The Majestic Tabla of Swapan Chaudhuri. 1993. Chhanda Dhara SNCD 71093. Compact disk.

Mallikarjun Mansur in Concert, Vol. 1: *Morning Ragas.* N.d. Pyramid Classical 7008. Compact disk. (Hindustani khyal performance of ragas Bibhas, Yamani Bilawal, and Bhairavi.)

Mallikarjun Mansur: The Legend Lives On. N.d. OMI Magnasound D4HV 0589. Compact disk. (Hindustani khyal performance of ragas Savani and Shivmat Bhairav.)

Manilal Nag, Sitar—Dawn Raga Latit. 1989. Raga Records 213. Compact disk. (Hindustani sitar performance with Anand Gopal Bandopadhyay, tabla.)

Masters of Raga: Sarangi Solo—Ram Narayan in Concert. 1994. Wergo (Welt Musik) SM 1601. Compact disk. (Performance of ragas Marwa and Misra Pilu recorded in 1976. Suresh Talwalkar, tabla.)

Masters of Tala: Pakhawaj Solo. N.d. Raja Chatrapati Singh, 1989. Wergo SM1075-50. Compact disk.

Mehdi Hassan—Classical Ghazals. 1990. Navras Records NRCD 0001-0003. 3 compact disks. (The Pakistani ghazal singer presents ghazals and thumris, with Sultan Khan, sarangi; and Shaukat Hussain, tabla.)

Memories of Herat: Music of Afghanistan. N.d. Produced by Bob Haddad. Music of the World LAT50602. Compact disk. (Performed by Aziz Herawi, *dutār* and *rubāb* lutes; Siar Ahmad Hazeq, tabla; and Omar Herawi, *zirbaghali* drum.)

Middle Caste Religious Music from India: Musicians, Dancers, Prostitutes, and Actors. N.d. Recorded by Rosina Schlenker. Lyrichord LLST7323. LP disk.

Music from the Shrines of Ajmer and Mundra. N.d. Multicultural Media TSCD-911. Compact disk. (Reissue of recordings of the 1970s by John Levy.)

Music in Sikkim. 1971. Recorded by Fred Liebermann and Michael Moore. Command COMS 9002. LP disk.

Musiques du Pendjab pakistanais/Music from the Punjab Province of Pakistan, Vol. 2: *Le Ghazal.* 1995. Performed by Farida Khanum, vocal. Arion ARN 64301. Compact disk.

Musiques du toit du monde: Ladakh et Nepal/Roof of the World Musics. 1988. Recorded at the monastery of Hemis by Gérard Kremer. Sunset-France, Playa Sound PS 65021. Compact disk.

The Mystic Fiddle of the Proto-Gypsies: Masters of Trance Music. 1997. Recordings and notes by Jean During; produced by Theodore Levin. Shanachie SH 65013. Compact disk.

Najma—Qareeb. 1989. Shanachie SH 64009. Compact disk. (Pop ghazals.)

Nepal: Musique de fête chez les Newar. 1989. Recorded by Marguerite Lobsiger-Dellenbach (1952) and Laurent Aubert (1973). AIMP XIII, Archives Internationales de Musique Populaire. VDE/Gallo VDE CD 553. Compact disk.

Nikhil Bannerjee: Raga Misra Kafi. 1990. Raga Records 204. Compact disk. (Sitar performance with Swapan Chaudhuri, tabla.)

North India: Instrumental Music of Medieval India. N.d. Anthology of Traditional Musics Series. Auvidis Unesco D 8205. Compact disk. (Ustad Asad Ali Khan, rudra vina, performs ragas Darbari Kanada and Gunakali.)

Nusrat Fateh Ali Khan: Intoxicated Spirit. 1996. Shanachie SH 64066. Compact disk. (Qawwali music of Pakistan.)

Nusrat Fateh Ali Khan—Qawwali: The Vocal Art of the Sufis, 1–2. 1996–1997. JVC Music VICG 5029-2/5030-2. 2 compact disks.

The Other Side of Naushad—Aathwan Sur. 1997. Navras Records NRCD 0102. Compact disk. (Ghazals composed by the Hindi film music director Naushad Ali, sung by Hariharan and Preeti Uttam.)

Padmashree M. S. Gopalakrishnan: Raga Bhimpalasi/Raga Puriya. N.d. OMI Magnasound C5CI 5013. Compact disk. (Hindustani violin performance.)

Pakistan: The Music of the Qawal. 1990. Recorded and with notes by Alain Daniélou. Anthology of Traditional Musics. Auvidis Unesco D 8028. Compact disk.

Pakistani Music: The Rubab of Kashmir. N.d. World Music Library KICC-5109. Compact disk. (Subhan Rathore, rubab and vocal, with Abdul Ghani, turnbaknari.)

Pandit Bhimsen Joshi—Bhakti. 1992. Audiorec ACCD 1024. Compact disk. (Four devotional bhajans.)

Pandit Jasraj—Tapasya. 1995. Audiorec ACCD 1031. Compact disk. (Hindustani vocal performance with Anindo Chatterjee, tabla; ragas Marubihag, Des Ang Jaijaivanti, and Bhairavi.)

Pandit Kartick Kumar—Atma. 1990. Audiorec ACCD 1004. Compact disk. (Hindustani sarod performance in ragas Bihag and Jhinghoti, with Sukhvinder Singh, tabla.)

Pandit Kumar Gandharva—Raga Bhairav ke Prakar. 1978. Navras Records NRCD 0042. Compact disk. (House concert with Vasant Achrekar, tabla.)

Pandit Ravi Shankar, Sitar/Ustad Ali Akbar Khan, Sarod, in Concert, 1972, with Alla Rakha, Tabla. 1996. Apple/EMI 7243 8 53817 2. 2 compact disks.

Pandit V. G. Jog. 1991. Moment Records MRCD 1003. Compact disk. (Live recording of Hindustani violin performance in Berkeley, May 1991, with Zakir Hussain, tabla; ragas Jog and Rageshri.)

Playback—The Fifty Melodious Years: The Fabulous Years 1946–1956. 1991. Gramophone Company of India. CDF 1.30024. Compact disk. (Contains 23 Hindi film songs.)

Playback—The Fifty Melodious Years: The Melodious Decade 1956–1966. 1991. Gramophone Company of India. CDF 1.30025. Compact disk. (Contains 18 Hindi film songs.)

Playback—The Fifty Melodious Years: The Exciting Era 1976–1986. 1991. Gramophone Company of India. CDF PMLP 5407. Compact disk.

Prayer Music of Sikh: In Bangra Sabib Temple, Delhi. 1988. JVC Ethnic Sound Series 21, VID 25035. Compact disk.

Purushotamdas Jalota—Praising Krishna. 1993. Audiorec ACCD 1013. Compact disk. (Songs of the eight Astachap poet-musicians of the fifteenth and sixteenth centuries.)

Purushotamdas Jalota—Songs of Kabir. 1992. Audiorec ACCD 1012. Compact disk. (Songs of the Indian mystic and poet Kabir.)

Purushotamdas Jalota—Songs of Surdas. 1991. Audiorec ACCD 1011. Compact disk. (Krishna bhajans of the sixteenth-century Hindu poet-saint Surdas.)

Qawwali: Sufi Music from Pakistan. 1998. Sabri Brothers. Nonesuch Explorer 72080-2. Compact disk.

The Raga Guide: A Survey of Seventy-Four Hindustani Ragas. 1999. By Joep Bor. Nimbus Records NI 5536/9. 4 compact disks with book.

Raga Lalitadhvani: Sarod Maestro Amjad Ali Khan. N.d. JVC Music VICG-5451-2. Compact disk.

Ram Narayan: Raga Lalit. N.d. Indian Classical Masters Series. Nimbus 5183. Compact disk. (Hindustani sarangi performance.)

Ras Rang—Evolution of Thumri, Vol. 1. 1997. Navras Records NRCD 0081. Compact disk. (Collection of thumris sung by Parween Sultana Birju Maharaj, Sipra Bose, Shobha Gurtu, Ghulam Mustafa Khan, and others.)

Ras Rang—Evolution of Thumri, Vol. 2. 1997. Navras Records NRCD 0082. Compact disk. (Collection of thumris sung by Girija Devi, Birju Maharaj, Sipra Bose, Shobha Gurtu, Ghulam Mustafa Khan, and others.)

Ravi Shankar—Concert for Peace at the Royal Albert Hall. 1993. Moment Records MRCD 1013. 2 compact disks. (Live performance in London, 9 November 1993. Ravi Shankar, sitar; Partho Sarathy, sarod; and Zakir Hussain, tabla, perform ragas Jait, Kirwani, and Misra Khammaj.)

Ravi Shankar: Concerto for Sitar and Orchestra. 1990. Angel Classics 69121. Compact disk.

The Sabri Brothers: Greatest Hits. 1997. Shanachie SH 64090. Compact disk. (Qawwali performance.)

The Sabri Brothers: Ya Mustapha. 1996. Produced by Richard Blair. Green Linnet Records, Xeno 4041. Compact disk.

Sacred Ceremonies: Ritual Music of Tibetan Buddhism—Monks of the Dip Tse Chok Ling Monastery, Dharamsala. 1990. Fortuna Records 17074-2. Tucson, Ariz.: Celestial Harmonies (P.O. Box 30122, Tucson, AZ 85751), distributor. Compact disk.

Sargam: Santur, Shenai and Tabla—Tarun Bhattacharya. N.d. Produced by Bob Haddad. Music of the World MOW 132. Compact disk.

Satya Sai Baba Chants the Bhajans. N. d. Recorded at Prasanthi Nilayam and Vrindavan. Tustin, Calif.: Sathya Sai Book Center of America (305 First Street, Tustin, CA 92680), distributor. Stereo SC-002. Audiocassette.

Sharda Sahai—The Art of the Benares Baj. 1993. Audiorec ACCD 1034. Compact disk. (Tabla solo in the Banaras style.)

Sheila Chandra—Silk. 1991. Shanachie SH 64035. Compact disk. ("Indipop" fusion album of Chandra songs recorded 1983–1990.)

Shiva Mahadeva: Dagar Brothers—Dhrupad, Classical Vocal Music of North India. 1996. Pan Records 4001/02. 2 compact disks. (Nasir Zahiruddin Dagar and Nasir Faiyazuddin Dagar, vocal; ragas Malkauns, Darbari Kanada, Adana, and Bhatiyar.)

Shujaat Khan, Sitar; Shyam Kane, Tabla. 1992. India Archive Music IAM CD 1009. Compact disk. (Ragas Shahana Kanada and Pahari.)

Songs of the Bauls, 2: *Purna Chandra Das*. 1993. JVC World Sounds JVC VICG5267. Compact disk.

The Songs of Distant Sands. 1995. Navras Records NRCD 0059. Compact disk. (Music of the Langas and Manganihars of Rajasthan.)

The Soul of Tabla. 1993. Swapan Chaudhuri. Interworld Music CD 809092. Compact disk.

Sri Lanka: Musiques rituelles et religieuses. 1992. Reissue of Ocora 558 552. Ocora C580 037. Compact disk.

String Craft: Nishat Khan. N.d. JVC Music VICG 5452-2. Compact disk. (Hindustani sitar performance.)

Tabla Lahara. 1988. Pandit Shamta Prasad. Concord Records 05015. Audiocassette.

Tabla Lahara. 1991. Ustad Afaq Husain Khan. Concord Records 05023. Audiocassette.

Tabla Tarang: Melody on Drums. 1996. Recorded by Walter Quintus, with notes by Laura Patchen. World's Musical Traditions 10. Smithsonian/Folkways CD SF 40436. Compact disk. (Performed by Pandit Kamalesh Maitra, tabla Tarang—a set of tabla tuned to pitches of a musical scale—and Trilok Gurtu, tabla.)

Talking Tabla—Bikram Ghosh. N.d. Music of the World MOW 143. Compact disk.

Thumri and Dadra: Vocal Art of Hindustan [2]. 1994. JVC World Sounds JVC VICG 5347. Compact disk. (Rita Ganguly, vocal; Sabri Khan, sarangi; Rashid Mustafa, tabla; and Sajjad Ahmed, harmonium.)

Thumri: Vocal and Instrumental Light Classical Music of North India. 1994. Produced by Lyle Wachovsky, with notes by Peter Manuel. India Archive Music IAM CD 1012. Compact disk.

Tibet—Monks of the Sera Jé Monastery: Ritual Music and Chants of the Gelug Tradition. N.d. Recorded by Angelo Ricciardi (January 1997) at a monastery-in-exile in South India. With 96-page color booklet. Chappaqua, N.Y.: Amiata Media (P.O. Box 405, Chappaqua, NY 10514; http://www.amiatamedia.it), distributor. Compact disk.

Tibetan Buddhist Rites from the Monasteries of Bhutan. N.d. Recorded by John Levy. Lyrichord LYRCD 7255-58. 4 compact disks. (1, rituals of the Drukpa order; 2, sacred dances and rituals of the Nyingmapa and Drukpa orders; 3, temple rituals and public ceremonies; 4, Tibetan Bhutanese instrumental and folk music.)

Tibetan Music from Ladakh and Zanskar. 1982. Recorded by Eric Larson. Lyrichord LLST 7383. LP disk.

The Tradition of Dhrupad on Rudravina, 1. N.d. Makar Records 006. Compact disk. (Bahauddin Dagar performs ragas Bhairav and Komal Re Durga.)

The Tradition of Dhrupad on Rudravina, 2. N.d. Makar Records 033. Compact disk. (Bahauddin Dagar performs ragas Kanakangi and Ragvardhani.)

The Traditional Music of Herat. 1996. Recorded by John Baily. UNESCO Collection, Auvidis D8266. Compact disk with accompanying notes.

Trésors du Pakistan/Pakistan Treasures. 1991. Playa Sound PS 65082. Compact disk. (Includes performances on rabab, sarinda, sarangi, Baluchi sarinda, and tabla.)

The "Ultimate" in Taal-Vidya: Solo Masterpieces in Teentaal and Jhaptaal. Alla Rakha. 1989. OMI Magnasound D4H 10079. Compact disk.

Ustad Ali Akbar Khan—Passing on the Tradition. 1995. Alam Madina Music Production AMMP 9608. Compact disk. (Hindustani sarod performance of ragas Marwa and Puriya Kalyan, with Swapan Chaudhuri, tabla.)

Ustad Ali Akbar Khan Plays Alap. 1992. Alam Madina Music Production AMMP 9303. Compact disk. (Hindustani sarod performance of ragas Shri, Pilu Baroowa, and Iman Kalyan.)

Ustad Ali Akbar Khan—Signature Series. N.d. Vol. 1: Three ragas—Chandranandan, Gauri Manjari, Jogiya Kalingra (original recordings 1966–1969). Vol. 2: Medhavi, Khammaj, Bhairavi Bhatiyar with ragmala (original recordings 1969–1970). Alam Madina Music Productions AMMP CD 9001-9002. 2 compact disks.

Ustad Alla Rakha and Zakir Hussain, Tabla Duet. 1991. Moment Records MRCD 1001. Compact disk. (Live performance at Ramkrishna Mission Auditorium, Calcutta, January 1991. Duet in tintal.)

Ustad Amir Khan: The Legend Lives On. N.d. OMI Magnasound D3HV 0636. Compact disk. (Khyal vocal performance of ragas Nand, Bahar, and Darbari Kanada.)

Ustad Imrat Khan: Rag Madhur Ranjani. N.d. Produced by Bob Haddad. Music of the World MOW 123. Compact disk. (Sitar performance.)

Ustad Latif Ahmed Khan—The Great Tabla Wizard. c. 1983. Academy of Indian Music AIMCD 003a. Compact disk. (Tabla solo in tintal, Delhi Gharana style.)

Ustad Muhammad Umar—Robab-Music from Afghanistan. N.d. Academy of Indian Music AIMCD 004. Compact disk. (Classical and folk music.)

Ustad Munawar Ali Khan and Raza Ali Khan. 1990. Audiorec ACCD 1003-S. 3 compact disks. (Homage to Ustad Bade Ghulam Ali Khan, sung by his son and his uncle, with Tanmoy Bose, tabla. Ragas include Komal Rishabh Asavari, Gaud Sarang, Bhimpalasi, Megh, and Rageshwari.)

Ustad Nizamuddin Khan. 1994. India Music Archive IAM CD 1014. Compact disk.

Ustad R. Fahimuddin Dagar: Raga Kedar. N.d. Jecklin Disco JD635. Compact disk. (Hindustani vocal dhrupad performance.)

Ustad Sabri Khan: Raga Darbari/Raga Multani. N.d. Auvidis Ethnic B 6754. Compact disk. (Hindustani sarangi performance.)

Ustad Sabri Khan—The Family Tradition. 1991. Audiorec ACCD 1018. Compact disk. (Hindustani sarangi performance by Sabri Khan with his sons Kamal Sabri, sarangi; and Sarvar Sabri, tabla. Ragas Nat Bhairav, Shri, Shyam Kalyan, and a dhun in raga mand.)

Ustad Vilayat Khan: Raga Darbari Kanada. N.d. EMI India CDNF 150186. Compact disk. (Hindustani sitar performance.)

Ustad Vilayat Khan: Raga Jaijaivanti. N.d. India Archive of Music 1010. Compact disk. (Hindustani sitar performance.)

Ustad Zia Mohiuddin Dagan Raga Yaman. N.d. Nimbus/Indian Classical Masters 5276. Compact disk. (Hindustani rudra vina performance.)

Veena Sahasrabuddhe—Live in Concert. 1994. Navras Records NRCD 0031. Compact disk. (The khyal singer from Maharashtra performs the morning raga Bhupal Todi in the Gwalior Gharana style, with Sanjay Deshpande, tabla.)

Venu: Hariprasad—Zakir Hussain. 1989. Produced by Zakir Hussain and Mickey Hart. Rykodisc RCD 20128. Compact disk. (Hindustani flute performance of raga Ahir Bhairav, with Zakir Hussain, tabla.)

Vicitra Vina: The Music of Pandit Lalmani Misra. N.d. Distributed by Multicultural Media D-8267. Compact disk. (Performance of the evening raga Kausi Kanhada.)

Vishwa Mohan Bhatt, Guitar: Ragas Bihag and Desh. 1996. Raga Records 208. Compact disk. (Hindustani performance on guitar with Sukhvindar Singh, tabla, recorded live in Pittsburgh in 1989.)

Vocal Music of Rajasthan: Langas and Manganiyars. N.d. World Music Library KICC-5117. Compact disk.

Vocal Phenomenon: Sri Bhimsen Joshi Live. 1992. Produced by Shefali Nag. Chhanda Dhara SNCD 70392. Compact disk. (Ragas Lalit and Jogia, and bhajans.)

Zakir Hussain and Sultan Khan. 1987. Chhanda Dhara SNCD 4487. Compact disk.

Zarsanga: Songs of the Pashtu. 1993. Produced by Alain Weber and Armand Amar. Long-Distance Music 662295. Compact disk. (Songs of Pakistan, accompanied by *rabāb, ḍholak,* and tabla.)

Zia Mohiuddin Dagar: Live in Seattle 1981. 1999. Raga Records 219. Compact disk. (Hindustani rudra vina performance in ragas Todi, Ahir Lalit, and Pancham Kauns recorded live at the University of Washington, 27 February 1998.)

MUSIC IN SOUTHERN AREAS

An Anthology of South Indian Classical Music. 1990. Ocora/Radio France C590001-04. 4 compact disks. (Broad selection of vocal and instrumental performances by various artists, including Semmangudi Srinivasa Iyer, vocal; M. S. Subbulakshmi, vocal; L. Subramaniam, violin; T. R. Mahalingam, flute; and Palghat T. S. Mani Iyer, mridangam.)

Ariyakudi Ramanuja Iyengar. N.d. EMI India CDNF 147750. Compact disk. (Karnatak vocal performance with M. N. Krishnan, T. N. Krishnan, P. Subramania Pillai, and Bangalore Manjunath; an All India Radio release.)

Aruna Sayeeram: Chant Karnatique/Karnatic Song. N.d. Auvidis Ethnic B6747. Compact disk. (Karnatak vocal performance, with Sundar Rajan and Bombay S. Shankaranarayanan, recorded in France.)

Bombay Sisters: Mutthuswamy Dikshitar's Navagraha Kritis. N.d. EMI India CDNF 170503. Compact disk. (Karnatak vocal performance of Dikshitar's Navagraha kriti cycle on the planets, with Usha Rajagopalan, Kamala Vishwanathan, K. V. Prasad, and N. Govindarajan.)

Cascades of Carnatic Music: M. L. Vasanthakumari. 1990. Oriental 158–159. 2 compact disks. (The Karnatak vocalist and distinguished disciple of G. N. Balasubramaniam performs with T. Rukmani, Palghat T. S. Mani Iyer, S. D. Sridhar, S. V. Raja Rao, and Hari Shankar.)

Christian Bhajans. 1979. Sung by Joseph Palackal. Bangalore: Deccan Records LDEC 102. LP disk.

Christian Classical Music Concert. 1988. Performed by George Panjara. Nadopasana/ Thodupuzha NC 101. Audiocassette.

Connoisseurs Delight: V. Ramachandran. N.d. OMI Magnasound D5CV 5043. Compact disk. (Karnatak vocal performance with Nagai R. Muralidharan, Guruvayur Dorai, and T. H. Subashchandran.)

Divine Sounds of the Bamboo Flute, "Mali." N.d. Oriental 183/184. 2 compact disks. (Karnatak flute performance by T. R. Mahalingam, with

Dwaram Mangathayaru, Karaikkudi R. Mani, and Gurumurthy.)

D. K. Jayaraman. N.d. EMI India CDNF 168307. Compact disk. (Karnatak vocal performance, with T. Rukmini, Srimushnam V. Raja Rao, and T. H. Subnashchandran.)

D. K. Pattammal. N.d. EMI India CDNF 147729. Compact disk. (Karnatak vocal performance, with T. Veeraraghavan, Sivakurnar, and K. M. Vaidyanathan.)

The Doyen of Carnatic Music: Dr. Semmangudi Srinivasa Iyer. N.d. Oriental 163–164. 2 compact disks. (Karnatak violin performance with V. V. Subramaniam, Guruvayoor Dorai, and V. K. Krishnan.)

Dr. L. Subramaniam: Raga Hemavati. N.d. Nimbus NI 5227. Compact disk. (Karnatak violin performance.)

Dr. M. L. Vasanthakumari—Carnatic Concert. N.d. Super Audio (Geethanjali) 020. Compact disk. (Karnatak vocal performance, with Sudha Raghunathan, A. Kanyakumari, and R. Ramesh.)

Dr. N. Ramani: Classical Carnatic Flute. N.d. Nimbus 5257. Compact disk. (Karnatak compositions and a ragam Tanam pallavi ragamalika.)

Dr. S. Ramanathan. N.d. Karnatak vocal performance, with Karaikudi R. Mani and M. S. Gopalakrishnan. OMI Magnasound C5CV 5017. Compact disk.

Folk Music of Tamilnadu. N.d. Recorded by Shyamala Balakrishnan, Padma Subramanyam, K. S. Vasudevan, and N. Vasudevan. Gramophone Company of India ECSD 3233. LP disk.

Folk Songs of South India. N.d. Gramophone Company of India MOCE 1004. LP disk.

Guru Padam: K. V. Narayanaswamy. N.d. Koel 063. Compact disk. (Karnatak vocal performance, with Padma Narayanaswamy, G. Chandramouli, J. Vaidhyanatha, and H. Siwaramakrishnan.)

The Immortal Sounds of the Veena: Dr. S. Balachander. N.d. Oriental 119. Compact disk. (Karnatak vina performance, with S. V. Raja Rao,

R. Harishankar, Karaikudi R. Mani, and T. H. Vinayagaram.)

Inde du sud: Kerala—Le thayambaka/South India: Kerala—The Thayambaka. 1997. Performed by Mattanur Shankarankutty; recording and notes by Jean-Paul Auboux. Ocora C560 047. Compact disk.

Jon Higgins. c. 1970. Gramophone Company of India CDNF 147728. Compact disk.

Karaikudi R. Mani—Layapriya. 1995. Audiorec ACCD 1028. Compact disk. (Karnatak drumming by the mridangam player Karaikudi R. Mani, with violin, ghatam, kanjira, and morsing.)

Karnatak Music of Andhra. 1997. Recorded by Nazir Jairazbhoy. Apsara Media for Intercultural Education. Audiocassette. (Voleti Venkateswarlu, voice; R. Subba Rao, vina; K. Kannan, flute; Anawarupu Gopalam, mridangam, morsing; Yella Venkateswara Rao, mridangam; N. C. H. Krishnamacharyulu, violin; D. Pandurangaraju, violin; and A. Gopalan, ghatam.)

K. S. Narayanaswamy—Veena. N.d. Oriental AAMSCD 202. Compact disk. (Karnatak vina performance, with Trichur Narendran.)

Lalgudi G. Jayaraman: Live Concert at Sri Krishna Gana Sabha, Vol. 2. N.d. OMI Magnasound C5CI 5031. Compact disk. (Karnatak violin performance, with G. J. R. Krishnan, Trichy Sankaran, and G. Harishankar.)

Laya Vinyās: The South Indian Drumming of Trichy Sankaran. 1990. Music of the World CDT120. Compact disk.

L. Subramaniam—Distant Visions. 1991. Audiorec ACCD 1021. Compact disk. (Karnatak violin performance, including ragamalika, with K. Gopinath, mridangam, and K. M. Rajah, kanjira.)

L. Subramaniam—In Praise of Ganesh. 1992. Audiorec ACCD 1027. Compact disk. (Live Karnatak violin performance with Karaikudi Krishnamurti, mridangam; Anindo Chatterjee, tabla; and T. H. Subashchandran, ghatam. Ragas Abhogi and Kapi.)

The Lyrical Tradition of Carnatic Music, 1: *Aruna Sayeeram*. N.d. Makar Records 013. Compact disk. (Karnatak vocal performance, with B. Anantharaman and S. Shankaranarayam.)

Maharajapuram V. Santhanam. N.d. Music Today/Maestro's Choice C 91016. Compact disk. (Vocal performance by the late Karnatak vocalist.)

M. S. Gopalakrishnan. N.d. EMI India CDNF 168311. Compact disk. (Karnatak violin performance, with Srimushnam V. Raja Rao and E. M. Subrahmanyam.)

M. S. Subbulakshmi. 1991. EMI India CD PMLP 5306/07. 2 compact disks. (Live Karnatak vocal performance at the United Nations Building, Washington D.C., on 23 October 1966, with Radha Viswanathan, V. V. Subramanian, T. K. Moorthy, and T. H. Vinayakram.)

M. S. Subbulakshmi—Live at Carnegie Hall. N.d. EMI India CDNF 147808/09. 2 compact disks. (Karnatak vocal performance, with Radha Viswanathan, A. K. S. Alagiriswami, and Guruvayur Dorai.)

Music of South India—Karaikudi Veena Tradition: Surabi—Rajeswari Padmanabhan. N.d. SonicSoul Acoustics 60. Compact disk. (Karnatak vina performance, with Mannargudi Easwaran.)

Music of the Veena, 1: *S. Balachander*. 1990. Recorded in 1974. JVC World Sounds VICG-5036-2. Compact disk.

Music of the Veena, 2: *Raajeswari Padmanabhan*. 1990. JVC World Sounds VICG-5038. Compact disk. (Karnatak performance by Raajeswari Padmanabhan and Sreevidhya Chandramouli, vina, and Tanjore Upendran, mridangam.)

Naadha Manjari—Lalgudi G. Jayaraman. N.d. AVM Audio CD 1066. Compact disk. (Karnatak violin performance, with G. J. R. Krishnan, Karakudi R. Mani, and T. H. Vinayakram.)

Nadanubhava—Horizons of Carnatic Music. 1998. K. N. Shashikiran and Sowmya. Produced by Carnatica, Chennai (India). Houston, Tex.: KalaiOli Musicals (16806 Soaring Forest Drive, Houston, TX 77059-4006, telephone 888-376-3758, E-mail shrie@msn.com), distributor in the United States. CD-ROM.

Nadhaswaram: Sheik Chinna Moulana—Musical Herolds [sic] *from South India*. N.d. Wergo/Haus der Kulturen der Welt SM 1507. Compact disk. (Karnatak performance on the double-reed nagasvaram, with Sheik Kasim, Sheik Babu, and Sheik Subramaaniam.)

Nadopasana—My Own Carnatic Tutor. 1998. By K. N. Shashikiran and Sowmya. Produced by Carnatica, Chennai (India). Houston, Tex.: KalaiOli Musicals (16806 Soaring Forest Drive, Houston, TX 77059-4006, telephone 888-376-3758, E-mail shrie@msn.com), distributor in the United States. CD-ROM.

Pallavi South India Flute Music. 1973. Tanjore Viswanathan. Nonesuch Explorer Series H-72052. LP disk.

Ramnad Krishnan: Vidwan, Music of South India. N.d. Elektra/Nonesuch: Explorer Series 9 72023-2. Compact disk. (Vocal performance of three kritis and a ragam tanam pallavi. Originally released as LP disk, 1967.)

Sangeeta Kalanidhi V. Doreswamy Iyengar: Live at Music Academy Hall, Madras (1984). N.d. Karnatak vina performance with D. Balakrishna, K. Viswanatha Iyer, and K. S. Manjunathan. EMI India CDNF 147774. Compact disk.

Sangita Kalanidhi M. S. Subbulakshmi. N.d. EMI India CDNF 147701. Compact disk. (Karnatak vocal performance, with Radha Viswanathan, V. V. Subramanian, T. K. Moorthy, V. Nagarajan, and T. H. Vinayakram.)

Sangita Kalanidhi Semmangudi Srinivasa Iyer. N.d. Oriental AAMS 186. Compact disk. (Karnatak vocal performance, with Palghat T. S. Mani Iyer, mridangam; and L. Shankar, violin.)

Semmangudi R. Srinivasa Iyer. N.d. EMI India CDNF 147752. Compact disk. (Karnatak vocal performance, with P. S. Narayanaswami, T. N. Krishnan, and S. V. S. Narayanan. An All India Radio release.)

South Indian Classical Flute: Tanjore Viswanathan. N.d. JVC Music VICG 5453-2. Compact disk. (Karnatak flute performance, with V. Thyagarajan and Ramnad V. Raghavan.)

Sri Muthuswami Dikshitar's Sri Kamalamba Navavaranam: S. Rajeswari. N.d. EMI India CDNF 147782/83. 2 compact disks. (Karnatak vocal performance of Muttusvami Diksitar's Sri Kamalamba Navavaranam song cycle.)

Sri Lanka—Buddhist Chant: Mahâ Pirit—The Great Chant. 1990. Recorded by Wolfgang Laade in 1979. Jecklin-Disco JD 651-2. Compact disk and booklet in English.

Südindische Tempelinstrumente. 1969. Recorded by Joseph Kuckertz, ed. Dieter Christensen, Museum für Völkerkunde, Berlin. Klangdokumente zur Musikwissenschaft KM 0001. LP disk.

Sunada: Karaikudi S. Subramaniam and Trichy Sankaran. 1992. Produced by Bob Haddad. Music of the World CDT 127. Compact disk. (Vina and mridangam; music from the classical tradition of South India.)

Swara Bushani. N.d. Oriental AAMS 166/167. 2 compact disks. (Compilation by Balamurali Krishna of vocal performances by various artists.)

The Tradition of Carnatic Music on Veena, 1: *Shri R. Pichumani—Tanjore Vani*. N.d. Makar Records 024. Compact disk. (Karnatak vina performance, with S. Karthick.)

The Tradition of Carnatic Music on Veena, 2: *Ranganayaki Rajagopalam—Karaikudi Vani*. N.d. Makar Records 029. Compact disk. (Karnatak vina performance, with S. Karthick.)

A Tribute to Adolphe Sax: Kadri Gopalnath. N.d. Oriental 228/229. 2 compact disks. (Karnatak performance on saxophone, with A. Kanyakumari, T. Bhakthavatsalam, S. Kartik, and B. Rajasekar.)

Tribute to the Great Masters: Ravikiran. N.d. Chhanda Dhara 71194. Compact disk. (Karnatak performance on the citravina—got-tuvadyam—with Vellore Ramabhadran.)

Vadya Lahari: South Indian Instrumental Ensemble. 1992. Produced by Bob Haddad. Music of the World MOW 125. Compact disk. (Features A. Kanyakumari, violin.)

V. Doreswamy Iyengar. N.d. Music Today/Maestro's Choice C 91014. Compact disk. (Karnatak vina performance recorded in 1991, with Vellore Ramabhadran.)

Veena Virtuoso/Balachander. N.d. King World Music Library 5110. Compact disk. (Karnatak vina performance recorded in 1982, with R. Ramesh.)

Violin Virtuoso: Lalgudi G. Jayaraman. N.d. Oriental AAMS 125. Compact disk. (Karnatak violin performance, with G. J. R. Krishnan, Karaikudi R. Mani, and T. H. Vinayakram. Includes an extended ragam tanam pallavi in raga Simhendramadhyamam.)

The Vocal Artistry of Trichur V. Ramachandran. N.d. Oriental 230-231. 2 compact disks. (Karnatak vocal performance, with Delhi P. Sunder Rajan, Srimushnam V. Raja Rao, and Vaikom Gopalakrishnan.)

DANCE AND DRAMA

Ache Lhamo: Théâtre musical tibétain "Prince Norsang." 1985. Recorded by Ricardo Canzio. Disques Espérance (Paris) ESP-8433. LP disk.

Devadasi Murai: Remembering Devadasis. 1998. Coproduced by Saskia Kersenboom; coproduction of Cultural Informatics Group, Indira Gandhi National Centre for the Performing Arts, Delhi, and Parampara Foundation for Traditional Arts of South India, Utrecht. Utrecht, Netherlands: Parampara (Postbus 417, 3500 AK Utrecht, Nederland; E-mail

parampara@worldonline.nl.), distributor. CD-ROM.

Inde du sud: Musiques rituelles et théâtre du Kerala/South India: Ritual Music and Theatre of Kerala. 1990. Recorded and with notes by Pribislav Pitoëf 1981–1983. Chant du Monde LDX 274 910. Compact disk.

Indian Classical Dance. N.d. ICD-01. Distributed by Multicultural Media at http://www.worldmusicstore.com. CD-ROM for Windows only. (Includes 60 minutes of video

performances and more than 400 color photos on *bharata nāṭyam, kathakali, mōhini āṭṭam, kuchipuḍi, oḍissi, kathak,* and *manipuri*.)

Indian Dance: Bharata Natyam. 1996. Info-drive Sofware, Madras. CD-ROM for PC.

Orissi Dance Music: An Ancient Performance from Orissa. 1993. JVC World Sounds JVC VICG 5268. Compact disk.

Pandit Birju Maharaj—A Kathak Performance. 1991. Navras Records NRCD 0044. Compact disk. (Live Hindustani kathak performance, with Zakir Hussain, tabla.)

Le Râmâyana: Musiques, chants et rythmes du Kathakali. 1993. Recorded in 1978, with notes in English and French. Ethnic/Auvidis B 6779. Compact disk.

Raslila (*The Dance of Krishna*): *Folkloric Dance Play of India.* 1988. CD Ethnic Sound Series 19. JVC VID-25033. Compact disk.

Sri Lanka: Comédies et opéras populaires. 1995. Recorded and with notes by Henri Lecomte. Chant du Monde CMT 274 1006. Compact disk. (Performed by the Dhamma Jagoda ensemble and the T. W. Gunadasa ensemble.)

SOUTH ASIAN DIASPORA

Jaya, Jaya Devi: Traditional Tamil Songs from the Madrasis of Guyana. 1996. Recorded in New York City. Produced and distributed by Errol G. Virasawmi.

Musiques de l'Inde en pays creoles. 1991. Recorded by Monique Desroches and Jean Benoist. University of Montreal UMM 201. Compact disk.

Films and Videos of South Asian Music

GENERAL

Discovering the Music of India. 1994. Distributed by Multicultural Media. AIMS 8705. Videocassette.

Folk Performers of India. 1984. Produced by Nazir Ali Jairazbhoy. UCLA Ethnomusicology Publications. Videocassette.

There'll Always Be Stars in the Sky: The Indian Film Music Phenomenon. 1992. Jeremy Marre. Harcourt Films. Videocassette.

MUSIC IN NORTHERN AREAS

Adaptable Kingdom: Music and Dance in Nepal. N.d. Produced by Deben Bhattacharya. Distributed by Multicultural Media AFV 72534. Videocassette.

Ali Akbar Khan Allauddin Festival 1990. 1990. Sound Photosynthesis. Videocassette.

Amir: An Afghan Refugee Musician's Life in Peshawar, Pakistan. 1985. Produced by John Baily. National Film and Television School, Beaconsfield, Buckinghamshire, England. Videocassette, 16mm film.

Between Time: A Tibetan Village in Nepal. 1984. Produced by Ken and Ivory Levine. Seattle, Wash.: Iris Film and Video (720 Blane Street, Seattle, WA 98109). 16mm film. (On the Bhotia culture.)

The Bhands of Kashmir. c. 1980. Produced by Siddharth Kak. A Cinema Vision India film. 16mm film.

Bhimsen Joshi; Girija Devi. 1994. Alurkar Music House AV 132. Videocassette. (Hindustani vocal music.)

Bhimsen Joshi; Gangubai Hangal. 1992. Produced by Suresh Alurkar. Alurkar Music House AV 108. Videocassette. (Hindustani vocal performance at the Savai Gandharva Music Festival, Pune.)

The Dragon Bride. 1993. Directed by Joanna Head. Distributed by BBC Enterprises, London. Videocassette. (The wedding of a teenage girl to four brothers of the Nyimba people of the Nepalese Himalayas.)

Echoes from Tibet. N.d. Distributed by Multicultural Media. AFV-72336. Videocassette. (A Tibetan refugee settlement in the western Himalayas; includes an excerpt of a ritual dance drama staged for the Dalai Lama's visit.)

Faces of the Forest: The Santals of West Bengal. N.d. Distributed by Multicultural Media AFV 72533. http://www.worldmusicstore.com. Videocassette. (Music and dance in the daily life and religious ceremonies of this *ādivāsī* "tribal" community.)

The Fair at Dharamtalla. 1984. Calcutta: Sharpe Film Collective (172-3 Rash Behari Avenue, Calcutta). 16mm. (Acrobats, healers, and snake charmers at a market in India.)

Folk Musicians of Rajasthan. 1984. Recorded by Nazir Jairazbhoy, August 1980. UCLA Video Series in Ethnomusicology. UCLA Music Department, Los Angeles. Videocassette and booklet.

Hariprasad Chaurasia; Zakir Hussain. 1993. Alurkar Music House AV 111. Videocassette. (Hindustani performance by Hariprasad Chaurasia, flute; and Zakir Hussain, tabla at the Savai Gandharva Music Festival, Pune, 1992.)

Himalayan Herders. 1997. Directed by John and Naomi Bishop. Watertown, Mass.: Documentary Educational Resources, distributor. Videocassette. (Ethnographic video showing rituals in Buddhist temples, villages, and mountains of central Nepal.)

Hindustani Slide: Indian Classical Guitar by Debashish Bhattacharya. 1995. Mark Humphrey, project coordinator. Vestapol (division of Stefan Grossmann's Guitar Workshop). Cambridge, Mass.: Rounder Records, distributor. Videocassette.

India Cabaret. 1986. Filmmakers Library, New York. 16mm film, videocassette. (Film about a Bombay nightclub, by Mira Nair.)

Indian Classical Music. 1994. Princeton, N.J.: Films for the Humanities and Sciences (P.O. Box 2053, Princeton, NJ 08543; http://www.films.com), distributor. AYP5066. Videocassette. (Includes performances by Ali Akbar Khan, sarod; Alla Rakha, tabla; Amjad Ali Khan, sarod; Hariprasad Chaurasia, flute; and Ravi Shankar, sitar.)

The Instrumental Artistry of Vishwa Mohan Bhatt. 1997. Vestapol (division of Stefan Grossmann's Guitar Workshop) V-13068. Distributed by Multicultural Media and Rounder Records. Videocassette. (Mohan vina player, modified slide guitar.)

Khandan: The Musical Heritage of Shujaat Khan. 1998. Produced by Arundhati Neuman. India Performing Arts. Videocassette.

Krishna in Spring. 1992 [1988]. Directed by Deben Bhattacharya. Guilford, Conn.: Audio-Forum V72182, distributor. Videocassette. (Temple ceremonies in India celebrating spring.)

Lord of the Dance: Destroyer of Illusion. 1994 [1985]. Directed by Richard Kohn and Franz-Christophe Giercke. New York: Mystic Fire Video (P.O. Box 1092, Cooper Station, New York, NY 10003), distributor. Videocassette. (Documentary on Mani Rimdu, an ancient Tibetan Tantric ritual, as practiced in a Buddhist monastery in Nepal.)

Menri Monastery. 1993. Produced by Roslyn Dauber. Berkeley: Center for Media and Independent Learning, University of California Extension, distributor. Videocassette. (About the relocated religious center of the Bonpo, pre-Buddhist Tibetans, at Menri Monastery, Himachal Pradesh, India. Includes rarely performed ceremonies.)

Musical Instruments of Kacch and Its Neighbors. 1999. Nazir Jairazbhoy and Amy Catlin. Van Nuys, Calif.: Apsara Media for Intercultural Education. Videocassette.

Painted Ballad of India. 1992 [1988]. Directed by Deben Bhattacharya. Sussex Tapes V72183. Guilford, Conn.: Audio-Forum, distributor. Videocassette.

Pandit Jasraj. 1992. Alurkar Music House AV 109. Videocassette. (Hindustani vocal performance at the Savai Gandharva Music Festival, Pune, 1992.)

Raga. 1992. Directed by Deben Bhattacharya. Guilford, Conn.: Audio-Forum, distributor. Videocassette. (Includes performance of raga Sindh Bhairavi by Halim Jaffar Khan.)

Raj Gonds. 1982. Produced by Melissa Llewelyn-Davies. Chicago: Films Inc. (5547 Ravenswood Avenue, Chicago, IL 60640). 16mm film, videocassette. (Dandari festival of central India.)

Ravi Shankar in Concert. 1994. Princeton, N.J.: Films for the Humanities and Sciences (P.O. Box 2053, Princeton, NJ 08543; http://www.films.com), distributor. BVL5070. Videocassette. (Sitar performance with Alla Rakha, tabla.)

Ravi Shankar: The Man and His Music. 1994. Produced by Anne Schelcher and Pascal Bensoussan. Princeton, N.J.: Films for the Humanities and Sciences (P.O. Box 2053, Princeton, NJ 08543), distributor. BVL4345. Videocassette.

Ravi Shankar: Raga. 1991. Produced by Howard Worth. New York: Mystic Fire Video (P.O. Box 1092, Cooper Station, New York, NY 10003). MYS 76239. Distributed by Multicultural Media. Videocassette.

Retooling a Tradition: A Rajasthani Puppet Takes Umbrage at His Stringholders. 1994. Produced by Nazir Jairazbhoy and Amy Catlin. Van Nuys, Calif.: Apsara Media for Intercultural Education. Videocassette. ("Fictive documentary.")

Shivkumar Sharma and Gangubhai Hangal. 1994. Alurkar Music House AV 126. Videocassette. (Hindustani performance at the Savai Gandharva Music Festival, Pune.)

South Asia, 2. 1988. JVC Video Anthology of World Music and Dance, Vol. 12. C3525. Videocassette. (Hindu devotional songs, git, and bhajans; Sikh bhajan.)

South Asia, 3. 1988. JVC Video Anthology of World Music and Dance, Vol. 13. C3526. Videocassette. (Rudra vina; sitar; Pabuji-ki-phad of Rajasthan; kathputli puppets of Rajasthan; bhatiyali, sari-gan, and Baul folk songs of Bengal.)

South Asia, 4: Pakistan, Bangladesh. 1988. JVC Video Anthology of World Music and Dance, Vol. 14. C3527. Videocassette. (Qawwali, hamd, manqabat, trance ritual.)

South Asia, 5: Sri Lanka, Nepal, Bhutan. 1988. JVC Video Anthology of World Music and Dance, Vol. 15. C3528. Videocassette. (Tovil, kohomba kankariya ceremonial dance, Devol ritual dance, Vedda hunting song.)

The Story of a Musician: Ustad Yunus Husain Khan. 1994. Produced by Arundhati and Daniel Neuman. Van Nuys, Calif.: Apsara Media for Intercultural Education. Videocassette.

Tales of Pabuji: A Rajasthani Tradition. 1996. Directed by Axel Horn; produced by Joseph C. Miller et al. New York: Filmmakers Library, distributor. Videocassette.

There'll Always Be Stars in the Sky: The Indian Film Music Phenomenon. 1992 [1983]. Produced by Jeremy Marre. Beats of the Heart Series. Newton, N.J.: Shanachie Records (37 East Clinton Street, Newton, NJ 07860; http://www.shanachie.com), distributor. Videocassette.

Traditional Music and Dance of Sikkim. 1971. Produced by Fred Liebermann and Michael Moore. Seattle: University of Washington Press. 16mm color film.

Waves of Joy: Anandalahari. N.d. Distributed by Multicultural Media. AFV-72431. Videocassette. (The Bauls, religious poet-singers, at the annual celebration of the twelfth-century poet-composer Jayadeva in West Bengal.)

MUSIC IN SOUTHERN AREAS

Bake Restudy 1984. 1991. Produced by Nazir Jairazbhoy and Amy Catlin. Van Nuys, Calif.: Apsara Media for Intercultural Education. Videocassette with accompanying monograph.

Buddha and the Rice Planters. 1992. Directed by Deben Bhattacharya. Guilford, Conn.: Audio-Form, distributor. Videocassette. (The importance of Buddhism in Sinhalese life, religion, art, and music in Sri Lanka.)

The Flying Bird: A Portrait of Savitri Rajan, Vina Artist. 1989. Produced by Vishnu Mathur and C. S. Lakshmi. Montreal: Productions la Fête. Videocassette, 16mm film.

Shiva's Disciples. 1985. Produced by Simon Kurrian. Boulder, Colo.: Centre Productions (1800 30th Street, #208, Boulder, CO 80301). 16mm film. (On South Indian music and dance.)

South Indian Classical Music House Concert with M. D. Ramanathan, vocalist; T. N. Krishnan, violin; and Umayalpuram Sivaraman, mridangam. 1994. Produced by Fredric Lieberman and Amy Catlin. Van Nuys, Calif.: Apsara Media for Intercultural Education. Videocassette.

DANCE AND DRAMA

Balasaraswati: A Vintage Video of Balasaraswati Dancing "Krishna ni Begane Baro." 1998. Directed by John Frazer. Available from Middletown, Conn.: World Music Archives, Olin Library, Wesleyan University. Videocassette. (Originally filmed at Wesleyan University in 1968. Bharata natyam classical dance.)

Circles and Cycles of Kathak Dance: The Lucknow Tradition. 1989. Produced by Robert Gottlieb. R. and L. Gottlieb Productions. Also Berkeley: University of California, Extension Media Center (2176 Shattuck Ave., Berkeley, CA 94720). 16mm film, videocassette. (On kathak classical dance of North India.)

The Cosmic Dance of Shiva. 1992. Produced and directed by Deben Bhattacharya, Jose Montes-Baquer, and Mario Dublanka. Audio-Forum V72409. Barre, Vt.: Sussex Video/Multicultural Media (R.R. 3, Box 6655, Granger Road, Barre, VT 05641; http://www.worldmusicstore.com), distributor. Videocassette. (Documentary interpretation of Shiva's cosmic dance in Indian classical style by the dancers Raja and Radha Reddy.)

A Dance the Gods Yearn to Witness. 1997. New York: Filmmakers Library, distributor. Videocassette. (Documentary on the classical bharata natyam dance.)

Dancing Girls of Lahore. 1993. Produced by Ahmad Jamal. New York: Filmmakers Library, distributor. Videocassette. (Portrait of two courtesans of Lahore, Pakistan, contrasting their lives with courtesans' life under the Mughals.)

Given to Dance: India's Odissi. 1985. Produced by Ron Hess (South Asian Studies, 1216 Van Hise Hall, University of Wisconsin, Madison, WI 53706). 16mm film. (On Oriyan music and dance.)

India—The Cosmic Dance of Shiva. N.d. Distributed by Multicultural Media AIMS 8705. Videocassette.

Kalakshetra: Devotion to Dance. 1985. Produced by Anthony Mayer, Boulder, Colo.: Centre Productions (1800 30th Street, #208, Boulder, CO 80301). 16mm. (Documentary on the Kalakshetra academy of music and dance in South India.)

Music and Dance of the Baiga People of Madhya Pradesh, India. 1993. Produced by Roderic Knight. Original Music. Videocassette.

Radha and Raja Reddy: Kuchipudi Nritya. 1993. Alurkar Music House AV 117. Videocassette. (Kuchipudi classical dance performance at the Savai Gandharva Music Festival, Pune, 1992.)

South Asia, 1. 1988. JVC Video Anthology of World Music and Dance, Vol. 11. C3524. Videocassette. (Covers bharat natyam, kathakali, manipuri, kathak, Manipuri folk dance, and dhol cholam—drum dance.)

South Asia, 2. 1988. JVC Video Anthology of World Music and Dance, Vol. 12. C3525. Videocassette. (Includes the chhau of Purulia, the chhau of Seraikela, and yaksha-gana.)

SOUTH ASIAN DIASPORA

Two Homes, One Heart: Sacramento Sikh Women and Their Songs and Dances. Joyce Middlebrook (P.O. Box 120, Brownsville, CA 95919). Videocassette.

The Middle East

Publications on Middle Eastern Music

INTRODUCTION TO THE REGION

Abu Lughod, Lila. 1986. *Veiled Sentiments: Honor and Poetry in a Bedouin Society*. Berkeley and Los Angeles: University of California Press.

————. 1989. *Before European Hegemony: The World System A.D. 1250–1350*. Oxford: Oxford University Press.

Adler, Israel. 1975. *Hebrew Writings Concerning Music, in Manuscripts and Printed Books, from Geonic Times up to 1800*. Munich: G. Henle.

Angles, Higinio. 1943–1964. *La musica de las Cantigas de Santa Maria del rey Alfonso el Sabio*. Barcelona: Disputación Provincial de Barcelona, Biblioteca Central.

ʿArafa, ʿAbd al-Munʿim, and Ṣafar ʿAlī. 1942. *Kitāb dirāsat al-ʿūd*. Cairo: n.p.

Armbrust, Walter. 1996. *Mass Culture and Modernism in Egypt*. Cambridge: Cambridge University Press.

Barkechli, Mehdi. 1963. *La musique traditionnelle de l'Iran*. Tehran: Secretariat d'État aux Beaux-Arts.

Bates, Daniel G., and Amal Rassam. 1983. *Peoples and Cultures of the Middle East*. Englewood Cliffs, N.J.: Prentice-Hall.

Bayer, Bathyah. 1963. *The Material Relics of Music in Ancient Palestine and Its Environs: An Archaeological Inventory*. Tel Aviv: Israel Music Institute.

Blench, Roger. 1984. "The Morphology and Distribution of Sub-Saharan Musical Instruments of North African, Middle Eastern, and Asian Origin." *Musica Asiatica* 4:155–191.

Blum, Stephen. 1972. "Musics in Contact: The Cultivations of Oral Repertoires in Meshed, Iran." Ph.D. dissertation, University of Illinois.

Bohlman, Philip. 1987. "The European Discovery of Music in the Islamic World and the 'Non-Western' in Nineteenth-Century Music History." *Journal of Musicology* 5(2):147–164.

Cachia, Pierre. 1973. "A Nineteenth-Century Arab's Observations on European Music." *Ethnomusicology* 17:41–51.

Campbell, Kay Hardy. 1999. "Days of Song and Dance." *Aramco World* 50(1):78–87.

Caton, Margaret. 1983. "The Classical Tasnif: A Genre of Persian Vocal Music." Ph.D. dissertation, University of California, Los Angeles.

Caton, Steven C. 1990. *"Peaks of Yemen I Summon": Poetry as Cultural Practice in a North Yemeni Tribe*. Berkeley: University of California Press.

————. 1999. *Lawrence of Arabia: A Film's Anthropology*. Berkeley: University of California Press.

Christianowitsch, Alexandre. 1863. *Esquisse historique de la musique arabe aux temps anciens, avec dessins d'instruments et quarante melodies notées et harmonisées*. Cologne: M. Dumont-Schaubert.

Danielson, Virginia. 1997. *The Voice of Egypt: Umm Kulthum, Arabic Song, and Egyptian Society in the Twentieth Century*. Chicago: University of Chicago Press.

Dauer, Alfons. 1985. *Tradition afrikanischer Blasorchester und Entstehung des Jazz*. Beiträge zur Jazzforschung, 7. Graz: Akademische Druck- und Verlagsanstalt.

D'Erlanger, Baron Rodolphe. 1930–1959. *La musique arabe*. Paris: Geuthner.

Déscription de l'Égypte. 1809–1822. Paris: Imprimerie Imperiale.

Djumaev, Alexander. 1993. "Power Structures, Culture Policy, and Traditional Music in Soviet Central Asia." *Yearbook for Traditional Music* 25:43–50.

Doubleday, Veronica. 1999. "The Frame Drum in the Middle East: Women, Musical Instruments, and Power." *Ethnomusicology* 43(1):101–134.

During, Jean. 1984. *La musique iranienne: Tradition et evolution*. Paris: Recherche sur les Civilisations.

————. 1988a. *Musique et extase: L'audition spirituelle dans la tradition Soufie*. Paris: Albin Michel.

————. 1988b. *La musique traditionnelle de l'Azerbayjan et la science des muqams*. Baden-Baden: V. Koerner.

————. 1992. "L'oreille islamique: Dix années capitales de la vie musicale en Iran: 1980–1990." *Asian Music* 23(2):135–164.

————. 1994. *Quelque chose se passe: Le sens de la tradition dans l'Orient musical*. Lagrasse: Verdier.

During, Jean, Zia Mirabdolbaghi, and Dariush Safvat. 1991. *The Art of Persian Music*. Washington, D.C.: Mage.

Eickelman, Dale F. [1981] 1998. *The Middle East and Central Asia: An Anthropological Approach*, 3rd ed. Upper Saddle River, N.J.: Prentice Hall.

Elsner, Jürgen. 1997. "Listening to Arabic Music." *World of Music* 39(2):111–126.

Engel, Hans, 1987. *Die Stellung des Musikers im arabisch-islamischen Raum*. Bonn: Verlag für Systematische Musikwissenschaft.

Farhat, Hormoz. 1965. "The *Dastgah* Concept in Persian Music." Ph.D. dissertation, University of California Los Angeles.

Farmer, Henry George. 1925. *The Arabian Influence on Musical Theory*. London: H. Reeves.

————. 1929. *History of Arabian Music to the Thirteenth Century*. London: Luzac.

————. 1933. *An Old Moorish Lute Tutor, Being Four Arabic Texts from Unique Manuscripts in the Biblioteca Nacional, Madrid (No. 334) and the Staatsbibliothek, Berlin (Lbg. 516)*. Glasgow: Civic.

————. [c. 1939] *The Structure of the Arabian and Persian Lute in the Middle Ages*. London: s.n.

————. 1943. *Saʿadyah Gaon on the Influence of Music*. London: A. Probsthain.

————. 1957. "Janitscharemusik." In *Die Musik in Geschichte und Gegenwart*. Kassel: Bärenreiter.

————. 1978. *Historical Facts for the Arabian Musical Influence*. New York: Arno.

————. 1997. *Studies in Oriental Music*. Frankfurt am Main: Institute for the History of Arabic-Islamic Science at Johann Wolfgang Goethe University.

al-Faruqi, Lois Ibsen. 1979. "The Status of Music in Muslim Nations: Evidence from the Arab World." *Asian Music* 12(1):56–85.

————. 1985a. "The Suite in Islamic History and Culture." *World of Music* 27(3): 46–64.

————. 1985b. "Music, Musicians, and Muslim Law." *Asian Music* 17(1):3–36.

Feldman, Walter. 1996. *Music of the Ottoman Court: Makam Composition and the Early Ottoman Instrumental Repertoire*. Berlin: VWB (Verlag für Wissenschaft und Bildung).

Friedl, Erika. 1991. *Women of Deh Koh: Lives in an Iranian Village*. New York: Penguin.

Gavin, Carney. 1985. "The Earliest Arabian Recordings: Discoveries and Work Ahead." *Phonographic Bulletin* 43:38–45.

Gerson-Kiwi, Edith. 1980. *Migrations and Mutations of the Music in East and West: Selected Writings*. Tel-Aviv: Tel-Aviv University, Faculty of

Visual and Performing Arts, Department of Musicology.

Goitein, S. D. 1967–1993. *A Mediterranean Society: The Jewish Communities of the Arab World as Portrayed in the Documents of the Cairo Geniza.* Berkeley: University of California Press.

Goldschmidt, Arthur. [1979] 1999. *A Concise History of the Middle East*, 6th ed. Boulder, Colo.: Westview.

Guignard, Michel. 1975. *Musique, honneur, et plaisir au Sahara.* Paris: Paul Geuthner. (Includes 45-rpm record.)

Hage, Louis. 1972–1991. *Musique maronite.* 4 vols. Kaslik, Lebanon: Bibliothèque de l'Université de Saint-Esprit.

Al-Ḥā'ik, Muḥammad ibn al-Ḥusayn. 1999. *Kunnāsh al-Ḥā'ik.* Rabat: Akadimiyat al-Mamlaka 'l-Maghribiya.

Hassan, Scheherazade Qassim. 1980. *Les instruments de musique en Irak et leur rôle dans la société traditionelle.* Paris: Mouton.

Hickmann, Hans. 1949. *Instruments de musique.* Cairo: Impr. de l'Institut Français d'Archeologie Orientale.

Hourani, Albert H. 1991. *A History of the Arab Peoples.* Cambridge, Mass.: Harvard University Press.

Husmann, Heinrich. 1970. "Die oktomodale Stichera und die Entwicklung des byzantinischen Oktoëchos." *Archiv für Musikwissenschaft* 27:304–325.

Ibn Khaldūn. 1967. *The Muqaddimah: An Introduction to History, Translated from the Arabic by Franz Rosenthal.* 3 vols., 2nd ed. Princeton. N.J.: Princeton University Press.

al-Jabartī, 'Abd al-Raḥmān. 1993. *Napoleon in Egypt: Al-Jabartî's Chronicle of the French Occupation, 1798*, trans. Shmuel Moreh. Princeton and New York: Markus Wiener.

Al-Jāḥiz. 1980. *The Epistle on Singing-Girls of Jahiz*, ed. with trans. and commentary by A. F. L. Beeston. Warminster, Wiltshire, England: Aris and Phillips.

Jeffery, Peter, 1994. "The Earliest Christian Chant Repertory Recovered: The Georgian Witnesses to Jerusalem Chant." *Journal of the American Musicological Society* 47:1–38.

Jung, Angelika. 1989. *Quellen der traditionellen Kunstmusik der Usbeken und Tadshiken Mittelasiens: Untersuchungen zur Entstehung und Entwicklung des šašmaqam.* Hamburg: Karl Dieter Wagner.

Kiesewetter, Raphael Georg. 1842. *Die Musik der Araber, nach Originalquellen dargestellt.* Leipzig: Breitkopf and Härtel.

Kitāb mu'tamar al-Mūsīqā al-'Arabīya (Book of the Conference of Arab Music). 1933. Cairo: al-Maṭba'a al-Amīrīya.

Lachmann, Robert. 1929a. "Die Weise vom Löwen und der pythische Nomos." In *Musikwissenschaftliche Beiträge: Festschrift für Johannes Wolf*, 97–106. Berlin: M. Breslauer.

———. 1929b. *Musik des Orients.* Breslau: F. Hirt.

Lambert, Jean. 1997. *La medecine de l'âme: Le chant de Sanaa dans la société yemenite.* Nanterre: Société d'Ethnologie.

Lane, Edward William. [1836] 1978. *An Account of the Manners and Customs of the Modern Egyptians.* Reprint, The Hague: East-West Publications.

Lapidus, Ira M. 1988. *A History of Islamic Societies.* Cambridge: Cambridge University Press.

Lawergren, Bo. 1995–1996. "The Spread of Harps between the Near and Far East during the First Millennium A.D.: Evidence of Buddhist Musical Cultures on the Silk Road." *Silk Road Art and Archaeology* 4:233–275.

———. 1997. "To Tune a String: Dichotomies and Diffusions between the Near and Far East." In *Ultra Terminum Vagari: Scritti in onore di Carl Nylander*, ed. B. Magnusson et al., 175–192. Rome: Quasar.

Levin, Theodore. 1984. "The Music and Tradition of the Bukharan Shashmaqam in Soviet Uzbekistan." Ph.D. dissertation, Princeton University.

———. 1993. "Western Central Asia and the Caucasus." In *Ethnomusicology: Historical and Regional Studies*, ed. Helen Myers. New York: Norton.

Marcus, Scott. 1989. "Arab Music Theory in the Modern Period." Ph.D. dissertation, University of California Los Angeles.

Massoudieh, Muhammad. 1973. "Tradition und Wandel in der persischen Musik des 19. Jahrhunderts." In *Musikkulturen Asiens, Afrikas, und Ozeaniens im 19. Jahrhundert*, ed. Robert Günther, 73–96. Regensburg: Gustav Bosse.

———. 1995. *Radif-i avazi-i musiqi-i sunnati-i Iran.* Tehran: Instisharat-i Vizarat-i Farhang va Hunar, Anjuman Ishaah va Ala-i Musiqi.

———. 1996. *Manuscrits persans concernant la musique.* Munich: G. Henle.

Monroe, James T. 1970. *Islam and the Arabs in Spanish Scholarship (Sixteenth Century to the Present).* Leiden: Brill.

———. 1986–1987. "A Sounding Brass and Tinkling Cymbal: Al-Halīl in Andalus (Two Notes on the Muwaššah)." *Corónica* 15(2):252–258.

Mostyn, Trevor, and Albert H. Hourani, eds. 1983. *The Cambridge History of the Middle East and North Africa.* Cambridge: Cambridge University Press.

La musique arabe: Le congrès du Caire de 1932. 1992. Cairo: CEDEJ.

Nasr, Seyyed Hossein. 1987. *Islamic Art and Spirituality.* Albany: State University of New York Press.

Nelson, Kristina. 1985. *The Art of Reciting the Qur'an.* Austin: University of Texas Press.

Nettl, Bruno. 1992. *The Radif of Persian Music.* Champaign, Ill.: Elephant and Cat.

Neubauer, Eckhard. 1965. "Musiker am Hof der frühen Abbasiden." Inaug.-Diss., Frankfurt am Main, J. W. Goethe-Universität.

———. 1994. "Die acht 'Wege' der arabischen Musiklehre und der Oktoechos." *Zeitschrift für die Geschichte der arabisch-islamischen Wissenschaften* 9:373–414.

———. 1995–1996. "Al-Halīl ibn Ahmad und die Frühgeschichte der arabischen Lehre von den 'Tönen' und den musikalischen Metren." *Zeitschrift für die Geschichte der arabisch-islamischen Wissenschaften* 10:255–323.

———. 1997. "Zur Bedeutung der Begriffe Komponist und Komposition in der Musikgeschichte der islamischen Welt." *Zeitschrift für die Geschichte der arabisch-islamischen Wissenschaften* 11:307–363.

Newlandsmith, Ernest, 1931. *The Ancient Music of the Coptic Church.* London, 1931.

Petry, Carl F. 1991. *The Civilian Elite of Cairo in the Later Middle Ages.* Princeton, N.J.: Princeton University Press.

Picken, Laurence E. R., and Noël J. Nickson. 2000. *Some Ancient Connections Explored.* Vol. 7 of *Music from the Tang Court.* Cambridge: Cambridge University Press.

Poché, Christian, and Jean Lambert. 2000. *Musiques du monde arabe et musulman: Bibliographie et discographie.* Paris: Geuthner.

Racy, Ali Jihad. 1983a. "The Waslah: A Compound Form Principle in Egyptian Music." *Arab Studies Quarterly* 5:396–404.

———. 1983b. "Music in Nineteenth-Century Egypt: An Historical Sketch." *Selected Reports in Ethnomusicology* 4:157–179.

———. 1991. "Creativity and Ambience: An Ecstatic Feedback Model from Arab Music." *World of Music* 33(3):7–28.

Rahman, Fazlur. [1966] 1979. *Islam*, 2nd ed. Chicago: University of Chicago Press.

Ribera, Julian. 1912. *Discursos leidos ante la Real Academia Española.* Madrid: Iberica.

———. 1970. *Historia de la musica arabe medieval y su influencia en la Española.* New York: AMS.

———. 1975. *Music in Ancient Arabia and Spain: Being La musica de las Cantigas.* New York: Da Capo.

Robson, James, and Henry George Farmer, eds. 1938. *Ancient Arabian Musical Instruments, as Described by al-Muffaddal ibn Salama (Ninth Century) in the Unique Istanbul Manuscript of the Kitab al-malahi in the Handwriting of Yaqut al-Mustasimi (d. 1298).* Glasgow: Civic.

Robson, James. 1938. *Treatise on Listening to Music.* London: Royal Asiatic Society.

Roy Choudhury, M. 1957. "Music in Islam." *Journal of the Asiatic Society, Letters* 23(2):43–102.

Said, Edward. 1978. *Orientalism.* New York: Pantheon.

Salvador-Daniel, Francisco. 1879. *La musique arabe: Ses rapports avec la musique grecque et le chant gregorien.* Algiers: A. Jourdan.

Sawa, George Dimitri. 1989. *Music Performance Practice in the Early Abbasid Era 132–320 A.H./*

A.D. 750–932. Toronto: Pontifical Institute of Mediaeval Studies.

Schlesinger, Kathryn. 1925. *Is European Musical Theory Indebted to the Arabs? Reply to "The Arabian Influence on Musical Theory" by H. G. Farmer*. London: H. Reeves.

Schuyler, Philip D. 1990. "Hearts and Minds: Three Attitudes toward Performance Practice and Music Theory in the Yemen Arab Republic." *Ethnomusicology* 34:1–18.

———. 1997. "*Qat*, Conversation, and Song: A Musical View of Yemeni Social Life." *Yearbook for Traditional Music* 29:57–73.

Shihāb al-Dīn Muḥammad ibn Ismāʿīl. c. 1840. *Safīnat al-mulk wa-nafisat al-fulk*. Cairo: Maṭbaʿat al-Jamiʿa.

Shiloah, Amnon. 1979. *The Theory of Music in Arabic Writings (c. 900–1900): A Descriptive Catalogue of Manuscripts in Libraries of Europe and the U.S.A.* Munich: G. Henle.

———. 1992. *Jewish Musical Traditions*. Detroit: Wayne State University Press.

———. 1995. *Music in the World of Islam: A Sociocultural Study*. Aldershot, Hants, England: Scolar.

Smith, J. A. 1994. "First-Century Christian Singing and Its Relationship to Contemporary Jewish Religious Song." *Music and Letters* 75:1–15.

Strunk, Oliver. 1942. "The Tonal System of Byzantine Music." *Musical Quarterly* 28:190–204.

———. 1950. *Source Readings in Music History*. New York: Norton.

Touma, Habib Hassan. 1973. "Die Musik der Araber im 19. Jahrhundert." In *Musikkulturen Asiens, Afrikas, und Ozeaniens im 19. Jahrhundert*, ed. Robert Günther, 49–72. Regensburg: Gustav Bosse.

———. 1996. *The Music of the Arabs*, trans. Laurie Schwartz. Portland, Ore.: Amadeus.

Van Nieuwkerk, Karin. 1995. *A Trade Like Any Other: Female Singers and Dancers in Egypt*. Austin: University of Texas Press.

Volney, Constantin-François comte de. 1787. *Voyage en Syrie et en Égypte*. Paris: Desenne.

Werner, Eric. 1959–1984. *The Sacred Bridge: The Interdependence of Liturgy and Music in Synagogue and Church during the First Millennium*. 2 vols. London: Dobson; New York: Columbia University Press.

———. 1965. "Greek Ideas on Music in Judeo-Arabic Literature." In *The Commonwealth of Music*, ed. Gustav Reese and Rose Brandel. New York: Free Press.

West, M. L. 1994. "The Babylonian Musical Notation and the Hurrian Melodic Texts." *Music and Letters* 75:161–179.

Wright, Owen. 1992. *Words without Songs: A Musicological Study of an Early Ottoman Anthology and Its Precursors*. London: School of Oriental and African Studies, University of London.

———. 2000. *Demetrius Cantemir: The Collection of Notations*. London: School of Oriental and African Studies, University of London.

Yekta, Raouf. 1922. "La musique turque." In *Encyclopédie de la musique et dictionnaire du Conservatoire*, ed. A. Lavignac. Paris: Delagrave.

Zimmerman, Heidy. 2000. *Tora und Shira: Untersuchungen zur Musikauffassung des rabbinischen Judentums*. Bern: Peter Lang.

Zirbel, Katherine. 1999. "Musical Discursions: Spectacle, Experience, and Political Economy among Egyptian Performers in Globalizing Markets." Ph.D. dissertation, University of Michigan.

THEORY, COMPOSITION, AND PERFORMANCE

Adler, Israel. 1975. *Hebrew Writings concerning Music in Manuscripts and Printed Books from Geonic Times up to 1800*. RISM, B IX². Munich: G. Henle.

And, Metin. 1976. *Turkish Dancing*. Ankara: Dost Yayınları.

———. 1987. *Culture, Performance, and Communication in Turkey*. Performance in Culture, 4. Tôkyô: Institute for the Study of Languages and Cultures of Asia.

Andrews, Walter. 1976. *An Introduction to Ottoman Poetry*. Chicago: Bibliotheca Islamica.

Bakewell, Anderson. 1985. "Music." In *Studies on the Tihāmah*, ed. Francine Stone, 104–108. London: Longman.

Bartók, Béla. 1976. *Turkish Music from Asia Minor*, ed. Benjamin Suchoff with afterword by Kurt Reinhard. Princeton, N.J.: Princeton University Press.

Başgöz, İlhan. 1972. "Folklore Studies and Nationalism in Turkey." *Journal of the Folklore Institute* 9:162–176.

Beken, Münir Nurettin, and Karl Signell. Forthcoming. "Confirming, Delaying, and Deceptive Elements in Turkish Improvisations." In *The Maqām Traditions of the Turkic Peoples: ICTM Study Group "Maqam," Proceedings of the Fourth Meeting, Istanbul, 18–24 October 1998*, ed. Jürgen Elsner and Yalçın Tura. Istanbul: Istanbul Technical University.

Caron, Nelly, and Dariouche Safvate. 1966. *Les traditions musicales: Iran*. Buchet/Chastel: Institut International d'Études Comparatives de la Musique.

———. 1988. "Melodic Contour in Persian Music, and Its Connection to Poetic Form and Meaning." In *Cultural Parameters of Iranian Musical Expression*, ed. Margaret Caton and Neil Siegel, 18–26. Redondo Beach, Calif.: Institute of Persian Performing Arts.

Caton, Margaret. 1983. "The Classical Tasnif: A Genre of Persian Vocal Music." Ph.D. dissertation, University of California, Los Angeles.

———. 1984. "Bahá'í Influences on Mírzá 'Abdú'lláh, Qájár Court Musician and Master of the *Radíf*." In *From Iran East and West*, ed. Juan Cole and Moojan Monen, 30–64, 187–190. Los Angeles: Kalimát.

Chabrier, Jean-Claude. 1985. "Éléments d'une approche comparative des échelles théoriques arabo-irano-turques." *Revue de Musicologie* 71:39–77.

Connelly, Bridget. 1986. *Arab Folk Epic and Identity*. Berkeley: University of California Press.

Crow, Douglas Karim. 1984. "Samāʿ: The Art of Listening in Islam." In *Maqām: Music of the Islamic World and Its Influences*, ed. Robert H. Browning, 30–33. New York: Alternative Museum.

Donald, Mary Ellen. 1985. *Arabic Tambourine: A Comprehensive Course in Techniques and Performances for the Tambourine, Tar, and Mazhar*. San Francisco: Mary Ellen Books.

During, Jean. 1975. "Elements spirituel dans la musique traditionnelle iranienne contemporaine." *Sophia Perennis: Bulletin of the Imperial Iranian Academy of Philosophy* 1(2):129–154.

———. 1984. *La musique iranienne: Tradition et évolution*. Paris: Éditions Recherche sur les Civilisations.

———. 1987. "Acoustic Systems and Metaphysical Systems in Oriental Traditions." *World of Music* 29(2):19–28.

During, Jean, and Zia Mirabdolbaghi. 1991. *The Art of Persian Music*. Washington, D.C.: Mage.

Elsner, Jürgen. 1967. "Zu Prinzipien arabischer Musizierpraxis." *Jahrbuch für Musikalische Volks- und Völkerkunde* 3:90–95.

———. 1975. "Zum Problem des Maqām." *Acta Musicologica* 47:208–239.

———, ed. 1989a. *Maqam-Raga-Zeilenmelodik: Konzeptionen and Prinzipen der Musikproduktion. Materialien der 1. Arbeitstagung der Study Group "Maqām" beim International Council for Traditional Music vom 28. Juni bis 2. Juli 1988 in Berlin*. Berlin: National-Komitee.

———. 1989b. "Zum maqām-Prinzip. Tongruppenmelodik als Grundlage und Baustein musikalischer Produktion." In *Maqam-Raga-Zeilenmelodik*, ed. Jürgen Elsner, 7–39. Berlin: National-Komitee.

———. 1990. "Trommeln und Trommelensembles im Jemen." In *Beiträge zur traditionellen Musik*, ed. Andreas Michel and Jürgen Elsner, 18–37. Berlin: Humboldt Universität.

———. 1992. "Trommeln und Trommelspiel im Jemen." In *Von der Vielfalt der musikalischen Kultur, Festschrift für Josef Kuckertz*, ed. Rüdiger Schumacher, 183–205. Anif/Salzburg: Ursula Müller-Speiser.

Elsner, Jürgen, and Gisa Jänichen, eds. 1992. *Regionale Maqām-Traditionen in Geschichte und Gegenwart. Materialien der 2. Arbeitstagung der Study Group "Maqām" des International Council for Traditional Music vom 23. bis 28. März in Gossen bei Berlin*. 2 vols. Berlin: s.n.

Elsner, Jürgen, and Risto Pekka Pennanen, eds. 1997. *The Structure and Idea of Maqām: Historical Approaches. Proceedings of the Third Meeting of the ICTM Maqām Study Group, Tampere—Virrat, 2–5 October 1995*. Tampere: University of Tampere.

D'Erlanger, Baron Rodolphe. 1930–1959. *La musique arabe*. 6 vols. Paris: Librairie Orientaliste Paul Geuthner.

Farhat, Hormoz. 1990. *The Dastgāh Concept in Persian Music*. Cambridge: Cambridge University Press.

Farmer, Henry George. 1936. "Musiki." In *Encyclopedia of Islam*, 749–755. Leiden: Brill.

———. 1973. *A History of Arabian Music to the Thirteenth Century*. London: Luzac.

al-Faruqi, Lois Ibsen. 1975. "The Muwashshah: A Vocal Form in Islamic Culture." *Ethnomusicology* 19:1–29.

———. 1978. "Ornamentation in Arabian Improvisational Music: A Study of Interrelatedness in the Arts." *World of Music* 20(1):17–32.

———. 1979. "The Status of Music in Muslim Nations: Evidence from the Arab World." *Asian Music* 12(1):56–85.

———. 1981. *An Annotated Glossary of Arabic Musical Terms*. Westport, Conn.: Greenwood.

———. 1985a. "Structural Segments in the Islamic Arts: The Musical 'Translation' of a Characteristic of the Literary and Visual Arts." *Asian Music* 16(1):59–81.

———. 1985b. "Music, Musicians, and Muslim Law." *Asian Music* 17(1):3–36.

Feldman, Walter. 1990. "Jewish Liturgical Music in Turkey." *Turkish Music Quarterly* 3(1):10–13.

———. 1996. *Music of the Ottoman Court: Makam, Composition, and the Early Ottoman Instrumental Repertoire*. Berlin: VWB (Verlag für Wissenschaft und Bildung).

Finnegan, Ruth. 1979. *Oral Poetry*. Cambridge: Cambridge University Press.

Hassan, Scheherazade Qassim. 1980. *Les instruments de musique en Iraq et leur rôle dans la société traditionelle*. Paris: École des Hautes Études en Sciences Sociales.

Gerson-Kiwi, Edith. 1963. *The Persian Doctrine of Dastga-Composition: A Phenomenological Study in the Musical Modes*. Tel-Aviv: Israel Music Institute.

Karpat, Kemal. 1963. "The People's Houses in Turkey." *Middle East Journal* 17:55–67.

———. 1976. *The Gecekondu: Rural Migration and Urbanization*. Cambridge: Cambridge University Press.

Khatschi, Khatschi. 1962. *Der Dastgäh: Studien zur neuen persischen Musik*. Regensburg: Gustav Bosse Verlag.

Krüger-Wust, Wilhelm J. 1983. *Arabische Musik in europäischen Sprachen: Eine Bibliographie*. Wiesbaden: Otto Harrassowitz.

Laborde, Jean Benjamin de. 1780. *Essai sur la musique ancienne et moderne*, Vol. 1. Paris: Imprimerie de Ph.-D. Pierres.

Lambert, Jean. 1989. "Du 'chanteur' à 'l'artiste' vers un nouveau statut du musicien." *Yemen Sanaa, Peuples Méditerranéens* 46.

———. 1990. "La médecine de l'âme: Musique et musiciens dans la société citadine à Ṣanʿāʾ." Ph.D. dissertation, Paris.

Lewis, Bernard. 1968. *The Emergence of Modern Turkey*. London: Oxford University Press.

Lortat-Jacob, Bernard, ed. 1987. *L'improvisation dans les musiques de traditional orale*. Paris: SELAF.

Marcus, Scott. 1989a. "Arab Music Theory in the Modern Period," esp. 12–42. Ph.D. dissertation, University of California, Los Angeles.

———. 1989b "The Periodization of Modern Arab Music Theory: Continuity and Change in the Definition of the *Maqāmat*." *Pacific Review of Ethnomusicology* 5:35–49.

———. 1992. "Modulation in Arab Music: Documenting Oral Concepts, Performance Rules, and Strategies." *Ethnomusicology* 36(2):171–195.

———. 1993a. "Solo Instrumental Improvisation (Taqāsīm) in Arab Music." *Middle East Studies Association Bulletin* 27:108–111.

———. 1993b. "The Interface between Theory and Practice: The Case of Intonation in Arab Music." *Asian Music* 24(2):39–58.

Markoff, Irene Judyth. 1986a. "Musical Theory, Performance, and the Contemporary Bağlama Specialist in Turkey." Ph.D. dissertation, University of Washington, Seattle.

———. 1986b. "The Role of Expressive Culture in the Demystification of a Secret Sect of Islam." *World of Music* 28(3):42–56.

———. 1990–1991. "The Ideology of Musical Practice and the Professional Turkish Folk Musician: Tempering the Creative Impulse." *Asian Music* 22(1):129–145.

Martin, Richard. 1982. *Islam: A Cultural Perspective*. Englewood Cliffs, N.J.: Prentice-Hall.

Maʿrufi, Musá, comp. 1963. *Les systems de la musique traditionnelle de l'Iran (radif)*. Tehran: Ministry of Culture and Arts.

Massoudieh, Mohammad Taghi. 1968. *Āwāz-e Sur: Zur Melodiebildung in der persischen Kunstmusik*. Regensburg: Gustav Bosse Verlag.

———. 1996. *Manuscrits persans concernant la musique*. RISM B XII. Munich: G. Henle.

Modir, Hafez. 1986. "Model and Interpretation in Iranian Classical Music: The Performance Practice of Mahmoud Zoufonoun." Master's thesis, University of California, Los Angeles.

Nelson, Kristina. 1985. *The Art of Reciting the Qurʾān*. Austin: University of Texas Press.

Nettl, Bruno. 1987. *The Radif of Persian Music: Studies of Structure and Cultural Context*. Champaign, Ill.: Elephant and Cat.

Nieuwkerk, Karin van. 1995. *"A Trade Like Any Other": Female Singers and Dancers in Egypt*. Austin: University of Texas Press.

Ogger, Thomas. 1987. *Maqām Segāh/Sikāh. Vergleich der Kunstmusik des Iran und des Irak anhand eines maqām Modells*. Hamburg: Karl Dieter Wagner.

Pacholczyk, Josef. 1970. "Regulative Principles in the Koran Chant of Shaikh ʿAbdʾl Basit ʿAbdʾs-Samad." Ph.D. dissertation, University of California, Los Angeles.

Picken, Laurence. 1975. *Folk Instruments of Turkey*. London: Oxford University Press.

Powers, Harold S. 1980. "Mode." In *The New Grove Dictionary of Music and Musicians*, ed. Stanley Sadie, 12:376–450. London: Macmillan.

———. 1988. "First Meeting of the ICTM Study Group on Maqām." *Yearbook for Traditional Music* 20:199–218.

———. 1989. "International *segāh*' and Its Nominal Equivalents in Central Asia and Kashmir." In *Maqam-Raga-Zeilenmelodik: Konzeptionen und Prinzipen der Musikproduktion. Materialien der 1. Arbeitstagung der Study Group "Maqām" beim International Council for Traditional Music vom 28. Juni bis 2. Juli 1988 in Berlin*, ed. Jürgen Elsner, 40–85. Berlin: National-Komitee.

Racy, Ali Jihad. 1976. "Record Industry and Egyptian Traditional Music: 1904–1932." *Ethnomusicology* 20(1):23–48.

———. 1977. "Musical Change and Commercial Recording in Egypt, 1904–1932." Ph.D. dissertation, University of Illinois, Champaign-Urbana.

———. 1991. "Creativity and Ambience: An Ecstatic Feedback Model from Arab Music" *World of Music* 33(3):7–28.

Reckord, Thomas. 1987. "Chant in Popular Iranian Shi'ism." Ph.D. dissertation, University of California, Los Angeles.

———. 1988. "The Role of Religious Chant in the Definition of the Iranian Aesthetic." In *Cultural Parameters of Iranian Musical Expression*, ed. Margaret Caton and Neil Siegel. Redondo Beach, Calif.: Institute of Persian Performing Arts.

Reichow, Jan. 1971. *Die Entfaltung eines Melodiemodells im Genus Sikāh*. Regensburg: Bosse.

Reinhard, Kurt, and Ursula Reinhard. 1984. *Musik der Türkei*. Wilhelmshaven: Heinrichschofen's Verlag.

Roychoudhury, M. L. 1957. "Music in Islam." *Journal of Asiatic Society, Letters* 23(2):43–102.

Sadeghi, Manoochehr. 1971. "Improvisation in Nonrhythmic Solo Instrumental Contemporary Persian Art Music." Master's thesis, California State University, Los Angeles.

Saygun, A. Adnan. 1976. *Béla Bartók's Folk Musical Research in Turkey*, ed. V. Laszlo. Budapest: Akademia Kiado.

Schneider, Marius. 1962. "Ragā-Maqām-Nomos." In *Die Musik in Geschichte und Gegenwart* 10:1864–1868. Kassel: Bärenreiter.

Schuyler, Philip D. 1984. "Moroccan Andalusian Music." In *Maqām: Music of the Islamic World and Its Influences*, ed. Robert H. Browning, 14–17. New York: Alternative Museum.

Serjeant, Robert B. 1951. *Prose and Poetry from Hadramawt*. London: Taylor's Foreign Press.

Seroussi, Edwin. 1989a. *Mizimrat Qedem: The Life and Music of R. Isaac Algazi from Turkey*. Jerusalem: Renanot-Institute for Jewish Music.

———. 1989b. "The Turkish *Makam* in the Musical Culture of the Ottoman Jews: Sources and Examples." *Israeli Studies in Musicology* 5:55–68.

———. 1991. "The *Peşrev* as a Vocal Genre in Ottoman Hebrew Sources." *Turkish Music Quarterly* 4(3):1–9.

Shiloah, Amnon. 1974. "Le poète-musicien et la création poetico-musicale en Moyen-Orient." *Yearbook of the International Folk Music Council* 6:52–63.

———. 1979. *The Theory of Music in Arabic Writings (c. 900–1900). Descriptive Catalogue of Manuscripts in Libraries of Europe and the U.S.A.* RISM B X. Munich: G. Henle.

———. 1981. "The Arabic Concept of Mode." *Journal of the American Musicological Society* 34(1):19–42.

———. 1992. *Jewish Musical Traditions*. Detroit: Wayne State University Press.

———. 1995. *Music in the World of Islam*. Detroit: Wayne State University Press.

Signell, Karl. 1977. *Makam: Modal Practice in Turkish Art Music*. Seattle: Asian Music.

———. 1986. *Makam: Modal Practice in Turkish Art Music*. New York: Da Capo. See also: 1973. "Turkish Makam System in Contemporary Theory and Practice." Ph.D. dissertation. Ann Arbor, Mich.: UMI Research Press.

Simon, Artur, et al. 1997. "Modale Melodiekonzepte." In *Die Musik in Geschichte und Gegenwart*, 2nd ed., Sachteil 6:354–382. Kassel: Bärenreiter; Stuttgart: Metzler.

Stokes, Martin. 1992. *The Arabesk Debate*. Oxford: Clarendon.

Szabolcsi, Bence. 1965. "The Maqam Principle in Folk and Art-Music: The Type and Its Variants." In *A History of Melody*, 205–215. London: Barrie and Rockliff.

Touma, Habib Hassan. 1971. "The *Maqam* Phenomenon: An Improvisation Technique in the Music of the Middle East." *Ethnomusicology* 15:38–48.

———. 1975. "Die Koranrezitation: Eine Form der religiösen Musik der Araber." *Beiträge zur Musik des vorderen Orients und seinen Einflussbereichen, Baessler-Archiv* 23(1):87–120.

———. 1976. *Der Maqam Bayati im arabischen Taqsim*. Hamburg: Karl Dieter Wagner.

———. 1996. *The Music of the Arabs*, trans. Laurie Schwartz. Portland, Ore.: Amadeus.

Tsuge, Gen'ichi. 1972. "A Note on the Iraqi Maqam." *Asian Music* 4(1):59–66.

———. 1974. "Āvāz: A Study of the Rhythmic Aspects in Classical Iranian Music." Ph.D. dissertation, Wesleyan University.

Varzi, Mortezá. 1988. "Performance-Audience Relationships in the *Bazm*." In *Cultural Parameters of Iranian Musical Expression*, ed. Margaret

Caton and Neil Siegel, 1–9. Redondo Beach, Calif.: Institute of Persian Performing Arts.

Vigreux, Philippe, ed. *Musique arabe: Le Congrès du Caire de 1932*. Cairo: CEDEJ.

Wright, Owen. 1978. *The Modal System of Arab and Persian Music, A.C. 1250–1300*. London Oriental Series, Vol. 28. Oxford: Oxford University Press.

———. 1988. "Aspects of Historical Change in the Turkish Classical Repertoire." *Musica Asiatica* 5:1–108.

———. 1992a. *Demetrius Cantemir: The Collection of Notations*. London: School of Oriental and African Studies, University of London.

———. 1992b. "Segah: An Historical Outline." In *Regionale Maqām-Traditionen in Geschichte und Gegenwart. Materialien der 2. Arbeitstagung der Study Group "Maqām" des International Council for Traditional Music vom 23. bis 28. März in Gossen bei Berlin*, ed. Jürgen Elsner and Gisa Jähnichen, 480–509. Berlin: s.n.

Yammine, Habib. 1995. "Les hommes des tribus et leur musique (Hauts-plateaux yéménites, vallée d'al-Ahjur)." Ph.D. dissertation, Paris.

Yar-Shater, Ehsan. 1974. "Affinities between Persian Poetry and Music." In *Studies in Art and Literature of the Near East*, ed. Peter Chelkowski, 59–78. Salt Lake City: University of Utah.

Yekta, Rauf. 1921. "La musique turque." In A. Lavignac, *Encyclopedie de la musique et dictionnaire du Conservatoire*, part 1, 5:2945–3064. Paris: C. Delagrave.

Zonis, Ella. 1973. *Classical Persian Music: An Introduction*. Cambridge, Mass.: Harvard University Press.

MUSIC IN RELIGIOUS EXPRESSION

Abdel-Malek, Kamal. 1995. *Muhammad in the Modern Egyptian Popular Ballad*. Leiden: Brill.

Abu Mrad, Nidaa. 1989. "Musicothérapie chez les Arabes au Moyen-Age." Thesis, Académie de Paris, Université René Descartes.

Ackerman, Phyllis. 1938–1939. "The Character of Persian Music." In *A Survey of Persian Art*, ed. Arthur Upham Pope, 2805–2817. London and New York: Oxford University Press.

Adler, Israel. 1975. *Hebrew Writings concerning Music in Manuscripts and Printed Books from Geonic Times up to 1800*. München: G. Henle. RISM B IX².

———. 1982. "Problems in the Study of Jewish Music." In *Proceedings of the World Congress on Jewish Music, Jerusalem 1978*, ed. Judith Cohen, 15–26. Tel-Aviv: Institute for the Translation of Hebrew Literature.

Aflākī, Shams al-Dīn Aḥmad. 1978. *Les saints des derviches tourneurs (Manāqib ul-ʿārifīn)*, trans. Clément Huart. 2 vols. Paris: Sindbad.

Ashqar, Paul. 1939. *Mélodies liturgiques syro-maronites*. Jounieh, Lebanon.

ʿAṭṭār, Farīd al-Dīn. 1959. *The Tadhkiratu 'l-Awliya* (Memoirs of the Saints), ed. and trans.

Reynold A. Nicholson. 2 vols. London and Leiden.

Bayer, Bathja. 1986. "The Announcement of the Institute of Jewish Music in Jerusalem by A. Z. Idelsohn and S. Z. Rivlin in 1910." *Yuval* 5:24–35.

Ben-Ami, Issachar. 1998. *Saint Veneration among the Jews in Morocco*. Detroit: Wayne State University Press.

Ben Rafael, E., and S. Sharot. 1991. *Ethnicity, Religion, and Class in Israeli Society*. Cambridge and New York: Cambridge University Press.

Birge, John Kingsley. 1937. *The Bektashi Order of Dervishes*. London: Luzac Oriental.

Borrel, Eugene. 1947. "Les poètes Kizil Bach et leur musique." *Revue des Études Islamiques* 15:157–190.

Borsai, Ilona. 1970–1971. "Caractèristiques générales du chant de la messe copte." *Studia Orientalia Christiana Aegyptica: Collectanea* 14:412–442.

———. 1974. "Y-a-t'il un octoechos dans le système du chant copte?" *Studia Aegyptica* 1:39–53.

Bürgel, J. Christoph. 1988. *The Feather of Simurgh: The "Licit" Magic of the Arts in Medieval Islam*. New York: New York University Press.

Chottin, Alexis. 1938. *Tableau de la musique marocaine*. Paris: P. Geuthner.

Cody, Aelred. 1982. "The Early History of the Octoechos in Syria." In *East of Byzantium: Syria and Armenia in the Formative Period*. Washington, D.C.: Dumbarton Oaks.

Cohen, Boaz. 1935. "The Responsum of Maimonides concerning Music." *Jewish Music Journal* 2, no. 2:1–7.

Corbin, Henry. 1960. *Terre céleste et corps de résurrection de l'Iran mazdéen à l'Iran shī'ite*. Paris: Buchet/Chastel. See also: 1979. *Corps spirituel et Terre céleste: De l'Iran mazdéen à l'Iran shī'ite*. (2nd ed.)

———. 1993. *History of Islamic Philosophy*, trans. Liadain and Philip Sherrard. London and New York: Kegan Paul.

Dalmais, Irene Henri. 1957. "L'apport des églises syriennes à l'hymnographie chrétienne." *L'Orient Syrien* 2(3):243–260.

Danielson, Virginia. 1997. *The Voice of Egypt: Umm Kulthum, Arabic Song, and Egyptian Society in the Twentieth Century*. Chicago: University of Chicago Press.

Denny, Frederick. 1980."The Adab of Qur'ān Recitation: Text and Context." In *International Congress for the Study of the Qur'ān*, ed. Anthony Johns, 143–160. Canberra: Australian National University.

———. 1986. "The Great Indonesian Qur'ān Chanting Tournament." *The World and I* 6:216–223.

———. 1988. "Qur'ān Recitation Training in Indonesia: A Survey of Contexts and Handbooks." In *Approaches to the History of Interpretation of the Qur'ān*, ed. Andrew Rippin, 288–306. Oxford: Clarendon.

———. 1989. "Qur'ān Recitation: A Tradition of Oral Performance and Transmission." *Oral Tradition* 4(1–2):5–26.

Deshen, Shlomo, and Moshe Shokeid. 1984. "Cultural Ethnicity in Israel: The Case of Middle Eastern Jews' Religiosity." *AJS Review* 9(2):247–271.

During, Jean. 1977. "The 'Imaginal' Dimension and Art of Iran." *World of Music* 19(3–4):24–34.

———. 1982. "Revelation and Spiritual Audition in Islam." *World of Music* 4:68–84.

———. 1987. "Le samā' de Ruzbehān Baqli Shirāzi." *Connaissance Religieuse* 2(4):191–197.

———. 1988. *Musique et extase: L'audition mystique dans la tradition soufie*. Paris: Albin Michel.

———. 1989. *Musique et mystique dans les traditions de l'Iran*. Paris: Institut Français de Recherche en Iran. Leuven: Diffusion, Éditions Peeters.

———. 1990a. "L'autre oreille: Le pouvoir mystique de la musique au Moyen-Orient." *Cahiers des Musiques Traditionnelles* 3:57–78.

———. 1990b. "Der Mythos der Simorg." *Spektrum Iran* 3(3):3–19.

———. 1992. "What Is Sufi Music?" In *The Legacy of Persian Medieval Sufism*, ed. Leonard Lewisohn, 277–287. London: Khaniqahi Nimatullahi.

———. 2001. *L'âme des sons: La musique d'Ostad Elâhi (1895–1974)*. Paris: Éditions du Relié.

Eickelman, Dale. 1978. "The Art of Memory: Islamic Education and Its Social Reproduction." *Comparative Studies in Society and History* 20(4):485–516.

Erian, Nabila. 1986. "Coptic Music: An Egyptian Tradition." Ph.D. dissertation, University of Maryland, Park County.

D'Erlanger, Baron Rodolphe. 1930–1959. *La musique arabe*. 6 vols. Paris: P. Geuthner.

Farmer, Henry George. 1925–1926. "The Influence of Music from Arabic Sources." *Proceedings of the Musical Association* 52:89–124.

al-Farūqi, Lois Ibsen/Lamyā'. 1979. "Tartīl al-Qur'ān al-Karīm." In *Islamic Perspectives: Studies in Honor of Mawlāna Sayyid Abul 'A'lā Mawdūdi*, ed. Khurshid Ahmad and Zafar Ansari, 105–121. London: Islamic Foundation.

Feldman, Walter. 1992. "Musical Genres and Zikir of the Sunni Tarikats of Istanbul." In *The Dervish Lodge: Architecture, Art, and Sufism in Ottoman Turkey*, ed. Raymond Lifchez, 187–202. Berkeley: University of California Press.

———. 1993. "Mysticism, Didacticism, and Authority in the Liturgical Poetry of the Halvetī Dervishes of Istanbul." *Edebiyat* NS 4:243–65.

Frishkopf, Michael. 1996. "La voix du poète: Ṭarab et poésie dans le chant mystique soufi." *Egypte/Monde Arabe/CDEJ* 25:85–117.

Gastoué, Amédée. 1931. "La musique byzantine et le chant des églises d'Orient." In *Encyclopédie de la musique et dictionnaire du Conservatoire*, 1:541–556. Paris: Librairie Delagrave.

Gilsenan, Michael. 1973. *Saint and Sufi in Modern Egypt: An Essay in the Sociology of Religion*. Oxford: Clarendon.

Graham, William A. 1985. "The Qur'ān as Spoken Word: An Islamic Contribution to the Understanding of Scripture." In *Approaches to Islam in Religious Studies*, ed. Richard C. Martin, 23–40. Tucson: University of Arizona Pres.

———. 1987. *Beyond the Written Word: Oral Aspects of Scripture in the History of Religion*. Cambridge: Cambridge University Press.

Hage, Louis. 1963. "Réforme du chant maronite." *Cahiers de Philosophie et de Théologie* 2:7–27.

———. 1967. "Les mélodies-types dans le chant maronite." *Melto* 3:325–409.

———. 1969. "Le chant maronite." In *Encyclopédie des musiques sacrées* 2:218–222. Paris: Éditions Labergerie. See also English translations: *Maronite Music*. 1978. London: Longman for the University of Essex; "Music of the Maronite Church." 1971. *Parole de l'Orient* 2(1):197–206.

———. 1972–. *Musique maronite*. Kaslik, Lebanon: Bibliothèque de l'Université de Saint-Esprit. Vol. 1: *Le chant syro-maronite* (1972). Vol. 2: *Le chant maronite* (1995). Vols. 3a and 3b: *Monuments du chant maronite* (1990–1991). Vols. 4a and 4b: *Analyse, classement, et références* (1990–1991).

———. 1980. "Lebanon." In *The New Grove Dictionary of Music and Musicians*, 10:573–576. London: Macmillan.

———. 1984a. "Siriaco, Canto." In *Dizionario enciclopedico universale della musica e dei musicisti, il lessico*, 4:308–309. Turin: UTET.

———. 1984b. "Les églises orientales non byzantines." In *Précis de musicologie*, ed. Jacques Chailley, 114–119. Paris: Presses Universitaires de France.

———. 1986. *Les strophes-types syriaques et leurs mètres poétiques du patriarche maronite Etienne Douayhi*. Kaslik, Lebanon: Bibliothèque de l'Université Saint-Esprit.

———. 1987. *The Syriac Model Strophes and Their Poetic Meters, by the Maronite Patriarch Stephen Douayhi*. Kaslik, Lebanon: University of the Holy Spirit.

———. 1997. *Précis de chant maronite*. Kaslik: Université Saint-Esprit de Kaslik.

———. 1997? Vol. 7: *Les strophes-types syriaques: Analyse, références, et classification*.

———. c. 1998. Vol. 8: *Écrits relatifs au chant syriaque et maronite*.

Hajdu, Andre. 1971. "Le niggun Meron." *Yuval: Studies of the Jewish Music Research Centre* 2:73–114.

Hajdu, Andre, and Yaacov Mazor. 1971. "Hasidim: The Musical Tradition of the Hasidim." In *Encyclopedia Judaica*, 7:1421–1432. Jerusalem: Encyclopedia Judaica; New York: Macmillan.

Halper, Jeff, Edwin Seroussi, and Pamela Squires-Kidron. 1989. "Musica Mizrahit: Ethnicity and Class Culture in Israel." *Popular Music* 8:131–142.

Hannick, Théodose. 1969. "Syriens occidentaux et Syriens orientaux." In *Traditions chrétiennes des premiers siècles aux cultes révolutionnaires*. Vol. 2 of *Encylopédie des musiques sacrées*, ed. Jacques Porte, 214–217. Paris: Éditions Labergerie.

Hodgson, M. G. S. 1974. *The Venture of Islam*, Vol. 1. Chicago: University of Chicago Press.

Hoffman, Valerie. 1995. *Sufism, Mystics, and Saints in Modern Egypt*. Columbia: University of South Carolina Press.

Horowitz, Amy. 1994. "Israeli Mediterranean Music: Cultural Boundaries and Disputed Territories." Ph.D. dissertation, University of Pennsylvania.

Hujvīrī, 'Alī ibn 'Uṣmān. 1976. *The "Kashf al-mahjub": The Oldest Persian Treatise on Sufiism*, trans. Reynold A. Nicholson. Lahore: Islamic Book Foundation.

Husman, Heinrich. 1967. *Die Melodien des chaldäischen Breviers Commune, nach den Traditionen Vorderasiens und der Malabarküste*. Rome: Pontificio Istituto per gli Studi Orientali.

———. 1969. "Die Tonarten der chaldäischen Breviergesänge." *Orientalia Christiana Periodica* 35:215–248.

———. 1969–1971. *Die Melodien der Jakobitischen Kirche*. Wien: Bohlau Kommissionsverlag.

———. 1970. "Arabische Maqamen in ostsyrischer Kirchenmusik." In *Musik als Gestalt und Erlebnis: Festschrift Walter Graf*, 102. Vienna: Böhlau.

———. 1971. "Hymnus und Troparion." In *Jahrbuch des Staatlichen Institutes für Musikforschung Preussischer Kulturbesitz Berlin*, 7–86. Berlin.

———. 1974. "Eine Konkordanztabelle syrischer Kirchentöne und arabischer Maqamen in einem syrischen Musiknotizbuch." In *Symposium Syriacum 1972*. Rome: Pont. Institutum Orientalium Studiorum.

———. 1976. "Madraše und Seblata—Repertoireuntersuchungen zu den Hymnen Ephraems des Syrers." *Acta Musicologica* 48:113–150.

Iamblichus (c. 250–c. 330). 1993. *Les mystères d'Egypte*, trans. Édouard des Places. Paris: Les Belles Lettres.

Ivánka, Endre von, et al., eds. 1971. *Handbuch der Ostkirchenkunde*. Düsseldorf: Patmos-Verlag.

Jargy, Simon. 1952. "La musique liturgique syrienne." In *Atti del Congresso Internazionale di Musica Sacra*, 166–169. Rome, Tournai, Paris: Desclée.

———. 1961. "Syrienne (musique)." In *Encyclopédie de la musique*, ed. François Michel, 3:992–993. Paris: Fasquelle.

———. 1971. *La musique arabe*. Paris: Presses Universitaires de France.

———. 1978. "The Folk Music of Syria and Lebanon." *World of Music* 1:79–89.

Jeannin, Jules, et al. 1924–1928. *Mélodies syriennes*. Paris: Leroux.

Kahn, Aharon. 1986–1989. "Music in Halakhic Perspective." *Journal of Jewish Music and Liturgy* 9:55–72, 10:32–49, 11:65–75.

Katz, Ruth. 1968. "The Singing of *Baqqashot* by Aleppo Jews." *Acta Musicologica* 40:65–85.

Kedem, Peri. 1991. "Dimensions of Jewish Religiosity." In *Tradition, Innovation, Conflict: Jewishness and Judaism in Contemporary Israel*, ed. Z. Sobel and B. Beit-Hallahmi, 251–272. Albany: State University of New York Press.

Khs-Burmester, O. H. E. 1967. *The Egyptian or Coptic Church: A Detailed Description of Her Liturgical Services and the Rites and Ceremonies Observed in the Administration of Her Sacraments*. Cairo: Publications de la Société d'Archéologie Copte.

Kuckertz, Josef. 1969. "Die Melodietypen der westsyrischen liturgischen Gesänge." *Kirchenmusikalisches Jahrbuch* 53:61–98.

Levi, Leo. 1957. "Les neumes, les notations bibliques, et le protochrétien." In *La musique sacrée au IIIème Congrès international de musique sacrée*, 147–155 [*La Revue musicale*, nos. 239–240]. Paris: Éditions Richard-Masse.

Lièvre, Viviane, and Jean-Yves Loude. 1990. *Le chamanisme des Kalash du Pakistan*. Paris: Éditions Recherche sur les Civilisations.

MacDonald, Duncan, ed. 1901–1902. "Emotional Religion in Islam as Affected by Music and Singing. Being a Translation of a Book of the *Ihyā 'Ulūm ad-Dīn* of al-Ghazzālī, with Analysis, Annotations, and Appendices." *Journal of the Royal Asiatic Society* (1901):195–252, 705–748; (1902):1–28, 195–252.

Martin, B. G. 1972. "A Short History of the Khalwati Order of Dervishes." In *Scholars, Saints, and Sufis*, ed. Nikki R. Keddie, 275–306. Berkeley: University of California Press.

Meinardus, Otto Friedrich August. 1989. *Monks and Monasteries of the Egyptian Deserts*, rev. ed. Cairo: American University in Cairo Press.

Ménard, René. 1952. "Notes sur les musiques Arabes et Coptes." *Cahiers Coptes* 2:48–54.

———. 1969. "Tradition copte." In *Traditions chrétiennes des premiers siècles aux cultes révolutionnaires*. Vol. 2 of *Encylopédie des musiques sacrées*, ed. Jacques Porte, 229–233. Paris: Éditions Labergerie.

Moftah, Ragheb. 1958. "The Coptic Music." *Bulletin de l'Institute des Études Coptes*.

Moftah, Ragheb, Margit Toth, and Martha Roy. 1998. *The Liturgy of St. Basil of the Coptic Orthodox Church*. Cairo: American University at Cairo Press.

Molé, Marijan. 1963. "La danse extatique en Islam." In *Les danses sacrées*, 145–280. Paris: Éditions du Seuil.

Nelson, Kristina. 1985. *The Art of Reciting the Qur'ān*. Austin: University of Texas Press.

Neubauer, Eckhard. 1990. "Arabische Anleitungen für Musiktherapie." *Zeitschrift für Geschichte der Arabisch-Islamischen Wissenschaften* 6:227–272.

Nieten, Ulrike. 1998. "Syrische Kirchenmusik." In *Die Musik in Geschichte und Gegenwart*, 9:185–200. Kassel: Bärenreiter.

Parisot, Dom Jean. 1899. *Rapport sur une mission scientifique en Turquie d'Asie*. Paris: E. Leroux.

———. 1901. "Les huit modes du chant syrien." *Tribune de Saint-Gervais* 7:258–262.

———. 1898. "Essai sur le chant liturgique des églises orientales." *Revue de l'Orient Chrétien* 3:221–231.

Poché, Christian. 1978. "Zikr and Musicology." *World of Music* 20:59–73.

Qureshi, Regula. 1969. "Tarannum: The Chanting of Urdu Poetry." *Ethnomusicology* 13(3):425–468.

———. 1995. *Sufi Music of India and Pakistan*. Chicago: University of Chicago Press.

Rasmussen, Anne K. 2001. "The Qur'ān in Indonesian Daily Life: The Public Project of Musical Oratory." *Ethnomusicology* 45:30–57.

Robertson, Marian. 1984–1985. "The Reliability of the Oral Tradition in Preserving Coptic Music: A Comparison of Three Musical Transcriptions of an Extract from the Liturgy of St. Basil." *Bulletin of the Coptic Archaeology Society* 26 and 27.

———. 1986. "Vocal Music in the Early Coptic Church." *Coptologia* 6:23–28.

Robson, James, ed. 1938. *Tracts on Listening to Music, Being Dhamm al-malāhī, by Ibn abī'l-Dunyā, and Bawāriq al-ilmā', by Majd al-Dīn al-Tūsī al-Ghazālī*. London: Royal Asiatic Society.

Rouanet, J. 1922. "La musique arabe." In *Encyclopédie de la musique et dictionnaire du Conservatoire*, ed. A. Lavignac, 1(5):2676–2812. Paris: C. Delagrave.

Ṣafi al-Dīn. [1346] 1967. *Biḥjat al-Rūḥ*, ed. Rabino de Borgomale. Tehran.

Sarrāj, Abū Naṣr 'Abd Allāh ibn 'Alī. 1914. *The Kitāb al-luma' fī 'l-Taṣawwuf of Abū Naṣr 'Abdallah b. 'Alī al-Sarrāj al-Ṭūsī*, ed. Reynold Alleyne Nicholson. Leyden: Brill; London: Luzac.

Schleifer, Eliyahu. 1995. "Current Trends of Liturgical Music in the Ashkenazi Liturgy." In *Jewish Musical Culture—Past and Present*. Vol. 37(1) of *World of Music*, ed. Uri Sharvit, 59–72. Basel, Kassel: Bärenreiter.

Schreiber, Baruch David. 1984–1985. "The Woman's Voice in the Synagogue." *Journal of Jewish Music and Liturgy* 7:27–32.

Sells, Michael. 1991. "Sound, Spirit, and Gender in *Sûrat al-Qadr*." *Journal of the American Oriental Society* 111(2):239–259.

———. 1993. "Sound and Meaning in *Surat al-Qari'a*." *Arabica* 40:403–430.

———, ed. 1999. *Approaching the Qur'ān—The Early Revelations*. Ashland, Ore.: White Cloud.

———. 2000. "A Literary Approach to the Hymnic Suras of the Qur'ān." In *Literary Structures of Religious Meaning in the Qur'ān*, ed. Issa Boullata, 3–25. London: Curzon.

Seroussi, Edwin. 1986. "Politics, Ethnic Identity, and Music in the Singing of *Bakkashot* among Moroccan Jews in Israel." *Asian Music* 17(2):32–45.

Sharvit, Uri. 1986. "Diversity within Unity: Stylistic Change and Ethnic Continuity in Israeli Religious Music." *Asian Music* 17(2):126–146.

El-Shawan, Salwa. 1975. "An Annotated Bibliography on Coptic Music." M.A. thesis, Columbia University.

Shiloah, Amnon. 1965, 1967. "L'épître sur la musique des Ikhwân al-Safâ." *Revue des Études Islamiques* 33:125–162; 37:159–193.

———, ed. 1972. *La perfection des connaissances musicales (al-Ḥasan ibn Aḥmad ibn 'Alī al-Kātib)*. Paris: P. Geuthner.

Slobin, Mark. 1989. *Chosen Voices: The Story of the American Cantorate*. Urbana and Chicago: University of Illinois Press.

Touma, Habib Hassan. 1975a. "Die Koranrezitation: Eine Form der religiösen Musik der Araber." *Bessler-Archiv*, Neue Folge, 23:87–133.

———. 1975b. *Die Musik der Araber*. Wilhelmshaven: Heinrichshofen's Verlag.

———. 1976. "Relations between Aesthetics and Improvisation in Arab Music." *World of Music* 18(2):33–36.

Tucci, Giuseppe. 1974. *Théorie et pratique du mandala*. Paris: Fayard.

Waugh, Earl H. 1989. *The Munshidīn of Egypt: Their World and Their Song*. Columbia: University of South Carolina Press.

Wegner, Ulrich. 1986. "Transmitting the Divine Revelation: Some Aspects of Textualism and Textual Variability in Qur'ānic Recitation." *World of Music* 27(3):57–78.

Weiss, Bernard, Morroe Berger, and M. A. Rauf, trans. 1975. *The Recited Koran: A History of the First Recorded Version by Labib as-Sa'id*. Princeton, N.J.: Darwin.

Wellesz, Egon. 1954a. "Early Christian Music." In *The New Oxford History of Music*, 2:1–13. London, New York, and Toronto: Oxford University Press.

———. 1954b. "Music of the Eastern Churches." In *The New Oxford History of Music*, 2:14–52. London, New York, and Toronto: Oxford University Press.

Werner, Eric. 1952. "The Common Ground in the Chant of Church and Synagogue." In *Atti del Congresso Internazionale di Musica Sacra*, ed. Igino Angles, 134–148. Tournai: Desclée.

———. 1959. *The Sacred Bridge: The Interdependence of Liturgy and Music in Synagogue and Church during the First Millennium*. London: Dobson; New York: Columbia University Press.

Yalcin, Warda, and Esther Lamandier. 1997. *Chants de l'église d'Orient en araméen*. Paris: Alienor.

POPULAR MUSIC AND THE MEDIA

Abraham, Sameer Y., and Nabeel Abraham. 1983. *Arabs in the New World: Studies on Arab-American Communities*. Detroit: Wayne State University Press, Urban Studies Center.

Alterman, Jon. 1998. *New Media, New Politics? From Satellite Television to the Internet in the Arab World*. Washington, D.C.: Washington Institute for Near East Policy.

Armbrust, Walter. 1996. *Mass Culture and Modernism in Egypt*. Cambridge: Cambridge University Press.

———. 1998. "When the Lights Go Down in Cairo: Cinema as Secular Ritual." *Visual Anthropology* 10(4):413–442.

———. 2000. "Farid Shauqi: Tough Guy, Family Man, Cinema Star." In *Imagined Masculinities: Male Identity and Culture in the Modern Middle East*, ed. Mai Ghoussoub and Emma Sinclair-Webb. London: Saqi.

Aswad, Barbara C., ed. 1974. *Arabic Speaking Communities in American Cities*. New York: Center for Migration Studies of New York.

Ayalon, Ami. 1995. *The Press in the Arab Middle East: A History*. Oxford: Oxford University Press.

Azzam, Nabil Salim. 1990. "Muhammad 'Abd al-Wahhab in Modern Egyptian Music." Ph.D. dissertation, University of California, Los Angeles.

Bourgeot, André. 1989. "Cultures, langues berbères, et folklorisation chez les Touaregs." In *Tradition et modernité dans les sociétés berbères*, ed. Tassadit Yacine, 33–52. Paris: Awal.

Brett, Michael, and Elizabeth Fentress. 1996. *The Berbers*. Oxford and Cambridge, Mass.: Blackwell.

Chaker, Salem. 1989a. *Berbères aujourd'hui*. Paris: L'Harmattan.

———. 1989b. "Une tradition de résistance et de lutte: La poésie berbère kabyle—Un parcours poétique." *Revue du Monde Musulman et de la Méditerrannée* 51(1):11–31.

Coon, Carleton Stevens. 1966. *Caravan: The Story of the Middle East*, rev. ed. New York: Holt.

Danielson, Virginia. 1988. "The Arab Middle East." In *Popular Musics of the Non-Western World*, ed. Peter Manuel, 141–160. New York: Oxford University Press.

———. 1996. "New Nightingales of the Nile: Popular Music in Egypt since the 1970s." *Popular Music* 15(3):299–312.

———. 1997. *The Voice of Egypt: Umm Kulthum, Arabic Song, and Egyptian Society in the Twentieth Century*. Chicago: University of Chicago Press.

Davis, Eric. 1983. *Challenging Colonialism: Bank Misr and Egyptian Industrialization, 1920–1941*. Princeton, N.J.: Princeton University Press.

Djaad, Abdelkrim. 1979. "Idir, entre l'aède et le show." *Algérie Actualité* (August 2–8):22–23.

Djura. 1990. *Le voile du silence*. Paris: M. Lafon. See also: 1992. *The Veil of Silence*, trans. Dorothy Blair. London: Quartet.

Ezzedine, Salah. 1966. "The Role of Music in Arabic Films." In *The Cinema in the Arab Countries*, ed. Georges Sadoul. Beirut: Interarab Center of Cinema and Television.

Gross, Joan E., and David A. McMurray. 1993. "Berber Origins and the Politics of Ethnicity in Colonial North African Discourse." *PoLAR: Political and Legal Anthropology Review* 16(2):39–57.

Gross, Joan E., D. McMurray, and Ted Swedenburg. 1996. "Arab Noise and Ramadan Nights: Rai, Rap, and Franco-Maghrebi Identities." In *Displacement, Diaspora, and Geographies of Identity*, ed. Smadar Lavie and Ted Swedenburg, 119–155. Durham, N.C.: Duke University Press.

Halper, Jeff, Edwin Seroussi, and Pamela Squires-Kidron. 1989. "Musica Mizrahit: Ethnicity and Class Culture in Israel." *Popular Music* 8:131–142.

Hirschkind, Charles. 2000. "Technologies of Islamic Piety: Cassette-Sermons and the Ethics of Listening." Ph.D. dissertation, Johns Hopkins University.

Hoogland, Eric, ed. 1987. *Crossing the Waters: Arabic-Speaking Immigrants to the United States before 1940*. Washington, D.C., and London: Smithsonian Institution Press.

Horowitz, Amy. 1994. "Israeli Mediterranean Music: Cultural Boundaries and Disputed Territories." Ph.D. dissertation, University of Pennsylvania.

Howell, Sally. 1998. "Picturing Women, Class, and Community in Arab Detroit: The Strange Case of Eva Habib." *Visual Anthropology* 10(2–4):209–226.

Kayal, Philip M., and Joseph M. Kayal. 1975. *The Syrian-Lebanese in America: A Study in Religion and Assimilation*. Boston: Twayne.

Lacoste-Du Jardin, Camille. 1978. "Chansons berbères, chansons pour vivre." *L'Histoire* 5:104–105.

Lefebure, Claude. 1984. "Ousman: La chanson berbère reverdie." *Annuaire de l'Afrique du Nord* 23:189–208.

Mandell, Joan. 1988. "Cultural Resilience through Change: Finding the Theme for *Tales from Arab Detroit*." *Visual Anthropology* 10(2–4):189–208.

Manuel, Peter. 1988. "The Non-Arab Middle East." In *Popular Musics of the Non-Western World*, ed. Peter Manuel, 161–170. New York: Oxford University Press.

———. 1993. *Cassette Culture: Popular Music and Technology in North India*. Chicago: University of Chicago Press.

Matoub, Lounes. 1995. *Rebelle*. Paris: Stock.

el-Mazzawi, Farid. 1966. "The U.A.R. Cinema and Its Relations with Television." In *The Cinema in the Arab Countries*, ed. Georges Sadoul. Beirut: Interarab Center of Cinema and Television.

McCarus, Ernest. 1984. *The Development of Arab-American Identity*. Ann Arbor: University of Michigan Press.

McDermott, Anthony. 1988. *Egypt from Nasser to Mubarak: A Flawed Revolution*. New York: Croom Helm.

Mehenni, Ferhat. 1983. "La chanson kabyle depuis dix ans." *Tafsut, Série Spéciale "Etudes et Débats"* 1:65–71.

Naaf, Alexa. 1985. *Becoming American: The Early Arab Immigrant Experience*. Carbondale: Southern Illinois University Press.

Racy, Ali Jihad. 1977. "Musical Change and Commercial Recording in Egypt, 1904–1932." Ph.D. dissertation, University of Illinois at Champaign-Urbana.

———. 1984. "Arab Music—An Overview." In *Maqam: Music of the Islamic World and Its Influences*, ed. Robert Browning, 9–13. New York: Alternative Museum.

———. 1991. "Creativity and Ambience: An Ecstatic Feedback Model from Arab Music." *World of Music* 33(3): 7–28.

Rasmussen, Anne. 1991. "Individuality and Musical Change in the Music of Arab Americans." Ph.D. dissertation, University of California Los Angeles.

———. 1996. "Theory and Practice at the 'Arabic Orq': Digital Technology in Contemporary Arab Music Performance." *Popular Music* 15(3):345–365.

———. 1997. "The Music of Arab Detroit: A Musical Mecca in the Midwest." In *Musics of Multicultural America: A Study of Twelve Musical Communities*, ed. Kip Lornell and Anne K. Rasmussen, 73–100. New York: Schirmer.

———. Forthcoming. "The Sound of Culture, The Structure of Tradition: Musicians' Work in Arab America." In *Creating a New Arab World: Life on the Margins of Multicultural America*, ed. Andrew Shryock and Nabeel Abraham. Detroit: Wayne State University Press.

Regev, Moti. 1992. "Israeli Rock: Or a Study in the Politics of 'Local Authenticity.'" *Popular Music* 11:1–14.

Reynolds, Dwight F. 1998. "From the Delta to Detroit: Packaging a Folk Epic for a New Folk." *Visual Anthropology* 10(2–4):145–164.

Robins, Kevin, and David Morley. 1996. "Almanci, Yabanci." *Cultural Studies* 10(2):248–254.

Schuyler, Philip D. 1984. "Berber Professional Musicians in Performance." In *Performance Practice: Ethnomusicological Perspectives*, ed. Gérard Béhague, 91–148. London: Greenwoode.

———. 1993. "A Folk Revival in Morocco." In *Everyday Life in the Muslim Middle East*, ed. Donna Lee Bowen and Evelyn A. Early, 287–293. Bloomington: Indiana University Press.

Seroussi, Edwin. 1996. *Popular Music in Israel: The First Fifty Years*. Cambridge, Mass.: Harvard College Library.

Shafik, Viola. 1998. *Arab Cinema: History and Cultural Continuity*. Cairo: American University in Cairo Press.

el-Shawan, Salwa Aziz. 1980. "Al-Musika al-Arabiyyah: A Category of Urban Music in Cairo, Egypt, 1927–1977." Ph.D. dissertation, Columbia University.

———. 1987. "Some Aspects of the Cassette Industry in Egypt." *World of Music* 29(2):32–45.

Shiloah, Amnon. 1992. "Eastern Sources in Israeli Music." *Ariel* 88:4–19.

Shiloah, Amnon, and Erik Cohen. 1983. "The Dynamics of Change in Jewish Oriental Music in Israel." *Ethnomusicology* 27(2):222–251.

Shiloah, Amnon, and Erik Cohen. 1985. "Major Trends of Change in Jewish Oriental Music in Israel." *Popular Music* 5:199–223.

Shryock, Andrew. 1998. "Mainstreaming Arabs: Filmmaking as Image Making in *Tales from Arab Detroit*." *Visual Anthropology* 10(2–4):165–188.

Stokes, Martin. 1992. *The Arabesk Debate: Music and Musicians in Modern Turkey*. Oxford: Clarendon.

Swedenburg, Ted. 1997. "Saida Sultan/Danna International: Transgender Pop and the Polysemiotics of Sex, Nation, and Ethnicity on the Israeli-Egyptian Border." *Musical Quarterly* 81:81–108.

Tekelioğlu, Orhan. 1996. "The Rise of a Spontaneous Synthesis: The Historical Background of Turkish Popular Music." *Middle Eastern Studies* 32(1):194–215.

Virolle-Souibès, Marie. 1995. *La chanson raï: De l'Algérie profonde à la scène*. Paris: Karthala.

Wallis, Roger, and Malm Krister. 1984. *Big Sounds from Small People: The Music Industry in Small Countries*. New York: Pendragon.

Waterbury, John. 1978. *Egypt: Burdens of the Past, Options for the Future*. Bloomington: Indiana University Press.

Yacine, Tassadit. 1989. *Ait Menguellat chante . . .* Paris: La Découverte/Awal.

Zogby, James, ed. 1984. *Taking Root, Bearing Fruit: The Arab-American Experience*. Washington, D.C.: American-Arab Anti-Discrimination Committee.

Zoulef, Boudjemaa, and Mohamed Dernouny. 1981. "L'identité culturelle au Maghreb à travers un corpus de chants contemporains." *Annuaire de l'Afrique du Nord* 20:1021–1051.

GENDER AND MUSIC

'Abd ar-Raziq, Aḥmad. 1973. *La femme au temps des Mamlouks en Ägypte*. Cairo: Institut Français d'Archéologie Orientale du Caire.

Abu-Lughod, Lila. 1986. *Veiled Sentiments: Honor and Poetry in a Bedouin Society*. Berkeley: University of California Press.

———. 1990. "Shifting Politics in Bedouin Love Poetry." In *Language and the Politics of Emotion*, ed. Catherine A. Lutz and Lila Abu-Lughod, 24–45. Cambridge: Cambridge University Press, Éditions de la Maison des Sciences de l'Homme.

Basset, Henri. 1920. *Essai sur la littérature des Berbères*. Alger: Jules Carbonel.

Brandily, Monique. 1986. "Qu'exprime-t-on par et dans la musique traditionnelle? Quelques exemples libyens." *Maghreb Review* 2(2–4):53–57.

———. 1997. *Introduction aux musiques africaines*. Musiques du Monde. Cité de la Musique/Actes Sud. (Compact disk included.)

Caussin de Perceval, A. 1873. "Notices anecdotiques sur les principaux musiciens arabes des trois premiers siècles de l'islamisme." *Journal Asiatique*, 7th series, 2:397–592.

Danielson, Virginia. 1991. "Artists and Entrepreneurs: Female Singers in Cairo during the 1920s." In *Women in Middle Eastern History: Shifting Boundaries in Sex and Gender*, ed. Nikki R. Keddie and Beth Baron, 292–309. New Haven and London: Yale University Press.

———. 1997. *The Voice of Egypt: Umm Kulthūm, Arabic Song, and Egyptian Society in the Twentieth Century*. Chicago: University of Chicago Press.

Farmer, George Henry. [1929] 1994. *A History of Arabian Music to the Thirteenth Century*. London: Luzac Oriental.

Doubleday, Veronica. 1988. *Three Women of Herat*. London: Cape.

Ferchiou, Sophie. 1972. "Survivances mystiques et culte de possession dans le maraboutisme tunisien." *L'Homme* 12(3):47–69.

Hassan, Schéhérazade Qassim. 1980. *Les instruments de musique en Irak et leur rôle dans la société traditionnelle*. Paris: Mouton (Cahiers de l'Homme).

Herndon, Marcia, and Susanne Ziegler, eds. 1990. *Music, Gender, and Culture*. Wilhelmshaven: Florian Noetzel Verlag.

Huart, Clément. 1884. "Étude biographique sur trois musiciennes arabes." *Journal Asiatique*, 8th Series, 3:141–187.

JaFran Jones, Lura. 1987. "A Sociohistorical Perspective on Tunisian Women as Professional Musicians." In *Women and Music in Cross-Cultural Perspective*, ed. Ellen Koskoff, 69–83. Urbana and Chicago: University of Illinois Press. (Originally published 1987. New York: Greenwood.)

al-Jāḥiẓ (d. 868). 1980. *The Epistle on Singing-Girls of Jahiz*, ed. and trans. A. F. L. Beeston. Warminster, Wiltshire: Aris and Phillips.

Jamous, Raymond. 1981. *Honneur et baraka: Les structures sociales traditionnelles dans le Rif*. Paris: Éditions de la Maison des Sciences de l'Homme.

Jansen, Willy. 1987. *Women without Men*. Leiden: Brill.

Jargy, Simon. 1971. *La musique arabe*. Paris: Presses Universitaires de France.

Koskoff, Ellen, ed. 1989. *Women and Music in Cross-Cultural Perspective*. Urbana and Chicago: University of Illinois Press. (Originally published 1987. New York: Greenwood.)

Kulthūm, Umm. 1976. "Umm Kulthūm." In *Middle Eastern Women Speak*, ed. Elizabeth

Warnock and Basima Qattan Bezirgan. Austin: University of Texas Press.

Lambert, Jean. 1997. *La médecine de l'âme. Hommes et musiques*. Nanterre: Société d'Ethnologie. (Compact disk included.)

Lortat-Jacob, Bernard. 1980. *Musique et fêtes au Haut-Atlas*. Paris: Mouton (Cahiers de l'Homme). (Compact disk included.)

———. 1994. *Musiques en fête. Hommes et musiques*. Nanterre: Société d'Ethnologie.

Mahfoufi, Mehenna. 1991. "Le répertoire musical d'un village berbère d'Algérie (Kabylie)." 2 vols. Ph.D. dissertation, Paris X-Nanterre University.

Meyers Sawa, Suzanne. 1987. "The Role of Women in Musical Life: The Medieval Arabo-Islamic Courts." *Canadian Woman Studies/Cahiers de la Femme* 8(2):93–95.

Nieuwkerk, Karin van. 1990. *Female Entertainment in Nineteenth- and Twentieth-Century Egypt*. Amsterdam: Middle East Research Associates.

———. 1995. *"A Trade Like Any Other": Female Singers and Dancers in Egypt*. Austin: University of Texas Press.

Rouget, Gilbert. 1980. *La musique et la transe: Esquisse d'une théorie générale des relations de la musique et de la possession*. Paris: Gallimard.

Rovsing-Olsen, Miriam. 1984. "Chants de mariage de l'Atlas marocain." 2 vols. Ph.D dissertation, Paris X-Nanterre University.

———. 1989. "Symbolique d'un rituel de mariage berbère: Une approche ethnomusicologique." *Anuario Musical* 44:259–291.

———. 1996. "Modalités d'organisaton du chant berbère: Paroles et musique." *Journal of Mediterranean Studies: History, Culture, and Society in the Mediterranean World* 6(1):88–108.

———. 1997. *Chants et danses de l'Atlas (Maroc).* Cité de la Musique/Actes Sud. (Compact disk included.)

Rowson, Everett K. 1991. "The Effeminates of Early Medina." *Journal of the American Oriental Society* 111(4):671–693.

Sakata, Hiromi Lorraine. 1983. *Music in the Mind: The Concepts of Music and Musician in Afghanistan.* Kent, Ohio: Kent State University Press.

———. 1987. "Hazara Women in Afghanistan: Innovators and Preservers of a Musical Tradition." In *Women and Music in Cross-Cultural Perspective,* ed. Ellen Koskoff, 85–95. Urbana and Chicago: University of Illinois Press. (Originally published 1987. New York: Greenwood.)

Sarkissian, Margaret. 1992. "Gender and Music." In *Ethnomusicology: An Introduction,* ed. Helen Myers, 337–348. The New Grove Handbooks in Music. London: Macmillan.

Sawa, George Dimitri. 1989. *Music Performance Practice in the Early 'Abbāsid Era 132–320 A.H./ A.D. 750–932.* Toronto: Pontifical Institute of Mediaeval Studies.

Schuyler, Philip D. 1984. "Berber Professional Musicians in Performance." In *Performance Practice: Ethnomusicological Perspectives,* ed. Gerard Béhague, 91–148. Westport, Conn.: Greenwood.

Shapiro, Anne Dhu. 1991. "A Critique of Current Research on Music and Gender." *World of Music* 33(2):5–13.

Siala, Mourad. 1994. "La hadra de Sfax: Rite soufi et musique de fête." 2 vols. Ph.D dissertation, Paris X-Nanterre University.

Stigelbauer, Michael. 1975. *Die Sängerinnen am Abbasidenhof um die Zeit des Kalifen al-Mutawakkil.* Vienna: Verband der Wissenschaftlichen Gesellschaften Österreichs.

Stokes, Martin. 1994. "Introduction: Ethnicity, Identity, and Music." In *Ethnicity, Identity, and Music: The Musical Construction of Place,* ed. Martin Stokes, 1–27. Oxford and Providence, R.I.: Berg.

Villoteau, Guillaume André. 1812. *De l'état actuel de l'art musical en Egypte, ou relation historique et descriptive des recherches et observations faites sur la musique en ce pays.* Vol. 14 of *Description de l'Egypte ou recueil des observations et des recherches qui ont été faites en Egypte pendant l'expédition de l'armée française.* Paris: Imprimerie de C.L.F. Panckoucke.

Wright, Owen. 1983. "Music and Verse." In *Arabic Literature to the End of the Umayyad Period,* 433–489. Cambridge: Cambridge University Press.

Yammine, Habib. 1995. "Les hommes des tribus et leur musique (Haut-plateaux yéménites, vallée d'al-Ahjur)." 2 vols. Ph.D. dissertation, Paris X-Nanterre University.

LEARNING AND TRANSMISSION

Başgöz, Ilhan. 1952. "Turkish Folk Stories about the Lives of Minstrels." *Journal of American Folklore* 65:331–339.

———. 1967. "Dream Motif in Turkish Folk Stories and Shamanistic Initiation." *Asian Folklore Studies* 26:1–18.

Blum, Stephen. 1972. "The Concept of the *'Asheq* in Northern Khorasan." *Asian Music* 4:27–47.

Chadwick, Nora K., and Victor Zhirmunsky. 1969. *Oral Epics of Central Asia.* Cambridge: Cambridge University Press.

Davis, Ruth. 1986a. "Modern Trends in the *Ma'lūf* of Tunisia: 1934–1984." Ph.D. dissertation, Princeton University.

———. 1986b. "Modern Trends in the Arab-Andalusian Music of Tunisia." *Maghreb Review* 11:58–63.

———. 1992. "The Effects of Notation in the Performance Practice of Tunisian Art Music." *World of Music* 34(1):35–114.

D'Erlanger, Rodolphe. 1917. "Au sujet de la musique arabe en Tunisie." *Revue Tunisienne* 24:91–95.

———. 1930–1959. *La musique arabe.* 6 vols. Paris: Librairie Orientaliste Paul Geuthner.

Hanaway, William L. 1971. "Formal Elements in the Persian Popular Romances." In *Iran: Continuity and Variety,* ed. Peter Chelkowski, 139–160. New York: Center for Near Eastern Studies.

———. 1978. "The Iranian Epics." In *Heroic Epic and Saga: An Introduction to the World's Great Epics,* ed. Felix J. Oinas, 76–98. Bloomington: Indiana University Press.

Hassan, Scheherazade. 1987. "Le makam irakien: Structures et realisations." In *L'improvisation dans les musiques de tradition oral,* ed. Bernard Lortat-Jacob, 143–149. Paris: SELAF.

———. 1989. "Some Islamic Non-Arabic Elements of Influence on the Repertory of al Makam al 'Iraki." In *Maqam, Raga, Zeilenmelodik: Konzeptionen und Prinzipien der Musikproduktion. Materialen der 1. Arbeitstagung der Study Group "Maqām" beim International Council for Traditional Music vom 28. Juni bis 2. Juli 1988 in Berlin,* ed. Jürgen Elsner, 148–155. Berlin: [Nationalkomitee DDR des International Council for Traditional Music in Verbindung mit dem Sekretariat Internationale Nichtstaatliche Musikorganisationen].

———. 1992a. "Choix de la musique et de la representation irakienne au Congrès du Caire en 1932: Vers une étude de contexte." In *Musique Arabe: Le Congrès du Caire de 1932,* ed. Philippe Vigreux, 123–145. Cairo: CEDEJ.

———. 1992b. "Survey of Written sources on the Iraqi *Maqām.*" In *Regionale Maqam-Traditionen in Geschichte und Gegenwart. Materialien der 2. Arbeitstagung der Study Group "Maqam" des International Council for Traditional Music vom 23. bis 28. März in Gosen bei Berlin,* ed. Jürgen Elsner and Gisa Jähnichen, 252–275. Berlin: s.n.

Lane, Edward. 1895. *An Account of the Manners and Customs of the Modern Egyptians.* London: East-West.

Lord, Albert B. 1960. *The Singer of Tales.* Cambridge, Mass.: Harvard University Press.

Marcus, Scott. 1989. "Arab Music Theory in the Modern Period." Ph.D. dissertation, University of California Los Angeles.

Moyle, Natalie K. 1990. *The Turkish Minstrel Tale Tradition.* New York: Harvard Dissertations in Folklore and Oral Tradition.

Page, Mary Ellen. 1977. "*Naqqāli* and Ferdowsi: Creativity in the Iranian National Tradition." Ph.D. dissertation, University of Pennsylvania.

Parry, Milman. 1987. *The Making of Homeric Verse,* ed. A. Parry. Oxford and New York: Oxford University Press.

Racy, Ali Jihad. 1977. "Musical Change and Commercial Recording in Egypt." Ph.D. dissertation, University of California Los Angeles.

Reichl, Karl. 1985. "Oral Tradition and Performance of the Uzbek and Karakalpak Epic Singers." In *Fragen der mongolischen Heldendichtung,* ed. W. Heissig, 613–643. Wiesbaden: Otto Harrassowitz.

———. 1992. *Turkic Oral Epic Poetry: Traditions, Forms, Poetic Structure.* New York: Garland.

Reinhard, Ursula, and Tiago de Oliveira Pinto. 1989. *Sänger und Poeten mit der Laute: Turkische Aşik und Ozan.* Berlin: Dietrich Reimer Verlag.

Reynolds, Dwight F. 1995a. *Heroic Poets, Poetic Heroes: The Ethnography of Performance in an Arabic Oral Epic Tradition.* Ithaca, N.Y.: Cornell University Press.

———. 1995b. "Musical Dimensions of an Arabic Oral Epic Tradition." *Asian Music* 26(1):51–92.

———. 1996. "Crossing and Recrossing the Line." In *The World Observed: Reflections on the Fieldwork Process,* ed. Bruce Jackson and Edward Ives, 100–117. Chicago: University of Illinois Press.

el-Shawan, Salwa Aziz. 1980a. "*Al-Mūsīka al-Arabiyyah:* A Category of Urban Music in Cairo, Egypt, 1927–1977." Ph.D. dissertation, Columbia University.

———. 1980b. "The Sociopolitical Context of al-Musiqa al-'Arabiyyah in Cairo, Egypt: Policies, Patronage, and Musical Change (1927–1977)." *Asian Music* 12(1):86–128.

———. 1982. "The Role of Mediators in the Transmission of al-Musika al-Arabiyyah in Twentieth-Century Cairo." *Yearbook for Traditional Music* 21:56–74.

———. 1984. "Traditional Arab Music Ensembles in Egypt since 1967: 'The Continuity of Tradition within a Contemporary Framework.'" *Ethnomusicology* 22(2):271–288.

Slyomovics, Susan E. 1987. *The Merchant of Art: An Egyptian Hilali Oral Epic Poet in Performance.* Berkeley and Los Angeles: University of California Press.

HISTORICAL ROOTS

Adler, Israel. 1975. *Hebrew Writings concerning Music in Manuscripts and Printed Books from Geonic Times up to 1800.* RISM B IX². München: G. Henle.

Anati, Emmanuel. 1968. *Rock-Art in Central Arabia.* Louvain: Institut Orientaliste.

Arberry, Arthur J., trans. [1935] 1977. *The Doctrine of the Ṣūfīs* (Kitāb al-Taʿarruf li-madhab ahl al-taṣawwuf). (From the Arabic of Abū Bakr al-Kalābādhī.) Cambridge: Cambridge University Press.

Baffioni, Carmela. 1984. "La scala pitagorica in al-Kindī." In *Studi in onore di Francesco Gabrieli nel suo ottantesimo compleanno*, ed. R. Traini. Rome: Università di Roma "La Sapienza," Dipartimento di Studi Orientali.

Barker, Andrew, ed. 1989. *Greek Musical Writings*, 2. Cambridge and New York: Cambridge University Press.

Beeston, A. F. L., ed. and trans. 1980. *The Epistle on Singing-Girls of Jāḥiz.* Warminster: Aris and Phillips.

Beichert, Eugen. 1931. *Die Wissenschaft der Musik bei al-Fârâbî.* Regensburg: Pustet.

Berque, Jacques. 1995. *Musiques sur le fleuve: Les plus belles pages du Kitâb al-Aghânî.* Paris: Michel.

Berthier, Annie, and Amnon Shiloah. 1985. "À propos d'un 'Petit livre arabe de musique,' Oxford, Bodleian Library, Manuscrits Turcs XLII. Paris, Bibliothèque Nationale, Arabe 2480." *Revue de Musicologie* 71:164–177.

Bohlman, Philip V. 1987. "The European Discovery of Music in the Islamic World and the 'Non-Western' in Nineteenth-Century Music History." *Journal of Musicology* 5:147–163.

Braune, Gabriele. 1990. "Puls und Musik: Die Wirkung der griechischen Antike in arabischen medizinischen und musikalischen Traktaten." *Jahrbuch für Musikalische Volks- und Völkerkunde* 14:52–67.

Bürgel, Johann Christoph. 1979. "Musicotherapy in the Islamic Middle Ages as Reflected in Medical and Other Sources." In *History and Philosophy of Science*, ed. Hakim Mohammed Said. Islamabad: Hamdard Foundation Press.

Burnett, Charles. 1993. "European Knowledge of Arabic Texts Referring to Music: Some New Material." *Early Music History* 12:1–17.

Carlisle, Roxane Connick. 1973. "Women Singers in Darfur, Sudan Republic." *Anthropos* 68:758–800.

Carra de Vaux, Baron. 1891a. "Notice sur deux manuscrits arabes." *Journal Asiatique*, 8th Series, 17:295–322.

———. 1891b. "Le traité des rapports musicaux ou l'Épître à Scharaf ed-Dîn, par Safi ed-Dîn

'Abd el-Mumin Albaghdâdî." *Journal Asiatique*, 8th Series, 18:279–355.

Caussin de Perceval, A. 1873. "Notices anecdotiques sur les principaux musiciens arabes des trois premiers siècles de l'Islamisme." *Journal Asiatique*, 7th Series, 2:397–592.

Centre des Musiques Arabes et Méditerranéennes, ed. 1992. *Les instruments de musique en Tunisie.* Tunis: Ministère de Culture.

Chabrier, Jean-Claude. 1985. "Éléments d'une approche comparative des échelles théoriques arabo-irano-turques." *Revue de Musicologie* 71:39–78.

———. 1996. "Musical Science." In *Encyclopedia of the History of Arabic Science*, ed. Roshdi Rashed. London and New York: Routledge.

Christianowitsch, Alexandre. 1863. *Esquisse historique de la musique arabe aux temps anciens.* Cologne: Dumont-Schauberg.

Clement of Alexandria. 1954. "Paedagogos (Christ the Educator)." In *Fathers of the Church*, Vol. 23. Washington: Catholic University of America Press.

Corriente, Federico, ed. and trans. 1988. *Poesía estrófica (cejeles y/o muwaššaḥāt) atribuida al místico granadino Aš-Šuštari (siglo XIII d.C.). (Preedición, traducción, estudio e índices).* Madrid: Consejo Superior de Investigaciones Científicas. Instituto de Filología. Departamento de Estudios Árabes.

Cortés García, Manuela. 1988. "Revisión de los manuscritos poético-musicales árabes, andalusíes, y magrebíes de la Biblioteca Nacional de Madrid." in *IV Congreso Internacional de Civilización Andalusí. Universidad de El Cairo*, 95–108. Cairo.

———. 1993. "Vigencia de la transmisión oral en el Kunnāš al-Ḥāʾik (Cancionero de al-Ḥāʾik)." *Revista de Musicología* 16:1942–1952.

———. 1995. "Nuevos datos para el estudio de la música en al-Andalus de dos autores granadinos: Aš-Šuštari e Ibn al-Jaṭīb." *Música Oral del Sur* 1:177–194.

———. 1996. "Sobre la música y sus efectos terapéuticos en la 'Epístola sobre las melodías' de Ibn Bāyya." *Revista de Musicología* 19:11–23.

Cowl, Carl, trans. 1966. "The Risāla fī ḥubr taʾlīf al-alḥān of Jaʿqūb ibn Isḥāq al-Kindī (790–874)." *Consort* 23:129–166.

Cruz Hernándes, Miguel. 1981. "La teoría musical de Ibn Sīnā en el Kitāb al-Šifāʾ." In *Milenario de Avicena*, ed. A. Badawi et al. Madrid: Instituto Hispano-Árabe de Cultura.

D'Erlanger, Baron Rodolphe. 1930–1959. *La musique arabe.* Paris: Librairie Orientaliste Paul Geuthner.

Dieterici, Friedrich. 1865. *Die Propaedeutik der Araber im zehnten Jahrhundert.* Berlin: Mittler. Reprints: 1969. Hildesheim: Olms; 1999. Frankfurt: Institute for the History of Arabic-Islamic Science.

Doughty, Charles. 1888. *Travels in Arabia Deserta.* Cambridge: Cambridge University Press.

Ehrenkreutz, Stefan. 1980. "Medieval Arabic Music Theory and Contemporary Scholarship." *Arab Studies Quarterly* 2:249–265.

Elsner, Jürgen, and Paul Collaer. 1983. *Nordafrika.* Musikgeschichte in Bildern, Band 1: Musikethnologie, Lieferung 8. Leipzig: Deutscher Verlag für Musik.

Elsner, Jürgen. 1969. "Remarks on the Big Argul." *Yearbook of the International Folk Music Council* 1:234–239.

al-Fārābī, Abū Naṣr (d. 950). 1967. *Kitāb al-Mūsīqī al-Kabīr*, ed. Ghaṭṭās ʿAbd-al-Malik Khashaba. Revision and introduction by Maḥmūd Aḥmad al-Ḥifnī. Cairo: Dār al-Kātib al-ʿArabī.

———. 1968–1969. "Die Theorie von Īqāʿ. 1: Übersetzung des Kitāb al-Īqāʿāt von Abū Naṣr al-Fārābī," trans. Eckhard Neubauer. *Oriens* 21–22:196–232.

———. 1994. "Die Theorie von Īqāʿ. 2: Übersetzung des Kitāb Iḥṣāʾ al-Īqāʿāt von Abū Naṣr al-Fārābī," trans. Eckhard Neubauer. *Oriens* 34:103–173.

Farmer, Henry George. [1929] 1973. *A History of Arabian Music to the Thirteenth Century.* London: Luzac.

———. 1929–1930. "Greek Theorists of Music in Arabic Translation." *Isis* l3:325–333. Reprint: 1997. In H. G. Farmer, *Studies in Oriental Music.*

———. 1930. *Historical Facts for the Arabian Musical Influence.* London: Reeves.

———. 1931. *The Organ of the Ancients. From Eastern Sources (Hebrew, Syriac, and Arabic).* London: Reeves. Reprint: 1997. In H. G. Farmer, *Studies in Oriental Music.*

———, ed. and trans. 1933. *An Old Moorish Lute Tutor: Being Four Arabic Texts from Unique Manuscripts in the Biblioteca Nacional, Madrid (No. 334) and the Staatsbibliothek, Berlin (Lbg. 516).* Glasgow: Civic. Reprint: 1997. In H. G. Farmer, *Studies in Oriental Music.*

———, ed. and trans. 1934. *Al-Fārābī's Arabic-Latin Writings on Music in the Iḥṣāʾ al-ʿulūm (Escorial Library, Madrid, No. 646), De scientiis (British Museum, Cott. MS. Vesp. B.X., and Bibl. Nat., Paris, No. 9335), and De ortu scientiarum (Bibl. Nat., Paris, No. 6298, and Bodleian Library, Oxford, No. 3623), etc.* Glasgow: Civic. Reprint: 1997. In H. G. Farmer, *Studies in Oriental Music.*

———. [1935] 1997. "A Maghribī Work on Musical Instruments." In *Studies in Oriental Music*, 2:151–165. Frankfurt am Main: Institute for the History of Arabic-Islamic Science.

———. [1937] 1997. "The Lute Scale of Avicenna." In *Studies in Oriental Music*, 2:175–187. Frankfurt am Main: Institute for the History of Arabic-Islamic Science.

———. 1941. "The Jewish Debt to Arabic Writers on Music." *Islamic Culture* 15:59–63. Reprint: 1997. In H. G. Farmer, *Studies in Oriental Music*.

———, trans. 1942. *Music: The Priceless Jewel. From the "Kitāb al-'iqd al-farīd" of Ibn 'Abd Rabbihi (d. 940)*. Bearsden: Author. Reprint: 1997. In H. G. Farmer, *Studies in Oriental Music*.

———. 1943. *Sa'adyah Gaon on the Influence of Music*. London: Arthur Probsthain. Reprint: 1997. In H. G. Farmer, *Studies in Oriental Music*.

———. 1945. *The Minstrelsy of "The Arabian Nights." A Study of Music and Musicians in the Arabic "Alf Laila wa Laila."* Bearsden: Author. Reprint: 1997. In H. G. Farmer, *Studies in Oriental Music*.

———. [1952] 1997. "The Religious Music of Islām." In *Studies in Oriental Music*, 1:123–128. Frankfurt am Main: Institute for the History of Arabic-Islamic Science.

———. 1955. "The Song Captions in the *Kitāb al-aghānī al-kabīr*." *Transactions of the Glasgow University Oriental Society* 15:1–10. Reprint: 1997. In H. G. Farmer, *Studies in Oriental Music*.

———. 1957. "Al-Kindī on the 'Ethos' of Rhythm, Colour, and Perfume." *Transactions of the Glasgow University Oriental Society* 16:29–38. Reprint: 1997. In H. G. Farmer, *Studies in Oriental Music*.

———, trans. 1959. "The Science of Music in the *Mafātīḥ al-'Ulūm*." *Transactions of the Glasgow University Oriental Society* 17:1–9. Reprint: 1997. In H. G. Farmer, *Studies in Oriental Music*.

———, trans. 1959–1961. "Tenth Century Arabic Books on Music: As Contained in 'Kitāb al-Fihrist' of Abu 'l-Faraj Muḥammad ibn al-Nadīm." *Annual of Leeds University Oriental Society* 2:37–47. Reprint: 1997. In H. G. Farmer, *Studies in Oriental Music*.

———. 1965. *The Sources of Arabian Music: An Annotated Bibliography of Arabic Manuscripts Which Deal with the Theory, Practice, and History of Arabian Music from the Eighth to the Seventeenth Century*. Leiden: Brill.

———. [1965a] 1997. "The Old Arabian Melodic Modes." In *Studies in Oriental Music*, 1:429–432. Frankfurt am Main: Institute for the History of Arabic-Islamic Science.

———. 1965b. *The Sources of Arabian Music*. Leiden: Brill.

———. 1966. *Islam: Musikgeschichte in Bildern*. ed. Heinrich Besseler and Max Schneider. Leipzig: VEB Deutscher Verlag für Musik.

———. [1986] 1997. *Studies in Oriental Music*. Vol. 1: *History and Theory*. (Reprint of writings published in 1925–1966.) Vol. 2: *Instruments and Military Music*. (Reprint of writings published in 1925–1969.) Frankfurt: Institute for the History of Arabic-Islamic Science. (First published 1986.)

al-Faruqi, Lois Ibsen. 1981. *An Annotated Glossary of Arabic Musical Terms*. Westport, Conn.: Greenwood.

———. 1982a. "Al Ghazālī on Samā'." In *Essays in Islamic and Comparative Studies. Papers Presented to the Islamic Studies Group of the American Academy of Religion*, ed. Isma'il Raji al Faruqi and Abdullah Omar Nasseef. Washington, D.C.: International Institute of Islamic Thought.

———. 1982b. "The Shari'ah on Music and Musicians." In *Islamic Thought and Culture*, ed. Ismail R. al Faruqi. Herndon: International Institute of Islamic Thought.

———. 1985. "The Suite in Islamic History and Culture." *World of Music* 27(3):46–64.

Fischer, August. 1918. *Das Liederbuch eines marokkanischen Sängers. Nach einer in seinem Besitz befindlichen Handschrift herausgegeben, übersetzt und erläutert*. Leipzig: B. G. Teubner.

Frolova, Olga B. 1995. "Egyptian Folk Songs in the Unique Manuscripts of the St. Petersburg University Library." *Studia Orientalia* (Helsinki) 75:87–93.

García Gómez, Emilio. 1962. "Estudio del Dār al-ṭirāz, preceptiva egipcia de la muwaṣṣaḥa." *Al-Andalus* 27:21–104.

Gramlich, Richard, trans. 1978. *Die Gaben der Erkenntnisse des 'Umar as-Suhrawardī ('Awārif al-ma'ārif)*. Wiesbaden: Steiner.

———, trans. 1989. *Das Sendschreiben al-Quṣayrīs über das Sufitum*. Wiesbaden: Steiner.

———, trans. 1990. *Schlaglichter über das Sufitum. Abū Naṣr as-Sarrāǧs Kitāb al-luma'*. Stuttgart: Steiner.

———, trans. 1994. *Die Nahrung der Herzen. Abū Ṭālib al-Makkī's Qūt al-qulūb*. Stuttgart: Steiner.

Graziosi, P. 1964. "New Discoveries of Rock Painting in Ethiopia." *Antiquity* 150:96.

Gribetz, Arthur. 1991. "The *Samā'* Controversy: Sufi versus Legalist." *Studia Islamica* 74:43–62.

Guardiola, María Dolores. 1990. "Biografías de músicos en un manuscrito de al-Udfuwī." *Estudios Onomástico-Biográficos de al-Andalus* 3:335–350.

———. 1991. "La figure de la ḳayna dans les sources musicales." In *Le patrimoine andalou dans la culture arabe et espagnole*. Tunis. (Actes du VIIe Colloque Universitaire Tuniso-Espagnol. Tunis 3–10 février 1989.)

———. 1995. "Licitud de la venta de esclavas cantoras." In *Homenaje al Profesor José María Fárneas Besteiro*, 2:938–996. Granada: Universidad de Granada.

Guettat, Mahmoud. 1980. *La musique classique au Maghreb*. Paris: Sindbad.

Guignard, Michel. 1975. *Musique, honneur, et plaisir au Sahara*. Paris: Geuthner.

Gulisaschwili, Boris A. 1967. "Ibn Sina und die reine Stimmung." *Beiträge zur Musikwissenschaft* 9:272–283.

Haas, Max. 1989. "Antikenrezpetion in der arabischen Musiklehre: Al-Fārābī über musikalische Fantasie." In *Kontinuität und Transformation der Antike im Mittelalter*, ed. Willi Erzgräber, 261–269. Sigmaringen: Jan Thorbecke.

Hammerstein, Reinhold. 1986. *Macht und Klang: Tönende Automaten als Realität und Fiktion in der alten und mittelalterlichen Welt*. Bern: Francke.

Haq, Sirajul. 1944. "Samā' and Raqṣ of the Darwishes." *Islamic Culture* 18:111–130.

al-Hassan, Ahmad Y., and Donald R. Hill. 1986. *Islamic Technology: An Illustrated History*. Cambridge: Cambridge University Press; Paris: UNESCO.

Hassan, Scheherazade Qassim. 1980. *Les instruments de musique en Irak et leur role dans la société traditionnelle*. Mouton, Paris, Lahaye, and New York: Cahiers de l'Homme.

Hickmann, Hans. 1954. "Ägyptische Volksinstrumente." *Musica* 8:49–52, 97–100.

el-Hefny, Mahmoud, ed. and trans. 1931. *Ibn Sina's Musiklehre hauptsächlich an seinem "Naǧāt" erläutert*. Berlin: Hellwig.

al-Heitty, Abd al-Kareem. 1990. "The Contrasting Spheres of Free Women and Jawārī in the Literary Life of the Early 'Abbāsid Caliphate." *Al-Masāq* (Leeds) 3:31–51.

Hill, Donald R., ed. and trans. 1974. *Al-Ǧazarī: Kitāb fī ma'rifat al-ḥiyal al-handasiyya. The Book of Knowledge of Ingenious Mechanical Devices*. Dordrecht and Boston: Reidel.

Huart, Clément. 1884. "Étude biographique sur trois musiciennes arabes." *Journal Asiatique*, 8th Series, 3:141–187.

Ibn Ghaybī, 'Abd al-Qādir (d. 1435). *Jāmi' al-Alḥān*. Oxford: Oxford University, Bodleian Library Marsh 282.

Ikhwān al-Ṣafā. 1976. *The Epistle on Music of the Ikhwān al-Ṣafā. Risāla fī al-Mūsīqī*, trans. Amnon Shiloah. Tel-Aviv: Tel-Aviv University.

al-Iṣbāhānī, Abū al-Faraj (d. 967). 1927–1974. *Kitāb al-Aghānī*. 24 vols. Cairo: Dār al-Kutub.

Jahn, Alfred. 1902. *Die Mehri-Sprache in Südarabien*. Vienna: A. Hölder.

Jenkins, Jean, and Røvsing-Olsen, Poul. 1976. *Music and Musical Instruments in the World of Islam*. London: Horniman Museum.

Kartomi, Margaret. 1990. "National Identity and Other Themes of Classification in the Arab World." In *On Concepts and Classifications of Musical Instruments*, 122–134. Chicago: University of Chicago Press.

Kazemi, Elke, ed. and trans. 1999. *Die bewegte Seele: Das spätantike Buch über das Wesen der Musik (Kitāb 'Unṣur al-mūsīqī) von Paulos/Būlos in arabischer Übersetzung vor dem Hintergrund der griechischen Ethoslehre*. Frankfurt: Institute for the History of Arabic-Islamic Science.

Kennedy, Ph. F. 1998. *The Wine Song in Classical Arabic Poetry: Abū Nuwās and the Literary Tradition*. Oxford: Clarendon.

el-Kholy, Samha A. 1984. *The Function of Music in Islamic Culture in the Period up to 1100 C.E.* Cairo: General Egyptian Book Organization.

Kiesewetter, Raphael Georg. 1842. *Die Musik der Araber, nach Originalquellen dargestellt.* Leipzig: Breitkopf und Härtel.

Kilpatrick, Hilary. 1997. "Cosmic Correspondences: Songs as a Starting Point for an Encyclopaedic Portrayal of Culture." In *Pre-Modern Encyclopaedic Texts (Proceedings of the Second COMERS Congress, Groningen, 1–4 July 1996),* ed. P. Binkley. Leiden: Brill.

———. 1998. "The Transmission of Songs in Medieval Arabic Culture." In *Philosophy and Arts in the Islamic World (Proceedings of the Eighteenth Congress of the Union Européenne des Arabisants et Islamisants held at the Katholieke Universiteit Leuven [September 3–September 9, 1996]),* ed. U. Vermeulen and D. de Smet. Leuven: Peeters.

———. 1999. "Princes, musiciens, et musicologues à la cour abbasside." In *Les intellectuels en Orient musulman: Statut et fonction,* ed. F. Sanagustin. Cairo: Institut Français d'Archéologie Orientale.

Kosegarten, Johann Gottfried Ludwig. 1844. "Die moslemischen Schriftsteller über die Theorie der Musik." *Zeitschrift für die Kunde des Morgenlandes* (Bonn) 5:137–163.

Lachmann, Robert, and Mahmud el-Hefni, eds. 1931. *Ja'qūb Ibn Isḥāq al-Kindī: Risāla fī ḫubr tā'lif al-alḥān. Über die Komposition der Melodien.* Leipzig: Kistner and Siegel.

Land, Jan Pieter Nicolaas. 1885. "Recherches sur l'histoire de la gamme arabe." In *Actes du Sixième Congrès International des Orientalistes tenu en 1883 à Leide.* Deuxième partie, section 1, Sémitique:37–168. Leiden: Brill.

———. 1892. "Remarks on the Earliest Development of Arabic Music." In *Transactions of the Ninth International Congress of Orientalists. (Held in London, 5th to 12th September 1892.),* 2:155–163. London.

———. 1922. "Tonschriftversuche und Melodieproben aus dem muhammedanischen Mittelalter." *Sammelbände für vergleichende Musikwissenschaft* 1:79–85.

Lane, Edward W. 1981. *Manners and Customs of the Modern Egyptians 1833–1835.* The Hague and London: East-West; Cairo: Livres de France.

Lerner, Ralph, and Muhsin Mahdi, ed. 1972. *Medieval Political Philosophy: A Source Book.* Ithaca, N.Y.: Cornell University Press.

Lyall, Sir Charles. 1913. *The Diwâns of 'Abīd ibn al-Abraṣ of Asad.* Leiden: Brill.

MacDonald, Duncan Black, trans. 1901–1902. "Emotional Religion in Islam as Affected by Music and Singing: Being a Translation of a Book of the *Ihyā' 'Ulūm ad-Dīn* of al-Ghazzālī." *Journal of the Royal Asiatic Society* (1901):195–252, 705–748; (1902):1–28.

al-Mallah, Issam. 1993. "The Increasing Role of Instrumental Music and Its Influence on Musical Life in Egypt." In *Actas del XV Congreso de la SIM. Revista de Musicología* 16:1246–1249.

———. 1997. *Arab Music and Musical Notation.* Tutzing: Hans Schneider.

Manik, Liberty. 1969. *Das arabische Tonsystem im Mittelalter.* Leiden: Brill.

———. 1979. "Zwei Fassungen einer von Ṣafī al-Dīn notierten Melodie." *Baessler-Archiv,* Neue Folge 23:145–151.

Marcus, Scott. 1989. "Arab Music Theory in the Modern Period." Ph.D. dissertation, University of California Los Angeles.

Margoliouth, David Samuel, trans. 1935–1938, 1945–1948. "The Devil's Delusion [*Talbīs iblīs*] by Ibn Al-Jauzi." *Islamic Culture* 9–12, 19–22, passim.

Menander. 1862. *Scriptorum Graecorum Bibliotheca Aristophanis, Menandri, et Philemoni.* Paris: Firmin Didot.

Michot, Jean R. 1988. "L'Islam et le monde: al-Ghazâlî et Ibn Taymiyya à propos de la musique (samâ')." In *Figures de la finitude: Études d'anthropologie philosophique,* ed. G. Florival et al. Louvain-la-Neuve: Éditions de l'Institut Supérieur de Philosophie, Librairie Peeters; Paris: Vrin.

———. 1991. *Musique et danse selon Ibn Taymiyya: Le Livre du Samâ' et de la Danse (Kitāb al-Samâ' wa l-Raqs) compilé par le shaykh Muḥammad al-Manbijī.* Paris: Vrin.

Mokri, Mohammad. 1995. "La mélodie chez al-Fârâbî: Rôle, fondement, et définition." In *Persico-Kurdica: Contributions scientifiques aux études iraniennes,* ed. M. Mokri. Paris, Louvain: Peeters.

Monroe, James T. 1989. "Aḥmad al-Tīfāshī on Andalusian Music." *Modern Philology* 125:35–44.

Müller, Hans. 1980. *Die Kunst des Sklavenkaufs nach arabischen, persischen, und türkischen Ratgebern vom 10. bis zum 18. Jahrhundert.* Freiburg: Klaus Schwarz.

Neubauer, Eckhard. 1965. "Musiker am Hof der frühen 'Abbāsiden." Ph.D. dissertation, J. W. Goethe-Universität.

———. 1968–1969. "Die Theorie vom *īqā'.* 1. Übersetzung des *Kitāb al-Īqā'āt* von Abū Naṣr al-Fārābī." *Oriens* 21–22:196–232. Reprint: 1998. In E. Neubauer, *Arabische Musiktheorie* (with facs. ed. of text).

———. 1987–1988. "Das Musikkapitel der *Gumal al-falsafa* von Muḥammad ibn 'Alī al-Hindī (1135 n.Chr.)." *Zeitschrift für Geschichte der arabisch-islamischen Wissenschaften* 4:51–59. Reprint: 1998. In E. Neubauer, *Arabische Musiktheorie* (with facs. ed. of text).

———. 1990. "Arabische Anleitungen zur Musiktherapie." *Zeitschrift für Geschichte der arabisch-islamischen Wissenschaften* 6:227–272.

———. 1993. "Der Bau der Laute und ihre Besaitung nach arabischen, persischen, und türkischen Quellen des 9. bis 15. Jahrhunderts." *Zeitschrift für Geschichte der Arabisch-Islamischen Wissenschaften* 8:279–378.

———. 1994. "Die Theorie vom *īqā'.* 2. Übersetzung des *Kitāb Iḥṣā' al-īqā'āt* von Abū Naṣr al-Fārābī." *Oriens* 34:103–173. Reprint: 1998. In E. Neubauer, *Arabische Musiktheorie* (with facs. ed. of text).

———. 1995–1996. "Al-Ḫalīl ibn Aḥmad und die Frühgeschichte der arabischen Lehre von den 'Tönen' und den musikalischen Metren. Mit einer Übersetzung des *Kitāb an-Naġam* von Yaḥyā ibn 'Alī al-Munaǧǧim." *Zeitschrift für Geschichte der arabisch-islamischen Wissenschaften* 10:255–323. Reprint: 1998. In E. Neubauer, *Arabische Musiktheorie* (with facs. ed. of text).

———. 1998. *Arabische Musiktheorie von den Anfängen bis zum 6./12. Jahrhundert. Studien, Übersetzungen und Texte in Faksimile.* Frankfurt: Institute for the History of Arabic-Islamic Science.

———. 2000. "Glimpses of Arab Music in Ottoman Times from Syrian and Egyptian Sources." *Zeitschrift für Geschichte der Arabisch-Islamischen Wissenschaften* 13:317–365.

Neubauer, Eckhard, and Elsbeth Neubauer. 1987–1988. "Henry George Farmer on Oriental Music: An Annotated Bibliography." *Zeitschrift für Geschichte der Arabisch-Islamischen Wissenschaften* 4:219–266.

Odeimi, Bechir. 1991. "Kitāb al-Imtā' wa-l-intifā': Un manuscrit sur la musique arabe de Ibn al-Darrāǧ." *Arabica* 38:40–56.

Pellat, Charles, trans. 1954. *Le livre de la couronne. Kitāb at-Tāǧ . . . attribué à Ǧāḥiẓ.* Paris: Les Belles Lettres.

———. 1955. *Le Kitāb at-Tarbī' wa-t-Tadwīr de Ǧāḥiẓ.* Damascus: Institut Français de Damas.

———, trans. 1963. "Les esclaves-chanteuses de Ǧāḥiẓ." *Arabica* 10:121–147.

Plumley, A. Gwendolen. 1976. *El Tanbur: The Sudanese Lyre or the Nubian Kissar.* Cambridge: Town and Gown.

Poché, Christian. 1984. "'Arṭaba," "Duff," "Ghirbāl," "Kinnārāt," "Mi'zaf," "Mizmār," "Qinīn," "Rabāba," "Ṭunbūr." In *The New Grove Dictionary of Musical Instruments,* ed. Stanley Sadie. London: Macmillan.

———. 1989. "Le partage des tâches: La femme dans la musique arabe." *Cahiers de l'Orient* 13:11–21.

———. 1993. "Un nouveau regard sur la musique d'al-Andalus: Le manuscrit d'al-Tīfāshī." *Revista de Musicología* 16(1):367–379.

Poché, Christian, and Jean Lambert. 2000. *Musiques du monde arabe et musulman: Bibliographie et discographie.* Paris: Geuthner.

Pollux, Julius. 1967. *Pollucis Onomasticon. Lexicographi Graeci,* Vol. 9, ed. Ericus Bethe. Stuttgart: Teubner.

Pourjavady, Nasrollah. 1990. "Zwei alte Werke über Samā'." *Spektrum Iran* (Bonn) 3(2):37–59; 3(3):36–61.

Pouzet, Louis. 1983. "Prises de position autour du samâ' en Orient musulman au VIIe/XIIIe siècle." *Studia Islamica* 57:119–134.

Qureshi, Regula Burckhardt. 1991. "Sufi Music and the Historicity of Oral Tradition." In *Ethnomusicology and Modern Music History,* ed. Steven Blum, Philip V. Bohlman, and Daniel M. Neuman, 103–120. Urbana: University of Illinois Press.

Racy, Ali Jihad. 1988. *Tanbura Music of the Gulf.* Doha: Arab Gulf States Folklore Center.

———. 1991. "Historical Worldviews of Early Ethnomusicologists: An East-West Encounter in Cairo, 1932." In *Ethnomusicology and Modern Music History*, ed. Steven Blum, Philip V. Bohlman, and Daniel M. Neuman, 68–91. Urbana: University of Illinois Press.

———. 1994. "A Dialectical Perspective on Musical Instruments: The East Mediterranean Mijwiz." *Ethnomusicology* 38:37–57.

Randel, Don M. 1976. "Al-Fārābī and the Role of Arabic Music Theory in the Latin Middle Ages." *Journal of the American Musicological Society* 29:173–188.

Rashid, Subhi Anwar. 1984. *Mesopotamien. Musikgeschichte in Bildern, Band 2: Musik des Altertums, Lieferung 2.* Leipzig: Deutscher Verlag für Musik.

Rasmussen, Anne. 1996. "Theory and Practice at the 'Arabic Orq': Digital Technology in Contemporary Arab Music Performance." *Popular Music* 15:345–365.

Rat, Gustave. 1899–1902. *Al-Mostaṭraf: Recueil des morceaux choisis ça et là dans toutes les branches de connaissances réputées attrayantes par Šihâb-ad-dîn Aḥmad al-Abšîhî. Ouvrage philologique, anecdotique, littéraire, et philosophique traduit pour la première fois.* 2 vols. Paris and Toulon.

Reinert, Benedikt. 1979. "Das Problem des pythagoräischen Kommas in der arabischen Musiktheorie." *Asiatische Studien* 33:199–217.

———. 1990. "Die arabische Musiktheorie zwischen autochthoner Tradition und griechischem Erbe." In *Die Blütezeit der arabischen Wissenschaft*, ed. Heinz Balmer and Beat Glaus. Zürich: Verlag der Fachvereine.

Reynolds, Dwight. 1995. *Heroic Poets, Poetic Heroes: The Ethnography of Performance in an Arabic Oral Epic Tradition.* Ithaca, N.Y.: Cornell University Press.

Ribera, Julián. 1929. *Music in Ancient Arabia and Spain: Being La música de las Cantigas.* London: Oxford University Press; Stanford, Calif.: Stanford University Press.

Rice, David Storm. 1958. "A Drawing of the Fatimid Period." *Bulletin of the School of Oriental and African Studies* 21:31–39.

Rimmer, Joan. 1969. *Ancient Musical Instruments of Western Asia in the British Museum.* London: Trustees of the British Museum.

Robson, James, ed. and trans. 1938. *Tracts on Listening to Music: Being* Dhamm al-malāhī *by Ibn abī 'l-Dunyā and* Bawāriq al-ilmā' *by Majd al-Dīn al-Ṭūsī al-Ghazālī.* London: Royal Asiatic Society.

Robson, James, and Henry George Farmer. (Facs., trans.) 1938. *Ancient Arabian Musical Instruments: As Described by Al-Mufaḍḍal ibn Salama (Ninth Century) in the Unique Istanbul Manuscript of the* Kitāb al-malāhī *in the Handwriting of Yāqūt al-Mustaʿsimī (d. 1298).* Glasgow: Civic.

Robson, James, trans. 1947–1953. "The Meaning of Ghinā'." *Journal of the Manchester University Egyptian and Oriental Society* 25:1–8.

———. 1952. "A Maghribi Ms. on Listening to Music." *Islamic Culture* 26:113–131.

———. 1957. "Muslim Controversy about the Lawfulness of Music." *Islamic Literature* 9:305–314.

———. 1958. "Some Arab Musical Instruments." *Islamic Culture* 32:171–185.

———. 1961. "Muslim Wedding Feasts." *Transactions of the Glasgow University Oriental Society* 18:1–14.

Ronzevalle, Louis, ed. and trans. 1913. "Un traité de musique arabe moderne." *Mélanges de la Faculté Orientale, Université Saint-Joseph* 6:1–120.

Rosenthal, Franz, trans. 1958. *Ibn Khaldûn. The Muqaddimah. An Introduction to History.* New York: Pantheon.

———. 1966. "Two Graeco-Arabic Works on Music." *Proceedings of the American Philosophical Society* 110:261–268. Reprint: 1991. In F. Rosenthal, *Science and Medicine in Islam.* Aldershot: Variorum.

Rowson, Everett K. 1991. "The Effeminates of Early Medina." *Journal of the American Oriental Society* 111:671–693.

Ryckmans, Gonzague. 1934. *Les noms propres sud-sémitiques.* 3 vols. Louvain: Bureaux du Muséon.

Sachs, Curt. 1913. *Real-Lexikon der Musikinstrumente.* Berlin: J. Bard.

———. 1940. *The History of Musical Instruments.* New York: Norton.

Saint-Saëns, Camille. 1913. "Lyres et cythares." In *Encylopédie de la musique et dictionnaire du conservatoire*, 1:538–540, ed. Albert Lavignac. Paris: C. Delagrave.

Salem, Elie A. 1977. *Hilāl al-Ṣābi'.* Rusūm Dār al-Khilāfah (*The Rules and Regulations of the 'Abbāsid Court*). Trans. from Arabic. Beirut: American University of Beirut.

Sawa, George Dimitri. 1981. "The Survival of Some Aspects of Performance Practice of Medieval Arabic Music." *Ethnomusicology* 25(1):73–86.

———. 1982. "Bridging One Millennium: Melodic Movement in al-Fārābī and Kolinski." In *Cross-Cultural Perspectives on Music*, ed. R. Falk and T. Rice. Toronto: University of Toronto Press.

———. 1983–1984. "Al-Fārābī's Theory of Īqāʿ: An Empirically Derived Medieval Model of Rhythmic Analysis." *Progress Reports in Ethnomusicology* 1(9):1–32.

———. 1984. "Musical Humour in the *Kitāb al-Aghānī* (Book of Songs)." In *Logos Islamikos: Studia Islamica in Honorem Georgii Michaelis Wickens*, ed. Roger M. Savory and Dionisius Agius, 35–50. Papers in Mediaeval Studies, 6. Toronto: Pontifical Institute of Mediaeval Studies.

———. 1985. "The Status and Role of the Secular Musician in *Kitāb al-Aghānī*." *Asian Music* 17(1):69–82.

———. 1989a. *Music Performance Practice in the Early 'Abbāsid Era, A.D. 750–932.* Toronto: Pontifical Institute of Medieval Studies.

———. 1989b. "The Differing World of the Music Historian and the Music Illuminator in Medieval Islamic Manuscripts." *Imago Musicae* 6:7–22.

———. 1989c. "Oral Transmission in Arabic Music, Past and Present." *Oral Tradition* 4(1–2):254–265.

———. 1990. "Paradigms in al-Fārābī's Musical Writings." In *Paradigms in Medieval Thought: Applications in Medieval Disciplines*, ed. Nancy van Deusen and Alvin E. Ford, 81–92. Lewinstone, N.Y.: Edwin Mellen.

———. 1997. "Editing and Translating Medieval Arabic Writings on Music." In *Music Discourse from Classical to Early Modern Times: Editing and Translating Texts*, ed. Maria Rika Maniates, 45–70. Toronto: University of Toronto Press.

Sezgin, Fuat. 1974. *Geschichte des arabischen Schrifttums.* Vol. 5, *Mathematik bis c. 430 H.* Leiden: Brill.

Shehadeh, Kamal, Donald R. Hill, and Richard Lorch, eds. and trans. 1994. "Construction of a Fluting Machine by Apollonius the Carpenter." *Zeitschrift für Geschichte der arabisch-islamischen Wissenschaften* 9:326–356.

Shehadi, Fadlou. 1995. *Philosophies of Music in Medieval Islam.* Leiden: Brill.

Shawqi, Yusuf. 1994. *Dictionary of Traditional Music of Oman.* Rev. and expanded by Dieter Christensen. Intercultural Music Studies 6, International Institute for Traditional Music. Wilhelmshaven: Florian Noetzel Verlag.

Shiloah, Amnon. 1962. "Réflexions sur la danse artistique musulmane au moyen âge." *Cahiers de Civilisation Médiévale* 5:463–474.

———. 1963. *Caractéristiques de l'art vocal arabe au moyen-âge.* Tel-Aviv: Israel Music Institute.

———, trans. 1964–1966. "L'épître sur la musique des Ikhwān al-Ṣafā'." *Revue des Études Islamiques* 32:125–162; 34:159–193.

———, ed. and trans. 1968. "Deux textes arabes inédits sur la musique." *Yuval* 1:221–248. (Reprint: Shiloah 1993.)

———, ed. and trans. 1971a. "Un 'Problème Musical' inconnu de Thābit ibn Qurra." *Orbis Musicae* 1:25–38. (Reprint: Shiloah 1993.)

———. 1971b. "Les sept traités de musique dans le manuscrit 1705 de Manisa." *Israel Oriental Studies* 1:303–315.

———. 1972a. "The Simsimiyya: A String Instrument of the Red Sea." *Asian Music* 4:15–26.

———, trans. 1972b. *Al-Ḥasan ibn Aḥmad ibn 'Alī al-Kātib: La perfection des connaissances musicales.* Paris: Geuthner.

———. 1972c. "Ibn Hindū: Le médecin et la musique." *Israel Oriental Studies* 2:447–462. (Reprint: Shiloah 1993.)

———, trans. 1974. "Un ancien traité sur le *'ūd* d'Abū Yūsuf al-Kindī." *Israel Oriental Studies* 4:179–205.

———, trans. 1978a. *The Epistle on Music of the Ikhwān al-Ṣafā'*. Tel-Aviv: Tel-Aviv University. (Reprint: Shiloah 1993.)

———. 1978b. "Reflets de la musique des divers peuples dans les écrits arabes sur la musique." In *Actes du Deuxième Congrès International d'Études des Cultures de la Méditerranée Occidentale*, ed. Micheline Galley, Vol. 2. Alger: Société Nationale d'Édition et de Diffusion.

———. 1979. *The Theory of Music in Arabic Writings (c. 900–1900): Descriptive Catalogue of Manuscripts in Libraries of Europe and the U.S.A.* München: Henle.

———. 1986. "Music in the Pre-Islamic Period as Reflected in Arabic Writings of the First Islamic Centuries." *Jerusalem Studies in Arabic and Islam* 7:109–120. (Reprint: Shiloah 1993.)

———. 1990. "Techniques of Scholarship in Medieval Arabic Musical Treatises." In *Music Theory and Its Sources: Antiquity and the Middle Ages*, ed. André Barbera. Notre Dame, Ind. (Reprint: Shiloah 1993.)

———. 1991. "Musical Modes and the Medical Dimension: The Arabic Sources (c. 900–c. 1600)." In *Metaphor: A Musical Dimension*, ed. Jamie Croy Kassler. Sydney. (Reprint: Shiloah 1993.)

———. 1993. *The Dimension of Music in Islamic and Jewish Culture*. Aldershot: Variorum.

———. 1994. "Notions d'esthétique dans les traités arabes sur la musique." *Cahiers de Musiques Traditionnelles* 7:51–58.

———. 1997a. "L'approche humaniste et métaphorique dans les premiers écrits arabes sur la musique." In *Festschrift Walter Wiora zum 90. Geburtstag*, ed. Christoph-Hellmut Mahling and Ruth Seiberts, 446–456. Tutzing: Hans Schneider.

———. 1997b. "Music and Religion in Islam." *Acta Musicologica* 69:143–155.

Smith, Eli, trans. 1847. "A Treatise on Arab Music, Chiefly from a Work by Mikhâ'il Meshâkah, of Damascus." *Journal of the American Oriental Society* 1:171–217.

Sobh, Mahmud. 1995. "La poesía árabe, la música y el canto." *Anaquel de Estudios Árabes* 6:149–184.

Stigelbauer, Michael. 1975. *Die Sängerinnen am Abbasidenhof um die Zeit des Kalifen Al-Mutawakkil: Nach dem Kitāb al-Aġānī des Abu-l-Faraġ al-Iṣbahānī und anderen Quellen dargestellt*. Vienna: VWGÖ.

el-Tawil, M. A. 1992. "Ibn Sina and Medieval Music (370–428 A.H./A.D. 980–1038): A New Edition of the Musical Section of Kitab al-Shifa and Kitab al-Najat plus a Comprehensive Study of His Life and Works on Music." Ph.D. dissertation, University of Exeter.

Terés, Elías, trans. 1971. "La epístola sobre el canto con música instrumental, de Ibn Ḥazm de Córdoba." *Al-Andalus* 36:203–214.

Vajda, Georges. 1980. "Un libelle contre la danse des soufis." *Studia Islamica* 51:163–177.

Valderrama, Fernando. 1986. "La música arábigo-andaluza." In *Actas del XII Congreso de la U.E.A.I. (Malaga, 1984)*. Madrid: Huertas.

Van den Branden, Albert. 1966. *Histoire de Thamoud*. Beirut: Publications de l'Université Libanaise.

Vigreux, Philip. 1985. *La derbouka: Technique fondamentale et initiation aux rhythmes arabes*. Aix-en-Provence: Eddisud.

Villoteau, G. A. 1809–1822. *De l'état actuel de l'art musical en Égypte*. Paris: Panckoucke.

———. 1813. "Description historique, technique, et littéraire des instruments de musique des orientaux." Vol. 14 of *Description de l'Egypte*. Paris: Pancoucke.

Weil, Jürgen W. 1975–1978. "Epigramme auf Musikerinnen [Parts 2 and 3: Künstlerinnen] in der Gedichtsammlung *Alf ġāriya wa-ġāriya*." *Rocznik Orientalistyczny* 37 (1975):7–12; 39 (1977):137–141; 40 (1978):83–93.

Werner, Eric, and Isaiah Sonne. 1941–1943. "The Philosophy and Theory of Music in Judaeo-Arabic Literature." *Hebrew Union College Annual* 16(1941):251–319; 17(1942–43):511–573.

Werner, Eric. 1965. "Greek Ideas on Music in Judeo-Arabic Literature." In *The Commonwealth of Music: In Honor of Curt Sachs*, ed. Gustave Reese and Rose Brandel. New York: Free Press; London: Collier Macmillan.

Wiedemann, Eilhard, and Fritz Hauser. 1918. "Byzantinische und arabische akustische Instrumente." *Archiv für die Geschichte der Naturwissenschaften und der Technik* 8:140–166. Reprint: 1984. In Wiedemann, *Gesammelte Schriften zur arabisch-islamischen Wissenschaftsgeschichte* 3:1580–1606. Frankfurt.

Wiedemann, Eilhard. 1910a. "Über die Herstellung von Glocken bei den Muslimen." *Mitteilungen zur Geschichte der Medizin und der Naturwissenschaften* 9:475–476. Reprint: 1984. In Wiedemann, *Gesammelte Schriften zur arabisch-islamischen Wissenschaftsgeschichte* 1:475–476. Frankfurt.

———. 1910b. "Über Musikautomaten bei den Arabern." In *Centenario della nascita di Michele Amari*, Vol. 2. Palermo: Virzì. Reprint: 1984. In Wiedemann, *Gesammelte Schriften zur arabisch-islamischen Wissenschaftsgeschichte* 1:451–472. Frankfurt.

———. 1914. "Über Musikautomaten." *Sitzungsberichte der Physikalisch-Medizinischen Societät in Erlangen* 46:17–26. Reprint: 1970. In Wiedemann, *Aufsätze zur arabischen Wissenschaftsgeschichte* 2:47–56. Hildesheim and New York: Olms.

Wiedemann, Eilhard, and Wilhelm Müller. 1922–1923. "Zur Geschichte der Musik. 1. Abschnitt über die Musik aus den Schlüsseln der Wissenschaft. 2. Angaben von al Akfânî über die Musik." *Sitzungsberichte der Physikalisch-Medizinischen Societät in Erlangen* 54–55:7–22. Reprint: 1970. In Wiedemann, *Aufsätze zur arabischen Wissenschaftsgeschichte* 2:580–595. Hildesheim and New York: Olms.

Wright, Owen. 1966. "Ibn al-Munajjim and the Early Arabian Modes." *Galpin Society Journal* 19:27–48.

———. 1978. *The Modal System of Arab and Persian Music A.D. 1250–1300*. Oxford: Oxford University Press.

———. 1983. "Music and Verse." In *Arabic Literature to the End of the Umayyad Period*, ed. A. F. L. Beeston et al. Cambridge: Cambridge University Press.

———. 1995. "A Preliminary Version of the *Kitāb al-Adwār*." *Bulletin of the School of Oriental and African Studies* 58:455–478.

Yammine, Habib. 1999. "L'évolution de la notation rythmique dans la musique arabe du IXᵉ à la fin du XXᵉ siècle." *Cahiers de Musiques Traditionnelles* 12:95–121.

Zenkowsky, S. 1950. "*Zār* and *Tambūra* as Practised by the Women of Omdurman." *Sudan Notes and Records* 31:65–81.

Ziegler, Christiane. 1979. *Les instruments de musique égyptiens au musée du Louvre*. Paris: Éditions de la Réunion des Musées Nationaux.

NORTH AFRICA: THE MAGHRIB

Abassi, Hamadi, et al. 1991. *Tunis chante et danse: 1900–1950*. Éditions de la Méditerranée. Tunis: Alif.

'Abd al-Wahhāb, Ḥassan Ḥusnī. 1918. "Le développement de la musique arabe en Orient, Espagne, et Tunisie." *Revue Tunisienne* 25:106–117.

Abun-Nasr, Jamil M. 1975. *A History of the Maghrib*, 2nd ed. Cambridge: Cambridge University Press.

———. 1987. *A History of the Maghreb in the Islamic Period*. Cambridge: Cambridge University Press.

Arberry, A. J. 1965. *Arabic Poetry*. London: Cambridge University Press.

Aydoun, Ahmed. 1995. *Musiques du Maroc*. Casablanca: EDDIF.

Bourgeot, André. 1989. "Cultures, langues berbères, et folklorisation chez les Touaregs." In

Tradition et modernité dans les sociétés berbères, ed. Yassadit Yacine, 33–52. Paris: Awal.

Bouzar-Kasbadji, Nadya. 1988. *L'emergence artistique algérienne au XXe siècle*. Algiers: Offices des Publications Universitaires.

Brandes, Edda. 1989. *Die Imzad Musik der Kel-Ahaggar-Frauen in Süd-Algerien*. Göttingen: Edition Re.

Brett, Michael, and Elizabeth Fentress. 1996. *The Berbers*. Oxford and Cambridge, Mass.: Blackwell.

Brown, Kenneth L. 1985. "The Discrediting of a Sufi Movement in Tunisia." In *Islamic Dilemmas: Reformers, Nationalists, and Industrialization*, ed. Ernest Gellner, 146–168. The Southern Shore of the Mediterranean: Religion and Society, 25. Amsterdam, Berlin, and New York: Mouton.

Brunel, René. 1926. *Essai sue la confrérie religieuse des Aîssâoûa au Maroc*. Paris: Geuthner.

Centre des Musiques Arabes et Méditerranéennes. 1992. *Les instruments de musique en Tunisie*. Tunis: Centre des Musiques Arabes et Méditerranéennes.

Chaker, Salem. 1989a. *Berbères aujourd'hui*. Paris: L'Harmattan.

———. 1989b. "Une tradition de résistance et de lutte: La poésie berbère kabyle—Un parcours poétique." *Revue du Monde Musulman et de la Méditerrannée* 51(1):11–31.

Chottin, Alexis. 1931–1933. *Corpus de musique marocaine*. Paris: Au Ménestrel Heugel.

———. 1938. *Tableau de la musique marocaine*. Paris: Librairie Orientaliste Paul Geuthner.

Collaer, Paul, and Jürgen Elsner. 1983. *Nordafrika: Musikgeschichte in Bildern*, 1(8), ed. Werner Bachman. Leipzig: Deutscher Verlag für Musik.

Compton, Linda Fish. 1976. *Andalusian Lyrical Poetry and Old Spanish Love Songs: The Muwashshah and Its Kharja*. New York: New York University Press.

Daoudi, Bouziane, and Hadj Miliani. 1996. *L'aventure du rai*. S.n.: Éditions du Seuil.

Davis, Ruth. 1985. "Songs of the Jews on the Island of Djerba: A Comparison between Two Surveys." *Musica Judaica* 7:23–33.

———. 1986a. "Modern Trends in the *Ma'lūf* of Tunisia: 1934–1984." Ph.D. dissertation, Princeton University.

———. 1986b. "Some Relations between Three Piyuṭim from Djerba and Three Arab Songs." *Maghreb Review* 11:134–144.

———. 1989. "Links between the Baron Rodolphe d'Erlanger and the Notation of Tunisian Art Music." In *Ethnomusicology and the Historical Dimension*, ed. Margot Lieth Philipp, 47–59. Ludwigsburg: Philipp Verlag.

———. 1992a. "The Tunisian Nūba as a Cyclic Genre: A Performance Analysis." In *Regionale Maqām-Traditionen in Geschichte und Gegenwart. Materialien der 2. Arbeitstagung der Study Group "Maqām" des International Council for Traditional Music vom 23. bis 28. März in Gossen bei Berlin*, ed. Jürgen Elsner and Gisa Jähnichen, 83–114. Berlin: s.n.

———. 1992b. "The Effects of Notation on Performance Practice in Tunisian Art Music." *World of Music* 34(1):85–114.

———. 1993a. "Tunisia and the Cairo Congress of Arab Music, 1932." *Maghreb Review* 18:83–102.

———. 1993b. "Melodic and Rhythmic Genre in the Tunisian *Nūba*." In *Ethnomusicologica*, 2, ed. F. Giannattasio and G. Giuriati, 71–87. Siena: Accademia Musicale Chigiana.

———. 1996. "The Art/Popular Music Paradigm and the Tunisian Ma'lūf." *Popular Music* 15:313–323.

———. 1997a. "Cultural Policy and the Tunisian Ma'lūf: Redefining a Tradition." *Ethnomusicology* 41:1–21.

———. 1997b. "Traditional Arab Music Ensembles in Tunis: Modernizing al-Turāth in the Shadow of Egypt." *Asian Music* 28(2):73–108.

———. In press. "*Piyuṭ* Melodies as Mirrors of Social Change in Djerba, Tunisia." *Musica Judaica* 14.

D'Erlanger, Rodolphe. 1917. "Au sujet de la musique arabe en Tunisie." *Revue Tunisienne* 24:91–95.

———. 1930–1959. *La musique arabe*. 6 vols. Paris: Librairie Orientaliste Paul Geuthner.

———. 1937. *Mélodies tunisiennes, hispano-arabes, arabo-berbères, juive, nègre*. Paris: Librairie Orientaliste Paul Geuthner.

Dermenghem, Emile, and Léo Barbès. 1951. "Essai sur la hadhra des Aïsaouia d'Algérie." *Révue Africaine* 84:289–314.

Djura. 1990. *Le voile du silence*. Paris: M. Lafon. See also: 1992. *The Veil of Silence*, trans. Dorothy Blair. London: Quartet.

Elsner, Jürgen. (1985) 1990. "Der Rhythmus Inṣirāf: Zum Problem quantitativer Rhythmik." In *Schriftenreihe des Mecklenburgischen Folklorezentrums, Abteilung Tanz*, ed. Rosemarie Ehm-Schulz, 59–74. Neubrandenburg: Mecklenburgisches Folklore-Zentrum. Also in *Rhythmik und Metrik in traditionellen Musikkulturen*, ed. Oskár Elschek, 239–249. Bratislava: VEDA, Verlag der Slowakischen Akademie der Wissenschaften.

———. 1991a. "Formation of New Music Traditions in the Arab Countries of North Africa." In *Studies in Ethnomusicology*, Vol. 1, ed. Jürgen Elsner and Gisa Jähnichen, 33–45. Berlin: Humboldt-Universität.

———. 1991b. "The Forms of Classical Algerian Instrumental Music." In *Studies in Ethnomusicology*, Vol. 1, ed. Jürgen Elsner and Gisa Jähnichen, 20–32. Berlin: Humboldt-Universität.

———. 1992 (1993). "Présentation de la musique algérienne au Congrès du Caire." In *Musique arabe, Le Congrès du Caire de 1932*, ed. Sheherazade Qassim Hassan, 191–208. Cairo: CEDEJ. German version as "Zur Darstellung der algerischen Musik auf der ersten Konferenz für arabische Musik Kairo 1932." In *Studies in Ethnomusicology*, Vol. 3, ed. Jürgen Elsner and Gisa Jähnichen, 111–136. Berlin: Humboldt-Universität.

———. 1993. "Some Remarks on New Developments in the Music of Algerian Cities." *Revista de Musicología* 16(3):1240–1245.

———. 1997. "Bashraf und Cambar in Algerian Art Music." In *The Structure and Idea of maqām, Historical Approaches, Proceedings of the Third Meeting of the ICTM Maqām Study Group Tampere—Virrat, 2–5 October 1995*, ed. Jürgen Elsner and Risto Pekka Pennanen, 65–85. Tampere: Department of Folk Tradition, University of Tampere.

Farmer, Henry George. 1929. *A History of Arabian Music to the Thirteenth Century*. London: Luzac.

Gross, Joan E., and David A. McMurray. 1993. "Berber Origins and the Politics of Ethnicity in Colonial North African Discourse." *PoLAR: Political and Legal Anthropology Review* 16(2):39–57.

Guettat, Mahmoud. 1980. *La musique classique du Maghreb*. Paris: Sinbad.

———. 1986. *La tradition musicale arabe*. S.n.: Ministère de l'Education Nationale.

———. 1992. "La Tunisie dans les documents du Congrès du Caire de 1932." In *Musique Arabe: Le Congres du Caire de 1932*, ed. Philippe Vigreux, 69–86. Cairo: Editions CEDEJ.

Johnson, Pamela Ryden. 1979. "A Sufi Shrine in Modern Tunisia." Ph.D. dissertation, University of California, Berkeley.

Jones, Lura JaFran. 1977. "The 'Isawiyya of Tunisia and Their Music." Ph.D. dissertation, University of Washington.

———. 1982. "The Role of Sufi Brotherhoods in the Preservation of Tunisian Art Music." In *Essays in Islamic and Comparative Studies*, ed. Isma'il Raji al-Faruqi, 109–120. Herndon, Virginia: International Institute of Islamic Thought.

———. 1987. "A Sociohistorical Perspective on Tunisian Women as Professional Musicians." In *Women and Music in Cross-Cultural Perspective*, 2nd ed., ed. Ellen Koskoff, 69–83. Champaign-Urbana: University of Illinois Press.

———. 1991. "Women in Non-Western Music." In *Women and Music: A History*, ed. Karin Pendle, 314–330. Bloomington: Indiana University Press.

Jouad, Hassan. 1995. *Le calcul inconscient de l'improvisation: Poésie berbère, rythme, nombre, et sens*. Paris: Peeters.

Jouad, Hassan, and Bernard Lortat-Jacob. 1978. *La saison des fêtes dans une vallée du Haut-Atlas*. Paris: Seuil.

Julien, Charles-André. 1970. *History of North Africa from the Arab Conquest to 1830*. New York: Praeger.

Kacem, Abdelaziz. 1973. "La politique culturelle tunisienne." *Annuaire de l'Afrique du Nord* 12:29–44.

Kapchan, Deborah. 1999. "*Zajal* Poetry: A Preface." *Méditerranēans/Méditerrannéennes* 11:45.

Kárpáti, J. 1961. "Mélodie, vers, et structure strophique dans la musique berbère (imazighen) du Maroc Central." *Studia Musicologica* 1(3-4):451–473.

Keddie, Nikki R., ed. 1972. *Scholars, Saints, and Sufis: Muslim Religious Institutions since 1500*. Berkeley: University of California Press.

Laade, Wolfgang. 1962. *Tunisia*. Vol. 2, *Religious Songs and Cantillations from Tunisia*. Folkways FW 8862.

Lachmann, Robert. 1940. *Jewish Cantillation and Song in the Isle of Djerba*. Jerusalem: Azriel, Archives of Oriental Music, Hebrew University.

———. 1974. *Die Musik im Volksleben Nordafrikas und orientalische Musik und Antike*. Vol. 1 of *Posthumous Works*, ed. Edith Gerson-Kiwi. Jerusalem: Magnes.

Lachmann, Robert, and Edith Gerson-Kiwi, eds. 1978. *Gesänge der Juden auf der Insel Djerba*. Yuval Monograph Series 7. Jerusalem: Magnes Press, Hebrew University.

Lacoste-Du Jardin, Camille. 1978. "Chansons berbères, chansons pour vivre." *L'Histoire* 5:104–105.

Laoust, Emile. 1993. *Noces berbères: Les cérémonies du mariage au Maroc*. Aix-en-Provence: Edisud.

Lefébure, Claude. 1977. "Tensons des ist—εṬa: La poésie féminine beraber comme mode de participation sociale." *Littérature Orale Arabo-Berbère* 8:109–142.

———. 1987. "Contrat mensonger, un chant d'*amdyaz* sur l'émigration." *Études et Documents Berbères* 3:28-46.

Liu, Benjamin M., and James T. Monroe. 1989. *Ten Hispano-Arabic Strophic Songs in the Modern Oral Tradition: Music and Texts*. Berkeley and Los Angeles: University of California Press.

Lortat-Jacob, Bernard. 1980. *Musique et fêtes au Haut-Atlas*. Paris: Mouton-EHESS.

———. 1994. *Musiques en fêtes*. Nanterre: Société d'Ethnologie.

Louati, Ali. 1995. *Le Baron d'Erlanger et son palais Ennajma Ezzahra à Sidi Bou Said*. Tunis: Editions Simpact.

el-Mahdi, Salah. 1972. *La musique arabe*. Paris: Alphonse Leduc.

Marcus, Scott. 1989. "Arab Music Theory in the Modern Period." Ph.D. dissertation, University of California Los Angeles.

Marouf, Nadir, ed. 1995. *Le chant arabo-andalou: Essai sur le rurbain ou la topique de la norme et de la marge dans le patrimoine musical arabe. Colloque international, Lille 6–8 décembre 1991*. Paris: Éditions L'Harmattan.

Matoub, Lounes. 1995. *Rebelle*. Paris: Stock.

Mehenni, Ferhat. 1983. "La chanson kabyle depuis dix ans." *Tafsut, Série Spéciale "Etudes et Débats"* 1:65–71.

Ministère de la Culture (Tunisia). 1995. *Centre des Musiques Arabes et Méditerranéenes*. Tunis: Simpact.

Monroe, James T. 1974. *Hispano-Arabic Poetry: A Student's Anthology*. Berkeley: University of California Press.

———. 1986–1987. "A Sounding Brass and Tinkling Cymbal: al-Halīl in Andalus (Two Notes on the Muwaššaha)." *Corónica* 15:252–258.

———. 1987. "The Tune or the Words? (Singing Hispano-Arabic Poetry)." *Al-Qantara* 8:265–317.

Moussali, Bernard. 1988. "Tunisia: Urban Music of Tunis." In *Congrès du Caire 1932*, 145–151. France: Édition Bibliothèque Nationale avec le concours de l'Institut du Monde Arabe.

Nylk, A. R. 1946. *Hispano-Arabic Poetry and Its Relations with the Old Provençal Troubadours*. Baltimore: Furst.

Pacholczyk, Josef. 1983. "The Relationship between the Nawba of Morocco and the Music of the Troubadours and Trouvères." *World of Music* 25(2):5–14.

Paris, André. 1921. "Haouach à Télouet." *Hespéris* 1:209-216.

Peyron, Michaël. 1991. *"Isaffen ghbanin (rivières profondes)": Poésies du Moyen-Atlas marocain traduites et annotées*. Casablanca: Wallada.

———. 1994. "Danse." *Encyclopédie Berbère* 14:2204–2213.

Plenckers, Leo J. 1989. *De muziek van de algerijnse muwashshaḥ*. Alkmaar: Rapporta B.V.

———. 1993. "Changes in the Algerian *san'a* Tradition and the Role of the Musicologist in the Process." *Revista de Musicología* 16(3):1255–1260.

Poché, Christian. 1995. *La musique arabo-andalouse*. S.n.: Cité de la Musique/Actes Sud.

Racy, Ali Jihad. 1991. "Historical Worldviews of Early Ethnomusicologists: An East-West Encounter in Cairo, 1932." In *Ethnomusicology and Modern Music History*, ed. Stephen Blum, Philip V. Bohlman, and Daniel M. Neuman, 68–91. Urbana and Chicago: University of Illinois Press.

Ribera, Julián. 1929. *Music in Ancient Arabia and Spain*. Stanford, Calif.: Stanford University Press.

Rouanet, Jules. 1913–1922. "La musique arabe" and "La musique arabe dans le Maghreb." In *Encyclopédie de Lavignac (Histoire de la musique)*, 5:2676–2812, 2813–2942. Paris: Delagrave.

Røvsing Olsen, Miriam. 1997. *Chants et danses de l'Atlas (Maroc)*. Pares: Cité de la Musique/Actes Sud.

Saadallah, Rabah. 1981. *Le chaâbi d'el-hadj M'hamed el-Anka*. Algiers: Dār al-kutub (Maison des Livres).

Salvador-Daniel, Francisco. 1986. *Musique et instruments de musique du Maghreb*. Paris: Boîte à Documents.

Schade-Poulsen, M. 1994. "Music and Men in Algeria. An Analysis of the Social Significance of Rai." Ph.D. dissertation, University of Copenhagen.

Schuyler, Philip D. 1978a. "*Rwais and Aḥwash*: Opposing Tendencies in Moroccan Berber Music and Society." *World of Music* 21(1):65–80.

———. 1978b. "Moroccan Andalusian Music." *World of Music* 21(1):33–46.

———. 1979a. "A Repertory of Ideas: The Music of the Rwais, Berber Professional Musicians from Southwestern Morocco." Ph.D. dissertation, University of Washington.

———. 1979b. "Music Education in Morocco: Three Models." *World of Music* 22(3):19–31.

———. 1984a. "Berber Professional Musicians in Performance." In *Performance Practice: Ethnomusicological Perspectives*, ed. Gérard Béhague, 91–148. London: Greenwood.

———. 1984b. "Moroccan Andalusian Music." In *Maqam: Music of the Islamic World and Its Influences*, ed. Robert Browning. New York: Alternative Museum.

———. 1985. "The *Rwais* and the *Zawia*: Professional Musicians and the Rural Elite in Southwestern Morocco." *Asian Music* 17(1):114–131.

———. 1993a. "A Folk Revival in Morocco." In *Everyday Life in the Muslim Middle East*, ed. Donna Lee Bowen and Evelyn A. Early, 287–293. Bloomington: Indiana University Press.

———. 1993b. "Entertainment in the Marketplace." In *Everyday Life in the Muslim Middle East*, ed. Donna Lee Bowen and Evelyn A. Early, 276–280. Bloomington: Indiana University Press.

el-Shawan, Salwa Aziz. 1980. "Al-Mūsīka al-arabiyyah: A Category of Urban Music in Cairo, Egypt, 1927–1977." Ph.D. dissertation, Columbia University.

Speight, R. Marston. 1966. "Tunisia and Sufism." *Muslim World* 26:58–59.

Stern, Samuel M. 1964. "Andalusian Muwashshahs in the Musical Repertory of North Africa." In *Actas del Primer Congreso de Estudios Árabes e Islámicos, Córdoba, 1962*, 319–327. Madrid: Maestre.

———. 1974. *Hispano-Arabic Strophic Poetry*, ed. L. P. Harvey. Oxford: Clarendon.

Touma, Habib Hassan. 1998. *Die Nūbah Māyah: Zur Phänomenologie des Melos in der arabisch-andalusi Musik Marokkos*. Hildesheim: George Olms Verlag.

Trimingham, J. Spencer. 1971. *The Sufi Orders in Islam*. Oxford: Clarendon.

Udovitch, Abraham L., and Lucette Valensi. 1984. *The Last Arab Jews: The Communities of Jerba, Tunisia*. Chur, London, Paris, and New York: Harwood Academic.

Vocke, Sibylle. 1990. *Die markkanische Malhun-poesie*. Wiesbaden: Otto Harrassowitz.

Wansbrough, John. 1969. "Theme, Convention, and Prosody in the Vernacular Poetry of North Africa." *Bulletin of the School of Oriental and African Studies* 32:477–495.

Wulstan, David. 1982. "The Muwaššah and Zaǧal Revisited." *Journal of the American Oriental Society* 102:247–264.

Yacine, Tassadit. 1989. *Aït Menguellat chante . . .* Paris: Découverte/Awal.

Yafil, Edmond-Nathan. 1904–1924. *Repertoire de musique arabe et maure.* Nos. 1–29. Algiers.

Yelles-Chaouche, Mourad. 1986. *Le Ḥaufi: Poésie féminine et tradition orale au Maghreb.* Algiers: Office des Publications Universitaires.

Zoulef, Boudjemaa, and Mohamed Dernouny. 1981. "L'identité culturelle au Maghreb à travers un corpus de chants contemporains." *Annuaire de l'Afrique du Nord* 20:1021–1051.

THE EASTERN ARAB WORLD: THE MASHRIQ

Abdun, Salih, ed. 1971. *Genesi della "Aida": Con documentazione inedita.* Quaderni dell' Istituto di Studi Verdiani, Vol. 4. Parma: Tipografia "La Nazionale."

Abu-Haidar. 1988. "The Poetic Content of the Iraqi Maqam." *Journal of Arabic Literature* 19:128–141.

Alexandru, Tiberiu, and Emile A. Wahba. 1967. *The Folk Music of Egypt.* Cairo: Ministry of Culture.

Armbrust, Walter. 1996. *Mass Culture and Modernism in Egypt.* Cambridge: Cambridge University Press.

Azzam, Nabil. 1990. "Muḥammad 'Abd al-Wahhāb in Modern Egyptian Music." Ph.D. dissertation, University of California, Los Angeles.

Bailey, Clinton. 1974. "Bedouin Weddings in Sinai and the Negev." In *Studies in Marriage Customs,* ed. Issachar Ben-Ami and Dov Noy, 117–132. Jerusalem: Magnes.

al-Barghoti, 'A. 1963. "Arab Folk Songs from Jordan." Ph.D. dissertation, University of London.

Barker, John. 1876. *Syria and Egypt under the Last Five Sultans of Turkey.* London: Tinsley.

Berger, Morroe. 1961. "A Curious and Wonderful Gymnastic . . . ." *Dance Perspectives* 10:4–41.

Berner, Alfred. 1937. *Studien zur arabischen Musik auf Grund der gegenwärtigen Theorie und Praxis in Ägypten.* Leipzig: Kistner and Siegel.

Braune, Gabriele. 1987. *Die Qasida im Gesang von Umm Kultum: Die arabische Poesie im Repertoire der grössten ägyptischen Sängerin unserer Zeit.* Hamburg: Karl Dieter Wagner.

———. 1992. "Maqāmāt and Western Harmony in Egypt with Musical Examples of Sayyid Darwīš and Farīd al-'Atrāš." In *Regionale Maqām-Traditionen in Geschichte und Gegenwart. Materialien der 2. Arbeitstagung der Study Group "Maqām" des International Council for Traditional Music vom 23. bis 28. März in Gossen bei Berlin,* ed. Jürgen Elsner and Gisa Jähnichen, 75–82. Berlin: s.n.

Buonaventura, Wendy. 1989. *Serpent of the Nile: Women and Dance in the Arab World.* London: Saqi.

Clot-Bey, Antoine Barthelemy. 1840. *Aperçu général sur l'Egypte.* Paris: Fortin, Massin et Cie.

Dalman, G. 1901. *Palästinisher Diwan.* Leipzig.

Danielson, Virginia. 1989. "Cultural Authenticity in Egyptian Musical Expression." *Pacific Review of Ethnomusicology* 5:51–61.

———. 1991a. "Artists and Entrepreneurs: Female Singers in Cairo during the 1920s." In *Women in Middle Eastern History,* ed. Nikki R. Keddie and Beth Baron, 292–310. New Haven and London: Yale University Press.

———. 1991b. "Min al-Meshayikh: A View of Egyptian Musical Tradition." *Asian Music* 22(1):113–128.

———. 1997. *The Voice of Egypt: Umm Kulthūm, Arabic Song, and Egyptian Society in the Twentieth Century.* Chicago: University of Chicago Press.

D'Arvieux, Laurent. 1735. *Mémoires du Chevalier d'Arvieux.* 6 vols. Paris: Charles Jean-Baptiste Delespine.

De Laborde, Jean Benjamin. 1780. *Essai sur la musique ancienne et moderne.* 4 vols. Paris: Chez Eugene Onfroy.

D'Erlanger, Baron Rodolphe. 1930–1959. *La musique arabe.* Paris: Paul Geuthner.

Elsner, Jürgen. 1973. *Der Begriff des maqām in Ägypten in neuerer Zeit.* Leipzig: VEB Deutscher Verlag für Musik.

Collangettes, D. M. 1906. "La musique d'Alep." *Revue Musicale* 6:142.

Fahmy, Farida Melda. 1987. "The Creative Development of Mahmoud Reda, a Contemporary Egyptian Choreographer." M.A. thesis, University of California Los Angeles.

Fakhri, Ahmed. 1973. *The Oases of Egypt,* Vol. 1. Cairo: American University in Cairo Press.

Farmer, Henry George. [1929] 1973. *A History of Arabian Music to the Thirteenth Century.* London: Luzac.

al-Faruqi, Lois Ibsen Lamya'. 1976–1977. "Dances of the Muslim Peoples." *Dance Scope* 11(1):43–51.

———. 1978. "Dance as an Expression of Islamic Culture." *Dance Research Journal* 10(2):6–13.

———. 1979. "The Status of Music in Muslim Nations: Evidence from the Arab World." *Asian Music* 12(1):56–85.

Fernea, Elizabeth, and Robert A. Fernea (with Aleya Rouchdy). 1991. *Nubian Ethnographies.* Prospect Heights, Ill.: Waveland.

Fernea, Robert A. 1966. "Initial Adaptations to Resettlement: A New Life for Egyptian Nubians." *Current Anthropology* 7(3):349–354.

———. 1973. *Nubians in Egypt: Peaceful People.* Austin: University of Texas Press.

Graham-Brown, Sarah. 1988. *Images of Women.* London: Quartet.

Granqvist, Hilma. 1931–1935. *Marriage Conditions in a Palestinian Village.* Helsingfors: Akademische Buchhandlung.

Haddad, M. 1986. *Palestinian Folk Heritage between Obliteration and Revival.* Taybih.

Hassan, Scheherazade Qassim. 1980. *Les instruments de musique en Irak et leur rôle dans la societé traditionelle.* Paris: Mouton.

———. 1987. "Le makam irakien: Structures et réalisations." In *L'improvisation dans les musiques de tradition orale,* ed. Bernard Lortat-Jacob, 143–149. Paris: SELAF.

———. 1989. "Some Islamic Non-Arabic Elements of Influence on the Repertory on al-Maqām al-'Irāqī in Bagdad." In *Maqam-Raga-Zeilenmelodik: Konzeptionen and Prinzipen der Musikproduktion. Materialien der 1. Arbeitstagung der Study Group "Maqām" beim International Council for Traditional Music vom 28. Juni bis 2. Juli 1988 in Berlin,* ed. Jürgen Elsner, 148–155. Berlin: National-Komitee.

———. 1992. "Survey of Written Sources on the Iraqi Maqam." In *Regionale Maqām-Traditionen in Geschichte und Gegenwart. Materialien der 2. Arbeitstagung der Study Group "Maqām" des International Council for Traditional Music vom 23. bis 28. März in Gossen bei Berlin,* ed. Jürgen Elsner and Gisa Jähnichen, 252–275. Berlin: s.n.

Haydar, 'Adnan. 1989. "The Development of Lebanese *Zajal*: Genre, Meter, and Verbal Duel." *Oral Tradition* 4(1–2):189–212.

Jargy, Simon. 1970. *La poésie populaire traditionelle chantée au Proche-Orient Arabe.* Paris: Mouton.

———. 1978. "Kasida." *Encyclopaedia of Islam* 4:713–714. Leiden: Brill.

Kennedy, John G. 1967. "Nubian Zar Ceremonies as Psychotherapy." *Human Organization* 26(4):185–194.

Al-Kholy, Samha, and John Robinson, eds. 1993. *Festschrift for Gamal Abd Al-Rahim.* Cairo: Binational Fulbright Commission in Egypt.

Koskoff, Ellen, ed. 1989. *Women and Music in Cross-Cultural Perspective.* Urbana and Chicago: University of Illinois Press.

Lagrange, Frédéric. 1996. *Musiques d'Egypte.* Paris: Cité de la Musique/Actes Sud.

Landau, Jacob M. 1958. *Studies in the Arab Theater and Cinema.* Philadelphia: University of Pennsylvania Press.

Lane, Edward W. 1936. *The Modern Egyptians.* London: Dent.

Linder, Sven. 1952. *Palästinische Volksgesänge.* Uppsala: Lundequistska Bokhandeln.

Marcus, Scott Lloyd. 1989. "Arab Music Theory in the Modern Period." Ph.D. dissertation, University of California Los Angeles.

McPherson, J. W. 1941. *The Moulids of Egypt.* Cairo: Ptd. N. M. Press.

Molé, Marijan. 1963. "La danse extatique en Islam." In *Les danses sacrées*, ed. Jean Cazeneuve. Paris: Éditions du Seuil.

Murray, G. W. 1935. *Sons of Ishmael*. London: Routledge.

Nelson, Kristina. 1985. *The Art of Reciting the Qur'ān*. Austin: University of Texas Press.

Nettl, Bruno, and Ronald Riddle. 1973. "Taqsīm Nahawand: A Study of Sixteen Performances by Jihad Racy." *Yearbook of the International Folk Music Council* 5:11–50.

Neubauer, Eckhard. 1989. "Musique arabe en France 1630–1830." In *Le monde arabe dans la vie intellectuelle et culturelle en France*. Paris: Institut du Monde Arabe.

Nieuwkerk, Karin van. 1995. *"A Trade Like Any Other": Female Singers and Dancers in Egypt*. Austin: University of Texas Press.

Poché, Christian. 1995. *La musique arabo-andalouse*. Arles, Paris: Actes Sud et Cité de la Musique.

Racy, Ali Jihad. 1976. "Record Industry and Egyptian Traditional Music: 1904–1932." *Ethnomusicology* 20(1):23–48.

———. 1977. "Musical Change and Commercial Recording in Egypt, 1904–1932." Ph.D. dissertation, University of Illinois at Urbana-Champaign.

———. 1981. "Music in Contemporary Cairo: A Comparative Overview." *Asian Music* 13(1):4–26.

———. 1982. "Musical Aesthetics in Present-Day Cairo." *Ethnomusicology* 26:391–407.

———. 1983a. "Music in Nineteenth-Century Egypt: An Historical Sketch." *Selected Reports in Ethnomusicology* 4:157–179.

———. 1983b. "The Waṣlah: A Compound-Form Principle in Egyptian Music." *Arab Studies Quarterly* 5(4):396–403.

———. 1988. "Sound as Society: The Takht Music of Early Twentieth Century Cairo." *Selected Reports in Ethnomusicology* 7:139–170.

———. 1991. "Creativity and Ambience: An Ecstatic Feedback Model from Arab Music." *World of Music* 33(3):7–28.

———. 1992. "Music." In *The Genius of Arab Civilization: Source of Renaissance*, 3rd ed., ed. John R. Hays, 151–171. New York: New York University Press.

———. 1996. "Heroes, Lovers, and Poet-Singers: The Bedouin Ethos in Music of the Arab Near-East." *Journal of American Folklore* 109 (434):404–424.

———. 1998. "Improvisation, Ecstasy, and Performance Dynamics in Arab Music." In *In the Course of Performance: Studies in the World of Musical Improvisation*, ed. Bruno Nettl and Melinda Russell, 95–112. Chicago and London: University of Chicago Press.

Russell, Alex[andre], and Pat[rick] Russell. 1794. *Natural History of Aleppo*. 2 vols. London: G. G. and J. Robinson.

Saarisalo, Aapeli. 1932. *Songs of the Druzes*. Helsinki.

Said, Edward. 1993. *Culture and Imperialism*. New York: Vintage.

Said, Mohamed Sayyid. 1999. "Cosmopolitanism and Cultural Autarky in Egypt." In *Cosmopolitanism, Identity, and Authenticity in the Middle East*, ed. Roel Meijer. Surrey: Curzon.

St. John, Bayle. 1973. *Village Life in Egypt*. New York: Arno.

Saleh, Magda. 1979. "A Documentation of the Ethnic Dance Traditions of the Arab Republic of Egypt." Ph.D. dissertation, New York University.

Saleh, Maher. 1965. "Horsemanship and the Horse Dance." *Al Funun al Shaabiya* (Folk Arts) 2:68–81.

Savary, [Claude Etienne]. 1785. *Lettres sur l'Egypte*. 3 vols. Paris: Chez Onfroy.

Sawa, George. 1989. *Music Performance Practice in the Early 'Abbasid Era, 132–320 A.H./A.D. 750–932*. Toronto: Pontifical Institute of Mediaeval Studies.

Sbait, Dirgham. 1982. "Improvised Folk-Poetry of the Palestinians." Ph.D. dissertation, University of Washington.

———. 1986. "Poetic and Musical Structure in the Improvised-Sung Colloquial *Qasidah* of the Palestinian Poet-Singers." *Al-'Arabiyya* 19:75–108.

———. 1989. "Palestinian Improvised-Sung Poetry: The Genres of *Hida* and *Qarradi*—Performance and Transmission." *Oral Tradition* 4:213–235.

———. 1993. "Debate in the Improvised-Sung Poetry of the Palestinians." *Asian Folklore Studies* 52:93–117.

Schiff, Ze'ev and Ya'ari, Ehud. [1989] 1991. *Intifada: The Palestinian Uprising—Israel's Third Front*, ed. and trans. Ina Friedman. New York: Simon and Schuster, Touchstone.

el-Shawan, Salwa. 1980a. "The Sociopolitical Context of *al-Musika al-'Arabiyyah* in Cairo, Egypt: Policies, Patronage, Institutions, and Musical Change (1927–1977)." *Asian Music* 12(1):86–129.

———. 1980b. "Al-Musika Al-'Arabiyah: A Category of Urban Music in Cairo, Egypt, 1927–1977." Ph.D. dissertation, University of Illinois at Urbana-Champaign.

———. 1982. "The Role of Mediators in the Transmission of Al-Musiqa Al-'Arabiyyah in Twentieth Century Cairo." *Yearbook for Traditional Music* 14:55–74.

———. 1984. "Traditional Arab Music Ensembles in Egypt since 1967: The Continuity of Tradition within a Contemporary Framework." *Ethnomusicology* 28(2):271–288.

———. 1985. "Western Music and Its Practitioners in Egypt (c. 1825–1985): The Integration of a New Musical Tradition in a Changing Environment." *Asian Music* 27(1):144–153.

Shelemay, Kay Kaufman. 1998. *Let Jasmine Rain Down: Song and Remembrance among Syrian Jews*. Chicago: University of Chicago Press.

Shiloah, Amnon. 1974. "A Group of Arabic Wedding Songs from the Village of Deyr al-Asad." In *Studies in Marriage Customs*, ed. Issachar Ben-Ami and Dov Noy, 267–296. Jerusalem: Magnes.

———. 1979. *The Theory of Music in Arabic Writings (c. 900–1900)*. Munich: G. Henle Verlag.

Simon, Artur. 1972. *Studien zur ägyptischen Volksmusik*. 2 vols. Hamburg: Karl Dieter Wagner.

Slyomovics, Susan. 1988. *The Merchant of Art: An Egyptian Hilali Oral Epic Poet in Performance*. Berkeley: University of California Press.

Sowayan, Saad A. 1989. "'Tonight My Gun Is Loaded': Poetic Dueling in Arabia." *Oral Tradition* 4(1–2):151–173.

Spector, Johanna. 1970. "Classical *'Ud* Music in Egypt with Special Reference to Maqamat." *Ethnomusicology* 14:243–257.

Sulaiman, Khalid A. 1984. *Palestine and Modern Arab Poetry*. London: Zed.

Touma, Habib Hassan. 1996. *The Music of the Arabs*. Portland, Ore.: Amadeus.

Tsuge, Gen'ichi. 1972. "A Note on the Iraki Maqam." *Asian Music* 4(1):59–66.

Vatikiotis, P. J. 1985. *The History of Egypt from Muhammad Ali to Mubarak*, 3rd ed. Baltimore: Johns Hopkins University Press.

Villoteau, M. [Guillaume A.] 1823. *Description historique, technique, et littéraire des instruments de musiques des Orientaux*. Vol. 13 of *Description de l'Egypte*. Paris: Panckoucke.

———. 1826. *De l'état actuel de l'art musical en Egypte*. Vol. 14 of *Description de l'Egypte*. Paris: Panckoucke.

Waugh, Earle H. 1989. *The Munshidin of Egypt: Their World and Their Song*. Columbia: University of South Carolina Press.

Wegner, Ulrich. 1982. *Abūdiya und mawwāl: Untersuchungen zur sprachlich-musikalischen Gestaltung im südirakischen Volksgesang*. 2 vols. Hamburg: Karl Dieter Wagner.

Wood, Leona. 1976. "Danse du ventre: A Fresh Appraisal." *Dance Research Journal* 8(2):18–30.

Zuhur, Sherifa, ed. 1998. *Images of Enchantment: Visual and Performing Arts of the Middle East*. Cairo: American University in Cairo Press.

MUSIC OF THE ARABIAN PENINSULA

Abbeele, Georges Van Den. 1992. *Travel as a Metaphor: From Montaigne to Rousseau*. Minneapolis: University of Minnesota Press.

Adler, Guido. 1903. "Sokotri-Musik." In *Die Mehri- und Soqotri-Sprache. 2. Südarabische Expedition der Akademie der Wissenschaften*, ed. David Heinrich Müller, 6:377–382. Vienna: A. Hölder.

Adra, Najwa. 1982. "Qabyala: The Tribal Concept in the Central Highlands Yemen Arab Republic." Ph.D. dissertation, Temple University.

———. 1993. "Tribal Dancing and Yemeni Nationalism: Steps to Unity." *Revue du Monde Musulman et de la Méditerranée* 67(l):161–168.

———. 1998. "Dance and Glance: Visualizing Tribal Identity in Highland Yemen." *Visual Anthropology* 11(1–2):55–101.

'Ali, Khalīl Husayn. 1988. "*Al-'idda* Dance in Yemen." *Al Ma'thūrāt al-Sha'biyya* 12:8–15.

Altorki, Soraya. 1986. *Women in Saudi Arabia*. New York: Columbia University Press.

Arom, Simha, and Uri Sharvit. 1994. "Plurivocality in the Liturgical Music of the Jews of San'a (Yemen)." *Yuval* 6:34–67.

Bahat, Naomi, and Avner Bahat. 1980. "Traditional Scriptural-Reading Hand Movements as a Dance Source for Yemenite Jews." *Israel Dance* 5:22–23.

———. 1995. *Saperi Tama: The Diwan Songs of the Jews of Central Yemen, as Sung in the Manakha Community, Poetry-Music-Dance*. Tel-Aviv: Beth Hatefutsoth.

Bahat-Ratzon, Naomi. 1975–1976. "Le saff-procession dansé dans les cérémonies du mariage druze." *Orbis Musicae* 5:45–65.

Bakewell, Anderson. 1985. "Music of the Tihamah." In *Studies on the Tihamah: The Report of the Tihama Expedition 1982*, ed. F. Stone, 104–108. London: Longman.

Barth, Fredrik. 1983. *Sohar, Culture and Society in an Omani Town*. Baltimore: Johns Hopkins University Press.

Burckhardt, John Lewis. 1830. *Notes on the Bedouins and Wahabys*. 2 vols. London: Coburn and Bentley.

Campbell, Kay Hardy. 1979. "Arabian Wedding Nights." *Arab News* (August 1).

———. 1985. "Saudi Arabian Women's Music." *Habibi* 9(3).

———. 1977. "The Lives and Literary Patronage of 'Aishah Bint Talhah Ibn 'Ubayd Allah and Sukaynah Bint al-Husayn Ibn 'Ali in *Kitab al-Aghani*." Summa cum laude thesis, University of Minnesota.

———. 1980. "Why Sarah Uthman Wants to Expand beyond Wedding Party Audiences." *Arab News* (August 4).

Caton, Steven. 1991. *Peaks of Yemen I Summon: Poetry as Cultural Practice in a North Yemen Tribe*. Berkeley: University of California Press.

Christensen, Dieter. 1991. "Traditional Music, Nationalism, and Musicological Research." In *Music in the Dialogue of Cultures*, ed. Max Peter Baumann, 215–223. Wilmhelmshaven: Noetzel.

———. 1992. "Worlds of Music, Music of the World: The Case of Oman." In *World Music, Musics of the World*, ed. Max Peter Baumann, 107–122. Wilhelmshaven: Noetzel.

Deaver, Sherri. 1978. "Concealment versus Display: The Modern Saudi Woman." *Dance Research Journal* 10(2):14–18.

Dickson, Harold Richard Patrick. 1967. *The Arab of the Desert*, 4th ed. London: Allen and Unwin.

Elsner, Jürgen. 1990. "Trommeln und Trommelensembles im Jemen." In *Beiträge zur traditionellen Musik*, ed. A. Michel and Jürgen Elsner, 18–37. Berlin: Humboldt Universität.

Farmer, Henry G. 1929. "Meccan Musical Instruments." *Journal of the Royal Asiatic Society* 3:489–505. Reprint: 1997. In H. G. Farmer, *Studies in Oriental Music*, ed. Eckhard Neubauer, 2:79–100. Frankfurt am Main: Institute for the History of Arabic-Islamic Science at the Johann Wolfgang Goethe University.

———. [1929] 1967. *A History of Arabian Music to the Thirteenth Century*. London: Luzac.

Fox, Edward. 1990. "Arabian Delights." *Folk Roots* 86:21–23.

Galley, Micheline. 1996. "Creativity and Tradition: Mediterranean Folk Poetry in Sung Form." *Journal of Mediterranean Studies* 6(1).

Gavin, Carney E. S. 1985. "The Earliest Arabian Recordings: Discoveries and Work Ahead." *Phonographic Bulletin* (September):38–45.

Grandguillaume, Gilbert. 1982. "Valorisation et dévalorisation liées au contacts de cultures en Arabie Saoudite." In *Péninsule arabique aujourd'hui: Études par pays*, ed. P. Bonnenfant, 623–654. Paris: Éditions du CNRS.

al-Harbi, Salih. 1980. "Hommes et société des pêcheurs de perles au Koweit." Diplome, École des Hautes Études, Paris.

Hassan, Scheherazade Qassim. 1976. "Musical Instruments among the Yezidi of Iraq." *Yearbook of the International Folk Music Council* 8:53–72.

Hofman, Shlomo. 1968. "The Density of a Yemenite Folk Tune." *Yearbook of the International Folk Music Council* 20:25–29.

Hood, Mantle. 1992. "Voiceprints of Traditional Omani Music." In *African Musicology: Current Trends*, 191–244. Los Angeles: University of California Press; Atlanta: Crossroads, African Studies Center.

Hurgronje, Snouck. [1888] 1931. *Mekka in the Latter Part of the Nineteenth Century*, trans. James Henry Monahan. Leiden: Brill.

Jargy, Simon. 1970. *La poésie populaire traditionnelle chanté au Proche-Orient arabe*. Paris: Mouton.

———. 1986. "Comments on the Concept and Characteristics of the Folk Music in the Gulf and Arabian Peninsula." *Al-Ma'tūrāt al-sha'biyya* (1 January).

———. 1987. "Aspects de la poésie chanté dans la tradition orale de la péninsule arabique." *Revue Musicale de la Suisse Romande* 40(1):2–12.

———. 1988. *La musique arabe*, 3rd ed. Paris: Presses Universitaires de France.

———. 1989. "Sung Poetry in the Oral Tradition of the Gulf Region and the Arabian Peninsula." *Oral Tradition* 4(1–2):174–188.

Jenkins, Jean, and Poul Røvsing-Olsen. 1976. *Music and Musical Instruments in the World of Islam*. London: World of Islam Festival Publishing.

Kanafani, Aida Sami. 1983. *Aesthetics and Ritual in the United Arab Emirates*. Beirut: American University in Beirut.

Kerbage, Toufic. 1983. *The Rhythms of Pearl Diver Music in Qatar*. Doha: Culture and Art Directorate, Ministry of Information.

———. 1986–1987. "Tonernes univers." *Dansk Musik Tidsskrift* 61(4):162–168.

al-Kholaifi, Aisha. 1986. "Al-Muradah: The Female Dance in the Arabian Gulf." *Al-Ma'thurat al sha'biyyah* 3:104–129.

al-Khulayfi, Samia. 1995. *Le chant des femmes du Koweit*. Paris: DEA, Université de la Sorbonne-Paris IV.

al-Khusaibi, Said bin Nasser. 1985. *The Use of Traditional Music in the Development of Mass Media in Oman*. Beverly Hills, Calif.: University of Beverly Hills.

Lambert, Jean. 1993. "Identité nationale et régionalisme musical." In *Revue d'Études du Monde Musulman et Méditerranéen*, 67(1), *Le Yémen, passé et présent de l'unité*, 171–186. Aix-en-Provence.

———. 1995. "La musique dans la Maison-tour: Harmonies et Dissonances." In *Sanaa, architecture domestique et société*, ed. P. Bonnenfant, 165–173. Paris: CNRS-Éditions.

———. 1997. *La médecine de l'âme: Le chant de San'ā' dans la société yéménite*. Hommes et Musiques. Nanterre: Societé d'Ethnologie.

———. 2000. "Yemen." In *The New Grove Dictionary of Music and Musicians*, 2nd ed., 27:652–657. London: Macmillan.

Lonnet, Antoine, and Marie-Claude Simeone-Senelle. 1987. "Rābūt: Trance and Incantations in Mehri Folk Medicine." *Proceedings of the Seminar for Arabian Studies* 17:107–115.

el-Mahdi, Salah. 1976. "Les formes improvisés de la musique arabe." *World of Music* 18(3):42–45.

el-Mallah, Issam. 1990. "Some Observations on the Naming of Musical Instruments and on Rhythm in Oman." *Yearbook of the International Folk Music Council* 22:123–126.

———. 1992. "Die Vorbereitung des Felles als Teil musikalischer Darbietungen in den arabischen Golfländern." In *Von der Vielfalt musikalischer Kultur: Festschrift für Josef Kuckertz—Zur Vollendung des 60. Lebensjahres*, 305–310. Anif/Salzburg: Müller-Speiser.

———. 1995. "Afrikanische Elemente in arabischen Musikkulturen." In *Altes im Neuen: Festschrift Theodor Göllner zum 65. Geburtstag*, 47–62. Tutzing: Hans Schneider.

———. 1996. *Arabische Musik und Notenschrift.* Münchner Veröffentlichungen zur Musikgeschichte, Vol. 53. Tutzing: Hans Schneider.

———. 1997. *Die Rolle der Frau im Musikleben Omans.* Tutzing: Hans Schneider.

Marks, Paul F. 1973. *Bibliography of Literature concerning Yemenite-Jewish Music.* Detroit: Information Coordinators.

Morris, M. 1983. "Some Preliminary Remarks on a Collection of Poems and Songs of the Batahirah." *Journal of Oman Studies* 6(1):129–44.

Ogger, Thomas. 1987. *Maqam segah/sikah: Vergleich der Kunstmusik des Irak und des Iran anhand eines maqam-Modells.* Hamburg: Verlag der Musikalienhandlung K.D. Wagner.

Poché, Christian. 1978. "Zikr [Dhikr] and Musicology." *World of Music* 20(1):59–71.

———. 1981. "Rhythme impair et danse boiteuse." *Cahiers Musique Culture Mémoire* (1981):97–101.

———. 1983. *Introduction à la musique de Djibouti.* Paris: Radio-France-Internationale, Centre de Documentation Africaine.

———. 1984. "Qanbūs." In *The New Grove Dictionary of Musical Instruments,* 3:168–169. London: Macmillan.

———. 1992. "Lyre of the Arab Gulf: Historical Roots, Geographical Link, and Social Context." *al-Ma'tūrā al sh'biyya* 27:7–17.

———. 1994a. "Pays du Golfe: De la frénésie sociale à l'accélération musicale." In *Adib,* ed. Y. Gonzales-Quijani and R. Boustani. Paris: IMA. (CD-ROM.)

———. 1994b. "De l'homme parfait . . . l'expressivité musicale: Courants esthétiques arabes au XXe siècle." *Cahiers de Musiques Traditionnelles* 7:59–74.

Pratt, Mary Louise. 1992. *Imperial Eyes: Travel Writing and Transculturation.* London: Routledge.

Ratzaby, Yehuda. 1986. "Yemenite *Qasid* Songs." *Yuval* 5:169–191.

al-Rifa'i, Hessa. 1985. "Sea Chanteys of Kuwait." *Arabian Studies* 7:88–95.

Rihani, Amin. 1930. "The Dance." In *Around the Coasts of Arabia.* Boston: Houghton Mifflin.

Rossi, Ettore. 1939. *L'arabo parlato a Sanaa: Grammatica, testi, lessico.* Rome: Istituto per l'Oriente.

Røvsing-Olsen, Poul. 1964. "Enregistrements faits à Kuwait et à Bahrein." In *Les colloques de*

Wegimont, 4—1958–1960, *Ethnomusicologie* 3, 137–170. Paris: Les Belles Lettres.

———. 1967. "La musique africaine dans le Golfe Persique." *Journal of the International Folk Music Council* 19:28–36.

———. 1974. "Six Versions de Taqsim en Maqam Rast." *Studia Instrumentorum Musicae Popularis* 3:197–202.

———. 1978. "The Vocal Bourdon in the Arab Gulf." *Anthropologiska Studier* 25–26:12–20.

———. 1980. "Arabian Gulf." In *The New Grove Dictionary of Music and Musicians,* 1:513–514. London: Macmillan.

al-Saud, Noura bint Muḥammad, al-Jawharah Muḥammad al-'Anqari, and Madeha Muḥammad al-'Atroush, eds. 1989. *Abha, Bilad Asir: Southwestern Region of the Kingdom of Saudi Arabia.* Riyadh: Published by the editors.

Schuyler, Philip. 1990. "Hearts and Minds: Three Attitudes towards Performance Practice and Music Theory in the Yemen Arab Republic." *Ethnomusicology* 34:1–18.

———. 1990–1991. "Music and Tradition in Yemen." *Asian Music* 22(1):51–71.

Serjeant, Robert B. 1951. *South Arabian Poetry and Prose of Ḥaḍramawt.* London: Taylor's Foreign Press.

Sharvit, Uri. 1980. "The Role of Music in the Yemenite *Heder.*" *Israel Studies in Musicology* 2:33–49.

Shawqi, Yusuf. 1994. *Dictionary of Traditional Music in Oman.* English ed., rev. and expanded by Dieter Christensen. Intercultural Music Studies, Vol. 6. Wilhelmshaven: F. Noetzel.

Shiloah, Amnon. 1972. "The *Simsimiyah*: A Stringed Instrument of the Red Sea Area." *Asian Music* 4(1):15.

———. 1980. "Arab Music: 2. Folk Music." In *The New Grove Dictionary of Music and Musicians,* 1:526–539. London: Macmillan.

———. 1991. "The Jewish Yemenite Tradition: A Case Study of Two Women Poet-Musicians." In *Tradition and Its Future in Music,* 447–450. Osaka: Mita.

Sillamy, Jean-Claude. 1987. *La musique dans l'ancien Orient, ou, La theorie musicale sumero-babylonienne.* 2 vols. Ajaccio: Jean Claude Sillamy.

———. 1991. *Le principe de la modulation dans le fragment babylonien d'Ur: U.7/80 (XVIIIème siècle av. J.C.) (à partir d'un instrument de l'époque non identifié, le "gis za-mi").* Ajaccio: Jean-Claude Sillamy.

Sowayan, Saad Abdullah. 1982. "The Prosodic Relationship of Nabati Poetry to Classical Arabic Poetry." *Journal of Arabic Linguistics* 8:72–79.

———. 1985. *Nabati Poetry: The Oral Poetry of Arabia.* Berkeley and Los Angeles: University of California Press.

———. 1989. "'Tonight My Gun Is Loaded': Poetic Dueling in Arabia." *Oral Tradition* 4(1–2):151–173.

Staub, Shalom. 1979. *A Review of the Literature and a Selective Bibliography of Yemenite Jewish Folklore and Ethnology with a Special Emphasis on Dance and Music, 1893–1978.* n.p.

Stone, Ruth. 1989. "Sound and Rhythm in Corporate Ritual in Saudi Arabia." In *Music and the Experience of God,* ed. Mary Collins et al. Edinburgh: Clark.

Tayash, Fahad. 1988. "Sameri Tradition and Zār Dance in Saudi Arabia." *Al-Ma'ṯūrāt al-Sha'biyya* 9:23–36.

Touma, Habib Hassan. 1975. *Die Musik der Araber.* Wilhelmshaven: Heinrichshofen.

———. 1977. "Le fidjri, forme de chant caractéristique des pêcheurs de perles de Bahrein." *World of Music* 19(3–4):128–132.

———. 1995. *The Music of the Arabs.* Portland, Ore.: Amadeus.

Wikan, Unni. 1982. *Behind the Veil: Women in Oman.* Baltimore: University of Chicago Press.

Wright, Owen. 1978. *The Modal System of Arab and Persian Music A.D. 1250–1300.* London: Oxford University Press.

———. 1992. "Segah: An Historical Outline." In *Regionale Maqam-Traditionen in Geschichte und Gegenwart,* 480–509. Berlin: Humboldt-Universität, Institut für Musikwissenschaft und Musikerziehung.

———. 1995. "'Abd Al-Qadir Al-Maraghi and 'Ali B. Muhammad Bina'i: Two Fifteenth-Century Examples of Notation. Part 2: Commentary." *Bulletin, School of Oriental and African Studies* 58(1):17–39.

Yammine, Habib. 1991. "Correspondances entre la musique tribale et la musique citadine (Sana) dans la région des hauts plateaux yéménites." In *Le chant arabo-andalou: Colloque, Lille, 1991,* 119–128. Paris: Harmattan.

———. 1995. "Les hommes de tribu et leur musique (Hauts plateaux yéménites, vallée d'al-Ahjur)." Ph.D. dissertation, Université de Paris X-Nanterre.

ARMENIA

At'ayan, Robert A. 1999. *The Armenian Neume System of Notation,* trans. V. N. Nersessian. Richmond, Surrey, England: Curzon.

Chabrier, Jean-Claude. 1986–1987. "Remarques sur l'interprétation du système de Limončean par Komitas Vardapet." *Revue des Études Arméniennes* 20:507–520.

Dowsett, Charles. 1997. *Sayat'-Nova: An Eighteenth-Century Troubadour: A Literary and Biographical Study.* Leuven: Peeters.

Ertlbauer, A. 1985. *Geschichte und Theorie der einstimmigen armenischen Kirchenmusik: Eine Kritik der bisherigen Forschung.* Vienna.

Kazandjian, Sirvart. 1984. *Les origines de la musique arménienne.* Paris: Éditions Astrid.

Kerovpyan, A. 1991. "Les *charakan* (*troparia*) et l'octoéchos arménien selon le *charaknots* (*tropologion* arménien) édité en 1875." In *Aspects de la musique liturgique au Moyen-Age,* ed. Christian Meyer, 93–123. Paris: Creaphis.

———. 1995. "Mündliche und schriftliche Überlieferung in der Musik der Armenier." In *Armenien: Wiederentdeckung einer alten Kulturlandschaft*, ed. K. Platt, 445–449. Bochum.

———. 1996. "Armenian Liturgical Chant: The System and Reflections on the Present Situation." *St. Nersess Theological Review* 1:25–42.

———. 1999. *Manuel de notation musicale arménienne moderne*. Vienna.

———. 1998. *Armenian Sacred and Folk Music*, trans. Edward Gulbekian. Richmond, Surrey: Curzon.

Komitas, Vardapet. 1986–1987. "La musique religieuse arménienne au XIXème siècle," trans. Léon Ketcheyan. *Revue des Études Arméniennes* 20:497–506.

Moses of Khoren. 1978. *History of the Armenians*, trans. Robert W. Thomson. Cambridge, Mass.: Harvard University Press.

Nersessian, Vrej, ed. 1978. *Essays on Armenian Music*. London: Kahn and Averill for the Institute of Armenian Music.

Sarafian, Krikor. 1959. *The Armenian Apostolic Church: Her Ceremonies, Sacraments, Main Feasts, and Prominent Saints*. Fresno, Calif.: Sunday School Council of the Armenian Diocese of California.

KURDISTAN

Allison, Christine. 1996. "Old and New Traditions in Badinan." In *Kurdish Culture and Identity*, ed. Philip G. Kreryenbroek and Christine Allison, 29–47. London and Atlantic Highlands, N.J.: Zed.

Blum, Stephen, and A. Hassanpour. 1996. "'The Morning of Freedom Rose Up'. Kurdish Popular Song and the Exigencies of Cultural Survival." *Popular Music* 15:325–343.

Bruinessen, Martin van. 1992. *Agha, Shaikh, and State: The Social and Political Structures of Kurdistan*. London: Zed.

Christensen, Dieter. 1961. "Kurdische Brautlieder aus dem Vilayet Hakkari. Süd-Ost Türkei." *Journal of the International Folk Music Council* 13:70–72.

———. 1963. "Tanzlieder der Hakkari-Kurden." *Jahrbuch für Musikalische Volks- und Völkerkunde* 1:11–47.

———. 1967a. "Die Musik der Kurden." *Mitteilungen der Berliner Gesellschaft für Anthropologie, Ethnologie, und Urgeschichte* 1:113–119.

———. 1967b. "Zur Mehrstimmigkeit in kurdischen Wechselgesängen." In *Festschrift für*

Walter Wiora zum 30. Dezember 1966, ed. Ludwig Finscher and Christoph-Hellmut Mahling, 571–577. Kassel: Bärenreiter.

———. 1975. "Musical Style and Social Context in Kurdish Songs." *Asian Music* 6:1–6.

During, Jean. 1989. *Musique et mystique dans les traditions de l'Iran*. Paris: Institut Français de Recherche en Iran; Leuven: Peeters.

Nezan, Kendal. 1979. "Kurdish Music and Dance." *World of Music* 21(1):19–32.

Tatsumura, A. 1980. "Music and Culture of the Kurds." *Senri Ethnological Studies* 5:75–93.

TURKEY

Ahrens, Christian. 1970. *Instrumentale Musikstile an der osttürkische Schwarzmeerküste, eine vergleichende Untersuchung der Spielpraxis davul-zurna, kemençe und tulum*. Munich: Kommissionsverlag K. Renner.

Ahrens, Christian, et al. 1984. "Weine meine Laute . . ." In *Gedenkschrift Kurt Reinhard*, ed. Christian Ahrens, Rudolf Maria Brandl, and Felix Hoerburger, 37–56. Regensburg: Laaber-Verlag.

Akdemir, Hayrettin. 1992. *Die neue türkische Musik*. Berlin: Hitit-Verlag.

Aksoy, Bülent. 1989. "Is the Question of the Origin of Turkish Music Not Redundant?" *Turkish Musical Quarterly* 2(4):1–8.

And, Metin. 1959. "Dances of Anatolian Turkey." *Dance Perspectives* 3:3–77.

———. 1976. *A Pictorial History of Turkish Dancing: From Folk Dancing to Whirling Dervishes—Belly Dancing to Ballet*. Ankara: Dost Yayınları.

———. 1986a. "Opera and Ballet in Modern Turkey." In *The Transformation of Turkish Culture: The Atatürk Legacy*, ed. Günsel Renda and C. Max Kortepeter. Princeton, N.J.: Princeton University Press.

———. 1986b. "Les rituals et les danses extatiques mystiques de la Confrérie des Bektachis et des Alevis d'Anatolie." In *Transe, chamanisme, possession: De la fête à l'extase; Actes des deuxièmes rencontres internationales sur la fête et la communication, Nice Acropolis, 24–28 avril 1985*. Nice: Éditions Serre, Nice-Animation.

———. 1987. *Culture, Performance, and Communication in Turkey*. Performance in

Culture, 4. Tokyo: Institute for the Study of Languages and Cultures of Asia.

Andrews, Walter. 1976. *An Introduction to Ottoman Poetry*. Chicago: Bibliotheca Islamica.

———. 1985. *Poetry's Voice, Society's Song: Ottoman Lyric Poetry*. Seattle: University of Washington Press.

Andrews, Walter, and Irene Markoff. 1987. "Poetry, the Arts, and Group Ethos in the Ideology of the Ottoman Empire." *Edebiyat* 1(1):28–70.

Bartók, Béla. 1976. *Turkish Folk Music from Asia Minor*, ed. Benjamin Suchoff. Princeton, N.J.: Princeton University Press.

Başgöz, Ilhan. 1952. "Turkish Folk Stories about the Lives of Minstrels." *Journal of American Folklore* 65:331–339.

———. 1967. "Dream Motif and Shamanistic Initiation." *Asian Folklore Studies* 1:1–18.

———. 1972. "Folklore Studies and Nationalism in Turkey." *Journal of the Folklore Institute* 9:162–176.

Beken, Münir Nurettin, and Karl Signell. In press. "Confirming, Delaying, and Deceptive Elements in Turkish Improvisations." *Proceedings of the ICTM Maqam Study Group*. Istanbul: Istanbul Technical University.

Bellah, Robert. 1958. "Religious Aspects of Modernization in Japan and Turkey." *American Journal of Sociology* 64:1–5.

Berkes, Niyazi, ed. 1981. *Turkish Nationalism and Western Civilization: Selected Essays of Ziya Gökalp*, trans. and ed. N. Berkes. Westport, Conn.: Greenwood.

Birge, John Kingsley. 1937. *The Bektashi Order of Dervishes*. London: Luzac.

Boratav, Pertev Naili. 1973. "La littérature populaire turque contemporaine." *Turcica* 5:47–67.

Brands, Horst Wilfrid. 1978. "Aytîş-Deyişme, Formen des Dichterwettstreits bei den Türkvölkern." In *Studies in Turkish Folklore*, ed. Ilhan Başgöz and Mark Glazer. Bloomington: [Indiana University].

Campbell, Richard G. 1968. *Zur Typologie der Schalenlanghalslaute*. Collection d'études musicologiques/Sammlung musikwissenschaftlicher Abhandlungen, 47. Strasbourg, Baden-Baden: Heitz.

Christensen, Dieter. 1963. "Tanzlieder der Hakkari-Kurden." *Jahrbuch für Musikalische Volks- und Völkerkunde* 1:11–47.

Eberhard, Wolfram. 1955. *Minstrel Tales from Southeastern Turkey*. Berkeley and Los Angeles: University of California Press.

Eliade, Mircea. 1974. *Shamanism: Archaic Techniques of Ecstasy*. Princeton. N.J.: Princeton University Press.

Emsheimer, E. 1956. "Singing Contests in Central Asia." *International Folk Music Journal* 8:26–29.

Erdener, Yıldıray. 1987. "Dueling Singers: Strategies and Interaction Processes among Turkish Minstrels." Ph.D. dissertation, Indiana University.

———. 1995. *The Song Contests of Turkish Minstrels: Improvised Poetry Sung to Traditional Music*. New York: Garland.

Erguner, Ahmed. 1990. "Alla turca—Alla franca: Les enjeux de la musique turque." *Cahiers de Musique Traditionnelles* 3:45–56.

Farmer, Henry G. 1937. *Turkish Instruments of Music in the Seventeenth Century*. Glasgow: Civic.

———. 1966. *Islam*. Musikgeschichte in Bildern, Vol. 3. Leipzig: Deutscher Verlag für Musik.

Feldman, Walter. 1990. "Jewish Liturgical Music in Turkey." *Turkish Music Quarterly* 3(1):10–13.

———. 1990–1991. "Cultural Authority and Authenticity in the Turkish Repertoire." *Asian Music* 22(1):73–111.

———. 1992. "Musical Genres and Zikir of the Sunni Tarikats of Istanbul." In *The Dervish Lodge: Architecture, Art, and Sufism in Ottoman Turkey*, ed. Raymond Lifchez, 187–202. Berkeley and Los Angeles: University of California Press.

———. 1993. "Ottoman Sources on the Development of the Taksîm." *Yearbook for Traditional Music* 25:1–28.

———. 1996. *Music of the Ottoman Court*. Intercultural Music Studies, 10. Berlin: International Institute for Traditional Music.

Finnegan, Ruth. 1979. *Oral Poetry*. Cambridge: Cambridge University Press.

Fisher, C. G., and A. W. Fisher. 1987. "Topkapı Sarayı in the Mid-Seventeenth Century: Bobovsk's Description." *Archivium Ottomanicum* 10:5–81.

Greve, Martin. 1995. *Die Europäisierung orientalischer Kunstmusik in der Türkei*. Frankfurt am Main: Peter Lang.

Hall, Leslie. 1989. "The Turlish *Fasıl*: Selected Repertoire." Ph.D. dissertation, University of Toronto.

Halman, Talât Sait, and Metin And. 1983. *Mevlana Celaleddin Rumi and the Whirling Dervishes*. Istanbul: Dost Yayınları.

Haq, Sirajul. 1944. "Samā' and Raqṣ of the Darwishes." *Islamic Culture* 18.2:111–130.

Inalcik, Halil. 1973. *The Ottoman Empire: The Classical Age 1300–1600*. New York: Praeger.

Jäger, Ralf Martin. 1996a. *Türkische Kunstmusik und ihre handschriftlichen Quellen aus dem 19. Jahrhundert*. Schriften zur Musikwissenschaft aus Münster, 7. Eisenach: K. D. Wagner.

———. 1996b. *Katalog der hamparsum-notası-Manuskripte im Archiv des Konservatoriums der Universität Istanbul*. Schriften zur Musikwissenschaft aus Münster, 8. Eisenach: K. D. Wagner.

James, D. W. 1946. "Some Turkish Folk Dances." *Dancing Times* (October):14–15.

Karpat, Kemal. 1963. "The People's Houses in Turkey: Establishment and Growth." *Middle East Journal* 17:55–67.

———. 1976. *The Gecekondu: Rural Migration and Urbanization*. Cambridge: Cambridge University Press.

Kusić, Dane. 1996. "Discourse on Three Teravih Namazı-s in Istanbul." Ph.D. dissertation, University of Maryland.

Lewis, Bernard. 1968. *The Emergence of Modern Turkey*. London: Oxford University Press.

Mardin, Şerif. 1984. "A Note on the Transformation of Religious Symbols." *Turcica* 16:119–120.

Markoff, Irene. 1986a. "Musical Theory, Performance, and the Contemporary Bağlama Specialist in Turkey." Ph.D. dissertation, University of Washington, Seattle.

———. 1986b. "The Role of Expressive Culture in the Demystification of a Secret Sect in Islam: The Case of the Alevis in Turkey." *World of Music* 28(3):42–45.

———. 1990–1991. "The Ideology of Musical Practice and the Professional Turkish Folk Musician: Tempering the Creative Impulse." *Asian Music* 22(1):129–145.

———. 1993. "Music, Saints, and Ritual: Samā' and the Alevis of Turkey." In *Manifestations of Sainthood in Islam*, ed. Grace Martin Smith and Carl. W. Ernst, 95–110. Istanbul: Isis.

———. 1995. "Introduction to Sufi Music and Ritual in Turkey." *MESA Bulletin* 29(2):157–160.

Mélikoff, Irène. 1974. "Le problème Kızılbaş." *Turcica* 6:49–67.

O'Connell, John M. 1996. "*Alaturka* Revisited: Style as History in Turkish Vocal Performance." Ph.D. dissertation, University of California Los Angeles.

Okyay, Erdoğan. 1976. *Melodische Gestaltelemente in den türkischen "Kırık hava."* Ankara: s.n.

Oransay, Gültekin. 1957. "Das Tonsystem der türkei-türkischen Kunstmusik." *Musikforschung* 10:250–264.

———. 1964. *Die traditionelle türkische Kunstmusik*. Ankara: Küğ-Veröffentlichung.

———. 1966. *Die melodische Linie und der Begriff Makam der traditionellen türkischen Kunstmusik vom 15. bis 19. Jahrhundert*. Ankara: Küğ-Veröffentlichung.

Öztürkmen, Arzu. 1993. "Folklore and Nationalism in Turkey." Ph.D. dissertation, University of Pennsylvania.

———. 1995. "The Alevi *Cem* Ritual and the Nationalization of *Semah* Dances." In *Dance and Ritual: Proceedings from the Eighteenth Symposium of the ICTM Study Group on Ethnochoreology*. Skierniewice.

———. 1994. "The Role of the People's Houses in the Making of National Culture in Turkey." *New Perspectives on Turkey* 11:159–181.

———. 1994. "Folk Dance and Nationalism in Turkey." In *Seventeenth Symposium of the Study Group on Ethnochoreology: 1992 Proceedings*, 83–86. Nafplion: Peloponnesian Folklore Foundation.

Picken, Laurence. 1975. *Folk Musical Instruments of Turkey*. London, New York, and Toronto: Oxford University Press.

Popescu-Judetz, Eugenia. 1981. *Studies in Oriental Arts: Dimitri Cantemir's Theory of Turkish Art Music*. Pittsburgh, Pa.: Institute of Folk Arts.

Radloff, V. 1885. *Proben der Volkliteratur der Türkischen Stamme*, Vol. 5. St. Petersburg: Akademie der Wissenschaft.

Reiche, Jens Peter. 1970. "Stilelemente südtürkischer Davul-Zurna-Stücke." *Jahrbuch für Musikalische Volks- und Völkerkunde* 5:9–54.

Reinhard, Kurt. 1956a. "Zustand und Wandel der bäuerlichen Musik in der türkischen Provinz Adana." *Sociologus*, Neue Folge, 6:68–78.

———. 1956b. "Types of Turkmenian Songs in Turkey." *Journal of the International Folk Music Council* 9:49–54.

———. 1960. "Ein türkischer Tanzliedtyp und seine außertürkischen Parallelen." *Baessler-Archiv*, Neue Folge, 8:131–169.

———. 1961a. "Trommeltänze aus der Süd-Türkei." *Journal of the International Folk Music Council* 13:19–26.

———. 1961b. "Zur Variantenbildung im türkischen Volkslied, dargestellt an einer Hirtenweise." In *Festschrift Heinrich Besseler zum 60. Geburtstag*, 21–34. Leipzig: Deutscher Verlag für Musik.

———. 1962. *Türkische Musik*. Berlin: Museum für Völkerkunde.

———. 1966a. "Türkische Musik." In *Die Musik in Geschichte und Gegenwart* 13:954–968. Kassel: Bärenreiter.

———. 1966b. "Musik am Schwarzen Meer: Erste Ergebnisse einer Forschungsreise in die Nordost-Türkei." *Jahrbuch für Musikalische Volks- und Völkerkunde* 2:9–58.

———. 1967. "Die Gegenwärtige Praxis des Epengesanges in der Türkei." In *Grazer und Münchener Balkanologische Studien: Beiträge zur Kenntnis Südosteuropas und des Nahen Orients*, 83–96. Munich: Trofenik.

———. 1967. "Die Quellensituation der türkischen Kunstmusik: Gedanken zur Frage mündlicher und schriftlicher Tradition und zum Problem Improvisation-Komposition." In *Festschrift Walter Wiora*, 578–582. Kassel: Bärenreiter.

———. 1969. "Cultivation and Encouragement of Traditional Music in Turkey: Creating a Wider Interest in Traditional Music." In *International Institute for Comparative Music Studies and Documentation, Berlin, 1969*, 160–169. Berlin.

———. 1970. "Strukturanalyse einer Hymne des türkischen Komponisten Itrî." In *Festschrift Walter Graf*, 158–177. Vienna: H. Böhlau.

———. 1972. "Grundlagen und Ergebnisse der Erforschung türkischer Musik." *Acta Musicologica* 44:266–280.

———. 1973a. "Vorderer Orient" and "Die Türkei im 19. Jahrhundert." In *Musikkulturen Asiens, Afrikas, und Ozeaniens im 19. Jahrhundert*, ed. Robert Günther, 17–48. Regensburg: Gustave Bosse.

———. 1973b. "Musikalische Gestaltungsprinzipien der *âyın*, dargestellt an der anonymen Komposition im Makam pençgâh." In *Uluslararası Mevlâna Semineri*, 315–333. Ankara: Türkiye İş Bankası Kültür Yayınları.

———. 1974. "Die türkische Doppelklarinette çifte." *Baessler-Archiv*, Neue Folge, 22:139–163.

———. 1975a. "Über die Beziehungen zwischen byzantinischer und türkischer Musik." In *Musica Antiqua 4, Acta Scientifica*, 623–632. Bydgoszcz.

———. 1975b. "Die Musikpflege türkischer Nomaden." *Zeitschrift für Ethnologie* 100:115–124.

———. 1976. "Über einige Beziehungen zwischen türkischer und griechischer Volksmusik." *Beiträge zue Ethnomusikologie* 4:9–18.

———. 1978. "Albert Bobovsky's Aufzeichnungen türkischer Musik als geschichtliche Quelle." In *Musica Antiqua 5, Acta Scientifica*, 373–382. Bydgoszcz.

———. 1979. "Spieltechnik und Musik der türkischen Kurzoboe mey." *Studia Instrumentorum Musicae Popularis* 6:111–119.

———. 1980a. "Turkey." In *The New Grove Dictionary of Music and Musicians* 19:165–179. London: Macmillan.

———. 1980b. "Türkei." In *Außereuropäische Musik in Einzeldarstellungen*, 165–179. Munich: Deutscher Taschenbuchverlag; Kassel: Bärenreiter.

———. 1981a. "Mozarts Rezeption türkischer Musik." In *Bericht über den Internationalen Musikwissenschaftlichen Kongress, Berlin 1974*, 518–523. Kassel: Bärenreiter.

———. 1981b. "Turkish Miniatures as Sources of Music History." In *Music in East and West: Essays in Honor of Walter Kaufmann*, 143–166. New York.

———. 1984a. "Gestalten südtürkischer Totenklagen." In *"Weine, meine Laute . . ." Gedenkschrift für Kurt Reinhard*, ed. Christian Ahrens, Rudolf Maria Brandl, and Felix Hoerburger. Regensburg: Laaber-Verlag.

———. 1984b. "Das Na't des İtrî und seine Versionen." *Jahrbuch für Musikalische Volks- und Völkerkunde* 11:9–13.

Reinhard, Kurt, and Ursula Reinhard. 1968. *Auf der Fiedel mein . . . Volkslieder von der osttürkischen Schwarzmeerküste*. Veröffentlichungen des Museums für Völkerkunde Berlin, Neue Folge, Vol. 14. Berlin: Museum für Völkerkunde.

Reinhard, Kurt, and Ursula Reinhard. 1969. *Turquie: Les traditions musicales*. Paris: Buchet-Chastel.

Reinhard, Kurt, and Ursula Reinhard. 1983. "Volksmusikelemente in der Türkischen Kunstmusik." In 2, *Milletlerarası Türk Folklor Kongresi Bildiriler* 3:225–239. Ankara: Kültür ve Turizm Bakanlığı.

Reinhard, Kurt, and Ursula Reinhard. 1984. *Musik der Türkei*. 2 vols. Wilhelmshaven: Heinrichshofen.

Reinhard, Ursula. 1965. *Vor seinen Häusern eine Weide . . . Volksliedtexte aus der Süd-Türkei*. Veröffentlichen des Museums für Völkerkunde Berlin, Neue Folge, Vol. 8. Berlin: Museum für Völkerkunde.

———. 1985. "Konstanz und Wandel im bağlama-Spiel und Gesang türkischer âşık und ihrer Lieder." *Studia Instrumentorum Musicae Popularis* 8:86–93.

———. 1985. "Das Musikleben in osmanischer Zeit." In *Türkische Kunst und Kultur aus osman-*

ischer Zeit, 1:159–163 and 213–222. Recklinghausen: A. Bongers.

———. 1987. "Westliche Einflüsse auf das türkische Musikleben einst und heute." In *Mozaik: Türkische Kultur in Berlin*, 37–44. Berlin: Arenhövel.

———. (1998, in press.) "Musik am türkischen Hof des 17. Jahrhunderts." Lecture, Akademie der Wissenschaften in Göttingen, June.

———. 1990. "The Veils Are Lifted." In *Music, Gender, and Culture*, ed. Marcia Herndon and Susanne Ziegler, 101–111. Wilhelmshaven: Florian Noetzel Verlag.

———. 1994a. "Epische Gesänge in der Türkei am Beispiel des Köroğlu-Epos." In *Historische Volksmusikforschung*, ed. Doris Stockmann and Annette Erler, 157–170. Göttingen: Edition Re.

———. 1994b. "Musik am Türkischen Hof des 17. Jahrhunderts." In *Höfische Kultur in Südosteuropa: Abhandlungen der Akademie der Wissenschaften in Göttingen*, ed. Reinhard Lauer and Hans Georg Majer, 174–204. Göttingen: Vandenhoeck und Ruprecht.

———. 1997a. "Eine alte nomadische Singtechnik in der Türkei und auf dem Balkan und ihre instrumentale Wiederbelebung." In *Historical Studies on Folk and Traditional Music*, ed. Doris Stockmann and Jens Henrik Koudal, 167–176. Copenhagen: Danish Folklore Archives.

———. 1997b. "Dichtersänger im Nordosten der Türkei, in Armenien und Aserbaidschan: Ein Vergleich." *Jahrbuch für Musikalische Volks- und Völkerkunde* 16:71–92.

———. 2001. "Die Musik der Alewiten." In *Aleviler/Alewiten*, ed. Ismail Engin and Erhard Franz, 199–220. Hamburg: Deutsches Orient-Institut.

Reinhard, Ursula, and Tiago De Oliveria Pinto. 1989. *Sänger und Poeten mit der Laute, Türkische Âşık und Ozan*. Veröffentlichungen des Museums für Völkerkunde Berlin, Abteilung Musikethnologie Berlin (with 2 cassettes). Berlin: Museum für Völkerkunde, Dietrich Reimer Verlag.

Robins, Kevin, and David Morley. 1996. "Almanci, Yabanci." *Cultural Studies* 10(2):248–254.

Roemer, Hans R. 1990. "The Qizilbash Turcomans: Founders and Victims of the Safavid Theocracy." In *Intellectual Studies on Islam: Essays Written in Honor of Martin B. Dickson*, ed. Michel M. Mazzaoui and Vera B. Moreen, 27–39. Salt Lake City: University of Utah Press.

Saygun, Adnan. 1948. *Les divers aspects de la musique turque*. Ankara.

———. 1950. "Des danses d'Anatolie et de leur caractère rituel." *Journal of the International Folk Music Council* 2:10–14.

———. 1976. *Béla Bartók's Folk Music Research in Turkey*, ed. László Vikár. Budapest: Akadémiai Kiadó.

Seroussi, Edwin. 1989a. *Mizimrat Qedem: The Life and Music of R. Isaac Algazi from Turkey*. Jerusalem: Renanot-Institute for Jewish Music.

———. 1989b. "The Turkish *Makam* in the Musical Culture of the Ottoman Jews: Sources and Examples." *Israeli Studies in Musicology* 5:55–68.

———. 1991. "The Peşrev as a Vocal Genre in Ottoman Hebrew Sources." *Turkish Music Quarterly* 4(3):1–9.

Sezgin, Paméla J. Dorn. 1994. "*Hakhamim*, Dervishes, and Court Singers: The Relationship of Ottoman Jewish Music to Classical Turkish Music." In *The Jews of the Ottoman Empire*, ed. Avigdor Levy, 585–632. Princeton, N.J.: Darwin.

Shaw, Stanford. 1976–1977. *History of the Ottoman Empire and Modern Turkey*. 2 vols. Cambridge: Cambridge University Press.

Shiloah, Amnon. 1992. *Jewish Musical Traditions*. Detroit: Wayne State University Press.

Sieglin, Angelika. 1975. *Untersuchungen in den Peşrev des Tanburi Cemil Bey*. Hamburg: Karl Dieter Wagner.

———. 1984. *Instrumentalkompositionen der türkischen Kunstmusik in ihrer Beziehung zum Makam*. Hamburg: K. D. Wagner.

Signell, Karl L. 1977. *Makam: Modal Practice in Turkish Art Music*. Seattle: Asian Music.

———. 1988. "Mozart and the Mehter." *Turkish Music Quarterly* 1(1):34–36.

Stokes, Martin. 1992. *The Arabesk Debate: Music and Musicians in Modern Turkey*. Oxford: Oxford University Press.

Van Bruinessen, Martin. 1996. "Kurds, Turks, and the Alevi Revival in Turkey." *Middle East Report* 200:7–10.

Wannig, Klaus-Detlev. 1980. *Der Dichter Karaca Oğlan. Studien zur türkischen Liebeslyrik*. Studien zur Sprache, Kultur, und Geschichte der Türkvölker, 1. Freiburg: Schwarz.

Wright, Owen. 1988. "Aspects of Historical Change in the Turkish Classical Repertoire." *Musica Asiatica* 5:1–108.

———. 1990. "Çargah in Turkish Classical Music." *Bulletin of the School of Oriental and African Studies (University of London)* 53:224–244.

———. 1992a. *Demetrius Cantemir: The Collection of Notations*. Musicology Series, 1. London: School of Oriental and African Studies (University of London).

———. 1992b. *Words without Songs: A Musicological Study on an Early Ottoman Anthology and Its Precursors*. Musicology Series, 2. London: School of Oriental and African Studies (University of London).

Yalman, Nur. 1969. "Islamic Reform and the Mystic Tradition in Eastern Turkey." *European Journal of Sociology* 10(1):41–60.

Yekta Bey, Raouf. 1922. "La musique turque." In *Encyclopédie de la musique*, ed. Albert Lavignac, 5:2045–3064. Paris: C. Delagrave.

Zimmermann, Cornelia-Kalyoncu. 1985. *Deutsche Musiker in der Türkei im 20. Jahrhundert*. Frankfurt am Main, Bern, and New York: Peter Lang.

IRAN

Albright, Charlotte F. 1976a. "The Music of Professional Musicians of Northwest Iran (Azerbaijan)." Ph.D. dissertation, University of Washington.

———. 1976b. "The Azerbaijani 'Ashiq and His Performance of a Dastan." Iranian Studies 9:220–247.

———. 1988. "The Azerbaijani 'Ashiq: A Musician's Adaptations to a Changing Society." Edebiyat n.s. 2(1–2):205–217.

Barkeshli, M. 1963. La musique traditionelle de l'Iran. Tehran.

Başgöz, Ilhan. 1952. "Turkish Folk Stories about the Lives of Minstrels." Journal of American Folklore 65:331–339.

Blum, Stephen. 1972a. "Musics in Contact: The Cultivation of Oral Repertoires in Meshhed, Iran." Ph.D. dissertation, University of Illinois.

———. 1972b. "The Concept of the 'Asheq in Northern Khorasan." Asian Music 4(1):27–47.

———. 1978. "Changing Roles of Performers in Meshhed and Bojnurd, Iran." In Eight Urban Musical Cultures, ed. Bruno Nettl, 19–95. Urbana: University of Illinois Press.

———. 1996. "Musical Questions and Answers in Iranian Xorāsān." EM: Annuario degli Archivi di Etnomusicologia, Accademia Nazionale di Santa Cecilia 4:145–163.

Boratav, Pertev Naili. 1965. "L'épopée et la 'hikâye.'" In Philologiae Turcicae Fundamenta, 2:11–44. Wiesbaden: Franz Steiner.

Borel, François. 1986. "La vièle, le tambour, et les génies du mal." In Le mal et la douleur, ed. J. Hainard and R. Kaehr, 199–205. Neuchâtel: Musée d'Ethnographie.

Caferoğlu, Ahmet. 1965. "Die Aserbaidschanische Literatur." In Philologiae Turcicae Fundamenta, 2:635–698. Wiesbaden: Franz Steiner.

Caron, Nelly. 1975. "The Ta'zieh: The Sacred Theatre of Iran." World of Music 17(4):3–10.

Caron, Nelly, and Dariouche Safvate. 1966. Iran: Les traditions musicales. Paris: Buchet/Chastel.

Chadwick, Nora K., and Victor Zhirmunsky. 1969. Oral Epics of Central Asia. Cambridge: Cambridge University Press.

Chelkowski, Peter J., ed. 1979. Ta'ziye: Ritual and Drama in Iran. New York: New York University Press.

———. 1991. "Popular Entertainment, Media, and Social Change in Twentieth-Century Iran." In The Cambridge History of Iran. Vol. 7, From Nadir Shah to the Islamic Republic, ed. Peter Avery, Gavin Hambly, and Charles Melville, 765–814. Cambridge: Cambridge University Press.

Chodzko, Alexander. 1842. Specimens of the Popular Poetry of Persia. London: Oriental Translation Fund.

De Warren, Robert, and Peter Williams. 1973. "Discovery in Persia." Dance and Dancers (January):28–32.

During, Jean. 1984. La musique iranienne: Tradition et évolution. Paris and Tehran: Institut Français d'Iranologie de Téhéran.

———. 1988a. Musique et extase: L'audition mystique dans la tradition soufie. Paris: Albin Michel.

———. 1988b. "Emotion and Trance: Musical Exorcism in Baluchestan." In Cultural Parameters of Iranian Musical Expression, ed. M. Caton and N. Siegel, 36–46. Redondo Beach, Calif.: Institute of Persian Performing Arts.

———. 1989a. Musique et mystique dans les traditions de l'Iran. Paris: Institut Français de Recherches en Iran-Peeters.

———. 1989b. "Les musiques d'Iran et du Moyen-Orient face à l'acculturation occidentale." In Entre l'Iran et l'Occident: Adaptation et assimilation des idées et techniques occidentales en Iran, ed. Yann Richard, 195–223. Paris: Éditions de la Maison des Sciences de l'Homme.

———. 1990. "Der Mythos der Simorg." Spektrum Iran 3(3):3–19.

———. 1991. Le répertoire-modèle de la musique persane: Radif de târ et de setâr de Mirzâ 'Abdollâh. Tehran: Sorūsh.

———. 1992a. "The Organization of Rhythm in Baluchi Trance Music." In European Studies in Ethnomusicology: Historical Developments and Recent Trends, ed. Max Peter Baumann 282–302. Wilhelmshaven: Florian Noetzel.

———. 1992b. "L'oreille islamique: Dix années capitales de la vie musicale en Iran: 1980–1990." Asian Music 23(2):135–164.

———. 1994. Quelque chose se passe: Le sens de la tradition dans l'Orient musical. Lagrasse: Verdier.

———. 1996. "La voix des esprits et la face cachée de la musique: Le parcours du maître Hâtam 'Asgari." In Le voyage initiatique en terre d'Islam: Ascensions célestes et itinéraires spirituels, ed. Mohammad Ali Amir-Moezzi, 335–373. Louvain and Paris: Peeters.

———. 1997a. "African Winds and Muslim Djinns: Trance, Healing, and Devotion in Baluchistan." Yearbook for Traditional Music 29:39–56.

———. 1997b. "Rhythmes ovôdes et quadrature du cycle." Cahiers des Musiques Traditionelles 10:17–36.

During, Jean, with Zia Mirabdolbaghi and Dariush Safvat. 1991. The Art of Persian Music. Washington: Mage.

Farhat, Hormoz. 1990. The Dastgāh Concept in Persian Music. Cambridge Studies in Ethnomusicology. Cambridge: Cambridge University Press.

Fatemi, Sasan. 1997. La musique et la vie musicale du Mazanderan: Le problème du changement. Thesis, Université de Paris-X.

Gobineau, Joseph-Arthur, comte de. [1859] 1983. Trois ans en Asie (de 1855 à 1858). Reprint: In Oeuvres, ed. Jean Gaulmier, 2:27–401. Paris: Gallimard.

Hamada, Geoffrey Mark. 1978. "Dance and Islam: The Bojnurdi Kurds of Northeastern Iran." M.A. thesis, University of California, Los Angeles.

Hassan, Schéhérazade Qassim. 1980. Les instruments de musique en Irak et leur rôle dans la société traditionnelle. Paris: Mouton.

Hill, Derek, and Oleg Grabar. 1964. Islamic Architecture and Its Decoration. Chicago: University of Chicago Press.

Hourani, Albert. 1991. History of the Islamic Peoples. Cambridge, Mass.: Harvard University Press.

Ivanov, Vladimir. 1926. "Notes on the Ethnology of Khurasan." Geographical Journal 67:143–158.

———. 1927. "Notes on Khorasani Kurdish." Journal of the Asiatic Society of Bengal, n.s. 23:166–235.

Jackson, Peter. 1989. "Bakši." In Encyclopaedia Iranica, ed. Ehsan Yarshater, 3:535–536. London: Routledge and Kegan Paul.

Kuckertz, Josef, and Mohammad Taghi Massoudieh. 1976. Musik in Bušehr (Süd-Iran). 2 vols. Ngoma: Studien zur Volksmusik und aussereuropäischen Kunstmusik, 2. Munich and Salzburg: Katzbichler.

La Meri [Russell Merriweather Hughes]. 1961. "Learning the Danse du Ventre." Dance Perspectives 10:43–47.

Lewis, Geoffrey. 1974. The Book of Dede Korkut. Harmondsworth, England: Penguin.

Lièvre, Viviane, and Jean-Yves Loude. 1990. Le chamanisme des Kalash du Pakistan. Paris: Éditions Recherche sur les Civilisations.

Massoudieh, Mohammad Teqi. 1973. "Hochzeitslieder aus Balūčestān." Jahrbuch für Musikalische Volks- und Völkerkünde 7:59–69.

———. 1978. Radif vocal de la musique traditionelle de l'Iran. Tehran.

———. 1988. Musik in Balūčestān. Beiträge zur Ethnomusikologie, 20. Hamburg: Karl Dieter Wagner.

———. 1992a. "Der Begriff des Maqām in der persischen Volksmusik." In Von der Vielfalt musikalischer Kultur: Festschrift Josef Kuckertz zum 60. Geburtstag, ed. Rüdiger Schumacher, 311–334. Anif/Salzburg: U. Müller-Speiser.

———. 1992b. "Die Begriffe Maqām und Dastgāh in der turkmenischen Musik des Iran." In Regionale maqām-Traditionen in Geschichte und Gegenwart, ed. Jürgen Elsner and Gisa Jähnichen, 377–397. Berlin: Study Group "Maqām" of the International Council for Traditional Music.

Nettl, Bruno. 1972. "Persian Popular Music in 1969." Ethnomusicology 16:218–239.

———. 1974. "Aspects of Form in the Instrumental Performance of the Persian Āvāz." Ethnomusicology 18:405–414.

———. 1978. "Persian Classical Music in Tehran: The Processes of Change." In Eight Urban Musical Cultures, ed. Bruno Nettl, 146–185. Urbana: University of Illinois Press.

———. 1992 [1987]. The Radif of Persian Music: Studies of Structure and Cultural Context, rev. ed. Champaign, Ill.: Elephant and Cat.

Nettl, Bruno, and Bela Foltin, Jr. 1974. *Daramad of Chahargah: A Study in the Performance Practice of Persian Music*. Detroit, Mich.: Information Coordinators.

Nooshin, Laudan. 1996. "The Processes of Creation and Re-Creation in Persian Classical Music." Ph.D. dissertation, University of London.

———. 1998. "The Song of the Nightingale: Processes of Improvisation in *Dastgāh Segāh* (Iranian Classical Music)." *British Journal of Ethnomusicology* 7:69–116.

Perry, John R. 1975. "Forced Migration in Iran during the Seventeenth and Eighteenth Centuries." *Iranian Studies* 8:199–215.

Picken, Laurence. 1975. *Folk Musical Instruments of Turkey*. London: Oxford University Press.

Reichl, Karl. 1992. *Turkic Oral Epic Poetry: Traditions, Forms, Poetic Structure*. New York: Garland.

Reinhard, Ursula, and Tiago de Oliveira Pinto. 1989. *Sänger und Poeten mit der Laute: Türkische Aşık und Ozan*. Veröffentlichungen des Museums für Völkerkunde Berlin, n.F. 47, Musikethnologische Abteilung 6. Berlin: Museum für Völkerkunde.

Rezvani, Medjid. 1962. *Le théâtre et la danse en Iran*. Paris: Maisonneuve et Larose.

Safvat, Dariush. 1984. "Musique et mystique," trans. Jean During. *Études Traditionnelles* 483:42–54, 484:94–109.

Shay, Anthony. 1995a. "Dance and Non-Dance: Patterned Movement in Iran and Islam." *Iranian Studies* 28:61–78.

———. 1995b. "*Bazi-ha-ye Namayeshi*: Iranian Women's Theatrical Plays." *Dance Research Journal* 27(2):16–24.

———. N.d. "Choreophobia: Iranian Solo Improvised Dance as Transgressive and Potentially 'Out-of-Control' Behavior in the Southern California Diaspora." Ph.D. dissertation, University of California, Riverside.

St. John, Katherine. 1988. "Afghan Atan." *Viltis* 47(1):23–24.

———. 1989. "Afghan Dance." *Folk Dance Scene* 24(2):8–18.

Slobin, Mark. 1969. *Kirgiz Instrumental Music*. New York: Society for Asian Music.

———. 1976. *Music in the Culture of Northern Afghanistan*. Viking Fund Publications in Anthropology, 54. Tucson: University of Arizona Press.

Spector, Johanna. 1967. "Musical Tradition and Innovation." In *Central Asia: A Century of Russian Rule*, ed. Edward Allworth, 434–484. New York: Columbia University Press.

Talai, Dariush. 1999. *Traditional Persian Art Music: The Radif of Mirza Abdollah*. Costa Mesa, Calif.: Mazda.

Tsuge, Gen'ichi. 1974. "*Āvāz*: A Study in the Rhythmic Aspects in Classical Iranian Music." Ph.D. dissertation, Wesleyan University.

Varzi, Morteza. 1988. "Performer-Audience Relationships in the *Bazm*." In *Cultural Parameters of Iranian Musical Expression*, ed. Margaret Caton and Neil Siegel, 1–9. Redondo Beach, Calif.: Institute of Persian Performing Arts.

Yarshater, Ehsan. 1974. "Affinities between Persian Poetry and Music." In *Studies in the Art and Literature of the Near East*, ed. Peter Chelkowski, 59–78. Salt Lake City and New York: University of Utah and New York University.

Youssefzadeh, Ameneh. 1996. "Les bardes *bakhshī* du Khorassan iranien." Dissertation, Université de Paris X-Nanterre.

Yūsofī, Gholam Hosein. 1994. "Calligraphy." *Encyclopaedia Iranica*, 680–718. London: Routledge and Kegan Paul.

Zonis, Ella. 1973. *Classical Persian Music: An Introduction*. Cambridge, Mass.: Harvard University Press.

CENTRAL ASIA

Akiner, Shirin. 1995. *The Formation of Kazakh Identity: From Tribe to Nation-State*. London: Royal Institute of International Affairs, Russian and CIS Programme.

Bacon, Elizabeth E. [1966] 1980. *Central Asians under Russian Rule: A Study in Culture Change*. Ithaca, N.Y.: Cornell University Press.

Beliaev, Victor, M., ed. 1950–1958. *Shashmaqâm*, Vols. 1–4. Moscow: Gosudarstvennoe Muzykalnoe Izdatelstvo.

———. 1975. *Central Asian Music: Essays in the History of the Music of the Peoples of the U.S.S.R.*, ed. and annotated Mark Slobin; trans. from Russian by Mark Slobin and Greta Slobin. Middletown, Conn.: Wesleyan University Press.

Chadwick, Nora Kershaw, and Victor M. Zhirmunsky. 1969. *Oral Epics of Central Asia*. London: Cambridge University Press.

Czekanowska, Anna. 1983. "Aspects of the Classical Music of Uyghur People: Legend versus Reality." *Asian Music* 14(1):41–93.

Djumaev, Alexander. 1993. "Power Structures, Culture Policy, and Traditional Music in Soviet Central Asia." *Yearbook for Traditional Music* 25:43–51.

Dru, C. Gladney. 1991. "Sedentarization, Socioecology, and State Definition: The Ethnogenesis of the Uighur." In *Rulers from the Steppe: State Formation on the Eurasian Periphery*, ed. G. Seaman and D. Marks, 308–340. Los Angeles: University of Southern California, Ethnographics Press.

During, Jean. 1988. *La musique traditionnelle de l'Azerbayjan et la science des muqams*. Baden-Baden: Valentin Koener.

During, Jean, and Sabine Trebinjac. 1991. *Introduction à l'étude de la musique ouïgoure*. Bloomington: Indiana University Press.

Emsheimer, Ernest. 1956. "Singing Contests in Central Asia." *Journal of the International Folk Music Council* 8:26–29.

Farmer, Henry George. 1937. *Turkish Instruments of Music in the Seventeenth Century as Described in the Siyahat Nama of Ewliya Chelebi*. Glasgow: Civic.

———. 1962. "Abdalqadir ibn Gaibi on Instruments of Music." *Oriens* 5:242–248.

———. 1965. *The Sources of Arabian Music: An Annotated Bibliography of Arabic Manuscripts Which Deal with the Theory, Practice, and History of Arabian Music from the Eighth to the Seventeenth Century*. Leiden: Brill.

Jung, Angelika. 1989. *Quellen der traditionellen Kunstmusik der Usbeken und Tadshiken Mittelasiens*. Hamburg: Karl Dieter Wagner.

Kakuk, S. 1972. "Chants ouïghours de Chine." *Acta Orientalia Academiae Scientiarum Hungaricae* 25:415–429.

Karomatov, Faizula M., ed. 1966–1975. *Shashmaqâm*, Vols. 1–6. Tashkent.

Karomatov, Faizula M., V. A. Meskeris, and Tamara Vyzgo. 1987. *Mittelasien*. Band 2, Lieferung 9 of *Musikgeschichte in Bildern*. Leipzig: Deutscher Verlag für Musik.

Khashimov, Abd al-Aziz. 1978. "Structure du *muqam* ouïghour et les conditions de sa préservation." In *Mâqams, mugams, et composition contemporaine*, 130–138. Tashkent.

Kunanbaeva, Alma. 1990. "The Kazakh Epic: Modernization and Return." *Turkish Music Quarterly* 3(2–3):1–3.

———. 1995. "The Kazakh Zhyrau as the Singer of Tales." In *Ethnohistorische Wege und Lehrjahre eines Philosophen: Festschrift dedicated to Prof. Lawrence Krader*, ed. Dittmar Schorkowitz, 293–303. Frankfurt am Main: Peter Lang.

Levin, Theodore. 1996. *The Hundred Thousand Fools of God: Musical Travels in Central Asia (and Queens, New York)*. Bloomington: Indiana University Press.

———. 2001a. "Making Marxist-Leninist Music in Uzbekistan." In *Music and Marx: Ideas, Practice, Politics*, ed. Regula Burckhardt Qureshi. New York: Garland.

Levin, Theodore, and Razia Sultanova. 2001b. "Uzbekistan." In *The New Grove Dictionary of Music and Musicians*, 2nd ed., 26:180–189. London: Macmillan.

Mackerras, Colin. 1985a. "Traditional Uygur Performing Arts." *Asian Music* 16:29–58.

———. 1985b. "Uygur Performing Arts in Contemporary China." *China Quarterly* 101:58–77.

Mukhambetova, Asiya. 1990a. "Philosophical Problems of Being in the Art of the Kazakh Kuyshi." *Yearbook for Traditional Music* 22:36–41.

———. 1995. "The Traditional Musical Culture of Kazakhs in the Social Context of the Twentieth Century." *World of Music* 37(3):66–83.

Neubauer, Eckhard. 1969. "Musik zur Mongolenzeit in Iran und angrenzenden Ländern." *Islam* 54(3):233–260.

Olcott, Martha Brill. 1995. *The Kazakhs*, 2nd ed. Stanford, Calif.: Hoover Institution Press, Stanford University Press.

Porter, James, ed. 1997. *Folklore and Traditional Music in the Former Soviet Union and Eastern Europe*. Los Angeles: UCLA, Department of Ethnomusicology.

Powers, Harold S. 1980. "[Mode:] Modal Entities in Western Asia and South Asia." In *The New Grove Dictionary of Music and Musicians* 5(2, i):423–238. London: Macmillan.

Reichl, Karl. 1992. *Turkic Oral Epic Poetry: Traditions, Forms, Poetic Structure*. New York: Garland.

Slobin, Mark. 1976. *Music in the Culture of Northern Afganistan*. Tucson: University of Arizona Press, for Wenner-Gren Foundation for Anthropological Research.

Trebinjac, Sabine. 1989. "Musique ouïghoure de Chine: De l'authenticité la folklorisation." In *Actes du colloque ESCAS III: L'Asie Centrale et ses voisins—Paris, 1989*, 227–238. Paris: INALCO.

———. 1995. "Femme, seule et venue d'ailleurs: Trois atouts d'un ethnomusicologue au Turkestan chinois." *Cahier de Musiques Traditionnelles* 8:59–68.

———. 1998. *Le pouvoir en chantant*, Vol. 1. Nanterre: Société d'Ethnologie.

Utegalieva, Saule. 1993. "The System of Images in the Dombra Tradition of Kazakhs." In *Proceedings of the First International Conference on Cognitive Musicology*, 270–282. Jyvaskyla: Jyvaskylan Yliopisto.

Winner, Thomas Gustav. 1980. *The Oral Art and Literature of the Kazakhs of Russian Central Asia*. New York: Arno.

Wright, Owen. 1978. *The Modal System of Arab and Persian Music, 1250–1300*. Oxford: Oxford University Press.

Zeranska-Kominek, Slawomira. 1990. "The Classification of Repertoire in Turkmen Traditional Music." *Journal of the Society for Asian Music* 31(2):90–109.

———. 1992a. "The Turkmen *Bakhshy*: Shaman and/or Artist." In *European Studies in Ethnomusicology: Historical Developments and Recent Trends*, ed. Max Peter Baumann, 303–317. Berlin: International Institute for Traditional Music.

———. 1992b. "Mode: Process and/or Structure—Analytical Study of Turkmen *Mukam Gökdepe*." In *Studi e testi 1. Secondo Convegno Europeo di Analisi Musicale*, ed. Rossana Dalmonte and Mario Baroni, 249–259. Trento: Universitá degli Studi di Trento.

———. 1995. "The Turkmen Musical Tradition and the Soviet Culture." In *Lux Oriente: Begegnungen der Kulturen in der Musikforschung—Festschrift Robert Günther zum 65. Geburtstag*, ed. K. W. Niemöller, 419–427. Kassel: Gustave Bosse Verlag.

Zeranska-Kominek, Slawomira, with Arnold Lebeuf. 1997. *The Tale of Crazy Harman: The Musician and the Concept of Music in the Türkmen Epic Tale "Harman Däli."* Warsaw: Dialog.

Zhirmunskii, Viktor. 1960. *On the Comparative Study of the Heroic Epic of the Peoples of Central Asia*. Moscow: Oriental Literature Publishing House.

ISRAEL

Adler, Israel. 1966. *La pratique musicale savante dans quelques communautés juives en Europe aux XVIIe et XVIIIe siècles*. Paris: Mouton.

———. 1974. *Musical Life and Traditions of the Portuguese Jewish Community of Amsterdam in the Eighteenth Century*. Jerusalem: Magnes Press, Hebrew University.

———. 1975. *Hebrew Writings Concerning Music in Manuscripts and Printed Books from Geonic Times Up to 1800*. RISM B IX². München: G. Henle.

———, ed. 1977. *A Directory of Music Institutions in Israel*. Jerusalem: Israel Section of the International Music Council.

———. 1982. "Problems in the Study of Jewish Music." In *Proceedings of the World Congress on Jewish Music, Jerusalem 1978*, ed. Judith Cohen, 15–26. Tel Aviv: Institute for the Translation of Hebrew Literature.

———. 1989. *Hebrew Notated Manuscript Sources Up to c. 1840: A Descriptive and Thematic Catalogue with a Checklist of Printed Sources*. Munich: Henle Verlag.

Adler, Israel, Bathyah Bayer, and E. Schleifer. 1986. *The Abraham Zvi Idelsohn Memorial Volume*. *Yuval* Studies of the Jewish Music Research Center, 5. Jerusalem: Magnes.

Adler, Israel, and Judith Cohen. 1976. *A. Z. Idelsohn Archives at the Jewish National and University Library: Catalogue*. Jerusalem: Magnes Press, Hebrew University.

Alvarez-Pereyre, F., T. Alexander, I. Benabu, I. Ghelman, O. Schwarzwald, and S. Weich-Shahak. 1991. "Towards a Typology of the Judeo-Spanish Folk Song: Gerineldo and the Romance Model." *Yuval* 6.

Armistead, Samuel G., and Joseph H. Silverman. 1973. "El cancionero judeo-español de arruecos en el siglo XVIII (Incipits de los Ben Cur)." *Nueva Revista de Filología Hispánica* 22(2):280–290.

Armistead, Samuel G., and Joseph H. Silverman. 1977. *Romances judeo-espanoles de Tanger recogidos por Zarita Nahon*. Madrid: Catedra Seminario Menedez Pidal.

Armistead, Samuel G., and Joseph H. Silverman. 1981. "El antiguo cancionero sefaradí: Citas de romances en himnarios hebreos (siglos XVI–XIX)." *Nueva Revista de Filología Hispánica* 30(2):453–512.

Armistead, Samuel G., Joseph H. Silverman, and Iacob M. Hassan. 1974. "Four Moroccan Judeo-Spanish Folksong Incipits (1824–1825)." *Hispanic Review* 42(1):83–87.

Armistead, Samuel G., Joseph H. Silverman, and Israel J. Katz. 1986. *Judeo-Spanish Ballads from Oral Tradition*. 1, *Epic Ballads*. Berkeley: University of California Press.

Avenary, Hanoch. 1963. *Studies in the Hebrew, Syrian, and Greek Liturgical Recitative*. Tel-Aviv: Israel Music Institute.

———. 1972. "Music." In *Encyclopaedia Judaica* 12:554–678. Jerusalem: Encyclopedia Judaica; New York: Macmillan.

———. 1978. *The Ashkenazi Tradition of Biblical Chant between 1500 and 1900: Documentation and Musical Analysis*. Tel Aviv: Tel Aviv University; Council for Culture and Art, Ministry of Education and Culture.

———. 1979. *Encounters of East and West in Music: Selected Writings*. Tel Aviv: Faculty of Visual and Performing Arts, Deptartment of Musicology, Tel Aviv University.

———. 1986. "Persistence and Transformation of a Sephardi Penitential Hymn." *Yuval* 5:181–232.

Avenary, Hanoch, Walter Pass, and Nikolaus Vielmetti. 1985. *Kantor Salomon Sulzer und seine Zeit: Eine Dokumentation*. Sigmaringen: Jan Thorbecke Verlag.

Bahat, Avner. 1986. "The 'Hallelot' in the Yemenite Diwan." *Yuval* 5:139–168.

Bar-Yosef, Amatzia. 1998. "Traditional Rural Style under a Process of Change: The Singing Style of the *Hadday*, Palestinian Folk Poet-Singers." *Asian Music* 29(2):57–82.

Bayer, Bathyah. 1963. *The Material Relics of Music in Ancient Palestine and Its Environs: An Archeological Inventory*. Tel Aviv: Israel Music Institute.

———. 1968. "The Biblical Nebel." *Yuval* 1:89-131.

———. 1980. "Creation and Tradition in Israeli Folksongs: Some Specimens." In *Aspects of Music in Israel*, 52–60. Tel Aviv.

———. 1982. "The Titles of the Psalms." *Yuval* 4:29-123.

———. 1986. "The Announcement of the Institute of Jewish Music in Jerusalem by A. Z. Idelsohn and S. Z. Rivlin in 1910." *Yuval* 5:24–35.

Ben-Ami, Issachar. 1975. "La qasida chez les juifs marocains." In *Le Judaisme Marocain: Études Ethno-Culturels*, 105–119. Jerusalem: Rubin Mass.

———. 1984. "The Ziara and Hillula Songs." In *Saint Veneration among the Jews of Morocco*, 99–146. Jerusalem: Magnes.

Bensky, Tova. 1989. "Ethnicity and the Shape of Musical State Patterns in an Israeli Urban Community." *Social Forces* 67:731–750.

Bensky, Tova, Joachim Braun, and Uri Sharvit. 1986. "Towards a Study of Israeli Urban Musical Culture: The Case of Kiryat Ono." *Asian Music* 17(2):168–209.

Bohlman, Philip V. 1989. *The Land Where Two Streams Flow: Music in the German-Jewish Community in Israel*. Urbana: University of Illinois Press.

Bohlman, Philip V., and Mark Slobin, eds. 1986. *Music in the Ethnic Communities of Israel*. Asian Music 17(2, special issue).

Brauer, Erich. 1933–1934. "Die Juden Jemens." *Ḳiryat Sefer* 10:119, 236, 515.

———. 1934. *Ethnologie der jemenitische Juden*. Heidelberg: C. Winter.

Brod, Max. [1951] 1976. *Die Musik Israels*, rev. ed. Kassel: Bärenreiter.

Burstyn, Shai. 1989–1990. "The 'Arabian Influence' Thesis Revisited." *Current Musicology* 45–47:119–146.

Chottin, Alexis. 1939. *Tableau de la musique marocaine*. Paris: Geuthner.

Cohen, Boaz. 1935. "The Responsum of Maimonides concerning Music." *Jewish Music Journal* 2(2):1–7.

Cohen, Dalia, and Ruth Katz. 1978. *The Israeli Folk Song: A Methodological Example of Computer Analysis of Monophonic Music*. Jerusalem: Magnes Press, Hebrew University.

Cohen, Eric, and Amnon Shiloah. 1985. "Major Trends of Change in Jewish Oriental Ethnic Music." *Popular Music* 5:199–223.

Cohen, Judith. 1988. "Judeo-Spanish Songs in the Sephardic Communities of Montreal and Toronto: Survival, Function, and Change." Ph.D. dissertation, Université de Montreal.

———. 1989. "The Impact of Mass Media and Acculturation on the Judeo-Spanish Song Tradition in Montreal." In *World Music, Politics and Social Change*, ed. Simon Frith, 90–97. Manchester: Manchester University Press.

Cohen, Judith, and Oro Anahory-Librowicz. 1986. "Modalidades expresivas de los cantos de boda judeo-españoles." *Revista de Dialectología y Tradiciones Populares* 41:189–209.

Eliram, Talila. 1995. "*Shirei Eretz Israel*: The Formation and Meaning of a Popular Music Repertory at the End of the Twentieth Century." M.A. thesis, Bar-Ilan University.

Etzion, Judith. 1989. "The Spanish and the Sephardi Romances: Musical Links." *Ethnomusicology* 32(2): 1–37.

———, ed. 1996. *El cancionero de la Sablonara*. London: Tamesis.

Etzion, Judith, and Susana Weich-Shahak. 1988. "The Music of the Judeo-Spanish Romancero: Stylistic Features." *Anuario Musical* 43: 221–250.

Fenton, Paul. 1975. "Les baqqasot d'orient et d'occident." *Revue des Études Juives* 134:101–121.

Flam, Gila. 1986. "Bracha Zephira—A Case Study of Acculturation in Israeli Song." *Asian Music* 17:108–125.

Fleisher, Robert Jay. *Twenty Israeli Composers: Voices of a Culture*. Detroit: Wayne State University Press.

Flender, Reinhard. 1992. *Hebrew Psalmody*. Yuval Monograph Series, 9. Jerusalem: Hebrew University.

Gerson-Kiwi, Edith. 1963. *The Persian Doctrine of Dastgah-Composition: A Phenomenological Study in the Musical Modes*. Tel-Aviv: Israel Music Institute.

———. 1965. "Women's Songs from the Yemen: Their Tonal Structure and Form." In *The Commonwealth of Music, in Honor of Curt Sachs*, 97. New York: Free Press.

———. 1967. "Migrating Patterns of Melody among the Berbers and Jews of the Atlas Mountains." *Journal of the IFTM* 19:64–73.

———. 1968. "Vocal Folk Polyphonies of the Western Orient in Jewish Tradition." *Yuval* 1:169–193.

———. 1974. "Robert Lachmann: His Achievement and His Legacy." *Yuval* 3:100–108.

———. 1980. *Migrations and Mutations of the Music in East and West: Selected Writings*. Tel Aviv, Israel: Tel Aviv University, Faculty of Visual and Performing Arts, Department of Musicology.

Goitein, S. D. F. [1937] 1973. *From the Land of Sheba: Tales of the Jews of Yemen*. New York: Schocken.

———. 1955. "Portrait of a Yemenite Weavers' Village." *Jewish Social Studies* 17:3.

Gradenwitz, Peter. 1963. *Wege zur Musik der Gegenwart*. Stuttgart: W. Kohlhammer.

———. 1977. *Musik zwischen Orient und Okzident*. Wilhelmshaven: Heinrichshofen.

———. 1978. *Music and Musicians in Israel: A Comprehensive Guide to Modern Israeli Music*, 3rd ed. Tel Aviv: Israeli Music Publications.

Halper, Jeff, Edwin Seroussi, and Pamela Squires-Kidron. 1989. "Musica Mizrahit: Ethnicity and Class Culture in Israel." *Popular Music* 8:131–142.

———. 1992. "Musica Mizrahit and the Realignment of Israeli Society: The Case of Hayyim Moshe." In *1789–1989 Musique, historie, democratie*, ed. Antoine Hennion, 3:669–672. Paris: Éditions de la Maison des Sciences de l'Homme.

Hajdu, Andre, and Yaacov Mazor. 1971. "Hasidim: The Musical Tradition of the Hasidism." In *Encyclopedia Judaica*, 7:1421–1432. Jerusalem: Encyclopedia Judaica; New York: Macmillan.

Herzog, Avigdor. 1963. *The Intonation of the Pentateuch in the Heder of Tunis*. Tel-Aviv: Israel Music Institute.

Hirshberg, Jehoash, and David Sagiv. 1978. "The 'Israeli' in Israeli Music: The Audience Responds." *Israel Studies in Musicology* 1:159–173.

Hirshberg, Jehoash. 1987. "Jerusalem Symphony Orchestra," "Israel Philharmonic Orchestra." In *Symphony Orchestras of the World: Selected Profiles*, ed. Robert Craven, 200–207. New York: Greenwood.

———. 1990. *Paul Ben-Haim: His Life and Works*. Jerusalem: Israeli Music Publications.

———. 1995. *Music in the Jewish Community of Palestine 1880–1948: A Social History*. Oxford: Clarendon; New York: Oxford University Press.

Horowitz, Amy. 1994. "Israeli Mediterranean Music: Cultural Boundaries and Disputed Territories." Ph.D. dissertation, University of Pennsylvania.

———. 1997. "Performance in Disputed Territory: Israeli Mediterranean Music." *Musical Performance* 1(3):43–53.

Høst, George Hjersing. 1781. *Nachrichten von Morokos und Fes, im Lande selbst gesammelt in der Jahre 1760 bis 1768*. Copenhagen.

Ibbeken, Ida, and Tzvi Avni. 1969. *An Orchestra Is Born*. Tel Aviv: Israel Philharmonic Orchestra.

Idelsohn, Abraham Zvi. 1914–1932. *Hebräisch-orientalischer Melodienschatz*. Leipzig: Breitkopf and Härtel.

———. 1918. "The Jews of Yemen: Their Poetry and Music." *Reshumot* 1:3–66.

———. [1929] 1992. *Jewish Music in Its Historical Development*. New York: Dover.

Kahn, Aharon. 1986–1989. "Music in Halakhic Perspective." *Journal of Jewish Music and Liturgy* 9:55–72, 10:32–49, 11:65–75.

Katz, Israel J. 1973. "The 'Myth' of the Sephardic Musical Legacy from Spain." *Proceedings of the Fifth World Congress of Jewish Studies* 4:237–243.

———. 1979. "Manuel Manrique de Lara and the Tunes of the Moroccan Sephardic Ballad Tradition: Some Insights into a Much-Needed Critical Edition." In *El Romancero hoy: Nuevas Fronteras*, ed. Antonio Sánchez Romeraldo, Diego Catalán, and Samuel G. Armistead, 75–87. Madrid: Catedra Seminario Menendez Pidal.

———. 1982. "On the Music of Three Romances from Tangíer," *Estudios Sefardies* 1:129–131.

———. 1986. "'Contrafacta' and the Judeo-Spanish Romancero: A Musicological View." In *Hispanic Studies in Honor of Joseph H. Silverman*, ed. Joseph V. Recapito, 169–187. Newark, Del.: Juan de la Cuesta.

Katz, Ruth. 1968. "The Singing of *Baqqashot* by Aleppo Jews." *Acta Musicologica* 40:65–85.

Keren, Zvi. 1980. *Contemporary Israeli Music: Its Sources and Stylistic Development*. Ramat-Gan, Israel: Bar-Ilan University Press.

Lachmann, Robert. 1940. *Jewish Cantillation and Song in the Isle of Djerba*. Jerusalem: Archives of Oriental Music, Hebrew University.

———. 1974, 1978. *Posthumous Works*, ed. Edith Gerson-Kiwi. 2 vols. Jerusalem: Magnes Press, Hebrew University.

————. 1978. *Gesänge der Juden auf der Insel Djerba*, ed. Edith Gerson-Kiwi. Jerusalem: Hebrew University.

Landman, Leo. 1972. *The Cantor: An Historical Perspective*. New York: Yeshiva University.

Larrea Palacín, Arcadio. 1952. *Romances de Tetuán*. 2 vols. Madrid: Instituto de Estudios Africanos.

————. 1954. *Canciones rituales hispano-judías*. Madrid: Instituto de Estudios Africanos.

Levy, Isaac. 1964–1980. *Antologia de la liturgia Judeo-Espanola*. 10 vols. Jerusalem: Author.

Lewis, Bernard. 1984. *The Jews of Islam*. Princeton, N.J.: Princeton University Press.

Loeb, Laurence D. 1972. "The Jewish Musician and the Music of Fars." *Asian Music* 4(1):3–14.

Marks, Paul F. *Bibliography of Literature concerning Yemenite-Jewish Music*. Detroit: Information Coordinators.

Mazor, Yacov. 2000. *The Klezmer Tradition in the Land of Israel*. Jerusalem: Jewish Music Research Center.

Nathan, Hans, ed. 1994. *Israeli Folk Music: Songs of the Early Pioneers*. Madison, Wisc.: A-R Editions.

Ne'eman, Amitay. 1980. "Light Music and Pop in Israel." In *Aspects of Music in Israel*, 61–65. Tel Aviv.

Ravina, Menashe. 1963. *Organum and the Samaritans*, trans. Alan Marbe. Tel Aviv: Israel Music Institute.

Regev, Moti. 1986. "The Musical Soundscape as a Contest Area: 'Oriental Music' and Israeli Popular Music." In *Media, Culture, and Society*, ed. Richard Collins et al., 8:343–355. London, Beverly Hills, and New Delhi: Sage.

————. 1989. "The Field of Popular Music in Israel." In *World Music, Politics and Social Change*, ed. Simon Frith, 145–155. Manchester: Manchester University Press.

————. 1992. "Israeli Rock, or a Study in the Politics of Local Authenticity." *Popular Music* 11(1):1–14.

Romero, Elena. 1981. "Las coplas sefardíes: Categorías y estado de la cuestión." In *Actas de las Jornadas de Estudios Sefaradíe*, 69–98. Cáceres: Universidad de Extremadura.

Sabbah, Dina. 1980. "Le chant religieux chez les marocains d'Israel." M.A. thesis, Université de Montréal.

Schleifer, Eliyahu. 1995. "Current Trends of Liturgical Music in the Ashkenazi Liturgy." In *Jewish Musical Culture—Past and Present*. Vol. 37(1) of *World of Music*, ed. Uri Sharvit, 59–72. Basel, Kassel: Bärenreiter.

Schreiber, Baruch David. 1984–1985. "The Woman's Voice in the Synagogue." *Journal of Jewish Music and Liturgy* 7:27–32.

Seroussi, Edwin. 1986. "Politics, Ethnic Identity, and Music in the Singing of *Bakkashot* among Moroccan Jews in Israel." *Asian Music* 17(2):32–45.

————. 1990a. "La musica arabigo-andaluza en las bakkashot judeo-marroquíes: Estudio histórico y musical." *Anuario Musical* 45:297–315.

————. 1990b. "The Growth of the Judeo-Spanish Folksong Repertory in the Twentieth Century." In *Proceedings of the Tenth World Congress of Jewish Studies*, 2:173–180. Jerusalem: World Union of Jewish Studies.

————. 1996. *Popular Music in Israel: The First Fifty Years*. Cambridge, Mass.: Harvard College Library.

Seroussi, Edwin, and Susana Weich-Shahak. 1991. "Judeo-Spanish Contrafacts and Musical Adaptations: The Oral Tradition." *Orbis Musicae* 10:164–194.

Sharvit, Uri. 1980. "The Role of Music in the Jewish Yemenite 'Heder.'" *Israel Studies in Musicology* 2:33–49.

————. 1981. "On the Role of Arts and Artistic Concepts in the Tradition of Yemenite Jewry." *Pe'amim* 10:119–130.

————. 1982. "The Musical Realization of Biblical Cantillation Symbols in the Jewish Yemenite Liturgy." *Yuval* 4:179–210.

————. 1986a. "Diversity within Unity: Stylistic Change and Ethnic Continuity in Israeli Religious Music." *Asian Music* 17(2):126–146.

————. 1986b. "The Music and Its Function in the Traditional Singing of the Qasid: 'Abda birabi di halak.'" *Yuval* 5:192–234.

————, ed. 1995. *Jewish Musical Culture—Past and Present*. Vol. 37(1) of *World of Music*. Basel, Kassel: Bärenreiter.

Sharvit, Uri, and Yehiel Adaqi. 1981. *A Treasury of Jewish Yemenite Chants*. Jerusalem: Israel Institute for Sacred Music.

Sharvit, Uri, and Simcha Arom. 1994. "Plurivocality in the Liturgical Music of the Jews of San'a (Yemen)." *Yuval* 6:34–67.

Sharvit, Uri, and E. Yaacov. 1984. "The 'Hallelot' of the Jews of Huggariyah and Those of Central Yemen." *Pe'amim* 19:130–162.

Shiloah, Amnon. 1969. "The World of a Yemenite Folk Singer." *Tatslil* 9:144–149.

————. 1972. "Africa, North: Musical Traditions." In *Encyclopaedia Judaica* 16:1257–1260. Jerusalem: Encyclopaedia Judaica.

————. 1977. *Music Subjects in the Zohar Texts and Indices*. Jerusalem: Magnes Press, Hebrew University.

————. 1980. "La muba et la celebration des bakashot en Maroc." In *Judaisme d'Afrique du Nord*, ed. Michel Abitbol, 108–113. Jerusalem: Ben-Zvi Institute.

————. 1983. *The Musical Tradition of Iraqi Jews*. Or Yehuda: Iraqi Jews' Traditional Culture Center.

————. 1984. "Impressions musicales des voyageurs européens en Afrique du Nord." In *Les relations intercommunautaires juives en Méditerranée occidentale*. Paris: Editions du C.N.R.S.

————. 1992a. *Jewish Musical Traditions*. Detroit: Wayne University Press.

————. 1992b. "Eastern Sources in Israeli Music." *Ariel* 88:4–19.

Shiloah, Amnon, and Eric Cohen. 1983. "The Dynamics of Change in Jewish Oriental Ethnic Music in Israel." *Ethnomusicology* 27:227–251.

Sikron, Moshe. 1957. *Immigration to Israel*. Jerusalem: Central Bureau of Statistics.

Slobin, Mark. 1989. *Chosen Voices: The Story of the American Cantorate*. Urbana and Chicago: University of Illinois Press.

Smoira-Roll, Michal. 1963. *Folk Song in Israel: An Analysis Attempted*. Tel Aviv: Israel Music Institute.

Spector, Johanna. 1952. "On the Trail of Oriental Jewish Music: Among the Yemenites." *Reconstructionist* 18:7–12.

Tischler, Alice. 1989. *A Descriptive Bibliography of Art Music by Israeli Composers*. Warren, Mich.: Detroit Studies in Music Bibliography.

Vinaver, Chemjo. 1985. *Anthology of Hassidic Music*, ed. Eliyahu Schleifer. Jerusalem: Jewish Music Research Center, Hebrew University of Jerusalem.

Weich-Shahak, Susana. 1989. *Judeo-Spanish Moroccan Songs for the Life Cycle*. Jerusalem: Jewish Music Research Center, Hebrew University of Jerusalem.

Weil, Daniel. 1994. *The Original Performance of the Tiberian Masoretic Accents: A Deductive Approach*. Jerusalem: ha-Universiṭah ha-'Ivrit.

Werner, Eric. 1976. *A Voice Still Heard: The Sacred Songs of the Ashkenazi Jews*. University Park: Pennsylvania State University Press.

Yurchenko, Henrietta. 1958. "The Music of the Jews in Morocco." In *Year Book of the American Philosophical Society*, 518–520. Philadelphia: American Philosophical Society.

Zafrani, Haim. 1977. *Poesie juive en Occident Musulman*. Paris: Geuthner.

Recordings of Middle Eastern Music

THE MAGHRIB

Aflak. 1994. *Marocain moderne/Aflak*. Paris: Les Artistes Arabes Associés, Club du Disque Arabe AAA102.

Ahouach, ahidous, et guedra. 1996. Les Artistes Arabes Associés, Club du Disque Arabe, AAA 131. Compact disk.

Alaoui, Amina. 1995. *Musique arabo-andalouse du Maroc*. Auvidis B 6806. Compact disk.

Amārg al-Maghrib: Mukhtārāt min ghinā' wa-mūsīqa al-ruwāyis / Maroc: Anthologie des rwâyes. 1991. Paris: Maison des Cultures du Monde, W260023. 4 compact disks.

Antūlūjīyat al-alāh / Anthologie al-ala: Musique Andaluci-Marocaine. 1989–. Paris: Maison des Cultures du Monde and Rabat: Ministère de la Culture.

Vol. 1 (1989). Haj Abdelkrim al-Raïs and the Orchestre al-Brihi de Fès: *Nūbat gharībat al-ḥusayn*. W260010. 6 compact disks.

Vol. 2 (1990). Haj Mohamed Toud and the Orchestre Moulay Ahmed Loukili de Rabat: *Nūbat 'ushshāq*. W260014. 6 compact disks.

Vol. 3 (1992). Mohammed Larbi-Temsamani and the Orchestre du Conservatoire de Tètouan: *Nūbat iṣbahān*. W260024. 6 compact disks.

Vol. 4 (1992). Ahmed Zaytouni Sahraoui and the Orchestre de Tanger: *Nūbat raṣd*. W260027. 6 compact disks.

Vol. 5 (1992). Haj Abdelkrim al-Raïs and the Orchestre al-Brihi de Fès: *Nūbat istihlāl*. W260028. 7 compact disks.

Vol. 6 (1992). Haj Mohamed Toud and the Orchestre Moulay Ahmed Loukili de Rabat: *Nūbat raṣd al-dhil*. W260029. 6 compact disks.

Vol. 7 (1992). Ahmed Zaytouni Sahraoui and the Orchestre de Tanger: *Nūbat 'irāq 'ajam*. W260030. 7 compact disks.

Vol. 8 (1997). Haj Abdelkrim al-Raïs and the Orchestre al-Brihi de Fès: *Nūbat al-ḥijāz al-kabīr*. W260031. 7 compact disks.

Vol. 9 [c. 1990.] Mohammed Larbi-Temsamani and the Orchestre du Conservatoire de Tètouan: *Nūbat ramal al-māya*. W260032. 8 compact disks.

Vol. 10 (1992). Haj Abdelkrim al-Raïs and the Orchestre al-Brihi de Fès: *Nūbat al-ḥijāz al-mashriqī*. W260033. 5 compact disks.

Vol. 11. [c. 1990.] Ahmed Zaytouni Sahraoui and the Orchestre de Tanger: *Nūbat al-māya*. W260034. 7 compact disks.

Vol. 12 [c. 1990.] Mohammed Brioual and the Ensemble al-Āla du Ministère de la Culture du Maroc: *Mīzān quddām bawākir al-māya* and *Mīzān al-quddām al-jadīd*. W260035. 2 compact disks.

Arab Music. Music of the Near East. 1968. Lyrichord LLST 7186, 7198. LP disk.

Archives de la musique arabe. 1987–. Ocora C558678. Compact disk.

Augier, Pierre, comp. 1975. *Algeria (Sahara): Music of Gourara*. EMI Odeon 3C 064 18079. LP disk.

Aux sources du raï. Les cheikat: Chants de femme de l'ouest algérien. 1996. Les Artistes Arabes Associés, Club du Disque Arabe AAA 132. Compact disk.

Azem, Slimane. 1995. *Meltiyid matchfam*. Les Artistes Arabes Associés, Club du Disque Arabe AAA 135. Compact disk.

Ben Mahmoud, Abderrahman Sheikh. n.d. *La Sulâmiyya: Chants soufis de Tunis*. Institut du Monde Arabe 321025. Compact disk.

Ben Sari, Elarbi. 1995. *Gharnata: Congrès du Caire 1932*. Les Artistes Arabes Associés AAA 098. Compact disk.

Bent el Hocine, Fatna. 1999. *Barbès café: Trois cheikhates mythiques du Maroc*. Night and Day BAC 104. Compact disk.

Bin 'Ashūr, Daḥmān. 1990. *La Nouba*. Les Artistes Arabes Associés, Club du Disque Arabe AAA 022. Compact disk.

Bin Ḥasan, Muḥammad. 1994. *Malouf tunisien: Congrès du Caire 1932*. Les Artistes Arabes Associés, Club du Disque Arabe AAA 094. Compact disk.

Bilkhayyāt, 'Abd al-Hādī. 1990. *La chanson moderne au Maroc*. Paris: Les Artistes Arabes Associés, Club du Disque Arabe, AAA 012. Compact disk.

Bin 'Ashūr, Daḥmān. 1990. *Nouba*. Vol. 4. Les Artistes Arabes Associés, Club du Disque Arabe AAA 143. Compact disk.

Boniche, Lili. [c. 1997.] *Trésors de la chanson judéo-arabe*. Blue Silver 79 102 2 BS. Compact disk.

Bowles, Paul, comp. 1972. *Music of Morocco*. Washington, D.C.: Library of Congress Recording Laboratory, AFS L63–64. 2 LP disks.

Būshnāk, Luṭfī. 1993. *Mālūf Tūnisī*. Paris: Maison des Cultures du Monde W260053. Compact disk.

Chants de traverse: Récital de musiques judéo-marocaines. Paris: Atoll Music. 2 compact disks.

Chants sacrés du Sahara Algérien: Ahallil de Gourara. 1994. Institut du Monde Arabe REF 50306–2. Compact disk.

Chaouli, Nacer Eddine. 1996. *Musique classique algérienne: Hawzi*. Les Artistes Arabes Associés AAA 149. Compact disk.

Chaouqi, Mohamed. 1995. *Les gnawa du Maroc: Ouled el 'abdi*. Auvidis B 6805. Compact disk.

Chawqi, Ahmed. 1995. *Ahmed (oud)* and *Souad (qanoun) Chawki*. Paris: Les Artistes Arabes Associés, Club du Disque Arabe, AAA 133. 2 compact disks.

Cheikha, Cherifa and Hanifa. 1996. *Chants berbères: Cherifa and Hanifa*. 1996. Les Artistes Arabes Associés AAA 146. Compact disk.

Chekroun, Alain. 2000. *Chants des synagogues du Maghreb*. Magda MGD027. Compact disk.

Cherkauoi, Abdeslam. 1988. *The Arabic Tradition in Morrocan* [sic] *Music/Musique de tradition arabe*. Paris: Audivis, D 8002. Compact disk.

Congrès du Caire 1932: Musique arabe savante et populaire. 1988. Édition Bibliothèque Nationale—France/Institut du Monde Arabe, APN 88–9, 88–10. 2 compact disks.

Dali, Abdelkrim. 1998. *École de Tlemcen*. Vol. 2, *Abdelkrim Dali*. Les Artistes Arabes Associés AAA 147. Compact disk.

Dances and Trances: Moroccan Sufi Brotherhoods, Berber Street Musicians. 2000. World Arbiter 2002. Compact disk.

La daqqa: Tambours sacrés de Marrakech/Sacred drums from Marrakesh. 1999. Paris: Institut du Monde Arabe, 321028. Compact disk.

Le diwân de Biskra. 1996. Ocora/Radio France C 560088. Compact disk.

El Din, Hamza. 1964. *Music of Nubia*. Vanguard VSD-79164. LP disk.

Ezzahi, Ammar. 1996. *La chaâbi*. Les Artistes Arabes Associés, Club du Disque Arabe AAA 124. Compact disk.

Fergani, Hadj Mohamed Tahar. 1993. *La nuba maya*. Harmonia Mundi/Ocora C 560002. Compact disk.

Le folklore Kabyle: Musique et traditions. 1990. Les Artistes Arabes Associés AAA 033, Club du Disque Arabe CDA 401. Compact disk.

Gharnâti de Tlemçen. 1993. Ocora/Radio France C 560004. Compact disk.

Groupe Lemchaheb. 1989. *La chanson populaire marocaine.* Paris: Les Artistes Arabes Associés, AAA 008. Compact disk.

Haddarat. *Chants sacrés des femmes de Fez.* Al Sur CDAL 243. Compact disk.

Hâdra des gnaoua d'Essaouira. 1993. Ocora/Radio France C560006. Compact disk.

Halali, Salim, 1990a. *Salim Halali en Algérie.* Les Artistes Arabes Associés AAA 023. Compact disk.

———. 1990b. *Salim Halali en Tunisie.* Les Artistes Arabes Associés AAA 036. Compact disk.

Hassan, Chalf. 1997. *Songs and Dances from Morocco.* EUCD 1393 ARC Music. Compact disk.

Le Hawzi: Sur des poèmes de Bentriki. 1994. Les Artistes Arabes Associés, Club du Disque Arabe AAA 081. Compact disk.

Hoggar: Musique des Touareg. 1994. Chant du Monde LDX 274974. Compact disk.

Kabyle chantée: Chants, rythmes, danses folkloriques de Kabylie. n.d. Les Artistes Arabes Associés AAA 160. Compact disk.

Khaznadji, Mohamed. 1993. *La nuba ghrib.* Harmonia Mundi/Ocora 560003. Compact disk.

Kheddam, Chérif. 1992. *Les maîtres de la chanson kabyle.* Vol. 4: *Chérif Kheddam.* Les Artistes Arabes Associés AAA060. Compact disk.

Krémer, Gérard. 1989. *Maroc: Documents recueillis au Maroc par Gérard Krémer.* Arion ARN 64079. Compact disk.

Kurd, Muḥammad. 1992. *La malouf Constantinois.* Vol. 1. Les Artistes Arabes Associés, Club du Disque Arabe AAA 051. Compact disk.

Laade, Wolfgang. 1962. *Tunisia.* Vol. 1: *The Classical Arab-Andalusian Music.* Vol. 2: *Religious Songs and Cantillations.* Vol. 3: *Folk Music.* Smithsonian Folkways FW 8861–8863. 3 LP disks.

Libye: Chants des oasis. n.d. Al-Sur CDAL 236-3. 3 compact disks.

Lortat-Jacob, Bernard. 1975. *Maroc: Musique berbère—Un mariage dans le Haut-Atlas oriental.* Vogue LDY 28.029. LP disk.

Lortat-Jacob, Bernard, and Hassan Jouad. 1979. *Berbères du Maroc "ahwash."* Collection CNRS/ Musée de l'Homme. Le Chant du Monde LDX 74705. LP disk.

Lortat-Jacob, Bernard, and Gilbert Rouget. 1971. *Musique berbère du Haut-Atlas.* Collection Musée de l'Homme. Vogue LD 786. LP disk.

Al-Maghrib: ʿAshr qaṣāʾid min ṭarab al-milḥūn/ Maroc: Anthologie d'al-melhûn. Traditions de Fes, Meknes, Salé, Marrakech. 1990. Morocco, Ministry of Culture, and Maison des Cultures du Monde, W260016. 3 compact disks.

Al-Maghrib: al-Ṭarab al-gharnāṭī: Nawbat al-ramal/Maroc: Musique gharnâtî. 1990. Paris: Maison des Cultures du Monde, W260017. Compact disk.

Mahieddine. 1996. *Musique classique arabo-andalouse.* Les Artistes Arabes Associés, Club du Disque Arabe AAA 138. Compact disk.

Le malouf tunisien Vol. 1. 1992. Les Artistes Arabes Associés AAA 054. Compact disk.

Le malhûn de Meknès: Musique et chants du Maroc. 1994. Institut du Monde Arabe 50305-2. Compact disk.

Maroc. 1980. 1. *Musique Tachelhit: Raïs Lhaj Aomar Ouahrouch.* 2. *Moyen Atlas: Musique sacrée et profane.* Paris: Radio-France OCORA OCR 558587, 558560. 2 LP disks.

Maroc: À Marrakech, sur la Djemâa el-Fna. 1994. Chant du Monde LDX 274973. Compact disk.

Moroccan Street Music. c. 1970. Lyrichord LLST 7263. LP disk.

Moroccan Sufi Music. c. 1970. Lyrichord LLST 7238. LP disk.

Moyen-Atlas: Musique sacrée et profane. 1989. Ocora/Radio France C 559057. Compact disk.

Music of Islam and Sufism in Morocco. 1999. Rounder CD 5145. Compact disk.

Music of Morocco. 1966. Folkways Records FE 4339. LP disk.

Musique arabo-andalouse classique: Ensemble Masano Tazzi. 1995. Chant du Monde CMT 274 1007. Compact disk.

Musique classique andalou-maghrébine. 1988. Ocora C559016. Compact disk.

Musique classique: Maroc. n.d. Les Artistes Arabes Associés AAA006. Compact disk.

La musique judéo-arabe. 1992–1993. Les Artistes Arabes Associés 062-072. 2 compact disks.

Musique tunisienne. Enregistrements du Congrès du Caire. Gramophone HC 40–55 and HC 83–86. 20 compact disks.

Nass el Ghiwan. 1997. *Nass el Ghiwane.* Paris: Blue Silver 50620–2. Compact disk.

Nawbat al-aṣbahān. 1992. Paris: Maison des Cultures du Monde W260024. 6 compact disks.

Nawbat al-aṣbahān. 1993. Paris: Maison des Cultures du Monde W260046. Compact disk.

Nawbat al-dhīl. 1992. Paris: Maison des Cultures du Monde W260044. Compact disk.

Nawbat al-ʿirāq. 1993. Paris: Maison des Cultures du Monde W260047. Compact disk.

Nawbat al-ramal. 1992. Paris: Maison des Cultures du Monde W260045. Compact disk.

Nawbat al-sīkāh. 1994. Paris: Maison des Cultures du Monde W260059. Compact disk.

Nûba çika. Nûba zidane. Nûba des înklabat', mode moual. 1994. Ocora/Radio France C560044/45. 2 compact disks.

Olsen, Miriam, and Bernard Lortat-Jacob. 1994. *Maroc: Musique berbère du Haut-Atlas et de l'Anti-Atlas.* Chant du Monde LDX 274991. Compact disk.

Poèmes de Benshala. 1993. Les Artistes Arabes Associés, Club du Disque Arabe AAA 071. Compact disk.

Rayīs, ʿAbd al-Karīm. 1993–1999. *Musique andalouse de Fès.* Paris: Institut du Monde Arabe, 321002–3. 2 compact disks.

Remitti, Cheikra. c. 1990. *Aux sources du raï.* Paris: Institut du Monde Arabe 503 09–2. Compact disk.

Rituel de transe: Les Assawa de Fès. 1999. Paris: Institut du Monde Arabe, 321011. Compact disk.

Sacred Music of the Moroccan Jews. 2000. Rounder CD 5087. 2 compact disks.

Sahara: Musiques du Gourara. 1991. Audivis D 8037. Compact disk.

Salah, Sadaoui. 1995. *Sadaoui Salah.* Vol. 1: *En Kabyle.* Les Artistes Arabes Associés AAA 106. Compact disk.

Saoudi, Nour-Eddine. 1998. *Nouba h'sine.* Les Artistes Arabes Associés AAA 167. Compact disk.

Saoula. 1993. *Hommage à [Amraoui] Missoum.* Les Artistes Arabes Associés AAA 086. Compact disk.

Schuyler, Philip D. 1978. *The Rwais: Moroccan Berber Musicians from the High Atlas.* Lyrichord LLST 7316. LP disk.

Tahar, Samir. 1996. *Oud.* Les Artistes Arabes Associés, Club du Disque Arabe AAA 136. Compact disk.

Tamar, Simone. 1993. *Malouf constantinois,* Vol. 3. Les Artistes Arabes Associés AAA 077. Compact disk.

Tazi, Massano. 1988. *Musique classique andalouse de Fès.* Ocora/Radio France C559035. Compact disk.

Tetma, Shaykhah. 1993. *École de Tlemcen: Cheikha Tetma.* Les Artistes Arabes Associés, Club du Disque Arabe AAA 067. Compact disk.

Tunisia. [c. 1970.] Musicaphon BM 30 L 2008. LP disk.

Zinelabidine, Mohamed. 1996. *Oud: De Carthage à Ifriqiya.* Les Artistes Arabes Associés, Club du Disque Arabe AAA 137. Compact disk.

THE MASHRIQ

ʿAbd al-Wahhāb, Muḥammad. [c. 1990.] *Fakka-rūnī.* Ṣawt al-Qāhira, Sīdī 94 SDCD 01B16. Compact disk.

———. c. 1990. *Aghaddan alqāk.* Ṣawt al-Qāhira, Sīdī 94 SDCD 01B25. Compact disk.

———. 1990. *The Music of Mohamed Abdel Wahab.* Axiom 422-846 754-2. Compact disk.

———. 1996a. *Min ghayr layh.* EMI Arabia 310511-2. Compact disk.

———. 1996b. *Waṭaniyyāt.* EMI Arabia 310607-2, 310608-2. 2 compact disks.

———. 1997. *The HMV Recordings*. EMI Arabia 0946 310963-2. Compact disk.

L'âge d'or de la musique égyptienne. 1991. Les Artistes Arabes Associés, Club du Disque Arabe AAA 043. Compact disk.

Aḥmad, Zakarīyā. c. 1990. *Al-āhāt, kalimāt: al-Ustādh Bayram al-Tūnisī, laḥn al musīqār*. Ṣawt al-Qāhira, Sīdī 94 SDCD 01B30. Compact disk.

———. c. 1990. *Anā fī intizārak kalimāt: Bayram al-Tūnisī, laḥn al-musīqār*. Ṣawt al-Qāhira, Sīdī 94 SDCD 01B58. Compact disk.

———. c. 1990. *Al-awwilah fīl-gharām*. Ṣawt al-Qāhira, Sīdī 94 SDCD 01B46. Compact disk.

———. c. 1990. *Ḥulm al-Amal*. Ṣawt al-Qāhira, Sīdī 94 SDCD 01B29. Compact disk.

Arabian Music: Maqam. 1971. Philips 6586 006. LP disk.

Arabic and Druse Music. 1956. Folkways P 480. LP disk.

Arabic Love Songs and Dances of Lebanon. 1957. Folkways FW 8815. LP disk.

Arabic Songs of Lebanon and Egypt. 1956. Folkways FW 6925. LP disk.

Archives de la musique arabe. 1987–. Ocora C558678. Compact disks.

Asmahān. 1988. *Asmahan*. Les Artistes Arabes Associés, Club du Disque Arabe AAA 004. Compact disk.

———. 1992a. *Asmahan: Archives des années 42/44*. Les Artistes Arabes Associés, Club du Disque Arabe AAA 049. Compact disk.

———. 1992b. *Asmahan*. Vol. 3: *Archives des années 30*. Les Artistes Arabes Associés, Club du Disque Arabe AAA 059. Compact disk.

Aṭrash, Farīd. 1992. *Farid el Atrache: Les années 30*. Baidaphon/Club du Disque Arabe, AAA053. Compact disk.

Barrayn, Shaykh Ahmad. *Sufi Songs*. Long Distance 592323. Compact disk.

Bashīr, Munīr. c. 1971. *Iraq: Oud classique arabe par Munir Bashir*. Ocora OCR 63. LP disk.

———. 1988a. *Munir Bachir en concert*. Maison des Cultures du Monde W260006. Compact disk.

———. 1988b. *Récital: Solo de luth-oud*. Les Artistes Arabes Associés AAA 003, Club du Disque Arabe CDA 401. Compact disk.

———. 1998. *L'art du 'ūd*. Ocora/Radio France C 580068. Compact disk.

———. 1993. *Maqamat*. Maison des Cultures du Monde W260050. Compact disk.

———. 1996. *Méditations*. Maison des Cultures du Monde W260071. Compact disk.

———. c. 1990. *Babylon Mood: Munir Bechir and His Quartet*. Voix de l'Orient, A. Cahine and Fils VDLCD 529. Compact disk.

Bashīr, Munīr, and Omar Bashīr. 1998. *Duo de 'ūd*. Auvidis B 6874. Compact disk.

Beduin Music of Southern Sinai. 1978. Folkways FE 4204. LP disk.

Bulos, Afif Alvarez. 1961. *Songs of Lebanon, Syria, and Jordan*. Folkways FW 8816. LP disk.

Cafés chantants du Caire. 1995–1996. Les Artistes Arabes Associés AAA 099, AAA 115, Club du Disque Arabe CDA 401. 2 compact disks.

Chants de Baghdad par l'ensemble al-Tchâlghî al-baghdâdî. 1996. Institut du Monde Arabe IMA-CD 18. Compact disk.

Coptic Music. 1960. Folkways FR 8960. LP disk.

Dāyikh, Adīb. 1994. *L'art sublime du Ghazal*. Notes by Bernard Mousali. Nanterre: Al Sur, ALCD 143–144. 2 compact disks.

Église Syrienne Orthodoxe: Liturgie d'Antioche. 1992. Auvidis D 8039. Compact disk.

Egypte: Ordre Chazili al-Tariqa al-Hamidiyya al-Chaziliyya'. 1992. Arion ARN 64211. Compact disk.

Ensemble David. 1999. *Liturgies coptes*. Institut du Monde Arabe 321022. Compact disk.

Fakhrī, Ṣabāḥ. 1990. *Ṣabāḥ Fakhrī*. Dūnyāfūn LPD CD 501. Compact disk.

———. 1995. *Sabah Fakhri au palais des congrès*. Les Artistes Arabes Associés, Club du Disque Arabe AAA110. Compact disk.

Fayrūz. 1988a. *Fairuz*. Ṣawt al-Sharq, Voix de l'Orient VDLCD 502. Compact disk.

———. 1988b. *Fayrūz fī al-Ūlimbiyā/Le Liban à l'Olympia gala Fairuz à Paris*. Ṣawt al-Sharq, Voix de l'Orient VDLCD 503-4. 2 compact disks.

———. 1993. *Al-aghānī al-khālida*. Ṣawt al-Sharq, Voix de l'Orient VDLCD 560. Compact disk.

———. 1997. *Ma'akoum*. EMI Music Arabia 0946 310964-2 6. Compact disk.

Firqat al-Tanbūrah. 1999. *La simsimiyya de Port Saïd*. Institut du Monde Arabe 321026. Compact disk.

Ghazālī, Nāẓim. 1994a. *Nāẓim al-Ghazālī al-juz' al-awwal*. Bou Zaid Phone, Digital Press Hellas BUZCD 515. Compact disk.

———. 1994b. *Nāẓim al-Ghazālī al-juz' al-thānī*. Bou Zaid Phone, Digital Press Hellas BUZCD 516. Compact disk.

Ḥāfiẓ, 'Abd al-Ḥalīm. 1996. *Kariat al Fengan*. EMI Arabia 310502-2. Compact disk.

———. 1997. *Abdel Halim Hafez: Live at the Royal Albert Hall, London*. Virgin 310968–2. Compact disk.

Hage, Louis. 1971–1973. *Traditions musicales du Proche-Orient*. Beirut: Kaslik. 13 45-rpm disks.

———. 1979a. *Florilège de chants maronites*. Paris: SM. LP disk.

———. 1979b. *Chants syriaques de l'Église Maronite*. Paris: SM. LP disk.

———. 1982a. *Noëls maronites*. Paris: SM. LP disk.

———. 1982b. *Chants de la Passion et de Pâques*. Paris: SM. LP disk.

———. 1983. *Gesänge der maronitischen Kirche*. Christophorus. LP disk.

———. 1993. *Chants maronites traditionnels*. Paris: SM. Compact disk.

Ḥamdī, Balīgh. [c. 1990.] *Ba'īd 'annak*. Ṣawt al-Qāhira, Sīdī 94 SDCD 01B63. Compact disk.

———. c. 1990. *Bitfakkar fī mīn*. Ṣawt al-Qāhira, Sīdī 94 SDCD 01B62. Compact disk.

———. c. 1990. *Al-ḥubb kulluh*. Ṣawt al-Qāhira, Sīdī 94 SDCD 01B48. Compact disk.

Ḥarrāshī, Daḥman. 1996. *Musique populaire algérienne: Dahmane Elharrachi*. Vol. 4: *Le chaâbi*. Les Artistes Arabes Associés AAA 142. Compact disk.

———. 1999. *Le chaâbi*. Vol. 5. Les Artistes Arabes Associés, Club du Disque Arabe AAA 183. Compact disk.

Ḥijāzī, Salāma. 1994. *Shaykh Salama Higazi*. Les Artistes Arabes Associés, Club du Disque Arabe AAA 085. Compact disk.

Ḥilmī, 'Abd al-Ḥayy. 1994. *Abd al-Hayy Hilmi*. Les Artistes Arabes Associés, Club du Disque Arabe AAA 075. Compact disk.

Iqa'at: Rythmes traditionnels. 1992. Auvidis D 8044. Compact disk.

Islamic Ritual Zikr in Aleppo/Rituel islamique zikr à Alep. 1989. Auvidis D 8013. Compact disk.

Jordanie: Chants bédouins, chants de mariage, chants des pêcheurs d'Aqaba. 1998. Maison des Cultures du Monde W260083. Compact disk.

Al-Kindī. 1998. *Le salon de musique d'Alep: L'art du chant classique Arabe*. Chant du Monde CML 5741108-9. 2 compact disks.

Laments of Lebanon. 1985. Folkways FE 4046. LP disk.

Mahmoud, Zein. 1997. *Chants sacrés de Haute-Egypte*. Paris: Institut du Monde Arabe IMA-CD 22. Compact disk.

Makkāwī, Sayyid. 1997. *Yā misahharnī*. Ṣawt al-Qāhira. Compact disk.

Manyālāwī, Yūsuf. 1993. *Shaykh Yûsuf Al-Manyalâwî (1847–1911)*. Les Artistes Arabes Associés AAA 065, Club du Disque Arabe CDA 401. Compact disk.

Mélodies judéo-arabes d'autrefois: Maghreb et Moyen Orient. 1997. Paris: Blue Silver Mélodie, 50556–2. Compact disk.

Mohamed, Matar. 1996. *Liban. Matar Muhammad (1939–1995): Hommage à un maître du buzuq*. Paris: Maison des Cultures du Monde W260068. Compact disk.

Moudallal, Sabri. 1994. *Chants sacrés et profanes de Syrie. Sabri Moudallal: Premier muezzin d'Alep*. Notes by Christian Poché. Paris: Institut du Monde Arabe, REF 303. Compact disk.

———. c. 1990. *Chants d'Alep*. Institut du Monde Arabe 321001. Compact disk.

Muezzins d'Alep. 1992. *Chants religieux de l'Islam*. Ocora 580038. Compact disk.

Muḥammad, Abū al-'Ilā. 1995. *Abu al-Ila Muhammad*. Les Artistes Arabes Associés AAA 114, Club du Disque Arabe CDA 401. Compact disk.

Music of the Nile Valley. c. 1980. Lyrichord LLST 7355. LP disk.

Musicians of the Nile. 1988. *Les musiciens du Nil*. Ocora C559006. Compact disk.

————. 1997. *Egypt: Music of the Nile from the Desert to the Sea.* Virgin 724384456924 LC 3098. 2 compact disks.

'Omar, Yusuf. n.d. *Iraq: Makamat par l'Ensemble al-Tchalghî al-Baghdâdî et Yusuf Omar.* Ocora OCR 79. LP disk.

————. 1995. *Le maqâm irakien.* Maison des Cultures du Monde W260063. 2 compact disks.

Qabbānjī, Muḥammad. 1994. *Le maqam en Irak: Congrès du Caire 1932.* Les Artistes Arabes Associés, Club du Disque Arabe AAA097. 2 compact disks.

Al-Qundarjī, Rashīd. 1996. *Musique savante d'Irak: Le fausset de Bagdad.* Nanterre: Al-Sur ALCD 183. Compact disk.

Racy, Ali Jihad. c. 1978. *Ancient Egypt: A Tribute.* Lyrichord LLST 7347. LP disk.

Redouane, Aïcha. 1993. *Egypte.* Ocora/Radio France C 560020. Compact disk.

Sabbāgh, Farḥān. 1992. *Recital de oud à Berlin.* Les Artistes Arabes Associés, Club du Disque Arabe AAA047. Compact disk.

Sāhir, Kāẓim. 1993. *al-'Azīz ghinā' wa-alḥān Kāẓim al-Sāhir.* Kuwait: Naẓā'ir NZR 08. Compact disk.

Sayyid Darwīsh. 1995. *Shaykh Sayyid Darwish.* Les Artistes Arabes Associés, Club du Disque Arabe AAA 096. Compact disk.

Shakkūr, Hamza. 1994. *Musique des derviches tourneurs de Damas.* Auvidis B 6813. Compact disk.

Shamma, Naseer. c. 1995. *Histoire d'amour orientale: Le luth de Baghdad.* Institut du Monde Arabe 50310-2. Compact disk.

Sunbāṭī, Riyāḍ. c. 1990. *Aghār min nasmat al-janūb.* Cairo: Ṣawt al-Qāhira, Sīdī 94 SDCD 01B31. Compact disk.

————. c. 1990. *Al-qalb ya'shaq kull jamīl.* Ṣawt al-Qāhira, Sīdī 94 SDCD 01B50. Compact disk.

————. c. 1990. *Aqbal al-layl.* Ṣawt al-Qāhira, Sīdī 94 SDCD 01B26. Compact disk.

————. c. 1990. *Aqūlak ayh.* Ṣawt al-Qāhira, Sīdī 94 SDCD 01B27. Compact disk.

————. c. 1990. *Arūḥ li-mīn.* Ṣawt al-Qāhira, Sīdī 94 SDCD 01B22. Compact disk.

————. c. 1990. *Dalīlī iḥtār.* Ṣawt al-Qāhira, Sīdī SDCD 01B19. Compact disk.

————. c. 1990. *Dhikriyāt.* Ṣawt al-Qāhira, Sīdī 94 SDCD 01B20. Compact disk.

————. c. 1990. *Ghanna al-rabī'.* Ṣawt al-Qāhira, Sīdī 94 SDCD 01B14. Compact disk.

————. c. 1990. *Ghulubt aṣaliḥ fī rūḥī.* Ṣawt al-Qāhira, Sīdī 94 SDCD 01B36. Compact disk.

————. c. 1990. *Hallit layālī al-qamar.* Ṣawt al-Qāhira, Sīdī 94 SDCD 01B77. Compact disk.

————. c. 1990. *Al-ḥubb kidah.* Ṣawt al-Qāhira, Sīdī 94 SDCD 01B47. Compact disk.

————. c. 1990. *Jaddidt ḥubbak layh.* Ṣawt al-Qāhira, Sīdī 94 SDCD 01B65. Compact disk.

————. c. 1990. *Lā yā ḥabībī.* Ṣawt al-Qāhira, Sīdī 94 SDCD 01B69. Compact disk.

————. c. 1990. *Lissah fākir.* Ṣawt al-Qāhira, Sīdī 94 SDCD 01B70. Compact disk.

————. c. 1990. *Udhkurīnī.* Ṣawt al-Qāhira, Sīdī 94 SDCD 01B21. Compact disk.

————. c. 1990. *Yā ṭūl 'adhābī.* Ṣawt al-Qāhira, Sīdī 94 SDCD 01B80. Compact disk.

————. c. 1990. *Yā ṭūlimnī.* Ṣawt al-Qāhira, Sīdī 94 SDCD 01B81. Compact disk.

Syria: Sunnite Islam. 1973. EMI Odeon 3C 064-17885. LP disk.

Syrie: Adīb Dāyikh et l'ensemble al-Kindī. 1995. Notes by Bernard Mousali. Paris: Institut du Monde Arabe REF 50314–2. Compact disk.

Touma, Habib Hassan. 1971. *The Music of the Syrian Orthodox Church.* UNESCO Collection, Musical Sources, Religious Psalmody, (4)2. LP disk.

————. 1996. *Église syriaque orthodoxe d'Antioche: Chants liturgiques du Carême et du Vendredi Saint.* Inédit W260072. Compact disk.

al-Tuḥāmī, Shaykh Yasīn. 1998. *The Magic of the Sufi Inshād: Sheikh Yasin al-Tuhami.* Long Distance 3039552 ARC 338. 2 compact disks.

Turāthīyāt: Munaqqa'āt 'Irāqīyah. c. 1990. Oak Park, Mich.: Spring Production 101. Compact disk.

Umm Kulthūm. 1989–. *Oum Kaltsoum.* 8 vols. Les Artistes Arabes Associés AAA005, 024–030, Club du Disque Arabe CDA 401. 8 compact disks.

————. c. 1990. *Aghānī waṭaniyyah. Juz'* 1–2. Cairo: Ṣawt al-Qāhira, Sīdī 94 SDCD 01B53–54. 2 compact disks.

————. c. 1990. *Anta al-ḥubb: Sayyidat al-ghinā' al-'arabī.* Sīdī 94 SDCD 01B59. Compact disk.

————. c. 1990. *Fīlm 'Āyidah.* Ṣawt al-Qāhira, Sīdī 94 SDCD 01B42. Compact disk.

————. c. 1990. *Fīlm Fāṭima.* Ṣawt al-Qāhira, Sīdī 94 SDCD 01B43. Compact disk.

————. c. 1990. *Fīlm Rābi'a al-'Adawiyyah.* Ṣawt al-Qāhira, Sīdī 94 SDCD 01B44. Compact disk.

————. c. 1990. *Qiṣṣat al-ams.* Ṣawt al-Qāhira, Sīdī 94 SDCD 01B17. Compact disk.

————. 1995–1997. *La diva.* 5 vols. EMI 352702, 310953-2, 310957-2, 310959-2, 310960-2. 5 compact disks.

————. 1998. *Sayyidat al-tarab.* EMI Arabia 310962-2. Compact disk.

Wasla d'Alep: Chants traditionnels de Syrie. 1988. Maison des Cultures du Monde MCM 260007. Compact disk.

Wenzel, Jochen, and Christian Poché. 1992. *Syrian Orthodox Church: Antioch Liturgy.* UNESCO/Audivis D 8039. Compact disk.

Yalcin, Warda, and Esther Lamandier. 1997. *Chants de l'Église d'Orient en araméen.* Alienor AL 1070. Compact disk.

THE ARABIAN PENINSULA

'Abduh, Muḥammad. 1991. *Sha'biyyāt.* Ṣawt al-Jazīra MACD 516-517. 2 compact disks.

Aman, Mohammed. 2001. *Arabie Saoudite. Mohammed Aman. Le majass, musique classique du Hijaz.* Ocora, Radio France. Compact disk.

Arabie Saoudite. Musique de 'Unayzah, ancienne cité du najd. 1999. Maison des Cultures du Monde W260087. Compact disk.

Archives de la musique arabe. 1987–. Ocora C558678. Compact disks.

Bahat, Noemi, and Avner Bahat. *The Yemenite Jews.* 1990. Auvidis D 8024. Compact disk.

Bakewell, Anderson. 1985. *The Afro-Arabian Crossroad: Music of the Tihama on the Red Sea, North Yemen.* Lyricord LLST 7384. LP disk.

Bhattacharya, Deben. n.d. (c. 1970). *Musique des bédouins.* Paris, Bam, Folklore et musiques de l'univers. LD 5783. LP disk.

Chant sacré du Yémen. 2000. Institut du Monde Arabe. Compact disk.

Chants du Hadramawt. 1998. Auvidis/UNESCO D 8273. Compact disk.

Christensen, Dieter. 1993. *Arts traditionels du Sultanat d'Oman.* Auvidis/UNESCO D 8211. Compact disk.

Congrès du Caire, 1932: Musique arabe, savante et populaire. 1988. Édition Bibliothèque Nationale, France APN 88-9, 88-10. 2 compact disks.

Fidjeri: Chants des pêcheurs de perles. 1992. Auvidis D 8046. Compact disk.

Hachlef, Ahmed. 1994. *La musique de Bahreïn: Anthologie de la musique arabe.* Club du Disque Arabe AAA 104. Compact disk.

Al-Hārithī, Muḥammad. 1997. *Le chant de Sanaa: Musique classique du Yémen.* Institut du Monde Arabe IMA-CD 26. Compact disk.

Hassan, Schéhérazade. 1998. *Yémen: Chants du Ḥaḍramawt.* Auvidis-UNESCO D 8273. Compact disk.

Ibn Faris, Muhammad, Dahi Ibn Walid, and Muhammad Zuwayid. 1994. *La musique de Bahreïn.* Les Artistes Arabes Associés, AAA 104. Compact disk.

Jargy, Simon. 1994a. *Les chants des femmes.* VDE CD 783. Compact disk.

———. 1994b. *Le sowt, musique des villes*. VDE CD 782. Compact disk.

Jargy, Simon, and Poul Røvsing-Olsen. 1994. *Poésie chantée des bédouins*. VDE-Gallo VDE CD-780. Compact disk.

Jargy, Simon, and Ali Zakariyya al-Ansari. 1994. *A Musical Anthology of the Arabian Peninsula*. Vol. 1: *Sung Poetry of the Bedouins*. Vol. 2: *Music of the Pearl Divers*. Vol. 3: *Ṣawt, Music from the City*. Vol. 4: *Women's Songs*. Geneva: VDE-Gallo, CD 758-61. 4 compact disks.

Jenkins, Jean, and Poul Røvsing-Olsen. 1976. *Music in the World of Islam*. 1. *The Human Voice*; 2. *Lutes, Strings*; 4. *Flutes and Trumpets*; 5. *Reeds and Bagpipes*; 6. *Drums and Rhythms*. Tangent Records, TGS 131–136. LP disks.

Johnson, Ragnar. [1975] 1999. *Music from Yemen Arabia: Sanaani, Laheji, Adeni*. Rounder CD 5156. Compact disk.

———. 1975. *Music from Yemen Arabia: Samar*. Lyrichord LLST 7284. LP disk.

Krémer, Gérard. 1996. *Yémen: Musiques des hauts plateaux*. PlayaSound PS 65179. Compact disk.

Lambert, Jean. 1997. *Mohammed al-Hārithī: Chant et luth de Ṣan'ā'*. Institut du Monde Arabe, Media 7 IMA-CD 26. Compact disk.

Maddāḥ, Ṭalāl. 1986. *Sīdī Qum*. Sharikat Ṣawt al-Jazīrah al-'Arabīyah LP ALJAZ 1. LP disk.

El-Mallah, Issam. 1994. *Die Musik einer alten Hochkultur: Das Sultanat Oman*. Oman: Ministry of Information. Compact disk.

The Music of Islām. Vol. 11: *Yémen*. 1998. Celestial Harmonies, 13151-2. Compact disk.

Music of South Arabia. 1951. Folkways P 421. LP disk.

Musiques traditionelles du Sultanat d'Oman. c. 1990. Paris: Buda Records 92703-2. Compact disk.

Poché, Christian. 1976. *Zaidi and Shafi'i: Islamic Religious Chanting from North Yemen*. UNESCO collection, Musical Sources, Philips 6586 040. LP disk.

Poché, Christian, and Jochen Wenzel. 1988. *Yémen du nord: Musique traditionnelle du nord*. Auvidis D 8004. Compact disk.

Racy, Ali Jihad. 1988. *Tanbura Music of the Gulf*, Vol. 2. Arab Gulf States Folklore Center. Cassette tape.

Røvsing-Olsen, Poul. 1968. *Pêcheurs de perles et musiciens du Golfe Persique*. Ocora OCR 42. LP disk.

Saint-Hilaire, Alain, and Karen Saint-Hilaire. 1971. *Les Emirats du Golfe Arabique*. Alvarès, Paris. C 471. LP disk.

Shiloah, Amnon. 1978. *Bedouin Music of Southern Sinai*. Ethnic Folkways Records EE 4204. LP disk.

Al-Tawḥīd. 1994. Maison des Cultures du Monde, Auvidis W260001. Compact disk.

Touma, Habib Hassan. 1979. *Fidjeri Songs of the Bahrain Pearl Divers*. Musical Sources, Vol. 23. UNESCO. Philips 064-18371. LP disk.

Yémen du nord: Musique traditionnelle du nord. 1988. Auvidis D 8004. Compact disk.

ARMENIA

Arménie: Chants liturgiques du moyen-âge. c. 1970. Ocora OCR 66. LP disk.

Arménie: Musique des Achough. c. 1972. Ocora OCR 59. LP disk.

Arménie: Musique instrumentale. c. 1972. Ocora OCR 67. LP disk.

Arménie: Musique de tradition populaire. c. 1970. Ocora OCR 50. LP disk.

Armianskaia dukhovnaia muzyka V–XIII vv (Armenian Sacred Music of the Fifth to Thirteenth Centuries). 1991. USSR: Melodiya 1000265. Compact disk.

Chants liturgiques arméniens: Chants liturgiques du Carême et des fêtes de Pâques (Armenian Liturgical Chant: Chant for Lent and Easter). 1989. Auvidis D 8015. Compact disk.

Chants liturgiques du moyen-age et musique instrumentale. 1988. Ocora C559001. Compact disk.

Gasparian, Djivan. 1996. *Apricots from Eden*. Traditional Crossroads CD 4276. Compact disk.

———. 1999. *Armenia*. WDR/World Network 32.377. Compact disk.

———. 2000. *Armenian Fantasies*. Frankfurt am Main: Network Medien 34.801. Compact disk.

Hagopian, Richard. 1993. *Armenian Music through the Ages*. Smithsonian/Folkways SF 40414. Compact disk.

Kalaschjan. 1992. *Rural and Urban Traditional Music from Armenia*. Wergo 281505-2. Compact disk.

Komitas, Vardapet. 1970. *The Music of Komitas*. KCC 100 Komitas Centennial Committee. 2 LP disks.

———. 1989. *Arménia: Chants et danses populaires d'Arménie*. Empreinte digitale ED 13002. Compact disk.

———. 1990. *Yerketsoghutuink srbo pataraki/Divine Liturgy*. New Albion Records NA 033. Compact disk.

———. 1995. *The Voice of Komitas Vardapet*. Traditional Crossroads CD 4275. Compact disk.

Manukian, Yeghish. c. 1995. *Arménie, sources*. Paris: Buda Records 92610-2. Compact disk.

Markarian, Varoujan. 1995. *Armenian Chant*. Holyland 17. Compact disk.

Music of the Russian Middle East. 1951. Folkways P 416. LP disk.

Musique de tradition populaire et des Achough. 1993. Ocora/Radio France C 580005. Compact disk.

KURDISTAN

Christensen, Dieter. 1965. *Kurdish Folk Music from Western Iran*. New York: Ethnic Folkways Library FE 3103. LP disk.

Groupe Koma Zozan. 1990. *Chants et musiques du Kurdistan*. Arion ARN 64263. Compact disk.

Groupe Musical du Kurdistan. 1994. *Chants du Kurdistan*. Nanterre: Al-Sur ALCD 125. Compact disk.

Kurdish Folk Songs and Dances. 1955. Folkways FE 4469. LP disk.

Kurdistan. [1974] 1989. UNESCO Collection Auvidis D8023. Compact disk.

Kurdistan: Zikr et chants soufis. 1994. Ocora/Radio France C 560071/72. 2 compact disks.

Music of Kurdistan. n.d. Koch 333362. Compact disk.

Musiques et chants du Kurdistan: Les espaces Kurdes. 1995. Les Artistes Arabes Associés AAA127. Compact disk.

Perwer, Şivan. 1989. *Chants du Kurdistan*. Auvidis B6145. Compact disk.

Temo. 1995. *Chants et musiques kurdes*. Auvidis B6815. Compact disk.

TURKEY

Archives de la musique turque. 1995. Ocora/Radio France C 560082. 2 compact disks.

Bacanos, Yorgo. 1998. *Udi Yorgo Bacanos, 1900–1977*. Traditional Crossroads CD 4287. Compact disk.

Bartók, Béla, comp. 1996. *Turkish Folk Music Collection*. Hungaroton HCD 18218-9. 2 compact disks.

Beken, Münir Nurettin. 1997. *The Art of the Turkish Ud*. Rounder CD 1135. Compact disk.

Cérémonie du djem alevi. 1998. Ocora/Radio France C 560125. Compact disk.

Chant des derviches de Turquie. 1988. Arion ARN 64061. Compact disk.

Çiçek, Ali Ekber. *Turkish Sufi Music: Folk Lute of Anatolia.* Lyrichord Stereo LLST 7392. Compact disk.

Les derviches de Turquie: Musique soufi. 1994. Playasound PS 65120. Compact disk.

Derviches tourneurs de Turquie: La cérémonie des Mevlevî. 1991. Arion ARN 64159. Compact disk.

Ensemble de Kudsi Erguner. 1990. *Fasl: Musique de l'empire ottoman.* Auvidis B 6737. Compact disk.

———. 1991. *Peshrev and Semai of Tanburi Djemil Bey.* CMP Records CMP CD 3013. Compact disk.

Erguner, Kudsi. 1979. *Meditation on the Ney.* Philips 6586 039. LP disk.

———. 1990. *Le ney turc.* Auvidis D 8204. Compact disk.

Firat, Ozan. 1992. *Musique des troubadours.* Auvidis B 6771. Compact disk.

Folk and Traditional Music of Turkey. 1956. Folkways FE 4404. LP disk.

Gençturk, Vedad. 1996. *L'art du 'ud turc.* Arion ARN 60265. Compact disk.

Great Voices of Constantinople, 1927–33. 1997. Rounder CD 1113. Compact disk.

Les janissaires: Musique martiale de l'Empire Ottoman. 1990. Auvidis B 6738. Compact disk.

Karaca, Kâni. 1998. *Cantillation coranique.* Ocora/Radio France C 560130. Compact disk.

Kartal, Göksel. 1994. *The Art of Taksim.* Traditional Crossroads CD TC4267. Compact disk.

Kenkulian, Hrant. 1994. *Udi Hrant.* Traditional Crossroads CD 4265. Compact disk.

———. 1995. *Udi Hrant: The Early Recordings.* Traditional Crossroads CD 4270-4271. 2 compact disks.

Makam: Musique classique ottomane. 1993. Al-Sur ALCD 114. Compact disk.

Masters of Turkish Music. 1990–1996. Rounder CD 1051, 1111. 2 compact disks.

Musique bektachi: Chants des Achik. 1996. Auvidis D 8069. Compact disk.

Musique de la cour ottomane: Ensemble Ulvi Erguner. 1992. Al-Sur ALCD 108. Compact disk.

Musique classique turque: Hommage à Yunus Emre. 1991. Auvidis D 8303. Compact disk.

Musique populaire et classique de Turquie. 1991. Playasound PS 65069. Compact disk.

Musique savante ottomane. 1996. Les Artistes Arabes Associés AAA 130. Compact disk.

Musique traditionnelle turque. Pièces instrumentales. 1971. Ocora OCR 56. LP disk.

The Mystic Flutes of the Sufis. 1988. JVC VID-25005. Compact disk.

Necdet Yaşar Ensemble. 1992. *Music of Turkey.* Music of the World CDT-128. Compact disk.

Özkan, Talip. 1980. *Turquie: L'art vivant de Talip Özkan.* Ocora C 558561. LP disk.

———. 1992. *The Dark Fire.* Axiom 314-512 003-2. Compact disk.

———. 1993. *L'art vivant de Talip Özkan.* Ocora/Radio France C 580047. Compact disk.

———. 1994. *Turquie: L'art du tanbûr.* Ocora/Radio France C 560042. Compact disk.

Reinhard, Kurt, comp. 1971. *The Music of Turkey: The Music of the Whirling Dervishes (Mevlevi).* Anthology AST 4003. LP disk.

The Road to Keşan: Turkish Rom and Regional Music of Thrace. 2000. Traditional Crossroads CD 6001. Compact disk.

The Sacred Koran: Recitations by Muezzins of Istanbul, the Ottoman Empire. 1988. JVC VID-25006. Compact disk.

Sağ, Arif. *Insan Olmaya Geldim.* Sembol Plak.

———, with Belkis Akkale. *Seher Yıldızı.* ASM Müzik Üretim.

Sağ, Tolga, Erdal Erzincan, and Ismail Özden. *Türküler Sevdamız.* ASM Müzik Üretim.

Şakır, Mehmet. 1998. *Le violon des yayla.* Ocora/Radio France C 560116. Compact disk.

Signell, Karl. 1970–1972. Turkish tape recordings. Signell collection, Archive of Folk Culture, Library of Congress, Washington, D.C. Recordings include concerts, interviews, mosque and Sufi musics, and many examples of *taksim, seyir,* and other genres. Index and copies available to qualified scholars.

Le sipsi des yayla/Sipsi of the Yayala. 1998. Ocora/Radio France C 560103. Compact disk.

Song Creators in Eastern Turkey. 1993. Smithsonian Folkways SF 40432. Compact disk.

Songs and Dances of Turkey. 1956. Folkways FW 8801. LP disk.

Sulukule: Rom Music of Istanbul. 1998. Traditional Crossroads CD 4289. Compact disk.

Tanbûrî Cemil Bey. 1994–1995. *Tanburi Cemil Bey.* Traditional Crossroads CD 4264, 4274. 3 compact disks.

Tanrıkorur, Cinuçen. 1986. *Turquie.* Ocora C558574. LP disk.

Tchinar, Feyzullah. 1995. *Chants sacrés d'Anatolie.* Ocora C 580057. Compact disk.

Tewari, Laxmi G. 1972. *Turkish Village Music.* Nonesuch H-72050. LP disk.

Turkey: A Musical Journey. 1975. Nonesuch H-72067. LP disk.

Turkey: An Esoteric Sufi Ceremony. n.d. JVC World Sounds. VICG-5345.

Turkey. 1: The Music of the Mevlevi. c. 1960. Bärenreiter-Musicaphon BM 30 L 2019. LP disk.

Turkey: Traditional Songs and Dances. c. 1977. Lyrichord LLST 7356. LP disk.

Turkish Folk Music. c. 1976. Lyrichord LLST 7289. LP disk.

Turkish Music. 2: Classical and Religious Music. n.d. Bärenreiter-Musicaphon BM 30 L 2020. LP disk.

Turquie: L'art du tanbûr ottoman. 1990. VDE VDE VD-586. Compact disk.

Turquie, aşik: Chants d'amour et de sagesse d'Anatolie. 1991. Maison des Cultures du Monde W260025. Compact disk.

Turquie: Cérémonie des derviches Kadiri. 1990. VDE VDE CD-587. Compact disk.

Turquie: Chants sacrés d'Anatolie. 1973. Ocora OCR 65. LP disk.

Turquie: Concert de musique classique ottomane. 1995. Chant du Monde CMT 2741013. Compact disk.

Turquie: Musique soufi. 1977. Ocora 558522. LP disk.

Turquie: Musique soufi, ilâhî, et nefes. 1991. Maison des Cultures du Monde W260021. Compact disk.

Turquie: Musique tzigane. 1984. Ocora 558649. LP disk.

Turquie: Musiques villageoises d'Anatolie. 1994. VDE VDE CD-797. Compact disk.

Turquie: Voyages d'Alain Gheebrant en Anatolie (1956–1957). 1985. Ocora 558634-558635. 2 LP disks.

Uzel, Nezih, and Kudsi Erguner. 1987. *Musique soufi.* Ocora C559017. Compact disk.

Women of Istanbul. 1998. Traditional Crossroads CD 4280. Compact disk.

The Works of Tatyos Efendi. 1996–. Traditional Crossroads TC4277-78. 2 compact disks.

IRAN

Akhbari, Djalal. 1996. *L'art du santûr persan.* Arion ARN 60351. Compact disk.

Alizādeh, Hossain. c. 1995. *Musique iranienne, improvisations.* Buda 92622-2 2 compact disks.

Alizādeh, Hossain, and Majdid Khaladj. 1998. *The Art of Improvisation.* Haus der Kulturen der Welt, Wergo 281530-2. Compact disk.

Anthology of Persian Music, 1930–1990. 1991. Washington, D.C.: Mage Publishers, Mage CD 22-1. Compact disk.

Bina, Sima. 1995. *Sima Bina: Persian Classical Music.* Nimbus NI 5391. Compact disk.

———. 1997. *Āvā-ye sahrā/Sounds from the Plain.* Canoga Park, Calif.: Caltex. Compact disk.

Chemirani, Djamchid. 1991. *Djamchid Chemirani, zarb.* Auvidis B 6752. Compact disk.

Dastgah nava. 1995. Traditional Crossroads CD 4273. Compact disk.

Digard, Jean-Pierre, comp. 1974. *Iran: Baxtyâri, nomades de la montagne.* SELAF-OROSTOM CETO 747. LP disk.

During, Jean, comp. 1979–1982. *Iran: Anthologie de la musique traditionnelle*. Ocora 558540, 558550, 558562, 558563. 4 LP disks.

———. [1981] 1992. *Baloutchistan: Musique d'extase et de guérison*. Ocora C580017-18. 2 compact disks.

———, comp. 1993. *Asie Centrale: Les maîtres du dotâr*. Geneva: Archives Internationales de Musique Populaire, AIMP 26. Compact disk.

———. 1997. *The Mystic Fiddle of the Proto-Gypsies, Masters of Trance Music*. Shanachie 65013. Compact disk.

Ensemble Moshtaq. c. 1992. *Musique savante persane*. Buda 92532-2. Compact disk.

Folk Music of Iran: The Luristan and Fars Provinces. c. 1970. Lyrichord LLST 7261. LP disk.

Googoosh. 2000. *Googoosh*. Pars Video, Caltex CLX 2046. 4 compact disks.

Ilāhī, Nūr ʿAli. 1996. *La musique céleste d'Ostâd Elâhi: Au luth sacré tanbûr*. Chant du Monde CMT 274 1026. Compact disk.

———. 1997. *Les chemins de l'amour divin/Paths of Divine Love. Ostad Elahi*. Chant du Monde CMT 2741083. Compact disk.

———. 1999. *Harmonies célestes*. Chant du Monde CMT 274 1122. Compact disk.

Iran. c. 1970. Bärenreiter Musicaphon BM 30 L 2004-5. 2 LP disks.

L'Iran: Le ney. 1973. CBS 65.414. LP disk.

Iran: Persian Classical Music. 1974. Elektra Nonesuch 72060. Compact disk.

Iranian Dastgah. 1971. Philips 6586 005. LP disk.

Izadi, Souroush. 1995. *La musique persane savante*. Auvidis B 6808. Compact disk.

Kalhor, Kayhan. 1997. *Ghazal: Lost Songs of the Silk Road. Persian and Indian Improvisations*. Shanachie 64096. Compact disk.

———. 1998. *Scattering Stars Like Dust*. Traditional Crossroads CD 4288. Compact disk.

The Kamkars. 1997. *Nightingale with a Broken Wing*. London: Womad WSCD 009. Compact disk.

Khaladj, Madjid. 1994. *Iran, l'art du tombak (zarb)*. Buda 92594-2. Compact disk.

———. c. 1997. *Le repertoire fondamental de Maître Tehrâni*. Buda 92672-2. Compact disk.

Kīānī, Majīd. 1991. *Majid Kiâni, santur*. Auvidis B 6756. Compact disk.

———. 1992. *Haft dastgāh-e mūsīqī-e Irān* (Seven *Dastgāh-hā* of Iranian Music). Tehran: Iran Seda SITC-126. Compact disk.

Kurdish Folk Music from Western Iran. 1966. Folkways FE 4103. LP disk.

Les maîtres de la musique traditionnelle. 1991–1992. Ocora/Radio France C 560024–560026. 3 compact disks.

Malek, Hossein. n.d. *Classical Music of Iran*. Lyrichord LLST 7403. LP disk.

Manahedji, Behnam. 1993. *Master of Persian Santoor*. Wergo SM 1508-2. Compact disk.

Marzīyah. 1995. *Monadjat: Musique traditionnelle persane*. Auvidis B 6825. Compact disk.

Morādi, Shahmirza. 1994. *The Music of Lorestan, Iran: Shahmirza Morādi, Sornā*. Wyastone Leys, Monmouth, England: Nimbus NI 5397. Compact disk.

Musavi, Mohammad. c. 1995. *Iran: Le ney de Mohammad Musavi*. Buda 92645-2. Compact disk.

Music of Iran: The Tar. 1968–1970. Lyrichord LLST 7201, 7220. 2 LP disks.

Mūsīqī-ye navāḥī-ye Irān (Regional Music of Iran). 1998. Tehran: Anjoman-e Mūsīqī-ye Irān. 16 albums, each with 6 cassettes and a booklet.

Musique iranienne. 1992. Harmonia Mundi HMA 190391. Compact disk.

Musique persane. [1971] 1987. Ocora/Radio France C559008. Compact disk.

ʿOmoumi, Hossein. 1993. *Persian Classical Music: Hossein Omoumi, Ney*. Nimbus NI 5359. Compact disk.

———. 2000. *The Song of the Ney*. Nimbus NI 7061. 2 compact disks.

Pāyvar, Farāmarz. 1995. *Musique classique iranienne*. Al-Sur ALCD 164. Compact disk.

A Persian Heritage: Classical Music of Iran. 1974. Nonesuch H-72060. LP disk.

The Persian Santur: Music of Iran. 1970. Nonesuch H-72039. LP disk.

Persische Kunstmusik. 1972. Harmonia Mundi 1C 065-99 632. LP disk.

Rastigār-Nizhād, Nāṣir. 1964–1966. *Santūr Recital*. Lyrichord LL 7135, 7165, 7166. 3 LP disks.

Shadjariān, Mohammad Rezā. 1990. *Musique classique persane*. Ocora/Radio France C 559097. Compact disk.

Shadjariān, Mohammad Rezā, and Kayhan Kalhor. *Night Silence Desert*. Traditional Crossroads CD 80702-4299-2. Compact disk.

Shenāsā, Masʿoud. 1996. *Santour*. Les Artistes Arabes Associés AAA 140. Compact disk.

Shūshā. c. 1972. *Persian Love Songs and Mystic Chants*. Lyrichord LLST 7235. LP disk.

Sulaymānī, Qurbān. 1995. *Mūsīqī shamāl Khurāsān/Music of the Bards from Iran, Northern Khorasan*. Los Angeles: Kereshmeh Records, KCD-106. Compact disk.

The Tar: Music of Iran. n.d. Lyrichord LLST 7201. LP disk.

Tārif, Sadiq. 1995. *Chants et musiques classiques persans*. Institut du Monde Arabe 50315-2. Compact disk.

Youssefzadeh, Ameneh, comp. *Bardes du Khorassan*. 1998. Ocora C 560136. Compact disk.

Zonis, Ella Mahler, and Ruhallah Khaleqi. 1991. *Classical Music of Iran: The Dastgah Systems*. Smithsonian Folkways CD SF 40039. Compact disk.

CENTRAL ASIA

Alimatov, Turgun. 1995. *Ouzbekistan: Turgun Alimatov*. Ocora/Radio France C 560086. Compact disk.

Asie Centrale: Traditions classiques. 1993. Ocora/Radio France C 560035–36. 2 compact disks.

At the Bazaar of Love: The Ilyas Malayev Ensemble. 1997. Shanachie Records 64081. Compact disk.

Azerbaijan 1. n.d. A Musical Anthology of the Orient, 24. Kassel: Bärenreiter-Musicaphon, BM 30 L 2024. LP disk.

Badakhshan: Pamir, chants et musiques du toit du monde. 2000. Buda 92744-2. Compact disk.

Bukhara: Musical Crossroads of Asia. Smithsonian Folkways 40050. Compact disk.

During, Jean. 1989. *Azerbaidjan: Musique et chants des ashiqs. Ashiq Hasan. Emran Heydari, Alim Qasimov*. Geneva: Archives Internationales de Musique Populaire, AIMP XIX, VDE-Gallo CD-613. Compact disk.

———. 1993. *Asie Centrale: Les maîtres du dotâr*. 1993. Geneva, AIMP 26; VDE VDE CD-735. Compact disk.

———. 1998. *Musiques d'Asie Centrale: L'esprit d'une tradition*. Paris: Cité de la Musique/Actes Sud. Compact disk.

During, Jean, and Eldar Mansurov. 1989. *Azerbayjan: Musique traditionnelle*. Chant du Monde LDX 274 901. Compact disk.

Dvenadtsat uygurskikh mukamov (The Twelve Uighur *Muqam*). 1983–1986. Tashkent: Melodiya Records, S-30. LP disks.

Les grandes voix du passé (1940–1965) (Uzbekistan: Great Voices of the Past, 1940–1965). 1999. Ocora/Radio France C 560142. Compact disk.

Hamidov, Abdorahim. 1997. *L'art du dotâr*. Recording and notes by Jean During. Ocora/Radio France C 560111. Compact disk.

Huun-Huur-Tu. 1993. *Sixty Horses in My Herd: Old Songs and Tunes of Tuva*. Shanachie 64050. Compact disk.

———. 1994. *The Orphan's Lament*. Shanachie 64058. Compact disk.

Ilyas Malayev Ensemble. 1997. *At the Bazaar of Love: Timeless Central Asian Maqâm Music*. Shanachie 64081. Compact disk.

Kholov, Davlatmand. 1992. *Davlatmand: Musiques savantes et populaires du Tadjikistan*. Maison des Cultures du Monde/Auvidis W260038. Compact disk.

Kirghizes et Kazakhs: Maîtres du komuz et du dombra. 1997. Ocora/Radio France C 560121. Compact disk.

Levin, Theodore. 1999. *Tuva: Among the Spirits. Sound, Music, and Nature in Sakha and Tuva.* Smithsonian Folkways SFW 40452.

Maqâm Navâ. 1997. Ocora/Radio France C 560102. Compact disk.

Mongolie: Chants Kazakhs et tradition épique de l'Ouest. 1993. Ocora/Radio France C 580051. Compact disk.

Morita, Minoru. 1992. *Music of Kazakhstan. 1: Songs Accompanied on Dombra and Solo Kobyz.* King Records (Tokyo, Japan), KICC 5166. Compact disk.

———. 1995. *Music of Kazakhstan. 2: Dombra Music of Kazakhstan and Songs Accompanied on Dombra.* King Records (Tokyo, Japan), KICC 5199. Compact disk.

Music of Central Asia: Uzbekistan. 1991. Tokyo: World Music Library KICC 5108. Compact disk.

Music of Khorezm. 1996. Auvidis/UNESCO D 8269. Compact disk.

Music of the Russian Middle East. 1951. Folkways P 416. LP disk.

Musique sur les routes de la soie. 1992. Auvidis B 6776. Compact disk.

Musique tadjike du Badakhshan. 1993. Auvidis D 8212. Compact disk.

Musiques du Kirghizstan. [c. 1995.] Buda 92631-2. Compact disk.

Musiques traditionnelles d'Asie centrale: Chants harmoniques touvas. 1995. Silex 225222. Compact disk.

Ouzbékistan: Musique classique instrumentale. 1998. VDE-Gallo VDE CD-974. Compact disk.

Songs and Dances of the S.S.R. Middle East. 1956. Folkways FP 916. LP disk.

Songs and Melodies of the Uighurs. 1995. PAN Records 2027. Compact disk.

Tadjikistan: Chants des bardes. 1998. VDE-Gallo VDE CD-973. Compact disk.

Tadjikistan-Ouzbékistan: Tradition savante shash maqam. c. 1995. Buda 92639-2. Compact disk.

Trebinjac, Sabine, and Jean During. 1990. *Turkestan chinois/Xinjiang, Musiques ouigoures.* Ocora/Radio France C 559092-3. 2 compact disks.

Turkmenistan: Chants des femmes bakhshi. 1995. Maison des Cultures du Monde W260064. Compact disk.

Tuva: Voices from the Center of Asia. Smithsonian Folkways 40017. Compact disk.

Uzlyau: Guttural Singing of the Peoples of the Sayan, Altai, and Ural Mountains. 1993. Pan Records PAN 2019CD. Compact disk.

Voyage en URSS: Anthologie de la musique instrumentale et vocal des peuples de l'URSS. c. 1985. Chant du Monde LDX 74001-74010. 10 LP disks.

Yultchieva, Monâjât. 1994. *Ouzbekistan: Monâjât Yultchieva (Maqam d'Asie Centrale. 1: Ferghana).* Ocora/Radio France C 560060. Compact disk.

Zerańska-Kominek, Slawomira. 1992. *Turkmenistan: Music of the Bakhshy.* VDE-Gallo CD-651. Compact disk.

———. 1994. *Turkmen Epic Singing: Köroglu.* Auvidis/UNESCO D 8213. Compact disk.

ISRAEL

Argov, Zohar. 1988. *Zohar Argov's Greatest Hits.* ACUM C.D.R. 990. Compact disk.

Ben, Zehava. 1999. *Best of Zehava Ben.* Paris: Atoll Music 521660-2. Compact disk.

Ben-Haim, Paul. 1962. *The Sweet Psalmist of Israel.* Columbia ML 5451. LP disk.

Bhattacharya, Deben. c. 1960. *In Israel Today: Songs of the Jews from Morocco.* New York: Westminster W-9806. LP disk.

———. c. 1960. *In Israel Today: Songs of the Jews from Yemen, the Atlas Mountains, Tunisia, and Spain.* New York: Westminster W-9810. LP disk.

———, comp. 1971. *Music from Israel.* Argo ZFB 50. LP disk.

Boniche, Lili. c. 1997. *Trésors de la chanson judéo-arabe.* Blue Silver 79 102 2 BS. Compact disk.

Braun, Yehezkiel. 1996. *Yetsirot le-makhelah/ Choral Works.* Tel Aviv: Bet ha-tefutsot BTR 9602. Compact disk.

Burning Bush. 1999. *Folksongs from Israel.* West Sussex: ARC Music EUCD1513. Compact disk.

Chants de traverse: Récital de musiques judéo-marocaines. Paris: Atoll Music. 2 compact disks.

Chants Hébreux d'Israël et d'Orient. 1995. Al Sur ALCD 139. Compact disk.

Chekroun, Alain. 2000. *Chants des synagogues du Maghreb.* Magda MGD027. Compact disk.

Damari, Shoshana. 1995. *Israeli, Yiddish, Yemenite, and Other Folk Songs.* Omega Vanguard Classics OVC 6025. Compact disk.

Danna International. 1998. *Diva.* Tel Aviv: Dancepool DANA1PCD. Compact disk.

Diaspora Yeshiva Band. 1998. *Land of Our Fathers/Erets avotenu.* Tel Aviv: RARE Productions. Compact disk.

Easter Ceremonies in Jerusalem. 1957. Folkways FR 8951. LP disk.

Einstein, Arik. [1969] 1995. *Puzy.* Tel Aviv: Phonokol 4070-2. Compact disk.

Ethnix. 1995. *Ha-Osef shel Etnix: Sefer disk.* Tel Aviv: Helicon HL8115. Compact disk.

Festival ha-zemer ha-Hasidi 1985/Israeli Chassidic Festival 1985. Tel Aviv: Isra-Art Productions FEST-85. LP disk.

Fleischer, Tsippi. c. 1999. *Israel at Fifty.* Greenville: Opus One CD175. Compact disk.

Folk Music of Palestine. 1951. Folkways FE 4408. LP disk.

Gadalnu yahad: Osef ha-yovel shel Yisrael, ha-musikah/Israel's 240 Greatest Songs in Celebration of Its Fiftieth Anniversary. 1998. Tel Aviv: Hed Arzi. 11 compact disks.

Ga'on, Yehoram. 1996. *Yehoram Ga'on.* Hed Arzi CD 15813. Compact disk.

———. 2000. *Osef ha-ladino ha-gadol/Ladino Masterpieces.* NMC Gold 20383-2, 20384-2, 20385-2. 6 compact disks.

Gavrielov, Miki. 1998. *Ha-Osef Miki Gavri'elov.* Phonokol 4138-2. Compact disk.

Gerson-Kiwi, Edith. c. 1960. *Oriental Music, Israel.* American Zionist Council E4 K1 5996. LP disk.

Great Artists Perform Israeli Music. 1975. Musical Heritage Society MHS 3241. LP disk.

Gronich, Shlomo. c. 1994. *Shelomoh Gronikh ve-makehlat.* Ramat Gan: Hed Arzi 15615. Compact disk.

Hadar, Joseph. 1997. *Erev shel shoshanim/Evening of Roses.* Tel Aviv: Phonokol 5125-2. Compact disk.

Ha-Festival ha-Yisre'eli le-shire yeladim mispar. 14: The Israeli Children's Song Festival Number 14. 1983. Tel Aviv: Isradisc. LP disk.

Halonot ha-gevohim. 1967. *The High Windows.* Ramat Gan: Hed Arzi BAN 49-47. LP disk.

Hanokh, Shalom. 1993. *Shalom Hanokh be-hofa'ah hayah/Shalom Hanoch in Concert.* Tel Aviv: NMC NMC-82270-2. Compact disk.

Haran, Michael. 1988. *Israeli Music for Cello.* Israel Music Publications MII-CD-7. Compact disk.

Haza, Ofra. 2000. *Melody of the Heart.* Hed Arzi 64027. 3 compact disks.

Hirsh, Nurit. 1992. *Nurit Hirsh.* Ramat Gan: Hed Arzi CD 15508. Compact disk.

Hora: Songs and Dances of Israel. 1961. Elektra EKL 186. LP disk.

Israel. Vol. 1: Traditions liturgiques des communautés juives. Les jours du Kippour. 1977. Ocora 558529. LP disk.

Israel. Vol. 2: Les Juifs d'Ethiopie. 1986. Ocora 558670. LP disk.

Jerusalem Great Synagogue Choir. 1994. *Jerusalem Great Synagogue Choir.* Studio Christal SCACD 11161. Compact disk.

Jewish and Israeli Folk Songs. 1959. Folkways FW 8740. LP disk.

Les juifs yémenites: Diwan judéo-yéménites. 1990. Auvidis D 8024. Compact disk.

Kaspi, Mati. 1992. *Mati Kaspi.* Tel Aviv: CBS Records 80779-2. Compact disk.

Kaveret. [1973.] 1989. *Sipure Pugi/Poogy Tales.* Hed Arzi. Compact disk.

Kraus, Shmulik. 1992. *Galgal mistovev/Spinning Wheel.* Ramat Gan: Hed Arzi 14950. Compact disk.

Lahaḳat ha-Naḥal. 1989. *Lahaḳat ha-Naḥal: Ha-lehiṭim ha-gedolim, 1963–1972*. Hed Arzi 15408. Compact disk.

Leyris, Raymond. 1994. *Cheikh Raymond: Chant d'exil*. Tel Aviv: Magda Music MGD023. Compact disk.

Mazor, Y., ed. 1998. *The Klezmer Tradition in the Land of Israel*. Anthology of Music Traditions in Israel, AMTI CD 9802. Jerusalem: The Jewish Music Research Centre. Compact disk.

Melamed, Nissin Cohen. 1980. *Pirḳe ḥazanut u-fiyuṭim: Be-nusaḥ Yehude Sefarad ha-Yerushalmiyim*. IMI Records 2002/3. 2 LP disks.

Mi-shire tenu'ot ha-no'ar / Songs of Israel's Youth Movements. 1991. Hed Arzi 14469. Compact disk.

Morasha: Traditional Jewish Musical Heritage. 1978. Folkways FE 4203. LP disk.

La musique judéo-arabe. 1992–1993. Les Artistes Arabes Associés 062-072. 2 compact disks.

'Ofrah Ḥazah, Shoshanah Damri, Lahaḳat ha-Naḥal, ha-Geva'ṭron, Shelishiyat Gesher ha-Yarḳon, Ariḳ Einstein ve-aḥerim: Sharim et shirehem ha-mefursamim shel Mosheh Vilenski, Na'omi Shemer ve-Shayḳeh Paiḳov. 1994. Hataḳlit C-3-071/73. 3 compact disks.

Osef festival shire yeladim. 1995–1996. Phonokol 4102-2, 4121-2. 4 compact disks.

Rinat Choir. 1993. *Rinat—Makhelah ḳamerit Yisre'elit: Haḳlaṭot meha-shanim 1972–1956/ Recordings from the Years 1956–1972*. Tel Aviv: NMC 1032-2. 3 compact disks.

Sacred Music of the Moroccan Jews. 2000. Rounder CD 5087. 2 compact disks.

Shalom ḥaver/Good-Bye, My Friend. 1996. Phonokol, Hed Arzi 20197-2. 2 compact disks.

Shemer, Naomi. 1991. *Artsi moladeti: Shireha ha-yafim shel No'omi Shemer/The Beautiful Songs of Naomi Shemer*. Haifa: Hataklit CD 201. Compact disk.

Un siècle de chansons judéo-arabes. 2000. Paris: NFB World NFB 160899. Compact disk.

Sulam. 1992. *Klezmer Music from Tel Aviv*. Wergo 281506-2. Compact disk.

Voice of the Turtle. 1997. *Full Circle: Music of the Spanish Jews of Jerusalem*. Titanic Ti-251. Compact disk.

Wilensky, Moshe. 1993. *Shalekhet ba-lev: Ha-shirim ha-ahuvim shel Mosheh Vilenski/ The Favorite Songs of Moshe Wilensky*. Haifa: Hataklit CD 156. Compact disk.

World Music from Israel. 1998. Frémeaux FA079. 2 compact disks.

Yemenite Passover. 1957. Folkways FW 8921. LP disk.

Yurchenco, Henrietta. 1994. *The Bride's Joys and Sorrows: Songs and Ballads of the Moroccan Jews as Sung by the Women of Tetuan, Morocco*. New York: Global Village CD 148. Compact disk.

Zahavi, David. 1980. *Yesh maḳom ba-'Eden shire David Zehavi li-yeladim/Children's Songs by David Zahavi*. Tel Aviv: CBS Records, 84316. LP disk.

Films and Videos of Middle Eastern Music

Ali, Aisha. 1991. *Dances of Egypt*. Los Angeles: Araf. Videocassette.

———. 1995. *Dances of North Africa*. Los Angeles: Araf. Videocassette.

Basic Middle Eastern Drums and Rhythms, Vol. 1. 1992. Portland, Ore.: Brothers of the Baladi. Videocassette.

Belic, Roko. 2000. *Genghis Blues*. Medium/New Video. Videocassette.

Bhattacharya, Deben. 1992. *Ecstatic Circle*. Guilford, Conn.: Distributed by Audio-Forum. Videocassette.

Cultural Fest. 1988. Jerusalem: Israel Film Service. Videocassette.

Dumon, Dirk. 1996. *I Am a Sufi, I Am a Muslim*. Princeton, N.J.: Films for the Humanities and Sciences. Videocassette.

Eeif perahim: Festival Dalyah 1968. 1987. Jerusalem: Israel Film Service. Videocassette.

Fayrūz. *Fayrūz fī 'l-Qāhira 67*. 1993. Santa Monica, Calif.: Sufian Video Company. Videocassette.

Genini, Izza. 1987. *Hymns of Praise: Les confréries religieuses au moussem Moulay Idriss Zerhoum*. First Run/Icarus Films. Videocassette.

———. 1989. *Malhoune: la parole chantée*. First Run/Icarus Films. Videocassette.

———. 1990. *Gnaouas*. New York: First Run/ Icarus Films. Videocassette.

———. 1993. *Airs en terre berbère: Vibrations en Haut-Atlas*. New York: First Run/Icarus Films. 2 videocassettes.

———. c. 1994. *Lutes and Delights*. First Run/ Icarus Films. Videocassette.

———. c. 1990s. *Aita*. New York: First Run/ Icarus Films. Videocassette.

Going on Fifty: The Israel Philharmonic Orchestra with Zubin Mehta. 1986. West Long Branch, N.J.: Kultur International Films. Videocassette.

Goldman, Michal. 1996. *Umm Kulthūm: A Voice Like Egypt*. Waltham, Mass.: Filmmakers Collaborative. Videocassette.

Goodman, Ruth. 1985. *Night on the Sea of Galilee: Israel Folk Dance Festival*. Long Branch, N.J.: Kultur. Videocassette.

Grabias, David. 1996. *Asiklar: Those Who Are in Love*. Watertown, Mass.: Documentary Educational Resources. Videocassette.

Great Cantors in Cinema. 1993. Waltham, Mass.: National Center for Jewish Film. Videocassette.

Green Voices: A Program of Songs with Artists from Israel's Kibbutsim. 1988. Jerusalem: Israel Film Service. Videocassette.

Haza, Ofra. 1988. *Ofra Haza: From Sunset till Dawn*. Teaneck, N.J.: Ergo Media. Videocassette.

Israel: Sounds in Search of a Home. 1999. Teaneck, N.J.: Ergo Media. Videocassette.

JVC Video Anthology of World Music and Dance. 1988. Tokyo: JVC. 30 videocassettes.

Landoff, Brita. 1995. *Shiwayyah li-qalbī wa-shiwayyah li-rabbī/Lite för mitt hjarta och lite för min Gud*. New York: Filmmakers Library. Videocassette.

el-Mallah, Issam. 1997. *The Role of Women in Omani Musical Life*. Tutzing: Hans Schneider. Includes videocassette.

Mandell, Joan. 1995. *Tales from Arab Detroit*. Detroit and Los Angeles: ACCESS and Olive Branch Productions. Videocassette.

Montgomery, Steve. 1995. *Morocco: The Past and Present of Djemma el Fna*. New York: Filmmakers Library. Videocassette.

Racy, Ali Jihad. 1983. *The Master Musicians of Jahjouka*. Long Beach, Calif.: Mendizza and Associates. Videocassette.

Smith, Huston. 1998. *Islamic Mysticism: The Sufi Way*. Wellspring Media. Videocassette.

Tlalim, Asher. 1994. *Morocco: The Music of the Jews of Morocco*. Teaneck, N.J.: Ergo Media. Videocassette.

Toub, Martin D. 1998. *Exploring the World of Music*. South Burlington, Vt.: Annenberg/CPB Project. 12 videocassettes.

Umm Kulthūm. [1970] 1982. *Sahrah ma'a al-Sayyidah Umm Kulthūm: Inta 'umrī & Yā msahharnī/Oum Kalsoum Concert: Ita Omry, Yam Sahreney*. Anaheim, Calif.: Ṣawt wa-Ṣūrah, Arabian Video Entertainment. Videocassette.

Under African Skies. Vol. 3, *Algeria*. 1989. London: BBC Videos for Education and Training. Videocassette.

Wickett, Elizabeth. 1990. *For Those Who Sail to Heaven*. New York: First Run/Icarus Films. Videocassette.

Wilets, Bernard. [1968] c. 1955. *Discovering the Music of the Middle East*. Huntsville, Tex.: Educational Video. Videocassette.

Zehavah Ben: The Solitary Star. 1988. Teaneck, N.J.: Ergo Media. Videocassette.

East Asia: China, Japan, Korea, and Inner Asia

Publications on East Asian Music

CHINA

Western-language publications

Note: For dissertations, see Kwok (1994) and the "Current Bibliography" section in the journal *Ethnomusicology*.

Addison, Don. 1974. "Elements of Style in Performing the Chinese P'i-p'a. *Selected Reports in Ethnomusicology* 2(1):119–139.

Amiot, Joseph-Marie. [1779] 1973. *Mémoire sur la musique Chinois*. Geneva: Minkoff Reprint.

Balasa, Marin Marian. 1997. "Chinese Diary." *East European Meetings in Ethnomusicology* 4:91–203.

Banu, Georges. 1986. "Mei Lanfang: A Case against and a Model for the Occidental Stage." *Asian Theatre Journal* 3(2):153–178.

Birrell, Anne M. 1989. "Mythmaking and *Yüeh-fu*: Popular Songs and Ballads of Early Imperial China." *Journal of the American Oriental Society* 109:223–235.

———. 1993. *Popular Songs and Ballads of Han China*. Honolulu: University of Hawaii Press.

Bodman, Helene Dunn. 1987. *Chinese Musical Iconography: A History of Musical Instruments Depicted in Chinese Art*. Taipei: Asian-Pacific Cultural Center.

Boltz, Judith Magee. 1996. "Singing to the Spirits of the Dead: A Daoist Ritual of Salvation." In *Harmony and Counterpoint: Ritual Music in Chinese Context*, ed. B. Yung, E. S. Rawski, and R. S. Watson, 177–225. Stanford, Calif.: Stanford University Press.

Brace, Tim. 1991. "Popular Music in Contemporary Beijing: Modernism and Cultural Identity." *Asian Music* 22(2):45–65.

Brace, Tim, and Paul Friedlander. 1992. "Rock and Roll on the New Long March: Popular Music, Cultural Identity, and Political Opposition in the People's Republic of China." In *Rockin' the Boat: Mass Music and Mass Movements*, ed. Reebee Garofalo, 115–127. Boston: South End.

Brandes, Edda, and Schu-Chi Lee. 1994. "Musikalische Feldforschung bei den *Aini, Lahu*, und *Bulang*—Drei nationale Minderheiten in Xishuangbanna/China." *Jahrbuch für musikalische Volks- und Völkerkunde* 15:44–73.

Brandl, Rudolf M. 1991. *Nuo-Geistermasken aus Anhui (China)*. Ausstellung des musikwissen-

schaftlichen und Ostasiastischen Seminars der Universitat Gottingen. Göttingen: Edition Re.

Brook, Tim. 1979. "The Revival of China's Musical Culture." *China Quarterly* 77:113–121.

Brösicke, Blandina. 1999/2000. "The Ideal of Sound in Fujian Nanyin." *CHIME* 14–15:82–88.

Bryant, Daniel. 1994. "Messages of Uncertain Origin: The Textual Tradition of the *Nan-T'ang Erh-Chu Tz'u*." In *Voices of the Song Lyric in China*, ed. P. Yu, 298–348. Berkeley: University of California Press.

Chan, Sau Y. 1991. *Improvisation in a Ritual Context: The Music of Cantonese Opera*. Hong Kong: Chinese University Press.

———. 1998. "Exploding the Belly: Improvisation in Cantonese Opera." In *In the Course of Performance: Studies in the World of Musical Improvisation*, ed. Bruno Nettl with Melinda Russell, 199–218. Chicago: University of Chicago Press.

Chang, Kang-i Sun Chang. "Liu Shih and Hsü Ts'an: Feminine or Feminist?" In *Voices of the Song Lyric in China*, ed. P. Yu, 169–187. Berkeley: University of California Press.

Chang, Peter M. 1991. "Tan Dun's String Quartet *Feng-ya-song*: Some Ideological Issues." *Asian Music* 22(2):127–158.

Charter, Vernon, and Jean DeBernardi. 1998. "Towards a Chinese Christian Hymnody: Processes of Musical and Cultural Synthesis." *Asian Music* 29(2):83–113.

Chen, Yingshi. 1988–1989. "Temperamentology in Ancient Chinese Written Records." *Musicology Australia* 11–12:44–64.

———. 1991. "A Report on Chinese Research into the Dunhuang Music Manuscripts." *Musica Asiatica* 6:61–72.

———. 1999. "Fundamental Theories of Chinese Traditional Music in Ancient Writings." Translated by Zhou Qinru. *Journal of Music in China* 1(1):55–76.

Cheng, Daofa. 2000. "Number Sequences in the Structure of Some Instrumental Ensemble Music Collected from Hubei Province," trans. Meng Qiu. *Journal of Music in China* 2(1):83–96.

Cheung, Hung-nin Samuel. 1996. "Songs and Rhymes: Cantonese Phonology as Reconstructed from Popular Songs." *Journal of Chinese Linguistics* 24(1):1–53.

Chong, Woei Lien. 1991. "Rock Star Cui Jian, Young China's Voice of the 1980s." *CHIME* 4:4–22.

Chou, Oliver K. 1999. "Maestro Li Delun and Western Classical Music in the People's Republic of China: A Personal Account." *Association for Chinese Music Research (ACMR) Reports* 12:23–46.

Chou, Wen-chung. 1999. "Music by Asian Composers." *Journal of Music in China* 1(1):111–115.

Chow, Rey, 1990. "Listening Otherwise, Music: A Different Type of Question about Revolution." *Discourse* 13(1):135.

Chow, Yiu Fai, and Jeroen de Kloet. 1997. "Sounds from the Margin: Beijing Rock Scene Faces an Uncertain Future." *CHIME* 10–11:123–128.

Collinge, Ian. 1993. "He Dra-nyen (The Himalayan Lute): An Emblem of Tibetan Culture." *CHIME* 6:22–33.

———. 1996–1997. "Developments in Musicology in Tibet: The Emergence of a New Tibetan Musical Lexicon." *Asian Music* 28(1):87–114.

Cook, Scott Bradley. 1995. "*Yue ji* (Record of Music): Introduction, Translation, Notes, and Commentary." *Asian Music* 26(2):1–96.

Dahmer, Manfred. 1988. *Die grosse Solosuite Guanglingsan: Das berühmteste Werk der frühest notierten chinesischen Instrumentalmusik*. Frankfurter China-Studien, Vol. 3. Frankfurt am Main: Peter Lang.

Dai, Xiaolian. 1998. "Plum Blossom: Three Variations—A Study of the Guqin Piece *Meihua san nong*." *CHIME* 12–13:124–141.

Dai, Yanjing, Keith Dede, Qi Huimin, Zhu Yongzhong, and Kevin Stuart. 2000. "'Laughing on the Beacon Tower' Spring Festival Songs from Qinghai." *Asian Folklore Studies* 58(1):121–187.

DeWoskin, Kenneth J. 1982. *A Song for One or Two: Music and the Concept of Art in Early China*. Michigan Papers in Chinese Studies, No. 42. Ann Arbor: Center for Chinese Studies, University of Michigan.

———. 1988. "Sources for the Study of Early Chinese Music and Music Culture: An Introductory Essay and Select Bibliography." *Archaeologia Musicalis* 2(2):70–97.

Dibello, Michelle. 1996. "*Longing for Wordly Pleasures*: An Example of the Sacred versus the Profane in Contemporary Chinese Drama." *CHINOPERL Papers* 19:67–78.

Dolby, William. 1976. *A History of Chinese Drama*. London: Paul Elek.

Du, Yaxiong. 1998. "A Tradition Shared by Many Ethnic Groups: Shaonian, Courtship Songs from Northwest China." *CHIME* 12–13:70–86.

———. 1999. "*Baban* and Its Form: A Study in Aesthetics." *Journal of Music in China* 1(1):95–100.

Egan, Ronald. 1994. "The Problem of the Repute of *Tz'u* During the Northern Sung." In *Voices of the Song Lyric in China*, ed. P. Yu, 191–225. Berkeley: University of California Press.

———. 1997. "The Controversy over Music and 'Sadness' and Changing Conceptions of the *Qin* in Middle Period China." *Harvard Journal of Asiatic Studies* 57(1):5–66.

Falkenhausen, Lothar von. 1993. *Suspended Music: Chime-Bells in the Culture of Bronze Age China*. Berkeley: University of California Press.

Fang, Kun. 1981. "A Discussion on Chinese National Musical Traditions." *Asian Music* 12(2):1–16.

Ferguson, Daniel. 1993. "The Shândông Highwayman: Mechanisms of Inclusion and Resistance and the Predication of Cantonese Identity through Cantonese Opera." *Yearbook for Traditional Music* 25:67–80.

Fong, Grace S. 1994. "Engendering the Lyric: Her Image and Voice in Song." In *Voices of the Song Lyric in China*, ed. P. Yu, 107–144. Berkeley: University of California Press.

Friedlander, Paul David. 1990. "Rocking the Yangtze: Impressions of Chinese Popular Music and Technology." *Popular Music and Society* 14(1):63–73.

———. 1991. "China's 'Newer Value' Pop: Rock-and-Roll and Technology on the New Long March." *Asian Music* 22(2): 67–81.

Gao, Houyong. 1989. "On Qupai." *Asian Music* 20(2):4–20.

Gao, Zhixi. 1992. "Shang and Zhou Period Bronze Musical Instruments from South China." *Bulletin of the School of Oriental and African Studies* 55(2):262–271.

Gild, Gerlinde. 1998. "Dreams of Renewal Inspired by Japan and the West: Early Twentieth-Century Reforms in Chinese Music." *CHIME* 12–13:116–123.

Gild-Böhne, Gerlinde. 1991. *Das Lü Lü Zheng Yi Xubian: Ein Jesuitentraktat über die europäische Notation in China 1713*. Göttingen: Edition Re.

Goormaghtigh, Georges. 1988. "'L'air du roi Wen' et 'l'Immortel des eaux': Aspects de la musique des lettres chinois." *Cahiers de Musiques Traditionnelles* 1:144–55.

———. 1990. *L'art du qin: Deux textes d'esthétique musicale chinoise*. Bruxelles: Institut Belge des Hautes Études Chinoises.

———. 1994. "La vertu de l'instrument: À propos de quelques inscriptions gravées sur des qin anciens." *Cahiers de Musiques Traditionnelles* 7:95–102.

———. 1998. "Propos de quatre auteurs chinois sur le qin." *Cahiers de Musiques Traditionnelles* 11:163–174.

Guo, Xin. 1999. "Eastern and Western Techniques in Chen Yi's *Qi*." *Journal of Music in China* 1(1):121–131.

Guy, Nancy. 1998a. "Peking Opera as 'National Opera' in Taiwan: What's in a Name?" *ACMR Reports* 11:67–88.

———. 1998b. "Writing about Chinese Opera (*Xiqu*) in English: One Hundred Flowers Bloom, One Hundred Terms Contend." *ACMR Reports* 11:89–94.

———. 1999. "Governing the Arts, Governing the State: Peking Opera and Political Authority in Taiwan." *Ethnomusicology* 43(3):508–526.

Halson, Elizabeth. 1966. *Peking Opera: A Short Guide*. London: Oxford University Press.

Hamm, Charles. 1991. "Music and Radio in the People's Republic of China." *Asian Music* 22(2):1–42.

Han, Kuo-Huang. 1978. "The Chinese Concept of Program Music." *Asian Music* 10(1):17–38.

———. 1979. "The Modern Chinese Orchestra." *Asian Music* 11(1):1–43.

———. 1980. "Three Chinese Musicologists: Yang Yinliu, Yin Falu, Li Chunyi." *Ethnomusicology* 24:483–529.

———. 1988. "J. A. van Aalst and His Chinese Music." *Asian Music* 19(2):127–130.

———. 1989. "Folk Songs of the Han Chinese: Characters and Classifications." *Asian Music* 20(2):107–128.

———. 1990. "Recent Developments in Minority Music Research." *CHIME* 2:24–27.

———. 1994. "Khapsaibi Music: A Preliminary Study." In *Themes and Variations: Writings on Music in Honor of Rulan Chao Pian*, ed. B. Yung and J. S. C. Lam, 260–277. Cambridge, Mass.: Department of Music, Harvard University.

———. 1999. "The *Daguashe* Music of Xi'an." *ACMR Reports* 12:103–121.

———. 2001. "Taiwan: Western Art Music." In *The New Grove Dictionary of Music and Musicians*, ed. Stanley Sadie and John Tyrrell, 2nd ed., 25:8–10, 13. New York: Grove. Available: http://www.grovemusic.com.

Han, Kuo-Huang, and Lindy Li Mark. 1980. "Evolution and Revolution in Chinese Music." In *Musics of Many Cultures: An Introduction*, ed. Elizabeth May, 10–31. Berkeley: University of California Press.

Han Kuo-Huang, and Patricia Shehan Campbell. 1996. *The Lion's Roar: Chinese Luogo Percussion Ensembles*, 2nd ed. Multicultural Materials for Educators. Danbury, Conn.: World Music. (With 1 audiocassette.)

Harbeck, James. 1996. "The Quaintness—and Usefulness—of the Old Chinese Traditions: *The Yellow Jacket* and *Lady Precious Stream*." *Asian Theatre Journal* 13(2):238–247.

Harris, Rachel. 1999–2000. "From Shamanistic Ritual to Karaoke: The (Trans)migrations of a Chinese Folksong." *CHIME* 14–15:48–60.

Ho, Edward. 1997. "Aesthetic Considerations in Understanding Chinese Literati Musical Behaviour." *British Journal of Ethnomusicology* 6:35–50.

Ho, Wai-Chung. 2000. "The Political Meaning of Hong Kong Popular Music: A Review of Sociopolitical Relations between Hong Kong and the People's Republic of China since the 1980s." *Popular Music* 19(3):341–353.

Holm, David. 1984. "Folk Art as Propaganda: the Yangge Movement." In *Popular Chinese Literature and Performing Arts in the People's Republic of China, 1949–1979*, ed. B. McDougall, 3–35. Berkeley: University of California Press.

———. 1991. *Art and Ideology in Revolutionary China*. Oxford: Clarendon; New York: Oxford University Press.

Hrdlickova, Venceslava. 1968. "The Chinese Storytellers and Singers of Ballads." *Transactions of the Asiatic Society of Japan, Third Series* 10:97–115.

Hsu, Tsang-Houei, and Cheng Shui-Cheng. 1992. *Musique de Taiwan*. Paris: Éditions Guy Trédaniel. (With 1 audiocassette.)

Hsu, Tsang-Houei, and Lu Yu-Hsiu. 2001. "Taiwan: Introduction." In *The New Grove Dictionary of Music and Musicians*, ed. Stanley Sadie and John Tyrrell, 2nd ed., 25:1, 10–11. New York: Grove. Available: http://www.grovemusic.com.

———. 2001. "Taiwan: Aboriginal Music." In *The New Grove Dictionary of Music and Musicians*, ed. Stanley Sadie and John Tyrrell, 2nd ed., 25:1–7, 11–12. New York: Grove. Available: http://www.grovemusic.com.

Hu, Jiaxun. 1999. "Miao *Lusheng* Speech of Northwestern Guizhou and Its Musical Presentation," trans. Cui Yanzhi. *Journal of Music in China* 1(1):39–54.

———. 2000. "Historical Data on Music and Dance in Ancient Yi Writing," trans. George Flournoy and Cui Yanzhi. *Journal of Music in China* 2(1):29–52.

Huang, Bai. 1992. "Haozi—Working Cries Turned into Art—A Discussion of Two Shanghai Work Songs," trans. Antoinet Schimmelpenninck. *CHIME* 5:42–49.

Huang, Jinpei. 1989. "Xipi and Erhuang of Beijing and Guangdong Operas." *Asian Music* 20(2):152–195.

Huang, Yi-Ping. 1998. "The Parting of the Way: Three Generations of Qin Performance Practice." *ACMR Reports* 11:15–44.

Huangpu, Chongqing. 1992. "Dixi: Chinese Farmers' Theatre." *TDR* 36(2T134):107–117.

Hughes, David, and Stephen Jones. 2001. "East Asia." In *The New Grove Dictionary of Music and Musicians*, ed. Stanley Sadie and John Tyrrell, 2nd ed., 7:837–841. New York: Grove. Available: http://www.grovemusic.com.

Hung, Chang-tai. 1996. "The Politics of Songs: Myths and Symbols in the Chinese Communist

War Music." *Modern Asian Studies* 30(4):901–930.

Huot, Claire. 2000. *China's New Cultural Scene: A Handbook of Changes*. Durham, N.C.: Duke University Press.

I-To, Loh. 1980. "Taiwan." In *The New Grove Dictionary of Music and Musicians*, ed. Stanley Sadie, 2nd ed., 18:529–533. London: Macmillan; Washington: Grove's Dictionaries of Music.

Ishida, Hidemi. 1987. "An Introduction to Musical Thought in Ancient China: Sound, Order, Emotion." *Contemporary Music Review* 1(2):75–84.

Jaivin, Linda. 1995. "Beijing Bastards: The New Revolution." *CHIME* 8:99–103.

———. 1996. "Hou Dejian and the Rise of Pop Music in Taiwan in the Seventies." *CHIME* 9:118–123.

Jiang, Jing. 1991. "The Influence of Traditional Chinese Music on Professional Instrumental Composition." *Asian Music* 22(2):83–96.

Jiayong, Qunpei. 2000. "Social Context and Musical Characteristics of Tibetan *Changlu* Songs of Banditry," trans. Cui Yanzhi. *Journal of Music in China* 2(1):73–82.

Jin, Jingyan. 1989. "Musikforschung in der Volksrepublik China (1949–1988)." *Acta Musicologica* 61(3):264–326.

Jin, Zhi. 1988. "Huangmei Opera—A Folk Drama." *Chinese Literature*: 177–182.

Johnson, David, ed. 1989. *Ritual Opera, Operatic Ritual: "Mu-Lien Rescues His Mother" in Chinese Popular Culture*. Publications of the Chinese Popular Culture Project 1. Berkeley: University of California.

Jones, Andrew F. 1992. *Like a Knife: Ideology and Genre in Contemporary Chinese Popular Music*. Cornell East Asia Series 57. Ithaca, N.Y.: East Asia Program, Cornell University.

———. 1994. "The Politics of Popular Music in Post-Tiananmen China." In *Popular Protest and Political Culture in Modern China*, ed. Jeffrey N. Wasserstrom and Elizabeth J. Perry, 148–165. Boulder, Colo.: Westview.

———. 2001. *Yellow Music: Media Culture and Cultural Modernity in the Chinese Jazz Age*. Durham, N.C.: Duke University Press.

Jones, Stephen. 1989. "The Golden-Character Scripture: Perspectives on Chinese Melody." *Asian Music* 20(2):21–66.

———. 1996. "Source and Stream: Early Music and Living Traditions in China." *Early Music* 24(3):374–388.

———. [1995] 1998. *Folk Music of China: Living Instrumental Traditions*. Oxford: Clarendon; New York: Oxford University Press. (With 1 compact disk.)

———. 1999. "Chinese Ritual Music under Mao and Deng." *British Journal of Ethnomusicology* 8:27–66.

———. 2001. "China 4: Religious Music." In *The New Grove Dictionary of Music and Musicians*, ed. Stanley Sadie and John Tyrrell, 2nd ed.,

5:669–671. New York: Grove. Available: http://www.grovemusic.com.

Jones, Stephen, Han Mei, and Wu Ben. 2001. "China 4: Instrumental Music." In *The New Grove Dictionary of Music and Musicians*, ed. Stanley Sadie and John Tyrrell, 2nd ed., 5:671–684. New York: Grove. Available: http://www.grovemusic.com.

Jones, Stephen, et al. 1992. "Field Notes 1991: Funeral Music in Shanxi." *CHIME* 5:4–29.

Jones, Stephen, and Xue Yibing. 1991. "The Music Associations of Hebei Province, China: A Preliminary Report." *Ethnomusicology* 35(1):1–29.

Judd, Ellen R. 1996. "Ritual Opera and the Bonds of Authority: Transformation and Transcendence." In *Harmony and Counterpoint: Ritual Music in Chinese Context*, ed. B. Yung, E. S. Rawski, and R. S. Watson, 226–246. Stanford, Calif.: Stanford University Press.

Jun, Hu, and Kevin Stuart. 1992. "The Guanting Tu (Mongour) Wedding Ceremonies and Songs." *Anthropos* 87(1–3):109–132.

Kagan, A. L. 1963. "Music and the Hundred Flowers Movement." *Musical Quarterly* 49:417–430.

Kaufmann, Walter. 1967. *Musical Notations of the Orient: Notational Systems of East, South, and Central Asia*. Bloomington: Indiana University Press.

———. 1976. *Musical References in the Chinese Classics*. Detroit Monographs in Musicology 5. Detroit: Information Coordinators.

Kisibe, Shigeo. 1965. "A Chinese Painting of the Tang Court Women's Orchestra." In *The Commonwealth of Music*, ed. Gustav Reese and Rose Brandel, 104–117. New York: Free Press.

Kloet, Jeroen de. 2000. "Let Him Fucking See the Green Smoke Beneath My Groin—The Mythology of Chinese Rock." In *Postmodernism and China*, ed. A. Dirlik and X. Zhang. Durham, N.C.: Duke University Press.

Kouwenhoven, Frank. 1990. "Chinese Music Research in Europe: West Meets West." *CHIME* 1:5–9.

———. 1990a. "Mainland China's New Music." *CHIME* 2:58–93; 3:42–75; 4:76–134.

———. 1990b. "Music Research in China: Signs of Change." *CHIME* 1:51–58.

———. 1991. "An Interview with Laurence Picken: Bringing to Life Tunes of Ancient China." *CHIME* 4:40–65.

———. 1992. "Redonner vie aux mélodies de la Chine ancienne: Laurence Picken et les secrets de la musique médiévale d'Extreme-Orient." *Cahiers de Musiques Traditionnelles* 5:217–245.

———. 1997. "New Chinese Operas by Qu Xiaosong, Tan Dun, and Guo Wenjing." *CHIME* 10–11:111–122.

Kouwenhoven, Frank, and Antoinet Schimmelpennick. 1992. "Chasing a Folk Tune in Southern Jiangsu, China." In *European Studies in Ethnomusicology: Historical Developments and Recent Trends*, ed. Artur Simon, Ulrich Wegner,

and Max Peter Baumann, 247–268. Wilhelmshaven: Noetzel.

———. 1993. "The Shanghai Conservatory of Music: History and Foreign Students' Experiences." *CHIME* 6:56–91.

———. 1997. "Guo Wenjing, a Composer's Portrait: 'The Strings Going *Hong Hong Hong* and the Percussion *Bong Kèèh*—That's My Voice!'" *CHIME* 10–11:8–49.

———. 2001. "China 4: Folksong and Dance." In *The New Grove Dictionary of Music and Musicians*, ed. Stanley Sadie and John Tyrrell, 2nd ed., 5:667–669. New York: Grove. Available: http://www.grovemusic.com.

Kraus, Richard Curt. 1988. *Pianos and Politics in China: Middle-Class Ambitions in the Struggle over Western Music*. New York: Oxford University Press.

Kuo, Chang-Yang. 1996. *Chinese Art Song: A Melodic Analysis*. Taiwan: Yueh-Yuhn.

Kuttner, Fritz A. 1989. *The Archaeology of Music in Ancient China: 2000 Years of Acoustical Experimentation, c. 1400 B.C.–A.D. 750*. New York: Paragon.

Kwok, Theodore J. 1994. "Chinese Music Theses and Dissertations: A Preliminary List." *ACMR Newsletter* 7(1):18–33.

Lai, Eric. 1993–1994. "Toward a Theory of Pitch Organization: The Early Music of Chou Wen-chung." *Asian Music* 25(1–2):177–207.

———. 1999. "Old Wine in New Bottles: The Use of Traditional Chinese Music in New Chinese Music." *ACMR Reports* 12:1–22.

Lam, Joseph S. C. 1993. "Analyses and Interpretations of Chinese Seven-String Zither Music: The Case of the *Lament of Empress Chen*." *Ethnomusicology* 37(3):353–385.

———. 1994. "Notational Representation and Contextual Constraints: How and Why Did Ye Tang Notate His Kun Opera Arias?" In *Themes and Variations: Writings on Music in Honor of Rulan Chao Pian*, ed. Bell Yung and Joseph S. C. Lam, 31–44. Cambridge, Mass.: Department of Music, Harvard University.

———. 1994. "'There Is No Music in Chinese Music History': Five Court Tunes from the Yuan Dynasty (A.D. 1271–1368)." *JRMA* 64(2):165–188.

———. 1995a. "Chinese Music Historiography: From Yang Yinliu's 'A Draft History of Ancient Chinese Music' to Confucian Classics." *ACMR Reports* 8(2):1–45.

———. 1995b. "Musical Relics and Cultural Expressions: State Sacrificial Songs from the Southern Song Court (A.D. 1127–1279)." *Journal of Sung-Yuan Studies* 25:1–27.

———. 1995c. "The *Yin* and *Yang* of Chinese Music Historiography: The Case of Confucian Ceremonial Music." *Yearbook for Traditional Music* 27:34–51.

———. 1996a. "Ritual and Musical Politics in the Court of Ming Shizong." In *Harmony and Counterpoint: Ritual Music in Chinese Context*, ed. B. Yung, E. S. Rawski, and R. S. Watson, 35–53. Stanford, Calif.: Stanford University Press.

———. 1996b. "Transnational Understanding of Historical Music: State Sacrificial Music from the Southern Song, China (A.D. 1127–1279)." *World of Music* 38(2):69–83.

———. 1998. *State Sacrifices and Music in Ming China: Orthodoxy, Creativity, and Expressiveness.* SUNY Series in Chinese Local Studies. Albany: State University of New York Press.

Lam, Joseph S. C., and Jonathan P. J. Stock. 2001. "China 2: History and Theory." In *The New Grove Dictionary of Music and Musicians*, ed. Stanley Sadie and John Tyrrell, 2nd ed., 5:637–654. New York: Grove. Available: http://www.grovemusic.com.

Lau, Frederick. 1995. "'Lost in Time?' Sources of the Twentieth-Century *Dizi* Repertory." *Pacific Review of Ethnomusicology* 1:31–56.

———. 1996a. "Forever Red: The Invention of Solo *Dizi* Music in Post-1949 China." *British Journal of Ethnomusicology* 5:113–131.

———. 1996b. "Individuality and Political Discourse in Solo *Dizi* Compositions." *Asian Music* 27(1):133–152.

———. 1998a. "Little Great Tradition: Thoughts on Recent Developments in *Jiangnan Sizhu*." *ACMR Reports* 11:45–66.

———. 1998b. "'Packaging Identity through Sound': Tourist Performances in Contemporary China." *Journal of Musicological Research* 17(2):113–134.

———. 2001. "Performing Identity: Musical Expression of Thai-Chinese in Contemporary Bangkok." *Sojourn* 16(1):38–70.

Lee, Byong-won. 1988. "Musical Identity and Acculturation in the Yanbian Korean Autonomous Region of the People's Republic of China: An Overview." In *Papers of the Fifth International Conference on Korean Studies: Korean Studies, Its Tasks and Perspectives*, 2. Songnam: Academy of Korean Studies.

Lee, Elsa. 1997. "An Introduction to the *Gushi* Drummer of the *Chuanju* Percussion Ensemble." *Asian Music* 28(2):1–26.

Lee, Gregory. 1995. "The 'East Is Red' Goes Pop: Commodification, Hybridity, and Nationalism in Chinese Popular Song and Its Televisual Performance." *Popular Music* 14(1):95–110.

———. 1996. *Troubadours, Trumpeters, Troubled Makers: Lyricism, Nationalism, and Hybridity in China and Its Others*. London: Hurst.

Lee, Joanna Ching-Yun. 1992. "All for Freedom: The Rise of Patriotic/Pro-Democratic Popular Music in Hong Kong in Response to the Chinese Student Movement." In *Rockin' the Boat: Mass Music and Mass Movements*, ed. Reebee Garofalo, 129–147. Boston: South End.

———. 1992. "Cantopop Songs on Emigration from Hong Kong." *Yearbook for Traditional Music* 24:14–23.

———. 1999–2000. "Interview with Composer Han Yong." *CHIME* 14–15:89–102.

———. 2001a. "Hong Kong: Popular Music." In *The New Grove Dictionary of Music and Musicians*, ed. Stanley Sadie and John Tyrrell, 2nd ed.,

11:686. New York: Grove. Available: http://www.grovemusic.com.

———. 2001b. "Taiwan: Popular Music." In *The New Grove Dictionary of Music and Musicians*, ed. Stanley Sadie and John Tyrrell, 2nd ed., 25:10, 13. New York: Grove. Available: http://www.grovemusic.com.

Lee, Schu-chi. 1992. *Die Musik in daoistischen Zeremonien auf Taiwan*. Frankfurt am Main: Peter Lang.

Lee, Tong Soon. 2000. "Professional Chinese Opera Troupes and Street Opera Performance in Singapore." *Asian Music* 31(2):35–70.

Lei, Daphne Pi-Wei. 1996. "Wang Zhaojun on the Border: Gender and Intercultural Conflicts in Premodern Chinese Drama." *Asian Theatre Journal* 13(2):229–237.

Levy, Jim. 1989. "Joseph Amiot and Enlightenment: Speculation on the Origin of Pythagorean Tuning in China." *Theoria* 4:63–88.

Li, Jichang. 2000. "Bouyei Love Song: Traditional Practices and Relationships with Bouyei Marital Systems," trans. Guo Xin. *Journal of Music in China* 2(2):221–234.

Li, Ping-Hui. 1996. "Processional Music in Traditional Taiwanese Funerals." In *Harmony and Counterpoint: Ritual Music in Chinese Context*, ed. B. Yung, E. S. Rawski, and R. S. Watson, 130–149. Stanford, Calif.: Stanford University Press.

Li You-Zheng. 1989. "Ingarden's 'Strata-Layer' Theory and the Structural Analysis of Traditional Chinese Kunqu Opera." *Semiotica* 74(1–2):25–41.

Liang, Maochun. 1996. "Tianhua Liu: A Contemporary Revolutionary of the Erhu." *Sonus* 17(1):44–52.

Liang, Ming-yüeh [Liang Mingyue]. 1972. *The Chinese Ch'in: Its History and Music*. San Francisco: Chinese National Music Association, San Francisco Conservatory of Music.

———. 1975. "Neo-Taoist Implications in a Melody for the Chinese Seven-Stringed Zither." *World of Music* 17(2):19–28.

———. 1980. "The Artistic Symbolism of Painted Faces in Chinese Opera: An Introduction." *World of Music* 22(1):17–85.

———. 1985a. *Music of the Billion: An Introduction to Chinese Musical Culture*. New York: Heinrichshofen.

———. 1985b. "Performance Process as a Recreative Process in Chinese Zheng Zither Music." *World of Music* 27(1):48–67.

Liang, Ming-yüeh, Tsun-Yuen Lui, and Colin Mackerras. 1980. "China 5: Instruments." In *The New Grove Dictionary of Music and Musicians*, ed. Stanley Sadie, 4:262–279. London: Macmillan; Washington: Grove's Dictionaries of Music.

Lieberman, Fredric. 1979. *Chinese Music: An Annotated Bibliography*, 2nd ed. Garland Reference Library of the Humanities, Vol. 75. New York: Garland.

———. 1983. *A Chinese Zither Tutor: The Mei-An Qinpu*. Seattle: University of Washington Press.

Lin, Shuen-fu. 1994. "The Formation of a Distinct Generic Identity for *Tz'u*." In *Voices of the Song Lyric in China*, ed. P. Yu, 3–29. Berkeley: University of California Press.

Liu, Chunjo. 1978. "Five Major Chant Types of the Buddhist Service *Gong-tian*." *CHINOPERL Papers* 8:130–50.

Liu, Guiteng. 2000. "Embodiment of Universal Sagacity: Making Forms, Deployments, and Cultural Features of Manchu Shaman Musical Instruments," trans. Cui Yanzhi and Zhou Qinru. *Journal of Music in China* 2(2):193–220.

Liu, Marjory Bong-Ray. 1974. "The Influence of Tonal Speech on K'unch'u Opera Style." *Selected Reports in Ethnomusicology* 2(1):63–86.

Lo, Kii-Ming. 1993. "New Documents on the Encounter between European and Chinese Music." *Revista de Musicología* 16(4):1896–1911.

Lowry, Kathryn. 1990. "Between Speech and Song: Singing Contests at Northwest Chinese Festivals." *Cosmos* 6:61–79.

Lü, Chuikuan, and Lu Yu-Hsiu. 2001. "Taiwan: Han Chinese Traditional Music." In *The New Grove Dictionary of Music and Musicians*, ed. Stanley Sadie and John Tyrrell, 2nd ed., 25:7–8, 12–13. New York: Grove. Available: http://www.grovemusic.com.

Lü, Guoqing. 1989. "Pei Yanling, Performer Extraordinary." *Chinese Literature* 168–173.

Lui Tsun-yuen. 1968. "A Short Guide to Ch'in." *Selected Reports in Ethnomusicology* 1(2):179–204.

Lum, Casey Man Kong. 1996. *In Search of a Voice: Karaoke and the Construction of Identity in Chinese America*. Mahwah, N.J.: Erlbaum.

Luo, Zhongrong. 2000. "A Composer's Note on 'Chang'e,'" trans. Zhou Qinru. *Journal of Music in China* 2(1):97–119.

Mackerras, Colin. 1964. "Folksongs and Dances of China's Minority Nationalities: Policy, Tradition, and Professionalization." *Modern China* 10(2):187–226.

———. 1972. *The Rise of the Peking Opera, 1770–1870*. Oxford: Clarendon.

———. 1975. *The Chinese Theatre in Modern Times: From 1840 to the Present Day*. Amherst: University of Massachusetts Press.

———. 1980. "China 3: Musical Drama and Narratives." In *The New Grove Dictionary of Music and Musicians*, ed. Stanley Sadie, 4:253–260. London: Macmillan; Washington: Grove's Dictionaries of Music.

———. 1981. *The Performing Arts in Contemporary China*. London: Routledge and Kegan Paul.

———. 1984. "Folksongs and Dances of China's Minority Nationalities: Policy, Tradition, and Professionalization." *Modern Music* 10(2):187–226.

———. 1996. "Chinese Traditional Theatre: A Revival in the 1900s?" *CHINOPERL Papers* 19:79–94.

———. 2001. "China 4: Living Traditions: Musical Drama and Narrative." In *The New Grove Dictionary of Music and Musicians*, ed. Stanley Sadie and John Tyrrell, 2nd ed., 5:660–

667. New York: Grove. Available: http://www.grovemusic.com.

Mao, Yu Run. 1991. "Music under Mao, Its Background and Aftermath." *Asian Music* 22(2):97–125.

Marett, Allan. 1985. "Togaku: Where Have the Tang Melodies Gone, and Where Have the New Melodies Come From?" *Ethnomusicology* 29:409–431.

———. 1986. "In Search of the Lost Melodies of Tang China: An Account of Recent Research and Its Implications for the History and Analysis of Togaku." *Musicology Australia* 9:29–38.

Mark, Lindy Li. 1966. "Speech-Tone and Melody in Wu-ming Folk Songs." In *Essays Offered to C. H. Luce*, ed. Ba Shin, 167–186. Ascona, Switzerland: Artibus Asiae.

———. 1996. "Conference Report: International Workshop on Oral Literature in Modern China, Copenhagen, August 29–31, 1996." *CHINOPERL Papers* 19: 109–122.

McDougall, Bonnie S., ed. 1984. *Popular Chinese Literature and Performing Arts in the People's Republic of China, 1949–1979*. Berkeley: University of California Press.

McLaren, Anne, and Chen Qinjian. 2000. "The Oral and Ritual Culture of Chinese Women: Bridal Lamentations of Nanhui." *Asian Folklore Studies* 59(2):205–238.

Miao, Jing. 1996. "The Role of Traditional Chinese Music in Music Education Today." *Sonus* 17(1):6–13.

Micic, Peter. 1995. "'A Bit of This and That': Notes on Pop/Rock Genres in the Eighties in China." *CHIME* 8:76–95.

———. 1997. "A Selected Annotated Discography of Pop and Rock Albums in the People's Republic of China." *Asian Studies Review* 20(3):63–78.

———. 1999–2000. "Pop 'n' Rock Loan Words and Neologisms in the PRC." *CHIME* 14–15:103–123.

Micic, Peter, and D. Stokes. 1996. "A Selected Annotated Discography of Pop and Rock Albums in the People's Republic of China (1989–1995)." *ACMR Reports* 9(2):37–52.

Mittler, Barbara. 1996a. *Chinese New Music as a Politicized Language: Orthodox Melodies and Dangerous Tunes*. Indiana East Asian Working Paper Series on Language and Politics in Modern China, 10. Bloomington, Ind.: East Asian Studies Center.

———. 1996b. "The Politics of Identity in New Music from Hong Kong and Taiwan." *CHIME*: 4–44.

———. 1997. *Dangerous Tunes: The Politics of Chinese Music in Hong Kong, Taiwan, and the PRC since 1949*. Wiesbaden: Harrassowitz Verlag.

Modirzadeh, Hafez. 2000. "Spiraling Chinese Cyclic Theory and Modal Jazz Practice across Millenia: Proposed Sources and New Perceptions for John Coltrane's Late Musical Conceptions." *Journal of Music in China* 2(2):235–264.

Moule, A. C. 1989. *A List of the Musical and Other Sound-Producing Instruments of the Chinese*.

Source Materials and Studies in Ethnomusicology 3. Buren: Frits Knuf.

Myers, John E. 1992. *The Way of the Pipa: Structure and Imagery in Chinese Lute Music*. Kent, Ohio: Kent State University Press.

Nickson, Noel. 1988. "Structural Design of 'Chinese' Melodies Known in Japan before 841." *Miscellanea Musicologica: Adelaide Studies in Musicology* 15:58–73.

Nygren, Christina. 1999/2000. "Report from a Chinese Village: A Traveling Theatre Group in Rural Shanxi." *CHIME* 14–15:61–69.

Oki, Yasushi. 1997. "Women in Feng Menglong's 'Mountain Songs.'" In *Writing Women in Late Imperial China*, ed. Ellen Widmer and Chang Kang-i Sun, 131–143. Stanford, Calif.: Stanford University Press.

Olivova, Lucie. 1998. "Storytelling in Yangzhou: Impressions from the Eighteenth-Century Book *Yangzhou huafang lu*." *CHIME* 12–13:98–108.

Owen, Stephen. 1994. "Meaning the Words: The Genuine as a Value in the Tradition of the Song Lyric." In *Voices of the Song Lyric in China*, ed. P. Yu, 30–69. Berkeley: University of California Press.

Perris, Arnold. 1983. "Music as Propaganda: Art at the Command of Doctrine in the P.R.C." *Ethnomusicology* 27:1–28.

———. 1986. "Feeding the Hungry Ghosts: Some Observations on Buddhist Music and Buddhism from Both Sides of Taiwan Strait." *Ethnomusicology* 30(3):428–448.

Pian, Rulan Chao. 1967. *Song Dynasty Musical Sources and Their Interpretation*. Cambridge, Mass.: Harvard University Press.

———. 1970. "Rewriting an Act of the Yuan Drama, *Lii Kwei Fuh Jing*, in the Style of the Peking Opera: A Fieldworker's Experiment." *CHINOPERL News* 2:19–39.

———. 1971. "The Function of Rhythm in the Peking Opera." In *The Musics of Asia*, ed. Jose Maceda, 114–131. Manila: National Music Council of the Philippines.

———. 1972. "Text Setting with the *Shipyi* Animated Aria." In *Words and Music: The Scholar's View*, ed. Laurence Berman, 237–270. Cambridge, Mass.: Department of Music, Harvard University.

———. 1975. "Aria Structural Patterns in the Peking Opera." In *Chinese and Japanese Music Drama*, ed. J. I. Crump and W. P. Malm, 65–86. Ann Arbor: Center for Chinese Studies, University of Michigan.

———. 1977. "*Feng Yeu Guei Jou* 'Boat Return in the Rain': A Transcription with Commentary." *Journal of Far Eastern Studies* 23(24):389–403.

———. 1979a. "Musical Analysis of the Medley Song 'The Courtesan's Jewel Box.'" *CHINOPERL Papers* 9:9–31.

———. 1979b. "Rhythmic Texture in the Peking Opera *The Fisherman's Revenge*." *Asian Cultural Quarterly* 7(4):19–26.

———. 1980. "China 1: General—Introduction." In *The New Grove Dictionary of Music and Musicians*, ed. Stanley Sadie, 4:245–250. London: Macmillan; Washington: Grove's Dictionaries of Music.

———. 1993. "Text Setting and the Use of Tune Types in Chinese Dramatic and Narrative Music." In *Text, Tone, and Tune: Parameters of Music in Multicultural Perspective*, ed. B. C. Wade, 201–233. New Delhi: Oxford and IBH Publishing.

———. 1997. "Music and the Confucian Sacrificial Ceremony." In *Enchanting Powers: Music in the World's Religions*, ed. Lawrence E. Sullivan, 237–262. Cambridge, Mass.: Harvard University Press.

Picard, François. 1991. "Chine: Le *xiao*, ou souffle sonorisé." *Cahiers de Musiques Traditionnelles* 4:17–26.

———. 1991. *La musique chinoise*. Paris: Minerve.

Picken, Laurence E. R. 1966. "The Origin of the Short Lute." *Galpin Society Journal* 8:32–42.

———, ed. 1977–. *Musica Asiatica*. London: Oxford University Press.

———. 1997. "The Dunhuang Lute-Manuscript." *Musicology Australia* 20:15–60.

Picken, Laurence E. R., et al. 1981–. *Music from the Tang Court: A Primary Study of the Original Unpublished, Sino-Japanese Manuscripts Together with a Survey of Relevant Historical Sources, both Chinese and Japanese, and a Full Critical Commentary*. London: Oxford University Press.

Picken, Laurence E. R., et al. 1997. "'West River Moon': A Song-Melody Predicted by a Lute Piece in Piba Tablature." *CHIME* 10–11:172–185.

Pratt, K. 1993. "Change and Continuity in Qing Court Music." *CHIME* 7:90–103.

Qi, Huimin, Zhu Yongzhong, and Kevin Stuart. 2000. "Minhe Mangghuer Wedding Songs: Musical Characteristics." *Asian Folklore Studies* 58(1):77–120.

Raben, Estelle M. 1992. "Peking Opera: The Persistence of Tradition in the People's Republic of China." *Journal of Popular Culture* 25(4):53–61.

Rao, Nancy Y. 2000. "The Role of Language in Music Integration: *Poème Lyrique II* by Chen Qigang." *Journal of Music in China* 2(2):273–295.

Rault-Leyrat, Lucie. 1987. *Le cithare chinoise zheng ku: Un vol d'oies sauvages sur les cordes de soie*. Paris: Leopard d'Or.

———. 1989. "Autour du zheng: Un essai de filiation de quelques cithares d'Asie orientale." *Cahiers de Musiques Traditionnelles* 2:63–73.

———. 1992. "L'harmonie du centre: Aspects rituels de la musique dans la Chine ancienne." *Cahiers de Musiques Traditionnelles* 5:111–125.

———. 2000. *Musiques de la tradition chinoise*. Arles: Actes Sud and Paris: Cité de la Musique. (With 1 compact disk.)

Rawski, Evelyn S. 1996. "The Creation of an Emperor in Eighteenth-Century China." In *Harmony and Counterpoint: Ritual Music in*

Chinese Context, ed. B. Yung, E. S. Rawski, and R. S. Watson, 150–174. Stanford, Calif.: Stanford University Press.

Rea, Dennis. 1993. "A Western Musician's View of China's Pop and Rock Scene." *CHIME* 6:34–55.

Rebollo-Sborgi, Francesca. 1994. "The Musicality of Oral Performance: the Case of Tianjin Shidiao and the Musical Expression of Urban Identity." *Asian Music* 26(1):9–52.

Rees, Helen. 1991. "An Annotated Bibliography on Shuochang (Narrative Singing)." *CHIME* 3:88–96.

———. 1994. "Unity in Diversity: Musical Promotion of Socialist Unity in Ethnically Diverse China." *MACSEM Newsletter* 13(2):3–6.

———. 1995–1996. "The Many Musics of a Chinese County Town: A Case-Study of Coexistence in Lijiang, Yunnan Province." *Asian Music* 27(1):63–102.

———. 1996. "Musical Assertion of Status among the Naxi of Lijiang County, Yunnan." In *Harmony and Counterpoint: Ritual Music in Chinese Context*, ed. B. Yung, E. S. Rawski, and R. S. Watson, 76–104. Stanford, Calif.: Stanford University Press.

———. 1998. "'Authenticity' and the Foreign Audience for Traditional Music in Southwest China." *Journal of Musicological Research* 17(2):135–161.

———. 2000. *Echoes of History: Naxi Music in Modern China*. Oxford and New York: Oxford University Press. (With 1 compact disk.)

Rees, Helen, and Sabine Trebinjac. 2001. "China 4: Minority Traditions." In *The New Grove Dictionary of Music and Musicians*, ed. Stanley Sadie and John Tyrrell, 2nd ed., 5:684–692. New York: Grove. Available: http://www.grovemusic.com.

Riddle, Ronald. 1983. *Flying Dragons, Flowing Streams—Music in the Life of San Francisco's Chinese Community*. Westwood, Conn.: Greenwood.

Riggs, Peter. 1991. "Up from Underground: Sound Technologies, Independent Musicianship, and Cultural Change in China and the Soviet Union." *Popular Music and Society* 15(1):1–23.

———. 1992. "Rock-and-Roll in China: A Samizdat Document." *Popular Music and Society* 16(4):37–39.

Riley, Jo. 1997. *Chinese Theatre and the Actor in Performance*. Cambridge: Cambridge University Press.

Robinson, Kenneth. 1980. *A Critical Study of Chu Tsai-yü's Contribution to the Theory of Equal Temperament in Chinese Music*. Wiesbaden: Steiner.

Ryker, Ana. 2001. "Hong Kong: Art Music." In *The New Grove Dictionary of Music and Musicians*, ed. Stanley Sadie and John Tyrrell, 2nd ed., 11:685–686. New York: Grove. Available: http://www.grovemusic.com.

Ryker, Harrison, ed. 1991. *New Music in the Orient: Essays on Composition in Asia since World War II*. Buren: Frits Knuf.

Salter, Denis. 1996. "China's Theatre of Dissent: A Conversation with Mou Sen and Wu Wenguang." *Asian Theatre Journal* 13(2):218–228.

Samson, Valerie. 1991. "Music as Protest Strategy: The Example of Tiananmen Square 1989." *Pacific Review of Ethnomusicology* 6:35–64.

———. 1999. "Chinese Music in the San Francisco Bay Area." *ACMR Reports* 12:47–102.

Sargent, Stuart H. 1994. "Contexts of the Song Lyric in Sung Times: Communication Technology, Social Change, Morality." In *Voices of the Song Lyric in China*, ed. P. Yu, 226–256. Berkeley: University of California Press.

Schaberg, David. 1999. "Song and the Historical Imagination in Early China." *Harvard Journal of Asiatic Studies* 59(2):305–361.

Schaffrath, Helmut. 1993. *Ein hundert chinesische Volkslieder: Eine Anthologie*. Studien zur Volkslied-Forschung 14. Bern: Peter Lang.

Schimmelpenninck, Antoinet. 1990a. "Hundred Years of Folk Song Studies in China." *CHIME* 2:4–23.

———. 1990b. "Report on Fieldwork—Jiangsu Folk Song." *CHIME* 1:16–29.

———. 1995. "Recherches dans la province du Jiangsu." *Cahiers de Musiques Traditionnelles* 8:33–57.

———. 1997. *Chinese Folk Songs and Folk Singers: Shan'ge Traditions in Southern Jiangsu*. Leiden: *CHIME*. (With 1 compact disk.)

Schimmelpenninck, Antoinet, and Frank Kouwenhoven. 1993. "The Shanghai Conservatory of Music: History and Foreign Students' Experiences." *CHIME* 6:56–91.

Schimmelpenninck, Antoinet, and Frank Kouwenhoven. 1995. "Female Folk Singers in Jiangsu, China." In *Ethnomusicology in the Netherlands: Present Situation and Traces of the Past*, ed. Wim van Zanten and Marjolijn J. van Roon, 261–274. Leiden: Center of Non-Western Studies, Leiden University.

Schönfelder, Gerd. 1972. *Die Musik der Peking-Oper*. Leipzig: Deutscher Verlag für Musik.

Scott, Adolphe Clarence. 1971. *Mei Lanfang: The Life and Times of a Peking Opera Actor*. Hong Kong: Hong Kong University Press.

———. 1980. "China 6: Since 1949." In *The New Grove Dictionary of Music and Musicians*, ed. Stanley Sadie, 4:279–283. London: Macmillan; Washington: Grove's Dictionaries of Music.

———. 1981. *Literature and the Arts in Twentieth Century China*. Westport, Conn.: Greenwood.

Shen, Qia. 1999. "Ethnomusicology in China," trans. Jonathan Stock. *Journal of Music in China* 1(1):7–38.

Shen, Yao. 1988. "Dramatic Suggestions in Traditional Chinese Opera." *Chinese Literature* 161–169.

Shigeo, Kishibe. 1980. "China 2: Court Traditions (Ya-Yüeh)." In *The New Grove Dictionary of Music and Musicians*, ed. Stanley Sadie, 4:250–

253. London: Macmillan; Washington: Grove's Dictionaries of Music.

Siu, Wang-Ngai, and Peter Lovrick. 1997. *Chinese Opera: Images and Stories*. Vancouver: UBC Press; Seattle: University of Washington Press.

Standifer, James A. 1986. "China's Multicultural Population: Insights from Minority Nationalities and Their Music." *International Journal of Music Education* 8(2):17–24, 30.

———. 1986. "Everyday Music in a Chinese Province." *Music Educator's Journal* 73(3):32–34, 39–40.

Steen, Andreas. 1996. *Der Lange Marsch des Rock 'n' Roll: Pop- und Rockmusik in der Volksrepublik China*. Berliner China-Studien 32. Hamburg: LIT-Verlag.

———. 1998. "A New Music Style? Buddhism and Rock Music." *CHIME* 12–13:151–164.

———. 1999–2000. "Zhou Xuan: 'When Will the Gentleman Come Back Again?'" *CHIME* 14–15:124–153.

Stevens, Catherine. 1990. "The Slopes of Changban: A Beijing Drumsong in the Liu Style." *CHINOPERL Papers* 15:69–83.

Stock, Jonathan P. J. 1992a. "Constructive Techniques in Music for Chinese Two-Stringed Fiddles." *CHIME*: 5:65–74.

———. 1992b. "Contemporary Recital Solos for the Chinese Two-Stringed Fiddle Erhu." *British Journal of Ethnomusicology* 1:55–88.

———. 1993a. "An Ethnomusicological Perspective on Musical Style, with Reference to Music for Chinese Two-Stringed Fiddles." *Journal of the Royal Musical Association* 118(2):276–299.

———. 1993b. "A Historical Account of the Chinese Two-Stringed Fiddle *Erhu*." *Galpin Society Journal* 46:83–113.

———. 1993–1994. "Three *Erhu* Pieces by Abing: An Analysis of Improvisational Processes in Chinese Traditional Instrumental Music." *Asian Music* 25(1–2):145–176.

———. 1995. "Reconsidering the Past: Zhou Xuan and the Rehabilitation of Early Twentieth-Century Popular Music. *Asian Music* 26(2):119–135.

———. 1996a. *Musical Creativity in Twentieth-Century China: Abing, His Music, and Its Changing Meanings*. Rochester: University of Rochester Press. (With 1 compact disk.)

———. 1996b. "Musical Narrative, Ideology, and the Life of Abing." *Ethnomusicology* 40(1):49–73.

———. 1997. "*Huju* and Musical Change: The Rise of a Local Operatic Form in East China, to 1920." *ACMR Reports* 10(1):14–38.

———. 1999. "A Reassessment of the Relationship between Text, Speech Tone, Melody, and Aria Structure in Beijing Opera." *Journal of Musicological Research* 18(3):183–206.

Stock, Jonathan S. C., and Joanna C. Lee. 2001. "China 4: Western-Influenced Styles." In *The New Grove Dictionary of Music and Musicians*, ed. Stanley Sadie and John Tyrrell, 2nd ed., 5:692–

695. New York: Grove. Available: http://www.grovemusic.com.

Stuart, Kevin, and Hu Jun. 1993. "That All May Prosper: The Mongour (Tu) *Nadun* of the Guanting/Sanchuan Region, Qinghai, China." *Anthropos* 88(1–3):15–27.

Tan, Shzr Ee. 1999/2000. "The Real Amis Enigma: Life History of a Taiwanese Aboriginal Musician." *CHIME* 14–15:70–81.

Tan, Sooi Beng. 2000. "The *Huayue Tuan* (Chinese Orchestra) in Malaysia: Adapting to Survive." *Asian Music* 31(2):107–128.

Tang, Jianping. 1999. "Tradition Is Alive: A Study of the Chamber Music Compositions *Duo Ye* and *Sparkle* by Chen Yi," trans. Yang Ruhuai. *Journal of Music in China* 1(1):133–145.

Tang, Yating. 2000. "Influence of Western Ethnomusicology on China: A Historical Reevaluation." *Journal of Music in China* 2(1):53–72.

Thrasher, Alan R. 1978. "The Transverse Flute in Chinese Traditional Music." *Asian Music* 10(1):92–114.

———. 1981. "The Sociology of Chinese Music: An Introduction." *Asian Music* 12(2):17–53.

———. 1985. "The Melodic Structure of Jiangnan Sizhu." *Ethnomusicology* 29:237–263.

———. 1988. "Hakka-Chaozhou Instrumental Repertoire: An Analytic Perspective on Traditional Creativity." *Asian Music* 19(2):1–30.

———. 1989. "Structural Continuity in Chinese Sizhu: The *Baban* Model." *Asian Music* 20(2):67–106.

———. 1990. *La-Li-Luo Dance-Songs of the Chuxiong Yi, Yunnan Province, China*. Danbury, Conn.: World Music.

———. 1993. "East Asia: China." In *Ethnomusicology*, Vol. 2: *Historical and Regional Studies*, ed. Helen Myers, 311–344. London: Macmillan Norton.

———. 1995. "The Melodic Model as a Structural Device: Chinese *Zheng* and Japanese *Koto* Repertories Compared." *Asian Music* 26(2):97–118.

———. 2000. *Chinese Musical Instruments*. Hong Kong: Oxford University Press.

———. 2001a. "China 1: Introduction: Historical, Regional and Study Perspectives." In *The New Grove Dictionary of Music and Musicians*, ed. Stanley Sadie and John Tyrrell, 2nd ed., 5:631–637. New York: Grove. Available: http://www.grovemusic.com.

———. 2001b. "China 3: Musical Instruments." In *The New Grove Dictionary of Music and Musicians*, ed. Stanley Sadie and John Tyrrell, 2nd ed., 5:654–660. New York: Grove. Available: http://www.grovemusic.com.

Tian, Qing. 1994. "Recent Trends in Buddhist Music Research in China." *British Journal of Ethnomusicology* 3:63–72.

———. 1999/2000. "The Sinicization of Buddhist Music (Part 1)." *CHIME* 14–15:8–30.

Tong, Kin-woon. 1983–1984. "Shang Musical Instruments." *Asian Music* 14(2):17–182; 15(1):103–184; 15(2):68–143.

Trebinjac, Sabine. 1990. "Chine: Le pouvoir en chantant." *Cahiers de Musiques Traditionnelles* 3:109–117.

———. 1995. "Femme, seule et venue d'ailleurs: Trois atouts d'une ethnomusicologue au Turkestan chinois (A Woman, a Woman Alone, and an Outsider: Three Assets of an Ethnomusicologist in Chinese Turkestan)." *Cahiers de Musiques Traditionnelles* 8:59–68.

Tsao, Pen-yeh. 1986. "Training of T'an-tz'u Performers: The Process of Oral Transmission in the Perpetuation of the Su-chou Singing-Narrative." In *The Oral and the Literate*, ed. Yoshihiko Tokumaru and Osamu Yamaguti, 221–231. Tokyo: Academia.

———. 1988. *The Music of Su-chou T'an-tz'u: Elements of the Chinese Southern Singing-Narrative*. Hong Kong: Chinese University Press.

———. 1989a. "Structural Elements in the Music of Chinese Story-Telling." *Asian Music* 20(2):129–151.

———. 1989b. *Taoist Ritual Music of the Yu-lan Pen-hui (Feeding the Hungry Ghost Festival) in a Hong Kong Taoist Temple*. Hong Kong: Hai Feng.

———. 1992. "Media Technology and Its Impact on the Dynamics of Musical Culture: The Hong Kong/China Phenomena." In *World Music—Musics of the World: Aspects of Documentation, Mass Media, and Acculturation*, ed. Max Peter Baumann, 243–356. Wilhelmshaven: Noetzel.

———. 1998. *Tradition and Change in the Performance of Chinese Music*. Amsterdam: Harwood Academic.

Tsao, Pen-yeh, and Daniel P. L. Law, eds. 1989. *Studies of Taoist Rituals and Music of Today*. Hong Kong: Society of Ethnomusicological Research.

Tsao, Pen-yeh, and Shi Xinming. 1992. "Current Research of Taoist Ritual Music in Mainland China and Hong Kong." *Yearbook for Traditional Music* 24:118–125.

Tuohy, Sue. 1991. "Cultural Metaphors and Reasoning: Folklore Scholarship and Ideology in Contemporary China." *Asian Folklore Studies* 50:189–220.

———. 1999. "The Social Life of Genre: The Dynamics of Folksong in China." *Asian Music* 30(2):39–86.

———. 2001. "The Sonic Dimensions of Nationalism in Modern China: Musical Representation and Transformation." *Ethnomusicology* 45(1):107–131.

Utz, Christian. 1998. "Tan Dun's Art for a New Generation: 'Extreme Crossover, Extremely Personal Music.'" *CHIME* 12–13:142–150.

Van Aalst, J. A. 1964. *Chinese Music*. Reprint. New York: Paragon.

Van Gulik, Robert Hans. 1951. "Brief Note on the Cheng, the Chinese Small Zither." In *Tōyō onagaku kenkyū*, ix.

———. 1969a. *Hsi Kang and His Poetical Essay on the Lute*. Monumenta Nipponica. Tôkyô: Sophia University; Rutland, Vt.: Tuttle.

———. 1969b. *The Lore of the Chinese Lute: An Essay in the Ideology of the Ch'in*. Tôkyô: Sophia University; Rutland, Vt.: Tuttle.

———. 1986. "On Wings of Song: The Lute and the Crane in Chinese Tradition." *Courier* 39(4):18–20.

Wang, Ying-fen. 1992. "The 'Mosaic Structure' of Nanguan Songs: An Application of Semiotic Analysis." *Yearbook for Traditional Music* 24: 24–51.

———. 1996. "For Better or for Worse: State Involvement in the Transmission of Nanguan in Taiwan." In *Dynamics of Asian Music: Tradition and Its Modification*, ed. Tomoaki Fujii. Ôsaka: National Museum of Ethnology.

Wang, Ch'iu Kuei. 1995. "Studies in Chinese Ritual and Ritual Theater: A Bibliographical Report." *CHINOPERL Papers* 18:115–130.

Wang, Hong. 1990. "The Big Anthology of Chinese Folk Music." *CHIME* 2:43–51.

Wang, Zichu. 1996. "The Marquis Yi of Zeng Stand of Bells." *Sonus* 17(1):14–19.

Ward, Barbara E. 1985. "Regional Operas and Their Audiences: Evidence From Hong Kong." In *Popular Culture in Late Imperial China*, ed. David Johnson, Andrew J. Nathan, and Evelyn S. Rawski, 161–187. Berkeley: University of California Press.

Watson, Rubie S. 1996. "Chinese Bridal Laments: The Claims of a Dutiful Daughter." In *Harmony and Counterpoint: Ritual Music in Chinese Context*, ed. B. Yung, E. S. Rawski, and R. S. Watson, 107–129. Stanford, Calif.: Stanford University Press.

Wei, Li. 1992. "The Duality of the Sacred and the Secular in Chinese Buddhist Music: An Introduction." *Yearbook for Traditional Music* 24:81–90.

———. 1997. "Life Cycle Rituals and Their Music among the Mosuo of Yongning." *CHIME* 10–11:153–156.

Wells, Marnix St. J. 1991. "Rhythm and Phrasing in Chinese Tune-Title Lyrics: Old Eight-Beat and Its 3-2-3 Meter." *Asian Music* 23(1):119–183.

———. 1998. "The Operatic Three-Line Coda: Three-Line Tail Sounds." *CHIME* 12–13:41–69.

Wichmann, Elizabeth. 1991. *Listening to Theatre: The Aural Dimension of Beijing Opera*. Honolulu: University of Hawaii Press.

Witzleben, J. Lawrence. 1987. "*Jiangnan Sizhu* Music Clubs in Shanghai: Context, Concept, and Identity." *Ethnomusicology* 31:240–260.

———. 1994. "An Ethnomusicological Perspective on the Development of Chinese Instrumental Music." In *History of New Music in China: The Development of China's Music*, ed. Liu Ching-chih and Wu Ganbo, 485–492. Hong Kong: University of Hong Kong, Center of Asian Studies.

———. 1995. *"Silk and Bamboo" Music in Shanghai: The Jiangnan Sizhu Instrumental Ensemble Tradition*. Kent, Ohio: Kent State University Press.

———. 1999. "Cantopop and Mandapop in Pre-Postcolonial Hong Kong: Identity Negotiation in the Performances of Anita Mui Yim-Fong." *Popular Music* 18(2):255–272.

———. 2001. "Musical Systems and Intergenre Relationships in Hong Kong." *World of Music* 42(3):79–91.

———. 2002. "Music in the Hong Kong Handover Ceremonies: A Community Re-Imagines Itself." *Ethnomusicology* 46(1):120–133.

Wixted, John Timothy. 1994. "The Poetry of Li Ch'ing-Chao: A Woman Author and Women's Authorship." In *Voices of the Song Lyric in China*, ed. P. Yu, 145–168. Berkeley: University of California Press.

Wolpert, Rembrandt F. 1990. "A Talk at the Kingston Seminar: Student of Chinese Music?" *CHIME* 1:10–15.

Wong, Cynthia. 1996. "Cui Jian: Rock Musician and Reluctant Hero." *ACMR Reports* 9(1):21–32.

Wong, Isabel K. F. 1984. "Geming Gequ: Songs for the Education of the Masses." In *Popular Chinese Literature and Performing Arts in the People's Republic of China, 1949–1979*, ed. B. McDougall, 112–143. Berkeley: University of California Press.

———. 1991. "From Reaction to Synthesis: Chinese Musicology in the Twentieth Century." In *Comparative Musicology and Anthropology of Music*, ed. Bruno Nettl and Philip V. Bohlman, 37–55. Chicago: University of Chicago Press.

Wong, James. 1997. "Popular Music and Hong Kong Culture." In *Asian Music with Special Reference to China and India—Music Symposia of 34th ICANAS*, ed. Liu Ching-chi, 95–110. Hong Kong: University of Hong Kong Centre of Asian Studies.

Wu, Ben. 1997. "Music Scholarship, West and East: Tibetan Music as a Case Study of Asian Music." *Asian Music* 29(2):31–56.

Wu, Tsu-kuang, et al. 1981. *Peking Opera and Mei Lanfang: A Guide to China's Traditional Theatre and the Art of Its Great Master*. Beijing: New World.

Wu, Zhao. 1996. "The Music and Ritual of the Luobowan M1 Tomb's Occupant." *Sonus* 17(1):27–43.

Xiang, Yang. 2000. "Music Households in Feudal China: A Report on the Data of Yuehu Collected from Shanxi Province," trans. Zhou Qinru and Cui Yanzhi. *Journal of Music in China* 2(1):7–28.

Xu, You-nian. 1986. "A Comparison of Malay Pantuns and Chinese Folk Songs." *Revue de Littérature Comparée* 60(238):149–167.

Xue, Jinyan. 1999. "Baban: A Long-Standing Form in Chinese Traditional Music," trans. Sun Hai. *Journal of Music in China* 1(1):77–94.

Yang, Daniel Shih-P'eng. 1967. *An Annotated Bibliography of Materials for the Study of the Peking Theatre*. Wisconsin China Series 2. Madison: University of Wisconsin.

Yang, Jinhe, and Li Hanjie. 1998. "Music History of the Dai." In *History of Music of Chinese Ethnic Minorities* (1), ed. Yuan Bingchang and Feng Guangyu, chap. 10. Beijing: Central Nationality University.

Yang, Mu. 1988–1989. "The *Ediang* of Hainan Island: A Variant of the Folksong Tradition of the Han People of China." *Musicology Australia* 11–12:65–86.

———. 1993. *Chinese Musical Instruments: An Introduction*. Canberra: Coralie Rockwell Foundation, Australian National University.

———. 1994a. "Academic Ignorance or Political Taboo? Some Issues in China's Study of Its Folk Song Culture." *Ethnomusicology* 38(2):303–320.

———. 1994b. "On the *Hua'er* Songs of Northwestern China." *Yearbook for Traditional Music* 26:100–116.

———. 1995–1996. "Music Loss among Ethnic Minorities in China: A Comparison of the Li and Hui Peoples." *Asian Music* 27(1):103–131.

———. 1997. "On Musical Instruments of the Li People of Hainan, China." *World of Music* 39(3):91–112.

———. 1998. "Erotic Musical Activity in Multiethnic China." *Ethnomusicology* 42(2):199–264.

Yao, Hai-hsing. 1990. "The Relationship between Percussive Music and the Movement of Actors in Peking Opera." *Asian Music* 21(2):39–70.

Yeh, Chia-ying. 1994. "Wang Kuo-Wei's Song Lyrics in the Light of His Own Theories." In *Voices of the Song Lyric in China*, ed. P. Yu, 257–297. Berkeley: University of California Press.

Yeh, Nora. 1988. "Nanguan Music Repertoire: Categories, Notation, and Performance Practice." *Asian Music* 19(2):31–70.

———. 1990. "Wisdom of Ignorance: Women Performers in the Classical Chinese Music Traditions." In *Women, Gender, and Culture*, ed. Marcia Herndon and Susanne Ziegler, 157–172. Wilhelmshaven: Florian Noetzel Verlag.

Yeung, Angela. 1999. "The Right Question for Chance: *I Ching* and Cage Revisited." *Journal of Music in China* 1(1):101–110.

Ying, Youqin. 2000. "The *Gamelan Slendro* Scales Reevaluated," trans. Tang Yating. *Journal of Music in China* 2(2):165–192.

Yu, Hui. 1997. "Discontinuity in *Guqin* Temperament Prior to the Fifteenth Century: An Investigation of Temperament of *Guqin* Music as Evidenced in Shen Qi Mi Pu." *CHIME* 10–11:79–110.

Yu, Pauline. 1994a. "Song Lyrics and the Canon: A Look at Anthologies of *Tz'u*." In *Voices of the Song Lyric in China*, ed. P. Yu, 70–103. Berkeley: University of California Press.

———, ed. 1994b. *Voices of the Song Lyric in China*. Berkeley: University of California Press.

Yu, Shiao-Ling. 1997. *Chinese Drama since the Cultural Revolution: An Anthology*. China Studies, Vol. 3. Lewiston, N.Y.: Edwin Mellin.

Yu, Siuwah. 1994. "Creativity in Musical Adaptation: A Hakka Zither Melody in a Cantonese Opera." In *Themes and Variations: Writings on Music in Honor of Rulan Chao Pian*, ed. Bell Yung and Joseph S. C. Lam, 111–144. Cambridge, Mass.: Department of Music, Harvard University.

Yuan, Jingfang. 1996. "The Capital Music of the Zhihua Temple." *Sonus* 17(1):20–26.

Yung, Bell. 1976. "Reconstructing a Lost Performance Context: A Field Work Experiment." *CHINOPERL Papers* 6:120–143.

———. 1980. "China 4: Theory." In *The New Grove Dictionary of Music and Musicians*, ed. Stanley Sadie, 4:260–262. London: Macmillan; Washington: Grove's Dictionaries of Music.

———. 1983a. "Creative Process in Cantonese Opera." *Ethnomusicology* 27(1):29–47; 27(2):297–318; 27(3):439–456.

———. 1983b. "The Role of Speech Tone in the Creative Process of the Cantonese Opera." *CHINOPERL News* 5:157–167.

———. 1984a. "Choreographic and Kinaesthetic Elements in Performance of the Chinese Seven-String Zither." *Ethnomusicology* 28:505–517.

———. 1984b. "Model Opera as Model: From Shajiabang to Sagabong." In *Popular Chinese Literature and Performing Arts in the People's Republic of China, 1949–1979*, ed. B. McDougall, 144–164. Berkeley: University of California Press.

———. 1987. "Historical Interdependency of Music: A Case Study of the Chinese Seven-String Zither." *Journal of the American Musicological Society* 40:82–91.

———. 1989a. *Cantonese Opera: Performance as Creative Process*. Cambridge Studies in Ethnomusicology. Cambridge: Cambridge University Press.

———. 1989b. "La musique du *guqin*: Du cabinet du lettré à la scène de concert." *Cahiers de Musiques Traditionnelles* 2:51–61.

———. 1994. "Not Notating the Notable: Reevaluating the *Guqin* Notational System." In *Themes and Variations: Writings on Music in Honor of Rulan Chao Pian*, ed. Bell Yung and Joseph S. C. Lam, 45–58. Cambridge, Mass.: Department of Music, Harvard University.

———, ed. 1995. *Celestial Airs of Antiquity: Music of the Seven-string Zither of China*. Recent Researches in the Oral Traditions of Music 5. Madison, Wisc.: A-R Editions.

———. 1996. "The Nature of Chinese Ritual Sound." In *Harmony and Counterpoint: Ritual Music in Chinese Context*, ed. B. Yung, E. S. Rawski, and R. S. Watson, 13–31. Stanford, Calif.: Stanford University Press.

———. 1998. "Music of *Qin*: From the Scholar's Study to the Concert Stage." *ACMR Reports* 11:1–14.

Yung, Bell, et al., eds. 1998. *Gems of Ancient Chinese Zithers: Shum's Collection of Ancient Qin from the Last Millenium*. Hong Kong: Department of Music and University Museum and Art Gallery, University of Hong Kong and Deyin Qing Society.

Yung, Bell, and Joseph S. C. Lam, eds. 1994. *Themes and Variations: Writings on Music in Honor of Rulan Chao Pian*. Cambridge, Mass.: Department of Music, Harvard University; Hong Kong: Institute of Chinese Studies, Chinese University of Hong Kong.

Yung, Bell, Evelyn S. Rawski, and Rubie S. Watson, eds. 1996. *Harmony and Counterpoint: Ritual Music in Chinese Context.* Stanford, Calif.: Stanford University Press.

Zevik, Emma, and Zhou Xiangping. 1998. "Sichuan Street Songs." *CHIME* 12–13:87–97.

Zha, Jianying. 1995. *China Pop: How Soap Operas, Tabloids, and Bestsellers Are Transforming a Culture.* New York: New Press.

Zhang, Boyu. 1997. "Chinese Music and Ethnomusicology." *Etnomusikologian Vuosikirja* 9:227–257.

Zhang, Xingrong. 1997. "A New Discovery: Traditional Eight-Part Polyphonic Singing of the Hani of Yunnan," trans. Helen Rees. *CHIME* 10–11:145–152.

Zhang, Wei-hua. 1992. "Music in Ming Daily Life, as Portrayed in the Narrative Jin Ping Mei." *Asian Music* 23(2):105–134.

———. 1993–1994. "Fred Wei-han Ho: Case Study of a Chinese-American Creative Musician." *Asian Music* 25(1–2):81–114.

———. 2000. "Notes on the Current Jazz Scene in China." *Journal of Music in China* 2(2):265–272.

Zhang, Z., and H. Schaffrath. 1991. "China's Mountain Songs." *CHIME* 4:23–33.

Zhao, Feng. 1988. "Chinese Traditional Music and Music Education." *ISME Yearbook* 15:81–89.

Zheng, Ruzhong. 1993. "Musical Instruments in the Wall Paintings of Dunhuang." *CHIME* 7:4–56.

Zheng, Su. 1990. "Music and Migration: Chinese Traditional Music in New York City." *World of Music* 32(3):48–67.

———. 1993. "From Toisan to New York: *Muk'yu* Songs in Folk Tradition." *CHINOPERL Papers* 16:165–205.

———. 1994. "Music Making in Cultural Displacement: The Chinese American Odyssey." *Diaspora* 3(3):273–288.

———. 1997. "Female Heroes and Moonish Lovers: Women's Paradoxical Identities in Modern Chinese Songs." *Journal of Women's History* 8(40):91–125.

———. 1999. "Redefining Yin and Yang: Transformation of Gender/Sexual Politics in Chinese Music." In *Audible Traces: Music, Gender, and Identity*, ed. Elaine Barkin and Lydia Hamessley, 153–176. Zurich: Carciofoli.

———. 2001. *Claiming Diaspora: Music, Transnationalism, and Cultural Politics in Asian/Chinese America.* Oxford: Oxford University Press.

Zhu, Jiajun. 1994. "Stylistic Changes of National Music through the Reception of Western Music: Cases in China." In *Music Cultures in Interaction: Cases between Asia and Europe*, ed. Mabuchi Usaburō and Yamaguti Osamu, 138–145. Tokyo: Academia Music.

Zhu, Yongzhong, Qi Huimin, and Kevin Stuart. 1997. "Minhe Mangghuer *Kugurjia* Songs: 'Mirror-Bright Hearts and Poor Lives.'" *CHIME* 10–11:62–78.

Zuo, Chang-yang. 1996. *Chinese Art Song: A Melodic Analysis.* Taipei: Yueh Yuhn.

Chinese-language publications

Cai, Zhongde. 1988. *Zhongguo yinyue meixue shilun* (Historical Studies of Chinese Music Aesthetics). Beijing: Renmin yinyue chubanshe (People's Music Publishing Company).

Cao, Zheng. 1980. "Guanyu ersi pu he ersi pu yu gongche pu guanxi de tantao (Discussion on 2-4 Notation and Its Relation to Gongche Notation)." *Yinyue Yanjiu* (Music Research) 4:87–94.

———. 1985. "Chaozhou guzheng liupai de jieshao (Introduction to Styles of Chaozhou Guzheng)." *Minzu Minjian Yinyue* (Chinese Folk Music) 1:28–30, 48; 2:21–24.

Chan, Sauyan [Chen Shouren]. 1996a. *Yishi, xinyang, yanzou: Sheng'gongxi yueju zai Xiang gang* (Ritual, Belief System, Performance: Cantonese Ritual Opera in Hong Kong). Hong Kong: Chinese University of Hong Kong, Cantonese Opera Research Project.

———. 1996b. *Shengongxi zai Xiang gang: Yueju, Chaoju ji Fulaoju* (Ritual Opera in Hong Kong: Cantonese Opera, Chaozhou Opera, and Fulao Opera). Hong Kong: Joint Publishing Company.

———. 1998. *Xiang gang yuequ daolun* (Introduction to Cantonese Opera in Hong Kong). Hong Kong: Chinese University of Hong Kong, Cantonese Opera Research Project.

Chen, Deju. 1957. *Guangdong yinyue de goucheng* (Structure of Cantonese Music). Guangzhou: Guangdong renmin chubanshe.

Chen, Di. 1986. "Dui liuxing yinyuede guancha (Observations on Popular Music)." *Yinyue Yanjiu* (Music Research) 3:51–60.

Chen, Geng, Zeng Xuewen, and Yan Zihe. 1997. *Gezaixi shi* (The History of Gezaixi). Beijing: Guangming ribao chubanshe.

Chen, Guoquan. 1998. *"Qing gen wo lai": Tongsu yinyue xinshang* ("Please Follow Me": An Appreciation of Popular Music). Wuhan: Huazhong ligong daxue chubanshe.

Chen, Huanjun. 1982. "Chaozhou miaotang yinyue jieshao (Introduction to Chaozhou Temple Music)." *Minzu Minjian Yinyue* (Chinese Folk Music) 4:50–53.

Chen, Huazhuo, Zhou Changbiao, and Huang Ruo. 1990. *Zhongguo youxiu min'ge xuan* (The Best of Chinese Folk Song). Guangdong: Zhongshan daxue chubanshe.

Chen, Junlin, Cai Shengtong, et al. 1989. *Chaozhoushi minjian yinyue zhi* (History of the Folk Music of Chaozhou City). Chaozhou: Chaozhou Wenhuaju.

Chen, Lei, Liu Xiangyu, and Lin Ruiwu. 1997. *Fujian difang xiju* (Fujian Regional Opera). Fuzhou: Fuzhou remin chubanshe.

Chen, Leishi. 1978. *Chaozhou yuepu ersi pu yuanliu kao* (Study of the Origin and Development of Chaozhou 2-4 notation). Hong Kong: Hong Kong Book Store.

Chen, Tianguo. 1981. "Guangdong minjian yinyue huayin gailun (Survey of Embellishments in Guangdong Folk Music). *Guangzhou Yinyue Xueyuan Xuebao* (Journal of the Guangzhou Conservatory) 4:7–8.

———. 1992. "Jin shinian lai Chaozhou yinyue yanjiu gaikuang (Survey of Research on Chaozhou Music in the Last Ten Years)." In *Zhongguo yinyue nianjian* (Yearbook of Chinese Music), ed. Zhongguo yishu yanjiu yuan and Yinyue yanjiu suo, 57–68.

Chen, Wei. 1986. "Yetan Chaozhou yinyue de 'ersipu' ji jige diao de 'qing,' 'zhong,' 'huo' he diaoxing wenti (A Discussion of *Ersipu* and Issues Relating to the Modal Attributes of Some Pieces of Chaozhou Music)." *Yinyue Yanjiu* (Music Research) 1:99–103.

Chen, Yingshi. 1985. "Gongche puzi yuanli zhi caixiang (Conjectures on the Principles of the Signs of Gongche Notation)." *Minzu Minjian Yinyue* (Chinese Folk Music) 1:44–48.

———. 1988. "Dunhuang yuepu xinjie (Reinterpretation of the Dunhuang Tablature)." *Yinyue Yishu* (The Art of Music) 1:1–24; 2:1–23.

Chen Yongzhi. 1992. "Zhongguo xin yinyue yanjiufa duili (An Overview of Contemporary Chinese Music)." In *Zhongguo xin yinyue shilunbian: Huigu yu fansi 1885–1995* (A History of New Music in China: A Critical Review 1885–1995), ed. Liu Ching-chih, 289. Hong Kong: University of Hong Kong.

Chen, Yugang. 1982. *Zhongguo guyuelü de yunshuang yu zhexi* (A Mathematical Calculation and Analysis of Ancient Chinese Tone Systems). Taipei: Shengyun.

Cheng Yun. 1988. "Zhongguo dangdai tongsu yinyue huanshi lu (An Overview of Contemporary Chinese Popular Music)." *Renmin Yinyue* (People's Music) 2:2–6.

Chen, Zemin. 1989. "Pudong pipa pu (Study of the Dating of the Pudong Pipa Score)." *Zhongguo Yinyuexue* (Musicology in China) 2:116–123.

Chu Yiuwai [Chu Yaowei]. 1998. *Xianggang liuxing geci yanjiu: Qiling niandai zhongqi zhi jiuling niandai zhongqi* (Study of Hong Kong Popular Song Lyrics: From the Mid-1970s to the Mid-1990s). Hong Kong: Joint Publishing Company.

Dai, Ning. 1997. "Ming Qing shiqi Qinhuai qinglou yinyue wenhua chutan (A Preliminary Study of Qinhuai Pleasure Quarters' Musical Culture in Ming and Qing)." *Zhongguo Yinyuexue* (Musicology in China) 3:40–54.

Dong, Weisong. 1982. "Cong yinyue fazhan luoji kan 'Baban' de jiegou (The Structure of 'Baban' as Seen through the Logic of Its Musical Development)." *Zhongguo Yinyue* (Chinese Music) 2:23–24.

Dongfang Yinyue Xuehui. 1989. *Zhongguo minzu yinyue daxi: Qiyue juan* (Compendium of Chinese Music: Instrumental Music). Shanghai: Shanghai yinyue chubanshe.

Du, Yaxiong. 1986. *Zhongguo shaoshu minzu yinyue* (The Music of China's Minorities). 2 vols. Beijing: Zhongguo wenlian chubanshe.

———. 1993. *Zhongguo de shaoshu minzu minjian yinyue gaishu* (An Outline of the Folk Music of All Minority Nationalities of China). 3 vols. Beijing: Renmin yinyue chubanshe (People's Music Publishing Company). (Includes sound recording.)

———. 1994. "Caifeng he caifengzhe de pinde (Fieldwork and Fieldworkers' Ethics)." *Zhongguo Yinyue* (Chinese Music) 56:17–19.

———. 1995. *Zhongguo minzu jiben yueli* (The Fundamentals of Chinese Music Theory). Beijing: Zhongguo wenlian chuban gongsi.

Du, Yaxiong, and Zhou Ji. 1997. *Sichou zhi lu de yinyue wenhua* (The Music of the Silk Road). Beijing: Minzu chubanshe.

Encyclopedia Sinica. 1989. *Zhongguo dabaike quanshu: Yinyue wudaojuan* (Encyclopedia Sinica: Music and Dance). Beijing: Zhongguo dabaike quanshu chubanshe.

Feng, Jiexuan, and Qin Xu. 1992. "Zhongguo yinyue gudai bufen wenxianxue jianshe (The Establishment of Bibliographic Studies of Ancient Chinese Music)." *Zhongguo Yinyue Nianjian* 1992:43–51.

Feng, Ling. 1994. *Liuxing zhi feng* (Pop Is a Fad). Shanghai: Shanghai yuandong chubanshe.

Fu, Xihua, ed. 1961. *Gudian xiqu shengyun lunji chongbian* (Collected Essays on the Vocal Music of Classical Drama), 2nd reprint. Beijing: Yinyue chubanshe.

Gan, Tao. 1985. *Jiangnan sizhu yinyue* (Silk and Bamboo Music). Nanjing: Jiangsu renmin chubanshe.

Gao, Houyong. 1981. *Minzu qiyue gailun* (Survey of Chinese Instrumental Music). Nanjing: Jiangsu renmin chubanshe.

Gao, Pei. 1984. "Henan sheng ji qi yanzou tese (The Henan Sheng and Its Performance Characteristics)." *Yueqi* 5:21–22.

———. 1986. "Sheng de yange he fazhan (The Evolution and Development of the Sheng)." *Yueqi* 1:1–4; 2:3–5.

Gao, Shaocheng. 2000. "Chuanxi dipu Daojiao yinyue gaishu (Survey of Daoist Music in Western Sichuan)." *Zhongguo Daojiao* (Chinese Daoism) 4:15–22.

Gao, Ziming. 1959. *Xiandai guoyue* (Present-Day National Music). Taipei: Zhengzhong shuju.

Gu, Baozi. 1994. *Yangbanxi chutai neimo* (The Inside Story of the Making of Model Plays). Beijing: Zhonghua gongshang lianhe chubanshe.

Gu, Guangjian. 1988. "Liaonan guchui de gutao tedian (Percussion Patterns in the Drumming and Blowing Music of Southern Liaoning)." *Zhongguo Yinyue* (Chinese Music) 4:11–15.

Guan, Lin, ed. 1984. *Shengyue yishu de minzu fengge* (The National Style in Vocal Arts). Beijing: Wenhua yishu chubanshe.

Guan, Ying. 1995. *Yaogun wangzu* (The Kings of Rock). Beijing: Shenghuo dushu xinzhi sanlian shudian.

Guangzhou Shi Xiqu Gaige Weiyuanhui. [1955] 1975. *Guangdong yinyue* (Cantonese [Instru-mental] Music). Guangzhou: Guangdong renmin chubanshe. Hong Kong: Taiping shuju.

Guo, Lin. 1990. "Zhongguo gudai yinyue wen-xian gaiyao (An Outline of Primary Sources for Ancient Chinese Music History)." *Sichuan Tushu-guan Xuebao* 5:63–68.

Han, Kuohuang [Han Guohuang]. 1990. "Zhongguo de diyige Xiyang guanxian yuedui—Beijing Hade yuedui (China's First Western Orchestra, Hart's Orchestra in Beijing)." *Yinyue Yanjiu* (Music Research) 2:43–53.

———. 1992. *Zhongguo yueqi xunli* (Parade of Chinese Musical Instruments). Taipei: Wenjianhui.

Han, Shude, and Chang Zhinian. 1985. *Zhongguo pipa shigao* (History of the Chinese Pipa). Chengdu: Sichuan renmin chubanshe.

He, Changlin. 1984. "Qinyue yu Chaoyue (The Music of Shaanxi and Chaozhou)." *Jiaoxiang* (Journal of the Xi'an Conservatory) 3:10–18.

———. 1985. "Nanyin de xingcheng fazhan yu fenqi (The Formation, Development, and Period-ization of *Nanguan*)." *Minzu Minjian Yinyue* (Chinese Folk Music) 3:19.

———. 1990. "Quyuan cun sangli gezan yanjiu (Study of the Funeral Liturgy of Quyuan Village)." In *Zhongguo yinyue guoji yantao hui luwenji, 1988, Xiang gang* (Collected Essays from the International Symposium on Chinese Music, 1988, Hong Kong), ed. Qian Jianzhong and Tsao Pen-yeh, 109–147.

Hu, Dengtiao. 1982. *Minzu guanxian yuefa* (National Wind-String Music Method). Shanghai: Wenyi chubanshe.

Hu, Ji, and Liu Zhizhong. 1989. *Kunju fazhanshi* (History of Kun Opera). Beijing: Zhongguo xiju chubanshe.

Huang, Jinpei. 1982. "Lun Guangdong yinyue de xingti (A Discussion of the Waxing and Waning of Cantonese Music)." *Guangzhou Yinyue Xueyuan Xuebao* (Journal of the Guang-zhou Conservatory) 1:8–17.

———. 1984. *Guangdong yinyue xinshang* (Appreciation of Cantonese Music). Guangzhou: Guangzhou yinyue xueyuan.

———. 1989. "Qinqiang de kuyin yu Guang-dong yinyue de yifan xian (The *Kuyin* in Qinqiang and the *Yifan* Scale in Cantonese Music)." *Xinghai Yinyue Xueyuan Xuebao* (Journal of the Xinghai Conservatory) 2:15–18.

Huang, Liaoyuan, et al. 1997. *Shinian—1986–1996 Zhongguo liuxing yinyue lishi* (A Chronology of Ten Years of Popular Music in China, 1986–1996), ed. Beijing Hantang wenhua fazhan youxian gongsi. Beijing: Zhongguo dian-ying chubanshe.

———. 1998. "Shinian yaogun shizang chang-pian zhi xin changzheng lushangde yaogun (Rock 'n' Roll on the New Long March: Ten Rock Albums over the Last Ten Years)." *Yinyue Sheng-huobao* (Musical Life) 19(February):5.

Huang, Qinghe, et al., eds. 1957. *Yunnan minjian gequ xuan* (Selection of Folk Songs from Yunnan Province). Beijing: Yinyue chubanshe.

Huang, Tipei. 1983. *Zhonghua yuexue tonglun* (A Complete Discussion in Chinese Music). 10 vols. Taipei: Xingzhengyuan wenhua jianshe weiyuanhui.

Huang, Xiangpeng. 1979. "Xian Qin yinyue wenhua de guanghui chuangzao—Zeng Houyi mude gu yueqi (Brilliant Creations of Early Qin [Dynasty] Music Culture—Ancient Instruments from the Tomb of Zeng Houyi)." *Wenwu* 7:32–39.

———. 1998. "On the Preservation and Devel-opment of Traditional Chinese music." *Zhongguo Yinyuexue* (Musicology in China) 1–32. (English edition.)

Huang, Zhaohan. 1988. "Muyu kao (Study of the *Muyu*)." In *Daojiao Yanjiu Lunwen Ji* (Collected Essays on Daoist Research), 237–262. Hong Kong: Chinese University of Hong Kong.

Huang Zhihua. 1990. *Yueyu liuxing qu sishi nian* (Fifty Years of Cantonese-Language Popular Song). Hong Kong: Joint Publishing Company.

Jiang, Mingdun. 1982. *Hanzu mingge gailun* (An Introduction to Folk Songs of the Han People). Shanghai: Wenyi.

Jin, Jianmin. 1981. "Datong minjian qiyue diao-cha (Survey of Folk Instrumental Music in Datong)." *Yinyue Yishu* (The Art of Music) 3:58–64.

Jin, Wenda. 1988. "Waiguo xuezhe dui Zhongguo gudai yinyue lishi fazhan di mouxie wujie (Foreign Scholars' Misunderstandings about the Development of Ancient Chinese Music)." *Yinyue Yanjiu* (Music Research) 2:60–67.

Jin, Zhaojun. 1989. "Cui Jian yu zhongguo yaogunyue (Cui Jian and Chinese Rock Music)." *Renmin Yinyue* (People's Music) 4:32–33.

———. 1993. "Zhongguo xinshiqi liuxing yinyue chuangzuo de meixue guannian (Aesthetic Concepts in the Composition of Popular Songs in the New Era)." *Zhongyang Yinyue Xueyuan Xuebao* (Journal of the Central Conservatory of Music) 3:5–8.

Jin, Zuli, and Xu Ziren. 1983. "Shanghai minjian sizhu yinyue shi (History of Silk and Bamboo Music in Shanghai)." *Zhongguo Yinyue* (Chinese Music) 3:28–31.

Ke, Yang. 1983. *Hua'er lun ji* (Selected Papers on Flower Songs). Lanzhou: Gansu renmin chubanshe.

Leung, Pui-chee [Liang Peichi]. 1988. *Nanyin yu yue'ou zhi yanjiu* (A Study of Nanyin and Yueou). San Francisco: Asian American Studies, San Francisco State University.

Li, Fusheng. 1969. *Zhonghua Guoju Shi* (History of Chinese National Opera). Taipei: Guofangbu yinshua.

Li, Guangdi, et al., eds. [1714] 1974. *Yuzhi lülü zhengyi* (Imperially Approved Standard Interpre-tation of Music Theory). Taipei: Commercial Press.

Li, Huanzhi, ed. 1997. *Dangdai Zhongguo yinyue* (Contemporary Chinese Music). Beijing: Dangdai Zhongguo chubanshe.

Li, Ling. 1984. "Guangdong yinyue de guoqu he weilai (The Past and Future of Cantonese

Music)." *Guangzhou Yinyue Xueyuan Xuebao* (Journal of Guangzhou Conservatory) 3:1–2, 36–43.

Li, Minxiong. 1982. *Minzu qiyue gailun* (Survey of Chinese Instrumental Music). Shanghai: Shanghai Conservatory of Music.

———. 1983. *Chuantong minzu qiyue qu xinshang* (Appreciation of Traditional Chinese Instrumental Pieces). Beijing: Remin yinyue chubanshe (People's Music Publishing Company).

———. 1984. "Woguo minjian yingyong de jidiao guding changming fa (The Fixed-Pitch System of Keys Used by Chinese Folk Musicians)." *Jiaoxiang* (Journal of the Xi'an Conservatory) 4:11–19.

Li, Minxiong, et al., eds. 1989. *Zhonggou minzu yinyue daxi: Minzu qiyuejuan* (The Chinese Traditional Music Series: Volume on Instrumental Music). Shanghai: Shanghai yinyue chubanshe.

Li, Minxiong, Gu Guanren, and Tang Wenqing, eds. 1997. *Shanghai sizhu quji* (A Collection of Shanghai *Jiangnan Sizhu* Pieces). Beijing: Renmin yinyue chubanshe.

Li, Wan. 1993. "Turan yinyue shidai (An Age of Unexpected Music)." *Dushu* 12:79–81.

———. 1996. "Liuxing yinyue bushi liuxingde yinyue (Pop Music Is Not Popular Music)." *Dushu* 2:123–127.

Li, Wan, and Shi Wenhua. 1998. *Minyao liuyu* (The Sphere of Influence of Folk Songs). Beijing: Yuwen chubanshe.

Li, Xiangting. 1993. *Tangdai guqin yanzuo meixue ji yinyue sixiang yanjiu* (Research on Performance Aesthetics and Musical Thought of Tang Dynasty *Guqin* Music). Taipei: Taiwan xinzhengyuan wenhua jianshe weiyuanhui (Taiwan Cultural Construction Committee).

Li, Xiaotian, Chen Deju, et al., eds. [1952] 1971. *Yueyue mingquji* (Collection of Famous Cantonese Pieces). Shanghai: Guoguang (1952–1955 edition, 10 vols.); Hong Kong: Xincheng (1971 edition, 3 vols.).

Li, Yan. 1983. "Xian lun (Discussion of String Temperament)." *Guangzhou Yinyue Xueyuan Xuebao* (Journal of the Guangzhou Conservatory) 3:12–22.

Liang, Maochun. 1988. "Dui woguo liuxing yinyue lishi de sikao (Thoughts on the History of Chinese Popular Music)." *Renmin Yinyue* (People's Music) 7:32–34.

———. 1993. *Zhongguo dangdai yinyue, 1949–1989* (Chinese Music of Today, 1949–1989). Beijing: Beijing guangbo xueyuan chubanshe (Beijing College of Broadcasting Press).

Lin, Keren, and Chang Dunming. 1993. *Zhongguo xiao di* (Chinese Horizontal and Vertical Bamboo Flutes). 3 vols. Nanjing: Nanjing daxue chubanshe.

Lin, Qiansan [Hayashi Kenzo]. 1962. *Dongya yueqi kao* (Study of Musical Instruments in Eastern Asia). Beijing: Yinyue chubanshe.

Ling, Xuan. 1989. "Xibeifeng yu 'Qiuge' (The Northwest Wind and 'Prison Songs')." *Remin Yinyue* (People's Music) 5:37–38.

Liu, Ching-Chih [Liu, Jingzhi]. 1982. "Zhongguo yishu kequ he Kangri kequ: Zhongguo jindai yinyue shi shengyue zuopin zhan ting hou (Art Songs and Anti-Japan Songs of China: A Review of the Parade of Vocal Works in Chinese Contemporary Music History)." *Ming Bao* 17(11):42–43.

———, ed. 1986. *History of New Music in China, 1885–1919: Collected Essays.* Hong Kong: University of Hong Kong, Center of Asian Studies.

———, ed. 1988. *History of New Music in China, 1920–1945: Collected Essays.* Hong Kong: University of Hong Kong, Center of Asian Studies.

———, ed. 1990. *History of New Music in China, 1846–1976: Collected Essays.* Hong Kong: University of Hong Kong, Center of Asian Studies.

———, ed. 1992a. *History of New Music in China: A Critical Review, 1885–1985.* Hong Kong: University of Hong Kong, Center of Asian Studies.

———. 1992b. *Zhongguo xin yinyue shilunbian: Huigu yu fansi 1885–1985* (A History of New Music in China: A Critical Review 1885–1985). Hong Kong: University of Hong Kong.

Liu, Ching-Chih, and Wu Ganbo, eds. 1994. *History of New Music in China: The Development of Chinese Music.* Hong Kong: University of Hong Kong, Center of Asian Studies.

Liu, Dongsheng, and Yuan Quanyou. 1988. *Zhongguo yinyueshi tujian* (A Pictorial Guide to the History of Chinese Music). Beijing: Renmin yinyue chubanshe (People's Music Publishing Company).

Liu, Dongsheng, Hu Chuanfan, and Hu Yanjiu. 1987. *Zhongguo yueqi tuzhi* (A Pictorial Record of Chinese Musical Instruments). Beijing: Qinggongye chubanshe.

Liu, Guowei. 1998. *Taiwan sixiang qu* (Taiwan's Thought in Song). Taipei: Huafeng wenhua.

Liu, Jidian. 1981. *Jingju yinyue gailun* (An Introduction to the Music of Peking Opera). Beijing: Renmin yinyue chubanshe (People's Music Publishing Company).

Liu, Kai. 1995. *Xibu hua'er sanlun* (On Flower Songs of West China). Nanning: Gansu minzu chubanshe.

Liu, Wei, and Shi Jie, eds. 1988. *Yiwu suoyou: Liuxing gequ ji* (I Have Nothing: A Collection of Popular Songs). Wuhan: Changjiang wenyi chubanshe.

Liu, Yiran. 1988. "Yaogun qingnian (Rockin' Youth)." *Qingnian Wenxue* 10:4–11.

Liu, Zaisheng. 2000. "Lun zhongguo yinyue de lishi xingtai (On Historical Patterns of Chinese Music)." *Yinyue Yanjiu* (Music Research) 2:41–53.

Lü, Bingchuan. 1984. "Taiwan chuantong yinyue (Traditional Music of Taiwan)." *Minzu Minjian Yinyue* (Chinese Folk Music) 3:14–24.

Ma, Shaobo, et al. 1991. *Zhongguo jingju fazhanshi* (Chinese Peking Opera's History of Development). Taipei: Shangding wenhua chuban.

Mao, Jizeng. 1964. *Baisha Xiyue*. Beijing: Zhongguo yinyue yanjiusuo. (Mimeograph.)

———. 1986. "Guanyu Beishi xili de diaocha baogao (Report on an Investigation into Baisha Xiyue)." In *Naxizu shehui lishi diaocha* (Investigation of Naxi Social History), Vol. 2, 109–150. Kunming: Yunnan minzu chubanshe.

Qiao, Jianzhong. 1987. "Suzhong jian ya—Qingyin yong cun (On Finding the Elegant within the Common—The Enduring Quality of Pure Music)." *Renmin Yinyue* (People's Music) 8:16–17.

———. 1990. "Qupai lun (On Qupai)." In *Zhongguo yinyue guoji yantao hui luwenji, 1988, Xiang gang* (Collected Essays from the International Symposium on Chinese Music, 1988, Hong Kong), ed. Qian Jianzhong and Tsao Penyeh, 319–336.

———. 1998. *Tudi yu ge—Chuantong yinyue wenhua yu qi dili lishi beijing yanjiu* (Earth and Song: Study of Traditional Music Culture and Its Geographical and Historical Background). Shandong: Shandong Wenyi chubanshe (Shandong Arts Publishing Company).

Qin, Yongcheng, and Wei Li, eds. 1989. *Zhongguo minzu yinyue daquan* (A Magnificent Display of Chinese Folk Music). Shenyang: Shenyang Publishing House.

Qiu, Hechou, ed. 1917. *Xian'ge bidu* (Essential String and Vocal Music). Guangzhou.

Sun, Wei. 1989. "Dachaozhong de wenhua fangzhou: yishude shangyehua wenti (Cultural Ark in the Flood: The Question of Commercialization in the Arts)." In *Zhongguo shehui datoushe* (An Overall Perspective on Chinese Society). Beijing: Zhongguo shehui kexue chubanshe.

Sun, Yude. 1958. *Dongxiao chuizoufa* (The Playing Techniques of Dongxiao). Beijing: Renmin yinyue chubanshe (People's Music Publishing Company).

Tang, Zhongliu. 1993. *Qinge* (Qin songs). Beijing: Wenhua yishu chubanshe.

Tao, Yabing. 1994. *Zhongxi yinyue jiaoliu shigao* (History of Musical Exchange between China and the Western World). Beijing: Zhongguo dibaike quanshu chubanshe.

Tian, Liantao. 1989. "Zangzu yinyue (Tibetan Music)." In *Zhongguo dabaike quanshu: Yinyue wudaojuan* (Encyclopedia Sinica: Music and Dance), 843–845. Beijing: Zhongguo dabaike quanshu chubanshe.

Tian, Qing. 1984. *Zhongguo gudai yinyue shihua* (Historical Essays on Ancient Chinese Music). Shanghai: Wenyi chubanshe.

———. 1992. "Cong 'Jin ping mei' kan Mingdao Fojiao yinyue (Buddhist Music of the Ming Dynasty as Seen in the *Jin ping mei*)." *Zhongguo Yinyue Xue* (Musicology in China) 2:76–83.

Tian, Qing, ed. 1997. *Zhongguo zongjiao yinyue* (Chinese Religious Music). Beijing: Zongjiao wenhua chubanshe.

Wang, Fengtong, and Zhang Lin. 1992. *Zhongguo yinyue jiepaifa* (The Meters of Chinese Music). Beijing: Zhongguo wenlian chuban gongsi.

Wang, Ningyi, and Yang Heping, eds. 1996. *Ershi shiji Zhongguo yinyue meixue wenxuan juan, 1900–1949s* (Documents on Chinese Music Aesthetics in the Twentieth Century, 1900–1949). Beijing: Xiandai chubanshe.

Wang, Qiang. 2000. *Huiguan xitai yu xiqu* (The Performance Stage of Regional Associations and Opera). Taipei: Wenjin chubanshe.

Wang, Wenhe. 1995. *Zhongguo dianying yinyue xunzong* (Traces of Chinese Film Music). Beijing.

Wang, Xiaodun. 1989. "Yinyue wenxianxue he Zhongguo yinyuexue di kexue jianshe (Bibliographic Studies of Music and the Scholarly Construction of Chinese Music Studies)." *Huangzhong* 4:1–7.

Wang, Yaohua. 1989. "Xianguan yanjiu de lishi he xianzhuang (The History and Present Outlook of Nanguan Research)." In *Zhongguo yinyue nianjian* (Yearbook of Chinese Music), ed. Zhongguo yishu yanjiu yuan and Yinyue yanjiu suo, 103–116.

Wang, Yi. 1994. *Yinyue zai shijimo de Zhongguo* (Music at the End of the Century in China). Beijing: Shehui kexue chubanshe.

Wang, Yuhe. 1984. *Zhongguo jinxiandai yinyueshi* (The Contemporary Music History of China). Beijing: Renmin yinyue chubanshe (People's Music Publishing Company).

Wang, Yuhe, ed. 1991. *Zhongguo xiandai yinyue shigang* (The History of Contemporary Chinese Music). Beijing: Huawen chubanshe.

———. 1992. *Zhongguo jinxiandai yinyuejia pingzhuan* (Biographical Studies of Contemporary Chinese Composers). Beijing: Wenhua yishu chubanshe.

Wang, Zhongguo. 1992. *Shijie liuxing tongsu yinyue zhixhuang* (A Window into Popular Music). Harbin: Heilongjiang chubanshe.

Wong, Chiwah [Huang Zhihua]. 1990. *Yueyu liuxingqu sishinian* (Forty Years of Cantonese Popular Songs). Hong Kong: Joint Publishing Company.

———. 2000. *Zaoqi Xiang gang yueyu liuxingqu, 1950–1974* (Early Cantonese Popular Songs in Hong Kong, 1950–1974). Hong Kong: Joint Publishing Company.

Wu, Ben. 1987. "Chuantong pipa xiaoqu yanjiu (Study of the Traditional 'Small Piece' for Pipa)." *Yinyue Yanjiu* (Music Research) 3:60–73.

———. 1991. "Abing yanzou de yuequ zhong you ¾ yin ma? (Are Three Quarter Tones in the Pieces Played by Abing?)." *Jiaoxiang* (Journal of Xi'an Conservatory) 1:19–22.

Wu, Guodong. 1991. "Cong huangwu zou xiang fanmao: Shaoshu minzu yinyue yanjiu sishi nian (From Wasteland to Florescence: Forty Years of Research on Minority Nationality Music)."

Zhongguo Yinyuexue (Musicology in China) 24: 4–12.

Wu, Tongbingrenmin, and Zhou Yaxun. 1991. *Jingju zhishi cidian* (Dictionary of Peking Opera), ed. Xu Lixian et al. Tianjin renmin chubanshe.

Wu, Zhao, and Liu Dongsheng. 1983. *Zhongguo yinyue shilue* (A Historical Sketch of Chinese Music). Beijing: Renmin yinyue chubanshe (People's Music Publishing Company).

Xia, Ye. 1989. *Zhongguo gudai yinyueshi jianbian* (Concise History of Ancient Chinese Music). Shanghai: Shanghai wenyi chubanshe.

Xiang, Yang. 1996. "Shanxi 'yuehu' kaoshu (Study of Hereditary Family of Entertainers in Shanxi)." *Yinyue yanjiu* (Music Research) 1:76–88.

Xiang, Zuhua. 1981. "Yangqin de yuanliu jiqi fazhan (The Origin and Development of the Yangqin)." *Zhongguo Yinyue* (Chinese Music) 3:26–28.

———. 1990. "Guangdong yinyue yangqin liu pai jiqi fengge (*Yangqin* Traditions in Cantonese Music and Their Styles)." *Zhongguo Yinyue* (Chinese Music) 4:27–29.

Xiao, Yaotian. 1985. *Chaozhou xiqu yinyuezhi* (The Chronicle of Chaozhou Opera and Music). Penang: Tianfeng chubanshe.

Xiu, Jun, and Jian Jin. 1993. *Zhongguo yueji shi* (History of Chinese Female Music Entertainers). Beijing: Zhongguo wenlian chuban gongsi.

Xu, Chaoming. 1991. "Sheng de heyin yu jieheyin (Sheng Harmony and Combined Tones)." *Yinyue Yishu* 4:6–9.

Xu, Jian. 1982. *Qinshi chupian* (An Introduction of the History of the Qin). Beijing: Renmin yinyue chubanshe (People's Music Publishing Company).

Xu, Muyun, and Huang Liaheng, eds. 1980. *Jingju ziyun* (Words and Rhymes in Peking Opera). Shanghai: Shanghai wenyi chubanshe.

Xue, Ji, ed. 1993. *Yaogun xunmeng: Zhongguo yaogunyue shilu* (In Search of the Rock 'n' Roll Dream: The True Story of Chinese Rock). Beijing: Zhongguo dianying chubanshe.

Xue, Yibing. 1985. "Yang'ge yuanliu bianxi (Study of the Origins of *Yang'ge*)." *Wudaoyishu* (The Art of Dance) 4:123–136.

———. 1990. "Jieshao yizhong Zangwen gongche pu (Introducing a Type of Gongche Notation in Tibetan)." *Huangzhong* (Yellow Bell) 4:28–30.

Yan, Haideng, et al. 1975. *Sheng de yanzoufa* (Performance Method for *Sheng*). Beijing: Renmin yinyue chubanshe (People's Music Publishing Company).

Yang, Hua. 1997. *Xian qin liyue wenhua* (Ritual and Music before the Early Qin Dynasty). Wuhan: Hubei jiaoyu chubanshe.

Yang, Minkang. 1992. *Zhongguo min'ge yu xiangtu shehui* (Chinese Folk Song and Local Society). Changchun: Jilin jiaoyu chubanshe.

Yang, Ruiqing. 1989. "Xibeifeng gequ heyi chengchao? (Why Does the Northwest Wind

Wave?)." *Yinyue wudao yanjiu* (Music and Dance Research) 5:8.

Yang, Wenyong, ed. 1990. *Zhongguo gexing gegu lu* (Chinese Pop Stars and Pop Songs). 2 vols. Beijing: Dongfang chubanshe.

Yang, Yinliu. 1953. *Zhongguo yinyue shigang* (An Outline of the History of Chinese Music). Shanghai: Wanye shudian.

———. 1962. *Gongche pu qianshuo* (Elementary Notes on *Gongche* Notation). Beijing: Yinyue chubanshe.

———. [1974] 1986. "Sheng yu kao (Examination of *Sheng* and *Yu*)." *Yueqi Keji Jianxun*, Vol. 3. In *Yang Yinliu yinyue lunwen xuanji*, 360–384. Shanghai: Wenyi chubanshe.

———. 1981. *Zhongguo gudai yinyue shigao* (A Draft History of Ancient Chinese Music). Beijing: Renmin yinyue chubanshe (People's Music Publishing Company).

Ye, Dong. 1983. *Minzu qiyue de ticai yu xingshi* (The Form and Structure of Chinese Instrumental Music). Shanghai: Wenyi chubanshe.

Yip, Ming Mei [Ye Mingmei]. 1991. *Guqin yinyue yishu* (The Art of *Guqin* Music). Hong Kong: Commerical Printing House.

Yu, Xunfa, and Wu Ximin. 1990. *Zhongguo zhudi* (The Chinese Bamboo Flute). Taiwan: Danqing tushu gongsi (Pictorial Book Company).

Yuan, Bingchang, and Mao Jizeng, eds. 1986. *Zhongguo shaoshu minzu yueqi zhi* (Musical Instruments of China's National Minorities). Beijing: Xin shijie chubanshe.

Yuan, Jingfang. 1983. "Minjian luoguyue jiegou danwei: Dui shifan luogu zhong luoguyue de fengxi yanjiu (An Introduction to the Structure of Folk *Luogu* Music: An Analytical Study of the *Luogu* Music of *Shifan Luogu*)." *Zhongyang yinyue xueyuan xuebao* (Journal of the Central Conservatory of Music) 2:15–24.

———. 1986. *Minzu qiyue xinshang shouce* (Handbook for the Appreciation of Chinese Instrumental Music). Beijing: Zhongguo wenlian chuban gongsi.

———. 1987. *Minzu qiyue* (Chinese Instrumental Music). Beijing: Renmin yinyue chubanshe (People's Music Publishing Company).

———. 1999. *Yuezhong xue* (The Study of Musical Genre). Beijing: Huayue chubanshe.

Zeng, Huijia. 1998. *Cong liuxing gequ kan Taiwan shehui* (Looking at Taiwan Society through Popular Songs). Taipei: Guiguan chuban gongsi.

Zeng, Suijin. 1988. "Gangtai liuxing gequ zhongjihou de huigu (A Look Back at the Influx of Popular Songs from Hong Kong and Taiwan)." *Zhongguo Yinyuexue* (Musicology in China) 2:44–51.

———. 1997. *Yinyue shehuixue gailun* (An Introduction to the Sociology of Music). Beijing: Wenhua yishu chubanshe.

Zeng, Wan, Ai Qun, and Jin Hua, eds. 1992. *Zhongguo minjian ertong gequ ji* (Anthology of Popular Chinese Children's Songs). Beijing:

Renmin yinyue chubanshe (People's Music Publishing Company).

Zhang, Bojie. 1981. "Chaozhou yinyue de lishi yange, yanzou xingshe he yishu tedian (The Historical Development, Performance Practice, and Musical Characteristics of Chaozhou Music)." *Minzu Minjian Yinyue* (Chinese Folk Music) 1:29–33.

Zhang, Faying. 1991. *Zhongguo xiban shi* (History of Chinese Theater Troupes). Shenyang: Shenyang chubanshe.

Zhang, Geng, ed. 1981. *Zhongguo xiqu tongshi* (A General History of Chinese Drama). Beijing: Renmin yinyue chubanshe (People's Music Publishing Company).

Zhang, Wen. 1981. "Xinmin'ge yundong yu minjian wenxue (The New Folk Song Movement and Folk Literature)." In *Minjian wenyi jikan* (A Collection of Articles on Folk Arts), ed. Wang Wenhua. Shanghai: Shanghai wenyi chubanshe.

Zhao, Jianwei. 1992. *Cui Jian zai Yiwusuoyou zhong nahan: Zhongguo yaogun beiwanglu* (Cui Jian Shouting 'Nothing to My Name': China's Rock 'n' Roll Memoir). Beijing: Beijing shifan daxue chubanshe.

Zhao, Songting. 1985. *Diyi chunqiu* (Spring and Autumn of the Art of the Di). Hangzhou: Zhejiang renmin chubanshe (Zhejiang People's Publishing Company).

Zheng, Jinwen. 1924. *Xiaodi xinpu* (New Music for Xiao and Di). Shanghai: Shanghai wenming shuju.

Zheng, Jinyang. 1988. "Zhongguo yinyue shixue di disan jieduan (The Third Stage of Historical Studies of Chinese Music)." *Yinyue Yanjiu* (Music Research) 3:12–21.

———. 1990. "Zhongguo yinyueshi di hongguan shikong siye (The Purview of a Macro View of Chinese Music History)." *Zhongguo Yinyue* (Chinese Music) 1:33.

Zheng, Xiangqun. 1988. "Yaobaiyue jiqi tezheng (Rock Music and Its Characteristics)." *Renmin Yinyue* (People's Music) 10:3–4.

Zhongguo Gudai Tonggu Yanjiuhui. 1988. *Zhongguo gudai tonggu* (Ancient Bronze Drums of China). Beijing: Wenwu chubanshe.

Zhongguo gudai yinyue tupian (Picture Collection of Ancient Chinese Music). 1959. Beijing: Renmin yinyue chubanshe (People's Music Publishing Company).

Zhongguo minzu, minjian qiyuequ jicheng: Shaanxi juan (Anthology of Chinese National and Folk Instrumental Music: Shaanxi Volume). 1992. Beijing: Renmin yinyue chubanshe (People's Music Publishing Company).

Zhongguo yinyue cankao tupian (A Pictorial Illustration of Chinese Music History), Vols. 1–3 (1954), 4–5 (1955), 6–7 (1956), 8 (1959), 9 (1964). Beijing: National Music Institute of the Central Conservatory of Music.

Zhongguo yinyue cidian (Dictionary of Chinese music). 1985. Ed. Zhongguo yishu yanjiu yuan Yinyue yanjiu suo Zhongguo yinyue cidian bianki bu. Beijing: Renmin yinyue chubanshe (People's Music Publishing Company).

Zhongguo yinyue shupu zhi (Bibliography on Chinese Music). 1984. Ed. Zhongguo yishu yanjiu yuan Yinyue yanjiu suo ziliao shi. Beijing: Remin yinyue chubanshe (People's Music Publishing Company).

Zhongguo Yinyuejia Xiehui Guangdong Fenhui, ed. 1963. *Jiefangqian Guangdong yinyue yanzou qumu huibian* (Edited Listing of Guangdong Music before the Liberation). Guangzhou.

Zhongguo yishu yanjiuyuan yinyue yanjiusuo (Research Institute of Music, Chinese Academy of Arts), ed. 1983. *Minzu yinyue gailun* (An Outline of National Music), rev. ed. Beijing: Renmin yinyue chubanshe (People's Music Publishing Company).

———. 1984. *Zhongguo yinyue cidian* (Dictionary of Chinese Music). Beijing: Renmin yinyue chubanshe (People's Music Publishing Company).

———. 1994. *Zhongguo jinxiandai yinyuejia zhuan* (Biographies of Musicians in Modern China). Shenyang: Chunfeng wenyi chubanshe.

———. 1995. *Yinyuexue wenji* (Collection of Articles in Musicology). Ji'nan: Shandong youyi chubanshe.

Zhongguo yishu yanjiuyuan yinyue yanjiusuo ziliaoshi. 1984. *Zhongguo yinyue shupu zhi: Xian Qin–1949 nian yinyue shupu quanmu* (Bibliography of Chinese Music Books and Notated Sources: A Complete List of Music Books and Notated Sources from Antiquity to 1949). Beijing: Renmin yinyue chubanshe (People's Music Publishing Company).

Zhongyang yinyue xueyaun (Central Conservatory), ed. 1986. *Minzu yinyue jiegou yanjiu lunwenji* (Study of the Structure of Traditional Music). Beijing: Zhongyang yinyue xueyaun bianjibu.

Zhou, Chunyi. 1996. *Renshi guqin kaifa xinling* (Understanding the *Guqin* and Exploring Your Heart and Spirit). Taipei: Xueding chubanshe.

Zhou, Hui, Zhou Hao, and Ma Shenglong, eds. 1986. *Jiangnan sizhu chuantong badaqu* (The Traditional Eight Great Pieces of *Jiangnan Sizhu*). Shanghai: Wenyi chubanshe.

Zhou, Jingbao. 1987. *Sidiao zhi lu de yinyue wenhua* (Music and Culture of the Silk Road). Urumqi.

Zhou, Min. 1991. "Zhongguo gudai yinyue lishi fenqi wenti pingshu (A Critical Description of the Problems in the Periodization of Ancient Chinese Music History)." *Zhongguo Yinyue* (Chinese Music) 1(41):15–18.

Zhu, Zaiyu. [1596] 1968. *Lülü jingyi* (Essential Interpretation of the Tone System). In *Yuelü quanshu* (Comprehensive Book on Music Theory, 1606). Taipei: Commercial Press.

JAPAN

General references

Amano, Dentyû [Denchû], et al., eds. 1995. *Bukkyô ongaku ziten* (A Dictionary of Buddhist Music). Kyôto: Hôzôkan.

Atumi [Atsumi], Seitarô, ed. 1956. *Hôgaku buyô ziten* (A Dictionary of Japanese Music and Dance Repertoire). Tôkyô: Huzanbô.

Gamô, Satoaki, Sibata Minao, Tokumaru Yosihiko, Hirano Kenzi, Yamaguti Osamu, and Yokomiti Mario, eds. 1988. *Iwanami kôza, nihon no ongaku, azia no ongaku* (Iwanami Series: Musics in Japan, Asia and Oceania). 7 vols. and 2 suppl. vols. Tôkyô: Iwanami Shoten.

Gunzi [Gunji], Masakatu [Masakatsu]. 1975. *Kabuki no bigaku* (Aesthetics of *Kabuki*). Tôkyô: Engeki Syuppansya.

———. 1977. *Nihon butô ziten* (A Dictionary of Japanese Dance). Tôkyô: Tôkyôdô Shuppan.

———, ed. 1999. *Nihon buyô zukan* (A Picture Book of Japanese Dance). Tôkyô: Kokusyo Kankôkai.

Gunzi, Masakatu, and Sibasaki [Shibasaki] Sirô. 1977. *Nihon butô meikyoku ziten* (A Dictionary of the Japanese Dance Repertoire). Tôkyô: Syôgakkan.

Hattori, Yukio. 1983. *Kabuki ziten* (An Encyclopedia of Kabuki). Tôkyô: Heibonsha.

Misumi, Haruo. 1981. *Minzoku geinô ziten* (An Encyclopedia of Japanese Folk Performing Arts). Tôkyô: Tôkyôdô Shuppan.

Heibonsha, ed. 1982. *Ongaku daiziten* (Encyclopedia of Music), 2nd ed. Tôkyô: Heibonsha.

Hirano, Kenzi [Kenji], Kamisangô Yûkô, and Gamô Satoaki, eds. 1989. *Nihon ongaku daiziten* (Encyclopedia of Japanese Music). Tôkyô: Heibonsha.

Hirano, Kenzi, et al., eds. 1987. *Nihon koten ongaku bunken kaidai* (Annotation of Literature Dealing with Traditional Musics of Japan). Tôkyô: Kôdansha.

Hosikawa [Hoshikawa], Kyôzi [Kyôji], and Tanaka Takahumi [Takafumi], eds. 2000. *Hôgaku disuku gaido* (Compact Disk Guide for Japanese Music). Tôkyô: Ongaku no tomosha.

Kikkawa, Eisi [Eishi], ed. 1984. *Hôgaku hyakka ziten: Gagaku kara Min'yô made* (Encyclopedia of Japanese Music: *Gagaku*, Folk Songs, and Others). Tôkyô: Ongaku no tomosha.

Nihon Hôsô Kyôkai, NHK (Japan Broadcasting Corporation), ed. 1944–1993. *Nihon min'yô taikan* (Anthology of Japanese Folk Song). 13 vols. Tôkyô: Nihon Hôsô syuppan kyôkai.

Nisino [Nishino], Haruo, and Hata Hisasi [Hisashi]. 1987. *Nô kyôgen ziten* (An Encyclopedia of Nô and Kyôgen). Tôkyô: Heibonsha.

Ono, Ryôya, and Tôgi, Masatarô, eds. 1989. *Gagaku ziten* (Encyclopedia of *Gagaku*). Tôkyô: Ongaku no tomosha.

Sibata, Minao, and Tôyama Kazuyuki, eds. 1993–1994. *Nyû Gorovu sekai ongaku daiziten* (The New Grove Dictionary of Music and Musicians). 23 vols. Tôkyô: Kodansha. (Japanese translation.)

Tanabe, Hisao, ed. 1975. *Hôgaku yôgo ziten* (A Dictionary of Japanese Musical Terms.) Tôkyô: Tôkyôdô Shuppan.

Tsuge, Gen'ichi. 1986. *Japanese Music: An Annotated Bibliography*. London: Garland.

Usuda, Zingorô, ed. 1985. *Nihon kayô ziten* (A Dictionary of the Japanese Song Repertoire). Tôkyô: Ôhûsya.

References in English and other Western languages

Abraham, Otto, and Erich M. von Hornbostel. 1902–1903. "Studien über das Tonsystem und die Musik der Japaner." *Sammel bände der Internationalen Musikgesellschaft* 4:302–360. (Reprinted in: Klaus Wachsmann et al., eds. 1975. *Hornbostel Opera Omnia* 1:1–84. The Hague: M. Nijhoff.)

Ackermann, Peter. 1986. *Studien zur Koto-Musik von Edo. Studien zur traditionellen Musik Japans*, Vol. 6. Kassel: Bärenreiter.

———. 1990. *Kumiuta: Traditional Songs for Certificates—A Study of Their Texts and Implications*. Swiss Asian Studies Monographs, Vol. 10. New York: Peter Lang.

Adriaansz, Willem. [1965] 1973. *The Kumiuta and Danmono Traditions of Japanese Koto Music*. Berkeley: University of California Press.

———. 1978. *Introduction to Shamisen Kumiuta*. Buren: Fritz Knuf.

Asai, Susan Miyo. [1988] 1989. "Music and Drama in Nomai of Northern Japan." Ph.D. dissertation, University of California.

———. 1997. "Origins of the Musical and Spiritual Syncretism of *Nômai* in Northern Japan." *Asian Music* 28(2):51–71.

Ashihara, Eiryô. 1964. *The Japanese Dance*. London: Macmillan.

Averbuch, Irit. 1990. "Yamabushi Kagura: A Study of a Traditional Ritual Dance in Contemporary Japan." Ph.D. dissertation, Harvard University.

———. 1995. *The Gods Come Dancing: A Study of the Japanese Ritual Dance of Yamabushi Kagura*. Ithaca, N.Y.: Cornell University East Asia Program.

Berger, Donald. 1969. *Folk Songs of Japanese Children*. Rutland, Vt.: Tuttle.

———. 1970. "The *Shakuhachi* and the Kinko *Ryu* Notation." *Asian Music* 1(2):32–72.

———. 1972. *Folk Songs of Japan*. New York: Oak.

Berlin, Zeke. 1988. "Takarazuka: A History and Descriptive Analysis of the All-Female Performance Company." Ph.D. dissertation, New York University.

Bethe, Monica, and Karen Brazell. 1982. *Dance in Nô Theatre*. 3 vols. Ithaca, N.Y.: China-Japan Program, Cornell University.

———. 1990. "The Practice of Noh Theatre." In *By Means of Performance*, ed. Richard Schechner and Willa Appel, 167–193. New York: Cambridge University Press.

Blasdel, Christopher Yohmei, and Yûkô Kamisangô. 1988. *The Shakuhachi: A Manual for Learning*. Tôkyô: Ongaku no tomosha.

Bowers, Faubion. 1974. *Japanese Theatre*. Rutland, Vt.: Tuttle.

Boxer, Charles Ralph. 1951. *The Christian Century in Japan*. Berkeley: University of California Press.

Coaldrake, Kimi A. 1997a. "Female *Tayû* in the *Gidayû* Narrative Tradition of Japan." In *Women and Music in Cross-Cultural Perspective*, ed. Ellen Koskoff, 151–161. New York: Greenwood.

———. 1997b. *Women's Gidayû and the Japanese Theatre Tradition*. New York: Routledge.

Cohen, Selma Jeanne, and Masakatsu Gunji. 1983. "Virtuosity and the Aesthetic Ideals of Japanese Dance and Western Classical Dance." *Dance Research Annual* 14:88–95.

Cowell, Mary-Jean. 1994. "East and West in the Work of Michio Ito." *Dance Research Journal* 26(2):11–23.

Embree, John. 1944. *Japanese Peasant Songs*. Philadelphia: American Folklore Society.

Eppstein, Ury. 1994. *The Beginnings of Western Music in Meiji-Era Japan. Studies in the History and Interpretation of Music*, Vol. 44. Lewiston, N.Y.: Mellen.

Frith, Simon, and Tôru Mitsui, eds. 1991. "The Japan Issue." *Popular Music* 10(3).

Fritsch, Ingrid. 1979. *Die Solo-Honkyoku der Tozan-Schule: Musik für Shakuhachi zwischen Tradition und Moderne Japans. Studien zur traditionellen Musik Japans*, Vol. 4. Kassel; Basel; London: Bärenreiter.

———. 1996. *Japans blinde Sänger in Schutz der Gottheit Myoon-Berzaiten*. Munich: Iudicium.

Fujie, Linda K. 1983. "Effects of Urbanization on *Matsuri-Bayashi* in Tôkyô." *Yearbook for Traditional Music* 15:38–44.

———. 1986a. "*Matsuri-Bayashi* of Tôkyô: The Role of Supporting Organizations in Traditional Musics." Ph.D. dissertation, Columbia University.

———. 1986b. "The Process of Oral Transmission in Japanese Folk Performing Arts: The Teaching of *Matsuri-Bayashi* in Tôkyô." In *The Oral and the Literate in Music*, ed. Tokumaru Yosihiko and Yamaguti Osamu, 231–238. Tôkyô: Academia Music.

———. 1989. "Popular Music." In *Handbook of Japanese Popular Culture*, ed. Richard Powers and Hidetosi Katô, 197–220. Westport, Conn.: Greenwood.

———. 1992. "Popular Music." In *Worlds of Music: An Introduction to the Music of the World's People*, ed. Jeff Todd Tilton, 360–375. New York: Schirmer.

Fukushima [Hukusima], Kazuo. 1990. *Descriptive Catalogue of the Twelve Exhibitions (1975–1988)*. Tôkyô: Ueno Gakuen Nihon Ongaku siryôsitu (Research Archives for Japanese Music). Ueno Gakuen College.

———. 1986. "Source Materials of Music in Japan." *Fontes Artis Musicae* 35(2):129–134.

———, ed.. 1995. *Anthology of Sources for Japanese Music in Facsimile*. Vol. 1, *Early Printed Shoomyoo [Syômyô] Notations*. Tôkyô: Tôkyô Bizyutu.

———. 1996. "The Documentary Sources of Japanese Music." *Fontes Artis Musicae* 43(2):177–193.

Fukushima [Hukusima], Kazuo, and Steven G. Nelson. 1983. *Musical Notations of Japan: Sixty Representative Examples, Ranging from an Eighth-Century Biwa (Lute) Tablature to a Nineteenth-Century Tablature Collection of English Military Tunes*. Tôkyô: Research Archives for Japanese Music.

Galliano, Luciana. 1998. *Yôgaku. Percorsi della musica giapponese nel Novecento*. Venezia: Cafoscarina.

Garfias, Robert. 1959. *Gagaku: The Music and Dances of the Japanese Imperial Household*. New York: Theatre Arts Books.

———. "The Togaku Style of Japanese Court Music: An Analysis of Theory in Practice." M.A. thesis, University of California Los Angeles.

———. 1975. *Music of a Thousand Autumns: The Togaku Style of Japanese Court Music*. Berkeley: University of California Press.

Gay, Jesús Lópes. 1976. "Christian Music—Introduction to Western Music in Japan." *Kirishitan Kenkyû* 16.

Gerstle, C. Andrew. 1986. *Circles of Fantasy: Convention in the Plays of Chikamatsu*. Harvard East Asian Monographs 116. Cambridge, Mass.: Council on East Asian Studies, Harvard University. Distributed by Harvard University Press.

Gerstle, C. Andrew, Kiyoshi [Kiyosi] Inobe, and William P. Malm. 1990. *Theater as Music: The Bunraku Play "Mt. Imo and Mt. Se: An Explanatory Tale of Womanly Virtue."* Ann Arbor: Center for Japanese Studies, University of Michigan.

Gondô, Atuko [Atsuko]. 1988. "The Reception of Western Music in the *Enka* of the Meiji and Taisho Periods." *Tôyô Ongaku Kenkyû* (Journal of the Society for Research in Asian Music) 53:4–6. (English summary of Japanese original.)

Groemer, Gerald. 1991. *The Autobiography of Takahashi Chikuzan: Adventures of a Tsugaru-Jamisen Musician*. Warren, Mich.: Harmonie Park.

———. 1993. "An Analysis of Improvisational Elements in *Tsugaru Jamisen* Performance." *Tôyô Ongaku Kenkyû* (Journal of the Society for Research in Asian Music) 57:4. (English summary of Japanese original.)

———. 1994a. "Fifteen Years of Folk Song Collection in Japan: Reports and Recordings of the 'Emergency Folk Song Survey.'" *Asian Folklore Studies* 53(2):200–209.

———. 1994b. "Singing the News: *Yomiuri* in Japan during the Edo and Meiji [Meizi] Periods." *Harvard Journal of Asiatic Studies* 54(1):233–261.

———. 1994c. "Songs of Blind Female Performers (*Goze*) of the *Kaga* Domain. *Tôyô Ongaku Kenkyû* (Journal of the Society for Research in Asian Music) 59:2–3. (English summary of Japanese original.)

———. 1995. "Edo's 'Tin Pan Alley': Authors and Publishers of Japanese Popular Song during the Tokugawa Period." *Asian Music* 7(1):1–36.

———, trans. and ed. 1997. *Edo Culture: Daily Life and Diversions in Urban Japan, 1600–1868*. Honolulu: University of Hawaii Press. (Originally in Japanese.)

Gunji [Gunzi], Masakatsu [Masakatu]. 1970. *Buyô: The Classical Dance*. New York: Walker Weatherhill.

Günther, Robert. 1973. *Musikkulturen Asiens, Afrikas, und Ozeaniens im 19. Jahrhundert*. In *Studien zur Musikgeschichte des 19. Jahrhunderts*, Vol. 31. Regensburg: G. Bosse.

Gutzwiller, Andreas. 1983. *Die Shakuhachi der Kinko-Schule. Studien zur traditionellen Musik Japans*, Vol. 5. Kassel: Bärenreiter.

Halford, Aubrey S., and Giovanna M. Halford. 1956. *The Kabuki Handbook*. Tôkyô: Tuttle.

Harich-Schneider, Eta. 1953. "The Present Condition of Japanese Court Music." *Musical Quarterly* 39:49–74.

———. 1954. *The Rhythmical Patterns in Gagaku and Bugaku. Ethno-musicologica*, Vol. 3. Leiden: Brill.

———. 1965. *Roei: The Medieval Court Songs of Japan*. Tôkyô: Sophia University Press.

———. 1973. *A History of Japanese Music*. London: Oxford University Press.

Havens, Thomas. 1983. "Rebellion and Expression in Contemporary Japanese Dance." *Dance Research Annual* 14:159–163.

Heard, Judith Ann. 1989. "The Neonationalist Movement: Origins of Contemporary Japanese Music." *Perspectives of New Music* 27(2):118–163.

Heifetz, Robin J. 1978. "Post-World War II Japanese Composition." D.M. dissertation, University of Illinois, Urbana-Champaign.

———. 1986–1987. "European Influence upon Japanese Instrumental and Vocal Media: 1964–1977." *Music Review* 47(1):29–43.

Hirano, Kenji [Kenzi]. 1998. "Philology and Music Source Materials in Japan," trans. Steven G. Nelson. *Dokkyô Daigaku Kyôyô Syogaku Kenkyû* (Dokkyo University Bulletin of Liberal Arts) 23:98–113.

Hoff, Frank. 1971. *The Genial Seed: A Japanese Song Cycle*. New York: Grossman.

———. 1978. *Song, Dance, Storytelling: Aspects of the Performing Arts in Japan*. Cornell University East Asia Papers 15. Ithaca, N.Y.: China-Japan Program, Cornell University.

Holvik, Leonard C. 1990. *Japanese Music: Another Tradition, Other Sounds*, ed. Jackson H. Bailey. Occasional Papers, Institute for Education on Japan 1(5). Richmond, Ind.: Earlham College Press.

How, Deborah H. 1992. "Geza Music of Kabuki: Scenic Design through Music." M.A. thesis, University of California Los Angeles.

Howe, Sondra Wieland. 1997. *Luther Whiting Mason: International Music Educator*. Detroit Monographs in Musicology/Studies in Music 21. Warren, Mich.: Harmonie Park.

Hsu, Francis L. K. 1975. *Iemoto: The Heart of Japan*. New York: Halsted.

Hughes, David. 1981. "Japanese Folk Song Preservation Societies: Their History and Nature." In *International Symposium of the Preservation and Restoration of Cultural Property: Preservation and Development of the Traditional Performing Arts*, 29–45. Tôkyô: Tôkyô National Research Institute of Cultural Properties.

———. n.d. "The Heart's Home Town: Traditional Folk Song in Modern Japan." Ph.D. dissertation, University of Michigan.

———. 1990. "Japanese 'New Folk Songs,' Old and New." *Asian Music* 22(1):1–51.

———. 1992a. "'Esashi Oiwake' and the Beginnings of Modern Japanese Folk Song." *World of Music* 34(1):35–56.

———. 1992b. "2. Japan." In *Ethnomusicology: Historical and Regional Studies*, ed. Helen Myers, 345–362. New York: Norton. (Norton/Grove Handbooks in Music.)

Iacovleff, A., and S. Elisseeff. 1933. *Le théâtre japonais (kabuki)*. Paris: Jules Meynial.

IASPM-Japan, ed. 1991. *A Guide to Popular Music in Japan*. Kanazawa: IASPM-Japan. Tôkyô National Research Institute of Cultural Properties, ed. *International Symposium on the Conservation and Restoration of Cultural Property: Preservation and Development of the Traditional Performing Arts: 6–9 August 1980*. 1981. Tôkyô: Tôkyô National Research Institute of Cultural Properties.

Immoos, Thomas. 1974. *Théâtre japonais*. Geneva: Les Éditions de Bonvent.

Isaku, Patia. 1973. "An Introduction to Japanese Folk Song." Ph.D dissertation, Wesleyan University.

———. 1981. *Mountain Storm, Pine Breeze: Folk Song in Japan*. Tucson: University of Arizona Press.

Johnson, Henry M. 1991. "Is There a Symbolism of the *Koto*?" In *Tradition and Its Future in Music: Report of SIMS 1990 Ôsaka*, ed. Tokumaru Yoshiko et al. Tôkyô; Ôsaka: Mita.

———. 1993. "The Symbolism of the *Koto*: An Ethnomusicology of the Form and Function of a Traditional Japanese Musical Instrument." Ph.D. dissertation, Exeter College.

———. 1996–1997. "A *Koto* by Any Other Name: Exploring Japanese Systems of Musical Instrument Classification." *Asian Music* 28(1):87–114.

Kamisangô, Yûkô. 1986. "Oral and Literate Aspects of Tradition Transmission in Japanese Music: With Emphasis on *Syôga* and *Hakase*." In *The Oral and the Literate in Music*, ed. Tokumaru Yoshiko and Yamaguti Osamu, 288–299. Tôkyô: Academia Music.

Kaneshiro [Kanesiro], Atsumi [Atumi]. 1990. "A Review of the Ryukyu Scale." *Tôyô Ongaku Kenkyû* (Journal of the Society for Research in Asian Music) 55:8–9. (English summary of Japanese original.)

Kawada, Junzo [Zyunzô]. 1986. "Verbal and Nonverbal Sounds: Some Considerations of the Basis of Oral Transmission of Music." In *The Oral and the Literate in Music*, ed. Tokumaru Yoshiko and Yamaguti Osamu, 158–172. Tôkyô: Academia Music.

———. 1998. *La voix, étude d'ethno-linguistique comparative*. Paris: Éditions de l'École des Hautes Études en Sciences Sociales.

Kikkawa, Eishi [Eisi]. 1984. *Vom Charakter der japanischen Musik. Studien zur traditionellen Musik Japans*, Vol. 2. Kassel: Bärenreiter.

———. 1997. *A History of Japanese Koto and Ziuta*, trans. Leonard Holvik, ed. Yamaguti Osamu. Tôkyô: Mita. (With 2 compact disks.)

Kishibe [Kisibe], Shigeo [Sigeo]. 1966. *The Traditional Music of Japan. Series on Japanese Life and Culture*, Vol. 12. Tôkyô: Kokusai Bunka Shinkokai.

———. 1970. "Means of Preservation and Diffusion of Traditional Music in Japan." *Asian Music* 2(1):8–13.

———. [1982] 1984. *The Traditional Music of Japan*. Tôkyô: Ongaku No Tomosha.

Kishibe [Kisibe], Shigeo [Sigeo] and Leo Traynor. 1951. "On the Four Unknown Pipes of the Shô." *Tôyô Ongaku Kenkyû* (Journal of the Society for Research in Asian Music) 9:26–53.

Klein, Susan B. 1988. *Ankoku Butoh: The Premodern and Postmodern Influence on the Dance of Utter Darkness*. Ithaca, N.Y.: East Asia Program, Cornell University.

Koizumi, Fumio [Humio]. 1965. "Towards a Systematization of Japanese Folk Song." *Studia Musicologica Hungarica* 7:309–313.

———. [1977] 1983. "Musical Scales in Japanese Music." In *Asian Musics in an Asian Perspective: Report of Asian Traditional Performing Arts 1976*, ed. Fumio Koizumi et al., 73–79. Tôkyô: Japan Foundation and Heibonsya. Tôkyô: Academia Music.

———. [1980] 1983. "Rhythm in Japanese Folk Music." In *Musical Voices of Asia: Report of Asian Traditional Performing Arts 1978*, ed. Minegishi [Minegisi] Yuki et al., 108–119. Tôkyô: Japan Foundation and Heibonsya. Tôkyô: Academia Music.

Koizumi, Fumio, and Kazuo Okada. 1974. *Gagaku: The Noble Music of Japan* (Publikation zu Wissenschaftlichen Filmen). Göttingen: Institut für den Wissenschaftlichen Film.

Koizumi, Fumio, Yoshiko Tokumaru, and Osamu Yamaguti, eds. 1977. *Asian Musics in an Asian Perspective: Report of Asian Traditional Performance Arts 1976*. Tôkyô: Heibonsya.

Komiya, Takayoshi [Takayosi], ed. 1956. *Japanese Music and Drama in the Meiji Era*, trans. E. Seidensticker and D. Keen. Tôkyô: Obunsha.

Komoda, Haruko. 1990. "Heike Mabushi in the Collection of Kyoto University—Its Compilation and Source Annotations." *Tôyô Ongaku Kenkyû* (Journal of the Society for Research in Asian Music) 55:6–7. (English summary of Japanese original.)

———. 1997. "On the Heikyoku Tradition in Nagoya." *Tôyô Ongaku Kenkyû* (Journal of the Society for Research in Asian Music) 62:1. (English summary of Japanese original.)

Landy, Pierre. 1970. *Musique du Japon*. Paris: Buchet/Chastel.

Lee, Riley Kelly. 1993. "Yearning for the Bell: A Study of Transmission in the Shakuhachi Honkyoku Tradition." Ph.D. dissertation, University of Sydney.

Liou, Lin-Yu. "The Shôka Education of Colonial Taiwanese in the Meiji Period: As Reflected in the Periodical of Taiwan's Educational Academy." *Tôyô Ongaku Kenkyû* (Journal of the Society for Research in Asian Music) 62:4. (English summary of Japanese original.)

Loeb, David. 1975. *Solo and Chamber Music for Traditional Japanese Instruments*. New York: Performing Arts Program of the Asia Society.

Luo, Chuankai. 1991. "Double Cultural Contact: Diffusion and Reformation of Japanese School Songs in China." In *Tradition and Its Future in Music: Report of SIMS 1990 Ôsaka*, ed. Tokumaru Yosihiko et al., 11–14. Tôkyô; Ôsaka: Mita.

Malm, Joyce Rutherford. 1977. "The Legacy of Nihon Buyô." *Dance Research Journal* 9(2):12–24.

Malm, William P. 1963. *Nagauta: The Heart of Kabuki Music*. Rutland, Vt.: Tuttle.

———. 1967. *Music Cultures of the Pacific, the Near East, and Asia*. Englewood Cliffs. N.J.: Prentice Hall.

———. [1959] 1968. *Japanese Music and Musical Instruments*. Tôkyô: Tuttle.

———. 1971. "The Modern Music of Meiji Japan." In *Transition and Modernization in Japanese Culture*, ed. D. H. Shively, 257–300. Princeton, N.J.: Princeton University Press.

———. 1972. "Personal Approaches to the Study of Japanese Art Music." *Asian Music* 3(1):35–39.

———. 1973. "Layers of Modern Music and Japan." *Asian Music* 4(2):3–6.

———. 1975. *Chinese and Japanese Music-Dramas*. Michigan Papers in Chinese Studies 19. Ann Arbor: Center for Chinese Studies, University of Michigan.

———. 1986. *Six Hidden Views of Japanese Music*. Berkeley: University of California Press.

———. 2000. *Traditional Japanese Music and Musical Instruments*. Tôkyô: Kodansha International.

Marett, Allan. 1977. "Tunes Notated in Flute Tablature from a Japanese Source of the Tenth Century." *Musica Asiatica* 1:1–59.

———. n.d. "Tôgaku: Where Have the Tang Melodies Gone, and Where Have the New Melodies Come From?" *Ethnomusicology* 29(3):409–431.

———. 1988. "An Investigation of Sources for Chû Ôga Ryûteki Yoroku-fu, a Japanese Flute Source of the Fourteenth Century." *Musica Asiatica* 5:210–267.

Markham, Elizabeth J. 1983. *Saibara: Japanese Court Songs of the Heian Period*. Cambridge: Cambridge University Press.

Masumoto, Kikuko. 1981. "Transmission of Gagaku." In *International Symposium on the Conservation and Restoration of Cultural Property: Preservation and Development of the Traditional Performing Arts*, 29–46. Tôkyô: Tôkyô National Research Institute of Cultural Properties.

Matsushita [Matusita], Hitoshi [Hitosi]. 1989. *A Checklist of Published Instrumental Music by Japanese Composers*. Tôkyô: Academia Music.

Matsuyama [Matuyama], Yoshio [Yosio]. 1980. *Studien zur Nô-Musik: Eine Untersuchung des Stückes "Hagoromo" (das Federgewand)*. Hamburg: Karl Dieter Wagner.

May, Elizabeth. 1958. "Japanese Children's Music before and after Contact with the West." Ph.D. dissertation, University of California Los Angeles.

———. 1963. *The Influence of the Meiji Period on Japanese Children's Music*. University of California Publications in Music, Vol. 6. Berkeley: University of California Press.

McClure, Steve. 1998. *Nipponpop*. Tôkyô: Tuttle.

McFadden, Elizabeth A. n.d. "Gidayû Shamisen Music: An Introductory Study of Its Presentation in Bunraku." M.A. thesis, University of Hawaii.

Minegishi [Minegisi], Yuki. 1980. "Discography of Japanese Traditional Music." In *Performing Arts of Japan*, 1. Tôkyô: Japan Foundation.

Mitani, Yôko, and Laurence Picken. 1979. "Finger-Techniques for the Zither *Sô-No-Koto* and *Kin* in Heian Times." *Musica Asiatica* 2:89–114.

Mitsui, Tôru. 1993a. "Copyright and Music in Japan: A Forced Grafting and Its Consequences." In *Music and Copyright*, ed. Simon Frith, 125–145. Edinburgh: Edinburgh University Press.

———. 1993b. "The Interaction of Imported and Indigenous Musics in Japan: A Historical Overview of the Popular Music and Its Industry." In *Whose Master's Voice? Music Industries in Twenty Countries*, ed. Alison Ewbank and Fouli Papageorgiou, 152–174. Westport, Conn.: Greenwood.

———. 1993c. "The Reception of the Music of American Southern Whites in Japan." In *Transforming Tradition: Folk Music Revivals Examined*, ed. Neil Rosenberg, 275–293. Urbana: University of Illinois Press.

Miyazaki, Mayumi. 2000. "The *Mosô-Biwa* 'Kasugano' Handed Down to Old-Myouonzan-Chokuji: A Commentary on the *Biwa* Closely Connected with Kagekiyo. *Tôyô Ongaku Kenkyû* (Journal of the Society for Research in Asian Music) 65:3. (English summary of Japanese original.)

Motegi, Kiyoko. 1984. "Aural Learning in Gidayû-Bushi Music of the Japanese Puppet Theater." *Yearbook for Traditional Music* 16:97–108.

Müller, Gerhild. 1971. *Kagura: Die Lieder der Kagura-Zeremonie am Naishidokoro*. Wiesbaden: Otto Harrassowitz.

Naka, Mamiko. 1994. "Intersecting Sounds in the Reception of Christian Music in China around the Dawn of the Twentieth Century." *Tôkyô Ongaku Kenkyû* (Journal of the Society for Research in Asian Music) 59:3. (English summary of Japanese original.)

Nakamura, Yasuo. 1971. *Noh: The Classical Theater*, trans. Don Kenny. New York: Weatherhill; Tôkyô: Tankosya.

Nelson, Steven G. 1983. *Nihon no gakufuten: Tenpyo biwafu kara Bakumatsu no kotekifu made—Kaidai mokuroku* (Japanese Music Scores from the Ancient to Modern Times: An Annotated Catalog). Tôkyô: Ueno Gakuen Nihon Ongaku Shiryoshitsu.

———. 1986a. *Documentary Sources of Japanese Music*. Tôkyô: Research Archives for Japanese Music.

———. 1986b. "The Gogen-Fu, a Japanese Heian-Period Tablature Score for Five Stringed Lutes—Concentrating on the Fret System and Tunings of the Instrument." *Tôyô Ongaku Kenkyû* (Journal of the Society for Research in Asian Music) 50:4–9. (English summary of Japanese original.)

———. 1990. "*Gagaku*: Its Past and Present." In *Gagaku no dezain* (The Designs of Gagaku), 264–273, ed. Tadamaro Ono [Ôno] Fohtani. Tôkyô: Shôgakkan.

Nishiyama, Matunosuke. 1997. *Edo Culture: Daily Life and Diversions in Urban Japan, 1600–1868*, ed. and trans. Gerald Groemer. Honolulu: University of Hawaii Press.

Ohtani [Ôtani], Kimiko. 1981. "The Okinawan Kumiodori: An Analysis of Relationships of Text, Music, and Movement in Selections from Nidô Tekiuchi." M.A. thesis, University of Hawaii.

Ohtani [Ôtani], Kimiko, and Tokumaru Yoshihiko. 1983. "Ethnomusicology in Japan since 1970." *Yearbook for Traditional Music* 15:155–159.

Okada, Maki. 1991. "Musical Characteristics of *Enka*." *Popular Music* 10(3):283–303.

Ortolani, Benito. 1969. "Iemoto." *Japan Quarterly* (16):297–306.

———. [1990] 1995. *The Japanese Theatre: From Shamanistic Ritual to Contemporary Pluralism*. Princeton, N.J.: Princeton University Press.

Oshio, Satomi. 1993. "A Tonal Structure in Nagauta." *Ongakugaku* (Journal of the Musicological Society of Japan) 38(2):85–97.

———. 1999. "The Concept of '*Gaku*' in Nagauta." *Tôyô Ongaku Kenkyû* (Journal of the

Society for Research in Asian Music) 64:1–2. (English summary of Japanese original.)

Park, Miri. 1992. "The Chordal Transition and Hand Movement of Playing Shô, a Japanese Mouth Organ: Theory and Practice." M.A. thesis, University of California Los Angeles.

Péri, Nöel. 1934. *Essai sur les gammes japonaises*. Bibliothèque Musicale de Musée Guimet, Series 2, No. 1. Paris: Geuthner.

———. 1944. *Le nô*. Tôkyô: Maison Franco-Japonaise.

Picken, Laurence. 1985–1987. *Music from the Tang Court* 2–4. Cambridge: Cambridge University Press.

Picken, Laurence, et al. 1981. *Music from the Tang Court* 1. London: Oxford University Press.

Piggott, Francis. [1893] 1971. *The Music and Musical Instruments of Japan*. New York: Da Capo.

Prescott, Anne Elizabeth. 1997. "Miyagi Michio, the Father of Modern Koto Music: His Life, Works, and Innovations, and the Environment Which Enabled His Reforms." Ph.D. dissertation, Kent State University.

Pronko, Leonard C. 1985. "*Shin Buyô* and *Sôsaku Buyô*: Tradition and Change in Japanese Dance." *Dance Research Annual* 15:111–121.

Reid, James Larry. 1977. "The Komagaku Repertory of Japanese Gagaku (Court Music): A Study of Contemporary Performance Practice." Ph.D. dissertation, University of California Los Angeles.

Robertson, Jennifer. 1998. *Takarazuka: Sexual Politics and Culture in Modern Japan*. Berkeley: University of California Press.

Sakamoto, Mamiko. 1987. "*Gagaku* at the Fifteenth-Century Imperial Court and Ayanokoji Aritoshi." *Tôyô Ongaku Kenkyû* (Journal of the Society for Research in Asian Music) 51:5–8. (English summary of Japanese original.)

Sakata, Lorraine. 1966. "The Comparative Analysis of *Sawari* on the *Shamisen*." *Ethnomusicology* 10(2):141–152.

Scauwecker, Detlev. 1994. *Musik und Politik, Tôkyô 1934–1944*. Monographien aus dem deutschen Institut für Japanstudien der Phillip Franz-von-Siebold-Stiftung 8(1):211–256. München: Iudicium Verlag.

Serper, Zvika. 2000. "*Kotoba* ('Sung' Speech) in Japanese Nô Theater: Gender Distinctions in Structure and Performance." *Asian Music* 31(2): 29–166.

Sesoko Seiken et al. 1998. *Musical Dramas of Ryukyu Court*. Tôkyô: Seven Seas.

Shehan, Patricia. 1987. "The Oral Transmission of Music in Selection of Asian Cultures." *Bulletin of the Council for Research in Music Education* 92:1–14.

Shiba [Siba], Sukehiro. 1955–1956. *Gagaku*. 2 vols. Tôkyô: Ryûgin-sya.

Signell, Karl L. 1976. "The Modernization Process in Two Oriental Music Cultures: Turkish and Japanese." *Asian Music* 7(2):72–102.

Suda, Naoyuki. 1998. *The Birth of Tsugaru Shamisen Music: The Origin and Development of a Japanese Folk Performing Art*. Aomori, Japan: Aomori University Press. (Original in Japanese: *Tsugaru syamisen no tanzyô: Minzoku geinô no seisei to ryûsei*.)

Sugiyama, Makoto, and Fujima [Huzima] Kanjuro [Kanzyûrô]. 1937. *An Outline History of the Japanese Dance*. Tôkyô: Kokusai Bunka Shinkôkai.

Takahashi, Chikuzan. 1998. *The Spirit of Tsugaru: Takahashi Chikuzan, Tsugaru-Jamisen, and the Folk Music of Northern Japan (With the Autobiography of Takahashi Chikuzan)*, trans. Gerald Groemer. Detroit Monographs in Musicology/Studies in Music 24. Warren, Mich.: Harmonie Park.

Takakuwa, Izumi. 1990. "'Kaidô-Kudari,' a Piece for *Nôkan* and *Kyôgen* Singing—One Example of Musical Intercourse between *Nôkan* and *Hitoyogiri*." *Tôyô Ongaku Kenkyû* (Journal of the Society for Research in Asian Music) 55:4–5. (English summary of Japanese original.)

———. 2000. "Transition of Shape of *Tsuzumi*." *Tôyô Ongaku Kenkyû* (Journal of the Society for Research in Asian Music) 65:1–2. (English summary of Japanese original.)

Tamba, Akira. 1974. *La structure musicale du nô*. Paris: Klincksieck.

———. 1981. *The Musical Structure of No [Nô]*. Tôkyô: Tokai University Press.

———. 1988. *La théorie et l'esthétique musicale japonaises*. Paris: Publications Orientalistes de France.

Tanabe, Hisao. [1938, 1959] 1960. *Japanese Music*. Kokusai bunka shinkokai Publication, Series B, No. 26. Tôkyô: Kokusai Bunka Shinkokai (Society for International Cultural Relations).

Terauchi [Terauti], Naoko. 1991. "A Study on the Arrangement of Togaku Pieces—Concerning Dokyoku Pieces in *Jinchi-Yoroku*." *Tôyô Ongaku Kenkyû* (Journal of the Society for Research in Asian Music) 56:3–4. (English summary of Japanese original.)

———. 1995. "A Study of the Metrical Specifications *Nobe* and *Haya* in the Late Heian to Early Kamakura Periods—Through an Analysis of *Kofu Ryoritsu-no-maki*." *Tôyô Ongaku Kenkyû* (Journal of the Society for Research in Asian Music) 60:1–2. (English summary of Japanese original.)

———. 1998. "On the Function of *Wagon* (Zither) in *Saibara* and *Sôgaku*: Observations in Light of an Analysis of Sources of the Ayanokôji Family." *Tôyô Ongaku Kenkyû* (Journal of the Society for Research in Asian Music) 63:2. (English summary of Japanese original.)

Thornbury, E. Barbara. 1995. "Behind the Mask: Community and Performance in Japan's Folk Performing Arts." *Asian Theatre Journal* 12(1):143–163.

Thrasher, Alan R. "The Melodic Model as a Structural Device: Chinese Zheng and Japanese Koto Repertoires Compared." *Asian Music* 26(2):97–118.

Tiba [Chiba], Nobuhiko. 1996. "The Melodic Structure of Ainu Songs." *Tôyô Ongaku Kenkyû* (Journal of the Society for Research in Asian Music) 61:1. (English summary of Japanese original.)

Tiba [Chiba], Zyunnosuke [Junnosuke]. 1988. "The Composition of Miyagi Michio's 'Haru no yo' and Its Periphery." *Tôyô Ongaku Kenkyû* (Journal of the Society for Research in Asian Music) 53:6–7.

Togi [Tôgi], Masataro [Masatarô]. 1971. *Gagaku: Court Music and Dance*. In *Performing Arts of Japan*, Vol. 5. New York: Walker/Weatherhill.

Tokita, Alison. 1989. "The Narrative Tradition in Japanese Music: Kiyomoto-Bushi as an Accompaniment of Kabuki Dance." Ph.D. dissertation, Monash University, Melbourne.

———. 1999. Kiyomoto—Bushi Narrative Music of the Kabuki Theatre. *Studien zur traditionellen Musik Japans*, Vol. 8. Kassel: Bärenreiter.

Tokumaru, Yosihiko [Yoshihiko]. 1977. "Some Remarks on the Shamisen and Its Music." In *Asian Musics in an Asian Perspective*, ed. Koizumi Fumio et al., 90–99. Tôkyô: Heibonsha.

———. 1991a. "The ATPA Project in Retrospect." In *Music in the Dialogue of Cultures: Traditional Music and Cultural Policy*, ed. Max Peter Baumann, 136–143. Wilhelmshaven: Florian Noetzel Verlag.

———. 1991b. "Intertextuality in Japanese Traditional Music." In *The Empire Signs: Semiotic Essays on Japanese Culture*, ed. Ikegami Yoshihiko, 139–155. Amsterdam and Philadelphia: Benjamins.

———. 1991c. "Le timbre dans la musique japonais." In *Le timbre: Métaphore pour la composition*, ed. Jean-Baptiste Barrière. Paris: Christian Bourgeois.

———. 2000. *L'aspect mélodique de la musique de syamisen*. Paris: Peeters.

Tokumaru, Yosihiko, et al., eds. 1991. *Tradition and Its Future in Music: Report of SIMS 1990 Ôsaka*. Tôkyô and Ôsaka: Mita.

Tokumaru, Yosihiko, and Yamaguti [Yamaguchi] Osamu. 1986. *The Oral and the Literate in Music*. Tôkyô: Academia Music.

Tsuge [Tuge], Gen'ichi [Gen'iti]. 1981. "Symbolic Techniques in Japanese *Koto-Kumiuta*." *Asian Music* 12(2):109–132.

———. 1983. *Anthology of Sôkyoku snd Jiuta Song Texts*. Tôkyô: Academia Music.

———. 1986. *Japanese Music: An Annotated Bibliography*. New York: Garland.

Wade, Bonnie C. 1967. "A Selective Study of *Honte-Kaete Tegoto-Mono* in Nineteenth-Century Japanese *Koto* Music." M.A. thesis, University of California Los Angeles.

———. 1976. *Tegotomono: Music for the Japanese Koto*. Westport, Conn.: Greenwood.

Waley, Arthur. [1920] 1957. *The Nô Plays of Japan*, 2nd ed. New York: Grove.

Wolz, Carl. 1971. *Bugaku: Japanese Court Dance*. Providence, R.I.: Asian Music.

Yamaji [Yamazi], Kôzô. 1983. "Early Kabuki Dance." *Dance Research Annual* 14:105–112.

Yano, Christine Reiko. 1995. "Shaping Tears of a Nation: An Ethnography of Emotion in Japanese Popular Song." Ph.D. dissertation, University of Hawaii.

Zou, Jì Cheng. "Relationship between Japanese Hichiriki-Fu and Chinese Koshaku-Fu—A Doubt about the Origin of Hichiriki Shiko-Fu and a New Theory about the Origin of Koshaku-Fu." *Tôyô Ongaku Kenkyû* (Journal of the Society for Research in Asian Music) 56:5–6. (English summary of Japanese original.)

Japanese-language publications

Abe, Suehisa. [1690] 1935. *Gakkaroku* (A Note from a *Gagaku* Musician's Family). Tôkyô: Koten zensyû kankôkai.

Akiyama, Kuniharu. 1978–1979. *Nihon no sakkyo-okuka tati: Sengo kara sinno sengoteki miraie* (Composers in Japan: From the End of the War to the Actual Future after the War). 2 vols. Tôkyô: Ongaku no tomousha.

Asakawa, Gyokuto. 1955. *Nagauta no Kiso Kenkyû* (An Elementary Study of *Nagauta*). Tôkyô: Hôgakusya.

Dentô geizyutu no kai, ed. 1969a. *Hôgaku hôbu* (Traditional Music and Dance of Japan). Tôkyô: Gakugeisyorin.

———. 1969b. *Ningyô sibai* (Puppet Theaters). Tôkyô: Gakugeisyorin.

Ebisawa, Arimiti [Arimichi]. 1983. *Yôgaku denrai si* (History of Western Music Imported into Japan). Tôkyô: Nihon kirisuto kyôdan syuppankyoku.

Gamô, Satoaki. 2000. *Nihon koten ongaku tankyû* (Investigations on the Classical Music of Japan). Tôkyô: Syuppangeizyutusya.

Geinôsi, Kenkyûkai, ed. 1969. *Kagura: Nihon no koten geinô* (Japanese Classical Performing Arts). Tôkyô: Heibonsya.

———. 1970a. *Buyô: Nihon no koten geinô* (Japanese Classical Performing Arts). Tôkyô: Heibonsya.

———. 1970b. *Gagaku: Nihon no koten geinô* (Japanese Classical Performing Arts), Vol. 2. Tôkyô: Heibonsya.

———. 1970c. *Kyôgen: Nihon no koten geinô* (Japanese Classical Performing Arts). Tôkyô: Heibonsya.

———. 1970d. *Nô: Nihon no koten geinô* (Japanese Classical Performing Arts). Tôkyô: Heibonsya.

———. 1970e. *Zyôruri: Nihon no koten geinô* (Japanese Classical Performing Arts). Tôkyô: Heibonsya.

———. 1971. *Kabuki: Nihon no koten geinô* (Japanese Classical Performing Arts). Tôkyô: Heibonsya.

———. 1985. *Nihon geinôsi* (History of Performing Arts in Japan). 7 vols. Tôkyô: Hôsei daigaku syuppankyoku.

Gunzi [Gunji], Masakatu [Masakatsu]. 1957. *Odori no bigaku* (Aesthetics of Dance). Tôkyô: Engeki Syuppansya.

Gurômâ, Zyerarudo (Groemer, Gerald). 1995. *Bakumatu no hayariuta: Kudoki-busi to dodoitu no sin kenkyû* (Japanese Popular Songs in the Late Edo Period: A New Study on Kudoku-Busi and Dodoitu). Tôkyô: Meityo Syuppan.

Hanayagi, Tiyo [Chiyo]. 1981. *Zitugi, Nihon buyô no kiso* (Fundamental Practice of Japanese Dance). Tôkyô: Tôkyô Shoseki.

Hayasi [Hayashi], Kenzô. 1964. *Syôsôin gakki no kenkyû* (A Study of Musical Instruments Preserved in Syôsôin). Tôkyô: Kazama Syobô.

———. 1973. *Higasi Asia gakki kô* (Studies on Musical Instruments of East Asia). Tôkyô: Kawai gakuhu.

Hayasiya, Tatusaburô, ed. 1973. *Kodai tyûsei geizyuturon* (Theories of Arts in Ancient Medieval Japan). Tôkyô: Iwanami shoten.

Hirano, Kenzi [Kenji]. 1987. *Syamisen to koto no kumiuta* (*Kumiuta* for *Syamisen* and *Koto*). Tôkyô: Hakusuisya.

———. 1990. *Sôkyoku/ziuta no kayô: sono hyôsyô bunkaron* (Songs of *Koto* Music and *Ziuta*: Their Representations). Tôkyô: Hôgakusya.

Hirano, Kenzi, and Kamisangô Yûkô, eds. 1978. *Nihon kayô kenkyû syûsei* (A Collection of Source Materials for the History of Japanese Songs). 7 vols. Tôkyô: Benseisya.

Honda, Yasuzi [Yasuji]. 1993–2001. *Honda Yasuzi tyosakusyû* (Collected Works of Honda Yasuzi). 20 vols. and 1 suppl. vol. for index. Tôkyô: Kinseisya. (To be completed.)

Horiuti [Horiuchi], Keizô. 1968. *Ongaku Mezji hyakunen si* (One Hundred Years of Japanese Music). Tôkyô: Ongaku no tomousha.

Hukusima [Fukushima], Kazuo. 1995. *Nihon ongaku siryô syûsei 1: Kohan syômyôhu* (Anthology of Sources for Japanese Music History in Facsimile, Vol. 1: Early Printed Shoomyoo Notations). Tôkyô: Tôkyô Bizyutu.

Iba, Takasi [Takashi]. 1928. *Nihon ongaku gairon* (An Outline of Japanese Music). Tôkyô: Kôseikaku Syoten.

———. [1934] 1950. *Nihon ongakusi* (History of Japanese Music). Tôkyô: Ongaku no tomo sha.

Inobe, Kiyosi [Kiyoshi]. 1991. *Zyôrursi kôsatu* (Studies on the History of Zyôruri). Tôkyô: Kazama.

———. 1998. *Nihon no ongaku to bunraku* (Music of Japan and Bunraku). Ôsaka: Izumi syoin.

Inobe, Kiyosi [Kiyoshi], and Mario Yokomiti et al. 1986. *Gidayû busi no yôsiki tenkai* (Stylistic Developments in Gidayû Busi). Tôkyô: Academia Music.

Isawa, Syûzi [Shuji]. 1971. *Yôgaku kotohazime: Ongaku torisirabe seiseki sinpôsyo* (Introduction to Western Music: Report of the Music Study Committee), ed. and supplemented by Yamazumi Masami.Tôkyô: Heibonsha.

Iwahara, Taisin [Taishin]. 1932. *Syômyô no kenkyû* (A Study of *Syômyô*). Kyôto: Fuzii Sahee.

JASRAC. 1990. *Nihon ongaku tyosakuken si.* (A History of Musical Copyright in Japan). 2 vols. Tôkyô: JASRAC.

Kaneko, Atuko [Atsuko]. 1995. *Taisyôgoto no sekai* (The World of Taisyô Goto). Tôkyô: Ongaku no tomo sha.

Kanetune [Kanetsune], Kiyosuke. 1913. *Nihon no ongaku* (Music of Japan). Kyôto: Hattori Syoten.

Katô, Yasuaki. 1974. *Nihon môzin syakai kenkyû si* (A History of Studies of the Japanese Blind Persons' Society). Tôkyô: Miraisya.

Kawatake, Sigetosi [Shigetoshi]. 1943. *Kabuki si no kenkyû* (A Study on the History of *Kabuki*). Tôkyô: Tôkyôdô.

Kikkawa, Eisi [Eishi]. 1952. *Hogaku kansyô* (The Appreciation of Japanese Music). Tôkyô: Hôbunkan.

———. 1965. *Nihon ongaku no rekisi* (A History of Japanese Music). Tôkyô: Sôgensya.

———. 1979. *Nihon ongaku no seikaku* (The Nature of Japanese Music). Tôkyô: Ongaku no tomo sha.

———, ed. 1989. *Nihon ongaku bunkasi* (A History of the Musical Culture of Japan). Osaka: Sôgensya.

———. 1997. *Syamisen no bigaku to Geidai hôgakuka tanzyôhiwa* (Aesthetics of the Syamisen [Samisen] and a Secret Story of the Birth of the Development of Japanese Traditional Music at the Tôkyô University of Fine Arts and Music). Tôkyô: Syuppangeizyutusya.

Kikkawa, Shûhei. 1989. "Nihonbuyô no riron, buyô no yôso, kôzô, dôsa no bunseki (Theory of Japanese Dance, Analysis of Elements, Structures and Movements of Dance)." In *Nihon no ongaku, Azia no ongaku* (Musics of Japan, Asia, and Oceania), ed. Gamô Satoaki et al., 5:155–184. Tôkyô: Iwanami Shoten.

Kindaiti [Kindaichi], Haruhiko. 1997. *Heikyoku kô* (Treatise on Heikyoku). Tôkyô: Sanseidô.

Kisibe [Kishibe], Sigeo [Shigeo]. 1982. *Kodai siruku rôdo no ongaku* (Musics along the Silk Road in Ancient Times). Tôkyô: Kodansha.

Kodera, Yûkiti [Yukichi]. 1922. *Kindai buyô si ron* (A Modern History of Dance). Nihon Hyôronsya.

———. 1928. *Buyô no bigakuteki kenkyû* (Aesthetic Study of Dance). Tôkyô: Syun'yôdô.

———.1941. *Kyôdo buyô to bon odori* (Folk Dance and *Bon* Dance). Tôkyô: Tôkei Syobô.

Koizumi, Humio [Fumio]. 1958. *Nihon dentô ongaku no kenkyû* (Studies on Traditional Music of Japan), Vol. 1. Tôkyô: Ongaku no tomo sha.

———. 1977. *Nihon no oto: Sekai no naka no Nihon no ongaku* (Sound of Japan: Japanese Music in the World). Tôkyô: Seidosya.

———. 1984a. *Koizumi Fumio fîrudo wâku: Hito wa naze uta o utauka* (Koizumi Fumio Fieldwork: Why Do People Sing a Song?). Tôkyô: Tozyusya.

————. 1984b. *Nihon dentô ongaku no kenkyû 2: Rizumu* (Studies on Traditional Music of Japan. Vol. 2, Rhythm). Tôkyô: Ongaku no tomo sha.

Kokugeki Kojôkai Publications, eds. 1953. *Geinô Ziten* (A Dictionary of Theater Arts). Tôkyô: Tokyô-dô.

Kokuritu bunraku gekizyô, ed. 1991. *Bunraku no butaibizyutu* (Stage Arts of Bunraku). Tôkyô: Nihon geizyutubunka sinkôkai.

Kokuritu Gekizyô [National Theater of Japan], ed. 1994. *Kodai gakki no hukugen* (Reconstructed Music Instruments of Ancient East Asia). Tôkyô: Ongaku no tomo sha.

Koma, Tikazane. [1233] 1928. *Kyôkunsyô* (On Music Education in the Medieval Period in Japan). Tôkyô: Koten zensyû kankôkai.

Kurata, Yosihiro [Yoshihiro]. 1979. *Nihon rekôdo bunka si* (A History of Phonograph Culture). Tôkyô: Tôkyô Syoseki.

————, ed. 1988. *Geinô* (Performing Arts). Tôkyô: Iwanami shoten.

Mabuti [Mabuchi], Usaburô. 1992. *Sitiku syosinsyû no kenkyû: Kinsei hôgakusi kenkyû zyosetu.* (Study of *Sitiku Syosinsyû*: An Introduction to the Music History of Premodern Japan). Tôkyô: Ongaku no tomo sha.

Masui, Keizi [Keiji]. 1984. *Nihon no opera: Meizi kara Taisyô e* (Japanese Opera: From Meizi to Taisyô).Tôkyô: Min'on ongaku siryô kan.

Masumoto, Kikuko. 1968. *Gagaku: Dentô ongaku eno atarasii apurôti* (A New Approach to *Gagaku*, a Traditional Music). Tôkyô: Ongaku no tomo sha.

Matusita [Matsushita], Hitosi [Hitoshi], ed. 1998. *Ibunka kôryû to kindaika: Kyôto kokusai seminâ 1996* (Cultural Encounters in the Development of Modern East Asia: International Conference of 1996 in Kyôto). Tôkyô: Ôzorasya.

Misumi, Haruo. 1968. *Nihon buyô si no kenkyû: Kabuki buyô to minzoku buyô* (A Study of Japanese History of Dance: *Kabuki* Dance and Folk Dance). Tôkyô: Tôkyôdô.

Mizuno, Yûko. 1998. *Sirarezaru geinôsi musume gidayû* (An Unknown Historical Aspect of Performing Arts in Japan: *Gidayû Busi* Performed by Girls). Tôkyô: Tyûô kôronsya.

Motizuki, Tainosuke. [1975] 1999. *Kabuki no geza ongaku* (Offstage Music of *Kabuki*). Tôkyô: Engekisyuppannsya.

Nakagawa, Aihyô. 1941. *Sangen gaku-si* (A History of *Syamisen* Music). Tôkyô: Dainippon Geizyutu Kyôkai.

Nakagawa, Masami. 1991. *Genzi monogatari to ongaku* (The Tale of Genzi and the Music Described Therein). Ôsaka: Izumi Syoin.

Nakamura, Kôsuke. 1987. *Seiyô no oto, nihon no mimi: Kindai nihon bungaku to seiyô ongaku* (Sounds of the West and Ears of Japan: Modern Japanese Literature and Western Music). Tôkyô: Syunzyûsya.

Nakamura, Rihei. 1993. *Yôgaku dônyûsya no kiseki: Nihon kindai yôgaku si zyosetu* (A Locus of Introducers of Western Music in Japan). Tôkyô: Tôsui Syobô.

————. 1996. *Kirisutokyô to Nihon no yôgaku* (Christianity and Western Music in Japan). Tôkyô: Ôzomsya.

Nakayama, Tarô. 1934. *Nihon môzin si* (A History of Blind People in Japan). Tôkyô: Syôwa Syobô.

Nihon Hôsô Kyôkai, NHK (Japan Broadcasting Corporation), ed. 1965. *Ainu dentô ongaku* (Traditional Ainu Music). Tôkyô: Nihon hôsô syuppan kyôkai.

————. 1974. *Nihon to sekai no gakuhu* (Musical Notation of Japan and the World). 3 vols. Tôkyô: Nihon hôsô syuppan kyôkai.

Nihon Kindai Yôgasuki Kenkyûkai [Society for Japanese Modern Western Music Research], ed. *Meizi ki Nihonzin to ongaku* (Meizi Period Japanese and Music). 2 vols. Tôkyô: Ôzorasya.

Nisigata [Nishigata], Setuko [Setsuko]. 1980. *Nihon buyô no kenkyû* (A Study of Japanese Dance). Tôkyô: Nansôsya.

Nisiyama [Nishiyama], Matunosuke [Matsunosuke]. 1959. *Iemoto no kenkyû.* (A Study of *Iemoto*). Tôkyô: Azekura Syobô.

Nisiyama [Nishiyama], Matunosuke [Matsunosuke] et al., eds. 1972. *Kinsei geidôron* (Theories of Arts in Premodern Japan). Tôkyô: Iwanami shoten.

Nisizawa [Nishizawa], Sô. 1990. *Nihon kindai kayô si* (A History of Modern Japanese Songs). 3 vols. Tôkyô: Ôhûsya.

Ogi, Mituo [Mituso]. 1977. *Nihon kodai ongaku si* (History of Music in Ancient Japan). Tôkyô: Yosikawa kôbunkan.

————. 1994. *Heian tyô ongaku seido si* (A History of Musical Institutions in the Heian Period). Tôkyô: Yosikawa Kôbunkan.

Okuyama, Keiko. 1979. "Nô to zyosei enzya (Female Performers in *Nô*)." In *Zyosei to bunka* 1:311–331. Tôkyô: Hakuba syuppan.

————. n.d. "Meizi no hôgaku kyôiku: Kiyomoto Oyô no baai." (Education in the Traditional Music of Japan during the Meizi Period: A Case Study of *Kiyomoto Oyô*). In *Zyosei to bunka* 2:105–124. Tôkyô: JCA syuppan.

Ôno, Tadamaro, ed. 1990. *Gagaku no dezain* (The Designs of *Gagaku*). Tôkyô: Syôgakukan.

Osida [Oshida], Yosihisa [Yoshihisa]. 1969. *Gagaku kansyô*. Tôkyô: Bunkendô.

————. 1984. *Gagaku e no syôtai* (An Invitation to *Gagaku*). FM Sensho (FM Selection Books). Tôkyô: Kyôdô Tûsinsya.

Ôsiro [Ôshiro], Manabu. 2000. *Okinawa geinôsi gairon* (An Introduction to the History of Performing Arts in Okinawa). Tôkyô: Sunagoya Shobô.

Otuka [Ôtsuka], Haiko. 1995. *Syamisen ongaku no onkô riron* (Pitch Theory in the Music of the *Syamisen*). Tôkyô: Ongaku no tomo sha.

Sakai, Taizyun [Taijun]. 1980. *Nihon bukkyô geinô si kenkyû* (A History of Buddhist Performing Arts of Japan). Tôkyô: Kazama Syobô.

Siba [Shiba], Sukehiro. 1967. *Gagaku tûkai* (Theory of *Gagaku*). Tôkyô: Kunitati ongakudaigaku syuppanbu.

————. 1969. *Gosenhu ni yoru gagaku sôhu* (*Gagaku* Music Transcription in Western Staff Notation). Tôkyô: Kawai Gakuhu.

Sibata [Shibata], Minao. n.d. *Ongaku no gaikotu no hanasi* (On the Skeletons of Music). Tôkyô: Ongaku no tomo sha.

————. 1985. *Ongaku si to ongaku ron* (History of Music and Music Theory).Tôkyô: Hôsô Daigaku Kyôiku Sinkô Kai.

Simohusa [Shimofusa], Kan'iti [Kan'ichi]. 1954. *Nihon Min'yô to onkai no kenkyû* (A Study of Japanese Folk Songs and Music Scales). Tôkyô: Ongaku no tomo sha.

Singonsyû [Shingonshu] Buzan-ha Bukkyô Seinenkai, ed. 1998. *Singi-Singon syômô syûsei* (Buddhist Chant of Shingi-Shingon). 2 vols. Tôkyô: Singonsyû Buzan-ha Bukkyô Seinenkai. (With 4 compact disks.)

Soeda, Tomomiti [Tomomichi]. 1963. *Enka no Meizi Taisyô si.* (A History of *Enka* during the Meizi and Taisyô Periods). Tôkyô: Iwanami Shoten.

Takano, Tatuyuki [Tatsuyuki]. 1926. *Nihon kayô si* (The History of Japanese Songs). Tôkyô: Syunzyûsya.

————. 1929. *Nihon kayô syûsei* (A Collection of Japanese Songs). Tôkyô: Syunzyûsya.

Takeuti [Takeuchi], Mititaka [Michitaka] 1982. *Kinsei geinôsi no kenkyû* (Studies on the History of Performing Arts in Premodern Japan). Tôkyô: Nansôsya.

————. 1989. *Kinsei hôgaku kenkyû nôto* (Research Notes on the Music of Premodern Japan). Tôkyô: Meityokankôkai.

————. 1998. *Kinsei hôgaku kô* (Research on the Music of Premodern Japan). Tôkyô: Nansôsya.

Tanabe, Hisao. 1919. *Nihon ongaku kôwa* (Lectures on Japanese Music). Tôkyô: Iwanami Syoten.

————. 1934. *Syûkyô ongaku* (Religious Music). Tôkyô: Tôhô Syoin.

Tanaka, Kenzi. 1998. *Densi gakki sangyôron* (Industry of Electronic Music Instruments). Tôkyô: Kôbundô.

Tanimoto, Kazuyuki. 2000. *Ainu e wo kiku* (Listening to Ainu Paintings). Sapporo: Hokkaidô Daigaku Tosyo Kankôkai.

Terauti [Terauchi], Naoko. 1996. *Gagaku no rizumu kôzô* (The Rhythmic Structure of *Gagaku*). Tôkyô: Daiiti Syobô.

Tôdô Ongakukai [Todo Music Society], ed. 1990. *Yoku wakaru sôkyoku ziuta no kiso tisiki* (Vandemecum of *Sôkyoku* and *Ziuta*). Tôkyô: Hakusuisha.

Tokumaru, Yosihiko [Yoshihiko]. 1991. *Minzoku ongakugaku* (Ethnomusicology). Tôkyô: Hôsô Daigaku Kyôiku Sinkô Kai.

————. 1996. *Minzokuongakugaku riron* (Theories of Ethnomusicology). Tôkyô: Hôsôdaigaku kyôiku sinkôkai.

Tôkyô Kokuritu Bunkazai Kenkyûsyo, ed. 1960. *Hyôzun nihon buyô hu* (The Standard Notation of Japanese Dance). Tôkyô: Sôgensya.

Toyohara no Muneaki. 1935 [1511]. *Taigensyô* (A Note on *Gagaku* Performance). Tôkyô: Koten zensyû kankôkai.

Tôyô ongakugakkai, ed. *Tôyô ongaku sensho* (Research in Asian Music Series). 1, *Nihon no min'yo to minzoku geinô* (Folk Songs and Folk Performing Arts of Japan, 1967). 2, *Tôdai no gakki* (Musical Instruments of the Tang Dynasty, 1968). 3, *Sôkyoku to ziuta* (*Koto* Music and *Ziuta*, 1967). 4, *Nô no hayasi goto* (Instrumental Music of *Nô*, 1990). 5, *Nan'yô, Taiwan, Okinawa ongaku kikô* (Music Expeditions in Micronesia, Taiwan, and Okinawa, 1968). 6, *Bukkyô ongaku* (Buddhist Music, 1972). 7, *Syamisen to sono ongaku* (*Syamisen* and Its Music, 1978). 8, *Tônan Azia no ongaku* (Music of Southeast Asia, 1970). 9, *Nihon no onkai* (Musical Scales of Japan,

1982). 10, *Gagaku* (*Gagaku*, 1969). 11, *Tyûgoku, Tyôsen ongaku tyôsa kikô* (Music Expeditions in China and Korea, 1970). 12, *Kabuki ongaku* (Music of *Kabuki*, 1980). Tôkyô: Ongaku no tomo sha.

Tuda [Tsuda], Mitiko [Michiko]. 1998. *Kyôto no hibiki: Yanagawa syamisen* (Yanagawa *Syamisen*: The Sound Proper to Kyôto). Kyôto: Kyôto tôdôkai.

Tukahara [Tsukahara], Yasuko. 1993. *19 seiki no nihon ni okeru seiyôongaku no zyuyô* (Reception of Western Music in Nineteenth-Century Japan). Tôkyô: Taga syuppan.

Tukitani [Tsukitani], Tuneko [Tsuneko]. 2000. *Syakuhati koten honkyoku no kenkyû* (Study of the Classical *Syakuhati Honkyoku*). Tôkyô: Syuppan Geizyutu Sya.

Tunoda [Tsunoda], Itirô [Ichiro]. 1980. *Ningyô butaisi* (History of Puppet Theater Stages). 2 vols. Tôkyô: Kokuritugekizyô.

Utida [Uchida], Ruriko. 1989. *Okinawa no kayô to ongaku* (Songs and Ballads in Okinawa): *Ethnomusicological Considerations*. Tôkyô: Daiichi Shôbô.

Watanabe, Hirosi [Hiroshi]. 1999. *Takarazuka kageki no hen'yô to Nihon kindai* (Transformation of Takarazuka *Kageki* and Modern Japan). Tôkyô: Sinsyokan.

Yamada, Yosio [Yoshio]. [1934] 1969. *Genzimonogatari no ongaku* (Music in the Tale of the Genzi). Tôkyô: Hôbunkan syuppan.

Yokomiti [Yokomiti], Mario. 1986. *Nôgeki no kenkyû* (Research on the Nô Plays). Tôkyô: Iwanami Syoten.

Yokomiti [Yokomiti], Mario, et al., eds. 1987–1990. *Iwanami kôza, nô, kyôgen* (Iwanami Series on *Nô* and *Kyôgen*). 7 vols. Tôkyô: Iwanami shoten.

KOREA

English-language and other Western-language sources

Ahn, Byung-Sup [An Pyŏngsŏp]. 1988. "Na Ungyu's Film *Arirang*." *Korea Journal* 28(7):48–51.

Ahn, Sook-Kyung [An Sukkyŏng]. 1974. "The Education of Musicians in the Republic of Korea." *ISME Yearbook* 2:21–28.

Anderson, Sara May. 1940. "Korean Folk Songs." M.A. dissertation, Eastman School of Music.

Boots, J. L. 1940. "Korean Musical Instruments and an Introduction to Korean Music." *Transactions of the Korea Branch of the Royal Asiatic Society* 30:1–31.

Burde, Wolfgang. 1989. "The Korean Poeple's Attitude to Music." *Koreana* 3(2):48–51.

———, ed. 1985. *Korea: Einführung in die Musiktradition Koreas*. Mainz: Schott.

Chang, Sahun. 1975. "Korean Traditional Music." *East Asian Review* 2(3):317–337.

———. 1976. "Transmutation of Korean Music." *Korea Journal* 16(12):15–19.

———. 1978. "Korean and Chinese Chongjae." *Korea Journal* 18(2):14–25.

———. 1980. "Education in Classical Korean Music, Past and Present." *Korea Journal* 20(11):39–45. (Also published in *Traditional Korean Music*. 1983. Seoul: Si-sa-yong-o-sa.)

———. 1983. "Nongak." In *Traditional Performing Arts of Korea*, 27–34. Seoul: National Academy of Arts.

Cho, Dong-il [Cho Tongil]. 1986. "The General Nature of P'ansori." *Korea Journal* 26(4):10–22.

———. 1997. *Korean Literature in Cultural Context and Comparative Perspective*. Seoul: Jipmoondang.

Cho, Euiyon [Cho Ŭiyŏn]. 1989. "Traditional Korean Music, *Nong-ak*, and *Pansori*: Their History and Features." *Asian Culture Quarterly* 17(3):30–35.

Cho, Oh Kon [Cho Ogon]. 1979. *Korean Puppet Theatre: Kkoktu Kaksi*. East Lansing: Michigan State University Asian Studies Center.

———. 1986. "East Asian Performance: Korea." In *Theatrical Movement: A Bibliographical Anthology*, ed. Bob Fleshman, 443–452. Metuchen, N.J.: Scarecrow.

———. 1988. *Traditional Korean Theatre*. Studies in Korean Religions and Culture, Vol. 2. Berkeley Calif.: Asian Humanities.

Codecasa, Maria Silvia. 1975. "Kaya-go and Other Korean String Instruments." *Korea Journal* 15(4):63–65. (Also published in *Traditional Korean Music*. 1983. Seoul: Si-sa-yong-o-sa.)

Condit, Jonathan. 1977. "The Evolution of *Yŏmillak* from the Fifteenth Century to the Present Day." In *Tongyang ŭmakhak nonch'ong: Chang Sa-hun paksa hoegap kinyŏm*, 231–262. Seoul: Hanguk kugak hakhoe.

———. 1978. "Uncovering Earlier Melodic Forms from Modern Performance: The *Kasa* Repertoire." *Asian Music* 9(2):3–20.

———. 1979. "A Fifteenth-Century Korean Score in Mensural Notation." *Musica Asiatica* 2:1–88.

———. 1981. "Two Song-Dynasty Chinese Tunes Preserved in Korea." In *Music and Tradition: Essays on Asian and Other Musics Presented to Laurence Picken*, ed. D. R. Widdess and R. Wolpert, 1–39. Cambridge: Cambridge University Press.

———. 1984. "Korean Scores in the Modified Fifteenth-Century Mensural Notation." *Musica Asiatica* 4:1–116.

———. 1984. *Music of the Korean Renaissance: Songs and Dances of the Fifteenth Century*. Cambridge: Cambridge University Press.

Eckardt, Andreas. 1930. *Koreanische Musik*. Tokyo: Deutsche Gesellschaft für Natur. Völkerkunde Ostasiens.

———. 1968. *Music—Lied—Tanz in Korea*. Abhandlungen zur Kunst-, Music- und Literaturwissenschaft, Vol. 51. Bonn: H. Bouvier Verlag.

Hahn, Man-young [Han Manyŏng]. 1974. "Nongak." In *Survey of Korean Arts: Folk Arts*, 286–294. Seoul: National Academy of Arts.

———. 1974. "Traditional Music of Korea." In *Aspects of Korean Culture*, ed. Suh Cheong-Soo and Pak Chun-kun. Seoul: Soodo Women's Teachers College Press.

———. 1975. "Religious Origins of Korean Music." *Korea Journal* 15(7):17–22. (Also published in *Traditional Korean Music*. 1983. Seoul: Si-sa-yong-o-sa.)

———. 1978a. "*Cho* (Mode-Scale) of *Hyangak*." *Korea Journal* 18(2):26–29.

———. 1978b. "Folk Songs of Korean Rural Life and Their Characteristics Based on the Rice Farming Songs." *Asian Music* 9(2):21–28.

———. 1990. "Chŏngak, ŭmakhak: The Rise of Music for the Middle Classes." *Minjok umakhak* 12:1–12.

———. 1991. *Kugak: Studies in Korean Traditional Music*. Seoul: Tamgudang.

Han, Myong-hee [Han Myŏnghŭi]. 1993. "Musical Instruments: Conveying the Korean Spirit through Nature." *Koreana: Korean Art and Culture* 8(4):38–43.

———. 1994a. "Sounds of the Mountains, Sound of the Heart." *Koreana: Korean Art and Culture* 8(4):26–33.

———. 1994b. "What Makes Korean Music Different: A Study of Its Roots and Branches." *Koreana: Korean Art and Culture* 8(3):6–9.

———. 1998a. "Music, Dance, Drama and Games." In *Kyongju: City of Millennial History*, ed. Korean National Commission for UNESCO. Elizabeth, N.J.: Hollym International.

———. 1998b. *The Study of Musical Instruments in Korean Traditional Music*. Seoul: National Center for Korean Traditional Performing Arts.

Han, Young-sook [Han Yŏngsuk, and Lee Mi-kyong [Yi Migyŏng]. 1974. "Traditional Dances of Korea." In *Aspects of Korean Culture*, ed. Suh Cheong-Soo and Pak Chun-kun. Seoul: Soodo Women's Teachers College Press.

Harvey, John H. T., ed. 2000. *Korean Intangible Cultural Properties*. Vol. 3: *Traditional Music and Dance*. Elizabeth, N.J.: Hollym International.

Hesselink, Nathan. 1996. "*Changdan* Revisited: Korean Rhythmic Patterns in Theory and Contemporary Performance Practice." *Han'guk Ŭmak yŏn'gu* (Studies in Korean Music) 24:143–155.

———. 1998. "Of Drums and Men in Chollabuk-do Province: Glimpses into the Making of a Human Cultural Asset." *Korea Journal* 38(3):293–326.

———. 2000. "Kim Inu's '*P'ungmulgut* and Communal Spirit': Edited and Translated, with an Introduction and Commentary." *Asian Music* 31(1):1–34.

Heyman, Alan C. 1966. *Dances of the Three-Thousand-League Land*. Seoul: Dong-A.

———. 1987. "P'an-sori—The Narrative-Epic Folk Drama of Korea." *Asian and Pacific Quarterly of Cultural and Social Affairs* 19(2-60):51–56.

———. 1989. "Han Yong-suk (1920–1989)." *Korea Journal* 29(12):51–55.

———. 1990. "The Psyche and Unique Character of Korean Dance." *Korea Journal* 30(11):61–68.

———, ed. 1993. *The Traditional Music and Dance of Korea*. Seoul: Korean Traditional Performing Arts Center.

Howard, Keith, 1983. "*Nongak*, the *Changgo*, and Kim Pyŏng-sŏp's *Kaein Changgo Nori*." *Korea Journal* 23(5):15–31; 23(6):23–34.

———. 1986. "Bands and Songs: Historical Precedents for the Contemporary Confluence of Rural and Urban Folk Music Styles in Korea." *World of Music* 28(2):14–25.

———. 1987. "An Introduction to Korean Folk Bands and Folk Songs." *Korea Journal* 27(8):28–48.

———. 1988. *Korean Musical Instruments: A Practical Guide*. Seoul: Se-Kwang Music Publishing.

———. 1989. "*Namdo tŭl norae*: Ritual and the Intangible Cultural Asset System." *Journal of Ritual Studies* 3(2):203–216.

———. 1990a. *Bands, Songs, and Shamanistic Rituals: Folk Music in Korean Society*. Seoul: Royal Asiatic Society, Korea Branch.

———. 1990b. "A Detailed Look of the Komun'go and Tanso." *Korean Culture* 11(2):18–21.

———. 1990c. "Tashiraegi: En Corée, pas de retour après la mort si ce n'est dans un trésor culturel intangible." *Cahiers de Musiques Traditionnelles* 3:119–139.

———. 1991a. "Samul Nori: A Reinterpretation of a Korean Folk Tradition for Urban and International Audiences." In *Tradition and Its Future in Music: Report of SIMS 1990 Osaka*, ed. Tokumaru Yosihiko, 539–546. Tokyo: Mita.

———. 1991b. "Why Do It That Way? Rhythmic Models and Motifs in Korean Percussion Bands." *Asian Music* 23(1):1–59.

———. 1992. "Musicology as a Science? Thirty Years of Indigenous Korean Music Studies." In *European Studies in Ethnomusicology: Historical Developments and Recent Trends,* ed. Max Peter Baumann, Artur Simon, and Ulrich Wegner, 52–66. Wilhelmshaven: Florian Noetzel Verlag.

———. 1993. "Where Did the Old Music Go?" *Minjok Ŭmakhak* 15:122–151.

———. 1995a. "Gender Issues in the Conservation of Korean Music: Presumptive Observations." In *Lux oriente: Begegnungen der Kulturen in der Musikforschung—Festschrift Robert Gunther zum 65. Geburtstag,* 181–195. Kassel: Bosse.

———. 1995b. *Korean Musical Instruments*. New York: Oxford University Press.

———. 1996a. "A Compact Discography of Korean Traditional Music." *Korea Journal* 36(3):115–132; 36(4):120–140.

———. 1996b. "Juche and Culture: What's New?" In *North Korea in the New World Order*, ed. Hazel Smith, Chris Rhodes, Diana Pritchard, and Kevin Magill, 169–195. Basingstoke: Macmillan.

———. 1997. "Different Spheres: Perceptions of Traditional Music and Western Music in Korea." *World of Music* 39(2):61–67.

———. 1998. "Blending the Wine and Stretching the Wine Skins: New Korean Music for Old Korean Instruments." In *Essays in Musicology: An Offering in Celebration of Lee Hye-Ku on His Ninetieth Birthday,* 501–536. Seoul: Kŭktong Munhwasa.

———, ed. 1998. *Korean Shamanism: Revivals, Survival, and Change*. Seoul: Seoul Press; Royal Asiatic Society, Korea Branch.

———. 1999. *Korean Music: A Listening Guide*. Korean Music Resources Series 3. Seoul: National Center for Korean Traditional Performing Arts.

———. 1999. "*Minyo* in Korea: Songs of the People and Songs for the People." *Asian Music* 30(2):1–37.

Howard, Keith, Joachim Bühler, and Chu Kyŏngsun. 1996. "Korea." In *Die Musik in Geschichte und Gegenwart* 5:733–756. Kassel: Barenreiter and Stuttgart: Metzler.

Hughes, David W. 1991. "Oral Mnemonics in Korean Music: Data, Interpretation, and a Musicological Application." *Bulletin of the School of Oriental and African Studies* 54(2):307–335.

Hwang, Byong-ki [Hwang Pyŏnggi]. 1978. "Aesthetic Characteristics of Korean Music in Theory and in Practice." *Asian Music* 9(2):29–40.

Jang, Yeonok [Chang Yŏnok]. 2000. "Development and Change in Korean Narrative Song, P'ansori." Ph.D dissertation, SOAS, University of London.

Kang, Sukhi [Kang Sŏkhŭi]. 1981. "Einige Aspekte traditioneller Musik in Korea." *Neue Zeitschrift für Musik* 142(4):348–352.

Kaufmann, Walter. 1967. *Musical Notations of the Orient*. Bloomington: Indiana University Press.

Killick, Andrew P. 1990. "New Music for Korean Instruments: An Analytical Survey." M.A. dissertation, University of Hawaii.

———. 1991. "Nationalism and Internationalism in New Music for Korean Instruments." *Korea Journal* 31(3):104–16.

———. 1992. "Musical Composition in Twentieth-Century Korea." *Korean Studies* 16:43–60.

———. 1997. "Putting *P'ansori* on the Stage: A Re-Study in Honor of Marshall R. Pihl." *Korea Journal* 37(1):108–130.

———. 1998a. "The Chŏson Songak Yŏn'guhoe and the Advent of Mature *Ch'anggŭk* Opera." *Review of Korean Studies* 1:76–100.

———. 1998b. "The Invention of Traditional Korean Opera and the Problem of the Traditionesque: *Ch'anggŭk* and Its Relation to *P'ansori* Narratives." Ph.D. dissertation, University of Washington.

Kim, Byong-Kon [Kim Pyŏnggon]. 1989. "Aesthetics in Kagok: The Musics of Yi Intellectuals." *Yesurwŏnbo* 33:149–172.

Kim, Ch'ang-nam [Kim Ch'angnam]. 1987. "The Spirit of Folksongs and Realism in Song: The Musical World of Kim Min-gi." *Korea Journal* 27(3):28–41.

Kim, Chong-il [Kim Chŏngil]. 1990. *On the Art of Opera*. Pyongyang: Foreign Languages Publishing House.

Kim, Chong-ja [Kim Chŏngja]. 1981. "Melodic Embellishment in Korean Royal Ancestral Shrine Music." *Hanguk Umak Yongu* 2:53–68.

Kim, Jin-gyun [Kim Chin'gyun]. 1974. "The Influence of Christianity in Korea's Development: Viewed from Aspect of Music (*Kyemyong taehak tongso munhwa yonguso*)." *Tongso Munhwa* 7:213–248.

Kim, Jungnyu. 1981. "The Character and Aesthetic Value of Seong Moo." *Han'guk umak yon'gu* 2:71–75.

Kim, Mi-yon [Kim Miyŏyon]. n.d. "Musical Organizations in an Ethnic Student Group: The Korean Church Choir and the *Samulnori Pae*." In *Community of Music: An Ethnographic Seminar in Champaign-Urbana*, ed. Melinda Russell et al., 84–92. Champaign, Ill.: Elephant and Cat.

Kim, Shi-op [Kim Siŏp]. 1988. "*Arirang*, Modern Korean Folk Song." *Korea Journal* 28(7):4–19.

Kim, Wŏn-yong [Kim Wŏnyong], et al. 1972. *Traditional Culture in the Nineteen-Sixties and Its Prospect*. Seoul: Ministry of Information and Culture.

Kim, Woo Ok [Kim Uok]. 1980. "P'ansori: An Indigenous Theater of Korea." Ph.D. dissertation, New York University.

Kim, Yang-kon [Kim Yanggon]. 1967. "Farmers' Music and Dance." *Korea Journal* 7(10):4–9, 29.

Kim, Yersu [Kim Yŏlsu]. 1976. *Cultural Policy in the Republic of Korea. Studies and Documents on Cultural Policies.* Paris: UNESCO.

Kim, Yŏlgyu, 1992. "A Study of the Present Status of Folklore and Folk Arts in North Korea." *Korea Journal* 32(2):75–81, 88–89.

Kim, Yong-mann [Kim Yongman]. 1989. "Korean Traditional Music: The History of Its Relations with Chinese Music (Part 1)." *Korean Culture* 10(4):22–27.

———. 1990. "Korean Traditional Music: The History of Its Relations with Chinese Music (Part 2)." *Korean Culture* 11(2):12–17.

Kim, Youn-Gap [Kim Yŏn'gap]. 1988. "The Origin of *Arirang* and *Meari* as Its Original Form." *Korea Journal* 28(7):20–34.

Kim, Young-woon [Kim Yŏngun]. 1998. "The Origin and Structure of the *Kayagum*." *Korea Journal* 38(2):287–317.

Kim, Young-Youn [Kim Yŏngyun]. 1999. "Traditional Korean Children's Songs: Collection, Analysis, and Application." *International Journal of Music Education* 33:38–45.

Korean National Commission for UNESCO. 1983. *Korean Dance, Theater, and Cinema.* Korean Art 4. Seoul: Si-sa-yong-o-sa; Arch Cape, Ore.: Pace International Research.

———. 1983. *Traditional Korean Music.* Seoul: Si-sa-yong-o-sa; Arch Cape, Ore.: Pace International Research.

———. 1996. *Methodologies for the Preservation of Intangible Heritage.* Seoul: Korean National Commission for UNESCO.

———. 1999. *UNESCO International Training Workshop on the Living Human Treasures System.* Seoul: Korean National Commission for UNESCO.

Lee, Baik-chun [Yi Paekchun]. 1964. "Jazz in Postwar Korea." *Korea Journal* 4(9):21–23.

Lee, Bo-hyung [Yi Pohyŏng]. 1997. "From *P'ansori* to *Ch'anggŭk*." In *Korean Cultural Heritage* 3, *Performing Arts,* ed. Joungwon Kim, 64–69. Seoul: Korea Foundation.

Lee, Byong Won [Yi Pyŏngwŏn]. 1977. "Structural Formulae of Melodies in the Two Sacred Buddhist Chant Styles in Korea." *Korean Studies* 1:111–96.

———. 1980. "Perspectives on the Problems of Ethnomusicological Research of Korean Music." *Korea Journal* 20(11):32–38.

———. 1981. "Korean Court Music and Dance." *World of Music* 23(1):35–49.

———. 1982. "Micro- and Macro-Structure of Melody and Rhythm in Korean Buddhist Chant." *Korea Journal* 22(3):33–38. (Also published in *Traditional Korean Music.* 1983. Seoul: Si-sa-yong-o-sa.)

———. 1987. *Buddhist Music of Korea.* Traditional Korean Music Series 3. Seoul: Jungeumsa.

———. 1993. "Contemporary Korean Musical Cultures." In *Korea Briefing,* ed. Donald C. Clark, 121–138. Boulder, Colo.: Westview.

———. 1997. *Styles and Esthetics in Korean Traditional Music.* Seoul: National Center for Korean Traditional Performing Arts.

———. 2000. "The Current State of Research on Korean Music." *Yearbook for Traditional Music* 32:143–149.

Lee, Duhyun [Yi Tuhyŏn]. 1990. "Korean Shamans: Role Playing through Trance Possession." In *By Means of Performance: Intercultural Studies of Theatre and Ritual,* ed. Richard Schechner and Willa Appel, 149–166. Cambridge: Cambridge University Press.

Lee, Duhyun [Yi Tuhyŏn], et al. 1997. *Korean Performing Arts: Drama, Dance, and Music Theater.* Korean Studies Series 6. Seoul: Jipmoondang.

Lee, Hye-Ku [Yi Hyegu]. 1962. "Historical Mensural Notation in Korea." *Korean Affairs* 1(3):267–274.

———. 1970. "Traditional Music." In *Korean Studies Today: Development and State of the Field,* ed. Sung-nyong Lee. Seoul: Institute of Asian Studies, Seoul National University.

———. 1976. "Introduction to Korean Music." *Korea Journal* 16(12):4–14. (Also published in *Traditional Korean Music.* 1983. Seoul: Si-sa-yong-o-sa.)

———. 1977. *An Introduction to Korean Music and Dance.* Seoul: Royal Asiatic Society, Korea Branch.

———. 1978. "Difference between *Hyangak* and *Tang-ak*." *Korea Journal* 18(2):4–13.

———. 1981a. *Essays on Traditional Korean Music,* trans. and ed. Robert C. Provine. Seoul: Royal Asiatic Society, Korea Branch.

———. 1981b. "Quintuple Meter in Korean Instrumental Music." *Asian Music* 13(1):119–129.

———, ed. 1982. *Korean Musical Instruments.* Seoul: National Classical Music Institute of Korea.

———. 1986. "Sung Dynasty Music Preserved in Korea and China." *Korean Studies* 10:69–92.

Lee, Kang-sook [Yi Kangsuk]. 1978. "An Essay on Korean Modes." *Asian Music* 9(2):41–47.

———. 1980. "Certain Experiences in Korean Music." In *Musics of Many Cultures: An Introduction,* ed. Elizabeth May. Berkeley: University of California Press.

———. 1983. "Korean Music Culture." In *Traditional Korean Music.* Seoul: Si-sa-yong-o-sa.

Lee, Sang-Man [Yi Sangman]. 1976. "The Essential Characteristics of Korean Traditional Music." *Asian and Pacific Quarterly of Cultural and Social Affairs* 8(3):40–44.

———. 1991. "South Korea." In *New Music in the Orient: Essays on Composition in Asia since World War II,* ed. Harrison Ryker, 249–264. Buren: Frits Knuf.

Lee, Wha-Byong [Yi Hwabyŏng]. 1991. *Studien zur Pansori-Musik in Korea.* Europaische Hochschulschriften, Reihe 36, Musikwissenschaft, Vol. 61. Frankfurt am Main: Peter Lang.

Lee, Yong-il [Yi Yŏngil]. 1990. "A Study of Korean Music Education and Its Improvement." In *Music Education: Facing the Future,* ed. Jack Dobbs, 260–266. Helsinki: International Society for Music Education.

Lee, Young-min [Yi Yŏngmin]. 1987. "The Development of Western-Style Orchestral Music in Korea: The Early Years." *Songshin Yoja Taehakkyo Yongu Nonmunjip* 25(2):357–387.

Lim, Mi-sun [Lim Misŏn]. 1998. "The Function of Music in Court Ceremonies of the Choson Period." In *Perspectives on Korea,* ed. Sang-Oak Lee and Duk-Soo Park. Sydney: Wild Peony.

Loken-Kim, Christine J. 1989. "Release from Bitterness: Korean Dancer as Korean Woman." Ph.D. dissertation, University of North Carolina.

Loken-Kim, Christine, and Juliette T. Crump. 1993. "Qualitative Change in Performances of Two Generations of Korean Dancers." *Dance Research Journal* 25(2):13–20.

Mackerras, Colin. 1984. "Theatre in the Democratic People's Republic of Korea." *Asian Theatre Journal* 1(1):76–89.

Maliangkay, Roald Heber. 1999. "Handling the Intangible: The Protection of Folksong Traditions in Korea." Ph.D. dissertation, University of London.

Malm, William P. 1980. "The Unique Position of Korea in the Study of East Asian Music." In *Che-1 hoe kukche haksulhoe ui nonmunjip: Papers of the First International Conference on Korean Studies.* Sŏngnam: Han'guk chŏngshin munhwa yŏn'guwŏn.

———. 1995. *Music Cultures of the Pacific, the Near East, and Asia,* 3rd ed. Englewood Cliffs, N.J.: Prentice-Hall.

Moon, Kwi-ok [Moon Kwiok]. 1974. "Folk Songs of Korea." In *Aspects of Korean Culture,* ed. Suh Cheong-Soo and Pak Chun-kun. Seoul: Soodo Women's Teachers College Press.

Nam, Unjung. 1998. "Pitch Distributions in Korean Court Music: Evidence Consistent with Tonal Hierarchies." *Music Perception* 16(2): 243–247.

National Academy of Arts (Yesurwŏn). 1973. *Survey of Korean Arts: Traditional Music.* Seoul: National Academy of Arts.

———. 1974. *Survey of Korean Arts: Folk Arts.* Seoul: National Academy of Arts.

Nellen, Frank. 1983. "Westernization of Korean Music or Koreanization of Western Music." *Korea Journal* 23(11):28–33.

———. 1984. *Bibliographie zu Musik und Tanz im traditionellen Korea,* Teil A: *Literatur in Europäischen Sprachen, Kleine Schriften zur Koreaforschung,* 1. Bochum: Verlag Norbert R. Adami.

Oh, Ruth K. 1985. "Improvisation in P'ansori: A Vocal Genre of Korea." In *Improvisation in the Performing Arts,* ed. Ricardo Trimillos and William Feltz, 23–35. Honolulu: East-West Center, Institute of Culture and Communication.

Paek, Inok. 1998. "Transmission Processes of Korean Traditional Music." Ph.D. dissertation, Queen's University of Belfast.

Park, Il-young [Pak Iryŏng]. 1991. "Communion Feast in Korean Shamanism." *Korea Journal* 31(1):73–86.

Park, Jeong-hye [Pak Chŏnghye]. 1997. "The Court Music and Dance in the Royal Banquet Paintings of the Choson Dynasty." *Korea Journal* 37(3):123–140.

Park, Mikyung [Pak Migyŏng]. 1980. "Confucian Symbolism in the Court Ritual Music of Korea." *Journal of Asian Culture* 4:143–153.

———. 1998. "What Is Ethnomusicology in Korea: An Evaluation of Its Current Status." *Tongyang Ŭmak* 20:61–91.

Pihl, Marshall R. 1991. "Putting *P'ansori* on the Stage." *Korea Journal* 31(1):110–119.

———. 1994. *The Korean Singer of Tales.* Harvard-Yenching Institute Monograph Series 37. Cambridge, Mass.: Council on East Asian Studies. Distributed by Harvard University Press.

Pratt, Keith L. 1976. "Music as a Factor in Sung-Koryŏ Diplomatic Relations, 1069–1126." *T'oung Pao* 62(4-5):199–218.

———. 1977. "Some Aspects of Diplomatic and Cultural Exchange between Korea and Northern Sung China." In *Chang Sahun paksa hoegap kinyŏm tongyang ŭmakhak nonch'ong,* 313–323. Seoul: Han'guk kugak hakhoe.

———. 1981. "Sung Hui Tsung's Musical Diplomacy and the Korean Response." *Bulletin of the School of Oriental and African Studies* 47(3):509–521.

———. 1987. *Korean Music: Its History and Its Performance,* Traditional Korean Music, Vol. 4. London: Faber Music and Seoul: Jungeumsa. (With 1 sound cassette.)

Provine, Robert C. 1975a. "Brief Introduction to Traditional Korean Folk Music." *Korea Journal* 15(1):29–31. (Also published in *Traditional Korean Music.* 1983. Seoul: Si-sa-yong-o-sa.)

———. 1975b. "The Sacrifice to Confucius in Korea and Its Music." *Transactions of the Korea Branch of the Royal Asiatic Society* 50:43–69.

———. 1978. "Who's in Charge Here? The Musical Bureaucracy in the Early Yi Dynasty Court (1392–1466)." *Asian Music* 9(2):48–58.

———. 1980a. "'Chinese' Ritual Music in Korea: The Origins, Codifications, and Cultural Role of Aak." In *Che-1 hoe kukche haksul hoeŭi nonmunjip* (Papers of the First International Studies. Hoeŭi, Sŏngnam: Han'guk chŏngsin munhwa yŏn'guwŏn.

———. 1980b. "'Chinese' Ritual Music in Korea: The Origins, Codifications, and Cultural Role of Aak." *Korea Journal* 20(2):16–25. (Also published in *Traditional Korean Music.* 1983. Seoul: Si-sa-yong-o-sa.)

———. 1982. "The Korean Courtyard Ensemble for Ritual Music (Aak)." *Yearbook for Traditional Music* 24:91–117.

———. 1985a. "Drumming in Korean Farmers' Music: A Process of Gradual Evolution." In *Music and Context: Essays for John M. Ward,* ed. Anne Dhu Shapiro, 441–452. Cambridge, Mass.: Department of Music, Harvard University.

———. 1985b. "Korean Music in Historical Perspective." *World of Music* 27(2):3–13.

———. 1985c. "Tracing the Ta-sheng yueh-p'u, a Progenitor of Korean Aak." In *Segye-sok ŭi Han'guk munhwa: Yulgok 400 chugi e chŭŭm hayŏ—Che-3 hoe kukche haksul hoeui nonmunjip* (Korean Culture and Its Characteristics on the Occasion of the 400th Anniversary of Yi Yulgok's Death: Papers of the Third International Conference). Hoeŭi Sŏngnam: Han'guk chŏngsin munhwa yŏn'guwŏn.

———. 1986. "Vocal and Instrumental Music in Sacrifical Rites Performed at the Korean Royal Court: A Case History." In *Actes du XIIIe Congrès de la Société Internationale de Musicologie, Strasbourg, 29 Aout–3 Septembre 1982: La musique et le rite sacré et profane,* 1, ed. Marc Honegger et al. Strasbourg: Association des Publications près les Universités de Strasbourg.

———. 1987. "The Nature and Extent of Surviving Chinese Musical Influence on Korea." *World of Music* 29(2):5–16.

———. 1988a. *Essays on Sino-Korean Musicology: Early Sources for Korean Ritual Music.* Traditional Korean Musics 2. Seoul: Iljisa.

———. 1988b. "Thoughts on Translating the Akhak Kwebŏm into English." In *Han'gukhak ŭi kwaje wa chŏnmang: Che-5 hoeŭi kukche haksul hoeui segye Han'gukhak taehoe nonmunjip 2 (Yesul—sasang—sahoe p'yŏn)* (Korean Studies, Its Tasks and Perspectives 2: Papers of the Fifth International Conference on Korean Studies). Sŏngnam: Han'guk chŏngshin munhwa yŏn'guwŏn.

———. 1989. "State Sacrificial Rites and Ritual Music in Early Chosŏn." *Kugagwŏn Nonmunjip* 1:239–307.

———. 1992a. "King Sejong and Music." In *King Sejong the Great: The Light of Fifteenth-Century Korea,* ed. Young-Key Kim-Renaud. Washington, D.C.: International Circle of Korean Linguistics.

———. 1992b. "The Korean Courtyard Ensemble for Ritual Music (*Aak*)." *Yearbook for Traditional Music* 24:91–117.

———. 1993. "Korea." In *Ethnomusicology: Historical and Regional Studies,* ed. Helen Myers, 363–376. New York: Norton.

———. 1996. "State Sacrificial Music and Korean Identity." In *Harmony and Counterpoint: Ritual Music in Chinese Context,* ed. Bell Yung, Evelyn S. Rawski, and Rubie S. Watson, 54–75. Stanford, Calif.: Stanford University Press.

———. 1998a. "Korean Music: Percussion, Power, History, and Youth." *East European Meetings in Ethnomusicology* 5:61–71.

———. 1998b. "Musical Information in the *Kukcho oryeŭi* and *Kukcho orye sŏrye* of 1474: An Exercise in Historical Ethnomusicology." *Han'guk Ŭmaksa Hakpo* (Journal of the Society for Korean Historico-Musicology) 10:631–650.

———. 1998c. "Rethinking Authenticity in Korean Traditional Music." In *Essays in Musicology: An Offering in Celebration of Lee Hye-ku*

on His Ninetieth Birthday, 585–596. Seoul: Kŭktong Munhwasa.

———. 2000. "Investigating a Musical Biography in Korea: The Theorist/Musicologist Pak Yŏn (1378–1458)." *Yearbook for Traditional Music* 32:1–14.

Provine, Robert C., with Keith Howard and Okon Hwang. 2000. "Korea." In *The New Grove Dictionary of Music and Musicians,* ed. Stanley Sadie, 2nd ed. London: Macmillan.

Rockwell, Coralie J. 1972. *Kagok: A Traditional Korean Vocal Form.* Providence, R.I.: Asian Music Publications.

———. 1974a. "Kayago: The Origin and Evolution of the Korean Twelve-String Zither." *Transactions of the Korea Branch of the Royal Asiatic Society* 49:26–47.

———. 1974b. "Trends and Developments in Korean Traditional Music Today." *Korea Journal* 14(3):15–20.

Shin, Yong-ha [Sin Yongha]. 1985. "Social History of Ture Community and *Nongak* Music." *Korea Journal* 25(3):4–17; 25(4):4–18.

Song, Bang-Song [Song Pangsong]. 1971. *An Annotated Bibliography of Korean Music.* Providence, R.I.: Asian Music Publications.

———. 1974a. "Korean *Kwangdae* Musicians and Their Musical Traditions." *Korea Journal* 14(9):12–19. (Also published in *Traditional Korean Music.* 1983. Seoul: Si-sa-yong-o-sa.)

———. 1974b. "Supplement to an Annotated Bibliography of Korean Music." *Korea Journal* 14(12) to 15(4). (Five installments.)

———. 1975. "The Etymology of the Korean Six-Stringed Zither, Komun'go." *Korea Journal* 15(10):18–23. (Also published in *Traditional Korean Music.* 1983. Seoul: Si-sa-yong-o-sa.)

———. 1976. "A Discography of Korean Music." *Korea Journal* 16(12):53–67.

———. 1977a. "A Discography of Korean Music." *Asian Music* 8(2):82–121.

———. 1977b. "History of Korean Music." *Ethnomusicology* 21(1):138–149.

———. 1977c. "Ritual Tradition of Korea." *Asian Music* 8(2):26–46.

———. 1977d. "Subject Index of Discography." *Korea Journal* 17(6):57–66.

———. 1978. "Korean Music: An Annotated Bibliography, Second Supplement." *Asian Music* 9(2):65–112.

———. 1980a. "Korean Musicology: Its Historical Development and Problems." *Korea Journal* 20(11):11–26. (Also published in *Traditional Korean Music.* 1983. Seoul: Si-sa-yong-o-sa.)

———. 1980b. *Source Readings in Korean Music.* Korean Traditional Music 1. Seoul: Korean National Commission for UNESCO.

———. 1981. "The Tradition of Confucian Ritual Music of Korea: A Historical Survey." *Han'guk Ŭmak Yŏn'gu* 43–50.

———. 1982. "Sanjo versus Raga: A Preliminary Study." In *Cross-Cultural Perspectives on Music,* ed. Robert Falck and Timothy Rice, 101–116. Toronto: University of Toronto Press.

———. 1985. "Present State of Research on Korean Traditional Music." *World of Music* 27(2):63–77.

———. 1986. *The Sanjo Tradition of Korean Kŏmun'go Music.* Traditional Korean Musics 1. Seoul: Jung Eum Sa.

———. 1991. "Music Exchange between Korea and Central Asia in Ancient Times." *Korea Journal* 31(2):33–40.

———. 1993. "Korean Music and the Silk Road." In *Festschrift zum 60. Geburtstag von Wolfgang Suppan*, ed. Bernhard Habla, 185–195. Tutzing: Hans Schneider.

———. 2000. *Korean Music: Historical and Other Aspects.* Historical Studies Series 13. Seoul: Jimoondang.

Song, Bang-song, and Keith Pratt. 1980. "The Unique Flavor of Korean Music." *Korean Culture* 1(3):4–14.

Song, Kyong-nin [Song Kyŏngnin]. 1976. "Korean Court Dance." *Korea Journal* 16(12):20–24.

Song, Soo-nam [Song Sunam]. 1990. "*Shinmyong* in Korean Group Dance Performance." *Korea Journal* 30(9):32–35.

Suh, Yon-Ho [Sŏ Yŏnho]. 1991. "The Revolutionary Operas and Plays in North Korea." *Korea Journal* 31(3):85–94.

Suhr, Moon Ja Minn [Sŏ Munja Min]. 1989. "Confucian Ritual Ceremony in Korea: Music and Dance." *Korean Culture* 10(1):29–39.

Sung, Kyung He [Sŏng Kyŏnghŭi]. 1984. "Trends and Developments in School Music Education." In *Music for a Small Planet: Papers from the XVIth International Conference, Eugene, Oregon, U.S.A. 1984*, ed. Frank Dobbs, 109–112. Nedlands, Western Australia: International Music Education.

Sur, Donald. 1978. "Introduction to the Classical Music of Korea." *World of Music* 20(2): 53–55.

———. 1980. "Tonal Arrangements in Korean Classical Music." *Korean Culture* 1(3): 15–18.

Sutton, R. Anderson. 1987. "Korean Music in Hawaii." *Asian Music* 19(1):99–120.

Uchida, Ruriko. 1979. "Rice-Planting Music of Chindo (Korea) and the Chugoku Region (Japan)." In *The Performing Arts: Music and Dance*, ed. John Blacking and Joann W. Kealiinohomoku, 109–117. The Hague: Mouton.

Um, Hae-kyung (Ŏm Hye-gyŏng). 1992. "Making P'ansori: Korean Musical Drama." Ph.D. dissertation, Queen's University, Belfast.

Van Erven, Eugène. 1988. "Resistance Theatre in South Korea: Above the Underground." *TDR: The Drama Review* 32(3):156–173.

Van Leest, Hyung-a Kim. 1991. "Political Satire in *Yangju Pyŏlsandae* Mask Drama." *Korea Journal* 31(1):87–109.

Van Zile, Judy. 1987. "*Ch'oyongmu*: An Ancient Dance Survives." *Korean Culture* 8(2):4–19.

———. 1991. "Chinju Kommu: An Implement Dance of Korea." *Studia Musicologica Academiae Scientiarum Hungaricae* 33(1–4):359–366.

———. 2001. *Perspectives on Korean Dance.* Middletown, Conn.: Wesleyan University Press.

Walraven, Boudewijn. 1985. *Muga: the Songs of Korean Shamanism.* Leiden.

———. 1994. *Songs of the Shaman: The Ritual Chants of the Korean Mudang.* London: Kegan Paul International.

Waterhouse, David. 1986. "Korean Music, Trick Horsemanship, and Elephants in Tokugawa Japan." In *The Oral and the Literate*, ed. Yosihiko Tokumaru and Yamaguti Osamu, 353–370. Tokyo: Academia.

———. 1991. "Where Did Toragaku Come From?" *Musica Asiatica* 6: 73–94.

Willoughby, Heather. 2000. "The Sound of Han: P'ansori, Timbre, and a Korean Ethos of Pain and Suffering." *Yearbook for Traditional Music* 32:15–30.

Yamamoto, Osamu. 1994. "The Use and Combination of Vocal and Instrumental Sounds in *Kut* (Shamanistic Ritual) in Heoanghaedo, Korea." In *Music Cultures in Interaction: Cases between Asia and Europe*, ed. Mabuchi Usaburŏ and Yamaguti Osamu, 106–115.

Yang, Jongsung [Yang Chongsŏng]. 1988. "Korean Shamanism: The Training Process of Charismatic 'Mudang.'" *Folklore Forum* 21(1):20–40.

Yi, Bo-hyong [Yi Pohyŏng]. 1973. *P'ansori: Survey of Korean Arts: Traditional Music.* Seoul: National Academy of Arts.

———. 1980. "Performing Styles of Korea Traditional Music." *Korea Journal* 20(11):11–26. (Also published in *Traditional Korean Music.* 1983. Seoul: Si-sa-yong-o-sa.)

———. 1988. "Musical Study on *Arirang*." *Korea Journal* 28(7):35–47; 52–58.

Yi, Sung-chun [Yi Sŏngch'ŏn]. 1997. "The Identity of Traditional Korean Music." *Korea Journal* 37(3):110–22.

Zong, In-sob [Chŏng Insŏp]. 1961. "The Classical Music and Dance of Korea." *Chungang Taehakkyo Nonmunjip* 6(12):5–25.

Korean-language publications

Akhak kwebŏm (Standard Music Treatise). 1493. (*See* Sŏng, Hyŏn, 1968).

An, Hwak. 1980. *Chosŏn ŭmak ŭi yŏn'gu* (Studies in Korean Music). Seoul: Korean Musicology Society.

An, Sang. [1572] 1974. *Kŭmhapchabo* (Handbook of Kŏmun'go Tablature). Seoul: Seoul National University.

Chang, Sahun. 1969. *Han'guk akki taegwan* (Korean Musical Instruments). Seoul: Korean Musicological Society.

———. 1974. *Yŏmyŏng ŭi tongsŏ ŭmak.* Seoul: Pojinje.

———. 1975. *Han'guk chŏnt'ong ŭmak ŭi yŏngu* (Studies in Korean Traditional Music). Seoul: Pojinjae.

———. 1982. *Hwajŏng'ae wa hwaryut'ae.* Seoul: Susŏwŏn.

———. 1984. *Kugak taesajŏn* (Dictionary of Korean Music). Seoul: Segwang ŭmak ch'ulp'ansa.

———. 1989a. *Yŏmmyŏng ŭi kugakkye.* Seoul: Sekwang ŭmak ch'ulp'ansa.

———. 1989b. "Kugak kyouk ŭi yoram." *Minjok Ŭmakhak* 11:1–8.

Chang, Sahun, and Hahn Man-yŏng [Han Manyŏng]. n.d. *Kugak kaeron* (Introduction to Korean Music). Seoul: Korean Musicology Society.

Cho, Dong-il [Cho Tongil]. 1978. "*P'ansori-ŭi chŏnbanjŏk sŏnggyŏk* (The General Nature of P'ansori)." In *P'ansori-ŭi ihae* (Understanding P'ansori). Seoul: Ch'angjak-kwa Pip'yŏngsa.

Cho, Dong-il [Cho Tongil], et al., eds. 1978. *P'ansori-ŭi ihae* (Understanding P'ansori). Seoul: Ch'angjak-kwa Pip'yŏngsa.

Ch'oe, Pyŏngsam, and Ch'oe Hŏn. 1992. *SamulNori.* In *Han'guk ŭmak*, 27. Seoul: Kungnip kugagwŏn.

Chŏn, Inp'yŏng. 1987. "Ch'angjak kugak (Newly Composed Music)." In *Han'guk ŭmak onŭl ŭi ŭmak*, 165–189. Seoul: Han'guk ŭmak yŏn'guhoe.

Chŏng, Hansuk, ed. 1992. *Munye yŏng'am.* Seoul: Han'guk munhwa yesul chinhŭngwŏn.

Chŏng, Hoegap. 1968. "Kyŏnggido nongak ŭi yŏn'gu (Studies in Kyŏnggi Province Folk Band Music)." *Ŭmdae hakpo* 4:18–23.

Chŏng, Inji. 1976. *Koryŏsa* (History of Koryŏ Dynasty). Seoul: Tongbanghak yŏn'guso, Yonsei University.

Chŏng, Nosik. 1955. *Chosŏn ch'anggŭksa* (A History of Korean P'ansori). Seoul: Chosŏn ilbosa.

Chŏng, Pyŏngho. 1985. *Han'guk ch'um* (Korean Dance). Seoul: Ilchogak.

———. 1986. *Nongak* (Korean Folk Band Music). Seoul: Yŏrhwadang.

Chŏng, Pyŏngho, and Yi Pohyŏng. 1985. *Nongak. Chungayo muhyŏng munhwajae chonghap pogosŏ*, 164. Seoul: National Academy of Arts.

Chŏng, Pyŏnguk. 1981. *Han'guk ŭi p'ansori* (Korean P'ansori). Seoul: Chimmundang.

Chosŏn wangjo sillok (Annals of the Yi Dynasty). 49 vols. 1972. Seoul: T'amgudang.

Ha, T'aehŭng, and Grafton K. Mintz, trans. 1972. *Yŏngyŏk Samguk yusa* (Legends and History of the Three Kingdoms). Seoul: Yongsei University Press.

Hahn, Man-young [Han Manyŏng]. 1979. "P'ansori ŭi ujo (*U* Mode in *P'ansori*)." *Han'guk Ŭmak Yon'gu* (Studies in Korean Music) 2:67–88.

———. 1985. "Hyŏndae kugak (Contemporary Korean Music)." In *Han'guk ŭmaksa*, 409–476. Seoul: Taehan min'guk yesurwŏn.

Ham, Hwajin. 1948. *Chosŏn ŭmak t'ongnon* (Introduction to Korean Music). Seoul: Ŭryu munhwasa.

Han'guk minsok chonghap chosa pogosŏ (A Report of Korean Folklore). 1969. Seoul: Munhwajae kwalliguk.

Han'guk ŭmakhak charyo ch'ongsŏ (Anthology of Source Materials for Korean Musicology). 1979–. Seoul: Kungnip Kukagwŏn.

Hwang, Byong-gi [Hwang Pyŏnggi]. 1978. "Chŏnt'ong ŭmak kwa hyŏndae ŭmak (Traditional Music and Contemporary Music)." In *Han'guk ŭi minjok munhwa: kŭ chŏnt'ong kwa hyŏndaesŏng*, 218–236. Sŏngnam: Han'guk chŏngshin munhwa yŏn'guwŏn.

Hwang, Junyon [Hwang Chun-yŏn]. 1993. "Han'guk ch'ŏnt'ong ŭmak ŭi akcho (The *Akcho* of Traditional Korean Music)." *Kugagwŏn Nonmunjip* (Journal of the National Center for Korean Traditional Performing Arts) 5:113–136.

Im, Chaehae. 1981. *Kkoktu kakshi norŭm ŭi ihae* (Understanding Korean Marionette Shows). Seoul: Honsŏngsa.

Iryŏn. [c. 13th century] 1973. *Samguk yusa* (Memorabilia of the Three Kingdoms). Seoul: Minjok munhwa ch'unjinhoe. (For translation see Yi Pyŏng-do 1962 and Ha, T'aehŭng, and Grafton K. Mintz 1972.)

Kang Hanyŏng. 1969. *Sin Chaehyo p'ansori chŏnjip* (Anthology of Korean *P'ansori* by Sin Chaehyo). Seoul: Yŏnsei University Press.

———. 1971. *Sin Chaehyo p'ansori sasŏljip* (*P'ansori* Texts of Sin Chaehyo). Seoul: Minjung sogwan.

———. 1977. *P'ansori*. In *Kyohyang kuksa ch'ŏngsŏ* 28. Seoul: Sejong taewang kinyŏm saŏphoe.

Kim, Chonggwŏn, trans. 1960. *Wanyŏk Samguk Sagi* (A Complete Translation of the History of the Three Kingdoms). Seoul: Sŏnjin munhwasa.

Kim, Haesuk. 1987. *Kayagŭm, ajaeng, tanso sanjo* (*Sanjo* for *Kayagŭm*, *Ajaeng*, and *Tanso*). Seoul: Segwang ŭmak ch'ulp'ansa.

Kim, Hŏn-sŏn. 1988. *SamulNoriran muŏshin'ga*. Seoul: Kwiinsa.

———. 1995. *Samulnori iyagi* (A Discussion on *Samulnori*). Seoul: P'ulbit.

Kim, Kijong, ed. 1986. "Chŏnt'ong yesul ŭi ihae (Understanding Korean Traditional Art)." In *Uri munhwa* 1. Seoul: Uri madang.

———. 1986. "Kkoktu kakshi norŭm (Korean Marionette Show)." In *Uri munhwa* 2. Seoul: Uri madang.

Kim, Kisu. 1972. *Kugak inmun* (Introduction to Korean Traditional Music). Seoul: Han'guk kojŏn ŭmak ch'ulp'ansa.

Kim, Kisu, and Choi Chungwong. 1974. *Kayagŭm chongak* (Correct Music for *Kayagŭm*). Seoul: Eunha.

Kim, Pusik. 1971. *Samguk sagi* (History of the Three Kingdoms). Seoul: Minjok munhwa ch'ujinhoe. (For translation see Yi, Pohyŏng, and Chonggwŏn Kim 1960.)

Kim, Tonguk. 1961. *Han'guk kayo ŭi yŏn'gu* (Studies in Old Korean Songs). Seoul: Ŭryu munhwasa.

Kim, Uhyŏn. 1984. *Nongak kyobon*. Seoul: Segwang ŭmak ch'ulp'ansa.

Korean Traditional Performing Arts Center, ed. 1968–present. *Han'guk ŭmak* (Anthology of Traditional Korean Music). Seoul: Kungnip kugagwŏn.

———. 1974–. *Kugak chŏnjip* (Complete Collection of Korean Music). Seoul: Kungnip kugagwŏn.

———. 1992. *Kugak yŏnbo*. Seoul: Kungnip kugagwŏn.

———. n.d. *Chŏnt'ong sŏngak ch'angpŏp chido t'ŭkkang* (Guide to Traditional Solo Vocal Music Practices). Seoul: Kungnip kugakwŏn.

Kwŏn, Hŭidŏk. 1981. *Nongak. Sŏnye kut. Akki nori*. Seoul: Huban'gi ch'ulp'ansa.

———. 1995. *Nongak kyobon. Nongak, samulnori ŭi yŏksa, iron, silche*. Seoul: Seilsa.

Kwŏn, Osŏng. 1977. "Minyo rŭl t'onghan manbukhan minjok tongjilsŏng hoebok (Restoration of Homogeneity by Studying Folk Song of North and South Korea)." In *Han'guk ŭmak san'go* 8:27–44. Seoul: Hanyangdae chŏnt'ong ŭmak yŏn'guhoe.

———. 1998. *Pukhan ŭi minjok sŏngak ŭi kaenyŏm kwa silche* (Concept and Present State of National Vocal Music of North Korea), 27–44. Seoul: Mandang haksulsang unyŏng wiwŏnhoe.

Lee, Bo-hyung. (See Yi Pohyŏng.)

Lee, Hye-ku [Yi Hyegu]. 1957. *Han'guk ŭmak yŏn'gu* (Studies in Korean Music). Seoul: Kungmin ŭmak yŏn'guhoe.

———. 1967. *Han'guk ŭmak sŏsŏl* (Topics in Korean Music). Seoul: Seoul National University Press.

———. 1976. *Han'guk ŭmak nonch'ong* (Essays on Korean Music). Seoul: Sumundang.

———. 1978. "Kugakhak e taehayŏ (On the Term *Kugakhak*, Korean Musicology)." In *Kwangjang*, 21–32. Seoul: Segye p'yŏnghwa kyosu hyŏbŭihoe.

———. 1985. *Han'guk ŭmak nonjip* (Essays in Korean Music). Seoul: Sewang ŭmak ch'ulp'ansa.

———. 1987. *Chŏngganbo ŭi chŏnggan taegang mit changdan* (A Study of Korean Rhythmic Notation). Seoul: Segwang ŭmak ch'ulp'ansa.

Lee, Hye-ku [Yi Hyegu], et al. 1965. *Kugaksa* (History of Korean Music). Seoul: Korean Musicological Society.

No, Tongŭn. 1988. "Pukhan ŭmak sahoe ŭi chŏnt'ong haesŏk (Interpretation of Tradition in the Musical Society of North Korea)." *Yesul Kwa Pip'yŏng* 16:36–54.

———. 1989a. "Pukhan ŭi ŭmak munhwa (Musical Culture of North Korea)." *Silch'ŏn Munhak* (Summer):135–138.

———. 1989b. *Han'guk minjok ŭmak hyŏndangye*. Seoul: Segwang ŭmak ch'ulp'ansa.

Paek, Taeung, Chŏn Sunhŭi, Kim Hŭijo, and Yi Pyŏnguk. 1993. *Kyagŭm samjungju kokchip*. Seoul: Tosŏ ch'ulp'ansa.

Pak, Hŏnbong, and Yu Kiryŏng. 1965. *Nongak sibi c'a. Muhyŏng munhwajae chonghap pogosŏ* 9. Seoul: Munhwajae kwalliguk.

Pak, Hwang. 1987. *P'ansori ibaengnyŏnsa* (*P'ansori*'s Two-Hundred-Year History). Seoul: Tosŏ ch'ulp'ansa.

Pak, Kŭmae. 1972. *Kugak*. Seoul: Kyŏdansa.

Ryu, Muyŏl. 1983. *Han'guk ŭi nongak* (Korean Folk Band Music). Ch'unch'ŏn: Kangwŏn ilbosa.

———. 1986. *Nongak* (Korean Folk Band Music). Seoul: Minjok munhwa mun'go kanhaenghoe.

Samguk sagi (History of Three Kingdoms). 1145. (See Kim, Pusik, 1971.)

Samguk yusa (Memorabilia of the Three Kingdoms). c. 13th century. (See Iryŏn 1973.)

Sejong sillok (Annals of King Sejong). (See *Chosŏn wangjo sillok* 1972.)

Sim, Usŏng. 1974. *Namsadang p'ae yŏn'gu*. Seoul: Tonghwa ch'ulp'ansa.

———. 1976. *Minsok munwha wa minjung ŭishik*. Seoul: Tongmunsŏn.

Sin, Chaehyo. *Kwangdaega* (Song of the *P'ansori* Singers). (See Kang, Hanyŏng, 1969.)

Siyong hyangakpo (Currently Performed Korean Music). c. 1500.

Sŏ Yugu. 1969. *Yuyeji* (Monograph on Amusement with the Arts). Seoul: Korean Musicological Society.

Song, Bang-song [Song Pangsong]. 1980. *Akchang tŭngok yŏn'gu* (A Study of the *Akchang tŭngok*). Kyŏngsan: Yeungnam University Press.

———. 1982. *Han'guk ŭmaksa yŏn'gu* (Studies in Korean Music History). Kyŏngsan: Yeungnam University Press.

———. 1984. *Han'guk ŭmak t'ongsa* (A History of Korean Music). Seoul: Ilchokak.

———. 1985. *Han'guk kodae ŭmaksa yŏn'gu* (Studies in Ancient History of Korean Music). Seoul: Ilchisa.

Sŏng, Hyŏn. 1968. *Akhak kwebŏm* (Standard Music Treatise). Yonsei University Press and Seoul: Minjok munhwa ch'ujinhoe.

Sŏng, Kyŏngnin. 1947. *Chosŏn ŭmak tokpon* (Introduction to Korean Music). Seoul: Ŭryu munhwasa.

———. 1976. *Han'guk ŭmak non'go* (Essays in Korean Traditional Music). Seoul: Tonghwa ch'ulp'ansa.

Yang, Tŏksu. [1610] 1959. *Yanggŭm sinbo* (Yang's New *Kŏmun'go* Notation Book). Seoul: T'ongmun'gwan.

Ye, Yonghae. 1963. *In'gan munhwajae*. Seoul: Ômun'gak.

Yi, Chaesuk. 1998. *Chosŏn kunjung ŭirye wa ŭmak* (Court Ceremonies and Music in the Chosŏn Period). Seoul National University, Asian Music Research Center, Research Monograph 1. Seoul: Seoul National University Press.

Yi, Kangsuk. 1985. *Ŭmak ŭi ihae* (Understanding Korean Music). Seoul: Minŭmsa.

Yi, Kŏnyong. 1987. *Han'guk ŭmak ŭi nolli wa yulli*. Seoul: Sewang ŭmak ch'ulp'ansa.

Yi, Kwangsik. 1981. *Han'guk kaehwasa yŏn'gu.* Seoul: Ilchogak.

Yi, Pohyŏng. 1970a. "Charyo, nongak ŭi yongŏ hoesŏl." *Munhak Sasang* 72:260–280.

———. 1970b. "Soe karak ŭi ch'undonggwa kŭ tayangsŏng." *Munhak Sasang* 72:242–249.

———. 1978. *P'ansori sasŏl-ŭi kŭkchŏk sangwhang-e ttarŭn changdan* (Composition of Rhythmic and Modal Patterns According to Dramatic Situations in the Text of *P'ansori*). In *P'ansori-ŭi ihae.* Seoul: Ch'angjak-kwa Pip'yŏngsa.

———. 1982. *P'ansori tasŏt madang* (Annotated P'ansori Text with English Introductions): *Haesol-kwa chusŏk-ŭl tan sasŏljip, purok—Yŏngmun haesŏl.* Seoul: Han'guk bŭrit'aenik'ŏ hoisa (Korea Britannica Corporation).

———. 1992. *Kyŏngsŏt'ori ŭmak yuhyŏng yŏn'gu* (A Study on Pattern in the *Kyŏngsŏt'ori* Tonal System). Seoul: Cultural Properties Office.

Yi, Pongsŏp. 1983. "Chwado kut kwa udo kut." In *Han'guk ŭi palgyŏn: Cholla pukto*, 108–117. Seoul: Han'guk pŭritaenik'ŏ.

Yi, Pyŏngdo, trans. 1962. *Yŏkchu Samguk yusa* (A Translation of the Samguk Yusa). Seoul: Tongguk Munhwasa.

———. 1977. *Kugyŏk Samguk sagi* (A Translation of the Samguk Sagi). Seoul: Ŭryu munhwasa.

Yi, Pyŏnguk. 1993. *Ŏullim: Sillaegok yŏnju kokchip.* Seoul: Segwang ŭmak ch'ulp'ansa.

Yi, Sangman. 1976. "Ŭmak kyegwan." In *Munye chonggan*, 329–352. Seoul: Munye yesul chinhŭngwŏn.

———. 1984. "Han'guk ŭi sŏyang ŭmak paengnyŏn (One Hundred Years of Western Music in Korea)." *Kaeksŏk* 1(1):160–163; 1(2) 94–98.

Yi, Sŏngchŏn. 1987. "Han'guk ŭmak ch'angjak ŭi yŏksa wa Kim Kisu ŭi ŭmak (The History of Korean Newly Composed Music and Kim Kisu's

Music)." In *Han'guk ŭmak* 23:3–4. Seoul: Kungnip kugagwŏn.

Yi, Tuhyŏn. 1969. *Han'guk kamyŏn'gŭk.* Seoul: Han'guk kamyŏng'uk yŏnguhoe/Munhwajae kwalliguk.

Yi, Yusŏn. 1976. *Han'guk yangak paengnyŏnsa.* Seoul: Chungang taehakkyo ch'ulp'anbu.

———. 1985. *Han'guk yangak paengnyŏnsa*, expanded ed. Seoul: Chungang taehakkyo ch'ulp'anbu.

Yi, Yusŏn, and Yi Sangman. n.d. "Hyŏndae yangak." In *Han'guk ŭmaksa*, 477–608. Seoul: Taehan min'guk yesulwŏn.

Yu, Kiryŏng. 1978. "Nongak. Minsok ŭmak yongŏ hoesŏl." *Wŏlgan Munhwajae* 8/1(73):17–20; 8/4(76):30–32; 8/5(77):16–19; 8/7(79):16–18.

Yun, Miyong, ed. 1984. *Kugak kyoyuk 30-nyŏn.* Seoul: Kungnip kugak kodŭng hakkyo.

INNER ASIA

Aalto, Petti. 1962. "The Music of the Mongols: An Introduction." In *Aspects of Altaic Civilization*, ed. Denis Sinor. Uralic and Altaic Series 23. Bloomington: Indiana University Publications.

Aksenov, A. N. [1964] 1973. "Tuvin Folk Music." *Asian Music* 4(2):7–18.

Attisani, Antonio. 1996. "Facets of Tibetan Traditional Theatre." *Tibet Journal* 21(2):128–139.

Batzengel. 1978. "Mongolia." In *Musical Voices of Asia*, ed. Y. Minegishi and R. Emmert, 45–53. Tokyo: Heibonsha.

———. 1980. "Urtyn Duu, Xöömii, and Morin Xuur." In *Musical Voices of Asia, Report of Asian Traditional Arts 1978*, ed. R. Emmert and Y. Minegushi. Tokyo: Heibonsha.

Beliaev, V. M. [1962] 1975. *Central Asian Music: Essays in the History of the Music of the Peoples of the U.S.S.R.* Middletown, Conn.: Wesleyan University Press.

Blum, Stephen. 1980. "Central Asia 2: Western." In *The New Grove Dictionary of Music and Musicians*, ed. Stanley Sadie, 4:67–75. London: Macmillan; Washington: Grove's Dictionaries of Music.

———. 2001. "Central Asia." In *The New Grove Dictionary of Music and Musicians*, ed. Stanley Sadie and John Tyrrell, 2nd ed., 5:363–372. New York: Grove. Available: http://www.grovemusic.com.

Bolsokhoyeva, Natalia D., and Kalsang Tsering. 1995. *Tibetan Songs from Dingri: Tibetan Text and Paraphrastic English Translation.* Opuscula Tibetana 24. Rikon: Tibet-Institut.

Browning, H., R. H. Browning, et al. 1982. *Music of the Middle East, Central Asia, and Greece.* New York: Alternative Museum.

Canzio, Ricardo O. 1986. "The Bonpo Tradition: Ritual Practices, Ceremonials, Protocol, and Monastic Behavior." In *Zlos-Gar: Performing Traditions in Tibet*, ed. J. Norbu, 45–57. Dharm-

sala, India: Library of Tibetan Works and Archives.

Canzio, Ricardo, Mireille Helffer, and Mona Schremp. 2001. "Tibetan Music 2: Monastic Music." In *The New Grove Dictionary of Music and Musicians*, ed. Stanley Sadie and John Tyrrell, 2nd ed., 25:441–449, 458–459. New York: Grove. Available: http://www.grovemusic.com.

Chabros, Krystyna. 1992. "Two Zaxcin Dance Texts: Jangar and the Hero's Journey." In *Fragen der mongolischen Heldendictung*, ed. Walther Heissig, 207–213. Wiesbaden: Harrassowitz.

Chahartugchi, Urna. 1995. *Tal Nutag: Lieder aus dem mongolischen Grasland.* Germany: Klangräume Musikproduktion.

Collinge, Ian. 1993. "He Dra-nyen (The Himalayan Lute): An Emblem of Tibetan Culture." *CHIME* 6:22–33.

———. 1996-1997. "Developments in Musicology in Tibet: The Emergence of a New Tibetan Musical Lexicon." *Asian Music* 28(1):87–114.

Crossley-Holland, Peter. 1967. "Form and Style in Tibetan Folk Song Melody." *Jahrbuch für Musikalische Volks- und Völkerkunde* 3:9–69, 109–126.

———. 1970. "Gya-gling Hymns of the Karma-Kagyu: The Rhythmitonal Architecture of Some Tibetan Instrumental Airs." *Selected Reports in Ethnomusicology* 1(3):80–114.

———. 1980. "Central Asia 1: Eastern." In *The New Grove Dictionary of Music and Musicians*, ed. Stanley Sadie, 4:61–67. London: Macmillan; Washington: Grove's Dictionaries of Music.

———. 1980. "Tibet." In *The New Grove Dictionary of Music and Musicians*, ed. Stanley Sadie, 18:799–811. London: Macmillan; Washington: Grove's Dictionaries of Music.

———. 1986. "The State of Research in Tibetan Folk Music." In *Zlos-Gar: Performing Traditions*

in Tibet, ed. J. Norbu, 105–124. Dharmsala, India: Library of Tibetan Works and Archives.

Damdinsüren, Ts. 1985. "On the New Edition of the Mongolian Version of 'Geseriada.'" In *Asiatische Forschungen* 91. Wiesbaden: Harrrassowitz.

Desjacques, Alain. 1990. "La dimension orphique de la musique mongole." *Cahiers de Musiques Traditionnelles* 3:97–107.

Diószegi, Vilmos. 1963. "Ethnogenic Aspects of Darkhat Shamanism." *Acta Orientalia Academiae Scientiarum Hungaricae* 16:55–81.

Djumaev, A. 1993. "Power Structures, Culture Policy, and Traditional Music in Soviet Asia." *Yearbook for Traditional Music* 25:43–50.

Dor, Rémy. 1982. *Chants du toit du monde: Textes d'orature kirghize suivis d'un lexique kirghiz-français.* Les Littératures populaires de toutes les nations 30. Paris: G. P. Maisonneuve and Larose.

During, Jean. 1988. *La musique traditionnelle de l'Azerbayjan et la science des muqâms.* Collection d'études musicologiques, Vol. 80. Baden-Baden: V. Koerner.

———. 1993. "Musique, nation, and territoire en Asie interieure." *Yearbook for Traditional Music* 25:29–42.

During, Jean, and Sabine Trebinjac. 1991. *Introduction au muqam ouïgour.* Papers on Inner Asia 17. Bloomington: Indiana University, Research Institute for Inner Asian Studies.

Ellingson, Ter. 1979a. "Dancers in the Marketplace: Tibetan Religious Dances." *Asian Music* 10(2):159–178.

———. 1979b. "The Mathematics of the Tibetan Rol Mo." *Ethnomusicology* 23(2):225–244.

———. 1990. "Nasadya: Newar God of Music." *Selected Reports in Ethnomusicology* 8:221–272.

Emsheimer, Ernst. 1971. "Preliminary Remarks on Mongolian Music and Instruments." In *The Music of the Mongols*: Part 1, *Eastern Mongolia*, comp. Henning Haslund-Christensen, 69–100. New York: Da Capo.

———. 1988. "On the Ergology and Symbolism of a Shaman Drum of the Khakass." *Imago Musicae* 5:145–166.

Gunji, S. 1978. "An Acoustical Consideration of Xöömij." In *Musical Voices of Asia*, ed. Y. Minegishi and R. Emmert, 135–141. Tokyo: Heibonsha.

Hamayon, Roberte. 1980. "Mongol Music." In *The New Grove Dictionary of Music and Musicians*, ed. Stanley Sadie, 12: 482–485. London: Macmillan; Washington: Grove's Dictionaries of Music.

Harvilahti, Lauri. 1983. "A Two-Voiced Song with No Words." *Journal de la Société Finno-Ougrienne* 78:43–56.

Haslund-Christensen, Henning. 1971. "On the Trail of Ancient Mongol Tunes." In *The Music of the Mongols: Part 1, Eastern Mongolia*, comp. Henning Haslund-Christensen, 3–38. New York: Da Capo.

Hasumi, H. 1978. "Understanding Mongolian Music." In *Musical Voices of Asia*, ed. Y. Minegishi and R. Emmert, 142–148. Tokyo: Heibonsha.

Heissig, Walter. 1986. "Banishing of Illnesses into Effigies in Mongolia." *Asian Folklore Studies* 45(1):33–43.

Helffer, Mireille. 1986. "Preliminary Remarks Concerning the Use of Musical Notation in Tibet." In *Zlos-Gar: Performing Traditions in Tibet*, ed. J. Norbu, 69–90. Dharmsala, India: Library of Tibetan Works and Archives.

———. 1989. "Organologie et symbolisme dans la tradition tibétaine: Le cas de la clochette *dril-bu* et du tambour." *Cahiers de Musiques Traditionnelles* 2:33–50.

———. 1995a. *Chod-rol: Les instruments de la musique tibétaine*. Paris: Maison des Sciences de l'Homme Centre National de la Recherche Scientifique. (With 1 compact disk.)

———. 1995b. "Quand le terrain est un monastère tibétain" (When the Field Is a Tibetan Buddhist Monastery). *Cahiers de Musiques Traditionnelles* 8:69–84.

———. 1998. "Du son au chant vocalisé: La terminologie tibétaine à travers les âges (VIIIe–XXe siècle)." *Cahiers de Musiques Traditionnelles* 11:141–162.

Henrion-Dourcy, Isabelle, and Geoffrey Samuel. 2001. "Tibetan Music 3: Traditional Music." In *The New Grove Dictionary of Music and Musicians*, ed. Stanley Sadie and John Tyrrell, 2nd ed. 25:449–460. New York: Grove. Available: http://www.grovemusic.com.

Hodgkinson, Tim. 1996. "Siberian Shamanism and Improvised Music." *Contemporary Music Review* 14(1–2):59–66.

Höfer, András. 1997. *Tamang Ritual Texts 2: Ethnographic Studies in the Oral Tradition and Folk-Religion of an Ethnic Minority*. Stuttgart: Franz Steiner Verlag.

Horloo, P. 1985. "Traditions and Peculiarities of Mongolian Heroic Epics." In *Asiatische Forschungen*, 91. Wiesbaden: Harrassowitz.

Jung, A. 1989. *Quellen der traditionellen Kunstmusik der Usbeken und Tadshiken Mittelasiens: Untersuchungen zur Entstehung und Entwicklung des sasmaqam*. Hamburg: K. D. Wagner.

Kara, György. 1970. *Chants d'un barde mongol*. Budapest: Akadémiai Kiadó.

Karmay, Samten G. 1986. "Three Sacred Bon Dances (*Cham*)." In *Zlos-Gar: Performing Traditions in Tibet*, ed. J. Norbu, 58–68. Dharmsala, India: Library of Tibetan Works and Archives.

Karomatov, F. 1972. "On the Regional Styles of Uzbek Music." *Asian Music* 4(1):48–58.

Karomatov, F. M., V. A. Meskeris, et al. 1987. *Mittelasien*. Leipzig: VEB Deutscher Verlag für Musik.

Lazar, Katalin. 1988. "Structure and Variation in the Ob-Ugrian Vocal Music." *Studia Musicologica Academiae Scientiarum Hungaricae* 30(1–4):281–296.

Lecomte, Henri. 1996. "À la recherche de l'authenticité perdue (In Search of Lost Authenticity)." *Cahiers de Musiques Traditionnelles* 9:115–129.

Levin, Theodore C. 1979. "Music in Modern Uzbekistan: The Convergence of Marxist Aesthetics and Central Asian Tradition." *Asian Music* 12(1):149–158.

———. 1993. "The Reterritorialization of Culture in the New Central Asian States: A Report from Uzbekistan." *Yearbook for Traditional Music* 25:51–59.

———. 1996. *The Hundred Thousand Fools of God: Musical Travels in Central Asia (and Queens, New York)*. Bloomington: Indiana University Press. (With 1 compact disk.)

Luzi, Laetitia. 2001. "Tibetan Music 4: Contemporary Pop Music." In *The New Grove Dictionary of Music and Musicians*, ed. Stanley Sadie and John Tyrrell, 2nd ed., 25:458. New York: Grove. Available: http://www.grovemusic.com.

MacKerras, Colin. 1985. "Traditional Uygur Performing Arts." *Asian Music* 16(1):29–58.

Matyakubov, O. 1993. "The Traditional Musician in Modern Society: A Case Study of Turgun Alimatov's Art." *Yearbook for Traditional Music* 25:60–66.

Muhambetova, A. I. 1995. "The Traditional Musical Culture of Kazakhs in the Social Context of the 20th Century." *World of Music* 37(3):66–83.

Nakagawa, S. 1978. "A Study of Urtiin Duu: Its Melismatic Elements and Musical Form." In *Musical Voices of Asia*, ed. Y. Minegishi and R. Emmert, 149–161. Tokyo: Heibonsha.

Nebesky-Wojkowitz, René de. 1976. *Tibetan Religious Dances: Text and Translation of the 'Chams yig*, ed. Christoph von Fürer-Haimendorf. The Hague: Mouton.

Nimri Aziz, B. 1985. "On Translating Oral Traditions: Ceremonial Wedding Poetry from Dingri." *Soundings in Tibetan Civilization*, ed. Barbara Nimri Aziz and Matthew Kapstein, 115–131. New Delhi: Manohar.

Norbu, Jamyang. 1986. "The Role of the Performing Arts in Old Tibetan Society." In *Zlos-Gar: Performing Traditions in Tibet*, ed. J. Norbu, 1–6. Dharmsala, India: Library of Tibetan Works and Archives.

———, ed. 1986. *Zlos-Gar: Performing Traditions in Tibet*. Dharmsala, India: Library of Tibetan Works and Archives.

Norbu, Jamyang, and Tashi Dhondup. 1986. "A Preliminary Study of Gar, the Court Dance, and Music of Tibet." In *Zlos-Gar: Performing Traditions in Tibet*, ed. J. Norbu, 132–142. Dharmsala, India: Library of Tibetan Works and Archives.

Ojamaa, Triino. 1995. "The Musical and Ritual Functions of the Nganasan Shaman Drum." In *Folk Belief Today*, ed. Mare Koiva and Kai Vassiljeva, 351–356. Tartu: Estonian Academy of Sciences; Institute of Estonian Language and Estonian Museum of Literature.

Oppitz, Michael. 1990. "Le tambour re et son pouvoir." *Cahiers de Musiques Traditionnelles* 3:79–95.

Pegg, Carole A. 1989. "Tradition, Change, and Symbolism of Mongol Music in Ordos and Xilingol, Inner Mongolia." *Journal of the Anglo-Mongolian Society* 7(1–2):64–72.

———. 1991. "The Revival of Ethnic and Cultural Identity in West Mongolia: The Altai Uriankhai *Tsuur*, the Tuvan *shuur*, and the Kazakh *Sybyzgy*." *Journal of the Anglo-Mongolian Society* 8(1–2):71–84.

———. 1992a. "The Epic Is Dead, Long Live the Üliger?" In *Fragen der mongolischen Heldendictung*, Vol. 5, ed. Walther Heissig, 194–206. Wiesbaden: Harrassowitz.

———. 1992b. "Mongolian Conceptualizations of Overtone Singing (*Xöömii*). *British Journal of Ethnomusicology* 1:31–55.

———. 1995. "Ritual, Religion, and Magic in West Mongolian (Oirad) Heroic Epic Performance." *British Journal of Ethnomusicology* 4:77–99.

———. 2000a. "Mongolia and Tuva: Sixty Horses in My Herd." In *World Music: The Rough Guide* 2, ed. Simon Broughton, 189–198. London: Rough Guides.

———. 2000b. "The Power of Performance: West Mongolian Heroic Epics." In *The Oral Epic: Performance and Music*, ed. K. Reichl. Intercultural Music Studies 12, ed. Max Peter Baumann. Berlin: Verlag für Wissenschaft und Bildung.

———. 2001a. "Mongol Music." In *The New Grove Dictionary of Music and Musicians*, ed. Stanley Sadie and John Tyrrell, 2nd ed., 16:922–934. New York: Grove. Available: http://www.grovemusic.com.

———. 2001b. *Mongolian Music, Dance, and Oral Narrative: Performing Diverse Identities*.

Seattle: University of Washington Press. (With 1 compact disk.)

———. 2001c. "Tibetan Music 1: Background, History and Research." In *The New Grove Dictionary of Music and Musicians*, ed. Stanley Sadie and John Tyrrell, 2nd ed., 25: 441, 458. New York: Grove. Available: http://www.grovemusic.com.

Pertl, Brian G. 1992. "Some Observations on the Dung Chen of the Nechung Monastery." *Asian Music* 23(2):89–96.

Porter, James, ed. 1997. *Folklore and Traditional Music in the Former Soviet Union and Eastern Europe*. Los Angeles: Department of Ethnomusicology, University of California Los Angeles.

Potapov, L. P. 1978. "The Shaman Drum as a Source of Ethnographical History." In *Shamanism in Siberia*, ed. V. Diószegi and M. Hoppál, 169–180. Budapest: Akadémiai Kiadó.

Rintchen, B. 1965. *Folklore Mongol 4*. In *Asiatische Forschungen*, 15. Wiesbaden: Harrassowitz.

———. 1966. "Manai Ardyn Tuul's (Our People's Epics)." In *Mongol Ardyn Baatarlag Tuul'syn Uchir*, ed. U. Zagdsüren and S. Luvsanvandan. Ulaanbaatar: Academy of Sciences.

Sadokov, R. L., and L. A. Grenoble. 1970. *The Musical Culture of Ancient Chorasmia*. Moscow: Nauka.

Samuel, Geoffrey. 1976. "Songs of Lhasa." *Ethnomusicology* 20:407–449.

———. 1986. "Music of the Lhasa Minstrels." In *Zlos-Gar: Performing Traditions in Tibet*, ed. J. Norbu, 13–19. Dharmsala, India: Library of Tibetan Works and Archives.

Scheidegger, Daniel A. 1988. *Tibetan Ritual Music: A General Survey with Special Reference to the Mindroling Tradition*. Opuscula Tibetana 19. Rikon: Tibet-Institut.

Skal Bzang Nor Bu and Kevin Stuart. 1996. "The Rdo Sbis Tibetan Wedding Ceremonies." *Anthropos* 91(4–6):441–453.

Slobin, Mark. 1969. *Kirgiz Instrumental Music*. New York: Society for Asian Music.

———. 1971. "Conversations in Tashkent." *Asian Music* 2(2):7–13.

———. 1977. *Music of Central Asia and the Volga-Ural Peoples*. Bloomington: Indiana University, Asia Studies Research Institute.

Stoddard, Heather. 1986. "A Note on Vajra-Dance Choreography in the Snow in the Early Eighteenth Century A.D." In *Zlos-Gar: Performing Traditions in Tibet*, ed. J. Norbu, 125–131. Dharmsala, India: Library of Tibetan Works and Archives.

Tethong, Rakra. 1979. "Conversations on Tibetan Musical Traditions." *Asian Music* 10(2):5–22.

Tran, Quang Hai. 1989. "Le chant diphonique: À propos du chant Xoomij." In *Dossier: Le chant diphonique*, 15–16. Limoges: Institut de la Voix.

Tran, Q. H., and D. Guillou. 1978. "Original Research and Acoustical Analysis in Connection with the Xöömij Style of Biphonic Singing." In *Musical Voices of Asia*, ed. Y. Minegishi and R. Emmert, 162–175. Tokyo: Heibonsha.

Trebinjac, Sabine. 1990. "Chine: Le pouvoir en chantant." *Cahiers de Musiques Traditionnelles* 3:109–117.

———. 1995. "Femme, seule et venue d'ailleurs: Trois atouts d'une ethnomusicologue au Turkestan chinois (A Woman, a Woman Alone, and an Outsider: Three Assets of an Ethnomusicologist in Chinese Turkestan)." *Cahiers de Musiques Traditionnelles* 8:59–68.

Trewin, A. M. 1995. "On the History and Origin of Gar, the Court Ceremonial Music of Tibet." *CHIME* 8:4–31.

Trewin, Mark. 1992. "Musical Studies in Western Tibet (Ladakh): Some Historical and Comparative Aspects of the Pioneering Work of August Hermann Francke." In *European Studies in Ethnomusicology: Historical Developments and Recent Trends*, ed. Artur Simon, Ulrich Wegner, and Max Peter Baumann, 69–86. Wilhelmshaven: Noetzel.

Tserensodnom, D. 1976. "On the Origin of 'Connected Verse' in Mongolian." *Journal of the Anglo-Mongolian Society* 3(1):51–57.

Tsukanoto, Atsuko. 1983. "Tibetan Buddhism in Ladakh." *Yearbook for Traditional Music* 15:126–140.

Uray-Kohalmi, Kathe. 1995. "Zwolf Lieder der Kamniganen." *Acta Orientalia Academiae Scientiarum Hungaricae* 48(3):473–478.

Vainshtein, S. I. 1996. "The Tuvan (Soyot) Shaman's Drum and the Ceremony of Its Enlivening." In *Folk Beliefs and Shamanistic Traditions in Siberia*, ed. V. Diószegi and M. Hoppál, 127–134. Budapest: Akadémiai Kiadó.

Van Oost, P. J. 1915–1916. "La musique chez Mongols des Urdus." *Anthropos* 10–11:358–396.

Vertkov, K., G. Blagodatov, and E. Yazovitskaya. [1963] 1975. "Musical Instruments of the Peoples Inhabiting the U.S.S.R." In *Atlas muzikal'nikh instrumentov naradov S.S.S.R.* (Atlas of the Musical Instruments of the Peoples of the U.S.S.R.). Moscow: State Publishers Music.

Walcot, Ronald. 1974. "The Chöömij of Mongolia: A Spectral Analysis of Overtone Singing." *Selected Reports in Ethnomusicology* 2(1):54–61.

Wu, Ben. 1997. "Music Scholarship, West and East: Tibetan Music as a Case Study of Asian Music." *Asian Music* 29(2):31–56.

CHINA

Ambush: Chinese Plucked Instrumental Music. 1989. Hugo HRP724-2. Compact disk.

The Ancient Art Music of China. 1990. (Lily Yuan, *yangqin*.) Lyrichord LYRCD7409. Compact disks.

An Anthology of Chinese Traditional and Folk Music: A Collection of Music Played on the Dizi. 1994. Shanghai: China Record Corporation, CCD–94/350–357. Compact disk.

L'art du qin. 1990. (Li Xiangting, *qin*.) Ocora C560001. Compact disk.

Aspects of Chinese Music. 1992. (Teashop courtship dialogues recorded in 1987 by Jack Body and Gong Hong Yu in Guiyang, and vocal polyphony recorded by Zhou Deyi in 1982 in Nan Ning, Guangxi Province.) New Zealand: Asia Pacific Archive. Sound cassette (analog) plus booklet.

Baishibai Songs of the Minority Nationalities of Yunnan. 1995. Anthology of Music in China 4. (Field recordings by Zhang Xingrong made in Yunnan Province between 1982 and February 1994.) Pan Records PAN2038CD. Compact disk.

The Beauty of Chinese Folk Opera. 1998. (Historic recordings made in the 1950s and 1960s.) Wind Records TCD-1021. Compact disk plus booklet.

The Best of Northern Style Dizi Music, Vol 1. 1990. (Li Zheng, Yang Ming, Li Zengguang, Zeng Yongqing, and the Beijing Philharmonic Traditional Orchestra conducted by Chu Shiji.) Linfair Magnet Sound, ROC20017.

Buddhist Music of the Ming Dynasty: Zhihuasi Temple, Beijing. 1993. (Recorded in 1992 in Beijing.) JVC VICG-5259. Compact disk.

Buddhist Music of Tianjin. 1994. (Recorded in 1993. Notes by Stephen Jones.) Nimbus NI5416. Compact disk.

Celestial Airs of Antiquity: Music of the Seven-String Zither of China. 1997. (Recorded in Shanghai, 1981–1982.) A-R Editions. Compact disk.

Chaozhou Drums Music. 1997. (Linhai Ensemble of Traditional String and Woodwind Instrumental Music. Recorded in Shantou in 1991.) Hugo HRP7149-2. Compact disk.

China/Chine. 1996. UNESCO Collection: Musical Anthology of the Orient. Auvidis D8071. Compact disk.

China. 1998. UNESCO Collection: Anthology of World Music, Musical Anthology of the Orient. Rounder CD5150. Compact disk.

China: Chuida Wind and Percussive Instrumental Ensembles/Chine: Sonneurs et batteurs chuida. 1992. UNESCO Collection: Musiques et musiciens du monde. Auvidis D8209. Compact disk.

China: Music of the Pipa. 1991. (Lui Pui-Yuen, *pipa*. Recorded at the University of Illinois in 1979. Notes by Isabel K. F. Wong.) Elektra Nonesuch H-72085. Compact disk.

China: Shantung Folk Music and Traditional Instrumental Pieces. n.d. (Lu-sheng Ensemble of Taiwan, with *sheng*.) Nonesuch H72051.

China: Time to Listen. 1998. (Joseph Bombak, producer.) Roslyn, N.Y.: Ellipsis Arts, CD3590-CD3593. 3 compact disks and booklet.

China's Instrumental Heritage. 1989. (Liang Tsai-Ping, *zheng*.) Lyrichord LYRCD792. Compact disk.

Chine. 1990. (Program notes by Tran Quang Hai.) Playasound PS65048. Compact disk.

Chine. 1998. (Wang Weiping, *pipa*.) Ocora C560128. Compact disk.

Chine: Chen Zhong. 1996. (Recorded November 1995.) Ocora C560090. Compact disk.

Chine: L'art de la cithare qin. 1992. (Dai Xiaolian, *qin*.) Auvidis B6765. Compact disk.

Chine: L'art de la viele erhu/China: The Art of the Erhu Fiddle. 1992. (Wu Suhua, *erhu*. Recorded by Julien Jauny. Notes by Francois Picard.) Auvidis Ethnic B6764. Compact disk.

Chine: L'art du pipa. 1993. (Lin Shih-ch'eng, *pipa*. Recorded in 1988.) Ocora C560046. Compact disk.

Chine Fanbai: Chant liturgique bouddhique; hymnes aux trios joyaux. 1997. (Recorded in 1996.) Ocora C560109. Compact disk.

Chine Fanbai: Chant liturgique bouddhique—Leçon du soir au Temple de Quanzhou. 1989. (Recorded in 1987, Temple Kaiyuan.) Ocora C559080. Compact disk.

Chine: Fanbai, chant liturgique bouddhique—Leçon du matin à Shanghai. 1995. (Recorded by Tian Qing.) Ocora C560075. Compact disk.

Chine, hautbois du Nord-Est—Shawms from Northeast China. 1994. Musique du monde. (Recorded by François Picard in 1994. Historical and descriptive notes by François Picard.) Buda Records 92612-2-92613-2. 2 compact disks.

Chine Ka-lé: La cérémonie du bonheur. 1996. Archives Internationales de Musique Populaire AIMP 47. (Recorded by Errol Maibach and François Picard in 1994 and 1995.) VDE-Gallo VDECD-911. Compact disk.

Chine: Musique ancienne de Chang'an. 1991. Ensemble du Conservatoire Superieur de Xian (Chang'an). Inédit. (Recorded 1991.) Maison des Cultures du Monde W 260036. Compact disk.

Chine: Musique classique. 1988. (Recorded between 1957 and 1971 in the People's Republic of China. Notes by Jacques Pimpaneau and Francois Picard.) Ocora C559039. Compact disk.

Chine: Traditions populaires instrumentales/China: Folk Instrumental Traditions. 1995. Archives Internationales de Musique Populaire AIMP 36-37. (Field recordings from Music Research Institute, Chinese Academy of Arts, Beijing. Recorded by Stephen Jones and others, 1930–1992.) VDE-Gallo VDE CD 822-823. 2 compact disks.

The Chinese Cheng Ancient and Modern. 1990. (Liang Tsai-ping, *cheng*.) Lyrichord LYRCD7302. Compact disk.

Chinese Han Music—Zheng Melodies: Above the Clouds. 1995. Interra IN5701. Compact disk.

Chinese Music of the Han and the Uighurs. 1988. World Music Library 41. (Recorded in 1985 in Tokyo.) King Records KICC6141. Compact disk.

Chinese Music of the Han People. 1987. World Music Library 40. (Recorded in 1985 in Tokyo.) King Records KICC5140. Compact disk.

Chinese Pipa. 1988. (He Shu-Feng, *pipa*.) World Music Library 43. King Records/Seven Seas KICC5143. Compact disk.

Chinese Traditional and Contemporary Music. 1993. (Wu Man, *pipa*. Recorded in 1993. Notes by Stephen Jones and Wu Man.) Nimbus NI5368. Compact disk.

Chinese Tung-Hsaio: The Art of Tong Ku-Chiun [Dong Kejun]. Taipei: Wind Records TCD1007.

Classical Chinese Pipa. 1991. (Cheng Yu, *pipa*. Recorded in Sussex, United Kingdom.) ARC Music EUCD1176. Compact disk.

Commemoration of the Renowned Folk Musician Hua Yanjun (Abing). 1996. Hong Kong: ROI Productions, RC-961992-2C. 2 compact disks.

Cui, Jian. 1998. *The Power of the Powerless.* World Beat Records. Compact disk.

Da desheng: Jinbei guyue (Triumphal Command: Wind and Percussion Music of Northern Shanxi). 1997. (Dingxiang Eight Note Troupes, Shanxi. North Chinese wind music from central Shanxi recorded in the provincial studio in 1992.) Hong Kong: Hugo, HRP759-2. Compact disk.

Dongjing Music in Yunnan, China. 1995. (Recorded in Kunming, Yunnan Province, China, in 1994. Notes by Wu Xueyuan and Suzuki Hideaki.) King Records/Seven Seas: KICC5189-5190. 2 compact disks.

Drums: Chinese Percussion Music. 1990. (Recorded in 1989 in Shanghai.) Hugo HRP719-2. Compact disk.

The East Is Red: Song and Dance Epic of the Chinese Revolution. 1994. (Recorded in 1965.) Bailey Record BCD-94072–BCD-94073. 2 compact disks.

Eleven Centuries of Traditional Music of China: Music from the Tang, Sung, Yuan, and Ming Dynasties (600–1600). 1983. Legacy International CD311. Compact disk.

Gongs and Drums for Celebration. II: Chinese Percussion Music. 1993. (Orchestra of Chinese Central Music College; Wang Fu-Jiang, conductor.) Wind Records TCD-1014. Compact disk.

Guangdong Folk Tunes. 1988. Guangdong Music, Vol. 1. (Recorded in 1987 in Guangzhou, China.) Hugo HRP706-2. Compact disk.

Guangling Qin Music. 1988. (Recorded in 1986 in Shanghai.) Hugo HRP718-2. Compact disk.

High Mountain and Flowing Water. 1990. (Cao Guifen, *zheng.* Recorded in 1990 in Shanghai.) Hugo HRP733-2. Compact disk.

Hong Kong Instrumental Music / Musique instrumentale. [1974] 1990. UNESCO Collection: Anthologie des musiques traditionnelles. Auvidis D8031. Compact disk.

The Hugo Masters: An Anthology of Chinese Classical Music. 1992. Celestial Harmonies 13042-2–13045-2. 4 compact disks.

The Imperial Bells of China. 1990. (Hubei Song and Dance Ensemble of the People's Republic of China; Peng Xiancheng, conductor. Recorded at the Cathedral of Saint John the Divine in New York, 1989.) Fortuna Records 17075-2. Compact disk plus booklet.

Liu, Yuan. 1992. *The Legend of Shadier: The Lin Yuan Collection.* (Recorded in Shanghai in 1990.) Yellow River 82001. Compact disk.

Love Songs—Chants d'amour. 1996. UNESCO Collection: Listening to the World/À l'ecoute du monde. Auvidis/UNESCO. Compact disk.

The Magic "Di" of Yu Xunfa: The Expression of Taiwan, Vol. 1. 1992. (Yu Xunfa and the Shanghai Film Studio Orchestra.) Pop Arts Production Company PAC-9105.

Minzu qiyue duzou xuan (Selection of National Instrumental Solos), Vol. 1. (Solos and duets performed in North China in the 1950s.) Hong Kong: Art-Tune, ATC-146.

The Monkey King: The World of Peking Opera. 1997. (Chinese Academy of Peking Opera. Recorded in Kokuritsu Gekijo Hall, Tokyo, in 1979.) JVC VICG-5016. Compact disk.

Moon and Lanterns. n.d. (Jiangnan *sizhu* performed by Shanghai Minzu Yuetuan with *sheng.*) Hong Kong: Bailey, NS-61 (cassette tape), NRS-33 (LP disk).

Moonlit River in Spring. 1991. (Recorded 1986–1989 in Hong Kong, Shanghai, and Beijing.) Hugo HRP747-2. Compact disk.

Music of the Aboriginal Tribes. 1991. (Wolfgang Laade, collector.) Jecklin Musikhaus [Music of Man Archive] JD 653-2. Compact disk.

Music of Chinese Minorities. 1988. World Music Library 42. (Recorded in Tokyo, 1981–1985.) King Records KICC5142. Compact disk.

Music from the People's Republic of China: Sung and Played on Traditional Instruments. [1976] 1991. Rounder Records CD-4008. Compact disk.

Music of the Qin. 1992. (Wu Wenguang, *qin.* Recorded in Beijing, China, in 1991.) JVC VICG-5213. Compact disk.

The Music of Small Ethnic Groups in Yunnan, China. 1995. World Music Library 87. (Recorded in Kunming, Yunnan Province, China, in 1994.) King KICC 5187. Compact disk.

The Music of Small Ethnic Groups in Yunnan, 2. 1996. World Music Library 114. (Recorded in Kunming, Yunnan Province, China, in 1994. Notes by Wu Xueyan and Suzuki Hideaki.) Seven Seas/King KICC 5214. Compact disk.

The Music of Yi People in Yunnan, China. 1995. World Music Library 88. (Recorded in Kunming, Yunnan Province, China, in 1994.) King KICC5188. Compact disk.

The Music of Yi People in Yunnan, 2. 1996. World Music Library 113. (Recorded in Kunming, Yunnan Province, China, in 1994.) Seven Seas/King Record. Compact disk.

Musical Creativity in Twentieth-Century China: Abing, His Music, and Its Changing Meanings. 1996. (Recorded c. 1930 and 1996.) Jonathan P. J. Stock. (Compact disk accompanying a book.)

Musique classique vivante. 1989. (Recorded in 1988.) Ocora C559049. Compact disk.

Nan-Kouan: Musique et chant courtois de la Chine du sud. 1988–. (Ballads sung by Tsai Hsiao-yueh with the Nan Sheng-She Ensemble.) Ocora C559004. 6 compact disks.

Naxi Music from Lijiang. 1997. (Performed by the Dayan *guyuehui;* program notes by Helen Rees.) Nimbus Records NI5510. Compact disk.

Opera du Sichuan: La legende de serpent blanc. [1994.] Musique du monde/Music of the World. (Recorded in Pixian, Sichuan Province, and in Chengdu in 1992.) Buda 92555-2. 2 compact disks.

Opera de Pekin: La forêt en feu, La princess Cent-fleurs/Peking Opera: The Forest on Fire, Princess Hundred-Flowers. 1995. Musique du monde/Music of the World. (Recorded by François Picard in 1994 at the Dalian Opera, Liaoning Province, China.) Buda Records 92618-2. Compact disk.

Orchidee: Traditional Zheng and Qin Music. 1992. (Xiaoyong Chen, *qin;* Huihong Ou, *zheng.*) Wergo Spectrum 281603-2; Welt Musik SM1603-2. Compact disk.

The Phoenix on the Wing: Sheng Solos by Hu Tianquan. (Music of the 1950s and later, composed and performed by Hu Tianquan.) China Record Company, HL-278. Cassette tape.

Polyphonies vocales des aborigines de Taiwan. 1989. Maison des Cultures du Monde W260011. Compact disk.

Qin Music on Antique Instruments. 1998. Department of Music, University of Hong Kong HKU-001. Compact disk.

Rain Dropping on the Banana Tree: Anthology of Chinese Classical Music. 1996. (Recordings from China and America made between 1902 and 1930. Notes by Dick Spottswood and Annie Mui.) Rounder CD1125. Compact disk plus booklet.

Reminiscences of Yunnan. 1991. (Recorded in Beijing and Shanghai, 1986–1990.) Hugo HRP737-2. Compact disk.

The Ruse of the Empty City: A Traditional Peking Opera. 2000. (Originally issued in 1960.) Smithsonian Folkways Records F-8882. Compact disk plus text.

Shuo chang: The Ultimate Art of Storytelling. (Historic recordings made in the 1950s and 1960s.) Wind Records TCD-1022. Compact disk plus booklet.

Sichuan Folksong and Ballad, Vol. 1. 1990. (Recorded in Chengdu, Sichuan, in 1989.) Hugo HRP731-2. Compact disk.

Sizhu Silk Bamboo: Chamber Music of South China. 1994. Anthology of Music in China 3. (Recorded by Alan R. Thrasher: Shanghai, Guangzhou, and Xiamen, 1986; Shanghai 1990; Vancouver 1994.) Pan Records PAN2030CD. Compact disk.

The Song of the Phoenix: Sheng Music from China. 1982. (Several styles, including traditional Shandong, *kunqu* opera accompaniment, and *guoyue* solos. Album edited by Terry E. Miller.) Lyrichord LLST-7369.

Sorrow of Lady Zhao-jun. 1991. Kuang-tung yin yueh 3. Hugo HRP745-2. Compact disk.

A Spray of Flowers. 1989. Chung-kuo ch'ui kuan yueh ch'u ching hsuan, Chinese Wind Instrumental Music, Vol. 2. (Recorded in China, 1986–1989.) Hugo HRP714-2. Compact disk.

Spring of Jiangnan: Special Collection of Dizi Master Lu Chunling in Celebration of His Sixty Years of Artistic Life. 1991. (Lu Chunling and the Shanghai Traditional Orchestra.) China Record Company HL-631.

The Spring Orchid. 1989. Chung-kuo ch'ui kuan yueh ch'u ching hsuan, Vol. 1. (Recorded in Shanghai in 1988.) Hong Kong: Hugo Productions HRP725-2. Compact disk.

Taiwan: Musique des peuples minoritaires. 1989. (Cheng Shui-cheng, collector.) Arion ARN64109. Compact disk.

Taiwan, Republic of China: The Confucius Temple Ceremony. 1991. Music of Man Archive. (Wolfgang Laade, collector.) Jecklin Disco JD652-2. Compact disk.

T'ang, Hsien-tsu. 1995. *Le pavillon aux pivoines: Opéra chinois kunqu/The Peony Pavilion: Chinese Classical Opera*. Inédit. (Recorded in 1994 by Joël Beaudemont.) Maison des Cultures du Monde W260060. 2 compact disks.

Thundering Dragon. 1994. *Thundering Dragon Percussion Music from China*. (Recorded in 1993. Notes by Thierry Chervel.) Welt Musik SM1519-2. Compact disk.

Tibetan Song-and-Dance Music. 1995. (Notes in English and Chinese. Includes performances of Nang-ma and Stod-gzhas.) Wind Records TCD 1603. Compact disk.

Tolling of Buddhist Temple. 1990. Kuang-tung yin yueh 2. (Recorded at Xinhai Conservatory of Music, Guangzhou, in 1989.) Hugo HRP729-2. Compact disk.

T'u ti yü ko: Songs of the Land in China. 1996. Tien ts'ang Chung-kuo yin yüeh ta hsi 2. (Qiao Jianzhong, director. Recorded 1953–1996.) Wind Records TCD-1020. 2 compact disks.

The Treasury of Xiao Tunes. 1987. (Recording and commentary by Zhang Weiliang.) China Record Company AL-14.

Triumphal Command: Shanxi Wind and Percussion Music. 1997. (Recorded in 1992.) Hugo HRP759-2. Compact disk.

A Wanderer's Autumn Grief: Au Kwan-cheung Sings Nanyin. 1996. (Recorded in Hong Kong in

1995.) Hugo Productions HRP7120-2. Compact disk.

Yang, Hsiu-ming. 1992. *Buddhist Chant: Chaozhou Zheng Music*. Cheng ti shih chieh 6. (Recorded in Beijing in 1991.) Hugo HRP753-2.

Yaomen Qin Music. 1991. (Recorded in Shanghai in 1957 and 1989.) Hugo HRP748-2. Compact disk.

Yeh shen ch'en: Night Thoughts. 1989. Chung-kuo la hsien yueh chu ching hsuan 1. (Recorded 1986–1989.) Hugo HRP723-2. Compact disk.

Zheng Music. 1989. Treasury of Zheng Music, Vol. 2. (Jiao Jinhai, *zheng*. Recorded in Hong Kong in 1987. Notes in Chinese and English by Jiao Jinhai.) Hugo HRP715-2. Compact disk.

Zollitsch, Robert, comp. 1997–1998. *Tibetan Folk Music*. (Urban and rural secular music with program notes. Recordings made in Lhasa in 1997–1998.) Lhasa/Nagchu: Saydisc CD-SDL427. Compact disk.

JAPAN

Anthologie de la musique traditionelle japonaise. 1960. Paris: Ducretet-Thomson 320 C137-138. 2 LP disks.

Best Take Series, 1989. (1: Yamamoto Hôzan, *shakuhati*. 2: Sawai Tadao, *koto*. 3: Sunazaki Tomoko, *koto*. 4: Mitsuhashi Kifû, *syakuhati*.) Tôkyô: Victor VDR5291-4. 4 vols. Compact disk.

Biwa no sekai (The World of *Biwa*). 1996. Tôkyô: Nippon Columbia, COCF13887. Compact disk.

Biwa: The World of Tusurta Kinshi. 1995. Tôkyô: King Records, World Music Library.

Buddhist Chant: A Recorded Survey of Actual Temple Rituals. 1960s. New York: Lyrichord, LLST118. 2 LP disks.

Bugaku: Bugaku no sekai. 1993. (Compiled by Ôno Tadamaro.) Tôkyô: Columbia Records COCF10888-9. 2 compact disks.

Chikamatsu Monzaemon no sekai. 1980. (Performed by Takemoto Oritayû and Tsuruzawa Seiji.) Tôkyô: Denon WX-7081/7090. 10 LP disks.

Classical Music of Japan. 1965. (Kyoto Kabuki Orchestra.) New York: Elektra Records, EKL-286. LP.

Classical Songs of the Ryukyu Court. 1998. Japan: Seven Seas/King Records, KICC5243. Compact disk.

The Far East. 1970s. New York: Lyrichord, LLST 7287. LP.

Festival of Japanese Music in Hawaii. 1964. Washington, D.C.: Folkways Records FW8885-8886. LP.

Folk Music of the Amami Islands, Japan. 1954. Washington, D.C.: Folkways Records, F-4448. Compact disk.

Folk Music of Japan. 1952. Washington, D.C.: Folkways Records, F-4429. Compact disk.

Folk Songs of Okinawa. 1994. (Performed by Rinsho Kadekaru.) JVC World Sounds. Compact disk.

Fumon Yoshinori: Satsuma Biwa, Japan's Noble Ballads. 2001. Celestial Harmonies 13207-2. Compact disk.

Gagaku. 1991. *Nihon no dentô*, Vol. 1. (Tenri University Gagaku Ensemble.) Tôkyô: Sony Music Entertainment, SRCL 2116. Compact disk.

Gagaku (Court Music). 1957. (Performed by Kunaicho Gakubu.) Japan: Columbia CL16. LP.

Gagaku (Court Music). 1958. (Performed by Kunaicho Gakubu, Gakuyu Kai.) Japan: Columbia CL62. LP.

Gagaku (Court Music): *Taiheiraku*. 1955. (Performed by Kunaicho Gakubu.) Kawasaki, Japan: Columbia, BL 29. LP.

Gagaku: The Imperial Court Music of Japan. 1964. (Performed by the Kyoto Imperial Court Music Orchestra.) New York: Lyrichord LL 126. LP.

Gagaku (*Kangen*). 1958. (Performed by Kunaicho Gakubu.) Japan: Columbia, CL34. LP.

Gagaku: Nihon no kodai kayô o tazunete. 1974. (Performed by Nihon Gagakkai.) Minoruphone HC-7001/7003. 6 LP disks.

Gagaku no sekai. 1990. (Compiled by Ôno Tadamaro.) Tôkyô: Columbia Records COCF6194-7. Two 2-CD vols. Compact disks.

Gagaku/Tôkyô Gakuso. 1986. Tôkyô: Nippon Columbia, Denon 30CF-1318. Compact disk.

Gendai sôkyoku senshû Japan (Selection of Contemporary Koto Music). 1979. (Compiled by Tsutomu Sakamoto.) Teichiku Records NC-6. LP.

Hagoromo/Kantan: Noh Plays of Japan. 1959. Caedmon TC2019. LP.

Harmony of Japanese Music. 1991. Tôkyô: King Records KICH2021. Compact disk.

A History of Japanese Music. 1973. (Edited by Eta Harich-Schneider.) London: Oxford University Press, OUP111. 3 LP disks.

Hogaku (Classical Music of Japan). 1964. Yokohama: Victor JL22. LP.

Kagura. 1966. Polydor SMN9003. LP.

Kamigami no ongaku (Music of Sintô). 1976. Tôkyô: Toshiba EMI TW800004-7. LP.

Japan: Its Music and Its People. 1970. Desto D501.

Japan: Semiclassical and Folk Music. 1974. Odeon 3C064-17967. LP.

Japan: Traditional Vocal and Instrumental Music—Shakuhachi, biwa, koto, shamisen. 1976. (Soloists of the Ensemble Nipponia; Minoru Miki, director.) Nonesuch H-72072. LP.

Japanese Buddhist Ritual. [1954.] Washington, D.C.: Folkways Records FE4449. Compact disk.

Japanese Dance Music. 1991. Tôkyô: King Records, KICH2022. Compact disk.

Japanese Koto Classics. 1966. (Performed, and sung in part, by Shinichi Yuize.) Nonesuch Records H-72008. LP.

Japanese Koto Music with Shamisen and Shakuhachi. 1960s. (Performed by master musicians of Ikuta-Ryu.) Lyrichord LL131. LP.

Japanese Koto Orchestra. 1967. (Koto ensemble of the Ikuta-ryu.) Lyrichord 7167. LP.

The Japanese Koto/Shin'ichi Yuize. Washington, D.C.: Folkways Records, C-1132. Compact disk.

Japanese Music. 1958. Yokohama: Victor of Japan, JL9. LP.

Japanese Noh Music. 1964. Lyrichord LL137. LP.

Japanese Work Songs. 1991. Tôkyô: King Records, KICH2023. Compact disk.

Japon 1. 1977. (Performed by Kinshi Tsuruta, *biwa*; Katsuya Yokoyama, *syakuhati*.) Ocora 558.518. LP.

Japon 3: Gagaku. 1980. (Performed by Gagaku Kai Society.) Paris: Radio-France. LP.

Japon 4: Jiuta. 1981. (Performed by Yonin no koi: Kozô Kithahara, *syakuhati*; Sumiko Goto, *koto* and *syamisen*; Mitoko Takahata, *koto*; Setsuko Kakui, bass *koto*.) Paris: Radio-France. LP.

Japon: Chants des Ainou. 1993. Auvidis: Paris. UNESCO Collection.

Japon: Gagaku. 1988. (Performed by Ono Gagaku-kai Society.) Paris: Ocora, C559018. Compact disk.

Japon: Musique millénaire: Biwa et shakuhachi. 1980. Chant du Monde LDX74473. LP.

Japon: Le shakuhachi de Reibo Aoki. 1980s. (Reibo Aoki, *syakuhati*, with accompaniment by *syakuhati*, *sangen*, or *koto*.) France: Playa Sound PS33526. LP.

Jin Jin: Firefly (Folk Songs from Okinawa). 2000. (Performed by Hirayasu Takashi and Bob Brozman.) World Music Network.

Kabuki Nagauta Music. 1960s. (Kyoto Kabuki Orchestra.) Lyrichord LL134. LP.

Kagura: Japanese Shinto Ritual Music. 1990. Hungary: Hungaroton, HCD18193. Compact disk.

Ki-sui-an honkyoku: Zen Shakuhachi Music/Ronnie Nyogetsu Seldin. 1981–1982. Flushing, N.Y.: Hogaku Society Records, HS201c–HS 202c. 2 sound cassettes.

Kodo: Heartbeat Drummers of Japan. 1985. Santa Barbara, Calif.: Sheffield Lab CD-KODO. Compact disk.

Koto Master. 1963. (Performed by Kimio Eto.) Hollywood, Calif.: World Pacific, WP-1428. LP.

The Koto Music of Japan. n.d. (Performed by Master Hagiwara, Master Hatta, Master Kitagawa, and Master Kikusui, *koto*.) Nonesuch 72005. LP.

Koto: Music of the One-String Ichigenkin. 1967. (Isshi Yamada, *ichigenkin* and vocals; in part with Fuzan Sato, *syakuhati*.) Folkways Records. Compact disk.

Koto no mudo / Shindo Takery. 1962. Yokohama: Victor of Japan SLV 27.

Min'yo: Folk Songs from Japan—Takahasi Yûjiro and Friends. 1999. Nimbus NI5618. Compact disk.

Miyagi Michio sakuhinshû (Collected Works of Miyagi Michio [Mitio]). 1989. Tôkyô: Victor VDR5302-4. 3 compact disks.

Music of Japanese Festivals. 1991. Tôkyô: King Records, KICH 2028. Compact disk.

Music of the Shakuhachi/Yasuda Shimpu. 1975. Washington, D.C.: Folkways Records, F-4218. Compact disk.

Music of the Shigin: Chanting to Chinese Poetry/ Abe Shufû I and Hal Gold. 1975. Washington,

D.C.: Folkways Records, F-M4220. Compact disk.

Music for Zen Meditation, and Other Joys. 1965. (Tony Scott, clarinet; Shinichi Yuize, *koto*; Hôzan Yamanmoto, *syakuhati*.) Verve V6/8634. LP.

Nagauta Music: Original Music and Arrangements from Older Classics. 1954. (Azuma Kabuki Musicians, with Katsutoji Kineya and Rosen Tosha.) New York: Columbia, ML 4925. LP.

Nakanosima Kin'ichi zenshû (The Complete Works of Nakanoshima Kin'ichi). 1972. Tôkyô: Victor, SJL25172-9. 8 LP disks.

Near and Far East: Twelve Modes and Melodies of the Orient. 1966. Provo, Utah: East-West Records. LP.

Nihon koten ongaku taikei (A Thousand Years of Japanese Classical Music). Tôkyô: Kôdansha, 10980-81. 74 LP disks.

Noh and Kyogen Plays Live. 1969. Washington, D.C.: Folkways Records, F9572. 2 compact disks.

Nô no ongaku (Nô Music). 1963. (Compiled by Mario Yokomiti.) Tôkyô: Victor Records, SJ-3005-1-3. LP.

O-Suwa-daiko: Japanese Drums. 1983. Paris: Waira, CSM 029. Cassette.

The Rough Guide to the Music of Japan. 1999. World Music Network RGNET1031. Compact disk.

Sankyoku / The Group Atarasii Kaze. 1997. (Compiled by Yosihiko Tokumaru.) Tôkyô: ALM Kojima Recordings, Ebisu-2. Compact disk.

The Shakuhachi Honkyoku: Japanese Flute. 1980. (Played by Riley Kelly Lee.) Washington, D.C.: Folkways Records, FE 4229. Compact disk.

Shakuhachi: The Japanese Flute. 1977. (Kohachiro Miyata, *syakuhati*.) Nonesuch H72076. CD.

Sôkyoku to ziuta no rekisi (History of *Sôkyoku* and *Ziuta*.) 1997. (Notes by Kikkawa Eisi.) Tôkyô: Victor, SLR510-13. 4 disks.

Sôkyoku ziuta taikei. (Collection of *Sôkyoku* and *Ziuta*). 1997. Tôkyô: Victor, VICG40110-40169. 60 disks.

The Soul of the Koto. 1970. Lyrichord LLST 7218. LP.

Soul of Nippon. 1960s. (Toshiko Yonekawa, Hideo Fujimoto, and the King Recording Orchestra.) Tôkyô: Nippon, SKJ-6002. LP.

Syamisen kohu no kenkyû (A Study of Old Samisen Notations). 1983. (Compiled by Hirano Kenzi.) Tôkyô: Toshiba EMI, THK-90212-90217. 6 compact disks.

Syamisen kumiuta zensyû. 1974. (Compiled by Hirano Kenzi.) Tôkyô: CBS Sony, SOJZ59-72. 16 compact disks.

Syômyô taikei (Compendium of *Syômyô*). 1983–1984. Nippon Columbia. Compact disk.

Takahashi Chikuzan: Iwaki no gensô. 1989. CBS Sony 30DG 5048. Compact disk.

Taikei nihon no dentô ongaku (Complete Collection of Japanese Music). 1990. Tôkyô: Victor Records, KCDK.

Tazima Keiko / Syamisen no sekai (Tazima Keiko: Her World of Samisen). 1994. Tôkyô: Nippon Columbia, COCF-11754. Compact disk.

Tozanryu shakuhachi gaku. 1960s-a. (Compiled by Tozan Nakao. Performed by Hoshida Ichizan et al.) Tôkyô: Toshiba Records, JHO-1068/1072. 5 LP disks.

Tozanryu shakuhachi gaku. 1960s-b. (Performed by Nagata Shozan et al.) Tôkyô: King Records, LKD. 16 LP disks.

Traditional Folk Dances of Japan. 1959. Washington, D.C.: Folkways Records, F-4356. Compact disk.

Traditional Folk Songs of Japan. 1961. Washington, D.C.: Folkways Records, F-4534. 2 compact disks.

The Traditional Music of Japan. 1965. Yokohama: Victor JL. 3 LP disks.

Tugaru zyongara busi kyôen syû (Tsugaru Jongara-bushi Competition). 1998. Tôkyô: King Records, KICH 2220. Compact disk.

Waka and Other Compositions: Contemporary Music of Japan. 1960. Washington, D.C.: Folkways Records, F-8881. Compact disk.

Wakana: Sato no akatsuki / Matsuura Kengyo. 1981. (New York Sankyoku Kai, Traditional Japanese Music Ensemble of New York.) Flushing, N.Y.: Hôgaku Society Records, HS101. LP.

The Way of Eiheiji: Zen Buddhist Ceremony. 1959. Washington, D.C.: Folkways Records, F-8980. Compact disk.

Yagi Keiji zenshû. 1982. (Yagi Keiji with Sawai Tadao, Uemura Kayoko, Saito Yoshino, Yokota Nobuko, Ota Hisako, Yamaguchi Goro, Iwata Kinya, Yokoyama Katsuya, Yoshiromoto Hisakao, Kawahara Naoko, Koyama Mariko, Yamamoto Hozan, Ogata Yaeko, Fujii Jido, Yonekawa Toshiko, Aoki Reibo, and Kawase Junsuke.) Tôkyô: Toshiba Records, THX-90152/90162. 11 LP disks.

Yonekawa Tosiko: Koto no miryoku (Yonekawa Tosiki: The Charm of the *Koto*). 1997. Tôkyô: King Records, KICH2054-57. 5 compact disks.

Yonekawa Tosiko no sekai: Musical Cosmos of Yonekawa Tosiko. 1995. (Compiled by Yamaguti Osamu.) Tôkyô: Victor Entertainment, VICG-40104-5. 2 compact disks.

Yoshimura Nanae: The Art of Koto. 2000. Celestial Harmonies 13186-2. Compact disk.

Yukar: The Ainu Epic Songs. 1997. Tôkyô: King Records, KICC-5217. Compact disk.

KOREA

Note: Romanizations of Korean and English-language titles are given as printed, with translations in brackets and McCune-Reischauer romanization of Korean titles in brackets only where needed. Among Korean companies, Samsung issues recordings under the labels Nices, Samsung Music, and Samsung Nices; Seoul Records controls Cantabile; Synnara (also spelled Syn-Nara and also known as Synnara Music), controls King/King Records. National Center is the National Center for Korean Traditional Performing Arts, formerly the Korean Traditional Performing Arts Center, and before that the National Classical Music Institute.

This discography does not list North Korean materials. There are currently no recordings of North Korean "improved" traditional instruments available. Audio and video recordings of revolutionary operas published by the state-run Mokran and KMC companies are intermittently available through government agencies.

Ahn Sook-Sun: Knowing the Sound (An Suksŏn: Chiŭm). 1994. (Vocal improvisations by respected Korean soloists and a Japanese bass player.) Nices SCO-021CSS. Compact disk.

Ahn Sook Sun: Choon Hyang Ga (An Suksŏn: Ch'unhyangga). 1997. (Ahn is the main disciple of the late Kim Sohŭi. The box contains a complete *p'ansori* performance.) Samsung SCO-093AHN. 6 compact disks.

Ahn Sook Sun, Kim Dae Ryeh Live Concert. 1998. (An Suksŏn, *p'ansori* expert; and Kim Taerye, shaman.) Samsung Music SCO-166CSS. Compact disk.

Ahn Sook Sun, Park Byung Chon, Ascend. 1998. (An, *p'ansori* expert; and Pak Pyŏngch'ŏn, shaman.) Samsung Music SCO-167CSS. Compact disk.

Anthology of Korean Music 1–6. 1996. (Recordings of court and folk music by the Seoul Ensemble.) M People HPTD-0001–HPTD-0006. 6 compact disks.

Anthology of Korean Traditional Folksongs (Han'guk minyo taejŏn). 2000. (Includes 336-page book, in Korean—213 pages, including song texts—and English: 123 pages. Taken from a much larger 103-CD set, *Han'guk minyo taejŏn*.) Kirin Music Publishing/MBC Radio. 12 compact disks.

Arirang: The Essence of Korean Spiritual Songs. 1999. Synnara Music NSSRCD-011. Compact disk.

Arirang of Korean Peninsula (Hanbando ŭi Arirang). 1994. Versions of *Arirang* collected throughout Korea. Synnara SYNCD-089–SYNCD-092. 4 compact disks.

Art World of Yi, Jiyoung's Kayagum (Yi Chiyŏng kayagŭm segye). 2000. (Live solo recordings of court and literati music.) Top TOPCD-032. Compact disk.

Bearer's Song (Man'ga). 1994. (*P'ansori* segments and funeral songs.) Seoul Records SRCD-3281. Compact disk.

Buddhist Temple Bells of Korea. 1966. (Historical recordings packaged in a wooden box.) KCTI, Han'guk munhwajae yŏn'guhoe. 5 LPs. Reissued 1996, as *Han'guk ŭi pŏmjong*. King SYNCD-118 and SYNCD-119. 2 CDs. Reissued 1999, as *The Great of Shilla Dynasty*. Synnara NSSRCD-025. 2 compact disks.

Cheong Dae-Seog Plays Komungo (Chŏng Taesŏk kŏmun'go tokchu kokchip). 1995. (Compositions written and played by Cheong for zither.) Sung Eum DS0067. Compact disk.

Choi Kyung-man's Pi-ri Plays (Ch'oe Kyŏngman ŭi p'iri yŏnju kokchip). 1994. (Folk music for *p'iri* 'oboe'.) King SYNCD-094–SYNCD-095. 2 compact disks.

Chŏng Kwŏnjin ch'ang Shimch'ŏngga. 1992. (Chŏng, 1927–1985, was one of the most masterful *p'ansori* singers of his generation; 124-page booklet with fully annotated libretto.) King SYNCD-030–SYNCD-032. 3 compact disks.

The Choongang Traditional Korean Orchestra (Chungang kugak kwanhyŏn aktan yŏnju kokchip) 4–6. 1990. (Creative traditional music.) Oasis ORC-1224–ORC-1226. 3 compact disks.

Chung Chae Kook piri recital (Chŏng Chaeguk p'iri tokchuhoe). 1994. (Live oboe recital.) Cantabile SRCD-1180. Compact disk.

Ch'unhyangga. In'gan munhwajae Sŏng Ch'angsun p'ansori taejŏn chip. 1994. (Sŏng, b. 1934, is a "holder" of the *p'ansori* Intangible Cultural Asset.) Sung Eum SEM DS0052. 4 compact disks.

The Complete Edition of Korean Traditional Female Lyric Songs Sung by Cho Soon-Ja (Cho Sunja yŏch'ang kagok chŏnjip). 1998. (Cho works at the National Center and is a disciple of one of the twentieth century's greatest literati singers, Yi Chuhwan.) Synnara NSSRCD-002. 6 compact disks.

Corée/Korea: Chants rituels de l'île de Chindo/Ritual Songs from the Island of Chindo. 1993. (Three folk song repertoires.) VDE/Archives Internationales de Musique Populaire VDE-756. Compact disk.

Corée: Musique instrumentale de la tradition classique. (Recorded for a radio broadcast in 1982 by the group *Chŏngnong akhoe*.) Ocora Radio France C558701. Compact disk.

Creative Traditional Orchestral Music (Ch'angjak kugak kwanhyŏnak). 2000. (12 disks packaged in three slipcases, with three 12-page booklets.) Korean Traditional Music and Publishing SRCD-8396–SRCD-8399, SRCD-8473–SRCD-8476, SRCD-8658–SRCD-8661.

The Deep-Rooted Tree P'ansori Collection (Ppuri kip'ŭn namu p'ansori). 1982. (Five boxed sets containing complete versions of the five *p'ansori* repertoires performed by four master singers: Han Aesun, Cho Sanghyŏn, Pak Pongsul, Chŏng Kwŏnjin.. Five illustrated booklets, 403 pages in all, with annotated libretti, music notations, and background articles in Korean and English.)

Korea Britannica Corporation/Jigu JLS1201622–JLS1201627. 23 LPs.

The Deep-Rooted Tree Collection of Korean Folksongs (Ppuri kip'ŭn namu palto sori). 1984. (Three boxed sets featuring more than 30 folksingers. Packaged in a single slipcase with three illustrated booklets, 368 pages in all, containing annotated texts and background articles in Korean and English.) Korea Britannica Corporation/Jigu JLS 1201867–JLS1201876. 10 LPs.

The Deep-Rooted Tree Collection of Korean Songs of Sorrow (Ppuri kip'ŭn namu hanbando ŭi sŭlpŭn sori). 1989. (Recorded from more than 20 singers. A 98-page introductory booklet contains complete music transcriptions and texts, with English and Korean introductory articles.) The Deep-Rooted Tree/Sung Eum SELRO 138. 3 LPs. Reissued on CD in 1994 and in 1996 as The Deep-Rooted Tree/King Records CDD-010–CDD-012.

The Deep-Rooted Tree Sanjo Collection (Ppuri kip'ŭn namu sanjo chŏnjip). 1989. (Wonderful recordings by senior musicians, many of whom have now died, of *sanjo* schools for *kayagŭm*, twelve-stringed zither; *kŏmun'go*, six-stringed zither; *taegŭm*, transverse flute; *p'iri*, oboe; *ajaeng*, bowed zither; and *haegŭm*, fiddle. Accompanied by a 256-page illustrated book containing music transcriptions and introductory articles in both Korean and English.) The Deep-Rooted Tree/Sung Eum SELRO 137. 9 LPs. Reissued on CD in 1994 and in 1996 as The Deep-Rooted Tree/King Records CDD-001–CDD-009.

The Deep-Rooted Tree P'ansori Tasŏt Pat'ang (Ppuri kip'ŭn namu p'ansori tasŏt pat'ang). 1990–1992. (The five *p'ansori* repertoires, sung by O Chŏngsuk, Chŏng Kwangsu, Kim Sŏnggwŏn, Cho Sanghyŏn and Ch'oe Sŭnghŭi. In five boxes with five booklets, 780 pages in all, containing commentaries in Korean and English, annotated libretto, and music notations.) The Deep-Rooted Tree/Sung Eum OL3241, OL 3245, SELRO 593, SELRO 596 and SELRO 668. 22 LPs. Selections reissued on CD as *The Five Nuns of P'ansori tasŏt pat'ang* in 1994 and 1996 as The Deep-Rooted Tree/King Records CDD-013.

East Wind (Nopsae param). 1994. (The shaman ritualist Kim Suk-Chul [Kim Sŏkch'ul]). Nices SCO-023CSS. Compact disk.

Eurasian Voices. 1996. (Korean and Japanese traditional musicians and jazz artists.) Samsung Music SCO-070CSS. Compact disk.

Experiencing the Spiritual World of the Haegŭm Sanjo Performed by Park Chŏng-sil: The Haegŭm Sanjo of Four Ryu (Pak Chŏngshil, Haegŭm sanjo yuram). 1999. (Four schools of *sanjo* for fiddle.) TOPCD-014. Compact disk.

Folk Songs 1. 1990. (Studio recordings of Kyŏnggi folk songs.) JVC World Sounds VICG-5022-2. Compact disk.

Folk Songs 2. 1990. (Studio recordings of Chŏlla folk songs.) JVC World Sounds VICG-5023-2. Compact disk.

From Korea, P'ansori, the Art of the Cosmic Voice. 1999. (The featured singer is Yoojin Chung

[Chŏng Ujin].) World Music Gallery L382. Compact disk.

Gayakum. Gumoongo: A-Jaing Sanjoh Collection (*Kayagŭm. Kŏmun'go: Ajaeng sanjo moŭm*). 1988. (Musicians from earlier times.) Meari SISCD-017. Compact disk.

Great Voices of the P'ansori 2 (*Im Pangul. Han'guk ŭi widaehan p'ansori myŏngch'angdŭl*) 2. 1991. (Historical recordings of Im Pangul, 1904–1961.) Synnara SYNCD-010. Compact disk.

Han'guk minyo taejŏn [Korean Folk Song Collection]. 1992–1996. (Boxed sets for each Korean province, with nine Korean books giving lyrics and music notations. MBC.) 103 compact disks.

Hung-bo ga sung by Park Chowol (*In'gan munhwajae Pak Ch'owŏl ch'ang Hŭngboga*). 1998. (A *p'ansori* recording made in the 1960s. With libretto.) Synnara Music NSSRCD-001. 2 compact disks.

Iri Region Local String Ensemble (*Iri Hyangje chul p'ungnyu*). 1994. (Local instrumental ensemble, designated as part of Intangible Cultural Asset number 83.) Jigu JCDS-9042. Compact disk.

Jeokbyuk-ga sung by Kim Dong-Jun (*Kim Tongjun ch'ang Chŏkpyŏkka chŏnjip*). 1998. (A *p'ansori* recording made in the 1960s, with annotated libretto.) Synnara Music NSSRCD-003. 2 compact disks.

Kang Jung Sook: Kayagum byong ch'ang (*Kang Chŏngsuk: kayagŭm pyŏngch'ang*). 1994. Oasis ORC-1471–ORC-1472. 2 compact disks.

Kasa and Sijo, Kim Ho Sung, the Korean Traditional Classic song (*Kim Hosŏng Kasa, Shijo*). 1996. (*Kasa*, narrative songs; and *shijo*, sung poems. Performed by a disciple of one of the twentieth century's greatest literati singers, Yi Chuhwan.) King Records SYNCD-111–SYNCD-113. 3 compact disks.

Kayagŭm Masterpieces by Hwang Byung-ki. 1993. (Hwang's compositions. Three of the four albums were originally issued on LP in 1978, 1979, and 1983.) Sung Eum DS0034–DS0037. 4 compact disks.

Kayagum Sanjo by Ji Aeri (*Chi Aeri Kayagŭm Sanjo*). 1993. (Now a celebrated performer in her own right, Ji Aeri is a disciple of Byung-ki Hwang.) Cantabile SRCD-1137. Compact disk.

Kayagŭm Sanjo by Moon, Chae-suk (*Mun Chaesuk kayagŭm sanjo*). 1993. (Mun is a disciple of the late Kim Chukp'a and traces her lineage back to the founder of the *sanjo* genre, Kim Ch'angjo.) Sung Eum SEM DS0043. Compact disk.

KBS-FM Series for the Twenty-First Century/ Korean Traditional Music 40–44. 1999. (Subtitles indicate content: "40, Chamber Music That Expresses Korea's Four Seasons," compositions; "41, New Compositions for the Twenty-Five-String *Kayagŭm*"; "42, Hidden *Minyo* Singers of Our Generation"; "43, Sugunga 1 by Pak Chowol," *p'ansori*; "44, Sugunga 2 by Pak Chowol.") KBS/Synnara Music NSC-018–NSC-022. 5 compact disks.

Kim Chi-ha Pansori (*Kim Chiha ch'angjak p'ansori*). 1993. (Sung by Im Chint'aek.) Seoul

Records SRCD-3262, SRCD-3263. 2 compact disks.

Kim Duk Soo SamulNori. 1995. (Ensemble versions of the core repertoire.) King SYNCD-114 and SYNCD-115. 2 compact disks.

Kim Duk Soo SamulNori and Red Sun: From the Earth to the Sky. 1997. (Jazz collaborations.) Samsung SCO-123ABN. Compact disk.

Kim Duk Soo with His Friends. 1997. (Korean percussion, with jazz and pop collaborators.) Samsung SCO-137NAN. Compact disk.

Kimsohee Chunghyangka (*Kim Sohŭi Ch'unhyangga wanch'ang*). 1995. (Reissues of LPs of a complete repertoire performance. Kim, 1917–1995, was the greatest female *p'ansori* singer of the twentieth century.) Seoul Records SRCD-1293–SRCD-1298. 6 compact disks.

Kimsohee Shimchongka (*Kim Sohŭi Shimch'ŏngga wanch'ang*). 1995. Seoul Records SRCD-1299–SRCD-1301. 4 compact disks.

Kim Soochul, Best Music of Films 1 and 2. 1997. Samsung Music SCO-124KSC and SCO-125KSC. 2 compact disks.

Kim Sohŭi Kuŭm (*Ipsori*). 1991. (The subtitle translates as mouth music. Segments from *p'ansori* and folk songs, and a wordless improvisation.) SEM CDS 0019. Compact disk.

Kim Suk Chul: Final Say (*Kyŏljŏngp'an*). 1997. (The shaman ritualist Kim Sŏkch'ul joined by saxophonists.) Samsung Music SCO-121CSS. Compact disk.

Kim Yong Woo: Kwenari. 1998. (Kim Yongu sings; *Sulkidoong* and jazz musicians accompany.) Samsung Music SCO-165KYW. Compact disk.

Kim Young Dong: Flute Performance Collection (*Taegŭm yŏnju chip*). 1983. Reissued as Seoul Records SRCD-3009. Compact disk.

Kim Young Dong: Chakp'um chip [Composition Collection]. 1983. Reissued as Seoul Records SRCD-3010. Compact disk.

Kim Young Dong: Mŏn'gil [Long Road]. 1987. Seoul Records SRCD-3012. Compact disk.

Kim Young Dong: Meditation Music (*Sŏn*). 1989. Seoul Records SRCD-3013. Compact disk.

Kim Young Dong, Music World 1: The National Anthem (*Ŭmak segye 1: Aegukka*). 1993. King KSC-4036A. Compact disk.

Kim Young Dong: Windsongs (*Param ŭi sori*). 1999. (Korean ambient music, mixing Korean, Peruvian, and North American instruments.) Woongjin Music WJCC-0276. Compact disk.

Kim Young Dong: Reconciliation (*Hwahae*). (Ambient music.) 2000. Woongjin Music WJCC-0398. Compact disk.

Kim Young Jae: The Sound of the Peninsula. 1996. (Folk song arrangements.) Samsung SCO-101CSS. Compact disk.

Kim Yŏnsu toch'ang: Ch'anggŭk Ch'unhyangjŏn. 1997. (Originally recorded in 1967.) Jigu JCDS-0577. 3 compact disks.

Korea/Corée: Musiques et musiciens du monde. 1972. (Issued in a UNESCO series. Musicians from the National Center.) Philips 6586-011. LP.

Reissued in 1998 as Auvidis D8010. Compact disk.

Korea: Seoul Ensemble of Traditional Music. 1992. (The Seoul Ensemble; mostly court music for small ensemble.) World Network LC6759. Compact disk.

Korean Buddhist Music. 1968. (Recordings made at Pongwŏn Temple in 1964 and notes by John Levy.) Vogue LVLX-253. LP.

Korean Buddhist Music by Pop Hyun: Scent of Serenity. 1999. Asia ACD-571. Compact disk.

Korean Buddhist Music by Pop Hyun: Rhythm of Rainbow. 1999. Asia ACD-572. Compact disk.

Korean Court Music. 1969. (Recordings and notes by John Levy featuring musicians from the National Center.) Lyrichord LL7206. LP. Reissued as LLST7206. LP. Reissued as LYRCD7206. Compact disk.

Korean Folksong Collection. 1988. (Venerable recordings; all songs have orchestral accompaniment.) Seorabul SISCD-013, SISCD-014. 2 compact disks.

Korean Folksongs Collected by Yim Suk-jay (*Im Sŏkchae ch'aerok han'guk kubi minyo*). 1995. (Field recordings from the 1960s and 1970s with a 143-page booklet.) Cantabile SRCD-1227–SRCD-1231. 5 compact disks.

Korean Kayagum Music (Sanjo): Chukp'a. (Recordings of Kim Chukp'a, 1911-1989.) King KICC-5144. Compact disk.

Korean Social and Folk Music. 1969. (Recordings and notes by John Levy.) Lyrichord LL7211. LP. Reissued as LLST7211. LP.

Korean Traditional Music, 1: Court Music Highlights (*Chŏngak*). 1987. (Includes excerpts from the rites to the royal ancestors and Confucius and vocal and instrumental ensemble pieces.) SKC SKCD-K-0004. Compact disk.

Korean Traditional Music, 2: Folk Music Highlights (*Sogak*). 1987. (Vocal and instrumental pieces.) SKC SKCD-K-0005. Compact disk.

Korean Traditional Music, 3: Ryong-san-hoi-sang (*Yŏngsan hoesang*). 1987. SKC SKCD-K-0007. Compact disk.

Korean Traditional Music, 4–8 (*Sanjo moŭm 1–5*). 1987. (*Sanjo* for *p'iri*, oboe; *ajaeng*, bowed zither; *kayagŭm*, zither; *kŏmun'go*, zither; and *haegŭm*, fiddle.) SKC SKCD-K-0009,–0010,–0011,–0012,–0060. 5 compact disks.

Korean Traditional Music, 10: The Royal Ancestral Shrine Music (*Chongmyo cheryeak*). 1987. SKC SKCD-K-0059. Compact disk.

Korean Traditional Music (Saenghwal kugak taejŏnjip). 1994. (Featuring musicians from the National Center and "holders" of Intangible Cultural Assets.) Cantabile SRCD-1207–SRCD-1211 and SRCD-1216–SRCD-1220. 10 compact disks.

Korean Traditional Music, 1–2. 1997 and 1998. (Various genres, all performed within the National Center. Sleeve notes in English.) National Center/Seoul Records SRCD-7525 and SRCD-7526. 2 compact disks.

Korean Traditional Music (Han'guk ŭi chŏnt'ong ŭmak). 1992 and 1994. (Subtitled "Music for the

Twenty-First Century." Includes court, folk, and new compositions.) Korean Broadcasting System KIFM-001–KIFM-009 and Hae Dong 110–119. Nineteen compact disks.

Korean Traditional Music: Yi Sŏngch'ŏn chakp'um chip. 1995. (Compositions by Lee Sung Chun.) KBS SRCD-1277. Compact disk.

Kugak ŭi hyangyŏn [Banquet of Korean Music]. 1988. (Five Korean-language booklets by assorted authors. Senior musicians, vocalists, and orchestras and ensembles of the National Center.) Chungang Ilbosa G169–G218. 50 LPs.

Kury Regional String Chamber Suite (*Kurye Hyangje chul p'ungnyu*). 1994. (Local instrumental ensemble, designated as part of Intangible Cultural Asset number 83.) Jigu. Compact disk.

Lee Chae Suk Kayagum Sanjo, Traditional Folk Art Music (*Yi Chaesuk kayagŭm sanjo*). 1997. (Lee is a senior teacher at Seoul National University.) TOP JCTOP-008. Compact disk.

Lee Kwangsu: The Sound of Arirang (*Arario*). 1996. (Vocal improvisations and versions of the *Arirang*.) Samsung Music SCO-100CSS. Compact disk.

Lee Sae Hwan Kŏmun'go Recital (*Yi Saehwan kŏmun'go yŏnjuhoe*). 1994. (Live recital of old and new pieces for six-stringed zither.) Cantabile SRCD-1195. Compact disk.

Lee Seng Gang: Taegŭm Sanjo. 1997. (Seven-movement *sanjo*.) Samsung Music SCO-109LSK. Compact disk.

Lee Yang-hee Kayagum Collection: Recital at the Tokyo Suntory Hall. 1996. (Primarily a *sanjo* performance.) Columbia GES-10867-CP. Compact disk.

The Legendary Artists of Korean Kayagŭm Sanjo (*Kayagŭm sanjo myŏngindŭl*). 1993. (Taken from SP and EP recordings of the 1920s–1950s.) King SYNCD-059B–SYNCD-063B. 5 compact disks.

Lim Dong Chang. 1993. (Compositions for *samullori* and piano.) Synnara SYNCD-064B. Compact disk.

Moon Hyun's Shijo (*Mun Hyŏn ŭi kyŏngje shijo*). 1999. (Selected *shijo*, sung poems.) Arch/Polyphony Classics AH-90001. Compact disk.

Muak. 1994–1997. (Studio recordings of shaman rituals: *Tong-hae-mu-sok-sa-mul* from the east coast; *Kyeong-gi-do-Do-dang-kut* from Kyŏnggi Province *Todang kut*; *Chin-do-Ssit-kkim-kut* from Chindo island *Ssikkim kut*; *Donghae Ogu kut* from the east coast; *Cheju chilmeri dang kut* from Cheju Island *Ch'ilmŏri tang kut*; *Seoul Chaesu kut*; and *Haenamgut* from the southwest.) Nices SCO-041CSS, SCO-042CSS, SCO-043CSS, SCO-058CSS, SCO-066CSS; and Samsung Nices SCO-102CSS, SCO-141CSS.

Music of the Kayagum. 1990. (*The Memories of Kayagum* in the North American market.) Devoted to the music of Sŏng Kŭmyŏn, 1923–1986.) JVC World Sounds VICG-5018-2. Also released as JVC VID-2508. Compact disk.

Nam Do Folk Song Collection (*Namdo minyo moŭm*). 1988. (Professional singers present the southern repertoire.) Seorabul SISCD-016. Compact disk.

Oh Kap Soon Ga Ya Kum Byeng Chang and Korean Folk Song Collection (*O Kapsun kayagŭm pyŏngch'ang kwa minyo moŭm*). 1988. (Five episodes of *p'ansori* and thirteen folk songs, all accompanied by zither.) Meari SISCD-015. Compact disk.

One Sound: Traditional Buddhist Music. 2000. (Track 1 is a Korean monk, Seung Sahn, recorded in Rhode Island.) Ellipsis CD4015. Compact disk.

Orchestra Asia, 1993.9.24. Seoul, Korea. 1993. (Korean, Japanese, and Chinese musicians performing new compositions.) Synnara SYNCD-065B. Compact disk.

Orchestra Asia, Ch'angdan yŏnjuhoe. 1994. Synnara SYNCD-074, SYNCD-075. 2 compact disks.

Ŏulim Live, 1 and 2. 1996. (Subtitled "*Ch'ŏng*" and "*Hŭng*." Creative traditional music mixing Korean and Western instruments.) Cantabile SRCD-1334, SRCD-1349.

Orinirŭl wihan kugak. 1998. (Children's songs, newly composed.) Sound Lab Z+Sound-008–Z+Sound-011. 4 compact disks.

Park Bum-Hoon: The Music of Play and Screen (*Pak Pŏmhun yŏn'gŭk, yŏngsang ŭmak 1*). (Two compositions, one for theater and one for film.) King SYNCD-049. Compact disk.

Park Jong Sun Ajaeng Sanjo. 1994. (Live recording of Pak Chongsŏn playing the *ajaeng*, a bowed zither.) Cantabile SRCD-1190. Compact disk.

P'ansori: Korean Epic Vocal Art and Instrumental Music. 1988. (Featuring Kim Sohŭi, with notes in English.) Nonesuch Explorer 72049-2. Compact disk.

P'ansori Yŏlsaga. 1994. (New music, sung by Yi Sŏnggŭn and Chŏng Sunim.) Synnara SYNCD-047–SYNCD-048. 2 compact disks.

Percussion Ensemble Puri (*P'uri*). (Percussion quartet, with Chinese and Thai instruments added.) Sori CMICD-1005. Compact disk.

A Petal (*Kkonip*). 1996. (Film score by Wŏn Il.) Samsung Music SCO-088WIN. Compact disk.

Red Sun/SamulNori. 1989. (The first album mixing *SamulNori* with Linda Sharrock, Wolfgang Puschnig, Jamaaladeen Tacuma, and Uli Scherer.) Amadeo 841 222-1. LP. Reissued in 1997 with Korean notes as Polygram DZ-2433. Compact disk.

Red Sun/SamulNori: Then Comes the White Tiger. 1994. (Definitive jazz collaborations mixed in Europe.) ECM ECM-1499. Compact disk.

The Road to Hwangchon (*Hwangch'ŏn kil*). 1994. (Compositions by Kim Soo Chul [Kim Such'ŏl].) Nices SCO-057KSC. Compact disk.

Saeul Kayagŭm Trio, Seoul. 1992. (Arrangements and compositions for zither trio.) SKC SKCD-K-0436. Compact disk.

Salp'uri. 1994. (Shamans, *p'ansori* singers, and Korean and Japanese instrumentalists.) Cantabile SRCD-1161. Compact disk.

Samullori: Korean Traditional Fork Music Series 1. 1986. (Unfortunately, *folk* is spelled *fork*; sleeve notes in Korean and English by Suzanna Samstag.) Jigu JLS 1201988. LP. Jigu JCDS-0050. Compact disk.

Samul-Nori: Drums and Voices of Korea. 1983. (The first recording, with notes by Alan Heyman.) Nonesuch Explorer 72093-1. LP. Reissued 1991 with Korean commentary as Oasis ORC-1041. Compact disk.

SamulNori. 1986. (Notes in Japanese.) Sony 32DG64. Compact disk.

SamulNori: Master Drummers/Dancers of Korea. 1987. (Notes in English by Kim Duk Soo and Suzanna Samstag.) SKC SKCD-K-0236.

SamulNori—Nanjang: A New Horizon. 1995. (*SamulNori* and *Red Sun*, mixed in Korea.) King KSC-4150A. Compact disk.

SamulNori: Record of Changes. 1988. (Recorded in New York, featuring shaman-inspired music.) CMP CD3002. CD. Reissued 1989 (with notes in Japanese) as Rhizome Sketch RZF 1002. Compact disk.

A Selection of Korean Traditional Music (*Han'guk ŭi chŏnt'ong ŭmak*). 1991. (Celebrating the fortieth anniversary of the National Center. Three contemporary recordings and one disk of historical recordings.) Jigu JCDS-0194–Jigu JCDS-0197. 4 compact disks.

The Selection of Korean Traditional Music (*Uri sori uri karak*). 1996. Historical and new recordings, accompanied by a 210-page book. Korean Traditional Music and Publishing. 20 compact disks.

Selections of Korean Classical Music (*Han'guk ŭmak sŏnjip*). 1972–1998. (Standard recordings of the court, *sanjo*, and *p'ansori* repertoire in Vols. 1–19; folk repertoire in Vols. 20–21; shaman ritual music in Vols. 22–23. The recordings match staff notation books in the series *Han'guk ŭmak* 'Anthology of Korean Music.') National Center/Jigu/KBS. 38 LPs and 16 compact disks.

Selections of Korean Classical Music (*Han'guk ŭmak sŏnjip*). 1985–1988. (Twelve sets, all reissues of National Center recordings except Vol. 11, which is devoted to solo pieces.) Sung Eum CS054–CS065. 36 cassette tapes.

Setting a Bridge between Tea and Music in Korean Tea Music: Tea Music (*Taak*) 1–3. (Compositions to accompany the tea ceremony.) Seoul Records SRCD-1423, SRCD-1424, SRCD-1429. 3 compact disks.

Shamanistic Ceremonies of Chindo. 1993. (Studio recording of Intangible Cultural Asset number 72, *Chindo Ssikkim kut*.) JVC World Sounds VICG-5214. Compact disk.

Shamanistic Ceremonies of the Eastern Seaboard. 1994. (Studio recording of Intangible Cultural Asset number 82a, *Tonghaean pyŏlshin kut*.) JVC World Sounds VICG-5261. Compact disk.

Shibi kasa sung by Yi Yang-gyo, Government-Designated Important Intangible Cultural Asset Number 41 (*Chungyo muhyŏng munhwajae che-41 ho*). 1992. (Definitive renditions of the entire repertoire of *kasa*, narrative song.) Jigu JCDS-0273–JCDS-0275. 3 compact disks.

Shimch'ŏngga: The Epic Vocal Art of P'ansori. 1990. (Abbreviated version of repertoire sung by Chŏng Chŏngmin.) JVC World Sounds VICG-5019-2. Compact disk.

Shimch'ŏngga. In'gan munhwajae Sŏng Ch'angsun p'ansori taejŏn chip. 1994. (Sŏng, b. 1934, is a "holder" of the *p'ansori* Intangible Cultural Asset.) Sung Eum SEM DS0051. 3 compact disks.

Shin Myong (*Shinmyŏng*). 1993. (Improvisations by Korean soloists and a Japanese bass player.) Cantabile SRCD-1088. Compact disk.

Short Kayagŭm Sanjo Collection of Chŏng Nam-hŭi and Hwang Byungki School (*Tchalbŭn kayagŭm sanjo moŭm, Chŏng Namhŭi-je Hwang Pyŏnggi ryu*). 1998. (Hwang reconstructs a *sanjo* from the 1930s, adding his own elements.) Sung Eum DS0234. Compact disk.

Sinawi and Sanjo: The Folkloric Instrumental Traditions, 1. 1990. (Studio recordings, one ensemble and two solo.) JVC World Sounds VICG-5020-2. Also released as JVC VID-25020 and as Seoul Records SRCD-1120. Compact disk.

Sinawi Music of Korea. 1984. (Three scorings of *sinawi* and one *p'iri*—oboe—*sanjo*.) King KICC-5143. Also released as Seoul Records SRCD-1307. Compact disk.

Sinawi, Sanjo, and Taepungnyu: The Folkloric Instrumental Traditions, 2. 1990. (One *sanjo*, one *sinawi*, and an instrumental quartet.) JVC World Sounds VICG-5021-2. Also released as JVC VID-25021. Compact disk.

Sŏp'yŏnje. 1993. (Film soundtrack by Kim Soo Chul [Kim Such'ŏl].) Seoul Records SRCD-3215. CD. Reissued in 1994 as Nices SCO-046KSC. Compact disk.

Sori for Invocation (*Pullim sori*). 1994. (Compositions by Kim Soo Chul.) Nices SCO-059KSC. Compact disk.

Sŏul kugak taegyŏngyŏn [Seoul Traditional Music Contest]. 1995. (Assorted selections, with an illustrated booklet in Korean and English.) Nices SCO-080CTM. Compact disk.

The Story of Patriot Ryu Kwan-Soon (*Yu Kwansun chŏn*). 1991. (Updated *p'ansori* sung by O Chŏngsuk.) Reissued 1998 as Synnara NSSRCD-006. Compact disk.

The Strings of 1,000 Years 1 and 2 (*Ch'ŏnnyŏn ŭi sori*). 1998. (A youthful string ensemble playing modified traditional instruments.) Korean Music Promotion. 2 compact disks.

Suh Yong Seok Taegŭm Sanjo (*Sŏ Yongsŏk taegŭm sanjo*). 1993. (Live recording.) Cantabile SRCD-1179. Compact disk.

Sulkidoong: From the Evening Tide till the Coming Dawn. 1996. (Songs and ensemble compositions.) Samsung Music SCO-127TAC. Compact disk.

Sulkidoong: Han'guk ch'angjak muyong kokchip. 1998. (Instrumental arrangements of songs and compositions, ostensibly for dancing.) Yedang YSCS-277. Compact disk.

SXL Live in Japan. 1987. (The first collaboration between *SamulNori* and jazz musicians, here featuring Bill Laswell, Shankar, Ronald Shannon Jackson, and Aiyb Dieng.) Terrapin 32DH824. Compact disk.

Taebaek Range of Mountains (*T'aebaeksan maek*). 1994. (Compositions by Kim Soo Chul.) Nices SCO-051KSC.

Traditional Music from Korea. 1999. (Featuring recent graduates of Tan'guk University in a live concert.) ARC EUCD1561.

Traditional Music of Korea (*Han'guk chŏnt'ong ŭmak*). 1980. (Court and folk music, played by members of the National Center, packaged with an English-language booklet in two boxes within a slipcase.) New York: Korean Cultural Service. 15 LPs.

Two-Stringed Love: Byun, Jong-hyuk (*Pyŏn Chonghyŏk haegŭm: Ijul ŭi sarang*). 1999. (*Sanjo*, literati music, and new compositions for the *haegŭm*, a fiddle.) Seoul Records SRCD-7227. Two compact disks.

Unrestrained Sound (*Kuŭm tasŭrŭm*). 1994. (The shaman Park Byung Chon [Pak Pyŏngch'ŏn].) Nices SCO-024CSS. Compact disk.

West End. 1996. (Shamans, jazz musicians, and *p'ansori* singers.) Samsung Music SCO-105CSS. Compact disk.

Whimoree (*Hwimori*). 1994. (Compositions, improvisations, and a segment of *p'ansori*.) Seoul Records SRCD-3281. Compact disk.

Won Chang-hyun Taegum Sanjo (*Wŏn Changhyŏn taegŭm sanjo*). 1992. Synnara SYNCD-003. Compact disk.

Yang Seung-hee, Gayagum Sanjo (*Juk-pa Version*) (*Yang Sŭnghŭi, kayagŭm sanjo*). 1997. (A disciple of the late Kim Chukp'a who traces her lineage back to the founder of the *sanjo* genre, Kim Ch'angjo.) Seoul Records SRCD-1399. Compact disk.

Yŏngsan hoesang. 1981. (Four versions of the literati suite performed immaculately by the leading classical group, Chŏngnong akhoe. 56-page booklet, with English notes by Lee Hye-Ku.) Sung Eum SEL-100122. 4 LPs.

Yong Woo Kim: Chige Sori. 1996. (Kim Yongu sings; *Sulkidoong* accompanies.) Seoul Records SRCD-1354. Compact disk.

INNER ASIA

Amdo: Monastère tibetain de Labrang. 1996. (Recorded by Tian Qing and Tian Miao in 1995.) Ocora C560101. Compact disk.

The Art of Morin Khuur. 1991. World Music Library 65. (Recorded in Tokyo in 1992.) King Records KICC5165. Compact disk.

Buddhist Liturgy of Tibet. 1991. King Records KICC-5137. Compact disk.

Chants chamaniques et narratifs de l'arctique siberien. [1992.] Musique du monde/Music of the World: Siberie/Siberia 1. (Recorded in 1992.) Buda Records 92564-2. Compact disk.

Chants épiques et diphoniques: Asie centrale et Sibérie. 1996. (Recorded between 1983 and 1995. Notes by François Grund and Pierre Bois.) Inédit-MCM W260067. Compact disk.

Chants kazakhs et tradition epique de l'Ouest. 1993. (Recorded by Alain Desjacques in 1984.) Ocora C 580051. Compact disk.

Chirgilchin. 1996. *The Wolf and the Kid.* Shanachie 64070. Compact disk.

Chöömej Throat-Singing from the Center of Asia. 1993. World Network 21. Compact disk plus booklet.

Deep in the Heart of Tuva: Cowboy Music from the Wild East. 1996. Ellipsis Arts 4080. Compact disk.

The Diamond Path: Rituals of Tibetan Buddhism—Yamantaka Trochu Rite of Khampagar Monastery. 1998. (Recorded in 1994 at Khampagar Monastery, Kangra Valley, by David Lewiston.) Shanachie 66006. Compact disk.

Höömii and Urtin Duu: The Folk Music Traditions. 1992. (Recorded at Mongolian Folk Music Theater, Ulanbator, in 1991. Notes in Japanese by Jagvaralyn Burenbekh and Hideaki Suzuki; notes in English by Robin Thompson.) JVC VICG-5211. Compact disk.

Huun-Huur-Tu. 1993a. *Old Songs and Tunes of Tuva.* Shanachie 64050. Compact disk.

———. 1993b. *Sixty Horses in My Herd.* Shanachie 64050. Compact disk.

———. 1994. *The Orphan's Lament.* Shanachie 64058. Compact disk.

———. 1996. *If I'd Been Born an Eagle.* Shanachie 64080. Compact disk.

———. 1998. *Where Young Grass Grows.* Shanachie 66018. Compact disk.

Inner Mongolia (China) Morin Huur: The Folk Music Traditions (II). 1992. (Ci Bulag, *morin huur*.) JVC VICG-5212. Compact disk.

Instrumental Music of Turkmenistan. 1994. World Music Library 75. (Recorded in 1993.) King Records KICC5175. Compact disk.

Instrumental Music of the Uighurs. 1991. World Music Library 38. (Recorded in 1989.) King Records. Compact disk.

Ladakh: Musique de monastère et de village. 1989. (Recorded in 1976.) Chant du monde LDX 274662. Compact disk.

The Lama's Chant: Songs of Awakening. 1996. (Performed by Lama Gyurme and Jean-Philippe Rykiel.) Sony SK 62591. Compact disk.

Levin, Ted. 1999. *Tuva, among the Spirits: Sound, Music, and Nature in Sakha and Tuva.* Smithsonian Folkways SFW 40452. Compact disk.

Melodies of the Steppes. White moon. Tsagaan sar: Traditional and Popular Music from Mongolia. 1992. Pan Records PAN 2010CD. Compact disk.

Menggu zu yin yue: The Music of Mongol Nationality. 1998. Zhongguo shao shu min zu yin yue ji cheng 4. Yao lan chang pian CRCD-9040. Compact disk.

Mongolia: Living Music of the Steppes—Instrumental Music and Song of Mongolia. 1997. (Recorded by Haruo Hasumi.) Multicultural Media MCM 3001. Compact disk.

Mongolia: Traditional Music. 1991. (Field recordings made by Alain Desjacques.) Auvidis D8207. Compact disk.

Mongolian Epic Song: Zhangar. 1991. World Music Library 36. (Recorded in 1985.) King Records KICC5136. Compact disk.

Mongolian Instrumental Music. 1988. (Musicians of the Mongolian People's Republic National Dance Troupe.) Seven Seas KICC 5134. Compact disk.

Mongolian Morin Khuur. 1987. (Ci Bulag, *morin khuur.* Recorded in 1985.) Seven Seas/King Records KICC 5135. Compact disk.

Mongolian Songs of Ottoman Empire. 1988. Min On/Seven Seas KICC 5133. Compact disk.

Mongolie: Chamans et lamas. 1999. (Field recordings made by Alain Desjacques, 1991–1993.) Ocora C560059. Compact disk.

Mongolie: Chants kazakhs et tradition épique de l'Ouest. 1993. (Recorded between 1984 and 1990. Field recordings by Alain Desjacques.) Ocora C580051. Compact disk.

Mongolie: Musique et chants de tradition populaire. 1986. GREM G7511. Compact disk.

Mongolie: Musique vocale et instrumental. 1989. Inédit. (Recorded in 1988.) Maison des Cultures du Monde W 260009. Compact disk.

The Music of Tibetan Buddhism. 1999. Anthology of World Music. (Recorded in 1961 in Tibet by Alain Danielou.) Rounder CD 5129-31. 3 compact disks plus booklet.

Musiques de Mongolie. 1993. (Recorded in 1993.) Buda BCD 92591–2. Compact disk.

Musiques ouïgoures. 1990. (Field recordings by Sabine Trebinjac and Jean During. Recorded in 1988 and 1989, Xinjiang.) Ocora 559092-93. 2 compact disks.

Musiques sacrées. 1989. (Notes by Georges Luneau Recorded by Georges Luneau, April–June 1971 at monasteries in Nepal.) Ocora C559011.

Musique sur les routes de la soie. 1992. (Live recordings from a broadcast series in Basel and Geneva, 1991. Notes by Laurent Aubert.) Auvidis Ethnic B 6776. Compact disk.

Naxi Music from Lijiang. 1997. (Performed by the Dayan Ancient Music Association. Recorded at Saint Jude's on the Hill, London, in 1995. Notes by Helen Rees.) Nimbus NI 5510. Compact disk.

Ozum (Sprouts): Young Voices of Ancient Tuva. 1991. Window to Europe SUM 90008. Compact disk.

Sainkho. 1993. *Out of Tuva.* CramWorld CRAW6CD. Compact disk.

———. 1998. *Naked Spirit.* Amiata ARNR2298. Compact disk.

The Secret Museum of Mankind: Ethnic Music Classics, 1925–1948: Central Asia. 1996. (Recorded 1929–1950, Noginskii, Aprelyevka, Soviet Union.) Yazoo 7007. Compact disk.

Shu-De. 1994. *Voices from the Distant Steppe.* Realworld CDRW41. Compact disk.

Songs and Music of Tibet. 1999. (Recorded in Kathmandu by Howard Kaufman.) Smithsonian Folkways Records F-04486. Compact disk.

Songs of Turkmenistan. 1997. World Music Library 130. (Recorded in 1993.) King Records KICC 5230. Compact disk.

Tajik Music of Badakhshan/Musique tadjike du Badakhshan. 1993. Musiques et musiciens du monde. (Field recordings made by Jean During in southern Tajikistan in June 1991 and in Sinkiang, China, June 1988.) Auvidis D 8212. Compact disk.

Tibet, the Heart of Dharma: Buddha's Teachings and the Music They Inspired. 1996. (Field recordings by David Lewiston.) Ellipsis Arts CD 4050. 4 compact disks plus booklet.

Tibet: Musiques sacrées. 1987. (Notes by Georges Luneau. Recorded in April–June 1971 in Nepal.) Ocora C559011. Compact disk.

Tibet—Traditions rituelles des Bonpos. 1993. (Recorded by Ricardo Canzio, 1981–1983.) Ocora C580016. Compact disk.

The Tibetan Buddhist Chant. 1992. (Sung by the monks of Namgyal Monastery.) World Music Library 64. Seven Seas/King. Compact disk.

Tibetan Buddhist Rites from the Monasteries of Bhutan. 1990s. (Recorded by John Levy in 1971.) Lyrichord LYCD7255–LYCD7258. Four compact disks.

Tibetan Ritual/Rituel tibetain. 1991. (Sung and played by the lamas of the Nyingmapa Monastary of Dehra Dun. Recorded by Manfred Junius and P. C. Misra.) Auvidis D 8034. Compact disk.

Tibetan Ritual Music. 1990. (Recorded in 1961 by Peter Crossley-Holland.) Lyrichord LYRCD7181. Sound disk.

Turkestan Chinois/Xianjiang: Musiques ouigoures. 1990. (Uighur music recorded in Xinjiang, 1988–1989.) Ocora C559092–C559093. 2 compact disks.

Turkmenistan: Chants des femmes bakhshi. 1995. Inédit. (Recorded 1988–1990.) Maison des Cultures du Monde W260064. Compact disk.

Turkmenistan: La musique des bakhshy/The Music of the Bakhshy. 1991. Archives Internationales de Musique Populaire 22. (Recorded 1988-01990.) VDE CD-651. Compact disk.

Tuva, Echoes from the Spirit World. 1992. Pan Records PAN2013CD. Compact disk.

Tuva, Voices from the Center of Asia. 1990. (Produced by Theodore Levin, Eduard Alekseev, and Zoya Kirgiz.) Smithsonian/Folkways CDSF40017. Compact disk.

Tuva, Voices from the Land of Eagles. 1991. Pan Records PAN2005CD. Compact disk.

Uzlyau: Guttural Singing of the Peoples of the Sayan, Altai, and Ural Mountains. 1993. (Notes by Vyacheslav Shchurov.) Pan PAN2019CD. Compact disk.

Vocal and Instrumental Music of Mongolia. 1994. (Recorded in 1974 by Jean Jenkins in various locations in Mongolia.) Topic TSCD909. Compact disk.

Vocal Music of the Uighurs. 1991. World Music Library 39. (Recorded in 1989.) Seven Seas KICC5139.

Virtuosos from the Mongol Plateau. 1994. (Recorded in 1992.) King Records KICC5177. Compact disk.

Films and Videos of East Asian Music

CHINA AND INNER ASIA

Le chant des harmoniques/The Song of Harmonics. 1989. (Produced by Hugo Zemp and Tran Quang Hai.) Paris, France: Centre National de la Recherche Scientifique (CNRS). Motion picture (37 minutes).

China: Unleashing the Dragon 3, The Soul of the Master. 1995. (Producer, Richard Hall. In English and Chinese with English subtitles and voiceovers.) First Run/Icarus Films. Videocassette (52 minutes).

Cui, Jian. 1989. *No More Disguises.* (Produced by Pamela Yates; directed by Tom Sigel and Boryana Varbanov. Filmed in China in January 1989.) Skylight Pictures, distributed by Icarus/First Run. Videocassette.

Echoes from Tibet. 1992. (Directed by Deben Bhattacharya. Originally produced as motion picture in 1980.) London: Sussex Tapes. Distributed by Audio-Forum V72336. Videocassette (27 minutes).

The Education of a Singer at the Beijing Opera. 1994. (Leone Jaffin.) Top Films and National Research Center, Paris. Films for the Humanities and Sciences, distributor. Videocassette.

Female College Students in China. c. 1991. (Director, Tian Zhuang Zhuang. Performers: Gao Jun, Cao Yan, Yang Lien, Wei Hua. In Chinese with English subtitles.) South Productions for Channel Four in association with RTVE (Spain) and SBS (Australia). First Run/Icarus Films. Videocassette (26 minutes).

Folk Music from Inner Mongolia. 1994. (Directed by Deben Bhattacharya.) London: Sussex Tapes. Audio-Forum V72186. Videocassette.

Genghis Blues. 1999. (Produced and directed by Roko and Adrian Belic.) DocuDrama, distributed by New Video. Vodeocassette (90 minutes).

The Herders of Mongun-Taiga. 1989. (Director-producer, John Sheppard.) London: Granada Television International, distributed by Shanachie Entertainment. Videocassette (52 minutes).

The Internationale. 2000. (Producer-director, Peter Miller.) First Run/Icarus Films. Videocassette (57 minutes).

JVC Video Anthology of World Music and Dance: East Asia. 1990. (Producer, Ichikawa Katsumori. Produced in collaboration with the National Museum of Ethnology, Osaka; and Smithsonian/Folkways Records.) JVC Video Anthology of World Music and Dance, Vols. 1–5. JVCVTMV-31–VTMV-35. 5 videocassettes.

Living Music for Golden Mountains. 1981. (Produced by Arthur E. Dong and Elizabeth J. Meyer, directed by Arthur E. Dong.) University of California Extension Media Center. Videocassette (27 minutes).

Lord of the Dance: Destroyer of Illusion. 1985. (Director, Richard Kohn; producer, Franz-Christoph Giercke.) First Run Features. Videocassette (114 minutes).

Love Songs of the Miao in China. 1990. (Produced by NHK.) Filmmakers Library. Videocassette (45 minutes).

Monkey King Looks West. 1989. (Producer, Renee Tajima; director, Christine Choy.) Filmmakers Library. Videocassette (42 minutes).

The Musical Steppes of Mongolia. 1994. (Produced and directed by Heidi Draper.) Filmmakers Library. Videocassette (51 minutes).

No. 17 Cotton Mill Shanghai Blues: Music in China. 1984. (Produced and directed by Jeremy Marre. Harcourt Films for Channel Four Television. Shanachie SH1212. Videocassette (60 minutes).

Performing Arts of China: Folk Music. 1992. (Directed by Deben Bhattacharya. Originally filmed in 1983.) London: OET Foundation for Culture, distributed by Audio-Forum V72188. Videocassette.

Performing Arts of China: Instruments and Music. 1992. (Originally produced and copyrighted in

1983. Directed by Deben Bhattacharya.) Audio-Forum V72185. Videocassette (27 minutes).

Performing Arts of China: The Opera. 1992. (Directed by Deben Bhattacharya. Originally produced and copyrighted in 1983.) Audio-Forum V72187. Videocassette (27 minutes).

The Perfumed Handkerchief: A Chinese Opera. 1981. (In Mandarin and English, with English and Chinese subtitles.) Kultur 1149. Videocassette (70 minutes).

Resonance of the Qin. 2000. (Yuan Jung-ping, *qin.* Written and directed by Willow Hai Chang.) New York: China Institute in America. Videocassette (33 minutes).

Silk and Strings: A Tale of Taiwan. 1990s. (Producer, John Seabourne; director, Deben Bhattacharya. Originally released by Sussex Tapes, London, in 1973.) Video-Forum V72544. Videocassete (26 minutes).

Songs of the Mountains, Dances of the Sea: Music and Dances of Taiwan's Indigenous People. 1997. (Producers, Daw Ming Lee and Robert Tzong-jen Shih; director, David Tawei Lee.) Distributed by Kwang Hwa Mass Communications. Videocassette (30 minutes).

Tan, Dun. 1997. *Hong Kong Symphony: Heaven, Earth, Mankind.* (Director, Larry Weinstein; producers, Charles Wang and Niv Fichman.) Bullfrog Films. Videocassette (57 minutes).

Tantra of Gyüto: Sacred Rituals of Tibet. 1985. (Mark Elliott and David Lewiston.) New York: Mystic Fire Video. Videocassette.

Tantric Voices and Thighbone Trumpets: A Look at Tibetan Buddhist Music and Culture. 1994. (Produced by Washington Commission for the Humanities. Directed by Brian Pertl.) Seattle, Wash.: Perspectives and Reality. The Inquiring Mind IM-16. Videocassette (58 minutes).

Uighurs on the Silk Route. 1985. (Directed by Deben Bhattacharya.) London: Sussex Video. Videocassette (27 minutes).

JAPAN

Azia no ongoku to bunka (Music and Cultures of Asia), 1998. (Directed by Yamaguti Osamu et al.) Tôkyô: Victor Entertainment. 6 LDs.

Aspects of the Kabuki Theatre of Japan. 1987. New York: Institute of Advanced Studies in the Theatre Arts (IASTA). VHS Video.

Bugaku. 1970s. (Performance of Osaka Garyo-Kai.) New York: Asia Society. VHS video.

Bugaku. 1998. (Performance of Osaka Garyo-Kai.) N.p. VHS video.

Bunraku: Bbuyo. 1980s. Tôkyô: Nippon Hôsô kyôkai (Japan broadcasting Corporation.) VHS video.

Bunraku Performance: Tsuri Onna. 1997. Tôkyô: KBS. VHS video.

Bunraku: Puppet Theatre of Japan. 1983. New York: Japan Society. VHS video.

Discovering the Music of Japan. 1987. (Directed by Bernard Willets. Originally released as a motion picture in 1967.) Pasadena, Calif.: Barr Films; North Hollywood, Calif.: Hollywood Select Video. Our Musical Heritage Series HSV 4006. VHS Video.

The Edo Stage: Kabuki and Bunraku. 1977. Tôkyô: Japan Foundation. VHS video.

Gagaku. 1976. Honolulu: University of Hawaii College of Continuing Education and Community Service. VHS video.

Gagaku, the Court Music of Japan. 1989. (Written and hosted by William P. Malm. Early Music Television Series, originally broadcast in 1989.) Norman: University of Oklahoma. VHS video.

Gagaku: An Important Intangible Cultural Property of Japan. 2000. (Produced by Shimonaka Memorial Foundation.) Tôkyô: Cinema Inc./ Heibonsha. 10 VHS videocassettes.

Hayashi: Nihon buyo; nagauta. 1980. Asian Performing Arts Summer Institute, UCLA Office of Instructional Development. VHS video.

Japanese Theatre in the World. 1998. Tôkyô: Sihizai. VHS video.

Kodo: Heartbeat Drummers of Japan. [1991– 1983] 1997. (Produced and directed by Jacques Holender.) Lyme, Conn.: Rhapsody Films. VHS video.

Kyogen—Sambaso; kabuki bayash; naguata. 1980. Asian Performing Arts Summer Institute, UCLA Office of Instructional Development. VHS video.

Living Treasures of Japan. 1988. National Geographic Special. Pittsburgh, Pa.: National Geographic Society. VHS video.

Music of Bunraku. 1991. (Written and hosted by William P. Malm. Early Music Television Series.) Norman: University of Oklahoma. VHS video.

Music of Modern Japan. 1984. (Presented by the Ministry of Foreign Affairs of Japan.) Tôkyô: Yomiuri Eigasha. VHS video.

Nagauta: The Heart of Kabuki Music. 1994. (Written and hosted by William P. Malm. Early Music Television Series, originally broadcast in 1993.) Norman: University of Oklahoma. VHS video.

Nihon Buyo—Ryogen Hisho; Kyogen—Fukuro; Shimai. 1980. Asian Performing Arts Summer Institute, UCLA Office of Instructional Development. VHS video.

On to eizô ni yoru Nihon koten geinô taikei (Anthology of Japanese Classical Performing Arts in Sound and Film). [1991] 1997. (Editors, Kishibe Shigeo et al.) 1: *Kyutei geinô to sinzi geinô* (Court and Shinto Music). 2: *Bukkyô gyôzi to bukkyô geinô* (Buddhist Music). 3–4: *Nô to kyôgen* (*Nô* and *Kyôgen*). 5–8: *Kabuki.* 9–10: *Bunraku.* 11: *Katarimono no ongaku* (Music for Narratives). 12: *Edo nagauta to kabuki buyo/Kamigatauta to zashikimai* (*Nagauta* and *Kabuki*). 13: *Sankyoku.* 14 (supplement): *Bekkan.* Two accompanying books, subtitled *Sôron hen* (General Reference) and *Eizô kaisetsu* (Handbook for Video). Tôkyô: Japan Victor Corporation (JVC), VTML 301– 314. 14 videodisks.

On to eizo ni yoru Nihon koten geino taikei (Anthology of Japanese Classical Performing Arts in Sound and Film). [1991] 1997. (Editors, Kishibe Shigeo et al.) 1–2: *Kyûtei geino to sinzi geinô* (Court and Sintô Music). 3–4: *Bukkyô gyôzi to bukkyô geinô* (Buddhist Music). 5–7: *Nô to kyôgen* (*Nô* and *Kyôgen*). 8–11: *Kabuki.* 12–13: *Bunraku.* 14–15: *Katarimono no ongaku* (Music for Narratives). 16: *Edo nagauta to kabuki buyo.* 17: *Kamigatauta to zashikimai* (Nagauta and Kabuki). 18: *Sankyoku.* Supplement: *Bekkan.* Two accompanying books, subtitled *Sôron hen* (General Reference) and *Eizô kaisetsu* (Handbook for Video). Tôkyô: Japan Victor Corporation (JVC), VTMV-100–VTMV-125. 25 videocassettes. VHS video, stereo or mono.

The Performing Arts. 1976. Great Plains National Instructional Television Library: Japan, the Living Tradition Series 11–12. Lincoln, Neb.: University of Mid-America. 2 VHS videos.

Shinto Festival Music. 1993. (Written and hosted by William P. Malm. Early Music Television Series, originally broadcast in 1989.) Norman: University of Oklahoma. VHS video.

The Soloists of the Ensemble Nipponia. 1998. (Originally produced at Brooklyn College in cooperation with the Performing Arts Program of the Asia Society.) VHS video.

Taikei nihon rekisi to geinô (Folk Performing Arts of Japan). 1991–1992. 15 vols. Tôkyô: Japan Victor, VTMT 81-94. VHS video.

The Tradition of the Performing Arts in Japan: The Heart of Kabuki, Noh, and Bunraku. 1989. Tôkyô: Nippon Steel Human Resources Development. VHS Video.

Video Series of Japanese Music. 1989. Tôkyô: Hôgaku Journal. VHS video, hi-fi.

KOREA

Aak, Korean Court Music and Dance. 1970. (Beate Gordon, producer and director.) Asia Society. Videocassette (30 minutes).

Arirang. 1990. (Directed by Lee Young Ho.) Korea Film Production. Videocassette (18 minutes).

Best of Seoul City Dance Theatre. 1995. Korean Broadcasting Services. Videocassette (60 minutes).

The Buddhist Dance. 1994. KBS Yongsang Saoptan Videocassette (36 minutes).

Changgu. 1995. KBS Yongsang Saoptan. Videocassette.

Ch'unhyangjŏn (The Story of Ch'unhyang). 2000. (Director: Im Kwŏn-taek.) T'ae Hung Productions.

Five Generations of Musicians. 1990. Korea Film Production. Videocassette (38 minutes).

Han'guk chŏnt'ong ŭmak kwa muyong / Korean Traditional Music and Dance. 1996. National Center for Korean Traditional Performing Arts. Videocassette.

Han'guk ŭi chŏnt'ong munhwa yesul minsogak. 1980s. MBC. Videocassette.

Images of Korea. 1990s. Korea Foundation. Videocassette (18 minutes).

Images of Korea, 2. 1996. Korea Foundation. Videocassette (14 minutes).

Images of Korea, 3. 1990s. (Editor, Hyung Bo.) Korea Foundation. Videocassette (22 minutes).

The JVC Video Anthology of World Music and Dance. East Asia 1, Korea 1. 1988. (Ichikawa Katsumori, producer; Fujii Tomoaki, editorial director.) JVC Video Anthology of World Music and Dance, Vol. 1. JVC, Victor Company of Japan; Rounder Records (distributor). Videocassette (49 minutes) with booklet.

The JVC Video Anthology of World Music and Dance. East Asia 2, Korea 2. 1988. (Ichikawa Katsumori, producer; Fujii Tomoaki, editorial director.) JVC Video Anthology of World Music and Dance, Vol. 2. JVC, Victor Company of Japan; Rounder Records (distributor). Videocassette (50 minutes) with booklet.

Kayagŭm/The Kayagŭm. 1995. Kungnip Yonghwa Chejakso. Han'guk Kyoyuk Yŏn'guso. Videocassette (26 minutes).

Kim Tŏksu ŭi samul nori kyosil/Kim Duk Soo "Samulnori." 1997. Konggŭbwŏn A and C K'oorong. 6 videocassettes with booklet.

Kŏmun'go Hyŏn'gum. 1995. KBS Yongsang Saoptan. Videocassette.

Korean Culture through the Arts: A Comparative View. 1984. (Directed by Dean M. Baldwin.)

Korean Dances. 1977. Korea Film Production. Videocassette (23 minutes).

A Korean Festival of Music and Dance. 1991. Korea Film Production. Videocassette (17 minutes).

Korean Traditional Dance: Chŏnt'ong muyong. 1993. Produced for the National Institute for International Education Development. Korean Film Production. Videocassette (43 minutes).

The Mask Dances of Korea. 1984. Korea Film Production. Videocassette (20 minutes).

P'ansori: Korean Dramatic Songs. 1991. (Director, Lee Chi-wan.) Korea Film Production. Videocassette (38 minutes).

P'ansori (Opera) and Chamber Music from Korea. 1970s. Asia Society. Videocassette (30 minutes).

Poch'on Pogyong Ŭmaktan. 1991. (Recorded in 1991 at a concert in Japan.) Koryo Trading Company. Videocassette (75 minutes).

Puk sori Ching. 1995. KBS Yongsang Saoptan. Videocassette.

Sŏp'yŏnje. 1993. (Directed by Im Kwŏn-taek.) Seoul: T'ae Hung Productions.

Sound from Antiquities and Melody of Nature: A Grand Stage of the Korean Court Music and Dance. Seoul: Kungnip kugagwŏn (National Center for Korean Traditional Performing Arts).

The Sound of Millennia: A Korean Festival of Music and Dance. 1991. (Recorded in 1991 at the Shrine Auditorium in Los Angeles.) Pacific Mountain Network. Korea Foundation. Videocassette (60 minutes).

The Survey of Korean Music. 1996. (Supervision by Byongwon Lee.) National Center for Korean Traditional Performing Arts; Artsource Library (distributor). 2 videocassettes (115 minutes) with booklet.

Taegum. 1995. KBS Yongsang Saoptan. Videocassette.

Uri ŭmak ŭi ihae. 1997. Kugak kyoyuk sich'ŏnggak charyo 4. Kungnip Kugagwŏn (National Center for Korean Traditional Performing Arts). Videocassette (113 minutes).

Europe

Publications on European Music

Note: This guide is a highly selective list of English-language books covering mainly traditional and popular music and associated arts, such as dance, ritual, and sung poetry.

OVERVIEWS

Bohlman, Philip V. 1988. *The Study of Folk Music in the Modern World*. Bloomington: Indiana University Press.

Grout, Donald Jay, and Claude V. Palisca. 1996. *A History of Western Music*, 5th ed. New York: Norton.

Karpeles, Maud. 1956. *Folk Songs of Europe*. London: Novello.

Ling, Jan. 1997. *A History of European Folk Music*. Rochester, N.Y.: University of Rochester Press.

Lund, Cajsa. 1974. *The Sound of Archeology*. Stockholm: Musikmuseet.

Sárosi, Balint. 1978. *Gypsy Music*, trans. Fred MacNicol. Budapest: Corvina.

Wallis, Roger, and Malm, Krister. 1984. *Big Sounds from Small Peoples: The Music Industry in Small Countries*. London: Constable.

West, M. L. 1992. *Ancient Greek Music*. Oxford: Clarendon.

Wiora, Walter. 1966. *European Folk Song: Common Forms in Characteristic Modifications*, trans. Robert Kilben. New York: Leeds Music.

MUSICAL INSTRUMENTS

Andersson, Otto. 1930. *The Bowed-Harp*. London: William Reeves.

Anoyanakis, Fivos. 1979 [1965]. *Greek Popular Musical Instruments*. Athens: National Bank of Greece.

Arbatsky, Yuri. 1953. *Beating the Tupan in the Central Balkans*. Chicago: Newberry Library.

Baines, Anthony. 1960. *Bagpipes*. Oxford: Oxford University Press.

Bentzon, Andreas F. W. 1969. *The Launeddas: A Sardinian Folk Musical Instrument*. Copenhagen: Akademisk Forlag.

Bessaraboff, A. 1941. *Ancient European Musical Instruments*. Cambridge: Harvard University Press.

Bezic, Jerko, et al., eds. 1975. *Traditional Folk Music Instruments of Jugoslavia*. Zagreb: Kolska Knjiga.

Collinson, Francis. 1975. *The Bagpipe: The History of a Musical Instrument*. London: Routledge and Kegan Paul.

Galpin, Francis. 1937. *A Textbook of European Musical Instruments: Their Origin, History, and Character*. London: Williams and Nowgate.

Harrison, Frank L., and Joan Rimmer. 1964. *European Musical Instruments*. London: Norton.

Ling, Jan, et al. 1991. *The Nyckelharpa: Present and Past*. Stockholm: Svea Fonogram.

Müller, Mette. 1972. *From Bone Pipe and Cattle Horn to Fiddle and Psaltery*. Stockholm: Musikhistoriska Museum.

Rimmer, Joan. 1977 [1969]. *The Irish Harp*. Cork: Mercier.

COLLECTIONS

Adler, Israel. 1986. *Epic Ballads*. Judeo-Spanish Ballads from Oral Tradition, 2, Part 1. Berkeley and Los Angeles: University of California Press. (Musical transcriptions and studies by Israel J. Katz.)

Bartók, Béla. 1954. *Serbo-Croatian Heroic Songs*, trans. Albert B. Lord. Cambridge: Harvard University Press.

Bartók, Béla, and Albert B. Lord. 1951. *Serbo-Croatian Folk Songs*. New York: Columbia University Press.

———. 1978. *Yugoslav Folk Music*, ed. Benjamin Suchoff. Albany, N.Y.: State University of New York Press. (Foreword by George Herzog.)

Bronson, Bertrand H. 1959–1972. *The Traditional Tunes of the Child Ballads*. Princeton: Princeton University Press.

Chianis, Sotirios (Sam). 1965. *Folksongs of Mantinea, Greece*. Berkeley: University of California Press.

Erdely, Stephen. 1994. *The Music of Four Serbo-Croatian Heroic Songs: A Study*. New York: Garland.

Holmboe, Vagn. 1988. *Danish Street Cries: A Study of Their Musical Structure, and a Complete Edition of Tunes with Words Collected before 1960*. Acta Ethnomusicologica Danica, 5. Copenhagen: Forlaget Kragen.

MacColl, Ewan, and Peggy Seeger. 1977. *Travellers' Songs from England and Scotland*. Knoxville: University of Tennessee Press.

Nielsen, Svend. 1982. *Stability in Musical Improvisation: A Repertoire of Icelandic Epic Songs (Rimur)*. Acta Ethnomusicologica Danica, 3. Copenhagen: Forlaget Kragen.

Slobin, Mark, ed. and trans. 1982. *Old Jewish Folk Music: The Collections and Writings of Moshe Beregovski*. Philadelphia: University of Pennsylvania Press.

Traerup, Birthe. 1970. *East Macedonian Folk Songs: Contemporary Traditonal Material from Malesevo, Pijanec, and the Razlog District*. Copenhagen: Akademisk Forlag.

Werner, Eric. 1976. *A Voice Still Heard: The Sacred Songs of the Ashkenazic Jews*. University Park: Pennsylvania State University Press.

MUSIC ETHNOGRAPHIES AND SPECIALIZED STUDIES

Bohlman, Philip V. 1989. *"The Land Where Two Streams Flow": Music in the German-Jewish Community of Israel*. Urbana: University of Illinois Press.

Boyes, Georgina. 1994. *The Imagined Village*. Manchester: Manchester University Press.

Cooke, Peter. 1986. *The Fiddle Tradition of the Shetland Isles*. Cambridge: Cambridge University Press.

Cowdery, James. 1990. *The Melodic Tradition of Ireland*. Kent, Ohio: Kent State University Press.

Finnegan, Ruth. 1989. *The Hidden Musicians. Music-Making in an English Town*. Cambridge: Cambridge University Press.

Flam, Gila. 1992. *Singing for Survival: Songs of the Lodz Ghetto, 1940–1945*. Urbana and Chicago: University of Illinois Press.

Goertzen, Chris. 1997. *Fiddling for Norway*. Chicago: University of Chicago Press.

Hopkins, Pandora. 1986. *Aural Thinking in Norway: Performance and Communication with the Hardingfele*. New York: Human Sciences.

Lortat-Jacob, Bernard. 1994. *Sardinian Chronicles*. Chicago: University of Chicago Press.

Mitchell, Timothy. 1994. *Flamenco Deep Song*. New Haven, Conn.: Yale University Press.

Porter, James, and Herschel Gower. 1995. *Jeannie Robertson: Emergent Singer, Transformative Voice*. Knoxville: University of Tennessee Press.

Rice, Timothy. 1994. *May It Fill Your Soul: Experiencing Bulgarian Music*. Chicago: University of Chicago Press.

Shields, Hugh. 1993. *Narrative Singing in Ireland: Lays, Ballads, Come-All-Yes, and Other Lyric Songs*. Dublin: Irish Academic.

Starkie, Walter. 1933. *Raggle-Taggle: Adventures with a Fiddle in Hungary and Romania*. London: John Murray.

Sugarman, Jane. 1997. *Engendering Song: Singing and Subjectivity at Prespa Albanian Weddings*. Chicago: University of Chicago Press.

Suojanen, Päivikki. 1984. *Finnish Folk Hymn Singing: Study in Music Anthropology*. Tampere: University of Tampere, Institute for Folk Tradition.

Washabaugh, William. 1996. *Flamenco: Passion, Politics, and Popular Culture*. Oxford and Washington, D.C.: Berg.

COUNTRY SURVEYS

Bartók, Béla. 1931. *Hungarian Folk Music*. London: Oxford University Press.

Breathnach, Breandán. 1977. *Folk Music and Dances of Ireland*. Dublin: Mercier.

Collinson, Francis. 1966. *The Traditional and National Music of Scotland*. London: Routledge and Kegan Paul.

Karpeles, Maud. 1987 [1973]. *An Introduction to English Folk Song*. London: Oxford University Press.

Kodály, Zoltán. 1960. *Folk Music of Hungary*, trans. Ronald Tempest and Cynthia Jolly. London: Barrie and Rockliff.

Lloyd, A. L. 1967. *Folk Song in England*. London: Lawrence and Wishart.

Purser, John. 1992. *Scotland's Music: A History of the Traditional and Classical Music of Scotland from Earliest Times to the Present Day*. Edinburgh: Mainstream.

Sárosi, Balint. 1986. *Folk Music: The Hungarian Music Idiom*. Budapest: Corvina.

Sharp, Cecil. 1907. *English Folk-Song: Some Conclusions*. London: Novello, Simpkin.

Warner, Elizabeth, and Evgenii Kustovskii. 1990. *Russian Traditional Folk Song*. Hull, U.K.: Hull University Press.

Williams, W. S. Gwynn. 1933. *Welsh National Music and Dance*. London: J. Curwen.

RITUALS AND CUSTOMS

Alexiou, Margaret. 1974. *The Ritual Lament in Greek Tradition*. Cambridge: Cambridge University Press.

Bendix, Regina. 1985. *Progress and Nostalgia: Silvesterklausen in Unäsch, Switzerland*. Berkeley: University of California Press.

Danforth, Loring. 1989. *Firewalking and Religious Healing: The Anastinaria of Greece and the*

American Firewalking Movement. Princeton, N.J.: Princeton University Press.

Glassie, Henry. 1982. *Passing the Time in Ballymenone: Culture and History of an Ulster Community*. Philadelphia: University of Pennsylvania Press.

Kligman, Gail. 1981. *Căluş: Symbolic Transformation in Romanian Ritual*. Chicago: University of Chicago Press.

———. 1988. *The Wedding of the Dead: Ritual, Poetics, and Popular Culture in Transylvania*. Berkeley: University of California Press.

DANCE

Cowan, Jane. 1990. *Dance and the Body Politic in Northern Greece*. Princeton, N.J.: Princeton University Press.

Flett, J. F., and T. M. Flett. 1985. *Traditional Dancing in Scotland*. London: Routledge and Kegan Paul.

Katsarova, Raina, and Kiril Djenev. 1976. *Bulgarian Folk Dances*. Cambridge, Mass.: Slavica.

Petrides, Ted. 1975. *Folk Dances of the Greeks*. Jericho, N.Y.: Exposition.

Popescu-Judetz, Eugenia. 1979. *Sixty Folk Dances of Romania*. Pittsburgh: Duquesne University Tamburitzans, Institute of Folk Arts.

Sharp, Cecil, and A. P. Oppé. 1924. *The Dance: An Historical Survey of Dancing in Europe*. London: Halton and Truscott Smith.

Torp, Lisbet. 1990. *Chain and Round Dance Patterns: A Method for Structural Analysis and Its Application to European Material*. 3 vols. Copenhagen: University of Copenhagen, Museum Tusculanum Press.

SONG POETRY

Aulestia, Gorka. 1995. *Improvisational Poetry from the Basque Country*. Reno: University of Nevada Press.

Bailey, James, and Tatiana Ivanova. 1998. *Anthology of Russian Oral Epics*. New York: M. E. Sharpe.

Beissinger, Margaret H. 1991. *The Art of the Lautar: The Epic Tradition of Romania*. New York: Garland.

Entwhistle, William J. 1939. *European Balladry*. Oxford: Clarendon.

Kolsti, John. 1990. *The Bi-Lingual Singer: A Study in Albanian and Serbo-Croatian Oral Epic Traditions*. New York: Garland.

Lord, Albert B. 1960. *The Singer of Tales*. Cambridge: Harvard University Press.

———. 1991. *Epic Singers and Oral Tradition*. Ithaca, N.Y.: Cornell University Press.

Vargyas, Lajos. 1983. *Hungarian Ballads and the European Ballad Tradition*. Budapest: Akadémiai Kiadó.

Zguta, Russell. 1978. *Russian Minstrels: A History of the Skomorokhi*. Oxford: Clarendon.

POPULAR MUSIC

Butterworth, Katherine, and Sarah Schneider. 1975. *Rebetika: Songs from the Old Greek Underworld*. Athens: Kolomboi.

Cushman, Thomas. 1995. *Notes from Underground: Rock Music Counterculture in Russia*. Albany: State University of New York Press.

Hebdige, Dick. 1979. *Subculture: The Meaning of Style*. London: Methuen.

Holst, Gail. 1977. *Road to Rembetika: Music of a Greek Sub-Culture: Songs of Love, Sorrow, and Hashish*. Limni and Athens: Denise Harvey.

———. 1980. *Theodorakis: Myth and Politics in Modern Greek Music*. Amsterdam: Adolf M. Hakkert.

Larkey, Edward. 1993. *Pungent Sounds: Constructing Identity with Popular Music in Austria*. Austrian Culture, 9. New York: Peter Lang.

Mitchell, Tony. 1996. *Popular Music and Local Identity*. London: Leicester University Press.

Oliver, Paul, ed. 1990. *Black Music in Britain: Essays on the Afro-Asian Contribution to Popular Music*. Milton Keynes: Open University Press.

Prendergast, Mark J. 1987. *Isle of Noises: Rock and Roll Roots in Ireland*. New York: St. Martin's.

Ramet, Sabrina Petra, ed. 1994. *Rocking the State: Rock Music and Politics in Eastern Europe and Russia*. Boulder, Colo.: Westview.

Ryback, Timothy. 1990. *Rock Around the Bloc: A History of Rock Music in Eastern Europe and the Soviet Union*. New York: Oxford University Press.

Smith, Gerald. 1984. *Songs to Seven Strings: Russian Guitar Poetry and Soviet "Mass" Song*. Bloomington: Indiana University Press.

Starr, S. Frederic. 1994. *Red and Hot: The Fate of Jazz in the Soviet Union, 1917–1991*. New York: Limelight Editions.

Taylor, Timothy. 1997. *Global Pop: World Music, World Markets*. New York: Routledge.

Troitsky, Artemy. 1987. *Back in the USSR: The True Story of Rock in Russia*. Boston and London: Faber.

Recordings of European Traditional Music

COLLECTIONS

Europe. 1994. Le monde des musiques traditionnelles/The World of Traditional Music/Musikkulturen der Welt/El mundo de las músicas tradicionales, 6. Produced by Christian Poché. Ocora/Radio France C560066. Booklet in French, English, German, Spanish. Compact disk.

Musique à la croisée des cultures/Music at the Crossroads. 1995. Artistic direction by Laurent Aubert. Archives Internationales de Musique Populaire and Disques VDE-GALLO CD 828–29. 75-page booklet in French and English. 2 compact disks.

Unblocked: Music of Eastern Europe. 1997. Ellipsis Arts CD 3570. *Eastern Voices, Northern Shores* (CD 3571), *From the Danube through the Carpathians* (CD 3572), *The Balkans* (CD 3573). 72-page booklet. 3 compact disks.

World Network. 1991–1997. Recordings made in Germany at concerts, festivals, and studios, and in the field. Edited by Christian Scholze and Jean Trouillet with Jan Reichow of WDR Westdeutscher Rundfunk. Network Medien GmbH, D-6-316 Frankfurt. Distributed by Zweitausendeins Versand, Frankfurt. Notes in German,

English, and French. Vol. 2 (1991; Nr. 52.985), Georgia; Vol. 4 (1991; Nr. 52.987), Crete; Vol. 11 (1992; Nr. 54.038), Portugal; Vol. 15 (1993; Nr. 55.832), France; Vol. 16 (1993; Nr. 55.833), Ireland; Vol. 24 (1994; Nr. 56.982), The Alps; Vol. 25 (1994; Nr. 56.983), Spain; Vol. 26 (1994; Nr. 56.984), Russia; Vol. 31 (1995; Nr. 58.393), Corsica/Sardinia; Vol. 32 (1995; Nr. 58.394), Scotland; Vol. 41 (1997; Nr. 28.300), Romania. 42 compact disks.

TRANSNATIONAL GROUPS

Atlan, Françoise. N.d. *Françoise Atlan: Romances Sefardies—Entre la rose et le jasmin/Sephardic Songs—From the Rose to the Jasmine*. Musique de monde/Music from the World. Notes and texts in French and English by Sami Sadak. Buda 92574-2. Compact disk.

Basque Country: Traditional and Contemporary Songs. N.d. Ocora/Radio France C 559083. Compact disk.

Chants du pays basque/Songs from the Basque Country. 1993 [1977]. Arion ARN 64223. Notes in French and English by Jean Haritschelhar. Compact disk.

Chants populaires Yiddish/Popular Yiddish Songs. N.d. Musique de monde/Music of the World. Notes and texts in French and English by Sami Sadak. Buda 92595-2. Compact disk.

Klezmer à la russe: Musiques juives d'Europe orientale. 1996. Recording by Christian Feldgen. Maison des Cultures du Monde W260066. Notes in French and English by Andreas Karpen and Kasbek. Compact disk.

Klezmer Music: A Marriage of Heaven and Earth. 1996. Musical Expeditions. 64-page booklet with essays by Michael Alpert, Frank London, and Andy Statman. Ellipsis Arts 4090. Compact disk.

Máramoros: The Lost Jewish Music of Transylvania—Muzsikás. 1993. Produced by Daniel Hamar and Muzsikás. Notes in English by Muzsikás and Judit Frigyesi. Hannibal Records HNCD 1373. Compact disk.

Musiciens Manouches en Roussillon/Gypsy Manouches from Roussillon: Zaïti. 1992. Recorded by Clément Ziegler. Notes by Pierre Parce, Daniel Elziere, and Hermine Duran. Al Sur ALCD 107. Compact disk.

Rubin and Horowitz: Bessarabian Symphony—Early Jewish Instrumental Music. 1994. Notes in German and English. Wergo Sm 1606-2. Spectrum 281606-2. Compact disk.

BRITAIN AND IRELAND

Bannal: Waulking Songs. 1996. Produced by Jim Sutherland. Notes and texts in Gaelic and English. Greentrax CDTRAX 099. Compact disk.

Bowen, Robin Hue. 1993. *Telyn Berseiniol fy Ngwlad/The Sweet Harp of My Land*. Notes in Welsh and English. Flying Fish FF 70610. Compact disk.

Ceol Mor, Ceol Beag: Iain MacFadyen. 1996. Produced by Robin Morton. Temple Records COMD2018. Compact disk.

The Drones and the Chanters: Irish Pipering, Vol. 2. 1994. Claddagh Records CC61 CD. Compact disk.

England. 1998. World Library of Folk and Primitive Music, 1. Recorded by Alan Lomax, Maurice Brown, Douglas Cleverdon, and others between

1939 and 1951. Rounder ROUN 1741. Compact disk.

English Roots Music: The Rough Guide. N.d. Rough Guide/World Music Network RGNET 1018CD. Compact disk.

From Galway to Dublin: Early Recordings of Traditional Irish Music. 1993. Recorded in Ireland, England, and America between 1921 and 1959. Rounder CD 1087. Compact disk.

The Gentlemen Pipers. 1994. Notes by Ron Kavana. Globestyle CDORBD 084. Compact disk.

Green Linnet Records: The Twentieth Anniversary Collection. 1996. Notes by Myron Bretholz and Wendy Newton. Green Linnet GLCD 106-1–106-2. Compact disk.

Ireland: Irlande. 1997. Traditional Musics of Today/Musiques traditionnelles d'aujourd'hui. UNESCO Collection. Recording and notes in English and French by Rionach Ui Ógáin. Auvidis and Unesco D 8271. Compact disk.

Irish Music: The Rough Guide. N.d. Rough Guide/World Music Network RGNET 1006CD. Compact disk.

McDonagh, John. 1994. *An Spailpín Fánach: Traditional Songs from Connemara*. Notes and texts in Irish and English. Cló-Iar-Chonnachta CICD 006. Compact disk.

The Muckle Sangs: Classic Scots Ballads. 1992. Scottish Tradition Series, 5. Produced by School of Scottish Studies, University of Edinburgh. Greentrax Records CDTRAX 9005. Compact disk.

Music at Matt Molloy's. 1992. Realworld and Caroline CAROL 2324-2. Compact disk.

The Northumbrian Small Pipes. 1996. Produced by Tony Engle. Notes by Colin Ross. Topic Records TSCD 487. Compact disk.

Scotland: Tunes from the Lowlands, Highlands, and Islands. 1995. World Network, 32. Notes by Thomas Daun. World Network WDR 58.394. Compact disk.

Scottish Music: The Rough Guide. N.d. Rough Guide/World Music Network RGNET 1004CD. Compact disk.

SCANDINAVIA, FINLAND, AND THE BALTIC STATES

Årsringar: Swedish Folk Music 1970–1990. 1990. Notes in Swedish by Per Gudmundson and Ale Möller. 2 compact disks. Musiknätet MNWCD 194–195. Compact disk.

Bjørkum, Per Saemund. 1994. *Den våre fela.* Produced by Hans Fredrik Jacobsen. Notes in Norwegian and English. Heilo HCD 7094. Compact disk.

Buen, Knut. 1996. *Knut Buen: As Quick as Fire.* Produced by Peter K. Siegel. Henry Street Records HSR 0002. Compact disk. (Norway: Hardanger fiddle.)

Ensemble Rasa. 1995. *Lettonie: Musiques des rites solaires/Latvia: Music of Solar Rites.* Inédit. Notes and texts by Valdis Muktupāvels, in French and English. Maison des Cultures du Monde W 260062. Compact disk.

Finlande: Musique traditionnelle/Finland: Traditional Music. 1996. Recorded by Yleisradio (National Radio of Finland) between 1941 and 1995. Notes by Sirkka Halonen. Ocora C600004. Compact disk.

Föregdångare. 1993. Folk-music recordings from the Archive of Swedish National Radio, 1949–1967. Notes by Märta Ramsten in Swedish and English. MNW CD 240–242. 3 compact disks.

JPP: Devil's Polska: New Finnish Folk Fiddling. 1994. Green Linnet GLCE 4012. Compact disk.

JPP: Kaustinen Rhapsody. 1994. Green Linnet GLCD 4019. Compact disk.

Kuulas Hetki. 1993. Sibelius-Akatemian Kansanmusiikin Osaston Äänitteitä, 1. OMCD-46. Compact disk.

Lien, Annbjørg. 1995. *Annbjørg Lien: Felefeber—Norwegian Fiddle Fantasia.* Shanachie 64060. Compact disk.

Lituanie: Le pays des chansons/Lithuania: The Country of Songs. 1997. Recorded by Luetuvos Radijas between 1958 and 1995. Notes by Antanas Fokas in English and Lithuanian. Ocora C 600005. Compact disk.

Lockrop och Vallåtar: Ancient Swedish Pastoral Music. 1996. Musica Sveciae/Folk Music in Sweden, 8. Recorded mainly between 1949 and 1964, with additional contemporary performances. Notes by Anna Ivarsdotter, in Swedish and English. Caprice CAP 21483. Compact disk.

Musica Sveciae: Folk Music in Sweden. 1994–1997. Produced by Anna Frisk. Notes in Swedish, English, and Finnish. Caprice Records CAP 21474-85. 25 compact disks.

Nordisk Sang: Music of Norway. 1991. Produced by Hans Wendl. New Albion Records NA 031. Compact disk.

Suède-Norvège: Musiques des vallées scandinaves. 1993. Notes by Jean-Pierre Yvert in French, English, and German. Distributed by Harmonia Mundi. Ocora C 560008. Compact disk.

The Kalevala Heritage: Archive Recordings of Ancient Finnish Songs. 1995. Compiled from recordings in the Archives of the Finnish Literature Society. Notes in English. Ondine ODE 849-2. Compact disk.

Valimik Eesti Rahvalaule/Anthology of Estonian Folk Songs. 1994. Compiled and annotated by Ingrid Rüütel, Estonian Folklore Archives. Forte FD 0012/2. Compact disk.

Värtinä: Seleniko. 1993. Green Linnet GLCD 4006. Compact disk.

Voix des pays baltes/Baltic Voices: Chants traditionnels de Lattonie, Lituanie, Estonie. 1994. Inédit. Compiled from recordings in radio archives, 1937–1985. Notes by Mārtiņ Boiko, Daiva Račiunaite-Vičiniene, and Vaike Sarv, in French and English. Maison des Cultures du Monde W 260055. Compact disk.

WESTERN EUROPE

Andalusian Flamenco Song and Dance: Lomas, DeMalaga. N.d. Lyrichord 7388. Compact disk.

Arnaud Maisonneuve: Songs of Lower Brittany. N.d. Ocora C559082. Compact disk.

Ballads, Songs, and Dances from Flanders and Wallonia. N.d. Ocora C580061. Compact disk.

Coeur de France: Music from Central France. 1997. Music from Limousin, Berry, Bourbonnais, Cenre, and Auvergne. Notes in English and French. Ethnic/Auvidis B 6848. Compact disk.

Corsica: Traditional Songs and Music. 1990. Music of Man Archives. Recorded by Wolfgang Laade in 1958 and 1973. Jecklin-Disco JD 650-2. Compact disk.

Donnisultana Per Agata: Polyphonies Corses. 1992. Notes by Ghjermana de Zerbi and Ghjacumu Fusina, in Italian, English, and French. Silex Y225019. Compact disk.

Duende: From Traditional Masters to Gypsy Rock. 1994. Ellipsis Arts ELLI CT 3350. 3 compact disks.

Duende: Passion: Voices of Flamenco. 1996. Produced by Angel Romero. Notes by A. Romero. Ellipsis Arts ELLI CD 3351. Compact disk.

El Barullo [and] Maraito: Plazuela. 1995. Flamenco Vivo. Notes in Spanish, English, and French. Auvidis/Ethnic B 6814. Compact disk.

Eriik Marchand and Thierry Robin: Songs of Central Brittany. N.d. Ocora C559084. Compact disk.

Fados de Lisboa 1928–1936. 1992. Fados from Portugal, 1. Notes by Paul Vernon. Heritage HT CD 14. Compact disk.

Flamenco: The Rough Guide. N.d. Rough Guide/World Music Network RGNET 1015CD. Compact disk.

France: Landes de Goscogne—La Cornemuse. 1996. Notes in French by Lothaire, with English and German translations. Ocora Radio France C560051. Compact disk.

Het daghet inden Oosten: It's Dawning in the East, Bagpipes of the Low Countries. 1995. Notes by Bert Lotz, in English. Pan Records PAN 2025CD. Compact disk.

In Dialetto Sardo: Music of Sardinia 1930–1932. 1993. Notes by Paul Vernon. Translation of lyrics by Maria Teresa Orru Babbage. Heritage HT CD 20. Compact disk.

Italia: Donne della pianura del Po/Italie: Femmes de ka Plaune du Pô/Italy: Women of the Po Valley.

1997. Notes in English and French. Ethnic B 6846. Compact disk.

Italian Treasury: Folk Music and Song of Italy—A Sampler. 1999. Recordings by Alan Lomax and Diego Carpitella. Rounder ROUN1801. Compact disk.

Italie: Polyphonie Génoise/Italy: Genoese Polyphony. N.d. Musique du monde/Music of the World. Notes by Franck Tenaille in English and French. Buda Records 92514-2. Compact disk.

Melis, Efisio. 1995. *Efisio Melis: Les Launeddas en Sardaigne 1930–1950.* Notes by Roberto Leydi and Pietro Sassu, in Italian, French, and English. Silex Memoire Y225106. Compact disk.

The Music of Portugal: The Rough Guide. N.d. Rough Guide/World Music Network RGNET 1025CD. Compact disk.

Musical Traditions of Portugal. 1994. Traditional Music of the World, 9. Recorded by Tiago de Oliveira Pinto and Max Peter Baumann in 1988. Notes by Salwa El-Shawan Castelo-Branco, in English and Portuguese. Distributed by KOCH International. Smithsonian Folkways CD SF 40435. Compact disk.

Musique populaire de la Belgique/Volksmuziek uit Belgie/Folk Music from Belgium. 1997. Recorded by Hubert Boone. Notes by Piet Chielens, with English and French translations. Ethnic/Auvidis B6844. 2 compact disks.

Les musiques de Bretagne/The Sounds of Brittany. 1991. Notes by E. Lehtela. Keltia Musique KMCD 19. Compact disk.

Planet Flanders: Music of Allochthones in Flanders/ Muziek van Allochtonen in Vlaanderen. 1996. Notes by Al de Boeck. Presented by the Intercultural Centre for Migrants. Distributed by Arhoolie. PAN POCC 1006. Compact disk.

Polyphonies de Sardaigne. 1992. Chant du Monde/Musée de l'Homme LDX 274760. Compact disk.

Portugal: Chants et Tamboures de Beira-Baixa/ Portugal: Songs and Drums from Beira-Baixa. 1992. Musique du monde/Music of the World. Notes by Murielle Mignon and Manuel Gomes. Buda Records 92542-2. Compact disk.

Portugal: Les voix de l'Alentejo/Voices of Alentejo. 1994. Notes in French and English. Distributed by Auvidis. Ethnic B6796. Compact disk.

Portugal, a Spirit of Fado: Fado Instrumental. 1993. Un Parfum de Fado, 5. Distributed by Auvidis. Playa Sound PS 65705. Compact disk.

Portuguese Traditional Music. N.d. Auvidis 8008. Compact disk.

Quand les Bretons passent à table/Kanomp ouzh taol. 1994. Tradition vivante de Bretagne, 2. Notes with texts in Breton and French. Dastum DAS 121. Compact disk.

Sacred Music of Corsica: The Chants of Holy Week, Bonifacio. N.d. Ocora C 559086. Compact disk.

Sanacore. N.d. *Sanacore—All' aria—Italie: Cants populaire/Italy: Popular songs.* Musique du monde/ Music of the World. Notes by Tania Pividori, in French and English. Texts in Italian, with translation. Buda 92626-2. Compact disk.

Sardaigne: Les maîtres de la musique instrumentale. 1995. Produced by Michel Pagiras. Notes by Roberto Leydi. Al Sur ALCD 157. Compact disk.

Skolvan: Kerzh Ba'n' Dans/Entrez dans la danse/ Come to the Dance. 1991. Keltia Musique KMCD 16. Compact disk.

Soñj: Kanticõu E Vro Briez/Musiques sacrées de Bretagne/Sacred Music of Brittany. 1991. Keltia Musique KMCD 17. Compact disk.

Storvvan: Digor'n Abadenn: Ouvrons la ronde/Join in the Round. 1991. Keltia Musique KMCD 24. Compact disk.

Suspiro del Moro: Flamenco and Moorish Roots. 1995. Musique du monde/Music of the World.

Notes by Marc Loopoyt, in French, Spanish, and English. Buda Records 92625-2. Compact disk.

Tenores di Bitti: S'amore 'e mama. 1996. A WOMAD Production. RealWorld CAR 2362-2. Compact disk.

Triskell-Servat: L'albatros fou/The Foolish Albatross. 1991. Keltia Musique KMCD 22.

Utrera, Fernando de. 1987. *Cante Flamenco: Fernando et Bernarda de Utrera*, Vols. 1–2. Notes by Antonio Espana, in Spanish with English and French translations. Ocora C558642/43. 2 compact disks.

La vielle en France: Les maîtres de la vielle à roue/ Hurdy-Gurdy in France: Hurdy-Gurdy Masters. N.d. Notes in English and French. Recorded between 1930 and 1991. Silex Memoire Y 225109. Compact disk.

Zampogne en Italie: Enregistrements 1969–1989. Produced by André Ricros. Notes by Roberto Leydi, with English translation by Mary Pardoe and French translation by Maria Costa. Silex France Y225111. Compact disk.

Zampogne en Italie/Zampogne Italian Bag-Pipes. N.d. Music of Latium, Molise, Campania, Basilicate, Calabria, and Sicily. Recorded between 1969 and 1989. Notes in English, French, and Italian. Silex Memoire Y 225111. Compact disk.

CENTRAL EUROPE

Austrian Folk Music, Vols. 1 and 2. N.d. Arhoolie 3003. Compact disk.

Austrian Zither. N.d. Playasound 65067. Compact disk.

Burgenland. 1993. Tondokumente zur Volksmusik in Österreich, 1. RST Records 915572-2. 2 compact disks.

Czechoslovakia. N.d. Planett 242003. Compact disk.

Fire in the Mountains: Polish Mountain Fiddle Music, Vols. 1 and 2. 1997. Compiled from 78-RPM recordings issued in 1928 and 1929. Yazoo 7012/7013. Compact disk.

Hungary and Romania: Descendants of the Itinerant Gypsies—Melodies of Sorrow and Joy. 1997.

Music of the Earth. Recording and notes by Minoru Morita. Produced by Stephen McArthur. Recordings drawn from *Music of the Earth: Fieldworkers' Sound Collections* (Victor Company of Japan, JVC, 1992). Multicultural Media MCM 3010. Compact disk.

Juuzli: Muotatal Jodel. N.d. Chant du Monde 274716. Compact disk.

Moskowitz, Joseph. 1996. *The Art of the Cymbalom: The Music of Joseph Moskowitz 1916–1953.* Recorded in the United States. Rounder CD 1126. Compact disk.

Mountain Songs and Yodeling of the Alps. N.d. Smithsonian Folkways 8807. Compact disk.

Music of the Tatra Mountains: Gienek Wilczek's Bukowina Band. 1996. Nimbus NI 5464. Compact disk.

Musiques traditionnelles de Hongrie/Hungarian Traditional Music: Tanchaz. 1993. Distributed by Auvidis. Playa Sound PS 65117. Compact disk.

Pologne: Chansons et danses populaires/Poland: Folk Songs and Dances. 1993. AIMP, 29. Recorded between 1972 and 1992. Notes by Anna Czekanowska. VDE CD 757. Compact disk.

Pologne: Danses. 1992. Texts in French and English. Arion ARN 64188. Compact disk.

Sebö: Hungarian Folk Music. 1993 [1980]. Originally issued by Hungaroton. Rounder CD 5005. Compact disk.

EASTERN EUROPE

Byelorussia. N.d. Auvidis 8005/8805. Compact disk.

Chants des bords de la Mer Noire/Songs from the Shores of the Black Sea: Georgians, Crimean Greeks, Kuban Cossacks. 1994. Produced by Tamara Pavlova and Ekaterina Dorokhova. Chant du Monde CDM LDX 274980. Compact disk.

Chants traditionnels de l'Ukraine/Traditional Songs of the Ukraine. 1993. Notes in French and English. Distributed by Auvidis. Ethnic/Auvidis B6780. Compact disk.

The Dmitri Pokrovsky Ensemble: The Wild Field. N.d. Researched, adapted, and arranged by Dmitri

Pokrovsky. A WOMAD production. RealWorld CD RW 17. Compact disk.

Georgia: The Real Polyphony of the Caucausus. 1997. Produced by Stephen McArthur. Music of the Earth. Recording and notes by Minoru Morita. Recordings drawn from *Music of the Earth: Fieldworkers' Sound Collections* (Victor Company of Japan, JVC, 1992). Multicultural Media MCM 3004. Compact disk.

Géorgie: Polyphonies de Svanétie/Georgia: Polyphony of Svaneti. 1994. Collection CNRS—Musée de l'Homme. Recordings by Sylvie Bolle-Zemp. Notes by Sylvie Bolle-Zemp, in French and English. Distributed by Harmonia Mundi

France. Chant du Monde LDX 274990. Compact disk.

Journey to the USSR. N.d. Chant du Monde 274920–274925. 6 compact disks.

The Music of Eastern Europe: The Rough Guide. N.d. Rough Guide/World Music Network RGNET 1024CD. Compact disk.

Music of the Tatar People. N.d. Tangent 129. Compact disk.

Musics of the Soviet Union. 1989. Smithsonian Folkways 40002. Compact disk.

Musique traditionnelles d'Ukraine, 1ère partie/ *Traditional Music from the Ukraine*, 1. 1993. Music of Steppe, Carathians, Western Podolie, and Boykivshchena. Notes in French, English, and Ukrainian. Silex 225211. Compact disk.

Old Believers: Songs of the Nekrasov Cossacks. 1995. Compiled and annotated by Margarita Mazo, with Olga Velichkina. Notes with texts in English translation. Smithsonian Folkways CD 40462. Compact disk.

Polyphonic Work Songs and Religious Chants. N.d. Ocora C559062. Compact disk.

Rustavi Choir. *Georgian Voices.* 1989. Nonesuch 79224. Compact disk.

The Terem Quartet: Terem. 1992. RealWorld CD RW 23. Compact disk.

Trio of Bandura Players: Ukrainian Folk Songs. 1992. MCA Classics. Distributed by MCA. Art and Electronics AED 10479. Compact disk.

Ukraine. N.d. Auvidis 8206. Compact disk.

Ukrainian Village Music: Historic Recordings 1928–1933. 1994. Produced by Chris Strachwitz. Edited by Dick Spottswood. Arhoolie/Folklyric CD 7030. Reissue. Compact disk.

THE BALKANS

A Harvest, a Shepherd, a Bride: Village Music of Bulgaria: Songs and Dances from the Regions of Pirin-Macedonia (Southwest), Rhodope (South), Thrace (Southeast), and Shope (Midwest) and *In the Shadow of the Mountain: Bulgarian Folk Music: Songs and Dances of Pirin-Macedonia.* 1988 [1970, 1971]. Recorded and produced by Ethel Raim and Martin Koenig in Bulgaria in 1968. Notes by Martin Koenig with Vergilii Atanasov, in English. Elektra/Asylum/Nonesuch Records 9 79195-2. Reissue of Nonesuch H-72034 (1970) and H-72038 (1971). Compact disk.

Balkana: The Music of Bulgaria. 1987. Produced by Joe Boyd and Rumyana Tsintsarka. Hannibal Records HNBL 1335. Compact disk.

Bosnia: Echoes from an Endangered World: Music and Chant of the Bosnian Muslims. 1993. Recorded, compiled, and annotated by Ted Levin and Ankica Petrović. Distributed by Koch International. Smithsonian Folkways CD SF 40407. Compact disk.

Bulgarian All Star Orchestra. 1997. *Dushá: The Soul of Bulgaria.* Produced by Christian Scholze and Jean Trouillet. Network Medien 25.829. 2 compact disks.

Bulgarie: Rhodope-Dobroudja. 1994. Anthologie de la musique bulgare, 2. Chant du Monde CDM LDX 274975. Compact disk.

Chants et danses croates/Croatian Folksongs and Dances. 1992. Recordings by Hungarian Radio Broadcasting between 1953 and 1985. Edited by Gábor Eredics. Distributed by Harmonia Mundi. Quintana QUI 903071. Compact disk.

Croatie: Musiques d'autrefois/Croatia: Music of Long Ago. 1997. Recordings by Hrvatski Radio, 1958–1993. Notes by Grozdana Marošević, in Croatian and English. Ocora C 600006. Compact disk.

Ensemble Vocal de Gjirokastër. 1995. *Albanie: Polyphonies Vocales du Pays Lab.* Collected by Françoise Gründe, Notes by Pierre Bois, in French, with English translation by Judith Crews. Maison des Cultures du Monde. Compact disk.

Fanfare Paysanne de Zece Prăjini/Žese Prăjini's Peasant Brass Band. N.d. Musique du monde/Music of the World, 2, Roumanie. Notes by Speranţa Rădulescu, in English and French. Buda 92655-2. Compact disk.

Folk Music of Bulgaria. 1994 [1966]. Topic World Series. Collected and edited by A. L. Lloyd. Topic TSCD 905. Compact disk.

Folk Music of Yugoslavia (Croatia, Bosnia-Hercegovina, Serbia, and Macedonia). 1994. Topic World Series. Collected and edited by Wolf Dietrich. Topic TSCD 906. Compact disk.

Gaida Orchestra: Bagpipe Music from the Rhodope Mountains. 1992. JVC World Sounds. JVC VICG 5224. Compact disk.

Greek Traditional Village Music and Dance. 1994. World Music Library, 76. Notes in English. Seven Seas/King Records KICC 5176. Compact disk.

Hungary and Romania: Descendants of the Itinerant Gypsies—Melodies of Sorrow and Joy. 1997. Music of the Earth. Recordings and notes by Minoru Morita. Produced by Stephen McArthur. Recordings drawn from *Music of the Earth: Fieldworkers' Sound Collections* (Victor Company of Japan [JVC], 1992). Multicultural Media MCM 3010. Compact disk.

Jova "Besir" Stojiljkovic and His Brass Orkestar. 1995. *Blow "Besir" Blow!* Globestyle GSUS038. Compact disk.

Kalesijski Zvuci. 1992. *Bosnian Breakdown: The Unpronounceable Beat of Sarajevo.* Notes by Kim Burton. Globestyle CDORBD 074. Compact disk.

King Ferus Mustafov. 1995. *Macedonian Wedding Soul Cooking.* Globestyle GSUS089. Compact disk.

Krächno Horo. 1994. *Musiques populaires de Bulgarie.* Produced by André Ricros. Notes by Erik Marchand, in French. Silex Mosaique 225217. Compact disk.

L'orient des Grecs/The Orient of the Greeks. N.d. Rebetika music in the Smyrna style, compiled mainly from historical recordings. Musique du monde/Music of the World. Notes by Philippe Zani, in English and French. Buda 92659-2. Compact disk.

Laver Bariu. 1995. *Laver Bariu: Songs from the City of Roses.* Produced by Ben Mandelson and Kim Burton. Notes by Kim Burton. Globestyle CDORBD 091. Compact disk.

Music From Albania. 1999. Anthology of World Music. Rounder ROUN 5151. Compact disk.

Musique de la Grèce continentale/Music from Continental Greece. 1995. Produced by Michel Pagiras and Clement Ziegler. Notes in French and lyrics in French, English, and Greek. Al Sur ALCD 138. Compact disk.

Muzar, Virgil. 1996. *Roumanie/Romania: Virgil Muzar: Le maître du violon roumain/Master of the Romanian Fiddle.* Notes in English and French. Ethnic/Auvidis B6821. Compact disk.

Narodne pjesme i plesovi iz Banije/Folk Songs and Dances from Banija. 1987–1989. Notes with texts by Grozdana Marošević and Svanibor Pettan, in English and Croatian. Jugoton ULP-2050/2286/2464. Compact disk.

Papasov, Ivo. 1989. *Ivo Papasov and His Bulgarian Wedding Band: Orpheus Ascending.* Produced by Joe Boyd and Rumyana Tzintzarska. Hannibal Records HNCD 1346. Compact disk.

Reflections of Romania: Village and Urban Folk Traditions. N.d. Nonesuch 72092. Compact disk.

Rembetica: Historic Urban Folk Songs from Greece. 1992. Produced by Charles Howard and Dick Spottswood. Translations and transcriptions by Charles Howard. Rounder CD 1079. Compact disk.

Roumanie: La vraie tradition de Transylvanie. 1989. Recordings and notes by Herman C. Vuylsteke. Reissue of Ocora 558596. Ocora C 559070. Compact disk.

Serbie: Danses et melodies pastorales—Musiques traditionnelles de la Serbie orientale/Serbia: Pastoral Dances and Melodies—Traditional Music from Eastern Serbia. 1991. Notes in French and English. Distributed by Auvidis. Ethnic B6759. Compact disk.

Sestri Bisserovi: Pirin Wedding and Ritual Songs. 1995. Choral Series. Notes by Elena Stoin and Lyubimka Bisserova, in English. Pan Records PAN 7005 CD. Compact disk.

Song of the Crooked Dance: Early Bulgarian Traditional Music, 1927–1942. 1998. Produced by Lauren Brody. Compiled from 78-RPM recordings. Yazoo 7016. Compact disk.

Songs and Dances of Yugoslavia. N.d. Playasound 65044. Compact disk.

Taraf de Haïdouks. 1998. *Dumbala Dumba.* 1998. Crammed Discs CRAW 21. Compact disk.

Taraf: Romanian Gypsy Music. 1996. Music from villages in the Danube Plain, Muntenia Province. Recorded by Speranţa Rădulescu, Valeriu Rădulescu, and Adrian Hotoiu. Produced by Martha Lorantos and Bob Haddad. Notes by Speranţa Rădulescu. Music of the World CDT-137. Compact disk.

Village Music of Yugoslavia: Songs and Dances from Bosnia-Herzegovina, Croatia, and Macedonia. 1995. Explorer Series. Recorded by Martin Koenig in 1968. Notes by Martin Koenig. Lyrics in Serbo-Croatian with English translations. Reissue of Nonesuch H-72042 (1971). Nonesuch 9 72042-2. Compact disk.

Wild Sounds from Transylvania, Wallachia, and Moldavia. 1997. Romania, 41. Notes in English, French, and German. World Network WDR 28.300. Compact disk.

Films and Videos of European Traditional Music

GENERAL

Encyclopaedia Cinematographica. Distributed by Pennsylvania State University. (Dozens of short black-and-white films on music from Albania, Austria, Czech Republic, Italy, Germany, Montenegro, Norway, Portugal, Romania, Slovakia, and Spain.)

JVC/Smithsonian Folkways Video Anthology of Music and Dances of Europe. 1996. Directed by Hiroshi Yamamoto. Barre, Vt.: Multicultural Media, distributor. 2 parts. 108 min. (Footage from Belgium, Czech Republic, Faroe Islands, Denmark, England, France, Hungary, Iceland, Ireland, Italy, Romania, Scotland, Spain, and Wales.)

Social Dance Music. 1975. University of Minnesota. 60 min. 16mm.

TRANSNATIONAL GROUPS

At the Crossroads: Jews in Eastern Europe Today. 1990. Oren Rudavsky and Yale Strom. New York: Arthur Cantor Prods. 58 min. 16mm.

T'an Bakhtale! (*Good Fortune to You!*): *Roma (Gypsies) in Russia*. 1996. Alaina Lemon and Midori Nakamura. New York: Documentary Educational Resources. 75 min.

The Last Klezmer. 1995. Yale Strom and Bernard Berkin. New York: New Yorker Films. 84 min. VHS.

The Romany Trail, Part 2: *Gypsy Music into Europe*. 1992 [1983]. Jeremy Marre. Newton, N.J.: Shanachie Records. 60 min. VHS.

We Have No War Songs. 1994. Abrahami Netz. New York: Filmakers Library. 53 min.

BRITAIN AND IRELAND

The Bagpipe. 1970. World Mirror—Realist Productions. University of Illinois. 22 min. 16mm.

Ireland's Whistling Ambassador: Micho Russell of Doolin, County Clare. 1993. Bill Ochs. Hinesburg, Vt.: Pennywhistler's Press. 34 min. VHS.

'Oss, 'Oss, Wee 'Oss. N.d. Peter Kennedy, Alan Lomax, and George Pickow. Indiana University. 20 min. 16mm.

Sing of the Border. 1967. British Transport Production. International Film Bureau, Extension Media Center, University of California. 20 min. 16mm.

Song of Seasons. 1978. New York: Canadian Travel Film Library. 27 min. 16mm.

The Story of the Clancy Brothers and Tommy Makem. 1991. David Hammond and Derek Bailey. Newton, N.J.: Shanachie Entertainment. 60 min. VHS.

SCANDINAVIA, FINLAND, AND THE BALTIC STATES

Bingsjölåtar i Pekkosgården. 1963. Lars Egler and Bengt Nordwall. Swedish Broadcasting Corporation. 20 min. 16mm.

Jijk: Da, när var mannen pa Oulavuoli (Joik: The Art of Recall). 1965–1966. Matts Arnberg and Pål-Nils Nilsson. Stockholm: Swedish Broadcasting

Corporation; Lidingö: Pål-Nils Nilsson. 17 min. 16mm.

Leticke, Leticke, Korna är hemma (Leticke, Leticke, the Cows Are Home). 1964. Lars Egler and Bengt Nordwall. Stockholm: Swedish Broadcasting Corporation. 24 min. 16mm.

Norwegian Folk Dances. 1962. Jan Wikbor. National Film Board of Norway and Dance Films. 13 min. 16mm.

Taiga Nomads: The School and the Village. 1991. Heimo Lappalainen and Jouko Aaltonen. Helsinki: Fin Image. 50 min. 16mm.

WESTERN EUROPE

Antonio and Rosario. 1961. Janus Films. Pennsylvania State University. 18 min. 16mm.

Danza flamenco de hoy. 1991. Pilar Perez de Guzman. New York: Alegrías Productions. 60 min. VHS.

Danzas regionales españolas. 1966. Encyclopaedia Britannica Educational Corporation. Extension Media Center, University of California. 17 min. 16mm.

Fiesta gitana! 1994. Rafael Fajardo and Pilar Perez Guzman. New York: Alegrías Productions. 39 min.

Flamenco. N.d. Sueva Films. Brandon Films. 79 min. 16mm.

La guitarra española. 1973. Walter H. Berlet. International Film Bureau, Boston University. 10 min. 16mm.

La jota aragonesa. 1996. Madrid: Videos de la Luz. 53 min.

Le carnaval de Binche. 1963. Studio de Balenfer. Gérard Maton, Binche. 49 min. 16mm.

Musica sarda. 1990. Georges Luneau. France: Centre National de la Recherche Scientifique, Meudon cedex. 70 min. VHS.

Of Pipers and Wrens: De souffle et de roseau. 1997. Lois Kuter, Michael Bailey, and Gei Zantzinger. Devault, Pa.: Constant Spring Productions: Brittany, France: Dastum. 58 min.

The Spanish Guitar. 1992. Rafael Fajardo. New York: Alegrías Productions. 45 min. VHS.

CENTRAL EUROPE

Beruf: Wandermusiker. 1994. Sabine Piechura and Eckhard Schenke. Göttingen, Germany: Institut für den Wissenschaftlichen Film. 46 min.

Kindertänze türkischer Kinder in Deutschland. 1993. Helmut Segler and Andrée Göttingen,

Germany: Kleindienst. Institut für den Wissenschaftlichen Film. 20.5 min.

Message from Gyimes. 1996. Györ, Hungary: Jeno Hartyandi. Mediawave Foundation. 49 min.

My Blood, Your Blood: The Rock Generation in Today's Poland. N.d. New York: Brighton Video. 52 min. VHS.

Village Life and Music in Hungary. 1992. Deben Bhattacharya. Guilford, Conn.: Audio-Forum. 27 min.

EASTERN EUROPE

Discovering Russian Folk Music. 1975. BFA Educational Media. 23 min. l6mm.

Soviet Union: Epic Land. 1971. Encyclopaedia Britannica Educational Corporation. Extension

Media Center, University of California. 29 min. 16mm.

Soviet Union: Faces of Today. 1972. Encyclopaedia Britannica Educational Corporation. Extension

Media Center, University of California. 29 min. 16mm.

USSR and R: Rock on a Red Horse. N.d. Ken Thurlbek. New York: Tapestry International. 88 min. 16mm and VHS.

THE BALKANS

Anastenaria. 1969. Peter Haramis. Extension Media Center, University of California. 17 min. 16mm.

Bryllup i bjergene (Wedding in the Mountains). 1966. Erik Elias. Copenhagen, Denmark: Erik Elias Film Production. 45 min. 16mm.

Dances of Macedonia. N.d. Julian Brian, Kenneth Richter, and Shirley Richter. Contemporary Films. 10 min. 16mm.

Dancing Songs. 1967. Contemporary Films. 10 min. 16mm.

Fire Dancers. 1974. Fleetwood Films. University of Illinois. 11 min. 16mm.

Jakub. 1992. Jana Sevikova. Watertown, Mass.: Documentary Educational Resources. 65 min.

Jugoslav Folk Dances. 1965. Dennis Boxell Films. Extension Media Center, University of California. 55 min. 16mm.

Kalogeros. 1969. Peter Haramis. Extension Media Center, University of California. 12 min. 16mm.

The Mask of the Other Face. 1991. Plamen Sjarov. Prague, Czech Republic: Plamen Sjarov. 18 min. 16mm.

Other Voices, Other Songs: The Greeks. N.d. New York: Sapphire Productions. 30 min. VHS.

Piemule. 1992. Jana Sevikova. Watertown, Mass.: Documentary Educational Resources. 43 min.

Yugoslav National Folk Ballet. 1965. Dennis Boxell Films. Extension Media Center, University of California. 51 min. 16mm.

Australia and the
Pacific Islands

Publications on the Music of Oceania

GENERAL WORKS

The Arts and Politics. 1992. *Pacific Studies* 15(4). Special issue, ed. Karen L. Nero.

Bellwood, Peter, et al., eds. 1995. *The Austronesians: Historical and Comparative Perspectives*. Canberra: Australian National University.

Beloff, Jim. 1997. *The Ukulele: A Visual History*. San Francisco: Miller Freeman.

Chenoweth, Vida. 1972. *Melodic Perception and Analysis: A Manual on Ethnic Melody*. Ukarumpa, Papua New Guinea: Summer Institute of Linguistics.

Finnegan, Ruth, and Margaret Orbell, eds. 1995. *South Pacific Oral Traditions*. Bloomington: Indiana University Press.

Fischer, Hans. 1986. *Sound-Producing Instruments in Oceania*, ed. Don Niles; trans. Philip W. Holzknecht. Boroko: Institute of Papua New Guinea Studies.

Goodenough, Ward H., ed. 1996. *Prehistoric Settlement of the Pacific*. Philadelphia: American Philosophical Society.

Götzfridt, Nicholas J. 1995. *Indigenous Literature of Oceania: A Survey of Criticism and Interpretation*. Westport, Conn., and London: Greenwood.

Hiroa, Te Rangi [Peter H. Buck]. 1953. *Explorers of the Pacific: European and American Discoveries in Polynesia*. Special Publication 43. Honolulu: Bishop Museum.

Irwin, Geoffrey. 1992. *The Prehistoric Exploration and Colonisation of the Pacific*. Oakleigh, Victoria, Australia: Cambridge University Press.

Johnson, L. W. 1983. *Colonial Sunset: Australia and Papua New Guinea 1970–1974*. St. Lucia: University of Queensland Press.

Kaeppler, Adrienne L., and H. Arlo Nimmo, eds. 1976. *Directions in Pacific Traditional Literature: Essays in Honor of Katharine Luomala*. Special Publication 62. Honolulu: Bishop Museum Press.

Linnekin, Jocelyn, and Lin Foyer. 1990. *Cultural Identity and Ethnicity in the Pacific*. Honolulu: University of Hawaii Press.

McLean, Mervyn. 1995. *An Annotated Bibliography of Oceanic Music and Dance*, rev. and enlarged 2nd ed. Detroit Studies in Music Bibliography, 74. Detroit, Mich.: Harmonie Park.

Moyle, Alice Marshall, ed. 1992. *Music and Dance of Aboriginal Australia and the South Pacific: The Effects of Documentation on the Living Tradition*. (Papers and discussions of the Colloquium of the International Council for Traditional Music, held in Townsville, Queensland, in 1988.) Oceania Monograph 41. Sydney: University of Sydney.

Siikala, Jukka, ed. 1990. *Culture and History in the Pacific*. Helsinki: Finnish Anthropological Society.

Smith, Bernard. 1992. *Imagining the Pacific: In the Wake of the Cook Voyages*. New Haven: Yale University Press.

Wendt, Albert, ed. 1995. *Nuanua: Pacific Writing in English since 1980*. Honolulu: University of Hawaii Press.

AUSTRALIA

Barwick, Linda, Allan Marett, and Guy Tunstill, eds. 1995. *The Essence of Singing and the Substance of Song: Recent Responses to the Aboriginal Performing Arts and Other Essays in Honour of Catherine Ellis*. Oceania Monograph 46. Sydney: University of Sydney.

Berndt, R. M., and E. S. Phillips, eds. 1973. *The Australian Aboriginal Heritage: An Introduction through the Arts*. Sydney: Australian Society for Education through the Arts and Ure Smith.

Borsboom, Adrianus P. 1978. *Maradjiri: A Modern Ritual Complex in Arnhem Land, North Australia*. Nijmegen: Katholieke Universiteit.

Breen, Marcus, ed. 1989. *Our Place, Our Music: Aboriginal Music*. Australian Popular Music in Perspective, 2. Canberra: Aboriginal Studies.

Chatwin, Bruce. 1987. *The Songlines*. Harmondsworth, England: Penguin.

Clunies Ross, Margaret, and Stephen A. Wild. 1982. *Djambidj: An Aboriginal Song Series from Northern Australia*. Canberra: Australian Institute of Aboriginal Studies.

Covell, Roger. 1967. *Australia's Music. Themes of a New Society*. Melbourne: Sun.

Dixon, Robert M. W., and Grace Koch. 1996. *Dyirbal Song Poetry: The Oral Literature of an Australian Rainforest People*. St. Lucia: University of Queensland Press.

Elkin, A. P., and Trevor A. Jones. 1953–1957. *Arnhem Land Music (North Australia)*. Oceania Monograph 9. Sydney: University of Sydney.

Ellis, Catherine J. 1985. *Aboriginal Music: Education for Living*. St. Lucia: University of Queensland Press.

Grieve, Ray. 1995. *A Band in a Waistcoat Pocket: The Story of the Harmonica in Australia*. Sydney: Currency.

Hayward, Philip, ed. 1992. *From Pop to Punk to Postmodernism: Popular Music and Australian Culture from the 1960s to the 1990s*. North Sydney: Allen and Unwin.

Johnson, Bruce. 1987. *The Oxford Companion to Australian Jazz*. Melbourne: Oxford University Press.

Mitchell, Ewen. 1996. *Contemporary Aboriginal Music*. Port Melbourne: Ausmusic.

Moyle, Alice M. 1974 [1967]. *Songs from the Northern Territory*. Canberra: Australian Institute of Aboriginal Studies.

————. 1978. *Aboriginal Sound Instruments*. Australian Institute of Aboriginal Studies AIAS 14. (LP disk.)

Moyle, Richard M. 1979. *Songs of the Pintupi: Musical Life in a Central Australian Society*. Canberra: Australian Institute of Aboriginal Studies.

Narogin, Mudrooroo. 1990. *Writing from the Fringe: A Study of Modern Aboriginal Literature*. Melbourne: Hyland House.

Neuenfeldt, Karl William. 1996. *The Didjeridu: From Arnhem Land to Internet*. Sydney: Perfect Beat and John Libbey.

Smith, Jazzer, ed. 1984. *The Book of Australian Country Music*. Sydney: BET Publishing Group.

Sutton, Peter, ed. 1989. *Dreamings: The Art of Aboriginal Australia*. Ringwood, Australia, and London: Viking Penguin.

Turner, Ian. 1969. *Cinderella Dressed in Yella: Australian Children's Play-Rhymes*. Melbourne: Heinemann Educational.

von Brandenstein, C. G., and A. P. Thomas. 1975. *Taruru: Aboriginal Song Poetry from the Pilbara.* Honolulu: University Press of Hawaii.

Walsh, Michael, and Colin Yallop, eds. 1993. *Language and Culture in Aboriginal Australia.* Canberra: Aboriginal Studies.

Wild, Stephen A., ed. 1986. *Rom: An Aboriginal Ritual of Diplomacy.* Canberra: Australian Institute of Aboriginal Studies.

NEW GUINEA

Brennan, Paul W. 1977. *Let Sleeping Snakes Lie: Central Enga Religious Belief and Ritual.* Adelaide: Australian Association for the Study of Religions.

Chenoweth, Vida, ed. 1976. *Musical Instruments of Papua New Guinea.* Ukarumpa: Summer Institute of Linguistics.

———. 1979. *The Usarufas and Their Music.* Publication 5. Dallas: Summer Institute of Linguistics Museum of Anthropology.

———. 1980. *Music for the Eastern Highlands.* Ukarumpa: Summer Institute of Linguistics.

Crawford, Anthony L. 1981. *Aida: Life and Ceremony of the Gogodala.* Bathurst: National Cultural Council and Robert Brown.

Feld, Steven. 1990. *Sound and Sentiment: Birds, Weeping Poetics, and Song in Kaluli Expression,* 2nd ed. Philadelphia: University of Pennsylvania Press.

Gell, Antony Francis. 1975. *Metamorphosis of the Cassowaries: Umeda Society, Language and Ritual.* London: Athlone.

Goodale, Jane C. 1995. *To Sing with Pigs Is Human: The Concept of Person in Papua New Guinea.* Seattle: University of Washington Press.

Harrison, Simon. 1982. *Laments for Foiled Marriages: Love-Songs from a Sepik River Village.* Boroko: Institute of Papua New Guinea Studies.

Herdt, Gilbert H. 1981. *Guardians of the Flutes: Idioms of Masculinity.* New York: McGraw-Hill.

Kasaipwalova, John, and Ulli Beier, eds. 1978. *Yaulabuta: The Passion of Chief Kailaga—An Historical Poem from the Trobriand Islands.* Port Moresby: Institute of Papua New Guinea Studies.

Kunst, Jaap. 1967. *Music in New Guinea: Three Studies,* trans. Jeune Scott-Kemball. Verhandelingen van het Koninklijk Instituut voor Taal-, Land-, en Volkenkunde, 53. The Hague: Martinus Nijhoff.

Lohia, Simon, and Raka Vele. 1977. *Central Guitar Songs.* Boroko: Institute of Papua New Guinea Studies.

McLean, Mervyn. 1994. *Diffusion of Musical Instruments and Their Relation to Language Migrations in New Guinea.* Kulele: Occasional Papers on Pacific Music and Dance, 1. Boroko: Cultural Studies Division, National Research Institute.

Paia, Robert, and Andrew Strathern. 1977. *Beneath the Andaiya Tree: Wiru Songs.* Boroko: Institute of Papua New Guinea Studies.

Schieffelin, Edward L. 1976. *The Sorrow of the Lonely and the Burning of the Dancers.* New York: St. Martin's.

Strathern, Andrea, ed. 1974. *Melpa Amb Kenan.* Port Moresby: Institute of Papua New Guinea Studies.

Talyaga, Kundapen. 1975. *Modern Enga Songs.* Boroko: Institute of Papua New Guinea Studies.

Van Arsdale, Kathleen O. 1981. *Music and Culture of the Bismam Asmat of New Guinea: A Preliminary Investigation.* Hastings, Neb.: Crosier.

Waiko, John D. D. 1993. *A Short History of Papua New Guinea.* Melbourne: Oxford University Press.

Wassmann, Jürg. 1991. *The Song to the Flying Fox: The Public and Esoteric Knowledge of the Important Men of Kandingei about Totemic Songs, Names, and Knotted Cords (Middle Sepik, Papua New Guinea),* trans. Dennis Q. Stephenson. Apwïtïhïre, 2. Boroko: National Research Institute.

Webb, Michael. 1993. *Lokal Music: Lingua Franca Song and Identity in Papua New Guinea.* Apwïtïhïre, 3. Boroko: National Research Institute.

Webb, Michael, and Don Niles. 1986. *Riwain: Papua New Guinea Pop Songs.* Goroka and Bomko: Goroka Teachers College and Institute of Papua New Guinea Studies.

———. 1990. *Ol Singsing Bilong Ples.* Boroko: Institute of Papua New Guinea Studies. (IPNGS 010. Book with 2 cassettes.)

Weiner, James F. 1991. *The Empty Place: Poetry, Space and Being among the Foi of Papua New Guinea.* Bloomington: Indiana University Press.

Williams, Francis Edgar. 1940. *Drama of Orokolo: The Social and Ceremonial Life of the Elema.* Oxford: Clarendon.

Yamada, Yoichi. 1997. *Songs of Spirits: An Ethnography of Sounds in a Papua New Guinea Society.* Apwïtïhïre, 5. Boroko: Institute of Papua New Guinea Studies.

Zahn, Heinrich. 1996. *Mission and Music: Jabêm Traditional Music and the Development of Lutheran Hymnody,* ed. Don Niles; trans. Philip W. Holzknecht. Apwïtïhïre, 4. Boroko: Institute of Papua New Guinea Studies.

MELANESIA

Ammann, Raymond. 1994. *Les danses Kanak: Une introduction.* Nouméa: Agence de Développement de la Culture Kanak.

———. 1997. *Kanak Dance and Music: Ceremonial and Intimate Performance of the Melanesians of New Caledonia, Historical and Actual.* Nouméa: Agence de Développement de la Culture Kanak. (Book with compact disk.)

Bonnemaison, Joël, Kirk Huffman, Christian Kaufmann, and Darrell Tryon, eds. 1997. *Arts of Vanuatu.* Bathurst, Australia: Crawford House.

Chenoweth, Vida. 1984. *A Music Primer for the North Solomons Province.* Ukarumpa: Summer Institute of Linguistics.

Hesse, Karl, with Theo Aerts. 1982. *Baining Life and Lore.* Boroko: Institute of Papua New Guinea Studies.

Layard, John. 1942. *Stone Men of Malekula: Vao.* London: Chatto and Windus.

Lindstrom, Lamont, and Geoffrey White. 1995. *Culture, Kastom, Tradition: Developing Cultural Policy in Melanesia.* Suva: Institute of Pacific Studies, University of the South Pacific.

Stella, Regis. 1990. *Forms and Styles of Traditional Banoni Music.* Apwïtïhïre, 1. Boroko: National Research Institute.

Suri, Ellison. 1980. *Ten Traditional Dances from the Solomon Islands.* Honiara: Solomon Islands Centre, University of the South Pacific.

Tjibaou, Jean-Marie. N.d. *Kaneké: The Melanesian Way,* trans. Christopher Plant. Papeete: Éditions du Pacifique.

Zemp, Hugo. 1995. *Écoute le bambou qui pleure: Récits de quatre musiciens mélanésiens.* Collection L'Aube des Peuples. Paris: Éditions Gallimard.

Zemp, Hugo, and Daniel de Copper. 1978. *'Aré'aré: Un peuple mélanésien et sa musique.* Paris: Éditions du Seuil.

MICRONESIA

Browning, Mary. 1970. *Micronesian Heritage.* Dance Perspectives, 43. New York: Dance Perspectives Foundation.

Burrows, Edwin G. 1963. *Flower in My Ear.* Seattle: University of Washington Press.

Fischer, John L. 1970 [1957, 1966]. *The Eastern Carolines*, rev. ed. New Haven, Conn.: Human Relations Area Files.

Grimble, Arthur Francis. 1989. *Tungaru Traditions: Writings on the Atoll Culture of the Gilbert Islands*, ed. H. E. Maude. Pacific Islands Monograph Series, 7. Honolulu: University of Hawaii Press.

Hijikata, Hisakatsu. 1996. *Myths and Legends of Palau*, ed. Hisashi Endo. Collective Works of Hijikata Hisakatsu. Tôkyô: Sasakawa Peace Foundation.

Maude, Honor. 1971. *The String Figures of Nauru Island.* Adelaide: Libraries Board of South Australia.

Tanabe, Hisao. 1968. *Nanyo, Taiwan, Okanawa Ongaku Kiko* (A Musical Journey to the South Seas, Taiwan, and Okinawa), ed. Toyo Ongaku Gakkai. Tôkyô: Ongaku no Tomosha.

POLYNESIA

Andersen, Johannes C. 1933. *Maori Music with Its Polynesian Background.* Polynesian Society Memoir 10. New Plymouth, New Zealand: Thomas Avery.

Barrère, Dorothy B., Mary Kawena Pukui, and Marion Kelly. 1980. *Hula: Historical Perspectives.* Pacific Anthropological Records, 30. Honolulu: Bishop Museum.

Burrows, Edwin. 1933. *Native Music of the Tuamotus.* Bulletin 109. Honolulu: Bishop Museum.

———. 1945. *Songs of Uvea and Futuna.* Bulletin 183. Honolulu: Bishop Museum.

Christensen, Dieter, and Gerd Koch. 1964. *Die Musik der Ellice-Inseln.* Veröffentlichungen des Museums, Neue Folge 5, Abteilung Südsee 2. Berlin: Museum für Völkerkunde. (Book with 45-rpm record.)

Davey, Tim, and Horst Puschmann. 1996. *Kiwi Rock: A Reference Book.* Dunedin: Kiwi Rock.

Dix, John. 1982. *Stranded in Paradise: NZ Rock 'n' Roll 1955–1988.* Wellington: Paradise.

Elbert, Samuel H., and Noelani Mabee. 1970. *Nā Mele o Hawai'i Nei: 101 Hawaiian Songs.* Honolulu: University of Hawaii Press.

Elbert, Samuel H., and Torben Monberg. 1965. *From the Two Canoes: Oral Traditions of Rennell and Bellona Islands.* Copenhagen: Danish National Museum.

Firth, Raymond, with Mervyn McLean. 1991. *Tikopia Songs: Poetic and Musical Art of a Polynesian People of the Solomon Islands.* Cambridge Studies in Oral and Traditional Culture, 20. Cambridge: Cambridge University Press.

Handy, E. S. Craighill, and Jane Lathrop Winne. 1925. *Music in the Marquesas Islands.* Bulletin 17. Honolulu: Bishop Museum.

Harding, Mike. 1992. *When the Pakeha Sings of Home: A Source Guide to the Folk and Popular Songs of New Zealand.* Auckland: Godwit.

Hayward, Philip, Tony Mitchell, and Roy Shuker, ed. 1994. *North Meets South: Popular Music in Aotearoa/New Zealand.* Umina, Australia: Perfect Beat.

Hereniko, Vilsoni. 1995. *Woven Gods: Female Clowns and Power in Rotuma.* Honolulu: University of Hawaii Press.

Highland, Genevieve A., Roland W. Force, Alan Howard, Marion Kelly, and Yoshiko H. Sinoto, eds. 1967. *Polynesian Culture History: Essays in Honor of Kenneth P. Emory.* Special Publication 56. Honolulu: Bishop Museum Press.

Jonassen, John. 1991. *Cook Islands Drums.* Rarotonga: Ministry of Cultural Development, Cook Islands.

Jones, Pei Te Hurinui. 1995. *Nga Iwi O Tainui: Traditional History of the Tainui People*, trans. Bruce Biggs. Auckland: Auckland University Press.

Kaeppler, Adrienne L. 1993a. *Hula Pahu: Hawaiian Drum Dances*, Vol. 1: *Ha'a and Hula Pahu: Sacred Movements.* Bishop Museum Bulletin in Anthropology 3. Honolulu: Bishop Museum Press.

———. 1993b. *Poetry in Motion: Studies of Tongan Dance.* Nuku'alofa: Vava'u Press, in association with the East-West Center's Pacific Islands Development Program.

Kaho, Tu'imala. 1988. *Songs of Love by Tu'imala Kaho of the Kingdom of Tonga.* Nuku'alofa, Tonga: Vava'u Press.

Kanahele, George S. ed. 1979. *Hawaiian Music and Musicians: An Illustrated History.* Honolulu: University of Hawaii Press.

Kirtley, Bacil F. 1971. *A Motif-Index of Traditional Polynesian Narratives.* Honolulu: University of Hawaii Press.

Love, Jacob Wainwright. 1991. *Sāmoan Variations: Essays on the Nature of Traditional Oral Arts.* Harvard Dissertations in Folklore and Oral Tradition, ed. Albert B. Lord. New York and London: Garland.

Mayer, Raymond. 1976. *Les transformations de la tradition narrative à l'Île Wallis (Uvea).* Publications de la Société des Ocanistes, 38. Paris: Musée de l'Homme.

McLean, Mervyn. 1991. *The Structure of Tikopia Music.* Occasional Papers in Pacific Ethnomusicology, 1. Auckland: Archive of Maori and Pacific Music.

———, ed. 1995. *Catalogue of Maori Purposes Fund Board Recordings Recorded by W. T. Ngata 1953–1958.* 2nd ed. Auckland: Archive of Maori and Pacific Music, Anthropology Department, University of Auckland.

———. 1996. *Maori Music.* Auckland: Auckland University Press.

McLean, Mervyn, and Margaret Orbell. 1979. *Traditional Songs of the Maori.* Auckland: Auckland University Press.

Moulin, Jane Freeman. 1979. *The Dance of Tahiti.* Papeete: Christian Gleizal/Éditions de Pacifique.

———. 1994. *Music of the Southern Marquesas Islands.* Occasional Papers in Pacific Ethnomusicology, 3. Auckland: Department of Anthropology, University of Auckland.

Moyle, Richard M. 1985. *Report on Survey of Traditional Music of Northern Cook Islands.* Working Papers in Anthropology, Archaeology, Linguistics, Maori Studies, 70. Auckland: Department of Anthropology, University of Auckland.

———. 1987. *Tongan Music.* Auckland: Auckland University Press.

———. 1988. *Traditional Samoan Music.* Auckland: Auckland University Press.

———. 1995. *Music of Takuu (Mortlock Island), Papua New Guinea.* Occasional Papers in Pacific Ethnomusicology, 5. Auckland: Archive of Maori and Pacific Music, Department of Anthropology, University of Auckland.

Quain, Buell Halvor. 1942. *The Flight of the Chiefs: Epic Poetry of Fiji.* New York: J. J. Augustin.

Roberts, Helen H. 1926. *Ancient Hawaiian Music.* Bulletin 29. Honolulu: Bishop Museum.

Rossen, Jane Mink. 1987. *Songs of Bellona Island.* 2 vols. Language and Culture of Rennell and Bellona Islands, 6. Copenhagen: Forlaget Kragen.

Stillman, Amy Ku'uleialoha. 1987. *Report on Survey of Music in Mangareva, French Polynesia.* Working Papers in Anthropology, Archaeology, Linguistics, Maori Studies, 78. Auckland: University of Auckland, Department of Anthropology.

Tatar, Elizabeth. 1982. *Nineteenth Century Hawaiian Chant.* Pacific Anthropological Records, 33. Honolulu: Department of Anthropology, Bernice P. Bishop Museum.

———. 1987. *Strains of Change: The Impact of Tourism on Hawaiian Music.* Special Publication 78. Honolulu: Bishop Museum Press.

———. 1993. *Hula Pahu: Hawaiian Drum Dances*, Vol. 2: *The Pahu: Sounds of Power.* Bulletin in Anthropology, 4. Honolulu: Bishop Museum.

Thomas, Allan. 1996. *New Song and Dance from the Central Pacific: Creating and Performing the Fatele of Tokelau in the Islands and in New Zealand.* Dance and Music, 9. Stuyvesant, N.Y.: Pendragon.

Thomas, Allan, and Takaroga Kuautoga. 1992. *Hgoro Futuna: Report of a Survey of the Music of West Futuna, Vanuatu.* Occasional Papers in Pacific Ethnomusicology, 2. Auckland: Department of Anthropology, University of Auckland.

REFERENCES ON RECORDINGS OF OCEANIC MUSIC

Ammann, Raymond. 1997. *Kanak Dance and Music: Ceremonial and Intimate Performance of the Melanesians of New Caledonia, Historical and Actual.* London: Kegan Paul.

Barwick, Linda, and Allan Marett. 1996. "Selected Audiography of Traditional Music of Aboriginal Australia." *Yearbook of Traditional Music* 28:174–188.

Crowe, Peter. 1995. "Melanesian Music on Compact Disc: Some Significant Issues." *Pacific Studies* 18(3):147–159.

Elkin, A. P., and Trevor A. Jones. 1953–1956. *Arnhem Land Music (North Australia).* Oceania monograph 9. Sydney: University of Sydney.

Furness, William Henry. 1910. *The Island of Stone Money: Uap of the Carolines.* Philadelphia: J. B. Lippincott.

Hayward, Philip. 1996. *Music at the Borders: Not Drowning, Waving and Their Engagement with Papua New Guinean Culture (1986–1996).* Sydney: John Libbey.

Herzog, George. 1932. "Die Musik auf Truk." In *Truk,* Part 2, by Augustin Krämer. Ergebnisse der Südsee Expedition 1908–1910, II.B.5. Edited by Georg Thilenius. Hamburg: Friedrichsen de Gruyter.

———. 1936. "Die Musik der Carolinen-Inseln." In *Westkarolinen,* by Anneliese Eilers. Ergebnisse der Südsee Expedition 1908–1910, II.B.9. Edited by Georg Thilenius. Hamburg: Friedrichsen de Gruyter.

Hopkins, Jerry. 1979. "Record Industry in Hawai'i." In *Hawaiian Music and Musicians: An Illustrated History,* ed. George S. Kanahele, 325–334. Honolulu: University Press of Hawaii.

Mitchell, Tony. 1994. "Flying in the Face of Fashion: Independent Music in New Zealand."

In *North Meets South: Popular Music in Aotearoa/ New Zealand,* ed. Philip Hayward, Tony Mitchell, and Roy Shuker, 28–72. Sydney: Perfect Beat Publications.

Moyle, Alice M. 1966. *A Handlist of Field Collections of Recorded Music in Australia and Torres Strait.* Canberra: Australian Institute of Aboriginal Studies. Occasional Papers in Aboriginal Studies, 6. Ethnomusicology Series, 1.

———. 1968–1969. "Aboriginal Music on Cape York." *Musicology* 3:1–20.

Niles, Don. 1984. *Commercial Recordings of Papua New Guinea Music: 1949–1983.* Boroko: Institute of Papua New Guinea Studies.

———. 1985. *Commercial Recordings of Papua New Guinea Music: 1984 Supplement.* Boroko: Institute of Papua New Guinea Studies.

———. 1987a. *Commercial Recordings of Papua New Guinea Music: 1985 Supplement.* Boroko: Institute of Papua New Guinea Studies.

———. 1987b. *Commercial Recordings of Papua New Guinea Music: 1986 Supplement.* Boroko: Institute of Papua New Guinea Studies.

———. 1988. *Commercial Recordings of Papua New Guinea Music: 1987 Supplement.* Boroko: Institute of Papua New Guinea Studies.

———. 1991. *Commercial Recordings of Papua New Guinea Music: 1988 Supplement.* Boroko: National Research Institute.

———. 1992. "The Chinese and Music in Papua New Guinea." *Association for Chinese Music Research Newsletter* 5(2):31–35.

———. 1993. *Commercial Recordings of Papua New Guinea Music: 1989 Supplement.* Boroko: National Research Institute.

Niles, Don, and Clement Gima. 1993a. *Commercial Recordings of Papua New Guinea Music: 1990 Supplement.* Boroko: National Research Institute.

———. 1993b. *Commercial Recordings of Papua New Guinea Music: 1991 Supplement.* Boroko: National Research Institute.

———. 1994. *Commercial Recordings of Papua New Guinea Music: 1992 Supplement.* Boroko: National Research Institute.

Sheridan, Ray. 1972. "Music (2)." In *Encyclopaedia of Papua New Guinea,* ed. Peter Ryan, 817–821. Melbourne: Melbourne University Press.

South Pacific Commission. 1956. *Clearing House Service for Broadcast Recordings.* Technical paper 93. Nouméa: South Pacific Commission.

———. 1957. *Clearing House Service for Pacific Broadcast Recordings.* Technical paper 93, supplement 1. Nouméa: South Pacific Commission.

———. 1959. *Pacific Islands Broadcast Recordings Service.* Technical paper 93, supplement 2. Nouméa: South Pacific Commission.

Tatar, Elizabeth. 1979a. "Radio and Hawaiian Music." In *Hawaiian Music and Musicians: An Illustrated History,* ed. George S. Kanahele, 320–325. Honolulu: University Press of Hawaii.

———. 1979b. "Selected Discography." In *Hawaiian Music and Musicians. An Illustrated History,* ed. George S. Kanahele, 419–482. Honolulu: University Press of Hawaii.

Webb, Michael. 1993. *Lokal Musik. Lingua Franca Song and Identity in Papua New Guinea.* Apwitihire, 3. Boroko: National Research Institute.

REFERENCES ON FILMS AND VIDEOS OF OCEANIC PERFORMING ARTS

Aoki, Diane, ed. *Moving Images of the Pacific Islands: A Catalogue of Films and Videos.* Occasional Paper 38. Honolulu: Center for Pacific Island Studies, School of Hawaiian, Asian, and Pacific Studies, University of Hawaii at Manoa.

Barclay, Barry. 1988. "The Control of One's Own Image." *Centerviews* 6(5):1, 4.

Blanton, Casey, ed. 1995. *Picturing Paradise: Colonial Photography of Samoa, 1875 to 1925.* Daytona Beach, Fla.: Daytona Beach Community College in collaboration with Rautenstrauch-Joest-Museum of Ethnology, Cologne, Germany.

Blythe, Martin. 1988. "From Maoriland to Aotearoa: Images of the Maori in New Zealand Film and Television." Ph.D. dissertation, University of California, Los Angeles.

Calder-Marshall, Arthur. 1963. *The Innocent Eye: The Life of Robert J. Flaherty.* London: W. H. Allen.

Douglas, Norman. 1981. "Films for Pacific Studies: A Select List." *Pacific History Association Newsletter* 4 (May).

Filmkatalog: Ethnologie—Australien/Ozeanian. 1990. Göttingen: Institut für den Wissenschaftlichen Film.

Hanson, Allan. 1989. "The Making of the Maori: Culture Invention and Its Logic." *American Anthropologist* 91(4):890–902.

Hayward, Philip. 1995. "A New Tradition: Titus Tilly and the Development of Music Video in Papua New Guinea." *Perfect Beat* 2(2):1–19.

Heider, Karl G. 1976. *Ethnographic Film.* Austin: University of Texas Press.

Heider, Karl G., and Carol Hermer. 1995. *Films for Anthropological Teaching,* 8th ed. Special Publication 29. Arlington, Va.: American Anthropological Association.

Loizos, Peter. 1993. *Innovations in Ethnographic Film: From Innocence to Self-Consciousness, 1955–1985*. Chicago: University of Chicago Press.

Pike, Andrew, and Ross Cooper. 1980. *Australian Film 1900–1997*. Melbourne: Oxford University Press.

Poignant, Roslyn, with Axel Poignant. 1996. *Encounter at Nagalarramba*. Canberra: National Library of Australia.

Reyes, Luis I. 1995. *Made in Paradise: Hollywood's Films of Hawaii and the South Seas*. Honolulu: Mutual.

Rollwagen, Jack R., ed. 1988. *Anthropological Filmmaking*. Chur, Switzerland: Harwood Academic.

Schmitt, Robert C. 1988. *Hawaii in the Movies 1898–1959*. Honolulu: Hawaiian Historical Society.

Volkman, Toby Alice. 1986. *Expressive Culture in Papua New Guinea: A Guide to Three Films Produced by Chris Owen*. Watertown, Mass.: Documentary Educational Resources.

Recordings of Oceanic Music

MULTICULTURAL RECORDINGS

Australia and New Guinea. N.d. Recordings by A. P. Elkin, Australian Broadcasting Commission, and André P. Dupeyrat; notes by A. P. Elkin and André P. Dupeyrat. Columbia World Library of Folk and Primitive Music, comp. and ed. Alan Lomax. Columbia SL-208. LP disk.

The Gilbert and Ellice Islands Festival Company. N.d. Hibiscus HLS 49. LP disk.

Gilbert and Ellice Islands Songs. N.d. Music from Kiribati and Tuvalu. Viking VE 218. LP disk.

Gilbert and Ellice Spectacular: Gilbert and Ellice Dance Group. 1973. Viking VP 365. LP disk.

Island Music of the South Pacific. 1981. Recordings and notes by David Fanshawe. Explorer Series. Nonesuch Records H-72088.

Music of Micronesia: Songs from the Gilbert and Ellice Islands. NA Viking VP 205. LP disk.

Music of the Orient in Hawaii: Japan/China/Korea/Philippines. 1963. Recorded by Jacob Feuerring. Folkways FW 8745. LP disk.

Musical Mariner: Pacific Journey. 1989. Music of the Highlands Region and Sepik Province of Papua New Guinea, Wagi Brothers Bamboo Band, Solomon Islands, Tahiti, and Rapa Nui. Recordings by David Fanshawe. Compact disk.

Musics of Hawai'i: "It All Comes from the Heart": An Anthology of Musical Traditions in Hawai'i. 1994. Folk Arts Program, State Foundation on Culture and Arts. Booklet and 5 cassettes.

Puerto Rican Music in Hawai'i: Kachi-Kachi. 1989. Recordings and notes by Ted Solís. Smithsonian Folkways 40014. Compact disk.

Puerto Rico in Polynesia: Jíbaro Traditional Music on Hawaiian Plantations. 1994. Original Music OMDC 020. Compact disk.

Tsounis, Demeter. 1990. *Shoulder to Shoulder.* Greek music in Australia. Adelaide: Multicultural Artworkers Committee of South Australia. Cassette.

Visions of the Pacific. 1992. Music at the sixth Pacific Festival of Arts: Papua New Guinea, Guam, Rotuma, Tonga, Tokelau, French Polynesia (Tahiti), Cook Islands, Hawai'i, Aotearoa. Recorded by Te Reo O Aotearoa (Maori and Pacific Islands Programme Unit, Radio New Zealand). Distributed by Ministry of Cultural Development, Rarotonga, Cook Islands. Cassette.

AUSTRALIA

Traditional Aboriginal music

Aboriginal Sound Instruments. 1981. Recordings by Alice M. Moyle. Australian Institute of Aboriginal Studies AIAS 14. Cassette, LP disk.

Arnhem Land: Authentic Australian Aboriginal Songs and Dances. N.d. Recordings by A. P. Elkin. His Master's Voice/E.M.I. Australia. OALP 7504–7505. 3 LP disks.

Australia: Songs of the Aborigines. c. 1965. Recordings and notes by Wolfgang Laade. Lyrichord LYRCD 7331. Compact disk.

Bunggridj-Bunggridj: Wangga Songs from Northern Australia by Alan Maralung. 1993. Recordings and notes by Allan J. Marett and Linda Barwick. International Institute for Traditional Music: Traditional Music of the World, 4. Smithsonian Folkways CD 40430. Compact disk.

Dargin, Alan. N.d. *Bloodwood: The Art of the Didjeridu.* Compact disk.

Didgeridoos: Sounds of the Aborigines. N.d. Produced by Murdo McRae and Harry Wilson. Nesak International 19812-2. Compact disk.

Djambidj: An Aboriginal Song Series from Northern Australia. 1982. Australian Institute of Aboriginal Studies AIAS 16. Cassette.

Goyulan the Morning Star: An Aboriginal Clan Song Series from North Central Arnhem Land. 1988. Recordings and notes by Margaret Clunies Ross and Johnnie Mundrugmundrug. Australian Institute of Aboriginal Studies AIAS 18. Cassette.

Modern Music of Torres Strait. 1981. Recordings by Jeremy Beckett. Australian Institute of Aboriginal Studies AIAS 15. LP disk.

Songs of Aboriginal Australia. 1987. Recordings by Paddy Naughton. Australian Institute of Aboriginal Studies AIAS 17. Cassette.

Songs of Aboriginal Australia and Torres Strait. 1964. Recordings by Geoffrey N. O'Grady and Alix O'Grady; musicological notes by Alice M. Moyle; ed. George List. Ethnic Folkways FE 4102. LP disk.

Songs from the Kimberleys. 1977 [1968]. Recordings and notes by Alice M. Moyle. Australian Institute of Aboriginal Studies AIAS 13. Cassette.

Songs from the Northern Territory. 1964. Recordings and notes by Alice M. Moyle. Monograph Series, 3. Institute of Aboriginal Studies M-001-5. 5 LP disks.

Songs from North Queensland. 1977 [1966]. Recordings and notes by Alice M. Moyle. Australian Institute of Aboriginal Studies AIAS 12. LP disk.

Songs from Yarrabah. 1970. Recordings and notes by Alice M. Moyle. Australian Institute of Aboriginal Studies AIAS 7. Cassette.

Traditional Music of the Torres Strait. 1981 [1972]. Recordings by Jeremy Beckett and Trevor Jones. Australian Institute of Aboriginal Studies AIAS 11. LP disk, cassette.

Tribal Music of Australia. 1953. Recordings and notes by A. P. Elkin. Ethnic Folkways FE 4439. LP disk.

Walley, Richard. N.d. *Bilya.* SMACD-06. Compact disk.

———. N.d. *Boolong.* Reissue of 13 remastered tracks from most of Walley's earlier CDs. SMACD-18. Compact disk.

Wandjuk Marika. 1977. *Wandjuk Marika in Port Moresby: Didjeridu Solo.* Notes by Jennifer Issacs. Larrikin Records LRE 014. EP disk.

Pop Aboriginal music

AIDS! How Could I Know? 1989. CAAMA Music 203. Cassette.

Anu, Christine. 1995. *Stylin' Up.* Mushroom Records D 24325. Compact disk.

Areyonga Desert Tigers. 1988. *Light On.* Imparja Recordings 21. Cassette.

Blekbala Mujik. 1995. *Blekbala Mujik.* CAAMA Music 245. Compact disk.

Casso and the Axons. 1987. *Australia for Sale.* Mantree Industries. Cassette.

Coloured Stone. 1987. *Black Rock from the Red Centre.* Rounder Records 5022. LP disk.

———. 1989. *Crazy Mind*. CAAMA M207. Cassette.

Desert Oaks Band. 1989. *Titjikala*. CAAMA Music. Cassette.

Geia, Joe. 1988. *Yil Lull*. Gammin Records D3129. LP disk.

Hermannsburg Ladies Choir. N.d. CAAMA M115. Cassette.

In Aboriginal. 1994. CAAMA Music 241. Compact disk.

No Fixed Address and Us Mob. 1981. *Wrong Side of the Road*. Black Australia Records PRC 196. Cassette.

Roach, Archie. 1990. *Charcoal Lane*. Mushroom 30386. Cassette.

Shillingsworth, Les, et al. 1988. *Justice Will Be Done*. Privately published. Cassette.

Stompem Ground: Highlights from the 1992 Kimberley Aboriginal Arts and Cultural Festival. 1993. Australian Broadcasting Corporation 518 0202. Cassette, compact disk.

Sunrize Band. N.d. *Sunset to Rise*. CAAMA M069. Cassette.

Tiddas: Sing about Life. 1993. Id Phonogram 518 3482. Cassette, compact disk.

UPK: Uwankara Palyanka Kanyinijaku (A Strategy for Well-Being). 1989. CAAMA Music 208. Cassette.

Warumpi Band. 1987. *Go Bush!* Festival Records C38707. Cassette.

Yothu Yindi. 1989. *Homeland Movement*. Mushroom Records. Cassette, compact disk.

———. 1991. *Tribal Voice*. Mushroom 30602. Cassette, compact disk.

———. 1993. *Freedom*. Hollywood Records HR-61451-2. Compact disk.

———. 1995. "Jailbreak." In *Fuse/Box: The Alternative Tribute*. BMG 74321 286814. Compact disk.

Young, Dougie. 1994. *The Songs of Dougie Young*. National Library of Australia, Aboriginal Studies Press 19. Cassette, compact disk.

NEW GUINEA

Collections

Australia and New Guinea. 1954. Recordings by A. P. Elkin and A. P. Dupeyrat; ed. A. P. Elkin. Columbia World Library of Folk and Primitive Music, 5. Columbia Masterworks KL-208. LP disk.

Indonesia. 1954. Recordings by André Dupeyrat and J. Hobbel; ed. Jaap Kunst. Columbia World Library of Folk and Primitive Music, 7. Columbia Masterworks KL-210. LP disk.

Music of the Anga. 1983. Recordings by Bergh Amos, Ilaita Gigimat, Lisa Lawson, and Don Niles. Institute of Papua New Guinea Studies IPNGS 006. Cassette.

Music of New Guinea: The Australian Trust Territory: An Introduction. 1958. Recordings by Ray Sheridan and W. E. Smythe; ed. Ray Sheridan. Wattle Recordings D2. LP disk.

New Guinea and Papuan Native Music. 1949. Recordings by Colin Simpson and John Cunningham. Australian Broadcasting System NAT 14. Seven 78-RPM disks.

Ol Singsing Bilong Ples. 1990. Recordings by Michael Webb and Don Niles. Boroko: Institute of Papua New Guinea Studies IPNGS 010. Book with 2 cassettes.

Papua New Guinea Music Collection. 1987. Ed. Don Niles and Michael Webb. Institute of Papua New Guinea Studies IPNGS 008. Book with 11 cassettes.

Primitive Sounds: An Authentic Sound Picture of New Guinea. 1971. Recordings by James L. Anderson. Hibiscus Records HLS 31. LP disk.

This Is New Guinea: A Recorded Sound Picture. N.d. Recordings by James L. Anderson. Hibiscus Records HLS 19. LP disk.

Popular music

Amazil Local. 1981. *Amazil Local*. Walter Bay Trading Company. Vista NGK 6028. Cassette.

The Best of PNG Pidgin Rock. 1991. Institute of Papua New Guinea Studies IPNGS 220.

Delapou Band, The Rainbows, and The Kopy Kats. 1968. *New Guinea Music Today*. Viking VP 266. LP disk.

Hollie Maea Band. N.d. *Mangi Moresby*. CHM Supersound 702. LP disk.

The New Guinea Scene. 1969. Recordings by the Australian Broadcasting Commission. Viking Records VP 318. LP disk.

Papua/New Guinea Independence Celebrations: Song Contest Finalists. 1975. Viking VPS 392. LP disk.

Riwain! Papua New Guinea Pop Songs. 1986. Compiled by Michael Webb and Don Niles. Institute of Papua New Guinea Studies IPNGS 007. Book with 2 cassettes.

Papuan region

The Coast of the Western Province, Papua New Guinea. 1993. Recordings and notes by Wolfgang Laade. Music of Man Archive. Jecklin-Disco JD 655-2. Compact disk.

Kamu Mariria: Music of the Maopa and Aloma. 1981. Recordings by Les McLaren and Ilaita Gigimat; compiled by Don Niles. Institute of Papua New Guinea Studies IPNGS 003. Cassette.

Music from the D'Entrecasteaux Islands. 1983. Recordings by Lisa Lawson, Hape Haihavu, Charles Asshy, and Pio Renssy. Produced in collaboration with the National Arts School. Institute of Papua New Guinea Studies IPNGS 005.

Music from South New Guinea. 1971. Recordings and notes by Wolfgang Laade. Folkways AHM 4216. LP disk.

Traditional Music of the Gizra and Bine People: Papua New Guinea, Western Province. 1978. Recordings and notes by Frédéric Duvelle, assisted by Billai Laba. Larrikin Records LRF 031. LP disk.

Highland region

Chimbu Music: Kukane Traditions. 1975. Recordings and notes by Frédéric Duvelle, assisted by Paul Kuange. Papua New Guinea, 1. Institute of Papua New Guinea Studies. LP disk.

Enga Traditional Music. 1974. Recordings by Frédéric Duvelle. Notes by Kundopen Talyaga. Institute of Papua New Guinea Studies. LP disk.

The Huli of Papua Niugini. 1986. Recordings by Jacqueline Pugh-Kitingan. Bärenreiter Musicaphon BM 30 SL 2703. LP disk.

The Kaluli of Papua Niugini: Weeping and Song. 1985. Recordings by Steven Feld. Bärenreiter Musicaphon BM 30 SL 2702. LP disk.

Music of the Kaluli. 1981. Recordings by Steven Feld. Institute of Papua New Guinea Studies IPNGS 001. LP disk.

Voices of the Rainforest: Bosavi, Papua New Guinea. 1991. Recordings and notes by Steven Feld. Rykodisc RCD 10173. Compact disk.

Mamose region

The Iatmul of Papua Niugini. 1980. Recordings by Robert MacLennan and Gordon Spearritt; notes by Meinhard Schuster and Gordon Spearritt. Bärenreiter Musicaphon BM 30 SL 2701. LP disk.

Kovai and Adzera Music. 1981. Recordings by Bergh Amos, Thomas Lulungan, Don Niles, and Jesse Pongap; Adzera translations by Soni Timo Maraba. Institute of Papua New Guinea Studies IPNGS 002. Cassette.

Papua Niugini: The Middle Sepik. 1980. Recordings by Robert MacLennan, Fred Gerrits, and Gordon Spearritt; notes by Meinhard Schuster and Gordon Spearritt. Bärenreiter Musicaphon BM 30 SL 2700. LP disk.

Rhythms and Music of Oceanic Islands, Following N. N. Miklouho-Maclay. 1978. Recordings by Boris N. Putilov. Leningrad: Melodiya M80-39597-39602. 3 LP disks.

Sacred Flute Music from New Guinea: Madang. 1977. Recordings by Ragnar Johnson and Jessica Mayer. Quartz Publications: !Quartz 001. LP disk.

Windim Mambu: Sacred Flute Music from New Guinea: Madang. 1978. Recordings by Ragnar Johnson and Jessica Mayer. Quartz Publications: !Quartz 002. LP disk.

Irian Jaya

Musik aus dem Bergland West-Neuguineas (Irian Jaya): Eine Klangdokumentation untergehender Musikkulturen der Eipo und ihrer Nachbarn/Music from the Mountainous Region of Western New Guinea (Irian Jaya): A Documentation in Sound of the Vanishing Musical Cultures of the Eipo and Their Neighbors. 1993. Recordings and notes by

Artur Simon. Museum Collection Berlin CD 20, Vols. 1 and 2. 6 compact disks.

Music of Biak, Irian Jaya. 1996. Recordings by Philip Yampolsky; notes by Danilyn Rutherford and Philip Yampolsky. Produced in collaboration with the Indonesian Society for the Performing Arts. Music of Indonesia, 10. Smithsonian Folkways CD 40426. Compact disk.

MELANESIA

Multicultural recordings

Manus; Bougainville. 1975. Recordings by Charles Duvelle and Frédéric Duvelle; notes by Kakah Kais and Leo Hannett. Ocora OCR 86. LP disk.

Island Region of Papua New Guinea

Music and Sounds of Melanesia. 1962. Music of the Duke of York Islands. Recordings and notes by Sandra LeBrun Holmes. HMV OELP 9189. LP disk.

Tolai Traditional Music from the Gazelle Peninsula. 1977. Recordings and notes by Frédéric Duvelle, assisted by Jacob Simet and Apisai Enos. Larrikin Records LRF 013. LP disk.

ToUna, Blasius. 1978. *Guitar Songs of Papua New Guinea.* Recordings and notes by Frédéric Duvelle. Larrikin Records LRF 030. LP disk.

Tribal Heart. 1994. Popular music of Rabaul. Larrikin Entertainment AIM 1042. Compact disk.

Solomon Islands

Fataleka and Baegu Music: Malaita: Solomon Islands. 1990 [1973]. Recordings and notes by Hugo Zemp. Augmented reissue. Auvidis-Unesco D 8027. Compact disk.

Îles Salomon: Ensembles de flûtes de pan 'Are'are. 1994. Recordings and notes by Hugo Zemp. Chant du Monde LDX 274 961–62. 2 compact disks.

Meja, Nelson, and His Bamboo Band, with Solomon Dakei. N.d. *Bamboo Beat.* Notes by Ron Calvert. Viking VE 163. LP disk.

Melanesian Music, 'Are'are, Vol. 3. 1973. Recordings and notes by Hugo Zemp. Collection Musée de l'Homme. Vogue LDM 30106. LP disk.

Musique de Guadalcanal-Solomon Islands. 1994. Recordings and notes by Hugo Zemp. Ocora Radio France C 5580049. Compact disk.

Polyphonies of the Solomon Islands (Guadalcanal and Savo). 1990. Recordings and notes by Hugo Zemp. Augmented reissue. Collection Centre National de la Recherche Scientifique and Musée de l'Homme. Chant du Monde LDX 274663. Compact disk.

St. Joseph's Temaru: Pan Pipers. 1986. Produced by St. Joseplis Temaru. Cassette.

Solomon Islands: 'Are'are Intimate and Ritual Music. 1995. Recordings and notes by Hugo

Zemp. Collection Centre National de la Recherche Scientifique and Musée de l'Homme. Chant du Monde CNR 274 963. Compact disk.

The Solomon Islands: The Sounds of Bamboo: Instrumental Music and Song of the 'Are'are People of Malaita. N.d. Recordings by the MABO Project. Music of the Earth MCM 3007. Compact disk.

New Caledonia

Bwanjep. 1993. *Vie.* Nouméa: Studio Mangrove. Cassette, compact disk. (Popular music by a band from northern Grande Terre.)

Cada et ayoii: Chants de Hienghène. 1992. Recordings by Jean-Michel Beaudet. Nouméa: Agence de Développement de la Culture Kanak. Cassette.

Chants kanaks: Cérémonies et berceuses. 1990. Recordings by Jean-Michel Beaudet and Lionel Weiri; notes by Jean-Michel Beaudet and Kaloonbat Tein. Collection Centre National de la Recherche Scientifique and Musée de l'Homme. Chant du Monde LDX 274909. Compact disk.

Chants et musiques Drehu. 1994. Recordings and notes by Raymond Ammann. Collection Musiques Kanak, 2. Nouméa and Maré: Centre Culturel Yéiwéné Yéiwéné and Agence de Développement de la Culture Kanak. Cassette.

Chants et musiques Iaaï. 1994. Recordings and notes by Raymond Ammann. Collection Musiques Kanak, 1. Nouméa and Maré: Centre Culturel Yéiwéné Yéiwéné and Agence de Développement de la Culture Kanak. Cassette.

Chants et musiques Nengone. 1994. Recordings and notes by Raymond Ammann. Collection Musiques Kanak, 3. Nouméa and Maré: Centre Culturel Yéiwéné Yéiwéné and Agence de Développement de la Culture Kanak. Cassette.

Gurejele. 1993. *Wabeb bulu.* Nouméa: Studio Mangrove. Cassette, compact disk. (Popular music by a band from Maré Island.)

Kaneké: Musiques canaques de Nouvelle-Calédonie: Festival Melanesia 2000. 1984 [1975]. Nouméa. LP disk, cassette.

Kanak Modern Music. 1987? Recordings by Warawi Wayenece, with the participation of l'Association Boenando. Amakal Productions. Cassette.

Mexem. 1995. *Kadely.* Nouméa: Studio Mangrove. Cassette, compact disk. (Popular music by a band from Lifou Island.)

Nouvelle-Calédonie: Danses et musiques kanak/New Caledonia: Kanak Dance and Music. 1997. Recordings by Raymond Ammann. Geneva: Musée d'Ethnographie, AIMP XLVIIL VDE CD923. Compact disk.

Pilou-Pilou: Songs and Dances of New Caledonia—Authentic Folk Music from New Caledonia, the Isle of Pines, and Loyalty Islands. 1969. Viking Records VP 278. LP disk.

Shabatan. 1995. *Waica ri kae deng.* Nouméa: Studio Mangrove. Cassette, compact disk. (Popular music by a band from Maré Island.)

Vamaley. 1993. *Echos du passé.* Nouméa: Studio Mangrove. Cassette, compact disk. (Popular music by a band from northern Grande Terre.)

Vanuatu

Black Brothers. N.d. *Best of the Black Brothers.* Vila: Sound Centre AGP 15. Cassette.

Black Revolution. 1986. *Everyday.* Studio Vanuwespa SAEP 8611. Cassette.

Magawiarua. 1992. *Magawiarua.* Vanuatu Productions V-PRO 92-11. Cassette.

Nahabau. NA *Radio Vanuatu and the Sound Centre.* Alain Gault Productions. TC AGP 17. Cassette.

New Hebrides Music Today. 1969. Recordings by Radio Nouméa. Viking VP 284. LP disk.

Noisy Boys. 1982. *Fes Tua.* Main Gault Productions. TC AGP 10. Cassette.

———. 1986. *1986 Tanna Inta Distrik Gems.* Vanuata [sic] Production Société de Promotion de Musique Mélanésienne. VP 24. Cassette.

Les Nouvelles-Hébrides. N.d. Recordings by Maurice Bitter. Musique Folklorique du Monde. Musidisc 30 CV 1273. LP disk.

Songs and Dances of the New Hebrides. 1969. Recordings by Radio Nouméa. Viking VP 280. LP disk.

Traditional Music of Vanuatu (New Hebrides) from the Cultural Centre Archives. 1977. Recordings by Joseph Boe, James Gwere, and Kirk Huffman. Cultural Centre. Cassette.

Vanuatu: Custom Music/Singsing-Danis Kastom. 1994. Recordings and notes by Peter Crowe and other participants in the New Hebrides Oral Traditions Project. Geneva: Musée d'Ethnographie, AIMP XLVIII. VDE 796. Compact disk.

Western Boys. c. 1992. *Again.* Vila: Sum Productions SP 160. Cassette.

MICRONESIA

Multicultural recordings

Enchanted Evening in Micronesia: Songs and Dances from Marshalls, Ponape, Truk, Yap, and Palau. 1960. Performed by Micronesian Club of Honolulu at the University of Hawai'i. 7-inch LP disk.

Guam, Northern Marianas, Federated States of Micronesia, Marshall Islands. 1994. Recordings and notes by Hikaru Koide. JVC World Sounds Special, Music of Micronesia. JVC VICG-5277. Compact disk.

Micronesia: A Musical Glimpse. N.d. Trutone Records for J. C. Tenorio Enterprises, Saipan, Northern Marianas. LP disk. (Six island cultures spanning Palau in the west to the Gilberts in the east.)

The Music of Micronesia, the Kao-Shan Tribes of Taiwan, and Sakhalin. c. 1978. Side A: recordings by Hisao Tanabe in Palau, Truk, Ponape, and the Marshall Islands. Side B: Taiwan and Sakhalin. Toshiba TW-80011. LP disk.

Spirit of Micronesia, Traditional Music Recorded between 1978–1984: Chants, Hymns, Dances from Kiribati, Marshall Islands, Kosrae, Pohnpei, Chuuk, Yap, and Palau. 1995. Recordings by David Fanshawe. Saydisc Records SDL-414. Compact disk.

West Micronesia

Call of the Morning Bird: Chants and Songs of Palau, Yap, and Ponape, Collected by Iwakichi Muranushi, 1936. 1985. Ed. Elizabeth Tatar. Honolulu: Bishop Museum, ARCS 2. Cassette.

Waab-Palau Trio (Rodol Ruethin, Kasiano Kelulau, Josino Joseph). c. 1983. *Kasinoma.* MRM Productions MRMC-1001. Cassette. (Palau and Yap.)

Palau

Bekebekmad, Johnny "B." N.d. *Johnny B.* Gem Records CS-1113. Cassette.

Eriich, Halley. N.d. *Ai Sa Nangyo.* ET Records. Cassette.

———. N.d. *Manterang.* ET Records. Cassette.

———. N.d. *Ngerbuus.* ET Records. Cassette.

Kanai, Virian. 1995. *Bertau.* BKE 10995. Cassette.

Yap

Wallow, led by Jesse Maw. 1995. *Wallow.* Recorded at the radio station. Cassette.

Pohnpei

Danpei Youth Choir of Ponape, Micronesia: On Tour. 1980. Produced by Rev. Elden Buck, tour director. Triad Recording Studio. LP disk.

Mariana Islands: Guam

Bias, Jesse. 1985. *Guam on My Mind.* Alifan Productions 85-12-001. LP disk and cassette.

———. N.d. *Language of Love.* LP disk and cassette.

———. N.d. *We Are One.* LP disk and cassette.

Biggest Chamorro Stars: Greatest Chamorro Hits, Vol. 2. 1994. Naou Records International VA-CS. Cassette.

Guerrero. 1987. *Chamorro Songs [Guam/Saipan]: Palao'an Matulaika Hao.* Produced by Tony R. Guerrero. Cassette.

Makpo. 1990. Songs composed or arranged by Maria Santos Yatar. Cassette.

The Music and Legends of Guam. 1978. Produced and directed by Jack de Mello for Guam Economic Development Authority. Notes by Jack de Mello. 2 LP disks, 2 cassettes.

Musikan Guahan. 1992. Ed. Judy Flores. Agaña: Guam Council on the Arts and Humanities. Cassette.

Sablan, Johnny. 1960s. *Dalai Nene.* Hafa Adai Records HAC 3300. Cassette.

———. N.d. *Chamorro Country-Western.* Hafa Adai Records HAC 3313. Cassette.

———. N.d. *Feliz Navidad!* Hafa Adai Records HAC 3315. Cassette.

———. 1982. *Shame 'n' Scandal.* Hafa Adai Records HAC 3325. Cassette.

Northern Mariana Islands

AFETNAS II. 1984. *Maila Ta Na' Mames Este Na Momiento.* Saipan: Tenda Store Production. TS4802. Cassette.

Cabrero, Joe. N.d. *Fiesta.* Saipan: A and E Productions. Cassette.

The Commonwealth. N.d. *Marianas Despedida.* CM1980-01. Cassette.

De la Cruz, Eddie. 1991. *Edwardo.* Guam: Doe Productions. Cassette.

De la Cruz, Frank. N.d. *Tinian.* Guam: Ke Productions. Cassette.

Diaz, Joseph M. N.d. *Fan Respeta Gi Manaina Mu.* Saipan: Tenda Store Production TS4812. Cassette.

Dinana i familian "Camacho." 1989. *Dinana i familian Camacho.* Saipan: S. D. Camacho Quality Productions. Cassette.

Indelecio, Cindy. N.d. *Un Tunoco Va.* Tinian: Guam Sirena Production. Cassette.

Kunados Tinian II. 1984. *Lao Hu-ouive Hao.* Tinian: Kunados Tinian Productions Enterprises. Cassette.

Muna, Jesse. 1990. *Fiestan Luta.* Rota: LJ's Production. Cassette.

Pangelinan, Frank M. N.d. *Chikko Va.* Saipan: N.p. Cassette.

———. N.d. *Memorias Marianas.* Saipan: Tenda Store Production TS6809. Cassette.

Sablan, Alesandro. 1993? *Jose Maria.* Saipan: Chamorro Hit Radio FM. Cassette.

Tropicsette. N.d. *Nobia.* Saipan: Tropicsette. Cassette.

East Micronesia

Marshall Islands

Bwil 'm Molo. 1994. *Ebwil!* Majuro: privately produced. Cassette.

Jabe in Nebar. N.d. *Jej family eo an Iroij.* V7AB Recording Studio. Cassette.

Kakinono. 1996. *Kakinono kein kaiuon.* Chaninway KK-I. Cassette.

Likajer. 1995. *Inedral.* Manufactured in Fremont, Calif. Cassette.

Skate-Em-Lā. 1985. *Mour Ilo Aelōñ Kein.* Recorded in Majuro by Bill Graham in association with Marshall Islands Yacht Club. Remastered in Honolulu by Academics Hawaii. Cassette.

Songs from Micronesia. N.d. Reissue of an untitled LP disk produced and recorded by Lee Webb in the Marshall Islands. Viking VP 265. LP disk.

Kiribati

Foon, Peter. 1986. *Bata Peter: Bibitakin te Moanoua.* Suva: Foon's Home Studio CPR 10. Cassette.

Nenem, Isaia. 1986. *Te Roro N Rikirake.* Suva: Foon's Home Studio CPR 17. Cassette.

POLYNESIA

Multicultural recordings

Pacific Rhythm, Vol. 1: *The First Compilation of the Pacific Islands Top Dance Hits.* 1997. Music of Fiji, Tonga, Samoa, Rarotonga. Produced by Kennedy Tau. Evander Kennedy Music EKM 00 1. Cassette.

Polynesian Panorama: Twenty Authentic Songs and Chants of the Southern Polynesian Islands Performed by Native Islanders Representing the Polynesian Institute at Laie, Oahu, Hawaii. N.d. Recordings by Jacob Feuerring. Produced by Bob Bertram. Polynesian PM 700. LP disk. (Music from Fiji, Tonga, Samoa, Tokelau, Cook Islands, Aotearoa.)

Songs and Dances of the Cook Islands. N.d. Viking Records VP 135. (Music from Tokelau and the Cook Islands.)

West Polynesia

Music of Marginal Polynesia: Fiji, Wallis and Futuna, Tuvalu. 1994, recorded in 1977–1985. JVC World Sounds Special, Music of Polynesia, 5. VICG-5276-2. Compact disk.

Samoa, Tonga. 1988, recorded in 1977–1985. JVC World Sounds Special, Music of Polynesia, 4. VICG-5274. Compact disk.

Fiji

Chet, Titau, and the Chequers Gold Band. 1996. *Titau Chet and the Chequers Gold Band*. South Pacific Recordings SPR 733. Cassette. (Banaban music.)

Drola Entertainment Group of Na Cula Village, Yasawa. 1997. *Traditional Fijian Songs and Mekes*. Procera DRO 2059.

Fiji Calls. N.d. Viking Records VP 47. LP disk.

Fiji on Parade: The Band of the Fiji Police Force. N.d. Viking VP 351. LP disk.

Garden Island Resort Band. 1997. *Garden Island Resort Band: Taveuni—Fiji*. South Pacific Recordings. Compact disk.

High Lights Music Man. 1991. Reggae by Epeli Kurualeba. South Pacific Recordings SPR 450. Cassette.

Kumar, Ashok. 1997. *Bhakti Kirtan*, Vol. 3. South Pacific Recordings SPR 316H. Cassette. (Fiji-Indian music.)

Matasiga Choral Group. 1995. *Jisu Jisu*. Procera. MCG 2118. Cassette.

Nawaka Entertainment Group. 1991. *Bula Fiji Bula*. South Pacific Recordings. Compact disk.

Rawasese Entertainment Group. 1991. *Mana Island*. South Pacific Recordings. Compact disk.

Serevi, Seru. 1993. *Vude Mai!* South Pacific Recordings. Compact disk.

———. 1997. *The Best of Seru Serevi*. Procera. Compact disk.

Wai Koula ni Gauna Vou Kei Tavua. 1996. *Oceie-Bolei Au*. South Pacific Recordings SPR 732. Cassette.

Wilson, Eddie. 1996. *Eddie Wilson's Tarana*. Fiji-Indian popular music. South Pacific Recordings SPR 284H. Cassette.

Tonga

Bill Sevesi and the Royal Tongans. 1965. *Tunes from Tonga*. Viking VE 103. EP disk.

Ifi Pak: Tongan Brass. 1994. Recordings by Ad Linkels and Lucia Linkels; notes by Ad Linkels. Anthology of Pacific Music, 4. PAN Records 2044. Compact disk.

Kaho, Tu'imala. 1988. *Songs of Love*. Warrior Records Pacific Division WARC 2011. Cassette.

Music from Tonga: The Friendly Islands. 1976. Recordings by Lavinia 'A. Finau. Tangent Records TGM 122. LP disk.

Music of Tonga. N.d. Recordings by Tonga Broadcasting Commission; notes by R. MacDonald. Viking Records VP 108. LP disk.

The Music of Tonga. 1972. Recordings and notes by Luis Marden. National Geographic Society 3516. LP disk.

Nuku'alofa Wanderers. c. 1972. *The Friendly Islands: Music from Tonga*. Viking Records VP 263. LP disk.

Tauhola, Fola 'Ofa, and Siale Hae Vala. 1973. *Tonga Spectacular*. Viking Records VP 353. LP disk. (Artists are groups.)

Tongan Coronation 1967. 1967. Viking VE 237. LP disk.

Tongan Festival Contingent, led by the Honourable Ve'ehala. 1972. *Music of Tonga*. Recordings by John Ruffell. Hibiscus Records HLS-39, 40. Two LP disks.

Traditional Music of Tonga: An Authentic Sound Picture. 1975. Recordings and notes by Richard M. Moyle. Hibiscus Records HLS-65. LP disk.

Tui Mala Group, Queen Salote College Choir, and Tongan Entertainers. N.d. Recordings by Tonga Radio and James Siers; notes by James Siers. Hibiscus Records HLS-4. LP disk.

Sāmoa

Choir of the American Samoa Arts Council. 1972. *American Samoa Spectacular*. Viking Records VP 360. LP disk.

Fa'a-Samoa: The Samoan Way . . . between Conch Shell and Disco. 1995. Recordings by Ad Linkels and Lucia Linkels. Anthology of Pacific Music, 6. Pan Records. Pan 2066CD. Compact disk.

The Music of Samoa: An Authentic Sound Picture. 1973. Recordings and notes by Richard M. Moyle. Hibiscus HLS-55. LP disk.

Popular Songs of Samoa. 1996. Five Stars Collection, 3. Hibiscus Records CD HLS160. Compact disk.

RSA Band, Vol. 4: *Apia W. Samoa*. 1996. RSA. Cassette.

Samoan Songs: A Historical Collection. N.d. Musicaphon BM 2705. LP disk.

Songs and Dances of Samoa. N.d. Viking Records VP 134. LP disk.

Western Samoa Teachers Training College. 1972. *Samoan Song and Rhythm*. Hibiscus Records TC HLS-24. Cassette.

'Uvea and Futuna

Chants et danses des Îles Wallis. c. 1972 [c. 1963.] Recordings by Maurice Bitter. Disque BAM LD 5749. LP disk.

Dance to the Wallis Island Beat. c. 1969. Recorded by Radio Nouméa. Viking VP 304. LP disk.

Songs and Dances of Wallis Island. c. 1969. Viking Records VP 293. LP disk.

Niue

Festival Company of Niue. 1972. Recorded at the South Pacific Festival of Arts. Hibiscus HE-10. EP disk.

Niue Island Magic: South Seas Souvenir. 1973. Viking Records VP 347. LP disk.

Niue Island Spectacular. Souvenir Record of the South Pacific Arts Festival. 1973. Viking Records VP 354. LP disk.

Rotuma

Island Drifters. 1996. *Kato'aga Helava Fau 150 Ne Rotu Katolike 'E Rotuma*. South Pacific Recordings 740. Cassette.

Tuvalu

An Evening in the Ellice Islands. N.d. Salem Record Company XP 5033. LP disk.

Tuvalu: A Polynesian Atoll Society. 1994. Recordings and notes by Ad Linkels. PAN 2055CD. Compact disk.

Polynesian outliers

Fatuana Matua. c. 1987. *Mi Laikem Yu . . . Long Fasin Blong Yu*. Music of West Futuna. Vanuata [sic] Productions VP 45. Cassette.

Ouvea: Chants, danses, et documents. c. 1972. Music of West 'Uvea. Recordings by Maurice Bitter. Disque BAM LD 5754. LP disk.

Polynesian Dances of Bellona (Mungiki): Solomon Islands. 1978. Recordings by Jane Mink Rossen and Hugo Zemp; notes by Jane Mink Rossen. Folkways FE 4274. LP disk.

Polynesian Songs and Games from Bellona (Mungiki): Solomon Islands. 1976. Recordings and notes by Jane Mink Rossen. Folkways FE 4273. LP disk.

Polynesian Traditional Music of Ontong Java (Solomon Islands). 1971. Recordings and notes by Hugo Zemp. Collection Musée de l'Homme. Vogue LD 785 and LDM 30.109. 2 LP disks. (Music of Luangiua.)

Tikopia Songs: Poetic and Musical Art of a Polynesian People of the Solomon Islands. 1991. Recordings and notes by Raymond Firth, with Mervyn McLean. Cassette.

East Polynesia

Easter Island, Marquesas Islands. 1994, recorded in 1977–1985. JVC World Sounds Special, Music of Polynesia, 3. VICG-5273. Compact disk.

The Gauguin Years. Songs and Dances of Tahiti. c. 1966, recorded in 1965. Recordings by Francis Mazière; notes by Jane Sarnoff. Explorer Series. Nonesuch H-72017. LP disk. (Music of the Marquesas, Society Islands, and Tuamotus.)

Îles Marquises et Tuamotu: Chants et musique. 1976. Recordings by Henri Lavondes. Orstom SETO 755. LP disk.

1980—Année du patrimoine: Îles Marquises—Tahiti. 1980. Manuiti 3038. LP disk.

Tahiti, Dream Island. N.d. Productions Musicales Polynésiennes. Manuiti/Playa Sound PS 65007. Compact disk. (Tracks 1–9 are Tahitian; 10–23, Marquesan.)

Tahiti Society Islands. 1988. JVC World Sounds Special, Music of Polynesia, 1. VICG-5271. Compact disk.

Tuamotu, Austral Islands. 1994, recorded in 1977–1990. JVC World Sounds Special, Music of Polynesia, 2. VICG-5272. Compact disk.

Society Islands

Le Ballet Polynésien Heiva. N.d. *O Tahiti*. Directed by Madeleine Moua. Chant du Monde LDX 74342. LP disk.

Chants et rythmes du Pacifique sud: South Pacific Songs and Rhythms. 1968. Productions Musicales Polynésiennes. Manuiti/Playa Sound PS 65018. Compact disk.

Coco et Son Groupe Folklorique Temaeva. N.d. *Tiurai: Tahiti Festival*. Manuiti 3 203. LP disk.

Drums of Bora Bora and Songs of Tahiti. 1993. Tracks 1–17 recorded by Gaston Guilbert in 1956; tracks 18–32 produced by Yves Roche for Criterion Records in 1993. Crescendo Records GNPD 2214. Compact disk.

Escale à Tahiti: A Journey to Tahiti. 1994. Productions Musicales Polynésiennes. Manuiti/Playa Sound PS 66501. Compact disk.

Heiva à Tahiti, 1: Himene, ute, toere—Les plus beaux moments du Heiva. N.d. Recorded at Vai'ete by Francis Teai. Produced by OTAC—Te Fare Tauhiti Nui. JMC Production Rama R016. Cassette.

Hiriata et Son Choeur, Salamon et ses Batteurs, and Maono et le Groupe de Patutoa. N.d. *Eddie Lund Presents . . . Aparima et Otea*. Tahiti Records EL 10 17. LP disk.

Joël et Son Groupe Folklorique Maeva Tahiti. 1976. *Pirogues tahitiennes: Ballet-Aparima*. Editions Manuiti 1712. EP disk.

Lund, Eddie, and His Tahitians and Mila. N.d. *Eddie Lund Presents . . . To the South Seas with the Tahiti Yacht Race*. Tahiti Records EL-1003. LP disk.

Manuia and Maeva. 1965? *Otuitui Tahiti: Et d'autres grands succès de Tahiti*. Produced by Michael H. Goldsen. Reo Tahiti Records/Criterion Records RTS 520. LP disk.

Moua, Madeleine, and Les Ballets Heiva. N.d. *À vous Tahiti*. Philips 844.915. LP disk.

L'Orchestré [sic] Hotel Tahiti, Paulina et Salamon, and Les Mama Ruau Ma. N.d. *Eddie Lund Presents . . . Tahiti—Mon Amour*. Tahiti Records EL 1016. LP disk.

Pahu Tahiti! Authentic Drums of the South Seas. N.d. Recordings by Gaston Guilbert. Criterion Records SRT-560. LP disk.

Paparai: Himene Tarava, Ute, Tuki. 1991. Océane Production OCN CD11. Compact disk.

Percussions polynésiennes: South Pacific Drums. 1990, recorded from 1965 to 1990. Productions Musicales Polynésiennes. Manuiti/Playa Sound PS 65066. Compact disk.

Royal Folkloric Troupe of Tahiti. 1992, recorded in 1966, 1970, and 1972. *Coco's Temaeva*. Manuiti Productions Musicales Polynésiennes. S 65808. Compact disk.

———. 1994, recorded in 1966, 1970, 1972, and 1987. *Coco's Temaeva, Vol. 2*. Manuiti Productions Musicales Polynésiennes. S 65815. Compact disk.

Royal Tahitian Dance Company. 1974. *Royal Tahitian Dance Company*. 1974. Monitor Records MCD 71758. Compact disk.

Tahiti, belle époque: All-Time Tahitian Favorites. 1991, recorded from 1940 to 1967. Productions Musicales Polynésiennes. S 65807. Compact disk.

Tahiti, belle époque, 3: Original Barefoot Boys from the 1960s—Ensemble original du Bar Lea. 1992, recorded in 1967 and 1968. Productions Musicales Polynésiennes. S 65811. Compact disk.

Tahiti, belle époque, 4: Songs of the Atolls and the Islands. 1994. Recordings by Gaston Guilbert in 1955–1959 and 1966. Productions Musicales Polynésiennes/Playa Sound PS 65816. Compact disk.

Tahiti fête! Authentique folklorique. c. 1997. Criterion Records SST-1800. LP disk.

Tahiti: Islands of Paradise: Authentic Tahitian Music Recorded by Gaston Guilbert in Papeete during the Filming of "Mutiny on the Bounty." c. 1956. MGM E 4082. LP disk.

Tahiti variétés. 1986. Océane Production OCN CD01. Compact disk.

Temaeva and Coco Hotahota. N.d. *Te Vahine Maohi*. Tupuna Production/Editions JMC Rama R012. Cassette.

Les Voix des Atolls and Le Zizou Bar Trio. N.d. *Ta'u Tahiti (Mon Tahiti)*. Recordings by Gaston Guilbert. Criterion Records STT-2000. LP disk.

Austral Islands

Pupu Himene no Rurutu, 1. c. 1980. Recorded by Studio Hei Tiare. Rama R-002. Cassette.

Pupu Himene no Rurutu, 2. c. 1980. Recorded by Studio Hei Tiare. Rama R-003. Cassette.

The Rurutu Choir: Polynesian Odyssey. 1996. Recordings by Pascal Nabet-Meyer. Shanachie Entertainment SH-64065. Compact disk.

The Tahitian Choir: Rapa Iti. 1992. Recordings by Pascal Nabet-Meyer. Triloka Records 7192-2. Compact disk.

The Tahitian Choir, Vol. 2. 1994. Recordings by Pascal Nabet-Meyer. Shanachie Entertainment SH-64055. Compact disk.

Tamarii Manureva no Rurutu. 1980s. Océane Production C-008. Cassette.

The Tubuai Choir. 1993. Recordings by Pascal Nabet-Meyer. Shenachie Entertainment SH-64049. Compact disk.

Tuamotu Islands

Lund, Eddie, and his Hahitians. N.d. *Paumotu Drums, Songs and Chants*. Viking Records VP 56.

Mariterangi. N.d. *Ua Reka*. Music arranged by Eddie Lund. Tahiti Records EL 108. LP disk.

Paumotu: Teaitu Mariterangi. N.d. Produced by Michael H. Goldsen. Criterion Records RT-419. EP disk.

Marquesas Islands

Kanahau Trio. 1990s. *Haavei i Ua Huka, Vol. 2*. Recordings by Here Recording. Océane Production STT 40. Compact disk.

Rataro. 1990s. *Kaoha, les Marquises*. Recordings by Here Recording. Océane Production A063. Cassette.

———. 1994. *Marquises terre sauvage*. Océane Production OCN CD38. Compact disk.

Salomon et Son Groupe avec Kapuhia. N.d. *Polynesian Primitive*. Tahiti Records EL 1035. LP disk.

Te Eo Hiva Oa. 1990s. Recorded at Studio JMC Production. Te Eo, 1. Océane Production. Cassette.

Te Hakamanu: La danse de l'oiseau. 1990. Légende marquisienne avec musique et chants du Festival des Arts des Îles Marquises. Haere Po no Tahiti. Rama 013. Cassette.

Te Ka 'ioi. 1991. Recorded at Studio de l'I.C.A. Océane Production CO13. Cassette.

Îles Marquises et Tuamotu: Chants et musique. 1981. Recordings by Henri Lavondès. Collection Traditionale Orale. ORSTOM-SELAF. Cassette.

Cook Islands

Cook Islands Musical Spectacular, Silver Anniversary 1965–1990. 1990. Recorded by Capricorn Studios. Produced by the Ministry of Cultural Development and Capricorn Studios. Capricorn CPR 206. Cassette.

Imene Tuki: Cook Islands Traditional Singing. 1990. Recorded by Capricorn Studios. Produced by the Ministry of Cultural Development and Capricorn Studios. Capricorn CPR 207. Cassette.

Tapuahua Boys. 1990. Recorded by the T and A Onu Studio. T and A Onu Studio TO25. Cassette.

Tumutevarovaro Live—Rarotonga, Cook Islands. 1990. Recorded by Capricorn Studios. Capricorn CPR 202. Cassette.

Hawai'i

Aloha Hula Hawaiian Style. 1995. Remastered recordings. Vintage Hawaiian Treasures, 9. HanaOla. HOCD 26000. Compact disk.

Apaka, Alfred. N.d. *The Golden Voice of the Island*. Hula Records C-HS408. LP disk.

———. 1984. *Hawaiian Paradise*. Capitol Records 541-56636. LP disk.

Beamer, Keola. 1995. *Moe'uhane Kīkā: Tales from the Dream Guitar*. Dancing Cat Records 08022-38023. Compact disk, cassette.

Bruddah Waltah and Island Afternoon. 1990. *Hawaiian Reggae*. Platinum Pacific Records PPR 1005CD. Compact disk.

Cazimero, Brothers. 1977. *The Brothers Cazimero in Concert*. Produced by Jack DeMello. Music of Polynesia 32672. Cassette.

———. 1987. *The Best of the Brothers Cazimero*. Mountain Apple MACD-2011. Compact disk.

———. 1997. *Twenty Years of Hōkū Award-Winning Songs*. Mountain Apple MACD-2042. Compact disk.

Chuck Machado's Luau Inc.: Recorded Live on the Beach at Waikiki. NA Recording by Sounds of Hawaii. CPM-9318. LP disk.

Denny, Martin. 1996. *Exotica: The Sounds of Martin Denny*. Scampi SCP 9712. Compact disk.

Edwards, Webley. 1997 [1975]. *Hawaii Calls: Hawaii's Greatest Hits*. Hawaii Calls, Inc. HCS 921A, 922A. 2 compact disks.

The Extraordinary Kui Lee. 1997. Remastered recordings. Hawaiian Legends, 2. HanaOla HOCD 28000. Compact disk.

Felix Mendelssohn and His Hawaiian Serenaders. 1997. Remastered recordings. Music of Hawaii, 5. Harlequin HQ CD 93. Compact disk.

Folk and National Music Recordings, Vol. 1: *Foreign Countries*. 1958. Recordings by British Broadcasting Commission. Recorded Programmes Permanent Library, 239–243, record 23176. LP disk.

Hapa Haole Hawaiian Hula Classics. 1993. Remastered recordings. Vintage Hawaiian Treasures, 1. HanaOla HOCD 17000. Compact disk.

Hawaiian Chants, Hula, and Love-Dance Songs. 1989 [1972]. Vocals by Kaulaheaonamoku Hiona. Recorded by Jacob Feuerring. Reissued with revised notes by Elizabeth Tatar. Smithsonian Folkways 4271. LP disk.

Hawaiian Chant, Hula, and Music. 1989 [1962]. Vocals by Kaulahcaonamoku Hiona. Recorded by Jacob Feuerring. Reissued with revised notes by Elizabeth Tatar. Smithsonian Folkways 8750. LP disk.

Hawaiian Drum Dance Chants: Sounds of Power in Time. 1989. Notes by Elizabeth Tatar. Smithsonian Folkways SF-40015. Cassette, compact disk.

Hawaiian Festival Contingent. 1976. *Festival Music from Hawaii*. Hibiscus Records HLS-71. LP disk.

Hawaiian Masters Collection, Vol 1. 1991. Remastered recordings. Tantalus Records TRCD 1002. Compact disk.

Hawaiian Masters Collection, Vol. 2. 1993. Remastered recordings. Tantalus Records TRCD 1003. Compact disk.

Hawaiian Slack Key Guitar Masters: Instrumental Collection. 1995. Dancing Cat Records 08022-38032-2. Compact disk.

Hawaiian Song Bird Lena Machado. 1997. Remastered recordings. Hawaiian Legends, 3. HanaOla HOCD 29000. Compact disk.

Hawaiian Style Band. 1994. *Rhythm of the Ocean*. Top Flight Records 2936. Compact disk.

The History of Slack Key Guitar. 1995. Remastered recordings. Vintage Hawaiian Treasures, 7. HanaOla HOCD 24000. Compact disk.

Ho'opi'i Brothers. 1975. *No Ka Oi*. Poki Records SP 9006. Cassette.

———. 1996. *Ho'opi'i Brothers: Ho'omau—To Perpetuate*. Produced by Jay W. Junker and Diane Sunada Koshi for Honu Productions. Notes by Jay W. Junker. Mountain Apple. Compact disk.

Hula Hawaiian Style. 1994. Remastered recordings. Vintage Hawaiian Treasures, 2. HanaOla HOCD 18000. Compact disk.

Kahumoku, George Jr. 1997. *Drenched by Music*. Produced by George Winston and George Kahumoku Jr. Dancing Cat Records 08022-38038-2. Compact disk.

The Kalima Brothers and the Richard Kauhi Quartette. 1996. Remastered recordings. Hawaiian Legends, 1. HanaOla HOCD 27000. Compact disk.

Kamakawiwo'ole, Israel. 1993. *Facing Future*. Bigboy Record Company BBCD 5901. Compact disk.

Kanaka'ole, Aunty Edith. 1978. *Ha'aku'i Pele i Hawai'i!* Produced by Don McDiarmid Jr.; notes

by Kalani Meinecke. Hula Records HS-560. LP disk.

———. 1979. *Hi'ipoi i ka 'Āina Aloha: Cherish the Beloved Land*. Hula Records HS-568. LP disk.

Kāne, Raymond. 1988. *Music Recorded for the Robert Mugge Film "Hawaiian Rainbow."* Produced by Robert Mugge. Rounder Records 6020. LP disk.

———. 1994. *Punahele*. Dancing Cat Records 08022-38001-2. Compact disk.

Kapena. 1992. *The Kapena Collection*. Remastered recordings. KDE Records KDE-1059CD. Compact disk.

KCCN's Twenty-Fifth Anniversary Collection: Twenty-Five of Hawaii's Most Beloved Songs. 1991, recorded between 1957 and 1990. 2 cassettes.

Kodak Hula Show. N.d. Produced by Tommy Kearns. Waikiki Records WC-302. Cassette.

Kotani, Ozzie. 1995. *Kani Hō'alu (The Sound of Slack Key)*. Dancing Cat Records 08022-38013. Compact disk.

Ku, Tony, accompanied by Tomomi Sugiura. 1979. *Original Hawaiian Steel Guitar*. Notes by Isami Uchizaki. Folkways FW 8714. LP disk.

Maiki Ain Lake and the Kahauanu Lake Trio and Singers. 1992. *Maiki: Chants and Mele of Hawaii*. Hula Records CHDS-588. Compact disk.

Mele-Hula. N.d. Produced by H. Skippy Hamamoto. Collectors Series, 1–2. Noelani Records NRS 102–103. 2 LP disks.

Mehe Hula Hawaiian Style. 1994. Remastered recordings. Vintage Hawaiian Treasures, 4. HanaOla HOCD 20000. Compact disk.

The Music of Hawaii. 1974. Recordings by Marc J. Aubort; notes by Mary McPeak and Robert E. Pullman. National Geographic Society 706. LP disk.

Musics of Hawai'i: It All Comes from the Heart. 1994. Folk Arts Program, State Foundation on Culture and Arts. Five cassettes.

Nā Leo Hawai'i Kahiko: Voices of Old Hawai'i. 1981. Notes by Elizabeth Tatar. Audio-Recording Collection Series, 1. Bishop Museum ARCS-1. Two LP disks.

Na Mele Ho'oheno: A Musical Tradition. 1997. Kamehameha Schools/Bernice Pauahi Bishop Estate. 2 compact disks. (Retrospective of seventy-five years of the choral-singing contest.)

Nahenahe Singers. c. 1960s. *Hawaii's Folk Singers*. Tradewinds-Records TS-115. LP disk.

Na Mele Paniolo: Songs of Hawaiian Cowboys. 1992 [1987]. Notes revised by Ricardo D. Trimillos, with an introduction by Lynn Martin. Folk Arts Program, State Foundation on Culture and the Arts. 2 cassettes.

Naope, George. 1985. *The Other Side of Hawaii's Golden Treasure: Na Mele o Kawa Kahiko (Chants of Hawaii)*. 1985. MDL-6430. Compact disk.

Nature's Mystic Moods: The Sounds of Hawaii. 1975. Recorded by Brad Miller. Bainbridge Entertainment BT6240. LP disk.

Night Club Hula Hawaiian Style. 1995. Remastered recordings. Vintage Hawaiian Treasures, 6. HanaOla HOCD 23000. Compact disk.

On the Beach at Waikiki (1914–1952). 1995. Remastered recordings. Music of Hawaii, 3. Harlequin HQ CD 57. Compact disk.

On a Coconut Island. 1994. Remastered recordings. Music of Hawaii, 2. Harlequin HQ CD 46. Compact disk.

Pahinui, Gabby. 1972. *Gabby*. Panini Records PS-1002. LP disk.

Peter Moon Band, with David Choy, Martin Pahinui, and Palani Vaughan. 1994. *Iron Mango*. Kanikapila Records KCD-1014. Compact disk.

Reichel, Keali'i. 1994. *Kawipunahele*. Punahele Records PP001. Compact disk.

———. 1997. *Lei Hali'a*. Punahele Records. Compact disk.

Rhythm of the Islands, 1913–1952. Remastered recordings. Music of Hawaii, 4. Harlequin HQ CD 92. Compact disk.

Royal Hawaiian Band: Live at Carnegie Hall. N.d., recorded in 1988. FRB CD 002-003. 2 compact disks.

Santa's Gone Hawaiian. 1995. Remastered recordings. Vintage Hawaiian Treasures, 8. HanaOla HOCD 25000. Compact disk.

Show Biz Hula Hawaiian Style. 1995. Remastered recordings. Vintage Hawaiian Treasures, 5. HanaOla HOCD 22000. Compact disk.

Sons of Hawaii: The Folk Music of Hawaii in Book and Record. 1971. Produced by Steve Siegfried, Witt Shingle, and Lawrence Brown; notes by Carl Lindquist. Island Heritage KN 1001. LP disk.

Ta'ua, Keli'i. 1977a. *Kamehameha Chants*. Pumehana Records PS-4918. Compact disk.

———. 1977b. *The Pele Legends*. Pumehana Records PS-4903. Compact disk.

Tickling the Strings, 1929–1952. 1993. Remastered recordings. Music of Hawaii, 1. Harlequin HQ CD 28. Compact disk.

Topolinski, Kaha'i. 1986. *Nou E, Kawena: For You, Kawena*. Pumehana Records PS-4926. LP disk.

Traditional Music from Hawai'i: Music from the Motion Picture Soundtrack "Troubled Paradise." 1992. Flying Fish Records FF70607. Compact disk.

We Are Hawaii. N.d. Hula Records P 21. Two LP disks.

Wong, Kaupena, and Pele Pukui. 1974. *Mele Inoa: Authentic Hawaiian Chants*. Poki Records SP 9003. LP disk.

Aotearoa

Authentic Maori Chants. N.d. Recordings prepared by the Maori Purposes Fund Board. Kiwi EC 8-10. Three EP disks.

Maori Songs of New Zealand: Haka, Tangi, Oriori, Waiata, Maemae, Karakia, Apakura. 1952. Recordings by the New Zealand Broadcasting Service. Ethnic Folkways P433. LP disk.

Polynesian Studies Group. N.d. *The Magic of Maori Song*. Salem XP 5025. LP disk.

Putiki Maori Club. N.d. *Maori Action Songs*. M3D-I. EP disk.

Te Wiata, Inia. N.d. *The Maori Flute: The Hinenmoa Legend in Song and Story*. Kiwi EA-120. EP disk.

Turakina Maori Girls' College Choir, Marton, New Zealand. N.d. *The Maori Girls of Turakina*. Viking VP 255. LP disk.

Rapa Nui

The Easter Island. 1976. Recordings by Claude Jannel; ed. Ariane Segal. Peters International FARN 91040. LP disk.

Isla de Pascua. 1965. Recordings by Jorge di Lauro. Odeon Chilena/EMI LDC-36547/36548. Two LP disks.

Ka Oho Mai. N.d. Contemporary music by Sergio Teao and friends. Private issue. Cassette.

Música de Isla de Pascua. 1991. Recopilación Ramón Campbell. Collección Música Chilena, Serie 1, Música Vernácula. Sección de Musicología, Facultad de Artes, Universidad de Chile. Cassette.

Musiques de l'Île de Pâques (Rapa-Noui). 1976. Recordings by Christos Clair-Vasiliadis. Société Française de Productions Phonographiques AMP 7 2908. LP disk.

Rapa Nui: Music and Natural Sounds. 1995. Recordings and notes by Jürg Hertel. Noiseworks 130. Compact disk.

Tepano, Tomás Tepano. 1996. *Rapa Nui*. Arion ARN 64345. Compact disk.

CONTEMPORARY CROSS-CULTURAL SYNTHESES

Anthill, John. 1977. *Corroboree: Symphonic Ballet*. Sydney Symphony Orchestra, conducted by John Lanchbery. EMI Records Australia OASD 7603. LP disk.

Atherton, Michael. N.d. *Windshift*. Compact disk.

Australia: Reconciliation—Two Stories in One. N.d. Compact disk.

Cooder, Ry, with Gabby Pahinui. 1975. *Chicken Skin Music*. Reprise Records K54083. LP disk.

Gabby Pahinui Hawaiian Band, with Ry Cooder. *Volume One*. 1977, recorded in 1974–1975. Warner Brothers BS 3023. LP disk.

Laurens, Guy. c. 1995. *Fenua*. Tahitian techno. Océane Production OCN CD58. Compact disk.

Manahune. 1995, recorded in 1992. *The Nurturing Hand*. Recorded at Studio Hei Tiare. Hula Records International CDHS-1001. Compact disk. (Tahitian world beat.)

Not Drowning, Waving, and the Musicians of Rabaul, PNG (featuring Telek). 1990. *Tabaran*. WEA 903172999. 2 compact disks.

Polynesian Music Festival 1993. 1994. Music from Fiji, Tonga, Sāmoa, Tuvalu, Tahiti, Cook Islands, Hawai'i, Aotearoa, Rapa Nui. Produced by Nigel Stone. Raging Goose Productions PMFT 001. Cassette, compact disk.

Rasta Nui. 1995. *Tahiti Reggae Beat*. Tahitian reggae. Recorded at Studio Hei Tiare. Produced by Tupuna Production. Hula Records CD HS-1002. Compact disk.

Royal Band. 1995. *Royal Band Live: En direct du Royal Papeete*. Océane Production OCN CD 55. Compact disk.

Telek, George. 1997. *Telek*. Origin OR 030. Compact disk.

Yothu Yindi. 1996. *Birrkuta: Wild Honey*. Mushroom Records. Compact disk.

Films and Videos of Oceanic Performing Arts

PACIFIC FESTIVALS OF ART

First festival: Suva, Fiji, 1972

South Pacific Arts and Crafts. 1972. Pacific Educational Network. 30 min. Video. (Melanesia, Micronesia, Polynesia.)

South Pacific Festival. 1972. Produced by Allen Keen for the government of Fiji. 53 min. Film.

Third festival: Papua New Guinea, 1980

Wantok. 1980. Commentary in English. Produced and directed by Ellen Umlauf. West Germany: Mana. Film. 60 min. Video. (New Guinea, Melanesia, Micronesia, Polynesia.)

Fourth festival: Tahiti, French Polynesia, 1985

A Koe No Na Pua: Hawai'i's Delegations to the Pacific Arts Festivals. 1985. Produced by Alu Like Library. 30 min. Film video. (Performers discuss their plans and experiences.)

Contemporary Music of the Arts Festival. 1985. Institut de la Communication Audiovisuelle de Polynésie Française. 57 min. Video.

Mélanésie. (Part 1, Solomon Islands and New Guinea; part 2, Australia, New Caledonia, Fiji.) 1985. Institut de la Communication Audiovisuelle de Polynésie Française. Video.

Micronésie. (Part 1, Guam, Federated States, and Tuvalu; part 2, Nauru and Northern Marianas.) 1985. Produced by Institut de la Communication Audiovisuelle de Polynésie Française. 2 parts, 55 min. each. Video.

Official Film of the Fourth Arts Festival of the Pacific. 1985. Institut de la Communication Audiovisuelle de Polynésie Française. 52 min. Video. (Summarizes each delegation's show.)

Polynésie. (Part 1, French Polynesia and Cook Islands; part 2, Hawai'i, Aotearoa, and Rapa Nui; part 3, American Sāmoa and Tokelau.) 1985. Produced by Institut de la Communication Audiovisuelle de Polynésie Française. 3 parts, totaling 220 min. Video.

The Tradition Bearers: Fourth Festival of Pacific Arts. 1985. Produced and directed by Summer Banner. Pape'ete, Tahiti. 28 min. Video.

Fifth festival: Townsville, Queensland, 1988

Dance Highlights from the Fifth Festival of Pacific Arts, 1988. 1989. Produced by Coral Sea Imagery. 30 min. Video.

Dancing in the Moonlight. 1988. Produced by Yarra Bank Films and Islander Media Association. Video. (Participants from various cultures perform and discuss political issues.)

Fifth Festival of the Pacific Arts. 1989. Produced by the UCLA World Arts and Culture Program. 68 min. Video.

Fifth Festival of the Pacific Arts: The Melanesians. 1989. Produced by Nā Maka o Ka 'Āina. 60 min. Video. (Participants from Melanesia and New Guinea.)

Fifth Festival of the Pacific Arts: The Polynesians. 1989. Produced by Nā Maka o Ka 'Āina. 60 min. Video. (Participants from Polynesia.)

Nā Mamo O Hawai'i. 1988. Produced by Nā Maka o Ka 'Āina. 60 min. Video. (Hawaiian delegation.)

New Caledonia. 1988. Produced and distributed by Coral Sea Imagery. 65 min. Video. (New Caledonian contingent.)

Papua New Guinea Delegation. 1988. Queensland: Coral Sea Imagery. 30 min. Video. (Oro and West Sepik provinces, Trobriand Islands, Manus, West New Britain, Gogodala, Mekeo, Pari, Sia; Raun Raun Theatre and Dua Dua Dance Group.)

Tahiti at the Festival. 1988. Produced by Nā Maka o Ka 'Āina. 60 min. Video.

Sixth festival: Rarotonga, Cook Islands; 1992

Maire Nui Vaka. 1992. Directed by Gundolf Krüger. Institut für den Wissenschaftlichen Film. 43 min. Video.

Tanz der Cook-Inseln. 1994. Directed by Andrea Weisser. Cologne: Deutsche Sporthochschule. 45 min. Video. (Cook Islands National Arts Theatre.)

Visions of the Pacific. c. 1992. Produced by Kenzo for the Ministry of Cultural Development, Cook Islands. 60 min. Video. (Australia, Papua New Guinea, New Caledonia, Guam, Samoa, Niue, Tahiti, Cook Islands, Hawai'i, Aotearoa.)

Seventh Festival: Apia, Samoa; 1996

Opening Ceremony. 1996. Produced by Televise Samoa. Video.

Performing Arts. 1996. Produced by Televise Samoa. Video.

MULTICULTURAL FILMS AND VIDEOS

Aus den Hamburgische museum für Völkerkunde: Völkerkunde Filmdokumente aus der Sudsee aus den Jahren 1908–1910. N.d. Edited by Hans Tischner. Hamburg: Museum für Völkerkunde. Film. (Dances from the Mortlock Islands, Chuuk, and the Bismarck Archipelago.)

Dancing in One World. 1993. Directed by Stephanie Bakal and Mark Obenhaus. New York: RM Arts, BBC-TV, and Thirteen/WNET. 57 min. Film. ('Uveans, Hawaiians, and others.)

JVC Video Anthology of Music and Dance, Vol. 29. 1990. Ed. Tomoaki Fujii, in collaboration with the National Museum of Ethnology, Ōsaka. Produced by Nakagawa Kunihiko and Yuji Ichihashi. Cambridge, Mass.: Rounder Records, distributor. 92 min. Video. Australia: Djinang, of Arnhem Land; New Guinea: Iatmul, Sawos, Eipo; Melanesia: New Caledonia (Tiga, Ouvea, and eastern Grande Terre); Micronesia: Federated States (Pohnpei), Northern Marianas (Saipan);

Polynesian outlier: Bellona. The New Caledonian, Micronesian, and Bellonese performances were shot at the fifth Festival of Pacific Arts.

Pacific Passages. 1997. Produced and directed by Caroline Yacoe, Wendy Arbeit, and G. B. Hajim. Pacific Pathways. 30 min. Video.

South Pacific. 1957. CBS/Fox. 150 min. Film, video. (Rodgers and Hammerstein musical, starring Rossano Brazzi and Mitzi Gaynor; island scenes filmed on Kaua'i, Hawai'i.)

AUSTRALIA

Note: Some films are marked with an asterisk (*). Aboriginal people consider that these films, because they show secret rites, should not be screened publicly in Australia; the Australian Institute of Aboriginal and Torres Strait Islander Studies prefers that they not be screened anywhere.

Multicultural films and videos

The Coolbaroo Club. 1996. Directed by Robert Scholes; research funded by Australian Institute of Aboriginal and Torres Strait Islander Studies. Ronin Films and Coolbaroo Club Productions. 55 min. Film, video. (Aboriginal dance club in Perth, popular from 1946 to the 1960s.)

Harold. 1994. Directed by Steve Thomas. 56 min. Film. (Documentary portrait of the Aboriginal singer Harold Blair, Australia's last great concert-hall tenor of the 1940s and 1950s.)

MIMI: Aboriginal Islander Dance Theatre. c. 1980s. Kim Lewis Marketing. 58 min. Video. (Interviews with and demonstrations by the troupe's principal dancers.)

Sunny and the Dark Horse. N.d. Directed by David MacDougall and Judith MacDougall. Canberra: Ronin Films. 86 min. Film, video. (Biography of an Aboriginal station manager; music by Harry and Wilga Williams and the Country Outcasts.)

The Wrong Side of the Road. 1981. Directed by Ned Lander; produced by Ned Lander and Graeme Isaac. Australian Film Institute, with assistance from Department of Aboriginal Affairs. 80 min. Film. (Two days in the lives of the Aboriginal bands No Fixed Address and Us Mob.)

Northern Australia

Aboriginal Dances. 1969. Directed by Alice M. Moyle and E. C. Snell. Groote Eylandt Field Project, 8.3. Australian Institute of Aboriginal Studies. 30 min. Film. (Anindilyaugwa, Groote Eylandt, Arnhem Land.)

Djalambu—Ceremonial Disposal of Human Remains in a Hollow Log Coffin. 1963. Directed by C. Holmes. Australian Institute of Aboriginal Studies. 47 min. Film. (Arnhem Land.)

* *The Djunguan of Yirrkala*. 1966. Directed by Roger Sandall. Australian Institute of Aboriginal Studies. 56 min. Film. (Yolngu, Arnhem Land.)

Eight Aboriginal Songs with Didjeridu Accompaniment. 1969. Directed by Alice M. Moyle and E. C. Snell. Groote Eylandt Field Project, 8.6. Australian Institute of Aboriginal Studies. 20 min. Film. (Anindilyaugwa, Groote Eylandt, Arnhem Land.)

Five Brolga Dances. 1969. Directed by Alice M. Moyle and E. C. Snell. Groote Eylandt Field Project, 8.4. Australian Institute of Aboriginal Studies. 15 min. Film. (Anindilyaugwa, Groote Eylandt, Arnhem Land.)

Good-Bye Old Man. 1977. Directed by David MacDougall. Australian Institute of Aboriginal Studies. 70 min. Film. (Tiwi mortuary rites, Melville Island.)

* *Gunabibi: An Aboriginal Fertility Cult*. 1966. Directed by Roger Sandall and Nicolas Peterson. Australian Institute of Aboriginal Studies. 54 min. Film. (Arnhem Land.)

Madarrpa Funeral at Gurka'wuy. 1979. Directed by Ian Dunlop. Sydney: Film Australia. 88 min. Film. (Yolngu, Arnhem Land.)

Mourning for Mangatopi. 1975. Directed by Roger Sandall. Australian Institute of Aboriginal Studies. 56 min. Film. (Tiwi mortuary rites, Melville Island.)

Primitive People: Australian Aborigines. 1950. University of California Extension Media Center. 33 min. Film, video. (The Mewite people, Arnhem Land; includes mortuary rites.)

Waiting for Harry. 1980. Directed by Kim McKenzie. Australian Institute of Aboriginal Studies. 57 min. Film. (Anbarra, north-central Arnhem Land.)

Gulf of Carpentaria

Dance on Your Land. 1991. Produced by SBS TV, Sydney, with the Woomera Aboriginal Corporation. 28 min. Film, video. (Fifty Yanyuwa, of Mornington Island, and Borroboola perform in fourteen Aboriginal communities; songs in Garawa and Lardil.)

Ka-Wayawayama—The Aeroplane Dance. 1994. Directed and produced by Trevor Graham. Film Australia 01269756. 56 min. Film. (Yanyuwa.)

Lurugu. 1974. Directed by Curtis Levy. Australian Institute of Aboriginal Studies. 59 min. Film. (Lardil, Mornington Island.)

Queensland

Dances at Aurukun. 1962. Directed by Ian Dunlop. Australian Institute of Aboriginal Studies. 31 min. Film. (Cape York.)

Five Aboriginal Dances from Cape York. 1966. Directed by Ian Dunlop. Sydney: Australian Commonwealth Film Unit. 8 min. Film.

The House Opening. 1980. Directed by Judith MacDougall. Australian Institute of Aboriginal Studies. 45 min. Film. (Aurukun, a place in Cape York.)

Lockhart Dance Festival. 1974. Directed by Curtis Levy. Australian Institute of Aboriginal Studies. 30 min. Film. (Cape York.)

Western Australia

Bran Nue Dae. 1991. Produced by Tom Zubrycki, with Bran Nue Dae Corporation. Ronin Films. 55 min. Film, video. (The life of Jimmy Chi, with the Broome band Kuckles.)

Milli Milli. 1993. Directed by Wayne Barker. Ronin Films. 53 min. Film, video. (Kimberleys.)

Central Australia

* *The Mulga Seed Ceremony*. 1966. Directed by Roger Sandall. Australian Institute of Aboriginal Studies. 25 min. Film.

* *The Native Cat Ceremonies* of *Watarka, Loritja Tribe*. 1950. Directed by T. G. H. Strehlow. Adelaide: Adelaide University. 21 min. Film. (Central Australian totemic rites.)

Peppimenarti. c. 1980s. Produced by Film Australia. 50 min. Video. (Aboriginal ranching; features sacred rites.)

A Walbiri Fire Ceremony: Ngatjakula. 1977. Directed by Roger Sandall. Australian Institute of Aboriginal Studies. 21 min. Film. (Walpiri.)

* *Walbiri Ritual at Gunadjari*. 1967. Directed by Roger Sandall and Nicolas Peterson. Australian Institute of Aboriginal Studies. 29 min. Film. (Walpiri.)

* *Walbiri Ritual at Ngama*. 1966. Directed by Roger Sandall and Nicolas Peterson. Australian Institute of Aboriginal Studies. 26 min. Film. (Walpiri.)

Southeastern Australia

Eelarmani. 1988. Produced by Lorraine Mafi-Williams. Sydney: Australian Film Institute. Film, video.

Torres Strait Islands

Islanders. N.d. Distributed by Film Australia. 22 min. Video. (Instruments and dances.)

Wame: Traditional String Figures from Saibai Island, Torres Strait. 1965. Directed by Wolfgang Laade and Roger Sandall. Australian Institute of Aboriginal Studies. 26 min. (Includes singing.)

NEW GUINEA

General and multicultural films and videos

Dances of New Guinea. 1965. Produced by the Australian Broadcasting Corporation. 7 min. Film.

Festival of the Pig. 1950. Produced by Peerless Films. 11 min. Film.

Governor General's Tour of Papua New Guinea. 1964. Produced by Commonwealth Film Unit for Australian Department of External Affairs. 25 min. Film.

Neu-Guinea 1904–1906: In Memoriam Prof. Dr. Rudolf Pöch. 1958. Ed. P. Spinder. Vienna:

Austrian Federal Institute of Scientific Film. 16 min. Film. (Includes clips filmed by Rudolf Pöch in 1904–1906.)

Port Moresby: Coronation Celebrations. 1953. Produced by Pacifilm. 15 min. Film. (Marking the crowning of Queen Elizabeth II.)

Songs of a Distant Jungle. 1985. Distributed by the University of California Extension Media Center. 20 min. Video. (A visitor's musical experiences in Western Province and the Trobriand Islands, Milne Bay Province.)

Songs from Papua New Guinea. 1986. University of California Extension Media Center. 21 min. Video. (Bultem and Tifalmin, West Sepik; Kopiri, Southern Highlands.)

When Headhunters Reigned. 1954. Produced by W. A. Deutscher. 42 min. Film.

Yesterday, Today, and Tomorrow: The Women of Papua New Guinea. 1987. Produced by Center Productions. Distributed by Barr Films. 27 min. Video. (Examines the place of custom in modern society; includes Mendi women's self-mutilation and girls' courtship rituals.)

Yumi Yet. 1977. Film Australia and Ronin Films. 54 min. Film, video. (Celebrations of Papua New Guinean political independence, 1975.)

Papuan region

Bespannen von Trommeln. 1963. Directed by E. Schlesier. Institut für den Wissenschaftlichen Film. 8 min. Film. (Me'udana, Milne Bay Province.)

Gogodala: A Cultural Revival? 1977. Directed by Chris Owen. Institute of Papua New Guinea Studies. 90 min. Film. (Gogodala, Western Province.)

Kama Wosi: Music in the Trobriand Islands. 1979. Directed by Les McLaren. Focal Communications. 49 min. Film, video. (Milne Bay Province.)

Mailu Story. 1962. Produced by the Commonwealth Film Unit. 25 min. Film. (Mailu, Central Province.)

Man without Pigs. Directed by Chris Owen. 90 min.; short version, 50 min. Film. (Binandere, Oro Province: Professor John Waiko returns home to Tabara Village.)

Sagari-Tänze. (Me'udana, Milne Bay Province.) 1963. Directed by Erhard Schlesier. Institut für den Wissenschaftlichen Film. 10 min. Film.

The Spirit World of Tidikawa. 1974. Produced by Jef Doring and Sit Doring. Distributed by Documentary Educational Resources. 50 min. Film. (Nomad, Western Province.)

Tidikawa and Friends. 1973. Produced by Jef Doring and Su Doring. Distributed by Focal Communications. 84 min. Film. (Nomad, Western Province.)

Trobriand Cricket: An Ingenious Response to Colonialism. 1973. Directed by Jerry W. Leach and Gary Kildea. Produced by Office of Information, Government of Papua New Guinea. Distributed by the University of California Extension Media Center. 54 min. Film. (Milne Bay Province.)

The Trobriand Islanders. 1951. Directed by H. A. Powell. London: Anthropology Department, Royal Anthropological Institute, University College. Film. (Milne Bay Province.)

Highland region

Bark Belt. 1987. Produced by the Institute of Papua New Guinea Studies. 35 min. Video. (Southern Highlands: manufacture of and dance with a bark belt.)

Bugla Yunggu. 1973. Directed by Gary Kildea. Distributed by Office of Information. 44 min. Film. (Chimbu, Chimbu Province.)

Gisaro: The Sorrow and the Burning. c. 1986. Produced by Yasuko Ichioka. Distributed by Nippon A-V Productions. 43 min. Video. (Kaluli, Southern Highlands.)

Guardians of the Flutes. 1994. Produced by Raul Reddish. New York: Filmmakers Library. 55 min. Video. (Sambia, Eastern Highlands.)

Maring in Motion. 1968. Directed by Allison Jablonko. College Park: Pennsylvania State University. Film. (Maring, Western Highlands.)

Moka Festival. 1951. Produced by Peerless Films. 10 min. Film. (Melpa, Western Highlands.)

Ongka's Big Moka. 1976. Granada Productions. 52 min. Film. (Melpa, Western Highlands.)

Sinmia; Haus Bilas Bilong Manmeri Bilong Baruya. 1985. Directed by Kumain. Distributed by Skul Bilong Wokim Piksa. 40 min. Film. (Baruya, Eastern Highlands.)

Songs of the Rainbow. N.d. Directed by Albert Falzon; produced by Beyond, Australia. Festivals of the World Series. 27 min. Video. (Singsing at Mount Hagen, Western Highlands.)

Tidikawa and Friends. 1972. Vision Quest. 82 min. Film. (Bedamini; includes initiatory and mortuary rites.)

Tighten the Drums: Self-Decoration among the Enga. 1983. Directed by Chris Owen. Institute of Papua New Guinea Studies. 58 min. Film. (Enga, Enga Province.)

Towards Baruya Manhood Series. 1972. Directed by Ian Dunlop and Maurice Godelier. 465 min. in 9 parts. Film. (Baruya, an Angan people of the Eastern Highlands.)

Turnim Hed: Courtship and Music in Papua New Guinea. 1992. Produced by James Bates and Phil Agland. Princeton, N.J.: Films for the Humanities and Sciences. 52 min. Film. (Chimbu Province.)

Usarufas: Music from the Eastern Highlands. 1985. Produced by John Caldwell and Vida Chenoweth. 22 min. Video. (Usarufa, Eastern Highlands.)

Werberitual (Amb Kanant). 1972. Directed by Irenäus Eibl-Eibesfeldt. Institut für den Wissenschaftlichen Film. 28 min. Film. (Melpa, Western Highlands.)

Werbetanz ("Amb Kenan"/"Tanim Het"). 1972. Directed by Irenäus Eibl-Eibesfeldt. Institut für den Wissenschaftlichen Film. 16 min. Film. (Melpa, Western Highlands.)

Mamose region

Auftritt der "Mai"-Masken in Korogo. 1984. Directed by Hermann Schlenker and Milan Stanek. Institut für den Wissenschaftlichen Film. 7 min. Film. (Iatmul, East Sepik.)

Aus dem Leben der Kate auf Deutsch-Neuguinea: Aufnahmen aus dem Jahre 1909. Directed by Richard Neuhauss. 1939. Filmed in 1909. Institut für den Wissenschaftlichen Film. 10 min. Film. (Kate, Morobe.)

Bespannen und Herrichten einer Handtrommel. 1984. Directed by Hermann Schlenker and Milan Stanek. Institut für den Wissenschaftlichen Film. 6 min. Film. (Iatmul, East Sepik.)

Cannibal Tours. 1987. Directed by Dennis O'Rourke. Direct Cinema, Los Angeles. 77 min. Film. (Mostly East Sepik.)

Fadenspiele "Ninikula." 1987. Directed by Irenäus Eibl-Eibesfeldt. Institut für den Wissenschafflichen Film. 21 min. Film. (Kaile'una, Trobriand Islands.)

Fertigstellung eines Lieder-Memorierstabes, Gesänge und Schlitztrommelschlagen bei einer Kanuweihe in Yindabu. 1988. Directed by Hermann Schlenker and Milan Stanek. Institut für den Wissenschaftlichen Film. 22 min. Film. (Iatmul, East Sepik.)

Fest zur Kanueinweibung in Kanganamun, Auftritt von Waldgeistern und Ahnfrauen. 1984. Directed by Hermann Schlenkjer and Milan Stanek. Institut für den Wissenschaftlichen Film. 21 min. Film. (Iatmul, East Sepik.)

Flötenorchester auf einem sakralen Felsen (7 Bambusflöten, 2 Schlagstcke). 1984. Directed by Hermann Schlenker. Edited by D. Kleindienst-Andrée. Institut für den Wissenschaftlichen Film. 18 min. Film. (Whom, East Sepik.)

Flötenorchester in Männerhaus. 1984. Directed by Hermann Schlenker; ed. D. Kleindienst-Andrée and M. Schuster. Institut für den Wissenschaftlichen Film. 16 min. Film. (Aibom, East Sepik.)

Herstellen und Spielen der einsaitigen Stielzither "Tagarangau." 1984. Directed by Hermann Schlenker and Milan Stanek. Institut für den Wissenschaftlichen Film. 11 min. Film. (Iatmul, East Sepik.)

Herstellen und Spielen der einsaitigen Stielzither "Woragutngau." 1984. Directed by Hermann Schlenker; ed. D. Kleindienst-Andrée and Milan Stanek. Institut für den Wissenschaftlichen Film. 6 min. Film. (Iatmul, East Sepik.)

Initiationsfest. 1958. Directed by Carl A. Schmitz. Institut für den Wissenschaftlichen Film. 16 min. Film. (Pasum, Morobe Province.)

Kandem erzählt von Schlitztrommel und Kopfjagd-trompete: Spiel auf beiden Instrumenten. 1984. Directed by Hermann Schlenker and Milan Stanek. Institut für den Wissenschaftlichen Film. 13 min. Film. (Iatmul, East Sepik.)

Kopfjägertanz in Chambri aufgeführt vor Touristen. 1984. Directed by Hermann Schlenker; ed. D. Kleindienst-Andrée and Milan Stanek. Institut für den Wissenschaftlichen Film. 11 min. Film. (Aibom, East Sepik.)

Männerinitiation in Japanaut: "Novizen in der Urzeit." 1984. Directed by Hermann Schlenker;

ed. D. Kleindienst-Andrée and Jürg Wassmann. Institut für den Wissenschaftlichen Film. 90 min. Film. (Iatmul, East Sepik.)

Männerinitiation in Japanaut: "Tod der Novizen." 1984. Directed by Hermann Schlenker; ed. D. Kleindienst-Andrée and Jürg Wassmann. Institut für den Wissenschaftlichen Film. 51 min. Film. (Iatmul, East Sepik.)

Männerinitiation in Takgei. 1984. Directed by Hermann Schlenker; ed. D. Kleindienst-Andrée, Jürg Wassmann, and J. Schmid-Kocher. Institut für den Wissenschaftlichen Film. 51 min. Film. (Iatmul, East Sepik.)

Männerinitiation in Tamanumbu. 1984. Directed by Hermann Schlenker; ed. D. Kleindienst-Andrée, Jürg Wassmann, and J. Schmid-Kocher. Institut für den Wissenschaftlichen Film. 18 min. Film. (Iatmul, East Sepik.)

Maultrommelspielen beim abendlichen Zusammensein. 1984. Directed by Hermann Schlenker; ed. D. Kleindienst-Andrée and Milan Stanek. Institut für den Wissenschaftlichen Film. 9 min. Film. (Iatmul, East Sepik.)

Mythologischer Gesang über die Vorfahren der Klane Mbowi-Semal. 1984. Directed by Hermann Schlenker and Milan Stanek. Institut für den Wissenschaftlichen Film. 11 min. Film. (Aibom, East Sepik.)

Namekas: Music in Lake Chambri. 1979. Directed by Les McLaren. Canberra: Ronin Films. 53 min. Film, video. (Pondo, East Sepik.)

The Red Bowmen. 1976. Directed by Chris Owen. Institute of Papua New Guinea Studies. 130 min.; short version, 58 min. Film. (Umeda, West Sepik: the *ida* ritual.)

Riten bei Knabeninitiation. 1963. Filmed in 1930. Directed by Felix Speiser and C. A. Schmitz. Institut für den Wissenschaftlichen Film. 6 min. Film. (Kambrambo, East Sepik.)

Le sang du Sagou. c. 1985. Produced by Bernard Juillerat, Centre Nationale de Recherche Scientifique. 60 min. Film. (Yafar, West Sepik.)

Singsing Tumbuan (*Mask Dance*). 1992. Asples Productions. 48 min. Video with 64-page booklet. (Birap Village, Madang.)

Tanzfest mit der Flöte "Yawanganamak" in Palimbei. 1984. Directed by Hermann Schlenker and Milan Stanek. Institut für den Wissenschaftlichen Film. 38 min. Film. (Iatmul, East Sepik.)

Totenfest in Gaikorobi: Anrufung und Tanz der Ahnen, Gesänge und Flötenspiel. 1979. Directed by Hermann Schlenker and Markus Schindlbeck. Institut für den Wissenschaftlichen Film. 18 min. Film. (Sawos, East Sepik.)

Irian Jaya

Asmat. 1990. Produced by Dea Sudarman. 52 min. Film. (Study of a six-week funerary ritual.)

Dead Birds. 1963. Directed by Robert Gardner. Cambridge: Harvard University. 83 min. Film, video. (Dani.)

Herstellen einer Maultrommel. 1976. Directed by F. Simon. Institut für den Wissenschaftlichen Film. 12 min. Film. (Eipo.)

Herstellen einer Sanduhrtrommel. 1961. Directed by Adrian A. Gerbrands. Institut für den Wissenschaftlichen Film. 16 min. Film. (Asmat.)

Ornamentieren eines Blashorns aus Bambus. 1961. Directed by Adrian A. Gerbrands. Institut für den Wissenschaftlichen Film. 5 min. (Asmat.)

Singen bei der Arbeit. 1976. Volker Heeschen. Eipo people. Institut für den Wissenschaftlichen Film. 9 min. Film. (Eipo.)

Spielen einer Maultrommel. 1976. Directed by F. Simon. Institut für den Wissenschaftlichen Film. 8 min. Film. (Eipo.)

Wow. 1975. Directed by William Leimbach, Jean-Pierre Dutilleux, and Peter Van Arsdale. London: Survival Films. Film. (Asmat.)

MELANESIA

Island region of Papua New Guinea

Cultural Performances at the 1989 West New Britain Provincial Show. 1989. Produced by Asples Productions. 60 min. Video.

The Drum and the Mask: Time of the Tubuan. 1996. Produced by Caroline Yacoe. Pacific Pathways. 30 min. Video.

Malangan Labadama: A Tribute to Buk-Buk. 1982. Directed by Chris Owen. Institute of Papua New Guinea Studies. 58 min. Film. (Mandak mortuary rites, New Ireland.)

Nausang Masks: Performance. 1973. Directed by Adrian A. Gerbrands. Institut für den Wissenschaftlichen Film. 35 min. Film. (Kilenge, West New Britain.)

The Sharkcallers of Kontu. 1982. Directed by Dennis O'Rourke. 54 min. Film, video. (Kontu, New Ireland.)

Sia Chorus. 1971. Directed by Adrian A. Gerbrands. Institut für den Wissenschaftlichen Film. 21 min. Film. (Kilenge, West New Britain.)

Tui; Wokim Garamut. 1983. Produced by Divisin Bilong Infomesin. 60 min. Video. (Arawa, North Solomons.)

Vukumo, Mask: Construction and Performance. 1971. Directed by Adrian A. Gerbrands. Institut für den Wissenschaftlichen Film. 17 min. Film. (Kilenge, West New Britain.)

Solomon Islands

Anlegen des Tanzschmuckes und Tänze. 1971. Directed by Gerd Koch. Institut für den Wissenschaftlichen Film. 35 min. Film. (Ndende, Santa Cruz Islands, Temotu Province.)

'Are'are Maasina. 1971. Produced by Daniel de Copper and Christa de Copper. Sound by Hugo Zemp. Axe Films. 33 min. Film. ('Are'are, Malaita Province.)

'Are'are Music and *Shaping Bamboo.* 1993. Produced by Hugo Zemp. Audiovisual Series, 1. Society for Ethnomusicology. Video. ('Are'are, Malaita Province.)

In Mi Nao: Solomon Islands Regains Independence. 1979. Directed by Graham Chase and Martin Cohen. Film Australia. 50 min. Film, video. (Various groups.)

Kwaio Artists. 1985. University of Hawai'i. 360 min. Video. (Kwaio, Malaita Province: manufacture of musical instruments and costumes.)

Totora and Siwa. 1980. Solomon Islands Culture series. Film Australia. 10 min. Film. (Feasts of Malaita Province: *totora* for courting, *siwa* for a murdered person.)

Wogasia. 1980. Solomon Islands Culture series. Film Australia. 53 min. Film. (Santa Catalina Island, Makira Province: garden-blessing rite.)

New Caledonia

Ae-ae se chante la nuit. 1994. Produced by Brigitte Travant. Noumea: Agence de Développement de la Culture Kanak. Film. (Arhâ area of Grande Terre.)

Chants kanak: Ayoii et cada. 1995. Produced by Gilles Dagneau. Nouméa: Agence de Développement de la Culture Kanak and RFO. 58 min. Film. (Rehearsals and the making of costumes and percussion instruments as performers from Hienghène prepare for a concert in Nouméa.)

Le cricket en Nouvelle-Calédonie. 1990. Produced by Michel Bironneau. Nouméa: Centre Territorial de Recherche Pédagogique. 12 min. Film.

La danse bua. 1994. Produced by Brigitte Whaap and André Ravel. Nouméa: Agence de Développement de la Culture Kanak and Centre Culturel Provincial Yéiwéné Yéiwéné. 10 min. Film.

La danse drengeju cileje trohemi. 1994. Produced by Brigitte Whaap and André Ravel. Nouméa: Agence de Développement de la Culture Kanak and Centre Culturel Provincial Yéiwéné Yéiwéné. 15 min. Film.

La danse tchap. 1994. Produced by Brigitte Whaap and André Ravel. Nouméa: Agence de Développement de la Culture Kanak and Centre Culturel Provincial Yéiwéné Yéiwéné. 10 min. Film.

Danse de Ti Ga. 1994. Produced by Raymond Ammann. Nouméa: Agence de Développement de la Culture Kanak. 18 min. Film. (Performances by Ti Ga, a troupe from Tioumidou and Galilé Villages, central Grande Terre.)

La danse de Wetr. Produced by Marc-Arnaud Boussat and Raymond Ammann. Nouméa: Agence de Développement de la Culture Kanak. 26 min. Film. (Structure and content of a dance of Lifu, created in 1992–1993.)

Danser avec les lutins. 1992. Produced by Auguste Cidopua. Nouméa: Agence de Développement de la Culture Kanak. 15 min. Film. (Paicî area of Grande Terre.)

Les danses drui et trutru abo. 1994. Produced by Brigitte Whaap and André Ravel. Nouméa: Agence de Développement de la Culture Kanak and Centre Culturel Provincial Yéiwéné Yéiwéné. 11 min. Film.

Jêmââ. 1992. Produced by Jean-François Lalié. Nouméa: Agence de Développement de la Culture Kanak. 19 min. Film. (The Kaneka band Jêmââ, from Poindimié, central Grande Terre, Paicî area.)

Kanak et fier de l'être. N.d. Produced by Office Cultural Scientifique et Technique Kanak. 55 min. Video.

La légende de Mwaxrenu. 1992. Produced by Élie Peu. Nouméa: Agence de Développement de la Culture Kanak. 16 min. Film. (Drubéa and Nouméa areas of Grande Terre.)

Levée de deuil à Tiaoué. 1995. Produced by Gilles Dagneau. Nouméa: Agence de Développement de la Culture Kanak and RFO. 20 min. Film. (Fwâi and Nemi areas of Grande Terre.)

Mélanésia 2000. 1975. Produced by Georges Ravat and Guy Chanel. Chanel Production. 17 min. Film. (Festival performances.)

Mwakheny. 1992. Produced by Brigitte Whaap. Nouméa: Agence de Développement de la Culture Kanak. 17 min. Film. (Fwâi and Nemi areas of Grande Terre.)

Nouvelle-Calédonie, Terre Missionaire. 1931. Produced by Alphonse Rouel. Society of Mary. 37 min. Film.

Remember New Caledonia. 1996. Produced by Gilles Dagneau. Nouméa: R.F.O. Film. (Films made by U.S. soldiers in 1942–1945, including excerpts of Kanak dancing.)

Vanuatu

Blong Save Hu Nao Yumi. 1986. Produced by Film Australia. 52 min. Video. (Activities of the Arts Festival held by the people of Malakula in 1986.)

Taem Bifo—Taem Nao. 1980. Film Australia. 27 min. Film. (First National Arts Festival, Vila, 1979: crafts, singing, dancing.)

Vanuatu. 1983. Radharc Films. 26 min. Film. (Celebrations of political independence.)

Vanuatu: Struggle for Freedom. 1981. Film Australia. 75 min. Film. (Celebrations of political independence.)

MICRONESIA

Celebrating the Arts of Micronesia. 1986. Produced by Carl Hefner. 30 min. Video. (Palau, Chuuk, Pohnpei, Marshalls; performances at the Micronesian Cultural Fair, University of Hawai'i.)

Micronesia. 1954. Produced by Oceania Films. 10 min. Film. (Carolines, Marshalls.)

West Micronesia

Palau

Beldeklel a Ngloik: The Process. 1993. Directed by Lynn Kremer Babcock. Worcester, Mass.: Lynn Kremer Babcock, Holy Cross College. 62 min. (Palauan-language version), 47 min. (English version). Film.

Federated States

Kamadipw. 1983. Produced by Steve Arvisu and Joseph R. Camacho. 60 min. Film. (Dances by performers from the Net Cultural Center, Pohnpei, and synchronized pounding of kava by twenty-four pounders.)

Kosrae Singing Group: Christmas. 1987. Alele Museum, Majuro. 198 min. Video. (Kosraean performances in Uliga Church, Majuro, Marshall Islands.)

Lamotrek: Heritage of an Island. 1988. Directed by Eric Metzger. Triton Films. 27 min. Video. (Lamotrek Atoll, Yap: studies *rong* "special skill and knowledge"; songs translated in subtitles.)

Mwan Mwich. 1979. Produced by Triton Films. Micronesian Transitions series. 30 min. Video. (Moen, Chuuk.)

The Navigators: Pathfinders of the Pacific. 1983. Directed by Sanford Low; produced by Public Broadcasting System. Distributed by Documentary Educational Resources. 59 min. Film, video. (Satawal, Chuuk.)

Satawalese Canoe Departure from Saipan, Spring 1988, and Traditional Dances. 1988. Produced by M. L. Kenney. 90 min. Video. (Festivities for a canoe departing for home in Satawal; includes dancing by the crew and Carolinean residents of Saipan.)

Spirits of the Voyage. 1996. Directed by Eric Metzger. Triton Films. 88 min. Video. (Studies *pwo*, a navigator's rite of passage.)

Mariana Islands (Guam and the Northern Marianas)

Belembaotuyan. 1980. Directed by Lee Soliwada. Agaña: Guam Council on the Arts and Humanities Agency. 30 min. Video. (Chamorro.)

Chamorro Music. 1990. Produced by Kathy Coulehan for KGTF-TV. Portraits of Guam, 8. 30 min. Video. (*Kentan chamorrita* and *belembaotuyan*.)

Guam's History in Songs. 1993. Script by Carmen L. Santos and Anthony P. Sanchez; produced by Carmen L. Santos. Underwritten by the Guam Quincentennial Commission. Shooting Star Production. 30 min. Video.

East Micronesia

Marshall Islands

Alele Festival. 1986. Alele Museum, Majuro. Video.

Alele Festival. 1994. Alele Museum, Majuro. Video.

Interview with Cultural Expert, Laimaaj Barmoj. 1988. Alele Museum, Majuro. Video. (About the *jebwa*—a dance—and Marshallese navigational singing.)

Kiribati

Batere-Tanz. 1967. Directed by Gerd Koch. Institut für den Wissenschaftlichen Film. 3 min. Film. (Nonouti.)

Bino-Tanz. 1965. Directed by Gerd Koch. Institut für den Wissenschaftlichen Film. 3 min. Film. (Tabiteuea.)

Ruoia-Tanz Kamei. 1967. Directed by Gerd Koch. Institut für den Wissenschaftlichen Film. 3 min. Film. (Nonouti.)

Ruoia-Tanz Kawawa. 1967. Directed by Gerd Koch. Institut für den Wissenschaftlichen Film. 3 min. Film. (Tabiteuea.)

Ruoia-Tänze. 1965. Directed by Gerd Koch. Institut für den Wissenschaftlichen Film. 4 min. Film. (Tabiteuea.)

Tirere-Tanz Ngeaba. 1967. Directed by Gerd Koch. Institut für den Wissenschaftlichen Film. 3 min. Film. (Nonouti.)

POLYNESIA

General

Islands of Light: South Pacific Dance. c. 1980s. Huia Films. (Sāmoa, Cook Islands, Aotearoa.)

JVC Video Anthology of Music and Dance, Vol. 30. 1990. Ed. Tomoaki Fujii, in collaboration with National Museum of Ethnology, Ôsaka. Directed by Nakagawa Kunihiko and Yuji Ichihashi. Cambridge, Mass.: Rounder Records, distributor. 92 min. Video. (Fiji, Tonga, Western Sāmoa, Tokelau, Tuvalu, Tahiti, Marquesas, Cook Islands, Aotearoa. Performances from Fiji and Aotearoa were shot in Japan, other performances at the fifth Festival of Pacific Arts.)

Song of the South Seas. 1992. Distributed by the New Zealand National Film Unit. 25 min. Film. (Cross-cultural musical experiences: Tonga and Aotearoa.)

Story Telling. 1990. Directed by Jeff Gere. Honolulu: KHET Television. 30 min. Video. (Tonga, Samoa, Hawai'i.)

West Polynesia

Fiji

Fijian Things. 1972. 13 min. Film. (Children's games and dances.)

South Pacific Island Children. 1951. Produced by Educational Films. 11 min. Film. (Viti Levu.)

Tonga

The Honourable Out-of-Step. 1976. British Broadcasting Corporation. 50 min. Film. (Music and dance at the centennial celebration for the Tongan constitution, November 1975.)

Kawa-Gesellschaft und Tänze. 1954. Directed by Gerd Koch. Dorfleben im Tonga-Archipel, 3. Institut für den Wissenschaftlichen Film. 13 min. Film.

Laumatanga, Pride of Locality in Tongan Poetry. 1986. Distributed by University of Hawai'i. 30 min. Video.

From Mortal to Ancestor: The Funeral in Tonga. 1994. Produced by Wendy Arbeit. Palm Frond Productions. Video.

Tonga Royal. 1977. Produced by Journal Library. 20 min. Film.

Village Life in Tonga. Produced by Tony Ganz for Harvard University. 20 min. Film. (Hoi Village; natural sounds and music.)

Samoa

Fa'a Samoa: The Samoan Way. N.d. Directed by Lowell D. Holmes. 17 min. DFA. Film.

Moana: A Romance of the Golden Age. 1926. Directed by Robert Flaherty; produced by Paramount. Distributed by Museum of Modern Art. 66 min. Silent film.

Moana of the South Seas. 1980. Directed by Robert Flaherty; sound added by Monica Flaherty Frassetto. Brattleboro, Vt.: Monica Flaherty Frassetto. 83 min. Film.

Samoa. c. 1948. Directed by F. W. Murnau and Robert Flaherty. 16 min. Film.

Tokelau

Tokelau Tafaoga: Games. 1995. Directed by Allan Thomas. Asia Pacific Archive, School of Music, Victoria University of Wellington. Video.

Tuvalu

Fakanau-Tänze. 1961. Directed by Gerd Koch. Institut für den Wissenschaftlichen Film. 6 min. Film.

Fatele-Tänze. 1961. Directed by Gerd Koch. Institut für den Wissenschaftlichen Film. 9 min. Film.

Siva-Tanz. 1961. Directed by Gerd Koch. Institut für den Wissenschaftlichen Film. 3 min. Film.

Viiki-Tanz. 1961. Directed by Gerd Koch. Institut für den Wissenschaftlichen Film. 3 min. Film.

East Polynesia

French Polynesia

Aroha Mai. 1986. Produced by Institut de la Communication Audiovisuelle de Polynésie Française. 49 min. Video. (Show staged by Coco Hotahota, with commentary in French by Coco.)

Heiva i Tahiti: Tahiti July Festival. 1993. Produced by Institut de la Communication Audiovisuelle de Polynésie Française. 90 min. Video.

Heiva i Tahiti: Tahiti July Festival. 1994. Institut de la Communication Audiovisuelle de Polynésie Française. 59 min. Video.

Island Dreaming. The Heiva i Tahiti Fête. c. 1980s. Directed by Albert Falzon. 26 min. Video.

Place of Power in French Polynesia. 1983. Produced by Film Australia. 30 min. Video. (A Tahitian dancer's view of the cultural renaissance.)

Religious Songs. 1986. Institut de la Communication Audiovisuelle de Polynésie Française. 26 min. Video. (At the Heiva, choirs of Adventist, Mormon, and Sanito churches perform.)

Sacred Ceremony of Umu-Ti. 1988. Soundtrack recorded by David Fanshawe. Coral Sea Imagery. 27 min. Video. (Sacred singing, ritualizing, dancing, firewalking; filmed on Magnetic Island.)

Tahiti Fête of San Jose: A Polynesian Dance Extravaganza. 1992. Produced by the Polynesian Cultural Association. Playback Memories, San Jose, California. 4 parts, about 135 min. each. Video.

The Tahitian Choir Rapa Iti. 1995. Produced by Pascal Nabet-Meyer. Shanachie SH 105. 60 min. Video.

Tahitian Scenes and Dancing. 1937. Bishop Museum. 15 min. Silent film.

Tarava. N.d. Filmed by Harris Aunoa. Text by Henri Hiro. OTAC. 60 min. Film.

Te Moana Nui. N.d. Institut de la Communication Audiovisuelle de Polynésie Française. 58 min. Video. (Performances at the OTAC Grand Theater.)

Cook Islands

Moana Roa. N.d. Distributed by Indiana University Audio Visual Center. 32 min. Film. (Singing, dancing, fishing, basketry.)

Sex and Social Dance. 1993. Directed by Stephanie Bakal and Mark Obenhaus. New York: RM Arts, BBC-TV, and Thirteen/WNET. 57 min. Film.

Turou Aere Mai. 1974. New Zealand National Film Unit. 9 min. Film. (Presentations welcoming Queen Elizabeth II.)

Hawai'i

Act of War: The Overthrow of the Hawaiian Nation. 1993. Directed by Puhipau and Joan Lander; produced by Nā Maka o Ka 'Āina; with singing by the activist Didi Lee Kwai. Video.

The 'Āina Remains. 1983. Narrated by Auntie Ma'iki Aiu Lake. Produced by Clarence Ching and Jeannette Paulson. Video.

Aloha 'Āina Concert. 1988. Produced by Nā Maka o Ka 'Āina, 120 min. Video. (Speeches and music at Andrews Amphitheatre, University of Hawai'i.)

And Then There Were None. 1995. Directed by Elizabeth Kapu'uwailani Lindsey. Honolulu: Pacific Islanders in Communication. 21 min. Video.

Beamer, Keola. N.d. *The Art of Hawaiian Slack Key Guitar*. Homespun Tapes VD-KEO-GT01. Video. (Instructional video.)

Blue Hawaii. 1961. Paramount. 100 min. Video. (Elvis Presley sings fourteen songs.)

Danny Kaleikini. 1985. Media Resources International. 45 min. Video. (Includes performances on nose-blown flute *and 'ukulele*.)

Don Ho: In Love with Hawaii. 1984. Media Resources International. 30 min. Video. (Music and commentary.)

First Two Aloha Week Celebrations. 1948. Bishop Museum. 15 min. Video. (Crafts, *hula*, parades.)

Fourteenth Annual King Kamehameha Hula Competition. 1987. Media Resources International. 90 min. Video.

Gift-Giving Ritual of Old Hawaii. 1973. Cine Pic Hawaii. 10 min. Film. (Re-created pageant staged at Pu'ukohola *heiau*.)

Hawaiian Rainbow. 1988. MugShot. 85 min. Video. (Ricardo Trimillos and George S. Kanahele narrate the history of Hawaiian music; the slack-key guitarist Raymond Kāne, the singers Auntie Genoa Keawe, the Ho'opi'i brothers, Jerry Santos, and others.)

The Hawaiian Way: The Art and Tradition of Slack Key Music. 1993. Directed by Eddie Kamae; produced by Myrna J. Kamae and Rodney A. Ohtani. Honolulu: Hawaii Sons. 68 min. Video.

Hawai'i Ponoi. 1970. Bishop Museum. 60 min. Video. (Hana Music Festival: 'Iolani Luahine, Auntie Genoa Keawe, the Sons of Hawai'i, Palani Vaughan, and others.)

Ho'āla: Awakening. 1992. Produced by Heather Haunani Giugni and Juniroa Productions. Video.

Ho'okupu Mele: Hawaiian Song Offerings. 1987. Alu Like Library. 30 min. Video. (Kawai Cockett and others.)

Ho'olaule'a: The Traditional Dances of Hawaii. 1965. Honolulu Academy of Arts. 33 min. Film. ('Iolani Luahine performs *hula*.)

Hula Dancers, Surf Riding at Waikiki, Native Life. Bishop Museum. 15 min. Silent film. (Dancing, surfing, crafts.)

Hula Dancing Steps. Bishop Museum. 15 min. Video. (Pat Bacon demonstrates.)

Hula: The First Thirty Years—Merrie Monarch Festival, a Collection of Memorable Performances. 1994. Produced and directed by Roland Yamamoto. KITV4, TAK Communications. Video.

Hula Ho'olaulea: Traditional Dances of Hawaii. 1960. Directed by F. Haar. Honolulu Academy of Arts. 22 min. Film.

Hula Hou: A Program on Hula Auwana. 1985. Alu Like Library. 31 min. Video. (Choreographers discuss modern *hula.*)

Hula Pa'aloha. The Beamers. 1930–1935. Bishop Museum. 20 min. Silent film. (Members of the Beamer family perform.)

Kāne, Raymond. N.d. *Kī Hoʻalu: Play and Learn.* Video, with lyrics and tablature for 12 songs. (Instructional video.)

Ka Poʻe Hula Hawaii Kahiko. 1984, filmed 1930–1935. Directed by Vivienne Huapala Mader; ed. Elizabeth Tatar. Bishop Museum. 16 min. Film.

Kī Hōʻalu: That's Slack Key Guitar. 1994. Directed by Susan Friedman. Half Moon Bay: Studio on the Mountain. 58 min. Video.

Kukahi 1996. 1996. M005-US. Video. (Performances by Kealiʻi Reichel and others on 16 March 1996 at the Waikīkī Shell.)

Kuoha Mele Aloha. Inspiring Songs of Love. 1987. Alu Like Library. 26 min. Video. (Frank Kawaikapua Hewett and women of Kuhai Hālau Kawaikapua Pā ʻOlapa Kahiko.)

Kuʻu Home: Hawaiian Songs of Home. 1991. KGMB Television (Hawaiʻi), channel 9. Video.

Kumu Hula: Keepers of a Culture. N.d. RHAP-80363. Video.

Lia. 1988. Directed by Eddie Kamae. Honolulu: Hawaii Sons. 60 min. Video.

Malie: The Peter Moon Band. 1981. Media Resources International. 20 min. Video. (Interviews; songs from the album *Malie.*)

Merrie Monarch Hula Festival, Auwana. 1985. Media Resources International. 240 min. Video. (Modern-style performances at the twenty-second festival.)

Merrie Monarch Hula Festival: Highlights. 1985. Media Resources International. 60 min. Video. (Performances at the twenty-second festival.)

Merrie Monarch Hula Festival Kahiko. 1985. Media Resources International. 240 min. Video. (Ancient-style performances at the twenty-second festival.)

Merrie Monarch Hula Festival: Miss Aloha Hula. 1985. Media Resources International. 240 min. Video. (Female soloists at the twenty-second festival.)

Molokai Ka Hula Piko. 1985. Alu Like Library. 28 min. Video. (John Kaimikaua's version of the origin of ancient Hawaiian dance.)

1987 Merrie Monarch Festival, Auwana. 1987. Media Resources International. 3 parts, 120 min. each. Video. (Modern-style performances at the twenty-fourth festival.)

1987 Merrie Monarch Festival: Highlights. 1987. Media Resources International. 120 min. Video. (Performances at the twenty-fourth festival.)

Pacific Sound Waves. 1987. Produced by Nā Maka o Ka ʻĀina. 60 min. Video. (Music of political protest and power.)

Paniolo o Hawaiʻi: Cowboys of the Far West. 1997. Produced and directed by Edgy Lee; written by Paul Berry and Edgy Lee. Film.

Papakōlea: A Story of Hawaiian Land. 1993. Directed by Edgy Lee and Haskell Wexler. 57 min. Video.

Paradise, Hawaiian Style. 1966. Distributed by CBS/ Fox. 91 min. Video. (Elvis Presley's second Hawaiian film.)

Puamana. 1990. Directed by Les Blank; sound by Chris Simon; produced by Meleanna Aluli Meyer. 37 min. Video. (Life and Music of Auntie Irmgard Farden Aluli.)

The Slack Key Secrets of Ray Kane. 1995. Lonetree Productions. 110 min. Video.

Sovereignty: A Celebration of Life. 1993. Produced by Henry Kapono. Honolulu: KHON-TV. 60 min. Video. (Performances by Roland Cazimero, Hula Hālau Olana, Israel Kamakawiwoʻole, and Cyril Pahinui.)

The Story of the Struggle of the Native Hawaiian People for Self-Determination. 1988. Directed by Puhipau and Joan Lander; produced by Nā Maka o Ka ʻĀina. 22 min. Honolulu. Video.

A Tour of the Hawaiian Islands. 1939–1940. Bishop Museum. 25 min. Silent video. (Views of Kauaʻi, Oʻahu, and the Kodak Hula Show.)

Tropical Storm: The Peter Moon Band. 1983. Media Resources International. 30 min. Video. (Interviews; songs from the album *Tropical Storm.*)

Ula Nōweo. 1966. Directed by Dorothy Kahananui Gillette and Barbara B. Smith; performed by Eleanor Leilehua Hiram. Committee for the Preservation and Study of Hawaiian Language, Art, and Culture, University of Hawaiʻi. 30 min. Film, with booklet and 7-inch 45-RPM disk. (Instruction for the *hula Ula Nōweo.*)

Aotearoa

Heritage of Maori Song. NA Distributed by Myriah's Polynesian Bazaar. 56 min. Video. (23 songs performed by various ensembles.)

Hirini Melbourne. 1994. Produced by Television New Zealand. 39 min. Video. (Life and music of the Maori composer Hirini Melbourne of Ngāti Tuhoe.)

Kapa Haka: The People Dance. 1996. Directed by Allison Carter; produced by Derek Kotuku Wooster. Distributed by Television New Zealand. 46 min. Video.

The Maori: Featuring Ngati-Rangswewehi of Rotorua. N.d. New Zealand Video Tours. 20 min. Video.

Mawai Fillers. 1978. New Zealand National Film Unit. 21 min. Film. (Mawai Hakona Maori Group sings and dances myths and legends.)

The Power of Music. 1988. Directed by John Day and Lee Tamahori. Distributed by Matte Box Films. 24 min. Video. (The all-Māori band Herbs promotes its new album in a rural town.)

Scenes of Maori Life on the East Coast: He Pito Whakaatu i te Noho a te Maori i te Tairawhiti. 1923. Directed by Johannes Andersen, Elsdon Best, and James McDonald, with Te Rangi Hiroa. New Zealand Film Archive. 26 min. Film. (Ngāti Porou's crafts and customs, including singing.)

Scenes of Maori Life on the Whanganui River: He Pito Whakaatu i te Noho a te Maori i te Awa o Whanganui. 1921. Directed by Johannes Andersen, Elsdon Best, and James McDonald, with Te Rangi Hiroa. New Zealand Film Archive. 48 min. Film. (Whanganui River people's crafts and customs, including string games and divinatory rites.)

Scenes at the Rotorua Hui: He Pito Whakaatu i te Hui i Rotorua. 1920. Produced by James McDonald. 24 min. Film. (Performances welcoming the Prince of Wales to the Rotorua Racecourse: singing, dancing, playing flutes and games.)

Songs of the Maori. 1963. Produced by the New Zealand National Film Unit. 19 min. Film. (Maori Mormon Choir.)

Tangi and Funeral of Te Rauparaha's Niece, Heeni Te Rei, Otaki, New Zealand. 1921. Produced by New Zealand Moving Picture Company and Maoriland Films. New Zealand Film Archives. 10 min. Silent film. (Maori mortuary rites.)

Te Amokura a te Aronui-A-Rua. N.d. New Zealand Maori Arts and Crafts Institute. New Zealand Video Tours. 30 min. Video.

Te Maori: A Celebration of the People and Their Art. 1985. New Zealand National Film Unit. 58 min. Film. (Exhibit of Maori culture, including singing and orations.)

Waituhi: The Making of a Maori Opera. 1985. New Zealand National Film Unit. 59 min. Film. (Tracks the production of *Waituhi* through rehearsals to the premiere at the State Opera House, Wellington.)

Rapa Nui

Easter Island. 1934. Produced by Franco-Belgian Expedition to Easter Island, sponsored by Trocadéro Museum (Paris) and Musée Royale (Brussels). Museum of Modern Art. 25 min. Film.

General Index

Notes: Volume numbers are in **boldface**.

Page numbers in *italics* indicate illustrations or musical examples.

For some specific instruments and genres, see also glossaries.

Aaj Kal (periodical), **5**:786
Aali, Jamiluddin, **5**:746
A and M label, **3**:749
Aavik, Juhan, **8**:497–98
Ababda bedouin, **6**:624
Abadía Morales, Guillermo, **2**:385, 398
al-Abadi, Ibrahim, **1**:571
al-Abadiya, Mahla, **1**:571
Abad, Juan, **4**:130, 871
Abadzekhian people, **8**:854–56
Abae ŭi kajok (television show), **7**:958
Abaev, Sulkhan-Bev, **8**:858
Abai (Zhubanov/Khamidi), **6**:958–59
Abakuria people, **1**:624
Abaluhya people, **1**:304, 624, 625, 627, 630. *See also* Luhya people
"*Abanico*" (Puente), **3**:794
Abarca Puma, Nicanor, **2**:473
Abasin Arts Council (Peshawar), **5**:791
Al-Abasy, Salama, **6**:608
Abayie, Charles Emmanuel Graves, **1**:211, 216, 220–21
ABBA (musical group), **8**:207, 216, 446
Abbāla people, **1**:560
'Abbās Ibn al-Niṣārī, **6**:442
'Abbās I, shah of Persia, **6**:851
Abbas, Aşiq, **6**:929
'Abbasid dynasty, **6**:131, 293, 294, 296–97, 311, 447, 456, 539–42, 543, 564; **7**:23
Abbassiya, **6**:270
Abbey Theatre (Dublin), **8**:391
Abbott, O. J., **3**:1082
'Abdul Qadir Jilani, Sheikh, veneration of, **5**:281
'Abd al-Ghanī al-Nābulusī, **6**:372–73
'Abd al-Ḥakīm, Mamluk sultan, **6**:298
'Abd al-Ḥayy ibn Muḥammad al-Ṭāluwī al-Dimashqī al-Ḥanafi, **6**:370
'Abd al-Ḥayy, Ṣāliḥ, **6**:570
'Abd al-Majīd, Ḥassan, **6**:643
'Abd al-Malik, caliph, **6**:539
'Abd al-Mālik ibn 'Abd al-Wahhāb al-Fattanī al-Makkī al-Madanī, **6**:371
'Abd al-Mun'in 'Arafa, **6**:45
Abdal Musa, **6**:794, 799

Abdal, Pir Sultan, **6**:81, 765, 768, 796, 798, 799
'Abd al-Qādir al-Marāghī, **6**:11, 17, 129, 177, 365, 835, 859, 860, 869, 910, 922, 924–25
'Abd al-Qādir ibn Maḥmūd al-Qādirī, **6**:366
'Abd Al-Rahim, Gamal, **6**:612
'Abd al-Raḥīm, Sha'ban, **6**:239
'Abd al-Raḥmān 'Ammār al-Jushamīy, "al-Qass," **6**:291
'Abd al-Raḥmān al-Ānisī, **6**:686
'Abd al-Rahman Djami, **6**:998
'Abd al-Raḥmān II, Umayyad ruler of Spain, **6**:442
'Abd al-Wahhāb (*muezzin*), **6**:352
'Abd al-Wahhāb, Muḥammad, **1**:220; **6**:39, 168, 235–37, *548*, 552–53, 558, 560, *599*, 601, *601*, 616
  collaboration with Umm Kulthūm, **6**:553, 603–5
  influence on Jewish liturgical music, **6**:201
  international popularity and influence of, **6**:269, 283, 529, 548, 1039
  life and works of, **6**:*597*, *598*, *599*, *600*
Abd El-Massih, Matilda and Sophie, **6**:610
Abdel-Wahab, Mohammed. *See* Abd al-Wahhāb, Muḥammad
'Abdolqāder Jilānī, **6**:889, 942
Abdōlqader al-Marāghī. *See* 'Abd al-Qādir al-Marāghī
Abdón, Bonifacio, **4**:859, 864, 866, 869, 870
'Abduh, Fīfī, **6**:*537*
'Abduh, Muḥammad, **6**:*537*
'Abdul-Haqq, Wajiha, **6**:421
Abdülaziz, Ottoman sultan, **6**:771
Abdülbaki Dede (d. 1935), **6**:108
Abdülbaki Nâsir Dede (d. 1820), **6**:109, 110, 118, 119
Abdülhamid II, Ottoman sultan, **3**:1181; **6**:116, 757
Abdul Latif, Shah (Sufi saint), **5**:753, 754, 757–59
Abdülmecid, Ottoman sultan, **6**:780
Abd-ul-Muman, **5**:690
Abdulqadir Jilani. *See* 'Abdolqāder Jilānī
Abdur Rahman, Afghan ruler, **5**:805
Abel, Charles, **9**:194
Abelam people, **9**:546, 549–52, 977
Abelardo, Nicanor, **3**:1025; **4**:870, 871, 872, 873
Abelardo Orchestra, **4**:883
Abelhak, **6**:271
Abelo, Losta, **1**:359

Abenaki Indian nation, **3**:1073, 1074
Abeni, Queen Salawa, **1**:474
Aberdeen Folk Club, **8**:371
Aberle, Juan, **2**:736
Abe Suehisa, **7**:587
Abeyta, Don Norberto M., **3**:762
Abhinavabhāratī (treatise), **5**:24, 25, 29–30, 71–72, 313
Abhinavagupta, **5**:24, 25, 29–30, 71–72, 313
Abhinaya Chandrika (Mahapatra), **5**:519
Abhinaya Darpana (treatise), **5**:522
Abhiramisundari, T., **5**:389
Abiam, Nana Danso, **1**:211
'Abīd al-Abraṣ, **6**:359
Abi fauqa al-Shajara (Egyptian film), **6**:238
Abilem Lum (Temiar shaman), **4**:*567*, 573, 579–84
Abing, **7**:139, 140, 177–78, 349
Abioro, Chief Bọlarinwa, **1**:481–82
Abjean, René, **8**:320
Abkhazian people, **8**:827–28, 850, 851–54, 857
  dance traditions of, **8**:853
  instruments, **8**:852–53
  research on music of, **8**:853–54
  vocal music of, **8**:852–53
Åbo Akademi (Turku), **8**:488
abolitionist movement (North America), **3**:66–67, 184, 307, 308
Aboriginal and Islander Dance Theatre, **9**:60, 229, 230, 415, 443, 452
Aboriginal Broadcast Network, **3**:1278
Aboriginal Land Rights (Northern Territory) Act, **9**:62, 467
Aboriginal peoples of Australia, **9**:418–47. *See also* Australia; *specific peoples*
  body decoration, **9**:349
  ceremonies, women's, **9**:244–45
  clansongs
    Baratjarr series, **9**:418
    Djambidj series, **9**:418, 421, 422
    Goyulan series, **9**:418
    Murlarra series, **9**:418, 421, *423–24*
  concepts of pitch, **9**:292–94
  concepts of time, **9**:289
  country music performers, **9**:413
  dance, **9**:314, 450–67
    notation of, **9**:317
    sexual differentiation in, **9**:243
  early writings about, **9**:408
  epigrammatic song texts, **9**:331
  films on, **9**:1010–12

Aboriginal peoples of Australia (*continued*)
  gender constructs, **9:**241–45
  initiation schools, **9:**251–52
  instruments, **9:**371
    didjeridu, **9:**393–98
    swung slat, **9:**392
  musical textures of, **9:**301
  political songs, **9:**212
  popular music of, **9:**60–61, 134, 144–46, 414, 1005
  regional music styles, **9:**410–12
  relation to New Guinean peoples, **9:**474
  religious rituals of, **9:**185, 187–88, 345
  research on, **9:**975–76
  singing as communication, **9:**321
  song composition of, **9:**355–57
  sound recordings of, **9:**985–89
  theatrical performers, **9:**226–29
Aboriginal Triplet (Ihukube), **7:**732
Abraham and Isaac (Stravinsky), **6:**1030
Abraham, Edru, **4:**886
Abraham, Rebecca Demetillo, **4:**886
Abreu, Zequinha de, **2:**305
absolute music, concept of, **8:**82, 192
Abū ʿAbd Allāh, **6:**443
Abū ʿAbd al-Munʿim ʿIsá ibn ʿAbdallāh. *See* Ṭuways
Abū ʿAbd al-Raḥmān al-Sulamī, **6:**372
Abu Ali Ebn-e Sinā. *See* Ibn Sīnā
Abū Bakr al-Mazzāḥ, **6:**686
Abū Bakr Ibn Bājja, vizier, **6:**12, 443, 447, 448, 456
Abu Dhabi. *See* United Arab Emirates
Abudulai, Mohamudu, IV, **10:**148
Abu Fazl, **5:**46, 48
Abū Ḥasan ʿAlī Ibn Nāfiʿ. *See* Ziryāb
Abū ʾl-Ḥasan, Sīdī (Bel-Aḥsan), **6:**515
Abuhatzira, Rabbi Yiśraʾel (Baba Sali), **6:**203
Abu Lughod, Janet, **6:**21
Abu-Lughod, Lila, **6:**5, 7
Abū Manṣūr al-Iṣbahānī. *See* Iṣbahānī, Abū Manṣūr al-
Abū ʾl-Mawāhib al-Tūnisī, **6:**370, 372
Abu Nasr al-Fārābi. *See* al-Fārābī, Abū Naṣr
Abung people, **4:**622, 627
Abun people, **9:**580
  composition of, **9:**360–61
  singing of, **9:**583
  songs of, **9:**589
Abu Saayid, **5:**690
Abū Ṣadaqa, **6:**297
Abū al-Ṣalt Umayya Ibn ʿAbd al-ʿAzīz, **6:**443
Abū Ṭālib al-Makkī, **6:**372
Abū Tammān, **6:**444
Abū ʿUbayda, **6:**353
Abū Zayd ʿAbd al-Raḥmān al-Mālikī, **6:**367
Abū Zayd al-Hilālī, **6:**545
Abū Zayd, Shaykh Ṭāhā, **6:**343
Abyssinia (Johnson), **3:**619
Academia Nacional del Tango, **2:**264–65
Academia Nacional de Música (Colombia), **2:**394, 397
Academia Porteña del Lunfardo, **2:**264
Academic Folklore Ensemble of France Marolt, **8:**920

Academy of Arts and Sciences (Bosnia-Hercegovina), **8:**970
Academy for Bear Training (Lithuania), **8:**280
Academy of Music of Manila, **4:**123, 870
Academy of Music (New York), **3:**60
Academy of Music (Padang Panjang), **4:**602
Academy of the Pear Garden (*Liyuan*), **7:**59, 89, 392
Academy of Sciences of the Soviet Union, **9:**23
Acadia, **3:**7, 9, 1115, 1135–36. *See also* Nova Scotia
Acadia University (Wolfville), **3:**1116, 1119
Acadie et Québec (Matton), **3:**1167
Acagba, Majaro, **1:**474
Accademia Nazionale di Santa Cecilia, **8:**621
ACCESS. *See* Arab Community Center for Economic and Social Services (Detroit)
accordions
  accordéon jurassien, **8:**693
  acordeon, **8:**880
  akordeon, **4:**628
  Albania, **8:**286, 997
  amirzakan, **8:**853
  in Arab music, **6:**422
  in Arctic music, **3:**380
  Argentina, **2:**237, 251, 253, *257*, 258, 259, 269
    in *cuarteto* music, **2:**273, 274
  Austria, **8:***673*, 674, 676; **10:***159*
  Azerbaijan, **6:**925
  Bahamas, **2:**805, 809
  baian, **8:**811
  bandoneón, **2:**89, 251, 512, 520; **3:**730, 899; **8:**170, 657
    in tango, **2:**253, 263, 264, 511, 519
  Barbados, **2:**816
  Basque region, **8:**314
  bayan, **8:**771, *798*
  Belize, **2:**677
  Bolivia, **2:**284, 288, 293, 297
  Bosnia-Hercegovina, **8:**965, 966
  Brazil, **2:**325, 330–33, 334
  Brittany, **8:**560
  Bulgaria, **8:***164*, 284, 894, 896, 902
  buzika, **8:**840, 841
  Chile, **2:**360, 368
  Colombia, **2:**402, 407
  concertina, **9:**413
    Africa, **1:**430, 761, 762
    Antigua, **2:**799
    Costa Rica, **2:**695
    England, **8:***329*, 330
    Europe, **8:**170, 197
    Germany, **8:**657
    Ireland, **8:**383, 385, 389, 391
    North America, **3:**231, 762, 842, 893, 894, 898, 1189
    Poland, **8:**707
    Puerto Rico, **2:**939
    Scotland, **8:**372
    Uruguay, **2:**512
    Wales, **8:**348, 355
  Corsica, **8:**572
  Croatia, **8:**927, 932, 933
  Cyprus, **8:**1031
  Denmark, **8:***136*, 454–55, *456*, 457, 458

  deutsche Harmonika, **8:**657
  Dominica, **2:**842
  Dominican Republic, **2:**849, *851*, *852*, 857
  Egypt, **6:**548, 559, 616, 627
  El Salvador, **2:**715
  Estonia, **8:***180*, 494
  Europe
    chromatic, **8:**544, 560, 615
    development of, **8:**168
    diatonic, **8:**383, 385, 544, 560
    dissemination of, **8:**9, 170
    double-action, **8:**531
    hybrid types, **8:**531
    pedal, **8:***705*
    piano, **8:**330, 385
    in rural traditions, **8:**228
    single-action, **8:**531
    Western, **8:**517
  Faroe Islands, **8:**468
  Finland, **8:**479, 483, 484, 486, 487
  fisarmonica, **3:**860–61, 865; **8:**627
  fisarmonica a nümar, **8:**694
  foot bass, **8:**531
  frajtonarica, **8:**918, 920, *920*
  France, **8:**544, 546, 547, 551
  gaita, **2:**309
  garmon, **8:**840
  garmon' (also *garmoshka*; *garmonika*), **8:**771, *771*, 774
  Georgia, **8:**836, 838
  Germany, **8:**656, 657–58
  gorodao, **1:**783
  Greece, **8:***1011*, 1020
  Guadeloupe, **2:**877
  Handäoline, **8:**657
  harmoniia, **8:**811, 819
  harmonik, **8:**797
  harmonika, **4:**621, 625
  harmonika (also *ramonika*), **8:**918, 931
  Honduras, **2:**742
  Hungary, **8:**743, 744
  Inuit performance of, **3:**1275
  Ireland, **8:**390, 391
  iron-kandzal-fandir, **8:**860–61
  Israel, **6:**1019, 1020, 1072
  kekhat-pondur, **8:**862, 863
  Kenya, **1:**625
  khromka, **8:**771
  kinanda, **1:**627
  klavirka, **8:**918
  komuk, **8:**862, 863
  Kosovo, **8:**286
  Latvia, **8:**504
  lindanda, **1:**423
  Lithuania, **8:**510, 512
  Low Countries, **8:**522, 527, 530–31
  Macedonia, **8:***144*, 281, 282, 976–77, *977*, 980, 983
  Madagascar, **1:**789
  Malta, **8:**639, 640
  in Maronite church music, **6:**216
  Maya culture, **2:**655
  melodeon, **8:**330, 331, *381*, 385
  Mexico, **2:**613, *614*, 622
  in Middle Eastern music, **3:**1218
  Montenegro, **8:**959, 960

Montserrat, **2:**924, 926
Nepal, **5:**705
Netherlands Antilles, **2:**930
Newfoundland, **3:**1070, 1124–25, 1139
Nicaragua, **2:**753
North America
    in Albanian bands, **3:**927
    in Basque music, **3:**731, 849–50
    in Bulgarian music, **3:**1199
    Cleveland makers of, **3:**901
    in *conjunto* music, **3:**522, 723, 772,
        773–74, *773–74*, 775–78,
        781
    in contra dance bands, **3:**231
    in Danish music, **3:**882–83
    in Dominican *merengue*, **3:**731
    in Estonian music, **3:**878–79, 1196
    in Finnish music, **3:**873, 875
    in French music, **3:**855, 857–58, *858*,
        1075, 1164
    in German music, **3:**889, 891, *891*
    in Hispano music, **3:**761, 762
    as identity symbol, **3:**826
    in Irish music, **3:**842, *843*, 845
    in Lithuanian music, **3:**875
    in Macedonian bands, **3:**925, 926
    Métis performance of, **3:***11*
    in Mexican ensembles, **3:**9
    in Norwegian music, **3:**868
    in polka bands, **3:**529, 824, 893, 894, 895,
        897, 902, 1195
    in Russian music, **3:**1199
    Russian Old Believer playing of, **3:**887
    in Slovak music, **3:**900
    in Swedish music, **3:**871, 1196
    in *tamburitza* orchestra, **3:**920
    in Ukrainian music, **3:**914
    in Volga German music, **3:**890
North Caucasia, **8:**851, 857
in Nubian music, **6:**642
Oceania, **9:**41, 134, *135*, 198, 413, 441, 817,
    881
    button, **9:**99, 102–3, 159, 745, 905, 907,
        909, 952
    piano, **9:***81*
Ontario, **3:**1189
organetto, **3:**860, 861, 864; **8:**608–9, *610*,
    614, 614–15
Ossetian people, **8:**197, 859
Panama, **2:***57*, 775, 777, 778, *779*
Peru, **2:**212, 474–75
plonarca, **8:**918
Poland, **8:**707
Portugal, **8:**580, 582
pshine, **8:**855
in *rai*, **6:**270
Réunion Island, **5:**609
Romania, **8:**277, 872, 879
Russia, **8:**134, 155, 768
sanfona, **2:**309
Sardinia, **8:**631
schwyzerörgeli, **8:**689, 696
Scotland, **8:**297, 365, 366
Serbia, **8:**946–47, 949, 952
Slovenia, **8:**914
sonettu, **8:**626, 627, 630, *631*

South America, **2:**39–40
    button types, **2:**73, 89–90
    piano, **2:**89
South Asia, in film music, **5:**347
Southeast Asia, **4:**432, 435, 605
    in Subarctic music, **3:**391
Surinam, **2:**508
Sweden, **8:**152, 435, 441
Switzerland, **8:**206, 689, 690, 693, 696
technological innovations, **3:**240
in Tibetan culture, **5:**715
in Tohono O'odham *waila*, **3:**436, 490
trekkspil, **8:**420
in Tunisian Jewish music, **6:**527
in Tunisian *ma'lūf*, **6:**329
in Turkish arabesk, **6:**257
in Turkish music, **6:**816
Ukraine, **8:**811
Uruguay, **2:**511, 512, 519
Yukon, **3:**1277
Yuma culture, **2:**598–99
Ziehharmonika, **8:**657

*Account of the Manners and Customs of the Modern
    Egyptians, An* (Lane), **6:**544
acculturation and assimilation. *See also* fusion
        genres and border crossings; Western
        culture and music
    Africa, **1:**9, 21, 46–47, 293, 322–24
        popular music styles, **1:**416
    African-American music, **3:**66, 595, 597–99
    African composition, **1:**214–16, 219, 222–23
    Aka people, Christianity, **1:**691–96
    Andean region, **2:**220–21
    Argentina, **2:**261
    Aymara culture, **2:**357
    Bahamas, **2:**807
    Bolivia, **2:**296–98
    Brazil, **2:**307
    Bribri and Cabécar cultures, **2:**631, 635
    Brunka and Teribe cultures, **2:**685
    Cameroon, xylophone tuning, **1:**661
    Central African music and instruments,
        1:666–67
    Central African Republic, *zokela*, **1:**686
    China, **7:**227–28
    East Africa, popular music, **1:**608
    East Asia, **7:**6
    Egypt, Nubian people, **6:**645
    Ethiopia, **1:**151
    Ewe repertoire, **1:**398
    French Guiana, **2:**439
    Guaraní culture, **2:**201
    Honduras, **2:**738
    Irish-Americans, **3:**845
    Japan, **7:**538
    Jewish populations, **8:**11, 260
    Kenya, **1:**626, 630
    Kuna culture, **2:**647–48
    Latin America, **1:**383–84
    Macedonia, *čalgija* bands, **8:**281–82
    Madagascar, **1:**783, 790–92
    Maleku culture, **2:**683
    Mapuche culture, **2:**237–38, 357
        of songs, **2:**236
    Middle East, **6:**12–13
    Nicaragua, **2:**755

Nigeria, composed music, **1:**233–38, 243–44,
    251
North Africa, **6:**438–39
North America, **3:**22
Peru, **2:**483, 491
Q'ero music, **2:**230–31
Rom people, **8:**271
Shona people, **1:**745, 755–57
South Africa, **1:**759–60, 762, 767
    miners, **1:**762, 766–67
South America, **2:**67, 70–75, 245
    tropical-forest region, **2:**123–24
southern Africa, **1:**716–20
Sudan, urban music, **1:**570–72
Suyá culture, **2:**149
Tanzania, **1:**634, 643–44
Tuareg people, **1:**574, 579
Uruguay, **2:**522
Vai people, **1:**340–49
Venezuela, **2:**525, 543
Waiãpí culture, **2:**162–63
Warao culture, **2:**188–89, 197
Wayana culture, **2:**164, 167
West Africa, instruments, **1:**449
Yaqui culture, **2:**592
Yuma culture, **2:**598–99
Aceh (kingdom), **4:**601
Acehnese people, **4:**603–5
Acevedo, Jorge L., **2:**635, 704
Acevedo, María Luisa, **2:**568
Acevedo, Memo, **3:**1085
Achanak (film), **5:**540
Achang people. *See* De'ang people
Acharian people, **8:**827–28
    dance traditions of, **8:**836
    instruments of, **8:**840
Aché-Guayakí culture, **2:**455–56
Achiary, Bena, **8:**315
Achimota College, **1:**216
Achinivu, Achinivu Kanu, **1:**40, 236
Achleitner, Hubert, **8:**676
Acholi people
    bwola orchestra, **1:**227
    melodic style, **1:**224
Achumawi Indian nation, **3:**415
Achva (record company), **6:**1071
A Cirnea (musical group), **8:**574
Ackah, Jewel, **3:**1213
Acker, Gregory, **3:**1018
Ackerman, Will, **3:**346
ACMR Reports (periodical), **7:**136
Acosta, Victor, **2:**370
Acoustic (musical group), **3:**1199
acoustics, **3:**237, 264
    aerophones, **9:**392–93
    Chinese experiments in, **7:**98
    didjeridu, **9:**395–97
    fission of the fundamental, **1:**185, 187–97
    flute, **1:**173–74, 190–91
    frequency modulation, **1:**192–93
    fusion of the fundamental, **1:**186, 194–95,
        197–99
    guitar, **1:**175–77
    hardingfele, **8:**415–16
    inanga, **1:**173–77
    inanga chuchotée, **1:**168–77

acoustics (*continued*)
as instrument classification principle, **5**:20–21
instruments, **1**:172–77; **5**:322
Japan, of *nô* stages, **7**:630
lounuat, **9**:381–82
membranophones, **9**:382–83
musical bow, **1**:305
nkangala mouth bow, **1**:321
overtone singing, **7**:1004–5, 1009–10
panpipes, **9**:393, 399–400
'au waa, **9**:398
psychoacoustics, **5**:289, 290–91, 293–94
recording studio, **3**:238, 249
research on, **8**:25, 26, 35, 36, 178
stretched strings, **9**:385–87
timbre and, **1**:165
treatises on, **5**:43
Turkish folk music, **6**:82–83
Tuvan music, **6**:981–82
'ūd, **6**:364
whispering, **1**:168–71, 184
Acquaah, Daniel, **1**:355
"Across the Valley from the Alamo" (Mills Brothers), **3**:708
Across the Yellow Earth (album), **7**:358
Act of War: The Overthrow of the Hawaiian Nation, **9**:222
Acuff, Roy, **3**:77, 79, 80, 520
Acuff-Rose Publishers, **3**:80
Acuña, Manuel, **3**:739
Acuña Jiménez, Hugo, **2**:697
Ada (Mota singer), **9**:701
Adalid y Gamero, Manuel, **2**:745
Adam, Adolphe, **8**:161
Adam de le Halle, **8**:*539*, 540, 550
Adam, V., **9**:*711*
Adamič, Emil, **8**:921
"Adams and Liberty," **3**:305
Adams, Bryan, **3**:251, 266, 315, 1097
Adams, Charles R., **1**:134
Adams, Charlie, **3**:1275, 1280
Adams, Henry, **9**:20, 797
Adams, Joe, **3**:743
Adams, John (composer), **3**:176, 254, 541; **4**:132
Adams, John (United States president), **3**:305
Adams, John Quincy, **3**:305
Adams, Leslie, **3**:610
Adams, Robert, **3**:465
Adán y Eva (*pastorela*), **3**:759
Adaskin, Harry, **3**:*1184*
Adaskin, Murray, **3**:1091
Adawīyya, Aḥmad, **6**:239–40
Addeo, Leo, **3**:1050
Addicted to Rock 'n' Roll (album), **8**:802
Addison, Joseph, **8**:17
Addo, Jonathan S., **1**:216
Adedeji, Joel A., **1**:400
Ade, Ebier G., **4**:110
Ade, "King" Sunny, **1**:46, 364, 481–82, 484
Adelaide Centre of the Performing Arts, **9**:416
Adepoju, Demola, **1**:364; **3**:339
Adesh, H. S., **5**:591
al-Adfuwī, Kamāl al-Dīn, **6**:372, 373
Adgate, Andrew, **3**:289
adhān. See chant (Muslim)
Adi Dravidian caste, **5**:866, 872

Adighian people, **8**:850, 854–56, 857
dance traditions of, **8**:855–56
instruments, **8**:855
research on music of, **8**:856
vocal music of, **8**:828, 854, 855–56
Ādi Granth Sāhib (Sikh holy book), **5**:314, *315*
Adi Karnataka caste, **5**:866, 872
Ading (Maceda), **4**:875
Adio, Kasumu, **1**:475
Aditya, Jamie, **10**:48
Adiwinata, Prince, **4**:676
Adiyappayya, Paccimiriyam, **5**:215, 217, 228
Adler, Guido, **3**:69
Adler, Hugo, **3**:939
Adler, Israel, **6**:1062, 1063, 1065
Adler, Larry, **9**:1931
Adlešič, Jure, **8**:922
Admiralty Islands (Papua New Guinea), **9**:178, 600, 602
funerals in, **9**:23
music and dance of, **9**:983
USO performances in, **9**:149
Admon-Gorochov, Yedidyha, **6**:1026, 1071
'Adnan, Abu, **6**:*666*
ADO (musical group), **7**:364
Adolph & the Boys (musical group), **3**:897
Adonara, **4**:786, 796
Adonay, Marcelo, **4**:862, 869
Adonis (musical comedy), **3**:193
Adorno, Theodor W., **3**:45; **8**:188, 445
Adurehim, Abdulla, **7**:468
Adventures of Robin Hood (film), **3**:203
advertising. *See* economics
Advocate (periodical), **3**:109, 110
Adzera people, **9**:548
A. E. Bizottság (musical group), **8**:746
Aegean Forces (musical group), **8**:1021
Aegukka (Kim), **7**:961
Aeka people
dance-dramas of, **9**:489
kundu ensembles, **9**:489
Aembu people, **1**:625
Aeolian Company, **3**:259
aerophones. *See also* double-reed instruments; flutes; free aerophones; free-reed instruments; mirlitons; multiple-reed instruments; organs; panpipes; single-reed instruments; trumpets or horns; whistles
acoustics of, **5**:322
Akan people, **1**:465
'arab, **5**:692
Arab world, **6**:413–16
automobile horns, *Martinshorn*, **8**:659
bajahteh, **5**:692
Borneo, **4**:835–37
China
early, **7**:88
notation for, **7**:124–25
south and southwestern minority cultures, **7**:490–92
classification of, **6**:396, 397, 398
Colombia, ancient, **2**:183
Congo, 1500s, **1**:77
Dan people, **1**:466
dekhnabāj, **5**:692

Dogon people, **1**:455
East Asia, **7**:5
Edo people, **1**:461
Europe, prehistoric, **8**:39
Ewe people, **1**:462
Finno-Karelian classification of, **8**:179
Hausa people, **1**:449
Hindustani, **5**:339–41
Java, **4**:642
Karnataka, **5**:874
Kasena people, **1**:455
Kazakh people, **7**:460
Khmer people, **4**:172–74
Korea, **7**:827–28
Kurdistan, **6**:745–46
Kwa groups, **1**:469
Lombok, **4**:767–68
Madagascar, **1**:787–88
Mexico, ancient, **2**:8
Middle East, association with virility, **6**:306
Mongol people, **7**:1013–14
mūsīqār, **5**:693
New Caledonia, **9**:964
Oceania, **9**:392–402
Orang Asli peoples, **4**:565
Otopame culture, **2**:570
Peru, Andean region, **2**:207
Solomon Islands, **9**:962–63
South America, **2**:29–30
pre-Columbian, **2**:45
South Asian folk, **5**:345
Southeast Asia, **4**:66–67
tuning of, **4**:175
Tanzania, **1**:641–42
terminology for, **2**:29–30
Thailand, **4**:235–37
tubes, bamboo, **4**:52, 59
ai-damangu, **9**:23
gumbang, **4**:818
klông pút, **4**:534–35
pīlipè, **9**:299
pilipili, **9**:609
qieke, **7**:491
sukute, **9**:669
Tukano culture, **2**:151–53
Uighur people, **7**:459
Vietnam, **4**:475
upland regions, **4**:534–35
voice-modifying
ai-ghabrai, **9**:22–23
coconuts, **9**:609
ilol-ai gourd, **9**:22–23
krywá, **2**:455
Kuna culture, **2**:640, 641, *642*
kwarising coconuts, **9**:563
megaphones, Angola, **1**:673–74
Melanesia, **9**:598
mongi-ai coconuts, **9**:22–23
New Guinea, **9**:476–77
Papua New Guinea, **9**:547–48, 555–56, 558, 562–65, 601, 609
pina gourd, **1**:564
Vanuatu, **9**:689–90, 693
West Africa, **1**:453
whistling, as speech surrogate method, **1**:106
Aerosmith (musical group), **3**:356

Æsir religion, **8:**405
aesthetics, **2:**186–87
  accessibility and, **3:**44
  Affektion theory in Europe, **5:**64
  African-American popular music, **3:**622
  Afro-Brazilian music, **2:**110
  Ainu people, nature and music, **7:**787
  Andalusian music, **6:**446–47, 448
  Andean regions, **2:**206, 215–17
  Andhra Pradesh, of folk music, **5:**889
  Arab music, **6:**33
    ṭarab concept, **6:**149, 165, 166, 177, *281,*
      305, 313, 549, 550, 552, 554,
      558–59, 563, 594, 664
  Argentina, *cuarteto,* **2:**280
  art music and concept of progress, **8:**59–60,
    64–65
  art music styles, **2:**115
  Atacameño culture, **2:**360–61
  audience evaluation, **3:**236
  Australia, Central, **9:**439
  Austria, **8:**671
  Azerbaijan
    aşiq, **6:**929
    hal concept, **6:**149, 928
  Aztec culture, concepts of music, **2:**555–56
  Bahamas, **2:**807
  of Balinese music, **4:**730, 759
  ballad, **8:**137
  bebop, **3:**580–81, 658–59
  Belarus, vocal music, **8:**795
  Bengal, **5:**845, 856
  bluegrass, **3:**161, 168
  Bolivia, **2:**294–96
  Bosnia-Hercegovina
    epic songs, **8:**966
    ganga, **8:**112, 964
  Brazil, Afro-Brazilian, **2:**352
  Bulgaria, **8:**905
  Bunjevci people, **8:**953
  cassettes and, **5:**552
  Central Asia, **6:**900
  changing concepts of, **3:**302
  China, **7:**91, 97–104; **10:**22–23
    Cantonese music, **7:**240
    Chinese *vs.* Western music, **7:**375–76, 377,
      381–82
    ensemble music, **7:**240–41
    Guangdong yinyue, **7:**219
    Han culture, **7:**92
    Jiangnan sizhu, **7:**225
    localization of styles, **7:**417–18
    morality and, **7:**101, 103
    new music, **7:**351
    popular music, **7:**361
    qin music, **7:**89, 159–60, 161
    quyi, **7:**246, 248
    research on, **7:**136
    sheng-guan music, **7:**200
    socialist realism, **7:**340–41, 385–87
    yin and *yang,* **7:**99–100, 103, 240, 312,
      319, 545
  Chuuk, of dance, **9:**737–38
  class and, **3:**49, 269, 1035
  Classical period, folk and art commonalities,
    8:53

clothing and, **9:**347–48
club blues, **3:**669
concept of progress, **3:**27, 28
Confucian, **7:**97–98, 240, 336, 361, 547–48
cool jazz, **3:**660
Corsica, *paghjelle,* **8:**570
Cuba, **2:**829
cultural knowledge and, **3:**332
cultural relativism, **3:**71
Czech Republic, **8:**723
dance, *Saṅgītaratnākara* passage on, **5:**41
Daoist, **7:**97–98, 361
disco, **3:**229, 230
Dominica, **2:**841
early evidence of, **8:**68
East Asia, theater, **7:**73–75
economics and, **8:**188–89
Egypt
  Arab music, **6:**558–60
  mass media, **6:**233, 238
electronic media and, **8:**55
El Salvador, **2:**707
emic *vs.* etic views of, **9:**40–41
emotional theories in music, **5:**64; **7:**159–60,
  214–15, 240–41
emotions (*duende*), **8:**598
emotions (*rasa*), **3:**130; **5:**21, 26, 64, 263,
  298–99; **10:**48
  in Karnatak music, **5:**101
  Nāṭyaśāstra passage on, **5:**29–30, 484,
    508
  in raga, **5:**67, 69, 71–72, 90
  rāgmālā depictions of, **5:**313, 317–18
  Saṅgītaratnākara passage on, **5:**33, 40
  theological bases of, **5:**247
  in *tuḷḷal* performance, **5:**514
England, performance style and, **8:**334–35,
  338
European concepts of, **3:**10, 15, 22–23, 27,
  28, 31–32, 70, 143, 269, 270, 313,
  557–58, 885
European *vs.* Native American, **3:**7, 15
Fiji, **9:**779
filmī gīt, **5:**544
Finland, **8:**480–81
France, **8:**547, 550–51
French folk song, **3:**1164–65
Garífuna culture, **2:**734
Georgia, **8:**830
gospel music, **3:**585
Great Basin Indian groups, **3:**426–27
Greece, **8:**1025
Greek *mandinades,* **3:**931
group *vs.* solo performance, **9:**385
Guyana, **5:**604
Haitian music, **2:**893; **3:**804
Hawai‘i, **9:**925
  of timbre, **9:**299–300
Hindustani music, **5:**129
  complexity, **5:**136
hip-hop, **3:**697, 701–3
historical performance movement, **8:**55–56
Hong Kong, popular music, **7:**361
Hungary, **8:**739–40
ideal sound quality, **2:**33–34
India, goals of music, **5:**20

Iran, **6:**832–33
  aşiq performance, **6:**846
  ethos and mode, **6:**60, 72–73
  ḥāl concept, **6:**133, 139, 140, 855–56, 857,
    859, 863
  movement flow, **6:**878
  shīrīn navāzī, **6:**862
Iraq, *maqām,* **6:**315
Ireland, **8:**390
Italy, **8:**611, 613
Japan, **7:**64, 545–55
  biwa, **7:**645
  Buddhist, **7:**548–49
  Confucian, **7:**547–48
  dance, **7:**66
  five natural elements, **7:**547, 565
  form and, **7:**552–55
  ma concept, **7:**551, 553, 775
  male *vs.* female performance styles, **7:**765
  nature and music, **7:**550, 551, 554–55
  sankyoku, **7:**716–17
  satuma biwa, **7:**648
  Shinto, **7:**549–50
  sin gyô sô, **7:**546
  timbre and, **7:**550–52
  yin and *yang,* **7:**545–46, 565
Javanese music, **4:**634, 635, 656, 669; **10:**43
jazz, **3:**580, 583–84, 650, 661, 664–65
Jewish music, **8:**252, 257–58
  ethnicity and, **8:**262–63
Kapingamarangi, **9:**328–30, 838
Karnatak music, **5:**101, 138, 155–56, 209
  improvisatory strategies, **5:**148
Kerala, **5:**943–44
khyāl, **5:**195
Korea, **7:**813–16
  han emotion, **7:**885, 959
  p’ansori, **7:**906–7
  yin and *yang,* **7:**813, 816, 823, 834, 965,
    966
Kuna culture, **2:**648
Kurdistan, **6:**745
listener preferences, **5:**40
local criteria, **8:**112, 120–21
Lombok, **4:**763, 771
Macedonia, **8:**973
Madhya Pradesh, epic song performances,
  5:723–24
Martinique, **2:**914–20
masterpiece concept, **8:**52, 60, 63
Middle Eastern music, **6:**7–9
Mixtec culture, **2:**567
Montserrat, **2:**923
Morocco, *ḥāl* concept, **6:**492
Motown Sound, **3:**674, 709
music revival movements, **3:**56–57
Nepal, *ghāṭu,* **5:**703
New Age music, **3:**345, 346
New Caledonia, of dance, **9:**685–86
North Korea, socialist realism, **7:**962–63
nostalgia and, **8:**61
Oceania, **9:**282
Palau, of dance, **9:**725–26
Paluskar’s views on, **5:**52
Panama, vocal, **2:**780
Papua New Guinea, Banoni people, **9:**644

Volume Key: **6,** Middle East; **7,** East Asia; **8,** Europe; **9,** Australia and the Pacific Islands; **10,** The World's Music.

aesthetics (*continued*)
  Peru
    Afro-Peruvian music, **2:**501–2
    Indian *vs.* mestizo, **2:**483
  Poland, **8:**709
  Polynesia, **9:**768–69, 770
  popular music and, **2:**100; **8:**207–9
  punk, **8:**218
  Puritanism and, **3:**24–25
  Q'ero culture, **2:**229–30
  Québec, **3:**1076, 1147, 1149–50, 1151–53
  Quichua culture, **2:**429–31
  Qur'ānic recitation, **6:**158, 161, 162
  race and, **3:**70–71
  raga, gender associations, **5:**47
  rap, **3:**702
  reciprocity and, **8:**117–21
  repertoire selection, **8:**61
  research on, **8:**25
  rhythm and blues, **3:**672, 673, 708
  rock, **3:**230
  Romantic period, **8:**83
  Russia, folk polyphony, **8:**756
  Saami people, joiks, **8:**302
  Sāmoa, **9:**807
  Santa Cruz Islands, **9:**333
  Sardinia, **8:**631
  Serbia, **8:**949–50
  silence, **7:**553
  singing
    Nāradīyaśikṣā passage on, **5:**38
    Saṅgītaratnākara passage on, **5:**36
  Slovenia, **8:**914
  soul, **3:**586
  South America, tropical-forest region, **2:**130, 135
  South Asian communities in North America, **5:**580
  of Southeast Asian musics, **4:**13–14
  Soviet Union (former), socialist realism, **8:**287
  spirituals, **3:**629
  Sri Lanka, **5:**957
  Suyá culture, **2:**147, 149
  Sweden, performance style and, **8:**438–39
  tabla, **5:**124–25
  Taiwan, popular music, **7:**361
  tamburitza music, **3:**921
  Tanna, spatial, **9:**703
  tempo associations, **5:**192
  theater, **5:**483
  Tokelau, **9:**826
  Tonga, **9:**365, 367–68, 783, 785, 789
  traditional music festivals, **8:**149
  treatises on, **5:**34, 43
  Turkey
    makam, **6:**56
    vocal style, **6:**781–87
  '*ūd* performance, **6:**594
  Uighur *ikki muqam*, **6:**998
  Ukraine, **8:**807, 818
  Uruguay, **2:**520–21
  Uttar Pradesh, **5:**664
  Vanuatu, **9:**695, 698
  Vedic chant, **5:**30
  Vietnamese dance, **4:**501
  Vietnamese music, **4:**462–64

visual depiction and, **5:**303
Waiāpí culture, **2:**162
Warao culture, **2:**198
Wayana culture, **2:**167
Western, **5:**560
world music and, **8:**224–25
Yanomamö culture, **2:**174–75
Yekuana culture, **2:**181–82
Yemen, *al-ghinā' al-ṣan'ānī*, **6:**687, 689, 690
Afghanistan, **5:**744, 804–41; **6:**895
  Badakhshan, **5:**792, 813, 825, 826
    instruments, **5:**831
    vocal music, **5:**812, 827–29
  Baghlan, **5:**825, 828
  Balkh, **5:**825
  Baloch people in, **5:**773, 776
  barber-musicians in, **6:**304
  Chishtī order in, **3:**1044
  court music of, **5:**805–7, 820
  dance traditions of, **5:**506
  Fariab, **5:**825
  film industry in, **5:**531
  genre categories in, **5:**826–27
  geography of, **5:**817, 825, 833
  Hazarajat
    vocal music, **5:**812
    women's dances, **5:**814
  Herat, **5:**824
    court music, **5:**804
    professional musicians, **5:**822–23
    vocal music, **5:**812–13, 820
    women performers in, **6:**305
    women's bands, **5:**815, 822–23, *823*
    women's dances, **5:**814
  history of, **5:**238, 810–11, 817, 825–26
  history of music in, **5:**804–5
  instrument making in, **5:**831–32
  instruments in, **5:**336–37, 344, 345, 804, 820–22, 830–31, 835
    gender associations of, **5:**812
  Iranian dance traditions in, **6:**875–79
  Jozjan, **5:**825
  Kabul, **5:**805
  Kandahar, **5:**805
  Kunduz, **5:**825
  languages of, **5:**5, 804
  map of, **5:***3, 802*
  Mazar-e Sharif, **5:**811, 818, 825
  musical genres
    falak, **5:**812, 828, 831
    Kabuli *ghazal*, **5:**805–6, 807, 835
    naghma-ye kashāl, **5:**805, 806–7, 835
    Pashtun songs, **5:**834–40
  northern, **5:**825–32
  Persian regions of, **6:**823
  politics in, **5:**16, 804–11
  popular music in, **5:**809–10, 818, 820, 827
  population of, **5:**5, 804, 825, 833
  regional cassettes in, **5:**554
  religion in, **5:**10, 804, 817, 825
  research on music of, **5:**817, 825
  Samangan, **5:**825
  shashmaqām in, **5:**827
  southeastern, **5:**833–41
  Takhar, **5:**825
  theater in, **5:**489

Turkmen people in, **6:**967
vocal music, **5:**827–29, 834–35; **6:**301, 830
  folk songs, **5:**810
western, **5:**817–24
women's music in, **5:**812–16, 818
Afghan people. *See also* Pashtun people
  in North America, **3:**949
  in North West Frontier Province, Pakistan, **5:**785
  in Sri Lanka, **5:**954
  in United Kingdom, **5:**572–76
Afikpo people, **1:**117, 459
Aflatoon (film), **5:**540
Aflou (musical group), **6:**466
Afonja (Oyo general), **1:**401
Afonso Henriques, king of Portugal, **8:**576
Afonso III, king of Portugal, **8:**576
Afonso, José, **8:**584
Afrāḥ al-Yaman (musical group), **6:**284–85
al-Afriāt, Shaykh, **6:**527
Africa. *See also specific countries, regions, and topics*
  African-American musical influences in, **3:**587
  Americans in, **1:**87
  Arabs in, **1:**11, 75–76, 147, 219–20, 436, 533, 635
  cassette dissemination in, **1:**4
  colonialism in, **1:**3, 15, 17–19, 47, 58–59, 62–63, 97, 159–60, 415–16
  cultural preservation in, **1:**38
  cultural revival in, **1:**30, 33
  dance in, **1:**285–92
  drumming traditions, **3:**335, 338; **10:**29
  employment in, **1:**3–4
  ethnomusicological research in, **10:**55–65, 109–24, 137–55
  Europeans in, **1:**11, 76–99, 319–20, 351, 389, 436, 635
  fusion genres of, **3:**337
  geography of, **1:**2, 415–16
  guitar in, **1:**350–67
  healing rituals, **1:**273–74, 277
  historical studies, **1:**293–96, 301–7; **10:**120
  Indonesians in, **1:**295, 598, 605, 607, 700, 715, 781, 782–83, 786
  kingdoms in, **1:**4–5
  kinship systems in, **1:**5
  languages of, **1:**2–3
  Latin American influences in, **1:**383–88
  maps of, **1:***xvi, 440, 530, 596, 648, 651, 698*
  national boundaries in, **1:**415
  politics in, **1:**15
  population of, **1:**2
  religions in, **1:**5
  rural-urban interchange in, **1:**415
  secret societies in, **1:**5
  settlements in, **1:**5
  slave trade in, **1:**3, 81–85
  style areas in, **1:**8
  trade and transport in, **1:**4–5
  traditional musical elements, **3:**593
  writing systems in, **1:**3
  xylophones in, **4:**58
Africa '70, **1:**483
Africa Brass (Coltrane), **3:**662
Africa in Latin America, **2:**839

African-Americans. *See also specific musical genres*
  African heritage movement, **3:**327, 336, 621, 678, 714
  African retentions, **1:**412; **3:**67, 523, 585, 592–95, 601
    influence on blues, **3:**638–39, 642–43
  art music composers, **3:**29, 603–12
  blues traditions, **3:**637–49
  choral music, **3:**535–36
  class-based distinctions, **3:**578
  collective biography, **3:**29
  colonial-era music, **3:**64, 594–96
  community music-making, **3:**284
  Creole, **3:**600, 651–52, 858
  cries, calls, and hollers of, **3:**81–85
  cultural interactions, **3:**21–22, 836
  as disco audience, **3:**228, 687, 711
  discrimination against, **3:**13
  Double V campaign, **3:**656, 668
  enslavement of, **2:**804; **3:**8–9, 43, 64–68, 81–85, 239, 325, 331–32, 506, 523, 573, 592–601, 625
  European descriptions of, early, **3:**65–66, 573, 593, 597
  European performances of, **8:**233
  folk traditions, **3:**534–35, 579–81, 592–601
  Gullah, **3:**574
  Harlem Renaissance, **3:**71, 577–78
  in Hawai‘i, **9:**100
  historical concerts, **3:**33–34
  influence on African music, **1:**416
  influence on South African music, **1:**719, 764–66
  instruments, **1:**316; **3:**593, 595, 596–97, *597*
  in Los Angeles, **3:**742
  musical origins, controversy, **3:**573, 575–76
  musical styles of, **3:**12–13, 32, 34, 63–72, 325, 523–25, 705–15
  music incorporated into classical compositions, **3:**14, 539
  music industry and, **3:**705–15
  “Negro music” as concept, **3:**66–68
  nineteenth century, **3:**9
  population of, **3:**4, 143
  as radio audience, **3:**350
  religious music of, **3:**624–35
  religious practices of, **3:**104, 120, 125–27, 523, 625–26, 630, 631, 639, 802
  research on music of, **3:**14, 31, 83–85, 149, 510, 512, 572–87; **10:**137–55
  step dancing, **3:**218
  stereotypes of, **3:**63–64, 65–66, 185, 186, 187, 191–92, 582, 638, 651
  subjugation of, **3:**17
  theatrical composers and performers, **3:**194, 607, 608–9, 614–22
  time-motion concepts, **1:**127
  women composers, **3:**93
  women popular musicians, **3:**96
  work songs of, **3:**293
African Arts (periodical), **1:**285
African Beats, **1:**364
African-Canadians
  in Maritime Provinces, **3:**150, 332, 1063, 1068, 1072, 1132–34
  music of, **3:**73, 331–32

  in Ontario, **3:**1078, 1082, 1085, 1188, 1211–13
  population of, **3:**4, 73
  in Prairie Provinces, **3:**1086, 1091
  in Québec, **3:**1077, 1169–70
  settlement of, **3:**1057
African Caribbean Institute, **1:**32
African descendants (Asia and Maghrib)
  in Arabian peninsula, **6:**297, 304, 403–4, 405, 417, 539, 546, 657, 703; **10:**58
  in Iraq, **6:**304, 546
  in Karnataka, **5:**877
  in Maghrib region, **6:**304, 407, 408, 434–35, 437, 474, 523, 1035 (*See also* Gnāwa people)
  in Oman, **6:**672, 678–79
  in Sri Lanka, **5:**954–55, 970–71
African descendants (Europe)
  in England, **8:**231–32, 233
  in France, **8:**231–32, 233, 234–35, 238–39
African descendants (Mexico), **2:**564, 600, 603
African descendants (South and Central America and Caribbean). *See also* Garífuna culture; Maroon cultures; *specific cultures listed under* Afro
  in Anglophone areas, **2:**95
  in Antigua and Barbuda, **2:**798–800
  in Argentina, **2:**16
  in Aruba, **2:**927–28
  in Bahamas, **2:**801, 803, 807
  in Barbados, **2:**813–14
  in Bolivia, **2:**284
  in Caribbean, **2:**18, 792, 793
  in Carriacou, **2:**867
  in Central America, **2:**630
  in Colombia, **2:**34
  in Cuba, **2:**822, 823–27
  dance and movement of, **2:**44
  in Dominica, **2:**840
  in Dominican Republic, **2:**850–55
  emigration to Angola and Liberia, **2:**91
  in Francophone areas, **2:**95
  in Guyana, **2:**444–46
  in Haiti, **2:**881–88
  identity issues of, **2:**55, 60–61
  instruments of, **2:**32
  in Jamaica, **2:**896, 902, 903
  in Martinique, **2:**920
  Miskitu culture, **2:**659
  in Netherlands Antilles, **2:**927–28
  in Panama, **2:**771, 773, 779, 783
  in Paraguay, **2:**457, 464
  popular music of, **2:**93
  in Puerto Rico, **2:**937, 939
  relations with Amerindians and European descendants, **2:**71
  religions of, **2:**47–48, 68
  rhythmic style of, **2:**73–74
  in Trinidad and Tobago, **2:**952, 959
  in Uruguay, **2:**510, 513
  in Venezuela, **2:**524
  in Virgin Islands, **2:**968, 969
African Fiesta, **1:**363, 424, 669
African Fiesta Sukisa, **1:**363
African Grove Theater (New York), **3:**615
African Inkspots, **1:**771

African Jazz, **1:**361, 362–63, 386, 424
African Methodist Episcopal Church, **1:**764; **3:**624, 626–28
African music. *See also specific countries, peoples, and topics*
  compositional practices in, **1:**208–30
  concepts of, **1:**7–11
  content analysis of, **1:**102–4
  discographies of, **1:**59–61
  European misperceptions of, **1:**11
  fusion genres, **3:**338–39
  historical studies of, **1:**74–98
  in Hong Kong, **7:**432
  insiders’ *vs.* outsiders’ views, **1:**29–30
  interaction with dance, **1:**108–13
  interaction with other arts, **1:**7–8, 21, 27, 33–34, 102–21, 142, 676
  intra-African influences, **1:**293–324
  notation of, **1:**146–62
  politics and, **1:**7, 9
  preservation of, **1:**11
  therapeutic uses, **1:**80–81
  travelers’ accounts of, **1:**74–93
African Music (periodical), **1:**54
African Musicology (periodical), **1:**13
African musicology and scholarship
  1920–1950, **1:**16–26, 62
  1950–1960, **1:**26–38
  1960–1970, **1:**38–43, 63, 67
  1970–1980, **1:**43–48
  1990s, **1:**47–48
  academic training, **1:**18–19
  challenges for the future, **1:**66–69
  concept of, **1:**13
  Eurocentric views in, **1:**57
  fieldwork, **1:**50–51
  goals of, **1:**14–16
  historical studies, **1:**55
  history and development of, **1:**13–69
  Latin American interactions, **1:**68
  musician and scholar dialogue, **1:**62–68
  periods of, **1:**15–16
  politics and, **1:**59
  recording and documentation of, **1:**51–58
  research topics in, **1:**37–38, 41–42, 47–48, 55–57
  scholarly competence in, **1:**64–65
  textbooks, **1:**60–63
  Western research, **1:**47, 48–58
African Music on LP (Merriam), **1:**54
African Music Research Transcription Library, **1:**52
African Music Society, **1:**53–54, 359; **10:**111
African National Congress, **1:**764, 769
“*Africano, El*” (Ochoa), **2:**105
African slaves (South and Central America and Caribbean)
  in Antigua and Barbuda, **2:**798
  in Bahamas, **2:**809, 811
  in Barbados, **2:**813–14, 817
  in Belize, **2:**666, 668, 677
  in Brazil, **2:**303, 313, 323, 333–34, 335, 340, 345
  in Caribbean, **2:**791, 792, 795
  in Carriacou, **2:**868
  in Central America, **2:**630, 659

African slaves (*continued*)
  Christian conversion of, **2:**46–47
  in Colombia, **2:**377, 379–80, 385,
    400–401
  in Costa Rica, **2:**680, 687–88
  in Cuba, **2:**823–27
  in Dominican Republic, **2:**845, 850
  in El Salvador, **2:**708–9
  in Grenada, **2:**864
  in Guadeloupe, **2:**873
  in Guyana, **2:**442, 444–45
  in Haiti, **2:**882
  in Jamaica, **2:**896, 903, 905–6, 907, 909
  in Martinique, **2:**916
  in Nicaragua, **2:**749, 753
  in Panama, **2:**771, 779
  in Peru, **2:**466, 481, 491, 495
  in Puerto Rico, **2:**933
  in Surinam, **2:**504
  in Trinidad and Tobago, **2:**953
  in Uruguay, **2:**510
  in Virgin Islands, **2:**968, 969
Africans Own Entertainers, **1:**770
Africville (Nolan), **3:**1072, 1134
Africville Suite (Sealy), **3:**1134
Afrika Bambaataa, **3:**689, 694, 695, 697, 700,
    702, 713
Afro-American Folksongs (Krehbiel), **3:**576
Afro-American Music (James), **3:**85
Afro-American Symphony (Still), **3:**609
Afro-Beat, **1:**363, 482, 483–84
Afro-Bolivian culture, **2:**293, 297
Afro-Brazilian culture, **2:**110, 323, 340–54
  afoxés, **2:**338, 351–52
  associations in, **2:**312–13
  blocos-afros, **2:**338, 351, 352–54
  capoeira, **2:**24, 345–47
  choro, **2:**350
  dance in, **2:**309, 348–50
  dramatic traditions, **2:**304, 347–48
  history of, **2:**340–41
  instruments of, **2:**308–9, 343
  religious traditions of, **2:**341–44
  samba, **2:**313–14, 350–51
  secular traditions of, **2:**344–50
  urban popular traditions of, **2:**350–54
Afro-Caribbean culture
  in Costa Rica, **2:**687–93
  in North America, **3:**808–12
Afro-Colombian culture, **2:**400–12
  history of, **2:**400–401
  instruments of, **2:**401–3
  popular music of, **2:**409–11
  religious traditions of, **2:**403–4
  research on, **2:**411–12
  secular traditions of, **2:**404–9
Afro-Cuban music, **2:**371–72, 823–27;
    3:783–89, 1205
  in Egypt, **6:**644
  in Nicaragua, **2:**763
  religious genres, **3:**784–85
  secular genres, **3:**662, 720, 728–29, 732, 742,
    743, 785–89, 790–99, 1085
"Afro-Cuban Suite" (Pozo), **3:**797
Afro-Ecuadorian culture
  currulao in, **2:**427–28

instruments of, **2:**414–17
  research on, **2:**431
Afro-Haitian Dance Company, **3:**805
Afro-Honduran culture, **2:**740–41
Afro-Mexican culture, **2:**603, 610
Afro-Peruvian culture, **2:**491–502
  African heritage of, **2:**491–93
  children's wakes, **2:**423
  Creole genres, **2:**498–500
  influence on *cueca*, **2:**369
  instruments of, **2:**475–76
  musical genres, **2:**495–98
  research on, **2:**501–2
  revival of, **2:**481–82, 500–501
  Spanish heritage of, **2:**493–95
Afro-Venezuelan culture
  festival of Saint Benedict the Moor, **2:**536
  festival of Saint John the Baptist, **2:**535–36
  instruments of, **2:**526–31
  joropo styles in, **2:**541
  research on, **2:**544
  urbanization of, **2:**543
Afrūz, Majles, **6:**866
After Fallen Crumbs (Singleton), **3:**611
After Forty Long Years the Dream Is Broken, the
    Fragrance Faded (Tang), **7:**307
Afterimage (musical group), **4:**887
"After the Ball" (Harris), **3:**191, 544, 549
Afzelius, Arvid August, **8:**136, 447
Again (musical group), **7:**360
Against All Odds (film), **3:**204
Aga Khan, **5:**825
Aganman (musical group), **3:**1170
Agarabi people, **9:**526–33
Agari people, **5:**719, 727
Ağ Aşiq, **6:**929
Agasti, Aryan sage, **5:**726
Agate, A. T., **9:**20, *410*
Agawu, Kofi, **7:**443
Agbebi, Mojola, **1:**403
Agdyev-Gyjakchy, Güych Nury, **6:***969*
Agee, James, **3:**610
Agence de Développement de la Culture Kanak,
    9:964–65, 992, 1008
Agerkop, Terry, **2:**544, 660, 663
Aghamalyan, Melik, **6:**725
Aghānī al-sīqā wa-ma'ānī al-mūsīqā (al-Ribāṭī),
    6:367
Agharubw Dancers, **9:**92
Agile Running Bear (Kazakh piece), **7:**461
Aglukark, Susan, **3:**73, 1063, 1275, 1280
Agni (musical group), **5:**429
Agrenev-Slaviansky, Dmitry, **8:**775, 777
Agricola, Martin, **8:**705
agriculture. *See also* bamboo; rice
  Afghanistan, **5:**489
  Ainu people, **7:**786
  Akha people, **4:**540–41
  Albania, **8:**988, 999
  Andhra Pradesh, **5:**889, 891, 900
  Atacameño culture, **2:**356, 361
  Austria, **8:**670, 671
  Bahrain, **6:**708
  Bali, **4:**731
  Bangladesh, **5:**488
  Barbados, **2:**813

Belarus, **8:**791–92
Berber people, **6:**483–84
Bolivia, **2:**289–90, 292
Borneo, **4:**824, 827
Brazil, **2:**301, 303–4
Caribbean, **2:**791
Central Asia, **7:**12
China, **7:**15, 29, 458, 463, 496
Corsica, **8:**566
Cuba, **2:**823
Denmark, **8:**458
Dominican Republic, **2:**845, 849
East Asia, **7:**16
El Salvador, **2:**706
England, **8:**335
Europe, **8:**21, 139, 142, 150
  rituals for, **8:**4
  women's roles in, **8:**192
France, **8:**539
Georgia, **8:**834
Goa, **5:**735, 738
Great Basin Indian groups, **3:**420
Great Lakes Indian groups, **3:**451, 452, 453
Greece, **8:**1007
Guyana, **2:**442
Haiti, **2:**885
Hawai'i, **9:**96
Hmong people, **4:**550, 551
Ifugao people, **4:**917
Inner Asia, **7:**9, 12
Ireland, **8:**378
Jamaica, **2:**905
Karen people, **4:**544
Karnataka, **5:**881, 887
Kerala, **5:**934
Kmhmu people, **4:**546
Korea, **7:**929, 930–31, 938
Lahu people, **4:**538
Lhoba people, **7:**482
Lisu people, **4:**542
Lithuania, **8:**509
Low Countries, **8:**523
Luangiua, **9:**842
Madhya Pradesh, **5:**721
Maharashtra, **5:**726
Malaysia, **4:**422–23
Montenegro, **8:**957
Nepal, **5:**701
New Caledonia, **9:**685
Northeast Indian groups, **3:**461
Norway, **8:**412, 421
Nusa Tenggara Barat, **4:**762
Pakistan, northern, **5:**792
Papua New Guinea, **9:**474, 511, 514, 553
  Baluan, **9:**602
  Halia people, **9:**640
  Huli people, **9:**537
  Mamose region, **9:**549
  Melpa people, **9:**516
  Nissan Atoll, **9:**632
  Trans-Fly region, **9:**506
Philippines, **4:**892, 896, 914, 920
Pohnpei, **9:**739
Poland, **8:**701
Portugal, **8:**577, 578
Pueblo Indian groups, **3:**429, 430

Punjab (India), **5:**650
Qatar, **6:**708
Q'ero culture, **2:**225
Romania, **8:**870
Russia, **8:**754, 758
Sāmoa, **9:**795
Sardinia, **8:**626
Scotland, **8:**360
Serbia, **8:**940
Shan people, **4:**547–48
Solomon Islands
  'Are'are people, **9:**666
  Choiseul Island, **9:**654
  Guadalcanal, **9:**664
South Asia, **5:**5
  influence on theatrical presentations, **5:**481
Southeast Asia, **4:**48
  island regions, **4:**594
  modernization and, **4:**113–15
  prehistoric, **4:**34–36, 36–37
  spirit beliefs and, **4:**49–53
  upland peoples, **4:**537
  water and, **4:**47–48, 49–50, 53
Sumatra, **4:**609
Sumba, **4:**787–88
Sumbawa, **4:**778
Sunda, **4:**699, 711
Surinam, **2:**507
Sweden, **8:**434
Switzerland, **8:**682
Tamil Nadu, **5:**544
Thailand, **4:**298
Tibet, **7:**471
Trinidad and Tobago, **2:**953
Tripura, **5:**503
Turkmenistan, **6:**966
Ukraine, **8:**809
Uttar Pradesh, **5:**660
Vanuatu, **9:**694
Waiãpí culture, **2:**162
Wales, **8:**342
Warao culture, **2:**188
Yao people, **4:**549
Yuman Indian groups, **3:**433
Aguabella, Francisco, **3:**729, 798
Aguaruna culture, **2:**482
Agueda (de la Peña), **4:**881
Aguila Records, **3:**741
Aguilar, Freddie, **4:**886
Aguilar, Gerónimo, **4:**841
Aguilar, Ignacio, **2:**621
Aguilar y Adame, Juan, **3:**740
Aguilera, Christina, **3:**721, 733
Aguinaldo, Emilio, **4:**85
Agungan (Maceda), **4:**875
Agung, sultan of Mataram, **4:**83
Agustín, Remigio, **4:**864
Agwŏn kosa, **7:**856
Ahad, Abdul, **5:**858
Ahad, Tony Abdel, **3:**1032
Aharon, 'Ezra, **6:**1029, 1058
Ahemad, Ali, **5:**487
Ahīr caste, **5:**602, 666–67, 673
Ahlberg and Ohlsson (instrument maker),
  8:440
Ahl-e Ḥaqq, **6:**193, 746, 825

Åhlström, Olof, **8:**444, 447
Ahmad, Abbasuddin, **5:**855, 858
Aḥmad al-Ānisī, **6:**686
Aḥmad Bey, **6:**325
Ahmad ibn al-Rifāʿī, **6:**149
Ahmad, imam of North Yemen, **6:**711
Ahmad Jazzar Pasha, **6:**780
Ahmad, Shamim, **5:**460
Ahmad Yassawi, Hoja, **6:***937*, 940, 943–44, 945,
  946
Aḥmad, Zakariyyā, **6:**168, 552, 598, 599, 612
Ahmadov, Kamil, **6:**924
Ahmaogak, Roy, **3:**486
Ahmed, Akhlaq, **5:**768
Ahmed, Haji Maqbool, **5:**426
Ahmed, Hattaye ag Muhammed, **1:***546*
Ahmed I, Ottoman sultan, **6:**194
Ahmed, Nafis, **5:**768
Ahmed, Sidi, **6:**269
Ahmed, Vardakosta, **6:**121
Ahn, Eaktay, **7:**952, 976
Ahn Sook Sun (An Suksŏn), **7:**960, 972–73, 986
Ahobala, **5:**46
Ahrens, Lynn, **3:**200
"Ah! vous dirai-je, maman" (folk song), **8:**20
Ahwāk (Egyptian song), **6:**601
Ahyoung, Olivia, **2:***449*, *450*
Ahyoung, Selwyn, **2:**85
Aibom people, **9:**982
Aichi Art Center (Japan), **7:**761
Aida (Verdi), **6:**547, 610; **8:**60
Aidonidis, Chronis, **9:**73
Aiken, George, **3:**618
Aima, Mohanlal, **5:**684
Aimaq people, **5:**805
'Ain-i Akbarī (treatise), **5:**46, 48, 402
'Āina Remains, **9:**222
Aingo, George Williams, **1:**355, *356*
'Ain-i Akbarī (Abu Fazl), **5:**46, 48
Ain't Misbehavin' (musical), **3:**622
"Ain't Nobody Here but Us Chickens" (Jordan),
  3:668, 708
Ain't No Other (MC Lyte), **3:**696–97
Ain't Supposed to Die a Natural Death (Van
  Peebles), **3:**621
"Ain't Too Proud to Beg" (Temptations), **3:**674
Ainu people, **7:**783–87
  bear ritual of, **7:**784, 785–86, 1029
  history and origins of, **7:**783
  instruments of, **7:**787
  music of, **7:**540, 732, 784–87
  rekukkara singing, **7:**786, 1030
Aird, James, **8:**373
Air Force Cultural Work Troupe (China), **7:**399
Airlangga, King of Java, **4:**635
*Airs and Melodies Peculiar to the Scottish
  Highlands* (Fraser), **8:**373
Ai Sam, **7:**506
'A'isha Bint Ṭalḥa, **6:**701
Aitken, Robert T., **9:**24, 969
Ait-Ouarab, Mohamed Idir. *See* Anka, Mohamed
  El-
Aitutaki (Cook Islands), **9:**903, *956*, 978
Aiyankār people, **5:**284
Aizo people, **1:**37
Aja peoples, **1:**37, 461–63

'Ajfā', **6:**442
Ajib, Abdul, **4:**697
Aji Gurnita manuscript, **4:**733
Ajisafe, A. K., **1:**404
Ajmal, Muhammad, **5:**768
Ajo de Buenaventura family, **2:**835
al-Ājurrī, **6:**372
Aka people
  music of, **1:**681–82, 687–96
  research on, **1:**688
  vocal music, **1:**267–69
  yodeling, **1:**658
Aka, S., **1:**475
Akademie für Kirchen- und Schulmusik (Berlin),
  8:659
Akademi Seni Karawitan Indonesia, **4:**122, 678,
  684–85
Akademi Seni Rupa Indonesia, **4:**777
Akademi Seni Tari Indonesia, **4:**678, 683, 698,
  705, 723, 759
Akagi no komoriuta, **7:**745
Akaka, Alan, **9:**390
Akamatsu, **7:**985
Akamba people, **1:**624
Akan people, **1:**469; **10:**141
  abofoo dance, **1:**286
  in Carriacou, **2:**869
  fontomfrom (*fɔntɔmfrɔm* music, **1:**227
  harmonic practices, **1:**224
  healing rituals, **1:**290
  music of, **1:**463–65
Akarsu, Muhlis, **6:**790, *791*, 798, 799
Akasi Kakuiti, **7:**646
Akatangeghos, **6:**723
Akawaio culture, **2:**131
Akbar, Mughal emperor
  court of, **5:**72, 77, 163, 190, 252, 308, 337,
    376, 379, 769, 792
  reign, chronicles of, **5:**48, 301, 303–4, 402
  visual depictions of, **5:**303–5, *308*
Akbarnāma (chronicle), **5:**301, 303–4, *308*
Akbarov, I. A., **6:**918
Akbayram, Edip, **6:**249
A. K. C. Brothers, **5:**232
Akchang tŭngnok, **7:**854, 855
Akdemir, Hayrettin, **6:**775
Akers, Doris, **10:**138
Akhak kwebom (Sŏng), **7:**54, 813, 823, 833–34,
  847–48, 853, 856
Akhak p'yŏn'go (Yi), **7:**856
Akhak sŭmnyŏng (Yi), **7:**856
Akhand, Laki, **5:**428
Akha people, **4:**537, 540–42
  instruments of, **4:**540, *544*, *545*
Akhil Bharatiya Gandharva Sangeet
  Mahavidyalaya (Bombay), **5:**444
Akhmedov, Mahmud, **6:**943
Akhobadze, Vladimer, **8:**846, 853
Akhtar, Begum, **5:**381, 412, 413, 424
Akhtar, Najma, **5:**575; **8:**240
Akiba, **7:**985
Akikaze no kyoku (Mituzaki), **7:**698
Akikuyu people, **1:**630. *See also* Kikuyu people
Akimel O'odham. *See* Pima Indian nation
Akin, David, **9:**666, 962, 964, 977
Akin, Ferit Cenan, **6:**775

Aki no irokusa (*nagauta* piece), 7:672
Akit people, 4:614
Akiyama Kuniharu, 7:733, 736
Akkadian period, 6:8, 407
Akkale, Belkis, 6:792
Akkıraz, Sabahat, 6:799
Akoi, Robert, Jr., 9:972
Akoya koto zeme (*kabuki* piece), 7:712
Akpabot, Samuel, 1:39, 40, 44, 45, 47, 233, 251
Akpalu, Vinčkč, 1:222
Aksdal, Bjørn, 8:427
Akšencaŭ, Feliks, 8:802
Akses, Necil Kazım, 6:775
Aksö kojon (Chŏng), 7:856
Aksu, Sezen, 6:251–52, *252*
Akt'ong, 7:856
Akumo (Ocomayana) culture, 2:503
A-ku-ta, 7:31
Akutagawa Yasusi, 7:736, 750
Akwan (Wilson), 3:611
al-. *See next element in name*
Alaap (musical group), 5:574; 8:241
Alabama
    field hollers in, 3:83–84, 85
    Mobile, shanty singing, 3:600
    Native American groups in, 3:466
"Alabamy Bound," 3:544
Alacaluf (Halakwalup) culture, 2:357
Aladdin Records, 3:263, 350, 670
Aładoŭ, Mikoła, 8:800
"A la Eskola de la Aliança" (Sephardic song),
        3:1174
Alájá-Browne, Afọlábí, 1:353
Alake, Batile, 1:474
Ala-Könni Academy (Turku), 8:480, 482
Ala-Könni, Erkki, 8:488
Alakotila, Timo, 8:478
Alal, Corinne, 6:1074
Alam Ara (film), 5:532
Alam, Farid, 6:281
Alam, Gulzar, 5:791
Alam, Muhammad, 5:768
Alam, Sultan, 5:858
Alamblak people, 9:557, 560
'Alāmī, Rāghib, 6:283
al-'Alami, Sidi Qaddur, 6:497
Alamphon label, 6:281
Alan people, 8:850, 851, 859
Al Andalus (musical group), 3:847
Alapai, Nani, 9:924
Alard, Jean-Delphin, 3:606
Alas people, 4:601, 603, 605
Alaska
    acquired from Russia, 3:10, 915, 1255
    Arctic peoples in, 3:374–81; 7:1028
    European settlement of, 3:379
    geography of, 3:3
    Gwich'in people in, 3:405
    Japanese people in, 3:967
    Native American groups in, 3:394–96
    Pribilof Islands, 3:486
    Sitka, 3:486
    Subarctic peoples, 3:383–92
al-'Alawchī, 'Abd al-Ḥamīd, 6:364
'Alawite dynasty, 6:496
'Alayqāt people, 6:641

Albani, Emma, 3:1149
Albania, 8:986–1004
    art music in, 8:999
    Çamëri, 8:991, 1004
    ethnicization of music in, 8:12
    Geg people, 8:957, 986
    geography of, 8:986
    Gjirokastër folk festival, 8:150
    history of, 8:986
    instruments and instrumental music, 8:197
        makam use, 8:994, 996, 997
        nibet genre, 8:996–97
        northern region, 8:994–97
        southern region, 8:992–93
        taksim genre, 8:997
    Labëri, 8:991
    Lab people, 8:990–92
        vocal performers, 8:115
    map of, 8:866, *987*
    Muslims in, 8:11, 986, 988, 997, 1002
    Myzeqe, 8:991
    northern communities in, 8:994–99
    pastoral music of, 8:142
    population of, 8:986
    postsocialist period in, 8:1002–3
    research on music of, 8:1003–4
    Rom people in, 8:195, 285–86, 993, 996, 997
    southern communities in, 8:990–94
    state folk ensembles in, 8:999, 1000, 1002
    Sufism in, 6:115
    Toskëri, 8:991
    Tosk people, 8:986, 990–92
    vocal music, 8:118, 194, 195, 198, 987–92,
        994–95
        laments, 8:132, 144, 196
        polyphony, 8:10, 14, 847, 990–92, 1010
    women's music in, 8:145, 194, *195*, 987,
        1000
Albanian people
    emigration patterns, 8:986, 1002
    in Italy, 8:610, 617
    in Macedonia, 8:972, 979
    in Montenegro, 8:957, 959
    in North America, 3:517, 926–29, 1084;
        8:1004
        Tosk, 3:919, 926, 927–29
    in Turkey, 6:117
    in Yugoslavia, 8:12, *144*, 940, 942, 951–52
Albanian Philharmonia, 8:999
Āl Bā Ṣāliḥ (Zirbādī ensemble), 6:98, *98*
Albéniz, Isaac, 3:852; 6:449; 8:601
Alber, Hans, 8:676
Alberstein, Chava, 6:1074
Alberta, 3:383, 1223–51
    African-Canadians in, 3:1091
    Calgary
        musical life in, 3:1087, 1090–91, 1225,
            1227
        music instruction in, 3:279
    Christian minorities in, 3:1237–40
    Edmonton
        Chinese people in, 3:1247–48
        Indian-Muslim community, 3:1086, 1089
        musical life in, 3:17, 1087, 1090–91,
            1224–31
        popular music in, 3:109

    European settlers in, 3:1086, 1249–51
    First Nations groups in, 3:440–50, 1085–86
    folk song collecting in, 3:292, 1250
    history of musical life, 3:1085–91, 1224–31
    Hutterites in, 3:1240
    intercultural traditions, 3:342–45
    Lac La Biche, 3:1089–90
    Mennonites in, 3:1238
    Stoney reserve, 3:1086
    Swedish people in, 3:1088–89
    Ukrainian people in, 3:218, 1088–89, 1241
Alberta Culture and Multiculturalism, 3:1231
Alberta Lounge (Montréal), 3:1077
Albert Einstein Committee, 8:221
Alberti, Luis, 2:860
d'Albertis, Luigi, 9:506
Alberto, José, 3:799
Alberts, Arthur, 1:359
Album musical (Ruiz Rivas de Domínguez),
        2:463–64
Album of Negro Spirituals (Johnson), 3:607
Albyn's Anthology (Campbell), 8:373
Alcalá, Jerónimo de, 2:576
Alcántara, Pedro, 4:857
Alcantara, Reynaldo, 3:786
Alcaraz, Luis, 3:741
Alcazaba, Simón de, 2:250
Alcides, 2:266
alcohol, 9:177–83, 321, 709, 727, 845, 847
    aguardiente, 2:383
    caña, 2:461, 462
    ceremonial use of, 2:45, 46
    chicha (corn beer), 2:228–29, 255, 425, 683
    hiu, 2:670
    jack-iron rum, 2:870
    manioc beer, 2:130, 158, 161, 166, 435
    Mapuche culture, 2:236
    puput, 2:751
    tesgüino, 2:553, 586, 587
    trago, 2:428
    in Venezuelan religious celebrations, 2:533
Aldema, Gil, 6:1073
Alder (musical group), 8:698
Alder, Arnold, 8:698
Alder family, 8:696
Alderbuebe (musical group), 8:691
Alderman, Pauline, 10:3
Aldiss, Joseph, 9:728
Aldridge, Ira, 3:615
aleatoric music, 7:736, 737; 8:85
Alegría (*chicha* group), 2:485
Aleichem, Sholom, 3:943
Alejandro, Hajji, 4:885
Aleksandersen, Åge, 8:430
Aleksandrah (Avidom), 6:1030
Aleksandrov, Aleksandr, 8:777
Alekseyev, Eduard, 6:987
Alele Museum (Majuro), 9:748, 752, 753, 967,
        995
Alemán, William, 2:861
Alencar, Edgar de, 2:320
Alencar, José de, 2:305
Alesker, Aşıq, 6:850, 851, 929
Alevi group, 6:81, 190, 193, 568, 768, 789–92,
        793–800, 811
    aşiklar, 6:765–66

history of, **6:**793–94
music of, **6:**795–96
Alexander, Alex, **3:**915
Alexander, Bill, **1:**361
Alexander the Great, king of Macedonia, **5:**14, 804, 817; **8:**972
Alexander, Haim, **6:**1031, 1063
Alexander, Jane, **10:***83*, 84
Alexander, Kavi, **5:**529
Alexander, Lucretia, **3:**625
Alexander, Monty, **2:**911
Alexander, Peter. *See* Neumayer, Peter
Alexander VI, pope, **2:**242
"Alexander's Ragtime Band" (Berlin), **3:**196
Alexander's Ragtime Band (steelband), **2:**96
Alexandra Allstar Band, **1:**774
Alexandru, Tiberiu, **8:**886
Alexandry, Joseph, **8:**531
Alex Harvey's Big Soul Band, **8:**369
Alexiou, Charis, **9:**73
Alexiou, Haris, **8:**1018
Alexis, tsar of Russia, **8:**122
Alf, Johnny, **2:**351
Alfaro, Daniel, **2:**658
Alfonso X, king of Castile and León, **6:**444–45; **8:**600
Alfred, Jerry, **3:**489, 1063, 1277, 1278, 1280, *1280*
Alfredo (concertina player), **2:**939
Alfur people, **9:**581
Alfvén, Hugo, **8:**444
Algazi, İsak, **6:**57, 58, 117, 1066
Algeria. *See also* Berber peoples; Maghrib; North Africa; *specific peoples*
Algiers, **6:**407, 449, 450–51, *467*, 467–68, 1044
Andalusian repertoire in, **1:**534–36; **6:**449, 450–51, 454, 457, 467–72, 1044
Aurès mountains, **6:**273
Berber peoples, **1:**532, 533; **6:**273–77, 299, 300–301
circumcision ceremonies, **1:**539
Constantine, **6:**406, 407, 449, 450–51, 453–54, 467–68, *468*, 1044
dance in, **1:**544
Djanet, **1:**544
Djurdjura mountains, **6:**273
female musicians, **1:**541
festivals, **1:**538
French rule in, **6:**432
geography of, **6:**429, 465
*griot*s in, **1:**540
history of, **6:**466
instruments in, **1:**542–43; **6:**403, 406–11, 414–15, 416–20, 421
malhūn, **6:**500
map of, **6:***430*
Mzab oases, **6:**273
Oran, **6:**269
Ouled Naïl people, **1:**544
popular music of, **1:**545, 547
population of, **6:**466
Qādiriyya Sufi trance ritual, **6:**304
rai genre in, **6:**269–72, 477; **8:**210, 233, 234

Tlemcen, **6:**269, 407, 449, 450–51, *467*, 467–68, 470, 1044
Tuareg people, **1:**574, 578–79, 584, 588, 592; **6:**273
urban music of, **6:**465–77
Algerian people, in France, **8:**231, 234–35
"Algo-Bueno" (Pozo), **3:**797
Algonquian peoples, **3:**383–92, 451, 1056, 1073, 1074. *See also specific groups*
dream-songs, **3:**386
drumming style, **3:***385*
research on music of, **3:**392
song text and structures, **3:**389
Ālhā (epic), **5:**401–2, 668, 673, 679
Al Hamra Arts Council, **5:**747
'Alī (Egyptian epic singer), **6:**341
'Ali (son-in-law of Muhammad), **5:**818, 877; **6:**293, 884, 889, 931, 939, 942
Sufi veneration of, **6:**768, 793–96, 825
'Alī, Ṣafar, **6:**18
'Alī Akbar Farāhānī, **6:**130, 138, 859, 860, 861, 866
'Alī Akbar Sheydā, **6:**137
Ali Akbar School of Music (California), **3:**985; **5:**529, 566, 583
'Alī al-'Ansī, **6:**686
'Alī Aqā Almājoqī, **6:**837, *839*, 839–41
Ali, Babar, **5:**768
'Ali Cherif, **6:**496
Ali Efendi, Tanburī, **6:**758
Ali, Fahim, **5:**767
'Alī Ḥassan Kūbān, **6:**641–42, *642*
'Alī ibn 'Ubayd Allāh al-Saylakūnī, **6:**366
'Alī ibn Yaḥyá, **6:**297
Ali, Imtiaz, **5:**767
Ali Izzet, **6:**796
Ali, Javad, **5:**767
Ali, Naushad, **5:***535*, 537
Ali, Nazakat, **5:**746
Ali Nutkî Dede, **6:**780
Ali Pasha, **8:**284
Ali people, **1:**267
Ali, Riaz, **5:**767
Ali, Rustam Fateh, **5:***767*
Ali, Salamat, **5:**746
Ali Şīr-u Gani, **6:**194
Ali, Sultan Fateh, **5:**767
Äliuly, Sügir, **6:**958
Ali, Ustad, **5:**690
Alibakieva, Tamara, **6:**998
Alibamu (Alabama) Indian nation, **3:**466, 470
Alice in Chains (musical group), **3:**358; **4:**887
Alice's Adventures in Wonderland (Carroll), **3:**176
"Alice's Restaurant" (Guthrie), **3:**317
Alienz (musical group), **3:**750
Aliev, Habil, **6:**924
Alifuru people, **4:**818, 819
Alijabiev, Aleksandr, **8:**856
Alim Khan, emir of Bukhara, **6:**903, 916, 967
Alim, Ömärjan, **7:**469
Alimatov, Turgun, **6:**919
"All about Love" (White), **3:**693
All-African Church Music Association, **1:**218, 219

All-African Church Music Association Journal, **1:**217
Allah, Hussein Muhammed Wagiya, **1:**557
Allahar, Anton, **3:**51
Allaidad, **5:***784*
Allakarialak, Madeleine, **3:**1280
"All Along the Watchtower" (Hendrix), **3:**710
Allauddin Khilji, sultan of Delhi, **5:**76
All China Music Workers' Federation, **7:**386
"All Coons Look Alike to Me" (Hogan), **3:**650
Allegheny College (Pittsburgh), **10:**133
allemande, **8:**168
Allen, George, **2:***923*; **3:**298
Allen, Harry, **3:**586
Allen, Lillian, **3:**1213
Allen, Matthew, **5:**385
Allen, Michael, **9:**139, 992
Allen, Rance, **3:**634
Allen, Richard, **3:**624, 626–27
Allen, Sadie Harper, **3:**1070
Allen Theatre (Winnipeg), **3:**1091
Allen, Tony, **1:**483
Allen, Ward, **3:**1080, 1125, 1190, 1257
Allen, William, **1:**91–92
Allen, William Francis, **3:**29, 70, 506, 523–24, 574–75, 601
Allende, Pedro Humberto, **2:**238
Allende, Salvador, **2:**90, 103, 373; **10:**81
All Eyez on Me (Shakur), **3:**715
Alleyne, Archie, **3:**1212
Alleyne, Wendy, **2:**820
"All for Love" (Color Me Badd), **3:**715
"All for You" (Cole), **3:**669
All Hail the Queen (Queen Latifah), **3:**696
Alliance Israélite Universelle, **6:**526, 1038
"All I Could Do Was Cry" (James), **3:**673
"All of You" (Ross and Iglesias), **3:**713
Allor, Martin, **3:**1058
Allotey-Pappoe, Rev. Mr., **1:**23
All Pakistan Music Conference, **5:**529
"All Quiet Along the Potomac Tonight" (Hewitt), **3:**188
'Allūn, **6:**442
'Allūya, **6:**356
Almada Roche, Armando, **2:**464
Almanac Singers, **3:**48, 316
Almanzares, Apolinario, **3:**762
Almast (Spendiaryan), **6:**726–27
Almatov, Almas, **6:***952*
Almaty State Conservatory (Kazakhstan), **6:**959
Almaz, **6:**547
Almeida, Bira (Mestre Acordeon), **2:**24
Almeida, Pua, **9:**390
Almeida, Renato, **2:**320
Almohads, **6:**431, 441, 442, 455
Almoravids, **6:**431, 441, 442, 455, 456
Aloha Collection (Hopkins), **9:**919, 922
"*Aloha 'Oe*," **9:**43, 45, 159, 353
Aloha Oe (film), **9:**43
Aloha Week, **9:**55–56
Alonso, Pacho, **2:**835
Alor, **4:**786
"Alouette," **3:**528
Alouette (anthology), **3:**148
Alouette Vocal Quartet, **3:**1166
Ałoŭnikaŭ, Uładzimir, **8:**800

Alpamysh (epic), **6:**952
Alperin, Mikhail, **8:**226
Alpert, Herb, **3:**751
Alpha Boys School (Kingston), **2:**909–10
Alphonse X the Wise. *See* Alfonso X, king of
    Castile and León
alphorn. *See* trumpets or horns
Alpine Septet (Toronto), **3:**1198
Alston, Lettie Beckon, **3:**612
Altai Urianghai people, **7:**1004–20
Altamirano, Cristóbal, **2:**511
Altan Khan, **7:**35
Altarac, Isak Kalmi, **8:**968
Alta Vista Records, **3:**767
Altay people, epic songs, **6:**345
Alte Kameraden Band (Wisconsin), **3:**889
Alterman, Natan, **6:**266
Alternance pour percussion (Shinohara), **7:**737
Alternative Museum (New York), **3:**1037
Altınçağ, Umut, **6:**251
Altinho, Jorge de, **2:**333
Alu Island (Solomon Islands), **9:**655
Alu Kurumbas, **5:**909
Aluku culture, **2:**438–39. *See also* Boni culture
Alur people, **1:**601
Alvarado, Pedro de, **2:**721
Alvarenga, Oneyda, **2:**306
Alvares Lôbo, Elias, **2:**305
'Alvarez, Rafael, **2:**736
Āḷvārs, **5:**105, 260–61, 262
Alves, Ataúlfo, **2:**316
Alvorada (musical group), **3:**1197
"Always" (Berlin), **3:**196
Alyawarra people, **9:**433, 452
Amadeo Schallplatten, **8:**678
Amahl and the Night Visitors (Menotti), **3:**546
Ama lehuo (*zhanian* piece), **7:**477
Amampondo, **1:**778
Amandebele people, **1:**777
Ama no kazu uta (*yakumo goto* piece), **7:**610
Amanullah, Afghan ruler, **5:**805, 807, 808
Amar, Joe, **6:**204
Amar, Kelly Sultan, **3:**1173
Amar, Rahamim, **6:**205
"Amar Sonar Bangla (My Golden Bengal, I Love
    You)," **5:**436–37, 851, 859
Amara people, **9:**614
Amaraa, **7:**1020
Amaradeva, **5:**424
al-'Āmarī, Ḥabīb, **6:**328
Amateur Movement (Cuba), **2:**828–29, 837
amateur musicians
    Borneo, **4:**825
    for calypso, **3:**810
    Cantonese music, **7:**219, 220
    China, **7:**92, 195, 200, 211, 223–24, 225,
        252, 287, 301, 306, 381, 394, 396,
        411–12, 416, 419
    England, **8:**327
    Europe, **8:**78, 79, 81, 82, 199–200
    Germany, **8:**653–54
    Hong Kong, **7:**231, 307–8, 433, 434–35
    Iran, **6:**829
    Ireland, **8:**386
    Japan, **7:**51, 599, 601, 646, 682, 687, 691,
        759–60, 765, 767, 774

    Java, **4:**681–82; **10:**44
    Korea, **7:**926, 983–84
    Low Countries, **8:**523
    Maritimes, **3:**1117
    Middle East, **6:**5
    for Middle Eastern music, **3:**1218
    nineteenth century, **3:**556
    North America, **3:**95, 143, 827
    pianists, **3:**190; **8:**51
    Punjab, **5:**771
    Québec, **3:**1075, 1148
    in Renaissance, **8:**74
    rock bands, **3:**284–85
    South Asia, **5:**404–5
    Taiwan, **7:**424
    vs. professional, **4:**6–7, 538
    women, **3:**90, 190; **5:**410
Amauan Ensemble (New York), **3:**1026
Amazigh movement, **6:**273, 274
Amazil Local (musical group), **9:**138
"Amazing Grace," **3:**369, 533, 533, 1280
Amazonas (Villa-Lobos), **2:**115
Amba (deity), **5:**501
Ambae (Vanuatu), **9:**966
    composers of, **9:**361
    economics, **9:**694
    instruments of, **9:**689
    music and dance of, **9:**693, 695–97, 965
    oral tradition, **9:**259–60
    sawagoro songs, **9:**690
    sound recordings from, **9:**992
    Western influences in, **9:**26
Ambertones (musical group), **3:**746
Ambon, **4:**812, 813, 817–18
Ambonese people, in Sunda, **4:**700
Ambros, August Wilhelm, **6:**22; **8:**266
Ambros, Wolfgang, **8:**676–77
Ambrose, R. S., **3:**1180
Ambrosi, Alisandru (Lisandru di Rustinu), **8:**569
Ambrym (Vanuatu)
    instruments of, **9:**693
    music and dance of, **9:**966
    upright log idiophones in, **9:**691
Amdo people, opera of, **7:**452
Ameche, Jim, **3:**743
Ameed, **3:**1037
A-mei (Zhang Huimei), **7:**358
Ameling, Elly, **3:**1210
"America," **3:**309
American Ballads and Folk Songs (Lomax),
    3:293–94
American Band (Providence), **3:**564
American Bandstand (television show), **3:**211,
    672
American Board of Commissioners for Foreign
    Missions, **9:**720, 735, 739, 752, 756,
    763, 914
American Book Company, **3:**276
American Composers Orchestra, **3:**175
American Council of Learned Societies, **3:**294
American Dance Guild, **3:**221
American Federation of Musicians, **3:**263, 264,
    667, 708
American Folklife Center (Washington, D.C.),
    2:862; **3:**294, 299, 414, 416, 418,
    495–96, 498; **8:**823; **10:**73

American Folklife Preservation Act, **3:**294, 495
American Gamelan Institute, **3:**953, 1017
American Graffiti (film), **3:**204
American Gramophone Records, **3:**345
American Hellenic Educational Progressive
    Association, **3:**529
American Indian Art Magazine, **3:**311
American Indian Dance Theater, **3:**207
American Indian Religious Freedom Act (1978),
    3:444
American Indians. *See* Native American peoples;
    specific peoples
American in Paris, An (Gershwin), **3:**196, 539
American Institute of Indian Studies (Chicago),
    5:529
American Institute of Indian Studies (Delhi),
    5:57
American Museum of Natural History (New
    York), **3:**31; **9:**24–25, 974–75
American Music (periodical), **8:**210
American Music Oral History Project (Yale
    University, New Haven), **3:**33
American Negro Songs and Spirituals (Work),
    3:579
American Negro Spirituals (Johnson and
    Johnson), **3:**576
American Sāmoa, **3:**1047; **9:**218. *See also* Sāmoa
    music and dance of, **9:**980
    Pacific Islanders in, **9:**116
    pedagogy in, **9:**265–67
    sound recordings from, **9:**985
    theater in, **9:**225
American Sāmoan Cultural Choir, **9:**225
American Society for Eastern Arts, **3:**1013–14
American Society of Composers, Authors, and
    Publishers (ASCAP), **3:**260–61, 560,
    609, 706, 708
American Union of Swedish Singers, **3:**870
American Women Composers, **3:**91
Americans in Oceania, **9:**5, 148–49
    ethnographic expeditions, **9:**18–20, 24–25,
        769, 778, 795, 827
    Kapingamarangi, **9:**836
    Kosrae, **9:**742–43
    Marshall Islands, **9:**748, 751
    Micronesia, **9:**159–60, 715
    Sāmoa, **9:**797
    in World War II, **9:**25–33, 139, 149–50, 157,
        160, 614, 665, 751, 779
America's Music (Chase), **3:**511, 512
"America, the Beautiful," **3:**521
Amerindian Museum (Guyana), **2:**442
Amerindians (South and Central America). *See*
    also specific cultures and countries
    Christian conversion of, **2:**46–47
    identity issues of, **2:**60–61
    relations with European and African
        descendants, **2:**71, 81
    rhythmic style of, **2:**73
Ames, David W., **1:**517; **10:**56
Amezketara, Fernando, **8:**313–14
Amft, Georg, **8:**663
Amhara people, **1:**599
    begena lyre, **1:**303–4
Amici, **3:**1186
'Ami'el, Dhelomi, **6:**1044

Amilan, Bouchit bint Loki ag, **1:**_580_
Amin, Idi, **8:**236
Amina, **6:**438
Amina, Ben, **6:**269
al-Amīn, caliph, **6:**539
el-Amin, Muhammed, **1:**571–72
Amiot, Jean-Joseph-Marie, **7:**136
*Amir, an Afghan Refugee Musician's Life in
      Peshawar, Pakistan* (film), **5:**810, 835
Amira, John, **2:**839
Amiran (epic), **8:**834
Amiran, Emanuel, **6:**1072
Amirī, **6:**914
Amirouche, **6:**275
Amirov, Meşadi Camil, **6:**922–23
Amis people
    instruments of, **7:**528
    musical traditions of, **7:**92, 427–29, _428_,
        526–28
    popular music of, **7:**358, 428–29
Amish. *See* Old Order Amish
Amla, sao muang long (Dai love song), **7:**505
Ammal, Bangalore A. R. Ramani, **5:**425
Amman, Jacob, **3:**887
Ammann, Raymond, **9:**316, 964, 965,
        986, 992
Ammons, Albert, **3:**647
Amoaku, William, **1:**45
Amoco Renegades, **2:**86
Among the Indians (Minikes), **3:**935
Amonkar, Kishori, **5:**_177_, 413, 460
Amor Patria (Nakpil), **4:**871
Amponsah, Daniel, **1:**357–58
Amu, Ephraim, **1:**22–26, 34, 35
    compositions of, **1:**24, 216, 221, 223, 224,
        227, 229, 230
Amuriza, Xabier, **8:**312–14, _313_
Amuzgo culture, **2:**563
    funerals in, **2:**567
Amzallag, Salomon, **3:**1174
Amzulescu, Alexandru I., **8:**876, 886
An. *See* An *plus next element in name*
Anabaptists, **3:**886, 1237, 1240
Anabarrabarra (Bararra ceremonial leader), **9:**_420_
Anabasis (Xenophon), **8:**881
Anacani, **3:**751
Anacaona (Cuban all-woman *orquesta*), **2:**105
Anacaona (Taino princess), **2:**846
Anadalyp, Nurmukhammet, **6:**970
Anahory-Librowicz, Oro, **3:**_1173_
Anak Dalem people, **4:**622
Analects (Confucius), **7:**97, 401
Anaman, Rev. J. B., **1:**220–21
Anā Maṣrī (Darwish), **6:**598
Anandamath (Chatterji), **5:**435–36
Anand Lok Natya Mandal (theater company),
        5:_729_
Anania Shirakatsi, **6:**737
Anant Narkong, **4:**26
Anas Al-Wugud (El-Shawan), **6:**607–8
Anasazi culture, **3:**429
Anastasia (musical group), **8:**983
Anataka (Wayana singer), **2:**167
Anat Enchi Chuvash, **8:**772
Anati, Emmanuel, **6:**357
Anatolian Folk Dancers, **3:**1199

Anatom (Vanuatu), **9:**702, 966
Anatri Chuvash, **8:**772
Ancelet, Berry, **3:**858
ancestor worship
    Central Asia, **6:**936
    China, **7:**24, 329
    influence on Central Asian Islam, **6:**936
    Korea, **7:**24, 818, 863–64, 865–66, 869–70,
        982
    Siberia, **7:**1028
An Ch'angho, **7:**991
Anchieta, José de, **2:**302
Anchiskhati (musical group), **8:**845
Anciens Canadiens, Les (de Gaspé), **3:**1165
Ancient and Modern Scottish Songs (Herd), **8:**373
Ancient Future (musical group), **3:**955
Ancient National Airs of Gwent and Morganwg,
        8:345–46, 352
Ancient Orkney Melodies (Balfour), **8:**373
Ancient Scotish [*sic*] *Melodies* (Dauney), **8:**373
Ancient Voices of Children (Crumb), **7:**351
An Comunn Gaidhealach, **8:**371
d'Ancona, Alessandro, **8:**620
And, Metin, **6:**876
Andal, Saint, **5:**260–61, 274
"Andalucía" (Palmieri), **3:**795
Andalusia. *See* Spain
Andalusian repertoire, **1:**534–36; **6:**20, 202, 326,
        406–7, 433, 434, 441–54, 455–63,
        505
    in Algeria, **6:**450–51, 454, 467–72
    history of, **6:**12, 441–45
    influence of, **6:**448–49
    Jewish performers of, **6:**1016, 1017
    in Libya, **6:**452–53, 454
    mode in, **6:**446–47
    in Morocco, **6:**450, 454, 499
    mysticism in, **6:**448
    origins of, **6:**131, 455–56
    poetry and metrics in, **6:**447–48
    song texts, **6:**370, 371
    status of, **6:**436–37
    in Syria, **6:**564, 567
    transmission of, **6:**461–63
    in Tunisia, **6:**451–52, 454, 516, 518
Andaman Islands, **5:**5
Andani, Yakubu, **10:**148
Andersen, Arild, **8:**430
Andersen, Hans Christian, **8:**451
Anderson, Benedict, **4:**650; **10:**43
Anderson, Elijah, **3:**681
Anderson, Laurie, **3:**204, 335
Anderson, Lois, **1:**51, 56
Anderson, Marian, **3:**524, 537, 609, 610, 629,
        1210
Anderson, R. Alex, **3:**1050
Anderson, Robert, **8:**333
Anderson, T. J., **3:**610; **10:**139
Anderson, Tom, **8:**366
Anderson, W. H., **3:**1227
Anderson, William, **9:**14–15, 794
Andersson, Benny, **8:**446
Andersson, Nils, **8:**447
Andersson, Olof, **8:**447
Andersson, Otto, **8:**488
Andh people, **5:**727

Andhra Pradesh, **5:**889–902. *See also* Vijayanagar
    cave paintings in, **5:**298
    dance traditions of, **5:**515, 516–18
    devotional music of, **5:**259, 537, 842
    film music in, **5:**890–91
    folk music in, **5:**889, 891–92
    geography of, **5:**889
    Hyderabad, **5:**889
        cassette industry in, **5:**554
        Shia Muslims in, **5:**256
    instruments in, **5:**350, 351, 364, 367, 893–96
    Karnatak tradition in, **5:**89, 209, 230–32, 234,
        449
    kuchipudi dance-drama in, **5:**104
    map of, **5:**_864_
    Melattur, **5:**518
    mural painting in, **5:**300
    musical genres
        maro dandorā, **5:**556
        narratives, **5:**892–902
    music societies in, **5:**270
    population of, **5:**889
    temple music in, **5:**889
    Tirupati, devotional music in, **5:**246
    vidhinātak theater in, **5:**486
    Vijayawada, public concerts in, **5:**212
Andhra University, **5:**450
Andino, Luis Felipe, **2:**767
And Keep Your Powder Dry (Mead), **3:**511
Ando Drom (musical group), **8:**276
Ando Masateru, **7:**_695_
Andorra, **8:**12
    map of, **8:**_516_
Andô Yosinori, **7:**593–94
Andrade, Manuel J., **2:**862
Andrade, Mário de, **2:**306, 334, 347, 349
Andral, Maguy P., **8:**553, 622
Andrasfalvy, Bertalan, **8:**154
Andreev, Vasily, **8:**9, 775
Andrew, Andrew (Cook Islands performer),
        9:_899_
Andrew E. (rap artist), **4:**886
Andrew Law, American Psalmodist (Crawford),
        3:32
Andrews Sisters, **3:**898
Andreyev, Vassily, **3:**57–58
Andrianampoinimerina (Madagascar king),
        1:782, 789
Andrtová-Voŋková, Dagmar, **8:**730
And Then There Were None (film), **9:**42
And They Lynched Him on a Tree (Still),
        3:609
Anegada, **2:**968
Aneka Record, **4:**681
Anêm people, **9:**614–16
Añez, Jorge, **2:**396, 398
Angaataha people, **9:**512
Angaité culture, **2:**452
Angan people, **9:**489
    dance of, **9:**63
    instruments of, **9:**512
    secret flutes of, **9:**512
    singsings of, **9:**496–97
    songs of, **9:**491
Ang Buhay (Bonus), **4:**863
Ang Chan, king of Khmer, **4:**154

Ang Duong, king of Khmer, **4:**158, 187, 190
Angel, Paula, **3:**757
"Angel in Your Arms" (Hot), **3:**712
Ángeles, Juana, **4:**856
Angelite (Bulgarian choir), **7:**1025; **8:**226
Angelo, Michael, **1:**77–78
Angelopoulos, Manolis, **8:**285
Angelou, Maya, **1:**32
Angkola people, **4:**607
Angkor empire, **4:**62, 153, 187, 215, 219, 315
Anglés, Higinio de, **6:**24; **8:**601
Anglicans. *See also* Episcopalians
  in Anuta, **9:**860
  in Argentina, **2:**259
  in Barbados, **2:**816–17
  in Costa Rica, **2:**688
  in Hawai'i, **9:**918
  in Jamaica, **2:**901
  in Luangiua, **9:**842
  in Oceania, **9:**187
  in Papua New Guinea, **9:**88, 193–94, 197
  in Sikaiana, **9:**844–45, 847, 848
  in Solomon Islands, **9:**665, 667
  in Trinidad and Tobago, **2:**952, 956
  in Vanuatu, **9:**199, 698, 700
  in Virgin Islands, **2:**969
Anglo-African Magazine, **3:**604
Anglo-American Folksong Scholarship since 1898
    (Wilgus), **3:**510
Anglo-American Magazine, **3:**1179
Anglo-Americans/Canadians
  in British Columbia, **3:**1092, 1256–57
  Canadian class structure and, **3:**51, 1070
  dances of, **3:**223
  early settlers, **3:**43–44, 143, 563, 831–33,
    1056, 1114–15
  Episcopalians, **3:**123
  fiddle tunes, **3:**185, 186, 230–31, 232,
    837–38, 870
  folk music, **3:**7, 29, 31, 43, 48, 52, 70, 76–77,
    147–48, 153–58, 292–93, 510–11,
    519–20, 823, 824–25, 831, 833–34,
    1082, 1123–25, 1256–57
    performed by slaves, **3:**66, 68, 595–96
    tunes used for German songs, **3:**888
    used for contra dances, **3:**230
    used in minstrel shows, **3:**837–38
  Lutherans, **3:**120
  in Maritime Provinces, **3:**1068, 1069–71,
    1114–21, 1123–25
  in New Mexico, **3:**755
  in Ontario, **3:**1188–91
  population of, **3:**4–5
  in Québec, **3:**1146, 1148
  religion of, **3:**118–19, 506
  research on music of, **3:**147–48, 510, 511
  in Texas, **3:**770, 771
  in western Canada, **3:**11, 409
Angola. *See also* Central Africa; Southern Africa;
    specific peoples
  Afro-Brazilian immigrants to, **2:**91
  Bantu groups, **1:**670
  Cokwe people, lamellophones, **1:**318
  dance, ballroom, **1:**668
  Europeans in, **1:**717
  history of, **1:**672

instruments, **1:**669, 677
lamellophones, **1:**295–96, 317, *318,* 319–20
Luchazi people, sand ideographs, **1:**150–51
Luvale people, **1:**723
  makishi masks, **1:**309, 311
Mbwela people, **1:**741–42
mukanda institution, **1:**309,
    674–76; **10:**117
music industry in, **1:**435
music of, **1:**672–73, 713–15
music research in, **1:**49; **10:**117–18, 120
Nkhangala people, **1:**741–42
Ovimbundu people, **1:**700
popular music of, **1:**428, 435
San people, **1:**703–5
  music of, **1:**305–7, 744–45
xylophones in, **1:**660
Angolan people
  in North America, **3:**848
  in Portugal, **8:**576
Anguar (Palau), **9:**718
Anguilla, **2:**968
  steelbands in, **2:**97
Angus, Ian, **3:**1057
Anhalt, Istvan, **3:**1075
Anhuradhapura (kingdom), **5:**955
Aníbal, René, **2:**704
Aniceto de la Merced, Father, **4:**843
Ani Choir, **3:**1084
An Ikt'ae. *See* Ahn, Eaktay
Anikulapo-Kuti, Fela. *See* Kuti, Fela
animal choreography, **1:**544–45, 584–85
  Egyptian horse dancing, **6:**628
animal imitations and representations
  Ainu people, **7:**784, 787
  bird calls, **1:**108, 307
  in dance, **1:**116, 117–18
  !Kung people, **1:**307
  Lozi people, **1:**713
  Madhya Pradesh, **5:**474–75
  in masks, **1:**119, 120–21
  in Saami joiks, **8:**303
  Siberia, **7:**1029
  in songs, **1:**133
  as spirits, **1:**275
  Tuvan music, **6:**980–81, 983, 986
  in Welsh songs, **8:**342, 343–44
Animals (musical group), **3:**318; **8:**214, 221
animal sacrifice
  Africa, **1:**277, 333–34, 336, 504
  Ainu people, **7:**785–86, 1029
  Akha people, **4:**541
  Argentina, **2:**257
  Bolivia, **2:**294
  Bontok people, **4:**914, 915
  Borneo, **4:**807
  Cambodia, **4:**157
  Central Asia, **6:**942
  Egypt, **6:**632–33
  Georgia, **8:**834
  Hmong people, **4:**555
  Irian Jaya, **9:**580, 583
  Karnataka, **5:**878–79
  Kmhmu people, **4:**546
  Laos, **4:**341, 359
  Lisu people, **4:**543

Macedonia, Muslim Skopje Roma, **8:**280
Mapuche culture, **2:**233
Martinique, **5:**595, 597, *598*
Maya culture, **2:**657
Nepal, **5:**490, 702
North Africa, **6:**408
Papua New Guinea, **9:**547, 615, 617
  Huli people, **9:**298, 537
  Kuman people, **9:**522–23, 524
Peru, **2:**477
Réunion Island, **5:**609
Siberia, **7:**1029
Southeast Asia, **4:**35, 49, 60
Sulawesi, **4:**808
Sumatra, **4:**619, 807
Sumba, **4:**790
Tarahumara culture, **2:**585
Thailand, **4:**313
Trinidad, **2:**954
Turkic peoples, **7:**21
Tuvalu, **9:**829
Vanuatu, **9:**198, 361, 694–95, 705, 966, 992
  Tanna, **9:**363
Vietnam, **4:**533, 534
  in Vodou ceremonies, **3:**804
Yao people, **4:**549
Animaşaun, Peter, **1:**483
animism. *See also* shamanism
  Ainu people, **7:**784
  Akha people, **4:**541
  Batak people, **4:**607
  Bhutan, **5:**489
  Borneo, **4:**828
  Buddhism and, **4:**59
  Burma, **4:**372–73
  Cambodia, **4:**157
  Central Asia, **6:**900
  China, **7:**495–96
  Hawai'i, **9:**207–8
  Hmong people, **4:**553
  Ifugao people, **4:**917
  Indonesia, **4:**75
  Islam and, **4:**60
  Karen people, **4:**544
  Khmer people, **4:**168, 193–94, 203
  Kmhmu people, **4:**546
  Lahu people, **4:**538–39
  Lisu people, **4:**543
  LoDagaa peoples, **1:**457
  Malaysia, **4:**421, 430, 562
  Maluku, **4:**813, 821
  Middle East, **6:**180
  Mongol people, **7:**1008–9, 1015
  Nepal, **5:**696, 697, 701
  Orang Asli peoples, **4:**565–76
  Orang Melayu Asli people, **4:**586
  Philippines, **4:**839, 889–90
  Rajasthan, **5:**639
  Ryûkyû Islands, **7:**795, 796
  Saami people, **8:**117, 128, 303, 304–5, 306,
    428
  Shan people, **4:**548
  South Asia, **5:**482
  Southeast Asia, **4:**44, 48–53, 59–61, 89
  Sri Lanka, **5:**490, 955, 957, 960–65
  Sulawesi, **4:**804, 806–7

Sumatra
  northern, **4:**605
  Riau, **4:**614–16
  southern, **4:**622
Sumbawa, **4:**779
Tahiti, **9:**207–8
Tuva, **6:**980–81, 985, *987*
Vietnam, **4:**502
Yao people, **4:**549
Aning, Ben, **1:**26, 45; **10:**147
Anir (Papua New Guinea), **9:**639
Anishinaabeg (Anishnabek), **3:**451–59, 1074, 1079
Aniwa (Vanuatu), **9:**702, 833
Anjashah, **6:**362
Anjoman Okhovat (Society of Brothers), **6:**138
Ankamma (deity), **5:**892, 901
el-Anka, Mohamed, **6:**476, *476*
Anka, Paul, **3:**314, 355, 1081
Ankara State Conservatory (Ankara Devlet Konservatuvarı), **6:**77
Ankermann, Bernhard, **10:**120
An Kiok, **7:**960
An Kiyŏng, **7:**960
Anlo-Ewe people. *See under* Ewe people
An Lushan, **7:**29, 30
An Minyŏng, **7:**856, 921
Anna and the King of Siam (Landon), **4:**285
Annakkiḷi (film), **5:**544
Annals of the Chakchiquels, **2:**721–22, 732
Annals of King Sejo. See Sejo sillok akpo
Annamacharya, Tallapakka, **5:**105, 216, 265, 266, 270, 452
Annamalai University, **5:**450
Annapurna (deity), **5:**892
Annayev-*baggy,* Ilaman, **6:**977
Anne of Green Gables (Campbell and Harron), **3:**199, 1119
Annie Get Your Gun (Berlin), **3:**545
"Another One Bites the Dust" (Queen), **3:**689
Anoush (Tigranyan), **6:**726
Anoyanakis, Fivos, **8:**21, 1025
An Pich'wi, **7:**985
An Píobaire, **8:**394
An Sang, **7:**983, 984
Ansang Kŭmbo (collection), **7:**921
al-Anṣārī, **6:**443
"Anselma" (Los Lobos), **3:**750
Ansen, Veve, **9:**362
Anson, George, **9:**743
Anson, Joe, **2:**890
An Suksŏn, **7:**803, *803,* 900
'Antar 'Abd al-'Āṭī, Shaykh, **6:**342
al-'Antarī, **6:**685
Anthem in New England before 1800 (Daniel), **3:**32
anthems, **3:**531, 532. *See also* hymns; national anthems
Anthology of Canadian Music, **3:**1108–9
Anthology of Chinese Folk Music, **7:**200
Anthony, Marc, **3:**522, 733, 743
Anthrax (musical group), **3:**358
anthropology
  cultural, **10:**43
  cultural essentialism, **10:**43
  deculturation concept, **2:**67, 72, 749
  degeneration theory, **1:**84–85

Eurocentrism, **1:**97, 718, 720
evolutionary theory, **1:**87–88, 93–98, 293–94
  musical applications, **1:**11, 36–37
influence on ethnomusicology, **8:**20, 22, 23–25
insider-outsider concept, **1:**29, 63–64, 130, 139, 258–59; **10:**9–11, 22–23, 26, 71
music's role in anthropogenesis, **8:**35
performance, **10:**95
psychological studies, **10:**132
social evolution theories, **7:**441
Anthropology of Music (Merriam), **3:**517; **10:**42, 129
Anthropology Newsletter, **3:**497
"Anticipating the Spring Breeze" (Teng), **7:**357
Antient British Music, **8:**350, 352
Antigua and Barbuda, **2:**789, 798–800
  geography of, **2:**798
  immigrants to Dominica, **2:**840
  musical genres
    calypso, **2:**800
    soca, **2:**96
    steelbands, **2:**97
  population of, **2:**798
Antikirinya people, **9:**433
Antique Tribal Art Dealers Association, **3:**311, 313
Antoni, Lorenc, **8:**1004
Antos, Yannis, **8:***206*
Antunes, Jorge, **2:**306
Antwerp Songbook, **8:**533
Anu, Christine, **9:**146
Anuta (Solomon Islands), **9:**833, 856–61
  instruments of, **9:**378–79, 860
  mataavaka genre, **9:**290
  musical structures of, **9:**306–7
  music and dance of, **9:**856–61
  population of, **9:**856
  research on, **9:**976
  settlement of, **9:**835
  singing, falsetto, **9:**297
  social organization of, **9:**835
  songs of, **9:**336
  sung poetry, **9:**327
Anwar, Gazi Mazharul, **5:**859
Anyi people, **1:**316
Anyumba, Henry Awuor, **1:**626
Aoi no ue (*nô* play), **7:**632
Aoki Reibo I, **7:**709
Aoki Reibo II, **7:**707, 709; **10:**27–28
Aotearoa, **9:**865, 928–51. *See also* Māori people
  adminstration of Cook Islands, **9:**896
  administration of Sāmoa, **9:**218–19
  administration of Tokelau, **9:**823
  archives and museums, **9:**972–74
  brass bands in, **9:**128, 130
  British in, **9:**128
  Chinese people in, **9:**71
  Christianity in, **9:**208
  colonial wars in, **9:**128
  Dalmatian people in, **9:**928
  English people in, **9:**928
  European art music in, **9:**929, 931–32
  European exploration of, **9:**7
  Europeans in, **9:**46
  films on, **9:**1008, 1019–20

  geography of, **9:**928
  history of, **9:**928–29, 934, 947
  immigrants in, **9:**69, 928, 983–84
  instruments of, **9:**386, 393, 932–33
  multiculturalism in, **9:**278
  music and dance of, **9:**48
  Pacific Islanders in, **9:**111–14, 928
  pedagogy in, **9:**277–78
  pipe-and-drum ensembles in, **9:**135
  political songs, **9:**212
  popular music in, **9:**167–69
  Pukapukan people in, **9:**910
  research on, **9:**212, 932, 947
  Rotorua, **9:**936
  Scottish people in, **9:**114–16, 928
  songs of dissent, **9:**354–55
  sound recordings from, **9:**985, 999, 1004
  string figures in, **9:**253
  theater in, **9:**233–34
  theatrical societies, **9:**229
  Tokelauans in, **9:**823–24, 826
Aotearoa (reggae band), **9:**168
Aozko Literature (Lekuona), **8:**315
Apache Indian (rap artist), **5:**568, 575
Apache Indian groups, **3:**425, 428, 429, 431, 755
  girls' puberty ceremonies, **3:**371, 433
  instruments of, **3:**477, 478–79
Apaka, Alfred, **9:**164
àpàlà, **1:**222, 474, 475–77, 485
A-pao-chi, **7:**31
Apapocuva culture, **2:**204
Aparai culture, **2:**157, 164
Aparicio, Frances R., **3:**98
Apaşlar (musical group), **6:**249
Apelu, Logoitino Vaovai, **9:**972
Aphorismen (Ishii), **7:**737
ap Huw, Robert, **8:**349
Apodaca, Antonia, **3:**763
Apodaca, Macario (Max), **3:**763
Apodaca, Tonie, **3:**768
Apodimi Kompania (Melbourne), **9:**73
APO Hiking Society, **4:**885
Apolima (Sāmoa), **9:**795
Apollo Choirs/Clubs, **3:**1090
Apollonius, **6:**373
Apollo's Banquet, **8:**372
Apollo Theater (Harlem), **3:**787
Apostolic Church, **3:**874
  in Cook Islands, **9:**898
  in Papua New Guinea, **9:**516
Apostolov, Anton, **3:**1199
Appalachia. *See also specific states*
  "flat foot" dancing, **3:**213
  folk music of, **3:**159, 160, 325–26, 519–20, 834–35
  lining-out practices in, **3:**832
  research on music of, **8:**19
  rural churches in, **3:**120
Appalachian Spring (Copland), **3:**14, 135, 295, 327
Appar, Saint, **5:**215–16, 260
Appavoo, Rev. James Theophilus, **5:***923,* 925–27
Appetite for Destruction (Guns 'n' Roses), **3:**358
Appianing, **1:**356
Applebaum, Louis, **3:**1185

Appleby, David P., **2:**116, 320
Appo, William, **3:**603, 604
April Wine (musical group), **3:**265
Apsan t'aryŏng (Korean folk song), **7:**886
Apsara (heavenly beings), **5:**399
Apsati (god), **8:**857
Apte, Shanta, **5:**420, 533
Apthorp, William Foster, **3:**27
Āqā Gholām Ḥosein, **6:**866
Āqā Hoseynqoli, **6:**130, 865–66
al-'Aqīlī, Majdī, **6:**568
Aqsarniit (musical group), **3:**1280
Aquabella, Francisco, **3:**784
Aquarium (musical group), **8:**778
Aquarius (musical group), **3:**266
Aquelarre (musical group), **2:**373
Aquino de Belén, Father Gaspar, **4:**843
Aquino, Mr., **2:**934
Aquitani people, **8:**309
Arab-Andalucían culture. *See also* Andalusian
        repertoire
    influence on Chilean music, **2:**367, 369
    influence on Venezuelan music, **2:**524, 540
    in Spain, **1:**534
Arabatsis, Nick, **9:**75
Arab Community Center for Economic and
        Social Services (Detroit), **3:**1037;
        6:286
arabesk, **6:**118, 247, 248, 250, 251, 255–59,
        776; **8:**204
    Albania, **8:**1002
    Germany, **8:**237
    history of, **6:**255–56
    Kosova, **8:**286, 951
    musical organization of, **6:**256–57
    sociocultural context of, **6:**259
Arabesque Dance Academy (Toronto), **3:**1219
Arabesque Dance Company (Toronto), **3:**1220
Arabian peninsula, **6:**649–59. *See also* Bahrain;
        Kuwait; Oman; Qatar; Saudi Arabia;
        United Arab Emirates; Yemen
    aerophones in, **6:**414–16
    African peoples in, **6:**304, 644; **10:**58
    ancient civilizations of, **6:**401, 535
    archaeological and epigraphical research,
        6:357–62
    chordophones in, **6:**407, 409, 412–13
    dance traditions in, **6:**703–11
    drums in, **6:**416–20
    folk traditions in, **6:**545
    geography of, **6:**649
    Gulf region, **6:**545–46, 649, 651–52
    healing rituals in, **6:**359, 405, 412, 546, 706,
        710
    idiophones in, **6:**403–5
    lyres in, **6:**357–59
    map of, **6:**650
    pearl-diving culture, **6:**10, 404, 546, 649, 651,
        657, 697–98, 703
    research on music of, **6:**649
    sung poetry in, **6:**663–69
    urban music of, **6:**649, 657
    Western expatriates in, **6:**713–19; **10:**58
    women musicians
        contemporary, **6:**695–702
        historical, **6:**293–98, 695–96

Arab Music Institute. *See* Ma'had al-Mūsīqá al-
        'Arabiyyah
Arab peoples. *See also* Bedouin peoples; *specific*
        countries
    in Algeria, **6:**466
    in Belize, **2:**666
    in Dominican Republic, **2:**847
    in Egypt, **6:**240, 555, 623–24
    in Morocco, **6:**496
    in North Africa, **1:**532–36; **6:**273, 431–32
    in North America, **3:**12, 1028, 1029, 1037,
        1084, 1089–90, 1215, 1216, 1245–46;
        6:279–86, 285–86
    in Nusa Tenggara Timur, **4:**787
    in Palestine, **6:**1015, 1021
    in Paraguay, **2:**462
    in Sumatra, **4:**616
    in Vietnam, **4:**531
    in Virgin Islands, **2:**969
Arab travelers and traders, **1:**11, 75–76, 436,
        635; **6:**21
Araca la Cana, **2:***518*
Arada nation, **2:**869
Aradhana (film), **5:**537
'Arafa, 'Abd al-Mun'im, **6:**18
'Arafa, 'Alī ibn, **6:**502
Arago, Jacques, **9:**17
Aragon, Joaquín, **4:**859
Aragon jota, **6:**443
Arai Hakuseki, **7:**27
Araiza, Carmen, **3:**763
Araketu (*bloco afro*), **2:**353
Araki Kodo IV, **7:**707, 708
Arakishvili, Dimitri, **8:**843, 846, 853, 861, 864
Arana Martija, J. A., **8:**309
Arana, Miranda, **3:***994*; **4:**25
Arancibia, Mario, **2:**372
Aranda people, **9:**433, 437
Aranyak (theater group), **5:**489
Aranzamendi, Bernabe, **2:**939
Arapaho Indian nation, **3:**371, 421, 440, 445
    Ghost Dance songs, **3:**487
Aras Male Choir (Toronto), **3:**1196
Araújo, Alceu Maynard de, **2:**306
Araullo, Teodoro, **4:**865
Araura, **9:**901
Arawak culture, **2:**78. *See also* Taino culture
    in Barbados, **2:**813
    in Central America, **2:**668, 733
    ceremonies of, **2:**45
    in Cuba, **2:**822
    in Dominican Republic, **2:**846
    extermination of, **2:**791, 798
    in French Guiana, **2:**434
    in Guyana, **2:**442
    in Haiti, **2:**881
    instruments of, **2:**13, 435
    in Jamaica, **2:**896, 902
    in Montserrat, **2:**922
    in Netherlands Antilles and Aruba, **2:**927, 928
    in Puerto Rico, **2:**932
    relation to Warao culture, **2:**189
    in Surinam, **2:**503
    in Trinidad and Tobago, **2:**952
    in Virgin Islands, **2:**968
    vocal music of, **2:**437

Arawete culture, **2:**128
'*Araysaynā yā raytā ḥalqah mbārakih* (*mḥorabih*),
        6:589
Arbatsky, Yuri, **8:**1003
Arbeau, Thoinot (Jehan Tabourot), **8:**108,
        546
Arcand, John, **3:**410
Arcaño y sus Maravillas, **2:**835; **3:**795–96
Arcaraz, Luis, **2:**622
archaeology
    Africa, **1:**4–5
        cord-and-peg drums, **1:**316
        harps, **1:**301
        iron bells, **1:**310, 319
        lamellophones, **1:**319
        rock paintings and petroglyphs, **1:**294, 301,
            305, 635, 705
    Arabian peninsula, **6:**357–61
    Argentina, **2:**249–50
    Armenia, **6:**723
    Austral Islands, **9:**880
    Aztec culture, **2:**555–56
    Basque region, **8:**316
    Belize, **2:**667
    Bolivia, **2:**11–12, 282
    British Columbia, **3:**1254
    Brittany, **8:**558
    Cambodia, **4:**153
    Caribbean, **2:**8
    Celtic civilization, **8:**319
    Central Africa, **1:**670
    Central America, **2:**8–9
    Central Asia, **5:**689; **6:**936
    Chile, **2:**356
    China, **7:**99–101, 127, 131, 319, 407
        instruments, **7:**87–88, 105–11, 159, 188,
            191, 491
        research on, **7:**136
    Colombia, **2:**9–10, 183, 379
    Cook Islands, **9:**896
    Costa Rica, **2:**680–81
    Denmark, **8:**463
    Dominican Republic, **2:**846
    East Asia, **7:**15–16, 41–43, 79
    Ecuador, **2:**10, 413
    El Salvador, **2:**706–7, 719
    Europe, **8:**20, 34–42
    Finland, **8:**481
    Georgia, **8:**837, 839, 842
    Germany, **8:**651
    Grenada, **2:**864
    Guaraní culture, **2:**199
    India, **5:**215
    Indus Valley, **5:**319–20, 374
    Inner Asia, **7:**11–13
    Iraq, **6:**407
    Ireland, **8:**384
    Israel, **8:**258–59
    Jamaica, **2:**896
    Japan, **7:**20, 534, 535, 557–62
    Kashmir, **5:**689
    Korea, **7:**20, 805–6, 821, 833
    Low Countries, **8:**526, 527
    Malta, **8:**634
    Mapuche culture, **2:**232, 233–34, 252–53
    Mariana Islands, **9:**743

Mashriq, **6:**535
Maya culture, **2:**650–51
Mexico, **2:**8–9, 600, 601–3
Middle Eastern instruments, **6:**17–18, 413
Mixtec culture, **2:**563
New Caledonia, **9:**598
Nicaragua, **2:**747–48
Norway, **8:**422–23
Orissa, **5:**519
Otopame culture, **2:**570
Palestine, **6:**1061–62, 1065
Panama, **2:**773
Papua New Guinea, **9:**566
Paraguay, **2:**452
Peru, **2:**10–11, 207, 467, 470
Philippines, **4:**913
Poland, **8:**705–6
Polynesian outliers, **9:**833, 834–35
Puerto Rico, **2:**932
Purépecha culture, **2:**575
research on, **8:**25
Romania, **8:**881
Sāmoa, **9:**795
Sardinia, **8:**631
Scotland, **8:**366
Shona culture, **1:**744
South and Central America, **2:**6–12, 33, 45;
         10:97, 99–100
    tropical-forest region, **2:**125
Southeast Asia, **4:**32–46
Spain, **8:**600
Sudan, **1:**549, 555
Sweden, **8:**439
Switzerland, **8:**682, 687
Tanzania, drums, **1:**637
Tarahumara culture, **2:**582–83
Tibet, **7:**471
United States, **3:**366, 478, 493
'Uvea and Futuna, **9:**808–9
Vanuatu, **9:**688–89
Vietnam, **4:**445–46
Archaimbault, Charles, **4:**341
Archer, Violet, **3:**90, 93, 1090
Archimedes, **6:**373
architecture
    Akha people, **4:**540–41
    Asmat people, **9:**190
    Atacameño culture, **2:**356
    Atoni people, **4:**796
    Batak people, **4:**607
    Borneo, **4:**824
    Brazil, temporary structures, **2:**331
    Carriacou, **2:**871
    Cirebon, **4:**686
    Colombia
        marimba house, **2:**402, 404
        Tairona culture, **2:**183
    Dai people, **7:**496
    Ecuador, marimba house, **2:**427
    Egypt, Coptic Orthodox churches, **6:**220
    Ghana, Gã houses, **1:**103
    Guarijio culture, **2:**552
    Hawai'i, **9:***208*
    Hmong people, **4:**551
    Ifugao people, **4:**917
    Karen people, **4:**544

Kmhmu people, **4:**546
Kosrae, **9:***741*
Lisu people, **4:**542
Mariana Islands, **9:**743
Minangkabau people, **4:**608
North America
    performance spaces, **3:**237
    worship structures and churches, **3:**122, 124
Palau, *bai*, **9:**722, 723, 724, *725*, 743
Papua New Guinea, **9:***962*
    Eastern Highlands peoples, **9:**529
    Iatmul people, **9:**553
    Lolo people, **9:**612–13
    Yupno people, **9:**303
Q'ero culture, **2:**225
Senoi people, **4:**562
Shan people, **4:**547
Solomon Islands, Blablanga people, **9:**657
South America, **2:**245
Southeast Asia, megaliths, **4:**570, 619
South Indian temples, **5:**263
Sulawesi, **4:**806, 807–8
Tarahumara culture, **2:**582
Timiar people, **4:**573
Torajan people, **4:**807–8
Warao culture, **2:**188
Yao people, **4:**549
Archiv Productions label, **8:**55
Archive of American Folk-Song. *See* Library of
    Congress
Archive of the Center for Folklife Programs and
    Cultural Studies (Smithsonian
    Institution), **9:**977–78
Archive of Folk Culture. *See* Library of Congress
Archive of Maori and Pacific Music, **9:**932, 961,
    972–74
Archive of New Zealand Music, **9:**974
archives and museums. *See also specific institutions*
    Albania, **8:**1003
    Aotearoa, **9:**932, 944, 972–74
    Armenia, **6:**727
    Australia, **9:**415, 958–61
    Austria, **8:**18
    Barbados, **2:**814, 817
    Bolivia, **2:**284
    Brittany, **8:**563
    California, **3:**736–37
    Canada, **3:**226, 292, 1073, 1167
    China, imperial, **7:**393
    Cuba, **2:**838
    Czech Republic, **8:**724, 725
    Dominican Republic, **2:**862
    Europe, **9:**980–84
        role in pedagogy, **8:**179–81
    Fiji, **9:**968
    Finland, **8:**481
    France, **8:**18, 553
    Germany, **8:**18, 663
    Great Britain, **8:**18
    Greece, **8:**1025
    Hawai'i, **9:**915, 968–72
    Israel, **6:**1037, 1058–59, 1060, 1062,
        1063–64
    Italy, **8:**18, 622
    Karnataka, **5:**887
    Latvia, **8:**506–7

Macedonia, **8:**983
Malta, **8:**642
Micronesia, **9:**967–68
New Caledonia, **9:**964–65
New Mexico, **3:**767
Nicaragua, **2:**767
North America, **3:**29–31, 33, 34, 497
Oceania, **9:**853, 958–74
Pakistan, **5:**747
Panama, **2:**783
Papua New Guinea, **9:**961–62
Poland, **8:**712
Portugal, **8:**585
Romania, **8:**885
Russia, **8:**784
Slovakia, **8:**724, 725
Slovenia, **8:**922
Solomon Islands, **9:**962–64
sound recording, **2:**66, 251, 488, 511, 593;
    3:292; **5:**213; **6:**1037, 1057, 1058–59,
    1062, 1063–64; **8:**177; **10:**73, 88
South Asia, **5:**529–30
Spain, **8:**601
Sweden, **8:**448
Switzerland, **8:**18
Ukraine, **8:**823
United States, **9:**974–80; **10:**88
    dance, **3:**221
    ethnographic materials, **10:**73
    media, **3:**237, 243, 245
    repatriation of Native American materials,
        3:494–96
Vanuatu, **9:**965–67
Archives of Andean Traditional Music of the
    Catholic University (Peru), **2:**488
Archives and Research Center for
    Ethnomusicology (Delhi), **5:**529
Archives of Traditional Music (Indiana
    University), **1:**31; **2:**488, 649, 783;
    3:416, 449, 465, 470; **9:**975; **10:**63
Archuleta, José, **3:**763
Arciniegas, Ismael Enrique, **2:**394
Arctic peoples. *See also specific groups*
    culture of, **3:**374–75
    historical and cultural changes, **3:**379–80
    instruments of, **3:**472–79
    musical performance, **3:**375–77
    musical styles, **3:**377–78
    research on music of, **3:**380–81
    subsistence patterns, **3:**374–75
Arctic Rose (Aglukark), **3:**1280
Arden, Jann, **3:**1081
Ardévol, José, **2:**828
Ardhanarishvara (deity), **5:**497
Ardijah (Māori band), **9:**168
'Are'are people
    music and dance of, **9:**666–68
    panpipe music of, **9:**42, 156, 286, 292, 393,
        398–401, 665
Arecuna culture, **2:**442
A-R Editions, **10:**165
'Āref Qazvini, **6:**137
Arel, Bülent, **6:**775
Arel, Sâdeddin, **6:**48, 84, 772, 783
Arendt, Hannah, **3:**513–14
Arensky, Anton, **8:**764

Aretz, Isabel, **2:**32, 115, 123, 251, 488, 523, 524, 536, 543–44, 783
Arévalo, Tito, **4:**883
Arewa, Ojo, **1:**501
Areyonga Desert Tigers, **9:**145
Argentina, **2:**249–70. *See also specific peoples*
 Aboriginal inhabitants of, **2:**249–51
 Afro-Brazilian cults in, **2:**260
 Andes region, harvest celebrations, **2:**255
 art music in, **2:**112–16
 Aymara-speaking peoples, **2:**205–23
 Buenos Aires
  music conservatory, **2:**114
  tango in, **2:**263–65
 Catamarca province, **2:**258
 Chaco, **2:**249, 250–51, 259
  harvest celebrations, **2:**255
 children's wakes in, **2:**422
 Chinese people in, **2:**84–85
 Córdoba province
  Cosquín folkloric festival, **2:**261
  cuarteto music in, **2:**40, 273–80
 Cuyo, **2:**249
 folkloric music in, **2:**261–63
 geography of, **2:**249
 German people in, **2:**89
 Guaraní culture, **2:**199–204
 history of, **2:**245, 250–51
 immigrants in, **2:**261
 influence on Uruguayan music, **2:**522
 instruments of, **2:**31, 251–54
 Italian people in, **2:**89–90
 Japanese people in, **2:**86–87; **10:**99, 102
 Jujuy province, **2:**249–50, 256, 257, 258
 La Rioja province, **2:**258
 Mapuche culture, **2:**57, 232–38
 Maronite Church in, **6:**208
 military regime in, **2:**104
 Misiones, **2:**254–55
 Misiones province, **2:**251
 musical genres
  baguala, **2:**256
  chamamé, **2:**269, *270*
  cifra, **2:**261
  cuarteto, **2:**105, 273–80
  estilo, **2:**261
  milonga, **2:**261, 263, 274
  murga, **2:**261
  música tropical, **2:**265–66
  nueva canción, **2:**103
  ranchera, **2:**261
  rock, **2:**104, 266–68
  Roman Catholic, **2:**256–59
  tango, **1:**384; **2:**49, 75, 89, 101, 249, 263–65, 269–70, 274
 music video broadcasting, **2:**268; **3:**248, 252
 pampas region, **2:**249, 261
 Patagonia, **2:**249, 250, 251
 population of, **2:**249
 religion in, **2:**254–61
 Río de la Plata, **2:**250
 Salta province, **2:**258
 San Juan province, **2:**258
 Santiago del Estero province, **2:**258
 secular music in, **2:**261–69
 shamanism in, **2:**45
 sound recording industry, **2:**64
 Spanish people in, **2:**90
 Tierra del Fuego, **2:**250, 251, 259
 tourism in, **2:**50
Argentine people
 in Brazil, **2:**84
 in North America, **3:**730, 1201, 1204
Argov, Alexander, **6:**1072–73
Argov, Zohar, **6:***1033*, 1033–34, 1074, *1074*
Arguedas, José María, **2:**36, 484
Arhoolie (record company), **2:**106; **9:**998
Arianism, **6:**431
Arias Larreta, Abraham, **2:**501
Arias Larreta, Felipe, **2:**501
'Arīb, **6:**296–97
Arif, Muhammad Akram, **5:***765*
Arifamu people, **9:**983
Arikara Indian nation, **3:**440
Arima Daigorô, **7:**592
Arion Club's Male Voice Choir, **3:**1094
Ariosto, Ludovico, **8:**17, 573, 608, 611
Arirang (Korean folk song), **7:**880–81, *881*, 885, 988
Arista Records, **3:**714
Aristi, Cecilia, **2:**837
Aristide, Jean-Bertrand, **2:**895
Aristides Quintilian, **8:**46, 47
Aristotelian Academy of Greek Traditional Dances (Sydney), **9:**73
Aristotle, **6:**16, 19, 367–69, 396, 541; **8:**46, 48, 92
Aristoxenus, **6:**16, 368; **8:**46, 47–48
Ariunaa, **7:**1020
Ariyaratne, Sunil, **5:**959, 966
Arizona
 Amerindian cultures of, **2:**591–93
 Hano, **3:**428
 Hopi Indian nation, **3:**215, 216
 Latino peoples in, **3:**718–19
 Native American groups in, **3:**420–22, 425–27, 428–38
 Spanish dance dramas in, **3:**850–51
 Tucson, *zarzuela* companies, **3:**851
 Yaqui Indian nation, **3:**218
Ariztimuño, Jose "Aitzol," **8:**315
Arkansas, Native American groups in, **3:**440, 466
"Arkansas Traveler," **3:**409
Arkivet för Ljud och Bild (Stockholm), **8:**448
Arlen, Harold, **3:**196, 549
Ar Log (musical group), **8:**355
Armandinho (pseud. of Salgado Armando Freire), **8:**583
Armbrust, Walter, **6:**24
Armed Forces Radio Network, **3:**79
Armendáriz, Pedro, **3:**740
Armenia, **6:**723–37
 folk music, **6:**727–31
 history of music in, **6:**723–27
 Iranian dance traditions in, **6:**877
 Kurdistan region of, **6:**743–52
 map of, **6:***724*
 research on music of, **6:**726–27
 vocal music of, **8:**828
Armenian Apostolic Church, **6:**405
 in Israel, **6:**1021
 liturgical music, **6:**725, 736–37
Armenian people
 in Bulgaria, **8:**903
 in Cyprus, **8:**1029
 diaspora of, **6:**724–25
 in Georgia, **8:**840, 842
 in Iran, **6:**828, 843
 in Nagorno-Karabakh, **6:**726
 in North America, **3:**930, 1028, 1029–30, 1031, 1032, 1033, 1035–36, 1084
 in Syria, **6:**565
 in Turkey, **6:**115, 117
 in Ukraine, **8:**821
Armistead, Samuel G., **6:**1037; **8:**267
Armour, Leslie, **3:**1061
Armstrong, Alan, **9:**314–15
Armstrong, Louis, **1:**772; **3:**71, 550, 568, 652–53, 654, 656, 660, 706; **8:**675
Army Show (revue), **3:**198
Arnaiz, Ramón B., **3:**738–39
Arnaz, Desi, **2:**371; **3:**732
Arne, Thomas, **3:**180
Arnič, Blaž, **8:**921
Arnim, Ludwig Achim von, **8:**17–18, 663
'Arnītah, Y., **6:**580
Arno Atoll (Marshall Islands), **9:**751
Arnold, Alison Geldard, **3:**980; **5:**585
Arnold, Eddy, **3:**77
Arnold, Kokomo, **3:**645
Aroding (Maceda), **4:**875
Arogangan, Awole (Oyo ruler), **1:**401
Arom, Simha, **1:**51, 59, 688
 field rerecording technique of, **1:**254–55, 256
 transcription methodology of, **1:**154, 156
Aromăn people, **8:**986
Aromot Island (Papua New Guinea), **9:**572
Aroona, **9:**443
Arop Island (Papua New Guinea), **9:**572–73, 983
Arowe people, **9:**607
arpa. See harps
Arraymusic (Toronto), **3:**1186
Arrested Development (musical group), **3:**702, 715
Arrivillaga Cortés, Alfonso, **2:**737
Arrow (calypsonian), **2:**96, 924
Arroyo, Joe, **2:**102, 410
Arroyo, Martina, **3:**726
Ärsary tribe, **6:**966, 975
Arsen the Katholikos, **8:**843
Arsenault, Angele, **3:**1137
Arsenault, Eddy, **3:**1137
Arsenault, Georges, **3:**1136
Arshak Erkrard (Chukhadjian), **6:**725
ars musica, **8:**49–50
Ars Nova, **8:**65, 71, 726
Ar Soner (periodical), **8:**563, 564
Ars Subtilior, **8:**50, 73
Art Ensemble of Chicago, **3:**664
Art Forum (periodical), **8:**730
Arthur Godfrey Show (radio show), **3:**1050
Arthur M. Sackler Gallery (Washington, D.C.), **5:**529
Artigas, José Gervasio, **2:**457
"Artii-Sayir" (Tuvan song), **6:**982, *983*
Artis, Bob, **3:**159

art music, Western, **8:**68–86. *See also*
　　composition; Western culture and
　　music; *specific composers, countries, and*
　　genres
African-American composers, **3:**603–12
African-American influences on, **3:**523, 539
Albania, **8:**999
American use of Indian music, **5:**528
Armenia, **6:**725–27
Asian influences on, **3:**327, 335, 541, 953–54,
　　1015–16, 1019, 1021
Austria, **8:**663, 670–71
authority concepts in, **8:**73, 96
Barbados, **2:**814, 820
Belarus, **8:**800
blues and, **3:**648
Bolivia, **2:**284
Bosnia-Hercegovina, **8:**963, 969
Brazil, **2:**303, 305–6
British Caribbean consumers, **3:**812
Bulgaria, **8:**904–5
Canada, **3:**1108
　　British Columbia, **3:**1096–97
　　development of, **3:**14
　　gendering of, **3:**87
　　Maritimes, **3:**1072, 1118–21
　　Northwestern Territories, **3:**1278
　　Ontario, **3:**1079–80, 1179–86, 1209–10
　　patronage of, **3:**52
　　Prairie Provinces, **3:**1090–91
　　Québec, **3:**1076, 1148–53, 1166
　　Yukon, **3:**1278
Caribbean, **2:**112–16
Central America, **2:**112–16
China, **7:**341–42, 350–51, 377, 388
Chinese-American performers of, **3:**963–64
Colombia, **2:**396–98
concept of, **2:**112–14; **8:**2, 204
concept of classic in, **8:**93
conducting of, **8:**100–102
Costa Rica, **2:**693–94, 702
Croatia, **8:**933–34
Cuba, **2:**827–28, 829, 836–37
Czech Republic, **8:**727–30
Denmark, **8:**460–61
Dominican Republic, **2:**859, 862
economics and, **8:**188–89
Egypt, **6:**607–8, 610–13
El Salvador, **2:**708, 716
England, **8:**71–72, 76
Estonia, **8:**494–98
European, **2:**69
Europe, Northern, **8:**399
feminist studies, **3:**91, 92
Finland, **8:**482, 485
folk idioms in, **8:**4, 17, 19, 53, 82, 95–96,
　　227–28, 272–73, 332–33, 339, 366,
　　372–73
France, **8:**543, 550
French Guiana, **2:**437
Georgia, **8:**843–44
German-American performers of, **3:**885
Germany, **8:**646, 653–54, 655, 663
Great Britain, use of bagpipe in, **8:**366, 369
Greece, **8:**1008
Grenada, **2:**866

Guatemala, **2:**735–36
Guyana, **2:**446–47
Haiti, **2:**892, 894
Hawai'i, **3:**527; **9:**923–25
history of, **8:**68–86
Honduras, **2:**745
Hungary, **8:**273
Iceland, **8:**406–7
ideology and, **8:**186–88
Indonesian-American collaborations,
　　3:1016–17
influence on film music, **3:**203, 204
influence on rock, **3:**347
Ireland, **8:**378
Israel, **6:**1023–32, 1061, 1066
Italy, **8:**609, 617, 618, 658
Jamaica, **2:**910
Japan, **7:**540, 728–29, 731–33, 735–38,
　　760–61
Japanese research on, **7:**595
Jewish composers of, **8:**264
Jewish liturgical music settings, **8:**250, 263
Jewish patronage of, **8:**260
Jewish performers of, **8:**260
klezmer and, **3:**942
Korea, **7:**803, 946, 952, 994
Korean-American performers of, **3:**977
Latin American, **3:**740
literacy and, **8:**6
Lithuania, **8:**510
Low Countries, **8:**518
Macedonia, **8:**980–81
Malta, **8:**642–43
Maya culture, European Renaissance genres,
　　2:731
men's roles in, **8:**199
Mexico, **2:**112–16, 113–15, 600, 603–5, 622,
　　623, 651
Native American influences on, **3:**14, 291,
　　367, 539
Netherlands Antilles, **2:**931
Nicaragua, **2:**764–65
Nigeria, **1:**232–53
Norway, **8:**411, 424–28
notation of, **8:**50–56, 91–92, 93, 97–98
Panama, **2:**784
Philippines, **4:**868–82
Poland, **8:**710
Portugal, **8:**585
recomposition in, **8:**91–97
repertoire selection, **8:**61
research on, **2:**116
rock and, **8:**215, 219, 221
role of history of, **8:**58–65
Romania, **8:**881–85
Russia, **8:**775, 780–82, 856, 858, 861
Scotland, **8:**366–69, 370
Serbia, **8:**943, 948
Singapore, **4:**523
Slovakia, **8:**727–30
Slovenia, **8:**921
social class and, **3:**45, 46, 269; **8:**13,
　　52, 189
South America, **2:**112–16, 245
Southeast Asian influences on, **4:**130–32
Spain, **8:**600–601

Spanish-American composers and performers,
　　3:851
Spanish mission and cathedral music, **3:**755,
　　768, 848–49
Sweden, **8:**434, 443–45
Switzerland, **8:**696–97
temporal dimensions of, **1:**127–28
theory in, **8:**92–93
Ukraine, **8:**819–20
United States
　　Christian liturgical, **3:**534
　　in Christian services, **3:**122, 123
　　crossover genres in, **3:**334–35
　　development of, **3:**11, 14, 257, 535–41
　　development of institutions for, **3:**10
　　electronic music, **3:**252–55
　　folk tunes in, **3:**327, 538–39
　　marketing of, **3:**44–45, 268–71
　　nineteenth century, **3:**536–39
　　patronage of, **3:**70
　　popular music influences in, **3:**335
　　race and, **3:**70
　　twentieth century, **3:**173–77, 539–41
　　urban contexts of, **3:**143
Vietnam, **4:**510–12
Western-Indian collaborations, **5:**561, 584
Western tradition
　　in Goa, **5:**737, 740–41
　　in South Africa, **5:**616
women's roles in, **8:**197, 199–200, 368
world music and, **8:**225
Yiddish, **3:**940
Arts America, **3:**298
Arts et Traditions Populaires (periodical), **8:**554
Arts Indonesia (New York), **3:**1020
Arts Plan 21 (Japan), **7:**761
Art Tower Mito (Japan), **7:**761
Aru Archipelago, **4:**819, 820–21
Aruba, **2:**789, 927–31
　　art music in, **2:**931
　　history of, **2:**927
　　instruments of, **2:**928–29
　　musical genres, *tambú*, **2:**928, 929–30
　　musical traditions, **2:**928
　　political status of, **2:**792
　　popular music in, **2:**930–31
　　research on, **2:**931
Arun, Ila, **5:**421, 427
Arunachal Pradesh, **5:**504–5
Arunagirinadar, Saint, **5:**265
　　tiruppugal of, **5:**105, 107, 145, 216, 918
d'Arvieux, Chevalier, **6:**566
Arvizu, Juan, **2:**372
Aryabhushan Theater (Pune), **5:**424
al-'Aryān, Ibrāhīm, **6:**40
Aryans, **5:**14, 17, 261, 720
　　introduction of caste system, **5:**374–75, 398
　　social organization of, **5:**9
　　Vedas of, **5:**66, 238
Aryasa, I. W. M., **4:**733
Arya Subadha Natya Sabha (institute), **5:**491
Asadoğlı, Mirza Sadıx, **6:**925
Asaf'ev, Boris, **8:**756, 767, 783–84, 803
Asafud-Daula, Nawab, **5:**133
Asante people. *See* Ashanti people
Asare, Kwame, **1:**377

Āśāri caste, **5:**930
Asaro people, **9:**63, 526–33
'Asatrú religion, **8:**408
ASCAP. *See* American Society of Composers, Authors, and Publishers
Asch, Michael, **3:**392, 1276
Asch, Moses, **3:**300
Aschoff, Peter, **3:**104
Ascuez, Augusto, **2:**499
Ascuez, Elías, **2:**499
Asenjo Barbieri, Francisco, **8:**601
Aserrí culture, **2:**680
Aşgabat Dramatic Theater, **6:**976
Ash, Allen, **3:**1190
Ashanti (kingdom), **1:**4
Ashanti (Asante) people
 atumpan drums, **1:**316
 in Belize, **2:**668
 dance, **1:**109, 286
 historical studies, **1:**88–89
 music of, **1:**464; **10:**78, 79
 political organization of, **1:**463–64
 songs, **1:**89
 speech surrogate methods, **1:**107
 in Surinam, **2:**504, 505
 textile design, **1:**114
Al-Ashara 'l-Ṭayyiba (Darwīsh), **6:**598
Ashbourne, Peter, **2:**912
Ashikaga Yoshimitsu, **7:**639, 641
Ashikaga Yoshimochi, **7:**641
Ashikaga Yoshinori, **7:**641
Ashkar, Paul, **6:**209
Ashkenazi Tradition of the Biblical Chant between 1500 and 1900 (Avenary), **6:**1059–60
Ashkenazy, Vladimir, **7:**416
Ashkhabad (Turkmenistan), **6:**905
Ashley, Robert, **3:**253
Ashnan Togher (Melik'yan), **6:**726
Ashoka, Mauryan emperor, **5:**490, 720, 731; **7:**22
Ashot (*gusan*), **6:**734, 736
al-Ashraf Shaʿbān, Mamluk sultan, **6:**298
Ashvaghosha, **5:**457–58, 484
Asia Records, **4:**493
Asiama, Simeon, **1:**26
Asian-American Creative Music (San Francisco), **3:**971–72
Asian-American movement, **3:**970
Asian-Americans/Canadians. *See also specific groups*
 in Canada, **3:**4–5, 1057, 1078, 1082, 1083–84, 1086, 1092, 1095–96, 1186, 1215–17, 1231, 1245–48, 1258–59
 immigration of, **3:**512
 jazz genres, **3:**336, 345
 karaoke performances, **3:**98
 overview of musics, **3:**526–27, 948–56
 population of, **3:**4–5
Asian Art Museum (San Francisco), **3:**996
AsianImprov Arts, **3:**972
AsianImprov Records, **3:**965, 972
Asian Institute for Liturgy and Music, **4:**878
Asian Music (periodical), **5:**57
Asian Traditional Performing Arts Project, **7:**594
Asiatic Researches (periodical), **5:**49

Aşîk Garip and Shah Senem (Turkish fairy tale), **6:**803
Āsīm, Midḥat, **6:**235, 236
Asin (musical group), **4:**886
Asirgadh dynasty, **5:**721
Asita tenki ni nare (Japanese folk song), **7:**604
'Askar al-Ḥalabī al-Ḥanafī al-Qādirī, **6:**182, 366, 565–66
Askew, Greg, **3:**786
Aslanishvili, Shalva, **8:**846
Asli and Kerem (epic), **6:**766, 929
Asmahan, **6:**239
al-Aṣmaʿī, **6:**353
Asmat Museum of Culture and Progress (Agats), **9:**191, 591
Asmat people
 bis ceremony, **9:**580
 composition of, **9:**360
 dance of, **9:**486–87
 instruments of, **9:**582–83
 music and dance of, **9:**589–91
 religious beliefs and rituals of, **9:**189–91
 songs of, **9:**587
 sung poetry, **9:**326
As Nasty As They Wanna Be (2 Live Crew), **3:**714
Asociación Aires Costarricenses, **2:**703
Asociación de Grupos e Intérpretes de la Cultura Popular (Costa Rica), **2:**703
Aspiazu, Don, **3:**732
Āśrama-Bhajanāvalī (Kalelakar), **5:**632
Assam, **5:**7
 bhavana theater in, **5:**486
 dance traditions of, **5:**503
 ojapali theater in, **5:**486
 Tai people in, **4:**218
Assamese people, in Bhutan, **5:**489
Assembly of God
 in Marshall Islands, **9:**748
 in Papua New Guinea, **9:**516
 in Sāmoa, **9:**207
assimilation. *See* acculturation and assimilation
Assiniboine Indian nation, **3:**440, 1086
Associación Sandinista de Trabajadores de la Cultura, **2:**766
Associated Board of the Royal Schools of Music (London), **3:**277
Associated Musicians of Ontario, **3:**1182
Association for the Advancement of Creative Musicians (Chicago), **3:**662, 664
Association des Artistes (Saskatchewan), **3:**1088
Association of Canadian Women Composers/ Association des Femmes Compositeurs Canadiennes, **3:**91
Association of Chinese Dramatists, **7:**387
Association for Chinese Music Research, **10:**24
Association of Chinese Musicians. *See* Chinese Musicians' Association
Association for Corporate Support of the Arts (Japan), **7:**761
Association pour la Création et la Recherche Electroacoustiques du Québec, **3:**1152
Association du Disque et de l'Industrie du Spectacle et de la Vidéo du Québec, **3:**1161
Association of Indians in America, **3:**987; **5:**584

Association of Irish Musicians, **9:**79
Association for Music Studies (Vietnam), **4:**511
Association for the Promotion of Folk Dance, **8:**461
Association for the Religious Instruction of the Negroes, **3:**598
Association of Ukrainian Choirs of America, **3:**912
associations. *See* societies and organizations; *specific names*
Associazione Puglia, **9:**80
Associazione Toscana, **9:**80
Assunçao, Fernando, **2:**501
d'Assunção, Martinho, **8:**583
Assyrian-Americans/Canadians, **3:**1028, 1029
Assyro-Chaldean Church, **5:**944–45; **6:**227, 228, 229, 283–84, 403
Aṣṭachāp group, **5:**251, 643
Astaire, Fred, **3:**195
As Thousands Cheer (musical), **3:**620
Astita, I Komang, **3:**1017, 1019
Astor Place riot, **3:**46
Astor Place Theater (New York), **3:**46
astrology, **5:**955, 962; **6:**17, 130, 183; **7:**100, 472, 834
astronomy, **7:**117, 118
Aswad, **8:**215, 236
Atâ Bey, **6:**780
Atacameño culture, **2:**356
 instruments of, **2:**357
 religious rituals and genres, **2:**360–61
Atafu (Tokelau), **9:**823
"At a Georgia Camp Meeting" (Mills), **3:**548, *548*
Atagotaaluk, Phoebe, **3:**1280
Atahualpa (Inka king), **2:**292, 427
Atahuallpa, Mauryan emperor, see Ashoka
Atanasov, Georgi, **8:**904
Atanasovski, Pece, **8:**981, *982*, 983
Atanassov, Vergilij, **8:**21, 907
Ata people, **4:**925
'Aṭarrad, **6:**354–55
Atat, Mustapha, **3:***1037*
Atatürk, Mustafa Kemal, **3:**1030; **6:**57, 77, *77*, 108, 247, 782, 783, 797
Atayal people
 flutes of, **7:**529
 Jew's harps of, **7:**527
 music of, **7:**525
Atchin people, **9:**690
Atelier de Musique Contemporaine, **3:**1152
Ateneo Municipal, **4:**861
Ateneo Paraguayo, **2:**463
Athanasiou, Anestis, **8:**285
Athapaskan (Athabascan) peoples, **3:**383–92, 438, 1254, 1274, 1275–77. *See also specific groups*
 dances of, **3:**222
 drumming style, **3:***385*
 fiddling traditions of, **3:**405, 1277
 personal songs, **3:**386
 potlatches of, **3:**5
 relations with other cultures, **3:**384
 religious beliefs, **3:**391, 1276
 research on music of, **3:**392
 song text and structures, **3:**389
 Southwestern groups, **3:**428, 431–33, 755

al-ʿĀṭī, Khumais, **6:**502

ʿĀtika bint al-Shuhda, **6:**296, 297, 353

Atikal, Ilanko, **5:**24, 260, 319, 327

Atilla the Hun (calypsonian; Raymond
    Quevedo), **2:**96, 963

Atinogen, Saint, **8:**834

Atis Endepandan (Independent Artists), **3:**805–6

Atis, Kaindum Baiagk, **9:**966

Atiu (Cook Islands), **9:**896, 974

ʿAṭiyya, Suzan, **6:**239

Atkins, Chet, **3:**80, 353, 520

Atkinson, Jane, **7:**20

Atkinson, John M., **9:**324

Atlacatl (marimba ensemble), **2:**718

Atlaian people, **7:**1027–30

al-Aṭlāl (al-Sunbāṭī), **6:**599

Atlan, Edmond, **6:**1044

Atlanta Symphony Orchestra, **3:**611

Atlantic Association of Composers, **3:**1121

Atlantic Canada. *See* Maritime Provinces

Atlantic Records, **3:**350, 670–73, 708, 710, 711

Atlarchopa (god), **8:**853

Atlas Durán, **2:**557

Atlas Eclipticalis (Cage), **3:**175

Atlığ, Nevzat, **6:**117

"At My Front Door" (El Dorados), **3:**672

atonality, **1:**221, 229–30; **8:**65, 84–85

Atoni people, **4:**796–98

Atpatoun, Vianney, **9:**966

al-Aṭrash, Farīd (El-Atrach, Farid), **1:**220, 227;
    6:46, 201, 236, 239, 269, 283, 592,
    1039

Atre, Prabha, **5:**414

Atria, Jaime, **2:**372

Atsugewi Indian nation, **3:**415

Atta, Kwesi, **10:**33

Attali, Jacques, **3:**45

ʿAṭṭār, Farīd al-Dīn, **6:**187, 369

al-ʿAṭṭār, Muḥammad, **6:**367

Attentat, **8:**216

At the Road Crossing (Peking opera), **7:**73

Attic (musical group), **3:**266

Attikamek Indian nation, **3:**383, 1074

Attwenger (duo), **8:**676

Atumi, prince, **7:**588

Atumori (Zeami), **7:**630, 640

Atu of Longoteme (Tongan composer), **9:**788

Atwood, Margaret, **3:**1059

Atya, Hassan, **1:**571

Aua Island (Papua New Guinea), **9:**602

Auber, Daniel François Esprit, **4:**859

Auberjonois, René, **8:**697

Aubin, Eugene, **3:**1096

Auca culture, **2:**250, 504–6

Auckland University, **9:**932

audiences
    Adighian people, **8:**855
    Afghanistan, **5:**837
    Albania, **8:**1000
    Alberta, for Winnipeg festivals, **3:**1233–35
    Andalusia, **6:**444
    Andean region, **2:**219
    Andhra Pradesh, **5:**889
        for Golla Suddulu singers, **5:**902
        for Telugu narratives, **5:**894
        for Vīravidyavantulu singers, **5:**901–2

Arabian peninsula
    expatriate communities, **6:**716–18
    for women's music, **6:**698, 702

Argentina
    for *cuarteto*, **2:**275–76, 280
    for folkloristic music, **2:**263
    for rock, **2:**266, 268
    for tango, **2:**263–65

for art and popular theater, **5:**486

for art music, **3:**535–41; **8:**59–60, 61, 62, 63

Australia
    for Anglo-Irish music, **9:**140
    for country music, **9:**142
    for jazz, **9:**143
    for popular music, **9:**144
    for *rebetika*, **9:**73
    for Torres Strait island dance, **9:**429

for ballad opera, **3:**46

Balochistan, for *mālid* and *shēparjā*, **5:**780

Barbados, **2:**817

Basque region, **8:**315–16

Belarus, **8:**801

Bellona, **9:**849

for Berber popular music, **6:**276–77

for bluegrass, **3:**160–61, 162, 163, 168

for blues, **3:**583, 639–40, 643, 648

Brazil, for *cantoria*, **2:**327

Canada, for Cantonese opera, **7:**303–4

for Canadian radio, **3:**1101, 1102

Carriacou, for big-drum dance, **2:**869

Celtic music, **8:**321

Central Asia, for *maqām* performance, **6:**916

for *chansonniers*, **3:**1076, 1156–57

China
    age of, **7:**419–20
    for amateur performances, **7:**411–12
    for Cantonese opera, **7:**303, 305
    for *huju*, **7:**297
    for *kunqu*, **7:**290
    for minority musics, **7:**445
    for narrative singing, **7:**253, 255, 262, 269
    for opera, **7:**276–77, 278, 387
    for Peking opera, **7:**281
    for *pipa* music, **7:**170
    for popular music, **7:**355–56, 359, 389
    for *qin* music, **7:**159, 160–61, 164
    for rock, **7:**360, 399
    for *Suzhou tanci*, **7:**419
    for *tanhuang*, **7:**299
    tourist, **7:**414–15
    for Uighur opera, **7:**463
    for Western music, **7:**381

class/music targeting, **3:**49, 192, 269

for club blues, **3:**669

Colombia
    for *cumbia*, **2:**410
    for *décima* competitions, **2:**408
    for *dueto bambuquero*, **2:**383

for composed African music, **1:**227, 229–30

for country music, **3:**97, 341

court, **8:**199

Dai people, for popular music, **7:**505

for devotional music, **5:**425–26

for disco music, **3:**228, 229, 687–88, 689,
    711

Dolan people, for *mäsräp*, **6:**992

Dominica, **2:**841

East Asia, for theater, **7:**73, 74

Egypt
    for epic songs, **6:**342–43, 411
    for films, **6:**237
    for *ḥaḍra* performance, **6:**148
    for *inshād*, **6:**166
    interaction with performers, **6:**557, 558,
        559, 604–5
    for popular music, **6:**597–600
    radio, **6:**236

England, performance style and, **8:**334–35

Europe, immigrant communities, **8:**232

Finland, for *runonlaulu*, **8:**114–15

in folk clubs, **8:**153

folk contexts of, **8:**648

for folk dance troupes, **8:**166

for folk festivals, **8:**151

for folk music recordings, **8:**157–58

for folk music revival, **3:**13–14; **8:**228

for free jazz, **3:**663

for funk, **3:**681

Garífuna culture, **2:**733

gay, **3:**114, 228, 229, 687–88, 711

gendered listening, **3:**92

Germany, **8:**665

Greece, for *rebetika*, **8:**1019

Guadeloupe, for *léwòz*, **2:**875–76

Guatemala, for *bambuco*, **2:**387

for Gupta theater, **5:**25–26

Guruṅg people, **5:**704

Guyana, for calypso, **2:**446

Haiti, for popular music, **2:**893

for *hardingfele* music, **3:**869

Hawaiʻi, **9:**925

for heavy metal, **3:**111, 112, 114

for Hindustani music, **5:**81, 85, 169–70, 172,
    203, 204

Hong Kong
    for Cantonese opera, **7:**303, 305, 307–8,
        434–35
    for Cantopop, **7:**355–56, 431, 435–36

Hungary, **8:**739, 746

Iceland, for *rímur*, **8:**117–18, 402

interaction with performers, **1:**287; **9:**284–85

Iran
    for epic songs, **6:**344, 840
    for *radif*, **6:**140–41, 142, 832–33, 837

Iraq, for *maqām*, **6:**314

Ireland, for Traveller singing, **8:**295

Israel, **6:**1032
    for *muzika mizraḥit*, **6:**265–66, 1033–34
    for *shirei erets Yisrael*, **6:**1019

Italy, **8:**611

Jamaica
    participation of, **2:**897
    for popular music, **2:**910–11

Japan
    for *biwa* styles, **7:**651
    for dance, **7:**63
    for *kabuki*, **7:**661, 765
    Korean people, **7:**894
    for *nô*, **7:**553, 639, 640
    for popular music, **7:**747
    for Western music, **3:**969
    for women's theater, **7:**766

audiences (*continued*)
for jazz, **3:**652
for jump blues, **3:**668
Karnataka, for *kaṭṭaikkūttu,* **5:**516
for Karnatak music, **5:**107, 110, 139, 151, 154, 212, 218, 354, 384, 385
Kazakhstan, **6:**950, 952–53, 960
Kerala, **5:**943
Korea
for *ch'anggŭk,* **7:**946
for *chŏngak,* **7:**815
for *p'ansori,* **7:**895, 897, 900, 906
for *t'alch'um,* **7:**942
Kuna culture, **2:**648
for Kurdish music, **6:**752
Kurdistan, for narratives, **6:**746–47
for Lao popular music, **3:**1009
for Latin American music, **3:**1204
Macedonia, Debarca, **8:**117
Malta
for *fatt,* **8:**638
for *spirtu pront,* **8:**636
mass media and, **2:**51
Middle East, **6:**7, 10
Morocco, for *nūba,* **6:**455
for musicals, **3:**545, 619, 622
for narratives, **9:**337
Native American crossover genres, **3:**489
for Native American dances and ceremonies, **3:**370
for New Age music, **3:**341
North Africa, for Andalusian music, **6:**436–37
North West Frontier Province, **5:**791
Norway
for *hardingfele slått,* **8:**417
for *langeleik,* **8:**422
Oceania
interaction of, **9:**323–24
participation of, **9:**321
for opera, **3:**181
at Pacific Festival of Arts, **9:**58
Pakhtun people, **5:**786
Pakistan, northern, **5:**798
Palestinian wedding eve celebration, **6:**574–75
as performance component, **3:**236
Peru, for jazz, **2:**486
for polka bands, **3:**824, 894
Polynesia, **9:**768, 769–70
for pop *bhajan,* **5:**549
for pop *ghazal,* **5:**548
for popular music, **2:**49, 92, 94, 109; **3:**712, 863; **5:**418, 419–20, 428–29; **8:**205, 207–9
for popular theater, **5:**484
preference issues, **2:**54, 55
for primitive theater, **5:**481
Punjab, for *bhangra,* **5:**650
for punk rock, **8:**216
Purépecha culture, **2:**579
for Qur'ānic recitation, **6:**160, 161
radio, **3:**49, 244, 299
for folk music, **8:**156
for popular music, **8:**207
for rap, **3:**699
for *rās līlā* dance-drama, **5:**495
for regional music on cassettes, **5:**549

religion and, **2:**60
for religious theater, **5:**483
response of, **1:**164–65, 202
for rhythm and blues, **3:**349, 671, 708, 710
for rock, **3:**229–30, 348, 356; **8:**215, 216
for rock and roll, **3:**347, 348, 349
Romania, **8:**874
rural, **3:**46
Russia, Rom music, **8:**287
for Saami joiking, **8:**299
St. Lucia, for *jwé,* **2:**943
Sāmoa, for *fāgono,* **9:**799
Saudi Arabia, women's wedding party, **6:**692–93
Serbia, Kosovo, **8:**285
sexually segregated, **8:**198
social class and preference issues, **8:**189
social class of, **2:**59–60
South Asia
changes in, **5:**526
for classical dance, **5:**492
cultural context of, **5:**399, 404
for film, **5:**542, 545
spirit-possession and shamanic ceremonies, **5:**288–89, 780
South Asian diaspora communities in North America, **5:**578–79
Southeast Asia
for Cantonese opera, **7:**303–4
for Cantopop, **4:**101; **7:**355–56
Spain, flamenco, **8:**598
Sweden, for popular music, **8:**436
Switzerland, **8:**689
Syria, Aleppo, **6:**544
for Syrian music, **6:**563–64
Tahiti, for Western music, **9:**868
Taiwan
for Cantopop, **7:**355–56
for *nanguan,* **7:**425
for Peking opera, **7:**287
technology and, **3:**245
teenage consumers, **3:**80
television, **3:**244
television studio, **3:**251
Tibet
for court dances, **7:**481
for King Ge-sar epic, **5:**711–12
for Tibetan music, **5:**715
Tonga, for *lakalaka,* **9:**368
tourists, **2:**74–75
Turkey
for art music, **6:**758
for *âyîn,* **6:**109–11, 118
for *makam,* **6:**56
for national dances, **6:**813, 814
for song duels, **6:**806, 808
Turkmenistan, for *baggy* concert, **6:**970
for Tuvan music, **6:**986–87
for *'ud* performances, **6:**594
Uighur people, for *muqam,* **6:**999
Ukraine, Soviet period, **8:**818
United States
for Cantonese opera, **7:**303–4
for Chinese traditional music, **3:**959
for dance, **3:**219–20
demographics of, **3:**302

for eighteenth-century popular music, **3:**179
ethnic, **3:**950
growth of, **3:**237
for Haitian folklore, **2:**889
marketing to, **3:**264
at Middle Eastern *ḥafla* (*haflah*), **3:**1031–32, 1218
for Middle Eastern music, **3:**1036, 1219–20
for minstrel shows, **3:**573
for nineteenth-century concert music, **3:**556, 557, 558
for nineteenth-century popular music, **3:**181, 182
racial aspects, **3:**330, 349–50
urban, **3:**46
Uruguay
for carnival, **2:**516
for *payada,* **2:**512
preferences and participation of, **2:**520–21
Uttar Pradesh
for *birahā,* **5:**668, 669
for *kajalī,* **5:**670
veneration of, **5:**470
for vinyl records, **3:**169
Wales, **8:**354, 355
folk festivals, **8:**356
Western
for Indian music, **5:**560, 563, 566, 567, 573
for Pakistani music, **5:**748
world music, **8:**210
Yugoslavia (former), **8:**1001–2
Audiencia de Guatemala, **2:**721, 722, 735
Audiogram label, **3:**1160, 1161
Auerbach, Rabbi Meir, **6:**205–6
Auezov, Mukhtar, **6:**959–60
!Augab, Peter Joseph, **1:**428
Augundson, Torgeir (Myllarguten), **8:**411–12, 417, 424
Augustin, Frisner, **3:**805, *805*
Augustinian order, **4:**842, 868
in Mexico, **2:**555, 577, 600
in South America, **2:**23
"Auld Lang Syne," **3:**306
Auliya, Nizamuddin, **5:**294
AUM (record company), **5:**528
"Aura Lea," **3:**188
Aurangzeb, Mughal emperor, **5:**47, 434
Aurobindo, Sri, **5:**255
Austerlitz, Paul, **2:**93; **3:**800
Austin, General Hudson, **2:**867
Austral Islands, **9:**865, 879–82, 998. *See also* Ra'ivavae; Rapa; Rimatara; Rurutu; Tubua'i
American expeditions to, **9:**24
Christianity in, **9:**208–9
dance in, **9:**873
drums of, **9:**384
festivals in, **9:**55, 57
geography of, **9:**879
hīmene, **9:**209
hīmene tārava (also *tārava rurutu*), **9:**871, 881–82, *883*
history of, **9:**879
music and dance of, **9:**880–82, 969
population of, **9:**879

research on, **9**:880, 973
sound recordings from, **9**:1002
Australia, **9**:407–67. *See also* Aboriginal peoples
    of Australia; *specific peoples*
  Aboriginal rock, **9**:144–46
  administration of British New Guinea, **9**:475,
    479–80, 488
  administration of New Britain, **9**:488, 614
  Albanian people in, **8**:986
  Anglo-Irish folk music, **9**:140–41, 413
  archives and museums, **9**:958–61
  Arnhem Land
    Aboriginal music, **9**:412
    Central-Eastern, **9**:419–22
    ceremonies of, **9**:47
    clansongs of, **9**:355
    dance, **9**:451
    didjeridus in, **9**:394–95, 412–13
    djarada genre, **9**:419
    madayin (also *bilma*) genre, **9**:419
    mirrijpu dance, **9**:*406*
    research on, **9**:418–19
    Western, **9**:422–27
    Yolngu dance, **9**:457–60
  Bathurst Island, Tiwi dance, **9**:455–57
  Bentinck Island, songs of, **9**:430
  blues, **9**:143
  British in, **9**:408–9, 439
  bush music, **9**:142
  Cape York, **9**:507
    Aboriginal music, **9**:411, 428, 429–30
    dance, **9**:451–53
    wanam dance, **9**:462–64
  capoeira, **9**:84
  Caribbean people in, **9**:82–84
  Central, **9**:432–39
    Aboriginal music, **9**:411
    Aboriginal women's ceremonies, **9**:244–45
    concepts of pitch, **9**:292–93
    men's *vs.* women's songs, **9**:243
    Warlpiri dance, **9**:464–67
    women's ceremonies, **9**:451
  children's songs, **9**:256–57
  Chinese people in, **9**:70–71, 409
  country music, **9**:141–42
  Cypriot people in, **8**:1032
  dance in, **9**:49, 450–67
  dimotika, **9**:73
  documentary films from, **9**:46–47
  Europeans in, **9**:46
  festivals in, **9**:59–62
  films on, **9**:1010–12
  gender and music, **9**:241–45
  geography of, **9**:418, 428, 430, 439
  Georgian people in, **8**:845
  Greek people in, **9**:72–75, 409
  Groote Eylandt, **9**:46
  Gulf of Carpentaria, **9**:427–28
    Aboriginal music, **9**:412
    Yanyuwa dance, **9**:460–62
  gumleaf bands in, **9**:134–35, 442
  history of, **9**:408–9
  Hmong people in, **9**:75–77
  immigrants in, **9**:69
  Indian people in, **5**:449
  Irish people in, **9**:77–79, 409

Italian people in, **9**:79–81, 409
  jazz, **9**:142–43
  Kimberleys, **9**:423, 430–32
    Aboriginal music, **9**:412
    dance, **9**:451
    didjeridus in, **9**:394
    lildjin genre, **9**:356
  Latin American people in, **9**:82–84
  Maltese people in, **8**:634
  map of, **9**:*409*
  Maronite Church in, **6**:208
  Melville Island
    Tiwi bereavement ceremony, **9**:47
    Tiwi dance, **9**:455–57
  Mornington Island
    initiation ceremony, **9**:47
    songs of, **9**:430
  Murray Islands, **9**:507
  music and dance of, **9**:48, 981
  nisiotika, **9**:73
  Northern, concepts of pitch, **9**:293–94
  nurlu complex, **9**:431–32, 451
  Pacific Islanders in, **9**:84–87
  pedagogy in, **9**:253–57
  penal colonies in, **9**:77, 177
  pipe-and-drum ensembles in, **9**:135
  political songs, **9**:212
  popular music in, **9**:143–44, 413–14
  population of, **9**:408
  Pukapukan people in, **9**:910
  Queensland, **9**:428–30
    didjeridus in, **9**:394
    research on, **9**:430
    south, central, and western, **9**:430
  rebetika, **9**:73, 74
  research institutions, **9**:415
  research on, **9**:244–45, 256, 437, 451, 462,
    975, 976
  salsa, **9**:83
  samba, **9**:83–84
  Sir Edward Pellew Islands, **9**:460
  song composition in, **9**:355–57
  sound recordings from, **9**:985–86, 987–89
  Southeastern, **9**:439–42
    Aboriginal music, **9**:411
    dance, **9**:451
  Tasmania, **9**:440
    Aboriginal music, **9**:411
  theater in, **9**:226–29
  Torres Strait Islands, **9**:84–85, 428, 429, 479,
    488
    Aboriginal music, **9**:412
    adhi buin dance, **9**:*411*
    dance, **9**:452, 507
    early recordings from, **9**:284
    festivals in, **9**:61
    kundus of, **9**:489
    music and dance of, **9**:981
    theater in, **9**:225
    trade with Trans-Fly groups, **9**:506–7
  tourism in, **9**:253
  Vietnamese people in, **9**:416
  Western
    epigrammatic song texts, **9**:331
    Pilbara sung poetry, **9**:326
Australia Music Centre, **9**:415

Australian Broadcasting Corporation, **9**:959, 985,
  989
Australian Greek Choir (Melbourne), **9**:72
Australian Institute of Aboriginal and Torres
  Strait Islander Studies (AIATSIS),
  9:415, 440, 462, 958–59, 960, 985,
  987, 1010
Australian Institute of Aboriginal Studies (AIAS),
  9:46
Australian Music Centre, **9**:960
Australian Research Council, **9**:462
Austria, **8**:670–79
  art music in, **8**:663, 670–71
  Burgenland, **8**:674
    Jewish communities in, **8**:258
  cabaret in, **8**:252, 675
  Carinthia, **8**:674, 675
  dance traditions of, **8**:166, 673
  folk and art music, interactions, **8**:53
  folk music in, **8**:671–74
  fusion music, **8**:676
  geography of, **8**:670
  history of, **8**:670
  influence on Croatia, **8**:933
  instrument collections in, **8**:175, 181
  instruments, **8**:170, 672–74
    research on, **8**:35, 39
  Lower Austria region, **8**:673–74
  map of, **8**:*644*
  minorities populations in, **8**:674
  popular music in, **8**:671, 674–79
  population of, **8**:670
  research on music of, **8**:18, 19, 177
  rock in, **8**:216
  Rom people in, **8**:272, 289
  Salzburg, Christmas songs of, **8**:673
  Salzkammergut, **8**:673
  Styria, **8**:673
  Tyrol region, **8**:672–73
  Upper Austria region, **8**:673
  Vienna, **8**:670
    cabaret in, **8**:252
    central synagogue, **8**:263
    folk music in, **8**:673–74
    Jewish community, **8**:262
    Jewish dance schools, **8**:251
    light music in, **8**:205
  Vorarlberg, **8**:673, 678
Austrian Federal Institute of Scientific Film
  (Vienna), **9**:984
Austrian people
  in Aotearoa, **9**:983–84
  in North America, **3**:1195
Austro-Hungarian empire, **8**:10, 251, 257, 271,
  670, 716, 729, 732, 736, 868, 952,
  963
Aut'Chose (musical group), **3**:1158
authorship. *See* copyright and ownership
Autret, Frédérique, **5**:610
Autry, Gene, **3**:78, 520
Autumn (album), **3**:346
Auvidis (record label), **5**:529
Ava dynasty, **4**:378
Avah (record company), **6**:1019
Avakumovic, Ivan, **3**:1270
Avalokiteshvara (deity), mantra of, **5**:712

Avant Garde Arts Theater, **5:**487
avant-garde music
  Bulgaria, **8:**905
  China, **7:**350–51, 388, 420
  conducting of, **8:**101
  Europe, **8:**85
  Greece, **8:**1008
  Hong Kong, **7:**232
  Iceland, **8:**407
  Japan, **7:**537, 735–37
  notation of, **8:**91, 97, 98
  Russia, **8:**782
  Sweden, **8:**445
Avars, **8:**868
"*A Vava Inouva*" (Idir/Mohamed), **6:**274–75,
    276
Avāz Bakhshī, **6:**839
Avedon Ballroom (Los Angeles), **3:**740
Avempace. *See* Abū Bakr Ibn Bājja
Avenary, Hanoch, **6:**1059–60, 1062, 1063, 1064,
    1065, 1066; **8:**266, 267
Average White Band (musical group), **8:**369
Averill, Gage, **2:**93, 862
Averroes. *See* Ibn Rushd
d'Avezac-Macaya, Marie Armand Pascal,
    1:89–91, 93
Avicenne. *See* Ibn Sīnā
Avidom, Menahem, **6:**1028, 1030
Avni, Tsvi, **6:**1031
Avodat Hakodesh (Bloch), **3:**939
Avraham Ibn Musah, Rabbi, **6:**1043
Avramenko, Vasile, **3:**1229
"*Avramico y Davico*" (Sephardic song),
    3:1173
Avramov, Arsemi Avra, **8:**856
Avsenik, Slavko, **8:**675
Awa people, **9:**526–33
'Awaḍallah, **6:**341
'Awaḍ, Manṣūr, **6:**322
Awad, Muhammed, **1:**557
Awasthi, Sapna, **5:**541
Awatiñas (musical group), **2:**297
Awawe Island (Papua New Guinea), **9:**619
Awin people, **9:**490
Awlād al-dhawat (Egyptian film), **6:**236
Awonda, **1:**571
Axe (musical group), **5:**428
"Axes to Grind," **3:**184
Axon, Turdi, **6:**990
ayak. *See* makam
Ayala family, **3:**727
Ayala, George, **9:**101
Ayala, Joey, **4:**886
Ayala, José, **3:**740
Ayala, Maria Ignez Novais, **2:**320
Ayala, Pedro, **3:**775–76, *776*
Ayang (king of the Colo), **1:**568
Aya no Tsuzumi (Zeami), **7:**640
Aybergenov, Tolegen, **6:***961*
Ayers, Roy, **3:**701
Ayestarán, Lauro, **2:**511
Ayizan (musical group), **3:**806
Ayler, Albert, **3:**662, 663
Aymara culture, **2:**205–23, 356–57, 467;
    10:36–37
  aesthetics of, **2:**34, 215–17

instruments of, **2:**33, 34, 35, 206–14, 253,
    288, 357–58
musical contexts, **2:**217–21
musical genres
  tonos de sikuri, **2:**362
  tono y rueda, **2:**361
religious rituals and genres, **2:**361–62, 363
Aymers, Black Sam, **2:***926*
Ayoreo culture, **2:**452
Ayres, Mary Clifton, **9:**977
Aytälan, **7:**469
Ay te dejo en San Antonio, **3:**751
Ayurvedic medicine, **5:**25, 33
Ayuthaya (kingdom), **4:**248, 286, 304
  Burmese defeat of, **4:**11, 219, 229, 366, 378,
    382
  Chinese entertainment in, **4:**70, 222, 238
  defeat of Angkor, **4:**153, 187
Ayyar Brahmin community, **5:**387, 930
Ayyar, C. S., **5:**53
Ayyar, Santhi, **5:***233*
Ayyangar Brahmin community, **5:**387
Ayyangar, R., **5:**56
Ayyubid dynasty, **6:**366
Ayyuwan Chi Pita (Feliciano), **4:**878
'*Azafa* (Ibn Manẓūr), **6:**359
azān. *See* chant (Muslim)
Azande people
  harps of, **1:**655–56
  healing rituals, **1:**273
  instruments of, **1:**650, 656–57
  likembe tuning, **1:**299
  music of, **1:**570, 652–53
  tuning system, **1:**267
Azanian people, **1:**227
d'Azeglio, Massimo, **8:**620
Azerbaijan. *See also* Iran
  art music traditions, **6:**824, 861, 862, 921–22
  dastanlar in, **6:**929–30
  epic songs, **6:**345
  folk song and dance, **6:**931–32
  geography of, **6:**921
  Georgian people in, **8:**826
  history of, **6:**843, 921–22
  influence on Tusheti music, **8:**828
  instruments in, **6:**924–25
  Iranian dance traditions in, **6:**875–79
  khanates in, **6:**922
  map of, **6:***844*
  mugam in, **6:**8, 18, 23, 866, 926–29
  musical life in, **6:**922–24
  population of, **6:**921
  Saingilo district, **8:**828
  song duels in, **6:**809
  vocal music of, **8:**828
Azerbaijani people
  epic songs, **6:**345, 827, 829
  in Georgia, **8:**840, 842
  in North America, **3:**1199
Azeti Keizi, **7:**713
Azevedo, Geraldo, **2:**333
al-Azhar University (Cairo), **6:**161, 432
Azîz Dede, **6:**109
Aziz Mahmūd Hüdāyī, **6:**194
Aziz, Mohammed, **5:**421
'*Azîza bint al-Saṭḥī*, **6:**298

Azkue Aberasturi, Resurrección Maria de, **8:**317
Azmi, Ahmad, **4:**519
Aznavour, Charles, **8:**209
Azoulay, Dr., **8:**562
Azteca (musical group), **3:**733
Azteca Records, **3:**741
Aztec culture and empire, **2:**555–56, 563, 601–3,
    628. *See also* Mexica culture; Nahua
    culture
  archaeomusicological studies of, **2:**7
  historical accounts of, **2:**23
  iconographical record of, **2:**12, 15, *17*
  instruments of, **2:**8, 13, 33, 556–57, 601–3
Azuma hakkei (*nagauta* piece), **7:**672, *673*
Azuza Street Revival (Los Angeles), **3:**631
"*Az vashir Moshe*" (*piyyut*), **3:**1173
'Azza al-Maylā', **6:**295, 352, 538–39
Azzopardi, Francesco, **8:**642
Azzouz, Jalil, **6:**279–82

Baai Jurong, **7:**306
BaAka people. *See* Aka people
Baataryn Avirmed, **7:**1008
Baba, Rahman, **5:**834
Baba, Russel, **3:**336
Baba Sali. *See* Abuhatzira, Rabbi Yiśra'el
Baba's Records, **3:**1243
Babadzan, Alain, **9:**880
Bābākhān family, **6:**916
Bābākhānov, Ari, **6:***918*
Bābākhānov, Levi (Leviche), **6:**916
"Babalú" (Valdez), **3:**740
Baban (*qupai* melody), **7:**233, 237, 238
Babar, Agha, **5:**487
Babar archipelago, **4:**821
Bābā Rowshān (epic), **6:**840
Babayev, Sabir, **6:**918–19
Babbitt, Milton, **3:**14, 175, 176–77, 253, 540
Babeldoab (Palau), **9:**722
Ba-Benzele people, **1:**117–18
Babes in Toyland (Herbert), **3:**193
Babes in Toyland (musical group), **3:**358
Babinga people, **1:**131
Babiracki, Carol M., **6:**68; **10:**69
Babkina, Nadezhda, **8:**779
Babla, **5:**592
Babur, Mughal emperor, **5:**805
Baby Gaby (Gabriel Sánchez), **3:**765–66
"Baby, I Love You" (Franklin), **3:**710
"Baby, It's You" (Spaniels), **3:**671
"Baby Seals' Blues" (Seals), **3:**706
Babyford, **3:**691
Babylonia, **6:**8, 411
Bača Family Band, **3:**897
Baca, Próspero S., **3:**762
Bacan, **4:**813
Bach, Carl Philipp Emanuel, **8:**79
Bach family, **8:**646
Bach, Johann Christian, **8:**79, 370
Bach, Johann Sebastian, **3:**123; **6:**1030; **7:**540;
    8:55, 60, 77, 86, 93–94, 199, 654
  cantatas of, **8:**79
  electronic arrangments of, **3:**254
  organ works, **8:**78
  reworkings of Vivaldi compositions, **8:**91
  solo violin sonata, **8:**99

bachata, **2:**105, 861; **3:**731, 800, 1204
Bachata: A Social History of a Dominican Popular
     Music (Pacini Hernández), **3:**800
Bachchan, Amitabh, **5:**583
Bachetarzi, Mahieddine, **6:**469–70
Bachman-Turner-Overdrive (musical group),
     3:1091
Bachmann, Werner, **8:**22
Back, George, **3:**1164
Backer, Agathe Ursula, **8:**422
Backo, Njacko, **3:**1170, *1170*
"Backside Albany" (minstrel song), **3:**837
"Back Stabbers" (O'Jays), **3:**677, 711
Back Tuva Future (Ondar), **3:**339
Bacon, Patience Wiggin, **9:**979
Bacon, Pat Namaka, **9:**969–70
B'äc Son culture, **4:**445
Bactria, **5:**238; **6:**936, 965
Bad Boy (Aytälan), **7:**469
Bad Company (musical group), **3:**356
Baḍaga people, **5:**278–79
     ceremonies of, **5:**284, 909
     instruments of, **5:**366–67
     patronage of Kota people, **5:**283
Baddar qamarna (*dabkih*), **6:**583
Badauê (*bloco afro*), **2:**353
Bade Miyan Chote Miyan (film), **5:**540
Badev, Atanas, **8:**980
Badhl (early songstress), **6:**369
Badi people, **5:**697
Badr al-Dīn al-Mālikī, **6:**372
Badr, Karim, **6:**283
Badu, Kwasi, **1:**158; **10:**78, 79, 140, 141
Badu, Zelma, **3:**224
Baduy people, **4:**27, 703, 717
Ba-Dw Sa Ka-Poon-An (Santos), **4:**878,
     879–80
Baegu people, **9:**666, 668–69
Baek Dae Woong, **7:**957, 971
Baes, Jonas, **4:**881
Baez, Joan, **3:**14, 49, 316, *316*, 520, 551; **4:**98,
     885; **6:**275
Baffinland Inuit, **3:**374, 381
Baganda people. *See* Ganda people
Bagbag Island (Papua New Guinea), **9:**561
Baggāra people, **1:**560–61, 599
Baghubhai, Parmar Khorabai, **5:***236*
baǧlama. See lutes
Baglanova, Roza, **6:**961
Bagley, Fred, **3:**1090
Bagobo people, **4:**920
     epics of, **4:**927
     instrumental music of, **4:**906
Bagong Lumad (musical group), **4:**886
bagpipes
     Aotearoa, **9:**115–16
     Arab world, **6:**415
     baghalbīn, **5:***756*, 769
     Balkan region, **8:**13, 867
     Basque region, **8:***246*
     biniou, **8:**545, *560*, 561, 562–63
     biniou bihan, **8:**559
     biniou bras, **8:**559–60
     biniou koz, **8:**559
     bishnicë (also *mishnicë*), **8:**996
     Bulgaria, **8:**899, 900

byz, **8:**774
cabreta, **8:**545, 547
cabrette, **8:**560
caramusa, **8:**571
Celtic, **8:**321
chiboni (also *chimoni*), **8:**836, 840
cimpoi, **8:**878–79, *879*
Corsica, **8:**571, 573
czarny kozioł doślubny, **8:**707
Czech Republic, **8:***200*
Denmark, **8:**454
diple, **8:**169, 959–60
diple s mijehom, **8:**928
diple z mehom, **8:**915
duda, **8:**707, 719, 743, 744, 797, 813, 932,
     932
dude, **8:**915
dudka, **8:**813
Estonian, **3:**879
Europe, **8:***1*, 9, 168, *180*
     dissemination of, **8:**169, 170
     early history of, **8:**42
     folk and art uses of, **8:**169
     used by shepherds, **8:**8, 142
     women's playing of, **8:***200*, 201
fam, **8:**774
France, **8:**542, 543, 544–45, 546, 551
gaida, **8:**1009, 1012, 1013, 1015
gaita, **8:**560, 593
gaita-de-foles, **3:**1197; **8:**583
gajda
     Bulgaria, **8:**99, *164*, 169, *176*, 282–83,
          285, 892–93, *893*, 897, 902
     Macedonia, **8:**975, *976*, 981, *982*, 983
     North America, **3:**926, 1198
gajde
     Albania, **8:**993
     Serbia, **8:**944–45, *945*, 947, 950, 952
gajdy, **8:**707, 719
Georgia, **8:**840, *840*
Germany, **8:**651, 654, 656
Great Britain, **8:**325
gudastviri, **8:**840
gurba, **6:**415
habbān, **6:**415
Hercegovinian (*mih*), **3:**1083
hubbān, **6:**710
Hungary, **8:**274, 739
Ireland, **8:**152, 325
Italy, **8:**616–17
jirba, **6:**415
kaba gajda, **8:**896, *896*
karabe, **8:**950
koza, **8:**707, *707*
kozioł, **8:**706
kozioł biały, **8:**707
labanorų dūda, **8:**511
lalim uadindz, **8:**859
Latvia, **8:**504, 505
Low Countries, **8:**523, 528–29
Lowland Scottish, **8:**366
maśak, **5:**345
mizmār al-jarāb, **6:**395, 397
mizwed, **6:**415
mizwid, **1:**537; **6:**519
mješnice, **8:**928

musette, **8:**169, 545
North America, **3:**838
     as identity symbol, **3:**826
     military use of, **3:**563
     regimental uses, **3:**324
Northumbrian smallpipes, **3:**55; **8:**331, *331*,
     333
Nova Scotia, **3:**1128–29
Oceania, **9:**135–36
Ontario, **3:**1189
pibau cod, **8:**348, 354
piva, **8:**616, 694
pive, **8:**930
Poland, **8:**704
Portugal, **8:**582
puzyr', **8:**774
qurba, **6:**415
research on, **8:**22
säckpipa, **8:**439
Scottish Highland, **8:**169, *363*, 363–64, 366,
     559–60
     canntaireachd tradition, **8:**98, 106, *107*
     Oman, **6:**415, 679–80, *680*
shapar (also *sarnai*), **8:**774
shuvyr, **8:**774
sierszeński, **8:**707
skamóra, **8:**774
Slovenia, **8:**914
smallpipes, **3:**1129
South Asia, **5:**345
Spain, **8:**589, 593
śruti upaṅga, **5:**366
surdulina, **8:**169
Swedish, **8:**440, *440*
Tamil Nadu, **5:**913
titti, **5:**895–96, *896*, 901
torupill, **3:**1196; **8:**494, *495*
Trinidad, **2:**965
tsambouna, **8:**118, 1015, *1015*
tulum (also *tulup*), **6:**763, *763*, 925; **8:**840
uilleann (also union) pipes, **3:**326, 842, *842*,
     845; **8:**169, *383*, 384, 391, 392, 394
     ornamentation on, **8:**382
Ukraine, **8:**810
válonka, **8:**774
veuze, **8:**560
volynka, **8:**774
warpipes, **8:**383, 384, 385 (*See also* Scottish
     Highland)
Yugoslavia, **8:**279
zampogna, **3:**860, 861; **8:**36, 169, *171*, 616
zampogna a chiave, **8:***616*
zaqq, **8:**640, 641–42
zukra, **1:**543–44
"Bags' Groove" (Monk), **3:***659*, 659–60
Baha'i faith
     in Marshall Islands, **9:**748
     in North America, **3:**218, 1031; **10:**95
     in Papua New Guinea, **9:**607
Bahamadia, **3:**701
Bahamas, **2:**78, 789, 801–12
     dance in, **2:**808–11
     Family Islands, **2:**801, 804, 808
     festivals in, **2:**811–12
     geography of, **2:**801
     instruments of, **2:**803–4

Bahamas (*continued*)
  musical genres
    anthem, **2:**804
    goombay, **2:**806
    junkafunk, **2:**808
    junkanoo, **2:**806–8
    rake 'n' scrape, **2:**805–6
    rhyming spiritual, **2:**804–5
  popular music in, **2:**95, 808
  population of, **2:**801
  religious music of, **2:**804–5
  research on, **2:**812
  secular music of, **2:**805–8
Bahamas Musicians and Entertainers Union,
    2:801
Bahamen (musical group), **2:**808
Bahamonde, Luis, **2:**370–71
Bahār Ensemble, **6:**908
Bahar, Mahdi, **4:**603
Bahat, Avner, **6:**1063–64, 1066
Bahauddin (Ustad), **5:**830, 831
Bahauddin Naqshband, Shaykh, **6:**940, 943
Bahauddin Zakariyya, Sheikh, **5:**760
Bahe Huiguan (Guangzhou organization), **3:**1261
Bahía (Valdivia) culture, **2:**10, 413
  archaeomusicological studies of, **2:**7
Bahinemo people, **9:**557
Bahiroba (deity), **5:**728
Bahmani dynasty, **5:**104
Bahnar people, **3:**996; **4:**444, 529
  courtship songs of, **4:**532
  gong ensemble of, **4:**534
  narratives of, **4:**533
Bahrain. *See also* Arabian peninsula
  chordophones in, **6:**412
  dance traditions in, **6:**706, 708, 709, 710
  idiophones in, **6:**403–5
  maqām traditions in, **6:**552
  al-nuban ritual, **6:**405, 412, 546
  pearl-diving songs, **6:**546, 651
  ṣawt genre, **6:**651–52
  women's music, **6:**697, 701, 702
Bahshi (Uighur tune), **7:**459
al-Bahtīmī, Kāmil Yūsuf, **6:**168
Bahubachan (theater group), **5:**489
Bahucharajimata (deity), **5:**634–35
Bahula, Julian, **1:**777–78
Bahurūpi community, **5:**728
Bai, Banni, **5:**270
Bai Guang, **7:**90, 354, 357
Bai, Janki, **5:**412, 424
Bai people, **7:**509
  music of, **7:***451*, 485–92
  opera of, **7:**452
Bai Xuexian, **7:**307
Bai Zhuyi, **7:**123
Bai, Zohra, **5:**412
Baidaphon (record company), **6:**234, 236
Baier, Randal E., **4:**107, 701
Baifa people, **9:**983
Baiga people, **5:**720, 722
Bailey, Kim, **9:**728, 994
Baillergeon, Hélène, **3:**1167
Bailleux (Walloon song collector), **8:**534–35
Baillie, Joanna, **8:**368
Bailly, Edmond, **5:**563

Baily, John, **5:**576
Baimaonu (ballet), **7:**349, 350
Baima wenba (Tibetan opera), **7:**479
Bain, Aly, **8:**366
Baines, Anthony, **8:**22
Baining people, **9:**189
  dance of, **9:**600
  masks of, **9:**350
  music and dance of, **9:**983
  songs of, **9:**607
Baiocchi, Regina A., **3:**610
Bairamov, Habib, **6:**924
Baird's Mammoth Minstrels, **3:***47*
Bait people, **7:**1004–20
Baixue Guoyueshe (Beijing), **7:**229
Baixue yiyin (Hua), **7:**130, 154
Baizhanuly, Zhayau Musa, **6:**955
Baja culture, **2:**553
Baja, Mariano, **4:**859
Bajao people. *See* Sama-Bajao people
Bajau people, **4:**824, 826
Bājgī caste, **5:**291
Bajić, Isidor, **8:**948
Bajramović, Šaban, **8:**279, 951
Bajuk, Marko, **8:**922
Bak, Kirsten Sass, **8:**464
Bakare, Ayinde, **1:**359, 478, 479, 481
Bake, Arnold A., **5:**629, 706, 883
Baker, Chet, **3:**659
Baker, David, **3:**610, 612; **10:**139
Baker, David N., **10:**139
Baker, Houston A., **3:**582
Baker, Josephine, **3:**619; **4:**509
Baker, Kenny, **3:***159*, 743
Baker, LaVern, **3:**352, 354, 673
Baker, Michael Conway, **3:**1097
Baker, Theodore, **3:**444, 485, 509
Bakhleval, Sharan Rani, **5:**204–5, 466
Bakht, Ms., **6:***857*
Bakhtiar, Ustad, **5:**787
Bakiga people, **1:**210
Bakixanov, A., **6:**924
Bakka, Egil, **8:**427
Bakkarud, Odd, **8:**422
Bakoota, Luke, **3:**58
Bakota people, **1:**663–64
Baksh, Maula, **5:**563
Bakshu, Nayak, **5:**164
Baktaman people, **9:**188
balada, **2:**101, 102–3, 105, 109, 623, 862
Balagtas at Celia (Pájaro), **4:**875
Bala Joban (film), **5:**591
Balakirev, Mily, **8:**755, 780–81, 856, 858
balalaika. *See* lutes
Balalaika and Domra Association of America,
    3:58
Balalaika and Domra Society of New York, **3:**58
Balamuralikrishna, Dr., **5:**424, 425
Balan, S., **5:**556
Balanchine, George, **8:**161, 843
Balanchivadze, Meliton, **8:**843
Balaraman, V. V., **5:***936*
Balasaraswati, T., **5:**104
Balašević, Đorđe, **8:**949
Balasubramanium, S. P., **5:**422, 424
Baláž, Ján, **8:**731

Balaž, Janika, **3:**922
Balazs, Gusztav, **8:**276
Baldovinos, Salvador, **3:***723*
Baldwin sisters, **9:**742
Balfe, Michael William, **3:**181
Balfour, David, **8:**373
Balgandharva, **5:**424
Balgarka (musical group), **3:**1199
Bali
  bamboo agriculture in, **4:**52
  competitions in, **4:**141
  dance in, **4:**757–58
  Dutch in, **4:**731–32
  gong-chime ensembles in, **4:**20
  Hinduism in, **4:**65; **5:**10
  history of, **4:**731–33
  influence on East Javanese culture, **4:**630, 635
  influence on Lombok culture, **4:**762, 763–65,
    766, 769, 774–75
  instruments in, **4:**741–43
  Javanese influences in, **4:**11
  map of, **4:***730*
  musical genres (*See also* gamelan; vocal music)
    baleganjuran, **4:**753
    Bali pop, **4:**730, 761
    gangsaran, **4:**744
    gendèr wayang, **4:**597, 749
    gending, **4:**733
    gending gong, **4:**744
    gilakan, **4:**753
    kreasi baleganjur, **4:**730, 753–54, 759
    kreasi baru, **4:**729, 745–46, 749, 759, 773
    lelambatan, **4:**744, 749
    musik kontemporer, **4:**730, 759–60
    musik pop, **4:**761
    pemungkah, **4:**751
    petegak, **4:**751
    pop Indonesia, **4:**761
    tabuh, **4:**733, 735, 757
  parallels with Cirebonese culture, **4:**686
  population of, **4:**732
  prehistoric, **4:**731
  Ramayana in, **5:**261
  religion in, **4:**729
  research on music of, **4:**27, 28–29, 733
  spirit beliefs in, **4:**52–53
  tourism in, **4:**136–37, 732–33, 760–61
  traditional music in, **4:**140–41
  vocal music in, **4:**755–57
"Bali Hai" (Rodgers), **9:**45
Bali (Unea) Island (Papua New Guinea),
    9:607–12
Bali people (of Africa), **1:**117
Baliku, **9:**156
Balım Sultan, **6:**794
Balinese-American Dance Theater, **3:**1021
Balinese Music (Tenzer), **4:**28
Balinese music in North America, **3:**952, 953,
    955, 1012–13, 1015, 1017, 1018–20;
    10:128, 134–35. *See also* Indonesian
    music
Balinese people
  in Lombok, **4:**776
  relation to peoples of Lombok, **4:**762
  in Sumbawa, **4:**779
  in Sunda, **4:**700

Balkan Arts Center (New York), **10**:82
Balkan Connection (musical group), **3**:1199
Balkan peoples
  in North America, **3**:529
  in Southeast Asia, **4**:796
Balkan region. *See also* Albania; Bosnia-
      Hercegovina; Bulgaria; Croatia; Greece;
      Macedonia; Romania; Serbia; Slovenia;
      Turkey; Yugoslavia (former)
  animal bells in, **8**:142
  carnival in, **8**:140
  dance traditions of, **8**:163, *164–65*
  epic songs, **8**:198
  folk music in, **8**:13–14
  function of music in, **8**:121
  gender roles in, **8**:194
  instruments, **8**:41, 170
  Islamic rule in, **8**:12
  lazarovden in, **8**:140
  "luck visits," **8**:140
  map of, **8**:*866*
  Muslim people, **8**:11
    prohibitions on women's singing and
      dancing, **8**:145
  sacred and secular polyphony, **8**:145
  Sephardic Jews in, **8**:248, 962
  state folk ensembles in, **8**:201
  Turkish influences in, **6**:759
  two-part polyphony, **8**:134
  wars in, **8**:952, 962, 1011
Balkanton (record company), **8**:903
Balkarian people, **8**:850, 854, 856–59
  dance traditions of, **8**:858
  epic performance, **8**:851
  instruments, **8**:857
  research on music of, **8**:858–59
  vocal music of, **8**:856–59
Ball, Lucille, **3**:732
"Ball of Confusion" (Temptations), **3**:318, 677
Ballad of Baby Doe (Moore), **3**:546
"Ballad of Brian Tobin" (Elliot), **3**:1142–43
"Ballad of Medgar Evers" (Ochs), **3**:316
"Ballad of the Green Berets" (Sadler), **3**:317
ballad opera, **3**:46, 179–80, 182, 542, 837, 839,
    1079, 1118; **8**:17, 393
ballads. *See also* corridos; narratives
  African-American, **3**:524
  Albania, **8**:195
  Amish singing of, **3**:887
  Anglo-American, **3**:7, 29, 48, 70, 147–48,
      153–58, 510, 511, 519–20, 824–25,
      831, 833–34
    influence on country music, **3**:76
  Anglo-Canadian, **3**:7, 11, 1071, 1123–24,
      1188–89
  Austria, Tyrol region, **8**:672
  Belarus, **8**:795
  Belgium, **8**:136
  Bengal, *pālāgān*, **5**:859
  Bosnia-Hercegovina, **8**:195
    duge pjesme, **8**:963
  Brazil, **2**:327
  broadside, **3**:180, 834–35, 1124, 1139, 1188;
    8:296, 435, *520*, 664, 727
  Bulgaria, **8**:195
    Krali Marko, **8**:896, 898

Carriacou, **2**:868
Child, **3**:29, 511, 833–34, 1123–24, 1188,
    1256; **8**:136, 295, 296, 297, *327*,
    328–29, 343, 370, 380, 606
Costa Rica, **2**:695, *696*, 698
Czech Republic, broadside, **8**:727
Denmark, **8**:23, 131, 134, 136, 451–53, *454*,
    456–57, 458, 460, 463
  navvy and manor-house, **8**:458, 462
England, **8**:8, 136, 195, 327–29, 332–33
Europe, **8**:134–37, 517
  as dance forms, **8**:131
  dissemination of, **8**:8, 20
  research on, **8**:23
  women's performance of, **8**:195
Faroe Islands, **8**:131
  kempurvísur, **8**:469, 470–71
  kvæði, **8**:469–70
  tættir, **8**:469, 471
Finnish-American, **3**:873, 874
France, **8**:135, 545
French Canadian, **3**:7, 1075, 1136, 1193
Gaelic, **3**:1070
Germany, **8**:23, 136, 195, 664
Great Britain, **8**:134, 135
Greece, on bandit-heroes, **8**:1009, 1030
Hungary, **8**:135, 740, *742*
Iceland, **8**:117–18, 403–4
immigrant, **3**:825
influence on blues, **3**:639, 640
Ireland, **8**:379–80, 390
  Travellers, **8**:294
Italy, **8**:605–6, 611
Japan
  kuzure, **7**:645
  tikuzen biwa, **7**:649–50, 766
Lithuanian emigrant, **3**:875
Low Countries, **8**:520, *520*, 523
Low German, **3**:1250
Malta, **8**:635
  fatt, **8**:637–38
New England, **3**:153–58
Norway, **8**:106–7, 412, 413, 426
Norwegian emigrant, **3**:867
Orissa, *daskathia* and *pala*, **5**:733
Poland, **8**:709
popular, **3**:193
Portugal, **8**:195
  romanceiros, **8**:136–37
  romances, **8**:578
Rajasthan, **5**:641
rhythm and blues, **3**:671, 673
Romania, **8**:875–76, 879, 882
Russia, **8**:*759*
Scandinavia, **8**:135
Scotland, **8**:106–7, *135*, 136, 195,
    369–70
  broadside, **8**:296
  highland, **8**:367
  lowland, **8**:365
  Northern Isles, **8**:365
Sephardic *romances*, **3**:942, 1171, 1172, 1173;
    8:195
Slovakia, broadside, **8**:727
Slovenia, **8**:135, 136–37, 911
Spain, *romances*, **8**:134, 589, 592, 601

Sweden, **8**:136, 195, 435
Swedish emigrant, **3**:870
Switzerland, **8**:695
Turkey, *destân*, **6**:762–63
Ukraine, **8**:135, 136, 195
Ukrainian-Canadian, **3**:1256
United States, **8**:23, 135
Wales, **8**:343–44, 346
Ballads and Sea Songs from Nova Scotia
    (Mackenzie), **3**:1125
Ballanta, Nicholas J. George, **1**:18, 19–22, 26,
    63
Ballantyne, Andrew, **9**:479
Ballard, Jean-Baptiste-Christoph, **8**:17
Ballasteros, Aaron, **3**:748
Ballet Creole (Toronto), **3**:224
Ballet Folclórico Nacional (Costa Rica), **2**:703
Ballet Folklórico (El Salvador), **2**:715
Ballet Folklorico (United States), **3**:207
Ballet Folklórico Nacional (Dominican
    Republic), **2**:861
Ballet Hispanico, **3**:851
Ballets Russes, **8**:161
Balling, Michael, **9**:928
Balmaseda, Manuel, **8**:598
Baloch (also Baluchi) people, **5**:7, 773, 805
  in Iraq, **6**:415
  in Oman, **6**:672, 681–82
  in United Arab Emirates, **6**:415
Baloch, G. N., **5**:747
Baloch, N. A., **5**:759
Balochistan (also Baluchistan), **5**:7, 744, 773–84.
    See also Iran
  dance traditions of, **5**:776–81
  geography of, **5**:773
  instruments in, **5**:783; **6**:10, 825, 881, 887–88
  Iranian dance traditions in, **6**:877
  map of, **5**:*742*
  musical genres of, **6**:881
  music, trance, and therapy in, **6**:177, *178*,
    881–90
  performers in, **5**:781–82
  qalandarī genre, **6**:887–88
  vocal music of, **5**:773–76
  Zikri sect in, **5**:754
Balogh, Kalman, **8**:*156*
Balogun, C. A., **1**:480
Balok (periodical), **5**:436
Bāltayev, Nur Muhammad, **6**:908
Baltic Germans, in Estonia, **8**:495–96
Baltic Institute of Folklore, **8**:507
Baltic peoples, **8**:754. *See also* Estonian people;
    Latvian people; Lithuanian people
  in North America, **3**:875–80, 1078, 1082
  in Sweden, **8**:434, 446
Baltic States. *See also* Estonia; Latvia; Lithuania
  Ashkenazic Jews in, **8**:248
  map of, **8**:*398*
Baltimore Symphony Orchestra, **3**:537
Baltzar, Veijo, **8**:289
Baluan (Papua New Guinea), **9**:602–7
Baluchistan. *See* Balochistan
Balumarilikrishna, Dr., **3**:990
Balungan (periodical), **3**:953, 1017
Balustauly, Espai, **6**:958
Balusubramaniam, Mr., **3**:990

Balys, Jonas, **3:**875
Balzano, Giuseppe, **8:**642
Bamana (Bambara) people
    dance, **1:**120–21
    masks of, **1:**119
    praise singing, **1:**495
    textile design, **1:**115
"Bamba, La" (Valens), **3:**732, 733, 746
"Bamba, La" (*son*), **2:**606
Bamba, La (film), **3:**750
Bambara people
    instruments of, **1:**445
    puberty rites, **1:**111
    textile design, **1:**114
    wedding dances, **1:**111
Bambenjele people, **1:**658
Bambis (musical group), **8:**679
bamboo, **4:**7, 596
    cultivation of, **4:**47–48
    rice and, **4:**51–53, 711, 914
    seed of, **4:**52
Bamboo and Barbed Wire (multimedia production), **3:**973
Bambuco, El (Párraga), **2:**387
BaMbuti people
    dance, **1:**117
    dance accompaniment, **1:**113
    funeral ceremonies, **1:**111
Bamogu Union Band, **9:**138
Bamu people, **9:**179–80
Banaba (Kiribati), **9:***337*, 712, 715, 754, 755, 758, 764
Banaban people, in Fiji, **9:***71*, 712, 764, 998
Banān, Gholām Hoseyn, **6:**140, 141
Banaras Hindu University, **5:**447, 466
Banarasi, Raunak, **5:**487
Banarjee, Jayasri, **5:**446–47
Banat, **8:**868. *See also* Romania
Banbei shi, **7:**463
Banco Central de Costa Rica, **2:**681
Band (musical group), **3:**348
Band in Blue, **1:**771
Band of Company C, Kentucky Volunteers, **3:***565*
Band, Heinrich, **2:**89; **8:**657
Banda Blanca, **2:**741
Banda Brava, **3:**1085
Banda Filarmónica de Managua, **2:**766
Banda Islands, **4:**817
Banda Linda people, **1:**267
Banda Mbiyi people, **1:**267
Banda Mel, **2:**353
Banda Nacional de Bogotá, **2:**397
Bandana Land (musical), **3:**608, 619, *620*
Banda Ndokpa people, **1:**267
Bandanna Sketches (White), **3:**608
Banda Para'í, **2:**459
Banda people
    harp music, **1:**656
    tuning system, **1:**267
Banda Reggae, **2:**353
Banda, Robson, **1:**432
Bandar, Mahawalatenne, **5:**960
Bandella di Tremona (musical group), **8:***695*
"Bande Mātaram!", **5:**435–36, 437–38
Bandem, I Made, **3:**1013; **4:**733

Bandido (musical group), **3:**766
Bandinha Cultural, **2:***331*
Bandini, Don Arturo, **3:**736
bandleaders. *See* conductors; *specific names*
bandoneón. See accordions
bands. *See* ensembles, musical
bandurria. See lutes
Bandy, David Wayne, **9:**134
Bandyopadhyay, Abhijit, **5:**857
Bandyopadhyay, Chabi, **5:**254
Bandyopadhyay, Hemchandra, **5:**848, 849
Bandyopadhyay, Kanika, **5:**254
Bandyopadhyay, Pratima, **5:**857
Bandyopadhyay, Pulak, **5:**857
Bandyopadhyay, Rangalal, **5:**848, 849
Bandyopadhyay, Shivadas, **5:**857
Bandyopadhyaya, Krishnadhana, **5:**432, 433
Banerjee, Jitendra Nath, **5:**205
Banerjee, Nikhil, **5:**205, 466, 530, 560
Banerji, Sabita, **5:**576
Banff Center for the Arts, **3:**1090
Banfield, William Cedric, **3:**610, 612
Bangani, Banzi, **1:***771*
Bangarra Dance Theatre, **9:**60, *410*, 416–17, 443, 452
Bangladesh, **5:**8, 844–62. *See also* Bengal (region)
    dance traditions of, **5:**505
    Dhaka
        musical life in, **5:**857–58
        theater in, **5:**488–89
    emigration of Hindus to India, **5:**857
    film industry in, **5:**531
    founding of, **5:**437, 503, 744, 858
    history of, **5:**16, 844
    languages of, **5:**7
    map of, **5:***3*, *842*
    Naga people in, **4:**528
    patriotic songs in, **5:**858–59
    popular music in, **5:**428
    Rajshahi district, **5:**860–61
    Rangpur region, **5:**860
    regional cassettes in, **5:**550
    religion in, **5:**10
    theater in, **5:**488–89
    Western popularity of musical genres, **5:**568
BaNgombe people, **1:**119, 658
Bang on a Can All-Stars (musical group), **3:**177, *177*
Banika (Solomon Islands), **9:**662
Banisil, Sindao, **4:**908
Banisil, Sultan Otil, **4:**908
Banja Luka Center for Folk Songs, **8:**970
banjo
    Africa, **1:**300
    African precursor, **3:**593
    in Algerian music, **6:**475, 476
    Australia, **9:**441
    Bahamas, **2:**805
    banjo-guitar, **8:**288
    banjolin, **3:**1190
    Barbados, **2:**814, 815, 819
    Belize, **2:**677
    Brazil, **2:**337
    Carriacou, **2:**872
    Cook Islands, **9:**900
    Denmark, **8:**458

    England, **8:**331
    in Filipino string bands, **9:**95
    Germany, **8:**656
    Indonesia, **4:**103
    Ireland, **8:**152
    Jamaica, **2:**900, 906
    Low Countries, **8:**533
    Madhya Pradesh, **5:**723
    Melanesia, **9:**27
    Montserrat, **2:**926
    Nicaragua, **2:**753
    Nigeria, **1:**478
    North America
        in African-American music, **3:**67, 593, 595
        in bluegrass music, **3:**159–165, 1258
        in Cambodian music, **3:**999
        in country music, **3:**77, 836
        in Finnish music, **3:**874
        in folk revival, **3:**328
        in gospel music, **3:**535
        in Hispano music, **3:**761
        in Irish music, **3:**842, 844
        in Italian music, **3:**865
        in minstrel shows, **3:**184, 543, 616, 838
        in Norwegian music, **3:**868
        in polka bands, **3:**824, 893, 901
        in Ukrainian music, **3:**914
    Oceania, **3:***13*; **9:**413
    Ontario, **3:**1190
    Peru, **2:**475
    Réunion Island, **5:**609
    skroud (also *bwa pòyé*), **2:**945
    South Africa, **1:**762
    Sri Lanka, **5:**970
    technological innovations, **3:**239, 240
    tenor, **8:**385
    Wales, **8:**355
    Yukon, **3:**1277
Bankalawa people, **1:**289, 292
Bankole, Ayo, **1:**19, 221, 223, 224, 226, 232, 233, 237, 249
Bankole, T. A., **1:**19
Banks, Homer, **3:**676
Banks Islands (Vanuatu), **9:**688
    instruments of, **9:**693, 694
    music and dance of, **9:**695, 698–702
    songs of, **9:**690
    sung poetry, **9:**361
Banks, Sir Joseph, **9:**10, 34
Bannen, Charlie, **10:**160
Bannock (rap artist), **3:**1063
Bannock Indian nation, **3:**420, 421
Bannzil Kwéyòl, **2:**942
Bano, Iqbal, **5:**425, 750, 766
Banoni people, **9:**644–47
Bansomdej Chaopraya Teacher's College, **4:**226
Bansuri (periodical), **5:**58
bānsurī. See flutes
Banten (kingdom), **4:**779
Banton, Pato, **9:**167
Bantu peoples, **1:**635, 703
    in Brazil, **2:**341
    in Cuba, **2:**822, 823, 825
    interactions with San groups, **1:**305–8
    in Uruguay, **2:**515

Banū 'Abbād, **6**:442
Banū al-Aḥmar, **6**:442
Banu, Laila Arjumand, **5**:858
Banū Mūsā ibn Shākir, **6**:373
Banyankore people, **1**:210, 602
Banyarwanda people, **1**:210
Banza Duo, **3**:1197
Bao Đại, emperor of Vietnam, **3**:993; **4**:125,
    449, 510
Bao Nana, **7**:357
Baoulé people, **1**:465
Bapa, Alexander, **7**:1024
Bapa, Sayan, **7**:1024
Bapedi people. *See* Pedi people
Bapiuly, Mädi, **6**:955
Bapodara, Vittal Das, **5**:251
Baptie, David, **8**:374
Baptists. *See also* German Seventh-Day Baptists;
        Missionary Baptists; Old Regular
        Baptists; Primitive Baptists
    in Antigua and Barbuda, **2**:798–99
    black congregations, **3**:120, 631–32, 1212
    in Costa Rica, **2**:688
    in Estonia, **8**:491
    in Jamaica, **2**:901
    in Papua New Guinea, **9**:516
    in Paraguay, **2**:457, 463
Baptist Standard Hymnal, **10**:138
Barabas, **3**:688
Bara ga saita (Japanese popular song), **7**:746
Barak, **9**:440
Baraka, Amiri, **3**:132, 325, 582, 584, 663
Barakāt, M., **6**:592
Baran, Ilhan, **6**:775
Baran, Timir, **5**:536
Barandiarán, Daniel de, **2**:172
Bārbad, **6**:129, 131, 183, 834, *834*, 859, 860
Barbadian-Canadians, **3**:1132, 1169, 1170,
    1201
Barbados, **2**:789, 813–21
    art music in, **2**:814, 820
    Bridgetown, **2**:814
    early black music in, **3**:64
    geography of, **2**:813
    history of, **2**:813–14
    instruments in, **2**:814–16
    Landship movement, **2**:816, 817, 818–19
    musical genres
        calypso, **2**:819–20
        folk songs, **2**:817
        spouge, **2**:820
        steelbands, **2**:97
    popular music in, **2**:819–20
    population of, **2**:813
    religious music of, **2**:816–17
    secular music in, **2**:817–19
    tea meetings, **2**:817
"Barbara Allen" (ballad), **3**:7, 155, 511, 519,
    834, 1124, 1188; **8**:8, 20
Barbary pirates, **6**:431
Barbeau, Marius, **3**:31, 33, 146, 147, 148, 291,
    292, 343, 465, 1058, 1164, *1164*,
    1165–67
Barbecue Bob, **3**:644
Barber, Samuel, **3**:335, 541
Barbería del Sur, **8**:599

Barbieri, Gato, **3**:797
Barbosa, Rui, **2**:340
Barbot, Jean, **1**:81–82
Barbuda. *See* Antigua and Barbuda
Barbu Lăutaru Folk Orchestra, **8**:278
Barclay (record company), **8**:239, 241
Bard al-Fu'ād, **6**:296
Bardesanes, **6**:227
Bardo Male Chorus (Viceroy), **3**:1251
Bardophone (record company), **6**:548
Barenaked Ladies (musical group), **3**:1081,
    1104
Bärenreiter, **8**:732
Barés, Basil, **3**:606
Barfield, Thomas, **7**:29, 30
Barford, Vernon, **3**:1090, 1227
Barga people, **7**:1004–20
al-Barghotī, 'A., **6**:580
Bariba people, **1**:452–53
Barike, **9**:90, 154, 155
Bar-Ilan University, **6**:1061, 1063, 1064
Baring-Gould, Rev. Sabine, **8**:337
Barishnikov, Mikhail, **2**:265
baritone horn. *See* trumpets or horns
Barito people, **4**:825
Bariu, Laver, **8**:993
Bar-Kays (musical group), **3**:676, 684
Barkechli, Mehdi, **6**:135
Barker, Edward B. B., **6**:566
Barker, George T., **9**:24
Barker, Jimmy, **9**:442
Barker, Muhammad Abd-al-Rahman, **5**:776
Barkin, Elaine, **3**:1017; **10**:88
Barlow, Bill, **3**:349
Barlow, Kim, **3**:1277–78, 1280
Barlow, William, **3**:103–4, 582
Barmakid Ja'far ibn Yahyá, **6**:296
Barn Dance (radio show), **3**:243, 1080
Barnes, Gina, **7**:25
Barnum, P. T., **3**:537
Barodekar, Hirabai, **5**:413, 414
Baron, Maurice, **9**:43
Baron, Robert, **10**:85
Barone, Anna, **8**:622
Barons, Krišjāns, **8**:506
Baroque, **8**:76–79
    Czech Republic, **8**:727
    folk idioms in art music, **8**:227
    Germany, **8**:652–55
    improvisational elements in, **8**:93
    innovation in, **8**:65
    instrumental music in, **8**:78–79
    Poland, **8**:710
    Romania, **8**:881
    Slovakia, **8**:727
    Sweden, **8**:444
Bāroṭ (also Bhāṭ) caste, **5**:402, 403, 635, 640
Barra MacNeils (musical group), **3**:150, 1073
Barral, Basilio María de, **2**:197
Barrand, Anthony, **3**:322, 323, 324
Barrera, Ray, **3**:778
Barretto, Ray, **3**:732, 743, 788, 789, 794, 796,
    797
Barrière, Mireille, **3**:1148
"Barrio Suite" (Salas), **3**:748
Barrios Mangoré, Agustín, **2**:463, 464

Barrister, Alhaji, **1**:485–86
Barrister, Sikiru Ayinde, **1**:484
Barroco Andino, **2**:373
Barron, Bebe, **3**:253
Barron, Louis, **3**:253
Barros, Raquel, **2**:374
Barroso, Ary, **2**:316–17
Barrot, Adolphe, **9**:16–17
Barrow, Norman, **2**:820
Barrow, Steve, **2**:93
Barry, John, **3**:203
Barry, Phillips, **3**:147
Barsanti, Francesco, **8**:372
Barsegh Tchon, **6**:737
Bartenieff, Irmgard, **3**:221
Barth, Fredrik, **3**:512, 515; **6**:671, 672
Barthes, Roland, **8**:97
Barthold, Bonnie J., **1**:127
Bartholomew, Dave, **3**:670, *670*
Bartholomew, Doris, **2**:573
Bartlett, Wayne, **3**:1139–40
Bartók, Béla, **3**:327, 537; **6**:775; **7**:342, 347,
    350; **8**:26, 369, 445, 730, 737
    ethnomusicological studies, **1**:545; **6**:502, 766,
        767; **8**:18–19, 20, 23, 95, 122, 177,
        274, 338, 742, 885, 890, 932
    ideology of folk creation, **8**:188
    string quartets, **8**:85
    views on Hungarian and Rom identity issues,
        8:272, 273
Bartoli, Cecilia, **3**:271
Bartolomé, Miguel Alberto, **2**:204
Bartolomei, Ugo, **9**:*81*
Barton, Andrew, **3**:180
Barton, Roy, **4**:872
Bartoš, František, **8**:721
Baruya people, **9**:511
    ceremonial spaces, **9**:512
    music and dance of, **9**:526–33
    secret flutes of, **9**:512
Barwick, Linda, **9**:439, 986
Bar-Yohai, Simeon, **6**:1040
Baryshnikov, Mikhail, **8**:161
Barz, Gregory F., **3**:150
Barzizza, Pippo, **8**:619
Bašagić, Sahvet-beg, **8**:966
Basalenque, Diego, **2**:577–78
Basa people, **1**:659
Basava (also Basavanna), **5**:264–65, 866
Basedow, H., **9**:987
Basemah people, **4**:622–23
Başgöz, Ilhan, **6**:845
al-Bashank, **6**:568
Bā-Sharāḥīl, **6**:685
al-Basha, Tawfīq, **6**:554
Bashari, Gilah, **6**:1031
Bashir, Aboud, **6**:281
Bashir, Muhammad, **5**:768
Bashir, Munir, **6**:593–95
Bashkir people, **8**:11
    instruments, **8**:774
    rhythmic patterns of, **8**:773
    throat-singing, **8**:773
Bashlachev, Aleksandr, **8**:778
bashraf, **6**:452, 470, 550, 560
    rhythmic modes in, **6**:91

Bāshṭarzī, Muḥyi al-Dīn. *See* Bachetarzi, Mahieddine

Basie, William "Count," **3:**655, 656, *657*, 707, 793, 863, 969

Basile, Christopher, **4:**29

Basilio, Tomás, **2:**588

Başkale, Fïrat, **6:**251

Basker (musical group), **5:**610

Basoga people. *See* Soga people

Basohli painting, **5:**300

Basotho people. *See also* Sotho people
 events categorization, **1:**134
 famo genre, **1:**769
 music of, **1:**762, 767, 769

Basque Language Academy, **8:**316–17

Basque people, in North America, **3:**217, 731, 847, 849–50

Basque region, **8:**7, 247, 309–17, 595
 carnival in, **8:**140, 315
 choral societies, **8:**147, 315
 history of, **8:**309, 316
 instruments, **8:***47*, 171, *246*, 314, 316, 545, 594, 600
 map of, **8:***310, 516*
 musical genres
  bederatzi puntuko, **8:**311
  bertsu competitions, **8:**134, 311–14
  old *vs.* new, **8:**121
  zortziko, **8:**311
 research on music of, **8:**316–17
 separatist movement, **8:**12, 309, 315
 two-part polyphony of, **8:**542

bass drum. *See* drums: barrel, conical, or cylindrical

Bassa people, **1:**119

Bassara, Robert, **3:**954

Bassini, Carlo, **3:**864

Bassler, Gerhard, **3:**1249

Basso, Keith H., **3:**433

Bastar people, **5:**721

Bastian, C. Don, **5:**491, 970

Bastidas, Rodrigo de, **2:**770

Basu, Anandamohan, **5:**848

Basu, Hiren, **5:**855, 856

Basu, Manomohan, **5:**849

Basuli (deity), **5:**734

Basyô (flute piece), **7:**546

Basyô (Konparu), **7:**630, 632

Bata people, **1:**117

Batachanga, **3:**798

"*Bataille des Sept Chênes, La*" (Falcon), **3:**410

Batak people, **4:**591, 601, 605, 607–8, 920
 instrumental music of, **4:**924
 lutes of, **4:**599
 in Sunda, **4:**700
 use of Western musical material, **4:**601

Batanay, Kemâl, **6:**119

Batchuluun, **7:**1020

Batek people, **4:**560, 573

Bates, Katherine Lee, **3:**521

Batjala people, **9:**430

Bats (musical group), **9:**169

Batshan, Ḥamdi, **6:**239

al-Batsh, ʿUmar, **6:**550

Battig, Sister M. Baptista, **4:**870

Battisti, Lucio, **8:**619

Battle of Algiers (film), **3:**204

"Battle Cry of Freedom" (Root), **3:**188

"Battle Hymn of the Republic," **3:**188, 310, 317, 521

Battle of Manassas (Bethune), **3:**605

Battle, Rex, **3:**1080

Battlefield Band (musical group), **8:**226, 372

Batuka (salsa band), **9:**83

Batuque, **2:**259–61, 340, 341, 348

Batwèl Rada (musical group), **3:**806

Baucke, Florian, **2:**251

Baud-Bovy, Samuel, **8:**1010, 1025

Bauer, Robert, **3:**1072

Bāul sect, **5:**254, *328*, 405, 503, 859
 folk songs of, **5:**436, 850, 851, 853, 859–60
 instruments of, **5:**343, 344, 859, *860, 861*
 women performers, **5:**411

Baum, Hillel, **8:***255*

Bauman, Richard, **1:**494

Baumann, Gerd, **1:**601–2; **5:**574, 576

Bauré culture, **2:**137

Bausch, Pina, **2:**265; **8:**161

Bautista, Antonina, **4:**856

Bautista, Father San Pedro, **4:**841

Bauve, Adam de, **2:**158

Bauzá, Mario, **1:**387; **3:**787, 793

Bauzi people, **9:**583

Bauzō, Louis, **3:***786*

Bavanīlu singers, **5:**894, 901

Bavaria community, **5:**648

Bawang xiejia (*pipa* piece), **7:**168

Bawāriq al-ilmāʿ (Majd al-Dīn al-Ghazālī), **6:**373

Bawihka Sumu, **2:**750

Ba Xie (Tibetan writing), **7:**476

Baxter, Ivy, **2:**913

Baxter, Les, **3:**787

Bayadère, La (Petipa), **5:**562

Bayanihan Philippine Dance Company, **3:**1025

"Bayan Ko" (Guzman), **3:**1025

Bayard Dominick Expedition, **9:**24, 880, 969

Bayard, Samuel P., **3:**834; **8:**338

Bay Area New Gamelan, **3:**1017

Baybars, al-Ẓāhir, **6:**340

Bay City Rollers (musical group), **8:**369

Bayer, Bathya, **6:**17–18, 1061–62, 1063, 1065

Bayer, Natan, **6:**1066

Bayete, **1:**428, 778

Bayezid II, Ottoman sultan, **6:**194

al-Bayhaqī, **6:**357

Bayïndïr nomads, **6:**966

Bayou Seco (musical group), **3:**763

Bay Psalm Book, **3:**832

Bayt al-Hikmah, **6:**540

Bayyūmī, ʿAbd al-Samīʿ, **6:**168

Bāzigār caste, **5:**639

Bazin, François, **3:**1148

BBC Gramophone Library, **8:**18

BBC Scottish Orchestra, **8:**369

BCC Chinese Folk Orchestra, **7:**229–30, 232

Beach, Amy Marcy Cheney, **3:**90, *90*, 93, 538

Beach Boys (musical group), **3:**311, 318, 348, 355, 550

Beale Street Sheiks, **3:**645

Béaloideas, **8:**394

Beamer, Keola, **9:**389, 1008

Beami people, **9:**490

Beastie Boys (musical group), **3:**133, 552, 696, 714

Beat (periodical), **3:**812

Beaterio de Santa Catalina, **4:**853–54

Beatles (musical group), **3:**48, 244, 336, 347, 348, 355, 356, 550, 552, 840, 952, 955, 1002; **8:**61, 209, 214, 216, 446
 influence of, **3:**747, 1081; **4:**208; **7:**354, 360, 1020; **8:**218, 220, 221, 238, 619, 679, 845; **9:**137, 213, 739
 performances with Shankar, **5:**528, 566
 reggae-influenced songs, **2:**97
 study of transcendental meditation, **3:**133

Beaton, Roderick, **8:**1024

Beatrice (musical group), **8:**746

Beat Street (film), **3:**713

Beaudet, Jean-Michel, **3:**1150, 1151; **9:**965, 992

Beau Dommage (musical group), **3:**1158, 1168

Beaudry, Nicole, **3:**381, 392, 1275

Beaumont, Pablo de, **2:**577

"Beautiful Dreamer" (Foster), **3:**187

"Beautiful Island" (Li), **7:**357

Beauty and the Beast (Carlos), **3:**955

Beauty in the Beast (album), **4:**132

Beauty World (Lee), **4:**523

Beaux Arts Trio, **3:**1210

Beaverbrook Playhouse (Fredericton), **3:**1120

Beazley, Del, **9:**166

Bebe, Walter, **9:**966

Bebey, Francis, **1:**45, 131, 363; **10:**56

bebop. *See* jazz

Becaraji (deity), **5:**626

Becaud, Gilbert, **6:**249

Becerra Casanovas, Rogers, **2:**140

Becerra, Martín, **3:**739

Bechet, Sidney, **3:**550, 652

Beck, Ervin, **2:**679

Beck, Jean, **3:**1165

Beck, Jeff, **8:**214

Becke, Louis, **9:**36

Becker, Alton, **4:**638; **10:**43, 51

Becker, Bob, **5:**136

Becker, David, **9:**965

Becker, Judith, **3:**1013; **8:**58; **10:**43, 51, 71
 research on Burmese music, **4:**26, 380, 392–94
 research on Indonesian music, **4:**103, 637, 638–39, 657, 660, 677

Becker, Peter, **3:**904

Beckett, Jeremy, **9:**987

Beckett, Samuel, **8:**378

Beckwith, John, **3:**144, 1058, 1075, 1108, 1186

Beckwith, Martha, **2:**913

Beda community, **5:***712*, 712–13

Bedard, Mel, **3:**409

Bédard, Philéas, **3:**147

Bedekar, Vishram, **5:**532

Bedil, Mirza, **5:**805; **6:**914, 945

Bedouin peoples, **6:**299, 300. *See also specific countries*
 Arabian peninsula, **6:**403, 404, 649, 652–54, 663–69, 697–98, 701
 chordophones of, **6:**409, 410
 dances of, **6:**623–24
 folk traditions of, **6:**544–45

in North Africa, **6:**269, 410–11, 431, 432, 466
Bedreddin, Şeykh, **6:**794
Bedul, Shiro, **9:**32
Bee, Darlene, **9:**357–58
Beechey, Captain F. W., **9:**885
Bee Gees (musical group), **3:**688–89, 1002
Beekley, N., **3:**59
"Beer Barrel Polka," **3:**529
Be'er Sheba Sinfonietta, **6:**1030
Beethoven, Ludwig van, **2:**394; **3:**27, 28, 190, 1179; **4:**862; **7:**341, 540; **8:**80, 86, 93–94, 186, 646, 727
    piano sonatas, **8:**81
    popular songs of, **3:**181
    Scottish tune arrangements, **8:**367, 372–73
    String Quartet op. 130, *Grosse Fuge*, **8:**62
    symphonies, **8:**60, 82, *83*, 187
Before the Rain (musical group), **8:**983
Begay, Harrison, **3:**312
Beggar's Opera (Gay), **3:**180, 542, 839; **8:**17
Begin Again Again … (Machover), **3:**254
Begley, Eileen, **9:**79
Bego label, **3:**781
beguine, **2:**95, 98
    in Dominica, **2:**842
    in Guadeloupe, **2:**874, 877–78, 879
    in Martinique, **2:**915–16, *917*, 919
Begum, Chandra, **5:**413
Begum, Gulnar, **5:**791
Begum, Roshanara, **5:**413, 746
Begum, Shamshad, **5:**420, 533, 538
Béhague, Gerard H., **2:**93, 116, 320, 321, 398
Behjat al-Ruh (Ṣafi al-Din), **6:**75
Behrman, David, **3:**254
Behulā (epic), **5:**679
Beidelman, Thomas O., **1:**125
Beiderbecke, Bix, **3:**550
Beier, Ulli, **10:**114
Beierlein, Hans, **8:**679
Beijing Arts Academy, **7:**397
Beijing Dance Academy, **7:**62
Beijing Institute of Peking Opera, **7:**387
Beijing opera. *See* Peking opera
Beikman, Donald, **10:**129
Beinteinsson, Sveinbjörn, **8:**408
Beissel, Georg Conrad, **3:**904–6
Beissinger, Margaret, **8:**23
Béjart, Maurice, **2:**265
Beka-Record G.m.b.H., **4:**96, 483, 493
Bekebekmad, Johnny "B," **9:**160
Beken, Münir Nurettin, **6:**52
Bekker Codex, **2:**15
al-Bekri, **1:**75
Bel, Mbilia, **1:**425
Belafonte, Harry, **3:**809, 1202
Béland, Madeleine, **3:***1164*
Beland, Pier, **3:**1155
Bélanger, Daniel, **3:**1162
Belarus, **8:**790–804
    art music in, **8:**800
    blind musicians in, **8:**819
    Chernobyl, **8:**793
    geography of, **8:**790
    history of, **8:**790
    history of music in, **8:**799–800

instruments, **8:**796–99, 809–10
map of, **8:***752*
popular music in, **8:**801–3
population of, **8:**790
regions of, **8:**795–96
research on music of, **8:**803–4
state folk ensembles in, **8:**800
urban music in, **8:**800–803
vocal music, **8:**790–96
    collective wailing, **8:**793
Belarusan people
    in Estonia, **8:**491
    in Lithuania, **8:**509
    in North America, **3:**1082
    in Poland, **8:**701
    in Ukraine, **8:**821
Belarusan State Conservatory, **8:**803
Belasco, David, **9:**38
Belau National Museum Research Library, **9:**967
Beldeklel a Ngloik = Palauan Dance: The Process (film), **9:**47, 48
Bélè nou, **2:**919
Belep (New Caledonia), **9:**671
Belgium, **8:**518–36. *See also* Low Countries
    blind musicians in, **8:**532
    Brabant Province, minuet in, **8:**524
    dance traditions of, **8:**523–25, 535
    Flanders, **8:**12, 518
    Hainaut Province, bagpipe of, **8:**529
    instrument collections in, **8:**181
    instruments and instrumental music, **8:**170, 523–33, 535
    map of, **8:***516*
    popular music in, **8:**208
    population of, **8:**518
    research on music of, **8:**533–35
    vocal music of, **8:**136, 518–23
    Wallonia, **8:**12, 518, 534–35
        fife and drum ensembles in, **8:**528
    West-Vlaanderen Province, fife and drum ensembles in, **8:**528
Beliaev, Victor, **6:**903, 917, 918
"Believe Me If All Those Endearing Young Charms," **3:**182
Belisle, Raymond, **9:**976
Belí y sus Muchachos, **2:***852*
Belize, **2:**628, 630, 666–79
    creole music, **2:**677–79
    Garifuna culture, **2:**668–77, 733
    geography of, **2:**666
    history of, **2:**666–67
    map of, **2:***629*
    Maya culture, **2:**650–58, 667–68
    Mennonites in, **3:**1238
    musical genres
        brukdown, **2:**677–78
        cungo, **2:**678–79
    population of, **2:**666
    research on, **2:**679
Belize National Folklore Company, **2:**676
Belkacem, Sonia, **3:***1219*
Belkhayāt, Abd el-Wahab, **6:**269
Bell, Al, **3:**676, 678, 710
Bell, Diane, **9:**437
Bell Piano and Organ Co., **3:**1180
Bell, Robert, **3:**1180; **8:**337

Bell, Thom, **3:**711
Bell, William, **3:**676, 1180
Bella Bella (Heiltsuk) Indian nation, **3:**394
Bella Coola (Nuxalk) Indian nation, **3:**394
Bellamou, Messaoud, **6:**270
Bellboys (musical group), **8:**237
Belle of Newport (Johnson and Cole), **3:**608
Belle of New York (Kerker), **3:**193
belles soeurs, Les (Tremblay), **3:**1157
Bellini, Vincenzo, **3:**862, 1181; **4:**857
Bellman, Carl Michael, **8:**444
Bellman Quartet, **3:**1089
Bello, Haruna-Ishola, **1:**222
Bellona (Solomon Islands), **9:**833, 848–53
    Americans in, **9:**30
    children's music, **9:**267–69
    composition in, **9:**354
    geography of, **9:**848
    history of, **9:**852–53
    instruments, struck plaques, **9:**378
    music and dance of, **9:**850–53
    pati dance of, **9:**315
    performative concepts, **9:**849–50
    poetry, **9:**327, 328
        verbal meter in, **9:**324
    research on, **9:**853
    singing, falsetto, **9:**297
    social organization of, **9:**835
    struck plaques of, **9:**851
    suahongi genre, **9:**308–9
Bellosi, Giuseppe, **8:**607
Bellou, Sotiria, **8:**1020
bells and chimes
    adjá (also *sineta*), **2:**511, 515
    Africa, **1:**294, 295
        double, **1:**78
    agogô (also *agogo*)
        Africa, **1:**461, 476, 481, 485
        South America, **2:**308–9, 313, 330, 343, 346
    in Alaska churches, **3:**486
    Andhra Pradesh, **5:**901
    Apache Indian groups, **3:**431
    Arab world, **6:**404
    Argentina, **2:**249, 250, 260
    Aztec culture, **2:**602
    bell choir, **8:**101
    bells, animal
        Bahamas, **2:**803, 806–8
        Barbados, **2:**820
        Brazil, **2:**337
        cencerro, **2:**285, 414, 834–36
        ekón, **2:**826
        Europe, **8:**8, 142, 169
        Garifuna culture, **2:**677
        kaway, **2:**438
        Peru, **2:**476, 484
        Puerto Rico, **2:**933
        sinsiru, **2:**285, 291
    bianzhong (bell set), **7:**88, 98, 99–101, 108, 115–16, 117, 121, 137, 191, 431
    Bulgaria, **8:**894, 899
    campana, **2:**708
    campanilla, **2:**494
    carillons, **8:**170
    cascabeles, **8:**594

bells and chimes (*continued*)
Celtic culture, **8:**321
Central Africa, **1:**670
China, **7:**82, 88, *98*, 218, 336
chong, **7:**830
chuông báo chúng, **4:**504
chuông gia trì, **4:**467, 504
cìsi, **4:***376*
clarine, **8:**544
clopote, **8:**876
Corsica, **8:**572
crotals, **8:**615
dai hông chung, **4:**467, 504
Da people, **7:**499
daqing, **7:**330, *331*
dazhong, **7:**330
distribution of, **1:**308–11, 315; **8:**170
dôtaku, **7:**557, 560, *560*
dril-bu, **5:**714, *714*; **7:**1017
eduo, **7:**477
El Salvador, **2:**707, 708
Europe, **8:**168
fanxiang, **7:**191
France, **8:**544
genta, **4:**599–600, 619, 622
gentha (also *klinthing*, *byong*, *kempang delima*),
    4:644
gentorak, **4:**746, 750
ghol, **5:**728
ghunghrū (ankle bells), **5:**476, 494, 497, 498,
    506, 517, 646, 647, 648, 722, 727,
    728
Greece, **8:**1023
grelot, **8:**544
grung, **4:**590
Guatemala, **2:**724
Guinea coast, 1600s, **1:**83
gumanak, **4:**750
Guyana, **5:**605
honh, **7:**1017–18
Hungary, **8:**743
Ila people, **1:**712
Indian Shaker Church, **3:**488
Iran, **6:**825
iron, **3:**785
Italy, **8:**614, 615
Japan, **7:***551*
juljul, **6:**395
karinyan, **1:**489, 498
Karnataka, **5:**877
karong, **4:**590
kemanak, **4:**632, 642, 691, 750
khánh, **4:**468, 504
kicikan, **4:**625
Korea, **7:***826*, 872–73
kulekule, **9:**661
kyi-zi, **3:**954
linh, **4:**504
Lithuania, **8:**512
longa, **1:**667
Low Countries, **8:**525
Maharashtra, **5:**727
Malta, **8:**640
Manchu people, **7:**520, *520*
Mapuche culture, **2:**254
nao, **7:**107–9

naqus, **6:**489
nāqūs, **6:**215, *216*, 408
Native American types, **3:**475
    worn by dancers, **3:**456–57, 473, 484, 1079
Naxi people, **7:***513*
né, **1:**446
ngongi, **1:**712
njuga, **1:**638
nnawunta, **1:**211
nono, **1:**463
Oceania, **9:**371, 373–82, *374*
ogā, **1:**315
ogan, **2:**883
ol-tnalan, **1:**638
pangul (Korean bell tree), **7:**959
Plains Indian groups, **3:**445
p'yǒnjong (bell set), **7:**829, 862–63, 866, 867
rei, **7:**617
Réunion Island, **5:**607
šarkuny, **8:**797
shimolo, **1:**638
shouling, **7:**312, 323
shuangling, **7:**205
sjö, **5:**704
Slovenia, **8:**914, 919
South America, **2:**29
South Asia, **5:**248
Spain, **8:**593, 594
Sri Lanka, **5:**962
suzu, **7:**610
Switzerland, **8:**683, 684, *684*, 685
tambrin, **4:**625
Tanzania, **1:**638–39
taozhong, **7:**105
tatûm, **1:**311
temple, **5:**342
Tibet, **7:**479–80
tiěu chung, **4:**467
tintenelle, **8:**544
Tokelau, **9:**828
ton ito, **1:**654
Ukraine, **8:**816
Vietnam, **4:**446
Wayana culture, **2:**436
West Africa, **1:**446, 449
yong, **7:**107–9
zang-i kaftar, **5:**830
zhāng, **5:**782, 783
zhong, **7:**108, 312
zurgǎlǎi, **8:**876
zvanočak, **8:**797
zvon, **8:**797
Bells Band, **6:**284, *284*
Bellwood, Peter, **4:**37–38
Belnap, Jeffrey, **9:**972
Belo, Jane, **4:**733
Beltinška Banda (musical group), **8:**917, 921
Beltrán, Lola, **2:**623
Beltrán, Lupita, **3:**741
Belzner, William, **2:**431
Bemba people, **1:**671
    chisungu ritual, **1:**286
    dance, **1:**112, 117
    music of, **10:**29, 116, 120
    ngwayi drumming, **1:**312; **10:**111
    bembé, **3:**784, 785

Bembeya Jazz National, **1:**365
Bemelmans, Ludwig, **2:**423
"Be My Baby" (Ronettes), **3:**673
Ben, Zohava, **6:**1034, *1034*
Bena bena people, **9:**511, 526–33
Benade, Arthur B., **1:**190
Ben'aljīya, 'Abd al-Ḥamīd, **6:**329–30, 332, 336,
    512
Bena Luluwa people, **1:**217
Benary, Barbara, **3:**1014, 1016, 1018
Benayahu, M., **6:**1039
Benedict, Laura, **4:**872
Benedict, Paul, **4:**218
Benegal, Uday, **5:**428
Benesh notation, **9:**316–17, *461*, *466*
Ben Fāris, Muḥammad, **6:**651
Benfissa, **6:**270
Bengal (region), **5:**844–62. *See also* Bangladesh
    folk music of, **5:**859–62
    instruments in, **5:**328–29, 343, 344
    jātrā theater in, **5:**419, 486, 488–89, 503,
        505, 550
    partition of, **5:**436–37, 844, 849, 857
    views of music in, **5:**432
    vocal music
        ādhunik gīt, **5:**550, 854–55, 858
        bāul, **5:**436, 846, 850, 851, 853, 859–60
        dhrupad, **5:**250
        folk genres, **5:**859–62
        padāvali kīrtan, **5:**250, 253–54, 505,
            845–46
        patriotic songs, **5:**848–49, 852, 853–54,
            856–57
        Rabindra saṅgīt, **5:**550, 857
        śaktapada saṅgīt, **5:**846, 847
        tappā, **5:**847, 852, 853, 856
Bengali people, **5:**8–9
    in Great Britain, **5:**572–76; **8:**231, 236, 240
    in North America, **3:**981, 987; **5:**578
Bengal Music School (Calcutta), **5:**442–43
Benglong people. *See* De'ang people
Bengtsson, Ingmar, **8:**447–48
Ben-Haim, Paul, **6:**1027, 1029, 1066
Bénichou, Paul, **8:**554
Benin. *See also* West Africa; *specific peoples*
    drums, cord-and-peg tension, **1:**315–17
    historical studies, **1:**83–84, 86
    history of, **1:**422
    music of, **1:**458
    music research in, **1:**37
    popular music of, **1:**422
    Yoruba people, **1:**400, 459
        popular music of, **1:**471–87
Benin (kingdom), **1:**4, 5, 81–82, 316–17
Ben Ismā'īl, Shaykh Muḥammad, **6:**333, 335–36
Benítez, Joaquim, **7:**595
Benlolo, Jack, **3:**1173
Ben Mosh, Moshe, **6:**265
Bennani, Abdel Hadi, **6:**496
Bennett, Richard Bedford, **3:**296
Bennett, Tony, **3:**528, 862
Bennett, Wendell Clark, **2:**587
Bennett, Willie P., **3:**1080
Benny, Jack, **9:**149
Benny Moré Band, **2:**836
Benoit, Édouard, **2:**920

Benoit, Émile, **3:**1125, 1137
Benson, Bobby, **1:**46, 359, 477, 483
Bentoiu, Pascal, **8:**883
Bentsich-Yellin, Thelma, **6:**1025
Ben-Tsisi, Fordhaus, **6:**1025
Bentzon, Andreas Weis, **8:**622, 632
Benyamini, Daniel, **6:**1031
Benz, Albert, **8:**688
Benzoni, Giralmo, **2:**13, 748
Beothuk culture, **3:**1069
Béranger, Pierre-Jean, **8:**548
Beranič, Davorin, **8:**922
Berata, I Dewa Putu, **3:**1019
Berber peoples, **1:**443; **6:**273–77, 299, 429, 431,
        442, 1035. *See also specific groups*
    Algeria, **6:**466
    brotherhoods, **6:**437
    chordophones of, **6:**407, 408, 410
    dance, **1:**543
    drums of, **6:**419
    festivals, **1:**539
    history of, **1:**532–33
    idiophones of, **6:**404
    influence on Andalusian and European music,
        6:446
    languages of, **6:**429
    Morocco, **6:**483–90, 496, 1036
    music of, **1:**541–42, 547; **6:**300–301, 307,
        432
    oratorical matches, **6:**302–3
    popular music, **6:**273–77
    song motifs, **1:**135
    Tunisia, **6:**523
    wedding customs of, **1:**539; **6:**479–82
    writing system of, **1:**3
Bereczki, Gabor, **8:**773
Beregovsky, Moshe, **8:**772, 820, 822–23
Berendt, Joachim, **5:**56
Berg, Alban, **7:**348
Berg, Kirsten Bråten, **8:**430–31
Bergara, Jean, **8:**311
Berger, Carl, **3:**1058
Berger, Henry, **9:**132–33, 919, 923
Berggreen, Andreas Peter, **8:**461, 463
Bergheaud, Jean, **8:**550
Bergin, Mary, **8:**385
Bergman, Ingmar, **8:**434
Bergquist, Charles, **2:**411
Berico groups, **5:**794–95
Berik people, **9:**585
berimbau. See musical bows
Berio, Luciano, **8:**26, 85
Berioska (dance ensemble), **3:**1199
Berkeley Gamelan, **3:**1017
Berkenbaiuly, Estai, **6:**955
Berkmans, Father S. J., **5:**924
Berland, Jody, **3:**49, 52, 314, 315
Berlin, Edward, **3:**580
Berlin, Irving, **3:**12, 196, 261, 305, 310, 545,
        549, 651, 707, 938; **9:**26
Berlin Phonogramm-Archiv, **1:**50; **2:**251; **6:**23;
        8:18, 20; **9:**980–81
Berlin Phonogramm-Archiv Demonstration
        Collections (Indiana University), **9:**975
Berlin Singakademie, **8:**81
Berliner, Emile, **3:**243, 247, 265, 487, 1154

Berliner label, **3:**1077
Berliner, Paul, **1:**156, 746–47; **3:**587
Berlinskii, P., **7:**1013
Berlioz, Hector, **8:**83, 369
Bermuda Tavern (Toronto), **3:**1213
Bermudes, Pedro, **2:**735
Bermúdez, Egberto, **2:**31, 411, 412
Bermúdez, Lucho, **2:**102
Bernal, Paulino, **3:**777
Bernard, Henry, **8:**907
Bernard, Yves, **3:**1170
Berndt, Catherine H., **9:**437, 987
Berndt, R. M., **9:**440, 987
Berne Copyright Convention (1886), **3:**258, 289
Bernes, Mark, **8:**778
Bernice P. Bishop Museum (Hawai'i), **9:**24–25,
        729, 885, 921, 968–70, 997
Bernstein, Elmer, **3:**203; **9:**46
Bernstein, Leonard, **3:**197–98, 541, 545
Berroa, Ignacio, **3:**789
Berry, Chuck, **3:**348, 353, 552, 648, 672, 709,
        709, 840; **8:**214; **9:**137–38
Berry, Edwin, **3:**761, *761*, 763
Berry, Hyatt, **3:***260*
Berry, Keith, **9:**361
Bershadskaya, Tatyana, **8:**784
Berta people
    music of, **1:**551–52, 564–68
    tambura cult of, **1:**555
Bertini, Gary, **6:**1030
Bertolucci, Bernardo, **3:**204
Bertoni, Moisés, **2:**204
Bertonio, Ludovico, **2:**207, 467
Beruva caste, **5:**957, 961, 962
Berwald, Franz, **8:**444
Berwick, Thurso, **8:**371
Besançon, André, **8:**688, 697
Beslenevian people, **8:**854–56
Besmer, Fremont E., **1:**51
Besmil, Hassan, **5:**827, 829
Bessermian tribe, **8:**772
"Best of My Love" (Emotions), **3:**712
BET (U.S. television channel), **3:**586, 697, 712
Betab, Narain Prasad, **5:**487
Betancourt, Helia, **2:**704
Betancourt, Justo, **3:**743
"Betcha by Golly, Wow" (Stylistics), **3:**711
betel, **9:**177, 179, 602, 608, 636, 638
Betela Dance Troupe, **9:**901, *902*
Bété people, **1:**287, 469
Bethel Dramatic Society (Nigeria), **1:**403
Bethel, E. Clement, **2:**812
Bethencourt, Agustín, **2:**931
Beth-Gazō (collections), **6:**228
Bethune, Thomas Green Wiggins "Blind Tom,"
        3:605
Beti people, **1:**659–60
Betsileo people, **1:**783, 791
Betsimisaraka people, **1:**782
Betsin (Halia performer), **9:**640
Betta Kurumbas, **5:**287, 909
Better Days (New York), **3:**688
"Bewildered" (Brown), **3:**678
Bey (honorific). *See previous element in name*
Bey, Salome, **3:**1081, 1212
Beyâtî âyîn (Köçek Mustafa Dede), **6:**110

Beyāzid II. *See* Bayezid II, Ottoman sultan
Beyer, H. Otley, **4:**872
Beyiose (Ladipo), **1:**401
"Beyond the Reef" (Pitman), **3:**1050
Bezić, Jerko, **8:**937
B. G. Militia Band (Guyana), **2:**447
Bhagavad Gita, **3:**130
Bhāgavata Purāṇa, **5:**249, 263–64, 515, 633,
        897. *See also* Puranas
Bhagavatar, Harikesanallur Muthiah, **5:**394
Bhagavatar, Kalyanakrishna, **10:**41
Bhagavatar, Krishna, **5:**106, 270, 907–8
Bhagavatar, Narasimha, **5:**390, 391
Bhagavatar, Walajapet Krishnasvami, **5:**221
Bhagavatar, Walajapet Venkatarama, **5:**221
Bhagavati (deity), **5:**935–36
Bhagi, Mai, **5:**747
Bhagyachandra, king of Manipur, **5:**495
Bhagyalekshmy, S., **5:**46
Bhaironji (Shiva incarnation), **5:**641, 645
bhajan (also *bhajana*), **5:**11, 211, 249, 254–56,
        267–68, 401
    classification of, **5:**724
    composed by Tirunal, **5:**229
    concerts of, **5:**420
    Fiji
        bhajan kavvali, **5:**613, 614; **9:**93
        tambūrā bhajan, **5:**613–14
    film-song versions of, **5:**533, 534
    Gujarat, **5:**630–32
    Guyana, **2:**444; **5:**602–3, 605
    Indo-Caribbean people, **2:**85–86
    influence on Hindustani tradition, **5:**246
    instruments in, **5:**347, 364, 425
    Karnataka, **5:**867, 869
    Kerala, **5:**935, 947
    Madhya Pradesh, **5:**724
    Maharashtra, **5:**729
    Nepal, **5:**702
    nirguṇa, **5:**253, 345, 655, 671, 724
    North America, **5:**579, 581, 582
    Orissa, **5:**732
    performance contexts of, **5:**284
    performers of, **5:**425–26
    pop, **5:**255, 548–49
    Punjab (Pakistan), **5:**772
    raga in, **5:**89, 105–6
    Rajasthan, **5:**642–43, 645, 646
    Réunion Island, **5:**608
    Singapore, **4:**521
    South Africa, **5:**617–18
    sung at funerals, **5:**273
    Tamil Nadu, **5:**909, 918, 923–24
    Trinidad and Tobago, **2:**958; **5:**590
    United Kingdom, **5:**573, 575
    use of *śloka*, **5:**262
    Uttar Pradesh, **5:**664, 674
    women performers of, **5:**410, 411, 414, 416
Bhajan, Yogi, **5:**256
bhakti, **5:**2, 11, 76, 246, 247, 248, 256, 306
    avatar doctrine of, **5:**486
    Bāul sect, **5:**503
    as codified emotion, **5:**72, 101, 313
    dance in, **5:**518
    dhrupad performance in, **5:**163
    in Gujarat, **5:**629

bhakti (continued)
  influence on *kathak* dance, **5:**493
  in Kerala, **5:**929
  in Maharashtra, **5:**728–29
  musical genres of, **5:**220–30, 250, 254–56
  Orissa, **5:**732
  poetry, **5:**765–66
  in Punjab (Pakistan), **5:**772
  in Rajasthan, **5:**643
  in South India, **5:**15, 96, 106, 209, 260–61, 263–70
  in Uttar Pradesh, **5:**250–52
  women devotees, **5:**416
Bhaktivedanta, Swami Prabhupada, A. C., **5:**255
Bhāṇḍ (also Bhāṅḍ) caste, **5:**639, 640, 765
Bhanghī caste, **5:**639
bhangra, **5:**500, 506, 540, 574, 650–52, 656
  in Europe, **8:**207, 232, 236, 240–41
  in North America, **3:**73, 218, 337, 812, 982, 984, 1064, 1084, 1205; **5:**579, 584, 652
  in Pakistan, **5:**426–27
  research on, **5:**576
  in Singapore, **4:**521
  in United Kingdom, **5:**550, 568, 573, 574–75, 652
Bhanumathi, P., **5:**421
Bharain caste, **5:**476
Bharanpurkar, Govind Rao, **5:***207*
Bharata, **5:**314
  Nāṭyaśāstra, **5:**18, 25–30, 104, 262, 298, 372, 633, 731
    on audience contribution, **5:**470
    as basis for later treatises, **5:**43
    dance in, **5:**299, 363, 509, 515, 519, 521
    description of, **5:**23–24
    information on *mridangam*, **5:**356
    information on performers, **5:**228, 399
    instrument classification in, **5:**51, 319, 320, 321–26, 327, 329, 350, 351
    nātya concept in, **5:**507–8
    raga theory in, **5:**73–75
    rasa theory in, **5:**71–72, 313, 317
    references to temple dancers, **5:**408
    on *śruti*, **5:**67
    tala theory in, **5:**110, 139, 140–41
    theater in, **5:**480, 484, 492
Bharataśvarabāhubali (Salibhadra), **5:**637
Bharatayuddha (epic), **4:**756
Bharathi Kala Manram, **3:**1084, 1216
Bharathi, Subramania, **5:**437, 911
Bharati, Gopalakrishna, **5:**390
Bharatiya Kala Kendra (Delhi), **5:**381
Bharatiya Sangeet Vidyalaya (Baroda), **5:**443
Bharatiya Vidya Bhavan (London), **5:**576
Bhasa, **5:**484
Bhāṭ caste. *See* Bāroṭ caste
Bhatkhande Music College (Lucknow), **5:**134, 444, 447
Bhatkhande, Vishnu Narayan, **5:**56, 380, 444, 448
  Hindustānī Saṅgīt-Paddhati, **5:**46, 52, 445–46
  Kramik Pustak-Mālikā, **5:**46, 52
  ṭhāṭ system, **5:**67, 78–79, 445
  on time/raga associations, **5:**69
Bhatra people, **5:**720

Bhatt, Balwant Rae, **5:**466
Bhatt, Vishwa Mohan, **3:**339; **5:**207, 466–67, 529
Bhatta, Sri Krishna Caitanya, **5:**252, *252*
Bhattacarya, Kamalakanta, **5:**846
Bhattacharya, Ajay, **5:**855
Bhattacharya, Anil, **5:**855
Bhattacharya, Dhananjay, **5:**857
Bhattacharya, Pannalal, **5:**857
Bhaumakar dynasty, **5:**731
Bhavabhuti, **5:**484
Bhavāī community, **5:**476, 647
Bhavani, **5:**103
Bhave, Ashwini, **5:**421
Bhengu, John "Phuzhushukela," **1:**776, 779
Bheru (deity), **5:**292
Bhīl people, **5:**639, 646–47, 719, 720, 727
Bhilal people, **5:**720
Bhirāīn group, **5:**766–69, 771
Bhomiyaji (deity), **5:**645
Bhopā community, **5:**345, 640, 646, *647*
Bhosle, Asha, **5:**412, 414, 420, 421, 537, 538
Bhote (also Bhotiya) people, **5:**5, 501
Bhujangy (musical group), **5:**426
Bhumij people, **5:**732
Bhutan
  Buddhism in, **5:**12, 489
  geography of, **5:**489
  gzhas songs, **5:**710
  history of, **5:**489
  instrumental ensembles in, **5:**715
  King Ge-sar epic in, **5:**712
  languages of, **5:**5
  Mahayana Buddhism in, **5:**257
  map of, **5:***3, 680*
  musical repertoires in, **5:**715
  population of, **5:**5
  religion in, **5:**10, 489
  theater in, **5:**489
  Tibetan culture in, **5:**709–16
  Tibetan monasteries in, **5:**713
Bhutto, Zulfikar Ali, **5:**747
Biafra Armed Forces Entertainment Band, **1:**241
Biagiola, Sandro, **8:**622
Biak, **4:**138
Bialy Orzel (musical group), **3:**1197
Bianchi, Pietro, **8:**695
Bian guan diao (xiaodiao), **7:**152
Bianti xinsuiling (Liu arrangement), **7:**229
Biarbieraŭ, Uladzimir, **8:**801
BIBAK (Filipino organization), **3:**1026
Bibayak people, **1:**256
Bibb, Leon, **3:**1212
Bibbo, **5:**533
Biber, Heinrich, **8:**78, 654
Bible Chorus (Palestine), **6:**1025
Bible, instrumental music descriptions in, **8:**258
bibliographies
  African research, **1:**49
  China, **7:**136, 139
  Korea, **7:**856, 990
Biblioteca del Orfeo Catalá (Barcelona), **8:**602
Bibliothèque St.-Sulpice (Montréal), **3:**33, 146
Bichevskaya, Zhanna, **8:**767, 779
Bickert, Ed, **3:**1080, 1107
"Bicycle Built for Two" (Dacre), **3:**549

Bid'a, **6:**297
Bidayuh people, **4:**823, 824
  instruments of, **4:**829, 833, 835, 836
Bidde, Axmed Suleebaan, **1:**620
Bidyalankorn, prince of Thailand (Bidyalankarana), **4:**223, 259, 298
Biebuyck, Daniel, **1:**121
Biermann, Wolf, **8:**289, 662
Bigard, Barney, **3:**652
Big Band Combo, **3:***806*
Big Chill (film), **3:**204
Big Dish (musical group), **8:**369
Big Dudes, **1:**779
Bigger and Deffer (LL Cool J), **3:**713
Bigelow, Janie Rice, **4:**511
Biggie Smalls, **3:**698
Biggs, Bruce, **9:**968, 976
Biggs, Fred, **9:**441
Big Maybelle, **3:**646
BigO (periodical), **4:**523
Big Tabar (Papua New Guinea), **9:**628–29
Big Tyme (Heavy D. & the Boyz), **3:**713
biguine. See beguine
Bihar
  bidesia theater in, **5:**485
  birahā genre of, **5:**666–69
  chau dance-drama of, **5:**497
  dance traditions of, **5:**502
  immigrants to Guyana, **5:**600–605
  instruments in, **5:**120, 345
  map of, **5:***658*
  Mithila region, **5:**677–79
  regional cassettes in, **5:**550
  Singhbum princely state, **5:**497
Bihari, János, **8:**273, 737
Bihjat al-Rūḥ (anon.), **6:**183
Bikini Kill (musical group), **3:**358
Bikol people, **4:**907
Bilaan people, **4:**920
Bilādī, Bilādī (Darwīsh), **6:**598
Bilāl, **6:**362
Bilal Nazim, **6:**1003
Bilhanā (shaving song), **6:**589
Billah, **5:**768
Billava caste, **5:**885
Billboard (periodical), **3:**316, 338, 347, 351, 560, 618, 678, 688, 689, 709, 713; **8:**211, 224
Bill & Brod, **4:**106
Bill Haley and the Comets (musical group), **3:**353, 354; **8:**217
Billings, William, **3:**25, 44, 275, 531, *532*
Billy Bishop Goes to War (Gray), **3:**199
Billy Idol, **8:**215
Billy, Rokucho, **9:**92
Billy the Kid (Copland), **3:**14
Billy Ward and the Dominoes, **3:**351, 354
Biloxi Indian nation, **3:**466
Bilson, Francis Sinbad, **10:**33
Bimba, Mestre (*capoeira* master), **2:**346
Bime people, **9:**982
Binandere people
  ario dance of, **9:**499–501
  composition of, **9:**358–60

dance-dramas of, **9**:489
kundu ensembles, **9**:489
songs of, **9**:491
Binchois, Gilles, **8**:518; **10**:129
Binder, Abraham W., **3**:939
Bindi, Umberto, **8**:619
Binet, Jocelyne, **3**:1151
Bingham, Hiram, **9**:923
Binglue lucun (Yuan), **7**:374
Binhi ng Kalayaan (Pájaro), **4**:875
Binjhal people, **5**:732
Binkley, Thomas, **6**:24
Binneas is Boreraig (Ross), **8**:374
Binumarien people, **9**:526–33
Biocca, Ettore, **2**:155
Biograhies of Accomplished Artists (Thailand),
    4:225
Biography of King Gesa'er (Tibetan writing),
    7:472
Biography of Milariba (Tibetan writing), **7**:472
Biography of Poluonai (Tibetan writing), **7**:472
Biotzetik Basque Choir, **3**:849
Birch Mountain Boys, **3**:1133
bird calls. *See* animal imitations and
    representations
Bird, Charles S., **1**:491–92, 494–95, 498, 509
Bird of Paradise (Broadway musical), **9**:390
Bird of Paradise (film), **3**:1049; **9**:44
Birgui, Gonga Sarki (Kutin performer), **1**:654
Birifor people, **1**:451–52, 457
Birket-Smith, Kaj, **3**:381
Birmingham Conservatoire, **5**:576
Birth of a Nation (film), **3**:203
Biruba (Shiva incarnation), **5**:728
Birzhan and Sara (Tulebaev), **6**:959
Birzhan-Sara (epic), **6**:954
Bishop, Charles Reed, **9**:968
Bishop, Dalton "Manface" (Jackie Opel), **2**:820
Bishop, Maurice, **2**:865, 867, 868
Bishop Museum. *See* Bernice P. Bishop Museum
    (Hawai'i)
Bishop, Princess Bernice Pauahi, **9**:275
Bisirkhoev family, **8**:862
Bismam Asmat people, **9**:580, 583, 590
Bismarck Archipelago (Papua New Guinea),
    4:38; **9**:475, 600
    Lapita cultural complex in, **9**:2, 4
    music and dance of, **9**:981
Bisnauth, Dale, **2**:445
Bisquera, Leon, **3**:748
Bisser (musical group), **3**:1198
Bissoondath, Neil, **3**:73
Biswas, Anil, **5**:420
Biswas, Hemanga, **5**:857
Bitches Brew (Davis), **3**:663
Bit of Fear, A (film). *See Shay' mīn al-Khauf*
biwa. See lutes
Biwagaku Kyôkai (*biwa* society), **7**:649
Biwa syo tyôsi bon (*biwa* score), **7**:588
Bizet, Georges, **2**:831; **3**:791; **7**:743; **8**:367, 550
Biz Markie, **3**:699, 714
Bjelo Dugme (musical group), **8**:969
Björk, **8**:216
Björling, Jussi, **8**:434
Blablanga people, **9**:657–59
Black 47 (musical group), **3**:326

Black and Blue (musical), **3**:621
Black and Tan Fantasy (Ellington), **3**:654
Black Artists Group (St. Louis), **3**:662
Black Bart (pirate), **3**:1070
Black Bear Dance (Kazakh piece), **7**:461
Blackboard Jungle (film), **3**:353; **8**:217, 430
"Black Bottom Stomp" (Morton), **3**:653
Black Brothers (musical group), **9**:155, 986
Black, Clint, **3**:97
Black Consciousness Movement, **1**:777
Black Crook (musical comedy), **3**:193
Black Crowes (musical group), **3**:348
Black Death, **8**:248
Black List Workshop, **7**:358
Black Music Research Journal, **3**:581
Black Nationalism and the Revolution in Music
    (Kofsky), **3**:663
Black Nativity (musical), **3**:621
"Black Night" (Brown), **3**:669
Black Patti label, **3**:707
Black Patti Troubadours, **3**:618
Black Perspective in Music (periodical), **3**:581
Black Power movement, **3**:507, 512, 583, 663,
    674, 676, 678, 680, 683–84, 710
Black Rose (musical group), **7**:1020
Black Sabbath (musical group), **3**:357; **8**:215
Black Stalin (calypsonian), **2**:964
Black Swan label, **3**:609, 707
Black Tai people, **4**:526, 527, 529, 536, 537
Blackburn, Stuart H., **5**:673
blackface minstrelsy, **3**:61, 66–67, 68, 71, 182,
    184–86, 510, 542–44, 565, 573,
    615–16, 643, 839
    African-American performers, **3**:192, 543, 616,
        1133
    banjo in, **3**:77, 184, 836, 838
    British reception of, **3**:831
    in California, **3**:735
    in Canada, **3**:198, 1080
    characters in, **3**:543, 651
    folk music in, **3**:146, 837–38
    influence on musicals, **3**:194
    influence on vaudeville, **3**:544
    Jewish performers, **3**:938
    later groups, **3**:191–93
    show structure, **3**:185
    social class and, **3**:45, 46–47, 48, 185
    songs adapted for political campaigns, **3**:306,
        310
    in South Africa, **1**:351, 764–65, 770
    women performers, **3**:191
    Yukon, **3**:1277
Blackfoot Indian Musical Thought (Nettl), **3**:511
Blackfoot Indian nation, **3**:440, 445, 484, 492,
    511, 1085; **10**:41
Blackhall, Andro, **8**:367
Blacking, John, **1**:51, 54, 64, 708, 722; **4**:13,
    14; **8**:394; **10**:28–29, 60, 120, 129,
    164
    principle of harmonic equivalence, **1**:715, 742
Blackstone, Milton, **3**:1184
Blackwell, Scrapper, **3**:645
Blades, Rubén, **3**:732, 743, 789, 797, 799
Blaise, Michel, **2**:784
Blak, Kristian, **8**:472, *472*
Blake, Arthur "Blind," **3**:644, 707

Blake, Eubie, **3**:194, 619–20
Blake, James W., **3**:549
Blake, Michael, **3**:525
Blake, Seamus, **3**:1107
Blakeley, Phyllis, **3**:1069
Blakely, David, **3**:565
Blakely, Pamela, **1**:670
Blakey, Art, **3**:660, 662, 664
Blanchard, Terence, **3**:664
Blanchet, Jacques, **3**:1156
Blanck, Hubert de, **2**:837
Blanco, Ricardo, **2**:704
Bland, Bobby "Blue," **3**:583, 647
Bland, James, **3**:192, 543, 616
Blassingame, John, **3**:585
Blå Tåget, **8**:216
Blazonczyk, Eddie, **3**:894
Bibliothèque National du Québec (Montréal),
    3:289
Bledsoe, Jules, **3**:609
Blekbala Mujik, **9**:145, 146, 445, 446, 987
Blench, R., **1**:605
Blesh, Rudi, **3**:580; **10**:111
Bless (musical group), **8**:407
"Blessed Assurance" (Crosby), **3**:533
Bley, Carla, **10**:87
Bley, Paul, **3**:1077, 1107
Blige, Mary J., **3**:701
Bligh, Captain William, **9**:34
Blind Louis, **3**:1075
blind or handicapped musicians
    Belarus, **8**:819
    Belgium, **8**:532
    China, **7**:258, 269, 305, 403
    Europe, **8**:99
    Iran, **6**:140
    Italy, **8**:143, 611
    Japan, **7**:82, 644–45, 649, 687, 691, 693,
        696, 712, 716, 755–56, 757–58, 764,
        777, 778
    Korea, **7**:965
    Macedonia, **8**:975
    North America, **3**:640
    Serbia, **8**:942
    South Asia, **5**:671
    Taiwan, **7**:358, 424
    Uganda, **10**:113, 114–15
    Ukraine, **8**:809, 813–16, 819, 820
    Uzbekistan, **6**:899, *899*
Blind Pig (Champaign club), **3**:170–71
"Blind Tom." *See* Bethune, Thomas Green
    Wiggins
Blinde-Rasmus, **8**:419
Blinky and the Roadmasters, **2**:970
Bliss-Giving River Grand Song Cycle (Xiao et al.),
    7:387
Bliss, Philip P., **3**:534
Blitzstein, Marc, **3**:45, 545–46
Bloch, David, **6**:1063
Bloch, Ernest, **3**:939; **6**:1027; **8**:252, 264
Bloch, Maurice, **1**:790
Block, Julius, **8**:764
Blok, Aleksandr, **8**:777
Blomdahl, Karl-Birger, **8**:445
Blondie (musical group), **3**:357, 552; **4**:887
Blondy, Alpha, **8**:239

Blood and Sand (film), **3:**203
Blood, Sweat, and Tears (musical group), **3:**356
Bloom, Harry, **1:**219
Blow, Curtis, **3:**714
"Blowin' in the Wind" (Dylan), **3:**316, 552
Blowsnake, Sam, **3:**26
"Blueberry Hill" (Domino), **3:**552, 709
Blue Boy (calypsonian), **2:**963
bluegrass, **1:**361; **3:**149, 158–68, 520; **8:**204
    Anglo-Irish traditional influences in, **3:**43, 159, 325
    banjo in, **3:**77
    in British Columbia, **3:**1258
    in Canada, **3:**411, 1080, 1133
    economics of, **3:**263
    genres of, **3:**164
    history of, **3:**161–63
    insider conceptions of, **3:**160–61
    musical system of, **3:**163–64
    music and creativity in, **3:**167–68
    polka and, **3:**894
    research on, **3:**159
Blue Grass Boys, **3:**158–59, *159*, 161, 163
"Blue Grass Stomp" (Monroe), **3:**168
"Blue Hawaii," **9:**43
Blue Hawaii (film), **3:**1049; **9:**43, 1007
"Blue Moon of Kentucky" (Monroe), **3:**167
Blue Nile (musical group), **8:**369
Blue Note label, **3:**659
Blue Rhythm Combo, **2:**820
Blue Rhythm Syncopators, **1:**765
blues, **3:**10, 146, 325, 510, 524–25, 577, 601, 637–49. *See also* rhythm and blues
    art music and, **3:**609
    in Australia, **9:**143
    in Austria, **8:**675, 676
    in Barbados, **2:**819
    bar band, **3:**350
    barrelhouse piano style, **3:**646
    bluegrass and, **3:**160
    Canadian Aboriginal, **3:**1063
    club, **3:**350
    copyright problems in, **3:**705
    in Costa Rica, **2:**691
    country music influenced by, **3:**48, 520
    economics of, **3:**263
    in Europe, **8:**228
    field hollers and, **3:**85
    funk and, **3:**680, 684
    gospel music and, **3:**631–32
    in Guatemala, **2:**733
    historical background and context, **3:**637–40
    honky-tonk, **3:**648
    hula, **3:**337
    influence on heavy metal, **3:**357
    instruments used in, **3:**638, 641
    jazz and, **3:**650
    jump, **3:**350, 646, 668, 669
    Métis, **3:**411, 1087
    musical theater and, **3:**622
    Native American, **3:**345
    popularization of, **3:**643–44
    race and, **3:**63
    recordings, **3:***263*, 330, 579–80, 582, 706
    research on, **3:**579–80, 582–83, 587
    role in American popular music, **3:***647*, 648

role in folk revival, **3:**316
soul, **3:**647
styles of, **3:**103–4, 524, 578, 579, 707
Subarctic consumers, **3:**391
texts of, **3:**641
women performers of, **3:**96, 103–6, 578, 644, 707
"Blues at Sunrise" (Moore), **3:**669
Blue Silver Records, **8:**241
"Blue Skies" (Berlin), **3:**196, 549
"Blue Skirt Waltz" (Yankovic), **3:**902
Blue Sky Boys (musical group), **3:**78
Blues News (periodical), **8:**484
Blues People: Negro Music in White America
    (Jones), **3:**582, 663
"Blue Yodel" (Rodgers), **3:**78
Blum, Joseph, **3:**516
Blum, Stephen, **6:**24
Blume, Hermann, **8:***185*
Blumenbach, J. F., **1:**85
Blumenthal, Eileen, **4:**25
Blumenthal label, **6:**758
Blyden, Edward Wylmot, **1:**16–17
Blythman, Morris, **8:**371
BMG Corporation, **2:**107; **3:**244, 264, 1161
BMI. *See* Broadcast Music, Inc.
Bmus idh-dhahabiyyih (shaving song), **6:**589
Bnei Akiva youth movement, **6:**202
Bni Battu people, **1:**133
Board of Music Trade, **3:**257, 258
Boardwalk Records, **3:**748
Boas, Franz, **3:**31, 71, 291, 381, 444, 509, 511
Boateng, Geoffrey, **1:**26
Boateng, Otto, **1:**26
Boatner, Edward, **3:**606, 607
Boazi people, **9:**489
Bobbili Yuddha Katha, **5:**898
Bob Boyd and the Red River Playboys, **3:**1091
Bobby Amos Orchestra, **3:**741
Bob Marley and the Wailers, **2:**97
Bobo people, **1:**119
Bobo, Willie, **3:**733, 748, 787, 797
Bobowski, Wojciech. *See* Ufki Bey, Ali
Bocanegra, Juan Pérez, **2:**469
Boccaccio (von Suppé), **7:**743
Bocca, Julio, **2:**265
Bock, Jerry, **3:**943
Bocobo, Jorge, **4:**872
"Bo Diddley," **3:**672, 709
Bodie, Kirkland "K.B.", **2:**806
Bodmann, Maria, **3:**1020
Body, Jack, **9:**929, *931*
body percussion. *See also* hand clapping
    Australia, **9:**411, 427, 431, *433*, 446
    Borneo, **4:**826–27
    Chuuk, **9:**736, 737
    Cook Islands, **9:**899–900
    corpophone classification, **2:**31
    Guadeloupe, *bouladjèl* (mouth drum), **2:**875
    Hawai'i, **9:**928
    Kiribati, **9:**761, 762
    Kosrae, **9:**741–42
    Manihiki, **9:**906, 907
    Marquesas Islands, **9:**892, 894

Marshall Islands, **9:**751
Micronesia, **9:**716, 718
New Caledonia, **9:**674, 685
Oceania, **9:**247, 345, 371, 581–82
Papua New Guinea, **9:**563
Philippines, **4:**852
Polynesia, **9:**769
Sāmoa, **9:**104, 805
slapping, **9:**243
Solomon Islands, **9:**332–34
Sumatra, **4:**604, 605, 611, 613
Takuu, **9:**839
Tonga, **9:**11, 793
Vanuatu, **9:**695, 703–4, 708
West Timor, **4:**797
Boe, George, **9:**361, 692
Boers, history of, **1:**705
Boethius, **8:**69, 92
Bogan, Lucille, **3:**104
Bogdan, Zvonko, **3:**922
Boggs, Garrido, **2:**862
Boggs, Stanley, **2:**719
Boggs, Vernon W., **2:**839, 941
Boghigian, George K., **3:***1033*
Boghosian, Edward, **3:***1033*
Bogle, Eric, **8:**372
Bohannan, Paul, **1:**50
Bohee, George, **3:**1133
Bohee, James, **3:**1133
Bohème (album), **8:**225
Bohemia. *See* Czech Republic
Bohemian Girl (Balfe), **3:**61, 181
Bohemian Kingdom, **8:**716
Bohlman, Philip V., **3:**147, 828, 888; **8:**267;
    10:157–66, *159*, *162–64*
Böhme, Franz Magnus, **8:**656, 663
Bohor I (Xenakis), **4:**131
Bohra people, in Sri Lanka, **5:**954
Bohur al-Alḥān (Persian treatise), **6:**60
Boieldieu, Adrien-Louis, **3:**1148
Boigu Island (Australia), **9:**61
Boiko, Mārtiņš, **8:**507
Boilès, Charles, **2:**555, 623; **10:**56
Boislaville, Loulou, **2:**916
Boîte à Musique (record label), **8:**553
Bokilo, Jean, **1:**669
Bokwe, John Knox, **1:**216, 218, 763
Bolahenk Nûrî Bey, **6:**110, 119
Bolaños, César, **2:**32, 207, 215, 467; **10:**100
Bolcom, William, **3:**541
Bolden, Buddy, **3:**651
Bolduc, Madame (La), **3:**33, 94, 1154, 1166
Bolemba people, **1:**681–82, 695–96
bolero, **2:**102
    in Brazil, **2:**330, 331
    in Chile, **2:**372
    in Costa Rica, **2:**691
    in Cuba, **2:**829, 832, 834, 835, 836
    in Dominican Republic, **2:**860, 861–62
    in Ecuador, **2:**428
    in Mexico, **2:**619, 620
    in North America, **3:**737, 739, 775, 781, 793, 795
    in Peru, **2:**487
    in Puerto Rico, **2:**940
    in Virgin Islands, **2:**970

Boleyn, Anne, **8:**367
Bolick, Bill, **3:**78
Bolick, Earl, **3:**78
Bolívar, Father Juan, **4:**842
Bolívar, Simón, **2:**245, 387, 793
Bolivia, **2:**282–98. *See also specific peoples*
  acculturation in, **2:**293, 296–98
  aesthetics in, **2:**294–96
  archaeomusicological studies in, **2:**7, 11
  copyright issues in, **2:**65
  dance in, **2:**291–92
  early cities of, **2:**81
  geography of, **2:**137, 282
  Guaraní culture, **2:**199–204
  history of, **2:**245, 282–84, 356–57
  instruments of, **2:**31, 33, 34, 284–88
  Japanese people in, **2:**86–87; **10:**99, 102
  Moxo culture, **2:**137–42
  musical genres, **2:**289–91
    huayño, **2:**297
    north-south distinctions, **2:**222
    Roman Catholic, **2:**284
    saya, **2:**293, 297
    taquirari, **2:**297
    tropical music, **2:**293, 297
  performers' roles, **2:**292–93
  population of, **2:**282
  Potosí, **2:**284
  pre-Columbian, **2:**282–83
  Quechua- and Aymara-speaking peoples,
    2:205–23
  Sucre (La Plata), **2:**284
  tropical-forest region of, **2:**123–35
Bolivian people, in Chile, **2:**84
Bolle-Zemp, Sylvie, **8:**847
Bollig, P. Laurentius, **9:**737
Bolstad, Per Mathiasen, **8:**419
Bolwell, Jan, **9:**948–51
bombal plena, **2:**936–37, 941; **3:**337, 726, 727,
    799
  in Costa Rica, **2:**695–97
  in Ecuador, **2:**415, 425
  in El Salvador, **2:**711
Bombay Sisters, **5:**232, 424
Bon religion, **5:**709
Bonaire, **2:**789, 927. *See also* Netherlands
    Antilles
Bonamore, Alessandra, **2:**704
Bonanni, Filippo, **1:**319
Bonan people, **7:**455–58
Bonch-Bruevich, Vladimir, **3:**1270
Bondei people, **1:**639
Bonds, Gary "US," **3:**709
Boner, Packy, **8:**381
Bone Squash Diavolo (burlesque), **3:**61
Bone, Thugs-N-Harmony (musical group),
    3:702
Bonet, Carlos, **2:**540
Bonfiglioli, Carlo, **2:**573
Bonga, Kuenda, **1:**435
Bongo people, **1:**570
bongos (bongo drums). *See* drums: barrel,
    conical, or cylindrical
Boni (Maroon) culture, **2:**158, 163, 164,
    438–39, 504–6. *See also* Aluku culture
Bonifačić, Ruža, **8:**937

Bonne Chanson, La (series), **3:**148, 279, 1088,
    1155, 1167
Bonner, Simon, **3:**1110
"Bonnie Blue Flag" (Macarthy), **3:**188
Bono, S., **4:**683
Bontok people
  instrumental music of, **4:**914–16, 919
  vocal music of, **4:**920
Bonus, Ladislao, **4:**857, 859, 863, 869, 871
Boodram, Sharlene, **5:**591–92
Boogie Boys (musical group), **3:**696
"Boogie Chillen" (Hooker), **3:**708
Boogie Down Productions, **3:**695, 699, 700, 714
"Boogie Nights" (Heatwave), **3:**685
"Boogie Oogie Oogie" (Taste of Honey), **3:**712
boogie-woogie, **3:**350, 646–47, 667, 668, 670
  in Oceania, **9:**25, 90, 139, 149, 156, 387
Booker T. and The MGs, **3:**675, 675–76, 710
Book of American Negro Spirituals (Johnson),
    3:607
Book of Common Prayer, **3:**123
Book of Hawaiian Melodies (King), **9:**919, 922
Book of the Kuzari (Ha-Levy), **6:**9
Book of Odes. See Shijing
Book of Rites. See Liji
Boomtown Rats (musical group), **8:**216
Boone, Hubert, **8:**535–36
Boone, Pat, **3:**317, 352
Boonyong Gatekong, **4:**128
Boorji, Miskin, **6:**735
Boorstin, Daniel, **3:**511
Boos Brothers Cafeteria (Los Angeles), **3:**740
Boosey and Hawkes, **3:**284
Bootsy's Rubber Band, **3:**684
Bor, Joep, **5:**55, 307
Bora, Tanil, **6:**247
Bora Bora (Society Islands), **9:**867
  dance of, **9:**878–79
  Europeans in, **9:**41
Boral, Rai Chand, **5:**536, 855, 856
Boras, Kostas, **9:**73
Boratav, Pertev Naili, **6:**845
Borden, David, **3:**254
border crossings. *See* fusion genres and border
    crossings
Borders Books and Music (Rochester), **3:**269–71
Bordón, Luís, **2:**456
Borduas, Paul-Emile, **3:**1147
Borenius-Lähteenkorva, A. A., **8:**488
Borgolla family, **2:**835
Borgu (kingdom), **1:**452
Bori, Lucrezia, **3:**607
Borinquen, **2:**78, 846, 932
Borkin, Benjamin A., **3:**294
Borneo, **4:**823–37. *See also* Brunei; Indonesia;
    Malaysia; *specific peoples*
  Arabs in, **4:**890
  cultural relationships with southern
    Philippines, **4:**889, 898, 924
  geography of, **4:**823
  gong-chime ensembles in, **4:**20, 596
  Hoabinhian culture in, **4:**34
  instrumental music of, **4:**11, 828–37
  map of, **4:**824
  music research on, **4:**27, 29
  population of, **4:**823–25

prehistoric, **4:**33, 37–38
revival movement in, **4:**126
stamped tube ensembles in, **4:**597
tourism in, **4:**138–39
urbanization of, **4:**115
village life in, **4:**6
vocal music, **4:**825–28
Born in East L.A. (film), **3:**777
"Born in the U.S.A." (Springsteen), **3:**552
Börnstein, F., **9:**479
Bornu empire, **1:**4, 447, 449. *See also* Kanem-
    Bornu kingdom
Borobudur label, **4:**681
Borodin, Alexander, **8:**781, 981
Boromokot, king of Ayuthaya, **4:**255
Boromtrailokanart, king of Khmer, **4:**252
borrowing. *See* composition
Borrowing the Plantain Fan (Cantonese opera),
    7:308
Borsai, Ilona, **6:**20
Borsboom, Adrianus P., **9:**418
Bortnyansky, Dmitry, **8:**780
Börtz, Daniel, **8:**445
Borumand, Nur'ali, **6:**139
Borus, Shankar Shripad, **5:**466
Borzunāma (epic), **6:**344
Bosco, Mwenda-Jean, **1:**222, 322, 359, 366, 423,
    608, 672; **10:**118
Boskaljon, Rudolf Frederik Willem, **2:**931
Boskovitch, Alexander U., **6:**1027–28, *1028*,
    1029, 1031
Boškov, Todor, **8:**981
Bosman, William, **1:**82–83
Bosnia-Hercegovina, **8:**962–70
  art music in, **8:**969
  dance traditions of, **8:**963
  Dinaric Alps, **8:**962
  "ethnic cleansing" of, **8:**11, 962
  ethnicization of music in, **8:**10
  folk music of, **8:**962–63
  geography of, **8:**962
  history of, **8:**962–63
  instruments, **8:**959–60, 966–67
    Asian derivations of, **8:**168
  map of, **8:**866
  Muslims in, **8:**11, 957, 962, 963, 964–68
  popular music in, **8:**963, 969
  population of, **8:**962
  research on music of, **8:**970
  Rom people in, **8:**279–80, 966
  Sephardic Jews in, **8:**262–63, 962, 967,
    968
  state folk ensembles in, **8:**968–69
  Sufism in, **6:**107, 115
  urban music in, **8:**964–66
  vocal music, **8:**195, 664, 958, 959
    epic songs, **8:**94, 130–31, 198
    ganga, **8:**112, 964, *966*
    na bas, **8:**943
    novokomponovane narodne pjesme, **8:**969
    old *vs.* new genres, **8:**122
    rural genres, **8:**963–64
Bosnian people
  in Croatia, **8:**925
  in Macedonia, **8:**972
  in North America, **3:**921, 923, 1082

bossa nova, **2:**107, 108–9, 110, 310, 317–18, 351; **3:**522
Boss Brass (musical group), **3:**1107
Boston Brass Band, **3:**564
Boston, Roseina, **9:**135
Boston Symphony Orchestra, **3:**174, 537
Boston University, **10:**3
Boston Village Gamelan, **3:**324, 1018
Bothy Band (musical group), **3:**846; **8:**392
Bothy Songs and Ballads (Ord), **8:**373
Botoa, Enoch, **9:**644
Botocudo culture, **2:**302
Botswana. *See also* Southern Africa; *specific peoples*
    Herero people, **1:**715
        music of, **1:**428
    San people, **1:**703–5
    Sotho peoples, **1:**707
Boublil, Alain, **4:**131
Bouchard, Linda, **3:**1152
Bouchard, Lucien, **3:**1162
Boucher, Daniel, **3:**1162
Boudreau, Walter, **3:**1076, 1077, 1152
Bougainville (Papua New Guinea), **9:**472, 600
    dance costumes of, **9:**336
    instruments of, **9:**647, 648–49, 651, 653–54
    map of, **9:***473*
    music and dance of, **9:**630, 632
        Banoni people, **9:**644–47
        Buin people, **9:**649–54
        Nagovisi people, **9:**647–49
Bougainville, Louis de, **9:**33, 34, 630, 689, 795
Bouiller, Auguste, **8:**632
Boukman Eksperyans (musical group), **2:**891; **3:**806
Boukrab, **6:***466*
Boulanger, Georges, **8:**882
Boulanger, Gustave-Clarence-Rodolphe, **8:***74*
Boulanger, Nadia, **3:**174, 175, 610, 611; **8:**882
Boulet, Benoît, **9:**402
Boulez, Pierre, **3:**328, 1151; **7:**735; **8:**85, 188
Bouliane, Denys, **3:**1152
Boulton, Laura, **1:**51, 584, 590; **2:**593; **3:**292, 381, 498; **9:**975, 979, 994
Bouni, Vahagn, **6:**731
Bountong Insixiengmai, **4:**346, 361
Bouquet of Melodies (Holland), **3:**605
Bourgault-Ducoudray, Louis-Albert, **8:**177, 562
Bourguiba, Habib, **6:**437
Bournonville, August, **8:**161
Bourrienne, Louis Antoine Fauvelet de, **6:**22
Bouscatel, Antonin, **8:**547, 550
Bousseloub, **6:**876
Bouteldja, Belkacem, **6:**270
Boutet, Martin, **3:**1075
Bouvet, Père, **4:**70, 222, 225, 252
Bouvette, Reg, **3:**409
bouzouki. *See* lutes
Bova, Kallen, **9:**402
Bovet, Joseph, **8:**693
Bowdich, Thomas Edward, **1:**88–89, 93, 153
Bowers, Jane, **3:**506
"Bowery" (Gaunt), **3:**544
Bowie, David, **3:**357–58; **8:**215, 220
Bowie, Lester, **3:**664
Bowling Green State University (Ohio), **3:**953
Bowring, John, **4:**225, 247, 254–55

Boy George, **8:**215
Boy and His Family Troubadours, **9:**101, *102*
Boyash Roma, **8:**272
Boycott (musical group), **8:**217
Boyd, Bob, **3:**1091
Boyd, Millie, **9:**442
Boyer, Horace Clarence, **3:**630; **10:**145
Boyes, Georgina, **8:**339
Boyko, Yefim, **6:**1031
"Boyne Water" (folk song), **3:**837, 839
Boyoyo Boys, **3:**339
Boys' Brigade Band (Manihiki), **9:**906
Boys from Bouf (musical group), **3:**1198
Boys of the Lough (musical group), **3:**846; **8:**392
Boyz II Men, **3:**715
Boyz N the Hood (film), **3:**715
Bozdağ, Zekeriya, **6:**250
"Bozo-les-culottes" (Levesque), **3:**1156
Bozzoli, María E., **2:**635
Brabants Volksorkest (musical group), **8:***535*, 536
Braceland, Francis J., **3:**355
Brackett, Joseph, **3:**135
Bradbury, William, **3:**533
Brade, Christine, **8:**36, 37, 38, 39
Bradford, Joseph, **3:**617
Bradford, Perry, **3:**33, 578, 644, *644*, 707
Bradley, Harold, **3:**80
Bradley, Owen, **3:**80
Bradshaw, Stephen, **9:**948
Brady, Erika, **3:**495
Brady, Paul, **8:**392
Brady, William, **3:**604
Braga, Caroline, **10:**18
Braham, David, **3:**192–93, 544
Brahim, Anwar, **6:**438
Brahma dharma sect, **5:**847–48
Brahma (deity), **5:**247, 494, 732
    attributes of, **5:**249
    Sant worship of, **5:**253
    Sikh views of, **5:**256
Brahmanas, **5:**11
Brahmbhatt, Bali, **5:**421
Brahmendra, Sadashiva, **5:**267
Brahmin class, **5:**398, 557
    boy performers, **5:***440*, 495, 516–18
    ceremonies, marriage consummation, **5:**287
    function of, **5:**9
    in Goa, **5:**735
    instrument specializations of, **5:**389
    in Karnataka, **5:**881, 885
    life-cycle ceremonial music of, **5:**284
    in Mithila, **5:**678
    as musicians, **5:**10, 261, 386–88, 401, 632
    in Nepal, **5:**706
    in Rajasthan, **5:**639
    Smarta sect, **5:**220, 223
    as storytellers, **5:**401
    Telugu, girls' puberty rites, **5:**274
    Telugu literature of, **5:**893
    transmission of Vedas, **5:**66, 239–44
    at Tyagaraja festival, **5:**391–92
    vocal music of, **5:**910
    weddings of, **5:**274–76
Brahmo Samaj movement, **5:**254
Brahms, Johannes, **2:**394; **8:**62, 83, 273, 367, 646, 663

Brail, Joseph Carl, **3:**203
Brăiloiu, Constantin, **4:**457; **7:**524; **8:**19, 23, 24, 26, 117, 338, 885
Braimah, J. K., **1:**483
Brainerd, Maria, **3:**60
Braithwaite, Barrington, **2:***449*, 450
Braithwaite, J. R., **3:**627
Braman, Amasa, **3:**1070, 1115
Brambats, Karl, **8:**115
Brand, Dollar. *See* Ibrahim, Abdullah
Brandão, Carlos Rodrigues, **2:**320
Brandeis, Antonie, **9:**757
Brandel, Rose, **1:**50, 155, 157; **10:**56
Brandl, Maria, **9:**47
Brando, Marlon, **8:**675
Brandon, James R., **4:**650
Brandon, Phillip, **3:**1094
Brandt, Max H., **1:**51; **2:**544
Brandts Buys, J. S., **4:**603, 636
Brandts Buys-Van Zijp, A., **4:**603, 636
Branduardi, Angelo, **8:**626
Brandwine, Naftule, **3:**938
Bran Nue Dae, **9:**443
Bran Nue Day (Aboriginal musical), **9:**60
Brash, Nora, **9:**233
Brassard, François, **3:**1166
Brassens, Georges, **3:**1167; **8:**548
Brat (musical group), **3:**750
Brauer, Arik, **8:**676
Braun, Bartholomé, **2:**586
Braun, Joachim, **6:**1063, 1064, 1065
Braun, Peter Michael, **4:**876
Braun, Yehezkiel, **6:**1031
Brauneiss, Jean Chrysostome, **3:**1148
"Brave Wolfe" (ballad), **3:**155
Bravničar, Matija, **8:**921
Bravo, Joe, **3:**779–80
Bravo, Soledad, **2:**103, 543
Bravo, Uriel, **2:**581
Braxton, Anthony, **3:**664
Brazhnikov, Maksim, **8:**779
Brazil, **2:**300–54, 441. *See also specific peoples*
    African brotherhoods in, **2:**47
    Afro-Brazilian religious traditions in, **2:**32, 48, 69, 260, 341–44
    Afro-Brazilian traditions in, **2:**340–54
    Amerindian cultures, **8:**17
        relations with European and African descendants, **2:**324–25
    Argentine people in, **2:**84
    art music in, **2:**112–16
    Bahia
        Afro-Brazilian popular music in, **2:**351–54
        Candomblé rituals, **2:**32
        marujada genre, **2:**347–48
    Brasília, **2:**324
    carnival in, **2:**94, 335–38
    central and southern, **2:**300–21
    children's wakes in, **2:**422
    Chilean people in, **2:**90
    Chinese people in, **2:**84–85
    Congolese instruments in, **1:**668
    copyright issues in, **2:**65
    cord-and-peg tension drums in, **1:**316
    dance traditions
        baile pastoril, **2:**334

batuque, **2:**348
bumba-meu-boi, **2:**335, 347
capoeira, **2:**345–47
chegança, **2:**334
côco, **2:**349
maculelê, **2:**349–50
marujada, **2:**347–48
reisado, **2:**334–35
Saint Gonçalo dance, **2:**311, 329
ternos, **2:**312–13
emancipated slaves from, **1:**351, 401–2, 471, 478
geography of, **2:**300, 323
German people in, **2:**89
Gê-speaking Indian groups, social organization of, **2:**58
Guaraní culture, **2:**199–204
history of, **2:**126, 242, 300–306, 323–24, 340–41
immigrant clubs in, **2:**49
influence on Angolan music, **1:**435
instruments of, **2:**308–11, 329–30, 378
Italian people in, **2:**89–90
Japanese people in, **2:**61, 86–89; **10:**99, 102
Manaus, Teatro Amazonas, **2:**90, *113*
Maronite Church in, **6:**208
Maroon cultures in, **2:**2, 131
migrant communities in, **2:**318–20
military regime in, **2:**93, 109
Minas Gerais, **2:**302–3
musical genres
axé, **2:**110, 353–54
bossa nova, **2:**108–9, 310, 317–18, 351
brão, **2:**307
cantoria, **2:**307, 324–28
carangueijo, **2:**307
cateretê, **2:**307
charm, **2:**354
choro, **2:**49, 305, 310, 350
cururu paulista, **2:**307
dobrados, **2:**309
embolada, **2:**307
folia de reis, **2:**311–12
forró, **2:**330–33
frevo, **2:**336–37
frevo-baiano, **2:**338
fricote, **2:**354
ijexá, **2:**338
jongo, **2:**307, 309
lundu, **2:**304, 313
maracatú, **2:**337
maracatú rural, **2:**337
moda-de-viola, **2:**307, 319
modinha, **2:**304, 313
MPB, **2:**109–10, 318
música caipira, **2:**59, 133, 319
música sertaneja, **2:**110, 310, 318, 319–20
porfia, **2:**307
religious songs, **2:**328–29
samba, **1:**384; **2:**313–17, 348–49, 350–51
timbalada, **2:**354
toada paulista, **2:**308
trio elétrico, **2:**337–38
tropicália movement, **2:**318, 351
xácara, **2:**307

northeastern, **2:**301, 323–38
Afro-Brazilian culture in, **2:**340
caboclo musical tradition, **2:**324–33
parafolclore movement, **2:**41
Pernambuco, **2:**323, 333, 335
popular music in, **2:**40, 107–11
population of, **2:**300, 323
research on, **2:**320–21
Rio de Janeiro, **2:**304–6, 313–17
colonial paintings from, **2:**16
economics, **2:**354
music conservatory, **2:**114
samba schools, **2:**61–62, 351
Teatro Colón, **2:**90
Salvador, **2:**24, 323, 333, 335, 337–38
African-Brazilian culture in, **2:**110, 351
São Paulo
Afro-Brazilian culture in, **2:**340
Japanese descendants in, **2:**87–88
sound recording industry, **2:**40, 64
southeastern, Afro-Brazilian culture in, **2:**340
Suyá culture, **2:**143–49
tourism in, **2:**50
tropical-forest region, **2:**123–35
Tupi-Guaraní culture in, **2:**45
Waiãpí culture, **2:**157–63
Waiwai culture, **2:**71, 131–32
Wayana culture, **2:**164–67
Xingu region, **2:**125, 134, 143–49
women's Iamuricumã ceremony, **2:**129
Yanomamö culture, **2:**169–75
Brazilian Dramatic Company, **1:**401
Brazilian people
in French Guiana, **2:**434
in North America, **3:**730–31, 848, 1203, 1204
in Portugal, **8:**576
Brazilian Society of Contemporary Music, **2:**306
Brazil-Paraguay War, **2:**245, 331
breakdown, **3:**836, 855, 1125
"Breakdown" (Thomas), **3:**676
Breakin' (film), **3:**713
"Break Up to Make Up" (Stylistics), **3:**711
Breathing (musical group), **7:**364
Breathnach, Breandán, **8:**394, *394*
Breazul, George, **8:**885
Brébeuf, Father Jean de, **3:**484
Brecht, Bertolt, **8:**646, 659
Bredda David and Tribal Vibes, **2:**679
Breechah Pintawng, **4:**291
Bregman, Albert S., **1:**183–84, 187–88, 191–92, 194, 195
Bregović, Goran, **8:**969
Breizh (periodical), **8:**564
Brel, Jacques, **3:**1167; **6:**249; **8:**548
Bremer, Fredrika, **3:**600
Bremner, Robert, **8:**367, 372, 373
"Brendan Voyage" (Davey), **8:**387
Brenston, Jackie, **3:**351, 708
Brent, T. David, **10:**165
Brentano, Clemens, **8:**663
Breslauer, Emil, **8:**266
Bressani, Father Francesco Giuseppe, **3:**23, 1178
Bretón, Tomás, **3:**851
Breuer, Hans, **8:**655–56
Breuker, Willem, **3:**664

Bṛhaddeśī (treatise), **5:**24, 34, 53, 66, 75, 96
date of, **5:**22
on notes and intervals, **5:**39
raga classification in, **5:**47, 313, 400
on songs, **5:**36, 40–41
use of term "raga" in, **5:**73
on vocal quality, **5:**37–38
Brian Boru, king of Ireland, **8:**383
Bribri culture, **2:**631–35
instruments of, **2:**632–33
population of, **2:**632
research on, **2:**635, 703
ritual music of, **2:**633–34
secular music of, **2:**634–35
Briceño y Añez (Colombian duo), **2:**396
Brick (musical group), **3:**712
Brides of Funkenstein (musical group), **3:**684
"Bridge Over Troubled Water" (Simon and Garfunkel), **3:**552
Bridges, Cy M., **9:**972
Bridie, David, **9:**1005
Brief Introduction to the Skill of Musick (Playford), **3:**832
Brigadoon (Lerner and Loewe), **3:**545
Briggs, Charles L., **2:**198; **10:**88, 95
Briggs, Lloyd Cabot, **1:**574
Briggs, Pete, **3:**653
Brigham Young University (Lā'ie), **9:**103
Bright Moon Song and Dance Troupe, **7:**353–54
Brihaddhvani, **5:**213
Brillantes, Roman, **4:**866
Brinda, T., **5:**99, *99*, 389, 395
Bringemeier, Martha, **8:**24
Bring in 'da Noise/Bring in 'da Funk (musical), **3:**545, 621
Brinner, Ben, **10:**52
Brinton, Daniel, **2:**749
Brisbane Conservatory, **10:**87
Bristow, George Frederick, **3:**14, 538
British Arts Council, **3:**288
British Broadside Ballad and Its Music (Simpson), **8:**374
British Caribbean community. *See* Caribbean people
British Columbia, **3:**1253–71
British culture in, **3:**1094–95, 1256–57
Doukhobors in, **3:**1092, 1095, 1267–70
European explorers and settlers, **3:**1094, 1254–55
First Nations groups in, **3:**383, 394–97, 399–402, 509, 1092–94, 1254
geography of, **3:**1092, 1254
gold rush in, **3:**1255
history of musical life, **3:**1091–97, 1254–59
Kamloops, **3:**1094
Nanaimo, **3:**1094
Vancouver
Chinese people in, **3:**11, 224, 957, 1095–96, 1258, 1260–66
cultural diversity of, **3:**223
musical life in, **3:**17, 1094–95
music instruction in, **3:**279
Victoria, **3:**1092, 1094–95, 1255
British Columbia Old Time Fiddlers Association, **3:**1257
British Council, **3:**295
British Guiana. *See* Guyana

British Harmony (Parry), **8:**352
British Honduras. *See* Belize
British Institute of Recorded Sound, **2:**649; **8:**18
British Methodist Episcopal Church, **3:**1212
British Museum (London), **8:**182
British North America Act (1867), **3:**1057
British people. *See also* English people; Scottish
  people
 in Antigua and Barbuda, **2:**798
 in Barbados, **2:**813, 816, 817, 820
 in Central America, **2:**659
 in Dominica, **2:**840
 in Guyana, **2:**83, 441–42
 in Jamaica, **2:**896
 in Montserrat, **2:**922
 in Nicaragua, **2:**749, 753
 in Panama, **2:**773
 in South America, **2:**4
 in Surinam, **2:**503
 in Syria, **6:**565
 in Trinidad, **2:**83
 in Virgin Islands, **2:**968
British Virgin Islands, **2:**968, 971. *See also* Virgin
  Islands
British West Indies, **2:**441–42
Brito, Eduardo, **2:**861–62
Brittany, **8:**558–64
 Celtic people in, **6:**277; **8:**319–22
 dance traditions of, **8:**164, 559, 561
 folk music in, **8:**13
 folk music recordings, **8:**157
 geography of, **8:**558
 history of, **8:**558
 history of music in, **8:**561–62
 influence on Welsh music, **8:**355
 instruments, **8:**201, 545, 559–60
 map of, **8:***516*
 population of, **8:**558
 research on music of, **8:**552, 553, 561–62
 separatist movement, **8:**12
 vocal music of, **8:**552, 559, 561
Britten, Benjamin, **4:**132; **7:**630, 955; **8:**84
broadcasting, **1:**46
 Central African Broadcasting Station, **1:**33
 Central African Republic, **1:**684
 East Africa, **1:**608
 Ghana, **1:**31
 of guitar music, **1:**367
 history and development of, **1:**416–17
 Kenya, **1:**426, 628
 of Kru music, **1:**381
 Niger, **1:**592, 593
 Nigeria, **1:**31, 34–35, 39, 236, 474
 North Africa, **1:**533
 role in diffusion, **1:**322
 satellite, **6:**233, 240–41
 Somalia, **1:**619, 620
 South Africa, **1:**760, 777, 779
 Sudan, **1:**562, 571–72
 Tanzania, **1:**644–45, 646
 Zaïre, **1:**385, 424
 Zimbabwe, **1:**432, 755–57
Broadcast Music, Inc. (BMI), **3:**263, 560, 609,
  708
Broadlahn (musical group), **8:**676
Broadwood, John, **8:**337, 367

Broadwood, Lucy, **8:**337, 373
Brod, Max, **6:**1028, 1060
Brödl, Günter, **8:**678
Bródy, János, **8:**747
Brody, Joseph, **3:**936
Broken Wings (Gibran), **6:**279
Brom, Gustav, **8:**730
Brong people, **1:**287
Bronisławski, Jędrzej, **8:***708*
Bronner, Gerhard, **8:**674–75
Bronson, Bertrand H., **3:**511, 825; **8:**23, 136,
  328, 329, 338, 374; **9:**294
Brontë, Charlotte, **3:**200
Bronx DJs (musical group), **3:**694
Bronze Age, **8:**36, 38, 39–40, 319
Brook, Michael, **5:**760
Brooke, Rupert, poetry of, **9:**39
Brooklyn Academy of Music (New York),
  3:664
Brooklyn College of the City of New York,
  3:610, 612
Brooklyn College Orchestra, **3:**612
Brooklyn Museum, **3:**1037
Brooks, Garth, **3:**81
Brooks, Hadda, **3:**646
Brooks, Ike, **1:**771
Brooks, Phyllis, **9:**149
Brooks, Shelton, **3:**1212
Broonzy, Big Bill, **3:**579, 645, 707
Broquiere, Bertrandon de la, **6:**192
Brosseau, J.-M., **8:**548
Brother Noland Conjugacion, **9:**167
Brothers of Hargeysa, **1:**618–20
Brothers Johnson, **3:**684
Brouhaha (musical group), **3:**1194
Brounoff, Platon, **3:**939
Broven, John, **3:**858
Brown, Anna, **8:**135, 200, 370
Brown, Anthony, **3:**972
Brown Buddies (musical), **3:**620
Brown, Carlinhos, **2:**354
Brown, Charles, **3:**646, 669
Brown, Clarence "Gatemouth," **3:**647
Brown, Donald N., **2:**473
Brown, Ernest, **3:**585, 626
Brown, George, **9:**21, 146–47, 627
Brown, Henry, **3:**645
Brown, James, **3:**552, 647, 677, 678, 680, 683,
  701, 710, *710*; **6:**644; **10:**78
Brown, Nacio Herb, **9:**43
Brown, Peter, **3:**712
Brown, Riwia, **9:**233
Brown, Robert E., **3:**1013–14, 1018, 1019;
  5:161, 566; **10:**41
Brown, Roy, **3:**646, 708
Brown, Ruth, **3:***263*, 351, 670, 709
Brown, Saul, **3:**934
Brown, Sterling, **3:**579
Brown University (Providence), **10:**10
Brown, William Henry, **3:**615
Browne-Cave, Beatrice Cave, **3:**1258
Browner, Tara Colleen, **3:**497, 498
Browning, Kurt, **3:**207
Browning, Robert, **3:**1008
Brubeck, Dave, **3:**660
Bruckner, Anton, **8:**83, 84

Bruddah Waltah and Island Afternoon, **9:**167,
  220–21
"*Brüder, zur Sonne, zur Freiheit*" (Radin/
  Scherchen), **8:**659
'Brug-pa kun-legs, **5:**712
Brunei, **4:**594, 823
 Islam in, **4:**74, 79–80, 596
Brunet, François, **3:**1155
Brunet, Jacques, **4:**25, 160, 341, 357–58
Brunka culture, **2:**684–85
Brünning, Heinrich, **2:**487–88
Brunswick Records, **3:**737; **9:**998
Brunton, M., **9:**256
Brusilovskii, Evgeni, **6:**959
Bruyneel, Hendrik, **8:***530*
Bry, Theodor de, **2:**301
Bryan, E. H., **9:**25
Bryant, Herbert, **3:***647*
Bryant, William Cullen, **3:**599
Bryce, L. Winifred, **5:**675
Bṣīrī, Gaston, **6:**529
Bṣīrī, Jacob, **6:**527, 528, *528*, 529–31
Bua, Balkrishna, **5:**78
Bua, Mirashu, **5:***207*
Bua, Ramachandra, **5:**106
Buang people
 falsetto singing of, **9:**297
 music and dance of, **9:**566–67
 sung poetry, **9:**328
Buarque, Chico, **2:**109, 318
Buayan people, **4:**890
Bubblin' Brown Sugar (musical), **3:**621
"*Bu Bu,*" **9:**149
Bubu gao (Lü), **7:**220
Buchan, Norman, **8:**365, 371
Buchanan, James, **3:**308
Buck, David, **7:**379
Buck, Sir Peter H., **9:**24–25, 885–86, 969
Buckholz, Lester, **3:**883
Buckley, Ann, **8:**394
Buckley's New Orleans Serenaders (blackface
  troupe), **3:**61, 185
Bucovina, **8:**868. *See also* Romania
Bucşan, Andrei, **8:**886
Buczynski, Walter, **3:**1186
BUDA Musique (record company), **8:**241
Budapest Ethnographic Museum, Folk Music
  Department, **8:**274
Budapest String Quartet, **3:**538
Buddhism, **3:**5; **5:**480, 482. *See also* chant
  (Buddhist)
 Afghanistan, **5:**489
 animism and, **4:**59
 Arunachal Pradesh, **5:**504–5
 Asian-American communities, **3:**950
 Bengal, **5:**844
 Bhutan, **5:**489
 Burma, **4:**363
 caste structure and, **5:**10
 Chăm people, **4:**590
 Chan, **7:**327
 China, **7:**19–20, 32–33, 34, 327–33
  ritual music for, **7:**91, 212, 311–12, 416,
   420–21, 619
  sheng-guan ceremonial music, **7:**200–201,
   312

Dai people, 7:496–504
Dhammaruci sect, 5:957
Himachal Pradesh, 5:499–500
history of, 5:12–13; 7:22–23, 311
Hokke, 7:611–13
India, 5:374
Indonesia, 4:75, 76, 596
influence on American music, 3:129–33
influence on Central Asian Islam, 6:936–37
Inner Asia, 7:14, 19
instrument classification in, 5:319, 327–29
Japan, 7:24–25, 533, 535, 548–49, 611–18, 756
   ceremonies, 7:614–15, 645
   folk music of, 7:617–18
   history of, 7:611–13
Japanese-Americans, 3:970, 973
Java, 4:632
Karen people, 4:544
Kashmir, 5:689
Khmer people, 4:156–57, 205–7, 215
Korea, 7:24, 806, 807, 871, 941
   chant styles, 7:871–73
   dance traditions in, 7:66–67, 871, 873–74
Laos, 4:336, 342
Lombok, 4:764–65
Madhya Pradesh, 5:720
Mahayana tradition, 3:950; 5:13, 257, 960, 962, 964, 965, 966–67, 969; 7:311, 327
Mahima Samaj sect, 5:732
Malaysia, 4:401
mandala in, 6:185
Mongol people, 7:1008, 1016–19
musical ideology of, 7:327–28
Nara, 7:611–13
Nepal, 5:696, 697, 701
Oceania, 9:71, 97, 99, 720
Orissa, 5:731, 732
Pakhtun people, 5:785
pipa as iconographic symbol in, 7:167
Pure Land sect, 7:327
Ryûkyû Islands, 7:796
shamanism and, 7:20
Shan people, 4:547–48
Sikkim, 5:502
Singon sect, 7:567–68, 589, 611–13
South Asia, 5:257, 261
Southeast Asia, 4:62
Sri Lanka, 5:108, 350, 363–64, 490, 537, 955, 956–57, 960, 965–69
Sumatra, 4:599–600, 624
Sumbawa, 4:779
Sunda, 4:699
Tendai sect, 7:567–68, 611–14, 645, 646
Thailand, 4:231, 247, 256–57, 287–97, 304
Theravada tradition, 3:950; 4:6; 5:12–13, 108, 257, 955, 956–57, 965–69; 7:327, 495, 496–500, 501–4
Tibetan, 3:133; 5:12, 13, 257, 709, 711; 6:983; 7:32–33, 34, 67, 327, 472, 478, 479–80
   in Mongol regions, 7:1016
   musical traditions of, 5:713–15
   in northeastern China, 7:520
Uighur people, 6:995

urban areas, 4:5
Vietnam, 4:69, 444, 446, 464, 500–501, 502–5
Vietnamese-Americans, 3:996
Zen, 3:130, 335, 540, 954; 7:327, 548–49, 611–13
   dance and, 3:214
   Fuke sect, 7:46
   Huke sect, 7:548, 617, 702, 715, 755, 758–59, 777
   influence on nô theater, 7:64
   Ôbaku, 7:613, 617
   Rinzai sect, 7:612–13
   Sôto sect, 7:612–13
   Zyôdo, 7:611–13
Buddhism and the Spirit Cults in North-East Thailand (Tambiah), 4:287
Buddruss, Georg, 5:800
Buen, Hanne Kjersti, 8:412
Buen, Hauk, 8:418, 422, 427–28
Buen, Knut, 8:418, 420, 427–28, 430
Buenaño, Alfonso de, 2:933
Buena Suerte label, 3:781
Buenaventura, Alfredo, 4:875
Buenaventura, Antonino, 4:130, 872, 873
Buenaventura, B., 4:864
Buencamino, Francisco, 4:864, 865, 872
"Buffalo Jump" (7th Fire), 3:1063
bugalú, 3:799
Buganda (kingdom), 1:4, 311–12
Bugeja family, 8:642
Bughayth, 'Abd Allah, 6:651
Buginese people, 4:804–6
Bugis people, 4:414, 780
Bugis Street (Singapore musical), 4:524
Bugti tribe, 5:783
Buhagiar, Dion, 8:643
Buhaya people, 1:636
Buhr, Glenn, 3:1091
Buica, Nicolae, 8:882
Buick, Tommy, 3:1244
Buin people
   instruments of, 9:651, 653–54
   laments of, 9:326, 652–53
   music and dance of, 9:649–54
   panpipe ensembles of, 9:632
   sung poetry, 9:327
al-Bū'isāmī, Muhammad, 6:367
Buitrago, Pablo, 2:765
Buitrón, Aníbal, 2:423
Bùi Văn Hai, 4:509
Buka (Papua New Guinea), 9:639
   music and dance of, 9:630, 632, 640–42
   prehistoric, 9:474
   songs of, 9:635
Bukhara (khanate), 6:936
al-Bukhārī, 6:358, 359, 362
Bukhari, Z. A., 5:745
Bukid people, 4:920
Bukidnon people, 4:927
Bukoreshtliev, Angel, 8:906
Bula, chief of Lösi District, Lifou, 9:683
Bulang people, 7:485–92, 495
Bulawayo Sweet Rhythm Band, 1:772
Bulgan, 7:1020

Bulgaria, 8:890–907
   art music in, 8:904–6
   ballad dissemination in, 8:8
   carnival in, 8:140, 161, 897, 899
   children's games, 8:145, 897
   choral music of, 3:340
   dance traditions of, 8:161–62, 164, 891, 897, 900, 901
   Dobrudzha, music of, 8:897
   ethnic minorities in, 8:903
   folk music pedagogy, 8:155
   history of, 8:890–91
   history of music in, 8:903–6
   instruments, 8:21, 99, 169, 198, 201, 891–97
      research on, 8:38, 172
   Koprivshtitsa folk festival, 8:150
   Macedonian people in, 8:972
   map of, 8:866, 869
   May Day celebration in, 8:186
   Muslims in, 8:11
   northern region, instruments, 8:897
   peperuda ceremony, 8:278
   Pirin region
      dance of, 8:892
      folk festival in, 8:151
      instruments, 8:895–96
      lament performance, 8:901
      vocal music of, 8:895
      zurla and tapan ensembles, 8:280
   popular music in, 8:903
   population of, 8:890
   research on aesthetics, 8:25
   research on music of, 8:19, 906–7
   research on Slavic elements in music, 8:23
   Rhodope Mountains, vocal music of, 8:896
   Rila Monastery, 8:904
   rock in, 8:220
   Rom people in, 8:226–27, 272, 278, 282–84, 893–94, 903
      kjuček genre, 8:282, 284
   rule over Macedonia, 8:972
   sedyanka gatherings, 8:141, 900
   Sofia, musical life in, 8:905
   Sredna Gora, vocal music of, 8:896
   state folk ensembles in, 8:201, 220, 890–91, 902
   Strandzha Mountains, 8:896–97
      singing games, 8:900
   Sufism in, 6:107, 115
   suppression of rock groups, 8:217
   Thrace, vocal and instrumental music of, 8:892, 896
   Turkish people in, 8:11, 12
   urbanized folk music, 8:14
   verbal categories for performance, 8:112–13
   vocal music, 8:195, 200, 891, 896–99, 901
      laments, 8:23, 200
      polyphony, 8:14, 112, 225–26, 610
      table songs, 8:114, 897
   vocal performers, 8:115
   wedding ceremony in, 8:6, 144, 900–901
   wedding music, 8:283–84, 901–3
Bulgarian Music (periodical), 8:905
Bulgarian National Ensemble of Folk Songs and Dances, 8:201
Bulgarian Opera Society, 8:905

Bulgarian Orthodox Church, **3:**925, 1199
  musical style in, **3:**118
Bulgarian people
  in North America, **3:**919, 924, 1199
  in Turkey, **6:**117
  in Ukraine, **8:**821
Bulgaria State Radio and Television Female Vocal
    Choir, **8:**220
Bulgars, **8:**890
Bull and the Lion (album), **1:**779
Bull, Ole, **3:**537, 556, 1180; **8:**424
Bulleh Shah, **5:**753, 756–57
Bullen, Frank T., **9:**37
bullroarers. *See* free aerophones
Bully and the Kafooners, **2:**970
"Bully Song" (Trevathen), **3:**619
Bülow, Hans von, **3:**556; **8:**368, 422
Bulu people, **1:**659–60
Bulūgh al-munā fī tarājim ahl al-ghinā'
    (Muḥammad Efendī al-Kanjī), **6:**371
Bulungur, **6:**345
Būlus, **6:**368
Bumble Bee Slim, **3:**645
"Bump and Grind" (Kelly), **3:**715
Bundelkhand dynasty, **5:**721
Bundjalung people, **9:**441, 442
Buŋili people, **1:**663–64
Bunjevci people, **8:**952–53
Bunnett, Jane, **3:**1064, 1085, 1107
bunraku, **7:**75, 77, 536, 663–65, *669*
  dissemination of, **7:**539
  gidayû busi in, **7:**539, 583, 654, 657, 663,
      667, 675–77, 679
  hayasi in, **7:**665
  instruments in, **7:**712
  Meizi patronage of, **7:**777
  min'yô in, **7:**601
  music in, **7:**665
  notation for, **7:**538, 583, 589
  performance contexts of, **7:**775
  plays for, **7:**667–70
  puppets and stage of, **7:**664–65
  sources on, **7:**588
  structure of, **7:**663–64
  subjects of, **7:**663, 668–69
Bunraku za (Ōsaka), **7:**663
Bunting, Edward, **8:**321, 386, 393, 394
Buntong Insixiengmai, **3:**1008, *1008*
Bunun people
  mouth bow of, **7:**524, 528–29
  music of, **7:**525, 527, 528–29; **10:**28
Bunun people (Taiwan), **9:**257
Buppha Devi, Norodom, princess of Cambodia,
    4:188
Burada, Teodor T., **8:**885
Buraima, Kondeh, **1:**509
Burano, Michaj, **8:**277
Būrās, **6:**270
Burchell, William, **1:**151–53
Burda (devotional poem), **6:**437
Burdon, Eric, **3:**318
Bureau of American Ethnology, **3:**29, 291–92,
    294–95, 300, 444, 509
Buretiu, Taanea, **9:***364*
Burgenland Roma, **8:**289
Burgess, John D., **8:**363

Burghers, in Sri Lanka, **5:**108, 954, 955
Burhan, Al-Amin, **1:**571
burials. *See* funeral ceremonies
Burian, Emil František, **8:**729
Burke, Mary E. Lawson, **9:**967, 974, 994–95
Burkina Faso. *See also specific peoples*
  academic training in, **1:**38
  Bobo people, masks of, **1:**119
  music research in, **1:**60
  Tuareg people, **6:**273
Burleigh, Harry T., **3:**577, *577*, 606, 607, *629*,
    706
Burlin, Natalie Curtis, **3:**1069
Burma
  Akha people in, **4:**540–42
  bamboo agriculture in, **4:**52
  "classical" music traditions in, **4:**7
  competitions in, **4:**142
  composition in, **4:**127, 128
  cultural origins of, **4:**10–11
  geography of, **4:**363
  Hinduism in, **4:**64
  history of, **4:**365–66
  Indians in, **4:**68
  instruments and ensembles in, **4:**366–81
  Karen people in, **4:**543–46
  Lahu people in, **4:**538–40
  Lisu people in, **4:**542–43
  map of, **4:***364*
  minority cultures in, **4:**90
  modal system in, **4:**390–95
  mother of rice, **4:**51
  musical genres
    anyeiñ, **4:**374, 377, 385
    bala hsaiñ, **4:**374
  music research on, **4:**24, 25, 26, 150, 364,
      529
  pedagogy in, **4:**122
  politics and war in, **4:**90
  population of, **4:**363
  Rangoon, **4:**5
    Swe Dagon pagoda, **4:**44
  representative music of, **4:**22, 132–33
  salient musical features of, **4:**18–19
  Shan people in, **4:**547–49
  spirit beliefs in, **4:**49–50
  Tai people in, **4:**218
  Thai influences on, **4:**229
  theater in, **4:**395–96
  Theravada Buddhism in, **5:**968
  tourism in, **4:**138
  trance in, **4:**61
  transmission and change in, **4:**395–99
  tuning systems in, **4:**385–90
  upland peoples, **4:**537–59
    music research on, **4:**26
  village life in, **4:**6
  vocal music in, **4:**373–74, 381–85
  wars in, **4:**11
  Western influences in, **4:**82
Burman, Rahul Dev "R. D.", **5:**427, 537–38,
    538
Burman, Sachin Dev, **5:**537, 855
Burman-Hall, Linda, **3:**1020
Burman people, **4:**364–65, 528. *See also* Burma
Burnell, A. C., **5:**240

Burnett, George Jennings, **3:**1096
Burnett, Paula, **3:**312
Burnette, Johnny, **3:**352, 355
Burney, Charles, **6:**22; **8:**97, 265; **9:**14
Burney, James, **9:**14, 285
Burnham, Pres. Forbes, **2:**448
Burnham, Mark, **3:**1179
Burns, E. Bradford, **2:**767
Burns, Robert, **8:**18, 333, 367–68, 373, 374
Burnt Bridge Gumleaf Band, **9:**135
Burrows, Edwin G., **9:**372, 769, 771, 815, 853,
    869, 883, 994
Burs, Florsen, **8:**438–39
Burstow, Henry, **8:**332
Burstyn, Shay, **6:**1063, 1067
Burt, Ben, **9:**962
Burton, Deena, **3:**1020
Burton, Frederick, **3:**367, 457
Burton, Sir Richard Francis, **1:**85–86, 635
Burton's New Theater (New York), **3:**61
Buru, **4:**819
Burucac culture, **2:**681
Burundi, **1:**651. *See also* East Africa; *specific*
    peoples
  inanga chuchotée music, **1:**164–206
  music genres in, **1:**183, 198
  music of, **1:**607
  Nangayivuza cult, **1:**202–6
  royal ensembles, **1:**602, 603
  verbal arts, **1:**197–98
Burungi people, **1:**638
Burusho people, **5:**283
Burxanov, Mutavaqqil, **6:**904
Buryat people, **7:**1003–20, 1027–30
"Bury Me Under the Weeping Willow Tree"
    (Carter Family), **3:**78
"Bury My Heart at Wounded Knee" (Sainte-
    Marie), **3:**1063
Busacca, Cicciu, **9:**81
Buschmann, Friedrich, **8:**657
"*Buselik Makamina*" (MFÖ), **6:**250
Bush, George, **3:**48
Bush, Kate, **8:**220
Bushell, Frederick S., **3:**1096
"Bush Killa" (Paris), **3:**699
Bushmen, **1:**635, 703, 761. *See also* San people
Bushnak, Lotfi, **6:**513
Bushnell, David, **3:**470
Bushshūsha, Muṣṭafā, **6:**509
Busia, Kofi Abrefa, **1:**27
Bussine, Romain, **3:**1148, 1149
Bussy, Marquis de, **5:**891
Bustos Valenzuela, Eduardo, **2:***609*
Butaritari (Kiribati), **9:**40–41, 758, 761
Butch Cassidy and the Sundance Kid (film), **3:**204
Butcher, Robert, **8:***380*
But Do You Wanna Buy Some Thongs (dance
    production), **9:**416
Butig people, **4:**890
Butler, Angeline, **10:**141
Butler, Edith, **3:**1137
Butler, Helen May, **3:**566, *567*
Butler, Jerry, **3:**683, 711
Butler, Judith, **3:**89
Butler, Ronnie, **2:**806
Butocan, Aga Mayo, **4:**891

Butô kyoku (Miyagi), **7:**779
Butterfield, Eva Pedersen, **3:**883
Butterfly Lovers' Violin Concerto (Chen/He),
    7:348, 350, 432
Butterworth, George, **8:**333
Butts, Magnolia Lewis, **3:**632
Butu people, **1:**642
Buxtehude, Dietrich, **8:**78, 444
Buyi people
    music of, **7:**485–92
    opera of, **7:**452
    tonggu genre, **7:**192
Büyükburç, Erol, **6:**249–50, 251
Buzacott, Aaron, **9:**898
Buzaglo, R. David, **6:**1039
Bwaidoga people, **9:**489
Byelorussian people, *See* Belarusan people
Byrd, Jerry, **3:**80
Byrd, Roy "Professor Longhair," **3:**789
Byrd, William, **2:**819; **8:**76
Byrds (musical group), **3:**133, 316, 318, 348,
    552; **9:**169
Byrne, David, **3:**204, 338–39
Byron, Don, **3:**664, 665
Bystroń, Jan Stanisław, **8:**712
By the Hillside (Buenaventura), **4:**872, 873
By the Light of the Moon (Los Lobos), **3:**750
Bytown Troubadours (musical group), **3:**1166
Byzantine Chanters (Sydney), **9:**72
Byzantine empire, **8:**566, *972*, 986, 1007
    cheironomy in, **8:**100
    influence on Arab music, **6:**362
    in North Africa, **6:**431
Byzantine music, **6:**208–9, 373, 442, 535, 544
    in Bulgaria, **8:**903–4
    in Greece, **8:**1023
    in Romania, **8:**881
Bzhedughis people, **8:**854–56

Ca'aguá culture. *See* Cainguá culture
Caballero, Juan Julián, **2:**568
"Cabbage and Meat (The Half Hitch)" (ballad),
    3:*155–56*
Cab Calloway Orchestra, **3:**787
Cabécar culture, **2:**631–35
    instruments of, **2:**632–33
    population of, **2:**632
    research on, **2:**635, 703
    ritual music of, **2:**633–34
    secular music of, **2:**634–35
Cabeza de Vaca, Alvar Núñez, **3:**770
Cabiddu, Michele, **8:***170*
Cabinda, **1:**667, 668
Cabin Memories (White), **3:**608
Cabot, John, **3:**143, 1056
Caccamise, Roxy, **3:**865
Caccini, Francesca, **8:**199
Cachia, Pierre, **6:**21
Cacoyannis, Michael, **8:**1021
Cactus Mack and the Saddle Tramps, **3:**1091
Cadar, Usopay, **4:**29, 891
Caddo Indian nation, **3:**466, 467
    Ghost Dance songs, **3:**487
Cadena, Chano, **3:**776
cadences
    Abkhazian people, **8:**852

Afghanistan
    chahārbeiti, **5:**819
    Kabuli *ghazal*, **5:**806
    Pashtun songs, **5:**835
Arab *qafla*, **6:**148–49, 549, 550
Armenia, **6:**727
Austral Islands, *hīmene* genres, **9:**881
Azerbaijani *muğam*, **6:**928
Brazil, **2:***308*
    cantoria, **2:**326
Burma, **4:**390, 391, 394
Chechen people, **8:**862
Chile, *verso*, **2:**367
China, *Suzhou tanci*, **7:**264
Colombia, *bambuco*, **2:**387
Croatia, Istrian music, **8:**930
Georgia, **8:**831
Germany, **8:**653
Hindustani music, **5:**131
    mukhṛā, **5:**191, *193*, 197, 200
    tihāī, **5:**155
    tīyā formula, **5:**118
Ingush people, **8:**862
Irian Jaya, Asmat songs, **9:**587, 591
Japan
    gidayû busi, **7:**676, 677, 680
    heikyoku, **7:**680
Java, **4:**657
Karnatak music
    kōrvai, **5:**155–56, *158*, 158–59
    mōrā, **5:**155, *156–57*, 158–59
Kerala, **5:**945
    kalāśam, **5:**936–38
Kiribati, dance-songs, **9:**761
Korea, **7:**851
    in folk songs, **7:**881
    sinawi, **7:**891
in Lao *lam son* genre, **4:**344
Maleku culture, *curijurijanapuretec*, **2:**682
Malta, *spirtu pront*, **8:**636
Maya culture, ritual music, **2:**653
Montenegro, **8:**958
Papua New Guinea
    Abelam songs, **9:**551
    Baluan *kolorai*, **9:**603
    Karkar music, **9:**561
    Siasi music, **9:**575
Persian *forud*, **6:**62
Pukapuka, *pātautau*, **9:**913
Romania, **8:**874
Russia, **8:**757
    byliny, **8:**764–65
Southeast Asia, **4:**15
Suyá invocations, **2:**146
Tahiti
    hīmene rū'au, **9:**871
    hīmene tārava, **9:**871–72
Turkish *makam*, **6:**51
Vanuatu, **9:**699–700
Waiãpí culture, **2:**159
Wales, feminine, **8:**345
Warao culture, shamanic songs, **2:**194–95
West Futuna, **9:**862
Yanomamö culture, shamanic songs, **2:**171
Cadillacs (musical group), **3:**672
Cadman, Charles Wakefield, **3:**367, 539

Cadogan, León, **2:**204
Caesar, Julius, **8:**558
Café Marimba (Toronto), **3:**1080
Cafer Sādik (Jafar al-Sadiq), **6:**794
Cágaba culture. *See* Kogi culture
Cage, John, **3:**14, 130–31, 133, *175*, 175–76,
    252–54, 335, 540, 953, 954, 1015;
    4:132, 881; **7:**342, 708, 737; **8:**85;
    10:41
Cahitan Indian groups, **3:**428, 437–38
Cahuilla Indian nation, **3:**417; **10:**88–89
Cai Qin, **7:**356
Cai Yan, **7:**402, 406
Cai Yong, **7:**159
Cai Yuanding, **7:**119, 128
Cai Yuanpei, **7:**228–29, 376, 377, 381–82
Cai Zhongde, **7:**137
Căianu, Ioan, **8:**881
Cainguá culture, **2:**199, 201. *See also* Guaraní
    culture
Caird, John, **3:**200
Cairo National Conservatory, **6:**323–24
Cairo, Nauplion, Khartoum (album), **8:**1022
Cairo Opera House, **6:**547, *607–8*, 610–11
Cairo Symphony Orchestra, **6:**611, *611*
Cajas Castro, Juan, **2:**585, 587
Cajuns. *See* French-Americans
Cakchiquel Maya, **2:**721–22, 736
    instruments of, **2:**728, 729
    songs of, **2:**732
cakewalk, **3:**651
Cakkiliyar caste, **5:**911, 915
Cākyār caste, **5:**363, 399, 509, 510, 511, 931
Calabar Brass Band, **1:**477
Caldas Barbosa, Domingos, **2:**304
Caldas, Luís, **2:**354
Caldas, Waldenyr, **2:**320
Calderash, Hans, **8:**289
Calderón, Eduardo, **10:**100, *100*
Calderón, Juan Bustillo, **2:***192*
Calderón de la Barca, Frances, **2:**600
"Caldonia" (Jordan), **3:**668
Cale, John, **3:**204
Caledonian Pocket Companion, **8:**372
Calendar, Ebenezer, **1:**377, 380, 381
Calero, Bibiano, **4:**866
Calero, Leocadio, **4:**866
Calgary Opera Company, **3:**1230–31
Calgary Philharmonic Orchestra, **3:***1230*
Calgary Philharmonic Society, **3:**1090
California
    Arab people in, **3:**1029
    Armenian people in, **3:**1030
    Basque people in, **3:**217, 847
    blues in, **3:**639
    Filipino people in, **3:**1024
    Fresno
        Hmong people in, **3:**948
        Lao people in, **3:**1007–9
    Gujarati people in, **3:**980
    Gustine, **3:**732
    Hmong people in, **3:**1003–5
    hula dancing in, **3:**1051
    Indonesian people in, **3:**1011
    Iranian people in, **3:**1031; **6:**877–78
    Japanese people in, **7:**628

California (*continued*)
jazz in, **3:**651
Latino and Hispano peoples in, **3:**718–19, 721, 734–51; **10:**88–95
Long Beach, Cambodian people in, **3:**998
Los Angeles
Arab people in, **3:**1036
Asian communities in, **3:**949
as center for country music, **3:**76
Central American communities in, **3:**727
Chicano music, **3:**720
Chinese people in, **3:**957, 961
dance styles in, **3:**212
Estonian people in, **3:**878, 879
Filipino people in, **3:**1024
gospel music in, **10:**149–51, 154
Greek people in, **3:**929
Hawai'ians in, **3:**1050
history of musical life, **3:**735–51
Iranian popular music in, **3:**1031, 1034–35
Italian people in, **3:**860
Japanese people in, **3:**968–69, 970
Korean people in, **3:**975–79
Latin Caribbean community, **3:**790, 798–99
Mexican people in, **3:**734–51
rhythm and blues in, **3:**669
Santería in, **3:**784
Thai people in, **3:**950, 1010
Turkish people in, **3:**1030
zarzuela companies, **3:**851
Mendocino, Middle Eastern Music and Dance Camp, **3:**1037
Mexican people in, **3:**721, 734–51
Native American groups in, **3:**371, 394–96, 412–18, 420–22, 425–27, 428–38, 734–35
north-central, **3:**415–16
northeastern, **3:**415
northwestern, **3:**412–14
Orange County, Vietnamese people in, **3:**949, 993, 995, 996
Pasadena, country music radio broadcasts, **3:**560
Portuguese people in, **3:**848, 849, 851
rap in, **3:**698, 714
San Diego, Filipino people in, **3:**1025
San Francisco
Asian communities in, **3:**948–49
Chicano rock in, **3:**751
Chinese people in, **3:**527, 957, 958–59, *961*, 964–65
Estonian people in, **3:**878
Greek people in, **3:**929
Hawai'ians in, **3:**1050
Irish people in, **3:**842
Italian people in, **3:**860, 861
Japanese people in, **3:**968–73
Latin Caribbean community, **3:**790, 798
pan-Latin American culture in, **3:**746
public school music education, **3:**275
punk in, **3:**171
Santería in, **3:**784
Sufism in, **3:**1042–43
Turkish people in, **3:**1030
zarzuela companies, **3:**851
San Joaquin Valley Indian groups, **3:**416

San Jose
Cham people in, **3:**1010
Vietnamese people in, **3:**993
South Asian people in, **3:**981
southern Indian groups, **3:**417–18
Spanish settlement in, **3:**521, 734–35, 847
Tahitian dancing in, **3:**1052
western swing in, **3:**79
California Corazón (Reyes), **3:**749
California Folk Music Project, **3:**737
California Institute of the Arts (Valencia), **3:**1013, 1015
Calinago culture, **2:**78
calinda, **3:**596
Çalıntı (periodical), **6:**249
Caliponau culture, **2:**78
Callado, Joaquim Antonio da Silva, **2:**350
Callas, Maria, **8:**1008
Callawaya culture, **2:**283
Calleja, Father José, **4:**842
Callender, Charles, **3:**616
Callewaert, Felix, **8:**531
calligraphy. *See* visual arts
Call Me Madam (Berlin), **3:**310, 545
Call of the Morning Bird, **9:**969
Calloway, Cab, **3:**742
call to prayer. *See* chant (Muslim); language and music
Caló, Miguel, **2:**264
Caluza, Reuben T., **1:**218, 764, 769–70, 772
Calvin, Jean, **3:**118–19
Calvinism, **3:**118–119, 122, 124–25
Calvo, Luís A., **2:**394, 395
Calvo, Luz María, **2:**212
calypso, **1:**377, 380; **2:**86, 93, 95–96, 97; **3:**337; **8:**235
in Antigua and Barbuda, **2:**800
in Australia, **9:**443
in Bahamas, **2:**802
in Barbados, **2:**819–21
blue beat and *kaiso* styles, **2:**819
in Canada, **3:**1170, 1202, 1203, 1209, 1212–13
in Carriacou, **2:**868
in Costa Rica, **2:**691–93
development of, **2:**796
in Dominica, **2:**843
in Grenada, **2:**865, 866–67
in Guatemala, **2:**733, 734
in Guyana, **2:**445–46; **5:**604
in Jamaica, **2:**908
links to Belize brukdown genre, **2:**678
links to Martinican *zouk*, **2:**918, 920
links to Surinam *kaseko* genre, **2:**508
in Montserrat, **2:**923–24, 925, 926
in Panama, **2:**773
in St. Lucia, **2:**949–50
sound recordings of, **2:**52
in Sri Lanka, **5:**970
in Trinidad and Tobago, **2:**962, 963–64; **3:**813
Indian, **2:**957, 959
in Turkey, **6:**249
in United States, **3:**809–10, 811
in Virgin Islands, **2:**970, 973
Calypso Association of Canada, **3:**1085

Calypsonian Commander, **2:**820
Camacho, Gonzalo, **10:**88
Camacho, Manuel "El Perro," **3:**737
Camacho Fajardo, Gema, **2:**599
Camār caste. *See* Chamār caste
Camara, Sory, **1:**510
Camargo, Jorge, **2:**395
Camarón, **8:**599
Câmbio Negro, **2:**354
Cambodia. *See also* Khmer people
Akha people in, **4:**540–42
aristocracy in, **4:**118
Chăm people in, **4:**590–91
classical music traditions in, **4:**7
composition in, **4:**127
cultural origins of, **4:**10–11
foreign influences in, **4:**156–57
French in, **4:**154, 157
geography of, **4:**151
Hinduism in, **4:**64
Karen people in, **4:**543–46
map of, **4:***152*
monochords in, **4:**59
music research on, **4:**24, 25, 150, 160, 529
pedagogy in, **4:**119–20
Phnom Penh, **4:**5
popular music in, **4:**207–8
population of, **4:**151–52, 156
prehistoric, **4:**157
Ramayana in, **5:**261
representative music of, **4:**23, 133–34
revival movement in, **4:**123–24, 158–59
salient musical features of, **4:**17–18
snake cult in, **4:**52
upland peoples of, **4:**529
village life in, **4:**6
wars in, **4:**11, 90–91, 118, 151, 153–54, 187, 208–10
Western music in, **4:**81, 207
Cambodian American Heritage (Maryland), **3:**1001
Cambodian Network Council, **3:**953, 1001
Cambodian people
in Hawai'i, **9:**100
in North America, **3:***19*, 219, 948–49, 950, 998–1002
Chinese ethnic groups, **3:**961
court music performances, **3:**999–1000
folk arts of, **3:**1001
popular music, **3:**1002
Cambridge Expedition, **9:**429, 479, 960
Camelot (Lerner and Loewe), **3:**545
Cameo (musical group), **3:**684
Camerata Canada, **3:**1186
Cameron, G. F., **3:**1182
Cameron, John Allan, **3:**1129
Cameron, Moira, **3:**1277
Cameroon. *See also* Central Africa; West Africa; *specific peoples*
Angola ideographs and, **1:**150
Bali people, performance spaces, **1:**117
Bantu cultures of, **1:**659–63
Bata people, performance spaces, **1:**117
court music, **1:**313–14
dance, **1:**113, 116
Duala people, speech surrogate methods, **1:**106

Fulɓe kingdom, court music, **1:**311–12
guitars, **1:**363
harps, **1:**301–2
iron bells, **1:**310
lamellophones, **1:**318–19
Lokele people, speech surrogate methods, **1:**106
Lus people, funeral ceremonies, **1:**111
makossa, **1:**387, 422, 682
Mbem people, dance, **1:**110
music of, **1:**367, 659–63
music research in, **1:**49
popular music of, **1:**323
Vai people, writing system, **1:**147
xylophone ensembles, **1:**668
Yaounde people, speech surrogate methods, **1:**106, 107
Cameroonian people, in France, **8:**231
Camerton (musical group), **7:**1020
Cameu, Helza, **2:**123
Camilleri, Charles, **8:**642
Caminha, Pero Vaz de, **2:**301
Camoes Players of Maui, **9:**98
Campa, Arthur L., **3:**757, 762, 767
Campa culture, **2:**482
Campa, Gustavo, **2:**604
campaign music, American, **3:**304–11, 505
Campbell, Alexander, **8:**373
Campbell, Ambrose Adekoya, **1:**380
Campbell, Archibald, **8:**373–74
Campbell, Dan J., **3:**1071
Campbell, David, **3:**1094
Campbell, Donald, **8:**373
Campbell, Duncan, **8:**361
Campbell, Elaine, **3:**199
Campbell, J. G. D., **4:**330
Campbell, John, **8:**98
Campbell, John Lorne, **8:**371, 373
Campbell, Joshua, **8:**373
Campbell, Lucie, **10:**138
Campbell, Norman, **3:**199
Campbell, Patricia Shehan, **3:**276, 996
Campos, Augusto de, **2:**318, 320
Campos, Carlos M., **2:**704
Campos, Ronaldo, **2:**501
Camposeco, Jerónimo, **3:**728
Campsie, Alistair, **8:**374
Camrose Lutheran College (Alberta), **3:**1251
Can, Halil, **6:**119
"Can I Get a Witness" (Gaye), **3:**674
Canada. *See also specific provinces, peoples, and topics*
  Albanian people in, **3:**517; **8:**986
  Arctic peoples of, **7:**786, 1028
  Arctic regions, **3:**374–81
    European settlement of, **3:**379
  attitudes toward history, **3:**21–23
  ballads in, **8:**23, 135
  Barrens region, **3:**374, 384
  bhangra dance in, **5:**500
  Cantonese opera in, **7:**303
  Church of God and Saints of Christ in, **3:**127
  class structures in, **3:**50–53, 1070
  colonial musical life, **3:**7–9, 142–43, 144–45, 238–39, 1056–57, 1079

  cultural differences with United States, **3:**15–17
  cultural exchanges with Asia, **3:**129
  dance in, **3:**222–26
  East Asian people in, **7:**6
  ethnic musics in, **3:**97–98
  expulsion of Acadians, **3:**9, 856, 1115, 1135–36
  folk music revival in, **3:**94
  folk song collecting in, **3:**145–46, 292–93, 410, 1250
  French-English polarity, **3:**17, 51–52, 74, 143
  fusion genres in, **3:**331–33
  geography of, **3:**2, 3, 16–17, 245, 313, 1066
  Georgian people in, **8:**845
  governmental policies toward music, **3:**288–302
  history of education in, **3:**275–79
  history of musical culture, **3:**5–15
  instrument making in, **3:**1067, 1116, 1180–81
  Japanese people in, **2:**86
  jazz in, **3:**1105–7
  Jesuits in, **3:**484–85
  Jewish people in, **6:**1036
  Maltese people in, **8:**634
  maps of, **3:***xii–xvi*
  Maronite Church in, **6:**208
  musical profile of, **3:**2–20
  musical theater in, **3:**198–200
  North African emigrant communities in, **6:**438
  Nova Scotia, Gaelic music in, **8:**373
  political and social organization of, **3:**3–5
  popular music, nineteenth century, **3:**189
  population of, **3:**4–5, 246, 313, 1066
  Portuguese people in, **8:**576
  public school music education, **3:**275–76, 279–83
  racial issues in, **3:**72–74
  relations with Europe, **3:**17
  relations with United States, **3:**18–20
  rural, suburban, and urban contexts in music making, **3:**142–44
  Sikh community in, **3:**981
  singing schools in, **3:**7, 1069–70, 1115–16, 1179, 1180, 1189–90
  slavery in, **3:**8, 17, 1057, 1078, 1169
  South Asian community in, **5:**578–86
  South Asian population of, **5:**578
  steel guitar associations, **3:**1049
  Subarctic regions, **3:**383–92
    European settlement of, **3:**390–91
  urbanization of, **3:**10
  westward expansion of, **3:**9–11
  women composers in, **3:**93, 1152
Canada Council for the Arts, **3:**226, 292, 295–96, 301, 1066–67, 1120, 1151, 1185, 1216, 1231
Canadian Academy of Music, **3:**1079
Canadian Airs (Back), **3:**1164
Canadian-Arab Friendship Society, **3:**1090
Canadian Arts Council, **3:**288
"Canadian Boat Song" (Moore), **3:**1163–64
Canadian Brass (musical group), **3:**1080, 1186
Canadian Broadcasting Corporation, **3:**18, 52, 247, 249, 295–96, 315, 1101–3, 1121, 1184, 1185, 1228, 1278

Canadian Center for Folk Culture Studies, **3:**292
Canadian Chinese Folk Dance Institute, **3:**1217
Canadian Citizenship Act (1947), **3:**13
Canadian Composers' League, **3:**1151
Canadian Copyright Act, **3:**301
Canadian Electronic Ensemble, **3:**1080
Canadian Federation of Music Teacher Associations, **3:**276
Canadian League of Composers (Toronto), **3:**1185
Canadian Mennonite Bible College (Winnipeg), **3:**1239
Canadian Museum of Civilization (Ottawa/Hull), **3:**291, 1067
Canadian Music Centre, **3:**1067, 1068, 1151, 1185
Canadian Music Educators' Association, **3:**276
Canadian Musical Heritage series, **3:**1180
Canadian Musical Heritage Society, **3:**1108–9
"Canadian National Air" (Lazare), **3:**289
Canadian National Railways, **3:**1183–84
Canadian Opera Company, **3:**1120, 1184–85
Canadian Pacific Railway, **3:**146, 343, 1058, 1076, 1092, 1095, 1154, 1166, 1225, 1255
Canadian Radio Broadcasting Commission, **3:**247, 1067
Canadian Radio-Television and Telecommunications Commission (Canadian Radio-Television Commission, CRTC), **3:**247, 250, 290, 314–15, 1068, 1101, 1103, 1104, 1107
Canadian Ukrainian Opera Association, **3:**1082
Canadian Women's Association of Alberta, **3:**1247
Canainī (epic), **5:**667
Canales, Johnny, **3:**780
Canales, Laura, **3:**780
Canaro, Francisco, **2:**519
Canary Islanders, in Dominican Republic, **2:**847
Canary Islands, speech surrogate methods, **1:**106
Canberra School of Music, **9:**255
Canboulay Dance Theatre (Toronto), **3:**224
Can-Can (Porter), **3:**545
"Canción mexicana" (Guerrero), **3:**739
Cancionero Vasco (Manterola), **8:**316
Canciones de Mi Padre (Ronstadt), **3:**725, 745, 751
Candies (musical group), **7:**747
Candomblé (also *candomblé*), **1:**316
  in Argentina, **2:**260
  in Brazil, **2:**48, 69, 341, 342–43, 348, 351, 352–53
    instruments in, **2:**309
    transvestite performers, **2:**57
    use of drums, **2:**32
  Congo-Angola groups, **2:**341
  de Caboclo groups, **2:**341, 342, 344
  Gêge-Nagô groups, **2:**341, 342–43
  in Paraguay, **2:**457
  Sergipe groups, **2:**341
Cánepa, Gisela, **2:**36
Caner, Y., **6:**258
Cangyang jiacuo Love Song (Tibetan writing), **7:**472

Caninha (samba performer), 2:350
Cannibal and the Headhunters (musical group),
    3:746, 747
Cannibal Tours (film), 9:49
Cannon, Roderick D., 8:374
Cannon Stars, 1:684
Cannon's Jug Stompers, 3:645
CANO (musical group), 3:1194
Cano, Eddie, 3:741, 743, 799
Cano, Natividad, 3:724, 724–25, 744
Canon, Fernando, 4:870, 872
Canonge, Mario, 2:919
Canseco, George, 4:885
Canseco, José, 4:857, 862–63, 868
Cantares (musical group), 2:703
Cantares de Dzitbalché, 2:650
Il cantastorie (periodical), 8:613
cantata, 8:79, 654
    church performances of, 3:122
Canteloube, Joseph, 8:574
Cantemir, Demetrius (Dimitrie), 6:18, 56, 109,
    113, 119, 120, 122, 124–27, 569,
    771; 8:881, 885
Cantemos label, 3:765
Canterbury University, 9:932
Canti popolari abbruzzesi (Tosti), 8:618
Cantilena (Israeli ensemble), 6:1063
cantillation. *See* chant; language and music
Canto, danza, y música precortesianos (Martí),
    2:623
Cantonese opera, 7:303–9
    accompaniment of, 7:217–18
    avocational performers of, 7:396
    development of, 7:89
    diffusion of, 7:303–4
    Hawai'i and Australia, 9:70–71
    history and contexts, 7:304–8
    Hong Kong, 3:1261; 7:431, 433, 434–35;
        10:18, 21–24
    influence on popular music, 7:355
    narrative songs in, 7:273
    North America, 3:11, 527, 949, 951, 958,
        960, 1083, 1095, 1217, 1247, 1260
    performance schools of, 7:55
    repertoire of, 7:308–9
    research on, 7:139
    Thailand, 4:70–71
    Western elements in, 7:306
Cantor, Eddie, 3:544
Cantors Assembly, 3:940
Cantú, Norma, 10:94
Canyon Records, 2:593; 3:449, 484, 486, 498,
    1087
Cao Đài, 3:996; 4:444, 506
Cao Dongfu, 7:172
Cao Hanzai, 7:290
Cao Shanggang, 7:132
Caouan xiaojiemei (Wu), 7:349
Caoyuan qibing (Hu), 7:189
Cape Breton Fiddlers' Association, 3:1128
Cape Coast Sugar Babies, 1:477
Cape Malay people, 1:761, 762
Cape Verde, 2:844
Cape Verdean people
    in North America, 3:848
    in Portugal, 8:576

Capercaillie (musical group), 8:371
Capers, Valerie, 3:610
Capiba (Lourenço Barbosa), 2:337
Capitan, El (Sousa), 3:193
Capitol Records, 3:265, 352, 714, 741, 787;
    9:998
Capitol Theatre (Moncton), 3:1120
Cappa, Carlo, 3:564
Capuchin order, Venezuela mission schools of,
    2:188
Cara, Irene, 3:751
Carabalí (León), 3:612
Carabao, 4:98, 332
Caractéristiques de l'art vocal arabe au Moyen Age
    (Shiloah), 6:1062
Cāraṇ caste, 5:399, 402, 403, 405, 635, 641
Caravaglios, Cesare, 8:621
"Caravan" (Ellington and Tizol), 3:732
Caravan (musical group), 4:98, 332
Caraveli, Anna, 3:931; 8:120
Carby, Hazel, 3:104, 582
Cardenal Argüello, Salvador, 2:663, 764, 767
Cardenas, Jenny, 2:298
Cárdenas Pinelo, Augusto "Guy," 2:620
Cardew, Cornelius, 8:98
Cardiffian Georgian Choir, 8:845
Cardozo, Felix Pérez, 2:456
Cardozo Ocampo, Mauricio, 2:463
Carey, Iskandar, 4:569
Carey, Mariah, 3:712, 715
cargo cults, 9:189
    Papua New Guinea, 9:570
        Nissan Atoll, 9:639
    Vanuatu, John Frum movement, 9:32,
        214–15
Caribbean. *See also specific countries and cultures*
    Amerindian ceremonies, 2:45
    Anglophone areas, 2:95–98
    archaeomusicological studies in, 2:8
    cultural composition, 2:792–93
    economics, 2:791–92
    folklore of, 2:18–19
    Francophone areas, 2:95, 98
    geography of, 2:789
    historical accounts of, 2:22–23
    history of, 2:78, 81, 791–93
    iconographical record in, 2:13
    immigrant groups of, 2:83–91
    immigration in, 2:4
    maps of, 2:3, 788, 790, 794
    musical culture of, 2:793, 795–97
    native peoples of, 2:78, 81
    politics in, 2:795–96
    popular music of, 2:75–76, 920
    population of, 2:789
    tourism in, 2:50
Caribbean Council of Churches, 2:901
Caribbean Cultural Committee (Toronto),
    3:1208, 1209
Caribbean Currents (Manuel), 2:913
Caribbean Ecumenical Consultation for
    Development, 2:942
Caribbean people
    in Australia, 9:82–84
    in Europe, 2:791
    in France, 8:231–32, 234

    in Great Britain, 8:231–32, 235–36, 336
    in North America, 2:791; 3:13, 848, 1057,
        1063
        English-speaking communities, 3:808–12
        fusion genres of, 3:337
        hip-hop culture, 3:692–93, 701
        Maritimes, 3:1132
        Montréal, 3:1073, 1077, 1169, 1170
        Prairie Provinces, 3:1086
        Toronto, 3:17, 73, 223, 1078, 1082, 1085,
            1201–3, 1207–9, 1212–13
    in Panama, 2:771
Carib culture, 2:78
    in Barbados, 2:813
    in Carriacou, 2:867–68
    in Central America, 2:668, 733
    ceremonies of, 2:45
    in Dominica, 2:840
    in Dominican Republic, 2:846
    extermination of, 2:791, 798
    in Grenada, 2:864, 865
    in Guyana, 2:442
    instruments of, 2:13, 23
    in Montserrat, 2:922
    in Netherlands Antilles and Aruba, 2:927, 928
    in Surinam, 2:503
    in Trinidad and Tobago, 2:952
    in Virgin Islands, 2:968
Caribou Inuit, 3:374, 381
Caribou Records, 3:1278
Carignan, Jean, 3:1168
Carle, Rainer, 4:603
Carlebach, Shelomo, 6:202, 204
Carleton University (Ottawa), 3:1185
Carli, Denis de, 1:77–78
Carlisle, Earl of, 2:813
Carlisle, Roxane Connick, 1:51, 561
Carlos, Roberto, 2:103, 109
Carlos, Wendy, 3:254, 955; 4:132
Carluén, Alejo, 4:857, 859, 864, 866, 871
Carluén, Gavino, 4:859, 864, 865, 866
Carmen (Bizet), 3:791; 7:743
Carmichael, Hoagy, 3:196, 549
Carmichael, Mrs. J. B., 3:1228
Carmichael, Stokeley, 10:138
Carmina Burana, 8:652
Carmody, Kev, 9:443–44
Carmona Maya, Sergio Ivan, 2:783
Carnatic tradition. *See* Karnatak (Karnatic)
    tradition
Carnegie Corporation of New York, 3:1116
Carnegie Hall (New York), 3:578, 610, 647, 846,
    1107
carnival, 2:47, 94. *See also* festivals, celebrations,
    and holidays
    agriculture and, 8:140
    Andean regions, 2:215, 220, 221
    Antigua and Barbuda, 2:799
    Argentina, 2:258–59, 273, 522
    Atacameño culture, 2:360–61
    Balkan region, 8:140
    Basque region, 8:140, 314–15
    Belgium, 8:525, 527
    Bolivia, 2:210, 216–17, 287, 289–90, 292
    Brazil, 2:94, 108, 110, 133, 309, 324–25,
        335–38

Bahia, **2:**351–53
 Rio de Janeiro, **2:**62
 samba in, **2:**314–16, 350–51
Bulgaria, **8:**140, 161, 897, 899
Caribbean, **2:**795
Colombia, **2:**405, 406
Costa Rica, **2:**693
Croatia, **8:**925
Cuba, **2:**94, 836
Dominica, **2:**843
Dominican Republic, **2:**852, 859
Faroe Islands, **8:**469
France, Istres, **8:**551
Germany, **8:**649, 657
Goa, **5:**738, 740
Greece, **8:**1015, 1016
Grenada, **2:**866
Guadeloupe, **2:**876–77
Haiti, **2:**94, 890, 894
Italy, **8:**608
Low Countries, **8:**522
Martinique, **2:**915
Mixtec culture, **2:**566
Montserrat, **2:**925–26
New York, West Indian, **2:**796; **3:**507–8
opera and oratorio performances during,
  8:51
Otomí culture, **2:**573
Panama, **2:**772, 778, 782–83
Peru, **2:**211, 228–29, 470, 477
 son de los diablos performances, **2:**494
Poland, **8:**704
Purépecha culture, **2:**578
Russia, **8:**758, 759
Slovenia, **8:**911, 915
social class and, **8:**16
Spain, **8:**589–91
Switzerland, **8:**140, 161, 684–85, 686
Trinidad and Tobago, **2:**95–97, *787*, 796, 807,
  962, 964–66; **3:**810, 813; **5:**590
Uruguay, **2:**510, 511, 515–19, 520, 521, 522
Virgin Islands, **2:**973
Carolan, Nicholas, **8:**393, 394
Caroline Islands, **9:**712, 754. *See also* Palau
 Christianity in, **9:**720
 instruments of, **9:**716
 music and dance of, **9:**719, 739, 979
 research on, **9:**25
 settlement of, **9:**715
 slack-key guitar music, **9:**160
 sound recordings from, **9:**994
 theatrical societies, **9:**229
Carolinian people, in Saipan, **9:**746
carols and caroling. *See also villancico*
 aguinaldo genre, **3:**727
 Albania, **8:**194, 988
 Arabian peninsula, in expatriate communities,
  6:717
 Armenia, **6:**728, *730*
 Austria, **8:**673
  Tyrol region, **8:**672
 Barbados, **2:**819
 Belarus, **8:**791, 794, *795*
 Bulgaria, *koleda*, **8:**899
 England, **8:**132–33, 140, 331
  Yorkshire, **8:**328

Europe, **8:**5, 132–33, 139–40, 325
 France, *noëls*, **8:**542, 546
 Georgia, **8:**835
 Germany, **8:**651
 Great Lakes Indians, **3:**458
 Latvia, **8:**502
 Low Countries, **8:**522
 Macedonia, **8:**973
 Montenegro, **8:**958
 mumming traditions, **3:**1070
 North America, **3:**825, 1108
 Ontario, **3:**1178
 Romania, **8:**879
  colinde, **8:**131, *132*, 140, 869
 Romanian-American, **3:**911
 Russia, **8:**758–59
 Serbia, *koleda*, **8:**940
 Slovenia, **8:**917
  koledniki, **8:**912
 Spain, **8:**589, 592, 601
 Swedish-American, **3:**871–72
 Ukraine, *koliadky*, **8:**808, 812–13
 Wales, **8:**346
  May, **8:**343, 346–47
  plygain, **8:**343, 344, 347, 349–50, *351*
Caron, Nelly, **6:**70
Carousel (Rodgers and Hammerstein), **3:**197
Carpenter, Carole, **3:**1060
Carpenter, James Madison, **8:**371
Carpenter, Lynn, **3:**58
Carpenter Performing Arts Center (Long Beach),
  3:1053
Carpentier, Alejo, **2:**838
Carpitella, Diego, **8:**21, 607, *621*, 621–22,
  632
Carr, Benjamin, **3:**180, 289, 538
Carr, Emily, **3:**1093
Carr, Leroy, **3:**645
Carr, Vikki, **3:**732, 745, 751
Carrabré, Patrick, **3:**1091
Carranza Soriano, Juan, **10:***91*
Carrasco, Gonzal, **2:**453
Carrasco, René, **2:**861
Carreras, José, **2:**263; **3:**852
Carriacou, **2:**864, 867–72
 history of, **2:**867–68
 homemade instruments of, **2:**871
 instruments of, **2:**870, 871
 musical genres
  big-drum tradition, **2:**793, 868–70
  game songs, **2:**868
  parang, **2:**868, 871
  passplay, **2:**868
  quadrille, **2:**868
  vocal, **2:**868
Carricarte, Pedro, **2:**396
Carrillo, Julián, **2:**604
Carrington, J. F., **1:**663
Carrington, John, **10:**56
Carrión, Balbino, **4:**862, 866
Carrión, Isabel V., **2:**431
Carrol, Father K., **1:**36
Carroll, Diahann, **3:**621
Carroll, John, **3:**355
Carroll, Lewis, **3:**176, 541
Carroll, Liz, **3:***843*; **10:***83*

"Carry Me Back to Old Virginny" (Bland),
  3:192, 543, 616
Carson, Fiddlin' John, **3:**78, *263*
Carta, Maria, **8:**613
Cartagena, Antonio, **2:**487
Cartas anuas, **2:**200, 453
Cartel (rap group), **6:**247
Carter, Asa, **3:**354–55
Carter, Charles, **2:**805
Carter, Elliott, **3:**14, 367, 540; **8:**85
Carter Family, **3:**13, 78, *78*, 81, 240, 520
Carter, Hazel, **2:**898
Carter, Maybelle, **3:**78
Carter, Wilf, **3:**265, 1073, 1091
Carter, William G., **1:**32; **10:**140
Carthage, **1:**533
Carthaginian culture, in Spain, **8:**588
Cartier, Jacques, **3:**143, 392
Cartridge Music (Cage), **3:**253–54
Carus, Paul, **3:**130
Caruso, Enrico, **3:**195, 242, 528, 537, 861, 863;
  8:618, 728
Carvajal, José, **4:**864
Carvalho-Neto, Paulo de, **2:**431, 464
Carvallo, Jorge Isaac, **2:**764
Carver, Robert, **8:**366–67
"Car Wash" (Royce), **3:**712
Casa de la Cultura (Ecuador), **2:**414
Casa Paoli Folk Research Center (Puerto Rico),
  2:940
Casadesus, Robert, **3:**611
Casals, Pablo, **6:**1025
"Casey Jones" (ballad), **3:**639, 873
Cash, Johnny, **3:**520, 552
Cashibo culture, **2:**482
Cask of Amontillado (Perry), **3:**611
Cass, Lewis, **3:**307
Cass-Beggs, Barbara, **3:**411
Cassandra, **6:***693*
Cassette Cultures (Manuel), **10:**53
cassettes. *See* sound recordings
Cassiodorus, **8:**92
Casso and the Axons, **9:**145
Castañeda, Daniel, **2:**623
castanets. *See* concussion idiophones
caste, **5:**9–10, 397–98, 480. *See also* Harijans;
  specific caste names
 association with specific instruments, **5:**350–51
 Balochistan, **5:**775
 of *dēvadāsi*, **5:**386–87, 392
 development of, **5:**374–75
 Ḍholi people, **5:**280
 Goa, **5:**735–36, 737
 hereditary musicians, **5:**344–45, 350, 360,
  398–406
 importance of, **5:**405
 instrument specializations and, **5:**389–90
 Kerala, **5:**929, 930–34, 934
 Nepal, **5:**696–700
  Newār people, **5:**702–3
 Rajasthan, **5:**7
 relations in South India, **5:**383, 386–90,
  391–92
 role in artists' expectations, **5:**8–10
 scheduled, **5:**9, 866 (*See also* Harijans)
 South Africa, **5:**615

caste (*continued*)
Sri Lanka, **5:**961
Tamil Nadu, **5:**910–11, 922, 925, 927
thread-wearing, **5:**274
Caste War, **2:**666
Castel, Nico, **3:**852
Castellanos, Rafael Antonio de, **2:**735
Castelnuovo, Vittorio, **8:**694
Castelnuovo-Tedesco, Mario, **3:**367; **8:**252
Castilla, Alberto, **2:**395
Castillo, Bobby, **9:**101
Castillo, Father Lorenzo, **4:**842
Castillo, Jesús, **2:**736
Castillo, Rafael, **2:**736
Castle House (New York), **3:**651
"Castle House Rag" (Europe), **3:**651
Castle, Vernon and Irene, **3:**651, 706
Caston, Ineze, **10:**149–50
Castro, Fidel, **3:**719
Castro, Francisco, **2:***546*
Castro, Francisco "Capiro," **3:***765*
Castro, João de, **5:**740
Castro, Raúl, **2:**520
Cat Records, **3:**352
Catalans, **8:**12
Catalogue de la chanson folklorique française
(Laforte), **3:**1167
Catalonia. *See* Spain
Catamo, Nonna Spella, **8:***609*
Catatan-catatan Pengetahuan Karawitan
(Martopangrawit), **4:**637
Cataveryen (deity), **5:**599
Catawba Indian nation, **3:**466
Cathayans (musical group), **3:**970
Cáthedra de Flamenco, **8:**598
Catherine the Great, empress of Russia, **8:**286,
766
Catholic church music, Philippines, **4:**841–45,
861–62, 868
Catinica, **8:**277
Catío culture, **2:**379
Catlin, Amy, **4:**26; **10:**88, 90, 95
Cato, Pauline, **8:***331*
Caton, Margaret, **6:**23–24
Caton, Steven C., **6:**21, 24
Cats (Lloyd Webber), **3:**198, 200, 545
Caturdaṇḍī Prakāśikā (Venkatamakhi), **5:**46–47,
97
Caudamma (deity), **5:**878
Caudeiron, Mable "Cissie," **2:**840
Caudillo, Connie, **3:**798
Caudillo, Henry, **3:**798
Cavaliers (musical group), **3:**1213
Cavanagh, Beverley, **3:**381
Cavazzi, António Giovanni, **1:**667–68
Cavour, Ernesto, **2:**289, 298
Cawley, Colonel Harris N., **10:**152
Cayabyab, Ryan, **4:**881, 885
Cayapa culture, **2:**414
Cayetano, Pen, **2:**677
Cayetano, Sebastian, **2:**668
Caymmi, Dorival, **2:**351
Cayton, Horace R., **3:**624
Caytronics label, **3:**741
Cayuga Indian nation, **3:**462, 1078
Cayulef, Gregorii, **2:**238

Cazden, Norman, **3:***1189*
Cazimero, Brothers, **9:**1008
CBC-LM label, **3:**296, 1103
CBC Opera Company, **3:**296, 1184
CBC Québec Chamber Orchestra, **3:**296
CBC-SM label, **3:**296, 1103
CBC Symphony Orchestra (Toronto), **3:**296,
1102, 1184
CBC Vancouver Chamber Orchestra, **3:**296
CBC Vancouver Orchestra, **3:**1096
CBC Winnipeg Chamber Orchestra, **3:**296
CBC Winnipeg Orchestra, **3:**1228
CBS Corporation, **3:**264
CBS International, **3:**776
CBS Records, **3:**711
CC Music Factory, **3:**698
Ceaucescu, Nicolae, **8:**883
Ceballos, Carlos, **2:***379*
Cedeño Morales, Antonio, **2:***700–701*
Ceja, Richard, **3:**741
Celebes. *See* Sulawesi
Çelebi (honorific). *See previous element in name*
Celestin, Louis, **3:**805
Célini, Raymond, **2:**879
Cellālüddin (or Celaleddin) Rūmī. *See* Jalāl al-
Dīn Rūmī
Celli, Joseph, **3:**954
Celluloid/Mélodie, **8:**239, 241
Celtic Academy, **8:**552
Celtic label, **3:**1128
Celtic Mass for the Sea (Macmillan), **3:**1070
Celtic music and culture, **8:**226, 247, 319–22,
535. *See also* Brittany; Ireland;
Scotland; Wales
in Brittany, **8:**558, 560–61
in England, **8:**326
history of, **8:**319
in Iceland, **8:**400
ideology of, **8:**185
in North America, **3:**223, 326, 845–46,
1110
British Columbia, **3:**1096
Maritimes, **3:**150–51, 1071, 1121, 1123,
1127–30
Ontario, **3:**1081, 1082, 1188–91
research on, **8:**40, 41, 322
in Scotland, **8:**360, 364, 366, 372
in Spain, **8:**588
in Wales, **8:**354, 355
Celtic Pipes and Drums of Hawai'i, **9:**95
Cemal Efendi, **6:**109
Cemīl Bey, Tanburī, **6:**757–58, 771–72
Cemīl Tel, Mes'ūd, **6:**117, 121, 757
Cenerentola, La (Rossini), **3:**542, 1181
Censki, Imre and Sándor, **8:**274
censorship and bans. *See also* taboos
Afghanistan
on music, **5:**811
on music and dance, **5:**489, 823, 824
Albania
on religious observances, **8:**986
of song texts and Western popular music,
8:1000
Algeria, on Berber music, **6:**275
Argentina, **2:**269
of *cuarteto*, **2:**274

Austro-Hungarian empire, on Rom culture,
8:271
Azerbaijan, during Soviet era, **6:**924
Barbados
on instruments, **2:**814
Jean and Johnnie dance, **2:**816
Basque region, on dance, **8:**316
Belarus, **8:**790
Bellona, **9:**852
Brazil, of *cantoria*, **2:**326
Brittany, on pagan traditions, **8:**561
Buddhism, **7:**328
Bulgaria, on Rom music, **8:**284
Burma, **4:**90
Canada
on First Nations ceremonies and songs,
3:405, 1062, 1086, 1093–94, 1225
on Northwest Coast ceremonies and songs,
3:395
Caribbean, on drums, **2:**795
Central Asia, on *shash maqām*, **6:**915–16
Chile, **2:**90
of *nueva canción*, **2:**373–74
China, **7:**386, 392
on *bianwen*, **7:**246
of Cantonese opera, **7:**306
on Dai alphabet, **7:**507
on *Peony Pavilion* performance, **7:**295
of ritual or erotic elements in music, **7:**443
on rock, **7:**360, 367, 413
on Western art music, **7:**341
on women opera performers, **7:**407–8
Christianity, on female voice, **6:**19
Chuuk, **9:**737
Colombia, of *bunde*, **2:**386
Czechoslovakia, **8:**730–31
Denmark, Home Mission opposition to
dancing, **8:**459
Dominica, on African traditions, **2:**840
East Asia, on theater, **7:**76
East Polynesia, **9:**208–9
Europe, **8:**84, 93
on old forms of music, **8:**122
on popular music and rock, **8:**211, 217–21
on Rom culture, **8:**271
Finland, on Kalevala singing, **8:**481–82
France, on Celtic languages, **8:**319
Georgia
on American jazz, **8:**845
on church music, **8:**843
Germany, Nazi period, **8:**660–61
Great Britain
on Celtic languages, **8:**319
Musicians' Union ban on foreign
performers, **8:**233
Greece, on *rebetika*, **8:**1019
Greek Orthodox church, on instruments,
8:1023
Grenada, on African dances, **2:**865
Guyana, of African drumming, **2:**444
Hungary, on popular music, **8:**747–48
India
on harmonium, **5:**341, 364
on political cassettes, **5:**552
on *sati*, **5:**643
on temple dancing, **5:**15

Indonesia, **4:**92–93, 106, 108–9, 111
Iran
  on music, **6:**142, 841
  on solo improvised dance, **6:**875–76
Ireland, on crossroads dancing, **8:**390
Irian Jaya, **9:**592
Islam
  on female voice, **6:**19
  on instruments, **6:**768
Japan
  on American and British cultural products,
      7:729, 745, 750
  on Christianity, **7:**724, 756
  on women performers, **7:**764
Jewish use of instruments, **8:**258–59
Judaism, on female voice and instruments,
      6:19, 200–201, 205–6, 1043
Kiribati, **9:**763
Korea, on bands during Japanese occupation,
      7:932
Kosrae, **9:**740, 742
Louisiana, on interracial dating, **3:**354
Marshall Islands, **9:**752
Micronesia, **9:**720
on Native American ceremonial drumming,
      3:7
Nauru, **9:**756, 757
Nepal, prohibitions on women making music,
      5:702, 704
New Caledonia, **9:**672
Norway, on *hardingfele*, **8:**415, 420, 425
Oceania, **9:**229
Pakistan, prohibitions on women making
      music, **5:**749–50
Papua New Guinea, **9:**88, 194, 477–78, 507,
      572, 602
Philippines, **4:**874
Poland, on spring songs, **8:**702
Prince Edward Island, on fiddling contests,
      3:1071
Pueblo nations, on notes, photographs, and
      recordings, **10:**90
Réunion Island, on *maloya*, **5:**611
Russia, **8:**776, 782, 785
  on *chastushki*, **8:**768
  on Rom culture, **8:**271
  on traditional instruments and minstrels,
      8:755, 770
Saami people, on shamanic rituals, **8:**306,
      428
Sāmoa, **9:**235
San Francisco, on Chinese ceremonial gongs,
      3:958–59
Scotland, on bagpipes, **8:**363
Solomon Islands, **9:**157, 665, 667
South America, **2:**54, 60, 70
  of Amerindian music, **2:**125
  on *dēvadāsi* dedication, **5:**387, 409
  of drum playing, **2:**47
  mass media and, **2:**52
  of popular music, **2:**93
  of secular dance, **2:**44
Soviet Union, on *zikr* practice, **6:**938, 944
Spain
  on Basque culture, **8:**315
  on Rom culture, **8:**271

Switzerland, on instrumental music and
      dancing, **8:**693
Taiwan, on political commentary, **7:**356
Tamil Nadu, on women's participation in
      Tyagaraja festival, **5:**392–93
Thailand, **4:**98
Tokelau, **9:**823
Trinidad and Tobago
  of calypso, **2:**963
  carnival participants, **2:**965
  on drumming, **2:**957, 962; **8:**233
Turkey
  on Alevi activities, **6:**791, 793–94, 798, 799
  on arabesk, **6:**256, 776
  on dancers, **6:**116
  on Sufi activities, **6:**108, 118
  on Turkish art music, **6:**255
Tuvalu, **9:**829
Ukraine
  on blind minstrels, **8:**819
  on fieldwork, **8:**821–22
United States
  on African-American drumming and
      dancing, **3:**8–9, 325, 594–95, 626
  on eighteenth-century theater, **3:**838
  on Northwest Coast ceremonies and songs,
      3:395
  on Plains ceremonies and songs, **3:**443
  on rap, **3:**358, 714
Vanuatu, **9:**198
Wales, on harp playing, **8:**353
in Wayana culture, **2:**167
Yemen, on dance, **6:**711
Center for Black Music Research, **10:**144
Center for Ethnic Studies (Latvia), **8:**507
Center for Folklife Programs and Cultural
      Studies (Washington, D.C.), **3:**300
Center for Pacific Islands Studies (University of
      Hawai'i), **9:**971
Center for the Research and Development of
      Cuban Music, **2:**829, 838
Center for Southern Folklore (Memphis), **10:**82
Center for the Study of Rebetic Song, **8:**1020
Center for Traditional Music and Dance (New
      York), **10:**72, 82
Center for World Music (California), **3:**1013,
      1019
Central Africa. *See also specific countries and
      peoples*
  colonialism in, **1:**659
  geography of, **1:**650–52
  harmony in, **1:**723, 741–42
  history of, **1:**657–58, 670–71
  lamellophone distribution, **1:**679
  languages of, **1:**650–52
  maps of, **1:**648, 651
  performance spaces, **1:**677
  popular music of, **1:**216–17, 423–28
  Pygmy musical influences, **1:**658
  research in, **1:**659, 663, 670
Central African Republic. *See also* Central Africa;
      specific peoples
  academic training in, **1:**40
  Aka people, vocal music, **1:**267–69
  harps, **1:**301–2, 655–56
  history of, **1:**650

iron bells, **1:**311
lamellophones, **1:**320
Mpyɛmɔ people, **1:**664
  kembe tuning, **1:**299
  secret societies, **1:**309
music of, **1:**681–96
scales in, **1:**256, 259–69
Central America, **2:**628, 630. *See also specific
      countries and cultures*
  Amerindian cultures of, **2:**78, *80*, 81, 628,
      630
  Andalusian influences in, **6:**449
  archaeomusicological studies in, **2:**7, 8–9
  colonial era in, **2:**46–47
  cultural syncretism in, **2:**46
  folklore of, **2:**19–21
  geography of, **2:**2
  historical accounts of, **2:**23
  history of, **2:**78, 81, 628
  iconographical record in, **2:**13–16
  immigrant groups of, **2:**4, 83–91
  instruments of, **2:**37
  maps of, **2:***3, 80, 629*
  population of, **2:**628, 630
  tourism in, **2:**50
Central Americans. *See* Latino peoples; *specific
      groups*
Central Asia, **6:**895–6. *See also* Kazakhstan;
      Kyrgyzstan; Tajikistan; Turkmenistan;
      Uzbekistan; *specific peoples*
  Buddhism in, **7:**22
  cultural interactions with China, **7:**88
  geography of, **6:**895, 897; **7:**11
  influence on Chinese music and culture,
      7:102–3, 111, 112, 113–14, 167, 176,
      455
  influence on South Asian culture, **5:**14
  instruments in, **6:**900
  Iranian dance traditions in, **6:**875–79
  map of, **6:***896;* **7:***10*
  maqām traditions, **6:**11, 18, 184, 311, 900,
      909–20, 922
  musical mythology in, **6:**181
  nomadic peoples of, **7:**11–14, 23, 28–30
  North Caucasian forced immigration to,
      8:850, 856
  overtone singing in, **6:**193
  Persian regions of, **6:**823
  prehistoric, **7:**12–14
  religion in, **6:**181, 839, 897–901, 909–10,
      935–47, 949–50, 967, 980
  research on music of, **6:**23, 909, 917–18
  sacred music and chant in, **6:**935–47
  settlement patterns in, **6:**897, 901–2
  Turkic peoples in, **6:**77, 345–46, 793
  Turkmen people in, **6:**965–67
  women's religious genres and roles, **6:**945–47
Central Asian Music (Beliaev), **6:**903
Central Australian Aboriginal Media Association,
      9:443, 959, 986, 987
Central Committee Song and Dance Troupe
      (China), **7:**399
Central Conservatory. *See* Conservatory of Music
      (Peking University)
Central Nationalities Song and Dance Troupe
      (China), **7:**442

Central Nationalities University (China), 7:443
Central National Orchestra (Beijing), 7:972
Central Opera and Opera and Ballet Company
	(Beijing), 7:399
Central Organization for Folk Music, 8:480
Central People's Broadcasting Station Chinese
	Folk Orchestra, 7:230–31
Central Philharmonic Orchestra (Beijing), 7:399
Central Political Cadre School (Beijing), 7:397
Central Song and Dance Company (Beijing),
	7:399
Centre for Aboriginal Studies in Music
	(Adelaide), 9:145–46, 415, 442, 443
Centre Communautaire Juif (Montréal), 3:1174
Centre Culturel Yéiwéné Yéiwéné, 9:992
Centre de Documentation Africaine, 1:60
Centre of Folk Culture of the Polish Radio,
	8:712
Centre for National Culture (Ghana), 1:394
Centre National de la Recherche Scientifique
	(Paris), 9:997
Centre for Studies in Middle Eastern Music
	(Toronto), 3:1220
Centro de Artistas (Philippines), 4:861
Centro Artístico (Philippines), 4:861
Centro de Bellas Artes (Philippines), 4:861
Centro de Cultura Popular (Uruguay), 2:521
Centro Escolar University Conservatory of
	Music, 4:123, 870
Centro de Estudios Folklóricos (Guatemala),
	2:736
Centro Etnográfico de Documentación Joaquim
	Díaz (Valladolid), 8:182
Centro de Historia del Folklore y de la Danza
	(Madrid), 8:601–2
Centro Nacional de Artes (El Salvador),
	2:717–18
Centro Nazionale Studi di Musica Popolare,
	8:621
Ceol (periodical), 8:394
Ceol na hÉireann, 8:394
Ceol Tíre, 8:394
Ceoltóirí Chualann, 8:391–92
Cepeda family, 3:727
Cepeda, Jesús, 2:934
Cercles Celtiques, 8:560, 562
Cerdd Dant Society, 8:353
ceremonies. *See also* carols and caroling; courtship
	rituals; *dhikr*; festivals, celebrations,
	and holidays; funeral ceremonies;
	healing rituals; performance contexts;
	processions and parades; *samā'*;
	shamanism; weddings
	Abkhazian people, 8:853
	Adighian people, 8:855
	Afghanistan, 5:620, 818
		childbirth and pregnancy, 5:814
		circumcision, 5:814, 821, 826
	Africa
		birth, 1:110
		circumcision, 1:539–40, 631, 709
		dance in, 1:286–87
		death, 1:205
		divination, 1:113, 125, 278–79
		initiation, 1:119–20, 125–26, 287, 288,
			454, 466, 467, 671, 701; 10:117;

	mukanda school, 1:674–76, 723–25;
		10:29
	Islamic holidays, 1:345–46, 348
	naming, 1:110, 523
	puberty, 1:110–11, 115
	seasonal, 1:119, 329–30
	timing of, 1:125
African-American religious rituals, 3:614
Afro-Cuban, 3:783–85
agricultural, 2:49; 8:4–5, 8–9
Ainu people, bear rituals, 7:784, 785–86
Akha people, 4:541
Albania, 8:997
	muabet, 8:118
	seasonal, 8:988
Albanian-Americans, 3:927
Algeria, *dīwān*, 6:403
Algonquian peoples, shaking tent ceremony,
	3:386, 1074
Andalusia, 6:444
Andean regions
	fertility, 2:220
	north-south distinctions, 2:222
Andhra Pradesh, 5:890
Angola, royal, 1:673
Anlo-Ewe people, 1:389
Anuta, 9:856
Apache Indian groups, 3:431
Arabian peninsula
	lewa, 6:403–4, 546
	Sufi, 6:543, 706, 710–11
Arawak culture, 2:13
Argentina
	Chaco region, 2:251
	fertility rituals, 2:256, 257
	ñemongaraí, 2:254–55
	novena, 2:258
	rutichico, 2:258
	topamiento de comadres, 2:258–59
Armenia, 6:728
Asmat people, 9:190
Atacameño culture
	cauzúlor, 2:360–61
	talátur, 2:357, 360–61
Athapaskan peoples, potlatch, 3:384, 388,
	1276–77
Atoni people, 4:796–98
Australia
	Aboriginal peoples, 9:228, 410–12, 453
	Arnhem Land, 9:394, 418, 419–27
	Cape York *bora*, 9:411, 429
	Central, 9:436–39
	circumcision, 9:420, 424, 428, 460–61, 467
	dance in, 9:450
	Djungguwan, 9:394, 419
	films of, 9:47
	gender in, 9:241–42
	Gunabibi, 9:419
	Hmong people, 9:75–77
	initiation, 9:243, 440, 450, 460, 467
	initiation schools, 9:251–52
	Kimberleys, 9:431–32
	love-magic, 9:431, 438
	Madayin, 9:419
	Marradjiri, 9:420
	mortuary, 9:228, 420, 424, 456, 464

	Pitjantjatjara people, 9:434
	Rom, 9:47, 227–28, *346*, 420, *420*, 467
	Southeastern Aboriginal peoples, 9:440
	Tiwi people, 9:455–57
	Torres Strait Pacific Islanders immigrants,
		9:84–85
	Ubar (also Ngulmarrk), 9:394, 419
	Warlpiri people, 9:464–67
	women's, 9:244–45, 451
	Yabuduruwa, 9:419
	Yolngu people, 9:457–60, 462
Aymara culture
	enfloramiento, 2:361
	pachallampe, 2:361
Aztec culture, 2:556
	human sacrifice, 2:602
Bali, 4:729, 738–39, 744, 760
	use of *kaca-kaca* structure, 4:53
Balkan region, 8:867
Balkarian people, 8:857–58
Balochistan, 5:774, 782
	damāl, zekr, and *verd*, 6:881, 884, 885, 889
	gwātī-ē lēb, 5:780–81; 6:881–90
	mālid and *shēparjā*, 5:779–80
Barbados, African descendants, 2:814
Batak people, 4:607
Belarus, "Tereshka's marriage," 8:792
Belgium
	alion, 8:522
	ommegang pageant, 8:525
Bellona, 9:849
Bhīl people, *gauri*, 5:646–47
Bolivia
	child's first haircut, 2:291
	dance in, 2:291–92
	initiation, 2:291
	k'illpa, 2:289
	Misa de Ocho Dias, 2:291
	music's role in, 2:289
	tinku, 2:426
	Vespers service, 2:138–40
Bosnia-Hercegovina, 8:963
Brazil
	caboclo wakes, 2:329
	Candomblé initiation, 2:342
	ifá, 2:342
	novena, 2:330
	Xingú *iamuricuma*, 2:57
Bribri and Cabécar cultures
	life-cycle, 2:634
	sulàr, 2:634
Bulgaria, 8:899–901
	fire-walking, 8:897
	laduvane, 8:899
	lazarovden, 8:140, 161, 900
	peperuda, 8:*151*, 161, 278, 900
Burma, *na' pwè*, 4:61, 372–73, 394
Byzantine empire, 8:1023
California, Native American groups, 3:412–13,
	415, 417
Caribbean, African-derived, 2:795
Central Asia
	Buddhist, 6:936
	women's, 6:945–46
Chechen people, 8:864
Chichimec culture, wakes, 2:573

Chile, wakes, 2:368
China, 7:98–99
    Buddhist, 7:311–12, 328–30, 331
    Confucian, 7:335–37
    "crossing the pass," 7:259
    Daoist, 7:312–13, 322–24
    exorcisms, 7:416
    music for, 7:153
    northwestern minorities, 7:462
    ritual music in, 7:91, 131, 311–13
    Shang dynasty, 7:319, 406
    wind and percussion ensembles in,
        7:199–201, 203–4
Choctaw Ballgame ceremonial cycle, 3:469
Chorotega culture, 2:748
    human sacrifice, 2:681
Christian rituals, 8:69–70, 74
Cirebon, 4:688–89, 695–96
    kasinoman, 4:689
Coast Salish spirit dancing, 3:396–97
Colombia
    adult wakes, 2:404, 406
    Afro-Colombian traditions, 2:403
    children's wakes, 2:403–4
    Kogi culture, 2:185–86
    municipal band's role in, 2:383–84
    novenaria, 2:404
Colo people, 1:568
Cook Islands, 9:896
Corsica, charivari, 8:571
Costa Rica
    novena, 2:698
    quinceaño, 2:698
    Spanish religious, 2:693
    volador, 2:681
    wakes, 2:689–90
Cree Indian nation, 3:1074
Creek Green Corn ceremony, 3:467, 468–69
Croatia, 8:926
Dai people
    tansin, 7:501–2
    tantham, 7:502–3, 504
Delaware Indian Big House, 3:464
Dominica, lavèyé (wakes), 2:841
Dominican Republic
    banco, 2:855
    baquiné (wakes), 2:849
    fiesta quinceañera, 2:858
    novena, 2:853, 855
    wakes, 2:853
Ecuador
    chigualo, 2:424
    children's wakes, 2:49, 218, 221, 422–24
    currulao, 2:414
    ñavi maillai, 2:425
Edo people, 1:460
Egypt
    circumcision, 6:629
    ḥaḍra, 6:147–51, 171–75
    madīḥ, 6:173, 414
    Nubian, 6:629
    thaumaturgical feats of dervishes, 6:626–27
    wedding preparations, 6:627
El Salvador, life-cycle, 2:709
Europe
    art-music concert as, 8:61–63

auditions, 8:64
calendar customs, 8:4, 139–41, 194, 325,
    342–43
confirmation, 8:143
dance in, 8:161–63
fertility, 8:140
lessons, 8:63–64
life-cycle, 8:139, 143–45
performers as mediators, 8:117
rehearsals, 8:63–64
women's responsibilities in, 8:193
Europe, Western, 8:517
Ewe people, 1:462
Fiji, chief presentation, 9:348
First Nations peoples, 3:1062–63, 1078
Flores, 4:793, 794
France, 8:545–46
    charivari, 8:143, 544, 551
    Dauphiné Bacchu-Ber, 8:542
    réveillez, 8:545
Fulani people, castigation contests, 1:451
Futuna, 9:815
    tū ritual, 9:815–16
gaṇḍā bandhan (thread-tying), 5:377, 459
Gā people, 1:103, 463
Garífuna (Garifuna) culture, 2:734
    amuyadahani, 2:669
    arairaguni, 2:669
    beluria, 2:669, 672, 674–75
    chugú, 2:669
    dügü, 2:669–72, 673
    novenarios, 2:734
    walagayo (also walagallo), 2:669,
        752–53
Gayo people
    daboih, 4:604, 605
    saman, 4:601, 605, 647
Georgia
    birth ritual, 8:835
    chonaoba, 8:834
    kvelieri, 8:834
    murkvamoba-kviriaoba, 8:834
    rain-begging rituals, 8:834
Germany, 8:649
Ghana
    durbar, 1:137–38
    Easter holiday, 1:394
Goa, harvest rituals, 5:737
Great Basin Indian groups, 3:422–25
Great Britain, coronations, 8:186
Great Lakes Indian groups, 3:453, 1079
    initiation, 3:455
Greece, 8:1015–16
    anastenaria, 8:1011
    fire-walking, 8:1011
    Karpathos, glendia, 8:118, 120, 1015
Grenada, 2:865
Guadeloupe
    vénérés, 2:876
    vèyè boukousou (wake), 2:875–76
Guaraní culture, 2:200
    puberty and initiation, 2:203
Guarijio culture, túmari, 2:552–54
guru-pūjā, 5:150
Guyana, 5:601, 605
    mashramani, 2:442, 447, 448

que-que, 2:445
    wakes, 2:445
Haiti
    baptism, 2:884
    rara band consecration, 2:887
    seremoni (also dans), 2:883
Hausa people, 1:450
Hawai'i, 9:16
    Chinese people, 9:71
    Japanese O-Bon, 9:95, 97, 106, 317
    Tongan people, 9:104
Hmong people, 3:1003; 4:551–52, 553–54
Hong Kong, 7:433–34
    purification rituals, 7:307
Hopi Indian nation, dance in, 3:215, 216
Huavasupai Indian nation, 3:434
Hungary, 8:739–40
Igbo people, 1:459
India
    North, groom's ritual bath, 10:8–9
    South, paṭṭāpiṣēkam, 5:279
Ingush people, 8:864
Iran, hey'at, 6:826–27
Iraq, Shi'ite, 6:415, 417, 419
Ireland
    religious, 8:388
    Wren Boys ritual, 8:391
Irian Jaya, 9:580
    Asmat bis, 9:580, 590, 591
    Asmat people, 9:589–91
    circumcision, 9:486
    Dani people, 9:50
    Eipo mot, 9:592, 593
    headhunting, 9:583, 590
    initiation, 9:580, 582, 590
Italy
    Sega la vecchia, 8:608
    tarantismo, 8:609
Jahai people, pano', 4:570–71
Jamaica
    Kumina cult, 2:902–3
    wakes, 2:906
Japan
    Buddhist, 7:613, 614–15, 645
    huryû, 7:605
    okina, 7:629
    omusya, 7:783
    Shinto, 7:607–9, 619–20
    Zyômon period, 7:558–59
Japanese Bon Odori, 3:217, 527
Java, 4:646–47, 648–49, 650–51, 655
    ruwatan, 4:651
    use of kaca-kaca structure, 4:53
Jewish people, 3:935, 936; 6:200, 524, 525;
        8:250, 259, 264
    bakashot, 6:1039, 1041
    bar mitzvah, 8:143
    circumcision, 6:524, 525
    death anniversaries, 6:1040
Kajang people, ngayau, 4:826, 831
Kalina culture, mourning, 2:436
Karachaevian people, 8:857–58
Karnataka
    bhūta kōla, 5:882, 883, 886
    dakke bali (cobra worship), 5:883–84
    doḍḍāki, 5:885

ceremonies, Karnataka (*continued*)
  firewalking, **5:**878–79
  initiation, **5:**881
  madringi pāḍunu, **5:**885
  tummattāṭa, **5:**887
Kasena-Nankani people, **1:**455–56
Kashmir, **5:**685
  circumcision, **5:**683, 685
Kayan people, *huduk apa*, **4:**830–31
Kazakhstan, hospitality rituals, **6:**950
Kenyah people
  kui, **4:**827
  tatip kamang, **4:**833
Kerala, **5:**949
  araṅṅēttam, **5:**932, 941, 944
  firewalking, **5:**362
  for *kūṭiyāṭṭam*, **5:**510
  pāmpin tuḷḷal, **5:**931
  propitiation, **5:**936
  temple rituals, **5:**934–35
  teyyam, **5:**931, 932
  tiruvātira kaḷi, **5:**934
Khmer people, **4:**18, 155, 167, 193–97, 209
  arakk, **4:**18, 155, 159, 166, 172, 193–95,
    209, 213
  bonn, **4:**197–200
  pinn peat use in, **4:**183
Kiribati, **9:**758–60, 763
  kario, **9:**364
  mamira, **9:**760
Kmhmu people, **4:**546
Korea
  akchang, **7:**818, 820, 829, 835, 861–64,
    865–66, 869–70
  dance in, **7:**66–67
  kut, **7:**875–78
  maegut, **7:**931, *939*
  narye, **7:**982
  nongak in, **7:**938
  p'algwanhoe, **7:**941, 982, 984
  shamanic, **7:**986–87, 995
  Sŏkchŏn, **7:**861–64, 865, 982
  tea, **7:**972
  yŏndŭnghoe, **7:**982
Kosrae, **9:**743
Kuna culture, **2:**638
  puberty, **2:**644–45, 646–47
Kurdistan, women's rituals, **6:**751
Kwakiutl Winter Ceremony, **3:**399–401
Lacandón Maya, **2:**656
Lahu people, **4:**539–40
Laos, healing and possession, **4:**340–41
Latvia
  rotāšana, **8:**501
  vākēšana, **8:**502
Lisu people, **4:**543
Lombok, **4:**771–72, 776
Low Countries, luck-visit singing, **8:**522, 525,
    532
Lozi people, *kuomboka*, **1:**672, 713
"luck visits," **8:**139–40, 342–43
Macedonia, **8:**973
  instrumental music in, **8:**975
  Islamic, **8:**975
  Muslim Skopje Roma, **8:**280, 281
  religious, **8:**983

St. George's Day, **8:***194*
sobor, **8:**116
Madagascar, **1:**788–89
Madhya Pradesh, life-cycle, **5:**721
Maguindanao people, **4:**892
  kapagipat, **4:**894
  pagipat, **4:**889–90
Maharashtra, **5:**728
Malawi, Tumbuka healing rituals, **1:**271–83
Malaysia, **4:**423–24
  buka panggung, **4:**403, 428
  circumcision, **4:**423–24
  court, **4:**429–30
  dance in, **4:**412–13, 415
  main lukah, **4:**421
  main puteri, **4:**417, 421, 574
  main saba, **4:**421
  north, **4:**404
  randai, **4:**413
  use of *mak yong* in, **4:**406, 421
  use of *zikir* in, **4:**432
Maleku culture, *caza de la tortuga*, **2:**683
Maliseet Indian nation, **3:**1069
Maluku, **4:**812, 819, 821
  dabus, **4:**813, 816–17
  fertility rituals, **4:**821
  kahua, **4:**818–19
  kolokie, **4:**814
  nabar panas pela, **4:**821
  salai jin, **4:**813, 816
Manchu people, *tsam*, **7:**520
Manding people, divination, **1:**445
Manihiki, **9:**904, 907
Māori people, **9:**942–43, 946–47
Mapuche culture, **2:**233, 362
  katán kawil, **2:**233
  ŋillipún, **2:**234, 253, 254, *255*, 359
Maranao people, **4:**896
Maroon cultures, **2:**438–39
Marshall Islands, historical accounts of,
    9:752
Martinique, Bon Dyé Coolies (Sèvis Zendyen),
    5:594–99
Martinique, wakes, **2:**915
Mashriq
  ancient, **6:**536–37
  music in, **6:**538
Maya culture
  pig-slaughtering, **2:**657
  rainmaking, **2:**653
  Tenebrae services, **2:**652
  wakes, **2:**731
Melanesia, **9:**598
Mexico, **10:**90
  Amerindian cultures, **2:**549–50
  la rama, **2:**615
  life-cycle events, **2:**606–7
Micronesia, **9:**712, 715–16
Middle East
  Islamic ritual cleansing, **6:**154
  therapeutic, **6:**304–5
Mi'kmaq Indian nation, **3:**1069
Miskitu culture
  isingni ulan, **2:**662
  kwal taya (wakes), **2:**660, 663
  upla pruan bara (wakes), **2:**663

Mixtec culture
  childbirth, **2:**566
  initiation, **2:**564
  wakes, **2:**567
Montserrat, involving jumbies, **2:**923
Morocco
  gnāwa, **6:**403
  Jewish people, **6:**1041
  thaumaturgical feats of dervishes, **6:**403
Mortlock Islands, **9:**23–24
Mossi-Bariba peoples, **1:**453
Muslim people
  circumcision, **8:**143, *144*, 975, 980, 988
  performance of *qaṣīda*, **5:**284
Native American, **3:**5–6, 366–67, 368, 526
  early European accounts of, **3:**23
  puberty, **3:**6, 94, 371, 433, 474
Native American Church, **3:**425, 480
Nauru
  first birthday, **9:**260–61
  holidays, **9:**262–63
Navajo Indian nation, **3:**432–33
  Nightway, **3:**311–13
Nepal
  childbirth, **5:**284
  circumcision, **5:**284
  Damāi people in, **5:**699
  healing, **5:**290–91
  pūjā, **5:**698
New Caledonia, **9:**671
  mourning, **9:**673–75
New Guinea, **9:**472, 474
  singsings, **9:**477
New Mexico, dance in, **3:**760
Nicarao culture, **2:**748
Niue, **9:**816–17
Nivkhi and Uilta peoples, bear rituals, **7:**788
Nkoya people, **1:**713
North Africa, *hadra*, **1:**537
Northwest Coast Indian groups
  healing, **3:**395
  initiation, **3:**395
  potlatch, **3:**5, 395, 396, 397–99, 400,
    1093–94
Nubian people, **1:**556–57
Oceania
  compared with theater, **9:**224
  initiation schools, **9:**251–52
  kava use in, **9:**172–74
  ritual processes of, **9:**185–86
Ojibwa *mite* rituals, **3:**26
Oman, **6:**673, 674–75, 678
  circumcision, **6:**678
  lewa, **6:**403–4, 546, 679
  mālid, **6:**674–75, 677–78, 682
  washing the groom, **6:**682
Orang Asli peoples, **4:**568–77, 579–84
Otopame culture, **2:**573
  wakes, **2:**571
Pakhtun people, **5:**785
Pakistan
  chili-gari-ai, **5:**488
  dhamal, **5:**760–61
  mehṅdī, **5:**760–61
Palau, **9:**724–25
Palawan people, **4:**924

Palestine
  shaving the groom, **6:**578, 587–89
  wedding eve, **6:**573–78, 581–90
Pame culture, wakes, **2:**573
Papua New Guinea
  Amanab *yangis*, **9:**547, 548
  Anêm people, **9:**615–16
  Angan singsings, **9:**496–97
  Bali and Vitu islands, **9:**608–11
  Baluan, **9:**604–6
  Banoni people, **9:**644–45
  baptisms, **9:**646–47
  birth purification, **9:**528
  Buang people, **9:**566–67
  Buin people, **9:**650
  Buin *remuremu*, **9:**650–51
  Buka, **9:**640–41
  cannibalism, **9:**567
  circumcision, **9:**609
  death-marking, **9:**553–54
  Eastern Highlands, **9:**302–3, 526, 527
  Enga singsings, **9:**533
  for firstborn children, **9:**613
  guitar-song performances for, **9:**152–53
  headhunting, **9:**491
  Huli *màli*, **9:**537
  Iatmul feasts, **9:**553–57
  Iatmul *mwai*, **9:**555–56
  initiation, **9:**257, 477, 483, 508, 511–12,
    524, 526–27, 535, 540, 548, 549,
    551–52, 555, 557, 558, 615, 621, 644
  initiation, girl's, **9:**527, 626, *627*
  Irumu people, **9:**569–70
  kaangu, **9:**549
  Kaluli people, **9:**320
  Karkar people, **9:**560–61
  Kaulong people, **9:**617, 619
  Kuman food-exchange ceremony, **9:**523
  Kuman initiation ceremony, **9:**524
  Kuman pig-killing ceremony, **9:**522–23
  Lolo *narogo* cycle, **9:**612–13
  Mali Baining people, **9:**192–93
  Mamose region singsings, **9:**545–46
  Managalasi singsings, **9:**502–5
  Maprik region, **9:**551–52
  Maring people, **9:**514–15
  Meda *ida* ritual, **9:**484
  Melpa *moka* exchanges, **9:**516, 518–20
  Melpa mortuary ceremonies, **9:**245
  mortuary, **9:**245, 613, 615, 633–38
  mourning, **9:**535
  Nagovisi *lawanda*, **9:**647
  New Britain, **9:**621, 625
  New Ireland, **9:**626–27
  New Ireland *malanggan* complex, **9:**350,
    351, 601, 628
  Nissan *buai*, **9:**636–38
  Papuan Gulf region, **9:**483
  Papuan region, **9:**488–89
  performance spaces, **9:**512–13
  Rai Coast, **9:**563–64
  religious rituals, **9:**188–89
  sanggai, **9:**178
  sia, **9:**572–74
  singsings, **9:**245, 529–30
  sweating, **9:**528–29

tigul, **9:**633–36, 639–40
Umboi Island, **9:**574
Waina *ida*, **9:**547, 548
Waina-Sowanda fertility rituals, **9:**350
Waxei people, **9:**558
West Sepik region, **9:**546
Paraguay
  children's wakes, **2:**462
  masses, **2:**458
  quinceañera, **2:**461–62
Paya culture
  katik-ka, **2:**739
  maihnewa, **2:**739
Peru
  animal-marking (*marcación*; *wylancha*;
    herranza), **2:**471–72, 477–78
  ayahuasca, **2:**482
  building construction (*pirkansa*), **2:**478
  child's first haircut (*corte de pelo*), **2:**469
  cleaning of irrigation channels, **2:**478
  communal labor, **2:**213, 471, 477
  fertility, **2:**471, 477
  labor day, **2:**480
Philippines
  headhunting, **4:**914
  humenta, **4:**846
  kagong, **4:**852
  pamanhikan, **4:**851
  pangangaluluwa, **4:**849
  pasyon, **4:**843–45, 856
  putong, **4:**851–52
  puwasa, **4:**907
  salubong, **4:**845–46
  sanghiyang, **4:**852
  santacrusan, **4:**847–48
Piaroa culture, *warime*, **2:**525
Pima Indian nation, **3:**435
Plains Indian groups, **3:**441, 480, 1086–87
Pohnpei, competitive feasting, **9:**175–76
Polynesia, **9:**769
  kava, **9:**202
  state rituals, **9:**207–8
  use of *pahu*, **9:**385
Portugal
  pilgrimages, **8:**577
  religious, **8:**579
  practicing, **8:**63–64
Pueblo Indian groups, **3:**429–31
Puerto Rico
  rosario para los muertos, **2:**936
  rosario de promesas, **2:**935–36
  rosario a la Santa Cruz, **2:**936, 941
Punjab (Pakistan), circumcision, **5:**770–71
Purépecha culture, **2:**576–77
  levantamiento del Niño, **2:**578
Q'ero culture, **2:**225
  fertility rituals, **2:**226
Rajasthan
  firewalking, **5:**648–49
  jāgaran vigils, **5:**642–43
  life-cycle rituals, **5:**639
  sati, **5:**643
  of women, **5:**645
Rejang people, **4:**619
Renaissance, **8:**77
Réunion Island, firewalking, **5:**607, *607*, 608

Romania, **8:**869–70, 881
  căluş, **8:**161, *162*, 870
  dragaica, **8:**194
  paparuda, **8:**194, 278, 870
Roti, **4:**800
Rotuma, **9:**818
Russia
  borona, **8:**760
  calendrical, **8:**759–60
  koliada, **8:**758–59
  Volga-Ural peoples, **8:**774
Ryûkyû Islands, **7:**793
Saami people, shamanic rituals, **8:**304–7
St. Lucia
  kélé, **2:**949, 950
  wakes, **2:**943, 948–49
Saisiat people, **7:**427, 525
Sama-Bajao people, **4:**900
Sāmoa, **9:**202
  betrothal, **9:**349
  Christian worship service, **9:**205–6
  kava, **9:**348–49, 803
  pre-battle, **9:**215–16
  tōga, **9:**801–2
  visiting, **9:**802–3
Sardinia, *argismo*, **8:**609, 632
Semang people, **4:**569–71
Semelai people, **4:**586
Serbia, **8:**940
Shan people, **4:**548
Shona people, **1:**745, 753–55
Siberia
  bear rituals, **7:**1029
  shamanic, **7:**1028
Sikaiana
  mortuary customs, **9:**335
  te-ika-lle, **9:**846
Sindh
  circumcision, **5:**287
  healing, **5:**286
Slovenia, instruments in, **8:**914, 919
Solomon Islands
  Bellonese *suahongi*, **9:**308–9
  Isabel Province, **9:**660
  Russell Islands, **9:**662–63
  Santa Cruz songfests, **9:**332–35
  Shortland Islands, **9:**656
South, corn-shucking rituals, **3:**66, 599, 601
South Africa, **5:**617
  firewalking, **5:**617, *617*
South America
  birth and christening, **2:**49
  fifteenth-birthday (*quinceaño*), **2:**49
  first lesson, **5:**150, 211
  pre-Columbian, **2:**45
  shamanic, **2:**45–46
  tropical-forest region, **2:**128–30
South Asia
  appropriate music for, **5:**282–83
  bhakti, *āratī*, **5:**255
  childbirth, **5:**8, 273–74, 661; Mughal
    depiction of, **5:**303, *304*
  circumcision, **5:**274, 284, 287, 683, 685,
    770–71, 814, 821, 826
  dance in, **5:**498
  dedication of a play, **5:**20, 25–26

ceremonies, South Asia (*continued*)
    drum dedication, **5:**29
    gender-segregated, **5:**8
    goddess cults, **5:**291–93
    hierarchy of, **5:**285–86
    incantations in, **5:**469
    initiation, **5:**9
    life-cycle, **5:**273–76, 278–87
    performance rituals, **5:**472–73
    puberty, **5:**274
    pūjā, **5:**549, 556
    rainmaking, **5:**278
    ritual order in, **5:**281–82
    royal arrivals and departures, **5:**402
    sarasvatī pūjā, **5:**9, 211
    seasonal and calendrical, **5:**276–78, 278–87
    self-mortification, **5:**293
    upanayana (student initiation), **5:**86, 459
South Asian Americans, **3:**991
Southeast Asia
    animistic, **4:**60–61
    harvest, **4:**51–52
    village-cleansing, **4:**49
Southeast Indian groups, **3:**467
Sri Lanka
    bali, **5:**961, 962–63
    dēvālē, **5:**963
    dorakadarśane, **5:**969
    kohomba kankāriya, **5:**963–64
    raṭa yakuma, **5:**274
    tovil, **5:**961–62, 964
Subanun people, *mekanu*, **4:**923
Sudan, *karāma*, **1:**550–51
Sumatra
    asiek, **4:**618
    bedabus, **4:**626
    bedukun, **4:**615
    belian, **4:**615
    dabus, **4:**601, 602, 604, 606, 612, 616, 625
    Enggano, **4:**619–21
    Jambi, **4:**616, 617
    Lampung Province, **4:**628
    Minangkabau, **4:**612
    Muslim, **4:**605–6
    northern, **4:**607
    penobatan, **4:**600
    puaka, **4:**605
    southern, **4:**627
    Suku Dalem, **4:**619
    Suku Terasing, **4:**619–21
    tabot, **4:**621
    tabut, **4:**600, 602, 612–13
Sumba, **4:**788–91
    pasola, **4:**788
Sumbawa, **4:**780, 782–83
Sunda, **4:**705–6, 707, 719–21
    seni debus, **4:**701
Surinam
    slametan, **2:**507
    vodu (also *papagadu*), **2:**505
Suyá culture, **2:**145–47
    mouse, **2:**128
Switzerland, Haute-Gruyère, *rindja*, **8:**119
Syrian Jews, **3:**943
Syrian Orthodox, **6:***225, 226*
Tahiti, chief presentation, **9:**348

Taino culture, *areito* (also *areyto*), **2:**822,
        846–47, 881, 932–33
Taiwan
    exorcisms, **7:**426
    Saisiat people, **7:**427
Tamil Nadu
    dēvadāsi participation in, **5:**518
    nalunku and *pattiyam*, **5:**275
    puberty, **5:**920
Tanna, circumcision, **9:**64–65
Tarahumara culture, **2:**584–87
    bakánawi, **2:**585
    korima, **2:**585
    nawesari, **2:**585
    tutuguri, **2:**585–86
Tejano, **3:**773, 778
Temiar people, **4:**563–64, 572
    naga, **4:**579
    səlombaŋ, **4:**573–79
Temuan people, **4:**586–87
Thailand
    coronation, **4:**248
    fawn phi, **4:**313
    khwan, **4:**307
    lam phi fa, **4:**329
    northeastern, **4:**326
    southern, **4:**307
    sukhawn, **4:**64, 293–96
    tham khwan, **4:**259–60
    wai khru, **4:**64–65, 120–21, 227, 253, 258,
        278, 299, 307
Tibet, **7:**476
Tibetan Buddhist, **5:**713
Tiboli people, **4:**921
Tohono O'odham Indian nation, **3:**436
Tonga
    chief presentation, **9:**348
    coronation, **9:***791*
    firstfruits, **9:**791
    kātoanga, **9:**789
Trinidad and Tobago
    Orisa, **2:**954–55
    South Asian community, **5:**589
Tuamotu Islands, **9:**884
Tukano culture
    dabucurí, **2:**154
    yuruparí, **2:**153, 154
Tunisia
    ḥaḍra, **6:**520
    stambūlī, **6:**403
    thaumaturgical feats of dervishes, **6:**519–20
Turkey
    Alevi rituals, **6:**793, 794–95, 796, 798
    Bektaṣīye rituals, **6:**190
    Mevlevi rituals, **6:**109–11, 114, 118, 122,
        132, 184, 185, 190, 196, 779, 780,
        811; **8:**967
    religious, **6:**568, 768–69
    Şeb-i 'Arûs, **6:**109
Turkmenistan, *pata*, **6:**968
Uighur people, *erke-sama*, **7:**459
United States, ethnic music at, **3:**827
Uruguay, Iemanjá devotion, **2:**515
Vai people
    d'aa fortieth-day feast, **1:**332–34, 345
    fidao redemption ceremony, **1:**333, 345

Vanuatu, **9:**198, 688, 692, 694–95, 966
    circumcision, **9:**691, 708–9
    Mota Pentecost celebration, **9:**698
    Tannese *nupu*, **9:**702–4
Vedic, **5:**30, 33, 240
    agnicayana rite, **5:**238–39
    havan, **5:**590
    sandhyā, **5:**590
    soma sacrifices, **5:**33, 239, 261
Venda people, circumcision schools, **1:**709
Venezuela
    children's wakes, **2:**535
    mampulorio, **2:**535
    velorio, **2:**530, 534–35
Vietnam, **4:**466
    Buddhist, **4:**502–3
    chầu văn, **4:**60, 89, 500, 505–6
    kinh đàn, **4:**501
    of minority peoples, **4:**533
    rối bóng, **4:**505
    seasonal, **4:**449–51
Vietnamese-Americans, **3:**996
Vlah people, **8:**950
Waiãpí culture
    bumblebee, **2:**126, 128
    cannibalism, **2:**158, 164–65
Wales, **8:**352, 355
    Mari Lwyd (horse ceremony), **8:**342
    wren hunt, **8:**342
Warao culture, curing, **2:**193–96
Wayana culture, **2:**165–66
    marake, **2:**166, 437
West Africa, **1:**446–47
Western Arctic peoples, potlatch, **3:**376
West Futuna, *kaitarua* memorials, **9:**861–62
Yanomamö culture
    amoamo, **2:**174
    cannibalism, **2:**173
Yao people, **4:**549
Yaqui Indian nation, Easter Ceremony, **3:**438
Yemen, *rābūt*, **6:**656
Yoruba people, **1:**460, 461, 472
Yugoslavia, *paparuda*, **8:**278
Yuma culture, **2:**598
Zulu people, **1:**706
Ceribašić, Naila, **8:**937
Cervantes, Ignacio, **2:**837
Cervantes, Laura, **2:**635
Cervantes, Leopoldo, **3:**792
Cervantes, María, **2:**837
Cervantes, Sal, **3:**743
Çsar et ses Romains (musical group), **3:**1158
Český lid (periodical), **8:**733
Céspedes, Carlos M. de, **2:**831
Céspedes, Dario, **4:**856
Céspedes, Francisco de, **2:**453
C'était la plus jolie des filles (Deschênes),
        3:1136
Cetus (Wilson), **3:**611
Chacalón y la Nueva Crema, **2:**485
Chacha (god), **8:**864
cha-cha-chá, **2:**105; **3:**13, 522, 732, 788, 790,
        794, 796, 893, 995, 1203
    in Barbados, **2:**819
    in Chile, **2:**372
    in Cuba, **2:**827, 829, 832, 833, 835

in Mexico, **2**:622
in Nicaragua, **2**:763
in Peru, **2**:487
in rhythm and blues songs, **3**:673
in Turkey, **6**:249
Chacha, Din Mohammad, **5**:787
Cha-Cha Jiménez y Los Chacos (musical group), **3**:780
Chacha, Werema Masiaga, **1**:641
Chacobo culture, **2**:285
Chaco War, **2**:245, 460–61
Chad, **1**:301–2. *See also* North Africa; West Africa; *specific peoples*
"*Chad gadya*," **8**:261
Chadima, Mikoláš, **8**:731
Chadwick, George, **3**:538
Ch'ae Taehyŏn, **7**:963–67
Ch'ae Tongsŏn, **7**:952
Chagga people, **1**:636, 638
Chagnon, Napoleon A., **2**:170, 173
chahārmezrāb, **6**:67, 68, 69, 132, 134, 137
Chahar people, **7**:1004–20
Chahartugchi, Urna, **7**:1020
Chailley, Jacques, **8**:554
"Chain of Fools" (Franklin), **3**:710
"Chains of Love" (Turner), **3**:708
Chaitanya Mahaprabhu, Sri, **5**:253, 265, 502, 504, 505
"*Čhaje Šukarija*," **8**:282
Chajin hanip (Yi), **7**:953
Chajin san t'aryŏng (Korean folk song), **7**:886
Chaka (Zulu king), **1**:705
Chaka Chaka, Yvonne, **1**:431, 779
Chakravarti, Vishnu, **5**:848, 849
Chaksam-pa (Tibetan Dance and Opera Company), **3**:207, 219
Chalcedon, Council of, **6**:207, 227
Chaldean Church. *See* Assyro-Chaldean Church
Chalice (Jamaican band), **2**:910
Chalkdust (calypsonian), **2**:964
Chalson, Jefferson, **9**:91
Chamakoko culture, **2**:452
Chamang people, **7**:485, 491, 492
Chamār caste, **5**:613–14, 639, 679
Chamba nation, **2**:869
Chamba people, **1**:654–55
Chamber Symphony (Adams), **3**:254
Chambers, Iain, **3**:513
Chambers, Stephen. *See* Hakim, Talib Rasul
Chambri people, **9**:189, 552
Chaminade, Cécile, **3**:1148
Chamisso, Adelbert von, **9**:38–39, 285
Chamorro, Arturo, **2**:581
Chamorro people, in United States, **9**:116–17
Champa (state), **3**:1010; **4**:43, 62, 153, 447, 498, 590
Champagne, Claude, **3**:14, 1076, 1150
Champagne, Paul, **3**:246
Chăm (Cham) people, **4**:154, 156, 210, 447, 449, 528, 529, 531, 590–91
  instruments of, **4**:212, 590
  lullabies of, **4**:533
  narratives of, **4**:533
  in North America, **3**:951–52, *997*, 1007, 1010

spirit beliefs of, **4**:50
yike theater, **4**:200–201
Champéry 1830 (musical group), **8**:693
Champfleury (pseud. of Jules Husson), **3**:1164
Champlain, Samuel de, **3**:7, 143, 392, 1073
Champlin, John Denison, Jr., **3**:27
Chamunda Devi (deity), **5**:641
Chamzuk, Irene, **3**:1089
Chan Ka Nin, **3**:1186
Chaná-Charrúa culture, **2**:510–11
Chancay culture
  archaeomusicological studies of, **2**:7
  instruments of, **2**:30
Chanderi dynasty, **5**:721
Chandidas, **5**:249, 253, 254, 845
Chandra, Sheila, **5**:575; **8**:225, 240
Chandrabhanu, Dr., **9**:416
Chandralekha (film), **5**:544
Chanel, St. Peter, **9**:814
Ch'angbu t'aryŏng (Korean folk song), **7**:881, 957, 961
Chang Chabaek, **7**:899
Chang Chaknyŏng, **7**:894
Chang, Grace (Ge Lan), **7**:354
Chang, K. C., **4**:37
Chang Kyech'un, **7**:985
Chang, Louis, **3**:1262
Chang P'angae, **7**:899, 909
Chang Sahun, **7**:853–54, 855, 856, 989, 990
Chang, Sarah, **3**:977
Chang Tŏkchin, **7**:894
Chang Wŏljungsŏn, **7**:909–11
Changcheng suixiang (Liu), **7**:177, 231
changgo. *See* drums: hourglass
ch'anggŭk, **7**:43, 73, 452. *See also p'ansori*
  history of, **7**:899, 944–46, 967–69
  music in, **7**:77
  narrator in, **7**:75
  performers of, **7**:893–95, 909–10
  propaganda in, **7**:808
  yŏsŏng kukkŭk troupes, **7**:76, 895, 899, 910, 945, 946, 968
Ch'anggŭk chŏngnip wiwŏnhoe (organization), **7**:968–69
Ch'anggŭkchwa (*p'ansori* company), **7**:968
Changhen'ge (Huang), **7**:345
Changī, Darvīsh-Alī, **6**:17
Changkki T'aryŏng (*p'ansori* story), **7**:899
Changlun (Zi), **7**:115, 129–30
Ch'angsŏngŭn choha (Korean folk song), **7**:962
Chánguena culture, **2**:681
Changzheng jiaoxiangqu (Ding), **7**:347
Chanok Sakarik, **4**:227, 277
Chanson de Roland (epic), **8**:129, 651
Chansonnier franco-ontarien I, II, **3**:1192
Chansons d'Acadie (Chiasson), **3**:1136
Chansons du Dodecanèse (Baud-Bovy), **8**:1025
Chansons folkloriques françaises du Canada (Barbeau and d'Harcourt), **3**:1165
Chansons populaires du Canada (Gagnon), **3**:28, 145–46, 1165
Chansons populaires et historiques du Canada (LaRue), **3**:1165
Chansons de Shippagan (Matton and Gauthier), **3**:1167

chant. *See also* monophony; narratives; recitation; vocal music
  Algerian, **6**:1044
  in Asian religions, **3**:122, 982, 1246
  Australia, children's, **9**:256
  Bahamas, for dances and games, **2**:810–11
  Bengal, *puthipāṭh*, **5**:862
  bolgarski rospev, **8**:904
  Brazil, **2**:325
  Buddhist
    bonbai, **7**:611, 613
    China, **7**:312, 327–33
    Dai people, **7**:497–99, 503–4
    hwach'ŏng, **7**:871
    Khmer people, **4**:206
    Korea, **7**:80, 871–73, 959
    kôsiki, **7**:646
    Mongolia, **7**:1016
    pŏmp'ae, **7**:872–73
    South Asia, **5**:13, 257, 966, 968–69
    syômyô (*shômyô*): documentary sources on, **7**:587; genealogical charts for, **7**:768; influence on other genres, **7**:617–18; instrumental accompaniment of, **7**:615, 617; melodies for, **7**:615–17; modal theories in, **7**:565, 567–68; notation for, **7**:538, 582–83, 589, 613; origins of, **7**:81, 535–36; performance contexts for, **7**:775; schools of, **7**:611–13; source materials for, **7**:589; texts for, **7**:613–14; vocalization in, **7**:551
    Thailand, **4**:288–92
    Tibetan, **6**:983; **7**:479, 582, 872; **10**:71
    Vietnam, **4**:470, 503, 504–5
    yŏmbul, **7**:871, 984
  Byzantine, **8**:70, 881, 980
  Carolingian, **8**:69
  Celtic, **8**:366
  children's, **3**:285
  in Christian services, **3**:122; **6**:19–20
  Coptic Orthodox, **6**:221–22
  Daoist, **7**:312, 313, 321–23
  Eastern Orthodox, **8**:12
  in Episcopalian church, **3**:123
  Ethiopia
    melekket, **1**:159
    zēmā, **1**:147–50
  Flores, **4**:794
  Georgian, **6**:20, 442
  Glagolitic, **8**:929, 960
  Greek Orthodox, **6**:195, 544
  Gregorian, **2**:325, 651–52, 682, 933; **3**:122, 755, 887, 1075, 1148, 1165; **4**:841, 846, 862; **5**:29, 31, 75; **8**:69–70, 265–66, 652, 737, 881, 960
    antiphons, **8**:131
    internationalism of, **8**:227
    as melodic basis for polyphonic compositions, **8**:75
    recent popularity of, **8**:96, 225, 600
  Haiti, *priyè ginen*, **2**:884
  Hawai'i
    mele genres, **9**:163, 915–16, 917, 923, 927–28, 968
    mele hula, **3**:527; **9**:926, 928
    pule, **9**:926

chant (*continued*)
  Hebrew, **3:**335, 530
  Iban people, *timang,* **4:**828
  Iceland
    kvæði, **8:**117
    rímur, **8:**401–2, 407
  Inca culture
    saynata, **2:**468
    uaricza araui, **2:**468
  Ireland, lays, **8:**379
  Japan, in *nô,* **7:**546, 552, 554, 630, 632–34, 770
  Japanese Shi-gin, **3:**1084
  Jewish, **6:**19–20, 524, 525, 526, 1036, 1062, 1066; **8:**12, 70, 252, 265–66
    Turkey, **6:**57–58
    Yemenite practice, **6:**1048–56
  Khmer people, *saraphanh,* **4:**156
  Korea, shamanic, **7:**876–77, 890, 898
  Kuna culture, **2:**639, 644–45, 648
  Lombok, *azan,* **4:**769
  Malaysia
    azan, **4:**431, 825
    berzanji, **4:**415, 423, 431
    marhaban, **4:**431
    nazam, **4:**431
  Mangareva, **9:**886
  Maronite, **6:**208, 209–15
  Marquesas Islands
    ha'anaunau, **9:**890–91
    hahi (also *mave*), **9:**891–92
    haka manumanu, **9:**892
    mahitete, **9:**892
    matatetau, **9:**892
    mea kakiu, **9:**890–94
    putu, **9:**892–93
    ru'u, **9:**209
  Mozarabic, **6:**442
  Muslim, **3:**530; **5:**744–45, 877; **6:**636–38; **8:**12, 967
    Bukharan style, **6:**939, 940
    call to prayer (*adhān; azān; ezan*), **5:**745, 818, 827; **6:**57, 132, 153–55, 165–66, 167–68, 352, 372, 437, 475, 517, 525, 538, 649, 673, 713, 768, 937, 938, 939; **7:**416, 459, 462
    cantillation systems in, **8:**100
    Malaysia, **4:**423–24, 430–31
    Philippines, **4:**906–7
    poetry recitations, **3:**1246–47
    Qur'ān cantillation, **3:**982, 983–84, 1045, 1246; **5:**256, 259, 579, 581, 590, 745, 747–48, 772, 818, 827, 958
    soz, **5:**282, *283,* 284
    Sufi forms, **6:**191, 192–93, 517, 939, 943–45
  Nauru
    children's, **9:**260
    iruwo, **9:**755
  Naxi people, *dongba,* **7:**512
  Oceania, **9:**301, 321
  oral transmission of, **8:**49, 106
  Pakistan, *ginān,* **5:**794
  Philippines, **4:**927
    adhan, **4:**907
    bang, **4:**907

    fatiha, **4:**907
    langkit, **4:**908
    lasib, **4:**907
    luguh, **4:**906, 907, 908, 911
    pabasa (also *pasyon*), **4:**843–45
  Pukapuka
    mako genres, **9:**911–12
    tila, **9:**911
    wrestling, **9:**910, 911
  Rajasthan, in trance ceremony, **5:**292
  Rapa Nui, **9:**952
  recomposition and adaptation in, **8:**54
  Roti, *bapa,* **4:**798, 801
  Russia, **8:**779
  Serbian, **8:**943
  sermons in folk churches, **3:**119, 121, 124, 125–26
  Sri Lanka, **5:**959
  Sumba, **4:**791
  Sunuwari, **5:**290–91
  Suyá culture, **2:**146
  Syrian Orthodox, **6:**226–27, 228–29
  Syro-Maronite, **6:**209, 210–13
  Syro-Maronite-Arabic, **6:**210, 213–14
  Tamil Nadu, *vaṭṭakaḷi,* **5:**909
  Tujia people, **7:**487
  Tupinambá culture, **2:**300
  Vaishnava, **5:**260–61
  Vedic, **2:**958; **5:**14, 18, 21, 38, 66, 96, 238–45, 246, 261, 469, 590, 968
    Rāmaṇṇa school of, **5:**243–45
    relation to Sinhalese music, **5:**956
    studies of, **5:**56
    styles of, **5:**242–44
    treatises on, **5:**24, 25, 30–33, 71
  Yanomamö culture, *waiyamou,* **2:**173
"Chant" (Morton), **3:**653
Chant of Jimmie Blacksmith (film), **9:**46
Chant of the Marching (album), **1:**779
Chant du Monde (record label), **5:**529; **8:**554; **9:**997
Chantels (musical group), **3:**673
Chanterelle (musical group), **3:**855
chanteys. *See* shanties
Chantou people, **7:**1004–20
Chants d'église (Lagacé), **3:**28
Chants Libres (Montréal), **3:**1152
Chants Populaires du Pays Basque (Sallaberry), **8:**316
Chanyuan zhongsheng (Cui), **7:**220
Chao, Y. R., **7:**382
Chaozhou people
  ensemble music of, **7:**169, 217, 219, 233, 236, 238, 241, 415
  in Hong Kong, **7:**433
  modes of, **7:**235
  puppet theater of, **4:**70; **7:**426
  in Thailand, **4:**70–71
Chapbook (periodical), **8:**371
Chapin, Norman A., **2:**649
Chapman, Anne, **2:**251
Chapman, Tracy, **3:**340
Chappell, William, **8:**337
Chapple, Steve, **3:**586
Chappotín, **2:**835
Chapuis, Corinne, **8:**693

Chapuis, Fabienne, **8:**693
Charan Manophet (musical group), **4:**98
charanga, **1:**380; **2:**832, 833, 835; **3:**788, 790, 791–92, 795–96
Charanga América (musical group), **3:**797
Charanga del Caribe (musical group), **2:**265
Charanga Duboney (musical group), **3:**796
Charanga '76 (musical group), **3:**797
charango. See guitars
Chardó class, **5:**735, 739–40
Charfauros Brothers, **9:**160
Chariot Jubilee (Dett), **3:**607
Chariots of Fire (film), **3:**204
Charland, Hector, **3:**1154
Charlebois, Robert, **3:**1156, 1158, 1168
Charlemagne, emperor, **8:**69
Charlemagne, Manno, **2:**892, 895; **3:**805
Charles IV, Holy Roman emperor, **8:**716, 726
Charles V, Holy Roman emperor, **2:**881–82; **8:**634
Charles VI, Holy Roman emperor, **8:**727
Charles V, king of Spain, **2:**23
Charles, John, **9:**46
Charles, prince of Wales, **7:**431
Charles, Ray, **3:***263,* 535, 647, 673, 678, 709; **8:**446
Charleston (dance), **2:**485; **3:**233, 687; **6:**623; **8:**443, 483, 660
Charlevoix, Pierre François, **2:**250, 463
Charlton, Hannah, **2:**411
"Charmaine" (Rapee), **3:**262
Charo, **3:**751
Charpentier, Gabriel, **3:**1151
Charpentier, Jean-Michel, **9:**965
Charters, Samuel, **2:**593; **3:**582
Charvet, J. B., **9:**10
Chase, Gilbert, **3:**143, 144, 511, 512
Chassaing, Jean-François, **8:**554
Chastain, Paul, **3:**169
Chatahoochee Records, **3:**747
Chateaubriand, François René, **3:**1164
Chatham Islands (Aotearoa), **9:**865
Chat qui pêche, Le (Baker), **3:**612
Chatrapati Singh, Maharaja, **5:**120–21, *378*
Chatterjee, Anindo, **5:**137
Chatterji, Bankim Chandra, **5:**435–36
Chattopadhyay, Anal, **5:**857
Chattopadhyay, Kalidas, **5:**847
Chattopadhyay, Rabin, **5:**857
Chattopadhyay, Vishnurama, **5:**849
Chatu group, **5:**769
Chaturbhuj Das, **5:**251
Chatwin, Bruce, **9:**707
Chatybok, Freddie, **3:**1089
Chatzidakis, Manos, **9:**72
Châu Minh, **4:**512
Châu Văn Tú, **4:**493
Chaudenson, Robert, **5:**609
Chaudhuri, Abdul Gaffar, **5:**858
Chaudhuri, Abdul Halim, **5:**858
Chaudhuri, Devbrata, **5:**206
Chaudhuri, Mohini, **5:**857
Chaudhuri, Salil, **5:**857
Chaudhuri, Satya, **5:**855
Chaudhuri, Swapan, **5:**137
Chaudhuri, Tapan, **5:**428

Chaumont, Le Chevalier de, **4:**70
Chaurasia, Hari Prasad, **5:**205, 340, 424, 466, *536*
Chauriya, A., **5:**562
Chauveau, Joseph-Olivier, **3:**1164
Chauvet, Stephen, **1:**669
Chávez, Alex J., **3:**764, 767
Chávez, Augustín, **3:**763
Chávez, Carlos, **2:**115, 604–5; **3:**740
Chávez, César, **3:**722
Chávez, Gerardo, **4:**866
Chávez, Jesús, **2:**581
Chávez, Lino, **2:**622
Chávez y Lugo, **3:**737
Chavín culture, **2:**466, 467
Chawai people, **1:**289, 292
Chébere, **2:**274, 275, 280
Chebiga (Korean folk song), **7:**886
Chechen people, **8:**11, 850, 861–64
  dance traditions of, **8:**864
  epic performance, **8:**851
  instruments, **8:**863
  research on music of, **8:**864
  vocal music of, **8:**862–64
Chech-Kini (god), **8:**864
Checker, Chubby, **3:**709; **4:**884
Check-List of Recorded Songs in the English Language in the Library of Congress Archive of American Folk Song to July, 1940, **3:**294
"Checkmate" (Barabas), **3:**688
Cheechoo, James, **3:**410
Cheechoo, Sinclair, **3:**410
"Cheek to Cheek" (Berlin), **3:**196
cheironomy, **8:**100
  interaction with oral transmission, **8:**105
Chekhov, Anton, **5:**491
Chelebi (honorific). *See previous element in name*
Chelu group, **5:**815
Chemehuevi, **3:**435
Chemín, Dominique, **2:**573
Chemín Bössler, Heidi, **2:**573
Chen Da, **7:**424
Chen Deju, **3:**1261; **7:**220–21
Chen Gang, **7:**348, 350
Chen Jile, **7:**229
Chen Kaige, **7:**76, 203, 257–59
Chen, Kelly (Chen Huilin), **7:**355
Chen Li, **7:**128
Chen Mingzhang, **7:**358
Chen Minzi, **7:**120
Chen, Rubi, **6:***263*
Chen Suo, **7:**929–30
Chen Tienhe, **7:**398
Chen Wei, **7:**213
Chen Yang, **7:**113, 128, 188
Chen Yi, **3:**964; **7:**420
Chen Yuanjing, **7:**131
Chen Yuqian, **7:**261, 264
Chen Zijing, **7:**169
Cheng, Adam (Zheng Shaoqiu), **7:**355
Cheng Yanqiu, **7:**394
Chengalvarayan, N., **5:**327
Chenla (state), **4:**62, 153, 157, 186
Chenoweth, Vida, **2:**736; **9:**88, 153, 480, 512, 571, 626, 650, 973, *980*

Cherkessian people, **6:**1021; **8:**854–56
Chernomyrdin, Viktor, **8:**768
Cherny, Al, **3:**1242, 1257
"Cherokee," **3:**658
Cherokee Indian Choir, **3:**486
Cherokee Indian nation, **3:**368, 370, 466, 470, 511
"Cherry Pink and Apple Blossom White" (Prado), **3:**732
Chess Records, **3:**263, 350, 351, 352, 353, 708
"Chester" (Billings), **3:**531, *532*
Chestnut, Cyrus, **3:**664
Chestnut Horse (Kazakh piece), **7:**461
Chetri people, **5:**706
Chetrit, Joseph, **6:**1039, 1042
Chetties, **5:**954
Cheung, Jacky (Zhang Xueyou), **7:**355, 431, 435
Cheung, Leslie (Zhang Guorong), **7:**355
Cheung Sai-bung, **10:**18
Chevalier, Maurice, **3:**1174
Cheville, Lila R., **2:**783
Chewa people, **1:**227, 286
Chewong people, **4:**560
"Cheyenne" (Monroe), **3:**168
Cheyenne Indian nation, **3:**440, 444
Cheyronnaud, Jacques, **8:**554
Chhandha Dhara (record company), **5:**528
Chheng Phon, **4:**161, 184–85, 209
Chhieng Proeung, **4:**188
Chi Ch'unsang, **7:**996
Chi Ping Dance Group (Toronto), **3:**1217
Chi Yŏnghŭi, **7:**915
Chiang Kai-shek, **7:**356–57, 384, 385–86, 423
Chiangmai (kingdom), **4:**219, 310
Chiasson, Père Anselme, **3:**1136
Chibcha culture
  archaeomusicological studies of, **2:**7
  in Central America, **2:**8
  El Dorado myth and, **2:**10
Chic (musical group), **3:**228, 712
Chicago Art Ensemble, **3:**326–27
Chicago Defender (newspaper), **3:**580
Chicago, Roy, **1:**477
Chicago Symphony Orchestra, **3:**537, 609, 885
Chicago World's Fair. *See* World's Columbian Exposition (Chicago)
Chicano movement, **3:**722, 734, 747, 749–51, 760, 763, 772
"Chicano Power" (Thee Midniters), **3:**747
Chicco, **1:**779
chicha, **2:**101, 102, 105, 293, 297, 484–85
Chichimec culture, **2:**570–74
Chickasaw Indian nation, **3:**466, 467
"Chicken Shack Boogie" (Milburn), **3:**669, 708
Chickering Piano Manufactory, **3:**561
Chico, Igo, **1:**483
Chico y Chencho (musical group), **3:**738, 741
Chico Science, **2:**354
Chicoria (*trovo*), **3:**758, 762
Chieftains (musical group), **3:**846; **8:**9, 226, 372, 392
Chiffons (musical group), **3:**673
Chigiy, Carmen, **9:**732
Chijavadze, Otar, **8:**846
Chikamatsu (Tikamatu) Monzeamon, **7:***667*, 667–70

Child, Francis James, **3:**14, 29, 70, 147, 519, 825, 833, 1123; **8:**136, 328–29, 337, 606
Children of Peace, **3:**136–37, 1079
children's music
  Adighian people, **8:**856
  African-American, **3:**599
  Algeria, **6:**473
  Anuta, **9:**860
  Arctic regions, **3:**376
  Australia, **9:**255–57, 442, 452
    Central, **9:**436
  Bahamas, ring-play, **2:**810–11
  Balkarian people, **8:**858
  Baluan, **9:**259
  Bulgaria, **8:**897, 901
  Canada, **3:**1081
  Carriacou, passplay, **2:**868
  Chile, *ronda*, **2:**366, 367
  China, **7:**153, 417
  Colombia, *arrullo*, **2:**408–9
  Corsica, **8:**566, 571
  Costa Rica
    balimbo, **2:**689–90
    ronda infantile, **2:**695
  Czech Republic, **8:**720, 725
  Danish-American, **3:**882
  Denmark, **8:**453, 456, 459–60, 462
  Dominica, **2:**843
  Dominican Republic, **2:**849
  El Salvador, **2:**709
  England, **8:**336
  Estonian-American, **3:**878
  Europe, **8:**135, 139, 145, 168
    harps, **8:**389–90
  Fiji, **9:**775, 782–83
  Finland, **8:**476
  Flanders, **8:**520
  France, **8:**542
  gender issues in, **3:**89
  Georgia, **8:**841
  German-American, **3:**889
  Germany, medieval, **8:**650
  Haiti, **2:**885
  Hungary, **8:**737, 740, 741
  Jamaica, **2:**905
  Japan, **7:**569, 600, 601, 604, 627
  Jewish, **8:**250, 261–62
  Karachaevian people, **8:**858
  Kosrae, **9:**742
  Low Countries, **8:**522
  Madhya Pradesh, **5:**723
  Malta, **8:**638
  Marquesas Islands, **9:**894, 895
  Mexico, **2:**617–18
  Nauru, **9:**260–62, 755, 756
  North America, **3:**285–86
  Oceania, **9:**252–53, 321
  Okinawa, **7:**791
  Papua New Guinea
    Iatmul people, **9:**257–58
    New Britain, **9:**623
    Umboi Island, **9:**574
  Philippines, **4:**910–11
  Plains Indian groups, **3:**441
  play dances, **3:**211

children's music (*continued*)
Poland, **8:**702
Rapa Nui, **9:**952
Romania, **8:**869, 876
Sāmoa, **9:**251, *285*
Scotland, Travellers, **8:**296
Slovakia, **8:**720, 725
Slovenia, **8:**911, 918–19
Solomon Islands
Bellona, **9:**267–69
Shortland Islands, **9:**657
South America, **2:**44, 58, 68, 84
Spain, *infantiles*, **8:**589
Switzerland, **8:**693, 697
Tibet, **7:**474
Tokelau, **9:**828
Tonga, *hiko*, **9:**787
Tuareg people, **1:**593
Tuvalu, **9:**251
Uruguay, **2:**511, 516, 522
'Uvea, **9:**812
dances, **9:**814
Vanuatu, **9:**259–60, 691, 692
Venezuela, **2:**537, 542
Wayana culture, **2:**166
Chile, **2:**356–74; **9:**951–52. *See also specific peoples*
administration of Rapa Nui, **2:**2
archaeomusicological studies in, **2:**12
art music in, **2:**112–16
Bolivian people in, **2:**84
children's wakes in, **2:**422
Chiloé Island, **2:**366
German descendants on, **2:**89
emigrants and exiles from, **2:**84, 90
ethnomusicological research in, **10:**80–81
festivals in, **2:***26*
geography of, **2:**2, 4, 356
German people in, **2:**89
history of, **2:**245, 356–57
instruments of, **2:**357–60
Italian people in, **2:**89–90
Mapuche culture, **2:**57, 232–38
military regime in, **2:**75, 90–91, 93, 104
musical genres
canto nuevo, **2:**373–74
chamamé, **2:**269
cueca, **2:**368–70
folkloric music, **2:**370–71
nueva canción, **2:**32, 60, 81, 103, 373
nueva ola, **2:**374
rock, **2:**104
tonada, **2:**89, 367–68
nationalism and popular music, **2:**104
Quechua- and Aymara-speaking peoples, **2:**205–23
religious contexts and genres, **2:**360–68
research on, **2:**374
Santiago de Chile, music conservatory, **2:**114
secular contexts and genres, **2:**366–71
shamanism in, **2:**45
Tierra del Fuego, **2:**357
Selk'nam culture of, **2:**57
Chilean people
in Mexico, **2:**610
in North America, **3:**730, 1201, 1204

Ch'ilgae ŭi moŭmgok "Pŏlgŏbŏkkin Sŏul" (Lee), **7:**956
Chi-Lites (musical group), **3:**677, 711
Chills (musical group), **9:**169
Chilula Indian nation, **3:**412
Chimbetu, Simon, **1:**429, 432
Chimbu people, **9:**511
flutes of, **9:**189, 533
performances of, **9:**513
CHIME (periodical), **7:**136
Chimeigundeng (Tibetan opera), **7:**479
chimes. *See* bells and chimes
Chimes (musical group), **5:**428
Ch'imhyangmu (Hwang), **7:**955–56
Chimombe, James, **1:**433
Chimu culture, **2:**7
Chin people, **4:**52, 399
Chin Silapabanleng, **4:**277
China, **3:**949, 959, 964. *See also* East Asia; Hong Kong; Taiwan; Tibet; Uighur people; *specific dynasties*
aesthetics and philosophy in, **7:**97–104
Beijing
as capital, **7:**32
Zhihua temple music, **7:**125, 133, 203, 311, 333
Buddhism in, **5:**12
cheironomy in, **8:**100
civil war, **7:**385–86
Confucian ideals, **5:**64
court music, **7:**91, 407
Buddhist influences on, **7:**332
daqu, **7:**89, 132, 168, 407
yanyue, **7:**89, 321
cultural exchanges in, **7:**49–51, 79–80, 88, 91–92, 102–3, 111, 191, 340–41, 415–16, 447, 455, 463, 480, 486
cultural influence on Korea and Japan, **7:**24–28, 80, 112, 534–35, 536, 538, 587, 620, 711, 723–25, 806, 981–82
cultural influence on Ryūkyū kingdom, **7:**711, 725, 789–90
cultural preservation in, **7:**47
cultural relationships to Southeast Asia, **4:**10–11
cultural syntheses under non-Han rule, **7:**30–36
Dai people in, **4:**547–49
dance traditions of, **7:**59–63
Dian culture, **4:**41, 44–46
Dunhuang, **7:**14
cave paintings in, **7:**59, *60*, 111, 112, 124, 137, 168
musical notation in, **7:**137
folk music, **7:**89, 91, 149–56, 413
classification of, **7:**149–50
genres of, **7:**150–53
research on, **7:**139–41, 155–56
Fujian province
archaeological sites in, **7:**191
cultural influence on Japan, **7:**724–25
minority cultures of, **7:**486–92
nanguan genre, **7:**169, 205–9, 396
xiao in, **7:**186
Gansu province
archaeological sites in, **7:**105–6

history of music, **7:**88
Kazakh people in, **7:**460–61
minority cultures of, **7:**455–64
Mongol people in, **7:**1003–20
Tibetan people in, **7:**474
Gaoluo, village traditions in, **7:**315–18
geography and climate of, **7:**11, 14–15, 455, 457–58
Guangdong province, **3:**949, 958, 1260, 1261
Cantonese opera in, **7:**303–9
Chaozhou region, **7:**211–16
instrumental musical traditions, **7:**217–21
minority cultures of, **7:**486–92
research on music of, **7:**220–21
Guangxi province
archaeological sites in, **7:**111
Cantonese opera in, **7:**303–9
minority cultures of, **7:**486–92
Guchifeng, Mongolian people in, **7:**451
Guizhou province
Miao people in, **7:**451
minority cultures of, **7:**486–92
Hainan province, **4:**219, 529
Cantonese opera in, **7:**303–9
minority cultures of, **7:**486–92
Hebei province, *sheng-guan* ensembles, **7:**203
Heilongjiang province
Khitan empire in, **7:**31
minority cultures of, **7:**517–21
Henan province
archaeological sites in, **7:**105, 107, 108, 110, 191
string chamber ensembles in, **7:**199
history of, **7:**15–18
history of music in, **7:**41–43, 87–91
Hmong people in, **3:**1003; **4:**550–51
Hubei province
archaeological sites in, **7:**108, 191
minority cultures of, **7:**486–92
Hunan province
archaeological sites in, **7:**107–8, 110
folk and religious music, **7:**140
minority cultures of, **7:**486–92
influenced by Vietnamese culture, **4:**447
influence on Burmese culture, **4:**363
influence on Cirebonese culture, **4:**698
influence on early Southeast Asian civilization, **4:**39, 40–41, 43
influence on Khmer culture, **4:**157, 201
influence on Maluku culture, **4:**813
influence on Philippines, **4:**913
influence on Southeast Asian musics, **4:**69–73
influence on Thai culture, **4:**222–23
influence on Vietnamese culture, **4:**17, 446–49, 472, 490, 516
Inner Mongolia, **7:**1003–20
minority cultures of, **7:**517–21
narratives of, **7:**452
yangqin in, **7:**179
instrument classification system in, **5:**21
instruments in, **4:**58; **7:**79–83, 105–11, 157–90
Japanese occupation of, **7:**294, 380, 383, 384–85, 745, 797
Jiangnan region, **7:**223–25

Jiangsu province
    archaeological sites in, **7:**105, 108
    folk songs, **7:**139
Jiangxi province
    Daoism in, **7:**320
    minority cultures of, **7:**486–92
Jilin province
    Khitan empire in, **7:**31
    minority cultures of, **7:**517–21
Kazakh people in, **7:**6
Korean people in, **7:**6
Liaoning province
    Khitan empire in, **7:**31
    minority cultures of, **7:**517–21
Manchuria, ensemble music in, **7:**203
May Fourth movement, **7:**89, 101–2, 137,
    139–40, 172, 346, 376, 380–83, 385,
    389
metallurgy in, **4:**37
minority cultures, **7:**403, 413–14, 439–521
    historical writing on, **7:**447–48
    musical classification systems, **7:**448–49
    northeastern regions, **7:**517–21
    northwestern regions, **7:**455–64
    overview, **7:**447–53
    policies toward, **7:**441–42
    research on, **7:**444
    south and southwestern regions, **7:**485–92,
        495–521
    stereotypes of, **7:**443
musical demographics of, **7:**417–21
musical ensemble traditions, **7:**191–243
    categorization of, **7:**41–42
    Chaoyang ditao, **7:**186
    Chaozhou xianshiyue, **7:**5, 57, 180, 211–16
    chuida, **7:**189, 195–97, 236, 239, 240
    gong and drum ensembles, **7:**192–93
    Guangdong yinyue, **7:**89, 180, 217–21, 240
    guchui, **7:**189, 392
    Jiangnan sizhu, **7:**5, 57, 82, 89, 139, 169,
        180, 186, 223–25, 233, 236, 238,
        239, 242, 298, 404, 411, 419
    nanguan, **7:**88, 169, 186, 205–9, 239, 242,
        394, 396, 404
    qing yanyue, **7:**212
    research on, **7:**139
    shifangu, **7:**5, 196, 224, 239, 311
    Shifan luogu, **7:**55, 192–93, 196, 224, 239,
        311
    structures and performance practices in,
        7:233–43
    Zhedong luogu, **7:**55, 195–96
musical institutions in, **7:**45–47, 59, 88, 102,
    387–88, 391–99
musical life, current, **7:**411–21
musical preservation in, **7:**103–4
music research in, **10:**21–26
nanguan, **4:**876
narratives traditions, **7:**245–73
Ningxia province, minority cultures of,
    7:455–64
nomadic conquests of, **7:**28–30
nomadic peoples of, **7:**13–14, 23
northeastern, minority cultures of, **7:**517–21
northwestern
    history of, **7:**455–58
    minority cultures of, **7:**455–64

notation of music in, **7:**123–25, 130–33; **8:**90,
    103, 104
number symbolism in, **7:**100
Old Believers in, **3:**916
opera traditions, **7:**275–309
population of, **7:**447
prehistoric, **4:**32, 33, 35, 37–38
printing in, **7:**22
Qinghai province
    minority cultures of, **7:**455–64
    Mongol people in, **7:**1003–20
    Tibetan people in, **7:**474
religious music in, **7:**311–37
research on music of, **7:**87, 90, 128–30,
    135–42, 225, 444
ritual music, **7:**91
Russian musical influences in, **7:**340–41, 349,
    354
scholar-musician figure in, **10:**19
scholarship and source materials in, **7:**127–42,
    439, 444
Shaanxi province
    archaeological sites in, **7:**107
    ensemble music, **7:**203
    minority cultures of, **7:**455–64
    musical genres in, **7:**199
    narrative singing in, **7:**257–59
    Qinqiang opera, **7:**235
    Yan'an area, **7:**140, 384–85
    zheng in, **7:**171
shamanism in, **7:**20
Shandong province
    ensemble music, **7:**203, 242
    lüju opera, **7:**412, 417
    string chamber ensembles in, **7:**199
    suona music of, **7:**236
    zheng music of, **7:**133, 238
Shanghai
    ballet in, **7:**62
    current musical life in, **7:**411–12
    Jiangnan sizhu in, **7:**223–25, 411
    opera in, **7:**297–301
    pipa performance schools, **7:**169
    popular music in, **7:**353–54, 389
    Western music in, **7:**381
    women performers in, **7:**408
Shanxi province
    archaeological sites in, **7:**107, 191
    Dongye "eight great suites," **7:**125, 203
    ensemble music, **7:**203, 239
    Hequ region, **7:**140
Sichuan province
    archaeological sites in, **7:**113
    minority cultures of, **7:**485–92
southern
    bossed gong cultures of, **4:**891
    minority cultures of, **7:**485–92, 495–521
Sunan region, *Sunan chuida* genre, **7:**55, 133,
    196–97, 239
Suzhou, narrative traditions of, **7:**250, 261–64
Tai people in, **4:**218–19, 337
taoqu genre in, **7:**237–40
theatrical traditions in, **7:**89
theory of music in, **7:**115–23
Tianjin, narrative traditions of, **7:**250, 251–55
Tibeto-Burman peoples of, **4:**528

Uighur people in, **7:**6
Vietnamese music in, **4:**446–47
Western musical influences in, **7:**50, 91–92,
    136, 141–42, 204, 219–20, 227–32,
    300–301, 306, 339–68, 899
Western music in, **7:**56, 91, 341–42, 373–77,
    381, 382, 388, 397–99, 415–16, 420
women musicians in, **7:**401–8
writing in, **7:**32
Wutai shan temple music, **7:**203, 311
Xi'an, ceremonial drum music (*Xi'an guyue*),
    7:125, 131, 200, 203
Xinjiang province, **6:**895, 904, *996*
    archaeological sites in, **7:**113
    Buddhism in, **7:**22
    geography and climate of, **7:**9
    history of music, **8:**88, 448, 455
    Kazakh people in, **7:**451, 460–61
    minority cultures of, **7:**455–64
    Mongol people in, **7:**1003–20
    Muslim call to prayer in, **7:**416
    popular music in, **7:**467–69
    Uighur *maqam,* **7:**450
    Uighur people in, **6:**910, 989–93, 995; **7:**5,
        92, 458–60
    Xibe people in, **7:**518
    yangqin in, **7:**179
Yao people in, **4:**549
Yunnan province, **4:**41, 42, 44
    agriculture in, **4:**917
    Akha people in, **4:**540
    bowed lutes in, **7:**176
    Buddhism in, **7:**327
    Dai people in, **7:**62, 495–507
    Lahu people in, **4:**538, 540
    Lisu people in, **4:**542–43
    Miao people in, **4:**556; **7:**6
    minority cultures of, **7:**485–515
    Naxi people in, **7:**139, 509–15
    Yi people in, **7:**139, 417, 451
Zhejiang province
    archaeological sites in, **7:**105, 108
    chuida genre, **7:**239
    minority cultures of, **7:**486–92
    Zhedong luogu music, **7:**195–96
China Blue, **7:**358
China Conservatory (Beijing), **7:**387, 398
Chinai, Alisha, **5:**429
Chindo arirang (Korean folk song), **7:**881, 882,
    882
Chindŏk, Silla king, **7:**981
Chinese Art Society (Edmonton), **3:**1247
Chinese Benevolent Society, **3:**1096
Chinese Canadian Choir (Toronto), **3:**1083
Chinese Cantabile Chorus (Ottawa), **3:**1083
Chinese Cultural Center (Toronto), **3:**1083
Chinese Exclusion Act (1882), **3:***507*, 958
Chinese Immigration Act, **3:**1092
Chinese Music (periodical), **3:**953
Chinese Music Ensemble of New York, **3:**962,
    963
Chinese Music Society of North America, **3:**953
Chinese Musicians' Association, **7:**221, 386, 387
Chinese Opera Club in America, **3:**961
Chinese people
    in Argentina, **2:**269

Chinese people (*continued*)
  in Australia, **9**:409
  in Barbados, **2**:813–14
  in Belize, **2**:666
  in Borneo, **4**:825
  in Burma, **4**:363
  in Cambodia, **4**:154, 156
  in Caribbean, **2**:4, 793
  in Central America, **2**:4
  in Cirebon, **4**:685–87
  in Costa Rica, **2**:704
  in Cuba, **2**:84–85, 822, 827
  diaspora of, **7**:6, 396
  in England, **8**:336
  in Fiji, **9**:773
  in French Guiana, **2**:434
  in Guyana, **2**:442
  in Hawai'i, **9**:96–97, 163, 914
  in Indonesia, **4**:72–73
  in Jamaica, **2**:896
  in Japan, **7**:724–25
  in Java, **4**:630, 650
  in Malaysia, **4**:71–72, 401
  in Netherlands Antilles, **2**:928
  in North America, **3**:9, 11, 12, 948, 950,
        957–65
    British Columbia, **3**:1092, 1095–96, 1255,
        1258
    Cantonese-speakers, **3**:949, 951, 958–59,
        1217, 1247–48, 1260–66
    as composers, **3**:964
    dances of, **3**:216, 224
    discrimination against, **3**:13
    history of music, **3**:526, 958–60
    immigrants from British Caribbean,
        3:808
    jazz, **3**:964–65
    minyue music, **3**:962
    Ontario, **3**:1078, 1083, 1215, 1217
    opera styles, **3**:960–61
    performance contexts, **3**:960
    popular music, **3**:964
    Prairie Provinces, **3**:1245, 1247–48
  in Nusa Tenggara Timur, **4**:787
  in Oceania, **9**:69–72
  in Panama, **2**:771
  in Papua New Guinea, **9**:153
  in Philippines, **4**:73
  popularity of karaoke, **2**:41, 85; **7**:399, 412,
        431, 444, 514
  on Réunion Island, **5**:606
  in Singapore, **4**:518–19
  in South America, **2**:4, 83, 84–85
  in Sumatra, **4**:616
  in Sunda, **4**:700, 722
  in Surinam, **2**:503
  in Tahiti, **9**:868
  in Thailand, **4**:70–71, 222, 238–39
  in Trinidad and Tobago, **2**:953
  in Vietnam, **4**:70
Chinese Restriction Act (Canada), **3**:13
Chinese Song and Dance Troupe, **7**:353–54
Chinese University of Hong Kong, **7**:432
Chinggis (popular performer), **7**:1020
Chinggis (also Genghis, Chingiz) Khan, **6**:966;
        7:21, 31, 32, 35, 1004, 1006, 1016

Ching Won Musical Society (Vancouver),
        3:*1095*, 1262
Chinhŭng, Silla king, **7**:941, 981, 984
Chínipa culture, **2**:551
Chinle Galileans (Navajo musical group), **3**:486
Chinnayya, Tallapakam, **5**:216
Chinook Indian nation, **3**:394
CHINOPERL Papers (periodical), **7**:136
Chinx, Comrade, **1**:432
Chip E., **3**:690
Chipaya culture, **2**:213–14, 285, 286, 288, 295
Chipchangga (Korean folk song), **7**:886
Chippewa Indian nation, **3**:292, 451–59. *See also*
        Ojibwa
    fiddling traditions of, **3**:405
Chiricahua Indian nation, **3**:431
Chiriguano-Chané culture, **2**:251, 253
Chiriguano culture, **2**:199, 452
    instruments of, **2**:34, 201
chirimía. See double-reed instruments
Chirino, Father Pedro, **4**:841
Chirino, Willy, **3**:788
Chiripá culture, **2**:199, 200, 204
    dance of, **2**:202–3
    instruments of, **2**:201
Chiriquí culture, **2**:9
Chiriwano culture. *See* Chiriguano culture
Chisa Ramblers, **1**:772
Chisholm, Angus, **3**:1071
Chisholm, Erik, **8**:368–69
Chishtī, Hazrat Khwaja Muīnuddīn Ḥasan,
        3:1044–45
Chisti, Sufi Ahmed Murad, **3**:1042
Chitimacha Indian nation, **3**:470
Chitra, **5**:422
Chitrakār caste, **5**:702
Chitswami, **5**:251
Chiŭm (album), **7**:972
Chiute, Lubeleje Mkasa, **1**:640
Chivers, Thomas Holley, **3**:595
Chiverton "Primo," Theophilus, **2**:*853*
Chiweshe, Stella, **1**:433
Chizbatron (Israeli band), **6**:1072
Chkhikvazde, Grigol, **8**:846
Cho Hakchin, **7**:986
Cho Kongnye, **7**:996
Cho Sanghyŏn, **7**:900, 972
Cho Sangsŏn, **7**:960
Cho Sŏnu, **7**:855
Cho T'aekwon, **7**:69
Cho T'ongdal, **7**:900
Cho Yongp'il, **7**:967
Ch'o Han ga (Korean folk song), **7**:886
Chocho culture, **2**:563
Choco culture, **2**:771, 783
Chocolate City (Parliament), **3**:684
Chocolate Dandies (musical), **3**:620
Chocolate Dandies (musical group), **1**:477
Choctaw Indian nation, **3**:466, 467
    Drunk Dance, **3**:*470*
    Social Dance songs, **3**:469
Chodzko, Alexander, **6**:844–45
Ch'oe Chŏngshik, **7**:985
Ch'oe Chongsil, **7**:933, 963–67
Ch'oe Ikhwan, **7**:965
Ch'oe Kyŏngshik, **7**:989

Ch'oe Oksan, **7**:915
Ch'oe Oksŏn, **7**:960
Ch'oe Pyŏngsam, **7**:965
Ch'oe Sangil, **7**:994
Ch'oe Sŏndal, **7**:898, 986
Ch'oe Sŭnghŭi. *See* Ch'oi Seung-hee
Ch'oe Sunyŏng, **7**:989
Ch'oe Taehyŏn, **7**:969
Choen, Shelono, **6**:1039
Chögyan Trungpa, **3**:133
Ch'oi Seung-hee, **7**:68
Choi Suntarawathin, **4**:55
Choice, Harriet, **3**:106
"Choice of Colors" (Mayfield), **3**:677
Choinière, Michèle, **3**:855
choirs. *See* ensembles, musical
Choiseul Island (Solomon Islands), **9**:654–55,
        656
Choisy, François Timoléon, Abbé de, **4**:70, 225
Ch'ŏkpyŏkka (Korean folk song), **7**:886
Chŏkpyŏk-ga (*p'ansori* story), **7**:899, 986
Chol culture, **2**:651
Chola, Dārep, **6**:908
Chola (also Cōla) dynasty, **5**:299, 386, 490, 518,
        740
Chŏlmŭn nal ŭi ch'osang (film), **7**:958
Chŏlmŭn ŭi taehangno (Oulim), **7**:971
Cholo culture, **2**:379
Chomlak, Dan, **3**:1244
Chomyŏnggok (Kim), **7**:957
Chŏn Chedŏk, **7**:965
Chŏn Sudŏk, **7**:965
Chon Sunhi, **7**:971
Chŏn Yongsŏn, **7**:915
Chŏng Chaeguk, **7**:915
Chŏng Ch'angŏp, **7**:899
Chŏng Ch'ŏl, **7**:965
Chŏng Ch'ŏlgi, **7**:965
Chŏng Chŏngnyŏl, **7**:899, 906, 986, 989
Chŏng Ch'ŏro, **7**:915, 969
Chŏng Ch'un-p'ung, **7**:899
Chŏng Hoegap, **7**:955, 956, 976
Chŏng Kwangsu, **7**:900
Chŏng Kwŏnjin, **7**:900
Chŏng Kyŏngok, **7**:911
Chŏng Kyŏngt'ae, **7**:984
Chŏng Namhŭi, **7**:915, 956, 960, 975, 986
Chŏng Nosik, **7**:985–86
Chŏng Sain, **7**:951
Chŏng Sŏngch'ŏn, **7**:938
Chŏng Sunim, **7**:911, 969
Chŏng Taryŏng, **7**:915, 916
Chŏng Yagyong, **7**:856
Chŏngbaekhon (Kim), **7**:953, 992
Chŏngdaeŏp (Sejong), **7**:835, 848, 851, 870
Chŏngdongbanggok (*hyangak* piece), **7**:868
Chŏngdong Theater (Seoul), **7**:995
Ch'ŏnggu yŏngŏn (Kim), **7**:855–56, 921, 927
Chŏnggwajŏng (*kagok*), **7**:921
Chongmyo Shrine (Seoul), **7**:865, 869–70, 982,
        989
Chŏngnyŏm (Kim), **7**:957
Chŏngsŏn arirang (Korean folk song), **7**:881, 883
Ch'ŏngsŏnggok (flute piece), **7**:954
Ch'ŏngsonyŏnŭl wihan kugak kwahyŏnak immun
        (Lee), **7**:955

Ch'ŏnnyŏn manse (*chŏngak* piece), **7**:869
Ch'ŏnnyŏn ŭi sori (Korean Buddhist recording), **7**:959
Chonpairot, Jarernchai. *See* Jarernchai Chonpairot
Chonyi people, **1**:624
"Choo Choo Ch' Boogie" (Jordan), **3**:668
Choo Huey, **4**:523
Chopi people, **1**:707
  history of, **1**:709
  instruments of, **1**:715–16
  music of, **1**:709–10
  orchestral music, **1**:159, 227, 436
Chopin, Fryderyk, **3**:190; **8**:53, 60, 187, 378, 710, 711, 712
choral music. *See* ensembles, musical; vocal music
Chorale Kinor (Montréal), **3**:1174–75
Chorale Notre Dame d'Acadie (Moncton), **3**:1118
Chorale de l'Université Saint-Joseph (Memramcook), **3**:1118
chordophones. *See also* dulcimers, hammered; guitars; harp-lutes; harps; hurdy-gurdies; keyboard instruments; lutes; lyres; monochords; musical bows; pianos; pluriarcs; ukulele; variable-tension chordophones; violins and fiddles; zithers
  acoustics of, **5**:322
  Akan people, **1**:465
  Angola, **1**:677
  Arab world, **6**:405–13
  Bali, **4**:743
  Borneo, **4**:834–35
  China
    early, **7**:88
    south and southwestern minority cultures, **7**:490–92
  classification of, **5**:326; **6**:396, 397, 398
  Congo, 1500s–1700s, **1**:77, 79–80, 81
  Dan people, **1**:466
  development of, **8**:41
  as drone instruments, **8**:9
  East Asia, **7**:5
  ghoṣaka, **5**:326
  guduki, **5**:732
  harp or lyre, Norwegian *harpa*, **8**:423
  Hindustani, **5**:332–39
  Japan, Zyômon period, **7**:560
  Java, **4**:641–42
  Kazakh people, **7**:460
  Kenya, **1**:625
  Khmer people, **4**:169–71
  Korea, **7**:823, 827
  Kurdistan, **6**:746
  Kwa groups, **1**:469
  Lombok, **4**:768
  Madagascar, **1**:785–87
  Mongol people, **7**:1010–13
  North Caucasia, **8**:851
  Oceania, **9**:385–91
  single-stringed gourd, Carib culture, **2**:23
  Solomon Islands, **9**:962
  Sotho peoples, **1**:707
  South and Central America, **2**:30
  South Asian folk, **5**:343–45

Southeast Asia, Indian influences on, **4**:66
Tanzania, **1**:640–41
Thailand, **4**:237–40
Uighur people, **7**:459
Vietnam, **4**:17, 471–75
  Chinese influences on, **4**:70
  upland regions, **4**:535–36
West Africa, **1**:453
Chords (musical group), **3**:351, 352, 709
choreography. *See also* animal choreography; dance and movement
  African movements, **2**:44
  Amerindian movements, **2**:44
  analysis of, **9**:313
  Andean region, circular, **2**:222
  Antigua and Barbuda, Africanization of colonial dances, **2**:799
  Anuta, *mako* genres, **9**:857–59
  Aotearoa, *haka*, **9**:944–45
  Arabian peninsula
    al-hubbān, **6**:710
    line dances, **6**:705
    traditional dances, **6**:706–11
  Arctic drum dances, **3**:377
  Argentina
    candombe, **2**:261
    cuarteto, **2**:276
  Australia
    gendered, **9**:243
    modern dance, **9**:416–17
    sources of inspiration, **9**:456–57
    wangga, **9**:454–55
    Warlpiri dance, **9**:465–67
    Yolngu dance, **9**:459
  Bahamas, jump-in dance, **2**:809–10
  Balochistan
    chogān, **5**:778–79
    drīs, **5**:777
  Bellona, **9**:851
  bharata nātyam, **5**:104, 149, 521–22
  borrowing in, **3**:218
  Brazil
    baile pastoril, **2**:334
    batuque, **2**:303
    for Candomblé rituals, **2**:343
    capoeira, **2**:346–47
    circular formations, **2**:348
    côco, **2**:349
    Saint Gonçalo dance, **2**:329
    samba-lenço, **2**:349
    ternos ensembles, **2**:312–13
  Bulgaria, *horo*, **8**:897
  Carriacou
    big-drum dance, **2**:870
    "dancing the cake," **2**:872
    "fighting the flags," **2**:872
    quadrille, **2**:871
  chain dances, **8**:165
  Chichimec culture, *danza chichimeca*, **2**:572
  Chile, *cueca*, **2**:370
  China
    Dolan *mäsräp* dances, **6**:991
    Peking opera, **7**:60
  Choctaw Social Dances, **3**:469
  Chuuk, **9**:738

Coast Salish spirit dances, **3**:396
Colombia
  bambuco, **2**:388–89
  currulao, **2**:404–5
  mapalé, **2**:405
contra dances, **3**:230; **8**:442–43
Cook Islands, **9**:902–3
  gendered, **9**:271
  hip movements, **9**:224–25
Costa Rica, *punto guanacasteco*, **2**:697
Creek Stomp Dance, **3**:468–69
Croatia
  kolo, **8**:926, 929
  northwestern dances, **8**:933
  poskočica, **8**:929–30
Cuba, *contradanza*, **2**:832–33
Czech Republic
  danaj, **8**:717
  sousedská, **8**:717
  verbunk, **8**:717
disco, **3**:229
Dominica
  bélé, **2**:841–42
  quadrille, **2**:842
Dominican Republic, merengue, **2**:860
Ecuador
  culebrillando, **2**:426
  sanjuán, **2**:424
Egyptian dances, **6**:623–33
England, morris dancing, **8**:329
Europe
  presentational folk dances, **8**:166
  ritual dances, **8**:161–62
  set dances, **8**:165–66
European folk dancing, **3**:209–10
European movements, **2**:44
Faroe Islands, ballad dancing, **8**:470
Garifuna culture
  ámalihaní, **2**:672
  awangulahani, **2**:672
  chumba, **2**:676
  combination, **2**:676
  gunjéi, **2**:676
  hüngühüngü, **2**:676
  punta, **2**:675
  senbai, **2**:676
  ugulendu, **2**:672
Ghost Dance, **3**:422
Goa, **5**:737–38
  mussoll, **5**:740
Guadeloupe, quadrille, **2**:877
Guarijio culture, *tuburada*, **2**:553
Guaymí culture
  bugutá, **2**:686
  jehio, **2**:686
Gujarat
  garbā, **5**:626
  rās, **5**:629–30
Guyana, *que-que*, **2**:445
Haiti, folkloric dances, **2**:888
Hawai'i
  gendered, **9**:241
  hula, **9**:67, 274–75, 925–28
Iran
  folk dances, **6**:877
  solo improvised dances, **6**:878–79

choreography (continued)
Irian Jaya, **9:**486–87, 581–82
Eipo *mot*, **9:**592
Japan
bugaku, **7:**64, 624
kabuki, **7:**64–65
nô, **7:**64
Java
court and classical dance, **4:**649
kosèk patterns, **4:**675
kathak, **5:**493, 494, 522
kathakaḷi, **5:**513–14
K'ekchi Maya, circle dances, **2:**668
Khmer court dance, **4:**189
Khmer folk dance, **4:**204
Kiribati, **9:**761–62
Kogi culture, **2:**187
Korea
salp'uri, **7:**68
t'alch'um, **7:**942
Kuna culture, *gammu burui* dances, **2:**645
Kurdistan, *govend*, **6:**748–49
Macedonia
čoček, **8:**282
oro, **8:**978
Makah potlatch dances, **3:**398
Mapuche culture
lonkomeo, **2:**237
puel purrún, **2:**237
Marquesas Islands
haka, **9:**890
mahohe (also *maha'u*), **9:**892
Marshall Islands, *jebwa*, **9:**750
Martinique, *zouk*, **2:**918
Métis dances, **3:**344, 409
Mexica culture
corpus, **2:**561
danza de cuauileros, **2:**560–61
Malinche dance, **2:**560
xayácatl, **2:**561
Mexico, *conchero*, **2:**614
Micronesia, marching dances, **9:**718
Mongol people
biy, **7:**1014
mörgüül biy, **7:**1015
tsam, **7:**1019
Morocco, Berber *aḥidus*, **6:**487
Nauru, frigate bird dance, **9:**757–78
Netherlands Antilles
danza, **2:**930
tambú, **2:**929
tumba, **2:**930
New Caledonia
Kanak dance, **9:**685–86
Loyalty Islands, **9:**683
mimetic dances, **9:**674–75
round dances, **9:**675
oḍissi, **5:**520
Otopame culture, male dances, **2:**572
Palau, **9:**725–26
Panama
el tamborito, **2:**777–78
gran diablos, **2:**779
Papua New Guinea, **9:**481–82
Abelam *bira*, **9:**549
Abelam paired dances, **9:**551

Anêm dances, **9:**615–16
Baluan dances, **9:**502
Binandere *ario*, **9:**499–501
Buang dance, **9:**566
Buin *ture*, **9:**650
Foi dance, **9:**247
Halia dance, **9:**640
Irumu dance, **9:**566
island dances, **9:**507
Kaluli dance, **9:**485
kanaaza, **9:**574
kanant, **9:**515–16
Managalasi dance, **9:**502
Maring dance, **9:**484
Maring *kaiko*, **9:**515
Melpa dances, **9:**485
Nissan *tinoia*, **9:**636
sia, **9:**545–46
solomon, **9:**625
Umeda *ida* ritual, **9:**484
Peru
alcatraz, **2:**496–97
dance-dramas, **2:**479
escobillada technique, **2:**494, 497, 499
hatajos de negritos, **2:**494
ingá, **2:**497
landó, **2:**498
marinera, **2:**499
vals criollo, **2:**500
zapateado technique, **2:**494–95, 497
Plains Indian Gourd Dance, **3:**448, 483
Plains Indian Grass Dance (War Dance), **3:**482
Plains Indian powwow dances, **3:**446–48
Polynesia, **9:**769–70
poetry and, **9:**307
Portugal, fandango, **8:**582
Puerto Rico
bomba, **2:**937
seis, **2:**938–39
Punjab (India)
bhangra, **5:**651–52
giddhā, **5:**652–53
Rapa Nui, comparisons to Tahitian and Cook
Islands dance, **9:**953
Romania, Rom people, **8:**277
Rotuma
mak paki, **9:**820–21
sua, **9:**821
tiap forau, **9:**822
tiap hi'i, **9:**822
Russia, *khorovod*, **8:**769
St. Lucia
calypso, **2:**950
jwé dansé, **2:**943
kwadril, **2:**944–45
Sāmoa, **9:**798–99
Sardinia, *ballu* and *danza*, **8:**630–31
Serbia, *kolo*, **8:**947
Sikaiana, **9:**846
Slovakia, *verbunk*, **8:**717
Solomon Islands
Blablanga *ragi māgana*, **9:**657
island dance, **9:**157
Russell Islands *ragi*, *sale*, and *vivi*, **9:**663–64
Sirovanga dance, **9:**655
South Asia, acrobatic, **5:**498

Spain, flamenco, **8:**598
Switzerland
ländler, **8:**689–90
silvesterchläuse, **8:**683, *684*
Tahiti, **9:**867–68
'aparima, **9:**878
group dances, **9:**875
hivinau, **9:**879
innovations in, **9:**879
'ōte'a, **9:**876
pā'ō'ā, **9:**878
tāmūrē, **9:**874
Taino culture, *areito*, **2:**847
Tamil Nadu
kōḷāṭṭam, **5:**920
kummi, **5:**919
tango, **2:**265; **3:**1204
Tarahumara culture, *matachín*, **2:**583, 586
Tibetan dances, **7:**475, 481
Tikopia, **9:**855
Tonga, **9:**784–85
fola'osi, **9:**351–52
gendered, **9:**241, *242*
mā'ulu'ulu, **9:**789–90
me'elaufola, **9:**11–12
Tuamotu Islands, **9:**884–85
Turkey
folk dances, **6:**814, 815–16
sema, **6:**795
Tuvalu, **9:**829
'Uvea, *kailao*, **9:**812–13
Vanuatu
counterclockwise directionality in, **9:**691,
696–97, 703
lega, **9:**698–99
men's genres, **9:**699–700
na lenga, **9:**696–97
Tanna, **9:**363, 705–6
Tannese *nupu*, **9:**703–4
Venezuela
joropo, **2:**539
Saint John the Baptist dances, **2:**535
Vietnamese dance, **4:**501–2
Virgin Islands, quadrille, **2:**972
Yap, **9:**732–33
tāyoer, **9:**727
Yemen
bara', **6:**655
dasa', **6:**709
Yuma dance, **2:**597
Choris, Louis, **9:***38, 754*
choro, **2:**49, 108, 305–6, 309, 310, 313, 350
Chorote culture, **2:**251
Chorotega culture, **2:**9, 680, 681, 747–48, 755
archaeomusicological studies of, **2:**7
Chorotí culture, **2:**452
Chorti culture, **2:**738
Chorus Line, A (Hamlisch and Kleban), **3:**545
Ch'osaga (*kasa*), **7:**927
Chosŏn ch'anggŭksa (Chŏng), **7:**985–86
Chosŏn Ch'anggŭktan (*ch'anggŭk* troupe), **7:**910,
968
Chosŏn Chŏngak Chŏnsŭpso (Korean Court
Music Study Institute), **7:**988–89
Chosŏn dynasty, **7:**28, 41
aak in, **7:**807, 834, 863, 982

bands in, **7:**930
Chinese interactions in, **7:**27
Confucianism in, **7:**848–49
court music in, **7:**807, 865, 982
dynastic histories of, **7:**833, 854, 855
folk genres in, **7:**807
government music offices in, **7:**854, 982
itinerant performing troupes in, **7:**879, 984
religious folk music of, **7:**889–90
royal authority in, **7:**26–27
sijo in, **7:**925
social policies in, **7:**43
treatises in, **7:**856
Chosŏn Kamu Yŏn'guhoe (society), **7:**989
Chosŏn kayo 2,000 kokchip (collection), **7:**961
Chosŏn Minsokhakhoe (society), **7:**808
Chosŏn minyo wa akpohwa (An), **7:**960
Chosŏn Sŏngak Yŏn'guhoe (vocal society), **7:**945, 968, 989
Chosŏn state (old), **7:**18, 24, 25
Chosŏn Ŭmak Chŏnjip (periodical), **7:**961
Chosŏn Ŭmak Hyŏphoe (society), **7:**989
Chosŏn Ŭmnyul Hyŏphoe (musical group), **7:**989
Chosŏn wangjo sillok (dynastic history), **7:**855
Ch'osudaeyŏp (kagok), **7:**921
Chottin, Alexis, **6:**436, 489, 1039
Choualy Yang, **4:***558*
Choudhuri, Bhupal Ray, **5:***55*
Chou Wen-chung, **3:**541; **4:**876; **7:**388
Chowdiah, Mysore T., **5:**212, 233–34
Choy, Peggy, **3:**1020–21; **10:***45*
Choyang Kurakpu (institute), **7:**988
Christensen, Alfred, **3:**883
Christensen, Chris, **3:**883
Christensen, Dieter, **6:**23; **9:**980
Christensen, James, **10:**33
Christensen, Lynn, **3:**883
Christensen, Ron, **3:**883
Christian, Bradley, **2:**972
Christian, Charlie, **3:**655
Christian Community of Universal Brotherhood, **3:**1267–70
Christian, Freddy, **9:***135*
Christianity. *See also* Armenian Apostolic Church; Assyro-Chaldean Church; Coptic Orthodox Church; Eastern Orthodoxy; Ethiopian Orthodox Church; Greek Orthodox Church; hymns; Maronite Church; Protestantism; Roman Catholicism; Syrian Orthodox Church; *specific denominations and religious orders*
Africa, **1:**17
African-Americans, **3:**82, 104, 523, 624–35
African denominations, **1:**403–4
Afro-Christian sects, **3:**811, 1205
Aka people, missionaries and, **1:**691–96
animism and, **4:**59–60
Anuta, **9:**856, 859, 860–61
Aotearoa, **9:**932–33, 935–36, 950
Pacific Islanders, **9:**111–12
Scottish people, **9:**114
Arab groups, **3:**1029, 1035
Armenia, **6:**723, 736–37
art music and, **2:**112–13; **3:**534

Asian-Americans, **3:**527, 950–51
Atoni people, **4:**796
Australia, **9:**452, 464
gumleaf bands and, **9:**134
Austral Islands, **9:**879–82
Baluan, **9:**602
Barbados, **2:**814
Bellona, **9:**849, 852
Borneo, **4:**828
Bosnia-Hercegovina, **8:**963
Burma, **4:**363
Canada, minority groups, **3:**1237–40
Central Africa, Bantu groups, **1:**659
Central Asia, **6:**936
China, missionaries in, **7:**373–74
Chinese-Americans, **3:**950
Chinese people in Oceania, **9:**71, 97
Chuuk, **9:**734–35, 737
Congo, **1:**76–81
Cook Islands, **9:**224–25, 272, 494, 896–98
Czech Republic, **8:**726
decline of liturgical music in, **8:**80–81
disputes with other religions, **8:**11
early history of, **6:**207
early music of, **6:**19–20; **8:**12, 69
East Africa, **1:**598–99, 607
East Polynesia, **9:**207–9
emotional expression in, **3:**120–21, 325, 639
Estonia, **8:**491
Ethiopia, **1:**147–50, 603
European adoption of, **8:**5
Fiji, **5:**612; **9:**775–76, 779, 780–81
Filipino-Americans, **3:**950
Flores, **4:**791, 795
fugue's relation to, **8:**62
Futuna, **9:**809, 814–15
Georgia, **8:**826, 835–36
Germany, **8:**646, 651
Gujarat, **5:**736
Guyana, **2:**443
Haiti, Vodou and, **2:**884
Hawai'i, **9:**207–9, 914, 917–19, 923
history of, **5:**13
India, **5:**234, 257, 259, 350, 374, 557
influence on African composers, **1:**19, 22, 23, 36, 208–10, 214–16
influence on instrumentation, **2:**36–37, 212
integrated worship, **3:**66
Ireland, **8:**378, 385
Irian Jaya, **9:**578, 592
Jamaica, **2:**901
Japan, **7:**538, 724, 756
Japanese-Americans, **3:**950, 969
Kapingamarangi, **9:**836
Karen people, **4:**544, 546
Kenya, **1:**630
Kerala, **5:**509, 582, 929, 944–47
Kiribati, **9:**759, 763
Kongo kingdom, **1:**666–67
Korea, **7:**834, 933, 951
Catholic and Protestant church music in, **7:**855
missionaries in, **7:**807
Korean-Americans, **3:**950, 976
Korean people in Oceania, **9:**99
Kosrae, **9:**159, 729, 740, 742

Kru people, **1:**374
Lahu people, **4:**539, 540
Lebanon, **6:**545
life-cycle rituals of, **8:**143, 194
Lithuania, **8:**509
Luangiua, **9:**842–43
Madagascar, **1:**790–91
Malta, **8:**634
Maluku, **4:**83, 812, 817–18, 819, 821
Manihiki, **9:**904, 905, 907
Marquesas Islands, **9:**896
Marshall Islands, **9:**748–49, 752
Maya culture, **2:**650, 668
Micronesia, **9:**717, 719–21
Middle East, **6:**3
Middle Eastern communities, **3:**1089
missionaries, **2:**67; **3:**7, 484–85, 521; **9:**21–22
to African-American slaves, **3:**64–65, 626
in Antigua and Barbuda, **2:**798–99
Arctic regions, **3:**379–80, 381
in Argentina, **2:**250–51
in Barbados, **2:**816
in Central America, **2:**23
in China, **7:**373–74
in Costa Rica, **2:**681
documentation by, **5:**48–49
in Great Lakes region, **3:**454
in Guatemala, **2:**735
introduction of harmonium, **5:**364
in Japan, **7:**538, 724
in Korea, **7:**807, 834, 951
in Mexico, **2:**23, 551, 556, 577, 588, 595, 600, 603, 651
in New France, **3:**23, 1074
in Nicaragua, **2:**753–54
in Northeast region, **3:**465
in Ontario, **3:**1079, 1178
in Plains region, **3:**441
in South America, **2:**23, 245
in Subarctic regions, **3:**390–91
syncretic music of, **5:**257
in Venezuela, **2:**525, 532
Moxo people, **2:**137–40
Munda people, **5:**502
Native Americans, **3:**455, 484–86
Nauru, **9:**755, 756–57
New Caledonia, **9:**672, 673
New Guinea, **9:**193, 477–78
Nigeria, **1:**233, 234, 236, 238–39
Niue, **9:**816–17
North Africa, **1:**533; **6:**431
North America, **2:**46–47; **3:**116–28; **5:**579
Northeast Indian groups, **3:**463
Northwest Coast groups, **3:**395–96
Nubia, **1:**556
Oceania, **9:**5, 186–87, 229, 321
hymn pedagogy, **9:**287–88
influence on theater, **9:**232–33
Pacific Islander groups, in North America, **9:**117
Pacific Islander missionaries, **9:**84, 193, 195, 204, 412, 429, 494, 762, 823, 829, 842, 852, 861
Papua New Guinea, **9:**88–89, 91, 148, 150, 506, 533, 537–38, 568, 572, 574, 650
Bali and Vitu islands, **9:**609, 612

Christianity, Papua New Guinea (*continued*)
  Baluan, **9:**607
  Buka, **9:**646–47
  influence on popular music, **9:**128–29
  Melpa people, **9:**516
  Motu people, **9:**493–94
  New Britain, **9:**614, 620, 625
  Rai Coast, **9:**565–66
Philippines, **4:**85–86, 839, 841–66, 890, 913
Pohnpei, **9:**739
Poland, **8:**701
Polynesia, influence on music, **9:**127
Portugal, **8:**576
post-Reformation divisions in, **8:**16–17
Pukapuka, **9:**913
religious calendar, **2:**47, 56
religious genres and, **2:**60
role in musical enculturation, **2:**68–69
Romania, **8:**881
Roti, **4:**798, 801
Rotuma, **9:**818, 820, 823
Ryûkyû Islands, **7:**796
Saami people, **8:**306
Sāmoa, **9:**103–4, 202, 204–7, 218–19,
  795–96, 799, 803, 805, 807–8
Samoan-Americans, **3:**1052
Scandinavia, bans on Saami music, **8:**122
Scotland, **8:**360, 366
Shona people, **1:**755
Sikaiana, **9:**844–45, 848
Slovakia, **8:**726
Slovenia, **8:**914
Solomon Islands, **9:**155, 654, 660–61
  'Are'are people, **9:**667
  Guadalcanal, **9:**664
  Isabel Province, **9:**661
  Malaita, **9:**666
  Russell Islands, **9:**662, 664
  Shortland Islands, **9:**656
South Africa, **1:**763–64, 765, 769; **5:**615, 617,
  618
South America, **1:**40
  tropical-forest region, **2:**131–32
South Asia, **5:**480, 482
  caste structure and, **5:**10
South Asian Americans, **3:**982, 983, 984;
  5:581–82
southern Africa, **1:**717–18, 759
Spain, **8:**588, 589–91
Sri Lanka, **5:**490, 955
statistics on, **3:**5
Sulawesi, **4:**804, 810
Sumatra, **4:**601, 608
  southern, **4:**623
Sumbawa, **4:**779
syncretic compromises, **8:**122–23
Syria, **6:**544
Tahiti, **9:**187, 207–8, 868, 869–73
Tamil Nadu, **5:**903, 921–27
Tanzania, **1:**634, 643–44
Thailand, **4:**26
Tikopia, **9:**853
Tokelau, **9:**823
Tonga, **9:**104, 202–4, 788, 791
  brass bands in churches, **9:**130–31
Tuamotu Islands, **9:**885

Tuvalu, **9:**829, 831
Ukraine, **8:**806
United Kingdom, **5:**573
'Uvea, **9:**809, 811–12
Vanuatu, **9:**198, 214, 689–90, 691, 695, 699,
  700
Vietnam, **4:**80–81, 444, 506, 507
views on music, **6:**19–20, 371
Virgin Islands, **2:**969
West Futuna, **9:**861–64
women's roles in, **8:**197
Yap, **9:**199–200, 729
Yoruba people, **1:**402–6, 459, 472
Zaïre, **1:**671
  Catholic radio stations, **1:**385
Zambia, **1:**671
Christianowitch, Alexandre, **6:**22
Christie, Dean William, **8:**373
Christina, queen of Sweden, **8:**440, 444
Christodoulou, Savvas, **9:**75
Christo, Nuno, **3:**1197
Christov, Boris, **8:**890
Christy, June, **3:**354
Christy's Minstrels, **3:**184, 616
Chromamorph I (Takahashi), **7:**737
Chronicle of Job (Jessye), **3:**608
Chrysanthos, **8:**1018
Chu Fong, **3:**959
Chu Tŏk-ki, **7:**898
Chuang people, **4:**218
Chuanzhilian (*Shifan luogu* suite), **7:**239
Chubuzú (musical group), **2:**703
Chue Chang, **3:**1005
Chukchi people
  bear ritual of, **7:**1029
  music of, **7:**786, 1027–30
  pie eynen genre, **7:**1030
Chukchisa (*kasa*), **7:**927
Chukhadjian, Tigran, **6:**725
Chulalongkorn University, **4:**121, 226, 249, 258
Chulas Fronteras (film), **3:**777
Chuldum-ool, Andrei, **6:**985
Chulupí (Churupí) culture, **2:**452
  instruments of, **2:**251, 455
Chuluunbat, **7:**1020
CHUM Ltd., **3:**250
Ch'um sori (Kim), **7:**959
Chumak people, **8:**795
Chuncaotang qinpu (Cao), **7:**132
Chundaeyŏp (*kagok*), **7:**921
Chungang kugak kwanhyŏn aktan (orchestra),
  7:957
Chungang Traditional Music Orchestra, **7:**972
Chŭngbo Munhŏn pigo (encyclopedia), **7:**854
Chung-Chia people, **4:**218
Chung, Kyung-Wha, **3:**977; **7:**803
Chung, Myung-Wha, **7:**803
Chung, Myung-Whun, **3:**977; **7:**803
Chung, Soonyon, **7:**970
Ch'unhyang-ga (also *Ch'unhyangjŏn*) (*p'ansori*
  story), **7:**898, 899, *903–5*, 908, 960,
  968, 969, 986
Ch'unhyangjŏn (North Korean opera), **7:**962
Chunjiang huayueye (*Jiangnan sizhu* piece),
  7:225, 239
Chunjiang huayueye (*pipa* piece), **7:**224

Chunjiao shima (Chen), **7:**220
Ch'unmyŏn'gok (*kasa*), **7:**927
Church of England. *See* Episcopalians
Church of God in Christ, **3:**630, 634
Church of God in Christ Northern California
  State Youth Choir, **3:**634
Church of God and Saints of Christ, **3:**118,
  126–27
Church of South India, **5:**922
Church of the Western Evangelical Millennium
  Pilgrims, **2:**445
Churchill, Sir Winston, **5:**789
Churchward, C. Maxwell, **9:**818
Churgin, Bathia, **6:**1063, 1064, 1067
Churgin, Pinchas, **6:**1063
Chutamani, prince of Siam, **4:**225
chutney, **5:**591–92, 601, 604–5
chutney-soca, **2:**86, 96; **3:**812, 816–17, 1205;
  5:604–5
Chuuk Islands (Federated States of Micronesia),
  9:712, 758
  alcohol use in, **9:**178
  dance genres of, **9:**728
  geography of, **9:**726
  music and dance of, **9:**733–38, 981
  poetry, **9:**324
  rap in, **9:**160
  sung poetry, **9:**328
  tokia dance, **9:**91–92
  verbal meter, **9:**324
Chuvash people, **8:**772
  instruments, **8:**774
  pentatonicism in music, **8:**773
  vocal music, **8:**773
Chu Xian Shou Ping (sacrificial piece), **7:**125
Chwado nongak (SamulNori), **7:**966
Chwaluk, Mae, **3:**345
Chwana people. *See* Tswana people
Ch'wit'a (*hyangak* piece), **7:**868
Chyaba minyo (Baek), **7:**971
Chybiński, Adolf, **8:**19, 712
Ciareščanka, Valžyna, **8:**801
"Ciboleros, Los," **3:**757
Ciboney culture, **2:**881
Çiçek, Ali Ekber, **6:**797
Cícero, Padre (venerated Ceará priest), **2:**328–29,
  331
Cicum-Okhotsk peoples, **7:**783
Cid, El, **8:**134, 256
Cid, El (epic), **8:**129, 256
Cid, Le (Corneille), **4:**508
Cienfuegos (*trovo*), **3:**758, 762
Cieza de León, Pedro, **2:**467, 707
Cifuentes, Santos, **2:**397
Cigan, France, **8:**922
Cihangirli Ahmed, **6:**194
Cikker, Ján, **8:**725, 729
Cikocki, Jaŭhien, **8:**800
Cilappatikāram (Atikal), **5:**24, 38, 260, 319, 327,
  518
Cilicia. *See* Kilikia
Cilla, Max, **2:**919
cimbalom. *See* dulcimers, hammered
Çimen, Nesimi, **6:**799
Cimze, Jānis, **8:**505
Çınar, Feyzullah, **6:**798

Cincinnati Symphony Orchestra, **3:**537
Cinderella (musical group), **3:**357–58
Cinderella Band (Filipino group), **4:**885
"Cinderella" Overture (Abelardo), **4:**873
Cindi, Abbie, **1:**777–78
Cine Musicians Association, **5:**535
cinnamon sphere (Toronto club), **3:**1186
Cinque, Luigi, **8:**622
Ciobanu, Gheorghe, **8:**886
Cipriani, Giovanni Battista, **9:**8–10
Circassian people, **8:**854–56
Circle of Life (album), **7:**358, 429
circular breathing, **6:**545
    Australia, **9:**395, 396
    Cambodia, **4:**172, 591
    India, **5:**359, 670–71
    Mongol people, **7:**1013
    Nepal, **5:**699
    Philippines, **4:**904
    Sardinia, **8:**630, 996
    Scotland, **8:**366
    Sumatra, **4:**605, 610–11, 622
Circumcelliones, **6:**431
Cirebon, **4:**685–99
    history of, **4:**686
    influence on Sundanese culture and music,
        4:686, 705
    instrumental music of, **4:**687, 690–97
    musical genres
        dangdut, **4:**696, 697, 698
        jaipongan, **4:**697
        lagu, **4:**690, 694
        pop Cirebonan, **4:**696
        pop Sunda, **4:**697
        ronggeng, **4:**688
        tarling, **4:**696, 697
    population of, **4:**685–87
    royal courts of, **4:**686, 690
Cirebonese music, **3:**1012. *See also* Indonesian
    music
Cirese, Alberto M., **8:**621
Ciría Cruz, Andrés, **4:**857, 866
Ciría-Cruz, Eduardo, **4:**857
Cirque jeune Annam et ca ra bộ Sadec amis
    (Nguyễn Văn Thặn), **4:**493
"Cisco Kid" (Scott), **10:**78
Citizen Kane (film), **3:**203
Citizens Act (1942), **3:**13
Citizen's Band (Perth, Ontario), **3:***1181*
Citovič State Academic Folk Choir of Belarus,
    8:799, 803
Citron, Marcia J., **3:**506
cittern. *See* lutes
Citulsky Family, **3:**1089
City Called Heaven, A (Wilson), **3:**611
City Lore (New York), **10:**72
City Nights (Tierra), **3:**748
Citytv (Canadian television channel), **3:**250–52
Civilisation traditionnelle des Lavalois (Sr. Marie-
    Ursule), **3:**1167
civil rights movement, **3:**329, 354, 507, 512,
    581, 583, 609, 621, 650, 660–61,
    662–63, 672, 681, 709; **10:**138
Civil War, American, **3:**187–89, 564–65
Civil Works Administration, **3:**297
Ci Xi, empress, **7:**393

Ciyuan (Zhang), **7:**129
CJ Mackintosh, **3:**691
Claddagh Records, **8:**392
Claerhoudt, Alphonse, **4:**872
Clair-Vasiliadis, Christos, **2:**238
Clamor Público, El (newspaper), **3:**735
Clancy Brothers (musical group), **3:**844, 846;
    8:226, 391
Clancy, Willy, **8:***383*
Clannad (musical group), **8:**226, 392
clappers. *See* concussion idiophones
Clapton, Eric, **2:**97; **3:**356; **8:**214, 215, 236
Clara van Groenendael, Victoria, **4:**650
"Clare de Kitchen," **3:**306
Clare, Eva, **3:**1229
Clare, John, **8:**333
clarinets. *See* single-reed instruments
Clark, Dick, **3:**211
Clark, Frances E., **3:**277
Clark, I., **9:***754*
Clark, LaRena, **3:**94, 147, 1082
Clark Sisters, **3:**634
Clark, William, **3:**441
Clarke, Anselmo, **2:***970*
Clarke, C. B., **5:**561
Clarke, Herbert L., **3:**33, 536, 1180
Clarke, J. P., **3:**1179, 1180
Clarke, Kenny, **3:**658
Clarke, Robert, **1:**92
Clarke, Stephen, **8:**367–68
Clarke, William Horatio, **3:**1180
Claro, Samuel, **2:**138, 140, 374
Clàrsach Society, **8:**364
Clash (musical group), **3:**357, 689; **4:**888; **8:**215
class. *See* social organization
Classical Arabic Music Quintet, **3:**1219
classical music. *See* art music, Western
Classical Music for Dummies, **3:**270
Classical Music Research Cell (Pakistan), **5:**747
Classical period, **8:**79–84, 367–68
    Czech Republic, **8:**727–28
    Finland, **8:**482
    folk idioms in art music, **8:**227
    Poland, **8:**710
    Slovakia, **8:**727–28
    Sweden, **8:**444
Claude, Renée, **3:**1158
Claus, Peter J., **5:**883
Clausen, Raymond, **9:**697, 977
clausula, **8:**71
Clave (periodical), **2:**838, 839
clavichord. *See* keyboard instruments
Clay, Edwin, **8:***337*
Clay, Henry, **3:**306
Clay Minstrel; or, National Songster, **3:**306
Clay, Sherman, **3:**1048
Clayton, Stuart, **9:***135*
Clayton-Thomas, David, **3:**1081
Clean (musical group), **9:**169
Cleaver's World (musical group), **3:**344, 1088
Clef Club (organization), **3:**706
Clef Club Symphony Orchestra, **3:**578
clef des chansonniers, La (Ballard), **8:**17
Clegg, Jonathan "Johnny," **1:**365, 430–31,
    779–80
Clémençon, Jean, **8:**692

Clement of Alexandria, **6:**360
Clement, Ernest, **5:**53
Clementi, Sir Cecil, **7:**267
Clementi, Muzio, **3:**190; **8:**609
"Clementine," **3:**914
Cleonides, **8:**48
Cleveland, Grover, **3:**309
Cleveland Institute of Music, **3:**610, 612
Cleveland, James, **3:**125; **10:**150
Cleveland Orchestra, **3:**175, 537
Cleveland Quartet, **3:**538
Cleveland State University, **3:***950,* 988–89
Cleveland, W. S., **3:**616
Cliff, Jimmy, **2:**353, 912; **3:**318; **9:**166
Clifford, James, **3:**145
Cline, Leigh, **8:***206*
Cline, Patsy, **3:**81, 520
Clinton, Bill, **3:**311
Clinton, George, **3:**683–84, *684,* 686, 701
Clinton, Hillary Rodham, **10:***83*
Clive Trio, **9:**938
Cló Iar-Chonnachta (publisher), **8:**387
Clones of Dr. Funkenstein (Parliament), **3:**684
Clorindy: Or, The Origin of the Cakewalk (Cook),
    3:194, 608
Clot-Bey, A., **6:**609
clothing. *See* costumes and clothing
"Cloud Nine" (Temptations), **3:**677
Cloutier, Guy, **3:**1161
Clovers (musical group), **3:**670, 671, 673
Club Dance (television show), **3:**212
Club Finlandia (Calgary), **3:**1250
Club Roma Dancers (St. Catherines), **3:**1196
Clunies Ross, Margaret, **9:**47
Clutha (musical group), **8:**372
Clyde McPhatter and The Drifters, **3:**671
"Coal Black Rose," **3:**182, 615
Coaldrake, Kimi, **7:**595
Coalition of Black Artists, **3:**1085
Coard, Bernard, **2:**867
Coard, Phyllis, **2:**867
Coast, John, **3:**1013
Coast Salish Indian nation, **3:**394, 1094
    spirit dancing, **3:**395, 396–97
Coasters (musical group), **2:**105; **3:**672
Coates, Richard, **3:**136, 1180
Coates, Thomas, **3:**565
COBA (Collective of Black Artists), **3:**224
Coba Andrade, Carlos Alberto G., **2:**31, 431
Çobanoglu, Murat, **6:***801,* 802, *802,* 804
Cobo, Bernabé, **2:**38, 283, 467–68
Cobos, Rubén, **3:**767
Cobra (album), **7:**364
Cobra (musical group), **7:**360, 363–65
Cochevelou, Jord, **8:**561
Cockburn, Bruce, **3:**314, 1058, 1081
Cockburn, John, **2:**748–49
Coclé culture, **2:**16, *17*
Coco (Hotahota, Jean), **9:**875, 876
Cocopah Indian nation, **3:**428, 433
Code d'Accès (musical group), **3:**1152
Code, James, **3:**1072
Codex Azcatitlan, **2:**15
Codex Borbonicus, **2:**557
Codex Calixtinus, **8:**600–601
Codex Madrid, **2:**650

Codex nitriensis, **8**:726
Codex Paris, **2**:650
Codification and Textbook Project, **1**:61–62
Codrington family, **2**:799
Codrington, R. H., **9**:361
Coelho Netto, Marcos, **2**:303
Coello Ramos, Rafael, **2**:745
Coen, Jan Pieterszoon, **4**:83
Cogui culture. *See* Kogi culture
Cohan, George M., **3**:193–94, 196, 544,
 650–51, 844
Cohen, Dalia, **6**:1063, 1066, 1067
Cohen, Erik, **6**:1065
Cohen, Henry, **2**:704
Cohen, Jacob, **5**:948–49
Cohen, Joel, **6**:24
Cohen, Joseph, **6**:1038
Cohen, Judith R., **3**:847, *1173*; **6**:1063, 1067
Cohen, Samuel, **6**:1069–70
Cohen, Yardenah, **6**:1029
Cohen, Yehuda Walter, **6**:1060
Coirault, Patrice, **8**:19, 553
Coker, F. C., **1**:18, 220
Coker, Robert, **1**:402
Cokwe people
 history of, **1**:672
 lamellophones, **1**:318, 678–79
 masks of, **1**:672–73, 676–77
 music of, **1**:672–77
Colacicchi, Luigi, **8**:621
Colas et Colinette (Quesnel), **3**:189, 1075
Cold Chillin' Records, **3**:714
Cold Crush Brothers (musical group), **3**:694
"Cold Sweat" (Brown), **3**:680, 710
Cole, Fay Cooper, **4**:872
Cole, Hugo, **8**:108
Cole, Madikane, **1**:18
Cole, Nat "King," **3**:354, 660, 669, 708
Cole, Robert "Bob," **3**:194, 608, 616, 618, 650
Colegio Español de Educación de Señoritas
 (Philippines), **4**:854
Colegio de Manila, **4**:842
Colegio de Niños (Philippines), **4**:842
Colegio de Niños de la Santa Iglesia Catedral
 (Philippines), **4**:842, 860–61, 868
Colegio Seminario de San Bartolomé, **2**:396
Coleman, Michael, **3**:843; **8**:384
Coleman, Ornette, **3**:328, 336, 661, 662–63
Coleridge, Samuel Taylor, **9**:33–34
Coleridge-Taylor, Samuel, **1**:213–14, 220; **3**:607, 608
Collaer, Paul, **2**:931; **8**:535, 622, 847
Collan, Karl, **8**:482
Collangettes, D. M., **6**:568
Collazo, Julio, **3**:784
Collection Livre Rose (Bigelow/Lerolle), **4**:511
Collection of Irish Tunes (Neal), **8**:17, 393
Collection of Notations (Cantemir), **6**:18
*Collection of the Newest and Most Fashionable
 Country Dances and Cotillions*
 (Griffiths), **3**:232
collections. *See also* archives and museums; *specific
 institutions or titles*
 Abkhazian people, folk songs, **8**:853–54
 Albania, folk songs, **8**:1003
 Andhra Pradesh vocal music, **5**:891

Arabic poetry, **6**:363, 370–71
Arabic song texts, **6**:20–21, 363, 369–71
Armenian music, **6**:725, 737
bakashot, **6**:1039
Balkarian music, **8**:858
ballad, **8**:135–36
Barbados, **2**:817
Basque music, **8**:309, 311, 316–17
Bosnia-Hercegovina, folk songs, **8**:970
Brittany, folk songs, **8**:561–62
Bulgaria, folk songs, **8**:906–7
byliny, **8**:129
Canada, folk songs, **3**:145–46, 148, 279,
 292–93, 410, 1068, 1088, 1123, 1133,
 1155, 1163–67, 1188, 1190, 1250
Chechen music, **8**:864
China
 Cantonese music, **7**:217–18, 220–21
 Daoist music, **7**:321
 folk music, **7**:200
 folk songs, **7**:89, 91, 140–41, 155, 348
 imperial archives, **7**:393
 kunqu librettos, **7**:293
 manuscripts, **7**:381
 music research, **7**:128–30
 nanyin, **7**:269
 notation in, **7**:123–25, 130–33, 137
 Peking opera librettos, **7**:287
 pipa music, **7**:169, 170
 poetry, **7**:79
 qin music, **7**:159–60
 reference materials, **7**:139
 song registers, **7**:130
 songs, **7**:130
 yue'ou, **7**:267–69
Corsica, folk songs, **8**:573–74
Croatia, folk songs, **8**:933, 936–37
Cyprus, song texts, **8**:1032
Czechoslovakia, national songs, **8**:729–30
Czech Republic, folk music, **8**:732–33
Denmark
 dances, **8**:461
 folk music, **8**:463–65
England
 dance music, **8**:330
 folk songs, **8**:328–29, 332–33, 334–35,
 337–38
Estonia, folk songs, **8**:496, 498
Europe
 folk songs, **8**:228
 song texts, **8**:7, 16–18, 177, 185
Finland, vocal music, **8**:479–80, 482, 488
France, folk songs, **8**:553
Georgia, folk song, **8**:846
Germany
 folk materials, **8**:646–47
 folk song, **8**:649, 662–64
 medieval manuscripts, **8**:651
Greece, folk songs, **8**:1023–24
Hawai'ian music, **9**:919, 922
history and development of, **8**:16–18, 86
Hungary
 dance music, **8**:737
 Rom folk songs, **8**:274
Iceland, *rímur*, **8**:408
Ireland, traditional tunes, **8**:391, 393

Israel, *shirei erets Yisrael*, **6**:1019
Italy, folk songs, **8**:613
Japan
 folk songs, **7**:539, 592, 599–600
 min gaku, **7**:725
 music anthologies, **7**:588–89
 pedagogical, **7**:778
 source materials, **7**:587
Jewish cultural materials, **8**:266–67
Jewish folk songs, **8**:257, 258, 261, 263, 266
Karachaevian music, **8**:858
Korea
 folk songs, **7**:887, 988
 historical, **7**:856–57
 instrumental scores, **7**:983–84
 kagok, **7**:921
 kasa, **7**:927
 sijo, **7**:925
 song texts, **7**:855–56
Latvia, folk music, **8**:504, 507
Lithuania, song texts, **8**:512
Low Countries
 dance music, **8**:523, 524, 528
 folk songs, **8**:522–23, 533–34
Macedonia, folk music, **8**:954, 983–84
management and goals of, **8**:179–81
Māori songs, **9**:932
North America, **3**:*406*
 dance music, **3**:232
 oral histories, **3**:33
North Korea, revolutionary songs, **7**:961
Norway
 folk songs, **8**:424–25
 religious songs, **8**:414
nūba, **6**:20, 367, 370–71
Oceania, ethnographic, **9**:5, 22, 23, 591
operatic arias, **8**:79
Ossetian music, **8**:861
Papua New Guinea, **9**:480, 990
Poland, folk songs, **8**:710
Portugal, folk songs, **8**:585
raga, **5**:433
Romania, folk music, **8**:881–82, 885
Rom songs, **8**:287, 289
Russia
 ethnic minorities' music, **8**:773, 778
 folk music, **8**:755, 756–57, 758, 781,
 782–83
 pesenniki, **8**:766, 776
Ryûkyû Islands, *sansin* music, **7**:793
Saami joik melodies, **8**:307
Scotland
 folk songs, **8**:371, 372–74
 pibroch, **8**:373–74
Serbia, folk songs, **8**:954
Slovakia, folk music, **8**:732–33
Slovenia, folk songs, **8**:921–22
Spain, *cancioneros*, **8**:601–2
Sufi *âyîn* lyrics, **6**:109–10
Sweden
 folk music, **8**:435, 437, 447
 manuscript, **8**:444
Switzerland, **8**:697
 folk songs, **8**:695
Taiwan, Aboriginal songs, **7**:524
Tibetan Buddhist teachings, **7**:472

Tibetan children's music, **7**:474
traditional dance, **8**:160
Turkish art music, **6**:113
Turkish *makamlar*, **6**:56
Turkish song texts, **6**:370
Ukraine, village music, **8**:820–21
United States
    folk song, **3**:14–15, 147–48, 293–94,
        511–12, 573–75, 579–81, 707, 736,
        762, 763, 767, 823–24, 833
    spirituals, **3**:29, 82, 506, 523–24, 573–75,
        600, 601; **10**:145
Wales
    folk songs, **8**:352, 353
    harp music, **8**:350, 352
collections, instrument
    Arab instruments, **6**:363
    Argentina, **2**:251
    Ecuador, **2**:413–14
    Europe, **8**:175–82, 307, 481, 923
    Japan, **7**:79, 81, 112, 188, 585, 622, 643,
        644, 701
    Kuna instruments, **2**:649
    Oceanic instruments, **9**:962–63, 964, 974–75
    Philippines, **4**:872
    United States, **3**:300
College of Dramatic Arts (Bangkok), **4**:121, 226,
    227, 249
College of Piping (Summerside), **3**:*1071*, 1120,
    1129
College of San Pablo, **2**:493–94
College of William and Mary (Williamsburg),
    3:953
Collier, John, **3**:443; **10**:106
Collier, John, Jr., **2**:423
Collier, Malcolm, **10**:106
Collier, Simon, **2**:93
Collins, E. John, **1**:353, 356
Collins, Judy, **3**:49
Collins, Sam, **3**:644
Collinson, Francis, **8**:371, 373, 374
Colo (Shilluk) people
    dance, **1**:112, 115, 116
    music of, **1**:564, 568–69
    puberty rites, **1**:111, 115, 117
Collocott, E. E. V., **9**:21, 787
Colombia. *See also specific peoples*
    Afro-Colombian traditions in, **2**:400–12
    Andean region, **2**:376–98
    archaeomusicological research in, **2**:7, 9–10;
        10:100
    children's wakes in, **2**:422
    geography of, **2**:376
    history of, **2**:387, 400–401
    instruments of, **2**:8, 31, 33, 34, 36, 39,
        376–82, 401–3
    Kogi culture, **2**:172, 183–87
    Kuna culture, **2**:637–49
    musical ensembles, **2**:382–85
    musical genres, **2**:385–94
        arrullo, **2**:408–9
        art music, **2**:396–98
        bambuco, **2**:382–83, 384, 385–89, 392,
            394–96, 397, 398, 407, 620
        bullerengue (also *tambor*; *chandé*),
            2:405–6

bunde, **2**:386–87, 395, 404
caribeños, **2**:410
carrilera, **2**:105
copla, **2**:389–91, 398
corrido, **2**:385
cumbia, **2**:101, 102, 398, 403, 409–10
cumbiamberos, **2**:410
currulao, **2**:404–5, *406*
danza, **2**:387, 393, 394–96
danza de negro, **2**:405–6
décima, **2**:408
fandango, **2**:406–7
folkloric music, **2**:394–96, 397–98
galerón, **2**:385
garabato, **2**:405
guabina, **2**:387, 390–91, 394–95
joropo, **2**:385, 394, 397
jota, **2**:407
lumalú, **2**:404
mapalé, **2**:405
paseo, **2**:407, *408*
pasillo, **2**:382, 383, 384, 387, 391–93,
    394–96, 397, 398
porro, **2**:403, 406, 407
puya, **2**:406
rajaleña, **2**:385, 390
reggaespañol, **2**:410
sanjuanero, **2**:385, 387, 394
serenata, **2**:383, 393
vallenato, **2**:39, 105, 402, 407–8, 410
vals, **2**:387, 393, 394
vaquería, **2**:408
zafra, **2**:408
    popular music, **2**:394–96
    population of, **2**:376
    research on, **2**:398, 411–12
    Sinú culture, **2**:9–10
    Tairona culture, **2**:10
    tropical-forest region of, **2**:123–35
    Tukano culture, **2**:150–55
    Yukpa culture, **2**:127
Colombian-Americans/Canadians, **3**:730, 1201
Colonial Harmonist (Burnham), **3**:1179
Colón, Willie, **3**:732, 743, 789, 794, 797,
    799
Colón Zayas, Edwin, **3**:799
Coloquios de los Pastores (*pastorela*), **3**:759
Color Me Badd, **3**:715
Colorado
    Boulder, dance in, **3**:208
    Denver, *taiko* drumming groups in, **3**:971
    Hispano peoples in, **10**:88–95
    Japanese people in, **3**:969
    Latino peoples in, **3**:718–19, 756
    Native American groups in, **3**:420–27,
        428–38, 440
    Ute Mountain Indian Reservation, **3**:425
    Volga Germans in, **3**:890
Colorado Alliance of Research Libraries,
    9:970
Colorado College (Colorado Springs), **3**:953
Colorado, Juan, **3**:779
Colores! (television series), **3**:767–68
colotomic structure. *See* form and structure
Coloured Stone, **9**:145, 443, 987
Coltrane, Alice, **3**:133

Coltrane, John, **3**:132–33, 336, 337, 661, 662,
    663, 664; **5**:528
Columbia Broadcasting System, **3**:294
Columbia-Princeton Electronic Music Center
    (New York), **3**:253
Columbia Records, **1**:417; **3**:247, 351, 352, 696,
    707, 714, 732, 737, 739, 741, 751,
    795, 843, 874, 902, 922, 938, 1033,
    1243; **5**:548; **6**:548, 785; **8**:678; **9**:998
    Canadian subsidiary, **3**:265
    Hawai'ian music recordings, **3**:1048
Columbia University (New York), **3**:253; **5**:563;
    9:975; **10**:71–72, 73
Columbia World Library of Folk and Primitive
    Music, **8**:371, 554
Columbus, Christopher, **2**:78, 441, 524, 693,
    770, 798, 847, 864, 881, 896, 927,
    932, 952, 968
Columbus, Ferdinand, **2**:681
Columbus, Samuel, **8**:444
Colvig, William, **3**:954, 1015, 1017–18
Comanche Indian nation, **3**:440, 444
    Ghost Dance songs, **3**:487
    gourd dancing, **3**:448
    War dance, **3**:449
Comanches, Los (*pastorela*), **3**:759
Combo Audio (musical group), **3**:169
Combo Mestizo (musical group), **3**:798
Combs, Sean "Puffy," **3**:701, 715
"Come, Love, and List Awhile" (Williams),
    3:604
"Come See about Me" (Supremes), **3**:674
comedia, **3**:848
Comhaltas Ceoltóirí Éireann (Association of Irish
    Musicians), **3**:846; **8**:386, 391
"Comin' thro' the Rye" (Scottish song), **3**:145
Comișel, Emilia, **8**:886
Committee for the Examination and
    Standardization of Turkish Music,
    6:783
Committee of Folkloric Investigation, **2**:719
Common Ground (periodical), **3**:311
Communauté Sépharade du Québec, **3**:1171,
    1174
communism. *See* socialism
Como, Perry, **3**:528, 862; **4**:884
Comorian people, **5**:606
Comoros, **6**:407
Compagnia Folk, **9**:81
Company (Sondheim), **3**:197
Compère, Loyset, **2**:735
competitions, **2**:62. *See also* festivals, celebrations,
    and holidays
    African-Americans, verbal, **3**:692
    Ainu people, *rekukkara* singing, **7**:786
    American Sāmoa, music and dance, **9**:266
    Anuta, *tauaangutu*, **9**:856–57
    Aotearoa
        brass band, **9**:130, 930
        choral, **9**:935
        Māori, **9**:947
        Māori Cultural Competitions, **9**:930
        Māori performances, **9**:937
        Pacific Islander music and dance, **9**:111
    Arabian peninsula, poetry duels, **6**:705
    Argentina, at folkloric festivals, **2**:261–62

competitions (*continued*)
  Atacameño culture, *copla de carnaval*, **2:**361
  Australia
    Aboriginal peoples, **9:**453
    jazz, **9:**143
    for Pacific Islanders, **9:**86–87
    spear throwing, **9:**61
  Austria, *Schlager*, **8:**676
  Azerbaijan, *dəyişmə*, **6:**929–30
  Bahamas, junkanoo, **2:**811–12
  Bali
    gamelan, **4:**759
    gong kebyar, **4:**745
  Balkarian people, **8:**858
  Barbados, calypso, **2:**820
  Basque region
    improvised verse contests, **8:**311–14, 315, *316*
    vocal, **8:**134
  Bengal, song duels, **5:**862
  Berber peoples
    oratorical matches, **6:**302–3
    poetry duels, **6:**488
  Bhutan, archery, **5:**489
  Bolivia, **2:**292, 297, 298
  Brazil
    frevo, **2:**337
    songwriters', **2:**109
  British Columbia, rodeos, **3:**1256
  Brittany, **8:**563
  Canada
    Anglophone dances, **3:**223
    bluegrass, **3:**1258
    calypso, **3:**1202, 1213
    Calypso Monarch of Canada, **3:**1209
    Calypso Soca Queen Competition, **3:**810
    competitive music festivals, **3:**1090, 1117, 1118, 1129, 1226–27
    composition, **3:**296
    fiddling contests, **3:**1071, 1080–81, 1125
    International String Quartet Competition, **3:**1090
    Pan Trinbago Panorama, **3:**1208
    step dancing, **3:**1080
  Carriacou, *parang*, **2:**871
  China
    hua er, **7:**92
    Jiangnan sizhu music, **7:**225
    narrative singing, **7:**254
    song duels, **7:**412
    Western music, **7:**398
  Chinese singing contest, **3:**964
  Chuuk
    island songs, **9:**734
    song, **9:**736
  Colombia
    bambuco, **2:**389
    décima, **2:**408
    guabina, **2:**391
    vallenato, **2:**411
  Cook Islands, **9:**898, 904, 911
    theatrical, **9:**238
  Corsica, song duels, **8:**134, 517, 566, 568

Costa Rica
  calypso, **2:**691
  carnival, **2:**693
  Pleasant Sunday Afternoons, **2:**689
Czech Republic, Strážnice festival, **8:**723
Dai people
  singing contests, **7:**506
  song duels, **7:**507
Dominica, storytelling, **2:**843
El Salvador, **2:**715
  popular music, **2:**718
England, pibroch, **8:**368
Europe
  ballroom dancing, **3:**210–11
  band, **8:**146
  folklore festivals and, **8:**151–52
Finland, singing, **8:**481
Flores, dueling, **4:**793
France, **8:**546
Futuna, **9:**815
Georgia, **8:**833
  shairi, **8:**838
German choral groups, **3:**885
Great Basin Bear Dances, **3:**423
Greece, ancient, **8:**46
Grenada, carnival, **2:**866
Guaymí culture, *la balsería*, **2:**687
Gujarat, *garbā*, **5:**628
Guyana
  Guyana Festival of the Arts (Guyfesta), **2:**448
  during Mashramani, **2:**448
  Mass Games, **2:**447–48
  Music Festival, **2:**446–47
Haiti, **2:**890
Hawai'i, **9:**923
  beauty contests, **9:**107
  choral, **9:**919
  dance, **9:**106
  hula, **9:**66–67, 272, 915
  Tahitian music and dance, **9:**105
hip-hop, **3:**695, 702
Hmong-Americans, **3:**1005
hula dancing, **3:**219, 1051
Hungary, **8:**739
hymn-writing, **2:**46
Iceland, poetry contests, **8:**402, 407
Indo-Caribbean community, **3:**816–17
Ireland, **8:**325
  traditional music, **8:**391
Irish music, **3:**845
Israel, **6:**1030–31
Jamaica
  Bruckins, **2:**906
  junkunnu bands, **2:**907
Japan, *min'yô*, **7:**603
Java, **4:**679
  angklung caruk, **4:**646, 667
  gandrung, **4:**679
  lomba, **4:**656
Kapingamarangi, *langa*, **9:**838
Karachaevian people, **8:**858
in Karnatak music, **5:**388–89
Kazakhstan
  Aziya Dauysy, **6:**960–61
  for *kyui*, **6:**958
  poetry duels, **6:**952, 953–54, 955, 960

Kiribati, **9:**759–60
Korea, **7:**995–96
  folk song, **7:**884
  kugak, **7:**976
  p'ansori, **7:**900
  for *tongyo*, **7:**972
Kosrae, village-choir, **9:**720
Kurdistan, heroic song performances, **6:**748
Latvia
  apdziedāšanās, **8:**502
  dance, **8:**504
lumber camp singing, **3:**157
Madhya Pradesh, question-and-answer, **5:**470
Maguindanao people, *kulintang* playing, **4:**892
Malaysia, **4:**442
  pantun, **4:**435
Malta, song duels, **8:**517, 636–37, 639
Mangareva, **9:**886
Manitoba, dance, **3:**409
Marquesas Islands, *hīmene* singing, **9:**894
Montserrat, **2:**925
Morocco, poetry duels, **6:**482, 488
Nauru
  choral singing, **9:**756–57
  string-figure, **9:**758
Nepal, *dohori gīt*, **5:**701
Nicaragua, for *canciones románticas*, **2:**766
Norway
  kappleikar (fiddlers' competitions), **8:**150, *151*, 427
  kveðing, **8:**426
  stevleik, **8:**412
Oceania, dance and athletics, **9:**55
Ontario
  Caribbean music, **3:**1202
  fiddle and step-dancing contests, **3:**1190–91
Orissa, **5:**733–34
Otopame culture, vocal, **2:**571
Pakistan, *qir'at*, **5:**748
Palau, **9:**181–82
Palestine, poetry duels, **6:**573, 575–76, 577
Papua New Guinea
  dance, **9:**62–63
  hymn-singing, **9:**150
  local shows, **9:**478
  peroveta, **9:***196*
  singsings, **9:**148, 245
  string-band, **9:**139
Peru, **2:**480–81
  dance, **2:**218–19, 497
  décima, **2:**495
  jarana, **2:**499
Philippines
  pasyon debates, **4:**845
  for popular performers, **4:**884
  popular song, **4:**885
  Qur'ān reading, **4:**906
  song duels, **4:**850–51
Plains Indian powwows, **3:**447–48
Pohnpei
  competitive feasting, **9:**175–76
  ritualized exchanges, **9:**727
Polynesia, choral, **9:**202
Portugal
  A Aldeia mais Portuguesa, **8:**577

song duels, **8:**517, 581
    vocal, **8:**134
powwow dancing, **3:**211
Puerto Rico, **2:**941
Pukapuka, hymn-singing, **9:**910
Punjab (India), *bhangra*, **5:**650–51
Québec, singing, **3:**1155
Romania, **8:**879
    Cîntarea României, **8:**883
Russia, *chastushki*, **8:**768
Ryûkyû Islands, *tobarâma*, **7:**794
St. Lucia, fiddling, **2:**944
samba, **2:**62
Sardinia, song duels, **8:**517, 627, 628–29
Saudi Arabia, poetry duels, **6:**654
Scotland, National Mod, **8:**363, 371
Serbia, **8:**949–50
    Prva Harmonika Srbije, **8:**947
Sicily, song duels, **8:**142, 517
Singapore, **4:**519, 520, 524
Society Islands
    choral-singing, **9:**873
    dance, **9:**379
Solomon Islands
    Russell Islands, **9:**662–63
    Sirovanga people, **9:**654
South America, band, **2:**62
Southeast Asia, **4:**141–42
Spain
    cante jondo, **8:**598
    song duels, **8:**517
Sri Lanka, song duels, **5:**971
Sumatra
    daboih, **4:**604
    rapa'i drumming, **4:**604
Sumbawa, *lomba hadra*, **4:**784
Sunda, **4:**707
    angklung ensembles, **4:**711
    pop Sunda, **4:**718
Sweden, *spelmansstämmor*, **8:**150
Switzerland
    chlepfe, **8:**687
    yodeling, **8:**691, 692
Tahiti
    dance, **9:**65–66
    dance and athletics, **9:**47–48, 57
    music-and-dance, **9:**867
Tahitian dancing, **3:**1052
Takuu, **9:**839
Tanjavur court, Kesavayya/Syama Sastri
        contest, **5:**229
Tokelau, singing, **9:**825–26
Tonga, brass band, **9:**130
Trinidad and Tobago, **2:**953
    Best Village, **2:**796
    classical singing, **5:**591
    parang, **2:**960
    steelband, **2:**962
Tunisia, for national art music, **6:**330, 511,
        513
Turkey
    âyîn, **6:**118
    folk dance, **6:**814
    song duels, **6:**82, 83, 765–66, 801–9
Turkmenistan, **6:**975
Ukraine, Soviet period, **8:**818

Ukrainian *tsymbaly* contests, **3:**913, 1082
United States
    bluegrass, **3:**160, 163
    fiddling contests, **3:**77, 825, 835
    hardingfele contests, **3:**869
    hula, **9:**117
    school band, **3:**277
    song duels, **3:**757–58
    Tahitian dance, **9:**118
Uruguay
    carnival, **2:**516
    payada, **2:**512, 520
Uttar Pradesh
    birahā, **5:**667, 669
    song duels, **5:**591
Vanuatu, string band, **9:**864
Wales
    choral, **8:**356
    eisteddfod, **8:**147, 151, 185, 342, 349, 350,
        352, 352–54, 356, 890
    harp, **8:**347
    singing contests, **8:**344
World Pipe Band Championship, **8:**363
Yap, ritualized exchanges, **9:**727
Yemen, poetry duels, **6:**655, 656–57
*Compilation of Proper Music and Theories of the
        Qing*, **7:**131
Complaintes acadiennes de L'Ile-du-Prince-Édouard
        (Arsenault), **3:**1136
*Complete Catalog of Sheet Music and Musical
        Works, 1870*, **3:**605
Complete Encyclopaedia of Music (Moore), **3:**27
Compo label, **3:**1077
Composé (Keleman), **8:**99
Composers Association of New Zealand, **9:**932
Composer's Collective (New York), **3:**45
composition. *See also* art music, Western;
        copyright and ownership; popular
        music; *specific composers and genres*
    Adighian people, **8:**854
    Afghanistan, **5:**807, 809, 834–35, 836
    African, **1:**16, 19, 208–30
        fusion of elements, **1:**8
        history and development, **1:**214–16,
            218–19
        model-based approach, **1:**217
        prospects, **1:**227
        techniques of, **1:**223–27
        types of, **1:**221–22
    Albania, **8:**993, 999
    Aotearoa, **9:**931–32, 936
        by Pacific Islanders, **9:**112–13
    Arab *vs.* Western art musics, **6:**39–42
    Argentina
        cuarteto, **2:**277, 279–80
        nationalist, **2:**262–63
    Armenia, **6:**725–26
    Asian influences on, **3:**324, 327, 335, 540,
        541, 953–54, 1012, 1015–16, 1019,
        1021
    Australia, **9:**355–57, 409
        Anglo-Irish folk music, **9:**141
        country music, **9:**142
        Greek composers, **9:**74–75
        Italian composers, **9:**81
    Austria, **8:**674–79

authorship issues of, **8:**73, 96–97
    Bali, **4:**729–30, 745–46, 747, 759–60
    Balochistan, **5:**776
    Baluan, sources of inspiration, **9:**602
    Belarus, **8:**796, 800
    Bellona, **9:**850, 852
    Bengali, **5:**844–59
    bhajan, **5:**255
    Bolivia, **2:**219, 284, 294
    borrowing and contrafactum techniques,
        1:235, 242, 251; **3:**180, 305–10, 327,
        367, 521, 538, 832, 837, 839,
        942–43, 1142–43, 1173–74, 1189,
        1211–12, 1257; **6:**1040–41; **8:**85
    Bosnia-Hercegovina, **8:**969
    by Brahmins, **5:**389
    Brazil
        art music, **2:**303
        dodecaphonic and avant-garde, **2:**306
    Bulgaria, **8:**904–5
    Burma, **4:**128
    Canada, **3:**296, 1058
        British Columbia, **3:**1096–97
        history of, **3:**14
        Maritimes, **3:**1072, 1121
        Ontario, **3:**1179, 1186
        operetta, **3:**189
        Prairie Provinces, **3:**1090–91
        Québec, **3:**1076, 1149–52
    Central Africa, **1:**216–17, 659, 671
    Central Asia, **6:**904
    Chechen people, **8:**862
    Chile
        boleros, **2:**372
        folkloric music, **2:**370–71, 372–73
    China
        assemblage of preexisting tunes, **7:**275, 276,
            277, 291, 309
        borrowing and parody techniques, **7:**347
        Cantonese music, **7:**219–20
        nanguan music, **7:**207–8
        "new wave" group, **7:**342, 350, 388
        northern ensemble music, **7:**202
        orchestral music, **7:**229–30, 231–32,
            348–51
        structural variation, **7:**234–37
        twentieth century, **7:**50, 170, 172–73,
            177–78, 181, 184–85, 339–68, 382,
            384–90, 419, 420, 463
        xianshiyue music, **7:**214–16
    Chuuk
        gendered, **9:**738
        island songs, **9:**734
    Colombia
        art music, **2:**397–98
        of *bambuco*, **2:**387–88
        folkloric music, **2:**394–96
    concept of progress and, **8:**59–60, 61,
        64–65
    Cook Islands, **9:**368–69
    Coptic Orthodox music, **6:**221–22
    Corsica, **8:**573
    Costa Rica, *bomba*, **2:**697
    Croatia, **8:**933–34
    Cuba, **2:**827–28, 833
    Cyprus, **8:**1030

composition (*continued*)
Czech Republic, **8:**723, 725–26, 732
dhrupad, **5:**168–70
diachronic reproduction, **8:**55–56
Dominican Republic, **2:**859, 860, 861, 862
East Africa, **1:**217–18
East Asia
assemblage, **7:**77
Western styles, **7:**49, 50
Ecuador, **2:**430–31
Egypt, **6:**547, 552–53, 561, 598, 600, 603–5, 612
El Salvador, **2:**717, 718
England
folk performers, **8:**333–34, 337
national school, **8:**332–33, 337, 339
Estonia, **8:**497–98
Ethiopia, **1:**44
Europe
arrangements and adaptations, **8:**54–55
arrangements of folk music, **8:**156
folk creation, **8:**188
nineteenth-century innovations, **8:**83
Faroe Islands, **8:**471–72
Fiji, *meke*, **9:**774
Filipino-Americans, **3:**1025
film composers, **3:**203–4
filmī gīt, **5:**532–34, 536–38, 540, 543, 544, 556, 856
Finland, **8:**480, 482
France, contrafacta technique, **8:**550
Futuna, **9:**815
Garífuna (Garifuna) culture, **2:**673, 734
punta, **2:**675
gat, **5:**130–31, 191
Georgia, **8:**843–44
Ghana, **1:**23–24, 34, 44
Greece, **8:**1008, 1014, 1018, 1020, 1021–22
Guatemala, **2:**735–36
Guyana, **2:**447; **5:**601
Haiti, **2:**884, 885, 894
Hawai'i, **9:**922–25
hīmeni, **9:**919
Hindustani music
for *pakhāvaj*, **5:**117–19
raga, **5:**82–84, 445–46
for sitar, **5:**335
for *tabla*, **5:**130–32
Hmong-Americans, **3:**1005
Hong Kong, **7:**170, 231–32, 432, 436
Hungary, **8:**737–38, 739
instrumental music, **8:**745
Iceland, **8:**406–7
improvisation, performance, and, **8:**73, 91–92, 93–95, 97
Indonesia, **4:**129–30
Indonesian-American collaborations, **3:**1016–17
Ingush people, **8:**862
Iran, **6:**60–75
Ireland, **8:**386–88
traditional music, **8:**390, 391–92
Irian Jaya, **9:**360–61, 593
Israel, **6:**1026, 1027–30, 1031–32, 1063
of folk songs, **6:**1018

Oriental Jewish music, **6:**1071–72
popular songs, **6:**1072–74
Italy, **8:**618–20
Jamaica, **2:**901
Japan, **7:**539–40
gagaku and, **7:**627
intertextuality, **7:**539–40, 554, 636, 676
sankyoku, **7:**716
sin nihon ongaku, **7:**698–99
sôkyoku, **7:**698–99
twentieth century, **7:**713, 731–32, 735–37, 761
Western styles, **7:**537, 627, 649, 735–38, 778–79
women composers, **7:**764
zyo ha kyû concept, **7:**546–47, 554–55
Java, **4:**683–85
jazz, **3:**653–55, 658–60, 664
Jewish contrafacta technique, **8:**254–56, 257
Kapingamarangi, **9:**836, 838
Karnatak music, **5:**154–56, 215–30
Kazakhstan, lyrical songs, **6:**956
khyāl, **5:**172–73
Kiribati, **9:**364–65, 759
kīrtana, **5:**265–67
Korea, **7:**951–73
twentieth century, **7:**975–77
kriti, **5:**268–69, 387
Latin American, **3:**740
Lebanon, **6:**553–55
Lithuania, **8:**510
Lombok, **4:**770–71
Macedonia, **8:**981
Malta, **8:**640, 642–43
Māori people, **9:**277
Mapuche culture, of *kantún*, **2:**236
Maronite church music, **6:**210–15
Marshall Islands, **9:**753
Martinique, *kadans*, **2:**917
medieval, **8:**50–56
medieval Arab music, **6:**351–52, 365
Métis people, **3:**410–11
Mexico, **2:**604–5
popular song, **2:**620–21
Micronesia, religious songs, **9:**720
Middle East, **6:**9–11
Montenegro, **8:**961
Native American conceptions and sources of, **3:**369–70
Nauru, **9:**757, 758
New Britain, **9:**177
New England, **3:**833
New Mexico, **3:**755, 759
Nigeria, **1:**36, 39, 44, 232–53, 401–10
history and development, **1:**233
Niue, **9:**817
North Africa, **1:**219–20
North Korea, **7:**960–63
Norway, **8:**425–26
for *hardingfele*, **8:**417–18, 428
notation and, **8:**51–52
Oceania
commemorative songs, **9:**32–33
payment and status, **9:**354, 362–64, 809
sources of inspiration, **9:**353–54, 362, 364, 431, 451

orchestral music, **3:**536–37
ownership and authority, **2:**64–65, 147–48; **9:**354–55
Arnhem Land, **9:**421, 425–26
Australia, **9:**455–57, 460
Cape York, **9:**429
Central Australia, **9:**427, 437
Gulf of Carpentaria, **9:**427
Kimberleys, **9:**431–32
Manihiki, **9:**909
Māori *haka*, **9:**947
Micronesia, **9:**716
New Ireland, **9:**628
Northwest Coast songs, **3:**394–95
Papua New Guinea, **9:**491, 523, 525, 546, 564, 609, 615, 633
Pukapuka, **9:**911
Southeastern Australia, **9:**442
Subarctic peoples, **3:**386
Tokelau, **9:**827
Yolngu people, **9:**301
Pakistan, northern, **5:**795, 798–99
Panama, **2:**784
Papua New Guinea, **9:**357–60
attitudes toward, **9:**478
Banoni people, **9:**644
Christian songs, **9:**516
Eastern Highlands Province, **9:**303
Enga people, **9:**536
hymn, **9:**194–95
Melpa people, **9:**518
Nissan Atoll, **9:**633–37
Papuan province, **9:**491
purchase of music, **9:**525
Rai Coast, **9:**564
song texts, **9:**512
sources of inspiration, **9:**564, 569, 608, 622
Teop Island, **9:**644
Paraguay, **2:**456–57
Peru, **2:**469, 484
Philippines, **4:**130, 873–81
1800s, **4:**860, 862–65
c. 1900, **4:**868–69
1900s, **4:**871–72
by friars, **4:**842
popular music, **4:**884–88
Polynesia, **9:**768
popular music, **8:**204–5
Purépecha culture, **2:**579
pirekua, **2:**580–81
qā'ida, **5:**128–29
Q'ero culture, **2:**229
research on, **8:**25–26
Réunion Island, **5:**611
Romania, **8:**881–85
Rotuma, **9:**819
Russia, **8:**763, 775, 780–82
Saami people, **8:**428–29
Sāmoa, **9:**799, 807
hymns, **9:**205
Sanskrit drama, of prologue music, **5:**26
Scotland, **8:**366–69
bagpipe tunes, **8:**363
Traveller songs, **8:**297
Serbia, **8:**948–49
Shankar, R., **5:**566

Sikaiana, **9:**845
Singapore, **4:**128–29, 523
Slovakia, **8:**725–26, 732
　　Rom contrafacta technique, **8:**276
Slovenia, **8:**921
South Africa, **1:**218–19, 763, 769–70
South America
　　art music, **2:**245
　　tropical-forest region, **2:**130
South Asia, ritual aspects in, **5:**472–73
Southeast Asia, **4:**126–36
　　gong-chime ensemble music, **4:**21
Soviet Union, **7:**340–41, 349
Sri Lanka, **5:**972
Sumbawa, **4:**784
Sunda, **4:**723–24
Suyá culture, **2:**149
Sweden, **8:**439, 444–45
Switzerland, **8:**688, 692, 696–97
synchronic reproduction, **8:**54–55
Tagore, R., **5:**254, 562
Taiwan, **7:**346–47
　　twentieth century, **7:**170
Tamil Nadu, **5:**911–12
Tanzania, **1:**643–44
　　text painting technique in, **8:**76
Thailand, **4:**127–28, 275, 277–83, 286
Tikopia, **9:**853–54
Tokelau, **9:**827
Tonga, **9:**783
　　hiva kakala, **9:**793
Trinidad and Tobago, **2:**960, 962–63, 964
Trobriand Islands, sources of inspiration, **9:**491
Turkey, **6:**115, 116, 771–72, 779–80
　　Sufi, **6:**194–96
　　twentieth century, **6:**775, 797–98
Turkmenistan, **6:**976
Uganda, **1:**44, 607
United States
　　band music, **3:**536
　　bluegrass music, **3:**167–68
　　Chinese-American composers, **3:**964
　　economics of, **3:**263
　　extramusical aspects of, **3:**236
　　folk song, **3:**147
　　gospel music, **3:**585
　　history of, **3:**14
　　indeterminacy in, **3:**335, 540
　　Italian band music, **3:**862
　　nineteenth century, **3:**538
　　popular songs, **3:**180–81, 182–83, 186–89,
　　　196–97
　　Spanish-Americans, **3:**851–52
　　twentieth century, **3:**173–77, 297, 539–41
Uruguay, **2:**521
'Uvea, **9:**809
Vai people, Islamic music, **1:**348–49
Vanuatu, **9:**361–64
　　Tanna, **9:**706–7
Vietnam, **4:**127, 129, 449, 512
Wales, **8:**353, 356
West Africa, **1:**220–21
West Futuna, **9:**862
women composers
　　Buang people, **9:**567
　　dēvadāsi, **5:**386

Hawai'i, **9:**353, 924
Irian Jaya, **9:**593
North America, **3:**89–90, 93, 1076, 1096,
　　1152
Tonga, **9:**365–68
Vanuatu, **9:**361–62
Yoruba, **1:**19
Composition for Synthesizer (Babbitt), **3:**253
Compton, Carol, **4:**25, 337, 343–44
Compton's Most Wanted, **3:**698
computers. *See also* electrophones; Internet
　　musical uses of, **3:**244–45, 265
　　pedagogical uses of, **3:**279
　　use in research, **8:**24; **10:**64–65
"Comrades, Fill No Glass for Me" (Foster),
　　3:187
Comte, Gustave, **3:**1150
"Con Alma," **3:**659
Conati, Marcello, **8:**622
Concert for Bangladesh, **5:**563
Concert Ensemble (Palestine), **6:**1026
Concertgebouw Orchestra (Amsterdam), **8:**518
concert music. *See* art music, Western
Concert Paraphrases of Traditional Negro Melodies
　　(White), **3:**608
concertina. *See* accordions
concerto, **8:**78, 82
Concerto da Camera (Boskovitch), **6:**1031
Concerto for Samul and Orchestra (Kang), **7:**967
Concerto in Slendro (Harrison), **4:**132
conch shells. *See* trumpets or horns
Concord College (Winnipeg), **3:**1239
Concordia Choir (Kitchener), **3:**1195
Concord Sonata (Ives), **3:**14
Concumén, **2:**371
concussion idiophones (castanets, clappers,
　　concussion sticks)
　　aboso, **2:**897, 902
　　Africa, **1:**674–75, 714, 723
　　Andhra Pradesh, **5:**896
　　Argentina, **2:**250, 251
　　ayag, **7:**1015–16
　　bali, **1:**565–66
　　ban, **7:**235
　　　accompanying narratives, **7:**247, 253–54,
　　　　269
　　　in *Jiangnan sizhu* ensemble, **7:**224–25
　　　in opera ensembles, **7:**276, 285, 292
　　bars, wooden, *bangibang*, **4:**919–20
　　bhajana cekkalu, **5:**364
　　bola'bola', **4:**900
　　bones, **9:**134
　　　England, **8:**331
　　　Ireland, **8:**385
　　　in minstrel shows, **3:**184, 543, 616
　　　Ontario, **3:**1189
　　　Palaeolithic osteophones, **8:**37, 38
　　　South America, **2:**814
　　　zo, **2:**945, 948
　　boomerangs, **9:**412, 427, 429, 430, 431–32,
　　　　433, 436, 440, 446
　　Brazil, **2:**313
　　buhahay, **4:**921
　　buluŋ, **1:**565
　　bwa, **2:**874, 877
　　canoíta, **2:**854–55

castañuelas, **2:**772, 774, 781, *782*
catta, **2:**898, 903
cekkai, **5:**364
cerek, **4:**408, 411, 412
chappar, **5:**753–54
chaprī, **5:**506
chumta, **5:**684
Chuuk, **9:**737
cimṭā, **5:**347, 651, 655, 762–63, 765, 769
ciplā, **5:**267, 364, 728
ciṭike, **5:**867, 869
clapsticks
　　North America, **3:**371, 415, 416
　　Oceania, **9:**61, 243, 301, 357, 373, 395,
　　　411, 412, 419, 421–22, 426, 445,
　　　454–55, 461
claves, **2:**709, 753, 830, 834–36, 930, 933
　　North America, **3:**280, 729, 786, 788,
　　　792–93
Corsica, **8:**572
dalupal, **4:**904
daru tālam, **5:**368
El Salvador, **2:**706
Europe, **8:**168, 169, 170
Fiji, **9:**19
Germany, **8:**656
Guatemala, **2:**726
hangar, **4:**919
hanske knap, **8:**525, *525*
hyôsigi, **7:**553, 659
Iran, **6:**879
Italy, **8:**609, 615
itones, **2:**826
jhāñjh, **5:**505, 665, *665*, 667
kālā'au, **9:**917, 928
kalutang, **4:**846
kapkaep, **4:**211, 213, 319
kartāl, **5:**347, *403*, 497
　　Fiji, **5:**613, *614*
　　Guyana, **5:**602
　　Karnataka, **5:**869
　　Madhya Pradesh, **5:**723
　　Rajasthan, **5:**641, 642, *644*
　　South America, **2:**958
　　Uttar Pradesh, **5:**665, *665*, 667
kartāḷa, **5:**364
kartsganag, **8:**860
kaṣik, **6:**763
kaṭṭai, **5:**368, *907*
katupi, **4:**852
kayamba, **1:**624, 625, 627
klt, **4:**547
knaptand, **8:**525
kołatki, **8:**704
krab, **4:**211
krap, **4:**228–29, *250*, 299, 305
krap khu, **4:**257
krapp, **4:**163
krap phuang, **4:**266
krap sepha, **4:**229, 259, 266
Low Countries, **8:**525
Luangiua, **9:**843
mai ngop ngep, **4:**339, 345, 346, 469
Manihiki, **9:**906
marabo, **9:**178
Marshall Islands, **9:**753

concussion idiophones (*continued*)
  metal rods, **4:**404
    agan, **2:**929, 930
    anak becing, **4:**806
    breng, **4:**616
    danda tal, **9:**94
    daṅda tāl, **5:**613
    dandtal, **2:**958
    dantal, **2:**85–86; **3:**814, 815, *815*
    ḍhantāl, **5:**589, 603, 604
    felu-ko-felu, **2:**505
    klentang, **4:**767
    kuria, **6:**630, 631
    sinna, **4:**613–14
  Micronesia, **9:**716, *718*
  muban, **7:**212
  Native American types, **3:**386, 397, 463, 474
  Nauru, **9:**756
  New Caledonia, **9:**213, 679, 681
  North America, **3:**475
  Oceania, **9:**373
  paiban, **7:**123, 205, 206, 235
  pak, **4:**229; **7:**829, 837, 959
  palipal, **4:**919
  palitos, **3:**786
  phách, **4:**465, 468, 481, 483
  phệch, **4:**469
  Polynesia, **9:**865
  popygua'i, **2:**200
  Portugal, **8:**582
  qairqa, **6:**898
  qarqabu, **1:**537
  Rapa Nui, **9:**952
  rhythm sticks, **3:**280, 595
  saffāqatān, **6:**395
  ṣahṣah, **6:**925
  sanba, **9:**99
  sanh, **4:**469
  shanbaal, **1:**611
  sinh tiên, **3:**994; **4:**468–69, 479
  Slovenia, **8:**918, 919
  Solomon Islands, **9:**668–69
  sonajas de azófar, **8:**594
  song lang, **4:**468, 474, 495
  South America, **2:**29
  South Asia, use in devotional music, **5:**248
  Spain, **8:**593, 594
  stones, concussive, **9:**373
    'ili'ili, **9:**917, 928, *929*
    Kosrae, **9:**742
    Micronesia, **9:**717
    New Caledonia, **9:**679
    Oceania, **9:**173
    Pohnpei, **9:**740
    Rapa Nui, **9:**952
    Vanuatu, **9:**694
  syaku byôsi, **7:**607–8, 620, 625
  taaw taaw, **4:**547
  Taino culture, **2:**22, 881
  taku, **7:**617
  talampi, **4:**852
  taqtuqa, **8:**640
  terkotki, **8:**704
  tibwa, **2:**915, 918, 943, 946–47, 948
  tiqrqqawin, **6:**487

tock-tock, **2:**959
tōkere, **9:**933
Tonga, **9:**792
triccaballacche, **3:**860
tuitin, **7:**617
tukegi, **7:**659
Vanuatu, **9:**708
Venezuela, **2:**528
wà, **4:**378, 379–81
wale'hkou', **4:**371
zilli maş, **6:**765
Condhong Raos, **4:**684
"*Cóndor Pasa, El,*" **2:**75
conducting, **8:**100–102
  Egypt, of Arab music, **6:**319, 559, 560–61
  Ethiopia, coordination in liturgical music, **1:**150
  by signal coordination, **1:**118
conductors and bandleaders
  African-American, **3:**564, 608
  bandleaders, **3:**891
  Chinese orchestras, **7:**6, 227
  Colombia, **2:**383
  Europe, **8:**62, 80
  Finnish, **3:**874
  German, **3:**885, 886
  Haiti, **2:**894
  Italian, **3:**862
  women, **3:**89, 608
conductus, **8:**71, 366
Cone, James H., **3:**582
Conestoga Congregation, **3:**904
Confederation Centre for the Arts (Charlottetown), **3:**1120
Conference on Chinese Oral and Performing Literature (organization), **10:**24
conferences and symposia. *See also specific organizations*
  Africa, **1:**43
  China
    on modern Chinese music history, **7:**138
    on new Chinese opera, **7:**387
  Egypt, Cairo Congress of 1932, **6:**18, 318, 323, 326, 421, 432–33, 502, 503, 508, 551, 557, 1058
  Europe, **8:**22, 25, 553, 847, 883
  France, International Congress of Jewish Music, **6:**1058, 1062
  Ghana Music Society, 1958, **1:**35
  International Folk Music Council, Ghana, 1966, **1:**31, 32, 65
  Israel, "East and West in Music," **6:**1061
  Japan
    International Musicological Society symposium, **7:**595
    Second Conference of Asian Traditional Performing Arts, **7:**525
  North America
    on contemporary music, **3:**1151
    on dance, **3:**221
    on music education, **3:**286
    on women in music, **3:**91
  Taiwan, First International Conference on Ethnomusicology, **7:**525
Confessions of a Justified Sinner (Wilson), **8:**369

Confucianism
  Buddhism's influence on, **7:**22
  China, **7:**34–35, 103, 335–37; **10:**22
    aesthetics and philosophy in, **7:**97–98, 240, 336, 361, 547–48
    discussions on music, **7:**128
    Han dynasty, **7:**88
    history of, **7:**335–36
    ritual music for, **7:**131, 186, 416
  dance and, **7:**59
  doctrine and principles of, **7:**17, 41, 101–2, 328, 401, 406, 547–48
  East Asia, **7:**7
  Japan, **7:**27, 28, 535, 547–48
  Korea, **7:**20, 24, 27, 28, 806, 833, 848, 861, 900, 941
    dance traditions in, **7:**66–67
    ritual music for, **7:**42, 59, 81, 807, 818, 829, 861–64, 982
  shamanism and, **7:**20
  Vietnam, **4:**448, 505
Confucius, **7:**17, 88, 97–98, 335–37, 861
  as *qin* player, **7:**159, 160
Con Funk Shun (musical group), **3:**684
Cong Su, **3:**204
conga, **2:**371; **3:**793
  cuarteto and, **2:**280
"Conga" (Miami Sound Machine), **3:**733
conga drums. *See* drums: barrel, conical, or cylindrical
Conger, Edwin H., **7:**373–74
Conger, Sarah Pike, **7:**373–74
Congo. *See also* Central Africa; *specific peoples*
  Bantu cultures of, **1:**659–63
  drums of, **2:**529
  guitar music, **1:**377
  historical studies, **1:**87–88
  instruments, **1:**664–66
  iron bells, **1:**310
  music of, **1:**659–69, 663–66
  popular music of, **1:**360–62, 363, 423–26, 669
  Portuguese in, **1:**76–81, 351, 667, 669
  Pygmies in, **1:**688
Congo (kingdom). *See* Kongo (kingdom)
Congo culture, **2:**105, 668
Congo, Fabián, **2:**430
Congo, Germán, **2:**417, 430
Congo Success, **1:**424
Congolese people, in France, **8:**231
Congregationalists
  in Hawai'i, **9:**208
  in Kapingamarangi, **9:**836
  in Kosrae, **9:**729
  in Micronesia, **9:**720
  in Nauru, **9:**756
  in Sāmoa, **9:**117
Congress on Research in Dance, **3:**221
Congress of South African Trade Unions, **1:**780
Congress of Vienna, **2:**441
Coniff, Ray, **3:**1050
Conjunto Casino, **2:**835
Conjunto Hueyapan, **3:**724
Conjunto Ilumán, **2:**428, *429*
Conjunto Libre, **3:**798

conjunto music, **3:**9, 16, 98, 284, 517, 522, 723, 772–78, 897–88
   in Mexico, **2:**613, *614*
   in New Mexico, **3:**756, 766
Conjunto Nacional de Folklore (Peru), **2:**501
Conklin, Harold, **4:**873
Conklin, Harold C., **1:**722; **3:**472
Conley, Arthur, **3:**710
Connecticut. *See also* New England
   Election Day celebrations, **3:**595
   Estonian people in, **3:**879
   Hungarian people in, **3:**908
   Lithuanian people in, **3:**876
   Pinkster Day celebrations, **3:**614
Connelly, Marc, **3:**621
Conner, Charles, **3:**671–72
Conners, Agnes, **3:***835*
Con Nhện Giăng Mùng, **4:***457, 460, 463*
Connolly, Matty, **3:***842*
Connor, Aaron J. R., **3:**603, 604
Connors, Stompin' Tom, **3:**1073
Conradh na Gaeilge (Gaelic League), **8:**390
Conrad, Joseph, **9:**44
Conseil des Arts et des Lettres du Québec, **3:**1151
"Consejos al maje" (Nevárez), **3:**737, 738
Conservatoire Artistique Territorial (Pape'ete), **9:**270
Conservatoire Française d'Extrême-Orient, **4:**510
Conservatoire de Musique du Québec, **3:**1150
Conservatorio Castella (Costa Rica), **2:**702
Conservatorio Municipal (Argentina), **2:**269
Conservatorio Nacional de Música (Colombia), **2:**397
Conservatorio Nacional de Música (El Salvador), **2:**717
Conservatorio Nacional de Música (Uruguay), **2:**522
Conservatory and School of Fine Arts (Colombia), **2:**398
Conservatory Canada, **3:**1182
Conservatory of Music (Peking University), **7:**376–77, 386, 397, 398, 416
Conservatory of Music of the University of the Philippines, **4:**870
Consiglio, Sandy, **3:**865
consonance and dissonance
   Belarus, two-part singing, **8:**794
   Bulgaria, two-part singing, **8:**896
   Chechen and Ingush polyphony, **8:**862
   Lithuania, **8:**510, 511
   Montenegro, two-part singing, **8:**958
   treatises on, **5:**33, 68, 74; **6:**368, 541
Constantino, Ernesto, **4:**873
Constitution Act (1982), **3:**1056
Consul (Menotti), **3:**546
Contant, Alexis, **3:**14, 1076, 1108, 1149
Contemporary Chamber Ensemble, **3:**175
Contemporary Music Project, **3:**281
Conte, Paolo, **8:**209
Conti, Bill, **3:**204
Conti, Manuel, **2:**397
Continental Six (musical group), **3:**1196
Continuing Story of Counterpoint (Borden), **3:**254
Contours for Orchestra (Smith), **3:**611

contredanse (*contradanza*, contra dance), **2:**98, 100, 795, 930; **3:**227, 230–34; **8:**165, 168
   clubs for, **3:**213, 233–34
   in Colombia, **2:**400, 407
   in Corsica, **8:**571
   in Costa Rica, **2:**697
   in Cuba, **2:**827, 829, 832–33, 835, 940; **3:**790, 791, 795, 802
   in Dominican Republic, **2:**860
   in France, **8:**546
   German, **3:**888
   in Guarijío culture, **2:**553–57
   in Honduras, **2:**744
   in Louisiana, **3:**802
   in Low Countries, **8:**524
   Métis, **3:**213, 332, 344
   music for, **3:**230–31, 836
   in New England, **3:**232–34, 323
   in Panama, **2:**773
   in Québec, **3:**1075, 1164
   in Southwest Pueblos, **3:**430
   in Spain, **8:**594
   Spanish, **3:**848
   in Sweden, **8:**442
   twentieth-century revival, **3:**233–34
Contreras, José, **4:**870
Contreras Arias, Guillermo, **10:**88, *91*, 91–95
Contursi, Pascual, **2:**263
Convite, **2:**861
Conway, Patrick, **3:**566
Conzemius, Eduard, **2:**660, 662, 739
Cooder, Ry, **3:**339, 777; **5:**529; **7:**1025; **9:**390, 1005
Cook, Al, **8:**675
Cook, Edwin, **9:**977
Cook, Captain James, **3:**527, 1092, 1255; **9:**7–15, 33–35, 128, 173, 285, 331–32, 589, 688, *766, 788, 791,* 794–95, 816, 896, 914, 933, 947
Cook, Ramsay, **3:**1147
Cook, Will Marion, **3:**194, 606, 608, 618–19, 620, 650, 706
Cook Islanders, in Aotearoa, **9:**112–13
Cook Islands, **9:**824, 865, 896–913. *See also* Aitutaki; Atiu; Mangaia; Manihiki; Mauke; Mitiaro; Nassau; Penrhyn; Pukapuka; Rakahanga; Rarotonga
   alcohol use in, **9:**178
   American expeditions to, **9:**24
   Chinese people in, **9:**71
   choral singing of, **9:**881
   Christianity in, **9:**208–9
   composition in, **9:**368–69
   cultural contacts with Aotearoa, **9:**929
   dance-drama, **9:**231
   dance, notation of, **9:***316*
   drumming, **9:**114
   films on, **9:**1008, 1018
   geography of, **9:**896
   hīmene tārava genre, **9:**872
   history of, **9:**896–97
   immigrants to Australia, **9:**85–86
   instruments, **9:**288, 898–901, 906–7, 913
     drums, **9:**384
     log idiophones, **9:**374
     struck tins, **9:**379

   missionaries in, **9:**21
   music and dance of, **9:**49, 278, 879, 902–3, 947, 973, 978
   'īmene genre, **9:**209, 898
   outsiders' influence in, **9:**5
   pedagogy in, **9:**271–72
   research on, **9:**114
   singing of, **9:**961
   sound recordings from, **9:**985, 999, 1002
   sung poetry, **9:**327
   theater in, **9:**224, 225, 233
   theatrical societies, **9:**229
   vocal music of, **9:**896–98
Cook Islands Christian Church, in Manihiki, **9:**905
Cook Islands National Archives, **9:**961
Cook Islands National Arts Theatre, **9:**225, 901
Cook Islands National Dance Company, **9:***898*
Cook Islands Youth Council, **9:**901
Cooke, Peter, **1:**256, 265
Cooke, Sam, **3:**709
Cooksey, Robert, **3:**645
Cool Hand Luke (film), **3:**203
Cool Stars, **1:**684
Cooley, Timothy J., **3:**150; **9:**640
Coolio, **3:**700, 701
Coomaraswamy, Ananda, **3:**130
Cooper, Alice, **8:**215
Cooper, Gary, **9:**149
Cooper, George, **3:**190
Cooper, James Fenimore, **3:**525
Cooper, John M., **3:**392
Cooper, Rachel, **3:**1013, 1019
Cooper, Ross, **9:**1008
Coopersmith, J. M., **2:**22, 862
"Cop Killer" (Ice-T), **3:**552
Copeland, Stewart, **9:**46
copla. See poetry; vocal music
Coplan, David B., **1:**218, *778*
Copland, Aaron, **2:**114; **3:**14, 33, 45, 135, 295, 297, 327, 521, 534, 539, 546, 797
"Coplas de las flores," **3:**1173
Coplas de la Tora (Jewish multilingual song), **6:**1043
Coppélia (Delibes), **8:**161
Coppens, Walter, **2:**178–79, 180, 544
Copper Age, **8:**38
Copper, Bob, **8:**327, 332, 338
Copper family, **8:**332, 334
Copper Inuit, **3:**374, 381
Copper, Ron, **8:**327
Coptic Orthodox Church, **6:**20, 219–23, 544
   instruments in, **6:**222, 403, 405
   in Israel, **6:**1021
   liturgies of, **6:**219, 220–21, 223
   Offices and hymns of, **6:**219, 221–22
   research on music of, **6:**223
Coptic Theological Seminary (Cairo), **6:**221, 223
copyright and ownership
   Afghanistan, **5:**832
   African-American music, **3:**705–6
   Argentina, *cuarteto*, **2:**279
   Belarus, **8:**796
   Bosnia-Hercegovina, epic songs, **8:**966

copyright and ownership (*continued*)
Canada, **3:**256, 289, 1068
of broadcasting companies, **3:**290
economics of, **3:**257
El Salvador, **2:**717
European cultural standards, **3:**256
film music, **5:**540
Finland, **8:**480
folk and traditional music issues, **3:**329, 339
Georgia, **8:**833
Haiti, **2:**891
intellectual property lawsuits, **3:**240–41, 301
issues in world music, **8:**225–26; **10:**152
Jamaica, **2:**909
legislation, **3:**242, 256–57, 259, 260–61, 288–90, 705
Métis fiddle tunes, **3:**405–6
music-licensing organizations, **3:**609
Native American cultural objects, **3:**311–13, 491–99
Northwest Coast songs, **3:**394–95
Pakistan, northern, **5:**798
in rock and roll, **3:**349
Russia, *byliny* tunes, **8:**764
South America, **2:**64–65, 74
Subarctic songs, **3:**386
Suyá culture, **2:**146–47
Taiwan, **7:**428
Turkey, **6:**252
United States, **3:**239, 289–90, 293, 838
Cora culture, **2:**573
Coral Records, **3:**352
Corbeille, Father, **1:**671
Cordas a Cannas (musical group), **8:**626
Cordel, Nando, **2:**333
Córdoba, Hernando de, **2:**748
Córdova, Arcenio, **3:**759
Córdova Cantú, José, **3:**740–41
Core (musical group), **5:**428
Corea, Chick, **3:**664, 797
Corelli, Arcangelo, **8:**51, *78*
Cormier, Charlotte, **3:**1136
"Cornbread" (Singer), **3:**669
Corneille, Pierre, **4:**508
Cornejo, Rodolfo, **4:**872
Cornelius, Don, **3:**211
Cornelius, Steven, **2:**839; **3:**790
Cornell University (Ithaca), **3:**953, 1014
Corner, Philip, **3:**1016
cornet. *See* trumpets or horns
Cornets de Groot, A. D., **4:**636
Coro Nacional Nicaragüense, **2:**765, 766
Coro San Marco (Toronto), **3:**1196
Coro Verdi (Toronto), **3:**1196
Corobicí culture, **2:**681
Corona, Manuel, **2:**831
Coronation of the Virgin (Gentile de Fabriano), **8:***70*
Coronel, Don Antonio, **3:**736
Coronel, Ignacio, **3:**735
Coronel, Soledad, **3:**735
corpophones. *See* body percussion; hand clapping
Corporation for Public Broadcasting, **3:**299
Corpus, Ramón L., **4:**864, 865, 870
Correa, Lani (Hawaiian performer), **9:***372*
Corréa de Oliveira, Willy, **2:**306

Correctional Institutional Services pipe band, **9:**136
Corri, Domenico, **8:**372
Corridos (Valdez), **3:**745, 749
corridos, **2:**101
in Chile, **2:**367, 371
in Colombia, **2:**385
in Guatemala, **2:**735
in Honduras, **2:**744–45
in Mexico, **2:**599, 605, 613, 616–17, 686–87
in Nicaragua, **2:**758–59, 767
in Philippines, **4:**853, 855
in United States, **2:**617; **3:**9, 13, 16, 522, 721–22, 723, 737–38, 771, 848, 849
New Mexican, **3:**755, 756, 757, 765, 768
in Venezuela, **2:**540
in Yaqui culture, **2:**591, 593
Corridos y canciones de Aztlán, **3:**749
Corries (musical group), **8:**391
"Corrina, Corrina" (Turner), **3:**673
corroborees, **9:***8*, 60, *410*, 426, 430, 440–41, 461. *See also* festivals, celebrations, and holidays
Corrow, Richard Nelson, **3:**311–13
Corsica, **8:**566–74
dance traditions of, **8:**571, 572, 573
geography of, **8:**566
history of, **8:**566
history of music in, **8:**573
independence movement, **8:**566
instruments, **8:**571–72, 573
map of, **8:***516*
population of, **8:**566
research on music of, **8:**573–74
separatist movement, **8:**12
song competitions, **8:**134, 517, 566, 568
vocal music, **8:***22*, *142*, 144–45, 196, 517, 566–71
polyphony, **8:**145, 542, 566, 569–70
Cortes, Araci, **2:**316
Cortés, Hernán, **2:**560, 600, 601, 603, 628, 666, 721; **3:**771
Cortesi, Santiago, **2:**457
Cortijo, Rafael, **3:**799
Cory, Daniel, **3:**137
Cosby (television show), **3:**715
Cosma, Octavian L., **8:**886
Cosma, Viorel, **8:**886
Cosmographia (Münster), **8:**504
cosmology. *See also* myths
Balinese, **4:**736–37, 739–41
Bolivia, **2:**289
China, **7:**81–82, 99–100, 128, 240, 312, 319, 391, 401, 547
Faŋ people, **1:**663
history of, **2:**232
Japan, **7:**547, 565, *566*
Korea, **7:**813, 823
Lombok, **4:**765
Mapuche culture, **2:**234, 252
Maya culture, **2:**650–51, 723
Middle Eastern, **6:**179–81, 186–88, 535–36, 537, 541, 543
Q'ero culture, **2:**229–30
South America, tropical-forest region, **2:**128–29

Suyá culture, **2:**148
Tarahumara culture, **2:**584
Tungus peoples, **7:**21
Warao culture, **2:**195, 198
Yaqui culture, **2:**589
Cossacks, **8:**755, 778
in Belarus, **8:**795
choral *byliny* singing, **8:**130
vocal polyphony of, **8:**757
Cossetto, Emil, **8:**933–34
Costa-Gavras, Constantin, **8:**1021
Costanzo, Jack, **3:**743
Costa Rica, **2:**628, 630, 680–704
Afro-Caribbean music in, **2:**687–93
archaeomusicological studies in, **2:**7
Aztec, Maya, and Chibcha cultures in, **2:**8
Bribri and Cabécar cultures of, **2:**631–35
Brunka and Teribe cultures, **2:**684–85
Diquís region, **2:**9
Guaymí culture, **2:**685–87
history of, **2:**681–82, 693–94
iconographical record in, **2:**16
instruments of, **2:**13, 694–95
Maleku culture, **2:**682–83
map of, **2:***629*
Miskitu culture, **2:**659–64
musical genres, Spanish and mestizo, **2:**695–98
performance contexts in, **2:**698–702
population of, **2:**680
research on, **2:**703–4
Spanish, criollo, and mestizo music, **2:**693–702
Costa Rican-Americans/Canadians, **3:**727
Costea, Constantin, **8:**886
Costello, Elvis, **8:**215
costumes and clothing. *See also* masks
Africa, **1:***8*, 114–17, 277
mtindo fashion, **1:**427
sapeur fashion, **1:**424–25
in African-American theater, **3:**614
Akha people, **4:**541
Andean regions, **2:**218
Antigua and Barbuda, Old Time masquerade bands, **2:**799
Aotearoa, **9:**974
Arabian peninsula
for dance, **6:**706
jingles on, **6:**405
Argentina, *cuarteto* performers, **2:**277
art-music concert performers, **8:**63
Asmat people, **9:**190
Atoni people, **4:**796
Austral Islands, **9:**880
Australia
Bentinck and Mornington islands, **9:**430
Torres Strait island dance, **9:**429
Aztec culture, **2:**556
Bahamas, junkanoo, **2:**811–12
Baiga people, **5:**722
Balkan region, for ritual dancing, **8:**161–62
Bangladesh, *jātrā*, **5:**505
Barbados, **2:**817
Basque region, carnival characters, **8:**315
Belarus, **8:**801
rusalka, **8:***791*

Belgium, **8:**525
  gille character, **8:**525
Bellona, **9:**849
Bhutan, for archery competitions, **5:**489
blackface minstrelsy, **3:**185
Bolivia, *machetero* dancers, **2:**139, 292
Bontok people, **4:**915
Bougainville, dance costumes, **9:**336
Brazil
  caboclos de lança, **2:**337
  northeastern, **2:**325
Brittany, *bagad* uniforms, **8:**562–63
Bulgaria
  kukeri, **8:**140, 897, 899
  for *Lazarovden*, **8:**900
California, Native American, **3:**415
Canada, Toronto Caribana festival, **3:**1207–9,
  1213
for Cantonese opera, **3:**1262
Caribbean, carnival, **2:**795
Carriacou, for big-drum dance, **2:**870
chau dance-drama, **5:***497–98*
Chile
  baile troupes, **2:**362
  huaso, **2:**368, *369*
China
  huju, **7:**298
  minority groups, **7:**443
  opera, **7:**279
  Peking opera, **7:**281
Chorotega culture, **2:**681, 748
Chuuk, **9:**738
Coast Salish Indian nation, **3:**396
Colombia
  for *bambuco*, **2:**389
  danza de negros congos, **2:**405
  for folkloric music, **2:**396
conjunto performers, **3:**777
Cook Islands, **9:**902
Costa Rica, **2:**701
Croatia, **8:**933, 935
  kolo, **8:**929
Denmark, folk dancing, **8:**461
disco, **3:**229
Dominican Republic, carnival, **2:**859
East Asia, for theater, **7:**73, 76
Ecuador, for San Juan festival, **2:**426
Egypt
  dancing girls, **6:**625
  for *haḍra* performance, **6:**147
  Nubian, **6:**629
El Salvador, dance, **2:**710–15
European folk dancing, **3:**209–10
Fiji, **9:**776–78
Flores, **4:**791, 794
funk, **3:**684, 685
Garifuna culture, *wárini*, **2:**674
Gilbert Islands, **9:**105
glam rock, **3:**357
glitter rock, **8:**215
Goa, **5:***736*, 738
Grenada, carnival, **2:**866
Gujarat, **5:**626
Guyana
  Jordanites, **2:**445
  for masquerades, **2:**446

Guyana, for *nagāṛā*, **5:**605
Haiti, **2:**888
  carnival, **2:**890
  rara, **2:**885–86
Hawai'i, **9:**21, 66, 105
  for *hula ku'i*, **9:**920
heavy metal, **3:**113
Hmong people, **4:**550, 551, 556
Hungary, Rom people, **8:***272*, *738*
India
  North, folk dance, **5:**497
  South, theatrical performances, **5:**104, 508
Irian Jaya, **9:**487
  Asmat people, **9:**590
Irish showbands, **3:**845
Italy, **8:**615
Jamaica, *jonkunnu* (also *buru*; horse head),
  2:907
Japan
  gagaku, **7:**624
  for *nô*, **7:**640
  Shinto, **7:**609
Java, **4:**647, 648, 653
jazz performers, **3:**551
Karen people, **4:**544
Karnataka, **5:**875–76, 877
  for *yakṣagāna* drama, **5:**401
Kayan people, **4:**830
Kerala
  kathakaḷi, **5:**511, 513, *513*
  kṛṣṇāṭṭam, **5:**511, *512*
  kuchipuḍi, **5:**517
  kūṭiyāṭṭam, **5:**509–10
  teyyam dancers, **5:**287
  tuḷḷal, **5:**514
Khmer court dance, **4:**189
Kiribati, **9:**349, 762, 764
Korea, **7:**970
  band musicians, **7:**930, 931–32, 935
  in *ch'anggŭk*, **7:**899
  for *p'ansori*, **7:**897
  in *samullori*, **7:**964
Kuna culture, **2:**772
Kurdish people, **6:**745
Kwakiutl Indian nation, **3:**400, *400*
Lahu people, **4:**538
Lisu people, **4:**542
Luangiua, **9:**843
Madia people, **5:**721–22
Maharashtra, **5:**728
Makah Indian nation, **3:**398
Malaysia
  in *bangsawan*, **4:**426
  in *dabus*, **4:**415
  in *hadrah*, **4:**409
  in *mak yong*, **4:**406
  in *randai*, **4:**413
  in *rodat*, **4:**410
Manipur, for war dances, **5:**504
Mapuche culture, **2:**238
Maranao people, **4:**896
Marquesas Islands, **9:**48, 892
Marshall Islands, **9:**749
Martinique, *zouk*, **2:**918
Maya culture, **2:**656, 731
Melanesia, **9:**599

Mexica culture, for *xayácatl* dance, **2:**561
Mexico, *conchero*, **2:**614
Micronesia, **9:**718
Mongol people, **7:**1016, 1018–19
Montserrat, **2:**925–26
Morocco, Berber, **6:**489
Native American, **3:**366
Naxi people, **7:***513*
Netherlands Antilles, Cuban-style orchestras,
  2:930
New Caledonia, **9:**681
New Guinea, **9:**22, 472, 478
Nicaragua
  for *la vaquita*, **2:**761
  los chinegros, **2:**760
Nusa Tenggara Timur, **4:**786–87
Oceania, **9:**345–52
  status and, **9:**348, 349
Palau, **9:**48
Palestine, **6:**576
Panama, **2:**784
  congos, **2:**778
  devil dancers, **2:**772, 781, *781–82*
Papua New Guinea, **9:**336, 482–83
  Anêm people, **9:**615
  Angan people, **9:**496
  Baluan, **9:**602
  Buang dance, **9:**566
  Eastern Highlands peoples, **9:**529
  Enga *mali lyingi*, **9:**534
  Erave people, **9:***537*
  Foi people, **9:***247*
  Fuyuge people, **9:**490
  Gulf Province, **9:**495
  Highlands peoples, **9:**484–85
  Irumu people, **9:**569
  Kaulong people, **9:**617
  Kiwai people, **9:***490*
  Kuman people, **9:**523–24
  Managalasi people, **9:**502
  Maring people, **9:**515
  Melpa people, **9:***513*, 518–20
  Milne Bay Province, **9:**490
  New Britain, **9:**621, 625
  Nissan Atoll, **9:**636
  njaguo, **9:**304
  Oro Province, **9:**332
  sia dance, **9:**545
  Siasi dancers, **9:**573–74
  Teop Island, **9:**644
Paraguay
  for folkloric dances, **2:**461
  promeseros, **2:**458
Peru
  hatajos de negritos, **2:**494–95
  for *son de los diablos*, **2:**494
Philippines, **4:**846
Plains powwow dancers, **3:**222, 482, 483
Polynesia, West, **9:**773
popular music, **3:**108
Portugal, **8:**577
Pueblo Indian groups, **3:**214, 430, 431
Punjab, **5:**500
  for *bhangra*, **5:**651
  for *giddhā*, **5:**653
punk, **3:**357

costumes and clothing (*continued*)
  Purépecha culture, **2:**578
  Rajasthan, **5:**648
  rap, **3:**700–701
  Rapa Nui, **9:***953*
  rock performers, **3:**551
  Romania, *paparuda*, **8:**870
  Roti, **4:**798
  Rotuma, **9:**821–22
  Ryûkyû dance dramas, **7:**66
  St. Lucia, masquerade, **2:**947–48
  Sāmoa, **9:**236, 237
  Saudi Arabia
    men's, **6:**693
    thōb nashal women's dancing dress, **6:**692–93
  Senufo people, **1:**115
  Society Islands, **9:**17
  Solomon Islands, **9:**157, 963
    Russell Islands, **9:**663
    Sirovanga people, **9:**655
  South America, tropical-forest peoples, **2:**126
  Sri Lanka
    for devil dance, **5:**490
    for Kandyan dances, **5:**363, 490–91
  Sufi, **6:**515
  Sunda, **4:**700, 709
  Switzerland
    fife-and-drum bands, **8:**685
    nüssler, **8:**684
    silvesterchläuse, **8:**683, *684*
    tschäggätä, **8:**685
  Tahiti, **9:**10
    group dances, **9:**875
    'ōte'a, **9:**876–77
  Takuu, **9:**839
  Tamil Nadu, **5:**909
    bharata nātyam, **5:**517, 522
    odissi, **5:**521
  Tarahumara culture, **2:**584, 586, 587
  Thailand, in *li-ke*, **4:**301–2
  Tibetan *a-lce lha-mo* troupes, **5:**712
  Tokelau, **9:**238, 826–27
  Tonga, **9:**14, 792
    politics and, **9:**351–52
  Trinidad and Tobago
    carnival, **2:**796, 964–66
    Orisa participants, **2:**955
    Spiritual Baptists, **2:**957
  Trobriand Islands, **9:***498*, 499
  Tuamotu Islands, **9:**882–83
  Tukano culture, **2:**155
  Turkey
    concert dress, **6:**786
    dance, **6:**816
  Uttar Pradesh, *rās līlā* dance-drama, **5:***495*
  Vanuatu, **9:**199, 699
    Tanna, **9:**705
  Virgin Islands, **2:**973
  Wales, **8:**343
  Wattal people, **5:**498
  Wayana culture, *okoma*, **2:**166
  Western Arctic peoples, **3:**376
  Western Athapaskan peoples, **3:**388
  world music performers, **8:**226

Yap, **9:**727, 732
Zouave, **3:**565
Côte d'Ivoire. *See also* West Africa; *specific peoples*
  academic training in, **1:**40
  Bété people, dance, **1:**287
  goumbé dance, **2:**803
  instruments of, **1:**465
  iron bells, **1:**310
  Kwa groups, **1:**468–69
  masks of, **1:**119
  music of, **1:**458, 466
  popular music of, **1:**419–20, 421
Côte d'Ivoire people, in France, **8:**231
Côté, James, **3:**51
Coté, René, **3:**1194
cotillion, **3:**522, 755, 760
Coto culture, **2:**681
Cotton Club (Harlem), **3:**655, 707
Coudreau, Henri Anatole, **2:**158, 164
Cougars (musical group), **3:**1213
"Could It Be I'm Falling in Love" (Spinners), **3:**711
Coulthard, Jean, **3:**1096
Council for the Development of French in Louisiana, **3:**859
counterpoint. *See also* texture
  Baroque, **8:**78–79
  California Indian vocal music, **3:**415, 418
  Ephrata Cloister use of, **3:**906
  Japan, in *dan mono*, **7:**697
  medieval, **8:**50, 71
  polyphonic, **8:**52
  Renaissance, **8:**75
  in Thai music, **4:**272, *273–75*, 276
Counter-Reformation, **8:**74
Country Dance and Song Society of America, **3:**323
Country Gentlemen (bluegrass group), **3:**159
Country Joe and the Fish, **3:**317
country music, **3:**10, 76–81, 514; **8:**204. *See also* country and western music
  African-American influences on, **3:**523
  Anglo-Irish traditional influences in, **3:**43, 48, 76, 520
  Anuta, **9:**861
  Aotearoa, **9:**167–69
  Arctic consumers, **3:**380
  audiences for, **3:**341
  Australia, **9:**141–42, 409, 413–14, 442, 443
  Barbados, **2:**819
  bluegrass and, **3:**160, 161, 163
  blues and, **3:**648
  Brazil, **2:**134
  Canada, **3:**52, 411, 1063, 1091, 1109–10, 1277–78
    Newfoundland, **3:**1070
    Nova Scotia, **3:**1133
    Ontario, **3:**1080, 1189, 1190
    Prairie Provinces, **3:**1087, 1091
    Québec, **3:**1155
    Subarctic consumers, **3:**391
    Ukrainian, **3:**345, 1110, 1242
  Christian, **2:**60
  commercial covers of, **3:**352
  corporate marketing of, **3:**81
  Czech/German influences in, **3:**897

  development of, **3:**13, 243
  economics of, **3:**263
  El Salvador, **2:**718
  gender coding in, **3:**108–10
  Guam, **9:**745, 746
  Hawai'i, **9:**107
  influence on African music, **1:**416
  instruments in, **3:**77–78, 240
  Micronesia, **9:**719
  Nashville studio system, **3:**80
  Papua New Guinea, **9:**388
  performers of, **3:**77–81
  political songs, **3:**317, 318
  pop music and, **3:**81
  Puerto Rico, **2:***938*
  recordings, **3:***263*
  religion in, **3:**531
  rockabilly genre, **3:**80, 326, 1081
  roots of, **3:**76–77
  Sāmoa, **9:**808
  social class and, **3:**45, 48, 1110
  steel guitar in, **3:**1049
  in Wales, **8:**355
  women in, **3:**79, 81, 97
Country Music Association, **3:**163
Country Music Television (U.S. cable station), **3:**290
Country Music, U.S.A. (Malone), **3:**1109
Country Network (Canadian cable station), **3:**290
Country Not Considered, A (Wayman), **3:**1061
Country Outcasts, **9:**413
Country Roads Refugee Arts Group (Boston), **3:**1001
country and western music, **3:**18, 79–80, 97, 325–26, 520. *See also* country music; western swing
  in British Columbia, **3:**1256
  dances, **3:**213
  in Maritimes, **3:**1073
  in Québec, **3:**1077
courante, **8:**168
Courlander, Harold, **2:**839; **3:**83, 84–85
Courrier du Canada, Le (newspaper), **3:**28
Courteen, Sir William, **2:**813
courtship rituals
  Akha people, **4:**541
  Andean regions, **2:**215
  Argentina, **2:**253, 254
  Australia, Hmong people, **9:**76
  blues in, **3:**640
  Bolivia, **2:**293
    dance in, **2:**291
    use of *charango*, **2:**288
  China, **7:**417
    northwestern minorities, **7:**462, 463
    southwestern minorities, **7:**492
  chordophones' use in, **9:**385
  Colombia, **2:**383, 389, 393
  Costa Rica, **2:**698
  Croatia, **8:**926
  Dai people, **7:**499
  Denmark, **8:**458
  Dominican Republic, **2:**849, 860
  El Salvador, **2:**711
  Europe, **8:**139, 145

France, **8:**545–46
Great Lakes Indian groups, **3:**455
Greece, **8:**1015
Hmong people, **3:**1003–4; **4:**552–53, 555–56,
  557–58
Ireland, **8:**388
Irian Jaya
  Asmat people, **9:**590
  Yali people, **9:**581
Karen people, **4:**544–45
Kmhmu people, **4:**546–47
Lahu people, **4:**539
lamellophones' use in, **9:**374
Latvia, **8:**503
Lisu people, **4:**543
Lombok, **4:**775
Macedonia, **8:**973
Mexico, **2:**618
Naxi people, **7:**511
Northwest Coast Indian nations, **3:**395
Palawan people, **4:**925
Panama, **2:**778
Papua New Guinea, **9:**153
  Angan people, **9:**497
  Buang people, **9:**567
  Chimbu Province, **9:**49–50
  Eastern Highlands peoples, **9:**528
  Eastern Highlands region, **9:**531
  Enga people, **9:**534–35
  Highlands region, **9:**297, 478, 512–13
  Huli people, **9:**537
  Irumu people, **9:**570
  Kaulong people, **9:**617
  Kuman people, **9:**326, 524–25
  Maring people, **9:**515
  Melpa people, **9:**516–18
  Nissan Atoll, **9:**640
  Papua New Guinea, **9:**484
Paraguay, **2:**462
Peru, **2:**213, 478, 485, 498–99
Philippines, **4:**849–50, 851, 905
  Bontok people, **4:**914–15
Plains Indian groups, **3:**441, 445
Pohnpei, **9:**739
Portugal, **8:**579
rock music and, **3:**96
Rotuma, **9:**819
Russia, **8:**761
Shan people, **4:**548
social dancing in, **8:**164
Solomon Islands, use of panpipes, **9:**400
songs in, **8:**196
South America, **2:**49
Southeast Asia, **4:**6
Spain, **8:**196, 589, 596
Sumba, **4:**790
Taiwanese Aboriginal peoples, **7:**527
Thailand, **4:**299, 313, 321, 539
Tikopia, **9:**247
Vietnam, **4:**216, 477, 532
Wales, **8:**145, 343
Yao people, **4:**549
Coushatta (Koasati) Indian nation, **3:**466
Coussemaker, Edmond de, **8:**534
Couture, Guillaume, **3:**1076, 1108, 1149
Covarrubias, Miguel, **4:**733

Cowan, Edward J., **8:**374
cowboy songs, **3:**78, 293, 510, 520, 1256
Cowboy Songs and Other Frontier Ballads
  (Lomax), **3:**293
Cowdery, James, **8:**394
Cowell, Henry, **1:**31; **3:**174, 327, 540, 953–54,
  1015; **5:**528; **7:**708
Cowley, John, **2:**965
Cox, Harry, **8:**327, 332
Cox, Ida, **3:**644, 707
Coxone, Sir, **3:**693
"Cradle Song" (Manchu folk song), **7:**518
Cradle Will Rock (Blitzstein), **3:**545
Craig, Adam, **8:**372
Crammed Discs, **8:**241
Cramner, Dan, **3:**1093
Crampton, Henry, **9:**869
Cranberries (musical group), **8:**392
Crane, Julia Ettie, **3:**277
Crash Test Dummies (musical group), **3:**1091
Crasson, Henri, **8:**527
Craven, David, **2:**767
Crawdaddy (periodical), **3:**348
Crawford, Michael, **4:**639
Crawford, Neelon, **2:**431
Crawford, Richard, **3:**32, 143, 512–13
Crawford, Ruth. *See* Seeger, Ruth Crawford
Crawfurd, John, **4:**225, 247
Crawley, David, **9:**89, 129
Crayner, John B., **10:**37
Crayton, Pee Wee, **3:**647
"Crazy Blues" (Bradford), **3:**263, 644, *644*, 707
Cream (musical group), **3:**263, 347, 356; **8:**214
Creation (Haydn), **3:**1179; **9:**203
Creation Records, **3:**169
creative process. *See* composition
Creatore, Giuseppe, **3:**566
Cree Indian nation, **3:**344, 383, 384, 392, 1073,
  1074, 1079
  fiddling traditions of, **3:**405
  intermarriages with French people, **3:**404
Creedence Clearwater Revival (musical group),
  3:348, 1002; **9:**154
Creek Indian nation, **3:**466
  Green Corn ceremony and dances, **3:**468–69
Crehan, Junior, **8:**387
Creighton, Al, **2:**446
Creighton, Helen, **3:**15, 147, 148, *148*, 149,
  292, 1068, 1072, 1125, 1133, 1136
Crémazie, Octave, **3:**1148
Cremo, Lee, **3:**52, 150, 1069
Cremo, AB, **3:**1213
Creoles. *See* French-Americans
Crescent (Coltrane), **3:**662
Crespo, Elvis, **3:**800
Crew Cuts (musical group), **3:**265, 352, 1081
Cringan, Alexander, **3:**465
"Cripple Creek," **3:**168
Crisanto Meléndez, Armando, **2:**740
Crisóstomo, Juan, **2:**581
Cristobal, Valente, **4:**866
Criterion Records, **9:**998
criticism, music, **5:**43; **8:**445
  arabesk, **6:**256
  Arabic writings on, **6:**364
  blues, **3:**579

dance, **3:**220
disco, **3:**229–30, 689
feminist issues in, **8:**192
Hungary, **8:**748
Japan, **7:**729, 750
jazz, **3:**579, 580–81, 583–84, 587, 663
Macedonia, **8:**973
nineteenth century, **3:**28
role of recordings in, **5:**526
Crivillé i Bargalló, Josep, **8:**602
Croatia, **8:**925–37
  art music in, **8:**933–34
  Baranja, **8:**925
    musical traditions of, **8:**931–32
  Cres island, **8:**930
  Dalmatia
    instruments, **8:***47*, 176, *244*
    musical traditions of, **8:**929–30
    polyphony, **8:**610
  dance traditions of, **8:**163, 926, 929, 931,
    932, 933, 935–36, 937
  Dinaric Alps, musical traditions of, **8:**927–29
  ethnic minorities in, **8:**925
  geography of, **8:**925
  history of, **8:**925
  Hungarians in, **8:**736
  instruments, **8:**169, 198, *926–27*, 928, 930,
    931–32, 959–60
    Asian derivations of, **8:**168
  Istria, **8:**925
    musical traditions of, **8:**930–31
  Krk island, **8:**930
  Kvarner Gulf, **8:**929
    musical traditions of, **8:**930–31
  Lošinj island, **8:**930
  map of, **8:***866*
  Međimurje
    bands in, **8:**927
    musical traditions of, **8:**932
  northwestern region, musical traditions of,
    8:932–33
  Omiš *klapa* festival, **8:**149–50, 929, 936
  Pannonia, musical traditions of, **8:**931–32
  Podravina, musical traditions of, **8:**932
  popular music in, **8:**209, 934
  population of, **8:**925
  Rab island, **8:**930
  religious music in, **8:**929
  research on music of, **8:**936–37
  Rom people in, **8:**279–80
  Slavonia, **8:**925, 926
    musical traditions of, **8:**931–32
    na bas style in, **8:**927, 931
    tamburica ensembles, **8:**927
  state folk ensembles in, **8:**151–52, 935–36
  vocal polyphony, **8:**610, 926, 930
  Zagreb folk festival, **8:**150, 935
Croatia (musical group), **3:**1198
Croatia Records, **8:**936
Croatian Folklore Federation, **3:**1083
Croatian Peasants' Party, **8:**935
Croatian people
  in Austria, **8:**674, 937
  in Bosnia-Hercegovina, **8:**962
  in Hungary, **8:**736, 937
  in Kosovo, **8:**951

Croatian people (*continued*)
  in Montenegro, **8:**957
  in North America, **3:**826, 919–24, 1082–83,
    1198; **8:**937
    choral music, **3:**919
    tamburitza orchestras, **3:**920–24
  in Romania, **8:**868
  in Serbia, **8:**952
  in South America, **2:**83–84
Croce, Giulio Cesare, **8:**608
Crocombe, Marjorie, **9:**233
Crofut, Bill, **3:**330
Cromanti nation, **2:**869–70
Cromwell, Harry, **3:**1133
Crónica, La (newspaper), **3:**735
Cronk, M. Sam, **3:**465
Crook, Larry, **2:**93, 839
Cros, Charles, **8:**18, 177
Crosby, Bing, **3:**77, 195, 844, 863, 898, 1049;
  9:26, 43
Crosby, Fanny, **3:**10, 533
Crosby, Stills, Nash, and Young, **3:**318
Cross, Lowell, **3:**254
Cross, William M., **3:**1096
Crossley-Holland, Peter, **2:**623; **5:**711; **10:**79,
  140
Crossley, Pamela, **7:**34
crossover. *See* fusion genres and border crossings
"Cross over the Bridge" (Page), **3:**352
Crotalan (Villalon), **6:**449
Crouch, Andrae, **3:**125, 634; **10:**150
Crow Indian nation, **3:**440, 445
Crowded House (musical group), **9:**169
Crowdy, William Saunders, **3:**126
Crowe, Peter, **9:**965, 973, 986
Crowley, Aleister, **3:**356
Crowley, Daniel J., **2:**812
Crows (musical group), **3:**351, 709
Croze, Austin de, **8:**573–74
Crucible (Ward), **3:**546
Crudup, Arthur "Big Boy," **3:**645, 708
Cruel Tears (Mitchell), **3:**199
Cruickshank, Brodie, **1:**84, 86
Cruikshank, Julie, **3:**1277
Crumb, George, **3:**175; **7:**351, 388
Crushin' (Fat Boys), **3:**713
Crutcher, Betty, **3:**676
Cruz, Celia, **3:**98, *98*, 732, 741, 743, 751, 789,
  794, 797, 798, 799
Cruz, José, **9:***26*
Cruz, Katy de la, **3:**1026
Cruz Mena, José de la, **2:**765
Cruz, Miguel, **3:**799
Cruz, Pedro, **9:***26*
Cruz, Ramiro de la ("Snowball"), **3:**780
Cruz, Ricardo, **9:***26*
Cruz-Sáenz, Michèle S. de, **2:**704
Cruz, Santiago, **4:**883
Cruz, Willie, **4:**884
"Cry" (Ray), **3:**351
"Crying in the Chapel" (Orioles), **3:**671, 709
Crystals (musical group), **3:**673, 709
Csermák, Antal György, **8:**737
Cuadra, Pablo Antonio, **2:**767
cuarteto, **2:**105, 265–66, 273–80
  electronic amplification of, **2:**40

Cuarteto Imperial, **2:**265
Cuarteto Leo, **2:**266, 273
cuatro. See guitars
Cuauhtémoc (nephew of Moctezuma), **2:**601
Cuba, **2:**789, 822–39
  archaeomusicological studies in, **2:**8
  art music in, **2:**827–28, 829, 836–37
  carnival in, **2:**94
  children's wakes in, **2:**422
  Chinese people in, **2:**84–85
  cord-and-peg tension drums in, **1:**316
  education in, **2:**836–37
  emancipated slaves from, **1:**351, 401–2, 471,
    478
  geography of, **2:**822
  governmental patronage, **2:**93
  Haitian dances in, **3:**802
  Haitian people in, **2:**793
  Havana, **2:**828, 837
  history of, **2:**822–23, 827–28
  industries of, **2:**791
  influence on African-American music, **3:**612
  influence on African guitar music, **1:**361
  influence on African music, **1:**416, 424; **2:**105
  influence on Angolan music, **1:**435
  influence on Filipino dance, **4:**854
  influence on Senegalese popular music,
    1:421–22
  influence on Tanzanian music, **1:**643
  instruments of, **2:**824–25, *825*
  musical genres, **1:**384, 385; **2:**829–33
    bolero, **2:**832, 834–35
    bolero-son, **2:**834
    canción, **2:**831–32
    canción protesta, **2:**103
    canción trovadoresca, **2:**831, 834
    cha-cha-chá, **2:**835
    claves, **2:**832, 834, 835
    columbia, **2:**831, 836
    comparsas, **2:**827
    contradanza, **2:**100
    criolla, **2:**832, 834
    danza, **2:**835
    danzón, **2:**832–33, 835, 838
    danzonete, **2:**833
    guaguancó, **2:**831, 836
    guajira, **2:**832, 834
    guaracha, **2:**835
    guaracha-son, **2:**834
    guarija-son, **2:**834
    habanera, **2:**49
    nueva canción, **2:**60
    nueva trova, **2:**829
    punto campesino, **2:**827
    punto guajiro, **2:**829, 833
    rumba, **2:**830–31, 836
    son, **2:**101, 827, 829–30, 835
    tumba francesa, **2:**839
    yambú, **2:**831, 836
  musical links with Venezuela, **2:**524
  popular music in, **2:**101, 796, 827–28
  population of, **2:**822
  research on, **2:**828–29, 838–39
  Santería in, **2:**32, 48, 69
  Santiago de Cuba, **2:**837
  tours of Bull, **8:**424

Cuba, Joe, **3:**788, 799
"Cuban Fire" (Kenton), **3:**797
Cuban Fire Suite (Richards), **3:**787
Cuban Institute of Music, **2:**837–38
Cuban people. *See also* Afro-Cuban music
  in North America, **2:**91; **3:**337, 719, 733,
    790–800, 1060, 1085
    African heritage, **3:**783–89
    musical genres of, **3:**728–29
    population of, **3:**718
  in Panama, **2:**84
Cuban Revolution, **2:**793
"Cubana Be—Cubana Bop," **3:**659
Cubanacán, **2:**372
Cubeo culture, **2:**151, 153
  mourning ceremony of, **2:**154–55
Cubero, Alejandro, **4:**856
Cucapá culture, **2:**595, 596, 599
  instruments of, **2:**598
"Cuckoo" (Scottish song), **3:**835
Cuckoo Namjil (Mongol legend), **7:**1008
Cucu, Pa, **4:***132*
Cudjoe, Seth, **1:**35
cueca
  in Bolivia, **2:**284, 292
  in Chile, **2:**100, 236, 361–62, 365, 368–70
  in Mexico, **2:**610
Cuéllar, Augusto, **2:***379, 381*
Cuéllar, Fernando, **2:***380, 381*
Cuenco, Ernani, **4:**885
cue-systems, **8:**92, 97–108. *See also* notation
  aural, **8:**104–8
  gestures, **8:**100–102
  tactile, **8:**99
Cuevas Maldonado, Rubén, **2:***612*
Cugat, Xavier, **2:**371; **3:**13, 521, 732, 794; **4:**883
Cuicatec culture, **2:**563
  dance of, **2:**564
  festivals of, **2:**566
Cui, Cesar, **8:**781
Cui Jian, **7:**259, 359, 360, 361, 363, 367–68,
  413, 436
Cui Weilin, **7:**220
Cui Zundu, **7:**119–20
Culata, Pepe (José Matallanes), **3:**731
Culina culture, **2:**482
Cullavagga, **5:**965
Cultier, Marius, **2:**919
cultural policies. *See* ideology; politics
Cumanana, **2:**501
cumbia, **2:**39, 101, 102, 105; **3:**728, 745–46,
  800, 1085, 1204
  in Argentina, **2:**265–66
  in Bolivia, **2:**293, 297
  in Chile, **2:**361, 372
  in Colombia, **2:**384, 398, 402–3, 406, 409–10
  in Costa Rica, **2:**685
  in Ecuador, **2:**428
  in Mexico, **2:**619, 622
  in Nicaragua, **2:**762, 763
  in Panama, **2:**778
  in Peru, **2:**483, 484–85
  Tohono O'odham, **3:**436, 490
  in Uruguay, **2:**520
cumbia andina. See chicha
Cummeragunga Concert Party, **9:**134

Cumming, Angus, **8**:373
Cummings, Andy, **9**:164
Cuna culture. *See* Kuna culture
Cuneta, Sharon, **3**:1025
Cuney-Hare, Maud, **3**:581
Cunha, A. R. "Sonny," **9**:919, 922
Čun, Medo, **8**:282
Cunningham, Arthur, **3**:610; **10**:139
Cunningham, Jamie, **3**:397
Cunningham, John, **9**:989
Cunningham, Merce, **3**:175
Cuntarar, Saint, **5**:260
"Cupid's Boogie" (Otis), **3**:669
Curaçao, **2**:789, 927. *See also* Netherlands
    Antilles
    industries of, **2**:791
    musical links with Venezuela, **2**:524
Curbelo, José, **3**:787, 796
Cure (musical group), **8**:215
Curime (musical group), **2**:703
curing. *See* healing rituals
Curlew River (Britten), **7**:630
Curonian people, **8**:499
Currasco, René, **2**:13, 861
Curriabá culture, **2**:680
Curtis, Edward, **3**:1093
Curtis Institute of Music (Philadelphia), **3**:611
Curtis, Johnny, **3**:486
Curtis, Natalie, **3**:92, 367, 444
Curtola, Bobby, **3**:1081
Curwen, John, **1**:160; **3**:1116; **8**:350
Curzon, George Nathaniel, Lord, **5**:849
Cuscatlán, **2**:718
Cutliff, Jimmy, **1**:241
Cuvier, Georges, **1**:85, 94
Cuyler, Dr., **3**:575
Čvara, Danilo, **8**:921
Cwezi people, **1**:598
cybernetics, **8**:24
Cyclopedia of Music and Musicians (Champlin
        and Apthorp), **3**:27
cymbals
    Andhra Pradesh, **5**:517, 901
    Arabian peninsula, **6**:360
    Armenia, **6**:736
    attached to drums, **8**:810, 946, 977
    in bands, **3**:563
    Barbados, **2**:814
    Batak people, **4**:607
    bhuchyāh, **5**:702
    bo, **3**:960; **7**:191, 201, 202, 312, 323
    Brazil, **2**:309, 337
    bujian, **7**:477, 478, 479–80
    çağana, **6**:767
    čampareta, **8**:967
    Canadian manufacture of, **3**:246, 1116
    in Cantonese music, **7**:218
    çapare, **8**:997
    ceng-ceng, **3**:1012; **4**:67, 742–43, 754–55, 767
    ceng-ceng kopyak, **4**:744–45, 753
    cha, **3**:961
    chabara, **7**:830
    chap, **4**:228, 299, 302, 303, 548
    chăp bạt, **4**:468
    chăp chòa, **4**:468
    chap lek, **4**:266

chegŭm, **7**:873
chhap, **4**:163
chhing, **3**:1001; **4**:67, 157, 162–63, 181, 183,
        194, 196, 203
China, **7**:450
chinchir, **5**:774, 783
    in Chinese opera ensembles, **7**:285–86, 292
    in Chinese shawm and percussion groups, **7**:201
ching, **4**:16, 17, 46, 67, 96, 211, 228, 244,
        246, 250, 251, 257, 265, 270, 272,
        299, 302, 303, 308, 309, 412
chùm chọe, **4**:468
chumpārāt, **6**:403
dabi-dabi, **4**:814, 815
Dai people, **7**:499
    depiction of, **5**:299
finger, **3**:1220
gini, **5**:733
gujih, **4**:623, 627
    in Gupta theater ensemble, **5**:25
halīle, **6**:192, 769
hatu, **7**:617
hazi, **7**:330
hi-hat, **2**:509; **3**:656, 658
iḷatāḷam, **5**:360, 362, 363
Iran, **6**:879
jālra, **5**:364, 368, 914, 914
jārī, **5**:665, 665
jhajh, **9**:93
jhāl, **5**:590, 600, 602, 604, 665
jhāñjh, **5**:347
    Caribbean, **2**:85, 444, 959
    Fiji, **5**:613
    Gujarat, **5**:625, 629, 633, 634, 635
    Guyana, **5**:601
    Madhya Pradesh, **5**:724
    in *naubat khānā*, **5**:279, 280
    Rajasthan, **5**:643
    use in devotional music, **5**:248, 251
    use in film music, **5**:534
jhyāli, **5**:505, 699, 704
kaimaṇi, **5**:364
kaitala, **4**:228
kamsāḷe, **5**:872, 874
kanci, **5**:887
kangsi, **4**:750
karākīb, **6**:403, 408
Karen people, **4**:546
karkabūs, **6**:403
Karnataka, **5**:874
kartāl, **5**:248, 251, 644, 732–33
kās, **1**:552
kāsījoḍa, **5**:629
kecèr, **4**:646
kecer, **3**:1012
kecicèr, **4**:644
Kerala, **5**:324, 514, 931, 933
kerincing, **4**:404
kesi, **4**:404, 411, 412, 416, 421, 428
khanjanī, **5**:505
khartāl, **5**:495, 503
Malta, **8**:640
mangera, **2**:897
mañjīrā, **5**:236, 342, 347, 400
    Bangladesh, **5**:505
    Fiji, **5**:612

Gujarat, **5**:625, 629, 633, 635
Maharashtra, **5**:728
North America, **3**:984; **5**:582
Rajasthan, **5**:647
Trinidad, **2**:958; **5**:589
Uttar Pradesh, **5**:665
    in Maronite church music, **6**:215, 216
Middle East, in religious ceremonies, **6**:403
nao, **7**:201, 202
não bạt, **4**:468
al-naqūs, **6**:222
nuiqsāt, **6**:403, 490
Oceania, **9**:96
Oman, **6**:403, 679
para, **7**:798, 826, 830, 873
platillos, **2**:403
Poland, **8**:707
pratos, **2**:330
qarqaba, **6**:491
Rajasthan, **5**:642
rincik (also *ricik*), **4**:742–43, 745, 748, 750,
        751, 754, 767, 771–74
rojèh, **4**:644
rujih, **4**:628
saeng, **4**:319
sagāt, **6**:403
sagāt tūra, **6**:626, 633
sajat, **6**:545
ṣanj, **6**:360, 395, 566
Santal people, **5**:502
sap, **4**:338, 355
sa-wa, **4**:312
sa-wae, **4**:312
sbug-chal, **5**:714, 714
sèlí, **1**:474
shae, **4**:540
    in *sheng-guan* ensemble, **7**:201, 315
shikshakāt, **6**:403
shing, **4**:228
sì, **4**:67, 371, 378, 379–81
sichyāh, **5**:702
sil-snyan, **5**:714
sing, **4**:67, 319, 338, 355, 358
South Asia
    played by women, **5**:8
    use in devotional music, **5**:253, 582
    use in Mahayana Buddhism, **5**:257
    use in Nepali shamanic ritual, **5**:291
    use in *oḍissi* ensemble, **5**:520
    in Sufi devotions, **6**:19
ṣunūj, **6**:403
ṣunūj al-aṣābi, **6**:403
suspended, **3**:348, 658
tāl, **5**:347, 728, 815, 831
tāla, **5**:305, 322–23, 324, 342, 877, 885
tāḷam, **5**:270, 323–24, 358, 366, 368, 607,
        608, 907
    in *cinna mēḷam* ensemble, **5**:104, 149, 360,
        913
    in *periya mēḷam* ensemble, **5**:103, 359, 912
    in Southeast Asia, **4**:67
    in Sri Lanka, **5**:956, 967
    use in devotional music, **5**:364, 557
tālampoṭa, **5**:329
Tamil Nadu, **5**:913
Tibetan, **5**:712, 713

cymbals (*continued*)
tongbo, 7:111
tōra, 6:170, *170*
tsan, 7:1017
tura, 6:403
tūrya, 5:327
ṭūs, 6:653
ṭwaysāt, 6:651
Uruguay, 2:511, 518
u siê, 4:536
Uttar Pradesh, 5:671
wo paheli, 4:802
yakwiñ, 4:371
zel, 6:403
zil, 6:767, 774
zili, 8:960, 967
zilia, 8:1019; 9:73
zils, 3:210, *210*
zunūj, 6:476
Cypress Hill (musical group), 3:750
Cypriot people, 8:1032
Cyprus, 8:12, 1029–32
geography of, 8:1029
history of, 8:1029
instruments, 8:1030–31
map of, 8:*866*
Maronite Church in, 6:208
population of, 8:1029
refugee camps in, 8:1031
research on music of, 8:1032
Turkish people in, 8:11, 12
vocal music of, 8:1029–30
Cyril, Saint, 8:726
Czechoslovakia (former), 8:716. *See also* Czech
Republic; Slovakia
dance-house movement, 8:153
ideology in, 8:723–24, 729–30
instruments, 8:21
jazz and popular music in, 8:730–31
nationalist movement, 8:59
research on music of, 8:18
suppression of rock groups, 8:217
Czechoslovak State Folk Ensemble of Songs and
Dances, 8:726
Czech people
in Mexico, 3:9
in North America, 3:529, 826, 896–99
Bohemian polka style, 3:890–91
community music-making, 3:284
Ontario, 3:1078, 1197–98
polka bands, 3:897, 898–99
western Canada, 3:292, 1250
wind bands, 3:897–99
in Poland, 8:701
in Ukraine, 8:821
Czech Republic, 8:716–33. *See also*
Czechoslovakia (former)
art music in, 8:727–30
Bohemia, 8:716
instruments, 8:172
musical styles in, 8:721–22
research on music of, 8:18
Chodsko district, 8:717, *718*, 719, 725
dance traditions of, 8:122, 166, 717–18
ethnographic districts in, 8:721–22
geography of, 8:716, 717

history of, 8:716
history of music in, 8:726–30
instruments, 8:170, 201, 719
research on, 8:172
map of, 8:*644*
Moravia, 8:716
Goral culture in, 8:717
instruments, 8:172
musical styles in, 8:721–22
old *vs.* new genres, 8:122
polyphonic singing in, 8:720
research on rhythm, 8:23
rhythmic use in, 8:718–19
population of, 8:717
Prague
Jewish community, 8:262
Second World Youth Festival (1947), 8:151
research on music of, 8:724, 732–33
Rom people in, 8:272, 276
Czekanowska, Anna, 8:23
Czerny, Al, 3:1190
Czinka, Panna, 8:199, 273

Da (*also* De, Di, Do, Du). *See* Da (*etc.*) plus next
element in name
el-Dabh, Halim, 1:220; 3:953
Da Brat, 3:697, 702
Daɓalo, Musa (Hausa drummer), 1:524–28
Da Capo Chamber Players, 3:175
Dacca Drama (theater group), 5:489
Dacian people, 8:868, 881
Da Costa, Paulinho, 3:340
Dacre, Harry, 3:549
da Cruz, Clement, 1:37
Dadap, Jerry, 4:875
Dadawa, 7:444
Dadey, Father José, 2:396
Dādhī caste. *See* Ḍhāḍhī
Dadibi people, 9:511
Dadi jiao (shawm band piece), 7:203
Dadi's Family (film), 5:661
Dad Mohammad, 5:806
"Da Doo Ron Ron" (Crystals), 3:673
dādrā, 5:162, 179, 183
development of, 5:373
Punjab, 5:766
women performers of, 5:412, 424
Dadson, Philip, 9:929, *930*
Dadu, Saint, 5:253
Daendels, Herman Willem, 4:83–84
Daeng Mile, Abdul Muin, 10:46, 49, *50*, 51
Daetwyler, Jean, 8:688, 697
da Gama, Vasco, 1:76
Dagar family, 5:136, 378, 640
Dagar, N. Faiyazuddin, 5:*165–66*, *167–68*
Dagar, N. Zahiruddin, 5:*165–66*, *167–68*
Dagar, Zia Mohinuddin, 5:207, *378*
Dagari people, 1:289
Dagbamba people
instruments of, 1:452–53, *454*
music of, 1:453; 10:141, 143, 154
Dagbani people, 1:109
Dagomba people, 1:116
Dagron, Gustave Charles, 7:727
Dahae nomads, 6:965
Dahl, Steve, 3:689

Dahl, Tracy, 3:1239
Dahle, Gunnar, 8:417
Dahle, Johannes, 8:417–18, *419*, *429*
Dahle, Knut, 8:417, 425
Dahlgren de Jordan, Barbro, 2:568
Dahlhaus, Carl, 6:1067; 8:52
Dahmen-Dallapiccola, Anna L., 5:318
Dahomey. *See* Benin
Dahomey (kingdom), 1:461–62, 464
Daik (kingdom), 4:615
Dai lamevin ki zehu helo be-elohav (*bakashot*),
6:*1040*
Daimi, 6:796, 798
Dainamaito busi (*sôsi enka*), 7:739–40, *740*
Dai Nihon siryô (collection), 7:587
Dai Ning, 7:142
Dai people, 7:495–507. *See also* Shan people
Buddhist music of, 7:496–500
dance of, 7:62
Haovassa festival, 7:501–4
music of, 7:485–92
opera of, 7:452
popular music of, 7:444, 505–7
population of, 7:495
Daio, Ekun, 1:377
Dairi people, 4:607
Dairo, Isiah Kehinde, 1:480–81, 482
Daja, Ferial, 8:1003
Dajo people, 1:562
Da kaimen (*qupai* melody), 7:233
Dakota Indian nation, 3:452, 454–55
Dakshabrahma (deity), 5:878
Dakwakada Dancers, 3:1277
Dala (god), 8:864
Dalai Lama, fifth, 7:480
Dalai Lama, sixth, 5:710
Dalai Lama, fourteenth, 3:133, 219; 5:709
al-Dalāl, 6:296
Dalaras, Giorgios, 9:73
Dalaras, Yorghos, 8:1018, 1020
Dalen, Kari, 8:421
Dal gCais, 8:394
Dalhart, Vernon, 9:390
Dalhousie University (Halifax), 3:1119
Dalila, 6:270
Dalīl al-anghām li-ṭullāb al-maqām (Ibrāhīm),
6:316
Dalits. *See* Harijans
Dall, Bobby, 3:97
Dall, William H., 3:381
Dallapiccola, Luigi, 3:611
Dallappé (musical group), 8:483
Dallara, Tony, 8:619
Dallas Journal, 3:578
Dalman, G., 6:580
Dalmatian people, in Aotearoa, 9:928
Dal'ona (*dabkih*), 6:583, 587
Daly, Robert Ilyerre, 9:*427*
Daly, Ross, 8:1018
Dalyell, Sir John Graham, 8:373
Dalzel, Archibald, 1:83–84
Damāi people, 5:273, 280–81, 697
musical repertoires of, 5:284, 286, 698–700
origin of, 5:698–99
Damāmī caste, 5:641
Damas, David, 3:381

Damaso, Jimeno, **4**:866
Damian, Cyrillys, **3**:773
Da Ming jili (collection), **7**:131
Daming yuzhi xuanjiao yuezhang (Daoist work), **7**:321
Daming zhengtong daozang (Daoist work), **7**:321
Dam-Jensen, Elsemarie, **8**:464
Đàm Linh, **4**:512
Damm, Hans, **9**:736–37
Damned (musical group), **3**:357
Damodara, **5**:46, 47–48, 314
Damone, Vic, **3**:528, 862
Dampier, William, **2**:662
Damrong, Prince (Rajanubhap), **4**:223, 240, 246, 254
Damrosch, David, **10**:68
Damrosch, Leopold, **3**:535
Damrosch, Walter, **3**:277, 563
Dan people, **1**:466
Dan the Guard (Lavry), **6**:1029
Dana, Richard Henry, **9**:40
dàn tranh. See zithers
Danbrook, Debbie, **3**:1217
dance and movement. *See also bhangra*;
    cheironomy; choreography; *hula*;
    martial arts; performers; powwows;
    theater; *specific international genres, such*
    as polka, tango, waltz
  Abkhazian people, **8**:853
  accoutrements of, **9**:345–52
  Adighian people, **8**:855–56
  aerobic, **3**:214–15, 225
  Afghanistan, **5**:506, *620,* 813
    atan, **5**:506, 814
    āushārī, **5**:823
    chubbāzi, **5**:823
    khattak, **5**:506
    peshpu, **5**:814
  Africa, **1**:108–13, 285–92; **3**:596
    at birth ceremonies, **1**:110
    chica, **2**:98
    costumes in, **1**:114–17, *277*
    cross-rhythms in, **1**:33–34
    cult, **1**:290
    dhikr, **6**:437
    at funeral ceremonies, **1**:111–12
    historical studies, **1**:85
    integration with other arts, **1**:287
    kalenda, **2**:96, 98
    masked, **1**:117–21, 287, 308–9, 329, *330,* 338–39, 469
    medicinal uses of, **1**:112–13
    mime, **1**:117–18, 121, 289, 307
    naming ceremonies, **1**:110
    pedagogy, **1**:290
    proscriptions on, **1**:112
    puberty ceremonies, **1**:110–11, 115, 117
    research methodologies, **1**:108–9
    rhythmic patterns, **1**:10
    self-accompaniment in, **1**:115–16
    stock movements in, **1**:113
    team, **1**:289
    temporal organization in, **1**:131
    types of, **1**:287–90
  African-American
    early descriptions, **3**:573, 594–97, 598

    patting juba, **3**:595, 802
    religious, **3**:625, 627, 630
    ring shouts, **3**:626, 628
    step dancing, **3**:218
  age and genre, associations, **8**:145
  Ainu people, **7**:784, 785–86
  Aka people, **1**:688–91, 692–93
  Akha people, **4**:542
  Alas people, **4**:605
  Albania, **8**:990
    kcim, **8**:994
    Rom people, **8**:285
  Albanian-American, **3**:927, 929
  Algeria, **1**:544
    religious, **6**:474
  Aluku culture, *aleke,* **2**:439
  Amish set dancing, **3**:887
  analytic systems for, **9**:312–13
  Andalusia, **6**:444
  Andean region, **2**:221
    north-south distinctions, **2**:222
    wifala, **2**:220
  Andhra Pradesh
    bhāgavata melām, **5**:516, 517
    bhamakalapam, **5**:516
    kuchipuḍi, **5**:104, 270, 358, 515, 516–18, 521
  Anglo-American styles, **3**:835–38
  Angola, **1**:306, 668
    masked, **1**:676–77
  anthropology of, **3**:221
  Antigua and Barbuda
    Highland fling, **2**:799
    maypole, **2**:799
    open-air dances, **2**:798
    stilt-dancers, **2**:799
    subscription balls, **2**:798
  Anuta, **9**:378
    mako genres, **9**:857–59
    mori complex, **9**:859
  Aotearoa
    ballet, **9**:947
    Cook Islander, **9**:112
    haka, **9**:10, 944–45
    haka peruperu, **9**:946
    haka poi, **9**:945, 946
    haka pōwhiri, **9**:943, 946
    kapa haka, **9**:935
    kopikopi, **9**:947
    modern, **9**:947–48
    Scottish, **9**:116
    travelers' descriptions of, **9**:9–10
    waiata-a-ringa, **9**:945, 946
  Apache Indian groups, **3**:431
  Arab-American, *dabka,* **3**:1035, 1037; **6**:283, 284
  Arabian peninsula, **6**:657, 703–11
    agricultural, **6**:708
    'arḍa, **6**:546, 653–54, 657, *659, 665,* 667, 706–7
    'ayāla, **6**:403
    devotional, **6**:710–11
    early references to, **6**:361
    entertainment, **6**:708–10
    exhibition, **6**:706
    expatriate communities, **6**:716

    farīsa, **6**:709
    līwa, **6**:710
    sea dances, **6**:707–8
    zafan, **6**:652
  Arab societies, **6**:373
  Arctic peoples
    drum dances, **3**:213, 376–77, 1062, 1275
    freeze dances, **3**:213
  Argentina
    candombe (also *charanda; ramba*), **2**:260–61
    chacarera, **2**:261
    Chaco, **2**:255
    chamamé, **2**:236, 256, 257, 259, 261, 269
    cuarteada, **2**:257
    cuarteto, **2**:273, 275–76
    cumbia, **2**:265–66
    gato, **2**:261, 422
    gato polceado, **2**:89
    ranchera, **2**:256, *256,* 261
    rasgueado doble, **2**:257, 269
    schools for, **2**:269
    tarantela, **2**:273
    vals, **2**:256
    zamba, **2**:259
  Armenia, **6**:729
  Aruba, *tambú,* **2**:928, 929–30
  Arunachal Pradesh
    cham, **5**:505
    ngonpae don, **5**:505
    sha cham, **5**:505
    shanag, **5**:505
  Ashanti people, *adowa,* **10**:78, 141
  Asmat people, **9**:190
  Assam
    ankia nat, **5**:503
    bihu, **5**:503
    deodhani, **5**:503
    mahā rās nritya, **5**:503
    satriya, **5**:503
  Austral Islands, genres of, **9**:880–81
  Australia, **9**:49, 415–17, 442–43, 450–67
    Aboriginal peoples, **9**:243
    Arnhem Land, **9**:355, 426
    Arnhem Land *mirrijpu,* **9**:406
    Bentinck and Mornington islands, **9**:430
    Cape York *kugu-nga'a-wu,* **9**:463
    Cape York *minha punka,* **9**:463
    Cape York shake-a-leg, **9**:429
    Cape York *wanam,* **9**:430, 462–64
    Cape York *wuungk,* **9**:464
    Central, **9**:437
    Central Arnhem Land, **9**:421
    Central women, **9**:436
    films of, **9**:47
    Greek, **9**:73–74
    Irish, **9**:78–79
    at Irish *céilí,* **9**:78
    Kimberleys *nurlu,* **9**:451
    Latin American and Caribbean styles, **9**:82–83
    Māori people, **9**:314–15
    modern, **9**:410
    Northern *wangga,* **9**:453–55
    pedagogy, **9**:228–29, 253–55
    research on, **9**:451–53

dance and movement, Australia (*continued*)
    samba, **9:**83
    Southeastern Aboriginal peoples, **9:**441
    Tiwi people, **9:**455–57
    Torres Islands island dance, **9:**429
    Torres Strait *adhi buin*, **9:***411*
    Torres Strait Pacific Islanders immigrants,
      9:84–85
    Yanyuwa island dance, **9:**461
    Yanyuwa *kalwanyarra*, **9:**461
    Yanyuwa *ngadiji*, **9:**461
  Austria
    Schuhplattler, **8:**166
    Stierische, **8:**673
  Azande people, *kponingbo*, **1:**657
  Azerbaijan, **6:**931
  Aztec culture, **2:**556, 602
  Bahamas, **2:**808–11
    ring dances, **2:**809–11
    rushin', **2:**804
  Bahrain, **6:**706, 708, 709
    murādā, **6:**710
  Bajau people, *berunsai*, **4:**826
  Bali, **4:**756, 757–58
    accompaniment for, **4:**734
    arja, **4:**757
    baris, **4:**758
    Calonarang, **4:**758
    daratan, **4:**758
    gambuh, **4:**757
    gandrung, **4:**757–58
    janger, **4:**743
    joged, **4:**754, 757–58
    joged bumbung, **4:**758
    kebyar, **4:**757
    kebyar trompong, **4:**757
    légong, **4:**747, 757
    légong kraton, **4:**747
    lepas, **4:**757
    onying, **4:**758
    parwa, **4:**757
    rejang, **4:**758
    sanghyang, **4:**758
    sanghyang dedari, **4:**758
    topeng, **4:**753, 757
    wayang wong, **4:**757
  Balkan-American, **3:**213, 529
  Balkarian people, **8:**858
  ballet, **3:**218, 224–25; **6:**817; **8:**77, 79,
    160–61, 460
    portrayals of South Asia, **5:**562
    in Turkey, **6:**817
  ballroom dancing, **3:**60, 210–11, 212, 668,
    1002
    Canada, **3:**225
    Vietnam, **3:**995
  Balochistan, **5:**776–81
    ambā, **5:**777–78, *778*
    chāp (also *suhbat*; *drīs*), **5:**777, 778–79
    chogān, **5:**778–79, *779*
    gwātī-ē lēb, **5:**780–81
    lēwā, **5:**777
    mālid and *shēparjā*, **5:**779–80
  Bangladesh
    jāri-nṛtya, **5:**506
    kṛṣṇa līlā, **5:**505

Barbados
  African descendants, **2:**814, 817
  British people, **2:**817
  hornpipe, **2:**819
  Jean and Johnnie dance, **2:**816
  jig, **2:**819
  maypole, **2:**819
  military marches, **2:**819
Basque-American, **3:**849
Basque region, **8:**314
  arinarin, **8:**314
  fandango, **8:**314
  jota, **8:**314
  Renaissance, **8:**316
  zortziko, **8:**311
Belarus, **8:**792
  karahody, **8:**792, 794
Belgium, **8:**533, 535
  branle, **8:**523
  crâmignon, **8:***519*, 522
  danse des pèlerins, **8:**523, 526
  trawantel, **8:**523, 526
  Wallonia, **8:**535
Belize, **2:**677–78
Bellona, **9:**849–52
belly dancing, **3:**210, *210*, 1033; **6:**115, 616,
  622, 624–25, 711; **8:**1019
Bengal region, **5:**859
Berber people, **1:**543; **6:**483, 484–89
  urar, **6:**307
bharata nātyam, **5:**400, *478*, 911, 941
  cinna mēḷam ensemble, **5:**104, 360, 390, 910
  dissemination in Sri Lanka, **5:**108
  instruments for, **5:**366
  in North America, **3:***223*, 951, 953, 1216,
    1246
  performance of *Gīta Govinda*, **5:**262
  raga performance in, **5:**104
  relation to *decknni* genre, **5:**738
  relation to *padam* genre, **5:**410
  songs for, **5:**149
  time-keeping percussion for, **5:**358
Bhotiya people, *dhurang*, **5:**501
Bolivia, **2:**291–92
  during carnival, **2:**290, 292
  chiquit, **2:**291
  ch'unchu, **2:**286
  chuqila (also *chokela*), **2:**292
  cueca, **2:**292
  diablada, **2:**292
  European genres, **2:**138
  huayño, **2:**292
  julajula-dances, **2:**292
  machetero, **2:**138–40, 287, 292
  morenada, **2:**292
  Moxo people, **2:**138
  suna, **2:***285*
  takirari, **2:**292
  tinku, **2:**290, 292
  waka tokori, **2:**292
  zapateo, **2:**290, 291
Bontok people, **4:**915–16
Bora Bora, **9:**41
Borneo
  datun julud, **4:**835
  mouth organ accompaniment of, **4:**836–37

  musuh, **4:**835
  ngajat lasan, **4:**834–35
  vocal accompaniment of, **4:**826–27
  borrowing in, **3:**218
Bosnia-Hercegovina
  kolo, **8:**963
  lindo, **8:**966
Bosnian-American, **3:**921–22
Brazil
  abaianada, **2:**330
  aldeia, **2:**337
  arrasta-pé, **2:**330, 331, 332–33
  baiano (also *baião*), **2:**330, 331, 332, 348
  bailados, **2:**347–48
  baile pastoril, **2:**334
  barca, **2:**334
  batuque, **2:**303, 304, 313, 348
  bumba-meu-boi, **2:**335, 347
  capoeira, **2:**24, 57, 336, 345–47, 349–50
  caretta, **1:**478
  carimbó, **2:**354
  cateretê, **2:**301, 302, 303, 311
  caxambu, **2:**348
  chegança, **2:**329, 334; **3:**850
  chegança de marujo, **2:**334
  côco, **2:**327, 348, 349
  congada, **2:**347
  congo, **2:**347
  dramatic dances, **2:**324–25, 329, 334–35
  emboscada, **2:**337
  fandango, **2:**309, 334
  forró, **2:**319, 324, 330–33
  fricote, **2:**354
  habanera, **2:**350
  jongo, **2:**348
  lambada, **2:**354
  lundu, **2:**348, 350
  maculelê, **2:**349–50
  maracatú rural, **2:**337
  marujada, **2:**347–48
  maxixe, **2:**350
  moçambique, **2:**309
  nau catarineta, **2:**334
  quadrilha, **2:**309, 331
  quilombo, **2:**334
  reisado, **2:**329, 334–35
  Saint Gonçalo dance, **2:**301, 311, 329
  samba folk dance, **2:**348–49
  sarambeque, **2:**348
  social, **2:**348–50
  toré, **2:**337
  xote, **2:**332–33
break dancing, **3:**692, 695; **4:**708; **5:**545
Bribri and Cabécar cultures
  bulsique, **2:**635
  muakuke, **2:***632*, 635
  sörbö, **2:**634–35
  sulàr, **2:**634
British Columbia, **3:**1256–57
Brittany, **8:**559, 561
Bulgaria, **8:**891, 897, 900
  horo, **8:**891, 897
  kyuchek, **8:**903
  ritual, **8:**161–62
  rŭchenitsa, **8:**897, 901
Bulgarian-American, **3:**926, 1199

Burma, **4:**19, *367*
  spirit possession, **4:**372
Burundi, **1:**179
Cajun dances, **3:**213
California, Native American types, **3:**412–15
Cambodia, prehistoric survivals, **4:**157
Cambodian court traditions, **3:**207, 219,
  999–1000
Cambodian folk traditions, **3:**1000
Canada, **3:**222–26
  African styles, **3:**224
  Anglo-Celtic styles, **3:**223, 1190
  Asian styles, **3:**223–24
  French styles, **3:**223, 1075, 1194
  Western theatrical forms, **3:**224–25
Caribbean, **3:**222
  ballet folklórico, **2:**796
  bamboulá, **2:**795
  calenda, **2:**795
  in Dominican Republic, **2:**860
  in El Salvador, **2:**718
  juba, **2:**795
  limbo, **2:**97
  in Netherlands Antilles, **2:**930
  ring games, **2:**795, 843
Carib culture, **2:**13
Carriacou
  big-drum dance (nation dance), **2:**793,
    868–70
  chumba, **2:**676
  "dancing the cake," **2:**872
  "fighting the flags," **2:**872
  lancers, **2:**872
Catalonia, *sardana,* **8:**123
Central African Republic, **1:**682, 683, 687,
  695
Central Asia, **6:**899, 900–901
  Sufi, **6:**937, 944
chain (also line) dances, **8:**162, 164–65, 314,
  442, 468–69, 522, 546, 631, *631,* 745
Chaldean, **6:**283–84
Chăm people, **4:**590
Chechen people, **8:**864
Cherokee Stomp Dances, **3:**368, 369, 370
Chichimec culture, **2:**572
of children, **2:**58
Chile
  bailes de paso, **2:**362, 363
  bailes de salto, **2:**362, 363
  cachimbo, **2:**373
  Chiloé Island, **2:**366
  cueca, **2:**368–70
  cueca chilenera, **2:**360, 369
  cueca porteña, **2:**360, 369
  for festival of Virgin of the Candelaria,
    2:364–65
  tango, **2:**371
  trote, **2:**373
  zamacueca chilena, **2:**499
  zamba, **2:**371
China, **7:**59–63
  ballet and modern dance, **7:**62–63, 90, 349,
    388, 411
  in Confucian ritual, **7:**336
  Dai people, **7:**506
  Dolan people, **6:**991, 1000

folk and minority dances, **7:**61–62, 419–20,
  421, 450, 457
  huaguxi, **7:**297–98
  lion dances, **7:**297
  in narrative performance, **7:**247
  in opera, **7:**279–80, 281, 292, 298
  theatrical, **7:**60
Chinese, in Tahiti, **9:**874
in Chinese *kunqu,* **3:**961
Chiriguano-Chané culture, **2:**252
Chopi people, *ngodo,* **1:**709–10
Chorotega culture, **2:**681
Chuuk, **9:**734, 737–38
Cirebon
  dangdut, **4:**689
  ketuk telu, **4:**689
  new works for, **4:**698
  randu kentir, **4:**687
  ronggeng, **4:**688
  rudat, **4:**695
  sidapurna, **4:**687, 695
  tayuban, **4:**689, 691
  wayang topèng, **4:**689, *691,* 696
Coast Salish spirit dancing, **3:**395, 396–97
Colombia
  bambuco, **2:**388–89, 697
  conquest dances, **2:**405
  contradanza, **2:**400, 407
  cumbia, **2:**406
  currulao, **2:**404–5
  danza de negros, **2:**405–6
  danza de negros congos, **2:**405
  fandango, **2:**400, 406–7
  joropo huilense, **2:**389
  pasillo, **2:**391–93, 697
  rajaleña, **2:**381
  sanjuanero, **2:**381, 389
  torbellino, **2:**387, 391
Colo people, **1:**568–69
community uses of, **3:**215
compas direct (konpa), **3:**803
Congo, **1:**77
contexts for, **2:**43–45
Cook Islands, **9:**49, 901–3
  comparisons to Rapa Nui dance, **9:**953
  genres of, **9:**902–3
  hupahupa, **9:**271
  kaparima, **9:**271, 902, 911
  notation of, **9:***316*
  ura pa'u, **9:**902
  ūtē, **9:**911
Corsica, **8:**571, 572, 573
  saltarello, **8:**571, 572
  tarantella, **8:**571
  tarascona, **8:**571, 572
Costa Rica
  callejera (also *parrandera*), **2:**698
  cuadrille, **2:**690
  danza (also *contradanza*), **2:**697
  fandango, **2:**693
  jota, **2:**697
  punto guanacasteco, **2:**697
  sarocla, **2:**684
  son suelto (also *baile suelto*), **2:**698
  tambito, **2:**698
  zarabanda, **2:**688

Creek Stomp Dances, **3:**468–69
Croatia, **8:**935–36, 937
  balun, **8:**931
  csárdás, **8:**926, 932
  Dalmatia, **8:**929–30
  drmeš, **8:**932
  kolo, **8:**926, 929, 931, 932, *932*
  lindo, **8:**929, 934
  northwestern region, **8:**933
  slavonsko kolo, **8:**932
Croatian genres, **3:**920, 921–22, 923
Cuba
  danzón, **2:**795, 829, 832–33, 860, 862,
    940
  folkloric genres of, **2:**829
  guaracha, **2:**930
  makuta, **2:**825
  son, **2:**796
  tumba francesa, **2:**793, 826, 937
  zapateo, **2:**833
Cuban-American, **3:**786–88, 790–99, 802
Cyprus, **8:**1030–31
  kartzilamades, **8:**1030, *1031*
Czech-American, **3:**897, 898
Czech Republic, **8:**717–18
  furiant, **8:**718
  matenik, **8:**166
  obkrocák, **8:**721
  sousedská, **8:**717, 721
  zelenyj kúsek, **8:**718, 721
Dances of Universal Peace, **3:**1042–43
Dang people, **5:**501
Danish-American, **3:**882
Dan people, **1:**466
Daur people, **7:**519
Denmark, **8:**457, 465
  ballad dancing, **8:**461–62
  polska, **8:**454, 457
Dinka people, **1:**569–70
Dogon people, masked, **1:**455
Dominica
  bélé, **2:**841–42
  flirtations, **2:**842–43
Dominican Republic
  baile de palos, **2:***851,* 854
  ballet folklórico, **2:**861
  bambulá, **2:**856
  carabiné, **2:**856
  danza (also *vals*), **2:**856
  drum dance, **2:**856
  mangulina, **2:**856
  merengue, **2:**796, 856
  merengue redondo, **2:**856
  merengue típico (also *perico ripiao*), **2:**856,
    857, 860, 861, 892
  priprí, **2:***852,* 856
  sarandunga, **2:**855
  social dances, **2:**859–60
  tumba dominicana, **2:**856
  zapateo, **2:**856
East Africa, European influences, **1:**603
East Asia, **7:**59–69
  ballet and modern dance, **7:**60
  masked dances, **7:**6
Eastern Athapaskan drum dance and tea dance,
  3:388, 1276

dance and movement (*continued*)
Ecuador
aruchicos, **2:**426
baile de respeto, **2:**428
bambuco, **2:**428
bomba, **2:**415, 425
culebrillando, **2:**426
currulao, **2:**427–28
el yumbo, **2:**210
pareja, **2:**423–25
sanjuán, **2:**417, 422, 423–25, 426–27
Egypt, **6:**623–33
bambūtiyya, **6:**623
burmīyya, **6:**624
dhikr, **6:**625–27, 630
kaff, **6:**627–28, *628*
kaff al'arab, **6:**624
Nubian, **6:**643
raqs al-khayl (horse dancing), **6:**628
raqs al-sham'ïdān, **6:**625
raqs bil-'aṣá, **6:**631, *631*
raqs iskandarānī, **6:**627
raqs sharqī, **6:**624–25
rongo, **6:**630–31
sham'idān, **6:**619
Sinai region, **6:**361, 654
tit, **6:**616
El Salvador, **2:**709–15
baile de la chabelona, **2:**713
baile de los chiraguaquitos, **2:**713, 715
baile de los diablitos, **2:**713–14
baile de los emplumados, **2:**715
baile de la garza, **2:**713
baile de los herodes, **2:**713–14
baile de los moros y cristianos, **2:**715
baile de la partesana, **2:**715
baile de los pastores o machines, **2:**713–14
baile de los pastores machos, **2:**713–14
baile de la soguilla, **2:**713
baile del zope, **2:**713
bailes burlescos, **2:**712–13
bailes de cacería, **2:**710–11
bailes de cortejo, **2:**711
bailes festivos, **2:**713
bailes guerreros, **2:**715
bailes navideños, **2:**713
bailes de ofrenda, **2:**711
bailes propiciatorios, **2:**711
bailes taurinos, **2:**712
chapetones, **2:**712–13
dance of Saint Benedict, **2:**711
dance of Saint Tingo, **2:**711
dance of the big box, **2:**711
dance of the flea and the louse, **2:**711
giganta, **2:**712–13
tapujeados, **2:**713
England, **8:**329–32
Cotswold morris dancing, **8:**329, *329,* 331, 338
gesticulations while singing, **8:**334
medieval round, **8:**133
research on, **8:**338
women's roles in, **8:**336
Ethiopia, liturgical, **1:**603
Europe
bonfire dances, **8:**162, 522, 561

ceremonial, **8:**162–63, 338
competitive dances, **8:**166, 198
couple dances, **8:**7, 165–66, 228
folk dance houses, **8:**153, 739
hora, **8:**254
men's dances, **8:**198
old *vs.* new genres, **8:**122
popular dance, **8:**161
prehistoric depictions of, **8:**38
Renaissance, **8:**76
set dances, **8:**165–66, 227, 524
social or participant dances, **8:**163–66
sword dances, **8:**162, 198, 338, 504, 523, 526, *610*
traditional, **8:**161–66
women's dances, **8:**197
European or North American genres
in Africa, **1:**358
in Algeria, **6:**475
in Aotearoa, **9:**947–48
in Argentina, **2:**256, 273
in Brazil, **2:**303, 305, 313, 330, 331, 334, 350
in Caribbean, **2:**795
in Colombia, **2:**396
in Costa Rica, **2:**691
in Cuba, **2:**835
in Dominican Republic, **2:**856
in East Asia, **7:**60
electric slide, **6:**643
in El Salvador, **2:**718
in French Guiana, **2:**437–38
in Guadeloupe, **2:**873–74, 877–78
in Guatemala, **2:**733, 735
in Haiti, **2:**888
in Hawai'i, **9:**106–7, 109–11
in Honduras, **2:**744, 745
in Israel, **6:**1019
in Mapuche culture, **2:**236–37
in Melanesia, **9:**26
in Mexico, **2:**89, 603–4, 613
in Montserrat, **2:**924
in Netherlands Antilles, **2:**930
in Peru, **2:**481, 485, 493
shimmy, **8:**443
in South and Central American and Caribbean, **2:**100, 107, 114, 269
Southeast Asia, **4:**426, 427
in Tahiti, **9:**874
in Uruguay, **2:**516
Evenki people, **7:**519
Faroe Islands, ballad dancing, **8:**413, 468–71
Federated States of Micronesia, **9:**726–29
Fiji, **9:**20
meke, **9:**774–75, 780–81
meke wau, **9:**18–19
seasea, **9:**780–81
taralala, **9:**157, 162, 779–80, 782
Filipino-American, **3:**1025
film recordings of, **9:**313–14, 317
Finland, **8:**482, 485–86
polska, **8:**477
First Nations groups, **3:**222–23, 1093–94
Flanders, **8:**535
Flores, **4:**793
gawi, **4:**794, *795*

France, **8:**546–47
branle, **8:**546–47
farandole, **8:**546, 573
rigaudon, **8:**547
ronde, **8:**546–47
French-American genres, **3:**528, 855, 857–58
French-Canadian genres, **3:**1137
French Guiana
belya, **2:**437
gragé, **2:**437, 438
kamougé, **2:**437
kaséko, **2:**437, 438
lérol, **2:**437
Fulani people, **1:**451
Futuna, **9:***773,* 815–16
Gabon, **1:**87
Gadaba people, **5:**485
Garífuna (Garifuna) culture, **2:**733, 753
abeimahani, **2:**673
ámalihani, **2:**672
awangulahani, **2:**672
charikanari, **2:**673–74
chumba, **2:**676, 734
combination, **2:**676
culeado, **2:**734
gunjéi (also *gunyei*), **2:**676, 734
hüngühüngü, **2:**676, 677
paranda (also *parranda; zarabanda*), **2:**675, 677, 734
pia manadi, **2:**673–74
punta, **2:**675, 677
sambay (also *senbai*), **2:**676, 734
seti, **2:**733
ugulendu, **2:**672
wárini, **2:**673–74
yankunú (also *iancunú*; John Canoe; *wanaragua*), **2:**673–74, 734, 740
Gayo people, **4:**605
gender roles in, **3:**98
Georgia, **8:**836, 841
dideba, **8:**834
German-American, **3:**888, 889, 897
Germany
Baroque, **8:**654
Zwiefache, **8:**166, 655
Ghana, **1:**39
Goa, **5:**737–40
Great Basin Indian groups, **3:**420
Bear Dance, **3:**422–25; **10:**89
Sun Dance, **3:**371, 422
Great Britain, **8:**325
Great Lakes Indian groups
Drum Dance, **3:**454–55, 456, 1079
Medicine Dance (*Midéwiwin*), **3:**454, 1079
Greece, **8:**1016–17
baiduska, **8:**1013
ballos, **8:**1014
hasapikos, **8:**1021
karsilamas, **8:**1009
kotsari, **8:**1011
mainland types, **8:**1009
omal, **8:***1012*
pentozali, **8:**1015
pidhiktos, **8:**1015
rebetika, **8:**1020

serra, **8:**1011
sousta, **8:**1015
studies of, **8:**1026
syrtos, **8:**1015
tik, **8:**1011
trigona, **8:**1011
tsifte teli (belly dance), **8:**1019
zeibekiko, **8:**1009, 1015, 1019
zonaradhiko, **8:**1013
Greece, ancient, **8:**160
Greek-American, **3:**213, 529, 926, 930, 931,
   1199
Grenada
   belair, **2:**865
   big-drum dance (nation dance), **2:**865
   chumba, **2:**676
   kalenda, **2:**865
Guadeloupe
   bamboula, **2:**873–78
   beguine, **2:**98
   compas direct, **2:**878–79
   léwòz, **2:**874–75
Guam, **9:**744–45
Guaraní culture
   ñembo'é kaagüy, **2:**202–3
   soul dances, **2:**203–4
   tangará, **2:**200, 201
Guarijio culture
   pascola, **2:**554, 587, 592
   tuburada, **2:**553–54
Guatemala
   baile del tun, **2:**653
   baile de los veinticuatro diablos, **2:**727
   baile del venado, **2:**723
   deer dance, **2:**729
   son chapín, **2:**726
   son guatemalteco, **2:**726
Guaymí culture
   bugutá, **2:**686
   jehio, **2:**686
Gujarat, **5:**8
   dance-dramas of, **5:**633
   dāṇḍiā rās, **5:**347, 405, 427, 501, 629
   disko dāṇḍiā, **5:**405
   garbā and *garbī*, **5:**277, 427, 501, 550,
      624–26, 628
   rās, **5:**501, 550, 629–30
   ṭīpaṇī, **5:**474, *475*, 501
Gumuz people, **1:**564
Guyana, **5:**605
   que-que, **2:**445
   rajdhar, **5:**605
   stilt dancers, **2:**446
Haiti
   anba tonèl, **2:**890
   djouba, **2:**883, 885
   folkloric companies, **2:**887–88
   kadans ranpa, **2:**892
   kèmès, **2:**889–90
   konpa, **2:**893
   konpa-dirèk, **2:**892
   lancers, **2:**888
   mereng (also *meringue*), **2:**795
   méringue, **2:**98
   for Vodou, **2:**883
Haitian folkloric troupes, **3:**805

hand gestures
   abhinaya, **5:**104, 267, 411, 513, 520,
      521
   in dance, **5:**498
   samāj gāyan, **5:**251
   tala, **5:**26, 27, *28*, 37, 39, 110, 138–46,
      152, 164, 169–70, 212, 219, 299,
      324, 358
   Vedic chant, **5:**30, 32–33, 242, 243–44
Haryana
   dhamyal, **5:**500
   holī, **5:**500–501
   lahū, **5:**500
Hawai'i, **9:**16–17, 49, 106–11, 317
   ballet, **9:**107, 109–10
   ballroom, **9:**106, 276
   Chinese, **9:**108
   Chinese lion dance, **9:**71, 96, 106, 109
   European, **9:**107
   Filipino, **9:**109
   fusion, **9:**110–11
   ha'a, **9:**925–26
   Japanese, **9:**106, 107, 108, 109
   Japanese *nihon buyo*, **9:**110
   kāholo, **9:**879
   Korean, **9:**107, 108, 109, 110
   Laotian, **9:**109
   mele ho'oipoipo, **9:**927–28
   mele inoa, **9:**927–28
   modern, **9:**107, 109–10
   notation of, **9:**315
   Okinawan, **9:**107, 108, 109
   Polynesian, **9:**108
   popular, **9:**111
   Puerto Rican, **9:**99, 101–2
   Sāmoan, **9:**104
   Scottish, **9:**106–7
   Spanish, **9:**108
   Vietnamese, **9:**109
Haya people, **1:**637
heteronomous dances, **3:**214–17
Himachal Pradesh
   parāsa, **5:**500
   singhi, **5:**499–500
Holiness churches, **3:**215
Honduras
   baile de los diablitos, **2:**741, 744
   el guancasco, **2:**741, 742, 743
   fandango, **2:**741, 744
   honoring Santa Lucía, **2:**743
   la correa, **2:**743
   la lanza, **2:**741
   la maroma, **2:**741
   moros y cristianos, **2:**743–44
   xique, **2:**744
Ho people, **5:**502
Hopi Indian nation, **3:**215, 216
   Snake Dance, **3:**430
Hungarian-American, **3:**1197
Hungary, **8:**739, 744–45
   verbunkos, **8:**162, 273–74, 737–38,
      745
   Vlach Roma, **8:**275
Iban people, **4:**830, 833, 834
ice dancing, **3:**207
identity issues in, **1:**109–13; **3:**215–16

Ila people, **1:**711–12
Inca (Inka) culture, **2:**468
   cashua taki, **2:**230
   uaricza araui, **2:**468
India, temple dancing, British disapproval of,
   5:15
India, East, **5:**496–97
India, North, folk dance, **5:**497–505
India, South, **5:**507–23
   disco style, **5:**543
   in films, **5:**543
   interpretations of Ksetrayya *padam*,
      5:266–67
   temple dancing, **5:**913
Indo-Caribbean community, **3:**812, 816–17,
   1205
Indonesia
   censorship of, **4:**93
   disco dangdut, **4:**105–6
Indonesian-American, **3:**1020–21
Ingush people, **8:**864
Inuit peoples, **3:**213
Iran, **6:**875–79
   Khorasan, **6:**837
   Lorestan, **6:**837
   regional folk dances, **6:**877
   solo improvised dances, **6:**878–79
   Sufi *charkh*, **6:**825
Iraq
   'ardha, **6:**419
   mijāna and *dal'lūna*, **6:**409
   sās, **6:**403
Ireland, **8:**198, 325, 382, 391
   crossroads dances, **8:**390
   revival of, **8:**387
Irian Jaya, **9:**486–87, 581–82, 583
Irish-American, **3:**842–43, 845
   step dancing, **3:**284, 846
Iroquois Social Dances, **3:**6, 463–64, 1062,
   1078
Islamic religious contexts, **6:**876–77
Isneg people
   tadek, **4:**918
   talip, **4:**918
Israel
   dabka, **6:**1073
   Hasidic, **6:**203, 1060
Italian-American, **3:**861
Italy
   danza dei coltelli, **8:***610*
   monferrina, **8:**609
   saltarello, **8:**608, 609, 614
   tammuriata, **8:**609, 614
   tarantella, **8:**197, 207, 609
Jamaica
   business dances, **2:**902
   genres of, **2:**906–10
   kromanti, **2:**902
   in Kumina cult rituals, **2:**902–3
   lancers, **2:**907
   limbo, **2:**909
   maypole, **2:**906, 908
   mento, **2:**906
   modern dance, **2:**909
   Rastafarian music, **2:**904
   stick dancing, **2:**908

dance and movement (*continued*)
Jammu and Kashmir, **5:**498–99
  bānde pāther, **5:**498–99
  kud, **5:**499
Japan, **7:**59–60, 63–66
  ballet and modern dance, **7:**736
  bon, **7:**605
  bugaku, **7:**63–64, 547, 621, 624–25, 627,
    635, 775
  butô, **7:**66
  dengaku, **7:**605, 641, 653
  folk dances, **7:**65
  gigaku, **7:**723
  huryû, **7:**605
  in *kabuki*, **7:**658–59, 679
  kabuki odori, **7:**764
  kagura, **7:**610
  min'yô in, **7:**600
  minzoku geinô genres, **7:**605
  ninzyô, **7:**609
  in *nô*, **7:**635
  puppet, **7:**669
  Shinto genres, **7:**607–8
  sira byôsi, **7:**764
Japanese-American
  bon, **3:**217, 527
  butoh, **3:**207
Java
  bedhaya, **4:**649; **10:**47–48
  court and classical, **4:**649
  èbèg, **4:**635, 646
  gambyong, **4:**647, 649
  jaranan, **4:**646
  jathilan, **4:**646
  kuda képang, **4:**646, 648
  ngrémo, **4:**649
  réyog Ponorogo, **4:**639, 646, 648, 679
  srimpi, **4:**649
  tayuban, **4:**648–49, 662
  wayang topèng, **4:**653–54
Jewish people, **3:**213, 939; **8:**251, 254
  wedding dance, **8:**250, 251
Kadazan people, **4:**829
Kalinga people, **4:**916–17
Kapingamarangi, **9:**836
Karachaevian people, **8:**858
Karnataka, **5:**514–16
  costumed performances, **5:**875–76, 883
  Koḍagu people, **5:**887
  regional genres, **5:**867, 876–79
  yakṣagāna, **5:**90, 270, *362*, 401, 515,
    885–86; instruments in, **5:**361, 362;
    transmission of, **5:**476; varieties of,
    5:104–5
Kasena-Nankani people, **1:**456
Kashmir
  bacha naghma, **5:**683, *683*
  rūf, **5:**684
  wanawun, **5:**685
kathak, **5:**180, 325, 493–94, 495, 522, 564,
  687
  development of, **5:**640
  in North America, **3:**953, 1216
  in Pakistan, **5:**487
  relation to *ṭhumrī*, **5:**410
  songs accompanying, **5:**179

tabla music for, **5:**131–32
use of instruments in, **5:**119, 123, 342
kathakaḷi, **5:**90, 324–25, 511, 513–14, 516,
  542, 933–34, 935, 941, 944
  instruments in, **5:**351, 361, 362–63
  in North America, **3:**207, 209
  raga performance in, **5:**104
  talas for, **5:**939
Kazakh people, **7:**461
K'ekchi Maya, **2:**668
Kenya, **1:**624, 627
Kenyah people
  kanjet (also *kancet*; *tu'ut*), **4:**833
  lekupa, **4:**826–27
  pangpagaq, **4:**831
Kerala, **5:**509–14 (See also *kathakaḷi*)
  bālē, **5:**934
  Christian genres, **5:**945
  jatisvaram, **5:**104, 512
  kōlkkaḷi, **5:**947
  kṛṣhṇāṭṭam, **5:**351, 362, 363, 510–11, *512*,
    934
  kūṭiyāṭṭam, **5:**361, 363, 399, 484, 509–10,
    510, 931, 933, 941
  kūttu, **5:**511
  mārgamkaḷi, **5:**945, *946*
  mōhini āṭṭam, **5:**358, 511, 512–13, 521,
    933–34, 935, 941–42
  muṭiyettu, **5:**362
  oppana, **5:**947, *948*
  padam, **5:**512
  paricamuṭṭukaḷi, **5:**947–48
  rāmanāṭṭam, **5:**510, 511
  teyyam, **5:**287, 511
  tillāna, **5:**512
  tuḷḷal, **5:**514
  varṇam, **5:**512
Khmer people
  court, **4:**155, 186–90, 200
  folk, **4:**155, 184, 203–4
  popular, **4:**208
  in Thailand, **4:**213
  transmission of, **4:**161
  in Vietnam, **4:**215–16
Khoikhoi people, **1:**703
Kiribati, **9:**845
  censorship of, **9:**763
  genres of, **9:**761–62
  in Rotuma, **9:**823
  social dances, **9:**758
  travelers' descriptions of, **9:**40–41
Kogi culture, **2:**187
  animal imitation, **2:**186
  chicote, **2:**185
Korea, **7:**59–60, 66–69
  in *aak*, **7:**862
  ballet and modern dance, **7:**68–69
  Buddhist drum dances, **7:**959
  chakpŏp, **7:**871, 873–74
  changgoch'um, **7:**947
  court dances, **7:**67
  folk dances, **7:**67
  kanggangsullae, **7:**885, 988
  masked dances, **7:**930, 935
  mugo, **7:**829
  nongak, **7:**934

  ritual dances, **7:**66–67
  salp'uri, **7:**68, 889, 891, 914
  shaman, **7:**876
  songp'a sandae nori, **7:**995
  sŭngmu, **7:**829
  t'alch'um, **7:**59, 68, 798, 805, *805*, 807,
    809, 942–43, *943*, 946
  tŏppoegi, **7:**933
Korean-American, **3:**977
Kosrae, **9:**741–42
Kpelle people, **1:**131
Kru people, **1:**373
Kumaon people, **5:**501
Kuna culture, **2:**772
  dramatic dances, **2:**641, *642*
  gammu burui dances, **2:**645
!Kung people, **1:**307
Kurdistan, **6:**748–51
Kuwait, **6:**706, 709, 710
Kwakiutl Indian nation
  cannibal dances, **3:**398, 400
  Cedar Bark Dance, **3:**399–401
Lahu people, **4:**539
Lao people, **3:**1007–9
Laos
  Luang Phrabang, **4:**357
  Vientiane, **4:**357–58
Latin American genres, **3:**13, 212, 225,
  521–22, 720, 725–27, 728, 743, 851,
  1077
Latvia
  četrpāru dancis, **8:**504
  diždancis, **8:**504
  iet rotaḷās, **8:**503
  krusta dancis, **8:**504
  sudmaliņas, **8:**504
Lebanese-American, **3:**1072
Lebanon
  dabka, **6:**545, 553–54
  mijāna and *dal'lūna*, **6:**409, 545
Lenca culture, **2:**739
Lisu people, **4:**543
LoDagaa people, **1:**456–57
Lombok
  batek baris, **4:**772
  cepung, **4:**768
  gandrung, **4:**773
  gendang beleq, **4:**768, 772
  rudat, **4:**774
  telek (also *batek*), **4:**772
Louisiana, African genres, **3:**802
Low Countries, **8:**523–24
  rozenhoed, **8:**522
  't patertje, **8:**522
  zevensprong (also *danse des sept sauts*), **8:**522
Lozi people, **1:**713
Luangiua, **9:**843–44
Luvale people, masked, **1:**725
Macedonia, **8:**978, 982
  age/genre associations, **8:**116
  čoček, **8:**282, 979, 983
  karsilama, **8:**979
  lambada, **8:**980
  notations of, **8:**984
  Rom dancers, **8:**281
Macedonian-American, **3:**922, 923, 926

Madagascar, **1:**789
Madhya Pradesh
  bhīmul pandum, **5:**721–22
  thandahar, **5:**721
  tribal, **5:**721–22
Maguindanao people, **4:**895
Maharashtra, **5:**727
  vāsudev gīt, **5:**728
Makah potlatch types, **3:**398
Makonde people, **1:**637
Malawi, **1:**271–83
Malaysia
  asyek, **4:**427, 428
  barongan, **4:**412–13
  dabus, **4:**414–15
  inai, **4:**415–16, 417, 424, 427
  joget, **4:**436–37, 825
  joget gamelan, **4:**417, 427, 428–29
  kuda kepang, **4:**412–13
  mak inang, **4:**437
  masri, **4:**437
  Orang Asli peoples, **4:**568–77, 579–84
  ragam, **4:**407
  randai, **4:**413–14
  ronggeng, **4:**82, 436
  silat, **4:**422
  social, **4:**82
  tarian lupa, **4:**421
  taridra, **4:**423
  Temiar people, **4:**563–64
  zapin, **4:**437, 825
Maleku culture
  nakikonarájari, **2:**682
  napuratengeo, **2:**682
Malta, **8:**637, 641–42, *642*
Maluku
  angkosi, **4:**821
  badansa, **4:**814
  badendang, **4:**821
  bambu gila, **4:**818
  cakalele, **4:**814, 817, 818, 819
  dalair, **4:**821
  dana, **4:**816–17
  hasa, **4:**814
  hasa bunga, **4:**814
  kibas, **4:**819
  lala (also *yon*), **4:**813
  lego, **4:**819
  lego-lego, **4:**815
  lulya, **4:**821
  nam, **4:**820
  ronggeng, **4:**813, 816
  samroh, **4:**813, 816–17
  sasoi, **4:**820
  sawat, **4:**820
  soya-soya, **4:**814
  t'nabar, **4:**821
  t'nabar mpuk-ulu, **4:**821
  ular, **4:**819
  usali, **4:**818–19
Manchu people, *tsam,* **7:**519–20
Mandinka people, **1:**136
Mangareva, **9:**886–89
Manihiki, **9:**904–5, 907, 908
Manipur, **5:**494–95
  gop rās (also *sanjenba*), **5:**504

khartāl cholom, **5:**504
lai hāroba, **5:**494, 504
pung cholom, **5:**504
rās, **5:**504
rās līlā, **5:**440, 494–95
thabal chongbi, **5:**504
thang-ta, **5:**504
Mapuche culture
  lonkomeo, **2:**236–37, 254, *255*
  puel purrún, **2:**236–37
Mariana Islands, **9:**743
Maroon cultures, **2:**506
Marquesas Islands, **9:**35–36
  haka genres, **9:**890, 894
  haka manumanu, **9:**892
  mahohe (also *maha'u*), **9:**892
  Tahitian genres of, **9:**894, 895
Marshall Islands
  biit, **9:**748
  genres of, **9:**750–51, 753, 754
  historical accounts, **9:**752–53
Martinique
  balakadri, **2:**918
  bal granmoun, **2:**918
  bigin bélè, **2:**915–16, 920
  biguine, **2:**98, 795
Mashriq, Sufi, **6:**543
Maya culture, **2:**667
  baile del tun, **2:**724
  baile de moros y cristianos, **2:**731
  cabeza del cochino (also *okot pol*), **2:**657
  dance of the conquest, **2:**731
  deer dance, **2:**731
  mestizo influences, **2:**657
  xtoles, **2:**656
Mayo culture
  deer dance, **2:**592
  pascola, **2:**592
Mbwela people, *makisi,* **10:**117–18
Meghalaya, **5:**504
Melanesia, **9:**598
  rhythmic clothing and, **9:**349–50
Métis, **3:**344, 405, 408, 411
  clogging patterns, **3:**406–7
  step dancing, **3:**409–10
Mexica culture
  corpus, **2:**561, 562
  danza de cuauileros, **2:**560–61, 562
  danza de Malinche, **2:**560, 562
  son, **2:**560–62
  xayácatl (also *xayacates*), **2:**561, 562
Mexican-American, **3:**745–46, 751, 772
Mexico
  conchero, **2:**559
  danza azteca, **2:**614
  jarabe, **2:**603, 604, 606, 611–12, 619
  jarana, **2:**613
  maromero acrobats, **2:**564
  polca, **2:**697
  vals, **2:**603–4
Micronesia, **9:**715–16, 721
  marching dances, **9:**717–19, 733, 737
  tokia, **9:**91
Middle East
  samrī, **6:**409
  zafn, **6:**396

Middle Eastern, **3:**1218, 1219
Miri people, **1:**561–63, 601
Miskitu culture, **2:**661–62
Mixtec culture, **2:**566–67
  baile del volador, **2:**564
Mizoram, **5:**504
modern dance, **3:**207, 224–25, 852; **6:**817;
  8:161
Moinba people, **7:**482
Mongol people, **7:**519–20
  biy, **7:**1005, 1008, 1011, 1012, *1014,*
    1014–15, 1016
  garuda, **7:**1003
  tsam, **7:**1017, 1018–19
Montenegro, **8:**958
Montserrat
  country dance, **2:**924
  jumbie, **2:**924–25
  Jump-up Day, **2:**925
Morocco, **1:**543
  ahidus, **6:***300,* 486, 486–87, 489
  ahwash, **6:**301, 303, 480, 486–89
  Gnāwa people, **6:**491–93
  warrior dances, **6:**489
Muṇḍa people, **5:**415, 502
  bhajan, **5:**502
Murut people, **4:**826
Nagaland, **5:**504
Naga people, **5:**485
Nahua culture, **2:**608
Native American groups, **3:**5, 367–68, 526
  attitudes toward self-expression in, **3:**214
  body sounds in, **3:**473–74
  Ghost Dance, **3:**421–22
  at powwows, **3:**211
  role of, **3:**207
  women's roles, **3:**371
Nauru, **9:**262, 757
Naxi people, **7:**510
Nepal, **5:**701
  caritra, **5:**704
  Damāi people, **5:**284
  ghāṭu, **5:**703, 705
  lakhe, **5:**505
  mahākālī pyakhan, **5:**505
  serga, **5:**704
  shamanic, **5:**291
  sorathī, **5:**704, 705
  ya-rakma, **5:**701
Netherlands, **8:**535
  vlöggelen, **8:**522
Netherlands Antilles
  joropo, **2:**930
  pasillo, **2:**930
  tambú, **2:**928, 929–30
  tumba, **2:**930
  wapa, **2:**930
New Caledonia, **9:**316, 672, 684–86
  bua and *cab,* **9:**678–79
  Lifou *bua,* **9:**683–84
  Loyalty Islands, **9:**683–84
  mimetic dances, **9:**674–75
  pilu, **9:**213
  pilupilu, **9:**23
  wahai, **9:**685
Newfoundland step dancing, **3:**223, 1125

dance and movement (*continued*)
New Guinea, **9:**477, 480–87
  mun-koror, **9:**22
  mun-sel, **9:**22
New Mexican Hispano genres, **3:**755, 756,
  759–60, 763
Ngoni people, **1:**320
Nicaragua
  baile de la marimba, **2:**761
  baile de las inditas, **2:**761
  baile de las negras, **2:**761
  cristianos y moros, **2:**760
  el gigante, **2:**756
  el toro huaco, **2:**756, 761
  la mazurka segoviana, **2:**757
  la vaquita, **2:**761
  los chinegros, **2:**760
  maypole, **2:**754
  moros y cristianos, **2:**761
  palo de mayo, **2:**754–55, 765
  tulu lulu (also *tulululu*), **2:**754
  yegüita, **2:**760
Nigeria, ballroom orchestras, **1:**477
Niue, **9:**817
North America
  country dancing, **3:**212–13, 225, 598–99
  European immigrant groups, **3:**825–26
  folk dancing, **3:**209–10
  improvisational, **3:**213, 214
  morris dancing, **3:**322, 323–24
  teenagers, **3:**211–12
Northeastern Algonquian feast dance, **3:**388,
  389
North West Frontier Province, **5:**789, 791
Norway, **8:**415
  ballad dancing, **8:**413
  bygdedansar, **8:**417
  gammaldansane, **8:**419–20, 427, 431
  halling, **8:**166
  local practices, **8:**121
  springar, **8:**417, *418*, 426
Norwegian-American, **3:**866–67
Norwegian genres, **3:**868–69
notation of, **9:**314–17
Nova Scotia, step dancing, **3:**1128
Nyungwe people, **1:**711
Oceania, **9:**311–17
  in storytelling, **9:**337
Oman, **6:**706
  'ayyāla, **6:**419, 654, 680
  bum, **6:**679
  lewa, **6:**403–4, 546, 679, 681
  line dances, **6:**673
  in *mālid* ritual, **6:**675
  qaṣṣafiyya, **6:**673, 676, *676*, 680
  sabāta, **6:**679
  wahhābiyya, **6:**676, *677*, 680, 681
Ontario
  early settlers, **3:**1188
  step dancing, **3:**1080, 1190–91
Orissa
  folk genres, **5:**733–34
  karam, **5:**732
  oḍissi, **5:**519–21
  performance of *Gīta Govinda*, **5:**519–20
Oroqen people, **7:**519

Ossetian people, **8:**861
Otomí culture
  concheros, **2:**572
  rayados contra franceses, **2:**572
Otopame culture, **2:**572
Ovimbundu people, **1:**714
Paiute Indian nation, **3:**435
Pakistan, **5:**506
  chogān, **5:**754, 761
  dhamal, **5:**754, 760–61
  Sufi genres, **5:**754
  tamāshā, **5:**795, 797–98, 799
  thari, **5:**488
Palau, **9:**48, 724
  aesthetics of, **9:**725–26
  matmatong, **9:**159
Palawan people, **4:**924
Palestine
  dabka, **6:**545, 576–77, 578
  dabkih shamāliyyih, **6:**582–83, 587, 591
  hora, **6:**1029
  mijāna and *dal'lūna*, **6:**409
  ṣaff saḥjih, **6:**583–85, 591
Palikur culture, **2:***436*
Pame culture
  malinche, **2:**572
  mitote, **2:**573
  monarca, **2:**572
  ropa del muerto y el arco, **2:**572–73
  xancaa (also *mitote*), **2:**570
Panama
  bullerengue, **2:**773, 778
  bunde, **2:**773, 778
  congos, **2:**775, 778–79
  contra dance, **2:**773
  cuenecué, **2:**773
  cumbia, **2:**773, 777, 778
  décima, **2:**772, 777
  el tamborito, **2:**773, 774, 777–78, 782
  gran diablos (also *los diablos de los espejos*),
    2:773, 774, 779
  los diablicos sucios, **2:**774
  marching bands, **2:**782
  mejorana, **2:**772, 777, 778
  punto, **2:**772, 776, 777, 778
  quadrille, **2:**773
Papua New Guinea, **9:**475
  Abelam *bira*, **9:**549
  Abelam people, **9:**551
  Anêm people, **9:**615–16
  Angan people, **9:**496–97
  Baining people, **9:**350
  Bali-Vitu genres, **9:**610–11
  Bali-Vitu *maghu*, **9:**610
  Bali-Vitu masked dances, **9:**608
  Baluan, **9:**602
  Banoni *ganini*, **9:**647
  Binandere *ario*, **9:**499–501
  Buang people, **9:**566–67
  Buin *aabi*, **9:**650
  Central Province *kitoro*, **9:**490
  in Christian music, **9:**197
  competitions, **9:**62–63
  Eastern Highlands peoples, **9:**529–30
  Enga *mali lyingi*, **9:**534
  Erave people, **9:***537*

  Highlands region, **9:**484–85, 512–13
  Hohodai Koita *maginogo*, **9:**316
  Iatmul people, **9:**555
  Irumu people, **9:**566–70
  island dances, **9:**507–8
  Kaulong people, **9:**617
  Kiwai dance, **9:**490
  Kuman *kundu kaima*, **9:**525
  lowlands areas, **9:**483–84
  malanggan, **9:**601
  màli, **9:**299
  Manus, **9:**601
  Maring *kaiko*, **9:**514–15
  Maring *kanant*, **9:**514, 515–16
  masked, **9:**489
  Melpa *mörl* and *werl*, **9:**485, 518–20
  Nagovisi people, **9:**647
  New Britain *sasanga*, **9:**621–23
  New Britain *tumbuan*, **9:**621–22, 625
  New Ireland, **9:**600, 626
  Nissan *bot*, **9:**635–36
  Nissan *tinoia*, **9:**636–37, 639–40
  njaguo konggap, **9:**304
  in *peroveta* genre, **9:**195
  sia, **9:**545–46, 572–74, 610, 616, 619
  Siasi *kai*, **9:**573–74, 610
  Siasi *kanaaza*, **9:**574
  Siasi *lou*, **9:**574
  solomon, **9:**625
  Tolai people, **9:**600
  Trans-Fly *badra*, **9:**507
  Trobriand Islands *kasawaga* and *mweki*
    genres, **9:**499
  tubuan, **9:**619
  tumbuan, **9:**601, 623
  Umboi Island, **9:**574
  Vitu *kakaparagha*, **9:**608, 610
Paraguay, **2:**463–64
  danza de las botellas, **2:**461
  galopa, **2:**459, 461
  genres of, **2:**461
  golondriana, **2:**459
  polca, **2:**89, 461
  polca paraguaya, **2:**459
  toro candil, **2:**459
Peru
  agua 'e nieve, **2:**497
  alcatraz, **2:**496–97
  bailes, **2:**485
  cachua, **2:**468
  carnaval, **2:**476
  carnival dances, **2:**470
  choquela, **2:**470
  dance-dramas, **2:**479–80, 481, 483
  dansaq (also *danza de tijeras*), **2:**207, 212,
    218, 222, 481
  hatajos de negritos, **2:**494–95, 497
  ingá (also *ungá*; *baile del muñeco*),
    2:496–97
  los majeños, **2:**483
  marinera, **2:**481, 499
  moros y cristianos, **2:**494
  penalivio (also *panalivio*), **2:**495
  polka, **2:**481
  resbalosa, **2:**499
  son de los diablos, **2:***493*, 494, 496

tondero, **2:**481, 499
zamacueca, **2:**498–99
zapateo criollo (also *pasada*), **2:**497
Philippines
annafunan, **4:**854
instrumental accompaniment for, **4:**854
jota, **4:**854
kumintang, **4:**850
leron-leron sinta, **4:**854
mascota, **4:**854
modern adaptations, **4:**881
pamulinawen, **4:**854
pandanggo, **4:**853, 854
rigodón, **4:**854
sainita, **4:**854
waltzes, **4:**864
Western, **4:**854, 868, 883, 884
Pima Indian nation, **3:**435
Plains Indian groups, **3:**445, 482–83
gourd dancing, **3:**448, 475, 483
Grass Dance (War Dance), **3:**480–83
powwow dances, **3:**211, 222, 446–48, 1087
Sun Dance, **3:**222, 371, 441, 443, 444, 1086–87
Pohnpei, **9:**739–40
Poland, **8:**703, 707–8, 710
krakowiak, **8:**708–9
oberek, **8:**704, 708, 710
old *vs.* new genres, **8:**122
Polish genres, **3:**529, 892, 1197, 1250
Polynesia, **9:**55, 769–70, 873–79
East, **9:**865, 867
ritual, **9:**385
West, **9:**771, 773
Polynesian outliers, **9:**836
Portugal, **8:**577, 581–82
chula, **8:**581–82
corridinho, **8:**582
fandango, **8:**198, 582, 583
fofa, **8:**583
lundum, **8:**583
malhão, **8:**582
vira, **8:**581–82
Portuguese-American, **3:**848
Prince Edward Island, step dancing, **3:**1128
Pueblo Indian groups, **3:**217–18, 429–31
Butterfly Dance, **3:**368
matachines, **3:**430, 614, 759, 850–51
women's participation, **3:**371
Puerto Rican genres, **3:**726–27
Puerto Rico
bomba, **2:**936–37
danza, **2:**795, 860, 862, 940, 941
plena, **2:**796, 939–40
seis, **2:**938–39
Pukapuka, **9:**910–11
Punjab (India), *giddhā*, **5:**500, 652–54, 656
Punjab (Pakistan), *giddhā*, **5:**506
Purépecha culture
parakata uarakua, **2:**576
zapateado, **2:**578–79
Pygmies, **1:**310
Qatar, **6:**706, 708, 709
murādā, **6:**710
Q'ero culture
chunchu, **2:**29

corn beer festival, **2:**229
kius, **2:**228
tinquy, **2:**228
ukuku, **2:**229
Ra'iatea, **9:**8–9, 10
Rajasthan
charī (also *charwā*), **5:**647
gauri, **5:**646–47
ghūmar, **5:**647, 648
ghumer, **5:**647
jasnāthi agni, **5:**648–49
khyāl dance-drama, **5:**646
men's dances, **5:**647–48
panīhārī, **5:**647
shankariā, **5:**647–48
terā tālī, **5:**647
Rapa Nui, **9:**349, 952–53
research on, **3:**98, 221, 226; **8:**23, 26, 35
resources for, **3:**226
Réunion Island, **5:**609
Romania, **8:**870, 872
călușul, **8:**198, 870
hora, **8:**870
manea, **8:**278
Rom people, **8:**277–78
Transylvania, **8:**88
Romanian-American, **3:**910, 911–12
Roti, **4:**800
e'ea, **4:**798, 800–801
foti, **4:**800
kaka musu, **4:**800
mudipapa, **4:**800
tae beno, **4:**800
Rotuma, **9:**819–22
Russia
circle dances, **8:**758
khorovod, **8:**769
Russian Old Believers, **3:**917
Ryûkyû Islands
Amami *hatigatu odori*, **7:**795
eisâ, **7:**796
kumi odori, **7:**789–90, 796
nisai odori, **7:**794
Okinawan *katyâsî*, **7:**795
onna odori, **7:**793
rôzin odori, **7:**793
zô odori, **7:**790
Saami people, **8:**302, 303
St. Lucia
débòt, **2:**943, 948
jwé dansé, **2:**943
lakonmèt, **2:**945, 946
manpa (also *maynan*), **2:**946, 947
omans, **2:**946
salsa, **3:**212
Sama-Bajao people, **4:**900
duldang-duldang, **4:**900, 901
magigal jin, **4:**889–90, 900
tariray, **4:**900
Sāmoa, **9:**236, 796, 797–99
in church, **9:**207
fa'ataupati, **9:**805, 806
mā'ulu'ulu, **9:**803, 823
sāsā, **9:**805, 806, 823
siva, **9:**20

soa, **9:**802–3, 806
taualuga, **9:**231, 349, 798–99, 802
Saṅgītaratnākara passage on, **5:**41
San people, **1:**704
Santal people, **5:**415
Sardinia, **8:**630–31
ballu, **8:**627, 630–31
Barbagia, **8:**121
danza, **8:**630–31
Saudi Arabia
furaysa, **6:**653
women's dancing, **6:**653, 692–93
Savu, **4:**802
Scandinavia, **8:**140
Scotland, **8:**166, 198, 360, 367, 370, 372
Serbia, **8:**947, 954
csárdás, **8:**947
kolo u šest, **8:**950
lambada, **8:**951
momačko kolo, **8:**953
Rom *čoček*, **8:**951
Serbian-American, **3:**921–22, 923, 926, 1198
Shakers, **3:**135
Sherpa people, **5:**490
Shona people, **1:**751, 752–53
Siberia, **7:**1030
Sikaiana, **9:**845
Sikkim
cham, **5:**502
shanag, **5:**502
Sindh
jamalo, **5:**506
lehrā, **5:**286
Singapore, **4:**519, 520
bhangra, **4:**521
branyo, **4:**522
joget, **4:**520
kuda kepang, **4:**520
Slovak-American, **3:**900
Slovakia, **8:**717–18
čardáš, **8:**721
karicka, **8:**721
Slovenia, **8:**920
Solomon Islands
Bellonese *pati*, **9:**315
Blablanga *gragi nifu*, **9:**658
Blablanga *ragi māgana*, **9:**657
Buka and Bougainville, **9:**632
Fataleka and Baegu peoples, **9:**669
gongala, **9:**157
hula, **9:**157
Isabel Province, **9:**659–60
island dance, **9:**157
Russell Islands, **9:**663–64
Santa Cruz Islands, **9:**332–34
Savo, **9:**666
Shortland Islands, **9:**656
Sirovanga people, **9:**654, 655
venga boru, **9:**156
Somalia, **1:**617–18
Sotho peoples, **1:**707
South Africa, **5:**617–18
European, **1:**761
popular, **1:**770
step, **1:**772–73
tickey draai, **1:**763, 767

dance and movement (*continued*)
  South America
    ritualized movements, **2**:44
    social dances, **2**:62
  South Asia
    chutney dances, **2**:86
    classical idioms, **5**:492
    devotional, **5**:493
    folk idioms, **5**:492
    movement as category in early Indian music, **5**:20, 21
    treatises on, **5**:33, 44
    visual depictions of, **5**:298–310
    Western performances of, **5**:564
  Southeast Asia
    aesthetic approach, **4**:67, 389
    hand gestures in, **4**:10
    Indian epics as source material, **4**:66, 67
    Indian influences on, **4**:67
    lowland *vs.* upland peoples, **4**:538
  Spain
    Andalusian influences, **6**:449
    coplas, **8**:198
    fandango, **8**:589, 594
    jota, **2**:422, 481, 613, 654, 657, 697; **8**:588, 592, 594–95, 596
    moros y cristianos, **2**:561
    religious, **8**:596
    ruedas, **8**:593
    sardana, **8**:594
    seguidilla, **8**:589, 592, 593, 594
  Spanish genres, **3**:735, 848, 851
  square dancing, **3**:213, 233, 802
    Arctic peoples, **3**:380
    bluegrass and, **3**:160
    Canada, **3**:223, 225, 1256–57
    Costa Rica, **2**:691
    German-Americans, **3**:888
    Nova Scotia, **3**:1128
    Prince Edward Island, **3**:1128
    Subarctic peoples, **3**:391
  Sri Lanka
    bailā, **5**:427, 556, 956, 970–71, 972
    bali, **5**:962–63
    devil dance, **5**:490
    kaffriñgnā, **5**:970
    Kandyan traditions, **5**:363–64, 490, 969
    at *kohomba kankāriya* ceremonies, **5**:963
    lī-keḷi, **5**:969
    naiyadi, **5**:490
    sanni yakku, **5**:490
    udekki, **5**:490
    ves, **5**:490
  state of, **3**:221–22
  Subarctic peoples, **3**:388–89
  Sufism, **3**:1043–44
  Sulawesi
    bosara, **4**:805
    mikki, **4**:805
    pajaga, **4**:805
    pakarena, **4**:805–6; **10**:51
    pakurru sumangga, **4**:805
    salongreng, **10**:51
    tidi, **4**:810
  Sumatra
    Aceh, **4**:604–5

benang setukal, **4**:624
Bengkulu, **4**:619–21
bines, **4**:605
burung andam, **4**:619
cakter, **4**:626
canget, **4**:627
dana, **4**:617, 621, 625
didong, **4**:605
early forms, **4**:601
erai-erai, **4**:625
galombang, **4**:611
gamat, **4**:613
gandai, **4**:613
gegerit, **4**:624
gelombang duobale, **4**:613
gilo lukah, **4**:613
guwel, **4**:605
inai, **4**:605, 615, 616
inang, **4**:606
indang, **4**:601, 611, 612–13
iyo-iyo, **4**:618
Jambi, **4**:617, 618–19
joget, **4**:606, 616, 617, 621, 628
kain, **4**:613
kain panjang, **4**:621
kipas, **4**:621, 628
lelalawan, **4**:619
ma'inang, **4**:606, 616
Minangkabau, **4**:609
nasit, **4**:612
nenet, **4**:613
Nias Island, **4**:608
northern, **4**:605–8
nugal, **4**:626
nyambai, **4**:627
olang, **4**:615
payung, **4**:613, 620
pedang, **4**:621
piring, **4**:613, 617, 621, 624
randai, **4**:611, 621
rantak kudo, **4**:613
rendai, **4**:621
Riau, **4**:616
ronggeng, **4**:606, 616
saman, **4**:601
saputangan, **4**:613
seka pur sirih, **4**:628
selendang, **4**:626
sembah, **4**:628
semut, **4**:621
serampang duabelas, **4**:606, 616, 626, 628
seudati, **4**:604
sikambang, **4**:607, 613
sinandung, **4**:606
sirih layang, **4**:619
slendang, **4**:621
southern, **4**:621–22, 623, 624
tuber, **4**:626
western, **4**:611, 612–13
zapin (also *bedana*), **4**:605, 606, 616, 625, 628, 691
Sumba, **4**:790
Sumbawa
  baleba, **4**:783
  barapan kebo, **4**:784

  berampakan, **4**:781
  dadara bagandang, **4**:784
  dadara nesek, **4**:781
  dahalira, **4**:783
  fatininu, **4**:783
  joge bungin, **4**:781
  kanja, **4**:783
  kosok kancing, **4**:781
  lanca, **4**:780
  lenggo, **4**:783
  lilin, **4**:785
  martial, **4**:763
  mpaa kantao, **4**:783
  naka, **4**:783
  nguri, **4**:781
  parise, **4**:780
  rebana, **4**:785
  sere, **4**:783
  tanak, **4**:781
Sunda, **4**:725
  female dancers, **4**:721
  gamelan saléndro accompaniment of, **4**:704–5
  jaipongan, **4**:93, 107, 111, *138*, 684, 697, 703, 704, 708, 721, 725
  kuda renggong, **4**:701
  kursus, **4**:705, 708
  ronggèng, **4**:104, 106
  sendratari, **4**:703
  sisinggaan, **4**:701
  tayuban, **4**:705
  topeng, **4**:705, 725
  topeng banjet, **4**:126, 708
Suyá culture, **2**:145
  pantomimes, **2**:147
Swahili people, **1**:631
Sweden, **8**:435–36, 442–43
  dance-suites, **8**:444
  gammeldans, **8**:436, 441
  jazz balett, **8**:443
  polska, **8**:434–35, 442–43
Swedish-American, **3**:233, 871, 872, 1196, 1251
Switzerland
  French styles, **8**:693–94
  German styles, **8**:689–90
  Italian styles, **8**:696
  monfrina, **8**:696
Syria
  mijāna and *dal'lūna*, **6**:409
  samāḥ, **6**:568
Tahiti, **9**:10–11, 307
  'aparima, **9**:875, 877–78, 879, 998
  group, **9**:874–75
  Hawaiian *hula 'auana*, **9**:879
  hīmene tuki, **9**:872
  hivinau, **9**:875, 878–79
  Māori *poi*, **9**:879
  'ori tahiti, **9**:874
  'ōte'a, **9**:875, 876–77, 998
  outside influences, **9**:879
  pā'ō'ā, **9**:875, 878
  pedagogy, **9**:270–71
  research on, **9**:869
  Sāmoan fire dance, **9**:879
  tāmūrē, **9**:874, 952

Volume Key: **1**, Africa; **2**, South America, Mexico, etc.; **3**, United States and Canada; **4**, Southeast Asia; **5**, South Asia

Tahitian
  comparisons to Rapa Nui dance, **9:**953
  competitions, **9:**47–48
  in Mangareva, **9:**888–89
  in Marquesas, **9:**894, 895
  in North America, **3:**1052; **9:**118–19
  in Pukapuka, **9:**910
  in Rapa Nui, **9:**952
  in Rotuma, **9:**823
Taino culture, **2:**13, 881
  areito, **2:**847
Tajik people, **5:**506
Tamil Nadu, **5:**485, 518–19
  ārati, **5:**275
  aṣṭapadī, **5:**522
  bhāgavata mēḷā, **5:**270, 908
  bharata nāṭyam, **5:**517, 520, 521–23
  cadir, **5:**910, 913
  cēyvaiyāṭṭam, **5:**915
  kaikkottikkali, **5:**518
  karakam, **5:**518, *519,* 914
  kaṭṭaikkūttu, **5:**515, 516
  kautuvam, **5:**522
  kāvaṭi, **5:**518, 914
  kāvaṭiyāṭṭam, **5:**921
  kōlāṭṭam, **5:**518, 909, 920, 969
  kummi, **5:**277, 278, 918, *919,* 919–20, 925
  kuravanji, **5:**518, 519
  *kuravan-ku*ratti, **5:**914
  kutirai, **5:**518
  oyilāṭṭam, **5:**919–20
  poy kāl kutirai, **5:**914
  pushpāñjali, **5:**522
  shamanic, **5:**259–60
  tēvarāṭṭam, **5:**915
  tillāna, **5:**522
  varṇam, **5:**522
Tanzania, **1:**643
Tarahumara culture
  ceremonial, **2:**585
  matachín, **2:**583, 586, 587
  pariseo, **2:**584, 586–87
  sontárusi, **2:**586–87
  yúmari, **2:**583
Tejano genres, **3:**212, 773
Thailand, **4:**19
  lakhawn, **4:**253–57
  northern, **4:**310, 314
  popular, **4:**328, 331
  ramwong, **4:**82, 91
  social, **4:**82
  in theatrical performances, **3:**618, 621;
    8:160–61; **9:**231
  as therapy, **3:**215
Tibetan culture, **3:**207, 219; **7:**474–77
  Buddhist, **7:**479–80
  ’cham, **5:**715
  court, **7:**480–81
  skor-gzhas, **5:**711
Tikar people, **1:**658
Tikopia, **9:**855–56
  mako, **9:**247
Toba culture, in Pentecostal worship, **2:**259
Tohono O'odham
  pascola, **2:**593
  waila, **3:**213, 489–90, 851

Tokelau, **9:**828
  fātele, **9:**379–80, 828
  genres of, **9:**825–26
  hake, **9:**827
  hiva hahaka, **9:**824
  tafoe, **9:**824
Tonga, **9:**11–14, 307, 317, 784–85
  ’eke, **9:**809
  fa’ahiula, **9:**791–92
  faiva, **9:**313
  kailao, **9:**379, 792, 809
  lakalaka, **9:**241, *242,* 783, 789
  mā’ulu’ulu, **9:**789–90
  me’elaufola, **9:**12, 241
  me’etu’upaki, **9:**13, 316, 790–91
  sōkē, **9:**792
  tāpaki, **9:**791, 809
  tau’olunga, **9:**231, 313, 787, 793, *794*
  ula, **9:**14
Tonga people (of Africa), **1:**711–12
Totonac culture
  danza de los voladores, **2:**549
  huahua, **2:**564
  los voladores de Papantla, **2:**564
Trinidad and Tobago
  bélè, **2:**959, 963
  kalenda, **2:**959, 963
  reel, **2:**959
Tsonga people, **1:**710
Tuamotu Islands, **9:**884–85
Tuareg people, **1:**593–94
  tende, **1:**585–87
Tunisia, **1:**543–44
Turkey
  ballet, **6:**817
  folk dance movement, **6:**815–16
  folk dance regions, **6:***78,* 814
  folk dances, **6:**80, 812–16, 844
  halay, **6:**80, 814, 816
  horon, **6:**80, 87, 812, 814
  identity issues, **6:**811–17
  karşılama, **6:**80, 87, 814
  Ottoman entertainment dances, **6:**115,
    812
  research on, **6:**812–13
  Sufi religious, **6:**19, 107–11, 184, 190, 568,
    768, 795, 811
  zeybek, **6:**80, 87, 812–13, 814, 816
Turkish-American, **3:**1199
Turkmenistan, **6:**943
Turkmen people, **5:**506
Tuvalu
  fakanau and *onga* genres, **9:**829
  fātele, **9:**762
Uganda, **1:**605
Uighur people, **7:**459
  muqam, **6:**995–1008
Ukraine
  at *dosvitky,* **8:**808
  hutsul’ka, **8:**812
  kolomyka, **8:***810*
  perepelka, **8:**808
  for weddings, **8:**807
Ukrainian-American, **3:**913, 1088, 1241, 1243
United Arab Emirates, **6:**706, 710
  ’ayyāla, **6:**419, 420, 654

United States, **3:**206–22
  dance fads of 1960s and '70s, **3:**676
  dancing as vocation, **3:**207–9
  disco styles, **3:**227, 229, 687–91
  ethnic, **3:**210, 216–17, 223
  funk, **3:**680
  fusion in, **3:**224
  in heavy metal, **3:**113
  jazz, **3:**214, 551
  longways dances, **3:**223, 232, 233
  multicultural approaches to, **3:**221–22
  New England social dances, **3:**158
  nineteenth century, **3:**555
  physical education curriculum, **3:**233
  reactionary movements in, **3:**218–19
  recreational, **3:**211–13
  scope of, **3:**206
  self-expression in, **3:**214
  slam dancing, **3:**211
  "slow drag," **3:**639
  tap dancing, **3:**207, 214
Uruguay
  candombe, **2:**515–16
  carangueijo, **2:**516
  chimarrita, **2:**516
  creolization of, **2:**522
  polka, **2:**516, 522
  ranchera (mazurka), **2:**516, 522
  at religious festivals, **2:**512
  tango, **2:**519
  tirana, **2:**516
Uttar Pradesh
  goddess cult dances, **5:**291–92
  kajalī, **5:**669–70
  kedār, **5:**501
  rāmlīlā dance-drama, **5:**495–96, 673
  rāslīlā dance-drama, **5:**673–74
'Uvea, **9:**49, 313
  ’eke (also *sokē*), **9:**792, 809, 813–14
  genres of, **9:**812–14
  kailao, **9:**379, 809, 812–13
  lakalaka, **9:**813, 814
  mā’ulu’ulu, **9:**814
  sāsā, **9:**813
  soāmako and *niutao,* **9:**813, *814*
Uzbek people, **5:**506
Vanuatu, **9:***316*
  bolo Ambae, **9:**259
  counterclockwise direction in, **9:**198, 691
  lakalaka, **9:**698
  lega, **9:**698–99
  men's genres, **9:**699–700
  na bolo, **9:**696
  na lenga, **9:**696
  na polo, **9:**198
  pedagogy of, **9:**260
  sawagoro, **9:**695–96
  syncretic elements, **9:**361–62
  Tanna, **9:**63–65, 702–6, 708, 863
  tieksas, **9:**26, 706, 709
Venda people, **1:**708
Venezuela
  fandango, **2:**539
  joropo, **2:**539–41, 542
  "La Batalla," **2:**536
  la perrendenga, **2:**533

dance and movement, Venezuela (*continued*)
  masked devil dancers, **2:**537, 544
  Parranda de San Pedro, **2:**530
  Saint John the Baptist dances, **2:**535–36
  tamunangue, **2:**536, 539
  video preservation of, **2:**41
Vietnam
  court, **4:**497–98
  folk, **4:**499–500
  masked, **4:**56
  popular, **4:**515
  religious, **4:**500–501
  theatrical, **4:**501–2
Virgin Islands
  bamboula, **2:**973
  masquerade jig, **2:**972–73
Volga Germans, **3:**890
Waiãpí culture, **2:**160, 161
Wales, **8:**353, 354
  May Day, **8:**343
  maypole, **8:**140
Warao culture
  habi sanuka, **2:**189
  nahanamu, **2:**189, 191
Wayana culture, **2:**166
West African, **3:**210, 214, 222, 224
West Bengal, **5:**502–3
  bolan, **5:**503
  kālī nāch, **5:**503
  nagar kīrtan, **5:**503
Western Athapaskan potlatch, **3:**388
West Futuna
  genres of, **9:**862, 863
  pohpokiga, **9:**861, 863
Xavante culture, **2:**127
Xhosa people, **1:**706, 769
Yakan people, **4:**900
Yanomamö culture, **2:**174
Yao people, **4:**549
Yap
  genres of, **9:**728, 731–33
  tãyoer, **9:**726–27, 732–33
Yaqui culture
  deer dance, **2:**549, 589, 590; **3:**218, 438,
    485, 851
  matachines, **2:**591; **3:**436, 437–38, 850–51
  pascola, **2:**590, 591; **3:**218, 437–38, 485,
    851
Yekuana culture, **2:**181
Yemen, **6:**303
  bar'a (also *bara'*), **6:**101, 105, 302, 655,
    657, 707, 707
  dasa', **6:**709
  la'ba, **6:**303
  lāl al-'ūd, **6:**676, 680
  lu'b, **6:**711
  lu'ba, **6:**656
  sharḥ, **6:**709
  zerbādī, **6:**657
Yoruba people, **1:**460, 461
Yukon, step-dancing, **3:**1277
Yuma culture, **2:**597
  nimbé, **2:**595
Zaghawa people, **1:**561
Zaramo people, **1:**637
Dance in America (television series), **3:**219

Dance Collection Danse (Toronto), **3:**226
Dance Critics Association, **3:**220, 221
"Dance, Dance, Dance" (Chic), **3:**712
dance-drama. *See* dance and movement; theater
Dance Educators of America, **3:**221
Dance Fever (television show), **3:**712
"Dance Floor," **3:**685
dance hall (dancehall) genre, **2:**95, 96, 98, 906,
    912; **3:**341, 702, 811, 1064, 1203;
    8:214
"Dance with Me" (Brown), **3:**712
"Dance with Me" (Drifters), **3:**673
"Dance to the Music" (Sly and the Family
    Stone), **3:**681, 710
Dance Notation Bureau (New York), **3:**221
Dance Ontario, **3:**226
Dance in Place Congo (Gilbert), **3:**14, 521
Dance Saskatchewan, **3:**226
Dance/USA, **3:**221
Dancel, Andrés, **4:**866
Dancemakers, **3:**224
Dancer Transition Resource Centre (Canada),
    3:226
Dances at Aurukun (film), **9:**47
Dances We Dance Company, **9:**109
Dances with Wolves (Blake), **3:**525
Dancin' Grannies (dance group), **3:**214
Dancing (video series), **3:**218
Dancing Fool (Molina), **4:**873
Dancing in One World (film), **9:**47, 48–49
"Dancing in the Street" (Martha and the
    Vandellas), **3:**674, 709
Danckert, Werner, **8:**20
Dande Lenol (performing group), **1:**8
Dane (Teop performer), **9:**644
Dane, Barbara, **3:**105, 106, 317
Dan Emmett and the Rise of Early Negro Minstrelsy
    (Nathan), **3:**32
dan Fodio, Osman, **1:**314
Dangan (Eipo performer), **9:**592
*Danger in the Dark: A Tale of Intrigue and
    Priestcraft* (Kelso), **3:**121
Dāngi people, **5:**639
Dan giri no senritu (*gidayû busi* piece), **7:**677
Dang people, **5:**501
Dani people, **9:**50
  composition of, **9:**360
  dance of, **9:**486–87
  songs of, **9:**583–84, 587
Dani-Hürel (legendary hero), **7:**1016
Dania Club (Edmonton), **3:**1251
Daniel Lapp Fiddleharmonic, **3:**1256
Daniel, Linda, **3:**315
Daniel, Ralph, **3:**32
Daniele, Pino, **8:**620
Daniélou, Alain, **4:**25, 160, 176; **5:**53, 57, 529
Daniels, Charles N., **3:**262
Danielson, Larry William, **3:**871
Danielson, Virginia, **6:**24, 235
Danielsson, Bengt, **9:**969
Danilov, Kiril, **8:**763
Danilov, Kirsha, **8:**129
  Russian folk song compilation, **8:**18
Danish Canadian Club (Winnipeg), **3:**1251
Danish Day Players (musical group), **3:**883
Danish Folk-Dancers, **8:**461

Danish Folk-Dancers' Association of Fiddlers,
    8:461, 465
Danish Folklore Archives, **8:**463, 464, 465;
    9:853
Danish people
  in North America, **3:**882–83, 1251
  in Virgin Islands, **2:**968
Dank, H. P., **3:**190
Dankó, Pista, **8:**273
Dannemann, Manuel, **2:**238, 374; **10:**80
Danpei Youth Choir, **9:**995
"Dans mon chemin j'ai rencontré" (*voyageur*
    song), **3:**1164
Danses et légendes de la Chine ancienne (Granet),
    7:60
Danso, Robert, **1:**25, 26
Dante Alighieri, **8:**573, 608
Danzan Ravjaa, **7:**1016
Danzas Negros del Perú, **2:**501
Danzas paraguayas, método de enseñanza (Rivas de
    Domínguez), **2:**463
Danzer, Georg, **8:**677
Danzhu'er (Tibetan collection), **7:**472
danzón, **2:**795, 829, 832–33, 835, 838
  in Dominican Republic, **2:**860, 862
  in Mexico, **2:**622
  in North America, **3:**742, 788, 790, 795–96,
    798
  in Puerto Rico, **2:**940
Danzon cubano (Copland), **3:**521
Dao An, **7:**329
Dao Chenwai, **7:**261
Dao chui lian (*yangqin* piece), **7:**180
Đào Cừ, **4:**480
Daodejing (Daoist work), **7:**97, 100, 321
Đào Duy Từ, **4:**498
Dao Mai (musical group), **7:**506
Dao Rong, **7:**611
Đào Tấn, **4:**449
Đào Thị, **4:**447
Daoism
  Buddhism's influence on, **7:**22
  China, **7:**311, 319–24; **10:**22
    aesthetics and philosophy in, **7:**97–98, 361
    history of, **7:**312, 319–22
    ritual music for, **7:**91, 131, 212, 312–13,
      322–24, 416, 420–21
    sheng-guan ceremonial music, **7:**200–201,
      203
  Hong Kong, ritual music for, **7:**434
  influence on American music, **3:**129–33
  Oceania, **9:**71, 97
  Quanzhen sect, **7:**312–13, 321, 322–23
  shamanism and, **7:**20
  Southeast Asia, **4:**549
  theology of, **7:**320–21
  Vietnam, **4:**444, 505
  Zhengyi sect, **7:**201, 312–13, 320, 321,
    322–23
Daoud, Rageh, **6:**612
Daoud, Reinette Sultana, **6:**1044
Daozang (collection), **7:**131, 319
Da Ponte, Lorenzo, **3:**181
Dapper, Olfert, **1:**81, 82
Da Qing huidian (dynastic history), **7:**480
darabukka. See drums: goblet

al-Darārī al-sabʿ ay al-muwashshaḥāt al-andalusiyya (Karāmī), **6:**567

Darashe, Mackay, **1:***771*

Ḍarb al-Baraʿ (Turba dance), **6:**105, *105*

Ḍarbat Sayyārī (Ḍāliʿ composition), **6:***93*, 100, 105

Darbazi (musical group), **8:**845

Darbo, Seni, **1:**497

Darby, William Sinkler, **5:**190

Dardzin-Nana (god), **8:**864

Darhat people, **7:**1004–20

Dariganga people, **7:**1004–20

Darius I, Persian Achaemenid emperor, **5:**14

Dark, Phillip, **9:**349

Dark City Sisters, **1:**771

Dark and Light in Spanish New Mexico (Chavez), **3:**767

Darkest America (musical), **3:**618

"Dark-Eyed Sailor" (ballad), **3:**1124

"Darktown Is Out Tonight" (Johnson), **3:**619

Darktown Negroes (musical group), **1:**770

Darktown Strutters (musical group), **1:**770, 771

"Darktown Strutters Ball" (Brooks), **3:**1212

Darkydom (musical), **3:**608

Darnuchans, Eduardo, **2:**520

Darrell, Jeannie, **9:**149

Dartington College (England), **5:**563

Dârülelhân Conservatory, **6:**117

Darütta'limi Musiki Cemiyeti, **6:**785

Darvish, Gholàm Hoseyn. *See* Darvīsh Khān

Darvīsh Khān, **6:**137, 138–39, 861, 862

Darvishi, Mohammad Reza, **6:**835

Darwin, Charles, **1:**11, 94, 95

Darwīsh, Sayyid, **1:**571; **6:**168, 547, 598, *599*, 600, 612

al-Darwīsh, Shaykh Nadīm Alī, **6:**326, 327, 328–29, 502–3, 508, 550, 564, 567, 910

Das Efx (musical group), **3:**700

Das, Joanna, **3:**1216

Das, Mukunda, **5:**849

Das, Purushottam, **5:**120

Das, Ram Shankar "Pagal Das," **5:**120

Das, Ritesh, **3:**1216; **5:**136

Das, Samar, **5:**858

Dāsa people, **5:**238

Dāsari singers, **5:**900–901

Das Gupta, Buddhadev, **5:**207

Dasgupta, Kamal, **5:**855, 856

Dasgupta, Sudhin, **5:**857

Dasgupta, Suval, **5:**855

Dasheng yuepu (Lin), **7:**863

Dashiki, **1:**778

Dashper, Mark, **9:**933

Dāstāngoh group, **5:**476, 770, 771–72

Dastum (organization), **8:**563

Dasyu people, **5:**238

Data Ganj Bakhsh (Sufi saint), death anniversary of, **5:**755

Date Records, **3:**747

Datong Guoyuehui (Shanghai), **7:**229

Dattagupta, Sailesh, **5:**855

Datta, Himamsu, **5:**855

Datta, Madhusudan, **5:**848

Dattila, **5:**313

Dattilam (treatise), **5:**24, 67, 73–75
    passage on tala hand gestures, **5:**39
    passage on tempo, **5:**40

Daucje (god), **8:**857

Daud Bandagi Kirmani (Sufi saint), death anniversary of, **5:***752, 763, 765*

Daud Khan, Mohammad, **5:**810

Daugavina (dance ensemble), **3:**1196

Daunais, Lionel, **3:**1166

Dauney, William, **8:**373

Dauphin, Claude, **2:**885

Daur people, **7:**518–19, 1004–20

Daura people, **1:**291

Davāmī, ʿAbdollāh, **6:**139, 856, 866, 867

Davashe, Mackay, **1:**774, 775

Dave Clark Five (musical group), **3:**348, 355, 840; **8:**214

Davenport, Charles "Cow Cow," **3:**645

Davenson, Henri, **8:**553

Davey, Shaun, **8:**387

David, A. B., **1:**406

David, Carina Constantino, **4:**886

David, Mrs. Edgeworth, **9:**830

David, king of Israel, **6:**359

David Lee Garza y Los Musicales, **3:**780

David Lee Garza y Su Conjunto, **3:**776

David, Mordecai ben, **6:**205

David Superstar (Zim), **3:**943

Davidenko, Aleksander, **8:**864

Davidson, Alexander, **3:**1179

Davidson, Harry C., **2:**398

Davidson, Janet, **9:**835

Davidson, Robert, **3:**1093

Davie, Cedric Thorpe, **8:**369

Davies, E. H., **9:**987

Davies, Sir Henry Walford, **2:**819

Davies, James, **9:**285

Davis, Angela, **3:**104, 582

Davis, Anthony, **3:**612

Davis, Charles K. L., **9:**924

Davis, Chip, **3:**345

Davis, Don, **3:**676

Davis, Eddie, **3:**747–48

Davis, Ewing, **3:***414*

Davis, Jefferson, **3:**308

Davis, Martha, **10:**85

Davis, Martha E., **2:**941

Davis, Miles, **3:**356, 659–664; **5:**528

Davis, Ossie, **3:**622

Davis, Possum, **9:**135

Davis, Roland, **3:**1077

Davis, Ruth, **6:**1036

Davis, Sammy, Jr., **3:**621, 713

Davis, Sunday, **1:**376, 379–80

Davis, Susan, **3:**892

Davis, Walter, **3:**645

Davis, William Heath, **3:**735

Davit Anhakht, **6:**723

Davit Kerakan, **6:**723

Davudiv-*Baggy*, Ashyrmämmet, **6:***969*

Davut Suları, **6:**796

Davydov, Sasha, **8:**776

Dawenkou culture, **7:**17

Dawes, Neville, **1:**32

Dawn (musical group), **4:**887

"Dawn of Correction" (Spokesman), **3:**317

Dawning of Music in Kentucky (Heinrich), **3:**538

Dawson, James, **3:**1116

Dawson, Peter, **3:**1125

Dawson, William, **3:**607, 629

Dayak peoples, **4:**823, 835. *See also specific peoples*
    funerals of, **4:**807

Dayan Ancient Music Association, **7:**414, 415, *415*, 445, *450*, 513, *514*

Daya Ram Kachroo "Khushdil," **5:**691–93

Day, Captain Charles R., **1:**92–93; **5:**50

al-Dāyikh, Muḥammad, **6:**567

Dayton (musical group), **3:**684–85

Dayton, Daryl, **4:**876

Dayuanmen (*Zhedong luogu* piece), **7:**195–96

Dayue lülü yuansheng (Li), **7:**128

Dazai Syundai, **7:**548

Dazey, Turner, **3:**618

"Dazz" (Brick), **3:**712

Dazz Band, **3:**684

De, Krishna Chandra, **5:**855, 856

De, Manna, **5:**857

Deacon, A. B., **9:**690

Deacon Blue, **8:**369

"Deacon's Hop" (McNeely), **3:**669, 708

Dead Birds (film), **9:**50, 487

Dead Kennedys (musical group), **3:**357

Dead Man Walking (film), **3:**340; **5:**753

Dean, Beth, **9:**314

Dean, chief of Mota, **9:**698

De'ang people, **7:**485–92, 495

Dear Brothers (musical group), **7:**364

Death (musical group), **3:**358

Death of Cook (ballet), **9:**34

"Death Letter Blues" (Yancey), **3:**105

Death of Rhythm and Blues (George), **3:**584

debate de las flores, El (Judeo-Spanish song), **6:**1042

Debs, Eugene, **3:**309–10

Debussy, Claude, **3:**335, 1076, 1149, 1150; **4:**13, 131, 873, 876; **5:**563; **6:**1027; **7:**341, 347, 736; **8:**26, 85, 161, 273, 370, 425

Debut Atlantic, **3:**1120

De Caro, Julio, **2:**263

Deccani painting, **5:**300

Decca Records, **3:**352, 737, 776, 843, 898, 1071; **9:**998

December (album), **3:**346

Dechênes, Marcelle, **3:**1152

Dechepare, Bernat, **8:**316

décima. See poetry; vocal music

Décimus, Pierre-Edouard, **2:**918

De Cock, Alfons, **8:**534

De Danann (musical group), **8:**392

Dede (honorific). *See previous element in name*

Dédé, Edmond, **3:**606

"Dede khudāke nāmse" (film song), **5:**532

Dede Qorqut (epic), **6:**851

Dedicated label, **3:**169

Deejays, **9:**155

Deep Forest, **8:**225

"Deep in the Heart of Texas" (American folk song), **9:**150

Deep Purple (musical group), **3:**357; **6:**250; **8:**215, 218, 220

"Deep River" (spiritual), **3:**607, 629

Deep River Boys (musical group), **3:**351
Défi québécois (Dufour), **3:**51
Def Jam, **3:**696, 714
Def Jef, **3:**714
Def Leppard, **8:**215
Defter-i Derviân (Ali Nutkî Dede), **6:**780
DeGaulle, Charles, **3:**1157
Degeyter, Pierre, **8:**659
de Graf, Nick, **3:**1280
De Gregori, Francesco, **8:**619–20
De Groen, Fonx, **8:**531
Dehiya, **6:**275
Dehong Dai and Jingpo Autonomous Prefecture
    Song and Dance Troupe, **7:**443
Dehoux, Vincent, **1:**256
Dehqan, Aşıq, **6:**845, *850*
Dehune (Japanese popular song), **7:**744
Dehuneno minato (Japanese popular song), **7:**744
Dei people, **1:**467
Deinbock, Heli, **8:**675, *675*
Deirdre (Willan), **3:**1184
Deiwá Eiñda Ù Mauñ Mauñ C̱ì, **4:**378
Deixa Falar (samba association), **2:**315
Dejardin (Walloon song collector), **8:**534–35
DeJarlis, Andy, **3:**344, 409, 1242, 1257
Déjà Vu, **9:**76
Deke, Musa (Vai Poro leader), **1:**337
De Koven, Reginald, **3:**544
Dela (god), **8:**864
Delacroix, Eugène, **6:**1043
Delahaye, Guy, **3:**1147
Dela-Molkh (god), **8:**864
Delamont, Arthur W., **3:**1094
Delaporte, Philip A., **9:**756
De La Soul, **3:**714
Delaware
    Chinese people in, **3:**957
    Native American groups in, **3:**461
Delaware Indian nation, **3:**462, 1078
    Big House songs, **3:**464
    instruments of, **3:**463
del Barco Centenera, Martín, **2:**250,
    453, 510
del Barco, Miguel, **2:**599
del Carmen, Guadalupe, **2:**371
De León, Oscar, **3:**743
Delfino, Clod, **4:**884
Delgadillo, Luis A., **2:**765, 767
"Delgadina, La" (*romance*), **3:**849
Delgado Aparicio, Jaime, **2:**485–86
Delgado, Miguel, **3:**749
Delhi
    drum traditions of, **5:**131
    gat traditions in, **5:**189–90
    map of, **5:***622*
    Mughal court in, **5:**15, 163, 744
    public concerts in, **5:**212
    sitar in, **5:**335
    tabla in, **5:**133–34, 136
Delhi University, **5:**447; **10:**5, 9
Delibes, Léo, **8:**161; **9:**38
Delicious Vinyl, **3:**714
Delius, Frederic, **8:**333
Dellâlzâde Ismail, **6:**779
Delmet, Paul, **3:**1148
Delmore Brothers (musical group), **3:**78

Delos Mars, Louisa Melvin, **3:**617
Deloume family, **3:**1096
Delphic Study Club (Montréal), **3:**1150
Delphonics (musical group), **3:**711
del Río, Dolores, **3:**740
Delson, Robert, **3:**1011
Delta Cats (musical group), **3:**351
Deltas (musical group), **4:**884
Del Tredici, David, **3:**176, 541; **10:**20
Deluxe Café (Chicago), **3:**652
Deluxe Swing Rascals, **1:**477
del Vecchio, Rosita, **3:**1181
"Demain l'hiver" (Charlebois), **3:**1156
DeMars, James, **3:**498
Demeter, Mrs. Jano Anna, **8:***742*
Demeter, P. S., **8:**287
Demeter, R. S., **8:**287
DeMille, Cecil B., **9:**43
Demir, Ilhami, **6:**804, *806*
Demirel, Hasan Hüseyin, **6:**251
Demme, Jonathan, **3:**204
"Democracy Bumpkin" (Chen), **7:**358
Democratic Party, **3:**306–9, 310
Demont, Madeleine, **1:**385
Dempster, Stewart, **9:**397
Dempwolff, Dr. Otto, **9:**981
Dene Indian nation, **3:**1274, 1275–76, 1280
Deng Lijun (Teresa Teng), **7:**356, 357, 359
Deng people, **7:**471, 483
Deng Xiaoping, **7:**90, 295, 317, 388, 467, 499
Dengzhebanjue, **7:**474, 475
Denis, Jean-François, **3:**1152
Denis, Joël, **3:**1158
Denisov, Edison, **8:**782
Denmark, **8:**451–65. *See also* Faroe Islands
    Anholt, **8:**464
    art music in, **8:**460–61
    Caribbean territories of, **2:**791, 968–69
    Copenhagen, ballet in, **8:**161
    dance traditions of, **8:**457, 465
    Fanø, **8:**465
        fannike dance, **8:**457
    folk revival in, **8:**461–62
    geography of, **8:**451
    influence on Swedish music, **8:**435
    instruments, **8:**198, 454–56
        research on, **8:**39–40, 41
    Jutland, **8:**464
        hymn-singing style, **8:**459
    Læsø, **8:**457
    map of, **8:***398*
    popular music in, **8:**458
    population of, **8:**451
    psalm singing in, **8:**3
    research on music of, **8:**18, 463–65
    rule over Iceland, **8:**400, 404
    rule over Norway, **8:**411, 413–14
    rule over Sweden, **8:**435
    Sønderho, figure dances in, **8:**457
    Thy, figure dances in, **8:**457
    vocal music, **8:**142, 451–53, *454*, 458–60,
        463–64
        ballads, **8:**23, 131, 134, 136
Denny, Frederick, **6:**162
Denny, Martin, **3:**1050; **9:**164

Densmore, Frances, **2:**593, 599, 649, 783; **3:**14,
    31, 70–71, 92, 291–92, 367, 426,
    444, 455, 457–58, 470, 478, 485,
    493, 509; **4:**872
Denton, Sandi "Pepa," **3:**696
D'Entrecasteaux Islands (Papua New Guinea),
    9:498
De nuptiis Mercurii et Philologiae (Martianus
    Capella), **8:**48
Deodhar, B. R., **5:***207,* 461–64, 466
Department of Anthropology (University of
    Auckland), **9:**974
Department of Canadian Heritage, **3:**296
Department of Performing Arts (Ilorin, Nigeria),
    1:216
Department of World Arts and Cultures (Los
    Angeles), **9:**976
Depeche Mode, **3:**690; **8:**215
De Philip, Addis, **6:**1030
De Poesi Fennica (Porthan), **8:**487–88
Deppe, Ludwig, **4:**870
Deren, Maya, **2:**883
Dérochers, Clémence, **3:**1156
Derrida, Jacques, **8:**192
Dertli, **6:**796
Derungs, Gion Antoni, **8:**692
Dervişan (musical group), **6:**250
dervishes, whirling. *See* Sufism (Mevlevî order)
Deryami of Artvin (*aşîk*), **6:**803
Desai, Morarji, **5:**624
Desai, Vasant, **5:**537
Desana culture, **2:**150–53
Desaulniers, Lucy, **3:**1280
"Descendants of the Dragon" (Hou), **7:**356, 357
Deschamps, Yvon, **3:**1158
Deschênes, Donald, **3:**344, 1136
Deschênes, Marcelle, **3:**1076
Descriptio Moldaviae (Cantemir), **8:**885
Déscriptions de l'Égypte, **6:**21–22, 609
Desert Oaks Band, **9:**145, 146
Desert Song (Romberg), **3:**544
"Desesperadamente" (García), **3:**739
Dêsíngurāju Katha, **5:**900
De Sio, Teresa, **8:**620
Desjarlais, Edgar, **3:**411
Desmond, Paul, **3:**660
Despard, George Pakenham, **2:**250
Desrochers, Clémence, **3:**1167
Desroches, Monica, **2:**920
Dessane, Antoine, **3:**28, 1076, 1148
Dessau, Paul, **8:**659
Destinnová, Ema, **8:**728
Destutt de Tracy, Antoine Louis Claude, **8:**184
"desvalido, El" (Garcia), **3:**737
Detroit Symphony Orchestra, **3:**611
Dett Collection of Negro Spirituals, **3:**607
Dett, R. Nathaniel, **3:**577, *578,* 606, 607, 629,
    1212
Detudamo, Timothy, **9:**756
Deuchler, Martina, **7:**24
Deutsch, Walter, **8:**672
Deutsche Marine Expedition, **9:**479
Deutsche Messe (Schubert), **8:**655
Deutsche Volkslied, Das (periodical), **8:**19
Deutsche Volkslieder mit ihren Melodien
    (anthology), **8:**649

Deutsche Volkslieder mit ihren Originalweisen
(Kretzschmer), **8:**656
Deutscher Liederhort (Erk/Böhme), **8:**656, 663
Deutsches Volksliedarchiv, **8:**663
deux meuniers, Les (Rigel), **6:**609
Deva, B. Chaitanya, **5:**327, 732
Deva, Hrdaya Narayana, **5:**47
Deva, Indra, **5:**675
Deva, Prabhu, **5:**545
Deval, K. B., **5:**53
DeVale, Sue Carole, **1:**135, 155, 158
Devarieux, Jacob, **2:**918
DeVeaux, Scott, **3:**580–81, 656
Devereaux, Kent, **3:**1017
Devi (deity), **5:**291–92
    portrayed in dances, **5:**493
    worship of, **5:**247, 643, 897–98
Devi, Annapurna, **5:**204, 205, 414, 466
Devi, Girija, **5:**181, *182,* 670
Devi, Kanan, **5:**855
Devi Mahātmya (text), **5:**505
Devi, Neelum, **5:**972
Devi, Nirmala, **5:**414
Devi, Rukmini, **5:**104
Devi, Saila, **5:**855
Devi, Sarasvati (daughter of Tansen), **5:**190, 378
Devi, Saraswati (film music director), **5:**420, 536
Devi, Siddeshwari, **5:**413, 670
Dević, Dragoslav, **8:**954
Devil and Daniel Webster (Moore), **3:**546
Deville, C. C., **3:**97
Devil to Pay (ballad opera), **3:**180
"Devil's Dream," **3:**409
De Vlier (musical group), **8:**535
Devon (musical group), **8:**472
devotional songs and singing (Hindu and
    Muslim). *See also bhajan; bhakti;
    dhrupad;* hymns; *kīrtan; qawwali;
    tēvāram*
    Hindu, **5:**2, 11, 376
        abhaṅg, **5:**250, 253, 549
        Andhra Pradesh, **5:**892
        Bengal, **5:**844–46
        bhakti genres, **5:**250, 265–66
        bheṇt, **5:**247
        caryā gīti, **5:**844, 859
        drone instruments for, **5:**343
        functions of, **5:**287
        gāyan, **5:**729
        Gujarat, **5:**501
        havelī saṅgīt, **5:**250–51, 401, 632,
            633, 643
        Karnataka, **5:**867–68
        Madhya Pradesh, **5:**724
        Maharashtra, **5:**728–29
        North America, **3:**814, 981, 983, 988–92,
            1084, 1205, 1246; **5:**579
        North India, **5:**247–56
        Orissa, **5:**732–33
        padāvali kīrtan, **5:**250, 253–54, 505
        Rajasthan, **5:**642–43, 645
        repertoire differences, **5:**284
        samāj gāyan, **5:**250, 251–52, 390
        sankīrtan, **5:**504, 729
        South India, **5:**105, 107, 145, 259–70, 351,
            556–57

Tamil Nadu, **5:**905–6, 918
Trinidad, **5:**590–91
Uttar Pradesh, **5:**663–64
vina as accompaniment, **5:**301
Muslim, **5:**2, 12, 259, 557
    Afghanistan, **5:**826–27
    Africa, **1:**536–37, 552–54
    ibtihālāt, **6:**167–68
    ilahije, **8:**968, 969
    inshād dīnī, **6:**19, 147, 148, 165–75, 321,
        372
    majlis, **5:**256, 284, 286
    marsīya, **5:**794
    milād, **5:**256, 411
    naʿt, **5:**748, 826–27
    Pakistan, **5:**748, 751–61, 769–70, 772
    Rajasthan, **5:**644
    Sri Lanka, **5:**958
    Sufi, **5:**256, 289, 339, 376, 401, 568,
        682–83, 686–88, 689, 694–95, 745,
        750, 751–61, 772; **6:**19, 114–15, 122,
        179, 190, 191, 193–95, 413, *770,*
        780, 795–96, 944
    tawāshīḥ, **6:**168, *169*
    Trinidad and Tobago, **2:**957
    performance practice, **5:**248–49
    Sikh, **5:**16, 256–57, 655–56, 762
        gurbāṇī, **5:**426
    South Africa, **5:**617
    in South Indian films, **5:**542
    studies of, **5:**56
Dewantara, Ki Hadjar, **4:**676–77
Dewar, Patricia, **3:**381
Dewetter, Jaroslav, **8:**723
Dewey, John, **3:**278
Dewey, Thomas, **3:**310
Dewit, Herman, **8:**535
Dexiaole, Tibetan king, **7:**472
Dexter, Noel, **2:**901
Dey, Manna, **5:**255, 420, 539
Dey, Suresh Chandra, **5:**56
Deyhim, Sussan, **6:**828
Ḍhāḍhī caste, **5:**403, 476, 639, 640, 641, 655
Dhākir, **6:**321
dhamār, **5:**170, 250
    development of, **5:**373
Dhamm al-malāhī (Ibn Abī 'l-Dunyā), **6:**372
Dhanakoti, **5:**103
Dhanammal, Vina, **5:**103, 233, 385, 389, 414
"Dhanam's Daughters," **5:**388–89
Dhangar community, **5:**728
Dhani Nivat, Prince, **4:**190, 223, 253
Dhanit Yupho, **4:**26, 223, 228, 229, 233, 238,
    240, 249, 254–55, 303
Dhanuk caste, **5:**679
d'Harcourt, Marguerite, **2:**24, 231, 467, 487;
    3:1165
d'Harcourt, Raoul, **2:**24, 231, 467, 487; **3:**1165
Ḍharhī caste, **5:**122–23, 133
dhikr (also *zikr; zekr*), **6:**184–86, 543
    Afghanistan, **5:**813, 818
    Africa, **1:**344–45, 537–38, 550–51, 593
    Central Asia, **6:**901, 937, 938, 939, 942–44,
        945–46
    Egypt, **6:**147–51, 170, 625–27, 630
    Iran, **6:**825, 833

Kurdistan, **6:**180–81
North Africa, **6:**437
North America, **3:**1043, 1044–45
Pakistan, **5:**754, 761, 794
Tunisia, **6:**516–20
Turkey, **6:**114, 189, 190–96, 768, 795
Dhlamini, Ezekial "King Kong," **1:**775
Ḍholā (epic), **5:**673
dholak. See drums: barrel, conical, or cylindrical
Ḍholī caste, **5:**7, 280, 403, *415,* 476, 640, 641,
    644–45
dhrupad, **5:**132, 162, 163–70, 253, 335–36, 342
    Afghanistan, **5:**805
    ālāp section of, **5:**198–99, 336
    composed by Tagore, **5:**850–51
    composed by Tirunal, **5:**229
    composition of, **5:**83, 168–70, 847–48
    Dagar *bānī,* **5:**378
    development of, **5:**15, 250, 373, 640, 845
    etymology of, **5:**83
    Gujarat, **5:**632
    Guyana, **5:**602
    history of, **5:**163–64
    improvisation in, **5:**202
    influence on Diksitar, **5:**224
    influence on Hindustani tradition, **5:**246
    influence on *khyāl,* **5:**125
    influence on sitar repertoire, **5:**190
    instrumental performance of, **5:**196–97, 202
    as men's genre, **5:**410–11
    Mithila women's genres and, **5:**678
    notation of, **5:**252
    patronage of, **5:**435
    performance of, **5:**164–70
    raga realization in, **5:**84–85
    ragas for, **5:**69
    recordings of, **5:**136
    similarities to *kīrtana,* **5:**42
    status of, **5:**196, 379
    as structure for *havelī saṅgīt,* **5:**633
    talas in, **5:**116–17
    Trinidad, **5:**591
    use of *bīn* in, **5:**119, 164, 188, 207, 333
    use of *pakhāvaj* in, **5:**116–19, 120
dhun, **5:**194, 198, 203
Dhyāb, 'U., **6:**592
Diabaté, Boubakar, **3:**1170
Diabaté, Sékou, **1:**365
Diablos Danzantes de Venezuela (Ortiz), **2:**544
Diaghilev, Sergei, **8:**161
Diaguita culture, **2:**356
    archaeomusicological studies of, **2:**7
    instruments of, **2:**12
Dial (journal), **3:**130
Diallo, Yaya, **3:**1170
Diamond, Beverley, **3:**50, 72, 74, 143, 144, 149,
    150, 392, 465, 473, 1072
Diamond, Jody, **3:**1017
Diamond, Neil, **3:**938; **4:**886
Diamonds (musical group), **3:**265, 314, 1081
Dian culture, **4:**41, 44–46
Dian Rucheng, **7:**261
"Diane" (Rapee), **3:**262
Dianyue people, **7:**495
Diary of Simeon Perkins 1766–1780, **3:**1070
Dias, António Jorge, **10:**117, 120

Días, Luis, **2:**861

Dias, Margot, **10:**117, 120

Diatta, Pascal, **1:**366

Díaz, Aniceto, **2:**833

Diaz, Augusto, **9:**390

Díaz del Castillo, Bernal, **2:**23, 557

Diaz Gainza, José, **2:**31

Díaz de Guzmán, Ruy, **2:**250, 453

Díaz, Porfirio, **2:**604

Díaz, Santo, **2:**780

Díaz Zelaya, Francisco Ramón, **2:**745

Dibango, Manu, **1:**415; **3:**228, 688; **8:**234

Dibia, I Wayan, **3:**1013, 1017, 1019; **4:**733

Dibrova Men and Women's Choir (Toronto),
        3:1082, 1200

Diccionario de Música (Osorio y Ricaurte), **2:**386

Dicey Doh Singers, **2:**805

Dick, J. C., **8:**374

Dickason, Olive P., **3:**1085, 1093–94

Dickson, Mary Henderson Flett, **3:**1209

Diddley, Bo, **3:**353, 354, 648, 672, 709, 789

Diderot, Denis, **3:**596; **9:**34

Didier, André, **1:**658, 663

didjeridu. *See* trumpets or horns

"Did You Ever Did See a Devil, Uncle Joe"
        (fiddling tune), **3:**77

Diego, Juan, **2:**613

Diegueño (Ipai and Tipai) Indian nation, **3:**417,
        418

Die Kreuzen (musical group), **3:**171

Die lustigen Tölzer (musical group), **8:***652*

Diero, Pietro, **3:**865

Difang Duana (Kuo Yingnan), **7:**358, 428–29

Difang Ignay (Kuo Shinchu), **7:**358, 428–29

Different World, A (television show), **3:**715

Digable Planets, **3:**699

Digenis Akritas, **8:**130

Diggs, Ronald, **10:**61–62

Digital Underground, **3:**714

Digo people, **1:**624, 627

Dihal, **5:**602, *603*

Dik Dik (musical group), **8:**619

Diksitar, Balusvami, **5:**224, 227, 338, 389

Diksitar, Chinnasvami, **5:**227

Diksitar, Muttusvami, **3:**989; **5:**15, 210, 220,
        223, 223–27, 228, *268*, 389,
        390, 508

    Brahmin class of, **5:**387

    compositions of, **5:**97, 223–27, 269

    Mīnākṣī mēmudam, **5:**145–47

    students of, **5:**386, 389

    Tyāgarāja yoga vaibhavam, **5:***148*

Diksitar, Ramasvami, **5:**219, 223, 227

Diksitar, Subbarama, **5:**46, 52, 227, 262

Di Lazzaro, Eldo, **8:**618

Dil Se (film), **5:**540–41

Dilbar, **6:***899*

Dillner, Johannes, **8:**440

Dilthey, Wilhelm, **1:**272–78

Dimas, Eddie, **3:**760

Dimitrov, Georgi, **8:**905

Dimitrova, Ghena, **8:**890

Dinā-Bhadrī (epic), **5:**679

"Dinah," **3:**544

Dindirri (musical group), **8:**315

Diné. *See* Navajo Indian nation

Dinesen, Isak, **8:**451

Dinesh "Leon," **5:**428

Ding Dusai, **7:**407

Ding Shande, **7:**347, 350

Ding Wu, **7:**365–67

Dingji liyue beikao (Qiu), **7:**336

Đinh dynasty, **4:**447, 480, 489

Đinh Lễ, **4:**480

Đinh Nhu, **4:**510

Đinh Tiên Hoàng, king of Vietnam, **4:**498

Dinicu, Grisoraş, **8:**882

Dinka people, **1:**568, 569–70

Dion, Céline, **3:**251, 252, 266, 315, 1161, 1168,
        1169

Dionysus (dance ensemble), **3:**1199

Dionysus, cult of, **8:**46

"*Dió que mate a la grega*" (Sephardic song),
        3:1174

Dioquino, Corazon, **4:**29

Diori Sinn (musical group), **3:**1170

Dirasat al-ʿūd (ʿAbd al-Munʿin ʿArafa), **6:**45

Directory for Publick Worship, **3:**125

Diriangén (Chorotegan chief), **2:**748

Dirty Dancing (film), **3:**200

Dirty Mind (Prince), **3:**685

Disappointment, or The Force of Credulity
        (Barton), **3:**180

Di Sarli, Carlos, **2:**264

Disciples of Massenet (Montréal), **3:**1150

disc jockeys (also disk jockeys, DJs)

    for African music, **1:**681–82

    for disco, **3:**228, 229–30, 687–88, 711, 712

    for gospel, **3:**585

    in hip-hop, **3:**552, 689, 690, 692–93, 694–95

    for Latin music, **3:**798

    on radio, **3:**263, 350, 560, 708, 709, 742, 743

    for reggae, **3:**809, 1202

disco, **2:**49–50; **3:**227–30, 323, 683, 684,
        687–91, 711–12, 1026; **8:**204, 674

    Aotearoa, **9:**168

    China, **7:**412, 444, 514

    Futuna, **9:**815

    Guatemala, **2:**735

    Hawai'i, **9:**928

    Manihiki, **9:**907

    Montserrat, **2:**926

    Papua New Guinea, **9:**179

    Uruguay, **2:**520

Disco Deewane (album), **5:**427

"Disco Lady" (Taylor), **3:**712

Disco Magic (television show), **3:**712

Discoteca di Stato (Italy), **8:**18

Discussion of Music, A (Jiu), **7:**473

Dishesangjiejiacuo, **7:**474, 475

disk jockeys. *See* disc jockeys

Disques Doubles, **3:**1160

Dissenten (musical group), **8:**225

Dissidenten, **8:**210

Di Stefano, Giuseppe, **8:**618

Distemperament (Maceda), **4:**876

Ditfurth, Franz-Wilhelm von, **8:**663

Dittersdorf, Karl Ditters von, **8:**881

Divadlo na zabradli, **8:**730

Divân-i Shams-i Tabrîzî, **6:**109

Divine Life Society, **5:**256

Divya Prabandham, **5:**260–61

Dīwān (Abū 'l-Mawāhib al-Tūnisī), **6:**370

Dix, John, **9:**932

"Dixie" (?Emmett), **3:**185, 188, 369, 543, 835

Dixie Hummingbirds (gospel quartet), **3:**633

"Dixie Moon" (Blake), **3:**619

Dixon, Archie, **3:**1133

Dixon, Boysie, **3:**1133

Dixon, George Washington, **3:**182, 184, 615–16

Dixon, James, **8:**337

Dixon, Luther, **3:**673, 709

Dixon, Willie, **3:**112, 583

Diyab, Amr, **3:**1220

Diyāb, ʿAmru, **6:**240, 283

Dizdancis (dance ensemble), **3:**1196

dizi. *See* flutes

Dizon, Camilo, **4:**865

Djaad, Abdelkrim, **6:**276

Djaambi, **9:**444

Djakoeb, Jakub, **4:**636

Djamal ʿAllām (musical group), **6:**270

Djang (musical group), **8:**287

Djaniya, **6:**270

Djaul (Papua New Guinea), **9:**626

Djawa (periodical), **4:**636

DjeDje, Jacqueline Cogdell, **10:**88, 137–55, *150*

Djenda, Maurice, **1:**304, 658, 663; **10:**119

Djerma people, **1:**588

DJ International, **3:**691

Djivani (*ashugh*), **6:***735*, 735–36

Djongi (BaAka woman), **1:**690

DJ Pierre, **3:**690

Djuka culture, **2:**438, 508–9. *See also* Auca
        culture

Djurdjura (musical group), **6:**270, 275

Dlaikan, Nadim, **3:***1037*; **6:**283

D'Leon, Oscar, **2:**102

Dnipro Ensemble (Edmonton), **3:**343, 1241

Dnishev, Alibek, **6:**961

Dnu Huntrakul, **4:**128

Dobiáš, Václav, **8:**729–30

Dobričanin, Dušan, **8:***942*

Dobrizhoffer, Martin, **2:**251, 463

Dobrovolski, Ivan, **8:**864

Dobrovolsky, Boris, **8:**784

Dobrowen, Issai, **6:**1026

Dobu people, **9:**489

Dock Rmah, **3:***994*

Doctor Jazz (musical), **3:**622

Dodd, Baby, **3:**653

Dodd, Clement ("Sir Coxsone"), **2:**97, 911

Dodds, Johnny, **3:**652–53

Dodge, Charles, **3:**254

Dodô (Bahian musician), **2:**337

Dodworth, Allen, **3:**564

Dodworth Band (New York), **3:**564

Dodworth, Charles, **3:**564

Dodworth, Harvey, **3:**564

Dodworth, Thomas, **3:**564

Dodworth, Thomas, Jr., **3:**564

Doe, Samuel, **10:**61

Dôgen, **7:**612

DoggyStyle (Snoop Doggy Dogg), **3:**715

Dogon people

    dance, **1:**109, 112

    dance as medicine, **1:**113

    masks of, **1:**119

music of, **1**:454–55
speech origin beliefs, **1**:108
Dogrib Indian nation, **3**:494, 1276
Doherty, Jim, **3**:*1189*
Doherty, Seán, **9**:79
"Doing the Dog" (Thomas), **3**:676
Dois Irmãos, **2**:*329, 331*
Dokta, Andrew, **9**:522
Dokugo (Dazai), **7**:548
Dolan people, **6**:990–93, 997
Dolgan people, **7**:1027–30
Dolidze, Viktor, **8**:843
Doliner, Gorana, **8**:937
Dolman, Ashley, **9**:*416*
Dolorier Abregu, Fausto, **2**:*473*
Ḍom groups, **5**:641, 794–95, 798–99, 800
Dombrowski, Norm, **3**:*896*
Domingo, Plácido, **3**:852; **8**:618
Domingo Sol, José, **2**:736
Domínguez Agurcia, Roberto, **2**:745
Domínguez, Francisco, **2**:*593*
Dominica, **2**:789, 840–44
  geography of, **2**:840
  musical genres
    bélé, **2**:841–42
    cadence-lypso, **2**:844, 879, 920
    cadence-rampa, **2**:844
    chanté mas, **2**:843
    quadrille, **2**:842–43
  popular music in, **2**:98
  population of, **2**:840
Dominica Folk Singers, **2**:843–44
Dominican-Americans/Canadians, **3**:337, 731, 790, 800
Dominican order
  in Mexico, **2**:600
  in South America, **2**:23
Dominican Republic, **2**:845–62; **3**:788
  African heritage, **2**:850–55
  archaeomusicological studies in, **2**:7, 8
  art music in, **2**:859, 862
  Baní, **2**:855
  children's wakes in, **2**:422
  creole culture, **2**:855–57
  geography of, **2**:845
  Haitian people in, **2**:792–93
  history of, **2**:792, 793, 845–47
  industries of, **2**:791
  military regime in, **2**:104
  musical genres, **2**:848–49, 851, 859–62
    bachata, **2**:105, 861
    balada, **2**:862
    merengue, **2**:*73*, 93, 98, 101, 104–5
    merengue, **1**:384, 424
    merengue típico, **2**:857
    salve, **2**:856–57
  musical links with Venezuela, **2**:524
  popular music in, **2**:861–62
  Puerto Plata, **2**:857
  rará societies of, **2**:795
  research on, **2**:862
  San Pedro de Macorís, **2**:857
  Santiago, **2**:857
  Santo Domingo, **2**:857
  Siboney culture of, **2**:78
  Spanish heritage, **2**:847–49

Taino culture, **2**:846–47
urban music, **2**:857–67
Villa Mella, **2**:*852*, 854, 855
Dominion Educational Association, **3**:276
Dominion label, **3**:1268
Dominion Land Act (1871), **3**:1088
Dominion Lands Act (1872), **3**:1249, 1255
Dominion Song Book, **9**:277
Dominion Telegraph Company, **3**:1182
"Dominique," **3**:1173
Domino, Antoine "Fats," **3**:351, 353, 552, 648, 670, 708, 709, 741, 789
Dominoes (musical group), **3**:671
Domnérus, Arne, **8**:446
Domo Mata (Chikamatsu), **7**:669
Don Messer and the Islanders, **3**:1125, 1190, 1257
Don Messer's Jubilee (television show), **3**:1257
Donald of the Burthens (Whyte), **8**:369
Donaldson, Lou, **3**:701
Donaldson, Tamsin, **9**:451
Donaldson, William, **8**:374
Donati, Giuseppe, **8**:616
Donatists, **6**:431
Don Bueso y su hermana (romance), **6**:1042
Donegan, Lonnie, **8**:369; **9**:938
Dones, Angie, **3**:798
Dong people
  folk songs of, **7**:449
  music of, **7**:485–92
  opera of, **7**:452
Dong Yue, **7**:985
Donga (Ernesto dos Santos), **2**:350
Đồng Đậu culture, **4**:36
Don Giovanni (Mozart), **3**:181; **8**:60
Dongjin (Eastern Jin) dynasty
  Buddhism in, **7**:329
  Daoism in, **7**:312, 320
Đồng Sơn culture, **4**:10, 40–41, 43, 44, 445
  bronze drums from, **4**:45–46, 58, 446, 467, 485, 596, 598–99, 632, 791–92, 819
Dongxiang people, **7**:455–58
Dongxiao chuizoufa (Sun), **7**:186
Đỗ Nhuận, **4**:512
Donizetti, Gaetano, **3**:1181; **4**:857, 863; **8**:367, 604, 618
Donizetti, Giuseppe, **6**:771, 779
Donkoo (Mongol song), **7**:1007
"Donna" (Valens), **3**:746
Donnelly, Dick, **9**:441
Donnelly, Sean, **8**:394
Donner, Philip, **8**:489
Donner, William, **9**:327
Donostia, José G. de Zulaika Arregi de, **8**:317
Donovan, **3**:317
Donovan, Mishi, **3**:1063, 1087
Don't Be Weary Traveler (Dett), **3**:607
"Don't Call Me Nigga, Whitey" (Stone), **3**:681
"Don't Leave Me This Way" (Houston), **3**:712
Don't Play Us Cheap (Van Peebles), **3**:621
"Don't You Know I Love You" (Clovers), **3**:670
Doobie Brothers, **4**:887
Doornbosch, Ate, **8**:523, 534
Doors (musical group), **3**:318, 348, 550
Doppio Teatro, **9**:81
Dopyera, John, **3**:240

Đorđevic, Tihomir, **8**:961
Dora Stratou Theater, **8**:1017
Dörbet people, **7**:1004–20
Dore, Giovanni, **8**:627
"Do, Re, Mi" (Rodgers and Hammerstein), **5**:224
Doret, Gustave, **8**:697
D'Or, Georges, **3**:1156
"Do Right Woman—Do Right Man" (Franklin), **3**:677
Ðorlaksson, Guðbrandur, **8**:404
Dornan, Angelo, **3**:147
Dorsenne, Jean, **9**:38
Dorset culture, **3**:1069
Dorsey, Henry, **1**:127
Dorsey, James Owen, **3**:444
Dorsey, Jimmy, **3**:742
Dorsey, Thomas A. "Georgia Tom," **3**:12, 534, 631–32, 645, 648; **10**:138, 145
Dorsey, Tommy, **3**:655, 863, 969
Þorsteinsson, Bjarni, **8**:401
dos Santos, Jão, **1**:319
Dostoevsky, Fyodor, **8**:781
"Do the Funky Chicken" (Thomas), **3**:676
"Do the Push and Pull" (Thomas), **3**:676
Do the Right Thing (film), **3**:715
Dot Records, **3**:352
Dotto, Gabriele, **10**:165
double bass. *See* violins and fiddles (bowed lutes)
Doubleday, Veronica, **6**:18, 305; **10**:69
Double Descent among the Fanti (Christensen), **10**:33
Double Exposure, **3**:688
Double Music (Harrison and Cage), **3**:953; **4**:132
double-reed instruments. *See also* bagpipes
  algaita (or *algeita*), **1**:313, 449
  Arab world, **6**:415
  aulos, **1**:550; **6**:360; **8**:39, 46–47, *47*, 1031
  bajón (bassoon), **2**:577–78
  balaban, **6**:10, 845, *845*, 846, 848, 851
    Azerbaijan, **6**:925, 930
  bassoon, **3**:563; **8**:330, 420, 454
  becu, **2**:929
  biko, **2**:929
  bili, **7**:42, 80, 111, 125, 491
  bishgüür, **7**:1017–18
  bombarde, **8**:528, 559–60, *560*, 561, 562–63
  botanical, **8**:456, 481
  chirimía, **2**:33, 36
    Bolivia, **2**:283
    Colombia, **2**:396
    Costa Rica, **2**:682
    Guatemala, **2**:726, 727, 729, 731
    Mexico, **2**:550, 558, 577–78
    Nicaragua, **2**:748, 758
    Paraguay, **2**:453
    Peru, **2**:472, 475, 476, 478, 481, 494
  chirisuya, **2**:33, 36, 472
  ciaramella, **3**:860, 861
  crumhorns, **8**:653
  cu tu, **4**:536
  diple, **8**:915, 928, 959–60
  disuona, **7**:231
  Dudey, **8**:654
  düdük, Azerbaijan, **6**:848

double-reed instruments (*continued*)
duduk, **8:**840, 842
  Armenia, **6:**729
Europe, early history of, **8:**42
gaita, **8:**314, 315
ghaita, **1:**536, 537, 541, 544; **6:**415, 498
guan (also *guanzi*), **7:**111
  in Buddhist rituals, **7:**312, 331
  in Daoist rituals, **7:**323
  mythical origins of, **7:**402
  in northern Chinese ensembles, **7:**199–204, 315
haidi, **7:**201
hitiriki (*hichiriki*)
  in *gagaku*, **7:**620, 622, 625
  in *mikagura*, **7:**607–8
  notation for, **7:**54, 626
  syôga vocables for, **7:**626
hnè, **4:**370–71
hojŏk, **7:**824, 825, 889, 933, 958
houguan, **3:**961; **7:**218
hyang-p'iri, **7:**822, 867, 868
jialing, **7:**477, 479–80, 481
karamoutza, **8:**1009
kèn đôi, **4:**475
kèn bầu, **4:**475
kèn bóp, **4:**475, 492
kèn mộc, **4:**475
kèn thau, **4:**475
kokal, **5:**949
koḷ, **5:**278, 366, 912, 915, *915*
kulal, **5:**360, 363, 938, 943
kungkuvak, **4:**837
kurnetta, **8:**640
kurum kulal, **5:**931, 932, 933
leaf oboes
  blùng, **4:**536
  China, **7:**450, 490, 491, 492, 511
  kèn lá, **4:**475
  Manihiki, **9:**906
  Marquesas Islands, **9:**895–96
  New Caledonia, **9:**680
  pu'i kikau, **9:**901
  Vanuatu, **9:**693
  Yap, **9:**730
mei, **6:**10
mey, **6:**81, 764, 799, 848
mimi, **7:**462
mizmār, **6:**395, 397, 398
  Arabian peninsula, **6:**360, 705
  Egypt, **6:**154, 415, 545, 628, 631
  in North America, **3:***1037*
  Oman, **6:**679, *679*
  Yemen, **6:**303, 306, 656, 709
mizmār baladī, **6:**415
mohurī (also *mahurī*; *mohorī*), **5:**346, 733
mukhavīṇā, **5:**366, 387, 879, 913
mu suona, **7:**491
mwali, **5:**505
nafiri, **4:**615
nāgasvaram, **5:**210, 212, 270, 275, 286, 323–24, 355, 544
  caste and, **5:**389, 390, 392
  Karnataka, **5:**876, 886
  in Karnatak music, **5:**90, 103, 161, 230, 234, 350, 352, 354, 393–94, 452, 556–57

Kerala, **5:**932, *933*
North America, **3:**990
in *periya mēḷam* ensemble, **5:**234, *359*, 359–60, 387, 912
Sri Lanka, **5:**108, 958
Tamil Nadu, **5:**915, 926
nallari (*See t'aep'yŏngso*)
narslon, **5:**608, *608*
nāyaṇam, **5:**914, *914*, 920, 921
Niger, **1:**538
nzumari, **1:**606, 624
oboe, **3:**563; **8:**9, 420, 454, 594
orlo (krummhorn), **2:**577–78
ottu, **5:**103, 359, 360, 912, 914
pey-aw, **4:**172, 212, 213
pey prabauh, **4:**172–73, 194, 196, 197
pi, **4:**236, 358, 411, 412
pi aw, **4:**236–37
pi chanai, **4:**66, 237, 249
pi chawa, **4:***235*, 237, 264, 307, 308, 309, 312
pí đôi, **4:**535
piffero, **8:**616
pi kaeo, **4:**355
pi ka law, **4:**304–5
pi klang, **4:**264
pi mawn, **4:**237
pi nai, **4:**17, *242*, 251, 261, 262, 264, 271, 272, 305
pi nawk, **4:**264
pipahī, **5:**679
pí pặp, **4:**535
pipiza, **8:**280, 1009
p'iri, **7:***824*, 828, 989
  contemporary music for, **7:**954, 959, 960
  modifications to, **7:**961
  sanjo repertoire, **7:**913–17
  in shaman rituals, **7:**986
  in *sijo*, **7:**925
  in *sinawi*, **7:**890
  in *t'alch'um*, **7:**942
  vocal imitation of, **7:**817
preret, **4:**743, 767–68, 771, 772, 773, 774, 776
pua, **4:**536
p'ulp'iri, **7:**890
puwí-puwí, **4:**806
qarnāta, **6:**415
rāsa śahnāī, **5:**700
rgya-gling, **5:**714
roženice, **8:**930
śahnāī, **5:**273, *274*, *304*, 336, 340, *341*, 346, 360, 362, 401, 496, *496*, 497, 506
  depictions of, **5:**305
  in film music, **5:**347
  Gujarat, **5:**625
  Karnataka, **5:**878
  in Karnatak music, **5:**351
  Kerala, **5:**948
  Laṅgā performers of, **5:**402
  Nepal, **5:**280, *699*, 699–700
  Pakistan, **5:**283, 285, *756*, 795
  Punjab, **5:***764*
  Rajasthan, **5:**280
  repertoire for, **5:**188, 195

as solo instrument, **5:**207
Uttar Pradesh, **5:**670, 671
sannāyi, **5:**896
saranai, **3:***997*, 1010; **4:**590
sarunai, **4:**237
sarunai kayu, **4:**613
sarunai nenet, **4:**620
sarune, **4:**609
sarune batang padi, **4:**609
sarunei, **4:**607–8
selumprit, **4:**413
se-p'iri, **7:**822, 866, 921, 927
serone, **4:**780, 783
serunai, **4:**66, 404, *405*, 407, 411, *415*, *419*, 429, 587, 615, 616, 619, 623
serune, **4:**605, 768, 780, 781, 782, 784
seurune kalëe, **4:**604
sez, **6:**745, *745*, 749
shahnai, **4:**237
shawm, **8:**168, 517
  Germany, **8:**651, 653, 654, 656
  Norway, **8:**420
  Spain, **8:**589, 593
shedag, **8:**863
shenai, **4:**66–67
sib-saba, **6:**415
silu, **4:**780, 783, 785
sirijna, **8:**857
slomprèt, **4:**646
soaenap (also *soenap*), **7:**933, 961
sona, **4:**698
sopile, **8:**930
sornā, **5:**814, 820–22; **6:**828, 839
sornāīe, **5:**789
sounai batang padi, **4:**615
South Asia, use in funerals, **5:**273
Southeast Asia, **4:**74
  in gong-chime ensembles, **4:**20–21
sralai, **3:**1001; **4:**17, 157, 173–74, 213, 236
sralai klang khek, **4:**173–74, 197, 202–3
sralai tauch, **4:**173–74, 183
sralai thomm, **4:**173–74, 183
ṣrnāj, **6:**415, *415*
sronèn, **4:**646, 668, 675
suona, **7:**80, *81*, 217, *512*
  in *bayin* groups, **7:**427
  in *beiguan* groups, **7:**425
  in Buddhist rituals, **7:**312
  in Chinese orchestra, **7:**230
  in Daoist rituals, **7:**323
  in North America, **3:**961, 1260
  in northeastern music, **7:**520
  in northern Chinese ensembles, **7:**199–204, 235, 242, 259
  notation for, **7:**125
  in opera ensembles, **7:**285
  origins, **7:**113
  performance techniques for, **7:**236
  in *shifangu* ensemble, **7:**196, *197*
surle (also *curle*; *zurle*; *cingonë*), **8:**996, 1000, 1001
surnā, **5:**340, 712, *712*, 774, 777, 781, 783
surnāī, **5:**346, 499, *499*, 506, 641, 642, 692, 795–96, *797*; **6:**898
ṣurnāy, **6:**546, 708, 710

surnāy, **5:**340, *685*, 685–86; **6:**1002
t'aep'yŏngso (also *nallari*), **7:**67, 822, *824, 825,* 828, 870, 873, 933, 944, 959
taletenga, **1:**465
Tamil Nadu, **5:**916
tang-p'iri, **7:**822, 867
tarompet, **4:**67, 709, 710
tarpe, **5:**727
terompet, **4:**67
terompet Cina, **4:**626
tètèt, **4:**645
trompet, **4:**655
tūtī, **5:**346
two-pipe instruments, **8:**39, 926
txanbela, **8:**314
xi u, **4:**536
xralày, **4:**215
yat, **4:**549
yuai, **7:**205
zamr, **6:**444, 445
zenga, **6:**415
zorna, **6:**263
zorne, **6:**745, 749
zourna, **8:**1008, 1009, 1011–12
zūkra, **6:**306, 415, 519
zummār, **6:**566
zurla, **8:***280, 977*
  Balkan region, **8:**168, 201, 280–81, 285, 951, *966*, 975–76, 978
  Canada, **3:**1198
zurna, **6:**10
  Azerbaijan, **6:**925, 931
  Balkan region, **8:**170, 279, 280, 284–85, 893, 895, 960, 966
  Egypt, **6:**415
  Georgia, **8:**836, 840, 842
  Syria, **6:**566
  in Turkish music, **6:**115, 257, 764, *764,* 767, 816
z'urna, **6:**729
"Double Vie" (Séguin), **3:**1161
Doucet, Suzanne, **3:**345, 346, 347
Doug E. Fresh, **3:**698
Dougall-Kudjardikudjardi, Jimmy, **9:**331
Dougan, Nadine, **8:**937
Doughty, Charles, **6:**21, 361–62
Douglas, James, **3:**1255
Douglas-Klotz, Neil, **3:**1043
Douglas, Norman, **9:**1008
Douglass, Frederick, **3:**26, 592
Douglass, John Thomas, **3:**617
Doukhobors, **3:**12, 292, 915, 1086, 1092, 1095, 1267–70
Doukhobors (Woodcock and Avakumovic), **3:**1270
Doula (musical group), **3:**1220
Doŭnar-Zapolski, Mitrafan, **8:**803
Doura people, **9:**492
Dow, Donald, **8:**367
Dowland, John, **8:**76
"Down in the Alley" (Clovers), **3:**673
Down Beat (periodical), **3:**1105; **8:**211
Down in the Delta (Ferris), **3:**583
"Down Home Rag" (Europe), **3:**651
"Down in Mexico" (Coasters), **3:**672
"Down Mexico Way," **9:**25

Downing, David L., **3:**564
"Do Ya Think I'm Sexy?" (Stewart), **3:**689
Dôzyôzi (*nô* drama), **7:**553
Dpir, Paghtasar, **6:**734
Dr. Dre, **3:**698, 700, 701
Dr. Kurt Ostbahn (musical group), **8:**678
Dr. No (film), **3:**203
Dr. Sun Yat Sen Classical Chinese Garden (Vancouver), **3:**1096
"Draft Dodger Rag" (Ochs), **3:**316
"Draft Resister" (Steppenwolf), **3:**318
Dragoumis, Markos, **8:**1025
Drake, Francis, **2:**250
Drake, Raleigh, **3:**278
Drake, St. Clair, **3:**624
Dramatic Mirror (periodical), **3:**618
Dramatics (musical group), **3:**676
Dranes, Arizona, **3:**631
"*Drapeau de Carillon*" (Crémazie), **3:**1148
Draper, David, **3:**470
Draumkvædet, **8:**413
Draupati (deity). *See* Shakti
Dravidian peoples, **5:**5, 14, 17, 238, 261, 720, 722, 726, 867
Drayton, Joseph, **9:***19*
Draytons Two, **2:**820
Dread, Marty, **9:**166
Dread Beat and Blood (musical group), **9:**168
Dreadfulwater, J. B., **3:**486
Dream Dances (ballet), **3:**498
Dreamgirls (musical), **3:**622
Dreamland Café (Chicago), **3:**652
Dream N. the Hood (Walker), **3:**612
Dream Warriors (rap group), **3:**73
'Dre-dkar community, **5:**711
Drehavicans, **8:**790
Drenica, Tahir, **8:**996
Dresden Codex, **2:**650
Dresher, Paul, **3:**1017–18
Dresser, Paul, **3:**191, 305, 549
Drewal, Margaret, **1:**121
Dreyfus Publishers, **3:**262
Dried Millet Breaking (Stone), **10:**59
Drifters (musical group), **2:**105; **3:**351, 671, 673, 709
"Drifting Blues" (Moore), **3:**669
"Drink to Me Only with Thine Eyes," **3:**839
Drinker, Sophie, **3:**93
Dripsody (Le Caine), **3:**1185
Drive, **1:**779
Driver, Harold E., **3:**473, 474
D'Rivera, Paquito, **3:**789
Drolet, Patricia Lund, **2:**783
drone
  Africa, **1:**542, 543, 579, 585, 591–92
  Andean music, **2:**216
  Arabian peninsula, **6:**546, 651
  Armenian music, **6:**731
  in art music, **8:**227
  Australia, didjeridu, **9:**294, 395–98, 422
  Azerbaijan, **6:**925
  Bellona, **9:**850
  Borneo, **4:**827, 832, 833, 834
  Brazil, in *desafio*, **2:**327

Europe
  instrumental, **8:**9, 13, 36, *170,* 406, 414, 418, 493–94, 503, 511, 543, 568, 572, 630, 705, 918
  research on, **8:**22
Fiji, **9:**19
Flores, **4:**793
France, **8:**543
Hungary, **8:**274
Ireland, **8:**384, 385
Irian Jaya, **9:**584
in Karnatak music, **5:**91, 92, 101
Lebanon, **6:**554
Luangiua, **9:**843
Macedonia, **8:**281
Malaysia, **4:**435
Māori songs, **9:**933
Middle Eastern music, **6:**10
Mongol people, **7:**1004–5, 1009, 1013, 1024
Paiwan people, **7:**525
Papua New Guinea
  Rai Coast songs, **9:**565
  vocal, **9:**538–39, 603
Philippines, **4:**906, 922, 926
Poland, **8:**705
Q'ero music, **2:**229, 230
Rapa Nui, **9:**952
Rotuma, **9:**822
Solomon Islands, **9:**658, *665,* 666
South Asia
  in devotional music, **5:**249, 655–56
  hummed, **5:**345
  instruments for, **5:**74, 323, 331–32, 340, 343, 350, 351, 352, 355, 366, 384, 670–71, 700, 901
  origins of, **5:**29, 74, 307–8
  pitches included in, **5:**67
strings, **3:**838; **5:**199
Sumatra, **4:**613
Switzerland, **8:**683, 691
Tonga, **9:**14, 308, *309,* 784
Tuvan music, **6:**981, 983; **7:**1024
as vocal accompaniment, **8:**9, 13
  Albania, **8:**990–92
  Balkan region, **8:**867
  Bulgaria, **8:**895, 901
  Georgia, **8:**827, 828, 830, 833
  Greece, **8:***1010,* 1013
  Latvia, **8:**500, *500,* 505
  Macedonia, **8:**973
  North Caucasia, **8:**851, 852, 854, 855, 856–57, 859, 862
  Romania, **8:**879
  Russia, **8:**757
  Slovenia, **8:**913
  Southeast Asia, **4:**597
Drost, Herbert Mason, **3:**1094
Drown, Betty, **10:**18
"Drown in My Own Tears" (Charles), **3:**678
Droxy, **9:**154
Druckman, Jacob, **3:**176
"Drug Store Drug Drivin' Man" (Byrds), **3:**318
drugs (hallucinogens and narcotics). *See also* alcohol; betel
  cocaine, **2:**151, 153
  datura, **2:**20

drugs (hallucinogens and narcotics) *(continued)*
  Egypt, **6:**620
  epena, **2:**171, 174–75
  Iran, **6:**139
  jazz and, **3:**659
  kava, **9:**172–74, 179, 202
  music and, **2:**129
  narcotic drinks, **3:**416
  Peru, **2:**482
  peyote, **2:**585–86; **3:**425, 433, 487–88
  rap and, **3:**698
  rock and, **3:**710–11
  shaman's use of, **2:**45–46, 171, 174–75, 177
  Tukano culture, **2:**153–54
Drumbeat Records, **3:**486
drum machines. *See* electrophones
"Drummer Boy of Shiloh" (Hays), **3:**188
Drummond, Barry, **3:**1018
Drumond, Don, **2:**911
drums. *See also* idiophones; *specific types below*
  acoustics of, **5:**322
  Africa, in healing rituals, **1:**276–77, 281–82
  African, **3:**593, 596
  Akan people, **1:**465
  Andean regions, **2:**206–7, 216
  antelope skin, **1:**689
  Arab world, **6:**416–20
  Arawak culture, **2:**13
  Argentina, **2:**250, 260
  association with Shiva, **5:**247
  bajé, **1:**562
  baka-baka, **4:**814
  Bali, **4:**743
  bamba, **1:**562; **4:**788
  baranung, **4:**590
  batak, **4:**572, 573, 585
  baydam, **2:**444
  bendu, **4:**788, 789
  bɔranɔʔ, **4:**572, 573, 585
  biankomé, **2:**826
  Buddhist classification of, **5:**327–29
  Central Africa, **1:**677
  chack, **4:**540
  Cham people, **3:**1010
  China
    clay, Zhou dynasty, **7:**82, 191
    early, **7:**88, 105, 107, 108, 111
    in opera ensembles, **7:**276, 285–86, 292
    south and southwestern minority cultures,
      7:490–92
  chua, **4:**536
  classification of, **5:**325–26
  Cokwe people, **1:**672
  Congo, 1600s–1700s, **1:**80–81
  cord-and-peg tension, **1:**314–17
  dabu-dabu, **4:**895, 898, 907
  Dan people, **1:**466
  dawilpaz, **7:**460
  deliro, **4:**788, 789
  dere, **4:**802
  distribution of, **2:**32
  durum, **2:**750
  e (Tibetan drum), **7:**477, 479–80
  early treatises on, **5:**21, 29
  East African royal, **1:**600–601
  East Asia, **7:**5

Edo people, **1:**461
ehti, **1:**561
empa-empal, **4:**821
engoma, **1:**218
euku, **9:**500
European depictions of, **9:**11, *12*
European types of, **8:**169
Ewe people, **1:**462
Gabon, 1800s, **1:**87
gaka, **1:***323*
gambyak, **4:**643, 655, 675
Gā people, **1:**463
ggageng, **9:**566
in gong-chime ensembles, **4:**20–21
gourd
  bentere, **1:**465
  Southwest Indian types, **3:**437
Guinea coast, 1600s, **1:**83
gumbay, **1:**419
Guyana, **2:**443
Haitian sacred drums, **3:**804
hala, **7:**460
halam, **1:**447
hari kawina, **2:**508
Hindustani, **5:**341–42
Hmong people, **4:**555
hun, **2:**826
huncito, **2:**826
hunga, **2:**826
hunguedde, **2:**826
Igbo people, **1:**459
Indus Valley civilization, **5:**320
Irian Jaya, **9:**585
iyà'lù, **1:**460, 472, 476
Java, **4:**642
jing'oma, **1:**678
jochana, **2:**206
jumbie drum (also *woowoo;* French reel), **2:**924
Karnataka, **5:**874
Kasena people, **1:**455
Kazakh people, **7:**460
kempol, **4:**768
Kenya, **1:**624, 625
kès, **2:**887
Khmer people, **4:**166–69
khong, **4:**548
kinang, **4:**590
klawng chatri, **4:**307
klawng khaek, **4:**66, 234, 266–68
kodeq, **4:**773
kola, **1:**562
Korea, **7:**828–29
koti kawina, **2:**508
kuchí-yeremá, **2:**826
kŭrkeh, **5:**692
Kwa groups, **1:**469
langoro, **1:**784
leng, **1:**569
Lithuania, **8:**512
LoDagaa people, **1:**457
log
  African-American types, **3:**595
  Native American types, **3:**476
  Southwest Indian types, **3:**429
  tombé, **3:**761, 763

Lombok, **4:**768–69
loor, **1:**569
Madagascar, sacred drums, **1:**784
makawa, **2:**358
maoma, **1:**713
meng jiao, **7:**451
Mexico, ancient, **2:**8
mhito, **1:**751
mortar, New Britain, **9:**623
mugonguê, **2:**349
Neolithic clay, **8:**36–37
ngamba, **1:**667
ng'oma, **1:**281, 312, 637, 709, 712
Nguni peoples, **1:**706
Nigeria, 1800s, **1:**91
Nkhumbi people, **1:**714
n'lapa, **1:**785
nōba, **1:**552
Northeast Indian groups, **3:**463
obi-apá, **2:**826
Oceania, **9:**381–85
oʃŋ, **1:**316
pahu matatahi, **9:**904, 906
Peru, ceramic, **2:**11, *13*
Plains Indian groups, **3:**445
prehistoric, **8:**39
pwita, **1:**678
Queensland, **9:**430
Saami shamanic drums, **8:**122, 428
sabar, **1:**422
sacred, **2:**48
Senufo people, **1:**454
Shona people, **1:**751
shougu, **7:**323
sintren, **4:**697
skor klang khek, **4:**167, 197, 203
skor klong khek, **4:**66
skor sangna, **4:**197
Somalia, **1:**611
South America, **2:**29
  made from human skin, **2:**35
  segon, **2:**883
  tropical-forest region, **2:**127
South Asia, use in funerals, **5:**273
South Asian folk, **5:**346
Southeast Asia, Indian influences on,
  4:66
southeastern Africa, **1:**708
Southeast Indian types, **3:**468
southern Africa, double-headed, **1:**719
ṭabl (general term), **6:**395, 398, 444
tabula, **1:**342
taḍ (pressure drum), **5:**770
tambora, **4:**843
tambur (also *tambu*), **4:**780, 783
tambura, **1:**555
tanbou ich, **2:**949
tanbou kongo, **2:**887
tanbou manman, **2:**949
tanbou petro, **2:**887
Tanzania, **1:**637–38
tembere, **5:**882
tende, **1:**538, 545, 575, 582–87, 594
Thailand, **4:**233–35
timbal, **2:**508
timbales, **9:**103

titir, **4:**820
tom, **1:**568
trống bụng, **4:**469
trống chầu ca trù, **4:**481
trống đạo, **4:**470, 504
trống ngũ bộ, **4:**470
Tsonga people, **1:**710–11
tufu, **4:**797
tugtugan, **4:**848
Uighur people, **7:**459
umva, **1:**562
Vietnam, **4:**469–70
    upland regions, **4:**534
West Africa, **1:**446, 453
    double-headed, **1:**449
    single-membrane, **1:**449
Yoruba people, **1:**460, 461
yūlu mǎlai, **9:**537, 541
zhegu, **7:**212
drums: barrel, conical, or cylindrical
    adaul, **8:**853
    Africa, prehistoric, **1:**549
    agida, **2:**505, 509
    àkúbà, **1:**474, 476, 479
    alcahuete (also *adulón*), **2:**854–55
    anabera, **5:**364
    apesin, **1:**461
    Arab world, **6:**419–20, 420
    Argentina, **2:**251, 256
    atabales, **2:**757, 851, 853, 854; **8:**314 (*See also under* kettledrums)
    atabaque, **2:**309, 343, *345*, 346, 349, 511, 515
    atumpan, **1:**106, 211, 316, 464
    B-52, **2:**803
    baboula, **2:**865
    balsié, **2:***852*, 855
    baraban, **8:**704, 810–11, *811*
    barabanče, **8:**977
    baraban z talerkami, **8:**797
    bass drum
        Antigua, **2:**799
        Argentina, **2:**261
        Barbados, **2:**815
        Brazil, **2:***59*
        Carriacou, **2:***871*, 872
        Dominican Republic, **2:***853*
        Jamaica, **2:**904, 907
        Moxo culture, **2:***139*, 140
        North America, **3:**400, 445, 484, 563, 674
        Oceania, **9:**382
        Otopame culture, **2:**571
        Peru, **2:***480*
        Quechua and Aymara culture, **2:**207, 210, 211, 212
        Serbia, **8:**946
        South Asia, **5:**589–90, 671
        Surinam, **2:**509
        Switzerland, **8:**686
        Trinidad and Tobago, **2:**959
        Uruguay, **2:**511, 518
        Virgin Islands, **2:**973
    bàtá, **1:**404, 471, 485
    bedam, **5:**601
    bedhug, **4:**642, 644, 673
    bedug, **2:**507; **4:***75*, 692, 695, 701, 743, 768–69

bélè, **2:**915, 918–19
beleq, **4:**772, *773*
bemba (also *bembe*), **2:***955*
bembé, **2:**824
bembe, **1:**404, 413
bengri, **6:**487
bherī, **5:**328
bhoom, **2:**446
biqi gu, **7:**224–25
boben, **8:**916
bocus, **2:**836
boeng mang, **4:**235
bomba, **2:**934; **3:**727
bomber, **2:**803
bombo, **4:**847; **8:**582
    Andean regions, **2:***76*, 207, 252, 253
    Argentina, **2:**252, 259, 260
    Bolivia, **2:**285
    Brazil, **2:**334
    Chile, **2:**360, 373
    Colombia, **2:**402, 404, 406
    Ecuador, **2:**414, 415, 421–22, 424, 427, *429*
    Nicaragua, **2:**757
    North America, **3:**730
    Peru, **2:**469, 478, 486
    Venezuela, **2:**528
bongos
    Africa, **1:**481
    Barbados, **2:**815
    Costa Rica, **2:**693
    Cuba, **2:**828, 830, 834–36
    Germany, **8:**656
    Netherlands Antilles, **2:**930
    Nicaragua, **2:**753
    North America, **3:**633, 726, 787, 792–93, 797
    in Nubian music, **6:**644
    Peru, **2:**476, 484, *485*
    Puerto Rico, **2:**934, 938
    South Asia, **5:**603, 652, 913
bonkó-enchemiyá, **2:**826
boom, **2:**925
botijas de barro, **2:**492
boula, **2:**870, 874–75, 876, 883, 959
boulè, **2:***916*, 918–19
bouñcì, **4:**375
boy, **1:**454–55
bubanj, **8:**950, 966
bubnjevi, **8:**967
būga, **6:**420
bul, **1:**568–69
bumbo, **2:**309
burburi, **5:**367, *367*
burro, **2:**528
buru, **2:**898
byò, **4:**375
cachimbo, **2:**825
caixa, **2:**309, 312, 313; **8:**582
caj, **2:**654
caja
    Argentina, **2:**252
    Bolivia, **2:**285, *287*
    Colombia, **2:**407
    Costa Rica, **2:**685, 686
    Cuba, **2:**825

Ecuador, **2:**415, 422
Guatemala, **2:**727
Panama, **2:**774–75
Peru, **2:**469, 478
Quechua and Aymara cultures, **2:**207, 210
caja chapaca, **2:**287
caja chayera, **2:**357, 361
Carib culture, **2:**23
cenţa, **5:**350, 351, 362, *362*, 363, 511, 513, 515, 885–86, 931, *932*, 936–39, 940–41, 943, 950
chenepri, **1:**316
chimbanguele, **2:**530–31, 536
China, **7:**201, 292
chin'go, **7:**829, 862
chinki, **2:**285
chivita, **2:**855
chǒlgo, **7:**829, 862
chwago, **7:**867
Cirebon, **4:**697
condonqueiro, **2:**309
conga (also *tumba*, *tumbador*), **3:**522, 726, 729, 785, 786, 788, 793, 803, 984
    in Barbados, **2:**815
    Costa Rica, **2:**691, 693
    Cuba, **2:**828, 830–31, 834–36
    Germany, **8:**656
    Guyana, **2:**445
    Netherlands Antilles, **2:**930
    Peru, **2:**476, 484
    Puerto Rico, **2:**934
    South Asia, **5:**347, 544, 582, 652, 970
    Surinam, **2:**509
    Virgin Islands, **2:**970
congo, **2:**775, 855, 955
Costa Rica, **2:**689
coupé, **2:**437
cruzao, **2:**530
cumaco (also *tambor grande*), **2:**528–29, 530, 536
cununo, **2:**34, 402, 404, 407, 414, 427
curbata, **2:**528, 530
cutter, **2:**959
cyas, **2:**898, 902–3
dadaiko, **7:**623–24
ḍaḍaň, **5:**795, 796, *797*
dāhinā, **5:**122, 339, 341–42
damāmeh, **5:**692
dammām, **6:**420, 653
danbolin, **8:**314
dandi, **1:**751
dannān, **6:**420
daouli, **8:**285, 1008, 1011–12
darabana, **8:**877
daulbas, **8:**960
daule, **5:**329, 363–64, 964, 967, *968*
daulle, **8:**993, 996
davil, **5:**949
davul, **3:**1199; **5:**360, 363; **6:***764*, 764–65, 767, 768, 816; **8:**280, 285
dehol, **6:**745, *745*, 749
dhāp, **5:**601
dhimay, **5:**702
dhog-dhog, **4:**646

drums: barrel, conical, or cylindrical (*continued*)
ḍhol, **5:***8, 273, 280,* 328, 346, 347, 360, *415,* 497; **6:**415
    Afghanistan, **5:**506
    Bhutan, **5:**489
    Europe, **8:**236
    Fiji, **5:**612–13, 614, *614*
    Gujarat, **5:**501, 625, 629
    Kashmir, **5:**685
    Madhya Pradesh, **5:**722
    Maharashtra, **5:**728
    North America, **3:**984; **5:**582
    North West Frontier Province, **5:**789–90
    Oceania, **9:**93–94
    Orissa, **5:**733
    Pakistan, **5:**275–76, 281, *282,* 283, 506, 755, *756*
    Punjab, **5:**500, 651, *651,* 763, *763,* 767, 768, 771
    Rajasthan, **5:**280, 640, 641, 647, 648
    Southeast Asia, **4:**521
    use in *bhangra,* **5:**426
    Uttar Pradesh, **5:**279
d'hol, **6:**729
ḍholak, **5:***115, 123, 236,* 342, 346, *403,* 472, 496, *496, 499,* 549, *549*
    Afghanistan, **5:***809*
    Bengal, **5:**505, *846*
    Bihar, **5:**502
    Gujarat, **5:**625, 629, 635
    Guyana, **5:**601, 602–3, *603*
    influence on *tabla,* **5:**123, 131, 133
    Kashmir, **5:**499
    Madhya Pradesh, **5:**723, 724, *724*
    Nepal, **5:**705
    North America, **3:**814, 815, *815,* 984, 1246; **5:**582
    Pakistan, **5:**506
    Punjab, **5:**500, 769, 77.1, 772
    Rajasthan, **5:**640, *640,* 641, 645
    South America, **2:**85–86, 443, 899, 958
    Tamil Nadu, **5:**913
    Trinidad, **5:**589, 590, 591
    use in *bhangra,* **5:**574
    use in devotional music, **5:**248, 644, 655
    use in film music, **5:**347, 534, 535
    Uttar Pradesh, **5:**660, 664–65, *665,* 666–67, 669–70, 673
ḍholakī, **5:**699
ḍholkī, **5:**651, 654, 656; **8:**236
dhool, **2:**899
dhopar, **5:***915*
dhūmsa, **5:**280
dīwī, **6:**420
dogdog (also *dog-dog*), **4:**697, 710
dohol, **5:**806, 835; **6:**828, 835, 839
doholak, **6:**881
dol, **4:**609, 611, 612, 621
doli (also *daphdaphi*), **8:**836, 838, 840, 842
ḍōlu, **5:**875, 876, 878, 884
Dominican Republic, **2:**859
doùpá, **4:**375
ḍuhl, **5:**774, 777, *778,* 780, 781, 782, 783
ḍukkur, **5:**774, 783
dumbak, **4:**829
dup, **2:**871

engalabi, **1:**218
fa'atete, **9:**869, 876–77, 880
fontomfrom, **1:**138, 227, 316, 464; **10:**29–36
foulé, **2:**437
fundeh, **2:**898, 904, 907
gaan doon, **2:**438
gagóma, **9:**508
galāl (also *gallāl*), **6:**270, 416
gandang, **4:**604, 609, 613, 898
gandang panjang, **4:**615, 619
ganga, **1:**313, 536, 541, 584, 591, 592, 594; **6:**487
gángan, **1:**475, 479
gangan, **1:**561
ganrang, **4:**805, 806
garaón, **2:**733
garavón, **2:**741, 752, *753*
garawoun, **2:**669, 671, 672, 674, 675, 676, 677
gâṭa bera, **5:**329, 364, 963, 964, *964*
gaval, **8:**863
geduk, **4:**404, 407, 412
gelāl, **6:**416
gendang
    Lombok, **4:**768–69, 772, 773
    Malaysia, **4:**104, 234, *405,* 407, 412, 413, 416, 421, 422, 424, 428, 429, 430, 433, 434, 436, 439, 829
    Singapore, **4:**520
    Sulawesi, **4:**806
    Sumatra, **4:**615, 617, 623, 624, 625, 626, 628
gendang anakna, **4:**607
gendang dua, **4:**625
gendang indungna, **4:**607
gendang lanang, **4:**768
gendang panjai (also *kandang panjai*), **4:**830
gendang panjang, **4:**615, 623
gendang penganak, **4:**615
gendang wadon, **4:**768
gendeang, **4:**618
Germany, **8:**656
geundrang, **4:**604
gimbal, **4:**924
gindang, **4:**628
goombay, **2:**803, 805–6, 808, 809–10
gordang, **4:**607
grande, **2:**530
grandy, **2:**897–98
gu, **7:**79, 312, 323, 330, *331*
gullu, **1:**455
gumbeh (also *boom drum*), **2:**677
ḥāgir, **6:**94, 95, *96, 97*
hājar, **6:**404, 420
hajir, **4:**625
hājir, **6:**657
Hawai'ian, **3:**527
Hmong funeral drum, **3:**1004
huancar, **2:**468
huéhuetl, **2:**550, 557–59, 601–2
ikko, **7:**623
iyesa, **2:**824
jènbe, **1:**489, 498
jidhor, **4:**655
jidur, **4:**413, 617, 625, 768, 774, 780
jiegu, **7:**111

jondo, **2:**774
ka, **2:**943, *944,* 946–47, 948–49
ka (also *gwoka*), **2:**877
kaḍime, **5:**916
kakko, **7:**572, 580, 621, 623, 626
kandang, **4:**829
kāsar, **6:**420
kāsir, **6:**676, *676–77,* 677
kata, **2:**870
katabung, **4:**615
katāngo, **6:**417
kateobak, **4:**613–14
katindiek, **4:**414
katuba, **8:**640
kbandu, **2:**898, 902
kendang, **2:**507; **3:**1012
    Bali, **4:**746, 748–49, 750, 751, 753, 754, 755
    Cirebon, **4:**692, 696, 697
    Sumatra, **4:**625
    Sumbawa, **4:**780, 781, 783, 784–85
    Sunda, **4:**701, 703, 706, 707, 709, 710, 718
kendang lanang, **4:**743, 744, 745
kendang mabarung, **4:**743
kendang wadon, **4:**743, 744, 745
kendhang, **4:**234, 470, 644, 645, 646, 648, 655, 666, 673–75
kendhang batangan, **4:**642, 649
kendhang bem, **4:**642
kendhang ciblon, **4:**103, 642, 649, 654, 661, 673, 674–75
kendhang gedhé, **4:**642
kendhang gendhing, **4:**642, 644, 662, 673–74
kendhang penunthung, **4:**642
kendhang wayang, **4:**643, 661, 674
kete, **1:**461, 464; **10:**78, 141
ketebong, **4:**829
ketipung, **4:**623, 624, 625, 627, 628, 642, 643, 644, 662, 675, 692
ketobung, **4:**615
kham, **5:**346
khīn, **5:**702
khol, **5:**346, 503, 732
    etymology of, **5:**356
khole, **5:**248, 253
kilu, **9:**384–85
kimbal, **4:**918
kinpar, **5:***915*
kirang, **1:**562
Kiribati, **9:***760,* 763
kirikaṭṭi, **5:**914
kittle, **2:**446
klawng chana, **4:**234–35, 249
klawng chum, **4:**311
klawng malayu, **4:**234
klawng nang, **4:**305
klawng pu ja, **4:**311
klawng seng (also *klawng jing; klawng tae*), **4:**319
klawng taphon, **4:**234
klawng that, **4:**233, 251
klawng tum, **4:**319
Kogi culture, **2:**185, 186
k'ojom (also *tampor*), **2:**653–54, 721, 722, 723, 726–27, *728*

kong, **4:**338
kong nyao, **4:**339, 341
kŏn'go, **7:**829
kong taphone, **4:**355
kong that, **4:**355, 358
kulanter, **4:**643
kungbi, **2:**661, 662
kuntalam, **5:**914
kutiridingo, **1:**136
kyobanggo, **7:**829
laba, **4:**793
laba dera, **4:**794
laba toda, **4:**794
laba wai, **4:**794
labu, **4:**800, 801
"Lambeg" drums, **8:**385
Landsknechttrommel, **8:**656
lanigi garawoun, **2:**669–73
lê, **2:**343, *345*
llamador, **2:**774, 778 (See also *tambor menor)*
lodër, **8:**996, 1001
ludag, **4:**918
mādal, **5:**703, *703,* 704, *704, 705,* 734, 862
maddalam, **5:**360, *360,* 361, 513, 514, 515, 931, 932–34, *933,* 950
maddale, **5:**885
makab, **6:**99
makè, **2:**918–19
makyè, **2:**874–75, 876
mandar, **5:**502
Manihiki, **9:**909
manman, **2:**883
maram, **5:**931, 933
marawis, **4:**624, 625
mardala, **5:**520
marwas, **4:**601, 605, 606, 616, 624, 625, 628, 816
mattalam, **5:**915
Maya culture, **2:**651
mba'e pu ovava'é, **2:**201
m'dinga, **1:**564
mewas, **4:**820
Mexico, **2:**14, 15
Middle East, **6:**7
military drums, **8:**331, 686
mina, **2:***527,* 528–29, 535
mirfa', **6:**94, *95,* 95–98, *97, 98*
mirwās, **6:**420, 546
     Bahrain and Qatar, **6:**404, 652
     Saudi Arabia, **6:**655
     Yemen, **6:**94, *95–98,* 657
Mixtec culture, **2:**565
molon, **5:**608, *608*
mongó (also *bongó),* **2:**855, 857
monkey, **2:**897–98
mrḍang, **5:**299, 342
mridang, **5:**503, 613–14, 693, 728, 733; **9:**94
mridangam, **5:**107, 149–59, *152,* 233, 235, 350, 356–58, *357,* 384, *391,* 513, 517
     as accompaniment instrument, **5:**157–58, 364, 522
     caste and, **5:**389
     in *cinna mēḷam* ensemble, **5:**104, 360, 913
     etymology of, **5:**356
     folk varieties, **5:**366
     functions of, **5:**324, 325

Goa, **5:**740
     North America, **3:**951, 983, 990, 1064, 1216
     organological studies on, **5:**307
     performance of, **5:**157–59, 326, 452
     relation to *pakhāvaj,* **5:**114
     sound recordings of, **5:**161
     Southeast Asia, **4:**66, 234, 470
     tani āvartanam solo, **5:**148, 158, 219, 223, 235, 356, 384
     training on, **5:**149–53, 157
     use in devotional music, **5:**222–23, 267, 581, 582
     use in film music, **5:**543, 555
     Uttar Pradesh, **5:**664
msondo, **1:**637
msōndō, **6:**417
mu'astī, **6:**420
mugulmānī, **5:**777, *778,* 780, 783
mula, **2:**825
mutumba, **1:**751
nafa, **9:**382, *383,* 790–91
nağara, **6:**925
nal, **3:**984
nāl, **5:**582
Native American types, **3:**6, 238, 367–68, 454–55, 456, 468, 476, 526, 1069
Nauru, **9:**716, 755–56
ngoma, **2:**825
nimaj k'ojom (also *tamborón),* **2:**727, 730
ninai daiko, **7:**623–24
nodo (pole drum), **7:***825,* 829
nogo, **7:**829
Oceania, **9:**96
     Western, **9:**41, 214
ôdaiko, **7:**654, 657, 659, 684
ògìdo, **1:**474, 479
okam, **9:**22
oulé (also *houlé; rouleur; ouleur),* **5:**609–10
oumalay (also *omele),* **2:**955
óuu, **2:**564
pahu, **9:**286, 289, *372,* 382, 384–85, 865, 869, 876–77, 880, 892, 895, 916, 917, 928, *956*
pahu matarua, **9:**904–5, 906
pahu tupa'i rima, **9:**869, 876
paigu, **7:**231
pailas, **2:**834–36
pakhāvaj, **5:**82, 111, *114–15,* 114–21, *121,* 122, 341, 342, *378*
     as accompaniment instrument, **5:**119, 164, 169
     etymology of, **5:**114
     Gujarat, **5:**633, 634
     influence on *tabla,* **5:**123, 131, 134
     Laṅgā performers of, **5:**402
     making of, **5:**114–15
     performance traditions of, **5:**120–21, 448
     Rajasthan, **5:**643
     recordings of, **5:**136
     repertoires for, **5:**117–19
     talas for, **5:**116–17
     use in devotional music, **5:**248, 251, 346
     use in *dhrupad* performance, **5:**197
     use in *kathak* ensemble, **5:**494

     use in *oḍissi* performance, **5:**520
     Uttar Pradesh, **5:**664
palo, **2:**104, 851, 853, 854
pa'má, **4:**369, 372
pampai, **5:**286, 911, 914, *914,* 915
par, **5:**912, 915
pashchima, **5:**505
pasu, **9:**827–28
pa'u, **9:**886, 900, 901, 902, 913
pa'u mangō, **9:**900, 901, 902, 913
petró, **2:***853,* 855
phon, **4:**305
phutu wankara, **2:**285
pikin doon, **2:**438
pipa, **2:**530
pole drums, **7:**98
Polynesia, East, **9:**384–85
pore, **5:**916
prenting, **2:**897–98, 902
prima, **2:**530
pujador, **2:**774–75
puk, **7:**67, *825,* 828–29, 873
     in *ch'anggŭk,* **7:**945
     in farmers' bands, **7:**828, 933–34
     notation for, **7:**937
     in *p'ansori,* **7:**828, 897, 944
     rhythmic patterns for, **7:**841–44
     in *samullori,* **7:**963–67
     in *sinawi,* **7:**890
pump, **2:**815
pumpu, **2:**285
pung, **5:**346, 494, 503, 504
pūniu, **9:***207,* 372, 382, 384–85, *956*
Purépecha culture, **2:**575–76
püt, **4:**305
quchana, **2:**285
quinjengue, **2:**348
quinto, **2:**831
qūs, **5:**692
rabga, **5:**502
raḥmānī, **6:**420, 676, *676–77,* 677
rebana ubi, **4:**424–25, 431
redoblante, **2:**511, 528, 537
repeater, **2:**898, 904, 907
repicador, **2:**774–75, 778, 937
repico, **2:**309
repique, **2:**309, 352
     in rock and roll, **3:**348
rum, **2:**32, 343, *345*
rumpi, **2:**343, *345*
sabak, **2:**632, 634, 635
sakhún, **4:**369
śakti, **5:**607, *607*
salidor, **2:**831
saliman, **2:**897–98
sambula, **2:**436
samhúda, **2:**177
sampho, **4:***164,* 168, 182, 183, 190, 203, 470
saŋba, **1:**329
sawng na, **4:**235, 266
seco, **2:**774
shkānga, **6:**417
side drum, **8:**364, 523, 527, 528, 810
sime daiko, **7:**684
sito, **4:**375–76
skin, **2:**903

drums: barrel, conical, or cylindrical (*continued*)
  skor chey, **4:**168
  skor thaun, **3:***999*
  skor thomm, **3:**1001; **4:***164*, 166–67, 183,
    190, 197
  skor yol, **4:**157
  snare drum
    Argentina, **2:**256, 258
    Barbados, **2:**815
    Brazil, **2:**329–30, 337, 352
    Europe, **8:**141
    Greece, **8:**1011, 1017
    Jamaica, **2:**907
    Mexico, **2:**558, 571, 572
    North America, **3:**385, 386, 463, 563, 564
    Oceania, **9:**382–83
    Peru, **2:**207, 210, 211, 478, *480*
    South America, **2:**34, *59*, 140
    Tamil Nadu, **5:**909, 926
    Uruguay, **2:**518
    Uttar Pradesh, **5:**671
    Virgin Islands, **2:**973
  sonador, **2:**937
  Southeast Asia, **4:**74
  śuddha maddaḷam, **5:**362
  sulibao, **4:**918
  surdo, **2:**309, 313, 330, 336, 337, 352; **9:**84
  suru, **2:***916*
  Switzerland, **8:**693
  tabıl, **6:**767
  ṭabl, **6:**415, 419–20, 665
    Arabian peninsula, **6:**360, 651, 653, *658*,
      659, 664, *666*
    Egypt, **6:**624, 628, 633
    Syria, **6:**566
    Turkey, **6:**115
    Yemen, **6:**94, 95, 656
  tabl, **1:**541
  ṭabla
    in Nubian music, **6:**642
    Palestine, **6:**636
  tabla, **1:**555, 571
  ṭabl al-leīwa, **6:**420
  al-ṭabl al-ṣaghīr, **6:**420
  ṭabl al-zār, **6:**420
  ṭabl baladī, **6:**283, 545, 631
  tabl baladi, **3:***1037*
  ṭabl bōga, **6:**99
  ṭabl marad, **6:**7, 99, *99*, 103–4
  ṭabl muʾaṣṭā, **6:**7, 99, *99*, 103–4
  ṭabl ṣāgh, **6:**99
  tabwrdd, **8:**348
  taiko, **7:**5, 551; **9:**97
    in *gagaku*, **7:**572, 623–24
    in *kabuki*, **7:**657
    in *nô*, **7:**634, 683
    North America, **3:**527, 970–71, 973, 1064,
      1096, 1248
    notation for, **7:**580, 624
    in Ryûkyû music, **7:**792
    syôga vocables for, **7:**626
    in *wayô gassô*, **7:**749–50
  taja, **2:**444
  tāla maddaḷe, **5:**879
  tali, **2:**682
  talot pot, **4:**311

  tambor, **2:**365, 469, 708, 728–29, 731, 742,
    757, 758, 759–61; **8:**593
  tambora, **3:**731, 773
    Brazil, **2:**285
    Colombia, **2:**378, 379, 384
    Dominican Republic, **2:***73*, *850*, *851*, 855,
      857, 860
    Puerto Rico, **2:**934
    Venezuela, **2:**528–30, 534, 536, 538–39,
      541
  tamboril, **2:**415, 511, 520; **3:**731, 849; **8:**171,
    583
  tamboril afrouruguayo, **2:**515–16
  tamborita, **2:**611
  tambor mayor (also *tambor macho*), **2:**402,
    405–6, *407*, 414
  tambor menor (also *tambor hembra*; *llamador*),
    2:402, 405–6, *407*
  tambor simple, **2:**706–7
  tambou (also *ka*), **2:**865
  tambour, **3:**1075; **8:**176–77
  tambourin, **8:**545
  tambou twavay, **2:**843
  tambú, **2:**928–29, 929
  tambu, **2:**307, 309, 348
  tambul, **4:**900, 917
  tambur, **4:**743
  tam-tam, **2:**445
  tamunango, **2:**536, 541
  tanbores, **2:**855
  tanbou bas a dé fas, **2:**876
  tanbou bas a yon fas, **2:**876
  tanbou bélé, **2:**841
  tanbou chan, **2:**876
  tanbou lélé, **2:**843
  tapan, **3:**926, 1198; **8:**201, *280*, 280–81, 285,
    944, 951, 975–76, 977, *977*, 981,
    982, 983
  taphon, **4:**233–34, *242*, 251–52, 253, 257,
    266, 302, 548
  taphone, **4:**354
  taphon mawn, **4:**234
  tapon, **4:**358
  tarija, **6:**489
  taʾriya, **1:**541
  tarol, **2:**329, 336
  tarola, **2:**565
  tavil, **5:**270, 323–24, 360, 363, 912, *914*,
    916, 926
    caste and, **5:**390
    in Karnatak music, **5:**161, 210, 212, 234,
      393–95, 452
    in *kēṭṭi mēḷam* ensemble, **5:**275, 286
    in *naiyāṇṭi mēḷam* ensemble, **5:**914
    in *periya mēḷam* ensemble, **5:**103, 359, *359*,
      387, 912, 932
    Sri Lanka, **5:**958
  tbel, **6:**498
  teng thing, **4:**311
  tenor drum, **8:**562, 654, 656
  tifa, **4:**812, 816–20
  tifa gila, **4:**814
  tifa kot, **4:***820*
  tifa laai, **4:***820*
  timbaletas, **2:**693
  ṭīmbuk, **5:**774, 777, *778*, 780, 782, 783

  tin drum, **2:**656
  tipung, **4:**413
  toba mare, **8:**877
  tom-tom, **2:**693, 803; **5:**909, 913
  toom, **4:**211
  toppi maddaḷam, **5:**513
  Torres Strait Islands, **9:**489, 508
  tres-dos, **2:**831
  trống bát nhã, **4:**467, 469, 504
  trống cái, **4:**469
  trống chầu (also *trống dại cổ*), **4:**469,
    492
  trống chầu ca trù, **4:**469–70
  trống chiến, **4:**470, 492
  trống cơm, **4:**470
  trống nhạc, **4:**470
  tumao, **2:**505, 506
  tumba; *tumbador* (*See* conga)
  tum-tum, **2:**815
  tun, **2:**438
  tŭpan, **8:***164*, 280, 284, *893*, 893–94, 895,
    897, 900, 902
  turi daiko, **7:**623–24
  in Ukrainian music, **3:**1242
  urume, **5:**880
  Virgin Islands, **2:**970
  vota, **8:**863
  wancar, **2:**37–38
  wankara, **2:**207, 285, 469
  xămphô, **4:**215
  yak bera (also *devol bera*; *ruhunu bera*), **5:***961*,
    961–62, 964
  yonggo, **7:***825*, 829
  yuka, **2:**825
  zabumba, **2:**329–30, 332, 335, 337, 347
  zambumbia (snare drum), **2:**714
drums: drum-chimes
  entenga, **1:**312, 601
  patt waìñ, **4:**548
  pa'waìñ, **4:***367*, *368*
  taganing, **4:**607
drum sets, **4:**606; **5:**582; **8:**225, 234
  Afghanistan, **5:**810
  Albania, **8:**286, 997
  in Arab music, **6:**422
  Argentina, **2:**274
  Bahamas, **2:**806, 808
  Barbados, **2:**815, 820
  Belgium, **8:**531
  in *bhangra*, **5:**574
  boeng mang kawk, **4:**235
  Bolivia, **2:**298
  Bulgaria, **8:**284
  with *changgo*, **7:**831
  Egypt, **6:**555
  Guyana, **5:**604
  hcau'loùnpa', **4:**369, *370*
  Ireland, **8:**390
  Israel, **6:**1073
  Kosovo, **8:**286
  Macedonia, **8:**282, 976–77, 980
  Mandailing people, **4:**607
  Mexico, **2:**613
  Montenegro, **8:**960
  Nepal, **5:**705
  Nicaragua, **2:**754

North America
  in Albanian bands, **3:**927
  in Arctic communities, **3:**380
  in Cajun and Creole music, **3:**858
  in Cambodian rock bands, **3:**1002
  in churches, **3:**125
  in *conjunto* music, **3:**723, 772, 773, 775, 776
  in Danish music, **3:**882
  in Finnish music, **3:**874
  in Greek bands, **3:**930
  in Hispano music, **3:**762
  in Iranian music, **3:**1035
  in Irish music, **3:**845
  in Lao popular music, **3:**1009
  in Macedonian bands, **3:**925, 926
  in Mexican music, **3:**746
  in *mini-djaz* groups, **3:**803
  in polka bands, **3:**529, 824, 891, 893, 894,
    895, 898, 901, 1195
  in rock, **3:**95, 285
  in rock and roll, **3:**80
  in salsa, **3:**788
  in Slovak dance bands, **3:**900
  in South Asian music, **3:**984
  in *tamburitza* orchestra, **3:**920
  in Tohono O'odham *waila*, **3:**436, 473, 490
  in Ukrainian music, **3:**914
  West African rhythms for, **3:***337*
  in Nubian music, **6:**642
  with *puk*, **7:***968*
  in *rebetika* ensembles, **8:**206
  Réunion Island, **5:**609
  Scotland, **8:**365
  Serbia, **8:**952
  Sri Lanka, **5:**971
  Sweden, **8:**442
  Tamil Nadu, **5:**924
  Ukraine, **8:**811
drums: frame
  adok, **4:**414, 609, 613
  adufe, **2:**329, 727; **3:**1197; **8:**577, *577*, 582,
    594
  Albania, **8:**194, *195*
  allun (also *tallunt*), **6:**486, 488, 489
  aluan, **4:**817
  Arab world, **6:**418–19
  aravāna, **5:**948
  Arctic types, **3:**375–76
  Argentina, **2:**251
  babala, **2:**924
  bandīr, **6:**326–27, 519, 633
  bangu, **3:**960, 961
  bas (also *tanbourin*), **2:**883
  bebana, **4:**616
  bebano, **4:**615
  bendêr, **6:**745
  bendir (also *bendīr*), **1:**537, 541, 543; **3:**1199;
    6:192, 276, 418, 476, 498, 799
  al-bendīr al-ʿĪsāwī, **6:**418
  binbir halka, **8:**967
  bodhrán, **3:**326, 842; **8:**354, 385, 391
  bombo (*See under* drums: barrel, conical, or
    cylindrical)
  brai, **4:**687, 695–96
  buben z brazhotkami, **8:**797, *798*
  bubon, **8:**810–11

caja (*See under* drums: barrel, conical, or
  cylindrical)
caṅg, **5:**671
cassella, **8:**571
cēvai palakai, **5:**915
Cham people, **3:***997*
chăṅg, **5:**642, 648
China, **7:**191, 292
cykace, **8:**704
ḍaf, **5:**346
daf, **1:**541; **5:**692, *813*, 828, 830, 831
daff, **5:**948, 958; **6:**418
  in Arab-American ensembles, **6:**282, 283
  Arabian peninsula, **6:**644
  in Arab music, **6:**180, 186, 692, 694, 698
  Iraq, **6:**8, 312
  Lebanon and Syria, **6:**91
  Palestine, **6:**586, 591
daff zinjārī, **6:**418
daflī, **5:***725*
dāʾirā, **5:**305, 310; **6:**566
daire, **6:**115, 192, 745
daire (also *dajre*), **8:**281, 282, 894, 895, 979,
  993, 994
dāire, **6:**8, 828, 833, 848
dairea, **8:**877
dāireh, **5:***620*, 812, 813, *813*, 815, 818, 820,
  822–23, *823*, 826, 828, 831
dāire-zangī, **6:**828
damḍi, **5:**869, *874*
dammām, **6:**419
dap, **4:**618; **6:**999
daph, **5:**500, 642, 671, 712
daphalā, **5:**671
daphi (also *daira*), **8:**837–38, 840
ḍappu, **5:**896
dappu, **5:**870
dara, **8:**877
dāya, **6:***898*
dāyere, **6:**138
dāyra, **6:**902, 919, 943, 946
deblek, **6:**763, 764, *764*, 765, *765*, 766
def
  Algeria, **6:**476
  Europe, **8:**285–86, 952, 960, 967, 993,
    994, 997
  Iran, **6:**825, 834
  Kurdistan, **6:**745
  in Turkish art music, **6:**774, *774*
  in Turkish folk music, **6:**763, 766
dəf, **6:**8, 925
deff, **6:**419, 498
deff qabāʾilī, **6:**419
defi, **8:**1010, 1012, 1019
dendoun toaurgī, **6:**419
dep, **4:**619–20
ḍhyāṅgro, **5:**290
doba, **8:**877, 880
dohol, **5:**814, 820–22
duff, **3:**1218; **5:**506, 722; **6:**395, 398
  Andalusia, **6:**445
  Arabian peninsula, **6:**295, 296, 359,
    360–61, *658*
  Syria, **6:**566
  Yemen, **6:**94
erebane, **6:**745

Europe, **8:**169
əkänzam, **1:**585, 591
folk varieties, **5:**365
galleta, **2:**836
gembyung, **4:**687, 695
genda, **4:**794
gendang hadrah, **4:**409
gendang ibu, **4:**408, *418*
gendang penganak, **4:**408, *418*
gendang peningkah, **4:**408, 409
genjring, **4:**687, 695
ghirbāl, **6:**360–61, 696
gievrie, **8:**305, 307
goombeh, **2:**897–98, 902, 903
grajcary, **8:**704
Gujarati, **5:**7
Gulf region, **6:**709
guwel, **4:**605
hadrah, **4:**519
Haiti, **2:**887
halage, **5:**878
hets, **7:**1015–16
iduffu, **1:**637
indang, **4:**611
Israel, **6:**1020
Jammu and Kashmir, **5:**499, *499*
Japan, **7:**617
jùjú, **1:**478
kahco, **7:**787
kajalī, **5:**613; **9:**94
kañcīrā, **5:**906
kāñjanī, **5:**732
kañjarī, **5:**346, 723
kañjīrā, **3:**984, *991*; **5:**149, 235, 357, 364,
  452, 582, *643*, 671
kāsir mufaltah, **6:**418–19
kencane, **4:**615
kerincingan, **4:**625
khanjarī, **5:**647–48
khanjiri, **5:**728
klawng dung, **4:**320
klawng düng nong, **4:**311
kompang, **4:**424, 431, 519, 520, 616
Kurdistan, **6:**745
Lithuania, **8:**512
Malta, **8:**639
Manchu people, **7:**520
mard, **6:**419
Martinique, **5:**595
mazhar, **3:**1218
  in Egyptian music, **6:**170, *170*, 171, 418,
    545, 626, 627
  in Turkish art music, **6:**774
  in Turkish folk music, **6:**763
Middle Eastern, **6:**18
mizhar, **6:**418
Mongol people, **7:**1017
Native American types, **3:**6, 425, 456,
  475–76, 526
ncomane, **1:**711
ngā, **5:**704
North America, **3:**1220
Northwest Coast types, **3:**396, 397, 399, 401
odap, **4:**608
Oman, **6:**679
pandareta, **2:**391

drums: frame (*continued*)
pandeireta, **8:**582
pandeiro, **2:**309, 312, 326, 327, 329, 334,
    336, 346, 349; **8:**582; **9:**84
pandereta, **2:**934; **3:***716, 726*, 727; **8:**593
pandero, **2:**609, *852*, 855, 857; **8:**314, 968
parai (also *pirai*), **5:**367, 910, 915–16, 926
pare, **5:**877
Poland, **8:***705*
puk, **9:**99
qanqa, **6:**419
qaval, **6:**845, *845*, 846, 848, 851, 925
rabana, **4:**815
rabāna, **5:**964–65, 969, 970
rabaneo, **4:**618
rabano, **4:**414, *609*, 611
rammana, **4:**233, *244, 246*, 266–68, 303, 309
rammana lam tat, **4:**299
rapaʾi, **4:**604, 611
rapaʾi daboïh, **4:**604
rapaʾi Pase (also *rapaʾi urok*), **4:**604
rapaʾi peulot (also *geurimphang*), **4:**604
ratip, **4:**783, 785
rebana
    Borneo, **4:**825
    Lombok, **4:**768
    Malaysia, **4:**408, 409, 410–11, 415, 420,
        421, 422, 423, 424, 427, 431, 433,
        434, 436, 439
    Maluku, **4:**812, 814, 816–17, 818
    Sulawesi, **4:**805, 806, 810
    Sumatra, **4:**598, 601, 606, 616, 617, 618,
        619, 624, 625, 628
    Sumbawa, **4:**780, 781–82, 783, 784
rebana kercing, **4:**431
redap, **4:**421, 619, 620, 621, 623
redep, **4:**625
rika, **1:**427
riqq, **1:**552, 556, 571; **6:**418
    in Arab-American ensembles, **3:**1032, 1218;
        6:282
    Egypt, **6:**8, 91, 148, 317, 547, 555, 559,
        561, 616, 623
    Lebanon, **6:**554
    Yemen, **6:**94
rnga, **5:**712, 713, 714, *714*
rumanea, **4:**168, 169, 175, 183, 184
ṣaḥfa, **6:**94, 419
sákárà, **1:**475
samā, **5:**780, 783
sámbà, **1:**478
samba, **1:**404
Siberia, **7:**1027–28
simbolo, **8:**930
skor rumanea, **3:***999*
skor yike, **4:**167
sogo, **7:***825*, 829, 886, 933–34
someak, **3:**476
South Asia, **5:***304*
in South Asian music, **3:**984
Southeast Asia, **4:**74
Spain, **8:**589, 593
Subarctic types, **3:**384–85, *385*, 386, 388,
    1063, 1276, 1280
in Sufi devotions, **6:**19
taar, **1:**556, 557

tabaṭk, **5:**912, 915, *915*
tabeteke, **5:**366
ṭabl al-ʿardha, **6:**418–19
tabuh rebana, **4:**628
tamaṭe, **5:**875, 876, 877
tamble (also *chamba; dar; daryal*), **5:**787, 789,
    790
tamborim, **2:**309, 313
tamboro, **4:**805
tambourin, **2:**437
tambourina, **2:**899
tambourine
    Antigua, **2:**798
    Argentina, **2:**259, 276
    Barbados, **2:**815, 817
    Belize, **2:**677
    Brazil, **2:**305, 327, 334–35
    Carriacou, **2:***871*, 872
    Chile, **2:**360
    Colombia, **2:**384
    Dominica, **2:**842
    Europe, **8:**142–43, 145, 170, *195*, 331,
        517, 656
    Grenada, **2:**865
    North America, **3:**184, 543, 563, 616, 674,
        981
    Puerto Rico, **2:**939–40
    South Asia, **5:**248, 579, 671
    Southeast Asia, **4:**438
    Trinidad and Tobago, **2:**959
tambur, **4:**772, 805
tamburello, **8:**609, *610*, 614, 615
tamburin, **4:**624
tamburini, **8:**609, 615
tampiang, **4:**815, 817
tampoutsia, **8:**1031
tamrin, **4:**625
tamurin, **4:**624
tanbou dibas, **2:**876–77
tanbouwen, **2:**946
tanbur, **8:**640
tapou, **5:**595, *595*, 607, *607*, 608–9
tappaṭṭai, **5:**904, 908, *908*, 910, 915
tappū, **5:**602
ṭār, **1:**552
ṭār (also *tar; tār*), **1:**535, 541, 546; **6:**418,
    519, 545, *545*
    Algeria, **6:**269, 270, 468, 470
    in Andalusian music, **6:**407, 454, 457, 460
    Arabian peninsula, **6:**651, 653, *659*, 664,
        666
    in Arab music, **6:**692, 693, 694, 698, 699,
        702
    Egypt, **6:**628, 629, *629*
    in Maghribi Jewish ensembles, **6:**1043
    Morocco, **6:**499
    North America, **3:**1045
    in Nubian music, **6:**641, 644, 645
    Oman, **6:**675, *678*
    Palestine, **6:**591, *1041*
    Saudi Arabia, **6:***657*
    Southeast Asia, **4:**410–11, 431, 433, 768
    in Tunisian Jewish music, **6:**527
    in Tunisian *maʾlūf*, **6:**326, 327, 328, 329,
        502
    Yemen, **6:**94

ṭbel, **6:**419
tep, **8:**863
terbang, **4:**623, 627, 628, 632, 634, 646, 647,
    655, 675, 687, 701, 710
terbangan, **4:**624, 625, 626
teueigan, **3:**1074
tinya, **2:**206, 211, 212, 218, 223, 469, 475,
    477, 478
toombah, **2:**798
trebang, **4:**687, 696
vuvă, **8:**877
wan, **7:**478
women's performance on, **8:**197
Yaqui culture, **2:**590
zap, **4:**625
zhirga, **8:**863
drums: friction, **8:**140, 169, 651
buhai, **8:**870, 877
burczybas, **8:**704
Central Africa, **1:**671
cuíca, **2:**309, 313, 378; **9:**84
dera, **5:**727
eltzagor, **2:**415
Flanders, **8:**544
furruco (also *furro*), **2:**378, 531, 538–39
Germany, **8:**655
gudalo, **8:**916–17
Hungary, **8:**743
Italy, **8:**609
juco, **2:**757
kinfuiti, **2:**825
llamador del tigre, **2:**740
onça, **2:**335
pignatu, **8:**571
puerca (also *marrano*), **2:**378, 384
puíta, **2:**309
putipù, **8:**615
rommelpot, **1:**703; **2:**378; **8:***526*, 526–27
rumlepotte, **8:**455
sacabuche (also *zambomba*), **2:**742
sarronca, **8:**582
Spain, **8:**589
tambor onça, **2:**347
ximbomba, **2:**415; **8:***590*
zambomba (also *zambumbia*), **2:**378, 391, 414,
    415, 531, 727
zavzava, **8:**640
drums: goblet
    Afghanistan, **6:**6
agwāl, **6:**489
apentemma, **2:**505
apinti, **2:**505–6
dabakan, **4:**892–93
dafbuka, **6:**1043
dalūka, **1:**555, 556, 558, 562, 606
darabuka, **4:**233; **8:**284–85, 894, 959, 960,
    979
    in Sephardi music, **6:**204
darabukka, **3:**953, 1032, 1037, 1199, 1218,
    1220
    in Andalusian music, **6:**457, 460
    in Arab-American ensembles, **6:**282
darbakke, in Palestinian music, **6:**576,
    578
darbeka, in Yemenite Jewish music, **6:**266
darbouka, **8:**233

darbuka, **8**:442
  in Arab music, **6**:692, 698, 699
  in Turkish music, **6**:250, 763, 799
darbūka, **6**:416, 519
  in Algeria, **6**:269, 407, 454, 468, 470, 474
  in Tunisian Jewish music, **6**:526, 527–28, 529
darbukka, **5**:748
  in Tunisian *ma'lūf*, **6**:326, 328, 329
deblek, **6**:763
derbuka, **1**:535, 541, 546; **6**:499
derbūka, **6**:*657*
djembe, **1**:420; **3**:1063
dombak, **4**:233
dombak (*tonbak*), **3**:953, 1034
dubakan, **4**:896–97
dumbah, **1**:427
dumbak, **3**:1045; **6**:682
dumbeg, **3**:1032
dumbuk, **6**:8, 312, 416, 552
dumbuq, **6**:94, *97*
durbakkih, **6**:586, 587, 589, 590, 591
gedombak, **4**:616
gedumbak, **4**:404, *405*, 412, *418*
gumaṭe, **5**:877
gumatt, **5**:737, *737*, 738, *739*
gummeṭa, **5**:893, *894*, 899, 900, 901
kantrüm, **4**:211, 213
Karen people, **4**:546
klawng yao, **4**:303, 319
kūbah, **6**:360
Lahu people, **4**:540
lamba, **4**:788, 789, *794*
Macedonia, **8**:980
madif, **6**:417
msōndō (also *msūndū*), **6**:417
òzi, **4**:304, *375*
pīpa, **6**:417
qypi, **8**:997
skor arakk, **4**:166, 194, 196, *197*
skor chhaiyaim, **3**:*19*; **4**:167, 199, 304
skor dai, **4**:194
ṭabla, **6**:416, 559
tabla, **6**:545, 552
tablih, **6**:586
tarabuka, **3**:926; **8**:*144, 176,* 281, *281,* 282, 286, 951, 997
t'arija, **6**:416, 499, 500
thap, **4**:265, 305, 412
thaun, **4**:168–69, 175, 183, 184
thon, **4**:233, *244, 246,* 265, 266–68, 299, 305
thon din paho, **4**:320
tifa podo, **4**:814, 816
tombak, **6**:138, 140
tuku, **1**:375
tumbaknarī, **5**:476, 683–84, 685
zarb (also *zarb*), **6**:8, 825, 828, 833, 925
zirbaghali, **5**:818, 820, *821*, 822, 828, 830, 831
drums: hourglass
  àdàmǫ, **1**:474, 476, 481, 484
  African, **5**:360
  asig, **9**:742
  Asmat people, **9**:191
  ban thaw, **4**:247

batá, **2**:32, 824; **3**:729, 785
bòng, **4**:469
Cape York (Australia), **9**:411, 412, 428, *429*, 430, 488
chaja, **9**:503
changgo (also *changgu*), **7**:798, *825, 842*
  construction of, **7**:828
  in court and *chŏngak* music, **7**:828, 866–69
  in farmers' bands, **7**:822, 828, 933–34
  in folk song accompaniment, **7**:880, 881, 885
  in *kagok*, **7**:921, 922
  in *kasa*, **7**:927
  in *kkoktu kakshi*, **7**:944
  notation for, **7**:55, 837, 937
  Oceania, **9**:99
  rhythmic patterns for, **7**:815–16, 841–44
  in *samullori*, **7**:963–67
  in *sanjo*, **7**:822, 913–17, 957
  in shaman rituals, **7**:986
  in *sijo*, **7**:925
  in *sinawi*, **7**:889–91
  sizes of, **7**:828, 831
  use in folk dances, **7**:67
  vocal imitation of, **7**:817
dakke, **5**:884
dalagu, **7**:111
damar, **7**:1017
ḍamaru, **4**:247; **5**:110, 325, 346, 365, *367,* *485,* 714, *714,* 722, 966
damaruo (skull drum), **7**:477
darabukka, **4**:623, 627, 630
dhāk, **5**:292
dhudak (also *dahanki*), **5**:722
donno, **1**:465
doodo, **1**:449
doumbeleki, **3**:930, 931
duḍi, **5**:887
dùndún, **1**:106–7, 404, 411, 413, 471, 472, 474, *477,* 480, 484
dutangu, **7**:111
ehuru, **2**:189, 191–92, 197
gendang keling, **4**:*415*
in goddess spirit-possession rituals, **5**:291
gomboy, **1**:455
gongs, **9**:582
gungonga, **1**:455
hudka, **5**:613; **9**:94
huḍki, **5**:291
huḍukka, **5**:346
huṛuk, **5**:*304,* 305
iḍakku, **5**:363
Irian Jaya, **9**:486, 581, 589, 591, 592
iṭaykka, **5**:360, 361, 363, 513, 931, 932, *932,* 933–34, 940–41
itótele, **2**:824
iyá, **2**:824
jauje, **1**:449
jiegu, **7**:42
kalangu, **1**:448, 449
kànàngó, **1**:136, 485
khashba, **6**:416
klawng düng nong (also *klawng ae*), **4**:311
klawng u je, **4**:311
kòotsoo, **1**:449, 524–28
kōṭānki, **5**:904

ko tuzumi, **7**:695
  in *kabuki*, **7**:657
  in *kyôgen*, **7**:636, 683
  in *nô*, **7**:551, 553, 624, 634, 683
  notation for, **7**:581, 590
  symbolism of, **7**:546
kuangruzai, **7**:499, *499*
kundus, **9**:*146*, 149, 152, 197, 245, 382, 476
  Anêm people, **9**:615
  Bali and Vitu islands, **9**:608, 609–11
  Buang people, **9**:566, 567
  Cape York, **9**:488
  clay, **9**:548
  distribution of, **9**:383, 570, 600–601, 630
  diwaka, **9**:489
  Eastern Highlands region, **9**:530, 532–33
  Enga people, **9**:50, *242,* 534
  Highland regions, **9**:512–13
  Huli people, **9**:299, 537
  Iatmul people, **9**:554–56
  Irumu people, **9**:568, 571
  Japanese ban on, **9**:28
  kaang, **9**:550
  Kaulong people, **9**:617, *618*
  Komba people, **9**:571–72
  Kuman people, **9**:523, 525
  laiyane, **9**:536
  lambu, **9**:619
  Mamose region, **9**:*280,* 547, 549
  Milne Bay Province, **9**:498
  napareaua, **9**:613–14
  nditing, **9**:518–20
  New Britain, **9**:600, 621, 623
  New Ireland, **9**:600–601, 626–27, *628,* 629
  Nissan Atoll, **9**:*596,* 632, 635–37, 639
  Oro people, **9**:332
  Papua New Guinea, **9**:*599*
  Papuan region, **9**:489, 490
  Rai Coast, **9**:563
  Sepik Hills people, **9**:558
  Sepik region, **9**:547
  tàbage, **9**:541
  Trans-Fly region, **9**:507–8
  Umboi Island, **9**:574–76
  use in Christian music, **9**:195
  use in dance, **9**:481–83
  wajuq, **9**:560
  waŋgäm, **9**:570
  Yupno people, **9**:304, 545
lunga, **1**:452, *454*
maoyuangu, **7**:111
Marshall Islands, **9**:753
Maya culture, **2**:651, 667
Micronesia, **9**:716
Middle Eastern, **6**:18
mukupela, **1**:670, 673
oggu, **5**:896
okonkolo, **2**:824
ô tuzumi
  in *kabuki*, **7**:657
  in *kyôgen*, **7**:636, 683
  in *nô*, **7**:551, 624, 634, 683
  notation for, **7**:581, 590
  symbolism of, **7**:546
pantañ (also *panatañ*), **2**:750, 751
Papua New Guinea, **9**:*470,* 496

drums: hourglass (*continued*)
redondo, **2:**528–30, 535, 539
san no tuzumi, **7:***47*, 621, 624, 626, *627*
in Shiva depictions, **5:**301
ṭabla, in Egyptian music, **6:**170, *170*, 616
tama, **1:**422, 446
timila, **5:**360, *360*, 931, 933, 940–41
Torres Strait Islands, **9:***412*
toubeleki, **8:**1015
toumberleki, **9:**73
uḍakkai, **5:**293
udakki, **5:**966
uḍukkai, **5:**368, 544, 904, 908, 926, 950
ulké (also *bobine*), **5:**607
urumi, **5:**544, *914*, 915
drums: kettledrums and pot drums
angu'á, **2:**200–201
Antigua and Barbuda, **2:**799
Arabian peninsula, **6:**405, 417–18
Argentina, **2:**251
atabales, **2:**589, 708, 724
ban, **1:**489
bayān, **5:**122, *328*, 339, 341–42
bāza, **6:**417, 626
bher, **5:**346, 760
bummâḍiya, **5:**367
cassella, **8:**572
Central African Republic, **1:**664–66
cifte-na'ire, **6:**115
damāhā, **5:**699
ḍāmal, **5:**795, 796, *797*
daman, **5:**712, *712*
dhamsa, **5:**497
dhankī, **5:**366
ḍigaṛī, **5:**679
diplipito, **8:**838
ḍuggī, **5:**340, 671
ḍugi, **5:**328, 503, 859, *860*
ḍukkaṛ, **5:**340
dul, **5:**692
duma, **1:**564
dumduma, **6:**7, 98–99, *99*, 103
El Salvador, **2:**707
ērtabaṭk, **5:**278, 915
əttebel, **1:**538
gaṭasiṅgāri, **5:**544
gendang nobat, **4:**615
gendang rebana, **4:**768, 774
gobdas, **8:**305, 307
gosha-nagara, **8:**838
gundwa, **6:**417
igba, **1:**459
k'ayum, **2:**656, 657
khurḍak, **5:**340, 671, 679
kös, **6:**115, 767
kudüm, **6:**192, 769, 774; **8:**967
kuenda, **6:**417
kultrún, **2:**234, 236, 238, 252, 254, 358–59
kurktu, **6:**418
leleng, **1:**569
marfa', **6:**655
Middle East, **6:**7
milāvu, **5:**363, *363*, 510, 511, 931, 933
mirfa', **6:**7, 94, 95, 98–99, *99*, 99–100, *101*, 103, 104–6, 417
mishkāl, **6:**417

musundu, **6:**678, *678*, 679
nagara, **1:**564; **2:**85; **8:**838
nagārā, **5:**602, 605
nagāṛā, **5:**342, 346, 496, *496*, 497, 502
Rajasthan, **5:**642
Uttar Pradesh, **5:***665*
in Uttar Pradesh, **5:**671, 674
nagarāt, **6:**468
nagare, **5:**700
nagarit, **1:**565, 601
naggaro, **1:**565–66, 568
naghāra, **6:**940
naghārāt, **6:**418, 454
nakkare, **6:**767
naqqāra, **1:**552, 558–59, 565; **6:**395, 417–18
Iraq, **6:**8, 312
Morocco, **6:**498
Syria, **6:**566
Tunisia, **6:**326, 327, 328, 329, 502
naqqāra, **5:***115*, 122, *123*, 279, 280, *304*, 346, 401
depictions of, **5:**305
influence on *tabla*, **5:**123, 131, 133
Kashmir, **5:**685
Laṅgā performers of, **5:**402
Pakistan, **5:**506, *764*
use in film music, **5:**347
naqqāre, **6:**835
naqrazān, **6:**631
nehara, **4:**429, 430
nihas, **1:**561
noggaara, **1:**554–55
Ocenaia, **9:**382
pañcamukha vādyam, **5:**365
pera, **5:**949
pūniu, **9:**916
qoṣa-nagara, **6:**925
rebana, **4:**768, 776, 780, 781–82
sarma, **1:**564
Senufo people, **1:**454
ṭabaīla, **6:**417
ṭabl, **6:**417
tablak (also *dumbul*), **8:**838, 840
ṭabla tījaniyya, **6:**417
ṭabl bāz, **6:**417
tāca, **5:**915
tācśe, **5:**886
tagennewt, **6:**417
talambas (also *dulbas*), **8:**960, 967
tambari, **1:**449
tambor, **2:**724
tammâṭṭa, **5:**329, 363, 364, 367, 967–68, *969*
tamukku, **5:**367, 914, *914*
ṭanjara, **6:**417
tāś, **5:**346
ṭāsa, **6:**94, 95, 99–100, *101*, 104–6, 417, 655
tasa, **4:**611, 612, 621
tāshā, **5:**279, *280*, 283, *285*, *299*
tassa, **2:**85–86, 444, 445, 899, 957, 959; **3:**815–16, *816*, 1208
tāssā, **5:**589–90, 601
tataun, **9:**500
tazâwat, **1:**541, 590
tbel, **1:**537, 540, 541, 543, 544
tbila, **6:**498
tegennewt, **1:**541, 591, 594

terbana, **4:**743, 768, 776
terbang, **4:**768, 776
timbale, **5:**428
timbales, **2:**353, 484, *485*, 708, 834–36; **3:**787, 788, 794–95, 797
timki, **5:**724
timpani, **3:**795
tumble, **1:**561
ṭungura, **6:**7, 99
tyāmko, **5:**699
Vanuatu, **9:**693
zevu, **1:**399
drums, log. *See* slit-drums
drums, paired
bàndiirii, **1:**521
kori, **1:**455
pambajōḍu, **5:**894–96, *895–96*, 901
sammēla, **5:**886
shatam, **1:**556
tabla, **5:***4*, *55*, *62*, *122*, *123*, *133*, *204*, *335*, *339*, 341–42; **10:***9*, *10*
as accompaniment instrument, **5:**132, 188, 195
Afghanistan, **5:**806, 815, 818, 822–23, *823*, 828, 830, 835, 837, 840
Andhra Pradesh, **5:**896
Balochistan, **5:**783
depictions of, **5:**307
in devotional music, **5:**248, 251, 364, 556–57, 582, 644, 655
in *dhrupad* performance, **5:**197
dokra, **5:**688, *688*, 694
dūkarah, **5:**693
Egypt, **6:**148
evolution of, **5:**121–23
in film music, **5:**534, 535, 543, 555
functions of, **5:**82, 325, 335
in *ghazal* performance, **5:**186
Gujarat, **5:**629, 633, 634, 635
Guyana, **2:**443–44; **5:**602, 604
Hindustani traditions of, **5:**111, 121–34
Jamaica, **2:**899
Karnataka, **5:**869
in Karnatak music, **5:**351
in *kathak* ensemble, **5:**494
Kerala, **5:**948
in *khyāl* performance, **5:**171–72
laggī performance, **5:**128, 181–83, 186, 198
Laṅgā performers of, **5:**402
Malaysia, **4:**427, 433, 438, 439
Nepal, **5:**702, 705
North America, **3:**339, 340, 951, 981, 983, 984, 1246
North West Frontier Province, **5:***791*
in Nubian music, **6:**644
Pakistan, **5:**746, *752*, 753
at Pakistani-American weddings, **5:**579
performance of, **5:**326, 448, 575
performance schools of, **5:**133–34
in pop *bhajan* genre, **5:**549
Punjab, **5:**762, 765, 768, 769, 771, 772
Rajasthan, **5:**642, *648*
in *rās līlā* dance-drama, **5:**495
recordings of, **5:**137
repertoires for, **5:**127–32
research on, **5:**136

Réunion Island, **5:**608
  in rock music, **5:**428
  in *śahnāī* ensemble, **5:**340
  Sikh use of, **5:**13, 257
  Singapore, **4:**520
  sound and technique of, **5:**124
  South Africa, **5:**618
  status of, **5:**378–79
  ṭabl, **5:**693
  Tamil Nadu, **5:**909, 913, 926
  in *ṭhumrī* performance, **5:**179–82
  Trinidad, **5:**591
  Uttar Pradesh, **5:**670
  women performers, **5:**207–8
drums: plucked, **5:**328–29
  ānandalaharī, **5:**328, 329, 365
  bārike caudike, **5:**873–74
  bhapang, **5:**647
  caudike, **5:**869, 872–73
  cawandgā, **5:***400*
  conkā, **5:**343
  dundhukī, **5:**343, 732
  ektārā, **5:**343, 347, 503, 859
  gopīyantra, **5:**328, *328,* 343, 859, *860–61*
  gubgubī, **5:**727
  jamiḍiki (also *jamikiḷi*), **5:**894, *895,* 901
  khamak, **5:**343
  premtāl, **5:**343
  pullavān kuḍam, **5:**365–66, *366*
  sruti caudike, **5:**872–73
  tokara, **5:**343
  tuntina, **5:**544, 908
  tuntune, **5:**343, 728
drums, water
  Apache Indian groups, **3:**431, 477
  Argentina, **2:**251
  Great Lakes Indian types, **3:**454, 455, 476–77
  Native American types, **3:**476–77
  Northeast Indian groups, **3:**463
  Paraguay, **2:**454–55
  in peyote ceremonies, **3:**487–88
  Seneca, **3:**472
  Southeast Indian types, **3:**468
  Yaqui Indians, **3:**485
Druskin, Michael, **8:**784
Druts, Efim, **8:**287
Druze people, **6:**544, 545, 1015, 1021
Drysdale, Learmont, **8:**368
Du Mingxin, **7:**349, 350
Du Royaume de Siam (La Loubere), **4:**225
Du Yaxiong, **7:**444
Duala people, **1:**659
  speech surrogate methods, **1:**106
Duan Anjie, **7:**129
Duangjai Thewtong, **4:**298
Duangpheng, **4:**344
Duan Yaocai, **7:***451*
Duany, Jorge, **2:**941
Duau people, **9:**489
dub, **2:**98, 910; **8:**235–36
Dubai. *See* United Arab Emirates
Dube, John, **1:**764
Düben, Gustav, **8:**444
Dubey, Chandrika Prasad, **5:***336*
Dubinskas, Frank, **8:**937
Dubois, Claude, **3:**1158

Dubois, Eugene, **4:**32
Dubois, Marie-Joseph, **9:**965, 992
Dubois, Paul-André, **3:**1147
Dubois, Théodore, **3:**1148, 1149
DuBois, W. E. B., **3:**68, 69, 71, 577
Dubrovački Trubaduri (musical group), **8:**934
Du Chaillu, Paul, **1:**87
Duchamp, Marcel, **3:**254
Du Chi Bà Lam, **4:**447
duCille, Ann, **3:**104
Duck, Stephen, **8:**333
Duda (Carlos Eduardo Cardoso Silva), **2:**354
Dudley, S. H., **3:***620*
"*Du, Du, Liegst Mir im Herzen*" (German song), **3:**888
Dueñas Perilla, Luís, **2:**393
Due South (television show), **3:**1059
Due Voci, **9:**81
Duet (film), **5:**545
Duet Club (Hamilton, Ontario), **3:**93, 1182, 1209
Dufay, Guillaume, **8:**71, 73, 75, 366–67, 518, 550
Duff, Alan, **9:**37
Duff Islands (Solomon Islands), **9:**833
Dufour, Christian, **3:**51, 52
du Fresne, Marion, **9:**7
Dugas, Marcel, **3:**1147
Duguay, Raoul, **3:**1077
Duguba people, **9:**537
Dugun (Akdemir), **6:**775
Duhamel, Maurice, **8:**562
Duhua (*Zhedong luogu* piece), **7:**195
Dui hua (*xiaodiao*), **7:**152
Dukas, Paul, **7:**346, 384–85
Dükenuly, Yqlas, **6:**957
Duke of York Islands (Papua New Guinea), **9:**147, 387
"Duke of York's March," **3:**839
Duke-Peacock Records, **3:**263
Dukhan (periodical), **6:**1061
al-Dukhī, 'Awad, **6:**552
Dukla, Franciszek, **3:**894
dūlāb, **6:**550, 551, 563, 569
Dularawan (Kasilag), **4:**875
dulcimers, hammered (struck zithers)
  anqā, **6:**395, 397, 398
  cembalo, **8:**609
  chang, **6:**919, 999
  cimbál, **8:**719, *720*
  cimbalom
    Hungary, **8:***156, 738,* 743, 744
    Lithuania, **8:**511
    North America, **3:**1197
    Romania, **8:**872, 876, 880
    Rom performers, **8:***272,* 273, 274, 275
    Slovenia, **8:**917
  cultural origins of, **4:**10
  cymbaly, **3:**826, 897, 1197, 1200; **8:**706–7, 796
  dàn tam thập lục, **4:**472, 490
  England, **8:**331
  Europe, **8:**168, 170
  Germany, **8:**653, 654, 656
  Hackbrett, **3:**890, *891;* **8:**615, 686–87
  hakkebord, **8:**532–33

  Ireland, **8:**385
  khim, **3:**1010; **4:**239–40, 282–83, 312, 350, 355
  khim lek, **4:**240
  khimm, **3:**1001; **4:**169, 183, 196
  Latvia, **8:**504
  Lithuania, **8:**511
  North America, **3:**838, 900
  nozheh, **6:**395, 398
  Ontario, **3:**1190, 1194
  oprekelj (also *cimprekelj; pretl; brana; male cimbale*), **8:**916
  qiang, **7:**113
  sandouri, **8:**1009, 1010, 1013, 1015, 1018, 1019
  santouri, **3:**930, 931; **8:**284–85; **9:**73
  santur (also *santūr; sanṭūr*), **1:**220; **6:**398, 411–12; **10:**79, 140
    Georgia, **8:**840
    Iran, **6:**8, 62, 64, 138, 828, 833, 867
    Iraq, **6:**8, 312, 552
    North America, **3:**1034
    South Asia, **5:**332, 338–39, *339,* 688, *688,* 693, *694;* use in Hindustani music, **5:**82, 207
    Syria, **6:**566
    Turkey, **6:**774, *774*
  Steirisch, **8:**673, *673*
  ṭambal, **8:**277, *277, 872,* 876, 877, 879, 880
  tsimbalo, **8:**1010, 1013
  tsymbaly, **3:**345, 826, 913, 914, 1082, 1089, 1242; **8:**809–12, *811,* 818
  tympanon, **8:**532–33
  velike cimbale, **8:**917
  yanggŭm, **7:**821, 827, 838, 866–69
  yangqin, **5:**715; **7:**80, 113, *179,* 179–81
    in Cantonese music, **7:**218, 242; **10:**18
    design and performance of, **7:**179–80
    in *Jiangnan sizhu* ensemble, **7:**224–25
    modernization of, **7:**181
    in narrative accompaniment, **7:**268, 269
    North America, **3:**960–61, 962, 1248, 1262
    Oceania, **9:**97
    in *qinshu* accompaniment, **7:**247
    repertoire for, **7:**180
    Southeast Asia, **4:**239
    in *Tianjin shidiao,* **7:**254
    Tibet, **7:**474, 480
    in *xianshiyue* ensemble, **7:**212
  yoochin, **7:**1013
Dulong people, **7:**485–92
Duluc, José, **2:**861
Dumaine, Brian, **10:***45*
Duman, Güler, **6:**799
Dumbells (revue group), **3:**198, 1080
Dumiyah ve-libbi yilhav (Hebrew song), **6:**1041
Dumont d'Urville, Jules-Sébastien-César, **9:**17, 598
Dun, Finlay, **8:**368, 373
Dunai Dancers (St. Catherines), **3:**1200
Duna people, **9:**537
  Christianity of, **9:**538
  narratives of, **9:**514
Dunayevsky, Isaak, **8:**779
Dunbar, Paul Laurence, **3:**608, 619
Duncan, Isadora, **3:**207, 214; **8:**161

Duncan, Rev. James B., **8:**371, 374
Duncan, Quince, **2:**703
Duncan, Todd, **3:**621
Duncan, William, **3:**1094
Dungidjau people, **9:**430
Dunham, Katherine, **3:**34, *34*
Duni, Egidio Romualdo, **2:**866
Dunin, Elsie Ivancich, **8:**937
Dunkards, **3:**884, 887
Dunlay, Kate, **3:**1071
Dunlop, Ian, **9:**42, 46–47, 419
Dunn, Ginette, **8:**25
Dunna-ze Indian nation, **3:**1094
Dunnel, E. G., **9:***410*
Dunnell, Ruth, **7:**31
Dunyā bint al-Uqba'i, **6:**298
Dunyue dunzhu (Tibetan opera), **7:**479
Duo di Piadena, Il, **8:**613
Duo Z, **8:**289
Dupeyrat, André, **9:**989
Dupuis, Joseph, **1:**88
Duquesne University Tamburitzans, **3:**921
Durán, Alejo, **2:**410
Durán, Anselmo, **2:**389
Durán, Diego, **2:**557, 602
Duran Duran, **8:**215, 220
Durán, Narciso, **3:**734–35
Durand, José, **2:**500–501
Durban, Irawati, **4:**705
Durcal, Rocio, **3:**746
Durch Alles (Singleton), **3:**611
D'Urfey, Thomas, **8:**17
Durga (deity), **5:***497*, 505, 617, 626
  worship of, **5:**247, 291, 471, 677, 846, 892
Durham, John George Lambton, Lord, **3:**1146
During, Jean, **6:**19, 23, 75
Duro-Ladipo, Abiodun, **10:**114
Durosier, Guy, **3:**803
al-Durr al-naqī fī 'ilm al-mūsīqī (al-Musallam al-
  Mawṣilī), **6:**367
Durrat al-tāj (encyclopedia), **6:**17
Duruma people, **1:**624
Dusādh caste, **5:**678–79
Dushi fengguang (film), **7:**345
Dushman (film), **5:***537*, 540
Dustam, General Abd ar-Rashid, **5:**811
Dusun people. *See* Kadazan people
dutar. See lutes
Dutch East India Company, **1:**760; **4:**633, 700
Dutch Guiana. *See* Surinam
Dutch people
  in Guyana, **2:**441–42
  in North America, **3:**1195
  in Sri Lanka, **5:**490, 954
  in Surinam, **2:**83, 503
  in Syria, **6:**565
  in Virgin Islands, **2:**968, 969
Dutch West Indian Company, **2:**441
Duthart, Alex, **8:**363–64
Dutt, Geeta, **5:**414, 420, 538
Dutton, Bertha P., **3:**428
Dutton, George, **9:**440
Duvalier, François "Papa Doc," **2:**882, 888, 894;
  3:803, 805–6
Duvalier, Jean-Claude "Baby Doc," **2:**882, 888,
  894; **3:**803

Duvelle, Charles, **9:**480, 992
Duvelle, Frédéric, **9:**480, 607, 992
Duverger, Marc, **2:**891
Duwayhi, Stephen, **6:**209
Duyse, Florimond Van, **8:**534
Dvaravati (kingdom), **4:**62, 153, 207
Dvořák, Antonín, **2:**114; **3:**538, 607; **8:**53, 60,
  84, 725, 728
Dwight, John Sullivan, **3:**542
Dwight's Journal of Music (periodical), **3:**28
Dyal, Susan, **3:**497
Dyck, Ralph, **3:**246–47
Dyen, Doris, **10:**85
"Dying Cowboy" (cowboy song), **3:**520
Dykema, Peter, **3:**278
Dylan, Bob, **3:**316, 348, 520, 551, 552, 840,
  970; **4:**98, 110, 885; **6:**275; **7:**746;
  8:356, 446, 677
dynamics. *See also* performance practice
  Arab music, medieval, **6:**392
  Bosnia-Hercegovina, **8:**964
  Burundi, *inanga chuchotée*, **1:**165
  China, *Jiangnan sizhu* music, **7:**225
  Greece, **8:**1011
  India, South, musical ensembles, **5:**279
  Kerala
    kathakaḷi ensembles, **5:**324–25
    Mappila songs, **5:**948
  Korea, vocal music, **7:**820
  Kota musical ensembles, **5:**278
  Macedonia, vocal, **8:**973
  Nepal, of instruments, **5:**699, 701
  Papua New Guinea, Managalasi songs, **9:**504
  qawwali, **5:**753
  Slovenia, **8:**912
  Ukraine, **8:**808
  Uttar Pradesh, *harikīrtan*, **5:**665
Dynamix (musical group), **3:**1197
Dyoko, Beauler, **1:**433–35
Dyula people, **1:**495
Dyunggayan, George, **9:**432, *433*
Dzakhord Orer (Djivani), **6:***735*
"*Dželem, Dželem*" (also "Đelem, Đelem"),
  8:279–80, 953
Dzhángar (epic), **8:**772
Dzhudzhev, Stoyan, **8:**906
Dzidzaria, K., **8:**853
Džipsi Aver (musical group), **8:**284
Dzugutov, Bibo, **8:**860
Dzungar people, **7:**35

Eagle, David, **3:**1186
Eagle Feather (musical group), **3:**1069
Eagle Records, **3:**1243
Eagles (musical group), **3:**81
Eakins, Thomas, **3:***520*
Eanes, Jim, **3:**164
Ear Magazine, **3:**1014
Earhart, Will, **3:**277
Earl Grey Orchestra Competition, **3:**1183
Earth (musical group), **3:**356
"Earth Angel" (Penguins), **3:**709
Earth, Wind, and Fire (musical group), **3:**682,
  685, 693, 711
Earthworks (record company), **8:**241
"Ease On Down the Road" (Smalls), **3:**622

East Africa. *See also specific countries and peoples*
  Arabs in, **1:**605–6
  Bantu line, **1:**599
  colonialism in, **1:**274, 426, 598, 602, 607,
    626, 633–36, 643
  culture of, **1:**598–99
  dance, European influences, **1:**603
  foreign influences, **1:**605–7
  geography of, **1:**598
  guitar in, **1:**351–52
  healing rituals, **1:**274
  map of, **1:***596*
  music of, **1:**598–608
  nomadic peoples of, **1:**604–5
  popular music of, **1:**423–28, 608
East African Music Research Scheme, **1:**18
East Asia. *See also* China; Hong Kong; Japan;
    Korea; Macao; Taiwan
  centralization and regionalism in, **7:**3
  cultural development in, **7:**15–16
  cultural exchange in, **7:**49–51
  dance traditions of, **7:**59–69
  geography and climate of, **7:**14–15
  geography of, **7:**9
  history of, **7:**15–18
  instruments in, **7:**79–83
  maps of, **7:***xxvii–xxxv*
  musical distinctions in, **7:**3
  musical historiography in, **7:**41–43
  musical institutions in, **7:**45–47
  musical transmission in, **7:**53–57
  pedagogical lineages in, **7:**46, 55–56
  theatrical traditions of, **7:**73–78
  transnationalism in, **7:**6
East Coast Music Association, **3:**1120
East European Meetings in Ethnomusicology, **8:**885
East Futuna. *See* Futuna
East India Company, **5:**15, 431
East Lote people, **9:**607
East Pakistan. *See* Bangladesh
East Side Story (Kid Frost), **3:**750
"East St. Louis Toodle-Oo" (Ellington), **3:**654
East Timor, **4:**796; **9:**416
East-West Trading Company (Santa Fe), **3:**312
Easter Island. *See* Rapa Nui
"Easter Parade" (Berlin), **3:**196
Eastern Jin dynasty
  Buddhism in, **7:**329
  Daoism in, **7:**312, 320
Eastern Orthodoxy, **6:**1021; **8:**881. *See also*
    Bulgarian Orthodox Church; Coptic
    Orthodox Church; Ethiopian
    Orthodox Church; Greek Orthodox
    Church; Macedonian Orthodox
    Church; Romanian Orthodox Church;
    Russian Orthodox Church; Serbian
    Orthodox Church; Syrian Orthodox
    Church
  Albanian people, **3:**926–27; **8:**986, 1002
  churches, **3:**122
  Georgia, **8:**826
  liturgical music, **3:**10, 939; **8:**5
  liturgy in, **3:**121
  Montenegro, **8:**957
  Ossetian people, **8:**859
  performance contexts in, **8:**11

research on, **3**:119
  South Asian peoples, **3**:984
Eastern Shoshones, **3**:421
Eastern Symphony Orchestra (Armenia), **6**:731
Eastern Timbira culture, **2**:134
Eastern Woodlands Indian groups, **3**:222–23,
        451, 461–65
  sound recordings of, **3**:291
Eastern Yueshi culture, **7**:17
Eastman, George, **3**:277
Eastman, Lloyd E., **7**:379
Eastman School of Music (Rochester), **3**:15, 536,
        610, 611, 953; **10**:133–35
Eastman Wind Ensemble (Rochester), **3**:567, *567*
Easton, Peter, **3**:1070
Easton, Sheena, **3**:751
Eastwood, Clint, **3**:204
Easy E, **3**:702
"Easy to Love" (Porter), **3**:549
Eazy E, **3**:714
Ebba Grön, **8**:216
Ebcioğlu, Fecri, **6**:249
Ebeling, Klaus, **5**:318
Eben, Petr, **8**:725
Ebeye (Marshall Islands), **9**:715
Ebisawa Bin, **7**:595
Ebony (*bloco afro*), **2**:353
"Ebony and Ivory" (Wonder and McCartney),
        3:713
Ebrāhīm Museli. *See* Ibrāhīm al-Mawṣilī
"*Echale Salsita*" (Piñeiro), **3**:788
Echezona, Wilberforce, **1**:15, 34, 40, 233, 251
Eckert, Franz, **7**:727, 728, 729, 951
Eckstine, Billy, **3**:743
Eclipse (Takemitsu), **7**:737
École Supérieure de Danse (Québec), **3**:225
economics. *See also* agriculture; mass media;
        music industry; sound recordings
  African-American community in the 1980s,
        3:685
  agrarian, **8**:193–98
  Albania, **8**:986, 987
  Albanian-Americans, **3**:929
  Amerindian cultures and, **2**:45
  Andhra Pradesh, mendicant performers, **5**:900
  Antigua and Barbuda, **2**:799, 800
  Arabian peninsula, **6**:703
  Argentina
    cuarteto performances, **2**:275, 277–78
    sound recording industry, **2**:64
    urbanization and, **2**:261
  artifacts and, **2**:7
  art music, **3**:268–71; **8**:188–89
  Asian-American communities, **3**:949–50
  Bahamas, **2**:801, 812
  Bali, **4**:760
  Barbados, **2**:813
  black empowerment, **3**:678
  blues musicians, **3**:640, 643
  Bolivia
    of fiestas, **2**:291
    mining communities, **2**:284
  Brazil, **2**:317, 318–19
    central and southern regions, **2**:301
    coffee growing, **2**:303–4
    gold mining, **2**:302–3

northeastern region, **2**:301, 323–24
    popular music and, **2**:354
    sound recording industry, **2**:107
    sugarcane growing, **2**:333–34
  Brunei, **4**:79–80
  Bulgaria, **8**:902
  Canada, **3**:1146
    colonialism and, **3**:50–51, 238–39
    fur trade, **3**:405, 452, 1056, 1074, 1086,
        1163, 1178, 1188, 1192, 1224
    Great Depression, **3**:1057, 1228, 1249,
        1250, 1267
    music industry, **3**:246–48, 265–67
    nineteenth century, **3**:1255
    relationship with United States, **3**:1061–62
  capitalism, **8**:200
  Caribbean, **2**:791–92, 793, 795
    sound recording industry, **2**:40–41, 52–53,
        796
  cassette technology, **5**:424, 547, 554
  Central America, sound recording industry,
        2:40–41, 52–53
  Central Asia, **6**:975; **7**:11
  China, **7**:389, 399, 444, 464, 467, 499
    acting troupes, **7**:394
    freelance musicians, **7**:419
    professional performers, **7**:419
  Colombia, **2**:397, 401, 409
    municipal budgets, **2**:383
  commercialism and music, **3**:44–45
  composers' royalties, **8**:51
  composers, twentieth-century, **3**:174
  consumer culture, **3**:49–50
  copyright and ownership issues, **2**:64–65;
        3:257; **8**:225
  Corsica, **8**:566
  Costa Rica, **2**:631, 689, 694
    pop orchestras, **2**:693
  country music, **3**:78, 560
  cross-cultural marketing, **3**:586
  Cuba, **2**:822–23, 827, 828
  Cyprus, **8**:1029
  Czechoslovakia, **8**:724
  dancers, **3**:207–8
  Denmark, **8**:451
    Great Depression, **8**:457
    instrumentalists, **8**:457
  disco, **3**:689
  Dolan people, **6**:990
  Dominican Republic, **2**:850
  Ecuador, fund-raising, **2**:427
  education and, **2**:69
  Egypt
    mass media, **6**:233, 239
    performers, **6**:618–19
    tipping, **6**:616–17, 619, 620
  employers of musicians, **2**:49–50
  England, professional musicians, **8**:336
  exchange values, **1**:517–18, 521–24, 525–28
  Faroe Islands, **8**:468
  Federated States of Micronesia, **9**:726
  film industry, **5**:539
  folk music and, **8**:2, 4
  France, **8**:539
    currency exchange with colonies, **8**:234
    song selling, **8**:550

Georgia, **8**:845
    Abkhazia, **8**:851–52
  Goa, **5**:735
  Great Lakes Indian groups, **3**:453
  Greece, **8**:1007
  Grenada, **2**:864, 866
  Guadeloupe, **2**:873–78, 879
  Gujarat, **5**:624
  Guyana, **5**:600
  Haiti, **2**:882, 889
  hip-hop culture and, **3**:693
  Hong Kong, **7**:433
  house music, **3**:691
  immigration and, **2**:83; **3**:719
  India, recording industry, **5**:560
  Indonesia
    cassette industry, **4**:101
    Muslim traders, **4**:75–76
    performers, **4**:720–21
  industrial revolution, **3**:143, 838; **8**:6–7, 13,
        147, 228, 326
  influence on traditional musics, **4**:3, 113–16
  Inner Asia, **7**:35
  Ireland, **8**:378, 390
  Israel, **6**:1021
  Jamaica, **2**:896, 910
    sound recording industry, **2**:97
  Japan
    biwa players, **7**:646
    kanzin method, **7**:653
    musicians, **7**:757, 758–59, 761, 769
  Jewish cantors, **3**:935
  Karnataka, **5**:881–82
  Kazakhstan, **6**:949
  Korea, fund-raising rituals, **7**:931
  Laos, **4**:335–36, 361
  Latino peoples, **3**:720
  Lithuania, **8**:509
  Low Countries, **8**:523
  Malaysia, **4**:442
  Mapuche culture, **2**:233
  Maritime Provinces, **3**:1068
  mass media and, **3**:12
  master-student relationship, **5**:86, 377, 943
  Maya culture, **2**:722–23
  Mexico, **2**:551–52, 567, 933
    sound recording industry, **2**:40–41, 52–53
  Micronesia, trade networks, **9**:716
  Montserrat, **2**:923
  musical innovation and, **2**:74
  musical theater, eighteenth-century, **3**:179
  music revival movements, **3**:55–56, 329
  Native American peoples, buffalo hunting,
        3:421, 440, 442, 1086
  Nauru, **9**:754, 755
  Navajo Indian nation, **3**:432
  Nepal, **5**:703
  New Caledonia, community music, **9**:678
  Newfoundland, **3**:1138–43
  Nicaragua, **2**:664, 749, 753, 754, 755,
        765–66
  North American Free Trade Agreement, **3**:266
  Northwest Coast Indian nations, whaling,
        3:395
  Norway, musicians' stipends, **8**:429
  Oman, **6**:672

economics (*continued*)
  O'odham peoples, **3:**435
  Pakistan, **5:**749, 792
  Palau, **9:**722
  Panama, **2:**770–71
  Papua New Guinea, **9:**494, 506, 561
    Enga singsings, **9:**533
    trade networks, **9:**53, 489, 492–93, 506–7,
      537, 545, 572, 573, 609–10, 621, 628
  patronage and, **5:**404–5
  performers' renumerations, **5:**380, 381
  Peru, **2:**466–67, 933
    sound recording industry, **2:**64
  Plains Indian groups, **3:**440–41
  Pohnpei, **9:**739
  Polynesia, trade networks, **9:**771
  popular music, **2:**63–64, 94, 104–5; **3:**95,
      838–39; **8:**188, 211
    nineteenth century, **3:**183
    Tin Pan Alley, **3:**197, 260, 548, 705
  prehistoric Southeast Asia, **4:**39
  publishing, **3:**241–42, 261
    nineteenth century, **3:**190–91, 257–59
    royalty disputes with radio, **3:**708
  Puerto Rico, **2:**933, 940
  Punjab (Pakistan), musicians, **5:**768
  Q'ero culture, **2:**230
  Québec, **3:**51, 1155, 1158–59
  radio, **3:**195, 349–50, 560
  radio performances and, **3:**244, 261–62
  religion and, **3:**120
  rock, **3:**355–56; **8:**216, 222
    benefit concerts, **8:**216
  rock and roll, **3:**349
  Rom people, **8:**271–72
  Russia, **8:**754
  Sāmoa, **9:**795
  Sardinia, **8:**626
  Scotland, **8:**360
    Hebrides, **8:**361
  Serbia, **8:**943
  slavery, **3:**65–66
  Society Islands, **9:**867
  Somalia, **1:**610
  South Africa, **1:**717, 759–60, 761–62, 766
  South America, **2:**245
    pre-Columbian trade routes, **2:**232
    sound recording industries, **2:**40–41,
      52–53
    tropical-forest immigrants, **2:**131–33
    tropical-forest region, **2:**123, 131
  South Asia, **5:**5
    studio musicians, **5:**535
  Southeast Asia, urban *vs.* rural areas, **4:**5–6
  southern Africa, **1:**700
  Southern African Development Community,
      1:428
  South Korea, **7:**983
  Soviet Union (former), state-sponsored rock
      groups, **8:**218–19
  Sri Lanka, **5:**954
  Subarctic peoples, **3:**384, 390–91
  Sudan, **1:**556, 571
  Surinam, **2:**504
  Suyá culture, **2:**143
  Taiwan, popular music, **7:**358–59

Tamil Nadu, **5:**910
  Nilgiri peoples, **5:**909
  Tyagaraja festival, **5:**391–92
Tarahumara culture, **2:**582
Thailand, **4:**221, 297, 329
  northern, **4:**315
  piracy, **4:**99
  popular music, **4:**97
  tourism, **4:**247, 249–50
Tibet, **7:**471
tourism, **2:**50–51, 75; **4:**135–41
Trinidad and Tobago, **2:**952–53, 964
Tunisia, **6:**526
Turkey, **6:**251, 256
Tuva, **6:**980
Ukraine, **8:**806, 812, 819
United States
  colonialism and, **3:**238–39
  Great Depression, **3:**45, 262, 725
  sound recording industry, **3:**48, 245, 261,
      329–30, 352–53; **6:**252
Uttar Pradesh, **5:**660
Vanuatu, **9:**694
Venezuela, **2:**542, 543, 933
Virgin Islands, **2:**969
Wales, **8:**342, 355
  industrial revolution, **8:**352–53
Warao culture, **2:**189
Wayana culture, **2:**165
world music and, **8:**225
Yap, **9:**729
Yaqui Indian groups, **3:**437
Yoruba popular music, **1:**473, 487
Yuman Indian groups, **3:**433
Ecos de México (Ituarte), **2:**604
Ecoutez tous petits et grands (Cormier), **3:**1136
Ecstasy of Rita Joe (Mortifee), **3:**199
Ecuador, **2:**413–31. *See also specific peoples*
  aesthetics in, **2:**429–31
  archaeomusicological research in, **2:**7, 10, 413
  children's wakes in, **2:**49, 422–24
  composition in, **2:**430–31
  festival of Saint John the Baptist, **2:**426–27
  geography of, **2:**4, 413
  Harvest in, **2:**425
  instruments of, **2:**31, 36, 379, 413–18, 431
  Japanese people in, **2:**86
  musical genres
    albazo, **2:**417, 424, 427
    currulao, **2:**427–28
    jaway, **2:**425
    pareja, **2:**418, 423–25
    pasacalle, **2:**417, 427
    pasillo, **2:**101, 392, 417, 427, 431
    Passion songs, **2:**419–20
    sanjuán, **2:**418, 423–25
    vacación, **2:**418, 424
  New Year's in, **2:**426
  performers, **2:**428–29
  processions
    Corpus Christi, **2:**420–22
    Holy Week, **2:**419–20
  Quechua- and Aymara-speaking peoples,
      2:205–23
  Quito, music conservatory, **2:**114
  research on, **2:**411, 431

shamanism in, **2:**419
Shuar culture of, **2:**127
tropical-forest region of, **2:**123–35
weddings in, **2:**424–25
Ecuadorian-Americans/Canadians, **3:**1201
Eddie Minnis and Da Brudders, **2:**808
Eddy, Nelson, **3:**544
Ede people, **3:**996
  ceremonies of, **4:**533
  narratives of, **4:**532–33
Edel, Yitshak, **6:**1071
Edelshtat, Dovid, **3:**939
Edelweiss Club (Toronto), **3:**1195
Edenhoffer, Gertrud, **3:**1250
Edéry, Jumol, **3:**1173
Edgar, Marjorie, **3:**873
Edinburgh Reel and Strathspey Society, **8:**370
Edinburgh University, **8:**371
Edison, Thomas Alva, **3:**242, 244; **8:**18, 177,
      755
Editorial Freeland, **2:**264
Edmonton Choral Society, **3:**1090
Edmonton Civic Opera Society, **3:**1228
Edmonton Male Choir, **3:**1227
Edmonton Opera Company, **3:**1230
Edmonton Philharmonic Society, **3:**1090
Edmonton Symphony Orchestra, **3:**1090, 1227,
      1228
Edmunds, Babyface, **3:**715
Edmundson, Morna, **3:**1096
Edna Manley Centre for the Visual and
      Performing Arts, **2:**910
Edo people (Africa), **1:**118, 459–60
Edo period (Japan)
  Ainu people in, **7:**783
  ban on women performers, **7:**764
  blind musicians in, **7:**755
  chamber music in, **7:**687
  gagaku in, **7:**625, 627, 757
  Heike narration in, **7:**646, 647
  kumiuta in, **7:**696
  mikagura in, **7:**607
  monks in, **7:**702
  narrative styles in, **7:**681–82
  qin music in, **7:**725
  syakuhati in, **7:**777
  syamisen in, **7:**760
  theater in, **7:**630, 653
  urbanization in, **7:**739
Edson, Lewis, **3:**532
Edström, Karl-Olaf, **8:**307
Ed Sullivan Show (television show), **3:**672
education. *See* oral tradition and transmission;
      pedagogy
Edu Pah (Rotinese performer), **4:***801*
Edward VII, king of England, **8:**186
Edwards, Charles L., **2:**812
Edwards, David "Honeyboy," **3:**583
Edwards, Gus, **3:**305
Edwards, Jane A., **9:**323
Edwards, Jimmy, **3:**780
Edwards, John, **2:***690*
Edwards, Norman, **2:***970*
Edwards, Ron, **9:**142
Edwards, Webley, **3:**1050
Edwin Hawkins Singers, **3:**633

Eekels, Cees, **8:**531
Eestlaste Laulu Selts (Estonian society), **3:**878
Efate (Vanuatu), **9:**691
Efe (kingdom), **1:**316–17
Efendi (honorific). *See previous element in name*
Effutu people, **1:**287
Efik culture, **2:**668
Efik people, **1:**107
Efimenkova, Borislava, **8:**785
Egana, Andoni, **8:**316
Eganghajie (*jialing* piece), **7:**480
Egba (musical group), **8:**446
Egberg, Gladys, **3:**1229
Ege, Akanbi, **1:**479
Egikov, Igor, **8:**782
Egypt
    ancient, **6:**401, 407, 413, 535, 537
    Arab music performance, **6:**553, 557–61,
        603–5
    art music (*turath*), **6:**8, 317–19, 558, 560–61
    Berber peoples, **6:**273
    British occupation of, **6:**547
    Cairo
        as Arab media capital, **6:**597–600
        Fāṭimids in, **6:**293, 294
        Mamluks in, **6:**293, 294, 297–98
        mawwāl performances, **6:**567
        Nubian music, **6:**239, 555, 641–45
        professional musicians, **6:**615–22
    cheironomy in, **8:**100
    composition in, **1:**219–20
    Coptic Orthodox Church in, **6:**219–23
    dance in, **6:**623–33
    early music of, **5:**17–18
    epic song traditions, **6:**10, 339–43
    film industry in, **6:**236–38, 255–56
    firqah orchestras, **1:**427, 645
    folk traditions in, **6:**545
    French occupation of, **6:**21–22
    Gurri people, dance as medicine, **1:**113
    influence on Arab music, **6:**362
    influence on Sudanese urban music, **1:**570–71
    inshād dīnī performance in, **6:**165–75
    instruments in, **1:**302, 303, 556; **6:**357, 358,
        403, 406, 407, 409–20
    Islamic call to prayer in, **6:**153–55
    layālī performances in, **6:**147–51
    Maronite Church in, **6:**208
    mass media's impact in, **6:**233–41
    musical genres of, **6:**550–52
    music industry in, **1:**571
    Nubian peoples, **6:**545, 555, 629–30, 641,
        645
    pedagogical institutions in, **6:**36, 43, 321–24,
        547
    popular song
        influence on Maghrib music, **6:**269,
            432–33, 475
        influence on Sephardi music, **6:**201–2
        influence on Tunisian Jewish music, **6:**526
    postmedieval musical life in, **6:**543–44
    Qur'ānic recitation in, **5:**747–48; **6:**158, 159,
        160–62, 626
    regional cassettes in, **5:**554
    research on music of, **6:**23, 371
    Ṣaʿīd, *ṣaʿīdī* rhythmic mode, **6:**92

    Sinai region, **6:**654
    Siwa oasis, **6:**273, 545, 624
    Sudanese people, **6:**630–31
    Suez region, **6:**623, 627
    ʿūd performance in, **6:**45–46
    Upper Egypt, **6:**627–28
    urban music in, **6:**552–53
    Wadi Natrun, **6:**219
    Western music in, **6:**546–48, 607–13
    women musicians in, **6:**305
    zār ritual, **1:**554; **6:**632–33
Egypt '80 (musical group), **1:**484
Egyptian Music Club, **1:**607
Egyptian people in North America, **3:**1218–20;
    6:282–83
Ehu, Vanina, **9:**270
"*Eibhlín a Rún*," **8:**389
Eichendorff, Joseph von, **8:**646
Eickelman, Dale F., **1:**133
Einarsson, Halldor, **8:**401
Einarsson, Magnus, **3:**1251
Eine Kleine Gamelan Music (Goode), **3:**1016,
    1017
Eipo people
    films on, **9:**48, 982
    mot genre, **9:**301, 592
    music and dance of, **9:**591–94
Eisai, **7:**612
Eisfeld, Theodore, **3:**60
Eisler, Hanns, **8:**659
Eji changmu (*zhanian* piece), **7:**477
Ekari (Kapauku) people, **9:**486
Ekiti state, **1:**401
Ekmalyan, Makar, **6:**725, 737
Eknath, Saint, **5:**253
Ekpo, Maurice, **1:**483
Ekstraphone (record company), **8:**777
Ekwueme, Lazarus Nyanyelu, **1:**40, 44, 47
    compositions of, **1:**210, *212*, 232, 233, 236,
        237, 251
el-, El. *See also next element in name*
El Ballet Garífuna, **2:**741
El Capitan (Sousa), **3:**544
El Chicano (musical group), **3:**733, 746, 747–48,
    749, 799
El Conjunto Bernal, **3:**777
El Conjunto Murrietta, **2:**592
El Cuarteto (Venezuelan group), **2:**543
El Dorados (musical group), **3:**672
El Quinto Olivo, **2:**940
El Salvador, **2:**628, 630, 706–19; **3:**719
    archaeological background of, **2:**706–7
    dances of, **2:**709–15
    geography of, **2:**706
    instruments of, **2:**706–9
    Lenca culture, **2:**739
    map of, **2:**629
    Maya culture, **2:**650–58
    musical life in, **2:**716–19
    population of, **2:**706
    religious music in, **2:**709
    research on, **2:**719
    son genre in, **2:**711
El Teatro Campesino, **3:**749
El Trío Imperial, **3:**741
El Trío de Taos, **3:**765

El Vez, **3:**522
Elatov, Viktor I., **8:**803
Elbert, Samuel, **9:**853
Eldridge, Roy, **3:**656
Ele (god), **8:**855
Eleanor of Aquitaine, **8:**199
Elebekov, Zhusupbek, **6:**955
Electrecord, **8:**883
electric guitars. *See* guitars, electric
electronic music
    Canada, **3:**246, 1185
    concert, **3:**252–55
    disco, **3:**228
    Europe, **8:**85
    Israel, **6:**1031, 1073–74
    Japan, **7:**735, 736, 751
    Nigeria, **1:**233
    notation and, **8:**97
    rock technologies, **3:**254, 357, 358, 540, 551,
        680
    Sweden, **8:**445
    United States, **3:**175
electrophones
    Canadian designs, **3:**246
    Colombia, **2:**403
    drum machines, **3:**552, 688, 845, 1035;
        5:946, 948; **6:**644
        in Arab-American ensembles, **6:**283
        in Arab music, **6:**422
    Bahamas, **2:**808
    China, **7:**468
    Palestine, **6:**586
    in *rai*, **6:**270–71
    in Yemenite Jewish music, **6:**266
El Salvador, **2:**719
    hyperinstruments, **3:**254
    India, in film music, **5:**347, 544
    in Karnatak music, **5:**235, 352
    keyboards, **2:**485
        in Arab music, **6:**699
        in Arctic communities, **3:**380
        Argentina, **2:**274
        Bahamas, **2:**805–6
        Cuba, **2:**835
        Egypt, **6:**616
        in ethnic bands, **3:**529
        Greece, **8:**1011, 1017
        Guyana, **5:**605
        in Hispano music, **3:**762
        in Irish showbands, **3:**845
        in Lao popular music, **3:**1009
        in Macedonian bands, **3:**926; **8:**976
        in Mexican music, **3:**746
        in Middle Eastern music, **3:**1033, 1034,
            1218
        Nicaragua, **2:**754
        North America, **3:**240
        in Nubian music, **6:**642, 644
        Palestine, **6:**586, 591
        in polka bands, **3:**895, 902
        in rock, **3:**285
        South America, **2:**73
        in Sufi *dhikr* ceremony, **3:**1045
        in Swedish music, **3:**871
        use in *bhangra*, **5:**574
        Venezuela, **2:**539

electrophones (*continued*)
  organ, electric, **2:**484; **3:**119, 254, 535, 1035,
    1185; **5:**604, 810; **8:**426, 895
    in Arab music, **6:**421
    in *rai*, **6:**270–71
  South America, **2:**30–31
  synthesizers, **2:**40, 274, 484; **3:**1033, 1185;
    5:364, 549; **8:**225, 234, 1032
    Albania, **8:**997
    in Arab-American ensembles, **6:**282, 283
    in Arab music, **6:**421, 636
    Bahamas, **2:**808
    Basque region, **8:**315
    in Berber music, **6:**276
    Bolivia, **2:**284
    Bulgaria, **8:**895
    China, **7:**468
    in concert music, **3:**253–55
    in disco, **3:**228, 688
    in Egyptian music, **6:**240, 555
    ethnomusicological use of, **1:**256, 258,
      259–69
    in funk, **3:**684
    Greece, **8:**1009
    in *grupo* music, **3:**780
    in Israeli *mizraḥit* music, **6:**261
    Japan, **7:**751
    in *kabuki*, **7:**661
    Kerala, **5:**946, 948
    Korea, **7:**958, 959, 960, 967
    Kosovo, **8:**286
    Macedonia, **8:***281*, 282, 980
    Nicaragua, **2:**754
    notation and, **8:**91
    in *rai*, **6:**270–71
    in rap, **3:**700
    in salsa, **3:**788
    Serbia, **8:**949
    Sri Lanka, **5:**971
    in Sufi *dhikr* ceremony, **3:**1045
    Sweden, **8:**442
    Turkey, **6:**257
    use in fusion styles, **5:**584, 652
    use in rock music, **5:**428
    Uttar Pradesh, **5:**674
  Ukraine, **8:**811
Eleish, Ebrahim, **3:**1219, *1219*
Elektra (musical group), **3:**1096
Elektra Records, **8:**241
Elements of Harmony (Aristoxenus), **8:**47–48
"Elevator Boogie" (Scott), **3:**669
Eleventh Symphony: 1905 (Shostakovich), **7:**347
Elfassiya, Zohara, **6:**1044
Elgar, Edward, **8:**186
Elgin County Male Choir, **3:***1182*
Elia (god), **8:**857
Elías, Manuel de, **2:**605
Elias, William, **6:**1030
Elie, Justin, **2:**892
Elijah (Mendelssohn-Bartholdy), **9:**203
Elin, Vladimir, **4:**870
L'Elisir d'Amore (Donizetti), **3:**1181
Elizabeth II, queen of England, **5:**698; **8:**186;
  9:795, 863, 938
Elizalde, Federico, **4:**870
Elkendeg (Mongol song), **7:**1007

Elkin, A. P., **9:**418, 986, 987, 989
Elk's Whistle (musical group), **3:**1087
Ellamma (deity), **5:**872, 901
Ellen Arise: A Ballad (Carr), **3:**289
Eller, Heino, **8:**498
Ellice Islands (Tuvalu), **9:**5, 758, 823, 828. *See
    also* Tuvalu
  films on, **9:**982
  music and dance of, **9:**719
  sound recordings, **9:**994
Elliman, Yvonne, **3:**712
Ellingson, Ter, **5:**327, 961, 967, 968
Ellington, Edward Kennedy "Duke," **3:**33, 550,
    621, 653, 654–55, 656, 664, 668,
    706, 707, 720, 732, 742, 793; **8:**288
Elliot, Jean Leonard, **3:**73
Elliot, Kirk, **3:**1142–43
Elliot, Missy, **3:**697
Ellis, Alexander J., **1:**261; **4:**225, 260, 285, 637;
    5:51
Ellis, Alfred Burdon, **1:**93
Ellis, Ben, **9:**909
Ellis, Catherine J., **9:**292–93, 415, 435, 437,
    439, 960, 987
Ellis, Henry T., **4:**858
Ellis, William, **9:**21
Ellstein, Abraham, **3:**937–38
Elmaghrebi, Sami, **6:**1044
Elman, Benjamin, **7:**26
Elman, Mischa, **4:**870
Elmas, Stepan, **6:**725
Elmhirst, Leonard, **5:**562–63, 564
Elmo and the Sparkplugs, **2:**971
Eloi, Saint, **8:**561
El Salvador. *See under* el, El
Elschek, Oskár, **8:**178–79, 721
Elscheková, Alica, **8:**178–79, 721
Elshinta label, **4:**681
Elsner, Józef, **8:**710
Elsnic, Joseph, **3:**897
Eluyemi, O., **1:**411
Elver, Süleyman, **6:**797
Elvis Brothers, **3:**169
Elworth, Steven, **3:**583
Elytis, Odysseus, **8:**1021
Emae (Vanuatu), **9:**833
Emancipation Proclamation (1863), **3:**606
Embers (musical group), **9:**138
"Embraceable You" (Gershwin), **3:**549, 659
Emek (Lavry), **6:**1029
Emerald Community Singers, **2:**923
Emerillon culture, **2:**164, 435–36
Emerson, Ida, **3:**549
Emerson, Lake, and Palmer (musical group),
    3:356; **8:**219
Emerson, Nathaniel B., **9:**915
Emerson Quartet, **3:**538
Emerson, Ralph Waldo, **3:**130
EMI Corporation, **2:**107; **3:**264, 270, 1280
EMI Pakistan (record label), **5:**528
EMI Records, **8:**678
Emigré, Viviane, **2:**438
Emin Dede, **6:**109
"Eminence Front" (The Who), **3:**689
Emini, Jima (Ajo) wult, **1:***542*
Emira (Papua New Guinea), **9:**626

Emmanuel, **3:**746, 751
Emmert, Richard, **10:***15*
Emmett, Daniel Decatur, **3:**185, 306, 543, 835
Emmons, Buddy, **3:**80
EMO label, **3:**1133
Emory, Kenneth P., **9:**24, 836, 883, 969, *970*,
    994
emotion. *See* aesthetics
Emotions (musical group), **3:**676, 712
Empire Band, **3:**898
Empreintes Digitales (publisher), **3:**1152
"Empty Heart" (Thee Midniters), **3:**747
Emrah, **6:**80, 249
"Emrah" (Apaşlar), **6:**249
Emrah and Selvi (Turkish fairy tale), **6:**803
Emsheimer, Ernst, **1:**558; **8:**178, 447, 847
Emunim arkhu shebah la-el (*piyyut*), **6:***1038*
En roulant ma boule (Barbeau), **3:**1166
Enadi Sisters, **5:**389
Encanto (musical group), **3:**781
Encarnacao, E. E., **7:**374
Encounters of East and West in Music (Avenary),
    6:1060
Encyclopedia of American Religions, **3:**116
Encyclopedia of Chinese Literature and Art, **7:**47
Encyclopedia of Music in Canada, **3:**343, 1066,
    1102, 1108
Encyclopedia of Music for Pictures (Rapee), **3:**202
Encyclopedia Sinica, **7:**246
"End" (Doors), **3:**318, 348
"End of the Road" (Boyz II Men), **3:**715
Endicott, Kirk, **4:**569
Endo, Kenny, **3:**336; **9:**97
Enemy Way Music (McAllester), **3:**511
Enescu, Georges, **8:**882
Enewetak Atoll (Marshall Islands), **9:**32
Enga people, **9:**178, 511
  festivals of, **9:**512
  music and dance of, **9:**484, 533–36
  narratives of, **9:**514
  performances of, **9:***242*, *289*, 513
Engel, Carl, **3:**293
Engel, Joel, **6:**1025, 1071; **8:**783
Engels, Friedrich, **7:**441; **8:**184
Enggano people, **4:**619
Engiraku (*komagaku* piece), **7:**625
England, **8:**326–39
  art music in, **8:**71–72, 76
  children's games, **8:**145
  Cornwall
    Celtic people in, **8:**319
    hobbyhorse dance procession, **8:**331
  Cypriot people in, **8:**1032
  dance traditions of, **8:**160, 165, 329–32, 338
  geography of, **8:**326
  ideology in, **8:**186, 188
  immigrant groups in, **8:**231, 336
  industrial revolution in, **8:**6, 326
  instruments and instrumental music of,
    8:329–31
  London
    immigrant music in, **8:**225, 231, 235–36,
      336
    Jewish community in, **8:**249, 265
    performance practice in, **8:**101
  map of, **8:***324*

Milton Keynes, folk clubs in, **8:**153
musical life in, **8:**333–36
Northumbria, dance music of, **8:**330, 331, 333
performance contexts, **8:**143, 331–32
population of, **8:**326
research on music of, **8:**19, 188, 327–29, 332–33, 337–39
Rom people in, **8:**296
solmization pedagogy in, **8:**106
transmission and education in, **8:**332–33
Travellers in, **8:**336
vocal music, **8:**326–29
  ballads, **8:**8, 136, 195, 327–29, 333
  carols, **8:**132–33, 140, 328, 331
  medieval secular songs, **8:**72
  motet, **8:**71
  Renaissance, **8:**76
  west gallery, **8:**328, 333, 336
  women's performances in, **8:**200, 335–36
  Yorkshire, carol singing in, **8:**328
England, Nicholas, **1:**51
Engländer, Richard, **8:**447
English-Americans/Canadians. *See* Anglo-Americans/Canadians
English and Scottish Popular Ballads (Child), **3:**833; **8:**328–29
English Beat, **8:**215
English Country Dance Society, **3:**323
English Dancing Master (Playford), **8:**17
English Folk Dance and Song Society, **8:**333, 338
English Folk-Song: Some Conclusions (Sharp), **8:**327–28, 337
English Governess at the Siamese Court (Léonowens), **4:**285
English people. *See also* Anglo-Americans/Canadians
  in Aotearoa, **9:**928
  in Australia, **9:**69, 140–41, 408–9
Enhbalsan, **7:**1012
Enhmanlai, **7:**1020
Enigma (performing group), **7:**358, 428
ENIGRAC (Nicaraguan recording label), **2:**765
"Enjoy Loneliness" (Xiao), **7:**364
Enlightenment, **8:**248–49
Ennaghem, **6:**512
Ennin, **7:**612
Ennis, Séamus, **8:**391, 393
Eno, Brian, **3:**347; **9:**1005
Enrique, Esmeralda, **3:**1197
Enrique, Louis, **3:**788
Enríquez, Luis, **3:**799
Enríquez, Manuel, **2:**605
Ensayos de Música Latinoamericana, **2:**839
Ensemble Aux Calabasses, **2:**889, 890
Ensemble Cadence Rempas de Wébert Sicot, **3:**803
Ensemble Compas Direct de nemours Jean-Baptiste, **3:**803
Ensemble Contemporain de Montréal, **3:**1152
Ensemble of Folk Instruments of Armenian Radio and Televsion, **6:**731
Ensemble for Folk Songs (Bulgaria), **8:**902
Ensemble Ibo Lélé, **2:**889
Ensemble Nemours Jean-Baptiste, **2:**98

Ensemble Nipponia (musical group), **7:**709
Ensemble Polonais, **8:**711
Ensemble Riviera, **2:**889
ensembles, musical. *See also* ensembles, musical (one-person); *gamelan*; instrumentation; klezmer music; *mariachi*; steelbands; string bands; *specific groups*
Acholi people, **1:**224, 227
Afghanistan, **5:**831
  Herat, **5:**822–23
  for Kabuli *ghazal*, **5:**806
  for *kharābāt*, **5:**828
  radio orchestras, **5:**809
  sāzdohol, **5:**818–19, 820–22
Africa
  bands, influence on rumba, **1:**424
  drum ensembles, **1:**33–34, 35; **10:**29–36
Afro-Cuban
  bembé, **3:**784, 785
  charanga francesca, **3:**788, 795–96
  güemilere, **3:**784, 785
Akan people, *ntahera* trumpet ensembles, **1:**465
Albania
  aheng, **8:**997
  brass bands, **8:**999
  čalgija, **8:**286
  dajre def, **8:**285
  Rom people, **8:**285
  saze, **8:**993, *993*, 997
  state folk ensembles, **8:**999, 1000, 1002
Algeria
  for Andalusian repertoire, **6:**406–7, *453*, 468–69
  nūba ensemble, **6:**407, 418
Andalusian *jawq* groups, **6:**460–61, 470
Andean folkloric, **2:**75, *76*, 135; **3:**730
Andean regions
  flute ensembles, **2:**209–11, 215–16, 219
  north-south distinctions, **2:**221–22
  panpipe ensembles, **2:**207–9, 216
Andhra Pradesh
  brass bands, **5:**896
  for *kuchipudi* dance-drama, **5:**517
Anlo-Ewe people, **1:**397–98
Aotearoa
  brass bands, **9:**130, 929, 930, 935
  fife-and-drum corps, **9:**935
  pipe-and-drum bands, **9:**115, 135
Arab-American, **6:**282–83
Arab-Andalusian music, **1:**535–36
Arabian peninsula
  expatriate communities, **6:**716–18
  'iddat al-lewa, **6:**404
  'iddat al-nubān, **6:**405, 412
  lyre ensembles, **6:**358–59
  for pearl-diving songs, **6:**546, 651
  for *sawt*, **6:**651–52
  women's *firqa*, **6:**698–99
Arctic rock groups, **3:**380
Argentina
  conjuntos, **2:**262
  cuarteto groups, **2:**273–80
  orquestas características, **2:**273–74
  orquestas típicas, **2:**273–74

panpipe ensembles, **2:**256
for tango, **2:**263
Australia
  Anglo-Irish folk-music bands, **9:**141
  brass bands, **9:**409
  céilí bands, **9:**78
  country music, **9:**142
  Greek bands, **9:**72–74
  gumleaf bands, **9:**134–35, 442
  Italian brass bands, **9:**80
  pipe-and-drum bands, **9:**135
  pop ensembles, **9:**144
Austria, **8:**671, *673*
  brass bands, **8:***671*
  Schrammel, **8:**676
  string ensembles, **8:**673
  tamburica, **8:**674
Aymara culture
  brass bands, **2:**362
  lichiwayo, **2:**362
  orquesta, **2:**361
  sikuri, **2:**362
  tarkeadas (also *tarqueadas*), **2:**358, 361
Azande people, flute and drum, **1:**657
Azerbaijan, **6:**925
  for *muğam*, **6:**8
  xanəndə-destesi, **6:**924, 925
Bahamas
  junkanoo, **2:**806–7
  rake 'n' scrape, **2:**805–6, 809
Bali, **4:**743–55
  gamelan jegog, **4:**754
  gamelan selundeng, **4:**755
  gegenggongan, **4:**754
  gendèr wayang, **4:**597, 735, 751–53, 754
  genggong, **4:**754
  gong suling, **4:**754
  joged kebyar, **4:**754
  pejogedan bumbung (also *gamelan joged*), **4:**754
Bangladesh, *jātrā*, **5:**505
Bantu peoples, choral, **1:**763
Barbados
  military bands, **2:**816
  tuk band, **2:**815
  use of trombone and trumpet, **2:**816
Basque region, **8:**314
  trikitixa, **8:**314, 315
Belarus
  arkiestry, **8:**798
  kalektyvy, **8:**796
  muzyki, **8:**798
  state ensembles, **8:**800
Belgium
  bands, **8:**524
  brass bands, **8:**522
  ocarina bands, **8:**528
Belize, brukdown ensemble, **2:**677–78
Bengal, *dohār*, **5:**861, 862
Bolivia
  brass bands, **2:**217, 284, 288, 291, 292, 293, 296
  conjuntos, **2:**295, 296, 297
  consorts, **2:**295
  flute-and-drum, **2:**286
  grupos autóctonos, **2:**297

ensembles, musical, Bolivia (*continued*)
    grupos folklóricos, **2:**297
    guitarrilla ensembles, **2:**213–14
    julajula ensembles, **2:**285
    musiñu ensemble, **2:**289
    panpipe-and-drum, **2:**285–86
    panpipe ensembles, **2:**211, 293
    pinkillo ensembles, **2:**210
    tropa recto, **2:**295
  Bosnia-Hercegovina
    narodni orkestar, **8:**968–69
    for *sevdalinke*, **8:**965
    state folk ensembles, **8:**968–69
    tamburaški orkestar, **8:**968–69
    tamburica, **8:**965
    Turkish *mehterhana*, **8:**967
    urban, **8:**966
  Brazil
    banda de pífanos (also *zabumba*), **2:**329–30
    bands, **2:**304, 309, 334
    baterias, **2:**309, 313
    batucada, **2:**350
    for *bumba-meu-boi*, **2:**335
    caipira band, **2:**55, *59*
    for *capoeira*, **2:**346
    choro, **2:**350
    conjunto nordestinos, **2:**330
    conjuntos regionais, **2:**330
    folias de reis, **2:**301, 311–12, 319
    for *frevo de bloco*, **2:**337
    for *frevo de rua*, **2:**336
    gagaku orchestras, **2:**88
    for Saint Gonçalo dance, **2:**329
    samba ensembles, **2:**309
    trio elétrico, **2:**337–38
    trios nordestinos, **2:**330–31
  British Columbia
    bands, **3:**1094, 1258
    choirs, **3:**1094
    orchestras, **3:**1094–95
  Brittany
    bagad, **8:**562–63
    bagpipe bands, **8:**560
  Brunei, *gulintangan*, **4:**830
  Brunka culture, **2:**685
  Buddhist, *tūryaugha*, **5:**327
  Bulgaria
    brass bands, **8:**894, *895*, 897, 904
    chift kavali, **8:**895–96
    female choirs, **8:**902, 905
    folkloric, **8:**895
    folk orchestras, **8:***176*, 892, 902
    state ensembles, **8:**901–2
    for urbanized folk music, **8:**14
    wedding ensembles, **8:**283–84, 894
    zurla and *tapan* ensembles, **8:**280
  Burma
    anyeíñ tìwaìñ, **4:**365
    boûñcì, **4:**375
    byò, **4:**375
    doùpá, **4:**375
    hsaìñwaìñ, **4:**13, 15, 18, 22, 128, 132–33, 366, 385, 388, 538, 548–49
    htwe'tomucì tìwaìñ, **4:**365
    indoor, **4:**366, 376–78

    modes for, **4:**390–92
    outdoor, **4:**366–76
    òzi, **4:**375
    pattwaìñ, **4:**235, 548
    pa'waìñ, **4:***368*
    sito, **4:**375–76, 385
  Burusho people, *harīp*, **5:**283
  Canada
    African-Canadian bands, **3:**1211
    African-Canadian choirs, **3:**1211, 1212
    Andean folkloric, **3:**1204
    Armenian choirs, **3:**1084
    bands, **3:**137, 1181, 1188
    big bands, **3:**1080
    bluegrass bands, **3:**1133
    Brazilian *batucada*, **3:**1208
    Cantonese opera ensembles, **3:**1083, 1260–61
    chamber music groups, **3:**1148, 1181, 1184, 1186
    Chinese traditional music, **3:**1095–96, 1247–48
    choirs, **3:**1090, 1181–82, 1184, 1225
    church choirs, **3:**1070
    early music groups, **3:**1186
    Estonian choirs, **3:**1196
    fife and drum groups, **3:**7, 240
    Finnish choirs, **3:**1196
    German choirs, **3:**1195
    gospel choirs, **3:**1169
    Inuit bands, **3:**1069, 1275
    Italian bands, **3:**1196
    Latvian choirs, **3:**1196
    Lithuanian choirs, **3:**1196
    Macedonian bands, **3:**1198
    mandolin orchestras, **3:**1089, 1241
    Mennonite bands, **3:**1082
    Mennonite choirs, **3:**1082, 1231, 1238, 1239
    multiethnic choirs, **3:**343
    New France, choirs in, **3:**275
    Norwegian choirs, **3:**1251
    orchestras, **3:**1120, 1148, 1183–84, 1186, 1228; high school, **3:**1228–29
    Polish polka bands, **3:**1197
    regimental bands, **3:**1069, 1079, 1115, 1179, 1224
    Russian choirs, **3:**1199
    Salvation Army bands, **3:**1118
    Serbian choirs, **3:**1198
    Serbian orchestras, **3:**1198–99
    Slovenian choirs, **3:**1198
    Slovenian polka bands, **3:**1198
    Swedish choirs, **3:**1196
    swing bands, **3:**1077, 1080, 1091
    taiko drummers, **3:**1096, 1248
    tamburitza orchestras, **3:**1198
    tassa drumming groups, **3:**1208
    Ukrainian, **3:**1242
    Ukrainian *bandura* orchestras, **3:**1082
    Ukrainian choirs, **3:**1082, 1199–1200, 1241
  Caribbean
    bands, **2:**50
    brass bands, **2:**62, 212
    military bands, **2:**32, 37–39, 60, 67, 114

  Carriacou
    for big-drum dance, **2:**870
    quadrille, **2:**871–72
  Catalonia, *sardana*, **8:**123
  Central America
    bands, **2:**50, 62, 212
    military bands, **2:**32, 37–39, 60, 67, 114
  Central Asia, *estrada* orchestras, **6:**904, 905
  Chile
    brass bands, **2:**364, 365, 369
    for *cueca*, **2:**369
    for *nueva canción*, **2:**373
    panpipe ensembles, **2:**369
    urban *tonada*, **2:**368
    for Virgin of Las Peñas festival, **2:**363
  China
    Chaoyang ditao, **7:**186
    Chaozhou xianshiyue, **7:**5, 57, 180, 211–16
    choral, **7:**386–87
    chuida, **7:**189, 195–97, 236, 239, 240
    cuchuida, **7:**196
    Daoist Zhengyi sect, **7:**313
    early groups, **7:**108
    gong and drum, **7:**192–93
    Guangdong yinyue, **7:**89, 180, 217–21, 240
    guchui, **7:**189, 392
    Jiangnan sizhu, **7:**5, 57, 82, 89, 139, 169, 180, 186, 223–25, 233, 236, 238, 239, 242, 298, 404, 411, 419
    for *kunqu*, **7:**292
    Manchurian *bajiao gu*, **7:**452
    military bands, **7:**88, 195, 374–75, 379, 386
    nanguan, **7:**88, 169, 186, 205–9, 239, 242, 394, 396, 404
    northern groups, **7:**199–204, 311
    northwestern minority cultures, **7:**457
    notation for, **7:**125
    orchestras, **7:**90, 170, 178, 227–32, 348, 377, 381, 382, 386–87, 389, 418–19
    for Peking opera, **7:**77, 285–86
    percussion groups, **7:**191–93
    pipa in, **7:**169
    qing yanyue, **7:**212
    school bands, **7:**417
    Shanxi ba datao, **7:**239
    shawm and percussion groups, **7:**199–204, 259, 416
    sheng-guan groups, **7:**199–204, 312, 315–18, 331
    shifangu, **7:**5, 196, 224, 239, 311
    Shifan luogu, **7:**55, 192–93, 196, 224, 239, 311
    sizhu, **7:**103
    structures and performance practices in, **7:**233–43
    Sunan chuida, **7:**55, 133, 196–97, 239
    Tianjin shidiao, **7:**254
    village percussion, **7:**315–18
    Zhedong luogu, **7:**55, 195–96
    Zhou dynasty, **7:**99–101
  Chopi people, **1:**227, 436
    xylophone ensembles, **1:**709–10, 715
  Cirebon
    genjring, **4:**695
    ketuk telu, **4:**696

sintren, **4:**689, 697, 698
trebang randu kentir, **4:**696
Colombia
 all-women ensembles, **2:**105
 banda municipal, **2:**383–84
 brass bands, **2:**403
 chirimía bands, **2:**384, 402–3, 406, 407
 conjunto de cumbia, **2:**403, *407*, 409
 conjunto de gaita, **2:**407
 conjunto guabinero, **2:**377–78, 384
 conjunto llanero, **2:**377, 382, 385
 conjunto de pito, **2:**406–7, 410
 currulao ensemble, **2:**404
 duetos bambuqueros, **2:**377, *381*, 382–83,
  387, 390, 393, 395–96
 estudiantina, **2:**382, 383, 394, 396
 Kogi *conjunto de carrizos*, **2:**185
 murgas, **2:**380–81, 384–85, 389
 national bands, **2:**397
 orquestas, **2:**102
 rajaleña, **2:**377, 384
 salsa, **2:**403
 tunas, **2:**39
 vallenato, **2:**39, 410
Cook Islands
 brass bands, **9:**901
 percussive, **9:**901
Costa Rica
 cimarrona, **2:**698, 701, *702*
 marimba ensembles, **2:**698
 military bands, **2:**694
 municipal bands, **2:**699–700
 pop orchestras, **2:**690, 693
 for song-dances, **2:**698
 tríos, **2:**694, 698
Croatia
 brass bands, **8:**927, 931
 gunci (also *gunjci*; *guci*), **8:**931
 tamburaški orkestri, **8:**927, 934
 tamburica, **8:***927*, 932, 936
Cuba
 all-women ensembles, **2:**105
 biankomeko, **2:**826
 chamber ensembles, **2:**837
 charanga, **2:**832
 charanga francesa, **2:**833
 charanga típica, **2:**835
 comparsa, **2:**831, 836
 conjunto, **2:**835
 cuarteto, **2:**834
 danzón ensembles, **2:**832
 dúo, **2:**834
 estudiantina, **2:**835
 gran combo (also *gran orquesta*), **2:**836
 guaguancó, **2:**836
 military bands, **2:**823, 837
 municipal bands, **2:**837
 ngoma ensemble, **2:**825
 orquesta típica, **2:**827, 832, 835
 piquete típico, **2:**835
 septeto de son, **2:**834–35
 sexteto de son, **2:**834
 son ensembles, **2:**830
 symphony orchestras, **2:**837
 trío, **2:**834
Cyprus, *vkiolarides*, **8:**1030–31

Czech Republic, **8:**719
 brass bands, **8:**719
 cimbalová muzika, **8:**719
 malá selcká muzika, **8:**719
 Moravian dulcimer band, **8:***720*
 slácíková muzika, **8:**719
 velké muzika, **8:**719
 zither bands, **8:**717
Dai people, **7:**504
Dan people, trumpet ensembles, **1:**466
Denmark
 dance groups, **8:**457
 pub ensembles, **8:**454
Dominica, jing ping band, **2:**842
Dominican Republic
 all-women ensembles, **2:**105
 brass bands, **2:**849, 862
 canuto, **2:**854–55
 congo ensemble, **2:***851*, 854, 855
 dance bands, **2:**849, 860
 fife-and-drum ensemble, **2:**851
 gagá ensemble, **2:**853
 longdrum ensembles, **2:**854–55
 merengue ensembles, **2:***851*, 854
 merengue típico (also *perico ripiao*), **2:***850*,
  857
 military bands, **2:**858
 mummers (also *momís*; *guloyas*), **2:***853*, 855,
  859
 municipal bands, **2:**858, 859
 priprí, **2:***852*, 855
 salve ensembles, **2:**855
East Africa
 bands, **1:**151, 602–3
 court musicians, **1:**601
 taarab orchestras, **1:**427, 607, 645–46
 trumpet ensembles, **1:**601
East Asia
 military bands, **7:**50
 orchestral, **7:**6, 83
Ecuador
 banda mocha, **2:**416
 brass bands, **2:**422
 currulao ensemble, **2:***405*, 414–15
 flute-and-drum, **2:**210
 orquesta de toros, **2:**415, 421
Egypt
 female orchestras, **6:**298
 firqa, **6:**8, 45–46, 147, 148, 317–19, 553,
  559–61, 612, 642
 military bands, **6:**321, 547, 608–9
 mizmār wa ṭābl baladī, **6:**415, 420, 545
 for *qiṣaṣ*, **6:**170, *170*
 takht, **6:**8, 148, 170, 413, 418, 547,
  550–51, 559, 612
 al-takht al-sharqī, **6:**406
 for *tawāshīḥ dīniyya*, **6:**168
El Salvador
 brass bands, **2:**708
 chilamate, **2:**714
 fife and drum, **2:**712
 for little devils dance, **2:**714
 marimba ensembles, **2:**718
 municipal bands, **2:**718
England
 bhangra bands, **8:**236

brass bands, **8:**327
concertina band, **8:***4*
German bands, **8:**336
Estonia, **8:**494
 amateur, **8:**497
 choral, **8:**495–96
 orchestras, **8:**497
Europe
 Baroque, **8:**76–77
 bell choir, **8:**101
 brass bands, **8:**517
 development of, **8:**9
 folk groups, **8:**152–54, 157–58
 folklore, in festival contexts, **8:**150–52
 four-part structures in, **8:**62
 interplayer signaling in, **8:**101
 Jewish chamber orchestras and ensembles,
  8:260
 orchestras, **8:**51–52, 82; cue systems in,
  8:97; repertoire of, **8:**80; social
  structures of, **8:**61–63
 radio folk music ensembles, **8:**156–57
 Renaissance, **8:**168
 Renaissance consorts, **8:**74, 75
 Renaissance music for, **8:**76
 rock-and-roll bands, **8:**299, *300*
 state folk ensembles, **8:**152, 153, *176*, 201,
  209, 228, 277, 513, 577, 860, 902
 string quartet, **8:**61, 82
 for weddings, **8:**144
 wind bands, **8:**62–63, 146–47
 world music, **8:**225
Faroe Islands, **8:**471
Fiji, **5:**612–13
Finland, **8:**485
 balalaika orchestra, **8:**487
 brass bands, **8:**6, 479
 horn ensembles, **8:**483, *483*
 Swedish groups, **8:**487
Flores
 feko genda, **4:**794, *795*
 laba go, **4:**793
 nggo lamba, **4:**794
 todagu, **4:**793–94
France
 bagpipe, **8:**548
 wind bands, **8:**543
Fur people, **1:**561
Garífuna culture, **2:**733
 brass bands, **2:**733
 dangbu, **2:**671
 drum ensembles, **2:**752–53
 flute and drum, **2:**674
 garavón ensemble, **2:**741
 punta-rock, **2:**676–77
Gaudeloupe, for carnival genres, **2:**876–77
Georgia, **8:**840–41, 842
 mtskobri, **8:**840
 sazandari, **8:**840
 state ensembles, **8:**840–41, 844–45
Germany
 bands, **8:**656–57
 Bavarian *Stubenmusi* (bar-music), **8:**143,
  656
 choirs, **8:**655
 folkloric chamber-music groups, **8:**656

ensembles, musical, Germany (*continued*)
    Posaunenchöre, **8:**657
    Turkish janissary bands, **8:**200
  Ghana
    drum ensembles, **10:**29–36
    military bands, **10:**33–35
    vufofo drumming, **1:**390
  Gogo people, choral, **1:**638
  Great Britain
    garage bands, **8:**214
    rock bands, **8:**214–15
  Greece
    amateur, **8:**1017
    brass bands, **8:**1012
    Dodecanese islands, **8:**1015
    klarino ensemble, **8:**1010
    koumpania, **8:**285, 1019, 1021
    for *laika*, **8:**1020
    mainland, **8:**1009
    military bands, **8:**1008
    rebetika, **8:**206
    Roumeli, **8:**1013
    Thrace, **8:**1013
    zournadhes and *daouli* ensembles, **8:**1008,
      1011–12, *1012*
    zurla and *tapan* ensembles, **8:**280–81
  Grenada, for carnival, **2:**866
  Guadeloupe, quadrille ensembles,
    2:877–78
  Guatemala
    marimba ensembles, **2:**726, 735
    for *son*, **2:**728
  Gupta theater ensemble, **5:**25–26
  Guyana
    masquerade bands, **2:**446
    military bands, **2:**447
    for *tān saṅgīt*, **5:**602, 604
    tāssā, **5:**601
  Haiti
    brass bands, **2:**894
    konpa bands, **2:**890, 894
    méringue band, **2:**894
    mini-djaz, **2:**892–93
    òkès bastreng, **2:**889
    rara bands, **2:**887, 890, 894
    twoubadou groups, **2:**891–92
  Hausa people, drum ensembles, **1:**291
  Hawai'i
    bands, **3:**527; **9:**132–34, 222
    gagaku, **9:**95
    hula 'auana accompaniment, **9:**66–67
    pipe-and-drum bands, **9:**95, 135
    taiko drum ensembles, **9:**97
  Honduras
    concert bands, **2:**745
    marimba ensembles, **2:**742
    pipe and tabor, **2:**739, 743
  Hong Kong, orchestras, **7:**435
  Hungary, Rom, **8:**143, *272*, 738, *738*, 742,
    744, 745–46
  Ibaloy people
    kulimbet, **4:**918
    sulibao, **4:**918
  Iban people
    gendang panjat (also *engkeromung*), **4:**830
    gendang Raya, **4:**23, 829

  India, North, **5:**163
    bagpipe bands, **5:**347
    brass bands, **5:**347–48
    dhrupad, **5:**164
    ghazal, **5:**186
    for *kathak*, **5:**494
    khyāl, **5:**171–72
    naubat, **5:**301, *303*, 305, 340, 342, 712
    śahnāī, **5:**340, 347
    ṭhumrī, **5:**180
  India, South, **5:**101
    ceṇṭa mēḷam, **5:**361, 362, *932*, 932–33,
      934, 935–39
    cinna mēḷam, **5:**104, 360, 383, 387,
      389–90, 509, 910, 913
    for light classical music, **5:**107, 543, 544
    nāgasvaram ensembles, **5:**90
    periya mēḷam, **5:**103, 234, 323–24, 351,
      358, 359, *359*, 383, 387, 389–90,
      509, 910–11, 912, 914, 932, 935
    temple ensembles, **5:**210, 212, 270, 910–11
  Iran
    for *radif*, **6:**8, 137–38, 833–34, 866–67
    for weddings, **6:**828
  Iraq
    al-chalghī al-baghdādī, **6:**8, 312, 315, 411,
      418, 551–52
    for *maqām*, **6:**312–13, 411, 552
    al-takht al-sharqī, **6:**8, 312, 406, 411
  Iraqi-American groups, **6:**283
  Ireland
    céilí bands, **8:**388, 390
    folk groups, **8:**152–53
    pipe bands, **8:**385
  Irian Jaya, flute ensembles, **9:**546
  Israel
    choruses, **6:**1030
    early music groups, **6:**1030, 1031
    military, **6:**1020, 1072, 1073
    for Sephardi *ḥazanut*, **6:**204
    synagogue choirs, **6:**205
  Italy
    alpine regions, **8:**615
    brass bands, **8:**617–18
    for *carnevale di Bagolino*, **8:**608
    choral groups, **8:**610, 613–14
    Viggianesi, **8:**618
  Jamaica
    big bands, **2:**97
    brass bands, **2:**899, 910
    junkunnu bands, **2:**907
    mento bands, **2:**899, 900, 906
    quadrille bands, **2:**907
  Japan
    amateur choruses, **7:**51
    for *etenraku imayo*, **7:**608
    fife and drum groups, **7:**725
    gagaku, **7:**42, 45, 607–8, 620–24, 625,
      701
    hayasi, **7:**655, 657, 659, 660, 665, 671,
      680, 683–85, 771
    for *kabuki*, **7:**77, 654, 657, 660–61, 712
    for *kyôgen*, **7:**636
    maturi bayasi, **7:**775
    military bands, **7:**721, 725, 727–28, *728*
    for *minzoku geinô*, **7:**605

    narimono, **7:**684
    for *nô*, **7:**551, 634–35
    orchestras, **7:**537, 732
    sankyoku, **7:**5, 82, 688, 692–93, 704, 705,
      712, 715–17, 777, 778–79; **10:**102
    for *sôkyoku*, **7:**696, 716
    tôgaku, **7:**609
    wayô gassô, **7:**722, 749–50
    for *ziuta*, **7:**673, 692, 696, 697, 716
  Java
    angklung, **4:**634
    angklung Banyuwangi, **4:**645–46, 656, 667,
      679
    Banyumas, **4:**645
    brass bands, **4:**633
    calung, **4:**634, 645, 656, 667, 669, 679,
      681
    gambang kromong, **4:**73
    gandrung, **4:**645, 656, 667
    réyog kendhang, **4:**646
    sronèn, **4:**646, 668, 675
    terbangan, **4:**646
    tetabuhan, **4:**632–33
  Jola people, choral, **1:**445
  Kalagan people, *tagunggo*, **4:**922
  Karnataka
    bands, **5:**886
    kaṛḍi majalu, **5:**874
    kombu kahaḷe, **5:**874–75
    mēḷa, **5:**867–68, *874*
    vādya, **5:**886
    for *yakṣagāna* dance-drama, **5:**515
  Kasena-Nankani people, **1:**455, 456
  Kashmir
    for *chakri*, **5:**683–84
    ṣūfyāna mūsīqī, **5:**688, *688*
    surnāy, **5:**685–86
  Kazakhstan, folk orchestras, **6:**959
  K'ekchi Maya, harp ensembles, **2:**668
  Kenya, **1:**626–28
    bands, **1:**626
    choral, **1:**629–30
    kiringoringo, **1:**624
  Kerala
    for *kathakaḷi* dance-drama, **5:**324–25, 513
    for *mōhīni aṭṭam*, **5:**513
    pañcavādyam, **5:**351, 360–62, 932–33, 935,
      940, 943–44
  Khmer people
    arakk, **4:**173, 194
    beepat khmer, **4:**214
    chhaiyaim, **4:**155, 165, 167, 199
    kantrüm, **4:**210–11, 213, 214–15
    kar, **4:**169, 173, 195–96
    klang chhnakk, **4:**167–68, 197
    klang khek, **4:**174, 197, 202
    korng skor, **4:**165, 197
    mahori, **4:**210
    mahori khmer, **4:**214–15
    mohori, **4:**168, 169, 176, 178, 183–85, 204
    mohori Samai, **4:**175, 184–85, 208
    pey keo, **4:**197
    pinn peat, **4:**134, 155, 157–58, 165, 168,
      173–74, 176–78, 183, 189–90, 191,
      215, 241, 533
    piphat, **4:**211
    thum mong, **4:**210, 214, 231

Korea
  for *aak*, **7:**822, 829, 862–63, 869–870
  for *ch'anggŭk*, **7:**77
  Chŏngnong akhoe, **7:**82
  chorach'i (also *kyŏngnaech'wi*), **7:**871, 873
  chulp'ungnyu, **7:**823, 866
  for court and *chŏngak* music, **7:**866–67
  farmers' bands (*nongaktae*, also
      p'ungmultae), **7:**5, 804, *804*, 807, 809,
      815–16, 817, 829, 873, 889, 929–39,
      942, 963–67, *965*
  for folk song accompaniment, **7:**880
  Hyangje chul p'ungnyu, **7:**983–84
  for *kagok*, **7:**921
  for *kasa*, **7:**927
  koch'wi, **7:**930
  kunak, **7:**930
  kwanhyŏnbang, **7:**982
  military bands, **7:**951
  samullori, **7:**963–67, *964*, *968*
  for *sijo*, **7:**925
  sinawi, **7:**817, 889–91, 914
  taep'ungnyu, **7:**823, 867
  t'aech'wit'a, **7:**873
  for *t'alch'um*, **7:**942
Kota people, *koḷvar*, **5:**278, 912
Kpelle people, **1:**467
Kuna culture, *gammu burui* ensemble, **2:**646
Kurdistan
  for dances, **6:**749
  dhol wa zurna, **6:**415
Laos, **4:**355–56
  khene vong, **4:**358
  maholi, **4:**356, 358
  pinpat, **4:**358–59
  piphat, **4:**356, 358
  sep noi, **4:**356
  sep nyai, **4:**356
Latvia, **8:**504
  state ensembles, **8:**505
Liberia, bands, **1:**376
Libya
  for Andalusian repertoire, **6:***453*
  women's groups, **6:**416
Lithuania, brass bands, **8:**512
Lombok, **4:**770
  cilokaq, **4:**768, 774
  gamelan grantang, **4:**767
  gamelan klentang, **4:**767
  gamelan Maulid, **4:**767
  gamelan rebana, **4:**773–74
  kamput, **4:**773
  kecimol, **4:**768, 774
  musik rudat, **4:**774
Low Countries
  fiddle-and-bass combination, **8:**523, 529,
      532
  fife and drum, **8:**528, *529*
  wind bands, **8:**529–30
Lozi people, royal ensembles, **1:**712
Luvale people, choral, **1:**726–43
Macedonia
  brass bands, **8:**976–78, 981
  čalgija, **8:**200, 281–82, 977, *979*, 979–80,
      981, 983
  choral, **8:**981

čift kavali, **8:**975
naroden orkestar, **8:**981, *982*
Rom people, **8:**280–82, 975–77
zurla and *tapan* ensembles, **8:**975–76, *977*,
    979, 982–83
Madagascar, choral, **1:**783, 791
Maguindanao people, *palabunibunyan*,
    4:892–95
Malaysia
  brass bands, **4:**440
  caklempong (or *taklempong*), **4:**414, 422,
      424
  gendang silat, **4:**417, 422
  gendang tarinai, **4:**415
  kulintangan, **4:**830
  nobat, **4:**427, 429–30
  ronggeng, **4:***427*
  RTM Orchestra, **4:**441
  taklempong pacik, **4:**414
Malta, **8:**639–40, *641*
Maluku, **4:**819–20
  gong-and-drum, **4:**812
  kulintang (also *kolintang*; *jalanpong*),
      4:814–15, 816
Manihiki, brass bands, **9:**906
Mapuche culture, *pifülka* ensembles, **2:**233–34
Maranao people
  kapanirong, **4:**905
  kulintang, **4:**896–98
Mariana Islands, brass bands, **9:**743
Maritimes, choirs, **3:**1120
Martinique, beguine orchestra, **2:**916, *917*
Mashriq region
  brass bands, **6:**548
  firqa, **6:**33, 552
  takht, **6:**33, 552, 553
  urkestr, **6:**552
Maya culture, **2:**651
  for *baile del tun*, **2:**724
  bandas, **2:**730–31
  brass band, **2:**655
  flute and drum, **2:**667
  marimba ensembles, **2:**655, 667, 730
  for saint's day processions, **2:**730
  string trio, **2:**655
  trumpet and drum bands, **2:**654
Melanesia, panpipe ensembles, **9:**598
Mexica culture, *conjunto azteca*, **2:**558
Mexico
  bandas, **2:**610, 622; **10:**90
  bandas del pueblo, **2:**604
  bandas sinaloenses, **2:**622
  bands, **2:**50, 62, 212
  brass bands, **2:**550
  chilena, **2:**610
  conchero, **2:**559
  conjunto de arpa grande, **2:***612*
  conjunto norteño, **2:**613, *614*
  dance orchestras, **2:**622
  marimba ensembles, **2:**610, 622
  military bands, **2:**32, 37–39, 60, 67, 114
  murza, **4:**854
  orquesta típica, **2:**622
  for *son*, **2:**606
  son guerrerense, **2:**611
  tamborazos zacatecanos, **2:**622

Miao people, *lusheng* bands, **7:**451
Micronesia, brass bands, **9:**719
Middle East, **6:**3, 7–8
  naqqāra-khāne, **6:**3
  ṭabl wa-zurna, **6:**415, 420
Mithila, *pipahī*, **5:**679
Mixtec culture, **2:**565
  bandas, **2:**549, 565, 567
  pre-Hispanic, **2:**564
Montenegro
  state folk ensembles, **8:**959
  tamburica, **8:**959
Mordvinian people, choral, **8:**773–74
Morocco
  for Andalusian repertoire, **6:***453*
  for *malḥūn*, **6:**498–99
Nauru, brass bands, **9:**261, 755
Nepal
  dhimaybājā, **5:**702
  nāykhīnbājā, **5:**702–3
  pāncai bājā, **5:**280–81, 286, 699–700
  urban orchestras, **5:**705
Netherlands Antilles
  Cuban-style orchestras, **2:**930
  jazz bands, **2:**930–31
Nguni people, choral, **1:**719
Nicaragua
  bandas de chicheros, **2:**749, 762, 767
  bandas filarmónicas, **2:**762
  brass bands, **2:**749
  guitar duos, **2:**757
  los atabales, **2:**757
  marimba ensembles, **2:**761–62, 767
Nigeria
  bands, **1:**234, 235–36
  choral, **1:**235, 236
  orchestras, **1:**233, 236
Niue, brass bands, **9:**817
Nkoya people, royal ensembles, **1:**712
North Africa
  European instruments in, **6:**435
  Jewish, **6:**1043
  Ottoman military bands, **6:**433
  women's groups, **6:**437
North Caucasia
  folk orchestras, **8:**859, 863
  state ensembles, **8:**851
Northwest Coast Indian groups, bands, **3:**11,
    1094
Norway, accordion, **8:**420
Nyungwe people, reed-pipe ensembles, **1:**711
Oceania
  brass bands, **9:**126, 128–34, 382–83
  log idiophone ensembles, **9:**374
Oman
  firāq al-dān, **6:**674, 677, *678*, 681–82
  firāq al-qurba, **6:**679–80, 681
  firāq al-razḥa and *al-razīf*, **6:**675–76, 680,
      681, 682
  firqat al-funūn al-sha'biyya lil-Ṣuḥār,
      6:680–81
  ḥalāq al-lewa, **6:**678–79
  ḥalāq al-mālid, **6:**677–78
Ontario
  orchestras, **3:**1079
  polka bands, **3:**1195

ensembles, musical (*continued*)
Orissa, *oḍissi*, **5:**520
Otomí culture, **2:**571
tunditos, **2:**571
Otopame culture
for *huapango arribeño*, **2:**571
música de golpe, **2:**571
pipe-and-tabor, **2:**572
Palawan people, *basal*, **4:**924
Panama
congo ensembles, **2:**775–76
conjuntos típicos, **2:**57, 774, *775*, 777, 783
drum-and-bugle corps, **2:**782
drum ensembles, **2:**774, 777
marching bands, **2:**782
military bands, **2:**772
Papua New Guinea
Baluan *garamut* ensembles, **9:**602, 604–6
bamboo bands, **9:**90, 155
bamboo pipe ensemble, **9:**609
Banoni panpipe and trumpet ensemble, **9:**647
brass bands, **9:**27, 89, 128–30, 147, 148, 196
Buin *garamut* ensemble, **9:**651
conch bands, **9:**89, 128–29, 195–96, *197*, 288, 393
flute ensembles, **9:**512, 546–47
garamut ensemble, **9:**376–77
gospel bands, **9:**90–91
Halia pipe and trumpet ensembles, **9:**640–41
Iatmul flute ensembles, **9:**556
kundu ensembles, **9:**489
Manus *garamut* ensembles, **9:**601
New Ireland *lounuat* ensemble, **9:**381–82
panpipes ensembles, **9:**512
pipe-and-drum band, **9:**89
power bands (also electric bands, live bands), **9:**90, 137–38, 139–40, 153, 246, 485–86
Saidor *tambaran* ensembles, **9:**548
Sepik Hills flute ensembles, **9:**558
side-blown flute ensembles, **9:**477
trumpet ensembles, **9:**477, 547, 548, 552, 609
vessel flute ensemble, **9:**609
Waxei flute ensembles, **9:**559
Paraguay
banda koyguá, **2:**459
brass bands, **2:**459
conjuntos, **2:**456–57, 458, 459, 461, 462
rock bands, **2:**459, 461, 463
Peru
ayarachi ensembles, **2:**35
bandas de guerra, **2:**471
banda típica, **2:**475
brass bands, **2:**63, 474, 480, 483
chiriwano ensembles, **2:**34
College of San Pablo band, **2:**493–94
conjunto, **2:**470, 474
conjunto de cuerdas, **2:**475
Cusco dance bands, **2:**212
estudiantina, **2:**474, 475
fiesta orchestras, **2:**209
flute-and-drum, **2:**210

flute ensembles, **2:**471, 475, 477–78
herranza, **2:**475
Inca military bands, **2:**37–38
orquesta típica, **2:**37, 474, 475, *479*, 483
panpipe ensembles, **2:**11, 468, 469, *470*, 483
roncadora, **2:**210
tarkeadas, **2:**471
tunas, **2:**39
use of accordion, **2:**474
Philippines
for alternative music, **4:**886–87
bands, **4:**859, 862–63, 868, 869
big bands, **4:**883–84
cumbanchero, **4:**883–84
cumparsa (also *comparsa*), **4:**854, 869
estudiantina, **4:**854, 869
kulintang, **4:**94, 876
musikong bumbong, **4:**860
orchestras, **4:**842, 859–60, 863, 868, 869, 870–71
rock bands, **4:**887–88
rondalla, **4:**854–55, 868, 869
show bands, **4:**886
Poland, **8:**705–6, 709
Polynesia, brass bands, **9:**771
Polynesia, *pahu* ensembles, **9:**385
Portugal, **8:**582–83
bagpipe-and-drum ensemble, **8:**579, 583
fado ensemble, **8:**116
polyphonic choral groups, **8:**581
ranchos folclóricos, **8:**577–78, 580–81, 582, 583
tunas, **8:**582, 583
wind bands, **8:**579–80
Puerto Rico
bands, **2:**940
jíbaro ensembles, **2:**935, 940
plena, **2:**939–40
Pukapuka, log-idiophone, **9:**913
Punjab (India), *bhangra*, **5:**651–52
Purépecha culture
brass bands, **2:**578
for *pirekuas*, **2:**579
for *sones*, **2:**579
Qatar, women's group, **6:***536*
Réunion Island, **5:**608
maloya ensemble, **5:**610
for *sega*, **5:**609
Romania, **8:**876
choral, **8:**882, *884*
collegium musicum, **8:**881
mehterhanes, **8:**881–82
taraf, **8:***872*, 880
tarafuri, **8:**878, 879
Roti
meko, **4:**798, 799–800
meko ai, **4:**800
Russia
balalaika orchestra, **8:***775*
folk instrument orchestras, **8:**9
rozhok ensembles, **8:**770
state ensembles, **8:**777
Tatar people, **8:***11*
vocal, **8:**757
Ryûkyû Islands, for *uta sansin*, **7:**792

St. Lucia
dance bands, **2:**950
kwadril ensemble, **2:**945
Sama-Bajao people
kulintang, **4:**900–901
pangongka'an, **4:**900–901
Sāmoa, brass bands, **9:**808
Sardinia, flute and drum, **8:**627
Saudi Arabia, female orchestras, **6:**653
Savu, gong-and-drum, **4:**802
Scotland, bagpipe bands, **8:**363
Scotland, skiffle bands, **8:**369
Serbia
amateur, **8:**950
brass bands, **8:**280, 946, *946*, 950–51, 953
Kosovan brass bands, **8:**285–86
Kosovan *čalgija*, **8:**286, 952, 997
Kosovan *dajre def*, **8:**285
Kosovan *zurla* and *tapan* ensembles, **8:**285, 951
Rom ensembles, **8:**951–52
tamburica, **8:**945, 946, 952, *953*
for urbanized folk music, **8:**14
Shona people
choral, **1:**755
ngororombe ensembles, **1:**751–52
Slovakia, **8:**719
brass bands, **8:**719
cimbalová muzika, **8:**719
dulcimer band, **8:***720*
slácikova muzika, **8:**719
Slovenia, **8:**914
brass bands, **8:**920
narodno-zabavni ansambli, **8:**920
tamburica ensembles, **8:**917
Solomon Islands
bamboo bands, **9:**156, 657
garamut ensembles, **9:**632
panpipe and trumpet ensemble, **9:**656, 658
panpipe ensembles, **9:**156, *283*, 398–401, 630, 632, 661, 665, 667, 668–69, *670*
Sirovanga panpipe and trumpet ensembles, **9:**654–55
urban bands, **9:**158
Songhai people, choral, **1:**450
Sotho peoples
choral, **1:**707
reed-flute ensembles, **1:**707
South Africa
bands, **1:**717, 765, 768, 769, 773
choral, **1:**218–19, 433, 718, 755, 763–64, 764, 765, 769–70, 770, 772; *mbholoho*, **1:**764; *ukureka*, **1:**770
jazz bands, **1:**765–66
royal ensembles, **1:**782
South America
bands, **2:**50, 62, 132, 212
estudiantinas, **2:**39–40
military bands, **2:**32, 37–39, 60, 67, 114
South Asia
avanaddha varga, **5:**323
bands, **5:**223, 347, 368; use at funerals, **5:**273
guitar bands, **5:**428
kutapa, **5:**323
medieval theater ensemble, **5:**33, 35, 40

naubat khānā, **5:**279–80; **6:**3
studio orchestras, **5:**108, 535–36, 543, 544,
545–46
tabla groups, **5:**136
Southeast Asia
Chinese *sizhu*, **4:**71, 73, 272
gong-chime ensembles, **4:**9, 11, 20–21, 27,
596
gong ensembles, upland regions, **4:**60
island regions, **4:**597
prehistoric, **4:**45–46
stamped tube ensembles, **4:**597
southern Africa, choral, **1:**227, 433
South Korea, orchestras, **7:**990
Spain, **8:**589
banda de música, **8:**594
for *cante jondo*, **8:**134
Catalonian *cobla* ensemble, **8:**593–94
rondalla, **8:**593, 594
Sri Lanka
centa mēlam, **5:**361
cinna mēlam, **5:**360
hēvisi, **5:**13, 329, 351, 361, 363–64, 958,
966, 967–68
pappara, **5:**966, 969
rabāna, **5:**964–65
for *sarala gī*, **5:**972
temple ensembles, **5:**958
Subanun people
gandang-gandang, **4:**923
gandingan, **4:**923
kinilisong, **4:**923–24
megayep, **4:**923
thanggunggu, **4:**923
Sudan, **1:**563–68
trumpet, **6:**416
Sulawesi
kolintang, **4:**810
Makassarese drum ensemble, **10:**46
mámarakka, **4:**809
orkes bea, **4:**810
orkes kacapi suling, **4:**806
pompang (also *bas*), **4:**806, *807*
rere, **4:**809–10
Sumatra
Bengkulu Province, **4:**619
calempong, **4:**609
canang, **4:**609, 615, 623, 628
canang situ, **4:**605
gamat moderen, **4:**613
gambang, **4:**615, 616, 617
gamulan, **4:**620
gendang, **4:**607
gendang sarunei, **4:**607
genderang, **4:**607
gondang, **4:**23, 607
gondang hasapi, **4:**608
gong-and-drum, **4:**598, 600, 602
gonrang, **4:**607
gonrang dagang, **4:**607
gordang lima, **4:**607–8
gordang sembilan, **4:**607–8
kelenongan, **4:**627
kelintang, **4:**616, 617, 619, 620, 621,
623–24, 628
kelintang kayu, **4:**616, 617

kelitang, **4:**623
kelittang, **4:**627, 628
keneo, **4:**621
keromong, **4:**627
keromongan, **4:**623, 624
kromong, **4:**616, 617, 619
kromongan, **4:**626
kulintang, **4:**627, 628
kulitang, **4:**627
nobat, **4:**600–601, 609, 615
nobat nafir, **4:**606
orkes gamat, **4:**601–2, 611, 621
orkes gambus, **4:**605, 621–22, 625
orkes Lampung, **4:**628
orkes Melayu, **4:**617, 621–22, 625
orkes sinandung timur, **4:**604–5
tabuhan, **4:**623, 624, 627
taganing ensemble, **4:**605
talempong, **4:**601, 609, 611, 612
tanjidor (brass bands), **4:**601, 626–27
tilempong, **4:**605
Sumbawa, **4:**781
ansambel musik Bima, **4:**783
ansambel musik Sumbawa, **4:**781
genda Mbojo, **4:**783, 785
gong genang, **4:**781
kareku kandei, **4:**783–84
rebana rea, **4:**781, 783
Sunda
angklung, **4:**710–11, 719–20, 725
arumba, **4:**712
calung, **4:**711–12, 724
kacapian, **4:**703, 712, 715–17
kacapi-suling, **4:**703, 712, 715, 724, 761
kendang penca, **4:**703, 709, 724
ketuk telu, **4:**696
ketuk tilu, **4:**107, 703, 707
rampak kendang, **4:**703, 709–10
Surinam, *gamelan* ensembles and *gamelan*
angklung, **2:**507–8
Sweden
bands, **8:**440–41
brass bands, **8:**435
fiddlers' ensembles, **8:**152
for *gammeldans*, **8:**441
orchestras, **8:**443
spelmanslag, **8:**441, *441*
Switzerland
bandella, **8:**694, 695
brass bands, **8:**683, 695
brass ensembles, **8:**688–89
fife-and-drum bands, **8:**685, 686
guggenmusige, **8:**684–85
ländlerkappelle, **8:**689–90, 693
orchestre champêtre, **8:**693
schwyzerörgeli quartetten, **8:**205–6
Syria
firqa, **6:**567
takht, **6:**566, 569, 570
Tahiti, brass bands, **9:**868
Taiwan
bayin, **7:**427
nanguan, **7:**425
orchestras, **7:**429
Tamil Nadu, **5:**912–16
for *bharata nātyam*, **5:**522

drum groups, **5:**914–15
naiyānti mēlam, **5:**913–14, *914*
percussion ensembles for possession rituals,
5:293
urumi mēlam, **5:**915
Tanzania, bands, **1:**643
Tarahumara culture, violin ensembles,
2:583
Tausug people, *kulintangan*, **4:**898
Thailand, **4:**226–27, 240–47
boeng mang kawk, **4:**235
brass bands, **4:**82, 330–31
bua loi, **4:**246
chuida, **4:**71
daluogu, **4:**71
historical, **4:**246–47
ka law, **4:**305
khap mai, **4:**247
khrüang, **4:**264
khrüang pra kom, **4:**312
khrüang sai, **4:**22, 133, 245–46, 261–62,
264, 331
khrüang sai khrüang khu, **4:**245
khrüang sai khrüang lek, **4:**245
khrüang sai phrasom, **4:**246
khrüang sai pi chawa, **4:**245–46
klawng chum, **4:**312
klawng khaek, **4:**246, 247, *250*
klawng u je, **4:**312
klawng yao, **4:**303
lao phan, **4:**247
mahori, **4:**17, 22, 133, 243–45, 255,
261–62, 264, 272, 548
mahori boran, **4:**243, 247
mahori khrüang hok, **4:**244
mahori khrüang khu, **4:**244–45
mahori khrüang yai, **4:**245
mahori maun, **4:**264
mahori wong lek, **4:**244
northern, **4:**312–13
penja duriyang, **4:**312
pi chum, **4:**312, 313
piphat, **4:**11, 17, 22, *121*, 133, 241–43,
247, 253, 255, 258–62, 269, 272,
286, 538, 548
piphat dükdamban, **4:**243, 256, 264
piphat khrüang ha, **4:**241
piphat khrüang khu, **4:**241
piphat khrüang yai, **4:**241–42, 251–52
piphat mai khaeng, **4:**241
piphat mai nuam, **4:**242, 257, 261, 264
piphat mawn, **4:**242–43, 247, 249, 264,
367
piphat nang hong, **4:**242, 264
pitch levels of, **4:**261
salaw süng pi, **4:**221
sizhu, **4:**238
southern, **4:**305–6
wong dontri lanna wong yai, **4:**312
Tibet
for *duolu*, **7:**480–81
for *nangma*, **7:**475
passim, **7:**873
for religious music, **7:**479–80
Tibetan culture, **5:**715
gar-pa troupes, **5:**713

ensembles, musical (*continued*)
Tinggian people
inila-ud, **4:**917
pinalaiyan, **4:**917–18
Tonga
brass bands, **9:**130–32, 793
conch bands, **9:**794
idiophone ensembles, **9:**784
Trinidad and Tobago
American congos, **2:**958–59
congos, **2:**965
film music, **5:**591
Orisa drum ensembles, **2:**955
parang ensembles, **2:**953, 959–60
soca bands, **2:**96
tamboo-bamboo bands, **2:**96, 962, 965
tāssā, **5:**589–90
Tunisia
for Andalusian repertoire, **6:**406–7, *453*
firqa, **6:**327
for Jewish weddings, **6:**527–28
for *ma'lūf* performance, **6:**327–29, 335–36,
418, 507, 508, 509, 511, 512
military bands, **6:**325–26
Turkey
arabesk orchestras, **6:**257, 776
choral, **6:**117
folk, **6:**764
janissary bands (*mehter*), **6:**21, 114–15, 190,
194, 767–68, 770
for *makam*, **6:**47
Ottoman court, **6:**108, 113–14
professional, **6:**785, 844
Western orchestra, **6:**771
Uganda
amakondere trumpet ensemble, **1:**312
Buganda court, **1:**601–2, 642
Uighur people, *naghira* drum music, **7:**459
Ukraine
brass bands, **8:**811
church choirs, **8:**806
folkloric, **8:**808, 819
folk music choirs, **8:**123
instrumental groups, **8:**810–11, 813
military bands, **8:**806
narodni muzychny instrumenty, **8:**816,
817–18
plucked lute ensembles, **8:**817
state ensembles, **8:**817
United States
African-American choirs, **3:**535–36, 577,
607
amateur bands, **3:**556, 557
Armenian ensembles, **3:**1032, 1033
balalaika orchestras, **3:**57–58, *59*, 529, 915,
920
Balinese *gender wayang*, **3:**1019
Balinese *kecak*, **3:**1019
banda orquesta, **3:**720, 778–80
banda típica, **3:**772
bands, **3:**60, 240, 536, 563–68, 604;
colonial period, **3:**563–64; nineteenth
century, **3:**556, 564–66; twentieth
century, **3:**566–67
Basque bands, **3:**849–50
batá ensemble, **3:**729

bell choirs, **3:**123
big bands, **3:**550, 654–56, 969; Latin,
3:720, 732, 741, 793–94; Tejano,
3:720, 778, 779–80
blackface minstrel groups, **3:**184, 543, 616
bluegrass bands, **3:**159, 161, 163–64
blues trios, **3:**669
bouzouki ensembles, **3:**930
café-aman orchestra, **3:**931
Cajun dance groups, **3:**857–58
Cambodian *mohori*, **3:**999
Cambodian *pinn peat*, **3:**1001, 1002
Cambodian rock bands, **3:**1002
Cambodian wedding ensembles, **3:**1000
Cantonese opera ensembles, **3:**527, 960–61
Celtic rock bands, **3:**845–46
chamber music groups, **3:**175, 537–38
Chaozhou percussion groups, **3:**961
children's choirs, **3:**284
Chinese silk and bamboo groups, **3:**961,
962
Chinese traditional music, **3:**949, 959
choirs, **3:**535–36
church choirs, **3:**119, 123, 125, 127
circus bands, **3:**568
club lounge trios, **3:**667
comparsa, **3:**729
composers' groups, **3:**176–77, 254
conjunto jíbara, **3:**726
conjuntos, **3:**9, 16, 522, 723, 897–88
contra dance bands, **3:**231
Croatian choirs, **3:**919
Czech bands, **3:**897
Czech choirs, **3:**898
dance orchestras, **3:**604
Danish groups, **3:**882–83
drum and bugle corps, **3:**899
early music groups, **10:**69–70
Estonian choirs, **3:**878
ethnic choirs, **3:**825
fife and drum groups, **3:**7, 240, 836
Filipino *rondalla*, **3:**1025
Finnish bands, **3:**874
French groups, **3:**855
funeral bands, **3:**568
gammeldans groups, **3:**868, 869–70, 871,
872
German bands, **3:**18, 888, 889
German choirs, **3:**528, 885–86
German groups, **3:**528
"girl groups," **3:**673, 709
gospel choirs, **3:**534–35, 585
gospel quartets, **3:**535, 585, 632, 670
Greek bands, **3:**929–30
grupo, **3:**780–81
Haitian *mini-djaz*, **3:**803–4
Harmoniemusik, **3:**563
hokum bands, **3:**645
Hungarian choirs, **3:**909
Iranian ensembles, **3:**1034, 1035
Irish showbands, **3:**845
Italian bands, **3:**861–62, 864–65
Italian ensembles, **3:**860–61
Japanese pop bands, **3:**968
Japanese traditional music, **3:**968–69, 972
jazz bands, **3:**524–25, 551, 651, 652–55

jazz combos, **3:**550, 644, 667, 668–69, 671
jazz ensembles, school, **3:**282–83
Jewish choirs, **3:**939, 943–44
jug bands, **3:**645
juke bands, **3:**645
kanklès ensembles, **3:**876
kantele ensembles, **3:**826, *826s*
Korean *samulnori*, **3:**977
kulintang ensemble, **3:**1025–26
Lao instrumental ensembles, **3:**1007–8
Lithuanian, **3:**875–77
Louisiana, bands in, **3:**802
luogu, **3:**279
Macedonian bands, **3:**925, 926
mandolin orchestras, **3:**920
marimba ensembles, **3:**723, 727–28, *728*,
746
merengue, **3:**731
Mexican *banda sinaloense*, **3:**746
Mexican bands, **3:**723
Mexican groups, **3:**745–46
Middle Eastern groups, **3:**1036–37
military bands, **3:**295
minstrel bands, **3:**568
mission choirs, **3:**735, 755
Navajo country and western bands, **3:**433
orchestras, **3:**536–37; colonial period, **3:**7;
government funding for, **3:**297, 299;
high school, **3:**277, 278, 282;
personnel, **3:**235; radio, **3:**559; theater,
3:555; women performers, **3:**89
Orff-Schulwerk instrumentarium, **3:**281,
1021
orquestas típicas, **3:**791, 795
for Peking opera, **3:**961
Plains Indian drum group, **3:**483
Polish choirs, **3:**891–92
polka bands, **3:**284, 529, 821, 824;
German, **3:**890–91; Polish, **3:**892,
893–96; Slovenian, **3:**901; at Swedish
events, **3:**871
quadrille bands, **3:**232
regimental bands, **3:**7, 563, 564–65
rock bands, **3:**284–85, 551, 943–44, 952
Russian church choirs, **3:**915
school bands, **3:**277, 278, 281–82, 536,
567
school choirs, **3:**276, 283, 536, 629
school percussion ensembles, **3:**279, 282,
342
Scottish highland bagpipe regiments,
3:324
in secondary schools, **3:**281–82
skiffle bands, **3:**645
Slovak bands, **3:**899, 900
society bands, **3:**564
son conjunto, **3:**792, 795
for South Asian music, **3:**984
for Spanish dance dramas, **3:**851
string quartets, **3:**538
for Sufi *dhikr* ceremony, **3:**1045
Swedish choirs, **3:**870–71
swing bands, **3:**668
Syrian ensembles, **3:**1032
taiko drummers, **3:**970–71, 973
tamburitza orchestras, **3:**529, 920–24

Tohono O'odham *waila*, **3**:436, 472–73, 489–90
tríos, **3**:777
Ukrainian *bandura* orchestras, **3**:10
Vietnamese rock bands, **3**:997
vocal harmony groups, **3**:350, 667, 670–71, 709
Volga German bands, **3**:890
washboard bands, **3**:645
wind band movement, **3**:536, 567, 826
women's bands, **3**:566
world music groups, **3**:948
Uruguay
  bands, **2**:516
  canto popular uruguayo, **2**:520
  fife-and-drum corps, **2**:511
  for tango, **2**:519
Uttar Pradesh
  amplified band with flatbed wagon, **5**:671
  for *birahā*, **5**:666–67
  brass bands, **5**:671
  for *kajalī*, **5**:670
  for *qawwali*, **5**:673
  śahnāī, **5**:671
Uzbekistan
  maqām, **6**:918–20
  nakkaraxāna military orchestra, **6**:940
  workers' choirs, **6**:918
Vanuatu
  idiophone ensembles, **9**:702
  log-idiophone ensembles, **9**:690, 694, 698
  Malakula *temes nainggol*, **9**:690
  panpipe ensembles, **9**:690
Venda people, *tshikona* ensemble, **1**:708–9
Venezuela
  aguinaldo ensemble, **2**:531, 538
  arpa llanera ensemble, **2**:540–41
  central-coastal harp ensembles, **2**:541
  chimbanguele, **2**:531, 536
  mina ensemble, **2**:528, 539
  redondo ensemble, **2**:527–30, 539
  tambora, **2**:528
  tamunangue, **2**:536
  tura ensembles, **2**:533
Vietnam
  avong, **4**:534
  brass bands, **4**:507, 511
  bronze gong ensembles, **4**:531, 533, 534
  chamber music, **4**:452, 454
  dại nhạc, **4**:70, 504
  gong ensembles, **4**:535
  ngũ tuyệt, **4**:467, 483
  nhạc bát âm, **4**:504
  nhạc huyền, **4**:448
  nhạc lễ, **4**:465, 467, 469, 470, 474, 475, 483, 504
  tam tấu, **4**:467
  tiểu nhạc, **4**:448
  trum, **4**:534
  ty bã lệnh, **4**:448
  xéc pùa, **4**:535
Virgin Islands
  dance bands, **2**:969
  fife-and-drum bands, **2**:973
  scratch bands (also *fungi* bands), **2**:969–71
Vlah people, *duduk* ensembles, **8**:950

Wales, skiffle bands, **8**:355
West Africa, **1**:355
  with guitar, **1**:358
West Timor, *sene tufu*, **4**:797
Yakan people, *tagunggu*, **4**:898–900
Yaqui culture
  conjuntos, **2**:592
  tríos románticos, **2**:592
Yemen, drum ensembles, **6**:7, 95–106, 420, 656
Yoruba people, drum ensembles, **1**:460, 472, 476, 485
Yugoslavia (former), state folk ensembles, **8**:1000–1002
Zaïre, bands, **1**:387
Zulu people, choral, **1**:706
ensembles, musical (one-person)
  Basque region, **8**:171, 314, 543, 545
  England
    mouth organ and tambourine, **8**:331
    whittle and dub, **8**:330–31
  pipe and rattle, **2**:14, *15*
    Mexico, **2**:8
    Panama, **2**:16, *17*
  pipe and tabor (flute and drum), **2**:16, 36–37, *38*, *62*; **8**:142
    Bolivia, **2**:287, *288*
    Ecuador, **2**:210, 415, 420
    El Salvador, **2**:708
    France, **8**:543, 545, 549
    Low Countries, **8**:528, 529
    Maya culture, **2**:653, 655
    Mexico, **2**:8, 550
    Nicaragua, **2**:749, 761
    Otomí culture, **2**:571
    Peru, **2**:471, 475, 477, 478, 481
    Spain, **2**:415; **8**:589, 593
    Tarahumara culture, **2**:583–84, 587
    Yaqui culture, **2**:590
  Spain
    bagpipe and drum, **8**:593
    shawm and drum, **8**:593
Ensemble Wébert Sicot, **2**:98
Entführung aus dem Serail, Die (Mozart), **6**:21
Entr (god; also Eter), **8**:864
d'Entrecasteaux, Bruni, **9**:13, 146, 788
Entsiklopediyah shel haḥasidut (Geshuri), **6**:1060
Envallsson, Carl M., **8**:447
E.O. 9066 (Brown), **3**:972
Ephesus, Council of, **6**:207
Ephraem the Syrian, St., **6**:227, 228, 544
Ephrata Cloister Chorus, **3**:907
Epic of Palnāḍu (*Palnāṭi Vīrula Katha*), **5**:895, 898, 900, 901–2
epics. *See* narratives; *specific titles*
Episcopalians. *See also* Anglicans
  Canada, **3**:1070
  churches, **3**:122
  liturgy of, **3**:121, 123
  missionaries, **3**:64–65, 390–91
  music of, **3**:123, 1132
  research on, **3**:119
  worship practices of, **3**:118
Epistle on Music of the Ikhwan al-Safa (Shiloah), **6**:1066
EPMD, **3**:699

Eppstein, Hans, **8**:447
Eppstein, Uri, **6**:1064
Eppu Normaali (musical group), **8**:217
Epstein, Dena, **3**:64, 83, 573, 574, 576
Epstein, Scarlett, **9**:153
Epthelia (Freeman), **3**:608
Epulef, Tomasa, **2**:*235*
Epullán, Andrés, **2**:234
Equatorial Guinea. *See also* West Africa; *specific peoples*
  Bantu cultures of, **1**:659–63
  Fernando Po, Kru people, **1**:374, 375
  music of, **1**:659–63
Equipe 84 (musical group), **8**:619
Eraserheads (musical group), **4**:887
Erazo, Norma, **2**:745
Erben, Karel J., **8**:721, 732
Erdahan, **6**:250
Erdely, Stephen, **3**:149, 828, 909
Erdman, Joah, **3**:980
Eresoinka (musical group), **8**:315
Ergun, Sadettin Nüzhet, **6**:780
erhu. *See* violins and fiddles (bowed lutes)
Eric B. and Rakim, **3**:698, 699
Ericson, Rolf, **8**:446
Erie Indian nation, **3**:1078
Erie Lads, **1**:770
Erikson, Erik H., **3**:515
Erkel, Ferenc, **8**:737
Erkin, Ülvi, **6**:775
Erk, Ludwig, **8**:656, 663
Erkomaishvili, Artem, **8**:841, 844
Erkomaishvili family, **8**:841
Erlach, Friedrich Karl von, **8**:663
d'Erlanger, Baron Rodolphe, **6**:18, 91, 326, 336, 433, 436, *501*, 501–3, 505, 506, 507–8, 535, 536
Erlitou culture, **7**:17
Erlmann, Veit, **1**:295; **10**:53
Ermatinger, Edward, **3**:1164
Ernst, Earle, **9**:109–10
Erodoğan, Özdemir, **6**:249
Eroğlu, Musa, **6**:790, *791*, 797, 798, 799
Eros I (album), **7**:1020
Erotokritos (Kornaros), **8**:1015, 1025
Erquan yingyue (Abing), **7**:177, 349
Erromango (Vanuatu), **9**:691, 702
Ersoy, Bülent, **6**:258
Erste Allgemeine Verunsicherung, **8**:676, 677
Ertegun, Ahmet, **3**:*263*
Ertegun, Nesuhi, **3**:*263*
Erya, **7**:187
Erzhanov, Manarbek, **6**:955
Erzia Mordvinians, **8**:772
Erzincan, Erdal, **6**:791, 799
Esasi oiwake (Japanese folk song), **7**:571, 602–3, *603*, 604
Escalator Over the Hill (Bley), **10**:87
Escamilla, Carlos "El Ciego," **2**:394, 395
Escandón, José de, **3**:770
Escape (Whodini), **3**:713
Escargot folk (periodical), **8**:554
Escobar, Alberto, **2**:395
Escola de Música de Margão (Madgaon), **5**:740
Escovedo, Coke, **3**:798
Escovedo, Pete, **3**:798

Escovedo, Sheila, **3:**789, 798
Escuela de Bellas Artes (Paraguay), **2:**463
Escuela para Instrumentistas de Música Popular
    de América Latina (Argentina), **2:**268
Escuela de Música (Nicaragua), **2:**766
Escuela de Música Victoriano López (Honduras),
    2:745
Escuela Nacional de Música (Honduras), **2:**745
Esei, Viliami, **9:**130
Eshāq Museli. *See* Isḥāq al-Mawṣilī
Esherick, Joseph, **7:**379
"*Eshet ne'urim*" (*piyyut*), **3:**1173
Eshpor-Zhe (god), **8:**864
Eskalieva, Nagima, **6:**961
Eskimo peoples, **3:**6, 509. *See also* Inuit; Inupiak;
    Yupik
    in Siberia, **7:**1027–30
    whale ritual of, **7:**1029
Esop, Lilian, **3:**879
Espace Musique (Ottawa), **3:**1080, 1186
Espinosa, Aurelio M., **3:**757, 762, 767
Espinosa, Eladio, **2:**395
Espinosa, Guillermo, **2:**397
Espinosa, Isidro Félix de, **2:**577
Espinosa, J. Manuel, **3:**762
Espirito Santo, Jose do, **9:**390
Espiritu Santo (Vanuatu), **9:**26, 689, 966
    music and dance of, **9:**696
    panpipe music of, **9:**689
Esprit Orchestra (Toronto), **3:**1080, 1186
Eṣrefoğlu Rumī, **6:**193
Essay for Orchestra (Banfield), **3:**612
Essays on Music and History in Africa
    (Wachsmann), **1:**294
Essig, David, **7:**976
Estampes (Debussy), **4:**131
Estancia (Ginastera), **2:**115
Estanislao, Aurelio, **4:**870
Esteban Anguita, Julio, **4:**870
Estefan, Emilio, **3:**733
Estefan, Gloria, **3:**720, 733, 751, 789, 799
Estella, José, **4:**857, 859, 864–65, 869, 871
Ester (Ponce de León), **2:**397
Esteva, José María, **2:**605–6
Estonia, **8:**491–98
    art music in, **8:**494–98
    geography of, **8:**491
    Hiiumaa Island, **8:**493
    history of, **8:**491
    instruments, **8:**170, *180*, 493–94, 496–98
    Kihnu Island, **8:**492
    map of, **8:***398*
    population of, **8:**491
    research on music of, **8:**498
    Setu, polyphonic songs of, **8:**492–93, *494*
    Tallin, folk music ensembles, **8:**154
    vocal music of, **8:**115, 491–93, 495–96, 773
Estonian-American Music Club (New York),
    3:878
Estonian people, **8:**475
    in North America, **3:**878–80, 1196
    in Russia, **8:**772
Estonian Workers' Club Choir (New York),
    3:878
Estornudo (periodical), **2:**267
Estrada, Julio, **2:**20
Estrada, Padre Pedro de, **4:**842

Estrellita de Los Angeles, La (newspaper), **3:**735
Estro poetico armonico (Marcello), **8:**255
Estudiantina Añez, **2:**396
Estudiantina Murillo, **2:**394–95
Estudios afros (Carvalho-Neto), **2:**464
Eswari, L. R., **5:**557
Etchecopar, Mixel, **8:***314*
Etenraku (*gagaku* piece), **7:**626
Etenraku (*koto* piece), **7:**574, *575*
Ethiopia, **8:**621. *See also* East Africa; *specific
    peoples*
    academic training in, **1:**40
    Amhara people, *begena* lyre, **1:**303–4
    composition in, **1:**44
    ethnomusicological research in, **10:**67–68, 71
    Falasha people, **1:**604; **10:**67
    Gumuz people, **1:**564
    Gurri people, dance as medicine, **1:**113
    influence on Arab music, **6:**362
    instruments, **1:**600
    kingdom of, **1:**600–601
    lyres in, **6:**357, 358, 359
    music in, **1:**601
    music notation system, **1:**147–50, 159
    Orchestra Ethiopia folklore ensemble, **1:**151,
        152
    religious institutions, **1:**603–4
    zār ritual, **1:**273–74, 277, 554, 604; **6:**632–33
Ethiopian-Americans/Canadians, **3:**1078
Ethiopian Orthodox Church, in Israel, **6:**1021
Ethiopian Serenaders, **3:**184
*Ethnic Groups and Boundaries: The Social
    Organization of Difference*, **3:**515
Ethnic Recordings in America, **3:**828
Ethnic Song and Dance Troupe (China), **7:**399
Ethnographic Czech-Slovak Exhibition, **8:**722
Ethnographic Museum (Bulgaria), **8:**906
Ethnological Institute for Oriental Jewish Music,
    6:1059
Ethnologie Française (periodical), **8:**554
Ethnomusicologist (Hood), **10:**42, 101
ethnomusicology, **5:**43, 44, 49–50, 213, 561;
    8:59, 394
    Abkhazian people, **8:**853
    academic programs in, **10:**3–5, 18–21, 27–29,
        41–44, 55–57, 62–64, 73–74, 78–79,
        87–88, 128–30
    Afghanistan, **5:**817
    Africa, **10:**27–38
        diffusion studies, **1:**31, 294, 296–300,
            301–4, 313, 314–14
        French research in, **8:**233
    approaches to art music, **2:**112–17
    archival and library research, **10:**11–12, 161
    Armenia, **6:**726–27
    Belarus, **8:**803–4
    bimusicality concept, **1:**34, 39; **3:**952, 1013;
        10:61, 79, 103–4, 139
    Bosnia-Hercegovina, **8:**970
    Brittany, **8:**563
    Bulgaria, **8:**906–7
    Canada, **3:**1059–60
        Doukhobor music studies, **3:**1268, 1270
        folk song collecting, **3:**14–15, 145–46,
            292–93, 410, 1123, 1125, 1133,
            1163–67, 1188, 1250
        urban studies, **3:**149

Chile, **2:**374
China, **7:**101–2, 137, 139–42, 172, 347, 381,
    382–83, 387–88, 397, 517–18
cognitive ethnocentrism concept, **1:**57–58
coinage of term, **8:**20
community-based research, **10:**89
comparative concepts of musical change,
    8:64–65
comparative studies, **1:**20; **10:**56, 154–55
Corsica, **8:**573–74
critical theory, **3:**149
Croatia, **8:**935, 936–37
cultural relativism ideology, **3:**71
cultural studies, **3:**149
Cyprus, **8:**1032
Czechoslovakia, **8:**724
definitions of, **10:**22, 77, 97, 101
Denmark, **8:**451–52, 458, 463–65
diaspora studies, **10:**154–55
discipline of, **5:**18–19; **10:**25–26, 55, 97–98,
    161–64
dissemination methods of, **10:**107
East Asia, **10:**3–15, 17–26
England, **8:**337–39
    melody classification, **8:**327–28
ethnicity and, **3:**515–17
ethnographic concerts and, **8:**154
feminist and gender studies, **3:**91–92, 149,
    586; **10:**131–32
field research, **10:**5–11, 28, 29–36, 42–43,
    44–53, 57–62, 68–71, 79–80, 83,
    88–95, 98–99, 100–105, 112–18,
    130–32, 133–34, 144–51, 160–61
    bias in, **10:**104–5
    culture bearers and, **10:**143, 145, 150–52
    equipment for, **10:**14, 30, 106, 145,
        150–51
    event as object, **10:**58–59
    feedback interviews, **10:**59–60
    field notes, **10:**60–61, 90–91, 103–4, 116,
        144–45
    living conditions and, **10:**6
    personal interactions, **10:**9–10
    preparations for, **10:**98, 141–44
Finland, **8:**484, 488–89
folklore as concept, **8:**326
folklore preservation, **8:**7
folk music as concept, **3:**147; **8:**2, 4, 7, 19–20,
    59, 204, 337, 436–37, 600, 646–50
France, **8:**551–54
Georgia, **8:**846–47
Germany, **8:**647–48, 663–64
Goa, **5:**741
Greece, **8:**1024–26
historical research, **10:**22
history and development of, **3:**11, 14–15,
    29–31, 149, 290–95, 324; **4:**24–25,
    27–28; **5:**51; **8:**18–26, 94–95, 326
Hungary, **8:**741–42
ideology and, **8:**187–89
Indonesia, **4:**123
insider/outsider issues, **8:**122; **10:**9–11, 22–23,
    26, 71, 154
interdisciplinary projects, **10:**23–24, 62,
    74–75, 91
Israel, **6:**1024, 1029, 1057–67
Italy, **8:**620–23

Japan, **7:**540, 591–95, 599–600
Jewish music studies, **3:**944; **8:**266–67
journals, **5:**57–58
Kazakhstan, **6:**958, 960
Korea, **7:**879–80, 988
laboratory work, **10:**105–6
Lithuania, **8:**513–14
Low Countries, **8:**534–35
Macedonia, **8:**983–84
mentorship in, **10:**81, 82–83, 163–64
methodologies, **1:**722–23, 742–43; **5:**53–56
Middle Eastern research avenues, **6:**22–24
multimedia projects, **10:**60
North Caucasia, **8:**861, 864
organological studies, **8:**172
outreach programs, **10:**133–34, 152–53
participant research, **10:**64, 149, 159
passive music-making, **10:**100–101
personal interactions in, **10:**12–13, 49–51,
    61–62, 68–71, 84, 91–95, 131–32,
    148–49, 152
Philippines, **4:**123
Poland, **8:**712
popular culture studies, **4:**95
Portugal, **8:**585
power structures studies, **3:**331
"primitive music," concept of, **1:**13, 74–75,
    95–97, 294; **8:**35
public sector work, **10:**81–85
race and, **3:**70–72
radio stations' role in, **8:**155–57
"real world" issues in, **10:**71–73
role models for ethnomusicologists,
    10:79–80
Romania, **8:**885–86
Russia, **8:**755–58, 772–73, 782–85
Saami music research, **8:**307
Sardinia, **8:**632
Scotland, **8:**373–74
Serbia, **8:**949, 954
Slovenia, **8:**922–23
social position of ethnomusicologists,
    10:13–15
sound recordings and, **3:**243
South America, tropical-forest research, **2:**123
South Asia, **10:**3–15
South Asian diaspora, **5:**576, 585–86
Southeast Asia, research on upland peoples,
    4:529–30
Spain, **8:**601–2
Sweden, **8:**435, 437, 447–48
Taiwan, **7:**524–25
team research, **10:**68–71, 143
textbooks for, **10:**10–11, 107, 164–65
Tibetan culture, **10:**26
traditional music as concept, **8:**4, 7, 20, 26,
    114, 339
"tune family" concept, **3:**834
Turkey, **6:**77
Ukraine, **8:**820–23
United States
    African-American music studies, **3:**572–87
    Arab music studies, **6:**285–86
    Arctic music studies, **3:**380–81
    Asian music studies, **3:**948, 952–53, 1258
    contextual research, **3:**142, 149–51

European-American folk music studies,
    3:827–29
folk song collecting, **3:**14–15, 82, 147–48,
    293–95, 511–12, 573–75, 579–81,
    707, 736, 762, 763, 767, 823–24, 833
gamelan music research, **3:**1012, 1013–14,
    1021
Hispano music studies, **3:**762, 767–68
identity issues studies, **3:**508–17
Mexican-American music studies, **3:**736
Native American music studies, **3:**291–92,
    367, 444–45, 465, 487, 493, 508–12
religious practices, **3:**117
rural subjects, **3:**149
South Asian music studies, **3:**980
Subarctic music studies, **3:**392
Tejano music studies, **3:**772
urban subjects, **3:**149
Western *vs.* Chinese scholarly approaches,
    10:25–26
Western *vs.* Indian scholarly standards, **5:**56
women's studies, **8:**192–93
world music and, **3:**341; **8:**224
Ethnomusicology (periodical), **2:**16, 238; **3:**576;
    10:85
Ethnomusicology Archive (Los Angeles), **9:**976
Ethnomusicology of the Flathead Indians
    (Merriam), **3:**511
ethos, concept of, **6:**60, 72–73, 549, 855; **8:**48,
    69. *See also* aesthetics
Etidloiee, Etulu, **3:**1275, 1279
Etno-Akademik (musical group), **8:**968
Etnografia Shqiptare (periodical), **8:**1003
Etrebü 'l āthār (Meḥmed Es'ad Efendi), **6:**371
Etruscans
    in Corsica, **8:**566
    instruments of, **8:**39–40
Ets, Tiina, **3:**879
"Etsi Shon" (Alfred), **3:**489
Ettu cult, **2:**901, 903
Ettyû owara busi (Japanese folk song), **7:**712
Etude Magazine, **3:**562
Études Tsiganes (periodical), **8:**288
Etzion, Judith, **6:**1066, 1067
Euayporn Kerdchouay, **4:**308
Euba, Akin, **1:**8, 39, 44, 413
    compositions of, **1:**220, 221, 223, 224, 226,
    227, 232–33, 237, 251
Eubie (musical), **3:**621
Euclid, **6:**16, 368, 388
Eurasian Association (Singapore), **4:**522
Eurasian people
    in Borneo, **4:**825
    in Singapore, **4:**522
    in Sri Lanka, **5:**954
Eurasian Voices (album), **7:**973
Euripik Atoll (Yap State, FSM), **9:**729
Európa Kiadó (musical group), **8:**746
Europe, James Reese, **3:**33, 578, 580, 651, 706
Europe. *See also specific countries, regions, and*
    topics
    Arab musical influences in, **6:**446, 448
    archaeomusicological studies, **8:**34–42
    Carpathian Mountains, Germans in, **8:**665
    Chilean people in, **2:**90
    class differences in, **8:**13–14, 188–89

    climate of, **8:**4
    concentration camps, **8:**661
    demography, c. 1600, **8:**17
    geography of, **8:**10
    immigrant music in, **8:**225, 231–41
    Indian people in, **5:**449
    industrial revolution in, **8:**13, 147
    Iranian emigrant communities, **6:**131–32
    Jewish music in, **8:**248–67; **10:**162–63
    map of, **8:***3*
    Maronite Church in, **6:**208
    minorities in, **8:**12–13
    music categories, **8:**2, 4
    North African emigrant communities, **6:**438
    pastoral regions
        organological traditions of, **8:**41
        women's music in, **8:**194
    prehistoric, **8:**35–40
    Rom people in, **8:**270–89
    shared musical culture, **8:**4–10
    Turkish military music in, **6:**767–68
    urban-rural differences in, **8:**13–14, 262
    village music in, **8:**7–10, 13
European Archaeological Convention (1969),
    3:492
European Economic Community, **8:**237
European Forum of Worldwide Music Festivals,
    8:241
European Seminar in Ethnomusicology, **8:**553
Europeans in North America, **3:**10, 820–29,
    1057, 1060. *See also specific groups and*
    genres
    cultural interactions, **3:**21–22
    dances of, **3:**209–10
    early settlers, **3:**143
    Jewish, **3:**933–35
    Native American views of, **3:**332
    parlor and salon music of, **3:**93
    population of, **3:**4
    research on, **3:**70, 827–29
Europeans in Oceania, **9:**5, 7–14, 88, 96, 100,
    158–59, 177–78, 237, 348, 474–75,
    516, 566, 568, 607, 620, 763–64,
    773, 823, 842, 844, 861, 885, 896,
    933–35. *See also* Christianity; *specific*
    countries
    British, **9:**7–13, 14–16, 33–34, 49, 69, 128,
        129–30, 193, 217, 408–9, 439, 506,
        689, 715, 719, 723, 754, 758, 773,
        780–81, 783, 786, 797, 816, 817–18,
        828, 861, 869, 885, 904, 914
    Dutch, **9:**191, 474–75, 589, 614, 795
    French, **9:**13–14, 16–17, 33, 34, 56–57, 128,
        146, 193, 671, 795, 861
    Germans, **9:**23–24, 128, 130, 159, 217, 475,
        479, 607, 614, 628, 715, 717–18,
        724, 728–29, 739, 748, 755
    Portuguese, **9:**390–91, 474, 689
    Spanish, **9:**158, 717, 720, 728–29, 745
Europeans in South America, **2:**84. *See also*
    specific groups
    in Argentina, **2:**261, 269
    relations with Amerindians and African
        descendants, **2:**71
    rhythmic style of, **2:**73
Euscaldun Anciña Anciñaco (Iztueta), **8:**316

694

Euskaldun Kantaria (Goyeneche), **8:**316
Euskitze, Xabier, **8:***316*
Euterpeiad (periodical), **3:**27
Eva Jessye Choir, **3:**535
Evald, Zinaida, **8:**757, 758, 783–84, 803
evaluation. *See* aesthetics
Evangelical Lutheran National Church, **3:**874
Evangelic Lectionary, **8:**881
Evangeline, **3:**1135
Evangeline (musical group), **3:**193
Evangelista, José, **3:**1151
Evans, Bill, **3:**661
Evans, David, **3:**83, 85, 579
Evans, Frank, **3:**743
Evans, Gil, **3:**335, 660
Evans, Ivor H. N., **4:**569
Evans, James, **3:**1086
Evans, Merle, **3:**568
Evans-Pritchard, E. E., **10:**36
Evans, Robert, **8:**355
"Eve of Destruction" (McGuire), **3:**316
Even people, **7:**1027–30
Evénéments du Neuf (new-music society), **3:**1151
Evenki people, **7:**518–19, 1027–30
Evergreen Club Gamelan Ensemble (Toronto), **3:**1064, 1084, *1084*, 1186, 1216
Evergreen State College (Olympia), **3:**953
Everly Brothers (musical group), **3:**80; **9:**137
"Everyday People" (Sly and the Family Stone), **3:**681, 710
"Evil Ways" (Santana), **3:**733
Evita (Lloyd Webber), **3:**545
Evit Koroll (periodical), **8:**564
Evliyâ Çelebi, **6:**21, 543, 768
Ewe Cultural Association, **3:**1213
Ewe culture, **2:**826
Ewe people, **10:**30–31, 141
  Anlo group, **1:**222
    dance, **1:**289
    rural-urban interchange, **1:**389–99
  dance, **1:**109
  drumming, **1:**35
  drums of, **1:**316
  history of, **1:**461–62
  instruments of, **1:**462
  konkoma music of, **1:**479
  music of, **1:**462–63
  oral notation, **1:**150
  song texts, **1:**137
  speech surrogate methods, **1:**107
Ewell, Don, **3:**105
Ewha Women's University, **7:**69, 990
Exclusion Act (1882), **3:**512
Exile One, **2:**98, 844
Exotica (Denny), **3:**1050
Ex-Panonia (musical group), **8:**934
explorers and expeditions, **8:**17. *See also* Spanish conquistadors; travelers' and missionaries' accounts; *specific names and expeditions*
  to Africa, **1:**85–88
  to North America, **3:**7, 9, 143, 437, 452, 596, 721, 754–55, 770–71, 1056, 1094, 1114–15, 1146, 1163–64, 1254–55

  to Oceania, **9:**7–25, 33–35, 128, 173, 285, 429, 479, 506, 589, 607, 671, 689, 722–23, 744, 752, 778, 788, 791, 794–95, 816, 842, 896, 914, 933, 947, 969, 977, 981, 983
Expo '67 (Montréal), **3:**1157
Expreso Imaginario (periodical), **2:**267
Eycken, Meen van, **8:**136
Eyuge qupu (Wang), **7:**132
Eyuphoro (musical group), **1:**436
Eyyubi Bekir Ağa, **6:**771
Ezar culture. *See* Chichimec culture
Ezgi Folk Music Ensemble, **3:**1199
Ezgija (musical group), **8:**983
Ezgi, Subhî, **6:**84, 197, 772, 783
Ezzedine, Salah, **6:**237

Fa Ngum, king of Lan Xang, **4:**353, 354, 356
Fa people, **9:**982
Fa'animo (Sāmoan elder), **9:**204, *959*
Fabbroni, Giovanni, **3:**22
Fadikka people, **6:**629, 641
fado, **3:**731–32, 851, 1197; **5:**737; **8:**204, 205, 577, 578, 583–84
  competitions, **8:**134
  ensemble for, **8:**116
  in Hawai'i, **9:**98
  international popularity of, **8:**7
Fage, J. D., **1:**83
Fagir, Hassan, **1:***558*
Fagnan, Grandy, **3:**407
Fagner, **2:**333
Fahd ibn 'Abdul al-'Azīz, king of Saudi Arabia, **6:**640
Fahnestock, Bruce, **9:**992
Fahnestock, Sheridan, **9:**992
Fai Lok San Chinese Music Society (Vancouver), **3:**1263
Failde, Miguel, **2:**833, 835
Fairfield Four (gospel quartet), **3:**633
Fairouz, **8:**637
Fais Atoll (Yap State, FSM), **9:**729
Faith, Percy, **3:**265, 314, 1081
Faithfull, Marianne, **3:**689
Faizabadi, Akhtari Bai. *See* Akhtar, Begum
Faiz, Faiz Ahmad, **5:**747
Fajardo, Emidio, **2:***378*
Fajar label, **4:**681
Fakaofo (Tokelau), **9:**823
Fakhrī, Ṣabāḥ, **3:**1220; **6:**550, 563–64, 592
Fakoli, **1:**509
Fa'lady, Joel, **9:***305*
Falasha people, **1:**604; **10:**67
Falatiya, Asha, **1:**571
Falco, **8:**679
Falcon, Pierre, **3:**410
Falig, Alex, **9:**160
Falk, Catherine A., **4:**701
Falkland Islands, **2:**2, 267
Fall Fret, **2:**919
Falla, Manuel de, **2:**114; **3:**1150; **4:**873; **6:**449; **7:**732; **8:**598, 601
Fallis, Mary Lou, **3:**1080
Fals, Iwan, **4:**110
Faltin, Richard, **8:**482
Falú, Eduardo, **2:**263

Fame (film), **3:**200
Fame Records, **3:**710
"Family Affair" (Sly and the Family Stone), **3:**710
Family Theatre (Dawson City), **3:**1277
Famintsyn, Aleksandr, **8:**780
Famous Chicago Novelty Orchestra, **3:**1169
Famous Hawaiian Songs (Cunha), **9:**919, 922
Fan Shange, **7:**172
Fan Sheng-E, **3:**1083
fandango, **2:**71, 334, 603, 744; **3:**735
Fandango (television show), **3:**741
Fandango USA (musical group), **3:**781
Faŋ (Fang) people, **9:**258
  dance, **1:**109–10, 117
  harps of, **1:**663
  music of, **1:**659–60
Fania All-Stars (musical group), **3:**797
Fania Records, **3:**788, 799
Fanshawe, David, **9:**968
Fantasia (Lee), **4:**523–24
Fantasia-Tahmeel (El-Dabh), **3:**953
"Fantastic Voyage" (Coolio), **3:**700
"Fantastic Voyage" (Lakeside), **3:**684
Fanti people
  dance, **1:**112
  konkoma music of, **1:**479
  research on, **10:**29–36
  songs, **1:**89, 211, 221, 224
Fantin, Francesco, **9:**80–81
Fanua, Tupou Posesi, **9:**113
Faqir, Lallan, **5:**747
Far East Side Band, **3:**973
Far West Club (Albuquerque), **3:**766
Fara, **3:**1094
Fara, Eli, **8:**993
Fara, Giulio, **8:**621, 632
al-Fārābī, Abū Naṣr, **6:**16, 17, 129, 135, 177, 368, 388–92, 395, 443, 502, 508, 541–42, 565, 772, 855, 859, 869, 910; **8:**92
  instrument classification system, **6:**373, 396–97, 398–99, 402
  philosophical writings, **6:**363, 367
  writings on metrics, **6:**365
Farah, Khalil, **1:**571
Faraj, 'Abdallah, **6:**651
Farewell My Concubine (film), **7:**76
Farhana, Faruqi, **5:**800
Farhat, Hormoz, **6:**24, 62, 67, 876
Farid, Haji Ghulam, **5:**426
Farid, Khwaja Ghulam, **5:**770
Farīda, **6:**354
Fariduddin Masud Ganj-i Shakar, Sheikh, **5:**753, 755, 779
  shrine of, **5:***756*
Farinas, Tak, **6:**275–76
Faris, J. C., **1:**134
Farley "Jackmaster Funk," **3:**690
Farmboys (musical group), **3:**169
Farmer, Henry George, **6:**22, 24, 364, 365, 367, 373, 535, 537, 539, 540, 541; **8:**374
"Farmer's Curst Wife" (ballad), **3:**519, 834
Farnon, Robert, **3:**1107
Faroe Boys (musical group), **8:**472
Faroe Islands, **8:**468–73
  carnival in, **8:**469

dance traditions of, **8:**164, 165, 413, 468–69
geography of, **8:**468
history of, **8:**468
international influences in, **8:**471–72
map of, **8:***398*
population of, **8:**468
research on music of, **8:**472
vocal music of, **8:**131, 469–71
Faroese Jazzband Triumf, **8:**471
Faron, Louis, **2:**238
al-Farrā', **6:**353
al-Farrān, Ibrāhīm, **6:**168
Farrar, Clair R., **3:**433
Farrell, Gerry, **5:**575
Fārsi people, **6:**942
al-Faruqi, Lois Ibsen, **1:**347; **6:**9, 162
Fārūz, Aḥmad, **6:**327
Farwell, Arthur, **3:**14, 367, 736, 737
"Fascinatin' Rhythm" (Gershwin), **3:**196
fascism, **8:**184–85, 187, 267
 Germany, **8:**660–61, 664
 Italy, **8:**618
 Spain, **8:**315
al-Fashnī, Shaykh Ṭaha, **6:**168, *169*
fāṣil (Syrian), **6:**551, 563, 569
fasıl (Turkish), **6:**11, 57, 111, 113–14, 116–17, 119–22, 185, 773, 779, 780
Fassie, Brenda, **1:**431, 779
el-Fassi, Mohammed, **6:**495
Fasu people, **9:**511, 512
Fat Boys (musical group), **3:**713
"Fat Man" (Domino), **3:**708
Fataleka people, **9:**301, 666, 668–69
Fatback Band, **3:**695
Father Is Up a Tree (film). *See Abi fauqa al-Shajara*
"Father on the Go" (Parent), **3:**1162
al-Fatḥiyya (al-Lādhiqī), **6:**502
Fatima, **6:**270
Fāṭimid dynasty, **6:**293, 294, 543
Fatme (musical group), **8:**1022
Fatuana, **9:**139–40
Fatu'ana (string band), **9:**863–64
Fatuiva (Marquesas Islands), **9:**889
Fauriel, Claude, **8:**1024
Fauro Island (Solomon Islands), **9:**655
Faurot, Albert, **4:**873
Fauset, Arthur Huff, **3:**1133
Faust (Goethe), **8:**646
Fauzi, Muḥammad, **6:**236, 239
Favara, Alberto, **8:**621
Favre, Gilberto "El Gringo," **2:**298
Fawa'd al-fu'ad (Auliya), **5:**294
Fayrūz, **6:**251–52, 283, 553–55, 592
al-Fayyūmī, Muḥammad, **6:**168
Faz, Roberto, **2:**835
Fazal Rabbi, **5:**790
Fazer Musiikki (record label), **8:**486
Fazisi (musical group), **8:***838*
Fazl Ahmad, **5:***806*
Fear of a Black Planet (Public Enemy), **3:**714
feasts. *See* ceremonies; festivals, celebrations, and holidays
Fedela, Chaba, **8:***234*
Federal Communications Commission, **3:**244, 559

Federal Cylinder Project, **3:**294–95, 495–96
Federal Music Project of the WPA, **3:**45, 297, 767
Federal Radio Commission, **3:**559
Federal Theater Project of the WPA, **3:**294, 297, 620–21
 Negro Unit, **3:**609
Federal Writers' Project of the WPA, **3:**926–27
Federated Slovak Societies, **3:**899
Federated States of Micronesia, **9:**116, 712, 726–43. *See also* Chuuk; Kapingamarangi; Kosrae; Nukuoro; Pohnpei; Yap
 Americans in, **9:**160
 films on, **9:**1016
 geography of, **9:**726
 music and dance of, **9:**726–43
 popular music in, **9:**160
 sung poetry, **9:**328
 tokia dance, **9:**91–92
 verbal meter, **9:**324
Federation of Canadian Music Festivals, **3:**1227
Fédération des Loisiers-Danse du Québec, **3:**223
Federazione Italiana Lavoratori Emigrati e Famiglie, **9:**80
Federico, Carlos, **3:**798
Fedon, Julien, **2:**865
Fedosova, Irina, **8:**763
Fedyk, Teodor, **3:**1088
Fée, Antoine Laurent Apollinaire, **8:**573
Feed Back (musical group), **5:**428
Fefita la Grande, **2:**105
Fei Shi (pseud.), **7:**379
Feild, Reshad, **3:**1044
Feinberg, Richard, **9:**290, 306–7, 327, 336, 378, 976
Feinstein, Alan, **3:**1014
Feiruz, **3:**1220
Fekete Föld, **3:**1197
Feldman, Walter, **6:**15
Feld, Steven, **3:**302, 340, 498; **9:**153, 976, 990; **10:**56
Feliciano, Francisco, **4:**130, 878
Feliciano, José, **3:**726, 751
Felicidad (musical group), **3:**780
Felipe, Julian, **4:**866, 871
Felix, María, **3:**740
Fellman, Jacob, **8:**307
Fellmann, Robert, **8:**692
Felo, Clement, **9:**28
Feltz, Kurt, **8:**679
Fender, Freddy, **3:**751
Fendrich, Rainhard, **8:**677
Feng Guangyu, **7:**137
Feng Jiexuan, **7:**137
Feng Menglong, **7:**130, 153–54
Feng Wenci, **7:**137
Feng ya shi'er shi pu (Zhao), **7:**125
Feng ya song (Tan), **7:**342, 343, 350
Feng Zicun, **7:**185
Feni Group (Papua New Guinea), **9:**626
Fennell, Frederick, **3:**536, 567
Fenton, John William, **7:**727, 728
Fenton, William, **3:**465, 497
Fenwick, John, **3:**199
Fenwick, Roy, **3:**277, 279

Fenyves, Lorand and Alice, **6:**1027
Ferdinand I, Holy Roman emperor, **8:**716, 727
Ferdowsī, **6:**344, 825, 827
Ferenado, S. H., Jr., **3:**586
Ferenczy, Oto, **8:**730
Ferera, Frank, **9:**390
Ferganian people, **6:**965
Ferguson, Cyril "Dry Bread," **2:**806
Ferguson, T. J., **3:**492
Ferguson, Walter "Mr. Gavitt," **2:**691–92
Fergusson, Alice, **9:**237
Fergusson, Maynard, **3:**1080
Ferianto, Djaduk, **10:**48
Ferland, Jean-Pierre, **3:**1156, 1158
Ferland, Marcien, **3:**411
Fernandes, Gaspar, **2:**735
Fernandes, Remo, **5:**427
Fernández, Arthur, **9:***102*
Fernández, Carmelo, **9:***102*
Fernández, Fernando, **3:**741
Fernández Guardia, Ricardo, **2:**704
Fernández, Julia, **4:**856
Fernández, León, **2:**704
Fernandez Magno, Susan, **4:**886
Fernández, Raymond, **9:***102*
Fernández, Sebastian, **9:***102*
Fernández, Tito, **9:***102*
Fernández, Tony, **9:***102*
Fernandez, Troy, **9:**165
Fernández, Vicente, **3:**721, 746
Fernando, C. T., **5:**427
Fernando, M. S., **5:**427
Fernie, Maxwell, **9:**929
Ferranti, Hugh de, **7:**595
Ferre, Boulou, **8:**288
Ferre, Elio, **8:**288
Ferré, Father, **2:**158
Ferreira, Alexandre Rodrigues, **1:**319
Ferreira, Nelson, **2:**337
Ferrer, Horacio, **2:**519
Ferrero, Luis, **2:**13, 16
Ferris, William, Jr., **3:**583
Fesov, Oleg, **6:**905
festivals, celebrations, and holidays. *See also* carnival; ceremonies; competitions; corroborees; Pacific Festival of Arts; powwows
 Abkhazian people, **8:**853
 Afghanistan
  country fairs, **5:**818–19, 821, 824
  Id, **5:**821
 Africa
  agricultural, **1:**119
  Muslim, **1:***454*, 485, 517, 524–27
  pan-African, **1:**38
 African-American
  Election Day, **3:**595
  holiday celebrations, **3:**594
  John Kuner (or John Canoe; Jonkonnu), **3:**614
  Pinkster Day, **3:**595, 614
 Akha people, **4:**541
 Albania, **8:**988, 997
  National Festival of Folklore, **8:**999, 1002
 Alberta
  Dalum Folkefest, **3:**1251

festivals, celebrations, and holidays, Alberta
    (*continued*)
    Lac La Biche, **3:**1087
    Vegreville Ukrainian festival, **3:**218
Aluku culture, **2:**439
American Sāmoa, Flag Day, **9:**235, 266
Amis people, **7:**427, 527
Andean regions, **2:**215, 220–21
    agricultural, **2:**35, 217
    All Saints, **2:**220
    brass bands at, **2:**212
    competitions in, **2:**62–63
    flute consorts in, **2:**210
    life-cycle, **2:**209
    north-south distinctions, **2:**222
    Santiago, **2:**220
Antigua and Barbuda, Old Time Christmas
    Festival, **2:**799
Aotearoa
    Aotearoa Arts Festival, **9:**936
    Constitution Day, **9:**112
    Hogmanay (New Year's Eve), **9:**115–16
    national festivals, **9:**937
    Niuean Constitution Day, **9:**113
    Pacific Drum Festival, **9:**114
    Polynesian Festival of Arts, **9:**937
    Sāmoan Independence Day, **9:**112
Arabian peninsula
    Christmas season in expatriate communities,
        6:716–18
    dance performances during, **6:**704
Arctic peoples, **3:**380
Argentina, **2:**256, 261
    Child-Mayor celebration, **2:**258
    festivales de folklore, **2:**261–62
    Holy Week, **2:**257–58
    jineteada, **2:**261
    minga, **2:**255
    National Folklore Festival, **2:**285
    patronal, **2:**257
    performance of *cuarteto*, **2:**273
    rock, **2:**267
    Saint Balthasar, **2:**260
    Saint James, **2:**257
    Saint John the Baptist, **2:**257
    señalada, **2:**237, 256
    Virgin of Punta Corral, **2:**256
    Virgin of Rosario de Andacollo, **2:**258
Arizona, *mariachi*, **3:**744
Aruba, **2:**929
Australia, **9:**59–62
    Aboriginal peoples, **9:**453
    Adelaide Festival, **9:**60
    Anglo-Irish, **9:**140
    Bondi Festival of South American Music
        and Dance, **9:**83
    Cape York, **9:**430, 464
    Cape York Dance Festival, **9:**464
    country music, **9:**141, 414
    Festival of Traditional Music, 1995, **9:**59
    folk, **9:**413
    Greek, **9:**72
    Italian, **9:**80
    jazz, **9:**143
    Kimberley Arts and Cultural Festival,
        9:60–61

Latin American and Caribbean, **9:**83
Melbourne Festival, **9:**60
National Australian Gamelan Festival, **9:**59
national-day celebrations for Pacific
    Islanders, **9:**86–87
Perth Festival, **9:**60
rock, **9:**443
Saint Patrick's Day, **9:**78
Sydney Festival, **9:**60
Sydney Festival del Sol, **9:**83
Torres Strait Islander Festival, **9:**61
WOMAD, **9:**155
Yolngu people, **9:**462
Aymara culture, **2:**357, 361–62
Aztec culture
    Xochilhuitl, **2:**556
    Xocotl Huetzi, **2:**556
Bahamas, junkanoo, **2:**811–12
Bali, **4:**738, 744, 755
Bali Arts Festival, **4:**759
Baltic states, choral, **8:**399
Barbados
    Christmas, **2:**819
    Crop Over, **2:**814, 817
    holidays, **2:**817
    national festival, **2:**819–20, *821*
Basque, **3:**217
Bastille Day, **8:**185
Belarus
    Maładečna, **8:**801
    Słavianski Bazar, **8:**801
Bellona, **9:**849–50, 852
Bengal, national expositions, **5:**848–49
Berber people, **1:**543
Berta people, **1:**565
Bolivia, **2:**218–21
    All Saints, **2:**210, 217, 290, 291
    fiestas, **2:**290–91
    Saint Michael, **2:**138–40
    seasonal, **2:**289–90
    timing of, **2:**290
Borneo, Chinese, **4:**825
Brazil
    Christmas, **2:**334–35
    Epiphany, **2:**312
    June celebrations, **2:**332–33
    nativista, **2:**318
    patronal, **2:**302, 303–4, 312, 330
    Pentecost, **2:***313*
    Rock-in-Rio, **2:**110
    Saint John the Baptist, **2:**301, 309
    saints' days, **2:**303, 331
    use of *cateretê*, **2:**302
Bribri culture, **2:**634–35
British Columbia, **3:**1097
    Chinese New Year, **3:**1263
    Doukhobors, **3:**1267
    May Day, **3:**1256
    Merritt Mountain Country Music Festival,
        3:1097
    North Vancouver Caribbean Festival,
        3:1097
    Vancouver Asia Pacific Festival, **3:**1265
    Vancouver Cityfest, **3:**1258–59
    Vancouver Exposition, **3:**1265
    Vancouver Folk Festival, **3:**1097

Vancouver Jazz Festival, **3:**1096, 1097, 1107
Victoria Symphony Splash, **3:**1097
Brittany
    fest noz, **8:**141, 563
    Fête Interceltique, **8:**322
    Fêtes de Cornouaille, **8:**563
    Interceltic Festival, **8:**563
    pardons, **8:**562
Brunka and Teribe cultures
    chichadas, **2:**685
    fiesta de los diablitos, **2:**684–85
    fiesta de los negritos, **2:**684
Buddhist, **4:**289; **7:**497, 499, 501–4
Bulgaria, Rom Music and Song, **8:**284
California
    Cahuilla Bird Song Festival, **10:**88–89
    Gustine Our Lady of Miracles Festival,
        3:850
    Los Angeles Festival, **9:**119
    Los Angeles Nisei Week Festival, **3:**527
    mariachi, **3:**744–45
    Monterey Pop Festival, **5:**566
    Pacific Islander festivals, **3:**1052–53
    San Francisco Asian American Jazz Festival,
        3:965
    San Francisco Ethnic Dance Festival, **3:**222;
        9:119
    Santa Barbara Obon Festival, **3:***971*
    Spanish, **3:**735
Cambodia, **4:**197–200
Canada, **3:**1185
    Canadian Pacific Railway festivals, **3:**146,
        1058, 1076, 1154, 1166
    Chinese, **3:**1083–84, 1217
    Du Maurier International Jazz Festivals,
        3:1091
    folk festivals, **3:**94, 149, 343
    heritage festivals, **3:**73, 1243
    jazz, **3:**1107
    northern regions, **3:**1278
    Prairie Provinces, **3:**1226–27
    Sangerfesten, **3:**1082, 1250
    Swedish, **3:**1089, 1251
    syncretic, **3:**1062–63
Caribbean, **2:**47, 68, 72, 795
Celtic Film and Television Festival, **8:**365
Celtic music, **8:**320, 322
Central America, **2:**47, 68, 72
Central Asia
    āsh, **6:**916–17
    Mavlud, **6:**942
    Muslim holidays, **6:**939, 940–42
    toi, **6:**897–98, 901, 968
    women's songs, **6:**946
Cham *kate*, **3:**1010
Chile
    Chiloé Island patronal festivals, **2:**360, 366
    Corpus Christi, **2:**365
    Cruz de Mayo, **2:**365
    Our Lady of the Rosary, **2:**365
    Saints Peter and Paul, **2:**365
    venerating Virgin Mary, **2:**362–65
    Virgin of Carmen, **2:**363–64
    Virgin of Guadalupe, **2:***26*
    Virgin of Las Peñas, **2:**363
    Virgin of the Candelaria, **2:**364–65

China, 7:91
  All-China Minority Nationalities Performing
    Arts Festival, 7:442
  Cantonese opera performances, 7:307
  dance in, 7:61
  gejie or *gehui*, 7:151–52
  "Hungry Ghosts" festival, 7:331
  Jiangnan sizhu performances, 7:225
  kunju, 7:294–95
  minority groups, 7:414, 442, 449, 450
  opera in, 7:278
Colombia, 2:411
  Afro-Colombian traditions, 2:403
  Cartagena Festival, 2:94
  dance in, 2:389
  Festival Nacional del Bambuco, 2:389
  Holy Week, 2:420
  municipal band's role in, 2:384
  murga in, 2:384–85
  rajaleña performance, 2:390
  Saint John the Baptist, 2:384
  Saints Peter and Paul, 2:384
  street ensembles in, 2:384
  Vélez *guabina* festival, 2:391
Colorado, World Syakuhati Festival, 7:707–9
Congo, 1:88
Cook Islands, *nuku*, 9:224
Costa Rica, 2:689, 698, 700–702
  Carnaval de Limón, 2:693
  Corpus Christi, 2:681, 693
  patronal, 2:688
  Somos Como Somos, 2:703
  Virgen de los Angeles, 2:693
Côte d'Ivoire, MASA trade fair, 1:419–20,
  437
Croatia, 8:925
  Festival of Village Singing Choruses, 8:935
  Omiš *klapa* festival, 8:929, 936
  Smotra Folkora, 8:949
Cuba, 2:829
  Epiphany, 2:836
Czech Republic, 8:717, 720, 722–23
  Strážnice, 8:723
Dai people, Buddhist, 7:497, 499, 501–4
Denmark
  New Year's, 8:455
  processions in, 8:458
Dominica, 2:844
  Fèt St.-Pierre and Fèt St.-Isidore, 2:841
  Jounen Kwéyòl, 2:841
  National Day Celebrations, 2:840–41
Dominican Republic, 2:851, 852, 853, 856,
  859
  velación, 2:848
Dominica, patronal, 2:841
Ecuador
  Corpus Christi, 2:415, 417, 420–22
  Fiesta del Coraza, 2:210
  Holy Week, 2:419–20
  New Year's Eve, 2:426
  radio festivals, 2:428–29
  Saint John the Baptist, 2:426–27
  Saints Peter and Paul, 2:426
Egypt
  al-mawlid al-nabawī, 6:414
  Muslim holidays, 6:166

saint's day (*mūlid*), 6:615, 616, 617–18,
  622, 625, 632
El Salvador
  Día de Santa Cruz, 2:709
  patronal, 2:709–10
  Saint Ursula, 2:711
England
  folk festivals, 8:332
  "Foreigners' Fêtes," 8:233
  Notting Hill Carnival, 8:235
Estonia, Estonian Song Festival, 8:495–96
Europe
  choral, 8:83
  Christian holidays, 8:5, 8–9, 139–41,
    342–43, 349, 388
  listings of, 8:241
  May Day, 8:185, *186*
  midsummer's eve, 8:399
  Muslim, 8:11–12
  traditional music festivals, 8:149–54, 158,
    175
Faroe Islands, Ólavsøka, 8:468, 471
Federated States of Micronesia, 9:726, 728
  Chuuk, 9:737
  Pohnpei, 9:719, 740
  Yap Day, 9:727, 729–30
Fiji, 9:780, 781–82
  Holī, 5:613
Finland, 8:486
  Kaustinen Folk Music Festival, 3:826
  May Day, 8:485
  Midsummer Eve, 8:485
Florida, Miami Reggae Festival, 3:809
France
  Africa Fête, 8:238, 241
  Universal Exposition of Paris, 8:175
French Guiana, 2:435
Futuna, 9:815
Gã people, 1:463
Georgia, 8:833, 834–35, 844
  jazz, 8:845
German Democratic Republic, rock, 8:219
Germany
  Bayreuth, 8:83
  children's participation in, 8:649
  Fasnacht, 8:649, 657
  Hamburg Rom Festival, 8:289
  Magneten festival, 8:272
  Saint Martin's Day, 8:649, 657
  tournaments, 8:653
  World Romani Congress, 8:289
Ghana
  Fetu Afahye, 10:30–36, 38
  national, 1:394–95
  Panafesta, 10:29–31
  Tsimsi Tsugu Festival, 10:145
Goa, 5:736–37
Great Britain
  Baisākhī, 5:574
  Festival of Britain, 1951, 8:235
  folk festivals, 8:153
Great Lakes Indians, Maple Sugar Festival,
  3:453
Greece, 8:1010, 1015–16
  country fairs, 8:1007–8, 1016
  Cycladic islands, 8:1015
  Macedonia, 8:1011

Guadeloupe, *balakadri*, 2:877–78
Gujarat
  Kutch folk festival, 5:7, *8*
  Navrātrī, 5:501, 550, 625, 628
Guyana, 2:447–48
  Caribbean Festival of the Arts, 2:447
  Christmas, 2:446
  Guyana Festival of the Arts, 2:448
  Hindu and Islamic, 2:443, 444
  Holī, 5:600
Haiti, 2:890
  rara, 2:885–87
Hanukkah, 8:250, 261
Hawai'i, 9:66–67
  Feast of the Holy Ghost, 9:97–98
  in Hawai'i-Tahiti Fête, 9:105
  hula genres for, 9:928
  Kamehameha Day, 9:95
  May Day, 9:109
  Merrie Monarch Festival, 3:218–19; 9:56,
    66–67, 923, 1008
  Prince Lot Hula Festival, 9:67
  Queen Lili'uokalani Keiki Hula Festival,
    9:67, 923, 1008
  Rizal Day, 9:100
  Sāmoan Flag Day, 9:104
  Santa Lucia Day, 9:95
  Scottish Highland Games, 9:106–7
  Tongan people, 9:104
Himachal Pradesh
  Dussehrā, 5:500
  Tushimig, 5:500
Hindu, 2:443, 444, 908, 959; 5:252
  Baisākhī, 5:500, 574, *579*, 650, *653*
  Divālī, 5:875
  Holī, 5:170, 276, 471, 473, 501, 590, 600,
    613, 642, *644*, 645, 648, 664, 665,
    877
  Navrātrī, 5:230, 277, 501, 550, 625, 628
Hmong people, 3:1003–4; 4:555–56
Honduras, *guancasco* (*paisanazgo*), 2:743–44
Hong Kong, 7:434
  Cantonese opera in, 7:307
Hungary, 8:739
  Rom musicians at, 8:274
  Vlach *mulatshago*, 8:275
  Vlach Rom gatherings, 8:276
Idaho, Jai-Aldi Festival, 3:849–50
Igbo people, 1:459
Illinois
  Chicago Asian American Jazz Festival, 3:965
  Ravinia Festival, 3:612
India
  audiences at, 5:419
  baha (flower festival), 5:415
  Basant, 5:276
  Dussehrā, 5:495–96
  Hindu, 5:252
  Hindustani music, 5:203
  kadam (karam tree festival), 5:415
  Krishna's birthday, 5:276
  Navrātrī, 5:230, 277
  Sawai Gandharva Music Festival, 5:4
  sohrae (harvest festival), 5:415
  spring festival, 5:497
  theatrical presentations at, 5:482

Volume Key: **6**, Middle East; **7**, East Asia; **8**, Europe; **9**, Australia and the Pacific Islands; **10**, The World's Music.

festivals, celebrations, and holidays (*continued*)
  Ingassana people, **1:**563
  Iran, cultural, **6:**823–24
  Ireland, **8:**325
    Fleadh Cheoil na hÉireann, **8:**391, 392
    harp festivals, **8:**393
    religious, **8:**388
    Willie Clancy Summer School, **8:**386
  Ireland, Northern, Belfast Harp Festival, **8:**321
  Israel
    art music, **6:**1030
    hilula pilgrimage, **6:**202–3
    Israeli Song Festival, **6:**204, 1020
    kibbutz, **6:**1030
    Mimuna, **6:**203
    mizraḥi Jews, **6:**263
    religious songs, **6:**204
  Italy
    Festival di Sanremo, **8:**619
    maggio, **8:**140, 607, 608, 614
  Jamaica
    birthday of Cudjoe, **2:**897–98
    Bruckins, **2:**906
    Hindu and Muslim, **2:**908
    Independence Festival, **2:**907–8
    Jonkunnu, **2:**907
    Reggae Sunsplash, **2:**94
  Japan
    bon, **7:**65, 603, 605
    Gion, **7:**639, 684
    Korean, **7:**798
    min'yô in, **7:**600
    setubun, **7:**610
    Shinto, **7:**607–9
    shrine, **7:**684
  Jewish people, **3:**936; **6:**200, 525, 1052;
        8:249–51, 261–62
    Mimunah, **6:**1040
    Passover, **8:**250, 251, 261
    Rosh Hashanah, **8:**250, 259
    Yom Kippur, **8:**250, 255, 259
  Kansas, Lindsborg Swedish festivals, **3:**871–72
  Kapingamarangi, songfests, **9:**838
  Karen people, **4:**544
  Karnataka, **5:**875, 881
    Divālī, **5:**875
    Gouri, **5:**875
    Holī, **5:**877
    Muharram, **5:**867, 875
    Purandara Dasa Festival (Mulubagilu),
        5:211
  Karnatak music, **5:**210–11
  Kashmir, *mi'rāj*, **5:**686
  Kazakhstan, **6:**954–55, 960
  Kenya, **1:**627, 629
  Kerala, **5:**930, 935–36, 949
    Puram Festival, **5:**360, 362
  Kiribati, **9:**758–59
  Korea
    band performances in, **7:**931, 938, 965
    harvest, **7:**884
    shamanic, **7:**889
  Kota people, Devr, **5:**272, 278, 281, 285
  Lahu people, **4:**539–40
  Laos, **4:**342, 357
    pong fai, **4:**341

Latvia
    Baltica '88, **8:**506
    Easter, **8:**501
    Jāṇi, **8:**501
    Latvian Song Festival, **8:**505
  Lisu people, **4:**543
  Lithuania, **8:**510
    Baltica, **8:**514
  Lombok, **4:**772, 776
  Louisiana, New Orleans Jazz and Heritage
        Festival, **9:**168
  Low Countries, **8:**522
  Luangiua, *sanga*, **9:**843
  Macedonia, **8:**982
    St. George's Day, **8:**282
    Vasilica, **8:**282
  Madhya Pradesh
    bhīmul pandum, **5:**721–22
    Janmashtami, **5:**724
    Maharashtra, **5:**726
    Mahāśivarātrī, **5:**725
  Maine, Portland Performing Arts Festival,
        3:999, 1001
  Malaysia, **4:**409
  Malta, **8:**639, 641
  Mangareva, **9:**886
  Manihiki, Christmas, **9:**908–9
  Manitoba
    Gimli Icelandic Festival, **3:**1089, 1225
    Islendinga Dagurinn, **3:**1251
    St. Boniface Festival de Voyageur, **3:**409
    Winnipeg Folk Festival, **3:**343, 1233–34
    Winnipeg Folklorama, **3:**1235–36
    Winnipeg New Music Festival, **3:**1091
  Mapuche culture, *ramada*, **2:**236
  Maritime Provinces, **3:**1117, 1118–19
  Marquesas Islands, Ko'ina Rare Festival, **9:**890,
        895
  Marshall Islands, **9:**748–49
  Martinique, International Creole Day,
        2:917–18
  Massachusetts
    Boston Asian American Creative Music
        Festival, **3:**965
    Boston peace jubilees, **3:**565
    Jacob's Pillow Dance Festival, **3:**221, 999,
        1001
    New Bedford Feast of the Blessed
        Sacrament, **3:**850
    Worcester Festival, **3:**535
  Maya culture, **2:**730–31
    Christian, **2:**667–68
    Holy Week, **2:**730–31
    Saint Sebastian, **2:**652, 653
    San Luís, **2:**667
  Mexica culture, **2:**562
  Mexico, **2:**607; **10:**91–95
    Encuento del Mariachi, **2:**623
    Virgin of Guadalupe, **2:**47, 559, 613–14;
        10:91–95
  Michigan
    Arab World Festival, **6:**284, 285
    Michigan Indian Day, **3:**453
  Micronesia, **9:**715–16
  Miskitu culture, *Krismis*, **2:**661–62
  Mithila, Durgā Pūjā, **5:**677

Mixtec culture, **2:**564, 565–66
  Mongol people, **7:**1003
  Montenegro, *guslari*, **8:**961
  Montserrat
    Boxing Day, **2:**925–26
    Jump-Up Day, **2:**925–26
  Morocco, Berber, **6:**484–85
  Muṇḍa people, Ind (also Indi), **5:***502*
  Muslim people, **1:**447, 517, 524–27, 538–39;
        2:908; **6:**939
    adhā, **6:**544
    Hosay, **2:**959; **5:**590
    Muhammad's birthday (Mavlud), **5:**278;
        6:942
    Muharram, **2:**85–86; **5:**276–77, 282, 284,
        285
    Ramadan, **1:***454*, 484, 536, 538, 542;
        2:507; **5:**277, 281, 684, 806, 816,
        824; **6:**673, 680, 940–42, 951;
        8:11–12
  Nauru, **9:**757
  Naxi people, **7:**510
  Nepal, **5:**490
    Damāi performances at, **5:**699
    Guruṅg people, **5:**705
    Indra Jātrā, **5:**505
    Sri Panchami festival, **5:**698
    Tij festival, **5:**702
  Netherlands Antilles, **2:**929, 930
    Simadan, **2:**930
  Netherlands, Tilburg, Derde Werde Festival,
        8:154
  New Brunswick
    International Baroque Music Festival,
        3:1119
    Miramichi Festival, **3:**1125
    Saint John Festival-by-the-Sea, **3:**1119
  Newfoundland
    St. John's Festival 500 Sharing the Voices,
        3:1119
    St. John's Sound Symposium, **3:**1119
  New Guinea, **9:**22
  New York
    Brooklyn *Mahrajan al-Fan*, **3:**1037
    Chinese New Year, **3:**958
    Italian people, **3:**861
    New York Asian Pacific American Heritage
        Festival, **3:**973
    New York O-Bon Dance Festival, **3:**973
    Staten Island Irish Traditional Music
        Festival, **3:**846
    West Indian Labor Day Carnival, **3:**507–8,
        806, 810, 811
    Woodstock Festival, **3:**551
  Nicaragua, **2:**762–63, 766
  Nigeria, **1:**34
    All-Eastern Nigeria Music Festival, **1:**14–15
  North Africa, **1:**538–39
  North Carolina
    Asheville folk festival, **3:**146
    Durham American Dance Festival, **3:**221
  Northern Marianas, **9:**92
  Northwest Territories, Yellowknife Folk on the
        Rocks, **3:**1278, 1281
  Norway, **8:**427
    jazz, **8:**430

Volume Key: **1**, Africa; **2**, South America, Mexico, etc.; **3**, United States and Canada; **4**, Southeast Asia; **5**, South Asia

Kalvoya Festival, **8**:430
Nordic Music Days, **8**:430
Sami Grand Prix, **8**:*306*
ULTIMA, **8**:430
World Music Days, **8**:430
Nova Scotia
   Annapolis Valley Apple Blossom Festival,
      3:1117
   Celtic Colours International Festival, **3**:1129
   Glendale Festival, **3**:1128
   Halifax Nova Scotia Tattoo, **3**:1119
   Halifax Scotia Festival of Music, **3**:1119
   Lunenburg Folk Harbour Festival, **3**:1119
   Musique Royale, **3**:1119
Oceania, **9**:53–67, 226, 321, 1008
Ohio
   Cincinnati May Festival, **3**:528, 535
   Tyagaraja Festival, **3**:*950*, 981, 988–92
Olympic Games, **8**:185
Oman
   end of Ramadan, **6**:673, 680
   Islamic feasts, **6**:680–681
Ontario, **3**:1186
   Afrofest Festival, **3**:1213
   Baltic song, **3**:1082
   French-Canadian music, **3**:1194
   German and Dutch, **3**:1195
   Mariposa Folk Festival, **3**:94, 149, 1186
   Middle Eastern, **3**:1219–20
   Oktoberfest, **3**:1082
   Ottawa Fête-Caribe, **3**:223
   Toronto AfriCaribeat, **3**:1203
   Toronto Caravan, **3**:223, 1216
   Toronto Caribana festival, **3**:17, 223, 1085,
      1186, 1202, 1203, 1207–9, 1212–13
   Toronto Centre Island Music Fest, **3**:1203
   Toronto Fringe Festival of Independent
      Dance Artists, **3**:225
   Toronto International Dragon Boat Race
      Festival, **3**:1217
   Toronto Panorama India, **3**:1216
   Toronto Reggaebana, **3**:1203
   Toronto Rhythms of the World, **3**:1216
   Toronto World of Music Arts and Dance
      Festival, **3**:1216, 1279
Orissa, **5**:733
Otomí culture, Saint Michael, **2**:573
Otopame culture, **2**:573
Ottoman empire, **6**:812
Pakistan, **5**:506, 794, 799–800
   qawwali, **5**:755
   'urs (saints' death anniversaries), **5**:751, *752*,
      754–55, 759, *763*, *765*, 769, 779
Palau, **9**:723
Pame culture, **2**:573
Panama, **2**:772, 781, *782*
   Carnaval de Colón, **2**:693
   Festival de la Mejorana, **2**:*775*, 783
   Independence Day, **2**:782–83
Papua New Guinea, **9**:62–63
   Abelam people, **9**:549, 550–51
   agricultural shows, **9**:148, 478
   Binandere people, **9**:359
   garamut signals for, **9**:377
   Highlands region, **9**:512
   Hiri Moale Festival, **9**:493, 494

Huli people, **9**:298–99
Melpa people, **9**:485
Mt. Hagen Festival, **9**:55
Nagovisi *pati*, **9**:649
Tolai Warwagira, **9**:139
Trobriand Islands *milamala*, **9**:498–99
Paraguay
   Holy Week, **2**:457–58
   patronal, **2**:458–59
   Saint Balthazar, **2**:457
   Saint John the Baptist, **2**:459
   San Blas, **2**:459
   Virgin of Caacupé, **2**:458–59
Pennsylvania
   Bethlehem Bach Festival, **3**:535
   Philadelphia Irish Music Festival, **3**:846
   regional German fairs, **3**:888
Peru, **2**:36, 218–21, 478–80
   Amancaes, **2**:483
   Christmas, **2**:494–95
   Corpus Christi, **2**:227, 468, 494
   Día de los Muertos, **2**:478
   Festival Negroide, **2**:501
   Huanchaco patronal festival, **2**:*38*
   Los Baños del Inca, **2**:*474*
   Palchasqa, **2**:228
   Saint John the Baptist, **2**:*37*, 226
   San Salvador, **2**:*63*
   Santiago, **2**:211
   Virgin of Carmen, **2**:*62*, *118*, *472*
   watermelon harvest, **2**:495
Philippines
   feast days, **4**:848–49
   flores de Mayo, **4**:847
   moriones, **4**:846
   Musics of Asia, **4**:876
   popular music, **4**:885
   regional, **4**:881
   Asian Composers League, **4**:876
Poland, **8**:702, 711
Polynesia, choral, **9**:202
Portugal, religious, **8**:577, 579
Prince Edward Island
   Acadian Jamboree, **3**:1137
   Charlottetown Festival, **3**:199, 1119
   Rollo Bay Fiddlers Festival, **3**:1128
Puerto Rico, *bomba* performances, **2**:937
Pukapuka, **9**:913
Punjab, Baisākhī, **5**:500, 574, 650, *653*
Purépecha culture
   chanántskua, **2**:578
   Corpus Christi, **2**:578
Purim, **8**:251, 261
Q'ero culture, **2**:225, 227–29
   Ahata Uhuchichis, **2**:229
Québec
   African and Caribbean, **3**:1170
   Montréal Carifiesta (CariFête), **3**:223, 1077,
      1170
   Montréal International New Music Week,
      3:1151, 1153
   Montréal Jazz Festival, **3**:1107, 1160, 1169,
      1170
   Montréal New Music America, **3**:1151
   St. Jean Baptiste Day, **3**:1075
   Uashat Innu Nikamu festival, **3**:1280

Rajasthan
   Holī, **5**:642, *644*, 645, 648
   'urs (saints' death anniversaries), **5**:644
Réunion Island, Fête de Dix Jours, **5**:608
Rhode Island
   Newport Folk Festival, **3**:149, 300
   Newport Jazz Festival, **7**:708
rock, **3**:551; **8**:216, 217
Rom music festivals, **8**:272
Romania, **8**:868, 883
   Cîntarea Românei, **8**:883
   International Week of New Music,
      8:883
Roti, **4**:801
Rotuma, **9**:818
Russia
   calendrical, **8**:760
   St. Petersburg Musical Spring, **8**:778
   Svyatki period, **8**:758–59
Ryûkyû Islands, **7**:794
St. Lucia, **2**:946
   Jounen Kwéyòl, **2**:942–43
   masquerade, **2**:947–48
Sāmoa, village celebrations, **9**:237
Saskatchewan, Craven Big Valley Jamboree,
   3:1091
Saudi Arabia, **6**:653
   Janādiriyya, **6**:702
Scotland
   Edinburgh International Festival, **8**:371
   People's Festival Ceilidhs, **8**:371
Serbia
   Belgrade Music Festival, **8**:949
   Kosovo, **8**:997
   Rom people, **8**:280
   Sabor Narodnog Stvaralastva, **8**:949
   Zlatna Truba, **8**:946
Sikaiana
   hakatoo pakupaku, **9**:844
   puina, **9**:844–45, 847
Sikkim, **5**:502
Simchas Torah, **8**:251
Singapore, **4**:519, 524
   Indian, **4**:521
   Peranakan, **4**:522
Slovakia, **8**:717, 720, 722–23
Slovenia, **8**:911–12, 915
Society Islands, **9**:873
   Chinese, **9**:868
   Heiva, **9**:56–57, 65–66, 867–68, 873,
      876–77, 880, 958
Solomon Islands
   independence, **9**:963
   Isabel Province, **9**:662
   Sirovanga *kelo*, **9**:654
South Africa, **1**:780
   "Cape Coon Carnival," **1**:765
   Johannesburg International Arts Alive
      Festival, **1**:431
   Karoo Festival, **1**:431
   Standard Bank Grahamstown Arts Festival,
      1:431
South America, **2**:47, 68, 72
   African brotherhoods' roles in, **2**:47
   birthday parties, **2**:58
   electronic recordings of, **2**:41

festivals, celebrations, and holidays, South
America (*continued*)
Japanese, **2:**87
national holidays, **2:**61
street music in, **2:**50
tropical-forest region, **2:**132
visual depictions of, **2:**12
South Asia, Holī, **5:**170, 276, 471, 473
Southern African Development Community,
1:428–29
Spain
Fiesta de los Diablos, **2:**414
fiestas, **8:**589, 596
flamenco, **8:**598
zambra, **6:**449
Sri Lanka, *perahēra*, **5:**491
Subarctic peoples, **3:**391
Sudan, Nuba mountains, **1:**563
Sumbawa, **4:**780
Surinam, Ramadan, **2:**507
Sweden
Falun Music Festival, **8:**154, 443
Järna, **8:**154, *155*
Switzerland, **8:**683–85, 698
chalandamarz, **8:**685
Fasnacht, **8:**685
Montreux Jazz Festival, **8:**698
Sechseläuten, **8:**685
Tahiti, Heiva Festival, **9:**56–57, 65–66,
867–68, 873, *875, 876–77,* 880, 958
Taino culture, harvest, **2:**22
Taiwan, **7:**424
Tamil Nadu, **5:**918
Dīpāvalī, **5:**277–78
Madras music festival, **5:**212
Mariyamman, **5:**277
Masinagudi Mariyamman festival, **5:**903–6
Srirangam Temple, **5:**261
Tyagaraja Festival (Tiruvaiyaru), **5:**269,
383–85, 390–95
Tarahumara culture, **2:**584–85, 586–87
Holy Week, **2:**586–87
Texas
Czech, **3:**898
mariachi, **3:**744
Thailand, **4:**293, 303
Buddhist, **4:**289
northeastern, **4:**326
northern, **4:**313
southern, **4:**309
Taejiu opera troups, **4:**71
thet mahachat, **4:**259
village, **4:**299
Tibetan culture, **7:**472
zho ston, **5:**712
Tokelau, *fiafia*, **9:**825–27
Trinidad and Tobago
Hindu and Muslim, **2:**959
Holī, **5:**590
Hosay, **5:**590
Indian, **2:**958
South Asian community, **5:**589
Tripura, Maimata, **5:**503
Tuareg people, **1:**545
camel, **1:**584–85
Tukano culture, *cachirí*, **2:**155

Tunisia
Jewish, **6:**524–25
Lag Ba'omer, **6:**523, 527, 528, 531
for national art music, **6:**330, 506, 511, 513
Testūr, **6:**332–36, 511
Turkey, **6:**765, 766
Alevi, **6:**799
aşîk, **6:**805, 807–8
founding of the People's Houses, **6:**813–14
Muslim holidays, **6:**794
Turkmenistan, **6:**975
Tuva, *khöömei*, **6:**987
Ukraine, patron saint, **8:**813
United States
Albanian, **3:**926–27
Arab music, **6:**285
Baisākhī, **5:***579*
bluegrass, **3:**162, 163
Cambodian, **3:**999, 1001
choral festivals, **3:**535
Croatian, **3:**922
dance festivals and workshops, **3:**210,
221–22, 225
Danish Christmas events, **3:**882
Estonian, **3:**878, 879, 880, 1196
ethnic, **3:**513, 822–23, 826–27
Filipino, **3:**1025
Finnish, **3:**872–73
folk festivals, **3:**149
French heritage festivals, **3:**856
German choral groups, **3:**885
Greek, **3:**529
Haitian, **2:**889; **3:**806
Indian communities, St. Tyagaraja Festival,
3:950, 951, 981, 988–92; **5:**579
Indian Independence Day, **3:**983
Indo-Caribbean community, **3:**814,
815–16
Indonesian music, **3:**1013, 1016
Inter-American Music Festivals, **2:**397
Irish, **3:**842, 845, 846
Japanese, **3:**527, 971, 973
Latvian, **3:**877
Lithuanian, **3:**875
mahrajān, **6:**280–81
mariachi, **3:**724–25, 744–45; **10:**79
Mexican-American, **3:**721, 735; *Cinco de
Mayo*, **3:**219, 721
Middle Eastern music, **3:**1037
polka, **3:**896
Polynesian music and dance, **3:**1052–53
Portuguese, **3:**850
Romanian, **3:**911
Sāmoan Flag Day, **3:**1052; **9:**117
Serbian, **3:**922
Slovak, **3:**899, 900
social and cultural contexts of, **3:**145
tamburitza orchestras, **3:**923
Tejano, **3:**773, 778
Ukrainian, **3:**912–13, 1088, 1231, 1243
Vietnamese, **3:**995
Uruguay, **2:**511–12
folk-music, **2:**516
San Cono, **2:**512
tango, **2:**519
Virgin of Verdun, **2:**511–12

Uttar Pradesh, **5:**668
Holī, **5:**501, 664, 665
Mirzapur, **5:**669
Ramlila, **10:**6–8
Tīj, **5:**669
'Uvea, **9:**809
Uzbekistan, **6:**905
Vanuatu
Independence Day, **9:**864
Malakula Arts Festival, **9:**966
National Arts Festival, **9:**966
Tanna, **9:**63–65, 363
Tannese *nakwiari*, **9:**703, 704–6
Tannese New Year's celebrations, **9:**706
Tannese *nieri*, **9:**703
Venezuela, **2:**526, 544
Corpus Christi, **2:**537
Parranda de San Pedro, **2:**530
Saint Anthony of Padua, **2:**536
Saint Benedict the Moor, **2:**530–31, 536
Saint John the Baptist, **2:**530, 535–36, 539
Yekuana *adaha ademi hidi*, **2:**181
Vietnam, **4:**450, 480, 497
dance in, **4:**499–500
Gối Village, **4:**486, 499–500
lê hội, **4:**476
Lim Village, **4:**477
during Lý dynasty, **4:**447
Mường people, **4:**535
upland regions, **4:**532
Virginia, Washington Irish Folk Festival, **3:**846
Virgin Islands, **2:**973; Cruz de Mayo, **2:**969
Waiāpí culture, Warikena, **2:**159
Wales
Cerdd Dant Festival, **8:**353–54
Cymanfa Ganu, **8:**350
folk festivals, **8:**356
"gray-mare" holiday, **8:**140, 342
Gŵyl Fair y Canhwyllau, **8:**343
gŵyl mabsant, **8:**353
jazz festival, **8:**356
Shrove Tuesday, **8:**343
Warao culture
habi sanuka, **2:**189
nahanamu, **2:**189, 191–93
Washington, Northwest Folklife Festival, **9:**119
Washington, D.C., Festival of American
Folklife, **2:**592; **3:**300, 823, 912;
9:*118*, 119, 978; **10:**80
West Africa, **1:**446–47
West Bengal
Durga Pūjā, **5:**503
Gajan, **5:**503
Western Arctic, **3:**376–77
Western Sāmoa, Independence Day, **9:**235
West Futuna, **9:**861, 863–64
Wisconsin
Milwaukee Holiday Folk Festival, **3:**216
Milwaukee Irish Music Festival, **3:**846
World of Music Arts and Dance (WOMAD),
1:418; **8:**225, 239–40, 241
world music festivals, **8:**154
World Romani Congress, **8:**282
Yami people, **7:**527
Yanomamö culture, *reaho*, **2:**173
Yoruba people, **1:**400, 411–13, 460, 461;
2:674

Volume Key: **1**, Africa; **2**, South America, Mexico, etc.; **3**, United States and Canada; **4**, Southeast Asia; **5**, South Asia

Yukon, Dawson City Festival, **3**:1278
Yuma culture, **2**:597–98
Zimbabwe, SADC Music Festival, **1**:437
Festival Singers of Canada, **3**:1079, 1184
Fétis, François-Joseph, **3**:28, 1165; **5**:50; **8**:176, 266
Feu'u, Fatu, **9**:112
Feux Follets, Les (folklore show), **3**:1076
Fewkes, Jesse Walter, **3**:243, 291, 485, 493, 509, 1069
Feynman, Richard, **3**:339; **7**:1023–24
Fiagbedzi, Nissio, **1**:26, 44–45
Fiberesima, **1**:251
Fiddler on the Roof (Bock and Harnick), **3**:940, 943
fiddles. *See* violins and fiddles (bowed lutes)
Fiddlesticks label, **3**:1071
fiddling traditions, North American. *See also* bluegrass; chordophones; country music
  African-American, **10**:142
  Anglo-Canadian, **3**:1080–81, 1082, 1256–57
  Athapaskan, **3**:391, 405, 1277
  Cape Breton (Gaelic), **3**:52, 74, 150–51, 1064, 1071, 1125, 1127–30, 1257
  country, **3**:160, 185, 186, 231, 520, 596, 835–39, 867, 1110
  French Canadian, **3**:1071, 1075, 1125, 1137, 1164, 1168, 1190, 1194
  Inuit, **3**:1275
  Métis, **3**:7, 332, 344, 405–10, 458, 1063, 1087, 1091, 1277
  Native American, **3**:326, 332, 405, 479, 1063
  Ukrainian, **3**:344–45, 1242
Field, John, **8**:378, 780
Field Museum of Natural History (Chicago), **9**:974; **10**:100
Fielden, Lionel, **5**:745
Fields, Al G., **3**:618
Fierro, Pancho, **2**:492, *493*, 494
Fiesta Araucana (Lavín), **2**:115
Fiestas Tradicionales de Venezuela (Hernández/ Fuentes), **2**:544
fife. *See* flutes
Figgy Duff (musical group), **3**:1071, 1121
"Fight the Power" (Public Enemy), **3**:715
Figueres, José, **2**:702
Figueroa, Alfredo, **3**:*722*
Figueroa, Alfredo, Jr., **3**:*722*
Figueroa, Charlie, **9**:101
Figueroa, Jesús, **3**:*722*
Figueroa, José María, **2**:682, 694
Figuš-Bystrý, Viliam, **8**:729
"*Fī jannati 'l firdawsi*" (*baṭāyḥī*), **6**:*333–35*
Fiji, **9**:771, 773–83. *See also* Kadavu; Lau Islands; Rotuma; Taveuni; Vanua Levu; Viti Levu
  adminstration of Rotuma, **9**:818
  American expeditions to, **9**:18–20, 24
  Americans in, **9**:27
  archives and museums, **9**:968
  Banaban people in, **9**:*71*, 764
  chief presentation ceremony, **9**:348
  Chinese people in, **9**:71–72
  Christian missionaries from, **9**:195
  composition in, **9**:353–54

cultural contacts with Sāmoa, **9**:795
cultural relationships with Malakula, **9**:689
drumming, **9**:114
films on, **9**:1017
geography of, **9**:773
history of South Asian people on, **5**:612
I-Kiribati in, **9**:760
immigrant groups in, **9**:69, 773, 782
immigrants to Australia, **9**:85–86
Indian people in, **3**:815; **9**:92–94
influence on Papua New Guinean string-band music, **9**:138
instruments imported to Papua New Guinea, **9**:508
instruments of, **9**:378, 776
kava use in, **9**:172–75, 176–77
map of, **9**:*772*
music and dance, **9**:20, 48, 774–83, 947, 980
  meke, **9**:161, 162, 774, 776–78, 780–81, 998
  meke wau, **9**:18–19
  sere ni cumu, **9**:161–62
  sere ni lotu, **9**:776, 779, 781
  sere ni vanua, **9**:781, *782*
  tāmūrē, **9**:211
  taralala, **9**:149, 157
  vakamalolo, **9**:823
  vakawelegone, **9**:263–65
Naloto Village, music and dance in, **9**:776–80
numeral notations in, **9**:287
outsiders' influence in, **9**:5
popular music in, **9**:161–62
population of, **9**:773
research on, **9**:976
social organization in, **9**:5
sound recordings from, **9**:985, 997–98, 999
South Asian population of, **5**:612–14
string figures in, **9**:263–65
sung poetry, **9**:328
theater in, **9**:233
tourism in, **9**:781–82
World War II troops, **9**:149
Fiji (Hawai'i band), **9**:165–66
Fiji Arts Club, **9**:233
Fiji Museum, **9**:968
Fijian Association (Australia), **9**:86
Fijian people
  in Aotearoa, **9**:114
  in United States, **9**:116–17
Fila (Vanuatu), **9**:833
Fil-Am Philippine Dance Company (Alhambra), **3**:1025
Filiasiana (Kasilag), **4**:875
Filibusterismo (Cayabyab), **4**:885
Filipinas para los Filipinos (Estella), **4**:864
Filipino Channel (television channel), **3**:1025
Filipino Heritage (periodical), **4**:29
Filipino people
  in Guam, **9**:*70*
  in Hawai'i, **9**:95, 96, 100, 109, 163, 914
  in Hong Kong, **7**:431–32
  in Mariana Islands, **9**:743
  in North America, **3**:527, 848, 948, 1024–26, 1215
  in Vietnam, **4**:531
Filip Kutev Ensemble, **8**:890

Fil-Layl ('Abd al-Wahhāb), **6**:600
Fillmore, John Comfort, **3**:29, 509
film and video. *See also* film music
  accompaniment for, **3**:262, 1183
  Afghanistan, **5**:531
  Africa, **1**:156
    use in transcription, **1**:254
  African-Americans in, **3**:715
  Albania, **8**:999–1000
  Andhra Pradesh, **5**:890–91
  Aotearoa, archives of, **9**:972–74
  Argentina, tango accompaniment for, **2**:264, 519
  Australia, archives of, **9**:958–61
  Bangladesh, **5**:531, 855, 858
  blaxploitation, **3**:711
  Bosnia-Hercegovina, **8**:969
  Caribbean, video recordings, **2**:41, 51, 52–53, 81
  cartoon depictions of African-Americans, **3**:71
  cartoons, **3**:202
  Central America, **2**:630
    video recordings, **2**:41, 51, 52–53, 81
  China, **7**:89–90, 399
  Chinese, **3**:951
  commercial, **9**:26, 42–47, 149, 390, 1007
  of dance and movement, **9**:313–14, 317
  decline in production of, **5**:539
  Denmark, videotapes of dances, **8**:465
  development of, **3**:244, 262, 861
  documentary, **3**:292; **9**:23, 42, 442
    Australia, **9**:46–47, 420
    Pacific Islands, **9**:47–50
  Egypt, **6**:233, 236–38, 239, 255–56, 432, 548, 552, 559, 597, 600
  ethnomusicological use of, **1**:267
  Fiji, archives of, **9**:968
  Haiti, video recordings, **2**:891
  Hawai'i
    archives of, **9**:968–72
    political videos, **9**:221–22
  Hawai'ian-themed, **3**:1049
  hip-hop culture in, **3**:586
  Hong Kong, **7**:354
    Cantonese operas, **7**:307
  India, North, **5**:531–33
  India, South, **5**:542, 543–44
  Japan, **7**:749–50
    animation, **7**:751
    nagauta accompaniment of, **7**:749
  Karnataka, **5**:883
  Kerala, **5**:950
  Korea, **7**:945
  Maharashtra, **5**:729
  Mexico, **2**:371, 605, 619, 620, 621, 622, 716
    video recordings, **2**:41, 51, 52–53, 81
  Micronesia, archives of, **9**:967–68
  Nepal, **5**:706
  New Caledonia, archives of, **9**:964–65
  Nicaragua, **2**:765
  Pakistan, **5**:531, 747, 790
  Papua New Guinea, archives of, **9**:961–62
  portrayals of Greeks in, **8**:1007
  Romania, **8**:886
  St. Lucia, video recordings, **2**:950
  silent, **3**:202–3, 262, 546

film and video (*continued*)
  Solomon Islands, archives of, **9:**962–64
  South America, video recordings, **2:**41, 51, 52–53, 81
  South Asia
    depictions of *giddhā*, **5:**654
    depictions of *qawwali* in, **5:**416
    depictions of religious mendicants in, **5:**347
  Sri Lanka, **5:**555
  survey of, **9:**1007–20
  Suyá culture, video recordings, **2:**145
  Turkey, **6:**255, 257–58, 259
  United States, **3:**202–4, 237; **8:**675
    archives of, **9:**974–80
    dominance of, **3:**18
    Jewish composers, **3:**12
    Latin music in, **3:**732, 794
    musicals, **3:**196, 200, 202, 544, 545; **6:**237
    music promotion in, **3:**260
  Vanuatu, **9:**965–67
  Yaqui dances, video recordings, **2:**593
  Yiddish, **3:**938
film music. *See also* film and video; film music, South Asian
  compilation soundtracks, **3:**204
  Egyptian, **1:**645; **6:**548, 552–53, 558
    in Algeria, **6:**269
    in Turkey, **6:**118, 255–56
  Greek music for, **8:**1021, 1022
  Hong Kong, **7:**355
  Japan, **7:**722, 732, 749–51
  Korea, **7:**958, 960
  United States, **7:**709
    African-American composers of, **3:**607, 609, 610
    composers of, **3:**203–4, 539, 541, 546
film music, South Asian (*filmī gīt*; also *cine*), **5:**2, 213, 419, 560
  Afghanistan, **5:**489, 809, 820, 827, 832
  Andhra Pradesh, **5:**890–91
  Bangladesh, **5:**858
  Bengal, **5:**853–54, 855–56, 857
  China, **7:**468
  Europe, **8:**240, 286, 951
  Fiji, **5:**614
  form of, **5:**533–34
  fusion trends in, **5:**540–41, 544–45
  genres of, **5:**533–34, 555–56
  Goa, **5:**737
  growth of, **5:**15, 405, 527, 547
  Guyana, **2:**444; **5:**603
  influence on *fiji*, **1:**485
  influence on *taarab*, **1:**427, 607, 631
  instruments in, **5:**347–48
  Kashmir, **5:**682
  Kerala, **5:**929, 950
  live performances of, **5:**421
  Mithila, **5:**679
  Nepal, **5:**696, 704
  North America, **3:**812, 817, 982, 987, 1005, 1205; **5:**579, 581
  North India, **5:**531–41
  orchestration in, **5:**338, 347, 368, 855, 950
  Pakistan, **5:**748, 799
  performers of, **5:**351, 420–23
  pop bhajans in, **5:**11, 255

raga in, **5:**107–8
South Africa, **5:**616
Southeast Asia, **4:**62, 68, 101, 601
South India, **5:**107–8, 368, 542–46, 555
South Indian religious music in, **5:**270
Sri Lanka, **5:**971
studies of, **5:**56
talas for, **5:**127
Tamil Nadu, **5:**906, 924
Tibetan culture, **5:**715
Trinidad and Tobago, **2:**958; **5:**591
United Kingdom, **5:**574
Uttar Pradesh, **5:**665, 667, 668
vocal style of, **5:**533
women performers of, **5:**407, 411, 412, 414
Filotei Sin Agai Jipei, **8:**881
Filothei Cozianul, **8:**881
"*Finada Pablita*," **3:**757
Findeizen, Nikolai, **8:**783
Fine Arts Department (Thailand), **4:**121, 219, 251, 255–56, 261, 277, 297
Fine Arts Quartet, **3:**175
Finestream Gamelan, **3:**1018
Finicio, Jacome, **5:**908
Finkelstein, Bernie, **3:**252
Finland, **8:**475–89
  art music in, **8:**482, 485
  brass bands in, **8:**6
  dance traditions of, **8:**477, 482, 485–86
  folk music pedagogy, **8:**155
  geography of, **8:**475
  healing ceremonies, **8:**196
  history of, **8:**475
  history of music in, **8:**481–84
  influence on Swedish music, **8:**435
  instrument collections in, **8:**181
  instruments, **8:**170, 478–79, 481
    research on, **8:**179
  Kaustinen, **8:**478
  map of, **8:**398
  music video broadcasting in, **3:**248, 252
  political music in, **8:**147
  popular music in, **8:**208, 217, 227, 483–86
  population of, **8:**475
  psalm singing in, **8:**482
  research on aesthetics, **8:**25
  research on music of, **8:**185, 487–89
  Rom people in, **8:**289, 487
  Saami people in, **8:**12, 299–307, 486–87
  Swedish people in, **8:**487
  tango in, **2:**75
  Turku, court music, **8:**481
  vocal music of, **8:**114–15, 196, 475–78
  weddings in, **8:**6, 144
  women's performances in, **8:**200
Finland-Swedish Archive of Folk Culture (Helsinki), **8:**481
Finlayson, George, **4:**225, 239
Finn, John Morris, **3:**1094
Finn, Julio, **3:**582
Finnegan, Ruth, **1:**133, 137
Finnish American Knights, **3:**823
Finnish Fiddlers' Club, **8:**480
Finnish Literature Society, **8:**481
Finnish people
  in Estonia, **8:**491

in North America, **3:**826, 872–75
  identity issues of, **3:**822–23
  instrumental music of, **3:**874–75
  Ontario, **3:**1078, 1082, 1196
  vocal music of, **3:**873
  western Canada, **3:**1250–51
in Russia, **8:**767, 772
in Sweden, **8:**434, 446
Finnish Socialist Federation, **3:**872
Finnish Society for Ethnomusicology, **8:**489
Finnish Society of Musicology, **8:**488
Finno-Ugric peoples, **8:**115, 736, 737, 754, 772–74
  vocal polyphony of, **8:**757, 774
Finsch, Otto, **9:**752–53
Finstrom, Matt, **3:**1018
Fipa people, **1:**637
Firdawsī. *See* Ferdowsī
"Fire" (Ohio Players), **3:**681, 711
Fire and Ice, **9:**158
Firestarter (film), **3:**204
Firqat al-Musiqa al-'Arabiyya (Cairo), **6:**45, 317–19, 553, 560, *560*
First Choice, **3:**689
First Nations peoples, **3:**143, 1097. *See also* Native American peoples; *specific groups*
  in British Columbia, **3:**1092–94, 1254, 1256
  ceremonial practices, **3:**1062
  citizenship legislation, **3:**13
  cultural policy views of, **3:**1067
  dance traditions of, **3:**222–23
  gender-role studies of, **3:**93–94
  history of musical culture, **3:**5–7, 366–67
  in Maritime Provinces, **3:**1069
  nineteenth century, **3:**9, 10–11
  in northern Canada, **3:**1274–80
  Northwest Coast, **3:**394–402
  in Ontario, **3:**1078–79, 1178
  popular music of, **3:**73
  population of, **3:**4, 1056
  in Prairie Provinces, **3:**1085–87, 1224, 1225
  in Québec, **3:**1074
  research on, **3:**509
  research on music of, **3:**31, 146, 149, 291
  social and musical interactions, **3:**480–90, 1056, 1062–63, 1069, 1114–15, 1135
  stereotyping of, **3:**73
  subjugation of, **3:**17, 51, 332
  trade networks of, **3:**3
Firth, J. R., **1:**27
Firth, Raymond, **9:**253, 835, 860
Fischer, Dudu, **6:**205
Fischer, Hans, **9:**371
Fischer, John L., **9:**739, 741
Fischer-Dieskau, Dietrich, **3:**1210
Fishbone, **9:**164–66
Fisher, Edward, **3:**1079
Fisher, Helen, **9:**947
Fisher, Miles Mark, **3:**627
Fisheries Broadcast (radio show), **3:**1139
"Fishers Hornpipe," **3:**839
"Fishers of Men," **9:**150
Fisk, Elliot, **3:**851
Fisk Jubilee Singers, **3:**10, 68, *69*, 524, *524*, 573, 575, 617, 628–29, 1133; **9:**929

Fisk University (Nashville), **3:**68, 524, 617, 632; **10:**137–39
Fistful of Dollars, A (film), **3:**204
Fitrat, Abdurauf, **6:**917
Fitzgerald, Ella, **3:**708
Fitzgerald, Tyrone "Dr. Offfff," **2:**808
Fitzgerald, Winston "Scotty," **3:**1071
Fitzpatrick, Sarah, **3:**625
Five Aboriginal Dances from Cape York (film), **9:**47
Five Blind Boys of Missisipy (gospel group), **3:**633
Five Dances (Alexander), **6:**1031
Five Dynasties period
  instruments in, **7:**111–12
  music theory in, **7:**118–19
Five Hand Reel (musical group), **8:**372
Five Keys (musical group), **3:**671
"5-10-15 Hours" (Brown), **3:**670
Five Windows on Africa (Stone), **10:**60, 61, 62
Fjellner, Anders, **8:**307
Flaherty, Frances Hubbard, **9:**975
Flaherty, Robert J., **9:**42, 44, 975, 1007
Flaherty, Stephen, **3:**200
Flam, Gila, **8:**267
flamenco, **6:**433; **8:**596–600
  aksak meters in, **8:**593
  Andalusian influences in, **6:**448–49
  Arab elements in, **8:**12
  guitar use in, **8:**594, 598
  history of, **8:**597–98
  international popularity of, **8:**7, 208
  in Judeo-Spanish repertoire, **6:**1042
  in North America, **3:**207, 209, 222, 338, 731, 851, 1197
  nuevo flamenco, **8:**599–600
  rai and, **8:**233
  Rom people and, **8:**272, 596–97
  in Uighur pop music, **7:**468
Flanders. *See also* Belgium; France; Low Countries
  broadside singers in, **8:**522
  burlesque fiddle imitations, **8:**532
  instruments and instrumental music, **8:**523–33, 535, 544
  research on music of, **8:**535
  vocal music of, **8:**519–20
Flannery, Kent V., **2:**568
Flannery, Regina, **3:**392
Flashdance (film), **3:**200, 204, 713
Flathead Indian nation, **3:**421, 511
Flatt, Lester, **3:**159, 166, 168
Fledermaus, Die (Strauss), **3:**193
Fleetwood Mac, **8:**215
Fleming, Alexander, **10:**122
Flemings, **8:**12, 518
Fleras, Augie, **3:**73
Fletcher, Alice Cunningham, **3:**29, 92, 291, 444, 457, 485, 487, 498, 509
Fletcher, Francis, **2:**250
Fleur du Rosier, (Creighton), **3:**1136
Fleurs de salon: 2 Favorite Polkas (McCarty), **3:**606
Fleurus, Jehan de, **8:**533
Fleurus, Noël de, **8:**533
Flight into Egypt (Harbison), **3:**541

Flintoff, Brian, **9:**933
Flonzaley Quartet, **3:**538, 1210
Flora, Reis, **5:**306
Florentine Codex, **2:**15, *17*, 557
Flores, **4:**762, 791–96
  geography of, **4:**791
  history of, **4:**791
  instruments of, **4:**792–93
  Lio people, spirit worship, **4:**61
  music research on, **4:**28, 29
  religion in, **4:**791–92
  textiles of, **4:**791, *792*
Flores, Bernal, **2:**704
Flores, Celedonio, **2:**263
Flores del Campo, Francisco, **2:**370–71, *372*
Flores Dorantes, Felipe, **2:**658
Flores García, Lorenza, **2:**658
Flores, José Asunción, **2:**460, 464
Flores, Juan, **2:**941
Flores, Julio, **3:***730*
"*Flores Negras*" (Flórez), **2:**392
Flores Solano, María Isabel, **2:**574
Flórez, Johnny, **3:**763
Flórez, Julio, **2:**392, 394
Florida
  acquired from Spain, **3:**9
  British Caribbean community, **3:**808
  Chinese people in, **3:**957
  Latino peoples in, **3:**719
  Masaryktown, **3:**900
  Miami
    Central American communities in, **3:**727
    Cuban people in, **3:**719
    disco in, **3:**228
    Estonian people in, **3:**878
    Haitian people, **3:**803
    Latin Caribbean community, **3:**790–800
    rap in, **3:**701–2, 714
    Santería in, **3:**784
    zarzuela companies, **3:**851
  Missionary Baptist Church in, **3:***126*
  Native American groups in, **3:**466
  St. Augustine, **3:**7, 847
  Spanish settlement in, **3:**521, 847
  Tampa, *zarzuela* companies, **3:**851
Florida International University (Miami), **3:**222
Florida, Nancy, **3:**1014
Florida State University (Tallahassee), **3:**952, 953; **10:**98–99
Florinda (Ponce de León), **2:**397
Floris, Peter, **4:**427
Florita, Keit, **9:**362
Florita, Paul, **9:**362
Flor y Canto (hymnal), **3:**759
"Flowers of Edinburgh," **3:**409, 839
Floyd, Carlisle, **3:**546
Floyd, Eddie, **3:**676
Floyd, Samuel A., Jr., **3:**581, *581*; **10:**144
flutes. *See also* panpipes; *subcategories below*; whistles
  acharpan, **8:**852–53
  adernaj, **7:**460
  ajabeba, **8:**594
  ajewwaq, **6:**276
  alghoza, **5:**7, 783
  alghozah, **5:**286

algojā, **5:**345
alma pinkillu, **2:**291
'ama (also *xul*; *zu*; *zubac*), **2:**654, 721, 722, 723, 726, 728–29, 730–31
Andean regions, **2:**215–16
Arab world, **6:**413–14
Argentina, **2:**249, 250, 251
Armenia, **6:**728
asiina, **9:**582–83
association with Krishna, **5:**247, 325, 339, 350, 354
atenteben, **1:**211, 465
Aztec culture, **2:**555
bal, **1:**563, 565–66, 568
Balkan region, **8:**867
Baluan, **9:**602
banci, **4:**836
bangdi, **7:**184
bangsi, **4:**605
bangsing, **4:**701
bānsarī, **5:**783
baṅsī, **5:**497
bāṅsurī, **5:**205, 339–40, *340*, 350
  Gujarat, **5:**633
  Madhya Pradesh, **5:***724*
  Nepal, **5:**705
  North America, **3:**984; **5:**582
  repertoire for, **5:**188, 194–95
  Trinidad, **5:**591
  use in film music, **5:**535, *536*
  Uttar Pradesh, **5:**670
bara, **2:**662, 750, 751
Barbados, **2:**815
  vine, **2:**815–16
beichulu, **7:**491
beitulu, **7:**491
Bellona, **9:**851
beluwat, **4:**607
belwêr, **6:**745–46
bengsi, **4:**619
bensi, **4:**605
bilbil, **8:**996
biliq, **7:**510
bilûlê asin, **6:**746
bi noi (also *pi noi*), **7:**496, 499
bisun, **7:**491
blûr, **6:**745–46
bobi, **4:**797
Bolivia, **2:**140, 282, 284
boo, **1:**467
bɔlo, **1:**565, 568
bosabosa, **9:**655
botija jugs, **2:**834, 836
bra-tara, **2:**661, 739–40, 750–51
Brazil, **2:**305, 324
buhbut, **4:**587
bulûl, **6:**745–46
bzhami, **8:**855
cacho (deer-skull), **2:**533
calambo, **2:**708
camil, **8:**855
caña, **2:**227
Carib culture, **2:**23
caval, **8:**875, 878, 879
Central America, **2:**8–9
chi, **7:***824*, 828

flutes (*continued*)
chiba, **7:**111–12
chirula, **8:**545
chiska, **2:**471
chivoti, **1:**624
chŏk, **7:***824*, 828
chokela, **2:**209
chöör, **7:**1005, 1014
chor, **7:**1005
chorumbal, **1:**445
chŏttae, **7:**890, 961
chunggŭm, **7:**827
chuqila, **2:**286
ch'utu, **2:**286
classification of, **8:**178–79
Colombia, **2:**9–10, 151, 384
Costa Rica, **2:**680
Cuba, **2:**834, 835
cwène, **8:**527
Czech Republic, **8:**719
da druzu shpelāi, **5:**788
damuk, **4:**619
dangli, **7:**491
Denmark, **8:**454, 456, 457
dizi (also *di*), **7:***81*, *183*, 183–85
    in Buddhist rituals, **7:**312
    in Chinese orchestra, **7:**230
    construction of, **7:**183–84
    in Daoist rituals, **7:**323
    early, **7:**108
    in Hong Kong Cantopop, **7:**355
    in *Jiangnan sizhu* ensemble, **7:**224–25
    modernization of, **7:**183, 229
    North America, **3:**961, 962, 1260
    notation for, **7:**125
    Oceania, **9:**97
    in opera ensembles, **7:**276, 292
    performance of, **7:**123, 184, 236, 242
    repertoire, **7:**184–85
    in *sheng-guan* ensemble, **7:**201, 315, 331
    in *shifangu* ensemble, **7:**196
    Southeast Asia, **4:**236, 475
    status of, **7:**89
    in Uighur music, **7:**459
dolo, **2:**640
Dominica, **2:**842
Dominican Republic, **2:***853*, 859
dongxiao, **7:**185, 205, 206–7, 242, 491, 702
    (*See also* xiao)
dru nörá, **2:**686–87
dudka, **8:**770, *793*, *797*, 816
düdük, **6:**11, 763, 765, *765*
duduk, **8:**836, 892, 897, 950, 960, 975
dudurejš, **8:**950
duosaiboluo, **7:**491
dutra, **8:**863
East Africa, **1:**601–2
Ecuador, **2:**419
élèt, **4:**717
El Salvador, **2:**707
encio, **4:**836
endere, **1:**218
England, **8:**330–31
ensuling, **4:**835
etka talacabe, **2:**633

Europe
    bark, **8:**168, 423
    dissemination of, **8:**170
    duct, **8:***1*, 143, 169
    shepherds', **8:**8, 142
    willow, **8:**41
falawatu (also *falawita*), **2:**211
feko, **4:**794
fhāl, **6:**413
fife
    Antigua, **2:**799
    Europe, **8:**385, 528, *529*, *530*, 654
    Guyana, **2:**446
    Jamaica, **2:**899, 906, 907
    Montserrat, **2:**924, 925, *926*
    North America, **3:**240, 563, 835, 836, 1190
    Virgin Islands, **2:**973
fifra, **8:**640
filinji, **9:**661
filutu, **4:**813
Finland, **8:**478, 481
fischju, **8:**571–72
flauta, **2:**286, 379–80, 471
flawta, **2:**286
Flores, **4:**793
floyera, **8:**1015, 1018
fluier, **8:**872, 875, 878, 879, 897
foi doa, **4:**793
foi dogo, **4:**793
foi mere (also *foi pai*), **4:**793
France, **8:**545
French Guiana, **2:**435
frula, **8:**897, 928, 931–32, 944, 947
fujara, **8:**171, 719, *719*
fujarka and *fulyrka*, **8:**704
fyell, **8:**992, 993, 996, 1000
fyelldrejti, **8:**996
gagaku syakuhati, **7:**701
gaita, **2:**329, 337, 402, 406
galabigbili, **2:**641
galoubet, **8:**545
gammu suid, **2:**641, 644
gargy tüydük, **6:**975
Garifuna culture, **2:**674
gasba, **1:**542
gaṣba, **6:**413–14, 466
Germany, **8:**651, 653, 654
gling-bu, **5:**710, 715
gorgigala, **2:**640
Guatemala, **2:**8
Guyana, **2:**443
hago, **9:**402
h'chul, **2:**657
hekido, **4:**802
hekunukabe, **2:**189, 192
hengdi, **7:**80, 218
hio, **9:**952
hito (also *wíchu*; *fhidyu*), **2:**178
hitoyogiri, **7:**701, 715
Honduras, **2:**743
hue, **7:**588, 601, 684, 792
huke syakuhati, **7:**702
Hungary, **8:**743
hurisia, **9:**503
Igofnemis kunu bogonim, **9:**559
insi, **4:**904

irasu, **2:**286
Ireland, **8:**152, 383, 384–85, 390, 391
Irian Jaya, **9:**580, 582–83
Italy, **8:**616, 618
jednojke, **8:**966
juak, **6:**489
jueli, **7:**491
jugs, **3:**631, 638
julü, **4:**543
juwwāk, **6:**407, 413
juwwāq, **6:**454
kagura bue, **7:**607–8, 620
kapika (also *taleli*), **4:**791
karakukua, **2:**682
katoŋuŋu, **9:**629
kau, **9:**615
kaval
    Bulgaria, **8:***164*, *176*, 282, 892, *893*, 895–96, 902
    Macedonia, **8:**975, 981, *982*, 983
    North America, **3:**926, 1198
    in Turkish art music, **6:**799
    in Turkish folk music, **6:**11, 81, *762*, 763, 765, 774
kavall, Albania, **8:**992, 996–97, 1000
kawadi dejë, **2:**178
kawala, **6:**170, *170*, 171
kesuling, **4:**835
khi, **9:**627
khloy, **4:**172, 183, 196, 197, 213, 236
    North America, **3:***999*, 1001
khlui, **4:**235–36, 256, 257, 271, 272, 312
khlui kruat, **4:**236
khlui lip, **4:**236, 264
khlui phiang aw, **4:**236, *244*, *246*, 261, 262, 264
khlui u, **4:**236, 264
Khoikhoi people, **1:**703
khui, **4:**338, 345, 350, 355, 358
khui lip, **4:**358
kiví, **2:**685
koa pela ming, **9:**521
kōauau, **9:**393, 932–33, 934
komabue, **7:**620, 621, 622, 627
kome, **1:**564
koncovka, **8:**719
Kru migrant music for, **1:**379–80
Kru people, **1:**376
kuakumba, **9:**523–24
kuísi, **2:**184–85, 186
kulal, **5:**107, 234, 350, 352, 354, 361–62
    caste and, **5:**389
    in *cinna mēḷam* ensemble, **5:**104, 360, 913
kuleru, **9:**661
kululu, **9:**536
kura, **7:**1014
kurai, **8:**773, 774
kuripeawa, **2:**157, 159–60
kwataratara, **9:**708
lantoy, **4:**924
lapulil, **9:**619
lawatu, **2:**286, 297
leizi bili, **7:***510*
Lenca culture, **2:**739
lichiwayo (also *lichiguayo*), **2:**209, 286, *287*, 289, 357–58, 362

liku, **2:**286
liling, **7:**482
limbe, **7:**1005, 1007, *1013*
limbi, **6:**987
Lithuania, **8:**511
Low Countries, **8:**530
lué, **2:**165
lué kôriró, **2:**165
luma, **1:**658
Madhya Pradesh, **5:**722
madrûf, **6:**93, 102, 657
malka kuñin (also *malaka kuñini, malaka kuñkana*), **2:**750
mangangan ra'anga, **2:**160
mataco, **2:**152
Maya culture, **2:**667
Mexico, **2:**8, 15
Micronesia, **9:**717
Middle Eastern, **6:**18
   in Sufi devotions, **6:**19
mimby, **2:**452, 455, 459
mimby kué, **2:**201
mimby pukú, **2:**201
minjayra, **6:**545
mitote, **2:**570, 573
Mixtec culture, reed, **2:**564, 565
Moche culture, **2:**207
muhusemoi, **2:**189, 192
mukululu, **2:**286
mulagala, **2:**640
mullu, **2:**286
musiñu (also *mohoceño*), **2:**286, *287*, 295
nabad, **4:**567
nabat, **4:**835
naḍ, **5:**775, 783
nai, **1:**427
nãʾī, **5:**305, 306
nal, **5:**775, 781
napiloli, **9:**614
nāṛ, **5:**345
Native American types, **3:**477, 489, 498
nausuneusun, **2:**682–83
nawa-wakal, **2:**750
nay
   Afghanistan, **5:**828, 830, 831
   Azerbaijan, **6:**925
   Palestine, **6:**591
   Uighur people, **6:**999, 1003
   Uzbekistan, **6:**919
nāy, **6:**8, 395, 398, 406, 413
   in Andalusian music, **6:**445, 454
   in Arab-American ensembles, **6:**282, 283
   Egypt, **6:**8, 155, 317, 547, 551, 559, 626
   Iraq, **6:**8, 312, 411
   North America, **3:**1034, 1218, 1220
   in Sephardi music, **6:**204
   Syria, **6:**566
   in Tunisian *ma'lûf,* **6:**327, 328, 329, 330, 407
New Caledonia, **9:**401–2, 679–80
   oblique, **9:**679
New Guinea, **9:**476
ney
   Afghanistan, **5:**804, 822
   in Iranian ensembles, **6:**138, 828, 833, 863, 866, 867

   in Mevlevî Sufi rituals, **6:**108, 138, 186, 413, 543, 769, *769*
   in Turkish arabesk, **6:**257
   in Turkish art music, **6:**114, 774, *774*, 798, 799
ney chāpuni, **5:**822
ngal, **9:**730
nhimia miti, **2:**160
nhimia mytare, **2:**160
Nicaragua, end-blown duct, **2:**748
nipjiiht, **2:**570–71
nôkan (also *fue*)
   in festival ensembles, **7:**684
   in *kabuki,* **7:**657
   in *kyôgen,* **7:**636, 683
   in *nô,* **7:**557–58, 624, 634–35, 683
   notation for, **7:**54, 55
North America
   in contra dance bands, **3:**231
   in dance music, **3:**835
   in Finnish music, **3:**874
   in Irish music, **3:**842
   in polka bands, **3:**893
   in quadrille band, **3:**232
   in salsa, **3:**788
North Caucasia, **8:**851
Northeast Indian types, **3:**463
northern Pakistan, **5:**794, 795, 796
Norway, wooden, **8:**420
Nyungwe people, **1:**711
Oceania, **9:**392–93, 601, 624
ôkurauro, **7:**702, 779
olimong, **4:**919
Ontario, **3:**1189
Otomí culture, **2:**571
pahu, **9:**848
pajupill (also *vilepill*), **8:**494
Palau, **9:**723
paldong, **4:**919
palendag, **4:**904, 924, *925,* 926
palwei, **4:**371, 377
Panama, ceramic, **2:**773
Papua New Guinea, **9:**188, 189, 245–46, 252, 258, 477, 489, 511–12, 531, 532, 546–47, 555, 556, 558, 563, 565
   cane pipes, **9:**533
   end-blown, **9:**477, 498, 508, 532–33, 546
pāwā, **5:**345
pennig'n yog'n, **4:**567
pennywhistle (also tin whistle)
   Africa, **1:**296, 376, 379, 430, 719, 773; **10:***119*
   Barbados, **2:**816
   Europe, **8:**330, 354, 383, 384–85, 391, 527
   North America, **3:**231, 326, 842, 1125
   Oceania, **9:**79, 413
pənsɔɔl, **4:**567
Peru, **2:**11, 476, 478
phalahuita, **2:**471
Philippines, **4:**925–26, 927–28
piccolo, **2:**906; **3:**563, 893; **8:**528, 654
pífano, **2:**210, 284, 286, 287, 325, 329, *331,* 415
pii, **4:**547
pīlipè, **9:**539
pincullo (also *pincullu; pingollo; pingullo;*

pinkillo; pinkillu; pinkullo; pinkullu; pinquillo), **2:**34, 35, 250
Bolivia, **2:**286, 289–90, 291, 293, 294
Ecuador, **2:**415, 421
Peru, **2:**468, 470–71, 475, 477, 478
Quechua and Aymara cultures, **2:**209, 210, 212, 215–19, 221, 223, 358, 361
pinculu, **2:**226–27, 228–30
pinkui, **2:**416
pinkullwe, **2:**358
pipe, three-holed, **8:**330
pipimemyra, **2:**159
pira ra'anga, **2:**160
pirula, **8:**571–72, 573
pisheh, **6:**395, 398
pito (also *pitu*)
   end-blown, **2:**212, 216, 475, 656, 742, 758, 759–61; **3:**759, 761
   transverse, **2:**211, 227, 364, 470, 471, 777, 781, *782*
pivana, **8:**572
pizhatka, **8:**770
Plains courting, **3:**441, 445, 455, 467, 478, 479
Polynesia, **9:**865
porutu, **9:**393
pōrutu, **9:**935
postranica, **8:**915
pulao, **4:**904
pulipuli, **2:**209
pumingi, **9:**526
puput, **4:**615
Purépecha culture, **2:**575
pūtōrino, **9:**393, 933, 934–35
qaṣaba, **1:**542; **6:**93
qawwāla, **6:**413–14
qina, **2:**286
qina-qina, **2:**286, 290
qudi, **7:**184
quena (also *kena*), **2:**35, *76*
   Argentina, **2:**253, 259
   Bolivia, **2:**286, 297, 298, 357–58
   Ecuador, **2:**416
   in *nueva canción* ensemble, **2:**90, 373–74
   Peru, **2:**467, 469, 470, 475, 478, 486
   Quechua and Aymara culture, **2:**209, 212, 221
quena (*kena*)
   in North America, **3:**730
   transverse, **2:**471
quenaquena, **2:**468
quri pinkillu, **2:**287, *288*
raj pus li, **4:**553
raj pus lim (also *chapuli*), **3:**1005
rayán, **2:**471
recorder
   Europe, **8:**168, 420, 426, 654, 656, 696
   Israel, **6:**1072
   Lebanon, **6:**554
   South America, **2:**283
rehu, **9:**393
rollano, **2:**286
Romania, **8:**870, 872
roncador, **2:**471
ruŋ, **9:**606

flutes (*continued*)
  ryûteki
    Chinese origin of, 7:81
    in *gagaku*, 7:620, 621, 622, 624–27
    notation for, 7:626
    syôga vocables for, 7:626
  sababa, 1:787–88
  sadam, 4:627
  Sagais kunu bogonim, 9:559
  salāmīyya, 6:413, 545
  salamuri, 8:833, 839, 841, 845
  salet, 4:567
  saluang, 4:610–11
  Santal people, 5:502
  sáo, 3:994, *994*; 4:472, 475, 490
  sarewa, 1:449, 591
  saripalka, 2:286, *287*
  satāra, 5:345, 641
  savarngil, 4:819, *820*
  Schwegel, 8:654
  schwegepfyfli, 8:687
  schwyzerpfyf, 8:687
  schyumbin, 9:22–23
  Scotland, 8:367
  seljefløyte, 8:416, 420
  sempelong, 4:614–15
  serdam, 4:619, 622, 623
  serndu, 1:445
  seruling, 4:424–25, 625, 835
  shabbāba, 6:407, 413, 545
  shbēb, 6:413
  shibāba, 6:636, *636*
  shöör, 7:1005
  shoor, 6:981, 987
  shpelāi, 5:788
  shubbābih, 6:582
  sibizgi, 8:857
  sibusié, 7:460
  siʔɔɔy, 4:567
  silbadora, 2:471
  silbote, 8:314
  simaku, 4:797
  simpelong, 4:611
  şimşal, 6:746
  sinobue, 7:684
  Slovakia, 8:719
  sobre requinto, 2:286, 295
  sogŭm, 7:827
  Solomon Islands, 9:667
  Songus kunu bogonim, 9:559
  so'o kangwera, 2:159
  sopel, 8:770
  sopilka, 8:816, 818
  Sotho peoples, 1:707
  South America, 2:29–30
    bamboo, 2:877
    distribution of, 2:34
    end-blown notched, 2:30
    pre-Columbian, 2:33; 10:103
    tropical-forest region, 2:127
    tubular, 2:33; 10:100
  South Asia, 3:1246; 5:*304*, 323
    in *bharata natyam* ensemble, 5:522
    in devotional music, 5:253, 557
    early treatises on, 5:21, 25, 29
    in film music, 5:347

  in *kathak* ensemble, 5:494
  in *oḍissi* ensemble, 5:520
Southeast Asia, 4:596
  European, 4:432, 435
  in gong-chime ensembles, 4:20–21
southeastern Africa, 1:708
Southeast Indian groups, 3:468
Southwest Indian groups, 3:434, 473
Spain, 8:593
spelpipa, 8:439
stabule, 8:503
stranščice, 8:915
suara, 2:640–41
suffarā, 6:413, 545, 633
sukwadi, 9:669
suling
  Bali, 4:743, 745, 746, 748–50, 751, 754,
    756–57
  Borneo, 4:835–36
  Cirebon, 4:692, 696, 697
  Java, 4:642, 645, 665, 672
  Lombok, 4:767–68, 771, 772, 773, *774*,
    775–76
  Maluku, 4:817, *818*
  In North America, 3:1012
  Philippines, 4:904, 924, 926
  Sulawesi, 4:806
  Sumatra, 4:625, 628
  Sumbawa, 4:780
  Sunda, 4:703, 714–15, 717
suling bambu, 4:819
suling degung, 4:707
suling lembang, 4:807, 809
suling loang telu, 4:768
suling miring, 4:692
suling pewayangan (also *selisir*), 4:768, 774
sulupgala, 2:640
supe, 2:640–41
šupelka, 8:975, *975*
sur, 2:657
surnāy, 6:395, 397, 705
suupi, 9:563
svirala, 8:928, 944, 950
svirka, 8:892
Swazi people, 1:707
Sweden, 8:439, 442
Switzerland, 8:141, 682, 687, 696
  wooden, 8:682
syakuhati (*shakuhachi*), 7:533, 536, *695*, 701,
    707, 827; 10:27–28, *99*, *101*, 102–3
  Chinese origin of, 7:81, 186
  construction of, 7:547, 701
  in folk song accompaniment, 7:705
  gaikyoku repertoire for, 7:704
  honkyoku repertoire for, 7:702–3, 705;
    10:102
  Huke sect music, 7:548–49, 617, 618, 702,
    703, 755–56, 758–59, 777
  international popularity of, 7:707–9
  Kinko-*ryû*, 7:579, 703, 704, 708, 717, 759;
    10:99, 102
  Kinpou-*ryû*, 7:708
  in *kumiuta*, 7:696
  modernization of, 7:537, 702, 704–5, 779
  in North America, 3:340, 346, 527, 968,
    970, 972, 973, 1084, 1217

  notation for, 7:54, 576–80
  Oceania, 9:97
  performance schools of, 7:46
  in *sankyoku*, 7:688, 692, 702, 705, 712,
    715–17, 779
  South America, 2:88
  Tikuho-*ryû*, 7:703
  timbre of, 7:554
  Tozan-*ryû*, 7:579–80, 703, 704, 716–17,
    720, 760, 777–78
  types of, 7:701–2
  Ueda-*ryû*, 7:703
  use in film music, 7:709
  in *ziuta*, 7:704
sybysghy, 6:956
sybyzgy, 7:1005
syôsôin syakuhati, 7:701
tabor pipe, 8:528
taegŭm, 7:824, 827, 989
  contemporary music for, 7:958–59, 960,
    971
  in court and *chŏngak* music, 7:822, 866–67
  in folk song accompaniment, 7:880
  in *kagok*, 7:921
  in *kasa*, 7:927
  sanjo repertoire, 7:822, 913–17, 957
  in *sijo*, 7:925
  in *sinawi*, 7:890
  in *t'alch'um*, 7:942
  vocal imitation of, 7:817
Taino culture, 2:22, 846, 932
Tairona culture, 2:183
Taiwanese Aboriginal peoples, 7:529
take bue, 3:972; 7:657
talacabe, 2:632–33
talawat, 1:541
tal'wwatt, 6:489
tambing, 1:445
Tamil Nadu, 5:924, 926
tampaleo, 3:438
tampoi, 4:619
tangjök, 7:867
tanso, 7:702, *824*, 827, 888, 970, 991
  in court and *chŏngak* music, 7:866
  in *kagok*, 7:921
  modifications to, 7:961
  sanjo repertoire, 7:915
Tanzania, 1:642
Tarahumara culture, 2:583
tarka
  Bolivia, 2:*288*, 289, 295
  Peru, 2:470, 471, 475
  Quechua and Aymara culture, 2:210, 212,
    216, 217, 219, 358
tarutaru ra'anga, 2:160
taẓammart, 1:542, 591–92
temïmbi-púku, 2:253
temimby ie piasá, 2:201
temja, 1:543
tenpuku, 7:701–2
Tibet, 7:475, 477
tiêu, 4:475, 490
tipanu, 4:843
tishbibt, 6:624
tlapitzalli, 2:601–2
tongali, 4:919

Torres Strait Islands, **9:**412, 428
tot, **4:**547
trà pua, **4:**536
trà pùn tử, **4:**536
tsuur, **7:**1005, *1013*, 1013–14
tula, **5:**828, 831
tulal, **9:**640
t'ungso, **7:***824*, 827, 890, 915
tura, **2:**533
turu, **9:**178
tütek, **6:**925
txirula, **8:**314, *314*, 316
txistu, **3:**731, 849; **8:**171, 314, 316, 600
tzijolah, **2:**654
tzijolaj, **2:**728
uasgala, **2:**640
'uffāta, **6:**413
ugege, **9:**178
uhuwep, **9:**570
Ukraine, **8:**811
una, **2:**750, 751
uo uoq (barley-stalk pipe), **7:**511
Uruguay, **2:**519
vaṃśa, **5:**326
vamzdis, **8:**511
vanjli, **5:**771
vaṅsī, **5:**345
Vanuatu, **9:**693, 697
vasdaṇda, **5:**350
Venda people, **1:**708–9
Venezuela, **2:**533
  end-blown, **2:**178
vēṇu, **5:**234, 350, 354
vijivijuku, **9:**655
vivo, **9:**906
wabi kain, **9:**554
wapi, **9:**546–47
weil enjiu, **7:**491
wenbeng, **7:**491
West Africa, **1:**445
whio, **9:**393
wua, **1:**455
xiao, **7:**111–12, *185*, 185–86, *186*, *413*, 827
  in Cantonese music, **7:**218
  in *Jiangnan sizhu* ensemble, **7:**224–25
  notation for, **7:**125
  in *shifangu* ensemble, **7:**196
xiongling, **7:**477, 481
xitiringo, **1:**711
xul (*See under* 'ama)
yak, **7:***824*, 828
Yaqui culture, **2:**589, 590
yarã'a, **6:**395, 397
yuruparí, **2:**153
zaowzaya, **1:**542
zhudi, **7:**462, 491
zigu, **4:**608
zi nasi syakuhati, **7:**705
zi nuri syakuhati, **7:**705
zongdi, **7:**529
Zulu people, **1:**707
zu; zubac (*See under* 'ama)
žvegla, **8:**915–16, *916*
flutes, aeolian, **9:**393
  Solomon Islands, **9:**664
  Vanuatu, **9:**693

flutes, bone, **2:***120*; **7:**79, 137; **8:**527
  Basque region, **8:**316
  Bolivia, **2:**12, 139–40
  Caribbean, **2:**8
  Carib culture, **2:**23
  Colombia, **2:**155
  current use of, **8:**41
  Finland, **8:**481
  Georgia, **8:**842
  Guaraní culture, **2:**199
  gudi, **7:**105
  Moxo culture, **2:**140
  Norway, **8:**420, 423
  Peru, **2:**10
  prehistoric, **8:**36, 37, 38, 39
  Sumu culture, **2:**750
  Switzerland, **8:**682
  Tupinambá culture, **2:**301
  Venezuela, **2:**170
  Warao culture, **2:**189, 192
  Yekuana culture, **2:**178
flutes, multiple-tubed, **8:**9
  biculë (also *cylëdyjare*), **8:**993
  binjak, **8:**996
  Croatia, **8:**926
  donal (also *giraw*; *alghoza*), **5:**783, *784*
  donelī, **6:**10, 881, 883, 887, 890
  dūnāy, **6:**395
  dviina fleita, **8:**816
  dvojanka, **8:**975
  dvojnice (also *dvojice*), **8:**928, 944, 960, 966
  El Salvador, **2:**707
  Europe, early, **8:**39
  Italy, **8:**616
  joṛi, **5:***763*, 770, 771
  Mexico, **2:**14, 15, 33
  Papua New Guinea, **9:**533
  pelqesë, **8:**996
  piszczałka, **8:**704
  Slovenia, **8:**912
  Vanuatu, **9:**693
flutes, nose-blown, **9:**393
  aangún (also *nikaangún*), **9:**736
  bidi, **7:**491, 529
  fagufagu, **9:**807, 816
  fangufangu, **9:***372–73*, *794–95*, *796*, *956*
  Fiji, **9:**769, 776
  kalaleng, **4:**914
  kofe, **9:**817
  kuripeawa, **2:**157, 159–60
  Marquesas Islands, **9:**36, 48
  Native American types, **3:**477
  New Caledonia, **9:**680
  nguru, **9:**393, 932, 935
  'ohe hano-ihu, **9:**916
  Papua New Guinea, **9:**606
  Peru, **2:**492
  poghi, **4:**791
  Polynesia, **9:**771
  pū ko'e, **9:**886
  Rotuma, **9:**819
  sangui, **4:**836
  selengut, **4:**836
  selingut, **4:**836
  South America, tropical-forest region, **2:**127
  tulali, **4:**806

  turali, **4:**836
  vivo, **9:**869, 895, 901, 902
flutes, piston, **9:**392
  El Salvador, **2:**707
  New Caledonia, **9:**679
  Papua New Guinea, **9:**477, 547, 563, 623
flutes, vessel
  akaryna, **8:**796–97, *797*
  Argentina, **2:**249–50
  Aztec culture, **2:**555
  Bolivia, **2:**11, 282
  Caribbean, **2:**8
  Central America, **2:**8–9
  China, **7:**88
  Colombia, **2:**9, 10; **10:**100
  Costa Rica, **2:**680
  dede, **2:**640
  deling, **7:**477
  Denmark, **8:**456
  dru mugata, **2:**686–87
  Ecuador, **2:**10, 413–14
  El Salvador, **2:**707
  feku, **4:**797
  hun, **7:**823, *824*, 828
  Indus Valley civilization, **5:**319
  ipu hōkiokio, **9:**393, *956*
  Japan, **7:**559, *559*
  ken, **7:**560
  liban, **2:**740
  lokarina, **8:**892
  Maleku culture, **2:**683
  Maya culture, **2:**651, 657, 667
  Mexico, **2:**8
  Moche culture, **10:***100*
  Native American types, **3:**477
  Nicaragua, **2:**748
  niwawu, **7:**462
  ocarina, **2:**932; **8:**511, 528, 616, 743
  Oceania, **9:**393
  okarina, **8:**816, 915, 917
  Panama, **2:**773
  Papua New Guinea, **9:**477, 533, 549–50, 551–52, 609
  Paraguay, **2:**455
  Peru, **2:**11, 470
  prehistoric, **8:**39
  South America, **2:**29, 33
    tropical-forest region, **2:**127
  Tairona culture, **2:**183
  taleot, **4:**701
  xun, **7:**105, 107, 109, 560
flutes, water, **9:**392, 477
Fluxus group, **3:**176
"Fly" (Checker), **3:**709
"Fly Girl" (Boogie Boys), **3:**696
"Fly Guy" (Peblee Poo), **3:**696
Flying Burrito Brothers (musical group), **3:**318
"Flying Home," **3:**669
Fo, Dario, **9:***81*
Fõ people, **1:**316
Fo'aanamae (Kwaio musician), **9:***964*
Foanaota, Lawrence, **9:**963
Fock, Niels, **2:**442
Foe people, **9:**511
  ceremonial spaces, **9:**512
  Christianity of, **9:**537, 539

Fogg Art Museum (Cambridge, Mass.), 5:529
Fogolar Furlan, 9:80
Foi people, 9:246–47, 339–40
Fokine, Michel, 8:161
Foley, Kathy, 3:1020
Foley, Kenan, 2:679
Foley, M. Kathleen, 4:701
Foley, Red, 3:77, 79
Folk and Traditional Music of Western Continents
        (Nettl), 3:828
Folklife Center News, 3:496
Folklore (periodical), 2:263
Folklore Archives of the Academy of Athens,
        8:1025
Folklore Institute (Ljubljana), 8:922
Folklore Institute of Scotland, 8:371
Folk Music and Modern Sound (Ferris and Hart),
        3:828
Folk Music Center (Latvia), 8:507
Folk Music Institute (Finland), 8:480, 486, 489
Folk Music Institute of Swedes in Finland, 8:489
Folk Music Journal, 8:339
Folk Music of the United States (recording
        project), 3:294
folk music revival, 3:13–14, 94, 149, 326, 520,
        730, 970; 8:228, 294, 296–97, 325,
        446
    autoharp in, 3:240
    bluegrass and, 3:162
    blues and, 3:582
    in Brittany, 8:563–64
    in Canada, 3:1081
    in Corsica, 8:569, 573
    in Denmark, 8:461–62
    in England, 8:332, 334–35, 338, 339
    in Finland, 8:480
    in France, 8:543–44, 546, 547–48, 549, 551,
        554
    in Germany, 8:656
    in Hungary, 8:739, 744
    in Ireland, 8:387, 390–92
    in Italy, 8:613–14, 615, 622
    in Latvia, 8:505–6
    in Lithuania, 8:509, 511, 512
    in Low Countries, 8:535–36
    in Malta, 8:641–42
    in Poland, 8:711
    politics and, 3:316, 551
    in Portugal, 8:584
    in Russia, 8:774–79
    in Scotland, 8:364–65, 366, 370–72, 374
    social class and, 3:45, 48–49
    sound recordings and, 3:243
    in Sweden, 8:437, 442
    in Switzerland, 8:695, 696
    in Wales, 8:353–55
Folk Music Society of Ireland, 8:394
Folk Research Centre (St. Lucia), 2:942
Folk Song in England (Lloyd), 8:338–39
Folk Song in Israel (Smoira-Roll), 6:1062
Folk-Song Society (Great Britain), 8:19, 326,
        337, 338
Folk Songs of Barbados (collection), 2:817
Folk Songs of Britain (recording series), 8:338
Folk Songs of French Canada (Barbeau and Sapir),
        3:1165

Folk-Songs of the Upper Thames (Williams), 8:329
Folk Song Weekly (periodical), 7:140
Folkways Records, 1:54; 2:593, 862; 3:300, 953,
        1125; 9:978, 985, 987, 997; 10:59.
        See also Smithsonian Folkways
"Follow the Drinking Gourd" (spiritual), 3:8,
        601
"Folsom Prison Blues" (Cash), 3:552
Fomin, Evstigney, 8:780
Fon culture, 2:341, 504, 668, 826
Fon people, 1:37, 461, 462
Fong Naam, 4:125–26, 128, 286
Fonoimoana, Blossom, 9:972
Fonseca, Julio, 2:704
Fonseca, Maria Amélia, 8:577
Fontana, Bernard, 2:587
Fontane Sisters, 3:352
Fonton, Charles, 6:120, 124
Fontonfrom Drum Ensemble, 3:1213
Fo'oa, Vili, 9:125
Fool's Mystery Play (Fo), 9:81
Foote, Arthur, 3:538
*Footnote to History: Eight Years of Trouble in
        Samoa*, (Stevenson), 9:40–41
Forbidden City (San Francisco club), 3:964
Forbidden Planet (film), 3:253
Force MDs (musical group), 3:713, 714
Ford, Clifford, 3:144, 1108
Ford Foundation, 3:281, 298, 495–96
Ford, Henry, 3:233
Ford, Lita, 3:358
Ford, Robert, 8:373
Forde, Anthony, 1:377
Forde, William, 8:393
Fore people, 9:511, 512, 526–33
Forehand, Blind Mamie, 3:631
Forestier, Louise, 3:1158
Forestiers et voyageurs (Taché), 3:1165
Forge, Anthony, 9:977
"Forgive and Forget" (Orioles), 3:671
"For God's Sake Give More Power to the People"
        (Chi-Lites), 3:677
"Forgotten Yesterday" (Donovan), 3:1063
Forkel, Johann, 6:22
form and structure
    Afghanistan
        falak, 5:828
        Kabuli *ghazal*, 5:805
        naghma-ye kashāl, 5:806
        Pashtun songs, 5:835
    Africa, 1:224
        cyclic, 1:701
        hymn refrains, 1:208–9
        hymns, 1:208–9
        phrasal variation, 1:465
        praise songs, 1:494–503
    analysis of, 9:300–309
    Andean music, 2:216
    Anglo-American ballads, 3:833
    antiphony (*See under* call-and-response)
    Anuta, choral songs, 9:306–7
    Apache songs, 3:431
    Arab music, 6:502
    Arctic songs, 3:378
    Armenia, *ashugh* songs, 6:735
    āstāī-antarā, 5:772, 806

Australia
    Aboriginal rock, 9:445
    Anglo-Irish music, 9:141
    Central, "other side," 9:433–35
    Central songs, 9:436, 438–39
    clansongs, 9:421–22
    country music, 9:142
    danced songs, 9:426–27
    history songs, 9:428
    popular music, 9:144
    Southeastern Aboriginal songs, 9:441
Azerbaijan
    folk songs, 6:931
    muğam-dəstgah, 6:927–29
Bahamas
    anthem, 2:804
    rhyming spiritual, 2:805
    ring-play, 2:811
Bali
    bapang, 4:735
    batel, 4:735
    gegaboran, 4:735
    gilak, 4:735, 746
    tabuh pat, 4:735
ballade, 8:72, 132
ballads, 8:135
Basque region
    songs, 8:311, 312
    zortziko, 8:121
Belize
    brukdown, 2:678
    creole music, 2:677
Bellona, vocal music, 9:850
bluegrass, 3:163
blues, 3:524, 638, 639, 642–43, 668
Bolivia, Moxo *machetero*, 2:140
Brazil
    Afro-Brazilian genres, 2:307
    in Candomblé music, 2:342
    of *cantoria*, 2:326–28
    for *capoeira* songs, 2:346
    central and southern genres, 2:306
    frevo de rua, 2:336
    marches, 2:330
    marujada songs, 2:348
    in religious music, 2:328
    samba, 2:314–15
    samba campineiro, 2:349
    samba de roda, 2:349
    samba-lenço, 2:349
Bulgaria, strophic songs, 8:891
Burma, 4:19
California, Native American music, 3:416, 417
call-and-response, 1:10, 243; 2:47, 74, 814;
        3:67, 678 (*See also specific forms*)
    in African-American music, 3:523, 573,
        599, 626
    in African music, 3:593
    Aka people, 1:695
    Bamana people, 1:121
    in Bengal, 5:862
    in big band music, 3:654, 656
    China, 7:150–51
    Colo people, 1:569
    Dan people, 1:466
    East Africa, 1:605, 608

East African hymns, **1:**607
Fulɓe people, **1:**115
Gumuz people, **1:**564
in Guyana, **5:**600
in Holiness churches, **3:**215
in Hui music, **7:**462
Igbo people, **1:**459
Igede people, **1:**111
in Iranian music, **6:**833
in Kashmir, **5:**682, 684–85
Kenya, **1:**622–23
in Kerala, **5:**945, 949–50
in Kurdistan, **6:**749
Luvale people, **1:**726
Madagascar, **1:**783
Mende people, **1:**468
in Native American music, **3:**368–69, 463,
    467
in Naxi music, **7:**510
in praise singing, **1:**499
in rap, **3:**699
Ryûkyû Islands, **7:**791, 795
San people, **1:**705
Shona people, **1:**750, 755
southeastern Africa, **1:**708
in Syria, **6:**563
in Taiwanese Aboriginal music, **7:**525–27
in Yemen, **6:**655
Yoruba people, **1:**411, 412
Yoruba popular music, **1:**472–73
in *ziuta*, **7:**693, 716
Zulu people, **1:**706
Carriacou, big-drum songs, **2:**870
Central Asia
    Bukharan *shash maqām*, **6:**900, 911, *912*,
        916, 920
    maqām, **6:**900
children's music, **3:**285
Chile
    cueca, **2:**369
    romance, **2:**367
    verso, **2:**367
    for Virgin Mary festivities, **2:**363
China
    bianzou process, **7:**234–37, 238
    Cantonese music, **7:**219
    chain form, **7:**239
    Confucian music, **7:**337
    cyclic, **7:**238–39
    dizi music, **7:**185
    Han folk song, **7:**154–55
    kunqu, **7:**291–92
    minority operas, **7:**452
    multipart music, **7:**489–90
    nanxi, **7:**276
    northern ensemble music, **7:**202
    northwestern musics, **7:**456
    orchestral music, **7:**348
    Peking opera, **7:**282–84
    of *qin* music, **7:**161–63
    shifan luogu, **7:**192–93
    Sunan chuida, **7:**197
    Suzhou tanci, **7:**262–63
    taoqu, **7:**237–40
    xianshiyue, **7:**214
    yangqin music, **7:**180
    zaju, **7:**275

Choctaw Social Dance songs, **3:**469
Chuuk, love songs, **9:**736
Cirebon, *renggong*, **4:**694, *695*
Colombia
    African-derived traits, **2:**401
    arrullo, **2:**403
    bambuco, **2:**387
    danza, **2:**393
    guabina veleña, **2:**391
    pasillo, **2:**392–93
colotomic structure, **4:**9, 16, 20–21, 576, 597
    in Balinese music, **4:**733–35, 737, 741, 747,
        753
    in Batak music, **4:**608
    in Cirebonese gamelan music, **4:**694–95
    in Iban music, **4:**830
    in Javanese music, **4:**659–63, 667
    in Lombok music, **4:**762, 767, 770
    in Malukun music, **4:**814, 816
    in Sumatran music, **4:**618
    in Sundanese *gamelan* music, **4:**701–2, 703,
        706
    in Sundanese *kacapi-suling*, **4:**715
    in Sundanese *kendang penca*, **4:**709
Corsica
    animal-drivers' songs, **8:**567
    chiam'e rispondi, **8:**569
Costa Rica
    balimbo, **2:**689–90
    romance, **2:**695
    song-dances, **2:**698
Creek Stomp Dance songs, **3:**468–69
Cuba
    contradanza, **2:**832–33
    criolla, **2:**832
    danzón, **2:**833
    rumba, **2:**831
    son, **2:**830
Cyprus, songs, **8:**1030
Czech Republic, **8:**722
    Moravian songs, **8:**718
Denmark
    ballads, **8:**453
    dance tunes, **8:**454, *455*
dhrupad, **5:**83, 84–85, 164, 168–69,
    250, 851
Dolan *muqam*, **6:**991, 1000
Dong *galao*, **7:**489
East Asian music, **7:**5
Ecuador, *currulao*, **2:**427
Egypt, *layla*, **6:**149, 150–51
England
    dance music, **8:**329
    songs, **8:**327
    variations, **8:**331, 333
Estonia
    devotional songs, **8:**492
    vemmalvärss, **8:**492
Europe
    agricultural songs, **8:**4
    canons, puzzle, **8:**98
    carol, **8:**132
    enumerative songs, **8:**541
    fugue, **8:**61–62, 78–79
    instrumental dance music, **8:**8–9
    laude spirituale, **8:**132

nonstrophic songs, **8:**127–31
    variations, **8:**52
Fiji, *meke*, **9:**775
Finland
    laments and songs, **8:**475
    runo, **8:**476
formes fixes, **8:**72
Garifuna culture
    bérusu, **2:**675
    paranda, **2:**675
    punta, **2:**675
    punta-rock, **2:**677
    vocal music, **2:**672, 734
    wanaragua, **2:**674
gat, **5:**189–98
Georgia, **8:**830
    vocal music, **8:**833
Germany
    medieval music, **8:**651
    periodic, **8:**655
Goa, *mandó*, **5:**739
Great Basin Bear Dance songs, **3:**423–24
Great Britain, songs, **8:**325
Guarijio culture
    contradanza, **2:**553–54
    son principal, **2:**553–54
Gujarat
    bhajan, **5:**630
    garbo, **5:**626
    havelī saṅgīt, **5:**633
    māṇ bhaṭṭ ākhyān, **5:**634
Haiti
    konpa, **2:**893
    Vodou songs, **2:**884
Hawai'i
    hapa haole song, **9:**922
    hula ku'i, **9:**920
    mele hula, **9:**917
Hindustani music, theme and variations in,
    5:127–29
Honduras, mestizo dance-music, **2:**744
Hungary, strophic songs, **8:**741
imitative, **8:**75
Iran, in *radif*, **6:**135–36, 137, 854, 855,
    862–63, 866
Iraq, *maqām*, **6:**311, 312
Ireland, **8:**382
    lyric songs and ballads, **8:**379–80
    songs, **8:**325
    Traveller songs, **8:**294–95
    variation, **8:**382, 387
Irian Jaya
    Asmat songs, **9:**591
    Eipo *mot*, **9:**592
    Mairasi songs, **9:**587, 589
    responsorial, **9:**583, 585, 587
    Sentani music, **9:**585–86
Iroquois Social Dance songs, **3:**464
Italy, Neapolitan song, **8:**618
Jamaica, *mento*, **2:**906
Japan
    aesthetics and, **7:**552–55
    biwa music, **7:**554
    gidayû busi, **7:**676
    koto music, **7:**554
    nô chant, **7:**554

form and structure, Japan (*continued*)
  rhythmic cycles, **7**:572
  westernized works, **7**:778
Java
  gendhing, **4**:659–63
  gendhing lampah, **4**:661, 666
  ketawang, **4**:660, 662
  ladrang, **4**:660–61, 662
  lancaran, **4**:660–61, 666, 667
  lancaran mlaku (also *bubaran*), **4**:660–61
  srepegan, **4**:654; **10**:51
  variation technique in melodies, **4**:670–73;
    10:43, 51
  in jazz, **3**:653–54, 661–62
Jewish music
  ethnic differences, **8**:263
  religious, **8**:252
jor, **5**:82, 199
kāfī, **5**:772
Karnataka
  katha, **5**:873
  pada genres, **5**:868
Karnatak music, theme and variations in,
  5:217–18
Kashmir
  chakri, **5**:682
  nande baeth, **5**:684
Kazakh songs, **7**:460
Kazakhstan
  epic songs, **6**:953
  lyrical songs, **6**:955, 960
Kenyah people, of *lekupa*, **4**:826
Kerala
  film songs, **5**:950
  temple drum compositions, **5**:936–39
Khmer music, **4**:180–81
Kiribati, dance-songs, **9**:761
Korea
  chŏngak, **7**:868–69
  contemporary music, **7**:957
  of folk songs, **7**:881
  kagok, **7**:922
  samullori pieces, **7**:964, 966–67
  sanjo, **7**:844
Kuna culture, *gammu burui* music, **2**:642–43
Latvia, *daina*, **8**:500
Lombok
  gamelan music, **4**:769
  janggel, **4**:769
  rangsangan, **4**:769
Low Countries
  instrumental music, **8**:524
  songs, **8**:519–20
Macedonia
  songs, **8**:974
  Turkish music, **8**:983
Malaysia
  asli, **4**:433
  dondang sayong, **4**:433
  theater and dance genres, **4**:406, 413, 417
Mapuche music, **2**:362
march form, **3**:651
Marquesas Islands
  putu, **9**:893
  tape'a, **9**:894
Marshall Islands, **9**:753

Martinique, beguine, **2**:916, *917*
Maya culture
  chaconne, **2**:652
  sarabande, **2**:652
Mende songs, **1**:468
Métis fiddle music, **3**:405
Mexico
  canciones rancheras, **2**:621
  children's songs, **2**:617
  corrido, **2**:686–87
  cumulative stories, **2**:617
  sones, **2**:550
  son michoacano, **2**:611
Middle Eastern music, **6**:9–11
Mongol people
  long-songs, **7**:1006, 1007
  short-songs, **7**:1007
Morocco
  Berber antiphonal songs, **6**:483, 485
  malhun, **6**:499–500
  wedding laments, **6**:481
Native American vocal music, **3**:367–68
New Caledonia, dance-songs, **9**:675–77
Nicaragua, *mento*, **2**:753
nonclassical traditions, use of variation in,
  5:474
Northwest Coast songs, **3**:401
Norway, *slått* variations, **8**:416–17, 426
nūba, **6**:450–53, 456–58
Ojibwe songs, **3**:458
Ontario, French-Canadian songs, **3**:1193
O'odham songs, **3**:435
Otopame culture, *minuete*, **2**:573
Papua New Guinea
  Baluan vocal music, **9**:603–4
  Binandere *guru*, **9**:358–60
  Binandere *ji tari*, **9**:358–59
  Binandere *yovero*, **9**:358
  Buin songs, **9**:650, 651–52
  Enga songs, **9**:536
  guitar songs, **9**:388
  Gulf Province, **9**:495
  Halia songs, **9**:641–42
  Iatmul *sagi*, **9**:554
  Irumu songs, **9**:568
  Karkar people, **9**:561
  Kaulong songs, **9**:617
  Komba music, **9**:572
  Lolo songs, **9**:614
  Managalasi *itiuri*, **9**:503
  Managalasi songs, **9**:504–5
  rounds, **9**:558
  Siasi music, **9**:574–76
Peru
  dance-dramas, **2**:479, 483
  harawi, **2**:476
  huayno, **2**:477
  Indian *vs.* mestizo aesthetics, **2**:483
  landó, **2**:498
  marinera, **2**:481
  resbalosa, **2**:499
  tondero, **2**:499
  yaraví, **2**:477
Philippines
  dance forms, **4**:854
  kulintang music, **4**:895–96

lebad, **4**:898–99
melody formulas, **4**:844
tukimug, **4**:897
in upland genres, **4**:927
Plains Indian songs, **3**:445, 483–84
Poland, **8**:707–8
  folk songs, **8**:703
popular songs
  eighteenth century, **3**:181
  nineteenth century, **3**:189
  twentieth century, **3**:194–95, 549, 1048
Pueblo Indian songs, **3**:429
Puerto Rico, *seis*, **2**:939
Pukapuka
  chants, **9**:912
  ula pau, **9**:910
ragtime, **3**:548, 651
rap, **3**:699
Renaissance, **8**:75
Romania, songs, **8**:874
rondeau, **8**:132
rondo, **8**:52
Roti, *bini*, **4**:799
Russia
  byliny, **8**:764–65
  chastushki, **8**:768
  village songs, **8**:755–56
Ryûkyû music, **7**:791
Saami people, joiks, **8**:300–301, 487
St. Lucia, *koutoumba*, **2**:948–49
Sāmoa
  choral songs, **9**:797
  of hymns, **9**:205
  tagi, **9**:799–801
Scotland
  Gaelic songs, **8**:360–61
  piobaireachd, **8**:363–64, 367
  Traveller songs, **8**:296
  variations, **8**:367
Serbia, **8**:942
Shona people, *mbira* songs, **1**:749–50
Slovakia, **8**:722
Society Islands
  hīmene tārava, **9**:872
  hīmene tuki, **9**:872
Solomon Islands
  Buka and Bougainville songs, **9**:632
  guitar songs, **9**:157
  Savo music, **9**:666
son, **3**:793
sonata-allegro, **8**:82, *83*
sonata principle, **8**:52
soul, **3**:678
South America
  repetition in shamanic ceremonies, **2**:46
  tropical-forest genres, **2**:135
South Asia
  ālāp, **5**:39–40, 48, 69, 82, 84–85, 119,
    164–68, 172, 177, 195, 196, 198–99,
    337
  ālāp-jor-jhālā, **5**:15, 198–99, 203, 206, 581
  cakkardār, **5**:118–19, 121
  early concept of, **5**:27
  filmī gīt, **5**:532, 544
  havelī saṅgīt, **5**:250–51
  khyāl, **5**:83, 84–85, 195

kīrtana, **5:**216, 262, 265–66, 517
kriti, **5:**36, 219, 221, 230, 269
laggī, **5:**128
pallavi, **5:**141, 145, 219, 544
paran, **5:**117–19, *120*, 121, 130–31, 132, 159
prabandha, **5:**164
qawwali, **5:**752–53
relā, **5:**119, 129
sthāī-antarā, **5:**169, 172, 532, 533–34
ṭhumrī, **5:**180–81
tihāī, **5:**201
uttara, **5:**27, *28*
varṇam, **5:**216–17
Southeast Asia, **4:**14–15
in gong-chime ensemble music, **4:**21
ostinato, **4:**597
Southeast Indian songs, **3:**467
Spain
jota, **8:**594–95
poetic forms, **8:**591–92
Sri Lanka, *sindu*, **5:**966
stichic, **8:**129–31, 539
strophic, **8:**8, 131–37, 284, 540–41; **9:**301, 330–35
Subarctic songs, **3:**389
suites in Middle Eastern music, **6:**10–11, 551
Sumbawa, **4:**781
Surinam, *kaseko*, **2:**508–9
Suyá songs, **2:**148
Syria, *muwashshaḥ*, **6:**550
Takuu, *tuki*, **9:**839
Tamil Nadu
cintu, **5:**920
kummi, **5:**920
Tarahumara culture, *tutuguri*, **2:**585
Tausug people
kuriri, **4:**898
lubak-lubak, **4:**898
sinug, **4:**898
Temiar people, **4:**577–78
Thailand, **4:**17, 274–75
Tibetan culture
Buddhist chant, **7:**479
of *dui xie*, **7:**475
folk songs, **7:**473
of *guo xie*, **7:**476
gzhas, **5:**710–11
of *nangma*, **7:**475
opera, **7:**478
vocal music, **5:**709
Tikopia, songs, **9:**854
Tonga
lakalaka, **9:**789
māʻuluʻulu, **9:**790
treatises on, **5:**44
Tuareg people, *anzad* music, **1:**578–79
Tunisia, *nūbat*, **6:**333–35
Turkey
âyîn, **6:**111, 118
fasıl, **6:**111, 113–14, 119–20, 773
peşrev, **6:**126–27
taksim sections, **6:**256–57, 773
Tuvan music, **6:**982–83
Uighur *ikki muqam*, **6:**989–90, 998
Uighur *muqam*, **6:**995

Ukraine, *dumy*, **8:**814
United States
black gospel music, **3:**534–35
parlor music, **3:**183
polka, **3:**895
variations, **3:**190
Uruguay, *murga*, **2:**517–18
Uttar Pradesh
birahā, **5:**667
women's songs, **5:**661
ʻUvea, *kupu*, **9:**809
Uzbekistan, Khorezm *maqām*, **6:**911, 913, 917
vamp, **3:**661
Vanuatu
Banks Islands, **9:**700–701
dance-songs, **9:**695
nupu, **9:**704
Venezuela
Amerindian music, **2:**525
in folk music, **2:**525
fulia, **2:**534
joropo, **2:**540, 541
revuelta (also *pasaje*), **2:**540
Vietnam, **4:**452, 454
virelai, **8:**132
Virgin Islands, *cariso*, **2:**972
Wales
bardic recitation, **8:**349
songs, **8:**343, 344–47
Warao culture, shamanic songs, **2:**194–95
Yemen, *al-ghināʼ al-ṣanʻānī*, **6:**687–89
Yiddish songs, **3:**936
Yuma vocal music, **2:**596; **3:**434
Formosa Aboriginal Dance Troupe, **7:**428
Fornaro Marita-Díaz, Antonio, **2:**511, 522
Føroya Fróðskaparfelag, **8:**472
Føroya Symphony Orchestra, **8:**472
Forrest, Edwin, **3:**46
Forry, Marki, **8:**937
"For Sentimental Reasons" (Cole), **3:**708
Forster, Georg, **8:**17, 653; **9:**35
Forster, Johann Reinhold, **9:**35
Forsyth, Malcolm, **3:**1090–91
Forsyth, W. O., **3:**1180, 1182
"Fort Hood Three" (Newman), **3:**317
Fortier, Achille, **3:**1149
Fortoul, Hippolyte, **8:**552
Fortune Teller (Herbert), **3:**544
Forty-Five Minutes from Broadway (Cohan), **3:**193
49th State Records, **9:**986, 998
For Whom the Bell Tolls (film), **3:**203
Foster, David, **3:**249
Foster, Makau, **9:**270
Foster, Nga, **9:**974
Foster, Stephen Collins, **3:***186*, 186–87, 192, 241, 257, 305, 308, 520, 527, 543, 547, *547*, 616, 617, 888; **7:**375; **8:**205
Fou Ts'ong, **7:**416, 420
Foucauld, Charles de, **1:**576
Foucault, Michel, **3:**89; **8:**192
Foula (musical group), **3:**806
Foundation of Chinese Folk Arts (Taiwan), **7:**524
Four Medical Tantras (Tibetan writing), **7:**473
4ʼ 33″ (Cage), **3:**130
Fournier, Pierre, **4:**870

"Four O'Clock Blues" (Yancey), **3:**105
Four Parodic Movements (Hukai), **7:**732
Four Saints in Three Acts (Thomson), **3:**545, 608
Fourteen (Cage), **3:**175
1492. Who Found Who? (Porter), **3:**1063
Four the Moment (musical group), **3:**1072, 1134
Four the Moment: Live (Four the Moment), **3:**1134
Four Tops (musical group), **3:**674, 709
Four Tunes (musical group), **3:**351
Four Works (Cardew), **8:**98
Fowke, Edith, **3:**15, 147, 1082, 1188, *1189*
Fowke, Francis, **5:**49
Fox, Della, **3:***195*
Fox, H. C. A., **9:**928–29
Fox Strangways, Arthur, **5:**52–53
fox-trot, **3:**706, 868, 893, 913, 914, 995
in Argentina, **2:**273
in Canada, **3:**408, 1195, 1256
in Costa Rica, **2:**691
dance competitions for, **3:**210
in Dominican Republic, **2:**860
in El Salvador, **2:**718
in Europe, **8:**443, 457, 483, 525, 660, 690, 812
in Guatemala, **2:**733, 735
in Israel, **6:**1019
in Peru, **2:**485
Foxy Brown, **3:**697, 699
Fracilor (musical group), **8:**276
Fra Diavolo (Auber), **3:**61
Frændur (musical group), **8:**472
Fragments (Feliciano), **4:**878
Fragments of Ancient Poetry (Macpherson), **8:**17, 186, 367, 370, 379, 460, 552
France, **8:**539–54. *See also* Basque region; Brittany; Corsica; Low Countries
Alsace-Lorraine, **8:**539
folk songs, **8:**664
wind bands, **8:**543
Aquitaine, medieval repertoire of, **8:**70
Arctic territories, **3:**379
art music in, **8:**69, 70–73, 75, 77, 543, 550
attitude toward colonized peoples, **8:**232
Aubrac, **8:**554
Auvergne
bagpipe in, **8:**560
drone performance, **8:**543, 545
Basque people in, **8:**12, 309
Béarn
instruments, **8:**176–77
two-part polyphony in, **8:**542, *543*
Beauvais, church bells, **8:**544
Berber peoples in, **6:**273, 276
Bretons in, **8:**12
Caribbean territories, **2:**791, 845, 864, 868, 953
Carolingian period in, **8:**69
Celtic people in, **8:**319
Corsicans in, **8:**12
court music, **8:**146, 199
dance traditions of, **8:**165, 546–47
Dauphiné, **8:**547
two-part polyphony in, **8:**542
Flanders, **8:**518
friction drums, **8:**544

France (*continued*)
France (*continued*)
  French Antillean peoples in, **2**:98
  immigrant groups in, **8**:231, 234–35,
      238–39
  influence on Greek island music, **8**:1009,
      1025
  influence on Québec art music, **3**:1148–50,
      1151
  influence on Québec *chansons*, **3**:1167–68
  instrument collections in, **8**:181, 182
  instruments, **8**:169, 170, 176, 543–45, 547
      research on, **8**:37–38, 39
  Jewish people in, **6**:1036
  Khmer people in, **4**:210
  Limousin
      bagpipe in, **8**:560
      drone performance, **8**:543
  Lorraine, **8**:539
  map of, **8**:*516*
  Massif Central, **8**:540
  Muslim immigrant communities in, **8**:11, 208
  North African colonies of, **6**:21–22, 274, 432,
      475, 505
  North African emigrant communities, **6**:438
  opera-ballet in, **8**:77, 160–61
  organ-building in, **8**:78
  Orléanais, dance in, **8**:547
  Paris
      Auvergnats in, **8**:547, 551
      ballet in, **8**:161
      Concerts Spirituels, **8**:80
      immigrant music in, **8**:210, 225, 231
      jazz in, **8**:233
      Jewish community of, **8**:265
      light music in, **8**:205
      Notre Dame cathedral, **8**:70–71
  popular music in, **8**:205, 207–8, 547–48
  population of, **8**:539
  Portuguese people in, **8**:576
  Provence, influence on Corsican culture, **8**:573
  Pyrenees, panpipes in, **8**:142, 544
  regional musics of, **8**:10
  Renaissance in, **8**:73
  research on music of, **8**:17, 177, 546, 547,
      551–54
  Rom people in, **8**:272, 288
  Roussillon, wind bands, **8**:543
  solfège pedagogy, **8**:106
  Soule
      Basque music, **8**:309, 311
      pastoral in, **8**:314–15
  tango in, **2**:101
  theatrical dance in, **8**:160
  viellée in, **8**:141
  Vietnamese people in, **4**:88
  vocal music of, **8**:71, 72, 75, 128, 132, 135,
      539–43, 546, 547, 548, 550
Francello, Elvira, **8**:606
Francini, Enrique Mario, **2**:264
Franciscan order
  in Costa Rica, **2**:631, 685, 695
  in Mexico, **2**:23, 555, 577, 582, 595, 600,
      656
  in North America, **3**:485, 755, 848–49
  in Peru, **2**:469
  in Philippines, **4**:841, 868

  role in music education, **2**:112
  in South America, **2**:23
  in Uruguay, **2**:511
Francis, Charles W., **10**:138
Francis, Daniel, **3**:1059
Francis, Hubert, **3**:1069
Francis Xavier, Saint, **8**:309
Francisco, Alejandro, **4**:866
Francisco de San José, Fray, **2**:681
Francisco, Juan R., **4**:881
Francisco, Lucia, **4**:870
Francke, Auguste H., **5**:712, 715
Franco. *See* Makiadi, Luambo "Franco"
Franco-Americans. *See* French-Americans
Franco-Belgian Easter Island Expedition,
      9:25
Franco, Francisco, **2**:102; **8**:185, 315, 588,
      598, 599
Franco, Hernando, **2**:735
François, Claude, **9**:213
François I, king of France, **6**:565
Franconian empire, **8**:38
Franke, Herbert, **7**:30
Frankel, Professor, **7**:348
"Frankie and Albert" (ballad), **3**:639
Frankie Lymon and the Teenagers, **3**:672
Franklin, Aretha, **3**:*263*, 535, 552, 677, 678,
      710, *710*, 713; **8**:61, 446; **10**:78
Franklin, John, **3**:392, 1164
Franklin, Kirk, **3**:635, *635*
Fransız Tiyatrosu (Istanbul), **6**:787
František Antonín, count of Kolovrat Libsteinsky,
      8:732
Fraser, Alasdair, **8**:371
Fraser, Simon, **3**:1255; **8**:373
Fraternidad Piadosa de Nuestro Padre Jesús
      Nazareno (religious brotherhood),
      3:757–58, 759
Frazer, James G., **9**:185
"Freaky Dancin'" (Cameo), **3**:684
Freddie label, **3**:781
Frederick, William, **4**:104–5
Fred Waring's Pennsylvanians (choral group),
      3:536
free aerophones
  bird quills, **3**:375, *375*
  bullroarers, **4**:810, 837; **8**:38, 655, 682
      Arctic regions, **3**:375
      Dogon people, **1**:455
      Great Basin area, **3**:425
      hvësegasse, **8**:455
      khirlee, **6**:981, 986
      kidiu, **4**:837
      Native American types, **3**:478
      Nkhumbi people, **1**:714
      Schwirrholz, **8**:655
      Subarctic regions, **3**:386
      svingbruse, **8**:455
      Tohono O'odham, **3**:473
      West Africa, **1**:445
      Yoruba people, **1**:460
      zingulca (also *brnkač*), **8**:919
  cicada, flying, **9**:615
  coconuts, *tagihuhu*, **9**:828
  combs, paper-covered, Jamaica, **2**:907
  disks, whirring

  kōrorohū, **9**:933
  New Caledonia, **9**:679
  leaf whizzers
      Irian Jaya, **9**:591
      New Britain, **9**:623
      New Caledonia, **9**:679
  nuts, whirring, **9**:393, 623
  plates, suspended, *waypülü*, **9**:681
  poiawhiuwhiu (swung gourd), **9**:933
  pole with attached bamboo strip, spun, **2**:751
  ribbon reeds
      New Britain, **9**:623
      New Caledonia, **9**:680
  stone slings, *maka*, **9**:901
  swung balls, *poi*, **9**:168, 933, 939, 945
  swung slats
      Australia, **9**:252, 436
      êlêŋî eni, **9**:615
      Irian Jaya, **9**:477, 591
      loblob-ai, **9**:23
      men's playing of, **9**:245
      Oceania, **9**:392, 512, 531
      Papua New Guinea, **9**:188, 381, 477, 489,
          508, 548, 549, 557, 563, 608, 611,
          623
      pūrerehua, **9**:168, 933
  tops, humming, **9**:393, 623
      kilakōla, **9**:655
      Vanuatu, **9**:693
  whips
      Hungary, **8**:743
      Low Countries, **8**:525
      Switzerland, **8**:683, 687
  whirled plaques
      nurá-mëe, **2**:153
      palo zumbador, **2**:706
Free Spirit (musical group), **3**:1069
Freebeats (musical group), **9**:138
Freed, Alan, **3**:349, 350, 353, 708
Freed, Arthur, **9**:43
Freed, Don, **3**:411
Freed, Ruth, **5**:674
Freed, Stanley, **5**:674
Freedman, Maurice, **1**:66
Freedman, Max, **3**:353
Freeman (newspaper), **3**:618
Freeman, Bud, **3**:652
Freeman, Derek, **9**:416
Freeman, Harry L., **3**:606, 608
Freeman, Robert, **10**:134
Freemasonry, **3**:126
free-reed instruments. *See also* accordions;
          harmonium; mouth organs; organs
  baosheng, **7**:189
  bilangdaomu, **7**:491
  buah padas, **4**:836
  cha mblay, **9**:76
  da paisheng, **7**:189
  datongsheng, **7**:231
  engkerurai, **4**:836
  fangsheng, **7**:189
  farara, **1**:788
  fulu, **4**:540, 543
  guoyue sheng, **7**:189
  he, **7**:108, 187, 188
  Hmong people, **4**:553

hnyìñ, **4:**365
hulusi, **7:**491
jiajian sheng, **7:**189–90
keledi (also *keluri*), **4:**836
kelulut, **4:**836
ken, **4:**172
kênh, **4:**536
khaen, **4:**22, 46, 61, 115–16, 141, 214, 215, 225, 316
    tuning and modes of, **4:**15, 67, 131, 321–24
khen, **4:**547
khene, **4:**18, 338, 342–49, 351–53, 355, 358, 361
    in North America, **3:**952, 954, 1008, *1008*
    playing styles of, **4:**339–40
    tuning of, **4:**339, 356
lachi, **4:**540, 541
lenglong, **7:**491, 492
lusheng, **7:**451, 491, *492*
m'baut, **4:**172
m'buôt, **4:**534
naw, **4:**539–40
New Caledonia, **9:**680
ngail mo, **7:**510
nokuma, **4:**540
oniya-niya, **4:**904
padi, **4:**743
pak bishur, **7:**1018
pey, **4:**197
pey pork, **4:**172, 194, 205
pi, **4:**345
pi-ankong, **4:**213
pi bap, **4:**338, 349
pi chum, **4:**310
pi luang, **4:**338
pi luk khaen, **4:**318
pi mon, **4:**349
pi-ngyen, **4:**213
ploy, **4:**157, 172
qeej (also *geng*), **3:**952, *1004*, 1004–5; **4:***59*, 551–52, 554–55; **9:**75–76
raj nplaim, **4:**553, *554*
raj nplaim (also *chamblai*), **3:**1005
rakle, **4:**590
saeng (also *saenghwang*), **7:**823, *824*, 828, 863
serunai, **4:**743
sheng, **7:**80, *187*, 187–90, *188*
    in Buddhist rituals, **7:**312, 331, 1018
    construction of, **7:**187, 189
    early, **7:**108
    history of, **7:**187–88
    in *Jiangnan sizhu* ensemble, **7:**224–25
    modern types, **7:**189–90
    mythical origins of, **7:**402
    in North America, **3:**962
    in northern Chinese ensembles, **7:**199–204, 242, 315
    in opera ensembles, **7:**292
    performance of, **7:**242
    in *shifangu* ensemble, **7:**196
    Southeast Asia, **4:**46, 475
    in *Tianjin shidiao*, **7:**254
shō (See *syô*)
sinh, **4:**475
sizhu sheng, **7:**188

sneng, **4:**155, 157, 172, 194, 205
Southeast Asia, **4:**596
    cultural origins of, **4:**11
    distribution of, **4:**58–59
śruti peṭṭi (drone box), **5:**355, 360, 582, 885, *914*
    in *cinna mēḷam* ensemble, **5:**913
    in North America, **3:**984, 990
    in *periya mēḷam* ensemble, **5:**103, *359*, 912
    use in devotional music, **5:**249, 364
sumbiling, **4:**836
sumpotan, **4:**836
surpeṭī, **5:**633
syō (*shō*), **4:**475; **7:**81, 621, 625–27, 770; **10:**27
tabarau, **4:**836
tolem, **4:**540
xiaosheng, **7:**188
    of Yao people, **4:**549
yu, **7:**79, 108, 187, 188
yuangsheng, **7:**189
zhongsheng, **7:**231
Freer Gallery of Art (Washington, D.C.), **5:**529
Fregozo, Teddy, **3:**739
Freie Deutsche Jugend, **8:**661
Freisinger Petruslied, **8:**650
Freitag, Léa Vinocur, **2:**320
Fremont culture, **3:**420
Frémont, John Charles, **3:**307
French-Americans, **3:**527–28, 835, 854–59
    Cajun music, **3:**326, 856–59
    Creole music, **3:**858
    early explorers and settlers, **3:**452
    in Louisiana, **3:**9, 505, 514, 527–28, 596, 791, 854, 856–59, 1135–36
        dances of, **3:**213
    in New England, **3:**527–28, 854–55
French and Indian War, **3:**9, 1056–57, 1073
French Antilles, **2:**95, 98. *See also* Guadeloupe; Martinique
French-Canadians, **3:**854
    Acadians, **3:**150, 1068, 1069, 1115, 1135–37
    class structure and, **3:**51
    cultural policy views of, **3:**1067
    dances of, **3:**223
    early explorers and settlers, **3:**7, 143, 452, 1056, 1114–15, 1146, 1163–64
    folk music, **3:**52, 145–46, 148, 265, 292, 1121
        used for contra dances, **3:**230
    influence on Métis culture and music, **3:**405, 408
    interminglings with Scottish-Canadians, **3:**325
    in Maritime Provinces, **3:**325, 1068, 1114–16, 1118, 1135–37
    in Ontario, **3:**1077, 1188, 1190, 1192–94
    popular music of, **3:**252, 265, 266
    population of, **3:**5
    in Prairie Provinces, **3:**343, 1086, 1087–88
    in Québec, **3:**1135, 1146–47
    research on music of, **3:**31
French Creoles, in Trinidad and Tobago, **2:**952–53
French Guiana, **2:**434–39. *See also specific peoples*
    Amerindian cultures of, **2:**434–37
    Asian descendants in, **2:**48

    Creole culture of, **2:**437–38
    geography of, **2:**434
    history of, **2:**242, 245
    instruments of, **2:**435–36
    Maroon cultures in, **2:**2, 131, 438–39
    musical genres
        musique folklorique, **2:**437–38
        musique typique, **2:**437–38
        musique véhiculaire, **2:**439
        vidé, **2:**438
    population of, **2:**434
    tropical-forest region of, **2:**123–35
    Waiãpí culture, **2:**157–63
    Wayana culture, **2:**164–67
"French Minuet," **3:**1190
French people
    in Cuba, **2:**822
    in Dominica, **2:**840
    in England, **8:**326, 336
    in French Guiana, **2:**434
    in Guyana, **2:**441
    in Mexico, **2:**613, 621
    on Réunion Island, **5:**606
    in Syria, **6:**565
    in Virgin Islands, **2:**968, 969
French Polynesia, **9:**865, 879. *See also* Austral Islands; Mangareva; Marquesas Islands; Society Islands; Tuamotu Islands
    brass bands in, **9:**128
    cultural contacts with Pukapuka, **9:**912
    cultural policies in, **9:**55
    films on, **9:**1017–18
    Mururoa Atoll, nuclear testing on, **9:**211, 346–47, 867
"Frenesí" (García), **3:**739
Frescobaldi, Girolamo, **8:**78
Fresedo, Osvaldo, **2:**263
Fresh Prince, **3:**699, 714, 715
Fresh Prince of Bel Air (television show), **3:**715
Freshko, Shemuel, **6:**1072
Freshley, Mary Jo, **9:**110, *111*
Freud, Sigmund, **3:**511; **8:**192; **10:**109, 111
Frey, Paul, **3:**1082
Freycinet, Captain Louis de, **9:**17
Frézier, Amédée François, **2:**469
friction idiophones
    blur cue armadillo shell, **2:**632, 634
    Europe, **8:**170
    lounuat, **9:**380–82
    oticonte (also *bote del diablo*; *arcuza*), **2:**565
    Papua New Guinea, **9:**374–75, 477, 601, 628–29
    sacabuche, **2:**709
    toá, **2:**285, 289
    tortoiseshells, **2:**150, 151
        gnelé, **2:**686
        kodedo, **2:**177
        morrocoyo, **2:**185
        pupu, **2:**157, 159
        zambumbia, **2:**709
Frictions, **4:**885
Fridolinons! (Gélinas), **3:**198
Frieberger, Buddy (Padhi), **10:**111–12
Fried, Abraham, **6:**205
Fried Rice Paradise (Lee), **4:**523
Friedenthal, Albert, **4:**857

Friedl, Erika, **6:**19
Friedman, Perry, **8:**662
Friedman, Robert, **3:**790
Friedsell, Louis, **3:**936
Friend (missionary periodical), **9:**21
"Friendship Train" (Gladys Knight and The
    Pips), **3:**677
Frigerio, Alejandro, **2:**260
Friml, Rudolf, **3:**193, 544
Frisbie, Charlotte J., **3:**428, 433, 492
Frische teutsche Liedlein (Forster), **8:**17, 653
Frith, Simon, **3:**45, 111, 114
Frizzell, Lefty, **3:**77, 79, *79*, 81
Frizzi, Ernst, **9:**479
Froberger, Jacob, **8:**78
Fróðskaparrit (periodical), **8:**472
Fróðskaparsetur Føroya, **8:**472
Frøhlich, Johann, **8:**460
From, Olof Jonsson (From Olle), **8:**439
"From the Beginning to the Present Time"
    (Doukhobor song), **3:**1268, *1269–70*
From Bulgaria with Love (album), **8:**225
"From Maine to Oregon" (Sousa), **3:**260–61
From Mao to Mozart (film), **7:**398
From Rice Paddies and Temple Yards (Nguyễn and
    Campbell), **3:**996
From Scratch (Aotearoan percussion ensemble),
    9:*930*
Fromm, Erich, **3:**130
Fromm, Herbert, **3:**939
Frontier label, **3:**169
Frost, Henry, **3:**1180
Fry, William Henry, **3:**538
Frye, Northrop, **3:**295
Frye, Theodore, **3:**632
FSB (musical group), **8:**220
FTA! Songs of the GI Resistance (Dane), **3:**317
Fu de ci (*xianshiyue* piece), **7:**215
Fu'ad I, king of Egypt, **6:**322
Fuat, **6:**249
"Fuchs Du Hast die Gans Gestohlen," **3:**889
"F— Tha Police" (NWA), **3:**699
Fueguino cultures, **2:**356, 357
Fuentas, Jovita, **4:**870
Fuentes C., Aurelio, **2:**431
Fuentes, Cecilia, **2:**544
Fuentes, Edgardo "Gary," **2:**277
Fuentes, Rubén, **2:**622; **3:**745
Fugazi, **9:**164
Fugees (musical group), **3:**701, 715, 806–7
fuging (fuguing) tunes, **3:**531, 532, 1070
"Fugitive Slave to the Christian," **3:**307
Fugs (musical group), **3:**317
fūjì, **1:**473, 474, 483, 484–87
Fujian Music College, **7:**398
Fujie, Linda, **3:**516; **7:**595, 775
Fujii Tomoaki, **7:**525
Fujita Takanori, **7:**594
Fujiwara house, **7:**27
Fukushima Kazuo, **7:**593, 736
Fulani people, **1:**518. *See also* Fulɓe people
    dance, **1:**289
    instruments of, **1:**448–49
    music of, **1:**447, 451, 588
Fulano (rock group), **2:**374
Fulayḥ ibn abī al-'Awrā', **6:**353

Fulɓe (kingdom), court music, **1:**311–12,
    313–14
Fulɓe people. *See also* Fulani people
    alternative designations for, **1:**443–44
    caste system, **1:**444
    dance, **1:**115, 116
    diaspora of, **10:**154
    gawlo (professional musician), **1:**444
    history of, **1:**443
    influence on Temne people, **1:**468
    instruments of, **1:**445–46, 448
    migration of, **1:**313–14
    music of, **1:**446
    textile design, **1:**114
Fuller, Blind Boy, **3:**645
Fuller, Paul, **4:**261
Fulson, Lowell, **3:**647
Fulton, Justin D., **3:**121
Fulup, Marc'harid, **8:**562
Funāfuti (Tuvalu), **9:**251, 829, 830
Funaki, 'Inoke F., **9:**972
Funan (state), **4:**43, 62, 153, 157, 304
Fund to Assist Canadian Talent on Record,
    3:1103
Fundação Nacional para a Alegria no Trabalho,
    8:577
Fundación de Etnomusicología y Folklore
    (FUNDEF, Venezuela), **2:**543
Fundación de las Humanidades (Puerto Rico),
    2:940
Fundación Interamericana de Etnomusicología y
    Folklore (Venezuela), **2:**488
Fundación Tango (Uruguay), **2:**519
Fun-da-mental, **5:**575
funeral ceremonies
    Abkhazian people, **8:**853
    Adighian people, **8:**855
    Admiralty Islands, **9:**23
    Africa, **1:**82
        dance at, **1:**111–12
        drums in, **1:**316
    Akha people, **4:**541
    Aluku culture, **2:**438–39
    Anlo-Ewe people, **1:**393–94, 396
    Anuta, **9:**858–59
    Arab societies, **6:**373
    Argentina, Santiago del Estero, **2:**258
    Australia
        Arnhem Land, **9:**419–20
        films of, **9:**47
        Hmong people, **9:**75–76
        Yanyuwa people, **9:**460
        Yolngu people, **9:**357
    Bahrain, **6:**403
    Bali, **4:**749, 752, 755, 807
    Barbados, African descendants, **2:**814
    Basque region, **8:**315
    Bribri and Cabécar cultures, **2:**632, 633, 634,
        635
    British Caribbean communities, **3:**811, 1205
    Burma, **4:**374
    California, Spanish, **3:**735
    Caribbean, **2:**795
    Central Asia, **6:**945
    China, **7:**91, 203, 416
        Buddhist, **7:**331
        village, **7:**315–18

    Colombia, **2:**384, 403–4
    Colo people, **1:**569
    Costa Rica, **2:**694
    Croatia, **8:**926
    Dagbamba people, **1:**453
    Dominican Republic, **2:**849
    El Salvador, **2:**709
    Europe
        performers as mediators, **8:**117
        women's and men's customs, **8:**194
    Gã people, **1:**117
    Georgia, **8:**835, 839
    Greece, Peloponnisos, **8:**1013–14
    Hausa people, **1:**523–24
    Hawai'i, **9:**132
    Hindu, performers at, **5:**286
    Hmong people, **3:**1004; **4:**554–55
    Hungary, **8:**739–40
        Rom musicians at, **8:**274
    Igbo people, **1:**459
    Iraq, **6:**403
    Irian Jaya, Dani people, **9:**50
    Jamaica, **2:**904, 906
    Japan, Kohun period, **7:**562
    Java, **4:**807
    Karen people, **4:**544–45
    Karnataka, **5:**886
    Kashmir, **5:**685
    Kazakhstan, **6:**951
    Kenya, **1:**626–28
    Kerala, **5:**949
    Khmer people, **4:**155, 167, 196–97, 231
        in Thailand, **4:**214
    Kiribati, *bomaki*, **9:**763
    Korea
        sangyŏsori songs in, **7:**988
        tashiraegi custom, **7:**985
    Kota people, **5:**278–79, 281
    Kuna culture, **2:**644
    Latin American communities, **3:**1205
    Latvia, **8:**502
    Lebanon, **6:**403, 545
    Liberia, **10:**61
    LoDagaa people, **1:**456–57
    Louisiana, African-Americans, **3:**802
    Madhya Pradesh, **5:**722
    Maleku culture, *fiesta de sufrimiento*, **2:**682
    Maliseet and Mi'kmaq nations, **3:**1069
    Mapuche culture, **2:**362
    Marquesas Islands, **9:**894
    Martinique, **2:**915
    Maya culture, **2:**731
    Miskitu culture, *sikru*, **2:**660–61, 662
    Mixtec culture, **2:**567
    Morocco, **1:**541
    Mường people, **4:**535
    Naxi people, **7:**511
    Nepal, **5:**701
        Gurung people, **5:**703–4
    New Caledonia, **9:**685
    New Guinea, **9:**22
    Nicaragua, **2:**762, 765
    Niue, **9:**816
    Otopame culture, **2:**573, 574
    Ovimbundu people, **1:**714
    Palau, **9:**723

Papua New Guinea
   Bali and Vitu *leleki* ritual, **9:**608–9
   Banoni people, **9:**645–46
   Binandere people, **9:**358
   Irumu people, **9:**570
   Lolo people, **9:**612–13
   Melpa people, **9:**520–21
   Nagovisi people, **9:**647
   New Ireland, **9:**381, 626
Paraguay, **2:**462
Paya culture, *tasnewa*, **2:**739
Peru, **2:**478
Philippines
   Islamic communities, **4:**911
   prehistoric, **4:**913
   wakes, **4:**845, 851
Polynesia, **9:**202
Puerto Rico, **2:**936
Pukapuka, **9:**910
Purépecha culture, **2:**577
Romania, **8:**871–72, 874, 879
Rotuma, **9:**819
St. Lucia, **2:**948–49
Sāmoa, **9:**805
Sardinia, **8:**627
Serbia, Kosovo, **8:**286
Shona people, **1:**753
Solomon Islands
   ʻAreʻare people, **9:**667
   Guadalcanal, **9:**664–65
   Malaita, **9:**668
South America, **2:**49
   shawm in, **2:**36
South Asia, **5:**273, 276
   appropriate music for, **5:**282–83, 286
Southeast Asia, prehistoric, **4:**35, 39, 42
Sri Lanka, **5:**967
Sulawesi, **4:**804, 806, 807–8
   Toraja, **4:**61
Sumatra, **4:**807
   Kerinci people, **4:**618
   Nias Island, **4:**608
   Rejang people, **4:**619
   Riau, **4:**616
Sumba, **4:**788, 789, 790
Sumu culture
   sau, **2:**750, 751
   sikro, **2:**739, 750–51
Taino culture, **2:**846, 881
Taiwan, **7:**424
Tajikistan, **6:**942
Takuu, **9:**841
Tamil Nadu, Nilgiri peoples, **5:**909
Thailand, **4:**242, 247, 248, 249, 291
Tikopia, **9:**855
Tokelau, **9:**824
Tonga, **9:**785
Tukano culture, **2:**154–55
Ukraine, **8:**806, 812
United States
   bands at, **3:**568
   ethnic music at, **3:**827
Vai people, **1:**332–34, 345
Vietnam, **4:**60, 450
   dance in, **4:**501
Vlah people, **8:**950

Western Arctic peoples, **3:**376
Xiaʼerba people, **7:**482
Yao people, **4:**549
Yuma culture, **2:**598
Yuman culture, **3:**433–34
Funk, Ray, **10:**144
funk, **2:**96, 98, 111; **3:**228, 680–86, 689, 701,
   711; **8:**204, 356
   black culture and, **3:**685–86
   Brazil, **2:**354
   disco and, **3:**688
   gospel music and, **3:**635
   influences on, **3:**680–81
   jazz and, **3:**665
   P-funk, **3:**683–84, 686
   techno-funk, **3:**684–85
Funkadelic (musical group), **3:**684, 686
Funkdafied (DaBrat), **3:**697
"Funkentelechy" (Clinton), **3:**684
"Funky Drummer" (Brown), **3:**701
Funky Four Plus One (musical group), **3:**694,
   696
"Funky President (People It's Bad)" (Brown),
   3:683, 701
"Funky Stuff" (Kool and the Gang), **3:**681, 711
Fur people, **1:**561
"Für Elise" (Beethoven), **7:**417
Furey, Finbar and Eddie, **8:**226
Furious Five (musical group), **3:**697
Furki (god), **8:**864
Furlong, Colonel Charles Wellington, **2:**251
Furness, William Henry, **9:**994
Fürniss-Yacoubi, Susanne, **1:**256
Furst, Peter, **2:**19–20; **3:**425
Fûshi Kaden (Zeami), **7:**640
fusion genres and border crossings. *See also* Afro-
   Cuban music; popular music;
   worldbeat; *specific genres*
   Africa, **1:**8, 34, 37, 370, 418, 471
   Algerian *ʻaçrî*, **6:**270
   Austria, **8:**676
   Bulgaria, **8:**903
   Canada, **3:**74, 331–33, 1062–64, 1077, 1084,
      1121, 1127, 1170, 1174, 1197,
      1202–3, 1277–78, 1279–81
   Central Asia, **6:**905
   Europe, **8:**209–10, 231–41
   Hawaiʻian dance, **9:**110–11
   hybridization, **3:**325–27; **8:**205–7
   Ireland, **8:**226, 392
   Israel, **6:**1074
   jazz, **7:**967, 972–73
   Korea, **7:**967, 969–73
   Macedonia, **8:**983
   Métis, **3:**344, 409
   Mexican-American popular music, **3:**739, 748,
      749–51, 777–78
   Middle East, **6:**406, 413
   multiethnic "old time" music, **3:**867
   Native American musicians, **3:**488–90
   new and experimental genres, **3:**334–37
   New Mexico, **3:**756, 763, 766
   North Africa, **6:**270–72, 435, 438
   Pakistan, **5:**748–49
   Scotland, **8:**226
   South America, **2:**46

South Asia, **5:**560–68
   film music, **5:**540–41, 544–45
   Hindustani tradition, **5:**136, 205, 206, 528,
      561
   Karnatak (Karnatic) tradition, **5:**529,
      544–45, 561
South Asian diaspora, **3:**73, 218, 986; **5:**568,
   574–75, 576, 582, 584–85
Sundanese popular music, **4:**717–18
tamburitza repertoire, **3:**922
Third Stream music, **3:**335, 583, 612
Tibetan music in, **3:**133, 340
transplantation, **3:**323–25
Turkey, **6:**791–92, 797–98
Tuvan music, **6:**979, 986–87; **7:**1014,
   1023–25
Ukrainian genres, **3:**344–45, 1110
United States, **3:**334–59
Futuna, **9:**771, 808–9, 814–16
   cultural contacts with Tonga, **9:**791
   history of, **9:**814
   instruments of, **9:**816
   kava use in, **9:**174, 202
   map of, **9:***772*
   music and dance of, **9:**59, 814–16, 969
   population of, **9:**808, 814
   sound recordings from, **9:**1000
   toka dance of, **9:**705
Fuyuge people, **9:**490
Füzuli, Mehmed bin Suleyman, **6:**922, 928, 931,
   943
Fynn, John, **10:**31

Gã people
   dance, **1:**109, 113, 114, 117
   history of, **1:**463
   music of, **1:**463
   song content, **1:**102–5
Gaál, Edith, **9:**983–84
Gaál, Károly, **9:**983–84
Gaanam, King, **3:**1257
Gaba Kaluks (musical group), **9:**138
Gabadi people, **9:**492
Gabashane, Susan, **1:**771
Gabb, William M., **2:**635
Gabbay, Shaul, **6:**314
Gabilondo Soler, Francisco, **2:**618
Gabilou, **9:**998
Gabon. *See also* Central Africa; *specific peoples*
   Bantu cultures of, **1:**659–63
   Bibayak people, scales of, **1:**256
   Fang people, dance, **1:**109–10
   harps in, **1:**302, 661–63
   historical studies, **1:**87
   music of, **1:**659–63
Gabree, John, **3:**348
Gabriel (Nissan composer), **9:**635–36
Gabriel, Gavino, **8:**621, 632
Gabriel, Juan, **2:**623; **3:**721, 746
Gabriel, Léona, **2:**916
Gabriel, Peter, **1:**418; **3:**338–39; **5:**568; **8:**225,
   239–40; **9:**155
Gabrielsson, Alf, **8:**448
Gadaba people, **5:**485
Ga da mei lin (Xi), **7:**347
Gadbois, Charles-Émile, **3:**1088, 1155

Gadd, May, **3:**323–24

Gaddar, **5:**556

Gaddi people, **5:**500

Gade, Anna, **6:**162

Gade, Niels W., **8:**460

Gadha dynasty, **5:**721

Gadolia Lothar people, **8:**271

Gadsden, Celeste, **10:**138

Gadsup people, **9:**526–33

Gadūliya Lohār people, **5:**639

Gaelic College (Baddeck), **3:**1120, 1130

Gaelic League, **3:**845

Gaelic Songs in Nova Scotia (Creighton), **3:**292

Gael-Linn, **8:**391, 392

gagaku, **7:**619–28, *720, 724, 757;* **10:**79

  azuma asobi repertoire, **7:**619, 620, 622

  bokkai gaku repertoire, **7:**723

  bugaku repertoire, **7:**624–25

  categorization of repertoire, **7:**42

  Chinese origins of, **7:**50, 59, 81, 89, 132, 535, 701, 808, 861

  Confucian views of, **7:**548

  dissemination of, **7:**539, 627–28

  documentary sources on, **7:**587–88

  genealogical charts for, **7:**768

  government bureau for, **7:**45

  kangen repertoire, **7:**621, 622, 624, 625, 720

  kibigaku repertoire, **7:**608–9

  komagaku repertoire, **7:**619, 620–25, 624, 756, 806

  kudaragaku repertoire, **7:**620, 756

  mikagura repertoire, **7:**607–8, 619, 622, 626–27, 768

  notation for, **7:**538, 574, 580, 590

  patronage of, **7:**687

  pedagogical lineages in, **7:**46

  performance contexts for, **7:**619, 775

  rhythmic cycles in, **7:**572

  rin'yû gaku repertoire, **7:**723

  saibara and *rôei* genres, **7:**619, 622, 625

  sankangaku repertoire, **7:**42, 723, 756

  siragigaku repertoire, **7:**620, 756

  sôkyoku genre of, **7:**574, 589, 618, 696

  theories in, **7:**565–68

  tôgaku repertoire, **7:**42, 609, 619, 620–25, 701, 756

  tora gaku repertoire, **7:**723

  tradition and change in, **7:**719, 721, 722

  transmission of, **7:**756–57, 759, 773, 775–76

  use in westernized art music, **7:**728, 732

  vocalization in, **7:**551

  wagaku repertoire, **7:**42

  zyo ha kyû concept in, **7:**554

Gagaku-ryô (institute), **7:**45, 626, 627, 723, 756–57, 761

Gagarin, G., **6:***923*

Gagime (Huli performer), **9:***372*

Gagnon, Ernest, **3:**28, 145–46, 465, 1165

Gahuku people, **9:**526–33

Gaidio people, **9:**559

Gāine people, **5:**697, 698, *698,* 706

Gaither, Bill, **3:**645

Gaither, Gloria, **9:**207

Gaither, William J., **9:**207

Gaixia ge (Peking opera song), **7:**282

Gakkaroku (Abe), **7:**587

Gakko (institute), **7:**757

Gakunin bunin (also *Gakuso bunin*), **7:**587

Galaev, Boris, **8:**860, 861

Galambawa people, **1:**289

Galán, Pacho, **2:**102

galant style, **8:**79, 435

Galarraga, Lazaro, **3:**784, *786*

Galavarishi (film), **5:**543

Galaxy Records, **3:**1243

Galdan, **7:**35

Gale, Albert, **4:**872

Gale, Marina, **2:***961*

Galea, John, **8:**643

Galeaʻi, Pulefanolefalasa F., **9:***972*

Galeano, Ignacio V., **2:**745

Galeyya, Alisetti, **5:**898

Galibi culture. *See* Kalina (Galibi) culture

Galich, Aleksandr, **8:**767, 778

Galicia, **8:**806

Galicians, **8:**12

Galilei, Vincenzo, **6:**366

Galin, Krešimir, **8:**937

Gallagher, Katherine, **3:**94

Gallardo, Carlos, **3:**798

Gallat-Morin, Elisabeth, **3:**1075, 1147

Gallego, Merced, **3:**787

Gallego, Teodoro, **4:**866

Gallery (New York), **3:**688

Galletti, Jean-Ange, **8:**572

"Galley Slave" (Reeve), **3:**180

galliard, **8:**367

Galli-Curci, Amelita, **3:**537; **7:**381

Gallini, Clara, **8:**632

Galloping Wild Horse (Kazakh piece), **7:**461

Galo Maigua, Segundo, **2:**427, 430

galop

  in Denmark, **8:**457

  in Low Countries, **8:**524

  in Sweden, **8:**435–36

  in Switzerland, **8:**690

Galron, Nurit, **6:**1074

Galván, Jorge, **3:**749

Galván, Ralph, **3:**778

Gama Pingcuolangijie, **7:**474–75

Gama, Rafael, **3:**739

Gama, Vasco da, **5:**15

Gambia. *See also* West Africa; *specific peoples*

  griot tradition in, **1:**419

  guitar in, **1:**365

  instruments of, **1:**445–46

  Mandinka people, **1:**444

    drumming, **1:**136

    modes of speech, **1:**498–99

    praise singing, **1:**506, 508

    Wolof people, **1:**444

Gambian people, in France, **8:**231

Gambier Islands, **9:**885

  Christianity in, **9:**208

Gambino, Joe, **3:**865

Gamble, Kenny, **3:**711

Gamboa, Emma, **2:**704

Gamboa, Sarmiento de, **2:**250

gamelan

  Balinese, **4:**729, 730–31

  in Canada, **3:**1216

    gamelan angklung, **4:**632, 736–37, 741–42,

743, 748–49, 752, 753; **10:**128, 134–35

    gamelan arja, **4:**743, 750–51, 753

    gamelan baleganjur, **4:**730, 753–54

    gamelan barong, **4:**754

    gamelan batel, **4:**753

    gamelan bebonangan, **4:**744, 753

    gamelan gambang, **4:**735, 752, 754–55

    gamelan gambuh, **4:**735, 736, 738–39, 743, 747, 749–50

    gamelan gong, **4:**734, 736, 744–46, 750, 753, 754, 758, 776

    gamelan gong beri, **4:**743

    gamelan gong gedé, **4:**744, 776

    gamelan gong kebyar, **4:**13, 18, 21, 23, 668, 729, 732, 735, 738, 741–43, 744, 745–46, 753, 759–60, 773

    gamelan luang, **4:**755

    gamelan pelégongan, **4:**736, 745, 747–48, 750, 757

    gamelan selundeng, **4:**755

    gamelan Semar pegulingan, **4:**736, 745, 746–47, 748, 750

    gamelan suling, **4:***133*

    in Hong Kong, **7:**432

    instrumentation, **4:**741–43

    kendang mabarung, **4:**754

    performances contexts, **4:**738–39

    tripartite division of, **4:**740

    in United States, **3:**952

  builders of, **3:**1015, 1017–18

  Canada, **3:**1084, 1216

    college programs, **3:**1216

  Cirebonese, **4:**686, 689–95, 697–98, 703

    colotomic structure in, **4:**694

    gamelan balé bandung, **4:**690

    gamelan denggung, **4:**690

    gamelan pélog, **4:**691–94

    gamelan prawa, **4:**691–94

    gamelan rénténg, **4:**690

    gamelan sekati, **4:**687, 690

    gamelan wanda anyar, **4:**697

    in United States, **3:**1020

  construction of, **4:**643–44

  Indonesian, **4:**596

  Japan, **7:**540

  Javanese, **4:**631, 639–40; **10:**43–53

    accompanying court dance, **4:**649

    Banyumas style, **4:**643, 667, 675; **10:**50, 51

    in Borneo, **4:**830

    broadcasts of, **4:**679–80

    in Canada, **3:**1216

    central, **4:**645

    concerts, **4:**656

    gambang in, **4:**58

    gamelan cara balèn, **4:**644, 647

    gamelan gadhon, **4:**645

    gamelan gedhé, **4:**644

    gamelan klenèngan, **4:**645

    gamelan kodhok ngorèk, **4:**644, 647

    gamelan lengkap, **4:**644

    gamelan mondrèng, **4:**645

    gamelan munggang, **4:**644, 647

    gamelan ringgeng, **4:**645

    gamelan sekati, **4:**644, 647, 673

    gamelan seprangkat, **4:**639

gamelan sléndro, **10**:44
gamelan sléndro-pélog, **4**:639
gamelan surabayan, **4**:636
gamelan thuk-brul, **4**:645
gendhing repertoire, **4**:659–63
in Hong Kong, **7**:432
influence on *kroncong* genre, **4**:103–4
in Kalimantan, **4**:825
klenèngan concerts, **4**:655, 675
lirihan, **4**:642
Malang style, **4**:667
melody in, **4**:669–73
new music for, **4**:684–85
notation for, **4**:676–77
at Paris 1889 exhibition, **4**:13, 131, 135
pedagogy, **4**:677–79
recordings of, **4**:680–81
regional repertoires, **4**:642–43, 667–68,
    678; **10**:51
rhythm and tempo in, **4**:668–69, 673–75
Semarang style, **4**:634, 667, 671, 675;
    10:51
Solonese style, **4**:633–34, *640*, 643, 644,
    659–60, 662, 667, 671, 673, 675, 683
soran, **4**:642
Surabaya style, **4**:680
tunings of, **4**:637, 656–59
in United States, **3**:952; **10**:42
uyon-uyon concerts, **4**:655, 675
variation in, **10**:43, 51
for *wayang kulit*, **4**:649
Yogyanese style, **4**:*640*, 643, 644, 659, 662,
    667, 669–70, 673
Lombok, **4**:762, 766, 771
    gamelan angklung, **4**:776
    gamelan baleganjur, **4**:776
    gamelan baris, **4**:768, 772
    gamelan barong tengkok, **4**:772
    gamelan beleq, **4**:772
    gamelan gendang beleq, **4**:771–72
    gamelan gong kuna, **4**:776
    gamelan gong Sasak, **4**:767, 772–73
    gamelan jerujeng, **4**:767, 772
    gamelan Maulid, **4**:767, 772
    gamelan tambur, **4**:772
    gamelan tawak-tawak, **4**:772
    gamelan wayang Sasak, **4**:774
    music for, **4**:769–71
Malaysia
    joget gamelan, **4**:428–29, 436
    Trengganu State, **4**:122
popularity of, **4**:28
Singapore, **4**:520
sonority of, **4**:13, 20
Sumbawa, **4**:781
Sundanese, **4**:701–7
    in Canada, **3**:1216
    colotomic structure in, **4**:694
    degung klasik, **4**:116
    gamelan degung, **4**:690, 702, 703, 706–7,
      715, 720, 723–24, 725, 761
    gamelan saléndro, **4**:703–6, 708, 710, 724,
      725
    in United States, **3**:1020
    village ensembles, **4**:707
timbre in, **5**:64

United States, **3**:327, 335, 338, 340, 541,
    1013–19, 1021, 1026; **10**:51–52, 128,
    134
    builders of, **3**:1017–18
    college programs, **3**:342, 1013–14, 1021
    community groups, **3**:324
    compositions for, **3**:1015–17
    gamelan angklung, **3**:1018, 1019
    gamelan kebyar, **3**:1019
    instrumentation of, **3**:1012
    Western popularity of, **4**:13, 28
Gamelan Amadindas, **3**:1018
Gamelan Galak Tika, **3**:1019
Gamelan Pacifica, **3**:1017
Gamelan Sekar Jaya, **3**:*1019*, 1019–20
Gamelan Son of Lion Ensemble, **3**:324, 953,
    1016, *1016*, 1018
Gamelan Toronto, **3**:1216
Gamelan Venerable Sir Voice of Thoom, **3**:1018
games and pastimes. *See also* martial arts; sports;
    string figures
    Ainu people, **7**:786
    Athapaskan *udzi*, **3**:387, *387*, 390
    Baluan, **9**:259
    Bellona, **9**:267–69
      babange'anga, **9**:850
    children's singing games, **3**:285–86
    China, Dolan *mäsräp*, **6**:992
    Cook Islands, **9**:897, 903
    Danish, **3**:882–83
    Fiji, **9**:263–65, 775
    Great Lakes moccasin games, **3**:456, 458
    Inuit juggling games, **3**:1275
    Inuit *katajjaq* (throat games), **3**:376, *377*,
      1063, 1275
    Kiribati, **9**:762
    Korea, **7**:930
    Kosrae, **9**:742
    Luangiua, **9**:843–44
    Marquesas Islands, **9**:892
    Marshall Islands, **9**:751
    Mongol people, **7**:1003
    Nauru, **9**:261, 755, 756
    New Caledonia, **9**:672
    New Mexican dancing games, **3**:760
    Oceania, **9**:252–53, 321
    Palau, **9**:723
    Papua New Guinea
      New Britain, **9**:623
      Nissan Atoll, **9**:638–39
      Nissan *tiko*, **9**:635
      Umboi Island, **9**:574
    Plains Indian groups, **3**:441, 449
    play-party games, **3**:598–99
    Rotuma, **9**:818–19
    Russian Old Believers, **3**:917
    Sāmoa, **9**:804–5
    Siberia, **7**:1030
    Solomon Islands, **9**:656
      Blablanga songs, **9**:657
      Isabel Province, **9**:661
      Sirovanga people, **9**:655
    Swedish, **3**:871
    Tokelau, **9**:827
    Tonga, **9**:787–88
    'Uvea, **9**:812

Vanuatu, **9**:691
West Futuna, **9**:862
Yokuts hand-game songs, **3**:416
Gami, **5**:687
Gamilaraay people, **9**:442
Gamilla, Alice Doria, **4**:884
Gammon, Vic, **8**:339
Gamô Satoaki, **7**:593
Gan Tao, **7**:229
Ganam, King, **3**:1091, 1125
Ganapathi, Krishnamoorthy, **3**:*988*
Gan-a-tsui (performing group), **7**:425
Ganbar, Baba, **6**:976
Ganbayar, **7**:1020
Gand, Hans in der, **8**:695
Ganda people
    amadinda playing, **1**:602
    dance, **1**:112
    ennanga harp, **1**:302
    lyres of, **1**:600
    rhythmic organization, **1**:210
    xylophone playing, **1**:36
Gandert, Miguel, A., **3**:849
Gandhara kingdom, **5**:14, 489; **7**:22
Gandharva (heavenly beings), **5**:399
Gandharva, Kumar, **5**:424
Gandharva Sangeet Mahavidyalaya (Bombay),
    5:444, 447, 466
Gandharva Sangeet Mahavidyalaya (Lahore),
    5:444, 466
Gandharva, Sawai, **5**:413
Gandhi, Mohandas K. (Mahatma), **2**:352; **5**:9,
    436, 624, 866
    favorite *bhajan* of, **5**:267
Ganesh (also Ganapati) (deity), **5**:*497*, 520
    visual depictions of, **5**:301
    worship of, **5**:120, 121, 150, 211, 216, 220,
      223, 225–26, 281, 494, 645, 738,
      892, 940
Gang dynasty, **5**:731
Ganga (deity), **5**:892, 898
Gangadharam, Nedunuri, **5**:891
Gangari people, **9**:441
Gangoly, Ordhendra Coomar, **5**:46, 56, 313, 318
Gann, Kyle, **3**:177
Gans, Herbert, **3**:302
Gansbourg, Hersh, **10**:130
Gansemans, Jas, **2**:931
Gant, Cecil, **3**:646
Gante, Pedro de, **2**:23
Ganzhouge (*shifangu* suite), **7**:239
Ganzhu'er (Tibetan collection), **7**:472
Gao, George, **3**:345, 1064, 1083, 1217
Gao Houyong, **7**:233, 242
Gao Yi, **7**:229
Gao Ziming, **7**:229–30
Gaoseng zhuan (Buddhist text), **7**:328
Gaos-i Azam, **5**:779–80
Gaozong, Qing emperor, **7**:480
Gaozu, Han emperor, **7**:335
Gap Band, **3**:684
Gapur, **5**:*783*
garamuts. *See* slit-drums
Garant, Serge, **3**:1076, 1151
Garasia people, **5**:639

Garay, Narciso, **2:**649, 783
Garay, Sindo, **2:**831
Garbarek, Jan, **8:**428–29, 430, 431
García, Adelina, **3:**739, 741
García, Aleixo, **2:**453
Garcia, Antonio (ethnomusicologist), **3:**429
García, Antonio (pianist), **4:**866, 868
García Caturla, Alejandro, **2:**828, 837
García, Charly, **2:**104, 268
García, Digno, **2:**456–57
García Flores, Raúl, **2:**573
García, Fulgencio, **2:**393, 394, 395
García, Hector, **10:**87
García, Jesús, **2:**529
García Jofré de Loaisa, Fray, **2:**250
García López, Patricia, **10:***91*
García Lorca, Federico, **4:**878; **8:**598
García, Manuel, **3:**181
Garcia, Manuela, **3:**736–37
García Matos, Manuel, **8:**601
García, Raúl, **3:**763
García, Silvia P., **2:**256–57
Garcías (*trovo*), **3:**758, 762
Garcilaso de la Vega, "El Inca," **2:**23, 37, 207,
    223, 467, 468
Gardel, Carlos, **2:**93, *245*, 263, 519
Garden, Mary, **8:**370
Gardissat, Paul, **9:**140
Gardner, Fletcher, **4:**872
Gardner, Newport, **3:**603
Gardner, Robert, **9:**50
Garfias, Robert, **2:**736; **4:**26, 383, 386–89,
    391–92, 394; **7:**595, 976; **10:**82
Garfinkle, Buena Sarfatty, **3:**1172
Gargi, Balwant, **10:**6–8
Garífuna (Garifuna) culture
    in Belize, **2:**666, 668–77
    in Guatemala, **2:**733–34, 737
    history of, **2:**668–69, 733, 740, 752
    in Honduras, **2:**668–69, 740–41
    musical genres
        chumba, **2:**733–34
        jungujugu, **2:**733, 734
        jungujugu de Chugu, **2:**733–34
        parranda (or paranda), **2:**675, 733–34
        punta, **2:**675, 733–34, 741
        punta rock, **2:**675, 676–77, 733
        sambay (or senbai), **2:**676, 733–34
        yankunú, **2:**733–34
    in Nicaragua, **2:**747, 749, 752–53
    research on, **2:**679
    ritual music of, **2:**669–73
    secular music of, **2:**673–76
Garip, **6:**80, 81, 82, 85
Garland, Judy, **3:**551
Garland, Phyl, **3:**584
Garlic Ballads (Mo), **7:**259
Garmana, Gan-gan, **4:***716*
Garnås, Agnes Buen, **8:**422, 427–28, 430–31
Garner, Loyal, **9:**167
Garofalo, Reebee, **3:**586
Garova, Ani, **8:**283
Garove Island (Papua New Guinea), **9:**607–8
Garranah, Rif'at, **6:**612
Garrett, Kenny, **3:**665
Garrido, Edna, **2:**861

Garrido Lecca, Celso, **2:**486
Garrido, Nelson, **2:**544
Garrison, Jimmy, **3:**662
Garrison, Lucy McKim, **3:**29, 506, 523–24,
    574–75
Garrison, Wendell, **3:**575
Garshāspnāma (epic), **6:**344
Garside, A. LaMoyne, **9:**972
Garst, Dan, **9:**699, 702
Garst, John, **3:**576
Garteveld, Wilhelm N., **8:**776
Gartz, Vladimir, **7:**377
Garvan, John, **4:**873
Garvey, Marcus, **2:**689, 904
Garvin, Paul, **9:**994
Garvi Valin caste, **5:**476
Gary (and his band), **2:**275, 276, 277, 280
Garza, David Lee, **3:**776
Garza Marcue, Rosa María, **2:**568
Garzón y Collazos (Colombian duo), **2:**387
Gasca, Luis, **3:**798
Gasher, Mike, **3:**1067
Gaskin, Jody Thomas, **3:**1063, 1087
Gaskin, Lionel John Palmer, **1:**49
Gáspár, Veriska, **8:**136
Gaspé, Philippe Aubert de, **3:**1164, 1165
Gassmann, Alfred Leonz, **8:**692
Gassyô no tameno konpozisyon (Mamiya), **7:**736
Gaston, Bruce, **3:**954; **4:**128, 286
Gaston, E. Thayer, **3:**278
Gastón Pérez, Rafael, **2:**766
gat, **5:**130–32, 135, 188–99
    ālāp section, **5:**199
    amīrkhānī, **5:**189
    concept of, **5:**189
    concert performances of, **5:**203–4
    do muhī, **5:**193
    firozkhānī, **5:**126, 189, 193–94
    jhālā section, **5:**194, 199, 203
    jor section, **5:**199
    masītkhānī, **5:**125, 126, 189–91, 197, 202,
        206
    razākhānī, **5:**126, 191–93, 197, 206
    styles of, **5:**133–34, 189–98
    tān kī, **5:**193
    zamzamā, **5:**193
Gāthā caste, **5:**702
Gathman, Beth, **9:**566
Gatica, Arturo, **2:**372
Gatica, Lucho, **2:**372
Gaua Island (Vanuatu), **9:**699
Gauda caste, **5:**738
Gaudīya sect, **5:**247–48, 253–54, 502–3
Gaugers (musical group), **8:**372
Gaughan, Dick, **8:**372
Gaulish culture, **8:**552, 558
Gaunt, Percy, **3:**193, 544
Gaup, Ingor Ántte Áitu, **8:***300, 301*, 429
Gauri (deity), **5:**646, 892, 898
Gauri kalyāṇam (song), **5:**274
Gautama, Siddhartha (Buddha), **5:**12, 399–400
Gauthier, Claude, **3:**1156
Gauthier, Conrad, **3:**1154, 1166
Gauthier, Dominique, **3:**1167
Gauthier, Eva, **3:**1149
Gavana (musical group), **5:***736*

Gavino, Joaquin, **4:**856
Gaviota label, **3:**781
Gavīt people, **5:**727
gavotte, **2:**396; **8:**559, 594
Gavriel, Shoni, **6:**1034
Gavrielov, Miki, **6:**1073
Gavrilin, Valery, **8:**782
Gay Gaieties, **1:**433
Gay, John, **3:**542; **8:**17
Gaye, Marvin, **3:**552, 674, 676, 677, 709, 711;
    10:78
Gayï nomads, **6:**966
Gaynor, Gloria, **3:**228, 711
Gayo people, **4:**601, 603, 647
    instruments of, **4:**605
Gayuma (Carluén), **4:**857
gazel, **6:**116, 117, 120, 121, 196, 773, 782. *See
    also ghazal*
Gazimihâl, Mahmut Ragıp, **6:**79, 83
Gazzaniga, Marietta, **3:**60
Gbalagume, Antoine, **1:***653*
Gbambiya people, **1:**267
Gbarbea, James, **10:**61
Gbaya people
    song texts, **1:**137
    tuning systems, **1:**257, 263, 267
Gbeho, Phillip, **1:**33–34, 35
Gbɔnda, Seku, **1:**333, *334*
Ge Hong, **7:**320
Gebusi people, **9:**173
    dance of, **9:**490
    music and dance of, **9:**977
    songs of, **9:**491
Geck, Adelheid, **8:**26
Geddes, John, **8:**369
Gedikli, Necati, **6:**775
"Gee" (Crows), **3:**351, 709
"Gee, Baby, Ain't I Good to You" (Cole), **3:**669
"Gee Whiz" (Thomas), **3:**676
Geedow, Caweys, **1:***614*
Geens, Hubert, **8:**522
Geering, Arnold, **8:**695
Ge'erxiangai jiefengjun (Yu), **7:**185
Geertz, Clifford, **1:**518; **10:**43
Geia, Joe, **9:**145, 146
Geijer, Erik Gustaf, **8:**136, 447
Geiringer, Karl, **10:**3
Geisser, Kasi, **8:**689
Geizyutuza (theatrical troupe), **7:**743
Gelao people, **7:**485–92
Geld oder Leben (album), **8:**677
Geldard, Alison. *See* Arnold, Alison Geldard
Geldof, Bob, **8:**216
Gelele, king of Dahomey, **1:**86
Gélinas, Gratiens, **3:**198
Gell, Alfred, **9:**314
"Gema" (Tierra), **3:**748
Gems for the Guitar (Holland), **3:**605
Genbaku syôkei (Hayasi), **7:**736
Genc Abdal, **6:**796
Gencebay, Orhan, **6:**256, 258
Gencebay, Osman, **6:**776
gender. *See also* sex and music; sexual
    differentiation
    Arab-Islamic concepts, **6:**299–307
    in Australian music, **9:**241–45

Berber concepts, **6:**299–303
chimbanguele sets, **2:**531
clothing and, **9:**348
concept of, **9:**127
of Cuban drums, **2:**831
"feminine" and "masculine" instruments, **3:**95
identity and, **3:**149, 506, 1061
instrument classification, **2:**653, 723, 733, 897; **5:**306
instrument pairs
    clarinets, **2:**178–79
    drums, **2:**402
    flutes, **2:**153, 184–85, 640–41
    panpipes, **2:**33–34, 151, 285, 295, 358
    rattles, **2:**526
Mongol instrument parts, **7:**1010, 1013
New Caledonia, botanical symbolism, **9:**685
in New Guinean music, **9:**245–46
Papua New Guinea
    of flutes, **9:**565
    of instruments, **9:**649
raga classifications, **5:**47, 72–73, 313
research on, **3:**87–99, 103–14, 561–63, 928
'Uvea, *hiva*, **9:**810
Vanuatu
    of directionality, **9:**691
    of instruments, **9:**693
    of vocal composition, **9:**692
Yemen, musical categories, **6:**305
Gendron, Bernard, **3:**583
General Allotment (Dawes) Act (1887), **3:**443
"General Green's March," **3:**839
"General Lafayette's Grand March" (Johnson), **3:**604
Generation X (musical group), **3:**357
Genesis (musical group), **3:**356; **6:**250
Genevieve, Saint, **8:**546
Genghis Khan. *See* Chinggis
Genmei, emperor of Japan, **7:**645
Genovese, Eugene D., **3:**84
"*gens de mon pays, Les*" (Vigneault), **3:**1156, 1173
Gente (Afro-Peruvian group), **2:**501
Gentile de Fabriano, **8:***70*
"Gentle Annie" (Foster), **3:**187
Gentle Shepherd (Ramsay), **8:***17*
Gentry, Howard S., **2:**554
Genzi (Genji) clan, **7:**586, 631, 646
Genzi [Genji] monogatari (Murasaki), **7:**28, 79, 550, *644*, 696
Geoffrey of Monmouth, **8:**186, 322
Geological and Natural History Survey of Canada, **3:**291
Georg-August-Universität (Göttingen), **8:**182
George IV, king of England, **8:**185
George V, king of England, **8:**186
George VI, king of England, **8:**186
George, Rev. Ezekiel, **5:**924
George, Graham, **3:**1135
George, Nelson, **3:**584, 586, 708, 713, 714
George, Sergio, **3:**799
George Wade and the Cornhuskers, **3:**1190
George Washington, Jr. (Cohan), **3:**544
George White's Scandals (Gershwin), **3:**545

Georgia (country), **8:**826–47. *See also* Abkhazian people
    Abkhazia, **8:**826, 851–54
    Achara, Ottoman rule in, **8:**826, 835–36
    art music in, **8:**843–44
    dance traditions of, **8:**165, 834, 836, 841
    ethnic minorities in, **8:**12
    ethnographic districts in, **8:**827–28
    geography of, **8:**826
    history of, **8:**826–27, 851
    history of music in, **8:**842–44
    instruments, **8:**837–41, 845, 846
    Iranian dance traditions in, **6:**877, 878
    map of, **8:***752, 827*
    music-making in, **8:***8*
    Ossetian people, accordions, **8:**197, 200
    pagan rituals, **8:**835–36
    popular music in, **8:**845
    population of, **8:**826
    research on music of, **8:**846–47
    state folk ensembles in, **8:**840–41, 844–45
    Tbilisi, instrumental music in, **8:**840
    urban music in, **8:**840, 841–42
    village music after collectivization, **8:**844–45
    vocal music, **8:**828–34, 842
        laments, **8:**196
        polyphony, **8:**14, 753, 827–30, *831–32*, 835, 836, 847
Georgia (state)
    African-American composers in, **3:**605
    Athens, indie music in, **3:**171
    Atlanta
        as center for country music, **3:**76, 559
        dance in, **3:**208
        South Asian people in, **3:**981
    gospel music in, **10:**145
    harvest celebrations, **3:**599
    Native American groups in, **3:**466
    Savannah, singing societies, **3:**275
    Sea Islands, **3:**574, 601
Georgia Minstrels, **3:**192
Georgia Satellites (musical group), **3:**348
"Georgia Tom." *See* Dorsey, Thomas A.
Georgian people
    in Azerbaijan, **8:**826
    in Turkey, **8:**826
Georgian Polytechnic Institute, **8:**845
Georgian State Ensemble of Folk Songs, **8:**845
Georgian Voices (musical group), **8:**845
Geoulah (musical group), **3:**1174
Gera, Azzaj, **1:**147
Geraghty, Paul, **9:**968
Gerard, Charlie, **2:**93
Gerbrands, Adrian A., **9:**976
Gerdan (musical group), **3:**1198
Gereformeerde Blues Band, **1:**780
Geri-Geri (god), **8:**857
Gerineldo (group), **3:**1077, 1173–75, *1173*
Gerini, G. E., **4:**285, 303
German Baptist Brethren, **3:**904
German Democratic Republic (former)
    cultural policies in, **8:**661–62
    music research in, **8:**664
    rock in, **8:**217, 219–20
German Federal Republic (former), folk revival in, **8:**661

German Folk-Song Archive, **8:**19
German people, **2:**4
    in Brazil, **2:**308, 309
    in Central America, **2:**660
    in Eastern Europe, **8:**664, *665*
    in Hawai'i, **9:**96, 100
    in Hungary, **8:**736
    identity issues of, **2:**61
    in Italy, **8:**617
    in Mexico, **2:**613; **3:**9, 213, 773
    in Nicaragua, **2:**753–54
    in North America, **3:**10, 528, 537, 828, 884–91
        Baltic Germans, **3:**878
        community music-making, **3:**284
        folk music of, **3:**884–85, 888
        Hawai'i, **3:**527
        Jewish, **3:**934
        Manitoba Mennonites, **3:**52–53, 1237–39
        Maritime Provinces, **3:**1114
        Ontario, **3:**1188, 1195
        Prairie Provinces, **3:**1086, 1249–50
        Québec, **3:**1073–74
        religion of, **3:**118–19
        religious music of, **3:**886–87
        secular music of, **3:**887–91
        singing societies, **3:**885–86
        Texas, **3:**213, 773
        Volga Germans, **3:**890, *891*
        western Canada, **3:**292
        Wisconsin, **10:**160
    in Paraguay, **2:**55, 462
    in Poland, **8:**701
    reimmigrants, **8:**664
    in Romania, **8:**868, 883, 886
    in Russia, **8:**767, 772
    in South America, **2:**38–40, 84, 89
    in Serbia, **8:**952
    in Ukraine, **8:**821
German Seventh-Day Baptists, **3:**904–7
German Society of Winnipeg, **3:**1249
Germania Choir (Hamilton), **3:**1195
Germania Musical Society, **3:**537, 1180
Germania Orchestra, **3:**556, 557
Germanisches Nationalmuseum (Nuremburg), **8:**182
Germano, Claudionor, **2:**337
Germany, **8:**646–65
    art music in, **8:**69, 75, 646, 653–54, 655, 663
    Baden-Württemberg, folk-music pedagogy, **8:**659
    Bavaria, **8:**646
        dance traditions of, **8:**166
        folk-music pedagogy, **8:**659
        guitar in, **8:**658
        Stubenmusi bar-music ensemble, **8:**143, 656
    Bayreuth, theater in, **8:**83
    Berlin
        cabaret in, **8:**252
        immigrant music in, **8:**231
        Jewish community of, **8:**257, 262, 266
    cabaret in, **8:**252, 659–60
    Carolingian period in, **8:**69
    court music, **8:**146
    dance traditions of, **8:**166, 655
    dissemination of music in, **8:**652

Germany (*continued*)
eastern *vs.* western cultures, **8:**12
Folklore und Mitmachen movement, **8:**153–54
Frankfurt
Jewish community of, **8:**257
world music in, **8:**210
geography of, **8:**646
Harz Mountains, yodeling in, **8:**651
history of, **8:**646
Hunsrück region, **8:**259
ideology in, **8:**185, 187, 659–62
immigrant groups in, **8:**231, 237
influence on Finnish songs, **8:**477
influence on Swedish music, **8:**435
instrumental music of, **8:**651–52, 653–54
instrument collections in, **8:**175, 182
instruments, **8:**170, 651–52, 653–55, 656
research on, **8:**35, 37, 38
map of, **8:***644*
modern dance in, **8:**161
Munich, cabaret in, **8:**252
nationalist movement, **8:**59
Nazism, **6:**1026; **8:**660–61, 664
treatment of Rom people, **8:**271, 276, 289
organ-building in, **8:**78
popular music, **8:**659–60
population of, **8:**646
research on music of, **8:**17, 18, 19, 662–65
reunification of, **8:**222
Rhineland, **8:**646
St. Martin's Day procession, **8:**657
rock in, **8:**216, 222
Rom people in, **8:**288–89
rule over Estonia, **8:**491
Russian Jews in, **8:**265
Sorb people in, **8:**172
theater, *liederspiele,* **8:**141
Turkish people in, **8:**11, 210, 237
unification of, **8:**10
urbanization of, **8:**13
vocal music, **8:**75, 133, 185, 650–51, 652–53
ballads, **8:**23, 136, 195
women's performances in, **8:**200
Worms, Jewish community of, **8:**248
Gero, Lorenzo, **2:**586
Gerrits, Egbert, **8:**136
Gerry and the Pacemakers, **8:**214
Gershwin, George, **2:**114, 962; **3:**174, 196, 530, 539, 545, 549, 608, 621, 648, 707
Gershwin, Ira, **3:**621
Gerson-Kiwi, Edith, **6:**524, 525, 1029, 1036, 1058–59, 1060, 1062, 1063, 1065, 1066; **8:**266
Gervaise, Nicolas, **4:**222, 225, 248, 284
Gesang, **4:**103
Gesäng der einsamen und verlassenen Turtel-Taube, Das (Ephrata Cloister), **3:**905
Geschichte der Musik (Ambros), **8:**266
Geschichte des transalpinischen Daciens (Sulzer), **8:**885
Gesellschaft der Musikfreunde (Vienna), **8:**81, 732
Gesellschaft für die Volksmusik in der Schweiz, **8:**696
Geser (epic). *See Tale of King Gesar*

Geshuri, Me'ir Shim'on, **6:**1060
Gessler, Aleksei, **8:**287
Gessner, Conrad, **8:**688
gestures. *See* dance and movement
"Get Off the Track" (Hutchinson Family), **3:**184
"Get Up, Get into It, and Get Involved" (Brown), **3:**677
Getek's Band, **4:**718
Geto Boys, **3:**699, 702
Getu, Chief, **9:**661
Getz, Russell P., **3:**907
Getz, Stan, **3:**659, 660; **8:**445
Gguq qil (Naxi song), **7:**511
Ghajar people, **6:**625
Ghalib, Mirza Asadullah Khan, **5:**184
Ghana. *See also* West Africa; *specific peoples*
academic training in, **1:**24–34, 39
Anlo Ewe people, dance, **1:**289
Ashanti kingdom in, **1:**4
Ashanti people
dance, **1:**109
speech surrogate methods, **1:**107
Brong people, *apoo* festival, **1:**287
composition in, **1:**22, 44, 220–21
"concert party" genre, **1:**407
dance, **1:**289, 290
drumming, notation of, **1:**158–59
drumming techniques in, **3:**335
drums, **2:**529
cord-and-peg tension, **1:**315–17
durbar ceremony, **1:**137–38
Effutu people, *aboakyere* festival, **1:**287
Ewe people, **1:**35
dance, **1:**109
rural-urban interchange, **1:**389–99
speech surrogate methods, **1:**107
Fanti people, **1:**112; **10:**29–36
Gã people, **1:**102–5, 463
dance, **1:**109, 113, 114, 117
guitar band competition, **1:**362
guitar in, **1:**355, 356, 366, 367
history of, **10:**31–36
independence of, **3:**336, 661, 662
iron bells, **1:**310
Kasena-Nankani people, dance, **1:**109
Kru people, **1:**373, 374–75, 377
LoDagaa people, **1:**456–57
musical scholarship in, **1:**22–26
music research in, **1:**47, 49; **10:**142–43, 145–49
national anthem of, **1:**34
national festivals, **1:**394–95
orchestral music in, **1:**226
Pan-African Orchestra, **1:**211
politics in, **1:**7, 24–25, 30, 34
popular music of, **1:**419, 422–23
processions, **1:**138
research on music of, **1:**285, 458
Tallensi people, masks of, **1:**119
Ghana (kingdom), **1:**4, 75, 456
Ghana Music Society, **1:**31, 35
Ghana National Dance Ensemble, **1:**395
Ghanaian people
in Canada, **3:**1213
in England, **8:**231
Ghanam, Victor, **6:**284

Ghānim, Kalthūm 'Alī, **6:**651
Ghānim, Muḥammad, **6:**502
Ghantasala, **5:**421
al-Gharabli, al-Hajj Ahmad, **6:**496
gharānā, **5:**15, 189, 377–78, 460, 465–67, 526, 746
Agra, **5:**443, 465
Agra *khyāl* style, **5:**83, 172, *174–76*, 177
Ajrara *tabla*, **5:**133–34, 136
Atrauli, **5:**460, 465
Banaras, **5:**494
Banaras *tabla*, **5:**133–34, 136, 137, 342
bānsurī, **5:***768*
clarinet, **5:***768*
compared with *bāj*, **5:**378–79
Dagar *bānī*, **5:**378
Delhi sitar, **5:**189–90
Delhi *tabla*, **5:**133–34, 136, 342
development of, **5:**373, 375
Faizabad *tabla*, **5:**133
Farrukhabad *tabla*, **5:**133–34, 136
Gwalior, **5:**206, 443–44, 465–66, *767*
Gwalior *khyāl* style, **5:**83, 177
Imdadkhan, **5:**465
Jaipur, **5:***493*, 494, 640
Jaipur *khyāl* style, **5:**83, 126, 410
Jaipur Seniyā sitar, **5:**190–91, 206, 378
Jhajjar *tabla*, **5:**133
kajalī, **5:**668
Khan, Amir, lineage, **5:**526
Khan, Ghulam Ali, lineage, **5:**194
Khan, Imdad, lineage, **5:**195, 196, 205–6
khyāl, **5:**83, 134, 176–77, 378
Kirana, **5:**465
Kirana *khyāl* style, **5:**177–78, 410, 413; **10:**10
Lahore *tabla*, **5:**133–34, 136
Laliyana *tabla*, **5:**134, 136, 137
Lucknow, **5:**494
Lucknow *tabla*, **5:**55, 123, *129*, 130–31, 132, 133–34, 136, 137, 342
Maihar, **5:**204, 206, 465–67
men's domination of, **5:**409
nonhereditary Hindu musicians, **5:**376
Papurthala, **5:***767*
Patiala, **5:**410, 465, *767*, 807
Punjab, **5:**766, *767–68*
raga conceptions in, **5:**83–84
raga theories, **5:**67
rubāb, **5:***768*
sārangī, **5:**368, *768*
sarod, **5:**337, *768*
Senī Baba Allauddin, **5:**204
Sham Chaurasi, **5:***767*
sitar, **5:***768*
studies on, **5:**57
success of system, **5:**381
tabla, **5:**133–34, 136, 342, 378–79, *768*
Talvandi, **5:***767*
vocal, **5:**379
Gharanon ki Gayaki (album), **5:**528
Gharibzadeh group, **5:**820–22
al-Gharīd, **6:**296
Ghatak, Anupam, **5:**857
Ghāyat al-maṭlūb fī 'ilm al-anghām wa-'l-ḍurūb (Ibn Kurr), **6:**366
Ghayyathī, Dān, **6:***413*

Volume Key: **1,** Africa; **2,** South America, Mexico, etc.; **3,** United States and Canada; **4,** Southeast Asia; **5,** South Asia

ghazal, **5:**107, 162, 179, 183–86, 192, 256; **8:**232, 240. *See also gazel*
Afghanistan, **5:**818, 819–20, 827, 828, *829*
Kabuli, **5:**805–7, 835
Bengal, **5:**853–54, 855, 856
dance performances of, **5:**494
decline of, **5:**376
development of, **5:**373
film-song versions of, **5:**533, 534, 540
Guyana, **5:**602
history of, **5:**184
influence on pop *bhajan,* **5:**255
international popularity of, **5:**748
Iran, **6:**60, 135–36, 140, 825, 833, 862, 863
Kashmir, **5:**687
Malaysia, **4:**438–39
North America, **5:**579, 581
Pakhtun people, **5:**786
patronage of, **5:**435
performance of, **5:**186
performers of, **5:**425, 749–50
pop, **5:**186, 381, 412, 534, 548–49
Punjab, **5:**766, 771
Rajasthan, **5:**644
Singapore, **4:**520
Sri Lanka, **5:**970
Sumatra, **4:**616
talas for, **5:**127
texts of, **5:**184–85
Trinidad, **5:**591
Uighur settings, **6:**1003
United Kingdom, **5:**573
Uzbekistan, **6:**944
women performers of, **5:**410, 411, 412, 424
Yemen, **6:**301, 685–86
al-Ghazālī, Abū Ḥamid, **6:**19, 360, 373
al-Ghazālī, Majd al-Dīn, **6:**19, 373
al-Ghazālī, Naẓīm, **6:**314–15
Ghaznavid empire, **5:**804
Ghaznavi, Rafique, **5:**420
Ghiās, Ata, **6:**917
Ghiaurov, Nikolai, **8:**890
Ghidinelli, Azzo, **2:**740
Al-ghinā' al-Yamanī al-qadīm wa mashāhiruh (Nājī), **6:**358
Ghoneim, Mona, **6:**612
Ghorbat group, **5:**815
Ghorid empire, **5:**804
Ghorwane (musical group), **1:**429, 436
Ghose, Aurobindo, **5:**436
Ghosh, Bikram, **5:**62
Ghosh, Jnan Prakash, **5:**136, 137, *207*
Ghosh, Manomohan, **5:**57
Ghosh, Mrinal Kanti, **5:**855
Ghosh, Nachiketa, **5:**857
Ghosh, Pannalal, **5:**205, 339–40
Ghosh, Rathin, **5:**254
Ghosh, Shankar, **5:**136
Ghost Dance Religion and the Sioux Outbreak of 1890 (Mooney), **3:**31
"Ghost Riders in the Sky" (Jones), **3:**490, 1142–43
Ghost Singer (Walter), **3:**493
Ghouri, Moulana Hasan, **5:**690
Ghrenassia, Sylvain, **6:**1044
Ghulam Hassan, **5:**807

Ghulmiyya, Walīd, **6:**554
Ghuzlūn, **6:**456
Giacometti, Michel, **8:**585
Giannattasio, Francesco, **1:**610–11
"Giant Steps" (Coltrane), **3:**337, 662
Giáo Tiên, **4:**473
Gibbon, John Murray, **3:**146, 343, 1166
Gibbons, Walter, **3:**688
Gibbs, Georgia, **3:**352
Gibbs, James, **1:**128–29
Gibøen, Håvard, **8:**412, 417
Gibran, Khalil, **6:**279
Gibril, Mohammad, **6:**162
Gibson, Don, **3:**80, 81
Gibson, Eric "King Eric," **2:**806
Gibson, "Jockey" Jack, **3:**708
Gibson, Richard, **3:**1072
Gidabal people, **9:**441
Gideon, Miriam, **3:**90
Giess, Michel, **6:**608
Gifford, E. W., **9:**24
Gifford, Kathie Lee, **3:**107
Giganti (musical group), **8:**619
Gigimat, Ilaita, **9:**480
gigue, **3:**223, 344; **8:**168. *See also* jig
"G.I. Jive" (Jordan), **3:**668
Gil, Gilberto, **2:**109–10, 318, 351
Ġila, Amare, **8:**289
Gilbertese people
in Guadalcanal, **9:**712
in Hawai'i, **9:**105, 847
in Sikaiana, **9:**845, 847
Gilbert, Mrs. H. E., **3:**1180
Gilbert, Henry F., **3:**14, 367, 521; **10:**128
Gilbert Islands (Kiribati), **9:**712, 715, 754, 758, 823. *See also* Kiribati
Christianity in, **9:**720
films on, **9:**982
music and dance of, **9:**719, 969
outsiders' influence in, **9:**5
settlement of, **9:**715
sound recordings from, **9:**994
Gilbert, Ronnie, **3:**328, *329*
Gilbert, William S., **2:**447; **3:**193, 544, 840, 1117, 1225, *1226*, 1228
Gilberto, João, **2:**317
Gilberto Pérez y Sus Compadres, **3:**776
Gilchrist, Anne, **8:**373
Gilday, Bill, **3:**1277, 1280
Gilday, Leela, **3:**1276, 1280
Gildo, Rex, **8:**208
Gill, William Wyatt, **9:**21
Gille, Philippe, **9:**38
Gillen, F. J., **9:**987
Gillespie, John Birks "Dizzy," **3:**34, *34*, 522, 658, 659, 732, 787, 793, 797; **4:**96; **8:**445
Gillett, Charlie, **3:**673, 709
Gillett, Dorothy K., **9:**315
Gilley, Mickey, **3:**81
Gilliat, Simeon, **3:**596
Gillies, Anne Lorne, **8:**363
Gillis, Frank, **10:**28
Gillis, Jackson, **3:**312
Gillis, Verna, **2:**862
Gillum, Jazz, **3:**645

Gilman, Benjamin, **3:**509; **8:**94
Gilmatam, John, **9:***305*
Gilmore, Patrick S., **3:**189, 277, 536, 556, 565, 604
Gilmore's Band, **3:**565
Gilroy, Paul, **3:**587
Gilyak people. *See* Nivkhi people
Gima, Clement, **9:**480, 986
Gimi people, **9:**526–33
Gina, Bill, **9:***27*
Ginastera, Alberto, **2:**115
Gingell, Judy, **3:***1277*
Ginling (Jinling) College, **7:**398
Ginn Publishing Company, **3:**276
Ginsberg, Allen, **3:**130
Ginsberg, Henry D., **4:**306
Ginsburg, S. M., **8:**266
Gintaras (dance ensemble), **3:**1196
Ginzburg, Semyon, **8:**784
Giobascus Vlachus, **8:**881
Gion Shrine (Kyôto), **7:**639, 684
Giorgetti, Filiberto, **1:**570
Gippius, Evgeny, **8:**757–58, 783–85, 803
Gipsy Kings (musical group), **3:**341; **8:**226, 276
Giraldus Cambrensis, **8:**349, 378, 393, 423
Giriama people, **1:**624, 627
Girl Crazy (Gershwin), **3:**545
"Girl I Left Behind Me," **3:**409
"Girl Is Mine" (Jackson and McCartney), **3:**713
Gironcourt, Georges de, **4:**26
Giroux, Robert, **3:**1076
Giselle (Adam), **8:**161
Gisi gakki zu (*min gaku* collection), **7:**725
Gisi gakuhu (*min gaku* collection), **7:**725
Gismonti, Egberto, **2:**108
Gisurdirāz, **6:**180
"Gitaa, Jonathan," **1:**353
Gītānjali (Tagore), **5:**850
Giurchescu, Anca, **8:***277*, 886
"Give My Regards to Broadway" (Cohan), **3:**193, 544
"Give Peace a Chance" (Lennon), **3:**318
"Give the People What They Want" (O'Jays), **3:**677
Gjurmime Albanologjike (periodical), **8:**1003
Glackemeyer, Frederick, **3:**1067, 1148
Gladys Knight and the Pips, **3:**677
Glanius, Mr., **4:**248
Glareanus, Heinrich, **8:**652
Glasnik Zemaljskog Muzeja u Sarajevu, **8:**970
Glass Orchestra (Toronto), **3:**1186
Glass, Philip, **3:**131, 176, 177, 204, 254, 335, 541, 953; **4:**132
Glasser, Stanley, **1:**219, 775
Glazer, Nathan, **3:**515
Gleason, Philip, **3:**504, 515
Gledhill, Edwin, **3:**1180
Glen family, **8:**373
Glinka, Mikhail, **6:**904; **8:**780
Glissant, Edouard, **2:**920
Global Unity Orchestra, **3:**664
GlobeStyle Records, **2:**106; **8:**240, 241
Globe Theatre (Barbados), **2:**819
Globokar, Vinko, **8:**26, 921
Glogauer Liederbuch, **8:**651
Glonar, Jože, **8:**922

Glover, J., **9**:*8*
Glover, Sarah, **8**:106
Gluck, Christoph Willibald, **8**:646, 727
Glutz, Alois, **8**:698
Glykeria, **8**:1020
Gnāwa people, **8**:233
    brotherhoods of, **1**:537
    history of, **1**:532
    in Morocco, **6**:403, 435, 487, 491–93
    music of, **1**:540, 542, 547
Gneist, W., **8**:661
Gnesin, Mikhail F., **8**:856
Goa, **5**:735–41, 881
    Chandor, **5**:740
    dhalo genre in, **5**:475
    geography of, **5**:735
    history of, **5**:735
    instruments in, **5**:737
    Jesuits in, **5**:257
    map of, **5**:*718*
    musical genres of, **5**:737–40
    population of, **5**:735
    research on music of, **5**:741
    studio musicians from, **5**:535
Goa, Sultanate of, **4**:779, 783
Goan people
    emigration patterns, **5**:735
    in Portugal, **8**:576
Goats (musical group), **3**:701
Goban Taiheiki (Chikamatsu), **7**:669
Gobbi, Alfredo, **2**:264, 519
Gobec, Radovan, **8**:921
Gobineau, Joseph-Arthur, Count, **6**:860
Godan ginuta (Mituzaki), **7**:698
Godard, Benjamin, **3**:1148
"God Be with You 'til We Meet Again," **9**:25
"God Bless America" (Berlin), **3**:196; **9**:25–26
Godelier, Maurice, **9**:42
Godfrey, Henry Herbert, **3**:1180
"Go Down, Moses" (spiritual), **3**:601
Godowsky, Leopold, **6**:1025
Godoy Aguirre, Mario, **2**:431
"God Save the King [Queen]," **3**:145, 521, 839;
    5:223, 433; **8**:186
Godzilla (film), **7**:751
Goebbels, Joseph, **8**:660
Goethe, Johann Wolfgang von, **8**:186, 646, 663;
    9:35
Goffin, Gerry, **3**:673
Go Go's (musical group), **3**:357
Go-Komatsu, emperor of Japan, **7**:641
Gogaji (deity), **5**:643
Gogo, Marie, **3**:*1280*
Gogo people, **1**:599, 635, 636; **10**:123
    lamellophones, **1**:317
    lutes of, **1**:641
    music of, **1**:604, 637, 638, 639
    ngoma drumming, **1**:312
    Tanzania, **1**:636
    zithers of, **1**:640
Gogodala people, **9**:491
Gogodala: A Cultural Revival? (film), **9**:42, 50
Gogol, Nicolai, **5**:487
Goilala people, **9**:491
Goisern, Hubert von, **8**:676
Goitein, S. D., **6**:21

Gojković, Andrijana, **8**:954
Gökalp, Ziya, **6**:782
Gokigen san yô tassya kane (Japanese popular
    song), **7**:746
Gokuraku zyôka (*syômyô* piece), **7**:617
Gola people, **1**:467
Golb, Norman, **6**:1065
Gold, Ann, **5**:674
Gold, Lisa, **3**:*1015*; **4**:733
Gold, Peter, **8**:847
Goldberg, Alan, **1**:134
Goldberg, Arthur, **3**:298
Gold Coast Spectator (periodical), **1**:355
Gold Coast Teachers' Journal, **1**:18–19, 24
Golden Boy (Odets), **3**:621
Golden Eagle, **3**:*6*
Golden Fleece (musical group), **8**:845
Golden Gate (gospel quartet), **3**:535, 632, *633*
Golden Keys (musical group), **3**:1195
Golden Star (musical group), **8**:241
"Golden Vanity" (ballad), **3**:834
Golder, Frank A., **3**:381
Goldfaden, Abraham, **3**:936
Goldman, Edwin Franko, **3**:566
Goldsmith, Jerry, **3**:204
Goldstein, Paul, **3**:257
Goldsworthy, David, **4**:603; **9**:973
Goleminov, Marin, **8**:905
Golla caste, **5**:898, 901, *902*
Golla Suddulu singers, **5**:902
Golob, Jani, **8**:921
"*Golondrina, La*" (Serradell), **2**:620
Golpasand, Ali Ahmad, **5**:822
Golpasand family, **5**:822–23
Golpasand, Gol Dasteh, **5**:*823*
Golpasand, Shahzadeh, **5**:*823*
Golpasand, Urak, **5**:*823*
Golynkin, Mark, **6**:1025
Gömbér, István, **8**:*742*
Gombert, Greg, **3**:428, 488
Gombitová, Marika, **8**:731
Gombrich, Ernst H., **8**:102
Gomburza (Monserrat/Lagdameo), **4**:885
Gomes, António Carlos, **2**:114, 115, 304, 305
Gomes, Edson, **2**:353
Gomes, Marcelina, **1**:306
Gomes da Rocha, Francisco, **2**:303
Gomme, Lady Alice, **8**:336
Gomon, Alla, **9**:23
Gò Mun culture, **4**:36, 40
Gon, David, **3**:1276, 1280
Gonashvili, Hamlet, **8**:845
Gond people, **5**:719, 720, 721–22, 727
Gonda, Jan, **5**:459
Gondinet, Edmond, **9**:38
Gong Hong-Yu, **9**:*931*
Gong 2000, **4**:110
Gong Zizhen, **7**:129
gongs
    aalakan, **4**:898
    Africa, **1**:107
    aguang, **4**:609
    agung, **4**:605, 615, *829*, 886, 892–93, 895,
        897–98, 899, 902, 924, *925*
    ahot, **4**:917
    ahuu, **4**:818

anamongu, **4**:788
anonan, **4**:897
arap, **4**:534
avong, **4**:534
babandil, **4**:892–93, 923
babandilanan, **4**:922
balbal, **4**:916
bandai, **4**:829, 830
bandil, **4**:830
basal, **4**:924
bendé, **4**:646
bende, **4**:623, 627, 709
bende (also *bebende*), **4**:742
benegulitok, **4**:921
blowon, **4**:921
bluck, **4**:540
bonang, **4**:20, 403, 644, 646, 656, 662, 685,
    690, 691, 692, *693*, 701, 704, 706–7;
    10:44, *45*, 47
bonang babok, **4**:641
bonang barung, **4**:641, 643, 669, 671–72, 677
bonang gambyong, **4**:644
bonang klènang, **4**:644
bonang panembung, **4**:643, 669
bonang panerus, **4**:641, 668, 671–72
Borneo, **4**:828–30
brass, **4**:602
bua, **4**:898, 900
bubundir, **4**:896–97
burnay, **4**:923
caklempong, **4**:422, 423
canang, **4**:404, 407, 412, *416*, 417, 421, 428,
    605, 623, 628, *829*
cĕkanti, **5**:915
celempong, **4**:615
cennala, **5**:360, 363
chiêng, **4**:467
chieng, **4**:590
Chinese, **3**:958–59, 961; **7**:*450*
    in Cantonese music, **7**:218
    in opera ensembles, **7**:285–86, 292
    in shawm and percussion groups, **7**:201
ching, **7**:67, *826*, 829, 870, 872–73, 933–34
    notation for, **7**:*936–37*
    in *samullori*, **7**:963–67
    in *sinawi*, **7**:890
ciwaiñ, **4**:367–68, *369*
còng, **4**:467
cultural origins of, **4**:11
dada, **4**:819, *820*
daldala, **4**:820
daluo, **3**:961
dang, **7**:312, 323
dangzi, **7**:201, 330
đầu, **4**:467
degung, **4**:107
didala ae, **4**:802
didala iki, **4**:802
doua neeb, **4**:*554*
duuduram, **7**:1017
duwahan, **4**:898
engkeromung, **4**:830
engkuk-kemong, **4**:642, 643, 659, 661
gagung pon, **4**:923–24
gagung thumbaga, **4**:923
gaha, **4**:802

galang, **4:**923
gandingan, **4:**892–93, 896, 923
gangha, **4:**917
gangsa, **3:**1026; **4:**23, 915
gelintang, **4:**623
geong, **4:**618
gereteh, **4:**414, 424
go, **4:**793
gong ageng
    Bali, **4:**740, 741, 742, 744, 745, 753, 755
    Cirebon, **4:**692
    Java, **4:**640, 641, 642, 643, 644, 654,
        659–60, 666
    Lombok, **4:**766
gong agung, **4:**403, *418,* 429
gong beleq, **4:**766
gong beri, **4:**741
gong gedhé, **4:**640
gong kodeq, **4:**767
gong lanang, **4:**741, 766
gong panimbul, **4:**626
gong penuntun, **4:**626
gong sabet, **4:**692
gong suwukan, **4:***418,* 429, 640
gong wadon, **4:**741, 766
go'ong, **4:**701, 703, 706, 707, 716
goujiao, **7:**205
gung, **4:**619, 624, 625, 628
hansa, **4:**918
haranga, **7:**1017
hibat, **4:**917
ho duc, **4:**534
Irian Jaya, **9:**582
in island Southeast Asia, **4:**596–97
Java, **4:**640–41
in jazz, **3:**132
jenglong, **4:**691, 706
kabolulu, **4:**789
kadua, **4:**916
kajar, **4:**742, 746, 749, 753, 767, 772, 774
kalsa, **4:**918
kane, **7:**617, 657, 684
kapat, **4:**916
Karen people, **4:**546
Karnataka, **5:**874
Kasena people, **1:**455
katala, **4:**789
katlo, **4:**916
kbolo, **4:**797
keb-ang, **4:**917
kebluk, **4:**691, 697
kelenang, **4:**755
kelintang, **4:**619, 627–28
kelitang, **4:**623
kelittang, **4:**627
kemong (also klentong), **4:**741–42, 767
kempli, **4:**742, 751, 753
kempul, **4:**403, 640, 641, 642, 645, 654, 659,
    703, 708, 767, 772
kempur, **4:**626, 740, 741–42, 745, 746, 748,
    749, 753, 754, 755
kempyang, **4:**641, 642, 644, 659, 661
kemyang, **4:**692, *693*
kenat, **4:**767, 772, 774
kenong
    Cirebon, **4:**691, 694

Java, **4:**641, 642, 644, 654, 659–60, 661,
    665, 666
Malaysia, **4:**403, 413, 429
Sumatra, **4:**626
Sunda, **4:**703
Kerala, **5:**324, 931
keromongan, **4:**623
kerumong, **4:**429
ketawa, **4:**625
ketawak, **4:**617
kethuk, **4:**641, 642, 644, 645, 654, 659–60,
    661, 666
ketuk, **4:**403, 691, 696, 697, 707
ketuk tilu, **4:**107
khah, **4:**534
khawng, **4:**230, 305, 311–12
khawng chai, **4:**230
khawng khu, **4:**230, 305, 307, 308
khawng kratae, **4:**230
khawng mawn, **4:**231
khawng meng, **4:**230
khawng mong, **4:**230, 266, 303, 309
khawng mong yai, **4:**305
khawng rang, **4:**230–31
khawng rao, **4:**230
khawng wong lek, **4:**231, 267, 270, 272
khawng wong yai, **4:**121, 231, *242,* 251, 262,
    270, 272, 277
khmuoh, **4:**165–66
khôngvông, **4:**215
khong vong, **4:**350, 354, 355, 358
kiwul, **4:**692, 694
kkwaenggwari, **7:**67, 817, *826,* 829, 933–34,
    944, *965*
    notation for, **7:***936–37*
    in *samullori,* **7:**963–67
klènang, **4:**691, 696
klentang, **4:**767
Kmhmu people, **4:**547
kolintang, **4:**810
kong thum, **4:**533
Korea, **7:**67
korng mong, **4:**165
korng tauch, **4:**183
korng thomm, **4:**183, 197
korng vung, **3:**1001; **4:**157, *158,* 197
korng vung tauch, **4:***164,* 165
korng vung thomm, **4:***164,* 165, 197
kulimbet, **4:**911
kulintang, **3:**1025–26; **4:**20, 628, 810, 886,
    891, 892–98, 908, 921
kundongan, **4:**897
kwintang, **4:**899
labuan, **4:**900
Lahu people, **4:**540
leko, **4:**802
lerukan, **4:**899
litokanan, **4:**922
luo, **7:**111, 276, 312, 323
magagung, **4:**828
Malaysia, **4:**19, 433
Maluku, **4:**820
mamongu, **4:**788
Manchu people, **7:**520
Mandailing sets of, **4:**607
matumusi, **7:**654

maùñ, **4:**371
maùñsaiñ, **4:**368–69, *370*
m'nhum, **4:**534
momo, **4:**814
momong, **4:**605
mong, **4:**211, 408, 412, 413, *416,* 428, 548,
    615, 616; **7:**499
mongmong, **4:**607
namangngu, **4:**802
nggaha, **4:**789
nggo, **4:**793, 794
ninai syôko, **7:**624
nyô, **7:**617
ogung, **4:**607
oncer, **4:**771
opop, **4:**916
orugôru, **7:**654
ô syôko, **7:**624
ote, **4:**797
palook, **4:**916
pamantikan, **4:**894
pan, **4:**312
pang hat, **4:**319
pangongka'an, **4:**900–901
paranjangu, **4:**789
patawaganan, **4:**922
patpat, **4:**917
pawwok, **4:**918
penagungguan, **4:**900
penanggisa-an, **4:**896–97
penontong, **4:**644
petuk, **4:**767, 771, 772, 773
Philippines, **4:**914–18, 921–24, *927*
pinsak, **4:**918
ponggang, **4:**643
power of, **4:**9–10
pulakan, **4:**898, 900
pumalsan, **4:**896–97
réong (also réyong), **4:**632, 690, 742, 745, 748,
    753, 767, 771, 772, 776
rincik, **4:**704, 706–7
Roti, **4:**800
rujih, **4:**623
rural areas, **4:**7
saliksik, **4:**918
sanang, **4:**924
sanj, **6:**395, 397
sapul, **4:**917
saragi, **4:**814
saua, **4:**414
Savu, **4:**802
selegai, **4:***829*
semagi, **4:**921–22
sembakung, **4:**921
sene, **4:**797
shiluo group, **7:**195
siyem, **4:**640, 641, 642, 654, 659, 661
slabon, **4:**923
soe, **7:**933–34
solembat, **4:**900–901
South Asia, **2:**29
Southeast Asia, **4:**20, 58
Sumatra, **4:**600
Sumba, **4:**788–89
Sumbawa, **4:**780–81
Surinam, **2:**507

gongs (*continued*)

syôko, **7:**572, 580, 624

tabaganan, **4:**922

tabuhan, **4:**623, 624

tagunggo, **4:**922, *923*

taklempong, **4:**414

tala, **4:**628, 788

tāla, **5:**885

talagutok, **4:**918

tale, **4:**623, 624

talempong, **4:**520, 609, 612

talo, **4:**628

talo balak, **4:**623, 627

talo tanggung, **4:**623, 627

tam âm la, **4:**467

tam-tam, **9:**96

tamuk, **4:**900

tang, **4:**921

tatabuang, **4:**815

tawag, **4:**830

tawak, **4:**615, 829–30

tawakan, **4:**617

tawak-tawak, **4:**615, 623, 772

tawa-tawa, **4:**742, 748

tembaga, **4:**921

tetawak

> Malaysia, **4:**404, 407, 411, 412, *416*, 417, *418*, 421, 428

> Sumatra, **4:**615, 617, 628

tetun, **4:**797

thanggunggu, **4:**923

thanh la, **4:**467

tilempong, **4:**605

tingkah, **4:**414

titir, **4:**821

tiyanggi, **4:**923

tobop, **4:**917

tonggu, **7:**108

topayya, **4:**916

totobuang, **4:**818, 819

trompong, **4:**20, 690, 734, 740, 742, 744, *745*, 746, 747, 755, 757

trompong barangan, **4:**745

trum, **4:**534

tsintsila, **8:**837

tulus, **4:**922

tunggalan, **4:**898

turi syôko, **7:**624

tutuntungan, **4:**898

ulla, **7:***826*, 830

unsaran, **4:**922

Vietnam, **4:**534

wenchang luo, **3:**960

wong khawng chai, **4:**230, 256

wo peibho abho, **4:**802

wuchang luo, **3:**960

wuluo group, **7:**195

xiangzhan, **7:**205

xiaoluo, **3:**961

yinqing, **7:**323, 330

yunluo, **7:**113, 191, 201, 203, 231, 315

> Tibet, **7:**480

> Yunnan, **7:***513*

Gonja people, **1:**222

"Gonna Find Her" (Tierra), **3:**748

Gonzaga, Chinquinha, **2:**305

Gonzaga, Luiz, **2:**332

Gonzales, Andy, **3:**799

Gónzales, Augusto, **2:**499

Gonzales, Bobby, **4:**884

Gonzales Holguín, Diego, **2:**467, 468

Gonzales, Jerry, **3:**799

Gonzales, Micky, **2:**486

González, Balde, **3:**778

González Dávila, Gil, **2:**680, 748

González, Ernesto, **2:**238, 374

González, Francisco, **3:**749

González, Leopoldo, **3:**739

González Malbrán, Armando, **2:**372

González, Pedro J., **3:**738

González "Piporro," Lalo, **2:**622

González Rodríguez, Luis, **2:**585–86, 587

González Sol, Rafael, **2:**719

Good, Kenneth, **2:**174

Good, the Bad, and the Ugly (film), **3:**204

"Good Lovin'" (Clovers), **3:**670

Good Rockin' Dopsie and the Twisters, **3:**339

"Good Rockin' Tonight" (Harris), **3:**669, 708

"Good Vibrations" (Beach Boys), **3:**348

Goodbye Columbus (film), **3:**204

Goodbye Old Man (film), **9:**47

Goode, Daniel, **3:**1016

Goodenough Island (Papua New Guinea), **9:**488, 489

Goodenough, Ward H., **9:**734–36

Goodman, Benny, **3:**45, 78–79, 329, 550, 655–56, 863, 969; **4:**96

Goodman, James, **8:**393

"Goodnight Irene," **3:**328

"Goodnight, Ladies," **3:**310

"Goodnite Sweetheart, Goodnite" (Spaniels), **3:**671

Goofalan (Yap dance expert), **9:**727–28

Goombeh cult, **2:**901, 903

Gopal, Nanu, **5:**462

Gopal, Nayak, **5:**76

Gopala Ayyar, Pallavi, **5:**100

Gopalnath, Kadri, **5:**424

Gopīcand (epic), **5:**674, 679

Gorali, Moshe, **6:**1061

Gordela (musical group), **8:**845

Gordo Enterprises, **3:**748

Gordon, Edwin E., **3:**278, 280, 281

Gordon, Lady Lucy Duff, **6:**21

Gordon, Michael, **3:**177

Gordon, Milton, **2:***970*

Gordon, Paul, **3:**200

Gordon, Robert Winslow, **3:**31, 146, 293

Gordon, Steve, **1:**437

Gordy, Berry, **3:**673–675, 677, 709–10

Górecki, Henryk Mikolai, **8:**210

Gore, Tipper, **3:**358

Gorkovenko, Aleksandr, **8:**784

Görkut atanyng kitaby (Oghuz tale), **6:**967, 969

Gorky, Maksim, **7:**47

Gorlinski, Virginia K., **4:**29

Gorman, Chester, **4:**33

Gorman, Larry, **3:**147, 1070, 1124

Görogly. See *Köroğlu*

Goroka Teachers College, **9:**480

Gosho Heinosuke, **7:**750

Gospel at Colonus (musical), **3:**621

Gospel Heirs (musical group), **3:**1133

Gospel Light Singers, **3:**486

gospel music, **3:**10, 12, 120, 125, 283, 510, 524, 531, 629–35; **10:**138. *See also* hymns

> Apache, **3:**433

> Barbados, **2:**817, 820

> black, **3:**534–35

> blues and, **3:**631–32, 648

> Canada, **3:**1072, 1077, 1085, 1133, 1134, 1169, 1212

> children's choirs, **3:**284

> contemporary, **3:**633–35

> early, **3:**629–31

> instruments in, **3:**632, 633

> jazz and, **3:**663

> musical theater and, **3:**622

> race and, **3:**63

> research on, **3:**584–85, 624; **10:**141–42, 144, 149–51, 154

> rural, **3:**630, 631

> soul and, **3:**535, 677–78

> traditional, **3:**631–33

> vocal harmony in, **3:**77

> white, **3:**533–34

> women performers of, **3:**96

Gospel Pearls (collection), **10:**138

Gospel Recordings, **9:**989

Gossen, Gary H., **2:**658

Gosvami, Kshetramohan, **5:**433, 434

Goswami, O., **5:**56

Goswami, Vinay, **5:**855

Gosyôraku (*bagaku* piece), **7:**625

Gosz, Paul, **3:**898

"Got My Mojo Working" (Muddy Waters), **3:**709

Götenberg Museum (Sweden), **2:**772

Goths, **8:**868

> in Corsica, **8:**566

Gotricke, Kacke, **1:**400

Gottlieb, Robert, **5:**136

Gottlund, Carl, **8:**488

Gottschalk, Louis Moreau, **2:**115, 837; **3:**14, 521, 537, *537*, 556, 1180

Göttsching, Manuel, **3:**690

Gottwald, Clement, **8:**723

Goudge, Helen, **3:**1210

Gould, Glenn, **3:***248*, 248–49, 1080, 1105, 1185

Gould, Morton, **3:**541

Gould, Stephen, **10:**120

Goulet, Jean-Guy, **3:**392, 1276

Goulet, Joseph-Jean, **3:**1149

Gounis, Thodoros, **8:**1022

Gounod, Charles, **3:**1148, 1182

Gourlay, Kenneth A., **1:**605, 722; **9:**372

Government Band (Hawai'i), **9:**133

Government College (Tonga), **9:**130

Govigama caste, **5:**957, 961

Govinda, Jai, **3:**223

Govinda Swami, **5:**251

Govindarajan, S., **5:**425, 557

Govindasvami Pillai, Malaikottai, **5:**383, 385, 389, 391–92, 393

Govshudov-Dutarchy, Aman, **6:***969*

Gow, Nathaniel, **8:**367, 373

Gow, Niel, **8:**364, 373

Gowan's Opera House (Ottawa), **3:**1181
Goyenche, Roberto, **2:**264
Goyeneche, A., **8:**316
Gozlan, Shlomo, **6:**1043
Graça, Fernando Lopes, **8:**585
Grace, Patricia, **9:**37
Graceland (album), **1:**364, 418, 431, 777, 781;
　3:338–39, 341
¡Gracias! América sin fronteras (Los Tigres del
　Norte), **3:**751
Gradante, William J., **2:**390, 398
Gradenwitz, Peter E., **6:**1029, 1030, 1060, 1063
Gradual romain, Le, **3:**1067
Graduate (film), **3:**204
Grady, Lottie, **3:***620*
Graebner, Fritz, **10:**120
Graf, Walter, **8:**25; **9:**983; **10:**112
Graff, Ola, **8:**307
Grafulla, Claudio, **3:**565
Graham, Billy, **3:**534
Graham Central Station, **3:**683
Graham, G. F., **8:**373
Graham, James E., Jr., **10:**31, 33
Graham, Larry, **3:**680–81, *681*, 683
Graham, Martha, **3:**135, 852; **4:**708; **7:**69; **8:**161
Graham, Shirley, **3:**606–7, 608–9
Graham, William A., **4:**330; **6:**162
Grainger Collection, **9:**961
Grainger Museum, **9:**959, 961
Grainger, Percy, **8:**18, 19, 327–28, 460, *461*,
　464; **9:**294, 961
　folk song research, **8:**337
　use of folk songs in compositions, **8:**333
Grame, Theodore C., **3:**828
Gramophone Company, **4:**96; **5:**527–28; **6:**234,
　548, 597, 599, 785; **8:**777
Gramophone Company of India, **5:**423, 528,
　531, 853–54; **8:**241
Gramophone and Phonography (periodical), **8:**783
Gramsci, Antonio, **8:**613
Gran Nicoya culture, **2:**13
Gran Teatro Coliseo de la Metrópoli (Mexico),
　2:603, 606
Granada, Gary, **4:**886
Granadino, David, **2:**718
Granados, Enrique, **3:**852, 1150; **6:**449; **8:**601
"Grand Hotel" (ballad), **3:**1257
Grand Ole Opry (Nashville), **3:**13, 79, 80, 243,
　520, 560, 1257
"*grand six pieds, Le*" (Gauthier), **3:**1156
Grand Terrace (Chicago), **3:**655
Grande Bande (bagpipe ensemble), **8:**548
"*Grande Gigue Simple,*" **3:**344
Grande Terre (New Caledonia), **9:**671–79, 965,
　981, 992
"Grandfather's Clock" (Work), **3:**190
Grandin, Ingemar, **5:**703
Grandmaster Flash, **3:**688, 694, 695, 697, 702,
　713
Grandmixer D. ST., **3:**695, *696*
"Grandpa's Spells" (Morton), **3:**653
Granet, Marcel, **7:**60
Grant, Mrs., **8:**368
Grant, Ulysses S., **3:**308, 454
Grappelli, Stephane, **8:**288
Grasso, Francis, **3:**687–88

Grateful Dead (musical group), **3:**339, 348
Gräter, Friedrich David, **8:**648
Gratton, Hector, **3:**1058, 1076, 1108
Grau, Andrée, **9:**317, 960
Grauman, Sid, **3:**740
Gravediggers, **9:**154
Graves, Buck "Uncle Josh," **3:**166
Graves, Charles. *See* Abayie, Charles Emmanuel
　Graves
Gray, John, **3:**199
Gray, Judith, **3:**495, 496
Gray, Merenia, **9:**948
Gray, Tanemahuta, **9:**948
Gray, William, **9:**363
Great Basin Indian nations, **3:**420–27, 438. *See
　also specific groups*
　dances of, **3:**371
　Ghost Dance movement, **3:**421–22, 487
　history and culture, **3:**420–21
　instruments of, **3:**425–26, 472–79
　performance contexts, **3:**422–25
　singing style, **3:**425–27
　women's game songs, **3:**371
Great Big Sea (musical group), **3:**1070, 1073
Great Britain. *See also* British people; England;
　Northern Ireland; Scotland; Wales
　administration of Egypt, **6:**547
　administration of Palestine, **6:**1024–26
　African-American performers in, **3:**604
　Arctic territories, **3:**379
　attitude toward colonized peoples, **8:**232
　ballad opera in, **3:**180
　ballads in, **8:**23, 134, 135
　BBC Light Programme broadcasts of folk
　　music, **8:**156
　bhangra dance in, **5:**500, 550, 568, 574–75
　Caribbean territories, **2:**791, 799, 802, 813,
　　868, 896, 942, 952–53, 968
　Church of God and Saints of Christ in, **3:**127
　colonial rule in South Asia, **5:**431–36, 650,
　　807, 853, 954; **6:**672
　　history of, **5:**15, 374, 375, 489, 720, 731,
　　　744, 849
　　influence on Diksitar family, **5:**223–24
　　influence on patronage, **5:**180, 331, 375,
　　　408–9, 435, 799
　　influence on pedagogy, **5:**442–43
　　influence on scholarship, **5:**44, 49–50,
　　　52–53, 433–34
　　infrastructure, **5:**403
　　introduction of Christianity, **5:**13
　contra dance in, **3:**232
　eighteenth-century popular music, **3:**831
　folk festivals in, **8:**153
　Georgian people in, **8:**845
　ideology in, **8:**186, 188
　immigrant music in, **8:**235–36, 239–41
　immigration laws in, **5:**572–73
　instrument collections in, **8:**182
　instruments, **8:**170
　Jewish people in, **6:**1036
　Maltese people in, **8:**634
　map of, **8:***324*
　musical exchange patterns in, **8:**336, 355
　Muslims in, **8:**11
　popularity of reggae, **2:**97–98

　popular music in, **8:**207, 210
　Protestantism in, **3:**119
　Punjabi people in, **8:**207
　research on music of, **8:**17, 188
　rock in, **8:**214–16
　Sephardic Jews in, **8:**248
　South Asian community in, **5:**561, 572–76
　South Asian musicians in, **5:**561–62, 572
　South Asian population of, **5:**573
　urbanization of, **8:**13
Great Lakes Indian nations, **3:**451–59
　belief systems, **3:**454–55
　history and social organization, **3:**451–52
　instruments of, **3:**472–79
　lifeways, **3:**452–54
　music of, **3:**455–59
　research on music of, **3:**457–58
　subsistence patterns, **3:**452
Great Lakes Intertribal Council, **3:**453–54
Great Moravian empire, **8:**716, 726
"Great Pretender" (Platters), **3:**672
Great Russian Orchestra of Folk Instruments,
　8:775
"Great Silkie of Sul Skerry" (ballad), **3:**833
Great Wall Capriccio (Liu), **7:**231, 432
Greater Perfect System, **8:**48
Grebe, María Ester, **2:**12, 238, 374
Grebenshchikov, Boris, **8:**778
Grebniov, Alexander F., **8:**856
Grebo people, **1:**91, 468–69
Grech, Pawlu, **8:**643
Greco, José, **3:**851
Greco, José, II, **3:**851
Greco, Juliette, **8:**208
Greece, **8:**1007–26. *See also* Byzantine empire
　Aegean islands, **8:**1014–15
　Albanian people in, **8:**986
　ancient
　　dance of, **8:**160
　　music of, **8:**46–48, 69, 1022–23
　　notational system of, **8:**49, 90
　art music in, **8:**1008
　Athens, **8:**1017
　Chios, **8:**1015
　Crete, **8:**1015, 1018
　　dance traditions of, **8:***164*
　　epic songs, **8:**130
　　instruments, **8:**39, *179*
　　laments, **8:**120
　　local traditions, **8:**123
　　mantinadhes, **8:**118–20
　　poetry of, **8:**1014
　Cycladic islands, **8:**1015
　　instruments, **8:**39
　dance traditions of, **8:**164–65
　Dodecanese islands, **8:**1015
　early music of, **5:**17–18, 19, 64
　Epirus
　　klarino style of, **8:**1009–10
　　laments, **8:**114, 1010
　　three-part vocal polyphony in, **8:**10, *1010*
　　Turkish court in, **8:**284
　　vocal performers, **8:**115
　ethnic minorities in, **8:**1010–11
　geography of, **8:**1007
　Halki, **8:**1015

Greece (*continued*)
history of, **8:**1007
history of music in, **8:**1022–23
improvised couplets, **8:**143
influence on Arab theory, **6:**15–16, 129, 540–41, 772
influence on medieval Arab society, **6:**396, 398–99
influence on Middle Eastern views of music, **6:**19, 181, 183
influence on South Asian culture, **5:**14
instruments, **8:**21, 1009–10, 1011, 1013, 1015
  research on, **8:**39
Ionian islands, *kantadhes* serenades, **8:**1008, 1014
island musical styles, **8:**1009, 1014–15, 1030
Judeo-Spanish music in, **8:**596
Kalymnos, **8:**1015
Karpathos, **8:**1015
Kasos, **8:**1015
Lesbos, **8:**1015
Macedonia, **8:**972, 1010–12
  zurla and *tapan* ensembles, **8:**280–81
  zurna playing, **8:**285
mainland musical styles, **8:**1009–14
map of, **8:**866
Mount Athos monasteries, **8:**943, 1023
music classification system, **5:**20
Naxos, **8:**1015
notational systems in, **8:**104
Peloponnisos, **8:**1013–14
Piraeus, hashish dens in, **8:**1019
Pontii people, **8:**1011
popular music in, **8:**204, 1008, 1021–22
population of, **8:**1007
research on music of, **8:**1023–25
Rhodes, **8:**1015
Rom people in, **8:**278, 284–85, 1008, 1011–12, 1017, 1019, 1023
Roumeli, **8:**1013–14
Saloniki, **8:**1011
Samos, **8:**1015
Sephardic Jews in, **6:**201; **8:**1011
Skyros, **8:**1015
Sufism in, **6:**107
Symi, **8:**1015
Thessaly, **8:**1013
  table songs, **8:**285
Thrace, **8:**1013
Turkish people in, **8:**11
vocal music
  ballads, **8:**1030
  dhimotika, **8:**206, 1008, 1017, 1018
  epic songs, **8:**129, 130, 198, 1024–25
  improvised couplets, **8:**1025
  ksenitias, **8:**1010
  laika, **8:**1008, 1018–19, 1020–21, 1030, 1031
  laments, **8:**9, 23, 120, 141, 144, 196, 1025
  rebetika, **8:**7, 143, 147, 204, 205–6, 207, 285, 1008, 1019–22
  smyrneika, **8:**1020
  table songs, **8:**114, 141, 285, 1013, 1015, 1016
women's dancing and singing styles, **8:**145

Greek culture, in Spain, **8:**588, 600
Greek Orthodox Church, **3:**529, 1029, 1088; **6:**195, 544; **8:**1007, 1023
  chant in, **3:**122
  Cyprus, **8:**1031
  in Israel, **6:**1021
  Karelia, **8:**481, 486
  music of, **3:**10
  Poland, **8:**710
Greek people
  in Australia, **9:**72–75, 409
  in Bulgaria, **8:**903
  in Corsica, **8:**566
  emigration patterns, **8:**1008
  expelled from Turkey, **8:**7, 1011, 1014, 1019
  in Hawai'i, **9:**100
  in North America, **3:**10, 529, 826, 919, 929–32, 1060, 1074; **8:**206
    dances of, **3:**213
    Ontario, **3:**1078, 1083, 1199
  in Panama, **2:**771
  in South America, **2:**84
  in Syria, **6:**565
  in Turkey, **6:**115, 116, 117
  in Ukraine, **8:**821
Greek Popular Musical Instruments (Anoyanakis), **8:**1025
Greeley, Horace, **3:**305, 308–9
Green, Al, **3:**677, 711
Green, Archie, **3:**47–48
"Green, Green Rocky Road," **3:**599
Green, John, **2:**593
Green, Karina Kahananui, **9:**972
Green, Lil, **3:**645
Green Linnet (record company), **8:**320
"Green Onions" (Booker T. and The MGs), **3:**675
Green Pastures (film), **3:**607
Green Pastures (musical), **3:**621
Green Pastures Spirituals (Johnson), **3:**607
Green, Richard, **3:**1110
Green Spot Band, **1:**481
Greenback Labor Songster, **3:**309
Greenback Party, **3:**309
Greenberg, David, **3:**1071
Greenberg, Joseph, **1:**2, 372, 515; **2:**232, 570, 575, 595
Greenday (musical group), **3:**358
Greene, Joseph, **3:**564
Greene, Victor, **3:**824, 826, 828
Greenfeld, Liah, **3:**504
Greenland, Arctic peoples in, **3:**374–81; **7:**1028
Greenmill Dance Project, **9:**415
Greenwich, Sonny, **3:**1212
Gregorc, Jurij, **8:**921
"Gregorio Cortez" (*corrido*), **3:**522
Gregor of Glenstrae, **8:**361
Gregor, Thomas, **2:**126
Gregory the Great, Pope, **8:**69
Greig-Duncan Folk Song Collection (Keith), **8:**374
Greig family, **8:**368, 374
Greig, Gavin, **8:**371
Greis, Yusif, **6:**612
Grenada, **2:**789, 864–72, 965. *See also* Carriacou
  art music in, **2:**866
  geography of, **2:**864

history of, **2:**864–65
musical genres
  belair, **2:**865
  calypso, **2:**865
  kalenda, **2:**865
  Petit Martinique, **2:**864, 867–68
  population of, **2:**864
  religious music and rituals, **2:**865–66
Grenadou, Ephraim, **8:**547
Grenet, Emilio, **2:**838; **3:**791
Grenier, Line, **3:**1076
Grétry, André Ernest Modeste, **2:**866
Grever, María, **2:**620
Grey, Earl, **3:**1226
Grey, Keti, **8:**1020
Grieg, Edvard, **2:**114; **8:**411, 425, 444
  Scottish ancestry of, **8:**368
Grierson, George A., **5:**675, 677, 678
Griffen, Johnny, **3:**336
Griffes, Charles Tomlinson, **3:**174, 367
Griffin, Margie, **9:**650
Griffith, D. W., **3:**203
Griffith, James S., **3:**851
Griffiths, John, **3:**232
Griffiths, Marcia, **2:**912
Grigor Narekatsi, **6:**736, 737
Grigor'ev, Aleksandr, **8:**764
Griles, Isidore, **2:**970
Grillo, Frank "Machito." *See* Machito
Grimaud, Ivette, **8:**847
Grimaud, Yvette, **1:**659
Grimm, Jacob, **3:**147
Grimm, Wilhelm, **3:**147
Grímsdóttir, Bára, **8:**407
Gringo Locos (musical group), **8:**217
Grinnell College (Iowa), **3:**953, 1014
griots, **1:**8, 415, 419; **3:**339, 638–39; **8:**232. *See also* praise songs, singing, poetry
  Fulɓe people, **1:**444
  Hausa people, *maròokii*, **1:**515
  itinerant, **1:**297
  Mali, **1:**420
  North Africa, **1:**540
  Senegal, **1:**421
    1600s, **1:**82
  Sierra Leone, *jeli*, **1:**489–512
  Wolof people, **1:**518, 523
Grixti, Pietro, **8:**642
Groneman, J., **4:**636, 677
Grönemeyer, Herbert, **8:**208
Gronich, Shlomo, **6:**1073
Gronow, Pekka, **8:**489
Groote Eylandt Field Project, **9:**47
"Groovallegiance" (Clinton), **3:**684
"Groove Line" (Heatwave), **3:**685, 712
Gros Ventre Indian nation, **3:**440, 445, 1086
Groshak, Alex, **3:**1243
Grossmann, Guido, **2:**751
Groulx, Chiga, **3:**406
Groven, Eivind, **8:**426
Growling Tiger (calypsonian; Neville Marcano), **2:**963
Gruber, Roman, **8:**784
Grünberg, Friedl, **2:**204
Grünberg, Georg, **2:**204
Grundlinien der Musikästhetik (Riemann), **7:**592

Grundtvig, Svend, **8:**136, 463
Grüner-Nielsen, Hakon, **8:**463
grunge rock, **2:**104; **3:**171, 358; **6:**248; **7:**361
Grunsky, Wolfgang, **3:**1186
Grunwald, Max, **8:**266
Grupo Coral da Caixa Social e Cultural da
    Câmara Municipal de Beja, **8:***578*
Grupo Ecuador de Los Hermanos Congo y
    Milton Tadeo, **2:**428, *429*, 430
Grupo Niche, **2:**102
Grupo de Renovación, **2:**828
Grupo da Velha Guarda, **2:**350
Gruuthuse Songbook, **8:**533
Gryphon Trio, **3:**1186
Gu Jian, **7:**277
Gu Zhong, **7:**365–67
Guadalcanal (Solomon Islands), **9:**630, 861
    'Are'are villages of, **9:**666
    Gilbertese in, **9:**712
    music and dance of, **9:**663, 664–66, 977
    research on, **9:**976
    Tikopia people in, **9:**833
Guadalupe Hidalgo, Treaty of, **3:**9, 718, 735
Guadeloupan people, in France, **8:**231, 234
Guadeloupe, **2:**789, 873–80
    balakadri, **2:**877–78
    carnival music (*mizik vidé; mizik a mas*),
        2:876–77, 879
    lèwòz, **2:**874–75
    Marie-Galante, **2:**874, 876, 877
    music of, **2:**873–78
    political status of, **2:**792
    popular music in, **2:**98
    population of, **2:**873
    zouk, **2:**93
guajira, **2:**832, 834; **3:**792
Guajiro culture, **2:**33, 380
Guam, **9:**712, 743
    Americans in, **9:**160
    archives in, **9:**968
    Chinese people in, **9:**71
    Christianity in, **9:**720
    Europeans in, **9:**158
    Filipino people in, **9:***70*
    films on, **9:**1016
    immigrants to Hawai'i, **9:**105
    instruments of, **9:**745–46
    music and dance of, **9:**744–46
    outsiders' influence in, **9:**5
    Pacific Islanders in, **9:**116
    popular music in, **9:**161, 721
    Russian exploration of, **9:**17
    settlement of, **9:**715
    sound recordings from, **9:**994, 995, 996
    Spanish in, **9:**717, 720
Guamán Poma de Ayala, Felipe, **2:**23, 207, 283,
    423, 467–68
Guambiano culture, **2:**379
Guamotzín (Ortega), **2:**114
Guana culture, **2:**452
Guandi (Han deity), **7:**513
Guangala culture, **2:**413
    archaeomusicological studies of, **2:**7
Guangdong Minjian Yinyue Tuan, **7:**220
Guangdong yinyue (Cantonese collection), **7:**220
Guangdong yinyue de goucheng (Chen), **7:**220–21

Guangdong yinyue xinshang (Huang), **7:**221
Guanglingsan (Xi), **7:**161–62; **10:**23
Guangxi Zhuang Autonomous Region Song and
    Dance Troupe, **7:**443
Guang Xu, Qing emperor, **7:**375
Guangzhou Conservatory of Music, **7:**220
Guan Hanging (Cantonese opera), **7:**308
Guanzi (treatise), **7:**115, 117–18
guaracha, **2:**372, 829, 835, 836, 862, 930;
        3:793, 795, 798
Guaraní culture, **2:**199–204, 452
    history of, **2:**199–200
    instruments of, **2:**200–202, 302, 454–56
    music and dance of, **2:**202–4
    research on, **2:**204
    shamanism in, **2:**200–204
    singing of, **2:**137, 453
Guarao culture. *See* Warao culture
Guarauno culture. *See* Warao culture
Guarco culture, **2:**680
Guarijio culture, **2:**551–54, 592
    contradanza, **2:**553
    research on, **2:**554
    son principal, **2:**553
    túmari ceremony, **2:**552–54
Guarín, José Joaquín, **2:**397
Guarnieri, Camargo, **2:**115, 306
Guasapa culture, **2:**551
Guatemala, **2:**628, 630, 721–37; **3:**719
    Antigua, cathedral in, **2:**735–36
    archaeomusicological studies in, **2:**7
    art music in, **2:**735–36
    early cities of, **2:**81
    emigrants to United States, **2:**91
    Garífuna culture, **2:**733–34
    history of, **2:**721–22
    instruments of, **2:**33, 36, 723–29
    Ladino culture, **2:**723, 734–35
    map of, **2:***629*
    Maya culture, **2:**650–58, 721–23, 729–33
    research on, **2:**736–37
    saint's-day celebrations in, **2:**46
    son guatemalteco, **2:**735
Guatemalan-Americans/Canadians, **3:**719,
        727–28
Guaykurú culture, **2:**452
    instruments of, **2:**454–55
Guaymí culture, **2:**681, 685–87, 771
    research on, **2:**783
Gua zhi'r (collection), **7:**155
Guazón, Domingo, **4:**857
Gubaidulina, Sofia, **8:**782
al-Gubantchī, **6:**314–15
Gubara, Mohamed, **1:**572
Guben zhushu jinian, **7:**447
Guðbjartsson, Þórður, **8:**117
Guðjohnsen, Pétur, **8:**406
Guðmundsdóttir, Björk, **8:**407
Guðmundsson, Karl, **8:**401, *402*
Guédon, Marie-Françoise, **3:**392
Guerin, Pierre, **3:**1233, 1234
"*Guernikako Arbola*" (Iparragirre), **8:**311
Guerra, Juan Luis, **2:**861; **3:**800
Guerra, Marcelino, **3:**787
Guerra-Peixe, César, **2:**306, 325
Guerrero, Francisco, **2:**735

Guerrero, Lalo, **3:**733, 739, 741, 749, 751
Guerrero, Raúl G., **2:**658
Guess Who (musical group), **3:**1091
Guettat, Mahmoud, **6:**505
Guevara, Rubén, **3:**742
Guguba people, **1:**289
Gugum Gumbira Tirasonjaya, **4:**93, 130, 708
Gui Ming-young, **3:**1261
Guiamalon, Mamaluba, **4:**896
Guiart, Jean, **9:**690
Guide (film), **5:**537
Guide to Caribbean Music History, A (Stevenson),
        2:931
*Guide to the Collections of the Human Studies Film
        Archives*, **9:**978–79
Guide to Native American Music Recordings, A,
        3:488
Guidonian hand, **8:***100*
Guignard, Silvain, **7:**595
Guigni, Heather Haunani, **9:**222
Guilbault, Jocelyne, **2:**93, 920; **10:**53
Guilcher, Jean-Michel, **8:**551, 554
Guinchard, Rufus, **3:**1125, 1137
Guinea. *See also* West Africa; *specific peoples*
    Fulani people, **1:**451
    guitar in, **1:**359, 365
    history of, **1:**81–83, 510–11
    instruments of, **1:**445
    Maninka people, **1:***444, 446*
Guinea Bissau, **1:**419
Guinean people, in France, **8:**231
Guiraud, Ernest, **3:**1149
güiro. *See* scrapers (rasps)
guitar music. *See under* chordophones
Guitar Player (periodical), **1:**364
Guitar Slim, **3:**352
guitar songs. *See* popular music
Guitarmen (musical group), **8:**679
guitars. *See also* banjo; guitars, electric; guitars,
        Hawaiian; lutes; ukulele
    acoustics of, **1:**175–77
    Africa, **1:**350–67
        in praise singing, **1:**489
    African musical styles
        Congolese style, **1:**322, 360–63, 365, 386,
            424, 608, 643, 644, 669
        jùjú, **1:**481
        Katanga style, **1:**322, 360, 423, 672
        maskanda, **1:**430
        palm-wine style, **1:**353, 358, 366, 370,
            376–79, 423, 478
        tickey draai, **1:**351, 762–63, 767
        two-finger style, **1:**376–79
    Albania, **8:**997
    Algeria, **6:**407, 435, 475
    American Sāmoa, **9:**266
    Amish playing of, **3:**887
    Andean regions, **2:**213–14
    Aotearoa, **9:**168, 937
    in Appalachian folk music, **3:***13*
    in Arctic communities, **3:**380
    Argentina, **2:**251, 255, 257, 258, 259, 261,
        263
    armadillo-shell, **2:**559, 572
    Austral Islands, **9:**880–81
    Australia, **9:**442

guitars (*continued*)
Austria, **8:**673
Bahamas, **2:**805, 809
bajo de unas (one-stringed bass), **4:**854, 884
bajo quinto, **3:**775, *775*
bajo sexto, **2:**613, *614*; **3:**723, 772, 773, *774*, 774–75, 778, 779, 781
banjo-guitar, **8:**288
banza, **3:**596
Barbados, **2:**815, 819, 820
Belize, **2:**677
Bellona, **9:**850
in Berber music, **6:**275
Bolivia, **2:**288, 297
bordonúa, **2:**934–35, 938
Bosnia-Hercegovina, **8:**965
braguinha, **9:**98, 136, 390
Brazilian bossa nova techniques, **2:**317–18
Canadian manufacture of, **3:**246
Carriacou, **2:**872
cavaquinho, **2:**305, 309, 311, 329, 335, 337, 350; **3:**1197; **8:**582, 582–83
charango (also *quirquincho*; *chillador*), **2:***76*
   Argentina, **2:**251, 253, 254, 259
   Bolivia, **2:**284, 288, 289–90, 291, 293, 295, 297, 298
   Ecuador, **2:**417
   North America, **3:**730
   in *nueva canción* ensembles, **2:**32, 90, 373
   Peru, **2:**469, 473, 475, 478, 486
   Quechua and Aymara culture, **2:**34, 213–14, 215, 221, 222, 382
Chechen people, **8:**863
Chilean performing techniques, **2:**367–68
chitara, **8:**880
chitarra battente, **8:**611, 615, *616*
Chuuk, **9:**734–36
cinco, **2:**531, 536, 541
cinco de seis cuerdas, **2:**531, 536
cinco y medio, **2:**531
Cirebon, **4:**696, 697
Colombia, **2:**381–83
contrabass, **8:**676
Cook Islands, **9:**238, 900, 902
Corsica, **8:**571, 572, 573
Costa Rica, **2:**691, 694, 698
cuatra, **2:**930
cuatro, **2:**30; **3:**726, 799; **9:**99, 102–3
   Carriacou, **2:**872
   Colombia, **2:**382, 385
   Dominican Republic, **2:**849
   Grenada, **2:**866
   Honduras, **2:**743
   Montserrat, **2:**926
   Puerto Rico, **2:**938–39
   St. Lucia, **2:**945
   Trinidad and Tobago, **2:**953
   Venezuela, **2:**170, 524, 530, 531, *532*, 534, 536, 538, 540–41, 542
cuatro (Puerto Rican ten-stringed), **2:**30, 934, *935*
cuatro con cinco cuerdas, **2:**531
cuatro de cinco cuerdas, **2:**536
cuatro y medio, **2:**531
Cuba, **2:**823, 830, 831, 833–36
Cyprus, **8:**1031

dàn ghi-ta, **3:**994; **4:**473–74, 508
Denmark, **8:**455, *456*, 458
development of, **1:**350–51
discante, **2:**531
dissemination of, **8:**170
Dobro (resonator guitar), **3:**79, 160, 164, 166, 240
Dominican Republic, **2:**849, 860, 861
East Africa, **1:**608
Ecuador, **2:**417, 426
El Salvador, **2:**712, 714–15
English guitar, **8:**331
Europe, **8:**169
Europe, Western, **8:**517
Fiji, **9:**161–62, 779
in Finnish music, **3:**874, 875
flamenco music for, **3:**338, 731
Futuna, **9:**815, 816
Garífuna (Garifuna) culture, **2:**673, 675, 753
Georgia, **8:**841
Germany, **8:**656, *657*, 658–59
gitar, **4:**797
gitara, **4:**854–55
Goa, **5:**737, *739*
Greece, **8:**1013, 1014, 1020
Grenada, **2:**866
Guadeloupe, **2:**877
Guam, **9:**745, 746
Guatemala, **2:**723, 727–28, 731
guitarillo, **8:**594
guitarra, **2:**360, 382, 392, 456, 708, 756, 757
guitarra portuguesa, **3:**1197; **8:**116, 583
guitarrilla, **2:**213–14, 222, 288, 708, 714, 723, 728, 743, 756, 761
guitarrón, **2:**288, 360, 367, *546*, 611, 612, *621*, 622; **3:**722, 737, 761, 765; **8:**594
Guyana, **5:**603, *604*
hanyani, **10:***119*
hạ uy cầm (steel guitar), **4:**474
Hawai'i, **9:**127–28, 166, 388–90, 920, 921–23
hichoch, **2:**657
in Hispano music, **3:**759–60, 761, 762
Honduras, **2:**741, 743
huapanguera (also *guitarra quinta*), **2:**571, 608; **3:***724*
Ingush people, **8:**863
Ireland, **8:**152
Irian Jaya, **9:**578, 591
Israel, **6:**261, 1019
Italy, **8:***5*, 608, 615
Jamaica, **2:**900–901, 906
jarana (also *guitarra de golpe*), **2:**559–60, 561, 564, 565–66, 608, 609, 610, 611, 612, 621; **3:**723, *724*
jitarrón, **2:**213
Kapingamarangi, **9:**836
Kazakhstan, **6:**961
K'ekchi Maya, **2:**667–68
Kenya, **1:**426–27
Kerala, **5:**948
kikā, **9:**163
kin, **2:**654–55
Kiribati, **9:**762
kitarra, **2:**288, 289–90
Korea, **7:**887–88, 958

Kru people, **1:**375–79
k'ullu charango, **2:**213
kuminjaré, **2:**201–2
Latvia, **8:**504
lira, **2:**536
Low Countries, **8:**533
Luangiua, **9:**843
lục huyền cầm, **3:**994; **4:**473–74
Macedonia, **8:**282
Malaysia, **4:**432, 438–39
Maleku culture, **2:**683
Malta, **8:**635, 637, 639–40
Mangareva, **9:**889
Manihiki, **9:**905, 907–9
Marquesas Islands, **9:**894, 896
Marshall Islands, **9:**748–49, 751, 753
Maya culture, **2:**654
mbaraká, **2:**456
mejorana, **2:**772, 776–77, 780
Melanesia, **9:**27, 598
Mexica culture, **2:**559
Mexico, **2:**550, 606, 611
Micronesia, **9:**719
Middle Eastern origin of, **8:**12
Mixtec culture, **2:**565
Montenegro, **8:**959, 960
Montserrat, **2:**926
Moorish, **6:**444
Mozambique, **1:**436
Native American use of, **3:**479
Nauru, **9:**261, 755
Nepal, **5:**705
Netherlands Antilles, **2:**930
New Caledonia, **9:**214, 679
Nicaragua, **2:**749, 761, 764
Nissan Atoll, **9:**640
North America
   in bluegrass music, **3:**160, 164, 165, 1258
   in blues performance, **3:**638, 642, 647
   in *chansonnier* movement, **3:**1155
   in churches, **3:**125
   in contra dance bands, **3:**231
   in country music, **3:**77–78, 520
   in Danish music, **3:**882–83
   in Estonian music, **3:**878
   in folk revival, **3:**328
   in French music, **3:**856
   in gospel music, **3:**535, 631
   in Greek bands, **3:**930
   in Iberian music, **3:**848
   in Irish music, **3:**844
   in Italian music, **3:**860
   in *mariachi* groups, **3:**722, 765
   in *matachines* dance, **3:**430, *757*, 759
   in Mexican music, **3:**735, 737
   music by African-American composers, **3:**605
   in Norwegian music, **3:**868
   in rhythm and blues performance, **3:**672
   in *son*, **3:**791
   in *son conjunto*, **3:**792
   in South Asian music, **3:**984
   in string bands, **3:**836
   in *tamburitza* orchestra, **3:**920
   in Tejano music, **3:**772
   in Texas-Czech bands, **3:**897

in Ukrainian music, **3:**914
in Volga German music, **3:**890
Oceania, **9:**372
Ontario, **3:**1190, 1194
Otopame culture, **2:**572
Panama, **2:**772, *773,* 781
Papua New Guinea, **9:**178, 195, 197, 387–88,
    516, 566, 571, 607, 612, 625, 649
Paraguay, **2:**461–63
Peru, **2:**473, 475–76, 486, 496, 497
Philippines, **4:**849, 928
Pohnpei, **9:**739–40
Polynesia, **9:**769, 771
Portugal, **8:**176, 582
Portuguese types of, **3:**850
Pukapuka, **9:**911
Purépecha culture, **2:**578
quinto, **2:**536
quirquincho, **3:**730
qunquta, **2:**288
Rapa Nui, **9:**952
requinto, **3:**761; **8:**594
    Argentina, **2:**251
    Colombia, **2:**381, 384, 385
    Costa Rica, **2:**694, 698
    Ecuador, **2:**417, *429*
    El Salvador, **2:**708, 712
    Honduras, **2:**743
    Mexico, **2:**609–10, 613
    Nicaragua, **2:**763
    Paraguay, **2:**457
    Puerto Rico, **2:**934
requinto jarocho, **3:**723
Réunion Island, **5:**609
Romania, **8:**277, 872, 879
Rotuma, **9:**818–19
Russian seven-stringed, **8:**287, 767, 840
Saami people, **8:**299
St. Lucia, **2:**946
Sāmoa, **9:**807–8
Sardinia, **8:**629–30
Scotland, **8:**366
seis, **2:**531
Sikaiana, **9:**335, 848
slack-key tuning of, **9:**136, 160, 387, 388–89,
    922
Slovenia, **8:**918
Solomon Islands, **9:**269, 654, 665
South Africa, **1:**351–53, 762–63, 775–76
South America, **2:**36
    distribution of, **2:**32
South Asia, **5:**582
    in *bhangra,* **5:**574
    in Hindustani music, **5:**207
    in Karnatak music, **5:**107, 351, 352
southern Africa, **1:**719
Spain, **8:**589, 593, 594, *594*
    rasgueado playing style, **8:**598
Sri Lanka, **5:**970
steel-string, **3:**77
Sumatra, **4:**625
Sunda, **4:**716
Sweden, **8:**152, 441
Switzerland, **8:**686–87, 694, 695–96
tabla charango, **2:**213
tablature for, **9:**286

Tahiti, **9:**868, 877
in Taiwanese pop music, **7:**356
Takuu, **9:**841
talachi, **2:**288
Tarahumara culture, **2:**583
in Tibetan culture, **5:**715
Tikopia, **9:**853
timple, **8:**594
tiple (also *tiplillo*), **8:**594
    Argentina, **2:**254
    Colombia, **2:**381, 382, 383, 384, 386–88,
        391, 392, 395
    Dominican Republic, **2:**849
    Honduras, **2:**743
    Puerto Rico, **2:**934, *935,* 938
    Trinidad and Tobago, **2:**953
    Venezuela, **2:**531
Tonga, **9:**793
Torres Strait Islands, **9:**429
tres, **2:**30, *31;* **3:**728, 792–93; **5:**428
    Costa Rica, **2:**693
    Cuba, **2:**828, 830, 833–36
    Dominican Republic, **2:**849, *850*
    Puerto Rico, **2:**934, 938
Trinidad and Tobago, **2:**953
triplo, **8:**594
Tuamotu Islands, **9:**883
tunings of, **1:**300
Turkey, **6:**248, 251, 257
Tuvalu, **9:**831
Ukraine, **8:**817
Uruguay, **2:**511, 512, 519, 520
'Uvea, **9:**809, 813, 814
Vanuatu, **9:**709
Vietnam, **4:**510
vihuela, **2:**284, 360, 494, 571, 708, 933
    Europe, **8:**170, 589, 594, 601
    North America, **3:**722, 723, 737, 765
vihuela (Mexican), **2:**611, 612, 621–22, 708
vihuela de mano, **2:**577–78
viola, **2:**309–10, 311–12, 319, 325, 326–27,
    329, 349
    Europe, **8:**116, 582, 583
    North America, **3:**1197
viola de arame, **3:**850
viola baixo, **8:**116, 583
viola caipira, **2:**310, 318
viola de cocho, **2:**309–10
viola dinâmica, **2:**310
violão, **2:**305, 309–10, 319, 325, 329, 330,
    335, 337, 350; **3:**850
violão-sete-cordas, **2:**310
violõe, **2:**305
Wales, **8:**354, 355
wandora (cuatro), **2:**189, 192, 197
Wayana culture, **2:**167
Yaqui culture, **2:**591; **3:**437, 485
Yúcatec Maya, **2:**667
Yukon, **3:**1277
Yuma culture, **2:**598
Zaïre, **1:**386–87, 669, 671–72, 683
Zambia, **1:**671–72
zongora, **8:**880
guitars, electric
    Afghanistan, **5:**810
    Albania, **8:**997

in Arab music, **6:**421
Argentina, **2:**264, 274
Barbados, **2:**815
Bolivia, **2:**284, 297–98
Brazil, **2:**329, 337
Bulgaria, **8:**894
Cyprus, **8:**1032
Europe, **8:***206,* 225, 234, 288
in funk, **3:**680
Garifuna culture, **2:**677
Germany, **8:**658–59
Guyana, **5:**604, *605*
Israel, **6:**1073
Japan, **7:**745
in Karnatak music, **5:**354
Kerala, **5:**946, 948
Low Countries, **8:**533
Macedonia, **8:**980, 983
North America, **3:**240
    in Albanian bands, **3:**927
    in Armenian ensembles, **3:**1033, 1034
    in blues, **3:**647
    in Cajun and Creole music, **3:**858
    in Cambodian rock bands, **3:**1002
    in country and western music, **3:**79–80
    in Greek bands, **3:**930
    in Hispano music, **3:**762
    in Iranian music, **3:**1035
    in Irish showbands, **3:**845
    in Lao popular music, **3:**1009
    in Macedonian bands, **3:**926
    in Mexican music, **3:**746
    in Middle Eastern music, **3:**1218
    in *mini-djaz* groups, **3:**803
    in Motown style, **3:**674
    in polka bands, **3:**895
    in rock, **3:**95, 111–12, 113, 285
    in rock and roll, **3:**351
    in salsa, **3:**788
    in Slovak dance bands, **3:**900
    in soul music, **3:**677
    in Tohono O'odham *waila,* **3:**436, 473, 490
in Nubian music, **6:**642
Palestine, **6:**586, 591
Peru, **2:**484, *485*
Romania, **8:**879
Serbia, **8:**949
South Asia, **5:**652
Southeast Asia, **4:**414, 439, 441
Sri Lanka, **5:**971
Sweden, **8:**442
Tamil Nadu, **5:**924
Turkey, **6:**248
Ukraine, **8:**811, 812
guitars, electric bass
    Brazil, **2:**329
    Colombia, **2:**39, 101
    Egypt, **6:**555
    Europe, **8:**225, 282, 284
    Germany, **8:**658–59
    in Israeli *mizraḥit* music, **6:**261
    Macedonia, **8:**980, 983
    Montenegro, **8:**960
    Nicaragua, **2:**754
    North America
        in Albanian bands, **3:**927

guitars, electric bass, North America (*continued*)
  in bluegrass music, **3:**164
  in blues, **3:**647
  in Cajun and Creole music, **3:**858
  in Cambodian rock bands, **3:**1002
  in *conjunto* music, **3:**522, 773, 775
  in gospel music, **3:**633
  in Greek bands, **3:**930
  in Hispano music, **3:**761, 762
  in Iranian music, **3:**1035
  in Irish showbands, **3:**845
  in Macedonian bands, **3:**926
  in Mexican music, **3:**746
  in *mini-djaz* groups, **3:**804
  in *plena* music, **3:**727
  in rock and roll, **3:**348
  in Texas-Czech bands, **3:**897
  in Volga German music, **3:**891
 in Nubian music, **6:**642
 Serbia, **8:**949
 South Asia, **5:**705
 in Sufi *dhikr* ceremony, **3:**1045
guitars, Hawai'ian (steel)
 Africa, **1:**353, 364, 481
 Australia, **9:**142
 in Cantonese music, **7:**219
 Egypt, **6:**600
 Hawai'i, **9:**127, 389–90
 mohan vīṇā, **5:**467
 North America, **3:**166, 337, 527, 984, 1049
  in Cajun music, **3:**858
  in Cantonese opera orchestra, **3:**1260
  in country and western music, **3:**79–80
 Oceania, **9:**136
 South Asia, **5:**339, 582
  in film music, **5:**347
Guízar, Pepe, **3:**732
Gujarat, **5:**7, 624–37
 bardic traditions of, **5:**635–37
 bhavāī theater in, **5:**419, 485, 634–35
 dance traditions of, **5:**277, 501, 629–30,
  634–35
 geography of, **5:**624
 history of, **5:**624
 instruments in, **5:**344, 347, 625, 629, 633
 Junagadh, **5:**636
  palace of, **5:**624
 Kutch region
  bardic traditions, **5:**635
  bird whistle of, **5:**476–77
 map of, **5:**622
 musical genres
  abhaṅg, **5:**250
  bhajan, **5:**630–32
  chand, **5:**636–37
  duho, **5:**635–36
  garbā, **5:**550, 624–28
  havelī saṅgīt, **5:**251, 632, 633
  khāṇḍana, **5:**274
  rās, **5:**550, 629–30
  soratho, **5:**636
  ṭīpaṇī, **5:**474, 475
 patronage in, **5:**402
 regional cassettes in, **5:**550
 Saurashtra (Kathiawar) region, bardic
  traditions, **5:**635

Somnath temple, **5:**624
Swaminarayan movement in, **5:**255
Vadodara (Baroda)
 court of, **5:**443
 palace of, **5:**624
Gujarati people
 in Fiji, **5:**612
 in North America, **3:**980, 981, 984; **5:**578
Gujarati Samaj, **5:**585
Gujin tusu jicheng, **7:**47
Gul Rooz, **5:**787
Gul Sanum, **5:**790
Gulik, Robert van, **7:**159, 595
Gullin, Lars, **8:**157, 446
Gülşenīzade Hayalī, **6:**193
Gültekin, Hasret, **6:**799
Guluo chenliu (Jiang), **7:**347
Gumbán, Eriberto, **4:**866
Gumboots (musical group), **3:**1277–78, 1280
Gummow, Margaret, **9:**430, 441, 451
Gumps Jazz Hounds, **3:**1106–7
Gumuz people, **1:**564
Gun people, **1:**461
 instruments of, **1:**462
 music of, **1:**462
Gunn, Russell, **3:**665
Gunn, William, **9:**861–62
Gunnar Hahn Folk Dance Orchestra, **8:**156
Gunong Sayang Association (Singapore), **4:**522
Guns 'n' Roses (musical group), **3:**356, 358
Gunsyo ruizyû (collection), **7:**587
Günther, Robert, **1:**51; **7:**595
Gunung Jati, Sunan, **4:**686
Gunyat al-Munyat (treatise), **5:**45
Guo Lun, **10:**18
Guo Maoqian, **7:**155
Guo yu (dynastic history), **7:**115, 117
Guoli Yinyue Yuan (Shanghai), **7:**339, 340, 345
Gupt (film), **5:**540
Gupta, Ishwar, **5:**848
Gupta kingdom, **5:**17, 720, 721
 theater of, **5:**18, 24, 25–30
Gupta, Ramnidhi (Nidhu Babu), **5:**847
Gupta, Shyamal, **5:**857
Gür Duuny Bichig (Mongolian Buddhist sources),
 7:1016–17
Gure Abendaren Ereserkiak (Donostia), **8:**317
Gurian people, **8:**827–28
 dance traditions of, **8:**836
 instruments of, **8:**838–39
 vocal music of, **8:**832–33, 841
Gurlitt, Wilibald, **6:**1059–60
Gurri people, **1:**113
Gurrufio (Venezuelan group), **2:**543
Gurtu, Trilok, **5:**136
Guru, **3:**699
Guru Granth Sāhib (Sikh holy book), **5:**314, 655
Guruh Gypsy, **4:**109
Gurung, Kishor, **5:**706
Guruṅg people, **5:**5, 700, 701, 703–5, 706
Gurung, Uma, **5:**428
Gurupañcāśikā (Ashvaghosha), **5:**457–58
Gurûpu ongaku (composers' group), **7:**737
Gurvin, Olav, **8:**426
Gusinde, Father (priest), **2:**251
gusle. *See* violins and fiddles (bowed lutes)

Gustav II Adolf, king of Sweden, **8:**444, 495
Gustav III, king of Sweden, **8:**443, 444
Gustav Vasa, king of Sweden, **8:**444
Gustin, Lyell, **3:**1229
Gusuxing (Jian), **7:**185
Guthrie, Arlo, **3:**317
Guthrie, Colonel, **2:**898
Guthrie, Malcolm, **10:**117
Guthrie, Woody, **3:**310, 316, 520; **8:**356
Gutiérrez, Bienvenido J., **3:**792
Gutiérrez, Efraín, **2:**626
Gutiérrez, Eugenio, **3:**779
Gutiérrez, Isidoro, **10:**80
Gutiérrez, Juan, **3:**727
Gutiérrez, Pedro Elías, **2:**540
Gutiérrez Villa, Ricardo, **2:**612
Gutzlaff, Charles, **4:**225
Guy, Buddy, **3:**582; **9:**165
Guyana, **2:**441–50. *See also specific peoples*
 African traditions in, **2:**444–46
 Amerindian cultures in, **2:**442–43
 Asian descendants in, **2:**48
 British traditions in, **2:**446–47; **3:**808
 East Indian people in, **2:**83, 85–86, 443–44,
  448, 792
 geography of, **2:**441
 history of, **2:**242, 245, 441
 instruments of, **2:**31–32
 Maroon cultures in, **2:**2, 131
 musical contexts and genres, **2:**447–50
 popular music in, **5:**603–5
 population of, **2:**443, 792
 research on, **2:**442
 South Asians (East Indians) in, **3:**813–17;
  5:600–605
 tropical-forest region of, **2:**123–35
 Warao culture, **2:**189
Guyana Police Force Band, **2:**447
Guyanese-Americans/Canadians, **3:**808–12, 1201
Guys and Dolls (Loesser), **3:**545; **7:**946
Guzmán, Carlos, **3:**780
Guzman, Constancio de, **3:**1025
Guzmán, Pablo "Yoruba," **3:**798
Gvishiani family, **8:**841
Gwalior dynasty, **5:**721
Gwangwa, Jonas, **1:**774
Gwashinda singers, **5:**782, 783
Gwero, James, **9:**966
Gwich'in Indian nation, **3:**391, 405, 1274, 1277
"Gwine to Run All Night [Camptown Races]"
 (Foster), **3:**186
Gwyllt, Ieuan. *See* Roberts, John
Gypsies. *See* Rom people; Travellers
Gypsies de Queens (musical group), **3:**803
"Gypsy" (Ink Spots), **3:**708
Gypsy Kings (musical group), **7:**468

Ha people, **1:**641
Ha Handam, **7:**986
Ha Kyuil, **7:**921, 925, 927, 985, 989
Ha Nhi people, **4:**535
Ha Peraḥ be-Gani, **6:**1033–34
Haarstrup, Ademuyiwa, **1:**403
Haas, Ain, **3:**879, 880
Haas, Gaby, **3:**343
Haazen, Father Guido, **1:**217

Hába, Alois, **8:**729
Ḥabāba, **6:**291–92, 295, 298
habanera, **2:**49
   in Brazil, **2:**313, 350
   in Colombia, **2:**393
   in Cuba, **2:**827, 831, 835
   in Guatemala, **2:**735
   in Mexico, **2:**604, 620
   in North America, **3:**13, 521, 783, 786, 790,
      791, 795, 797
Habenicht, Gottfried, **8:**886
Habibullah, Afghan ruler, **5:**805
Habudatta, **5:**462
Hacı Arif Bey, **6:**116, 779
Hacı Bayram Veli, **6:**193
Hacı Bektaş Veli, **6:**794, *794,* 799
Hacı Faik Bey, **6:**110, 779
Hacibekov, Uzeir, **6:**924, 927
Hacienda label, **3:**781
Hadādjī, **6:**270
Hadar, Joseph, **6:**1073
Haddow, Alexander John, **8:**374
Hadendowa people, **1:**558–60
Hadhi l-asiliyyih (jalwih), **6:**586–87
Hadjidakis, Manos, **8:**208
Ḥadriyya (Saiʾūn ensemble), **6:**97, 98
Hadzhiev, Parashkev, **8:**905
Hadzidakis, Manos, **8:**1021
Hadzis, Kostas, **8:**285
Haebang chŏnsa ŭi norae (An), **7:**960
Haebang chŏnsa ŭi norae (Ri), **7:**960
Haeberli, Joerg, **2:**467
Haedong kayo (Kim), **7:**856
Haefer, J. Richard, **3:**473
Haeffner, Johann Christian Friedrich, **8:**447
haegŭm. See violins and fiddles (bowed lutes)
Haegŭm hyŏpchugok (Kim), **7:**957
Haemada pomi omyŏn (North Korean aria),
      7:962–63
Haeryŏng (hyangak piece), **7:**867
Hāfez. *See* Ḥāfiẓ (Sufi poet)
Ḥāfiẓ (Sufi poet), **5:**687, 805, 828; **6:**132, 135,
      826, 914, 940, 945
Ḥāfiẓ, ʿAbd al-Ḥalīm, **6:**72, 237, 238, 239, 283,
      592, 599, 600–601, *601*
Ḥāfiẓ, Jihād, **6:**573–76
Ḥāfiẓ, Mūsā, **6:**573–76, *574*
Hafiz Post, **6:**194, 771
Ḥāfiẓ, Saʿīd, **6:**168
Hafiz, Sahajahan, **5:**858
Hafsid dynasty, **6:**444
Hagan, George, **10:**31
Hage, Louis, **6:**20, 209
Haggard, Merle, **3:**77, 81, 520
Hagibis (musical group), **3:**1026
Hahn, Gunnar, **8:**152, 156
Hahn, J. G. von, **8:**1003
Hahn Man-young. *See* Han Manyŏng
Hahn, Michael, **3:**565
Hahon people, **9:**644
Haibitan, Mahmad-i, **5:***782*
Haida Indian nation, **3:**5, 394, 1093–94, 1254
Haider, Ali, **5:**788, 790, 791
Haider, Ghulam, **5:**420
Haider, Musafer, **5:**790
Haifa Orchestra, **6:**1030

Haihaya people, **5:**720
al-Ḥāʾik, Muḥammad Ibn al-Ḥusayn, **6:**20,
      1039
Haiko Ôtsuka, **7:**570; **10:**13
Hailanda (album), **9:**155
Haʾilono Mele, **9:**915
"Haimatochare" (Hoffmann), **9:**39
Haîm Bey, **6:**110, 779
Haines, Paul, **10:**87
Haiqing na tianʾe (pipa piece), **7:**168
Hair (film), **3:**200
Hair (musical), **3:**198, 199
Haiti, **2:**845, 881–95
   African influences, **2:**881–88
   art music in, **2:**892, 894
   ban on drums, **2:**795
   carnival in, **2:**94
   cord-and-peg tension drums in, **1:**316
   Creole language of, **2:**4, 72
   folklore of, **2:**18–19
   history of, **2:**792, 850, 881
   industries of, **2:**791
   military regime in, **2:**93
   musical genres
      kadans ranpa, **2:**892
      konpa-dirèk, **2:**95, 98, 878, 879, 892, 920
      mereng koudyay, **2:**890
      mereng-vodou (also *vodou-jazz*), **2:**892, 893
      méringue genres, **2:**891–92
      mini-djaz, **2:**890, 892, 894
      mizik angaje, **2:**892
      mizik rasin, **2:**891, 892, 893
      nouvèl jenerasyon, **2:**892
      rará, **2:**795, 885–87
   musical links with Venezuela, **2:**524
   popular music in, **2:**95, 98, 889–93
   slave rebellions in, **3:**802
   Vodou in, **1:**134; **2:**48, 69
Haitian people
   in Belize, **2:**666
   in Canada, **3:**1077, 1085, 1169, 1170
   in Cuba, **2:**793, 826, 827, 828, 837
   in Dominican Republic, **2:**792–93, 850
   early immigrants, **3:**802–3
   in French Guiana, **2:**434, 437
   in United States, **2:**91, 888–89; **3:**791, 802–7,
      811
Haitian Revolution, **2:**792, 793, 826, 845, 882
Haïti Culturelle, **3:**805–6
Haiyun (Zhao), **7:**346
Hajdú, André, **6:**1031, 1064, 1065; **8:**274, 288
Hajduk Veljko (dance ensemble), **3:**1198
Hajibeyov, Uzeir, **6:**18
Hajiev, Şakir, **6:**930
Haji Murad (Tolstoy), **6:**6–7
El-Hajj, Ali A., **1:***553*
Ḥajjar, ʿAli, **6:**239
Hakala, Joyce, **3:**826
Hakalits, Ben, **9:**155, 1005
Ḥakam al-Wādī, **6:**353
al-Ḥakam I, emir of Córdoba, **6:**442, 540
Hakataya culture, **3:**429
Hakhverdyan (Armenian musicologist),
      6:734–35
Ḥakīm, **6:**240
Hakim, Talib Rasul, **3:**610

Hakka people
   ensemble music of, **7:**169, 217, 219, 233, 236,
      238, 241
   modes of, **7:**235
   musical aesthetics of, **7:**240
   in Oceania, **9:**69
   in Taiwan, **7:**423, 427
Hakuga no hue hu, **7:**588
Halabi (hava), **6:**850, *850*
Ḥalab people, **6:**625
Halāî, Salīm, **6:**1044
Halau ʾO Kekuhi, **3:**207
Hale, Albert, **3:**313
Hale, Horatio, **9:**778–79
ha-Levi, Judah, **6:**9, 19
Halévy, Jacques-François, **3:**606
Haley, Bill, **4:**884; **8:**430
Halfarḥah likbīrih lal-ʿarīs il-ghālī (farʾawī),
      6:590
Halia people, **9:**640–42
Halifax Conservatory (Nova Scotia), **3:**1116
Halili, Merita, **8:**999
Halkias family, **8:**284
Hall, Adelaide, **3:**620
Hall, Bon, **9:***135*
Hall, David, **9:**972
Hall, Doreen, **3:**1185
Hall, Frederick A., **3:**144, 1069, 1108
Hall, Hazel, **9:**256
Hall, James Norman, **9:**41, 45
Hall Johnson Choir, **3:**536, 607, 621
Hall, Juanita, **3:**621
Hall, Pauline, **8:**425–26
Hall, Reg, **8:**339
Hall, Stuart, **3:**587
Hall, Tom T., **3:**81, 317
Hall, Vera, **3:**579
Hallberg, Bengt, **8:**446
Halliday, Johnny, **9:**213
Hallowell, Irving, **3:**392
Hallstatt culture, **8:**35, 40, 319, 321
hallucinogens. *See* drugs (hallucinogens and
      narcotics)
Hallvarðsdóttir, Herdís, **8:**407
Halmahera, **4:**812, 813
Halpern, Ida, **3:**367
Halpern, Steve, **3:**346
Halpert, Herbert, **3:**294
Haluma, **6:**674
Halvorsen, Johan, **8:**425
Ham (musical group), **8:**407
Ham people, **1:**289
Ham Hwajin, **7:**830, 988, 989, 990
Hamada, **6:**270
Hamadjan (Kutin performer), **1:**654
Ḥamās movement, **6:**636, 637–38
Hamazkain Choir, **3:**1084
Hambourg, Boris, **3:***1184*
Hambourg Conservatory (Toronto), **3:**1182
Hambruch, Paul, **9:**739, 756, 757, 981
Hamburg Südsee-Expedition, **9:**23–24, 479, 722,
      741, 756, 836, 981, 994
Hamburger, Poul, **8:**460
al-Hamdānī, **6:**360
Ḥamdānid dynasty, **6:**565
Hamdi, Baligh, **6:**604

Ḥamdi, Saḥar, **6:**239
Hamel, Peter, **5:**56
Ḥamīda, 'Ali, **6:**239
Hamidov, Abdurahim, **6:***907*, 907–8
Hamilton, A. W., **4:**436
Hamilton, Bob, **3:**1280, *1280*
Hamilton, Carl, **3:**676
Hamilton, Iain, **8:**369
Hamilton Philharmonic Orchestra, **3:**1184
Hamilton Tamburitzan Ensemble, **3:**1083
Hamlet (Shakespeare), **3:**615; **7:**300
Hamlisch, Marvin, **3:**545
Hamm, Charles, **3:**32, 42, 143, 144
Ḥammād, **6:**353
Hammarskjöld, Dag, **3:**610
Hammer, Jan, **3:**204
Hammer, M. C., **4:**886
"Hammer Song" (Hays and Seeger), **3:**328
Hammershaimb, Venceslaus Ulricus, **8:**468
Hammerstein, Oscar, II, **3:**197
Hammond, James H., **3:**598
Hammond, John, **3:**580
Hammond, John, Jr., **3:**329
Hammond, Norman, **2:**658
Hamnigan people, **7:**1004–20
Hamparsum, Baba. *See* Limondjian,
    Hambardzum
Hampton Institute (Virginia), **3:**524, 575, 632
Hampton, Lionel, **3:**655, 668, 669, 742
Hamtai people, **9:**491
al-Ḥamūlī, 'Abduh, **6:**547, 570
Hamza 'Alā al-Dīn, **6:**641
Hamza El Din. *See* Hamza 'Alā al-Dīn
Hamziyya (devotional poem), **6:**437
Han (Kim), **7:**959–60
Han Chuhwan, **7:**915
Han du chun (Xibo song-dance), **7:**463
Han dynasty
    Buddhism in, **7:**311
    commanderies of, **7:**18, 24
    Daoism in, **7:**312, 320
    Donghan (Eastern Han) period, **7:**311, 312,
        320, 402
    gongs in, **7:**191
    hengchui music in, **7:**455
    instruments in, **7:**111, 112
    military music in, **7:**195
    musical institutions in, **7:**102, 103
    musical notation in, **7:**131
    musical revivals in, **7:**42
    music in, **7:**88, 396, 407, 480
    pipa in, **7:**167
    qin in, **7:**159
Han Ilsŏp, **7:**915
Han Indian nation, **3:**1274, 1277
Han Kaptŭk, **7:**915, 916
Han Manyŏng (Hahn Man-young), **7:**853, 854,
    855
Han Myŏnghŭi, **7:**853, 969
Han Nongsŏn, **7:**900
Han people. *See also* China
    banhu playing, **7:**176–77
    dances of, **7:**61
    folk songs of, **7:**149–56
    influence on minority cultures, **7:**464, 495–96,
        500, 509, 512–14, 518, 521

musical traditions of, **7:**92
music theory of, **7:**115–23
    in northwestern China, **7:**455
percussion genres of, **7:**192
population of, **7:**441, 447
relationship to Manchu rulers, **7:**379
Han Pŏmsu, **7:**915
Han Qixiang, **7:**258–59
Han Songhak, **7:**899
Han Sukku, **7:**913, 914
Han Sŭngho, **7:**900
Han ture (Kim), **7:**959
Hanahal (Israeli band), **6:***1072*
Ḥanahleh Hitbalbelah (Israeli song), **6:**266
Hana Ola Records, **9:**998
Hanawa Hokiiti, **7:**587
Hancock, Herbie, **3:**340, 664, 695; **7:**967
Hancock, Hunter, **3:**742
Handa people, **1:**651
Hand at the Gate (musical), **3:**621
Handbook of North American Indians, **3:**496
*Handbook of Research on Music Teaching and
    Learning*, **3:**286
Handbuch der europäischen Volksmusikinstrumente,
    8:172
hand clapping
    Afghanistan, **5:***620*, 813
    Africa, **1:**33, 118, 605
    in African-American music, **3:**595, 597, 625,
        627, 630
    Algeria, **6:**473
    Andalusia, **6:**444
    Anuta, **9:**857, 858–59, 860
    Arabian peninsula, **6:**546, 651, 652, *658*, 698,
        706
    Arab women, **6:**372
    Australia, **9:***433*, 446
        Aboriginal peoples, **9:**242
        Cape York, **9:**411, 429
        Central, **9:**437
        Gulf of Carpentaria, **9:**427
        Kimberleys, **9:**431–32
    Bahamas, **2:**804, 810
    Balochistan, **5:**774
    Bamana people, **1:**121
    Barbados, **2:**817
    Bellona, **9:**850, 852
    in black gospel music, **3:**534
    Bora Bora, **9:**41
    Borneo, **4:**826
    Brazil, **2:**311, 349
    in Cajun music, **3:**857
    in ceremonies, **5:**469
    Chuuk, **9:**737
    Colombia, **2:**401, 404, 406
    Congo, **1:**77
    in country dances, **3:**212
    Denmark, **8:**460, 462
    Dominica, **2:**841
    Dominican Republic, **2:***848*, 857
    Egypt, **6:**623, 624, 629
        Nubian people, **6:**641, 645
        saqfa suwaysī, **6:**627
    Ewe people, **1:**35
    Fiji, **9:**19, 173, 774, 776, 777
    in folk dances, **5:**498, 500–501

Guadeloupe, **2:**875
Gumuz people, **1:**564
Guyana, **2:**445; **5:**603
Iran, **6:**833
Jamaica, **2:**897, 901, 906
Japan, **7:**683
Kerala, **5:**934
Kiribati, **9:**761–62
Kosrae, **9:**741–42
!Kung people, **1:**112–13
Laos, **4:**350
Luangiua, **9:**843–44
Madagascar, **1:**789
Malaysia, **4:**423
Manihiki, **9:**905, 907
Maroon cultures, **2:**506
Marquesas Islands, **9:**892, 893, 894, 895
Micronesia, **9:**716
Middle East, **6:**398
    in Moroccan court music, **3:**65
    in Motown style, **3:**674
    for narratives, **9:**337
    in Native American music, **3:**473
Niue, **9:**817
Nubian people, **1:**557, 558
Pakistan, **5:**752
    northern, **5:**797
Palestine, **6:**574, 575, 578
Panama, **2:**778, 780
Papua New Guinea, **9:**197
    Binandere people, **9:**500
    Rai Coast, **9:**563
    Sursurunga people, **9:**627
Peru, **2:**496, 499
Philippines, **4:**852
Polynesia, **9:**769
Polynesian outliers, **9:**836
Pukapuka, **9:**911
Punjab, **5:**652, 765, 771
Rajasthan, **5:**644, *648*
Rom people, **8:**287
Rotuma, **9:**822
Ryûkyû Islands, **7:**791
St. Lucia, **2:**943
Sāmoa, **9:**20, 207, 798, 805
Saudi Arabia, **6:**653, 692, 693
Sikaiana, **9:**847
Solomon Islands, **9:**156, 267
    Isabel Province, **9:**660
Somalia, **1:**611
South Africa, **5:**617
South America, **2:**31
Spain, **8:***597*, 598
Sudan, **1:**555
in Sufi rituals, **6:**186, 543
Sumatra, **4:**604, 605, 611
Switzerland, **8:**691
Takuu, **9:**839
tala and, **5:**112, 119, 139–42, 212, 358,
    939
Tamil Nadu, **5:**919–20
Thailand, **4:**299, 300
Tikopia, **9:**853, 855
Tonga, **9:**11, 788, 793
Trinidad, **2:**957; **5:**590–91
Tuareg people, **1:**538, 585, 587, 590, 593

Tumbuka people, **1:**281
Tunisia
in Jewish women's songs, **6:**525, 526, 528
in *ma'lūf*, **6:**326, 507
Tuvalu, **9:**829
Uganda, **1:**602
Uttar Pradesh, **5:**665
'Uvea, **9:**809, 813
Vanuatu, **9:**695, 703
Tanna, **9:**708
in Vodou ceremonies, **3:**804
West Futuna, **9:**861
by women, **5:**8
Yap, **9:**732
Handel, George Frideric, **3:**27, 1179, 1225;
        6:1025, 1030; **8:**79, 86, 646; **9:**131,
        187, 203
conducting of, **8:**101–2
oratorios, **1:**763; **8:**17, 60, 62, 254
Handel and Haydn Society (Boston), **3:**28, 535
handicapped musicians. *See* blind or handicapped
        musicians
Handog ng Diyos (de León), **4:**881
Handoyo, **4:**698
Handsome Lake (Seneca prophet), **3:**7, 463–64,
        1078
Handy, E. S. Craighill, **9:**24, 869, 891, 892, 969
Handy, W. C., **3:**524, 578, 644, 706, 707, 787
Handy, Willowdean, **9:**24
Hangal, Gangubai, **5:**413
"Hangman's Reel," **3:**1075, 1164
Han'gong qiuyue (*Jiangnan sizhu* piece), **7:**225
Han'gong qiuyue (*pipa* piece), **7:**234
Han'guk akki taegwan (Chang), **7:**854
Han'guk ch'angjak ŭmak yŏn'guhoe (Korean
        society), **7:**972
Han'guk Chŏngshin Munhwa Yŏn'guwŏn
        (institute), **7:**990
Han'guk Kugak Hakhoe. *See* Korean
        Musicological Society
Han'guk Kugak Yesul Hakkyo (institute), **7:**990,
        991
Han'guk ŭmak (collection), **7:**993
Han'guk ŭmak (Kim), **7:**953
Han'guk ŭmakhak charyo ch'ongsŏ (collection),
        7:857, 993
Han'guk ŭmaksa (Chang), **7:**854
Han'guk Ŭmak Sahakpo (periodical), **7:**855
Han'guk ŭmaksa yŏnp'yo (Chang), **7:**854
Han'guk ŭmak sŏnjip (recording collection),
        7:993
Han'guk Ŭmak Yŏn'gu (periodical), **7:**855
Han'guk Ŭmanhak (periodical), **7:**855
Han'guk Ŭmbanhak (periodical), **7:**994
Hani people, **7:**485–92
Hank Ballard and the Midnighters, **3:**351
Hanks, Nancy, **3:**298
Hannaford Street Silver Band, **3:**1080
Hanna, Judith Lynne, **3:**221
Hannerz, Ulf, **3:**512, 677
Hanne ŭi sŭnch'ŏn (Kim), **7:**958
Hanno, **1:**74, 75, 635
Hannula, Tero, **8:**485
Han obaengnyŏn (Korean folk song), **7:**883
Hanoi Conservatory of Music, **4:**511–12. *See also*
        National Conservatory of Music

Hanoi Rocks (musical group), **8:**217
Hanokh, Shalom, **6:**1073, *1074*
Hanopol, Mike, **4:**885
Hansberry, Lorraine, **3:**622
Hansche Weiss Quintett, **8:**289
Hansell, Kathleen, **10:**165
Hansen, Georg Caspar, **8:**471
Hansen, Kathryn, **5:**675
Hansen, Ole Koch, **8:**460–61
Han shu (dynastic history), **7:**125
Hanslick, Eduard, **7:**341
Hanson, F. Allan, **9:**212, 880
Hanson, Howard, **3:**541, 609, 610
Hantang Yuefu (performing group), **7:**425
Hantian lei (Yan), **3:**1261; **7:**180, 219
Hanua xishui (*xianshiyue* piece), **7:***213*, 215–16
Hanuman (deity), **5:**897
vina playing of, **5:**353
worship of, **5:**645
Hanumāna mat, raga classification in, **5:**77, 314,
        316
Hanumān chālīsā, **5:**549
Hanuman, school of, **5:**47, 77, 314
Hanunóo people, **1:**722; **4:**920
Hanxleden, John Ernest, **5:**946
Hanzu diaoshi hesheng (Li), **7:**347–48
Hanzu min'ge gailun (Jiang), **7:**156
Hao Jiang Tian, **3:**959
al-Haouari, Belaoui, **6:**269
Hap Cats (musical group), **8:**237
"Happy Days Are Here Again" (Ager), **3:**310,
        505
Happy End (musical group), **7:**746
Happy Gang (radio show), **3:**1107
Happy Miao Family, A (album), **7:**443
Happy Notes (musical group), **3:***896*
Hapsburg empire. *See* Austro-Hungarian empire
Haq, Abdul, **5:**413
Harahap, Irwansyah, **3:**1020
Haralambos, Michael, **3:**584
Haranga (musical group), **7:**1019–20
Harant, Krištof, **8:**726
Harappan civilization, **5:**14, 238, 239, 298,
        319–20, 374
Harari, **1:**779
Ḥarbān, Jāsim Muḥammad, **6:**651
Harbhuji (deity), **5:**643
al-Harbi, Salih, **6:**651
Harbison, John, **3:**541
Harchin people, **7:**1004–20
d'Harcourt, Marguerite, **2:**24, 231, 467, 487;
        3:1165
d'Harcourt, Raoul, **2:**24, 231, 467, 487; **3:**1165
Harcourt-Whyte, Ikoli, **1:**233, 237
"Hard Rain's a-Gonna Fall" (Dylan), **3:**316
Hardanger fiddle. *See* violins and fiddles (bowed
        lutes)
Hardanger Violinist Association of America,
        3:869
Hard Day's Night, A (film), **8:**679
Hardie, Matthew, **8:**367
Hardin, Lil, **3:**652
Harding, Albert Austin, **3:**567
hardingfele. *See* violins and fiddles (bowed lutes)
*Harding's Collection of Jigs, Reels, and Country
        Dances*, **3:**1190

Hardison, O. B., **1:**492
Hardjosoebroto, **4:**130, 683
Hardy, Ron, **3:**691
Hare Krishna (ISKCON) movement, **3:**983;
        5:255, 581
Hare Rama Hare Krishna (film), **5:**427, 537
Hargrove, Roy, **3:**664
Haridas, Swami, **5:**252
Harihara II, king of Vijayanagar, **5:**740
Hariharan, K., **5:**545
Harijans (also Dalits; untouchables; scheduled
        castes), **5:**9
in Karnataka, **5:**866, 872, 875, 880
in Tamil Nadu, **5:**557–58, 910, 911, 922
Harimati, **5:**855
Haripunchai (kingdom), **4:**310
al-Ḥarīrī, Darwīsh, **6:**168
Harivyasdevacharya, Sri, **5:**252
Harjito, Denni, **3:**1014
Harjito, I. M., **3:**1014
Harker, Dave, **8:**339
Harlem Dynamites (musical group), **1:**477
Harlem Hamfats (musical group), **3:**645–46
Harlem Matinee (radio show), **3:**742
Harlem Swingsters (musical group), **1:**771
Harlequin label, **9:**998
Harlow, Larry, **3:**797
Härma, Miina, **8:**497
harmonicas. *See* mouth organs
Harmonic Choir (musical group), **7:**1023; **10:**71
Harmonicon (tunebook), **3:**1116
Harmonie Choir (Toronto), **3:**1195
Harmonie Orchestra (Curaçao), **2:**931
Harmonie Universelle (Mersenne), **8:**615
Harmonielehre (Adams), **3:**541
harmonium
Afghanistan, **5:**806, 815, 818, 820, 822–23,
        823, 828, 831, 835, 837
Africa, **1:**607
Andhra Pradesh, **5:**896
Balochistan, **5:**782, 783
Fiji, **5:**612–13, *614*
Finland, **8:***485*
Gujarat, **5:**633, 634, 635
Guyana, **2:**444; **5:**603, 604
Jamaica, **2:**900, 908
Japanese manufacturers, **7:**537
Karnataka, **5:**869
Kashmir, **5:**684
Kerala, **5:**945, 948
Khwarezm, **6:**946
in Korea, **7:**951, 988
Madhya Pradesh, **5:**723
Malta, **8:**640
in Maronite church music, **6:**216
Nepal, **5:**702, 704, 705
North America
        at Pakistani-American weddings, **5:**579
        in South Asian (East Indian) music, **3:**815,
        815, 981, 983, 984, 1246
North West Frontier Province, **5:**790
Oceania, **9:**93–94
Pakistan, **5:**746, 752, *752*, 753
Punjab, **5:**762, *765*, 769, 771
Rajasthan, **5:**641, *641*, 642, 643, 644, 645,
        648

harmonium (*continued*)
  Réunion Island, **5:**608, 609
  Scotland, **8:**297
  Sikh use of, **5:**13, 257
  South Africa, **5:**618
  South America, in South Asian music, **2:**85–86
  South Asia, **5:**338, 340–41, *496*, 563, 715
    in *bhangra*, **5:**426
    in *chau* dance-drama, **5:**497
    in devotional music, **5:**248, *248*, 251, 256, 257, 267, 364, 582, 655–56
    in film music, **5:**534, 535, 543, 555
    folk uses of, **5:**365
    in *ghazal* performance, **5:**186
    in Hindustani music, **5:**82, 188
    instruction on, **5:**575
    in *jātrā* theater, **5:**505
    in Karnatak music, **5:**235, 352
    in *kathak* ensemble, **5:**494
    in *khyāl* performance, **5:**171–72
    in *oḍissi* ensemble, **5:**520
    in pop *bhajan* genre, **5:**549, *549*
    in *rās līlā* dance-drama, **5:**495
    in *ṭhumrī* performance, **5:**180, 182
    in *yakṣagāna* ensemble, **5:**515
  Southeast Asia, **4:**432, 435, 438–39, 605, 620
  Sri Lanka, **5:**970
  Tamil Nadu, **5:**906, 909, 913, 924, 926
  Trinidad and Tobago, **2:**958; **5:**590–91
  in Tunisian *ma'lūf*, **6:**327, 329
  Uttar Pradesh, **5:**660, 665, 667, 670, 673, 674
Harmonium (Adams), **3:**176, 541
Harmonium (musical group), **3:**265, 1158, 1168
Harmonius, **6:**227
harmony
  Abkhazian people, **8:**852
  African composed music, **1:**229–30
  African hymns, **1:**209–10
  African music, **1:**21
  Andean regions
    flute ensemble music, **2:**211, 286–87, 295
    panpipe ensemble music, **2:**209, 210, 285
  Anuta, hymns, **9:**860
  Apache songs, **3:**431
  in art music, **8:**68
  Australia, Torres Strait island dance, **9:**429
  Austria, **8:**671–72
  Aztec culture, **2:**555
  Bantu peoples, **1:**763
  "blow harmony" and doo-wop, **3:**671, 672
  in bluegrass, **3:**161, 165
  in blues, **3:**638, 639, 642–43
  in bossa nova, **2:**108
  Brazil
    acculturation in, **2:**307
    bossa nova, **2:**108
    caboclo music, **2:**325
    central and southern genres, **2:**306
    dupla, **2:**307–8, 319
    in religious music, **2:**329
    samba-lenço, **2:**349
    ternos songs, **2:**313
  Bulgaria, in seconds, **8:**896
  Central Africa, **1:**673, 723, 741–42
  Chile
    cueca, **2:**369

    romance, **2:**367
    tonada, **2:**368
    urban *tonada*, **2:**368
    verso, **2:**367
  China
    Chinese-mode based, **7:**230, 231, 347–48
    minority cultures, **7:**490
    Russian music, **7:**457
    westernized music, **7:**229, 339, 443
  chromodal discourse, **3:**337
  Coast Salish spirit dancing songs, **3:**397, 401
  Colombia
    bambuco, **2:**382
    danza, **2:**393
  Congo, **1:**663–64
  Costa Rica, *romance*, **2:**695
  in country music, **3:**77
  Creek Stomp Dance songs, **3:**469
  Croatian songs, **3:**922
  Cuba
    canción, **2:**831
    criolla, **2:**832
  Czech Republic, **8:**719
    Moravia, **8:**721–22
  Denmark, ballads, **8:**453
  in Doukhobor music, **3:**1267–68
  England
    dance music, **8:**330
    songs, **8:**327
  Ephrata Cloister use of, **3:**906
  Estonia, **8:**492
  Fiji
    meke, **9:**775
    triadic, **9:**162
  in free jazz, **3:**662
  Garifuna culture
    bérusu, **2:**675
    paranda, **2:**675
  Georgia, **8:**830, 842
  German music, **3:**889
  Germany, **8:**653
  Ghana, guitar music, **1:**356–58
  Goa, **5:**737, 739, 741
  Gogo people, **1:**639
  Greece, *rebetika*, **8:**206
  Guarijio culture
    contradanza, **2:**554
    son principal, **2:**554
  Haiti, popular music, **2:**893
  harmonic equivalence principle, **1:**709, 715, 728, 742
  Hawai'i, **9:**914–28
    Jawaiian genre, **9:**166
  Honduras, mestizo dance-music, **2:**744
  Iceland, *tvísöngur*, **8:**403, 423
  Irian Jaya
    Asmat songs, **9:**587
    vocal music, **9:**583–84
  Italy, **8:**619
    Neapolitan song, **8:**618
    vocal music, **8:**610
  Jamaica, *mento*, **2:**906
  Japan, *syô* (*sho*), **7:**621
  in jazz, **3:**650, 654, 661–62
  Jewish modes, **8:**253, 258

  Kiribati, dance-songs, **9:**761–62
  Lithuania, in seconds, **8:**510, 511
  in liturgical music, **3:**67
  Low Countries, **8:**523
  Luvale people, **1:**726–43
  Mangareva, *īmene*, **9:**889
  Manihiki, **9:**907
  Marshall Islands, **9:**753
  Mexica culture, in *sones*, **2:**561
  Mexico
    corrido, **2:**616
    son, **2:**606
  Miskitu culture, *tiun*, **2:**663
  in modal jazz, **3:**661–62
  New Age music, **3:**345
  New Caledonia
    hymns, **9:**678
    kaneka, **9:**214
  Nguni peoples, **1:**706
  Nicaragua
    corrido, **2:**759
    guitar music, **2:**757
  nineteenth-century innovations, **8:**83
  North Korea, westernized music, **7:**961
  Norway, **8:**425
  Nsenga and Shona peoples, **1:**307–8
  Papua New Guinea
    Abelam people, **9:**550
    Baluan hymns, **9:**607
    cacophony, **9:**533
    four-part, in conch bands, **9:**195–96, 393
    guitar songs, **9:**387–88
    Gulf Province, **9:**495–96
    Irumu string bands, **9:**571
    Karkar people, **9:**561
    Managalasi songs, **9:**503, 505
    Orokolo people, **9:**489
    Siasi music, **9:**575–76
    string-band music, **9:**138
    Teop people, **9:**643–44
    thirds, **9:**490
    triadic, **9:**148, 196
    urban music, **9:**497–98
  parlor music, **3:**183
  Peru
    Indian *vs.* mestizo aesthetics, **2:**483
    tondero, **2:**481
    yaraví, **2:**477
  Pohnpei, **9:**739
  popular songs, **3:**195
    eighteenth century, **3:**181
    twentieth century, **3:**196, 549
  Portugal, **8:**581
  Pukapuka, *pātautau*, **9:**913
  in punk, **3:**357
  Purépecha culture
    pirekua, **2:**579
    son regional, **2:**579
  Rapa Nui, **9:**952
  Réunion Island, *sega*, **5:**609
  in rock, **3:**551
  Romania, **8:**879–80, 881
  Rotuma, *sua*, **9:**822
  Russia, **8:**771
  Sāmoa, hymns, **9:**204–5
  San people, **1:**704–5

Volume Key: **1**, Africa; **2**, South America, Mexico, etc.; **3**, United States and Canada; **4**, Southeast Asia; **5**, South Asia

Sardinia, *canto a chiterra*, **8:**629
Shona people, **1:**744, 747–48, 753
"skipping process" of, **1:**741
Slovakia, **8:**719
Solomon Islands
   Blablanga songs, **9:**658
   Western, **9:**155–56
in soul, **3:**678
South Africa
   composed songs, **1:**218
   thula n'divile format, **1:**767
South America, tropical-forest regions, **2:**131
southern African music, **1:**701
Spain, *jota*, **8:**595
Tahiti, *hīmene rū'au*, **9:**871
Tamil Nadu, **5:**924
Tonga, *hiva kakala*, **9:**783
Turkish rock and pop music, **6:**252
Tuvalu, **9:**831
twentieth-century American art music, **3:**174,
   539
twentieth-century innovations, **8:**85
two-part pentatonic, **1:**320
Ukraine, **8:**809
Vanuatu, **9:**690
Venezuela
   harp music, **2:**532–33
   two-part, **2:**534
in village music, **8:**9
Yiddish songs, **3:**936
Zande harp music, **1:**656
Harmony Brass (musical group), **3:**1195
Harnasie Highlanders (musical group), **3:**1197
Harner, Michael J., **2:**431
Harnick, Sheldon, **3:**943
Harold III (Sigurdarson), king of Norway, **8:**423
Harold Melvin and the Blue Notes, **1:**778;
   3:228, 711
"Harp That Once thro' Tara's Halls" (Moore),
   3:182, 520
harp-lutes
   ardin, **1:**302, 540
   kerân-non-konîng, **1:**467
   kora, **1:**8, 158, 159, 161, 364–65, 420,
      421–22, *437*, 445, 489, 498
      Europe, **8:***239*
      North America, **3:**339, 1063, 1170
   nkoni, **1:**445
   sanku, **1:**89, 351
   Senufo people, **1:**454
   seperewa, **1:**23, 351, 356, 367, 377, 465
   soron, **1:**445
   West Africa, **1:**445
harps
   Africa
      bow types, **1:**549–50
      diffusion of, **1:**301–2; **10:**120
   aijuma, **8:**853
   Andean regions, **2:**212, 222–23
   ardin, **6:**359, 409
   Argentina, **2:**251
   arpa, **2:**360
   arpa aragüeña, **2:**532
   arpa criolla, **2:**532–33
   arpa ecuatoriana-paraguaya, **2:**418
   arpa folclórica, **2:**418

arpa grande, **2:**611
arpa imbabureña, **2:**418
arpa india, **2:**456–57, 464
arpa indigena, **2:**473–74
arpa jarocha, **2:**609
arpa llanera, **2:**532, *532*, 540–41
arpa mirandina, **2:**532
arpa tuyera, **2:**532
Austria, **8:**672
Azande people, **1:**650
al-bakurbo, **1:**560
Baroque music for, **8:**78
bīṇ bājā, **5:**329
Bolivia, **2:**288
bolon, **1:**444, 445
Celtic, **8:**321
çeng, **6:**115, 774
Central Africa, **1:**655–56
chang, **5:**692–93; **6:**395, 398
changi, **8:**838–39, *839*, 840
Chile, **2:**368
citrā vīṇā, **5:**326
cláirseach, **8:**383–84, 393
clàrsach, **8:**362, 364, 366, 367
clarsach, **9:**116
classification of, **8:**41
Colombia, **2:**385
dissemination of, **8:**170
domingacha, **2:**473
duadastanon-fandir, **8:**860
early, **8:**39
ebani, **8:**838–39
Ecuador, **2:**212–13, 216, 218, 221, 417–18,
   423–24
Egypt, **8:**839
engkeratung, **4:**835
ennanga, **1:**302
fengshou konghou, **7:**112
Gabon, **1:**661–63
Germany, **8:**656
Greece, ancient, **8:**47
Guatemala, **2:**728
Guinea coast, 1600s, **1:**83
harppu, **8:**479
Hungary, **8:**743
Indus Valley civilization, **5:**320
Ireland, **8:**152, 389
Italy, **8:**197, 615, 618
jank, **6:**444
jank al-miṣrī, **6:**373
kamele ngoni, **1:**420
K'ekchi Maya, **2:**667–68
kingir-kobuz, **8:**857
knari, **8:**838–39
konghou, **7:**42, 455
krding, **1:**301
kundi, **1:**302, 570, 655–56
kurbi, **1:**560
Madhya Pradesh, **5:**306, 323, 329
magadis, **8:**47
Maya culture, **2:**655
Mayo culture, **2:**592
Mexica culture, **2:**559–60, 561
Mexico, **2:**550, 606, 610, 621–22
Minnesängerharfe, **8:**651
Native American use of, **3:**479

nebel (also *nevel*), **8:**36
ngombi, **1:**660, 663
North America
   in Iberian music, **3:**848
   in Irish music, **3:**326, 842
   in Mexican music, **3:**723, 735
   in Paraguayan music, **3:**730
ongnyugŭm, **7:***826*, 831, 961, 962
paracá, **2:**553
Paraguay, **2:**461–63
pedal, **8:**347–48
Peru, **2:***1*, 37, 209, 473–75, 483
pinn, **4:**157, 169
psalterion, **8:**47
Purépecha culture, **2:**577–78
ṣanj, **6:**397
saùñ, **4:**15, 132, 222, 377–78; **5:**329
Scotland, triangular, **8:**366
shu konghou, **7:**112
simbing, **1:**445
Slovenia, **8:**914
sogonghu, **7:***826*, 830
South America, **2:**36
   central-coastal harp, **2:**532, 541
sugonghu, **7:**830
Tanzania, **1:**641
telenn, **8:**560–61
telyn, **8:**347
trigonon, **8:**47
triple, **8:**347–48, 352, *355*
tünak, **4:**545
Uruguay, **2:**519
Venezuela, **2:**524, 531
vipañcī vīṇā, **5:***299*, 326
wagonghu, **7:**830
Wales, **8:**200, 342, 344, 347–48, 350–53,
   354, 355, 356
West Africa, arched, **1:**445
Yaqui culture, **2:**590, *591*; **3:**437–38, 485
harpsichord. *See* keyboard instruments
Harrán, Don, **6:**1063, 1066–67
Harrant, Oudi, **3:**1032
Harrell, Max Leigh, **4:**701
Harries, Jeanette, **1:**135
Harriet Tubman Center (Toronto), **3:**1085
Harrigan, Edward, **3:**544
Harrigan, Ned, **3:**192–93
Harris, Charles K., **3:**191, 544, 549
Harris, Ellen, **10:**71–72
Harris, Emmylou, **3:**81, 520, 777
Harris, Michael, **3:**630
Harris, Roy, **2:**114; **3:**174, 175, 297, 327, 539
Harris, Wynonie, **3:**646, 669, 708
Harrison, Benjamin, **3:**309
Harrison, Bill, **9:**130
Harrison, Daphne Duval, **3:**104, 582
Harrison, Frank L., **8:**22, 320, 321
Harrison, George, **3:**336, 952, 953; **5:**566; **8:**220
Harrison, Guy F., **4:**870
Harrison, Lou, **3:**327, 335, 541, 953, 954, 1015,
   1017–18, 1020; **4:**132; **7:**708, 954,
   976
Harrison, Regina, **2:**429–30
Harrison, William Henry, **3:**304, 305–6
Harron, Don, **3:**199
Harry, Debby, **2:**97

Harsa, King, **5:**509
Hart, C. W. M., **9:**987
Hart, George, **5:**930
Hart House String Quartet, **3:**1079, 1117, 1184, *1184*
Hart, Lorenz, **3:**197
Hart, Mickey, **3:**338, 339; **7:**1025
Hart, Sir Robert, **7:**374
Hart Rouge (musical group), **3:**1088
Hart, Tony, **3:**192–93, 544
Hartigan, Royal, **3:**337
Hartmann, Johann P. E., **8:**460
Hartwig, Gerald W., **1:**636
Hārūn al-Rashīd, caliph, **6:**294, 295–96, 297, 353, 447, 539
Haru no sirabe (*yakumo goto* piece), **7:**610
Haru no umi (Miyagi), **7:**779
Harvard University (Cambridge), **3:**173; **10:**17, 20, 69, 73
Harvest of Seven Years: Cropped and Chronicled (lang), **3:**108, 109, 111
Haryana, **5:**7, 650
    dance traditions of, **5:**500–501
    map of, **5:***622*
Has al'Ayamī, **6:***686*
Hasan, Aghan ("Amanat"), **5:**487
Hasan Hüseyn, **6:**796
Ḥasan ibn 'Ali (martyr), **6:**544, 826, 939, 942
Ḥasan, Mehdi, **5:**425, 534, 548, 766
Ḥasan, Muḥammad bin, **6:**502
Hasan, Riffat, **5:**437
Hashem, **5:**809
Hashimoto Toshie, **7:**647, *647*
Hashr, Agha, **5:**487
Hasimoto Kunihiko, **7:**732
al-Ḥaṣkafī al-Ḥiṣnī, al-Muẓaffar ibn al-Ḥusayn, **6:**366
Haskell, Russel, **3:**135
Hasluck, Margaret, **8:**285
Haslund-Christensen, Henning, **7:**1012
Ḥassan, Aḥmad Fu'ād, **6:**600
Hassan, Ghulam, **5:**807
Hassan II, king of Morocco, **6:**496
Hassan, Kamal, **5:**537
Hassan, Mehdi, **5:**425
Hassan, Mohamed Abdulla. *See* Xasan, Maxamed Cabdille
Hassan, Nazia, **5:**427
Hassan, Scheherazade Qassim, **6:**18, 23
Hassan, Zoheb, **5:**427
Hasselgård, Åke "Stan," **8:**445
Hassell, John, **9:**1005
Hassin, David ben, **6:**1038
Hassinen Kone (musical group), **8:**217
Hassler, Hans Leo, **8:**653
Hastanto, Sri, **4:**637, 656, 693; **10:**52
"Haste to the Wedding" (Métis fiddle tune), **3:***406*, 407–8
Hastings, Thomas, **3:**27, 532, *532*
Hatai, **6:**81, 796
Hatch, Martin, **3:**1014; **4:**102, 109, 637, 638, 639
Hatchett, Hattie Rhue, **3:**1063
Hatikvah (Herz-Imber), **6:**1069–70
Hatizyô kaden syo (Japanese philosophical text), **7:**546, 547

Hatton, Orin T., **3:**484
Hattori Ryôiti, **7:**745, 751
Haudricourt, André-Georges, **9:**402
Hauenschild, Walter, **9:**43
Ha Ŭndam, **7:**898
Hau'ofa, Epeli, **9:**37
Hauptmann, Gerhart, **8:**646
Hausa people, **10:**30–31
    court music, **1:**313–14, 515, 524–28
    dance, **1:**116, 289, 290–91
    Gnawa brotherhoods of, **1:**537
    healing rituals, **1:**273, 290
    history of, **1:**447–48, 518–19
    influence on Nupe people, **1:**452
    influence on Yoruba music, **1:**474
    instruments of, **1:**448–49, 450, 588
    interaction with Fur people, **1:**561
    marriage rules, **1:**523
    music of, **1:**447, 450, 451, 515–29
    praise songs, **1:**131, 291
    research on, **1:**517
    speech surrogate methods, **1:**106
Hausa states, **1:**313, 447, 452, 459
Hauser-Schäublin, Brigitta, **9:**990
Havana Mambo Orchestra, **3:**743
Havana Orchestra, **3:**795
Hà văn Cầu, **4:**25
Havasi (*gusan*), **6:***734*, 736
Havasupai Indian nation, **3:**417, 422, 433, 434
"Have Mercy, Baby" (Dominoes), **3:**671
Havergal, Frances, **9:**204
Haverly, J. H., **3:**616
Haverly's Genuine Colored Minstrels, **3:**1133
Havnar Jazzfelag, **8:**472
al-Hawa (*dabkih*), **6:**583
Hawai'i (also Hawaii), **3:**1047–53; **9:**865, 914–28
    alcohol use in, **9:**177
    annexation of, **3:**10
    archives and museums, **9:**968–72
    brass bands in, **9:**132–34
    Chinese people in, **3:**957; **7:**6; **9:**70–71, 96–97, 914
    Christianity in, **9:**207–9
    dance and music in, **9:**16–17, 49, 317, 865, 879, 925–28
        art song, **9:**923–25
        chalangalang, **9:**127–28
        dance-drama genres, **9:**231
        gendered, **9:**241
        hapa haole song, **9:**921–22
        hīmeni, **9:**187, 918–19
        hula, **3:**207, 209, 218–19, 527, 1051; **9:**17–18, 38, 163, *201*, 211–12, 272, 274–75, 925–28, *929*, 979
        hula 'ala'apapa, **9:**21
        hula 'auana, **9:**879, *930*
        hula kahiko, **9:**391
        hula ki'i, **9:**230–31
        hula ku'i, **9:**389, 390, 919–21, 928
        hula 'ōlapa, **9:***921*, 928
        hybrid genres, **3:**337
        island music, **9:**167
        Japanese *gagaku*, **9:**95
        Jawaiian, **9:**164, 166–67
        mele, **9:**299–300, 915–17
        mele hual'āla'apapa, **9:**918

    mele hula, **9:**917
    mele inoa, **9:**276
    Okinawan genres, **9:**98–99
    political songs, **9:**212, 219–22
    Puerto Rican genres, **9:**95, 99, 101–3
    seated, **9:**315
    dance competitions in, **9:**66–67
    ethnographic films on, **9:**42
    European exploration of, **9:**15–17
    European poetry on, **9:**39
    Europeans in, **9:**46
    festivals in, **9:**55–56, 66–67
    Filipino people in, **3:**1024–25; **9:**100, 914
    films on, **9:**1008, 1018–19
    geography of, **3:**3; **9:**914
    history of, **3:**527, 1047; **9:**914
    immigrants in, **9:**69, 95–111, 914
    instruments in, **9:**384–90, 916–17, 922
    Japanese people in, **3:**337, 967–68, 969; **7:**628; **9:**97, 914
    Jawaiian music genre, **3:**337, 811
    kava use in, **9:**173
    Korean people in, **9:**99; **10:**47
    missionaries in, **9:**21
    Okinawan people in, **2:**86; **9:**98–99; **10:**47
    outsiders' influence in, **9:**5
    Pacific Islanders in, **9:**103–5
    pedagogy, **9:**272–77
    pipe-and-drum ensembles in, **9:**135
    poetry, **9:**325–26
        metaphor in, **9:**336
        sung, **9:**327–28
    popular music in, **3:**1047–51; **9:**162–67
    Portuguese people in, **3:**848; **8:**582; **9:**97–98, 914
    Puerto Rican people in, **9:**99, 101–3
    religion in, **9:**200, *201*
    research on, **9:**212, 915, 968–72, 976
    Russian exploration of, **9:**17–18, 38–39
    singing, **9:**307
        falsetto, **9:**297
        timbral qualities, **9:**287, 289, 292
    sound recordings from, **9:**980, 983, 986, 998–99, 1002–4
    string bands in, **9:**136
    string figures in, **9:**253
    theater in, **9:**225, 233–34
    theatrical societies, **9:**229
    timbre and aesthetics, **9:**299–300
    tourism in, **9:**108
    yodeling, **9:**300
Hawaii (film), **9:**46
"*Hawai'i Aloha*," **9:**187
Hawai'i Archives of Ethnic Music and Dance (University of Hawai'i), **9:**971
Hawaii Calls (radio show), **3:**1050
Hawai'i Gagaku Kenkyukai ensemble, **9:**95
Hawai'i Okinawa Center, **9:**99
Hawai'i Pacific University, **9:**103
"*Hawai'i Pono'ī*," **9:**133
Hawaiian Collection (University of Hawai'i), **9:**971
Hawaiian National Band, **9:**133
Hawai'ian people, in U.S. mainland, **9:**116–18
Hawaiian Steel Guitar Association, **3:**1049
Hawaiian Style Band, **9:**167, *997*

Hawaiian Transcription Productions, **9:**998
"Hawaiian War Chant" (Leleiohoku), **3:**1050
Hawaiian Way: The Art and Tradition of Slack Key Music (film), **9:**42
"Hawaiian Wedding Song" (King), **3:**1050
Hawes, Bess Lomax, **3:**299; **10:**80, 81, 82, 84
ḥawfi, **6:**269, 473–74, *474*
Hawkins, Coleman, **3:**654, 656
Hawkins, Edwin, **3:**633–34
Hawkins, Ronnie, **3:**1081
Hawŏnch'un (Kim), **7:**953, 992
Hawthorne, Alice (pseud. of Septimus Winner), **3:**59–60, 190
ḥawzī, **6:**269, 407, 472–73, 475, 1044
Hax, Jebwen, **9:**749–50
Hayans, Guillermo, **2:**783
Haya people, **1:**637, 638
Hayasaka Humio, **7:**732, 750
Hayasi Hikaru, **7:**736–37
Hayasi Kenzô, **7:**581–82, 592
Haydar (Çiçek), **6:**797
Haydn, Franz Joseph, **3:**190, 1179; **6:**1025; **8:**53, 60, 80, 186, 199, 655, 727; **9:**203
    masses, **8:**84
    popular songs, **3:**181
    Scottish tune arrangements, **8:**367, 372–73
    use of *verbunkos* themes, **8:**273
Haydn, Michael, **8:**881
Hayes, Isaac, **3:**676, 711
Hayes, Roland, **3:**524, 537, 609, 629
al-Hāyik, **6:**450
Haynes, Mary Ann, **8:**336
Haynes, William, **3:**1094
Hayŏga (Seo), **7:**967
Hayre, Carlos, **2:**501
Hays, Lee, **3:**328, *329*
Hays, Terence E., **9:**511–12
Hays, Will S., **3:**188, 191
Hayward, Philip, **9:**986
Hayward, Victoria, **3:**342–43
Haza, Ofra, **8:**210
Hazara people, **5:**5, 805, 825, 828
Hazzard, Isaac, **3:**603, 604
He Baoquan, **7:**172
He Chengtian, **7:**118–19
He Dasha, **7:**220
He Gengji, **7:**511
He Liutang, **3:**1261; **7:**220
He Luting, **7:**90, 339, 341, 347, 382
He Zhanhao, **7:**348
Head of Christ (Sallman), **3:**122
"Head Hunter" (Otis), **3:**669
Headhunters (musical group), **3:**664
"Headhunting Ballad" (Puyuma), **7:**527
Healing Drum (Diallo), **3:**1170
healing rituals. *See also dhikr*
    Africa, **1:**204–5, 554–55, 557, 587
        diagnostic categories, **1:**280
        instruments' use in, **1:**80–81, 204–5
        musical modes and, **1:**535
        music in, **1:**587, 593
        use of dance in, **1:**112–13, 704, 706
        zār, **1:**113, 273–74, 277, 604
    Akan people, **1:**290
    Algeria, *līla,* **6:**408

Arabian peninsula
    nuban, **6:**405, 412, 546
    zār, **6:**359, 405, 412, 417, *535,* 656, 674, 706, 710
    Balochistan, *lēb* treatment, **6:**882–85
    Bribri and Cabécar cultures, **2:**632, 633–35
    California, Native American, **3:**371, 413–14
    Central Asia, *dhikr,* **6:**181
    Egypt, *zār,* **1:**554; **6:**632–33
    Europe, **8:**196, 304
    Guyana, **2:**442–43
    Hausa people, **1:**290
    Irian Jaya, **9:**594
    Laos, **4:**340–41
    Morocco, **6:**492–93
    Papua New Guinea, **9:**529, 560, 639
    South Asia, **5:**120, 272, 278
        power of music in, **5:**224, 693
    Sudanese ceremonies for, **1:**554–55, 557
    Taino culture, **2:**22
    Tamil Nadu, **5:**286, 287
    Tumbuka people, **1:**271–83
    Tunisia, *jeddeba* (also *stambūlī*), **6:**408
    Vanuatu, **9:**708–9
    Yanomamö culture, **2:**170–71
    Yekuana culture, **2:**179–80
Heard, Larry, **3:**690
Hearne, Samuel, **3:**392
Heart of Midlothian (Scott), **8:**368
Heartbeat of Africa, **1:**602
"Heartbreak Hotel" (Presley), **3:**552
Hearthill (musical group), **8:**217
Heath, Ted, **1:**773
"Heat Wave" (Berlin), **3:**196
Heatwave (musical group), **3:**685, 712
Heavy D. & the Boyz, **3:**698, 713
heavy metal, **2:**104; **3:**357–58; **8:**214, 215
    art music influences on, **3:**328
    in China, **7:**361, 365–67, 468
    gender construction in, **3:**111–14
    women performers of, **3:**95, 358
Hebdige, Dick, **2:**93, 913
Hébert, Donna, **3:**855
Hebräisch-orientalischer Melodienschatz (Idelsohn), **8:**266
Hebreos en Marruecos (Ortega), **6:**1036
Hebrew Disc and Cylinder Company, **3:**938
Hebrew Notated Manuscripts (Adler), **6:**1062
Hebrew Union College (Cincinnati), **6:**1058
Hebrew University (Jerusalem), **6:**1025, 1029, 1058, 1060, 1061, 1062, 1063
Hebrew Writings Concerning Music in Manuscripts and Printed Books (Adler), **6:**1062
Hebula, Hugo, **9:**661
Hecksher, August, **3:**298
Hector, George, **3:**1133
Hedāyat, Mehdī Qolī, **6:**867
Hedrick, Basil C., **2:**812
Heeger, Georg, **8:**663
Heer, Nicholas de, **1:**355
Heera (musical group), **5:**574; **8:**241
Hegamin, Lucille, **3:**644
Hegelian philosophy, **8:**184
Hehe people, **1:**635, 636, 640, 642
Heian period, **7:**586, 646
    aesthetics and philosophy in, **7:**545–55

gagaku in, **7:**565, 625, 626
poetry of, **7:**607
scales in, **7:**566–68
syômyô in, **7:**613
theater in, **7:**629
Heider, Karl G., **9:**1008
Heifetz, Jascha, **4:**870; **6:**1025; **7:**381
Heike clan, **7:**586, 631, 646
Heike mabusi (score), **7:**646
Heike monogatari (epic), **7:**586, 645, 646–47
Heiltsuk Indian nation. *See* Bella Bella (Heiltsuk) Indian nation
Heiman, Nahum, **6:**1019
Heimskringla (Sturluson), **8:**405
Heino, **8:**656, *675*
Heinrich, Anthony Philip, **3:**538
Heins, Donald, **3:**1183
Heins, Ernst L., **4:**103, 637, 701
Heinschink, Mozes, **8:**289
Heintzman firm, **3:**1183
Heintzman, Theodor August, **3:**1180
Heinze, R. von, **4:**603
Heisley, Michael, **3:**734, 737
Heiva (dance troupe), **9:**875, 998
Heki (Hirose), **7:**705
Hekmatyar, Gulbuddin, **5:**811
Hektorović, Petar, **8:**936
Hela-gee Maga (Makulloluwa), **5:**960
Helemano, Butch, **9:**166
Helen May Butler and Her Ladies Brass Band, **3:**566, *567*
Helfer, Erwin, **3:**105, *106*
Helffer, Mireille, **5:**698, 711
Helfman, Max, **3:**939
Helgas, **9:**90
Helgason, Gísli, **8:**407
Helgason, Hallgrímur, **8:**406–7
Helgeland, Sjur, **8:**417
Hellenic Musicians Association of South Australia, **9:**72
Hellenic Symphonia and Sirens (Adelaide), **9:**72
Hellenic Youth Dancers (Adelaide), **9:**73
Heller, André, **8:**272, 676
Hellerman, Fred, **3:**328, *329*
Hellman, Lillian, **3:**545
Hellmer, José Raúl, **2:**555
"Hello Central, Give Me Heaven" (Harris), **3:**191
"Hello! My Baby" (Howard and Emerson), **3:**549
"Hello Viet Nam" (Hall), **3:**317
Helm, George, **9:**164
Helm, June, **3:**392
Helmholtz, Hermann von, **7:**592
Helong people, **4:**796
Helpmann Academy, **9:***416*
Helsinki University, **8:**489
Helu, Futa, **9:**113
Hemba people, **1:**670
Hemetek, Ursula, **8:**289
Hemlandssånger (Swedish songbook), **3:**870
Hemmenway, James, **3:**603, 604
Hemphill, Sid, **3:**330
Hempson, Dennis, **8:**383
Ḥen, Nira, **6:**1072
Henderson, Donald, **2:***853*
Henderson, Fletcher, **3:**653, 654, 655, 656

Henderson, Hamish, **8:**295, 365, 371, 374
Henderson, Murray, **8:**363
Henderson, Rosa, **3:**644
Hendra, W. J., **3:**1227
Hendrix, Jimi, **3:**318, 335, 347, 356, 663, 710–11; **8:**218; **9:**139, 168
Heng Samrin, **4:**154, 187
Heni, Siaka, **9:**151
Henneberry, Ben, **3:**147
Henry and the Dumptrucks (musical group), **3:**199
Henry, Edward O., **5:**673, 674–75
Henry, Frances, **3:**1132, 1133
Henry, Ida, **9:***429*
Henry, Sam, **8:**393
"Henry's Cottage Maid" (Pleyel), **3:**180
Henwood, Major S. W., **2:**447
Henze, Hans Werner, **8:**646
Hep Stars (musical group), **8:**446
Heper, Sadettin, **6:**119
Hepner, Ben, **3:**1082, 1239
Herangi, Te Puea, **9:**929
Herawi, Amir Mohammad, **5:***836*
Herbert, Bert, **9:**43
Herbert, Victor, **3:**193, 260–61, 367, 530, 544
Herbs (musical group), **9:**168
Hercegovina. *See* Bosnia-Hercegovina
Herculords, **3:**695
Hercus, Luis, **9:**960
Herd, David, **8:**373
Herder, Johann Gottfried von, **3:**147, 538–39; **8:**2, 94, 186, 337, 655–56; **10:**158
   coinage of term *Volkslied*, **8:**17, 646–47, 662–63
   founding of comparative philology discipline, **8:**18, 19, 53
   Stimmen der Völker in Liedern, **8:**307
   Volkslieder, **8:**17, 512
"Here Comes Nixon," **3:**310
Hereniko, Vilsoni, **9:**37, 234
Herero people, **1:**713, 715
Heretic (Williamson play), **9:**416
Heritage Records, **3:**1243
Herman, Bogdana, **8:**920
Herman's Hermits, **8:**214
Hermannsburg Ladies Choir, **9:**987
Hermano Negro (Plá), **2:**464
Hermanson, Åke, **8:**445
hermeneutics, **6:**186–87; **8:**24
Hermer, Carol, **9:**1008
Hermit Islands (Papua New Guinea), **9:**602
Hernandez, Aaron, **3:**1281
Hernández, Clara, **2:**839
Hernández, Daria, **2:**544
Hernandez, José "Perico," **3:**745, 799
Hernandez, Juan, **4:**859, 864, 865, 870
Hernández, Julio Alberto, **2:**860
Hernández, Oscar, **3:**777
Hernández, Pedro, **3:**744
Hernández, Salvador Luis, **3:**739
Hernández Tziandón, Jesús, **2:**578
Herndon, Marcia, **3:**470, 511
Herodotus, **1:**75
Heron of Alexandria, **6:**373
Herrera family, **3:**724
Herrera, Johnny, **3:**779

Herrera, Ramiro "Ram," **3:**780
Herrmann, Bernard, **3:**203, 546
Herskovits, Frances S., **2:**24, 505, 954, 955
Herskovits, Melville J., **1:**31, 51; **2:**24, 70, 505, 954, 955; **3:**34, 72, 512, 576, *576*
Hertzainak (musical group), **8:**315
Herzfeld, Michael, **8:**123
Herz-Imber, Naphtali, **6:**1069
Herzog, Avigdor, **6:**1036, 1062, 1064, 1065, 1066
Herzog, George, **1:**31, 50, 51; **2:**599; **3:**367, 418, 421, 509, 512, 1165; **9:**975, 980, 994; **10:**62
"He's a Rebel" (Crystals), **3:**673, 709
"He's So Fine" (Chiffons), **3:**673
Hesheng de lilun yu yingyong (Sang), **7:**348
Hess, Myra, **3:**1210
Hester Hannah's Book, **3:**137
heterophony
   Africa, **1:**579
   in Andalusian music, **6:**436
   Andean regions, **2:**215, 216, 221
   Arab music, **6:**166, 167, 168
   Bali, **4:***746*
   Belarus, **8:**794–95, 796
   Bulgaria, **8:**896
   Burma, **4:**372
   China, **7:**169
      Buddhist chant, **7:**329–30
      ensemble music, **7:**203, 242–43
      huaguxi, **7:**298
      Jiangnan sizhu music, **7:**225
      kunqu, **7:**292
      minority cultures, **7:**490
      nanguan music, **7:**206–7
      xianshiyue, **7:**214
   in Christian churches, **3:**125
   East Asia, **7:**3, 82
   England, dance music, **8:**330, 333
   France, **8:**542
   Greece, **8:**1008
   Hungarian Rom music, **8:**274
   Hungary, **8:**744
   Indian Shaker hymns, **3:**488
   Ireland, **8:**382
   Japan, **7:**552–53
      dan mono, **7:**697
      gagaku, **7:**620–21
      sankyoku, **7:**716
   Java, **4:**669–73
   Kajang people, **4:**827
   Kashmir, *ṣūfyāna mūsīqī*, **5:**687
   Lombok, **4:**770–71
   Macedonia, **8:**281
   in Maguindanao *kulintang*, **4:**893–94
   Malaysia, **4:**417, 435
   Mashriq, **6:**552
   Mongol people, **7:**1005, 1007
   Native American songs, **3:**6, 526
   Naxi people, **7:**513
   Nepal, **5:**705
      Guruṅ people, **5:**704
   Peru, Amazonian region, **2:**482
   in psalm-singing, **3:**832–33
   Q'ero music, **2:**228–29, 230
   Romania, **8:**879

Russia, **8:**757
Scotland, in psalmody, **8:**363
Southeast Asia, **4:**538
   island musics, **4:**596–97
   Sumatra, **4:**611
   Thailand, **4:**272
   in Tunisian *ma'lūf*, **6:**327
   Vietnam, **4:**454, 467
   Waiãpí culture, **2:**436
Heth, Charlotte, **3:**470; **10:**88, 89, 95
Hethuska Indian nation, **3:**446
Hétu, Jacques, **3:**1151
Hewa people, **9:**511, 537
   ceremonial spaces, **9:**512
   kundus of, **9:**384
Hewitt, James, **3:**542
Hewitt, John Hill, **3:**182–83, 188, 189; **8:**205
Heyerdahl, Thor, **9:**42
Heyit, Abdurehim, **7:**469
Heyns, Pol, **8:**534
Hezhen people, **7:**518
Hiatt, Lester R., **9:**418
Hibatallāh, **6:**296
Hibbs, Harry, **3:**1070, 1125
Hibik Sa Karimlan (de León), **4:**881
Hibiscus Records, **9:**985, 997, 999
hichiriki. *See* double-reed instruments
Hickmann, Hans, **6:**17, 535
Hicks, Ivan, **3:**1125
Hidalgo, Felix Resurrección, **4:**866
Hidatsa Indian nation, **3:**421, 440, 444
Hidayatullah, **5:**791
Hideyoshi Toyotomi, **7:**756
al-Ḥifnī, Maḥmūd Aḥmad, **6:**18, 322–23, 422, 536, 611
Ḥigāzī, Salāma, **6:**570, 612
Higgins, Charlotte, **8:**296
Higgins, Chuck, **3:**742
Higgins, Clifford, **3:**1227
Higgins, Jon, **5:**54, 159, 231; **10:**41
Higgins, Lizzie, **8:**200, 296, 372
Higgs, Alphonso "Blind Blake," **2:**806
"High Hopes," **3:**310
"Higher Ground" (Wonder), **3:**677
Higher Institute of Art (Cuba), **2:**837
Higher Institute for Musical Theater. *See* Ma'had al-Mūsīqá al-Masraḥiyya (Cairo)
Higher Institute for Music Teachers (Cairo), **6:**323, 611
Highland Society of London, **8:**368
highlife, **1:**7, 322, 775; **2:**75; **3:**338, 1213; **8:**232, 233
   Ghana, **1:**355, 357, 358, 361, 377, 407, 419, 423; **10:**35, 38
   influence on composers, **1:**221, 227, 239–40, 242
   Liberia, **1:**379
   palm-wine, **1:**353
   Yoruba, **1:**407, 477–78
High Life Below the Stairs (play), **3:**614
Highlife World label, **3:**1213
High Noon (film), **3:**203
High Road of Song, **3:**279
High Voltage, **2:**808
Highway QCs (gospel quartet), **3:**633
Higi people, **1:**288–89, 291–92

"*Al-ḥigra al-Murra*" (al-'Aṭṭār), **6:**643
Hijacks (musical group), **4:**884
Ḥijāzi, Shaykh Salāma, **6:**168, 235, 547
Hijikata, Hisakatsu, **9:**25, 722
Hijos de la tierra (album), **2:**374
Hijras, **5:**493
Hikmat (Ahmad Yassawi), **6:**943, 944, 945
Hikmet, Nazim, **6:**243, 245, 250, 251
Hikôki gumo (album), **7:**746–47
Hila, Morea, **9:**151
Hilaire, Andrew, **3:**653
Hilālī, **6:**914
Hilandar Monastery, **8:**943
al-Hilbāwī, Shaykh Muḥammad, **6:**168, 172, *172*
Hilburn, Robert, **3:**750
Hildan, Ola, **8:**417
Hildebrand, Lee, **10:**144
Hildegard von Bingen, **8:**70, 197
Hi-Life Stars (musical group), **3:**1213
Hill, Alfred, **9:**392
Hill, Bertha "Chippie," **3:**644, 707
Hill, Donald C., **2:**869
Hill, Donald R., **2:**93
Hill, Emily, **3:**487
Hill, Joe, **3:**873, 1257
Hill, Lauryn, **3:**697, *697*
Hill, Noel, **8:**385
Hill, Stephen, **3:**346
Hillberg, Wilma, **4:**870
Hille, Veda, **3:**1280
Hillegeist, Helmut, **10:**114
Hiller, Lejaren, **3:**254
Hilme, Jorn, **8:**417
Ḥilmi, 'Abd al-Ḥayy, **6:**235, 548
al-Hiluw, Muḥammad, **6:**239
Hima people, **1:**607
Himachal Pradesh, **5:**650, *680*
    dance traditions of, **5:**499–500
    Dharamsala, Tibetan culture in, **5:**709, 712
    regional cassettes in, **5:**550
    Spiti region
        bag-ston gyi glu (marriage songs), **5:**710
        song text collections, **5:**715
    wedding music of, **5:**415
Himno de Riego (march), **4:**869
Himno Nacional de Filipinas (Felipe), **4:**871
Hindemith, Paul, **3:**33, 175, 610; **4:**131; **6:**775,
        1029; **7:**341, 346; **8:**93, 369, 406,
        426, 445, 646, 730
Hinderas, Natalie, **10:**138
Hindu (Madras newspaper), **5:**395
Hinduism, **2:**85; **3:**5, 983; **5:**480, 482. *See also*
        Shaivite traditions; Vaishnavite
        traditions; *specific sects*
    Andhra Pradesh, **5:**892, 897–98
    Asian-American communities, **3:**950, 1084
    attitudes toward Indian music, **5:**433–35
    Bali, **4:**632, 729, 731; **5:**10
    Bhutan, **5:**489
    Chăm people, **3:**1010; **4:**590
    Cirebon, **4:**686
    Fiji, **5:**612
    Goa, **5:**735–37
    Guyana, **2:**443
    Haridāsī tradition, **5:**251, 252, 262, 265–66
    Himachal Pradesh, **5:**500

history of, **5:**10–11
India, **5:**374
India, South, **5:**14, 259–70, 350
    temple ensembles, **5:**103, 210, 359–60
Indonesia, **4:**75, 76, 594, 596
influence on American music, **3:**129–33
Jamaica, **2:**901
Java, **4:**632, 807
karma concept, **5:**698
Karnataka, **5:**866, 880
Kashmir, **5:**682
Kerala, **5:**929, 934–36
Khmer people, **4:**153, 156–57, 206
Lombok, **4:**764
Madhya Pradesh, **5:**720
Maharashtra, **5:**727
Malaysia, **4:**401
mandala in, **6:**185
musician's role in, **5:**70
Nepal, **5:**490, 697, 701
Nimbārka tradition, **5:**251–52
North America, **5:**579, 581
oral transmission and, **5:**23
Orissa, **5:**731, 732, 733–34
Pakhtun people, **5:**785
philosophical systems in, **5:**34, 220
Rādhāvallabha tradition, **5:**251, 252
Rajasthan, **5:**639
religious music of, **5:**246–56
revival movement, **5:**380
Sant tradition, **5:**248, 249, 253
social order of, **5:**8–10, 39
South Africa, **5:**615, 617
Southeast Asia, **4:**62, 64–65
    urban areas, **4:**5
Sri Lanka, **5:**108, 350, 490, 955
    temple ensembles, **5:**359–60
Sumatra, **4:**599–600, 605, 615, 624
Sunda, **4:**699
Tamil Nadu, **5:**903
Thailand, **4:**256–57, 287
theology, **5:**246–47, 249–50
Trinidad, **2:**952, 956, 963; **5:**590
United Kingdom, **5:**573
views of gods in, **5:**400–401
views of music in, **5:**376, 933
views of treatises in, **5:**22
Hindustani Sangeet Mandal (Ottawa), **3:**1216
Hindustāni Saṅgīt-Paddhati (Bhatkhande), **5:**46,
        52, 445–46
Hindustani tradition, **3:**339, 950, 951, 955, 981,
        983, 1205, 1216, 1246; **5:**2. *See also*
        dādrā; *dhamār*; *dhrupad*; *gat*; *khyāl*;
        paran; *tarānā*; *ṭhumrī*
    Afghanistan, **5:**489
    as cultural export, **5:**380
    development of, **5:**42, 45, 77, 246, 375
    effects of internationalization on, **5:**566–67
    English scholarship on, **5:**50
    fusion trends in, **5:**136, 205, 206, 528, 561
    Goa, **5:**737, 741
    history of, **5:**14–15
    Hong Kong, **7:**431
    instrumental music, **5:**188–208
    instruments of, **5:**188, 331–43
    interaction with Karnatak tradition, **5:**47–48

Mughal period, **10:**11–12
Muslims as carriers of, **5:**375, 460, 746
Nepal, **5:**697
North America, **5:**581
Orissa, **5:**732
Pakistan, **5:**746
Persian influences on, **5:**18
peshkār genre, **5:**129
qā'ida genre, **5:**128–29, 130, 131
raga, **5:**64–87 (*See also* raga *heading*)
relā genre, **5:**119, 129
rhythmic divisions in, **5:**112–13
scholarly works on, **5:**44
Sikh use of, **5:**13
social order in, **5:**372–81
sound recordings of, **5:**57
supremacy of vocal music in, **5:**162, 322
tala, **5:**110–37 (*See also* tala *heading*)
United Kingdom, **5:**573
as urban phenomenon, **5:**397–98
vina in, **5:**207, 307
vocal music, **5:**15, 162–86, 847, 855; **10:**5
    Trinidad genres of, **5:**591
Western studies on, **5:**54–56, 57
Hines, Earl, **3:**653, 656
Hines, J. Earle, **10:**138
Hines, Jerome, **3:**537
Hines, Ron, **3:**1121
Hinson, Glenn, **3:**83, 85
Hinton, Thomas B., **2:**599
Hiotis, Manolis, **8:**1020
hip-hop, **2:**50, 98, 111, 133; **3:**17, 552, 687,
        688, 689, 692–703; **5:**584, 652;
        8:676, 802. *See also* rap
    1970s, **3:**694–95
    Aotearoa, **9:**168
    Canada, **3:**73, 1212–13
    cultural elements of, **3:**692, 713, 715
    dancing to, **3:**211, 225
    Filipino, **3:**1026
    fusions in, **3:**337, 522, 1203
    gospel music and, **3:**635
    Haitian, **3:**806, 807
    Hawai'i, **9:**165
    jazz and, **3:**665
    Native American, **3:**345
    northern Canada, **3:**1280–81
    reggae/dancehall and, **3:**811
    research on, **3:**586–87
    Samoan, **3:**1052
    women in, **3:**96, 586, 696–97, 714
Hipkins, A. J., **4:**225, 285
Hiragani Seisuiki (kabuki piece), **7:**657
Hirano Kenzi, **7:**593
Hiranyakasipu (mythical ruler), **5:**276
Hirao Kisio, **7:**732
Hiroa, Te Rangi. *See* Buck, Sir Peter H.
Hirose Ryôhei, **7:**705
Hiroshima (musical group), **3:**336, 972–73
Hīr Ranjha (romance), **5:**756, 771
Hirschberg, Walter, **1:**295
Hirsh, Nurit, **6:**1073
Hirshberg, Jehoash, **6:**1063, 1065, 1066, 1067
His Majesty's Band (Hawai'i), **9:**132
Hisao, Tanabe, **9:**159
Ḥishtron (Israeli band), **6:**1072

Hispanic Causing Panic (Kid Frost), **3:**750
Hispanic Folk Music of New Mexico and the Southwest (Robb), **3:**767
Hispanic music. *See* Latino peoples; *specific peoples and genres*
Hispaniola (Island), **2:**789, 845. *See also* Dominican Republic; Haiti
Hispano Folk Music of the Past, **3:**767
Hispavox (record company), **8:**601
Histoire illustré de la Corse (Galletti), **8:**572
Histoire du soldat (Stravinsky), **8:**697
Historia de la música en México (Saldívar), **2:**623
Historia general de las cosas de Nueva España (Sahagún), **2:**602
Historia general de las Islas Filipinas (Conceptión), **4:**858
Historia de la música popular mexicana (Morena Rivas), **2:**624
Historical Annals (Tibetan writing), **7:**472
Historical Anthology of Canadian Music, **3:**1109
historiography, **2:**21–24; **3:**508–13; **8:**38–39
    African-American music, **3:**64, 572–87, 707
    attitudes toward history, **3:**21–23
    biographies of musicians, **3:**27, 29; **6:**20, 364, 369–71, 535
    Canadian music, **3:**1059–60, 1062
    class and music, **3:**45
    concept of periods, **8:**60
    concept of progress, **3:**27, 28
    cultural interaction and, **3:**21–22
    East Asia, **7:**41–43
    European accounts of South Asian cultures, **5:**49–50
    European concepts of, **8:**58–61, 64–65, 93
    feminist, **3:**91
    historical concerts and, **3:**33–34
    interpretation and, **3:**26
    Jewish, **8:**259, 265–66
    Middle Eastern musics, **6:**15, 22
    popular music, **8:**60–61
    problems of, **4:**12
    Puritan influences on, **3:**24–26
    rural, suburban, and urban contexts in music making, **3:**142–44
History of Arabian Music to the Thirteenth Century (Farmer), **6:**537
History of Indian Music (Pringle), **5:**51
History of the Later Han (dynastic history), **7:**471
History of Music in British Columbia (McIntosh), **3:**1258
History of Music in Canada 1534–1914, A (Kallmann), **3:**32
History of Thai Music (Panya Roongrüang), **4:**224, 225
History of Thai Musicians (Jarernchai Chonpairot), **4:**277
Ḥīt, **6:**296
Hit Harivansh, Sri, **5:**252
Hit Parade (television show), **9:**938
Hita-Caurāsi (Hit Harivansh), **5:**252
Hitchcock, H. Wiley, **3:**32, 143
Hitchcock, J. T., **2:**866
Hitchiti Indian nation, **3:**466
Hiti Marama, **9:**896
hitiriki. *See* double-reed instruments
Hitler, Adolf, **8:**187, 660, 664

Hito-Atan family, **9:**952
Hitomi Tikudô, **7:**725
Hiva'oa (Marquesas Islands), **9:**889
    putu genre of, **9:**892–93
Hiver Hyvas, **1:**770
Hizikata Tatumi, **7:**66
Hızır Ilyas Bey, **6:**780
Hlebaŭ, Jaŭhieñ, **8:**800
Hmao people, **4:**550
Hmong people, **4:**550–59; **7:**6
    in Australia, **9:**75–77
    courtship songs of, **4:**532
    distribution of, **4:**528, 551
    instruments of, **4:**59, 535–36, *544*, 551–53
    in Laos, **4:**336, 338, 347, 537
    music research on, **4:**26
    narratives of, **4:**533
    in North America, **3:**948, 949, 952, 1003–5, 1007
    origins of, **4:**550–51
    resettlement of, **4:**360–61
    ritual music of, **4:**553–55
    secular music of, **4:**555–59
    song genres of, **4:**555, 556–59
    in Vietnam, **4:**444
Hmu people, **4:**550
HMV (record label), **1:**417, 426, 770; **5:**423, 547, 548
Hnatiuk, Peter, **3:**345
Ho people, **5:**502
Hồ Chí Minh, **3:**993
Hồ Chí Minh City Conservatory of Music, **4:**511–12
Ho Chunk Indian nation, **3:**454
Ho, Don, **9:**164
Ho, Fred Wei-han, **3:**328, 336, 965, *965*
Hŏ Kyu, **7:**969
Hoa people, in Vietnam, **4:**531
Hòa Bình culture, **4:**10, 33–34, 57, 445, 596
Ho'aikane, **9:**166, 167
Ho'āla: Awakening, **9:**222
Hoam Art Hall (Seoul), **7:**994
Hoàng Việt, **4:**512
Hobei Normal College (Tianjin), **7:**397
Hobsbawm, Eric, **9:**223
Hocart, A. M., **9:**992
hocketing. *See* texture, interlocking
Hodes, Art, **3:**105
Hodges, Johnny, **3:**660
Hodges, Teremoana, **9:**278
Hodgson, Harold, **2:**754–55
Hodgson, M. G. S., **6:**162
Hodgson, Samuel "Sabu," **2:***754*
Hodŭgi (Yi), **7:**957
Hodu ladonay kir'u bishmo (cantillation), **6:***1037*
Hoernle, Winifred, **1:**53
Hoffman, Marc, **3:**1020
Hoffmann, E. T. A., **9:**39
Hoffman, Stanley B., **4:**638, 660
Hoffman, Walter J., **3:**457
Hofman, Shlomo, **6:**1065
Hofmayr, Wilhelm, **1:**568
Hofstadter, Douglas R., **1:**182
Hogan, Ernest, **3:**616, 618, 619, *619*, 650
Hogg, James, **8:**373
Hograno people, **9:**659–62

Hohodai Koita people, **9:**316
Hohokam culture, **3:**429
Hokea, Ben, **9:**390
Hoklo people, in Hong Kong, **7:**433
Hokowhitu A Tu, **9:**931
Hokum Boys (musical group), **3:**645
Holdys, Zbiggy, **8:**221
Hole (musical group), **3:**358
Hole in the Head (film), **3:**310
Holguín, Rita, **3:**741
Holiday, Billie, **3:**656, 674, 743, 863
"Holiday for Skins," **3:**662
holidays. *See* festivals, celebrations, and holidays
Holland, Justin Miner, **3:**604–5, *605*
Holland's Comprehensive Method for the Guitar, **3:**605
Holland's Modern Method for the Guitar, **3:**605
Holle Holle (musical group), **8:**241
Hollie Maea, **9:**179
Hollies (musical group), **8:**214
Holliger, Heinz, **8:**697
Holly, Buddy, **3:**353, 732, 746, 840; **8:**214
Hollywood All Stars, **3:***647*
Hollywood Palladium (Los Angeles), **3:**741, 743, 798
"Hollywood Swinging" (Kool and the Gang), **3:**681
Holm, Ellev Ellevsen, **8:**419
Holman English Opera Company, **3:**1181
Holmboe, Vagn, **8:**463
Holmer, Nils M., **2:**649
Holo people, in Taiwan, **7:**423, 424–27
Holocaust, **3:**940; **6:**1013; **8:**11, 249, 263, 265, 266–67, 289, 1011; **10:**163
    Rom songs concerning, **8:**276, 289
Holst, Gustav, **1:**52; **2:**962; **8:**19, 186, 188, 333
Holt, Claire, **4:**603
Holý, Dušan, **8:**733
Holy Roman empire, **8:**716
Holzapfel, Otto, **10:**164
Holzmann, Rodolpho, **2:**231
Homage to Iran (Cowell), **3:**953
Homage to Vivaldi (Perry), **3:**611
Homaidan, Rana, **6:**282, *283*
Home Mission, **8:**459
"*Homenaje a John F. Kennedy*" (Morante), **3:**522
Homer, **6:**523; **8:**129, 130, 763, 941
homophony
    ancient Greek music, **8:**47
    Armenian music, **6:**725
    Brazilian art music, **2:**303
    Bunun people, **7:**525
    Dan people, **1:**466
    Zande music, **1:**652–53
homosexuality
    Afghanistan, transvestites, **5:**815
    Arabian peninsula, transvestites and transsexuals, **6:**296, 538, 651
    Brazil, transvestites, **2:**57
    disco and, **3:**228, 229, 687–88
    gay and lesbian scholarship, **3:**89–90, 107–11
    heavy metal and, **3:**114
    klezmer and, **3:**942
    Punjab, transvestites and hermaphrodites, **5:**770–71
    South Asia, transvestites, **5:**492, 515, 683, 685

Trinidad and Tobago, transvestites, **2:**965
Turkey
 in harems, **6:**115
 transvestites and transsexuals, **6:**258–59
Homunculus C.F. (Perry), **3:**611
Hon Sing Athletic Association, **3:**1265–66
Honam Yŏsŏng Nongaktan (musical group),
 7:938
Honda Yasuzi, **7:**605
Honderd jaar muziekleven op Curaçao (Boskaljon),
 2:931
Honduran people
 in Belize, **2:**666
 in North America, **3:**727
Honduras, **2:**628, 738–45
 Chorti culture, **2:**738
 dances of, **2:**743–44
 Garífuna culture, **2:**668–69, 733
 geography of, **2:**738
 instruments of, **2:**739–40, 741–43
 Jicaque-Tolupán culture, **2:**739
 Lenca culture, **2:**739
 map of, **2:**629
 Maya culture, **2:**650–58
 Maya murals in, **2:**15
 mestizo culture, **2:**741–45
 Miskitu culture, **2:**659–64, 740, 749
 musical genres, *son,* **2:**744
 Omoa, **2:**744
 Paya culture, **2:**739
 population of, **2:**738
 research on, **2:**745
 Sumu culture, **2:**739–40
Hone, Philip, **3:**305
Honegger, Arthur, **3:**1150; **7:**341; **8:**93, 550, 696
Honest Yorkshireman (ballad opera), **3:**180
Honey B & the T-Bones (musical group), **8:**217
"Honey Chile" (Jordan), **3:**708
"Honeydripper" (Liggins), **3:**669
"Honey Hush" (Turner), **3:**708
"Honey Love" (Drifters), **3:**351
Hong Chŏngsu, **7:**855
Hong Dongki, **7:**970
Hong, Hei-Kyung, **3:**977
Hong Kong, **7:**6; **9:**71
 Cantonese opera in, **3:**1261; **7:**303–5, 307–8,
  396, 431, 433; **10:**18, 21–24
 Chaozhou people in, **7:**211
 cultural exchanges in, **7:**49–51
 emigrés from, **3:**949, 959, 1057, 1078, 1082,
  1083, 1245, 1247, 1260, 1263
 history of music in, **7:**90–91
 influence on Southeast Asian culture, **4:**80
 instrumental musical traditions, **7:**217–21
 musical life in, **7:**431–36
 nanguan genre, **7:**205–9, 433
 narrative singing in, **7:**273
 pan-Chinese music in, **7:**432–33
 popular music in, **3:**964; **7:**354–56, 389, 433,
  435–36
 research on music of, **7:**220–21
 scholarship in, **7:**136, 139
 Temple Street market in, **7:**434–35
Hong Kong Chinese Orchestra, **7:**231–32, 431,
  432, 435
Hong Kong Coliseum, **7:**431, 435–36

Hong Kong Philharmonic, **7:**431
Hong Nanp'a, **7:**952, 988
Hong Shi (Tibetan writing), **7:**476
Hong Took Tong Chinese Dramatic Company,
  3:958
Hong Wŏn'gi, **7:**989
Hong Xian'nu, **7:**306
Hong Yifeng, **7:**357
Hong Yŏnghu, **7:**952
Hongloumeng (Chinese novel), **7:**246
Hongse niangzijun (ballet), **7:**349
Hongshan culture, **7:**17
Hongtaiji, **7:**33, 35
Honigmann, John, **3:**381
Honjo Hidetaro, **7:**695
*Honkers and Shouters: The Golden Years of Rhythm
  and Blues* (Shaw), **3:**584
*Honor the Earth Powwow: Songs of the Great Lakes
  Indians,* **3:**498
"Hoochie Coochie Man" (Muddy Waters), **3:**552
Hood, Mantle, **1:**31, 32; **3:**952, 1013; **4:**26, 131,
  637, 638, 657, 693, 733, 876; **10:**5, 6,
  9, 42, 51, 56, 77, 78–79, 97, 101,
  106, 129, 139, 140
Hook, James, **3:**180
Hooker, John Lee, **1:**366; **3:**647, 708
Hooker, Naomi, **1:**363
Hoola Bandoola (musical group), **8:**446
Hooley, Bruce, **9:**566
Hooper, Louie, **8:**327, 336
Ho'opi'i, Richard, **9:**922
Ho'opi'i, Solomon, **9:**390, 922
Hoopi, Sol, **3:**337
Hoorn Island. *See* Futuna
Hoosli Ukrainian Folk Ensemble (Winnipeg),
  3:343
Hoover, Cynthia, **3:**562
Hope, Bob, **9:**26, 149
Hopenko, Mosheh, **6:**1024
Hopewell cultures, **3:**478
Hopf, Ed, **3:**880
Hopi Indian nation, **3:**215, 216, 433
 Butterfly Dance, **3:**429
 kachina cycle, **3:**430
 reed instruments, **3:**478
 songs of, **3:**429
 use of popular songs, **3:**369
Hopkins, Charles, **9:**919, 922
Hopkins, Pandora, **8:**25
Hopkins, Pauline, **3:**617
Hopkins, Sam "Lightnin'," **3:**647
Hopkinson, Francis, **3:**275
Hopoate, Vaisima, **9:**793
Horchin people, **7:**1004–20
Horigome Genta, **7:**601
Horikawa Nami no Tsuzumi (Chikamatsu), **7:**669
Horiuchi, Glenn, **3:**336, 972
Horiuti Keizô, **7:**729, 750
Hornbostel, Erich M. von, **1:**10, 50, 74, 254,
  261; **2:**178, 180; **3:**576; **4:**224, 225,
  281, 285–86, 603, 636, 637; **6:**23;
  7:137; **8:**18, 20, 906; **9:**258, 650, 980;
  10:120, 139
 instrument classification system, **2:**28; **3:**473;
  5:20, 51, 322; **8:**40, 177–78, 803;
  9:371

Horne, Lena, **3:**621
Horney, Karen, **3:**130
Horniman Museum and Library (London), **8:**182
hornpipe, **3:**231, 596, 825, 836, 839, 855; **8:**168
 in Canada, **3:**1178
 in England, **8:**330, 331
 in Ireland, **8:**382
 Irish, **3:**843
 in Kosrae, **9:**742–43
 in Low Countries, **8:**524
 in Scotland, **8:**367
horns. *See* trumpets or horns
Horse (musical group), **8:**369
Horslips (musical group), **8:**322, 392
"*Horst Wessel-Lied*" (Blume), **8:**185
Horton, Christian, **1:**45
Horton, Robin, **1:**127
Hosakawa Shûhei, **7:**595
Hosein. *See* Husayn ibn 'Ali
Hoseyn Tehrāni, **6:**138
Hoshovsky, Volodymyr, **8:**23
Hoshut people, **7:**1004–20
Hosni, Daoud, **6:**612
Hot (musical group), **3:**712
Hot Air (radio show), **3:**1107
Hot Chocolate, **3:**712
Hot, Cool and Vicious (Salt-N-Pepa), **3:**696, 713,
  714
Hot Five (musical group), **3:**652–53
"Hot Fun in the Summertime" (Dayton), **3:**685
"Hot Fun in the Summertime" (Graham), **3:**681
"Hot Fun in the Summertime" (Sly and the
  Family Stone), **3:**710
"Hot House," **3:**659
Hot Jumpers (musical group), **8:**237
Hot Rize (bluegrass group), **3:**159
Hot Seven (musical group), **3:**652–53
Hotahota, Jean. *See* Coco
Hotdog Band, **4:**885
Hotel Vanderbilt (New York), **3:**260–61
Hothouse Flowers (musical group), **8:**392
Hoto, David, **9:**27
Hotogoid people, **7:**1004–20
Hoton people, **7:**1004–20
Hottentots, **1:**703, 761. *See also* Khoikhoi people
Hŏt'ŭn t'aryŏng (Oulim), **7:**971
Hou Dejian, **7:**356, 357
Houdini (calypsonian), **2:**963
Hougaku Journal (periodical), **7:**772
Hou han shu (dynastic history), **7:**117
Houle, Lawrence "Teddy Boy," **3:**344, 410, *410,*
  458
Houmpheng Boupha, **4:**357
Hourani, Albert, **6:**876
Hourdebise, Joseph, **1:**385
house music, **2:**50; **3:**230, 341, 355, 687,
  690–91, 702
House Opening (film), **9:**48
House Party Productions, **3:**1071
House, Son, **3:**645, 707
House Un-American Activities Committee, **3:**328
Houston, Thelma, **3:**712
Houston, Whitney, **3:**712
Houtu (goddess), **7:**317
Hovhaness, Alan, **5:**528; **7:**954, 976
Hovnat'an, Naghash, **6:**734

How to Change a Flat Tire (musical group), **3:**322, 324
"How Deep Is the Ocean" (Berlin), **3:**196
How It Happens (Johnson), **3:**255
"How Long Blues" (Yancey), **3:**105
"How Sweet It Is (To Be Loved by You)" (Gaye), **3:**674
How to Name It (album), **5:**544
"How Will the Wolf Survive?" (Los Lobos), **3:**750
Howard, Camille, **3:**647
Howard, George, **3:**618
Howard, Gregg, **9:**959–60
Howard, Harlan, **3:**81
Howard, James, **3:**367, 470, 484
Howard, John, **3:**865
Howard, John Tasker, **3:**508
Howard, Joseph E., **3:**549
Howard Morrison Quartet, **9:**938
Howard, Rosetta, **3:**645
Howard, Wayne, **5:**239
Howe, Edgar, **9:***135*
Howe, Elias, **3:**232, 840
Howe, James, **2:**649
Howe, Julia Ward, **3:**521
Howell, Sally, **6:**286
Howitt, A. W., **9:**440
Howkins, Alun, **8:**339
Howlin' Wolf, **3:**647
Howson, John, **8:**339
Hoxha, Enver, **8:**990, 1000
Hoyer, Matt, **3:**901
Hoyos, Rodolfo, **3:**739
Hoysala dynasty, **5:**300
Hrabalová, Olga, **8:**732
Hristov, Angel, **8:**906
Hristov, Dobri, **8:**891, 904, 906
Hrynblat, Mikhail, **8:**803
Hryniuk Family, **3:**1089
Hsia dynasty. *See* Xia dynasty
Hsiung-nu tribe, **6:**965
Hsu Tsang-houei, **7:**137, 524
Hu Defu, **7:**357
Hu Liezhen, **7:**229
Hu Tianquan, **7:**189
Hu Zhihou, **7:**204
Hua chuan luogu (*Zhedong luogu* piece), **7:**196
Hua'er hui (poetry collection), **7:**463
Hua Guangsheng, **7:**130, 154
Hua shan mian (*xiaodiao*), **7:**152
Hua Wenbin, **7:**133
Hua Wenyi, **3:**959
Hua Yanjun, **7:**170
Hua Yanjung. *See* Abing
Huahine (Society Islands), **9:**867
Huai gu (*Jiangnan sizhu* piece), **7:**225
Huaijiu (Huang), **7:**345
Huainan zi (treatise), **7:**118
Hualapai Indian nation, **3:**428, 434
Hua liuban (*yangqin* piece), **7:**180
Huambaly, **2:**372
Huang Di emperor, **7:**87
Huang Haidai, **7:**426
Huanghe (Yin et al.), **7:**349–50
Huanghe dahechang (*Yellow River Cantata*) (Xian), **7:**346, 384, 386

Huanghe de gushi (Shi), **7:**348
Huang Jinpei, **3:**1261, 1264, 1265–66; **7:**221
Huang Junxiong, **7:**426
Huang Wenhuan, **7:**474
Huang Xiangpeng, **7:**137
Huang Zhen, **7:**442
Huang Zi, **7:**345, 397
Huangzhong (periodical), **7:**141
Huanle ge (*Jiangnan sizhu* piece), **7:**225, 240
Huanle ge (*sheng* piece), **7:**188
Huan sha ji (Liang), **7:**290–91
huapango, **2:**571, 573; **3:**737, 746
Huaraijió culture. *See* Guarijío culture
Huari culture, **2:**467
huayno (also *huayño*; *wayno*), **2:**59, 101, 133
    in Argentina, **2:**256
    in Bolivia, **2:**293, 297
    in Chile, **2:**361, 363, 369
    form of, **2:**483
    influenced by *cumbia*, **2:**483
    in Peru, **2:**230, 473, 477, 478, 483
    sound recordings of, **2:**484
Huber, Ferdinand F., **8:**683
Huber, Kurt, **8:**664
Huberman, Bronislaw, **6:**1026
"Hucklebuck" (Checker), **3:**709
"Huckle-Buck" (Williams), **3:**669
Huddleston, Father Trevor, **1:**777
Hudie furen (Xi), **7:**301
Hudson, David, **9:**397
Hudson, Henry, **8:**385, 386–87, 393
Hudson, James "Pookie," **3:**671
Hudson, Karen, **9:**571
Hudson, Tom, **3:**1278
Hudson's Bay Company, **3:**9, 1164, 1178, 1188, 1255, 1276
Hudyana Widya Mardawa (musical group), **10:**44
Hue and Cry (musical group), **8:**369
Huế Conservatory, **4:**125, 138
Huehns, Colin, **5:**800
¡Huelga en general!, **3:**749
Huerta Ríos, César, **2:**568
Huesca, Andrés, **2:**622
Hues Corporation, **3:**688
Huetara culture, **2:**680
Huff, Leon, **3:**711
Huffman, Kirk, **9:**966
Hugg, Dick "Huggy Boy," **3:**742
Hughes, David, **4:**638; **7:**595
Hughes, H. G. A., **9:**994
Hughes, Langston, **3:**577–78, 610
Hughes, "Queen" Carolyne, **8:**336
Hughes, Rev. T. S., **8:**1024
Huh, Yoonjung, **7:**970
Huhm, Halla Pai, **9:**99, 110
Hui, Andy (Xu Zhi'an), **7:**355
Hui people, **7:**447, 455–58
    folk songs of, **7:**152, 449
    musical traditions of, **7:**461–62
    in southern China, **7:**485
    in Tibet, **7:**471
Huichol culture, **3:**425
    folklore of, **2:**20–21
    narratives of, **2:**19
Hüidae theater (Seoul), **7:**968

Huitoto culture, **2:**482
Huizong, Song emperor, **7:**81, 321, 807, 982
Hujia shibapai (Cai), **7:**123, 406
al-Hujwiri, Ali ibn 'Uthman al-Jullabi, **5:**754, 755
Hukai Sirô, **7:**732, 735
Hŭktam (Yi), **7:**957
Hukutahu, **9:**904
hula, **9:**163, *201*, 925–28, *929*, 979
    competitions for, **9:**66–67
    hula 'ala'apapa, **9:**21
    hula 'auana, **9:**66–67, 879, 923
    hula kahiko, **9:**66–67, 923
    hula ku'i, **9:**127, 919–21
    on mainland North America, **3:**207, 209, 218–19, 527, 1051
    pedagogy, **9:**211–12, 272, 274–75, 925
    Rockette-like presentations of, **9:**67
    Solomon Islands, **9:**157
    Tahiti, **9:**879
    travelers' descriptions of, **9:**16–18, 38
Hula people, **9:**983
Hula Records, **9:**998
Huli people
    gender in instrument terminology, **9:**241
    instruments of, **9:**286, *372*, *393*, 540–43
    music and dance of, **9:**484, 536–43
    narratives of, **9:**514
    yodeling of, **9:**298–99
Hülphers, Abraham Abrahmson, **8:**447
Hultkläppen (fiddler), **8:**439
Hum (musical group), **3:**169
Human Studies Film Archives (Smithsonian Institution), **9:**975, 978–79
Humardani, Gendon, **4:**684–85
Ḥumaydī bin Manṣūr, **6:**657
Humbert, Stephen, **3:**1067–68, 1070, 1115, 1116
Humbi people, **1:**713
Humeniuk, Pawlo, **3:**913–14
Humina (musical group), **8:***484*
Humperdinck, Engelbert, **3:**173
Humphrey, Doris, **3:**852
Humphrey, Judith, **3:**1179
Humpty Dumpty (Johnson and Cole), **3:**608
Huna Benkei (Kanze), **7:**630
Hunayda, **6:**456
Ḥunayn ibn Isḥāq, **6:**16, 368
Huneker, James, **3:**562
Hùng dynasty, **4:**445, 449
Hung Xiannu, **7:**55
Hungarian Academy of Sciences, Folk Music Research Group, **8:**274
Hungarian Canadian Cultural Council, **3:**1250
Hungarian Kapisztran Folk Ensemble, **3:**1250
Hungarian people
    in Aotearoa, **9:**983–84
    in Austria, **8:**674
    in Croatia, **8:**736, 925
    in England, **8:**336
    in North America, **3:**10, 223, 529, 530, 908–9
        Jewish, **3:**120
        Ontario, **3:**1078, 1197
        Prairie Provinces, **3:**1249–50
        western Canada, **3:**292

in Romania, **8:**736, *743*, 868, 883, 886
in Serbia, **8:**736, 952
Hungarian String Quartet, **3:**538
Hungaroton (record label), **8:**746
Hungary, **8:**736–48
  cabaret in, **8:**746
  dance traditions of, **8:**162, 273–74, 737, 739,
    744–45
  ethnomusicological research in, **8:**20, 23
  geography of, **8:**736
  history of, **8:**736
  history of folk music, **8:**736–39
  identity issues in, **8:**270, *272*, 273, 738–39,
    747
  instrumental music in, **8:**742–46
  instruments, **8:**21, 170, 743–44
    research on, **8:**37, 172
  Jewish communities in, **8:**258
  map of, **8:***644*
  nationalist movement, **8:**59
  popular music in, **8:**205, 746–48
  population of, **8:**736
  research on music of, **8:**18, 23, 177
  rock in, **8:**217, 220–21
  Rom orchestras, **8:**143
  Rom people in, **8:**199, 270, 272–76, 737–39,
    744, 745–46
  táncház movement, **8:**153, 739, 746
  vocal music, **8:**23, 273–74, 739–42, 773
    ballads, **8:**135
    laments, **8:**120, 128
Hüngboga (Yi), **7:**953
Hüngbo-ga (also *Hüngbojön*) (*p'ansori* story),
    7:899, 968, 969, 984, 986
Hungerford, James, **3:***601*
Hünggyö un ilt'ö (Korean *kayagŭm* piece), **7:**962
Hüng t'aryŏng (Korean folk song), **7:**882
Hunn Brothers, **3:**616
Huns, **5:**720; **6:**965, 995; **8:**868
Hunsberger, Donald, **3:***567*
Hunt (companion of Despard), **2:**250
Hunt, George, **3:**31
Hunt, Steve, **3:***212*
Hunter, Alberta, **3:**644
Hunter, Andy, **8:**365, 372
Hunter College (New York), **10:**56
Hunter, Ivory Joe, **3:**646, 669, 673, 708
Hunter, Ruby, **9:**244, 443–44
Hunter, Tommy, **3:**1080
Hupa Indian nation, **3:**371, 412
huqin. See violins and fiddles (bowed lutes)
hurdy-gurdies, **8:**22, 142, 169, 170, 176
  Denmark, **8:**454
  England, **8:**331
  France, **8:**543, 544–45
  Germany, **8:**651, 654, 656
  ghironda, **8:**615
  lajna, **8:**919
  laterna, **8:**1012, *1013*, 1015
  lira, **3:**1200; **8:**796, 813, *815*
  Low Countries, **8:**528, 529, 532
  Malta, **8:**640
  New York, **3:**864
  North America, **3:**1197
  Poland, **8:**706
  Québec, **3:**331

rela, **8:**796
tekerő, **8:**743
vevlira, **8:**439
vielle (also *vielle à roue*), **8:**532, 545, 560
viula di orbi, **8:**694
zampogna, **8:**36
zanfona, **8:**589, 594
Hüreller, Üç, **6:**249, 251
Hurley, Frank, **9:**479
Hurley, Steve "Silk," **3:**690
Huron Indian nation, **3:**451, 465, 484, 1073,
    1074, 1078
"Hurrah! Hurrah for Grant and Wilson," **3:**308
Hurricane (film), **9:**45
Hurricane, Al (Alberto Sánchez), **3:**756, 765–66,
    766, 767
Hurricane, Al, Jr., **3:**766, *767*
Hurricane Band, **3:***766*
Hürriyet (newspaper), **6:**249
Hurston, Zora Neale, **2:**812; **3:**34, 577, 579
Hurt, Jakob, **8:**498
Hurt, "Mississippi" John, **3:**707
Hurtado, Sebastián, **2:**726
Hus, Jan, **8:**726
Husain, Madholal, death anniversary
    commemoration, **5:**276
Husain, Shah, **5:**753
Husain Sharqi, sultan of Jaunpur, **5:**170
al-Husayn ibn 'Ali, **5:**256
  veneration of, **5:**277, 279, 772, 794; **6:**544,
    826, 840, 876, 931, 939, 942
Ḥusayn ibn Aḥmad al-Kubaysī al-Ḥanafi al-
    Shādhilī, **6:**371
Hüseyin Fahreddin Efendi, **6:**109
Hüseyin Fahrettin Dede, **6:**110
Hushang chunguang (Tan), **7:**229–30
Hushaym, **6:**353
Husioti (*gidayû busi* piece), **7:***676*
Husni, Daud, **6:**318
Husni, Kamal, **6:**318
Hussain, Akhtar, **5:**770
Hussain, Fida, **5:**791
Hussain, Imdad, **5:**768
Hussain, Rahdath, **5:**790
Hussain, Rehdat, **5:**791
Hussain, Salamat, **5:**768
Hussain "Tafu," Altaf, **5:**768
Hussain, Zakir, **3:**986; **5:***4*, 136, 137, 342, 380,
    424, 528, 560, 584
Hussein, king of Jordan, **6:**640
Hussein, Saddam, **6:**638–39
"Hustle" (McCoy), **3:**228, 711
"Hustlers' Convention" (toast), **3:**693, 698
Hutajulu, Ritathony, **3:**1020
Hutamura Teiiti, **7:**744
Hutatu no rento (Takemitsu), **7:**736
Hutchings, Eliza, **8:***327*
Hutchinson, Anne, **3:**25
Hutchinson, Edgar "Pitún," **2:**691
Hutchinson Family Singers, **3:**184, 308, 557
Hutchinson, John W., **3:**308
Hutchinson's Republican Songster, **3:**308
Hutchisson, Don, **9:**626
Hutiwaki Zyutyôin, **7:**647
Hutka, Jaroslav, **8:**730
Hutterites, **3:**1086, 1240, 1249

Hutton, Charles, **3:**1070
Hutu people, **1:**108
Huun-Huur-Tu (musical group), **7:**1019,
    1023–25; **8:**226
Huvaidā. *See* Khuvaido
Huw Bowen, Robin, **8:**355, *355*
Huyssen, Andreas, **3:**94
Huzi Keiko, **7:**747
Huziwara family, **7:**586
Huziwara no Moronaga, **7:**589
Huziwara no Sadatosi, **7:**588, 644
Huziwara no Yukinaga, **7:**646
Huziwara Yosie, **7:**733, 744
Huziyama Itirô, **7:**745
Hwach'o sagŏri (Korean folk song), **7:**886
Hwang Byung-ki, **7:**56, 803, 954–56, 957, 972,
    975, 975–77, 990; **10:***14*
Hwang Chini, **7:**969, 985
Hwang Chini (*ch'anggŭk* piece), **7:**969
Hwang Haech'ŏn, **7:**898
Hwang Ilbaek, **7:***932*
Hwangch'ŏn kil (Kim), **7:**959
Hwanggŭmsan ŭi paek toraji (Korean folk song),
    7:961, 962
Hwanggyesa (*kasa*), **7:**927
Hwanghwa mannyŏn chigok (Kim), **7:**953
Hwangsangsok ŭi kŭdae (Seo), **7:**967
Hwarang ch'anggŭktan (*p'ansori* company),
    7:968
Hwimori (Onŭrŭm), **7:**972
Hwong, Lucia, **3:**346
Hyatt, George Washington, **9:**132
Hyegong, Silla king, **7:**981
Hye-Kerkdal, Käthe, **9:**983
Hyers, Anna, **3:**617
Hyers, Emma, **3:***617*
Hykes, David, **10:**71
hymnals. *See also* tunebooks
  China, **7:**374
  Chuuk, **9:**735
  Fiji, **9:**775
  Hawai'i, *Na Himeni Haipule Hawaii*, **9:**919
  Hindu
    Samāj-Ṣṛṅkhalā, **5:**252
    Sri Krishna Kīrtan, **5:**845
    Śrī Rādhāvallabhjī kā Varṣotsav, **5:**252
  Iceland, **8:**404
  Low Countries, **8:**533–34
  Lutheran, **3:**886
  Mangareva
    E Katekimo Katorika no Magareva, **9:**889
    *Na mau purega me te takao kiritiano aka
      Magareva me te mau himene*, **9:**889
  Mennonite, **3:***1238*
  Methodist, **3:**485–86, 627
  Nauru, *Iriañ in Evangelium*, **9:**756
  New Mexican, **3:**759
  Papua New Guinea, **9:**88, 493
    Anglican, **9:**197
    Buk na Kakailai, **9:**150
    Conchshell-Hymnal, **9:**196, 288
    Lutheran, **9:**193, 197
    Lutheran Gae Buk, **9:**568, 570
    Romano Katoliko Katekismo, **9:**288
  Pennsylvania, Ephrata Cloister, **3:**905
  Québec, **3:**1148

Volume Key: **6**, Middle East; **7**, East Asia; **8**, Europe; **9**, Australia and the Pacific Islands; **10**, The World's Music.

hymnals (*continued*)
  Rotuma, *Him Ne Rot Uesli*, **9:**823
  Sikh
    Guru Granth Sahib, **5:**256–57
    Guruvani, **5:**257
  Sweden, **8:**444
  Tahiti
    Buke Himene (1974), **9:**870
    Buke Himene (1983), **9:**870
    Buke Himene Tahito, **9:**870
  Tonga, **9:**203
  Western
    *Boston Handel and Haydn Society's
      Collection*, **9:**918
    Christian Lyre, **9:**918
    Hymns Ancient and Modern, **3:**8; **5:**922
    Moody/Sankey, **9:**913, 919
    Scottish Psalter and Church Hymnary, **9:**114
    Tamil Church Hymnal and Christian Lyrics,
      5:923, 924–25
  Yap, *Ngadatanggad ku Samol*, **9:**199–200
"*Hymne au printemps*" (Leclerc), **3:**1156
hymns, **2:**46, 67, 131; **3:**534. *See also* devotional
    songs and singing (South Asian);
    psalmody; vocal music; *specific genres*
  African Christian, **1:**16, 693–95, 718, 755
    aladura movement, **1:**404–6
    composers of, **1:**19, 36, 208–10, 216, 221,
      234, 408, 607, 763
    East Africa, **1:**598–99
    influence on popular music, **1:**480, 482,
      485
    influence on rumba, **1:**424
    Kenya, **1:**626, 627
    Zambia, **1:**671
  Ahl-e Haqq, **6:**193
  alabados, **3:**9, 755, 756–57, 759, 761–62,
    848
  alabanzas, **3:**759
  Amish, **3:**887
  Anuta, **9:**860
  Aotearoa, **9:**935
  Arab Protestant, **6:**547
  Arctic peoples, **3:**380
  in art music, **3:**539
  Asia, **3:**527
  Asian Christian, **7:**49–50, 373–74, 951
  Austral Islands, **9:**881–82
  Australia, **9:**442
    Torres Strait Islands, **9:**412
  Austria, **8:**673–74
  Bahamas, **2:**804
  Barbados, **2:**816–17
  Bellona, **9:**849, 851
  Brazil, **2:**329
  Buddhist, **7:**329, 330
    boudha caryāgīt, **5:**731
    jayamaṅgala gāta, **5:**557
    mgur, **5:**711
  Bulgaria, **8:**904
  Byzantine *stichera*, **6:**11
  Canada, **3:**144, 1063, 1108, 1189
  Caribbean, **2:**795
  Carriacou, *sankeys*, **2:**868
  Children of Peace, **3:**136
  Chile, for Virgin Mary festivities, **2:**363

Christian
  cassette dissemination of, **5:**557
  Hindi translations of, **5:**257
  Kerala, **5:**945
  South Asian congregations, **5:**582
  Tamil Nadu, **5:**922–24
Chuuk, **9:**734–35
colonial period, **3:**7, 531, 831–33
Cook Islands, **9:**224
  'imene, **9:**898
Coptic Orthodox, **6:**219, 221–22
Costa Rica, **2:**688
Czech Brethren, **8:**726
Delphic, **8:**47
Denmark, **8:**452, 459, 460
Dominican Republic, **2:**859
Doukhobor, **3:**1268
East Polynesia, **9:**208–9
Episcopalian, **3:**123
Estonia, **8:**492, *493*
European immigrant groups, **3:**825
Faroe Islands, **8:**469
  kingosang, **8:**471
Fiji, **9:**775
  sere ni lotu, **9:**776, 779, 781
France, *cantiques*, **8:**546
Garifuna culture, **2:**669, 675
Georgia, **8:**843
German, **3:**885, 888
gospel, **3:**10, 118, 119, 121, 125, 576, 1169
Greek Orthodox, **8:**1007
Guyana, **2:**445
Hawai'i, **3:**527; **9:**923
  hīmene haipule, **9:**917–19
  reggae treatment of, **9:**166
  song texts of, **9:**187
Hebrew *piyuṭim*, **3:**1173; **6:**524–25, 526–27,
    528, 529–31, 1037, *1038*, 1039,
    1040–41; **8:**253–54, 257
Hutterite, **3:**1240
Indian Shaker Church, **3:**488
Jamaica, **2:**901, 903–4
Kiribati, **9:**758, 763
  kairi, **9:**762
Korean Protestant, **3:**976
Kosrae, **9:**159, 742
Kuna culture, **2:**644
Luangiua, **9:**843
Lutheran, **3:**886; **8:**5, 726
Malta, **8:**638
Mangareva, **9:**208
  īmene, **9:**889
Manihiki, *hīmene* genres, **9:**905, 907
Marquesas Islands, *hīmene*, **9:**894
Marshall Islands, **9:**753
  alin jar, **9:**749
Maya culture, **2:**653
Mennonite, **3:**886–87, 1238
Mexico, **2:**614
Micronesia, **9:**158, 720
Moravian, **3:**10
Native American, **3:**484–86, 1079
Nauru, **9:**755, 756–57
Newār people, **5:**702
New Caledonia, **9:**672
  temperance, **9:**678–79

New England, **3:**154–55
New Guinea, **9:**193
Nicaragua, **2:**748, 754
Oceania, **9:**321
  pedagogy of, **9:**287–88
Ojibwe, **3:**458
Palau, **9:**723
Papua New Guinea, **9:**88–89, 147, 150, 153,
    493
  Bali and Vitu islands, **9:**609, 612
  Baluan, **9:**607
  Buang people, **9:**566
  Huli people, **9:**538–39
  indigenization of, **9:**194–97
  New Britain, **9:**614, 625
  played by conch bands, **9:**128–29
Pennsylvania, Ephrata Cloister, **3:**905, 907
Philippines, **4:**845–46, 847
Pohnpei, **9:**739
political, **8:**185, 187
Polynesia, **9:**127
Protestant, **3:**531
psalmody, **8:**97–98
Pukapuka
  īmene āpī Sāpati, **9:**913
  īmene tapu, **9:**913
  īmene tuki, **9:**910, 913
Purépecha culture, **2:**577
Quechua, **2:**215
Rotuma, **9:**819
  mak pel, **9:**819, 823
rural, **3:**532–33
St. Lucia, **2:**948
Sāmoa, **9:**204–7, 803, 805, 807–8
Scotland, Orkney Islands, **8:**423–24
Shaker, **3:**135
Sikaiana, **9:**848
  aasi, **9:**847
Solomon Islands, **9:**155, 656
  Isabel Province, **9:**661
  Malaita, **9:**667
Spanish, sung by Native American
    congregations, **3:**849
Sri Lanka
  pasam, **5:**960
  praśasti (also *virudu*), **5:**960, 965, 966
Subarctic peoples, **3:**391
Syrian Christian, **3:**984
Syrian Orthodox, **6:**227, 228, 229, 544
Tahiti, *hīmene*, **9:**37–38, 869–71
Toba culture, **2:**259
Tokelau, **9:**824
Tonga, **9:**202–4, 790
Tuamotu Islands, *hīmene*, **9:**885
Turkey, **6:**769
  nefes, **6:**768
Tuvalu, **9:**830–31
United States, **3:**144
urban, **3:**532
'Uvea, **9:**811–12
Vanuatu, **9:**198, 214, 691
Vedic, **5:**24, 25, 30–33, 66, 238
Virgin Islands, **2:**973
Waiwai culture, **2:**71–72, 131–32
Wales, **8:**349–50
Wayana culture, **2:**166, 167

West Futuna, **9:**861
Yap, **9:**199–200, *729*
Hyojong, Chosŏn king, **7:**982
Hyŏn Chemyŏng, **7:**952
Hyŏn Ch'ŏl, **7:**990
Hyŏnak Yongsan Hoesang (*chŏngak* suite), **7:**848, 868
Hyŏn'gŭm oŭm t'ongnon (collection), **7:**856
Hyŏn'gŭm sinjŭng karyŏng (collection), **7:**856, 921
Hyŏn'gŭm tongmun yugi (collection), **7:**856
Hyonok Kim and Dancers, **9:**415
Hypocrisy (album), **7:**364
Hyslop, Graham, **1:**60, 644

Iā'Oe E Ka Lā Hula Competition, **9:**923
Ia Ora Tahiti, **9:**998
Iatmul people
    children's songs of, **9:**257–58
    films on, **9:**48, 982
    instruments of, **9:**289, 546; **10:**28
    music and dance of, **9:**258, 552–57
    myths of, **9:**340
Iba Takasi, **7:**592
Ibadan empire, **1:**471
Ibadite people, **6:**273
Ibagué Conservatory, **2:**395
Ibaloy people, **4:**914
    instrumental music of, **4:**918, 919
    music of, **4:**878
    vocal music of, **4:**920
Iban people, **4:**823, 824, 825
    instruments of, **4:**829–30, 835, 836
    music of, **4:**828
    spirit beliefs, **4:**51
Ibáñez, Paco, **8:**208
Ibarra, Leticia, **3:**749
Iberia (Georgian region), **8:**826
Iberian people. *See also* Basque people;
        Portuguese people; Spanish people
    in Corsica, **8:**566
    in North America, **3:**731–32, 847–52
Ibibio people, **1:**459
Ibidali (Huli panpipe player), **9:**393
Ibn 'Abbās, **6:**443
Ibn Abī 'l-Dunyā, **6:**19, 372
Ibn 'Ā'isha, **6:**291
Ibn al-Akfānī, **6:**367–68
Ibn al-'Arabī, **6:**372, 443
Ibn Bājja. *See* Abū Bakr Ibn Bājja
Ibn Baqqī, **6:**443
Ibn Battuta, Mohammed ibn Abdullah, **1:**11, 75–76, 138, 313
Ibn Baṭūṭa, **6:**21
Ibn al-Darrāj al-Sabtī, **6:**373
Ibn Faḍl Allāh al-'Umarī, **6:**370
Ibn al-Firnās, **6:**442
Ibn Fulayta, **6:**686
Ibn Gabirol, Salomon, **6:**19; **8:**255
Ibn Ghaybī, **6:**395, 398, 399
Ibn Ghazāla, **6:**353
Ibn Ḥajar al-Haytamī, **6:**372
Ibn Ḥanbal, **6:**358, 359, 360
Ibn Ḥāsib al-Mursī, **6:**443, 447
Ibn Ḥazm, **6:**372
Ibn Himāra, **6:**443, 447

Ibn Jāmi', **6:**353, 355
Ibn al-Jawzī, **6:**372
Ibn Jot, **6:**443
Ibn Jūadi, **6:**443, 447
Ibn al-Kalbī, **6:**372
Ibn al-Khāl. *See* 'Abd al-Ḥayy ibn Muḥammad
        al-Ṭāluwī al-Dimashqī al-Ḥanafī
Ibn Khaldūn, **6:**12, 20, 273, 364, 444, 1035
Ibn al-Khaṭīb al-Salmānī, **6:**20
Ibn al-Khaṭīb, Lisānu al-Dīn, **6:**443
Ibn Khurdādhbih, **6:**182, 297, 355, 369
Ibn Kurr, **6:**366
Ibn Li'būn, **6:**652, 657
Ibn Mājah, **6:**359, 360
Ibn Mālik, **6:**443
Ibn Manẓūr, **6:**359
Ibn Misjaḥ, **6:**12, 539
Ibn Msāyib, Muḥammad, **6:**472
Ibn Muḥriz, **6:**352, 539
Ibn-al-Muḥtār, **1:**313
Ibn al-Munajjim, **6:**364, 368, 541
Ibn Nāqiyā, **6:**370
Ibn al-Qaysarānī, **6:**372
Ibn Qayyim al-Jawziyyah, **6:**358, 372
Ibn Qudāma al-Maqdisī, **6:**372
Ibn Rushd, **6:**443; **8:**92
Ibn Ṣāfi, **6:**653
Ibn Sahla, Būmidyan, **6:**472
Ibn Sanā' al-mulk, **6:**370
Ibn Sīnā, **6:**17, 129, 177, 367, 369, 392, 395,
        502, 508, 542, 869, 910; **8:**92
    instrument classification system, **6:**373,
        397–98, 399
Ibn Surayj, **6:**295, 296, 297, 539
Ibn al-Ṭaḥḥān, **6:**362, 365, 373
Ibn al-Ṭawīl. *See* 'Abd al-Ḥayy ibn Muḥammad
        al-Ṭāluwī al-Dimashqī al-Ḥanafī
Ibn Taymiyya, **6:**372
Ibn al-Trīkī, Aḥmad, **6:**472
Ibn Tufayl, **6:**443
Ibn al-Walīd, Ḍāhi, **6:**651
Ibn Zayla, **6:**369, 373, 392, 395, 398, 399, 542
Ibn Zuhr, **6:**443
Ibo culture, in Belize, **2:**668
Ibo Dancers, **3:**805
Ibo people
    music research on, **1:**34–35, 40
    speech surrogate methods, **1:**106
Ibo Records, **2:**890–91; **3:**804
Ibragimova, Tamti, **6:**956
Ibrahim, Abdullah, **1:**430, 774, 778–79, 780
Ibrāhīm Adham (epic), **6:**840
Ibrāhīm al-Mawṣilī, **6:**131, 295, 352, 353, 355,
        539–40
Ibrahim Gülşeni, **6:**193
Ibrāhīm ibn al-Mahdī, **6:**294, 354, 355, 540
Ibrāhīm, Sha'ūbī, **6:**315–16
Ibu Sawitri (Cirebonese dancer), **4:**691
"I Can't Get No Satisfaction" (Rolling Stones),
        3:318, 552
"I Can't Help Myself" (Four Tops), **3:**674
"I Can't See Myself Leaving You" (Franklin),
        3:677
"I Cried a Tear" (Baker), **3:**673
Ice Cream Castles? (The Time), **3:**685
Ice Cube, **3:**699, 701, 714, 715

Iceland, **8:**400–408
    art music in, **8:**406–7
    court music, **8:**146, 405
    dance traditions of, **8:**164
    geography of, **8:**400
    healing ceremonies, **8:**196
    history of, **8:**400, 405
    instruments, **8:**405–6
    kvöldvaka gatherings, **8:**117, 141, 400, 401–2,
        407
    lausavísur performance, **8:**143, 402, 407, 408
    map of, **8:***398*
    popular music in, **8:**208
    population of, **8:**400
    psalmody in, **8:**122
    research on music of, **8:**408
    Reykjavík cathedral, **8:**406
    vocal music of, **8:**117–18, 129, 400–405
Icelandic Club (Calgary), **3:**1250
Icelandic Composers' Society, **8:**406
Icelandic people, in Manitoba, **3:**343, 409, 1086,
        1089, 1225, 1237, 1250, 1251
Iceland Symphony Orchestra, **8:**406
Icelar, Bo, **3:**312
Ice-T, **3:**552, 698, 699, 714, 715
Ichalkaranjikar, Balkrishnabuwa, **5:**461–62, 465
I Ching, **3:**130, 335; **7:**153, 823
Ichiyanagi Toshi, **7:**627, 736–37
iconography, **2:**12–16; **3:**562; **5:**43, 301–2. *See
        also* visual arts
    Andalusian instruments, **6:**444–45
    Arabian peninsula, instrument depictions,
        6:357–58
    bagpipe ensemble depiction, **8:**504
    Bali, of instruments, **4:**731
    Burma, of harps, **4:**378
    Byzantine music, **8:**1023
    Cambodia, of instruments, **4:**157–58, 173,
        183
    Chavín culture, **2:**467
    China, **7:**127
        depictions of instruments, **7:**111–12, 113
        depictions of women musicians, **7:**403–4
        minority cultures, **7:**447
        research on, **7:**136
    Denmark, **8:**463
    depictions of women instrumentalists, **5:**411
    dhrupad performance depictions, **5:**163
    early European sources, **8:**36, 39, 40, 42
    Ecuador, ceramic vases, **2:**413
    France, popular songs, **8:**548
    Georgia, **8:**842
    Germany, instrument depictions, **8:**651,
        654–55
    Greece, ancient, **8:**46
    Huari culture, **2:**467
    India, instrument depictions, **5:**322, 325, 331,
        332, 337, 341
    Indus Valley instrument depictions, **5:**320
    Iran, of dance, **6:**875
    Italy, harp depictions, **8:**615
    Java, of instruments, **4:**632
    Jewish sources, **8:**259
    Kashmir, instrument depictions, **5:**689
    Korea, **7:**806
        depictions of shamans, **7:**986

iconography (*continued*)
kundus, **9:**245
Laos, carvings of instruments, **4:**354–55
Low Countries, **8:**523
  bagpipes, **8:**529
  hurdy-gurdy, **8:**532
  pipe-and-tabor ensemble, **8:**528
Mashriq, **6:**536
Maya culture, **2:**650–51, 667
Mexico, colonial codices, **2:**557
Middle Eastern depictions of musical scenes,
  6:363
Moche culture, **2:**207, 467
Norway
  harpa, **8:**423
  langeleik depiction, **8:**414
Otomí culture, instrumental ensembles, **2:**571
Paraguay, instrument depictions in mission
  towns, **2:**454
prehistoric Southeast Asian cultures, **4:**44–46
problems of, **4:**12
Purépecha culture, Christian imagery, **2:**577
research on, **8:**26
Sardinia, **8:**631
Serbia, instrument depictions, **8:**945
South America, **10:**100
Sulawesi, of instruments, **4:**806
Sumatra, of instruments and dance, **4:**598–99,
  600
Sweden, instrument depictions, **8:**439–40
Tamil Nadu, carved dancer images, **5:***14*
Thailand, **4:**286
Tiwanaku culture, **2:**282
Uighur instrument depictions, **6:**998
Vietnam
  of dance, **4:**497–98
  of instruments, **4:**446, 472
iconology, **2:**6; **5:**302–6. *See also* iconography
Īḍāḥ al-dalālāt fī samā' al-ālāt (Abd al-Ghanī al-
  Nābulusī), **6:**373
Idaho
  Basque people in, **3:**847, 849–50
  Japanese people in, **3:**969
  Native American groups in, **3:**420–22, 425–27
"Ida Red," **3:**353
"I'd Be Satisfied" (Dominoes), **3:**671
Iddi, M., **10:**143
Iddrisu Goondze, Sulemana, **10:***150*
Ideal label, **3:**781
Idea of North (Gould), **3:**1105
Ideflawen, Ali, **6:**275
Idelsohn, Abraham Zvi, **6:**22, 23, 205, 535,
  1024, 1029, 1036, 1057–58, 1065,
  1066, 1071; **8:**266
identity issues. *See also* ideology; politics
  affinity groups, **3:**326–27
  Africa, dance and, **1:**109–13
  African-Americans, **3:**327, 583, 587, 625, 635
  African descendants in South and Central
    America, **2:**55
  Alevi Turks, **6:**790–91, 793–800
  American music, **3:**174, 184, 519, 538,
    552–53
  Arab-Americans, **3:**1035
  Asian-Americans, **3:**951–52
  Basque people, **8:**314–16

Berber peoples, **6:**274–75, 276–77
bluegrass, **3:**168
border crossings and, **3:**322–33
Breton people, **8:**558–59
Cajun and Creole peoples, **3:**858–59
Canada, **3:**16–17, 1056–64, 1067, 1146–47,
  1164–65
  European minorities, **3:**1060
  northern, **3:**1281
Canadian Aboriginal peoples, **3:**52
Canadian country music, **3:**1109–10
Caribbean, **2:**792–93
  immigrant groups, **2:**83–91
Celtic people, **8:**319–22
Central America
  Amerindians, **2:**60–61
  German people, **2:**61
  immigrant groups, **2:**83–91
  Italian people, **2:**61
  Spanish people, **2:**61
Central Asian peoples, **6:**895, 902–3
Cham people, **3:**951–52
Chicano, **3:**749
China, **7:**35–36, 92; **10:**25–26
  folk music and, **7:**229
Chinese-Americans, **3:**964–65
class and music, **3:**42–53
concept and evolution, **3:**505–8
Dai people, **7:**507
dances and, **3:**215–16
Dolan people, **6:**990
Dominicans, **3:**731, 800
dualism, **3:**512–13, 514, 821
East Asia, **7:**49–51
Egypt, **6:**557–61, 612
El Salvador, **2:**719
enculturation and, **3:**274, 284
ethnicity concept, **3:**11, 151, 192, 505,
  515–17, 587, 820–24, 1035
Europe, social organization and, **8:**247
Falasha people (Beta Israel), **10:**67
Filipino-Americans, **3:**1026
French-Americans, **3:**855
German-Americans, **3:**885, 886
Ghana, Cape Coast region, **10:**29–36
Greek-Americans, **3:**929
Haitian-Americans, **3:**805
historiography and, **3:**21
Honduras, **2:**738
Hong Kong, **7:**431, 435–36
Hungary, **8:**270, *272,* 273, 738–39, 747
hybridization, **3:**824
India, **5:**7; **8:**120–21
indie music, **3:**171
Inner Asia, **7:**35–36
Israel, **6:**199–200, 1016, 1069–70
  mizraḥi Jews, **6:**261–68
Italian-Americans, **3:**910
Jewish people, ideology and, **8:**258, 265–67
Korea, **7:**47, 804–5, 911, 938, 959
Korean-Americans, **3:**975–76, 977–78
Korean-Japanese people, **7:**797–98
Kurdish people, **6:**744–45, 747, 751–52
Maritime minority groups, **3:**150–51
Martinique, **2:**915–20
Métis, **3:**404

Mexico, immigrant groups, **2:**83–91
Mongol people, **7:**1004, 1014
multiple levels of identity, **3:**18–20
music and, **3:**508–17
music revivals, **3:**55–59
Native Americans, **3:**446, 480
New Mexican Hispanos, **3:**756
North America, **3:**504–17
Norwegian-Americans, **3:**866
Nubian people, **6:**645
Oceania, **9:**5, 211–22
  festivals and, **9:**55–57
Oman, **6:**682
Pacific Islanders, **3:**1052; **9:**117–18
Palestinians, **6:**638–40
place and, **3:**142, 149–51, 171
Polish-Americans, **3:**892
popular music and, **8:**206
Québécois, **3:**1058, 1061, 1158, 1166, 1167
religion and, **3:**117–18
for rock groups, **3:**113
Romanian-Americans, **3:**910
Ryûkyû peoples, **7:**790
Saami people, **8:**299, 302–3
Shona people, **1:**756–57
Siberian peoples, **7:**1030
societal aspects, **3:**328
South America
  Amerindians, **2:**60–61, 129
  German people, **2:**61
  immigrant groups, **2:**83–91
  Italian people, **2:**61
  Japanese people, **2:**86–89; **10:**102
  Portuguese people, **2:**61
  Spanish people, **2:**61
South Asian Americans, **3:**986–87
Subarctic peoples, **3:**391–92
Sweden, **8:**441
Switzerland, **8:**682
Taiwan, **7:**424, 425–26, 428–29
Tejanos, **3:**771
Tohono O'odham Indians, **3:**490
Tuareg people, **1:**574–75
Turkish people, **6:**247, 252, 781–87, 812–17
Tuvan people, **7:**1024–25
Uighur people, **6:**995
Ukrainian-Americans, **3:**914–15
United States, **3:**16–17
ideology. *See also* nationalism; politics
Afghanistan, **5:**807–10, 812, 814–16, 824,
  826, 829
African-American secular music, **3:**592
Albania, **8:**999–1000
Andhra Pradesh, **5:**901
art music and, **3:**269; **8:**58–61
Asian-American movement, **3:**964
Austria, **8:**670, 675
Balkan region, **8:**867
Bangladesh, **5:**503
Bulgaria, **8:***894,* 901–2
Cambodia, Khmer Rouge, **4:**90, 209
Canada, **3:**2, 15–17
Canadian Broadcasting Corporation
  programming, **3:**52
China, **7:**220, 380–81, 383–88
  aesthetics and, **7:**101

compositional content and, 7:340–41, 347–50, 396–97
cultural preservation, 7:47
Cultural Revolution, 7:47, 90, 102–3, 341
effect on scholarship, 7:136, 140
folk orchestras and, 7:230–31
narrative content and, 7:258–59, 262
opera content and, 7:294, 300
qin playing and, 7:163–65
Croatia, 8:933–35
cultural relativism, 3:71, 509–10
Czechoslovakia, 8:723–24, 725, 729–30
Denmark, folk revival, 8:461
East Asia historiography, 7:43
Egypt, 6:235–36, 611–12
Europe, central, 8:645
Faroe Islands, 8:470
Finland, 8:482–83, 484, 485
folk orchestras and, 8:176
folk song movement and, 8:19
France, 8:551
funk, 3:680–81, 683–84
gender, 3:89–90; 8:191
Germany, 8:659–62, 664
Great Britain, 8:186
Greece, 8:1008, 1018
Harlem Renaissance, 3:577–78
Hindu fundamentalism, 5:624
Hungary, 8:738–39, 747–48
Iceland, 8:404, 406
individuality, 3:44
Ireland, 8:186
Islam, 6:690
Islamic, 5:486
Israel-Palestine, 6:262, 263–64, 1013, 1015, 1018–19, 1023, 1025–26, 1027–28, 1029, 1070–72, 1074
Italy, 8:613–14, 618–19
Japan
min'yô styles, 7:601
propaganda songs, 7:745
Western music and, 7:536–37
Jewish identity issues, 8:258, 265–67
Judaism, vs. performance practice, 6:200–201
Korea, 7:807, 953
Liberia, Islam, 1:327–49
Macedonia, 8:981–82
Mapuche culture, 2:234
Marxist, 8:184, 188, 192, 338–39
masculinity, 3:87, 96, 97
melting-pot, 3:15–16, 313, 511, 513, 820, 991–92, 1061
modernism, 3:650
Mongolia, 7:1005–6
Montenegro, 8:959
mosaic, 3:72–73, 342–43, 513, 820, 1060
multiculturalism, 3:11, 14, 53, 73, 313, 1060, 1067, 1245–46
music and, 8:184–89
music revivals, 3:55–59
myth and, 8:26
nationalism and, 3:16, 504, 507, 511, 1164–65; 5:433–34; 8:10, 16, 82
Nepal, 5:696–97, 705–6
North Korea, 7:808, 960–63, 992, 997
Norway, 8:420, 429

Nusa Tenggara Barat, 4:766–69
Pakistan, 5:744–50
pan-Africanism, 1:38, 43
performance contexts and, 8:147
pluralism, 3:504, 512–14, 515
Poland, 8:709, 711
popular music and, 8:209
populist, 3:145–46, 147
Portugal, 8:577, 583
primitive vs. modern, in religion, 3:121–22
Q'ero culture, 2:229–30
race as concept, 3:63–64, 65–66, 69
rock and, 8:217
Romania, 8:874, 882–86
Russia, 8:764, 770, 778–79, 782
scholarship and, 5:49–50
Scotland, 8:186
Serbia, 8:949–50
Slovenia, 8:920–21
social class and preference issues in, 8:188–89
soul music, 3:676
Soviet, 8:753
in Azerbaijan, 6:924
in Belarus, 8:800
in Central Asia, 6:12, 903, 917–19, 938, 958–60
in Estonia, 8:498
in Georgia, 8:840–41, 844–45
in Latvia, 8:505–6, 507
in Lithuania, 8:513–14
in North Caucasia, 8:851, 853
in Ukraine, 8:817–18, 821
Spain, 8:598
state folk ensembles and, 8:152, 153, 228
Sweden, 8:441, 446
Switzerland, 8:128, 683
Tunisia, 6:510, 513
notation of Tunisian art music, 6:325–36
Turkey, 6:57, 77, 781–87, 796–97
United States, 3:2, 15–17
Vietnam, 4:88
Wales, 8:185
world music and, 8:225, 226
Yugoslavia (former), 8:1000–1002
Idεris (Sudanese lyrist), 1:303
IDG Books, 3:270
idiophones. See also bells and chimes; concussion idiophones; cymbals; friction idiophones; gongs; Jew's harps; lamellophones; lithophones; marimbas; metallophones; rattles; scrapers; slit-drums; triangles; xylophones
acoustics of, 5:322
Akan people, 1:465
Andean regions, 2:206–7
animal bladders, struck, vejiga, 2:380, 381, 774, 781
Arab world, 6:403–5
Bali, 4:741–43
barrels, copper, spilendz-churi, 8:840
barrels, kerosene
Futuna, 9:816
'Uvea, 9:812, 814
bottles, struck
Bahamas, 2:814

bottil, 5:612–13, 614; 9:93
Cook Islands, 9:900
Oceania, 9:140, 863–64
Trinidad and Tobago, 2:962
bowls or pots, struck
batil, 4:420, 421
cântaro com abano, 8:582
chunyu, 7:108
garvi, 5:769
geger, 5:684
ghada, 5:476
ghaṭam, 5:149, 150, 235, 357–58, 368, 452, 684
inkin, 7:617
jaltarang, 5:342–43
jaltarangam, 5:352, 354–55
kane, 7:617
kin, 7:617
kuḍam, 5:907
kūnzag, 5:774, 782, 783
māngāi (also garāi), 5:787, 789, 790
nūt, 5:683–84, 685
Papua New Guinea, 9:490
phinggian, 4:923
pu, 7:826, 829
qing, 7:312, 323
Sumbawa, 4:784
ṭāsa, 6:403
brake drums, naqūs, 6:404
broomsticks, Belize, 2:677
buzzers, bamboo
balingbing, 4:918–19
duri dana, 4:608, 809–10
pakkung, 4:919
rere, 4:809–10
buzzers, insect, 9:615, 655
cans, jars, tins, pails
Africa, 1:555, 594
apa, 9:828
Arabian peninsula, 6:403–4
Carriacou, 2:871
chegbe, 1:376
Cook Islands, 9:904
gula gending, 4:767
jaḥla, 6:404, 546, 651
Jamaica, 2:903
jermani, 1:591
kalenge, 1:455
Mangareva, 9:886
Marquesas Islands, 9:895
Marshall Islands, 9:750, 753–54
Niue, 9:817
Oceania, 9:41, 159, 378, 427
Papua New Guinea, 9:147, 508
Polynesia, 9:379–80
Pukapuka, 9:913
pulotu, 9:379
Sāmoa, 9:798
Sikaiana, 9:848
Takuu, 9:839
tanaka (also pāto), 6:403–4, 404
tini, 9:906, 908
Tonga, 9:792
Trinidad and Tobago, 2:962
China
early, 7:88, 191

idiophones, China (*continued*)
　south and southwestern minority cultures,
　　7:490–92
classification of, **6**:396, 398
clickers
　New Guinea, **9**:245
　Solomon Islands, **9**:651, 657
coins, rolled, Switzerland, **8**:686
combs, struck, **9**:563
Congo, 1500s–1600s, **1**:77, 78, 79
Cook Islands, **9**:899
Coptic Orthodox music, **6**:544
crystallophones, *ranat kaeo*, **4**:125, 230, 286
Cuba, **2**:836
Dan people, **1**:466
disks, struck, with body resonator, Papua New
　Guinea, **9**:490
Dogon people, **1**:455
drums, basket, **3**:434, 435–36, 472, 475
drums, box
　adakem, **1**:356
　Ainu people, **7**:784
　baoki, **9**:762, 763
　cajita, **2**:492, 494
　cajón, **2**:475, 481, 493, 496, 499, 500, 709;
　　3:786
　cajón de tapeo, **2**:565
　chestier, **7**:788
　chúc, **4**:448
　mugu, **7**:527–28
　Native American types, **3**:474–75, 477
　pōkihi, **9**:380, 825, 828
　tormento, **2**:360
　Western Arctic, **3**:375
drums, bronze
　China, **7**:108, 191, 491
　cultural origins of, **4**:11
　Java, **4**:632
　Kmhmu people, **4**:547
　mahorathük, **4**:231
　mahoratuk, **4**:545
　moko, **4**:791–92
　nakara, **4**:598–99
　nekara, **4**:819–20
　power of, **4**:9
　prehistoric, **4**:40–41, 43, 44–46
　Southeast Asia, **4**:58, 485, 497, 596
　trống đồng, **4**:467
　Vietnam, **4**:446, 535
drums, deerhide, Delaware Indian, **3**:463,
　464
drums, iron, *dama*, **7**:477, 480, 481
drums, sides of, Venezuela, **2**:526–27, 542
drums, steel (pans), **2**:29, 96–97, 796; **3**:1202,
　1213; **8**:235
　Grenada, **2**:866
　Guyana, **2**:446; **5**:604
　Montserrat, **2**:923
　Trinidad and Tobago, **2**:960–63
　Venezuela, **2**:528
drums, water
　Africa, **1**:446
　assakalabu, **1**:585, 587, 590–91
　baa wéhai, **2**:550
　ba kubahe, **2**:589, *590*
　bastel (also *seoe*), **2**:929

trotrobe, **1**:789
　Yaqui Indians, **3**:475
early treatises on, **5**:21
East Asia, **7**:5
Edo people, **1**:461
Ewe people, **1**:462
flabella
　k'shots, **6**:736
　mirwaḥa, **6**:405
Gã people, **1**:463
gourds, struck
　Africa, **1**:449, 451
　ahá, **1**:475
　angara, **2**:492–93
　bukhsa, **1**:562
　checo, **2**:492–93
　horde, **1**:446, 449, 546
　igbá, **1**:475
　ipu, **9**:21, 177, 391, 916, 917, 920, 923,
　　928, *956*
　larakaraka, **1**:224
　Papua New Guinea, **9**:498
　Sudan, **1**:564
Hindustani, **5**:342–43
hoes, struck, **3**:785
　Carriacou, **2**:870
　Cuba, **2**:824–25
　Haiti, **2**:885
Igbo people, **1**:459
Java, **4**:642
jingle rings
　chia nênh, **4**:536
　panteru, **5**:490, 966
jingling johnny (Turkish crescent), **8**:693
jugs, struck
　cántaro, **2**:707
　Mixtec culture, **2**:565
　Spain, **8**:593
Kenya, **1**:426
Khmer people, **4**:162–66
Korea, **7**:829–30
leaves, shaken
　didu, **9**:615
　kumpas, **4**:924
　napinapin, **9**:63
　New Caledonia, **9**:674, 682–83, 685
　Oceania, **9**:515, 530, 608, 615, 906
　Russell Islands, **9**:664
　Vanuatu, **9**:705, 708
Lombok, **4**:766–67
machete, struck
　adawo, **2**:897
　ispara almuk, **2**:660, 663
Madagascar, **1**:784–85
majira, **2**:85
mats, rolled, **9**:508
　fala, **9**:828
　fala and *tu'itu'i*, **9**:805–6
　Futuna, **9**:816
　Polynesia, **9**:771
　Polynesian outliers, **9**:836
　Rotuma, **9**:819, 821
　Sāmoa, **9**:797–98, 805
　Tonga, **9**:792
　Tuvalu, **9**:829
　'Uvea, **9**:813, 814

Mexico, ancient, **2**:8
Mongol people, **7**:1015–16
music boxes, *ka'i* (also *tingilingibox*), **2**:929
New Caledonia, **9**:964
pedagogical uses of, **3**:279, 280
penis sheaths, **9**:548
pestles and mortars
　antan, **4**:*418*, 423, 831–32
　Bolivia, **2**:285
　ch'uk, **7**:822–23, 829
　Colombia, **2**:150–51, 153
　đuống, **4**:535
　gandang lasuang, **4**:609
　hāwon, **6**:651
　lesung, **4**:423, 646, 675, 679, 831
　mahbash, **6**:654, *657*
　mihba, **6**:545
　mihbash, **6**:404
　mộc bảng, **4**:504
　quánh loông, **4**:535, *536*
　rantok, **4**:767, 780–81
　Shao and Bunun peoples, **7**:527
　Spain, **8**:589
　Sumatra, **4**:623
　Venezuela, **2**:537
pillows, struck, **9**:243, 440
planks (wooden), struck
　Bulgaria, **8**:894
　fa'aali'i lāiti (also *pulotu*), **9**:806–7
　Hopi Indians, **3**:430
　Kwakiutl, **3**:400
　Madagascar, **1**:785
　matrimonial, **2**:929
　mesa de ruidos (also *tamborete*; *tormento*),
　　2:492, 493
　mộc bảng, **4**:468
　napa, **9**:378–79, 857, 859, 860
　Native American types, **3**:474–75
　Northeast types, **3**:463
　Northwest Coast, **3**:401
　Oceania, **9**:267, 373
　papa, **9**:827–28, 850, 851, 852
　Polynesia, **9**:771
　Polynesian outliers, **9**:836
　tā, **9**:853, 855
　tagum, **9**:649
　taqasrah, **9**:702
　Tonga, **9**:14
　tubitubi, **9**:656
　txalaparta, **8**:171, 314, 315, *315*
　'Uvea, **9**:814
　Vanuatu, **9**:693, 699
planks (wooden), suspended
　kagul, **4**:924
　kwintangan kayu, **4**:899
　Oceania, **9**:375
　Philippines, **4**:928
　semāntron, **6**:222
　toaca, **8**:876
plaques (metal), struck
　ghadyal-tipru, **5**:727
　han, **7**:617
　kecrèk, **4**:107, 642, 652, 673, 675, 697
　kei, **7**:617
　kepyak, **4**:652
　ṣaḥn, **6**:94, 656

prehistoric, **8:**39
rumsterstang (barker's stick), Denmark, **8:**455
saw, musical, **3:**969
    Denmark, **8:**455, 458
    Sweden, **8:***440*
scissor blades, Peru, **2:**207, 481
Senufo people, **1:**454
shells, struck, **9:**681
    Marshall Islands, **9:**750
    Mexico, **2:**14, *15*
    Vanuatu, **9:**693
shields, struck, Papua New Guinea, **9:**617, *618*
shoes
    cutarras, **2:**774, 781
    tap, **3:**206
Solomon Islands, **9:**962
Southeast Asia, **4:**67
spurs, metal, *suila jut'as*, **2:**285
stamping tubes, **1:**113; **4:**542, 562, *564*, 565, 596, 794
    ʔawɛn, **4:**573–76
    bamba, **2:**929
    bavugu, **1:**307, 705
    bembu, **9:**23
    boompipe, **2:**899
    borépudearíyuhkë, **2:**150–51
    Borneo, **4:**830–33
    derua, **9:**776, 777
    gɔh, **4:**573, 585
    kesut, **4:**831
    lopu, **9:**853
    Luangiua, **9:**843
    makau taposa, **9:**647
    New Caledonia, **9:**680–81, 683, 685
    New Ireland, **9:**600
    Oceania, **9:**15, 213–14, *283*, 374
    pamploi, **1:**463
    Papua New Guinea, **9:**490, 491, 502, 503–5
    pemuli, **4:**924
    Peru, **2:**492
    Polynesia, **9:***766*, 771
    qaḍīb, **6:**395, 398
    quitiplás, **2:**527, 528
    Solomon Islands, **9:**962
    takuapú, **2:**200, 203, 454
    Teop Island, **9:**642–43
    thobo, **4:**793
    tingtung, **4:**697
    Tonga, **9:**14, 784
    tongatong, **4:**886, 919
    Trinidad and Tobago, **2:**962
    tsinguru, **9:**651
    'urutu, **9:**503
    Vanuatu, **9:**693
stool, struck, *kwakwa*, **2:**505, 508
Thailand, **4:**228–32
timelines played on, **1:**113
tops, humming, Kuna culture, **2:**640
tortoiseshells, struck
    ayotl, **2:**550, 601
    French Guiana, **2:**435
    Garífuna culture, **2:**673, *676*, 677, 733
    kuswa taya, **2:**660
    Maya culture, **2:**651

Mexico, **2:**13, *14*
    Purépecha culture, **2:**577
    tiyoo, **2:**563–64
    tortuga, **2:**653, 723–24
trays, metal
    berdah, **4:**616
    chinchāna, **6:**403
    ṣaḥn mīmiyeh, **6:**687, *687*
    ṣaḥn nuḥ ḥāsī, **6:**403, *403*
    salawek dulang, **4:**611–12, 613
    tāl, **5:**774, 782, 783
    tepsi, **8:**994–95, *995*
    tepsija, **8:**951
    thāl, **5:**727
    thālī, **5:**291, 292, 640, 647
    Trinidad and Tobago, **2:**962
tubes, struck (bamboo or cane)
    cana, **8:**582
    fagoigoi, **9:**863
    gandang, **4:**899
    goong teng leng, **4:**534
    ihara, **9:**869, 876
    kalatong, **4:**848
    kohe, **9:**895
    kongkong, **9:**563
    kongon, **9:**23
    kwat, **2:**897
    Madagascar, **1:**784
    mambu, **9:**570–71
    marap, **9:**508
    Marquesas Islands, **9:**892
    Martinique, **2:***916*
    Micronesia, **9:**716, *718*
    muṅgoose, **5:**544
    New Caledonia, **9:***214*, 674
    Oceania, **9:**19, 156, 189, 192
    Papua New Guinea, **9:**376, 600
    patang-ug, **4:**919
    peruncung (also *keruncung*), **4:**833
    piké, **5:**610
    pū'ili, **9:**916–17
    rawat, **9:**640
    sede, **9:**492–93
    shantu, **1:**449
    Solomon Islands, **9:**667
    sonbrer, **5:**610
    South America, **2:**96
    Southeast Asia, **4:**581, 583
    sukute, **9:**669
    Tabar Islands, **9:**629
    tamboo-bamboo, **2:**866
    tamlang agung, **4:**902
    tangbut, **4:**832
    tangianau (with attached coconut shell), **9:**900
    Tanna, **9:**64
    togunggak (also *togunggu*), **4:**833
    t'pol, **4:**534
    tukumal, **9:**664
    Vanuatu, **9:**362, 691, 698, 699
    vat ge uro, **9:**702
    Yap, **9:**733
Tukano culture, **2:**150–51
Uighur people, **7:**459
utensils, domestic, **2:***50*; **8:**655; **9:**134
    Albania, **8:**997

Belgium, **8:**525
Cook Islands, **9:**900
Denmark, **8:**455, 458
England, **8:**331
Fiji, **9:**777, 779
in French music, **3:**855, 857
Germany, **8:**656
Hungary, **8:**743
Ireland, **8:**385
Korea, **7:**830
koutalia, **8:**1019
łyžki, **8:**797
Madhya Pradesh, **5:**722
Manihiki, **9:**905
Morocco, **6:***303*
Ontario, **3:**1189
palmetas, **2:**401
prato-e-faca, **2:**349
Slovenia, **8:**918–19
spoons, **2:**384, 475
Ukraine, **8:**816
Vlach Rom music, **8:**275
Vietnam, **4:**467–69
    upland regions, **4:**534–35
water-stamped, **9:**245, 373, *374*, 477, 553
    paddles, Russell Islands, **9:**664
    Papua New Guinea, **9:**556–57
West Africa, **1:**453
whale's rib, *pākuru*, **9:**933
wind chimes, Korea, **7:**830
wooden noisemakers, Argentina, **2:**261
Yoruba people, **1:**461
Idīr, **6:**270, 274–75, 277
Idlout, Lucie, **3:**1275, 1280
Idne-Lolo people, **9:**612
Idol, Billy, **3:**357
"I Don't Believe You Want to Get up and Dance" (Gap Band), **3:**684
I Don't Know Band, **9:**160
"I Don't Want Nobody to Give Me Nothing" (Brown), **3:**677
Idrasingha, Sanant, **5:**424
"I Dreamt That I Dwelt in Marble Halls" (Balfe), **3:**181
Ifalik (Yap State, FSM), **9:**979
"I-Feel-Like-I'm-Fixin'-to-Die-Rag" (Country Joe and the Fish), **3:**317
"I Feel Love" (Summer), **3:**688
Ife state, **1:**401
"If I Can't Have You" (Elliman), **3:**712
"If I Had a Hammer" (Seeger), **3:**316
Ifugao people, **4:**914
    epics of, **4:**907
    instrumental music of, **4:**917, 919
    vocal music of, **4:**920
Ifukube Akira, **7:**751
"If You Don't Know Me by Now" (Harold Melvin and the Blue Notes), **3:**711
Igbo nation, in Grenada, **2:**869
Igbo people
    dance accompaniment, **1:**113
    historical studies, **1:**91–92
    masks of, **1:**119
    melodic practices, **1:**210
    music of, **1:**458–59
    secret societies, **1:**309

Volume Key: 6, Middle East; **7**, East Asia; **8**, Europe; **9**, Australia and the Pacific Islands; **10**, The World's Music.

Igede people, **1:**111–12
Iglesias, Julio, **2:**103; **3:**713, 746, 751
Iglulik Inuit, **3:**374, 381
Ignacio Cervantes Professional Music Upgrading
    Center, **2:**838
Ignacio de Jesús, Father, **4:**842
Ignacio, Leon, **4:**864, 865, 866, 871
Ignatius, Saint, **8:**309
Igneri culture, **2:**668
Igor's Tale (epic), **8:**763
"I Got a Woman" (Charles), **3:**709
"I Got My Eye on You" (Dayton), **3:**685
"I Got Rhythm" (Gershwin), **3:**658
"I Got You" (Brown), **3:**710
Igualada, Francisco de, **2:**155
Ihaia (Tokelau composer), **9:**354
"I Hate to See That Evening Sun Go Down"
    (Smith), **3:**632
"I Have a Silent Sorrow Here" (Reinagle), **3:**180
"I Have Nothing" (Cui), **7:**359, 367
"I Heard It through the Grapevine," **3:**685
Ihopu, Paloma Gilmore, **9:**974
Iḥṣā' al-'ulūm (al-Fārābī), **6:**367
Ihsani, Mevlüt, **6:**804
Ihukube Akira, **7:**732
Iḥyā' 'ulūm al-dīn (Abū Ḥamid al-Ghazālī),
    6:373
Ijebu people, **1:**474
Ijo people, **1:**459
Ika culture, **2:**183
Ikeda Mitsumasa, **7:**608
Ikenouti Tomozirô, **7:**732
Ikhwān al-Ṣafā (Brethren of Purity), **6:**19, 181,
    367, 368, 373, 392, 442, 448, 542
Ikiru yorokobi (Zikken kôbô), **7:**736
"*Ikliğ*" (Moğollar), **6:**250
al-Iklīl (al-Hamdānī), **6:**360
"I Knew You Were Waiting for Me" (Franklin
    and Michael), **3:**713
Ikuta *kengyô*, **7:**758
Ilagán, Hermógenes, **4:**865, 866, 871
Ilaiyaraja, Isaignani, **5:**422, 544–45, 555
Ila people
    composers, **1:**222
    history of, **1:**711
    instruments of, **1:**712
    kuyabilo music, **1:**216
    music of, **1:**711–12
Ilava caste, **5:**930
Ilaya Orchestra, **4:**883
Ilé Aiyê (*bloco afro*), **2:**352–53
Ilerici, Kemal, **6:**82, 84, 775
"*Il-Gharusa ta' Mosta*," **8:**637
Iliad (Homer), **8:**129, 130
Ilieva, Anna, **8:**907
Ilieva, Vaska, **8:**981
Ilieva, Yordanka, **8:***893*
"I Like Ike" (Berlin), **3:**310
Ilinden 1903 (musical group), **3:**1198
Iliyasu Mai Buta, **1:**521–23
Ilkanid dynasty, **6:**113; **7:**23–24
Illapu (musical group), **2:**373
"I'll Be Around" (Spinners), **3:**711
Illés (musical group), **8:**746, 747
Illinois
    Champaign-Urbana, indie pop in, **3:**168–71

Chicago
    Albanian people in, **3:**926, 927–29
    Asian communities in, **3:**948–49
    balalaika orchestra in, **3:**57
    blues in, **3:**105
    as center for country music, **3:**76, 560
    Chinese people in, **3:**957
    Estonian people in, **3:**878, 879
    Filipino people in, **3:**1024
    gospel music in, **3:**631–32
    Greek people in, **3:**929, 930
    house music in, **3:**690
    Hungarian people in, **3:**908
    Irish people in, **3:**324, 842, 845
    Italian people in, **3:**860
    jazz in, **3:**550, 652–53
    Jewish people in, **3:**935
    Latin Caribbean community, **3:**790–800
    Lithuanian people in, **3:**876
    public school music education, **3:**275
    Puerto Rican and Mexican peoples in,
        3:719
    Russian people in, **3:**915
    South Asian people in, **3:**980, 981, 982,
        984
    taiko drumming groups in, **3:**971
    Thai people in, **3:**950, 1010
    Turkish people in, **3:**1030
    zarzuela companies, **3:**851
    Evanston, South Asian people in, **3:**983
    Iranian people in, **3:**1031
    Latino peoples in, **3:**719
    Native American groups in, **3:**466
    Norwegian people in, **3:**866–70
    Rockford, Lao people in, **3:**948
    rural churches in, **3:**119–20
    South Asian people in, **3:**981
    Swedish people in, **3:**870–72
Illinois Indian nation, **3:**451
"I'll Take You Home Again, Kathleen"
    (Westendorf), **3:**190
Illyrian Movement, **8:**917, 936
Illyrians, **8:**40
Ilmu Karawitan (Sindoesawarno), **4:**636–37
Ilokano people, **4:**907
Ilonggot people, **4:**914, 920
I Love Lucy (television show), **3:**732
"I Love Music" (O'Jays), **3:**711
Ils Fränzlis da Tschlin (musical group), **8:**689
Ilu people, **9:**583
Ilustración Filipina, La (periodical), **4:**858
Il'ya Muromets, **8:**129
Ilyas Malayev Ensemble, **6:**920
"Il y avait une belle fille," **3:**344
Im Chint'aek, **7:**969
Im Kijun, **7:**927
Im Kwŏnt'aek, **7:**960, 969
Im Pangul, **7:**893, 895, 899, 909, 910, 911, 969,
    985
Im Sobang, **7:**990
Im Sohyang, **7:**960
Im Thurn, Sir Everard, **2:**442
Im Tonch'ŏl, **7:**965
Im Tonggwŏn, **7:**887
Im Ungsu, **7:**965
'Imādaddīn, **6:**922

"I'm Afraid to Come Home in the Dark" (Van
    Alstyne), **3:***195*
Images du Canada français (Champagne), **3:**14
*Imaging Sound: An Ethnomusicological Study of
    Music, Art, and Culture in Mughal
    India* (Wade), **10:**12
Imai Tutomu, **7:**647
Imakumano Shrine (Kyôto), **7:**639
Imam, Hakim Mohammad Karam, **5:**51, 123
"I'm a Yankee Doodle Dandy" (Cohan), **3:**514
Imazighen people, **6:**483–92. *See also* Berber
    peoples
Imbaquingo, Elías, **2:**418
Imeretian people, **8:**827, 841
Imjin haengjaengga (Kim), **7:**960
"I'm Just Here to Get My Baby Out of Jail,"
    3:78
"I'm Just Thinking about Coolin' Out" (Butler),
    3:683
"I'm Just Wild about Harry" (Blake), **3:**619
Immémoriaux (Ségalen), **9:**38
immigrants and immigration (to North America)
    Albanian, **8:**986
    Arab, **3:**1029, 1033, 1245
    Armenian, **3:**1029–30
    Asian, **3:**129, 526–27, 948–49, 1083, 1215,
        1245
    Basque, **8:**309
    British, **3:**43–44, 1227
    British Caribbean, **3:**808–9, 1201
    Bulgarian, **3:**924
    to Canada, **3:**9, 10, 13, 51, 223–24, 342, 854,
        933, 1057, 1072, 1078, 1083, 1146,
        1171, 1185, 1188, 1192, 1195, 1201,
        1215, 1217, 1218, 1225, 1227, 1245,
        1255
    Caribbean, **2:**84, 91, 102, 796–97
    Central American, **2:**84, 91
    changing patterns of, **3:**515
    Chilean, **2:**90
    Chinese, **3:**9, 11, 526–27, 957–59, 1217
    Croatian, **3:**919
    Cypriot, **8:**1032
    Czech, **3:**896
    dances of, **3:**216–17
    East Asian, **7:**6
    Estonian, **3:**878
    ethnic musics, **3:**97–98
    Filipino, **3:**1024; **4:**126
    Finnish, **3:**872
    French, **3:**854
    Garífuna, **2:**733
    Georgian, **8:**845
    German, **3:**884, 897
    Guatemalan, **2:**735
    Haitian, **2:**888–89, 889; **3:**803–5
    to Hawai'i, **3:**527
    Hmong, **3:**1003
    Hungarian, **3:**908
    Iberian, **3:**847
    identity issues and, **3:**505–7, *507*, 510–11,
        512–14, 820–24
    immigration laws, **5:**572–73
    Indo-Guyanese community, **5:**602, 604–5
    Indonesian, **3:**1011
    Iranian, **3:**1031

Irish, **3:**324, 842, 843
Italian, **3:**860, 864; **8:**622
Japanese, **2:**86; **3:**9, 11, 526–27, 967–68
Jewish, **3:**175, 933, 935, 936, 1171; **6:**1036; **8:**263
Khmer, **4:**187–88, 210
Korean, **3:**975
Lao, **4:**354, 358, 361
Latin Americans, **3:**522, 718–19, 720, 729–30, 746, 1201
Latvian, **3:**877
Lithuanian, **3:**875
Macedonian, **3:**924–25
Maltese, **8:**634
Maya, **2:**733
Mexicans, **3:**16, 734, 735–36, 744, 756, 770–71
to Mexico, **3:**9
Mixtec people, **2:**567–68
Nicaraguan, **2:**763
nineteenth century, **3:**9, 10, 11, 12
North African communities, **6:**438
Norwegian, **3:**866
Pacific Islanders, **9:**116–19, 712
Polish, **3:**893, 895
Portuguese, **8:**576
Romanian, **3:**910
Russian, **3:**908, 915
Serbian, **3:**919
Slovak, **3:**899–900
South American, **2:**84, 91
South Asian, **3:**986, 1215; **5:**449, 578–86
Thai Dam, **4:**349
Tibetan, **3:**129, 133
Trinidadian, **2:**96
Turkish, **3:**1030
twentieth century, **3:**11, 12
Ukrainian, **3:**908
Vietnamese, **3:**993; **4:**88
Yaqui people, **2:**589, 592–93
Yuma people, **2:**595, 597, 598
Immigration Act (1924), **3:**512, 968
Immigration Act (1990), **3:**290
Immigration and Naturalization Act (1952), **3:**844, 968, 1029
Immigration and Naturalization Act (1965 amendment), **3:**845, 959
Immutable System, **8:**48
Imperato, Pascal James, **1:**121
Imperial Gagaku Troupe (Japan), **7:***627*
Imperial Order of the Daughters of the Empire, **3:**1117
Imperial Records, **3:**350, 352, 670, 708, 739, 741
Imperial Theater (Japan), **7:**733
Imperial Theatre (Saint John), **3:**1120
impressionism, **3:**174; **7:**732, 736; **8:**85
Impressions (musical group), **3:**677
improvisation, **2:**74; **5:**20. *See also layālī; taqsīm*
Abkhazian people, **8:**852
Afghanistan
chahārbeiti, **5:**819
falak, **5:**828
of lullabies, **5:**813
naghma-ye kashāl, **5:**806
in African-American music, **3:**523, 601

Ainu people, **7:**784, 786
Akha people, **4:**541
Albania, **8:**993
taksim, **8:**997
Aluku culture, of songs, **2:**438
Arabian peninsula
dance, **6:**705, 707
in pearl-diving songs, **6:**651
sung poetry, **6:**667
Arabic poetry, **3:**1035
Arab music, medieval, **6:**291, 355, 388, 402, 444, 1062
Arab music, modern, **6:**38–42, 388, 406, 549, 550
Argentina, secular vocal music, **2:**261
in art music, **8:**68, 79, 85
Atacameño culture, **2:**360–61
copla de carnaval, **2:**361
Atayal people, song lyrics, **7:**525
Australia
Arnhem Land, **9:**413
clansongs, **9:**422
Hmong songs, **9:**76–77
Yolngu clansongs, **9:**301
Azerbaijan, *muğam*, **6:**927, 929
Bahamas
anthem, **2:**804
quadrille, **2:**809
rhyming spiritual, **2:**805
Bali, **4:**734
in *arja*, **4:**750–51
Balkarian people, **8:**857
Balochistan, text, **5:**774
Barbados, **2:**819
Basque region, text, **8:**311–14, 315
basso continuo, **8:**76
bedouin peoples, **6:**409
Belarus, instrumental music, **8:**799
bhajan, **5:**255
in bluegrass, **3:**160, 168
in blues, **3:**638
Brazil
in Candomblé music, **2:**342
cantoria, **2:**324–27
côco songs, **2:**349
forró, **2:**332
maracatú rural, **2:**337
samba verses, **2:**315
textual, **2:**307
Bribri culture, *ajkö̀yönuk*, **2:**634
Bulgaria, **8:**891
wedding music, **8:**284
Burma, **4:**385
California Brush Dance songs, **3:**414
cantus super librum, **8:**50
Cherokee Stomp Dance songs, **3:**369, 370
Chile
canto a lo pueta, **2:**367
contrapuntos, **2:**366
China, **7:**92, 202
Dolan verses, **6:**992
in *huju*, **7:**298
Jiangnan sizhu music, **7:**225
narrative singing, **7:**258–59, 270–71
Colombia
bambuco, **2:**389

copla, **2:**389–91
cumbia, **2:**406
on marimba, **2:**402
murga, **2:**384
composition, performance, and, **8:**73, 91–92, 93–95, 97
copla texts, **3:**758, 759
Corsica, vocal, **8:**566, 568–69
Costa Rica, text, **2:**695
Creek Stomp Dance songs, **3:**469
Crete, *mantinadhes*, **8:**120
Croatia
klapa singing, **8:**149–50
pismice, **8:**931
Cyprus, texts, **8:**1030
Czech Republic, **8:**719
Dai people, of song lyrics, **7:**507
in dance, **1:**113, 117, 120; **3:**213, 214
Dan people, **1:**466
Denmark, text, **8:**459
Dominican Republic, **2:**849
East Asia, **7:**5
Ecuador, *currulao*, **2:**427
Egypt
Arab music, **6:**558, 559, 599, 603–5
in epic songs, **6:**343
layla, **6:**149
taqāsīm, **6:**46
text, **6:**624
El Salvador, text, **2:**711
Faroe Islands, **8:**469
hymn singing, **8:**471
Finland
in *runonlaulu*, **8:**115
text, **8:**478
Gã people, songs, **1:**105
Garifuna culture, **2:**752
chumba, **2:**676
in *dügü* ritual music, **2:**671
gunjéi, **2:**676
gat, **5:**191
Georgia, vocal, **8:**831, 833
Germany, **8:**654
ghazal, **5:**186
gong-chime ensemble music, **4:**21–22
Greece
Aegean islands, **8:**1014
Crete, **8:**1015
Epirus, **8:**1010
Gypsy influences, **6:**116
in *rebetika*, **8:**206
taxim, **8:**1022
text, **8:**1025
Greek *amanedes*, **3:**930
Guadeloupe, **2:**879
léwòz, **2:**875
quadrille, **2:**877
Guam, *chamorrita*, **9:**744
Hadendowa people, **1:**559
in highlife, **1:**379
Hindustani music, **5:**127–28, 162–63
ālāp-jor-jhālā, **5:**198–99, 202, 203, 206, 581
ālāp section, **5:**39–40, 48, 164–68, 172, 174–75, 177, 195, 196, 198–99
bol banāo, **5:**197

improvisation, Hindustani music (*continued*)
  bolbānt, **5:**169, 175, *176*
  in *dhrupad*, **5:**164–70
  genre associations, **5:**202
  instrumental genres, **5:**198–202
  sargam, **5:**176, *178*, 179
  sitar, **5:**335
  tān, **5:**175–76, *177*, 197, 198, 199,
    200–201, 202, 642
  tihāī, **5:**198, 200, 201, 202
  toḍā, **5:**198, 200, 201–2
Hungary, **8:**740
  text, **8:**275
  verbunkos, **8:**273
Iceland
  on hymn tunes, **8:**404
  lausavísur, **8:**402
  poetry, **3:**1251
  rímur, **8:**118
  text, **8:**405
instrumental, **8:**9
Iran
  radif, **6:**129, 134, 139, 141, 854
  solo dances, **6:**875, 878–79
Iraq, *maqām*, **6:**311, 312–13, 315
Ireland
  Traveller singing, **8:**295
  vocal, **8:**387
Irian Jaya
  Abun people, **9:**361
  Asmat people, **9:**590
  Bismam Asmat people, **9:**580
  songs, **9:**583
Israel, **6:**1033
Italy
  lyric songs, **8:**606–7, 608, 611
  text, **8:**17
Jamaica, **2:**902–3, 905–6
  mento, **2:**906
  quadrille, **2:**907
Japan, **7:**600
  in *kabuki*, **7:**661
  satuma biwa narration, **7:**648
Java, **4:**638
in jazz, **3:**283, 550, 568, 648, 650, 651, 652
Jewish liturgical music, **8:**254
Kalinga people, **4:**916
Karachaevian people, **8:**857
Karen people, **4:**545
Karnataka, of *lāvṇi*, **5:**869–70
Karnatak music, **5:**98–103, 147–48, 214–15,
  384, 451
  ālāpana section, **5:**89, 90, 94, 98–103, 104,
    106, 218, 389, 912
  tānam, **5:**215, 218
  viruttam (also *padyam*), **5:**215, 218
Kashmir, text, **5:**685
Kazakh people, **7:**460
Kazakhstan, of poetry, **6:**952, 953–54, 955
Kerala, **5:**943
khyāl, **5:**173–76
Korea
  farmers' bands, **7:**933
  rhythmic, **7:**841, 842, 843
  in *salp'uri*, **7:**68
  sanjo, **7:**976

  sinawi, **7:**890, 891, 914
  theatrical, **7:**942
kriti, **5:**411
Kuna culture
  songs, **2:**645–47, 648
  text, **2:**639
Laos, text, **4:**347
Lombok, **4:**769
  text, **4:**775
lowland *vs.* upland peoples, **4:**538
Luvale music, **1:**732
Macedonia
  mane, **8:**281, 282
  taksim, **8:**976, 979
Madhya Pradesh, tribal music, **5:**721, 722
Malaysia
  asli, **4:**435
  dondang sayung, **4:**435
  text, **4:**426, 433, 440, 577
Malta, **8:**636–37
  text, **8:**635
Maluku, text, **4:**821
Mapuche culture, of songs, **2:**236
Maronite church music, **6:**214–15
Martinique, *bigin bélè*, **2:**915
Maya culture
  of ancestral songs, **2:**731
  text, **2:**652
melismatic, **1:**118
melodic, Central Africa, **1:**217
Mexico
  copla, **2:**608
  Michoacán region, **2:**561
  son jarocho, **2:**610
Middle Ages, **8:**146
Middle East, **6:**5–7, 9
Miskitu culture, text, **2:**661
Mixtec culture, text, **2:**567
in modal jazz, **3:**661
Mongol people, in narratives, **7:**1008
Montenegro, **8:**958–59
  epic songs, **8:**961
Morocco
  malhun, **6:**499
  nūba, **6:**450
in Native American music, **3:**370
Naxi people, of song lyrics, **7:**511
Nepal, text, **5:**701
Netherlands Antilles, *tambú*, **2:**928, 929
North Africa, **1:**541, 542
Norway, **8:**430
  religious singing, **8:**414
  stev, **8:**413
Palestine
  taqāsīm, **6:**576, 578, 582–83
  vocal, **6:**574, 579, 584–85, 591
Panama, vocal, **2:**780
Papua New Guinea
  Angan vocal music, **9:**497
  Baluan hymns, **9:**607
  Enga songs, **9:**535–36
  guitar songs, **9:**152
  Huli people, **9:**538
  Irumu flute music, **9:**570
  Managalasi songs, **9:**503
  songs, **9:**22

Paraguay, dance, **2:**461
  in pastoral songs, **8:**194
Peru
  dance, **2:**497
  marinera, **2:**499
  of text, **2:**495
Philippines
  duaya, **4:**849
  duruyanon, **4:**849
  oyayi, **4:**849
  yekyek, **4:**849
Poland
  Rom sung poetry, **8:**276
  text, **8:**703
in polka music, **3:**893
Portugal, text, **8:**581
of praise songs, **1:**489, 502–3
Puerto Rico
  bomba, **2:**937
  seis, **2:**939
Pukapuka, *pātautau*, **9:**912
qawwali, **5:**256
rāgam-tānam-pallavi, **5:**94, 100, 159, 215,
  217–18, 388–89
of religious music, **3:**122, 125
Réunion Island, **5:**608
rhythmic, **1:**113
Romania
  lament texts, **8:**871–72
  Rom dance, **8:**277–78
Rom music, **8:**271
Russia, laments, **8:**763
Ryûkyû Islands, **7:**794, 795
Saami people, joiks, **8:**300–301
Sāmoa, *tagi*, **9:**799–800
Saudi Arabia
  of poetry, **6:**654
  taqāsīm, **6:**692
Scotland
  psalmodic, **8:**97–98
  Travellers, **8:**296
Serbia
  epic singing, **8:**941–42
  Kosovo, text, **8:**286
  sokačke pesme, **8:**952
Shona people, **1:**747
  songs, **1:**749, 750, 753
Slovakia, **8:**719
  text, **8:**276
Slovenia, **8:**917, 919
song, **1:**131, 332, 346
South Asian music, **3:**132
Southeast Asia, **4:**14–15, 127
southern Africa, **1:**701
Spain
  flamenco, **8:**12
  joropo, **2:**540
Sulawesi, text, **4:**806
Sumatra, **4:**613
  cang-incang, **4:**623
Sumbawa, text, **4:**763, 782
Sunda, **4:**723
  in *jaipongan*, **4:**708
  in *kacapi-suling*, **4:**715
  in *kendang penca*, **4:**709

Volume Key: **1**, Africa; **2**, South America, Mexico, etc.; **3**, United States and Canada; **4**, Southeast Asia; **5**, South Asia

Syria
    mawwāl, **6:**566–67
    taqsīm, **6:**563, 567
Tahiti, **9:**877
Taiwan, of song lyrics, **7:**424
Thailand, **4:**276, 324
    on *ranat thum*, **4:**267
    treatises on, **5:**33, 36, 44
Trinidad and Tobago, verbal duels (*picong*),
    2:96
Tuareg people, **1:**540
    anzad music, **1:**579
Tunisia, in *ma'lūf*, **6:**328, 329, 331, 519
Turkey
    Gypsy influences, **6:**116
    makam, **6:**47, 56, 114, 120–22
    song competitions, **6:**765–66, 801–9
    in *taksim* sections, **6:**257, 758
Turkish music, **6:**782
twentieth-century decline of, **8:**52
Uruguay
    payada, **2:**512
    text, **2:**521
Vanuatu, of children, **9:**259
Venezuela
    joropo music, **2:**541
    tonos, **2:**534
Vietnam, **4:**17, 454, 463, 465, 481
    text, **4:**492
Waiāpí culture, **2:**162
Wales, vocal, **8:**342, 350, 352–53
Wayana culture, flute music, **2:**165
    in Western music, **4:**127
West Timor, Atoni music, **4:**797
    in work songs, **3:**599–600
Yemen
    al-ghinā' al-ṣan'ānī, **6:**687–89
    in drum ensemble music, **6:**100–106
Yoruba popular music, **1:**472
"I'm Still in Love With You" (Green), **3:**711
al-Imtā' bi-aḥkām al-samā' (Kamāl al-Dīn al-
    Adfuwī), **6:**372
Imula, Ferhat Imazighen, **6:**275
Imwŏn Kyŏngjeji (Sŏ), **7:**925
al-In'ām fī ma'rifat al-anghām (al-.Saydāwī al-
    Dimashqī), **6:**366
Inbal Dance Theater (Israel), **6:**1030
In C (Riley), **3:**175
Inca (Inka) culture, **2:**225, 231, 363
    archaeomusicological studies of, **2:**7
    ceremonies of, **2:**45, 258
    in Chile, **2:**356
    empire of, **2:**205, 232, 283, 357, 427, 466,
        468
    harvest songs, **2:**425
    high-pitched aesthetic of, **2:**34
    historical accounts of, **2:**23, 283, 468
    instruments of, **2:**20, 35, 207, 223
    military bands of, **2:**37–38
Inchcolm Antiphoner, **8:**366
In China (album), **8:**226
incidental music
    Japan, *hayasi*, **7:**655, 657, 659, 660, 665, 671,
        680, 683–85, 771
    Korea, **7:**958–59
    Sanskrit drama, **5:**25–26

Inconnu (musical group), **3:**1277–78, 1280
Incredible String Band (musical group), **8:**369
In Dahomey (musical), **3:**194, 608, 619
Indah Record, **4:**681
Independence Day (film), **3:**715
"Independent Woman" (Shanté), **3:**714
Index of Tonal Consistency, **9:**295
India. *See also* Andhra Pradesh; Arunachal
        Pradesh; Assam; Bihar; Goa; Gujarat;
        Haryana; Himachal Pradesh;
        Hindustani tradition; Jammu and
        Kashmir; Karnataka; Karnatak
        tradition; Kerala; Madhya Pradesh;
        Maharashtra; Manipur; Meghalaya;
        Mizoram; Nagaland; Orissa; Punjab;
        Rajasthan; Sikkim; Tamil Nadu;
        Tripura; Uttar Pradesh; West Bengal
    art music traditions of, **8:**59
    bamboo agriculture in, **4:**52
    Bhojpuri-speaking regions of, **3:**813
    cheironomy in, **8:**100
    classical music traditions of, **5:**372–73
    cultural interactions with China, **7:**88, 111,
        112, 191, 311
    cultural relationships to Southeast Asia,
        4:10–11
    early conceptions of music, **5:**19–21
    early history of, **5:**17
    epics of, **4:**66
    ethnic tensions in, **5:**374
    ethnomusicological research in, **10:**5–12
    film industry in, **5:**531–46
    geography of, **5:**7, 15–16
    historical studies of, **5:**56
    independence of, **5:**9, 375–76, 744, 911
    influenced by Vietnamese culture, **4:**447
    influence on Balinese culture, **4:**756
    influence on Burmese culture, **4:**363, 378
    influence on Chăm culture, **4:**590–91
    influence on early Southeast Asian civilization,
        4:38–39, 43
    influence on Javanese culture, **4:**632
    influence on Khmer culture, **4:**153, 156–57,
        189
    influence on Malaysian culture, **4:**402, 409,
        426–27, 428, 437, 438, 439
    influence on Southeast Asian culture, **4:**61–68,
        104
    influence on Southeast Asian spirit beliefs,
        4:52–53
    influence on Sumatran culture, **4:**599–600,
        625
    influence on Sundanese culture, **4:**719
    influence on Thai culture, **4:**222–23
    influence on Vietnamese culture, **4:**446
    instruments in, **5:**319–68; **8:**176
    languages of, **5:**5
    light classical music in, **5:**107–8, 162, 179–86,
        194, 373–74, 381, 409, 411, 532, 543
    map of, **5:**3
    metallurgy in, **4:**37
    Muslim culture in, **5:**42
    nonclassical traditions of, **5:**468–77, 534
    northwestern, as origin of Rom people, **8:**271
    notational systems in, **8:**90, 104
    partition of, **5:**403

popular music in, **5:**542–59
population of, **5:**5
princely states in, **5:**4, 312–13, 720
relationships with Western music, **5:**560–68
religion in, **5:**8–10, 403
rice origin myths, **4:**51
Samaveda treatise, **8:**90
self-mortification rituals in, **5:**293
Sino-Tibetan peoples of, **4:**528
Tai people in, **4:**218
theatrical genres, **5:**484–86
Tibetan culture in, **5:**709–16
Tiruvaiyaru, Tyagaraja festival, **3:**989–90
tribal populations, studies of, **5:**56
Western popularity of musical genres, **5:**568
India (salsa singer), **3:**522
India Archive Music (record company), **5:**528
India League of America, **3:**987
India Office Library, Vedic chant manuscripts,
    5:240
India Today (periodical), **5:**528
India West (periodical), **3:**992
Indian Antiquary, **5:**883
Indian Awareness movement, **3:**481
"Indian Cars" (Secola), **3:**458
Indian Civil Rights Act (1986), **3:**444
Indian Gaming Regulatory Act (1988), **3:**444
Indian House (record company), **3:**449, 484,
    1087
Indian Music Journal, **5:**58
Indian National Congress, **5:**849
Indian and Pakistan Leagues of America, **5:**584
Indian (South Asian) people. *See also* Bengali
        people; Gujarati people; Indo-
        Caribbean peoples; Pakistani people;
        Sikhs
    in Arabian peninsula, **6:**703
    in Barbados, **2:**813–14
    in Belize, **2:**666
    in Borneo, **4:**825
    in Burma, **4:**363
    in Caribbean, **2:**4, 71, 792
    in Central America, **2:**4, 71
    in Fiji, **9:**92–94, 773, 782, 998
    in Great Britain, **5:**572–76; **8:**231, 236, 240,
        336
    in Grenada, **2:**864
    in Guadeloupe, **2:**873
    in Guyana, **2:**83, 85–86, 442, 443–44, 448
    in Hawai'i, **9:**100
    in Jamaica, **2:**896, 897, 899, 904, 908
    in Malaysia, **4:**401
    in Martinique, **2:**919
    in Netherlands Antilles, **2:**928
    in North America, **3:**949, 950, 951, 980–87
        art music of, **3:**53
        Canada, **3:**1057, 1078, 1082, 1084,
            1215–16, 1245, 1255
        fusion genres of, **3:**73, 218, 986
        music and dance activities, **3:**223, 951,
            983–86, 988–92, 1215, 1246–47,
            1259
        research on, **3:**980
    in Nusa Tenggara Timur, **4:**787
    religions of, **2:**48
    in Singapore, **4:**521

Indian (South Asian) people (*continued*)
in South America, **2:**4, 71
in Southeast Asia, **4:**62, 68
in Surinam, **2:**85–86, 503
in Trinidad and Tobago, **2:**52–53, 83, 85–86, 952, 953, 958–59
in Vietnam, **4:**531
in Virgin Islands, **2:**969
Indian People's Theatre Association, **5:**856–57, 858
Indian Records, **3:**449
Indian Reorganization Act (1934), **3:**443
Indians for Indians Hour (radio show), **3:**444
Indian Shaker Church, **3:**395–96, 488
Indian Society of Record Collectors, **5:**530
Indians of the American Southwest (Dutton), **3:**428
Indian Students Association, **5:**584
Indian Telugu United Methodists, **5:**582
Indian Territory. *See* Oklahoma
Indian Theater of São Lourenço, **2:**302
"Indian Villages in London" Exhibition, **5:**561–62
Indian Wars, **3:**442
Indiana
Hungarian people in, **3:**908
Indianapolis
Estonian people in, **3:**879
Slovenian people in, **3:**901
Macedonian people in, **3:**925
Old Regular Baptists in, **3:**124
Richmond, high school orchestra in, **3:**277
Romanian people in, **3:**910
Indiana University (Bloomington), **3:**15, 221, 612; **10:**28, 56, 62–64
Indígena (León), **3:**612
Indira Kala Sangeet Viswavidyalaya (Khairagarh), **5:**447
Indispensable Harp (Schechter), **2:**464
Indo, Berta, **2:***240*
Indo-Caribbean peoples. *See also* Indian (South Asian) people
in Canada, **3:**1205
in United States, **3:**808–9, 812, 813–17, 983
Indonesia. *See also* Bali; Borneo; Cirebon; Flores; Irian Jaya; Java; Lombok; Maluku; Roti; Savu; Sulawesi; Sumatra; Sumba; Sumbawa; Sunda; West Timor; *specific peoples*
art music traditions of, **8:**59
Austronesian speakers, **4:**529; **9:**319
Chinese influences in, **4:**72–73
"classical" music traditions in, **4:**7
competitions in, **4:**142
composition in, **4:**129–30
cultural identity, **4:**765
cultural origins of, **4:**10–11
geography of, **4:**2, 594
influence on Madagascar, **1:**700, 715, 781, 782–83, 786
Islam in, **4:**73–74, 75–78
Jakarta, **4:**5
migration within, **4:**779
musical genres
dangdut, **4:**23, 68, 104–6, 110, 684, 717, 761, 778; **10:**48–49
gambang kromong, **4:**73
keroncong, **4:**439
kreasi baru, **4:**666
kroncong, **4:**102–4, 633, 717, 761, 774; **9:**150
musik pop, **4:**778
orkes melayu, **4:**439
pop Indonesia, **4:**778
music research on, **4:**24, 27, 28–29
Muslim cities in, **4:**5
notational systems in, **8:**103
pedagogy in, **4:**122–23
political divisions of, **4:**732
politics in, **4:**92–94
popular music in, **4:**8, 101–11
prehistoric, **4:**37–38, 43
prehistoric art, **4:**44
regionalism in, **4:**5
representative music of, **4:**23, 135
revival movement in, **4:**126
role in East Africa, **1:**295, 598, 605, 607
salient musical features of, **4:**20–22
snake cult in, **4:**52
touring ensembles, **4:**135
tourism in, **4:**136, 138–39
tuning systems in, **4:**14
village life in, **4:**6
wayang performance, **8:**56
Western influences in, **4:**83–85
Indonesian music in North America, **3:**327, 527, 1011–22, 1084, 1216
early performances, **3:**1012–13
Indonesian people, **2:**4, 71. *See also* Balinese people; Javanese people
in French Guiana, **2:**434
in Netherlands, **8:**231, 237–38
religions of, **2:**48
in Surinam, **2:**52–53, 503, 507–8, 792
in Vietnam, **4:**531
Indra (deity), **5:**278, *502*
Industrial Workers of the World, **3:**873, 1257
Indus Valley civilization, **5:**14, 374, 486
instruments of, **5:**319–20
d'Indy, Vincent, **2:**397; **3:**173; **7:**346; **8:**550
"I Need Someone" (Thee Midniters), **3:**747
"I Never Loved a Man" (Franklin), **3:**677
Infante, Pedro, **2:**621; **3:**740
information theory, **8:**24
Ingalla, José María, **4:**866
Ingalls, Gustavus, **3:**565
Ingano culture, **2:**379
Ingassana people, **1:**563–64, 601
Ingemann, Bernhard Severin, **8:**460
Ingen, **7:**613
Ingram, James, **3:**713
Ingrian people, **8:**475
Ingush people, **8:**850, 861–64
dance traditions of, **8:**864
epic performance, **8:**851
instruments, **8:**863
research on music of, **8:**864
vocal music of, **8:**862–64
Ingyô, emperor of Japan, **7:**723
Injegol, Mrs., **6:***857*
Injo, Chosŏn king, **7:**982
Ink Spots (musical group), **3:**670, 674, 708
Inka culture. *See* Inca culture
In Living Color (television show), **3:**715
Inlonshka Indian nation, **3:**446
In My Soul (Four the Moment), **3:**1134
Inner Asia. *See also* Central Asia; Mongolia; Siberia; *specific peoples*
development of culture in, **7:**11–13
geography and climate, **7:**9, 11
map of, **7:***10*
nomadic peoples of, **7:**11–14, 23, 28–30, 1003–20
"Inner City Blues" (Gaye), **3:**677
Innes, Frederick Neil, **3:**277
In Newport (Johnson and Cole), **3:**608
Innu Indian nation, **3:**383, 385, 392, 1073, 1074
In Old Kentucky (Dazey), **3:**618
Inoue Tokiko, **10:***14*
Inoue Yôsui, **7:**747
Inreco (record company), **5:**528
In Search of the Turtle's Navel (album), **3:**346
Insect World (Lam), **7:**232
Inspector General (Gogol), **5:**487
Inspirationists, **3:**904
Institut de l'Egypte (Cairo), **6:**609
Institut Français d'Afrique Noire (IFAN), **1:**51
Institut Kesenian Jakarta, **4:**683
Institut du Monde Arabe (Paris), **6:**23
Institut de Phonétique (Paris), **9:**992
Institut de Recherche et Coordination Acoustique/Musique (IRCAM), **8:**91
Institut Seni Indonesia (Yogyakarta), **4:**678
Institut für Völkerkunde (Vienna), **2:**950
Institut für den Wissenschaftlichen Film (Göttingen), **9:**982
Institute of Accordion Music (Finland), **8:**489
Institute of African Studies, **1:**32, 39; **10:**143, 145, 147
Institute for Arab Music. *See* Ma'had al-Mūsīqá al-'Arabiyyah
Institute of Art (Warsaw), **8:**712
Institute of Art, Folkloristics, and Ethnology (Kyïv), **8:**823
Institute of Art History (Romania), **8:**886
Institute of Art Studies, Ethnography, and Folklore (Belarus), **8:**803
Institute for Comparative Musical Documentation (Berlin), **5:**529
Institute of Correspondence Education (Madras), **5:**453
Institute of Ethnography and Folklore (Bucharest), **8:**883, 885
Institute of Ethnography and Folklore "C. Brăiloiu" (Bucharest), **8:**885
Institute for Ethnomusicology (UCLA), **10:**3, 5
Institute of Folklore and Ethnography (Prague and Brno), **8:**724
Institute of (Indigenous) People's Music (China), **7:**397
Institute of Jamaica, **1:**32
Institute of Jazz Studies (Rutgers University, Newark), **3:**33
Institute of Language Literature (Latvia), **8:**507
Institute for Music (Bulgarian Academy of Sciences), **8:**901–2

Institute for Musical Ethnography (Slovenia), **8:**922

Institute for Musical Folklore (Neuss), **8:**647

Institute of Musicology (Bratislava), **8:**724

Institute of Papua New Guinea Studies, **9:**480, 989–90

Institute for Polynesian Studies, **9:**971–72

Institute of Popular Music (Finland), **8:**489

Institute of Puerto Rican Culture, **2:**940–41

Institute of Russian Literature in Academy of Sciences, **8:**768

Institute of Sindhology, **5:**747

Institute Salvadoreano de Turismo, **2:**715

Institute Shirat Israel (Jerusalem), **6:**205

Institute for the Study of Folklore (Sarajevo), **8:**970

Instituto Español de Musicología (Barcelona), **8:**601

Instituto Indigenista de Guatemala, **2:**736

Instituto Interamericano de Etnomusicología y Folklore (INIDEF) (Venezuela), **2:**543, 783

Instituto de Investigaciones del Folklore Musical (Chile), **2:**374

Instituto Nacional de Antropología e Historia (Mexico), **2:**593

Instituto Nacional de Folklore (INAF) (Venezuela), **2:**543

Instituto Nacional Indigenista (Mexico), **2:**568, 574

Instituto Nacional de Musicología "Carlos Vega" (Argentina), **2:**251, 270, 488

instrumental ensembles. *See* ensembles, musical; instrumentation

instrumentation

  aak ensembles, **7:**862

  acculturation and, **2:**72–73

  Afro-Beat ensembles, **1:**483–84

  aguinaldo ensemble, **2:**538

  Andean ensembles, **2:**216

    north-south distinctions, **2:**222

  Antillean jazz bands, **2:**930–31

  àpàlà, **1:**476

  arakk ensemble, **4:**194

  bailā ensemble, **5:**970

  baile de la marimba, **2:**761–62

  Balinese *gamelan*, **4:**741–43

  banda de guerra, **2:**475

  banda orquesta, **3:**778–79

  bandas de chicheros, **2:**762

  banda típica, **2:**475; **3:**772, 773

  bandella, **8:**695

  bands, **3:**563–64

  barongan ensemble, **4:**413

  beepat khmer ensemble, **4:**214

  beguine ensembles, **2:**915–16, *917*

  Belarusan *muzyki*, **8:**798

  bhangra bands, **5:**574

  big bands, **3:**654

  blackface minstrel groups, **3:**184, 543, 616

  bluegrass bands, **3:**160, 164, 1258

  Brazil, central and southern genres, **2:**306

  brukdown ensemble, **2:**677–78

  Brunka culture, various ensembles, **2:**685

  bua loi ensemble, **4:**246

  Bukharan *maqām* ensembles, **6:**919

Bulgarian folk orchestras, **8:**902

Bulgarian wedding bands, **8:**284

café-aman orchestra, **3:**931

cài biên ensemble, **4:**513

cài lương ensemble, **4:**494–95

Cajun dance groups, **3:**857–58

caklempong ensemble, **4:**414, 422

čalgija ensemble, **8:**281–82, 286, 977, 980

Cambodian *pinn peat* ensemble, **3:**1001

Cantonese opera ensembles, **3:**960

Cantonese opera orchestra, **3:**1260

canto popular uruguayo, **2:**520

céilí bands, **9:**78

celempong ensemble, **4:**615

ceṇṭa mēḷam ensemble, **5:**362, 932–33

cha-cha-chá, **3:**796

charanga, **2:**832

charanga francesca, **3:**788, 795–96

charanga típica, **2:**835

chèo ensemble, **4:**490

China, shawm and percussion groups, **7:**201, 259

Chinese orchestras, **7:**229–31

chirimía bands, **2:**407

chorach'i, **7:**873

cimarrona ensemble, **2:**701

cimbalová muzika, **8:**719

cinna mēḷam ensemble, **5:**104, 360, 913

Cirebonese *gamelan*, **4:**690, 691–92

comparsas, **2:**836

conjunto, **3:**522, 772

conjunto (Cuban), **2:**835

conjunto azteca, **2:**558

conjunto de cuerdas, **2:**475

conjunto de cumbia, **2:**406

conjunto ensemble, **9:**103

conjunto llanero, **2:**385

contra dance bands, **3:**231

Costa Rica, pop orchestras, **2:**690, 693

cuarteto groups, **2:**273, 274, 834

Cuban-style orchestras, **2:**930

cuchuida ensemble, **7:**196

cueca ensembles, **2:**369

cumbancheros ensemble, **4:**884

currulao ensembles, **2:**404, 427

dance bands, **2:**212

Danish dance ensembles, **8:**457

dhrupad ensemble, **5:**164

dúo, **2:**834

duolu ensemble, **7:**480–81

English dance music, **8:**330

estudiantina ensemble, **2:**383, 475, 835

fátele ensemble, **9:**379

film studio orchestras, **5:**535, 543

firqa ensemble, **6:**8, 148, 317, 454, 559

frevo de bloco ensembles, **2:**337

frevo de rua ensembles, **2:**336

fújì, **1:**484–85

gambang kromong ensemble, **4:**73

gamelan, **3:**1012; **4:**631

gamelan angklung, **4:**748–49

gamelan arja, **4:**751

gamelan baleganjur, **4:**753

gamelan bebonangan, **4:**753

gamelan cara balèn, **4:**644

gamelan gambang, **4:**755

gamelan gambuh, **4:**749–50

gamelan gendang beleq, **4:**771

gamelan gong gedé, **4:**744–45

gamelan jegog, **4:**754

gamelan kodhok ngorèk, **4:**644

gamelan luang, **4:**755

gamelan munggang, **4:**644

gamelan pelégongan, **4:**747

gamelan saléndro, **4:**703

gamelan sekati, **4:**644

gamelan selundeng, **4:**755

gamelan Semar pegulingan, **4:**746

gammeldans ensemble, **8:**441

gandang-gandang ensemble, **4:**923

gandingan ensemble, **4:**923

gegenggongan ensemble, **4:**754

gendèr wayang, **4:**751–53

ghazal ensemble, **4:**438–39

golpe ensemble, **2:**541

gondang ensembles, **4:**607

gong-chime ensembles, **4:**9–10, 20

gong suling ensemble, **4:**754

gordang ensembles, **4:**607

gran combo (also *gran orquesta*), **2:**836

Greek bands, **3:**929–30, 930; **9:**73

guaguancó, **2:**836

Guangdong yinyue ensembles, **7:**218

hadharī ensemble, **6:**269

Harmoniemusik ensemble, **3:**563

herranza ensemble, **2:**475

hēvisi ensemble, **5:**967

highlife, **1:**477

Hindustani music ensembles, **5:**82

hsaiñwaiñ ensemble, **4:**367–71

Hungarian Rom string bands, **8:**274

Hungarian string ensembles, **8:**744

inila-ud ensemble, **4:**917

Iraqi *maqām* ensembles, **6:**8, 312–13, 552

Irelish *céilí* bands, **8:**390

Irish showbands, **3:**845

jaipongan ensemble, **4:**107

janissary bands (*mehter*), **6:**114–15, 767–68

jātrā ensemble, **5:**505

jawq ensemble, **6:**454, 460, 470

Jiangnan sizhu ensemble, **7:**224–25

jíbaro ensemble, **2:**935

joget ensemble, **4:**436

jùjú, **1:**478–79, 481

kacapian ensemble, **4:**716

kacapi-suling, **4:**715

kagok ensemble, **7:**921

kantrüm ensemble, **4:**213

kar ensemble, **4:**196

kathak ensemble, **5:**494

kathakaḷi ensemble, **5:**362–63, 513

kelittang ensemble, **4:**627

kethoprak ensemble, **4:**655

ketuk telu ensemble, **4:**696

khap thum ensemble, **4:**350

khrüang pra kom, **4:**312

khyāl ensemble, **5:**171–72

kinilisong ensemble, **4:**923–24

klang chhnakk ensemble, **4:**197

klang khek ensemble, **4:**197

klawng chum, **4:**312

klawng khaek ensemble, **4:**246, 247

instrumentation (*continued*)
  klawng u je, 4:312
  Korea, for ancestral ceremonial music, 7:869–70
  korng skor ensemble, 4:197
  kromongan ensemble, 4:626
  kroncong ensemble, 4:102–3
  kuchipuḍi ensemble, 5:517
  kuda kepang ensemble, 4:413
  kulintang ensemble, 4:892, 896
  kulintangan ensemble, 4:898
  kunqu ensembles, 7:292
  kūṭiyāṭṭam ensemble, 5:363
  kwadril ensemble, 2:945
  lam ban xok ensemble, 4:345
  lam genres, 4:351
  lam mahaxay ensemble, 4:346
  lam phu thai, 4:347
  lam salavane ensemble, 4:344–45
  lam tang vay ensemble, 4:345
  ländlerkappelle, 8:689
  Lao popular music genres, 4:360
  lirihan ensemble, 4:642
  Lombok *gamelan,* 4:762, 771–73, 776
  Macedonian brass bands, 8:976–77
  Macedonian *naroden orkestar,* 8:981
  mahori ensemble, 4:214, 243–45, 247
  main puteri ensemble, 4:421
  mak yong ensemble, 4:407
  Malaysia
    theatrical orchestras, 4:403
    urban folk music, 4:432–33
  malḥūn ensembles, 6:498–99
  maloya ensemble, 5:610
  manora ensemble, 4:411–12
  mariachi, 2:621, 622; 3:722, 737
  marimba ensembles, 2:742
  mek mulung ensemble, 4:408
  mento bands, 2:753, 906
  merengue ensemble, 3:731
  mereng-vodou ensembles, 2:892
  Mexican performing groups, 3:745–46
  mini-djaz groups, 2:892; 3:803
  mohori ensemble, 4:113
  mohori Samai ensemble, 4:175, 184–85
  murga ensemble, 2:384, 517–18
  nanguan, 7:205
  naubat khānā ensemble, 5:279
  nhạc huyền ensemble, 4:448–49
  nhạc mới ensemble, 4:513
  nhạc tài tử ensemble, 4:483–84
  nobat ensemble, 4:429, 601, 615
  nô ensemble, 7:634–35
  Norwegian *gammeldans* groups, 3:868
  Nubian ensembles, 6:644
  oḍissi ensemble, 5:520
  orchestration and, 8:54
  orkes gambus ensemble, 4:605
  orkes sinandung timur ensemble, 4:604–5
  orquesta típica (Cuban), 2:835
  pāncai bājā ensemble, 5:280, 286, 699–700
  pañcavādyam ensemble, 5:360–62
  pangongka'an ensemble, 4:900
  parang groups, 2:953, 959–60
  pejogedan bumbung ensemble, 4:754
  Peking opera orchestra, 7:285–86

  penja duriyang, 4:312
  periya mēḷam ensemble, 5:103, 359, 383, 387, 912
  pey keo ensemble, 4:197
  pi chum, 4:312
  pinn peat ensemble, 4:165, 168, 173–74, 183
  pinpat ensemble, 4:358
  piphat ensemble, 4:241–43, 247
  pirekua ensembles, 2:579
  plena ensembles, 2:939–40
  polka bands, 3:529, 895
    Bohemian-style, 3:890–91
    Chicago-style, 3:894
    Czech-style, 3:897, 898
    Eastern-style, 3:893
    Polish types, 3:893
    Slovenian-style, 3:824, 901–2
    swing style, 3:891
  in popular music genres, 2:101
  punta-rock, 2:676–77
  quadrille ensembles, 2:871–72, 877, 907; 3:232
  radif ensemble, 6:8, 137–38, 863
  rai, 6:270–71
  rajaleña ensemble, 2:384
  rake 'n' scrape, 2:805–6
  rebetika ensemble, 9:73
  rhythm and blues combos, 3:708
  Rom brass bands, 8:951
  Romanian *taraf* ensemble, 8:277
  rondalla ensemble, 3:1025; 4:854; 8:593
  ronggeng ensemble, 4:616
  Saint Gonçalo dance ensemble, 2:329
  sákárà, 1:475
  salsa, 3:788; 9:101
  sankyoku, 7:692, 712, 715, 779
  Schrammel, 8:676
  scratch bands, 2:970
  sega ensemble, 5:609
  septeto de son, 2:834–35
  sheng-guan groups, 7:201
  shifangu ensemble, 7:196
  Shifan luogu ensemble, 7:196
  sinawi, 7:890
  soca bands, 2:96
  son conjunto, 3:792, 795
  son ensembles, 2:101, 579
  son jarocho, 2:609
  soran ensemble, 4:642
  string bands, 3:836; 9:95
  Swiss brass ensembles, 8:689
  Swiss string bands, 8:690
  symphony orchestra, 8:*81*
  taarab orchestras, 1:427, 645
  takht ensemble, 6:8, 170, 406, 411, 413, 418, 547, 559
  talempong ensembles, 4:609
  tamburitza orchestra, 3:920
  tango ensembles, 2:263, 264, 519
  tanjidor (brass band) ensemble, 4:626
  tari inai ensemble, 4:416
  tembang Sunda, 4:714, 715
  thanggunggu ensemble, 4:923
  thum mong ensemble, 4:214
  Tianjin shidiao, 7:254
  Tohono O'odham *waila,* 3:436, 489–90

  Trinidad film music groups, 5:591
  trio elétrico, 2:337–38
  tropical music ensembles, 2:266
  tuồng ensemble, 4:492
  ty bā lệnh ensemble, 4:448
  Uighur *muqam,* 6:995–1008
  Ukrainian instrumental groups, 8:810–11
  urkestr, 6:552
  Uttar Pradesh brass bands, 5:671
  vallenato ensemble, 2:410
  Volga German wedding band, 3:890
  wàkà, 1:474
  wayang gedek ensemble, 4:404
  wayang melayu ensemble, 4:428
  wayang Siam ensemble, 4:404
  Western orchestra, 9:371–72
  wind bands, 8:529–30
  wong dontri lanna wong yai, 4:312
  xianshiyue ensemble, 7:212
  Yemeni drum ensembles, 6:7, *94*
  yikay ensemble, 4:548
  zaju ensemble, 7:276
  Zhedong luogu, 7:195
  zydeco ensembles, 3:858
Instrumentos musicales precortesianos (Martí), 2:623
instruments. *See also* aerophones; chordophones; drums; electrophones; ensembles, musical; idiophones; mirlitons
  Abkhazian people, 8:852–53
  Adighian people, 8:855
  Afghanistan, 5:336–37, 344, 345, 804, 820–22, 830–31, 835
    gender associations of, 5:812, 822
  African, 3:593, 596–97, *597*
    cataloguing and documentation, 1:54
    composers' uses of, 1:223
    intra-African connections, 1:437
    secret, 1:455
    as speech surrogates, 1:89, 105–7, 204–6, 451, 466, 472, 650–51
    symbolism of, 1:783–84
    timbral aspects of, 1:137
    timeline performance, 1:310
  Ainu people, 7:787
  Akan people, 1:464–65
  Akha people, 4:541–42
  Albania, 8:992–93, 994–95, 996
  Andalusia, 6:444–45, 449
  Andhra Pradesh, 5:893–96
  Angola, 1:669, 677
  Anuta, 9:860
  Aotearoa, 9:932–33
  Arab, 6:401–22
    ancient, 6:357, 407–8, 537
  Arabian peninsula, 6:651
  Argentina, 2:251–54
  Armenia, 6:729, 731
  Aruba, 2:928–29
  Atacameño culture, 2:357
  Austria, 8:672–74
  Aymara culture, 2:206–14, 357–58
  Azande people, 1:570
  Azerbaijan, 6:924–25
  Aztec culture, 2:556–57, 601–3
  Bahamas, 2:803–4

Bali, **4:**741–43
 early, **4:**731
Balkarian people, **8:**857
Balochistan, **5:**783
Barbados, **2:**814–16
Basque region, **8:**314, 316, 594, 600
Belarus, **8:**796–99, 809–10
Bellona, **9:**851
Bengali, **5:**328–29, 343, 344
 in blues, **3:**638, 641
Bolivia, **2:**284–88
Bongo people, **1:**570
Bosnia-Hercegovina, **8:**959–60, 966–67
Brazil, **2:**308–11
Bribri and Cabécar cultures, **2:**632–33
Brittany, **8:**559–60
Bulgaria, **8:**21, 891–97
Burma
 early, **4:**365
 sàndeyà (unidentified), **4:**365
Cambodian, **3:**998–99
Canada, manufacturing of, **3:**246, 1116, 1148,
  1180–81, 1183
Caribbean, archaeological finds, **2:**8
Carriacou, **2:**870, 871
Celtic culture, **8:**321
Central Africa, Bantu groups, **1:**659–63
Central America
 ancient, **2:**6–12
 symbolic interpretations of, **2:**32–40
Central Asia, **6:**3, 900
Chechen people, **8:**863
Chile, **2:**357–60
China
 archaeological finds, **7:**105–11
 Buddhist ritual, **7:**311, 312, 329, 330
 Daoist ritual, **7:**313, 320, 323–24
 early, **7:**87–88, 99–101
 foreign imports, **7:**41–42, 79–80
 minority cultures, **7:**450–51, 457, 459
 modernization of, **7:**90, 228–32, 389, 418,
  419
 northeastern minority groups, **7:**520–21
 south and southwestern minority cultures,
  7:490–92
Chuuk, **9:**736–37
classification of, **3:**472–73; **4:**161–62;
  5:20–21, 51, 319–29, 351–52, 966,
  968; **6:**5; **9:**372–73
 Africa, **1:**9–10, 49, 466–67, 783
 Andean regions, **2:**222
 'Are'are people, **9:**398, 667
 Central America, **2:**28–32
 China, **7:**107
 Europe, **8:**40–41, 177–79
 Java, **4:**639–40
 Khmer people, **4:**161–62
 Korea, **7:**823
 Laos, **4:**355
 medieval Middle Eastern, **6:**17, 395–99,
  401–2
 Oceania, **9:**371
 South America, **2:**28–32
 Thailand, **4:**228
 Tukano culture, **2:**150
 Tzutujil-Maya culture, **2:**653, 723

Colombia, **2:**376–82, 401–3
 archaeological finds, **2:**9–10
composite flute-rattles, Maya culture, **2:**667
Computer Musical Instruments (CMIs), **9:**144
Congo, **1:**664–66
Cook Islands, **9:**898–901, 906–7, 909, 913
Corsica, **8:**571–72, 573
Costa Rica, **2:**694–95
Croatia, **8:**926–27, 928, 930, 931–32, 959–60
Cuba, **2:**825
 locally made, **2:**828
 used in Santería, **2:**824–25
Cyprus, **8:**1030–31
Czechoslovakia, **8:**21
Czech Republic, **8:**719
Dai people, **7:**496, 499
Dan people, **1:**466
dating methods for, **2:**6–7
Denmark, **8:**454–56
dissemination of, **1:**299–323, 607; **2:**32; **6:**3
East Asia, **7:**5
 modernization of, **7:**82–83
 status of, **7:**81–82
Ecuador, **2:**413–18, 431
 pre-Columbian, **2:**413–14
Edo people, **1:**461
Egypt, **6:**547–48
 ancient, **6:**537
El Salvador, **2:**706–9
England, **8:**330–31
Estonia, **8:**493–94, 496–98
Ethiopia, **1:**600
Europe
 manufacturing of, **8:**81–82, 227, 228
 palaeo-organological studies, **8:**34–42
 Renaissance, **8:**74
 research on, **8:**21–22, 172
 traditional European, **8:**168–72, 175–82
 uses of, **8:**8–9
European, **2:**36–40
 in Africa, **1:**351, 416
 in Madagascar, **1:**789
 in North Africa, **1:**535, 545, 547
 in South Africa, **1:**356, 429, 761, 767
 in southern Africa, **1:**719
 in Sudan, **1:**570–71
Ewe people, **1:**462
Fiji, **9:**776
Finland, **8:**478–79, 481
Flores, **4:**792–93
Fon people, **1:**462
France, **8:**543–45, 547
French Guiana, **2:**435–36
Futuna, **9:**816
Gã people, **1:**463
gender associations, **8:**197, 201
Georgia, **8:**837–41, 845, 846
Germany, **8:**651–52, 653–55, 656
Goa, **5:**737
Greece, **8:**21, 1009–10, 1011, 1013, 1015
Greece, ancient, **8:**46–47
Guam, **9:**745–46
Guaraní culture, **2:**200–202
Guatemala, **2:**723–29
Gujarat, **5:**625, 629, 633
Gun people, **1:**462

Guyana, **2:**443–44, 445
Hawai'i, **9:**916–17, 922
Hindustani tradition, **5:**331–43
Hmong people, **3:**1004–5; **4:**551–53
Hui people, **7:**462
as human extensions, **1:**9–10
Hungary, **8:**21, 743–44
hyperinstruments, **3:**254
Iceland, **8:**405–6
as identity symbols, **3:**826
Igbo people, **1:**459
Ila people, **1:**712
India
 North, **5:**331–47
 South, **5:**350–68
 use in devotional music, **5:**248–49, 251
 use in film and popular music, **5:**347–48,
  368
Indus Valley civilization, **5:**319–20
Ingush people, **8:**863
Iran, **5:**321, 344, 345; **6:**834–35
Ireland, **8:**383–85
Irian Jaya, **9:**582–83
 Asmat people, **9:**591
Islamic views on, **4:**74
Israel, **8:**258–59
Italy, **8:**614–17
Jamaica, **2:**896–901
Japan
 archaeological finds, **7:**557–62
 in Buddhist rituals, **7:**617
 in *kabuki*, **7:**660
 manufacturing of, **7:**537
 modernization of, **7:**779
 in Shinto rituals, **7:**620
Java, **4:**639–43
 decoration of, **4:**643
 early, **4:**632
in Jewish liturgy, **8:**250, 257, 258–59
Karachaevian people, **8:**857
Karen people, **4:**545–46
Karnatak tradition, **5:**350–58
Karnataka, **5:**350–58
Kasena-Nankani people, **1:**455
Kashmir, **5:**189, 329, 335, 336, 339, 343–44,
  345, 683–84, 688, 692–93
Kazakh people, **7:**460–61
Kenya, **1:**624–25, 627
Kerala, **5:**931–32, 948
Khmer people
 materials used for, **4:**162
 solo music for, **4:**204–5
 tuning of, **4:**175
Khoikhoi people, **1:**703
Kiribati, **9:**717, 762–63
Kmhmu people, **4:**547
Kogi culture, **2:**184–85
Kongo kingdom, **1:**667
Korea, **7:**821–31, 854
Kosrae, **9:**742
Kpelle people, **1:**466–67
Kru people, **1:**375–80
Kuna culture, **2:**638, 640–43, 649, 772
Kurdistan, **6:**745–46
Kwa groups, **1:**469
Lahu people, **4:**540

instruments (continued)
Laos, 4:338–40, 354–55
  making of, 4:339
Latvia, 8:503–4
Lenca culture, 2:739
Lhoba people, 7:482
Lisu people, 4:543
Lithuania, 8:511–12
LoDagaa people, 1:456–57
Lombok, 4:766–69, 778
Low Countries, 8:523–33, 535
Macedonia, 8:975–77, 979–80
Madagascar, 1:783–89
Madhya Pradesh, 5:722, 723
Maharashtra, 5:727
Malaysia, Orang Asli peoples, 4:562–63, 567
Mali, Wassoulou music, 1:420
Malta, 8:639–40
Maluku, 4:813
Manchu people, 7:520–21
Mangareva, 9:886
Manihiki, 9:906–7
Mapuche culture, 2:233–34, 358–59
Maronite church music, 6:215–16
Marquesas Islands, 9:895–96
Marshall Islands, 9:716, 742, 753–54
Mashriq, 6:545–47
Maya culture, 2:651, 657–58, 667
Melanesia, 9:598
Mende people, 1:467
Mexica culture, 2:558–60
Mexico, 2:8–9, 600, 608–9, 611, 623
Micronesia, 9:716–17
Middle East, 6:3, 7–8
Miskitu culture, 2:660–61
Mixtec culture, 2:563, 565
Moinba people, 7:482
Mongol people, 7:1005, 1010–14, 1017
Montenegro, 8:959–60
Moxo culture, 2:137–38
Native American peoples, 3:238, 472–79
Naxi people, 7:511, 512, 513
Nepal, 5:290–91, 705
  Damāi people, 5:699–700
  Gāine people, 5:705
  Guruṅg people, 5:703–4
  Newār people, 5:702
  as signals, 5:701
Netherlands Antilles, 2:928–29
New Caledonia, 9:679–82, 964
New Mexican Hispanos, 3:761–62
Nguni peoples, 1:706–7
Nissan Atoll, 9:639–40
Niue, 9:817
Nkhumbi people, 1:714
noisemakers
  Low Countries, 8:525
  Macedonia, 8:975
  Romania, 8:876
  Slovenia, 8:918–19
  Switzerland, 8:683–84
North Africa, 1:542
North Caucasia, 8:851
Northeast Indian groups, 3:463
Northwest Coast Indian groups, 3:401
North West Frontier Province, 5:786–90

Norway, 8:414–20, 422–23
Nubian people, 1:556
Oceania, 9:371–402
  research on, 9:372–73
organological studies of, 5:306–7; 6:17–18, 373
Ossetian people, 8:859–60
Otopame culture, 2:570–71
Pakistan, 5:336, 344, 345
  northern, 5:795–96
Panama, 2:773–77
Papua New Guinea, 9:475–76
  Abelam people, 9:549–50, 552
  ai class of, 9:22
  Anêm people, 9:615
  Baluan, 9:604–6
  Banoni people, 9:647
  Chimbu people, 9:522
  Enga people, 9:536
  Highlands region, 9:511–12, 531–33
  Huli people, 9:540–43
  Iatmul people, 9:556–57
  Irumu people, 9:570–71
  Island region, 9:600–601
  Kaulong people, 9:619–20
  Lolo people, 9:613–14
  Mamose region, 9:546–48
  Managalasi people, 9:503
  Nagovisi people, 9:648–49
  New Britain, 9:623–25
  Papuan region, 9:489–90
  Rai Coast, 9:562–63
  Sepik Hills region, 9:558
  Sursurunga people, 9:627
  Tabar Islands, 9:628–29
  Trans-Fly region, 9:507–9
  Waxei people, 9:559–60
Paraguay, 2:454–57
Paya culture, 2:739
Peru, 2:469–76, 492–93
  pre-Hispanic, 2:468
Philippines
  bamboo, 4:914, 918–20, 924–26, 927
  early, 4:839, 913
Plains Indian groups, 3:445
Poland, 8:704–8, 809–10
Portugal, 8:21, 582–83
Puerto Rico, 2:933–35
  locally crafted, 2:933, 935
Pukapuka, 9:913
Punjab (India), 5:651
Punjab (Pakistan), 5:762–63
Pygmies, 1:658
Q'ero culture, 2:225–27
Quechua culture, 2:206–14
Rapa Nui, 9:952
in religious ceremonies, 3:118, 119, 121, 125
Romania, 8:870, 875, 876–79, 880, 885
Russia, 8:755, 770–71, 775
  Volga-Ural peoples, 8:774
Ryûkyû Islands, 7:792
Sāmoa, 9:805–7
Sardinia, 8:627, 630
Scotland, 8:363–64, 365–66, 367, 372
Sena people, 1:711
Senufo people, 1:454

Serbia, 8:943–47
Shan people, 4:548
Shona people, 1:751–52
Sikaiana, 9:848
Slovakia, 8:719
Slovenia, 8:21, 914–19, 920, 922
Solomon Islands
  'Are'are people, 9:667
  Baegu and Fataleka peoples, 9:669
  Banoni people, 9:647
  Blablanga people, 9:659
  Buin people, 9:651, 652–54
  Halia people, 9:641
  Isabel Island, 9:661
  Nagovisi people, 9:648–49
  Russell Islands, 9:664
  Shortland Islands, 9:656–57
  Sirovanga people, 9:655
Somalia, 1:611, 619
South Africa, played in shebeens, 1:429, 767
South America
  ancient, 2:6–12
  archaeological finds, 2:9–12; 10:97, 99–100
  inventory lists of, 2:31–32
  symbolic interpretations of, 2:32–40
South Asia
  associations with Hindu deities, 5:325
  folk, 5:343–47, 365–68
  geographical distribution of, 5:319–20
  scholarship on, 5:55
  treatises on, 5:33–34, 37, 43, 44, 321–29
Southeast Asia
  Indian sources for, 4:66–67
  indigenous, 4:11, 56
  Islamic, 4:74–75
  island, 4:596
  made in villages, 4:6, 7
  modification of, 4:55, 70
southeastern Africa, 1:708
Southeast Indian groups, 3:468
southern Africa, 1:701, 702
Southwest Indian groups, 3:429, 434, 435–36
Soviet Union, 8:21
Spain, 8:593–95
Sri Lanka, 5:350–68, 956, 958, 964–65
Subarctic region, 3:384–85, 391
Sudan, 1:600
Sumatra
  collections of, 4:603
  early, 4:600
Sumba, 4:788
Sumbawa, 4:780–81
Sumu culture, 2:739, 750–51
Surinam, 2:505–6
Sweden, 8:438, 439–42
Switzerland, 8:21, 682, 685–89, 693–96
Tahiti, 9:868–69
Taino culture, 2:22–23
Tamil Nadu, 5:907–8, 912–16, 924
Tanzania, 1:636–42
Tarahumara culture, 2:582–84
technological innovations, 3:236–37, 239–41, 246–47
terminology for, 2:28; 5:350
Thai, 3:999

Thailand, **4**:285
    early, **4**:284
    northeastern, **4**:316–20
    northern, **4**:310–12
    southern, **4**:304–5
Tibetan, **5**:710; **7**:474, 475, 477–78, 479–80
    Buddhist, **5**:714
Tokelau, **9**:827–28
Tonga, **9**:793–95
Tsonga people, **1**:710–11
Tukano culture, **2**:152–53
Tunisia, in Sufi performance, **6**:519
Turkey
    art, **6**:774–75
    folk, **6**:763–65
Tuva, **6**:985–86
Uganda, **1**:599–600
Uighur people, **6**:995
Ukraine, **8**:809–16
Uruguay, **2**:510, 511
'Uvea, **9**:814
Vanuatu, **9**:693–94, 701–2, 708–9
Venda people, **1**:708–9
Venezuela, **2**:524–25, 526–33, 544
Vietnam
    Chinese influences on, **4**:70
    early, **4**:446
    made of bamboo, **4**:532
    of minority peoples, **4**:533–36
    reforms to, **4**:508–9
Vietnamese, **3**:994
Vlah people, **8**:950
Waiãpí culture, **2**:159–61
Warao culture, **2**:189–93
Wayana culture, **2**:165
West Africa, **1**:445–46, 448–50, 452–57
Western, **4**:102, 103, 104; **9**:371–72
    in Aotearoa, **9**:937
    in Australia, **9**:413, 441
    in Aymara culture, **2**:358
    in Bahamas, **2**:804, 806, 807
    in Bali, **4**:743
    in Bolivia, **2**:284, 288
    in Brazil, **2**:303, 305, 309
    in Burma, **4**:372
    in Cambodia, **4**:175
    in Chuuk, **9**:737
    in Cirebon, **4**:696, 697
    in Colombia, **2**:396, 400, 402–3, 407
    in Cook Islands, **9**:901
    in Costa Rica, **2**:693–94, 701
    in Cuba, **2**:835, 836
    in Fiji, **9**:777
    in French Guiana, **2**:437–38
    in Garífuna culture, **2**:733
    in Guyana, **2**:446–47
    in Honduras, **2**:742
    in Irian Jaya, **9**:578
    in Jamaica, **2**:899, 901, 907
    in Java, **4**:646
    in Kiribati, **9**:763
    made by Guaraní, **2**:302, 454
    made by Mexican native peoples, **2**:553,
        559–60, 603
    made by Moxo people, **2**:137–38
    made in Costa Rica, **2**:694

made in El Salvador, **2**:708
    in Malaysia, **4**:426, 427, 432
    in Maluku, **4**:814, 816
    in Mangareva, **9**:889
    in Manihiki, **9**:905, 907, 909
    in Mapuche culture, **2**:237
    in Marquesas Islands, **9**:896
    in Marshall Islands, **9**:748–50, 753
    in Mexico, **2**:550
    in Micronesia, **9**:160–61, 719, 720
    in Mixtec culture, **2**:565
    in Nauru, **9**:261, 755–56
    in Netherlands Antilles, **2**:931
    in New Caledonia, **9**:213
    in Nicaragua, **2**:762
    on Nissan Atoll, **9**:640
    in Niue, **9**:817
    in Papua New Guinea, **9**:146, 195
    in Paraguay, **2**:453–54
    in Peru, **2**:469, 474–75, 493
    in Philippines, **4**:847, 854–60, 868, 884
    in Polynesia, **9**:127, 771
    in Pukapuka, **9**:911
    in Sāmoa, **9**:207, 807–8
    in Solomon Islands, **9**:26–27
    in Sumatra, **4**:601, 606, 613, 616, 623,
        626–27
    in Sunda, **4**:712, 717
    in Surinam, **2**:508
    in Tahiti, **9**:868
    in Thailand, **4**:82
    in Tonga, **9**:793
    in Tuvalu, **9**:831
    in Uruguay, **2**:511
    in Vanuatu, **9**:26–27
    in Vietnam, **4**:466, 473–75, 484, 494, 508,
        511, 513, 515
    in Virgin Islands, **2**:970
    in Yap, **9**:305
West Futuna, **9**:862
Yao people, **4**:549
Yap, **9**:730
Yaqui culture, **2**:589
Yekuana culture, **2**:176–79
Yemen, **6**:93–95
Yoruba people, **1**:460–61, 472
Yuma culture, **2**:598
Zaïre, **1**:664–66, 671
Instruments de musique traditionnelle (Desroches),
    2:920
Intá 'Umrī ('Abd al-Wahhāb), **6**:599, 603–5
Interlake Polka Kings, **3**:1242
intermedi, **8**:77, 160
International Alliance for Women in Music, **3**:91
International Archives of Traditional Music
    (Switzerland), **8**:18
International Association for Research in
    Vietnamese Music, **3**:953
International Bluegrass Music Association, **3**:163
International Brothers, **1**:482
International Conference of Composers, **3**:1185
International Council for Traditional Music,
    9:59, 227
International Dictionary of Black Composers, **3**:604
International Exhibition (Christchurch), **9**:947
International Fair (Hawai'i), **9**:67

International Folk Music Council (later
    International Council for Traditional
    Music), **1**:31, 32, 62, 65; **7**:524, 594;
    8:19–20, 22, 25, 155–56, 178
    study groups, **8**:21, 23, 178
International Institute for Comparative Music
    Studies and Documentation, **1**:33
International Library of African Music, **1**:54
International Music Council, **1**:33
International Musicological Society, **8**:22, 25
International Network for the Dances of
    Universal Peace, **3**:1043
International New Age Music Network, **3**:345
International Polka Association, **3**:896
International Society for Contemporary Music,
    7:732; **8**:427
International Society for Krishna Consciousness,
    3:983; **5**:581
International Society for Music Education,
    1:32–33
International Society for the Study of Time,
    10:64
International String Congress, **3**:1185
International Symphony Orchestra of Sarnia and
    Port Huron, **3**:1184
Internationale (anthem), **3**:939; **7**:347, 350, 383,
    414; **8**:659
Internet, **3**:245, 1279
    in China, **7**:360
    ethnomusicological uses of, **10**:64–65, 106–7
    in Japan, **7**:772, 774
    music transfers over, **3**:240–41, 289, 359
    websites on British Caribbean music, **3**:812
    websites on dance, **3**:222, 226
intervals. *See* scales and intervals; tuning and
    temperament
In the Bottoms (Dett), **3**:607
"In the Evening by the Moonlight" (Bland),
    3:543
In the Heat of the Night (film), **3**:203
In the South Seas (Stevenson), **9**:40
In Their Shoes (multimedia production), **3**:973
Intihar Ensemble, **3**:821, *821*, 824
Inti-Illimani (musical group), **2**:32, 40, 75, 293,
    373–74; **3**:730
"Intonation in Present-Day North Indian
    Classical Music" (Jairazbhoy/Stone),
    5:53
Intonation of the Pentateuch in the Heder of Tunis
    (Herzog), **6**:1062
intonation theory, **8**:23, 756, 783, 800, 804
Into the Heart of Borneo (O'Hanlon), **4**:29
Into the Woods (Sondheim), **3**:545
Introduction to Folk Music in the United States, An
    (Nettl), **3**:828
Introvoys, **4**:887
Intruders (musical group), **3**:711, 748
Inuit Artist World Showcase, **3**:1275, 1278
Inuit Broadcasting Corporation, **3**:1278
Inuit Land Use and Occupancy Project, **3**:1275
Inuit peoples, **3**:6, 374–81, 384, 1097, 1118,
    1274. *See also* Eskimo peoples
    dances of, **3**:213, 222–23, 1062, 1275
    drumming style, **3**:385
    in Maritime Provinces, **3**:1069
    music of, **3**:1275

Inuit peoples (continued)
  popular music of, 3:1279–81
  population of, 3:1056
  in Québec, 3:1074
Inuktitut Christmas and Gospel Songs, 3:1279–80
Inupiak peoples, 3:374–81
  drumming style, 3:385
  Whale Feast, 3:376
Invalids, 9:164
Inventor (calypsonian; Henry Forbes), 2:963
"In Walked Bud" (Monk), 3:659
Ioakimi, Apolo, 9:825
Ioane (Sāmoan comedian), 9:235
Ioannides, Christos, 9:75
Ioannides, Tassos, 9:75
Ioelu (Sāmoan comedian), 9:235
Iona, Andy, 9:390
Iowa
  Czech people in, 3:898
  Des Moines, Thai Dam people in, 3:948,
    1007–9
  Native American groups in, 3:440, 451
  Norwegian people in, 3:866–70
  Swedish people in, 3:870–72
  women's bands in, 3:566
Iowa Indian nation, 3:440
Iparragirre, José María, 8:311
Ipili people, 9:514
Ippolitov-Ivanov, Mikhail, 8:861
Ipsori (album), 7:972
īqā', 1:220; 6:89–92, 166, 352, 538, 549
  al-Fārābī's theories, 6:365, 369, 388, 389–90
  treatises on, 6:365
  in Tunisian art music, 6:329, 506
Īqā' al-Istimā' (Yemeni composition), 6:102, 103
Īqād al-shumū' li-ladhadhat al-masmū' bi-
  naghamāt al-ṭubū' (al-Bū'iṣāmī), 6:367
Iqbal, 5:687
Iqbal, Muhammad, 5:437, 746
Ira Doan's Book, 3:137
Irama, Rhoma, 3:338; 4:104–5
Iramudun Samayama (deity), 5:961
Iran, 6:823–37. See also Azerbaijan; Balochistan
  Afghan refugees in, 5:810
  Azerbaijan region, 6:921
    aşıq music in, 6:809, 843–52
    population of, 6:843
    relations with Anatolia, 6:113
  Baloch people in, 5:744, 773, 776; 6:881–90
  blind musicians in, 6:140
  classical music of, 5:820
  dance traditions in, 6:875–79
  epic song traditions, 6:340, 343–44
  geography of, 6:823
  influence on Arab music, 6:362
  influence on South Asian culture, 5:14
  instruments in, 5:321, 344, 345
  Isfahan, 6:351
  Khorasan, 6:839–41
  Kurdistan region, 6:743–52
  Lorestan, dance traditions in, 6:877
  map of, 6:824, 844
  Mashhad, 5:817
  Meshed, 6:24
  performers in, 6:827–29
  Persian art music (radif), 6:11, 129–42,

184–85, 824, 832–36, 853–63,
  865–74, 1062
change in, 6:137, 142, 859–63
compendiums of, 6:18
functions of, 6:141–42
gushehā in, 6:65–70, 71, 132–33, 134–37,
  140–41, 833, 836, 866–67, 868
history of, 6:129, 131, 865–66
instruments in, 6:8, 137–38
Jewish performances of, 6:1016
Kurdish performances of, 6:751
mode in, 6:59–75
modulation in, 6:135
musical style of, 6:134–37, 867–74
origins of, 6:859
performers of, 6:139–40
poetry for, 6:135–36
research on, 6:23, 24, 130–31, 142
schools of, 6:71–72
settings for, 6:140–41
transmission of, 6:138–39
Urmawī school, 6:365
popular music of, 5:810
postrevolutionary musical life, 6:19, 131, 142
Rayy (now Tehran), 6:351
regional cultures of, 6:823–24
research on music of, 6:824
traditions in music, 6:853–63
Turkmen people in, 6:967
venues for performance, 6:824–28
Iranian people
  in Arabian peninsula, 6:415, 703, 710
  in Georgia, 8:840, 842
  in Iraq, 6:415
  in North America, 3:1028, 1031, 1034–35,
    1215, 1216; 6:131–32, 875, 877–78
  in Sweden, 8:434
Irani, Ardeshir, 5:532
Iranun people, 4:890
Iraq
  aerophones in, 6:414–15
  African peoples in, 6:304
  archaeological studies in, 6:17, 407
  Baghdad
    'Abassid court in, 6:131, 293, 294, 296,
      297, 351, 456, 538, 936
    as center for Middle Eastern music,
      6:365–67, 442, 853
    tomb of 'Abdul Qadir Jilani, 5:281
    'ūd playing in, 6:402–3
  Balochi people in, 6:415
  Basra, 6:296, 351
  chordophones in, 6:406–12, 593–95
  drums in, 6:416–20
  idiophones in, 6:403–5
  Kufa, 'Abbasid court in, 6:293, 296
  Kurdistan region of, 6:743–52
  lyres in, 6:358
  maqām in, 6:8, 11, 12, 311–16, 403, 411,
    551–52, 1016
  popular music in, 6:229
  Rom people in, 6:304
  Samarra, 'Abbasid court in, 6:293, 294, 296
  Turkmen people in, 6:967
  wedding rituals in, 6:303
Iraqi-Americans/Canadians, 3:1199; 6:283–84

Ira-Record, 4:681
al-Irbilī, Ibn al-Khaṭīb, 6:366
Ireland, 8:378–94. See also Northern Ireland
  art music in, 8:378
  Celtic people in, 8:319–22
  concepts of music in, 8:387–88
  Connemara, sean-nós style of singing, 8:327,
    380, 382, 387, 389
  court music, 8:146
  dance traditions of, 8:198, 325, 382, 387,
    390–91
  Dublin, social life in, 8:389
  folk groups, 8:152–53
  folk music in, 8:13
  Gaeltacht regions, singing style, 8:380–81
  geography of, 8:378
  history of, 8:378
  ideology in, 8:186
  instruments, 8:169, 170, 383–85
    research on, 8:35, 36, 39, 41
  map of, 8:324
  musical exchanges with Great Britain, 8:336
  musical exchanges with Wales, 8:354, 355
  musical genres
    céilí, 8:141, 388, 390
    fusion, 8:226, 392
    instrumental, 8:382–85
    "symphonies," 8:393
  musical life in, 8:387–92
  nationalist movement, 8:59
  performance contexts, 8:388–89
  pubs, 8:143, 391
  population of, 8:378
  research on music of, 8:17, 393–94
  rock in, 8:214–16
  Tory Island, choral singing, 8:381
  transmission and deducation in, 8:385–86
  Travellers in, 8:294–95, 389
  vocal music, 8:378–82, 388, 389–90
    ballads, 8:294, 379–80, 390
    laments (caoineadh; keening), 8:23, 128,
      132, 143, 196, 295, 378–79, 387–89
    plow whistle, 8:379, 385, 388
    slow airs, 8:9, 141, 382
Irewowona people, 9:983
Irian Jaya, 4:2; 9:472, 486–87, 578–94, 715
  Asmat people, 9:189–91
  composition in, 9:360–61
  Dani people of, 9:50
  fanfare melodies of, 9:257
  films on, 9:982, 1014
  geography of, 9:578, 591
  history of, 9:578
  instruments, 9:374, 582–83, 591
    flutes, 9:546
    kundus, 9:384
    tube zithers, 9:385–86
  kundu tuning systems, 9:489
  map of, 9:579
  music and dance of, 9:486–87, 981
    fatiya, 9:360, 581, 583
    karame, 9:360
    kona, 9:360
    sukne, skuba, and sukrot songs, 9:360–61
  outsiders' influence in, 9:5
  politics in, 9:560

population of, **9:**578
sound recordings from, **9:**986, 991
tourism in, **9:**191, 591
Vogelkop region, **9:**587–89
yodeling in, **9:**297
Irigwe people, **1:**119
Irino Yosirô, **7:**735–36
Irirangi (Māori elder), **9:**950
Irish Descendants (musical group), **3:**1071
Irish Folklore Commission, **8:**393
Irish Folk Music Studies (periodical), **8:**394
Irish Melodies (Moore), **3:**182, 187, 520, 839
Irish people
    in Antigua and Barbuda, **2:**798
    in Australia, **9:**77–79, 140–41, 409, 413
    in Montserrat, **2:**922
    in North America, **3:**192–93, 544, 842–46,
        1057
        dances of, **3:**223, 284, 842–43
        folk music of, **3:**43, 76–77, 153–58, 182,
            322, 324, 520, 835, 839; used for
            contra dances, **3:**230
        fusion genres of, **3:**326
        identity issues of, **3:**822
        Maritimes, **3:**1070–71, 1123, 1125, 1128
        musical traditions of, **3:**10
        Ontario, **3:**1078, 1081, 1082, 1188, 1189,
            1190, 1191
        popular music of, **3:**844–46
        Québec, **3:**1146, 1148
        traditional music revival, **3:**846
        vocal music of, **3:**843–44
    in Virgin Islands, **2:**969
Irish Traditional Music Archive, **8:**393
"Irish Washerwoman," **3:**870
Irish World Music Centre, **8:**394
'Irisipau ('Are'are panpipe performer), **9:**400
Irmer, Wilhelm, **8:**663
Iron Age, **8:**38, 41
Iron Maiden, **8:**215
Iroquois Indian groups, **3:**11, 452, 462–64, 465,
        1056, 1073, 1074, 1078
    instruments of, **3:**477
    repatriation of sacred objects, **3:**492, 494
    Social Dance songs, **3:**6, 371, 463–64, 1062,
        1078
Irshād al-qāṣid (Ibn al-Akfānī), **6:**367–68
Irshick, Chad, **3:**1280
Irsoy, Zekâîzâde Ahmed, **6:**116, 118, 119, 786
Iruḷa people, **5:**903, 905–6, 909, 915–16
    ceremonies of, **5:**284
Irumu people
    falsetto singing of, **9:**297
    music and dance of, **9:**567–71
Iruska Indian nation, **3:**446
Iruva caste, **5:**887
Irvine, Andy, **8:**226, 392, *392*
Irwin, May, **3:**189
Irwin, Theodore, **3:**349
Isaacs, Barney, **9:**390
Isaacs, Bud, **3:**80
Isaacs, Jorge, **2:**385
Isaacson, Michael, **3:**940
Isabel de Bragança, Princess, **2:**349
Iśai Veḷḷāḷar caste, **5:**387, 910
Isak, Tanbûrî, **6:**121, 124

"Is All Not One?" (Scott), **3:**346
Isamitt, Carlos, **2:**115, 238
Isanvarman I, king of Chenla, **4:**153
Isawa Syûzi, **7:**728, 760
'Īsāwiyya brotherhood. *See* Sufism
al-Iṣbahānī, Abū al-Faraj, **6:**12, 20, 291, 293,
        351–56, 365, 370, 392, 396, *402,*
        565, 696
al-Iṣbahānī, Abū Manṣūr, **6:**372
Isba label, **3:**1160
iscathamiya, **1:**764, *772–73,* 777; **3:**338
Iseler, Elmer, **3:**1184
Iseler Singers, **3:**1079
Ise monogatari (Japanese novel), **7:**696
"I'se the B'y" (Morsden), **3:**1141
al-Iṣfahānī, Abū al-Faraj. *See* Iṣbahānī, Abū al-
        Faraj al-
Isham, John, **3:**618
Isḥāq al-Mawṣilī, **6:**8, 17, 131, 295–96, 297,
        352, 353, 355, 365, 369, 387, 442,
        456, 541
Ishii Maki, **7:**737
Ishimori, Shuzo, **9:**737
Ishq (film), **5:**540
Ishwari, L. R., **5:**421–22
Isidore of Seville, **6:**442
Isii Baku, **7:**68
Isik Dogudan Yükselir (Aksu), **6:**252
Isimura *kengyô,* **7:**692
Isirawa people
    composition of, **9:**360
    instruments of, **9:**582–83
    kona songs, **9:**580
    songs of, **9:**583, 587
al-Iskandarānī, Ibrāhīm, **6:**168
Iskandar Muda, Sultan, **4:**604
Iskhakova, Barno, **6:**919
Isla de Pascua. *See* Rapa Nui
Islam, **5:**480, 482. *See also* chant (Muslim);
        Muslim people; Sufism; *specific sects*
    Adighian people, **8:**854
    Afghanistan, **5:**804, 808, 810–11, 817, 824,
        825–26
    Africa, **1:**5
        diffusion of, **1:**313–14
    Albania, **8:**1002
    Albanian-Americans, **3:**926
    Algeria, **6:**474–75
    animism and, **4:**60
    Asian-American communities, **3:**950, 1084
    Bali, **4:**743
    Balkarian people, **8:**856, 858
    Black Muslims, **3:**663
    Borneo, **4:**825
    Bosnia-Hercegovina, **8:**962
    Brunei, **4:**79–80, 596
    Bulgaria, **8:**895
    Burma, **4:**363
    Canadian Prairie communities, **3:**1086,
        1089–90, 1246
    Caribbean, **2:**61, 85
    caste structure and, **5:**10
    Central Asia, **6:**897–901, 909–10, 935–47,
        949–50, 980; **7:**23–24
    Chăm people, **3:**1010; **4:**590
    Chechen people, **8:**861

China, **7:**19–20, 113–14, 152, 416, 458, 459,
        462
Cirebon, **4:**686, 687–88, 695–97
dance contexts in, **6:**876–77
East Africa, **1:**598, 599, 605–6
Egypt, **6:**165–75, 414, 612
Europe, **8:**11–12, 233
Fiji, **5:**612
Flores, **4:**791
Fulɓe people and, **1:**443
gender concepts in, **6:**299–307
Georgia, **8:**826, 835–36
Goa, **5:**735
Guyana, **2:**443
Hamadsha brotherhood, **1:**274
Hausa people, **1:**447, 450, 515, 519, 523–24,
        528
Hindu converts to, **5:**398
history of, in South Asia, **5:**11–12, 720,
        726–27
Ibadite branch, **6:**671, 682
India, **5:**374, 375, 486
India, South, **5:**350
Indo-Caribbean communities, **3:**1205
Indonesia, **4:**75–78, 92, 596
influence on dance traditions of Europe, **8:**163
Inner Asia, **7:**19, 23–24
Ismaili sect, **6:**177, 935
    in Afghanistan, **5:**825, 826, 828
    in Pakistan, **5:**792, *793,* 794, *797–98*
Jamaica, **2:**901
Java, **4:**630, 632–33, 647
Karachaevian people, **8:**856, 858
Karnataka, **5:**866, 877
Kashmir, **5:**682
Kenya, **1:**629, 631
Kerala, **5:**929, 947–48
Kharijite sect, **6:**431, 523
Kurdistan, **6:**743
legal schools of, **6:**130, 131, 371–73, 656, *936*
Liberia, **1:**327–49
LoDagaa people, **1:**457
Lombok, **4:**763, 764, 765, 768–69, 770, 774,
        775–76
Macedonia, **8:**983
Madhya Pradesh, **5:**720
Malaysia, **4:**78, 401, 409, 414–15, 430–32,
        586, 596
Mali, **1:**421
Mali empire, **1:**76
Malta, **8:**634, 635
Maluku, **4:**812, 813, 814, 816–17, 819, 820
Middle East, **6:**3
Mossi-Bariba peoples, **1:**453
Mozabite sect, **1:**536
Mozambique, **1:**297
Nigeria, **1:**413–14
North Africa, **1:**219, 416, 532, 533, 536–38;
        6:273, 431–32
North America, **3:**5, 120, 530, 982, 983;
        5:579, 581
North Caucasia, **8:**850
Nur Bakhshia sect, **5:**792, *793*
Nusa Tenggara Barat, **4:**762
Oman, **6:**671, 674–75, 677–78, 682
Orissa, **5:**731

Islam (*continued*)
   Ossetian people, **8**:859
   Pakhtun people, **5**:785
   Pakistan, **5**:743, 744–45
      northern, **5**:797–98, 799
   Philippines, **3**:1026; **4**:78–79, 94, 839,
      889–911, 913, 920, 921, 928
   Rajasthan, **5**:639–40
   Russia, **6**:935
   sama' polemic in, **6**:19
   Shi'ite branch, **3**:1031; **6**:403, 544, 671,
      793–800, 826–27, 844, 860–61,
      876–77, 935, 942
     in Afghanistan, **5**:817, 825
     attitude toward music, **6**:131, 139, 371,
      825, 868
     in Azerbaijan, **6**:921–22, 923, 931
     in Central Asia, **6**:899
     in Delhi, **5**:133
     hymns of, **5**:745
     in Iraq, **6**:415
     Muharram festival of, **5**:276–77, 282
     naubat khānā ensemble of, **5**:279–80
     nonliturgical music of, **5**:256
     in Pakistan, **5**:792, *793*
     in Turkey, **6**:114–15, 765–66
   Sierra Leone, **1**:504
   Somalia, **1**:610
   South Africa, **5**:615, 617
   Southeast Asia, **4**:73–80
     urban areas, **4**:5
   Sri Lanka, **5**:108, 955, 957, 958
   Sudan, **1**:549, 550–55, 556, 561, 565, 605–6
   Sulawesi, **4**:804, 806, 810
   Sumatra, **4**:600
     Aceh, **4**:603–5
     Jambi, **4**:616–17
     Lampung Province, **4**:628
     Minangkabau, **4**:611–12
     North Sumatra, **4**:605–6
     Riau, **4**:614, 616
     southern, **4**:624–25
   Sumbawa, **4**:779, 780, 782–83, 784
   Sunda, **4**:699, 719, 725
   Sunni branch, **3**:1029; **5**:779; **6**:371, 429,
      671, 935
     in Afghanistan, **5**:817, 825
     attitude toward music, **6**:131
     hymns of, **5**:745
     in Kazakhstan, **6**:949–50
     nonliturgical music of, **5**:256
     in Pakistan, **5**:792, *793*
     tāshā playing of, **5**:*285*
     in Turkey, **6**:768, 798–99
     Uighur people, **6**:995
     women's singing, **5**:411
   symbolic universe of music in, **6**:177–88
   Syria, **6**:570
   Tamil Nadu, **5**:903
   Tanzania, **1**:634, 637
   Thailand, **4**:79
   Trinidad, **2**:952; **5**:590
   Tuareg people, **1**:577, 581–82, 592–93
   Tunisia, **6**:523, 525–26
   Turkey, **6**:57, 798–99, 807
   Turkmenistan, **6**:967

   Uighur people, **6**:995
   United Kingdom, **5**:573
   Vietnam, **4**:444
   views on music, **2**:60; **5**:256, 273, 376, 486,
     744–45, 751, 772, 799, 810, 818,
     824, 826; **6**:19–20, 131–32, 165–66,
     177, 364, 371–73, 537–38, 539,
     915–16
   Voltaic region, **1**:451, 452
   Wahhabi movement, **6**:652, 654
   Yemen, **6**:656, 690
   Yemeni people, **6**:284
   Yoruba people, **1**:459, 472, 474–77, 484–85
   Zaydi sect, **6**:655
   Zikri sect, **5**:754, 761, 778–79
Islam and Music (Keldibeki), **6**:938
Islam, Kazi Nazrul. *See* Nazrul Islam, Kazi
Island Boiz (musical group), **3**:1052
Islander label, **3**:1071
Íslandica (musical group), **8**:407
Island Nights' Entertainments (Stevenson),
   9:36–37
Island Records, **3**:714; **8**:236, 241
"Island Wedding" (Lennon), **8**:387
Islas Malvinas, **2**:2
Isle of Man, **8**:319
Isle of Pines (New Caledonia), **9**:671, 674, 680,
   681, 686
Isley Brothers (musical group), **3**:677, 684, 709,
   711
Isma'il, khedive of Egypt, **6**:547, 609, 610
Ismā'īl, Shaykh Muṣṭafá, **6**:161
Ismail Dede Efendi, **6**:108, 109, 110, 115, 771,
   772, 779–80
Ismail Hakki Bey, **6**:196
Ismail, Mahi, **1**:571–72
Ismail, Shah (Hatâyî), **6**:794
Ismailov, M. S., **6**:927
Ism'tulla Mojizi, Mulla, **7**:447
Isneg people, **4**:914, 916, 918
Iṣóla, Alhaji Haruna, **1**:475, 476, 480
Ísólfsson, Páll, **8**:406
Isostasie III (Feliciano), **4**:878
Isouard, Nicolò, **8**:642
Isoz, Étienne, **8**:688
Is Paris Burning? (film), **3**:203
Isqī al-'itāsh (anon.), **6**:568–69
Israel, **3**:939, 940; **6**:1013–21; **8**:263; **10**:161.
     See also Jewish people; Judaism;
     Palestine
   ancient music of, **5**:17–18; **8**:249, 265
   Arab people in, **6**:1015
   Bukharan Jews in, **6**:905, 919–20
   cheironomy in, **8**:100
   folk songs, **6**:202, 1018–19, 1024, 1062,
     1066, 1069
   founding of, **8**:264, 266
   history of, **6**:1013, 1015
   intifāda revolt, **6**:635–40
   Jewish religious music in, **6**:199–206
   Maghribi Jews in, **6**:1036–43
   map of, **6**:*1014*
   musical life and institutions in, **6**:1023–32
   music scholarship in, **6**:1057–67
   muzika mizraḥit in, **6**:204, 205, 261–68,
     1016–18, 1020–21, 1033–34, 1074

   non-Jewish communities in, **6**:1021
   popular music in, **6**:1069–74
   Yemenite Jews in, **6**:1047–54
Israel Chamber Orchestra, **6**:1030
Israel Institute for Sacred Music, **6**:1060, 1061
Israel Music Institute, **6**:1030, 1061
Israel Music Publications, **6**:1030
Israel Philharmonic Orchestra, **6**:1021, 1026,
   1030
Israeli Andalusian Orchestra, **3**:1175; **6**:204,
   1021
Israeli Music Publications, **6**:1060
Israeli Opera, **6**:1030
Issiki Terukoto, **7**:610
Istanbul Conservatory, **6**:77, 109
Istranova (musical group), **8**:920
Isudaeyŏp (*kagok*), **7**:818, 921
'Itāb (Saudi singer), **6**:697
Italian Catholic Federation, **3**:823, 860
Italian Folk Ensemble (Adelaide), **9**:80–81, *82*
Italian people, **2**:4
   in Australia, **9**:79–81, 409
   in Brazil, **2**:331
   in Canada, **3**:1060, 1074, 1078, 1082, 1083,
     1196–97
   in Croatia, **8**:925
   in England, **8**:336
   in North America, **3**:10
   in Panama, **2**:771
   in South America, **2**:59–60, 61, 84, 89–90
   in Sweden, **8**:434
   in Switzerland, **8**:697
   in Syria, **6**:565
   in United States, **3**:528, 860–63, 864–65;
     8:622
   in Uruguay, **2**:510
Italy, **8**:604–23. *See also* Sardinia; Sicily
   Albanian people in, **8**:610, 617, 986
   art music in, **8**:69, 71–76, 80, 84, 609, 617,
     618, 658
   Basilicata
     canti all'altalena, **8**:116
     laments, **8**:119
     local traditions, **8**:123
   blind musicians in, **8**:143, 611
   Bolognese street violinist, **8**:*33*
   Carolingian period in, **8**:69
   Celtic people in, **8**:319
   court life in, **8**:199
   dance traditions of, **8**:160, 163, 197, 207, 609
   Emilia Romagna, **8**:621
   Ferrara, court of, **8**:199
   folk/art music interactions, **8**:53, 617–18
   folk music recordings, **8**:21
   Genoa, *trallalero* polyphony, **8**:134, 610
   geography of, **8**:604
   Germans in, **8**:617, 675
   history of music in, **8**:617–18
   influence on Croatia, **8**:933
   influence on Montenegrin music, **8**:959
   influence on northern Croatian music, **8**:930
   instruments, **8**:169, 170, 176, 197, 614–17
     research on, **8**:39
   Jewish people in, **6**:1035
   Ladin-speakers in, **8**:617
   Leghorn, **6**:434

Lombardy, *tiir* polyphony, **8**:610
Mantua, court of, **8**:264
map of, **8**:*516, 604*
Marche, accordion and violin ensemble, **8**:609
North African colonies of, **6**:432
North African emigrant communities, **6**:438
northern *vs.* southern cultures in, **8**:12
Occitans in, **8**:617
opera in, **8**:80, 84, 604, 617–18
Piedmont, **8**:604
    ballads, **8**:606
    Monferrato, **8**:*5*
popular music in, **8**:*141,* 204, 205, 207, 208,
    617–20
population of, **8**:604
Puglia, shepherds' music, **8**:*25*
Renaissance in, **8**:73–74, 75–76
research on music of, **8**:613, 620–23
Rome, world music in, **8**:210
rule over Ethiopia, **8**:621
Salento, **8**:207
Sardinians in, **8**:12
Sephardic Jews in, **8**:262
Slavs in, **8**:617
Trentino-Alto Adige (South Tyrol), **8**:675
    alpine choirs of, **8**:613–14
    choral societies, **8**:147
unification of, **8**:10
Val Camonica, rock carvings, **8**:36
Venice, influence on Greek island music,
    8:1009, 1014–15, 1025
vocal music, **8**:23, 24, 142, 145, 207, 517,
    605–8, 609–13, 617–18
    art music, **8**:71, 72–73, 75–76
    laments, **8**:120, 128, 196
    laude spirituale, **8**:132
    minorities, **8**:617
    polyphony, **8**:134, 610–11
    text improvisation, **8**:17
Italy, Kingdom of, **8**:632
Itasca Expedition, **9**:25
Itelmen people, **7**:1027–30
al-Ithnayn (periodical), **6**:233, 237
Itigetuzi Temple (Kanto), **7**:703, 758
ItitinKiribati (dance troupe), **9**:*760, 762*
Itrî, Buhurîzâde Mustafa, **6**:108, 110, 118, 196,
    769, 771
"It's Alright" (Graham Central Station), **3**:683
It's a Natural label, **3**:351
"It's Too Soon to Know" (Orioles), **3**:351, 671
It Takes a Nation of Millions to Hold Us Back
    (Public Enemy), **3**:714
Ittifâq, **6**:298
Ituarte, Julio, **2**:604
"It Was by Chance We Met" (Williams), **3**:604
"It Wasn't God Who Made Honkytonk Angels"
    (Wells), **3**:79
Itzhaki, Israel, **6**:1019
Ivančan, Ivan, **8**:936, 937
"I've Been Loving You Too Long" (Redding),
    3:677, 710
"I've Got a Woman" (Charles), **3**:678
Iverson, Ernest and Clarence ("Slim Jim & the
    Vagabond Kid"), **3**:869
Ives, Charles, **3**:14, 24, 33, 174, 539–40, 563;
    8:85

Ives, Edward, **3**:147, 1070, 1123, 1124
Ives, George, **3**:565
Ivey, Bill, **10**:82
Ivory Coast. *See* Côte d'Ivoire
Ivoti (musical group), **2**:*270*
Iwa-K, **4**:110–11
Iwami Baikyoku, **7**:708
Iwami, Tsuna, **2**:88–89; **10**:*99*
Iwan, Dafydd, **8**:322, 356
Iwanami kôza, Nihon no ongaku, Azia no ongaku
    (encyclopedia), **7**:525
"I Wanna Do Something Freaky to You," **3**:700
"I Wanna Take You Higher" (Stone), **3**:681
"I Want to Be a Cowboy's Sweetheart"
    (Montana), **3**:79
"I Want You to Be My Girl" (Lymon), **3**:672
Iwasimizu Hatimangû shrine (Kyôto), **7**:607
"I Would I'd Never Met Thee" (Williams), **3**:604
Ixcatec culture, **2**:563
Ixil Maya, **2**:721, 723, 736
Iyabora, Manuel, **9**:33
Iyagi (Lee), **7**:955
Iyer, Vijay, **3**:972
Iyŏdo sana (Korean folk song), **7**:883
Izenzaren (musical group), **6**:270, 275
Izgrev (musical group), **3**:1198
Izikowitz, Karl Gustav, **2**:31–32, 127, 152
Iztueta, Juan Ignacio de, **8**:121, 316
Izu, Mark, **3**:336, 972
Izumo no Okuni, **7**:764
Izutu (Zeami), **7**:553, *582,* 583, 630, 632, 640

Ja'aliyīn people, **1**:556
Jaamac, Cibaado, **1**:*615*
Jaap Kunst Museum (Netherlands), **2**:507
al-Jabaqjī, 'Abd al-Raḥmān, **6**:569
al-Jabartī, 'Abd al-Raḥmān, **6**:20, 22
Jabbarov, Kāmiljān, **6**:908
Jabbour, Alan, **3**:149, 299, 498
Jabêm people, **9**:326–27, 566
Jablonko, Alison, **9**:314
Jabo people, **1**:106, 468–69
Jabo, Sawung, **4**:110
Jabulka, Ululani Robertson, **9**:924
"Jack of Diamonds" (folk song), **3**:835
Jackson (Irish piper), **8**:386, 389
Jackson, Alan, **3**:81
Jackson, Andrew, **3**:305
Jackson, Aunt Molly, **3**:47
Jackson, Bruce, **3**:573
Jackson, D. D., **3**:1107
Jackson, George Pullen, **3**:575–76
Jackson, Henry Japeth, **3**:*10*
Jackson, Janet, **4**:111
Jackson, Jay, **3**:1212
Jackson, Jim, **3**:645
Jackson, Joyce Marie, **3**:632
Jackson, Mahalia, **3**:535, 631–32
Jackson, Michael, **3**:206, 712, 713, *713,* 733,
    1002; **4**:90, 100, 886; **5**:656; **6**:248;
    8:207, 220; **9**:207
Jackson, Papa Charlie, **3**:644, 707
Jackson, Raymond, **3**:676
Jackson, Tom, **3**:1087
Jackson, Tommy, **3**:80
Jacob the Mohawk, **3**:1179

Jacob of Serug, **6**:228, 229
Jacobe, Cayetano, **4**:866
Jacobite Song (Donaldson), **8**:374
Jacobo, Cruz, **2**:581
Jacobsen, H. N., **8**:472
Jacobson, Doranne, **5**:674
Jacquet de la Guerre, Elizabeth Claude, **8**:77, 199
Jacquet, Illinois, **3**:669
Jade Warrior (musical group), **3**:955
al-Jadhba, Ṣāliḥ, **6**:568
Jaegerhuber, Werner A., **2**:892
Jaëll, Alfred, **3**:556
Jaen, Tomasa, **2**:776
Ja'far, Umm, **6**:296
Jafar al-Sadiq. *See* Cafer Sādik (Jafar al-Sadiq)
al-Ja'farī, Shaykh Ṣāliḥ, **6**:173
Ja'far Qolī, **6**:840
Jafra wya harrabi (*dabkih*), **6**:583
Jafri, Àrif, **5**:768
Jafri caste, **5**:476
Jagannath (deity), **5**:731, 732
Jagatkishore, **5**:462
Jagger, Mick, **8**:226, 392
Jāghidār caste, **5**:639
Jagoda, Flori, **8**:*968*
Jagori (feminist organization), **5**:552
Jagwali, Santabai, **5**:*400*
Jah Hut people, **4**:560
Jahai people, **4**:569–71, *577*
Jahangir, Mughal emperor, **5**:308
Jahan, Nur, **5**:750
al-Jāḥiz, **6**:20, 360, 362, 664
Jahn, Brian, **2**:913
Jai, Rikki, **2**:86
Jaime (Warao elder), **2**:188
Jaiminīya school, **5**:242–43
Jainism, **5**:12, 259, 480, 482, 639, 731
    Digambara sect, **5**:13
    history of, **5**:13
    Karnataka, **5**:866
    Madhya Pradesh, **5**:720
    manuscript miniatures, **5**:300, 312
    music of, **5**:261, 280
    North America, **5**:579
    raga visualizations in, **5**:313
    Svetambara sect, **5**:13
    Tamil Nadu, **5**:903
    United Kingdom, **5**:573
Jairazbhoy, Nazir, **3**:980; **5**:53, 322, 673, 674,
    675; **10**:77, 90
Jairo Varela y Grupo Niche, **2**:410
Jakhai (deity), **5**:728
Jakun (Orang Hulu) people, **4**:560, 585–87
Jalakas, Mart, **3**:879
Jalāl, Ata, **6**:916, 917
Jalāl al-Dīn Rūmī, **3**:1044; **5**:687, 691; **6**:72,
    107–11, 119, 132, 138, 186, 187,
    769, 826, 831–32
Jalali, **5**:819
Jalalian, Boghos, **6**:554
Jalaluddin Rumi. *See* Jalāl al-Dīn Rūmī
Jalayrid dynasty, **6**:922
Jalbert, Laurence, **3**:1160
Jale, **3**:1073
Jalil, Ibrahim Abdul, **1**:571
Jalkanen, Pekka, **8**:489

Jallāl, **6:**271

Jalota, Anup, **5:**255, 425, 548, 549

Jalq'as culture, **2:**287

Jaluit (Marshall Islands), **9:**751

"Jam" (Graham Central Station), **3:**683

"Jam on Gerry's Rock" (ballad), **3:***157*

Jam, Jimmy, **3:**715

Jam Session Orchestra, **1:**477

Jama-Coaque culture, **2:**7, 413

Jamaica, **2:**789, 896–913; **3:**808
  art music in, **2:**910
  Church of God and Saints of Christ in, **3:**127
  dance and festivals in, **2:**906–10
  early black music in, **3:**64
  East Indians in, **3:**813–17
  education in, **2:**909–10
  history of, **2:**896
  industries of, **2:**791
  instruments of, **2:**896–901
  John Kuner celebrations, **3:**614
  Maroon cultures, **2:**2, 795; **10:**143, 152
  musical genres
    dance hall, **2:**912
    mento, **2:**678, 906
    ragga, **3:**806
    reggae, **2:**912; **3:**809
    religious, **2:**901–4
    secular, **2:**904–6
    ska, **2:**93
  popular music in, **2:**95, 97–98, 910–12
  population of, **2:**896
  research on, **2:**912–13
  sound recording industry in, **2:**40
  toasting genre, **2:**98; **3:**692–93, 694
  Yamaye culture of, **2:**78

Jamaica (musical), **3:**621

Jamaica Orchestra for Youth, **2:**910

Jamaica School of Music, **2:**910

Jamaican Canadian Association, **3:**1085

Jamaican people
  in Belize, **2:**666–67
  in Costa Rica, **2:**688, 690
  in Cuba, **2:**828
  in England, **8:**231, 232, 235
  in Nicaragua, **2:**753
  in North America, **3:**337, 808–12, 1085, 1170, 1201–2, 1203

al-Jamāl al-Muṭrib, **6:**366

Jama Mapun people, **4:**889

"Jambalaya," **3:**369, 1155

James A. Rubin Collection (Cambridge, Mass.), **5:**530

James, Billy T., **9:**933

James, Catheryne, **9:***416*

James, Cheryl "Salt," **3:**696

James Cleveland Gospel Music Workshop of America, **3:**632

James, Colin, **3:**1091

James, Elmore, **3:**647

James, Etta, **3:**673

James, Harry, **3:**863

James, Rick, **3:**684

James, Willis Laurence, **3:**84–85

Jāmiʿ al-alḥān (Ibn Ghaybī), **6:**398

Jamī, Abd al-Raman, **6:**914

Jamieson, Robert, **8:**371

Jamikiḷi singers, **5:**894, 901

Jamīla, **6:**291, 294–95, 297, 298

Jammu and Kashmir, **5:**682. *See also* Kashmir
  dance traditions of, **5:**498–99
  instruments in, **5:**343–44
  map of, **5:***680*

Jammu and Kashmir Academy of Arts, Culture, and Language, **5:**688

al-Jamoussi, Moḥammed, **6:**269

Jamunarani, **5:**421

Jan, Gauhar, **5:**412–13, 424

Jan from Jenstejn, Archbishop of Prague, **8:**726

Jan, Malang (Mohammad Amin), **5:**834–35, 836–40

Jan, Malka, **5:**412, 424

Janáček, Leoš, **8:**26, 725, 728, 732

Janai (deity), **5:**728

Janaki, S., **5:**421

Janapada Academy (Bangalore), **5:**881

Jančuk, Mikoła, **8:**803

Jane Eyre (Gordon and Caird), **3:**200

Jangam singers, **5:**900, 901

Janggar (epic), **7:**1008, 1014, 1015

Jang, Jon, **3:**336, 965, 972

Janis, Harriet, **3:**580

Janković, Danica, **8:**937, 954

Janković, Ljubica, **8:**937, 954

Janse, Olov, **4:**40

Jansen, Arlin D., **4:**603

Jansen, Manfred, **3:**1277–78

Jansen, Robbie, **1:**428

Jansons, Māris, **8:**507

Janssen, Johann Voldemar, **8:**495

Jansson, Lars, **8:**446

Japan. *See also* East Asia; *gagaku*; Ryûkyû Islands; *specific periods*
  aesthetics and philosophy in, **7:**545–55
  biwa traditions, **7:**643–51
  blind musicians in, **7:**82, 644–45, 649, 687, 691, 693, 696, 712, 716, 755–56, 757–58, 764, 777, 778
  Buddhism in, **5:**12; **7:**24–25, 548–49, 611–18
  chamber music traditions, **7:**687–717
    dan mono, **7:**696–97
    kokyû genres, **7:**711–13
    sankyoku, **7:**715–17
    sôkyoku, **7:**695–99, 716
    syamisen genres, **7:**688–89
    tukusi goto, **7:**687–88, 696, 698
    zither genres, **7:**689
    ziuta (*jiuta*), **7:**691–93, 697, 716
  cheironomy in, **8:**100
  Chinese influences in, **7:**24–28, 59, 80, 534–35, 536, 538, 587, 620, 711
  Chinese people in, **7:**724–25
  Confucianism in, **7:**28, 547–48
  continuity and authenticity in traditional music, **7:**767–72
  cultural exchanges in, **7:**49–51, 720–22
  cultural preservation in, **7:**46–47, 650–51
  dance traditions in, **7:**59–60, 63–66
  drumming traditions of, **3:**970
  ethnographic research of, **9:**25, 159, 739
  ethnomusicological research in, **10:**3–5, 12–15
  film and animation music in, **7:**749–51
  folk music in, **7:**595–604

foreign influences in, **7:**719–22, 723–25, 756

gender roles in, **7:**763–66

geography and climate of, **7:**15, 534

history of, **7:**15–18

history of music in, **7:**534–36

influence on Southeast Asian culture, **4:**80

instruments in, **7:**79–83, 557–62

keiko concept, **7:**768

Korean music in, **7:**797–98

Kyôto, **7:**535

minority cultures, **7:**540, 783–98
  cultural policies toward, **7:**796

musical institutions in, **7:**45–47

musical life, current, **7:**537–41

musical transmission in, **7:**773–76

music theory in, **7:**565–73

Nagasaki, "secret" Christians of, **7:**724, 756

nagauta genre in, **7:**5, 551, 654, 659, 671–74, 749, 759, 765, 773

Nara, **7:**535

narrative genres of, **7:**675–82

notational systems in, **7:**573–83; **8:**103

occupation of China, **7:**294, 380, 383, 384–85, 745, 797

occupation of Korea, **7:**797, 866, 899, 932, 951–52, 983, 989

occupation of Taiwan, **7:**423

overview of music in, **7:**533–41

popular music, **7:**354–55, 720, 739–40, 743–47
  in Kapingamarangi, **9:**836
  in Micronesia, **9:**126, 159, 724, 730, 739, 750
  in Papua New Guinea, **9:**150

printing in, **7:**22

research on music of, **7:**591–95

scholarship in, **7:**591–95

shamanism in, **7:**20

Shintoism in, **7:**549–50, 607–10

Simane Prefecture, archaeological sites in, **7:**557

social groups and institutions in, **7:**755–61

source materials in, **7:**585–90

syakuhati genres, **7:**701–5, 707–9

theatrical traditions in, **7:**6, 59, 63–65, 629–37, 639–41, 653–85

tradition and change in, **7:**719–20

Western musical influences in, **7:**698–99, 731–33, 735–37, 740, 743–47, 749–50, 777–79, 808

Western music in, **7:**49–51, 56, 536–37, 538, 540, 627, 721–22, 725, 727–29, 756, 760–61, 763, 774, 808; **10:**13–14

in World War II, **9:**25–32, 150, 475, 499, 607, 614, 620, 750, 758, 764

Japan Art Fund, **7:**761

Japan Symphonic Orchestra, **7:**732

Japanese Association for the Study of Popular Music, **7:**595

Japanese Canadian Cultural Center, **3:**1084

Japanese Columbia Company, **7:**894

Japanese Express, **1:**768

Japanese Harmonica Band, **3:**969

Japanese people, **2:**4, 71
  in Argentina, **2:**269; **10:**99, 102
  in Bolivia, **10:**99, 102

in Brazil, **2:**61; **10:**99, 102
in Caribbean, **2:**793
in Hawai'i, **7:**6, 707–8; **9:**95, 96, 97, 109,
 163, 317, 914
in Micronesia, **9:**305, 715, 719, 720, 728,
 729, 748
in North America, **3:**9, 11, 950, 967–73;
 7:707–8
 British Columbia, **3:**1092, 1096
 dances of, **3:**216–17
 discrimination against, **3:**13
 history of music, **3:**526
 internment of, **3:**969, 970, 972, 973
 issei, **3:**968–69
 nisei, **3:**968, 969–70
 Ontario, **3:**1083, 1084, 1215, 1217
 Prairie Provinces, **3:**1245, 1248
 sansei, **3:**970–73
in Oceania, **9:**5
in Paraguay, **2:**456, 462–63; **10:**99, 101, 102
in Peru, **10:**99, 102
popularity of karaoke, **2:**41, 87–88
religions of, **2:**48
in South America, **2:**83, 86–89; **7:**6, 707–8;
 10:99, 102–4
in Sumatra, **4:**616
Jaques-Dalcroze, Emile, **3:**280
Jara, Mauricio, **3:**741
Jara, Victor, **2:**60, 90, 373
"*Jarabe Tapatío, El,*" **2:**604, 619
Jarai people, **3:**996; **4:**444, 529
 gong ensemble of, **4:**534
 instruments of, **4:**535
 narratives of, **4:**533
Jaramillo, Julia, **3:**763
Jarawa people, **1:**289
Jarba, Oudam Zahram, **6:**270
Járdányi, Pál, **8:**23, 24
Jarernchai Chonpairot, **4:**25, 26, 224, 277, 316,
 321, 337, 340, 346
Jargy, Simon, **6:**301–2
Jarman, Joseph, **3:**664
Jarre, Maurice, **3:**203–4
Jaruud people, **7:**1004–20
Järvelä, Arto, **8:**478
Järvelä, Mauno, **8:**478
Jason, Kenny, **3:**691
Jasraj, Pandit, **5:**255
Jaṭ caste, **5:**639
Jat group, **5:**813, 815, 820–22
Jat, Nagoji, **5:**647
Jatin-Lalit (director duo), **5:**540
Jáuregui, Jesús, **10:**88, 95
Java. *See also* Cirebon; Indonesia; Sunda
 aristocracy in, **4:**118
 Baduy people, **4:**27
 Banyumas, **4:**630
 ciblon drumming, **4:**675
 repertoire, **4:**667
 Banyuwangi, **4:**645
 musical genres, **4:**679
 repertoire, **4:**667
 British in, **4:**633
 Central, **4:**630, 633–35; **10:**42–43
 Banyumas style, **4:**634–35, 658, 678
 regional repertoire, **4:**667

Semarang style, **4:**658, 675
Solonese style, **4:**633–34, 658, 675, 676,
 678, 680
Yogyanese style, **4:**634, 658, 675, 676, 678,
 680
cultural influences on Malaysia, **4:**428–29
Dutch in, **4:**77, 83–85, 633
East, **4:**630, 635, 655
 gendhing repertoire, **4:**667, 675
 instruments in, **4:**675
 musical genres, **4:**678
 rice cultivation in, **4:**48
ethnomusicological research in, **10:**41–53
gamelan music (*See also* gamelan heading)
 influence on Western composers, **4:**13,
 131–32, 135
 melody in, **4:**385
 sléndro tuning, **4:**387
geography of, **4:**630–31
gong-chime ensembles, **4:**20
history of, **4:**594, 596, 632–33
Indians in, **4:**68
influence on Balinese culture, **4:**731
influence on Lombok culture, **4:**763–64,
 775
influence on Sumatran culture, **4:**621, 626,
 627–28
Islam in, **4:**77
Jakarta, **4:**630
Madura, **4:**630, 635
 instruments in, **4:**675
 repertoire, **4:**668
 wayang topèng, **4:**654
map of, **4:**631
musical genres (*See also* vocal music *heading*)
 gendhing, **4:**639, 659–63, 667, 670,
 672–75, 676, 680, 683, 684–85
 gendhing Banyumas, **4:**662
 gendhing bonang, **4:**662, 667, 675
 gendhing gagahan, **4:**667
 gendhing Jawa timuran, **4:**662
 gendhing kemanak, **4:**666
 gendhing lampah, **4:**652, 653, 654, 655,
 659, 661–63, 666, 667, 675
 gendhing sekar, **4:**654, 655
 gendhing tayub, **4:**662, 667
 gendhing wayang, **4:**667
 jaipongan, **4:**107
 jineman, **4:**666
 klenèngan, **4:**680, 683
 kreasi baru, **4:**666, 684–85
 laras madya, **4:**646
 palaran, **4:**654, 655, 665
 prajuritan, **4:**646
 rambangan, **4:**655, 665
 santiswaran, **4:**646
 sekar gendhing, **4:**665
 sindhènan, **4:**683
musical performances in, **4:**646–48
music research on, **4:**27, 28–29
population of, **4:**631
Portuguese in, **4:**633
prehistoric, **4:**32, 34
Ramayana in, **5:**261
regional cassettes in, **5:**554
regional styles in, **4:**633–35

research on, **4:**635–39
spirit beliefs in, **4:**49–50, 52–53
Tengger, **4:**51
trance in, **4:**61
West, **4:**630 (*See also* Sunda)
Yogyakarta, **4:**630, 654
Javaanse Volksvertoningen (Pigeaud), **4:**636
Javae culture, **2:**131
Javakhishvili, Ivane, **8:**839, 846
jāvaḷi, **5:**103, 104, 389, 411, 414, 452, 517, 522
 texts of, **5:**107, 219–20
Javanese music in North America, **3:**952,
 1012–15; **10:**52. *See also* Indonesian
 music in North America
Javanese people, **4:**630. *See also* Indonesian
 people
 in Borneo, **4:**825
 in Malaysia, **4:**412
 in Nusa Tenggara Timur, **4:**787
 relation to peoples of Lombok, **4:**762
 in Sumatra, **4:**616
 in Sunda, **4:**700
Javits, Jacob, **3:**297
Jávor, Pál, **8:**746
Jawāhir al-niẓām fī maʿrifat al-anghām (al-Irbilī),
 6:366
jawbones. *See* scrapers (rasps)
Jawhar, Abū, **6:**576–78
jawharps, jaw's harps. *See* Jew's harps
Jaws (film), **3:**204
Jayadeva, **5:**105, 249, 253, 262, 452, 510,
 519–20, 522, 633, 844–45, 931
Jayakori, Edward, **5:**424
Jayamma, Eddie, **5:**491
Jayaraman, Lalgudi, **3:**981; **5:**384–85
Jayavarman II, king of Angkor, **4:**153, 252
Jayavarman I, king of Chenla, **4:**153
Jayavarman VII, king of Khmer, **4:**153, 187
Jay, Jaya, Devi (Jayaraman), **3:**981
al-Jazarī, **6:**373
jazz, **2:**49; **3:**325, 510, 577, 601, 650–65. *See
 also* swing
 African roots of, **1:**51
 Afro-Cuban music and, **3:**662, 720, 732, 783,
 786–87, 789, 791, 793, 797
 Algeria, **6:**475
 art music and, **3:**539, 609, 611
 Asian-American, **3:**336, 345, 527, 957,
 964–65
 Asian thought in, **3:**132–33, 663, 664
 Australia, **9:**142–43, 409
 Austria, **8:**674, 676; **10:**111
 bebop, **3:**550, 580–81, 583, 648, 656,
 658–60, 674, 732, 793, 797, 1077,
 1080
 big band, **3:**549–50, 654–56, 969
 Irish groups, **3:**844
 bluegrass and, **3:**160
 blues and, **3:**524–25, 648
 Brazil, **2:**110
 British Caribbean consumers, **3:**812
 Brittany, **8:**564
 Canada, **3:**296, 1105–7
 Maritimes, **3:**1072–73
 Northwestern Territories, **3:**1278
 Ontario, **3:**1080, 1186, 1205

jazz, Canada (*continued*)
   Prairie Provinces, **3:**1091
   Québec, **3:**1077, 1160
 China, **7:**353, 399
 cool, **3:**550, 660
 copyright problems in, **3:**705
 crossover genres in, **3:**335
 Cuba, **2:**827, 836
 Czechoslovakia, **8:**730–31
 dances, **3:**214, 233
 Denmark, **8:**462
 development of, **3:**13, 325, 550, 651–52, 707
 Dixieland, **3:**550, 580–81
 economics of, **3:**263
 England, **8:**232
 Europe, **8:**204, 228, 233, 903
   during Nazi occupation, **8:**661
 Faroe Islands, **8:**471
 feminist studies, **3:**91
 in film, **3:**203
 Finland, **8:**399, 485
   humppa, **8:**483–84, 485–86
 free, **3:**662–63, 1077, 1158
 funk and, **3:**684
 fusion genres, **3:**326–27, 663–64, 665, 799;
   7:967, 972–73
 Georgia, **8:**845
 Germany, **8:**659, 660
 government funding for, **3:**299
 Guyana, **2:**448
 Haiti, **2:**891, 917
 Haitian *mini-djaz*, **3:**803–4
 hard bop, **3:**583
 Hawai'i, **9:**163
 Hindustani drumming in, **5:**136
 Hungary, **8:**746, 747
 identity issues in, **3:**513
 influence on African music, **1:**416
 influence on Nubian music, **6:**642
 Israel, **6:**1074
 Italy, **8:**618
 Jamaica, **2:**910, 911, 912
 Japan, **7:**538, 744
 Japanese-Americans, **3:**971–72
 Jewish performers of, **8:**264
 Latin, **2:**797; **3:**513, 797
 Macedonia, **8:**983
 Manouch, **8:**288
 marketing of, **3:**269
 modal, **3:**661–62
 musical theater and, **3:**622
 Norway, **8:**427, 429, 430
 Peru, **2:**485–86
 Portugal, **8:**584–85
 progressive, **3:**550
 Puerto Rico, **2:**940
 race and, **3:**63, 707
 railroad train sounds in, **1:**127
 recordings, **3:**706
 research on, **3:**580–81, 583–84, 587
 revival movements, **3:**55
 rock compared with, **3:**550–51
 Romania, **8:**882
 Rom people, **8:**288
 Russia, **8:**777
 Scandinavia, **8:**399

 in schools, **3:**278–79, 282–83
 smooth genres, **3:**341
 soul, **3:**663
 South Africa, **1:**430, 764, 765–66, 767–75;
   5:616
   "society" bands, **1:**770
 Spain, **8:**593
 Surinam, **2:**509
 Sweden, **8:**437, 445–46
 Switzerland, **8:**688, 698
 tango's influence on, **3:**521
 Tanzania, **1:**644–45
 Thailand, **4:**96
 Third Stream, **3:**335, 583, 612
 use of didjeridu, **9:**397
 Wales, **8:**356
 Western-Indian collaborations, **5:**561, 584
 white performers of, **3:**578
 women performers of, **3:**95, 96
 women's performance of, **8:**201
 Yukon, **3:**1278
Jazz Dazzlers Orchestra, **1:**774, 775
Jazz Duvergé (musical group), **2:**890
Jazz Epistles (musical group), **1:**774
Jazz des Jeunes (musical group), **2:**98, 890, 892;
   3:803, 805
Jazz Maniacs (musical group), **1:**770, 771, 774
Jazz Masters Fellowships, **3:**301
Jazzmatazz (musical group), **3:**699
Jazz Messengers (musical group), **1:**779;
   3:660
Jazz Singer (film), **3:**196, 262, 938
Jazzy Jeff, **3:**699, 714
Jazzy M, **3:**691
J. Dufour (firm), **9:**10
Jean-Baptiste, Nemours, **2:**98, 892; **3:**803
Jean le Précurseur (Couture), **3:**1149
Jean Paul Sartre Experience (musical group),
   9:169
Jean, Wyclef, **3:**807
"Jeanie with the Light Brown Hair" (Foster),
   3:187, *187*, 547
Jeanne (de Tourdonnet), **3:**200
"Jeden Morgen geht die Sonne auf" (Marx), **8:**661
Jefferson Airplane (musical group), **3:**318, 552;
   4:885
Jefferson, Blind Lemon, **3:**524, 644, 707
Jefferson, Marshall, **3:**690
Jefferson, Randolph, **3:**595
Jefferson, Thomas, **3:**22, 295, 595; **8:**186
Jeffery, Peter, **6:**20
Jeffreys, Herb, **3:**743
Jehai people, **4:**560
Jehin-Prume, Frantz, **3:**1181
Jekyll, Walter, **2:**913
Jelly's Last Jam (musical), **3:**622
Jemec, Franciska, **8:**136
Jenaer Liederbuch, **8:**651
Jenček, Ljuba, **8:**921
Jenkins, Carol, **2:**675, 679
Jenkins, Travis, **2:**679
Jenness, Diamond, **3:**381; **9:**153, 479
Jennings, Tom, **3:***1112*
Jennings, Waylon, **3:**81, 520
Jensen, Jens Kristian, **8:***461*
Jepparov-*bagsy*, Sakhy, **6:**976

Jerábek, Bedřich, **8:**729
"Jersey," **3:**1190
Jerú culture, **2:**453
Jerusalem Music Center, **6:**1030
Jerusalem Music School, **6:**1025
"Jesous Ahatonhia" (carol), **3:**1178
Jesse Bias and the Taotao Tano Dancers, **9:**160
Jessye, Eva, **3:**535, 577, 606, 607, 608
Jesuit order
 in Argentina, **2:**250–51
 in Bolivia, **2:**137–38, 283–84
 in Brazil, **2:**301–2, 334
 in Chile, **2:**366
 in Colombia, **2:**396
 in Ecuador, **2:**417, 419, 421
 in Goa, **5:**257
 Guaraní culture and, **2:**199–200, 202, 453
 instruments introduced by, **2:**32
 in Japan, **7:**724
 in Mexico, **2:**582, 584, 588–89, 590, 599,
   600
 in North America, **3:**23, 390, 392, 484–85,
   848–49, 1056, 1063, 1074, 1108,
   1147
 in Paraguay, **2:**453, 463
 in Philippines, **4:**841–42, 868
 role in musical enculturation, **2:**69
 role in music education, **2:**112, 396
 in South America, **2:**23, 36–37
 in Uruguay, **2:**511
Jesuit Relations, **3:**23, 392, 485
Jesus Christ Superstar (Lloyd Webber), **3:**198,
   545; **8:**219
"Jesus Loves Me" (Bradbury), **3:**533
Jetarin Watthanasin, **4:**100
Jeter, Leonard, **3:**619
Jethro Tull (musical group), **6:**250; **8:**215, 369
Jets (musical group), **9:**55
Jeunesse d'aujourd'hui (television show), **3:**1158
Jewish-Americans/Canadians, **3:**530, 933–44,
   1057, 1074, 1077; **6:**600. *See also*
   Judaism
 Ashkenazic, **3:**12, 934, 1077, 1078
 dances of, **3:**213
 discrimination against, **3:**13
 Hasidim, **3:**942, 944; **10:**127–33
 Iranian, **3:**1031
 klezmer music, **3:**325, 530, 934, 938–39,
   941–42
 in Manitoba, **3:**343
 Sephardic, **3:**847, 934, 940, 942–43, 1077,
   1171–75
 Syrian, **3:**513, 943, 1029; **10:**69–71, 72–73,
   74–75
 twentieth-century immigrants, **3:**175
 women's roles, **3:**98, 940–41
Jewish Cantillation and Song in the Isle of Djerba
   (Lachmann), **6:**523–25, 1058
Jewish Choir (Helsinki), **8:**487
Jewish Folk Choir (Winnipeg), **3:**1090
Jewish Iraqi Musical Tradition (Shiloah), **6:**1066
Jewish Musical Traditions (Shiloah), **6:**1065
Jewish Music Center (Betha-Tefutsot),
   6:1063–64
Jewish Music in Its Historical Development
   (Idelsohn), **6:**1058

Jewish Music Research Center (Jerusalem), **6:**1037, 1062–63
Jewish National and University Library (Jerusalem), **6:**524; **8:**266–67
Jewish people, **8:**11, 12, 17, 26, 247. *See also* Israel; Jewish-Americans/Canadians; Judaism; klezmer music
   Algerian, **6:**1030, 1044
   Ashkenazi, **6:**199–200, 202, 203–4, 261, 526, 1013, 1015, 1016, 1018, 1024–25, 1065, 1070
     in Europe, **8:**248, 250, 253, 258, 262
     in North America, **3:**12, 934, 1077, 1078
   Azerbaijani, **6:**1016
   Balkan communities, **6:**1060, 1071
   bar mitzvah ceremony, **8:**143
   in Bosnia-Hercegovina, **8:**962, 967, 968
   Bukharan, **6:**905, 916, 919–20
   Bulgarian, **6:**1030; **8:**903
   in Caribbean, **2:**792, 793
   from Caucasus region, **6:**1016, 1018
   Central Asian, **6:**899, 1018, 1031, 1071
   in Costa Rica, **2:**704
   in Curaçao, **2:**927, 931
   in Dominican Republic, **2:**847
   Egyptian, **6:**1030
   in England, **8:**326, 336
   Ethiopian, **6:**1031–32
   ethnic issues, **8:**262–63
   European history of, **8:**248–49
   European populations of, **8:**11
   in Finland, **8:**487
   folk music of, **8:**252, 257, 258, 261, 263
   gender roles, **8:**261
   in Georgia, **8:**840
   in Germany, **8:**660
   in Greece, **8:**1023
   in Hawai‘i, **9:**100
   history of music, **8:**263–65
   in Hungary, **8:**736
   instrumental music of, **8:**257–61
   Iraqi, **6:**12, 263, 417, 1016, 1017, 1023, 1024, 1071
   in Jamaica, **2:**901
   Judeo-Hispanic ballads, **8:**23, 254, 266, 596
   Judeo-Spanish, **6:**116, 526, 1035–36, 1037, 1042
   Karaite, **6:**1032
   in Kerala, **5:**948–49
   Kurdish, **6:**203, 261, *263*
   in Lithuania, **8:**509
   Maghribi, **6:**1035–44
   medieval scholarship, **6:**15, 16
   Mediterranean communities, **6:**1060
   Moroccan, **6:**203, 261, 1016, 1017, *1018*, 1023, 1030, 1036–44, 1044
   music of, in Europe, **8:**248–67
   in North Africa, **6:**431–32, 434, 1035–44
   Oriental, **6:**202, 261, 1013, 1015, 1016–18, 1023, 1030, 1057–58, 1070, 1071
   Persian, **6:**203, 261, 1016, 1024, 1062
   in Poland, **8:**701
   as professional musicians in Muslim countries, **6:**12, 304, 313, 434, 470, 503, 506, 565, 828, 899, 1043, 1044
   Purim play, **8:**141, 251, 261

   religious music of, **6:**1047–54; **8:**249–51, 263–64
   research on music of, **6:**22, 1036–37, 1057–67; **8:**265–67; **10:**158–66
   in Romania, **8:**886
   in Russia, **8:**767, 771, 772
   Russian, **6:**1017–18, 1024
   Samaritan, **6:**1032, 1062, 1065
   Sephardi, **6:**58, 117, 195, 199–200, 201–2, 204, 206, 434, 1013, 1015, 1017, 1035–36, 1038, 1063, 1065–66, 1071, 1072
     in Europe, **8:**195, 248, 253–54, 258, 262–63, 266, 267, 962, 967, 968, 1011
     in North America, **3:**847, 934, 940, 942–43, 1077, 1171–75
   in Serbia, **8:**952
   in South America, **2:**83–84, 89
   in Spain, **8:**588
   in Surinam, **2:**503
   in Syria, **6:**226, 544, 565, 566
   Tunisian, **6:**431, 523–31, 1036–44, 1039, 1044, 1058, 1060
   Turkish, **6:**57–58, 115, 117, 195, 1060, 1071
   in Ukraine, **8:**810, 820, 821
   vocal genres of, **3:**513, 943; **6:**202, 1020; **8:**131, 252–57, 261
   Yemenite, **6:**205, 261, 263, 264, *264*, 265–66, 649, 1016, 1017, 1018, 1023, 1024, 1030, 1047–54, 1064, 1065, 1071
Jewish Theological Seminary (New York), **6:**1060
Jew's harps (also jawharps; jaw's harps; mouth harps)
   Ainu people, **7:***785*, 787
   aman huur, **7:**1013, 1015–16
   amplification of, **3:**241
   angkuoch, **4:**166, 205
   Arctic regions, **3:**375
   Argentina, **2:**254
   aruding, **4:**924
   ata, **4:**540
   awedeng, **4:**914
   begenggong, **4:**615
   berimbak, **4:**820
   bibaw (also *sturmant*), **8:**348
   bijambò, **8:**640
   bungkau, **4:**834
   Bunun people, **10:**28
   chang, **5:**781, 783, 812, 813–14, 831
   chang-kobuz, **6:**902
   changko'uz, **5:**812
   chau, **4:**541–42
   China, **7:**417, 491, *491*, 492
   Corsica, **8:**572
   cultural origins of, **4:**11
   dapchang, **5:**783
   Denmark, **8:**454
   distribution of, **4:**58–59
   drimba, **8:**876
   drumlica (also *drumelca*; *brnica*), **8:**917
   drymba, **8:**816
   Europe, **8:**143, 169, *170*
   European description of Pacific, **9:**36
   genggong, **4:**754, 767
   gengon, **4:**567

   Germany, **8:**651, 654, 656
   ginggong, **4:**619
   ginggung, **4:**622, 623, 627
   giwong, **4:**919
   gue gueq, **7:**511, 514
   harmonic structures of, **10:**28
   hun, **4:**318
   Hungary, **8:**743
   Ireland, **8:**385
   Italian performance of, **3:**864
   Italy, **8:**609, 615
   Japanese-Americans, **3:**969
   junggotan, **4:**834
   juring, **4:**627
   juring rangguin, **4:**567
   karinding, **4:**701, 717, *718*
   khomus, **6:**902, 981, 985, 986
   Kmhmu people, **4:**547
   knobe besi, **4:**797
   knobe oh, **4:**797
   kubing, **4:**886, 904–5, 924
   kulaing, **4:**904–5
   kumbing, **4:**924
   kuohuang, **7:**111, 527, *528*
   Low Countries, **8:**526
   morchang, **5:**641
   morsing, **5:**222–23, 235, 358
   mūhchang, **5:**692
   mukkuri, **7:**787
   ncas, **4:**552–53
   ncas (also *nja*; *guimbard*), **3:**1005
   nggunggi, **4:**791
   Nivkhi people, **7:**788
   onnat, **4:**919
   Ontario, **3:**1189
   Orang Asli people, **4:**587
   Québec, **3:**1075
   rangoyd, **4:**567
   rangun, **4:**567
   ribeba, **8:**615
   ruding (also *geruding*), **4:**834
   rural areas, **4:**7
   Sardinia, **8:**627
   scacciapensieri, **8:**615
   shang-qobyz, **6:**956
   Siberia, **7:**1029
   slober, **4:**767
   Southeast Asia, **4:**161, 596
   tebe, **4:**802
   tong, **4:**834, 835
   tromba degli zingari, **8:**615
   trompa (also *birimbao*), **2:**251, 528
   trompe, **2:**359, 366
   trump, **8:**366
   trunfa, **8:**615
   u cha, **4:**536
   Uilta people, **7:**788
   ulibao, **4:**919
   Vietnam, **4:**534
   yusap, **2:**750
   zampogna, **8:**36
Jeyifo, Biodun, **1:**409
Jež, Jakob, **8:**921
Jhanak Jhanak Payal Baje (film), **5:**493–94
Jharia, Kamala, **5:**855
Ji Liankang, **7:**137

Jian Jun, **7:**142
Jian Xianwei, **7:**185
Jiang Baishi, **7:**125
Jiang Dingxian, **7:**339
Jiang Fengzhi, **7:**177
Jiang Jianhua, **7:**177
Jiang Keqian, **7:**132
Jiang Kui, **7:**132
Jiang Mingdun, **7:**156
Jiang Qing, **7:**63, 90, 102, 306, 349, 388
Jiang Semin, **7:**431
Jiang Wenye, **7:**346–47
Jiang Yuequan, **7:**264
Jiangjun deshengling (*Zhedong luogu* piece), **7:**196
Jiang jun ling (*culuogu* piece), **7:**197
Jiang jun ling (*qupai* melody), **7:**233
Jiang jun ling (*yangqin* piece), **7:**180
Jiangnanchun (Lu), **7:**185
Jiangnan sizhu. See ensembles, musical
Jiannaisi (*jialing* piece), **7:**480
Jiao wo ruhe bu xiang ta (Zhao), **7:**346
Jiaoxiang (periodical), **7:**141
Jicaque-Tolupán culture, **2:**739
Jicarilla Apache, **3:**431
Jie, Xia emperor, **7:**406
Jie people, **1:**599
Jie'r ge (folk song), **7:**154
Jieshi diao youlan (*qin* piece), **7:**123, 132
jig, **3:**231, 825, 836, 843, 855. *See also* gigue
   African influences on, **3:**595–96
   in Canada, **3:**1075, 1081, 1125, 1164, 1178, 1190, 1191
   in England, **8:**330, 331
   Inuit, **3:**213
   in Ireland, **8:***381*, 382, 387
   in Low Countries, **8:**524
   Métis, **3:**407–10
   in Scotland, **8:**367
"Jigi Dou" (Inconnu), **3:**1280
Jijón, Inés, **2:**431
Jikki, **5:**421
Jilālī, **6:**270
Jilguero del Huascarán, el, **2:**484
Jim Crow laws, **3:**637, 651, 656, 667
Jiménez Borja, Arturo, **2:**35, 487, 501
Jiménez, Carlos "La Mona," **2:**274–75, *276*, 277, 279–80
Jiménez, Cha-Cha, **3:**780
Jiménez, José, **3:**740
Jiménez, José Alfredo, **2:**621; **3:**722
Jiménez, Leonardo "Flaco," **3:**751, 776–77
Jiménez, Manuel "Canario," **3:**799
Jiménez, Santiago "Flaco," **3:**775–76
Jiménez, Santiago, Jr., **3:**776
Jimi Hendrix Experience (musical group), **3:**710
Jimmy Dee and the Chamorritas, **9:**160
Jin dynasty, **7:**517
   Daoism in, **7:**312
   music in, **7:**88
   qingshang yue genre, **7:**41, 407
Jin (Jurchen) dynasty, **7:**29, 31, 32, 321, 517, 807
Jin Qinjiang, **7:**725
Jin Wah Sing Society (Edmonton), **3:**1247
Jin Wah Sing Society (Vancouver), **3:**1261, 1262, 1265

Jin Zuli, **7:**224
Jiŋama (Irumu performer), **9:***571*
Jinder, Åsa, **8:**446
Jindřich, Jindřich, **8:**725
Jing, Zhou king, **7:**115, 117
Jing Fang, **7:**118, 119
jingju. See Peking opera
Jing people, **7:**447, 485–92
Jingpo people, **7:**485–92
Jinling College, **7:**398
Jinnah, Mohammad Ali, **5:**858
Jin ping mei (Chinese novel), **7:**403
Jinshang tianhua (*sizhu* piece), **7:**236
Jinuo people, **7:**485–92
Jinzi jing (*qupai* melody), **7:**233
al-Jirari, Abbas, **6:**495, 496
Jirikaranani, **1:**501–9
Jiu Mipangjiacuo, **7:**473
Jiuge (Tan), **7:**351
Jiugong dacheng naubeici gongpu (collection), **7:**132
Jívaro culture, **2:**413. *See also* Shuar culture
"Jive Jive Pakistan," **5:**746
Jive Records, **3:**714
"Jive Turkey" (Ohio Players), **3:**681
Joachim, Otto, **3:**1151
Joanne, Chris, and Charlie (musical group), **3:**970
João, king of Portugal, **2:**242, 245, 304
Jobim, Antônio Carlos, **2:**108, 317–18
Jobson, Eddie, **3:**345
Jobson, Richard, **3:**593
Jocano, F. Landa, **4:**881
Jöde, Fritz, **8:**659
Jodeci, **3:**715
Joel, Billy, **7:**1020
Joest, W., **4:**812
Joffrey Ballet, **3:**852
Jog, V. G., **5:**207
Jogī caste, **5:**345, 405, 488, 640, 643, *644*, 671, *671*
Jogira sect, **5:**471
Joglekar, Archana, **5:***478*
Johan, Sikander, **5:***283*
Johansen, Bruce E., **3:**497
Johansen, Hans, **8:**463
Johanson, Selma, **3:**1089
Johansson, Jan, **8:**157, 446
Johansson, Lars-Jonas, **8:***301*
"John Brown's Body" (American folk song), **3:**308, 521; **7:**375
John Church Company, **3:**260
John, Elton, **7:**1020; **8:**215; **9:**179
"John Hardy" (ballad), **3:**47, 524
"John Henry" (ballad), **3:**47, 524
John Oxley Library (Brisbane), **9:**959
"John Tyler's Lamentation" (Appo), **3:**604
Johnny Albert Band, **9:**60
Johnny and the Self Abusers, **8:**369
Johnny and the Shamrocks, **8:**679
Johnny Belinda (Moore and Fenwick), **3:**199
"Johnny B. Goode" (Berry), **3:**709
Johnny Moore's Three Blazers, **3:**669
Johnson, Aili Kolehmainen, **3:**873
Johnson, Billy, **3:**618
Johnson, Blind Willie, **3:**631

Johnson, Bunk, **3:**568
Johnson, Charles, **3:**579; **10:**144, 149–50
Johnson, Edward, **3:**1186
Johnson, Ella, **3:**646
Johnson, Francis "Frank," **3:**564, 603–4, *604*
Johnson, George Washington, **3:**706
Johnson, Guy B., **3:**575–76
Johnson, Hall, **3:**536, 577, 606, 607, 619, 621
Johnson, Harold "Rankin Scroo," **9:**166
Johnson, Howard, **2:**913
Johnson, James, **8:**18, 367, 373
Johnson, James (African religious leader), **1:**403
Johnson, James Weldon, **3:**192, 576, 607, 608, 618, 650, 706
Johnson, J. deGraft, **1:**216
Johnson, John W., **1:**498
Johnson, J. Rosamond, **3:**576, 577, *577*, 606, 608, 618–19, 650, 706
Johnson, Lew, **3:**616
Johnson, Lil, **3:**645
Johnson, Lonnie, **3:**644
Johnson, Louise, **3:**104
Johnson, Lyndon B., **3:**298, 316
Johnson, Merline, **3:**645
Johnson, Osa H., **9:**844
Johnson, Osokale Tejumade, **1:**403
Johnson, Pete, **3:**647
Johnson, Ragnar, **9:**990
Johnson, R. K., **9:**969
Johnson, Robert, **3:**316, 329, 356, 524, 645, 707; **8:**367
Johnson, Samuel, **1:**403
Johnson, Scott, **3:**255
Johnson, Taj, **3:**1281
Johnson, Tommy, **3:**644–45
Johnston, Calum, **8:***363*, 371
Johnston, Kwesi, **10:**32
Johnston, Thomas F., **3:**381, 392
Johnstons (musical group), **8:**392
Joint Nordic Saami Institute, **8:**428
Joke (Kundera), **8:**730
Jola people, **1:**443, 445–46
Jolly Orchestra, **1:**380
Jolof states, **1:**444
Jolson, Al, **3:**12, 196, 262, 544, 938
Jolt (musical group), **8:**369
Joly, Luz Graciela, **2:**783
Joma Khan Qader, **5:**806
Jōmon period, instruments of, **7:**79
Jonassen, Jon Tikivanotau Michael, **9:**288, *902*, 972
Jones, Arthur Morris, **1:**51, 362, 671, 711; **10:**111, 112, 116, 120, 139
   Indonesian theories of, **1:**55, 605, 782–83
   transcription methodology of, **1:**47, 55–56, 154, 156, 157, 254
Jones, Betty, **9:**109
Jones, Brian, **3:**336
Jones, Chris, **3:**684–85
Jones, Cliff, **3:**199
Jones, Curtis, **3:**645
Jones, Edward, **8:**185, *347*, 348, 352
Jones, Elvin, **3:**662
Jones, George, **3:**81
Jones, Grace, **1:**422
Jones, Gwyneth, **3:**999

Jones, Jo, **3:**658

Jones, LeRoi. *See* Baraka, Amiri

Jones, Marshall, **3:**681, 684, 685

Jones, Oliver, **3:**1077, 1107, 1169

Jones, Pedro K., **2:**635

Jones, Quincy, **3:**203, 715

Jones, Rocky, **3:**691

Jones, Sissieretta, **3:**617, 618

Jones, Stephen, **7:**87

Jones, Tom, **4:**884; **8:**392

Jones, Trevor A., **9:**418, 976, 986

Jones, Sir William, **5:**49, 50, 561

Jongleur Songs of Old Québec (Barbeau and Beck), **3:**1165

Jonny spielt auf (Křenek), **8:**659

Jónsson, Benedict, **8:***403*

Jónsson, Jóhann Björn, **8:**407

Jónsson, Sigurður Rúnar, **8:***406*, 407

Jónsson, Sveinn, **8:**407–8

Joplin, Scott, **3:**12, 548, *549*, 650, 651, 705, 706

Jordan, **6:**409, 413. *See also* Mashriq

Jordán, Esteban (Steve Jordan), **3:**776, 777–78

Jordan, Joe, **3:**608

Jordan, Louis, **3:**668, 708, 742

Jordan, Nathaniel, **2:**445

Jordan, Vic, **3:***159*

Jordania, Mindia, **8:**846

Jorge, Bernarda, **2:**862

Jørgensen, Sven, **8:**465

Jorgi Quartett, **8:**711

Joropo y Sus Andanzas, El (Salazar), **2:**544

Jorrín, Enrique, **2:**833, 835

José de la Virgen, Father, **4:**841

José José, **2:**103; **3:**746

Josef, Aşıq, **6:**845

Joseph, Holy Roman emperor, **8:**271

Joseph (Coker), **1:**402

Joseph and His Brethren (Sternberg), **6:**1027

Josephs, Noel, **3:**243

Josephson, J. A., **8:**447

Joshi, Bhimsen, **5:**255

Joshibuwa, **5:**461–62

Josif (monk), **8:**904

Joslin, René, **3:**776

Josquin des Prez, **8:**73, 75, 518

Jost Van Dyke, **2:**968

Jothinatha, Mahadeva, **5:**970

Jouad, Hassan, **6:**497

Jourdan, Christine, **9:**962

Journal of the African Music Society, **1:**643

Journal of American Folklore, **3:**159

Journal of the Folk-Song Society, **8:**327, 334

Journal of the Indian Musicological Society, **5:**58

Journal of the International Folk Music Council, **8:**20

Journal of the Irish Folk Song Society, **8:**394

Journal of the Music Academy, Madras, **5:**58, 212

Journal of Music in China, **7:**136

Journal of Research in Music Education, **3:**286

Journal of the Society of African Music, **1:**160

Journal of the Welsh Folk-Song Society, **8:**346, 353

Journey to the West (Chinese novel), **7:**308

Jovanotti, Lorenzo, **8:**620

Jovanović, Jarko, **8:**279

Joventango (Uruguay), **2:**519

Joyce, James, **8:**378

Joyce, P. W., **8:**393

"Joyeux Paris" (Waldteufel), **8:**641

JPP (musical group), **8:***478*

J.S.D. (musical group), **8:**372

Jü Xixian, **7:**387

Juan de la Concepción, Father Juan, **4:**858

Juan de la Cruz Band, **4:**885

Juan de San Miguel, **2:**577

Juan de Santa Marta, Father, **4:**841

Juana Inés de la Cruz, Sor, **2:**113

Juárez Toledo, Manuel, **2:**736

Juarros, Domingo, **2:**725

juba, **3:**595, 802

Jubal, **8:**259

Jubany, Giuseppe, **8:**1003

Jubilee Records, **3:**351

Judaism, **2:**61; **3:**5, 120, 530; **5:**480, 509; **8:**11. *See also* Jewish Americans/Canadians; Jewish people

aesthetic views of, **8:**257–58

Central Asia, **6:**936

denominations of, **3:**939, 940–41

emotional expression in, **3:**120

Ethiopia, **1:**604

Hasidism, **6:**200, 202, 1024, 1060, 1065, 1071; **8:**249, 251, 254, 257

identity issues in, **3:**514

influence on early Christian music, **6:**19–20

Israel, **6:**199–206

Kerala, **5:**929, 948–49

liturgical music, **3:**934, 939–41, 1171–72; **6:**22, 195, 201–2, 1036, 1037–39, 1047–54, 1065

Middle East, **6:**3

Orthodox, **6:**199–206

rabbinical opinions on music, **6:**15, 205–6, 371

Reform movement, **6:**199

seasonal rituals of, **8:**250

Temple Beth-El, **3:**127

Turkey, **6:**57–58

use of American tunes in Simhat Torah ritual, **3:**514

views on music, **6:**19–20

women rabbis and cantors, **3:**98, 940–41

Judas Priest (musical group), **3:**358; **8:**215

Judds (musical group), **3:**81

Jüeh-chih tribe, **6:**965

Jugar con Fuego (zarzuela), **4:**856

Jugrue Quawal, **5:**591

Juice (film), **3:**715

Juilliard Quartet, **3:**175, 295, 538, 1210

Juilliard School of Music (New York), **3:**15, 175

jùjú, **1:**322, 358, 359, 364, 377, 423, 472, 473, 477, 478–83, 485; **2:**409, 410; **3:**338; **8:**232

Julien, Pauline, **3:**1156

Juluka, **1:**430, 779

"Jump Jim Crow," **3:**182

Junaro, Emma, **2:**298

Junayd, Shaykh, **6:**179

al-Jundī, 'Uthmān, **6:**569

Jung, Angelika, **6:**17

Jung, Carl Gustav, **10:**124

Jungar state, **7:**1004, 1007, 1014

"Jungle Boogie" (Kool and the Gang), **3:**681, 711

Jungle Rhythm Boys (musical group), **9:**28

Junior Unbelievers (musical group), **9:**154

"Jupiter Wise" (Parsons), **3:**1072

Jurado, Antonio de Torres, **1:**351

Jurchen people, **7:**27, 29, 30, 31, 32, 517, 807

Jürgens, Udo, **8:**679

Jurjāns, Andrejs, **8:**505, 506

Just Another Band from East L (Los Lobos), **3:**750

"Just Because" (Yankovic), **3:**902

"Just Behind the Times" (Harris), **3:**191

"Just Tell Them That You Saw Me" (Dresser), **3:**191

Juste, Farah, **2:**892; **3:**806

Justus, Domingo, **1:**355

Jutras, Monique, **8:**553

Juwo people, **9:**983

JVC/Smithsonian Video Anthology of Music and Dance of the Americas, **9:**48

JVC Video Anthology of World Music and Dance, **4:**134, 160–61; **7:**525; **9:**47–48

Ka Pao Her (Hmong shaman), **4:***554*

Ka'a, Keri, **9:**948–51

Ka'ai, Ernest, **3:**1049

Ka'ak, 'Uthmān, **6:**509

Kaalo, Hortto, **8:**289

Ka'au Crater Boys, **9:**164–65, 167

Kaa'ungken brothers, **9:**462–63, 464

Kabaivanska, Raina, **8:**890

Kabana people, **9:**614

Kabanova, Tatyana, **8:**778

Kabardian people, **8:**854–56

Kabasele, Joseph "Le Grand Kalle," **1:**386, 424

Kabeláč, Miloslav, **8:**729

Kabi Kabi people, **9:**430

Kabiosile (León), **3:**612

Kabir, Saint, **5:**471, 660, 671

bhajans of, **5:**253, 256, 724

Kabira sect, **5:**471

Kabra, Brij Bhushan, **5:**207

Kabu hinmoku (Ogawa), **7:**588

kabuki, **7:**6, 73, *74*, 533, *535*, 654, *654*, 655, 657–58, 657–61, 667

audiences for, **7:**774–75

dance scenes in, **7:**679–82

dissemination of, **7:**539

ensembles for, **7:**77, 654

female performers of, **7:**764

gidayû busi in, **7:**539, 657–58, 660, 675, 944

hayasi in, **7:**657, 659, 660, 671–72, 680, 684

influence on *kumi odori*, **7:**789–90

influence on *sibai uta*, **7:**693

instruments in, **7:**654, 660–61, 712

ma concept in, **7:**553

Meizi patronage of, **7:**777

min'yô in, **7:**601

movement in, **7:**59, 63, 64–65

music in, **7:**77, 657–59

nagauta in, **7:**657, 659, 660, 671, 679–82

narrator in, **7:**75

notation for, **7:**538, 659–60

onnagata actors, **7:**764–65

origins of, **7:**536, 657

plays by Chikamatsu (Tikamatu), **7:**668, 669

kabuki (*continued*)
    source materials for, **7**:589
    zyôruri styles in, **7**:657–59
Kabuki Scenes (Tillis), **3**:612
Kabuki Theater (Japan), **7**:774
Kabungsuan, Muhamad, **4**:890
Kabwa people, **1**:642
Kabyle people, **6**:273, 274–75, 276, 299,
        300–301, 307. *See also* Berber peoples
Kachamba, Daniel, **10**:118, *119*
Kachamba, Donald, **1**:296; **10**:*119*, 120
Kachin people, **4**:399, 537
Kachok people, **4**:156
Kachulev, Ivan, **8**:907
Kadavu (Fiji), **9**:773, 774, 776, 973
Kadazan (Dusun) people, **4**:51, 824, 828–29
Kadensho (Zeami), **7**:640
Kader, Cheb, **8**:239
Kadhalan (film), **5**:545
Kadiag, Ba-I, **4**:907–8
Kadman, Gurit, **6**:1059
Kaebŏlt'ŏ ŭi pangge kumŏngjiptŭl (Lee), **7**:956
Kaebyŏk (Kim), **7**:959
Kaech'ŏnbu (Kim), **7**:953
Kaeppler, Adrienne L., **3**:221; **9**:307, 313, 316,
        317, 915, 969, 976, 979
Kaf, Le Rwa, **5**:609
kâfi, **5**:12, 753–54, 756–57, 759, 772
Kafka, Franz, **10**:111
Kafui, **1**:223
Kafwale, Sanele, **1**:730
Kagaba culture. *See* Kogi culture
Kagok wŏllyu (Pak/An), **7**:856, 921
Kagoro people, **1**:289
Kaguru people, **1**:125
Kagyadehû busi (*gozen hû* piece), **7**:793
Kahar people, **5**:722
Kahauanu Lake Trio, **9**:164
Kahia (Halia performer), **9**:640
Kahle, Sigrid Nyberg, **5**:487
Kahn, Gane, **5**:*477*
Kaho, Tu'imala, **9**:136, 793
Kahukōkā (Māori composer), **9**:941–42
Kai Archipelago, **4**:812, 813, 819–20
Kaiabi culture, **2**:146
Kaibab Paiutes, **3**:435
Kaidô tôsei (Nobutoki), **7**:733
Kaimen (shawm band piece), **7**:203, 236
Kaimiloa Expedition, **9**:24
Kaipat family, **9**:160
Kaipo, Joe, **9**:390
Kaiser, Eva-Maria, **8**:676
Kaiserin-Augusta-Fluss Expedition, **9**:479
Kaiyuan Li (Confucian text), **7**:335
Kaja, Aloni (Basoga lyrist), **1**:304
Kajang people, **4**:824
    instruments of, **4**:829, 831, 834
    music and dance of, **4**:826, 827, 836–37
    singing of, **4**:825
Kajfeš, Davor, **8**:157
Kakala, Sofele, **9**:204
Kakaṛ tribe, **5**:791
Kakhetian people, **8**:827–28, 841, 843
Kakinoki Gorô, **7**:569
Kakka, Majid, **6**:284, *284*
Kakoma, George, **1**:222

Kakyô (Zeami), **7**:552, 553, 641
Kala Academy (Panjim), **5**:740
Kalagan people, **4**:922
Kalahari people (Bushmen; Africa), **8**:36
Kalai Kovil Academy (Toronto), **3**:1216
Kalākaua, king of Hawai'i, **3**:219; **9**:66, 127,
    128, 133, 136, 390, 919
Kalakshetra (Madras academic institution),
    5:104, 213
Kalanduyan, Danongan, **3**:1026
Kalānidhi (treatise), **5**:45
Kalapalo culture, **2**:21
Kalāvant group, **5**:171, 379, 409, 476, 641
Kalbeliā people, **5**:647, *648*
Kälberer, Oliver, **7**:1020
Kaldayakov, Shamshi, **6**:961
Kalderash Roma, **8**:276, 288
Kale (musical group), **8**:276
Kaleh, Nimeh, **1**:503, 505, 506
Kalelakar, **5**:632
Kalender, Sabahattin, **6**:775
Kalenjin people, **1**:624
Kalevala (epic), **3**:873, 1196; **8**:*187*, 476–77,
    488
Kalff, Gerrit, **8**:534
Kalgi-turra group, **5**:470
Kalhana, **5**:689
Kali (deity), **5**:607, 617
    worship of, **5**:247, 249, 461, 503, 846, 847,
        855, 876, 877–78
Kaliai people, **9**:609–10
Kalibobo Bamboo Band, **9**:139
Kālidās (film), **5**:543
Kalidasa, **5**:408, 484, 509, 721
Kalihi-Palama Culture and Arts Society, **9**:105
Kalijaga, Sunan, **4**:686
Kalimantan, **4**:48, 823–37. *See also* Borneo;
    specific peoples
Kalimba Kalimba (musical group), **3**:1170
Kalina (Galibi) culture, **2**:164, 435–36, 437, 668
Kalinak, Kathryn, **3**:204
Kalind (musical group), **5**:428
Kalinga people, **4**:914, 920. *See also* Tinggian
    people
    instrumental music of, **4**:916–17, 918–19, 919
    music of, **4**:878
    vocal music of, **4**:920
Kalinger dynasty, **5**:721
Kaḷḷar caste, **5**:557
Kallas, Oskar, **8**:498
Kalle, Aruna Narayan, **3**:1216, *1216*
Kallinatha, **5**:45, 314
Kallmann, Helmut, **3**:32, 143, 144, 145, 1067,
    1108
Kalmikoff, Michael, **3**:1270
Kalmyk people, **6**:966; **7**:1003–20; **8**:11, 767,
    772
Kaloo Qawwal, **5**:426
Kalpa Sūtra (manuscript), **5**:312
Kalthoum, Oum, **3**:338
Kaltsas, Nikos, **8**:*206*
Kaltŭng (Kim), **7**:959
Kaluli people, **9**:511
    audience-performer interaction, **9**:284–85
    ceremonial spaces, **9**:512
    dance of, **9**:350, 483, 484, 485

gisalo genre, **9**:189, 485
    language and music, **9**:320, 326, 336
    music theory of, **9**:514
    research on, **9**:976
    songs of, **9**:188
    status of composers, **9**:354
Kalyanji-Anandji (director duo), **5**:427, 537
Kalyanpur, Suman, **5**:420, 538
Kalyi Jag (musical group), **8**:276
Kam Kee Yong, **4**:129
Kam, Ruşen Ferîd, **6**:117
Kamae, Eddie, **9**:42, 164
Kamaka, Samuel, **9**:390
Kamakawio'ole, Israel, **9**:166, 167
Kamakshi (deity), **5**:227, 269
Kamakura period
    music theory in, **7**:547
    okina ceremony in, **7**:629
    theater in, **7**:653
Kamal, Abu Hena Mostafa, **5**:858
Kamāl, Ḥusayn, **6**:238
Kamalam, Tiruvarur, **5**:386
Kamano people, **9**:526–33
Kamara, Musa (*imam*), **1**:*331*, 343, 344
Kamara, Varni (*imam*), **1**:342
Kāmar caste, **5**:647
Kāmasūtra (Vatsyayana), **5**:407, 408, 551
Kama Wosi: Music in the Trobriand Islands (film),
    9:50
Kamba, Polo, **1**:669
Kambite, Andre "Damoiseau," **1**:386
Kambiu String Band, **9**:151–52
Kamehameha I, king of Hawai'i, **9**:38, 132, 275,
    914
Kamehameha V, king of Hawai'i, **9**:132
Kamehameha Schools (Hawai'i), **9**:275–77,
    299–300, 919
Kameol (Chuuk choreographer), **9**:*959*
Kami Kyôsuke, **7**:750
Kamien, Roger, **6**:1063, 1067
Kamieński, Łucjan, **8**:712
Kamikaze (Yamada), **7**:733
Kamisangô Yûkô, **7**:593
Kamitoni, Feke, **9**:130
Kamkam, **1**:356
Kamkar, Hooshang, **6**:751–52
Kammu people. *See* Kmhmu people
Kamo shrine (Kyôto), **7**:757
Kamockaja, Kacia, **8**:802
Kamocki, Aleś, **8**:801
Kampong Amber (Lee), **4**:523
Kampuchea. *See* Cambodia
Kamsa (deity), **5**:266
Kamu, Okko, **8**:485
Kamula people, **9**:483
Kanahele, Pualani Kanaka'ole, **3**:207
Kanak people, **9**:212, 213–14
Kanaka Dasa, **5**:266
Kanaka'ole, Edith, **3**:207
Kanaka'ole, Nalani, **3**:207; **9**:*201*
Kanaka'ole, Pualani, **9**:*201*
Kan'ami Kiyotsugu, **7**:629, 639, 640
Kananga people, **1**:119
Kanasiki kutibue (Japanese popular song), **7**:745
Kanazawa Masakata, **7**:595
Kanchan, **5**:592

Kancheli, Gia, **8:**844

Kanchni caste, **5:**476

Kanchwalla, Abdul Rahman, **5:**426

Kanda, Bata, **8:**951

Kandrian people, **9:**621

Kandy (kingdom), **5:**955
  dance traditions of, **5:**363, 490
  musical traditions of, **5:**957–58, 964

Kāne, Raymond, **9:**389, 1008

Kanem-Bornu kingdom, **1:**4

Kanetune Kiyosuke, **7:**592

Kang, Aminurta, **3:**224

Kang Chunhyŏk, **7:**967

Kang Chunil, **7:**967

Kang Hanyŏng, **7:**969

Kang, Hojoong, **7:**970

Kang Hyŏngju, **7:**900

Kang Kich'ang, **7:**962, 997

Kang Minsŏk, **7:**965

Kang Paekch'ŏn, **7:**915

Kang T'aehong, **7:**899, 915

Kang Xi, Qing emperor, **7:**206

Kangdongjiebu, **7:**478

Kangen ongi (treatise), **7:**547

Kanggangsullae (Kim), **7:**970

Kangnŭng Maehwajŏn (*p'ansori* story), **7:**899, 969

Kaniet Islands (Papua New Guinea), **9:**602

Kanikar caste, **5:**367

Kanite people, **9:**526–33

Kanjri group, **5:**476, 769

Kankanay people, **4:**914

Kannada Kuta, **5:**585

Kanoboism, **2:**189, 194

Kano Chronicle (manuscript), **1:**313

Kansa Indian nation, **3:**440

Kansanmusiikki Instituutti (Kaustinen), **8:**181, 481

Kansas
  Lindsborg, Swedish people in, **3:**871–72
  Mennonites in, **3:**1237
  Native American groups in, **3:**431, 440, 451
  Swedish people in, **3:**870–72
  Volga Germans in, **3:**890

Kantemiroğlu. *See* Cantemir, Demetrius

Kanté, Mory, **1:**419; **8:**232, 238, *239*

Kantor Salomon Sulzer und seiner Zeit (Avenary), **6:**1060

Kanum people, **9:**587

Kanŭn kil (Ri), **7:**960

Kanuri people, **1:**290–92, 447, 449

Kanyaka (martyr), **5:**898–99

Kanyakumari, A., **5:**161

Kanza (musical group), **3:**1170

Kanz al-tuḥaf (anon.), **6:**373, 395, 398, 399, 835

Kanze Motomasa, **7:**630, 641

Kanze Nobumitsu, **7:**630

Kanzintyô (*kabuki* piece), **7:***671*, 672

Kapalakiko Calendar of Hawaiian Events, **3:**1052

Kapela Domu Tańca, **8:**711

Kapelye (musical group), **3:**941

Kapena, **9:**167

Kaper, Bronislau, **9:**45

Kapinangan (Cayabyab), **4:**885

Kapingamarangi (Pohnpei State, FSM), **9:**715, 833, 836–38, 969
  history of, **9:**836

music and dance of, **9:**836–38
  sung poetry, **9:**327, 328–30

Kapirikitsa, Bulandisoni, **10:***119*

Kapleau, Philip, **3:**130

Kapon, Avram, **8:**968

Kapono, Henry, **9:**167, 1008

Kapoor, Mahendra, **5:**539

Kapp, Artur, **8:**497

Kappel, Johannes, **8:**497

Kapriman people, **9:**557, 560

Kapuge, Gunadas, **5:**424

Kaptori wa Kapsuni (Korean folk song), **7:**887

Karaca, Cem, **6:***243*, 243–45, 249–50

Karaca, Kâni, **6:**57

Karacaoğlan, **6:**765

Karachaevian people, **8:**850, 854, 856–59
  dance traditions of, **8:**858
  epic performance, **8:**851
  instruments, **8:**857
  research on music of, **8:**858–59
  vocal music of, **8:**856–59

Karachi Theater, **5:**487

Karadeniz, Ekrem, **6:**195, 772

Karády, Katalin, **8:**746

Karadžić, Vuk Stefanović, **8:**942, 954

Karagāttakkāraṅ (film), **5:**542

Karagounidhes, **8:**1013

Karagwe people, **1:**636

Karaïndrou, Eleni, **8:**1022

Karakalpak people, **6:**967
  epic songs, **6:**345
  Ramadan songs, **6:**941

Karakhanid dynasty, **7:**23, 30

Kara koyun (Turkish instrumental piece), **6:**11

Karamasani (deity), **5:**732

Karāmat-e mujrā (treatise), **5:**689–91, 693

Karāmī, Buṭrus, **6:**567

Karamojong people, **1:**599, 605

Kara-Murza, Khristofor, **6:**725

Karanga people, **1:**709

Karangu people, **1:**106

karaoke. *See* technology and music

Karapo (Buin musician), **9:**650

Karaponga, Mehau, **9:**909

Karasai-Qazi (epic), **6:**952

Karassery, M. N., **5:**947

Karatygin, Vyacheslav, **8:**783

Karavar people, **9:**188

Karawari people, **9:**557

Kardam, **6:**295

Kardanov, X., **8:**859

Kardaşlar (musical group), **6:**250

Kardec, Allan, **2:**344

Kardecism, **2:**344; **3:**784

Karelia, **8:**475. *See also* Finland; Russia
  instruments, research on, **8:**179
  laments, **8:**120, 132, 761
  musical traditions of, **8:**484, 488

Karelian people, **8:**475, 754
  in Finland, **8:**486
  instruments, **8:**774
  in Russia, **8:**772

Karen people, **4:**363, 528, 537, 543–46
  instruments of, **4:**545–46
  music research on, **4:**26

Karesau people, **9:**983

Kāretu, Tīmoti S., **9:**354–55, 949

Kariağdı, Cabbar, **6:**924, *924*

Karika, **9:**896

Karīmī, Maḥmūd, **6:**66, 67, 68, 70, 836, 866, 867

Karim, Makdum, **4:**890

Karīm, Muḥammad, **6:**236

Karjalainen, K. F., **8:**488

Karkar Island (Papua New Guinea), **9:**546, 561

Karkar people, **9:**560–61, 983

Karkoschka, Erhard, **4:**876

Karluq peoples, **7:**23

Karmenov, Zhanibek, **6:**955

Karnataka, **5:**866–87
  Bangalore
    cassette industry in, **5:**554
    public concerts in, **5:**212
  ceremonies, spirit possession, **5:**867, 886
  coastal regions, **5:**881–87
  dance traditions, **5:**361, 514–16
    yakṣagāna, **5:**104–5, 401, 486, *486*, 885–86
  devotional music of, **5:**259, 262, 265
  Dharwan district, *gīgī pada*, **5:**870, *871*
  geography of, **5:**866
  Hindustani influences in, **5:**104
  history of, **5:**866
  instruments, **5:**351
  Karnatak tradition in, **5:**89, 209, 230–32, 449
  map of, **5:***864*
  Mulubagilu, Purandara Dasa Festival, **5:**211
  music societies in, **5:**212, 270
  Mysore district
    ban on temple dancing, **5:**409
    court period in, **5:**89
    dance in, **5:**104–5, 401
    miniature painting in, **5:**300
    public concerts in, **5:**212
  population of, **5:**866
  princely states in, **5:**866
  regional music traditions in, **5:**866–68
  sabhā schools in, **5:**455
  Telugu-speakers in, **5:**889
  Tibetan culture in, **5:**709
  vocal music
    pada genres, **5:**868–70
    Tuluva genres, **5:**882–85

Karnatak (Karnatic) tradition, **5:**2. *See also jāvaḷi; kīrtana; kriti; padam; rāgam-tānam-pallavi; tillāna; varṇam*
  Andhra Pradesh, **5:**889–90
  concert performances in, **5:**384–85
  dance in, **5:**508–9
  development of, **5:**42, 45, 77, 246, 375
  effects of internationalization on, **5:**566–67
  English scholarship on, **5:**50
  fusion trends in, **5:**529, 544–45, 561
  hand gestures in, **5:**324
  history of, **5:**14, 15, 18
  influence on Orissan styles, **5:**732
  instrumental music, **5:**188, 209–35
  instruments of, **5:**350–58
  interaction with Hindustani tradition, **5:**47–48
  Kerala, **5:**929
  mallāri genre, **5:**234

Karnatak (Karnatic) tradition (*continued*)
North America, **3:**950, 951, 981, 983, 988–92, 1216; **5:**581
outside South Asia, **5:**210
periya mēļam ensemble, **5:**103, 323–24
raga, **5:**89–108 (*See also* raga *heading*)
recent developments in, **5:**232–35
relation to Kerala temple music, **5:**939–40
scale degrees in, **5:**67
scholarship on, **5:**52
social order in, **5:**383–95
songs in, **5:**40–41
sound recordings, **5:**57, 159–60, 213
supremacy of vocal music in, **5:**138, 322
svarajāti, **5:**228
svara kalpana improvisation in, **5:**98–99, 148, 218, 384
tala, **5:**138–61 (*See also* tala *heading*)
tālamālikā improvisation, **5:**215, 218
in Tamil Christian music, **5:**923–24
Tamil regional styles, **5:**906, 916
tani āvartanam, **5:**148, 158, 219, 223, 235, 356, 384, 940
as urban phenomenon, **5:**397–98
use in film music, **5:**543
vina in, **5:**307
violin in, **5:**338
vocal music, **5:**209–35
Western studies on, **5:**54–55
women's *vs.* men's performances of, **5:**103, 388–89
Karnika Devi (deity), **5:**733
Karok Indian nation, **3:**371, 412
Karoma, **1:**571
Karomatov, Faizula M., **6:**911
Karo people, **4:**607
Karon people, **9:**582
Karor, Amir, **5:**833–34
Karore people, **9:**617
Karp, Ivan, **10:**28
Kárpáti, János, **6:**487, 489
Karpeles, Maud, **1:**52; **3:**1256; **8:**19, 337
Karras, Simon, **8:**1017, 1025
Karsten, Rafael, **2:**419
Kartlian people, **8:**826, 827, 836, 840
Kartomi, Margaret, **4:**29, 603, 638, 639, 640, 701; **9:**256; **10:**52
Kartuli Ensemble, **8:**845
Karukaya (*sekkyô busi* piece), **7:**654
Karumulun (Solomon Islands), **9:**662–63
Karzhevsky, Hanina, **6:**1071
Kasagi Sizuko, **7:**745
Kasahara Kiyoshi, **7:**594
Kasai Akira, **7:**66
Kasā'ī, Ḥasan, **6:**866
Kasai people, **1:**217
Kasaipwalova, John, **9:**233, 234
Kasbi people. *See* Mīrāsī group
Kasena-Nankani people, **1:**109, 455–56
Kashf al-humūm wa-salwat al-maḥzūn (anon.), **6:**373
Kashf al-Mahjub (treatise), **5:**751, 755
Kashgar Song and Dance Troupe, **7:**445
Kashil, Kaya ruler, **7:**981
Kashinaua culture, **2:**128
Kashkin, Nikolai, **8:**783

Kashmir (region), **5:**682–95. *See also* Jammu and Kashmir; Northern Areas (Pakistan)
bhand-jashna theater in, **5:**485
geography of, **5:**682, 688–89
historical sources, **5:**688–95
history of, **5:**682
instruments in, **5:**189, 329, 335, 336, 339, 343–44, 345, 683–84, 688, 692–93
musical genres
chakri, **5:**475–76, 682–84
nande baeth, **5:**684
nande chakri, **5:**685
rūf, **5:**475, 684
ṣūfyāna mūsīqī, **5:**339, 682, 686–88, 689, 694–95
wanawun, **5:**685
political unrest in, **5:**16, 552
population of, **5:**682
Al-Kashshāf fī 'ilm al-anghām (al-Ḥaṣkafī), **6:**366
Kashtin (musical group), **3:**73, 1063, 1074, 1162
Kasilag, Lucrecia R., **4:**875
Kaska Indian nation, **3:**1274
Kaspi, Mati, **6:**1073, *1073*
'l-Kassar, George Abyaḍ 'Alī, **6:**598
Kassav' (musical group), **2:**98, 918; **8:**239
Kasseya, Souzy, **8:**238
Kastalsky, Aleksandr, **8:**783
Kasuga Grand Shrine (Nara), **7:**607, 608, 757
Kāṭamarāju Katha, **5:**895–96, 898, 902
Katana, Mbabi, **1:**217
Katari Taiko (musical group), **3:**1096
Katcha Sinsŏn T'aryŏng (*p'ansori* story), **7:**899
Kâte people, **9:**290–91
Kathak (theater group), **5:**489
Kathak caste, **5:**123, 641. *See also* Dholī
Kathmandu University, **5:**706
"Kathy I" (Aglukark), **3:**1063, 1280
Kati, **1:**313
al-Kātib, al-Ḥasan ibn Aḥmad, **6:**177, 365
Katidoki to heiwa (Yamada), **7:**731
Katjar (musical group), **3:**1077
Katlama (Khotan folk song), **7:**468
Katsarova, Raina, **8:**906, 907
Kāṭṭu Nāyakka, **5:**287, 909
Katutarô, **7:**745
Katyûsya no uta (Sinpei), **7:**743
Katz, Israel J., **3:**847; **6:**1037; **8:**23, 267
Katz, Ruth, **6:**1063, 1065, 1066, 1067
Kauffman, Robert A., **1:**217, 363
Kaufman, Dimitrina, **8:**907
Kaufman, Moe, **3:**1080
Kaufman, Nikolaj, **8:**23, *24*, 907
Kaufman, Robert, **10:**130, 133–34
Kaui, Billy, **9:**167
Kaukabi, **6:**910
Kaŭl (Hwang), **7:**955
"Kaulana nā Pua" (Prendergast), **9:**133, 219, 222
Kaulong people, **9:**617–20
Kaumann, Christian, **9:**982
Kaur people, **4:**619, 620
Kauraka, Kauraka, **9:**903
Kaurasi, Mosese, **9:**819
Kausar, Naeem, **5:**786
Kauthuma school, **5:**242, 243–45
kaval. See flutes
Kvæðamannafélagið Íðunn, **8:**407, 408

Kaveri (deity), **5:**887
Kavirayar, Arunachala, **5:**275
Kavkasia (musical group), **8:**845
Kavsadze family, **8:**841
Kavsadze, Sandro, **8:**844
Kavyu, **1:**223
Kawada Junzô, **7:**525
Kawaiisu Indian nation, **3:**420
Kawakami Otozirô, **7:**740
al-Kawākib (periodical), **6:**237
Kawase Junsuke, **7:**707
Kawczynski, Rudko, **8:**289
Kay, Ulysses, **3:**610
Kaya, Ahmet, **6:**251
Kaya state, **7:**24, 25, 821, 981
Kayabi culture, **2:**131
kayagŭm. See zithers
Kayah (Karenni) people, **4:**543
Kayamanan ng Lahi (Los Angeles), **3:**1025
Kayan people, **4:**823, 824, 825
instruments of, **4:**829, 830–33, 834
Kaygusuz Abdal, **6:**794
Kayoi Komachi (Zeami), **7:**640
Kayser, Aloys, **9:**756
Kazadi, Pierre Cary, **1:**217, 226
Kazadi wa Mukuna, **2:**313
Kazak (musical group), **3:**806
Kazakh Choir, **6:**959
Kazakh people, **6:**966; **7:**35
in Afghanistan, **5:**805
in China, **7:**6, 455–58, 460–61
conversion to Islam, **7:**24
epic songs, **6:**345
history of, **7:**460
in Mongolia, **7:**1004–20
musical traditions of, **7:**460–61
tanbur (*tämbur*) bands, **7:**451
Kazakhstan, **6:**895, 897, 949–61; **7:**36. *See also* Central Asia
epic songs and storytelling, **6:**844, 950, 952–53, 960
folk songs, **6:**950, 951–52
geography of, **6:**949
improvised poetry, **6:**950, 953–55
Islamic culture in, **6:**935–47
kyui genre, **6:**902, 956–58
lyric songs, **6:**955–56
mouth harp playing in, **5:**814
musical genres of, **6:**950–51
popular songs, **6:**961
population of, **6:**949, 959
Ramadan songs, **6:**941, 951
research on music of, **6:**958, 960
shamanism in, **6:**942, 967
Soviet period in, **6:**903–4, 958–60
Uighur people in, **6:**995
Kazakh State Philharmonia, **6:**959
Kazantzides, Stellios, **8:**1020
Kazel ha Kazel (periodical), **8:**564
Kazembe (kingdom), **1:**312, 671
KBS Kugak Kwanhyŏn Aktan (orchestra), **7:**954, 967, 970, 990
K.C. and the Sunshine Band, **3:**712
"Ke Kali Nei Au" (King), **9:**925
Kealiinohomoku, Joann W., **3:**221
Keating, Paul, **9:**414

Keats, John, **9:**39
Keawe, Genoa, **9:**164
Kéba (musical group), **3:**1170
Kébec-disques, **3:**1160
Kebede, Ashenafi, **1:**44
Kechua culture. *See* Quechua culture
Keeler, Ward, **4:**26, 639
Keeling, Richard, **3:**496, 506
Keen, Ian, **9:**418
"Keep on Pushing" (Mayfield), **3:**677
Keesing, Roger M., **9:**212, 962, 964, 977
Kehlonn (Alfred), **3:**1280
Keiko no yume wa your hiraku (Japanese popular song), **7:**747
Keil, Charles, **3:**149, 302, 583, 825, 901
Keil, Jared Tao, **9:**650
Keillor, Elaine, **3:**392, 1108
Keillor, Lenore Stevens, **3:***1182*
Keisei Hotoke no Hara (Chikamatsu), **7:**668
Keisei Mibu Nenbutsu (Chikamatsu), **7:**668
Keita, Salif, **1:**419, 420–21, 437; **8:**238
Keita, Soundiate, **1:**420
Keitadi, Jack, **9:**966
Keith, Alexander, **8:**374
Keith Vaudeville Circuit, **3:***198*
Keith, Victoria, **9:**222
Kekana, Steve, **1:**778, 779
Kekchí (K'ekchi) Maya, **2:**666, 667–68, 721, 736
Kekuku, Joseph, **3:**1049; **9:**389–90, 922
Kela people, **5:**732
Kelabit people, **4:**824
Kelao people, **4:**219
Kelaptrishvili, Omar, **8:**845
Keldibeki, Haji, **6:**938
Kele, Kotelano, **9:***825*, 973
Kele people, **1:**662
Keleier Kendalc'h (periodical), **8:**564
Keleier War'l Leur (periodical), **8:**564
Keleman, Milko, **8:***99*
Keli'i, David, **9:**390
Kelimālā (Haridas), **5:**252
Keller-Leuzinger, Franz, **2:**138–39, 140
Kelly, Clancy, **9:***135*
Kelly, John, **3:**313; **8:**390
Kelly, R., **3:**715
Kelly, Thomas, **10:**69
Kelly, Thomas Alexander Erskine, Earl of, **8:**367
Kelly, William, **2:**599
Kelso, Isaac, **3:**121
Kemanī Aleksan Ağa, **6:**758
Kemine, **6:**970
Kemp, Andrew, **8:**367
Kemu people, **7:**485
Kendalc'h, **8:**562
Kendall, Edward "Ned," **3:**564
Kendergi, Maryvonne, **3:**1151
Kendon, Adam, **9:**976
Kendro Dierhomeno (album), **8:**1021
Kennedy, Anne Gamble, **10:**138
Kennedy Center for the Performing Arts (Washington, D.C.), **3:**300, 846
Kennedy, David, **8:**370
Kennedy-Fraser, Marjory, **8:**368, 370, 373
Kennedy, John F., **3:**298, 310, 551, 1029
Kennedy, Norman, **8:**372

Kennedy, Peter, **8:**338, 371
Kennedy, Raymond, **9:**976
Kennedy, Robert F., **3:**551
Kennedy, Roy, **9:***135*
Kenneth E. Hill Collection of Pacific Voyages, **9:**977
Kenney, Mart, **3:**1091
Kenney, William, **3:**587
Kensiu people, **4:**560, 569
Kent, Ron, **3:**1280
Kent State University (Ohio), **3:**318, 952, 1010
Kentaq Bong people, **4:**560
Kentaq people, **4:**569
Kente, Gibson, **1:**219, 777
Kenton, Stan, **3:**335, 522, 787, 797
Kentucky
    bluegrass in, **3:**158–68
    camp meetings in, **3:**67
    Louisville
        German people in, **3:**528
        public school music education, **3:**275
    Native American groups in, **3:**466
    Old Regular Baptists in, **3:**123–24
Kentucky Minstrels, **3:**185
Kenuz people, **6:**629, 630, 641
Kenya. *See also* East Africa; *specific peoples*
    Abaluhya people, lyres, **1:**304
    composition in, **1:**217–18
    expulsion of South Asian community, **8:**236
    geography of, **1:**622
    guitar in, **1:**353, 358–59, 608
    instruments of, **1:**624–25, 627
    Kikuyu people, dance, **1:**109
    lamellophones, **1:**317
    Lamu Island, **1:**426, 427, 606, 607
    Luo people, **1:**362
        birth ceremonies, **1:**110, 116
        dance, **1:**110
    lyres in, **1:**303–4
    Maasai people, dance, **1:**109
    music, 1500s, **1:**76
    music industry in, **1:**426
    music of, **1:**607, 622–32
    popular music of, **1:**365, 423, 426–27, 626
    recording industry in, **1:**423
    religious music of, **1:**629–30
    Sunburu people, wedding dances, **1:**111, 115
    Swahili people, music of, **1:**631
    taarab music, **1:**607, 631–32
Kenyah people, **4:**823, 824, 825
    instruments of, **4:**834
    music and dance of, **4:**826–27, 831–33, 836–37
Kenyatta University College (Nairobi), **1:**216
Keo people, **4:**791
Keogh, Raymond D., **9:**432
Keota Ladies Band (Iowa), **3:**566
Kepler, Johannes, **8:**652
Keppard, Freddie, **3:**651
Keppeler, Ken, **3:**763
Kerala, **5:**929–50
    cavittunāṭakam theater in, **5:**485, *485*, 945–46
    dance traditions, **5:**361–63, 509–14, 933–34, 945
        teyyam, **5:**287
    devotional music of, **5:**259, 537, 944–49

folk music of, **5:**949–50
geography of, **5:**929
Hindu drumming traditions in, **5:**930
history of, **5:**929
instruments in, **5:**351, 360–63, 364, 365, 367, 931–32, 948
Karnatak tradition in, **5:**89, 209, 230, 232, 449
kathakaḷi dance-drama in, **5:**90, 104, 324–25, 361, 362–63, 542, 933–34, 935, 941, 944
Kozhikode, cassette industry in, **5:**554
kūṭiyāṭṭam drama in, **5:**361, 399, 484, 486, 931, 933, 941
map of, **5:***864*
mural painting in, **5:**300
musical genres
    eṇṇam, **5:**943
    kēḷi, **5:**933, 936, 939, 940
    koṭṭippāṭisseva, **5:**932, 940
    mēḷam, **5:**940, 943–44
    pāṇi, **5:**933, 934, 943–44
    sōpānam saṅgītam, **5:**230–31, 363, 931, 934, 940
    tāyampaka, **5:**362, 933, 935, 936, 939, 940, 941, 942, 943–44
Palghat, **5:**929
popular music in, **5:**929, 935
population of, **5:**929
Puthucode, Vedic chant in, **5:**243
Syrian Christians in, **5:**582
temple music in, **5:**929–36
Travancore, **5:**229
    ban on temple dancing, **5:**409
tribal music in, **5:**949
Trichur, **5:**929
    Vadakkunathan temple, **5:**509
Trivandrum, **5:**929
    Ayyar Brahmins in, **5:**930
Vedic chant in, **5:**239, 241–43
Kerala Kalamandalam, **5:**942
Kerala University, **5:**451
Kerebe people, **1:**636, 637
Kerek people, **7:**1027–30
Kerekere, Wiremu, **9:**932, 985
Kerem, **6:**80, 82
Kerkar, Kesarbai, **5:***207*, 413, 530
Kerker, Gustave, **3:**193
Kerkorrels (musical group), **1:**780
Kerman, Joseph, **3:**32; **8:**58
Kern Buam Band, **8:**675
Kern, Jerome, **3:**196, 530, 544, 549, 620
Kerr, Annie, **9:**390
Kersands, Billy, **3:**616
Kersey, Ken, **3:**1061
Kershner, Lidia, **8:**784
Kesavayya, **5:**229
Ketahun people, **4:**619
Ketama (musical group), **8:**599, 600
Ketan, Joseph, **9:**521
Ketu qiuhen (*nanyin*), **7:**270–71
Ketu state, **1:**401
Kevserî, Mustafa, **6:**109, 119, 127
Kewa people, **9:**514, 537
Key, Francis Scott, **3:**521
Key Kool (rap artist), **3:**973

Keyboard Book, 3:137
keyboard instruments. *See also* pianos
  clavichord, 8:200, 422, 440
  fortepiano, 8:367
  harpsichord, 3:55; 8:75, 391
    Baroque music for, 8:78
    conducting from, 8:101
    decline of, 8:82
    in Germany, 8:654
    in Norway, 8:422
    Renaissance music for, 8:76
    revival of, 8:55
    in Scotland, 8:367
    women performers of, 8:200
  spinets, 8:367
  virginals, 8:367
keyboards, electric. *See* electrophones
keyed fiddle. *See* violins and fiddles (bowed lutes)
Keyes, Cheryl L., 3:513, 586
Kgakgudi, Lazarus, 1:779
Kgalemang Tumediso Motsete, 1:428
Khachaturian, Aram, 6:726
Khada, 6:271
Khadan, Emir, 6:899
Khaddaj, Amer, 6:279–81
Khaddaj, Sana, 6:279–81
Khadīja al-Rihaābīya, 6:298
Khadīja bint Nuhayla, 6:298
khaen. See free-reed instruments
K'aenon (Baek), 7:971
Khairat, Abu Bakr, 6:612
Khakas people, 6:980; 7:1027–30
al-Khāl. *See* 'Abd al-Ḥayy ibn Muḥammad al-
    Ṭāluwī al-Dimashqī al-Ḥanafī
Khaldī, 6:270
Khaled, Cheb, 5:429, 545; 6:271; 8:210, 238
Khalifa, Marcel, 6:554
Khalil, Dahaba, 1:557
al-Khalīl ibn Aḥmad, 6:17, 387, 442
Khalīl, Mu'īn, 6:576–78, 577
Khalis (Sufi poet), 6:943
Khalkha people, 7:35, 1004–20
Khamidi, Latif, 6:958–59
al-Khamīsī, Muḥammad, 6:687
al-Khamouli, Abdu, 1:571
Khampa people, 5:504
Khampti people, 5:504
Khamseung Inthanone, 3:1008
Khamseung Syhanone, 4:361
Khamu people. *See* Kmhmu people
Khamvong Insixiengmai, 3:1008, 1008; 4:361
Khan, Abdul Aziz, 5:207, 334
Khan, Abdul Karim, 5:177, 410, 413
Khan, Abdul Rahiman, 5:414
Khan, Abdul Wahid, 5:177, 178, 413
Khan, Abid Husain, 5:134, 135
Khan, Adnan Sami, 5:748
Khan, Afaq Husain, 5:136, 137
Khan, Afzal, 5:767
Khan, Ahmad, 5:791
Khan, Ahmed Ali, 5:462–63, 767
Khan, Ali, 5:563
Khan, Ali Akbar, 5:4, 132, 204, 207, 337, 337,
    378, 466–67, 565, 566
  on *ālāp*, 5:82
  interest in unusual talas, 5:134, 194

music school of, 5:566
presentation style of, 5:203–4, 205
on raga, 5:65, 74–75
recordings of, 5:529
students of, 5:414, 537
Western performances of, 5:560, 563, 565
Khan, Alladiya, 5:126, 410, 413, 460
Khan, Allah Rakha, 5:768
Khan, Allauddin, 5:133, 204, 207, 337, 338,
    339, 340, 403, 461, 462–64, 564
  gharānā of, 5:204, 465
  presentation style of, 5:132, 342
  on role of musician, 5:70
  students of, 5:204–5, 414, 460, 466, 536, 564
Khan, Amir, 5:189, 526
Khan, Amir Ahmed, 5:767
Khan, Amir Hussain, 5:137
Khan, Amjad Ali, 5:206, 206–7, 337, 560
Khan, Asad Ali, 5:207, 333, 333, 746
Khan, Asad Amanat Ali, 5:767
Khan, Ashish, 5:4, 466
Khan, Ashraf Sharif, 5:768
Khan, Ata Hussain, 5:443
Khan, Ataullah, 5:425
Khan, Azam, 5:428
Khan, Bade Ghulam Ali, 5:410, 424, 746
Khan, Bakhtiar Ahmed, 5:768
Khan, Barkat Ullah, 5:190, 190–91, 206, 413
Khan, Basat, 5:192
Khan, Bhurji, 5:460
Khan, Bilas (son of Tansen), 5:190, 378
Khan, Bismillah, 5:207, 207, 340, 424, 670
Khan Bugti, Sachchu, 5:783
Khan, Bundu, 5:477, 746, 746
Khan, Chaka, 1:422
Khan Chea, 4:188
Khan, Dera Ghazi, 5:776
Khan Dharhi, Bakhshu, 5:133
Khan Dharhi, Sudhar, 5:121, 122, 133
Khan, Enayat, 5:205
Khan, Faiyaz, 5:175–76, 424, 443
Khan, Fateh Ali, 5:767, 768
Khan, Firoz, 5:189, 193
Khan, Ghulam Ali, 5:194, 206–7
Khan, Ghulam Bandagi, 5:336–37, 786
Khan, Ghulam Haider, 5:767
Khan, Ghulam Husain, 5:460
Khan, Ghulam Jafar, 5:767
Khan, Ghulam Raza, 5:192, 197
Khan, Ghulam Shabbir, 5:767
Khan-Girei, Sultan, 8:856
Khan, Habibuddin, 5:134, 136
Khan, Hafiz, 5:767
Khan, Hafiz Ali, 5:206, 207, 786
Khan, Haji Vilayat Ali, 5:133, 134
Khan, Hamid Ali, 5:767
Khan, Hassu, 5:465
Khan, Hazrat Inayat, 3:1044, 1044–45; 5:53,
    56, 307, 562, 563–64
Khan, Hidayat, 5:205, 563–64
Khan, Ilmas Husain, 5:136
Khan, Ilyas, 5:207
Khan, Imdad, 5:195, 196, 205–6
Khan, Imrat, 3:1216; 5:205, 336, 560, 563
Khan, Inam Ali, 5:136
Khan, Irshad, 3:1216; 5:205, 336

Khan, Kallu, 5:133
Khan, Kaukabh, 5:337
Khan, Keramatullah, 5:136, 137, 207
Khan Kharangui (epic), 7:1008
Khan, Khusrau, 5:189, 335
Khan, Latif Ahmad, 5:135, 563
Khan, Maheboob, 5:563
Khan, Mammu, 5:133
Khan, Mando, 5:767
Khan, Manji, 5:460
Khan, Manzoor Ali, 5:753
Khan, Masit, 5:135, 189–90, 192, 193
Khan, Mazhar Ali, 5:768
Khan, Miru, 5:133
Khan, Muhammad Ilyas, 5:767
Khān, Muhammed Jum'a, 6:656
Khan, Munir, 5:134
Khan, Munne, 5:207
Khan, Mushtaq Ali, 5:206
Khan, Mushtaq Hussain, 5:207
Khan, Natthu, 5:128–29, 134
Khan, Nazakat Ali, 5:767
Khan, Nazim Ali, 5:749, 768
Khan, Nisar Hussain, 5:207
Khan, Nishat, 5:205
Khan, Nizamuddin, 5:137
Khan, Noormohammad, 5:403
Khan, Nusrat Fateh Ali, 3:340; 5:256, 426, 568,
    748, 750, 753, 756, 760, 762, 766
Khan, Nyamat (Sadarang), 5:170–71, 189
Khan, Pathana, 5:753, 770
Khan, Pazeer, 5:788
Khan, Pyar, 5:192
Khan, Rafaqat Ali, 5:767
Khan, Rais, 5:205, 768
Khan, Rehmat Ali, 5:767
Khan, Sabz Ali, 5:791
Khan, Sadiq Ali, 5:768
Khan, Salamat Ali, 5:767
Khan, Samander, 5:787
Khan, Shafaat Ahmad, 5:339
Khan, Shafqat Ali, 5:767
Khan, Shammu, 5:414
Khan, Sharafat Ali, 5:767
Khan, Shaukat Hussain, 5:768
Khan, Shitab, 5:133
Khan, Shujaat, 5:205, 205
Khan, Tawakkal Ali, 5:767
Khan, Umrao Bundu, 5:296
Khan, Vidhan Ameer, 5:970
Khan, Vilayat, 5:198, 205, 207, 335, 460, 768
Khan, Vilayat Hussain, 5:57
Khan, Wahid, 5:205
Khan, Wajid Husain, 5:136
Khan, Wazir, 5:204, 206, 463–64
Khan, W. M., 5:532
Khan, Zafar Ali, 5:767
Khan, Zakir Ali, 5:767
Khan, Zarnoosh, 5:788
Khanam, Afsari, 5:858
Khanam, Farida, 5:750
Khandoba (deity), 5:728
Khandzteli, Giorgi, 8:843
K'angwŏndo arirang (Korean folk song), 7:883
Khants people, 8:488
  bear ritual of, 7:1029
  music of, 7:1027–30

Khantseguashe (god), **8:**855
Khanum, Farida, **5:**766
Khanzanchi, Deepak, **5:**427
Khāqānī, **6:**922
Kharkiv, Volodymyr, **8:**822
Khashaba, Ghattās, **6:**536
Khasi people, **5:**504
Khatā'ī, Shāh, **6:**922
Khatamov, Arifkhān, **6:**919
Khatchaturian, Aram, **4:**873
Khathīr, Sa'ib, **6:**538
Khattak, Kushal Khan, **5:**834
Khattak tribe, **5:**791
khayāl. See khyāl
Khayrī, Badī', **6:**598
Khayrī, Muḥammad, **6:**550
Kheddam, Cherif, **6:**269
Kheira, **6:**270
Khelvi, Ataulla Khan Isa, **5:**749, *749*
Khengar, Chaudasuma Ra, **5:**636
Khevian people, **8:**827–28
Khevsur people, **8:**827–28, 832
Khidr (legendary prophet), **6:**181
Khidr al-'Aṭṭār, **6:**643, *643*, 644
Khin Zaw, Ù, **4:**26, 392, 394–95
Khitan people, **7:**29, 30, 31, 32, 517
Khiva, khanate of, **6:**903, 967
Khmer people, **4:**151–216, 529
    court music
        ensembles, **4:**182–85
        genres, **4:**155
        repertoire, **4:**185–86
    cultural interactions, **4:**159
    cultural relationships with Laos, **4:**353–54,
        357
    dance
        court, **4:**186–90
        folk, **4:**203–4, 216
    folk music, **4:**155, 159, 193–205, 213–16
    history of, **4:**153–54, 156–59, 186–87
    instruments, **4:**161–74
    in Laos, **4:**151
    lullabies of, **4:**533
    music research on, **4:**159–61
    music system of, **4:**174–82
    narratives of, **4:**533
    in North America, **3:**1007
    religious genres of, **4:**156
    religious life of, **4:**205–7
    resettlement of, **4:**187–88, 210
    in Thailand, **4:**148, 151, 210–15, 221, 222,
        316
    theater of, **4:**190–93
    in Vietnam, **4:**148, 151, 215–16, 531, 532,
        533
Khmu people. *See* Kmhmu people
Khoikhoi people, **1:**761
    instruments of, **1:**703, 707
    music of, **1:**703, 719, 762
Khoisan peoples, **1:**702–3
Khoja people, in Sri Lanka, **5:**954
Khokhar, Mahfuz, **5:**767
Khomeinī, Ayatollāh Rūhollāh, **5:**820; **6:**19, 876
Khorasan, **5:**817; **6:**936; **7:**23
    Islam in, **6:**539, 793
Khosros II, king of Persia, **6:**129, 834

Khote, Durga, **5:**533
Khouri, Ken, **2:**911
Khoury, J., **6:**209
Khovalyg, Kaigal-ool, **6:***985*; **7:**1024
Khri-srong-lde-brtsan, **7:**478
Khubeka, Abagail, **1:**774
Khūbī al-'Awwāda, **6:**298
al-Khula'ī, Muḥammad Kāmil, **6:**321, 327, 371,
    551, 612
Khumalo, A. A., **1:**764
K'un Ch'ogo, Paekche king, **7:**24
Khün people, **4:**218
Khurasan. *See* Iran; Khorasan
Khurjawale, Altaf Hussain, **5:***207*
Khurshid, **5:**420
Khurtsia, Noko, **8:**844
Khushnawaz, Amir Jan, **5:**822
Khushnawaz, Amir Mohammad, **5:**822
Khushnawaz family, **5:**822
Khushnawaz, Mohammad Rahim, **5:**822
Khusrā caste, **5:**476, 770–71
Khusrau, Amīr, **3:**1044; **5:**76, 306, 335, 752,
    753, 755
    ghazals of, **5:**184, 256
    invention of *tabla*, **5:**121
Khuvaido (also Huvaidā; Sufi poet), **6:**943, 946
Khwaja Moinuddin Chishti, **5:**644
Khwaja Safi al-Din, **5:**690
Khwarezm, **6:**936, 942, 945, 965
Khyal (Afghan singer), **5:***809*
khyāl, **5:**162, 163, 170–78, 335, 336, 338, 381
    Afghanistan, **5:**805
    ālāp section of, **5:**172, 174–75, 177, 195, 196
    baṛā type, **5:**172–73, 175, 190, 195
    Bengal, **5:**847, 852–53
    choṭā type, **5:**172, 173–74, 180, 206
    composed by Tirunal, **5:**229
    composition of, **5:**83, 172–73
    development of, **5:**15, 333, 373
    dhrupad influences in, **5:**125
    form of, **5:**533
    gharānā for, **5:**176–77, 378
    history of, **5:**170–71
    improvisation in, **5:**202
    influence on Tagore, **5:**860
    instrumental performance of, **5:**195–96, 202,
        206, 207
    North America, **5:**581
    performance of, **5:**171–72
    qawwali influences in, **5:**125
    raga realization in, **5:**84–85
    ragas for, **5:**69
    research on, **10:**9–11
    similarities to *qawwali*, **5:**256
    status of, **5:**379
    tabla accompaniment of, **5:**123, 132
    talas in, **5:**125–27
    use of *pakhāvaj* in, **5:**119
    women performers of, **5:**410, 411, 413
*Khyal: Creativity within North India's Classical
    Music Tradition* (Wade), **10:**10
Ki no Kaion, **7:**668
Kiabig (Nissan composer), **9:**638
Kīānī, Majīd, **6:**855, 856, 857, 858, 859
Kiatamba, Kuna (*kengai*), **1:**329, *330*
Kickapoo Indian nation, **3:**451

Kid Frost (rap artist), **3:**750
Kidjo, Angélique, **1:**422; **8:**225
Kidson, Frank, **8:**337
Kiefer, Bruno, **2:**320
Kiefer, Thomas, **4:**891
Kierkegaard, Søren, **8:**451
Kiesewetter, Raphael, **6:**22
Kiganda people
    Angolan ideographs and, **1:**150
    instruments, **1:**218
    religious music, **1:**210
    song style, **1:**217
Kikkawa Eisi, **7:**545, 592, 603
Kiko (Los Lobos), **3:**751
Kikoak, Eddie, **3:**1275
Kikongo culture, **2:**898
Kikunaga *kengyô*, **7:**758
Kikuyu people, **1:**624, 627, 630
    dance, **1:**109
    instruments of, **1:**625
Kila Police Youth Band, **9:**89
Kilberry Book of Ceòl Mor (Campbell), **8:**373–74
Kilenge people, **9:**614
Kilgunak (*kasa*), **7:**927
Kilikia, **6:**724, 737
Kilimanjaro (Washington, D.C.), **3:**806
Kilivila people
    kundu ensembles, **9:**489
    performers, **9:**489
Kiliwa culture, **2:**595, 598, 599
"Kill for Peace" (Fugs), **3:**317
Killer Geishas A Go-Go (musical group), **3:**973
Killick, Andrew, **10:**105
Killin Collection of Gaelic Songs (Stewart), **8:**373
Killing Fields (film), **4:**159
"Killing Me Softly" (Fugees), **3:**715
Killoran, Paddy, **3:**843
Kimberley's Diamond Minstrels, **1:**765
Kimbu people, **1:**642
Kim Ch'anghwan, **7:**899, 906, 968
Kim Ch'angjin, **7:**986
Kim Ch'angjo, **7:**807, 907, 913, 914, 917, 986
Kim Ch'angnyong, **7:**899
Kim Ch'anŏp, **7:**899
Kim Chech'ŏl, **7:**898, 905
Kim Chiha, **7:**959, 969
Kim Chonggi, **7:**915
Kim Chŏnggun, **7:**899
Kim Chŏngmun, **7:**899
Kim Chongsu, **7:**853, 854
Kim Ch'ŏnhŭng, **7:**985, 989, 990
Kim Ch'ŏnt'aek, **7:**856, 921
Kim Chukp'a, **7:**915, 984
Kim Dae Ryeh, **7:**972
Kim Duk Soo, **7:**933, 963–67
Kim Haesuk, **7:**971
Kim Heejo, **7:**971, 972
Kim Hongsŭng, **7:**969
Kim Hŭijo, **7:**957
Kim Illyun, **7:**971
Kim Ilsŏng changgŭn ŭi norae (Kim), **7:**961
Kim Il Sung, **7:**797, 960, 961, 962, 991–92, 997
Kim Inshik, **7:**951
Kim, Jin Hi, **3:**954
Kim Jong Il, **7:**962
Kim Kibok, **7:**984

Kim Kilhak, **7:**997

Kim Kisu, **7:**952–53, 976, 989, 992

Kim Kwangsu, **7:**965

Kim Myŏnggon, **7:**960

Kim Oksŏng, **7:**961

Kim Pongho, **7:**969

Kim Pusik, **7:**79, 833

Kim Pyŏngho, **7:**915, 916

Kim Pyŏngsŏp, **7:**933

Kim Rinok, **7:**997

Kim Sejong, **7:**854, 899, 906

Kim Sohŭi, **7:**900, *900*, 909, 972, 986

Kim Sŏnghye, **7:**991

Kim Sŏngjin, **7:**989

Kim Sŏngok, **7:**906

Kim Soo Chul, **7:**958, 959–60, 969

Kim Sujang, **7:**856, 921

Kim Suk Chul, **7:**972

Kim Sunnam, **7:**952, 960

Kim T'aesŏp, **7:**989

Kim Talsŏng, **7:**955

Kim Vàn Kiêu (Trương Duy Toàn), **4:**493

Kim Wŏn'gyun, **7:**961, 962, *963*, 997

Kim Yongbae, **7:**933, 963–65, 966

Kim Yŏngjae, **7:**957, 989

Kim, Yongwoo, **7:**970

Kim Yŏn'gyu, **7:**997

Kim Yŏngyun, **7:**954

Kim Yŏnsu, **7:**899, 900, 906

Kim Yŏran, **7:**900

Kim Young Dong, **7:**958–59, 969, 970

Kim Yujago, **7:**983

Kim Yunbong, **7:**997

Kim Yundŏk, **7:**915, 916, 954, 975, 984, 986

Kimi koisi, **7:**744

Kimmelman, Michael, **3:**517

Kin ari (Korean folk song), **7:**883

Kin Nanbongga (Korean folk song), **7:**883

Kina, Shoukichi, **3:**339

Kincaid, Bradley, **3:**78

Kincaid, Jamaica, **2:**800

Kind of Blue (Davis), **3:**661

Kind, Theodor, **8:**1024

al-Kindī, **6:**16, 17, 18, 19, 365, 368, 373, 387, 442, 448, 541, 869

Kineya Sakiti IV, **7:**779

"King Alcohol," **3:**184

King and I (Rodgers and Hammerstein), **3:**197, 545, 1026; **4:**131, 285

King, Anthony V., **1:**51, 517

King, B. B., **3:**583, 647, 674, 709

King, Ben E., **3:**673

King, Carole, **3:**673

King, Charles E., **3:**1050; **9:**919, 922, 924–25

King Crimson (musical group), **3:**356; **8:**215

King, Cyprian, **2:***970*

King Elejigbo (Oyele), **1:**403

King Force Quintet, **1:**774

King Ganam and the Songs of the West, **3:**1091

King Kamehameha Traditional Chant and Hula Competition, **9:**67, 923, 1008

King Kong (film), **3:**203

King Kong (musical), **1:**773, 774, 775, 777

King, Martin Luther, Jr., **3:**316, *316*, 551, 682

King people, **9:**983

King Radio (calypsonian; Norman Span), **2:**963

King Records, **3:**263, 677, 708

"King Tim III" (Fatback Band), **3:**695

King, Tunde, **1:**377, 478–79, 481

King's Band (Hawai'i), **9:**132

King's Farewell to His Concubine (Peking opera), **7:**282

King's Threshold (Yeats), **8:**388

"Kingdom Coming" (Work), **3:**189, 835

Kingdom of Serbs, Croats, and Slovenes, **8:**940

King'ei, Geoffrey K., **1:**631–32

Kingman, Daniel, **3:**144

Kingo, Bishop Thomas, Gradual of, **8:**414, 459, 469, 471

Kingston Symphony, **3:**1079, 1184

Kingston Trio, **3:**14, 48, 49, 162, 520

Kink, Martin, **3:**880

Kinka hu (Japanese manuscript), **7:**581, *581*, 589

Kinks (musical group), **8:**214

Kinloch, George, **8:**371

Kinloch, William, **8:**367

Kinnaird, Alison, **8:**366

Kinnara School (California), **3:**985; **5:**565, 583

Kinnara Taiko (musical group), **3:**970, *971*

Kinnear, Michael, **5:**57

Kinney, Esi Sylvia, **1:**363

Kino (musical group), **8:**779

Kino, Eusebio Francisco, **2:**595

Kinuta (Zeami), **7:**640

Kiowa-Apache Indian nation, **3:**431, 440

Kiowa Indian nation, **3:**213, 440, 444, 445

    Ghost Dance songs, **3:**487

    gourd dancing, **3:**448

Kiowa Indian Tonkonga Society, **3:**448–49

Kippen, James R., **5:***55*, 136, 378–79

Kipsigis people, **1:**605

Kır Ismail, **6:**766

Kiran, Ravi, **5:**424

Kirby, Len "Busch," **9:***135*

Kirby, Percival R., **1:**51, 56, 355–56, 714

Kirch, Patrick V., **9:**835

Kircher, Athanasius, **6:**366; **8:**265

Kirghiz people. *See* Kyrgyz people

Kiribati, **9:**712, 758–64. *See also* Banaba; Butaritari; Gilbert Islands

    Christianity in, **9:**720

    composition in, **9:**353–54, 364–65

    costumes for dance, **9:**349

    emigrants from, **9:**664, 760, 762, 764

    epigrammatic song texts, **9:**331–32

    Europeans in, **9:**40

    films on, **9:**982, 1008, 1016

    geography of, **9:**758

    immigrants to Australia, **9:**84, 85–86

    instruments of, **9:**717, 762–63

    Japanese in, **9:**32

    kuaea and *maie* genres, **9:**365, 761–62

    music and dance of, **9:**231, *346*, 758–64

    outsiders' influence in, **9:**5

    Polynesian influences in, **9:**758, 762

    popular music in, **9:**721

    sound recordings from, **9:**985, 994, 997

Kiribati Ministry of Education, **9:**967

Kiribati Student Culture Club, **9:***105*

Kirikiri people, **9:**587

Kırmızıgül, Mahsun, **6:**248, *258*

Kirshenblatt-Gimblett, Barbara, **3:**944, 1109

Kirsti of Norbø, **8:**415

kīrtan, **5:**250, 253–54, 908. *See also kīrtana*

    Bengal, **5:**845, *846*, 853, 856

    dance in, **5:**503

    Gujarat, **5:**632–34

    instruments in, **5:**347

    Madhya Pradesh, **5:**724

    Maharashtra, **5:**729

    Orissa, **5:**732

    Rajasthan, **5:**642–43

    Sikh, **5:**13, 250, 257, 549, 655–56, 772

    Trinidad, **5:**590

    United Kingdom, **5:**573, 575

    Uttar Pradesh, *harikīrtan,* **5:**664–65

    women performers of, **5:**411, 416

kīrtana, **5:**42, 211, 216, 262, 263, 265–67, 517, 522. *See also kīrtan*

    group singing of, **5:**216

    in Kerala Christian music, **5:**947

    ragas in, **5:**97

    similarities to *dhrupad,* **5:**42

    structure of, **5:**262, 920

    in Tamil Christian music, **5:**922, 923–24, 925

Kirton, Jiggs, **2:**820

Kisaeng t'aryŏng (Korean folk song), **7:**886

al-Kisā'ī, **6:**353

Kisan Kol people, **5:**732

Kiselgof, Zusman, **8:**772

Kishibe Shigeo, **7:**524, 592; **10:**4, *4*

Kishwar Sultan, **5:**791

Kisii people, **1:**624

Kisimoto Yosihide, **7:**608

KISS (musical group), **8:**215

"Kiss Me Again" (Herbert), **3:**193

Kiss Me, Kate (Porter), **3:**545

Kitāb al-adwār (Ṣafī al-Dīn al-Urmawī), **6:**16–17, 365, 369, 502, 542

Kitāb al-aghānī (al-Iṣbahānī), **6:**12, 20, 291, 293, *293*, 294, 295, 351–56, 365, 370, 392, 396, 402, 541, 564, 565, 696

Kitāb al-an'ām bi-ma'rifat al-anghām (al-Ṣaydāwī al-Dimashqī), **6:**568–69

Kitab al-Bayan wa 'l-Tabiyhin (al-Jahiz), **6:**664

Kitāb al-Imtā' wa-'l-intifā' fi mas'alat samā' al-samā' (Ibn al-Darrāj al-Sabtī), **6:**373

Kitāb al-īqā' (al-Khalīl ibn Aḥmad), **6:**387

Kitāb al-īqā'āt (al-Fārābī), **6:**17, 388, 389–92

Kitāb al-jumū' fī 'ilm al-mūsīqā wa-'l-ṭubū' (Abū Zayd al-Mālikī), **6:**367

Kitāb al-malāhī wa-asmā'ihā (al-Mufaḍḍal ibn Salama), **6:**373

Kitāb al-muḥdath fī 'l-aghānī (Ibn Nāqiyā), **6:**370

Kitāb al-mūsīqā al-kabīr (al-Fārābī), **6:**17, 368, 388–89, 402, 443, 502, 541, 542; **8:**92

Kitāb al-mūsīqī (Thābit ibn Qurra), **6:**368

Kitāb al-mūsīqī al-sharqī (al-Khula'ī), **6:**551

Kitāb al-najāt (Ibn Sīnā), **6:**367, 369

Kitāb al-qiyān (Yūnus al-Kātib), **6:**369

Kitāb al-shifā' (Ibn Sīnā), **6:**367, 369, 502

Kitāb fī 'l-aghānī (Yūnus al-Kātib), **6:**369

Kitāb fī ta'līf al-nagham (Isḥāq al-Mawṣilī), **6:**387

Kitāb ibtidā' al-ghinā' wa-'l-'īdān (Ibn al-Kalbī), **6:**372

Kitāb iḥṣā' al-īqā'āt (al-Fārābī), **6:**388, 389–92

Kitāb mu'tamar al-mūsīqā al-arabiyya, **6**:326
Kitāb ṭabaqāt al-mughannīn (Ibn Khurradādbih), **6**:369
Kitâbu ilmi'l-mûsikî alâ vechi'l-hurûfât (Cantemir), **6**:771
Kitab ustadh al-musiqa l-'arabiyya ('Abd al-Mun'in 'Arafa), **6**:45
Kitahara Hakusyû, **7**:729, 732
Kitchener-Waterloo Symphony Orchestra, **3**:1079, 1184
Kitione, Rev., **9**:819–20
Kito na Taiko (musical group), **3**:1248
Kitoj culture, **8**:38
Kitsai Indian nation, **3**:440
Kittredge, George Lyman, **3**:147
Kittredge, Walter, **3**:188
Kituxe e os Acompanhantes (musical group), **1**:435
Kiwai people, **9**:178–79
  dance of, **9**:376, 490, 491, 507
  epic singing of, **9**:489
  songs of, **9**:326
  sound recordings of, **9**:981
  sung poetry, **9**:326
Kiwele, Joseph, **1**:671
Kiwi, **9**:999
Kiyomoto Enzyudayû, **7**:681
Kiyomoto Oyô, **7**:764
Kiyose Yasuzi, **7**:732, 735
Kiyoshi Nagata Taiko Drumming Ensemble, **3**:1217
Kiyotune (Zeami), **7**:632, 640
Kjarkas (musical group), **2**:293, *297*
Kjellberg, Erik, **8**:448
Kjellstad, Ivar, **8**:419
Kjellström, Rolf, **8**:307
Kjerulf, Halfdan, **8**:425
Kkaeŏjin t'osŏng (Oulim), **7**:971
Kkŏt p'anŭn ch'ŏnyŏ (North Korean opera), **7**:962–63
Klaasen, Lorraine, **3**:1170
Klaasens, Thandi, **1**:774
Klaaste, Sol, **1**:219, 774
Klaatu (musical group), **3**:1081
Klami, Uuno, **8**:482
Klassen, Doreen, **3**:52–53, 1250
Klaus und Ferdl (duo), **8**:675
Klave y Kongo (musical group), **3**:1085
Klein, Lothar, **3**:1186
kleine Nachtmusik, Eine (Mozart), **6**:52
Klezmatics (musical group), **3**:336
Klezmer Conservatory Band (Boston), **3**:941
klezmer music, **6**:202, 203, 1018, 1065
  Europe, **8**:251, 259, 263, 660
  international popularity of, **8**:11
  nigunei Meron repertoire, **6**:203
  North America, **3**:98, 325, 330, 336, 530, 934, 938–39, 941–42, 943, 944
  vocal imitations of, **6**:206
Klezmorim (Berkeley), **3**:941
Kliekske (musical group), **8**:535
Kligman, Mark Loren, **3**:943; **10**:69
Kliment of Ohrid, **8**:904
Kline, Patsy, **3**:108
Klondike Kate, **3**:1277
Klusen, Ernst, **8**:24, 26, 647, 664

Klymasz, Robert B., **3**:292, 344, 345, 914, 1088, 1110
Kmhmu people, **3**:1007; **4**:347, 537, 546–47
  khene playing, **4**:338
  in Laos, **4**:338
  resettlement of, **4**:360–61
Kmoch, František, **3**:897
Knaben Wunderhorn, Des (Arnim/Brentano), **8**:17–18, 663
Knauft, Bruce, **9**:977
Kneisel Quartet, **3**:538, 1210
Kneubuhl, John, **9**:233
Kneubuhl, Victoria, **9**:233, 234
Knight, Roderic, **1**:51, 56, 136, 158, 161, 488
Knights and Ladies of *Kaleva*, **3**:873
Knights of St. John of Jerusalem, Hospitaler (Knights of Malta), **8**:634–35
Kniš, Siarhiej, **8**:*219*
Knjaževsko-Srpska Banda, **8**:948
Knocks, Alfred J., **9**:961
Knopoff, Steven, **9**:418
Knott, Sarah Gertrude, **3**:823
Knox, John, **3**:118
Knuckles, Frankie, **3**:690
Knudsen, Thorkild, **8**:23, 461, 464
Ko Hŭnggon, **7**:956, 971
Ko Sugwan, **7**:898, 986
Ko Wimin, **7**:987
Koasati Indian nation. *See* Coushatta (Koasati) Indian nation
Kobayashi Yoshitake, **7**:595
Koch, Gerd, **9**:829–30, 980, 982, 994, 1008
Koch-Grünberg, Theodor, **2**:176, 178, 180
Koch Records, **8**:675
Koḍagu people, **5**:886–87
Kodalli, Nevit, **6**:775
Kodaly Ensemble (Toronto), **3**:1197
Kodály, Zoltán, **3**:279, 280–81; **8**:18, 19, 23, 274, 737, 742
Kodandapani Pillai, Lalgudi, **5**:391
Kodo (musical group), **3**:1215
Koegel, John, **3**:848
Koellreutter, Hans-Joachim, **2**:306
Koesana, Maurice, **9**:640
Koetting, James, **1**:137, 455
Kofi, Danhin Amagbenyō, **1**:315
Kofsky, Frank, **3**:584, 663
Kofun period, **7**:18, 24
Koga Masao, **7**:745
Kogi culture, **2**:10, 183–87, 188
  history of, **2**:183–84
  instruments of, **2**:184–85, 380
  shamanism in, **2**:172
  vocal music of, **2**:185–87
Kogo ch'ŏnbyŏn (*kayagŭm pyŏngch'ang*), **7**:908
Kogo ch'ŏnbyŏn (*tan'ga*), **7**:905
Kogŭm kagok (collection), **7**:927
Koguryŏ kingdom, **7**:18, 30, 41
  Chinese interactions in, **7**:24, 25, 27
  cultural influence on Japan, **7**:723
  instruments of, **7**:79, 821
  komagaku repertoire, **7**:620
  music in, **7**:806, 981
  puppet theater in, **7**:943
  tomb paintings in, **7**:955
Kohout, Josef, **8**:727–28

Kohun period, instruments of, **7**:559, 560–62
Kohyang ŭi tal (Hwang), **7**:956
Koiari people, **9**:492
Koita, Amy, **1**:366
Koita people, **9**:491, 492
Koitapu people, **9**:983
Koivun Kaiku, **3**:826, *826*
Koizumi Fumio, **7**:524, 568–71, 593, 603, 708; **10**:27
Kojima Shin, **7**:595
Kojo, Yeo, **1**:211, 213
Kojong, Chosŏn king, **7**:909
Kokana people, **5**:727
Kokazi (nô play), **7**:632
Ko Ko, Ù, **4**:19
"Koko," **3**:658, 658–59
Kököchu, **7**:21
Kokoro Dance Ensemble (Vancouver), **3**:224, 1096
Kokua, Hone, **9**:233
Kokuho Rose Prohibited, **3**:1096
Kokusenya Kassen (Chikamatsu), **7**:669
Kokyû sansyô (Makino), **7**:713
Kol people, **9**:607, 620, 621
Kolam people, **5**:727
Kolarić, Pajo, **8**:933
Kolarov, Mile, **8**:981
Kolas, Jacub, **8**:790
Kolberg, Oskar, **8**:18, 712, *712*, 803, 821
Kolchis, **8**:826
Köler, Johann, **8**:496
Kolessa, Filaret, **8**:803, 820, 822
Kolessa, Mykola, **8**:820
Kolhatkar, Bhaburao, **5**:423
Koli people, **5**:501
Kolinski, Mieczyslaw, **1**:31, 50; **8**:20; **9**:980
Kolla Suyu, **2**:232
Kollar, Jan, **8**:732
Kollington, Ayinla, **1**:484
Kolmarer Liederbuch, **8**:651
Kölner Markt, Der (Zangius), **8**:653
Kolo (musical group), **3**:1198
Kolo Club, **3**:922–23
Kololo people, **1**:712
Kolomoku, Walter, **9**:390
Kolonovits, Christian, **8**:677
Kolpakov Trio, **8**:287
Kolsti, John, **8**:1003
Koma family, **7**:627
Koma no Tikazane, **7**:547, 587
Komadina, Vojin, **8**:969
Komatsiutiksak (musical group), **3**:1280
Komatu Kôsuke, **7**:731
Komba people, **9**:571–72
Kombe people, **9**:609–10
Kombo t'aryŏng (Korean folk song), **7**:886
Kome (film), **7**:750
Komi people, **8**:754
  instruments, **8**:774
  vocal polyphony of, **8**:774
  wedding laments, **8**:754
Komi-Permiak people, **8**:757
Komi-Zyriane people, **8**:774
Komitas, **6**:725, *725*, 725–26, 737
Komitas State Conservatory of Music (Yerevan), **6**:727

Kŏmjŏng komusin (Oulim), 7:971
Komodo, 4:786
Komparu Zentiku, 7:549
kŏmun'go. See zithers
Kon, I. U., 6:918
Kon Tikis (musical group), 9:138
Koncz, Szuzsa, 8:747
Konde, Fundi, 1:426
Kondô Jô, 7:737–38
Kondo, Yoshio, 9:25
Kondrat'ev, Mikhail, 8:773
Kong Jifen, 7:336
Kong Kinam, 7:960
Kong Ros, 4:188
Kong Shangren, 7:336
Köngäs-Maranda, Elli, 9:962
Konggan Sarang (Seoul theater), 7:994
Kongmiao dacheng yuezhang (Jiang), 7:347
Kongmin, Koryŏ king, 7:982
Kongmyŏngga (Korean folk song), 7:886
Kongo (kingdom), 1:4, 660
    court music, 1:312
    history of, 1:666–67
Kongo nation, 2:869; 3:802
Kongque kaiping (He), 7:220, 241
Kŏn'guk haengjin'gok (Kim), 7:960
Kongzi. *See* Confucius
Koning, Jos, 8:394
Konishi, Junko Iwata, 9:994
Konitz, Lee, 3:660
Konkow Indian nation, 3:415
Konoe Hidemaro, 7:732
konpa-dirèk (*compas-direct*), 2:95, 98, 878–79,
    892–93, 920
Konparu Zenpô, 7:546
Konparu Zentiku, 7:565, 630, 641
Konservatori Karawitan Indonesia, 4:122, 677,
    678, 684, 758
Konservatori Tari Indonesia, 4:678
Kontaktnäten, 8:216
Konté, Mamadou, 8:238
Kontra-Gapi (musical group), 4:886
Kontroll Csoport (musical group), 8:746
Konuk, Ahmed Avnî, 6:110, 116, 118
Konzo people, 1:606
Konzyaku monogatari (collection), 7:645
Koo, Joseph (Gu Jiahui), 7:355
Kool and the Gang (musical group), 3:681,
    682–83, 684, 711
Kool DJ Herc, 3:688, 694–95, 697, 702, 713
Kool Moe Dee, 3:697, 700, 714
Kool Moe Dee and the Treacherous Three
    (musical group), 3:694
Koola Lobitos (musical group), 1:483
Koorn, Dirk, 2:398
Kootenayan Indian nation, 3:1254
Kopi Kats (musical group), 9:138
Kopytman, Mark, 6:1031, 1063
kora. See harp-lutes
Koraga caste, 5:884
Koraku people, 5:722
Korana people, 1:703
Koranda, Lorraine D., 3:381
Koranko people, 1:130
    instruments of, 1:446
    praise singing, 1:488–513

Koray, Erkin, 6:249, 250
Korea. *See also* East Asia; North Korea; South
    Korea; *specific dynasties*
    aesthetics and philosophy in, 7:813–16
    blind musicians in, 7:965
    Buddhism in, 5:12; 7:24, 871–74
    Cheju Island
        folk songs of, 7:880, 883, 988
        shamanism on, 7:876, 878
    Chindo Island
        farmers' bands, 7:935–36
        folk songs of, 7:988
    Chinese influences in, 7:24–28, 59, 80, 806,
        981–82
    Chŏlla provinces, folk songs of, 7:881–82,
        886, 890, 903, 957, 958
    chŏngak repertoire, 7:813, 849, 865–70
        form of, 7:844
        relation to *sanjo*, 7:913
        rhythmic patterns in, 7:841–42
        transmission of, 7:988–89
    Ch'ungch'ŏng province, folk songs of,
        7:881–82, 886, 891, 957
    composition in, 7:951–73, 975–77
    Confucianism in, 7:27, 28, 807, 848, 900,
        982
    court music, 7:865–70, 981–83
        aesthetics of, 7:813
        dance and, 7:67
        form in, 7:844
        hyangak, 7:42, 806–7, 822, 866, 867–68,
            869
        percussion instruments in, 7:5
        reform of, 7:43
        rhythmic patterns in, 7:841–42
        tangak, 7:806–7, 822, 866, 867, 869
        treatises on, 7:833–34
        vocal genres, 7:919–24
    cultural exchanges in, 7:49–51
    cultural influence on Japan, 7:723–24
    dance traditions of, 7:59–60, 66–69
    folk musicians in, 7:983–88
    folk regions of, 7:850, 880–83, 988
    folk song traditions of, 7:879–88
    form in, 7:844–45
    fusion music in, 7:967, 969–73
    geography and climate of, 7:15
    Hamgyŏng province, folk songs of, 7:883
    history of, 7:15–18, 25–26, 27, 805–9
    history of music in, 7:41–43
    Hwanghae province, folk songs of, 7:882–83,
        886
    instruments in, 7:79–83, 821–31
    Japanese occupation of, 7:797, 866, 899, 932,
        951–52, 983, 989
    Kangwŏn province, folk songs of, 7:883
    kugak in, 7:804–5, 808–9
    Kyŏnggi province, folk songs of, 7:881, 886,
        891, 904, 957
    Kyŏngsang province, folk songs of, 7:883, 891,
        957
    melody and modes in, 7:847–51
    musical institutions in, 7:45–47, 988–92
    musical profile of, 7:803–9
    musical transmission in, 7:988–92
    music theory in, 7:833–34

    nongak genre, 7:797–98, 929–39
    notation systems in, 7:834–35, 837–39; 8:103
    p'ansori in, 7:893–95, 897–908, 909–11
    printing in, 7:22
    P'yŏngan province, folk songs of, 7:882–83,
        886
    rhythmic patterns in, 7:841–44
    ritual music (*aak*), 7:806–7, 808, 816, 818,
        822, 834, 838, 848, 861–64, 865–66,
        869–70
    samulnori (also *samullori*) genre in, 7:5, 798,
        843, 933, 938, 947, 963–67
    sanjo repertoire, 7:913–17
    scholarship in, 7:853–57
    shamanism in, 7:20, 849, 850–51, 875–78,
        889–91, 942, 959, 972, 986–87
    sinawi repertoire, 7:817, 889–91, 914
    social and regional contexts in, 7:981–97
    theater in, 7:941–47
    vocal genres in, 7:919–28
    vocal techniques in, 7:817–20
    Western musical influences in, 7:807–8,
        887–88, 944, 951–53, 976
    Western music in, 7:803, 946, 951–52, 994
    writing in, 7:28
Korea Fantasy (Ahn), 7:976
Korean Classical Music Institute of America, 3:978
Korean Empire, 7:863–64
Korean Folk Performing Arts Center (Namwŏn),
    7:983
Korean Musicological Society, 7:853, 990
Korean people, 2:4
    in Belize, 2:666
    in China, 7:6, 447, 452, 519
    in Hawai'i, 9:96, 99, 109, 163; 10:47
    in Japan, 7:797–98, 894
    in North America, 3:949, 975–79
        British Columbia, 3:1096
        Ontario, 3:1215
        Presbyterians, 3:120
    in Paraguay, 2:462
Korean Traditional Music Institute of New York,
    3:978
Korean Traditional Performing Arts Center. *See*
    Kungnip Kugagwŏn
Korean War, 3:742, 975; 7:797, 899, 953, 975,
    983, 992
Korekore people, 1:745, 753
Koriak people, 6:980
Korku people, 5:720, 727
Korn (musical group), 3:359
Kornaros, 8:1015, 1025
Korngold, Erich Wolfgang, 3:203
Kornhauser, Bronia, 4:102–3
Koro Sutro (Harrison), 4:132
Köroğlu (epic), 6:82, 766
    Azerbaijani version, 6:929, 930
    Iranian version, 6:829, 840, 851
    Kazakh version, 6:952
    Turkmen version, 6:969, 970
Koror (Palau), 9:180–83, 722
Kortua, I., 8:853
Korwa people, 5:720
Koryak people
    bear ritual of, 7:1029
    music of, 7:1027–30

Koryjan, Viačaslaŭ, **8:***219*
Koryŏ dynasty, **7:**863
   Chinese influences in, **7:**27
   court music office in, **7:**981–82
   dynastic history of, **7:**855
   history of, **7:**806–7
   hwarang in, **7:**984
   instruments in, **7:**80–81, 807
   kagok in, **7:**921
   kunak in, **7:**930
   sijo in, **7:**925
   social policies in, **7:**43
Koryŏsa (dynastic history), **7:**41, 855, 982
Kos, Koraljka, **8:**25
Kosena-Awiyaana people, **9:**526–33
Koshetz, Oleksander, **3:**1089, 1229, 1241
Koskoff, Ellen, **3:**150, 506; **10:**127–35, *134*
Kosovo (Kosova). *See* Serbia
Kosrae (Federated States of Micronesia), **9:**712, 740–43
   Americans in, **9:**31
   Christianity in, **9:**729
   commemorative songs, **9:**32
   Europeans in, **9:**158
   geography of, **9:**726
   hymn-singing in, **9:**159
   instruments of, **9:**717, 742
   kava use in, **9:**172–73
   music and dance of, **9:**740–43
   poetry, **9:**328
      verbal meter, **9:**324
   settlement of, **9:**715
   village-choir competitions, **9:**720
Kosrae State Museum Archives, **9:**967
Kossar, Leon, **3:**223
Kossar, Zena, **3:**223
Košt'ál, Arnošt, **8:**725
Kostash, Myrna, **3:**1060
Kostric, Matjaz, **8:**136
Kosugi Takehisa, **7:**737
Koswara, Koko, **4:**715–16, 718, 723
Koswara, Mang Koko, **4:**697
Kota people, **5:**272, 903, *905*, 909
   ceremonies of, **5:**278–79, 281, 284, 285–86
   dance traditions of, **5:**905–6
   devr koḷ genre, **5:**278, 281
   instruments of, **5:**366, 912, 915–16
   musical repertoire, ethnic differentiation in, **5:**283
   weddings of, **5:**285
Kotafon people, **1:**37
Kōṭi-Chenayya Pāḍḍana, **5:**882–83, 885
Kotikova, Natalya, **8:**785
koto. See zithers
Kotosh culture, **2:**10–11
Kotte (kingdom), **5:**959
Kottonmouth Kings (musical group), **3:**359
ko tuzumi. See drums: hourglass
Kotzebue, August Friedrich Ferdinand von, **9:**17, 35
Kotzebue, Otto von, **9:**17, 38, 752
Kotzwara, Franz, **3:**839
Kou Qianzhi, **7:**312, 320–21
Koudal, Jens Henrik, **8:**464
Koukias, Constantine, **9:**75
Koùñbauñ dynasty, **4:**365, 378

Kourbelis, John, **9:**75
Koussevitzky Music Foundation, **3:**174
Kouyate, Djimo (*kora* player), **1:**8
Kouyaté, Mamadou, **1:**151
Kouyate, Tata Bambo, **1:**366
Kovach, K., **8:**853
Kovai (Managalasi flute player), **9:**503
Kovalcsik, Katalin, **8:**272, 274–75
Kovaleva, Olga, **8:**776, 777
Kove people, **9:**614
Kow, Michel Yieng, **9:**973
Koyaanisqatsi (film), **3:**204
Kozak, Joszef, **8:***155*
Koziki (Japanese history), **7:**59, 586
Kozima Tomiko, **7:**593
Kozina, Marjan, **8:**921
Kozlovsky, Alexei Fedorovich, **6:**904
Kôzyô no tuki (Taki), **7:**731
Kpamanda, Maurice, **1:***685*, 687
Kpelle people, **10:**55–56, 59–61
   choral singing of, **1:**10
   dance of, **1:**113
   epics of, **1:**107, 124, 128–29, 130–44, 488; **10:**59–60
   events timing, **1:**134–35; **10:**59–60
   history of, **1:**466
   instrument categories, **1:**10, 467
   music of, **1:**466–67
   performance concepts, **10:**57, 64
   sang concept, **1:**7
   time reckoning, **1:**125, 143–44
   writing system of, **1:**3
Kponton, Hubert, **1:***315*
Krader, Barbara, **3:***517*; **8:**907
Kraft-Ebbing, Richard, **3:**90
Kraftwerk, **3:**689, 690
Kraja, Marie, **8:**999
Krakatau, **4:**109–10
krakowiak, **3:**893, 894; **8:**708–9
Krall, Diana, **3:**1097, 1107
Krama (musical group), **8:**802, *802*
Krämer, Augustin F., **9:**23–24, 737, 751
Kramer, Billy J., **8:**214
Kramer, David, **1:**780
Kramer, Gorni, **8:**619
Kramik Pustak-Mālikā (Bhatkande), **5:**46, 52
Kranjska Čbelica (periodical), **8:**922
Kras (musical group), **8:**920
Krăstev, Venelin, **8:**905, 907
Kraučanka, Siarhiej, **8:***219*
Kraus, Alfredo, **3:**852
Kraus, Lili, **9:**929
Kraus, Shmulik, **6:**1073
Krause, E. R. W., **9:**908
Krause, Fritz, **9:**640
Krause, Tom, **8:**485
Krauss, Alison, **3:**159
Kreasi Baru (Macht), **3:**1016
Kreek, Cyrillus, **8:**498
Krehbiel, Henry Edward, **3:**510, 576
Kreisler, Fritz, **7:**381; **8:**96
Kreisler, Georg, **8:**675
Kreitner, Kenneth, **3:**826
Krek, Uroš, **8:**921
Kremenliev, Boris, **8:**121, 907
Křenek, Ernst, **8:**659

Kresánek, Josef, **8:**733
Kreslin, Vlado, **8:**921
Kretzschmer, Andreas, **8:**656
Krez, Geza de, **3:***1184*
Kriashen Tatars, **8:**772, 773
Kridha Beksa Wirama school, **4:**677
Krishna (deity), **5:***249*, 625
   association with Braj region, **5:**247, 550
   birthday of, **5:**276
   flute playing of, **5:**247, 306, 325, 339, 350, 354
   Guruṅg adaptation of, **5:**701, 704
   manifestations of, **5:**249
   portrayed in dances, **5:**132, *440*, 493, 494, 495, 501, 503, 504, 505, 511, 520
   songs about, **5:**163, 170, 173, 180, 219, 230, 252, 253, 266, 301
   visual depictions of, **5:**313
   worship of, **5:**72, 247–48, 249, 250, 251, 259, 401, 501, 512, 517, 551, 617–18, 629, 630, 632, 633, 643, 665–66, 677, 724, 844–45, 846, 855, 891
Krishna Ayyar, Mylattur, **5:***391*
Krishna Das, **5:**251
Krishna, M. Balamurali, **5:**232
Krishna Pillai, H. A., **5:**923
Krishnadevaraya, Vijayanagar emperor, **5:**263
Krishnamurthi, Kavita, **5:**421
Krishnan, Ramnad, **5:**159
Krishnappa, Bidaram, **5:**393
Kriss Kross, **3:**702
Kristen Kaset, **9:**989
Kristensen, Evald Tang, **8:**18, 460, *461*, 463–64, 465
Kristi, Leo, **4:**110
Kristofferson, Kris, **3:**81, 317
kriti, **5:**36, 94, 100, 218, 219, 268–69, 387
   composed by Diksitar, **5:**223–27
   composed by Syama Sastri, **5:**228–29
   composed by Tirunal, **5:**230
   composed by Tyagaraja, **5:**209, 211, 217, 220–23, 390–91, 393, 394–95
   development of, **5:**216
   niravall sāhitya prastāra improvisation in, **5:**98–99, 147–48
   rāgamālikā technique in, **5:**218–19
   ragas in, **5:**97
   sāhitya text in, **5:**385
   structure of, **5:**145–47
   svara kalpana improvisation in, **5:**98–99, 148
   tempo of, **5:**149
   women performers of, **5:**388–89, 410–11, 414
Krivan (dance ensemble), **3:**1197–98
Krivichi tribe, **8:**758, 760
Krivopolenova, M. D., **8:**130
Kroeber, Alfred L., **3:**418
Krohn, Ilmari, **8:**488, 937
Krohn, Julius, **8:**488
Krohn, Kaarle, **8:**488
Krolikowski, Ed, **3:**893
Krom Phra Nakhawn Sawan Waraphinit, Prince, **4:**330
Kroma, Senesee (Vai elder), **1:**344
Kronborg: 1582 (Jones), **3:**199
Kronos Quartet, **3:**335; **7:**1025
Kroo Young Stars Rhythm Group, **1:**380, 381

Kṛṣhṇalīlātaraṅgiṇī (Narayanatirtha), **5:**452
KRS-One, **3:**699
Kru people
  guitar music, **1:**353
  history of, **1:**370–75
  music of, **1:**375–82, 669
Krüger, Gundolf, **9:**982
Krukova, A. M., **8:**130
Krusenstern, Adam Johann, **9:**896
Kruta, Beniamin, **8:**990, 1003
Kryl, Bohumir, **3:**566
Kryvichans, **8:**790
Ksetrayya, **5:**219, 266–67, 269
Kshatriya class, **5:**386, 398
  function of, **5:**9
  in Goa, **5:**735
  life-cycle ceremonial music of, **5:**284
Kshemakarna, **5:**314, *315*
Ksidakis, Nikos, **8:**1022
KSMB (musical group), **8:**216
Kua people, **1:**468–69
Kuautoga, Takaroga, **9:**974
Kuba, Ludvik, **8:**18, 936–37, 961, 970
Kuba people, **1:**666
Kūbān, 'Alī Ḥassan, **6:**644
Kubelik, Jan, **4:**870; **6:**1025
Kubik, Gerhard, **1:**51, 56, 59, 68, 136, 150,
    364, 663, 713, 714, 730; **3:**585;
    10:28, 109–24, *113–14*
  on Bantu line, **1:**599
  impact notation and, **1:**254
  research on rhythm, **1:**10, 135, 156
  research on tuning, **1:**563, 570, 604, 635,
    715, 741–42, 744–45
  transcriptions of, **1:**157–58, *159*
Kubitschek, Juscelino, **2:**317
Kuchma, Alexander, **3:**58
Kuckles, **9:**443
Kucsan, Kathy, **3:**459
"*Kudala Kwetu Sasi Valela,*" **1:**218
Kudau Singh Maharaj, **5:**121
Kudumiyamalai rock inscription, **5:**24
Kugak chŏnjip (collection), **7:**953, 993
Kugak Hyŏphoe (society), **7:**990
Kugak Kŏnsŏl Ponbu (association), **7:**990
Kugak munhŏn charyo chipsŏng (Chang), **7:**854
Kugak taesajŏn (Chang), **7:**854
Kugak Yŏnbo (periodical), **7:**993
Kugaksa Yangsŏngso (institute), **7:**990
Kugu-nganhcharra people, **9:**430, 462
Kuhač, Franjo, **8:**933, 936, 961
Kuhlau, Friedrich, **8:**460
Kuhnau, Johann, **8:**654
Kui people, **4:**316
Kūkai, **7:**612
Kukcho oryeŭi (ceremonial book), **7:**982
Kukhwa yŏp'esŏ (Hwang), **7:**955
Kukkŭksa (*ch'anggŭk* troupe), **7:**910
Ku Klux Klan, **3:**354–55
Kukra Sumu, **2:**750
Kukuzel, Yoan, **8:**904
Kul Himmet, **6:**796
Kul Huseyn, **6:**796
Kulatillake, Cyril de Silva, **5:**957, 959, 960, 962,
    963–64, 965, 968
Kulesha, Gary, **3:**1091

Kuliev, Aliaqa, **6:**924
Kulkarni, Baburao, **5:**135
Kull layl wa-kull yawm (Hamdi), **6:**604
Kullapse (musical group), **3:**1052
Kullervo (Sallinen), **8:***187*
Kulliyat al-Tarbiyya al-Musiqiyya (Cairo), **6:**45
Kulthūm, Umm. *See* Umm Kulthūm
Kultura Popullore (periodical), **8:**1003
Kulumindini Band, **9:**444, 445, 446
Kulung (Kpelle epic performer), **1:***124, 127,*
    131–32
Kuluwaimaka, J. P. K., **9:**969
Kuman people
  courtship songs, **9:**326
  music and dance of, **9:**522–26
Kumano, Harry, **3:**1084
Kumano zyûnisyo zyûnitabi (Sibato), **7:**713
Kumaon people, **5:**501
Kumar, Arvind, **5:**429
Kumar, Hemant, **5:**537
Kumar, Kishore, **5:**420, 539
Kumar, Nita, **5:**674
Kumar, Vani, **5:**855
Kumara (deity), **5:**224
Kumari (deity), **5:**505
Kumasi Trio, **1:**353–54, 355, 356, 358
Kumbhakarna, king of Rajasthan, **5:**45
Kumbhan Das, **5:**251
Kumer, Zmaga, **8:**922
Kumgang Music Group, **7:**797
Kŭmgangsan ŭi sori (North Korean opera), **7:**962
Kŭm hapchabo (collection), **7:**835, 856, 983
Kumhār community, **5:**648
Kumiai culture, **2:**595, 598
Kumina cult, **2:**897–98, 901, 902–3
Kumu Kahua Theater (Honolulu), **9:**233
Kuna culture, **2:**188, 637–49, 771, 772
  aesthetics of, **2:**648
  history of, **2:**637–38
  instruments of, **2:**640–43, 772
  musical contexts and genres, **2:**644–47
  narratives of, **2:**19
  population of, **2:**637
  research on, **2:**649, 783
Kunaityô sikibu syokugakubu (organization), **7:**757
Kunanbaev, Abai, **6:**959–60
Kŭnariyŏ (Chŏong), **7:**969
Kunayza, **6:**296
Kunbam t'aryŏng (Korean folk song), **7:**881
Kunda, Touré, **8:**238
Kundera, Milan, **8:**730
kundus. *See* drums: hourglass
!Kung people. *See also* San people
  dance, **1:**115, 117
  healing rituals, **1:**112–13, 115, 274
  music of, **1:**305–7
Kungjung muyong mubo (dance notations), **7:**993
Kungla (dance ensemble), **3:**1196
Kungliga Musikaliska Akademien (Stockholm),
    8:448
Kungnip Ch'anggŭk Tan (National Ch'anggŭk
    Opera Troupe), **7:**968, 983
Kungnip Kugagwŏn (Korean Traditional
    Performing Arts Center), **7:**45, 56,
    804, 808, 855, 856–57, 861, 953,
    975, 977, 983, 989, 992–93

Kungnip Kugak Kodŭng Hakkyo (institute),
    7:989
Kungnip Muyong Tan (National Dance Troupe),
    7:983
Kungurtuk (musical group), **7:**1024
Kunnāsh al-Ḥā'ik (Tetouan), **6:**367, 371
Kunnbi caste, **5:**738
kunqu, **7:**91, 289–96
  all-female troupes for, **7:**407, 408
  avocational performers of, **7:**394, 396
  codification of, **7:**289–90
  decline of, **7:**278
  drama types in, **7:**290–92
  embellishment in, **7:**123
  history of, **7:**293–96
  Hong Kong, **7:**432–33
  influence on *Jiangnan sizhu*, **7:**224
  librettos for, **7:**292–93
  modernization of, **7:**399
  North America, **3:**961–62
  origins of, **7:**89, 277, 289
  Peking opera influenced by, **7:**283, 287
  qudi use in, **7:**184
  revival of, **7:**294–95, 381
  scales in, **7:**116
  schools of, **7:**55
  source materials on, **7:**129
  Taiwan, **7:**429
Kunqu Chuan Xi Suo (Suzhou), **7:**294
Kunqu Society (New York), **3:**962
Kunsthistorisches Museum (Vienna), **8:**529
Kunst, Jaap, **1:**261; **8:**19, 534, 535; **9:**372, 490,
    570; **10:**51
  research on Balinese music, **4:**733
  research on Balkan-Indonesian relationships,
    4:796
  research on Javanese music, **4:**28, 603, 634,
    636, 637, 645, 677
  research on Kai music, **4:**813
  research on Sumatran music, **4:**103
  research on Sundanese music, **4:**701, 703
Kunst-Van Wely, C. J. A., **4:**733
Kunthong Assunee, **4:**100
Künzig Institute for East German Folklore, **8:**664
Kuo, Kaiser, **7:**365–67
Ku'oko'a (newspaper), **9:**21–22
Kuoy people, **4:**154, 172
Kupala, Janka, **8:**790
Kupferberg, Tuli, **3:**317
Kuppuswami, K., **5:**912
Kuppuswamy, Pushpavanam, **5:**556
Kura people, **1:**624
Kurach'ŏlsagŭmbo (Yi), **7:**925
Kurai tobira (Yamada), **7:**731
Kurama people, **1:**289
Kuramayama (*nagauta* piece), **7:**673
Kuranko people. *See* Koranko people
Kurath, Gertrude Prokosch, **3:**221, 367, 429,
    457, 465, 484
Kurava people, **5:**519
Kurban-*baggy*, **6:**976
Kurdikar, Mogubai, **5:**413, *413*, 460
Kurdish people
  aerophones of, **6:**414, 415
  in Armenia, **6:**743–44
  chordophones of, **6:**408

in Georgia, **8:**840
in Iran, **6:**743–44, 839, 843
in Iraq, **6:**743–44
in North America, **3:**1028
in Syria, **6:**565, 743–44
in Turkey, **6:**251, 743–44
Kurdistan
  demography of, **6:**743
  geography of, **6:**743
  history of, **6:**743–45
  instruments in, **6:**415, 745–46
  Iranian dance traditions in, **6:**877
  map of, **6:**744
  Sufi ceremonies in, **6:**12, 180–81
  vocal music of, **6:**746–51
Kuria people, **1:**599, 641
Kurmangazy State Orchestra of Folk Instruments,
  6:959
Kurohune (Yamada), **7:**732
Kurosawa Akira, **7:**750
Kurosawa Kinko I, **7:**703
Kurosawa Takatomo, **7:**524; **10:**28
Kurpiński, Karol, **8:**710
Kurtág, György, **8:**744
Kurtis Blow, **3:**698
Kurumba people, **5:**284, 887, 903, 909, 915–16
Kurup, D. Parameswara, **5:***932*
Kuṟuppā caste, **5:**931, 932
Kusano Taeko, **7:**524
Kusen, Kurash, **7:**469
Kushans, **5:**720
Kushnarev, Christopher, **8:**784
Kuss, Malena, **2:**116
Kusturica, Emir, **8:**969
Kusudiardjo, Bagong, **4:**698
Kusumadinata, Machyar, **4:**702–3
Kusuma label, **4:**681
Kusumo, Amna S., **3:**1013
Kutamba Rhapsody (White), **3:**608
Kutayla Ibn Qurānghān, **6:**298
Kutché (album), **8:**238
Kutev, Filip, **8:**201, 890, 902, 905
Kuti, Fela Anikulapo, **1:**477, 483; **2:**410
Kutin people, **1:**654
Kuular, Anatoli, **6:***986;* **7:**1024–25
"*Ku'u Leialoha*" (King), **9:**925
Kuŭm (album), **7:**972
Kuŭm tasŭrŭm (album), **7:**972
Kuvezin, Albert, **7:**1024
Kuwait
  chordophones in, **6:**409, 412
  dance traditions in, **6:**654, 706, 709, 710
  maqām traditions in, **6:**552
  al-nuban ritual, **6:**546
  pearl-diving songs, **6:**546, 651
  ṣawt genre, **6:**651–52
  women's music, **6:**697, 701, 702
al-Kuwaytī, 'Abd-al-Laṭīf, **6:**651
Kuyateh, Hawa, **1:**497, 505
Kuyateh, Pa Sanasi, **1:**495, *500,* 501–2, 503,
  504, 506, 509, 511, 512
Kuzma-Demian (god), **8:**793
Kuzniacoŭ, Ivan, **8:**800
Kvæðamannafélag Siglufjardar, **8:**407
Kvæðamannafélagið Hafnarfjardar, **8:**407
Kværne, Elisabeth, **8:**430

Kvam, Janet, **3:**868
Kvitka, Klyment, **8:**19, 784–85, 803, 821
Kwa groups, **1:**468–69
Kwadwa, Byron, **1:**217–18
K'waejina ch'ingch'ing nane (Korean folk song),
  7:883, *883*
Kwai, Didi Lee, **9:**222
Kwaidan (film), **7:**751
Kwaio Cultural Centre, **9:**964
Kwaio people
  music and dance of, **9:**666, 962, 977
  panpipe music of, **9:**398, 401
Kwaiut people, **9:**982
Kwajalein Atoll (Marshall Islands), **9:**715
Kwak (*post-zouk* group), **2:**919
Kwakiutl (Kwá-kwa-kya-wakw) Indian nation,
  3:26, 394, 509
  winter ceremony, **3:**399–401
Kwalwasser, Jacob, **3:**278
Kwamin, **1:**356
Kwan, Leonard, **9:**389
Kwanak Yongsan Hoesang (*chŏngak* suite), **7:**848,
  868–69
Kwangdaega (Sin), **7:**814, 969, 985
Kwangdaega (Yi), **7:**953
Kwanhyŏn sigok "Na ŭi noguk" (Lee), **7:**956
Kwanjong, Koryŏ king, **7:**26
Kwanongoma College, **1:**40
Kwanuhui (Song), **7:**899, 905
Kwarekwareo people, **9:**401
kwela, **1:**219, 296, 322, 363, 387, 427, 430,
  608, 773–74; **10:**118, 119–20
Kwerba people, **9:**581
Kwok, Aaron (Guo Fusheng), **7:**355
Kwoma people, **9:**289, 982
Kwŏn Osŏng, **7:**853, 854
Kwŏn Samdŭk, **7:**898, 904, 906, 986
Kwon, Sungtaek, **7:**970
Kwŏnjuga (*kasa*), **7:**927
Kyagambiddwa, Joseph, **1:**36, 44, 210, 216, 217,
  223, 230, 607
Kyana Corroboree, **9:**60
Kyego, **7:**981
Kylander, Arthur, **3:**874
Kyōganoko musume dôzôzi (*kabuki* piece), **7:**671,
  673
kyôgen, **7:**76, 636–37
  female performers of, **7:**766
  hayasi in, **7:**683
  history of, **7:**536, 629–30
  huryu odori in, **7:**685
  interpolated melodies in, **7:**636
  patronage of, **7:**687
  stage in, **7:**630
  transmission of, **7:**759
Kyōkunsyô (Koma), **7:**547, 550, 587
Kyŏngbokkung t'aryŏng (Korean folk song), **7:**988
Kyŏngdŏk, Silla king, **7:**981
Kyrgyz people, **6:**995
  in Afghanistan, **5:**805
  in China, **7:**455–58
  epic songs, **6:**345
Kyrgyzstan. *See also* Central Asia
  Islamic culture in, **6:**935–47, 943
  mouth harp playing in, **5:**814
  performers in, **6:**844, 945

Ramadan songs, **6:**941
  shamanism in, **6:**967
  Soviet period in, **6:**903–490
  Uighur people in, **6:**995
Kyurkchijski, Krasimir, **8:**905
Kyzl-Orda University, **6:**960

La, Le (etc.). *See article plus next element in name*
Laade, Wolfgang, **6:**524; **7:**524; **8:**554, 574;
  9:509, 960, 974, 990, 992
La Argentina (dance group), **3:**851
Laba, Martin, **3:**1109
Laban, Rudolf von, **3:**221
Laban Institute of Movement Studies, **3:**221
La Banda de la Corona, **2:**396
La Banda de los Supremos Poderes, **2:**745
Labanotation, **1:**158, 161; **9:**316–17, *454, 466,*
  783, 926
LaBarbera, Joe, **3:**865
Labat, Jean Baptiste, **3:**596
LaBega, Carl, **2:**971
Labelle, Jean-Guy (Chuck), **3:**1194
LaBelle, Patti, **3:**107, 713
Labi, Gyimah, **1:**221, 226, 227, *228*
Laboe, Art, **3:**742
Labor Dance (Kazakh piece), **7:**461
Laborde, Jean Benjamin de, **6:**566
Labrador. *See* Newfoundland
Lacandón Maya, **2:**549, 656–58
Lacan, Jacques, **8:**192
Lach, Robert, **8:**846, 861
Lachmann, Robert, **6:**10, 22, 23, 502, 523–25,
  526, 529, 531, 1029, 1036, 1058–59,
  1066; **7:**569; **8:**266, 906
La Connexión Mexicana (musical group), **3:**780
Lacourcière, Luc, **3:**1167
La Croix, Pétis, **6:**566
Lacroix, Véronique, **3:**1152
La Cuadrilla Morena de Pancho Fierro, **2:**500
Lac Vieux Desert Indian nation, **3:**454
Lacy, Steve, **3:**131, 664
Ladake Genealogy (Tibetan writing), **7:**472
Ladakh
  bag-ston gyi glu (marriage songs), **5:**710
  Beda and Mon communities in, **5:**712–13
  instrumental ensembles in, **5:**715
  King Ge-sar epic in, **5:**712
  Mahayana Buddhism in, **5:**257
  map of, **5:***680*
  research on music of, **5:**715
  Tibetan monasteries in, **5:**713
Ladd, Edmund J., **3:**492
La De Das (musical group), **9:**167–69, *168*
Laderoute, Eugene, **3:**410
al-Lādhiqī, Muḥammad ibn 'Abd al-Ḥamīd,
  6:17, 365, 502, 508
Ladí, Estanislao, **3:**726
"Ladies First" (Queen Latifah), **3:**714
Ladies Ideal Band (Mauston, Wisconsin), **3:**566
Ladies Morning Musical Club (Montréal), **3:**1150
Ladies of Kaleva, **3:**823
La Diferenzia (musical group), **3:**780
Ladino (musical group), **8:**968
Ladipo, Duro, **1:**401, 408, *409,* 410–11; **10:**114
Ladipo, Gboyega, **10:**114
La Divina Pastora, **2:**960

Lado (musical group), **8:**152, 936, 937
La Dubonney (musical group), **3:**788
Lady in the Dark (Weill), **3:**545
"Lady Isabel and the Elf Knight" (ballad), **3:**519, 834, *834, 835*
Lady Macbeth of the Mtsensk District (Shostakovich), **7:**340
Ladysmith Black Mambazo, **1:**418, 431, 777, 779; **3:**339
La Fage, Adrien de, **5:**50
LaFarge, John, **9:**20
La Flesche, Francis, **3:**29, 31, 291, 498, 509
LaFontsee, Dane, **3:**498
Laforte, Conrad, **3:**1164, 1167; **8:**553, 554
LaFrance, Ron, **3:**465
Lagacé, Pierre-Minier, **3:**28
Lagdameo, Chinggay, **4:**885
Lagos City Orchestra, **1:**477
Lagos Philharmonic Society, **1:**233
La Grange, Anna de, **3:**60
Laguerre, Fédia, **3:**806
Lagueux, Cécile, **3:**1164
Lagzi Lajcsi (musical group), **8:**747
Lahiri, Tulsi, **5:**855
Lahjat-i Sikandar Shāhi (Yahya), **5:**45
Laḥn al-wafā' (Egyptian film), **6:**601
Lahu people, **4:**537, 538–40; **7:**485–92
     instruments of, **4:**540, *544, 545*
     Shehleh subgroup, **4:**540
Lai, Leon (Li Ming), **7:**355
Laïd, **6:**270
Laidlaw Foundation, **3:**1216
Laila, Runa, **5:**427–28
La India, **3:**743
Laing, David, **8:**373, 374
Laing, Irving, **3:**1077
Laird, Wayne, **9:***930*
Lais people, **4:**619
Laitinen, Heikki, **8:**486
Lajenn Etwal, **2:**843–44
Lajia people, **7:**486
Lakambini (Estella), **4:**871
Lake, Auntie Ma'iki Aiu, **9:**222
Lakeside (musical group), **3:**684, 700
Lake Tyers Gumleaf Band, **9:**134
Lakhe (deity), **5:**505
Lakmé (Delibes), **9:**38
Lakota Indian nation, **3:**484
     song sources, **3:**369
     Wounded Knee massacre, **3:**11, 421, 487, 494
Lakshadweep Islands, **5:**5
Lakshmana Pillai, **5:**90
Lakshmana Sena, king of Bengal, **5:**844–45
Lakshmanachariar, **5:***391*
Lakshmanan, B. V., **5:**232
Lakshmi (deity), **5:**277, 897
     worship of, **5:**503, 892
Lakshmi, K. R., **5:**226–27
Lakshmikant-Pyarelal (director duo), **5:**537, *537*
Lakshmiratnammal, Smt., **5:**389
L.A. Law (television show), **3:**1062
Lal Ded, **5:**689
La Lega, **9:**81
Lalemant, Father Gabriel, **3:**23
La Ley, **2:**374
Laliberté, Alfred, **3:**1150

La Lira (musical group), **8:**968
La Lira Colombiana, **2:**383
Lalitha, C., **5:**232
Lalla bint Salem, **1:***586*
Lalo, Édouard, **3:**1148
Lalonde, Bobby, **3:**1194
Lalonde, Pierre, **3:**1158
La Loubere, Simon de, **4:**70, 222, 225, 231, 233, 234, 236, 238, 251, 252, 254, 284
Lā'l Shahbāz Qalandar (Sufi saint), **5:**754, 759–61, 780; **6:**884, 889
Lam, Doming, **7:**232
Lam, Joseph, **7:**595; **10:**20–21, 24, 26
Lam Manyee, **7:**232
Lamadrid, Enrique R., **3:**757, 849; **10:**88, 89
La Mafia (musical group), **3:**780
Lamb, Joseph, **3:**651
lambada, **2:**94, 107, 354
Lambata, **4:**796
Lambert, Adélard, **3:**1166
Lambert, Charles, **3:**606
Lambert, Jean, **6:**23, 24
Lambert, Sidney, **3:**606
Lambeth Walk, **8:**660
Lambovič, Liza, **8:**801
Lambro (Rom *zurla* player), **8:**977
lamellophones (also lamellaphones)
     Africa, **1:**294, 295–96; **10:**118
     agidìgbo, **1:**317, 356, 474, 476, 479
     Azande people, **1:**650
     Baluan, **9:**602
     bambaro (or *bomboro*), **1:**449
     begube, **9:**178
     bekura (also *tagowande*), **9:**648–49
     bekuru, **9:**647
     belembaopachut, **9:**745
     bell-resonator, **1:**668–69
     benta, **2:**505
     bingkong, **9:**592
     biŋgoŋ, **9:**570
     Central Africa, **1:**678–79
     cisanji, **1:**320, 670, 678–79
     diffusion of, **1:**317–20
     gbèlee, **1:**467
     híriyùla, **9:**537–38, 540–41
     ikembe, **1:**172, 299
     Ila people, **1:**712
     Irian Jaya, **9:**487, 582, 591
     kadongo, **1:**299; **10:**114
     kahanzi, **1:**713
     kalimba, **1:**320; **3:***1170*
     karimba, **1:**624, 745
     kembe, **1:**299–300, 664
     kikau akatangi, **9:**900
     kondi, **1:**570
     koŋgoma, **1:**329, *334,* 356, 467
     kuleru, **9:**661
     likembe, **1:**295, 297, 299, 317, 320, 322, 608, 669, 678–79
     makomako, **9:**656
     malimba, **1:**711
     marímbola (also *marimba*), **2:**528, *850, 851,* 854, 857
     marímbula (also *marimba*), **2:**401, 834–35, 930, 933–34, 941, 960; **9:**103
     mbila dzamadeza, **1:**709

mbira, **1:**10, 136, 715–16, 744–50, 752–53, 756; **3:**132
mbira dzavadzimu, **1:**153, 319, 429, 432, 433–35, 745–47, 752
mbøŋgo, **1:**319
mokena, **9:**793
mucapata, **1:**318, 679
New Caledonia, **9:**679
nja, **9:**76
Nkhumbi people, **1:**714
Oceania, **9:***241,* 374, 476
olaiyole, **9:**536
origin of, **1:**715–16
pagur, **9:**640
Palau, **9:**723
Papua New Guinea, **9:**286, 508, 512, 530, 531–33, 548, 549, 556, 558, *571,* 606, 623, 630
prempresiwa, **1:**356
pupuaha, **9:**503
rhumba box, **2:**897, 906, 907
rōria, **9:**933
San people, **1:**705
Shona people, **1:**745–50
Sikaiana, **9:**848
South Aermica, **2:**16
southeastern Africa, **1:**708
southern Africa, **1:**702, 719
taimbagos, **9:**560
tambagle, **9:**525–26
taŋguxi, **9:**615
Tanzania, **1:**638–39
tembakl, **9:**521
timbrh, **1:**319
tioro, **9:**895
tita'apu, **9:**895
tukin, **9:**563
tuning of, **1:**715–16, 746–47
ulimba, **1:**317, 639
ūtete, **9:**816, 828
'ūtete, **9:**793
utete, **9:**807
Vanuatu, **9:**708
West Africa, **1:**449
West Futuna, **9:**863
Zaïre, **1:**423
Zimbabwe, **1:**719
laments
     Abkhazian people, **8:**852
     Albania, **8:**132, 144, 196, 990, 992
     Algeria, **6:**473
     Anuta, **9:**290, 297, 307
          puatanga, **9:**857, 858, 860
     Arabian peninsula
          naḥba, **6:**651
          nawḥ, **6:**696
     Azerbaijan, *mərsiyə*, **6:**924, 931
     Balkarian people, **8:**857
     Belarus, **8:**793, 794
     Bellona, *haingaa tangi*, **9:**850, 852
     Bolivia, **2:**292
     Bosnia-Hercegovina, **8:**963
     Bulgaria, **8:**901
     Carriacou, *hallecord*, **2:**869
     Central Asia, **6:**945
     China, marriage, **7:**421

Chuuk, *asangut*, **9:**734, 735
Chuvash people, **8:**773
Colombia, *guabina*, **2:**391
Corsica, **8:**144–45, 196, 566–67, 568
Crete, **8:**120
Croatia, *Gospin plač*, **8:**929
  in Eastern Orthodoxy, **8:**11
Ecuador, on Atahualpa, **2:**427
Egypt, Nubian, **6:**643
Europe, **8:**8, 127, 132–33, 143, 144–45, 196
  bridal, **8:**114, 132–33, 196, 475
  interactions with ballads, **8:**135
  intervallic range of, **8:**128
  men's performance of, **8:**198, 200
  performers of, **8:**114
  research on, **8:**23
Finland, **8:**475–76, 480
French Guiana, **2:**435
Georgia, **8:**196, 828, 834
Greece, **8:**9, 23, 120, 141, 144, 1010, 1025
  Epirus, **8:**114
Guadeloupe, *kantikamò*, **2:**876
Hmong people, **3:**1004
Holocaust songs, **8:**276, 289
Hungary, **8:**23, 120, 128, 737, 739, 740–41,
  744, 745
India, North, bride departure songs, **5:**275,
  414–15
Iran, **6:**942
  nowhe, **6:**826, 833, 840
Ireland, **8:**23, 128, 132, 143, 196, 295,
  378–79, 387, 388, 389
Irian Jaya, **9:**580, 583
  Asmat people, **9:**590
  Eipo *layelayana*, **9:**594
  Sentani people, **9:**587
  Yali people, **9:**584, *585*
Irish-American, **3:**843
Italy, **8:**23, 120, 128, 607
  Basilicata, **8:**119
Japan, *ruika*, **7:**620
Jewish, **8:**250
Kapingamarangi, *langa tangihangi*, **9:**838
Karachaevian people, **8:**857
Karelia, **8:**120, 132, 481, 488, 489
Kazakhstan, wedding, **6:**951
Kiribati, *bomaki*, **9:**763
Kuna culture, **2:**645–46
Lebanon, **6:**545
Luangiua, *huakanga* and *sa'a*, **9:**843
Macedonia, **8:**120
Malta, **8:**638
Mangareva, *tau* and *akareimarū*, **9:**887
Māori people, **9:**939, 940–42
Marquesas Islands, *uē tūpāpa'u*, **9:**894
Marshall Islands, **9:**752
Mashriq, **6:**537
Maya culture, **2:**653, 721–22, 731
Miskitu culture, *inanka*, **2:**660, 662–63
Montenegro, **8:**958
Morocco
  Berber *ladkar*, **6:**486
  Judeo-Arabic, **6:**1042
  wedding, **6:**301, 480
Muslim, **5:**772
  majlis genre, **5:**256, 284, 286; **6:**626, 840,
  937

Nepal, **5:**698
New Caledonia, **9:**23
Niue, **9:**817
North Caucasia, **8:**851
Ossetian people, **8:**859
Pakhtun people, **5:**785
Pakistan, bride departure songs, **5:**275–76
Papua New Guinea
  Anêm people, **9:**616
  Bali and Vitu islands, **9:**610
  Baluan, **9:**604
  Banoni *tanisi*, **9:**645–46
  Buang *susën*, **9:**567
  Buin people, **9:**326, 650–53
  Enga people, **9:**535
  Huli crying, **9:**539–40
  Huli people, **9:**538
  Managalasi people, **9:**504
  Manam people, **9:**245
  Nagovisi *marimari*, **9:**648
  Nissan *kirkiring*, **9:**638
  Titan *ndrilang* dirges, **9:**601
  Umboi *tingiizi*, **9:**574
Peru, *penalivio* (also *panalivio*), **2:**495
Philippines, **4:**911
Poland, **8:**702–3
Polish wedding, **3:**892
Polynesia, **9:**202
Portugal, **8:**579
Punjab (Pakistan), *nohā* and *marsīya*,
  5:772
Rapa Nui, **9:**952
Romania, **8:**23, 120, 871–72, 874, 879
Russia, **8:**23, 120, 758, 761–63
  aukan'e, **8:**760
  Rom people, **8:**287
  wedding, **8:**761, *762*, 774
Sardinia, **8:**631
Scotland, **8:**360–61, 367
Serbia, **8:**941
Sikaiana, *tani*, **9:**847
Slovenia, **8:**137, 911
Solomon Islands
  'Are'are people, **9:**667
  Bellonese, **9:**324–25
  Isabel Province, **9:**660
  Russell Islands *tatal*, **9:**664
  Sirovanga people, **9:**654
South Asia, **5:**272, 273
Sufi, **6:**795–96
Takuu, *lluu* and *sau*, **9:**841–42
Tamil Nadu, **5:**925
  oppāri (also *pilākkaṇam*), **5:**907
Tikopia, *fuatanga*, **9:**853–55
Tokelau, *haumate*, **9:**113, 824–25, *825*
Tonga, **9:**785–86
Trinidad and Tobago, *marseeha*, **2:**959
Tuamotu Islands, *fagu tutagi*, **9:**884–85
Turkey, **6:**80
  ağit, **6:**761–62, 766–67
  mersiye, **6:**768, 769
Umayyad era, **6:**295–96
Uttar Pradesh, **5:**661
'Uvea, *hiva*, **9:**810–11
Vep people, **8:**772
women's performance of, **8:**120, 200

La Meri (pseud. of R. M. Hughes), **6:**876
Lamond, Mary Jane, **3:**1073, 1127
Lamothe, Willie, **3:**1077, 1155
Lamotrek Atoll (Yap State, FSM), **9:**29, 712, 729
Lamour, Dorothy, **9:**45, 67
Lampel, Max, **6:**1025
Lampião (Brazilian bandit), **2:**327
Lan Xang (kingdom), **4:**350, 353, 354, 356
Lancefield, Robert, **3:**496
Lancere, Gita, **8:**507
Lanctot, Gustave, **3:**1166
"Land of a Thousand Dances" (Cannibal and the
  Headhunters), **3:**747
"Land of a Thousand Dances" (Pickett), **3:**710
"Land of a Thousand Dances" (Thee Midniters),
  3:747
"Land of the Sky-Blue Water" (Cadman), **3:**539
Landa, Diego de, **2:**557
Landau, Paul, **6:**1030
Landers, Joan, **9:**221
Landini, Francesco, **8:**72
ländler, **8:**168
  in Austria, **8:**672, 673, 674
  in Low Countries, **8:**524
  in Switzerland, **8:**689–90
Landon, Margaret, **4:**285
Landowska, Wanda, **3:**1210
Landry, Jeanne, **3:**1151
Landry, Ned, **3:**1125, 1257
Landslaget for Spelemenn, **8:**426–27
Landtman, Gunnar, **9:**479
Lane, Bobby, **9:**426
Lane, Edward, **6:**21, 340, 544
Lane, Frankie, **3:**862
Laneth (periodical), **6:**249
Laney College (Oakland), **3:**952
Laṅgā caste, **5:**345, 398, 401, 402–3, 476, *477*,
  639, 640–42
Lang, Andrew, **3:**147
Lang, David, **3:**177
lang, k. d., **3:***107*, 107–11, 252, 1091, 1110
Langapai (Buin musician), **9:**650
Lange, Francisco Curt, **2:**303
Langer, Suzanne, **3:**278; **7:**74
Langford, Andrew, **9:**397
Langi, Pāluki, **9:**113
Langley, Phillip, **9:***254*
Langrene, Bireli, **8:**288
Langsa (Tibetan opera), **7:**479
language and music
  Australia, children's songs, **9:**256–57
  cantillation, **1:**341, 346, 474
  China, theatrical delivery, **7:**279, 286,
  290
  curses, **1:**103
  glides, **1:**107
  Hawai'i, **9:**299–300
  herding calls, **8:**119–20
  Igbo people, **1:**459
  Irian Jaya, ceremonial languages, **9:**587, 591
  Islamic call to prayer (*adhān*; *azān*; *ezan*),
  1:332, *333*, 341, 348, 536; **6:**132,
  153–55, 352, 372, 517, 525, 538,
  649, 673, 937, 938, 939
    in Algeria, **6:**475
    in Arabian peninsula, **6:**713

Volume Key: **6**, Middle East; **7**, East Asia; **8**, Europe; **9**, Australia and the Pacific Islands; **10**, The World's Music.

language and music, Islamic call to prayer
(*continued*)
  in Egypt, **6:**165–66, 167–68
  in Turkey, **6:**57, 768
Islamic public sermons, **6:**937
Kuna culture, **2:**639
Mangareva, archaic languages, **9:**886
Māori *whaikōrero*, **9:**946
metaphor and symbolism, **6:**302–3; **9:**336–43
metaphorical terminology, **1:**257
metrics, **9:**324–25
Mongol people, animal communication,
  7:1003
multilingual countries, popular music in,
  8:209
narrative techniques, **1:**107–8
New Caledonia, ceremonial speech, **9:**672,
  673–74
Nicaragua, drum signals, **2:**757
North West Frontier Province, drum codes,
  5:789
Oceania, **9:**319–43
onomatopoeia, **1:**125, 131, 235
oration, **9:**297
Papua New Guinea
  Baluan ritual language, **9:**603
  ceremonial languages, **9:**637
phonemic play, **9:**326–30, 432, 569–70, 676,
  723, 836, 837
proverbs' use in musical performance, **1:**132
religious lyrics, **9:**188, 189
Sāmoa
  cheering and jeering, **9:**803–4
  verbal imagery, **9:**216–17
Siberia, shaman sound effects, **7:**1029
sonics, **9:**325–30
speech-song continuum, **9:**321
speech surrogates, **1:**89, 105–7, 204–6, 316,
  451, 466, 472, 650–51; **2:**505–6;
  4:554–55, 905; **7:**417, 491–92, 511,
  520; **9:**374
speech tone patterns, **1:**730–31; **7:**262–63,
  270–71
Tikopia, gender-based insults, **9:**247–49
Tonga, sung speeches, **9:**789
transcription of, **9:**322–24
tropical-forest discourse on music, **2:**127–28
tropical-forest oratory, **2:**128
Uttar Pradesh, drum codes, **5:**291
Vanuatu, secret languages, **9:**699
Yoruba "holy words," **1:**404
Language Movement (Bengal), **5:**858
languages. *See also* linguistics
Abkhazian, **8:**850, 854
Adamawa-Eastern group, **1:**650
Adighian, **8:**850, 854
African, **1:**2–3; **2:**902
Afrikaans, **1:**761
Agöb, **9:**506–9
Ainu, **7:**783
ajmi, **1:**537
Albanian, **3:**926; **8:**604, 986
Aleut, **3:**374
Algonquian (Algonkian) family, **3:**383, 440,
  451, 461, 462, 1074, 1085
Altaic family, **7:**18–19, 447, 517; **8:**772

Ambulas, **9:**549
Amuzgo, **2:**563
Anatom, **9:**702
Andean phylum, **2:**78
Angan family, **9:**494, 496
Anir, **9:**639
Arabic, **1:**532, 571; **6:**9, 12, 167, 213–14,
  273, 274, 322, 540, 902
  in Coptic texts, **6:**222–23
  Nubian use of, **6:**641, 643–44
  in Syria, **6:**565
  in Yemen, **6:**685–86
Arabi-Malayalam, **5:**947
Aramaic, **6:**225, 226, 1047–48
Araucanian, **2:**232
Arawak, **2:**125, 434, 668
'Are'are, **9:**664
Armenian, **6:**723
Assamese, **5:**6, 249, 503, 660
Athapaskan family, **3:**440, 1085, 1274
Athuva, **5:**959
Austral Islands, **9:**879
Australian indigenous, **9:**319, 423, 427, 428,
  431, 433, 439–40, 444
Austroasiatic family, **4:**529, 546–47, 560; **5:**5,
  480; **7:**19, 447
Austronesian family, **4:**529, 531, 594, 786,
  913; **7:**447, 523; **9:**319
  Eastern Oceanic, **9:**688
  Other Melanesian, **9:**688–89
  Papua New Guinea, **9:**488, 492, 498, 545,
    548–49, 560, 561, 566, 574, 600,
    602, 607–8, 614, 617, 620, 626, 632,
    642, 644
  Solomon Islands, **9:**664
  Vanuatu, **9:**688
Avadhi, **5:**247, 249, 495, 660
Aymara, **2:**205, 282, 283, 293, 466, 467–68
Azerbaijani, **6:**831, 843, 921
Bahasa Bima, **4:**779
Bahasa Samawa, **4:**779
Bajan, **2:**813
Balinese, **4:**739
Balkarian-Karachaevian, **8:**850
Balochi, **5:**5, 6, 744, 773, 778
Balti, **5:**792, *793*, 794
Baltic family, **8:**399, 509
Bandanese, **4:**817
Bantu group, **1:**650, 657, 700, 703, 712, 716,
  744
Basa Sunda, **4:**699
Bashkir, **8:**772
Basque, **3:**849; **8:**309, 315, 539, 595
Belarusan, **8:**790, 800, 802
Bellona, **9:**848
Belu, **4:**796
Bengali, **5:**6, 7, 247, 249, 254, 404, 533, 660,
  844
  in United Kingdom, **5:**573
Berber, **1:**575; **6:**273–74, 429, 497
Beurla-reagad, **8:**295
Bhojpuri, **2:**958; **5:**5, 183, 550, 600, 660
  in Fiji, **5:**612
  in Guyana, **5:**602
  in Trinidad, **5:**588–90
  in United States, **3:**813–14, 816

Bine, **9:**506–9
bini ritual language, **4:**799
Bislama, **9:**214, 690, 709, 861
Black English, **3:**1026
Braj Bhasha, **5:**5, 183, 247, 252, 256, 495,
  660
Brajbuli, **5:**247, 249
Breton, **8:**319, 539, 558, 561
Brythonic, **8:**319
Buin, **9:**649
Bundeli, **5:**724
Burmese, **4:**383
Burushaski, **5:**792, *793*, 794
Caddoan family, **3:**440, 466
Cahitan, **3:**437
Caló dialect, **3:**739, 742
Canadian Aboriginal, **3:**1056
Canarese, **5:**423
Cantonese, **3:**949, 951, 958; **4:**222; **7:**270–71,
  305, 433, 436
Carib, **2:**164, 176, 435, 668
Catalan, **8:**539, 604
Caucasian family, **8:**850, 854, 861
Cayuga, **3:**461
Celtic family, **8:**319, 320, 322
Central Africa, **1:**666, 670, 672
Central Amerind family, **2:**78
Chagatay Turkic, **6:**9
Chaozhou dialect, **3:**961; **4:**222; **7:**433
Chechen, **8:**850
Cheke Holo, **9:**659–62
Chibchan, **2:**78, 125, 127, 575
Chibchan-Paezan phylum, **2:**78, 188
Chimbu, **9:**522
Chinese, **3:**1057, 1215
  influence on Southeast Asian, **4:**69
Chinese (Mandarin), **3:**951; **7:**19, 22–23, 247,
  262–63, 424, 432, 497, 806, 833
Chinook, **3:**1258
Chuave, **9:**522
Chuvash, **8:**772
Cimbrian, **8:**617
Cirebonese, **4:**687
classification of, **2:**78, 81
Congo, **1:**663
Cook Islands Māori (Rarotongan), **9:**896, 898,
  908
Coptic, **6:**219–20, 223
Cornish, **8:**319, 558
Corsican, **8:**539, 566
Cree, **3:**344
Creole, **2:**4, 72, 242, 666, 678, 753, 792, 923,
  942–43, 968; **3:**813
Croatian, **8:**930, 933
Cuicatec, **2:**563
Czech, **8:**717, 726, 728
Dagbani, **10:**145
Dagestanian, **8:**850
Dai, **7:**496, 497, 498, 500, 503, 505–7
Danish, **8:**470
Dari, **5:**5, 6, 804, 808–9, 825
Delaware (Lenape), **3:**461
Deng, **7:**483
Ḍomaakí, **5:**800
Dorro, **9:**506–7
Dravidian family, **5:**5, 293, 350, 480, 508, 903

Drehu, **9**:682
Dutch, **2**:242, 927; **3**:813, 1057; **8**:518
Dzongkha, **5**:5, *6*
East African, **1**:598, 599
Eastern Abenaki, **3**:461
Eleman, **9**:494
Ellicean, **9**:834
Ende, **9**:506
Ende-Lio, **4**:791
English, **2**:242, 441, 630, 666, 772, 792, 813,
    840, 841, 923, 927, 932, 969; **3**:4,
    143, 820, 975–76, 1057, 1088, 1162;
    5:5, 7, 44, 49, 123, 375, 404, 443,
    487, 582, 588, 624, 736, 737, 745,
    911; **8**:342, 360, 378, 385–86, 389
English creole, **5**:601
Equatorial phylum, **2**:78
Equatorial-Tucanoan phylum, **2**:150
Erromango, **9**:702
Eskimo-Aleut family, **3**:374
Esselen-Yuman, **2**:595
Estonian, **8**:399, 491
Euskara (*See* Basque)
Fadikka, **6**:641, 644
Fagauvea, **9**:682
Faroese, **8**:468, 471, 472
Farsi, **3**:1035; **5**:44, 692, 766, 778, 804
Fiji Hindi, **5**:612
Finnish, **8**:399, 475, 480, 488, 772
Finno-Ugric family, **8**:399, 488, 491, 645,
    736, 772
Flemish, **8**:539
Folopa, **9**:494
Fon, **2**:342
French, **2**:242, 792, 873, 914, 947; **3**:4, 17,
    74, 143, 313, 315, 600, 1057, 1067,
    1073, 1154–62; **5**:44; **8**:539, 558, 682
French Creole (Kwéyòl), **2**:840, 841, 873,
    874, 878–79, 914, 916
Frisian, **8**:518
Futunic, **9**:834
Gaelic, **3**:150, 1070, 1127, 1128, 1129
Galician, **8**:595
Gallo dialect, **8**:558
Garhwali, **5**:291, 660
Garifuna, **2**:666, 675
Garove, **9**:608
Gê family, **2**:125, 127, 129–30, 143
Gê-Pano-Carib phylum, **2**:503
Georgian (Kartuli), **8**:826
German, **2**:666; **3**:52–53, 884, 886, 888, 889,
    1057; **5**:44; **8**:518, 604, 670
German dialects, **8**:539, 678, 682
Gidra, **9**:506
Gizra, **9**:506–9
Goidelic, **8**:319
Gondi, **5**:5
Greek, **3**:1057; **8**:604, 607, 617, 881
    in Egypt, **6**:219–20
    in Syria, **6**:227
Guaraní, **2**:282, 452, 458, 460
Guarijio, **2**:551–52, 553
Guayakí, **2**:452
Gujarati, **5**:6, 7, 247, 404, 533, 624
    in South Africa, **5**:615
    in United Kingdom, **5**:573

Gurumukhi, **5**:256
Hakka dialect, **7**:486
Hamito-Semitic family, **6**:273
Hausa, **1**:518; **6**:9
Hawai'ian, **3**:1051
Hebrew, **3**:939, 940; **5**:949; **6**:9, 12, 261,
    1015, 1023, 1024, 1047–48, 1070,
    1072; **8**:257, 258
Hindi, **2**:666; **3**:1215; **5**:5, *6*, 247, 249, 368,
    404, 427, 533, 624, 639, 660, 720,
    729, 736, 737, 866
    in Guyana, **5**:600
    in North America, **5**:581
    poetry and songs in, **5**:163, 219
    scholarly writings in, **5**:44, 45
    in South Africa, **5**:615
    in Trinidad, **5**:588, 591
    in United Kingdom, **5**:573
Hindustani, **5**:229, 534
Hiri Motu, **9**:488, 492, 494–95, 506
Hittite, **6**:358
Hmong, **4**:550
Ho, **5**:5
Hokan, **2**:78, 595; **3**:420, 433
Hoklo dialect, **7**:433
Hopi, **3**:428
Hungarian, **8**:272, 475, 736
Iaaï, **9**:682
Icelandic, **8**:404
Indian influences on, **4**:65
Indo-Aryan family, **5**:490, 660, 696, 700
Indo-European family, **5**:5, 731; **7**:19, 447;
    8:499, 509
Indo-Iranian family, **5**:480; **7**:13–14
Ingushian, **8**:850
Innu, **3**:73, 1162
Inupiak, **3**:374
Inupiat, **3**:486
Iranian, **6**:897, 965
Irish Gaelic, **8**:319, 378, 385–86, 389, 391
Iroquoian family, **3**:461, 462, 466
Irumu, **9**:567
Italian, **3**:1057; **8**:573, 682, 930
Japanese, **7**:19, 585, 731
Javanese, **4**:631–32, 635; **10**:44
Jopará, **2**:452, 460
Judeo-Berber, **6**:1035
Judeo-Spanish, **6**:1035
Jurchen, **7**:32
Kalmyk, **8**:772
Kambera, **4**:788
Kannada, **5**:5, *6*, 18, 89, 105, 211, 259, 350,
    368, 390, 508, 866, 868, 869, 881,
    883, 884, 885, 887, 906
    films in, **5**:542
    poetry and songs in, **5**:96, 219, 220, 231,
    264–65, 266, 452
Karib, **2**:125
Kartvelian family, **8**:826
Kashmiri, **5**:6, 683
Kâte, **9**:568
Kazakh, **6**:949; **7**:461
Kenya, **1**:622
Keresan, **3**:428
Kerewo, **9**:495
Khitan, **7**:32

Khmer, **4**:159
Khoisan, **1**:703
Khorasan Turkic, **6**:831, 839
Khowar, **5**:792, *793*, 794
Kiowa-Tanoan phylum, **2**:78; **3**:440
Kiwai, **9**:494, 495
Kodagu, **5**:886
Komi-Permiaki, **8**:772
Komi-Zyriane, **8**:772
Konkani, **5**:736, 737, 866, 881
Kope, **9**:495
Korean, **3**:975–76; **7**:19, 28, 871, 910
Kota, **5**:5, 905
Kudubi, **5**:877
Kuma, **9**:522
Kumaoni, **5**:291, 660
Kuna, **2**:639, 647
Kunza, **2**:356, 360
Kuot (Panaras), **9**:626
Kurdish, **6**:12, 743, 798
Kurmanji Kurdish, **6**:743
Kurukh, **5**:5
Kwaio, **9**:964
Kwakiutl, **3**:31
Ladin, **8**:617
Ladino, **3**:847; **6**:526; **8**:252, 254, 257, 258,
    596, 962, 968, 1011
Lamaholot, **4**:791
lanna thai, **4**:315
Lao, **3**:952
Latin, **8**:881
Latino-Faliscan, **8**:605
Latvian, **8**:399, 499
Lavukáleve, **9**:662
Lenca, **2**:739
levels of, **4**:65
Lhoba, **7**:482
Lithuanian, **8**:399, 509
Low German, **3**:52–53, 1238, 1250
Lozi, **1**:712–13
Lucumí, **3**:729, 785
lunfardo dialect, **2**:264
Luyana, **1**:713
Macedonian, **8**:972
Macro-Arawakan phylum, **2**:137
Macro-Carib phylum, **2**:78
Macro-Chibchan phylum, **2**:169, 183, 185,
    631, 659, 680, 750
Macro-Ge phylum, **2**:78
Macro-Panoan phylum, **2**:78
Macro-Tucanoan phylum, **2**:78
Madurese, **4**:635
Magadhi, **5**:5
Maipuran family, **2**:137
Maithili, **5**:5, 503, 677, 702
Malagasy, **1**:782
Malayalam, **3**:984; **5**:5, *6*, 18, 89, 350, 368,
    508, 509, 510, 513, 514, 887, 906,
    909, 929, 942, 945, 949, 950
    films in, **5**:421, 542
    poetry and songs in, **5**:219, 231, 452
    recordings in, **5**:423, 554
Malay-Indonesian family, **7**:523
Maleu, **9**:612
malḥūn dialect, **6**:472, 475
Maliseet, **3**:461

languages (*continued*)
Maltese, **8:**634, 635
Manchu, **7:**32, 34
Mande groups, **1:**465
Manggarai, **4:**791
Mangue, **2:**680, 747
Manihikian, **9:**908
Manipravala, **5:**513
Manx, **8:**319
Māori, **9:**928
Mapudungun, **2:**357
Marathi, **5:**6, 7, 247, 249, 413, 533, 550, 624, 729, 736, 866
Mari-Cheremis, **8:**772
Maskoy family, **2:**452
Massachusett, **3:**461
Mataco-Mataguayo family, **2:**251
Matako family, **2:**452
Matokki, **6:**641, 644
Maya, **2:**630, 666, 722
Mbïá-Guaycurú family, **2:**251
Mbwela, **10:**117
Megrelian (Megruli), **8:**826
Mehri, **6:**361
Melchas, **5:**689
Mexican Amerindian, **2:**549
Miao-Yao family, **4:**549–59; **7:**486, 491
Michif (Mitchif, Métchif), **3:**344, 404, 405, 410
Micmac, **3:**461
Micronesia, **9:**715
Minnan dialect, **7:**356, 396
Mīrāsī private language, **5:**764
Miskitu, **2:**659, 750
Mixteco, **2:**563
Mobilian trade, **3:**466
Mocheno-German, **8:**617
Mochica, **2:**488
Mohawk, **3:**461
Moinba, **7:**481
Mongolian, **7:**14, 18–19, 32; **8:**772
Mon-Khmer family, **3:**952; **7:**491
Mordvinian-Erzia, **8:**772
Mordvinian-Moksha, **8:**772
Mota, **9:**847
Moxo, **2:**282
Mundari, **5:**5
Mundua, **9:**608
Muskhogean family, **3:**466
Náhuatl, **2:**555–56, 558, 601, 680, 747–48
Nakho-Dagestanian group, **8:**861
Nanticoke, **3:**461
Narragansett, **3:**461
native American, **2:**28
Naxi, **7:**509
Nbula, **9:**574
Ndaoese, **4:**802
Nehan, **9:**632
Nengone, **9:**682
neo-Aramaic, **6:**283
Nepali, **5:**5, *6*
Newari, **5:**5, 702
New Caledonia, **9:**671, 682
New Guinea, **9:**472, 474
Ngada, **4:**791
Nginia, **9:**665

Niger-Congo groups, **1:**458
Nilotic family, **6:**641
Ŋola(m)banu Okamo, **9:**602
Nomane, **9:**522
non-Austronesian, **9:**662
 Irian Jaya, **9:**589, 591
 Kwomtari Phylum, **9:**545, 560
 Papua New Guinea, **9:**499, 514, 522, 536, 600, 607, 614, 620
 Sepik-Ramu Phylum, **9:**545, 546, 549, 560, 561
 Sko Phylum, **9:**545, 546, 560
 Solomon Islands, **9:**666
 Torricelli Phylum, **9:**545, 549, 560
 Trans-New Guinea Phylum, **9:**488, 511, 537, 545, 560, 561, 567
North Athapaskan, **3:**383
Norwegian, **8:**411
Numic, **3:**420
in Nusa Tenggara Timur, **4:**786
Ojibwa (Ojibwe), **3:**344, 1192–93
Okinawan dialect, **7:**789
Old Church Slavonic, **8:**726, 881, 903–4, 929, 960
Old Javanese, **4:**756
Oneida, **3:**461
Onondaga, **3:**461
Oriya, **5:**6, 660, 731
Orokolo, **9:**495
Osco-Umbrian, **8:**605
Ossetian, **8:**850
Oto-Mangue phylum, **2:**78, 563, 570
Owera, **9:**506–9
Palestinian Arabic, **6:**579
Pali, **4:**65, 259, 287, 288, 291, 292; **5:**257, 956, 959, 968; **7:**497, 498, 502–3
Pano, **2:**125
Papiamento, **2:**242, 927
Papua New Guinea
 Gulf Province, **9:**494
 Trans-Fly region, **9:**506
Pashto (also Pakhtu), **3:**981; **5:**5, 6, 506, 579, 744, 785, 804, 805, 808–9, 825, 833
Passamaquoddy, **3:**461
Penobscot, **3:**461
Penutian, **2:**78
Persian, **5:**57, 77, 179, 805, 817; **6:**9, 12, 108, 109, 120, 679, 823, 858
Persian-Tajik, **6:**939, 943
phasa isan, **4:**297
Piman, **3:**472–73
Pitjantjatjara, **9:**229
Polish, **3:**1057
Polynesian outliers, **9:**834, 839–40
Porome, **9:**494, 495
Portuguese, **2:**242, 342, 513; **3:**1057; **5:**736, 737
Powhatan, **3:**461
Prakrit, **5:**510
Proto-Polynesian, **9:**320, 328
Provençal, **8:**539, 604
Pukapukan, **9:**909, 912
Pukina, **2:**283
Punjabi (also Panjabi), **3:**1215; **5:**5, 6, 247, 256, 404, 574, 744, 751, 766
Purari, **9:**494

Pygmy, **1:**657
Quechua (Kechua), **2:**205–23, 258, 282, 283, 284, 293, 466, 467–68, 478, 482
Rajasthani, **5:**5, 247, 249, 639, 720
Rarotongan, **9:**896, 898, 908
Rhaetoromanisch, **8:**617, 682, 692
Romance family, **8:**517
Romani, **8:**271, 272, 276, 278, 283, 284, 285, 287, 295, 336, 776, 903, 983
Romanian, **8:**272
Romansh, **8:**682
Rumu, **9:**494, 495–96
Russian, **6:**897, 909; **8:**776
Saami, **8:**299, 399, 411
Sabellian, **8:**605
Sadani, **5:**5
Samoan, **3:**1051
Samoyed, **8:**475, 488
San, **1:**744
Sanskrit, **4:**65, 287; **5:**14, 247, 248, 255, 434, 503, 513, 517, 713, 893, 896, 899, 911, 956, 959, 964; **7:**613
 influence on raga classification structure, **5:**97
 poetry and songs in, **5:**104, 105, 163, 215, 219, 224, 226, 228, 254, 261–62, 269, 390, 452
 recordings in, **5:**423
 theater tradition in, **5:**484, 486, 510
 treatises in, **5:**17, 18, 25, 35, 44, 45, 49, 56–57, 77, 262–63
 in Trinidad, **5:**588, 590
Santali, **5:**5
Saraiki, **5:**751
Saranantogo, **2:**166
Sardinian, **8:**566, 626
Savosavo, **9:**666
Savunese, **4:**802
Scandinavian family, **8:**399
Scots, **8:**360, 365, 389
Scottish Gaelic, **8:**319, 360
Seneca, **3:**461
Serbo-Croatian, **3:**921; **8:**940, 962
Shao, **7:**527
Shilha, **6:**299, 301
Shina, **5:**792, *793*, 794, 799
Shona, **1:**708, 744
Shoshoni, **3:**435
Sicilian, **8:**566
Sierra Leone, **1:**495
Sikaianan, **9:**844, 846
Sikka, **4:**791
Sinasina, **9:**522
Sindhi, **5:**5, 6, 506, 744, 751, 759
Sinhalese (also Sinhala), **5:**5, 6, 7, 350, 368, 424, 959, 970
Sino-Tibetan family, **4:**528, 538–46; **5:**480; **7:**447, 471, 485, 491, 496, 509
Siouan family, **3:**440, 466
Siwai, **9:**649
Slovak, **8:**717
Slovenian, **8:**930
Somali, **1:**610
Sorani Kurdish, **6:**12, 743
Southeast Asia, musical characteristics of, **4:**11
southern African, **1:**700, 701–2

Spanish, **2:**242, 282, 284, 357, 452, 466, 549, 552, 579, 630, 647, 666, 772, 792, 822, 927, 932; **3:**720, 771, 942
Sranan, **2:**503
Sulawesi, **4:**804
Sumu, **2:**750
Sundanese, **4:**687
Sunuwari, **5:**290–91
Svanetian (Svanuri), **8:**826
Swahili, **1:**634; **5:**777; **6:**9, 710
Swedish, **8:**481, 483
Swiss-German, **8:**682
Syriac, **6:**207, 225, 227, 544
Tagalog, **3:**1025, 1026
Taglish, **3:**1026
Tai-Kadai family, **4:**11, 218, 529, 547–49; **7:**486, 491
Tajik, **6:**12, 903, 909, 917–18
Taki-taki, **2:**242
Tamazight, **6:**275, 483, 486
Tamil, **3:**1215; **5:**5, *6*, 18, 89, 223, 350, 368, 508, 866, 903, 906, 911–12, *917*, *922*
  Cankam literature, **5:**260, 293, 319, 326–27, 884
  in Fiji, **5:**612
  films in, **5:**421, 542
  in Martinique, **5:**594
  poetry and songs in, **5:**104, 105, 219, 228, 231, 260–61, 390, 452, 517
  recordings in, **5:**423
  in South Africa, **5:**615
  in United Kingdom, **5:**573
Tangut, **7:**32
Tanna, **9:**702
Tanzania, **1:**633–34
Tarascan, **2:**575, 579
Tashlhiyt, **6:**483, 486, 489–90
Tatar, **8:**772
Telugu, **3:**984, 989, 990; **5:**5, *6*, 89, 350, 368, 404, 508, 866, 869, 889–90, 892–93, 896, 899, 911
  in Fiji, **5:**612
  films in, **5:**421, 542
  in North America, **5:**582
  poetry and songs in, **5:**104, 105, 216, 219, 228–29, 231–32, 265–66, 269, 390, 452, 517
  recordings in, **5:**423, 554
  in South Africa, **5:**615
Teop, **9:**642
Tewa, **3:**428
Thai, **4:**221, 287, 296
  Khmer influence on, **4:**159
Thai-Austronesian family, **7:**496
Tibetan, **5:**5, *6*, 709; **7:**19, 471
Tibeto-Burman family, **5:**5, 696, 700, 702, 703
Tiwa, **3:**428
Toaripi, **9:**495
Toba, **2:**452
Tok Pisin, **9:**475, 488, 567
Tolai, **9:**620
Tonkawa, **3:**440
Towa, **10:**89
Trinitario, **2:**137
Trique, **2:**563

Tucano family, **2:**150
Tulu, **5:**5, 350, 866, 881, 887
Tungusic family, **7:**18–19, 31
Tupi-Guaraní family, **2:**125, 127, 157, 164, 435
Turkic family, **5:**5; **6:**827, 897, 902–3, 921, 939, 943, 949, 965, 967, 979; **7:**14, 18–19; **8:**772, 850, 858
Turkish, **6:**9, 12, 113, 120, 193, 773, 843
Tuscarora, **3:**461
Tuvan, **6:**979
Tuyu, **7:**460
Twi, **2:**902
Udmurt-Votyak, **8:**772
Uighur, **6:**995; **7:**32, 460
Ukrainian, **3:**1057
Uniapa, **9:**608
Uralic family, **8:**475
Urdu, **3:**814, 1215; **5:**5, *6*, 404, 425, 487, 624, 639, 660, 692, 736, 744, 745, 746, 749, 755, 766, 853, 866, 889; **6:**9
  poetry and songs in, **5:**183, 186, 256
  scholarly writings in, **5:**44, 57
  theater in, **5:**486–87
  in United Kingdom, **5:**573
Uruqilla, **2:**283
Uto-Aztecan family, **2:**78, 551, 555, 588; **3:**420, 435, 440
'Uvea, **9:**809
Uzbek, **6:**12, 903, 909, 918
Vagua, **9:**654
Varisi, **9:**654
Vedic, **5:**31
Venda, **1:**708
Venezuela, **2:**524
Vietnamese, **4:**69, 80, 451, *475*
Visayan, **3:**1025
Voltaic cluster, **1:**451
Wakashan, **3:**1094
Wakhi, **5:**792, *793*, 794
Warao, **2:**188
Welsh, **8:**319, 342, 345, 353, 354, 356, 558
West Africa, **1:**443
West Atlantic group, **1:**468
Western Abenaki, **3:**461
Xibe, **7:**518
Xibo, **7:**463
Yanomamö, **2:**169
Yaqui, **2:**589
Yele, **9:**488
Yemeni Arabic, **6:**685–86
Yiddish, **3:**530, 933, 935, 936–37, 940, 1077; **6:**1024, 1071; **8:**248, 251, 252, 256–57, 258, 263, 772
Yoruba, **1:**472; **2:**342, 352
Yuaga, **9:**672
Yuchi, **3:**466
Yupik, **3:**374
Yurakaré, **2:**282
Zaïre, **1:**663
Zamuko family, **2:**452
Zaza Kurdish, **6:**743
Zhejiang-Shanghai dialect, **3:**962
Zulu, **1:**706, 708
Zuni, **3:**428

Languriya (deity), **5:**551
Lanier, Jaron, **3:**954
Lanier, Sidney, **3:**595, *595*
Lanner, Joseph, **8:**205
Lanoh people, **4:**560, 569
Lanois, Daniel, **3:**249
Lansky, Paul, **3:**254
Lantis, Margaret, **3:**381
La Nuova Compagnia di Canto Popolare, **8:**613
Lao people
  in Cambodia, **4:**210
  in Hawai'i, **9:**100, 109, 163
  mouth organs of, **4:**59
  in North America, **3:***117*, 948–49, 950, 951–52, 1007–9
    Chinese ethnic groups, **3:**961
  resettlement of, **4:**360–61
  in Thailand, **4:**218, 221–22, 315–16, 321
Lao-tzu (Laozi), **7:**88, 312, 319, 320, 321
Lao Wu, **7:**366
Laocan Youji (Chinese novel), **7:**246
La Orquesta de Beto Villa, **3:**778–79
La Orquesta de Oscar Martínez, **3:**779
La Orquesta Típica de Las Vegas, **3:**763
Laos
  Champassak, **4:**356, 358–59
  classical music in, **4:**7, 353–60
  composition in, **4:**127
  court music in, **3:**1007–8
  cultural origins of, **4:**10–11
  geography of, **4:**2, 335
  Hinduism in, **4:**64
  history of, **4:**349–50, 353–54, 356, 358
  Hmong people in, **3:**1003; **4:**550–51
  influenced by Vietnamese culture, **4:**447
  Khmer people in, **4:**151
  Kmhmu people in, **4:**546–47
  Lahu people in, **4:**538–40
  lam ploen, **4:**353
  Luang Phrabang, **4:**11, 356–57
  map of, **4:***337*
  musical genres, **4:**18, 133, 341–52, 361
    eua ba, **4:**351
    joi yuan, **4:**351
    khap genres, **4:**18, 340, 451
    khap haw, **4:**351
    khap lam, **4:**351
    khap maen, **4:**351
    khap meuy, **4:**351
    khap ngeum, **4:**18, 22, 341, 347, 351
    khap ngom, **4:**351
    khap ong ga, **4:**351
    khap phuan, **4:**341, 347–48, 351
    khap sam neua, **4:**341, 348–49, 351
    khap thai dam, **4:**341, 349, 352
    khap thum, **4:**22, 349–51, 352
    khap thum luang phrabang, **4:**341
    lakhawn lam, **4:**353
    lam ban xok, **4:**341, 345, 351
    lam kae, **4:**342
    lam kawn, **4:**341
    lam khon savan, **4:**22, 337, 341, 345–46, 351, 352
    lam leuang, **4:**342, 353
    lam mahaxay, **4:**341, 346, 351, 352
    lam nithan, **4:**341–42

Laos, musical genres (*continued*)
  lam phu thai, **4:**341, 346–47, 351
  lam ploen, **4:**342
  lam salavane, **4:**18, 22, 341, 344–45, 351
  lam sithandone, **4:**341, 343, 351
  lam som, **4:**337, 341, 343–44, 351
  lam tang vay, **4:**18, 341, 345, 351, 352
  lam tat, **4:**341, 352
  lam top phanya, **4:**342
  lao phay, **4:**351
  seung pong fai, **4:**341
  music research on, **4:**24, 25–26, 150, 336–37,
    361, 529, 530
  pedagogy in, **4:**120
  politics and wars in, **4:**89, 118
  popular music in, **4:**360
  population of, **4:**335–36
  regional styles in, **4:**356–59
  representative music of, **4:**22–23, 133
  rituals in, **4:**340–41
  salient musical features of, **4:**18
  Tai people in, **4:**218
  theater in, **4:**342, 352–53, 357–58
  tourism in, **4:**138
  trance in, **4:**61
  upland peoples, **4:**529, 537–59
    music research on, **4:**26
  Vientiane, **4:**5, 336, 356, 357–58, 360
  village life in, **4:**6
  village music in, **4:**338–53
  vocal music in, **4:**340
  war in, **4:**551
  Western influences in, **4:**81
  Yao people in, **4:**549
Laotian people. *See* Hmong people; Lao people
Laozi (Lao-tzu), **7:**88, 312, 319, 320, 321
Laozi daode jing (Daoist work), **7:**319
La Peña, Verne de, **4:**881
La Perfekta, **2:**917
La Pérouse, Jean Francis de, **9:**795
Lapin, Viktor, **8:**784
Lapita cultural complex, **4:**38; **9:**2, 4, 598, 689,
    771, 809
La Poaseña, **2:**702
Lapointe, Jean, **3:**1158
Lapp, Daniel, **3:**1257
Lapponia (Schefferus), **8:**307
Lapps. *See* Saami people
Laqua people, **4:**219
Lara, Agustín, **2:**620; **3:**740
Lara, Manrique de, **6:**1037
La Rama, Rufo de, **4:**866
Lares (periodical), **8:**620–21
Lares, Oswaldo, **2:**544
Largam, **6:**270
Larionoff, Sergei, **3:**58
Laroche, Hermann, **8:**783
La Rosa, Esperanza de, **4:**870
Larrikin Records, **9:**989
Larrocha, Alicia de, **8:**601
Larry's Rebels (musical group), **9:**168
Larson, LeRoy, **3:**868
Larsson, Lars-Erik, **8:**445
LaRue, Hubert, **3:**1165
La Sagouine (musical group), **3:**1137
Las Casas, Father Bartolomé, **2:**846

Las Chicas del Can, **2:**105
Las Hermanas Padilla, **3:**738–39, 751
Lasisi, David, **9:**962
Las Musas, **2:**105
"*Lass Maro Tschatschepen*," **8:**289
Lasso, Orlando di, **8:**73–74, 75, 618
Last Dance (film documentary), **4:**354
Last Emperor (film), **3:**204
Last, James, **8:**210
Last of the Mohicans (Cooper), **3:**525
"Last Night" (Mar-Keys), **3:**675
Last Poets (spoken word trio), **3:**693
"Last Rose of Summer" (Moore), **3:**182, 520
Last Temptation of Christ (film), **5:**753
Last Virgin in Paradise (Hereniko), **9:**234
Last Wave (film), **9:**46
Laswell, Bill, **7:**967
Latcho Drom (film), **8:**272
"Lately" (Jodeci), **3:**715
La Tène culture, **8:**319, 321, 558
*Latent and Manifest Theory: A Maqam Tradition
    in Practice* (Cohen), **6:**1066
Latgalian people, **8:**499
Lath, Mukund, **5:**161
Lathief, A. Halilintar, **10:**46
Lati people, **4:**219, 537
Latif, Abdul, **5:**858
Latiff, **5:***603*
Latin Alliance (rap project), **3:**750
Latin American Center (Los Angeles), **10:**98
*Latin American Harp Music and Techniques for
    Pedal and Non-Pedal Harpists* (Ortíz),
    2:464
Latin American music. *See also* tango
  in Denmark, **8:**462
  influence on African guitar music, **1:**361
  influence on Angolan music, **1:**435
  influence on Cameroon music, **1:**661
  influence on Tanzanian jazz, **1:**644
  in Italy, **8:**619
  in Nigeria, **1:**317
  in Philippines, **4:**854, 883–84
  in Sierra Leone, **1:**363, 377, 380
  in Spain, **8:**208
  in Zaïre, **1:**380, 383–88, 669
Latin American Music Review (periodical), **2:**116
Latin Breed (musical group), **3:**780
Latin New York (periodical), **3:**788
Latinoamérica es Música (Salazar), **2:**544
Latino peoples. *See also* specific groups
  in Australia, **9:**82–84
  in Canada, **3:**718, 1078, 1085, 1201, 1203–5
  culture of, **3:**719–20
  as disco audience, **3:**687, 711
  migration of, **3:**13, 512, 718–19, 734, 848
  musics of, **3:**13, 16, 31, 98, 521–23, 720–33
  population of, **3:**718
  rap musicians, **3:**699
  stereotypes of, **3:**98, 740
  in Sweden, **8:**434, 443
Latin Quarter (Toronto), **3:**1213
Latin Time (television show), **3:**741
Latin Tinge (Roberts), **3:**732, 790
La Torre, Sylvia, **4:**884
Latraverse, Guy, **3:**1161
Latrobe, Benjamin Henry, **3:**597

La Tropa F (musical group), **3:**780
La Troupe Folklorique Nationale d'Haïti, L
    3:805; **2:**887
Lattimore, Owen, **7:**29, 30
Latvia, **8:**499–507
  geography of, **8:**499
  history of, **8:**499
  history of music in, **8:**504–6
  instruments, **8:**170, 503–4
  Kurzeme (Courland), **8:**499, 500–502, 505
  Latgale, **8:**499, 500–502, 505
  map of, **8:**398
  population of, **8:**499
  research on music of, **8:**506–7
  Vidzeme (Liefland), **8:**499
  vocal music of, **8:**499–503, 504–5
  vocal performers, **8:**115
  Zemgale (Semigallia), **8:**499, 502
Latvian Academy of Music, **8:**507
Latvian Folklore Repository, **8:**506–7
Latvian people, in North America, **3:**866, 877,
    1196
Latviešu mūzikas folkloras materiāli (Melngailis),
    8:507
Latviešu tautas mūzika (Vītoliņš), **8:**507
Latvju dainas (Barons), **8:**506
Latvju tautas mūzikas materiāli (Jurjāns), **8:**506
Lau, Andy (Liu Dehua), **7:**355
Lau, H., **8:**661
Lau Islands (Fiji), **9:**773
  kava use in, **9:**174
  music and dance of, **9:**973
  polotu genre of, **9:**775, 781
Lau, Tats (Liu Yida), **7:**355
Lau, William, **3:***224*
Lauati (Sāmoan leader), **9:**217
Laub, Thomas, **8:**460
Laubach, Frank, **3:**1227
Laufman, Dudley, **3:**233
"Laughing Song" (Johnson), **3:**706
launeddas. See single-reed instruments
Launis, Armas, **8:**307
Lauper, Cyndi, **3:**97
Laurendeau, Arthur, **3:**1149
Laurent, Donatien, **8:**561
Laurents, Arthur, **3:**198
"Laurett[e]" (Williams), **3:**604
Lauridsen, Jan, **9:**294
Lauritsen, Birgit, **8:**464
Lausanne, Treaty of, **8:**1011
Lăutaru, Barbu, **8:**882
Lautoka, Polikalepo, **9:**814–15
Lautrec, Donald, **3:**1158
Lauvergne, Barthelme, **9:**17, *18*
Lauzon, Jani, **3:**345, 1063
Laval University (Québec City), **3:**1150, 1167
Lavallée, Calixa, **3:**14, 144–45, 189, 1076, 1108,
    1109, 1148–49, 1181
Lavallee, Roland, **3:**1077
"*lavaplatos, El*" (Osorio), **3:**737–38
Lavelua, king of 'Uvea, **9:**811
Lavignac, Albert, **6:**24
LaVigna, Maria, **3:**495
La Villemarqué, Hersart de, **8:**552, 561
Lavín, Carlos, **2:**115, 238
Lavirinthos (musical group), **8:**1018

Lavista, Mario, **2:**605
Lavoe, Hector, **3:**789
Lavongai (Papua New Guinea), **9:**600, 626
Lavotta, János, **8:**737
Lavry, Marc, **6:**1029
Lawa people, **4:**537
"Lawdy Lawdy Blues" (Jackson), **3:**707
"Lawdy Miss Clawdy" (Price), **3:**708
Lawlor, Charles B., **3:**549
Lawrence, Helen Reeves, **9:**349, 973
Lawrence, T. E., **6:**21
Lawry, Walter, **9:**203
laws. *See* copyright and ownership; politics
Laws, G. Malcolm, **8:**338
Lawson, Doyle, **3:**159
layālī, **6:**34, 121, 147–51, 388, 550, 551, 559, 567, 569
Layard, John, **9:**316, 690, 977, 992
Laycock, Donald C., **9:**650
Layeni, A. Ajibola, **1:**406
Layla (female singer of Granada), **6:**443
Layla and Majnun. See Leyla and Mecnun
"Lay This Body Down" (spiritual), **3:**523
lays. *See* narratives
Lazare, Martin, **3:**289
Lazika, **8:**826
Lê Đức Mao, **4:**481
Lê dynasty (earlier), **4:**447, 472, 480, 489
Lê dynasty (later), **4:**448, 482, 489
Lê Lợi, **4:**480
Lê Nhân Tông, king of Vietnam, **4:**498
Lê Thái Tông, king of Vietnam, **4:**448
Le-Tsiyon, Rishon, **6:**1024
Lê Tuấn Hùng, **4:**25
Leacock, Eleanor, **3:**1074
Leacock, Stephen, **3:**199
Leadbelly (pseud. of Huddie Ledbetter), **3:**147, 293, 316, 328, 579, 707
Leader Music (recording company), **2:**266
League of Armenian Music Teachers, **6:**726
League of Filipino Composers (Philippines), **4:**875
League of the Iroquois, **3:**462
League of Leftist Writers of China, **7:**384, 385
Leahy, Michael, **9:**979
Leahys (musical group), **3:**1081, 1191
Leake, Jerry, **5:**136
learning. *See* oral tradition and transmission; pedagogy
Leary, James P., **3:**828, 899, 900
Leary, S. P., **3:***106*
Leavitt, Stephen, **9:**977
Lebanese people
    in Antigua and Barbuda, **2:**798
    in Barbados, **2:**813
    in Caribbean, **2:**793
    in French Guiana, **2:**434
    in Netherlands Antilles, **2:**928
    in North America, **3:**1029, 1032, 1036, 1072, 1073, 1218–20; **6:**279–81
    in Panama, **2:**771
    in South America, **2:**84
Lebanon. *See also* Mashriq
    aerophones in, **6:**414
    Beirut, as Arab media capital, **6:**597
    chordophones in, **6:**409

drums in, **6:**91, 554
folk traditions in, **6:**545
idiophones in, **6:**403
Iraqi people in, **6:**593–95
Maronite Church in, **6:**207–8, 544
popular music, **6:**229, 251
urban music in, **6:**553–55
Lebar, Frank M., **4:**528
Lebar, Matt, **3:**1198
Lebič, Lojze, **8:**921
Leb i Sol (musical group), **8:**983
Leblanc, Edward Olivier, **2:**840–41
Leblebiji (Chukhadjian), **6:**725
LeBronnec, Robert Te'ikitautua, **9:**974
Lebrun, Roland, **3:**1155
Leça, Armando, **8:**585
LeCaine, Hugh, **3:**246, 1185
Lechowia (musical group), **3:**1197
Leclair, Jean-Marie, **8:**78
Leclerc, Félix, **3:**1156, 1157, 1162, 1167
Leclere, Adhemard, **4:**190
Lecor, Tex, **3:**1077
Lecuona Cuban Boys, **3:**795
Lecuona, Ernesto, **3:**795; **8:**619
Ledang, Ola Kai, **8:**427
Ledbetter, Huddie ("Leadbelly"). *See* Leadbelly
Lederman, Anne, **3:**344, 405
Ledesma, Antonino, **4:**866
Ledesma, Kuh, **4:**885
Ledrú, André Pierre, **2:**936
Led Zeppelin (musical group), **3:**111–14, *263*, 348, 356, 357, 552; **4:**885; **6:**250; **7:**360; **8:**215, 218
Led Zeppelin, Rock Culture, and Subjectivity (Walser), **3:**114
Lee, Alain, **3:**1005
Lee Bing, **3:**1262
Lee Bing-chuen, **3:**1262
Lee Byong-Won, **7:**855
Lee, Byron, **2:**911, 912
Lee, Dennis, **3:**1081
Lee, Dick, **4:**523–24; **7:**355
Lee, Dorothy Sara, **3:**495; **9:**976
Lee, Edgy, **9:**42
Lee Geon-yong, **7:**956
Lee, Hope, **3:**1186
Lee Hye-Ku, **7:**853, 855, 856, 990
Lee, Johnny, **3:**81
Lee, Julia, **3:**646
Lee, Junho, **7:**970
Lee, Kui, **9:**126, 164
Lee, Ranee, **3:**1077
Lee, Riley Kelly, **7:**595, 709; **10:**13
Lee Saenggang, **7:**915
Lee, Spike, **3:**715
Lee Sung Chun, **7:**954–56, 957, 971, 972
Leecan, Bobbie, **3:**645
Leeds College of Music (England), **5:**575
Leegajus (musical group), **8:**154
Leenhardt, Maurice, **9:**965, 992
Lees, Ann, **3:**134–35
Leeuw, Ton de, **4:**876
Leeward Islands, **2:**789, 798
Lefebvre, Marie-Thérèse, **3:**1108
Lefkowitch, Henry, **3:**939
Left Hand, **3:**487

Légaré, Ovila, **3:**1154, 1166
Legas (Mota singer), **9:**701
Legaspi, Celeste, **4:**885
Legebokoff, Peter, **3:**1270
Legend of Sari-Manok (Kasilag), **4:**875
Le Groupe de la Place Royale, **3:**224
Lehár, Franz, **3:**193
Lehman College of the City University of New York, **3:**610
Lehman, F. K., **4:**52
Lehmann-Nitsche, Robert, **2:**251
Lehr, John, **3:**52
Leiber, Jerry, **3:**672–73, 709
Lei Haiqing, **7:**392
Leili vo Mecnun (Hacibekov), **6:**924
Leisiö, Timo, **8:**179, 489
Leitch, Peter, **3:**1107
Leiva, Victor Manuel, **2:**764
Le Jardin (New York), **3:**688
Le Jazz Libre du Québec, **3:**1158
LeJeune, Paul, **3:**1074
"Lekha dodi" (*piyyut*), **3:**1173
Lekis, Lisa, **2:**931
Lekuberri, Juana, **8:***312*
Lekuona, Manuel de, **8:**315
Leland, John, **3:**586
Lela, Remzi, **8:**993
"*Lele Devla*," **8:**283
Lélé, Granmoun, **5:**609
Leleiohoku, William Pitt, prince of Hawai'i, **3:**1050; **9:**919
Lelièvre, Sylvain, **3:**1156
Lelu Island (Kosrae State, FSM), **9:**740, 742
Lemaire, Alfred J. B., **6:**130, 867
Lemak (Nissan composer), **9:**637
Lemarias (Nissan composer), **9:**638
Lembata, **4:**786
Lem'i Atlı, **6:**772
Lemieux, Germain, **3:**1192–93
Lemmon, Alfred E., **2:**599
Lemper, Ute, **8:**209
Len, Billy Hew, **9:**390
Lenca culture, **2:**739
Lengge, Samuel, **9:**260
Lengua culture, **2:**452, 456
Leningrad Rock Club, **8:**219
Lenin, Vladimir I., **3:**1270; **6:**930
Lenje people, **1:**671
Lennon, Charlie, **8:**387
Lennon, John, **3:**318
Lenny Henry En De Funk (television show), **3:**680
"Lenox" (Edson), **3:**532
Lenox, Annie, **3:**97
Lenox Avenue (Still), **3:**609
Lenshina, Alice, **1:**671
Leo, the Royal Cadet (Telgmann), **3:**189, 1182, *1183*
León, Ageliers, **2:**839
León, Bayani de, **4:**130, 881
Leon, Florante de, **4:**886
Leonard, Charles, **3:**286
Leoncavallo, Ruggero, **6:**609
Leong Yoon Pin, **4:**129, 523
Leonhardt, Gustave, **10:**20

Leoni, the Gypsy Queen (Delos Mars), **3:**617
Leonin, **8:**71, 366
Leonora-Uitvlagt Indian Orchestra, **5:***604*
Léonowens, Anna Harriette, **4:**285
León, Tania, **3:**610, 612, *612*
Léothaud, Gilles, **1:**256; **9:**398
Leppert, Richard, **3:**562
Lerdo de Tejada, Miguel, **2:**622
Lerma, Dominique de, **10:**139
Lerma, Florencio, **4:**863, 866
Lerole, Aaron "Jake," **1:**773
Lerolle, Rouart, **4:**511
Leroux, Charles Édouard Gabriel, **7:**728
Léry, Jean de, **2:**300–301
Lesage, Jean, **3:**1156
Les Ambassadeurs (musical group), **1:**365, 420,
      421; **2:**892
Les Ambassadeurs Internationaux (musical
      group), **1:**421
LeSaunier, Jenny Lerouge, **3:**1229
Les Bantous (musical group), **1:**424
Les Baronets (musical group), **3:**1158
Les Berbères (musical group), **6:**275
Lescarbot, Marc, **3:**23, 1074, 1135
Les Classels (musical group), **3:**1158
Les Difficiles de Pétion-Ville (musical group),
      2:98
Les Disques Star (musical group), **3:**1160
Les Fantaisistes de Carrefour (musical group),
      2:98, 892
Les Frères Parent (musical group), **2:**892; **3:**805
Les Gants Blancs (musical group), **3:**1158
Les Grands Ballets Canadiens, **3:**224
Les Habitants (musical group), **3:**1136
Les Jeunesses Musicales (musical group), **3:**1118
Leskinen, Juice, **8:**485
Leslie, Charles, **2:**897; **8:**369–70
Les Loups Noirs (musical group), **2:**892
Lesmawan, I Made, **3:**1020
Les Méchants Maquereaux (musical group),
      3:1136, 1137
Lesotho, **1:**769. *See also* Southern Africa; *specific
      peoples*
   Matchappee people, dance, **1:**117
   music of, **1:**428
   poetry, *sefala*, **1:**218
   Sotho peoples, **1:**707
Les Redoutables (musical group), **1:**425
Lessa, William A., **9:**994
Lesser Antilles, **2:**789, 927, 968, 969. *See also
      specific countries and islands*
Lesser Perfect System, **8:**48
Les Sinners (musical group), **3:**1158
Lessons from the World (Campbell), **3:***276*
Les Sultans (musical group), **3:**1158
Les Tymeux de la baie (musical group), **3:**1137
Les Zed (musical group), **3:**344
"Let the Good Times Roll" (Jordan), **3:**668–69
Let the Inside Be Sweet (Stone), **10:**58–59
"Let It Whip" (Dazz Band), **3:**684
Letâif-i Enderûn (Hızır Ilyas Bey), **6:**780
Lete, Xabier, **8:**315
Letondal, Arthur, **3:**1149, 1150
Letondal, Paul, **3:**1149
Létourneau, Henri, **3:**411
Létourneau, Pierre, **3:**1156

Let's Dance (radio program), **3:**656
"Let's Have Another Cup of Coffee" (Berlin),
      3:196
"Let's Stay Together" (Green), **3:**677, 711
"*lettre de sang, La*" (Métis song), **3:**410
Leuven University, **8:**534
Leuzinger, Else, **10:**112
Levan, Larry, **3:**689, 690, *690*
Levant, **6:**535. *See also* Jordan; Lebanon;
      Mashriq; Palestine; Syria
Levantines, **6:**565
Léveillée, Claude, **3:**1076, 1156, 1167
Levesque, Raymond, **3:**1156
Lévesque, René, **3:**1157, 1159
Levi, Carlo, **8:**123
Levi, Isaac, **6:**1071
Levi, Leo, **8:**622
Levi, 'Ofer, **6:**267
Lévi-Strauss, Claude, **1:**517; **8:**102, 192, 1024
Levi-Tannay, Sarah, **6:**1030, 1071
Leviche. *See* Bābākhānov, Levi (Leviche)
Leviev, Milcho, **8:**903
Levin, Theodore, **6:**23, 990; **7:**1023–24
Levine, Lawrence, **3:**144, 258, 585
Levine, Nancy, **3:**104
Levine, Victoria Lindsay, **3:**470
Levy, Alexandre, **2:**306
Levy, Curtis, **9:**47
Lévy, Isaac Jack, **6:**1037, 1066; **8:**267
Levy, John, **5:**712
Levy, Leo, **6:**1060
Lévy, Solly, **3:**1173, *1173*, 1175
Levy, Yossi, **6:**265
Lewandowski, Louis, **3:**934
Lewerissa, Henry, **9:***151*
Lewin, Olive, **2:**913
Lewis and Clark College (Portland), **3:**1020
Lewis, Furry, **3:**645, 707
Lewis, Hou'olionalani, **9:***927*
Lewis, Jerry Lee, **3:**348, 648
Lewis, J. Lowell, **2:**24
Lewis, Meade Lux, **3:**647
Lewis, Meriwether, **3:**441
Lewis, Oscar, **5:**674
Lewis, Samuel L., **3:**1042–43, 1044
Lewis, Smiley, **3:**670
Lewis, Terry, **3:**715
Ley, Tabu "Rochereau," **1:**425, 669; **8:**234
Leydi, Roberto, **8:**24, 611, 613, 622, 623, 694
Leyla and Mecnun (epic), **6:**766
Leyrac, Monique, **3:**1156, 1167–68
Leyris, Raymond, **6:**1044
Leyva, Francisco S., **3:**762
Lhagvasüren, **7:**1020
L'Harmonie Kinoise (musical group), **1:**387
L'Herbier, Robert, **3:**1155
Lhoba (Lopa) people, **7:**449, 471, 482
Lhote, Henri, **1:**574
Li Binghui, **7:**358
Li Chenggan, **7:***450*
Li Chunyi, **7:**137
Lićviny (musical group), **8:**801
Li Daitong, **7:**185
Li Decai, **7:**180
Li Dou, **7:**129
Li Guinian, **7:**392

Li Ji (*Liji*, Book of Rites), **7:**120, 123, 127, 187,
      191, 587.
Li Jinguang, **7:**354
Li Jinhui, **7:**90, 353–54
Li Jinwen, **7:**258
Li Minxiong, **7:**234, 236
Li people, **4:**219; **7:**485–92
Li, Raymond, **3:**1262–63
Li Shigen, **7:**200
Li Shuangzi, **7:**357
Li Shutong, **7:**56, 375
Li Tianlu, **7:**425
Li Wenli, **7:**128
Li Wenmao, **7:**305
Li Xiangzhi, **7:**154
Li Yinghai, **7:**231, 347–48
Li Yu, **7:**402
Li Yuan Ki, **4:**447, 490
Li Zhengnian, **7:**455
Li Zhizao, **7:**131, 336
Lia (film), **9:**42
Lian Cheng-wu, **7:**588
Liang dynasty, **7:**27
Liang Maochun, **7:**87, 139
Liang Mingyue, **7:**87
Liang Shengyu, **7:**290–91
Liang Tsai-ping, **7:**172, 173, *173*
Liang Xingbo, **7:**307
Liangshanbo yu zhuyingtai (He), **7:**348
Liangzhu culture, **7:**17
Lianhua jin (Buddhist text), **7:**311
Liao dynasty, **7:**29, 31, 32, 321, 517
Liberal Republican Party, **3:**308
Liberati, Alessandro, **3:**564, 566
Liberation Choir (Toronto), **3:**1195
Liberia. *See also* West Africa; *specific peoples*
   African-American immigrants to, **1:**3; **2:**91
   Grébu people, historical studies, **1:**91
   guitar in, **1:**351
   highlife in, **1:**423
   Islam, **1:**327–49
   Jabo people, speech surrogate methods,
      1:106
   Kpelle people, **10:**55–56, 57, 59–61, 64
      epics, **1:**124, 128–29, 130–44, 488
      instrument categories, **1:**10
      sang concept, **1:**7
   Kru people
      history of, **1:**370–75
      music of, **1:**375–82
   Kwa groups, **1:**468–69
   Liberian English language of, **1:**3
   music of, **1:**9, 466, 468
   Vai people, concepts of music, **1:**347
Liberovici, Sergio, **8:**613
Liberty Minstrel, **3:**307
Liberty Party, **3:**307
Libornio, José Sabas, **4:**863; **9:**133
libraries. *See* archives and museums; *specific
      institutions*
Library of Congress (Washington, D.C.), **2:**488,
      593; **3:**292, 294; **8:**823; **9:**961, 975,
      979–80. *See also* American Folklife
      Center
   Archive of American Folk-Song, **3:**31, 293–94,
      495, 579, 707

Archive of Folk Culture, **3:**31, 294–95, 449, 465, 470, 484, 486, 511; **9:**979–80
  Music Division, **3:**295
  Recorded Sound Division, **3:**289–90
  Recording Laboratory, **3:**294
  as repository, **3:**289, 293, 295
Libya. *See also* Maghrib; North Africa; *specific peoples*
  aerophones in, **6:**414–15
  Andalusian repertoire in, **6:**415, 449, 452–53, 454, 457
  Berber peoples, **1:**533; **6:**273
  chordophones in, **6:**410, 411
  drums in, **6:**416–20
  festivals, **1:**538
  Fezzan oasis, wedding rituals in, **6:**306
  geography of, **6:**429
  hadra ceremony, **1:**537
  idiophones in, **6:**403
  Italian rule in, **6:**432
  Jewish people in, **6:**1044
  Judeo-Spanish music in, **8:**596
  map of, **6:**430
  Tuareg people of, **1:**574
Libyan people, in Corsica, **8:**566
Licad, Cecile, **4:**870
Licensed to Ill (Beastie Boys), **3:**696
Liceo Científico Artístico Literario, **4:**861, 866
Lichti, Daniel, **3:**1082
Lidholm, Ingvar, **8:**445
Lieb, Sandra, **3:**104
Liebenzell Mission, **9:**720
Lieberman, Baruj, **2:**624
Lieber, Michael, **9:**327
Liechtenstein, **8:**12
Lied von der Erde, Das (Mahler), **3:**953
Lien, Annbjørg, **8:**226, 421, 430
Lien, Matthew, **3:**1278
Lienert, Max, **8:**692
Lieth-Philipp, Margot, **2:**973
Lietuva (musical group), **8:**513
Lieu Da-Kun, **7:**375–76
Liễu Hạnh, **4:**505
Lieurance, Thurlow, **3:**367
Life of Christ in Negro Spirituals (Jessye), **3:**608
Life of Lam-Ang (Pájaro), **4:**874–75
"Life Let Us Cherish" (Nägeli), **3:**180
Life of Music in North India (Neuman), **5:**57
Lifou (New Caledonia), **9:**680, 682–84
"Lift Every Voice and Sing" (Johnson), **3:**608
Ligeti, György, **7:**737
Ligęza, Józef, **8:**712
Liggins, Jimmy, **3:**353, 742
Liggins, Joe, **3:**669, 742
Light, Enoch, **3:**1050
Light Up and Listen (radio show), **3:**1107
Lighter Shade of Brown, A (musical group), **3:**750
Lightfoot, Gordon, **3:**14, 314, 1058, 1081
Lighthouse (musical group), **3:**1081
Ligo, Hardy, **9:**966
Ligurians, in Corsica, **8:**566
Lihir Group (Papua New Guinea), **9:**626
Liji (Book of Rites), **7:**120, 123, 127, 187, 191, 587
Lika (musical group), **3:**1199

Likas-An (Santos), **4:**878
Likelike, Miriam, princess of Hawai'i, **9:**919
likembe. See lamellophones
Likona, Domingo, **8:**316
Lila Muni (musical group), **10:**134
Lila Wallace Reader's Digest Foundation, **3:**1037
Lilburn, Douglas, **9:**931, 932
Lili Fatale (musical group), **3:**1161
Lili'uokalani, queen of Hawai'i, **9:**133, 919, 923
  compositions of, **9:**43, 353, 924
Lil' Kim, **3:**697, 699, 701
Lilley, Joseph L., **9:**43
Lillo, Baldomero, **2:**423
Lim Dong Chang, **7:**965, 967
Lim Yau, **4:**523
Lima, Emirto de, **2:**398
Limba people, **1:**445
"Limbo Rock" (Checker), **3:**709
Limbu people, **5:**701
Limondjian, Hambardzum (also Limoncuyan, Hamparsum), **6:**18, 113, 125, 725, 727, 737, 771, 779
Limp Bizkit (musical group), **3:**359
Lin Dejian, **7:**725
Lin, Lady (legendary figure), **7:**402
Lin Qiang (Lim Giong), **7:**358
Lin Shengshi, **7:**346
Lin Shicheng, **7:**169, 170, 224
Lin Xue, **7:**363–65
Lin Yu, **7:**863
Linares, María Teresa, **2:**839
Lincoln, Abraham, **3:**308
Lincoln Center for the Performing Arts (New York), **3:**664–65; **7:**295–96
Lincoln Center Jazz Orchestra, **3:**664
Lind, Jenny, **3:**18, 537, 556, 557, 864, 1180; **8:**434
Linda, Solomon, **1:**772–73; **3:**328, 329
Lindeman, Ludvig Mathias, **8:**414, 424–25
Lindgren, Adolf, **8:**447
Lindner, Rudi, **7:**13
Lindsay, Jennifer, **4:**639
Lindsay, John (bass player), **3:**653
Lindsay, John (Cook Islands performer), **9:**899
Lindsay, Tom (Cook Islands performer), **9:**899
Lindsborg Swedish Dancers, **3:**871, 872
Lindsey, Elizabeth Kapu'uwailani, **9:**42
Line Islands (Kiribati), **9:**758
Lineva, Evgeniya, **8:**18, 133, 755, 756, 770, 783, 822
Ling, Jan, **8:**25, 437, 448
Ling, Pehr-Henrik, **8:**443
Lingāyat sect, **5:**265, 870, 881
Lingo (deity), **5:**721–22
Linguae Vasconum Primitiae (Dechepare), **8:**316
Lingual Singer (Kolsti), **8:**1003
linguistics, **8:**18, 24; **10:**56. *See also* language and music; languages
  African, **1:**27, 295
  analytical methods, **9:**321–22
  archives of, **9:**975
  Australian communities, **9:**439–40
  causative and reflexive forms, **1:**203
  content analysis, **1:**102–4
  Kirundi, **1:**167–68, 202–4
  Kiswahili, **1:**425–26

language distribution in Oceania, **9:**319–20
  Mandinka, modes of speech, **1:**498–99
  New Guinean languages, **9:**474
  phonology and, **7:**22
  Somali poetry, **1:**612–13
  southern African languages, **1:**716
Linnekin, Jocelyn, **9:**212
Linton, Ralph, **2:**70; **9:**24
Lipaev, Ivan, **8:**783
Lipan Apache Indian nation, **3:**440
Lipovšek, Marjan, **8:**921
Lippay, Alexander, **4:**870
Lippincott Magazine, **3:**574
Lipset, Seymour Martin, **3:**1060
Lipsker, Eli, **10:**130
Liqā' (al-Ṭawīl), **6:**601
Lira, Agustín, **3:**749
Lira Colombiana, **2:**395, 396
Lira Filipina, La (periodical), **4:**858
Lirophone (record company), **8:**777
Lisān al-'Arab (dictionary), **6:**222
Li Sao (Tan), **7:**350
Liscano, Juan, **2:**524, 535
List, George, **2:**4, 411, 431; **8:**20; **9:**287; **10:**56, 57
Listen to the Lambs (Dett), **3:**607
"Listen to the Mocking Bird" (Winner), **3:**59–60
Listopadov, Aleksandr, **8:**783
Lisu people, **4:**537, 542–43; **7:**509
  dances of, **7:**510
  instruments of, **4:**540, 544, 545
  music of, **7:**485–92
Liszt, Franz, **8:**83, 272, 368, 422, 737
  Hungarian Rhapsodies, **8:**746
Literatura guaraní del Paraguay, **2:**204
literature. *See also* narratives; poetry; treatises; *specific titles*
  Bali, **4:**756
  Beat Zen, **3:**130
  Belarusan, **8:**790
  Bengali, **5:**562
  Buddhist, **5:**319, 327–29, 965
    Jātaka stories, **5:**399–400
    sutras, **7:**478, 502–3
  Burma, **4:**366
    Maha Gitá, **4:**373
  Canadian, **3:**1059
  Cankam (also Sangam), **5:**260, 293, 319, 326–27, 884
  China
    novels, **7:**246, 286, 308, 403, 452
    opera librettos, **7:**287, 292–93
    qin music and, **7:**159–60
  France, **8:**550
  Germany, **8:**646
  Harlem Renaissance, **3:**71, 577–78
  Hindu, **5:**10–11
  Iceland, **8:**404–5
  Ireland, **8:**378, 388
  Islamic
    Barzanji, **4:**766, 776, 782–83, 784
    hikayat, **4:**775
    romances, **5:**496
  Italy, **8:**573
  Japan
    bunraku plays, **7:**663, 667–70
    nô plays, **7:**629–30, 640
  Java, **4:**632
    Pakem Wirama, **4:**636

literature, Java (*continued*)
   Panji, **4:**255
   Serat Centhini, **4:**635
   Smaradhana, **4:**632
  Kannada, **5:**515–16
  Karnataka, Tulu, **5:**883
  Khmer people, *Reamker*, **4:**189, 191, 192, 215–16
  Lao people
   Sang sin sai, **4:**329
   used in northeastern Thai theatrical genres, **4:**321
  Lombok, *Serat Menak*, **4:**774
  Malayalam, **5:**516, 942
  Malaysia
   in *joget gamelan*, **4:**429
   in *mak yong*, **4:**406
   in *wayang kulit*, **4:**404
  Oceania, Western writings on, **9:**33–42
  Oriya, **5:**731–32
  Philippines
   awit, **4:**853, 855
   Christian texts, **4:**841–42, 843–44, 846
   Islamic texts, **4:**907
   playwrights, **4:**864–66
  Sanskrit, **5:**515
  South Asian
   influence on Southeast Asian writing systems, **4:**65–66
   references to temple dancers, **5:**408
   references to women instrumentalists, **5:**411
   sacred musical texts, **5:**470
  Southeast Asia, **4:**65
  Sulawesi, **4:**805
   I La Galigo, **4:**805
  Sumbawa, **4:**784–85
  Tamil, **5:**516
  Telugu, **5:**516, 893
  Thailand, **4:**66, 309, 366
   in *hün*, **4:**257
   Inao, **4:**255
   Khrai Thawng, **4:**255
   Khun Chang Khun Phaen, **4:**255, 258–59, 302, 306
   in *lakhawn*, **4:**255, 256, 313
   in *manora*, **4:**411
   northeastern, **4:**325
   Phra Apai Mani, **4:**257, 306
   Phra Law, **4:**310, 313
   Ramakian, **4:**250–51, 252, 257
   Sang Thawng, **4:**306
   Suton Manora, **4:**254
  Tibet, **7:**472
  Uttar Pradesh, **5:**667
  Vaishnava, **5:**519–20
lithophones
  alu bakatentang, **4:**610
  bianqing (stone chimes), **7:**79, 82, 88, 98, 108, 191, 336
  duoding, **7:**451
  goong lu, **5:**320
  Karelia, **8:**481
  meko, **4:**800
  North America, **3:**475
  Orissa, **5:**320–21

p'yŏn'gyŏng (stone chimes), **7:**829, 862–63, 866, 867
qing, **7:**105, 106–7, 108
  rock gongs, Scotland, **8:**366
  temple pillars, **5:**210, 365
  Vietnam, **4:**56–57, 446, 534
Lithuania, **8:**509–14
  adoption of Christianity, **8:**5, 509
  art music in, **8:**510
  geography of, **8:**509
  history of, **8:**509
  history of music in, **8:**512–13
  instruments, **8:**170, 511–12
  map of, **8:***398*
  population of, **8:**509
  research on music of, **8:**513–14
  state folk ensembles in, **8:**513
  vocal music of, **8:**131, 509–11, 512–14
Lithuanian people
  in Canada, **3:**1196; **8:**514
  exiled to Siberia, **8:**509, 510–11
  in Poland, **8:**701
  in South America, **2:**84
  in United States, **3:**866, 875–77; **8:**514
   instrumental music of, **3:**876
   vocal music of, **3:**875–76
Lithuanian Varpas Choir, **3:**1082
Little Black Sambo (Graham), **3:**609
Little Egypt, **3:**1028, 1277
Little Esther, **3:**669
Little Eva, **3:**709
Little Island Cree (musical group), **3:**1087
Little, Jenny, **9:**974
Little, Jimmy, **9:**444
Little Joe (Tejano band leader), **3:**745
Little Joe and the Latinaires, **3:**780
Little Joe y La Familia, **3:**780
Little Johnny Jones (Cohan), **3:**193, 544
"Little Lucy" (Büyükburç), **6:**249
Little Night Music, A (Sondheim), **3:**197, 545
"Little Old Cabin in the Lane" (Hays), **3:**191
"Little Old Log Cabin in the Lane" (Carson), **3:**78, *263*
Little Richard, **3:**348, 353, 648, 671–72, 709; **4:**884; **8:**214
"Little Sailor Boy" (Carr), **3:**180, 289
"Little Sally Walker," **3:**599
Little Sisters of the Grassland (*pipa* concerto), **7:**170, 349
Little Trinidad Club (Toronto), **3:**1213
Little Walter, **3:**647
Littlecreek, "Grandpa" Hollis, **3:**455
Litva, Grand Duchy of, **8:**790
Liu Bang, **7:**168
Liu Ching-chih, **7:**139
Liu Dehai, **7:**170
Liu Guangyue, **7:**185
Liu Shikun, **7:**348–49
Liu Tianhua, **7:**50, 89–90, 140, 170, 177, 228–29, 232, 377, 382–83
Liu Wenjin, **7:**177, 231
Liu Xiumei, **7:***253*
Liu Yuan, **7:**367
Liu Yuxi, **7:**450
Liu Zaisheng, **7:**142
Liu Ziyun, **7:**299, 300

Liuban (*qupai* melody), **7:**233
Liu bo qiu (Sun), **7:**177
Liudkevych, Stanislav, **8:**820
Liuqing niang (*qupai* melody), **7:**218, 233, *234*, 235–38, *236–38*
Liushizhong qu (Mao), **7:**130
Liuyaojin (*qupai* melody), **7:**233
Live Aid concert, **1:**364; **8:**216
Live at the Plugged Nickel (Davis), **3:**662
Live Music Directory, **3:**1081
Liverpool, Hollis Urban, **2:**93
"Living for the City" (Wonder), **3:**677
Living Single (television show), **3:**715
Livingstone, David, **1:**635, 650, 717
"Livin' La Vida Loca" (Martin), **3:**733
Livonia, **8:**499
Livonian people, **8:**475
Livre d'orgue de Montréal (Gallat-Morin), **3:**1075
Lizardo, Fradique, **2:**861
Lizot, Jacques, **2:**170–72
Ljevaković, Zvonimir, **8:**151, 936
LL Cool J (musical group), **3:**696, 698, 713, 714
Llerenas, Eduardo, **2:**784
Lloyd, Albert Lancaster, **8:**188, 338–39, 1004
Lloyd, Richard, **9:**529
Lloyd, Thomas, **3:**1070
Lloyd Webber, Andrew, **3:**198, 200, 545; **8:**219
Loar, Lloyd, **1:**353; **3:**164
Loba Negra, La (Feliciano), **4:**878
Lobanov, Mikhail, **8:**785
Lobban, Bill, **4:**209
Lobi people, **1:**456
Lobo de Mesquita, José Joaquim Emérico, **2:**303
Lobo, Edu, **2:**109
Lobo y Melón (musical group), **3:**741
Local Import, **9:**81
Lochamer Liederbuch, **8:**651
Lochies (musical group), **8:**371
Locke, Alain, **3:**577
Locke, David, **1:**56
Lockel, Gérard, **2:**875
Lockhart Festival (film), **9:**47
Lockwood, Normand, **3:**553
"Loco-Motion" (Little Eva), **3:**709
Locomotiv GT (musical group), **8:**746
LoDagaa people, **1:**456–57
Lộ Địch (Ưng Bình Thúc Gịa), **4:**508
Loeb, David, **3:**954
Loeb, Edwin M., **9:**817
Loeffler, Charles Martin, **3:**538
Loeffler, Jack, **3:**757, 763, 767, 849
Loesser, Arthur, **3:**562
Loesser, Frank, **3:**545
Loewe, Frederick, **3:**545
Lofimbo Stars (musical group), **3:**1170
Loft (New York), **3:**688
Lofthouse, Charles, **2:**806
Log Cabin Songbook, **3:**305
log drums. See slit-drums
Logan, Wendell, **3:**610
Lohār group, **5:**769
Lohmann, Adolf, **8:**661
Loizos, Manos, **8:**1021; **9:**72
Lokananta, **4:**102
Lokananta label, **4:**681
Lokele people, **1:**106

Lok Mchah, **4:**193

Lok Virsa (National Institute for Folk Heritage, Islamabad), **5:**529, 747, *764*

Lole y Manuel (flamenco duo), **8:**599

Lô Lô people, **4:**533

Lolo people (New Guinea), **9:**612–14

Lô Lô people (Vietnam), **4:**535

Lolua, Dzuku, **8:**844, 853

Lomax, Alan, **1:**8, 54, 688; **3:**14, 31, 72, 85, 146, 293–94, 302, 310, 330, 510, 511, 576, 579, 707; **8:**21, 96, 338, 371, 613; **10:**79

  cantometrics project, **1:**518; **2:**231; **8:**20–21

  choreometrics project, **3:**221; **9:**314

  importance of, **10:**80

Lomax, John A., **3:**14, 31, 146, 147, 293–94, 299, 510, 511, 579, 707; **10:**80

Lombardo, Guy, **3:**265, 314, 1080

Lombards, in Corsica, **8:**566

Lombok, **4:**763–78

  Dutch in, **4:**764, 765

  geography of, **4:**765

  history of, **4:**731, 763–65

  instruments of, **4:**766–69

  musical genres (*See also* vocal music *heading*)

    dangdut Sasak, **4:**778

    orkes Melayu, **4:**778

    qasidah Sasak, **4:**778

  musical styles in, **4:**762–63

  performance traditions of, **4:**765–66

  population of, **4:**762

  research on, **4:**765

  tourism in, **4:**762, 778

  vocal music in, **4:**774–75

Lo Mejor de Lorenzo Martinez y sus Violines (Martínez), **3:**767

Lo Mejor de Los Reyes de Albuquerque, **3:**767

Lom, Jakup (Fel-Jakup; Loms-Jakup), **8:**419

Lon Nol, **4:**90, 154, 209

"London Bridge Is Falling Down," **8:**145, 900

London Civic Symphony Orchestra, **3:**1079, 1184

"Londonderry Air," **8:**380, 393

London, Jack, **3:**1047; **9:**37, 41, 44

London Missionary Society

  in East Polynesia, **9:**208

  in Kiribati, **9:**763

  in Manihiki, **9:**905

  in Micronesia, **9:**720

  in New Caledonia, **9:**682

  in New Guinea, **9:**193–94

  in Niue, **9:**816

  in Papua New Guinea, **9:**88, 195, 493–94, 506

  in Sāmoa, **9:**204, 206, 795

  in Tokelau, **9:**823

  in Torres Strait Islands, **9:**84, 412, 429

  in Tuvalu, **9:**828–29, 831

Lonely Child (Vivier), **3:**1151

Lonely M. L. Daughters, **9:**139

"Long Ago and Far Away" (Kern), **3:**549

Long, Bena, **10:**61

Long Black Veil (album), **8:**226

"Long Gone" (Thompson), **3:**669

Long Island (Papua New Guinea), **9:**561

Long, John Luther, **9:**38

"Long Lonely Nights" (McPhatter), **3:**673

Long Ngâm, **4:**457, *462–63*

"Long Tailed Blue," **3:**182

"Long Tall Sally" (Little Richard), **3:**672

Longfellow, Henry Wadsworth, **3:**532, 1135; **8:**307

Longfield, Jesse, **3:**1096

Longomba, Victor "Vicky," **1:**386

Longoria, Valerio, **3:**776

Longuda people, **1:**292

Longwhitecloudland (album), **8:**802

Longxiang (*qin* piece), **10:**18

Lönnrot, Elias, **8:**488

Lontará Bugis (manuscript), **4:**805

Lontará Makassar (manuscript), **4:**806

"Loobie Loo," **3:**599

"Lookin' for Love in All the Wrong Places," **3:**81

Loomer, Diane, **3:**1096

Lopa people. *See* Lhoba people

Lopars, **8:**754

Lopategui, Jon, **8:**312–14

Lopes, Duarte, **1:**77

Lopes de Souza, Pedro, **2:**510

López, Anselmo, **2:**531, 540

López, Braulio, **2:**520

Lopez, Donald, **3:**133

López, Eduardo, **2:**394, 396

López de Gómara, Francisco, **2:**602

López, Isidro, **3:**779, 796

López, Israel "Cachao," **3:**787, 789, 793, 796

López, Jennifer, **3:**733

López, Joe, **3:**780

López, Lisa, **3:**751

López, Manny, **3:**741, 743, 799

Lopez, Orestes, **3:**793

López, Pantaleón, **4:**864, 865

López, Sal, **3:**749

López, Sonia, **3:**743

Lopez, Tily, **3:**743

López, Wilmor, **2:**767

Loras, Jelaleddin, **3:**1044

Lord, Albert B., **6:**340, 342, 343; **8:**94, 95, 130, 896, 898, 1003, 1024; **10:**43

Lord Beginner (calypsonian; Egbert Moore), **2:**963

Lord Caresser (calypsonian), **2:**963

Lord Cobra (calypsonian), **2:**691

Lord of the Dance (dance show), **3:**846

Lord Executor (calypsonian; Phillip Garcia), **2:**96, 963

Lord Invader (calypsonian; Rupert Grant), **2:**96, 963

Lord Kitchener (calypsonian; Aldwyn Roberts), **2:**691, 963

Lord Pretender (calypsonian; Alric Farrell), **2:**963

Lord Radio and the Bimshire Boys, **2:**819, 820

Lord Rhaburn (Gerald Rhaburn), **2:**678

Lord Rhaburn Combo, **2:**678

Lord Silvers (calypsonian), **2:**819

Lord, You Brought Me a Mighty Long Way (anthology), **3:**1133

Lords (musical group), **8:**679

"Lorena," **3:**188

Lorenzo Martinez: Tocandoy Cantando (Martínez), **3:**767

Lorik (epic), **5:**673, 675

Lorimer, David L. R., **5:**800

Lorita Leung Dancers (Vancouver), **3:**224

Lorita Leung Dance Studio (Vancouver), **3:**1096

"*Lorke*" (Moğollar), **6:**250

Lortat-Jacob, Bernard, **6:**23; **8:**114, 622

Los Alacranes de Angel Flores (musical group), **3:**776

Los Alacranes Mojados (musical group), **3:**749

Los Alegres de Taos (musical group), **3:**763

Los Angeles Philharmonic Orchestra, **3:**537, 740

los Ángeles, Servando de, **4:**866

Los Angeles Times, **3:**739–40

Los Arlequines (musical group), **2:**517

Los Bárbaros del Ritmo (musical group), **2:**755

Los Bisturices Harmónicos (musical group), **2:**767

Los Bukis (musical group), **3:**746

Los Caifanes (musical group), **2:**104

Los Campesinos de Michoacán (musical group), **3:**723

Los Casinos (musical group), **3:**780

Los Corraleros de Majagual (musical group), **2:**409

Los Cruzados (musical group), **3:**750

Los Cuatitos Cantú (musical group), **3:**776

Los Cuatro Huasos (musical group), **2:**368

Los Doneños (musical group), **3:**776

Los Dos Gilbertos Los Guadalupanos (musical group), **3:**776

Los Fabulosos Cuatro (musical group), **3:**780

Los Flamingos (musical group), **3:**741

Los Folkloristas Nuevomejicanos (musical group), **3:**764

Los Freddys (musical group), **3:**746

Los Frejoles Negros (musical group), **2:**501

Los Gaiteros de San Jacinto (musical group), **2:**407

Los Girasoles (musical group), **2:**763

Los Guaraguaos (musical group), **2:**103

Los Hermanos (religious brotherhood), **3:**757

Los Hermanos Banuelos, **3:**737

Los Hermanos Cuatro, **2:**592

Los Hermanos Eliceiri, **3:**738

Los Hermanos Sánchez, **3:**741

Los Huasos Quincheros (musical group), **2:**368

Los Huastecos (musical group), **2:**371

Los Humildes (musical group), **3:**746

Los Illegals (musical group), **3:**750

LoSix (musical group), **1:**774

Los Jairas (musical group), **2:**298

Los Jaivas (musical group), **2:**32, 40, 104, 374

Los Lobos (musical group), **2:**105; **3:**339, 720, 721, 733, 750–51

Los Madrugadores (musical group), **3:**738–39, 741

Los Masis (musical group), **2:**297

Los Muñequitos (musical group), **2:**836

Los Muñequitos de Matanzas (musical group), **3:**786

Los Negros (Papua New Guinea), **9:**602

Los Panchos (musical group), **2:**372

Los Papines (musical group), **3:**786

Los Paraguayos (musical group), **5:**971

Los Pavos Reales (musical group), **3:**776

Los Peniques (musical group), **2:**372

Los Piratos del Centro (musical group), **2:**475

Los Pleneros de la 21 (musical group), **3:**727
Los Pleneros de la Veintitrés Abajo (musical group), **2:**940
Los Prisioneros (musical group), **2:**104, 374
Los Provincianos (musical group), **2:**368, *369*
Los Queretanos (musical group), **2:**371
Los Reyes de Albuquerque, **3:**767
Los Reyes de Albuquerque (musical group), **3:**765
los Reyes, Maximino de, **4:**864
Los Rock Angels (musical group), **3:**750
Los Soñadores de Sarawaska (musical group), **2:**758
Lost Horizon (film), **3:**609
Los Tigres del Norte (musical group), **3:**723, 751
Lost in the Stars (Weill), **3:**621
"Lost Lambs" (Xiao), **7:**364
Los Tres (musical group), **2:**374
Los Van Van (musical group), **2:**835
Los Veracruzanos (musical group), **2:**371
Los Yonics (musical group), **3:**746
Los Yuras (musical group), **2:**297
Lote people, **9:**620–25, 974
Lotring, **4:**130
Lott, Eric, **3:**67
Lotus (periodical), **3:**992
Lotus Sutra, **3:**130
Lou 'Ilima Koula 'o 'Amusia e 'A, **9:**136
Lou Zhongrong, **7:**346, 350
Loughnane, Victor, **9:**79
Louie, Alexina, **3:**1186
Louis Jordan and His Tympany Five, **3:**668, 708
Louis Riel (Somers), **3:**1058
Louis XIV, king of France, **8:**77, 160
Louisiade Archipelago (Papua New Guinea), **9:**177, 498, 983
Louisiana
   French people in, **3:**9, 505, 854, 856–59, 1135–36
   Haitians in, **3:**802–3
   Native American groups in, **3:**466, 470
   New Orleans, **2:**47, 49
      African-American composers in, **3:**606
      African-American theater in, **3:**615
      African traditions in, **3:**325, 596–97, 598, 786–87
      Afro-Creole culture in, **3:**600
      black-owned publishing houses in, **3:**644
      Congo Square, **3:**597, 802
      funeral bands, **3:**568
      jazz in, **3:**550, 580–81, 651–52
      street vendors, **3:**600
      Vietnamese people in, **3:**993
      zarzuela companies, **3:**851
   St. Bernard Parish, Isleños, **3:**849
Louisiana French Folk Songs (Whitfield), **3:**857
Louisiana Purchase, **3:**9, 441, 596
Loukinen, Michael, **3:**410
Loumoli, 'Ana, **9:**113
Loun Island (Solomon Islands), **9:**662–63
Lounes, Matoub, **6:**275
Loutherbourg, Philippe Jacques de, **9:**34
Louvain, Michel, **3:**1158
L'Ouverture, Toussaint, **2:**826
Louvin, Charles, **3:**80
Louvin, Ira, **3:**80

Lovae people, **4:**344
Lovara (also Lovari) Roma, **8:**276–77, 289
Love (rock album), **9:**446
Love and Money (musical group), **8:**369
"Love Child" (Supremes), **3:**677
"Love I Lost" (Harold Melvin and the Blue Notes), **3:**711
"Love Is the Message" (MFSB), **3:**688
Love, J. W., **9:**287, 307, 976
"Love to Love You Baby" (Summer), **3:**688, 711
Love, M'pongo, **1:**425
"Love of My Own, A" (Thomas), **3:**676
"Love Rap" (Spoonie Gee), **3:**699
love songs, **8:**133
   Afghanistan, **5:**819; **6:**301
   Akkadian period, **6:**8
   Albania, Rom people, **8:**285
   Austria, *Kärntnerlied*, **8:**674
   Azerbaijani, **6:**851–52
   Balochistan, *dastānag*, **5:**775, 781
   bedouin peoples, **6:**545
   Belarus, **8:**795
   Bengali
      composed by Nazrul Islam, **5:**855
      composed by Ray, **5:**852
      composed by Tagore, **5:**851
      ṭappā, **5:**847
   Berber peoples, **6:**301
   bluegrass, **3:**167–68
   Bosnia-Hercegovina, **8:**959, 963
   Bulgaria, **8:**900, 903
   China, northwestern minorities, **7:**462
   Czech Republic, **8:**720, 721
   Dai people, **7:**505
   Denmark, **8:**453, *454*, 463
   Finland, **8:***477*
      Rom people, **8:**289
   French-American, **3:**855, 858
   French Canadian, **3:**1193
   German-American, **3:**889
   Hmong people, **3:**1003–4
   Hungary, *nóta*, **8:**273
   Iran, **6:**851–52
   Iranian, **3:**1035
   Italy, *maggi a serenata*, **8:**608
   Japan, **7:**688, 740
   Jewish, **8:**250, 261
   Kurdistan, **6:**748
   Low German, **3:**1250
   Macedonia, **8:**973
   Native American, **3:**371
   Nepal, **5:**698
   Ojibwe, **3:**457
   Philippines, **4:**908–9
   Plains Indian, **3:**447
   popular music, **3:**109, 110–11, 195
   Punjab (India), **5:**656
   Romania, **8:***873*
   Ryûkyû Islands, **7:**791, 795
   Slovakia, **8:**720
   South Slav, **3:**923
   Trinidad, *kajarī*, **5:**590
   Turkey, **6:**761, 768, 851–52
   Uttar Pradesh, **5:**666
      caitī, **5:**277
   Vlah people, **8:**950

Wales, **8:**343
Xia'erba people, **7:**482–83
Love Supreme, A (Coltane), **3:**662
"Love Train" (O'Jays), **3:**711
"Love Will Find a Way" (Blake), **3:**619
Loveland, Jerry, **9:**971
"Lovely Hula Hands" (Anderson), **3:**1050
Loven people, **4:**344
Loven, Sven, **2:**13
Loverboy (musical group), **3:**1097
"Lovesick Blues" (Williams), **3:**79
Loving, Colonel Walter H., **4:**859
Lowcanes (runaway slave), **3:**1169
Low Countries, **8:**518–36. *See also* Belgium; Flanders; Luxembourg; Netherlands
   art music in, **8:**518
   geography of, **8:**518
   history of, **8:**518
   instruments and instrumental music, **8:**523–33, 535
   moving house customs, **8:**145
   organ-building in, **8:**78
   Renaissance in, **8:**73
   vocal music of, **8:**142, 195, 518–23
Low, John, **1:**359–60, 608
Lowell, James Russell, **3:**532
Lowens, Irving, **3:**32
Lowenstein, Herbert, **6:**1059
Lower Canada, **3:**9, 1073, 1146
Lower Rhine Folk-Song Archive, **8:**647
Lower Xiajiadian culture, **7:**17
Lowie Museum of Anthropology. *See* Phoebe Hearst Museum (Berkeley)
LoWilisi people, **1:**457
Lowry, Robert, **3:**534
Loy, Kim, **2:**85
Loyalists, **3:**8, 1057, 1060, 1069–70, 1072, 1078, 1079, 1114, 1115, 1179, 1188
Loyalty Islands (New Caledonia), **9:**833, 965, 992
   immigrants to Australia, **9:**84
   kaneka genre, **9:**214
   music and dance of, **9:**671–72, 674, 682–84, 981
   social organization of, **9:**835–36
Loyola, Margot, **2:**370–71
Loza, Steven, **3:**790; **10:**88
Lozano, Conrad, **3:**748
Lozano, Danilo, **3:**790
Lozano, Pedro, **2:**250
Lozi people, **1:**711
   dance as medicine, **1:**113
   history of, **1:**712
   music of, **1:**672–73, 712–13
Lu Bingchuan, **7:**524
Lu Chuansheng, **7:**357
Lu Chunling, **7:**185
Lu Dehua, **7:**224
Lü Ji, **7:**140, 382, 384, 385
Lü Nan, **7:**132
Lư Nhat Vu, **4:**25
Lu people, **4:**218
Lu state, **7:**101
Lu Siqing, **3:**959
Lu T'ai, **4:**284
Lü Wencheng, **3:**1261; **7:**220, 236

Lu Xiujing, **7:**312, 321
Lua, Pale, **9:**390
Luahine, Iolani, **9:***929*
Luang Phrabang (kingdom), **4:**350, 353, 354
Luang Pradit Phairoh, **4:**56, 128, 148, 227, 277, 280, 281
Luangiua (Solomon Islands), **9:**833, 842–44
  betrothal festivals, **9:**349
  cultural contacts with Takuu, **9:**839–40
  geography of, **9:**842
  history of, **9:**842
  music and dance of, **9:**843–44
  social organization of, **9:**835–36
  struck plaques of, **9:**378
Luba people, **1:**672
  farewell songs, **1:**217
  kasala mourning songs, **1:**217
  speech surrogate methods, **1:**107
Luba-Lunda empires, **1:**4, 723
  court music, **1:**312
  drums of, **1:**670
Lubej, Emil H., **8:**622
Lubelo, Daniel "De-la-Lune," **1:**386
Lubin (French Guianese songwriter), **2:**438
Lubogo, Waiswa, **10:**114–15
Luca family, **8:**277
Lucă, Fanica, **8:**277, 882
Lucas, Clarence, **3:**189, 1182
Lucas et Cecile (Quesnel), **3:**1075
Lucas, Maine, **3:***212*
Lucas, Sam, **3:**616
Lucaya culture, **2:**78
Lucero, **3:**746
Luchazi (or Lucazi) people, **1:**672–73
  sand ideographs, **1:**150–51
  vocal music of, **1:**674–76
Lục Hòn Nhung (unidentified country), **4:**498
Lucía, Paco de, **3:**851; **8:**150, 226, 599
Lucian Kaiso, **2:**950
"Lucille" (Little Richard), **3:**672
Lu-Ci-Yun, **4:**556
Luck Ngi Musical Club (Seattle), **7:***304*
Lucknowvi, Ahsan, **5:**487
luck-visit singing. *See* carols and caroling; ceremonies
Lucky Sambo (musical), **3:**620
Lúčnica (musical group), **8:**723
Lucrezia Borgia (Donizetti), **4:**863
Lucumí. *See* Santería
"Lucy, or Selim's Complaint" (Hook), **3:**180
Ludi caste, **5:**774, 776, 781, 782
Lüdig, Mihkel, **8:**497
Ludin, Fritz, **9:**109
Ludlam, Thomas, **1:**373
Ludwig, Christa, **3:**1210
Luengas Pérez, Rubén, **10:***91,* 91–95
Luening, Otto, **3:**253, 498, 1135
Luening, Paul, **3:**610
Lugbara people, **1:**286
Luguru people, **1:**638
Luhya people, **1:**624, 625
Lui, Christopher, **9:**361
Lui Pui-Yuen, **7:**170
Lui Tsun-Yuen, **7:**170
Luisa Fernanda (Moreno Torroba), **3:**851
Luiseño Indian nation, **3:**417

Lukács, Gyorgy, **8:**20
Lukashenko, Aleksandr, **8:**802
Lü li chu tong (Zhu), **7:**119
lullabies, **2:**68; **5:**274
  Abkhazian people, **8:**852
  Adighian people, **8:**856
  Afghanistan, **5:**813
  Ainu people, **7:**786
  Albania, **8:**988
  Algeria, **6:**473
  Andhra Pradesh, **5:**891
  Aotearoa, **9:**938–39
  Armenia, **6:**728, *729*
  Azerbaijan, **6:**931
  Balkarian people, **8:**858
  Balochi people, **5:**774; **6:**881
  Baluan, **9:**258–59
  Bosnia-Hercegovina, **8:**963
  Bulgaria, **8:**901
  Chechen people, **8:**863
  Chile, Chiloé Island, **2:**366
  Cook Islands, **9:**897
  Corsica, **8:**196, 566, 567
  Costa Rica, *arrullo*, **2:**695
  Croatia, **8:**926
  Czech Republic, **8:**720
  Denmark, **8:**453, 458
  El Salvador, **2:**709
  Europe, **8:**133, 139, 145
    interactions with ballads, **8:**135
    performers of, **8:**114
    research on, **8:**23
  European immigrant groups, **3:**825
  Fiji, **9:**775
  Finland, **8:**476
  Finnish, **3:**873
  France, *berceuse*, **8:**542
  French-American, **3:**855, 857, 858
  French Guiana, **2:**435
  Georgia, **8:**828, 833, 835, 847
  Greece, *nanarismata*, **8:**1015
  Gujarat, *hālad*, **5:**632
  Guyana, **5:**601
  Hmong people, **3:**1004
  Ingush people, **8:**863
  Ireland, **8:**388, 389
  Italy, **8:**606, 611
  Jamaica, **2:**904–5
  Japan, **7:**600, 601
  Jewish, **8:**250, 261
  Judeo-Spanish, **6:**1042
  Kabyle people, **6:**301
  Karachaevian people, **8:**858
  Kuna culture, **2:**640, 645–46, 647, 649
  Kurdistan, **6:**751
  Lacandón Maya, **2:**656
  Latvia, **8:**500
  Luangiua, *kangi*, **9:**843
  Malta, **8:**638
  Marquesas Islands, **9:**894
  Marshall Islands, **9:**751
  Maya culture, **2:**653
  Mexico
    Amerindian cultures, **2:**549
    arrullo, **2:**618
  Mongol people, **7:**1009

Native American, **3:**371
Nauru, **9:**260, 755
New Caledonia, **9:**672–73
North America, **3:**236, 285, 600
North Caucasia, **8:**851
Northwest Coast Indian groups, **3:**395
Norway, *bånsuller*, **8:**421
Ossetian people, **8:**859, 861
Palau, **9:**723
Papua New Guinea
  Banoni *watetamasi*, **9:**646
  Buin people, **9:**651
  Nagovisi *wate*, **9:**648
  New Britain, **9:**622
Plains Indian groups, **3:**441
Portugal, **8:**579
Punjab (Pakistan), **5:**771
Rajasthan, **5:**646
Romania, **8:**873, 874
Sāmoa, **9:**804
Sanskrit, **5:**262
Sardinia, **8:**631
Scotland, **8:**360–61
Slovakia, **8:**720
Solomon Islands
  'Are'are people, **9:**667
  Fataleka and Baegu *rorogwela*, **9:**669
  Isabel Province, **9:**660–61
  Russell Islands *guario*, **9:**664
  Shortland Islands, **9:**656
  Sirovanga people, **9:**654
South America, tropical-forest region, **2:**128
Spain, **8:**593
  cuñeros, **8:**589, 591
Subarctic peoples, **3:**386
Sweden, **8:**438–39
Switzerland, **8:**691
Tamil Nadu, **5:**910
  tālāṭṭu, **5:**556
Tuareg people, **1:**593
Turkey, **6:**766
Uruguay, **2:**511, 516
Uttar Pradesh, **5:**661
Venezuela, **2:**537
Virgin Islands, **2:**969
Warao culture, **2:**197, 198
Wayana culture, **2:**166
women's singing of, **8:**120
Yanomamo culture, **2:**173
Yuma culture, *arrullo*, **2:**596
Lullabies (He/Jiang), **7:**339
"Lullaby" (Storace), **3:**180
Lully, Jean-Baptiste, **8:**77, 79, 101, 160
Lulu, Tongan leader, **9:**130
Lulu and the Luvvers, **8:**369
Lülü jingyi (Zhu), **7:**119, 188
Lülü xinshu (Cai), **7:**128
Lülü zheng yi houbian (treatise), **7:**125
Luman, Jimmy, **3:**312
Lumbera, Bien, **4:**885
Lumer, Robert, **3:**48
Lumholtz, Carl, **2:**575
Lummis, Charles F., **3:**31, 736, 762, 767
Luna, Manuel, **4:**866
Lunceford, Jimmie, **3:**78–79, 656, 668, 743
Lund, Alan, **3:**199

Lund, Kristiane, **8**:421

Lunda empire. *See* Luba-Lunda empires

Lunda people, **1**:671, 672

Lundin, Bengt-Ake, **6**:*611*

Lun hanzu min'ge jinsi secaiqu-de guafen (Miao and Qiao), **7**:156

Lunn, Johathan, **3**:999

Lunny, Donal, **8**:392, *392*

Lunsford, Bascom Lamar, **3**:146

Lunsonga, Cajetan, **1**:217

Lunyu. See Analects

Luo Dayou, **7**:357–58

Luo people, **1**:624, 627, 630
   benga, **1**:365, 427
   birth ceremonies, **1**:110, 116
   dance, **1**:110
   fiddle music of, **10**:142
   instruments of, **1**:625
   lyres of, **1**:600
   music of, **1**:362

Luo Pinchao, **7**:306

Luogu sihe (Shanghai piece), **7**:224

Luohan qian (*huju* opera), **7**:300

Lương Đăng, **4**:448

Lupták, Anton, **8**:*719*

Lurås, Knut, **8**:417

Lurie, Nancy, **3**:1276

Lurugu (film), **9**:47

Lus people, **1**:111

Lush (musical group), **9**:169

Lü shi chun qiu (treatise), **7**:118, 151

Lu shi hou ji, **7**:447

Lush, Marion, **3**:895

Lusi people, **9**:614

Lussier, René, **3**:1077

Lustig, Eitan, **6**:1030

lustige Witwe, Die (Lehár), **3**:193

Lutcher, Nellie, **3**:646

lutes. *See also* banjo; guitars; ukulele; violins and fiddles (bowed lutes)
   abaj dombura, **7**:460–61
   achangur, **8**:853
   apandur, **8**:853
   Arab world, **6**:405–9
   bağlama, **3**:1199; **6**:*789*; **8**:993, 1019–20
      Alevi performers, **6**:789–92, 797–99
      recitals of, **6**:790
      in Turkish arabesk, **6**:257
      in Turkish folk music, **6**:80, 82–83, 85, 244, 763, 765
      in Turkish religious music, **6**:768, 795–96
   baglamas, **9**:73
   bakllama, **8**:993
   balalaika, **8**:22, 134, 155, 169, 176
      Belarus, **8**:796
      Finland, **8**:487
      North America, **3**:57–58, *59*, 529, 915, 917, 920, 1199
      North Caucasia, **8**:863
      Russia, **8**:768, *769*, 770, *775*
      Ukraine, **8**:816, 817
   balikan (also *blikan*), **4**:835
   bambirn, **6**:733
   bandol, **2**:953
   bandola
      Chile, **2**:358, 361

Colombia, **2**:382, 383, 387, 392–93, 394–95
   Venezuela, **2**:531, 540–41

bandola andina (also *bandurría*), **2**:531

bandolim, **2**:309, 311

bandolín, **2**:337, 417, 531

bandura, **3**:10, 1200; **8**:*99*, 815–16, 817, *817*

bandurria
   Cuba, **2**:823, 833–36
   Guatemala, **2**:728
   North America, **3**:1025
   Peru, **2**:213, 473, 475
   Philippines, **4**:849, 852, 854–55
   Spain, **8**:594

bappe, **1**:444

barbat (also *barbaṭ*), **5**:692; **6**:12, 131, 397, *834*

berde, **3**:920

bisernica, **3**:920; **8**:917

biwa, **7**:167, 643–51, 691, *711*
   construction of, **7**:547, 643
   in film scores, **7**:751
   in *gagaku*, **7**:588, 622, 625, *627*, 644
   in *heikyoku*, **7**:536, 624, 653
   North America, **3**:968, 969
   notation for, **7**:538, 574–78, 588–89, 626, *650*
   origins of, **7**:81, 622, 643
   performance techniques of, **7**:622
   status of, **7**:82
   syôga vocables for, **7**:626
   use in narrative accompaniment, **7**:75, 624, 643–51

bouzouki, **8**:169, 204, *206*, 285, 1015, 1019–20; **9**:73
   Cyprus, **8**:1031
   Germany, **8**:656
   Ireland, **8**:152, 385
   North America, **3**:529, 826, 842, 930, 1199
   Scotland, **8**:366
   Wales, **8**:354

bozuk, **6**:115

brač, **3**:920, 1198; **8**:917

bugari, **8**:997

bugarija, **3**:920, 1198; **8**:917, 966

bulbul taraṅg, **5**:674

buzuk, **8**:994

buzūkī, **6**:407

buzuq, **6**:407, 408, 554, 555, 1074

cannacione, **8**:615

cautārā, **5**:343

čelo, **3**:920

cetera, **8**:571, 572, *572*, 573, 632

chahārtār, **5**:822

chapey dang veng, **3**:999; **4**:66, 155, 171, 194, 196, 197, 202, 238

chishapshina, **8**:855

chitrāli sitār, **5**:787, *788*

chonguri, **8**:838, 840, 841, 845, 853

çifteli (also *çiteli*), **8**:285, 996, *996*, 997, 1000, 1002

citrā vīṇā, **5**:*299*, 306

cittern, **3**:842; **8**:367
   Germany, **8**:654, 656
   halszither, **8**:686–87
   Low Countries, **8**:533

Norway, **8**:422
   women performers of, **8**:200

cobza, **8**:277, 876, 877, 879, 880

çöğür, **6**:795

colascione, **8**:615

cümbüş, **6**:764

dai ba tiêu, **4**:509

dala-fandir, **8**:859–60

damboro, **5**:754, 759

dambura, **5**:828, 829, 830

damburā (also *dhambura*; *danburo*), **5**:344, 506

dambūrag, **5**:776, 781, *782*, 783, *783*, *784*

dàn đáy, **4**:467, 472, 481, 513

dàn nguyệt (also *dàn kim*), **3**:994, *994*; **4**:70, 238, 465, 472–73, 490, 505, *506*

dàn tam, **4**:473, 490

dàn tỳbà, **4**:70, 472, 473

dàn xến, **4**:473

daruan, **7**:231

dechik-pondur, **8**:863, 864

deśī sitar, **5**:344, *344*

dhrupad rabāb (barbed lute), **5**:337, 345

diassare, **1**:444, 445

diên xin, **4**:536

döm, **4**:541

dombira, **6**:345

dombra, **6**:901, 902, 953, *953*, 956–58, *957*, *959*, 961, 967

dombura, **7**:460–61

domra, **3**:57, 58, 920; **8**:155

đon xến, **4**:484

dongbula, **7**:451

dōtār, **6**:345

dotārā, **5**:344, *860*

dotāro, **5**:344

dungga (also *jungga*), **4**:791, 803

duru, **1**:460–61

dutar (also *dutār*; *dūtār*), **6**:6
   Afghanistan, **5**:344, 818, 819, *821*, 822, 830
   Central Asia, **6**:900, 901, *901*, 902, *902*
   Iran, **6**:825, *828*, 834–36, *839*, 839–41, 844
   Turkmenistan, **6**:968, 969, 971–74
   Uighur people, **6**:995; **7**:113, 459, 468–69
   Uzbekistan, **6**:907–8, 919, 946

dutār-e chārdeh jalau, **5**:820

džumbuš, **8**:281, 282, 286, 980

ekanāda, **5**:365, 366

ektār, **5**:344, 400, 769–70
   use in rock music, **5**:428

ektārā, **5**:343, 347

ēktāri, **5**:867, 869

elektrobağlama, **6**:257

Europe, **6**:449; **8**:169
   Baroque music for, **8**:78
   dissemination of, **8**:170
   Renaissance music for, **8**:74, 75, 76
   short-necked, **8**:12
   tablature for, **8**:*103*
   women performers of, **8**:200

faglong, **4**:886

faglung, **4**:924

gabusi, **1**:351

gagaku biwa, **7**:643, *644*, 644–45, *651*

gambaré, **1:**463
gambo, **4:**780, 781, 784
gambus
    Bali, **4:**743
    Lombok, **4:**768, 774
    Malaysia, **4:**432, 437, 438–39
    Maluku, **4:**806, 816, 817, 820
    Singapore, **4:**520
    Sumatra, **4:**598, 605, 606, 611, 612
gàraayàa (or *garaya*), **1:**273, 448, 521
gekkin, **4:**472; **7:**740
Germany, **8:**654, 656
geṭṭuvādyam, **5:**365
gidayû busi syamisen, **7:**674, 675, 692
ginbri (also *gimbrī; gumbrī; jumbrī*), **6:**269,
    403, 407, 408, 435
gingiru, **1:**113, 455
gumbri, **1:**75, 537
gurmi, **1:**448
hagelong, **4:**905
hagelung, **4:**924
han pipa, **7:**167
hasapi, **4:**599, 608
heike biwa, **7:**643, 646–47, *651*
hoddu, **1:**445
huobusi, **7:**114
husapi, **4:**66
hyang pip'a, **7:***826*, 830
igqonqwe, **1:**761
iktār, **5:**769–70, 772
internal spike, **1:**366
jamubul dombura, **7:**461
japey, **4:**212, 214
junbush, **6:**407
kabosa (or *kabosy*), **1:**351, 367, 787
kacapi, **4:***805*, 806, 810
kacaping, **4:**805
kacchapī, **4:**599–600; **5:**326
kachappi, **4:**338, 345, 346, 355, 358
kankala, **6:**395
kankara sansin, **7:**790
karadjuzen, **8:**966
kāsyapī, **4:**599
kerona, **1:**445
ketadu, **4:**802, 803
kil-kobuz, **8:**857
king, **5:**763, 769–70, 772
kitar, **2:**661, 663
kobza, **3:**1200; **8:**796, 813, 815, 818
kologo, **1:**367
komuz, **6:**844
koni, **1:**445
konting, **1:**444, 445
kopuz, **6:**80
kotyapi, **4:**905, 908
krajappi, **4:**66, 237–38
kucapi, **4:**599
kudlung, **4:**905, 925
kudyapi, **4:**66
kudyapiq, **4:**924
kulcapi, **4:**599, 607
kuntigi (or *kuntiji*), **1:**448, 450
kusyapiq, **4:**924–25
kutyapi (also *kutyapiq*), **4:**905
kwītra, **6:**405, 407, 454, 470
lagouto, **9:**73

Lahu people, **4:**540
laouto, **3:**930, 1199; **8:**118, 284–85, 1010,
    1013, 1015, 1019, 1025, 1030–31
laúd, **2:**475, 823, 833–36
laud, **3:**792, 1025; **4:**854–55; **9:**100
lavta, **6:**758
leku (also *pisu; bijol*), **4:**797
lginbri, **6:**489
lijerica, **8:**929
liuqin, **7:**231
llautë, **8:**993, 997, 1000
long-necked, **8:**12
longtou qin, **7:**474
lotār (also *loṭar*), **6:**410, 489
Low Countries, **8:**533
luc y cầm, **4:**509
Madagascar, **1:**787
Madhya Pradesh, **5:**323
makbas, **6:**651–52
mandole, **6:**421
mandolin, **2:**213, 222; **3:***13*
    Algeria, **6:**407, 421, 435, 475, 476
    Amish playing of, **3:**887
    Argentina, **2:**251, 254
    bandurria, **9:**100
    Belarus, **8:**796
    Cook Islands, **9:**900
    Croatia, **8:**936
    El Salvador, **2:**708
    Germany, **8:**658
    Goa, **5:**737
    Greece, **8:**1014
    Guyana, **5:**603, *604*
    Ireland, **8:**385
    Italy, **8:**608
    in Karnatak music, **5:**351, 352, 354
    Kru people, **1:**375
    Latvia, **8:**504
    Low Countries, **8:**533
    Malta, **8:**639, 640
    Marshall Islands, **9:**753
    Nepal, **5:**705
    Netherlands Antilles, **2:**930
    North America: in bluegrass music, **3:**159,
      160, 164, 166; in contra dance bands,
      3:231; in Finnish music, **3:**874; in
      gospel music, **3:**631; in Hispano
      music, **3:**761; in Irish music, **3:**842; in
      Italian music, **3:**861, 864, 920; in
      Norwegian music, **3:**868; in string
      bands, **3:**836; in *tamburitza* orchestra,
      3:920; in Ukrainian music, **3:**1200
    Ontario, **3:**1190, 1194
    Peru, **2:**473
    Portugal, **8:**583
    Réunion Island, **5:**609
    South Asia, **5:**234; **8:**169, 170; use in film
      music, **5:**347, 535, 544
    Sri Lanka, **5:**970
    Switzerland, **8:**687, 694, 695–96
    in Tunisian *ma'lūf*, **6:**327
    Ukraine, **8:**817
    Vietnam, **4:**508
    Wales, **8:**354
    Yukon, **3:**1277
mandolina, **2:**531, 572, 743

mandolin-guitarophone, **3:**1190
mandoll, **8:**997
manolin, **4:**743, 768, 774
meihuaqin, **7:**212
merrywang, **2:**900, 907
Middle Eastern, **6:**18
mizhar, **6:**295
móló, **1:**289, 445, 475, 588, 789
môsô biwa, **7:**617, 643, *645*, 645–46, 649,
    651
nagauta syamisen, **7:**673–74, 692, 715, 779;
    10:13, 27–28
narsyuk, **7:**1029
nash'at kār, **6:**570
ndere, **1:**445
nisiki biwa, **7:**648–49
North America, revival of, **3:**55
Norway, **8:**420, 422
nyanyuru, **1:**444, 445
octavina (also *oktavina*), **3:**1025; **4:**854–55
oūd (also *oud*), **1:**220, 427; **3:**931, 1072;
    6:586, 589 (*See also 'ūd*)
outi, **3:**930; **8:**285, 1013, 1019, 1021; **9:**73
panduri, **8:**8, *833*, 838, 840, 841, 845, 853,
    859
pararayki, **7:**787
penting, **4:**768
Peru, **2:**494
Philippines, **4:**924–25, 928
phin, **4:**18, 66, 316, 338
piccolo bandurria, **4:**855
pipa, **4:**70; **7:**42, *80, 81, 167*, 167–70;
    9:97
    Abing's performances, **7:**140
    in Buddhist rituals, **7:**312
    in Cantonese music, **7:**217
    construction of, **7:**167
    contemporary music for, **7:**170
    Dunhuang manuscripts for, **7:**132–33
    early history of, **7:**167–68, 455
    influence on *Jiangnan sizhu*, **7:**224
    in *Jiangnan sizhu* ensemble, **7:**224–25
    musical genres for, **7:**169–70
    in *nanguan* ensemble, **7:**205, 206–7
    in narrative accompaniment, **7:**254, 262,
      263, 267
    North America, **3:**962, 1248
    northern Chinese music for, **7:**199
    notation for, **7:**124, 168, 169, 170
    in opera ensembles, **7:**276, 292
    origins of, **7:**112
    performance schools of, **7:**55
    performance techniques, **7:**123, 242, 396
    precursors of, **7:**88
    repertoire sources for, **7:**168, 233
    in *shifangu* ensemble, **7:**196
    status of, **7:**82, 89, 168
    Vietnam, **4:**473
    in *xianshiyue* ensemble, **7:**212
pivačka tambura, **8:**965, 966
prim, **3:**920, 1198
qanbūs, **6:**405, 407, 654, 655, *686*, 686–87
qin pipa, **7:**81, 167
qinqin, **3:**1260; **4:**473; **7:**212, 218, 224–25
qubuz, **1:**787
quxiang pipa, **7:**80, 81, 112

Volume Key: **6**, Middle East; **7**, East Asia; **8**, Europe; **9**, Australia and the Pacific Islands; **10**, The World's Music.

lutes (continued)
rabāb, **5**:190, 196, 655, 692, 794
   Afghani, **5**:188, 193, 336–37, *337*, 344,
      506, 786–87, *787*, 789
   Balochistan, **5**:783; **6**:825, 881, 883
   Kashmiri, **5**:329
   Uzbekistan, **6**:907, 919
ramkie, **1**:351, 719, 761
rāmsāgar, **5**:*236*
rawap, **6**:998; **7**:113, 459
rebāb, **5**:310, 683–84; **8**:840
rebec, **2**:251, 254
robab, **4**:615
ruan, **4**:70, 238; **7**:112, 212, 292
ruanxian, **7**:112, 167, 229
rubāb (also *rubab*), **5**:506, *806*, 818, 820,
      822, 828, 830, 831, 835, *836*, 837;
      6:395, 398, 1002, *1004*
safe, **4**:66
saj, **7**:460
samica, **3**:920; **8**:926
samisen, **4**:473
sampi', **4**:833
sanhsien, **9**:97
sansin, **7**:691, 789, 792–93, 795; **9**:98–99
sanxian, **7**:*80*, 113, *258*, 691
   in Buddhist rituals, **7**:312
   in Cantonese music, **7**:218; **10**:18
   in Hui music, **7**:462
   influence on Ryûkyû *sansin*, **7**:792
   in *Jiangnan sizhu* ensemble, **7**:224–25
   in *nanguan* ensemble, **7**:205, 207, 242
   in narrative accompaniment, **7**:254, 262, 263
   North America, **3**:961
   notation for, **7**:124
   in opera ensembles, **7**:276, 292
   in *shifangu* ensemble, **7**:196
   Vietnam, **4**:473
   in *xianshiyue* ensemble, **7**:212
sapeh (also *sapi'*), **4**:66, 833, 834–35
sarangi, **2**:85
sarasvatī vīṇā, **5**:232–33, 350, 352–53, *353*
      (*See also bīn*; vina)
   as accompaniment instrument, **5**:324
   as solo instrument, **5**:325
šargija, **8**:966
sarod, **3**:951; **5**:*4*, *133*, *204*, *206*, 336–37,
      337, 462–63, *565*
   depictions of, **5**:307
   North West Frontier Province, **5**:786
   Punjab, **5**:762
   repertoire for, **5**:123, 188–208
   Sri Lanka, **5**:956
   use in film music, **5**:347, 543
   women performers of, **5**:411
sarod-banjo, **5**:337
sasa biwa, **7**:*645*
satuma biwa, **7**:643, 647–49, *648*, *649*, *651*
saw, **4**:547
saz (also *sāz*), **6**:407, *805*, *847*; **8**:168
   Albania, **8**:996, 997
   in Azerbaijani music, **6**:10, 843–52, 925,
      929–30
   Bosnia-Hercegovina, **8**:964, 966, *967*
   Bulgaria, **8**:893
   distribution of, **6**:405, 408

Georgia, **8**:840
Greece, **8**:1019
Macedonia, **8**:983
Montenegro, **8**:959
Serbia, **8**:951
Turkey, **6**:746, 751
Turkic cultures, **6**:345
   in Turkish *aşîklar* performances, **6**:803, 805,
      808
   in Turkish folk music, **6**:10, 82, 763, *763*,
      764, 816
   in Turkish religious music, **6**:768, 795
   in Turkish rock music, **6**:248, 250, 251
s'az, **6**:734, *734*
Scotland, **8**:367, 373
sehtār, **5**:693
setār (also *setar*), **5**:189, 335, 344
   Afghanistan, **5**:830
   Balochistan, **6**:10
   China, **7**:113
   in Iranian *radif*, **6**:137–38, 866, 868–71
   Kashmir, **5**:686, 688, *688*, 694
   North America, **3**:1034
sgra-snyan, **5**:710, 715
sharki, **8**:996, 997
shudraga, **7**:1005, 1011–12, 1014
sitar, **2**:901; **4**:66; **5**:*204*, *205*, 333, 334–35,
      334–35, 565, 582
   depictions of, **5**:307
   in film music, **5**:347, 535, 543
   functions of, **5**:325
   Guyana, **5**:602
   in Karnatak music, **5**:107, 351
   Kashmir, **5**:694
   in *kathak* ensemble, **5**:494
   North America, **3**:340, 951, 952, 953, 984,
      1246
   northern Pakistan, **5**:794
   North West Frontier Province, **5**:787
   in *oḍissi* ensemble, **5**:520
   origins of, **5**:335
   Pakistan, **5**:746
   performance of, **5**:464–65, 575
   popularity of, **5**:564–66
   Punjab, **5**:762
   repertoire for, **5**:123, 125, 126, 188–208
   as solo instrument, **5**:335
   Sri Lanka, **5**:956
   women performers of, **5**:411
sitār (Afghani), **5**:830
sixian, **7**:491
South America, tropical-forest region, **2**:127
Southeast Asia, **4**:74, 596
   rural areas, **4**:7
subü, **4**:543
Sudan, **1**:549, 571
sugudu, **7**:*513*
suisen (also *suisin*), **6**:407, 499
sundatang, **4**:835
süng, **4**:310, 316
surbahār, **5**:196–97, 204, 205, 335–36
sursiṅgār, **5**:196, 337
Sweden, **8**:440
syamisen (also *shamisen*; *samisen*), **7**:3, 536, 551,
      684, 688, 691, 695, *711*; **10**:*4*, 99
   in *bunraku*, **7**:663, 667

chamber music genres for, **7**:688–89
Confucian views of, **7**:548
construction of, **7**:547, 691
in film scores, **7**:750
in *gidayû busi*, **7**:675–77, 777
in *hyari uta*, **7**:739
in *kabuki*, **7**:654, 657, 658–59, 684
in *kumiuta*, **7**:696
in *kyôgen*, **7**:636
in *min'yô*, **7**:601
miyazono busi genre, **7**:760
modal theories for, **7**:568
modernization of, **7**:537
nagauta genre, **7**:671–74, 777
North America, **3**:527, 968–69, 970, 1084
notation for, **7**:54, 538, 576–78, 590, 660,
   675
Oceania, **9**:97
origins of, **7**:81, 691
relation to Ryûkyû *sansin*, **7**:688, 792
in *sankyoku*, **7**:692, 712, 715–17, 779
sawari, **7**:552
shin'nai busi genre, **7**:760
sinnai genre, **7**:553
South America, **2**:87, 88
syôga vocables for, **7**:776
timbre of, **7**:551, 552
use in narrative accompaniment, **7**:75, 654,
   679–82
in *utusie*, **7**:749
in *wayô gassô*, **7**:749–50
women performers, **7**:601, 649
yamatogaku genre, **7**:766
ziuta genre, **7**:673, 688, 691–93
in *zyôruri*, **7**:691
tahardent, **1**:540, 546, 575, 587–90, 593
ta in, **4**:535
tambūr, **5**:164, *308–9*, 308–310, 332, 344
tambura, **8**:168, 169, 198
   Bosnia-Hercegovina, **8**:963, 966
   Bulgaria, **8**:*176*, 283, 893, *893*, *894*, 895,
      896, 902
   Croatia, **8**:927, 933
   Hungary, **8**:743
   Macedonia, **8**:975, 981, *982*, 983
   Montenegro, **8**:959, *961*
   Serbia, **8**:945, 953
tambura (also, *tamburitza*), **3**:529, 826,
      920–24, 1198, 1199
tambūrā, **3**:990
   Afghanistan, **5**:804
   Fiji, **5**:613, *614*; **9**:94
   North Indian, **5**:*4*, 74, 165, *171*, 307, 310,
      332, 334, 343, *378*, 494, 633, 643,
      644, *647*, 723
   South Indian, **5**:104, 223, 232, *233*, 355,
      356, 360, 364, 384, 392, 522, 556,
      557, 893, *894*, 899, 900, 901, 913
   Trinidad, **2**:958; **5**:590
tambūri, **5**:869
tambūrī, **5**:343
tamburica, **8**:279, *279*, 674, 917, 981
ṭambūr khurasānī, **6**:408, 542
tanbīre, **6**:825, 883, 888
ṭanbūr, **6**:407–8
   Central Asia, **6**:900

distribution of, **6:**405
Syria, **6:**566
tanbur, **5:**830
Azerbaijan, **6:**925
Iran, **6:**130, 825
Kurdistan, **6:**746, 751
Turkey, **6:**82–83, 114, 115, 117, 758, 769, 774, *774*
Uighur people, **6:**999, 1003; **7:**113, 451, 459
Uzbekistan, **6:**919
tanbūr, **5:**692–93
tanburag, **6:**10
ṭanbūr baghdādī, **6:**407–8, 542
tandūro, **5:**647
tang pip'a, **7:***826*, 830
tānpūrā, **5:**74, 188, 310, 332, 465, *565*
Afghanistan, **5:**806
use in devotional music, **5:**249, 251
Tanzania, **1:**641
ṭār (also *tar*; *tār*), **6:**395
Afghanistan, **5:**822–23
Azerbaijan, **6:**8, 923, 924, *924*, 925–26, *931*
Central Asia, **6:**900, 902
Iran, **6:**8, 130, 138, 140, 828, 833, 866, 868–71
Israel, **6:***1018*
t'ar, **6:**725, 734
ṭarab, **6:**686, *686*
tembûr, **6:**746
tha, **4:**545
thà chinh, **4:**536
tidinit, **1:**540, 588; **6:**405, 408–9
tiêu ba tiêu, **4:**509
tikuzen biwa, **7:**643, 649–51, *650*, *651*, 766
tính tẩu, **4:**535–36
tinten, **4:**835
topshúr, **7:**1005
topshuur, **7:**1005, 1008, 1011, 1012, *1012*, 1014, 1016
toshpulúr, **7:**1005
tūmbī, **5:**651
ṭunbūr, **6:**395, 396, 397
tyû zao syamisen, **7:**658, 680
tzouras, **9:**73
'ūd, **1:**351, 535, 556, 571, 607; **4:**432; **5:**692, 804; **8:**281, 286 (*See also under* oud)
Albania, **8:**993
Algeria, **6:**269
in Andalusian music, **6:**444, 445, 460, 462
in Arab-American ensembles, **6:**282, 283
Arabian peninsula, **6:**651–52
in Arab music, **6:**16, 17, 279, 281, 395, 396, 397, 398, 405–7, 413, 537, 539–40, 566, 570, 705
in Arab treatises, **6:**364, 373
Azerbaijan, **6:**925
distribution of, **6:**406
Egypt, **6:**8, 45–46, 148, 170, *170*, 171, 317, 318, 406, 547, 551, 559
European lute and, **6:**449
in fusion music, **6:**438
Georgia, **8:**840
Iran, **6:**130, 833, 863, 868, 869

Iraq, **6:**8, 312, 402–3, 406, 411, 442, 593–95
Israel, **6:**263, *1018*, 1029, *1041*, 1074
in Lebanese popular music, **6:**554–55
in Maghribi Jewish ensembles, **6:**1043
manufacturing of, **6:**406
method book for, **6:**18
Morocco, **6:**499
North America, **3:**1032, *1032*, 1037, 1199, 1218, 1220
in Nubian music, **6:**641–42
Oman, **6:**682
Palestine, **6:**591
recitals of, **6:**403, 406, 593–95
in Sephardi music, **6:**204
Syria, **6:**406
transvestite performers, **6:**296
tuning of, **6:**36, 39, 541, 542
Tunisia, **6:**452
Turkey, **6:**257, 766, 774
women performers, **6:**291, 294–95, 297, 298, 352, 456, 691–93, 698, 699, 701
Xinjiang depictions of, **6:**1005
Yemen, **6:**656, 685, 686–87, 709, 711
Ziryāb's modifications, **6:**442, 448, 540
'ūd 'arbī, **6:**327, 328, 329, 405, 406–7, 454, 470, 502
'ūd sharqī, **6:**327, 328, 405–7, 454, 527, 528, *528*, 530
'ūd tūnisī, **6:**405
'ukarere, **9:**896
ut, **8:**979, *979*, 997
vina, **5:**332–34, *353*, *378*, 513, *582*, *721*
as accompaniment instrument, **5:**163, 355
association with Sarasvati, **5:***211*, 247, 301
in *cinna mēḷam* ensemble, **5:**104, 913
depictions of, **5:**301, *302*, 307, 313
early treatises on, **5:**21, 25, 29, 48, 261, 692
in film music, **5:**543, 555
history of, **5:**307
in Karnatak music, **5:**100, 101, 107, 218, 232–33, 352–53, 389, 522
North America, **3:**951, 984, 990, 1044, 1247; **10:**41
one-stringed, **5:**728
sound recordings of, **5:**161
women performers of, **5:**411
waina, **5:**786
West Africa, **1:**445, 448–49
wölgüm, **7:***826*, 830
woolkum, **4:**472
wuxian pipa, **7:**112
xalam, **1:**366, 444, 445
xhymbyz, **8:**997
yaktāro, **5:**753, 759
yueqin, **3:**961; **4:**70, 472; **7:**218, 285, 424, 740
zhanian, **7:**474, 475, 477, 480
zhongruan, **7:**231
ziuta syamisen (*shamisen*), **7:**692, 715
Lutfullah, M., **5:**530
Luth, Sissel, **8:**415
Luther, Martin, **8:**74, 145, 652
Lutherans, **3:**120, 528, 867, 872, 874, 884
in Canada, **3:**1249, 1251
chorales of, **3:**10, 1238

in Denmark, **8:**451
in Estonia, **8:**491
in Finland, **8:**481–82, 488
revivalists, **8:**478
in Hungary, **8:**736
hymn tunes, **8:**5
in Latvia, **8:**499
in Liberia, **10:**61
liturgy of, **3:**121
Missouri Synod, **3:**886
music of, **3:**886
in Oceania, **9:**187
in Papua New Guinea, **9:**88, 193–94, 195–96, 516, 533, 565–66, 568, 572, 607
research on, **3:**119
Suomi Synod, **3:**874
in Sweden, **8:**434
in Tamil Nadu, **5:**921–22
worship practices of, **3:**118
in Yap, **9:**199
Lutka, Petr, **8:**730
Lütke, Fyedor Petrovich, **9:***711*, 741–42
Luttazzi, Lelio, **8:**619
Lutz, Maija, **3:**381, 1275
Lưu Hữ Phưóoc, **4:**510
Luvale people
makishi masks, **1:**309
mukanda institution, **1:**723–25; **10:**29
music of, **1:**723–43; **10:**29
timelines of, **1:**678
Luxembourg, **8:**12, 518
map of, **8:***516*
Lüxue xinshuo (Zhu), **7:**119, 128
Luxun Academy of Fine Arts (Yan'an), **7:**339–40, 384
Luz, Ernst, **9:**43
Luzbetak, Rev. Louis, **9:**976
Luzel, François-Marie, **8:**561–62
Luzerner Chronik (periodical), **8:**686
L'vov, Nikolai, **8:**18
Lwalid, Mimoun, **6:**275
Lwena people, **1:**672–73
timelines of, **1:**678
vocal music of, **1:**674–76
Lý Anh Tông, king of Vietnam, **4:**498
Lý dynasty, **4:**447, 448, 467, 489, 498
Lý Nhân Tông, king of Vietnam, **4:**447
Lý Thái Tổ, king of Vietnam, **4:**480
Lý Thánh Tông, king of Vietnam, **4:**447, 498
Lyceum of Greek Women, **8:**1017
"Lydian Concept of Tonal Organization" (Russell), **3:**661
Lyle, Agnes, **8:**135, 370
Lyles, Aubrey, **3:**619
Lyman, Arthur, **9:**164
Lymon, Frankie, **3:**672
"Lyndon Johnson Told the Nation" (Paxton), **3:**316
Lynn, Loretta, **3:**81
Lyon, James, **3:**1070
Lyons, Rev. Lorenzo, **9:**187, 919
Lyra, Carlos, **2:**318
lyres
abangarang, **1:**565
Africa, **1:**549–50
distribution of, **1:**302–4, 600

lyres (continued)
  Arabia, ancient, **6:**357–59, 537
  Arab world, **6:**412–13
  barbitos (also *barbiton*), **8:**47
  bāsān-kōb, **1:**558, 560
  begana (or *begena*), **1:**303–4, 600
  begenna, **6:**357
  benebene (or *beriberi*), **1:**562
  bowl, **1:**303
  box, **1:**303
  Celtic culture, **8:**321
  crowd (also *crwth*), **8:**42, *347*, 348, 354, 355
  cruit, **8:**366, 383
  Egypt, **8:**839
  endongo, **1:**299
  enkana, **1:**304
  entongoli, **1:**218, 299
  fedefede, **1:**562
  Greece, ancient, **8:**47
  Illyria, **8:**40
  jaŋarr (or *jangar*), **1:***303*, 564
  kazandik, **1:**562
  kenniniur, **6:**358
  Kenya, **1:**624
  kinar, **6:**358
  kinnāru, **6:**358
  kinnor, **6:**358; **8:**839
  kisir, **1:**556, 557, 558
  kisr, **6:**412, 641
  kithara, **8:**39, 46–47
  knr, **6:**358
  krar, **6:**358
  litungu, **1:**304, 625, 641
  Middle East, **6:**17–18
  mi'zafa, **6:**295, 358–59, 395, 396, 397
  Norway, **8:**423
  nūbān, **6:**710
  obokano, **1:**304
  pagan, **1:**303, 304
  qinīn, **6:**358, 359
  qitāra, **6:**413
  rababa, **1:**554
  rabābah, **6:**357, 358
  rote, **8:**42
  samsamiyya, **6:**656
  sangwe, **1:**564
  shareero, **1:**611
  simsimiyya (also *simsimīyya*; *simsimīyyah*), **6:**93, 358, 412–13, 545
  sulyāq, **6:**395, 397
  ṭambūra, **6:**93, 405, 412–13
  tambura, **1:**554–55
  ṭanbūr, **1:**556, 571
  ṭanbūra (also *ṭanbūrah*), **6:**357, 546, 656, 705, 710
  tiompán, **8:**384
  tom, **1:**568
  ṭumbarah, **6:**357
  ṭunbūr, **6:**358, 359
  use in battle, **6:**359
lyres, bowed, **8:***180*, 485
  geśle, **8:**705
  hiiukannel (also *rootsikannel*), **8:**493–94
  jouhikantele, **8:**406, 423
  jouhikko, **8:**479
  talharpa, **8:**406, 423

Lyric Arts Trio, **3:**1186
Lyric Music Academy, **4:**123, 870
Lysenko Music Institute (L'viv), **8:**822, 823
Lysenko, Mykola, **8:**820
Lysloff, René, **4:**103, 639
Lyte as a Feather (MC Lyte), **3:**696

Ma, Anandamayi, **5:**255
Ma Huanzhang, **7:**224
Ma Ke, **7:**349
Ma Rufei, **7:**261, 264
Ma Shizeng, **7:**306
Ma Sitson, **7:**341
Ma, Yo-Yo, **3:**254; **7:**416, 431
Maacho, **9:**166
Maadai, **7:**1020
Ma'afu, Tongan chief, **9:**817
Maal, Baaba (pop musician), **1:**8, 419
Maan, Gurdas, **5:**426, 550
Maasai people, **1:**599, 605, 634, 635
  dance of, **1:**109, 110
  music of, **1:**623, 638
  trumpets of, **1:**642
Ma'bad, **6:**11, 12–13, 291, 294, 295, 352
Mabel's (Champaign club), **3:**170–71
Mabireh, Kofi, **1:**356
MABO Project, **9:**963
Mabruk iklīl il-'ursān (*far'awī*), **6:**590
Mabu (Huli musical bow performer), **9:***386*
"*Mabuhay Ang Pilipinas*" (Abad), **4:**130
Mabuse, Sipho "Hot Sticks," **1:**779
MacAllester, David, **3:**71; **10:**95
MacAloon, John J., **1:**506
MacAndrew, Hector, **8:**364
Macao
  Cantonese opera in, **7:**305
  Chaozhou people in, **7:**211
  scholarship in, **7:**139
macarena, **3:**522
MacArthur family, **8:**363
Macarthy, Harry, **3:**188
Macaulay, Herbert, **1:**402
Macaulay, O. E., **1:**159
MacBeath, Jimmy, **8:**372
MacColl, Ewan, **8:**296, 297, 338, 365, 371, 374
MacCormick, Kate, **8:***362*
MacCrimmon, Donal Ruadh, **8:**368
MacCrimmon family, **8:**363, 374
MacCrimmon Legend (Campsie), **8:**374
MacCunn, Hamish, **8:**368
MacDermot, Galt, **3:**198, 199
MacDiarmid, Hugh, **8:**368
MacDonald, Alexander, **8:**367
MacDonald, Allan, **8:**363
MacDonald, Captain Major Sir Claude Maxwell, **1:**92
MacDonald, Iain Luim, **8:**367
MacDonald, Jeanette, **3:**544
MacDonald, Joseph, **8:**373
MacDonald, Rev. Patrick, **8:**362, 373
MacDonald, Sileas, **8:**367, 374
MacDougall, David, **9:**47
MacDougall, Judith, **9:**47
MacDowell, Edward, **3:**14, 367; **7:**955
MacEachen, Frances, **3:**1129

Maceda, José, **4:**29, 123, 130, 316, 870, 873, 891, 895, 900
  compositions of, **4:**875–76, *877*
Macedonia, **8:**972–84
  Albanian people in, **8:**979, 986, 995–96, 1002–3
  art music in, **8:**980–81
  blind musicians in, **8:**975
  dance traditions of, **8:***162*, 201, 282, 979, 984
  Debar
    akil concept in, **8:**117
    çiteli playing, **8:**285
    fusion music in, **8:**983
  geography of, **8:**972
  history of, **8:**972
  instruments and instrumental music, **8:**975–77, 979–80
    Asian derivations of, **8:**168
    čalgija ensembles, **8:**979–80
    makam use, **8:**200, 281–82, 979–80
    wedding bands, **8:**146, 977, 979, 980, 982
    zurla and *tapan* ensembles, **8:**975–76, *977*, 979, 982–83
  Kostur, **8:**973–74
  map of, **8:***866*
  Muslim people in, **8:**975, 979
  popular music in, **8:**980, 983
  population of, **8:**972
  research on music of, **8:**983–84
  Rom people in, **8:**272, 280–82, 285–86, 951, 975–77, 979–80, 981–83, 984
  sobor ceremony in, **8:**116
  state folk ensembles in, **8:**981–82
  taksim genre, **8:**976, 979
  Turkish people in, **8:**11, 979
  urban music in, **8:**978–81
  vocal music, **8:**954, 973–74
    laments, **8:**120
    novokompanovani narodni pesni, **8:**980
    three-part polyphony, **8:**10
    women's songs, **8:***194*
  wedding ceremony in, **8:***13*, *144*
Macedonian Institute for Folklore, **8:**983
Macedonian Orthodox Church, **3:**925, 926, 1199; **8:**972, 983
Macedonian people
  emigration patterns, **8:**972, 973
  in North America, **3:**924–26, 1198
"*Macera Dolu Amerika*" (Rafet El Roman), **6:**252
MacEwen, John, **8:**368
MacFadyen, John, **8:**363
MacGregor, Chris, **1:**774
MacGregor, Gordon, **9:**24, 827
Machado, Loremil, **3:**731
Machado, Manuel, **8:**598
Machaut, Guillaume de, **8:**72, 104, *105*
Machedo, Sister Louisa, **5:**257
Machito (pseud. of Frank Grillo), **1:**387; **3:**732, 743, 787, 793, 794, 796–97, 798, 799
Machito and His Afro-Cubans, **1:**387; **3:**732, 787, 793
Machover, Tod, **3:**254
Macht, Robert, **3:**1016
Macias, Enrico, **6:**1044
Macias, Rudy, **3:**741, 799
Maciniyamman (deity), **5:**903

MacInnes, Mairi, **8**:363
Macintyre, Duncan Ban, **8**:367
MacIsaac, Ashley, **3**:150, 1127
Maciszewski, Amie, **10**:90
Mack, Cecil, **3**:706
Mackandal (dance troupe), **3**:805
MacKay, Angus, **8**:368, 373
MacKay brothers, **1**:417
Mackay, Rhona, **8**:366
Mackay, Rob Donn, **8**:367
Mackenzie, Alexander, **3**:392, 1255; **8**:368
Mackenzie Delta Inuit, **3**:374
MacKenzie, Roy, **3**:14, 1125
MacKenzie, Talitha, **8**:226, 369
MacKenzie, Tandy Kaohu, **9**:924
Mackenzie, William Lyon, **3**:137
MacLean, Calum, **8**:371
MacLennan, Pipe-Major L., **9**:135
MacLeod, Margaret Arnett, **3**:411
MacLeod, Mary, **8**:367
MacMahon, Bryan, **8**:391
MacMaster, Natalie, **3**:150, 151, 1127
Mac Mathúna, Ciarán, **8**:391
Macmillan Brown Library, **9**:974
MacMillan, Ernest, **3**:144, 343, 1058, 1079, 1108, 1166
Macmillan, James, **8**:369
Macmillan Publishing Company, **3**:294
Macmillan, Scott, **3**:1070
MacNamara, Frank "the Poet," **9**:77
MacNeacail, Iain, **8**:370
MacNeil, Flora, **8**:363, *363*, 371
MacNeill, Seamus, **8**:374
MacNeil, Rita, **3**:94
Macon, Uncle Dave, **3**:77, 78
Macpherson, James, **8**:17, 186, 367, 370, 379, 460, 552
Macready, William Charles, **3**:46
Macumba
    in Brazil, **2**:341
    in Uruguay, **2**:513, 515
Macushi culture, **2**:442
Madagascar. *See also* East Africa; *specific peoples*
    Austronesian speakers, **4**:529; **9**:319
    court music of, **1**:782–83, 789
    culture of, **1**:700
    education in, **1**:792
    guitar in, **1**:351–52
    history of, **1**:781–82
    Indonesians in, **1**:605, 607, 715
    instruments of, **1**:367
    Malagasy language of, **1**:3
    music of, **1**:782–92
    rija genre, **1**:786
    valiha in, **4**:59
Madagasha, Gervais, **1**:204–5
Madale, Nagasura, **4**:881
Madama Butterfly (Puccini), **3**:953; **7**:733; **9**:38
"Madam Butterfly" (Long), **9**:38
Madam Butterfly (Belasco), **9**:38
Madamu to nyôbô (film), **7**:750
Ma'dan al-Mūsīqī (treatise), **5**:51, 123
Madānī, **6**:270
Madari caste, **5**:639
Madarrpa Funeral at Gurka'wuy (film), **9**:47

Madau, Matteo, **8**:632
Maddix, Leah, **3**:1136
Maddy, Joseph, **3**:277
Made in Sweden (musical group), **8**:446
"*Madelón*" (Sephardic song), **3**:1173–74
Mader, Vivienne Huapala, **9**:969
Maderna, Osmar, **2**:264
Madero, Francisco, **2**:616
Madesa (deity), **5**:872
Madho Sangeet Mahavidyalaya, **5**:443
Madhumati (film), **5**:535
Madhvacharya, **5**:265
Madhwa, **5**:105
Madhya Pradesh, **5**:720–25
    arched harp in, **5**:306
    Avanti, **5**:720
    bardic traditions of, **5**:635
    Bastar region, **5**:471
    Chattisgadh region, **5**:723
    folk music of, **5**:722–24
    geography of, **5**:720
    Gwalior
        amīrkhānī gat in, **5**:189
        court patronage, **5**:163, 177, 206, 443–44
        Mughal court in, **5**:15
    history of, **5**:720–21
    instruments in, **5**:120, 345, 722, 723
    Malwa, performing castes of, **5**:476
    map of, **5**:*718*
    Pavaya, bas-reliefs in, **5**:299, 323, 328
    population of, **5**:720
    princely states in, **5**:720
    Sanchi, **5**:720
    Sironj district, **5**:720
    tribal music of, **5**:721–22
    Ujjain, **5**:720
    Vedic chant in, **5**:239
    vocal music, **5**:723–24
        animal and nature songs, **5**:474–75
Madia people, **5**:719, 720, 721–22
Madison, James, **3**:305
Madison Square Garden (New York), **3**:698
Madja-Pahi, **4**:802
Madness (musical group), **4**:887; **8**:215
Madonna, **3**:340, 1002; **4**:100, 111; **5**:429; **6**:248; **8**:207, 220; **9**:179
Madrahimov, Qāzi, **6**:908
Madrasi people, **5**:602
Madras Music Academy, **5**:106, 212, 270
madrigal
    Baroque, **8**:76
    Corsica, **8**:570
    Italy, **8**:75–76, 617
Madrigal (musical group), **8**:883
Madumere, Adele, **1**:35
Madurai Kamaraja, **5**:450
Madurese people, **4**:635, 646
Maegut (Kim), **7**:959
Maehwa T'aryŏng (kasa), **7**:927
Maeny, Urip Sri, **3**:1014
Maewo (Vanuatu)
    composition on, **9**:361
    instruments of, **9**:693
    music and dance of, **9**:691–97, 965
    oral tradition, **9**:259, 689
    secret societies of, **9**:694

songs of, **9**:690
upright log idiophones in, **9**:691
Mafātīh al-'ulūm (Muḥammad ibn Aḥmad al-Khwārazmī), **6**:367
Maffei, Elisa, **4**:870
Mafi-Williams, Lorraine, **9**:442
Magahum, Ángel, **4**:866
Magalona, Francis, **4**:886
Magar people, **5**:701, 702
Magdapio (Carluén), **4**:857, 871
Magellan, Ferdinand, **4**:85
Magenta (recording company), **2**:266
Maggid, Sofya, **8**:784
Maghrib (also Maghreb), **6**:429–39. *See also* Algeria; Libya; Morocco; Tunisia
    African peoples in, **6**:304, 407, 408, 434–35, 437, 474, 523, 1035
    Andalusian repertoire in, **1**:534–36, 545–46; **6**:449–54, 455, 1035
    art music (*turath*), **6**:317–19
    cultural influences in, **1**:533–34; **6**:432–35
    drums in, **6**:416–20
    Egyptian influences in, **6**:1035
    history of, **1**:533–34; **6**:429, 431–35, 1035–36
    Jewish people in, **6**:1035–44
    Judeo-Arabic folk song, **6**:1041–42
    musical treatises, **6**:367
Magic Flute (Mozart), **4**:523; **9**:371
Magic Stone label, **7**:358, 360, 365, 429
Magnasound (record company), **5**:528
Magnes, Judah L., **6**:1058
"Magnificent Dance" (Clash), **3**:689
Magno, Jacqui, **4**:885
Magnolia (Dett), **3**:607
Magnum Band (musical group), **2**:892; **3**:803
Magnússon, Árni, **8**:408
Magrini, Tullia, **8**:607, 622; **10**:164
Magrupi, Gurbanaly, **6**:969
Magsaiai Island (Solomon Islands), **9**:655–57
Maguindanao people, **4**:889, 920
    epics of, **4**:907
    instrumental music of, **4**:891–96, 901–4, 926
    vocal music of, **4**:907, 908, 911
Maguzawa people, **1**:287, 289, 291
Magyars, **8**:736
Mah Meri (Besisi) people, **4**:560
Mahabad Republic, **6**:744
Mahabharata (epic), **3**:1012; **5**:11, 399, 607, 633, 733, 872, 908; **7**:451, 477
    danced performances of, **5**:482–83, 497, *498*, 509, 513, 515–16, 723–24, 876, 879, 933
    firewalking ritual and, **5**:617
    mentions of transvestite performers in, **5**:492
    references to women performers, **5**:408
    saṅkha in, **5**:361
    in Southeast Asia, **4**:66, 428, 650, 705–6, 751, 753, 756
    Telugu renditions of, **5**:893, 897
Mahaboob, Khalishabi, **5**:234
Mahadeviakka, **5**:866
Mahadev Koli people, **5**:727
Ma'had al-'Ali li-l-Musiqa al-'Arabiyya (Cairo), **6**:45
Ma'had al-Dirāsāt al-Naghamiyya (Baghdad), **6**:315–16

Ma'had al-Funūn al-Jamīla (Baghdad), **6:**315
Ma'had al-Mūsīqá al-'Arabiyyah (Cairo), **6:**235, 322, 611, 621
Ma'had al-Mūsīqá al-Masrahiyya (Cairo), **6:**323, 611
Ma'had al-Mūsīqī al-Maṣrī (Cairo), **6:**322
Ma'had al-Qira'at (Cairo), **6:**321
Mahajan, Anup, **5:**428
Mahakali (deity), **5:**505
Mahalakshmi (deity), **5:**505
Mahalingam, T. R. "Mali," **5:**234
Mahama, Salisu, **10:**143, 145–48
Maha-Parinibbana-Sutta, **5:**965
Mahapatra, Maheshwar, **5:**519
Maharaj, Gokul Utsav, **5:**251
Maharaj, Janji, **5:**970
Maharaj, Kanthe, **5:***133, 207*
Maharaj, Kishan, **5:**134, 136, 137, *207*
Maharaj, Madan, **5:***493*
Maharaja Sayajirao University (Vadodara), **5:**443, 447
Maharashtra, **5:**7, 726–30
    Bombay (Mumbai), **5:**5, 444
        film industry in, **5:**531–32, 547, 591, 729–30
        public concerts in, **5:**212
        rock groups in, **5:**428
        theater in, **5:**486, 487
        as trade center, **5:**15
    cave paintings in, **5:**298, 299
    folk music of, **5:**727–28
    geography of, **5:**726–27
    instruments in, **5:**120, 343, 727
    map of, **5:***718*
    musical genres
        abhaṅg, **5:**250, 253, 549
        harikathā, **5:**106–7
        haveli saṅgit, **5:**251
        pad, **5:**162
        powada, **5:**474
    Nagpur, **5:**444
    popular music in, **5:**729–30
    regional cassettes in, **5:**550
    saṅgīt nāṭak theater in, **5:**729
    tamāśā theater in, **5:**419, 423–24, 485
    tribal music of, **5:**727
    Vedic chant in, **5:**241
Mahasarakham University, **4:**121, 226
Mahasona (deity), **5:**961
Mahāvāṇī (Harivyasdevacharya), **5:**252
Mahavira, Vardhamana, **5:**13
Mahavishnu Orchestra, **3:**356, 664, 955
al-Mahdī, 'Abbasid caliph, **6:**447, 539
al-Mahdī, Ṣāliḥ, **6:**325, 330–31, 335, 336, 511
al-Mahdīyya, Munīra, **6:**235, 548, 598
Mahendravarman I, Pallavan emperor, **5:**215
Mahesharam, **5:***647*
Mahi, Aaron David, **9:**133–34, 923
al-Mahi, Abdallah, **1:**571
El-Mahi, Maidub M. Hajj, **1:**552–53
Mahidol University, **4:**121, 226, 249
Mahillon, Victor-Charles, **5:**322; **8:**176, 178
Māhina, 'Okusitino, **9:**113
Mahlathini. *See* Nkabinde
Mahler, Elsa, **8:**23
Mahler, Gustav, **3:**953; **6:**1027; **8:**26, 83, 663, 781

Mahmood, Talat, **5:**420, 539
Mahmoud, Abd al-Azīz, **6:**270
Mahmud I, Ottoman sultan, **6:**771
Mahmud II, Ottoman sultan, **6:**110, 780
Maḥmūd, 'Alī, **6:**168
Mahmud, Altaf, **5:**858
Mahmud Aqa, **6:**923
Mahmud Bey, **6:**757
Mahmud of Ghazni, **5:**720
Mahommed, Pops, **1:***437*
Mahoney, Therese, **4:**25, 337–38
Mahotella Queens, **1:**430, *431*, 433, 776
Mahsuni, **6:**798
Mahuta, Harry, **9:**151
Mahwash, **5:**809, 816
Mai Zong Vue, **3:**1005
Mai'ao (Society Islands), **9:**867
Maidu Indian nation, **3:**415
Maikurohwon no ongaku (Akutagawa), **7:**736
Mailu people, **9:**489
Maimonides, **6:**19; **8:**265
Maine. *See also* New England
    Sabbathday Lake, Shaker community, **3:**135
    shanties in, **3:**158
Maine Pyar Kiya (film), **5:**540
Mair, Victor, **7:**19, 22; **10:**24
Mairasi people, **9:**580
    composition of, **9:**360
    dance of, **9:**582
    gong playing of, **9:**582
    songs of, **9:**583, 587–89
Mairire, Abraham, **1:**217
Maisin people, **9:**983
Maison des Cultures du Monde (Paris), **6:**23
Maisuradze, Nino, **8:**846–47
Maitra, Jyotirindra, **5:**857
Maitra, Radhika Mohan, **5:**207, *207*
Maîtrise des Chanteurs à la Croix d'Ébène (Ngumu), **1:**659
Maiwa people, **9:**983
Mai zahuo (*xiaodiao* tune), **7:**218
Majapahit (kingdom), **4:**62, 75–76, 594, 596, 600, 632, 686, 699, 731, 788, 802, 889
Majara, Majara, **1:**762
Mājid, Abū, **6:**576–78
Majikina, Yoshinae, **9:***96*
Majikina, Yoshino, **9:***96, 108*
Majumdar, Gauriprasanna, **5:**857
Majumdar, Pravir, **5:**857
Majumdar, Ronu, **5:***340*
Majumdar, S. N., **5:**852
Mak Shu-wing, **3:**1263
Maká culture, **2:**452, 454–56
Makah Indian nation, **3:**394
    potlatch ceremony, **3:**396, 397–99
    whaling rituals, **3:**395
makam. *See also* maqām; modal organization
    acemaşiran, **6:**49, *49*, 50, 52
    in Albanian music, **8:**994, 996, 997
    beyati, **6:**48, *49*, 50–52, 54, 55, *55*, 57
    beyati-araban, **6:**53–54
    in Bosnian music, **8:**964, 968
    buselik, **6:**780
    compound, **6:**53–54
    contemporary practice of, **6:**47–58

dügâh, **6:**110, 118
ehnâz, **6:**780
extramusical elements in, **6:**57–58
hüseyni, **6:**51–52, 110, 118
Jewish performers of, **6:**1016
karciğar, **6:**115
in Macedonian music, **8:**281, 282
melody in, **6:**51–52
modulation in, **6:**52–53
muhayyer, **6:**51–52
nihavent, **6:**49, *49*
pençgâh, **6:**110, 118, *770*
performance practice of, **6:**55–56
possible Greek derivation of, **8:**1022
rast, **6:**50, 50–51, 772, *772*
related repertoires, **6:**56–57
saba, **6:**49, *50*, 55
scales and intervals in, **6:**48–51
segah, **6:**48
şehnaz, **6:**49, *49*
in Serbian music, **8:**951
stereotyped motives in, **6:**54
suznak, **6:**837
tonal centers in, **6:**51
in Turkish music, **6:**48–51, 82–85, 114–18, 190, 194, 256, 771, 772, 782, 801
uşşak, **6:**54, 55, 110, 772
Makar Records, **5:**528
Makara, Teiroa, **9:**974
Makassarese people, **4:**804–6
Makatea (Tuamotu Islands), **9:**882
Makazi Band, **1:**429
"Make Me a Pallet on the Floor" (Yancey), **3:**105
Makeba, Miriam, **1:**430, 433, 771, 772, 774, 775, 780
Makedonija (musical group), **3:**1198
Makedonka (dance ensemble), **3:**1198
Makedonski Folklor (periodical), **8:**983
Makedonski Melos (musical group), **3:**1198
Mäkelä, Matti, **8:***478*
Makembe, **1:**684
Makem, Tommy, **3:**844, 846; **8:**391
Makerere University (Kampala), **1:**39, 216
makeup. *See* costumes and clothing
Makgalemele, Michael, **1:**779
Makhanbetov, Shazynda, **6:***953*
Makhtum Qolī, **6:**840
Makiadi, Luambo "Franco," **1:**361, 362, 386, 424; **8:**234
Makin (Kiribati), **9:**758, 761
Makino Yutaka, **7:**713
Makkuraji nondurŏnge ppajida (Lee), **7:**956
Makolekole, Kambazithe, **1:***323*
Makolkol people, **9:**607
Makonde people, **1:**599
    flutes of, **1:**642
    lamellophones of, **1:**317
    likumbi institution, **1:**309
    masks of, **1:**119
    music of, **1:**606, 637, 639
makossa, **1:**387, 422, 682; **8:**238
Makrani Balochis, **5:**754, 761, 773, 777
Makua people, **1:**119, 639, 642
Makuare, Karitua, **9:**112–13
Makulloluwa, W. B., **5:**960
Makushi culture, **2:**131

makwaya, **1:**33, 227, 433, 718, 755, 763–64, 765, 769–70
Malabe, Frank, **3:***786*
"Malagueña" (Palmieri), **3:**795
Malaita (Solomon Islands), **9:**963
   'Are'are panpipe music, **9:**42, 156, 286, 292, 393, 398–401, 665
   end-blown flute, **9:**398
   music and dance of, **9:**666–68, 977
   panpipe distribution, **9:**401
Malakula (Vanuatu), **9:**689, 966
   instruments of, **9:**693
   music and dance of, **9:**696–97
   panpipe music of, **9:**689
   temes nainggol ensembles, **9:**690
   upright log idiophones in, **9:**691
Malam Shu'aibu Mai Garaya, **1:**521–23
Malamusi, Moya Aliya, **10:**115, 118, *119*
Malamusi, Yohana, **10:***122*
Malamusi-Kubik, Lidiya, **10:***119*, 120
Malang, **5:**831
Malangan Labadama: A Tribute to Buk-Buk (film), **9:**50
Malang-fakir caste, **5:**476
Malanji people, **1:**667
Malaspina, D. Alejandro, **9:**7
Malawi. *See also* East Africa; Southern Africa; *specific peoples*
   Bantu groups, **1:**670
   beni music, **1:**426
   composition in, **1:**216–17
   Europeans in, **1:**717
   guitar in, **1:**359
   kwela, **1:**387; **10:**119–20
   lamellophones, **1:**320
   Marari people, masks of, **1:**119
   missionaries in, **1:**718
   music of, **1:**429, 640, 643
   Ngoni people, **1:**320–21, 705
   nkangala mouth bow, **1:***3*
   nyau masked societies, **1:**309, 311
   Nyau people, masks of, **1:**119
   Nyungwe people, **1:**711
   popular music of, **1:**323, 423, 436–37
   Sena people, **1:**711
   Swazi people, **1:**321
   Tumbuka people, healing rituals, **1:**271–83
   women's drumming, **1:**312
   Zulu people, **1:**321
Malay people, **4:**529
   in Borneo, **4:**824–25
   influence on Malukun dance, **4:**813
   in Philippines, **4:**855
   in Singapore, **4:**519–21
   in Sri Lanka, **5:**954
   in Sumatra, **4:**598, 600–601, 605–7, 614–19
Malayalam Eastern Orthodox Church, **5:**582
Malayan caste, **5:**931
Malayev, Ilyas, **6:**919–20
Malaysia, **3:**1260
   aristocracy in, **4:**118
   baby of rice, **4:**51
   British in, **4:**78
   ceremonies in, **4:**423–24
   Chinese influences in, **4:**71–72
   court music of, **4:**7, 427–30

cultural origins of, **4:**10–11
dance genres, **4:**412–16
Europeans in, **4:**134, 139, 401, 436
geography of, **4:**401
gong-chime ensembles in, **4:**596
healing rituals, **4:**421
Hoabinhian culture, **4:**34
Indian people in, **4:**68; **5:**449
influence on Sumatran music and dance, **4:**601, 604
Islam in, **4:**74, 78
island regions of, **4:**594–97
Kelantan State, **4:**579
Kuala Lumpur, **4:**5
map of, **4:***402*
martial arts in, **4:**422
Melaka (Malacca), **4:**78, 79, 134, 522, 596, 601
   cultural shows in, **4:**139
musical genres
   asli, **4:**424, 427, 433–36, 441
   asli langgam, **4:**435
   batitik, **4:**826
   bongai, **4:**424
   dangdut, **4:**439
   dondang sayang, **4:**433–35
   ghazal, **4:**438–39
   inang, **4:**437, 439, 441
   joget, **4:**436–37
   joget gamelan, **4:**402, 417, *418*, 427, 441
   keroncong, **4:**439, 442
   kugiran, **4:**441–42
   lagu-lagu rakyat, **4:**439–40, 442
   magagung, **4:**828–29
   main pulau, **4:**423
   masri, **4:**437, *438*, 441
   orkes Melayu, **4:**104
   ronggeng, **4:**19, 82, 436
   tumbuk kalang, **4:***418*, 423
   zapin, **4:**437, *439*, 441
   zikir rebana, **4:**431
music research on, **4:**24, 25, 26–27, 150, 529–30
Muslim cities in, **4:**5
Orang Asli of, **4:**560–87
pedagogy in, **4:**122
politics in, **4:**91–92
popular music, **4:**8, 433–39, 441–42
population of, **4:**401–2, 561
Portuguese in, **4:**78, 79
prehistoric, **4:**33
Qur'ānic recitation in, **6:**161
recitation, **4:**417–21
religious traditions in, **4:**430–32
representative music of, **4:**23, 134
revival movement in, **4:**125
Sabah, **4:**401, 823–37
salient musical features of, **4:**19–20
Sarawak, **4:**401, 823–37
   spirit beliefs in, **4:**49
storytelling in, **4:**417–21
theatrical genres, **4:**402–12, 416–17, 426–27
upland peoples, **4:**529
   music research on, **4:**26
urban folk music, **4:**432–40
village life in, **4:**6

Western music in, **4:**8, 82, 440
work songs, **4:**422–23
Malayu (kingdom), **4:**600
Malbars, **5:**606
"Malbrough s'en va-t-en guerre" (folk song), **8:**20
Malcolm X, **3:**661, 676
Maldevilin (deity), **5:**594–96, 598–99
Maldonado, Roberto, **3:***730*
Malê Debalê (*bloco afro*), **2:**353
Male and Female (film), **9:**43
Malecite Indian nation, **3:**291
Maleku culture, **2:**682–83
Malem people, **9:**740
Malhar people, **5:**727
malḥūn, **6:**416, 432, 472, 475, 495–500, 1041, 1044
Mali. *See also* North Africa; West Africa; *specific peoples*
   Bamana people, textile design, **1:**115
   banjo-like instrument in, **3:**77
   Dogon people
      dance, **1:**109, 112
      music of, **1:**454–55
   griots in, **1:**297, 419, 540
   guitar in, **1:**365
   instruments of, **1:**445
   Manding people, *dyeli* (professional musician), **1:**444
   music research in, **1:**60
   popular music of, **1:**420–21
   processions, **1:**138
   Tuareg people, **1:**546–47, 574, 584, 588; **6:**273
   Wassoulou, women musicians, **1:**420
Mali Baining people, **9:**189, 191–93
Mali caste, **5:**647
Mali empire, **1:**4, 314, 420, 456, 465, 488
   court music, **1:**11, 75–76, 313
   history of, **1:**443–44, 496–97, 508–9
Malian people, in France, **8:**231
Maliekkal, Rabban Thomas, **5:**946
Maliemen (deity), **5:**594, 596, 598, 599
Mālietoa (Sāmoan leader), **9:**204, 217, 795
al-Malik al-'Ādil, Ayyubid ruler, **6:**366
Malik, Anu, **5:**537, 540
Mālik ibn Abī al-Samḥ, **6:**291
Malika Shahi, Sultan, **5:**45
Malikmata (Molina), **4:**873
Malikov, Anželo, **8:**283
Malikov, Jašar, **8:**283
Malinke people, **1:**114, 465
Malinowski, Bronislaw, **9:**186, 479
Maliseet Indian nation, **3:**462, 463, 1069, 1135
Malisori people, **8:**957, 958, 959, 960
Mallat, Jean Baptiste, **4:**859
Mallick family, **5:**136
Mallik, K., **5:**855
Mallouliphone, **6:**512
Malm, Krister, **2:**93; **3:**828; **8:**96
Malm, William P., **4:**27, 125, 876; **7:**595; **10:**3–5, 71
Malmkvist, Siw, **8:**446
Malmsteen, Yngwie, **8:**216
Malmsten, Georg, **8:**487
Malo (musical group), **3:**733
Maloh people, **4:**825, 835

Malol people, **9:**983
Malombo, **1:**777–78
Malone, Bill C., **3:**1109
Malopoets, **1:**778
Malostranska beseda (organization), **8:**730
Malou (musical group), **8:**600
Malsol, Ngiraklang, **9:**724
Malta, **8:**634–43
   art music in, **8:**642–43
   band competitions, **8:**146
   dance traditions of, **8:**637, 641–42
   geography of, **8:**634
   history of, **8:**634–35
   instruments, **8:**639–40
   map of, **8:***516, 866*
   Mdina Cathedral, **8:**642
   opera in, **8:**643
   population of, **8:**634
   research on music of, **8:**642–43
   vocal music of, **8:**198, 517, 635–39
Maltese people
   in North Africa, **6:**435
   in Syria, **6:**565
Ma'lūf, Nasīm, **6:**422
Malukava, **9:**113
Maluku, **4:**812–21
   Dutch in, **4:**812, 817, 818
   Europeans in, **4:**83
   history of, **4:**813
   map of, **4:***805*
   musical genres, *keroncong*, **4:**439
   music research on, **4:**29
   Portuguese in, **4:**818
   prehistoric, **4:**819
   research on, **4:**812–13
   Tanimbar Islands, **4:**51–52
Malwa dynasty, **5:**721
Mam Maya, **2:**721, 736
"Mama, He Treats Your Daughter Mean"
   (Brown), **3:**709
Mamadaliev, Fatakhān, **6:**908, 919, *919*
Mamangakis, Nikos, **8:**1008, 1021
Mamaya African Jazz (performing group), **1:**8
Mambaso, Little Lemmy, **1:**773
mambo, **2:**93, 105; **3:**13, 337, 522, 732, 742,
      787, 788, 790, 793, 794, 796, 798,
      1203
   in Chile, **2:**371
   in Cuba, **2:**827, 832, 833
   in Nicaragua, **2:**763
   in Peru, **2:**487
   in Turkey, **6:**249
Mambo Boys (musical group), **3:**794
Mambo Girl (film), **7:**354
Mami, **6:**271
Mamiya Michio, **7:**736
Mamluk era, **6:**293, 294, 297–98, 543
Mammedov, Haci, **6:**924
"Mammy," **3:**544
Mamrun se fue a la guerra (Spanish ballad),
   6:1040
al-Ma'mūn, caliph, **6:**540
Mamusi people, **9:**620–25
Mán people, **4:**444
"Man on the Flying Trapeze," **3:**1188
Man with the Golden Arm (film), **3:**203

Man Singh, Raja, **5:**45, 163, 314
Mana (journal), **9:**233
Maná (musical group), **2:**104
Mana people, **4:**619; **8:**842
Managalasi people
   attitude toward song ownership, **9:**491
   falsetto singing of, **9:**297
   music and dance of, **9:**501–5
   songs of, **9:**491
Manahune, **9:**1005
Manambu people, **9:**545
Manam Island (Papua New Guinea), **9:**561
Manam people, **9:**245–46
Manana, the Jazz Prophet (musical), **1:**777
"Mañanitas, Las," **2:**613, 618; **3:**721; **10:**93
Manas (epic), **6:**345, 844, 903
Manasa (deity), **5:**503, 861
Mānasollāsa (treatise), **5:**22, 24
Manaus opera house (Brazil), **2:**90
Mančevski, Kiril, **8:**981
Manchukuo, **7:**383
Manchu people, **7:**27, 447, 1003
   music of, **7:**518
   opera of, **7:**452
   rule over China, **7:**29, 33–35, 103, 379, 517,
      518
   in southern China, **7:**485
Mancini, Henry, **3:**203
Manço, Barış, **6:**249, 251
Mancuso, Dominic, **3:**1197
Mandac, Evelyn, **4:**870
Mandaeyŏp (*kagok*), **7:**921
Mandailing people, **4:**607, 807
Mandala (musical group), **3:**1081
Mandan Indian nation, **3:**440, 444, 478
Mandara no hana (Yamada), **7:**731
Mandaya people, **4:**920
Mande people, **1:**456, 465–67
   influence on Bariba people, **1:**452
   influence on Mossi people, **1:**452
   popular music of, **1:**420
Mandel'shtam, Osip, **8:**777
Manding nation, **2:**869
Manding people, **1:**444, 445–46, 449
Mandingo people, **1:**445–46
Mandinka empire, **1:**420
Mandinka people
   balafon music, **1:**159
   drumming, **1:**136
   history of, **1:**443
   instruments of, **1:**445–46
   jali (professional musician), **1:**444
   praise singing, **1:**508
Mando folklórico paraguayo (Cardozo Ocampo),
   2:463
Mando, Sadiq Ali Khan, **5:**768
Mandŏk, **7:**981
Mandok Island (Papua New Guinea), **9:**572–73
mandolin. *See* lutes
Mane (Solomon Islands), **9:**662
Mane, Suresh Babu, **5:**414
Manfila, Kante, **1:**365
Mang Pe'i (Baduy instrumentalist), **4:***718*
Manga people, **9:**977
Mangaia (Cook Islands)
   choral songs, **9:**330
   instruments of, **9:**898, 901

Mangala Devi (deity), **5:**733
Man'ga (Onŭrŭm), **7:**972
Manganihār caste, **5:**7, 273, 281, *282,* 345, 476,
      639, 640, *641,* 641–42. *See also* Mīrāsī
      group
Mangareva, **9:**865, 885–89
   American expeditions to, **9:**24
   cultural contacts with Tuamotus, **9:**882
   geography of, **9:**885
   history of, **9:**885–86
   instruments of, **9:**384, 886
   music and dance of
      'akamagareva, **9:**208–9, 889
      indigenous, **9:**886–88
      pe'i, **9:**379
      Tahitian, **9:**888–89
   research on, **9:**885–86, 973
   theatrical societies, **9:**229
Mangareva Expedition, **9:**24–25, 885, 969
Mangbetu people, **1:**655–56, 658
Mangelsdorff, Albert, **3:**664
Mangeshkar, Dinanath, **5:**414, 424
Mangeshkar, Lata, **3:**338; **5:**255, 412, 414, 420,
      421, *421, 538,* 538–39, *539,* 540
Mangeshkar, Meena, **5:**538
Mangeshkar, Usha, **5:**538
Mangkunegaran court, **4:**633
Man'go Kangsan (*tan'ga*), **7:**905
Mango Records, **8:**241
Mangseng (Arowe) people, **9:**620, 621
Manhattan Brothers, **1:**771, 774, 775
Manhattan School of Music (New York), **3:**977
Man hua deng (*Zhedong luogu* piece), **7:**196
Mani Ayyar, Maduri, **5:**107
Mani Ayyar, Palghat, **5:***152,* 389
"Maniac" (Russell), **3:**183
Maniak (musical group), **3:**1136
"*manicero, El*" (Simon), **3:**732
Manichaeanism
   Central Asia, **6:**936
   Uighur people, **6:**995
"*manic, La*" (D'Or), **3:**1156
Manifold, John, **9:**142
Manigaro, Jack, **9:**664
Manihiki (Cook Islands), **9:**903–9
   costumes, **9:**349
   history of, **9:**904
   instruments of, **9:**906–7
   music and dance of, **9:**904–9
   population of, **9:**903
   research on, **9:**973
   theater in, **9:**238
Manik, Liberty, **4:**603
Manikkavasagar, *tiruvāsakam* of, **5:**105
Manilow, Barry, **4:**886
Maninka people
   instruments of, **1:**445–46
   jali (professional musician), **1:**444, 446
   komo secret society, **1:**445
   music of, **1:**491
   praise singing, **1:**488–513
Manipa community, **5:**712
Manipur
   dance traditions of, **5:**494–95, 504
   Imphal, Govindji temple, **5:**504
   instruments in, **5:**329, 345

Maniruzzaman, Mohammad, **5:**858
Manitoba, **3:**9, 1223–51
  Christian minorities in, **3:**1237–40
  European settlers in, **3:**1086, 1249–51
  First Nations groups in, **3:**440–50, *448*,
    1085–86
  folk song collecting in, **3:**292, 1250
  Gimli, Icelandic people in, **3:**1086, 1089,
    1251
  history of musical life, **3:**1085–91, 1224–31
  Hutterites in, **3:**1240
  intercultural traditions, **3:**342–45
  Mennonites in, **3:**52–53, 1225, 1237–39
  Métis people in, **3:**344, 405–11
  Swedish people in, **3:**1088–89
  Ukrainian people in, **3:**1088–89, 1241–44
  Winnipeg
    choirs in, **3:**343
    festivals in, **3:**343, 1232–36
    founding of, **3:**1224
    musical life in, **3:**1087, 1090–91, 1225–31
Manitoba Arts Council, **3:**1231
Manitoba Opera Association (Winnipeg),
  3:1230
Manitoba Registered Music Teachers Association,
  3:1229
Maniwong, Thongkhio, **3:**1008
Manker, Ernst, **8:**307
Mān Kutūhal (treatise), **5:**45
  raga classification in, **5:**314, *315*
Mankwane, Marks, **1:**365
Man liuban (*Jiangnan sizhu* piece), **7:**225, 236
Mann, Barry, **3:**673
Mannenburg (album), **1:**779
Mannette, Ellie, **2:**961
Mannheim, Bruce, **2:**231
Mannheim Steamroller, **3:**347
Manning, Frank, **2:**799, 800; **3:**1061, 1062
Manning, Frankie (dancer), **3:**212
Mannoia, Fiorella, **8:**620
Manny, Louise, **3:**1125
Manoa, Sunday, **9:**164
Manobala, Muhammad, **1:**342
Manobo people, **4:**905, 920
  epics of, **4:**907
  instrumental music of, **4:**906
Manolov, Emanuil, **8:**904
Manono (Sāmoa), **9:**795
Manouch Roma, **8:**288
Mansa (deity), **5:**476
Mansaka people, **4:**927
Man sanliu (*Jiangnan sizhu* piece), **7:**225
Mansareh clan, **1:**496–97, 499–500, 502, 504
Manseru caste, **5:**887
Mansilungan, Miguel, **4:**863
Mansi people, **8:**488
  bear ritual of, **7:**1029
  music of, **7:**1027–30
Mansukhani, G. S., **5:**655
Manṣūr al-Mughannī, **6:**442
Mansur, Malik Arjun, **5:**460
Mansur, Mirza, **6:**923
Mansurov, Bahram Suleimanğlı, **6:**923
Mansurov, Meşadi Melik, **6:**923
"Manteca" (Pozo), **3:**659, 797
Mantegazzi, Gian Battista, **8:**695

Manteño culture, **2:**413
  archaeomusicological studies of, **2:**7
Manterola, José, **8:**316
Mantingfan (*culuogu* piece), **7:**197
"Mantle So Green" (ballad), **3:**1124
Manto, Saadat Hassan, **5:**487
Manu, **5:**422
Manu'a (American Sāmoa), **9:**795
Manuae (Society Islands), **9:**867
Manuaud, Suzanne, **9:**815
Manuel, Arsenio, **4:**873, 881
Manuel I, king of Portugal, **6:**444
Manuel, Peter, **2:**93, 508, 839, 913; **3:**790, 828;
    4:104, 107; **5:**434, 674, 675;
    10:52–53
Manuela, **8:**208
Manus (Papua New Guinea), **9:**472, 602
  garamut ensembles, **9:**601
  map of, **9:**473
  sound recordings of, **9:**992
Manuvu people, **4:**927
al-Manyalāwi, Shaykh Yūsuf, **6:**548
Manza people, **1:**267
Manzai (Sibata), **7:**737
Manzairaku (*tôgaku* piece), **7:**625
Manzanares Aguilar, Rafael, **2:**740, 744
Manzanar Jive Bombers (musical group), **3:**970
Manzanero, Armando, **2:**623
Mao Jin, **7:**130
Mao Jizeng, **7:**439
Mao Shanyu, **7:**300
Mao Zedong, **6:**995; **7:**316–18, 340, 347, 350,
    383, 385–88
  death of, **7:**90
  writings of, **7:**102, 103, 350, 413, 960
Maonan people, **7:**449, 485–92
Maopa Band, **9:**130
Māori Agriculture College, **9:**935
Māori Hi Fives, **9:**938
Māori people
  in Australia, **9:**85
  body decoration, **9:**349
  Christian converts, **9:**208
  films on, **9:**1019–20
  instruments of, **9:**386, 393, 932–33
  musical performances, transcribed by Davies,
    9:285
  music and dance of, **9:**9–10, 314–15, 865,
    879, 933–51, 976, 983
    haka, **9:**287, 416, 931–32, *940*, 947,
      948–51, 961
    haka poi, **9:**945, 946
    mōteatea, **9:**938–44
    tangi, **9:**961
    wāiata, **9:**168
    wāiata-a-ringa, **9:**931, 945
    wāiata tawhito, **9:**933–34
  poetry, verbal meter, **9:**324
  political songs, **9:**212, 947, 948–51
  popular music of, **9:**277, 937–38
  revival of traditions, **9:**930–33, 943–44
  scales of, **9:**292
  singing of, **9:**961
  sound recordings of, **9:**985, 999
  status of composers, **9:**354
  touring theatrical troupes, **9:**225

*Mapa de los Instrumentos Musicales de Uso Popular
  en el Perú*, **2:**487
Mapfumo, Thomas, **1:**365, *366*, 432, 757
Maple Leaf Band (North Buxton), **3:**1080, 1212
"Maple Leaf Rag" (Joplin), **3:**548, *549*, 651, 706
Mapoma, Mwesa I., **1:**45, 671; **10:**29
Mapou Guinin (musical group), **3:**1170
Mappila people, **5:**947–48
maps
  Afghanistan, **5:***3, 802*
  Africa, **1:***xvi*
  Albania, **8:***866, 987*
  Algeria, **6:***430*
  Andhra Pradesh, **5:***864*
  Andorra, **8:***516*
  Arabian peninsula, **6:***650*
  Armenia, **6:***724*
  Australia, **9:***409*
  Austria, **8:***644*
  Azerbaijan, **6:***844*
  Bali, **4:***730*
  Balkan region, **8:***866*
  Balochistan, **5:***742*
  Baltic States, **8:***398*
  Bangladesh, **5:***3, 842*
  Basque region, **8:***310, 516*
  Belarus, **8:***752*
  Belgium, **8:***516*
  Belize, **2:***629*
  Bhutan, **5:***3, 680*
  Bihar, **5:***658*
  Borneo, **4:***824*
  Bosnia-Hercegovina, **8:***866*
  Bougainville (Papua New Guinea), **9:***473*
  Brittany, **8:***516*
  Bulgaria, **8:***866, 869*
  Burma, **4:***364*
  Cambodia, **4:***152*
  Canada, **3:***xii, xiv, xvi*
  Caribbean, **2:***3, 788, 790, 794*
  Central Africa, **1:***648, 651*
  Central America, **2:***3, 80, 629*
  Central Asia, **6:***896*
  Corsica, **8:***516*
  Costa Rica, **2:***629*
  Croatia, **8:***866*
  Cyprus, **8:***866*
  Czech Republic, **8:***644*
  Delhi, **5:***622*
  Denmark, **8:***398*
  East Africa, **1:***596*
  East Asia, **7:***xxvii–xxxv*
  El Salvador, **2:***629*
  England, **8:***324*
  Estonia, **8:***398*
  Europe, **8:***3*
  Faroe Islands, **8:***398*
  Fiji, **9:***772*
  Finland, **8:***398*
  France, **8:***516*
  Futuna, **9:***772*
  Georgia (country), **8:***752, 827*
  Germany, **8:***644*
  Goa, **5:***718*
  Great Britain, **8:***324*
  Greece, **8:***866*

maps (*continued*)
  Guatemala, **2:**629
  Gujarat, **5:**622
  Haryana, **5:**622
  Honduras, **2:**629
  Hungary, **8:**644
  Iceland, **8:**398
  India, **5:**3
  Inner and Central Asia, **7:**10
  Iran, **6:**824, 844
  Ireland, **8:**324
  Irian Jaya, **9:**579
  Israel, **6:**1014
  Italy, **8:**516, 604
  Jammu and Kashmir, **5:**680
  Java, **4:**631
  Karnataka, **5:**864
  Kerala, **5:**864
  Kurdistan, **6:**744
  Ladakh, **5:**680
  Laos, **4:**337
  Latvia, **8:**398
  Libya, **6:**430
  Lithuania, **8:**398
  Luxembourg, **8:**516
  Macedonia, **8:**866
  Madhya Pradesh, **5:**718
  Maharashtra, **5:**718
  Malaysia, **4:**402
  Malta, **8:**516, 866
  Maluku, **4:**805
  Manus (Papua New Guinea), **9:**473
  Mashriq, **6:**536
  Mexico, **2:**3, 80, 548
  Micronesia, **9:**713–14
  Middle East, **6:**4
  Mithila, **5:**658
  Montenegro, **8:**866
  Morocco, **6:**430
  Nepal, **5:**3, 680
  Netherlands, **8:**516
  New Britain (Papua New Guinea), **9:**473
  New Guinea (island of), **9:**473
  New Ireland (Papua New Guinea), **9:**473
  Nicaragua, **2:**629
  Niue, **9:**772
  North Africa, **1:**530; **6:**430
  North America, **3:**xii–xvi
  North Caucasia, **8:**752, 827
  Northern Areas (Pakistan), **5:**742
  North West Frontier Province (Pakistan),
    5:742
  Norway, **8:**398
  Nusa Tenggara Barat, **4:**730
  Nusa Tenggara Timur, **4:**730, 787
  Oceania, **9:**3
  Orissa, **5:**718
  Pakistan, **5:**3, 742
  Panama, **2:**629
  Philippines, **4:**840
  Poland, **8:**644
  Polynesia, **9:**772, 866
  Polynesian outliers, **9:**834
  Portugal, **8:**516
  Punjab (India), **5:**622
  Punjab (Pakistan), **5:**742

  Rajasthan, **5:**622
  Romania, **8:**866, 869
  Rotuma (Fiji), **9:**772
  Russia, **8:**752
  Sāmoa, **9:**772
  Sardinia, **8:**516, 604
  Scandinavia, **8:**398
  Scotland, **8:**324
  Sicily, **8:**516
  Sikkim, **5:**680
  Sindh, **5:**742
  Slovakia, **8:**644
  Slovenia, **8:**866
  Solomon Islands, **9:**631
  South America, **2:**3, 79, 122, 243–44,
    246–47
  South Asian diaspora, **5:**570
  Southeast Asia, **4:**4, 149, 595
  southern Africa, **1:**698
  Spain, **8:**516
  Sri Lanka, **5:**3, 952
  Sulawesi, **4:**805
  Sumatra, **4:**599
  Sweden, **8:**398
  Switzerland, **8:**644
  Tajikistan, **6:**910
  Tamil Nadu, **5:**864
  Thailand, **4:**220
  Tokelau, **9:**772
  Tonga, **9:**772
  Trobriand Islands (Papua New Guinea), **9:**473
  Tunisia, **6:**430
  Turkey, **6:**78, 760, 844
  Tuvalu, **9:**772
  Ukraine, **8:**752, 807
  United States, **3:**xii, xiii, xv
  Uttar Pradesh, **5:**658
  'Uvea, **9:**772
  Uzbekistan, **6:**910
  Vietnam, **4:**445
  Wales, **8:**324
  West Africa, **1:**440
  West Bengal, **5:**842
Mapuche culture, **1:**151; **2:**232–38, 356, 357,
    366
  acculturation in, **2:**237–38
  history of, **2:**232–33
  instruments of, **2:**233–34, 251–54, 358–59,
    366
  musical genres
    acculturated, **2:**237
    vocal, **2:**236–37, 366
  religious rituals and genres, **2:**254, 255, 362
  research on, **2:**238
  shamanism in, **2:**57, 268
maqām, **5:**64; **6:**11. *See also* makam; modal
    organization; *muǧam*; *muqam*
  in Afghanistan, **5:**804
  'ajam, **6:**42
  'ajam 'ushayrān, **6:**49
  in Arab music, **6:**33–44, 184, 283, 503,
    548–49, 594, 692, 699–701, 1066
  bayyātī, **6:**36, 37–38, 38–43, 39, 168, 283,
    574
  in Central Asian music, **6:**11, 12, 18, 184,
    311, 900, 909–20, 922, 937, 944

  in Egyptian music, **6:**46, 148, 166, 171, 318,
    604, 608, 612
  in European music, **8:**20, 591, 593
  ḥijāz, **6:**36, 38, 154, 168
  ḥusaynī, **6:**40, 41, 42, 43
  ḥuzām, **6:**38
  influence on Sephardi Jewish music, **6:**201–2,
    206
  in Iranian music, **6:**59, 75, 129, 866
  Iraqi, **6:**8, 11, 12, 311–16, 403, 411, 551–52,
    1016
  in Jewish cantillation, **6:**524, 1058
  in Kashmir, **5:**686, 687, 689, 693, 694
  khumāsī, **6:**644
  muḥayyar, **6:**43
  mythical origins of, **6:**182
  nahāwand, **6:**36, 38, 41–42
  number of, **6:**42–43
  in Oriental Jewish synagogue music, **6:**1017
  in Qur'ānic recitation, **6:**160
  rāst, **6:**36, 37, 37–38, 41, 154
  ṣabā, **6:**37, 37–38
  shūrī, **6:**41, 42
  in Syrian music, **6:**563, 568, 569
  in Syrian Orthodox music, **6:**228–29
  tunings in, **6:**18, 135
  in Tunisian art music, **6:**325, 329, 370, 506,
    512, 524
Maqamat (Partos), **6:**1031
al-Maqqarī, **6:**20
Maqralqyz (epic), **6:**952
al-Maqrīzī, **6:**20
Maqueda, Father Antonio de, **4:**841
Mar Thoma Church, **5:**945
marabi, **1:**387, 430, 767–70, 772, 778
maracas. *See* rattles
al-Marāghī, 'Abd-al-Qādir. *See* 'Abd al-Qādir al-
    Marāghī
Maralung, Alan, **9:**355–56, 426
Maramasike (Solomon Islands), **9:**666
Maranao people, **4:**889, 890, 920
  Darangen epic of, **4:**908, 910
  epics of, **4:**907
  instrumental music of, **4:**891, 896–98, 904–6
  vocal music of, **4:**908–9, 909–10
Maranda, Pierre, **9:**962
Marani (musical group), **8:**845
Marano, P. A., **4:**385
Mārār caste, **5:**351, 360, 361, 362, 930, 931–36,
    940–41, 944
Marari people, **1:**119
Marāṭhā rulers, **5:**263, 268, 390, 650, 720, 727,
    907–8
Marau (Solomon Islands), **9:**665
Maravi empire, **1:**670
Maravilla, Ricky, **2:**266
Marawi Band, **9:**138–39
Marc Records, **2:**891; **3:**804
Marcel-Dubois, Claudie, **3:**857; **8:**553, 622
Marcello, Benedetto, **8:**255
Marcelo de San Agustín, Fray, **4:**842, 861
Marceneiro, Alfredo, **8:**583
march, **3:**231, 548, 836, 839, 874
  in Austria, **8:**672
  in Barbados, **2:**819
  in Brazil, **2:**330

in Canada, **3:**1190
in China, **7:**340, 350, 379
in England, **8:**330
in Germany, **8:**659, 660
influence on jazz and ragtime, **3:**650–51
in Ireland, **8:**382
Irish, **3:**843
Italian, **3:**860
in Low Countries, **8:**524
meter in, **8:**9
in Micronesia, **9:**717–19, 733, 737
in Panama, **2:**782
Polish, **3:**892
in Scotland, **8:**363
in Switzerland, **8:**685
"March in the Battle of Prague" (Kotzwara),
   3:839
"March to Freedom," **3:**307
March, Richard, **3:**825; **8:**937
Marchand, Charles, **3:**1154, 1166
Marchand, Pierre, **3:**251
Marchiel, Taćciana, **8:**802
"Marching through Georgia" (Work), **3:**189
Marconi Dancers (London, Ontario), **3:**1196
Marcos, Ferdinand, **3:**1025; **4:**885
Marcoux, Omer, **3:**855
Marcu, George, **8:**115
Marcus Aurelius, Roman emperor, **4:**446
Marcus, George, **10:**95
Marcus, Joyce, **2:**568
Marcus, R., **4:**338
Marcus, Scott, **5:**675
Mardana, **5:**256
Mardusari, Nyi Bei, **4:**638, 684
Maré (New Caledonia)
   music and dance of, **9:**682–84, 965
   sound recordings from, **9:**992
Maré, de, **4:**603
Marek, P. S., **8:**266
Mareschal, Eric, **4:**556
Marett, Allan, **7:**595; **9:**418, 986
Maretzek, Max, **3:**60, 61
Márez, David Lee, **3:**780
Margianian people, **6:**965
Margi people, **1:**289
Margo, Alfredo, **3:**741
Marguste, Anti, **8:**498
Mari people, **8:**475, 772
   instruments, **8:**774
   pentatonicism in music, **8:**773
   rhythmic patterns of, **8:**773
Maria (Austral Islands), **9:**879
Maria (Isaacs), **2:**385
Maria Cafra Band, **4:**885
"Maria La O" (Palmieri), **3:**795
Maria Theresa, Holy Roman Empress, **8:**271
mariachi, **2:**57
   in Costa Rica, **2:**694
   in Mexico, **2:**547, 573, 592, 612, 621–22,
      623
   in Nicaragua, **2:**763
   in United States, **3:**284, 721, 722–23,
      724–25, 728, 732, 737, 744–45, 763,
      765, 772, 850; **10:**78, 79
Mariachi Las Adelitas, **3:**745
Mariachi Las Campanas de América, **3:**745

Mariachi Los Camperos de Nati Cano, **3:***724*,
   724–25, 744, 745
Mariachi Los Galleros de Pedro Rey, **3:**744, 745
Mariachi Las Reynas de Los Angeles, **3:**745
Mariachi Sol de México de José Hernandez,
   3:744, 745
Mariachi Uclatlán de Mark Fogelquist, **3:**744
Mariachi Vargas de Tecatitlán, **2:**622, 623; **3:**725,
   744, 745
María Escalón de Núñez Foundation, **2:**718
mariage de Loti, Le (Viaud), **9:**37–38
Mariamma (also Mariamman; Mariéman;
      Mariyamma; Mariyamman; deity),
      5:293, 367, 602, 607, 617, 876,
      879–80
   Masinagudi festival for, **5:**903–6
Marian Sobieski Phonographic Archive, **8:**712
Mariana Islands, **9:**712, 743–46. *See also* Guam;
      Northern Mariana Islands,
      Commonwealth of the
Mariang Makiling Overture (Padilla de León),
   4:872
Mariano, John, **2:**673
Mariano, Patricio, **4:**864, 865
Maricopa Indian nation, **3:**428, 433
Maridi, **3:**1020
al-Māridīnī, Jamāl al-Dīn, **6:**366
Marie de France, **8:**561
Marie de l'Incarnation, **3:**1075
Marie-Ursule, Sr., **3:**1167
Ma'rifat al-naghamāt al-thamān (anon.), **6:**367
Marifosqui, Vicente, **4:**863
Marigny Theater (New Orleans), **3:**615
Marimba Centroamericana, **2:**718
Marimba la Tica, **2:***699*
marimbas
   Bolivia, **2:**284
   Colombia, **2:**401, 404, *405*
   Costa Rica, **2:**693
   Ecuador, **2:**414–15, 427–28
   El Salvador, **2:**718
   Guatemala, **2:**32, 724–26, 735, 736
   Honduras, **2:**738, 742
   marimba criolla, **2:**708–9
   marimba cuache, **2:**726
   marimba de arco, **2:**708–9, 725, 749, 756,
      761–62, 765, 767
   marimba de ceras, **2:**725
   marimba de cinchos, **2:**726
   marimba de mesa, **2:**725
   marimba de tecomates, **2:**725
   marimba doble, **2:**726, 742, 756, 767
   marimba en escuadra, **2:**695
   marimba grande, **2:**655, 726
   marimba sencilla, **2:**725–26, *729*
   marimba simple, **2:**698
   marimba tenor, **2:**655
   Maya culture, **2:**655, 667, 730–31
   Mexico, **2:**610, *611*
   Nicaragua, **2:**755
   North America, **3:**723, 727–28, 731, 746
   Peru, **2:**492, 493
   South Amreica, **2:**29
marímbula. See lamellophones
Marín, Alfredo, **3:**738
Marín, Orlando, **3:**743

Marind people, **9:**506, 587
Marinella, **8:**1020
Mariner, William, **9:**786, 788
maringa, **1:**358, 377, 380, 381, 386–88
Maringe people, **9:**659–62
Maring in Motion (film), **9:**50
Maring people, **9:**50
   falsetto singing of, **9:**297
   music and dance of, **9:**314, 484, 514–16
Marini, Biagio, **8:**78
Marino, Salomone, **8:**611
Marinos, Tassos, **8:***206*
Mario, I, **4:**757
Marion, Virginia, **9:**994
Maritana (Wallace), **3:**181
Mariteragi, Raymond T., **9:**972
Maritime Folk Songs (Creighton), **3:**292
Maritime Provinces, **3:**1113–43. *See also* New
      Brunswick; Newfoundland; Nova
      Scotia; Prince Edward Island
   Acadians in, **3:**1069
   British in, **3:**1069–71
   early settlers, **3:**1114–15
   First Nations peoples in, **3:**1069
   folk song collecting in, **3:**148, 292, 1068,
      1123, 1125, 1133
   history of musical life, **3:**1068–73, 1114–21
   lumber camps in, **3:**1070, 1123, 1124
   multicultural programs in, **3:**1067
Maritime School for the Blind (Halifax), **3:**1116
Mariz, Vasco, **2:**320
Marketaki, Tonia, **8:**1022
marketing. *See* economics
Markevic, Evdokim, **8:***793*
Mar-Keys (musical group), **3:**675, *676*
Marko Kraljević, **8:**130
Markopoulos, Yannis, **8:**1018, 1021
Markova, Anna, **3:**1270
Marks, Dennis, **1:**366
Marks, Doreen, **9:**530
Marks, Edward B., **3:**259
Marks, J., **3:**348
Marks, Morton, **2:**862
Marl, Marly, **3:**714
Marlboro Morris Men (dance troupe), **3:**324
Marley, Bob, **2:**93, 97, 353, 410, 910, 912;
      3:809, 1202; **4:**887; **6:**644; **8:**236;
      9:145, 166, 168, 213
Marley, Rita, **2:**912
Marmontel, François-Antoine, **3:**1148–49
Marna, **5:**770
Marokaipipi, **9:**908
Marolt, France, **8:**922
Maron (saint), **6:**207, 544
Maronite Church, **3:**1029; **6:**20, 207–16, 227,
      228, 229, 544; **8:**1029
Maroon cultures, **2:**2, 71, 131, 134, 158, 163,
      164, 166–67
   in Belize, **2:**668
   in French Guiana, **2:**438–39
   in Haiti, **2:**881, 882
   instruments of, **2:**505–6
   in Jamaica, **2:**795, 896, 897–98, 900, 901–2;
      10:143, 152
   in Surinam, **2:**503, 504–6

Maroserana dynasty, **1**:781
Marošević, Grožđana, **8**:937
Maróthy, János, **8**:20, 188
Marotiri (Austral Islands), **9**:879
Maroyu (musical group), **2**:297
Maroz, Vitali, **8**:*798*
Marquesan people, in Tahiti, **9**:890
Marquesas Islands, **9**:865, 889–96. *See also*
　　　　Fatuiva; Hiva'oa; Nukuhiva; Tahuata;
　　　　'Uahuka; 'Uapou
　American expeditions to, **9**:24
　body decoration, **9**:349
　Christianity in, **9**:208
　composition in, **9**:353
　cultural contacts with Hawai'i, **9**:914
　Europeans in, **9**:40
　external influences on, **9**:894
　festivals in, **9**:55, 57
　French exploration of, **9**:17
　geography of, **9**:889
　instruments, **9**:895–96
　　drums, **9**:384
　　musical bows, **9**:386
　musical performances, transcriptions of, **9**:287
　music and dance of, **9**:35–36, 48, 873, 875,
　　　879, 969, 980
　　ha'anaunau (also *anaunau*), **9**:890–91
　　hahi (also *mave*), **9**:891–92
　　haka manumanu, **9**:892
　　mahitete, **9**:892
　　mahohe (also *maha'u*), **9**:892
　　matatetau, **9**:892
　　putu, **9**:892–93
　　rari (also *ru'u*), **9**:209, 890, 893
　　tape'a, **9**:894
　　vakahoa, **9**:894
　population of, **9**:889
　research on, **9**:974
　sound recordings from, **9**:1002
　string figures in, **9**:253
　theatrical societies, **9**:229
　vocal music in, **9**:321
Márquez, Alicia, **3**:741
Márquez, Pablo, **10**:91–95
Márquez, Samuel, **2**:500
Marquis Classics, **3**:1109
Marras, Piero, **8**:626
Marre, Jeremy, **2**:411
Marriage of Figaro (Mozart), **3**:181
Marrisyebin people, **9**:453–55
Marroquín, Salvador, **2**:719
Marsalis, Wynton, **3**:664, 665
Marseillaise, La (anthem), **3**:939
Marsh, Kathryn, **9**:256
Marshall, Bertie, **2**:961
Marshall-Deane, Deirdre, **9**:994
Marshall, Sir Don, **2**:819
Marshall, Ingram, **3**:954
Marshall Islands, **9**:712, 740, 748–54
　archives and museums, **9**:967
　Bikini Atoll, **9**:347
　Christianity in, **9**:720
　films on, **9**:1016
　geography of, **9**:748
　history of, **9**:748
　instruments of, **9**:716, 742, 753–54

music and dance of, **9**:748–54
popular music in, **9**:160, 721
population density of, **9**:715
research on, **9**:25, 974
Russian exploration of, **9**:17
settlement of, **9**:715
sound recordings from, **9**:996
tin-can performance, **9**:159
Marshall, Phyllis, **3**:1212
Marshall, William, **8**:367
Marteau, Henri, **6**:1025
Martel, Marcel, **3**:1155
Martel, Renée, **3**:1155
Martenot, Alain, **4**:891, 900
Martha and the Vandellas (musical group),
　　3:674, 709
Martí, Samuel, **2**:555, 623, 658; **3**:740
martial arts. *See also* dance and movement
　Australia, *capoeira*, **9**:84
　Bali, **4**:743
　Brazil
　　capoeira, **2**:24, 57, 336, 345–47, 349–50
　　maculelê, **2**:349–50
　Chinese communities, **9**:71
　Chuuk Islands, *tokia*, **9**:91–92
　Cook Islands, **9**:903
　Egypt
　　bedouin combat dances, **6**:624
　　horse training, **6**:628
　　taḥṭib, **6**:631–32
　Japan
　　chambala, **7**:426
　　karate, **7**:794
　Korea, *taekwŏndo*, **7**:956
　Malaysia, **4**:413, 422
　North America, **3**:214, 955
　　capoeira, **3**:730–31
　Roti, **4**:800
　Sulawesi, **4**:806
　Sumatra, **4**:606, 615, 618, 623
　Sumbawa, **4**:763, 780, 781, 783
　Sunda, **4**:703, 708, 709
　Taiwan, **7**:426
　Trinidad and Tobago
　　gatka, **2**:959
　　kalenda, **2**:959, 965, 966
Martial, David, **2**:917
Martianus Capella, **8**:48
Martica, **3**:751
Martin and Osa Johnson Safari Museum, **9**:975
Martin, Charles Amador, **3**:1075
Martin, Dave, **3**:1213
Martin, Dean, **3**:528
Martin, Frank, **8**:696
Martin, Grady, **3**:80
Martin, Jimmy, **3**:159
Martin, John, **3**:250
Martín, Juan, **2**:933
Martin, Mungo, **3**:1093
Martin, Ricky, **3**:522, 733
Martin, Roberta, **3**:631
Martin, Sallie, **3**:632; **10**:145
Martin, Sara, **3**:644
Martin, Sarah, **3**:707
Martínes, Ángel, **2**:762
Martínes, Marco, **2**:762

Martínes, Omar, **2**:*762*
Martínez, Alma, **3**:749
Martínez Compañón, Baltasar Jaime, **2**:468–69,
　492
Martínez Espinel, Vicente, **2**:937
Martínez, Freddie, **3**:780
Martínez, Johnny, **3**:743, 799
Martínez Landero, Francisco, **2**:739
Martínez, Lorenzo, **3**:760, 765, *765*, 767
Martínez Montoya, Andrés, **2**:397
Martínez, Narciso, **3**:775–76, *776*, 897
Martínez, Oscar, **3**:779
Martínez, Roberto, **3**:757, 765, *765*, 767
Martinez, Sabu, **3**:662
Martínez, Tony, **3**:743
Martínez y Coll, Fray Antonio, **2**:736
Martínez Zepeda, Jorge, **2**:599
Martinican people, in France, **8**:231, 234
Martinique, **2**:789, 914–20; **3**:596
　cultural identity, **2**:920
　East Indians in, **3**:813–17
　history of, **2**:914
　musical genres
　　beguine, **2**:915–16, 920
　　kadans, **2**:916–18
　　mazouk, **2**:915, 916
　　mizik chouval-bwa, **2**:879
　　rap and raggamuffin, **2**:919
　　zouk, **2**:93, 918–19
　political status of, **2**:792
　popular music in, **2**:98
　population of, **2**:914; **5**:594
　research on, **2**:920
　South Asian community in, **5**:594–99
Martino, Ernesto de, **8**:621
Martins, José de Souza, **2**:320
Martinů, Bohuslav, **8**:725, 729
Martinus ex Martinis, Johannes, **8**:692
Martopangrawit, R. L., **4**:130, 637, 683; **10**:43
Maru, Jeannine, **9**:270
Ma'rufi, Musá, **6**:62–65, 63, 67, 68, 69–70, 139,
　867
Maruloun (Solomon Islands), **9**:662–64
Marvelettes (musical group), **3**:674, 709
Marwari community, **5**:639
Marx, Karl, **8**:661
"Mary" (Stoddard), **3**:261
"Mary Had a Little Lamb," **3**:242
"Mary Mack," **3**:599
Mary, Queen of Scots (Musgrave), **8**:369
Maryam (female singer of Granada), **6**:443
Maryland
　Baltimore
　　Estonian people in, **3**:878, 879
　　orchestras in, **3**:536
　　Chinese people in, **3**:957
　　Native American groups in, **3**:461
　　theater in, **3**:189
"Mary's a Grand Old Name" (Cohan), **3**:193
Marzac, Nicole, **8**:547
Marzano, Gonzalo, **4**:866
Marzano, Leonor, **2**:273
Mas, Cokorda, **3**:1013
Maṣabnī, Badi'ā, **6**:570
Masacote, **3**:799
Masakado (*tokiwazu busi* piece), **7**:681

Masakin people, **1:**562

Masālik al-abṣār fī mamālik al-amṣār (Ibn Faḍl
    Allāh al-ʿUmarī), **6:**370

Masaoka, Miya, **3:**336, 972

Masaryk, Thomas, **8:**18

Más Canciones (Ronstadt), **3:**744, 745

Mascgani, Pietro, **8:**618

Masekela, Hugh, **1:**430, 774, *775*, 780

Maselall, Prahalad, **5:**603

Masengo, Edouard, **1:**359

Mashantucket Pequot Museum (Connecticut),
    3:494

"Mashed Potato Time" (Sharp), **3:**709

Mashiyane, Spokes, **1:**430, 773

Mashrab (Sufi poet), **6:**914, 940, 943, 945, 946

Mashriq, **6:**535–56. *See also* Bahrain; Egypt; Iraq;
    Israel; Jordan; Kuwait; Lebanon;
    Oman; Qatar; Saudi Arabia; Sudan;
    Syria; United Arab Emirates; Yemen
    history of, **6:**535–40
    liturgical and folk practices in, **6:**544–46
    map of, **6:***536*
    modal organization of music in, **6:**33–44,
        548–50
    musical genres of, **6:**33, 550–52
    music theory in, **6:**540–42
    postmedieval practices in, **6:**543–44
    research on music of, **6:**535–36
    Sufism in, **6:**543
    twentieth-century music in, **6:**553–56
    urban music in, **6:**546–48

Mashshaqa, Mikhāʾil, **6:**548

Mashughel, Hamid, **5:**834

Masikini, Abeti, **1:**425

Masio-Kwiek, Sylwester, **8:**277

Masiza, Hamilton, **1:**764

masks. *See also* costumes and clothing; dance and
    movement; visual arts
    African, **1:***8*, 110, 117–21, 309–10, 676–77;
        10:*117*, 117–18
    Arunachal Pradesh, **5:**504–5
    Australia
      Cape York, **9:**430
      Torres Strait Islands, **9:***412*, 429
    Bangombe, **1:**658–59
    Bhutan, **5:**489
    Bolivia, **2:**292
    Cambodian, **3:***19*
    Canada, for Toronto Caribana festival,
      3:1207–9
    Caribbean, **2:**795
    Cokwe, **1:**672
    Dan people, **1:**466
    Dominican Republic, **2:**859
    East Asia, **7:**6
    Ecuador, *blanco*, **2:**422
    El Salvador, **2:**713
    Garífuna culture, **2:**734
      wárini, **2:**674
    Guarijio culture, **2:**554
    Guyana, in masquerades, **2:**446
    India
      East, for *chau* dance-drama, **5:**497
      North, folk dance, **5:**497
    Jamaica, *buru*, **2:**907
    Jammu and Kashmir, *bhānd*, **5:**499

Japan, for *nô*, **7:**631, 640

Karnataka, **5:**876, 878–79, *879*

Kerala
    kathakaḷi, **5:**511
    kṛṣṇāṭṭam, **5:**361, 362, 511, *512*

Kogi culture, **2:**186

Korea, **7:***805*, 942
    in dance-dramas, **7:**59, 68

Kwakiutl Indian nation, **3:**400, *400*

Makah Indian nation, **3:**398

Melanesia, **9:**349–50, 598, *599*

Mixtec culture, **2:**566

Mongol people, **7:**1018–19

Mortlock Islands, *tapuanu*, **9:**23–24

Nepal, **5:**505, 702

New Guinea, **9:**474

New Mexico, Pueblo *matachines*, **3:**614

Northwest Coast groups, **3:**222

Oceania, **9:**232

Panama, **2:**772
    gran diablos, **2:**779

Papua New Guinea, **9:**234, 482, 489, 548,
    615
    Anêm people, **9:**608
    Bali Island, **9:***596*
    hevehe, **9:**483
    Iatmul people, **9:**553
    Kuman people, **9:**525
    Lolo people, **9:**613
    Mamose region, **9:**548
    Mwai people, **9:**555–56
    New Britain, **9:**600, 621–22
    New Ireland, **9:**350, *351*, 600
    Siasi Islands, **9:***545*

Peru, for *son de los diablos*, **2:**494

Pueblo Indian groups, **3:**214, 430, 431

Purépecha culture, **2:**579

Rajasthan, **5:**647

Sri Lanka, **5:**490–91, 964

Tibet, **7:***478*

Tibetan, **5:**711

Trinidad and Tobago, **2:**962

Tukano culture, **2:**154

Venezuela, for devil dancers, **2:**537

Western Arctic peoples, **3:**376

Yaqui culture, **2:**590; **3:**438

Maslama al-Majrītī, **6:**442

Maslov, Aleksandr, **8:**783

Masnavî (Jalāluddin Rûmî), **6:**107, 109,
    831–32

Mason, Alden, **3:**392

Mason, John Alden, **10:**100

Mason, Lowell, **3:**27, 44, 275, 532, *532*, 534

Mason, Luther Whiting, **3:**276, 527; **7:**722,
    728–29, 760

Mason, Mrs. Rufus Osgood, **3:**34

Mason and Risch firm, **3:**1183

Masrur, Shamsuddin, **5:**830, 832

mass
    Baroque, **8:**76, 77
    church performances of, **3:**122
    Classical, **8:**84
    mariachi, **3:**721
    Montenegro, **8:**960
    Native American performances of, **3:**735
    Portugal, **8:**579

Renaissance, **8:**75, 366–67
    Spain, **8:**596

mass media. *See also* film; popular music; radio;
    sound recordings; television
    acculturation and, **2:**123–24
    Afghanistan, **5:**832
    Algeria, **6:**467
    Argentina, **2:**262
    Austria, **8:**675
    Bali, dissemination of traditional music, **4:***140*
    Burma, **4:**399
    Central America, **2:**40–41, 51–53, 63, 92–94,
      100
    China, **7:**91, 104, 219, 278, 354, 360–61,
      412, 417, 420, 514
      dissemination of Cantonese opera, **7:**306,
        307
    Colombia, **2:**411
    Costa Rica, **2:**702–3
    cultural diffusion and, **8:**6, 228
    Cyprus, **8:**1031
    Denmark, **8:**462
    Dominican Republic, **2:**860, 861–62
    East Asia, role in transmission, **7:**51
    Egypt, **6:**233–41, 343, 597, 612, 621
    El Salvador, **2:**716–19
    Europe
      folk music and, **8:**155–58
      performance contexts and, **8:**147
      transmission of popular music, **8:**2, 204,
        205, 222
    France, **8:**546
    French Guiana, **2:**439
    Garífuna culture, **2:**734
    Germany, **8:**647, 657
    Guatemala, **2:**735
    Haiti, **2:**890–91
    Honduras, **2:**742
    Hungary, **8:**747
    Indonesia, role in dissemination of popular
      music, **4:**101, 111; **10:**51–52, 53
    Ireland, **8:**390
    Israel, **6:**266–68, 1013
    Jamaica, **2:**910–11
    Japan, **7:**537, 761, 775
    Java, **4:**633, 635, 647, 679–81
    Karnataka, **5:**880–81
    Kazakhstan, **6:**960
    Kurdistan, **6:**752
    Laos, **4:**360, 361
    Malaysia, **4:**440–41, 442
    Malta, **8:**638
    Morocco, **6:**1042
    Naxi people, **7:**511
    Nepal, **5:**696, 701
    New England, influence on musical
      participation, **3:**158
    Nicaragua, **2:**763, 765–66
    North America, **3:**11–12
      country music's involvement with, **3:**76
      dissemination of Asian music, **3:**956, 964,
        985–86
      dissemination of hip-hop culture, **3:**586–87
      social class and, **3:**45, 269
      tie-ins, **3:**271
    North West Frontier Province, **5:**785, 791

mass media (*continued*)
  Oman, **6:**672
  Pakistan, **5:**750
  Peru, **2:**475, 485–87
  Philippines, **4:**883, 884
  rock and, **2:**103–4
  Ryûkyû Islands, **7:**796
  South America, **2:**40–41, 51–53, 63, 92–94, 100
    tropical-forest region, **2:**132–33, 134
  South Asia, **5:**526–29
    broadcasts of folk cassettes, **5:**550–51
    regional artists and, **5:**405–6
    role in dissemination of Hindustani music, **5:**331
    role in dissemination of popular music, **5:**4, 15, 16
  Southeast Aisa
    influence on Khmer culture, **4:**209–10
    influence on traditional musics, **4:**115
  South Korea, **7:**900
  Sumatra, **4:**602
  Sunda, *pantun* broadcasts, **4:**713
  Thailand, **4:**226, 249, 296–97
    influence on traditional musics, **4:**116–17
    role in dissemination of popular music, **4:**99
  Tunisia, **6:**527
  Turkey, **6:**248, 252
  United States dominance of, **3:**18
  Uruguay, **2:**522
  Wales, **8:**355
  Wayana culture, **2:**167
  world music and, **8:**224
Massachusetts. *See also* New England
  Boston
    African-American composers in, **3:**604
    Albanian people in, **3:**926–27
    attitude toward theater, **3:**615
    bands in, **3:**565
    British regimental bands in, **3:**563
    Chinese people in, **3:**957, 958
    class structures in, **3:**44
    early music groups in, **10:**69–70
    Estonian people in, **3:**879
    Filipino people in, **3:**1025
    Greek people in, **3:**929, 930
    Irish people in, **3:**842, 845
    Italian people in, **3:**860
    Middle Eastern peoples in, **3:**1028
    orchestras in, **3:**536
    public schools, **3:**27, 275, 276, 532
    singing societies, **3:**275
    taiko drumming groups in, **3:**971
  Cambridge, morris dancing in, **3:**323
  Election Day celebrations, **3:**595
  Fall River, **3:**732
  Finnish people in, **3:**872–75
  Lithuanian people in, **3:**876
  Lowell, Cambodian people in, **3:**998
  Massachusetts Bay Colony, **3:**831–33
  Plymouth, **3:**831
    morris dancing in, **3:**323
  Portuguese people in, **3:**847
Massachusetts Institute of Technology (Cambridge), **3:**1019
Massagetae (Sakas) nomads, **6:**965

Massajoli, Pierleone, **2:**740
"Massa's in de Cold Ground" (Foster), **3:**187
Massenet, Jules, **3:**1148, 1182
Massey Music Hall (Toronto), **3:***52*
Massicotte, Édouard-Zotique, **3:**33, 146, 1165
Massoudieh, Muhammad, **6:**22, 70
Master Says (musical group), **7:**360
"Masters of War" (Dylan), **3:**316
Mastrolio, Giro "Jerry," **3:**865
Mastrolio, Peter "Al," **3:**865
Masucci, Jerry, **3:**788
Masuda, Akiko, **9:**110
al-Mas'ūdī, **6:**361
Masuku, Dorothy, **1:**771
Ma'sūm and Afrūzparī (epic), **6:**840
Masumi Kato, **7:**681
Masvesi, Padre Antonio, **4:**842
Mata Durga Bhavani (deity), **5:**291
Mata, Eduardo, **2:**605
Mata Guzmán, Nicomedes, **2:**387
Mata, Manuel, **4:**862, 866
Mata, Natalio, **4:**862
Matā'afa (Sāmoan leader), **9:**217
matachines, **3:**757, 761, 848, 850–51
  Hispano culture, **10:**89
  Mexico, **10:**89–95
  Pima culture, **2:**593
  Pueblo culture, **3:**430, 614, 759; **10:**89
  Tarahumara culture, **2:**583, 586, 587
  Yaqui culture, **2:**591, 593; **3:**436, 437–38
Mataco culture, **2:**251–52, 259
Matagalpan culture, **2:**747
Matagi Tokelau, **9:**824
Mataji (deity), worship of, **5:**625–29, 643
Matamoros, Miguel, **3:**792
Matanga, **5:**39
  Bṛhaddeśī, **5:**24, 34, 53, 66, 75, 96
    raga classification in, **5:**47, 313, 400
    on songs, **5:**36
    use of term "raga" in, **5:**73
Matangaro, **9:**904
Mataram (kingdom), **4:**76–77, 83, 632, 634, 686, 700
Mataram University, **4:**777
Maṭar, Būlūs, **6:**651
Matchappee people, **1:**117
Matenadaran Research Institute, **6:**727
Mateo, Joseíto, **3:**731
Material Relics of Music in Ancient Palestine and Its Environs (Bayer), **6:**1061–62
Mather, Bruce, **3:**1151
Mather, Cotton, **3:**24
Mathers Museum (Indiana University), **9:**975
Matheson, Karen, **8:**363
Matheson, William, **8:**363, 374
Mathews, Max, **3:**254
Mathews, R. H., **9:**440
Mathiassen, T., **3:**381
Mathieson, Willie, **8:**372
Mathieu, Rodolphe, **3:**1108, 1150
Mathieu, W. A., **3:**1043
Mathis, Johnny, **4:**884
Mathnawī (Jalāl al-Dīn Rūmī), **5:**691
Mathur, Sharan Rani, **5:**414
Matida Kasyô, **7:**592
Matilal, Nitai, **5:**855

Matinsky, Mikhail, **8:**780
Matiure, Sheasby, **10:***63*
Maton, Adolphe, **3:**1149
Matos Guerra, Gregório de, **2:**304
"Matriarch" (Shenandoah), **3:**489
Matshikiza, Meekley "Fingertips," **1:**765, 767, 768
Matshikiza, Pat, **1:**779
Matshikiza, Todd, **1:**219, 768, 774, 775
Matsievsky, Igor, **8:**784, 821
Matsikenyiri, Patrick, **1:**217
Matsudaira Yoriaki, **7:**737
Matsudaira Yoritsune, **7:**732, 735
Matsui Akira, **10:***15*
Matsushita Shin'ichi, **7:**736
Matt Lebar Ensemble (musical group), **3:**1195
Mattaka, Lina, **1:**433
Mattau, Joseph, **8:**526
Matthews, Washington, **3:**493
Mattila, Karita, **8:**485
Matton, Roger, **3:**1167
Matuda Seiko, **7:**747
Matui Sumako, **7:**743
Matukaze (*nô* play), **7:**632
Matumura Sinsin, **7:**793
Maturan, Diomedes, **4:**884
Matusky, Patricia, **4:**27, 29
Matyakubov, Matrasul, **6:***898*
Mauch, Carl, **1:**153
Maude, Honor, **9:**253
Maudgalaya, Vinay Chandra, **5:***207*
Maugham, Somerset, "Rain," **9:**37, 45
Mauke (Cook Islands), **9:**974
Mauléon, Rebecca, **3:**789
Maultsby, Portia, **3:**585, 627
Maupiha'a (Society Islands), **9:**867
Maupiti (Society Islands), **9:**867
Maurault, Olivier, **3:**1150
Maure people, **1:**108
Maurício, José, **2:**305
Mauritania. *See also* North Africa; *specific peoples*
  aesthetic distinctions in, **6:**8
  Berbers in, **1:**533
  black Africans of, **1:**532
  drums in, **6:**360
  griots in, **1:**540
  harps, **1:**302; **6:**359
  instruments of, **1:**588
  lutes in, **6:**405, 408–9
  music of, **1:**533, 542
  Wolof people, **1:**444
Mauritius, **1:**781, 789
  Indian people of, **5:**449
Maurset, Magne, **8:**419, 422
Maurset, Margrete, **8:**419, 421–22
Maurseth, Jens, **8:**419
Mauryas, **5:**720
Mauss, Marcel, **1:**522
Mavimbela, J. C. P., **1:**770
Ma wang ge (*xiaodiao*), **7:**152
Mawi, Pritak, **9:**983
Mawia people, **1:**638
al-Mawṣilī, Ibrāhīm. *See* Ibrāhīm al-Mawṣilī
al-Mawṣilī, Isḥāq. *See* Isḥāq al-Mawṣilī
mawwāl, **6:**388, 550, 687
  Egypt, **6:**34, 167, 170, 237–38, 551

Iraq, **6:**313
Israel, **6:**1033–34
Morocco, **6:**450, 499, 1041–42
Saudi Arabia, **6:**655, 699
Syria, **6:**544, 566–67, 569
Maxexe, Charlotte Manye, **1:**764
Maxfield, Richard, **3:**175–76
Maxwell Davies, Peter, **5:**136; **8:**366
May, Butler "String Beans," **3:**644
May, Elizabeth, **9:**976
May, Ricky, **9:**938
Maya (musical group), **3:**748
Maya culture, **2:**549–50, 563, 601, 628, 650–58
    archaeomusicological studies of, **2:**7
    in Belize, **2:**666, 667–68
    ceremonies of, **2:**45
    in Guatemala, **2:**721–23, 729–33, 736
    highland groups, **2:**651–55
    history of, **2:**650–51, 721–22
    in Honduras, **2:**738
    iconographical record of, **2:**12, 15
    instruments of, **2:**8, 13, 20, 32, 33, 653–55,
        657–58, 667
    lowland groups, **2:**655–58
    narratives of, **2:**19
    outmigrations to United States, **2:**91
    research on, **2:**658
"Maybe" (Chantels), **3:**673
"Maybelline" (Berry), **3:**353, 552, 672
Mayeda Akio, **7:**595
Mayer, Raymond, **9:**313
Mayer-Serra, Otto, **2:**623
Mayfield, Curtis, **3:**677, *677*, 711
Mayinda, Evarista, **1:***302*
Mayinda, Evarista (*ennanga* player), **1:**300
May It Fill Your Soul (Rice), **10:**52
Maynor, Dorothy, **3:**1210
Mayo-Butocan, Aga, **4:***893*
Mayo culture, **2:**554, 586, 588–93, 592. *See also*
        Yaqui Indian nation
Mays, Benjamin, **3:**624
Maytwayashing, Cliff, **3:**410
Mayuzumi Toshirô, **7:**627, 735–37, 750
Maza Meze (musical group), **3:**1220
Mazatec culture, **2:**563
Mazhar, **6:**249
Māzin family, **6:**625
Mazor, Ya'akov, **6:**1064, 1065
Mazovians, **8:**701
mazurka, **2:**100; **3:**529; **8:**166, 168
    in Argentina, **2:**269
    in Brazil, **2:**330, 331
    in Brittany, **8:**559
    Cajun, **3:**857
    in Caribbean, **2:**795
    in Corsica, **8:**571
    in Denmark, **8:**457
    dissemination of, **8:**7
    in Dominica, **2:**842
    in Dominican Republic, **2:**860
    in Finland, **8:**478
    in French Guiana, **2:**438
    in Guadeloupe, **2:**877
    in Guatemala, **2:**735
    in Honduras, **2:**744
    Irish, **3:**843

Italian, **3:**860, 861, 865
    in Jamaica, **2:**908
    in Low Countries, **8:**524, 527
    in Martinique, **2:**919
    Mexican/Hispano/Tejano, **3:**522, 755, 760,
        773, 775
    in Mexico, **2:**604, 613
    in Netherlands Antilles, **2:**930
    in Nicaragua, **2:**757, 764
    in Norway, **8:**419
    Norwegian, **3:**868
    in Peru, **2:**481
    for piano, **3:**190
    in Poland, **8:**703, 708, 709, *710*
    Polish, **3:**892
    in Spain, **8:**594
    in Sweden, **8:**443
    in Switzerland, **8:**690, 694, 696
    in Uruguay, **2:**516
    in Virgin Islands, **2:**970
Mazz (musical group), **3:**780
el-Mazzawi, Farīd, **6:**237
Mbabatsikos brothers, **3:**1199
Mbabi-Katana, Solomon, **1:**39, 45
Mbali, William "Sax-O-Wills," **1:**765
mbaqanga (*mbaquanga*), **1:**365, 430, 432, 772,
        773–79; **3:**338, 339, 1213
    jive, **1:**775–76, 779
Mbati people, **1:**681–82, 683, 686–87
Mbeere people, **1:**624
Mbem people, **1:**110
Mbeng, Daniel, **1:**660
mbira. See lamellophones
Mbojo (Bimanese) people, **4:**762, 763, 779, 781,
        783–85
"*Mbube*" (Linda), **1:**773
Mbuli, Letta, **1:**774
Mbunga, Stephen, **1:**643–44
Mbwela people, **1:**672
    drums of, **1:**677
    masked dancing, **1:***8*
    music of, **1:**741–42
Mbyá culture, **2:**199, 200, 204
    instruments of, **2:**201–2, 251
    religious genres of, **2:**254–55
MC (rap artist), **9:**169
MCA Corporation, **3:**264
MCA Records, **3:**739
McAdams, Stephen, **1:**191, 199
McAdoo, Orpheus "Bill," **1:**765
McAllester, David P., **1:**31; **2:**16; **3:**367, 496,
        511; **10:**24
McArthur, Patricia, **3:**1087
McBride, Christian, **3:**664
McCarthy, James, **9:***930*
McCarthy, Joseph P., **3:**58, 672
McCarthy, Michael "Mikeen," **8:**295
McCartney, Andra, **3:**1059
McCartney, Paul, **3:**713
McCarty, Victor-Eugène, **3:**606
McClain, Ernest, **9:**994
McClellan, George B., **3:**308
McClellan, Mike, **9:**389
McClintock, Walter, **3:**444
McColeman, Andrea, **3:**1280, *1280*
McComiskey, Billy, **3:***843*

McConnell, Rob, **3:**1080, 1107
McConnel, Ursula, **9:**429, 987
McCormack, John, **3:**195, 537, 607, 842; **8:**378
McCosker, Sandra Smith, **2:**783
McCoury, Del, **3:**159
McCoy, James, **2:**941
McCoy, Kansas Joe, **3:**645
McCoy, Ron, **3:**311
McCoy, Van, **3:**228, 711
McCoy, Viola, **3:**644
McCoy, William J., **3:**737
McCrae, George, **3:**688
McCue, George, **3:**144
McCulloh, Judith, **10:**164
McCullough, Lawrence, **8:**394
McDaniel, Susanne, **10:**137
McDermott, Vincent, **4:**637
McDonald, Michael, **3:**713
McEntire, Reba, **3:**81
McFarlane, Reuben, **3:**1115
McGee, F. W., **3:**631
McGee, Timothy, **3:**144
McGettrick, Paul, **8:**394
McGibbon, William, **8:**367, 372
McGill (musical group), **5:**429
McGill University (Montréal), **3:**15, 246, 1150
McGinn, Matt, **8:**371
McGlashan, Alexander, **8:**373
McGowan, Chris, **2:**93, 320
McGrath, Norman, **3:***148*
McGregor, Gaile, **3:**1059
McGregor, Sir William, **9:**147
McGuinn, Roger, **3:**133
McGuire, Barry, **3:**316–17
McGuire, Edward, **8:**369
McGuire Sisters, **3:**352
MC Hammer, **3:**698, 715
Mchunu, Sipho, **1:**430
McInnis, Dan Joe, **3:**1071
McIntire, Dick, **9:**390
McIntosh, Dale, **3:**1258
McIntosh, Ethel, **2:**972
McIntosh, James, **8:**364
McIntosh, Robert, **3:**1094, 1095
McIntosh, Sylvester "Blinky," **2:***970*
McIntyre, Paul, **3:**1212
McIsaac, Ashley, **3:**345, 1064
McKay, Tony "The Obeah Man," **2:**808
McKean, Thomas A., **8:**370
McKennan, Robert, **3:**392
McKennitt, Loreena, **3:**252, 326, 1081; **8:**322
McKenzie, Claude, **3:**1074
McKenzie, Kim, **9:**47, 419
McKenzie, Philip, **3:**1074
McKern, W. C., **9:**24
McKim, John, **3:**82
McKinley, Katherine, **3:**999
McKinley, Kathy, **4:**25
McKinley, William, **4:**85
McLachlan, Jessie, **8:**370
McLachlan, Murray, **3:**1080
McLachlan, Sarah, **3:**252, 315
McLaren, Les, **9:**50, 480
McLaughlin, John, **1:**777; **3:**664, 851, 955
McLaughlin, Les, **3:**1278
McLean, Mervyn, **9:**292, 372, 932, 973

McLearie, Jeannie, **3:**763
McLellan, Gene, **3:**1073
McLeod, Jenny, **9:**932, 947
McLeod, Norma, **1:**51, 782, 783
McLuhan, Marshall, **3:**334, 1061
MC Lyte, **3:**696–97, 714
McMahon, Charlie, **9:**397
McMahon, Tony, **8:**385
McMasier, Mary, **8:**364
McNaughton, Patrick, **10:**64
McNeely, Big Jay, **3:**669, 708
McNeil, Rita, **3:**1073
McNemar, Richard, **3:**135
McPartland, Jimmy, **3:**652
McPeek, Ben, **3:**1186
McPhatter, Clyde, **3:**671, 673
McPhee, Colin, **3:**335, 953, 1015, 1183; **4:**28, 131, 733
McRae, Tommy, **9:**440
McReynolds, Jesse, **3:**159, 166
McReynolds, Jim, **3:**159
McRobbie, Angela, **3:**111, 114
McTell, Blind Willie, **3:**329, 644, *645*, 707
Mdledle, Nathan, **1:**775
Me and Bessie (musical), **3:**621
Meacham, James, **3:**65
Meacham, Joseph, **3:**135
Mead, Margaret, **3:**511; **9:**416, 975
Mealing, Mark, **3:**1095
Meari (organization), **7:**970
Measures of Musical Talent (Seashore), **3:**278
Meccia, Gianni, **8:**619
Mechling, W. H., **3:**291
Mecmû'a-i Sâz ü Söz (Ufkî Bey), **6:**18, 113, 771
Međedović, Avdo, **8:**131
Medeiros, Anacleto de, **2:**305
Medevecky, Karol, **8:**18
Medici, Lorenzo dei, **8:**608
Medicine Beat (musical group), **3:**1280, *1280*
Medicine Fiddle (film), **3:**410
medieval period. *See* Middle Ages
Medina, Avihu, **6:***266*, 1033, 1074
Medina, Frank, **9:**132
Medina Silva, Ramón, **2:**20
Medina, Victoria, **4:**857
El-Medioni, Saoud, **6:**1044
Meditation: From Easter Celebration (Williams), **3:**612
Meditations on a Drama (Avni), **6:**1031
Mediterranean Sinfonietta (Avidom), **6:**1028
Medium (Menotti), **3:**546
Medly, John, **3:**1116
Medoff, David, **3:**938–39
Medtner, Nicholas, **3:**1150
Meer, Wim Van der, **5:**57
Meet the Navy (revue), **3:**198
Mega Metal (periodical), **6:**249
Megaw, J. V. S., **8:**321
Meghalaya, **5:**504–5
Meghwal caste, **5:***647*
Megrelian people, **8:**827, 840
"*Me gustas tal come eres*" (Easton and Miguel), **3:**751
Mehaji (deity), **5:**643
Mehetia (Society Islands), **9:**867

Mehinaku culture, **2:**128
 music and dance of, **2:**126
Mehmed II, "the Conquerer," Ottoman sultan, **6:**194
Mehmed III, Ottoman sultan, **6:**194
Meḥmed Es'ad Efendi, **6:**371
Mehta, Narsinh, **5:**630
Mehta, Zubin, **5:**566; **7:**803
Mei'an qinpu (handbook), **7:**159
Mei Baojiu, **7:**395
Mei Baoyue, **7:**395
Mei Lanfang, **3:**961; **7:**55, 60, 286, 394–95, *395*
Mei Qiaoling, **7:**394
Meida, Nining, **4:**718
Meido no Hikyaku (Chikamatsu), **7:**669
Meier, Ernst, **8:**648
Meier, John, **8:**19, 647–48, 663, *663*
Meihua cao (*nanguan* piece), **7:**239
Meiji era. *See* Meizi era
Meilleur, Marcel, **3:**409
Meintjes, Louise, **1:**419
Meissonnier, Martin, **1:**481
Meistersinger von Nürnberg, Die (Wagner), **8:**187
Meiteis, **5:**494
Meizi (Meiji) era
 abolition of *todô syoku yashiki* and *komusô* systems, **7:**756, 777
 abolition of Zen Huke sect, **7:**703, 715
 Ainu people in, **7:**783
 dance during, **7:**66
 gagaku in, **7:**625, 627, 757
 kabuki in, **7:**765
 kumiuta in, **7:**696
 minsin gaku in, **7:**725
 modernization during, **7:**46, 228, 565, 720–22, 727–29, 756, 760, 777–78
 nagauta concerts in, **7:**654
 nô in, **7:**630
 political songs in, **7:**739–40
 satuma biwa in, **7:**648
 sôkyoku in, **7:**698
Meizi sentei hu (collection), **7:**626, 627
Mejía Baca, José, **2:**501
Mejía Godoy, Carlos, **2:**103, 764, 767
Mejía Godoy, Luis Enrique, **2:**764, 767
Mejía, Libardo, **2:***381*
Mejía Sánchez, Ernesto, **2:**767
Mejit Island (Marshall Islands), **9:**751
Mek people, **9:**583
Mekeo people, **9:**63, 491
Mekhanadjian, Khoren, **6:**737
Mekong Band, **9:**76
Mekoro people. *See* Boni (Maroon) culture
Melamed, Nissan Cohen, **6:**1071
Melanau people, **4:**824
Melanesia, **9:**598–99. *See also specific countries, islands, and peoples*
 betel use in, **9:**177
 films on, **9:**1014–15
 geography of, **9:**598
 German expedition to, **9:**23
 initiation schools, **9:**251–52
 instruments, **9:**598
  log idiophones, **9:**374
  swung slat, **9:**392
 kava use in, **9:**172–73

 Lapita cultural complex in, **9:**4
 metrical traits in, **9:**289–90
 music and dance of, **9:**981
 prehistoric, **9:**598
 research on, **9:**296, 977
 rhythmic clothing and dance, **9:**349–50
 sound recordings from, **9:**991–94
Melanesian Archive (San Diego), **9:**977
Melanesian Resource Center (San Diego), **9:**964
Melbourne, Hirini, **9:**933
Mele, Giovanni, **8:***630*
Mele Hawaii (Berger), **9:**919
"*Mele of Kaho'olawe*" (Mitchell), **9:**220
Melebugnon people, **4:**889
Meléndez, Carlos, **2:**703
Melendez, Gilberto, **6:***878*
Melereda (god), **8:**863
Melgunov, Yuly, **8:**756–57, 783
Melik'yan, Spiridon, **6:**726
Melkite Christians, **3:**1029
Mellēna, Māta, **8:**507
Mellers, Wilfrid, **3:**143, 144
Melngailis, Emilis, **8:**505, 507
Melodiya (record company), **6:**940; **8:**287, 800
melodrama, **3:**182
melody
 Abung people, **4:**627
 Afghanistan, **5:**827
  falak, **5:**828
  gorgholi, **5:**828–29
  Kabuli *ghazal,* **5:**805
  Pashtun songs, **5:**835
 African music, **1:**20–21
  downdrift of, **1:**166, 171–72, 178, 198
  gapped, **1:**211
  "wandering," **1:**725
 Akha people, **4:**541
 Albania, **8:**993, 994, 996
  urban songs, **8:**997
 Algeria
  'arūbī, **6:**472
  ḥawzī, **6:**473
  tūshiya Zīdān, **6:**468
 analysis of, **9:**292–93
 Andalusian music, **6:**446, 453–54
 Andean music, **2:**216, 221
 Anglo-American ballads, **3:**834
 Anuta
  aro reo, **9:**306
  puatanga, **9:**860
  tungaunu, **9:**858
 Arabian peninsula
  ṣawt genre, **6:**652
  women's songs, **6:**701
 Arctic songs, **3:**378
 Argentina
  candombe, **2:**260
  secular music, **2:**261
 Armenian music, **6:**727
 Ashkenazic, **8:**253
 Atacameño culture, **2:**361
 Australia
  Cape York *bora,* **9:**429
  Central Aboriginal songs, **9:**411, 434–35, 438–39

children's songs, **9:**256–57
clansongs, **9:**422
Italian music, **9:**81, *82*
men's *vs.* women's songs, **9:**243
Mornington Island songs, **9:**430
Pitjantjatjara songlines, **9:**292–93
Southeastern Aboriginal songs, **9:**441
Torres Strait island dance, **9:**429
wangga, **9:**426
Yolngu *dhambu,* **9:**301–2
Austria, **8:**671–72
Azerbaijan
   dastanlar, **6:**930
   folk songs, **6:**931
Bahamas, *goombay,* **2:**806
Bajau people, *berunsai,* **4:**826
Bali, **4:**747, 755–56
   arja, **4:**751
   pokok, **4:**733–35, 737
Balkan region, **8:**867
Bantu peoples, **1:**763
Basque music, **8:**309, 311
Belarus
   instrumental music, **8:**799
   vocal music, **8:**793, 794, 795
Belize
   brukdown, **2:**678
   creole music, **2:**677
Bellona, **9:**850
Berber people, **1:**543
in bluegrass, **3:**161
in blues, **3:**639, 643
Bolivia, Westernization of, **2:**297
Bontok people, **4:**914
Borneo, *sapeh* music, **4:**835
Bosnia-Hercegovina, **8:**964
   Sephardic Jewish music, **8:**968
Brazil
   bossa nova, **2:**108
   caboclinho genres, **2:**337
   in Candomblé music, **2:**342
   cantoria, **2:**326
   central and southern genres, **2:**306
   côco songs, **2:**349
   folia de reis, **2:**312
   marujada songs, **2:**348
   for religious music, **2:**330
   samba campineiro, **2:**349
   ternos toadas, **2:**312–13, *314*
Bribri and Cabécar cultures, ritual songs,
   2:634
Bulgaria, **8:**891
Burma, **4:**18–19, 384–85, 386, 392–94
   hsaìñwaìñ, **4:**371, 372
   songs, **4:**383
California, Native American music, **3:**414,
   416, 417
Celtic music, **8:**321
Central Africa, improvisation, **1:**217
Central Asia, *maqām,* **6:**900, 911
Chăm people, **3:**1010; **4:**591
Chile
   cueca, **2:**369
   flautones music, **2:**359
   verso, **2:**367
   for Virgin Mary festivities, **2:**363

China, **7:**122–23
   Cantonese music, **7:**217–18, 309
   foqü Buddhist repertoire, **7:**331–33
   instrumental music, **7:**233–34
   nanguan music, **7:**207, 208
   nanyin, **7:**272
   Peking opera aria types, **7:**282–84, 286
   qupai, **7:**184, 196, 197, 201–2, 208, 224,
      225, 233–43, 249, 457
   shengqiang, **7:**277–79, 289
   Suzhou tanci, **7:**262–63
   xianshiyue, **7:**214–16
   yinqiang tunes, **7:**456
   zaju tunes, **7:**275–76
Chuuk
   dance-songs, **9:**738
   love songs, **9:**736
Colombia
   African-derived traits, **2:**401
   bordónes, **2:**404
   guabina veleña, **2:**391
   rajaleña, **2:**390
Coptic Orthodox music, **6:**221
Costa Rica
   "*La sangre de Christo,*" **2:**682
   ornamentation of, **2:**698
   romance, **2:**695
Creek Stomp Dance songs, **3:**469
Croatia
   epic songs, **8:**927
   Hungarian types, **8:**932
   pismice, **8:**931
Cuba, *tonadas,* **2:**833
Cyprus, **8:**1029–30
Czech Republic, **8:**721
   Moravia, **8:**721–22
Delaware Big House songs, **3:**464
Denmark
   fiddle music, **8:**454
   songs and ballads, **8:**453
Doukhobor music, **3:**1267–68
East Africa, nomadic peoples, **1:**605
Ecuador
   pingullo, **2:**422
   responsorial Passion song, **2:***421*
   vacación, **2:**424
Egypt
   in epic songs, **6:**343
   inshād, **6:**166
   layla, **6:**149
   tawāshīh, **6:**168
England, songs, **8:**327–28
Estonia, *regivärss,* **8:**492, 493
Ethiopia, modal categories, **1:**149
Europe
   agricultural songs, **8:**4
   ballad, **8:**135
   dissemination of, **8:**20
   laments, **8:**144
   in village music, **8:**9
Faroe Islands
   ballad dances, **8:**470
   ballads, **8:**469
Fiji, **9:**781
   bhajan kavvali, **5:**613
   cautal, **5:**613
   Indian *cautal,* **9:**94

Indian *kavvali,* **9:**93
   meke, **9:**775
Finland, **8:**481
   Kalevala songs, **8:***477*
   Rom people, **8:**289
   songs, **8:**478
France
   chanson de geste, **8:**539
   vocal music, **8:**542
Futuna, **9:**771
   fasi, **9:**815
Garifuna culture
   bérusu, **2:**675
   eremuna égi, **2:**675
German music, **3:**884–85
Germany, **8:**652–53, 655
   medieval music, **8:**650–51
Goa, *dhalo,* **5:**738
in gong-chime ensemble music, **4:**21
Great Basin Bear Dance songs, **3:**423–24
Great Basin Indian songs, **3:**426
Greece, **8:**1008
   strophic songs, **8:**284
Greek music, ancient, **8:**47
Gregorian chant, **8:**70
Guadeloupe
   quadrille, **2:**877
   vèyé boukousou, **2:**875
Guarijio culture
   contradanza, **2:**553–54
   son principal, **2:**553–54
Gujarat
   bhajan, **5:**632
   duho, **5:**636
   garbo, **5:**628
Haiti, Vodou songs, **2:**883
Hawai'i, **9:**16
   art songs, **9:**925
   hula ku'i, **9:**920
   Jawaiian genre, **9:**166
Hindustani music, raga and, **5:**67–69
Hmong people, **4:**552, 556–57
Hungary, **8:**737, 741–42, 743
   magyar nóta, **8:**738
   sirató, **8:**740–41
   string ensemble music, **8:**744
   strophic songs, **8:**131
   verbunkos, **8:**273
   Vlach Rom music, **8:**275
Iceland
   rímur, **8:**401, 402
   tvísöngur, **8:**403
inanga music, **1:**166–67, 178, 198
Iran
   Azerbaijani *havalar,* **6:**848–50
   for *bakshi* repertoire, **6:**840
   gharībī, **6:**829–31
   radif, **6:**59, 62–70, *71,* 134, 854, 855, 865,
      867
Iraq, *maqām,* **6:**311
Ireland
   laments, **8:**379
   lyric songs and ballads, **8:**379–80
Irian Jaya, **9:**257
   Abun songs, **9:**589
   Asmat songs, **9:**590–91

melody, Irian Jaya (continued)
  Eipo *mot*, **9:**592
  Isirawa songs, **9:**587
  Kiriki songs, **9:**587
  Mairasi songs, **9:**587–89
  Orya songs, **9:**589
  Sentani music, **9:**586–87
  tiled contour, **9:**585
  vocal music, **9:**583–89
Irish music, **3:**843
Iroquois Social Dance songs, **3:**464
Islamic call to prayer, **6:**154–55, 352
Italy, **8:**609–10
  ballads, **8:**606
Japan
  heike biwa, **7:**646–47
  min'yô, **7:**604
  nagauta, **7:**673
  in narratives, **7:**679–80
  nô, **7:**632–33
  satuma biwa music, **7:**648
  stereotyped, **7:**554, 616
  syômyô, **7:**613–14, 615–17
  theories concerning, **7:**569–70
jāti modes and, **5:**28, 73–74, 75
Java, **4:**669–73
  balungan, **4:**660, 661, 665, 673, *674*, 677
  cèngkok, **4:**657, 666, 672, 677
  gamelan, **4:**385; **10:**51
  garapan, **4:**669, 672–73, *674*, 677
  tembang, **4:**664–65
Jewish music, **6:**1052–54, 1057; **8:**252–53, 258
  contrafacta technique, **8:**254–56, 257
  Eastern European, **8:**131
  ethnic differences, **8:**263
  niggun, **8:**254, *255*
  Sephardic, **8:**253
jùjú, **1:**478
Kapingamarangi, *langa*, **9:**837
Karnataka, *pada* genres, **5:**868
Kashmir
  rūf, **5:**684
  ṣūfyāna mūsīqī, **5:**687
Kazakh people, **7:**461
Kazakhstan, *kyui*, **6:**958
Kenyah people, *kui*, **4:**827
Khmer people, **4:**17–18, 163, 179–80, 181
  modal organization, **4:**178
khyāl, **5:**172, 173–74
Kiribati, dance-songs, **9:**761–62
Kmhmu people, **4:**547
Korea, **7:**847–51
  Buddhist music, **7:**874
  him principle in, **7:**816
  kayagŭm pyŏngch'ang, **7:**908
  p'ansori, **7:**902–5
  pŏmp'ae, **7:**872
  sanjo, **7:**916–17
  shamanic chant, **7:**877–78
  sinawi, **7:**891, 914
Kosrae, **9:**741
Kpelle people, **1:**467
kriti, **5:**269
Kuna culture
  chants, **2:**644

gammu burui, **2:**642, 645
  lullabies, **2:**646
  paired flute, **2:**641
Kurdistan, *beyt*, **6:**748
Kwakiutl Winter Ceremony songs, **3:**400
Lahu people, **4:**540
Lao people, **4:**18
  khap ngeum, **4:**347
  khap phuan, **4:**348
  khap sam neua, **4:**349
  khap thum, **4:**350
  lam, **4:**342, 351
  lam khon savan, **4:**346
  salong sam sao, **4:**350
Latvia, *balss* formula, **8:**500, 503
Lisu people, **4:**543
Lithuania, **8:**510
Lithuanian *sutartine* genre, **3:**875–76
Lombok, **4:**769, 770
Low Countries, songs, **8:**520, 521
Luvale songs, **1:**727–32
Macedonia, dance music, **8:**978
Maguindanao people, lullabies, **4:**911
Makah potlatch songs, **3:**399
Malaysia, **4:**19, 67
  asli, **4:**433–34, 435
  dangdut, **4:**439
  dondang sayong, **4:**433–34, 435
  ghazal, **4:**439
  jikay, **4:**411
  mak yong, **4:**407, *419*
  masri, **4:**437, *438*
  rebana besar, **4:**420
  tarikh selampit, **4:**420–21
  theater and dance genres, **4:**417
  urban folk music, **4:**432
  wayang Siam, **4:**419
Malta
  bormliza, **8:**637
  fatt, **8:**637
  spirtu pront, **8:**636
Maluku, **4:**813, 814
Māori songs, **9:**933
Mapuche culture, **2:**362, 366
  tayil, **2:**235
Maronite church music, **6:**210, 212–15
Marquesas Islands, **9:**36
  rari, **9:**893
  tape'a, **9:**894
Marshall Islands, **9:**753
Martinique, beguine, **2:**916
Mashriq region, **6:**33
Maya culture
  of ancestral songs, **2:**731–32
  flute melodies, **2:**654
  multiple names for, **2:**652–53
  shamanic songs, **2:**652
Melanesia, tonal centers in, **9:**296
  in Mennonite hymns, **3:**1238
Métis fiddle music, **3:**405
Mexico
  "*Canto de San Sebastián*," **2:**652
  gusto, **2:**611
  "*La Rama*," **2:**615
  sones, **2:**550

Micronesia, **9:**716
Minangkabau people, **4:**611
Miskitu culture, *inanka*, **2:**663
Mithila, **5:**678
Mongol vocal music, **7:**1006–7
Montenegro, **8:**957
Morocco
  aḥwash, **6:**487, 1036
  wedding laments, **6:**481
Moxo culture
  machetero, **2:**140, *141*
  vespers, **2:**140, *142*
Murut people, in *lansaran*, **4:**826
naqamat, **1:**536
Native American Ghost Dance songs, **3:**421, 487
Nauru, **9:**755
Nepal, Guruṅg people, **5:**704
New Caledonia
  dance-songs, **9:**675–76
  side-blown flute, **9:**402
Nicaragua
  baile de las marimba, **2:**761, *762*
  corrido, **2:**758
Nigeria
  Igbo practices, **1:**210
  lyricism, **1:**243
Niue, **9:**817
North Caucasia, vocal music, **8:**851
Northeast Indian songs, **3:**463
Norway
  Draumkvædet, **8:**413
  hardingfele slått, **8:**416
nūba, **6:**436, 457–58
Oceania, structure of, **9:**300–301
Ojibwe love songs, **3:**457
O'odham songs, **3:**435
Orang Asli people, **4:**565–67
Orang Dalem people, **4:**619
organum, **8:**71
Otopame culture, *minuete*, **2:**573
Pakistan, northern, **5:**798
Palau, **9:**723, 726
Palawan people
  gong music, **4:**924
  in *Kudaman*, **4:**927
Panama
  mejorana, **2:**777
  violin, **2:**776
Papua New Guinea
  Abelam songs, **9:**550–51
  Angan vocal music, **9:**497
  Baluan *kolorai*, **9:**603
  Buang songs, **9:**567
  Buin songs, **9:**651–53
  Eastern Highlands Province, **9:**302–3, 530
  Enga songs, **9:**536
  guitar songs, **9:**152
  Gulf Province, **9:**495
  Halia songs, **9:**642
  Huli people, **9:**538–40
  Irumu people, **9:**568
  island dances, **9:**507
  Karkar people, **9:**561
  Komba music, **9:**572
  Lolo songs, **9:**614

Volume Key: **1**, Africa; **2**, South America, Mexico, etc.; **3**, United States and Canada; **4**, Southeast Asia; **5**, South Asia

Mali Baining people, **9:**192
Managalasi songs, **9:**503–5
New Britain panpipe music, **9:**625
New Britain *tumbuan,* **9:**622
New Ireland *kubak,* **9:**627
paired-flute, **9:***532*
Rai Coast, **9:**563–64, 565
sia, **9:**610–11
Siasi music, **9:**574–76
string-band music, **9:***138*
Sursurunga people, **9:**627
Teop people, **9:**644
tonal centers in, **9:**296
Paraguay, *coritos,* **2:**460
parlor music, **3:**183
Peru
    in courtship activities, **2:**213
    festejo, **2:**496
    hatajos de negritos, **2:**495
    landó, **2:**498
    vals criollo, **2:**500
    yaraví, **2:**477
Philippines
    awit and *corrido* formulas, **4:**853
    dance forms, **4:**854
    kumintang, **4:**850
    in *moro-moro,* **4:**856
    punto formulas, **4:**844, 847, 848
Plains Indian songs, **3:**445, 483
Pohnpei, **9:**739
Poland
    dance music, **8:**708
    stylistic changes, **8:**113–14
Polynesian music, **9:**769–70
Polynesian outliers, **9:**836
popular songs, **3:**195
    eighteenth century, **3:**180–81
    nineteenth century, **3:**187
    twentieth century, **3:**549
Portugal, **8:**581
Pueblo Indian songs, **3:**429
Puerto Rico, *seis,* **2:**939
Pukapuka, *amu,* **9:**912
Punjab, *giddhā,* **5:**654
Purépecha culture
    abajeño, **2:**578–79
    pirekua, **2:**579
    son regional, **2:**579
    torito, **2:**578
Q'ero culture, **2:**230
    pinculu, **2:**227
Qur'ānic recitation, **6:**159, 160
Rapa Nui, vocal music, **9:**952
research on, **8:**23
rock, **3:**551
Romania
    doina, **8:**873
    shepherds' music, **8:**875
Rotuma
    sua, **9:**822
    temo, **9:**820
Russia
    byliny, **8:**130, 764–65
    church music, **8:**779
    kant, **8:**767
    village music, **8:**756

Ryûkyû Islands, Okinawan *usudêku,* **7:**794
Saami joiks, **8:**301–2, 303, 307, 487
St. Lucia, *kwadril,* **2:**945
Sāmoa
    hymns, **9:**204
    tagi, **9:**799, *800*
Sardinia, *canto a chiterra,* **8:**629
Saudi Arabia, *dewīnih,* **6:**652
Scotland, formulas in, **8:**361
Serbia, *glas* concept, **8:**942
Shan people, **4:**548
Shuar culture, **2:**419
Slovakia, **8:**721
Slovenia, **8:**912
Solomon Islands, **9:**288
    Bellonese game-playing songs, **9:**268
    Blablanga *ragi māgana,* **9:**657
    Blablanga songs, **9:**658
    Guadalcanal, **9:**665
    Santa Cruz Islands songs, **9:**334
Somali music, **1:**613–14
South Asia
    early concepts of, **5:**19–20
    instruments designated for, **5:**322–23
Southeast Indian songs, **3:**467
southern Africa, **1:**701, 702
Spain, **8:**593
Sri Lanka, **5:**959–60
strophic songs, **8:**131
Subarctic songs, **3:**389–90
in Sufi *dhikr* ritual, **3:**1045
Sumatra, **4:**604
Sunda
    in *gamelan degung,* **4:**706
    gamelan music, **4:**701–2
    lagu, **4:**704
    in *pantun,* **4:**713
Suyá unison songs, **2:**146–47
Swahili, **1:**606
Sweden
    dance music, **8:**436
    folk music, **8:**435
    lullabies, **8:**439
Syrian Orthodox music, **6:**228
Tahiti
    hīmene rū'au, **9:**871
    hīmene tārava, **9:**872
Taiwan
    Hengchun tunes, **7:**424
    shange, **7:**427
Taiwan, Bunun people, **9:**257
Tamil Nadu
    folk *vs.* classical styles, **5:**916–17
    Kota people, **5:**916
    tēvāram, **5:**260
Tarahumara culture
    matachín, **2:**583
    tutuguri, **2:**585
Temiar people, **4:**574, 577–78, 581–84
Teribe culture, *pasodoble,* **2:**685, *686*
Thailand, **4:**17, 269–72, 313
    Buddhist chant, **4:**292
    northern, **4:**314–15
    village songs, **4:**299
thumrī, **5:**181
Tibetan Buddhist chant, **7:**479

Tibetan folk songs, **7:**473
Tibetan opera, **7:**478
Tibetan vocal music, **5:**709–10
Tiboli people, gong music, **4:**922
Tikopia, **9:**854
"tint affinity" studies, **8:**20
Tonga, **9:**14, 783
    hiva kakala, **9:**783
    nose-flute, **9:***796*
    treatises on, **5:**20, 33, 34, 43
Trinidad and Tobago
    byāh ke gīt, **5:**589
    in steelband music, **2:**961
Tuamotu Islands, **9:**884
Tuareg people, *anzad* (or *imzad*) music, **1:**542,
    578–79
Tunisia
    Jewish *piyuṭim* repertoire, **6:**529–31
    ma'lūf, **6:**332, 506, 517–18
Turkey
    arabesk, **6:**256
    art music, **6:**122–26, 128
    folk music, **6:**79–81, 82, 759–62
    makam, **6:**51–52
    seyir, **6:**52
Tuvalu, triadic songs, **9:**830
Tuvan music, **6:**982, 983
Uganda, **1:**210
Uighur people, **7:**459, 460
    muqam, **6:**995–1008
Ukraine
    ladkana, **8:**809
    ritual songs, **8:**807, *808*
Uruguay
    milonga, **2:**512
    murga, **2:**518
Uttar Pradesh, women's songs, **5:**661
'Uvea, **9:**771
    fasi, **9:**809–10, 813
Uzbekistan, *katta ashula,* **6:**944
Vanuatu
    Banks Islands, **9:**700–701
    dance-songs, **9:**695
    of songs, **9:**362, 697
Vedic chant, **5:**244, *245*
    gāyatra, **5:**239
Venezuela
    Amerindian music, **2:**525
    golpe, **2:**541
    joropo, **2:**540, 541
Vietnam, **4:**17, 456, 462
    cải lương, **4:**494
    in *chèo,* **4:**490
Wales
    hymns, **8:**350
    songs, **8:**343, 344
Warao culture, shamanic songs, **2:**194–95
Wayana culture, flute music, **2:**165
West African songs, **1:**446, 451
West Futuna, **9:**862
Xia'erba songs, **7:**483
Yanomamö culture, shamanic songs, **2:**171, *173*
Yao people, **4:**550
Yap
    teempraa, **9:**730
    wavy processes in, **9:**304–6

Volume Key: **6,** Middle East; **7,** East Asia; **8,** Europe; **9,** Australia and the Pacific Islands; **10,** The World's Music.

melody (*continued*)
  Yaqui culture, **3:**437
    deer songs, **2:**589
    matachín, **2:**591
    son, **2:**591
    sonim, **2:**590
  Yekuana culture, curing songs, **2:**180
  Yemen
    al-ghinā' al-ṣan'ānī, **6:**687, *688*
    drum ensemble music, **6:**101–2
  Yoruba music, **1:**461
  Yuman songs, **3:**434
  Yuma vocal music, **2:**596
Melody Kings (musical group), **3:**1077
Melody Maker (periodical), **8:**407
Melón, **3:**799
Melop Merlier Archives at the Center for Asia
      Minor Studies (Athens), **8:**1025
Melpa people, **9:**511
  festivals of, **9:**512
  music and dance of, **9:**484–85, 516–22
  performances of, **9:**513
  songs of, **9:**514
Melrose (musical group), **8:**217
Melville, Herman, **9:**35–36, 44
Membertou (Mi'kmaq), **3:**1069
membranophones. *See* drums *headings*; mirlitons
Memehusa Company (musical group), **9:**138
Memon people, in Sri Lanka, **5:**954
"Memorial Song" (Sioux song), **3:**526
Memorial University of Newfoundland (St.
      John's), **3:**1119, 1125
"*Memorias dolorosas*" (Garcia), **3:**737
Memoria sopra le cose musicali di Sardegna
      (Oneto), **8:**632
Memory (Kopytman), **6:**1031
"Memphis Blues" (Handy), **3:**524, 644, 706
Memphis Jug Band, **3:**645
Memphis Minnie, **3:**104, 645
Men in Black (film), **3:**715
Men at Work, **9:**414
Men, Women, and Pianos (Loesser), **3:**562
Mena Moreno, Juan Manuel, **2:**765
Menander, **6:**360
Menard, Paul, **3:**1194
Menck, Ric, **3:**169
Mendaña, Alvaro de, **9:**630
Mende people, **1:**467–68
Mendelson, Gerhard, **8:**678
Mendelssohn-Bartholdy, Felix, **3:**885; **6:**1025;
      8:55, 83, 93–94, 368, 646, 653; **9:**203
Mendelssohn Quintette Club (Boston), **3:**537–38
Mendes, Gilberto, **2:**306
Mendes Pinto, Fernão, **4:**224, 248, 284
Mendez, Alfredo, **3:**787
Méndez, Juan, **2:**581
Mendi people, **9:**511
  dance of, **9:**484
  festivals of, **9:**512
  performances of, **9:**513
Mendonça, Newton, **2:**318
Mendonsa, Eugene, **10:**36
Mendoza, Amalia, **3:**740
Mendoza Cruz, Luciano, **2:**568
Mendoza de Arce, Daniel, **2:**320
Mendoza, Eliseo, **4:**863

Mendoza, Lydia, **3:**733
Mendoza, Pedro de, **2:**453
Mendoza, Vicente T., **2:**606, 623–24; **3:**767
Mendoza, Virginia R. R. de, **3:**767
Mendriq people, **4:**560, 573
Mendt, Marianne, **8:**676
Menéndez Pidal, Ramón, **8:**266
Menestins (dance ensemble), **3:**1196
Menezes, Margareth, **2:**354
Menezes, Sister Noel, **2:**442
Mengal, Aquil Khan, **5:**776
Mengen people, **9:**974
  music and dance of, **9:**620–25
  songs of, **9:**607
Mengjiang nü (*xiaodiao*), **7:**233
Mengqi bitan (Shen), **7:**123, 129, 196
Mengrai, Prince, **4:**310
Menguellat, Lounes Ait, **6:**275–76
Mennin, Peter, **3:**541
Mennonite Brethren Bible College (Winnipeg),
      3:1239
Mennonite Children's Choir (Winnipeg), **3:**1249
Mennonite Oratorio Choir, **3:**1239
Mennonites, **2:**89; **3:**528, 884
  in Belize, **2:**666–67
  hymns of, **3:**886–87
  in Manitoba, **3:**52–53, 1086, 1225, 1231,
      1249
  in Ontario, **3:**1078, 1082
  in Paraguay, **2:**457, 463
  songs of, **3:**292
Mennonite Symphony Orchestra (Winnipeg),
      3:1249
Menominee Indian nation, **3:**451, 454, 455,
      457, 477
Menotti, Gian Carlo, **3:**546
Mensa, Kwabena, **1:**356
Mensah, Atta Annan, **1:**26, 31, 44, 45
Mensah, E. T., **1:**361
Mensah, Percy James, **1:**45, 216
Mensah, Sam, **3:**1213
mento, **2:**97
  in Belize, **2:**678
  in Jamaica, **2:**899, 900, 901, 906, 908, 910,
      912
  in Nicaragua, **2:**753, 754
Menu, Kwesi, **1:**356, 357–58
Menuhin, Yehudi, **3:**986; **4:**870; **5:**564, 584;
      7:416; **8:**96
Menya people, **9:**512
Meo people. *See* Hmong people
Mer, La (Debussy), **4:**131
Mera, Juan León, **2:**427
Meraliuly, Muhit, **6:**955
Mercadante, Saverio, **8:**618
Mercado, Pedro, **4:**869
Mercer, Jeanne Aiko, **3:**336
Mercer, Mabel, **3:**863
Merchule, Giorgi, **8:**843
Mercouri, Melina, **8:**1007
Mercure, Pierre, **3:**1076, 1151
Mercury, Daniela, **2:**354
Mercury Records, **3:**352, 672
Meredith, John, **9:**142
merengue, **2:**75, 93, 95, 98, 101, 104–5
  in Africa, **1:**361, 387, 416, 424, 435

  in Barbados, **2:**819
  in Brazil, **2:**338, 353
  in Colombia, **2:**384, 410
  cuarteto and, **2:**280
  in Dominica, **2:**842
  in Dominican Republic, **1:**384; **2:**796, 849,
      856, 860, 862
  in Guatemala, **2:**734, 735
  in North America, **3:**337, 728, 731, 791, 800,
      803, 1204
  in Puerto Rico, **2:**940
  in St. Lucia, **2:**947
  in Uruguay, **2:**520
  in Virgin Islands, **2:**969, 970
*Merengue: Dominican Music and Dominican
      Identity* (Austerlitz), **3:**800
Mergen Diyanci Lama, **7:**1018–19
Merina (kingdom), **1:**782, 783, 786, 789
Merino, Ignacio, **2:**493
Merino, Luis, **2:**238, 374
Merino de Zela, Mildred, **2:**480
Meritt label, **3:**707
Merkel, Una, **9:**149
Merkù, Pavle, **8:**921
Merlier, Melpo, **8:**1025
Merlier, Octavio, **8:**1025
Meroë (kingdom), **1:**550
Merolla, Girolamo, **1:**667–68
Merollo da Sorrento, Jerom, **1:**78–80
Merriam, Alan P., **1:**31, 50, 51, 54, 55, 57, 363,
      663, 670; **3:**71, 72, 159, 236, 367,
      426, 511, 517; **5:**18; **10:**28–29, 42,
      56, 57, 77, 111, 112, 118, 129, 130,
      139
  views on ethnomusicology, **1:**63, 64, 65
Merrill-Mirsky, Carol, **10:**143
Merrill, William L., **2:**585, 587; **3:**492
Merritt, Geoff, **3:**170, 171
Merry Blackbirds, **1:**770, 771
Merry Moonshiners, **9:**78
Merrymen (calypsonian), **2:**819
Merseburgh, William, **9:**132
Mersenne, Marin, **8:**615
Mersmann, Hans, **8:**659
Merta, Vladimír, **8:**730
Meru people, **1:**599
Merupu Kallalu (film), **5:**545
Merusvami, **5:**230
Mervar, Anton, **3:**901
Mes, Florencio, **2:**668
Mesa, Eddie, **4:**884
Mescalero Apaches, **3:**371, 425, 431
Mescher-Tatar people, **8:**487
  in Finland, **8:**487
Meshakarna. *See* Kshemakarna
Meshketian people, **8:**827
  dance traditions of, **8:**836
  instruments of, **8:**840
  vocal music of, **8:**846
Meshko, Nina, **8:**777
Mesnevi. See Masnavî
Mesolithic period, **8:**36, 38
Mesopotamia, **5:**321; **6:**227, 362, 401, 413
  cheironomy in, **8:**100
Mesplé, Raymond, **9:**869
Mesrop Mashtots, **6:**723

Messakh, Obbie, **4**:108

Messar, **6**:271

Messe Katangaise (Kiwele), **1**:671

Messenjah and the Satellites, **3**:1213

Messer, Don, **3**:74, 1071, 1073, 1110, 1125, 1133, 1242, 1257

Messiaen, Olivier, **3**:1076, 1151; **6**:330; **7**:342, 736

Messiah (Handel), **1**:763; **3**:1179, 1225; **8**:17, 60, 62; **9**:131, 187, 203

Messika, Raoul Journo Ḥabība, **6**:1044

Messner, Gerald Florian, **9**:983

Messomo, Albert Noah, **1**:659

Mestizo (Valdez), **3**:749

Metallica (musical group), **3**:358

metallophones. *See also* xylophones
  gangsa, **4**:742, 767
  gangsa gantung, **4**:742
  gangsa jongkok, **4**:742, *745*
  gendèr, **10**:18, 43–44, *44*, 47, 51
    in Bali, **4**:742, 745, 746, 747, 748, 751, 752–53, 755
    in Cirebon, **4**:691, 692
    in Java, **4**:164, 637, 644, 648, 656, 665, *674*, 682
    in Surinam, **2**:507
  gendèr babok, **4**:641
  gendèr barangan, **4**:*752*
  gendèr barung, **4**:641, 643, 672–73
  gendèr calung (also *jublag*), **4**:745
  gendèr gedé, **4**:751, *752*
  gendèr jegogan, **4**:742, 745
  gendèr kantilan, **4**:742, 745
  gendèr panembung, **4**:641
  gendèr panerus, **4**:641, 643, 665, 672–73
  gendèr pemade, **4**:742, 745, 751, *752*, 767
  gendèr rawat, **4**:*748*
  giying, **4**:745
  in gong-chime ensembles, **4**:20–21
  gong kemodhong, **4**:645
  in island Southeast Asia, **4**:596–97
  Java, **4**:641
  jegogan, **4**:767
  kantilan, **4**:767
  khawng fak, **4**:305
  Oceania, **9**:374
  pengugal, **4**:734, 745
  ranat ek lek, **4**:230, 260, 271
  ranat thum lek, **4**:230, 271
  roneat, **3**:1001
  roneat dek, **4**:164–65, 183
  roneat ek, **3**:*999*, 1001
  roneat thong, **4**:165
  Rotuma, **9**:819, 823
  saron, **4**:107, 164
    Bali, **4**:744, 745, 746, 755
    Cirebon, **4**:691, 694
    Java, **4**:637, 643, 644, 646, 648, 657, 660, 685
    Sumatra, **4**:626
    Sunda, **4**:701, 703–4, 707
    Surinam, **2**:507
  saron barung, **4**:429, 641, 668, 669–71
  saron demung, **2**:507; **4**:413, 641, 643, 668, 669–71
  saron panerus, **4**:641, 645, 704

saron peking, **4**:429, 641, 668, 671, 704

saron ricik, **4**:641

saron sanga, **4**:643

saron wayang, **4**:643, 671

sarunay, **4**:*67*, 891, *892*

slenthem, **4**:641, *642*, 643, 660, 669–71

titil, **4**:691

vibraphone, **3**:794, 893; **5**:544

metallurgy, **4**:43, 58, 596, 602, 603, 643
  prehistoric, **4**:36–37, 39–40

metamorphosis and transformation
  Bolivia, **2**:283
  shamanism and, **2**:45–46
  Suyá culture, **2**:143, 144, 148
  in tropical-forest ceremonies, **2**:128
  Waiãpí culture, **2**:161
  Warao culture, **2**:193
  Yanomamö culture, **2**:170

Metaxas, Ioannis, **8**:1019, 1020

meter. *See* rhythm and meter

Metfessel, Milton, **3**:71

Methodist Error (Watson), **3**:627

Methodists, **3**:1086; **8**:353
  in Barbados, **2**:816
  black congregations, **3**:120, 626–27, 630, 632
  in Costa Rica, **2**:688
  in Estonia, **8**:491
  in Fiji, **9**:780, 781
  in Jamaica, **2**:901
  liturgy of, **3**:121
  in Luangiua, **9**:842
  in Papua New Guinea, **9**:88, 146–47, 193–94
  research on, **3**:119
  in Rotuma, **9**:818–19, 823
  in Sāmoa, **9**:206–7, 795
  in Solomon Islands, **9**:665
  South Asian, **3**:984
  in Tonga, **9**:117, 202–4, 791
  in Virgin Islands, **2**:969
  in Wales, **8**:350

Methodius, Saint, **8**:726

Métis (people), **3**:*11*, 404–11, 452, 1086, 1097, 1224
  contredanses, **3**:213
  dances of, **3**:407–10
  early accounts of, **3**:405
  fiddling traditions of, **3**:7, 332, 405–10, 458, 1063, 1087, 1091, 1224, 1277
  fusion genres, **3**:344, 1087
  in Ontario, **3**:1188, 1192
  population of, **3**:1056
  in Québec, **3**:1163
  Red River Jig, **3**:408, 409–10
  separatist movement, **3**:11, 410

"*Métisse, La*" (Riel), **3**:344

Métraux, Alfred, **2**:883; **9**:25

Metró (musical group), **8**:746

Metronome (periodical), **3**:1105

Metropolis (film), **3**:204

Metropolitan Museum of Art (New York), **9**:975

Metropolitan Opera (New York), **3**:298, 542, 629

Metropolitan Toronto Reference Library, **3**:226

Metropol Jazz Centre, **8**:427

Metternich, Klemens, Fürst von, **8**:604

"*Me vaya kappará*" (Sephardic song), **3**:1173

Mevlevî dervishes. *See* Sufism

Mevlūt (Çelebi), **6**:196, 769

Mexica culture, **2**:555–62. *See also* Aztec culture; Nahua culture
  instruments of, **2**:8, 550, 558–60
  musical genres, *son*, **2**:560–62

Mexican-Americans/Canadians, **2**:91; **3**:13, 16, 719, 848. *See also* Latino peoples
  in California, **3**:734–51
  colonial period, **3**:734–35
  community music-making, **3**:284
  conjunto music, **3**:98, 522, 723, 766, 772–78, 797, 897–88
  dances of, **3**:219, *220*
  música ranchera, **3**:722, 744, 763, 765, 766, 775, 778, 781
  music of, **3**:721–25, 732, 734–51
    1830s–1930s, **3**:735–39
    1940s–50s, **3**:739–43
    1960s to present, **3**:743–51
  in New Mexico, **3**:754–68
  pachuco culture, **3**:739, 740, 742, 749, 798
  population of, **3**:718
  in Texas, **3**:770–81

Mexican Revolution, **3**:719, 756

Mexican Revolution (musical group), **3**:780

Mexican War, **3**:9, 718, 735, 770

Mexico, **2**:600–24, 845; **3**:770
  Amerindian cultures of, **2**:549–50
  Andalusian influences in, **6**:449
  archaeomusicological studies in, **2**:7, 8–9
  art music in, **2**:112–16
  cathedral choirs in, **2**:113
  Chamulá, **2**:20
  Chiapas, **2**:610, 622, 651, 652–53, 655–58
    Maya murals, **2**:15
  Chihuahua, **2**:551, 582, 592
  children's wakes in, **2**:422
  Chilean people in, **2**:84, 90
  Colima, **2**:8, 560
    figurines of musicians, **2**:13–14, *15*
  colonial period of, **2**:23, 46–47, 603
  Costa Chica region, **2**:610
  cultural syncretism in, **2**:46
  early cities of, **2**:81
  El Norte region, **2**:613
  folklore of, **2**:19–21
  geography of, **2**:551, 575, 582, 588, 608
  Guarijío culture, **2**:551–54
  Guerrero, **2**:563, *564*, 611
  history of, **2**:23, 78, 81, 600, 601–5, 628
  Huasteca region, **2**:608
  iconographical record in, **2**:13–16
  immigrant groups of, **2**:4, 83–91
  independence period in, **2**:603–4
  influence on Filipino dance and music, **4**:842, 843, 854
  instruments of, **2**:8, 33, 36, 37, 600, 608–9, 611
  Jalisco, **2**:8, 612, 621
  Japanese people in, **2**:86
  maps of, **2**:*3*, *80*, *548*
  Maya culture, **2**:650–58
  Mayo culture, **2**:588–93
  Mennonites in, **3**:1238
  Mexica culture, **2**:555–62

Mexico (*continued*)
  Mexico City, music conservatory, **2:**114
  Michoacán culture, **2:**560–61; **3:**723–24
  Mixtec culture, **2:**563–68
  musical genres
    aires nacionales, **2:**603
    arrullo, **2:**618
    balada, **2:**623
    black satirical, **2:**603
    bolero ranchero, **2:**621
    canción romántica, **2:**619, 620
    cantos de nana, **2:**618
    children's games and songs, **2:**617–18
    chilena, **2:**610
    corrido, **2:**101, 613, 616–17, 759
    cumbia, **2:**102
    jarabe, **2:**611–12, 621
    mariachi, **2:**573, 623
    minuetes, **2:**621
    música norteña, **2:**622
    nueva canción, **2:**103
    ranchera, **2:**101, 620–21, 622
    rock, **2:**103
    son, **2:**603, 605–13, 619, 621
    sonecitos del país, **2:**603
    son guerrerense (also *son calentano*), **2:**611
    son huasteco, **2:**608
    son istmeño (also *son oaxaqueño*), **2:**610
    son jalisciense, **2:**612–13
    son jarocho, **2:**608–10, 622; **10:**80
    son michoacano, **2:**611–12
    Spanish-derived, **2:**603, 606
    valona, **2:**607–8, 611–12
  música tropical in, **3:**741, 743, 797
  music printing in, **2:**23
  music video broadcasting in, **3:**252
  native peoples of, **2:**78, 81
  Nayarít, **2:**8, 621
    figurines of musicians, **2:**13–14
  norteño music, **3:**772–73
  Oaxaca, **2:**563, 610, 622
  Otopame culture, **2:**570–74
  popular music, **2:**101
  population of, **2:**600
  pre-Encounter music in, **2:**601–3
  Puebla, **2:**563
  Purépecha culture, **2:**575–81
  research on, **2:**623–24
  saint's-day celebrations in, **2:**46
  San Luis Potosí, **2:**570
  shamanism in, **2:**45
  Sinaloa, **2:**588
  Sonora, **2:**551–54, 588; **3:**428, 435–36
  sound recording industry in, **2:**40
  Tarahumara culture, **2:**582–87
  tourism in, **2:**50
  Veracruz, **2:**555, 560, 564, 605–6, 615; **3:**797
  Yaqui culture, **2:**588–93; **3:**417
  Yucatán, **2:**613, 655–58, 666
  Yucatec culture, **2:**620
  Yuma culture, **2:**595–99
Mexis, Themos, **9:**75
Mey, Reinhard, **8:**676
Meyer, Augusto, **2:**306
Meyer, Jeffrey T., **9:**650
Meyer, Leopold de, **3:**556

Meyerbeer, Giacomo, **8:**618
Meyrowitz, David, **3:**936
Mezzoforte (musical group), **8:**407
MFÖ (musical group), **6:**249, 250, 251
MFSB (musical group), **3:**688, 689, 711
MGM Records, **3:**352
Mgur-'bum (Mi-la ras-pa), **5:**711, 712
Mhu people, **4:**550
Mi Tierra (Estefan), **3:**733
"*Mi tormento*" (García), **3:**739
Mia, Aziz, **5:**426
Miami Bar Xylophone Band, **1:**323, 661, *662*
Miami Indian nation, **3:**451
Miami Sound Machine, **3:**733, 799
Miami Vice (television show), **3:**204
Miao Jing, **7:**156
Miao people, **4:**528; **7:**6. *See also* Hmong people
  folk songs of, **7:**449
  lusheng bands of, **7:**451
  music of, **7:**485–92
  opera of, **7:**452
Miatsela (god), **8:**863
Mịch Quang, **4:**25
Michael, George, **3:**713
"Michael, Row the Boat Ashore" (spiritual),
  3:523
Michaels, Bret, **3:***97*
Michel, Emeline, **2:**891; **3:**806
Michel, George, **6:**45–46, 318
Michel, Jacques, **3:**1158
Michelsen, Ralph C., **2:**599
Michener, James, **9:**37, 45
Michigan
  Ann Arbor, ONCE group, **3:**253
  Detroit
    Arab people in, **3:**1029, 1037; **6:**279–86
    Asian communities in, **3:**948
    balalaika orchestra in, **3:**57
    Greek people in, **3:**929
    Jewish people in, **3:**935
    Motown Sound, **3:**673–75, 677, 709–10
    Polish people in, **3:**892, 893
    Puerto Rican and Mexican peoples in, **3:**719
    Romanian people in, **3:**910
    Turkish people in, **3:**1030
    urban folk music in, **3:**828
    Finnish people in, **3:**872–75
    Lanham, Tamil people in, **3:**982
    Native American groups in, **3:**451–59
    Old Regular Baptists in, **3:**124
    Swedish people in, **3:**870–72
Michna, Adam, **8:**727
Mickey and Bunny (musical duo), **3:**345, 1242
"Mickey (Pretty Mickey)" (Daniels), **3:**262
Mickey of Ulladulla, **9:***8*, 440
Micmac (Mi'kmaq) Indian nation, **3:**52, 150,
  291, 462, 1069, 1074, 1135
Micronesia, **4:**38. *See also specific countries,
  islands, and peoples*
  archives and museums, **9:**967–68
  betel use in, **9:**177
  films on, **9:**1016
  geography of, **9:**712
  German expedition to, **9:**23
  instruments of, **9:**716–17
  map of, **9:***713–14*

  music and dance of, **9:**336, *337*, 712–21, 980
  popular music in, **9:**158–61
  population of, **9:**712, 715
  research on, **9:**975
  settlement of, **9:**715
  sound recordings from, **9:**994–97
  tourism in, **9:**160
  World War II in, **9:**159–61
Micronesia Expedition, **9:**25, 729, 969
Micronesian Area Research Center, **9:**968, 994
Micronesian peoples, in Hawai'i, **9:**105
Micronesia Seminar Library, **9:**968
Middle Ages, **8:**38
  art music in, **8:**68, 69–73, 197
  Basque region, **8:**316
  Brittany, **8:**560–61
  Bulgaria, **8:**890, 904
  Celtic music's possible origins in, **8:**321
  court music and poetry of, **8:**146
  Czech Republic, **8:**726
  epic and heroic songs, **8:**129
  Europe
    cheironomy in, **5:**32
    melodic color theories, **5:**64
  Faroe Islands, **8:**470
  Finland, **8:**481
  France, **8:**539–40, 549
  genres surviving from, **8:**127, 131, 134
  Georgia, **8:**842
  Germany, **8:**650–52
  Hungary, **8:**736, 740
  Iceland, **8:**405
  India, **5:**17, 76–77
    musical life of, **5:**35–36
  Ireland, **8:**378, 383–84, 388, 393
  Italy, **8:**617
  Jewish culture in, **8:**248, 251, 259, 261, 264,
    265
  Low Countries, **8:**518
  musical fusions and hybrids in, **8:**227
  music theory in, **8:**48, 49
  Poland, **8:**710
  recomposition and adaptation in, **8:**54
  Romania, **8:**881
  Scotland, **8:**365, 366
  secular music in, **8:**72–73
  Slovakia, **8:**726
  Spain, **8:**600
  Sweden, **8:**439–40, 443–44
  Wales, **8:**347
  women in, **8:**198–99
Middle East. *See also specific countries and regions*
  centrality of voice in, **6:**5–7
  cultural diversity in, **6:**12–13
  cultural links with European Muslims, **8:**12
  distinctive musical features, **6:**7–9
  drone in, **6:**10
  ethnomusicological research in, **10:**55–65
  improvisation in, **6:**5–7, 9
  influence on European instruments, **8:**168, 170
  influence on European music, **8:**20
  influence on Macedonian music, **8:**200–201
  instruments and ensembles in, **6:**3, 5
  map of, **6:***4*
  religions of, **6:**3
  Sephardic Jews in, **8:**248

Middle Eastern-Americans/Canadians, **3:**12, 530, 949, 1028–38, 1057, 1078, 1082, 1084, 1218–20, 1245–46. *See also* Armenian people; Egyptian people; Iranian people; Lebanese people; Syrian people; Turkish people
Midnight Oil, **9:**414
Midwest. *See also* specific states
   Armenian people in, **3:**1030
   blues in, **3:**639
   choral groups, **3:**283
   country music in, **3:**76
   Czech people in, **3:**897, 898–99
   German people in, **3:**884, 888–89
   Scandinavian people in, **3:**528, 866–80
   wind band movement, **3:**277
miedo llegó a Jalisco, El (film), **3:**740
Mielnikaŭ, Andrej, **8:**801
Miensk Philharmonic, **8:**801
"*Mientras tú duermes*" (Garcia), **3:**737
Miércoles, Los (periodical), **4:**858
Mierczyński, Stanisław, **8:**712
Mighty Chalkdust (calypsonian), **2:**96
Mighty Dragon (calypsonian), **2:**819
Mighty Gabby (calypsonian), **2:**819, 820
Mighty Jerry (Barbadian minstrel), **2:**819
"Mighty Lak' a Rose" (Stanton and Nevin), **3:**549
Mighty Romeo (calypsonian), **2:**819
Mighty Sparrow (Francisco Slinger; calypsonian), **2:**93, 96, 691, 800, 866–67, 963
Mighty Three Music, **3:**711
migration (African)
   diffusion and, **1:**296–97, 298, 301
   East Africa, **1:**635; **10:**120
   Ghana, rural to urban, **1:**390–92; **10:**31–36
   influence on popular music, **1:**436
   Kpelle people, **1:**466
   LoDagaa people, **1:**456
   Madagascar, **1:**781
   Malinke people, **1:**465
   Ngoni people, **1:**320–21
   North Africa, **1:**533, 546
   South Africa, **1:**705
   southern Africa, **1:**429, 700, 717
   West Africa, **1:**456
Migrations and Mutations of the Music in East and West (Gerson-Kiwi), **6:**1059
Miguel, Luis, **2:**623; **3:**746, 751
Migung (Hwang), **7:**956, 957
Mihasi Mitiya, **7:**746
Mihók, Mihály, **8:**744
Mijares, José, **4:**866
Mijikenda people, **1:**624
Mikalayi, Nicolas Kasanda Wa, **1:**362–63
Mikasuki Indian nation, **3:**466
Mike Di Amore Jazz Quartet, **9:**160
Mīkhā'īl Mushāqa, **6:**39–40, 43, 369
Mikhman (Ömärjan), **7:**469
Miki Minoru, **10:**12, 13
Miki Rohû, **7:**732
Mikise Yuriko, **7:**695
Miklouho-Maclay, Nikolai Nikolayevich, **9:**22–23, 570, 691
Mikroutsikos, Thanos, **8:**1021
Mikuli, Karol, **6:**725

Miladinov brothers, **8:**906
Miladinov, Naum, **8:**980
Milanés, Pablo, **2:**103
Mi-la ras-pa, **5:**711, 712
Milburn, Amos, **3:**669, 708
Milder, Joakim, **8:**446
Miles in Berlin (Davis), **3:**662
Miles, Elizabeth, **3:**271
Miles, Lizzie, **3:**644
Milestones (musical group), **8:**677
Miley, Bubber, **3:**654
Milhaud, Darius, **8:**161, 252
milhūn. See malhūn
Milladoiro (musical group), **8:**226
Millán, Saúl, **2:**573
Miller, Flournoy, **3:**619
Miller, Frankie, **8:**369
Miller, Glenn, **3:**550, 742; **10:**111
Miller, Harry, **9:**938
Miller, Mark, **3:**1110
Miller, Michael, **3:**1072
Miller, Neville, **3:**263
Miller, Terry E., **3:**828, 953; **4:**25, 26, 316
Millie, Jocelyn, y los Vecinos, **3:**731
Millima iyagi hara (North Korean opera), **7:**962
Millinder, Lucky, **3:**668
Million Dollar Theater (Los Angeles), **3:**740
Mills Brothers (musical group), **3:**670, 674, 708
Mills College (Oakland), **3:**953
Mills, Florence, **3:**619
Mills, Kerry, **3:**548
Mills, Stephanie, **3:**713
Milner, George B., **9:**992
Milojević, Miloje, **8:**961
Milošević, Vlado, **8:**969, 970
Miloš Obrenović, Prince, **8:**940, 947–48
Miloti, Luçije, **8:**999
Milton, Roy, **3:**669, 742
Milva, **8:**209
Milwaukee Ballet Company, **3:**498
Mimasi, **7:**723, 981
Mimes (musical group), **8:**679
Min Huifen, **7:**177
Min Youngch'i, **7:**970
Mina, **8:**619
Minagawa Tatsuo, **7:**595
Minahasan people, **4:**804, 810, 812
Minakshi (deity), **5:**228, 269
Mīnākṣī mēmudam (Diksitar), **5:**145–47
Minamoto no Hiromasa, **7:**587, 588
Minangkabau people, **4:**608–13
   dabus performance, **4:**414
   heart of rice, **4:**51
   in Malaysia, **4:**413, 422, 423, 424
Minang people, in Sunda, **4:**700
Mīna people, **5:**292, 639, 648
   bhopā priests, **5:**288
Mindanao. *See* Philippines; *specific peoples*
Mindanao State University, **4:**873
Mindon, king of Burma, **4:**366
Miner, Allyn, **5:**51, 192, 307, 337
Minerve, La (newspaper), **3:**1068
Minezaki *kôtô,* **7:**693
Ming dynasty, **7:**27
   Beijing as capital, **7:**32
   Buddhism in, **7:**312

   centralization in, **7:**26
   chuanqi in, **7:**276, 392–93
   chuida music in, **7:**195, 196
   Confucianism in, **7:**336–37
   Daoism in, **7:**319, 321
   erhu in, **7:**176
   literature in, **7:**246
   musical institutions in, **7:**392
   music in, **7:**89, 131, 132, 724–25
   opera in, **7:**289, 321–22
   patronage of Tibetan Buddhism, **7:**32–33
   pipa in, **7:**168, 169
   qupai melodies from, **7:**202
   tanci performances in, **7:**261
   theater in, **7:**291
   women performers in, **7:**407
Ming Hua Yuan, **7:**426–27
Ming Yi, **7:**125
Mingat people, **7:**1004–20
Mingo Saldívar y Sus Tremendos Cuatro Espadas, **3:**776
Mingus, Charles, **3:**661–62
Mini All Stars, **2:**891
Mini Records, **2:**891; **3:**804
minimalist music, **3:**175–77, 254, 541, 953
Minjian gequ gailan (Song), **7:**156
Minjok Akki Kaeryang Saŏpkwa (institute), **7:**992
Minjok Ŭmakhak (periodical), **7:**855
Min kunūzinā al-muwashshaḥāt al-andalusiyya (Rajā'ī), **6:**567
Minkus, Léon, **5:**562
Minmini, **5:**422
Minnah, Kobina, **10:**32, 34
Minnan people
   ensemble music of, **7:**238, 239, 242, 396
   modes of, **7:**235
   musical aesthetics of, **7:**240
Minneapolis Symphony Orchestra, **3:**537
Minnesota
   Czech people in, **3:**898
   Finnish people in, **3:**872–75
   Hmong people in, **3:**1003–5
   Mennonites in, **3:**1237
   Minneapolis
      Estonian people in, **3:**878
      funk in, **3:**685
      indie music in, **3:**171
      Russian people in, **3:**915
   Native American groups in, **3:**440, 451–59
   New Ulm, polka bands in, **3:**890, 898
   Norwegian people in, **3:**866–70
   Palo, Finnish-American community, **3:**823
   Slovenian people in, **3:**901
   Swedish people in, **3:**870–72
Minnis, Eddie, **2:**808
Minshall, Peter, **2:**966
al-Minshāwī, Shaykh Muḥammad Siddīq, **6:**161
"Minstrel's Return'd from the War" (Hewitt), **3:**183
Minstrelsy (Scott), **8:**370
Mintil people, **4:**560
Minton's Playhouse (Harlem), **3:**658
Minturn, Leigh, **5:**674
Mintz, Leo, **3:**350

minuet, **8:**168, 170
  in Canada, **3:**1164, 1188
  in Colombia, **2:**396
  in Denmark, **8:**454, 457
  in Low Countries, **8:**524
  in Spain, **8:**594
Minzu yinyue gailun, **7:**140, 155–56
Mira, Dario Marisičo, **8:**922–23
Mirabai, **5:**249, 591, 630, 643
Mirabdolbaghi, Zia, **6:**75
Mirabet, Mel, **3:**1197
Miracles (musical group), **3:**674, 709
Miranda, Agapito de, **5:**741
Miranda, Carmen, **2:**316
Miranda, Marlui, **2:**124, 135
Mīrāsī group, **5:**7, 123, 506. *See also* Manganihār
    caste
  gharānā of, **5:**379
  origins of, **5:**763–64
  in Punjab, **5:**273, *283,* 476, 763–66, 771
  in Rajasthan, **5:**345, 476, 641, 644–45
  relation to Bhirāīn group, **5:**766–69
  women, **5:**409–10
Mireku, **1:**356
Miri people
  dalūka songs, **1:**606
  music of, **1:**561–63
  sorek dance, **1:**601
Mirkelam, **6:**252
mirlitons
  Central Africa, **1:**673
  cobweb, **2:**570, 573
  Gbaya people, **1:**263–64
  Guatemala, **2:**725, 729
  kazoos, **1:**426; **3:**638; **8:**169, 919
    engwara, **1:**604
    kili, **4:**797
    klisang, **2:**660–61, 662
  Nicaragua, **2:***756*
  Senufo people, **1:**454
  turu-turu, **2:**660
  West Africa, **1:**445
  Yoruba people, **1:**460
  zumbador, **2:**564
Mīrs, **5:**402–3
Miryang arirang (Korean folk song), **7:**883
Mirza (romance), **5:**771–72
Mīrzā 'Abdollāh, **6:**130, 854, 859, 865–66
Mirza Khan, **5:**46, 48
Mirza, Traian, **8:**886
Misa (Cayabyab), **4:**885
Misa de Cataluña, **3:**735
Misa Pastorela (Mata), **4:**862
Misa Solemne (Adonay), **4:**862
Misa Vizcaina, **3:**735
Mischler, Craig, **3:**392
Miseducation of Lauryn Hill (Hill), **3:**697
Miserere, **8:**628
al-Misfir, Murbarak, **6:***665*
Mishar Tatars, **8:**772
Mishler, Craig, **3:**405, 1277
Mishra, Shridhar, **5:**675
Misiani, D. O., **1:**427
Miskitu culture
  history of, **2:**659–60
  in Honduras, **2:**659–64, 740

  instruments of, **2:**660–61
  in Jamaica, **2:**902
  in Nicaragua, **2:**747, 749, 750, 765
  population of, **2:**659
Miso, Pirro, **8:**1003
Misool Islands (Irian Jaya), **9:**581
Misora Hibari, **7:**745, 751
Misra, Daya Shankar, **5:**207
Misra, Gopal Shankar, **5:**207
Misra, Lalmani, **5:**207, 465
Missa Baba Yetu (Mbunga), **1:**643–44
Missa Luba, **1:**217
Missa Solemnis (Beethoven), **4:**862
Miss Godey's Lady's Book, **3:**562
"Miss Lucy Long" (Whitlock), **3:**185, 186
Miss Saigon (Schonberg/Boublil), **3:**1026; **4:**131
"Miss You" (Rolling Stones), **3:**689
missionaries. *See* Christianity; *specific*
    denominations and orders
Missionary Baptists, **3:**120–21, 125–26
Mississippi
  blues in, **3:**639
  folk song collecting in, **3:**294
  Native American groups in, **3:**466
Mississippi Sheiks (musical group), **3:**645
Mississippian culture, **3:**466–67, 468
Missoun, Maâmar, **6:**269
Missouri
  Kansas City, jazz in, **3:**550
  Native American groups in, **3:**440, 466
  St. Louis
    African-American composers in, **3:**605
    balalaika orchestra in, **3:**57
    German people in, **3:**528
    public school music education, **3:**275
Missouri Indian nation, **3:**440
Missud, Jean, **3:**566
"Mister Tambourine Man" (Byrds), **3:**552
Mitani Yôko, **7:**593
Mitchell, Uncle Harry Kunihi, **9:***122,* 220
Mitchell, Joni, **3:**14, 314, 1081, 1091
Mitchell, Ken, **3:**199
Mitchell Library (Sydney), **9:**959
Mitchell, Roscoe, **3:**664
Mitchell, William, **9:**990
Mithila, **5:**677–79
  geography of, **5:**677
  map of, **5:***658*
  ritual songs of, **5:**678–79
  women's song genres, **5:**677–78
Mitiaro (Cook Islands), **9:**974
Mitko, Thimi, **8:**1003
Mitoma, Judy, **3:**1020; **9:**976
Mitra, Jaganmay, **5:**855
Mitra, Navagopal, **5:**848–49
Mitra, Premendra, **5:**855
Mitra, Sucitra, **5:**254
Mitra, Syamal, **5:**857
Mitri, Amer, **3:**1220
Mitropoulos, Dimitri, **3:**610; **8:**1008
Mitsou, **3:**74
Mitsui, José, **10:**101
Mitsui Toru, **7:**595
Mitterrand, François, **2:**879; **8:**238
Mit-todŭri (*tangak* piece), **7:**867
Mitukuri Syûkiti, **7:**732

Mituzaki *kengyô,* **7:**698
Miu people, **9:**617
Miura Tamaki, **7:**733
Miville-Deschênes, Monique, **3:**1156
Miwok Indian nation, **3:**415
Mixco, Mauricio, **2:**599
Mixed Relations (musical group), **9:**60, 446
Mixtec culture, **2:**549, 563–68
  festivals and celebrations of, **2:**566–67
  history of, **2:**563–64
  immigrants to California and Mexico City,
    2:567–68
  instruments of, **2:**15, 565
  musical genres
    Afro-mestizo, **2:**567
    Euro-mestizo, **2:**567
    flor de nube, **2:**566
    flores, **2:**566
    katikubi, **2:**567
    tarantela, **2:**567
  research on, **2:**568
Miyagi Mitio, **7:**50, 575, 698–99, 713, 721,
    778–79
Miyako dori (*nagauta* piece), **7:**672
Miyakozi Sonohati, **7:**682
Miyasita Syûretu I, **7:**779
Miyazono Ranpôken, **7:**682
Miykodayu Ittyu, **7:**681
Miykozo Bungo, **7:**681
Mi-zimrat ḳedem (Seroussi), **6:**1066
Mizoram, **5:**504–5
Mizraḥi, Asher, **6:**1039, 1044
Mizraḥ u-Ma'arav be-Musiḳah (Cohen), **6:**1066
Mizu no hentai (Miyagi), **7:**779
Mkhar-mon community, **5:**712
Mkwawa, Pancras, **1:**640
Mlangeni, Babsi, **1:**778
Mlle. Modiste (Herbert), **3:**193, 544
Mnayn jibt il-hinna? (*tarawid*), **6:**581
Mncunu, Sipho, **1:**779–80
Mo Hŭnggap, **7:**898, 904, 986
Mo Yan, **7:**259
Moa (Rennellese evangelist), **9:**852
Moana and the Moahunters (musical group),
    9:168, 938
Moana Hotel Orchestra, **9:**163
Moana of the South Seas (film), **9:**42, 46
"Moanin'" (Blakey), **3:**660
Mo'azzez, Salar, **6:**867
Moberg, Carl-Allan, **8:**447
Moccasin Time (radio show), **3:**444
Moche (Mochica) culture, **2:**467
  archaeomusicological studies of, **2:**7
  iconographical record of, **2:**12
  instruments of, **2:**11, 16, *18,* 20, 207; **10:**100
Mock Doctor (ballad opera), **3:**180
Mockler-Ferryman, Captain, **1:**92
Mocoví culture, **2:**251
Moctezuma, emperor of the Aztecs, **2:**600, 601
Modal: La Revue des musiques traditionnelles
    (periodical), **8:**554
modal organization. *See also* ī*qā'; makam;*
    maqām; muğam; muqam; raga; rhythm
    and meter; scales and intervals; tuning
    and temperament
  African composed music, **1:**224

Andalusian music, **1:**535; **6:**20, 365, 367, 446–47, 450, 453–54
Arabian peninsula, **6:**657
   ṣawt genre, **6:**652
Arab music, **6:**16–17, 33–44, 183–84, 365–67, 502–3, 541–42
Armenia, *ashugh* songs, **6:**735
Azerbaijani music, **6:**926–27
Bali
   in *gambuh*, **4:**750
   patutan, **4:**735
   saih gendèr wayang, **4:**735–37, 751
   saih pitu, **4:**735–37, 755
Burma, **4:**15, 67, 381, 387–88, 390–95
Cambodia, **4:**67
China, **7:**120–22, 128, 137
   Cantonese music, **7:**218–19
   diaoshi, **7:**234–35, 347–48
   mood and, **7:**241
   nanguan music, **7:**208
   northern ensemble music, **7:**202, 203
   Peking opera melodies, **7:**282
   xianshiyue, **7:**213, 214–16
Cirebon, *patut*, **4:**692–94
Egyptian music, **6:**46, 365
   in Filipino dance forms, **4:**854
Greek modes, **8:**48, 69; **9:**73–75
Hui people, **7:**462
India (*See* raga)
Iran
   māye, **6:**59–75, 871–74
   radif, **6:**129–42, 854, 862, 865–74
Iraq, *maqām*, **6:**312, 551–52
Japan, theories, **7:**565–70
Java, *pathet*, **4:**15, 67–68, 387, 636, 637–38, 651–52, 653, 654, 657–59; **6:**47
Jewish music, **6:**1057–58, 1073
Khmer people, **4:**178–79
Korea, **7:**845, 847–51
   Cheju folk songs, **7:**883
   kagok, **7:**920, 921, 923
   kasa, **7:**928
   p'ansori, **7:**898, 902–5
   sijo, **7:**926
   sinawi, **7:**891, 914
Laos, *lai*, **4:**15, 67, 347, 348
Lombok, **4:**769
Maronite church music, **6:**212
Mashriq region, **6:**33–44
Middle East, **6:**8–9, 11
nūba, **6:**456, 461, 463
Southeast Asia, **4:**127
Syrian Orthodox music, **6:**228–29
Thailand, **4:**263–64
   lai, **4:**15, 67, 323–24
Tunisia, *ma'lūf*, **6:**332, 501, 517–18
Turkey
   folk music, **6:**82–85, 247
   makam, **6:**47–58, 771, 772
   Qur'anic recitation, **6:**769
Uighur music, **6:**989–90, 995–1008; **7:**456, 459–60
Vietnam, **4:**17, 454–59, 463–64, 482, 494, 496, 505–6
   điệu, **4:**15, 67, 455, 483, 491–92
Yemen, *al-ghinā' al-ṣan'ānī*, **6:**687

Modèle d'Haïti, **2:***887*
Modern Dance Association of Korea, **7:**69
Modern Jazz Club (Sophiatown), **1:***774*
Modern Jazz Quartet, **3:**335, 660
Modern Records, **3:**350, 708
modinha, **2:**107, 304, 305–6, 313, 350
   in Italy, **8:**619
   in Portugal, **8:**583
Modir, Hafez, **6:**69
Modirzadeh, Hafez, **3:**336–37
Modoc Indian nation, **3:**415
Modrekili, Mikael, **8:**843
Modugno, Domenico, **8:**209, 619
Modus (musical group), **8:**731
Moe, Tau, **9:**390
Moeata, **9:**270
Moedano, Gabriel, **2:**573
Moehau, Kuini, **9:**949
Moeketsi, Kippie "Morolong," **1:***771*, 774
Moeran, E. J., **8:**333
Moerane, Michael, **1:**764
Moerenhout, J. A., **9:**17
Moffat, Riley, **9:**972
Moffatt, Michael, **5:**911
Moftah, Ragheb, **6:**20, 223
Moğollar, **6:**249, 250
Mogollon culture, **3:**429
Mogulesco, Sigmund, **3:**936
Mohamad, Goenawan, **3:**1017
Mohamed, Ben, **6:**274–75
Mohammad "Dil," Munshi, **5:**487
Mohammad, Khyal, **5:**791
Mohammad Omar, **5:**806–7, *807*
Mohammad, Taj, **5:**790
Moḥammadī, Ṣohrab, **6:***828*
Mohan, Anuradha, **5:**544
Mohan, Prithvi, **3:***982*
Mohan, Shashi, **5:**466
Mohapeloa, Joshua, **1:**764, 769
Mohave Indian nation, **2:**598; **3:**417, 418, 422, 428, 433
Mohawk Indian nation, **3:**462, 1073, 1074, 1078
Mohd. Taib Osman, **4:**29
Mohe doule (Li), **7:**455
Mohenjo Daro civilization, **5:**14, 298, 319–20, 374
Mohini (deity), **5:**512
Moholo, Louis, **1:**774
Mohori (Ung), **4:**131
Mohyeddin, Zia, **5:**487
Moi people, **9:**582
Moinba (Monba) people, **7:**471, 481–82
Moinuddin, Khwaja, **5:**487
Moiseyev, Igor, **8:**151, 777
Moist (musical group), **3:**1097
Mokats Mirza (epic), **6:**728
Mokgaleng, Pinoccio, **1:***771*
Moko nation, **2:**869
Mokranjac, Stevan, **8:**954
Moksha Mordvinians, **8:**772
Mokuru people, **9:**983
Molachs, **9:**154
Moldavia, **8:**868. *See also* Romania

Moldes, Rhyna, **2:**13
Molière, **5:**491
Moli hua (xiaodiao), **7:**233
Molina, Antonio J., **4:**123, 865, 872, 873
Molina, Exequiel "Lito," **4:**884
Molina, José, **2:**592
Molina, Juan, **4:**869
Molina Orchestra, **4:**859
Molina, Ramón P., **2:**736
Molina, Titay, **4:**856
Molinare, Nicanor, **2:**370
Molla-Cuma, Aşiq, **6:**929
Mollanepes, **6:**970
Molokans, **3:**915
Moloney, Colette, **8:**394
Moloney, Mick, **8:**394
Moloney, Paddy, **8:**392
Moluccas. *See* Maluku
Moluche culture, **2:**232
Moment Records, **5:**528
Momizi gari (Kanze), **7:**630, 632
Momiziyama Gakuso (institute), **7:**757
Mon community, **5:**712–13, 794–95
Mon people, **4:**153, 382, 399, 529, 537
   in Burma, **4:**363
   piphat ensembles of, **4:**242
Mona, Eugène, **2:**916, 920
Monache Indian nation, **3:**416
Monaco, **8:**12
Monash University, **4:**603
Monberg, Torben, **9:**853
Moncada, José María, **2:**759
Moncrieff, Gladys, **9:**149
Monday Group, **8:**445
Mondo Trasho (periodical), **6:**249
Mondragón, Roberto, **3:**764
"Money" (Walker), **3:***674*
"Money Honey" (Drifters), **3:**671
Mong people, **4:**550
Monganga, Kaïda, **1:**683–85, 687
Mong Dong (Qu), **7:**351
Monge, María Eugenia, **2:**704
Monggŭmp'o t'aryŏng (Korean folk song), **7:**882, 882–83
Mongol people
   dance of, **7:**519–20, 1014–15
   histories and identities of, **7:**1003–6
   höömii singing, **7:**449, 1005, 1009–10
   instruments of, **7:**114, 1010–14
   invasion of Central Asia, **6:**965–66, 967
   invasion of Koryŏ kingdom, **7:**27
   invasion of Uighur territory, **6:**995
   invasion of West Asia, **6:**743
   matouqin playing, **7:**176
   musical ensembles of, **7:**451
   narratives of, **7:**451–52
   popular music of, **7:**444
   religious music of, **7:**1015–19
   rule over China, **7:**29, 30, 31, 89, 511
   shamanism of, **7:**1003, 1015–16
   vocal music of, **7:**1006–10
Mongolia, **7:**1003–20. *See also* Mongol people
   Buddhism in, **5:**12
   cultural exchanges in, **7:**49–51
   cultural preservation in, **7:**47
   geography and climate of, **7:**9, 11

Mongolia (*continued*)
  Khitan empire in, **7:**31
  languages of, **7:**18
  nomadic peoples of, **7:**13–14, 23
  overtone singing in, **6:**193
  popular music in, **7:**1014–15
  Russian and Chinese influences in, **7:**50
Mongolian empire, **7:**1004
Mongosso, Justin, **1:**694
Moni people, **9:**583–84
Monias, Ernest, **3:**1063, 1087
Moniuszko, Stanisław, **8:**710
"Monkey Woman [Monkey Man] Blues"
    (Yancey), **3:**105–6
Mon-Khmer peoples, **4:**215, 344–45, 529,
    560
  in Cambodia, **4:**157
  in Laos, **4:**336
  in Vietnam, **4:**531, 533
Monk, Meredith, **3:**335
Monk, Thelonious, **3:**335, 658, 659–60, 664
Monkhouse, Jonathan, **9:**9–10
Monks and Magic (Terwiel), **4:**287
Mono Island (Solomon Islands), **9:**655
monochords, **1:**255, 257, 261; **4:**59
  dàn bầu (also *dàn độc huyền*), **4:**59, 471
  khse muoy, **4:**18, 169, 194, 196
  kopil, **4:**590
  North America, **3:**638
  Oceania, **9:**498
  phin hai, **4:**317–18, 320
  phin nam tao, **4:**66, 311, 315
  say diev, **4:**169, 205
  Vietnam, **4:**466–67
Mononoke hime (animated film), **7:**751
monophony. *See also* chant; narratives; recitation;
    texture; vocal music
  Albania, **8:**994
  Amish church music, **3:**887
  Anuta, **9:**306–7
  Arab music, **6:**166, 167
  Arctic songs, **3:**377
  Armenian music, **6:**727, 737
  Belarus, **8:**794–95, 796
  Bosnia-Hercegovina, **8:**964–65
  Brazil, in Candomblé music, **2:**342
  China
      Buddhist chant, **7:**329
      northwestern musics, **7:**456
  Estonia, **8:**492
  Europe, Northern, **8:**399
  Europe, Western, **8:**517
  France, **8:**539
  Greece, **8:**1008
  Greece, ancient, **8:**1022
  Hungary, **8:**737, 739
  Irian Jaya, Berik and Sobei songs, **9:**585
  Japan, *syômyô*, **7:**615
  Korea, *pŏmp'ae*, **7:**872
  Low Countries, **8:**519–20, 523
  Māori songs, **9:**933
  Maronite church music, **6:**212
  medieval songs, **8:**72
  Montenegro, **8:**958
  Native American songs, **3:**6, 526
  Northwest Coast songs, **3:**401

Papua New Guinea
  Bali-Vitu islands, **9:**608
  Iatmul people, **9:**258
  Kaulong people, **9:**619
  Komba music, **9:**572
  Titan *ndrilang* dirges, **9:**601
Plains Indian songs, **3:**445
Polynesian outliers, **9:**836
Punjab, **5:**654
Romania, **8:**879
Russia, **8:**779
Serbia, **8:**953
Spain, **8:**589, 593
Suyá unison songs, **2:**146
Sweden, **8:**436
Taiwan, Aboriginal peoples, **7:**523–24
Ukraine, **8:**809
Uttar Pradesh, **5:**660
Monophysite doctrine, **6:**207
Monpa people, **5:**504
"Mon pays" (Vigneault), **3:**1156
"*Mon pays*" (Vigneault), **3:**1059
Monroe, Bill, **3:**48, 77, *77*, 158–59, *159*, 160,
    161–63, 167–68, 520
Monroe, James, **3:***159*, 305
Monroe, James T., **6:**24
Monroe's Uptown House (Harlem), **3:**658
Monserrat, Philip, **4:**885
Monson, Ingrid, **3:**513, 587
Montagnais Indian nation, **3:**383, 1069, 1074
Montague, Paul, **9:**992
Montagu, Lady Mary Wortley, **6:**21, 107
Montaigne, Michel de, **8:**17
Montana
  Japanese people in, **3:**969
  Native American groups in, **3:**440
Montana, Patsy, **3:**79
Montand, Yves, **8:**209
Montañés, Washington, **2:***513–14*
Montañez, Victor, **3:**799
Montcalm, Térez, **3:**1161
Monteiro, Alcymar, **2:**333
Montelibano, Miguela, **4:**866
Montenegrin people, in Kosovo, **8:**951
Montenegro, **8:**940, 957–61
  Albanian people in, **8:**986, 994–99, *995*
  dance traditions of, **8:**958
  geography of, **8:**957
  instruments, **8:**959–60
  map of, **8:***866*
  musical regions of, **8:**957
  population of, **8:**957
  religious music in, **8:**960
  research on music of, **8:**961
  rural folk music, **8:**957–59
  Sandžak region, vocal music, **8:**959, *960*
  state folk ensembles in, **8:**959
  urban folk music of, **8:**950, 959
Monteros, Raimundo M., **2:**431
Montes de Oca J., Ignacio, **2:**624
Monteverdi, Claudio, **6:**1031; **8:**60, 77, 79, 199
Montez, Bobby, **3:**743
Montez, Chris, **3:**751
Montgomery, Little Brother, **3:**105
Montgomery, Lokalia, **9:***929*
Montgomery, Lucy Maud, **3:**199

Montgomery, Wes, **1:**777
Montiel, Sarita, **3:**741
Montjarret, Polig, **8:**321
Montoya, Carlos, **3:**851
Montoya, Edwin, **2:**214
Montoya, Ernesto, **3:**763
Montoya, Luís, **2:**214
Montoya, Rodrigo, **2:**214
Montoya, Vicente, **3:**763
Montréal Black Community Youth Choir, **3:**73,
    1169
Montréal Jazz Big Band, **3:**1077
Montréal Jazz Workshop, **3:**1077
Montréal Jubilation Gospel Choir, **3:**73, 1077,
    1169
Montréal Philharmonic Society, **3:**1149
Montréal Symphony Orchestra, **3:**1149, 1150
Montreuil, Suzanne, **3:**1280
Montri Tramote, **4:**26, 125, 224, 278
Montserrat, **2:**789, 922–26
  celebrations, **2:**825–26
  geography of, **2:**922
  immigrants to Dominica, **2:**840
  jumbie, **2:**924–25
  musical contexts and genres, **2:**923–24
  population of, **2:**922
  soca in, **2:**96
Monumbo people, **9:**983
Monumenta Musicae Sveciae, **8:**447
Monument National (Montréal), **3:**33, 146,
    1166
Monyeh manuscript, **4:**756, 775
Mo O-chu, **7:**294
"Mood Indigo" (Ellington), **3:**654
Moody Blues (musical group), **8:**215
Moody, Clyde, **3:**164
Moody, Dwight, **3:**10, 534; **9:**919
Moog, Robert, **3:**254
"Moon of Manukoora," **9:**45
Moon, Peter, **9:**167, 1008
Moon, Tom, **3:**677
Mooney, Gordon, **8:**366
Mooney, James, **3:**31, 444, 470
Moonglows (musical group), **3:**352, 671
Moonstrucks (musical group), **4:**884
Mo'orea (Society Islands), **9:**867
Moore, Christy, **8:**392, *392*
Moore, Douglas, **3:**546
Moore, Hamish, **8:**366
Moore, Johnny, **3:**669
Moore, John Weeks, **3:**27
Moore, Lynette M., **4:**603
Moore, Mavor, **3:**198–99, 1061
Moore, Mrs. (folk singer), **3:***834*
Moore, Pryor, **3:**740
Moore, Thomas, **3:**182, 187, 520, 839,
    1163–64; **9:**77
Moore, Undine Smith, **3:**629
Moore, Victor, **9:**149
Moore, Wild Bill, **3:**669
Moors
  in Spain, **8:**588, 600
  in Sri Lanka, **5:**108, 954
Mooser, Ulrich, **8:**697
Mopán Maya, **2:**666, 667
Moquah Slovak Dance Group, **3:**901

Mora, Henry, **3:**799
Moraes, Vinícius de, **2:**317, 318
Moraid people, **9:**582
Morais, Megan Jones, **9:**314, 317
Morales, Bibiano, **4:**859, 866
Morales, Cristobal, **2:**735
Morales, Ignacio, **4:**866
Morales, Issi, **3:**741
Morales, José Alejandro, **2:**387–88, 395
Morales, Juan de Dios, **4:**866
Morales, Melesio, **2:**604
Morales Pino, Pedro, **2:**383, 387, 393, 394
Morante, José, **3:**522
Moras, Lorenzo, **2:**736
Moravanka (dance ensemble), **3:**1197–98
Moravian Brethren, **8:**495–98, 726
Moravians, **3:**884, 887
    in Barbados, **2:**816
    in Central America, **2:**660, 661, 662
    hymns of, **3:**10, 528
    in Jamaica, **2:**901
    missionaries, **3:**380, 1069, 1118, 1275
        in South Asia, **5:**715
    in Nicaragua, **2:**753–54
Mordasova, Maria, **8:**779
Mordisco (periodical), **2:**267
Mordva-Karatai, **8:**772
Mordvinian people, **8:**475, 488, 772
    instruments, **8:**774
    vocal music, **8:**757, 773
Moré, Benny, **3:**743, 792, 794, 798
"More Bounce to the Ounce," **3:**685
Moré culture, **2:**285, 289, 291, 293
Morel de Santa Cruz, **2:**748
Morel, François, **3:**1151
Morena (Afro-Peruvian group), **2:**501
Moreno Andrade, Segundo Luis, **2:**419, 431
Moreno, Rita, **3:**751
Moreno Rivas, Yolanda, **2:**624
Moreno Torroba, Federico, **3:**851
Morera, Enric, **6:**449
Moresby, John, **9:**506
Morey, Carl, **3:**1066, 1079
Morgan Brothers' Syncopated Jazz Band, **3:**1091
Morgan, Justin, **3:**44
Morgan, Lewis Henry, **3:**465; **7:**441
Morgan, Russ, **3:**743
Morganfield, McKinley (Muddy Waters), **3:**12, 552, 647, 709
Möricke, Eduard, **8:**646
Morin, Léo-Pol, **3:**1076, 1147, 1150
Morin, Paul, **3:**1147
Moriscos, **6:**456
Morissette, Alanis, **3:**251, 266, 315, 1081
Morlás Gutiérrez, Alberto, **2:**431
Morley, Thomas, puzzle canon, **8:**98
Mormons, **9:**117
    in Alberta, **3:**1086, 1237
    in Aotearoa, **9:**935, 936
    in Cook Islands, **9:**898
    folk music of, **3:**433
    in Hawai'i, **9:**918
    influence on Ghost Dance movement, **3:**421
    in Manihiki, **9:**905
    in Marshall Islands, **9:**748
    in Micronesia, **9:**720

in Niue, **9:**816
Polynesian communities of, **3:**1047, 1050
    in Sāmoa, **9:**795
Moro, Pamela A., **4:**26
Moro people, **1:**570
Moroccan people
    in Canada, **3:**1073, 1077, 1171–75
    in France, **8:**231
Morocco, **3:**336. *See also* Maghrib; North Africa;
    specific peoples
    aerophones in, **6:**415
    Andalusian repertoire in, **1:**534–36; **6:**202,
        449–50, 454, 455–63, 499
    Anti-Atlas region, **6:**273, 301, 302, 303, 483,
        484, 488
    Berber peoples, **1:**532, 533, 543; **6:**273–77,
        299–303, 479–82, 483–90, 496, 1036
    Bni Battu people, performance schedules,
        1:133
    chordophones in, **6:**407–11
    circumcision ceremonies, **1:**540
    court music of, **3:**65
    drums in, **6:**416–20
    female musicians, **1:**541
    festivals, **1:**538–39
    French and Spanish rule in, **6:**432
    geography of, **6:**429
    Gnāwa people in, **6:**435, 487, 491–93
    High Atlas region, **6:**273, 300, 301, 303, 306,
        483, 484, 485, 487, 488, 489
        disappearance of women's repertoires, **6:**306
    idiophones in, **6:**403
    'Īsāwiyya brotherhood in, **6:**403
    itinerant musicians, **1:**540–41
    Jewish people, **6:**203, 1036–44
    Judeo-Spanish music in, **8:**596
    malhun, **6:**495–500
    map of, **6:**430
    Middle Atlas region, **6:**273, 483, 487
    popular music in, **1:**546–47; **6:**269
    Rif region, **6:**273, 302–3, 483
        imdyazn musicians, **6:**306
    Sus Valley, **6:**273
    Tafilalet region, **6:**495–96
    wedding rituals in, **6:**303
Moroder, Giorgio, **3:**204, 228, 688
Moroi Makoto, **7:**705, 735–37
Moroi Saburô, **7:**732, 735
Morphy, Howard, **9:**47, 418
Morricone, Ennio, **3:**204
Morris, James, **3:**300
Morris, Kenneth, **10:**138
Morris, Peter T., **7:**267, 268
Morrison, Sir Howard, **9:**168, 938
Morrison, James, **3:**843
Morrison, Ruairidh Dall, **8:**362, 367, 374
Morrison, Van, **8:**215, 226, 392
Morsden, Owen, **3:**1141
Mort du Capitaine Cook, La (ballet), **9:**34
Morthenson, Jan W., **8:**445
Mortier, Pierre, **8:**523
Mortifee, Ann, **3:**199
Mortlockese people, immigrants to Northern
    Marianas, **9:**91–92
Mortlock Islands (Chuuk State, FSM), German
    expedition to, **9:**23–24

Morton, David, **3:**953; **4:**26, 91, 131, 223, 224,
    247, 286; **10:**140
    research on Thai ensembles, **4:**240
    research on Thai instruments, **4:**164, 228
    research on Thai musical elements, **4:**269, 274,
        276, 278, 281
    research on Thai tuning, **4:**261, 262
Morton, Ferdinand "Jelly Roll," **3:**13, 550, 579,
    652, 653–54, 787, 803
Mosafinn, Ola, **8:**417
Moser, Brian, **2:**155, 649
Moshe, Chaim, **6:**266
Moshoeshoe I (Lesotho leader), **1:**707
Mosonyi, Mihály, **8:**737
mosquito, El (Dimas), **3:**760
Mosquito Singers, **3:**1087
Moss, John, **3:**1059
Mossi people, **1:**452–53
Mossinik tribe, **8:**843
Most Happy Fella (Loesser), **3:**545
"Most of All" (Moonglows), **3:**671
Mota (Vanuatu)
    composition on, **9:**362
    instruments, **9:**693
    music and dance of, **9:**695, 698–702
Mota Lava (Vanuatu), **9:**693, 698
motet, **8:**71–72
    Baroque, **8:**76, 77, 654
    Renaissance, **8:**75, 727
    Scotland, **8:**366
Mother Goddess, **5:**291, 645, 931. *See also* Devi;
    Durga; Kali; Shakti
    worship of, **5:**211, 223, 228, 247, 493, 494,
        501, 505, 663, 724, 846, 935–36
Motherlode (musical group), **3:**1081
Mother Mallard Portable Masterpiece Co., **3:**254
Mother of Us All (Thomson), **3:**545
Mothership Connection (Parliament), **3:**684
Mothers of Invention (musical group), **3:**347
Motherwell, William, **8:**135, 370, 371
Motilón culture, **2:**380
Motion Picture Moods for Pianists and Organists
    (Rapee), **3:**262
Mötley Crüe (musical group), **3:**357–58
Motolinía, Toribio de, **2:**602
Motoori Nagayo, **7:**731
Motown Records, **3:**673–75, 677, 678, 709–10
Motoyoshi, **7:**641
Motsieloa, Griffiths, **1:**771
Motu Haka, **9:**890
Motu One (Society Islands), **9:**867
Motu people, **9:**492–94
    dance of, **9:**491
    music and dance of, **9:**983
    trade networks of, **9:**489, 492–93
Mouā, Madeleine, **9:**875
Mouffe, **3:**1158
Mouk people, **9:**614
Moulin, Jane Freeman, **9:**307, 315, 869, 891,
    974
Moulton, Rev. James Egan, **9:**203–4
Moulton, Tom, **3:**690
Moumen, **6:**271
Mounier, G., **1:**584
Mount Allison University (Sackville), **3:**1116,
    1119, 1121

Mountford, C. P., **9**:987
Mouquet, Eric, **8**:225
Mourning for Mangatopi (film), **9**:47
Mouskouri, Nana, **8**:1021
Mousseau, Willie, **3**:*406*
mouth harps. *See* Jew's harps
mouth organs (harmonicas)
 Argentina, **2**:251
 armónica, **2**:40
 Bahamas, **2**:805
 Barbados, **2**:816, 819
 dulzaina, **2**:40
 England, **8**:330, 331
 Estonia, **8**:494
 Europe, **8**:143
 France, **8**:545
 Garifuna culture, **2**:673–74
 Germany, **8**:658
 Honduras, **2**:742
 Ireland, **8**:385
 Jamaica, **2**:907
 Low Countries, **8**:530
 Malta, **8**:640
 Mixtec culture, **2**:565, 567
 Mundäoline, **8**:657
 mundharp, **8**:420
 mungiga, **8**:439
 musique à bouche, **8**:547
 Newfoundland, **3**:1125
 North America
  Amish playing of, **3**:887
  in blues performance, **3**:638, 642, 647
  in Danish music, **3**:882–83
  in Finnish music, **3**:874
  in French music, **3**:855
  in gospel music, **3**:631
  in Hispano music, **3**:761, 762
  in Norwegian music, **3**:868
  Russian Old Believer playing of, **3**:887
  in Volga German music, **3**:890
 Oceania, **9**:27, 134, 159, 361, 401, 441, 522,
   578, 591, 679, 718, 742, 745, 756,
   836, 901, 903, 905, 907, 908, 909
 Ontario, **3**:1189, 1194
 rondín, **2**:40
 sinfonía, **2**:40
 Sweden, **8**:435
 Switzerland, **8**:689, 693
 Uruguay, **2**:511, 512
 ustne orglic (also *ustne harmonike*), **8**:919
 Wales, **8**:348, 355
 Wayana culture, **2**:167
Mouton, Jean, **2**:735
El-Moutribia (Algerian society), **6**:1044
"Move It On Over" (Williams), **3**:353
movement. *See* dance and movement
Moving Away from Silence (Turino), **10**:52
Moving Hearts, **8**:392
Movius, H. L., **4**:32
Movses Khorenatsi, **6**:723, 732–33
Mowatt, Judy, **2**:912
Moxo culture, **2**:137–42
 harmony of, **2**:131
 research on, **2**:140
Moyer, Will D., **9**:286
Moyle, Alice M., **9**:418, 960, 986, 987, 1008

Moyle, Richard M., **9**:244, 960, 973, 974, 987
Moynihan, Daniel P., **3**:515
Moyo, Jonah, **1**:432
Moyzes, Alexander, **8**:729
Mozambican people
 in North America, **3**:848
 in Portugal, **8**:576
Mozambique. *See also* East Africa; Southern
   Africa; *specific peoples*
 Arab influences in, **1**:297, 700
 Bantu groups, **1**:670
 beni music, **1**:426
 culture of, **1**:700
 economy of, **1**:428
 Europeans in, **1**:717
 lamellophones, **1**:317, *318*
 likumbi institution, **1**:309
 Makonde people, **1**:119
 music of, **1**:429, 606, 640, 701, 720
 Ngoni people, **1**:320–21
 Nyungwe people, **1**:711
 popular music of, **1**:323, 435–36
 Sena people, **1**:711
 Shangaan people, **1**:705
 Shona people, music of, **1**:744–57
 Thonga people, blood sacrifice, **1**:277
Mozart, Wolfgang Amadeus, **2**:394; **3**:1179;
   6:21, 52, 767; **7**:540; **8**:62, 80, 86,
   186, 670, 727
 operas of, **3**:181; **8**:54, 60, 84; **9**:371
Mozdokian Kabardian people, **8**:854–56
Mparanyane, **1**:778
MPB, **2**:109–10
Mpompo people, **1**:658
Mpyɛmɔ̃ people
 kembe tuning, **1**:299, 664
 music of, **1**:658, 664, *665*
 secret societies, **1**:309
Mqayi, S. E. R., **1**:764
mridangam. See drums: barrel, conical, or
   cylindrical
Mroja (musical group), **8**:802
Mr. Wonderful (musical), **3**:621
Mshvelidze, Shalva, **8**:844
Msika, Ḥabība, **6**:527, 529
Mtatsminda (musical group), **8**:*837*
Mtatsmindeli, Ekvtime, **8**:843
Mtatsmindeli, Giorgi, **8**:843
Mtiebi (musical group), **8**:845
Mtired, Jilali, **6**:496, 499
Mtiyletian people, **8**:827
M'tukudzi, Oliver, **1**:432
MTV (U.S. music video channel), **2**:52, 374;
   3:96, 206, 211, 219, 244, 250, 551,
   586, 697, 712; **5**:427, 429; **10**:48–49
Mu'ain, Ismail Abdel, **1**:571
Muara Takus (kingdom), **4**:600
Mu'awiya I, caliph, **6**:539
Mubangizi, Benedikto K., **1**:208–9, 607
El-Mubarak, Abdel Aziz, **1**:571–72
Mubarak, Husni, president of Egypt, **6**:640
Mubarak, Susan, **6**:607
MuchMoreMusic (Canadian music video
   channel), **3**:252
MuchMusic (Canadian music video channel),
   3:74, 96–97, 248, 250–52, 266

Mud label, **3**:169
Mudaliar, Chinnasvami, **5**:225, 227, 561
Mudaliar, Chinnayya, **5**:223–24
Mudallal, Ṣabrī, **6**:568
Mudd Club (New York), **3**:689
Muddupalani, **5**:386
Muddy York (musical group), **3**:1189
Mudia people, **5**:720, 722
Muerte de Lucrezia (Canseco), **4**:863
Muezo, José, **4**:866
al-Mufaḍḍal ibn Salāma, **6**:17, 373
muğam, Azerbaijani, **6**:8, 18, 23, 311, 552, 834,
   866, 923, 927–29, 1016
 modal organization, **6**:926–27
 in opera and large ensembles, **6**:924, 930
Muggeru caste, **5**:887
Mughal empire, **5**:48, 307–8, 337, 350, 650,
   660, 731, 744, 881
 history of, **5**:11–12, 375; **10**:11–12
 painting style, **5**:300, 301, 303–6, 307, 332,
   333, 411
 patronage in, **5**:14–15, 47, 76–77, 121, 163,
   170–71, 188, 376, 402, 493, 745,
   792, 805; **10**:12
Mugiya busi (Japanese folk song), **7**:712
Muhamad, Salipada, **4**:*901*
Muhammad (Prophet), **5**:591; **6**:293
 'Ali and, **6**:794
 birthday of, **5**:278, 411
 gwatī songs to, **6**:889
 hymns to, **5**:748, 753, 770, 772, 778–79, 867,
   921, 947
 na'at songs to, **6**:940
 Qur'ān and, **6**:157
 recorded words of (*ḥadīth*), **6**:19, 131, 179,
   187, 294, 358, 359, 362, 371, 538,
   636
 views on cross-dressing, **6**:296
 views on dance, **6**:876
 views on music, **6**:130, 131, 180, 517, 538
 views on women's singing, **6**:696
Muḥammad 'Alī, viceroy and pasha of Egypt,
   6:233, 321, 547, 609, 625, 630
Muḥammad ben 'Īsā, Sīdī, **6**:516, 517
Muḥammad Efendī al-Kanjī (al-Ganjī), **6**:371
Muḥammad ibn 'Abd al-Ḥamīd al-Lādhiqī. *See*
   Lādhiqī, Muḥammad ibn 'Abd al-
   Ḥamīd al-
Muḥammad Ibn Abī 'Īsā, qāḍhī, **6**:443
Muḥammad ibn Aḥmad al-Khwārazmī, **6**:367
Muḥammad ibn Ibrāhīm Qarīḍ, **6**:297
Muḥammad Shah, Mughal emperor, **4**:601;
   5:121, 133, 163, 170, 189; **6**:130
Muḥammad Sharaf al-Dīn, **6**:686
Muḥammad, Shaykh Abū al-'Ila, **6**:168, 548
Muhammad Speaks (periodical), **3**:663
Muhiddin Uftade, **6**:193
Muhua, Mrs., **10**:*115*
Mui, Anita (Mei Yanfang), **7**:355, 435
Muizo, Sheikh, **6**:1044
al-Mūjī, Muḥammad, **6**:600–601
Muk Kyewŏl, **7**:985
Mukaiba, Ligali, **1**:475
Mukangi, Deyess, **1**:425
Mukesh, **5**:255, 420, 421, 539
Mukesh, Nithin, **5**:421

Mukharinskaia, Lidiia S., **8:**803

Mukhāriq, **6:**297, 354, 355, 356, 539

Mukherjee, Arun, **3:**1059

Mukherjee, Budhaditya, **5:**205

Mukhopadhyay, Dhirendranath, **5:**855

Mukhopadhyay, Hemanta, **5:**857

Mukhopadhyay, Manavendra, **5:**857

Mukhopadhyay, Sandhya, **5:**857

Mukhopadhyay, Satinath, **5:**857

Mukhopadhyay, Saurindra Mohan, **5:**855

Mukhpul, Yasin, **7:**468

Muko-muko people, **4:**619–20

Muktha, T., **5:**389, 395

Muktupāvels, Valdis, **8:**507

Mukuna, Kazadi wa, **1:**44, 68

"*Mula Bronca, La*" (Hurricane), **3:**766

Mulam people, **7:**485–92

Mulao people, **7:**449

Mules and Men (Hurston), **3:**34

Mūlidiyya (devotional poem), **6:**437

Mullaqand family, **6:**916

Müller, Fabian, **8:**698

Müller, Péter, **8:**746

Müller, Peter J., **8:**677

Muller, Sister Winfrieda, **4:**870

Müller-Egger, Paul, **8:**692

Mullick, Pankaj, **5:**420, 536, 855, 856

Mulligan, Gerry, **3:**335

Mulligan Guards' Ball (Harrigan and Hart), **3:**544

Mullu Kurumbas, **5:**909

Multani, Muhammad Baksh, **5:***283*

Multicultural History Society of Ontario, **3:**1060

Multiculturalism Act (Canada, 1988), **3:**14, 1067

multiple-reed instruments
　horanâva, **5:**329, 363, 366, 958, 964, 967–68
　jawarun ra'anga, **2:**160

Multitone (record company), **8:**241

Mulyani, S., **4:**103

Mumford, Jeffrey, **3:**612

Mumma, Gordon, **3:**254

Mun Chaesuk, **7:**986

Mun Paegyun, **7:**932

Mun Yusŏk, **7:**989

Münchner Stadtmuseum (Munich), **8:**182

Muṇḍa people, **5:**415, 720
　dance traditions of, **5:**502, *502,* 722

Mundo folklórico paraguayo (Cardozo Ocampo), **2:**463

Mundy, Jimmy, **3:**655

Munetada Shrine (Okayama), **7:**609

Mungiki. *See* Bellona

Municipal Conservatory of Music (Havana), **2:**837

Munīr, Muḥammad, **6:**239, 240

Munishi, Rexhep, **8:**1004

Munizaga, Carlos, **2:**238

Munjong, Koryŏ king, **7:**982

Munmyo Shrine (Seoul), **7:**861, 865

Munnelly, Tom, **8:**393, 394

Muñoz Camargo, Diego, **2:**557

Muñoz Tábora, Jesús, **2:**740

Munro, Ailie, **8:**374

Munro, Alexander, **8:**372

Münster, Sebastian, **8:**504

Muntenia, **8:**868. *See also* Romania

Munusvami Appa, Bangalore, **5:**392

Munye Kŭkch'ang (Seoul theater), **7:**994

Mường people, **4:**444, 529, 531
　ceremonies of, **4:**533
　courtship songs of, **4:**532
　gong ensembles of, **4:**533
　instruments of, **4:**467, 535
　narratives of, **4:**533

Muqaddima fī qawānīn al-anghām (al-Māridīnī), **6:**366

muqam, Uighur, **6:**184, 185, 909, 910, 989–93, 995–1008; **7:**5, 450, 457, 459

Muquinche, Don César, **2:**418

Murād, Layla, **6:**236, 239

Murad, Shah, **6:**899

Muranushi, Iwakichi, **9:**25, 159, 729, 969, 994

Muraqqa'-i Dihlī, **5:**121

Murasaki Sikibu, **7:**79, 550

Murdoch, John, **3:**381

Murdock, George Peter, **1:**2, 574–75, 701, 707

Müren, Zeki, **6:**118, 258

Murgiyanto, Sal, **3:**1020

Muriavai, **9:**901

Muriel, Inés, **2:**431

Murillo, Emilio, **2:**394–95

Mūristus (Mūristes), **6:**373

Murko, Matija, **8:**18

Murle people, **1:**601

Murnau, F. W., **9:**44

Muromati (Muromachi) period
　hayasi in, **7:**683
　heikyoku in, **7:**646, 757–58

Murphy, Dennis, **3:**1018, *1018*

Murray, Albert, **3:**582

Murray, Anne, **3:**314, 1073

Murray, Charlotte, **3:**609

Murray, David, **3:**664

Murugan (deity), **5:**259, 265, 608, 921

Murut people, **4:**824, 826, 833

Mūsā, Sayyid, **6:**168

Musahar caste, **5:**679

al-Musallam al-Mawṣilī, **6:**367

Musango, **1:**608

Mūsavī, Mohammad, **6:**857

Musée des Arts et Traditions Populaires (Paris), **8:**181, 182, 543, 554, 562, 574

Musée de l'Homme (Paris), **1:**51; **6:**23; **8:**182, 233, 553; **9:**992

Musée Instrumental (Brussels), **8:**176–77, 181, 526, 529, 535

Musée Royal de l'Afrique Centrale, **1:**670

Musée de Saint Boniface (Manitoba), **3:**411

Musée de Tahiti et des Îles, **9:**892, 958

Museo Arqueológico (Ecuador), **2:**413

Museo Arqueológico del Instituto Nacional de Seguros (Costa Rica), **2:**681

Museo di Etnografia Italiana (Museo Nazionale di Arti e Tradizioni Popolari), **8:**621–22

Museo Histórico Nacional (Uruguay), **2:**511

Museo Nacional de Costa Rica, **2:**681

Museu de la Música (Barcelona), **8:**176, 180, 182

Museu da Música Regional Portuguesa (Estoril), **8:**182

Museu Etnografico (Lisbon), **8:**181

Museum of Antiquities (Bucharest), **8:**885

Museum of the Belgian Congo (Belgium), **2:**529

Museum of the Bosnian Krajina, **8:**970

Museum of New Zealand, **9:**974

Museum für Völkerkunde (Berlin), **6:**524; **8:**182; **9:**994

museums. *See* archives and museums; *specific institutions*

Musgrave, Thea, **8:**369

Music (periodical), **8:**783

Music in America (Ritter), **3:**508

Music Archive of the Institute of Papua New Guinea Studies, **9:**961–62

Music in Aztec and Inca Territory (Stevenson), **2:**623

Music in Bali (McPhee), **4:**28

Music of Black Americans: A History (Southern), **3:**581

Music Box (Chicago), **3:**691

Music Box Revues, **3:**545

Music in Canada: A Research and Information Guide (Morey), **3:**1066

Music from China (organization), **3:**953

Music in the Cold (Schafer), **3:**1059

Music Conservatory (Brazil), **2:**305

Music Culture in West Asia, **7:**525

Music Department of Santa Isabel College, **4:**870

Music of the Earth, **7:**525

Music Educators Journal, **3:**276

Music Educators National Conference, **3:**276, 286, 302

Music from the Hearts of Space (radio program), **3:**346

Music in India: The Classical Traditions (Wade), **10:**11

Music India Ltd. (MIL), **5:**557

music industry (North America), **3:**256–67. *See also* audiences; copyright and ownership; economics; film; printing and publishing; radio; sound recordings; television
　African-American executives and producers, **3:**712–13, 715
　African-American music and, **3:**705–15
　Canada, **3:**246–48, 256–67, 314–15, 1067–68, 1080, 1178–86
　country music, **3:**78–81
　crosscultural marketing, **3:**586
　Tejano, **3:**781
　United States, **3:**256–65

Music in Java (Kunst), **4:**28, 636, 701; **10:**51

Music for Mallet Instruments, Voices, and Organ (Reich), **3:**954; **4:**132

Music in Mexico: A Historical Survey (Stevenson), **2:**623

Music Museum Collection (Grainger Museum), **9:**961

Music and Musical Thought in Early India (Rowell), **5:**69–70

Music and Musicians in Early America (Lowens), **3:**32

Music and Musicians in Israel (Gradenwitz), **6:**1060

Music of New Mexico: Hispanic Traditions, **3:**767

Music in the New World (Hamm), **3:**32

Music of the Orthodox Church in Alaska, **3:**486

Music Performance Trust Fund (Philadelphia), **3:**537–38

Music Research Institute of the Chinese Academy of Arts, 7:397
Music and Some Highly Musical People (Trotter), 3:29, 581, 606
Music Study Society (Peking University), 7:228, 376, 381
Music Supervisors Bulletin, 3:276
Music Supervisors National Conference, 3:276
Music Today (media company), 5:528
Music in Twelve Parts (Glass), 3:254
Music of the World (record label), 5:159–60
Music for Zen Meditation (Scott), 3:346
Musica e Dischi (periodical), 8:211
Musica Enchiriadis, 6:366; 8:50, 134
Música de la gente (film), 3:767
Musica getutscht und ausgezogen (Virdung), 8:654
Musica instrumentalis deudsch (Agricola), 8:705
Música Maya-Quiché, La (Castillo), 2:736
música popular de México, La (Reuter), 2:624
Música Viva, 2:306
Música de los Viejos, La (film), 3:763, 767
Musical Academy (periodical), 8:785
Musical Areas in Aboriginal North America (Roberts), 3:512
Musical Artifacts of Pre-Hispanic West Mexico (Crossley-Holland), 2:623
Musical Biography, A (Parker), 3:27
musical bows
  Africa, 1:305–8, 562, 702, 715, 719; 9:258
  Argentina, 2:250, 251
  baka aapa, 2:591, 593
  basoi (also *busoi*), 4:835
  belembaotuyan, 9:387, 745–46
  benta, 2:929
  berimbau, 1:435; 3:730–31; 8:442; 9:84
  berimbau de barriga, 2:346, *347*
  bijuela, 3:762
  Bolivia, 2:287–88
  Buka and Bougainville, 9:630, *634*
  cajuavé, 2:455
  caramba (also *zambumbia*), 2:694, 709, 738, 739, 743
  chipendani, 1:710, 752
  Colombia, 2:380
  cunculcahue, 2:253–54
  dàn bàu (also *dàn độc huyền*), 3:994
  dānda, 9:542
  dende, 1:709
  ehat waŋgäm (also *ende waŋgäm*), 9:570
  gáwa, 9:372, 537–38, 541–42
  gayumba, 2:855
  gongqin, 7:524, 528–29
  gora, 1:703, 707
  goura, 1:151–53
  gualāmbau (also *guyrambau*; *lambau*), 2:201, 457
  gubo, 1:320–21
  gulimmed, 4:920
  guyrapa-í, 2:201
  hìbulu báralu, 9:542
  hool, 2:658
  Huli people, 9:286
  kawayawaya, 1:677
  kha:s, 1:703
  khodili, 9:661
  Khoikhoi people, 1:703

  knobe kbetas, 4:797–98
  kongo, 9:655
  kòn-kpàla, 1:470
  kouxian, 7:462
  kū, 9:933
  kuṭam, 5:932
  kwadili, 9:669
  lesiba, 1:702, 707
  lungku, 2:661, *662*, 739
  luñku, 2:750
  makomako, 9:656
  marimba, 2:402
  mbulumbumba, 1:435, 714
  mouth-resonated, 9:512, *634*, 647, 649, 667, 851, 865
  Native American types, 3:478
  nganga, 1:640
  Nguni peoples, 1:706, 708
  nkangala (or *nqangala*), 1:*3*, 320–21, 430, 711; 10:*119*
  Nkhumbi people, 1:714
  ohonji (or *onkhonji*), 1:306, 714
  Papua New Guinea, 9:556
  paruntsi, 2:487
  Paya culture, 2:739
  Peru, 2:476, 492
  Pygmies, 1:659
  quijongo, 2:694, 698, 743, 757–58
  quinquerche (also *quinquercahue*), 2:234
  rapá, 2:455
  San people, 1:704–5, 708, 744
  sanu, 4:*60*
  sanu (musical bow), 4:317
  Shona people, 1:708, 752
  shukster, 2:815
  siloŋgote, 9:615
  South America, 2:73
    tropical-forest region, 2:127
  tambour maringouin, 2:855
  Tanzania, 1:640
  Tarahumara culture, 2:583
  tita'apu, 9:895
  trông quân, 4:471
  tshizambi, 1:709
  Tsonga people, 1:708, 710, 711
  tumank (also *tsayantur*), 2:416–17
  tunings, 1:663
  two-stringed, 9:386, 532
  ugubhu, 1:321, 706
  'ūkēkē, 9:386, *956*
  umakhweyana, 1:364, 706
  umrhubhe, 1:706
  Uruguay, 2:510–11
  Vanuatu, 9:693
  villādi vādyam, 5:*367*, 367–68
  villu, 5:*907*
  West Africa, 1:445
Musical Buxton (Robbins), 3:1212
Musical Cyclopedia (Porter), 3:27
Musical Expositor, A (Haskell), 3:135
Musical Homework (Fenwick), 3:277
Musical Institute for Folk Music Research (Cuba), 2:838
Musical Instruments Historic, Rare, and Unique (Hipkins), 4:225, 285
Musical Memoirs of Scotland (Dalyell), 8:373

Musical and Poetical Relicks of the Welsh Bards (Jones), 8:352
Musical Publications and Recording Studios (Cuba), 2:828, 838
Musical Self (Koskoff), 10:132
musical theater, popular, 3:193–94, 196–98, 200, 544–45, 943. *See also* opera; theater
  African-American composers, 3:194, 577, 607, 608–9, 618–20, 650
  Canada, 3:198–200
  China, 7:385
  forerunners, 3:544
  gospel, 3:585
  Hong Kong, 7:355
  Japan, 7:744
  Korea, 7:946
  Nigeria, 1:403
  South Africa, 1:773, 774, 775, 777, 780
Musical Union (Ottawa), 3:1181
Musicalisches Theatrum (Weigel), 8:654–55
musicians. *See* performers; *specific names and groups*
Musicians Omnibus (Howe), 3:232
Musick (Stuart), 8:372
Musicological Society of Australia, 9:415
Musicological Society of Japan, 7:729
Musicologica Slovaca (periodical), 8:733
musicology, 3:243; 5:213, 227, 849–50, 912; 8:59–60. *See also* African musicology and scholarship; ethnomusicology; treatises
  Armenia, 6:726–27
  Basque music research, 8:316–17
  biographies, 3:27, 29
  Bulgaria, 8:906–7
  Canada, 3:1059–60, 1108–9
  China, 7:135–39, 416, 444; 10:22–23
  Corsica, 8:573
  Cuba, 2:828–29, 838
  development of, 3:31–34, 293
  Estonia, 8:498
  Finland, 8:484, 487–89
  France, 8:551–54
  Georgia, 8:843–44, 846–47
  Greece, 8:1024–25
  historical performance movement, 8:55–56, 85–86
  Israel, 6:1057–67
  Italy, 8:620–23
  Japan, 7:540, 589, 591–93, 595, 729
  Korea, 7:853–57, 990–91, 993
  Low Countries, 8:534–35
  North Africa, 6:435
  North Caucasia, 8:853, 856, 861, 864
  Norway, 8:427
  Poland, 8:712
  popular music research, 3:95–96; 8:210–11
  race and, 3:69–72
  research on American music, 3:511
  research on Jewish music, 8:265–67
  revival movements and, 3:56
  Romania, 8:884, 885–86
  Russia, 8:782–85
  Sardinia, 8:632
  score-based, 8:52, 60, 86
  Spain, 8:601–2

Sri Lanka, **5:**956–57
studies of African-American music, **3:**572–87
Sweden, **8:**447–48
Tunisia, **6:**326, 329, 502–3, 508
  Jewish music, **6:**523–25
Turkey, **6:**79–81, 83, 108, 783
Ukraine, **8:**820–23
visual sources, **5:**307–310
Western *vs.* Indian scholarly standards, **5:**56
women's studies, **3:**91, 93; **8:**192–93
Musicology Australia (journal), **9:**415
Musiikin Suunta (periodical), **8:**489
Musiikki (periodical), **8:**488
Musik der Araber nach Originalquellen dargestellt
  (Kiesewetter), **6:**22
Musik und Bildung (periodical), **8:**210
Musik Israels, Die (Brod), **6:**1060
Musik des Orients (Lachmann), **6:**22
Musik zwischen Orient und Okzident
  (Gradenwitz), **6:**1060
Musikaliskt Tidsfördrif (periodical), **8:**444
Musikgesellschaft Speicher, **8:**689
Musikhistorisk Museum og Carl Claudius
  (Copenhagen), **8:**180–81
Musiki (musical group), **1:**683–84
Musikinstrumenten-Museum (Markneukirchen),
  8:182
Musikmarkt (periodical), **8:**211
Musikmuseet (Stockholm), **8:**448
Musil, Aloys, **6:**667
musique arabe, La (collection), **6:**326, 328, 501,
  502–3, 508
musique arabe, La: Le congrès du Caire de 1932
  (conference proceedings), **6:**23
Musique Bretonne (periodical), **8:**563
musique concrète, **3:**252–53, 540; **7:**735, 736
Musique en Polynésie (Tahiti), **9:**868
Musique Plus (Canadian music video channel),
  3:74, 250–52, 266
musique traditionnelle de la Martinique, La
  (Desroches), **2:**920
Muskogee Indian nation. *See* Creek Indian
  nation
Muslihiddin Merkez, **6:**193
Muslim people and culture (in Europe)
  circumcision ceremony, **8:**143, *144*, 975, 980,
    988
  European populations of, **8:**11–12, 143–45,
    195, 197
    Balkan region, **8:**280, 281, 895, 942, 951,
      957, 959, 962, 963, 964–68, 975,
      979, 986, 988, 1002, 1011, 1023
    Caucasus region, **8:**826, 835–36, 850, 854,
      856, 858, 859, 861
    Russian Tatars, **8:**774
  religious music, **8:**967–68, 969
Muslim people and culture (in South Asia). *See
  also* Islam; *specific topics*
  attitudes toward Indian music, **5:**433–35
  caste structure of, **5:**10
  ghazal poetry of, **5:**184
  influence in South India, **5:**76–77, 263, 265,
    280, 350, 374, 375, 408, 509
  in Kashmir, **5:**682
  as *nāgasvaram* and *tavil* players, **5:**234
  in Pakistan, **5:**743, 744–45, 792, *793*

in Rajasthan, **5:**639
on Réunion Island, **5:**606–7
in Sri Lanka, **5:**108, 954
as *tabla* players, **5:**123
Musnad (Ibn Ḥanbal), **6:**358, 359
Mussang shin'gu chapka, **7:**984
Mussau (Papua New Guinea), **9:**626
"Mussels in the Corner" (Newfoundland song),
  3:*1124*
Mussolini, Benito, **8:**187, 618
Mussorgsky, Modest, **2:**114; **8:**84, 764, 781, 800
Mussur people. *See* Lahu people
Mustafa Çavuş, Tanbûrî, **6:**115
Mustafa Dede, Köçek, **6:**108, 110, 118
Mustafa Nakî Dede, **6:**110
Mustafov, Ferus, **8:**983
Mustafov, Muzafer, **8:***982*
Musumali, Lithundu, **1:***306*
Musurgia Universalis (Kircher), **8:**265
Musurugwa, August, **1:**772
Mutakhar, Sumati, **10:**10
al-Muʿtamid, caliph, **6:**297
al-Muʿtaṣim, caliph, **6:**352, 356
al-Muʿtaṣim d'Alméria, **6:**443
Mutʿat al-asmāʿ fī ʿilm al-samāʿ (al-Tīfāshī), **6:**370
Mutiny on the Bounty (film), **9:**45
Mutong duangdi (He), **7:**339
Muttumariyamma (deity), **5:**558
Muttuttandavar, **5:**387, 452
Mutwa, Credo V., **1:**219
"*Mutya ng Pasig*" (Abelardo), **3:**1025
Muu-ökin (Maoyi Khan), **7:**452, 1008
muwal. See mawwāl
Muwarra (Yolngu leader), **9:**458
muwashshaḥ
  Andalusian, **1:**535; **6:**21, 436, 443, 447–48,
    452, 454, 458–59, 470, 475, 496,
    506, 540, 564, 567, 585
  collections of, **6:**370–71
  Egypt, **6:**167, 237, 550, 551, 560, 626
  influence on European music and poetry, **6:**24
  influence on Sephardi *baḳashot*, **6:**202, 1037
  rhythms in, **6:**91
  Syrian, **6:**283, 550, 551, 563, 567–68
  Yemen, **6:**686
muwwal. See mawwāl
Muyinda, Evaristo, **10:**113–14, 115–16
Muzenza (*bloco afro*), **2:**353
Muzeum Instrumentów Muzycznych (Poznań),
  8:182
Muzeum Ludowych Instrumentów Muzycnych
  (Szydtowiec), **8:**182
"*muzher que cale tomar, La*" (Sephardic song),
  3:1174
Muzicul Român, **8:**885
Muzsikás (musical group), **8:***227*
Müzük (periodical), **6:**249
Muzyka i Penie (periodical), **8:**783
Muzykalʹnyi Listok (periodical), **8:**780
Muzykalʹnyi Svet/Le Monde Musical (periodical),
  8:780
Mvele people, **1:**660
Mvome, André, **1:**663
Mwamba, Charles "Dechaud," **1:**386
Mwana, Tshala, **1:**425
"*Mwen désennd Sin Piè*" (beguine), **2:**916

Mwera people, **1:**317, 638, 639
M. Witmark and Sons (publishing firm), **3:**191,
  262
Mwokiloa Atoll (FSM), **9:**739
Myanmar. *See* Burma
Myáwadi Mîñcì (or Wuñcì) Ù Sá, **4:**366, 378
"My Blue Heaven" (American popular song),
  7:744
"My Bonnie Lies over the Ocean" (folk song),
  3:1136; **5:**737
"My Cherished Hope, My Fondest Dream"
  (Connor), **3:**604
"My Country 'Tis of Thee," **3:**521, 839
My Fair Lady (Lerner and Loewe), **3:**545
"My Faith Looks Up to Thee" (Mason), **3:**532
"My Favorite Things" (Rodgers), **3:**661
My Favorite Things (Coltrane), **3:**662
My Funny Valentine (Davis), **3:**662
My Fur Lady (revue), **3:**199
"My Gal Sal" (Dresser), **3:**191
"My Girl" (Temptations), **3:**674
"My Guy" (Wells), **3:**674
"My Happiness" (Fitzgerald), **3:**708
"My Lost Youth" (Longfellow), **8:**307
"My Mammy," **3:**196
My Music, My Life (Shankar), **5:**565
"My Old Kentucky Home, Good Night"
  (Foster), **3:**187
"My Own Paradise" (Cobra), **7:**364
"My Prayer" (Platters), **3:**672
"My Uncle" (Flying Burrito Brothers), **3:**318
"My Wild Irish Rose," **3:**520
Myerhoff, Barbara, **2:**19–20
Myers, Helen, **2:**744; **3:**828, 980
Myezini, Mazllum, **8:**999
Myint Maun, Ù, **4:***142*, 389–90
Myllarguten. *See* Augundson, Torgeir
  (Myllarguten)
Myôanzi Temple (Kyôto), **7:**703, 758
Myŏlchi chabi norae (Korean folk song), **7:**883
Myŏngchʼang Im Pangul (Kang), **7:**969
Myŏng Wanbyŏk, **7:**921
Myosotis, **4:**509
mystère des voix bulgares, Le (album), **7:**1025;
  8:890
Myth of the Negro Past (Herskovits), **3:**72, 512
myths, **2:**16–21. *See also* cosmology; narratives;
  recitation; *specific gods, epics, and
  narratives*
  Australia, **9:**442
    in Aboriginal theater, **9:**227–28
    about the Dreaming, **9:**187–88, *410*, 417,
      419, 431, 450–51, 456
    Cape York, **9:**429
    on Kaaʻungken brothers, **9:**462–63, 464
    Yolngu people, **9:**457–60
  autonomous work of art, **8:**184
  Bolivia, **2:**282–83
  Bribri and Cabécar cultures, **2:**631, 632, 633,
    634, 635
  Bulgaria, **8:**898
  Canadian, **3:**1059
  Caribbean, **2:**18–19
  Celtic, **8:**322
  Central America, **2:**19–21
  Chechen and Ingush people, **8:**863

myths (*continued*)
Cherokee, **3**:370
China, on instrument origins, **7**:402
Cook Islands, **9**:897
creation, **2**:19, 20; **4**:540
Cubeo culture, **2**:153
Datura Person, **2**:20
Desana culture, **2**:153
Egypt, initiatory dreams, **6**:341
El Dorado, **2**:9, 10, 441
El Salvador, **2**:709–10
Faroe Islands, **8**:469
Finland, **8**:475, 477, 481
Georgia, **8**:835
Germany, **8**:83
Greek, Kyknos, **6**:889
Guaraní culture, **2**:202, 203–4, 460
Hawai'i, **9**:915
Hindu, **5**:918
   gâṭa bera in, **5**:364
   Mohini in, **5**:512
   in *Nāradīyaśikṣā*, **5**:32
Hmong people, **4**:555
Iceland, **8**:400
Indian-influenced, **4**:52–53
India, South
   portrayal in films, **5**:543
   theatrical interpretations of, **5**:104, 490, 876
on instruments, **8**:41–42
Inuit, **3**:1275
Iran, **6**:142
   origins of music and instruments, **6**:835
Ireland
   heroic figures, **8**:379, 385
   preternatural beings, **8**:387–88
Irian Jaya, Asmat people, **9**:189–90, 589–90
Islamic
   origins of music and instruments, **6**:181–82
   samā', **6**:179
   sīmorgh bird, **6**:179–81, 889–90
Jubal as inventor of instrumental music, **8**:259
Karen people, **4**:545
Kashmir, **5**:689
K'ekchi Maya, **2**:668
Khalkha people, on origin of *höömii*, **7**:1009
King Arthur, **8**:186
Kuna culture, **2**:638, 644
Kwakiutl, **3**:400
Lakota, **3**:369
Maharashtra, **5**:727
Malaysia, **4**:412–13
Maleku culture, **2**:682
Maluku, **4**:821
Māori people, **9**:939
Marshall Islands, **9**:750
Mataco culture, **2**:251
Maya culture, **2**:650, 721, 731–32
Mexico, **2**:19–21
Mongol people, on instrument origins, **7**:1010
Navajo, **3**:369
New Guinea, on women's knowledge, **9**:477
Northwest Coast, **3**:1094
origin of rice, **4**:50–51, 53
origin of sacred flutes, **2**:129
Pakistan, northern, **5**:795, 796
Palau, **9**:722

and Palestinian *intifāḍa*, **6**:638–40
Papua New Guinea, **9**:23
   Huli people, **9**:537
   Iatmul people, **9**:340–42, 553, 557
   Lolo people, **9**:614
   Mali Baining people, **9**:192
   Manambu people, **9**:545
   Manam people, **9**:246
   Melpa people, **9**:521
   New Ireland, **9**:380
   Sepik region, **9**:479
   sia, **9**:572–73
   Waxei people, **9**:558–59
Pohnpei, **9**:739
Polynesian, **9**:200–201
research on, **8**:26, 36
Roti, **4**:798
Rotuma, **9**:817
Saami people, **8**:307
Sāmoa, **9**:201–2
Savu, **4**:802
Scotland
   heroic figures, **8**:362, 365
   preternatural beings, **8**:363, 365
Solomon Islands, on panpipes, **9**:400–401
South America, **2**:21
southern California Indian groups, **3**:417
Sumba, **4**:788
Suyá culture, **2**:144
Takuu, **9**:842
Tamil Nadu, **5**:904
Tonga, **9**:201–2
Transylvania, **8**:870
Trique culture, **2**:564
Tuamotu Islands, **9**:884
Tukano culture, **2**:151
Turkey, initiatory dreams, **6**:802–4
Turkic cultures, initiatory dreams, **6**:345, 845, 967–68
Vanuatu, **9**:689, 692, 693
   southern, **9**:702, 705
Waiāpí culture, **2**:158, 159
Wayana culture, **2**:165
Yekuana culture, **2**:177
Yuma culture, **2**:598
Mzayyin il-'arīs'arīs (shaving song), **6**:589
Mzetamze (musical group), **8**:845

Na Essayé (musical group), **5**:610
Na h-Oganaich (musical group), **8**:364, 371
Na Leo Pilimahana, **9**:167
Nā Maka o ka 'Āina, **9**:222
Na Píobairí Uilleann (Irish Pipers' Society), **8**:384, 386, 394
Na Waiho'olu'u O Ke Ānuenue, **9**:166
Nabi Gol, **5**:807
Nabi, Golam, **5**:847
Nabiyev, Jurabek, **6**:919
Nacaome (musical group), **2**:703
Nachang (epic), **5**:701
Nachtigal, Gustav, **1**:659
Nacken (mythical figure), **8**:439
nāda (primordial sound) concept, **5**:34, 69–70, 91, 221–22, 247, 912
Nadel, Siefried, **8**:846, 847
Nadi al-Mūsīqá al-'Arabiyyah (Cairo), **6**:*323*, 324

Nādī al-Mūsīqá al-Sharqī (Cairo), **6**:322
Nadir al-Aasri Ustad Sultan Muhammad Mauri, **5**:690
Nādir Qolīkhān Afshār, **6**:922
Nador, Mustapha, **6**:476
Nae sarang hanŭn kkot (collection), **7**:961
Naess, Ragnar, **7**:351
Naficy, Hamid, **3**:1035
Nag, Dipali, **5**:*174*
Naga (deity), **5**:931
Naga people, **4**:528; **5**:485
Nagai, Frank, **7**:746
Nagaland, **5**:7, 504–5
Nagaoka (Ichiyanagi), **7**:737
Nagarajan, **3**:*991*
Nagaratnammal, Bangalore, **5**:211, 270, 383, 386, 392–93
Nagārcī caste, **5**:641
Nagarjuna University, **5**:450
nāgasvaram. *See* double-reed instruments
Nagata Kinsin, **7**:648
Nagata, Shuichi, **4**:569
Nagauta Kenseikai (musical group), **7**:671–72
Nage people, **4**:791
Nägeli, Hans Georg, **3**:180
naghma. *See maqām*
Naghmāt-i Āsafi (Reza), **5**:46, 50–51
Nago cult, **2**:901, 903
Nagorik (theater group), **5**:489
Nagoulou Mila (deity), **5**:594
Nagovisi people, **9**:643, 644, 647–49
Nagraland (Lee), **4**:523
Nagui, Mustapha, **6**:*611*
Nagwŏn ŭi norae (collection), **7**:961
Nagy, Feró, **8**:746
Nagy, Peter, **8**:731
Nagyangch'un (*tangak* piece), **7**:867
Nahabau, **9**:709
Ñahñú culture. *See* Otomí culture
Nahua culture, **2**:550, 563, 576, 707. *See also* Mexica culture
   narratives of, **2**:19, 20
Nāī caste, **5**:291
Naicker, E. V. Ramasvami, **5**:393
Naidu caste, **5**:910–11
Naik, Raghunatha, **5**:46
Nā'ila bint al-Maylā', **6**:295
Nâ'ilî, **6**:115
Naimanbaiuly, Äset, **6**:955
Naiman, Joanne, **3**:50, 51
Naipaul, V. S., **5**:590
Nairne, Lady, **8**:368
Naiwi, Miu Lan, **9**:924
Najarian, Viken, **3**:*1032*
Najmuddin, Muhiuddin Hāji, **6**:908
Nakagawa Sin, **7**:594
Nakai, R. Carlos, **3**:498
Nakajima Miyuki, **7**:355
Nakane Genkei, **7**:568, 588
Nakao Tozan, **7**:698, 703, 720
Nakasone, Seisho "Harry," **9**:98
Nakayama Kotonusi, **7**:609, 610
Nakayama Sinpei, **7**:731, 743, 745
Nakazima Miyuki, **7**:747
Nakhaie, M. Reza, **3**:51
al-Nakhaylī, 'Abd al-'ālīm, **6**:174

Nakhcho (god), **8:**864
Nakorn Sawan, prince of Thailand, **4:**128
Nakpil, Julio, **4:**871
Nalke caste, **5:**882–83
Naluo faqu (*qin* piece), **7:**333
Nam Chung Musical Association, **3:**960, *961*
Nam Kihwan, **7:**984
Nam Kimun, **7:**965
Nam Sangsuk, **7:**853
Nam Sŏkhaeng, **7:**984
Nam Unyong, **7:**984
Nama people, **1:**703
Nambiar, Kunjan, **5:**514
Nambiśśan caste, **5:**931
Nambiyār caste, **5:**363, 510, 511, 931
Nambudiri Brahmins, **5:**239, 241–43, 509, 930
Namdev, **5:**249, 256
Namdo hwansanggok (Hwang), **7:**956
Namdo kutkŏri (Baek), **7:**957
Nā Mele Ho'ona'auao, **9:**275
Nā Mele Welo: Songs of Our Heritage, **9:**968
Namibia. *See also* Southern Africa; *specific peoples*
    Europeans in, **1:**717
    Herero people, **1:**715
    Khoikhoi people, **1:**703
    music of, **1:**428, 713–15, 717
    San people, **1:**703–5
Namiki Mitiko, **7:**745
Nammalvar, Saint, **5:**260–61
Namoluk Atoll (Chuuk State, FSM), **9:**733–37, *959*
Namonuito Atoll (Chuuk State, FSM), **9:**737–38
Namutin (Solomon Islands), **9:**662
Nanaimo Silver Comet Band, **3:**1094
Nanai people, **7:**12, 1027–30
Nanak (Sikh Guru), **5:**13, 256, 655, 772
Nanbei dynasty, **7:**191
Nanchao (kingdom), **4:**219
Nanda Das, **5:**251
Nanda Kishore Das, **5:**253
Nandamalini, **5:**422, *423*
Nandi (deity), **5:**357
Nandi people, **1:**605
Nandiwālā community, **5:**727
Nandu, Saint, **5:**253
Nangan, Butcher Joe, **9:***432–33*, 451
Nangiyār caste, **5:**399, 510, 511
Nangma Jidu, **7:**475
nanguan. See ensembles, musical
Nangû biwa hu (*biwa* score), **7:**588
Nani family, **8:**642
"*Nani Nā Pua*" (Lili'uokalani), **9:**924
Nanjing Arts Academy, **7:**398–99
Nan jiugong shisan diao qupu (Shen), **7:**130
Nannini, Gianna, **8:**209
Nant'a (theatrical production), **7:**946–47
Nanton, Tricky Sam, **3:**654
Nanumanga (Tuvalu), **9:**828–30
Nanumea (Tuvalu), **9:**829
Nanyadeva, king of Mithila, **5:**24, 72
Nanzhao state, **7:**30
Nao tai (*yangqin* piece), **7:**180
Nap Chum, **4:**193
Napata (Kush) Kingdom, **1:**550
Napier, Marie-Louise, **8:**366
Napoleon (Williams and Sabiston), **3:**200

Napoleon Bonaparte, **6:**21, 410, 544, 546, 608–9; **8:**186, 187, 286, 566
Napoleon in Egypt (al-Jabartī), **6:**22
Napuka (Tuamotu Islands), **9:**883
al-Naqshabandī, Sayyid, **6:**168
Nara period
    Chinese relations during, **7:**756
    gagaku in, **7:**626, 723
    instruments of, **7:**79, 561–62, 622, 701
Narada, **5:**24, 30, 47, 72, 86, 252, 313
    visual depictions of, **5:**301
Nāradīyaśikṣā (treatise), **5:**18, 23, 25, 71, 73
    content of, **5:**30–33
    description of, **5:**24
    passage on intonation, **5:**39
    passage on listener preferences, **5:**40
    passage on scales, **5:**38–39
    passage on singing, **5:**38
Narai, king of Siam, **4:**81, 225, 284
Naranappa, Kaivara, **5:**869
Naranjo, Bobby, **3:**777
Naranjo, Rubén, **3:**776
Narantsogt, **7:**1008
Narasimha (deity), **5:**230
Narayama busi kô (film), **7:**750
Narayan, Ram, **5:**55, 207, 338, 560
Narayan, Udit, **5:**540
Narayanaswamy, K. V., **3:***991*
Narayanatirtha, **5:**452
Nardi, Nachum, **6:**1071
Narendrasinghe, King, **5:**960, 965–66
Narimo, **10:***44*
Nariño culture, **2:**10, *11*
    archaeomusicological studies of, **2:**7
Narit, prince of Siam, **4:**128, 234, 276, 278, 281
Národopisné aktuality (periodical), **8:**733
Naropa Institute (Boulder), **3:**133
Narottama Thakur (Vaishnav saint), **5:**845–46
Narottam Das, **5:**253
narratives. *See also* ballads; *corridos*; literature; *p'ansori*; recitation; theater; vocal music; *specific titles*
    Adighian people, **8:**855
    Afghanistan
        epic songs, **5:**810
        gorgholi, **5:**827, 828–29
    Africa, **1:**117–18
        epics, **1:**107–8, 124, 130–44
    Ainu people, *kamuy-yukar*, **7:**784
    Albania, **8:**995
        epic songs, **8:**1004
        kângë kreshnikësh, **8:**989
    Andhra Pradesh, **5:**892–902
        burra katha, **5:**899, 901
        heroic epics, **5:**898
        piṭṭa katha technique in, **5:**894, 899
        topics for, **5:**896–99
    Anuta, *tangikakai*, **9:**857
    Arab
        mawāwīl, **6:**628
        shurūqi, **6:**545
        sīra, **6:**339–43, 628
    Armenia, **6:**723
        epic songs, **6:**728, 732–33
    Azerbaijan, *dastanlar*, **6:**929–30
    Bai people, *chuichuiqiang*, **7:**452

Balkarian people, **8:**857
Balochistan
    pahlawān, **6:**881
    shēr, **5:**776, 781, 783
Bellona, *tangi*, **9:**850, 851
Bengal
    jārigān, **5:**861
    maṅgala gān, **5:**846
    pālāgān, **5:**862
Bihar, *bidesia*, **5:**485
Bosnia-Hercegovina, epic songs, **8:**94, 130–31, 963, 965–66
Brazil, seafaring stories, **2:**334
Bribri and Cabécar cultures, *siwa' páköl*, **2:**633
Brittany, lays, **8:**561
Carriacou, genealogies, **2:**869
Central Asia
    dastān, **6:**900–902, 937, 945
    epic songs, **6:**900
Chechen people, **8:**864
China, **7:**91, 245–73
    accompaniment instruments for, **7:**247
    anthologies of, **7:**140
    banyan, **7:**273
    Buddhist, **7:**167
    Cantonese styles, **7:**267–73
    delivery styles of, **7:**246–47
    drumsong genres, **7:**253, 254, 395
    geyangqiang, **7:**452
    guquei, **7:**247
    kuaibanlei, **7:**246–47
    longzhou, **7:**273
    melody in, **7:**122
    minority groups, **7:**451–52, 463
    muyu, **7:**273
    nanyin, **7:**269–73
    northern traditions, **7:**251–55
    origins of, **7:**246
    overview of, **7:**245–50
    pinghualei, **7:**246–47
    pingtan, **7:**245
    pipa accompaniment, **7:**169
    schools of, **7:**55
    shuochang, **7:**6, 245, 346
    source materials on, **7:**129
    sung genres, **7:**247
    Suzhou tanci, **7:**261–64, 395, 411, 419
    Suzhou tanhuang, **7:**298
    teaching of, **7:**397
    women performers of, **7:**404, 407
    xiangshenglei, **7:**246–47
    yangqin accompaniment, **7:**180
    yue'ou, **7:**267–69
Cook Islands, *ura peu tupuna*, **9:**902–3
Corsica, *lamenti di banditi*, **8:**567, 568
Croatia, epic songs, **8:**927
Dai people, Buddhist sutras, **7:**503
Dominica, *kont* (storytelling), **2:**843
Egypt
    epic songs, **6:**10, 410–11, 545
    qiṣaṣ dīniyya, **6:**169–70
Europe, **8:**129–31
    epic songs, research on, **8:**23
    men's performance of, **8:**198
Faroe Islands, **8:**469
    historical ballads, **8:**399

narratives (*continued*)
Fiji
    Fiji kavvali, **5**:613
    meke, **9**:774–75
Finland, **8**:399
Finnish *Kalevala* performances, **3**:873, 1196
France, *complainte*, **8**:546
Georgia, epic songs, **8**:834
Germany, Nibelung and Hildebrand epics, **8**:651
Great Basin Indian groups, **3**:426
Greece
    epic songs, **8**:46, 129, 130, 198, 1024–25
    Karpathos, *syrmatika*, **8**:118
Guadeloupe, storytelling, **2**:876
Guaraní culture, *mborahéi pukú*, **2**:203
Gujarat
    ākhyān, **5**:632, 633–34
    chand, **5**:635, 636–37
    duho, **5**:635–36
    rāso epic, **5**:629
    soratho, **5**:636
Guyana, African storytelling traditions, **2**:444
Hawai'i, **9**:926
Hezhen people, **7**:518
Hindu, **5**:11, 261–62, 282
Hispano *indita*, **3**:757, 758, 762
Iceland
    epic poems, **8**:399
    heroic songs, **8**:129
    history of, **8**:404–5
    rímur, **8**:117–18, 400–403, 404, 407
Igbo people, **1**:459
India, North
    birahā, **5**:550
    kathā, **5**:549, 550
Ingush people, **8**:864
Inuit, **3**:1275
Iran
    dāstān, **6**:827, 840, 846, 851
    devotional, **6**:826–27
    epic songs, **6**:343–44, 829
    naqqāli tradition, **6**:344
    parde-dārī, **6**:827
    romantic, **6**:831
Ireland, lays, **8**:379, 385, 388
Irian Jaya, Asmat epics, **9**:590
Italy, epic songs, **8**:53, 607
Jamaica, storytelling, **2**:905
Japan, **7**:605
    bigin, **7**:650
    biwa accompaniment of, **7**:624
    bungo busi, **7**:681
    bun'ya busi, **7**:654
    gidayû busi, **7**:539, 551, 654, 657, 663, 667, 675–77, 719, 759, 765, 944
    heike biwa, **7**:586, 590, 617, 643, 646–47
    heike katari, **7**:82
    heikyoku, **7**:536, 624, 653, 680, 755–56, 757–58
    ittyû busi, **7**:679–82
    katô busi, **7**:658–59, 679–82, 697
    kiyomoto busi, **7**:658–59, 660, 679–82, 759
    kusemai, **7**:629, 653
    min'yô, **7**:600, 601
    miyazono busi, **7**:658–59, 679–82

    ôzatuma busi, **7**:658–59
    sekkyô busi, **7**:654
    sinnai busi, **7**:679–82
    tokiwazu busi, **7**:658–59, 660, 679–82, 759
    tomimoto busi, **7**:679–82
    zyôruri (*jôruri*), **7**:75, 546, 547, 551, 565, 617, 654, 657–59, 663, 675, 679–82, 691
Jewish people, **8**:256
    Haggadah, **8**:250, 251
Judeo-Hispanic *romanceros*, **8**:254, 256, 266, 968
Kajang people, *wa*, **4**:827
Kalmyks, Dzhángar epic, **8**:772
Karachaevian people, **8**:857
Karnataka
    caudike, **5**:872–74
    katha, **5**:867–68, 870, 872–74, *873*
    pāddana songs, **5**:415, 882–83, 885
    tāl-maddale, **5**:515–16, 879
Kashmir, *bhand-jashna*, **5**:485
Kazakh people, **7**:460
Kerala
    cākyār, **5**:510
    cavittunāṭakam, **5**:485
Kiribati, **9**:759
    te katake, **9**:762
Korea, *kasa*, **7**:807, 817, 818, 820, 866, 886, 919, 927–28
Kpelle Woi epic, **1**:124, 130–44; **10**:59–60
Kuna culture, **2**:644
Kurdistan, **6**:746–48
Kyrgyzstan, epic songs, **6**:903
Madhya Pradesh, epic songs, **5**:723–24
Malaysia, *selampit*, **4**:420
Maleku culture, **2**:682
Malta, **8**:637–38
Maluku, **4**:813
Mangareva, *atoga*, **9**:886
Marshall Islands
    bwebwenato, **9**:751
    iukkure, **9**:750, 752
Martinique, *krik-krac* tales, **2**:915
Mongol people
    baatarlag tuul', **7**:1005, 1007–8, 1011
    bengsenü-üliger, **7**:1004, 1008
    domog, **7**:1008, 1011
    qugur-un üliger, **7**:1004, 1008
Montenegro, epic songs, **8**:957–59, 961
Montserrat, storytelling, **2**:923
Mordvinian people, epic songs, **8**:773
Nahua culture, **2**:19, 20
Nauru, *iruwo*, **9**:755
Nepal, *karkhā*, **5**:698
New Mexican Hispano genres, **3**:757–58
Nivkhi people, **7**:788
North African epic tales, **6**:10, 431, 432, 1036
North Caucasia, Nart epic, **8**:851
Norway, **8**:412
    epic songs, **8**:413
Oceania, metaphor in, **9**:337–38
Oman, *riwāya*, **6**:678
Orissa, *chanda*, **5**:732–33
Ossetian people, **8**:860
Otopame culture, **2**:571–72
Pakistan, northern, **5**:795

Papua New Guinea
    Anêm people, **9**:616
    Banoni *wakekena*, **9**:646
    epic songs, **9**:488–89
    Huli people, **9**:540
    Iatmul mythological suites, **9**:340–42
    kang rom, **9**:514
    Kaulong people, **9**:619–20
    Melpa *kang rom*, **9**:521–22
    Nissan Atoll, **9**:638
Philippines, **4**:907–8, 908
    epics, **4**:852, 907–8, 910, 920, 927
    pabasa (also *pasyon*), **4**:843–45
Pohnpei, **9**:719
Poland, **8**:703
Polynesia, **9**:770
Punjab (Pakistan), **5**:770
Rajasthan
    epic songs, **5**:646
    in trance ceremony, **5**:292
    romance, **3**:757, 848, 849
Romania
    balade, **8**:875–76
    epic songs, **8**:23, 130, 874
    Rom epics, **8**:278
Russia, *byliny* (also *stariny*; *starinki*), **8**:23, 121, 129–30, 201, 754, 763–65
Ryûkyû Islands
    kudoki, **7**:791, 793–94, 795
    Miyako *tabi*, **7**:794
    Yaeyama *yunta*, **7**:794
Saami people, epic songs, **8**:486
St. Lucia, *listwa* (storytelling), **2**:943
Sāmoa, *fāgono*, **9**:799
Scotland
    lays (also *laoidh*; *duan*), **8**:361–62
    lowland, **8**:365
Serbia, epic songs, **3**:1199; **6**:342; **8**:14, 94, 129, 130–31, 941–42
Sicily, **8**:611
Sikaiana
    naha, **9**:846
    ttani kkai, **9**:847
Solomon Islands
    Fataleka and Baegu peoples, **9**:668
    Russell Islands, **9**:664
South Asia, **5**:480
    harikathā, **5**:89, 105, 106–7, 270, 390
    musicians in, **5**:399
    storytelling, **5**:401
    types of, **5**:485
Spain, *romance*, **8**:589
Sri Lanka, **5**:963
    virudu, **5**:965
Sumatra
    cerito (*kaba*), **4**:613
    guritan, **4**:623
    hikayat, **4**:615
    nyanyi panjang, **4**:616
    talibun, **4**:607
    warahan, **4**:627
Sumba, **4**:789–90, 791
Sunda, *pantun*, **4**:703, 712–13, 717
Taishan *muyu* genre, **3**:958, 960, 963
Taiwan, mainland genres, **7**:429
Takuu, *kkai*, **9**:842

Tamil Nadu, *kalakṣēpam*, **5:**262, 270, 907–8, 925

Thailand
  lam phün, **4:**325
  sepha, **4:**241, 250, 258–59, 264, 267, 272, 279

Tibetan culture
  King Gesar epic, **5:**710, 711–12, 715; **7:**451, 472, 477, 1008
  zhega and *lamamani*, **7:**477

Tikopia, *pese*, **9:**854

Tokelau, *kakai*, **9:**827

Tonga
  fakaniua, **9:**788
  fananga, **9:**786

Trinidad and Tobago, Indian, **2:**958

Tuamotu Islands, **9:**884

Turkey, **6:**80, 81–82
  destân, **6:**81–82, 762–63
  epic songs, **6:**766
  hikâye, **6:**851

Turkic epic songs, **6:**345–46, 967–70

Tuvalu, **9:**829

Uighur people, **6:**995; **7:**459

Uilta people, **7:**788

Ukraine, *dumy* (epic songs), **8:**99, 129, 813–14, *814*, 822

Uttar Pradesh
  birahā, **5:**667–68
  epics, **5:**673

'Uvea, *tagi*, **9:**811

Vanuatu
  sawagoro, **9:**695–96
  southern, **9:**706–8
  tanurnwe, **9:**695

Warao culture, **10:**97

West Futuna, *tagi* and *hkai*, **9:**862

Xibe people, **7:**518

Yaqui culture, **2:**591

Yoruba people, *álö* stories, **10:**114

Yuma culture, **2:**595–96

Nart epic, **8:**850, 851, 855, 857, 864

Nartosabdho, Ki, **4:**130, 666, 683, 684

Narváez, Peter, **3:**56–57

Nasca culture, **2:**467
  archaeomusicological studies of, **2:**7
  instruments of, **2:**11, *13*, 30, 207, 215

Nascimento, Milton, **2:**109, 124, 135, 318, 351

Nashashibi, Azmi, **6:**280

Nashenas, **5:**809

Nashīt, **6:**295

Nashuying qupu (Ye), **7:**132

Nashville Bluegrass Band, **3:**159

Nasīf, Zāki, **6:**554

al-Nāṣir, Jamāl 'Abd, **6:**601, 603–4

Naskapi Indian nation, **3:**383, 1074

Nasori (*komagaku* piece), **7:**624

Naṣr al-Dīn Shāh, **6:**861, 865

Nasrid dynasty, **6:**455

Nasriddinov, Muhammad Aminhon, **6:**899

Nassau (Cook Islands), **9:**909

Nasuhī Efendi, **6:**196

Nāṭ caste, **5:**476, *481*, 639, 640, 673

Natak (institute), **5:**487

Nataletti, Giorgio, **8:**621

Nataraja (deity), visual depictions of, **5:**110, 299, *300*, 301

Natarajan, A. K. C., **5:**232, 424

Natarajasundaram Pillai, **5:**392

Natasin School (Vientiane), **4:**352, 354, 357–58, 361

Natavan, **6:**928

Natchez Indian nation, **3:**466

"Natchez on the Hill" (fiddle tune), **3:**837, *837*

Natekar, Balkoba, **5:**423

Natesa Pillai, **5:**389

Nath, Pran, **10:**9–10

Nāth sect, **5:**476, 643, 648–49

Natha cult, **5:**253, 471, 733

Nathan, Hans, **3:**32

Nation (periodical), **3:**575

National Aboriginal and Islander Skills Development Association (NAISDA), **9:**228–29, 442–43

National Academy of Music (Bulgaria), **8:**905

National Academy of Music (Ghana), **1:**216

National Academy of Recording Arts and Sciences, **3:**714

National Academy of Tango (Argentina), **2:**519

National Academy of Tango (Uruguay), **2:**519

national anthems
  African, **1:**218, 222, 626, 764, 769
  Bangladesh, **5:**431, 436–37, 851
  Basque, **8:**311
  Bolivia, **2:**296
  Brazil, **2:**305
  Canada, **3:**14
  China, **7:**90, 346, 384
  Colombia, **2:**397
  Dominican Republic, **2:**858
  Egypt, **6:**598
  Estonia, **8:**496
  Finland, **8:**482
  France, **3:**939
  Great Britain, **3:**145, 521, 839; **5:**223, 433; **8:**186
  Guatemala, **2:**736
  identity and, **3:**505
  India, **5:**431, 437–38
  Israel, **6:**1069–70
  Korea, **7:**952, 976
  Malaysia, **4:**440
  Malta, **8:**638
  Nauru, **9:**262–63
  North Korea, **7:**961
  Oceania, **9:**321
  Papua New Guinea, **9:**129–30, 148
  Philippines, **4:**871
  Rom people, **8:**279–80
  South America, **2:**60
  Tlingit Indian nation, **3:**1277
  United States, **3:**305, 318, 521, 839
  Vietnam, **4:**510
  Western Sāmoa, **9:**219

National Anti-Slavery Standard, **3:**574–75

National Archives (Solomon Islands), **9:**963

National Archives of Music (Dominican Republic), **2:**862

National Arts Center (Ottawa), **3:**296

National Arts Center Orchestra (Ottawa), **3:**296, 1079, 1186

National Association for the Advancement of Colored People, **3:**608

National Association of Broadcasters, **3:**263, 708

National Association of Negro Musicians, **3:**608

National Ballet of Canada, **3:**224

National Ballet School (Canada), **3:**225

National Barn Dance (radio show), **3:**79, 560

National Black Theater of Harlem, **3:**621

National Bunraku Theater (Ōsaka), **7:**773, 775

National Center for Concert Music (Cuba), **2:**838

National Center for Higher Professional Education (Cuba), **2:**837

National Centre for the Performing Arts (Bombay), **5:**57, 529

National Ch'angguk Troupe, **7:**911, 945–46

National Classical Music Institute. *See* Kungnip Kugagwŏn

National Conservatory (Bolivia), **2:**284, 296

National Conservatory (Japan), **7:**56

National Conservatory of Music (Dominican Republic), **2:**858

National Conservatory of Music (Guatemala), **2:**736

National Conservatory of Music (Hanoi), **4:**89, *119*, *120*, 129

National Conservatory of Music (New York), **3:**538, 606

National Conservatory of Music (Tunisia), **6:**330, 332, 510–11, 512

National Conservatory of Music (Vietnam, planned), **4:**511

National Convention of Gospel Choirs and Choruses, **3:**632

National Council of Education (United States), **3:**276

National Council for the Traditional Arts (United States), **3:**823; **4:**354; **10:**82

National Dance Company of Ghana, **1:**39

National Dreams (Francis), **3:**1059

National Education Association, **3:**276

National Endowment for the Arts, **3:**119, 207, 222, 288, 295, 297, 298–99, 301, 513; **10:**81–85

National Endowment for the Humanities, **3:**298–99, 859, 1037

National Ensemble for Folk Song and Dance (Bulgaria), **8:**890, 902

National Federation of Music Clubs, **3:**1209

National Film and Sound Archive (Australia), **9:**415, 959

National Film Board (Canada), **3:**292, 1184, 1185

National Gramophone Company, **3:**487

National Heritage Fellowships, **3:**299, 301, 513

National History and Arts Council (Guyana), **2:**443

"National Interest March" (Kupferberg), **3:**317

National Library of Australia, **9:**415, 959

National Library of Canada (Ottawa), **3:**289

National Library of New Zealand, **9:**932, 974

National Library of Wales, **8:**353

National Lyric Opera (Brazil), **2:**305

National Museum (Bosnia-Hercegovina), **8:**970

National Museum (Panama), **2:**772, 783

National Museum (Papua New Guinea), **9:**962

National Museum of American History
    (Washington, D.C.), **3**:300
National Museum of Anthropology (Mexico),
    2:557
National Museum of Anthropology and
    Archaeology (Peru), **2**:467; **10**:100
National Museum of Australia, **9**:960
National Museum of Baghdad, **6**:358
National Museum of Canada (Ottawa), **3**:31,
    291, 292
National Museum of Cuban Music, **2**:829, 838
National Museum of Ethnology (Japan), **7**:525
National Museum of Finland, **8**:181, 481
National Museum of Natural History
    (Washington, D.C.), **3**:493
National Museum of the American Indian
    (Washington, D.C.), **3**:492
National Museum of the Solomon Islands,
    9:962–63
National Museum of Wales, **8**:353
National Museums of Scotland, **8**:182
National Music College (Nanjing), **7**:398
National Music Course (Mason), **3**:276
National Music Publishing House (Cuba), **2**:828
National Music Reform Society (Beijing), **7**:376
National Networked Facility for Research in
    Australian Music, **9**:960
National Nô Theater (Japan), **7**:766, 773
National Opera (Washington, D.C.), **3**:852
National Orchestra (Aotearoa), **9**:931
National Origins quota, **3**:*507*
National Public Radio, **3**:299
*National Republican Grant and Wilson Campaign
    Song Book*, **3**:308
National School of Art (Cuba), **2**:837
National School of Dance (Guyana), **2**:444
National School of Music and Theatrical Art
    (Saigon), **4**:511, 512
National Self Teacher for Hawaiian Ukulele . . .
    (Moyer), **9**:286
National Sound Archive (Jerusalem), **6**:1037
*National Standards for Arts Education: What Every
    Young American Should Know*, **3**:302
National Symphony Choir (Costa Rica), **2**:702
National Symphony Orchestra (Bolivia), **2**:284
National Symphony Orchestra (Costa Rica),
    2:702
National Symphony Orchestra (Washington,
    D.C.), **3**:300
National Temperance Songster, **3**:309
National Theater (Seoul), **7**:969, 983, 994
National Theater (Tokyo), **7**:761, 774, 775
National Theater of the Opera and Ballet
    (Tiranë), **8**:999
National Theatre Company (Papua New
    Guinea), **9**:235
National Tune Index, **3**:839
nationalism. *See also* ideology; politics
    Afghanistan, **5**:807–8, 834–35, 836–37, 840
    African-American, **3**:603, 609, 676–78
    Albania, **8**:1003
    Argentina, **2**:262
    art music and, **2**:113–15; **3**:327; **8**:4
    Bahamas, **2**:802, 808
    Baltic states, **8**:399
    Bangladesh, **5**:503, 858–59

Barbados, **2**:814
Basque region, **8**:309, *312*, 314–16
Belarus, **8**:796, 800
Bengal, **5**:846, 848–49, 853–55
Bolivia, **2**:284
Bosnia-Hercegovina, **8**:962
Brazil, **2**:305–6
    samba and, **2**:315–16
    tropical-forest region, **2**:134
Bulgaria, **8**:*894*, 904
Canada, **3**:16, 74, 314, 1058, 1061–62, 1086,
    1146–47, 1149, 1183
Central Asia, **6**:903, 904–6
Chile, **2**:104
China, **7**:89–90, 136, 139–40, 339, 347–48,
    379–82, 383, 385, 389
Colombia, **2**:397–98, 401
Cook Islands, **9**:896
Croatia, **8**:917, 927, 933–34
Cuba, **2**:827–28
Czech Republic, **8**:725–26
Denmark, **8**:460
Dominica, **2**:840–41, 844
Dominican Republic, **2**:845, 857–58, 860
East Asia, **7**:43
Egypt, **6**:235–36
England, **8**:332–33, 337, 339
Estonia, **8**:496
ethnicity and, **3**:505
Europe, **8**:184–88
European concept of, **8**:2
Finland, **8**:185, 227, 479, 482, 488
folk (traditional) music and, **8**:7, 16, 53, 59,
    82, 91, 95–96, 123–24, 155, 227
Georgia, **8**:843–44
Greece, **8**:1022, 1024
Guadeloupe, **2**:873–74, 879
Guyana, **2**:444, 448
Haiti, **2**:887–88, 892, 894
Hawai'i, **9**:220–22
Hungary, **8**:270, 737, 738–39, 747–48
identity issues and, **3**:505–7, 511
ideology and, **8**:10, 184–88
India, **5**:404, 444, 466, 624, 911
Indonesia, **4**:85
Inner Asia, **7**:36
Iran, **6**:860–61, 862
Ireland, **8**:390–92
Israel, **6**:263–64, 1015, 1069
Italy, **8**:618, 620
Japan, **7**:729, 733, 736
Jewish identity issues and, **8**:266
Kazakhstan, **6**:960–61
Korea, dance and, **7**:69
Kurdish people, **6**:751–52
Latvia, **8**:504–6
Lithuania, **8**:510, 512–14
Macedonia, **8**:972, 1011
Malaysia, **4**:78
Martinique, **2**:920
Mexico, **2**:600, 604–5, 619, 621
Montenegro, **8**:959
Morocco, **6**:496
Nepal, **5**:696–97, 705–6
Nicaragua, **2**:754, 765–66
Nigeria, **1**:402–3, 407–8

North Caucasia, **8**:851
Norway, **8**:411, 424–26
Nubian people, **6**:643
Oceania, **9**:212
Pakistan, **5**:404
Palestinian *intifāḍa*, **6**:635–40
Papua New Guinea, **9**:139
Paraguay, **2**:460–61
Peru, **2**:491, 498, 500
Philippines, **4**:85, 860, 871–72
popular music and, **2**:92–93, 100; **9**:126–27
Portugal, **8**:577, 583
Québec, **3**:51, 145–46, 314, 1059, 1067,
    1073, 1161–62, 1165–66
Réunion Island, **5**:610
rise of, **8**:10, 12, 82, 249
Romania, **8**:882
Russia, **8**:270, 755, 765, 775, 780
St. Lucia, **2**:946, 950
Scotland, **8**:365, 371
Serbia, **8**:954
Singapore, **4**:524
Slovakia, **8**:725–26
Slovene, **8**:921
South America, **2**:245
South Asian, **5**:431–38
Southeast Asia, **4**:2–3
South Korea, **7**:805, 808–9, 900, 958, 967,
    969, 972, 997
Spain, **8**:270, 601
spread of, **8**:5
Sri Lanka, **5**:971, 972
Sweden, **8**:437, 441, 444–45
Switzerland, **8**:682, 692
Taiwan, **7**:424
Tunisia, **6**:505–6, 510–11
Turkey, **6**:77, 79, 247, 255, 781–87, 812–14,
    816
Turkmenistan, **6**:976–77
United States, **3**:16
Uruguay, **2**:521
Venezuela, **2**:540
visual arts and, **2**:12
world music and, **8**:225
Yoruba people, **1**:407
Nationalteatern (rock group), **8**:216
Native American Bible Church, **3**:486
Native American Church, **3**:425, 426, 433, 443,
    455, 477, 480, 487–88
Native American Graves Protection and
    Repatriation Act (NAGPRA), **3**:311,
    491–99
Native American peoples. *See also* First Nations
    peoples; *specific groups*
    California, **3**:412–18
    citizenship legislation, **3**:13
    compositional techniques, **3**:369–70
    concepts of dance, **3**:214
    concepts of music, **3**:7, 15, 369–70
    cultural images of, **3**:525
    cultural interactions, **3**:21–22, 831
    early European accounts of, **3**:23, 332, 367
    fusion genres of, **3**:326, 337, 345
    gender-role studies of, **3**:93–94
    Ghost Dance movement, **3**:421–22
    Great Basin region, **3**:420–27

Great Lakes, **3:**451–59
Hawai'i, **9:**107
history of musical culture, **3:**5–7, 366–67
horse culture, **3:**421, 440, 1086
instruments of, **3:**238, 472–79
musical styles of, **3:**32, 367–68, 525–26
music incorporated into classical compositions, **3:**14, 291, 367, 539
nineteenth century, **3:**9, 10–11
"noble savage" image, **3:**23–24
Northeast region, **3:**461–65
Northwest Coast region, **3:**394–402
pan-Indian movement, **3:**215–16, 463, 467, 480
Plains region, **3:**440–50
population of, **3:**4, 143, 525
religious movements, **3:**421–22, 425, 426, 443, 449, 462–64
repatriation issues, **3:**294, 311–13, 491–99
research on music of, **3:**14, 29, 31, 70–71, 291–92, 367, 444–45, 465, 470, 508–10, 511–12
social and musical interactions, **3:**480–90
Southeast region, **3:**466–70
Southwest, **3:**428–38
subjugation of, **3:**17
trade networks of, **3:**3, 429
urban relocation program, **3:**481
Native American Rights Fund, **3:**492
Natividad, Alejo, **4:**857
Nat King Cole Trio Time (radio program), **3:**655
Na't Khwān group, **5:**770
Nattiez, Jean-Jacques, **3:**381
Natural History of Aleppo (Russell), **6:**566
Natural Man (musical), **3:**621
"Natural Woman" (Franklin), **3:**710
Nature Boys (musical group), **3:**1052
Nātyalochana (treatise), **5:**72
Nātyaśāstra (treatise), **5:**18, 104, 262, 298, 372, 633, 731
  on audience contribution, **5:**470
  as basis for later treatises, **5:**43
  contents of, **5:**25–30
  dance in, **5:**299, 363, 509, 515, 519, 521
  date of, **5:**22
  description of, **5:**23–24
  information on *mridangam*, **5:**356
  information on performers, **5:**228, 399
  instrument classification in, **5:**51, 319, 320, 321–26, 327, 329, 350, 351
  nātya concept in, **5:**507–8
  passage on drumming, **5:**41
  passage on theater ensemble, **5:**40
  raga theory in, **5:**73–75
  rasa theory in, **5:**71–72, 313, 317
  references to temple dancers, **5:**408
  relevance of, **5:**52
  on *śruti*, **5:**67
  tala theory in, **5:**110, 139, 140–41
  theater in, **5:**480, 492
Nau, Father François, **3:**23
Naughty Marietta (Herbert), **3:**193, 544
Naughty by Nature, **3:**699
Naukācaritram (Tyagaraja), **5:**452
Naumann, Hans, **8:**19
Naumann, Johann Gottlieb, **8:**444

Naumbourg, Samuel, **3:**934
Nauru, **9:**712, 715, 740, 754–58, 764
  children's music, **9:**260–63
  history of, **9:**754–55
  I-Kiribati in, **9:**760, 764
  immigrants to Australia, **9:**85–86
  instruments of, **9:**716
  music and dance of, **9:**231, 719, 754–58
  pedagogy in, **9:**261–62
  popular music in, **9:**721
  sound recordings from, **9:**995
  string bands of, **9:**388
  string figures in, **9:**755, *758*
  vocal music in, **9:**321
Nautu, Dorri, **9:**972
Nava, José María, **4:**866
Nava L., E. Fernando, **2:**568, 573–74
Navā'ī, Alishir, **6:**836, 914, 943
Navaira, Emilio, **3:**781
Navajita Plátea, **8:**599
Navajo Community College (Tsaile), **3:**496
Navajo Indian nation, **3:**428, 432–33, 755
  girls' puberty ceremonies, **3:**371, 433
  historical songs, **3:**368
  instruments of, **3:**475, 476, 477
  popular music of, **3:**433
  repatriation of sacred objects, **3:**311–13, 492, 496, 499
  song sources, **3:**369
  song subjects, **3:**526
  use of popular songs, **3:**369
Navajo Songs, **3:**498
Navajo Times, **3:**311
Navanitakrishnan, M., **5:**912
Navanitakrishnan, Vijayalakshmi, **5:**556, 912
Navaroji, Rev. Dinakaran Sara, **5:**924
Navarro, Fats, **3:**797
Navarro, Lea, **4:**885
Navarro, Ramón, **9:**43
Navasupai Indian nation, **3:**428
Naviso (Vanuatu), **9:**693
Navras Records, **5:**528
Navy Cultural Work Troupe (China), **7:**399
Nawa (musical group), **6:**1006
Nawahi, Benny, **9:**390
Nawāi. See Navā'ī, Alishir
Nawar people, **6:**625
al-Nawawī, **6:**372
Nawaz, Saz, **5:**694
nawba. See nūba
Nawba Na'imāt (Shiḥr ensemble), **6:**96, 97, 103
Nawmat al-Ḍuḥá, **6:**296
Naxi people, **7:**509–15
  Baisha xiyue genre, **7:**511
  dances of, **7:**450
  dianju opera, **7:**512
  dongjing repertoire of, **7:**445, 512–13
  folk songs of, **7:**511
  mass media influences on, **7:**444
  music of, **7:**415, 485–92
  population of, **7:**509
  research on music of, **7:**139
  ritual music of, **7:**512
nay. See flutes
Nāy caste, **5:**702

Nāyak rulers, **5:**220, 269, 907–8
Nāyakkar dynasty, **5:**960, 966
Nāyakkar people, **5:**284
Nāyanārs, **5:**105, 215–16, 260–61
Nāyar caste, **5:**509, 930, 931, 936
Nayarít culture, archaeomusicological studies and iconographic record of, **2:**7, 12
Nayeb Asadollāh, **6:**868
Nayî Osman Dede, **6:**108
Nayo, Nicholas Zinzendorf, **1:**26, 44, 221, 223, 224, 226, 227
Nazareth (musical group), **8:**369
Nazareth (Nazaré), Ernesto, **2:**305, 350
Nazario, Máximo, **4:**868
Nāẓeri, Shahrām, **6:**828
Nazîm, **6:**115
Nazir, Muhammad, **5:**901
Nazrul Islam, Kazi, **5:**437, 846, 849, 850, 853–55, 856, 857, 858
Nbanga, Edward "Edo," **1:**386
Ndao, **4:**786
Ndebele people, **1:**114, 673, 705, 757
Ndembu people, **1:**272
Ndlazilwane, Victor, **1:**779
Ndogo people, **1:**570
Ndoja, Bik, **8:**999
N'Dour, Youssou, **1:**365, 419, 422, 437; **3:**339, 341
Ndubuisi, Okechukwu, **1:**233, 237, 238–52
Neal, Larry, **3:**582
Neale, Frederick Arthur, **4:**225
Neal(e), John and William, **8:**17, 393
Near East Ensemble (Los Angeles), **3:**1036
"'Neath the Passion Vine: South Seas Serenade," **9:**43
Nebiki no Kadomatsu (Chikamatsu), **7:**669
Nebraska
  Native American groups in, **3:**440, 451
  Swedish people in, **3:**870–72
  Volga Germans in, **3:**890
Nebuchadnezzar, king of Babylonia, **6:**411
Necib Pasha, **6:**779
Ned A. Hatathli Cultural Center/Museum (Tsaile), **3:**496
Ned, Annie, **3:**1277
Nedbal, Oskar, **8:**729
Nedîm, **6:**115
Neduha, Jaroslav Jeroným, **8:**731
Neej Tshiab Band, **9:**76
Ne'eman, Amitai, **6:**1073
Ne'eman, Yehosh'a Lev, **6:**1065
Neff, Françoise, **2:**568
Negār, Baste, **6:**866
Negishi Kazuim, **7:**595
Negrete, Jorge, **2:**621
"*Negrita*" (Dueñas Perilla), **2:**393
Negrito, El (*trovo*), **3:**758
Negrito peoples, **4:**594
  Philippines, **4:**872, 913, 920
"Negro Boy Sold for a Watch," **3:**307
Negro Ensemble Theater, **3:**621
Negro Musicians and Their Music (Cuney-Hare), **3:**581
Negro Nuances (musical), **3:**608
Negro Philharmonic Society (New Orleans), **3:**615

Negro Slave Songs in the United States (Fisher), **3:**627
"Negro Speaks of Rivers" (Swanson), **3:**610
Negrón Rivera, Julio, **2:***935*
Negu Gorriak (musical group), **8:**315
Nehan kôkyôkyoku (Mayuzumi), **7:**737
Neho, Charles, **9:**948
Neill, Edward, **8:**622
Neimeng minge-zhuti xiaoqu qishou (Sang), **7:**348
Neja, Mindia, Kanak high chief, **9:**402
Nejep Oglan (folk story), **6:**969
Nejma, Elma'alma, **6:**1044
Nelson, David P., **5:**161
Nelson Davies, Kristina, **6:**19, 162
Nelson, Edward W., **3:**381
Nelson, Job, **3:**1094, 1096
Nelson, Johnny, **3:**799
Nelson, Sarah, **7:**15
Nelson, Steven G., **7:**595; **10:***15*
Nelson, Willie, **3:**81, 339, 520
Nelson's Cornet Band, **3:***1094*
Nelsova, Zara, **3:**1079
Nenets, **8:**754, 772
Neng Yang, **3:***1005*
Neni-kole, Feme, **10:***57*
Neoclassicism, **8:**85
Neolithic period, **5:**298; **7:**11–12, 17, 105–7; **8:**36–38, 682, 687, 704, 881
neoromanticism, **3:**176, 541
Nepal, **5:**696–707
    caste musicians in, **5:**696–700
    Damāi people, **5:**273, 280–81, 284, 286, 698–700
    dance traditions of, **5:**505, 701, 703–5
    ethnic musical traditions, **5:**700–705
    folk songs of, **7:**483
    Gāine people, **5:**697–98, 706
    Gandhaki zone, **5:**698
    geography of, **5:**489
    Guruṅg music, **5:**703–5
    history of, **5:**489–90, 696
    Humla, *bag-ston gyi glu* (marriage songs), **5:**710
    instruments in, **5:**291, 699–700, 702, 703–4, 705
    jātrā theater in, **5:**490
    Kathmandu, **5:**490, 706
        Hindustani music in, **5:**697
        musical life in, **5:**705, 706
        rock bands in, **5:**428
    languages of, **5:**5
    light classical music in, **5:**696
    Mahayana Buddhism in, **5:**257
    map of, **5:***3, 680*
    musical genres
        ādhunik gīt, **5:**705
        bhajan, **5:**254
        dhrupad, **5:**250
        Gāine song repertoire, **5:**698
        lok gīt, **5:**705–6
        rāṣṭrīya gīt, **5:**705–6
    Mustang region, vocal music, **5:**711
    Newār music, **5:**702–3
    popular music in, **5:**428, 705
    population of, **5:**5
    research on music of, **5:**697–98, 700

    shamanism in, **5:**289–91
    Shar-Khumbu region, **5:**713
    temple music, **5:**700
    theater in, **5:**489–90
    Thulung Rai people, **5:**288
    Tibetan culture in, **5:**709–16
    Tibetan monasteries in, **5:**713
    timing of ceremonies in, **5:**296
    weddings in, **5:**279
Nepalese people
    in Bhutan, **5:**5, 489
    in North America, **3:**949
    in United Kingdom, **5:**572–76
Nepia, Moana, **9:**947
Nepomuceno, Alberto, **2:**306
Nerses Shnorhali, **6:**724, 737
Neruda, Pablo, **8:**1021
Nerval, Gérard de (pseud. of G. Labrunie), **3:**1164; **8:**547
Neset, Neri, **8:**417, 419
Neshat, Shirin, **6:**828
Nesimi (contemporary *aşik*), **6:**796, *797*, 798
Nesimi, Seyid Imaddedin, **6:**791, 796, 922, 928
Nestorian Church, **5:**945
Nestorian doctrine, **6:**207, 843
Netherlands, **8:**518–36. *See also* Low Countries
    Amsterdam
        Sephardic and Ashkenazic synagogal traditions in, **8:**258, 262, 263
        world music in, **8:**210
    Caribbean territories, **2:**791, 927, 953
    dance traditions of, **8:**523–24, 535
    immigrant groups in, **8:**231, 237–38
    Indo-Caribbean community in, **3:**817
    instruments and instrumental music, **8:**170, 523–33, 535
        research on, **8:**35
    Jewish people in, **6:**1036
    map of, **8:***516*
    popular music in, **8:**208
    population of, **8:**518
    research on music of, **8:**533–35
    Rom people in, **8:**288
    Sephardic Jews in, **8:**248
    Tilburg, Derde Werde Festival, **8:**154
    vocal music of, **8:**518–23
    Volendam singing style, **8:**521
Netherlands Antilles, **2:**789, 927–31. *See also* Aruba; Bonaire; Curaçao
    art music in, **2:**931
    history of, **2:**927
    instruments of, **2:**928–29
    musical traditions, **2:**928
    political status of, **2:**792
    popular music in, **2:**930–31
    population of, **2:**927
    research on, **2:**931
    tambú in, **2:**928, 929–30
Netsilik Inuit, **3:**374, 381
Nettl, Bruno, **1:**63–64; **3:**367, 418, 445, 484, 511, 512, 517, 828; **5:**881; **6:**23, 67, 68; **7:**227–28; **8:**22; **10:**42, 56, 101, 139, 160, 164, 165
Neua people, **4:**218, 348
Neubauer, Eckhard, **6:**92
Neue deutsche Gesänge (Hassler), **8:**653

Neufeld, K. H., **3:***1239*
Neuhauss, Richard, **9:**479
Neukomm, Sigmund, **2:**305
Neuman, Daniel M., **3:**980; **5:**57, 136, 379, 380, 460–61, 567
Neumayer, Peter, **8:**679
Neutrals (First Nations people), **3:**1078, 1178
Nevada
    Basque people in, **3:**217, 847, 849–50
    Las Vegas, dance performances in, **3:**219
    Native American groups in, **3:**415, 428
Nevárez, E., **3:**738
"Never Can Say Good-Bye" (Gaynor), **3:**711
Nevermann, Hans, **9:**992
Nevermind (Nirvana), **3:**358
Never Mind the Bollocks (Sex Pistols), **7:**468
Never on Sunday (film), **8:**1007
Neves e Melo, Adelino António, **8:**585
Neves, José Maria, **2:**320
Nevin, Ethelbert, **3:**549
Nevis (island), **2:**97
Nəvvab, Mir Möhsun, **6:**927
Ne Win, **4:**398
New Age music, **3:**49, 133, 327, 345–47, 489, 954
    audience for, **3:**341
    in Korea, **7:**959, 971–72
    use of didjeridu, **9:**397
Newār people, **5:**5, 700, 706
    dance traditions of, **5:**505
    musical traditions of, **5:**702–3
"New Britain" (folk tune), **3:**533
New Britain (Papua New Guinea), **9:**472, 600, 607–25. *See also* Bali (Unea); Vitu; *specific peoples*
    betel use in, **9:**177
    geography of, **9:**607
    history of, **9:**607
    instruments, **9:**613–14, 615, 619, 623–25
        garamuts, **9:**547, 601
        log idiophones, **9:**376
        musical bows, **9:**386
        panpipes, **9:**401
    Lapita cultural complex in, **9:**4
    map of, **9:***473*
    missions on, **9:**21, 147
    prehistoric, **9:**474
    Rabaul, **9:**620
        buai magic of, **9:**636
        guitar playing, **9:**387–88
    research on, **9:**607, 974, 983
    sound recordings from, **9:**991, 992
    trade with Siasi Islands, **9:**573
New Brunswick
    Acadians in, **3:**1136
    African-Canadians in, **3:**1132
    First Nations groups in, **3:**291, 461
    history of musical life, **3:**1114–21
    Saint John, musical life in, **3:**1115, 1116
New Budapest Orpheum Society, **10:**159
New Caledonia, **9:**598, 671–87, 836. *See also* Grande Terre; Isle of Pines; Lifou; Loyalty Islands; Maré; Tiga; West 'Uvea
    Americans in, **9:**27
    archives and museums, **9:**964–65

dance, **9:**316
films on, **9:**1008, 1015
Futunans in, **9:**814–15
geography of, **9:**671
history of, **9:**671
immigrants in, **9:**69
immigrants to Australia, **9:**85
instruments, **9:**679–82, 964
  flutes, side-blown, **9:**401–2
Lapita cultural complex in, **9:**4
music and dance of, **9:**48, 671–87, 980
  kaneka, **9:**213–14, 965
  political songs, **9:**212
prehistoric, **9:**682, 684–85
Russian expedition to, **9:**23
social organization in, **9:**5
sound recordings from, **9:**992–93
New England. *See also* Connecticut; Maine;
    Massachusetts; New Hampshire; Rhode
    Island; Vermont
Armenian people in, **3:**1030
ballads in, **3:**153–58
contra dance in, **3:**230–34, 836–37
early attitudes toward music, **3:**24–26
folk music of, **3:**325
French-Americans in, **3:**854–55
lumber camps in, **3:**157
Native American groups in, **3:**461–65
psalmody in, **3:**831–33
singing schools in, **3:**7, 275
New England Conservatory of Music (Boston),
    3:15, 606–7, 1036
New England Foundation for the Arts, **3:**1001
Newfoundland
Acadians in, **3:**1137
comic songs, **3:***1124*
dance music, **3:**1124–25
fishing moratorium songs, **3:**1138–43
folk styles in, **3:**1063, 1070–71, 1121
history of musical life, **3:**1070, 1114, 1117–18
Labrador
  Algonquian peoples, **3:**383
  European voyagers, **3:**379
  Inuit in, **3:**374, 1069, 1074
  Jesuit missionaries in, **3:**390
  Moravian influences on Inuit music, **3:**380,
      1118, 1275
Norse contact in, **3:**7, 143, 1056, 1068, 1069
population of, **3:**5
St. John's, **3:**1118
step dancing in, **3:**223, 1125
swilin song genre, **3:**1124
New France, **3:**7, 9, 23–24, 275, 1056,
    1074–75, 1146, 1147, 1163
New Generation (musical group), **3:**1199
New Georgia (Solomon Islands), **9:**663
New Grove Dictionary of American Music, **3:**980
New Grove Dictionary of Music and Musicians,
    3:828; **8:**91
  Japanese translation, **7:**540
New Guinea (island of), **4:**2; **9:**471–87. *See also*
    Irian Jaya; Papua New Guinea
Chinese people in, **9:**69–70
Europeans in, **9:**474–75
films on, **9:**982
history of, **9:**474–75

Lapita cultural complex in, **9:**4
map of, **9:***473*
outsiders' influence in, **9:**5
population of, **9:**472
prehistoric, **9:**474
research on, **9:**975, 977
New Guinea Collection, **9:**962
New Guinea National Theatre Company, **9:**225,
    234
New Hampshire. *See also* New England
ballads in, **3:**153–58
New Hanover. *See* Lavongai
New Harvard Dictionary of Music, **8:**91
New Hebrides. *See* Vanuatu
New Image (musical group), **3:**1196
New Ireland (Papua New Guinea), **9:**472, 600,
    625–29
betel use in, **9:**177
ceremonies, *malanggan* complex, **9:**350, *351*,
    628
cultural links with Nissan, **9:**630, 632
geography of, **9:**626
instruments
  friction blocks, **9:**374, 380–82
  garamuts, **9:**601
  log idiophones, **9:**376
  musical bows, **9:**386
Lapita cultural complex in, **9:**4
lounuat repertoire, **9:**381
map of, **9:***473*
missions on, **9:**147
music and dance of, **9:**600, 625–29, 981
prehistoric, **9:**474
research on, **9:**983
sound recordings from, **9:**991
New Israeli Opera (Tel Aviv), **6:**1031
New Jack City (film), **3:**715
New Jersey
Armenian people in, **3:**1030
British Caribbean community, **3:**808
Chinese people in, **3:**957
Iranian people in, **3:**1031
Lakewood, Estonian people in, **3:**878, 879
Latino peoples in, **3:**719
Marlboro, South Asian people in, **3:**982
Native American groups in, **3:**461
Newark, African-American musicians in,
    3:604
New Brunswick, Hungarian people in, **3:**908
Pinkster Day celebrations, **3:**595
Portuguese people in, **3:**847–48, 851
Seabrook, Estonian people in, **3:**878
South Asian people in, **3:**981
New Kumaisa, **9:**179
Newlandsmith, Ernest, **6:**20, 223
Newlight movement, **3:**1132
Newman, Alfred, **3:**203, 546; **9:**45
Newman, Grace Mora, **3:**317
New Mexico
Acoma Pueblo, **3:**428
Albuquerque, **3:**756
  Comanchitos dance, **3:**761
Alcalde, *matachines* dance in, **10:**89
Cochiti Pueblo, **3:**428
cultural patrimony issues, **3:**311–13
cultural regions, **3:**756

Española, **3:**756
Hispano (Mejicano) music and traditions,
    3:718–19, 720, 721–25, 754–68, 849,
    850–51; **10:**88–95
history of musical life, **3:**754–56
Isleta Pueblo, **3:**428
Jemez Pueblo, **10:**89
  use of popular songs, **3:**369
Laguna Pueblo, **3:**428
Las Cruces, **3:**428, 756
Las Vegas, **3:**756
Nambé Pueblo, **3:**428
Native American groups in, **3:**368, 420–22,
    425–27, 428–38
Penitente sect, **3:**757, 759, 762, 848
Picurís Pueblo, **3:**428
Pojoaque Pueblo, **3:**428
Pueblo Indians, *matachines* dances, **3:**430,
    614, 759, 850–51
Sandía Pueblo, **3:**428
San Felipe Pueblo, **3:**428
San Ildefonso Pueblo, **3:***217*, 428; **10:**90
San Juan Pueblo, **3:**371, 428; **10:**89, 90
  Butterfly Dance, **3:**368, 429
Santa Ana Pueblo, **3:**428
Santa Clara Pueblo, **3:**428
Santa Fe, **3:**756
  zarzuela companies, **3:**851
Santo Domingo Pueblo, **3:**428
Spanish settlement in, **3:**9, 521, 754–55, 847
Taos, **3:**756
Taos Pueblo, **3:**213, 428
  Comanche dance, **3:**761
Tesuque Pueblo, **3:**428
Zia Pueblo, **3:**428
New Moon (Romberg), **3:**544
New Music (quarterly), **3:**174
New Music Concerts (Toronto), **3:**1080, 1186
New Music Group, **2:**306
New Musical Express (periodical), **8:**211
New Musical Grammar (Tans'ur), **3:**26
New Musical Resources (Cowell), **3:**174
New National Theater (Japan), **7:**761
New Orleans Brass Funeral Band, **3:**568
New Orleans Creole Band, **3:**1091
New Ottawa Carleton Male Choir, **3:**1195
New Rican Village Cultural Center (New York),
    3:799
New School for Social Research (New York),
    3:175, 176
Newsflash Sounds, **3:**1133
New Spain, **2:**603, 933; **3:**770, 771
Newsweek (periodical), **3:**354
New Symphony Orchestra (Japan), **7:**732
Newton-Davis, Billy, **3:**1212
Newton, Douglas, **9:**976
Newton, John, **3:**533
Newton-John, Olivia, **9:**414
New Vista Records, **3:**750
new wave, **3:**689; **8:**204, 218, 220, 674
New Westminster Choral Union, **3:**1094
New World Theatre (Charleston), **3:**179
New Year and Courtesy Cotillion (Hemmenway),
    3:604
New York, **2:**796–97
Armenian people in, **3:**1030

New York (*continued*)
　Buffalo, public school music education, **3:**275
　Catskill Mountains
　　Irish-American resorts, **3:**845
　　Jewish resorts, **3:**941
　Finnish people in, **3:**872–75
　Fire Island, **3:**228
　Iranian people in, **3:**1031
　Italian people in, **3:**861–62, 864–65
　Latino peoples in, **3:**719
　Livingston County, **3:**864–65
　Native American groups in, **3:**461–65
　New York City
　　African-American composers in, **3:**604
　　African-American theater in, **3:**615
　　Arab people in, **3:**1029, 1033
　　Asian communities in, **3:**948–49
　　avant-garde in, **3:**175–76
　　balalaika orchestra in, **3:**57
　　bands in, **3:**564
　　British Caribbean community, **3:**808–12
　　British regimental bands in, **3:**563
　　Broadway musicals, **3:**618–20
　　Bukharan Jews in, **6:**905, 919–20
　　Central American communities in, **3:**727
　　Chinatown Tet celebration, **3:***513*
　　Chinese Lion Dance organizations, **3:**955
　　Chinese people in, **3:**957, 958
　　dance performances in, **3:**219
　　dance styles in, **3:**212
　　disco clubs in, **3:**227–30, 687–88
　　East Harlem community, **3:**507
　　Estonian people in, **3:**878
　　ethnic musics in, **3:**97
　　Filipino people in, **3:**1024, 1025
　　Greek people in, **3:**929, 930
　　Greenwich Village, **3:**316
　　Haitian people, **3:**803, 805
　　Harlem Renaissance, **3:**607
　　hip-hop culture in, **3:**692, 693
　　Indo-Caribbean community in, **3:**817
　　Indonesian people in, **3:**1011
　　Irish people in, **3:**324, 842, 845
　　Italian people in, **3:**860–61, 861
　　Japanese people in, **3:**973
　　jazz in, **3:**550, 654–59, 662–65
　　Jewish people in, **3:**934, 935–39, 942–43;
　　　10:69–71, 72–73, 74–75, 131–32
　　Korean people in, **3:**975–79
　　Latin Caribbean community, **3:**790–800
　　Middle Eastern peoples in, **3:**1028
　　mid-nineteenth-century musical life in,
　　　3:59–61
　　musical theater in, **3:**193–95, 196–98,
　　　544–45, 935, 937–38, 943–44
　　operetta in, **3:**544
　　orchestras in, **3:**536–37
　　Puerto Ricans in, **3:**336, 719, 725–27, 794,
　　　798, 799
　　rap in, **3:**701, 713
　　Russian people in, **3:**915
　　salsa in, **3:**336, 788, 798–99
　　Santería in, **3:**784
　　Slovak people in, **3:**899–900
　　South Asian people in, **3:**981
　　taiko drumming groups in, **3:**971, 973

　　Thai people in, **3:**950, 1010
　　theater in, **3:**542
　　Tin Pan Alley, **3:**12, 194–95, 260, 548–49,
　　　705
　　Turkish people in, **3:**1030
　　West Indian carnival in, **3:**507–8
　　world music in, **10:**71–74
　　zarzuela companies, **3:**851
　Pinkster Day celebrations, **3:**595, 614
　Potsdam, teacher training in, **3:**277
　Rochester, high school orchestra in, **3:**277
　Saratoga Springs, African-American musicians
　　in, **3:**604
　Utica, Polish people in, **3:**892
　Yates County, Danish people in, **3:**882–83
New York Community Choir, **3:**634
New York Dolls (musical group), **3:**357
New York Estonian Male Chorus, **3:**878
New York Gaelic League, **3:**324
New York Oratorio Society, **3:**535
New York Philharmonic, **3:**60, 536, 564, 612,
　885
　performances of newly composed music,
　　3:175, 176, 610
New York Public Library for the Performing Arts,
　Dance Collection, **3:**221
New York Tribune, **3:**308
New York University, **10:**69, 133–35
New York World's Fair, **3:**1013
New Youth (periodical), **7:**383
New Zealand. *See* Aotearoa; Cook Islands; Tokelau
New Zealand Māori Chorale, **9:**936
Nexsus, **9:***305*
Nexus (musical group), **3:**1080
ney. See flutes
Neyzen Salih Dede, **6:**110
Nez Perce Indian nation, **3:**421
Nezāmī, **6:**922, 924, 928
Ng, Sheung Chi, **3:**963, *963*
Ng Taikong, **7:**232
Ngada people, **4:**791
Ngāhua, **9:**941–42
Ngai Lum Society (Vancouver), **3:**1262–63, 1266
Ngaju people, **4:**825
Ngā Mōteatea, **9:**932, 944
Ngangela peoples, **1:**672–73, 676–77
Ngansan people, **7:**1027–30
Ngata, Sir Apirana, **9:**277, 353, 354, 932,
　936–37, 939, *940*
Ngata, Reupena, **9:**314–15
Ngāti Pōneke Club, **9:**936–37
Ngāti Toa people, **9:**940–41
Ngatipa, Takai, **9:**908
Ngatirah, **4:**684
Ngawai, Tuini, **9:**277, 354, 931, 936
Ngbaka people, **1:**267, 655
Ngema, Mbongi, **1:**275, 276, 777
Nggela Island (Solomon Islands), **9:**630, 666
Ngiusanga, Jason, **9:***851*
Ngiyampaa people, **9:**441
Ngô dynasty, **4:**447
Ngoni people, **1:**635, 705
　history of, **1:**744
　Malawi invasion of, **1:**275
　migration of, **1:**320–21
　music of, **1:**638, 643

Ngozi, Winston Mankunku, **1:**779
Ngū, Wellington, prince of Tonga, **9:**130, *131*
Ngubane, Simon, **1:**29
Ngudya Wirama (musical group), **10:**44
Ngulu Atoll (Yap State, FSM), **9:**729
Ngumu, Pie-Claude, **1:**45, 659, 660–61
Nguni peoples
　blood sacrifice, **1:**277
　history of, **1:**705
　music of, **1:**705–6, 715, 719, 773
Nguyễn Bính, **4:**480
Nguyễn Đình Tấn, **4:**512
Nguyễn Du, **4:**493
Nguyễn dynasty, **4:**70, 448–49, 482, 492, 498,
　507
Nguyễn Hiền, **4:**480
Nguyễn, Phong T., **3:**953, *994*, 996; **4:**25
Nguyễn Trãi, **4:**448
Nguyễn Văn Bửu, **4:**452, 509
Nguyễn Văn Thận, André, **4:**493
Nguyễn Văn Thương, **4:**512
Nguyễn Văn Thuyên, **4:**509
Ngwenya, Devera, **1:**433
Nhac Viet (periodical), **3:**953
Nhang people, **4:**218
Nhật Lai, **4:**512
Nhia Ka Moua, **3:***1004*
Niaotou lin (Yi), **7:**220
Niblo's Garden (New York), **3:**60, 61
Nicaragua, **2:**628, 747–67; **3:**719
　archaeomusicological studies in, **2:**7
　art music in, **2:**764–65
　Atlantic Coast, **2:**749–55
　children's wakes in, **2:**422
　Creole people, **2:**753–55
　Garífuna culture, **2:**733, 747, 749, 752–53
　geography of, **2:**747
　Granada, **2:**757
　history of, **2:**747–49
　instruments of, **2:**8–9
　León, **2:**757
　map of, **2:**629
　mestizo people in, **2:**755
　Miskitu culture, **2:**659–64, 747, 749, 765
　Monimbó, **2:**757
　musical genres
　　mento, **2:**753, 754
　　nueva canción, **2:**103
　　palo de mayo, **2:**754–55, 765
　　purísima, **2:**762–63
　　romance, **2:**758
　　son, **2:**760, 761
　　sones de cacho, **2:**762
　　sones de pascua, **2:**765
　　sones de toro, **2:**762
　　son nica, **2:**764
　　villancico navideño, **2:**763
　　volcanto, **2:**764, 765
　musical life, **2:**765–66
　Pacific Coast, **2:**755–64
　popular music in, **2:**763–64
　population of, **2:**747, 749
　Rama culture, **2:**747, 749
　research on, **2:**767
　Sumu culture, **2:**739, 747, 749, 750–51
Nicaraguan-Americans/Canadians, **3:**719,
　727–28

Nicarao culture, **2:**9, 680, 747, 755
  archaeomusicological studies of, **2:**7
Nichang qu (*Jiangnan sizhu* piece), **7:**225
Ni chang yu yi ge (Bai), **7:**123
Nicholls, Robert W., **1:**112
Nicholson, Calum Ruadh, **8:**362, 370
Nicholson, Joseph, **3:**624
Nicholson, Ruby, **2:**690
Niciton (musical group), **7:**1020
Nico, Doctor, **8:**234
Nicobar Islands, **5:**5, 485
Nicola, Jean, **2:**50
Nicola, Narat, **2:**50
Nicolas, Arsenio, **4:**891
Nicolas, Francis, **1:**574, 584
Nicolas, René, **4:**306
Nicomachos of Gerasa, **6:**16, 360, 368
Niculescu, Stefan, **8:**883
Ní Dhomhnaill, Caitlín, **8:***389*
Nido Tituti (Tamagusuku), **7:**66
Nie Er, **7:**90, 346, 347, 350, 354, 384, 385
Niebelungenlied (epic), **8:**129
Niebuhr, Carsten, **6:**107, 108
Niedermeyer, Louis, **3:**28, 1165
Nielsen, Carl, **8:**444, 451, 460
Nielsen, Grüner, **8:**465
Nielsen, Selma, **8:**24, 464
Nielsen, Svend, **8:**25, 464
Nielson, Mataio, **9:***902*
Nieto, Ubaldo, **3:**662
Nievera, Bert, **4:**884
Nievera, Martin, **3:**1025; **4:**886
Nieves, Tito, **3:**743, 799
Niewindt, Martinus Joannes, **2:**928
Niger. *See also* North Africa; West Africa; *specific*
      peoples
  Agadez, **1:**538
  griots in, **1:**540
  Tuareg people, **1:**546–47, 574, 578–79,
     584–88; **6:**273
    curing ceremonies, **1:**537–38
    weddings, **1:**539
Niger Symphony (Tillis), **3:**612
Nigeria. *See also* West Africa; *specific peoples*
  academic training in, **1:**39–40
  Afikpo people, performance spaces, **1:**117
  Bankalawa people, dance, **1:**289
  Bantu cultures of, **1:**659–63
  Benin kingdom in, **1:**4, 5
  Chawai people, dance, **1:**289
  civil war in, **1:**408, 477–78
  composition in, **1:**44, 221, 222, 232–53
  court music, **1:**313–14
  Dagari people, dance, **1:**289
  dance, **1:**288–90
  drums, cord-and-peg tension, **1:**315–17
  Eastern Forest region, **1:**458
  Edo people, dance, **1:**118
  Efik people, speech surrogate methods, **1:**107
  Fulani people
    dance, **1:**289
    gime, **1:**451
  Fulɓe kingdom, court music, **1:**311–12
  Galambawa people, dance, **1:**289
  Guguba people, dance, **1:**289
  guitar in, **1:**351, 353, 364, 377

Ham people, dance, **1:**289
Hausa people, **1:**515–29
  dance, **1:**289
  healing rituals, **1:**273
  speech surrogate methods, **1:**106
  highlife in, **1:**423
Higi people, dance, **1:**289
Ibo people, **1:**34–35
  speech surrogate methods, **1:**106
Igbo people
  dance accompaniment, **1:**113
  historical studies, **1:**91–92
  masks of, **1:**119
  secret societies, **1:**309
Igede people, funeral ceremonies, **1:**111–12
instruments of, **1:**450
Irigwe people, masks of, **1:**119
iron bells, **1:**310
Islam in, **1:**413–14
Jarawa people, dance, **1:**289
jùjú, **1:**387
Kagoro people, dance, **1:**289
Kru people, **1:**373, 374–75, 377, 379–81
Kurama people, dance, **1:**289
Lagos, **1:**401–2, 471–73, 477
  guitar in, **1:**352–53, 359
lamellophones, **1:**317, 318–19
Maguzawa people, dance, **1:**287, 289
Margi people, dance, **1:**289
  masks of, **1:**119
music industry in, **1:**417
music research in, **1:**14–15, 46, 47, 49
nationalist movement in, **1:**402–3, 407–8
Niger Delta region, song, **1:**103
Nomana people, dance, **1:**289–90
Nyamalthu (Terawa) people, dance, **1:**288
Piti people, dance, **1:**289
popular music of, **1:**323
population of, **1:**2
Tiv people, inside-outside distinctions, **1:**130
Tshi people, historical studies, **1:**93
Ture people, *sasa-ture* dance, **1:**286–87
Yoruba people, **1:**19, 36–37, 89–91, 459
  dance, **1:**118
  festivals of, **1:**411–13
  historical studies, **1:**93
  inside-outside distinctions, **1:**130
  popular music of, **1:**471–87
  speech surrogate methods, **1:**107
  theater of, **1:**400–402, 406–9
Nigerian Institute of Music, **1:**14–15
Nigerian people, in England, **8:**231
Niggaz with Attitude (NWA), **3:**698, 699, 714
Nightingale, Maxine, **3:**712
Nightingale, Tunde Western, **1:**480, 481, 482
"Night in Tunisia," **3:**659
Night of a Hundred Stars (television program),
    7:367
"Night of the Thumpasorus Peoples"
    (Parliament), **3:**684
Nigog (periodical), **3:**1149–50
Nigra, Costantino, **8:**606, 620
Nihon cendai sakkyokuka renmei (society), **7:**732
Nihon kayô kenkyû siryô syûsei, **7:**589
Nihon Min'yô Kyôkai, **7:**603
Nihon ongaku (Kikkawa), **7:**545

Nihon ongakubunka kyôkai, **7:**733
Nihon ongaku gairon (Iba), **7:**592
Nihon ongakusi (Iba), **7:**592
Nihon ongaku siryô syûsei, **7:**589
Nihon sandai zituroku (dynastic history), **7:**586
Nihon syoki (also *Nihon gi*; chronicle), **7:**539,
    586, 723
Nijenhuis, Emmie te, **5:**56, 57
Nijinsky, Vaclav, **8:**161
Nijô Yoshimoto, **7:**639
Nikifaroŭski, Mikoła, **8:**803
Nikoaos Ağa, **6:**779
Niles, Don, **9:**372, 480, 570, 607, 986
Nilote people, **1:**599, 635
Nilsson, Birgit, **8:**434
Nilsson, Christine, **3:**556; **8:**434
Nimad dynasty, **5:**721
Nima Quiche, **2:**718
Nimbarkacharya, Sri, **5:**251–52
Nimbus (record company), **5:**529
Nimfa, Nana Kwamina, IX, **10:**31
Nimmons, Phil, **3:**1080
Nimo, Koo, **1:**366, 377
Nimri Dede, **6:**798
Nin Weijong, **7:***511*
Nine Days of Fortune, **7:**451
1989 (musical group), **7:**360
1999 (Prince), **3:**685
Ninigo Group (Papua New Guinea), **9:**602
Ninin wankyû (*nagauta* piece), **7:**673
Ninmyô, emperor of Japan, **7:**620
Niño Perdido, El (*pastorela*), **3:**759
Niosi, Bert, **3:**1107
Nippon Hôsô Kyôkai, **7:**599
Nippon Ongaku Gakkai, **7:**592
Nippon Pro Musica (musical group), **7:**972
Nipu, Nipu, **9:**909
Nirvana (musical group), **3:**358; **4:**887
Nisenan Indian nation, **3:**415
Nisga Indian nation, **3:**1093
Nishang qu (*Hangzhou sizhu* piece), **7:**239
Nishang xu-pu (poetry collection), **7:**154, 155
Nishigata Akiko, **7:**691
Nishumbha (deity), **5:**505
Nisio, Bert, **3:**1080
Nissan Atoll (Papua New Guinea)
  instruments of, **9:**630, 639–40
  music and dance of, **9:**632–40
Niu Longfei, **7:**137
Niu Tao, **7:**511
Niu Weijiong, **7:***513*
Niue, **9:**771, 816–17
  drumming, **9:**114
  history of, **9:**816
  instruments of, **9:**817
  map of, **9:***772*
  music and dance of, **9:**816–17, 947
  research on, **9:**817, 973
  sound recordings from, **9:**985, 1000
Niuean people
  in Aotearoa, **9:**113, *114*
  in Australia, **9:**84, 85
Niutao (Tuvalu), **9:**828
  films on, **9:**982
  music and dance of, **9:**829–30
Niuzai nü (*huju* opera), **7:**300

Nivkhi people, 7:787–88, 1027–30
Nixon, Richard, 3:310
Niyāzī-i Misri, 6:194
Nizami, Ghulam Farid, 5:768
Nizami of Ganja. *See* Nezāmī
Nizamuddin Auliya (Sufi saint), 5:752, 755
    tomb of, 5:*12*
Ni zheng pu (Liang), 7:172
Njoku, Jak, 10:62
Njoku, Johnston Akuma-Kalu, 1:233
Nkabinde, Simon "Mahlathini," 1:430, *431*,
    776–77, 779
Nketia, J. H. Kwabena, 1:25, 26–33, 137–38,
    221, 650, 723; 3:*581*, 585, 593;
    10:29, 112, 140, 142–43
    coining of term "timeline," 1:310
    compositions of, 1:8, 224, 227, 230
Nkhangala people, 1:672
    drums of, 1:677
    masked dancing, 1:8
    music of, 1:741–42
Nkhata, Alick, 1:33
Nkhumbi people, 1:651, 714
Nkonyane, Elijah, 1:*771*, 774
"*Nkosi Sikelel' iAfrika*" (Sontonga), 1:218, 626,
    764, 769
Nkosi, Zakes, 1:779
Nkoya people, 1:711, 712–13
Nkrumah, Kwame, 1:32; 3:336
nô, 7:533, 629–36, *631*
    actors in, 7:631
    aesthetics of, 7:73, 546
    asirai style in, 7:552
    Buddhist ideology in, 7:565
    calls in, 7:634–35
    in Canada, 3:1084
    chant in, 7:546, 552, 554, 630, 632–34,
        770–71
    chorus in, 7:631
    dissemination of, 7:539
    female performers of, 7:766
    hayasi in, 7:683
    history of, 7:76, 629–30
    influence on *kumi odori*, 7:789–90
    influence on *utai mono*, 7:693
    instrumental pieces in, 7:635
    instruments in, 7:624, 634–35, 771
    ma concept in, 7:553
    movement in, 7:59, 63, 64
    mugen nô, 7:629–30, 640
    music in, 7:77
    notation for, 7:538, 580–81, *582*, 583
    origins of, 7:75, 536
    patronage of, 7:687
    percussion mnemonics in, 7:55
    performance contexts of, 7:653, 774–75
    performance versions in, 7:635–36
    repertoire of, 7:631–32
    rhythmic cycles in, 7:572
    sarugaku and, 7:618, 629, 639
    stage in, 7:630, *630*
    structure of, 7:632
    theories in, 7:565
    transmission of, 7:759, 768, 776
    utai bon, 7:589–90, 617; 10:27
    vocalization in, 7:551, 552

    writings on, 7:588, 653–54
    Zen influences, 7:549
    zyo ha kyû concept in, 7:554
"No Coons Allowed!" (Cole), 3:616
No Fixed Address, 9:145, 146, 443
"*No me niegues*" (Garcia), 3:737
No me puso mi madre (Judeo-Spanish song),
    6:*1043*
No Sé Quien y No Sé Cuantos, 2:486
No Strings (Rodgers), 3:621
No Tongŭn, 7:854
No World Improvisations (musical group), 3:954
Noanama culture, 2:379
Noanime, Tannese Chief, 9:64
Noatsi people, 9:381
Nobat-*bagsy*, Ödenyaz, 6:976, 977
Nobili, Robert de, 5:923
Noble, Johnny, 9:163, 919, 922
Nobody Lied (*When They Said That I Cried Over
    You*) (Berry), 3:*260*
Nobre, Marlos, 2:306
Nóbrega, Manoel da, 2:302
Nobs, Claude, 8:698
Nobutoki Kiyosi, 7:731, 733
noche está serena, La" (Garcia), 3:737
Noel (Mota singer), 9:701
Noelia (*cuarteto* singer), 2:276
Nôgaku siryô syûsei, 7:589
Nogay people, 6:966
Nogŭm pangch'o (*kayagŭm pyŏngch'ang*), 7:908
noh. *See* nô
Noisy Boys, 9:32–33, 709
nôkan. *See* flutes
Nok Lae, 4:98–99
Noksaek ŭi pulkil (Kim), 7:959
Nolan, Dick, 3:1125
Nolan, Faith, 3:1134
Noli Me Tangere (Rizal), 4:881
Nollyang (Korean folk song), 7:886
Nolsøe, Napoleon, 8:471
Nomadi (musical group), 8:619
Nomads of the Wind (film), 9:47, 48–49
Nomana people, 1:289–90
Nomlaki Indian nation, 3:415
Nommensen University (Medan), 4:602
Nomura Antyô, 7:793
Nomura Kôiti, 7:729
Nomura kunkunsî (*sansin* collection), 7:793
Nonesuch Records, 8:241
Non'gae, 7:985
Nongbuga (Korean folk song), 7:882, 957
Nonouti (Kiribati), films on, 9:982
Noorjehan, 5:420, 538
Nootka Convention (1790), 3:1255
Nootka (Núu-chá-nulth; Westcoast) Indian
    nation, 3:394, 397
    potlatch ceremony, 3:396, 398
    whaling rituals, 3:395
Nopsae param (album), 7:972
Norae karak (Korean folk song), 7:881
Nordal, Jón, 8:407
Nordal, Sigurður, 8:407
Nordenskiöld, Erland, 2:649
Nordgren, Gösta "Snoddas," 8:445
Nordheimer, Abraham, 3:1179–80
Nordheimer firm, 3:1183

Nordhoff, Charles, 9:24, 41, 44–45
Nordic Cultural Centre, 8:472
Nordic Leikarring (Grand Forks), 3:867
Nordic Museum (Stockholm), 8:307
Norit'ŏ (Lee), 7:955, 956, 957
Norland, Sigurður, 8:407
Norlind, Tobias, 8:447
Norman, Jerry, 7:19
Norman, Jessye, 3:537
Norman, Karyl (pseud. of George Paduzzi),
    3:*260*
Normand, Mabel, 3:262
Normans, 8:326, 360
Norraena empire, 8:468
Norrøna Leikarring society (Minneapolis), 3:867
Norsk Folkemusikk (periodical), 8:427
Norsk Folkemusikk og Danselag, 8:427
Norsk Musikkgranskning (periodical), 8:427
Norsk Musikk-Kongress, 8:430
Norte de Potosí, 2:297
North. *See* North *plus next element in name*
North, Alex, 3:203
North, Richard, 3:1020
North Africa, 1:533–47. *See also* Algeria; Egypt;
    Libya; Maghrib; Morocco; Tunisia;
    specific peoples
    colonialism in, 1:532, 578
    emigrants to France, 8:208, 210, 237
    folk music traditions of, 6:437–38
    geography and population of, 1:532; 6:429
    Hamadsha brotherhood, healing rituals, 1:274
    history of, 1:533–34
    influence on European instruments, 8:168
    influence on European singing, 8:517
    influence on Maltese language, 8:634
    influence on Maltese singing style, 8:636
    influence on Portuguese music, 8:577
    influence on Sephardic music, 8:254, 265
    influence on Sicilian music, 8:610, 611, *612*
    influence on Spanish music, 8:594, 600
    influence on West African music, 1:447, 449,
        452
    Islam in, 1:416
    maps of, 1:*530*; 6:*430*
    music genres of, 1:533–34
    popular music of, 1:545–47
    professional musicians in, 1:540–41
    research on music of, 8:18
    Sahel region of, 1:532, 533
    Sephardic Jews in, 8:248
North Alabama Citizens' Council, 3:354–55
North America. *See* Canada; United States
North American Basque Organization, 3:849
North American Free Trade Agreement, 3:18,
    266, 290, 1061, 1068
North American Indian Musical Styles (Nettl),
    3:512
North Carolina
    Asheville, folk festival, 3:146
    blues in, 3:639
    Charlotte, as center for country music, 3:76
    dance programs in, 3:221, 222
    early African-Americans in, 3:598
    field hollers in, 3:85
    John Kuner celebrations, 3:614
    Moravians in, 3:528

Native American groups in, **3:**461, 466
Vietnamese minority groups in, **3:**996
North Caucasia, **8:**850–64. *See also* Abkhazian
    people; Adighian people; Balkarian
    people; Chechen people; Ingush
    people; Karachaevian people; Ossetian
    people
  Chechnya, **8:**850, 861–64
  history of, **8:**850
  instruments, **8:**851
  map of, **8:***752, 827*
  political struggles in, **8:**851, 862
  popular music in, **8:**851
  population of, **8:**850
  regional musical styles, **8:**851
  state folk ensembles in, **8:**851
  Turkmen people in, **6:**967
  vocal polyphony of, **8:**14, 753, 851
Northcott, William, **9:**132
North Country (Somers), **3:**1059
North Dakota
  German people in, **3:**891
  Native American groups in, **3:**440
  Norwegian people in, **3:**866–70
  Swedish people in, **3:**870–72
  Turtle Mountain, Métis in, **3:**344, 405–11
Northeast Indian nations, **3:**461–65
  Algonquian groups, **3:**384
  history and culture of, **3:**461–62
  instruments of, **3:**463, 472–79
  music of, **3:**463–64
  performance contexts, **3:**462–63
  research on music of, **3:**465
  women's musical roles, **3:**371
Northern Arapaho, **3:**445
Northern Areas (Pakistan), **5:**744, 792–800
  Astor, **5:**792
  Baltistan, **5:**682, 792, 800
  Diamar district, **5:**792
  geography of, **5:**792
  Gilgit district, **5:**682, 792, 797–98
  history of music in, **5:**799
  Hunza, **5:**682, 797–98, 800
  instrumental music of, **5:**794–98
  instruments in, **5:**795–96
  map of, **5:***742*
  Nager, **5:**800
  population of, **5:**792
  research on music of, **5:**799–800
  vocal music of, **5:**794
Northern Arts and Cultural Center (Yellowknife),
    3:1278
Northern Illinois University (Dekalb), **3:**953
Northern Ireland. *See also* Ireland
  parades and competitions in, **8:**385, 388
  pentatonic tunes in, **8:**378
  Protestantism in, **8:**378
  traditional music of, **8:**389
Northern Mariana Islands, Commonwealth of
    the, **9:**712, 743. *See also* Saipan
  Americans in, **9:**160
  belembaotuyan, **9:**387, 745–46
  betel use in, **9:**177
  Europeans in, **9:**158
  films on, **9:**1016
  Mortlockese people in, **9:**91–92

music and dance of, **9:**48, 59, 743–46
popular music in, **9:**721
sound recordings from, **9:**996
Spanish in, **9:**717
theatrical societies, **9:**229
Northern Ojibwa Indian nation, **3:**383
Northern Paiutes, **3:**420, 421, 435, 487
Northern Shoshones, **3:**421
Northern Skies (musical group), **3:**1280
Northern Song dynasty
  music in, **7:**89, 321
  music theory in, **7:**121
Northern-Southern dynasties, **7:**517
  Daoism in, **7:**312, 321
  music in, **7:**88
North Korea. *See also* Korea
  ch'anggŭk in, **7:**946
  composition and creativity in, **7:**960–63
  cultural policies in, **7:**804, 808, 991–92
  cultural preservation in, **7:**47, 997
  farmers' bands in, **7:**933, 938
  instrument modifications in, **7:**830–31, 961–62
  "Sea of Blood" operas, **7:**76, 946, 962–63, 992
Northrop, Henry D., **1:**85, 87
Northrup, Solomon, **3:**598
North Star Mennonite Church Band, **3:***1239*
North Sumatra University (Medan), **4:**602
North Tanami Band, **9:**445
Northumbrian Pipers' Society, **8:**331
Northwest Coast Indian nations, **3:**383,
    394–402. *See also specific groups*
  brass bands of, **3:**11, 1094
  dances of, **3:**222
  historical changes, **3:**395–96
  instruments of, **3:**472–79
  interaction with Athapaskans, **3:**384
  links with California groups, **3:**412
  musical characteristics, **3:**401–2
  musical genres, **3:**396–401
  performance contexts, **3:**5, 395
  song ownership, **3:**394
  sound recordings of, **3:**291
  trade language, **3:**1258
  trade networks, **3:**6
  women's songs, **3:**371
North West Company, **3:**1255
North West Frontier Province (Pakistan), **5:**744,
    785–91
  Chitral, **5:**800
  geography of, **5:**785
  instruments in, **5:**786–90
  map of, **5:***742*
  population of, **5:**785
  Tera region, **5:**788
  vocal music of, **5:**786
Northwest Mounted Police Band, **3:**1090
Northwest Territories, **3:**9, 1255, 1273–81. *See*
    also Nunavut
  Arctic peoples, **3:**374–81
  Athapaskan peoples, **3:**383, 1275–76
  European exploration and settlement, **3:**379
  geography of, **3:**1274
  musical life in, **3:**1097
  popular music in, **3:**1277–78
  population of, **3:**1274
  Yellowknife, **3:**1274

Norton, Barley, **4:**25
Norway, **8:**13, 411–31
  art music in, **8:**411, 424–28
  Bergen, **8:**420
  concert life in, **8:**427
  court music, **8:**146, 423
  dance traditions of, **8:**166, 417
  fiddlers' competitions, **8:**150, *151*, 427
  geography of, **8:**411
  Hallingdal region, **8:**422
  Hardanger region, **8:**417
  history of, **8:**411, 424
  history of music in, **8:**422–26
  Icelandic skalds in, **8:**405
  instrument collections in, **8:**182
  instruments and instrumental music, **8:**25, 99,
    141, 170, 176, *177*, 197, 414–20,
    422–23
  Kongsberg, **8:**420
  Lærdal, **8:**420
  local repertoires, **8:**121
  map of, **8:***398*
  Nordfjord, **8:**419, 422
  Norfjordeid, *landskappleik*, **8:**150
  Oslo, concert life in, **8:**427
  popular music in, **8:**205, 208, 430–31
  population of, **8:**411
  research on music of, **8:**427
  Røros, **8:**419
  rule over Faroe Islands, **8:**468
  Saami people in, **8:**12, 299–307, 428–29
  Setesdal region, **8:**417, 419
  Telemark, **8:**417–18, 422, 425
    hardingfele music, **8:**121
  trønderrock in, **8:**96, 430
  Trondheim Cathedral, **8:**423
  Valdres region, **8:**417, 421
  Valestrand, **8:**424
  vocal music of, **8:**106–7, 134, 363, 412–14
  Voss region, **8:**417
Norwegian Jazz Federation, **8:**427
Norwegian Opera Company, **8:**427
Norwegian people
  in Hawai'i, **9:**96, 100
  in Iceland, **8:**405
  in North America, **3:**826, 866–70
    dance music of, **3:**868–69
    hardingfele traditions, **3:**869–70
    vaudeville, **3:**869
    vocal music of, **3:**866–68
    western Canada, **3:**343, 1089, 1250–51
Norwegian Singers Association of America,
    3:867
Norwegian Song and Music Council, **8:**430
Norwegian State Academy of Music, **8:**427
Nosaka Keiko, **7:**779; **10:**13
"Nos braves habitants" (La Bolduc), **3:**1156
Nosotros (Latino association), **3:**751
Not Drowning, Waving, **9:**155, 1005
notation. *See also* Benesh notation; Labanotation;
    Tonic sol-fa; transcription
  African music, **1:**146–62
  alphabetic, **6:**18, 113, 771; **8:**49
  Angola, sand ideographs, **1:**150–51
  Babylonian, **6:**8
  Balinese, **4:**737

notation (*continued*)
  Bartók's views on, **8**:95
  basso continuo, **8**:*78*, 104
  biwa, **7**:538
  Braille, **8**:99
  Byzantine, **8**:886
  chant, **8**:70
  charango, **2**:289
  Chinese, **7**:123–25
    banzi pu, **7**:125
    Buddhist graphic, **7**:330, *332*
    cipher, **7**:124
    ersipu, **7**:213
    gongchepu, **3**:1260; **7**:54, 124–25, 130, 169,
      202, 207, 213, 217, 268, 287, 317,
      321, 513, *514*, 725, 793, 834
    jianzipu, **7**:125, 161
    lülüpu, **7**:54, 834
    luogujing, **7**:55, 123–24, 192
    mnemonic types, **7**:123–25, 202
    northern ensemble music, **7**:202–3
    prescriptive types, **7**:54, 92
    research on, **7**:136
    sources for, **7**:130–33, 965
    wenzipu, **7**:124, 161
    Western types, **7**:125
    yuyin fashi, **7**:321
  cipher, **10**:106, 115, *115*
  circle, **6**:*393*
  Colombia, of popular music, **2**:394
  composite systems, **1**:151
  conch-band, **9**:*197*
  dance, **1**:158, 161; **3**:221; **9**:314–17, *454*,
    460, *461*, *466*, *783*
  difficulties of, **1**:21
  of early ragas, **5**:24, 34–35, 48, 75
  East Asia, **7**:5, 50, 54–55
    Western, **7**:50
  ekphonetic, **6**:229, 723–24; **8**:881
  electronic, **9**:289
  Ethiopia, *melekket* system, **1**:147–50, 151,
    152, 159
  Europe, **8**:6, 90–92
    art music, **8**:68, 73
    authority and, **8**:93–94
  Ewe drumming, **1**:35
  "eye music," **8**:51
  fasola, **3**:*276*
  Fraktur calligraphy, **3**:905
  France, **8**:549
  Franconian, **8**:104, *105*
  graphic, **1**:136–37, 157–58, 161, *653*; **8**:91,
    99, 768; **9**:287
  Greece, ancient, **8**:1022
  of Greek music, **8**:69
  Hamparsum (Limondjian) system, **6**:18, 110,
    113, 119, 725, *727*, 771
  Hindustani (*svarlipi*), **5**:445
  history and development of, **8**:49–56, 59, 90,
    102–4
  Iceland, **8**:406
  ideographic, **8**:103–4, *105*
  Indian music, **5**:432–33, 434, 444, 464, 850,
    851
  interaction with oral transmission, **3**:22
  Ireland, manuscripts of lays, **8**:379

Japan, **7**:573–83
  bunka hu, **7**:578
  for *gagaku*, **7**:771
  hakase, **7**:582–83, 613
  for *kabuki*, **7**:659–60
  kari bakase, **7**:583
  katei siki (*miyagi hu*), **7**:575–77
  mnemonic types, **7**:55
  for percussion instruments, **7**:580–81
  philosophy of, **7**:768
  prescriptive types, **7**:54–55
  seihu, **7**:593
  for stringed instruments, **7**:574–78
  vocal, **7**:581–83, 589
  Western types, **7**:574, 577–78, 583, 778
  for wind instruments, **7**:578–80
Java, **4**:636, 660, 676–77, 683
Karnatak music, **5**:100–101
khaz, **6**:723–24, 737
Klavierskribo, **8**:*104*
Korea, **7**:834–35, 837–39
  gongche (*kongch'ŏk*), **7**:834, 838
  hapchabo, **7**:55, 839, 856
  kuŭm, **7**:817, 890
  mnemonic types, **7**:55
  oŭm yakpo, **7**:838, 856
  rhythmic (*chŏngganbo*), **7**:54, 55, 807,
    834–35, 837, 842, 856, 953, 965, 993
  for *samullori*, **7**:967
  verbal, **7**:935–36
  yŏnŭmp'yo, **7**:839
  yukpo, **7**:55, 838, 856
  yulchabo (*lu-lu*), **7**:54, 55, 834, 838, 856
Kuna culture, **2**:647, *648*
lead sheets, **8**:104
letter, **5**:79–81, 433; **6**:17; **8**:50–51
ligatures, **8**:103
Malaysia, *dai* system, **4**:430
mannerism in, **8**:98
Maronite chant, **6**:209
medieval, **8**:71, 73, 146
mensural, **8**:481
Miao people, **7**:452
mnemonic, **7**:55
Mongolian Buddhist, **7**:1017
multiple methods of, **9**:289
neumatic, **8**:49–50, 90–91, 100, 105, 650,
  841, 843, 903, 904, 1023
  karifu and *meyasu*, **8**:103
  kriuk, **8**:779
numeric, **3**:1237; **9**:203, 287–88, 753; **10**:146
oral, **1**:150
oral transmission and, **8**:130–31
Ottoman classical music, **6**:18, 109, 119, 194
Peru, of pre-Hispanic music, **2**:468–69
pictographic, **8**:102–3, *105*
of pitch, **1**:35, 36
Ranganathan-Brown transcription system,
  5:161
Regular singing of psalmody, **3**:25–26
of rhythm, **1**:35, 47
Ryûkyû Islands, **7**:792–93
sargam, **5**:52, 252
in scholarly works, **5**:43
score, **8**:50
Shaker music, **3**:135

shape-note, **3**:*10*, 119, 276, 532, 833
Shona *mbira* music, **1**:747
Southeast Asia, indigenous systems, **4**:127
staff, **1**:157; **9**:285–86, 808
  African use of, **1**:159–62
  of *bambuco*, **2**:385–86
stone inscriptions, **5**:215
Sundanese, **4**:702–3
svara, **5**:100–101
syllabic, **5**:111, 112, 214, 326
symbolic, **9**:288–89
tablature, **1**:158, *159*, 161; **7**:574, *575*; **8**:50,
  103, *104*, 349, 373, 572, 601, 710;
  9:286–87
  Japan, **7**:588, 644, *650*, 675
  Korea, **7**:835, 839, 856
  Ryûkyû Islands, **7**:793
  Thailand, **4**:91, 227, 261, 282–83
  of Third Stream jazz, **3**:335
Tibetan systems, **5**:713; **7**:452, 479, 480, 582,
  1016
timbral, **1**:135
time-unit box system, **9**:289
transcription and, **8**:95
uniphonic, **8**:103, 104, 106
Vedic chant, **5**:240, 243–44, *245*
Vietnam, **4**:451, *452–53*, 480, 509
Western, **5**:17
  in China, **7**:125
  early uses in Africa, **1**:298
  in East Asia, **7**:50
  in Japan, **7**:574, 577–78, 583, 778
  in Turkey, **6**:771
  use in transcribing Tunisian art music,
    6:325–36
Notes on the Book of Music (Tibetan writing),
  7:447
Notes on Siamese Musical Instruments (Verney),
  4:224, 225, 285
Notes on the Songs of Robert Burns (Dick), **8**:374
Notes on the State of Virginia (Jefferson), **3**:22
"Nothin' but a G Thang" (Snoop Doggy Dogg),
  3:*700*
Notker Balbulus, **8**:70
Notorious B.I.G., **3**:698, 715
Nôtomi Judô, **10**:99
Notosudirdjo, R. Franki S., **4**:639
Noudjoum el-Raï, **6**:271
al-Nour, Abd, **6**:285
Nouvel Ensemble Moderne, **3**:1152
Nova Generacija (musical group), **3**:1198
Nova Scotia. *See also* Acadia
  Acadians in, **3**:1135–37
  African-Canadians in, **3**:332, 1072, 1132–34
  ballad research in, **3**:148, 292, 1133
  Cape Breton
    cultural isolation of, **3**:331
    fiddle music, **3**:52, 74, 150–51, 230, 1064,
      1071, 1127–30
    Gaelic songs, **3**:1070
    Louisbourg, **3**:1072, 1115
    songwriting in, **3**:1125
  early black communities in, **3**:73
  Eskasoni reserve, **3**:150
  First Nations groups in, **3**:52, 461
  folk styles in, **3**:325, 1121

Halifax
    Africville, **3:**1072, 1132, 1133
    musical life in, **3:**1069–70, 1115, 1116,
        1120
    history of musical life, **3:**1114–21
    Port Royal, **3:**7, 223, 1056, 1069, 1114–15,
        1135
    slavery abolished in, **3:**8
Nova Scotia Mass Choir, **3:**1072, 1133
Nova Scotia Opera Association, **3:**1120
Nova Scotia Talent Trust, **3:**1120
Novaes, Guiomar, **3:**1210
Novaje Nieba (musical group), **8:**802
Novák, Jan, **8:**731
Novák, Vítezslav, **8:**728–29
November Steps (Takemitsu), **7:**649, 705, 708,
        737
Novi Fosili (musical group), **8:**934
Now (periodical), **3:**1081
"Now-Do-U-Wanta Dance" (Graham Central
        Station), **3:**683
Nowell, Wedgwood, **9:**43
"Now Is the Hour," **9:**931
Noy, Meir, **6:**1072
Nozawa Matunoseke, **7:**750
Nr. 1 des Wienerwalds, **8:**677
NRA (Not Really Anything), **9:**169
NRM (musical group), **8:**802
Nsenga people, **1:**286, 671
    harmonic systems, **1:**307–8
    music of, **1:**673
    nsogwe dance, **1:**286
Ntsikana (Xhosa prophet), **1:**763
Ntwumuru people, **1:**109
Nu people, **7:**485–92
Nü Wa (legendary sovereign), **7:**187
Nüa people, **4:**218
nūba
    aesthetics of, **6:**448
    Algeria, **6:**450–51, 470–72
    aṣbahān, **6:**327, 331–36
    collections of, **6:**20, 367, 370–71
    compared with *fāsil* and *wasla*, **6:**551
    formal structure of, **6:**436, 450–53, 456–58,
        470, 507
    inqilāb, **6:**470
    instruments for, **6:**407, 411
    jawq ensemble for, **6:**418, 460–61, 470
    Libya, **6:**452–53
    Morocco, **6:**450, 455–63, 1039
    oral transmission of, **6:**461–63
    organization of, **1:**534–35; **6:**11, 184, 185,
        443, 471–72
    origins of, **6:**441, 442, 447, 456, 540
    poetry of, **6:**447–48
    recordings of, **6:**512
    schools of, **6:**455
    al-sikah, **6:**512
    terms for, **6:**449
    Tunisia, **6:**331, 333–36, 451–52, 506,
        517–18, 519
    waslat, **6:**513
Nuba peoples, **1:**560–62
Nubia (kingdom), **1:**555–56
Nubian peoples
    in Cairo, **6:**555, 641–45

dance of, **6:**629–30
    in Egypt, **6:**23, 545
    music of, **1:**555–58
*Nuclear Theme as a Determinant of Patet in
    Javanese Music* (Hood), **10:**51
Nuet people, **1:**109
nueva canción, **2:**32, 60, 81, 90, 101, 103; **6:**277
    in Bolivia, **2:**298
    in Chile, **2:**373
    in Dominican Republic, **2:**861
    in Nicaragua, **2:**764, 766, 767
    in North America, **3:**730, 1204
    in Peru, **2:**486
nueva trova, **2:**103, 486, 796, 829, 831
Nuevo Mundo (marimba ensemble), **2:**718
Nügua (legendary figure), **7:**402
Nuić, Rada, **8:**969
Nukalatalli (deity), **5:**892
Nukufetau (Tuvalu), **9:**828, 829–30
Nukuhiva (Marquesas Islands), **9:**889
    mahohe dance of, **9:**892
Nukumanu (Papua New Guinea), **9:**378, 833
Nukunonu (Tokelau), **9:**823, 973
Nukuoro (Pohnpei State, FSM), **9:**715, 833
Nukuria (Papua New Guinea), **9:**833
Numan, Gary, **3:**690
Numbertwo, Jimmy, **9:**427
Nunatsiakmiut Native Communications Society,
        3:1278
Nunavut, **3:**3, 1074, 1273–81
    Arctic peoples, **3:**374–81
    geography of, **3:**1274
    Hudson's Bay communities, **3:**377
    Iqaluit, **3:**1274
    musical life in, **3:**1097
    popular music in, **3:**1277–78
    population of, **3:**1274
"Nunca jamás" (Guerrero), **3:**739
Nunes Garcia, José Maurício, **2:**304
Nunes, Manuel, **9:**390
Núñez de Balboa, Vasco, **2:**771
Núñez del Prado, Oscar, **2:**231
Núñez, Evangelina de, **2:**704
Nùng people, **4:**218, 537
    ceremonies of, **4:**533
    courtship songs of, **4:**532
Nunns, Richard, **9:**933
Nuosang (Tibetan opera), **7:**479
nuovo canzoniere italiano, Il (periodical), **8:**613
Nupe (kingdom), **1:**452, 459
Nupe people, **1:**452
Nuper rosarum flores (Dufay), **8:**71
"Nura" (Gubara), **1:**572
Nur, An-Naim Muhammed, **1:**571
Nur Mia Qawwal, **5:**426
Nur-ud-din (Nund Rishi), **5:**689
Nuratin, **6:**345
Nureyev, Rudolf, **8:**161
Nurgaci, **7:**33, 34, 518
Nuristani people, **5:**805
Nurmio, Hannu "Tuomari," **8:**217
Nürpeisqyzy, Dina, **6:**958
Nusantao people, **4:**42
Nusa Tenggara Barat, **4:**765, 778. *See also*
        Lombok; Sumbawa
    geography of, **4:**762–63

map of, **4:***730*
    population of, **4:**762
Nusa Tenggara Timur. *See also* Flores; Roti; Savu;
        Sumba; West Timor
    Dutch and Portuguese in, **4:**786
    geography of, **4:**786
    map of, **4:***730, 787*
    population of, **4:**786
    textiles of, **4:**786–87
Nusch-Nuschi, Das (Hindemith), **4:**131
Ñusta Huillac (Inca princess), **2:**363
NUTA Jazz Band, **1:**645
Nuttycombe, N. R., **9:**976
Núu-chá-nulth Indian nation. *See* Nootka (Núu-
        chá-nulth; Westcoast) Indian nation
Nuui (Tuvalu), **9:**828
Nuvellist (periodical), **8:**780
Nuwayra (Nuwera), 'Abd al-Halim, **6:**317,
        318–19, 560
Nuxalk Indian nation. *See* Bella Coola (Nuxalk)
        Indian nation
NWA. *See* Niggaz with Attitude (NWA)
Nwosu-Lo Bamiloko, Joy, **1:**241
Nwuba, Felix, **1:**237
Nxumalo, Gideon, **1:**774
Nyamalthu people, **1:**288, 291–92
Nyampala people, **1:**637
Nyamwezi people, **1:**636
    Arabic influences, **1:**606
    lamellophones, **1:**317
    musical bows of, **1:**640
    music of, **1:**637
Nyanga people, **1:**110–11
Nyangɔ-Bɛbɛnisangɔ (Mpyɛmɔ̃ performer),
        1:*665*
Nyaturu people, **1:**640
Nyau people, **1:**119
nyckelharpa. See violins and fiddles (bowed lutes)
Nyei, Braimah (Vai Islamic leader), **1:**344
Nyei, Momo (*imam*), **1:**337
Nyemba people, **1:**672
Nyerere, Julius, **1:**636
Nyerup, Rasmus, **8:**460, 463
Nyhus, Sven, **8:**427
Nyikang (king of the Colo), **1:**568
Nyman, Michael, **9:**46
Nynningen, **8:**216
Nystroem, Gösta, **8:**445
Nyumbu, Mwene, **1:**677
Nyungwe people, **1:**711
Nyzhankivs'kyi, Nestor, **8:**820
Nzakara people
    bird call imitations, **1:**108
    harps of, **1:**655–56
Nzewi, Meki, **1:**40, 45

O', Ó. *See* O', Ó *plus next element in name*
O Chŏnghae, **7:**960
O Chŏngsuk, **7:**900
O Sugwan, **7:**899
O T'aesŏk, **7:**899, 909–10, 911
Oakenfold, Paul, **3:**691
Oanh, Kim, **3:***994*
Obadia, Dahlia, **3:***1219*
Obadiah the proselyte, **6:**1065
Oba koso (Ladipo), **10:**114

Ó Baoill (also O'Baoill), Colm, **8:**374, 394
Obena people, **9:**537
oberek, **3:**892, 894, 1197; **8:***704,* 708, 710
Oberlin College (Ohio), **3:**277, 604–5, 606, 610,
    611, 953
Obey, Ebenezer, **1:**46, 482–83
Obi, Bredda David, **2:**679
Obituary (musical group), **3:**358
Oblivion (Piazzolla), **7:**972
oboe. *See* double-reed instruments
Obomsawin, Alanis, **3:**1074
Obrenović, Miloš, **8:**279
O'Brien, Frederick, **9:**41
O'Brien, Linda, **10:**140
O'Brien, Oscar, **3:**1166
O'Brien-Rothe, Linda, **2:**658, 736–37
Obrochta, Bartek, **8:**712
Obscure Records, **9:**1005
Obusa (kasa), **7:**927
Ocampo, Louie, **4:**885
Ocampo, Martín, **4:**869
"O Canada" (Lavallée), **3:**14
Ó Canainn, Tomás, **8:**104–5
ocarinas. *See* flutes, vessel
Ó Carolan, Turlough, **8:**24, 391–92, 394
O'Casey, Sean, **8:**378
Ocasio, Nydia, **3:***786*
occupational songs. *See* work music
Oceania. *See also specific countries, islands, peoples,*
    and topics
  children's games and pastimes, **9:**252–53
  clothing and costumes, **9:**345–52
  colonialism in, **9:**5
  cultural borrowings among Pacific Islanders,
    9:59
  cultural identity in, **9:**5
  dance, **9:**311–17
  drinking songs, **9:**321
  East Asian people in, **7:**6
  festivals in, **9:**53–67
  geography of, **9:**2
  immigrant groups of, **9:**69–121
  instruments, **9:**371–402
  invented traditions in, **9:**212
  linguistic and musical systems of, **9:**319–24
  map of, **9:***3*
  musical contexts in, **9:**282–84
  outsiders' influences on, **9:**5, 7–50
  pedagogy in, **9:**251–78
  politics in, **9:**211–22
  prehistoric, **9:**2–5
  string figures in, **9:**253
  theater in, **9:**224–26, 229–39
  tourism in, **9:**53–55
    role of touring troupes, **9:**225–26
  vocal music, war-era songs, **9:**28–32
  Western writings on, **9:**33–42
  World War II in, **9:**25–33
Ocean Island. *See* Banaba
Óc Eo (kingdom), **4:**156, 215
Ochanomizu University, **7:**594
Ochialbi, Dumitrache, **8:**882
Ochoa, Angeles, **2:**623
Ochoa, Calixto, **2:**105
Ochres (dance production), **9:***410,* 416–17
Ochs, Elinor, **9:**323
Ochs, Phil, **3:**316

Ochurte, Señor don Trinidad, **2:***597*
Ockeghem, Johannes, **8:**73, 518
Ó Conluain, Proinsias, **8:**391
O'Connor, Nuala, **8:**322
O'Connor, Sinéad, **8:**216, 226, 392
OCORA (Office de Coopération
    Radiophonique), **1:**54, 60
OCORA (record label), **5:**529; **8:**553, 554
Octobre (musical group), **3:**1158
Octoroon (musical), **3:**194
Odaiko New England (musical group), **3:**973
Odawa Indian nation. *See* Ottawa (Odawa)
    Indian nation
Odawara Symphony Orchestra, **7:***535*
Ode label, **9:**999
Odeon (record company), **1:**417; **4:**483, 493;
    6:234, 548, 597
Odéon Kinois, **1:**387
Odes (album), **8:**1018
ODILA (Orquesta de Instrumentos
    LatinAmericanos), **2:**543
Odilio Urfé Center for Promotion and
    Information on Cuban Music, **2:**838
Odoevsky, Vladimir, **8:**782
Odol ttogi (Korean folk song), **7:**883
Odsuren, **7:**1020
Ŏdum ŭi chasiktŭl (film), **7:**958
Oduvars, **5:**216
O'Dwyer, William, **3:**207
Odyssey (dance ensemble), **3:**1199
Odyssey (Homer), **6:**523; **8:**129, 130, 763
Oesch, Hans, **4:**26, 530, 565–78, 585, 586–87
O'Fake, Peter, **3:**604
Ofei, Patrick, **1:**26
"*O fetai o le Papa Lauina,*" **9:**294–95
Offenbach (musical group), **3:**1158
Offenbach, Jacques, **3:**193, 544; **8:**205
Office label, **3:**169
Office of Public Information (FSM), **9:**967
Office of War Information, **3:**297
Offices, in Coptic Orthodox Church, **6:**219, 221
Office Territoriale d'Action Culturelle (OTAC),
    9:958
Offir, **6:**1047
Offspring (musical group), **3:**358
Ó Floinn, Liam, **8:***392*
Ofo Indian nation, **3:**466
Of Thee I Sing (Gershwin), **3:**545
Ôga family, **7:**627
Oğanezaşvili, Saşa, **6:**924, *924,* 925
Ogawa Hiroshi, **7:**595
Ogawa Morinaka, **7:**588
Oghuz nama (epic), **6:**969
Oghuz people, **6:**965–66, 995; **7:**23
  epic songs, **6:**345, 967, 969–70
Ogilby, John, **1:**81, 126
Ôgimachi Kinmochi, **7:**667
Ogiński, Prince Michał Kleofas, **8:**710
Oglethorpe, Lady, **3:**64
Ognenovski, Tale, **8:**977
Oguaa Fetu Afahye (periodical), **10:**31, 33
Ogumefu, E., **1:**405
Ogunba, Oyinade, **1:**400, 411
Ogunde, Hubert, **1:**14, 401, 406–8
Ogunmola, Kola, **1:**408
Ogyû Sorai, **7:**548

Ohana, Hui, **9:**164
O'Hanlon, Redmond, **4:**29
"O Happy Day," **3:**633–34
O'Hara, Geoffrey, **3:**189, 1108
Ohara Otondo, **7:**609
"Oh Dem Golden Slippers" (Bland), **3:**616
"Oh Girl" (Chi-Lites), **3:**711
"Oh How I Hate to Get Up in the Morning"
    (Berlin), **3:**196
Ohia, Chinyere, **1:**233
Ohinemutu Quartet, **9:**938
Õhinemutu Rotorua Māori Choir, **9:**935
Ohio
  Cincinnati
    as center for country music, **3:**76
    German people in, **3:**528
    public school music education, **3:**275, 276
  Cleveland
    African-American composers in, **3:**605
    Chinese Lion Dance organizations, **3:**955
    Hungarian people in, **3:**908
    Lithuanian people in, **3:**876
    public school music education, **3:**275
    Romanian people in, **3:**910
    Slovenian people in, **3:**901–2
    South Asian people in, **3:**981
  Finnish people in, **3:**872–75
  Old Regular Baptists in, **3:**124
  rap in, **3:**702
  Russian Orthodox church in, **3:***117*
"Ohio" (Crosby, Stills, Nash, and Young), **3:**318
Ohio Magazine, **3:**992
Ohio Players (musical group), **3:**681, *682,* 684,
    685, 711
Oh Kyunghee, **7:**970
Ohlange Institute Choir, **1:**764
"Oh! Lemuel" (Foster), **3:**186
Ohrid (musical group), **3:**1198
"Oh! Susanna" (Foster), **3:**186, 293, 543, 547,
    616, 888, 1211–12
Ohtani Kimiko, **7:**525
Ohyŏn'gŭm (Lee), **7:**955
Oian people, **9:**983
Oinkari Dancers, **3:**849, *849*
Oirat people, **7:**35, 1014
Oistrakh, David, **7:**415
Oiwake (Japanese folk song), **7:**602–3
OJ (rap artist), **9:**169
O'Jays (musical group), **3:**228, 677, 683, 711
Ojeda, Alonso de, **2:**927
Ojibwa (Ojibwe, Ojibway) Indian nation, **3:**26,
    344, 451–59, 1079, 1192–93
  instruments of, **3:**476–77
  intermarriages with French people, **3:**404
  women's musical roles, **3:**371
"Ojibwe Air Force Song," **3:**458–59, *459*
Ojindo, **1:**475
Ojo, Dele, **1:**477
Ojŏk (Kim), **7:**969
Oju yŏnmun changjŏn san'go (Yi), **7:**855, 925
Ok people, **9:**491, 583
Ô kagami (Japanese history), **7:**586
Oka Masana, **7:**588
Oka, Seizo, **3:**969
Okamoto Bun'ya, **7:**654
Okara, Gabriel, **1:**142

Okazaki, Yoshiko, **4:**603
O'Keeffe, John, **9:**34
OKeh label, **3:**652, 707, 1243
Oke-Korpa (Melpa singer), **9:**521
Okell, John, **4:**374, 384
Okelo, Rev. Anthony, **1:**216, 224
Okena people, **9:**983
"Okie from Muskogee" (Haggard), **3:**81
Okie, Packard, **1:**378
Okina (flute piece), **7:**546
Okina sanbasô (nô play), **7:**793
Okinawa. *See* Ryûkyû Islands
Okinawa Band, **9:**158
Okinawa Prefectural University of Arts, **7:**796
Okinawa, Shuri court of, **9:**98
Okinawan people
    in Hawai'i, **9:**96, 98–99, 109; **10:**47
    in North America, **3:**216–17
    in South America, **2:**83, 86–89, 293
Okir (de León), **4:**881
Ôkishi Genkin, **7:**610
O.K. Jazz, **1:**360–61, 386, 424, 669
Okladnikov, A. P., **7:**11
Oklahoma
    Native American groups in, **3:**431, 440,
        448–49, 451, 462, 487
    Native American removal to, **3:**446, 467
Oklahoma! (Rodgers and Hammerstein), **3:**197,
        545
Oklahoma Indian Welfare Act (1936), **3:**443
Okongwu, David, **1:**233
Okonta, Edy, **1:**477
O. Koshetz Choir (Winnipeg), **3:**1241
OK Success, **1:**424, 425
Okudzhava, Bulat, **8:**767, 778
Ôkura Kisitirô, **7:**702
Ólafsson, Gísli, **8:**403
Olaiya, Victor, **1:**477, 483
Olajubu, Oludare, **1:**400, 410
Olajuwon, Akeem, **1:**486
Ola Na Iwi (Kneubuhl), **9:**234
Olarin Musiikki Oy, **8:**486
Olatunji, Yusufu, **1:**475; **3:**336
Old Believers, **3:**916–17; **8:**755, 764, 778, 780
"Old Black Joe" (Foster), **7:**375
"Old Dan Tucker," **3:**184, 305, 306, 307–8, *543*
"Old Folks at Home" (Foster), **3:**186–87, 190,
        543, 547
"Old Glory Raising on Iwo Jima" (Navajo song),
        3:526
"Old Granite State" (Hutchinson Family), **3:**184
"Old Home Ain't What It Used to Be" (White),
        3:192
"Old Hundredth" (psalm), **3:**531, 831
"Old Maid Boogie" (Vinson), **3:**669
"Ol' Man River" (Kern), **3:**514
Old Man's Jazz Band (Shanghai), **7:**102, *103*
Old Order Amish, **3:**118, 121, 528, 823–24,
        884, 887, 1082
*Old Plantation and What I Gathered There in an
    Autumn Month* (Hungerford), **3:**601
Old Regular Baptists, **3:**118, 122, 123–25
"Old Ship of Zion" (spiritual), **3:**523
Old Time Mas', **2:**960
Ole Bull Akademiet, **8:**427
Ole, Maren, **8:**24

Ole Smoke Seneca Singers, **3:**486
Olewale, Ojo, **1:**475
Oli caste, **5:**957, 961, 962
Olivas, Margarito, **3:**763
Oliver (Hawai'ian leader), **9:**132
Oliver, Douglas L., **9:**650
Oliver, Joe "King," **3:**13, 568, 652, 706
Oliver, Paul, **3:**582
Oliver, Robert, **9:**929
Oliveros, Pauline, **3:**93, 131, 253
Olle and His Playmates (musical group), **3:**1251
Oller y Cestero, Francisco, **2:**423
Olmec culture, **2:**601, 680
    archaeomusicological studies of, **2:**7
Olmos, Edward James, **3:**749
Olmstead, Frederick Law, **3:**83
Olodum (*bloco afro*), **2:**353
Olofsdotter, Elisabeth, **8:**200, 438–39
Olomana, **9:**164
Ölöt people, **7:**1004–20
Olp'yŏn (*kagok*), **7:**923
Olsava (musical group), **8:**723–24
Olsen, Christian, **8:**465
Olsen, Dale A., **2:**45, 128, 198, 231, 544;
        7:707–8; **10:**97–107, *99*
Olsen, Diane, **10:**99
Olshanetsky, Alexander, **3:**937
Olson sisters, **3:**869
Oltenia, **8:**868. *See also* Romania
Olude, Ola, **1:**19
Oluwa, Abibu, **1:**475
Om (album), **3:**132–33
Ó Madagáin, Breandán, **8:**394
Omaha Indian Music, **3:**498
Omaha Indian nation, **3:**29, 440, 446, 494,
        495–96, 509, 539
Omai (Tahitian traveler), **9:**34
Omai, or a Trip Round the World (pantomime),
        9:34
Oman, **6:**649. *See also* Arabian peninsula
    aerophones in, **6:**414–16
    chordophones in, **6:**407, 412
    concept of arts in, **6:**672–73
    dance traditions in, **6:**654, 703–11
    drums in, **6:**417–20
    geography and history of, **6:**671–72
    idiophones in, **6:**403–5
    al-nuban ritual, **6:**546
    Sohar, musical life, **6:**671–83
    wedding rituals in, **6:**674
    zār ritual, **6:**674
Omar Khayyam, **5:**687
Omar, Mohammed, **5:**603
Omar, Mrs. Mohammed, **5:**603
Omega (musical group), **8:**746
Omerzel-Terlep, Mira, **8:**920, 923
Omi Music (record company), **5:**528
Omibiyi, Mosunmola, **1:**40, 45
"Omie Wise" (ballad), **3:**835
Omondi, Washington, **1:**45
Omowura, Alhaji Ayinla, **1:**475, 477
Omwami, Joshua, **1:**304
"On the Banks of the Wabash" (Dresser), **3:**191,
        549
"On the Beach at Waikiki," **3:**1048
"On Broadway" (Drifters), **3:**673

On the Corner (Davis), **3:**663
On Emancipation Day" (Dunbar), **3:**619
"On My Own" (LaBelle and McDonald), **3:**713
"On the Musical Modes of the Hindus" (Jones),
        5:49, 50
"On the Musical Scales of Various Nations"
        (Ellis), **5:**51
"On the Reform of (Chinese) Music" (Fei),
        7:379
On Taoism (Tan), **7:**351
"On Top of Old Smoky," **3:**328
On the Trail of Negro Folk-Songs (Scarborough),
        3:71
"On the Vina or Indian Lyre" (Fowke), **5:**49
Ona (Selk'nam) culture, **2:**250, 357
    vocal music of, **2:**57, 251
Oñate, Cristóbal, **2:**577
Oñate, Juan de, **3:**721, 754
Oñate, Pedro de, **2:**453
ONCE group, **3:**253
"Once I Loved Thee" (Foster), **3:**187
Ondar, Kongar-ol, **3:**339
" *1 Mayıs* " (Dervişan), **6:**250–51
101 Strings (musical group), **3:**1050
Oneida Indian nation, **3:**454, 458, 462, 497,
        1078
O'Neil, Greg, **3:**1280
O'Neill, Francis, **3:**324; **8:**393
one-man bands. *See* ensembles, musical (one-
        person)
"One Mint Julep" (Clovers), **3:**670
One Mo' Time (musical), **3:**621
I of IV (Oliveros), **3:**253
"One's On the Way" (Cline), **3:**81
one-step, **2:**485; **3:**408; **8:**443, 690
"One Sweet Day" (Boyz II Men), **3:**715
Oneto, Nicolo, **8:**632
Ong, Walter, **10:**43
Ongaku daiziten: Encyclopaedia Musica, **7:**525
Ongaku Gakkai, **7:**592
Ongakugaku (periodical), **7:**592
Ongaku to Bungaku (periodical), **7:**729
Ongyoku kuden syo (Takemoto), **7:**546
Ongaku Torisirabe Gakari (organization), **7:**721,
        728, 756, 760–61, 778
Ongaku Zassi (periodical), **7:**729
Ongaku ziten (encyclopedia), **7:**525
Ongala, Remmy, **1:**427
Onggojip-chŏn (*p'ansori* story), **7:**899
Ongoongotau, Mele Nunia, **9:**972
Onimole, G. T., **1:**406
Onjob people, **9:**983
"Only You" (Platters), **3:**672
Onna Goroshi Abura Jigoku (Chikamatsu), **7:**669
Onnami, **7:**641
Ôno family, **7:**626–27
Ôno Kazuo, **7:**66
Ôno Tadatomo, **7:**627
Ono, Yoko, **3:**176
Onondaga Indian nation, **3:**462, 1078
Onotoa (Kiribati), films on, **9:**982
Ontario, **3:**1177–1221. *See also* Upper Canada
    African-Canadians in, **3:**1211–13
    Algonquian peoples, **3:**383
    Anglo-Celtic music, **3:**1188–91
    Arctic peoples in, **3:**374–81

Ontario (*continued*)
Asian peoples in, **3:**1215–17
early black communities in, **3:**73
ethnic newspapers in, **3:**1060
European groups in, **3:**1081–83, 1195–1200
festivals in, **3:**1186
First Nations groups in, **3:**461–65, 1078–79
Guelph, organ building in, **3:**1180
history of, **3:**1178, 1188, 1192
history of musical life, **3:**1077–85, 1178–86
Kingston, **3:**1179
Latin American and Caribbean peoples in, **3:**1201–5
lumber camps in, **3:**1082, 1189, 1193
Manitoulin Island, **3:**451
Mariposa Folk Festival, **3:**94, 149, 1186
Métis people in, **3:**405–11
Middle Eastern music in, **3:**1218–20
Ottawa, **3:**1178
concert life in, **3:**1181, 1183
Sharon (Hope), **3:**1179
Children of Peace community, **3:**136–37, 1079
Six Nations Reserve, **3:**462
Thunder Bay (Fort William), Czech and Slovak people in, **3:**1250
Toronto, **3:**1178
African-Canadians in, **3:**73
Albanian people in, **3:**926, 927–29
Caravan festival, **3:**223
Caribana festival, **3:**17, 223, 1085, 1186, 1202, 1203, 1207–9, 1212–13
Chinese people in, **3:**224, 957
concert life in, **3:**1182, 1183–86
cultural diversity of, **3:**223
ethnic musics in, **3:**97
Indo-Caribbean community in, **3:**817
musical life in, **3:**17
musical societies in, **3:**1179
musical theater in, **3:**200
music instruction in, **3:**279
Sephardic Jews in, **3:**1171
Ontario Arts Council, **3:**1185, 1216
Ontario Black History Society, **3:**1085
Ontong Java. *See* Luangiua
"*Onun Arabasi Var*" (Sandal), **6:**252
Onŭrŭm (musical group), **7:**972
"Onward, Christian Soldiers," **3:**310; **9:**150
Onyido, Udemesuo, **1:**14–15
Onyina, Kwabena, **1:**362
Onyx Club (Toronto), **3:**1080
O'odham Indian groups, **3:**428, 435–36
O'otam culture, **3:**429
opera. *See also* Cantonese opera; *ch'anggŭk*;
kunqu; Peking opera; theater; *tonadilla*;
zarzuela
adaptation and recomposition traditions in, **8:**54
Africa, native-air, **1:**406
African-American composers, **3:**617–18
Armenia, **6:**725, 726
Azerbaijan, **6:**924
Baroque, **8:**79
Bulgaria, **8:**904, 905
Canada, **3:**1069, 1090, 1095, 1181, 1182, 1184–85, 1186, 1230

China, **7:**6, 275–309
age of performers, **7:**420
Anhui, **7:**355
anthologies of, **7:**140
bangzi, **7:**184
chudiao, **7:**286
female performers, **7:**407
hanju, **7:**212
huadeng, **7:**411, *412*
huidiao, **7:**286
huju (Shanghai opera), **7:**297–301, *301*
instrumental accompaniment, **7:**176
lüju, **7:**412, 417
melody in, **7:**122
minority cultures, **7:**452
nanxi, **7:**75, 212, 276–77, 291
northern *vs.* southern styles, **7:**116
overview of, **7:**275–80
qinqiang, **7:**212, 235
qu arias, **7:**130
revolutionary, **7:**76, 90, 102, 341, 349, 387, 388, 413
role types in, **7:**276, 283–84, 291–92, 308–9
shengqiang types, **7:**277–79, 289
yangqin accompaniment, **7:**180
yiyangqiang, **7:**212
Yuan drama, **7:**102
yueju, **7:**411, 420, 433
zaju, **7:**89, 275–76, 291, 407
zhengzixi, **7:**212
Chinese
in Hawai'i and Australia, **9:**70–71
in North America, **3:**11, 527, 949, 951, 958, 960–61, 1083, 1095, 1217, 1247, 1260–66
in South and Central America, **2:**85
in Thailand, **4:**70–71
Classical and Romantic, **8:**80, 727–28
Croatia, **8:**933
Czech Republic, **8:**727–29
Denmark, **8:**460
Egypt, **6:**547, 607–8
English, **3:**61, 181, 542
European
in Australia and Oceania, **9:**38
in South and Central America, **2:**603, 694, 827, 866
Finland, **8:**484
French, **3:**542, 600
Georgia, **8:**843–44
German, **3:**542
Germany, **8:**659–60
Greece, **8:**1008
Guatemala, **2:**736
Iberian performers of, **3:**852
Israel/Palestine, **6:**1025, 1029, 1030, 1031
Italian, **2:**59–60, 61, 90, 114, 396–97, 736; **3:**181, 542, 839, 860, 861
Italy, **8:**84, 604, 617–18
Corfu, **8:**1014
Japan, **7:**733
Asakusa, **7:**732–33, 743–44
Kazakhstan, **6:**959–60
Korea, **7:**946, 953–54
Latin American, **2:**113, 114–15, 134, 305, 306, 397

Malta, **8:**643
Mexican, **2:**622
Moinba people, **7:**482
Naxi people, *dianju*, **7:**512
Nigeria, **1:**241
North America
government funding for, **3:**299
nineteenth century, **3:**181, 542
nineteenth-century popularity of, **8:**205
social class and, **3:**45, 46
touring concert troupes, **3:**557
twentieth century, **3:**545–46
North Korea, revolutionary, **7:**76, 946, 962–63, 992
Poland, **8:**710
Québec, **3:**1148
Renaissance, **8:**77
rock, **8:**215, 747
Romania, **8:**882
Romantic, **8:**83–84
Russia, **8:**759, 780–81
Scotland, **8:**369
Slovenia, **8:**921
South Africa, **1:**219
South Asia portrayed in, **5:**562
Spain
flamenco, **8:**597–98
tonadilla escénica, **8:**601
Sweden, **8:**444
Taiwan
gezaixi, **7:**425, 426–27
liyuanxi, **7:**425
mainland genres, **7:**429
o-pe-ra-hi, **7:**426
temporality of, Baroque period, **8:**55
texture in, **8:**61
Tibet, **7:**478–79
Turkey, **6:**775
Turkish plots in, **6:**21, 767
Uganda, **1:**217
Uighur, **7:**463
women performers in, **8:**199
Yoruba people, **10:**114
Opera Anonymous (Toronto), **3:**1186
Opera Atelier (Toronto), **3:**1080, 1186
opéra-comique, **8:**534, 728
Opera New Brunswick, **3:**1120
operetta, **2:**447; **3:**193, 544, 840, 861, 899, 921
Canada, **3:**189, 1090, 1095, 1117, 1182, 1184, 1225, *1226*, 1228
Croatia, **8:**933
Egypt, **6:**433, 547
Hungary, **8:**747
Japan, **7:**732
Ukrainian, **3:**912
Opie, Peter and Iona, **8:**336
Opinión, La (Martí), **3:**740
Opium War, **7:**228, 373
Oplenac Dancers (Mississauga), **3:**1198
Oppekepe busi (Kawakami), **7:**740
Oppenheimer, Joselito, **2:**939
Opposite Corner (musical group), **8:**446
Optimist (Moore), **3:**199
Opunui (Hawai'ian missionary), **9:**742
Opus, **8:**677, 679
Oquendo, Manny, **3:**798, 799

"Ora Sí Entiendo por Qué" (Ramos), **2**:388
oratorio
  church performances of, **3**:122
  Renaissance, **8**:77
Orain na'h Albain, **8**:373
oral histories, **2**:22. *See also* narratives
  Aotearoa, **9**:974
    Māori *mōteatea*, **9**:939
  of blues performers, **3**:105–6
  collections of, **3**:33
  Dominican Republic, **2**:862
  Grenada, **2**:865
  Hawai'i, **9**:915, 969–70, 978
  indie pop musicians, **3**:171
  Kuna culture, **2**:638
  Mapuche culture, **2**:232–33
  Native American, **3**:366–67, 1079
  New England, **3**:155
  Oceania, songs as, **9**:28–33
  South Asia, **5**:57
  Wayana culture, **2**:165
  women musicians, **3**:92
  Yukon First Nations performers, **3**:1277
Oral History Centre (Wellington), **9**:974
oral tradition and transmission. *See also gharānā*;
     pedagogy; transmission
  Abkhazian people, **8**:852
  Adighian people, **8**:854
  Afghanistan, **5**:825, 831–32
  Africa, historical value of, **1**:295, 296, 303,
    304
  African-Americans, **3**:43, 72, 239, 579–80,
    692, 693
  Albanian-Americans, **3**:928
  Andalusian repertoire, **6**:448–49, 455, 461–63,
    470
  Andhra Pradesh, of narratives, **5**:896
  Anglo-American ballads, **3**:155, 833
  Anglo-American fiddle tunes, **3**:837–38
  Arab-American music, **6**:283
  Arab epic traditions, **6**:339–43, 431, 432
  Arabian peninsula, **6**:663–67
  Argentina, **2**:258, 268
    secular vocal music, **2**:261
  Australia
    of folk music, **9**:141
    Gulf of Carpentaria, **9**:427
    Italian people, **9**:80
  Bahamas, **2**:802
  Bali, **4**:737, 738
  Balkarian people, **8**:857
  ballads, **3**:180
  Baluan, **9**:258–59
  Barbados, **2**:817, 821
  Berber music, **6**:432, 485
  Bhutan, of King Ge-sar epic, **5**:712
  bluegrass music, **3**:167
  Bolivia, **2**:289, 296
  Brazil, tropical-forest region, **2**:134
  British Caribbean folk and traditional music,
    3:811
  Brittany, **8**:559
  Bulgaria, **8**:898
    Rom people, **8**:282
  Burma, **4**:395–96, 397–98
  Byzantine music, **8**:1023

Cambodia, **3**:1001
Canada, **3**:1146, 1163
  rural areas, **3**:142, 147–48, 239
Celtic music, **8**:320–21
Central America, **2**:58, 68–70
  of myths, **2**:17
Central Asia, **6**:901–2, 911, 917
Chechen people, **8**:861
China, **7**:124, 127
  age and, **7**:420
  of Buddhist music, **7**:330
  of *kunqu*, **7**:289
  of *kunshanqiang*, **7**:277
  of local genres, **7**:395–96
  narrative singing, **7**:245–50, 253, 262
  northern ensemble music, **7**:202–3
  northwestern minorities, **7**:463
  pipa music, **7**:168–70
  of village rituals, **7**:317–18
  xianshiyue, **7**:213
Chuuk, **9**:734
Coptic Orthodox music, **6**:220–21, 222–23
Cyprus, **8**:1031
Dai people, **7**:499
Denmark, **8**:457
Dominica, **2**:841
Dominican Republic, **2**:861
East Asia, **7**:5, 51, 53–54
  mnemonics, **7**:55
Egypt, **6**:321
  of *inshād* repertoire, **6**:167
  'ūd music, **6**:45–46
England, **8**:332–33, 337
  of songs, **8**:328–29
  by women, **8**:336
Ethiopia, *zēmā* chant, **1**:149
Europe, **8**:17, 59
  of art music, **8**:68
  of epic songs, **8**:130–31
  folk music and, **8**:2
  invented texts for, **8**:480
  of song genres, **8**:127
  of village music, **8**:8
  vocalization, **8**:105–8
Faroe Islands, of ballads, **8**:469–70
Finland, **8**:479–80
France, **8**:541, 549
Georgia, **8**:841
German-Americans, **3**:889
Germany, **8**:647
Goa, **5**:737
Greece, Rom people, **8**:285
Guyana, of Hindi *bhajan*, **2**:444
Hawai'i, **9**:914
Hindustani music, **5**:66
Hmong people, **3**:1005
Hungary, **8**:736–37
Hutterite hymns, **3**:1240
Iceland, **8**:405
India, of Tyagaraja's biography, **5**:221
interaction with written music, **3**:22; **8**:52–54
Iran, **6**:834
  of narratives, **6**:827, 839–40, 845
  of *radif*, **6**:59, 61, 71–72, 130, 138–39,
    856–57, 859–60, 866
Iraq, of *maqām*, **6**:313–14

Ireland, **8**:186, 381, 385–86
Irish music, **3**:843
Islamic chant, **8**:967
Italy, **8**:604, 607, 618
Jamaica, **2**:909
Japan, **7**:538–39, 549, 565, 585, 722
  of folk music, **7**:599
  of *gagaku*, **7**:626–27, 757
  gidayû busi, **7**:677
  heike biwa, **7**:646
  kuden, **7**:771–72
Java, **4**:676–77
Jewish cantorial music, **6**:205
Jewish liturgical music, **8**:253
Jewish music, **6**:1059
Jewish *niggunim*, **8**:254
Karachaevian people, **8**:857
Karnataka, **5**:867
Karnatak music, **5**:213
  of ragas, **5**:97
Kashmir, of *ṣūfyāna mūsīqī*, **5**:687
Kazakhstan, **6**:950, 952, 960
Khmer music, **4**:160, 174, 181, 185
Kuna culture, **2**:639, 647
Latvian music, **3**:877
legitimate knowledge, **3**:26
Lithuania, **8**:509
Lombok, **4**:766
Malaysia, **4**:403
Malta, **8**:637, 641
Mangareva, of *ïmene*, **9**:889
Māori people, **9**:933
Maronite church music, **6**:211, 212
Martinique, **2**:914–15
Mashriq, **6**:536
medieval Arab music, **6**:297, 352–53
medieval chant, **8**:49
medieval songs, **8**:72
Mennonite hymns, **3**:887, 1237, 1238
Mexico, children's songs, **2**:618
Middle Eastern musics, **6**:15
mnemonic systems
  Africa, **1**:108, 118, 125, 310, 650; **10**:29
  Angola, **1**:677
  Ethiopia, **1**:149
  Europe, **8**:104–8, 130–31, 197, 311,
    363–64
  Ewe people, **1**:150
  Kpelle people, **1**:136–37, 143
  Mandinka people, **1**:136
  relation to Tonic Sol-fa, **1**:235
  South Asia, **5**:32, 239–40, 472, 494
  Tsonga people, **1**:710–11
Mongol people, of epics, **7**:1008
Morocco, *malhūn*, **6**:497–98
Native American music, **3**:7, 43, 239, 366–67,
  372
Nepal, of healing traditions, **5**:289–90
New Caledonia, dance-songs, **9**:677–78
Nivkhi people, **7**:788
North America
  European immigrant groups, **3**:825
  South Asian community, **5**:581
Norway, **8**:425
  of ballads, **8**:413
  of *hardingfele* music, **8**:416
  of *tralling*, **8**:421, 422

oral tradition and transmission (*continued*)
Oceania, **9:**6
oral-formulaic theory, **8:**94
Palestine, of wedding songs, **6:**579–80
Panama, **2:**777
Persian epic traditions, **6:**343–44
Poland, **8:**709
popular music and, **8:**205
of psychoacoustic phenomena, **5:**289
Punjab (India), of *bhangra* and *giddhā*, **5:**654
Qur'ān recitation, **6:**157–59
Rajasthan, **5:**640, 649
of epics, **5:**646
research on, **8:**22
role in preservation, **1:**11; **2:**66
Romanian emigrant songs, **3:**911
Romania, Rom people, **8:**278
Russia
of *byliny*, **8:**764
of lyric songs, **8:**766
Rom music, **8:**287
Saami people, of joiks, **8:**303–4
of *samāj gāyan*, **5:**252
Sāmoa, **9:**807
Sardinia, **8:**632
Scotland, **8:**186
of ballads and songs, **8:**365
canntaireachd, **8:**98, 106, *107*, 363
social class and, **3:**43
solmization syllables, **5:**32, 38–39, 67, 384
Solomon Islands, mnemonics, **9:**664
song texts about music, **5:**77–78
sound recordings and, **5:**57
South America, **2:**58, 68–70
of myths, **2:**17
tropical-forest region, **2:**125–27, 130
South Asian music, **3:**983, 984–86, 991–92;
5:14, 17, 399, 442, 464
communication channels in, **5:**473–77
documentation of, **5:**55
drum syllables, **5:**116, 151, *152*, 472, 522,
692, 702
guru's control over, **5:**459, 470–71
interaction between Hindustani and
Karnatak musicians, **5:**89
khyāl, **5:**173
of nonclassical traditions, **5:**468–77
of *sūtras*, **5:**471–72
transcriptions of, **5:**52
treatises and, **5:**21, 23, 29, 43
Southeast Asian musics, **4:**118
Spanish mission and cathedral music, **3:**849
Sunda, **4:**722–23
Sweden, **8:**443
of drinking and erotic songs, **8:**436
Switzerland, **8:**692, 696
Syrian Orthodox music, **6:**227–28, 229
Taiwan, **7:**424
Aboriginal peoples, **7:**523–24
Tarahumara culture, **2:**586
Thai music, **4:**277, 298
Tibet, of song-and-dance music, **7:**474
Tibetan Buddhist rituals, **5:**713
Tikopia, **9:**853
Travellers, **8:**295
Trinidad and Tobago, **2:**961

Tunisia, **6:**326, 329, 336, 506
Jewish music, **6:**524
of *ma'lūf*, **6:**518, 520–21
Turkey
of art music, **6:**771, 782
of folk music, **6:**759, 765–66, 784
Turkic epic traditions, **6:**339, 345–46, 969–70
Uilta people, **7:**788
Ukraine, of ritual texts and melodies, **8:**807
Ukrainian-Americans, **3:**915
United States, rural areas, **3:**142, 147–48, 239
Uruguay, **2:**521
use of tape recorders in, **3:**127
Vanuatu, **9:**259–60, 692, 694
Tanna, **9:**706–8
Vedic chant, **5:**239–40, 242–44
Venezuela, **2:**542
via ships, **9:**147
Vietnam, **4:**451
Wales, of ballads, **8:**343
Warao culture, **2:**198
West Africa, **1:**444
work music, **3:**47
Yoruba people, **1:**475; **10:**114
Yukon First Nations groups, **3:**1277
Yuma culture, **2:**598
Oral Traditions Collection Project (Vanuatu),
9:965–66
Orang Dalem (Kubu) people, **4:**598, 600, 616,
618–19
Orang Kanaq people, **4:**560
Orang Melayu Asli people
acculturated music of, **4:**585–87
instruments of, **4:**563
lifestyle of, **4:**560
physical characteristics of, **4:**561
Orang Selatar people, **4:**560
Orang Sungei people, **4:**824
Oransay, Gültekin, **6:**772
Oraon people, **5:**5, 502, 720
Oraq-Mamai (epic), **6:**952
d'Orbigny, Alcides, **2:**250
Orbis Musicae (periodical), **6:**1064
Orbison, Roy, **3:**80
Orchestra Dendera, **1:**429
Orchestra Makassy, **1:**427
Orchestra Matimila, **1:**427
Orchestra of the Shanghai Public Work Bureau,
7:381
Orchestra Super Matimila, **1:**427
orchestras. *See* ensembles, musical
Orchestre Casino Internationale, **2:**892
Orchestre Casino Nationale, **3:**803
Orchestre Maquis du Zaïre, **1:**645
Ord, John, **8:**373
Order of the Sons of Italy in America, **3:**823,
860
Ordering of Moses (Dett), **3:**607
l'Ordre du Bon Temps, **3:**1114
Ordway's Aeolian Vocalists (minstrel troupe),
3:565
Ore, Harry, **10:**18
Oregon
Astoria, Estonian people in, **3:**878
Finnish people in, **3:**872–75
Japanese people in, **3:**969

Native American groups in, **3:**394–96,
420–22, 425–27
Woodburn, Old Believers in, **3:**916–17
O'Reilly, Patrick, **9:**869
Orellana, Joaquín, **2:**736
Orera (musical group), **8:**845
L'Orfeo (Monteverdi), **8:**77
Orfeon label, **6:**758
Orff, Carl, **3:**279, 280, 281, 1185
Orford String Quartet, **3:**1079, 1186
Orgad, Ben-Zion, **6:**1031
Organization of Calypso Performing Artists,
3:1202
organizations. *See* societies and organizations
organs. *See also subcategories below*
African music for, **1:**221, 230
arghūn, **5:**692
Baroque, **8:**78
Byzantine texts on, **6:**373
Canada, **3:**28, 246, 1116, 1148, 1180–81,
1183, 1224
Colombia, **2:**396
Costa Rica, **2:**694, 698
electric, **8:**277
El Salvador, **2:**708
Europe, **8:***74*
development of, **8:**55
improvisation in liturgical music, **8:**73
Renaissance music for, **8:**75
synagogal use of, **8:**258
Finland, **8:**478, 479
Germany, **8:**654
Guatemala, **2:**735
Iceland, **8:**406
Jamaica, **2:**901
in Maronite church music, **6:**216
melodeon, **3:**1180
Netherlands Antilles, **2:**931
North America
in churches, **3:**9, 119, 123, 125, *136*, 530,
874, 1079, 1179
in German music, **3:**888
in Norwegian music, **3:**868
Shaker use of, **3:**135
in soul blues, **3:**648
in synagogues, **3:**934
reed, **3:**246
Romania, **8:**881
Russia, **8:**755
Sāmoa, **9:**205–6, 207
South Asia, in film music, **5:**535
Sweden, **8:**440
Switzerland, **8:**692
Tamil Nadu, **5:**922
urghanīn, **6:**395, 397
organs, barrel
Canada, **3:**136
Germany, **8:**654–55
órgano oriental, **2:**835
Russia, **8:**777
sharmanka, **8:**766
terrimaxka, **8:**640
organs, pump
in Coptic Orthodox music, **6:**222
Ontario, **3:**1190
organum, **8:**71, 403

Organum and the Samaritans (Ravina), **6**:1062
"Orgy in Rhythm," **3**:662
Ó Riada, Seán, **8**:321, 390, 391–92, 394
Oriental Records, **5**:528
Orientexpressen (musical group), **8**:*155, 229*
Origin and Development of Religious Sects (Tibetan
   writing), **7**:472
Original Dixieland Jazz Band, **3**:578, 706
Original Evening Birds (musical group), **1**:772–73
Original Fidelen Mölltaler (musical group), **8**:675
Original Music (record company), **2**:106, 931
Original Oberkrainer Band, **8**:675
Original Scotch Tunes, **8**:372
Original Shleu Shleu (musical group), **3**:803
Original Turtle Shell Band, **2**:677
Orioles (musical group), **3**:351, 670–71, *671*,
   709
Orisa (cult), **2**:952, 954–57. *See also* Shango
Orissa, **5**:731–34
   dance traditions of, **5**:519–21
   folk music of, **5**:732–34
   geography of, **5**:731
   history of, **5**:731–32
   instruments in, **5**:343, 345, 347
   jātrā theater in, **5**:486
   lithophone from, **5**:319, 320–21
   map of, **5**:*718*
   māyurbhanj chau dance-drama of, **5**:497
   pala theater in, **5**:486
   Puri, **5**:731
      Jagannātha Temple, **5**:262
   Tibetan culture in, **5**:709, 712
   tribal music of, **5**:732
Orkestar Politour (musical group), **3**:1195
Orkney Wedding, An (Maxwell Davies), **8**:366
Orlando, Tony, **3**:751
Orléans Theatre (New Orleans), **3**:606
Orloff, Count Grigory, **8**:286
Örn, Ralf, **8**:478
ornamentation
   Africa, *inanga* music, **1**:166–67
   Anuta, *puatanga*, **9**:860
   anzad music, **1**:578–79
   Arabian peninsula, women's songs, **6**:701
   Arab music, **6**:397
      of drum rhythms, **6**:90–91
   Arab music, medieval, **6**:369, 390–92
   Australia
      Central melodic, **9**:435
      Central secret songs, **9**:438
   Azerbaijan, vocal, **6**:931
   Balochistan, *qalandarī* music, **6**:887
   Batak people, **4**:608
   Belarus, vocal music, **8**:795, 796
   Bellona, **9**:851
   bluegrass singing, **3**:161
   Borneo, *sapeh* music, **4**:835
   Bosnia-Hercegovina
      Sephardic Jewish music, **8**:968
      vocal music, **8**:964
   Bulgaria
      harvest songs, **8**:*892*
      Krali Marko ballads, **8**:896
      regional differences, **8**:895
      table songs, **8**:891
      Thrace region, **8**:896

Burma, **4**:384–85, 398
Central Asian art songs, **6**:900
China, **7**:123
   Cantonese opera, **7**:309
   dizi music, **7**:184
   ensemble music, **7**:242–43
   instrumental, **7**:92, 235, 236–37
   Jiangnan sizhu, **7**:224
   kunqu, **7**:290
   nanguan music, **7**:206
   opera arias, **7**:282–83
   Suzhou tanci, **7**:264
   xianshiyue music, **7**:214
Coptic Orthodox music, **6**:221–22
Czech Republic, **8**:719
Dai Buddhist chant, **7**:498
Egypt
   Arab music, **6**:558
   in *btihālāt* performance, **6**:168
England, songs, **8**:327
Europe
   pastoral songs, **8**:194
   regional style differences, **8**:14
   in table songs, **8**:141
Faroe Islands, ballads, **8**:413
Finland, Rom people, **8**:289
Greece, **8**:1008
Gujarat, *bhajan*, **5**:632
Hawai'i
   hula ku'i, **9**:920
   vocal, **9**:916
Hindustani music, **5**:95
   genre associations, **5**:202
Hungary, **8**:741
   instrumental music, **8**:743
   Rom music, **8**:274
   string ensemble music, **8**:744
   verbunkos, **8**:273, 737
Iceland
   hymns, **8**:404
   rímur, **8**:401
Iran
   melodic, **6**:133, 141
   radif, **6**:855
Ireland
   dance music, **8**:382
   vocal music, **8**:380, 381
Irish *sean-nós* singing, **3**:843
Japan
   in narratives, **7**:679
   sankyoku, **7**:716
   syamisen, **7**:659
   syômyô, **7**:615, 616
   tôgaku, **7**:42–43, 622
Java, **4**:670
jazz, **3**:652
Karnataka, *pada* genres, **5**:868
Karnatak music, **5**:89, 93–95, *98–99*, 145,
   352, 924
Kerala, Jewish songs, **5**:949
Khmer people, **4**:179, 186
Korea, **7**:821, 851
   folk songs, **7**:883
   form and, **7**:844–45
   hyangak, **7**:868
   kagok, **7**:845, 923

kasa, **7**:927
p'ansori, **7**:902–5
pŏmp'ae, **7**:872
sijo, **7**:925, 926
sinawi, **7**:891
vocal, **7**:817
Lombok, **4**:763, 767
Low Countries, vocal music, **8**:*521*
Macedonia, *zurla* playing, **8**:281
Malaysia
   ghazal, **4**:439
   Islamic chant, **4**:430
   mak yong, **4**:*419*
   theater and dance genres, **4**:417
   urban folk music, **4**:432
   wayang Siam, **4**:*419*
Micronesian music, **9**:716
Minangkabau people, **4**:611
Mithila, **5**:678
Mongol vocal music, **7**:449, 1006–7
North America
   country music singing, **3**:77
   fiddle tunes, **3**:836
Northwest Coast songs, **3**:397, 399,
   400–401
Norway, herding calls, **8**:412
Papua New Guinea
   flute music, **9**:565
   Gulf Province, **9**:495
   Managalasi songs, **9**:503–4
Philippines, cadenzas, **4**:857
Poland, **8**:707
Qur'ānic recitation, **6**:160
Romania, *doina*, **8**:873
Ryûkyû Islands, Amami *sima uta*, **7**:795
sangati, **5**:217, 221–22
Sangītaratnākara passage on, **5**:39
Scotland
   piobaireachd (also pibroch), **8**:106, *107*,
      363, *364*, 367, 368
   psalm singing, **8**:362–63
Serbia, epic songs, **8**:941
Slovakia, **8**:719
South Asia, **5**:20
   alankāra, treatises on, **5**:36
   andohan (vibrato), **5**:82
   filmī gīt, **5**:533
   gamaka, **5**:36, 39, 93–95, *98–99*, 197, 232,
      924
   gat, **5**:193
   khyāl, **5**:83
   mīnd, **5**:191, 197, 199, 202
   raga, Hindustani, **5**:69
   sthāya, treatises on, **5**:36
   thumrī, **5**:181
   treatises on, **5**:33, 34, 36, 44
   varnam, **5**:149
   vina, **5**:29
Southeast Asia, gong-chime ensemble music,
   4:21
Spain, flamenco, **8**:12
Sunda, **4**:723
   pop Sunda, **4**:718
Switzerland, in yodeling, **8**:691
Tamil Nadu, folk music, **5**:910
Thailand, **4**:267, 270, 293, *294*

Volume Key: **6**, Middle East; **7**, East Asia; **8**, Europe; **9**, Australia and the Pacific Islands; **10**, The World's Music.

ornamentation (*continued*)
   Tibetan folk songs, **7:**473
   Tibetan music, **5:**711
   Tuamotu Islands, **9:**884
   Tuareg people, *tesîwit*, **1:**579
   Tunisia, in *ma'lūf*, **6:**328
   Turkey
      arabesk, **6:**776
      art music, **6:**773
      of drum rhythms, **6:**90–91
      vocal music, **6:**761–62, 786
   Turkmenistan, *baggy* music, **6:**974
   Tyagaraja *kriti*, **5:**268–69
   Uighur *muqam*, **6:**995–1008
   Ukrainian fiddle music, **3:**345
   Vedic chant, **5:**31, 261
   Vietnam, **4:**17, 55, 70, 456, *459*, 461–62,
      463, *464*
   Wales
      bardic music, **8:**349
      songs, **8:**344, 345–46
   West African songs, **1:**446, 451
   Yap, **9:**305
   Yemen, *tawshīḥ*, **6:**690
   Yoruba people, **1:**460
Ornaments (Boskovitch), **6:**1031
Ornelas, Mike, **3:**778
Ornstein, Ruby, **4:**733
Orochi people, **7:**1027–30
Orod people, **7:**1004–20
Orokaiva people, **9:**489
Oroko people. *See* Uilta people
Orokolo people, **9:**489, 492
Oromo Association, **3:**1213
Oromo people, **1:**605
Oroqen people, **7:**518–19
Orozalynuly, Seitek, **6:**958
Orpheon (record company), **8:**777
Orpheus Caledonius (Thomson), **8:**17, 372
Orpheus Chamber Orchestra (New York), **8:**102
Orpheus Operatic Society (Ottawa), **3:**1182
Orpheus Theatre (Vancouver), **3:**1096
orquesta music, **3:**756, 766, 778–80
Orquesta Aragón, **2:**835; **3:**743, 796, 798
Orquesta Broadway, **3:**788, 797
Orquesta de Cámara Nicaragüense (Nicaragua),
   2:766
Orquesta Experimental de Instrumentos Nativos
   (Bolivia), **2:**284
Orquesta Feminina de Pandacan, **4:**859, 863,
   869
Orquesta Gilberto Valdés, **3:**788
Orquesta Gris, **2:**835
Orquesta de La Luz, **3:**799
Orquesta Nacional (Nicaragua), **2:**766
Orquesta Nuevo Ritmo, **3:**788
Orquesta Sinfónica de la Ciudad de Asunción
   (Paraguay), **2:**463
Orquesta Sinfónica Nacional (Colombia), **2:**397
Orquesta Típica Mexicana, **3:**740–41
Orquestra Típica Pixinguinha-Donga, **2:**350
Orr, Robin, **8:**369
Orrego-Salas, Juan, **2:**238
Orsmond, John, **9:**21
Orsúa, Arzans de, **2:**284
Ortega, Aniceto, **2:**114

Ortega, Juan, **3:**759
Ortega, Manuel M., **6:**1036
Ortiga (musical group), **2:**373
d'Ortigue, Joseph, **3:**28, 1165
Ortiz (Cuban musican), **2:**836
Ortiz (violist), **2:**603
Ortíz, Alfredo Rolando, **2:**464
Ortiz, Andrés, **4:**866
Ortiz, Belle, **3:**724
Ortiz, Cleofes, **3:**763, 768
Ortiz de la Peña, José, **2:**741
Ortiz de Zárate, Juan, **2:**453
Ortiz, Fernando, **2:**838–39
Ortiz, Henry, **3:**760
Ortiz, Juan, **3:**724
Ortiz, Luis "Perico," **3:**797
Ortiz, Manuel Antonio, **2:**544
Ŏrŭndŭrŭn wae kŭraeyo? (Kim), **7:**959
Ory, Edmund "Kid," **3:**568, 652–53
Orya people, **9:**589
Osa, Sigbjørn, **8:**427
Osage Indian nation, **3:**29, 31, 440, 449
Ôsaka University, **7:**594; **9:**963
Osborne Brothers, **3:**159
Osbourne, Ozzy, **3:**356–57; **8:**215
Oscar, General Charles, **2:**890
Osei, James, **1:**357–58
Osgood, Cornelius, **3:**392
Oshima, Akira Mark, **10:***15*
"O Siem" (Aglukark), **3:**1280
Osing Javanese people, **4:**635
Osipov Orchestra, **3:**58
Oskorri (musical group), **8:**315
Osland, Len, **3:**1277–78
Oslin, K. T., **3:**81
Osman Dede, **6:**109, 110, 118, 119, 196
Osmar (Bahian musician), **2:**337
Os Oito Batutas, **2:**350
Osorio, Jesús, **3:**737–38
Osorio y Ricaurte, Juan Crisóstomo, **2:**386–87
Ospina, Simón, **2:**387
O ssei sseil (Naxi funeral song), **7:**510
Ossetia. *See* Georgia; North Caucasia
Ossetian Folk Songs (Galaev), **8:**861
Ossetian people, **8:**826, 850, 857, 859–61
   dance traditions of, **8:**861
   epic performance, **8:**851
   instruments, **8:**197, 200, 859–60
   research on music of, **8:**861
   vocal music of, **8:**859–61
Ossetian State Ensemble, **8:**860
Ossian. *See* Macpherson, James
Ossian (musical group), **8:**372
Ostanek, Walter, **3:**1198
Oster, Harry, **3:**858
Ostermayer, Hieronymus, **8:**881
Österreichisches Museum für Volkskunde
   (Vienna), **8:**181
Osterwald, Hazy, **8:**210
Ostjak people, **8:**128
Ostrovsky, Aleksandr, **8:**759
Ostyak people. *See* Khants people
Ó Súilleabháin, Mícheál, **8:**320, 394
O'Sullivan, Donal, **8:**391–92, 394
Osuna, Sonny, **3:**733
Oswald, James, **8:**367, 368, 372

Oswald, Olaf, **9:**24
Oswalt, Windell, **3:**381
Os Zimbos (musical group), **1:**428, 435
Otago University, **9:**932
Ôtaguro Motoo, **7:**729
Otake, Tomoyoshi, **4:**387–88
"O Tannenbaum," **3:**889, 943
Otarov, O., **8:**859
Otavalo culture, **2:**379, 413. *See also* Quichua
   culture
Othello (Shakespeare), **3:**615
Otis, Johnny, **3:**669, 742
Otoe Indian nation, **3:**440
Otomí culture, **2:**570–74
Otopame culture, **2:**570–74
   dances of, **2:**572–73
   instruments of, **2:**570–71
   musical genres
      huapango arribeño, **2:**571, 573
      huapango huasteco, **2:**573
      mestizo, **2:**573
      minuete, **2:**573
      son arribeño, **2:**573
   research on, **2:**573–74
   songs of, **2:**571–72
Otrar Sazy ensemble, **6:**960
Ottawa (Odawa) Indian nation, **3:**451–59, 1079
Ottawa Orpheus Glee Club, **3:**1181–82
Ottawa Symphony Orchestra, **3:**1079
Otter, Anne Sofie von, **8:**434
Ottley, Jerry, **9:**936
Otto, Steven, **4:**891
Ottoman empire, **3:**942, 1029–30; **6:**980; **8:**10.
     See also Turkey
   in Aleppo, **6:**566
   artistic legacy, **6:**77, 255, 757–58, 770–71, 781
   conflicts with Safavids, **6:**73
   dance in, **6:**811–12
   decline of, **6:**1013
   defeat of Mamluks, **6:**293
   Epirus court, **8:**284
   European slaves in, **6:**18, 770–71
   history of music in, **6:**113–28
   military music in, **6:**547, 767–68, 770
   milyet system, **8:**1023
   in North Africa, **6:**431, 433, 543–44, 547,
      1035
   rule over Albania, **8:**986, 997
   rule over Balkans, **8:**867
   rule over Bosnia-Hercegovina, **8:**962–63
   rule over Bulgaria, **8:**890, 895
   rule over Georgia, **8:**827, 835–36
   rule over Greece, **8:**1007, 1009–11, 1022,
      1023–24
   rule over Hungary, **8:**736, 737
   rule over Kurdistan, **6:**743
   rule over Macedonia, **8:**972, 973
   rule over Montenegro, **8:**957
   rule over Palestine, **6:**1023–24
   rule over Romania, **8:**868, 881
   rule over Serbia, **8:**940, 952
   Sephardi Jews in, **6:**201
   Sufism in, **6:**108–9, 189–90, 194, 769
Ouanga (White), **3:**608
Óučanok, Ihar, **8:**800
Ouda, Chaykha, **6:**269

Oude en Nieuwe Hollantse Boerenlieties en Contredansen, **8**:523
Ouighur (Huigu) people, **7**:458
Oulim (musical group), **7**:970–71
Öullimül wihan 1990 (Oulim), **7**:971
Oumarou, Watta, **1**:492
Our American Music (Howard), **3**:508
"Our Land Redeemed," **3**:309
Ouseph, Esthappan, **5**:*950*
Out from the Silence (Tonooka), **3**:972, 973
Out of Bondage (musical), **3**:617
Ôuta dokoro (institute), **7**:626, 757
Ouvéa. *See* West 'Uvea
Ovadia, Mony, **8**:210
Ovambo people, **1**:713, 714
Ovation Studios, **3**:339
Oven, Cootje van, **1**:60
Overd, Mrs., **8**:336
Övgön Shuvuu Hoyor (Buddhist dance-drama), **7**:1016
Ovid, **8**:608, 878
Oviedo y Valdés, Gonzalo Fernández de, **2**:13, 22, 183, 681
Ovimbundu people, **1**:700, *713*–14
Owen, Chris, **9**:42, 50, 1007
Owen, Roger C., **2**:599
Owens, Buck, **3**:81
Owens, Harry, **3**:1049, 1050
Owens Valley Paiutes, **3**:420
ownership issues. *See* copyright and ownership
Owöl Kwangju (Im), **7**:969
Owöl üi norae (Kim), **7**:953
"Oxford Town" (Dylan), **3**:316
Oxford University Press, **3**:284
Øyaland, Ola, **8**:418
"¿*Oye cómo va?*" (Puente), **3**:733, 751, 795, 798
Oyele, D. A., **1**:403
Oyo (kingdom), **1**:401, 459, 471
Özal, Turgut, **6**:248
Ozawa, Seiji, **7**:398, 416, 729, *729*
Özdemir, Cengiz, **6**:790, 791
Özden, Ismail, **6**:799
Özgen, Ihsan, **6**:121
Özkan, **6**:249
Ozomatli (musical group), **3**:750
Ozuna, Sunny, **3**:780

"*Pa los Rumberos*" (Puente), **3**:794
Paama (Vanuatu), **9**:690
Paasonen, Heikki, **8**:488
Pabuji (deity), **5**:643, 646
Pābujī kī par (epic), **5**:646
P'abungsön (Kim), **7**:953
Pacaca culture, **2**:680
Pace, Carmelo, **8**:642
Pace, Harry, **3**:707
Pacha (musical group), **2**:293
Pacheco, Aragon, **1**:422
Pacheco Areco, Jorge, **2**:517
Pacheco, Johnny, **1**:387, 422; **3**:732, 743, 788, 794, 796, 797
Pachev, Bekmurra, **8**:855
Pacholczyk, Jozef, **10**:140, 141
"Pachuco Hop" (Higgins), **3**:742
Paci, Mario, **7**:381
Pacific Coast Norwegian Singers Association, **3**:867

Pacific Collection (Fiji), **9**:968
Pacific Collection of the University of Hawai'i Library, **9**:970–71
Pacific Festival of Arts, **9**:48–49, 53, 199, 224, 232, *404*, 689, 973, 976, 979, 982, 997
    Austral Islands participants, **9**:880
    Australian participants, **9**:464
    Banaban participants, **9**:*71*
    Chamorro participants, **9**:*743*
    Chinese participants, **9**:868
    Cook Islands participants, **9**:*898*
    cultural policies and, **9**:57–59
    Enga participants, **9**:242, *289*
    Fijian participants, **9**:*774*, *780*
    films of, **9**:1008, 1009–10
    Futuna participants, **9**:*773*, *816*
    goals of, **9**:65
    Hawai'ian participants, **9**:67, 276
    instruments performed, **9**:*372*
    Kiribati participants, **9**:*346*, *721*
    Kosraean participants, **9**:743
    Loyalty Islands participants, **9**:*684*
    Māori participants, **9**:*946*, *948*
    Micronesian participants, **9**:721
    Mortlockese participants, **9**:92
    Nauru participants, **9**:262, *757*, *758*
    New Ireland participants, **9**:*351*
    Niue participants, **9**:817
    Papua New Guinea participants, **9**:*146*, *225*, *481*, *482*, *483*, *491*, *601*
    Pohnpei participants, **9**:*728*
    politics and, **9**:56
    Rapa Nui participants, **9**:953
    Sāmoan participants, **9**:*54*, *320*, *806*, *808*
    sound recordings from, **9**:985
    Tikopia participants, **9**:*1*, *855*
    Tokelauan participants, **9**:*826*
    Torres Strait Islander participants, **9**:*412*
    Tuvaluan participants, **9**:831
    'Uvea and Futuna participants, **9**:*816*
    West Futuna participants, **9**:*863*
Pacific Islander Americans: An Annotated Bibliography in the Social Sciences, **9**:972
Pacific Islander Council (Los Angeles), **3**:1052
Pacific Islanders. *See also specific groups*
    in Aotearoa, **9**:111–14, 928
    in Australia, **9**:84–87
    in Hawai'i, **9**:103–5
    in North America, **3**:4–5, 526, 1092
Pacific Islands Regiment Pipes and Drums Band, **9**:89
Pacific Manuscripts Bureau, **9**:959
Pacific Overtures (Sondheim), **3**:545
Pacific Studies (periodical), **9**:212, 971
Pacini Hernández, Deborah, **2**:93, 411; **3**:800
Pacius, Fredrik, **8**:482, 496
"Pack Up Your Troubles in Your Old Kit Bag," **9**:848
Pada (Lee), **7**:956
Pada, Lata, **3**:223, 1216
padam, **5**:100, 103, 104, 389, 410–11, 452, 512, 517, 522, 940
    composers of, **5**:229, 266–67
    text of, **5**:107, 219–20

Pada üi norae (Korean *kayagüm* piece), **7**:962
Paderewski, Ignacy, **8**:368
Padilla, Alonzo J., **3**:312
Padilla de León, Felipe, **4**:872, 874
Padilla, Rafael, **2**:387
Padmanabha (deity), **5**:230
Padmavathi Mahila Vishvavidyalaya, **5**:450
Paebijang T'aryŏng (p'ansori story), **7**:899
Pae Sŏlhyang, **7**:893, 909
Paek Nakchun, **7**:915
Paek Taeung, **7**:853, 854
Paek Tongjin, **7**:988
Paek Uyong, **7**:951
Paekche kingdom, **7**:18, 27, 41
    Chinese interactions in, **7**:24, 25
    cultural influence on Japan, **7**:723, 798
    kudara gaku repertoire in, **7**:620
    music in, **7**:806, 981
Paekkusa (*kasa*), **7**:927
Paeni, Mukhlis, **10**:46
Páez culture, **2**:379
Pagan (kingdom), **4**:62, 365, 376, 378
Pagan (film), **9**:43
Pagan Babies (musical group), **9**:167
"Pagan Love Song," **9**:43
Pagán, Ralfi, **3**:799
paganism. *See also* shamanism
    Armenia, **6**:736
    Belarus, **8**:793
    Europe, **8**:5, 122–23
    Georgia, **8**:835–36
    Hungary, **8**:704
    Latvian *dievturīc* movement, **8**:505
    North Caucasia, **8**:853, 855, 857–58, 863–64
    Russia, **8**:754
Pagdakila sa Kordilyera (Feliciano), **4**:878
Page, Frederick, **9**:928
Page, Jimmy, **3**:112–14, 356; **8**:214
Page, JoAnne, **9**:317
Page, Mary Ellen, **6**:344
Page, Patti, **3**:352
Page, Ralph, **3**:233
Page, Stephen, **9**:*410*, 417
Pageant (periodical), **3**:349
Pagpili ng Ministro (de la Peña), **4**:881
Pagsamba (Maceda), **4**:875–76
Paguía, Felipe, **4**:864
Pahelio, Fafie, **9**:*825*
Paheo, Monica, **9**:886, 973
Pahinui, Gabby, **3**:339; **9**:164, 389, 390, 1005
Pahlavi dynasty, **6**:142
Pahne, Helen, **9**:437
Pahor, Karel, **8**:921
Pahoturi people, **9**:507
Pai Indian groups, **3**:428
Paimier de chuntian (Li), **7**:185
"Pain in My Heart" (Redding), **3**:676
Paine, John Knowles, **3**:173, 538
Paine, Robert Treat, Jr., **3**:305
Painim Nabaut, **9**:179
Painim Wok, **9**:90
Painim Wok (album), **9**:154
Painter, Muriel Thayer, **3**:437, 438
Pai-pai culture, **2**:595, 598
Paisiello, Giovanni, **8**:618

Paí-Tavyterá culture, **2:**199, 204
Paiute Indian nation, **3:**420–421, 435
  songs of, **3:**426
Paiwan people, **7:**525–26, 529
Pajai (Pijie), **7:**451–52, 1008
Pajajaran (kingdom), **4:**62, 699, 715, 723
"Pájaro Campana," **3:**730
Pájaro, Eliseo, **4:**874–75, 878
Pajelança, **2:**341
Pak Chihong, **7:**986
Pak Chiwŏn, **7:**855
Pak Chonggi, **7:**915
Pak Chŏnghǔi. *See* Park Chung Hee
Pak Ch'osŏn, **7:**900
Pak Ch'owŏl, **7:**900
Pak Hŏnbong, **7:**963, 990
Pak Husaeng, **7:**985
Pak Huung, **7:**921
Pak Hyogwan, **7:**856, 921
Pak Hyŏnsuk, **7:**971
Pak Island (Admiralty Islands), **9:**983
Pak Kyesun, **7:**984
Pak Kyŏngni, **7:**959
Pak Mansun, **7:**899
Pak Nokchu, **7:**899, 989
Pak P'algwoe, **7:**899
Pak Pŏmhun, **7:**915
Pak Pongsul, **7:**900
Pak Sanggŏn, **7:**921
Pak Tongjin, **7:**900, 969, 986
Pak Tongsil, **7:**910, 960
Pak Ŭnha, **7:**938, 964–65
Pak Yŏn, **7:**833, 854
Pak Yujŏn, **7:**898, 906
Paka, July, **9:**390
Pakarati family, **9:**952
Pakem Wirama (Javanese manuscript), **4:**636
pakhāvaj. See drums: barrel, conical, or
  cylindrical
Pakhtun people, **5:**785, 786–90, 833. *See also*
  Pashtun people
Pakistan, **5:**743–800. *See also* Balochistan;
  Northern Areas (Pakistan); North West
  Frontier Province (Pakistan); Punjab
  (Pakistan); Sindh
  Afghan refugees in, **5:**810, 831, 840
  amateur music-making in, **5:**749
  Balochi people, **6:**881–90
  ceremonies, marriage consummation, **5:**287
  compilation of Ṛgveda in, **5:**238
  dance traditions of, **5:**506, 754, 760–61
  film industry in, **5:**531
  funerals in, **5:**283
  fusion music in, **5:**748–49
  geography of, **5:**744
  hereditary professional musicians, **5:**749
  history of, **5:**16, 744
  Hunza, **6:**181
  Indrasabha in, **5:**487
  instruments in, **5:**336, 344, 345
  Islamabad, **5:**746
    King Faisal Mosque, **5:***745*
  languages of, **5:**5
  map of, **5:***3, 742*
  musical genres
    bride departure songs, **5:**275–76

dhrupad, **5:**250
ghazal, **5:**256
qawwali, **5:**256
musical life in, **5:**403
Parsi theater in, **5:**487
popular music in, **5:**542–53, 810
population of, **5:**5
Qur'ānic recitation in, **6:**161
religion in, **5:**10, 16, 403
Tharparkar, **5:**488
theater in, **5:**486–88
Torbat, **6:**882, 883, 884
weddings in, **5:**277
Western popularity of musical genres, **5:**568
Pakistan-Canadian Association, **3:**1090
Pakistan League of America, **3:**987
Pakistani people
  in Arabian peninsula, **6:**703
  in Denmark, **8:**463
  in Great Britain, **5:**572–76; **8:**231, 236, 240,
    336
  in North America, **3:**980–88, 1218–20
  in Vietnam, **4:**531
"Pakiusap" (Santiago), **3:**1025
Pakkala, Alaine, **3:**874
Pakpak people, **4:**607
Pakualaman court, **4:**633
Palac (album), **8:**802
Palace Grand (Dawson City), **3:**1277
Palace Museum (Beijing), **7:**393
Palacin, Larrea, **6:**1037
Palacio, Andy, **2:**675, *676*
Palacios, Carlos, **2:***756*
Palacios, Juan, **2:***756*
Palaeolithic period, **8:**36–38, 600
Palais, James, **7:**26
Palama, Eddie, **9:**390
Palas, Peter, **7:**1014
Palästinischer Diwan (Dalman), **6:**580
Palau, **9:**712, 722–26, 743. *See also* Tobi Island
  archives in, **9:**967
  betel use in, **9:**177
  European exploration of, **9:**7
  films on, **9:**1016
  geography of, **9:**181, 722
  instruments of, **9:**717
  Japanese in, **9:**27, 32
  Koror Island, alcohol use in, **9:**180–83
  music and dance of, **9:**48, 159, 722–26, 979,
    981
  popular music in, **9:**160, 161, 721
  recitation, **9:**287
  research on, **7:**594; **9:**25, 722
  settlement of, **9:**715
  sound recordings from, **9:**994–95
Palawan people, **4:**920
  epics of, **4:**907, 927
  instrumental music of, **4:**924, 925
Paleolithic period, **5:**298
  Inner Asia, **7:**11–12
  Japan, **7:**534
Palestine, **6:**279–80, 434, 1013, 1015, 1021;
    8:254, 266. *See also* Israel
  aerophones in, **6:**414
  archaeological studies in, **6:**18, 1061–62, 1065
  drums in, **6:**417

folk traditions in, **6:**545
intifāḍa, **6:**635–40
Jewish people in, **6:**1035–36
lyres in, **6:**357, 358
musical life in, **6:**1023–30
research on music of, **6:**580
wedding eve celebrations in, **6:**573–78,
    579–92
Palestine Liberation Organization, **6:**636
Palestine Opera, **6:**1025
Palestine Orchestra, **6:**1026–27
Palestinian people
  in Caribbean, **2:**793
  in North America, **3:**1029; **6:**282
Palestrina, Giovanni Pierluigi da, **8:**74, *74*, 75
Paliashvili, Zakaria, **8:**843, 846
Paliau, John, **9:**607
Palikur culture, **2:**164, 434
  instruments of, **2:**435, *436*
  vocal music of, **2:**435, 437
Palisca, Claude, **1:**13
Paljetak, Vlaho, **8:**934
Palladium Ballroom (New York), **3:**13, 732, 787,
    793, 794
pallavi, **5:**141, 145, 217–18, 219, 520, 544. *See
    also rāgam-tānam-pallavi*
  women performers of, **5:**410
Pallivathucal, Leena, **5:***521*
Palm, Edgar, **2:**928, 931
Palm, Jan Gerard, **2:**931
Palm Wine Drunkard (Ogunmola), **1:**408
Palma, Precioso, **4:**866
Palmer, Gus, Sr., **3:**449
Palmer, Paula, **2:**703
Palmer, Robert, **3:**351
Palmieri, Charlie, **3:**732, 788, 796
Palmieri, Eddie, **3:**336, 732, 743, 789, 795, 797,
    798, 799
Palo Mayombe (religious system), **3:**785
"Paloma, La" (son), **2:**604, 606, 620; **3:**791, 797
Paluskar, D. V., **5:**255
Paluskar, Vishnu Digambar, **5:**52, 255, 380, 433,
    444–45, 466
Pälwan-*baggy*, **6:**970
Pambada caste, **5:**882–83
Pame culture, **2:**570–74
Pamoki, Ba-I, **4:**907–8
Pampa y la Puna (Ginastera), **2:**115
Pan Records, **9:**997
Pan-African Orchestra, **1:**211
Pan American Association of Composers, **3:**174
Pan-American Exposition (Buffalo), **3:**1048
Pan American Union, **2:**397; **3:**22
Panagoniak, Charlie, **3:**1275, 1279
Panama, **2:**628, 770–84
  African brotherhoods in, **2:**47
  African descendants, **2:**773
  archaeomusicological research in, **2:**7, 9
  art music, **2:**784
  Aztec, Maya, and Chibcha cultures in, **2:**8
  Bocas del Toro province, **2:**771
  calypso in, **2:**773
  children's wakes in, **2:**422
  Chiriquí province, **2:**771
  Choco culture, **2:**771
  Chorrera, **2:**779

Coclé province, **2:**771, 772–73
Colón province, **2:**773
congo in, **2:**773
Cuban people in, **2:**84
cumbia in, **2:**778
Darién province, **2:**771, 773
décima in, **2:**780
English people, **2:**773
festivals of, **2:**781–83
Garachiné, **2:**779
geography of, **2:**770
Guaymí culture, **2:**685, 771
Herrera province, **2:**771, 772–73
history of, **2:**770–71
iconographical record in, **2:**16
instruments of, **2:**773–77
Kuna culture, **2:**637–49, 771, 772
Los Santos province, **2:**771, 772–73
map of, **2:**629
music and dance of, **2:**777–81
Panamá province, **2:**773
Pearl Islands, **2:**773, 779
population of, **2:**771–72
punto in, **2:**776
research on, **2:**783–84
San Blas Islands, **2:**637–38, 771, 772
Spanish heritage in, **2:**772–73
Teribe culture, **2:**771
Veraguas province, **2:**771, 772–73
Panama-Pacific Exposition (San Francisco),
      3:1048
Panamá la Vieja, **2:**626
Panamaka Sumu, **2:**750, 751
Panamanian-Americans/Canadians, **3:**727
Pāṇan caste, **5:**931, 932
Panar caste, **5:**884
Panare culture, **2:**164
Panaxov, Panah, **6:**930
Panchamasārasamhitā (treatise), **5:**72
Panda Dance Theatre (Toronto), **3:**1217
Pandey, Shyam M., **5:**675
Pando Ch'anggŭktan (*p'ansori* company), **7:**968
Pando people, **5:**720
Panduranga, **5:**253
Pandya dynasty, **5:**260, 490
Pandyale (deity), **5:**607
Pandya, Sri Dharmiklal, **5:**633–34, *634*
Panei (kingdom), **4:**600
Pang Sŭnghwan, **7:**965
Pan'gap sŭmnida (collection), **7:**961
Panga t'aryŏng (Korean folk song), **7:**957
Panga t'aryŏngŭl chujero han haegŭm hyŏpchugok
      (Kim), **7:**957
Pangelinan, Max, **9:**160
Panggung, Pangeran, **4:**686
Panguan liyueshu (Li), **7:**131, 336
Pangwa people, **1:**640; **10:**123
Paṇi people, **5:**238
Panigrahi, Sanjukta, **5:**520
Panina, Varvara, **8:**776
Paṇiya people, **5:**903, 909, 916
Panjara, George, **5:**947
Panju Ayyar, **5:**390, 391, *391*
Pankow, **8:**219
Pann, Anton, **8:**881–82
Panneton, Isabelle, **3:**1152

Pannonia, **8:**736
Panopio, Fred, **4:**884
*Panorama de la música mexicana desde la
      independencia hasta la actualidad*
      (Mayer-Serra), **2:**623
panpipes
   Andean regions, **2:**207–9
   antara (also *andara*), **2:**35, 207–8, 467, 468,
         469
   Argentina, **2:**250
   'aulebi, **9:**964
   'au po'o, **9:**398, 400
   'au waa, **9:**398, 667
   'au ware, **9:**398, 400–401
   au ware, **9:**667
   ayarachi, **2:**469
   Baluan, **9:**602
   bèchöö, **9:**680
   bengo, **9:**570
   Bolivia, **2:**12, 282, 285–86, 295, 297
   Buka Island, **9:**640–41, 647
   busi, **9:**647, 648
   California, **3:**478
   canchis sipas, **2:**226, 230
   Carib culture, **2:**23
   carrizo, **2:**533
   chiriguano (also *chiriwanu*), **2:**216, 285, 469
   Colombia, **2:**155
   cornamusa, **8:**572
   dew-dew-as, **4:**919
   Ecuador, **2:**222
   ehu, **9:**656
   erebo, **2:**159, *160*, 161
   Europe
      bone, **8:**38
      early specimens, **8:**38–39
   fagovava, **9:**863
   Fiji, **9:**776
   firlinfeu, **8:**616
   flauta, **2:**365
   flautone, **2:**359, 365
   folotsy, **1:**788
   France, **8:**142, 544
   French Guiana, **2:**435
   gammu burui, **2:**640, 641–43
   goke, **2:**643
   Guaraní culture, **2:**201
   guli, **2:**643
   gùlungùlu, **9:**542–43
   gúlupòbe, **9:**393, 542–43
   Hawai'ian, **3:**527
   isong akakä, **9:**624–25
   isong akarigo, **9:**624–25
   julajula (also *julujulu*), **2:**285, 289, 290, 291
   kantus, **2:**216
   kugikly (also *kuvikly*), **8:**770
   laquita (also *lakita*), **2:**286, 362
   larasup, **9:**619–20
   lawi, **9:**619
   maremare, **2:**533
   Melanesia, **9:**598
   Mexico, **2:**8
   Micronesia, **9:**23
   mimby pú, **2:**201
   mimiha, **9:**794, *795*
   mıskal, **6:**108, 114, 115, 774

moráo, **2:**293
nai, **8:**277, 872, 878
nakerkuli, **9:**614
Nasca culture, **2:**467
nasomsom, **9:**614
ngororombe, **1:**751–52
nifu, **9:**658–59, 661
Oceania, **9:**146, 393, 398–401
   bundle types, **9:**393, 398–401, 508–9,
         542–43
   raft types, **9:**393, 498
Papua New Guinea, **9:**90, 481, 530, 537, 601
Peru, **2:**11, 16, *18*, 207, 476
perurupe, **9:**525
piago, **9:**178
piloilo, **2:**358
pito, **2:**365
pitucahue, **2:**233
pöliannez (also *pölian' ias*), **8:**774
porétépoqa, **9:**533
potoviso, **9:**629
púlugèla, **9:**542–43
pupe, **9:**536
quills, **3:**593
rondador, **2:**208, 416, *417*, 426
rondadorcillos, **2:**210
Rotuma, **9:**819
saggeypo, **4:**919
Sāmoa, **9:**956
shengo, **9:**655
siku, **2:**33, 34–35, *76*, 90
   Argentina, **2:**253, 256
   Bolivia, **2:**286
   Chile, **2:**357–58, 362, 373–74
   Peru, **2:**245, 486
   Quechua and Aymara culture, **2:**207, 212,
         216, *217*, 219
sikuri, **2:**469
skudutis, **8:**511
so, **7:**824, 828
Solomon Islands, **9:**42, 156, *283*, 286, 292,
      371, 630, 665, 666–69, 962
   raft types, **9:**632, 667
solpet, **9:**615
South America, **2:**29, *76*
   consorts of, **2:**208–9
   distribution of, **2:**34
   pre-Columbian, **2:**215
   Spanish views about, **2:**283
   tropical-forest region, **2:**127
stviri (also *soinari*; *sastsrapo*; *larchemi*),
      8:839–40
suduchu, **2:**178
syrinx, **8:**39, 47
takamasi, **9:**649
takamatsi, **9:**651, 653–54
tala 'au (also *susuku*), **9:**668–69
tarheinau, **9:**708
Torres Strait Islands, **9:**428
trstene orglice, **8:**915, *916*, 919
Uighur, **6:**1004
Vanuatu, **9:**690, 693
veó-páme, **2:**151–52
wek, **9:**640
wot, **4:**318, 320
yue, **7:**79, 108

Volume Key: **6**, Middle East; **7**, East Asia; **8**, Europe; **9**, Australia and the Pacific Islands; **10**, The World's Music.

panpipes (*continued*)
  yui, **9:**606
  zampoña, **2:**207, 221, 286, 291, 357, 365, 373; **3:**730
Panse, Nana, **5:**121
p'ansori, **7:**6, *818*, 897–908, 942, 944–46, 967–69. *See also* ch'anggŭk
  aesthetics of, **7:**73, 814, 906–7
  cadences in, **7:**851
  calls in, **7:**897
  cho concept in, **7:**902–5
  contemporary adaptations of, **7:**960
  female performers of, **7:**76
  folk songs in, **7:**879, 903–4, 988
  han emotion in, **7:**885
  history of, **7:**75–76, 898–900
  influence on *sinawi*, **7:**891
  kayagŭm pyŏngch'ang and, **7:**907–8
  origins of, **7:**75, 807
  performance lineages of, **7:**46, 55, 906, 985–86
  performers of, **7:**893–95, 897, 909–11, 985–86, 989
  punch'ang style, **7:**898
  rhythmic patterns in, **7:**842–43, 901–2
  sanjo and, **7:**914
  scales in, **7:**849
  schools of, **7:**905–6
  sound recordings of, **7:**972
  taehwa ch'ang style, **7:**968
  tan'ga songs in, **7:**897, 905, 908
  texts in, **7:**900–901
  vocal techniques in, **7:**817, 819–20, 882, 902–5, 906–7
  yŏnch'ang style, **7:**898, 968
P'ansori Hakhoe (organization), **7:**969
P'ansori inhyŏnggŭk Hŏsaengjon (Lee), **7:**955
Państwowe Muzeum Etnograficzne (Warsaw), **8:**182
Pantages Theatre (Toronto), **3:***198*
Pantaleoni, Hewitt, **1:**10, 135–36, 137, 158–59, 161
Pantar, **4:**786
Pan Trinbago Steelband Association, **3:**1202
Panya Roongrüang, **4:**26, 128, 224, 277, 278, 286
Paoli, Gino, **8:**619
Paoli, Pasquale, **8:**571
Paopuzi (Ge), **7:**320
Paotred an Dreujenn Gaol, **8:**560
Papadopoulos, Steve, **9:**75
Papago Indian nation. *See* Tohono O'odham Indian nation
Papakōlea: A Story of Hawaiian Land (film), **9:**42
Papakura, Maggie, **9:**936
"Papa's Got a Brand New Bag" (Brown), **3:**710
Papathanassiou, Vangelis, **8:**1018
Papayan, Nadezda, **6:**725
Papazov, Ivo, **8:**226–27, 284, 890, 903
"Paper Thin" (MC Lyte), **3:**714
"*Papillon, Le*" (Lavallée), **3:**1148–49
Papineau-Couture, Jean, **3:**1076, 1108, 1151
Papineau, Louis-Joseph, **3:**1146
Pappas, Irene, **8:**1018
Papua New Guinea, **9:**472–654. *See also* Admiralty Islands; Bali (Unea) Island; Baluan; Bismarck Archipelago;

Bougainville; Buka; Karkar Island; Louisiade Archipelago; Manus; New Britain; New Guinea (island of); New Ireland; Nissan Atoll; Nukumanu; Nukuria; Rossel Island; Siasi Islands; Takuu; Trobriand Islands; *specific peoples*
  alcohol use in, **9:**178
  Americans in, **9:**148–50
  archives and museums, **9:**961–62
  Australians in, **9:**149, 475
  Austronesian speakers, **9:**319
  bands in, **9:**27, 128–30
  betel use in, **9:**177
  Central Province, **9:**491–94
    kitoro dance, **9:**490
  Chimbu Province, **9:**511, 522–26
  Chinese people in, **9:**72
  Christian music in, **9:**88–89, 91
  cultural policies in, **9:**55
  cultural regions of, **9:**475
  dance in, **9:**480–87
  Daru Island, **9:**178–80, 506
    island dances, **9:**507
  documentary films on, **9:**49–50
  East New Britain Province, **9:**600, 620–21
  East Sepik Province, **9:**545, 548–60; **10:**28
    Iatmul mythological suites, **9:**340–42
    Kwoma signaling rhythms, **9:**289
    musical bows of, **9:**386
    myths of, **9:**479
    secret instruments of, **9:**477
    Sepik Hills region, **9:**557–58
  Eastern Highlands Province, **9:**511, 526–33
    melodic structures of, **9:**302–3
    performances of, **9:**513
    Usarufa composition, **9:**357–58
  Enga Province, **9:**511, 533–36
  ethnographic films on, **9:**42
  Europeans in, **9:**146–48, 153, 506, 516
  festivals in, **9:**62–63
  films on, **9:**48, 979, 1007, 1008, 1012–14
  garamut signals, **9:**376–77, 475, 478, 651
  gender and music, **9:**241, 245–46
  geography of, **9:**472, 475, 488, 494, 499, 505–6, 511, 514, 522, 545, 552–53, 560, 561, 566, 600, 607
  guitar songs, **9:**150–55
  Gulf Province, **9:**494–98
    instruments of, **9:**490
  Highlands regions, **9:**511–43
    body decoration in, **9:**349
    dance of, **9:**484–85
    falsetto singing in, **9:**297
    festivals in, **9:**55, 56
    secret instruments of, **9:**477, 511
  history of, **9:**488, 499, 506–7, 566, 568, 614, 620
  Hohodai Koita *maginogo* dance, **9:**316
  immigrants to Australia, **9:**85–87
  initiation schools, **9:**251–52
  instruments, **9:**372, 475–76
    garamuts, **9:**374, 375–77
    kundus, **9:**383–84
    panpipes, **9:**398
    swung slat, **9:**392

Island region, **9:**600–29
  flutes, **9:**392
  garamuts in, **9:**475
  Japanese in, **9:**25, 28, 475, 499
  kava use in, **9:**172–73
  Madang Province, **9:**545, 561–66
    dance, **9:**484
    Yupno *konggap*, **9:**303–4
  Mamose region, **9:**545–77
    garamuts in, **9:**475
    Iatmul children's songs, **9:**257–58
    instruments of, **9:**476, 546–48
  Manus Province, **9:**600, 602–7
    garamut ensembles, **9:**601
  Milne Bay Province, **9:**498–99
    epigrammatic song texts, **9:**331
    kundu ensembles, **9:**489
    Sudest *gia eledi* genre, **9:**177
    Trobriand festivals, **9:**498–99
  Morobe Province, **9:**545, 566–76
    Jabêm sung poetry, **9:**326–27
    song transcriptions, **9:**290–91
  mun genre, **9:**22
  national anthem of, **9:**129–30
  New Ireland Province, **9:**600, 625–29
  North Solomons Province, **9:**498, 600, 630–54, 833
    garamuts of, **9:**601
  numeral notations in, **9:**287
  Oro Province, **9:**499–505
    Binandere composition, **9:**358–60
    epigrammatic songs, **9:**332
    Hunjara *kasama*, **9:**332
    instruments of, **9:**490
    kundu ensembles, **9:**489
  Papuan region, **9:**488–509
    dance of, **9:**483
    instruments of, **9:**476
  Parama Island, dances of, **9:**507
  peroveta genre, **9:**88, 153, 187, 194–95, 494
  pipe-and-drum ensembles in, **9:**135–36
  political formation of, **9:**475
  population of, **9:**492, 505, 511, 514, 548, 560
  prehistoric, **9:**514, 566
  Rai Coast, **9:**561–66
    falsetto singing, **9:**297
    kundus, **9:**476
  religion in, **9:**188–97
  research on, **9:**23, 153, 296, 479–80, 511–12, 650, 976, 977, 983
  Russian expeditions to, **9:**22–23
  sound recordings from, **9:**980, 981, 985, 986, 989–93
  Southern Highlands Province, **9:**511, 536–43
    Foi memorial songs, **9:**246–47, 339–40
    Kaluli dance genres, **9:**485
    Kaluli people, **9:**284–85, 320
    Kaluli sung poetry, **9:**326
    yodeling in, **9:**297, 298–99
  string bands in, **9:**27, 137–39
  theater in, **9:**225, 233, 234–35
  tourism in, **9:**49
  Trans-Fly region, **9:**428, 506–9
  West New Britain Province, **9:**600
    music and dance of, **9:**607–20

West Sepik Province, **9:**545, 560–61
  dance, **9:**484
  epigrammatic song texts, **9:**331
  Umeda people, **9:**314
  Waina-Sowanda fertility rituals, **9:**350
  yaubug genre, **9:**331
Western Highlands Province, **9:**511, 514–22
  Maring dance, **9:**314, 484
Western Province, **9:**505–9
  instruments of, **9:**490
  Kiwai dance, **9:**376, 507
  Kiwai sung poetry, **9:**326
World War II in, **9:**149–50
Papua New Guinea Collection of the National
    Library, **9:**962, 989
Papua New Guinea Constabulary Band, **9:**89
Papua New Guinea Music Collection, **9:**480, 990
Papua New Guinea National Archives, **9:**962
Papua New Guinea Police Band, **9:**129
Papua New Guinea Service of the Australian
    Broadcasting Commission, **9:**962
Paquette, Robert, **3:**1194
Par un dimanche au soir (Arsenault), **3:**1136
Para Sa Intermisyon (Santos), **4:**878
"Para Vigo me Voy" (Palmieri), **3:**795
Paracas culture, **2:**11
Parachute Club (musical group), **3:**1081
parades. *See* processions and parades
Paradis, Mark, **3:***1280*
Paradise Garage (New York), **3:**689, 690
Paradise Lost and Regained (Jessye), **3:**608
Paraguay, **2:**452–64. *See also specific peoples*
  Afro-Brazilian cults in, **2:**260
  Asunción, **2:**452
  Chaco region, **2:**452
  children's wakes in, **2:**422
  dances of, **2:**461
  geography of, **2:**452
  German people in, **2:**55, 89
  Guaraní culture, **2:**199–204
  history of, **2:**245, 453
  instruments of, **2:**454–57
  Japanese people in, **2:**86–87; **10:**99, 101, 102
  Jesuits in, **2:**23
  music and dance of, **2:**460–62
  performers, **2:**462–63
  popular music of, **2:**463
  population of, **2:**452
  religious contexts in, **2:**457–60
  research on, **2:**463–64
  secular contexts in, **2:**460–62
  Yapeyú, **2:**453
Paraguayan-Americans/Canadians, **3:**730
Paraiyar caste, **5:**910, 911, 915
Paraja people, **5:**720
Paramaka culture, **2:**438
Paramananda Das, **5:**251
Paramana Strangers, **9:**90
Paramana Strangers (musical group), **9:**138
Paramida, Cici, **10:**48
Paramount Records, **3:**707
Param ŭi sori (Kim), **7:**959
paran
  Hindustani, **5:**117–19, *120*, 121, 130–31, 132
  Karnatak, **5:**158, 159
Paranoid (Black Sabbath), **3:**357

Paras, Parvez, **5:**767
Parasol Records, **3:**169–70, 171
Parast, Osman Moḥammad, **6:**836
Parasurama (deity), **5:**500
Parava caste, **5:**882–83
Parawoto, Pak, **10:**18
Parayan caste, **5:**931, 932
Pardesi (musical group), **5:***574*
Pardhi people, **5:**727
Pardo Tovar, Andrés, **2:**398
Pardon, Walter, **8:**334
Paredes, Americo, **3:**719
Parent, Kevin, **3:**1162
Parents' Music Resource Center, **3:**358
Paret-Limardo de Vela, Lise, **2:**736
Parhae kingdom, **7:**30, 31
Paridāna mīcitē (Subramania Ayyar), **5:***146*
Parikh, Arvind, **5:**205, 460
Parios, Yannis, **8:**1018
Paripāṭal, **5:**259–60
Paris (musical group), **3:**699
París, Juan, **2:**827
Paris Conservatory of Music, **3:**606, 1149
Paris, Treaty of (1763), **3:**1115, 1136
Parisot, Jean, **6:**209
Parizeau, Jacques, **3:**1162
Park Bum Hoon, **7:**957–58, 967, 972, 990
Park Byung Chon, **7:**972
Park Chung Hee, **7:**945, 953, 991, 996
Park Theatre (New York), **3:**615
Parker, Charlie, **3:**658–59, 793; **8:**445
Parker, Horatio, **3:**173, 538
Parker, James A., **3:**312
Parker, John Rowe, **3:**27, 29
Parker, Junior, **3:**583
Parker, Michael, **3:**1072
Parker, Wiremu, **9:**932, 985
"Parker's Mood," **3:**659
Parkinson, James, **9:**8–10
Parlak, Erol, **6:**791
Parlets (musical group), **3:**684
Parliament (musical group), **3:**684, 686
Parlier, Jim, **9:**502
Parlier, Judy, **9:**502
parlor and salon music (North America), **3:**93,
    179, 182–83, 186–88, 189–91, 197,
    241, 258, 617
  in Canada, **3:**1148
Parlow, Kathleen, **3:**1079, 1184
Paroliers Musique, **2:**880
Parra, Ángel, **2:**90, 373
Parra, Isabel, **2:**90, 373
Parra, Violeta, **2:**89, 103, 370–71
Párraga, Manuel María, **2:**387, 397
Parreiras Neves, Ignacio, **2:**303
Parrinder, E. G., **1:**410
Parry, Blind John, **8:**352
Parry, Hubert, **8:**186
Parry, Milman, **2:**431; **6:**340, 342, 343; **8:**94, 95,
    130, 1003, 1024
Parsi community
  in Sri Lanka, **5:**954
  theater of, **5:**423–24, 487, 491
Parsley, Sage, Rosemary, and Thyme (Simon and
    Garfunkel), **3:**317
Parsons, David, **3:**222

Parsons, Elsie Clews, **2:**423, 812
Parsons, Jack, **3:**767
Parsons, Scott, **3:**1072
Parsvadeva, **5:**24, 44, 45
Pärt, Arvo, **8:**498
Partbooks (Wood), **8:**367
Partch, Harry, **1:**31; **3:**335, 954
Parthia, **6:**936, 965
Parthian people, **7:**22
Parti Fronheulog, **8:***351*
Parti Québécois, **3:**1073, 1159, 1161–62
Parton, Dolly, **3:**77, 81
Partos, Oedoen, **6:**1027, 1031, 1066
"Party Song" (Slave), **3:**684
Parvati (deity), **5:**230, 277, 314, 875, 898
  visual depictions of, **5:**301
  worship of, **5:**702
Parveen, Abida, **5:**750, 753
Parvez, Anwar, **5:**859
Parvez, Shahid, **5:**205
Parvin, Shahida, **5:**767
Parvin, Zahida, **5:**767
Parwin, **5:**815–16
Pasai (kingdom), **4:**600
Pasaribu, Ben M., **3:**1020
Pascoal, Hermeto, **2:**108
Pascua Indian nation, **3:**437
Pashai people, **5:**805
Pashkevich, Vasily, **8:**780
Pashtun (also Pathan) people, **5:**5, 193. *See also*
    Pakhtun people
  in Afghanistan, **5:**804, 805–11, 815, 817, 824,
    825, 829, 833–41
  dance traditions of, **5:**506
pasillo, **2:**101
  in Colombia, **2:**382, 383, 384, 387, 391–96,
    397, 398, 697
  in Ecuador, **2:**417, 427, 431
  in Guatemala, **2:**735
  in Netherlands Antilles, **2:**930
pasodoble, **2:**735, 773
  in Argentina, **2:**273
  in Philippines, **4:**846, 847, 856, 869
  Teribe culture, **2:**685
Paspati, A. G., **8:**284
Pasquet, Alix "Dadou," **2:***892*
Passamaquoddy Indian nation, **3:**243, 291, 462,
    509
Passamonte, Frank, **3:**865
Passamonte, Gus, **3:**865
Passamonte, Nick, **3:**864
Passion (album), **8:**225
Passow, Arnold, **8:**1024
Pastorcita Huaracina, **2:**484
pastorelas, **2:**572; **3:**735–36, 759, 848, 850
Pastori, Niña, **8:**599
Pastori, Niña, **8:**599
Paswan, Mahavir, **5:**678, *679*
Patagone (Tehuelche) culture, **2:**357
Patakim (musical group), **3:**786
Patamona culture, **2:**131, 442
Pata Negra (flamenco duo), **8:**599
Patanella, Santo, **3:**865
Patani (kingdom), **4:**407
Patar caste, **5:**476
Pātea Māori Club, **9:**938
Pātē, Kiko, **9:**952

Patek, Joseph, **3:**897
Paterno, Dolores, **4:**866, 869
Paterno, Juan, **4:**866
Paterno, Pedro A., **4:**857, 864
Pathan, Dr. A. M., **5:**562, 563
Pathan people. *See* Pashtun people
"Patha Patha" (Makeba), **1:**772
Pathé-Marconi, **1:**417; **4:**483, 493; **6:**548, 785;
    8:239, 241, 777
Pathet Lao, **3:**1003
Patrice, Ilunga, **1:**360
Patrie, La (newspaper), **3:**1149
patriotic music, American, **3:**521, 531, 538, 939.
    See also campaign music, American
Patrocinio Carvajal, Candelaria Punzalán, **4:**856
patronage, **8:**145–46. *See also* politics; power and
    status
  'Abassid era, **6:**356
  Afghanistan, **5:**805–7
  Albania, government, **8:**999
  Andhra Pradesh, **5:**889
    of Jangam singers, **5:**900
    of mendicants, **5:**900
    of Piccukaguntlu singers, **5:**901
    of Telugu narrative song, **5:**893
  Aotearoa, government funding, **9:**169, 931
  Arabian peninsula, by women, **6:**701
  Australia
    of Aboriginal rock, **9:**144–45
    of Anglo-Irish folk music, **9:**141
    of dance, **9:**415
    of folk, **9:**141
    of immigrants' groups, **9:**87
    of jazz, **9:**143
    of popular music, **9:**414
    of Warlpiri dance, **9:**467
    of Yanyuwa dance, **9:**462
  Azerbaijan, **6:**922
  Bali, **4:**732, 747
  Balkan region, government support of village
    music, **8:**13
  Belarus, rock bands, **8:**802
  Bengal, **5:**432, 844–45
  Bhutan, of Tibetan monasteries, **5:**713
  British, of painting, **5:**300
  Bulgaria, government, **8:**901–2, 905–6
  Cambodia
    of *mohori,* **4:**183
    of *yike* theater, **4:**200–201
  Canada, **3:**52, 247–48, 250–51, 252, 1120,
    1151, 1184, 1185, 1216, 1227, 1231
  Canadian Pacific Railway, **3:**146, 1058
  China
    government, **7:**59, 294–95, 301, 386–88,
      391–93, 413–14, 513–14
    imperial, **7:**89
    by industrial complexes, **7:**399
    of *kunqu,* **7:**293–94
    in late twentieth century, **7:**389
    of narrative singing, **7:**253
    of opera, **7:**278, 286–87, 392–93
    of theater, **7:**394
  Chinese-Canadians, **3:**1264–65
  Cirebon, **4:**690
  Czech Republic, **8:**727
  Dalai Lama, of *gar-pa* troupes, **5:**713

East Asia, of theater, **7:**73, 75–76
Egypt
  of Arab art music, **6:**322, 547
  of popular performers, **6:**597, 600
  of Western art music, **6:**610
Europe
  of art music, **8:**68–69, 199
  in immigrant communities, **8:**232
  influence on musical style, **8:**186–87
  nineteenth-century decline of, **8:**51
  by women, **8:**200
France
  government, **8:**549
  support for African musicians, **8:**238
Fulani people, **1:**451
Guam, government, **9:**745–46
Gujarat, **5:**443
  of bards, **5:**635–37
Guyana, **5:**602
Hausa people, **1:**450
Hawai'i
  government, **9:**109–10, 921, 930
  royal, **9:**919, 925
Hungary, of Rom people, **8:**273, 274
Iceland, court, **8:**146, 405
India, **10:**12
Iran, **6:**834
  of Persian art music, **6:**139–40, 142,
    861–62, 865
Ireland, court, **8:**146
Irian Jaya, of Asmat music, **9:**591
Japan
  of chamber music, **7:**687–89
  of *gagaku,* **7:**626–27, 687
  government, **7:**59, 627, 761
  of *katô busi,* **7:**681
  of *kyôgen,* **7:**536, 687
  of *nagauta,* **7:**672
  of *nô,* **7:**536, 630, 639–41, 687
  of *satuma biwa,* **7:**647–48
  of *tomimoto busi,* **7:**681
Java, **4:**633, 653, 676, 682
Jewish patrons, **8:**260
Karnataka, **5:**881–82
  of *yakṣagāna,* **5:**885
Kashmir, **5:**689
Kerala, **5:**944
  Trivandrum court, **5:**508
  Vedic chant, **5:**243
Korea
  aristocracy, **7:**807, 813, 984–85
  Chinese imperial, **7:**81
  of *chŏngak,* **7:**813, 866, 913–14
  chungin, **7:**985
  government, **7:**59, 822, 945, 972, 981–83,
    988–90, 993–94, 996–97
  of *kagok,* **7:**919–20
  of *p'ansori,* **7:**898, 899, 900
  of *sanjo,* **7:**914
Kurdistan, of heroic narratives, **6:**747
Ladakh, of Mkhar-mon, **5:**712
Laos, royal, **4:**350
Lithuania, government, **8:**513
Louisiana, of New Orleans theaters, **3:**615
Madhya Pradesh, **5:**720, 721
Malaysia, royal, **4:**404, 427–30

Mashriq, royal, **6:**538–40
Middle Ages, **8:**71
Middle Eastern music, **3:**1036–37
Morocco, of *malhun,* **6:**496
Mughal empire, **5:**14–15, 76–77, 375, 402,
    493, 792; **10:**12
Nāyakkar dynasty, **5:**966
Nepal, **5:**703
  of North Indian classical music, **5:**697
North Africa, Ottoman rulers, **6:**433
Norway
  court, **8:**146, 423
  government, **8:**427, 431
Oceania, of popular theater, **9:**233
Oman, **6:**683
Ottoman empire, of Rom musicians, **8:**284
Pakistan, **5:**745, 748–49
  of Hindustani classical music, **5:**745–46
  of religious recitation, **5:**748
  of theater, **5:**487
Pakistan, northern, **5:**794, 795, 799
Poland, Rom people, **8:**276
Punjab (Pakistan), **5:**747
  of *Mīrāsī,* **5:**764
Rajasthan, **5:**7, 640–42
Rajputs, **5:**402, 639, 641
Renaissance, **8:**73, 75, 77, 160
Romania, government, **8:**882
Russia, **8:**755
  of Rom music, **8:**286–87
Sardinia, government, **8:**626
Scotland, of bards, **8:**362
Singhbum princely state, **5:**497
Slovakia, **8:**727
Solomon Islands, international, **9:**964
South Asia
  caste and, **5:**8–9, 476
  of classical traditions, **5:**372
  court, **5:**401–3
  of courtesans, **5:**373
  decline of, **5:**15, 212, 230, 331, 377, 433,
    526, 560, 649
  of *dhrupad* genre, **5:**163, 250
  of *khyāl* genre, **5:**163, 170, 177
  of Kota people, **5:**283
  of light classical music, **5:**435
  modern contexts, **5:**403–6
  of *pakhāvaj* performance, **5:**121
  of *pallavi* singers, **5:**217
  partition and, **5:**403
  of *rāgmālā* visualizations, **5:**312–13,
    318
  of regional caste artists, **5:**397–406
  sacred contexts of, **5:**400–401
  of scholarly work, **5:**45, 50–51, 387–88
  secular music and, **5:**33, 246
  of Sufi music, **5:**687
  of *tabla* performance, **5:**121, 133
  of theater, **5:**486
  of *thumrī* genre, **5:**179–80
  of Tibetan culture, **5:**715–16
  of Tyagaraja festival, **5:**390–91
  of women performers, **5:**408
Southeast Asia, **4:**9
  changes in, **4:**117–18
Spain, **8:**600

Sri Lanka
  of Buddhist chant, **5:**969
  of theater, **5:**490
Sumbawa, **4:**779
Sunda, **4:**700, 720, 722
Sweden, court, **8:**440, 444
Taiwan, government, **7:**429
Tamil Nadu
  of Cankam literature, **5:**260
  Nilgiri peoples, **5:**910–11
  Tanjavur court, **5:**220, 387–88, 390, 508, 518, 907–8
  by Toda people, **5:**909
  Travancore court, **5:**229
Thailand, **4:**225–26, 248
Tonga, of brass bands, **9:**130
Tunisia, of art music, **6:**503, 505–13
Turkey
  of art music, **6:**113, 116, 757, 770, 779
  janissaries, **6:**114–15
  Mevlevî Sufis, **6:**108, 110
Uighur *muqam*, **6:**995–1008
Umayyad dynasty, **6:**294
United States, **3:**43, 44, 70
  of Arab music, **6:**281
  of Cajun and Creole music, **3:**859
  of Chinese opera, **3:**961
  of dance, **3:**208, 221, 222, 226
  of ethnomusicological research, **3:**294; **10:**98
  government, **3:**30–31, 298–99; **5:**376, 404, 649; **10:**81–85
  of Hawai'ian dance, **3:**207
  of Indonesian music, **3:**1021
  of Iranian music, **3:**1034
  of music education, **3:**278
  of *pastorelas*, **3:**736
  of radio broadcasts, **3:**559
  of twentieth-century composers, **3:**174
Uttar Pradesh, of *rām līlā*, **5:**495–96
Uzbekistan, of *maqām* performers, **6:**916
Vanuatu, international, **9:**965
Victoria, queen of England, of Scottish customs, **8:**368
Vijayanagar kingdom, **5:**508
Wales, **8:**349, 352
West Africa, **1:**448
  of musicians, **1:**444–45
  of praise singers, **1:**492, 519–20
Yugoslavia (former), Kosovo region, **8:**1001
Pattamal, D. K., **5:**414
Patten, Christopher, **7:**431
Patten, Herbert, **9:**135
Patterson, H. O., **2:**897
Patti, Adelina, **3:**556, 1180
Pattini (deity), **5:**491, 963
Patton, Charley, **3:**524, 645, 707
Patwardhan, Vinayak Narayan, **5:***207*
Patwardhan, Vinayakrao, **5:***177*, 466
Patwin Indian nation, **3:**415
Paucke, Florian, **2:**463
Paudwal, Anuradha, **5:**421
Pauern-Kirchfahrt (Biber), **8:**654
Paul, Fred, **2:**891
Paul, Lawrence, **3:**1093
Paul, Margaret, **3:**1069
Paul, Norman, **2:**865

Paula Aguirre, Francisco de, **2:**540
Paunetto, Bobby, **3:**336
Paupers (musical group), **3:**1081
Pau'u, Tupou Hopoate, **9:**972
Pavarotti in Beijing (film), **7:**398
Pavarotti, Luciano, **3:**271, 528; **7:**398; **8:**618
Pavlova, Anna, **2:**619; **5:**564; **8:**161
Pavlović-Carevac, Vlastimir, **8:**949
Pavuvu (Solomon Islands), **9:**664
Pawnee Indian nation, **3:**440, 444, 446
  hand game, **3:**449
Paxton, Tom, **3:**316
"Pay Dirt" (lang), **3:**109–10
Paya culture, **2:**659, 739
Payawal, Serafín, **4:**883
Payne, Daniel Alexander, **3:**628
Payne, Jim, **3:**1121
Payne, Trevor W., **3:**1077, 1169
Pazisi (musical group), **8:**845
p'Bitek, Okot, **1:**603
Peabody Conservatory of Music (Baltimore), **3:**15
Peabody Museum of American Archaeology and Ethnology, **3:**29
Peabody Museums (Harvard University, Yale University, and Salem), **9:**974–75
Peacock, James, **10:**43
Peacock, Judith, **8:**366
Peacock, Kenneth, **3:**14–15, 292–93, 1096, 1125, 1212, 1250, 1270
Peacock Records, **3:**350, 708
"Peanut Vendor" (Simon), **1:**385; **3:**732, 787
Pearl Jam (musical group), **2:**267; **3:**358; **4:**887
"Pearly Shells" (Edwards and Pober), **3:**1050
Pearse, Andrew, **2:**958
Peart, Donald, **9:**976
Peblee Poo, **3:**696
Peck, James, **3:**1079
Peculiar Sam: or Underground Railroad (musical), **3:**617
Peda people, **1:**37
pedagogy. *See also gharānā*; oral tradition and transmission; *specific institutions*
  Africa
    dance, **1:**290
    institutional, **1:**38, 216, 230
    Western correspondence schools, **1:**19, 215–16, 234, 239
  Albania, **8:**999
  American Sāmoa, **9:**265–67
  Andalusia, **6:**442, 445–46
  Aotearoa, **9:**277–78
    Māori, **9:**933, 950–51
    mission schools, **9:**935
    of *mōteatea*, **9:**943–44
    Pacific Islander music and dance, **9:**114
  Arabian peninsula, Western music lessons, **6:**715–16
  Argentina, **2:**268–69
    for *cuarteto* performers, **2:**278
    enculturation, **2:**268–69
  Armenia, institutional, **6:**726–27
  Australia, **9:**253–57, 414–15, 443
    Central, **9:**437
    dance, **9:**228–29
    jazz, **9:**143
    popular music, **9:**144

Tiwi people, **9:**456
  Warlpiri dance, **9:**467
  Yolngu people, **9:**457
Azerbaijan, **6:**18, 845–46, 924
Aztec culture, *cuicalli* schools, **2:**603
Bali, **4:**730, 733, 758–60
Basque region
  bertsulari schools, **8:**311–12
  instrument instruction, **8:**314
Belarus, **8:**801
Bellona, **9:**851–52
Bolivia, **2:**284, 296
Bosnia-Hercegovina, **8:**970
Brazil, **2:**305
  of African slaves, **2:**333–34
  capoeira, **2:**346
Bribri and Cabécar cultures, **2:**631
Bulgaria, **8:**902, 905
  of folk music, **8:**155
Burkina Faso, **1:**38
Burma, **4:**122, 396–98
Cambodia, **4:**119–20
  Buddhist schools, **4:**206
  dance, **4:**188–89
Canada, **3:**275–79, 1180
  art music, **3:**173–74
  Asian performance studies, **3:**1258, 1264, 1265–66
  of Canadian music, **3:**1060
  Cantonese opera singing, **3:**1263
  Chinese music, **3:**1083
  early schools, **3:**275, 1116
  examining boards, **3:**1230
  gamelan programs, **3:**342, 1013–14
  jazz, **3:**1072
  music schools and conservatories, **3:**1119–20, 1182, 1185
  private instruction, **3:**1118, 1148, 1229
  private schools, **3:**1073, 1088, 1239
  public schools, **3:**275–77, 1117, 1119, 1150, 1228–29
  singing schools, **3:**7, 1069–70, 1070, 1115–16, 1179, 1180, 1189–90
  solmization and solfège, **3:**1180
  South Asian music, **3:**1216, 1246
  summer music camps, **3:**1119–20
  traditional music, **3:**1120, 1129–30
Central African Republic, **1:**40
Central America, **2:**68–69
  art music, **2:**112–13, 114
Central Asia, **6:**904
Chile, tango, **2:**371
China
  of actors, **7:**294, 393–95
  Cantonese opera, **7:**306
  conservatories and institutions, **7:**90, 339, 375–76, 381–82, 386, 397–99, 416, 420, 514, 756–57
  dizi, **7:**185
  erhu, **7:**177
  foreign-trained musicians, **7:**137, 346–49, 375–77, 382, 384, 386, 388, 416
  minority musics, **7:**445
  narrative singing, **7:**250, 252–53, 254–55, 397
  Naxi *dongjing* music, **7:**445

pedagogy, China (*continued*)
    northwestern minorities, 7:463
    pipa, 7:169–70
    private teachers, 7:399, 420
    qin, 7:164
    tanhuang, 7:299
    wind and percussion ensemble music, 7:204
    Yunnan province, 7:509
    zheng, 7:171–72
Cirebon, 4:688, 698–99
Colombia, 2:396
    art music, 2:397–98
    bambuco, 2:387
    currulao, 2:405, 406
Comprehensive Musicianship method, 3:280, 281
Cook Islands, 9:271–72
Costa Rica, 2:689, 694, 702–3
Côte d'Ivoire, institutional, 1:40
Cuba, 2:828–29, 836–37, 838
Cyprus, 8:1031
Czech Republic, 8:724–25, 727, 731, 733
Dai people, temple schools, 7:497, 507
Dalcroze method, 3:280
Denmark, 8:460
Dominica, 2:844
Dominican Republic, 2:857–58
East Asia, schools and institutions, 7:55–57
Egypt
    dance schools, 6:625
    of European music, 6:610, 611
    institutional, 6:36, 43, 321–24, 547, 610–12
    'ūd music, 6:45–46
El Salvador, 2:717–18
England, 8:337
    of South Asian music, 5:575–76
Estonia, Moravian Brethren, 8:495
Ethiopia, institutional, 1:40
Europe
    folk music instruction, 8:154–55
    of Indian music, 5:561
    Jewish educational settings, 8:252, 257
    music history, 8:85–86
    national conservatories, 8:82
    role of museums, 8:179–81
    singing schools for psalmody, 8:97
    solmization and solfège, 8:106
Faroe Islands, 8:472
Fiji, courses on Indian culture, 9:782–83
Finland, 8:480, 482, 484, 486
France, 8:549
Garífuna culture, 2:734
Georgia, 8:841
Germany, 8:649, 653–54
    folk music, 8:659
    Liederschulen, 8:653
Ghana, institutional, 1:27, 30–31, 33, 39–40, 216
Goa, 5:736–37, 740–41
Gordon method, 3:280, 281
Greece, 8:1016
Guadeloupe, 2:879
Guyana, 2:450
    British traditions of, 2:446–47
Haiti, 2:894

Hawai'i, 9:272–77
    dance, 9:106, 108–9
    hula schools, 9:923, 925
    by missionaries, 9:918–19
Hmong music, 3:1005
Hungary, of Rom people, 8:273–74
India
    nonclassical traditions, 5:468–77
    North, institutional, 5:442–48, 466
    South, institutional, 5:449–56
Indonesia, 4:122–23
    pesantren Islamic schools, 4:76
Iran, 6:130, 858
    of *radif*, 6:138–39, 142
Iraq, *maqām*, 6:315–16
Ireland, 8:385–86, 389, 394
Irian Jaya, 9:580
    Asmat people, 9:591
Israel
    cantorial schools, 6:200, 205
    musicology departments, 6:1060–61, 1063–67
    rabbinical academies, 6:200
Jamaica, 2:909–10
Jammu and Kashmir, 5:688
Japan, 7:538–39
    conservatories and institutions, 7:535, 536–37, 731–32, 755–61, 774, 778
    contemporary music, 7:736
    continuity and authenticity in traditional music, 7:767–72
    foreign-trained musicians, 7:731–32
    iemoto system, 7:719–20, 755–56, 760–61, 769–70
    imitative and rote methods, 7:767, 770–71, 775
    Korean music, 7:798
    min'yô, 7:601
    nagauta performance schools, 7:674
    Protestant hymns in, 7:49–50
    syakuhati, 7:709, 759
    traditional music, 7:540–41
    Western-style, 7:50–51, 728–29, 808
    women students, 7:687, 764
Java, 4:676–79, 682–83
Karnataka, 5:881
Karnatak music, 5:96, 100–101, 138
Kazakhstan, 6:959, 960
Kenya, institutional, 1:216, 628, 629–30
Kerala
    of drumming, 5:940–41, 942–43
    Vedic schools, 5:243
Kindermusik method, 3:284
Kiribati
    composition, 9:364
    mission schools, 9:763
Kodály method, 3:279, 280–81, 1119; 8:100–101
Kogi culture, 2:185–86
Korea
    institutional, 7:804, 808, 910, 988–92
    kwŏnbŏn system, 7:894, 909
    sanjo, 7:808
    Western-style, 7:952
Kuna culture, 2:647
Laos, 4:120, 358

Lombok, 4:766, 777
Macedonia, 8:981
Madagascar, 1:792
    institutional, 1:792
Malaysia, 4:122
    apprenticeship, 4:403
    of Orang Asli people, 4:586
Maleku culture, 2:683
Martenot method, 3:1119
master-disciple relationship, 5:66
    in Afghanistan, 5:832
    in Africa, 1:291
    in Andhra Pradesh, 5:889
    in Azerbaijani Iran, 6:845
    in Central Asia, 6:904, 917, 950, 968, 974
    in China, 7:252–53, 262, 299, 393–95; 10:22
    in Egypt, 6:341–43
    institutional adaptation of, 5:446–47
    in Iran, 6:59, 61, 71–72
    in Iraq, 6:314–15
    in Japan, 7:759–60, 769–71, 773
    in Java, 10:44–45, 49–50
    in Kerala, 5:940–43
    in Korea, 7:985–86
    in Malaysia, 4:403
    in Maya culture, 2:668
    in Muslim culture, 5:459–61
    in Nepal, 5:697
    in North America, 5:582–83
    in northern Pakistan, 5:794, 795
    in Sardinia, 8:630
    in Saudi Arabia, 6:665
    in South Asia, 5:65, 86–87, 100–101, 150–51, 213, 220, 231, 259, 376–80, 442, 457–67, 470–71; 10:10
    in Southeast Asia, 4:118, 120–21, 123, 160, 161, 174, 227, 258, 299, 395–96
    in Sri Lanka, 5:957, 959
    in Turkey, 6:801
    in Uzbekistan, 6:345
    for women, 5:373, 378
Maya culture, apprenticeship, 2:668
medieval Arab music, 6:352–53
Mexico, 2:604–5, 619
    mission schools, 2:600, 603
Micronesia, 9:721
Middle East, institutional, 6:43
Middle Eastern music, 3:1036–38
mission schools, 2:46–47, 131–32, 188, 283, 325, 453, 600, 603, 748; 3:734–35, 755; 9:763, 935
Morocco, *malḥūn*, 6:497–98
Nauru, 9:261–62
    Christian school, 9:756
Nicaragua, 2:749, 766
    mission schools, 2:748
Nigeria
    of composers, 1:234–35
    institutional, 1:14–15, 39–40, 216, 241
North Africa, 6:432, 433, 435
North Korea, 7:991–92
North West Frontier Province, 5:791
Norway
    cathedral schools, 8:423
    institutional, 8:427

Oceania, **9:**127, 251–78
Orff method, **3:**279, 280, 281, 1119
Pakistan, northern, **5:**799
Palestine, institutional, **6:**1024, 1025
Papua New Guinea, **9:**480
    initiation schools, **9:**527
Paraguay, **2:**453, 462
Philippines, **4:**123, 853–54, 860–61, 868,
    869–71
    friars' schools, **4:**841–42
Puerto Rico, **2:**940–41
Rajasthan, **5:**649
Renaissance and Baroque, **8:**79
research trends, **3:**286–87
Romania, **8:**882, 883
Roti, **4:**798
Russia, **8:**780
    Rom people, **8:**287
Ryûkyû Islands, traditional music, **7:**796
St. Lucia, **2:**950
Sāmoa, **9:**808
Scotland, **8:**363–64
    bagpipe, **8:**368
Senegal, institutional, **1:**38, 40
Shan people, **4:**548
Singapore, **4:**524
    Indian music, **4:**521
Slovakia, **8:**724–25, 727, 731, 733
Solomon Islands, Blablanga people, **9:**657
South Africa, **5:**616
South America, **2:**68–69
    Andean regions, **2:**222–23
    art music, **2:**112–13, 114
    electronic preservation and, **2:**41
    enculturation, **2:**67–70
South Asia
    Hindustani music, **5:**65, 87, 372–73
    institutional, **5:**15, 376, 380–81, 432, 565
    Karnatak music, **5:**213
    regional music in, **5:**405
    role of recordings in, **5:**526–27
    sabhā schools, **5:**454–55
    Western models for, **5:**561–62, 563
    of Western music, **5:**449–50
    for women, **5:**380–81, 454
    women's musical education, **5:**409–10, 412
southern Africa, European, **1:**718, 719
Sudan, institutional, **1:**40, 571–72
Sumatra, **4:**602
    Islamic schools, **4:**625
Sumbawa, **4:**784
Sunda, **4:**721, 722–23
    penca silat schools, **4:**709
Suyá culture, **2:**149
Suzuki method, **3:**280, 281
Sweden, **8:**443
Switzerland, **8:**692, 696, 697–98
Tahiti, **9:**269–71
    Chinese schools, **9:**868
Tanzania, institutional, **1:**644
Thailand, **4:**120–22, 226–27, 249, 261, 287,
    299, 323
    westernized, **4:**82
Trobriand Islands, *kundu* rhythms, **9:**489
Tunisia
    Djerban Jewish communities, **6:**526–27

of national art music, **6:**325, 326, 328–29,
    330, 501–2, 508–9, 511–12, 521
Turkey, **6:**784–85
    art music, **6:**775
    bağlama, **6:**789–92
    folk music, **6:**77, 79, 783
    Halk Eğitim Merkezleri, **6:**77, 79
    Halk Evleri, **6:**77, 797, 813–14, 817
    institutional, **6:**117
    Mevlevî Sufis, **6:**108, 109, 119
    Western music and dance, **6:**817
Turkmenistan, **6:**975–76
Uganda, institutional, **1:**18, 39, 216
Ukraine, **8:**817, 818
United States, **3:**274–87
    academic institutions, development of, **3:**11,
    14, 27, 173–74, 532
    African-American composers, **3:**603, 604–5,
    606–7, 610
    art music, **3:**173–74
    Asian performance studies, **3:**952–53
    bluegrass music, **3:**167
    cantorial training programs, **3:**940
    children's songs, **3:**89
    community-based, **3:**283–85
    dance, **3:**220, 222, 225
    dance notation, **3:**221
    elementary school practices, **3:**279–81
    ethnomusicology, **10:**3–5, 18–21, 27–29,
    41–44, 55–57, 62–64, 73–74, 78–79,
    81, 87–88, 128–30
    European bias in, **3:**15
    European ideology and, **3:**70, 173–74
    gamelan programs, **3:**342, 1013–14
    German-American schools, **3:**885
    history of, **3:**275–79
    hula schools, **9:**117
    of Indian music, **5:**561
    instrumental music, **3:**277
    Italian teachers, **3:**862
    jazz, **3:**278–79, 282–83
    Korean-Americans, **3:**977–78
    mariachi, **3:**724–25, 751
    mass education, **3:**44
    multicultural trends in, **3:**279
    physical education, **3:**233
    private instruction, **3:**190, 239, 258, 277,
    284
    public schools, **3:**275–77
    secondary school practices, **3:**281–83
    singing masters, **3:**67
    singing schools, **3:**7, 44, 77, 275, 531, 603
    of South Asian music, **3:**984–86; **5:**582–84
    summer camps, **3:**210
    tamburitza orchestras, **3:**923
    teacher training, **3:**277–78
    testing and assessment, **3:**278
    transmission and, **3:**241
    types of, **3:**274
    Vietnamese music, **3:**996
Uruguay, **2:**521–22
Uzbekistan, **6:**18
    apprenticeship system, **6:**345
    religious colleges, **6:**935, 940
Vanuatu, **9:**259–60
    church schools, **9:**198–99

Venezuela, **2:**542
Vietnam, **4:**119, 451, 509, 510–12
    Buddhist chant, **4:**504
    early, **4:**480
    Westernized, **4:**81
Virgin Islands, **2:**969
Wales, **8:**353
Yanomamö culture, enculturation, **2:**173–74
Yap, **9:**730
    dances, **9:**732
Zaïre, institutional, **1:**40
Zimbabwe, **1:**755, 757
    institutional, **1:**40
Pedero, Nonong, **4:**885
Pedi people, **1:**707, 767, 768
Pedrell, Felipe, **6:**449, 1042
Pedro I, emperor of Brazil, **2:**245, 305
Pedro II, emperor of Brazil, **2:**305
"Pedro Navaja" (Blades), **3:**799
Pedro Pablo Traversari Collection of Musical
    Instruments (Ecuador), **2:**414
Peebles, David, **8:**367
"Peek-A-Boo" (Cadillacs), **3:**672
Peekna, Andres, **3:**880
Peer, Ralph, **3:**78, *263*, 707
Peerce, Jan, **3:**530
Peeters, Theophiel, **8:**523, 528
Peets, Gottlieb, **3:**880
Pegu (kingdom), **4:**62
Peirce, Charles Sanders, **3:**517
Pekin Club (Chicago), **3:**652
Peking opera (*jingju*), **7:**5, 88, 275, 281–87,
    393; **10:**21
    aesthetics of, **7:**73, *73*
    avocational clubs, **7:**396
    categories of, **7:**279
    cross-dressing in, **7:**408
    development of, **7:**89
    ensembles for, **7:**77
    female performers of, **7:**76
    history of, **7:**76, 294
    in Hong Kong, **7:**432–33
    influences on, **7:**287
    interpolated melodies in, **7:**283
    librettos for, **7:**287
    modernization of, **7:**399
    movement in, **7:**59, 60
    notation in, **7:**55
    orchestra in, **7:**285–86
    origins of, **7:**278
    performance elements in, **7:**281–82
    politicization of, **7:**413
    research on, **7:**139
    rural performances of, **7:**417
    schools of, **7:**55
    stories for, **7:**287–88
    structure of, **7:**282–84
    in Taiwan, **7:**429
    text setting in, **7:**284–85
    in Yunnan, **7:**512
Peking University, **7:**228, 376, 381, 383,
    397
Peking Women's Normal College, **7:**397
Pekkan, Ajda, **6:**249–50, 251
Pekkilä, Erkki, **8:**25
Pelen, Jean-Noël, **8:**554

Pelinski, Ramon, **3:**381
Pelléas et Mélisande (Debussy), **8:**370
Pelletier, Frédéric, **3:**1150
Pelletier, Wilfrid, **3:**1076, 1150
Pelo (periodical), **2:**267
Pelón, El (*trovo*), **3:**758, 762
Peloponnesian Folklore Society, **8:**1018
Pemberton, John, **3:**1014; **10:**18
Peña, Angél, **4:**875, 884
Pena Branca and Xavantinho, **2:**319
Peña Hernández, Enrique, **2:**767
Peña, Jorge, **2:**90
Peña, Manuel, **3:**517, 736, 737, 738
Penan people, **4:**824
Pen Cayetano and the Turtles, **2:**677
Penderecki, Krzysztof, **4:**878
Penderecki String Quartet, **3:**1186
Peng Xiuwen, **7:**231
Peng Yongshan, **7:***512*
Penguins (musical group), **3:**671, 709
Penina o le Pasefika (Samoan cultural troupe),
    3:1052
Pennekamp, Peter, **3:**299
Penner, Fred, **3:**1081
Pennies from Heaven (film), **3:**609
Pennsylvania
    Amish in, **3:**887
    Armenian people in, **3:**1030
    Bedford County, Salemville congregation, **3:**907
    Chinese people in, **3:**957
    Ephrata Cloister, **3:**904–7
    Finnish people in, **3:**872–75
    Franklin County, Snow Hill congregation,
        3:907
    German people in, **3:**884, 887–88
    Johnstown, ethnic groups in, **3:**821–22, 824
    Lithuanian people in, **3:**875–77
    Mennonites in, **3:**1237
    Moravians in, **3:**528, 904–7
    Native American groups in, **3:**461
    Philadelphia
        African-American composers, **3:**564, 603–4
        attitude toward theater, **3:**615
        balalaika orchestra in, **3:**57
        British regimental bands in, **3:**563
        Cambodian people in, **3:**998
        gospel music in, **3:**630
        hip-hop in, **3:**701
        Irish people in, **3:**842
        Italian people in, **3:**860
        Jewish people in, **3:**935
        Lithuanian people in, **3:**876
        orchestras in, **3:**536
        Romanian people in, **3:**910
        singing societies, **3:**275
        soul in, **3:**689, 711
        theater in, **3:**180
        Turkish people in, **3:**1030
    Pittsburgh
        Hungarian people in, **3:**908
        Italian people in, **3:**860
        Lubavitcher community in, **10:**127–28
        public school music education, **3:**275
    Pocono Mountains, Irish-American resorts,
        3:845
    Slovak people in, **3:**899–900

Pennsylvania Gazette, **3:**180
pennywhistle. *See* flutes
Penobscot Indian nation, **3:**462
Penrhyn (Cook Islands), **9:**973
Pentecost (Vanuatu)
    ceremonies of, **9:**691
    instruments of, **9:**693
    music and dance of, **9:**695–97, 966
Pentecostals
    in Argentina, **2:**259
    in Barbados, **2:**817
    in Jamaica, **2:**901
    in Paraguay, **2:**457
    Rom people, **8:**274, 288
Pentikäinen, Juha, **8:**307
Pentland, Barbara, **3:**90, 1096, 1184
Peony Pavilion (*chuanqi* play), **7:**295–96
People (periodical), **3:**712
"People Everyday" (Arrested Development),
    3:715
"People Get Ready" (Mayfield), **3:**677
People's Republic of China. *See* China
"*pepa, La*" (Garcia), **3:**737
Pepera, Kwesi, **1:**356
Pépin, Clermont, **3:**1151
Pepper, Art, **3:**659
Pepper, Herbert, **1:**50, 59
Peppermint Lounge (New York), **3:**227
Peps (musical group), **8:**216
Pepusch, Johann Christoph, **3:**542
Pequenino (mouth bow player), **1:***306*
Perahia, Murray, **3:**1210
Peranakan people, **4:**522
Peraza, Armando, **3:**787
perception. *See also* acoustics
    ambiguity and, **1:**195–96
    Balochistan, of *qalandarī* music, **6:**887–88
    component harmonicity and, **1:**189
    cultural, **8:**58–65
    figure-ground phenomenon, **1:**180–82, 193,
        195–97, 201
    frequency proximity of partials, **1:**189–92
    illusory, **1:**185–86, 198–99, 201
    inherent rhythms in African music, **1:**155
    of Javanese modes, **4:**657–58
    listening as transmission process, **5:**470
    Luvale people, **1:**726–43
    of melody and tonality, **9:**292
    methodology of studies on, **1:**722–23,
        742–43
    of microtones, **5:**39
    musical, **9:**282
    offset synchronicity, **1:**188–89
    onset synchronicity, **1:**187–88
    of pitch, **1:**255–69, 604
    psychoacoustics, **5:**289
    research on, **8:**25
    schema-based sound analysis, **1:**194, 198–99
    selective process of, **1:**165, 166, 183, 187, 201
    of Southeast Asian music, **4:**14–16
    of tempo, **9:**290–91
    of timbre, **8:**91; **9:**296–97
    of tuning, **1:**734–37
    universal change, **8:**64–65
    veridical, **1:**183–85
    whispering *vs.* voiced speech, **1:**169–71

percussion instruments. *See* drums; idiophones
Percy, Thomas, **8:**17, 177
Perdomo Escobar, José Ignacio, **2:**380, 398
Perea, Lilia, **2:**776
Peregrinacão (Pinto), **4:**224, 284
Peretti, Burton, **3:**587
Pérez de Arce, José, **2:**374
Pérez Arregui, D. Ignacio, **8:***312*
Pérez, Diego C., **4:**866, 869
Pérez Estrada, Francisco, **2:**767
Pérez, Gilberto, **3:**776
Perez, Iohefo, **9:***825*
Pérez Jiménez, Marcos, **2:**540
Perez, Luciano, **9:***102*
Pérez Prado, Dámaso, **2:**371, 833
Pérez de Ribas, Andrés, **2:**588
Pérez de Zárate, Dora, **2:**783
Perfect (musical group), **8:**221
perfection des connaissances musicales, La (Shiloah),
    6:1066
"Perfidia" (García), **3:**739
performance contexts. *See also* ceremonies;
        festivals, celebrations, and holidays;
        performance places; weddings
    Abkhazian people, **8:**853
    adaptation and change in, **3:**92
    Adighian people, **8:**855–56
    Afghanistan
        dancing-boy parties, **5:**815
        northern region, **5:**826–28
        western region, **5:**818–19
    Africa, **1:**21–22
        concepts of, **1:**7, 8–11, 21
        events categorization, **1:**134–35
    Albania, **8:**987–88
        men's gatherings, **8:**118, 996–97
    Albanian music, **3:**927–29
    Amish music, **3:**887
    Aotearoa, concert parties, **9:**168, 936–37
    Arabian peninsula
        dance, **6:**703–4, 711
        gender-segregated, **6:**657
        women's music, **6:**697–98
    Arab music, **3:**1031–32, 1033, 1090
    Argentina, **2:**261–63
    Armenian music, **3:**1032, 1033
    Australia
        Aboriginal peoples, **9:**419–21, 424, 431
        Aboriginal theater, **9:**227
        Irish *céilí*, **9:**78
        Latin American people, **9:**83
    Aymara culture, **2:**217–21
    Azerbaijan, **6:**922–23
    Bali, **4:**738–39
    Balkarian people, **8:**857–58
    Barbados, tea meetings, **2:**817
    Basque region, **8:**314–15
    Belarus, instrumental music, **8:**798–99
    for *bhajan*, **5:**284
    for bluegrass, **3:**160, 161, 168
    for blues, **3:**103–5, 639–40, 643–44, 647
    Bolivia, **2:**289–92
    Brazil, **2:**313
    British Caribbean folk and traditional music,
        3:811
    Brittany, **8:**563–64

Bulgaria, **8:**891, 899–901
  sedyanka, **8:**141, 900
Bulgarian music, **3:**925
Burundi, *inanga chuchotée,* **1:**179–80
California, Native American groups, **3:**412–13
Cambodian music and dance, **3:**998–99
Canada, band concerts, **3:**1181
Caribbean, **2:**54–55
Celtic music, **8:**322
Central African Republic, **1:**685, 687
Central America, **2:**54–55
changes in, **5:**376
Chechen people, **8:**863–64
Chile, **2:**366–67
China
  Cantonese opera, **7:**304–8
  Dolan *mäsräp,* **6:**991–93
  entertainment music, **7:**411–13
  Jiangnan sizhu, **7:**223–24, 225
  nanguan music, **7:**209
  narratives, **7:**245–46
  northern narratives, **7:**251–52
  Peking opera, **7:**287
  present-day, **7:**411–17
  qin music, **7:**160
  shan'ge, **7:**151–52
  temple fairs, **7:**257–59
  women musicians, **7:**405–8
  xiaodiao, **7:**152
  yue'ou, **7:**269
Chinese music, **3:**960
Cirebon, **4:**688–89
concerts
  Asian music, **3:**1215–17
  band, **3:**536
  benefit, **3:**1175
  British Columbia, **3:**1096–97
  Central African Republic, **1:**685, 687
  chamber music, **3:**740
  charity rock, **3:**341, 713
  Egypt, **6:**319, 616, 621
  ethnographic, **8:**154, 166, 778
  Europe, **8:**61–63, 80
  historical, **3:**33–34, 146, 1154, 1166
  India, **5:**205, 351, 380
  Korea, **7:**994–95
  Lithuania, **8:**512–14
  Maritimes, **3:**1117, 1118
  mass, **3:**145
  multiethnic Canadian, **3:**343
  nineteenth century, **3:**183–84, 554–58
  North America, **3:**43
  Ontario, **3:**1079
  outdoor, **3:**1095, 1097; **6:**566
  popular music, **3:**1160
  popular performers, **3:**551
  Québec, **3:**1076, 1148, 1151
  rap, **3:**698
  in schools, **3:**283
  South Asia, **5:**212, 331
  subscription, **3:**180
  Syria, **6:**570
  touring groups, **3:**557
  Turkey, **6:**786–87
contra dance event, **3:**231
Corsica, **8:**573

Costa Rica, **2:**698–702
Croatia, **8:**925–26
Croatian *becar* events, **3:**923
Czech Republic, **8:**720
Dai people, Buddhist music, **7:**496–97, 501–4
Danish music, **3:**882–83
Denmark, **8:**457, 462
  twilighting, **8:**458
for disco, **3:**687–88
Ecuador, **2:**418–19
Egypt, **6:**616–18
  for epic songs, **6:**411
  inshād, **6:**167–75
  Nubian music, **6:**642–44
  for *qiṣaṣ,* **6:**170
  sahbra, **6:**551
England, **8:**331–32, 334
  folk clubs, **8:**153, 331
Estonian music, **3:**880
Europe
  1800s–1900s, **8:**146–47
  contemporary, **8:**149–58
  court life, **8:**199
  domestic, **8:**199–200
  folk music, **8:**648–50
  immigrant music, **8:**232–41
  Middle Ages, **8:**70–72, 168
  Renaissance, **8:**73–75
  rural music concerts and festivals, **8:**8
  sexually segregated, **8:**197, 198, 854
  traditional, **8:**139–47, 194
European-American music, **3:**826–27
Faroe Islands, **8:**469–70
  domestic devotionals, **8:**471
Fiji, **5:**612–14
  Indian people, **9:**93–94
Finland, **8:**480–81, 485–86
  iltamat, **8:**483
  public concerts, **8:**482
Finnish music, **3:**873
France, **8:**545–47
  after-dinner singing, **8:**546
  viellée, **8:**141
French-Americans, evening parties, **3:**854–55, 857
Georgia, **8:**832–33, 834–37, 837
German choral groups, **3:**885
Germany, hootenannies, **8:**662
Ghana, Anlo-Ewe, **1:**393–95
Goa, **5:**736–37
Great Basin Indian groups, **3:**422–25
Great Britain, **8:**325
Greece, folk music, **8:**1015–18
Greek *glendi,* **3:**931–32
Greek music, **3:**931–32
Guaraní culture, **2:**202–4
Gujarat
  bardic poetry, **5:**635
  bhajan, **5:**631
  kīrtan, **5:**632
Haitian *spèktak,* **3:**804
Hawai'i
  dance and, **9:**106–8
  Puerto Rican people, **9:**101–2
Hindustani music
  instrumental, **5:**202–4
  vocal genres, **5:**163

Hong Kong, **7:**432, 433–35
  for Cantonese opera, **7:**307
Hui people, **7:**462
Hungarian music, **3:**908–9
Hungary, **8:**739–40
  instrumental music, **8:**742–43
  Vlach Rom music, **8:**275
Iceland, *kvöldvaka,* **8:**117, 141, 400, 401–2
India
  jugalbandī concerts, **5:**205, 351, 380
  mehfil, **5:**493, 527, *694,* 694–95
India, South
  cinna mēḷam ensembles, **5:**387
  nonclassical, **5:**105
  periya mēḷam ensembles, **5:**103, 323, 359, 383, 387
Ingush people, **8:**863–64
Iran
  for Azerbaijani *aşıqlar,* **6:**846
  for *bakhshi* performances, **6:**840
  radif, **6:**130, 140–41, 142
Iranian music, **3:**1034–35
Ireland, **8:**325, 388–89
Irian Jaya, **9:**578, 580
Irish music, **3:**842
Israel
  bakashot and *tish,* **6:**202
  henna party, **6:**202
  Jewish religious music, **6:**201–4
  shirei erets Yisrael, **6:**1019
Italian music, **3:**861, 864–65
Italy, singing, **8:**604
Japan
  audience development and, **7:**774–75
  festival drumming, **7:**606
  for folk songs, **7:**599
  for *gagaku,* **7:**619
  hayasi, **7:**683–85
  Heian period *gyoyû,* **7:**625
  for *kokyû,* **7:**712
  for *minzoku geinô,* **7:**605–6
  for *nagauta,* **7:**654, 671–72, 765
  for puppet theater, **7:**665
for jazz, **3:**551, 580
Jewish music, **3:**933–34, 1171–74, 1175
  Lubavitcher Hasidim, **10:**132
  religious, **8:**249–52
  secular, **8:**252
Karachaevian people, **8:**857–58
Karnataka
  for *kombu kahaḷe* ensemble, **5:**875
  regional genres, **5:**868–70
Karnatak music, **5:**90, 209–12, 351
  arangētram concert, **5:**157
Kashmir
  for *chakri,* **5:**683
  mehfil, **5:**683, 686
  for Sufi music, **5:**686
Kenya, **1:**629–32
Kerala, **5:**934–36
  Mappila songs, **5:**948
Kogi culture, **2:**185–86
Korea, **7:**808
  concerts, **7:**994–95
  farmers' bands, **7:**929, 933–35
  folk songs, **7:**884–85

performance contexts, Korea (*continued*)
  kut, 7:875–76
  vocal techniques and, 7:820
Kota people, *devr koḷ*, 5:281
Kuna culture, 2:644
Lao music, 3:1009
Latvia, 8:501–3
Lithuania, 8:511
  choral concerts and festivals, 8:512–14
Low Countries, 8:522–23
Macedonia, 8:973
  čalgija ensembles, 8:979
  instrumental music, 8:975–76
Macedonian music, 3:925
Malaysia, 4:402
Malta, 8:639, 640
Manitoba, Mennonite Plautdeutscha Owend,
  3:52–53
Mapuche culture, 2:234–37
Maya culture, 2:652–53
Mexico, 2:54–55
Middle Eastern peoples, 3:1033–35
  ḥafla (*haflah*), 3:1031–32, 1033, 1218;
    6:280–81, 691–94
  outdoor instruments, 6:3, 415
Mongol people, 7:1003, 1009, 1014, 1015
Montenegro, epic song, 8:959
Morocco, *līla*, 6:493
Native Americans, 3:5–6, 370–72
Nepal, 5:706
  Damāi people, 5:699–700
New Caledonia, 9:672–75
New England
  community singing, 3:154–55
  social dances, 3:158
North America
  balls, 3:564, 598, 1075
  barn dances, 3:868, 887
  camp meetings, 3:67, 68, 533, 575–76, 1132
  community-based, 3:284
  dance parties, 3:213
  hootenannies and sing-ins, 3:13–14
  house parties, 3:868, 900, 1070
  jam sessions, 3:669, 1170
  music performance model, 3:236–37
  for piano music, 3:239
  picnics, 3:640, 882–83, 890, 900, 922–23,
    925, 929, 931, 1031–32
  place as determinant, 3:142, 149–51,
    232–33, 322–23
  popular songs, eighteenth century, 3:180
  private homes, 3:179, 258, 283–84, 927–28
  research on, 3:144–45
  tamburitza music, 3:921, 922
Northeastern Indians, 3:462–63
Northwest Coast Indian groups, 3:395
North West Frontier Province, 5:791
Norway
  domestic devotionals, 8:414
  hardingfele concerts, 8:417, 420
  for *langeleik*, 8:415, 422
  Sunday-evening concerts, 8:415
Norwegian folk music, 3:866–68
Nova Scotia
  Cape Breton fiddle music, 3:1128
  Gaelic song, 3:1070, 1129

Nusa Tenggara Barat, 4:762
Oceania
  concert parties, 9:149
  Latino peoples, 9:83–84
Oman, 6:680–82
Ontario
  Anglo-Celtic music and dance, 3:1190
  Asian music, 3:1215–16
  concert societies, 3:1179
Ossetian people, 8:860–61
Pakistan, 5:745–50
  bāzum, 5:797
  majlis, 5:745
  mehfil, 5:747
  mehfil-e samā', 5:752, 755
  mushāira (poetry recitals), 5:749, 750
  of Muslim devotional music, 5:751, 772
Pakistan, northern, 5:796–97, 799
  amateur music-making, 5:794
Palestine, *henna* party, 6:581
Papua New Guina, 9:477–78, 511–12,
  526–27
Poland, 8:702, 711
Polish engagement parties, 3:892
Polynesian music and dance, 3:1051–53
Portugal, 8:578–81
Prince Edward Island, fiddling, 3:1128
Q'ero culture, 2:227–29
Quechua culture, 2:217–21
for rap, 3:694
rock, 3:551
Romania, 8:868–72
Romanian music, 3:911–12
Rotuma, 9:818–19
Russia
  posidelki, 8:765
  staged performances, 8:775–76
  village music, 8:755, 778
Russian music, 3:915
Russian Old Believers, 3:916
Ryûkyû Islands, traditional music, 7:796
Saami people, joiks, 8:302–5, 306
St. Lucia
  jwé, 2:943
  kwadril evenings, 2:944–45
Sāmoa, 9:799–805
  concert parties, 9:237
Sardinia, 8:626
  canto a chiterra, 8:629
Saudi Arabia, women's wedding party,
  6:691
Scotland, 8:369–70
  ceilidh, 8:371
  Traveller songs, 8:297
Serbian *becar* events, 3:923
Slovakia, 8:720
Slovenia, 8:911–12
South Africa
  balls, 1:761
  for jazz, 1:767–69
  for popular music, 1:429–30
South America, 2:54–55
South Asian
  film music concerts, 5:368
  foreign concert tours, 5:379–80
  mushaira, 3:1246–47

in North America, 3:980–82; 5:578–80
  qaṣīda, 5:284
  religious theater, 5:482
  ritual *vs.* incidental music, 5:20
  scholarly works on, 5:43
  ṭhumrī, 5:179
  visual depictions of, 5:305–6
  women's performances, 5:407–16, 413
Southeast Indian groups, 3:467
Spain, 8:589–91
  flamenco, 8:598
Sri Lanka
  nightlong stage shows, 5:961, 970
  popular music, 5:971
  temple ensembles, 5:108, 359
Susak music, 4:771–72
Suyá culture, 2:145–48
Sweden, 8:444
Swedish music, 3:1251
Switzerland, 8:682–85
Syrian music, 6:563–64
Tamil Nadu
  for cassettes, 5:558
  for dance, 5:919–20
  for songs, 5:917–18
Thailand, 4:247–50
Tokelau, 9:824–27
Trinidad, classical singing, 5:591
Tukano culture, 2:153–55
Tunisia, *ma'lūf*, 6:335, 501, 502, 506–7,
    508–9, 517–18, 519
Turkey, Ottoman court, 6:113, 767–68
Turkmenistan, *baggy* concerts, 6:968–69
Uighur people
  ikki muqam, 6:990
  muqam, 6:995–1008
Ukraine, 8:806
  dosvitky, 8:196–97, 808, 809, 810, 812
  instrumental music, 8:809
  Soviet period, 8:817–19
Ukrainian music, 3:912–13, 1242–43
Uttar Pradesh
  birahā, 5:668
  for *kajalī*, 5:670
Vietnam
  chamber music, 4:480
  minority peoples, 4:532–33
Vietnamese-American music, 3:995
Waiãpí culture, 2:162
Wales, 8:342–44
  folk clubs, 8:354, 355, 356
Warao culture, 2:193–97
West Africa, 1:450–51
West Futuna, 9:861–62
Yekuana culture, 2:181–82
Yoruba people, for popular music, 1:472
Zaïre, concerts, 1:387–88
performance places. *See also* performance contexts
  Afghanistan, teahouses, 5:830, 831
  Africa, 1:117, 131
    spatial concepts, 1:120, 121
    time-space relationships, 1:126, 150–51
  Algeria, for Andalusian music, 6:469–70
  Andhra Pradesh, for mendicants, 5:900
  Arabian peninsula
    coffeehouses, 6:651

for dance, **6:**704
dar, **6:**668
taverns, **6:**294
Western expatriates, **6:**713–19
Argentina, **2:**262
   bailantas, **2:**275
   cantinas, **2:**90
   for *música tropical*, **2:**265–66
   for tango, **2:**263, 264, 273
   theaters, **2:**90
Australia, **9:**345, 437
   Aboriginal performances, **9:**226–27,
      450–51, 453, 458–59, 464
   ancestral space, **9:**458–60
   bars, **9:**140
   community centers, **9:**140
Azerbaijan, **6:**922–23
Bahamas, nightclubs, **2:**801–2
Bali, temples, **4:**738–39
Bali people (of Africa), **1:**117
Barbados
   plantation homes, **2:**814
   theaters, **2:**819
Belize, for punta-rock, **2:**677
Bellona, **9:**849
Bengal, for *pālāgān*, **5:**862
Berber popular music, **6:**276
Bihar, for *chau*, **5:**497
Bolivia
   for fiestas and dances, **2:**291–92
   machetero dance, **2:**139
   music clubs, **2:**298
   theaters, **2:**284
Brazil
   for *cantoria*, **2:**326, 327
   forró clubs, **2:**333
   native American theaters, **2:**302
   nightclubs, **2:**317
   opera houses, **2:**334
   pickup trucks, **2:**337–38
   social class and, **2:**313
   temporary structures, **2:**331
   theaters, **2:**90, *113*
Caribbean, **2:**44–45, 56
   bars, **2:**49
   dance halls, **2:**49–50, 76
   nightclubs, **2:**49
   street, **2:**50, 63
   urban venues, **2:**49–50
Central African Republic, bars, **1:**681–82
Central America, **2:**44–45, 56
   bars, **2:**49
   dance halls, **2:**49–50, 76
   nightclubs, **2:**49
   street, **2:**50, 63
   urban venues, **2:**49–50
Central Asia, Sufi *khānaqāl*, **6:**937, 940, 943
China
   for Cantonese narratives, **7:**261, 269
   for Cantonese opera, **7:**305
   Daoist ritual space, **7:**322
   nanguan music, **7:**209
   for northern narratives, **7:**251–52, 253–54
   parks, **7:**411
   rock clubs, **7:**363–68
   Shanghai singing halls, **7:**353

Tang dynasty entertainment houses, **7:**402
tanhuang singers, **7:**298–99
teahouses, **3:**1261; **7:**261, 407, 411
Chuuk, for love serenades, **9:**736
Colombia
   bailaderos, **2:**411
   casetas, **2:**411
   discoteca, **2:**411
   for folkloric music, **2:**395–96
   piqueteaderos, **2:**394–95
   for *serenata*, **2:**383
   theaters, **2:**395
Cook Islands, **9:**901
Costa Rica, **2:**699–700
   theaters, **2:**694, 702
   town plazas, **2:**694
Cuba, theaters, **2:**828
Dai people
   for Buddhist music, **7:**504
   for popular music, **7:**505
Denmark, Folk-Music Houses, **8:**461, 464
Dominican Republic, **2:**856, 858–59
   bars and brothels, **2:**856
   theaters, **2:**858
East Asia, for theater, **7:**73
Egypt
   cafés, **6:**234
   coffeehouses, **6:**411
   for *ḥaḍra*, **6:**174
   nightclubs, **6:**555, 616, 620–21
   for *qiṣaṣ*, **6:**170
El Salvador, theaters, **2:**718
Europe, **8:**81
   cabarets, **8:**252, 257, 264, 544, 659–60,
      675
   coffeehouses and taverns, **8:**198
   concentration camps, **8:**661
   dance halls, **8:**251
   rock clubs, **8:**216
   salons, **8:**260, 261
Fiji, *meke*, **9:**777
Finland, **8:**486
   lakeshore dance pavilions, **8:**485
   rock clubs, **8:**217
Germany, **8:**654
Great Britain, **8:**325
Greece
   bouzoukia, **8:**1020
   café aman, **8:**285, 1014
   coffeehouses, **8:**1016
   Naxos, **8:**1015
   for *rebetika*, **8:**1019–21
Guadeloupe, nightclubs, **2:**878
Guarijio culture, *pascola ramada*, **2:**553, 554
Guatemala, **2:**736
   for popular music, **2:**735
   theaters, **2:**736
Gujarat, *rāj darbār*, **5:**635
Haiti
   peristil, **2:**887
   for popular music, **2:**893
   for public dances, **2:**889–90
   theaters, **2:**890
Hawai'i, clubs, **9:**162–66
Hong Kong
   for Cantonese opera, **7:**305, 307–8

concert halls, **7:**434
teahouses, **7:**434
Hungary
   culture houses, **8:**746
   táncház, **8:**744–45
India, South
   homes, **5:**211–12
   maṇḍapam, **5:**212
   temples, **5:**210–11, 910–11
Iran
   coffeehouses, **6:**340, 344
   concert halls, **6:**130
   indoor *vs.* outdoor, **6:**140, 142
   khāneqāh, **6:**823, 824–26, 829
   teahouses and coffeehouses, **6:**827, 829, 846
   zūr-khāne, **6:**825–26
Ireland, **8:**325
Irian Jaya
   for dance, **9:**581–82
   Eipo *mot*, **9:**592
Israel
   concert halls, **6:**203–4
   nightclubs, **6:**1034
   synagogues, **6:**201–2, 1016–17
   wedding hall, **6:**202
Japan
   for *bugaku*, **7:**621, 624
   for *bunraku*, **7:**664–65
   concert halls, **7:**533, 601
   karaoke bars, **7:***534*
   min'yô bars, **7:**601
   temporary structures, **7:**653
for Karnatak music, **5:**351
Kashmir, **5:**682
   for *chakri*, **5:**683
Kenya, nightclubs, **1:**631
Kerala, *kūttambalam*, **5:**509
Korea
   indoor *vs.* outdoor, **7:**822, 823, 994–95
   for *kagok*, **7:**920
   for *p'ansori*, **7:**898
   public theaters, **7:**944
Low Countries, singing pubs, **8:**522
Macao, for Cantonese opera, **7:**305
Macedonia, coffeehouses, **8:**281
Manihiki, **9:**907
Māori communities, **9:**277, 936, 946
Mapuche culture, **2:**237, 254
Maritimes, theaters, **3:**1120
Martinique, **2:**920
   street music, **2:**915, *916*
Mbyá culture, **2:**255
Mexico, **2:**44–45, 56
   bars, **2:**49
   dance halls, **2:**49–50, 76
   nightclubs, **2:**49
   quioscos, **2:**604
   street, **2:**50, 63
   street performers, **2:**568
   theaters, **2:**603, 606
   urban venues, **2:**49–50
Middle East, **6:**5
Mongol people, **7:**1005
Montserrat, rum shops, **2:**926
Nepal, Newār people, **5:**702
New Caledonia, *wahaï* dance, **9:**685

performance places (*continued*)
Nicaragua, theaters, **2:**766
North America
  acoustics of, **3:**237
  ballrooms, **3:**668
  barrelhouses, **3:**644
  bars, **3:**316, 890
  beer gardens, **3:**897
  for bluegrass, **3:**162
  cabarets, **3:**199, 578, 652
  café concerto, **3:**861
  cantinas, **3:**773
  catering halls, **3:**935
  churches, **3:**283
  circuses, **3:**182, 568, 643
  for classical concert music, **3:**10
  coffeehouses, **3:**211–12, 316, 317, 931,
    1032, 1204
  concert halls, **3:**46, 173–76, 181
  for country fiddling, **3:**77
  for dance, **3:**207
  dance clubs, **3:**211, 216, 227–30, 687–91
  dance halls, **3:**211–12, 258, 868–69
  discothèques, **3:**227
  eighteenth century, **3:**180
  ethnic clubs, **3:**822–23
  Finnish halls, **3:**872–73
  folk music clubs, **3:**1204
  for Great Basin Bear Dances, **3:**423
  homes, **3:**180, 868, 887, 900, 936, 995,
    1070, 1090, 1246, 1264–65
  for house music, **3:**690–91
  Indian temples, **5:**580
  juke joints, **3:**640, 644
  karaoke clubs, **3:**964
  Korean *noraebang*, **3:**978–79
  lodge halls, **3:**898
  lofts, **3:**176
  nightclubs, **3:**211–12, 652, 711, 725, 1169;
    Croatian and Serbian, **3:**923; Middle
    Eastern, **3:**1028, 1033–34, 1035,
    1036; *peñas*, **3:**730
  nineteenth century, **3:**181
  opera houses, **3:**46, 181
  outdoor locations, **3:**157, 251, 773, 1095,
    1097
  as performance determinant, **3:**236, 237–38
  pleasure gardens, **3:**180, 189
  Pueblo Indian groups, **3:**430
  rent parties, **3:**644
  rock clubs and bars, **3:**170–71, 551
  saloons, **3:**181, 258, 1277
  segregated, **3:**46, 619, 652, 660–61
  settlement houses, **3:**93
  for Southeast Indian Green Corn ceremony,
    3:468
  speakeasies, **3:**551
  swing clubs, **3:**551
  taverns, **3:**888
  tent and medicine shows, **3:**103, 640, 643,
    836, 868
  theaters, **3:**542–46; black ownership of,
    3:619; nineteenth century, **3:**181
  Western Arctic men's houses (*kasigi*), **3:**377
Oceania, **9:**345, *404*
Pakhtun people, **5:**786

Pakistan
  northern, **5:**797
  Sufi shrines, **5:**754–55
Palau, **9:**724, *725*
Palestinian wedding eve celebrations, **6:**576
Papua New Guinea
  Abelam initiation ceremonies, **9:**549, 552
  Angan singsings, **9:**497
  Bali and Vitu islands, **9:**611
  for ceremonies, **9:**512–13
  Highlands Region, **9:**478
  Iatmul death-marking ceremony, **9:**553–54
  Iatmul people, **9:**555
  inside *vs.* outside, **9:**512–13
  Maring ceremonies, **9:**514–15
  Nissan Atoll, **9:**633
  Papuan Gulf region, **9:**483
  Papua region, **9:**490
  singsings, **9:**529–30
Paraguay
  kermese, **2:**459
  parrilladas, **2:**461
Peru
  chicódromos, **2:**485
  coliseos, **2:**484
  peñas criollas, **2:**501
  peñas folklóricas, **2:**486
  salsódromos, **2:**487
  theaters, **2:**500–501
for popular music performances, **2:**92
popular music venues, **2:**63
Punjab (India), for *bhangra*, **5:**650
Q'ero corn beer festival, **2:**229
Québec, *boîtes à chansons*, **3:**1076, 1156,
  1168
Rajasthan, *devrā*, **5:**292
Rotuma, **9:**818
Russia
  for lyric songs, **8:**765–66
  piatachki, **8:**767
St. Lucia, private homes, **2:**944–45
Serbia, Vojvodina, **8:**952
Society Islands, **9:**873
Solomon Islands, Santa Cruz Islands,
  9:332–34
South Africa
  for popular music, **1:**429–30
  shebeens, **1:**766–68
  taverns and dance halls, **1:**761, 767–68
South America, **2:**44–45, 56
  bars, **2:**49
  dance halls, **2:**49–50, 76
  nightclubs, **2:**49
  street, **2:**50, 63
  tropical-forest region, **2:**132
  urban venues, **2:**49–50
South Asia
  for dances, **5:**498
  gosthi, **5:**408
  influence on performance practice, **5:**567
  for popular music, **5:**428–29
South Korea, **7:**994–95
Spain
  cafés cantantes, **8:**597
  dance clubs, **8:**600
  tablaos, **8:**598

Sweden
  folkparker, **8:**443
  outdoor dance pavilions, **8:**443
Switzerland, **8:**694–95
Syria
  coffeehouses, **6:**570
  music halls, **6:**570
  religious institutions, **6:**570
Tahiti, **9:**229
Taiwan, for *gezaixi* opera, **7:**426
Takuu, **9:**839
Trinidad and Tobago, calypso tents, **2:**96
Tukano culture, **2:**151
Tunisia
  coffeehouses and cafés, **6:**506, 509
  diyār al-thaqāfa, **6:**330, 511
  indoor *vs.* outdoor, **6:**519
  zāwiya, **6:**516–20
Turkey
  coffeehouses and taverns, **6:**116, 802, 805–8
  Halk Evleri, **6:**77, 797, 813–14
  indoor *vs.* outdoor, **6:**115
  nightclubs, **6:**57, 117–18, 121, 243–45,
    259, 758
  Sufi *tevhīd-hane*, **6:**191
Ukraine, village clubs, **8:**817
Uruguay
  cafés, **2:**521
  dance halls, **2:**521
  for popular music, **2:**520
  tablados, **2:**516
  tanguerías, **2:**520
Uttar Pradesh, for *kajalī*, **5:**670
'Uvea, for *kailao*, **9:**812
Vietnam, Chinese cultural clubs, **4:**70
Virgin Islands
  for quadrille, **2:**971–72
  theaters, **2:**969
Wales, *twmpath*, **8:**355
Yap, **9:***717*
Yoruba people, for popular music, **1:**472
performance practice. *See also specific topics and*
  peoples
Afghanistan, **5:**813
  chahārbeiti, **5:**819
  concert positions, **5:**830
  Kabuli *ghazal*, **5:**805–6
  tanbur, **5:**830
African-American worship, **3:**626–28
Albania, **8:**991–92
Algeria, Andalusian repertoire, **6:**450–51, 454,
  468, 470–72
Anglo-American ballads, **3:**833–34
Arabian peninsula
  changes in, **6:**355–56
  lyre playing, **6:**357–59
  sung poetry, **6:**664–65, 667–68
  women's songs, **6:**699–701
Arab music, **6:**548–50
  medieval, **6:**16, 354–56, 397, 535–42
  modes in, **6:**38–42
  rhythmic modes, **6:**89–92
Belarus, calendric and family-ritual songs,
  8:793–94
Belgium, violin, **8:**532
Berber popular music, **6:**276

Brittany, responsorial singing, **8:**559
Bulgaria
　regional styles, **8:**895–97
　wedding music, **8:**284
Celtic music, **8:**321–22
Central Asia, Bukharan *shash maqām*, **6:**903,
　　911, 919–20
China
　Buddhist chants, **7:**329–30
　dapu, **10:**19
　ensemble music, **7:**240–41
　instrumental melody, **7:**123
　Jiangnan sizhu, **7:**224
　nanguan music, **7:**208–9
　opera productions, **7:**279–80, 287
　orchestras, **7:**227
　pan-Chinese performance style, **7:**419, 443,
　　514
　Suzhou tanci, **7:**261–62
　traditional genres, **7:**91, 92
　xianshiyue, **7:**214–16
　xiaodiao, **7:**152
Coptic Orthodox music, **6:**221–22, 544
Czech Republic, parlando-rubato style, **8:**721
Denmark, street musicians, **8:**458
dizi, **7:**184
Egypt
　of Arab music, **6:**557–61
　epic songs, **6:**342–43
　inshād, **6:**166–67, 171–74
　'ūd, **6:**45–46
England
　folk music, **8:**333–35
　vocal, **8:**326–29
erhu, **7:**175–76
Europe
　composition, improvisation, and, **8:**73,
　　91–92, 93–95, 97
　cue systems in, **8:**97–98
　deviations from notation in, **8:**95–96
　historical performance movement, **8:**60,
　　85–86
　historicism and, **8:**55–56
　mediated folk music performances, **8:**156
　notation and, **8:**50–56, 93–94
　popular music, **8:**204–5
　revival movements and, **8:**228
　traditional music in festival contexts,
　　8:149–54
　village music, **8:**8–9
Finland, Rom people, **8:**289
France
　drone instruments, **8:**543
　picotage technique, **8:**543
　variation processes, **8:**550
　vocal music, **8:**542–43
Georgia
　antiphonal, **8:**833
　Soviet influences on, **8:**844–45
Goa, Konkani song repertoire, **5:**737–38
Great Britain, **8:**325
Greece, Rom music, **8:**285
Gujarat
　bhajan, **5:**631–32
　duho, **5:**636
Guyana, *chowtal* singing, **5:**600–601

Hindustani music
　gāyakī aṅg style, **5:**195–96
　instrumental concert programs, **5:**203–4
　raga in, **5:**64–66, 79–87
　savāl-javāb (question-answer), **5:**132, 204
　tala gestures, **5:**169–70
　tala in, **5:**119
　vocal genres, **5:**162–63
Hong Kong, Cantonese opera and
　　instrumental music, **7:**435
Hungary
　folk music, **8:**739
　parlando-rubato style, **8:**740, 741, 746, 747
　Rom ensembles, **8:**745–46
　Rom string bands, **8:**273–74
Iceland, *rímur*, **8:**401–2
Iran, **6:**832–34
　authenticity and, **6:**858–59
　radif, **6:**61–62, 129–42, 836, 855–57,
　　862–63
Iraq, *maqām*, **6:**312–13
Ireland, **8:**325
　instrumental music, **8:**382, 384–85, 387
　keening, **8:**378–79
　Travellers, **8:**295
　vocal music, **8:**380–81
Islamic call to prayer (*adhān*), **6:**154–55
Israel, synagogue music, **6:**1017, 1048–54
Italy, vocal music, **8:**610–11, 613
Japan
　aesthetics and, **7:**550–55
　gidayû busi, **7:**675
　kyôgen instrumentalists, **7:**636
　mikagura, **7:**619
　nô, **7:**640
　performance posture, **7:**548, 644, 647
　source materials on, **7:**585
　syô, **7:**621
　syômyô, **7:**615
　tôgaku repertoire, **7:**42–43
Java, **4:**668–75
Jewish liturgical, **6:**200–201
Karnatak music, **5:**230–35, 323–24, 351,
　　384–85
　jōḍipaṭṭu, **5:**227, 232
　koraippu trading section, **5:**159, *160*
　raga traditions, **5:**97
　tala gestures, **5:**138–39, 152, 358
Kashmir
　maqām, **5:**689–90
　ṣūfyāna mūsīqī, **5:**694–95
Kazakhstan
　antiphonal songs, **6:**951
　epic genres, **6:**952–53
　kyui, **6:**902, 957–58
　lyrical songs, **6:**955–56
Kerala, Vedic chant, **5:**241–42
Korea
　aak, **7:**816, 863
　farmers' bands, **7:**931–32
　kagok, **7:**920–21
　kasa, **7:**927
　kut, **7:**876
　sijo, **7:**925
　sinawi, **7:**890–91
Libya, Andalusian repertoire, **6:**454

Malta
　bormliza, **8:**637
　fatt, **8:**638
　spirtu pront, **8:**636
Maritime fiddling, **3:**1071
Martinique, Tamil ceremonies, **5:**596–98
Métis fiddling, **3:**406–7
Middle Ages, **8:**70
Morocco
　Andalusian repertoire, **6:**450, 454
　malhun, **6:**499–500
mridangam, **5:**151–53, 157–59
North America
　bluegrass, **3:**161
　country music, **3:**77
　music revivals, **3:**55–59
　organ music, **3:**28
North Caucasia, epic song, **8:**851
Norway
　hardingfele, **8:**417
　nystev singing, **8:**413
pakhāvaj, **5:**115–16
Pakistan, northern, instrumental music, **5:**796
Palestine, wedding eve music, **6:**574–75, 577
Parsi theater, **5:**487
pipa, **7:**168
Poland
　apocope, **8:**703
　change in, **8:**711
　fiddlers, **8:**706
Portugal, *fado*, **8:**583–84
psalmody, **3:**832–33
　lining-out practices, **3:**119, 121, 125,
　　832–33; **8:**97–98, 145
qin, **7:**158–59, 163–65
Qur'ānic recitation, **6:**159–62
recomposition and adaptation, **8:**54–55
recording technology and, **3:**243, 244
regional style differences, **8:**14
research on, **8:**56
Réunion Island, *maloya*, **5:**609–10
Romania, **8:**879–80
　nai, **8:**878
　Rom epic performance, **8:**278
Russia
　byliny, **8:**764
　lyric songs, **8:**765
　znamenny rospev, **8:**779
Ryûkyû Islands, **7:**791
Saami people, joiking, **8:**302
Sanskrit drama, **5:**25–26, 29, 40
Sardinia
　launeddas, **8:**630
　a tenore singing, **8:**627, *628*
Saudi Arabia, antiphonal songs, **6:**653–54
Scandinavian folk music, **3:**867
Scotland
　circular breathing, **8:**366
　psalm singing, **8:**362–63
Serbia, *gajde*, **8:**944–45
sheng, **7:**187, 188–90
Slovakia, parlando-rubato style, **8:**721
Slovenia, **8:**912–13
　violin playing, **8:**917
South Asia
　bhajan, **5:**254–55, 267–68

performance practice, South Asia (*continued*)
　bhajana, **5:**106
　drumming, **5:**325–26, 328
　gat, **5:**189, 192, 198–202
　ghazal, **5:**186
　Hindu devotional singing, **5:**248–49
　kathak, **5:**494
　khyāl, **5:**171–78
　musicians seated on stage, **5:**483
　qawwali, **5:**752–53
　scholarship since 1300, **5:**42–58
　treatises on, **5:**33, 35–36, 41, 44, 51, 54–56
Suyá culture, **2:**148–49
Sweden, folk songs, **8:**436
Switzerland, yodeling, **8:**690–91
tabla, **5:**133–34, 136, 342
Tamil Nadu, *kēṭṭi mēḷam*, **5:**275, 286
technology's impact on, **5:**567
television demands on, **8:**157
ṭhumrī, **5:**180–83
Tunisia
　Andalusian repertoire, **6:**454
　of national art music (*ma'lūf*), **6:**326–27, 329–30, 331–36, 507, 509
Turkey
　art music, **6:**113–14, 117, 119–28
　makam, **6:**55–56
　rhythmic modes, **6:**89–92
　song duels, **6:**806–7
　taksim sections, **6:**257
　vocal, **6:**781–87
Turkmenistan, *baggy* music, **6:**971–75
Uighur music, **6:**995–1008; **7:**456
Ukraine, vocal music, **8:**808–9
Vedic chant, **5:**30–33, 241–44
Vīravidyavantulu singers, **5:**901
Vlach Rom music, **8:**275
Wales
　canu gyda'r tannau, **8:**350, 352–54
　songs, **8:**345–47
yangqin, **7:**180
Yemen
　al-ghinā' al-ṣan'ānī, **6:**687–90
　drum ensemble music, **6:**100–106
zheng, **7:**172–73
performers. *See also* amateur musicians; blackface
　　minstrelsy; blind or handicapped
　　musicians; conductors and bandleaders;
　　disc jockeys; ensembles, musical;
　　gharānā; *griots*; *specific names and
　　groups*
　acrobats, **2:**564; **5:***481*, 484, 488, 498, 501, 519, 640, 673, 878; **6:**627, 812
　Afghanistan
　　professional musicians, **5:**818, 822–23, 831–32
　　sāzdohol, **5:**818–19, 820–22, *821*
　　women, **5:**809, 814–15; **6:**305
　Africa, professional families, **1:**8
　African-American
　　fiddlers, **3:**66, 596, 598–99; **10:**142, *151*
　　popularity in Europe, **8:**233
　　theater, **3:**616–22
　Afro-Cuban music, **3:**793–99
　age and genre, associations, **2:**57–58; **8:**116, 145

Albania
　kryeplak and *kryetar*, **8:**118
　Labs, vocal, **8:**115
　Rom people, **8:**285–86
Algeria
　gawwāl, **6:**466
　maddaḍāt, **6:**305
　rai, **6:**270–71
Andalusia, singing slave girls, **6:**12, 364, 370, 445–46
Andean regions, **2:**218
　north-south distinctions, **2:**222
Andhra Pradesh
　mendicants, **5:**899–900
　narrative singers, **5:**899–902
animals, **5:**769
　trained bears, **8:**142–43, 280, *283*, 893, 950, 953
animal trainers, **5:**481, 484, 727
Antigua and Barbuda, Old Time masquerade bands, **2:**799
Arab-American, **6:**283
Arabian peninsula
　dancers, **6:**703–11
　dangers of arrest in, **6:**354–55
　joqa, **6:**667
　mukhannathūn, **6:**296, 538
　muṭriba, **6:**698–99, 701
　nahhām, **6:**546, 651
　qiyān, **6:**537, 539, 696, 697
　singing slave girls, **6:**20, 293–96, 297, 360, 361, 364, 456
　women musicians, **6:**20, 293–97, 695–702
Argentina
　cuarteto groups, **2:**274–80
　locutor, **2:**274
　payadores, **2:**262
　professionalization of, **2:**262–63, 268
Armenia
　ashughner, **6:**724, 734–36
　gusanner, **6:**723, 731–33
　vipasanner, **6:**723, 732
Australia
　Aboriginal vaudeville troupes, **9:**134
　Arnhem Land, **9:**412
　Central, **9:**437
　dancers, **9:**456
　Greek musicians, **9:**72–73
Azerbaijan
　aşiq, **6:**827, 829, 922, 924, 925, 929–30
　xanəndə, **6:**924, 929
Bahamas, **2:**802
　basser, **2:**804–5
　rhymer, **2:**804
Bali, **4:**737–38
　dalang, **4:**751
　joged, **4:**754, 757–58
　juru tandak, **4:**750
　professional, **4:**760
Balkan region, Rom people, **8:**867
Balochistan
　Gwashinda, **5:**782, 783
　instrumentalists, **5:**781
　mālid and *shēparjā* dancers, **5:**780
　motk-kashsh, **5:**776
　naḍī, **5:**775

Pahlawān and Ḍomb minstrels, **5:**776, 781, *782*
　sarogān, **5:**777
　shāir, **5:**778–79
　sherward, **6:**881
　singers, **5:**781–82
　Sotī, **5:**782
　surrī, **5:**775
Basque region
　bertsulari, **8:**311–14, 315, *316*
　joaldunak, **8:**314–15
　txistulari, **8:**314, 316
Bāul sect, **5:**503
Belarus
　bardy, **8:**801
　skamarochi, **8:**799
Bengal, *kīrtan* singers, **5:**254
Berber
　poets, **6:**274, 489
　rways, **6:**410, 448, 489–90
blues musicians, **3:**524, 638–640, 643–48, 707
　white, **3:**644
Bolivia, **2:**292–93
Borneo, **4:**825
Brazil
　alabê drummers in Candomblé rituals, **2:**343, *345*
　caboclinhos, **2:**337
　caboclos de lança, **2:**337
　for carnival, **2:**335–36
　chorões, **2:**305, 313, 350
　emboladores, **2:**327
Bribri and Cabécar cultures, **2:**635
　stsóköl, **2:**633–34
Brittany, bards, **8:**561
Bulgaria, **8:**112–13
　Greece, vocal, **8:**115
　kukeri, **8:**140, 897, *899*
　Rom people, **8:**282–84
Burma, **4:**399
Caribbean
　gender of, **2:**57
　kinship and, **2:**58
　mummers, **2:**795
　occupation and, **2:**58–59
　popular musicians, social backgrounds of, **2:**104–5
　social context of, **2:**55–57
Carriacou, *chantwell*, **2:**870
castrati, **8:**77
cathedral musicians, **2:**113, 507, 603, 651–52, 693, 735
Central America
　gender of, **2:**57
　kinship and, **2:**58
　occupation and, **2:**58–59
　popular musicians, social backgrounds of, **2:**104–5
　social context of, **2:**55–57
Central Asia
　ashiq, **6:**901
　bacha (boy dancers), **6:**899
　bakhshī (also *baxšī*), **6:**345, 901, 967
　jrau, **6:**901
　maddāh, **6:**901
　mavrighikhān, **6:**899

qalandarlar, **6:**901, 937, *938*, 939, 942, 945
qawwāl, **6:**937
women, **6:**946
Chechen people, *illancha*, **8:**864
Chile, *bailes*, **2:**362–65
China
age of, **7:**419–20, 511
amateur singers, **7:**287
Buddhist preceptor, **7:**329
Cantonese opera, **7:**306–7
Daoist cantors, **7:**322
dizi players, **7:**184–85
drum singers, **7:**395
female impersonators, **7:**394–95, 407–8
minjian yiren, **7:**90
narrative singers, **7:**252, 255, 269, 404, 408, 451–52
opera role types, **7:**276, 283–84, 291–92, 308–9
opera troupes, **7:**304–5, 407–8
pipa players, **7:**82, 90, 167, 168, 169–70
professional, **7:**418–19
qin players, **7:**159, 160
of *quyi*, **7:**252
in *sheng-guan* ensembles, **7:**200
song and dance troupes, **7:**297–98, 353–54, 442–43, 513–14
storytellers, **7:**245–50, 420
suona players, **7:**204
tanhuang singers, **7:**299
theatrical troupes, **7:**394–96
women, **7:**82, 171, 172, 252, 255, 269, 363–65, 401–8, 421
xianshiyue, **7:**211
xiao players, **7:**186
yangqin players, **7:**181
zheng players, **7:**171, 172, *173*
Chinese-American, **3:**959–60, 961–62
Chinese-Canadian, **3:**1247–48, 1263–65, 1266
Cirebon
gamelan, **4:**689
ronggèng, **4:**688
traditional families of, **4:**686, 699
Colombia
bordonero, **2:**402
dueto bambuquero, **2:**383
tiplero (also *requintador*), **2:**402
Corsica, *paghjelle* singers, **8:***570*
Costa Rica, *payasos*, **2:**701, *702*
Croatia
guslači (also *guslari*), **8:**927
zvončari, **8:**925
Cuba
censor, **2:**835
church musicians, **2:**836
clarina, **2:**835
decimista, **2:**835
tonista, **2:**835
trovadores, **2:**831
Cyprus, *poietarides*, **8:**1030, 1032
Czechoslovakia, **8:**724
folkníci, **8:**730
Czech Republic
jokulatori, **8:**726
town trumpeters, **8:**727

Dai people, *zhangkhap*, **7:**506
dalang puppet master, **3:**1012, 1020
dancers, **3:**206–26
avocational, **3:**209–20, 233
ballet, **3:**207–8
Canada, **3:**223–24
self-accompanying, **3:**206
Denmark
ballad singers, **8:***136*
fiddlers, **8:**457
instrumentalists, **8:**457
street musicians, **8:**455, *456*, 457–58, 462–63
tavern musicians, **8:**458
Dominica
chantwèl, **2:**841
danm, **2:**842
kavalyé, **2:**841–42
lavwa, **2:**841
Dominican Republic, *trovadores*, **2:**860
East Asia, musicians' guilds and lineages, **7:**46, 55–56, 65
economics and, **3:**45, 68, 82
Ecuador
danzantes, **2:**421–22
glosador, **2:**427
golpeador, **2:**212–13
paki, **2:**425
respondedoras, **2:**427
Egypt
'awālim, **6:**305, 547, 567, 615–16, 618, 625
Cairo, **6:**615–22
film stars, **6:**236–38
ghawāzī, **6:**305, 545, 625, *626*
male dancers, **6:**625
muḥaddithīn, **6:**340
munshidīn, **6:**165–75, 543, 623
mustaftiḥ, **6:**171
muṭrib, **6:**167
popular, **6:**235–36, 239–41, 269, 597–600, 603–5
professionalization of, **6:**621–22
professional mourners, **6:**298
professional poets, **6:**340
'ūd players, **6:**45–46
women musicians, **6:**297–98
El Salvador, **2:**715–16
England
blackface minstrels, **8:**331
folk singers, **8:**332–36
Italian street musicians, **8:**336
Europe
ballad singers, **8:**135–36, 142, 195
ballet dancers, **8:**160–61
Baroque, solo singers, **8:**76
chain-dance leader, **8:**164–65
church and synagogue musicians, **8:**145, 253
church choirs, **8:**81
church organists, **8:**81
courtesans, **8:**199
folk troupes, **8:**7, 166
in immigrant communities, **8:**232
instrumental, **8:**198
itinerant, **8:**142–43

Middle Ages, **8:**71
orchestral, **8:**62
popular music, **8:**204–5
popular musicians in socialist countries, **8:**209
professionalization of, **8:**150, 199–200
professional lamenters, **8:**196
Renaissance, instrumentalists, **8:**75
Renaissance, women, **8:**77
separation from composers in art music, **8:**93
specialists, **8:**121–22
Fiji, clowns, **9:**230–31
Finland, **8:**485
fiddlers, **8:**480
of *runonlaulu*, **8:**114–15
wedding musicians, **8:**476
Finnish professional entertainers, **3:**874–75
Flanders, broadside singers, **8:**522
France
chansonniers, **8:**544, 548
jongleresses, **8:**199
jongleurs, **8:**72, 542
vielleur, **8:***544*
women, **8:**548
gamelan, **3:**1017–20, 1021–22
Garifuna culture, *gayusa*, **2:**672
Georgia, families of, **8:**841
Germany
amateur, **8:**653–54
Bänkelsänger, **8:**16
guilds, **8:**651–52
Stadtpfeifer, **8:**653
traveling musicians, **8:**652, 653
Greece, **8:**1016–17
Epirus, vocal, **8:**115
Karpathos, *meraklis*, **8:**118
professional mourners, **8:**1013–14
of *rebetika*, **8:**1019–21
Rom people, **8:**284–85
Greece, ancient, **8:**40, 46
aedes, **6:**953
Guadeloupe
chantè, **2:**874
konmandè, **2:**876, 877
répondè, **2:**874
Guarijio culture, *turélo*, **2:**552–53
Gujarat
bhajan singers, **5:**631
kīrtankār, **5:**632–33
māṇ bhaṭṭ, **5:**7, 633–34
Guyana, calypsonians, **2:**445
Haiti
onjènikon, **2:**884
sanba, **2:**885
twoubadou, **2:**890, 891
hautboys, **3:**563
Hawai'i, dancers, **9:**110
Hindustani music, **5:**204–8
Hispano-American, **3:**762–66
Hungary, **8:**739
instrumentalists, **8:**742–43
Rom people, **8:**272–76
Iban people, *lemambang*, **4:**828
Iceland
kvæðamaður, **8:**117–18, 401
skalds, **8:**146, 405, 423

performers (*continued*)
  India
    sectarian musicians, **5:**248
    South, *naṭṭuvanār*, **5:**104, 522
  Ingush people, *illancha*, **8:**864
  Iran, **6:**827–31
    'āsheq (also *aşıq*), **6:**827, 829, 839, 843–52
    bakhshī (also *baggy*), **6:**827, *828*, 829, 835, 837, 839–41, 844
    daste-ye moṭreb, **6:**827–28, 829
    itinerant, **6:**831
    morshed, **6:**825–26
    motreb, **6:**139, 868
    naqqāl, **6:**827
    Persian art music, **6:**861–62
    Persian court musicians, **6:**131
    radif musicians, **6:**138–39, 868
    rowẓe-khān, **6:**826–27
    storytellers, **6:**344
  Iraq
    of *maqām*, **6:**313
    qurrā', **6:**551
  Ireland, **8:**386–88, 390–92
    bards, **8:**146
    traveling schoolmasters, **8:**143
    ullagoner, **8:**295
  Irian Jaya, Eipo *mot winye*, **9:**592
  Irish-American, **3:**842, 843–46
  Israel, popular music, **6:**1020, 1033–34, 1074
  Italian-American, **3:**861–63, 864
  Italy, **8:**611
    cantastorie, **8:**143, 611
    cantautori, **8:**619
    cantimbanchi, **8:**16
    female wailers, **8:**607
    gondolieri, **8:**53
    poeti a braccio, **8:**611
    urlatori, **8:**619
  Jamaica, *bomma*, **2:**905
  Jammu and Kashmir, *bhānd* (also *bhagat*), **5:**498–99
  Japan
    bensi (also *katuben*), **7:**749
    biwa players, **7:**643–46
    entertainers, **7:**601
    gakun'in, **7:**756–57
    geisya, **7:**602, 739, 745
    komosô and *komusô* monks, **7:**701, *702, 703,* 755–56
    narrative singers, **7:**681–82, 759
    onnagata actors, **7:**764–65
    satuma biwa players, **7:**648–49
    syakuhati players, **7:**705, 707–9
    tayû, **7:**667
    tugaru zyamisen players, **7:**600
    women, **7:**601, 602, 648–49, 650–51, 682, 687, 763–66
    yomiuri, **7:**739
    for *zyôruri*, **7:**675
  Java
    amateur, **4:**681–82
    andhong, **4:**648
    dhalang, **4:**638, 642, *650,* 652, 654
    gambyong, **4:**647
    of *gamelan* music, **4:**681–82
    gandrung, **4:**645

  gérongan, **4:**642, 646, 673, *674*
  itinerant, **4:**647–48
  lènggèr, **4:**645, 648
  pesindhèn, **4:***640,* 642, 666–67, 672–73, *674,* 682–83, 684; **10:**44
  ronggèng, **4:**645, 648
  singer-dancers, **4:**648–49
  talèdhèk, **4:**648, 682–83
  tandhak, **4:**648, 682–83
  jazz musicians, **3:**551, 656, 658, 662
    white, **3:**578
  Jewish people
    in Arab countries, **6:**303, 313, 434, 470, 506, 565, 828, 1016, 1017, 1029, 1043, 1044
    ba'al tokeah, **8:**259
    cantors, **3:**530, 933, 934, 935, 940; **6:**201–2, 205, 1053; **8:**253–54, 261, 263, 264; in Turkey, **6:**57–58
    instrumentalists, **8:**249, 251–52, 257–58, 259–60
    instrument/gender associations, **8:**261
    klezmorim, **3:**934, 938, 941–42; **8:**11, 259–60, *260*
    paytan, **6:**1037, 1039
    popular music, **8:**264–65
    wedding musicians, **8:**250
  Karnataka
    kamsāḷe, **5:**872, *874*
    lāvṇi singers, **5:**869–70
    mendicants, **5:**867, 870
    women, **5:**455
  Karnatak music, **5:**103, 230–35
    comparative status of, **5:**393–95
    leadership role, **5:**384–85
  Kashmir
    dervishes, **5:**683
    ḥāfiẓa, **5:**687
    ṣūfyāna musicians, **5:**687
  Kazakhstan
    aqyn, **6:**951, 953–55, *961*
    epic singers, **6:**844, 952–53
    kyuishi, **6:**957–58
    lyric singers, **6:**955–56
  Kerala, *kūṭiyāṭṭam*, **5:**510
  Korea
    band musicians, **7:**932–33
    chaein, **7:**985, 986
    folk musicians, **7:**983–88
    hwarang, **7:**930, 941, 984
    hyŏmnyulsa, **7:**893, 910
    itinerant troupes, **7:**879, 933, 939, 984, 988
    kagok singers, **7:**925
    kisaeng, **7:**893–95, 909–11, 945, 984–85
    kwangdae, **7:**814, 893–95, 897, 984–85
    p'ansori, **7:**898–900
    shamans, **7:**986–87
    toch'ang, **7:**968
    women, **7:**893–95, 945, 985
  Korean-American, **3:**977
  Kuna culture, chanters, **2:**643–44
  Kurdistan
    mitirp, **6:**745–46, 748, 749, 750
    of narratives, **6:**746–48
  Kyrgyzstan
    akin (also *manaschi*), **6:**844
    duwan, **6:**945

Laos, *molam*, **4:**340, 343, 361
Latino women, **3:**98
Latvia
  budeḷi, **8:**502
  vocal, **8:**115
Lombok, *pepaosan*, **4:**775
Low Countries
  amateur, **8:**523
  bagpipers, **8:**529
  hurdy-gurdy, **8:**532
Macedonia
  guslari, **8:**975
  Rom people, **8:**975–77, 979–80, 981–83
Madhya Pradesh, mendicants, **5:***725*
Maharashtra, **5:**727–28
  kīrtanakāra, **5:**106
Malaysia
  dalang, **4:**405
  theatrical, **4:**403
Malta, *gannej*, **8:**640–41
Maluku, *ngufa ngufa*, **4:**817
Mandinka people, *jali*, **1:**444
Maninka people, *jali*, **1:**444, 446
Maranao people, *pabubayok*, **4:**910
Maronite cantors, **6:**214–15
Martinique
  kadans musicians, **2:**917
  Tamil drummers, **5:**599
Mashriq
  qawwāl, **6:**545
  shā'ir, **6:**545
Mexico
  concheros, **2:**614
  danzantes, **10:**92–95
  depictions of, **2:**13–15
  gender of, **2:**57
  kinship and, **2:**58
  maestros cantores, **2:**656
  occupation and, **2:**58–59
  popular musicians, social backgrounds of, **2:**104–5
  social context of, **2:**55–57
Middle East, **6:**5–7
  professional musicians, **6:**303, 364
  women, **6:**19
minnesingers and meistersingers, **8:**146, 650, 726
Mīrāsī people, **5:**7, 273, 283, *283,* 763–66
Mixtec culture, *tejorones*, **2:**566
Mongol people, bards, **7:**1008, 1016
Montenegro, *guslar*, **8:**959, 961
Montserrat, musickers, **2:**924
Morocco
  Berber musicians, **6:**489–90
  Berber poets, **6:**485
  raysat, **6:**490
Mughal depiction of, **5:**305
Muslim, **4:**74; **6:**939–40, 945
  mu'adhdhin, **6:**153–55
Nepal
  Badi people, **5:**697
  caste musicians, **5:**697–700
  Damāi people, **5:**273, 697
  ethnic groups, **5:**701–2
  Gāine people, **5:**697, 698

Guruṅg *ghāṭu* dancers, **5:**703
studio musicians, **5:**706
New England, professional folk singers, **3:**158
Nicaragua
dance troupes, **2:**766
national institutions, **2:**766
North Africa, sub-Saharan Africans, **6:**435
North America
blackface minstrels, **3:**191, 615–16, 1133
bluegrass, **3:**160–68
celebrity, **3:**271
chansonniers, **3:**855, 1059, 1076, 1154–58, 1167–68
conjunto musicians, **3:**775–78
country music, **3:**77–81
disco dancers, **3:**229
ethnic music, **3:**827
field musicians, **3:**563
folk musicians, **3:**48, 147–48; female, **3:**94
harmonium players, **5:**581
pompom girls, cheerleaders, and drill teams, **3:**215
popular singers, **3:**195
professional, **3:**143
street musicians, **3:**864
tabla players, **5:**581
virtuosos, nineteenth century, **3:**537, 556
Norway
skalds, **8:**146, 423
spelemann, **8:**417
women instrumentalists, **8:**419, 421–22
Oman
muṭrib, **6:**682
women's *dān* groups, **6:**674, 677, *678*, 681–82
Ontario
Anglo-Canadian, **3:**1190–91
French-Canadian, **3:**1194
organ-grinders, **3:**59–60
Ossetian people, *kadeganag*, **8:**860
Pakistan
chogān, **5:**761
ghazal singers, **5:**749–50
hereditary professionals, **5:**749
northern, hereditary professionals, **5:**794–95
qāri (Qur'ān reciters), **5:**748
Qawwāl, **5:**748, 765
Palau, dancers, **9:**724
Palestine, **6:**1025
professional, **6:**585–86
Panama
cantalante, **2:**780
decimero, **2:**780
gran diablos, **2:**779
mejoraneros, **2:**777
revellín, **2:**780
segundas, **2:**780
Papua New Guinea
Baluan, **9:**602, 604
instrumentalists, **9:**246
Nissan dukduks and tubuans, **9:**632, *634*
Paraguay, **2:**462–63
galoperas, **2:**461
Peru
Afro-Peruvian genres, **2:**500

black dance masters, **2:**493
chunginos, **2:**479
harawiq, **2:**476
responseros, **2:**478
semiprofessional creole groups, **2:**500
tamborero, **2:**474, 475
tunantadas, **2:**479
Philippines
band musicians, **4:**862–63
church, **4:**861–62
epic singers, **4:**908
instrumentalists, **4:**866
mambabasa, **4:**845
onor, **4:**910
popular music, **4:**883–88
theatrical musicians, **4:**863–65
Poland
fiddlers, **8:**709
Rom people, **8:**276
Polynesia, **3:**1050–53; **9:**769–70
Portugal, in *fado* ensemble, **8:**116
Puerto Rico
cantaor, **2:**937, 939
trovador, **2:**937
Punjab (India)
rabābī, **5:**655
raggī, **5:**655, *656*
Punjab (Pakistan)
amateur, **5:**771
dāstāngoh storytellers, **5:**770
faqīr, **5:**769–70, *772*
garvivāliāṅ, **5:**769
gavayyā, **5:**766
ghazalgoh, **5:**766, 771
mendicants, **5:**769–70
professional, **5:**762, 763–71
puppeteers, **5:**769
Qalandar, **5:**769
sāīṅ, **5:**769–70, 772
sāzindā, **5:**766
Rajasthan, professional caste musicians, **5:**344–45, 640–42
rhythm and blues musicians, **3:**667–76
rock and roll, **3:**352–53
rock guitarists, **3:**111–12, 113, 358
rock musicians, **3:**551
Romania
cāluṣari, **8:***871*
lāutari, **8:**122, 873, 877
Rom people, **8:**277–79
Rom people
bear trainers, **8:**142–43, 280, *283*, 893, 950, 953
professional musicians, **8:**270–71
Roti, *manahelo*, **4:**799, 800–801
Rotuma, *hân mane'àk*, **9:**231
Russia
bardy, **8:**778
bylina singers, **8:**130
epic singers, **8:**764
poiushchii poet, **8:**776
raspevshchiki, **8:**765
skomorokhi, **8:**122, 770
starinshchik, **8:**121
St. Lucia, *chantwèl*, **2:**946
Sāmoa, *usu* (leaders), **9:**797

Saudi Arabia
rawi, **6:**667
shā'ir, **6:**653, 664, 665–67
Scotland, **8:**369–71
bards, **8:**362, 367, 370
pipers, **8:**368
Serbia, *guslari*, **8:***941*, 941–42
Shona people, **1:**752–53
Sindh
faqīr, **5:**753–54, 759
Manganihār people, **5:**181, 273, 281, *282*
singing families and groups, **3:**183–84
Slovakia
jokulatori, **8:**726
town trumpeters, **8:**727
Slovenia, **8:**914
Solomon Islands, Sirovanga people, **9:**655
South America
gender of, **2:**57
kinship and, **2:**58
occupation and, **2:**58–59
popular musicians' backgrounds, **2:**104–5
social context of, **2:**55–57
tropical-forest region, **2:**127–28
South Asia, **5:**273
bhāgavatar, **5:**270, 390, 515, 885
bhajan singers, **5:**401
buffoons, **5:**765
of classical Indian music, **5:**424
courtesans, **5:**407–8; British disapproval of, **5:**15, 122–23, 338, 374, 375
dancers, merits of, **5:**41
devadāsī (also *dēvadāsi*), **5:**211, 263, *263*, 386–87, 392–93, 400, 407–8, 409, 518, *518*, 521, 738, 872
devotional singers, **5:**251, 425–26
dhrupadīyā, **5:**169
drummers, merits of, **5:**41
family lineages of, **5:**8, 373, 377–78
film "playback" singers, **5:**420–23, 531, 538–39, 543, 555, 855, 950
film-studio musicians, **5:**535–36
fortune-tellers, **5:**488, 867, 870
ganika, **5:**408
gotipua, **5:**519–20
havelī saṅgītkār, **5:**401
huṛukīyā, **5:**305, 306
itinerant, **5:**5, 867, 884; instruments of, **5:**347, 350
jogī, **5:**488
jugglers, **5:**481, 484, 501, 640
kathakkaṛ, **5:**493
magicians, **5:**481, 484
mahari, **5:**519
medicine men, **5:**488
mēḷakkāran, **5:**387, 388
mixed-sex groups, **5:**273
narrative singers, **5:**7
nauṭaṅki, **5:***410*
nautch (*nāc*) dancers, **5:**122, *335*, *370*, 409, 561–62
niyukta, **5:**407
pakhāvaj, **5:**120
pāṭini, **5:**518
patronage and, **5:**398–99
popular artists, **5:**418–29

performers, South Asia (*continued*)
    Qawwāl, **5:**426, 644
    rājadāsi, **5:**518
    regional caste artists, **5:**397–406
    Sangītaratnākara descriptions of, **5:**35–36
    Sanskrit drama, stage director, **5:**26
    sārangī, status of, **5:**378
    snake charmers, **5:***1,* 345, 350, 365, *469,*
        488, 519, 640, 647, *648,* 670–71,
        732, 861, *897,* 899
    storytellers, **5:**401, 770
    studio musicians, **5:**527
    sūtradhāra, **5:**517
    tawāif, **5:**424, 476, 644–45
    virali, **5:**518
    whistlers, **5:**235
    women instrumentalists, **5:**8
    wrestlers, **5:**484
Spain
    flamenco musicians, **8:**596–600
    medieval Andalusian women, **6:**442, 443,
        444
Spanish-American, **3:**851
Sri Lanka, chant and drumming specialists,
    5:955, 960–61
Sulawesi, *to mábadong* dancers, **4:**807
Sumatra, **4:**602
    sintren, **4:**626
Sumba, *touta liyo,* **4:**789–90
Sunda, **4:**719–21
    dalang, **4:**706
    juru kawih, **4:**706
    kliningan, **4:**703, 725
    of *pantun,* **4:**712
    pasindén, **4:**704
    ronggeng, **4:**707–8
Surinam
    dalang, **2:**507
    dukun, **2:**507
    lèdèk, **2:**507
Sweden, fiddlers, **8:**439
Switzerland, *cantastorie,* **8:**695
Tahiti, *'arioi* troupes, **9:**229, 769, 875
Taino culture, *tequina,* **2:**847
Taiwan, age of, **7:**425
Takuu, *purotu,* **9:**839
Tamil Nadu
    community and itinerant musicians,
        5:905–6
    kōtti, **5:**918
Thailand, **4:**247
    chang saw, **4:**313
Tibetan
    a-lce lha-mo troupes, **5:**712
    mendicant musicians, **5:**711–13
Tonga, *vāhenga* dancers, **9:**351
transvestite, **5:**492–93, 515, 683, 685,
    770–71, 815, *815*
Trinidad and Tobago, chantwells, **2:**95–96,
    965
troubadours and trouvères, **6:**446, 448; **8:**72,
    146, 168, 199, 550, 726
trovadores, **3:**757–58
Turkey, **6:**757–58
    ağit singers, **6:***766*
    Alevi, **6:**796–98, 799

    ancient, **8:**40
    arabesk, **6:**258–59
    aşıklar, **6:**114–15, 762, 765–66, 771, 791,
        796, 799, 801–9, 844, 845
    bağlama virtuosos, **6:**789–92, 797–99
    çengiler, **6:**115, 812
    curcunabaz, **6:**812
    eğitim, **6:**77, 79
    hafiz, **6:**121
    halk hikayecileri, **6:**766
    köçekler, **6:**115, 116, 765, 779, 812
    of *makam,* **6:**55–56
    minstrels, **6:**80, 81–82, 83
    ozanlar, **6:**80, 81, 765–66, 796, 844
    soytarı, **6:**812
    tasbaz, **6:**812
    whirling dervishes, **6:**107–11
    zākirler dervishes, **6:**191
Turkic cultures, epic singers, **6:**345–46
Turkmenistan, *bagsy,* **6:**967–77
Tuva, *khöömeizhi,* **6:**982–84
Uighur people, **6:**989, 995
Ukraine
    kobzari, **8:***99,* 809, 813–16, 819, 820, 822
    lirnyky, **8:**143, 809, 813–16, *815,* 819,
        820, 822
    part-time specialists, **8:**809–12
    starchykhy, **8:**816
    startsi, **8:***813, 815,* 816, 818
    trembitary, **8:**812
    women, **8:**807–8
Uruguay, *murgas,* **2:**511
Uttar Pradesh, *birahā* singers, **5:**668–69
'Uvea, *pulotu,* **9:**809
Uzbekistan
    aşyk, **6:**967
    Bukharan Jews, **6:**916
    female entertainers, **6:**899
    yallachi, **6:**902
Venezuela, **2:**542
    guía, **2:**534
    maraquero, **2:**541
    paleros, **2:**536
Vietnam, **4:**452, 480
Waiāpí culture, **2:**162
Wales, **8:**353–56
    bards, **8:**146, 347, 348–49
    fiddlers, **8:**348
    harpists, **8:**347–48
Warao culture, **2:**198
Wayana culture, specialists, **2:**167
Wolof people, *gewel,* **1:**444
women
    in Afghanistan, **5:**809, 814–15; **6:**305
    Andalusian, **6:**12, 364, 370, 442, 443, 444,
        445–46
    in Arabian peninsula, **6:**20, 293–97,
        695–702; singing slave girls, **6:**20,
        293–96, 297, 360, 361, 364, 456
    in Bengali theatrical presentations, **5:**488
    in blues, **3:**96, 103–6, 578, 644, 707
    castes of, **5:**402–3
    in Central Asia, **6:**946
    in China, **7:**82, 171, 172, 252, 255, 269,
        363–65, 401–8, 421
    as church musicians, **8:**197

    in country music, **3:**79, 81
    courtesans: in Europe, **8:**199; in South Asia,
        5:15, 122–23, 338, 374, 375, 407–8
    dancers, **5:**407–9, 492, 495
    devadāsī (also *dēvadāsi*), **5:**211, 263, *263,*
        386–87, 392–93, 400, 407–8, 409,
        518, *518,* 521, 738, 872
    in Egypt, **6:**297–98
    European instrumentalists, **8:**197, 200
    in France, **8:**548
    of Hindustani music, **5:**205, 207, 466
    in Italy, **8:**607
    in Japan, **7:**601, 602, 648–49, 650–51,
        682, 687, 763–66
    in Karnataka, **5:**455
    of Karnatak music, **5:**103, 232, 385–86,
        388–89
    in Korea, **7:**893–95, 945, 985
    Latino, **3:**98
    of light classical genres, **5:**179, 373–74, 376,
        381, 409, 411
    in Middle East, **6:**19
    North American folk musicians, **3:**94
    in Norway, **8:**419, 421–22
    in Oman, **6:**674, 677, *678,* 681–82
    in orchestras, **3:**89
    Persian dancers, **5:**493
    in popular entertainments, **3:**95
    of popular music, **5:**381
    in Renaissance Europe, **8:**77
    in South Asia, **5:**8
    in Ukraine, **8:**807–8
    in Uzbekistan, **6:**899
Yap, dancers, **9:**732
Yemen
    mughannī, **6:**686
    nashshād, **6:**13, 689
    professional musicians, **6:**303
Yuma culture, **2:**599
Pergolesi, Giovanni Battista, **8:**618
"*Perico, El*" (*son*), **2:**606
periodicals. *See also specific titles*
    Africa, colonial, **1:**17–18
    Asian music, **3:**953
    on bluegrass, **3:**163
    Brittany, **8:**564
    Canada, **3:**246
    China, **7:**141
    Chinese music, **7:**136
    Corsica, **8:**573
    Czech Republic, **8:**733
    Egypt, **6:**233
    ethnomusicological, **4:**27, 701; **5:**57–58; **8:**20
    France, **8:**554
    Germany, **3:**885
    Israel, **6:**1061, 1062–63
    Japan, **7:**729
    on Karnatak music, **5:**213
    Korea, **7:**855
    Middle East, **6:**24
    nineteenth century, **3:**557
    Ontario ethnic newspapers, **3:**1060
    popular music, **8:**210–11
    on popular music, **3:**95–96
    rock, **3:**348; **8:**217
    Romania, **8:**885–86

Russia, **8:**783
Slovakia, **8:**733
Turkey, rock and pop, **6:**249
Ukraine, **8:**820, 821
Periplus (Hanno), **1:**74, 75, 635
Peristeris, Spyros, **8:**1025
Perkins, Carl, **3:**80, 353, 648
Perkins, Kathy, **3:**609
Perkins, Simeon, **3:**1070
Perlak (kingdom), **4:**600
Perlman, Itzhak, **3:**330, 942
Perlman, Marc, **4:**638; **10:**52
PERMIAS (Association of Indonesian Students), **3:**1011
Perna group, **5:**769
Pernot, Humbert, **8:**18
Perón, Juan, **2:**269
Perotin, **8:**71, 366
Peroz, **5:***784*
Perrone, Charles A., **2:**320, 321
Perry, Hubert, **2:***754*
Perry, Julia, **3:**610, 611
Perry Mason (television show), **3:**609
Perry, Matthew, **3:**969
Persen, Mari Boine, **8:**429
Persia. *See* Iran
Persian culture, in India, **5:**42, 77, 332, 346, 350, 374, 375
Persian Doctrine of Dastgah-Composition (Gerson-Kiwi), **6:**1059, 1062
Persian people. *See* Iranian people
Person, John, **8:**428
Persson, Åke, **8:**446
Peru, **2:**466–88, 491–502, 845. *See also specific peoples*
 Afro-Peruvian traditions of, **2:**491–502
 Amazonian region
  instruments of, **2:**476
  musical genres of, **2:**482
 Andean area, **10:**36–37
  instruments of, **2:**469–75
  musical genres of, **2:**476–81
 Andean migrants in urban areas, **2:**483–85
 archaeomusicological research in, **2:**7, 10–11, 467; **10:**100
 art music in, **2:**112–16
 Aymara-speaking peoples, **2:**205–23
 children's wakes in, **2:**422
 Chinese people in, **2:**84–85
 Christian holidays in, **2:**46
 coastal region, musical genres of, **2:**481–82
 early cities of, **2:**81
 geography of, **2:**466, 467
 historical accounts of, **2:**23
 history of, **2:**245, 357, 466–69
 iconographical record in, **2:**16
 immigrant clubs in, **2:**49
 instruments of, **2:**32, 33, 34, 35–36, 39, 468, 469–76, 492–93
 Japanese people in, **2:**86–87; **10:**99, 102
 Jesuits in, **2:**23
 Lima, **2:**467
  Andean music in, **2:**483–85
 mingas (work parties), **2:**36, 48
 musical genres
  carnaval (also *wifala; puqllay; araskaska; pumpín, pasacalle*), **2:**230, 473, 476

chicha, **2:**101, 102, 105, 484–85
cumbia, **2:**483
festejo, **2:**496–97, 501
folkloric, **2:**486–87
harawi, **2:**476
harp performance styles, **2:**474
hatajos de negritos, **2:**494–95, 501
haylli, **2:**476, 483
huayla, **2:**476
huayno (also *wayno*), **2:**59, 101, 133, 230, 477, 478, 483
kashwa, **2:**213, 476–77
kh'ajhelo, **2:**213, 215
landó, **2:**497–98, 501
marinera, **2:**475, 481, 483
muliza, **2:**477
nueva canción, **2:**486
polka, **2:**481
pre-Encounter, **2:**468
salsa, **2:**487
santiago, **2:**476
tondero, **2:**481
triste, **2:**477
tuta kashwa, **2:**478
vals, **2:**475
vals criollo, **2:**89, 101, 475, 481, 499–500
walina, **2:**476, 478
wanka, **2:**476
yaraví, **2:**473, 477, 483
zamacueca, **2:**498–99
music printing in, **2:**23
popular music in, **2:**415–17
population of, **2:**466, 482
Q'ero culture, **2:**225–31
Quechua-speaking peoples, **2:**205–23
religious processions, **2:***62, 118*
research on, **2:**487–88, 501–2
social organization in, **2:**482–83
sound recording industry, **2:**64
tropical-forest region of, **2:**123–35
Perú Negro, **2:***492, 498,* 501
Peruvian people, in Mexico, **2:**610
Perwer, Şivan, **6:**752
Pesch, Ludwig, **5:**231
peşrev, **6:**11, 80, 110, 114, 116, 118, 120–23, 126–27, 773
 Persian *pishdarämad* and, **6:**137
 rhythmic modes in, **6:**91, 194
 in Turkish military music, **6:**767
Pessanha, Ricardo, **2:**320
Pestalozzi, Johann Heinrich, **3:**275, 278
Petalangan people, **4:**600
Peteke (Paraguayan band), **2:**459
Petelo (Sāmoan comedian), **9:**235
"Peter Amberley" (ballad), **3:**157
Peter, Brigitte, **9:**983
Peter the Great Museum of Anthropology and Ethnography (St. Petersburg), **9:**22
Peter, Hanns, **9:**983
Peter Moon Band, **9:***997*
Peter, Paul, and Mary (musical group), **3:**316; **4:**885; **9:**167
Peters, Friday, **1:**376
Peters, Karl, **1:**635
Peters, Kun, **1:**381
Peterson-Berger, Wilhelm, **8:**444

Peterson, Bernard, **3:**618
Peterson, Daisy, **3:**1169
Peterson, Hjalmar, **3:**872
Peterson, Nicolas, **9:**47
Peterson, Oscar, **3:**1077, 1106, 1107, *1107*, 1169
Peterson, Richard, **3:**302
Peters, "Sir" Shina, **1:**483
Peters, Wilfred, Jr., **2:**678–79
Petipa, Marius, **5:**562; **8:**161
"*petit mari, Le*" (French song), **3:**1193
Petitot, Emile, **3:**392
Petrarch, **8:**573
Petrescu, Ioan D., **8:**886
Petri, Michala, **3:**1210
Petrie, George, **8:**393
Petrillo, James, **3:**263
Petritsi, Ioane, **8:**830
Petropoulos, Elias, **8:**1020
Petros the Peloponnesian, **6:**109
Petrović, Boško, **8:**157
Petrović, Radmila, **8:**25, 954
Petrucci, Ottaviano, **8:***104*
Petry, Carl F., **6:**21
Pettan, Svanibor, **8:**937
Petterson, Allan, **8:**445
Petun Indian nation, **3:**1078
Peurt-a-Baroque (musical group), **3:**1070
Pew Foundation, **3:**221
Peyroux, Simone, **9:***416*
Peyton, Dave, **3:**580
Phadali caste, **5:**476
Phalèse, Pierre, **8:**523
Phạm Duy, **4:**25
Phạm Thị Trân, Lady, **4:**447, 489
Phan, P. Q., **4:**127
Phango, Peggy, **1:**774
Phantom of the Opera (Lloyd Webber), **3:**198, 545
Phantoms (musical group), **3:**806
Pharaohs (musical group), **3:**1212
Phaulkon, Constance, **4:**225
phenomenology, **10:**121–24
 healing rituals, **1:**272–73, 280–83
 viscerality of music, **1:**282
Philadelphia International Records, **3:**228, 711
Philadelphia Orchestra, **3:**537
Philbin, Regis, **3:**107
Philby, St. John, **6:**21
Philharmonic Choir (Israel), **6:**1030
Philharmonic Orchestra (England), **8:***81*
Philharmonic Organization of Havana, **2:**838
Philharmonic Society (minstrel troupe), **1:**765
Philharmonic Society of London, **8:**102
Philip II, king of Macedonia, **8:**972
Philip III, king of Spain, **2:**362
Philip Glass Ensemble, **3:**254
Philippine Educational Theater Association, **4:**885
Philippine Performing Arts (Florida), **3:**1025
Philippine Sociological Review (periodical), **4:**29
Philippine Suite (Tapales), **4:**873
Philippine Women's University, **4:**875
Philippines. *See also specific peoples*
 Americans in, **3:**1024; **4:**859–60, 864, 869–71, 883

Philippines (*continued*)
Austronesian languages of, **4:**529; **9:**715
Chinese influences in, **4:**73
composition in, **4:**130
concerts and recitals in, **4:**857–58, 870–71, 876
Cordillera highlands, **4:**878, 906, 913, 914–20, 927, 928
cultural origins of, **4:**10–11
dance in, **4:**854
foreign influences in, **4:**56
geography of, **4:**2, 594, 839, 913
gong-chime ensembles in, **4:**596
highland groups, **4:**58
history of, **4:**839, 841–42, 889
Hoabinhian culture, **4:**34
instrumental music in, **4:**858–60
instruments of, **9:**717
Islam in, **4:**74, 78–79, 889–911
Japanese occupation of, **4:**873–74, 883
Luzon, **4:**839
Manila, **4:**5
bands in, **4:**859
theaters in, **4:**856
map of, **4:***840*
Marinduque, **4:**839, 846, 851–52
Mindanao, **4:**79, 889, 913, 920–21
epics of, **4:**907–8
geography of, **4:**891–92, 896
instrumental music in, **4:**891–98, 901–6, 921–26
vocal music in, **4:**906–11, 927
Mindoro, **4:**839, 913, 920–21
musical genres (*See also* vocal music *heading*)
art music, **4:**868–82
bago, **4:**897
barikata, **4:**902
Christian, **4:**842–49
falliwes, **4:**915
gangsa topayya, **4:**916
kulintang, **4:**20, 21, 894–96, 897
kulintangan, **4:**900
kuriri, **4:**898
lellang, **4:**900
linggeng, **4:**924
marcha, **4:**856
minuna, **4:**896
pasodoble, **4:**846, 847, 856, 869
patriotic music, **4:**871–72
pattung, **4:**916–17
punebre, **4:**846, 847, 856
sambulayang, **4:**901
semagi genres, **4:**922
serangsang, **4:**924
sinaguna, **4:**896, 902
takik, **4:**915–16
te-ed, **4:**898
titik jin, **4:**900
titik tabawan, **4:**900
titik tagunggu, **4:**900
titik to'ongan, **4:**901
turambes, **4:**924
musical life
1800s, **4:**853–66
1900s, **4:**868–82
music research on, **4:**27, 29

Northern Luzon (*See* Cordillera highlands)
opera in, **4:**857, 863, 865, 868, 869, 871, 885
Palawan Island, **4:**905, 913, 920–21, 924, 927–28
pedagogy in, **4:**123
politics and war in, **4:**94
popular music in, **4:**8, 883–88
pre-Christian traditions in, **4:**839, 841
prehistoric, **4:**33, 34, 37–38, 42, 43, 56, 913
prehistoric art, **4:**44
regionalism in, **4:**117
representative music of, **4:**23, 135
research on, **4:**872–73, 875, 891
revival movement in, **4:**126
rice cultivation in, **4:**48
Roman Catholicism in, **4:**85
salient musical features of, **4:**20–22
sound recording production in, **9:**161
Spanish in, **4:**841–42, 857, 865, 890, 913
Sulu Archipelago, **4:**79, 889, 913, 924
epics of, **4:**907–8
instrumental music of, **4:**833, 891, 898–906, 921, 927–28
vocal music of, **4:**906–11
tourism in, **4:**139, 881
upland peoples, **4:**594, 913–28
musical styles, **4:**927–28
urbanization of, **4:**115
village life in, **4:**6
Visayan Islands, **4:**839
vocal music, secular, **4:**849–53
Western music in, **4:**7, 85–86
Yaqui Indians in, **3:**437
Philips, T. K. E., **1:**216, 230, 233
Phillips, Ekundayo, **1:**18, 19, 36–37, 405–6
Phillips, Nigel, **4:**603
Phillips, Sam, **3:**351
philology, **2:**21–22; **8:**18
philosophy. *See also* aesthetics; cosmology; ideology; *specific schools*
China, **7:**81–82, 88, 97–104, 319, 391–93, 462; **10:**22
ethics
Greek views on, **6:**19
Iranian views on, **6:**857
Islamic *ta'hīr* doctrine, **6:**177
role of epic performance in, **6:**952
gnosticism, **6:**186–87
Greek, **6:**19, 181, 367, 540–41
Japan, **7:**545–55
Jewish medieval, **6:**19
Korea, **7:**813–16
Muslim medieval, **6:**19, 367–69
Nigeria, *oboratze* concept, **1:**103
South Asia, **5:**34
Sufi, **6:**61
Phimmasone, **4:**346
Phippard, John, **3:**1141–42
Phiri, Ray, **1:**779
Phoebe Hearst Museum (Berkeley), **3:**414, 416, 418, 496
Phoenicians, **1:**533
in Corsica, **8:**566
in North Africa, **6:**431
in Sardinia, **8:**631–32
in Spain, **8:**588

Phoenix Islands (Kiribati), **9:**758
Phonogram Archives (Jerusalem), **6:**1029
Phonogrammarchiv der Österreichische Akademie der Wissenschaften, **6:**1057; **8:**18, 937; **9:**982–84
Phonothèque Nationale (Paris), **8:**18, 574
Phoon Yew Tien, **4:**523
Phoxay Sunnalath, **4:**26
Phra Apai Mani (Sunthon Phu), **4:**257, 306
Phra Chen Duriyanga (Peter Feit), **4:**26, 223, 330–31
Phra Pin-klao, **4:**230
Phrygians, **8:**39
Phuan people, **4:**218, 322, 338, 347, 529
Phulambrikar, Krishnarao, **5:**424, 536
P'ungmu (Yi), **7:**957
P'ungmul (Kim), **7:**960
Phùng Nguyên culture, **4:**36–37
Phuthai people, **4:**218, 316, 322, 338
Phya Anuman Rajadhon, **4:**223
Pi (Kim), **7:**957
PIA Arts Academy, **5:**746
Piae Cantiones, **8:**481
Piaf, Edith, **8:**209
Piamenta Brothers, **3:**943–44
Pian, Rulan Chao, **10:**20–21, *22*, 24
Piano (film), **9:**46
Pianoi culture, **2:**164
pianos, **8:***85*
Algeria, **6:**407
American manufacture of, **3:**239
Aotearoa, **9:**937
Arabian peninsula, **6:**715–16
in Arab music, **6:**421
Argentina, **2:**273
arrangements of orchestral music, **8:**54–55
Bolivia, **2:**298
Brazil, **2:**305
Burma, **4:**388, 390
Canadian manufacture of, **3:**246, 1067, 1116, 1148, 1183
Chile, **2:**360
China, **7:**388
Colombia, **2:**397
Costa Rica, **2:**694
Cuba, **2:**834
Denmark, **8:**455, 457
development of, **8:**82
Egypt, **6:**548, 610
El Salvador, **2:**708
England, **8:**331
Estonia, **8:**494
Finland, **8:**479
Goa, **5:**737
Greece, **8:**1020
Hawai'i, **9:**925
in Iranian *radif*, **6:**863
Ireland, **8:**390
Jamaica, **2:**901
Japanese manufacturers, **7:**537
Lebanon, **6:**554
Madagascar, **1:**783
mass production of, **3:**95
Mexico, **2:**603, 619
North America
in *banda orquesta*, **3:**779

in bluegrass music, **3:**1258
in blues performance, **3:**638, 642, 646, 647
in churches, **3:**119, 125, 874
in Danish music, **3:**882
in German music, **3:**889
in gospel music, **3:**535, 585, 631
in Irish music, **3:**842
in Norwegian music, **3:**868
as parlor instrument, **3:**190, 561–63, 936
in polka bands, **3:**891, 893, 894, 897
in quadrille band, **3:**232
in rock and roll, **3:**348
in salsa, **3:**788
Shaker use of, **3:**135
in Slovak dance bands, **3:**900
in *tamburitza* orchestra, **3:**920
in Tejano music, **3:**772
Norway, **8:**422
Ontario, in folk music, **3:**1190, 1194
player piano, **3:**239, 257, 259–60, 276–77, 1183; **8:**694
prepared, **3:**954
in *rebetika* ensembles, **8:**206
Russia, **8:**767
Scotland, **8:**365, 368
South Africa, **1:**762, 767–78
South America, **2:**114, 115
South Asia
  in film music, **5:**535, *537,* 544
  in Hindustani music, **5:**82
Switzerland, **8:**689
in Tunisian *ma'lūf,* **6:**327
Wales, **8:**353
women performers of, **8:**200
Pianta, Bruno, **8:**622
Piaroa (Wothuha) culture, **2:**525
Piartal culture, **2:**413
  archaeomusicological studies of, **2:**7
Piasah, **1:**356
Piatnitsky, Mitrofan, **8:**774
Piazzolla, Astor, **2:**264; **7:**972
Picadilly Boys (musical group), **3:**794
Picaflor de los Andes, **2:**484
Picard, Bernard, **2:**13
Picasso, Pablo, **8:**161, 309
piccolo. *See* flutes
Piccukaguntlu singers, **5:**901
Piché, Jean, **3:**1076
Piché, Paul, **3:**1160, 1162
Pichel, Wenzel, **8:**881
Picken, Laurence, **4:**323; **7:**42–43, 595
Pickering, Michael, **8:**339
Pickett, Wilson, **3:**710
Picon, Molly, **3:**938, *938*
Picts, **8:**40, 366
Pictures at an Exhibition (Emerson, Lake and Palmer), **8:**219
Picu, Nicolae, **8:**882
Piekha, Edita, **8:**779
Pierce, Franklin, **3:**307
Pierce, Webb, **3:**80
Pierpont, John, **3:**597
Pierre Rassin Orchestra, **2:**916
Pieśni ludu polskiego (Kolberg), **8:**712
Pietism, **3:**867, 870, 904
Pietsch, Rudolf, **8:**937; **10:**164

Pigafetta, Antonio, **2:**250; **4:**839
Pigeaud, T., **4:**634, 636, 645
Pigeon Inlet Productions, **3:**1071, 1125
Pigot, J. E., **8:**393
Piggott, Vincent, **4:**36
Pike, Andrew, **9:**1008
Pikunche culture, **2:**357
Pilagá culture, **2:**251
Pilapil, Father Mariano, **4:**843
Pilbara people, **9:**326
Pileni (Solomon Islands), **9:**833
Pilgrim, Philip, **2:**447
Pilgrims, **3:**831
Piliso, Ntemi, **1:***771,* 774, 779
Piḷḷai (caste suffix), **5:**387
Pillay, Savatri, **5:***616*
Pills to Purge Melancholy (D'Urfey), **8:**17
Pilolevu, princess of Tonga, **9:***125,* 351–52
Pima culture, **2:**596
  matachín dance of, **2:**593
Pima Indian nation, **3:**428, 433, 435–36
  instruments of, **3:**475, 477
"*Pimienta, La*" (*habanera*), **3:**791
Pin Chao Luo, **3:**959
Pinari (SamulNori), **7:**966
Pindar, Islene, **3:**1021
Pineaha, Kahu, **9:**938
Pineda, Alonso de, **3:**770
Pineda, Fortunato, **4:**865
Piñeiro, Ignacio, **2:**835; **3:**788, 792
Piñeros Corpas, Joaquín, **2:**398
Pines, Jim, **2:**913
Pingelap Atoll (FSM), **9:**739
Pinghu qiuyue (*Jiangnan sizhu* piece), **7:**225
Pinghu qiuyue (Lü), **7:**219, 220
Pinipel (Pinipir) Atoll (Papua New Guinea), **9:**632
Pink Floyd (musical group), **3:**356; **6:**248, 250; **8:**215
Pink Lady (musical group), **7:**747
Pink Panther (film), **3:**203
Pinnell, Richard, **2:**320
Pino, Geraldo, **1:**483
Pinochet, Augusto, **3:**730
Pinochet Ugarte, Augusto, **2:**90, 103
Pinon, Roger, **8:**535
Piñón, Salvador, **4:**868
Pinson, Jean-Pierre, **3:**1147
Pinto, Joaquín, **2:**422
Pintupi people, **9:**433, 452, 467
Piobaireachd Society, **8:**368
Pioneers (Weinberg), **6:**1026
pipa. *See* lutes
P'i pada (North Korean opera), **7:**946, 962–63, 992
Pipapu (Hua), **7:**133
Pipa yin (Cantonese tune), **7:**217
Pipers and Dancers Association of New Zealand, **9:**115
Pipers' Club (Dublin), **8:**390
Pipes and Drums of the Pacific Islands Regiment, **9:**135–36
Pipkov, Lyubomir, **8:**905
Pîr Adil Çelebi, **6:**108
Pir 'Omar, **6:**889
Pir, Rafi, **5:**487

Pirak, Lars, **8:***302*
Pirates, or The Calamities of Capt. Bligh (pantomime), **9:**34
p'iri. See double-reed instruments
P'iri hyŏpchugok (Park), **7:**957
Piriaki (musical group), **3:**1199
Pirkova-Jakobson, Svatava, **3:**826
Pisni imigrantiv prostaryi I novyi krai (Fedyk), **3:**1088
Piščaci (musical group), **8:**920
pistola y el corazón, La (Los Lobos), **3:**751
Piston, Walter, **3:**175
Pitcairn Island, **9:**951
Pitch Black Follies, **1:**771
"Pithecanthropus Erectus," **3:**662
Piti people, **1:**289
Pitjantjatjara people
  dance, **9:**451–52, 464
  musical concepts of, **9:**433–35
  songlines, intervals in, **9:**292–93
Pitman, Jack, **3:**1050
Pitraji (deity), **5:**645
Pittsburgh Symphony Orchestra, **3:**537
Piva people, **9:**644
Pixinguinha (Alfredo da Rocha Viana), **2:**305, 350
Piya Kiya To Darna Kya (film), **5:**540
Pizarro, Francisco, **2:**400
P. J. Meertens Institute, **8:**534
Plá, Josefina, **2:**464
Plaatjie, Solomon, **1:**764
Plain-Chant for America (Still), **3:**609
Plainfield Village Gamelan (Vermont), **3:**1018
Plains Cree Indian nation, **3:**440, 1086
Plains Indian nations, **3:**440–50, 1085–87. *See also specific groups*
  ceremonies of, **3:**11, 477
  dances of, **3:**222, 371
  drum manufacture, **3:**238
  early contact with Europeans, **3:**440, 441–42
  Ghost Dance movement, **3:**11, 487
  history and culture of, **3:**440–44
  instruments of, **3:**472–79
  men's organizations, **3:**480
  music of, **3:**445–46
  performance contexts, **3:**446–49
  powwows, **3:**211, 446–48, 480–84
  recordings sources, **3:**449
  relations with Athapaskans, **3:**384
  research on music of, **3:**444–45
  song sources, **3:**369
  sound recordings of, **3:**291
  vocal music of, **3:**5, 368–69
"Plains of Waterloo" (ballad), **3:**1124
Plains Ojibwa Indian nation, **3:**440, 1086
Plakun Trava (Tarasoff), **3:**1270
Planalp, Jack, **5:**674
Planet Drum (Hart), **3:**338, 339
Planet of the Apes (film), **3:**204
"Planet Rock" (Afrika Bambaataa), **3:**689
Plankerdown Band, **3:**1071
Plant, Robert, **3:**111, *111,* 112–14
Planxty (musical group), **3:**846; **8:**392
Plastic People of the Universe (musical group), **8:**730–31

Plato, **6:**16, 19, 180, 181, 368, 540–41, 835; **8:**46, 48
Platters (musical group), **3:**672; **4:**884
Play of Daniel, **6:**1030
"Play That Funky Music" (Wild Cherry), **3:**712
Playa Sound, **9:**997
Playford, John, **3:**832; **8:**17, 165
Playford (firm), publication of Scottish tunes, **8:**372
Please Hammer Don't Hurt 'Em (Hammer), **3:**715
"Please Mr. Postman" (Marveletts), **3:**674
"Please, Please, Please" (Brown), **3:**678
Pleasure Dome of Kubla Khan (Griffes), **3:**174
Pleazers (musical group), **9:**167–69
Plebs, Milena, **2:**44, 265
plena. See bomba/plena
Plevitskaya, Nadezhda, **8:**776, 777
Pleyel, Ignaz, **3:**180
Plotkin, Mark J., **2:**504
Plow that Broke the Plains (Thomson), **3:**14
Plúmm (musical group), **8:**472
Plummer, Levi S., **3:**127
Plunkett, Al, **3:**1080
Plunkett, Merton, **3:**1080
pluriarcs
    agwado, **2:**438
    chihumba, **1:**714
    Gabon, **1:**661–63
    gbegbetêle, **1:**467
    Nkhumbi people, **1:**714
    nsambi, **1:**667
    West Africa, **1:**445
Pnong people, **4:**154, 157
Pober, Leon, **3:**1050
Poblete, Pascual, **4:**871
Pöch, Rudolf, **9:**479, 983
Pococí culture, **2:**681
Pocomía, **2:**688
Podolak, Mitch, **3:**1233
Poe, Edgar Allan, **3:**595
"Poem for Bali" (Carlos), **4:**132
Poetic Edda, **8:**405
Poetics (Aristotle), **6:**16
Poétiques de la chanson traditionnelle française (Laforte), **3:**1167
poetry. *See also mawwāl; muwashshaḥ; qaṣīda; songs, texts; zajal*
    Afghanistan, **5:**823–24
        falak, **5:**828
        ghazal, **5:**805, 818, 828, *829*
        kharābāt, **5:**828
        Pashtun, **5:**833–37, 840–41
    Africa, panegyric, **1:**491–92, 493
    Algeria, *ḥawzī*, **6:**472–73
    Andalusian, **1:**535; **6:**443–44, 447–48, 454, 540
    Arabian peninsula, **6:**663–69
        dance accompaniment to, **6:**705, 707, 709
        al-sāmirī, **6:**709, 710
        ṣawt genre, **6:**652
    Arabic, **1:**606; **6:**173, 301, 396–97, 540, 651, 652, 663–69, 696
        'aṭaba, **6:**283, 545
        collections of, **6:**363, 370–71
        didactic, **6:**366, 367

epic rhyme schemes, **6:**342–43
improvised genres, **3:**1035
influence on European forms, **6:**24
meter in, **6:**9, 17, 313, 387, 389, 944
Argentina, **2:**262
    payada, **2:**495
Azerbaijan, **6:**922, 924, 928, 931
    aşıq, **6:**845–46, 851–52, 929
    dastanlar, **6:**930
Bali, **4:***140*, 731, 751, 756
    tembang, **4:**756
Balochi, **5:**776
    shēr, **6:**881
bedouin peoples, **6:**409
Bellona, **9:**850, 851
Bengal, **5:**845, 850–51
Berber, **6:**274, 301, 485, 490
Binandere people, metaphor in, **9:**359–60
Bolivia, Quechua, **2:**296
Borneo, *pantun*, **4:**827
Brazil
    cantoria, **2:**324–27
    sextilha, **2:**326–27
Brittany, **8:**561
Bulgaria, **8:**903
Burma, **4:**383
Burundi, **1:**198
Cameroon, **1:**660
Caribbean, *décima*, **2:**795–96
Central Asia, **6:**901
Chagatay Turkic, **6:**914
    meter in, **6:**9
Chile
    cogollo, **2:**368
    copla, **2:**369–70
    décima, **2:**368
    pareado, **2:**369–70
    quintilla, **2:**368
    romance, **2:**367, 368
    seguidilla, **2:**369–70
    tonada, **2:**368
    verso, **2:**367
China
    ci, **7:**129–30, 132, 407, 867
    collections of, **7:**132
    in narraatives, **7:**248
    northwestern minorities, **7:**463
    settings of, **7:**153–54
    Song dynasty, **7:**402
    Tang dynasty, **7:**129, 163, 402
    xinshi, **7:**346
Colombia, **2:**394
    copla, **2:**389–91, 398
    décima, **2:**408
    romance, **2:**389–90
Corsica, *currente*, **8:**568, 573
Costa Rica
    bomba, **2:**695–97
    retahila, **2:**695
Croatia, **8:**933
    deseterac, **8:**927
Cuba
    cuarteta, **2:**823
    décima, **2:**823, 833
Cyprus, **8:**1030
Dai people, **7:**506

Dominican Republic
    décima, **2:**849, 861
    poesía coreada, **2:**859
Eddic, **8:**405, 423
Egypt
    for *inshād*, **6:**167
    sīra, **6:**628
    used in bedouin dances, **6:**624
England, **9:**39
Europe
    formes fixes, **8:**72
    Renaissance, **8:**77
    stichic composition, **8:**129
    troubadour, **6:**446, 448
Fiji
    meke, **9:**775
    meke ni yaqona, **9:**176–77
    serekali and *vucu*, **9:**778–79
France
    chanson en laisse rhyme scheme, **8:**540–41
    medieval, **6:**24
Gabon, **1:**660
Georgia, **8:**832, 838
German, chamber settings of, **8:**83
Germany, **8:**646
Greece, **8:**1021
    Crete, **8:**1014, 1015
    mainland *vs.* island types, **8:**1009
Gujarat, *rāso* structure, **5:**635
Guyana, **2:**447
    calypso, **2:**445–46
Hausa people, **1:**451
    meter in, **6:**9
Hawai'i, **9:**299, 325–26
    art, **9:**923–25
    mele genres of, **9:**915, 920–21
    mele hula 'āla'apapa, **9:**917
    Puerto Rican *décimas*, **9:**101
    shigin, **9:**97
Hebrew, **6:**1036, 1038
    meter in, **6:**9
Hindi, **3:**1246–47
Hindu devotional, **5:**247, 250, 665–66
Hmong people, **3:**1003
Honduras, *copla*, **2:**744
Hungary, **8:**737
Icelandic, **3:**1251
    lausavísur, **8:**143, 402, 407, 408
    sléttubönd, **8:**402, 407
India, South, *śloka*, **5:**104, 107, 218
Iran, for *radif*, **6:**135–36, 140–41, 867
Iraq, for *maqām*, **6:**311, 313
Ireland, **8:**378–82, 393
Irian Jaya, Asmat people, **9:**591
Israel, **6:**266
Italian *stornello*, **3:**861
Italy, **8:**607–8
Jamaica, chanted genres, **2:**98
Japan
    haiku, **7:**555
    hauta, **7:**647
    kudoki, **7:**601
    renga, **7:**639
    saibara, **7:**625
    tanka, **7:**555
    waka, **7:**607, 768

Java
  parikan, **4:**667
  pupuh, **4:**711
  tembang, **4:**632, 659
  wangsalan, **4:**666
Kannada, **5:**220
Kashmir, *nande baeth*, **5:**684
Kazakhstan
  epic songs, **6:**953
  improvised, **6:**953–54, 955
  qara öleng, **6:**951–52
Khmer people, *yike* songs, **4:**201
Korea
  sa, **7:**867
  sijo, **7:**921–22, 924–27, 985
Kurdish, **6:**748, 840
Laos, **4:**342
  kon, **4:**346
Latvia, *apdziedāšanā*, **8:**502
Lombok, **4:**768, 775–76, 776
Madagascar, **1:**786
Malaysia
  Orang Asli, **4:**577
  pantun, **4:**423, 424, 435–36, 440
Malta, *spirtu pront*, **8:**636
Maluku
  pantun, **4:**813
  pantun saut, **4:**816
Mangareva, types of, **9:**886–87
Māori *mōteatea*, **9:**938–44
Mexico
  copla, **2:**606, 607–8, 610, 612, 613, 616
  décima, **2:**607–8, 612, 616, 795
  quintilla, **2:**608
  seguidilla, **2:**607
  sextilla, **2:**608
Mithila, **5:**677–78
Mongol people, **7:**1006–7, 1008–9
Morocco, **6:**485, 1044
  malhūn, **6:**496–97
Muslim
  devotional, **6:**437
  na't, **5:**278, 772
  qaṣīda, **5:**278, 284, 753, 827; **6:**458, 506, 563, 569, 626, 678
New Caledonia, assonance in, **9:**678
Nicaragua
  copla, **2:**757
  romance, **2:**758
North Africa, **1:**541–42
Norway, *stev* and *nystev*, **8:**134, 413, 426
Nusa Tenggara Timur, ritual oration, **4:**787
Oceania
  epigrammatic, **9:**331–32
  on kava, **9:**174–75, 176–77
  metaphor in, **9:**336–43
  metrics in, **9:**324–25
  phonemic play in, **9:**326–30
  rhyme in, **9:**325–26
  timbre in, **9:**297
Oman, **6:**675–76, 677–78
Oriya, **5:**731
Otopame culture
  copla, **2:**571
  décima, **2:**571
  valona, **2:**571

Pakhtun people, *dīvāni ghazal*, **5:**786
Pakistan, **5:**749
  kāfī, **5:**753–54
Palestine
  'atābā, **6:**409, 574–76, 577, 582, 584, 591
  āwīhā, **6:**582, 587, 591
  far'āwī, **6:**574, 575, 577
  ḥidā, **6:**584
  m'annā, **6:**588, 591
  murabba', **6:**574, 575, 577
  muthamman, **6:**575
  oral duels, **6:**573–76, 577, 584
  qarrādī, **6:**588, 591
  yā ḥalālī yā mālī, **6:**574
Panama, *décima*, **2:**772, 780
Papua New Guinea
  Banoni *tanisi*, **9:**646
  Buin *pia*, **9:**652–53
  Enga lyrics, **9:**535–36
  Foe people, **9:**514
  Foi people, **9:**246–47
  Huli people, **9:**538, 542
Persian, **6:**60, 61, 72, 120, 823, 825, 840, 914, 917
  in Azerbaijan, **6:**921–22
  dīwān, **6:**773
  meter in, **6:**9, 136, 137, 141, 829–30, 836, 944
Peru
  amor fino, **2:**495
  cumanana, **2:**495
  décima, **2:**495
Philippines, **4:**843–45, 850, 851
  pop ballads, **4:**885–86
Polynesia, **9:**768–69
  choreography and, **9:**307
  performed at kava ceremonies, **9:**202
Polynesian outliers, **9:**836
Puerto Rico
  copla, **2:**935
  cuarteta, **2:**938
  décima, **2:**935, 937–38
  decimilla, **2:**935, 937–38
Punjab (India), *bolī* couplets, **5:**500
Rajasthan, *duhā*, **5:**642
Romania
  cîntece, **8:**874
  strigături couplets, **8:**119, 165, 870
Roti
  bini, **4:**799, 800
  oration rituals, **4:**798
Russia, **8:**777
Ryûkyû Islands, **7:**791
Sāmoa, **9:**807
  solo, **9:**799, 803
  solo'ava, **9:**173
Sanskrit, **5:**105, 107, 249, 261–62, 520
  svarakṣara device, **5:**224
Saudi Arabia, contests, **6:**654
Scotland, **8:**367, 368
  lays, **8:**362
Serbia, *deseterac*, **8:**129, 941
Sikaiana, **9:**335
Singapore, *pantun*, **4:**520, 522
Society Islands, **9:**873
Solomon Islands, Bellonese songs, **9:**324–25

Somalia, **1:**125, 610–21
Sotho people, *sefala*, **1:**218
South Asia
  aesthetics and emotions in, **5:**317
  bhakti, **5:**263–64
  birahā, **5:**668–69
  ghazal, **5:**184, 548, 853
  marsiya, **5:**277
  meter in, **5:**20
  nauḥa, **5:**277
  padam, **5:**219
  stotra, **5:**261–62, 268
  theatrical presentations of, **5:**482
Southeast Asia, rural competitions, **4:**7
Spain
  Andalucían *zejel*, **2:**367
  coplas, **8:**591–92, 594, 598, 601
  cuarteta (also *copla de seguidilla*), **8:**592
  décima, **2:**540
  medieval, **6:**24
  romance, **2:**540
Sufi, **5:**687, 751–53, 756–60, 765–66, 769–70; **6:**132, 133, 149, 518, 543, 900, 914, 940, 943, 945
  ilāhī, **6:**193–94
Sulawesi, **4:**807
  pantun, **4:**806
Sumatra
  cang-incang, **4:**623
  pantun, **4:**604, 605, 606, 611, 615–16, 617, 618, 619, 620
  syair, **4:**615
  talibun, **4:**621
Sumbawa, **4:**763, 781, 782, 784
Sunda, *tembang Sunda*, **4:**714–15
Swahili, **1:**606
  meter in, **6:**9
Syria, **6:**568–69
Syriac, **6:**208–9
Tamil, **5:**105, 259–61, 437, 930
Tanzania, *taarab*, **1:**427–28
Thailand, **4:**298
  aeo sao, **4:**313
  klawn, **4:**325
  northeastern, **4:**321
  thet lae, **4:**293
Tibet, **7:**472
Tikopia, **9:**853
Tonga, **9:**783, 785
  lakalaka, **9:**789
  me'etu'upaki, **9:**790–91
  pō sipi, **9:**793
Trinidad and Tobago
  parang, **2:**960
  speech mas', **2:**965
Tuamotu Islands, **9:**882
Tuareg people, **1:**575, 593
Tunisian *ma'lūf*, **6:**506
Turkey, **6:**120, 796
  Alevi *deyişler*, **6:**790
  aşik, **6:**250, 765–66, 801–9
  folk forms, **6:**81–82
  mesnevi, **6:**769
  meter in, **6:**9
  strophic, **6:**115
  Sufi religious, **6:**107–11, 796

Volume Key: **6**, Middle East; **7**, East Asia; **8**, Europe; **9**, Australia and the Pacific Islands; **10**, The World's Music.

poetry, Turkey (*continued*)
　　türkü, koşma, and mani, **6:**762–63, 767, 768
　　Turkic, **6:**840
　　Tuvalu, **9:**830
　　Uighur people, *muqam* texts, **6:**1003
　　United States
　　　coplas, **3:**758, 759, 848, 849
　　　décima, **3:**757, 848, 849
　　　dub, **3:**1212–13
　　　psalms, **3:**831
　　　rap, **3:**699, 700
　　Urdu, **3:**1246–47; **5:**256
　　　meter in, **6:**9
　　Uttar Pradesh, *caubolā*, **5:**674
　　Vanuatu, **9:**361
　　Venezuela, *décima*, **2:**534, 544, 795
　　Vietnam
　　　ca huế, **4:**482
　　　ca trù, **4:**480–81
　　　nói lối, **4:**454
　　　phường vải, **4:**477
　　Wales, **8:**344–45, 349–50, 354
　　　declamation of, **8:**347, 348–49
　　　llatai concept, **8:**343
　　Yaqui culture, *corrido*, **2:**591
　　Yemen, **6:**651, 655, 711
　　　al-ghinā' al-ṣan'ānī, **6:**690
　　　ghazal, **6:**301, 685–86
　　　homaynī, **6:**685–86
　　Yuma culture, **2:**596
Pogues (musical group), **8:**226, 392
Pohlin, Marko, **8:**921
Pohnpei (Federated States of Micronesia), **9:**712, 739–40. *See also* Kapingamarangi
　alcohol use in, **9:**178
　dances of, **9:**719, 727, 728, 733, 739
　Europeans in, **9:**158
　geography of, **9:**726
　instruments of, **9:**717
　Japanese *bon* dance in, **9:**739
　Japanese in, **9:**29
　Kapinga people in, **9:**833, 836
　kava use in, **9:**172–76, 719, 740
　music and dance of, **9:**719, 739–40
　poetry, **9:**328
　　verbal meter in, **9:**324
　popular songs of, **9:**159
　research on, **9:**25
　settlement of, **9:**715
　songs of, **9:**739–40
　sound recordings from, **9:**994, 996
Pohöja (*tangak* piece), **7:**842, 867, 869
Pohösa, **7:**866
Poiana, Lou, **9:**82
Poirier, Lucien, **3:**1108
Poison (musical group), **3:**97, 357–58
Pokoman Maya, **2:**721
Pokot people, **1:**599, 605, 623
Pokrovsky, Dmitri, **8:**154, 757, 778
Poland, **8:**701–12
　art music in, **8:**710
　Ashkenazic Jews in, **8:**248
　carnival in, **8:**704
　Carpathian Mountains, **8:**707, 711
　　Rom people in, **8:**276

dance traditions of, **8:**703, 707–8, 710
ethnic minorites in, **8:**701
geography of, **8:**701
Goral culture in, **8:**717
Hasidic Jews in, **8:**254
history of, **8:**701
history of music in, **8:**709–10
independence movement in, **8:**187
instrument collections in, **8:**182
instruments, **8:**170, 704–8, 809–10
　research on, **8:**35, 38
Kieleckie, **8:**703
klezmorim performances at weddings, **8:**11
Kurpie, **8:**703
Małopolska (Little Poland), **8:**701, 703
map of, **8:**644
Mazowsze (Mazovia), **8:**701, 703
musical genres
　categories of, **8:**113–14
　old *vs.* new, **8:**122
Podhale, **8:**703, 706, 707, 710, 711
Pomerania, **8:**704
Pomorze (Pomerania), **8:**701
　religious songs, **8:**702–3
popular music in, **8:**205, 711
population of, **8:**701
research on music of, **8:**18, 19, 712
research on rhythm, **8:**23
rock in, **8:**220–21
Rom people in, **8:**272, 276–77
rule over Lithuania, **8:**509
Silesia, **8:**701, 707, 711
　wedding songs, **8:**131
Tatra Mountains, **8:**19
Ukrainian people in, **8:**810
vocal music of, **8:**113–14, 276, 701–4
Warsaw, cabaret in, **8:**252
Wielkopolska (Great Poland), **8:**701, 703, 707, 711
Żywiec, **8:**707
Polans, **8:**701
Polatov Wind Band, **8:**730
Poliakov family chorus, **8:**287
Police (musical group), **3:**357; **8:**215
Poligar chieftains, **5:**921
Polish people
　in England, **8:**336
　in Hawai'i, **9:**100
　in Mexico, **2:**613
　in North America, **3:**529, 891–96
　　Alberta, **3:**1249–50
　　Catholics, **3:**120
　　choirs, **3:**825
　　choral groups, **3:**891–92
　　community music-making, **3:**284
　　Detroit, **3:**517
　　Manitoba, **3:**343, 1088, 1249–50
　　Ontario, **3:**1078, 1082, 1197
　　polka styles, **3:**892–96
　　weddings of, **3:**892
　in South America, **2:**84
　in Ukraine, **8:**821
Polish Singers' Alliance of America, **3:**892
politics
　Afghanistan, **5:**489, 804–11, 816, 824, 834–35, 840–41

Africa
　arts and, **1:**7, 9, 15, 24–25, 30, 38, 43
　musicology and, **1:**59, 62–63
　sanctioned criticism, **1:**120, 287, 450, 710
　stateless societies, **1:**5
Albania, **8:**990, 1002
Algeria, **6:**271–72, 274
Antigua and Barbuda, **2:**800
Aotearoa, **9:**212, 947, 948–51
　cultural policies, **9:**169
　Māori, **9:**942–43
　popular music and, **9:**168
　songs of dissent, **9:**354–55
Arabian peninsula
　'Abassid era, **6:**354–55
　support of women's music, **6:**701–2
Argentina, **2:**52, 104
　cuarteto and, **2:**274
　cultural policies, **2:**263, 269
　music and, **2:**261
　tango and, **2:**263
Ashanti people, **1:**463–64
Australia, **9:**212
　Aboriginal ownership disputes, **9:**61–62
　Arnhem Land, **9:**47
　cultural policies, **9:**80, 87, 141, 143, 144–45, 228–29, 253–55, 414–15, 442–43, 462, 467
　immigration policies, **9:**85
　rock and, **9:**443–44, 445
　White Australia Policy, **9:**84
Austria, **8:**670, 671, 675, 677
Bahamas, **2:**801–2
Bali, **4:**731–33
Balkan region, **8:**867
Baluan, **9:**259
Bangladesh, **5:**503, 858–59
Barbados, cultural policies, **2:**819–20
Basque region, **8:**314–15
Belarus, **8:**796, 801–3
Belize, **2:**677
　cultural policies, **2:**676
Bengal, **5:**848–49
Berber peoples, **6:**274
Bolivia, **2:**205
　cultural policies, **2:**297
Brazil, **2:**52, 109, 317, 318
　cantoria and, **2:**326
　cultural policies, **2:**158
　Movimento Negro Unificado, **2:**352
　samba and, **2:**315–16
Bulgaria, **8:**220, 283, 891, *894*
　Bulgarization campaign, **8:**284
Burma, **4:**90, 398
　Shan State, **4:**548
Cambodia, **3:**998
　popular music and, **4:**207–8
　war in, **4:**11, 90–91, 118, 123–24, 151, 153–54, 187, 208–10
Canada, **3:**143
　cultural policies, **3:**18, 30–31, 72–74, 226, 247–48, 250–52, 265, 288–302, 1066–67, 1151, 1185
　foreign relationships, **3:**1060–62
　policies toward music conservation, **3:**290–93

policies toward music education, **3:**278, 302
policies toward music presentation, **3:**295–97, 297–301
policies toward popular music, **3:**314–15
Québec separatist movement, **3:**17, 313, 314, 1059, 1067, 1073, 1147, 1155–57, 1159, 1161–62, 1167
Caribbean, **2:**787, 791–92, 793, 795–96
Central African Republic, **1:**684, 686–87
Central America, **2:**630
Chechen people, **8:**861
Chile, **2:**52, 75, 90–91, 104, 373–74; **10:**81
China, **4:**337–38; **7:**17, 25–30, 32–36, 89–90, 379–90, 412–13
Anti-Rightist campaign, **7:**441
Boxer Rebellion, **7:**317, 379, 398
boycott of American goods, **7:**380
cultural policies, **6:**990; **7:**230–31, 413–14, 441–42, 499–500, 510–11
Cultural Revolution, **6:**995; **7:**47, 59, 63, 90, 102–3, 140, 141, 164, 201, 204, 255, 258–59, 294, 316–18, 333, 341, 349–50, 388, 413, 420, 441, 499, 510–11, 1006
Dai people, **7:**499–500
effect on scholarship, **7:**136, 138–39
effect on village traditions, **7:**316–18
Great Leap Forward, **7:**203, 204, 317, 341, 348–49, 441
Hundred Flowers movement, **7:**41, 961
Inner Mongolia, **7:**1005–6
musical institutions in, **7:**45–47, 59, 88, 396–99
"open door policy," **7:**90, 141, 359, 388–89
oral performance and, **7:**245–46, 253
repression of Cantonese opera, **7:**306
Taiping rebellion, **7:**305
Tiananmen Square demonstrations, **7:**367–68
Xinjiang province, **7:**468–69
Zhou dynasty, **7:**98, 101
Chuuk, **9:**734
Colombia, **2:**388, 397, 409
Corsica, **8:**566
election songs, **8:**571, 573
Costa Rica, **2:**681, 682
Croatia, **8:**933–35
Cuba, **2:**791, 796, 827, 828–29, 861
cultural policies, **2:**93, 828, 837–39
Cyprus, **8:**1029, 1032
Czechoslovakia, **8:**724, 729–31
Denmark, **8:**461
Dominica, **2:**840–41
cultural policies, **2:**841, 844
Dominican Republic, **2:**796, 861
cultural policies, **2:**104, 845–46
East Africa, **1:**600
East Asia, **7:**6
Ecuador, **2:**205
Egypt
cultural policies, **6:**560–61, 611–13
policies toward Nubian music, **6:**645
Umm Kulthūm's involvement in, **6:**599–600
El Salvador, **2:**716–17, 719
cultural policies, **2:**717

ethnomusicology and, **10:**148–49, 152, 163
Europe
ballads in, **8:**137
central, **8:**645
"ethnic cleansing" and, **8:**11
music and, **8:**184–85, 187–88
nationalism and, **8:**10, 16
rock and, **8:**216–22
social structures in, **8:**62
Faroe Islands, **8:**468, 470–71
satirical songs, **8:**471
Federated States of Micronesia, **9:**726
Fiji, **9:**773, 781
cultural policies, **9:**72
nuclear testing protests, **9:**211, 347
popular theater and, **9:**233
Finland, **8:**6, 147, 479, 482–83, 484–85
fourth-world cultures, **9:**212
France
cultural policies, **8:**549
support for African musicians, **8:**238
French Guiana, **2:**435
Futuna, **9:**814
Georgia, **8:**843–44, 851–52
German Democratic Republic, **8:**219–20
Germany, **8:**83, 659–62, 664
policy of liberal asylum, **8:**288
Ghana, **1:**389–90, 393, 396; **10:**33–36, 148–49, 152
Great Britain
bhangra and, **5:**575
rock and, **8:**215
Greece, **8:**1007, 1008, 1018, 1020, 1022, 1024
Grenada, **2:**864–65
Guadeloupe, cultural policies, **2:**879–80
Guam, cultural policies, **9:**745–46
Guatemala, **2:**91, 723
native American movements, **2:**81
Guyana, cultural policies, **2:**448, 450
Haiti, **2:**93, 792, 845, 885, 888, 892; **3:**805–6
cultural policies, **2:**887–88, 894–95
Hausa people, **1:**450, 518–19, 520
Hawai'i, **9:**212, 219–22
brass bands and, **9:**133–34
cultural policies, **9:**100–101, 109–10, 211–12
Hong Kong, **7:**431, 436
Hungary, **8:**736, 738, 746, 747–48
Iceland, **8:**400, 408
India, **5:**380
in films, **5:**544
independence, **5:**375–76
militant Hindu movement, **5:**552
"scheduled castes" in, **5:**9
state restructuring in, **5:**7, 15–16
Indonesia, **4:**83–85, 92–94
arts policies, **4:**86
cultural policies, **9:**191, 486–87, 591
relations with Surinam, **2:**507–8
social criticism, **4:**110
Inner Asia, **7:**29–30, 35
Iran, **6:**860–61
cultural policies, **6:**142, 823–24, 861–62
Ireland, **8:**388
musical idioms and, **8:**388, 393

Irian Jaya, **9:**560
cultural policies, **9:**578
Israel, **6:**264–66
cultural policies, **6:**1021, 1030
Italy, **8:**618–19, 620
Jamaica
reggae and, **2:**97
social protest, **2:**93
Japan, **7:**25–28, 535, 562
cultural policies, **7:**756, 761, 796
intangible cultural properties system, **7:**46–47, 784, 796
pop-folk movement, **7:**746
Java, **4:**633
support of Sundanese arts, **4:**116
Jewish Americans, **3:**939
Kenya, **1:**628–29, 631
Korea, **7:**25–28
Laos, **4:**89, 336, 343, 350, 353–54, 358, 360–61, 551
Latvia, **8:**505–6
Lithuania, **8:**512–14
Lombok
cultural policies, **4:**763, 765, 777–78
revolts in, **4:**764
Macedonia, **8:**972, 983
Madagascar, **1:**792
Malaysia, **4:**91–92, 426, 440–41
cultural policies, **4:**561–62, 579–84, 586
Maluku, **4:**815
cultural policies, **4:**821
Martinique, **2:**919
Mexico, **2:**616
cultural policies, **2:**567–68, 604–5, 619
independence period, **2:**603–4
native American movements, **2:**81
Micronesia, **9:**719
cultural policies, **9:**721
Middle Eastern embassies, **6:**21
Middle Eastern peoples, **3:**1035–36
Mongolia, **7:**1005–6
Morocco, **6:**274
Mozambique, **1:**429, 436
Native American leagues and confederacies, **3:**462
Nepal, **5:**705–6
New Caledonia, **9:**212, 213–14
Newfoundland, fishing moratorium, **3:**1138–43
New Guinea, **9:**472
Nicaragua, **2:**754, 758–59
cultural policies, **2:**663–64, 765–66
Sandinista period, **2:**754–55, 764, 765–66
Nigeria, **1:**407–9, 477–78, 483–84
North Caucasia, **8:**850, 851
North Korea, **7:**804
Flying Horse movement, **7:**961
Norway, cultural policies, **8:**429–30
Nusa Tenggara Barat, cultural policies, **4:**762
Nusa Tenggara Timur, **4:**786
Oceania
cultural policies, **9:**5, 55–59
foreign powers in, **9:**5
popular music and, **9:**126–27
theater and, **9:**234
World War II, **9:**25–33

Volume Key: **6**, Middle East; **7**, East Asia; **8**, Europe; **9**, Australia and the Pacific Islands; **10**, The World's Music.

politics (*continued*)

Oman, policies toward arts, **6:**681

Pakistan
cultural policies, **5:**744–49
Pashtunistan movement, **5:**834

Palau, **9:**181

Palestinian *intifāda*, **6:**635–40

Panama, cultural policies, **2:**784

Papua New Guinea, **9:**475
Buin people, **9:**650
cultural policies, **9:**153–54, 480
independence, **9:**148
kakaparagha, **9:**608
Maring people, **9:**514–15
Melpa people, **9:**518
New Britain, **9:**388

Paraguay, cultural policies, **2:**460

Peru, **2:**466–67, 486, 491, 502

Philippines, **3:**1025; **4:**94, 857, 865, 871–72,
885–86
arts policies, **4:**86
cultural policies, **4:**860
Japanese occupation of, **4:**873–74
revolutionary music, **4:**860

Pohnpei, **9:**739
kava and, **9:**176

Poland, **8:**221, 701, 709

Polynesia, **9:**768
outlier societies, **9:**836

Portugal, **8:**584–85
cultural policies, **8:**577

Réunion Island, **5:**610–11

Rom people, **8:**271–72, 279

Romania, **8:**882
homogenization policy, **8:**278
post-revolution, **8:**279

Rotuma, **9:**818

Russia, **8:**19, 767, 768, 776
Russification program, **8:**287

St. Lucia, **2:**942
cultural policies, **2:**946, 950

Sāmoa, **9:**215–19, 795
satire, **9:**235

Saudi Arabia, **6:**652, 654
cultural policies, **6:**23, 667

Scotland, protest music, **8:**364–65, 368, 371,
374

Serbia, Kosovo, **8:**1002

Sikaiana, **9:**846

Singapore, cultural policies, **4:**524

Slovenia, **8:**921

socialist governments, **8:**147, 211
suppression of rock, **8:**217–18, 219–20
suppression of Rom music, **8:**271, 278, 283,
284
use of folklore ensembles as propaganda,
8:152

Solomon Islands, cultural policies, **9:**963

Somalia, **1:**618–20

South Africa, **1:**776–78, 779–80

South America
cultural policies, **2:**245, 248
identity and, **2:**129
independence movements, **2:**242, 245
popular music and, **2:**92–93
rallies, **2:**50, 55
wars in, **2:**245

South Asia, **5:**14–16, 374
cassettes and, **5:**434, 551–52, 557
music and, **2:**60; **5:**431–38
partition and, **5:**403–4
princely states, **5:**4, 402

Southeast Asia, **4:**87–94, 365–66
Chinese incursions into, **4:**69
ethnic groups, boundaries, and, **4:**148
influence on music research, **4:**24, 27
influence on traditional music, **4:**119
prehistoric, **4:**39, 41
refugee peoples, **4:**529
wars in, **4:**11, 118

South Korea
democracy movement, **7:**809, 938, 959–60,
969, 997
intangible cultural properties system, **7:**47,
804, 808, 899–900, 911, 932, 938,
969, 976, 984, 988, 991, 993, 996–97

southern Africa, **1:**718–20

Soviet Union (former), **8:**84
cultural policies in Central Asian republics,
6:903–4, 915–17, 959–60
cultural policies in Tuva, **6:**986–87
glasnost, **8:**218–19

Spain, **2:**102; **8:**588, 598, 599

Sri Lanka, **5:**108, 971

Sudan, **1:**572

Sumatra, cultural policies, **4:**602, 627

Sumbawa, cultural policies, **4:**784

Sunda, **4:**700
patriotic songs, **4:**710–11
social criticism, **4:**717

Surinam, **2:**504, 509
relations with Indonesia, **2:**507–8

Sweden, **8:**446
administrative units of, **8:**437

Switzerland, **8:**683, 685, 698
cultural policies, **8:**697

Tahiti, **9:**867
cultural policies, **9:**56–57

Taiwan, **7:**356–58, 423–24, 429

Tamil Nadu, caste and, **5:**393

Tanzania, **1:**642–43

Thailand, **4:**91, 286, 296
arts policies, **4:**99–100
coup of 1932, **4:**249, 255, 331
social criticism, **4:**98–99, 332

Tikopia, **9:**853

Tokelau, **9:**824

Tonga
clothing and, **9:**351–52
Niua Islands, **9:**211
songs of dissent, **9:**354

Trinidad and Tobago, **2:**952–53, 963, 966
calypso and, **2:**96
during carnival, **2:**796
cultural policies, **2:**953

Tuareg people, **1:**578

Tunisia, **6:**437
policies toward art music, **6:**330, 505–13

Turkey, **6:**116, 243–44, 247, 248, 250–51,
252, 255, 781–87, 791, 796, 798
cultural policies, **6:**744
Tanzimat reforms, **6:**108, 757–58, 781

Ukraine, **8:**19, 806, 816–17

United States
African-Americans, **3:**13, 354, 606, 609,
617, 637, 656, 662–63, 667, 668–669,
672, 680–83, 685
Asian-Americans, **3:**948–49, 967–68, 970
campaign music, **3:**304–11
charity rock, **3:**341, 713
Chicanos, **3:**734, 749
Cold War, **3:**297–98
cultural policies, **3:**29–31, 58, 222,
288–302, 328, 513–14, 951; **10:**81–85
dance and, **3:**219
democracy *vs.* aesthetics, **3:**44
ethnic communities and, **3:**822
folk music revival and, **3:**13–14, 49, 94
Mexican farmworker movement, **3:**721–22
Native American rights, **3:**311–13, 491–99
Native Americans, **3:**442, 443–44, 467
nineteenth-century social reform, **3:**184
Pan-Indian movement, **3:**512
Pan-Latino movement, **3:**512
policies toward music conservation,
3:290–95
policies toward music education, **3:**278,
302
pre-Civil War, **3:**616
protest music, **3:**315–18, 520, 551,
600–601
relationship with Canada, **3:**1061–62
religion in, **3:**119
rock and roll opponents, **3:**354–55
tax policies, **3:**290

Uruguay, **2:**104, 516, 517–18, 521

Uttar Pradesh, **5:**667

Uzbekistan, cultural policies, **6:**905

Vanuatu
John Frum movement, **9:**214–15
Nagriamel movement, **9:**361–62
string bands and, **9:**139, 140
Tanna, **9:**706

Venda people, **1:**708–9

Venezuela, cultural policies, **2:**540

Vietnam, **4:**496, 497, 507
cultural policies, **4:**512–13, 515
influence on traditional music, **4:**129
revolutionary songs, **4:**510, 511, 514
satirical theater, **4:**489
wars in, **4:**446, 449, 497, 510, 529

Western Sāmoa, **9:**112

West Futuna, **9:**861

Yugoslavia (former), **8:**920, 1000–1002

Zaïre, **1:**671

Zambia, **1:**671

Zimbabwe, **1:**365, 432–33, 718–19, 756–57

Politis, Nikolaos, **8:**1024

Polk, James K., **3:**306–7

polka, **2:**71, 89, 100, 107, 114; **3:**149, 212, 232,
233, 529, 836, 850, 855; **8:**166, 168,
170, 228
in Argentina, **2:**256, 257, 269
in Austria, **8:**672, 674
band arrangements, **3:**874
in Belarus, **8:**792, 799
in Brazil, **2:**305, 313, 330, 331, 350
in Brittany, **8:**559
Cajun, **3:**857

in Canada, **3:**408, 1190, 1195, 1196, 1197, 1198
in Caribbean, **2:**795
Chicago-style, **3:**894
Croatian, **3:**921
in Cuba, **2:**835
Czech, **3:**897
in Czech Republic, **8:**721
Danish, **3:**882
in Denmark, **8:**457
development of, **3:**893
dissemination of, **8:**7
in Dominica, **2:**842
in Dominican Republic, **2:**860
"Dutchman" style, **3:**890–91
Eastern-style, **3:**893–94
in England, **8:**329, 330, 331
in Finland, **8:**483, 484
Finnish, **3:**874–75
in Guatemala, **2:**735
in Haiti, **2:**888
in Honduras, **2:**744
in Ireland, **8:**382
Irish, **3:**843
Italian, **3:**860, 861, 862, 865
in Jamaica, **2:**908
krakowiak and, **3:**893, 894
in Low Countries, **8:**524, 527
in Mapuche culture, **2:**236–37
meter in, **8:**9
Mexican-Hispano-Tejano, **3:**9, 213, 522, 723, 745, 755, 760, 773, 774, 775, 778, 779, 781
in Mexico, **2:**604, 613
in Netherlands Antilles, **2:**930
Newfoundland, **3:**1125
in Norway, **8:**419
Norwegian, **3:**868
in Paraguay, **2:**459, 461
Paraguayan, **3:**730
in Pennsylvania, **3:**821, 824
in Peru, **2:**481
for piano, **3:**190
Polish styles, **3:**892–96
recent trends, **3:**895
in Russia, **8:**766
in St. Lucia, **2:**945
Slovak, **3:**900
in Slovenia, **8:**920
Slovenian, **3:**901–2
in Spain, **8:**594
styles of, **3:**825–26
in Sweden, **8:**435–36, 443
Swedish, **3:**872
in Switzerland, **8:**690, 694, 696
Tohono O'odham, **3:**436, 473, 490
in Ukraine, **8:**812
Ukrainian, **3:**913, 914, 1088
in Uruguay, **2:**516, 522
Volga German, **3:**890–91
Polka Music Hall of Fame and Museum (Chicago), **3:**896
Pollak-Eltz, Angelina, **2:**865
Pollap Atoll (Chuuk State, FSM), **9:**737–38
Pollard, Maseelall, **5:**603
Pollux, Julius, **6:**360

"Polly Ann" (lang), **3:**109
polonaise, **8:**168
Polonnaruwa (kingdom), **5:**955
Polopa people, **9:**490
Polowat (Chuuk State, FSM), **9:**737
Pol Pot, **3:**219, 998; **4:**154
Polydor (record company), **5:**528; **8:**55, 678
PolyGram (record company), **2:**107; **3:**264, 270; **5:**548
Polynesia, **4:**38. *See also specific countries, islands, and peoples*
    cultural influences in Kiribati, **9:**762
    dance in, **9:**55
    East, **9:**865–67
    ethnic revival movement in, **9:**211–12
    European exploration of, **9:**7–20
    films on, **9:**1017–20
    geography of, **9:**768, 833
    history of, **9:**771
    instruments, **9:**372
       log idiophones, **9:**374
       nose flutes, **9:**393
       struck tins, **9:**379–80
    kava use in, **9:**172–74
    Lapita cultural complex in, **9:**4
    map of, **9:**772, 866
    metrical traits in, **9:**289
    multipart singing, **9:**307–9
    pan-Polynesian festival participation, **9:**65–66
    prehistoric, **9:**768, 771
    religion in, **9:**200–209
    sound recordings from, **9:**997–1006
    West, **9:**771–73
Polynesian Cultural Center, **9:**972
Polynesian music in North America, **3:**811, 1047–53
    tiki culture, **3:**1050
Polynesian outliers, **9:**598, 630, 671–72, 682, 702, 715, 833–64
    archaeology on, **9:**835
    map of, **9:**834
    prehistoric, **9:**835
    sound recordings from, **9:**1000–1001
polyphony. *See also* texture
    Abkhazian people, **8:**852
    Adighian people, **8:**854
    Africa, pentatonic, **1:**454
    Ainu people, **7:**785
    Aka people, **1:**268
    Albania, **8:**10, 14, 847, 990–92, 1010
    Armenian music, **6:**726
    in art music, **8:**68
    Austria, **8:**674
    Balkan region, **8:**134, 867
    Balkarian people, **8:**856–57
    Belarus, **8:**794–95
    Bosnia-Hercegovina, **8:**964
    Bulgaria, **8:**610
       Pirin region, **8:**895
       Shop region, **8:**896
    Chechen people, **8:**862
    China, minority cultures, **7:**449, 490
    Chuvash people, **8:**773
    Corsica, **8:**542, 566, 569–70
    Croatia, **8:**926, 930, *931*
    Czech Republic, **8:**719–20

Dan people, **1:**466
early New Mexican composers, **3:**755, 768
Estonia, **8:**492–93
Europe, Eastern, **8:**753
Europe, Western, **8:**517
Ewe people, **1:**463
France, **8:**542
Gã people, **1:**463
Georgia, **8:**827–30, *831–32*, 835, 836, 847
    church music, **8:**843
Germany, **8:**75
Greece, Epirus, **8:**10, 1010, *1010*
Iceland, **8:**399, 423
improvisation in, **8:**73
Ingush people, **8:**862
Irian Jaya, coordinate, **9:**583
Italy, **8:**610–11
    choral, **8:**610
    trallalero and *vatoccu* styles, **8:**134
Japan, syncretic music, **7:**779
Karachaevian people, **8:**856–57
Kasena-Nankani people, **1:**456
Korea, *sinawi*, **7:**891
!Kung people, **1:**307
Latvia, **8:**500–501
Lithuania, **8:**510
Macedonia, **8:**973–74, 995
Madagascar, **1:**783
medieval, **8:**49–50, 70–71
Montenegro, **8:**958
Mordvinian people, **8:**773–74
Naxi people, **7:**510
New Caledonia
    Grande Terre, **9:**675
    Ouvéa *seloo*, **9:**684
North Caucasia, **8:**851
Norway, **8:**423–24
organum, **8:**71
Ossetian people, **8:**859, 861
Papua New Guinea
    Abelam people, **9:**550
    Baluan, **9:**602
    Buka and Bougainville vocal music, **9:**630
    children's music, **9:**257
    five-part, **9:**331
    Halia songs, **9:**641–42
    Sepik Hills peoples, **9:**558
    vocal, **9:**491
    Waxei *lefen* genre, **9:**560
Philippines, **4:**841
Plains Indian peyote songs, **3:**445
Poland, **8:**705
    Carpathian region, **8:**703
Polynesia, **9:**307–9
    East, **9:**865
Portugal, **8:**578–79, 581
Pygmies, **1:**658, 659
Renaissance vocal, **8:**74, 75–76
Romania, **8:**879
Russia, **8:**756–58, *759,* 767
sacred and secular comparisons, **8:**145
San people, **1:**659
Sardinia, **8:**134, 145, 542, 570, 626, 627–28, *628,* 632
Serbia, **8:**942–43, 951
    Kosovo, **8:**995
Shona people, **1:**308

polyphony (*continued*)
Slovakia, **8:**719–20
Slovenia, **8:**610, 913
Solomon Islands
'Are'are songs, **9:**668
Fataleka and Baegu panpipe ensemble music, **9:**669
Guadalcanal, **9:**665
panpipe music, **9:**398, 630
Spain, **8:**600–601
Sweden, **8:**443–44
Taiwan, Aboriginal peoples, **7:**524
Tonga, **9:**14–15, 131–32, 784
Tuamotu Islands, **9:**884
Turkey, **6:**192–93, 775
Udmurt people, **8:**773
Ukraine, **8:**809
vocal, **8:**134
Yemen, **6:**99
Pom (Korean work), **7:**962
Pomaks, **8:**895, 896
Pombo, Rafael, **2:**394, 397
Pomeranians, **8:**701
Pomerantz, James, **5:**565
Pommer, Josef, **8:**19, 647, 664
Pomo Indian nation, **3:**371, 420
Pomory class, **8:**755
Pompili, Claudio, **9:**81
Ponape. *See* Pohnpei
Pona-wɛni (Liberian singer), **1:**9
Ponca Indian nation, **3:**440, 444, 446, 449
Ponce, Daniel, **3:**789
Ponce de León, José María, **2:**397
Ponce, Manuel M., **2:**604
Pondicherry, Karnatak tradition in, **5:**449
Pondler, Barry, **2:**754
Ponēke, Ngāti, **9:**277, 937
Pongjiga (Kim), **7:**970
Pŏngŏri Samnyong (television show), **7:**958–59
Pongsŏn Temple (Korea), **7:**959
Pongsŏnhwa (Hong), **7:**952
Ponhea Yat, king of Khmer, **4:**154
Ponnusvami Pillai, Madurai, **5:**392
Ponselle, Rosa, **3:**537
"Pony Time" (Checker), **3:**709
Poole, Charlie, **3:**78
Poole, Deborah A., **2:**480
Poonchwala, Sharif Khan, **5:**746
Poong Mool Nori (musical group), **7:**965
Poor Soldier (Shield), **3:**837
Pop, Iggy, **3:**357
Pop Mechanix (musical group), **9:**168
Pop, Mihai, **8:**886
Pŏpchi, **7:**981
Popoloca culture, **2:**563
Popol Vuh, **2:**650, 721–22, 732
Popo, Sundar, **5:**592
Popovich Brothers' Yugoslavian Tamburitza Orchestra, **3:**529
Popsicle label, **3:**169
popular music. *See also* bhangra; film music; rock; technology and music; *specific genres and performers*
Afghanistan, **5:**809–10, 818, 820, 827

Africa, **1:**415–37; **2:**75
cassette dissemination of, **1:**4, 367, 417, 420, 436, 533, 543
commercialization of, **1:**416–18
diffusion of, **1:**322
genres of, **1:**227
intra-African connections, **1:**436–37
African
European popularity of, **8:**208, 210, 225, 238–39
in Portugal, **8:**585
Albania, **8:**1002
Alberta, **3:**1091
Algeria, **1:**545, 547; **6:**269–72, 475–77
Anglo-American, **3:**838–40
Angola, **1:**435
Aotearoa, **9:**167–69, 931–32, 937–38
sound recordings of, **9:**999
Arab, influence on Sephardi music, **6:**201–2, 206
Arabian peninsula, **6:**667
mu'alleyā, **6:**651
Arctic peoples, **3:**73, 380
Argentina, **2:**263–68
cuarteto, **2:**273–80
Asian-American, **3:**951
Asian influences on, **3:**955
Australia, **9:**143–44, 413–14
Aboriginal rock, **9:**60–61, 144–46, 414, 442, 443–47
Hmong and Laotian bands, **9:**76
Latin American and Caribbean styles, **9:**83
music-hall songs, **9:**409, 413
rebetika, **9:**73–74
salsa, **9:**83
sound recordings of, **9:**987–89
use of didjeridu, **9:**394, 397
Austria, **8:**674–79
Austropop, **8:**676–78
volkstümlichemusik, **8:**671, 675–76
Bahamas, **2:**808
Bali, **4:**760–61
Barbados, **2:**819–20
Belarus, **8:**801
Belgium, **8:**208
Belize, *cungo*, **2:**678–79
Benin, **1:**422
Berber peoples, **6:**273–77
bhajan, **5:**255
blues as, **3:**643–44
Bolivia, **2:**297–98
Bosnia-Hercegovina, **8:**963, 969
Brazil, **2:**61, 107–11, 313–19
African traits in, **2:**340
Bribri and Cabécar cultures, **2:**635
British Caribbean peoples, **3:**809–11
British Columbia, **3:**1096
Bulgaria, **8:**903
Burma, **4:**398–99
Cambodian, **3:**999, 1002; **4:**207–8
Cameroon, **1:**323
Canada, **3:**296, 314–15, 1058, 1186
First Nations peoples, **3:**1063–64, 1279–81
nineteenth century, **3:**189
Caribbean, **2:**75–76, 796
age and preference issues, **2:**58
Anglophone areas, **2:**95–98

in Argentina, **2:**265–66
in Bahamas, **2:**802
in Barbados, **2:**819
in Bolivia, **2:**297
in Chile, **2:**371–72
in Costa Rica, **2:**693, 703
Francophone areas, **2:**95, 98
in Guadeloupe, **2:**879
in Guatemala, **2:**733, 734–35
in Honduras, **2:**744
issues in, **2:**92–93
in Martinique, **2:**920
in Mexico, **2:**622–23, 653
in Montserrat, **2:**923
in New York, **2:**796–97, 797
in Nicaragua, **2:**763
in Paraguay, **2:**463
in Peru, **2:**487
transnational influences on, **2:**75–77
in Uruguay, **2:**520
in Virgin Islands, **2:**969
Central Africa, **1:**216–17, 423–28, 681–87, 695–96
Central America
age and preference issues, **2:**58
issues in, **2:**92–93
transnational influences on, **2:**75–77
Central Asia, **6:**905
Chile, **2:**368, 372–74
China, **3:**964; **7:**90, 353–68, 389, 399, 408, 412–13, 417, 444, 514
1950s to present, **7:**359–61
history of, **7:**353–61
"northwest wind" movement, **7:**359
tongsu style, **7:**259
Chinese-Americans, **3:**964, 1266
Chuuk
guitar songs, **9:**735–36
polka, **9:**736
Cirebon, **4:**696, 697–98
Colombia, **2:**394–96, 409–10
commodification of, **8:**188
concept of, **8:**2, 20, 204, 436–37
Costa Rica, **2:**699
Côte d'Ivoire, **1:**419–20, 421
Croatia, **8:**209, 934
Cuban, **2:**486–87, 827–28; **9:**103
Cyprus, **8:**1030
Czechoslovakia, **8:**730–31
Dai people, **7:**505–7
Denmark, **8:**458
Dominica, **2:**843–44
Dominican Republic, **2:**861–62
East Africa, **1:**423–28, 608
Egypt, **6:**235–41, 548, 552–53
aghāni shabābiyya, **6:**555
influence on Maghrib music, **6:**269–70, 432–33
ughniyya, **6:**558, 559
El Salvador, **2:**715–19
England, folk influences on, **8:**339
Europe, **8:**204–12
cultural diffusion and, **8:**6
historiography of, **8:**60–61
hybrid repertoires, **8:**205–7
local traditions of, **8:**60, 205–9, 226

preference issues, **8:**207–9
social class and, **8:**13
"evergreens," **8:**209–10
feminist studies, **3:**91
Fiji, **9:**161–62
   sere ni cumu, **9:**779–80, 781
Filipino-Americans, **3:**1025
Finland, **8:**208, 483–84
   women's performance of, **8:**200
France, **8:**205, 207–8, 547–48
   chanson, **6:**249, 275
French Antilles, **2:**98
French Guiana, **2:**437–38, 439
gāna style, **5:**557
Garífuna culture, **2:**675, 676–77, 733
gender studies of, **3:**94–97
Georgia, **8:**845
Germany, **8:**659–60
Ghana, **1:**419, 422–23
global styles in indigenous languages, **5:**427
Great Britain, **8:**207, 210
Greece, **8:**1008, 1021–22
   elafra, **8:**1014
Greek *rebetika*, **3:**930
Guadeloupe
   beguine, **2:**877–78
   zouk, **2:**879–80
Guam, **9:**745
   Chamolinian, **9:**746
Guatemala, **2:**723, 728
Guyana, **5:**601, 603–5
Haiti, **2:**98, 889–93
Hawai'i, **9:**162–67, 389–90, 921–22
   karaoke, **9:**99, 164
   Puerto Rican salsa, **9:**101
Hawai'ian, in Aotearoa, **9:**936
Hindustani drumming in, **5:**136
Hmong-Americans, **3:**1005
Hong Kong, **7:**354–56, 359, 361, 389, 431, 433, 435–36
Hungary, **8:**205, 746–48
Iceland, **8:**208, 407–8
identity issues in, **3:**19; **8:**206
India, North, **5:**547–53
India, South, **5:**554–59
Indonesia, **4:**10, 68, 101–11, 717, 778; **10:**48–49
   influence on Irian Jayan music, **9:**585
   kroncong, **9:**150
   internationalization of, **2:**93–94, 101, 134
Inuit, **3:**1059, 1063, 1279–81
Iranian-Americans, **3:**1031, 1034–35
Iraq, **6:**229
Ireland, folk revival, **8:**391–92
Irish-Americans, **3:**844–45
Islamic views on, **4:**74
Israel, **6:**1019, 1020–21, 1069–74
   muzika mizrahit, **6:**204, 205, 261–68, 1020–21, 1033–34, 1074
   neo-Hasidic, **6:**202, 1071, 1073, 1074
   religious, **6:**202, 204, 205
Italian-Americans, **3:**528, 860, 865
Italy, **8:**205, 208, 617–20
Jamaican, **2:**97–98, 910–12; **8:**204, 207, 215
Japan, **7:**354–55, 533, 538, 720
   folk-pop, **7:**746

hayari uta, **7:**739, 743
hayasi mono (medieval street entertainment), **7:**684–85
   pre-twentieth century, **7:**739–40
   syosei busi, **7:**743
   twentieth century, **7:**722, 743–47
Japanese-Americans, **3:**969–70
Java, **4:**684
Jewish, **3:**943–44; **8:**263, 264–65
Kashmir, **5:**682
Kenya, **1:**365, 423, 426–27, 626
Kerala, **5:**929, 935
Khmer people, **4:**156
Kiribati, **9:**721
Korea, *yuhaengga*, **7:**952
Kosrae, **9:**743
Kurdish, **6:**251
Lao-Americans, **3:**952, 1009
Laos, **4:**18, 360
Latin American, **3:**521–22, 720–21, 732–33
Lebanon, **6:**229, 251
lesbian, **3:**92, 107–11
Lombok, **4:**778
Macedonia, **8:**980, 983
Maharashtra, **5:**729–30
Malawi, **1:**323, 423, 436–37
Malaysia, **4:**433–39, 441–42
Mali, **1:**420–21
Manihiki, *hīmene māpū*, **9:**905, 907–8
Mariana Islands, **9:**743
Maritimes, **3:**1072–73
Marshall Islands, **9:**749
Martinique, **2:**918–20
   orchestral beguine, **2:**916
   zouk and *post-zouk*, **2:**918–20
Mashriq, *mijāna*, **6:**283
Maya culture, **2:**652
Mexican
   in Chile, **2:**371
   in Costa Rica, **2:**703
   in Dominican Republic, **2:**861
   in El Salvador, **2:**708, 716, 718, 719
   in Guatemala, **2:**728
   in Nicaragua, **2:**763
   in Peru, **2:**485
Mexican-American, **3:**734, 756
Mexico, **2:**619–23, 653
Micronesia, **9:**158–61, 719, 721
   guitar songs, **9:**719
Mongolia, **7:**1019–20
Morocco, **1:**546–47; **6:**269
Mozambique, **1:**323, 435–36
Nauru, **9:**721
Navajo, **3:**433
Netherlands, **8:**208
Netherlands Antilles, **2:**930–31
New Caledonia, **9:**213–14
   kaneka, **9:**213–14, 965
New Mexico, **3:**756
Nicaragua, **2:**754–55, 763–64
Niue, **9:**817
North Africa, **1:**545–47
North Caucasia, **8:**851
Northwest Territories, **3:**1277–78, 1279–81

Norway, **8:**205, 208, 430–31
Nunavut, **3:**1277–78, 1279–81
Oceania, **9:**126–69
Ontario, **3:**1080
Pakistan, **5:**547–53, 748–49
Palestine
   intifāḍa, **6:**635–40
   sung at weddings, **6:**579, 591–92
pan-European trends in, **8:**211–12
pan-Pacific pop, **9:**127, 137, 139, 198, 598–99, 667, 823, 843, 894
Papua New Guinea, **9:**72, 89–91, 146–55
   Baluan, **9:**607
   dance and, **9:**485–86
   guitar songs, **9:**150–55, 625, 633, 639
   Gulf Province, **9:**495
   Rai Coast, **9:**565–66
Paraguay, **2:**463
Peru, **2:**485–87
Philippines, **4:**883–88
Poland, **8:**205, 711
Portugal, **8:**204, 205, 584–85
Puerto Rico, **2:**940
Pukapuka
   hīmene māpū, **9:**911
   īmene lōpā, **9:**910
Punjab (India), **5:**656
Québec, **3:**1154–62
research on, **2:**93; **3:**584, 587; **8:**210–12
Réunion Island, **5:**609–11
role of blues in, **3:**648
Romania, **8:**882, 885
Rotuma, foreign styles, **9:**823
Russia, **8:**778
Saami people, joiks in, **8:**306
Sāmoa, **9:**808
Sardinia, **8:**626
Saudi Arabia, **6:**655
Scotland, **8:**367–68
   American influences on, **8:**369
   folk influences on, **8:**364–65
Senegal, **1:**365, 421–22
Serbia, **8:**209, 279, 948–49
   Kosovo, **8:**286, 1002
Shona people, **1:**755
Sicily, **8:**208
Singapore, **4:**523
Slovenia, **8:**209
Solomon Islands, **9:**155–58
   guitar songs, **9:**156–57, 654, 665
   Sirovanga people, **9:**654
South Africa, **1:**216–17, 219, 296, 322, 429–31, 433, 759–80, 772, 775; **5:**616
South America
   age and preference issues, **2:**58
   issues in, **2:**92–93
   transnational influences on, **2:**75–77
   tropical-forest region, **2:**133
South Asian, **5:**418–29
   dissemination of, **2:**40–41; **5:**4, 15, 16, 107–8, 368
   economics of, **2:**63–64
   in Europe, **8:**240–41
   growth of, **5:**15, 376
   in North America, **5:**580–81

Volume Key: **6**, Middle East; **7**, East Asia; **8**, Europe; **9**, Australia and the Pacific Islands; **10**, The World's Music.

popular music, South Asian (*continued*)
    social mobility and, **5:**8
      in Southeast Asia, **4:**62, 68, 101, 601
      in Trinidad and Tobago, **5:**591–92
    Southeast Asia, **4:**8
    southern Africa, **1:**428–37, 720
    Spain, **8:**204, 205, 208, 226, 593, 599–600
    Spanish-American, **2:**100–106
    Sri Lanka, **5:**961, 969–72
    Sudan, **6:**644
    Sumatra, **4:**601–2, 602–3
      pop Melayu, **4:**606
    Sunda, **4:**703, 712, 717–19
    Sweden, **8:**208, 445–46
    Switzerland, **8:**208, 209, 698
    Syria, **6:**229
    Taiwan, **7:**356–59, 361, 389
      campus folk song movement, **7:**356, 357
      protest songs, **7:**358
    Tanzania, **1:**423, 427–28, 644–45
    Thailand, **4:**18, 95–101, 222, 297, 316,
        320–21, 327, 329–33, 514; **7:**506
      northern, **4:**315
    Trinidad and Tobago, **2:**95–97
      South Asian community, **5:**591–92
    Tunisia, **6:**269, 527
    Turkey, **6:**117–18, 243–45, 247–52, 255–59,
        776
      arabesk genre, **6:**255–59
    Uganda, **1:**423, 426
    Uighur people, **7:**467–69
    United States, **3:**547–53
      cross-cultural marketing, **3:**586
      dance music of the 1980s, **3:**355
      eighteenth century, **3:**179–81, 547, 838–39
      folk revival, **8:**391
      Hawai'ian-themed, **3:**1048
      independent production, **3:**168–71
      Jewish influences, **3:**530
      Latin American influences, **2:**105
      nineteenth century, **3:**181–94, 547, 839–40;
        8:205
      rural South, **3:**13
      seventeenth century, **3:**179
    Uruguay, **2:**519–20
    Vanuatu, **9:**709
    Venezuela, **2:**543
    Vietnam, **4:**81, 509–10, 513
    Vietnamese-Americans, **3:**949, 995
    Virgin Islands, **2:**969
    Wales, **8:**356
    West Africa, **1:**419–23
    Western, **9:**28
      adapted by Australian Aboriginal peoples,
        9:442
      in Aotearoa, **9:**936
      in Bahamas, **2:**802
      in Barbados, **2:**820
      in China, **7:**359, 360, 363, 399, 412, 416,
        468
      in Chuuk, **9:**737
      in Cook Islands, **9:**897
      in Egypt, **6:**612
      in Futuna, **9:**815
      guitars in, **9:**387
      in Guyana, **2:**445, 447

      Hawai'ian-themed, **9:**43, 389–90, 922
      in Indonesia, **4:**111
      influence on Southeast Asian culture, **4:**90,
        92–93
      influence on Southeast Asian musics,
        4:80–86
      in Kosrae, **9:**743
      in Niue, **9:**817
      in Oceania, **9:**25–26
      in Peru, **2:**485–86
      in Philippines, **4:**883–88
      in Pohnpei, **9:**739
      in Rapa Nui, **9:**952
      in Sāmoa, **9:**207, 808
      in Sikaiana, **9:**848
      in Taiwan, **7:**357
      in Thailand, **4:**97–100, 545
      in Turkey, **6:**248–49
      in World War II, **9:**25–26
    women performers of, **5:**412; **8:**201
    world music and, **8:**225–26, 234
    Yap, **9:**730
    Yemen, **6:**656–57
    Yoruba people, **1:**471–87
      wákà, **1:**474
    Yukon, **3:**1277–78, 1279–81
    Zaïre, **1:**385–87, 419, 423–26, 669, 671–72,
        683, 687
    Zambia, **1:**423, 436, 671–72
    Zimbabwe, **1:**423, 432–33, 756–57
    Zulu people, **1:**419, 430–31
Popular Music and Society (periodical), **8:**210
popular songs, North American. *See also* vocal
    music
    Arab, **3:**1033
    campaign songs, **3:**304–11
    Civil War, **3:**187–89
    "coon" songs, **1:**765; **3:**650, 706
    eighteenth-century, **3:**180–81, 831
    in films, **3:**204
    Italian, **3:**865
    nineteenth-century, **3:**189–91, 547, 834–35,
        1108
      influence on country music, **3:**76
      women composers of, **3:**95
    protest music, **3:**14, 315–18, 520, 551,
        600–601, 730, 749, 1204
    Québec, *chansons*, **3:**17, 265, 1059, 1154–62
    Serbo-Croatian, **3:**922
    Thai people, **3:**1005
    Tin Pan Alley, **3:**12, 194–95, 260, 310,
        348–49, 548–50, 622, 705, 707, 837,
        863, 891
      Hawai'ian-themed, **3:**1048
    twentieth-century, **3:**194–95, 196–97, 706,
        862–63
    Vietnamese genres, **3:**994–95
Por people, **4:**154, 157, 172
Porcaro, Dino, **9:**82
Porehoods (musical group), **9:**138
Poreporena Village Choir, **9:**88–89, 151, 493
Porgy and Bess (Gershwin), **3:**196, 539, 545, 608,
    621
Poriķis, Jānis, **8:**504
Porno Indian nation, **3:**415
Porter, Charles, **3:**1116

Porter, Cole, **3:**196–97, 545, 549
Porter, David, **3:**676
Porter, James, **3:**828; **8:**25, 296, 297
Porter, John, **3:**51
Porter, Murray, **3:**345, 1063
Porter, William Smith, **3:**27
Porthan, Henrik Gabriel, **8:**114–15
Porthan, H. G., **8:**487–88
Portibi (kingdom), **4:**600
Portugal, **3:**527; **8:**576–85
    Alentejo, polyphonic songs, **8:**578–79, 581
    Andalusian influences in, **6:**449
    Arab-Andalusian influences in, **6:**444
    art music in, **8:**585
    Azores, **8:**134, *146*, 576, 585
    band competitions, **8:**146
    colonization of South Asia, **5:**15, 735, 921,
        944, 954
    dance traditions of, **8:**163, 198, 581–82
    fado, **8:**7, 116, 204, 205, 577, 578, 583–84
    function of music in, **8:**121
    geography of, **8:**576
    history of, **8:**576
    instrument collections in, **8:**181, 182
    instruments, **8:**21, 197, 582–83
    Madeira Islands, **8:**576
      braguinha of, **8:**582
    map of, **8:**516
    popular music in, **8:**204, 205, 584–85
    population of, **8:**576
    research on music of, **8:**585
    song duels, **8:**134, 581
    vocal music of, **8:**132, 136–37, 195, 517,
        578–79, 581
Portugal, Marcos, **2:**304–5
Portuguese Federation of Folklore, **8:**578
Portuguese people
    in Antigua and Barbuda, **2:**798
    in Brazil, **2:**300–306, 323
    in Caribbean, **2:**793
    in Goa, **5:**735–36
    in Grenada, **2:**864
    in Guyana, **2:**441–42
    in Hawai'i, **9:**96, 97–98, 163, 390–91, 914
    identity issues of, **2:**61
    in North America, **3:**731–32, 847–48, 848,
        850, 1074, 1078, 1197, 1204
    in Sri Lanka, **5:**490, 954, 970–71
    in Surinam, **2:**503
    in Trinidad and Tobago, **2:**953
Poryŏm (Korean folk song), **7:**886
Posad class, **8:**755
posadas, **2:**614–15, 653–54, 724; **3:**736, 848,
    850; **4:**843
Posadas, Artemio, **3:**724, *724*
Posadas, Romy, **4:**884
Posen, Sheldon, **3:**1081
Posen, Shelly, **3:**1189
Postels, A., **9:***711*, *741*
Poster Children (musical group), **3:**169, 171
Post, Hafiz. *See* Hafiz Post
Postlewaite, Joseph William, **3:**605
Poston Sonata (Horiuchi), **3:**972
Pot'aep'yŏng (Sejong), **7:**835, 848, 870
"Potato Head Blues," **3:**652, *653*
Potawatomi Indian nation, **3:**451–59, 498, 1079

Potes, Teófilo, **2**:406
Pothuval caste, **5**:351, 361, 362
potlatch. *See* ceremonies
Potlatch: A Strict Law Bids Us Dance (film), **3**:1093
Pottier, Eugène, **8**:659
Potts, Seán, **8**:390
Potts, Tommy, **8**:387, 390
Pouesi, Ioselani, **9**:207
Pougatchov, Emanuel Amiran, **6**:1026
Poulenc, Francis, **4**:131
Pound, Louise, **3**:147
"*Pour quelques arpents de neige*" (Léveillée), **3**:1156
Pousse-Café (Ellington), **3**:621
Powdermaker, Hortense, **9**:153
Powell, Baden, **2**:108, 351
Powell, Bud, **3**:658
Powell, Jarrad, **3**:1017
Powell, John, **2**:813
Powell, John Wesley, **3**:291
Powell, Maud, **3**:536
Powell, Mrs., **8**:*328*
Powell, Thomas, **9**:21
power and status. *See also* caste
  Abkhazian people, healing power of music, **8**:853
  Adighian people
    of *bzhami* whistle, **8**:855
    magical power of music, **8**:855–56
  Afghanistan, **5**:815
    of Jat groups, **5**:820–22
  Africa
    age-related, **1**:140
    dance as indicator, **1**:112, 114
    dancers and musicians, **1**:291–92
    influence on composers, **1**:219, 229–30
    kings' courts, **1**:311–14
    masks as indicator, **1**:119
    of musicians, **10**:61
    nyama concept, **1**:499–500, 502
    of objects, **1**:509; **4**:9
    of praise songs and singers, **1**:503, 509–11
    religion as, **1**:718
    secret societies and, **1**:311
    of spirits, **1**:329
  of African-American music, **3**:64, 68, 82
  Algeria, of performers, **6**:470
  Angola, royal instruments, **1**:673
  Arabian peninsula
    dance as equalizer, **6**:707
    of dancers, **6**:703
    expatriate communities, **6**:715–16
    of *mukhannathūn*, **6**:296
  of art music, **2**:114; **3**:557–58; **8**:58–60, 63
  Asante chief installation, **1**:286
  Australia
    Cape York dance and song, **9**:430
    ceremonial participants, **9**:459–60
    dance and song, **9**:450
    of musical knowledge, **9**:435
    women, **9**:438–39
  Baggāra people, royal drums, **1**:561
  Bali
    caste system, **4**:739–40
    of gamelans, **4**:731, 747
    of *gamelan selundeng*, **4**:755

  Balochistan, music and, **6**:885–86
  Bantu groups, royal xylophones, **1**:660
  Beja people, royal drums, **1**:558–59
  Belarus, of calendric songs, **8**:792–93
  Bengal, of Muslims, **5**:435
  of blues performers, **3**:638
  Bolivia, of instruments, **2**:289
  Borneo, of gongs, **4**:828
  Brittany, traditional performers, **8**:564
  Burma, of musicians, **4**:399
  Burundi, **1**:198
  Central Africa, royal instruments, **1**:670–71
  Central America, of instruments, **2**:20, 35, 152–53, 251
  Central Asia
    maqām performers, **6**:913
    of reciters, **6**:939
  China
    of actors, **7**:294, 393, 395, 397
    of avocational performers, **7**:396
    of musicians, **10**:19
    of opera, **7**:276–77
    of performers, **7**:131, 418–19
    social classes, **7**:98–99
    of *yueji*, **7**:406
  Chopi people, xylophone ensembles, **1**:710
  Christianity, **8**:306
  Cirebon, royal courts, **4**:686
  Colo people, **1**:568–69
  of *conjunto* music, **3**:775
  copresence, **8**:117
  East African kingdoms, **1**:600–601
  East Asia
    of instruments, **7**:81–82
    of musicians, **7**:46
  East Polynesia, **9**:209
  Ecuador, of musicians, **2**:428
  Egypt
    of performers, **6**:544, 597, 618, 620–21, 622
    of piano playing, **6**:548, 610
  ethnomusicological interest and, **10**:73
  of ethnomusicologists, **10**:9–11, 13–15
  Europe
    of folk musicians, **8**:155
    of local genres, **8**:122
    medieval women, **8**:199
    of musicians, **8**:53
    notated music, **8**:102
    orally transmitted music, **8**:52, 53, 59
    of Renaissance instrumentalists, **8**:75
    of traditional music, **8**:188–89
  Fiji, Indian castes, **9**:94
  Finland
    of accordion, **8**:479
    magical power of music, **8**:478–79, 480–81
    of Swedish-speakers, **8**:483–84
    of violin, **8**:479
  Flores, of gongs, **4**:794, 796
  France, magical power of music, **8**:550–51
  gender relations and, **3**:87–88
  Germany, of folk instruments, **8**:654
  Ghana
    durbar ceremony, **1**:137–38
    of musicians, **1**:390, 397–98
  Goa, **5**:741

  Greece
    of instrumentalists, **8**:1017
    of *zournadhes* and *daouli* ensemble, **8**:1011–12
  Guadeloupe, of musicians, **2**:880
  Haiti, musical genres, **2**:893
  Hausa people, **1**:515–16, 525–28
    of musicians, **1**:517–21, 524–28
  Hawai'i, **9**:15–16, 925
    of *pahu*, **9**:385
  Iceland, magical power of music, **8**:405
  India, North, of music and musicians, **5**:372–81
  Iran
    of art musicians, **6**:139–40, 861–62
    Azerbaijani musicians, **6**:845
    of *bakhshi*, **6**:841
    of court musicians, **6**:131
    daste-ye moṭreb, **6**:828
    mendicant dervishes, **6**:827
    of musicians, **6**:829
  Iraq, of performers, **6**:313
  Ireland, magical power of music, **8**:388
  Irian Jaya, **9**:578
    compositions, **9**:360
  Islamic debates on music's power, **6**:132, 183
  Japan, **7**:27
    Kohun period, **7**:562
    of *koto*, **7**:764
  Java
    of gamelans, **4**:644
    of musicians, **4**:682
  Karnataka
    regional artists, **5**:881
    of regional musicians, **5**:867
  Kazakhstan
    of oral culture, **6**:959
    of performers, **6**:950
  Kerala, of *āśān*, **5**:942–43
  Kimbu people, royal horns, **1**:642
  Kogi culture, of musical knowledge, **2**:186
  Korea, **7**:26–27
  Ladakh, of Beda and Mon communities, **5**:712
  Laos
    classical music, **4**:354
    molam, **4**:343
  Low Countries, pipe-and-tabor ensemble, **8**:528
  Lozi people, **1**:672
    royal music, **1**:712–13
  Madagascar
    royal instruments, **1**:783, 785
    royal music, **1**:789
  Maguindanao people, of *kulintang*, **4**:892
  Mali, of musicians, **1**:421
  Manganihār caste, **5**:641
  Manihiki, **9**:904
  Mapuche culture, **2**:234
  Maritime folk music, **3**:1070
  Martinique, *kadans* musicians, **2**:917
  Martinique, of Tamil community, **5**:596, 599
  Maya culture
    of music, **2**:721–33
    of musicians, **2**:657
  Mexica culture, of dancers, **2**:561
  Middle East, of instrumental ensembles, **6**:3

power and status (*continued*)
  of Middle Eastern musicians, **3**:1038
  Mongol people, **7**:1005
  Motu people, **9**:493
  Mozambique, royal xylophone ensembles,
    1:720
  music as emotive power, **8**:74, 93
  Native American women, **3**:94
  Nepal, **5**:697
    of Gāine people, **5**:698
    of musicians, **5**:706
  New Caledonia, side-blown flutes, **9**:401–2
  New Guinea, **9**:472
  New Ireland, friction block players, **9**:381
  Nkoya people, royal music, **1**:712–13
  Nyamalthu people, dance differentiation,
    1:288
  Oceania
    of chordophones, **9**:385
    clothing and, **9**:348, 349
    of composers, **9**:354
    kava use and, **9**:172
    musical display of, **9**:127
  Oman, **6**:682
  Pakistan, **5**:746
    northern, of musicians, **5**:798–99
  Palau, **9**:183
  Papua New Guinea
    Baluan *kolorai* sponsorship, **9**:603
    Halia people, **9**:640
    Nissan Atoll, **9**:632
    Sepik River flutes, **9**:245–46
    of Usarufa composers, **9**:358
  Plains powwow and, **3**:446
  Polynesia, **9**:768
  popular music singers *vs.* composers, **8**:204–5
  Punjab (Pakistan), of musicians, **5**:762, 763,
    765
  Q'ero culture, **2**:229
  race and, **3**:88, 329–30
  rock genres, **8**:218
  of rock guitarist, **3**:112
  Romania, Rom *lăutari*, **8**:278
  Roti, clans, **4**:798
  Russia
    of *byliny*, **8**:763
    of *khorovod*, **8**:769
    magical power of music, **8**:760
  Saami people, of animals, **8**:303
  Saharan cultures, **1**:302
  St. Lucia, of *kwadril* participants, **2**:944
  Scotland, Travellers, **8**:295
  Shona people
    music as power, **1**:752–53
    royal instruments, **1**:753
  Sierra Leone, of praise singers, **1**:492
  social class and, **3**:330
  Solomon Islands, Shortland Islands, **9**:655–56
  Sotho peoples, reed-flute ensembles, **1**:707
  South America
    of instruments, **2**:20, 35, 152–53, 251
    of music, **2**:21
    of shamans, **10**:101–2
    tropical-forest region, **2**:129–30
  South Asia
    of accompanists, **5**:378–79, 567

  of *bāī* women, **5**:379, 381
  of *bīn* players, **5**:333
  changes in, **4**:117–18
  of drumming, **5**:884
  of guru, **5**:457–59, 470–71
  of international musicians, **5**:567
  of intervals, **5**:39
  of *kathak* dance, **5**:493
  of *khyāl*, **5**:170
  of *mridangam*, **5**:356
  musical volume and, **5**:279
  of music, in Sufi thought, **5**:755
  of *nāgasvaram* players, **5**:392, 393–95
  pain, self-inflicted, and, **5**:876
  of *pakhāvaj*, **5**:120
  performers, **5**:8, 10
  repertoire depth and, **5**:83, 189
  of *sāraṅgī* players, **5**:171, 207, 338
  of *tabla* players, **5**:122–23, 132, 134, 342,
    378–79, 380
  of *tavil* players, **5**:393–95
  of vocal music, **5**:321–22
  Southeast Asia
    influence on urban geography, **4**:5
    networks of, **4**:8–10
    prehistoric, **4**:39
    relation to Western art music tradition, **4**:7
    representational control of traditional music,
      4:132–41
    wars as culture-shapers, **4**:11
  southern Africa, royal instruments, **1**:701
  Spain, flamenco musicians, **8**:596
  Sri Lanka, **5**:961
  Sumatra
    of bronze drums, **4**:599
    of gongs, **4**:609
    of *nobat* ensemble, **4**:615
  Sumba, of instruments, **4**:788–89
  Sunda
    class distinctions, **4**:699, 719
    of gamelans, **4**:703
    of musical genres, **4**:719–20
  Sweden, of lurs, **8**:439
  Switzerland, magical power of music, **8**:683
  Tagbanua people, **4**:927
  Tamil Nadu, Nilgiri peoples, **5**:909, 910–11
  Tanzania, royal drums, **1**:637
  Thailand, royal processions, **4**:248
  Tibet, of narrative singers, **7**:477
  Tonga, clothing and, **9**:352
  Trinidad and Tobago, Spiritual Baptists, **2**:957
  Tuamotu Islands, **9**:884
  Tunisia
    'Īsāwiyya brotherhood, **6**:516
    of *ma'lūf*, **6**:503, 508–9
  Turkey
    alaturka vocal music, **6**:785
    Ottoman court dancers, **6**:812
  Ukraine
    of female lead singers, **8**:808
    on instrumentalists, **8**:812
  Vai women, **1**:339–40
  Venda people, social stratification, **1**:708–9
  Wales
    bards, **8**:348
    of instruments, **8**:348, 354

  West Africa, **1**:446
    of musicians, **1**:444–45, 452, 455
    royal instruments, **1**:452
    women as consumers, **3**:93
    women as leaders, **3**:93
    women's music, **3**:90
  Yemen, of musicians, **6**:656
  Yoruba people, **1**:411–12
    of musicians, **1**:460
  Yuma culture, of musicians, **2**:599
Powerplant (Chicago), **3**:691
Powers, Harold S., **4**:637; **5**:318, 466; **6**:911
  on Western *vs.* Indian scholarly standards,
    5:56–57
Powers, Henry, **10**:87
Powers, William, **3**:367, 484
powwows, **3**:6, 43, 149, 222, 368, 372, 456,
    480–84, 525
  British Columbia, **3**:1256
  California, **3**:415, 418
  competitive dancing at, **3**:211, 214
  context and structure of, **3**:370–71, 446
  drums at, **3**:477, 1069
  Great Basin, **3**:424–25, 425, 426
  identity issues in, **3**:215–16
  intertribal, **3**:238, 454–55
  Ojibwe styles, **3**:458–59
  Ontario, **3**:1079
  Plains, **3**:368–69, 446–48, 1087
    Northern type, **3**:481–83
    Southern type, **3**:483
  research on, **3**:484
  Southeast, **3**:467
  Southwest, **3**:438
  women's roles in, **3**:94, 370
Pozo, Chano, **3**:34, 659, 732, 787, 797
Prabhakar, Sharon, **5**:428
Prabowo, Tonny, **3**:1017
Prach, Ivan, **8**:18
Prado, Felipe, **4**:866
Prado, Pérez, **3**:732, 741, 743, 787, 796, 798
Praetorius, Michael, **1**:662; **8**:177–78, 654
Prairie Provinces. *See* Alberta; Manitoba;
    Saskatchewan
praise songs, singing, and poetry
  Africa, **1**:119–20
    1600s, **1**:82
    Islamic, **1**:536–37
  Algeria, **6**:475
  Arabian peninsula, **6**:304, 353, 696
  Colo people, **1**:569
  content of, **1**:508–12
  form of, **1**:494–503
  Fulani people, **1**:451
  function of, **1**:503–8
  Ghana, **1**:357
  Ham people, **1**:289
  Hausa people, **1**:131, 291, 450, 451, 515, 517
  historical and genealogical, **1**:446
  Iran, **6**:831, 835, 844
  Kasena-Nankani people, **1**:456
  Kenya, **1**:626, 628–29
  Kurdistan, **6**:747
  Maasai people, **1**:110
  Madagascar, *antsa*, **1**:789
  Mongol people, **7**:1008–9, 1011

Morocco, **6:**490
Mossi-Bariba peoples, **1:**453
Ngoni people, **1:**320
Nigeria, **1:**313
North Africa, **1:**539, 540–41
Nubian people, **1:**556
Oman, **6:**673, 675–76, 678
research on, **1:**488
Senegal, **1:**445
Sierra Leone, **1:**488–513
Turkey, **6:**196, 768, 769
United Arab Emirates, **6:**700
Vai people, **1:**332, 340, 345–46
West Africa, **1:**447–48
Xhosa people, **1:**762
Yoruba people, **1:**409–10, 461, 472, 475
Yoruba popular music, **1:**472–73
Prajasudirja, **10:**44, 48, 50
Prajnanananda, Swami, **5:**56
Prakash, Khemchand, **5:**537
Prakempa manuscript, **4:**733, 736–37, 740, 747
Prasad, Rajender, **5:**207
Prasad, Shanta, **5:**137, *204*
Prasad, Subhagia Devi, **5:**602
Pratap Singh, maharaja of Jaipur, **5:**46, 50, 386, 687
Pratella, Francesco Balilla, **8:**621
Pratique musicale savante dans quelques communautés juives en Europe (Adler), **6:**1065
Pratt, George, **9:**21
Prawatasaputra (Prawotosaputro), **3:**1018; **10:**42
Práxedes, María Cárpena, **4:**856
Precious P., **5:**427
Precision label, **3:**691
Prefontaine, Jean, **3:**1077
Prele (Hungarian scholar), **8:**858
"Prelude to 'Romances of the Seven Seas,'" **9:**43
Prema Desam (film), **5:**545
Prema Satsangh, **2:**904
Premanand, **5:**633–34
Premiata Forneria Marconi, **8:**619–20
Premysl family, **8:**716
Prendergast, (Ellen) Kekoa[ohiwai]kalani, **9:**133, 219, 222
Prenjak, **4:**684
Presbyterians, **3:**120, 1070, 1132
in Jamaica, **2:**901
liturgy of, **3:**121
research on, **3:**119
in Scotland, **8:**360
in West Futuna, **9:**861
Prešeren, France, **8:**922
President Go Home (album), **8:**802
Presley, Elvis, **3:**48, 80, 108, 109–10, 114, 244, 329, 348, 350, 352, 353, 354, 356, 522, 550, 552, 648, 689, 709, 845; **4:**884; **7:**1020; **8:**61, 214, 446; **9:**43, 138, 1007
Presser, Gábor, **8:**747
Prestán, Arnulfo, **2:**649
Preston, Denis, **8:**235
Preston, Richard, **3:**392
Preston, William, **3:**1090
Pretenders (musical group), **8:**215
"Pretty Fair Maid" (ballad), **3:**1124

"Pretty Girl Is Like a Melody, A" (Berlin), **3:**196
"Pretty Mama Blues" (Hunter), **3:**669
"Pretty Thing" (Diddley), **3:**672
Prévost, André, **3:**1151
Price, Dorothy, **9:**560
Price, Enrique, **2:**397
Price, Florence, **3:**606, 607, 609
Price, Harry F., **3:**286
Price, Jorge W., **2:**397
Price, Leontyne, **3:**609, 1210
Price, Lloyd, **3:**670, 708
Price of Love (film), **8:**1022
Prieto, Arturo, **2:**372
Prieto, Emilia, **2:**703
Prihodko, Vassily, **4:**870
Prime, Dalvanius, **9:**168, 938
Prime Time Country (television show), **3:**212
Primitive Baptists, **3:**120–21, 124
Primitive Music (Wallaschek), **3:**575–76
Primov, Kurban, **6:**924, *924*
Primrose, Christine, **8:**363
Primus, **9:**164
Primus, Pearl, **3:**34
Prince (rock musician), **3:**685, 712; **8:**220
Prince Edward Island
Acadians in, **3:**1135–37
Charlottetown, **3:**1072
comic songs, **3:**1124
fiddle music, **3:**1071, 1125, 1127–30
history of musical life, **3:**1114–21
Lebanese community, **3:**1072
Prince, Irma, **9:**998
Prince of Hawaii (operetta), **9:**924–25
Prince of the Pagodas (Britten), **4:**132
Princess Wencheng (Tibetan writing), **7:**472
Princeton University, **3:**175
Pring Gading, **4:**698
Pringle, B. A., **5:**51
printing and publishing, **2:**23; **3:**241–42
African-American compositions, **3:**705–6
African-American-owned firms, **3:**644, 711
of American art music, **3:**539
Belgium, **8:**523, 533–34
broadside sheets and chapbooks, **8:**17, 137, 142
Brittany, **8:**561
Bulgaria, **8:**903
Czech Republic, **8:**727
Denmark, **8:**452–53, *453*, 458
England, **8:**328–29, 332, 336
Finland, **8:**289, 479–80
France, **8:**548, 549
Ireland, **8:**386, 387
Italy, **8:**606, 611
Jewish, **8:**257, 263
Low Countries, **8:**519, 522
Russia, **8:**755
Scotland, **8:**365, 368, 369
Slovakia, **8:**727
Sweden, **8:**435
United States, **3:**835
Wales, **8:**343
Canada, **3:**258, 1067–68, 1179–80
Children of Peace community, **3:**137
Maritimes, **3:**1116

China, **7:**22
choral music, **3:**284
contra dance tunes, **3:**232
of country music, **3:**80
Czech music, **3:**897
development of, **8:**6, 51, 59, 73, 81, 647
educational materials, **3:**276
Egypt, **6:**548
Faroe Islands, **8:**472
gospel music, **3:**534, 585
growth of, **3:**43
Hawai'ian popular music, **3:**1048
Iceland, **8:**404
India, **5:**445, 454, 674
Iran, **6:**867
Ireland, **8:**384, 385–86
Traveller ballads, **8:**295
Israel, **6:***1070*
Japan, **7:**538, 589–90
Jewish presses, **8:**257, 263
Latvia, **8:**504
marketing strategies, **3:**258
Middle East, **6:**18
minstrel songs, **3:**182
Nigeria, **1:**237
Pennsylvania, Ephrata Cloister, **3:**905
piano music, **3:**190
popular songs
eighteenth century, **3:**180, 181
nineteenth century, **3:**190–91
psalm books, **8:**97–98
quadrille call-books, **3:**232
Québec, **3:**1148, 1152
Romania, **8:**881, 885
royalty disputes with radio, **3:**708
Russia, **8:**776
scholarly materials, **10:**69, 164–66
sheet music industry, **3:**95, 194–95, 196, 239, 241, 257–59, 263, 547, 705–6, 838–39, 897, 912, 936–37, 1068, 1148
songbooks, **3:**925
songsters, **3:**305–6, 307, 308–9
spirituals, **3:**524
Sweden, **8:**444
Ukrainian music, **3:**912
'ukulele method books, **3:**1049
of women composers, **3:**91
Yiddish music, **3:**936
Priority Records, **3:**714
Prisdang, Prince, **4:**260
Prism (musical group), **3:**1097
Prithvīrājrāso (epic), **5:**401–2
Priya (film), **5:**544
Pro Arte String Quartet, **3:**538
Pro Musica (Tahiti), **9:**868
Probyn, Elspeth, **3:**1061
Proca-Ciortea, Vera, **8:**886
Procera, **9:**997–98
processions and parades
Africa, **1:**75, 79, 90–91
African-American participants, **3:**66, 598
Andalusia, wedding, **6:**444
Argentina, religious, **2:**256, 258
Aymara culture, for patronal festivals, **2:**362
Azerbaijan, ceremonial mourning, **6:**923

processions and parades (*continued*)
Bahamas, junkanoo parade, **2:**804, 806–8,
    811–12
Bali, **4:**753–54
Balkarian people, **8:**857
Barbados, **2:**815
    Landship parades, **2:**818–19
Basque region, **8:**314, 315
Belarus, **8:**791
Belgium, **8:**529
Bolivia, **2:**289
    Moxo people, **2:**138, 140
    pilgrimages, **2:**291
    suna, **2:**285
Bosnia-Hercegovina, **8:**963
Brazil, **2:**309
    for carnival, **2:**336–38
    dance in, **2:**347
    fife-and-drum bands in, **2:**330
    folias de reis, **2:**312
    pilgrimages, **2:**328
    religious processions, **2:**334
    samba, **2:**314–16
Bribri and Cabécar cultures, **2:**634
Bulgaria, **8:**897, 899
Canada
    Emancipation Day parades, **3:**1211
    Montréal CariFête, **3:**1170
    Toronto Caribana festival, **3:**223, 1202,
        1203, 1207–9, 1212–13
China
    aesthetics in, **7:**240
    bands in, **7:**201, 202, 258–59
    funeral processions, **7:**331, 375
Colombia, municipal band's role in,
    2:384
Costa Rica, **2:**701
    Afro-Caribbean people, **2:**688
    Carnaval de Limón, **2:**693
    Corpus Christi, **2:**681
    Virgen de los Angeles festival, **2:**693
Cuba, **2:**836
Cuban *comparsa*, **3:**729
Denmark, **8:**458
Dominican Republic, **2:**852
    alborada, **2:**859
    morano, **2:**855
    parranda, **2:**859
Ecuador, **2:**419–22
    Corpus Christi, **2:**417
Egypt
    hinna al-suwaysī, **6:**627
    saint's shrine procession, **6:**630
    wedding, **6:**415
    zaffa, **6:**616, 626, 643
England, Cornwall, Padstow, **8:**133, 331
Europe
    bells in, **8:**572
    during carnival, **8:**140
    municipal bands in, **8:**146
Flanders, **8:**535
Garífuna (Garifuna) culture, **2:**673–74,
    733–34
Georgia, **8:**834
Germany, **8:**649, 656–57, 659
Ghana, **1:**138; **10:***30*, 33, *34*, *34–35*, 35

Greece, Thrace, **8:***1013*
Grenada, carnival, **2:**866
Guatemala, **2:**729
Gujarat, rain rituals, **5:**278
Haitian *rara*, **2:**885–87; **3:**805
Himachal Pradesh, **5:**500
India
    nāgasaṅkīrtana, **5:**267–68
    South, temple, **5:**210
Iran, ceremonial mourning, **6:**826
Ireland, **8:**385
Jamaica
    Christmas masquerade, **2:**898
    jonkunnu (also *buru* or horse head),
        2:907–8
Japan, Buddhist, **7:***534*
Karachaevian people, **8:**857
Kerala, **5:**930, 934–35
    for Puram Festival, **5:**360
Korea
    farmers' bands, **7:**822, 828, 929, 930–31,
        934
    t'aech'wit'a, **7:**822, 828
Kota people, **5:**278
Kumaon people, **5:**501
Kurdistan, for weddings, **6:**750
Latvia, **8:**502
Louisiana, **3:**600
    for funerals, **3:**802
Mali, **1:**138
Malta, **8:**640
Martinique, **2:**915
    vidé, **2:**918
Maya culture, **2:**727
    posadas, **2:**653–54
    for saints' days, **2:**730
    San Luís patronal festival, **2:**667
Mexico
    Chiapas, **2:**652
    Virgin of Guadalupe festival, **2:**614
Mixtec culture, **2:**565
Montserrat, **2:**925
Morocco
    Berber, **6:**483
    wedding, **6:**480, 498
Muslim Matkor procession, **2:**85
Nepal, **5:**490
    sībājā, **5:**702–3
New York, Jewish protest marches, **3:**939
Nicaragua, **2:**762
Oman
    'āzī, **6:**675, 680
    zaffa, **6:**682
Pakistan, northern, **5:**795
Palestine
    mhorbih, **6:**585, 589
    wedding day, **6:**590–91
Panama
    congo visits, **2:**776
    dirty little devils, **2:**781
    Independence Day, **2:**782–83
    tunas, **2:**772
Paraguay
    Holy Week, **2:**458
    patronal festivals, **2:**458–59
    promeseros, **2:**458

Peru
    in children's wakes, **2:**423
    cofradías in, **2:**491
    Corpus Christi, **2:**468
    pilgrimage to Collariti, **2:**227
    religious, **2:***62, 118*
Plains powwows, **3:**481
Portugal, **8:***578*, 579, *580*
Rajasthan, **5:**642, 648
Romania, **8:**869–70
Russia, **8:**760
St. Lucia, masquerade and *séwinal*, **2:**947–48
Sardinia, **8:**627
Saudi Arabia
    military, **6:**653
    wedding, **6:**693
Slovenia, **8:**911–12
South Africa, *nayyandi mēlam*, **5:**617
South America, **2:**50, 62, 63
    movement in, **2:**44
    shawm's use in, **2:**36
South Asia, bands in, **5:**368
Spain, **8:**591
Sri Lanka, **5:**965, 966, 969
    Buddhist, **5:**364
Switzerland, **8:**683–84, 686, 692
Taino culture, **2:**881
Taiwan, **7:**425
Tamil Nadu, **5:**221, 293, 904–5
    bhajan, **5:***918*
    uñcavritti bhajana, **5:**211, 391, 393,
        394–95
Tarahumara culture, **2:**586
Thailand, **4:**248
Tokelau, **9:**824
Trinidad and Tobago, **2:**959; **5:**590
    parang, **2:**953
    road march, **2:**96
    steelbands, **2:**961–63
Tunisia, *kharja*, **6:**520
Turkey, Ottoman court, **6:**767
United States
    Bahamian *junkanoo* groups in, **2:**811
    circus parades, **3:**568
    nineteenth century, **3:**555
    political, **3:**304
Uruguay, role of Black Lubolos, **2:**515
Uttar Pradesh, **5:**671
Vai people, **1:**333, 345
Venezuela
    parranda, **2:**538
    Parranda de San Pedro, **2:**530
    Saint John the Baptist, **2:**535–36
Virgin Islands, **2:**973
Wales, **8:**342
Warao culture, traveling music, **2:**197
    wedding, **8:**144
Yemen, **6:**656
    zaffa, **6:**102
Procol Harum, **8:**215
Proctor, George, **3:**144, 1058
Prodigal Son (musical), **3:**621
Production Guy Cloutier, **3:**1160
Profazio, Otello, **8:**613
"Professor Bop" (disc jockey), **3:**708
Progessive Party, **3:**310

program music
  Bali, for *wayang kulit*, **4**:751
  Belarus, **8**:799
  Burma, **4**:374
  Cambodia, in *pinn peat*, **4**:183, 189–90
  Central Asia, *kyui*, **6**:902
  China
    aesthetics of, **7**:240–41
    Guangdong yinyue, **7**:219
    Jiangnan sizhu, **7**:224
    for *qin*, **7**:159–60
    for *zheng*, **7**:172–73
    concept of, **8**:82–83
  East Asia, **7**:3, 5
  Java, in wayang genres, **4**:652, 653, 661
  Korea, **7**:959
  Malaysia, **4**:403
    in *mak yong*, **4**:407
    in *wayang melayu*, **4**:428
    in *wayang Siam*, **4**:404–6
  Middle Eastern suites, **6**:10–11
  Philippines, in *kulintang*, **4**:895
  Romania, **8**:875
  Thailand, **4**:275–76, 318
  Tuva, **6**:985–86
Progressive Church of God in Christ Radio
    Choir, **3**:633
Prohibition movement, **3**:309, 578
Prokofiev, Sergei, **3**:537; **4**:873; **8**:781
Prokopetz, Josef, **8**:676–77
Prokop, Skip, **3**:1081
Proletenpassion (album), **8**:677
Prólogo (Durán), **3**:734–35
"Promised Anthem" (Gardner), **3**:603
PromoFACT, **3**:252
Prose Edda, **8**:405
"Prosifunkstication" (Clinton), **3**:684
Próspero, Salvador, **2**:581
Protestant Church Music in America (Stevenson),
    3:32
Protestantism. *See also* Christianity; *specific sects
    and denominations*
  Antigua and Barbuda, **2**:798–99
  Antinomian heresy, **3**:25
  Argentina, **2**:259, 269
  Bahamas, **2**:804
  bluegrass and, **3**:162, 168
  Brazil, **2**:329
  Canada, Ontario, **3**:1179
  Caribbean, **2**:795
  Central America, **2**:630
  China, **7**:416, 420
  Costa Rica, **2**:688
  Czech Republic, **8**:726
  Denmark, **8**:459
  Dominican Republic, **2**:859
  East Asia, **7**:49–50
  El Salvador, **2**:709
  Estonia, **8**:495
  Europe, Northern, **8**:399
  evangelical, **2**:47; **3**:533–34
    camp meetings, **3**:67, 68, 533, 575–76,
      1132
    Holiness and Pentecostal churches, **3**:215,
      630, 631, 632, 1212
    Prohibition movement and, **3**:309
  Finland, **8**:477, 479, 480, 485

  Germany, **8**:646, 652, 660–61
  Hallelujah sect, **2**:47, 131, 443
  Hmong-Americans, **3**:1005
  Hungary, **8**:736
  Iceland, **8**:404
  India, **5**:257
  Jamaica, **2**:901
  Kerala, **5**:944–45
  Korean-Americans, **3**:976
  liturgical music, **3**:10, 530–35; **8**:5, 145
    chorales, **8**:74, 131, 255, 413–14, 726
    New England, **3**:24, 831–33
  Maritime Provinces, **3**:1115–16
  Maya culture, **2**:653, 722
  Miskitu culture, **2**:660
  missionaries, **3**:379, 390–91, 435, 1086
  Netherlands Antilles, **2**:927, 931
  Nicaragua, **2**:753
  North America, **3**:118–19, 506
  Northern Ireland, **8**:378, 389
  Norway, **8**:420, 425
  Paraguay, **2**:459–60
  performance contexts in, **8**:11
  psalmody in, **8**:97–98
  Québec, **3**:1148
  Romania, **8**:868
  Scotland, **8**:360, 367
  South Africa, **5**:618
  South America, **2**:46, 60, 69, 89, 131, 167
  South Asian Americans, **3**:984
  statistics on, **3**:5
  Surinam, **2**:503–4
  Sweden, **8**:444
  Switzerland, **8**:693
  Tamil Nadu, **5**:921–27
  Wales, **8**:349–50, 353
Proud Scum (musical group), **9**:168
Provincial Freeman (newspaper), **3**:1211
Provine, Robert C., **7**:43
Prowse, Juliet, **3**:211
Proyart, Abbé, **1**:80–81
Prudence (musical group), **8**:430
Prussia, **8**:702
Pryor, Arthur, **3**:536, 566
Psaila, Dun Karm, **8**:638
Psalma Bok (Þorláksson), **8**:404
psalmody
  Armenian, **6**:736–37
  Coptic Orthodox, **6**:221
  Doukhobor, **3**:1095, 1267–70
  Europe, **8**:73, 97–98, 145
  Finland, **8**:477–78, 482, 488
  Hungary, **8**:737, 742
  Iceland, **8**:122
  Jewish, **8**:252
  Jewish Maghribi, **6**:1037–38
  Latvia, **8**:502
  North America, **3**:7, 24–26, 119, 275, 531,
    831, 1070, 1179
  Scotland, **8**:97–98, 362–63, 367
  Syrian Orthodox, **6**:226
  Transylvania, **8**:742
  Wales, *halsingod*, **8**:349
psaltery. *See* zithers
Psaltichia Româneasca (Filotei Sin Agai Jipei),
    8:881

  Pshav people, **8**:827–28, 840
Pshimazitkhe (god), **8**:855
Psychedelic Aliens, **1**:363
psychology
  cognitive studies, **10**:74–75, 115–16, 120–24,
    132
  dreaming, **10**:121–22
  research on, **3**:286; **8**:25
Ptolemy, **6**:16, 368; **8**:46, 47, 48
Pu Yi, Qing emperor, **7**:383, 393
Public Enemy (musical group), **3**:696, 699, 714,
    715
Public Folklore (Baron/Spitzer), **10**:85
Puccini, Giacomo, **3**:953; **4**:857; **7**:733; **8**:60,
    84; **9**:38
Puceanu, Romica, **8**:278
Pu di jing (*xiaodiao*), **7**:152
"Pueblito Viejo" (Morales), **2**:393
Pueblo Indian groups, **2**:591; **3**:428, 429–31,
    438, 755. *See also specific pueblos*
  Christianity and, **3**:485
  dances of, **3**:214, *217*, 217–18
  instruments of, **3**:474, 476
  matachines performances, **3**:430, 614, 759,
    850–51; **10**:89
  music composition of, **3**:370
  repatriation of sacred objects, **3**:492
  songs of, **3**:213, 368
  Spanish influences on, **3**:217–18
  women's musical roles, **3**:371
Pueblo Revolt of 1680, **3**:755
Puente, Tito, **3**:13, 720, 726, 732, 733, 741,
    743, 751, 787, 789, 793, 794–95,
    796, 797, 798, 799
Puerta, Ramiro, **3**:1085
Puerto Rican Heritage Society, **9**:101
Puerto Rican people, **2**:91; **3**:98, 337, 790
  in Hawai'i, **9**:95, 96, 99, 101–3, 163
  música jíbara, **3**:726–27
  musical genres of, **3**:725–27, 799
  in New York, **3**:336, 719, 725–27, 794, 798,
    799
  population of, **3**:718
  role in Afro-Cuban music, **3**:792, 794
  role in salsa, **3**:798–99
  in Virgin Islands, **2**:969
Puerto Rico, **2**:789, 932–41, 969; **3**:3, 788
  archaeomusicological studies in, **2**:8
  Borinquen culture of, **2**:78
  children's wakes in, **2**:422
  geography of, **2**:932
  history of, **2**:932–33
  industries of, **2**:791
  instruments of, **2**:933–35
  musical genres
    bomba, **2**:936–37, 941
    cumbia, **1**:384
    danza, **2**:100
    décima, **2**:937–38
    plena, **2**:939–40, 941
    seis, **2**:934, 936, 938–39
  musical links with Venezuela, **2**:524
  political status of, **2**:792
  popular music in, **2**:940
  religious contexts and genres, **2**:935–36
  research on, **2**:941

Volume Key: **6**, Middle East; **7**, East Asia; **8**, Europe; **9**, Australia and the Pacific Islands; **10**, The World's Music.

Pugacheva, Alla, **8**:779
Pugh-Kitingan, Jacqueline, **9**:286, 990
Pugliese, Osvaldo, **2**:264
Puheketama, Mrs. D., **9**:973
Puhipau, **9**:221
puk. See drums: barrel, conical, or cylindrical
Pukapuka (Cook Islands), **9**:909–13
  cultural contacts with Tokelau, **9**:827
  dance of, **9**:910–11
  history of, **9**:909–10
  instruments of, **9**:913
  poetry, **9**:327
    verbal meter, **9**:324
  population of, **9**:909
  vocal music of, **9**:911–13
Pukapukan people
  in Aotearoa, **9**:910
  in Australia, **9**:910
  singing of, **9**:307
Pukch'ŏng saja nori üi t'ungso karage wihan saegok (Yi), **7**:957
Pukch'ŏng saja norŭm (Baek), **7**:957
Pukerua, Totini, **9**:908
Pukerua, Tutai, **9**:909
Pukhraj, Malka, **5**:750
Pukko, **2**:903
Pukt, Ryhor, **8**:800
Pukui, Mary Kawena, **9**:968, 969–70
Pula people, **4**:920
Pulavar, Acan Ali, **5**:921
Pulawa, Hwâdo, **9**:677
Pulaya caste, **5**:367, 930
Pulido, Roberto, Jr., **3**:781
Pulikowski, Julian, **8**:712
Pullan, Usman, **5**:*775*
Pullim sori (Kim), **7**:960
"Pullin' Back the Reins" (lang), **3**:110–11
Pulḷuva caste, **5**:350–51, 931, 932
Pumi people, **7**:485–92, 509
Pump Records, **3**:750
Punan people, **4**:824
Punchvale, Sharif Khan, **5**:768
Pünhani of Kars (*aşîk*), **6**:803–4
Punjab (India), **5**:7, 650–56, 744
  Amritsar, Golden Temple in, **5**:257
  dance traditions, **5**:500
    bhangra, **5**:426–27, 574, 579
    giddhā, **5**:652–54
  entertainment music in, **5**:656
  geography of, **5**:650
  history of, **5**:650
  instruments in, **5**:651
  map of, **5**:*622*
  Patiala, **5**:177
  political unrest in, **5**:552
  regional cassettes in, **5**:549–50
  vocal music, **5**:475, 651, 653–55
Punjab (Pakistan), **5**:7, 744, 762–72
  Baloch people in, **5**:773, 776
  dance traditions, **5**:506
    bhangra, **5**:426–27, 574, 579
  geography of, **5**:762
  Gujranwala, manufacture of harmoniums, **5**:762
  Harappa institution, **5**:319
  Hīr Ranjha romance of, **5**:756–57, 771

history of, **5**:762
instruments in, **5**:762–63
Lahore
  dhol playing in, **5**:281, 283
  Muharram festival in, **5**:285
  patronage in, **5**:747
  tabla in, **5**:133–34, 136
  theater in, **5**:487
map of, **5**:*742*
Mīrāsī people, **5**:273, 283, *283*, 763–66
Multan, *thari* horse-dance in, **5**:488
musical genres of, **5**:771–72
Pakpattan, **5**:755
performers in, **5**:476, 763–71
regional cassettes in, **5**:549–50
Sufi shrines in, **5**:765, 769–70
theatrical traditions, **5**:765
  bhand, **5**:488
  puppet theater, **5**:769
weddings in, **5**:277
Punjabi by Nature (musical group), **3**:1064, 1084
Punjabi people, in Great Britain, **8**:207, 232, 236, 240–41
punk
  in Austria, **8**:676
  in Bulgaria, **8**:220
  in China, **7**:361
  in Europe, **8**:214, 215, 216, 217, 218, 236
  fusion in, **3**:327
  in Hawai'i, **9**:164–66
  in Hungary, **8**:220–21, 746, 747–48
  New Wave, **3**:357
  in North America, **3**:92, 323, 348, 357, 689
  in Poland, **8**:221
  in San Francisco, **3**:171
  in Scotland, **8**:369
  in South America, **2**:97, 104
  in Turkey, **6**:248
  women performers of, **3**:95
Puno, Rico J., **4**:885
punta-rock, **2**:675, 676–77, 733, 741
puppet theater. *See* theater, puppet
Pupunu, Sunia Tuineau, **9**:786–87
Purakayastha, Subodh, **5**:855
Puranas, **5**:11, 497, 511, 513, 633, 726, 731, 733, 872, 896
Purandara Dasa, **3**:989; **5**:15, 96, *216*, 262, 265, 386, 508
  Brahmin class of, **5**:387
  compositions of, **5**:105, 216, 219, 266, 452
  festival honoring, **5**:211, 270
  lyrics of, **5**:264, 265
  tala scheme of, **5**:139–42
Puran Mal (epic), **5**:674
Purari people, **9**:491, 492
Purba, Arie W. and Jonathan, **4**:106
Purba, Mauly, **4**:603
Purépecha culture, **2**:550, 575–81
Purevdash, **7**:1020
P'uri (musical group), **7**:970
Puri Kip'ŭn Namu (organization), **7**:969
Puritans, **3**:24, 531, 831–33
Purlie (musical), **3**:622
Purlie Victorious (Davis), **3**:622
Purna, **5**:*724*

Purnananda, Swami, **5**:590
"Purple Haze" (Hendrix), **3**:710
Purple Rain (Prince), **3**:685
Púrpura de la Rosa, La (Torrejón y Velasco), **2**:113
Purser, John, **8**:374
Purupuru, Samson, **9**:642
Puryear, Mark, **9**:994
Pusan Traditional Music Orchestra, **7**:959
Puschnig, Wolfgang, **7**:967
Pushkin, Aleksandr, **8**:286
Push Push (musical group), **9**:169
Puso (de León), **4**:881
"Put Your Little Foot" (mazurka), **3**:760
Put3ska, **4**:887
Putnam, Herbert, **3**:293
Putro, Widiyanto S., **3**:1020
"Puttin' on the Ritz" (Berlin), **3**:196
Putz, Adalbert, **10**:*163*
Puya y Ruiz, Adolfo, **4**:858
Puyuma people, **7**:527, 528
Pwahalu, Noel Pwanee, **9**:672–73
P'wo people, **4**:543
Pyaasa (*Pyāsa*; film), **5**:537, 543
Pyar Kiya To Darna Kya (film), **5**:540
Pyar To Hona Hi Tha (film), **5**:540
Pyatnitsky, Mitrofan, **8**:776, 777
Pygmies. *See also specific peoples*
  asymmetric timeline, **1**:309–10
  culture of, **1**:652
  music of, **1**:657–59, 660, 664, 681–82, 687–96, 744
  origin of term, **1**:688
  research on, **1**:688
  use of masks, **1**:309
Pyne, Louisa, **3**:61
Pynten, Berit, **8**:415
Pyogül nŏmŏsŏ (Hwang), **7**:956
Pyŏlgok (*chŏngak* piece), **7**:869
Pyŏn'gangsoega (Sin), **7**:969
Pyŏn'gangsoe t'aryŏng (*p'ansori* story), **7**:899
P'yŏngjo ioesang (*chŏngak* suite), **7**:869
P'yŏnsudaeyŏp (*kagok*), **7**:923
P'yŏngyang Minjok Ŭmak Tan (musical group), **7**:992
P'yŏngyang Muyong P'yogibŏp Yŏn'gusil (institute), **7**:992
P'yŏngyang, P'yŏngyang ch'insŏn üi tosiyŏ (collection), **7**:961
Pyŏn'gangsoe t'aryŏng (*p'ansori* story), **7**:984
Pyragi, Magtymguly, **6**:970
Pythagoras, **6**:16, 181, 183, 368, 540; **8**:47, 48, 93
Pyu (kingdom), **4**:365, 378
Pyykönen, Tommi, **8**:*478*

al-Qabbānī, Aḥmad Abū Khalīl, **6**:547, 550
Qabus bin Said, sultan of Oman, **6**:640, 672
Qais, Fazle Rabbi, **5**:791
Qajar dynasty, **6**:130, 137, 138, 140, 865
Qalandar group, **5**:769
Qalawūn, al-Nāsir M. B., Mamluk sultan, **6**:298
Qambar (saint), **6**:835
Qamrojana, **5**:791
Qand, **6**:296
Qantati Ururi, **2**:483

qanun (also *qānūn*). *See* zithers
Qānūn al-asfiyā' fī 'ilm naghamāt al-adhkiyā' (Siyāla), **6:**367
Qaraqalpaq people. *See* Karakalpak people
Qareeb (album), **8:**240
Qari'at al-Finjān (Egyptian song), **6:**601
Qāri-Yakubov, Muhiddin, **6:**939
Qarwashī, Monjī, **6:**336
al-Qaṣabjī, Muḥammad, **6:**548, 599
Qasem, **5:**807–8
Qashaubaiuly, Ämre, **6:**955
Qashqa'i people, **6:**827
qaṣīda, **1:**535; **6:**9, 409
   Afghanistan, **5:**827
   Algeria, **6:**470, 475
   collections of, **6:**371
   Egypt, **6:**149, 167, 173, 237–38, 547, 550, 551, 599, 600, 626
   form of, **6:**447, 454, 458, 540
   Iraq, **6:**313
   Israel, **6:**203
   Java, **4:**634
   Jewish performance of, **6:**1039
   kāfī and, **5:**753
   Lombok, **4:**776, 778
   Mashriq, **6:**545
   Morocco, **6:**496–97, 498, 499–500, 1041–42
   Oman, **6:**678
   Palestine, **6:**584–85, 591
   South Asia, **5:**278, 284
   Sumatra, **4:**606
   Syria, **6:**563, 569
   Tunisia, **6:**452, 506, 519
al-Qass. *See* 'Abd al Raḥmān 'Ammār al-Jushamīy, "al-Qass"
Qatar
   chordophones in, **6:**412
   dance traditions in, **6:***546*, 654, 706, 708, 709, 710
   idiophones in, **6:**403–4
   pearl-diving songs, **6:**546, 651
   women's music, **6:***536*, 697, 702
   zār ceremony in, **6:***535*
Qatrān Tabrīzī, **6:**922
qawwali, **5:**12, 256, 403, 416, 568, 751–53, 756–57
   Afghanistan, **5:**817
   Central Asia, **6:**937
   concerts of, **5:**420
   etymology of, **5:**751
   festivals of, **5:**755
   Fiji, **5:**613; **9:**782
   film-song versions of, **5:**533, 534, 535, 540
   influence on *khyāl*, **5:**170
   influence on *tarānā*, **5:**179
   instruments in, **5:**347
   international popularity of, **5:**748
   Kashmir, **5:**682, 695
   Mashriq, **6:**545
   North America, **3:**338, 340, 981, 1044, 1215; **5:**579, 581
   Pakistan, **5:**746, 748, 750
   performers of, **5:**423, 426
   Punjab (India), **5:**651, 656
   Punjab (Pakistan), **5:**765–66, 772
   Rajasthan, **5:**644

research on, **5:**576
   rhythm in, **5:**125
   United Kingdom, **5:**573
   Uttar Pradesh, **5:**668, 673
Qawwāl musicians, **5:**426, 476, 644, 748, 765–66, 769, 772
Qazanghapuly, Tättimbet, **6:**958
Q'ero culture, **2:**225–31
   instruments of, **2:**225–27
   musical genres, *chunchu*, **2:**227
   research on, **2:**231
Qeşem, Aşıq, **6:**845
Qi kingdom, **7:**319, 517
Qi Lainfang, **7:**264
Qi Rushan, **7:**279, 280, 286
Qi Shufang, **3:**959
Qian Decang, **7:**130
Qian Lezhi, **7:**118
Qian Nanyang, **7:**290
Qiang people, **7:**29, 30, 485–92
Qianlong emperor, **7:**34, 35, 294
Qiao (*Jiangnan sizhu* piece), **7:**225
Qiao Jianzhong, **7:**156
Qiao Jifu, **7:**229
Qijia culture, **7:**17
qin. *See* zithers
Qin dynasty, **7:**25, 88
   building of Great Wall, **7:**28–29
   instruments in, **7:**111–12
   musical revivals in, **7:**42
   xianshiyue music in, **7:**211
Qin fa wei hu (Chen), **7:**120
Qin jian (Cui), **7:**120
Qin kingdom, *zheng* in, **7:**171
Qin lü shuo (treatise), **7:**115
Qinding Gujin Tushu Jicheng (encyclopedia), **7:**129
Qinding shijing yuepu, **7:**132
Qinfu (Xi), **7:**159
Qing dynasty, **4:**447
   Buddhism in, **7:**322
   centralization in, **7:**26
   Confucianism in, **7:**336
   Daoism in, **7:**321–22
   dissolution of, **7:**379, 380
   instruments in, **7:**113–14, 176
   Korean-Japanese relations during, **7:**27, 28, 711, 725
   literature in, **7:**246
   Manchu origins of, **7:**517, 518, 1003
   musical institutions in, **7:**392
   music in, **7:**89, 103, 131
   nanguan ensemble in, **7:**206
   opera in, **7:**278, 289
   patronage of Tibetan Buddhism, **7:**34–35
   pipa in, **7:**169
   Taiping rebellion, **7:**305
   tanci performances in, **7:**261
   theater in, **7:**291
   unification in, **7:**33–35
   westernization during, **7:**228, 373
   women performers in, **7:**407–8
   yangqin in, **7:**180
Qing huidan tu (dynastic history), **7:**129
Qinglou Ji (Xia), **7:**403, 407
Qingnian (Liu), **7:**348–49

Qing Shan, **7:**357
Qing yang zhuan (*xiaodiao*), **7:**152
Qinqu jicheng, **7:**140
Qinshu daquan (Jiang), **7:**132
Qintong (Xu), **7:**117, 120
Qinxue rumen (*qin* piece), **7:**162–63
Qinxue rumen (Zhang), **7:**132
Qionghua Huiguan (society), **7:**304
Qishouban (*nanguan* piece), **7:**239
Qiu Hechou, **7:**217, 220
Qiu Ming, **7:**124, 132, 161
Qiu Zhilu, **7:**336
Qizilbash, Asad, **5:**768
Qo Hsiong people, **4:**550
Qoli, Aga Hoseyn, **6:***858*
Qolla culture, **2:**207, 223
Qomri, **6:**931
Qoramsinuly, Akhan-seri, **6:**955
Qorbani, Aşıq Rasul, **6:**845, *849*, 851–52
Qozhaghululy, Birzhan-sal, **6:**954, 955
Qozy Körpesh-Bayan Sulu (epic), **6:**952
Qu Qiubai, **7:**383
Qu Wei, **7:**349
Qu Xiaosong, **7:**351
quadrille, **2:**98, 100, 795; **3:**232, 407, 528; **8:**165–66
   in Antigua and Barbuda, **2:**798, 799
   in Bahamas, **2:**805, 809
   in Brazil, **2:**305, 330, 331
   in Canada, **3:**1190, 1196
   in Carriacou, **2:**868, 871–72
   in Corsica, **8:**571
   in Croatia, **8:**931
   in Dominica, **2:**842–43
   in Dominican Republic, **2:**860
   in France, **8:**546
   in Grenada, **2:**865
   in Guadeloupe, **2:**874, 877–78
   in Honduras, **2:**744
   in Ireland, **8:**382
   Italian, **3:**860, 864
   in Jamaica, **2:**900–901, 907–8
   in Louisiana, **3:**802, 857
   in Low Countries, **8:**524
   Mexican, **3:**735, 755
   in Montserrat, **2:**924–25
   in Netherlands Antilles, **2:**930
   New Mexican, **3:**760
   in Panama, **2:**773
   in Russia, **8:**766
   in St. Lucia, **2:**944–45
   in Virgin Islands, **2:**969, 970, 971–72
Quain, Buell Halvor, **9:**778
Quakers, **3:**136
Quality Records, **3:**1243
Qualtinger, Helmut, **8:**674–75
Quan Tangshi zhong di yuewu ziliao (collection), **7:**129
"*Quando quando*" (Renis), **8:**209
Quapaw Indian nation, **3:**440
Quarkoo, **2:**800
Quarkango (musical group), **3:**1077
Quashie, Harry Eben, **1:**355
Quatuor de Jazz Libre du Québec, **3:**1077
al-Qubbanji, Muḥammad, **6:**551
Qubilai (Kubilai Khan), **7:**32, 35

Québec, **3:**9, 1145–75. *See also* Lower Canada;
    New France
  Algonquian peoples, **3:**383
  Arctic peoples, **3:**374–81, 381
  Asian peoples in, **3:**1073
  Breton music in, **3:**331
  colonial life in, **3:**1148
  cultural isolation of, **3:**331
  dance in, **3:**223
  dance music in, **3:**1164, 1190
  First Nations groups in, **3:**461, 1162
  folk music in, **3:**325, 1075–76, 1163–68
  folk song collecting in, **3:**145–46, 148
  French-English polarity in, **3:**51–52, 313,
    1146, 1152, 1156
  historical concerts in, **3:**33, 1154, 1166
  history of musical life, **3:**1073–77, 1146–53
  Jesuit missionaries in, **3:**390
  Laurentian Mountains, **3:**1077
  Maliotenan reserve, **3:**73
  Montréal
    African-Canadians in, **3:**73, 1169–70
    chansonnier movement in, **3:**1059, 1076,
      1154–62, 1167–68
    cultural diversity of, **3:**223, 1073
    festivals in, **3:**223, 1170
    first music school in, **3:**275
    jazz in, **3:**1077
    light opera in, **3:**189
    L'Osstidcho concert, **3:**1157–58
    musical life in, **3:**17, 1148, 1149–53
    radio in, **3:**247
    Sephardic Jews in, **3:**1171–75
    settlement of, **3:**1056
  organ music performance controversies, **3:**28
  popular music in, **3:**1154–62
  population of, **3:**5
  Québec City
    1879 commemorative concert, **3:**145
    musical life in, **3:**1075
    settlement of, **3:**1056
  separatist movement in, **3:**17, 313, 314, 1059,
    1067, 1073, 1147, 1155–57, 1159,
    1161–62, 1167
  sound recording industry in, **3:**247, 1154,
    1159–61
Québec Act (1774), **3:**1073, 1146
Quechan Indian nation, **3:**428, 433
Quechua culture, **2:**205–23, 467
  aesthetics of, **2:**34, 215–17
  instruments of, **2:**35, 206–14
  musical contexts, **2:**217–21
  song traditions of, **2:**214–15
Queco, **8:**208
Queen, **3:**689; **8:**220
Queen Latifah, **3:**96, 97, 696, 714
Queen Victoria Girls School (Auckland), **9:**277
Queen's University (Belfast), **8:**394
Queers (musical group), **9:**164
Queiros, Pedro Fernandez, **9:**688
"quejas de Jimena, Las," **8:**256
Quellen deutscher Volkskunde (sound recording
    series), **8:**664
Quepo culture, **2:**681
"¿Qué será mi china?" (Puente), **3:**795
Quesnel, Joseph, **3:**189, 1075

Quest for Music Divine (Dey), **5:**56
Quest of the Ballad (Mackenzie), **3:**1125
Quetzal (musical group), **3:**750
Quevedo, Marcos de, **2:**735
Quevedo Rachadell, Nicolás, **2:**396
Quiché Maya, **2:**650, 651–52, 721–22, 736
  songs of, **2:**732
Quiché Vinak (Castillo), **2:**736
Quichua culture
  aesthetics of, **2:**429–31
  children's wakes in, **2:**423–24
  Holy Week processions of, **2:**419–20
  instruments of, **2:**414–18
  male performers in, **2:**428
  New Year's Eve celebration, **2:**426
  shamanism in, **2:**419
  weddings in, **2:**424–25
Quicksilver (bluegrass group), **3:**159
quickstep, **3:**1190; **8:**525
Quiet One (film), **3:**610
Quiet Revolution, **3:**1073, 1076, 1155–57,
    1167–68
Quigley, Sam, **3:**1018
Quilapayún (musical group), **2:**32, 75, 373;
    3:730
Quileute Indian nation, **3:**394, 395
Quilici, Félix, **8:**22, 574
Quinault Indian nation, **3:**394, 395
Quinlan, Julian, **9:**288
Quinn, Anthony, **8:**1007
Quinn, Frank, **3:**414
Quinn, Freddy, **8:**679
Quinn, Frederick, **10:**36
Quintana, Manuel, **2:**499
Quintana, Mr., **2:**933
Quintanar, Héctor, **2:**605
Quintanilla, Selena. *See* Selena
Quintero Rivera, Ángel G., **2:**941
Quinteto Contrapunto, **2:**543
Quintette Club (Ottawa), **3:**1181
Quintette du Hot Club de France, **8:**288
Quiroz, Manuel José de, **2:**735
Quisqueya, **2:**846
Quissaq, Tumasi, **3:**1275
Quissa (Quitsaq), Tumasi, **3:**1280
Qulie wenxiankao (Kong), **7:**336
Qulü (Wang), **7:**122, 130
Qur'ānic recitation. *See* recitation
Quraysh tribe, **5:**763
Qurbani (film), **5:**427
Qurbani, Aşiq, **6:**929
Qürbati (hava), **6:**849, 849–50, 851
Qureshi caste, **5:**476
Qureshi, Regula, **3:**1090, 1096; **5:**403, 585, 675
al-Qushayrī, **6:**372
Quṭb al-Dīn al-Shīrāzī, **6:**17, 73, 181, 365, 869,
    922
Qyz-Jibek (Brusilovskii), **6:**959
Qyz-Zhibek (epic), **6:**952

Raamlaxman, **5:**540
Rabāb (Kuwaiti singer), **6:**697
Rabagliati, Alberto, **8:**619
Rabai people, **1:**624
Rabelais, François, **8:**17
Rabi (Fiji Islands), Banabans in, **9:**712

Rabia, **6:**270
Rabinal culture, **2:**736
Rabindra Bharati, **5:**447
Rabinowitz-Ravina, Menashe, **6:**1025
Rachabane, Barney, **1:**779
Rachian people, **8:**827–28
  dance traditions of, **8:**841
  instruments of, **8:**840
Rachmaninov, Sergei, **3:**537; **7:**350; **8:**84, 776,
    781
racial issues (North America)
  African-American music scholarship, **3:**572–87
  blackface minstrelsy, **3:**185–86, 191–92
  blues and, **3:**579–80, 637–38, 644, 647
  Canada, **3:**72–74
  Chinese-Americans, **3:**958–59
  disco, **3:**688–89
  ethnomusicology and, **10:**139–40, 153–54
  gender and, **3:**88
  hip-hop and, **3:**697–99
  jazz and, **3:**578, 650, 652, 655–56, 660–61,
    663, 664
  Louisiana, racial classification, **3:**651–52
  musicality and, **3:**22–23
  musical theater, **3:**619
  music industry, **3:**329–30, 705–15
  Native Americans, **3:**525
  popular music, **3:**584
  pre-Civil War, **3:**616
  race riots of 1967, **3:**674
  ragtime and, **3:**651
  religion, **3:**120, 122, 123, 124, 125
  rhythm and blues and, **3:**349–50, 667, 668,
    671, 672, 675–76
  rock and roll and, **3:**354, 550–51
  swing, **3:**656
  United States, **3:**63–72
  white as racial category, **3:**67
Racines (Martinican group), **2:**919
Racy, Ali Jihad, **3:**1036, 1037; **6:**22, 24, 40, 235,
    285, 286; **10:**88
Rácz, Aladár, **8:**744
Rada (musical group), **3:**1170
Rada, Rubén, **2:**520
Radama I (Madagascar king), **1:**789
Radano, Ronald, **10:**164
Radcliffe-Brown, A. R., **9:**440, 987
Radebe, Marks, **1:**764
Raden, Franki, **3:**1013
Radha (deity)
  portrayed in dances, **5:**440, 493, 494, 495,
    503, 520
  visual depictions of, **5:**313
  worship of, **5:**132, 163, 249, 251, 252, 253,
    643, 665, 677, 844–45, 846, 855
Radharani, **5:**254, 855
Radhika Santwanam (Muddupalani), **5:**386
Radić, Antun, **8:**935, 937
Radić, Stjepan, **8:**935, 937
radif. See Iran
Radin, Leonid P., **8:**659
Radin, Paul, **3:**26
radio, **2:**40–41, 51–52; **3:**12, 237, 243–44. *See
    also* mass media
  Afghanistan, **5:**807–10, 811, 815–16, 820,
    825, 827, 831, 832, 835

Albania, **8:**999, 1000
Algeria, **6:**271, 475, 476
American military, **9:**26, 27
Aotearoa, **9:**931, 935, 944, 985
    Māori broadcasts, **9:**168
Arabian peninsula, **6:**667, 697, 701, 702
Arab music programming, **3:**1037
Arctic stations, **3:**380
Argentina, **2:**263, 265, 266, 267, 269, 270,
        276, 278
Australia, **9:**60, 414, 985
    Aboriginal rock broadcasts, **9:**145
    Aboriginal stations, **9:**443
    Anglo-Irish folk music broadcasts, **9:**141
    country music broadcasts, **9:**142, 413
    folk programming, **9:**413
    Greek-community programs, **9:**73
Austria, **8:**671
Azerbaijan, *aşıq* broadcasts, **6:**846
Bali, **4:**733
Bangladesh, **5:**527, 858–59
    archives of, **5:**529
Barbados, **2:**814, 819
Belarus, **8:**801
Belize, **2:**678
Bellona, **9:**852
Bolivia, **2:**288–89, 293, 297
Bosnia-Hercegovina, **8:**968–69
Brazil, **2:**107, 316, 326
Brunka culture, **2:**685
Bulgaria, **8:**903
Canada, **3:**18, 247–48, 265, 295–96, 1063,
        1066, 1101–5, 1185
    Anglo-Celtic broadcasts, **3:**1071, 1190
    art works for, **3:**1105
    broadcasts of South Asian music, **5:**583
    cable, **3:**1105
    campus–community, **3:**1104
    Canadian content rules, **3:**247–48, 250–51,
        265–66, 290, 314–15, 1068, 1103–4,
        1159
    Chinese programming, **3:**1261, 1265
    commercial stations, **3:**1103–4
    community, **3:**1104
    concert broadcasts, **3:**52, 1102–3, 1183–84,
        1228–29
    format, **3:**1103
    French-language programming, **3:**315,
        1088, 1103–4, 1150, 1154, 1157,
        1159
    jazz programming, **3:**1107
    Maritimes, **3:**1117, 1121, 1125, 1128
    native, **3:**1094, 1104
    northern regions, **3:**1278
    Québec, **3:**52
    Ukrainian broadcasts, **3:**1244
Caroline Islands, military stations, **9:**160
Central America, **2:**630
Chile, **2:**371
China, **7:**219, 354, 399
    folk music broadcasts, **7:**229
    orchestral music broadcasts, **7:**231
    shenqu broadcasts, **7:**300
Chuuk, **9:**736, 737
Colombia, **2:**382–83, 409
Cook Islands, **9:**897

copyright issues and, **2:**65
Corsica, **8:**573
Costa Rica, **2:**690, 691, 702–3
Croatia, **8:**936
Cuba, **2:**828
Czechoslovakia, **8:**724, 730
Denmark, **8:**464
Dominica, **2:**844
Dominican Republic, **2:**860, 861–62
Ecuador, **2:**428–29
educational role of, **2:**69–70
Egypt, **6:**166, 168, 233, 234–36, 239, 559,
        597–600, 604, 612, 616
El Salvador, **2:**716, 718
England, **8:**334, 338
Europe
    "evergreen" programming, **8:**209–10
    folk music broadcasts, **8:**155–57
    popular music programming, **8:**205, 207
Faroe Islands, **8:**471, 472
Federated States of Micronesia, **9:**160
Fiji, **5:**612
    Indian-community programming, **9:**93
Finland, **8:**217, 484, 486
    Saami stations, **8:**306
France, **8:**239
Georgia, **8:**844
Great Britain, **8:**210
Greece, **8:**1009, 1016
Guadeloupe, **2:**879–80
Guam, military stations, **9:**160
Guatemala, **2:**723
Gujarat, **5:**624
Guyana, **2:**448
Haiti, **2:**889, 890, 893
Hawai'i, **9:**163, 985
    reggae, **9:**166
Hungary, **8:**738–39, 746
Iceland, **8:**406
India, All India Radio, **5:**57, 527
    archives of, **5:**529
    ban on harmonium, **5:**341, 364
    ban on *tawāif* singing, **5:**374
    broadcasts from Tyagaraja festival, **5:**394
    broadcasts of *bhajana*, **5:**106
    broadcasts of *birahā*, **5:**667
    broadcasts of film music, **5:**737
    broadcasts of folk cassettes, **5:**550
    broadcasts of *havelī saṅgīt*, **5:**251
    broadcasts of Hindustani music, **5:**741
    broadcasts of Karnatak music, **5:**213
    broadcasts of ragas, **5:**854, 855
    broadcasts of regional music, **5:**405
    broadcasts of South Indian religious music,
        5:270
    broadcasts of *ṣūfyāna mūsīqī*, **5:**686
    broadcasts of Western music in Kashmir,
        5:682
    employment opportunities, **5:**454, 649
    National Programme of Music, **5:**527
    staff artists, **5:**379
India, South, **5:**543
Indonesia, **4:**102, 679–80, 682, 683, 685, 722
    broadcasts of *gamelan* music, **4:**655–56;
        10:44
Iran, **6:**142, 824, 861–62
    aşıq broadcasts, **6:**846

Ireland, **8:**386, 387, 388, 391
Irian Jaya, **9:**578, 591
Israel, **6:**263–64, 1017, 1020, 1029, 1069,
        1071
    ḥazanut on, **6:**204
    religious popular music on, **6:**204
Italy, **8:**613–14, 620, 621
Jamaica, **2:**97, 910–11
Japan, **7:**537, 732
Karnataka, **5:**880
Kashmir, **5:**684
    broadcasts of *ṣūfyāna mūsīqī*, **5:**686–87
Kiribati, **9:**760
Korea, **7:**880
Kuna culture, **2:**648
Latvia, **8:**507
Macedonia, **8:**974, 976, 978–79, 980, 981,
        1003
Maharashtra, **5:**729, 730
Maleku culture, **2:**683
Malta, **8:**639, 640
Mariana Islands, military stations, **9:**160
Marshall Islands, **9:**751–52
Martinique, **2:**917, 920
Maya culture, **2:**653
Mexico, **2:**567, 599, 605, 619, 620, 621, 622,
        623
Micronesia, **9:**719, 721, 994
Miskitu culture, **2:**663
Montenegro, **8:**961
Nepal, **5:**696, 697, 701, 704, 705–6
Netherlands Antilles, **2:**931
New Caledonia, **9:**672, 678
Nicaragua, **2:**663, 763, 765–66
North West Frontier Province, **5:**790–91
Norway, **8:**426, 427
Oceania, archives, **9:**958
Pakistan, **5:**527, 745–46, 748
    archives of, **5:**529, 747
    northern, **5:**798, 799
Palestine, **6:**279–80
Panama, **2:**783
Papua New Guinea, **9:**91, 149, 516, 985
    broadcasts of Motu choirs, **9:**493
    guitar songs, **9:**155
    Gulf Province, **9:**495
    Rai Coast, **9:**566
Paraguay, **2:**460, 463
Peru, **2:**484, 485–86, 487
Pohnpei, **9:**739–40
Portugal, **8:**578, 584
Punjab (India), **5:**656
Qur'ānic recitation broadcasts, **6:**161
Radio Free Europe, **8:**218
Radio Luxembourg, **8:**218
Romania, **8:**880, 883, 884
Ryûkyû Islands, **7:**795
St. Lucia, **2:**950
Scandinavia, Saami stations, **8:**306
Scotland, **8:**371, 374
Serbia, **8:**949
Sikaiana, **9:**848
Slovenia, **8:**919–20, 922
Solomon Islands, **9:**158, 667
South Africa, **5:**616
South Asia, **5:**420

Volume Key: **6,** Middle East; **7,** East Asia; **8,** Europe; **9,** Australia and the Pacific Islands; **10,** The World's Music.

radio (*continued*)
South Korea, **7:**952, 988, 993–94
Spain, **8:**600
Sri Lanka, **5:**969, 970, 972
Surinam, **2:**504
Suyá culture, **2:**145, 149
Sweden, **8:**152
Switzerland, **8:**209, 697
Tahiti, **9:**958
Tonga, **9:**958
Trinidad, **5:**591
Tunisia, **6:**437, 509, 512, 527
Turkey, **6:**79, 117, 119, 121, 248, 250, 256, 785, 797
aşîk performances, **6:**808
Ukrainian programming, **3:**1244
United States
Asian programming, **3:**951
big band broadcasts, **3:**655–56, 707
black-appeal, **3:**349–50, 353, 560–61, 670, 692, 742
bluegrass broadcasts, **3:**161, 163
California, Los Angeles, **3:**742–43, 746
chutney-*soca* programming, **3:**816
concert broadcasts, **3:**277, 559
country music broadcasts, **3:**13, 76, 79, 80, 243, 315, 520, 559–60, 1073, 1077
development of, **3:**195
disco programming, **3:**688, 712
diversity of programming on, **3:**504
economic issues of, **3:**261–62, 263
ethnic, **3:**558–61
exclusion of black artists, **3:**707
folk-song broadcasts, **3:**294
format, **3:**49, 559
gospel music broadcasts, **3:**534, 634; **10:**144
government funding for, **3:**299
Hawai'ian-themed programming, **3:**1050
house music programming, **3:**691
Illinois, Champaign-Urbana, **3:**170
Latin music programming, **3:**743
New Age programming, **3:**346
payola scandal, **3:**355, 709
pedagogical uses, **3:**277
Plains Indian programming, **3:**444
rap programming, **3:**552, 713, 714
reggae programming, **3:**809, 1202
rock programming, **3:**348
rock and roll programming, **3:**349
royalty disputes, **3:**708
South Asian programming, **3:**985–86; **5:**583
Spanish-language programming, **3:**522, 737, 738–39, 740, 744, 746, 747, 781
top-forty, **3:**355, 356, 559, 683
traditional music affected by, **3:**148, 149
urban contemporary format, **3:**712
Uruguay, **2:**520, 522
'Uvea and Futuna, **9:**814–15, 958
Uzbekistan, **6:**918, 919
Vanuatu, **9:**140, 694
Virgin Islands, **2:**969
Voice of America, **8:**619
Warao culture, **2:**193
West Futuna, **9:**863
Yap, **9:**730
Yugoslavia (former), **8:**279, 1001

Radio Ballads (MacColl), **8:**371
Radio-Canada, **3:**1121
Radio City Music Hall (New York), **3:**219
Radio Kings of Harmony, **3:**1212
Radio *ma'lûf* ensemble (Tunisia), **6:**329–30, 331–32
Radio Télé Tahiti, **9:**958
Radya Pustaka (Surakarta), **4:**677
Radzimichans, **8:**790
Rafael (Spanish singer), **2:**102; **3:**746
Rafet El Roman, **6:**252
Raffi, **3:**1081
Raffles, Thomas Stamford, **4:**84, 518, 636
Rafi, Mohammad, **5:**420, 421, 539
Rafu Shimpo (newspaper), **3:**968
raga, **4:**15; **6:**47. *See also* ragas
Afghanistan, **5:**827
ancestors of, **5:**28, 66, 96
authorship concepts in, **5:**83
brass band performances of, **5:**671
classification systems
by family, **5:**47, 48, 68, 72–73, 76, 77, 79, 313–14, *315–16*
by scale type, **5:**45, 46–47, 51, 52, 77, 78–79, 94, 96–97, 262, 314, 445–46
collection prepared for Queen Victoria, **5:**433
in devotional music, **5:**250, 252, 253
dhunî style, **5:**194, 203
early, **5:**96
âlâp section, **5:**40, 48
paṇ, **5:**216
etymology of, **5:**90
for *filmî gît*, **5:**532
ghana, **5:**100, 217, 218
Hindustani, **5:**64–87 (*See also* ragas, below)
âlâp section, **4:**67; **5:**69, 84–85, 119, 164–68, 172, 177, 195, 196, 198–99, 337
alpatva/bahutva relationships, **5:**64, 68
for *caryâ* songs, **5:**844
characters of, **5:**69
compared with Karnatak, **5:**89, 92, 95
composition in, **5:**82–84
concert performances of, **5:**203–4
created by Nazrul Islam, **5:**855
for *dhrupad*, **5:**164–68
emotion and, **5:**64, 69, 71–72
extramusical associations of, **5:**66, 69–73
gharânâ styles of, **5:**83–84
in Kabuli *ghazal*, **5:**805
letter notation for, **5:**79–81
in light classical genres, **5:**179, 192
meaning of, **5:**64–66
performance of, **5:**79–87
performance styles of, **5:**66
pitch configurations in, **5:**66
pitch theory in, **5:**73–76
râgmâlâ (garland of ragas), **5:**197, 203
realization of, **5:**84–86
sandhiprakâs, **5:**69, 79
śruti/svara distinctions, **5:**67
suitability factors, **5:**69
theoretical terms and concepts in, **5:**66–69
for *ţhumrî*, **5:**180–81
transmission of, **5:**66, 86–87
used by Sikhs, **5:**13
vâdî/samvâdî relationships, **5:**64, 68, 74–75

institutional transmission of, **5:**447–48
Karnatak, **5:**89–108, 209, 260, 261 (*See also* ragas, below)
âlâpana section, **5:**89, 90, 94, 98–103, 104, 106, 214–15, 218, 384, 389
as basis for Brahmin song, **5:**910, 916
characteristics of, **5:**89–90
compared with Hindustani, **5:**89, 92, 95
components of, **5:**90–96
created by Tyagaraja, **5:**269
in dance and drama performances, **5:**104–5
emotion and, **5:**90
improvised forms, **5:**98–103, 214–15
in light classical music, **5:**107–8
meanings of, **5:**89–90
in nonclassical traditions, **5:**105–6
pitch configurations in, **5:**93
râgamâlikâ 'garland of ragas,' **5:**97, 99, 107, 215, 217, 218–19, 225
in Sri Lanka, **5:**108
śruti/svara distinctions, **5:**93
in Tamil Nadu theater, **5:**913
tonal hierarchy in, **5:**95–96
use in film music, **5:**545
in *vâdya*, **5:**886
Kashmiri, **5:**692
"large" *vs.* "small," **5:**85
local traditions of, **5:**20, 33, 400
medieval, **5:**76–77
Newâr concept of, **5:**702
Orissa, **5:**733
"parent" *vs.* "derived," **5:**97
performance of, **6:**42
poetic descriptions of, **5:**73
râgiņî, **5:**47, 73, 313
râgmâlâ iconographical personifications, **5:**44, 46–47, 73, 301–2, 307–8, 312–18, *692*
tonal possibilities in, **5:**64–65
transmission of, **5:**373
treatises on, **5:**24, 33, 34–35, 38, 40, 43, 44, 45, 50–51, 52, 66, 313, 445–46
Raga Records, **5:**530
ragas, (H = Hindustani; K = Karnatak)
aḍânâ (H), **5:**81, 85
ahîr bhairav (H), **5:**78, 80
alhaiyâ bilâval (H), **5:**80
ânandabhairavi (K), **5:***148*, 224, 229
anandi kedar (H), **5:***177*
ârabhi (K), **5:**100, 217
âsâvari (H), **5:**80
âsâvari family (H), **5:**81
âsâvêri (K), **5:**90
bâgeshrî (H), **5:**74
bahâduri toḍî (H), **5:**85
bairâgî (H), **5:**80
bairâmi (Afghan), **5:**827
begaḍa (K), **5:**217
behâg (K), **5:**917
beiru (Afghan), **5:**827
bhairav (H), **5:**77, 80, 85, 314
bhairavî (H), **5:**181, *182*, 194, 197
bhairavî (K), **5:**107, 217
bhairavî (Trinidad), **5:**591
bhâtiâli (H), **5:**860
bhîmpalâsî (H), **5:**81

bhūpālī (H), **5:**78
bhūp kalyāṇ (H), **5:**190, 190–91
bihārī (H), **5:**194
bilahari (K), **5:**217
bilāskhānī ṭoḍī (H), **5:**68–69
bilāval family (H), **5:**80
chārūkauns (H), **5:**190
citrañjani (K), **5:**221–22, *223*
darbārī kānaḍā (H), **5:**66, 72, 73, 74, 75, *76*,
    78, 81–82, 85
deś (H), **5:**81, 85, 194, 436
devgandhār (H), **5:**633
devgiri bilāval (H), **5:**80
dhulia malhār (H), **5:**85
ṭoḍī (H), **5:**315, *317*
durgā (H), **5:**80
gārā (H), **5:**194, 197
gauḷa (K), **5:**100, 217
hamsadhvani (K), **5:**225, *227*
harikambhōji (K), **5:**354
hemant (H), **5:**80
imān kalyāṇ (H), **5:**85
jaijaivantī (H), **5:***175–76*
jaunpurī (H), **5:**66, 72, 74, 75, *76*, 78, 81,
    85, *177*
kāfī (H), **5:**74, 181, 197, 753
kāfī (Trinidad), **5:**591
kalyāṇi (K), **5:**217, 282
kāmbhōji (K), **5:**107, 217
kanada (H), **5:**73
kedār (H), **5:**633
kedaram (K), **5:**217
kesturi (Afghan), **5:**827
ketāragoula (K), **5:**107
khamāj (H), **5:**85, 180–81, 194, *196*, 197
kīravāni (K), **5:**90
kuraṇji (K), **5:**275, 910
lalit (H), **5:***174*
lalitha (K), **5:**229
madhuvanti (H), **5:**81
madhyamāvati (K), **5:***98*, 220, 275
mālaśrī (Nepalese), **5:**699
mālkauns (H), **5:***73*, 633
māṇḍ (H), **5:**642
mānjh khamāj (H), **5:**194
mārvā (H), **5:**80
megh (H), **5:**81
megh malhār (H), **5:***47*, 313
miyāṅ kī ṭoḍī (H), **5:**68–69, *165–66, 167–68*
miyāṅ malhār (H), **5:**81
mōhanam (K), **5:**217
mukhāri (K), **5:**282
multānī (H), **5:**81, *178*
nārāyaṇī (H), **5:**80
nāṭa (K), **5:**100, 217
nāṭadurañji (K), **5:**225
nat bihāg (H), **5:**849
nīlāmbari (K), **5:**90, 910
pahārī (H), **5:**194
pāri (Afghan), **5:**827
paṭdīp (H), **5:**81
pilu (Afghan), **5:**827
pīlū (H), **5:**180, 194, 197
punnāgavarāli (K), **5:**90
pūriyā dhanāshrī (H), **5:**80, 85
pūrvī (H), **5:**80

pūrvikalyāṇi (K), **5:**99
rāmkalī (H), **5:**80
śankarābharaṇa (K), **5:**93, 94–96, 97, 217
sāraṅg (H), **5:**633
sāwani kalyāṇ (H), **5:**85
śrī (K), **5:**100, 217
ṭhumrī aṅg (H), **5:**194, 203
tilak kāmod (H), **5:***201*
varāli (K), **5:**100, 217
vasanta (K), **5:**90
yadukulakāmbhōji (K), **5:**90, 217
Raga (Vanuatu), **9:**697
Ragamala (album), **5:**528
Rāgamālā (Kshemakarna), **5:**314, *315*
Rāgamālā (Vitthala), **5:**48, 52, 314
Raga-Mala Societies, **3:**1084, 1216
Rāgamañjarī (Vitthala), **5:**48
rāgam-tānam-pallavi, **5:**94, 100, 159, 213, 215,
    217–18, 388–89
ragamuffin, **8:**207
Rāgasāgara (treatise), **5:**313
Rāgavibodha (Somanatha), **5:**46, 48
Rage Against the Machine (musical group),
    3:133, 750
ragga, **2:**96, 98, 893
Raghavan, M. D., **5:**964
Raghavan, V., **5:**225
Ragi (Nissan composer), **9:**639
ragtime, **3:**12, 510, 547–58, 601, 650–51; **8:**228
    in Africa, **1:**218
    Afro-Cuban music and, **3:**783
    band performances of, **3:**568
    blues and, **3:**640, 644, 648
    in Finland, **8:**483
    in Guatemala, **2:**733
    musical theater and, **3:**193, 618, 622
    publishing of, **3:**705
    research on, **3:**580
    in South Africa, **1:**218, 764, 765–66, 767,
        769, 770
    tango's influence on, **3:**521
    in West Africa, **1:**358
Ragtime (Flaherty and Ahrens), **3:**200
Ragu'el, Azzaj, **1:**147
Raguer, Elisea, **4:**856
Rāḥ al-jām fī shajarat al-anghām (Askar al-Ḥalabī
    al-Ḥanafī al-Qādirī), **6:**366, 565–66
Raḥbānī brothers, **6:**251–52, 553–55
Raḥbānī, Ziyād, **6:**555
Raheja, Gloria, **5:**674
"*Rahél lastimosa*" (Sephardic song), **3:**1173
Rahim, Gamel Abdel, **1:**220
Rahimov, Farukh Abdul, **6:***931*
Rahka, Alla, **3:**953
Raḥma, **6:**296
Rahman, Azizur, **5:**858
Rahman, Jusuf, **4:**603
Rahman, Sheik Lutfar, **5:**858
rai, **1:**422, 547; **3:**338; **5:**429; **6:**269–72, 438,
    477; **8:**210, 233, 234–35, 238, 239
Rai, I Wayan, **3:**1019; **4:**733
Ra'iatea (Society Islands), **9:**867
    Chinese in, **9:**868
    dance in, **9:**7–9, 10
Raichev, Alexander, **8:**905
Raidma, Karl, **3:**880

Raijua, **4:**786, 802
Rail Band, **1:**420, 421
"Railroad Bill" (ballad), **3:**639
Railway Cultural Work Song and Dance Group
    (China), **7:**399
Räimo Ärvenpää (musical group), **3:**1196
Rain (film), **9:**45
Raïna Raï, **6:**271
Rainbow Stage Opera (Winnipeg), **3:**1230
Rainer Family, **3:**183–84
Rainey, Gertrude "Ma," **3:**103, 524, 631, 644
Rainger, Ralph, **9:**43
Raipur dynasty, **5:**721
Ra'iqa, **6:**295
Raisin (musical), **3:**622
Raisin in the Sun (Hansberry), **3:**622
Raising Hell (Run-D.M.C.), **3:**713
Ra'ivavae (Austral Islands), **9:**879–82
Raj, Dilber, **5:**790
Raja, A. M., **5:**421
Raja, C. Kunhan, **5:**57
Raja, Hasan, **5:**859
Rajabī, Yunus, **6:**918, 919
al-Rajab, Muḥammad Hāshim, **6:**536
Rajabov, Yuri, **6:**911
Rajā'ī, Fu'ād, **6:**567
Rājā Jaitsīno Chand, **5:**637
Rajalakshmiammal, Smt., **5:**389
Rajammal, **5:**905
Rajam, N., **5:**207, 466
Rāja Pārvai (film), **5:**544
Rajaraja, Chola king, **5:**263
Rajarattinam Pillai, T. N., **5:**393–94
Rajasimha, King, **5:**960
Rajasthan, **5:**639–49
    Bikaner court, **5:**640
    ceremonies, spirit possession, **5:**292
    dance traditions of, **5:**646–49
    devotional music of, **5:**642–44
    folk music, popular arrangements of, **5:**427
    geography of, **5:**639
    history of, **5:**639
    instruments in, **5:**343–45, 347
    Jaipur court, **5:**640
    Jodhpur court, **5:**640
    Kishangarhi painting style of, **5:**300, 307
    map of, **5:**622
    Mīna people, spirit possession rituals, **5:**288
    Nathdvara, *naubat khānā* in,
        5:280
    patronage in, **5:**7, 639–42
    performing castes of, **5:**476, 640–42
    population of, **5:**639
    rāgmālā painting in, **5:**314
    regional cassettes in, **5:**550
    Udaipur court, **5:**640
    vocal music
        epic songs, **5:**635, 646
        gālī insult songs, **5:**642, 645, 646, 648
        havelī saṅgīt, **5:**251, 643
        keśyā, **5:**277, 645
        khyāl (folk song genre), **5:**645
        men's genres, **5:**646
        pad, **5:**643
        swing songs, **5:**645–46
        women's genres, **5:**644–46

Rājataraṅgiṇī (Kalhana), **5**:689
Rajendra-Coladewa (South Indian ruler), **4**:600
Rajneesh, Osho, **5**:557
Rajpur dynasty, **5**:721
Rajputs, **5**:305, 402, 411, 720
  dances of, **5**:647
  epics of, **5**:646
  patronage of performing arts, **5**:7, 639, 641
  relation to Laṅgās, **5**:640
  religion of, **5**:643
Raju, U. P., **5**:234
Rakahanga (Cook Islands), **9**:909
  history of, **9**:904
  music and dance of, **9**:904–7
  population of, **9**:903
Rakha, Alla, **5**:134, 136, 137, 380, 566
Rakhine people, **4**:363
Raks-PolyGram, **6**:252
Ralambo (Madagascar king), **1**:789
Ram (musical group), **3**:806
Ram, Sita, **10**:10
Rama (deity), **5**:261, 701
  association with Ayodhya, **5**:247
  portrayed in dances, **5**:495–96, 503, 511, 673
  worship of, **5**:220–21, 230, 247, 249, 253, 259, 268–69, 279, 589, 617, 661, 891
Rama I, king of Siam, **4**:225, 251, 255
Rama II, king of Siam, **4**:225, 235, 251, 255, 258
Rama III, king of Siam, **4**:229, 231, 286
Rama IV, king of Siam (Mongkut), **4**:91, 219, 225, 230, 248, 285, 287–88, 304
Rama V, king of Siam (King Chulalongkorn), **4**:219, 230, 234, 255, 277, 285
Rama VI, king of Siam (Vajiravudh), **4**:223, 255, 277
Rama VII, king of Siam (Prajadhipok), **4**:225, 276, 277–78
Rama IX, king of Thailand (Bhumibol Adulyadej), **4**:96, 219, 225
Rama culture, **2**:747, 749
Rama Hari (Cayabyab), **4**:881, 885
Rama Tibodi II, king of Ayuthaya, **4**:250
Ramachandran, M. G., **5**:555, *555*
Ramadas, **5**:264, 266, 270
Ramadas, Bhadrachala, **5**:216
Ramakrishna movement, **5**:256
Ramakrishna, Sri, **3**:130
Ramalho, Elba, **2**:326, 333
Ramalingasvami, **5**:216
Ramamatya, **5**:46, 77, 262
Ramamurthy, T. K., **5**:544
Raman, B. V., **5**:232
Raman, V. P., **5**:327
Ramanandi sect, **5**:247
Ramanathan, G., **5**:543
Ramanathan, Geetha, **5**:*233*
Ramanathan, M. D., **5**:217, 224–25
Ramanathan, S., **5**:326–27
Ramanaŭ, Jeŭdakim, **8**:803
Ramani, N., **3**:*985*, 990
Rāmaṇṇa school, **5**:243–45
Ramanuja, **5**:105
Ramaraju, Biruduraju, **5**:891
Ramaromanompo (Madagascar chief), **1**:782

Ramayana (epic), **3**:*1000*, 1012, 1019; **5**:11, 220, 261–62, 353, 613, 633, 667, 668, 733, 919
  danced performances of, **5**:282, 482–83, 490, 497, 509, 513, 515–16, *618*, 723–24, 876, 879, 933
  firewalking ritual and, **5**:617
  references to Sri Lanka in, **5**:490
  references to women performers, **5**:408
  saṅkha in, **5**:361
  in Southeast Asia, **4**:66, 650, 654, 705–6, 753, 756
  Telugu rendition of, **5**:897
Ramazzotti, Eros, **8**:620
Ramblin' Thomas, **3**:645
Rambolamasonadro (Madagascar princess), **1**:789
Rambutjo (Papua New Guinea), **9**:602
Rāmcaritmānas (Tulsi Das), **5**:253, 495–96, 589, 673
Ramchandra, C., **5**:537, 540
Ramdevji (deity), **5**:643, 647
Rameau, Jean-Philippe, **8**:160, 550
Ramel, Povel, **8**:445
Ramérez, Agustín, **3**:780
Ramgoonai, Drupatee, **2**:86
Rāmī, Aḥmad, **6**:552, 605
Raminsh, Imant, **3**:1097
Ramírez de Arellano, Enrique, **2**:784
Ramírez, Ariel, **2**:263
Ramirez, Bruno, **3**:1083
Ramírez, Louis, **3**:789
Ramirez, Tina, **3**:851
Ramkhelawan, Kries, **2**:86
Ramnagar, maharajah of, **10**:6–8, 12
Ramón y Rivera, Luís Felipe, **2**:488, 523, 524, 540, 544, 744, 783
Ramos, Alfonso, **3**:780
Ramos, Daniel, **10**:80
Ramos, Ignacio, **4**:856
Ramos, Rubén, **3**:780
Ramovš, Mirko, **8**:922
Rampal, Jean-Pierre, **3**:986, 1210; **5**:584
Rampart label, **3**:748
Rampling, Danny, **3**:691
Ramprasad, **5**:249
Ramsay, Allan, **8**:17, 372
Ramseyer, Urs, **4**:733
Ramsey, S. Robert, **7**:28
Ramuneles Singers, **3**:1082
Ramuva movement, **8**:513
Ramuz, Alphonse, **8**:697
Rānā caste, **5**:641
Rana family, **5**:697
Rana, Sohail, **5**:746
Ranade, Ashok, **5**:423
Raṇamalla Chand, **5**:637
Ranavalona I (Madagascar queen), **1**:789
Rāṇāyanīya school, **5**:242, 243
ranchera, **2**:101
  in Argentina, **2**:256, 261
  in Chile, **2**:371
  in Costa Rica, **2**:703
  in Dominican Republic, **2**:861
  in El Salvador, **2**:708, 716, 718, 719
  in Guatemala, **2**:728

  in Mexico, **2**:101, 620–21, 622
  in Nicaragua, **2**:763
  in Peru, **2**:485
  in United States, **3**:722, 744, 763, 765, 766, 775, 778, 781; **10**:78
  in Uruguay, **2**:516, 522
Rancho Abandonado, El (Williams), **2**:115
Rancho Folclórico das Lavradeiras de Mosteiró, **8**:*577*
Randall, A. G., **3**:1090
Randall, Bob, **9**:443–44
Randia, **8**:277
Rane, Sarasvatibai, **5**:414
Ranganathan, T., **5**:161, 561
Rang, Sada, **5**:767
Rangel, Irma, **3**:749
Ranger, Terence O., **1**:603, 636; **9**:223
Rangiwewehi, Ngāti, **9**:*946*
Ranglin, Ernie, **2**:911, 912
Rani, Devika, **5**:420
"Ran-Kan-Kan" (Puente), **3**:794
Rankin family, **3**:150, 1073, 1127
Ransome-Kuti, Fela. *See* Kuti, Fela
Ransome-Kuti, Funmilayo, **1**:483
Ransome-Kuti, I.O., **1**:483
Ransome-Kuti, Rev. J. J., **1**:19, 405
"*Ranz des vaches fribourgeois*" (Bovet), **8**:693
Ranzini, Paul, **10**:165
Rao, A. S. Sadashiva, **5**:437
Rao, S. Ramachandra, **5**:*264*
rap, **2**:96, 98, 111; **3**:17, 18, 323, 341, 513, 552, 689, 713–15
  Afrocentricity and, **3**:714
  Aotearoa, **9**:168, 169, 999
  Belarus, **8**:802
  bhangra and, **5**:427, 575
  blues and, **3**:648
  Brazil, **2**:354
  British Caribbean consumers, **3**:812
  Bulgaria, **8**:284
  Cambodian, **3**:1002
  Canada, **3**:73, 1205
  Chicano, **3**:750
  China, **7**:361, 368
  cuarteto and, **2**:280
  dancing to, **3**:211, 225
  deejays for, **3**:230
  early history of, **3**:692–93
  East Coast, **3**:701
  Egypt, **6**:555
  Europe, **8**:214, 228
  in film music, **5**:545
  fusions in, **3**:337, 1064
  gangsta, **3**:552, 697, 698, 701, 714
  gospel music and, **3**:635
  Haitian, **2**:893; **3**:806
  Hawai'i, **9**:165, 220, 928
  ideology and, **3**:621
  influence on rock, **3**:359
  Japanese-American, **3**:973
  Korean, **3**:513; **7**:967
  Macedonia, **8**:983
  Martinique, **2**:919
  Miami style, **3**:701–2
  Micronesia, **9**:160
  Midwest, **3**:702

Volume Key: **1**, Africa; **2**, South America, Mexico, etc.; **3**, United States and Canada; **4**, Southeast Asia; **5**, South Asia

Mongolia, **7:**1020
Nepal, **5:**705
Oceania, **9:**211
Peru, **2:**486
plena-rap, **2:**797
Portugal, **8:**585
Puerto Rico, **2:**940
race and, **3:**63
reggae-dancehall and, **3:**811, 1203
Samoan, **3:**1052
South Asia, **5:**429, 568, 652
southern fried, **3:**702
stylistic features of, **3:**699–701
subgenres of, **3:**698–99
West Coast, **3:**698, 701, 714
women performers of, **3:**95, 96, 714
Rapa (Austral Islands), **9:**879–82, *998*
Rapa Nui, **2:**2, 356; **4:**529; **9:**46, 319, 336, 865,
          951–53
  body decoration, **9:**349
  films on, **9:**1020
  history of, **9:**951–52
  music and dance of, **9:**951–53
  rongorongo genre, **9:**885
  sound recordings from, **9:**1004–5
  Tahitian, Sāmoan, and Chilean genres in,
          9:952
Rapa-Nui (film), **9:**46
Rapee, Erno, **3:**202, *262*
Raphaelson, Samson, **3:**938
Rappaport, Charley, **3:**58
Rappaport, Roy A., **9:**185
"Rappers Delight" (Sugar Hill Gang), **3:**695, 699
Raqq al-Ḥabīb (al-Qaṣabjī), **6:**599
Raqṣat al-Ghall (Zabīd dance), **6:**99, *100*
Raqṣat al-Mansarī (Zabīd dance), **6:***104*
al-Raqūtī, **6:**443
Rara Machine (musical group), **3:**806
Rarámuri culture. *See* Tarahumara culture
Raroia (Tuamotu), **9:**969
Rarotonga (Cook Islands)
  Christian missionaries from, **9:**195
  cultural contacts with Rotuma, **9:**823
  dance of, **9:**951
  hīmene raroto'a, **9:**872
  history of, **9:**896
  music of, **9:**961
  popular music in, **9:**897
  theater, **9:**238
Rasā'il (Ikhwān al-Ṣafā), **6:**367
Rās Dhāria (Mīrāsī subgroup), **5:**765
al-Rashīd Bey, Muḥammad, **6:**325, 433, 505,
          506, 507
Rashid, Hasan, **6:**612
Rashīdiyya Institute (Tunis), **6:**325, 326–32, 336,
          407, 433, 502, 505–6, 508–9, 510,
          511–12, 513
Rashīd, Subhi Anwar, **6:**535
Rashomôn (film), **7:**750
Rasito, **4:**683; **10:**50
Rasmussen, Anne K., **6:**162
Rasmussen, Knud, **3:**381
Rasmussen, P. E., **8:**460
Rasmussen, Sunleif, **8:**471
Rasool, Ghulam, **5:***549*
Rasoolanbai, **5:**413–14

rasps. *See* scrapers (rasps)
Rastafarianism, **2:**76, 97, 353, 795
  in Antigua and Barbuda, **2:**799
  in Barbados, **2:**817
  in Belize, **2:**666–67, 677
  in Canada, **3:**1205
  in Europe, **8:**235–36
  in Jamaica, **2:**898–99, 904, 910
  in United States, **3:**811
Rastriya Nachghar (institution), **5:**705
Rasul Mir, **5:**687
Rasūlī dynasty, **6:**685–86
Rātana Church, **9:**935
Ratanpur dynasty, **5:**721
Ratbeat (periodical), **8:**484
Rathebe, Dolly, **1:***771*, 774
Rathole, Vinod, **5:**421
Ratia, Alfredo, **4:**856
Ratna Recording Company, **5:**705
Ratnayaka, Victor, **5:**424
Rätta Hemlandet, Det (periodical), **3:**870
rattles
  abwe, **2:**824
  Africa, **1:**554, 785
    worn in dance, **1:**111, 113, 115–16, 118,
          277, 565, 605, 624, 625, 638, 707,
          752
  agé, **2:**511
  ainkjaga, **8:**853
  akapkap, **8:**853
  alfandoque, **2:**377, 414
  Andean regions, **2:**206
  angkalung, **4:**232
  angklung, **3:**954, 1018
    Bali, **4:**748–49
    Cirebon, **4:**697
    Java, **4:**634, 645, 646, 655
    Malaysia, **4:**413
    Singapore, **4:**520–21
    Sunda, **4:**52, 114–15, *138*, 710–11, 717
  Anuta, **9:**860
  Argentina, **2:**249, 250, 251–52, 256
  asæzaghu, **1:**565
  ason, **2:**883
  asoso, **1:**555
  atitish, **1:**565
  Australia, **9:**411, 412
  ayacachtli, **2:**601
  ayam, **2:**589, *590*
  Aztec culture, **2:**556
  beer-bottle cap, **9:**179
  beiraq, **6:**404–5
  bèri, **4:**691
  Bolivia, **2:**139
  brazhotki, **8:**797
  Brazil, **2:**144, 324
  buta (or *buutàa*), **1:**273, 521
  California Indian groups, **3:**417
  carángano, **2:**377, 384
  Carib culture, **2:**13, 23
  cascabeles, **2:**494
  caxixí, **2:**346, *347*
  chac-chac, **2:**866, 870–71, 953, 955, 959
  chacha, **2:**874, 877, *916*, 918
  chacha-lérol, **2:**437
  chairígoa, **2:**554

  chakchak, **2:**841, 945, 946, 948
  chaworó, **2:**824
  chéqueres, **2:**828
  chilchil, **2:**414, 748
  chinchin (also *jícara*), **2:**741
  chiquít, **2:**291
  chischiles, **2:**748, 761
  chocalhos, **2:**337
  chorimori, **2:**357, 361
  chucho, **2:**376–77, 384, 391
  chunan, **2:**234
  clay, **7:**559; **8:**169
  coconut-leaf, **9:**909
  cocoons, **3:**416, 438, 473
  cog-ratchet
    Austria, **8:**655
    batidorcito, **2:**715
    carraca, **2:**708
    Europe, **8:**140, 169, 170
    matraca, **2:**251, 285, 347, 348, 708, 724,
          730, 742; **3:**759, 762
    Switzerland, **8:**682, 685–86
  Colombia, **2:**150–51, 155
  Corsica, **8:**572
  coyole, **2:**554
  coyole belt, **3:**473
  coyolim, **2:**590, *591*
  coyolli, **2:**601
  de shot and rattle, **2:**814–15
  Dogon people, **1:**455
  döleng, **9:**566
  duruitoare, **8:**876
  Ecuador, **2:**414
  eglīte, **8:**503
  El Salvador, **2:**706
  ensasi, **1:**218
  erikindi, **2:**826
  fao, **1:**463
  France, **8:**544
  ganzá (also *guaiá*), **2:**308, 313, 326, 327, 330,
          337, 348, 349
  Garífuna culture, **2:**674, 733
  gema (also *gemanash*), **8:**863
  Great Lakes Indian groups, **3:**454, 456
  guacho (also *gauche*), **2:**377
  Guam, **9:**744
  guasá (also *guacho*; *guazá*), **2:**377, 401, 404,
          406, *407*, 414–15, 427
  Guatemala, **2:**723, 724, 729
  guaya, **2:**762
  gwaj (also *syak*), **2:**842
  habi sanuka, **2:**189
  Haiti, **2:**18, 19, 887
  hali', **2:**553
  hamadao, **7:**520
  Hawai'i, **3:**527; **9:**21
  hebu mataro, **2:**189–91, 192, 194
  hoof, **3:**396, 397, 401, 425, 474; **6:**546, 706,
          710
    rihhutiam, **2:**589, *590*
    Yuma culture, **2:**598
  hosho, **1:**432, 752
  huada, **2:**234
  hwin krā, **2:**144
  illacu, **2:**734
  Indus Valley civilization, **5:**319, 321

rattles (*continued*)
Ingassana people, **1:**563
insuba (also *simbaika*), **2:**660, 662, 663
jalajala, **2:**377, 384
Japan, **7:**79
jawbones, in Oceania, **9:**952
jeke, **1:**329, *334*
jhika, **5:**613
jiqmaqn, **3:**1069
kabbāde, **6:**825
kalai, **9:**489
ka:lawa:si, **2:**435
kars, **8:**857
kaskawilla, **2:**358–59
kayamb (also *kayamn*; *caimbe*), **5:**609–10
khirkhāsha, **6:**404–5
kiji'i, **9:**503
korare, **9:**178–79
kūpe'e niho'īlio, **9:***375*
kuwai, **2:**165
lagerphone, **9:**413
leŋaleŋa, **9:**629
Low Countries, **8:**525
Madagascar, **1:**785
madaka, **2:**177, 179
magavhu, **1:**752
makich, **2:**414
malakach, **2:**877
mangour, **6:**633
mangūr, **1:**554
manjūr, **6:**405, 412, 546
manyanga, **1:**638
maracas, **1:**481; **4:**438; **5:**604, 671
Brazil, **2:**302, 334
Brunka and Teribe cultures, **2:**685
Colombia, **2:**385, 401
Cuba, **2:**830, 834–36
Dominican Republic, **2:**846–47, *851*, 854–55
Ecuador, **2:**414
Garífuna culture, **2:**675, 753
Kogi culture, **2:**186
Lenca culture, **2:**739
Maleku culture, **2:**682
Maya culture, **2:**655
Mexico, **2:**620
Netherlands Antilles, **2:**930–31
North America, **3:**280, 788, 792
Panama, **2:**774
South America, **2:**29
Taino culture, **2:**822, 932
Trinidad and Tobago, **2:***961*
Venezuela, **2:**526, 529, 530, 534, 536, 537, 538, 540–41
maraka (also *marari*), **2:**159, *160*, 161
marwaha (metallic disk), **6:**215–16, *216*
Maya culture, **2:**651, 656, 731
mbaraká, **2:**200, 202, 203, 453, 454
melê (also *afoxé*), **2:**308
Métis use of, **3:**344
Mexico, **2:**13, 550
Mixtec culture, **2:**563–64, 565
nasis, **2:**640, *641*, 644
Native American, **3:**367–68, 371, 474, 526
Navajo, **3:**432
New Caledonia, **9:**681

new types, **3:**475
Nkhumbi people, **1:**714
nkocho, **1:***323*
noanipiripa, **9:**64
North America, **3:**474
in dances, **3:**206
worn by dancers, **3:**370, 468
Northeast Indian groups, **3:**463
Northwest Coast Indian groups, **3:**395, 1093
nutshells, **9:**622, 623, 625
nyahsánu, **2:**150–51
nyisi, **1:**277
Oceania, **9:**440, 531
in Christian music, **9:**195, 197
men's playing of, **9:**245
types of, **9:**374
worn by dancers, **9:**374, 481–82, 552
oksh, **6:**633
orlan-ai, **9:**22
Otopame culture, **2:**571
paiá, **2:**309, 313
paichochi, **2:**285
Panama, **2:**774
Papua New Guinea, **9:**350, 476, 485, 490, 523, 530, 563, 610
Paraguay, **2:**454
in peyote ceremonies, **3:**487
pkhachich, **8:**855
Plains Indian groups, **3:**445
Polynesia, **9:**865
prehistoric, **8:**38
Puerto Rico, **2:**933
pū'ili, **9:**373, 374, 928, *956*
Purépecha culture, **2:**575, *576*
puškaitis, **8:**503
quiribillo (also *quiriviño*, *piribique*, *triviño*), **2:**377, 391
raganelle, **8:**615
raglja, **8:**919
rangle, **8:**422–23
rumba, **8:**656
safail, **6:**943, 945
sasaa, **1:**329, 339, 340
sea-urchin, **9:**701–2
seed, **9:**247, 508, 563, 693, 698, 701–2
şèkèrè, **1:**461, 474, 478, 481, 483, 485
sewei, **2:**189, 192
shaka, **2:**677
shakap, **2:**414
shakhshākah, **6:**631
shakka, **2:**897
shak-shak, **2:**677, 803, 805, 814–15; **5:**589
shark, **9:**693
sha-sha, **2:***916*
shekere, **2:**824; **3:**785
shell, **9:**350, 512, 515, 602, 694
sísira (also *chíchira*; *magara*), **2:**670, 672, *673*, 675, 733
Slovenia, **8:**919
snail-shell, **8:**682
Solomon Islands, **9:**334, 663, 668–69
sonaja (also *chin-chin*), **2:**377, 680, 722, 723, 741, 743, 755–56, *760*, 761
soot, **2:**657
Sotho peoples, **1:**707
South America, **2:**200
tropical-forest cultures, **2:**127

South Asian music, **3:**984
Southeast Indian types, **3:**468
Southwest Indian types, **3:**429, 431, 434, 435, 438, 472
Subarctic types, **3:**386
Sumu culture, **2:**750
Surinam, **2:**505, 508
Switzerland, **8:**684
syakuzyô, **7:**617
Taino culture, **2:**22, 822, 846–47, 881
tani, **2:**184, 185
Tanzania, **1:**638
Tarahumara culture, **2:**582–83, 585, 586
tarasa, **9:**647
tchatcha, **2:**881, 883, 887
teneboim, **2:**554, 589, 590, *591*
thermos bottle, **2:**726
tobo, **9:**629
tön, **2:**686, *687*
tôndáxin, **2:**563
tönö, **2:**632, 634
Torres Strait Islands, **9:**429
tricceballacche, **8:**615
trīdeksnis, **8:**503
trù nênh, **4:**536
tsikatray, **1:**784, 785
tsu neeb, **4:**554
tswawo, **1:**752
Tupinambá culture, **2:**301
turtle shell, **3:**472
uaitúge, **2:**151
'ūlili, **9:**374, *956*
'ulī'ulī, **9:**374, *375*, 916, 928, *956*
ū sēru, **9:**853
Vanuatu, **9:**701–2
Venezuela, **2:**537
wada, **2:**358–59
Waiāpí culture, **2:**159
Warao culture, **2:**189, 191
wasaha, **2:**177
waw, **2:**435
Wayana culture, **2:**165
West Africa, **1:**446
wooden, **3:**401
xekeres (also *shekeres*), **2:**73
xichat, **2:**572
Yaqui culture, **2:**589; **3:**485
Yuma culture, **2:**596, *597*, 598
zaabia, **10:***151*
zangūleh, **5:**692
rattles, bell. *See* bells and chimes
rattles, *sistrum*
Argentina, **2:**249, 250, 251
ayacaste, **2:**741, 744
Dogon people, **1:**455
Ethiopia, **1:**603
jhika, **9:**93
kebele, **1:**455
kuluk-kuluk, **4:**911
lala, **1:**446
Saudi Arabia, **6:**361
senasawim, **2:**590
senasum, **2:**554
txia neeb, **4:**554
West Africa, **1:**446
Yemen, **6:**359

Rattles (musical group), **8**:679
Raudkivi-Stein, Walter, **3**:879, 880
Raukawa, Ngāti, **9**:942–43, 943
Raun Raun Theatre (Papua New Guinea), **9**:225, 233, 234
Rauni (Brazilian Indian leader), **2**:124, 134
Rauvazi (god), **8**:858
Ravana (deity), vina playing of, **5**:353
rave, **6**:248
Ravel, Maurice, **3**:196, 1076, 1150; **4**:873; **6**:1027; **7**:732; **8**:161, 309, 425
Ravenel, Henry W., **3**:596
Ravens (musical group), **3**:351, 670
Ravicz, Robert S., **2**:568
Ravikiran, Chitravina, **5**:233, *233*
Ravina, Menashe, **6**:1062, 1065
Ravitz, Judith, **6**:1074
Rāwal caste, **5**:476, 641
Rawḍat al-mustahām fī 'ilm al-anghām (al-Jamāl al-Muṭrib), **6**:366
Rawski, Evelyn, **10**:23
Ray, Anjali, **5**:858
Ray, Bharat Chandra, **5**:846
Ray, Bimal, **5**:858
Ray, Chitta, **5**:855
Ray, Dewan Kartikayachandra, **5**:852
Ray, Dilip Kumar, **5**:856
Ray, Dwijendralal, **5**:849, 850, 852, *852*, 856, 858
Ray, Govindachandra, **5**:849
Ray, Hemendra Kumar, **5**:855
Ray, Johnny, **3**:351
Ray, Juthika, **5**:855
Ray Norris Quintet, **3**:1107
Ray, Pranab, **5**:855
Ray, Raja Rammohan, **5**:847–48
Ray, Sailen, **5**:855
Ray, Vinay, **5**:857
Raymond, Jack, **3**:58
al-Raynāwi, Tawfiq, **6**:576
Rayner's Big Six, **1**:770
Rayseen dynasty, **5**:721
Rayyā, **6**:291
Rayyiq, **6**:355
Razakov, Shuhrat, **6**:*901*
"*Raza, La*" (Kid Frost), **3**:750
Razmik (*gusan*), **6**:736
Razumovskaya, Elena, **8**:785
Razzi, Guido, **8**:621
RCA (RCA Victor), **3**:169, 261, 264, 268, 352, 709, 714, 741, 1033, 1167. *See also* Victor
RCI label, **2**:880; **3**:296, 1103
Rea, John, **3**:1151
Read, Ezra, **3**:1096
Reade, John, **3**:465
Ready to Die (Notorious B.I.G.), **3**:715
Reagan, Albert B., **3**:457
Reagan, Ronald, **3**:311, 685
Reagon, Bernice Johnson, **3**:626; **10**:144
Real Escuela Superior de Arte Dramático y Danza (Madrid), **8**:601–2
Real World Records, **8**:225, 241
Rebecca Cohn Auditorium (Halifax), **3**:1120
Rebel without a Cause (film), **3**:203
Rebetico (film), **8**:1021

rebetika, **8**:*7*, 143, 147, 204, 205–6, 207, 285, 1008, 1019–22
Rebetika Tragoudhia (Petropoulos), **8**:1020
Rebirth of Hindu Music (Rudhyar), **5**:53
Rebman, Rao, **1**:353
reception theory, **8**:19, 647–48
Rechmenski, Nikolai, **8**:864
Rechter, Yony, **6**:1073
recitation. *See also* chant; narratives; vocal music
    Afghanistan, *zikr*, **5**:818
    biblical, **6**:1037, 1048–49
    Chuuk, *ngor*, **9**:734
    Cook Islands, **9**:902–3
    Dai people
        of Buddhist scripture, **7**:497–99
        of Buddhist sutras, **7**:503–4
    Fiji, **9**:778
    genealogy of patron, **5**:402, 403, 901
    Guyana, in healing rituals, **2**:442–43
    Hawai'i, **9**:286
        mele pule, **9**:915
        of prayers, **9**:208
    Irian Jaya, Eipo people, **9**:594
    Japan
        of Buddhist sutras, **7**:613
        rôei, **7**:619, 622, 625
        sigin, **7**:650
    Jewish religious, **8**:252
    Kapingamarangi, **9**:837
    Khmer people, *smaut*, **4**:206–7
    Kiribati, **9**:364
    Kosrae, **9**:743
        usok, **9**:741
    Malaysia, **4**:417–21
        awang batil, **4**:420
        jubang linggang, **4**:420
        kaba, **4**:413, 420
        tambo alam minangkabau, **4**:413
    Maleku culture, *poora* and *jalacomapacuaper*, **2**:682
    mantras, **5**:221, 469
    Māori *tau*, **9**:939
    Muslim poetry, **5**:278
    Nepal, *pé*, **5**:703
    Nicaragua, *la gigantona*, **2**:757
    Niue, **9**:817
    Oceania, **9**:301
    ōm, **5**:239, 255
    Oman, *jalāla*, **6**:678, 682
    Pakistan, **5**:744–45, 747–48, 749, 750
        zikr, **5**:754, 761, 794
    Palau, **9**:287, 724
    Panama, declamations, **2**:781
    Papua New Guinea
        Huli people, **9**:538, 540
        Iatmul *sagi*, **9**:553–54
        New Britain magic spells, **9**:622
    Philippines
        awit and *corrido*, **4**:853
        Islamic communities, **4**:906, 911
    Pohnpei, *ngis*, **9**:740
    Polynesia, **9**:769
        of prayers, **9**:202
        use of *pahu*, **9**:385
    Punjab (Pakistan), of genealogies, **5**:764

Qur'ānic, **6**:157–62, 372, 517, 649
    Algeria, **6**:475
    Central Asia, **6**:900, 937, 938, 939–40, 943
    Egypt, **6**:148, 165–68, 170, 321, 626
    Iran, **6**:839, 840
    Mashriq, **6**:538
    mujawwad style, **6**:160–62, 321
    murattal style, **6**:159–60, 161–62
    North Africa, **6**:437, 501
    Oman, **6**:678
    research on, **6**:162
    Turkey, **6**:192, 768–69
    women reciters, **6**:19, 291, 292, 295, 305
Rapa Nui, *kaikai*, **9**:951–52
Rotuma, **9**:819–20
Sāmoa
    'auala, **9**:805
    juggling chants, **9**:804–5
    of prayers, **9**:205
Sikaiana, **9**:845
    kaitae, **9**:846
Slovenia, prayers, **8**:912
Sumatra
    daboih, **4**:604
    dabus, **4**:604
    kaba, **4**:611, 613
Tahiti, *pāta'uta'u*, **9**:878
Takuu, **9**:839, 842
Thailand
    khao, **4**:313
    in *manora*, **4**:307
    sukhawn, **4**:295–96
    theatrical, **4**:251, 253
    thet, **4**:292–93, 321
    thet mahachat, **4**:250, 259, 313
Tibetan culture, **5**:711–12
Tonga
    children's games, **9**:787–88
    hiko, **9**:*253*
Tuamotu Islands, **9**:884
Tuva, **6**:981, *987*
Tuvalu, **9**:830
Vedic, **5**:70, 240–41, 469, 509, 956
Vietnam, minority peoples, **4**:532–33
Wales
    hwyl declamatory technique, **8**:345
    poetic declamation, **8**:347, 348–49
Warao culture, in shamanic songs, **2**:195
Reck, Tommy, **8**:390
Recollet order, **3**:23, 1056; **4**:868
Record of Changes (album), **7**:967
Record of Tibet's Kingly Lineage, **7**:472
Record Retailer and Music Industry News (periodical), **8**:211
recorder. *See* flutes
Recuay culture, **2**:11
Recuerdo de Filipinas y Sus Cantares (Pérez), **4**:869
Red Army Base Grand Vocal Cycle (Jü), **7**:387
Red Army Ensemble of Songs and Dances, **8**:777
Red Bowmen (film), **9**:42, 50, 314, 484
Red Bull Singers, **3**:1087
Red Detachment of Women (ballet), **7**:63, 349
Red Heat (film), **3**:204
Red Hot Chili Peppers (musical group), **3**:359
Red Mill (Herbert), **3**:193

Red Moon (Johnson and Cole), **3:**608, 619
Red Plastic Bag (calypsonian), **2:**820
"Red River Jig," **3:**344, *410*
Red Star Productions label, **7:**364
Red Sun (musical group), **7:**967
Red Tai people, **4:**218, 529, 537
Red Turbans, **7:**863
Reda Dance Troupe, **3:**1220
Reḍḍi caste, **5:**901
Redding, Otis, **3:**676, 677, 710; **10:**78
Reddiyar, Annamalai, **5:**921
Redfeather, Princess Tsianina, **3:**539
Redfield, Robert, **2:**70
Redman, Don, **3:**653, 654
Redondo Largo, El (Martínez), **3:**760, 765
redowa, **3:**522, 773, 775
Redpath, Jean, **8:**372
Redžepova, Esma, **8:**282, *282*, *953*, 983
Reed, Jimmy, **3:**647
Reed, Larry, **3:**1020
Reed, Lou, **3:**357
Reed, Preston, **6:**791–92
Reef Islands (Solomon Islands), **9:**833
Reeks, Dori, **2:**138, 139
reel, **3:**231, 825, 836, 855, 888; **8:**168
    Cajun, **3:**857
    in Canada, **3:**1075, 1081, 1125, 1137, 1164,
        1178–79, 1190, 1191
    in England, **8:**330, 331, 336
    Inuit, **3:**213
    Irish, **3:**843; **8:**382, *383*, 391
    in Low Countries, **8:**524
    Métis, **3:**407
    in Scotland, **8:**367, 370
Rees, Stephen, **8:**355
Reese, Della, **3:**535
Reese, Helen, **10:**23
Reeve, William, **3:**180
Reeves, David, **3:**566
Reeves, Jim, **1:**608; **3:**77
Refik Bey, **6:**757
Reflections (Babbitt), **3:**253
Reflexu's (samba-reggae group), **2:**353
Reformed Church, **3:**884; **8:**413–14
Refus Global, Le (Borduas), **3:**1073, 1147, 1151
Regalado, Rudy, **3:**799
Regent label, **6:**758
reggae, **2:**75–76, 93, 95, 97–98, 104
    in Africa, **1:**363, 416, 432, 570, 778
    in Aotearoa, **9:**166, 168, 931, 999
    in Australia, **9:**145–46, 414, 442, 443
    in Belarus, **8:**802
    in Belize, **2:**678
    in Brazil, **2:**317, 338
    in Canada, **3:**1085, 1201–2, 1212–13
    in Colombia, **2:**409, 410
    in Costa Rica, **2:**693
    in Europe, **8:**204
    in Fiji, **9:**162
    fusion in, **3:**327, 1064, 1174
    in Great Britain, **8:**215, 232, 235–36, 356
    in Guatemala, **2:**733, 734
    in Guyana, **5:**604
    in Hawai'i, **9:**166–67, 220, 928
    influence on Brazilian samba music, **2:**353–54
    instruments used in, **9:**372

    in Jamaica, **2:**904, 910, 912, 913
    Jamoan style, **9:**160
    Jawaiian music genre, **3:**337, 811
    links to Martinican *zouk*, **2:**918, 920
    in Melanesia, **9:**599
    in Montserrat, **2:**923
    in New Caledonia, **9:**213, 679
    in Nicaragua, rasta, **2:**755
    in North America, **3:**212, 318, 337, 338, 522,
        809
    in Oceania, **9:**126, 211
    in Papua New Guinea, **9:**155, 388
    in Peru, **2:**486
    in Punjab, **5:**652
    reggae resistência, **2:**353
    in Sāmoa, **9:**166
    sound recordings of, **2:**52
    in Sri Lanka, **5:**971
    in Surinam, **2:**508
    in Tahiti, **9:**166
    in Tonga, **9:**166
    in Uighur pop music, **7:**468
    in Virgin Islands, **2:**969
Regina (Blitzstein), **3:**545
Regina Philharmonic and Orchestral Society,
    3:1227
Regina Symphony Orchestra, **3:**1228
Reginella campagnola (Di Lazzaro), **8:**618
Regional Resource Centre for Folk Performing
    Arts (Udupi), **5:**887
Regis Records, **3:**1243
Regla de Ochá. *See* Santería
Regnoni-Macera, Clara, **8:**606
Regroupement des Artistes Del 'Ouest Canadien,
    3:343
Rehber-ī Mūsikī (Tanburī Cemīl Bey), **6:**758
Rehman, A. R., **5:**540–41, 545, 554, 555
Rehnqvist, Karin, **8:**445
Reich, Steve, **3:**176, 177, 335, 541, 953; **4:**131,
    132
Reichardt, Johann Friedrich, **8:**653
Reichel-Dolmatoff, Gerardo, **2:**152–53, 155,
    186–87
Reichel, Hapa, **9:**165
Reichel, Keali'i, **9:**165, 986, 1008
Reid, Bill, **3:**1093; **9:**442
Reid, Duke, **2:**97, 911; **3:**693
Reid, LA, **3:**715
Reigaku sentei (Tomokiyo), **7:**549
Reihōzi Temple (Tôkyô area), **7:**703
Reilly, John "Jacko," **8:**295
Reily, Suzel Ana, **2:**320, 321
Reinagle, Alexander, **3:**180, 538
Reinhard, Kurt, **9:**980
Reinhardt, Babik, **8:**288
Reinhardt, Django, **8:**288
Reinhardt, Lousson, **8:**288
Reinhardt, Schnuckenack, **8:**288
Reis, Sérgio, **2:**318
Reisenburg, S. H., **3:**474
Rejang people, **4:**619–29, 622
Rejcha, Antonín, **8:**728
Rejebov-*Baggy*, Mukhammet, **6:***968*
Rejuvenation Club, **5:**849
Rekhteen, Sidiqullah, **5:**787
Relata I (Babbitt), **3:**175

"Release Yourself" (Graham Central Station),
    3:683
Relics of Jacobite Poetry (Hogg), **8:**373
Relief statique (Takemitsu), **7:**736
religion. *See also* ancestor worship; animism;
        'Asatrú religion; Asir religion; Bon
        religion; Buddhism; Candomblé; Cao
        Đài; cargo cults; Christianity;
        Confucianism; Daoism; Hinduism;
        Islam; Jainism; Judaism;
        Manichaeanism; Native American
        Church; Orisa; paganism;
        Protestantism; Rastafarianism; Roman
        Catholicism; Santería; shamanism;
        Shango; Shinto; Shintoism; Sikhs;
        spirit possession; Sufism; Tenrikyō;
        Vedic religion; Vodou; Zoroastrianism;
        *specific Christian sects and
        denominations*; *specific gods, cults, and
        genres*
    Africa, **1:**5
        spirit tutors, **1:**8–9
        use of masks in, **1:**119
    African-derived, **2:**47–48, 793
        in Argentina, **2:**259–61
        in Barbados, **2:**817
        in Belize, **2:**669
        in Brazil, **2:**338, 340, 341–44
        in Costa Rica, **2:**688
        in Cuba, **2:**822
        in Dominican Republic, **2:**852–53, 856
        in Grenada, **2:**865
        in Haiti, **2:**882–84
        in Jamaica, **2:**897–98, 902
        in Paraguay, **2:**457
        in St. Lucia, **2:**949
        in Surinam, **2:**506
        in Trinidad and Tobago, **2:**954–57
        in Uruguay, **2:**512–16, 521
    Afro-Cuban systems, **3:**783–85
    Aka people, **1:**692–93
    Akan people, **1:**464
    Amerindian, **2:**45–46
    Arawak culture, **2:**13
    Arctic peoples, **3:**380
    Argentina, **2:**254–61
    Asian, **3:**11
        influence on American music, **3:**129–33
    Atacameño culture, **2:**356, 360–61
    audiences and, **2:**60
    Australia, **9:**301, 355–57
        Aboriginal peoples, **9:**187–88, 227–28, 321,
            411, 418, 419, 431, 434, 435, 451,
            453, 465–67
    Aymara culture, **2:**357
    Aztec culture, **2:**15, 556
    Bellona, **9:**849
    Bolivia, **2:**289
    cantillation systems in, **8:**100
    Carib culture, **2:**13
    China, **7:**311–37, 416, 420–21
        Houtu worship, **7:**317
    class and ethnicity factors, **3:**120
    Colombia, **2:**403–4
    Colo people, **1:**568
    dance in, **3:**220

definition of, **3:**116
East Africa, **1:**603–4
East and Inner Asia, **7:**19–24
Edo people, **1:**460
emotion and evangelicalism in, **3:**120–21
ethnic identity and, **2:**84
European disputes over, **8:**10–11
Faŋ people, **1:**663
Fiji, **9:**773
Garifuna culture, **2:**669
Greece, ancient, **8:**46
Guaraní culture, **2:**200, 203–4, 452
Guaymí culture, *mamanchí,* **2:**686
Gumuz people, **1:**564
Guyana, syncretic, **2:**445
Hausa people, **1:**448, 450–51, 515
Hawai'i, **9:**926
Irian Jaya, Asmat people, **9:**190, 589–90
Jamaica, **2:**901–4
Japan, *keiko* ascetic training concept,
        7:768
Kapingamarangi, **9:**836–37, *838*
Kasena-Nankani people, **1:**455
Kiribati, **9:**759–61, 763
Kogi culture, **2:**183, 185, 186
Kosrae, **9:**740–41
LoDagaa people, **1:**456
Madagascar, **1:**788–89
Manus, **9:**186
Marshall Islands, **9:**752
Maya culture, **2:**650
Mayo culture, **2:**589
Mixtec culture, **2:**564
Montserrat, **2:**924
myth and, **2:**17
Native American
    Athapaskan prophets, **3:**391, 1276
    Bole-Maru cult, **3:**415
    Christian, **3:**437, 484–86, 488
    Ghost Dance movement, **3:**11, 415, 418,
        421–22, 426, 443, 449, 480, 487,
        1086, 1094
    Kuksu, **3:**415
    Longhouse (Handsome Lake) religion, **3:**7,
        462–63, 463–64, 1078
    Medicine Lodge, **3:**451, 454, 456, 1079
    peyote religion, **3:**425, 433, 438, 443, 445,
        486, 487–88
    Plains groups, **3:**441, 1086
    syncretic, **3:**217–18
New Caledonia, **9:**672
New Guinea, **9:**478
North America, **3:**116–28, 530–35
    identity issues and, **3:**117–18, 506, *507,*
        822
    liturgy *vs.* spontaneity in, **3:**121
    mainstream *vs.* folk, **3:**119
    musical performance styles in, **3:**122
    political issues, **3:**301
    primitive *vs.* modern ideologies, **3:**121–22
    racial segregation in, **3:**120
    research on, **3:**117, 119–22
    statistics on, **3:**5
    urban *vs.* rural contexts, **3:**119–20
Oceania, magic and, **9:**186, 200, 453
Palau, Modekngei, **9:**720

Papua New Guinea
    Baluan, **9:**602, 604–5
    Enga sorcery, **9:**535
    Huli people, **9:**537–38
    Iatmul people, **9:**553
    Lolo people, **9:**612
    Mali Baining Pomio Kivung, **9:**191–93
    masks and, **9:**350
    Nissan Atoll, **9:**636–39
    Rai Coast, **9:**561–63
    sorcery, **9:**540
    tambaran belief system, **9:**546–48, 561–62
    Waxei people, **9:**558–59
Paraguay, **2:**457
Polynesia, **9:**200–209
pre-Columbian, **2:**81
Purépecha culture, **2:**576
Rapa Nui, **9:**951–52
role in musical enculturation, **2:**68–69
Roti, Songo, **4:**801
Russia, syncreticism in, **8:**122–23
Shona people, **1:**710, 752, 753–55, 757
Sikaiana, **9:**846
Solomon Islands
    Russell Islands, **9:**663
    Santa Cruz Islands, **9:**334
spirit communication (*See* shamanism)
Subarctic peoples, **3:**391
Sulawesi, Aluk To Dolo, **4:**806–7
Sumba, Marapu, **4:**788–90
Surinam, Maroon cultures, **2:**504–5
Tairona culture, **2:**185
Takuu, **9:**842
Tanzania, **1:**634
Tsonga people, **1:**710–11
Tuareg people, **1:**587, 594
Tukano culture, **2:**153–54
Tuvalu, **9:**829
Vai people, **1:**334–36
Vanuatu, **9:**198–99
    John Frum movement, **9:**32, 214–15
    southern, **9:**702
    Tanna, **9:**708–9
Venda people, **1:**709
Warao culture, **2:**194
Wayana culture, **2:**165
West Africa, forest region, **1:**458
Winti, **2:**508
Yaqui culture, **2:**589
Yoruba people, **1:**39, 400, 403–6, 459
*Religious Folksongs of the Negro as Sung at
        Hampton Institute* (Dett), **3:**607
religious music. *See bhajan; bhakti;* chant;
        devotional songs and singing; *dhrupad;*
        hymns; *kīrtan;* psalmody; *qawwali;*
        tēvāram; specific religions
Reliques of Ancient English Poetry (Percy), **8:**17
Relle, Moritz, **3:**1180
Relocation (XIT), **3:**489
R.E.M. (musical group), **7:**436; **8:**210
Remaidanjue (Sajiabanzhida Gonggajianzan),
        7:472–73
Rembang, I Nyoman, **4:**733
Rembrandt Trio, **3:**1186
Reményi, Eduard, **4:**857, 870
Remignard, Gilles, **8:**551

Ren Huichu, **7:**180
Ren Jianhui, **7:**307
Ren Tongxiang, **7:**204
Rena Rama (musical group), **8:**446
Renacimiento (periodical), **4:**857
Renaissance, **8:**73–76
    art music in, **8:**69, 199
    Brittany, **8:**561
    Corsica, **8:**573
    Czech Republic, **8:**726–27
    dance in, **8:**160
    education and theory in, **8:**79
    Finland, **8:**481
    Germany, **8:**652–54
    historical consciousness in, **8:**59
    Hungary, **8:**736, 737, 740
    Italy, **8:**608, 617
    Jewish culture in, **8:**248, 259
    Low Countries, **8:**518
    musical fusions and hybrids in, **8:**227
    Poland, **8:**710
    Romania, **8:**881, 882, 886
    Scotland, **8:**366–67, 373
    Slovakia, **8:**726–27
    Spain, **8:**601
Renesa (musical group), **5:**428
reng, **6:**132, 137, 834, 863, 879
Renis, Tony, **8:**209
Renmin Yinyue (periodical), **7:**141
Rennell (Solomon Islands), **9:**833, 835, 849,
        852, 853
Rennock, Mrs. Marie, **2:***902*
Reno Club (Kansas City), **3:**707
Reno, Don, **3:**159
Reno, Ginette, **3:**1158, 1168
Renoir, Pierre-Auguste, **8:***85*
Rent (musical), **3:**545
Rentak Melayu, **4:**520
Renuka (deity), **5:***400,* 500, 901
*Répertoire de la chansons folkloriques françaises au
        Canada* (series), **3:**1165–66
Rephann, Richard, **2:**414, 431
Replacements (musical group), **3:**171
Report on Agricultural Products of Korea, **7:**929
Reptiles (musical group), **8:**407
Republican Party, **3:**307–9, 310, 505
requinto. See guitars
Reru (Managalasi elder), **9:**502–3
Research Institute of Music (Beijing), **7:**137–38
Resetarits, Willi, **8:***216,* 678
"Respect" (Franklin), **3:**552, 710
"Respect" (Redding), **3:**677
"Respect Yourself" (Staple Singers), **3:**677
Respighi, Ottorino, **8:**618
Restrepo Duque, Hernán, **2:**398
Restrepo L., Pablo, **2:**395
"Resurrection of Billy Adamache" (Gilday),
        3:1280
Retrograde Company (musical group), **8:**1021
Rettore, Donatella, **8:**620
Return to Forever (musical group), **3:**356, 664
"Return to Innocence" (Enigma), **7:**428
Reuben, Alben, **9:**966
Reunion (Cage), **3:**254
Réunion Island, **1:**781
    history of South Asian people in, **5:**606

Réunion Island (*continued*)
  maloya genre of, **5:**609–11
  plantation temple music on, **5:**606–8
  sega genre of, **5:**609, 611
  self-mortification rituals, **5:**293
  South Asian community in, **5:**606–11
  urban temple music on, **5:**608–9
Reupena (Sāmoan comedian), **9:**235
Reuter, Jas, **2:**624
Reuveni, Asher, **6:**265–66
Reuveni, Meir, **6:**265–66
Revelli, William D., **3:**567
Revista de Etnografi și Folclor (periodical), **8:**886
Revista de Folclor (periodical), **8:**884, 885, 886
Revista Musical Chilena (periodical), **2:**238
Revival cult, **2:**901, 903–4, 908, 910
revival movements (North America), **3:**13–14,
     55–59. *See also* folk music revival
  blues, **3:**582
  Celtic music, **3:**1189
  Irish traditional music, **3:**846
  klezmer, **3:**941–42
  Maritimes, **3:**1121, 1125
  social class and, **3:**45
Revolutionary Army (Zou), **7:**379
Revolutionary Association of the Women of
     Afghanistan (RAWA), **5:**840–41
Revolutionary War, **3:**563, 1060, 1078, 1115
Revolver (Beatles), **3:**347, 955
Revueltas, Silvestre, **2:**115, 605
Revuts'kyi, Lev, **8:**820
Rexha, Fitnete, **8:**999
REX Records, **8:**802
Rey, Cemal Reşit, **6:**775
"*rey, El*" (Jiménez), **3:**722
Reyes, Al, **3:**749
Reyes Bautista, Juan, **4:**856
Reyes, Crispino, **4:**865, 866
Reyes, Lucha, **3:**739
Reyes, Luis I., **9:**1008
Reyes, Roman, **4:**857
Reyes Schramm, Adelaida, **3:**149, 516; **10:**71
Reyes, Severino, **4:**857, 864, 871
Reyes Tolentino, Francisca, **4:**872
Reyhani of Erzurum (*aşîk*), **6:**804
Reyna, Cornelio, **2:**622
Reyna, Fredy, **2:**531, 543
Reyna, Juan, **3:**738
Reynolds, Dwight F., **6:**24
Reynolds, Roger, **3:**253; **4:**881
Reza (martyr), **6:**826
  shrine of, **5:**817
Reza, Mary Helen, **3:**759
Reza, Mohammad, **5:**46, 50–51
Rezazî, Nasir, **6:**752
RFO Wallis et Futuna, archives of, **9:**958
Rhade people, **4:**529
Rhapsodietta on a Manobo Theme (Buenaventura),
    4:873
Rhapsody in Blue (Gershwin), **3:**174, 196, 539
Rheinberger, Joseph, **3:**173
Rheinhardt, Django, **1:**361
rhetoric, concept of, **8:**74–75, 79
Rhettmatic (deejay), **3:**973
Rhino Band, **1:**358–59, 426

Rhode Island. *See also* New England
  Election Day celebrations, **3:**595
  Newport Folk Festival, **3:**149, 300
  Pinkster Day celebrations, **3:**614
  Portuguese people in, **3:**847, 851
  Providence, bands in, **3:**564
  Woonsocket, French-Americans in, **3:**854
Rhodes, Steve, **1:**236
Rhodes, Willard, **1:**31, 51; **3:**423, 488
rhythm and blues, **2:**97; **3:**149, 667–76, 708,
    741, 858; **10:**78
  British Caribbean consumers, **3:**812
  Canada, **3:**1205
  club blues style, **3:**669
  cocktail music, **3:**669
  country and western music and, **3:**325–26
  crossover formulas in, **3:**672–73
  disco and, **3:**228–30
  Europe, **8:**214, 369, 619
  funk and, **3:**684
  jazz and, **3:**663–64
  Memphis Sound, **3:**673, 675–76
  Motown Sound, **3:**673–75, 677, 709–10
  Ontario, **3:**1081
  rap in, **3:**693
  recordings, **3:**263, 350, 354, 560
  research on, **3:**584, 587
  as rock and roll precursor, **3:**349–51,
    550, 584
  white covers of, **3:**329–30, 352–53, 354
  women performers of, **3:**96
Rhythm and Blues (musical group), **8:**221
rhythm and meter. *See also* *īqā'*; tala; timelines;
    usûl
  acculturàtion and, **2:**73–74
  Afghanistan, **5:**827
    chahārbeiti, **5:**819
    Kabuli *ghazal*, **5:**805–6
    Pashtun songs, **5:**835, 836
  African music, **1:**23–24; **2:**73–74; **3:**593
    additive, **1:**35
    asymmetrical, **1:**666
    concepts of, **1:**128
    duple, **1:**558
    duple *vs.* ternary, **1:**21
    inherent, **1:**155
    interlocking, **1:**312
    metered music, **1:**701
    mnemonic patterns for, **1:**677
    modes of, **1:**534–35
    modes used in healing rituals, **1:**276–77,
      281–82
    moraic, **1:**167–68
    movement and, **1:**10
    in multipart textures, **1:**11
    parallel layers, **1:**498
    polyrhythms, **1:**446, 701, 708, 749
    rhythmic ostinato, **1:**11; **6:**98, 101, 103
    in speech surrogate methods, **1:**106–7
    synchronization methods, **1:**125, 143
    timbre and, **1:**136–37
    transcription of, **1:**261
  Afro-Cuban music, **3:**783, 785, 789
  Akha people, **4:**541
  Albania, **8:**990, 994
    urban songs, **8:**997

Algeria
  Andalusian repertoire, **6:**468, 470
  'arūbī, **6:**472
  ḥawzī, **6:**473
  sha'bi, **6:**472
Amerindian music, **2:**73
Amish hymns, **3:**887
Andalusian music, **6:**448
Andean music, **2:**216
Anglo-American ballads, **3:**833
Anuta, **9:**307
  mori, **9:**859
  struck plaque rhythms, **9:**378–79
  tungaunu, **9:**858
Apache songs, **3:**431
Arabian peninsula
  hand clapping patterns, **6:**651, 657
  polyrhythmic music, **6:**546
  ṣawt genre, **6:**652
Arab music
  mawwāl, **6:**567
  medieval theories, **6:**7, 8, 16–17, 364, 366,
    387–93
  rhythmic modes, **6:**89–92, 184, 502, 549,
    568
Arctic songs, **3:**378
Argentina
  candombe (also *charanda*; *ramba*), **2:**260
  tunga-tunga, **2:**273, 274, 280
Armenian music, **6:**727
art music
  Europe, **8:**68
  twentieth-century American, **3:**174
Australia, **9:**357
  Anglo-Irish music, **9:**141
  Arnhem Land songs, **9:**426–27
  Central Aboriginal songs, **9:**411, 435–36,
    438
  children's songs, **9:**256–57
  clansongs, **9:**422
  country music, **9:**142
  didjeridu music, **9:**395, 396–97
  Greek dance, **9:**73
  Kimberleys *nurlu*, **9:**432, *433*
  Pitjantjatjara structures, **9:***434*
  popular music, **9:**144
  Yolngu clansongs, **9:**301–2
Austria, **8:**671–72
  alpine style, **8:**610
Azerbaijan, **6:**693
  dastanlar, **6:**930
  muğam, **6:**927, 928
back-beat, **3:**680
Bahamas
  junkanoo, **2:**807
  rake 'n' scrape, **2:**806
baion rhythm, **3:**673
balabolo pattern, **1:**489, 490–91, 494–504,
    509, 511–12
Bali, **4:**745
  angsel, **4:**734, 745
  gambangan, **4:**755
Balkan region
  additive, **6:**85, 760; **8:**867
  polymeter, **8:**165
Balkarian people, **8:**856

Balochistan, *qalandarī* music, **6:**887, 888
Barbados
    African influences, **2:**819
    spouge, **2:**820
Basque music, **8:**309
    zortziko, **3:**849; **8:**311
Batak people, **4:**607
Belize, brukdown, **2:**677
Bellona, **9:**850, 851
Berber people, **1:**543
bhajan, **5:**255
bhangra, **5:**574
bharata nāṭyam, percussive footwork in,
    5:149
bluegrass, **3:**161, 166
blues, **3:**638
Bolivia, vespers music, **2:**140
Borneo
    kidiu music, **4:**837
    in stamping tube music, **4:**830, 831–32
Bosnia-Hercegovina, **8:**964
    aksak meters, **8:**964
Brazil
    Afro-Brazilian genres, **2:**307
    baião de viola, **2:**332
    bossa nova, **2:**108–9, 317
    caboclinho genres, **2:**337
    caboclo music, **2:**325
    in Candomblé music, **2:**342–44
    cantoria, **2:**327
    capoeira songs, **2:**346
    cateretê, **2:**307
    côco songs, **2:**349
    embolada, **2:**327, *328*
    forró, **2:**332
    frevo de rua, **2:**336
    habanera, **2:**350
    ijexá, **2:**352
    maxixe, **2:**350
    samba, **2:**313, 315
    samba campineiro, **2:**349
    samba-lenço, **2:**349
    samba-reggae, **2:**353
    ternos songs, **2:**313
    toque afro-primitivo, **2:**352
    zabumba patterns, **2:**332
Bribri and Cabécar cultures, ritual songs,
    2:634
Bulgarian music, **3:**926; **8:**890, 891
    aksak (asymmetrical) meters, **6:**85; **8:**226,
        891
    kjuček, **8:**282
    regional differences, **8:**895
Burma, **4:**18–19
    percussive patterns, **4:**379–81
California Native American music, **3:**413, 414,
    415–16, 418
Cambodian music, **3:**1002
Carriacou, big-drum dance, **2:**870
Celtic music, **8:**321
Central Asia
    asymmetrical meters, **6:**85
    Bukharan *shash maqām*, **6:**911
    in poetry, **6:**914–15
Chaldean *jūrjuna* pattern, **6:**284
Chechen people, **8:**862

Chile
    cueca, **2:**369
    romance, **2:**367
    tonada, **2:**368
China
    Confucian music, **7:**337
    ensemble music, **7:**235–36
    nanguan music, **7:**207–9
    nanyin, **7:**272–73
    northern ensemble music, **7:**202, 203
    northwestern musics, **7:**456
    opera arias, **7:**282–83
    pai concept, **7:**123
    Peking opera percussion patterns, **7:**286
    qupai melodies, **7:**233
    shan'ge, **7:**151
    shifan luogu, **7:**192–93
Chuvash people, **8:**773
Colombia
    African-derived traits, **2:**401
    bambuco, **2:**385–86, 409
    cumbia, **2:**101, 406
    for *currulao*, **2:**404
    danza, **2:**393
    pasillo, **2:**392
    vallenato, **2:**407–8
    conjunto music, **9:**103
Cook Islands, percussion music, **9:**901
Coptic Orthodox music, **6:**221
Corsica, Italian songs, **8:**571
Costa Rica
    song-dances, **2:**698
    son suelto, **2:**698
    zarabanda, **2:**688
    country music, **3:**77
Creek Stomp Dance songs, **3:**469
Croatia, Hungarian types, **8:**932
cross-rhythms, **1:**33–34, 35, 156,
    378, 563
    conducting of, **8:**101
    notation of, **1:**47
    waza trumpet ensembles, **1:**566–67
Cuba
    criolla, **2:**832
    danzón, **2:**833
    makuta, **2:**825
    in Santería, **2:**823–24
Czech Republic, **8:**717–18, 721
Damāi band music, **5:**700
Delaware Big House songs, **3:**464
Denmark, dance music, **8:**454
Dominican Republic
    bomba-e, **2:**855
    criolla, **2:**860
    jacana, **2:**855
    palo abajo and *palo arriba*, **2:**854
    palo corrido, **2:**854–55
    palos de muerto, **2:**854–55
    salve con versos, **2:**856
    sarandunga, **2:**855
    dunya, **1:**497–98
Ecuador
    bomba, **2:**415, 428
    currulao, **2:**428
    pareja, **2:**424
    in Passion songs, **2:**420

Egypt
    layla, **6:**149, 150–51
    wah'da wa-nuss, **6:**631
England
    dance music, **8:**330
    songs, **8:**327, 328
Ephrata Cloister use of, **3:**906
Estonia, **8:**492
Ethiopia, *zēmā* chant, **1:**149–50
Europe
    in dance music, **8:**9–10
    duple-triple alternation, **8:**166
    work music, **8:**141
Faroe Islands
    ballad dances, **8:**470
    ballads, **8:**413
Fiji, **9:**775, 778
    lali patterns, **9:**777
    popular music, **9:**162
    taralala, **9:**780
    vakawelegone, **9:**264
Finland
    ethnic preferences, **8:**487
    Kalevala meter, **8:**476–77, 480–81, 486
    rekilaulu, **8:**477
folk spirituals, **3:**626
France
    alpine style, **8:**610
    vocal music, **8:**541
French Guiana, *kamougé*, **2:**437
Futuna, *fasi*, **9:**815
Garifuna culture
    chumba, **2:**676
    combination, **2:**676
    in *dügü* ritual, **2:**670–71
    eremuna égi, **2:**675
    of *garavón* drum music, **2:**753
    gunjéi, **2:**676
    hüngühüngü, **2:**676
    punta, **2:**675, 677
    senbai, **2:**676
    wanaragua, **2:**674
Georgia, **8:**832
Germany
    marches, **8:**660
    medieval music, **8:**651
    Zwiefache, **8:**655
gong-chime ensembles, **4:**20
Great Basin Bear Dance songs, **3:**423–24
Great Basin Indian songs, **3:**426
Greece
    aksak (asymmetrical) meters, **6:**85; **8:**1008
    island music, **8:**1009
    Macedonia, **8:**1012
    mainland music, **8:**1009
    in *rebetika*, **8:**206
Greece, ancient, **8:**47, 1022
Greek-American music, **3:**529, 926, 930
Guadeloupe
    beguine, **2:**878
    carnival music, **2:**876
    léwòz, **2:**874–75
    quadrille, **2:**877
    zouk, **2:**879
Guarijio culture
    contradanza, **2:**553
    son principal, **2:**553

rhythm and meter (*continued*)
  Guatemala, *son guatemalteco*, **2:**726
  Gujarat, *garbo*, **5:**628
  Guyana, *tāssā* ensemble music, **5:**601
  habanera, **3:**791; **8:**619
  Hadendowa people, **1:**560
  Haiti
    kase, **2:**883, 888
    mereng koudyay, **2:**890
    Vodou ritual music, **2:**883
  Haitian-American music, **3:**802, 805
  Hawai'i
    Jawaiian genre, **9:**166
    mele hula, **9:**916, 926
    percussion patterns, **9:**916
  Hindu devotional poetry, **5:**249
  Hindustani music
    divisions in, **5:**112–13
    laykārī performance, **5:**111, 136, 169, 175,
        178, 200
    nom-tom ālāp, **5:**168, 175, 215
    raga, **5:**82
  Honduras
    mestizo dance-music, **2:**744
    xique, **2:**744
  Hui people, **7:**462
  Hungary, **8:**745
    aksak meters, **8:**744, 745
    esz-tam, **8:**932
    instrumental music, **8:**743
    popular music, **8:**747
    rubato or *giusto* rhythm, **8:**739, 741, 742,
        746
    verbunkos, **8:**737
  Iban people, **4:**830
  Iceland, *rímur*, **8:**401
  India, tala system, **4:**68
  Indonesia, *dangdut* genre, **4:**104, 105
  Ingush people, **8:**862
  Iran
    Azerbaijani *havalar*, **6:**850–51
    dance music, **6:**879
    poetic meter, **6:**829–30, 834, 836
    in *radif*, **6:**134, 136–37, 854, 855, 863
    reng, **6:**137
  Iranian popular music, **3:**1035
  Iraq, for *maqām*, **6:**311
  Ireland, dance music, **8:**382
  Irian Jaya
    Asmat songs, **9:**591
    conch signals, **9:**583
    Mairasi songs, **9:**587
  Irish-American music, **3:**843
  Iroquois Social Dance songs, **3:**464
  irregular, mixed, and additive, **6:**85, 87, 389;
      8:10
  Islamic views of, **6:**183
  isorhythms, **1:**220; **8:**71
  Israel, *dabka*, **6:**1073
  Italy, **8:**610
    alpine style, **8:**610
  Jamaica
    for *buru*, **2:**907
    cult rhythms, **2:**910
    goombeh rhythms, **2:**897
    in Kumina cult drumming, **2:**898, 902

    limbo, **2:**909
    mento, **2:**906
    in Revival music, **2:**903
    ska, **2:**97
  Japan
    kudoki poetic meter, **7:**601
    min'yô, **7:**603
    nô, **7:**633–34, 653
    in *syakuhati* music, **7:**703
    theories of, **7:**570–73
    utazawa, **7:**688
  Java, **4:**660, 668–69
    drum patterns, **4:**661–64
    macapat, **4:**664
    percussion patterns, **4:**673–75
    tembang, **4:**665
    in *tembang Sasak*, **4:**775
    triple meter, **4:**684
    wayang kulit, **4:**653
  jazz, **3:**551, *551*, 660, 662
  Jewish music, **8:**252–53, 258
  jig, **8:***381*
  juba, patting, **3:***595*
  Judeo-Spanish songs, **6:**1042
  Kajang people, **4:**827
  Kalinga people, **4:**916
  Kapingamarangi, **9:**836
    langa, **9:**837
  Karachaevian people, **8:**856
  Karen people, **4:**545
  Karnataka, *pada* genres, **5:**868
  Karnatak music
    internal beat structure in, **5:**142–44
    kaṇakku strategy, **5:**148, 153, 154–56
    konakkol system, **5:**214
    rhythmic shape (*yati*), **5:**147
    sarvalaghu strategy, **5:**148, 153–54
  Kashmir
    chakri, **5:**683
    rūf, **5:**684
    ṣūfyāna mūsīqī, **5:**687, 694
    treatises on, **5:**689–90, 692
    turushka, **5:**689
  kathak, percussive footwork in, **5:**494
  Kazakh songs, **7:**460, 461
  Kenyah people, **4:**827
  Kerala
    Jewish songs, **5:**949
    Mappila songs, **5:**947
    temple drum compositions, **5:**936–39
  Khmer people, **4:**18, 159, 168, 180–82
    smaut, **4:**206
  Kiribati, dance-songs, **9:**761–82
  Kmhmu people, **4:**547
  Korea
    folk songs, **7:**519
    hwach'ŏng, **7:**871
    kagok, **7:**922–23
    kasa, **7:**927–28
    nongak, **7:**932, 935–36, *937*, 938
    p'ansori, **7:**898, 901–2
    pŏmp'ae, **7:**872
    rhythmic patterns (*changdan*), **7:**815–16,
        821, 841–44, 881–83, 890–91, 897,
        898, 901–2, 913, 915–16, 922–23,
        926, 927–28, 932, 955

    shamanic chant, **7:**877–78
    sijo, **7:**926
    sinawi, **7:**890–91, 914
    taeak, **7:**813
  kriti, **5:**269
  !Kung people, **1:**307
  Kuwaiti, **6:**692, 693
  Kwakiutl Winter Ceremony songs, **3:**400
  Lao people, **4:**18
    khap phuan genre, **4:**348
    khap thum genre, **4:**350
    lam genres, **4:**352
    lam tang vay, **4:**345
  Latin American dance music, **3:**522
  Latvia, *daina*, **8:**500
  Lisu people, **4:**543
  Lithuania, **8:**510
  Lithuanian-American songs, **3:**876
  liturgical accents, **8:**100
  Lombok, *lederang*, **4:**769
  Low Countries, songs, **8:**521
  Lozi people, **1:**713
  mabo, **1:**689
  Macedonia
    asymmetrical meters, **6:**85
    čoček, **8:**983
    dances, **8:**978
    songs, **8:**974
    usul modes, **8:**979
  Macedonian-American dance music, **3:**926
  Maguindanao people, rhythmic modes,
      4:894–95
  majika, **1:**436
  Malaysia, **4:**19, *416*, *417*, *418*
    asli, **4:**434
    ghazal, **4:**438, *439*
    inang, **4:**437
    joget, **4:**436
    masri, **4:**437, *438*
    tumbuk kalang, **4:**423
    zapin, **4:**437, *439*
  Malta, *spirtu pront*, **8:**636
  Maluku, **4:**818
  Manihiki, percussion, **9:**904–5
  Māori people
    haka, **9:**951
    songs, **9:**933
  Mapuche culture, *pifülka* music, **2:**234
  Maritime fiddle music, **3:**1071
  Maronite church music, **6:**212
  Marquesas Islands, *tape'a*, **9:**894
  Marshall Islands, **9:**753
  Martinique
    beguine, **2:**915, *916*, *917*
    kadans, **2:**917
    mazouk, **2:**915
  Martinique, drumming patterns, **5:**596–98
  Maya culture
    of ancestral songs, **2:**732
    jota, **2:**657
  Mennonite hymns, **3:**887, 1238
  Métis fiddle music, **3:**405
  Mexica culture, **2:**561
    sones, **2:**561
  Mexico
    Amerindian music, **2:**549

canciones rancheras, **2:**621
compás, **2:**610
corrido, **2:**616
gusto, **2:**611
habanera, **2:**620
polka, **2:**613, 616
son, **2:**606
son jalisciense, **2:**613
son jarocho, **2:**609
zapateado, **2:**610
Micronesian music, **9:**716
Middle Eastern music, **6:**9, 10, 121
Miskitu culture, *tiun*, **2:**663
Mongol people
    Buddhist music, **7:**1017
    short-songs, **7:**1007
    urtyn duu, **7:**1006
Montenegro, *aksak* meters, **8:**959
Morocco
    Berber *ahidus*, **6:**487
    serraba, **6:**499
    tazrrart, **6:**487
Native American songs, **3:**367
Nātyaśāstra passage on, **5:**26–27, 322
Nepal, **5:**705
Netherlands Antilles
    tambú, **2:**928, 929
    waltz, **2:**930
New Caledonia
    dance-songs, **9:**676, 685–86
    kaneka, **9:**213
    mimetic dances, **9:**674
Nicaragua
    baile de la marimba, **2:**761–62
    mazurka, **2:**757
    mento, **2:**753
    son nica, **2:**764
North Caucasia, **8:**851
Northwest Coast songs, **3:**401–2
Norway, **8:**425
    bygdedansar, **8:**417
    hardingfele slått, **8:**416–17
nūba, **6:**436, 451, 457–58, 461–62
Nubian music, **6:**644
oberek, **3:**892
Oceania
    interlocking, **9:**376
    metrics, **9:**324–25
    transcription of, **9:**285
organum, **8:**71
Ossetian people, **8:**859
Palauan music, **9:**723
Panama
    el tamborito, **2:**782
    mejorana, **2:**778
    punto, **2:**778
Papua New Guinea
    Abelam *bira*, **9:**549
    Abelam songs, **9:**550
    Baluan *kileŋ* formulas, **9:**605–6
    Binandere *ario* dance, **9:**500
    Buin *garamut* signals, **9:**651
    children's music, **9:**257
    costumes and, **9:**482–83
    garamut ensembles, **9:**376
    Gulf Province, **9:**494, 495

Halia songs, **9:**641
Iatmul *mariuamangi*, **9:**554, *555*
Komba music, **9:**572
kundu music, **9:**384, 489
Kwoma people, **9:**289
Mali Baining people, **9:**192
Managalasi songs, **9:**504–5
    paired-flute melody, **9:***532*
    string band music, **9:**388
Sursurunga songs, **9:**627
Tolai music, **9:**155
Trans-Fly island dances, **9:**508
Paraguay
    guaránia, **2:**460
    polca, **2:**461
Peru
    cumbia, **2:**483
    festejo, **2:**496
    huayno, **2:**477
    landó, **2:**498
    marinera, **2:**481
    yaraví, **2:**477
Philippines
    in dances, **4:**854
    kulintangan music, **4:**898
    kulintang music, **4:**897
    tagunggu music, **4:**899
    in upland genres, **4:**927–28
Plains Indian songs, **3:**445, 484
Pohnpei, kava beating, **9:**173, 740
Poland
    dance music, **8:**708
    wiskanie, **8:**702
Polynesia, **9:**289, 769–70
    outlier islands, **9:**836
    pahu rhythms, **9:**385
popular songs, **3:**195
    eighteenth century, **3:**181
    twentieth century, **3:**196
Portugal, **8:**581, 582
Pueblo Indian songs, **3:**429
Puerto Rico
    bomba, **2:**937
    seis, **2:**939
Pukapuka, chants, **9:**911, 912
pulse *vs.* beat, **1:**747
Punjab, ethnic differentiation of, **5:**283
punk, **3:**357
Purépecha culture
    abajeño, **2:**579
    cuatrillo, **2:**579
    pirekua, **2:**579
    son regional, **2:**579
    torito, **2:**578
quintuple meter, **9:**289–90, 307
racial categories in, **3:**68, 72
rap, **3:**552
Rapa Nui, vocal music, **9:**952
research on, **8:**23
Réunion Island, **5:**607–8, 609–10
rhythm and blues, **3:**670
ride rhythm, **3:**658
rock, **3:**337, 551, *551*
rock and roll, **3:**348
Romania
    asymmetrical meters, **6:**85

čiftečeli, **8:**278
dance music, **8:**875
polyrhythm, **8:**872
ţiituri, **8:**880
Rotuma
    sua, **9:**822
    tiap forau, **9:**822
rumba, **3:**786
Russia, **8:**785
    village songs, **8:**755–56
    Volga-Ural region, **8:**773
Ryûkyû music, **7:**791, 794
Saami people, joiks, **8:**301–2, 303
St. Lucia
    kwadril, **2:**945
    La Rose musical styles, **2:***947*
Sāmoa, **9:**289
    hymns, **9:**205
Sardinia
    ballu, **8:**631
    danza, **8:**631
Saudi Arabia
    dewīnih, **6:**652
    women's wedding party music, **6:**692, 693, 699
Scotch snap, **8:**14
Scotland
    lays, **8:**362
    Traveller songs, **8:**296
Serawai people, **4:**619
Serbia
    dance music, **8:**947
    Kosovan *talava* genre, **8:**286
    usul modes, **8:**951
Serbian-American dance music, **3:**926
Shona people, **1:**747–49
Shuar music, **2:**419
shuffle rhythms, **3:**668
Sindh, *dhamāl*, **5:**281
Slovakia, **8:**717–18, 721
Slovenia, **8:**912, *913*, 919
Somalia, polyrhythms, **1:**254–55, 614
son, **3:**791, 792–93
soul, **3:**678
South Asia
    time-marking instruments, **5:**322–24
    treatises on, **5:**20, 43
Southeast Asia
    cyclic systems, **4:**10, 68
    island musics, **4:**597
Southeast Indian songs, **3:**467
Spain, **8:**593, 598
    aksak meters, **8:**593
    flamenco, **8:**597
Sri Lanka, **5:**956, 959
    akasara-vrutta, **5:**963–64
    bali, **5:**962
    Buddhist ritual music, **5:**363
    drum patterns, **5:**961, 967
Subanun people, gong music, **4:**923
Sumatra, **4:**613, 623
    dendang, **4:**620
    indang, **4:**611
    joget, **4:**616
    Muslim music, **4:**606
    rapdorap, **4:**624
    ronggeng, **4:**616

rhythm and meter (continued)
Sunda
gamelan music, **4:**702
ketuk tilu, **4:**707
pantun, **4:**713
pop Sunda, **4:**717
tembang Sunda, **4:**714
Suyá unison songs, **2:**146
Sweden, *polska*, **8:**435
swing, **3:**650
Switzerland, dance music, **8:**690, 694
syncopation
in African music, **1:**211
in concert music, **3:**539
in *contradanza*, **3:**791
in fiddle tunes, **3:**836
in Haitian dance music, **3:**802–3
in jazz, **3:**196, 650
in minstrel music, **3:**182, 543, 616
in musical theater, **3:**193, 194
in ragtime, **3:**547–48, 651
in rhythm and blues, **3:**668
in Vietnam, **4:**17
Syrian Orthodox music, **6:**228
table songs, **8:**9–10
tahardent music, **1:**589–90
Tahiti, *'ote'a* accompaniment, **9:**876–77
Tamil Nadu
in folk music, **5:**913
for *karakam* procession and dance,
5:904–5
Kota people, **5:**916, *916*
noṇṭi cintu, **5:**921
Tuticorin fishermen's songs, **5:***907*
tango, **3:**791
Temiar people, **4:**574, 583
Thailand, **4:**16, 17, 264–69, 292
khaen music, **4:**324
northern, **4:**315
village songs, **4:**299
Tibet, Buddhist chant, **7:**479
Tikopia, **9:**854–55
Tonga
fa'ahiula, **9:**792
fakaniua, **9:**788
Trinidad and Tobago
Orisa drumming, **2:**955
tāssā ensemble music, **5:**589–90
Tsonga people, **1:**710
Tsou music, **7:**525
Tuareg people, **1:**545
anzad music, **1:**579
curing ceremonies, **1:**587
tende n-əmnas, **1:**585–87
Tunisia
baṭāyḥī, **6:**331, 333–36
in *ma'lūf*, **6:**518
Turkey
aksak meters, **6:**115, 190, 760, 796
Alevi music, **6:**796
arabesk, **6:**256–57, 776
art music, **6:**128
aşîk performance, **6:**808
çiftetelli, **6:**567
folk music, **6:**79–80, 85–87, 760–62
Qur'anic recitation, **6:**769

rhythmic modes, **6:**89–92, 122, 194, 767,
772–73
Sufi music, **6:**122, 194
Tuvan music, **6:**982
Uighur music, **6:**995–1008; **7:**456–59
Uruguay, tango, **2:**519
Uttar Pradesh
birahā, **5:**667
naubat khānā music, **5:***280*
'Uvea
fasi, **9:**809–10, 813
kailao, **9:**812
Vanuatu
dance-songs, **9:**697–98
of hymns, **9:**199
pedagogy of, **9:**260
of songs, **9:**362
Vedic chant, *jaṭāmātrā*, **5:**241, 242
Venezuela
Amerindian music, **2:**525
chimbanguele, **2:**531
cyclic, **2:**527–28
joropo, **2:**540
"*La Batalla*," **2:**536
malembe, **2:**528, 535
Yekuana curing songs, **2:**180
Vietnam, **4:**16, 452, 454, 464–66, 478
Wales
hwyl declamation, **8:**345
snap, **8:**346
wǫ́rǫ̀, **1:**476
work music, **3:**83
world beat, **3:**337
Xia'erba songs, **7:**483
Yanomamö culture, shamanic songs, **2:**171
Yao music, **4:**550
Yap, **9:**304
churuq, **9:**731
Yaqui songs, **3:**437
Yemen, **6:**284–85
drum ensemble music, **6:**93–106
in drum music, **6:**656
al-ghinā' al-ṣan'ānī, **6:**687, *688*, 689–90
Yuma culture, dance-songs, **2:**596; **3:**434
Zande harp music, **1:**656
Rhythm Brothers, **1:**477
Rhythm Kings, **1:**770
Rhythm Music (periodical), **8:**211
Rhythm Slave (musical group), **9:**169
Ri Chŏngŏn, **7:**997
Ri Kŏnu, **7:**960
Ri Myŏngsang, **7:**961
Riabinin, Ivan, **8:**764
Riabinin, Trofim G., **8:**764
Riau-Lingga (kingdom), **4:**428
Ribary family, **8:**696
al-Ribāṭī, Ibrāhīm ibn Muḥammad al-Tādilī,
6:367
Ribera, Julian, **6:**22, 24, 535
Ricardo Palma (Peruvian ensemble), **2:**500
Ricci, Matteo, **4:**10, 472
rice
bamboo and, **4:**51–52, 711, 914
cultivation of, **4:**3, 6, 35, 38, 47, 48, 113–15,
594
in Borneo, **4:**830

in Burma, **4:**547
in China, **7:**153, 495, 496
in Indonesia, **4:**630, 731, 760, 762
in Japan, **7:**560, 605, 794, 795
in Korea, **7:**930, 942, 988
in Laos, **4:**546
in Malaysia, **4:**423, 575
in Philippines, **4:**914, 917, 920–21
in Thailand, **4:**300–301
goddess of, **4:**52–53
mother or soul of, **4:**51
origin myths about, **4:**50–51
spirit of, **4:**51
Rice, Thomas Dartmouth, **3:**182, 184
Rice, Timothy, **3:**15, 1082–83; **8:**25, 99,
112–13, 116; **10:**52
Richard and Pringle, **3:**616
Richard III (Shakespeare), **3:**615
Richard, Maurice, **3:**1157
Richard, Michèle, **3:**1158
Richard, Zacharie, **3:**1136
Richards, Cliff, **4:**331
Richards, Johnny, **3:**743, 787
Richards, Nansi, **8:**348
Richards, Zaneta Ho'oūlu, **9:**917, *918, 921*
Richardson, Major-General Sir George, **9:**219
Richardson, J. P. "Big Bopper," **3:**732, 746
Richie, Lionel, **3:**712, 713, 1002
Richmond, Jeff, **10:**143
Richter, František Xaver, **8:**727
Richter, Sviatoslav, **7:**415
Ricks, George Robinson, **3:**585; **10:**145
Riḍā, Muṣṭafá, **6:**235, 322
Ridder, Allard de, **3:**1095
Ride (musical group), **9:**169
Rideman, Peter, **3:**1240
Riding the Black Horse (Kazakh piece),
7:461
Riding the Date-Red Horse (Kazakh piece), **7:**461
Ridington, Robin, **3:**392, 1094
Ridout, Elizabeth H., **3:**1180
Ridout, Godfrey, **3:**1075, 1184
Riedel, Johannes, **2:**431
Riego de Dios, Emiliano, **4:**869
Riel, Louis, **3:**11, 344, 410, 1058, 1086
Riemann, Hugo, **7:**592
Riesenfeld, Hugo, **9:**44
Riesman, David, **3:**515
Riesman, Michael, **3:**254
Rifai cult, **5:**779
Rif'at, Shaykh Muḥammad, **6:**161
Rigden, Veda, **9:**560
Rigel, Henri-Jean, **6:**609
"Right Back Where We Started From"
(Nightingale), **3:**712
Right On: From Blues to Soul in Black America
(Haralambos), **3:**584
Right Said Fred, **9:**179
"Right Time" (Charles), **3:**673
Rigoletto (Verdi), **6:**547, 610
al-Rīhānī, Najīb, **6:**598
Riho (musical group), **8:***839*
Rihtman, Cvjetko, **8:**969, 970
Rikkokusi (Japanese history), **7:**586
Riley, Billy Lee, **3:**353

Riley, Terry, **3**:175, 335, 953; **4**:132; **10**:10
Rim Taesik, **7**:962
Rimatara (Austral Islands), **9**:879–82
Rime of the Ancient Mariner (Coleridge), **9**:33–34
Rimiti, **6**:270
Rimmer, Joan, **8**:22, 394
Rimsky-Korsakov, Nikolai, **2**:962; **3**:953; **5**:64; **6**:904; **8**:84, 85, 497, 759, 764, 772, 781
Rinaldi, Susana, **2**:264
Rinat Chamber Choir (Israel), **6**:1030
Rincah, **4**:786
Rin-chen bzang-po, **5**:713
Rindai seigaiha (*bugaku* piece), **7**:625
Ring, Oluf, **8**:460
Ring des Nibelungen, Der (Wagner), **8**:60
Ring Shout Concerto (Tillis), **3**:612
Ringer, Alexander, **6**:1063
Ringling-Barnum Band, **3**:568
Ringo no uta (Japanese popular song), **7**:745
Ringo oiwake (Japanese popular song), **7**:745
Ringve Museum (Trondheim), **8**:182, 427
Rinzler, Ralph, **3**:300
Ríos, Alberto, **3**:*730*
Rios, Orlando "Puntilla," **3**:784
Ríos Yáñez, Ovaldo, **2**:*612*
Riot Grrrls, **3**:92, 358
Ripley, S. Dillon, **3**:300
al-Risāla al-sharafiyya (Ṣafī al-Dīn al-Urmawī), **6**:369, 393, 502
al-Risāla al-shihābiyya (Mushāqa), **6**:369
Risāla fil-mūsīqā (Abū Bakr Ibn Bājja), **6**:443
Risālat rawḍ al-massarāt fī 'ilm al-naghamāt (al-Jundī), **6**:569
Risāle-i Musīqī (Changī), **6**:17
Rishon Le-Tsiyon Orchestra, **6**:1031
Risky Business (film), **3**:204
Rita, Jacinto, **2**:581
Rite of Spring (Stravinsky), **3**:1150; **8**:60; **10**:20
Ritmo y Juventud, **2**:372
Ritson, Joseph, **8**:*373*
Ritsos, Yannis, **8**:1021
Rittai hôsô no tameno myuzîku konkurêto (Sibata), **7**:736
Ritter, Frederic Louis, **3**:508
rituals. *See* ceremonies
Ritugen hakki (Nakane), **7**:568, 588
Ritwal ng Pasasalamat (Santos), **4**:878
Rivals (musical group), **3**:1213
Rivard, Michel, **3**:1160
Rivas de Domínguez, Celia Ruiz, **2**:463–64
Rivas, Inés, **2**:*609*
River of Krishna's Sports (Tirtha), **5**:267
Rivera, Danny, **2**:103
Rivera, Hipolito, **4**:866
Rivera, Ismael, **3**:799
Rivera, Jerry, **3**:788
Rivera, Reynaldo, **3**:*786*
Rivera, Tito, **3**:743
Rivera y Rivera, Roberto, **2**:658
Riverdance (dance show), **3**:846
Rivero, Edmundo, **2**:264
Rivers, W. H. R., **9**:992
Riverson, Isaac Daniel, **1**:35, 221, 223, 224, 230
Rivista Italiana delle Tradizioni Popolari (periodical), **8**:620

Rivlin, Zalman, **6**:205
Riwäyat (musical group), **7**:468
Riza, Ymer, **8**:997
Rizal Glorified (Adonay), **4**:862
Rizal, José, **4**:73, 85, 881, 885
Rizitika (album), **8**:1018
R. J. and the Riots, **4**:884
"R. M. Blues" (Milton), **3**:669
Roach, Archie, **9**:443–44, 987
Roach, David, **5**:136
Roach, Max, **3**:336, 658, 663
Roaring Lion (calypsonian; Hubert de Leon), **2**:96, 963
Roast, Ron, **3**:869
Robb Archives of Southwestern Music (Albuquerque), **10**:88
Robb, Ian, **3**:1189
Robb, John Donald, **3**:763, 767
Robb, Morse, **3**:1185
Robbins, James, **2**:839; **3**:149, 790, 1061
Robbins, Jerome, **3**:943
Robbins, Marty, **3**:80, 1050
Robbins, Vivian, **3**:1212
Robert and Frances Flaherty Study Center, **9**:975
Robertino, **8**:208–9
Roberto Pulido y Los Clásicos (musical group), **3**:781
Roberts, Christopher, **9**:979
Roberts, Donald, **3**:367
Roberts, Edmund, **4**:225
Roberts, Helen Heffron, **3**:29, 367, 381, 418, 473, 493, 495–96, 512; **9**:915, 968
Roberts, John (Ieuan Gwyllt), **8**:350
Roberts, John Storm, **2**:93, 862, 931; **3**:732, 790, 795, 796
Roberts, Marcus, **3**:664
Roberts, Rocky, **8**:209
Robertson, Carolina, **10**:56, 71, 130
Robertson, Dale B., **9**:*972*
Robertson, Eck, **3**:78
Robertson, Jeannie, **8**:24, 136, 200, 296, 297, 370, 372
Robertson-Wilson, Marian, **6**:20
Robeson, Paul, **3**:524, 619
Robey, Don, **3**:708
Robidoux, Fernand, **3**:1155
Robin et Marion (play), **8**:540
Robin Hood (De Koven), **3**:544
Robin, Leo, **9**:43
Robinson, Alan, **3**:1018
Robinson, Alfred, **3**:735
Robinson, Anne, **3**:345, 346
Robinson, Bill "Bojangles," **3**:207, 620
Robinson, Gertrude, **3**:1013
Robinson, Harry, **3**:1094
Robinson, Ken, **2**:844
Robinson, Smokey, **3**:676, 709
Robinson, Tumata, **9**:270
Robles, Fred, **4**:884
Robles, Valentín, **3**:751
Robley, Stanley, **9**:101
Rob Roy (film), **8**:369
Rocco, Emma S., **3**:826
Rocha, Otto de la, **2**:764
Rochberg, George, **3**:176
Rochefort, Cesar de, **2**:23

Rochereau. *See* Ley, Tabu "Rochereau"
Rochester Philharmonic (New York), **3**:609
rock. *See also* heavy metal; popular music; rock and roll; *specific genres such as* punta rock; *specific groups*
Africa, **1**:416
African-American performers of, **3**:17
alternative, **8**:214
amateur performances, **3**:284–85
Aotearoa, **9**:168, 929, 931, 937–38
Arctic consumers, **3**:380
Argentina, **2**:262, 266–68, 269, 463
"art rock," **8**:215
Australia, **9**:142, 144–46, 414, 442, 443–47
Austria, **8**:676
Belarus, **8**:801–3
blues and, **3**:648
Bolivia, **2**:293, 297
Bosnia-Hercegovina, **8**:969
Brazil, **2**:109, 110, 134, 318, 338, 354
British groups, **3**:840
Bulgaria, **8**:903
Cambodian, **3**:1002
Caribbean, **2**:103–4
Celtic, **3**:845–46; **8**:322
Central America, **2**:103–4
Chicano, **3**:749–51
Chile, **2**:32, 40, 374
China, **7**:359–61, 363–68, 399, 413, 468
Christian, **2**:60
Costa Rica, **2**:693, 699
Croatia, **8**:934
dancing to, **3**:227
Denmark, **8**:462
disco and, **3**:229–30
early, **3**:355–56
El Salvador, **2**:716, 718–19
Europe, **8**:204, 228
    Eastern, **8**:217–22
    Western, **8**:214–17
in film, **3**:204
Finland, **8**:480, 484, 485
funk and, **3**:680, 684
Futuna, **9**:815
Georgia, **8**:845
glitter, **8**:215
Greece, *elliniko*, **8**:1008
Haiti, **2**:892
Hawai'i, **9**:164, 220
history of, **3**:347–59
Hungary, **8**:746–48
indie markets and groups, **3**:168–71
instruments used in, **9**:372
Ireland, **8**:392
Israel, **6**:1021, 1073, 1074
Italy, **8**:619–20
    Neapolitan, **8**:204, 207
Japan, **7**:540, 746–47
jazz compared with, **3**:550–51
Jewish, **3**:943–44
Latin, **3**:721, 732–33, 751, 789, 798
local genres of, **8**:96
Macedonia, **8**:983
Maritimes, **3**:1073
Melanesia, **9**:599
Métis, **3**:411

rock (*continued*)
 Mexico, **2:**103–4, 623
 minimalism in, **3:**254
 mizik rasin and, **3:**806
 Mongolia, **7:**1019–20
 musical theater and, **3:**622
 Nepal, **5:**705
 Netherlands, **8:**238
 new wave, **3:**750
 Nicaragua, **2:**763
 North Caucasia, **8:**851
 Norway, **8:**421, 429, 430
 Oceania, **9:**126
 Ontario, **3:**1081
 Pakistan, **5:**748
 Papua New Guinea, **9:**154–55
  New Britain, **9:**614
 Paraguay, **2:**459, 462, 463
 Peru, **2:**486
 Portugal, **8:**584
 progressive, **3:**356
 Puerto Rico, **2:**940
 punk, **3:**750
 rap-influenced, **3:**359
 rhythm in, **3:**337
 Romania, **8:**882
 Russia, **8:**778
 Scotland, **8:**369
 Serbia, **8:**949
 South America, **2:**103–4
 South Asia, **5:**427–29
 Spain, **8:**593, 600
 style components of, **3:**551
 Subarctic consumers, **3:**391
 Sweden, **8:**446
 Switzerland, **8:**698
 Turkey, **6:**247–52, 256
 United States dominance of, **3:**18
 Uruguay, **2:**521
 use of didjeridu, **9:**397, 446–47
 Vietnamese, **3:**997
 Virgin Islands, **2:**969
 Wales, **8:**356
 women performers of, **3:**95, 96–97
 world music in, **3:**338–39
"Rock of Ages" (Hastings), **3:**532, *532*
"Rock the Boat" (Hues Corporation), **3:**688
"Rock around the Clock," **3:**353
rock en español, **2:**101, 104, 486, 716; **3:**522–23
Rock, Jenny, **3:**1158
Rock and Jokes Extempore Band, **8:**731
Rock, Joseph, **7:**511
Rock Machine (musical group), **5:**428
"Rock Me" (Tharpe), **3:**535
Rock and Other Four Letter Words (Marks),
  3:348
Rock & Pop (periodical), **2:**267
Rock against Racism, **8:**215
rock and roll, **3:**149, 197, 671
 Africa, **1:**362
 Austria, **8:**674
 blues and, **3:**648
 Chicano, **3:**734, 742
 country music and, **3:**163
 development of, **3:**326, 550–51, 561
 early reactions to, **3:**353–55

early references to, **3:**349
economics of, **3:**48, 263
history of, **3:**347–56
in Hong Kong, **7:**354
influence on country music, **3:**80–81
Italy, **8:**619
Mexican-American peformers, **3:**746–48
musical characteristics of, **3:**348
musical theater and, **3:**621
Native American popular music and, **3:**489
Netherlands, **8:**237–38
protest songs, **3:**316–18
Québec *yé-yé*, **3:**1076, 1158, 1161, 1162
rhythm and blues and, **3:**330, 584, 708
sound recordings and, **3:**243
Turkey, **6:**249
Rock and Roll on the New Long March (Cui),
  7:367
Rock 'n' Roll Is Here to Pay (Chapple and
  Garofalo), **3:**586
Rock 'n' Roll Trio, **3:**352
Rock 2000 (periodical), **8:**730
"Rock Your Baby" (McCrae), **3:**688
rockabilly, **1:**361
Rockabye Hamlet (Jones), **3:**199
"Rocket 88" (Brenston), **3:**351, 708
Rockett, Rikki, **3:***97*
Rocking Beijing (album), **7:**364
Rockin' Rembets (Adelaide), **9:**73
"Rockit" (Hancock), **3:**695
rock-steady, **2:**910, 912; **8:**235
Rockwell, John, **3:**144
Rocky (film), **3:**204
Rodd, Francis, **1:**584, 590
Rodeheaver, Homer, **3:**534
Rodeo Records, **3:**1128
Rodgers, Frankie, **3:**1257
Rodgers, Jimmie, **3:**13, 78, 520, 648; **8:**369;
  9:390
Rodgers, Richard, **3:**196, 197, 530, 545, 621
Rodrigo, Joaquín, **8:**601
Rodrigues, Amália, **8:**583
Rodrígues, Eva, **9:**101
Rodrigues, Jair, **2:**351
Rodrigues, Julio, Jr., **9:**101
Rodríguez, Arsenio, **3:**787, 792–93, 795
Rodríguez, Bobby, **3:**797
Rodríguez, Diane, **3:**749
Rodríguez, Eddie, **3:**741
Rodríguez, Fabian, **2:**736
Rodríguez, Jesús, **2:***532*
Rodríguez, José Luís (El Puma), **2:**103; **3:**746
Rodríguez, José Napoleón, **2:**718
Rodríguez, Juan Ángel, archbishop of Manila,
  4:842
Rodríguez, Lalo, **3:**743, 799
Rodríguez, Luis, **3:**747
Rodríguez, Miguel Ángel, **2:**464
Rodríguez, Olavo Alén, **2:**839
Rodríguez, Pete, **3:**741
Rodríguez, Rodri, **3:**745
Rodríguez, Russell, **3:***724*
Rodriguez, Sylvia, **10:**88, 90
Rodríguez, Sylvio, **2:**103
Rodríguez, Tito, **3:**732, 743, 787, 793, 794, 796,
  798

Rodríguez, Wesceslao, **2:**718
Rodriquez, Georges, **3:**1170
Roe, Paddy, **9:**432
Roediger, David, **3:**67
Roelli, Gilles, **8:**698
Roelli, Hans, **8:**698
Roesli, Harry, **4:**109
Rogefelt, Pugh, **8:**216
Roger and Zapp, **3:**685
Roger, Charles, **3:**1181
Roger, Estienne, **8:**523
Rogers, Benny, **9:**390
Rogers, Bernard, **3:**610
Rogers, David Feet, **9:**390
Rogers, Kenny, **3:**713
Rogers, Nile, **3:**715
Rogers, Roy, **3:**520
Rogers, Shorty, **3:**749
Rogers, Tim, **3:**1080
Roggeveen, Jacob, **9:**795, 951
Roghair, Gene, **5:**898
Rogie, S. E., **1:**366, 377
Roh Tae Woo, **7:**960
Roi boit, Le, **3:**1166
Róise Rua, **8:**387
Roja (film), **5:**545, 555
Rojas, Nydia, **3:**745
Rokeri s Moravu (musical group), **8:**949
Roknaddin Khan Mokhtāri, **6:**137
Rokudan (*dan mono*), **7:**696–97
Rokudan no sirabe (Yatuhasi), **7:**688
Roland, Edward de, **3:**604
Roldán, Amadeo, **2:**828, 837
*Role of Music in the Interaction of Black Americans
  and Hispanos in New York City's East
  Harlem* (Schramm), **3:**149
"Roll Jordan, Roll" (spiritual), **3:**523, *523*
"Roll Over Beethoven" (Berry), **3:**672
Rolling Along in Song (Johnson), **3:**607
Rolling Stone (periodical), **3:***96*, 689; **8:**211
Rolling Stones (musical group), **2:**911, 923;
  3:*263*, 318, 336, 348, 355, 550, 552,
  689, 777, 840, 1002; **8:**214, 216
 influence of, **4:**208, 885; **7:**1020; **8:**220, 619,
  679
 reggae-influenced songs, **2:**97
Rollins College (Winter Park), **3:**34
Rollins, Sonny, **3:**133, 659
Rolmo'i bstan-bios (Sakya Pandita), **7:**447
Rom people (Gypsies), **8:**7, 12, 17, 26, 247,
  270–89. *See also* Travellers
 in Albania, **8:**285–86, 993, 996, 997
 appellations for, **8:**270
 in Austria, **8:**289
 in Balkan region, **8:**140, 867
 as blacksmiths, **6:**361
 in Bosnia-Hercegovina, **8:**279–80, 966
 in Bulgaria, **8:**226–27, 278, 282–84, 893–94,
  903
 in Croatia, **8:**279–80
 in Czech Republic, **8:**276
 in Egypt, **6:**625
 in England, **8:**296
 in Finland, **8:**289, 487
 in France, **8:**288
 in Germany, **8:**288–89

in Greece, **8:**206, 278, 284–85, 1008, 1011–12, 1017, 1019, 1023
history of, **8:**271–72
in Hungary, **8:**19, 143, 199, 272–76, 736, 737–39, 744, 745–46
in Iraq, **6:**304, 408, 416
in Kurdistan, **6:**745–46
in Lebanon, **6:**554
in Macedonia, **8:**13, 116, *144, 162,* 200–201, 280–82, 285–86, 951, 972, 975–77, 979–80, 981–83, 984
misconceptions about, **8:**270
musical styles of, **8:**271
in Netherlands, **8:**288
in North America, **3:**530, 851, 909, 922, 923, 927, 1197, 1198
in Poland, **8:**276–77, 701
research on, **8:**24
in Romania, **8:**194, 196, *198,* 200, 277–79, 868, *872,* 873, 874, 877, 881, 884, 886
in Russia, **8:**199, 286–87, 765, 775–76
in Scotland, **8:**295
in Serbia, **8:**945, 950–52
in Slovakia, **8:**276
in Slovenia, **8:**914, 917
in Spain, **8:**270
  flamenco music, **8:**7, 596–600
in Syria, **6:**408
trained bears of, **8:**142–43, 280, *283,* 893, 950, *953*
in Turkey, **6:**57, 116, 763, 764, 784
in Ukraine, **8:**821
use of *rabāba,* **6:**409
in Wales, **8:**347, *348*
in Yugoslavia, **8:**279–80
Romafolk (musical group), **8:**276
Román, Father (Jesuit priest), **2:**176
Roman, Johan Helmich, **8:**444
Roman, Kenny, **3:**748
Roman Catholicism. *See also* Christianity; *specific orders, such as* Jesuit order
Afro-Cuban syncretism, **3:**784
Albanian people, **3:**926; **8:**986, 1002
American suspicion of, **3:**121, 506
Andean regions, **2:**206, 209, 220–21
Antigua and Barbuda, **2:**799
Argentina, **2:**256–59
Aruba, **2:**927
Australia, **9:**455
Austria, **8:**670
Basque region, **8:**316
Bolivia, **2:**137–40, 283, 289, 290–91
Bosnia-Hercegovina, **8:**962
Brazil, **2:**300–303, 307–8, 309, 310, 311–13, 324–25, 328–29, 333
  syncretism with African religions, **2:**341, 344, 347–48
Brittany, **8:**558
Caribbean, **2:**46–47, 795
censorship of traditional music and ceremonies, **2:**131
Central America, **2:**46–47, 630
Chile, **2:**356–57, 362–66
China, **7:**416
churches, **3:**122

Colombia, **2:**384, 400, 403–4
confirmation ceremony, **8:**143
Cook Islands, **9:**898
Corsica, **8:**574
Costa Rica, **2:**681, 688, 693–702
Croatia, **8:**925
Cuba, **2:**822, 823, 827, 836
Dominica, **2:**840
Dominican Republic, **2:**847–49, 852–53
Eastern European Americans, **3:**529
Ecuador, **2:**419–24
El Salvador, **2:**708, 709–11
Estonia, **8:**491
Europe, Western, **8:**517
Finland, **8:**481
France, **8:**539
French-Americans, **3:**854, 1056
French Canadians, **3:**146, 275, 1073, 1074–75, 1114, 1116, 1146, 1154–55, 1164, 1167
Futuna, **9:**814–15
Garífuna culture, **2:**734, 740
gender issues, **2:**57
Georgia, **8:**826
Germany, **8:**646, 655, 660–61
Goa, **5:**735–37, 740–41
Guarijío culture, **2:**552–53
Guatemala, **2:**735, 737
Guaymí culture, **2:**686
Haiti, **2:**882, 884
Hawai'i, **9:**918
Hmong-Americans, **3:**1005
Honduras, **2:**744–45
Hungary, **8:**736, 740
Ireland, **8:**378, 389
Irian Jaya, **9:**191
Jamaica, **2:**901
Kapingamarangi, **9:**836
Karnataka, **5:**881
Kiribati, **9:**762, 763
Latino peoples, **3:**720, 721
Latvia, **8:**499
Lithuania, **8:**399
liturgical music, **8:**5, 84, 106
  for organ, **3:**28
liturgy in, **3:**121
Malta, **8:**635, 640, 642
Mangareva, **9:**885, 886, 889
Manihiki, **9:**905
Marquesas Islands, **9:**894
Marshall Islands, **9:**748
Maya culture, **2:**651–52, 656, 730–31
Mexica culture, **2:**558, 562
Mexican people, **3:**735
Mexico, **2:**46–47, 556, 603, 613–16
Micmac Indian nation, **3:**1069
Micronesia, **9:**719–20
missionaries, **3:**23, 379, 390–91, 484–85, 721, 734–35, 847, 848–49, 1056, 1063, 1069, 1074–75
  New France, **3:**1115, 1147
  Southwest, **3:**755
Montenegro, **8:**957, 960
Montserrat, **2:**924
Nauru, **9:**756

Netherlands Antilles, **2:**927
New Mexico, **3:**755, 756–57, 758–59
Nicaragua, **2:**748, 762–63
Niue, **9:**816
North America, **3:**120
Oceania, **9:**187
Papua New Guinea, **9:**88, 193–94, 288, 516, 565–66, 572, 607, 612, 614, 632–33, 647, 650
Paraguay, **2:**457–59
passion plays, **8:**140
patronage of art music, **8:**69, 145
performance contexts in, **8:**11
Peru, **2:**214, 478–79, 491
Pohnpei, **9:**739
Poland, **8:**702, 709–10
Portugal, **8:**579
Pueblo Indian groups, **3:**217–18, 430
Puerto Rico, **2:**933
Pukapuka, **9:**913
Purépecha culture, **2:**575, 577–78
Rapa Nui, **9:**951–52
research on, **3:**119
Romania, **8:**868
Rotuma, **9:**818, 823
St. Lucia, **2:**942, 946, 949
Saipan, **9:**92
Sāmoa, **9:**206–7, 795
Scotland, **8:**360
Serbia, **8:**952
Society Islands, **9:**208
Solomon Islands, **9:**662, 665, 667
South America, **2:**46–47
South Asian Americans, **3:**984
Spain, **8:**596
statistics on, **3:**5
Switzerland, **8:**693
Tamil Nadu, **5:**921–27
Tokelau, **9:**823
Tonga, **9:**117, 791, 792
Trinidad and Tobago, **2:**952, 956–57
Ukrainian-Canadians, **3:**1088
Uruguay, **2:**511–12, 515
'Uvea and Futuna, **9:**809
Venezuela, **2:**533–37
Virgin Islands, **2:**969
women religious, **8:**197
worship practices of, **3:**118
Yap, **9:**199–200, 729, 730
Yaqui Indians, **2:**589; **3:**437, 438
Roman empire, **8:**38, 248
research on instruments of, **8:**39–40
rule over Albania, **8:**986
rule over Corsica, **8:**566
rule over France, **8:**558
rule over Great Britain, **8:**321, 326, 360
rule over Greece, **8:**1007
rule over Macedonia, **8:**972
rule over Malta, **8:**634
rule over North Africa, **1:**533; **6:**431
rule over Romania, **8:**868, 881
Romance (musical group), **3:**781
Romancero du Canada (Barbeau and d'Harcourt), **3:**1165
Romanelli, Samuel, **6:**1043
Romani Yag (musical group), **3:**1198

Romania, **8:**868–86
  Alba, instruments of, **8:**880
  Arad, instruments of, **8:**877, 880
  art music in, **8:**881–82
  Banat
    instruments of, **8:**876–78, 880
    rituals of, **8:**870–71
    Serbian-influenced music, **8:**884
    vocal music of, **8:**871–72, 875, 879
  Bihor
    instruments of, **8:**877
    vocal music of, **8:**874, 879
  Bucovina
    instruments of, **8:**878
    rituals of, **8:**869–72
    vocal music of, **8:**872, 873, 875
  Carpathian Mountains, instruments of,
      8:877–78
  dance-house movement, **8:**153
  dance traditions of, **8:**161–62, 198, 870, 872
  Dobruja, **8:**881
    instruments of, **8:**878–79
    rituals of, **8:**870–71
    vocal music of, **8:**873, 875
  ethnic minorities in, **8:**868, 883
  geography of, **8:**868
  Gyimes, funeral ceremony of, **8:**745
  history of, **8:**868
  history of music in, **8:**881–85
  Hunedoara
    instruments of, **8:**877, 880
    rituals of, **8:**870
    vocal music of, **8:**874, 879
  Hungarians in, **8:**736
  instrumental music of, **8:**874–86, 879–80
  instruments, **8:**870, 875, 876–79, 880, 885
    research on, **8:**172
  klezmorim performances at weddings, **8:**11
  map of, **8:**866, 869
  Maramureş
    instruments of, **8:**876–77, 880
    rituals of, **8:**870–71
    vocal music of, **8:**873, 874
    weddings, **8:**119
  Moldavia
    history of music in, **8:**881
    instruments of, **8:**877, 878–79, 880
    old-style songs, **8:**740
    rituals of, **8:**869–72
    Rom people in, **8:**271, *743*
    taraf ensemble, **8:**277
    vocal music of, **8:**872, 873, 874, 875, 879
  Muntenia
    dragaica ritual, **8:**194, 870
    instruments of, **8:**877, 878–79, 880
    rituals of, **8:**869–70
    taraf ensemble, **8:**277
    vocal music of, **8:**871, 873, 874, 875
  Năsăud, vocal music of, **8:**873, 874
  Oltenia
    instruments of, **8:**876–77, 878–79, 880
    old *vs.* new genres, **8:**121–22
    rituals of, **8:**870–71
    vocal music of, **8:**869, 871, 873, 874, 875,
      879, 950
    women performers, **8:**277

  popular music in, **8:**882, 885
  population of, **8:**868
  research on music of, **8:**18, 885–86
  rock in, **8:**217
  Rom people in, **8:**194, 277–79, 873, 874,
      877, 881, 884
    musica lăutarească genre, **8:**277
    muzica orientala genre, **8:**278
  state folk ensembles in, **8:**277, 278
  Transylvania
    history of music in, **8:**881
    Hungarian people and music in, **8:**736,
      739–42
    instruments of, **8:**877–78, 880
    Kalotaszeg, **8:**88
    old-style songs, **8:**740
    rituals of, **8:**870–72
    Rom people, **8:**275
    Székely people, **8:**274, 744
    violin and *gardon* ensemble, **8:**744
    vocal music of, **8:**869, 871–72, 873, 874,
      875, 879
  Turkish influences in, **8:**278
  vocal music, **8:**23, 120, 872–74, 879–80
    bocete, **8:**196, 871
    cîntece ceremoniale, **8:**196, 871
    cîntece de mahala, **8:**277
    colinde, **8:**131, *132*, 140, 869
    doina, **8:**9, 278, 872–73, 879, 882
    epic song, **8:**23, 130, 873
    hora lunga, **8:**128, *129*, 873
  Vrancea, instruments of, **8:**877
  Wallachia
    old *vs.* new genres, **8:**121–22
    Rom people in, **8:**271
Romanian Orthodox Church, **3:**911; **8:**868, 881
Romanian people
  in North America, **3:**910–12
  in Serbia, **8:**952
Romano, İsak Fresko, **6:**57
Romanovskaya, Elena E., **6:**941
Romantic Canada (Hayward), **3:**342–43
Romantic period, **8:**79–84, 368–69
  Denmark, **8:**460
  Estonia, **8:**495–96
  Finland, **8:**482
  Poland, **8:**710
  Spain, **8:**601
  Sweden, **8:**444
"Romany Life" (Herbert), **3:**530
Romathan (musical group), **8:**276
Romberg, Sigmund, **3:**193, 544
Rome in America (Fulton), **3:**121
Rome, Treaty of, **8:**237
Römer, Markus, **8:**574
Romero, Brenda M., **3:**849, 851; **10:**87–96, *89,
      91*
Romero, Fernando, **2:**501
Romero, Luis Casas, **2:**832
Romero, Ray, **3:***786*
Romero, Sílvio, **2:**313
Romet, Cheryl, **9:**256
Romeu, Antonio María, **3:**792
"Romish Lady" (ballad), **3:**121
Romodin, Aleksandr, **8:**778
Romualdez, Justice Norberto, **4:**123, 872

Romungre Roma, **8:**272–74, 276
Roncal, Simeón, **2:**284
Ronderos (librettist), **4:**863
Ronettes (musical group), **3:**673
Ronga people, **1:**214, 708
Ronli-Riklis, Shalom, **4:**523
Ronstadt, Linda, **3:**81, 713, 725, 732, 744, 745,
      751; **8:**220
Ronström, Owe, **8:**448
Room Rockers (musical group), **8:**237
Roos, Jaime, **2:**520
Roosevelt, Franklin Delano, **3:**310, 738
Roosevelt, Theodore, **3:**310, 967
Root, Deane, **3:**46
Root, George F., **3:**25, 188
Roots (musical group), **3:**701
Roots II (Baker), **3:**612
roots music (*mizik rasin*), **2:**95
Ropati (Sāmoan performer), **9:**807
Roper, Dee Dee "Spinderella," **3:**696
Rore, Cipriano de, **8:**76
Rorem, Ned, **3:**541
Roro people, **9:**491
Rosa, José de la, **3:**736
Rosa, Noel, **2:**316
Rosa, Tony de la, **3:**776
Rosario, Conrado del, **4:**878
Rosario-Villanueva, Nena del, **4:**870
Rosas, Fernando, **3:**741
Rosas, Juventino, **2:**604
Rose, Axl, **3:**358
Rose, Deborah B., **9:**419
"Rose of Ontario Waltz" (Stisted), **3:**289
"Rose in Spanish Harlem" (Drifters), **2:**105
"Rose Tree" (Scottish fiddle tune), **3:**837,
      837
Rose, Tricia, **3:**586
Rosebashvili, Kakhi, **8:**846
Rosellini, Jim, **1:**59
Roseman, Marina, **3:**790; **4:**26, 565–66, 572,
      577, 579
Rose-Marie (Friml), **3:**193, 544
Rosenberg, Hilding, **8:**445
Rosen, Franziska von, **3:**465
Rosenberg, Neil V., **3:**55, 56, 74, 146, 1063,
      1072, 1133
Rosenberg, Stochelo, **8:**288
Rosenberg, Tornado, **8:**289
Rosenberg Trio (musical group), **8:**288
Rosenblum, Ephraim, **10:**130
Rosenblum, Miriam, **10:**130
Rosenblum, Yair, **6:**1073
Rosenfeld, Morris, **3:**939
Rosengren, Bernt, **8:**446
Rosenman, Leonard, **3:**203
Rosi Tambir, **6:**1006
Rosina (Shield), **3:**839
Rosman, Abraham, **1:**517, 518
Rosnes, Renee, **3:**1107
Rosolio, David, **6:**1025
Rosowsky, Solomon, **6:**1025
Ross, Diana, **3:**693, 713
Ross, Robert, **8:**373
Ross, Roderick, **8:**374
Ross, William, **8:**368, 373
Rossburn Cymbaly Ensemble, **3:**1089

Rossel Island (Papua New Guinea), **9:**488, 498
  music and dance of, **9:**490, 983
  singing of, **9:**491
Rossen, Jane Mink, **9:**315, 853
Rossi, Annabella, **8:**24, 622
Rossi, Salomone, **6:**1067; **8:**263
Rossi, Tino, **4:**509
Rossi, Vasco, **8:**620
Rossi, Vittorio, **7:**733
Rossignol y chante, **3:**1166
Rossini Club (Portland, Maine), **3:**1209
Rossini, Gioacchino, **2:**736; **3:**542, 862, 1181,
    1182; **4:**854, 859; **8:**84, 367, 370
Rostocker Liederbuch, **8:**651
Rota (Northern Marianas), **9:**743, 744
Roter Frontkämpferbund, **8:**659
Roth, Juliana, **8:**907
Roth, Klaus, **8:**907
Roth, Walter E., **2:**24, 32, 442
Roti, **4:**798–801
Rotinese people, in West Timor, **4:**796, 798
Rotokas people, **9:**644
Rotuma (Fiji), **9:**490, 771, 817–23
  American expeditions to, **9:**24
  geography of, **9:**817
  haʻi, **9:**818
  history of, **9:**817–18
  map of, **9:***772*
  music and dance of, **9:**59, 818–23
  sound recordings from, **9:**1000
  tautoga, **9:**507, 819, 821–22
  theater, **9:**231, *232*
Rotuman people
  in Australia, **9:**84
  in Fiji, **9:**818, 998
Rouget, Gilbert, **1:**50, 51, 131, 658, 659, 663,
    783; **3:**1044–45; **10:**111, 112, 121
"Rough and Ready," **3:**307
Rough and Ready Songster, **3:**307
Rouland, Henri, **8:**542–43
Roulez Fillettes (musical group), **8:**548
Rounder Records, **3:**1128; **8:**241; **9:**998
"Round Midnight" (Monk), **3:**659
Rouse, Irving, **2:**13
Rousseau, Jean-Jacques, **3:**70, 275, 278
Roussel, Alain, **6:**608
Roussel, Albert, **3:**1150; **7:**732
Rovsing-Olsen, Miriam, **6:**23
Røvsing-Olsen, Poul, **6:**651
Row of Lodges, **3:**487
Rowe, "Doc," **8:**339
Rowe, Mann O., **10:**152
Rowell, Lewis, **1:**128; **5:**56, 69–70, 400
Rowland, Steve, **3:**683–84
Rowsome, Leo, **8:**390
"Roxanne, Roxanne" (UTFO), **3:**696
"Roxanne's Revenge" (Shante), **3:**696
Roxas, Francisco, **4:**866
Roxette, **8:**216
Roy, Carmen, **3:**292
Roy Choudhury, M., **6:**19
Roy, Martha, **6:**20, 223
Roy, Ram Mohan, **5:**254
Roy, U., **3:**693
Royal (marimba ensemble), **2:**718
Royal Academy of Dancing (Canada), **3:**225

Royal Academy of Performing Arts (Bhutan),
    5:715
Royal Alexandra Theatre (Toronto), **3:***200*
Royal Anthropological Institute (London), **1:**55
Royal Beauty (Tang), **7:**307
Royal Cambodian Dancers, **3:**207, 219
Royal Canadian Air Farce (television show),
    3:1059
Royal Canadian College of Organists, **3:**1119
Royal Collection of Hawaiian Songs (Noble),
    9:919, 922
Royal College of Music (London), **5:**740
Royal Commission on Bilingualism and
    Biculturalism (Canada), **3:**14
Royal Conservatory Chongakwon (Korea), **7:**56
Royal Conservatory of Music (Toronto), **3:**1079,
    1182
Royal Conservatory Opera School (Toronto),
    3:1184
Royal Corps of Musicians (Tonga), **9:**130
Royal Danish Ballet, **8:**161
Royal Hawaiian Band, **9:**133–34, 222, 923
Royal Jesters (musical group), **3:**780
Royal Musicians of Hindustan (group), **5:**563
Royal Nepal Academy, **5:**705
Royal Papuan Constabulary Band, **9:**27
Royal Schools of Music (London), **2:**909
Royal Tahitian Ballet, **9:**998
Royal, Taiaroa, **9:**948
Royal University of Fine Arts (Phnom Penh),
    3:998, 999; **4:**90, 119–20, 124, 156,
    161, 183, 190, 191, 193, 200–201,
    207, 209
Royal Winnipeg Ballet, **3:**224
Royce, Anya Peterson, **3:**151, 221
Royce, Rose, **3:**712
Royl, Ekkehard, **9:**980
Rozdol's'kyi, Iosyf, **8:**822
Rozsa, Miklos, **3:**203, 546
Rózsavölgyi, Mark, **8:**737
R. S. Williams firm, **3:**1183
Rualath (Yap dance expert), **9:**727
Rüang Tham Kwan (suite), **4:**260
Ruatoka (Cook Islands missionary), **9:**494
Rubalcava, Alfred, **3:**748
Rubayiat of ʻUmar Kahyyām (Alexander), **6:**1031
"Rubberband Man" (Spinners), **3:**711
Rubel, Paula, **1:**517, 518
Rubén Darío Theater (Nicaragua), **2:**766
Rubén Naranjo y Los Gamblers (musical group),
    3:776
Rubin, Edgar, **1:**180–81, 184
Rubin, Rick, **3:**696
Rubin, Ruth, **3:**944
Rubinstein, Anton, **3:**1180; **8:**780, 781
Rubinstein, Arthur, **6:**1025
Rubinstein, Nikolai, **8:**780
Rubio, Hilarión, **4:**872
Rubio, Miguel Ángel, **2:**573
Rubtsov, Feodosy, **8:**23, 784
"Ruby My Dear" (Monk), **3:**659
Rudaki, **6:**131
Rudd, Nick, **3:**169–70
Rudder, Antonio "Boo," **2:**820
Rudder, David, **2:**964
Rudež, Jože, **8:**921

Rudhyar, Dane, **5:**53
Rudichenko, Tatyana, **8:**778
Rudiments of Music (Adgate), **3:**289
Rudra (deity), **5:**238
Rudy, Paul, **3:**423–24
Ruffinel (French Guianese songwriter), **2:**438
"Ruffneck" (MC Lyte), **3:**697
Rugalo, Pete, **3:**743
Ruggles, Carl, **3:**174
Ruhunu (kingdom), **5:**955, 960
Ruíz, Eduardo, **2:**578
Ruiz Espadero, Nicolás, **2:**837
Rukai people, **7:**526
Rukmana, Rukruk, **4:***132*
rumba, **2:**100, 371; **3:**13, 521, 732, 742, 743,
    783, 785–86, 790, 791, 793, 794,
    797, 798, 893, 995, 1203
  Africa, **1:**386–88, 415
  Algeria, **6:**270
  Angola, **1:**435
  Barbados, **2:**819
  Benin, **1:**422
  Cameroon, **1:**661
  Central African Republic, **1:**683
  Congo-Zaïre, **1:**361, 423–26, 432; **8:**234
  Cuba, **2:**827, 829, 830–31, 836
  dance competitions for, **3:**210
  Honduras, **2:**744
  influence on rhythm and blues, **3:**669, 670
  Kenya, **1:**427
  Nicaragua, **2:**763
  Peru, **2:**487
  Spain
    flamenco-style, **8:**204, 205
    rumba catalán, **8:**204, 205
  styles of, **3:**729, 786
  Tanzania, **1:**643, 644
Rumba (periodical), **8:**484
Rūmī. *See* Jalāl al-Dīn Rūmī
Rumillajta, **2:**297
"Rumpofsteelskin" (Parliament), **3:**684
Rumshinsky, Joseph, **3:**937–38
Run-D.M.C. (musical group), **3:**552, 696, 700,
    713
Run-D.M.C. (album), **3:**713
Run, Little Children (Johnson), **3:**607
Runfola, Charlie, **3:**865
"Running with the Devil" (Van Halen), **3:**552
Runnin' Wild (musical), **3:**620
Runrig (musical group), **8:**322, 364–65, 371
Rururu (Austral Islands), **9:**879–82
Ruschenberger, W. S. W., **4:**225, 251
Rush (musical group), **3:**1081; **4:**887
Ruslanova, Lidiya, **8:**777, 779
Russell, Albert "Diz," **3:**670
Russell, Alexander, **6:**544, 566
Russell, Andy (Andrés Rábago), **3:**732, 741, 742,
    751
Russell, Anna, **3:**1080
Russell, Craig, **3:**848
Russell, George, **3:**659, 661
Russell, Henry, **3:**183, 184, 839; **8:**205
Russell, Ian, **8:**339
Russell Islands (Solomon Islands), **9:**28, 861
  music and dance of, **9:**662–64

Russell Islands (Solomon Islands) (*continued*)
　research on, **9**:963
　songs of, **9**:30
　Tikopia people in, **9**:833
Russell, Kelly, **3**:1121
Russell, Mark, **3**:311
Russell, Micho, **8**:385
Russell, Patrick, **6**:566
Russia, **8**:754–85. *See also* Karelia; North
　　Caucasia; Siberia; Soviet Union
　　(former)
　Archangelski district, *byliny*, **8**:764
　Arctic territories, **3**:379, 479
　art music in, **8**:780–82, 856, 858, 861
　Ashkenazic Jews in, **8**:248
　Astrakhan region, **6**:967; **8**:772
　balalaika orchestra in, **3**:58
　ballet in, **8**:161
　ban on *skomorokhi*, **8**:122
　Belgorod district
　　panpipes in, **8**:770
　　vocal polyphony, **8**:757
　Bryansk district
　　panpipes in, **8**:770
　　vocal polyphony, **8**:757
　court life in, **8**:199, 755
　Dagestan, **8**:828
　　Iranian dance traditions in, **6**:877
　ethnic minorities in, **8**:12, 766–67, 771–74,
　　778
　folk instrument orchestras, **8**:9, 154, 775
　folk music, use in world music recordings,
　　8:226
　geography of, **8**:754
　healing ceremonies, **8**:196
　history of, **8**:754–55
　history of music in, **8**:754–55, 779–82
　Ingermanlandia region, **8**:772
　instruments, **8**:770–71, 775
　　research on, **8**:38
　　Volga-Ural peoples, **8**:774
　jazz in, **8**:777
　Jewish people in, **8**:772
　Kalmykia, **7**:1003
　Kasimov, **8**:772
　Kola peninsula, Saami in, **8**:299
　Kursk district, panpipes in, **8**:770
　Lake Onega region, *tirade byliny*, **8**:765
　map of, **8**:*752*
　Mordvinia, vocal music, **8**:773
　Moscow, **8**:780
　Muslim peoples in, **8**:11
　Ob-Ugrian peoples, **8**:488
　Oka river region, vocal polyphony, **8**:757
　participants' obligations, **8**:114
　Pomorie region, **8**:754
　popular music in, **8**:778
　Povolzh'e region, **8**:754
　Pskov district, *pod draku*, **8**:768
　regional genres in, **8**:758–69
　research on music of, **8**:18, 19, 763–64, 773,
　　775
　Riazan district, vocal polyphony, **8**:757
　Rom people in, **8**:199, 270, 286–87, 765,
　　775–76
　Saami people in, **8**:12, 299–307

St. Petersburg, **8**:755, 780
　ethnic minorities in, **8**:766–67
Setu region, **8**:772, 774
Smolensk district, vocal polyphony, **8**:757
Stavropol' region, **6**:967
suburban vocal genres, **8**:6–7
Tatarstan, **6**:897
Tot'ma, laments, **8**:120–21
Tula region, accordions in, **8**:771
Udmurtia, vocal music, **8**:773
Ural Mountains, vocal polyphony, **8**:757
urban revivalism in, **8**:774–79
village music, **8**:778
　structures of, **8**:755–58
Vladimir district, *rozhok* ensembles, **8**:770
vocal music, **8**:755–69
　byliny, **8**:23, 121, 129–30, 201, 763–65
　calendrical songs, **8**:24, 758–61
　chastushki, **8**:6–7, 134, 761, 768, 779
　kant, **8**:755, 767, *768*, 780
　laments, **8**:23, 120, 761–63
　lyric songs, **8**:765–67
　noviny, **8**:130
　protiazhnaia pesnia, **8**:9, 133, 756, 765
　three-voice polyphony, **8**:757, *759*, 767
　two-voice polyphony, **8**:753, 757
Volga region, *stradaniia*, **8**:768
Volga-Ural region, **6**:935; **8**:772–74
Vologda district
　laments, **8**:758
　weddings, **8**:774
Voronezh district
　stradaniia, **8**:768
　vocal polyphony, **8**:757
Yaroslavl district, *rozhok* ensembles, **8**:770
Russian Court Singing Cappella, **8**:780
Russian empire, **8**:753, 806
　rule over Belarus, **8**:790
　rule over Central Asia, **6**:897, 903, 937–38,
　　967, 975
　rule over Estonia, **8**:491
　rule over Finland, **8**:475
　rule over Georgia, **8**:826, 843
　rule over Latvia, **8**:499
　rule over Lithuania, **8**:509
　rule over North Caucasia, **8**:850, 862
Russian Institute for the History of the Arts,
　　8:783, 784
Russian Musical Gazette (periodical), **8**:783
Russian Musical Society, **8**:780
Russian Orthodox Church, **3**:1267; **8**:772, 779,
　　850
　Alaska Native churches, **3**:486
　Estonia, **8**:491
　musical style in, **3**:118
　music of, **3**:10, 529, 915
　Poland, **8**:710
　in Siberia, **7**:1030
　support of balalaika orchestras, **3**:57
　Yupik people, **3**:380
Russian people. *See also* Volga Germans
　in Central Asia, **6**:897, 905
　in China, **7**:354, 398, 455–58
　in Estonia, **8**:491
　explorers, **3**:1255; **9**:17–18, 22–23
　in Finland, **8**:487

　in Lithuania, **8**:509
　in North America, **3**:529, 915–17, 1267–70
　　Ontario, **3**:1199–1200
　in North Caucasia, **8**:850
　in Oceania, **9**:100
　in Paraguay, **2**:462
　in Siberia, **7**:20–21
　in South America, **2**:84
　in Ukraine, **8**:821
Russian Song (musical group), **8**:779
Russkii Fol'klor (periodical), **8**:764, 785
Russo-Iranian war, **6**:922
Russo-Japanese War, **7**:383, 648, 728, 740, 743
Rustavi (musical group), **8**:845
Rustembekov, Bidas, **6**:*957*
Rustembekov, Zhienbay, **6**:*954*
Rutgers University (New Jersey), **3**:610
Ruthenian people, in Serbia, **8**:952
Rutherford, Paul, **3**:1061
Rüütel, Ingrid, **8**:498
al-Ruzayqī, Shaykh Aḥmad, **6**:*157*
Rwanda, **1**:602, 603, 607, 651. *See also* East
　　Africa; *specific peoples*
Ryabinin, Trofim G., **8**:130
Ryan, Sean, **8**:*385*
Ryan's Mammoth Collection, **3**:*406*, 1190
Rybner, Dr. P. M. C., **5**:563
Rybnikov, Aleksei, **8**:782
Rybnikov, P. N., **8**:130
Rycroft, David, **1**:51, 359, 363–64; **10**:112, 120
Rydving, Håkan, **8**:307
"Rye Waltz," **3**:1190
Ryerson, Egerton, **3**:275, 1180
Ryga, George, **3**:199
Rykodisc, **3**:498; **8**:241
Rymbaeva, Roza, **6**:961
RYO (Rural Youth Orchestra), **9**:158
Ryôô (*tôgaku* piece), **7**:624
Rypdal, Terje, **8**:430
Ryûkyû gumi (*kumiuta*), **7**:692
Ryûkyû Islands, **7**:9, 789–96
　Amami island group, **7**:789, 791, 795
　classical music of, **7**:793–94
　dance in, **7**:65–66
　folk songs of, **7**:794–95
　geography of, **7**:789
　history of, **7**:789–90
　instruments of, **7**:688, 711, 792
　kumi odori genre, **7**:789–90, 796
　Miyako island group, **7**:789, 791, 794
　music of, **7**:540
　Okinawa island group, **7**:789, 791, 794–95
　research on music of, **7**:593
　Yaeyama island group, **7**:789, 791, 794
Ryûkyû kingdom, **7**:725, 789–90, 792, 795
Ryûsen (*biwa* piece), **7**:644, 645
ryûteki. See flutes
Rzaev, Asad, **6**:930

Saada, Nadia Mécheri, **1**:545
Sa'āda, Muḥammad, **6**:330, 332, 336
Saadya Gaon, Rav, **6**:16, 541
Saafi, Sione, **9**:113
Saami Musicians Association, **8**:428
Saami people, **8**:12, 247, 299–307, 475, 486–87
　Christian bans on shamanic music, **8**:122

drums of, **8:**305
Fjeld group, **8:**487
Inari group, **8:**486–87
joiks of, **8:**96, 117, 127, 128, 143, 299–307,
    428–29, 447, 487, 488
lev'dd genre, **8:**486, 488
in Norway, **8:**411, 428–29
research on, **8:**306–7
in Russia, **8:**772
Skolt group, **8:**486
in Sweden, **8:**434, 435, 446–47
Saar, Mart, **8:**497–98
Saari, Wimme, **8:***487*
Saarisalo, A., **6:**580
Saatcï, Ercan, **6:**248
Ṣabā, Abdolhassan, **6:**62, 139, 862, 866
Saba Island, **2:**927
Ṣabāḥ, **6:**592
Sabanga people, **1:**267
Sabanisdze, Ioane, **8:**843
Sabas (French Guianese songwriter), **2:**438
Sabater, Jimmy, **3:**788
Sabatier, Charles Wugh, **3:**1076, 1148
al-Ṣabbāgh, Tawfīq, **6:**548, 568
Sabbah, Dina, **6:**1037
Sabbatarianism, **3:**904–5
Sabbat Cantata (Seter), **6:**1029
Saber, Ahmed, **6:**269
Saber, Mamitua, **4:**881, 907–8
Sabian Ltd. (cymbal manufacturer), **3:**246,
    1116
Sabir, **6:**931
Sabiston, Andrew, **3:**200
Sablan, David, **9:**160
Sablan, Johnny, **9:**160
Sablosky, Irving, **3:**511
"*Sabor a mi*" (El Chicano), **3:**748
Sabri Brothers, **3:**1215; **5:**426, 746, 753
Sabri, Ghulam Farid, **5:**746, 748
Sabum people, **4:**560
Sacasa, Juan Bautista, president of Nicaragua,
    2:759
Sac-Fox Indian nations, **3:**451
Sachal Sarmast (Sufi saint), **5:**753
    death anniversary of, **5:**759
Sachdev, G. S., **5:**529
Sachs, Curt, **1:**31; **2:**28; **3:**473; **5:**213; **6:**361,
    535, 1058; **7:**137, 603; **8:**20, 177,
    178, 266, 803; **9:**371; **10:**56
    instrument classification system, **5:**20, 51, 322;
    8:40
Sachs, Hans, **8:**650
Sacramento, Lucino, **4:**872
Sacred Bridge (Werner), **6:**19
Sacred Harmony (Davidson), **3:**1179
Sacred Harp (tunebook), **3:**533
Sacred Service (Bloch), **6:**1027
Sadai, Yizhak, **6:**1031
Sadat, Anwar, president of Egypt, **6:**619
Sadayasu, prince, **7:**588
Sadeghi, Manoochehr, **6:**67, 70; **10:**79, 140
Sa'di (Sufi poet), **5:**687, 805; **6:**72, 132, 135,
    826
Sādiqov, Fakhriddin, **6:**908
Sadler, Barry, **3:**317
Sadrāga-candrodaya (Vitthala), **5:**46, 48

Saebelmann-Kunileid, Aleksander, **8:**495
Saek people, **4:**316
Sae nara (Kim), **7:**953
Sáenz, Anselmo, **2:**736
Sáenz de A., Benedicto, **2:**736
Sáenz, Guido, **2:**704
Saenz, Tony, **3:**739
Sae t'aryŏng (Korean folk song), **7:**882
Saeul Kayagŭm Trio, **7:**971, *971*
Safavid dynasty, **6:**73, 113, 130–31, 183, 794,
    843, 859, 922; **7:**24
Safedimova, Katja, **8:**283
Ṣafi al-Din, 'Abd al-Mo'men, **6:**75
Safi al-Dīn of Ardabil, **6:**794
Ṣafi al-Dīn al-Urmawī (Safiaddin Ormavi),
    6:16–17, 35, 73, 75, 129, 135, 183,
    184, 365, 366, 369, 392–93, 502,
    508, 542, 772, 855, 859, 869, 910,
    922
al-Ṣāfi, Wadī', **3:**1220; **6:**529, 554, *554*, 592
Safina (Ḥusayn ibn Aḥmad al-Kubaysī al-Ḥanafī
    al-Shādhilī), **6:**371
Safinat al-mulk wa-nafisat al-fulk (Muḥammad
    Shihāb al-Dīn), **6:**371, 567–68
Safinaz (Karaca), **6:**250
Ṣafvat, Dariūsh, **6:**70, 75, 857
Sağ, Arif, **6:***789*, 789–92, *791*, 797–98, 799
Sağ, Tolga, **6:**791, 799
Sagard-Théodat, Gabriel, **3:**23
Sagimusume (*nagauta* piece), **7:**674
Sagye (musical group), **7:**972, *972*
Sagye (Lee), **7:**956
Sáha culture, **2:**183
Sahag Partev, **6:**723
Sahagún, Bernardino, **2:**15, *17*, 557, 602
Sahai-Achuthan, Nisha, **5:**675
Sahai, Ram, **5:**133
Sahai, Sharda, **5:**136; **10:**10, *10*
Sahasrabuddhe, Vina, **5:***171*, 466
Saheb, Nana, **5:**866
Saheb, Sharif, **5:**866, 869
Sahibinin Sesi (company), **6:**787
Ṣaḥiḥ (al-Bukhārī), **6:**358
Šahinpašić, Hamdija, **8:***961*
al-Saḥīr, Kādhem, **6:**240, 592
al-Sahir, Kazim, **3:**1220
Şahkullu Sultan, **6:**794
Sahl, Michael, **3:**45
Sahlins, Marshall, **9:**835
Sahmasi, Naseer, **5:**487
šahnāī. See double-reed instruments
Sahô no mai, uhô no mai (Hayasaka), **7:**732
Sahraoui, Cheb, **8:***234*
Sahriya people, **5:**639
Sahul Land, **9:**2
Sa Huynh culture, **4:**42–43
Sai Baba, Sathya, **3:**983; **5:**267–68, 425, 557,
    579, 581, 590–91
Sai Hseng Mao, **7:**506
Saibai Island (Australia), **9:**61
Sā'ib Khāthir, **6:**294, 295
al-Sa'īd, Labīb, **6:**162
Said bin Timur, sultan of Oman, **6:**672
Ṣa'īd Ibn Yūsuf. See Saadya Gaon, Rav
Said, Edward, **6:**21–22

Saigal, Kundan Lal, **5:**420, 533, *533*,
    539, 855
Saigô Takamori, **7:**648
"Saigon Bride" (Baez), **3:**316
"Sail On Boogie" (Walker), **3:**669
Sail the Midnight Sun (Kasaipwalova), **9:**234
Sailong duojin (He), **3:**1261; **7:**220
Sain Record Company, **8:**354, 356
Sainson, de, **9:**947
"St.-Adèle P.Q." (Ferland), **3:**1156
St. Andrews Music Book, **8:**366
St. Croix, **2:**968–73
St. Croix Heritage Dancers, **2:**972
St. Cyr, Johnny, **3:**652–53
St. Denis, Ruth, **3:**1042; **5:**563; **8:**161
Saint-Dominigue. *See* Haiti
"Sainte Anne's Reel," **3:**409, 1190
Sainte-Marie, Buffy, **3:**14, 73, *73*, 1063, 1081,
    1087
St. Francis Xavier University (Antigonish),
    3:1072, 1119
St. George's Episcopal Church (New York),
    3:629
St. James Anglican Church (Toronto), **3:**1079
St. John (island), **2:**968
St. John the Baptist Society (Québec), **3:**1148
St. John's Choral Society (Victoria), **3:**1094
St. John's Orchestral Society (Newfoundland),
    3:1118
St. John's Spiritual Baptist Church (Brooklyn),
    3:8
St. Kitts, **2:**97, 939
St. Lawrence String Quartet, **3:**1186, 1210
"St. Louis Blues" (Handy), **3:**524
"St. Louis Greys Quick Step" (Postlewaite),
    3:605
St. Louis University, **4:**873
St. Louis World's Fair, **9:**225
St. Lucia, **2:**789, 942–50
    African brotherhoods in, **2:**47
    history of, **2:**942
    La Rose and La Marguerite societies in, **2:**946
    musical genres
        calypso, **2:**949–50
        jwé, **2:**943–44
        kwadril, **2:**944–45
        masquerade, **2:**947–48
        séwinal, **2:**948
    popular music in, **2:**98
    research on, **2:**950
    tourism in, **2:**51
St. Lucian people, in French Guiana, **2:**437
Saint-Marcoux, Micheline Coulombe, **3:**1076,
    1152
St. Martin (island), **2:**789, 927
Saint Matthew Passion (Bach), **6:**1030; **8:**55, 60
St. Matthias Group (Papua New Guinea), **9:**600,
    626
Saint-Méry, Moreau de, **3:**596
St. Paul's Anglican Church (Halifax), **3:**1070
St. Petersburg Philharmonic Society, **8:**780
St. Petersburg Society of Chamber Music, **8:**780
Saint-Saëns, Camille, **3:**1148, 1149; **6:**49,
    357–58
St. Scholastica's College, **4:**123, 869–70
St. Thomas, **2:**939, 968–71

St. Vincent, **2:**789, 864
  Garífuna emigrants from, **2:**668, 733, 740, 752
St. Vincent's College (Los Angeles), **3:**736
Saipan (Northern Marianas), **9:**712, 743, 746, 995
Saisiat people, **7:**427, 525
Saitô Gessin, **7:**588
Saityô, **7:**612
Sajiabanzhida Gonggajianzan, **7:**472–73
Sajia Maxim (Tibetan writing), **7:**472
Saka, Pierre, **8:**548
Sakad (musical group), **3:**806
Sakae zisi (*kokyû* piece), **7:**712
Sakai people, **4:**598, 600, 614
Sakai Tikuho I, **7:**703
Sakalava kingdoms, **1:**781–83, *784*
Sakaloski, Niescer, **8:**800
Sakamoto, Ryuichi, **3:**204
sákárà, **1:**474–75, 478, 485
Sakas. *See* Massagetae
Sakata, Hiromi Lorraine, **6:**301, 305
Sake wa namidaka tameikika (Koga), **7:**745
Sakha people, **6:**980; **7:**14, 1027–30
Sakhat-*baggy,* Nobat Aman, **6:**976
Sakhile, **1:**778, 779
Sakiusa, **9:**138
Saktaeyŏp (*kagok*), **7:**921
Sakti, Tanjung, **4:***623*
Sakurai Tetuo, **7:**594
Sakuramento teiyô (Christian manuscript), **7:**724
Sakya Pandita, **7:**447
Ṣalāḥ al-Dīn, **6:**615, 638
Salamah, Gamal, **6:**612
Salangai Oli (film), **5:**544
Salar people, **7:**449, 455–58, 463
Salas, Rudy, **3:**748
Salas, Steve, **3:**748
Salas y Castro, Esteban, **2:**827, 836
Salasaca culture, **2:**415
"Salauma" (Cambodian piece), **3:**1001
Salaw, **4:**98
Salazar, António de Oliveira, **8:**576, 577, 583
Salazar, George, **3:**759
Salazar, Rafael, **2:**523, 544
Salazar, Rodrigo, **2:**635, 703
Saldívar, Gabriel, **2:**605, 623–24
Saldívar, Mingo, **3:**776
Sale (Sāmoan comedian), **9:**235
Salesian order, **2:**238
Salgán, Horacio, **2:**264
Salheś (epic), **5:**678, *679*
Salibhadra, **5:**637
Ṣāliḥ, 'Abbūd, **6:**643
Ṣāliḥ, Muḥammad 'Abduh, **6:**604
Salihović, Selim, **8:***967*
Salim, Abdel Gadir, **1:**571–72
Salim, Mohamed Al Hassan, **1:**572
Salinas, Elena, **3:**739
Salinas, Francisco de, **8:**601
Salisbury, Kevin, **9:**307, 973
Salish Indian nation, **3:**5, 509, 1094, 1254
Sallaberry, Jean-Dominique-Julien, **8:**316
Sallāma (film), **6:***291,* 292
Sallāmā, Shaykh Muḥammad, **6:***160*

Sallāma al-Qass, **6:**291–92, 295–96
Sallāma al-Zarqā', **6:**295, 297
Sallée, Pierre, **1:**256
"Sallie Gooden" (Robertson), **3:**78
Sallinen, Aulis, **8:***187*
Sallman, Warner, **3:**122
Sālma yā Salāma (Darwīsh), **6:**598
Salmen, Walter, **3:**45; **8:**251, 259, 267
Salmerón, Francisco, **2:**581
Salón México, El (Copland), **3:**797
salon music. *See* parlor and salon music
Salonen, Esa-Pekka, **8:**485
Sālote, queen of Tonga, **9:**351, 353, 366–68, 793
Salp'o kanŭn kil (television show), **7:**958–59
Salpvuri (Onŭrŭm), **7:**972
salsa, **1:**416, 424; **2:**75, 93, 101, 102, 105, 133
  in Argentina, **2:**265
  in Brazil, **2:**353
  in Canada, **3:**1085, 1204
  in Colombia, **2:**383, 410, 411
  in Costa Rica, **2:**693
  in Cuba, **2:**829, 839
  dancing to, **3:**212, 213
  development of, **3:**325, 336, 743, 788, 794–95, 797–99
  ensemble members, **2:**57
  identity issues in, **3:**513
  in Mexico, **2:**622
  in North America, **3:**16, 98, 228, 516, 522, 728, 729, 732, 781, 785, 790, 793
  in Nubian music, **6:**644
  in Peru, **2:**487
  in Puerto Rico, **2:**940, 941
  in United States, **2:**101, 102
  in Uruguay, **2:**520
"Salsa y Bembé" (Sabater), **3:**788
"Salsa Na Ma" (Velasquez), **3:**788
Salsiology (Boggs), **2:**839
salsoul, **3:**513
Salsoul Records, **3:**748
"Salt Peanuts," **3:**659
Salt-N-Pepa (musical group), **3:**696, 713, 714
Salter, Joseph, **5:**562
Salvadoran-Americans/Canadians, **3:**719, 727–28, 1201, 1204
Salvador-Daniel, Francisco, **6:**22
Salvatierra, Juan María, **2:**595
Salvation (New York), **3:**688
Salvation Army, **2:**798; **3:**1118
  in Aotearoa, **9:**930, 935
  in Japan, **7:**728
Salvatti, Federico, **3:**741
Salve Patria (Nakpil), **4:**871
Salve Regina, **2:**847–48
Salyr people, **6:**966
"Sam" (Ghanaian guitar composer), **1:**356–57
Sam, Chan Moly, **4:**25
Sam and Dave, **3:**676, 677, 710
Sam Hui (Xu Guanjie), **7:**354
Sam Jack's Creole Burlesque Company, **3:**618
Sam, Jacob, **9:**966
Sam On Soth, **4:**188
Sam, Sam-Ang, **4:**25
samā' (also *sema*), **6:**179, 184–86, 187–88, 543; **10:**160
  Algeria, **6:**474–75

Balochistan, **6:**885, 888–89
Central Asia, **6:**937, 939, 942–43, 945
Egypt, **6:**158
history of, **6:**19
Iran, **6:**132
Tunisia, **6:**517
Turkey, **6:**109, 114, 118–19, 190, 768, 769, 795, 796, 798
Sama people, **4:**920
  epics of, **4:**908
  instrumental music of, **4:**902
  vocal music of, **4:**911
Sama-Bajao people, **4:**889, 920
  instrumental music of, **4:**891, 898, 900–901
Samad, **5:***783*
al-Samad, Shaykh 'Abd al-Bāsiṭ 'Abd, **6:**161
Samadhi (film), **5:**540
samā'ī, **6:**550–51
  bayyātī, **6:**40
  Egypt, **6:**45, 560
  Husaynī Ṭātyos, **6:**43
  Muḥayyar Jamīl Bey, **6:**43
  rhythmic modes in, **6:**91
  Syria, **6:**563, 569
Samal people, **4:**889
Samanid dynasty, **6:**131
Samapol Piwapongsiri, **4:**100
Samarakoon, Ananda, **5:**972
Samaroff, Olga, **3:**1210
Samaroo, Jit, **2:**86
Samawa (Sumbawanese) people, **4:**762, 763, 779, 781–83
samba and samba schools, **2:**61–62, 71, 93, 107–8, 110, 111
  in Algeria, **6:**270
  in Barbados, **2:**819
  in Brazil, **2:**313–17, 334, 338, 350–51
  electronic amplification of, **2:**40
  folk genres of, **2:**348–49
  in Guatemala, **2:**735
  influence on *jùjú,* **1:**478
  influence on Umbanda music, **2:**344
  in North America, **3:**522, 731, 1203
  in Nubian music, **6:**644
  samba baiana, **2:**313, 315, 316
  samba campineiro, **2:**349
  samba-canção, **2:**313, 316
  samba carioca, **2:**351
  samba carnavalesca, **2:**313, 315, 316
  samba-choro, **2:**313
  samba corrido, **2:**313, 316
  samba da cidade, **2:**313
  samba de breque, **2:**313
  samba de gafieira, **2:**317
  samba de morro, **2:**109, 313, 350
  samba de partido-alto, **2:**313, 316, 351
  samba de roda, **2:**349
  samba de terreiro, **2:**313, 316
  samba de viola, **2:**349
  samba-enredo, **2:**313, 315–16, 351
  samba-lenço, **2:**313, 314, 349
  samba-reggae genre, **2:**107, 317, 353–54
  samba rural, **2:**313, 314
  sound recordings of, **2:**52
Sambaa people, **1:**639
Sambamurthy, Pichu, **5:**22, 56, 98, 161, 213, 215, 324, 365, 453–54

Sambandhar, Tirujnana, **5:**260
Samberigi people, **9:**537
Sambia people, **9:**511
　　secret flutes of, **9:**189, 512
Sambleben, Kanny, **8:**472
Samburski, Daniel, **6:**1071
Samburu people, **1:**112, 115, 605, 623
Samdech Chaufea Thiounn, **4:**190
Samdo sŏl changgo (SamulNori), **7:**966–67
Samegrelian people, **8:**838–40, 841
Samer Theater Group, **3:**1220
Samfund for Musikkgranskning, **8:**427
Samguk sagi (Kim), **7:**41, 79, 813, 833, 855, 981
Samguk yusa (dynastic history), **7:**855
Samiou, Domna, **8:**1010, 1017–18; **9:**73
Samjuk kŭmbo (collection), **7:**856, 927
Şamkirli, Hüseyn, **6:**930
al-Sammān, Ibrāhīm, **6:**659
Sammy Mendoza Orchestra, **3:**741
Sāmoa, **3:**4; **9:**771, 795–608. *See also* American
　　Sāmoa
　　American expeditions to, **9:**20, 25
　　audience-performer interaction, **9:**323
　　body decoration, **9:**349
　　ceremonies
　　　　kava, **9:**348–49
　　　　nuptial, **9:**342–43, 348
　　children's performances, **9:**251
　　Christianity in, **9:**204–7
　　Christian missionaries from, **9:**195
　　composition in, **9:**354
　　cricket matches, **9:**231
　　cultural contacts with Cook Islands, **9:**903
　　cultural contacts with Gilbert Islands, **9:**758
　　cultural contacts with Pukapuka, **9:**909
　　cultural contacts with Takuu, **9:**842
　　cultural contacts with Tokelau, **9:**827
　　cultural contacts with Tuvalu, **9:**830–31
　　cultural contacts with 'Uvea and Futuna,
　　　　9:808
　　drumming, **9:**114
　　early recordings from, **9:**284
　　European poetry on, **9:**39
　　Europeans in, **9:**41, 217, 236–37
　　festivals in, **9:**55
　　films on, **9:**1017
　　history of, **9:**795
　　immigrants to Australia, **9:**84, 85–86
　　instruments, **9:**805–7
　　　　imported to Papua New Guinea, **9:**508
　　　　struck plaques, **9:**378
　　　　struck tins, **9:**379
　　kava use in, **9:**172–75
　　map of, **9:***772*
　　metrical traits in, **9:**289
　　missionaries in, **9:**21
　　music and dance of, **9:**48, 307, 796–808, 969,
　　　　973, 979, 980
　　　　biblical plays, **9:**236
　　　　fāgono, **9:**338
　　　　faleaitu, **9:**229–30, 235–36
　　　　koniseti, **9:**235, 237
　　　　laulausiva, **9:**797, 825
　　　　malaga, **9:**53
　　　　mā'ulu'ulu, **9:**278, 803, 823
　　　　political songs, **9:**215–19

salamo, **9:**205
siva, **9:**20
soa, **9:**802–3
taualuga, **9:**231
　　New Zealand administration of, **9:**218–19
　　poetry, **9:**327–28
　　　　timbre in, **9:**297
　　　　verbal meter, **9:**324
　　prehistoric, **9:**795
　　religion in, **9:**201–2
　　research on, **9:**975, 976
　　singing, falsetto, **9:**297
　　song transcriptions, **9:**294–95
　　sound recordings from, **9:**999, 1000
Samoan Advisory (Australia), **9:**86
Samoan Centre for Arts and Culture (Australia),
　　9:86
Sāmoan people
　　in Aotearoa, **9:**112, 235, 238
　　in Hawai'i, **9:**103–4, 163, 235
　　in North America, **3:**1047, 1050, 1052;
　　　　9:116–17, 235, 238
Samo kok (Lee), **7:**955
Samori, Almamy, **1:**504, 506, 508, 509, 510–11
"*S'amours ne fait*" (Machaut), **8:**104, *105*
Samoyed peoples, **8:**488
Sampaguita, **4:**885
Sampradaya (organization), **5:**213
Sampson, Adam, **3:***469*
Sampson, Peggy, **3:**1186
Samre people, **4:**154
Samson (Teop performer), **9:**644
Samson and Delilah (Saint-Saëns), **6:**49
Samsudaeyŏp (*kagok*), **7:**921
Samudragupta, Emperor, **5:**721
Samullori (Baek), **7:**971
SamulNori (musical group), **7:**933, 938, 939,
　　963–67, *964*
SamulNori Hanullim (organization), **7:**965
Samut, Robert, M.D., **8:**638
Samwell, David, **9:**794–95
San people, **1:**761
　　interactions with Bantu groups, **1:**305–8
　　music of, **1:**659, 703–5, 715, 744–45
San (= Saint). *See* San *plus next element in
　　name*
San Mah Si-jang, **7:**307
San, Samuel Ting Chu, **4:**129
Sanabria, Bobby, **3:**789
Sanapana culture, **2:**452
San baofuo (Cantonese tune), **7:**217
Sánchez, Alberto. *See* Hurricane, Al (Alberto
　　Sánchez)
Sanchez, Armando, **3:**788
Sánchez Chavaleis, Alfonso, **3:**741
Sánchez de Fuentes, Eduardo, **2:**831, 837
Sánchez, Edis, **2:**861
Sánchez, Jesús, **3:**738; **10:**78, 79
Sánchez, José "Pepe," **2:**831, 832
Sánchez Labrador, Joseph, **2:**250
Sánchez, Lorenzo Antonio, **3:**766
Sánchez, Michel, **8:**225
Sánchez, Miguel, **3:**741
Sánchez, Poncho, **3:**797, 799
Sánchez, Victor, **3:**738
Sánchez, Walter, **2:**213

Sancho Dávila, Bartola, **2:**499
Sancho IV, king of Castile and León, **6:**444
Sanctuary (New York), **3:**687, 688
Sand, George (pseud. of A. Dudevant), **3:**1164;
　　8:128
Sandágerði, Pauli í, **8:**471
Sandal, Mustafa, **6:**252
Sandall, Roger, **9:**46–47
Sandanam, Maharajapuram, **5:**424
Sandawe people, **1:**635, 640
San Diego State University, **3:**1013, 1020
Sandimba (BaAka woman), **1:**690–91, 692–93
Sandino, Augusto C., **2:**758–59
San Diu people, **4:**532
Sandô (Zeami), **7:**641
Sandoval, Alfonso, **2:***381*
Sandoval, Arturo, **3:**789
Sandoval, Chris, **3:**779
Sandrie, George, **3:**1096
Sandro (Argentine singer), **2:**103
Sands, William Franklin, **7:**968
Sandugong Panaginip (Bonus), **4:**857, 863, 869,
　　871
Sandybaiuly, Ibrai, **6:**955
Sandžak, Krstan, **8:**980
Sane, Dan, **3:**645
Sanemori (Zeami), **7:**632, 640
San Francisco Ballet, **3:**218
San Francisco Symphony Orchestra, **3:**537
San Francisco Tape Music Center, **3:**253
Sang (Yi), **7:**957
Sang Tong, **7:**348, 350
Sanga, Glauco, **8:**622
Sanga, Zar, **5:**791
Sangare, Oumou, **1:**420
Sangeetha (record company), **5:**528
Sangeet Natak Akademi (New Delhi), **5:**57,
　　529
Sangeet Natak Akademi Bulletin, **5:**58
Sangeet Research Academy (Calcutta), **5:**529
Sanghistorisk Arkiv (Århus), **8:**464
Sangil people, **4:**889
Saṅgītadarpaṅa (Damodara), **5:**46, 47–48, 314
Saṅgītamakaranda (Narada), **5:**47, 72
Saṅgītāñjalī (Thakur), **5:**52, 56
Saṅgītapārijāta (Ahobala), **5:**46
Saṅgītarāja (treatise), **5:**45
Saṅgītaratnākara (treatise), **5:**18, 25, 69, 70, 114,
　　262
　　commentaries on, **5:**44–45
　　contents of, **5:**33–37
　　date of, **5:**22
　　description of, **5:**24
　　influence on later treatises, **5:**43–44, 47
　　information on *mridangam*, **5:**356
　　instrument classification in, **5:**324–25
　　passage on *ālāp*, **5:**198
　　passage on dancing, **5:**41
　　passage on emotion in performance, **5:**40
　　passage on ornaments, **5:**39
　　passage on raga, **5:**40
　　passage on sound, **5:**37
　　raga theory in, **5:**75–76, 96, 215
　　relevance of, **5:**52
　　talas listed in, **5:**111
　　translation of, **5:**56

Saṅgītasamayasāra (Parsvadeva), **5:**22, 24, 36, 44, 45
Saṅgīta Sampradāya Pradarśinī (Diksitar), **5:**46, 52, 227
Saṅgītasāramṛta (treatise), **5:**46, 47
Saṅgītasārasaṅgraha (Tagore), **5:**46, 51
Saṅgītaśiromaṇi (treatise), **5:**45
Saṅgītaśudha (Naik), **5:**46
Saṅgīt-gyoṇ ke saṃsmaraṇ (Khan), **5:**57
Saṅgītopaniṣad-sāroddhāra (Sudhakalasa), **5:**44, 45, 47, 313
Saṅgītsār (treatise), **5:**46, 50–51
Sangju moshimgi norae (Baek), **7:**971
Sango yôroku (Huziwara), **7:**589
Sangsabyŏlgok (*kasa*), **7:**927
Sangu people, **1:**640
Sanguma, **9:**90, 155, 384
Sanguozhi (Chen), **7:**886, 929
Sanguozhi yanyi (Chinese novel), **7:**452
Sanima culture, **2:**169–75
Sanio people, **9:**557
Sanjan Nagar Institute (Lahore), **5:**529
Sanjar, Seljug sultan, **6:**922
Sanjilang (Cantonese tune), **7:**219
sanjo, **7:**5, 909, 913–17
  contemporary compositions, **7:**956, 957
  development of, **7:**807, 907, 977
  form of, **7:**844
  instruments for, **7:**822, 823, 910, 913
  melodic patterns in, **7:**816, 916–17
  origins of, **7:**913–14
  performance schools of, **7:**46, 56, 986
  performers of, **7:**985–86
  rhythmic patterns in, **7:**842–43, 915–16
  scales in, **7:**849–50
  schools of, **7:**916
  sinawi and, **7:**889, 890
  transmission of, **7:**5, 975
San Jorge Island (Solomon Islands), **9:**659–62
San Juan, Aura, **3:**741
San Juan de Letrán, **4:**861
"*Sanjuanero Huilense, El*" (Durán), **2:**389
Sankara, **5:**105
Sankaradeva. *See* Shankardev
Sankaran, Trichy S., **3:**1064, 1216; **5:**159, 161, 385
Sankey, Ira David, **2:**688, 795; **3:**10, 534; **9:**919
Sāṅkhya philosophy, **5:**34
Sanliu (*Jiangnan sizhu* piece), **7:**224, 225, 239
Sanliu (*yangqin* piece), **7:**180
San Luis, Teodora, **4:**857
San Marino, **8:**12
San Martín, José de, **2:**245
Sanmenxia changsiqu (Liu), **7:**177
Sanna, Antonio, **8:**622
Sano Kôzi, **7:**595
San Pedro culture, **2:**356
  archaeomusicological studies of, **2:**7
  instruments of, **2:**12
San Pedro, Lucio, **4:**872
Sansei Choir (Ontario), **3:**1084
Sanskritik Sansthan, **5:**705
Sansyô dayû (*sekkyô busi* piece), **7:**654
Santa Anna, Cosme, **2:**621
Santa Cecilia Chorus (Toronto), **3:**1196

Santa Cruz Islands (Solomon Islands), **9:**688
  films on, **9:**982
  instruments of, **9:**693
  research on, **9:**963
  songfests of, **9:**322, 332–35
Santa Cruz, Nicomedes, **2:**481–82, 501
Santa Cruz, Victoria, **2:**481–82, 499, 501
"Santa Fe Blues" (Yancey), **3:**105
Santa Fe Desert Chorale, **3:**768
Santa Isabel College, **4:**123
Santa Isabel Island (Solomon Islands), **9:**29
  music and dance of, **9:**659–62, 663
  songs of, **9:**30
Santal people, **5:**415, 734
  dance traditions of, **5:**502, 732
  musical genres
    bapla (marriage songs), **5:**474
    dasae songs, **5:**471
    jan (charm song), **5:**476
    jhumur, **5:**855, 861–62
Santamaría, Mongo, **3:**729, 787, 788, 797
Santana (musical group), **3:**1002
Santana, Bruno, **4:**859
Santana, Carlos, **2:**105; **3:**721, 732–33, 751, 789, 795, 798; **4:**208; **9:**168
San t'aryŏng (Korean song cycle), **7:**886
Santería, **2:**32, 48, 69, 793, 823–25; **3:**220, 720, 728–29, 784, 1205
Santiago, Ángel, **9:**101
Santiago del Nuevo Extremo, **2:**374
Santiago, Eddie, **3:**788, 799
Santiago, Francisco, **3:**1025, 1026; **4:**123, 860, 864, 865, 870, 871, 872
Santiago, Jess, **4:**886
Santiniketan (institution), **5:**562
Santoro, Cláudio, **2:**306
Santos, Artur, **8:**585
Santos, John, **3:**789, 798
Santos, Primitivo, **3:**731
Santos, Ramón Pagayon, **4:**29, 130, 876, 878, 879–80
Santos, Rosendo, **4:**875
Sant Tukaram (film), **5:**60
santur. *See* dulcimers, hammered
Santuri Edhem Efendi, **6:**771
Sanu, Kumar, **5:**540
Sanwuqi (Zhao), **7:**185
sanxian. *See* lutes
Sanyuhwa (Kim), **7:**960
sanza. *See* lamellophones
Sanzyûnisô honkyoku (*syômyô* piece), **7:**617
Saoch people, **4:**156
Sao da bai fon muang haw (Dao Mai), **7:**506–7
São Tomé and Principe, **1:**76
São Vicente Captaincy, **2:**302
Sapardai group, **5:**769
Saperā caste. *See* Jogī caste
Sapir, Edward, **3:**291, 1165
Sapper, Carl, **2:**635
Sapporo (Ichiyanagi), **7:**737
Saprapason, Basilius, **10:**114
Sap-sang-khit (Montri Tramote), **4:**224
Sapwuahfik Atoll (Pohnpei State, FSM), **9:**727
Saqafat (periodical), **5:**747
sarabande, **8:**168
Sarabhai, Gita, **3:**130

Sarabhoji, Tanjavur king, **5:**230
Saracens, in Corsica, **8:**566
Sarachandra, Ediriwira, **5:**491
Saracini, Giuliano, **3:**1196
Sarafina! (musical), **1:**777
Sarahang, **5:**807
Sarakatsani people, **8:**1010–11
Sarala Devi (deity), **5:**733
Saramaka culture, **2:**438, 504–6
Sarangga (*kayagŭm pyŏngch'ang*), **7:**908
sāraṅgī. *See* violins and fiddles (bowed lutes)
Saran Höhöönii Namtar (Buddhist dance-drama), **7:**1016
Sarasate, Pablo de, **8:**368
Saraste, Jukka Pekka, **8:**485
Sarasvati (deity), **5:**277, 494
  vina playing of, **5:**247, 325, 352–53
  visual depictions of, **5:***211*, 301
  worship of, **5:**9, 223, 892
Sarasvatīhṛdayālaṅkāra (Nanyadeva), **5:**24, 72
Sarcee Indian nation, **3:**440
Sardinia, **8:**604, 626–32
  Barbagia, **8:**627
    local repertoires, **8:**121
  Cagliari, **8:**627
  Catalan-speakers in, **8:**604, 617
  dance traditions of, **8:**609, 630–31
  geography of, **8:**626
  history of, **8:**631–32
  history of music in, **8:**631–32
  improvised sung witticisms, **8:**143
  instruments, **8:**22, *47*, 170, *170*, 627, 630
  research on, **8:**39
  map of, **8:***516*, *604*
  Nuoro, **8:**627
  Oristano, **8:**627
  popular music in, **8:**626
  research on music of, **8:**621, 622, 632
  Sassari, **8:**627
  vocal music, **8:**517, 627–30, 632
    polyphony, **8:**134, 145, 542, 570, 626, 627–28, *628*
Sarfert, Ernst, **9:**736–37, 741–42, 981
Sarfi, **5:**687
Sargara community, **5:**648
Sargon II, king of Assyria, **8:**842
Sarhadi, Ijaz, **5:**788, *789*
Sarhadi, Munir, **5:**788
Sarievski, Aleksandar, **8:**981
Sariredjo, Diyat, **4:**684
"Sarisinim" (Kirimizigul/Caner), **6:***258*
Sarısözen, Muzaffer, **6:**79, *79*, 82, 85, 87, 790
Sarkar, Dilip, **5:**857
Sarkar, Suprabha, **5:**855
Sarkessian, Leo, **3:**1032
Sarkissian, Margaret L., **3:**1084; **4:**27, 139, 393
Sarma, Harihara, **5:**161
Sarmadee, Shahab, **10:**11
Sarmanto, Heikki, **8:**485
Sarmatian people, **7:**13
Sarmientos de León, Jorge Álvaro, **2:**736
Sarngadeva, *Saṅgītaratnākara*, **5:**18, 24, 25, 33–37, 69, 70, 114, 262
  date of, **5:**22
  extract from, **5:**37
  influence on later treatises, **5:**43–44, 47

information on *mridangam*, **5:**356
instrument classification in, **5:**324–25
raga theory in, **5:**75–76, 96, 215
talas listed in, **5:**111
sarod. See lutes
Saroja, C., **5:**232
Sárosi, Bálint, **8:**272–73
Sarr, Ndiouga, **3:**1170
al-Sarrāj, **6:**372
Sarrāj, Abū Naṣr, **6:**180
Sarugaku dangi (Zeami), **7:**641
Sarvāye Pāpaḍu, **5:**900
Sarwat, Johnny, **6:**283
Sarweh, Ramon, **3:**1220
Sary-Arga (shertpe-kyui), **6:**958
Sary Aşiq, **6:**929
Saryev-baggy, Puli, **6:**976, 977
Saryglar, Alexei, **7:**1025
Saryk tribe, **6:**966
Sas, Andrés, **2:**115, 467
Sasak people, **4:**762, 779. *See also* Lombok
    origins of, **4:**763–64
    popular music of, **4:**778
    religion of, **4:**763–65
Sasi p'unggyŏng (Kim), **7:**957
Saskatchewan, **3:**1223–51
    African-Canadians in, **3:**1091
    European settlers in, **3:**1086, 1249–51
    First Nations groups in, **3:**440–50, 1085–86
    folk song collecting in, **3:**292, 1250
    French Canadians in, **3:**74
    history of musical life, **3:**1085–91, 1224–31
    Huttcrites in, **3:**1240
    intercultural traditions, **3:**342–45
    Mennonites in, **3:**1238
    Métis people in, **3:**405–11
    Regina, **3:**1225, 1227
        musical life in, **3:**1087
    Saskatoon, **3:**1227
        musical life in, **3:**1087, 1090
    Swedish people in, **3:**1088–89
    Ukrainian people in, **3:**1088–89, 1241–44
Saskatchewan Arts Board, **3:**1231
Saskatchewan Indian Cultural Center, **3:**1086
Saskatoon Opera Company, **3:**1231
Saskatoon Philharmonic Society, **3:**1090
Sassanian dynasty, **6:**129, 131, 834, 921
Sassu, Pietro, **8:**622, 631, 632
Sastrapustaka, **10:**44, 45, *45*, 47, 50
Sastri, Sarabha, **5:**389
Sastri, Syama, **3:**989; **5:**15, 210, 217, 220,
        227–29, *228*, 268, *268*, 390, 508
    Brahmin class of, **5:**387
    compositions of, **5:**97, 228–29, 269, 451
Sastriar, Tanjore Vedanayakam, **5:**923
Sastrigal, Sri Sesadri, **5:**245
Sastrigal, T. S. Balakrishna, **5:**270
Sasui Punhun (romance), **5:**757–58
Sasŭm (Lee), **7:**956
Satavahana dynasty, **5:**720, 731
Satawal (Yap State, FSM), **9:**737
Sathe, Ravindra, **5:**540
Sati Mata, **5:**643, 645
Satô Keizirô, **7:**736
"Satori" (Scott), **3:**346
Sattar, **6:**922

Satuma clan, **7:**647, 727, 790, 795
Saturday Night Fever (film), **3:**200, 229, 684,
        688–89
"Saturday Night Fish Fry" (Jordan), **3:**668, 708
Saturn (deity), **5:**867
Satyapir (deity), **5:**733
Saudi Arabia. *See also* Arabian peninsula
    aerophones in, **6:**414
    Asir, **6:**652
    chordophones in, **6:**409, 412
    Ḥijāz, **6:**12–13, 407, 412–13, 538, 652,
        654–55
        compositional school, **6:**365
        dance, **6:**703–11
        women patrons, **6:**701
    idiophones in, **6:**405
    Jidda, **6:**691–94
    Mecca, **6:**293, 294, 351
        transvestite entertainers in, **6:**296
        women entertainers, **6:**696
    Medina, **6:**293, 294, 351, 538
        transvestite entertainers in, **6:**296
        women entertainers, **6:**442, 696
    musical genres of, **6:**652–55
    Najd region, **6:**652–54
    Qur'ānic recitation in, **6:**161–62
    research on music of, **6:**23, 649, 652
    rhythmic modes, **6:**92
    wedding rituals in, **6:**691–94, 699
    women's music, **6:**695–702
    women's wedding party in, **6:**691–94
Saulteaux Indian nation, **3:**405, 1086
Saumaiwai, Chris, **9:**968
Saumaiwai, Vula, **9:**968
Saumell, Manuel, **2:**827, 833
Saunders, Jesse, **3:**690
ṣaut al-Rubūṭ (Yemeni wedding piece), **6:**97, *98*,
        101
Sauvageau, Charles, **3:**1148
Sauvlet, Guillaume, **7:**729
Sava, Saint, **8:**943
Savaglio, Paula, **3:**517, 825, 891–92
Savai'i (Sāmoa), **9:**795, 803
Savang Vatthana, king of Laos, **4:**350, 354
Savard, Félix-Antoine, **3:**1167
Savard, Rémi, **3:**392
Savary, Claude Etienne, **6:**567
"Save the Last Dance for Me" (Drifters), **3:**709
Savia Andina, **2:**297, 298
Savin, Risto, **8:**921
Savo Island (Solomon Islands), **9:**666
Savoy Ballroom (New York), **3:**655, 787
Savoy Records, **3:**708
Savoy Theatre (Glace Bay), **3:**1120
Sǎvremenna Muzika (Bulgaria), **8:**904
Savu, **4:**801–3
    Dutch in, **4:**802
    population of, **4:**802
Savuka, **1:**431, 779; **6:**277
Savunese people, in West Timor, **4:**796
Savvopoulos, Dionysis, **8:**1021
Sawa, George, **3:**1216, 1219, *1219*, 1220; **6:**535
Sawa, Suzanne Meyers, **3:**1219
Sawi (Yi), **7:**957
Sawos people, **9:**48, 552, 982
Sawyer, Pam, **3:**677

Sax, Adolphe, **3:**564; **8:**530
Saxonia Band, **3:**556
Saxons, **8:**326
saxophones
    Albania, **8:**286
    Arab music, **6:**422
    bamboo, **2:**899
    Barbados, **2:**816, 820
    Belgium, **8:**530
    Bolivia, **2:**284
    Bulgaria, **8:**284, 895
    Cantonese music, **7:**219
    Cantonese opera orchestra, **3:**1260
    Costa Rica, **2:**691
    Dominican Republic, **2:**860
    Egyptian music, **6:**616
    Europe, **8:**281, 281–82
    Guyana, **5:**604, *605*
    Ireland, **8:**392
    Karnataka, **5:**886
    Kosovo, **8:**286
    Macedonia, **8:**976–77, 980
    North America
        in Armenian ensembles, **3:**1033
        in *banda orquesta*, **3:**779
        in Finnish music, **3:**874, 875
        in Greek bands, **3:**930
        in Hispano music, **3:**761
        in Italian music, **3:**865
        in Macedonian bands, **3:**926
        in merengue, **3:**731
        in *mini-djaz* groups, **3:**804
        in polka bands, **3:**891, 893, 897, 1195
        in rhythm and blues, **3:**668
        in salsa, **3:**788
        in Slovak dance bands, **3:**900
        in Ukrainian music, **3:**914
        in zydeco, **3:**858
    in Nubian music, **6:**642
    Oceania, **9:**27
    Peru, **2:**33
    Punjab, **5:**652
    in *rai*, **6:**270
    Scotland, **8:**366
    Serbia, **8:**952
    South America, **2:**59
    South Asia, **5:**347, 368
        in *bhangra*, **5:**574
        in film music, **5:**535, *537*, 544
        in Hindustani music, **5:**82
        in *jātrā* theater, **5:**505
        in Karnatak music, **5:**235, 352, 354
    Sri Lanka, **5:**970
    Sweden, **8:**442
    Switzerland, **8:**689
    tenor, **3:**337, 348, 350, 668, 669
    in Tohono O'odham *waila*, **3:**436, 472–73,
        490
    Tonga, **9:**131
    Ukraine, **8:**811
    Uruguay, **2:**519
Saxton, Alexander, **3:**46
Sayajirao III, maharaja of Baroda, **5:**443
"Say Brothers, Will You Meet Us," **3:**521
"Say It Loud—I'm Black and I'm Proud"
        (Brown), **3:**552, 677, 710

"Say It with Music" (Berlin), 3:261
"Say Say Say" (Jackson and McCartney), 3:713
Sayat-Nova, 6:734–35
al-Ṣaydāwī al-Dimashqī, Shams al-Dīn, 6:366, 568–69
Sayf al-Dawla, 6:565
Saygun, Adnan, 6:775
Sayın, Neyzen Niyazi, 6:54, 121
Saykao, Dr. Pao, 9:76
Saythara, 9:76
Sayyad, 6:851
al-Sayyid, Lutfī, 6:24
Sayyid Muhammad Ibrahim (Sufi saint), death anniversary of, 5:752, 763, 765
saz (also sāz). See lutes
Saz Nawaz, 5:694
saz semai, 6:116, 120–22, 550–51, 773
rhythmic modes in, 6:91
Sbait, Ḍirghām Ḥ., 6:580
Sbornik Kirshi Danikova (anthology), 8:763
Scala, Francis, 3:564
scales and intervals. See also modal organization; tuning and temperament
Adighian people, 8:854
Afghanistan, 5:827, 835–36
for chahārbeiti, 5:819, 823
falak, 5:828
African music, 1:20–21; 3:593; 10:123
Ainu people, 7:787
Akha people, 4:541
Albania, 8:992–93, 994, 996, 997
analysis of, 9:292–93
Andalusian music, 6:446, 454; 8:593, 596
Andean music, 2:217, 221
of panpipes, 2:208
Anglo-American ballad modes, 3:833
anhemitonic, 1:268
anhemitonic pentatonic, 1:558, 652
Anuta, 9:306–7
Arab music, 6:18, 34–38, 366, 502–3, 548–49
quarter-tone system, 6:35, 369
Argentina, 2:258, 269
Armenian music, 6:727
Atacameño culture, 2:360
Australia
Central, 9:439
Yolngu clansongs, 9:301–2
Austria, 8:671–72
Azerbaijan, 6:926–27
dastgāh and āvāz, 6:184, 924
Babylonian and Sumerian music, 6:8
bagpipe, Highland, 8:363
Bali
pélog, 4:753
saih, 4:735
saih angklung, 4:736–37, 751
saih gendèr wayang, 4:751
saih gong, 4:736, 751, 753, 769
saih lima, 4:769
saih pitu, 4:750
selisir, 4:736, 746–47, 750–51, 769
tembung, 4:746
Balkarian people, 8:856
Basque music, 8:309
Bellona, 9:850
in blues, 3:539, 638, 641–42, 648; 10:123

Bolivia
panpipes, 2:285, 286
Westernization of, 2:297
Bontok people, 4:914
Bosnia-Hercegovina, 8:964, 968
Sephardic Jewish music, 8:968
Brazil
caboclo music, 2:325
cantoria, 2:326
frevo de bloco, 2:337
in religious music, 2:328
Bṛhaddeśī passage on, 5:39
Bulgaria, 8:891, 896, 897
Burma, 4:385–90
Byzantine modes, 6:227; 8:1023, 1029–30
California, Native American music, 3:414, 416, 417
Celtic music, 8:321
Central African Republic, 1:256, 259–69
Central Asian music, 6:900
Cham people, 3:1010
Chechen people, 8:862
Chile, for Virgin Mary festivities, 2:363
China, 7:115–17, 128, 172, 208, 212–13, 234–35, 263, 339, 347–48
minority cultures, 7:449
research on, 7:137
south and southwestern systems, 7:485–89
church modes, 3:759, 833
Colombia, bambuco and bunde, 2:387
Coptic Orthodox music, 6:221
in country music, 3:77
Croatia
Medimurje region, 8:932
na bas music, 8:931
northwestern region, 8:933
cwène horn-flute, 8:527
Cyprus, 8:1029–30
Czech Republic, 8:721
Moravia, 8:721
Delaware Big House songs, 3:464
Denmark, ballads, 8:453
diatonic, 1:462–63
dodekachordon scheme, 8:652
Ecuador, 2:420, 421
for pingullo melodies, 2:422
England
dance music, 8:330
songs, 8:327–28
equiheptatonic, 1:323, 711, 715
equipentatonic, 1:266–67, 268, 604
Estonia, 8:492
Finland, 8:475
Rom music, 8:289, 487
Flanders
children's music, 8:520
songs, 8:520
Georgia, 8:830–31, 832, 844
German-American music, 3:884–85, 889
Germany, 8:655
medieval music, 8:650
Goa, mussoll songs, 5:740
grāmal jāti system, 5:45, 96
Great Britain, 8:325
Greece, 8:1008, 1013, 1020
Epirus, 8:1010

Greek modes, 8:47–48, 48, 69, 1022
Guadeloupe, léwòz songs, 2:875
Guarijio culture, 2:554
Haiti, Vodou songs, 2:883–84
hardingfele, 8:416
heptatonic
Africa, 1:358, 456, 463, 465, 466, 709, 726, 741
China, 7:116–17, 212–13
Japan, 7:566–68
Korea, 7:866
heptatonic equidistant, 1:489, 710
heptatonic equitonal, 1:446, 746
herding calls, 8:128
hexatonic, Kajang people, 4:827
Hmong people, 4:556
Hungary, 8:737, 742
verbunkos, 8:273
Iceland, in rímur, 8:401
Ingush people, 8:862
Iran
Azerbaijan, 6:849–50
dāng, 6:869–71
dastgāh, 5:820
dastgāh and āvāz, 6:11, 59–75, 129, 131, 133, 134, 135, 137, 140–41, 142, 184, 185, 824, 825–26, 833–34, 836, 854, 867, 871–74, 1016, 1062
ḥāl and, 6:855–56
rāst scale, 6:369
saz, 6:847–48
seven Khusrovania, 6:129, 131, 834
Ireland, 8:325, 378
in laments, 8:379
Istrian
in Croatia, 8:930, 931
in Slovenia, 8:912
Italy, 8:609–10
ballads, 8:606
canto a vatoccu, 8:607
Jamaica, 2:906
Japan, 7:592, 688
in kyôgen, 7:636
min'yô, 7:603–4
post-Meizi theories, 7:568–70
pre-Meizi theories, 7:565–68
zoku tyô, 7:588
jāti modes and, 5:27–28, 33, 34, 73–74, 75
Java, 4:634, 637, 656–59
pélog, 4:639
sléndro, 4:639
Jewish music, 3:530; 6:1070; 8:253, 258
Kajang people, 4:827
Karachaevian people, 8:856
Karen people, 4:545
Karnatak music, 5:90–93
mela scheme, 5:47, 219
Kashmir, melodic modes, 5:687
kaval, 8:892
Kazakh people, 7:461
Kenyah people, 4:826, 833
Khmer people, 4:176–77
Kiribati, dance-songs, 9:761–62
Kmhmu people, 4:547
Kogi songs, 2:185

Korea, **7:**847–51, 866
  for folk genres, **7:**849–51, 881–83
  for *kagok*, **7:**849
Kuna culture, **2:**641
Lahu people, **4:**540
Lao people
  san, **4:**339, 343, 345, 346
  yao, **4:**339, 343, 344, 345, 346, 348, 349
Lisu people, **4:**543
Lithuania, **8:**510, 511
  sutartine genre, **3:**876
Lombok, **4:**769–70, 773
Low Countries
  sacred songs, **8:**533–34
  secular songs, **8:**520
lowland *vs.* upland peoples, **4:**538
Macedonia, **8:**973–74
  makam system, **8:**281, 282
makam system, possible Greek derivation, **8:**1022
Malaysia, **4:**417, *419–20*
Mapuche music, **2:**362
maqam structures in European music, **8:**20,
  591, *593*
Maronite church music, **6:**212
microtones, **1:**542; **5:**39, 73–74, 81–82, 92,
  445; **6:**775; **7:**488–89
Middle Eastern music, **3:**1034; **6:**8–9
Mongol people, *urtyn duu*, **7:**1006
Montenegro, **8:**957
Morocco, **6:**487
Nāradīyaśikṣā passage on, **5:**38–39
Nāṭyaśāstra passage on, **5:**27–28
Nepal, **5:**699, 700
  Guruṅg people, **5:**704
"neutral thirds," **1:**676–77, 741
New Ireland, Sursurunga songs, **9:**627
Nguni peoples, **1:**706
nonequitonal heptatonic, **1:**446
North Caucasia, **8:**851
Northeast Indian songs, **3:**463
Northwest Coast songs, **3:**401
Norway, **8:**425
notation of, **8:**104
Orang Asli people, **4:**565–67, 587
Ossetian people, **8:**859
Ostjak music, **8:**128
Palawan people, **4:**925
Panama, *torrentes*, **2:**777, 780
Papua New Guinea
  badra melodies, **9:**507
  Buin songs, **9:**653
  Enga songs, **9:**536
  Iatmul songs, **9:**257–58
  Irumu songs, **9:**568
  Lolo songs, **9:**614
  Siasi music, **9:**575–76
  Western systems, **9:**195–96
pentatonic, **1:**21; **3:**833; **8:**9
  Ainu people, **7:**787
  Argentina, **2:**258
  Bontok people, **4:**914
  Central Africa, **1:**268, 652, 656
  China, **7:**100, 115–17, 172, 208, 212, 231,
    234–35, 263, 273, 353, 486–88
  Dai people, **7:**498
  East Africa, **1:**604, 605, 613, 635, 639

Ecuador, **2:**420, *421*
Japan, **7:**566–68, 740, 743, 744, 750
Kenyah people, **4:**826, 833
Korea, **7:**823, 851, 866, 881, 971
Lombok, **4:**773
Mongol people, **7:**1006
North Africa, **1:**543, 585
Palawan people, **4:**925
Philippines, **4:**928
Roti, **4:**799
Russia, **8:**773
Ryûkyû types, **7:**790–91, 793
  in southeastern Europe, **8:**10
Southern Africa, **1:**707, 709
West Africa, **1:**406, 446, 453, 454, 463,
  466, 467
perfect consonances, **8:**71
Persian, **5:**819, 820, 823
Peru
  Amazonian region, **2:**482
  landó, **2:**498
  of panpipes, **2:**226, 467, 468, 469, 483
Philippines, **4:**928
pitch measurement methods, **1:**255–69
pitch names, **5:**66, 67, 79, 176, 215
pitch organization systems, **5:**20
Plains Indian songs, **3:**445, 483
Poland, **8:**703
Portugal, **8:**581
Pueblo Indian songs, **3:**429
Punjab, *giddhā*, **5:**654
ragas classified by, **5:**46–47, 51, 52, 67, 77,
  78–79, 85, 262, 445–46
Romania, songs, **8:**874
Roti, **4:**799
Russia
  glas modes, **8:**779
  laments, **8:**763
  pentatonicism, **8:**773
  village music, **8:**756
  vocal music, **8:**760
Ryûkyû Islands, **7:**790–91, 793
Saami people, **8:**128
  joiks, **8:**301, 487
  lev'dd songs, **8:**486
Sāmavedic hymns, **5:**31, 38–39
Sāmoa
  political songs, **9:**215
  tagi, **9:**799
Sardinia, **8:**631
Scotland, **8:**373
  modal tunes, **8:**367, 372–73
  Traveller songs, **8:**296
secular scale, **5:**31, 38–39
Serbia, **8:**942, 951
Shan people, **4:**548–49
Sicily, **8:**610
Sikaiana, **9:**847
Sindh, **5:**758–59
Slovenia, **8:**912, 920
Solomon Islands
  'Are'are songs, **9:**668
  Blablanga songs, **9:**658
  Malaita, **9:**666
  panpipes, **9:**400
  Western, **9:**155–56

South America, early flutes, **10:**103
Southeast Indian songs, **3:**467
Spain, Andalusian scale, **8:**593, 596
Sri Lanka, **5:**956, 963, 968
śruti and *svara*, distinctions, **5:**31–32
  in Hindustani music, **5:**67
  in Karnatak music, **5:***93*
Sumatra, **4:**625
  Burai, **4:**623
  northern, **4:**605, 606
Sumbawa, **4:**763, 781
Sunda, **4:**702
Sweden
  dance music, **8:**436
  folk music, **8:**435
Switzerland, in *betruf*, **8:**128
Syrian Christian modes, **3:**984; **5:**582
Taiwanese Aboriginal musics, **7:**525–27
Tamil Nadu, in folk melodies, **5:**917
Temiar people, **4:**577–78, 584
tetratonic, **1:**635, 703, 704–5; **4:**769–70
Thailand, **4:**263, 270, 292, 299, 313, 323
  northern, **4:**314
thirds, in Luvale music, **1:**728–37
Tibetan music, **5:**711
Tikopia, **9:**854
tonal structure of early modes and ragas, **5:**29,
  38
Tonga, of nose flutes, **9:**795
transilience concept, **5:**64, 75
transmigration of, **4:**456, 457, *463*
treatises on, **5:**33, 53
Trinidad and Tobago, for calypso, **2:**96
Turkey, **6:**48–51, 82–85, 772
  in popular music, **6:**247
Tuvalu, **9:**830
Tuvan music, **6:**982
Uighur people, **7:**459
Ukraine, ritual songs, **8:**809
'Uvea and Futuna, **9:**771
Vanuatu, **9:**691, 697, 700
Venezuela, Yekuana curing songs, **2:**180
Vietnam, **4:**14, 456–61, *463*, 464
  of *kênh*, **4:**536
Vietnamese music, **3:**993–94
Wales
  bardic music, **8:**349
  songs, **8:**344
Warao culture, shamanic songs, **2:**194–95
Yao people, **4:**550
Yap, **9:**304–5
Yuma vocal music, **2:**596
Scandinavia. *See also* Denmark; Iceland; Norway;
  Sweden
  healing ceremonies, **8:**196
  herders of, **8:**119
  instruments, **8:**170, 181
    research on, **8:**35, 36, 41
  map of, **8:***398*
  midsummer bonfire dances, **8:**140
  musical genres, ballads, **8:**135
  rock in, **8:**216–17
  Travellers in, **8:**295
Scandinavian Center of Calgary, **3:**1250
Scandinavian people
  in Hawai'i, **9:**100

Scandinavian people (*continued*)
   in North America, **3:**10, 528, 866–75, 1086,
      1089, 1250–51 (*See also specific groups*)
Scandinavian Program (radio program), **3:**1250
Scarborough, Dorothy, **3:**71
"Scarborough Fair/Canticle" (Simon and
      Garfunkel), **3:**317
Scarlatti, Alessandro, **8:**618
Scars (musical group), **8:**369
Schaareman, Danker, **4:**733
Schade, Michael, **3:**1210
Schaefer, Jacob, **3:**939
Schaeffer, Pierre, **7:**735
Schaeffner, André, **1:**51; **8:**178
Schafer, R. Murray, **3:**14, 279, 345, 1059, 1105,
      1219
Schalit, Heinrich, **3:**939, 940
Schallehn, Henry, **3:**1180
Schanachie (record company), **2:**106
Schantz, Filip von, **8:**482
Schebesta, Paul, **1:**688; **4:**569, 570
Schechter, John M., **2:**431, 464; **10:**95
Schedelsches Liederbuch, **8:**651
Scheepers, Will, **8:**534
Scheerlinck, Vital, **8:**531
Schefferus, Johannes, **8:**307
Schein, Johann Hermann, **8:**653
Schellenberg, Henriette, **3:**1239
Scherchen, Hermann, **8:**659
Scherzo (Zhou), **7:**339
Scheutz, Wilfried, **8:**676
Schieffelin, Edward, **9:**976
Schifrin, Lalo, **3:**203, 751
Schiller, Friedrich, **8:**646
Schimmel, Annemarie, **5:**757
Schindler, Kurt, **6:**1042; **8:**601
Schindler's List (Spielberg), **4:**101
Schiørring, Nils, **8:**464
Schlager, Ernst, **4:**733
Schlaginhaufen, Otto, **9:**981
Schlatter, Richard, **1:**68
Schleifer, Eli, **6:**1065
Schlesinger, Kathryn, **6:**24
Schlesinger, Michael, **3:**861
Schlose, Professor, **7:**348
Schmalz, Oskar Friedrich, **8:**692
Schmaus, Alois, **8:**1003
Schmetterlinge (musical group), **8:***216*,
      677, 678
Schmidt, Daniel, **3:**1017–18
Schmidt, Robert, **3:**1150
Schmidt, Wilhelm, **9:**983
Schmiedel, Ulrich, **2:**453
Schmitt, Adam, **3:**169
Schmitt, Robert C., **9:**1008
Schmitt, Werner, **8:**697
Schmitz, Carl A., **9:**568
Schneeberger, Andreas (Andrew Snowberger),
      3:907
Schneider, Albrecht, **1:**558; **8:**394
Schneider, Marius, **1:**50; **8:**20, 622, 846, 847;
      9:980
Schneider-Trnavsky, Mikuláš, **8:**725
Schneller, Hans Walter, **8:**692
Schnittke, Alfred, **8:**85, 782
"Schnitzelbank," **3:**889

Schoenberg, Arnold, **3:**174, 175, 540, 1184;
      6:1029; **7:**341, 342, 350; **8:**84–85,
      250, 264, 445
Schofield, Robert, **4:**870
Schola Cantorum, **4:**123, 870
Schonberg, Claude-Michel, **4:**131
schöne Müllerin, Die (Schubert), **8:**60
School of Arts Instructors (Cuba), **2:**837
School of Dramatic Arts (Hanoi), **4:**488
School of Fine Arts (Vientiane), **4:**89, 120, 138,
      353
School of Music of Vietnam (Hanoi), **4:**511
School of Scottish Studies (Edinburgh), **8:**371
School of Theatrical and Cinematographic Arts
      (Vietnam), **4:**511
Schorr, David, **6:**1025
schottische, **2:**71, 89, 107, 114; **3:**212, 825, 843;
      8:166, 168
   band arrangements of, **3:**874
   in Brazil, **2:**305, 330, 331, 350
   in Brittany, **8:**559
   in Canada, **3:**408, 1125, 1196
   in Corsica, **8:**571
   Czech, **3:**897
   Danish, **3:**882
   in Denmark, **8:**457
   dissemination of, **8:**7
   in Dominica, **2:**842
   in Finland, **8:**484
   Finnish, **3:**874–75
   in French Guiana, **2:**438
   German, **3:**891, 892
   in Guatemala, **2:**735
   Italian, **3:**860
   in Jamaica, **2:**908
   in Low Countries, **8:**524, 527
   in Mapuche culture, **2:**237
   Mexican/Hispano/Tejano, **3:**522, 760, 773,
      775
   in Mexico, **2:**604, 613
   in Netherlands Antilles, **2:**930
   Norwegian, **3:**868
   for piano, **3:**190
   in St. Lucia, **2:**945
   in Sweden, **8:**435–36, 443
   Swedish, **3:**872
   in Switzerland, **8:**690, 694, 696
   Tohono O'odham, **3:**436, 473, 490
   Ukrainian, **3:**913
   Volga German, **3:**890
Schrammel, Hans, **8:**676
Schrammel, Josel, **8:**676
Schrecker, John, **7:**379
Schreiner, Claus, **2:**320
Schubert, Franz, **8:**83, 367, 670
   Lieder, **8:**60, 656
   masses, **8:**84, 655
   use of *verbunkos* themes, **8:**273
Schuller, Gunther, **3:**335, 583, 612, 663
Schultz, Chester, **9:**144
Schumacher, Rüdiger, **4:**638
Schuman, William, **3:**297, 541
Schumann, Clara, **8:**200
Schumann-Heink, Ernestine, **3:**607
Schumann, Robert, **8:**83, 367, 646, 663;
      9:39

Schunda, Jozsef V., **8:**877, 879
Schünemann, Georg, **8:**664, 846
Schupman, Edwin, Jr., **3:**470, 495
Schuster, Meinhard, **9:**982
Schutz, Alfred, **1:**127–28
Schütz, Heinrich, **8:**77, 646
Schuursma, Ann Briegleb, **9:**976
Schuyler, Philip, **6:**24, 490
Schwab, Gilbert, **8:**693
Schwartz, Abe, **3:**938
Schweinfurth, Georg August, **1:**87–88, 650
Schweizerischer Tambourenverband, **8:**686
Schwob, Marcel, **9:**41
Schwörer-Kohl, Gretel, **4:**26
Scindia, Madhavrao, maharaja of Gwalior,
      5:443–44
Scorpions (musical group), **6:**248
Scotish [*sic*] *Minstrel* (Smith), **8:**373
Scotland, **8:**360–74
   art music in, **8:**366–69, 370
   ballad dissemination in, **8:**8, 365
   Celtic people in, **8:**319–22, 360
   dance traditions of, **8:**166, 198, 360, 367,
      370, 372
   folk music revival in, **8:**364–65, 370–72
   geography of, **8:**360
   Hebrides, **8:**322
      heterophonic singing of Gaelic psalms,
         8:134
      instrumental music, **8:**363–65
      vocal music, **8:**360–63
   Highlands
      instrumental music, **8:**363–65
      vocal music, **8:**360–63, 373
   history of, **8:**360, 362, 365
   history of music in, **8:**366–69
   ideology in, **8:**186
   instrument making in, **8:**367
   instruments and instrumental music, **8:**169,
      201, 363–64, 365–66, 367, 372
      fusion, **8:**226
      piobaireachd (also pibroch), **8:**98, 106, *107*,
         363, 367, 368, 373–74
      research on, **8:**40
   Lowlands
      instrumental music, **8:**365–66
      vocal music, **8:**365, 373
   map of, **8:***324*
   Northern Isles
      instrumental music, **8:**365–66
      vocal music, **8:**365
   Orkney Islands, **3:**407–8
      hymn to St. Magnus, **8:**423–24
   popular music in, **8:**367–68
   population of, **8:**360
   research on music of, **8:**18, 371, 372–74
   Rom people in, **8:**295
   Scotch snap in, **8:**14
   Shetland Islands, **3:**407–8
      fiddle playing, **8:**365–66
   Travellers in, **8:**295–97, 370, 371, 372, 374
   vocal music
      ballads, **8:**106–7, *135*, 136, 195, 296, 365,
         367, 369–70
      bothy songs, **8:**296–97, 365, 373
      psalmody, **8:**97–98, 362–63, 367

waulking songs, **8:**133, 141, 197, 361–62, 373

women's performances in, **8:**200

Scots Musical Museum (Burns/Johnson), **8:**18, 367, 373

Scott, Francis George, **8:**368

Scott, Gina, **2:**677, 679

Scott, Howard, **10:**78

Scott, James, **3:**651

Scott, Joe, **3:**147, 1070

Scott, Mabel, **3:**669

Scott-Pascall, Marin, **3:***225*

Scott, Shirley, **3:**663

Scott, Tony, **3:**346

Scott, Sir Walter, **8:**135, 367, 368, 370

Scott, Willie, **8:**372

Scott, Winfield, **3:**307

Scottish Free Church, **9:**114

Scottish Music (Purser), **8:**374

Scottish Opera, **8:**369

Scottish people

in Antigua and Barbuda, **2:**798

in Aotearoa, **9:**114–16, 167, 928

in Australia, **9:**140

in Carriacou, **2:**867

in Hawai'i, **9:**106–7

in Jamaica, **2:**900

in North America, **3:**826

dances of, **3:**223

folk music of, **3:**76–77, 153–58, 823, 824–25, 833–35; used for contra dances, **3:**230, 332; used in minstrel shows, **3:**837–38

influence on Métis culture and music, **3:**405, 407–8

interminglings with French Canadians, **3:**325

Maritime Provinces, **3:**150, 292, 1123, 1127–30

Nova Scotia, **3:**325, 1070

Ontario, **3:**1178, 1188, 1190

Québec, **3:**1146, 1148

religion of, **3:**118–19

in Virgin Islands, **2:**969

Scottish Songs (Ritson), **8:**373

scrapers (rasps)

armadillo shell, **2:**185

Brazil, **2:**330, 335

Bulgaria, **8:**894

cacho, **2:**709

cadacada, **2:**234

carpenter's saw, **2:**803, 805–6, 809

carraca llanera, **2:**414

carrasca (also *raspador*), **2:**377–78, 384, 741–42

cassuto, **1:**668

charrasca, **2:**528, 538, 565

coconut grater, **2:**689

El Salvador, **2:**706

Europe, **8:**170

garakot, **4:**904

graj, **2:**887

grater, **2:**897

Great Basin types, **3:**422, 474

guacharaca, **2:**39, 391, 401, 406, 407

Guatemala, **2:**724

güira (also *guayo*), **2:**834–36, *850, 851, 852,* 854–55, 857

güiro

Colombia, **2:**377

Costa Rica, **2:**683, 693

Cuba, **2:**830, 834–36

Dominican Republic, **2:***73*, 854

Ecuador, **2:**414

Europe, **8:**656

Mexico, **2:***611*, 620

Nicaragua, **2:**762

North America, **3:***726*, 731, 785, 788

Oceania, **9:**99, 102–3

Panama, **2:**57, 774, *775*

Puerto Rico, **2:**932, 933, 938–39

Trinidad, **2:**960

gwaj (also *syak*), **2:**842, 877, 946

hair comb, **2:**803, 805

hirukiam, **2:**589, *590*

jawbones

aras napat, **2:**660, 663

Belize, **2:**677

Costa Rica, **2:**689

cumbamba, **2:**377

Garífuna culture, **2:**753

quijada (also *carraca*; *carachacha*; *charassga*), **2:**834; Chile, **2:**360; Colombia, **2:**377, 384, 385, 391; Ecuador, **2:**414; El Salvador, **2:**709, 714; Peru, **2:**476, 492, 493, 494, 496

kagul, **4:**904

kokkara, **5:**367

Kongo kingdom, **1:**667–68

krita, **2:**660, 663

Madagascar, **1:**785

mai ngop ngep, **4:***339*, 345, 346

martellu, **8:**572

Maya culture, **2:**651, *731*

Métis performance of, **3:***11*

Mexico, **2:**13, *14*

Middle East, **6:**405

Mixtec culture, **2:**563

morache, **3:***423*, 425

Native American types, **3:**475

ngŭ (crouching tiger box), **4:**448; **7:**5

Nicaragua, **2:**753

Northeast types, **3:**463

notched stick, **2:**492

ŏ (crouching tiger box), **7:**5, 823, *826*, 829

Oceania, **9:**412, 431

omichicahuaztli, **2:**601

Peru, **2:**492, 493

prehistoric, **8:**38

pseudo-bass, **8:**526, 531

ragana, **8:**572

raspu, **2:**928

rêco-rêco, **2:**308, 313, 329

reque reque, **8:**582

ridged bottle, **2:**803, 805

rook jaw, **2:**814–15

sinh tiên, **4:**468–69, 479

South America, **2:**29

Southwest types, **3:**371, 429, 436, 437, 472, 474

squash, **2:**969–70

śuktivādya, **5:**367

taccule, **8:**572

tagutok, **4:**924

tatarizo, **1:**638

tortoiseshells, El Salvador, **2:**706

traccule, **8:**572

Vanuatu, **9:**693

Venezuela, **2:**534

washboards, **3:**638; **8:**355

frottoir, **3:***362*, 858

West Africa, **1:**446

wiri, **2:**929

Yaqui Indians, **3:**485

Screaming Mee Mees (musical group), **9:**168

Scriabin, Aleksandr, **3:**1150; **5:**64, 563; **7:**341; **8:**781

Scripps Institution of Oceanography, **9:**977

Scripps, Louise, **3:**1013–14

Scripps, Sam, **3:**1013–14

Scriven, Joseph, **9:**203

Scruggs, Earl, **3:**77, 159, 165, 166, 168

Scruggs, T. M., **2:**767

Scythian people, **7:**13, 28

"*Se acabó el WPA*" (Marín), **3:**737, 738

Seal, Sydney, **6:**1025

Seals, Arthur, **3:**706

Sealy, Joe, **3:**1134, 1169

Searchers (musical group), **8:**214

"Searching" (Coasters), **3:**672

Searching the Academy (Cantonese opera), **7:**308

Sears, Laurie Jo, **4:**650

Seashore, Carl, **3:**278, 286; **8:**91, 95–96

Seasons (Cage), **3:**130

Seaweed, Joe, **3:***400*

Sebestyén, Marta, **8:**226, *227*

Sechan, Sarah, **10:**48

Seckar, Alvena, **3:**900

Secola, Keith, **3:**458

Second Book of Negro Spirituals (Johnson), **3:**607

Second Great Awakening, **3:**123, 533, 575–76

Secret History of the Mongols, **7:**31

secret societies. *See* societies, secret

Sectio canonis (Euclid), **6:**368

Secunda, Sholom, **3:**937–38

Secundino, Agapito, **2:**580

Sedaka, Neil, **4:**884

Sedang people, **4:**533, 534

Seddon, Patsy, **8:**364

Sedeño, Joseph "Boy," **9:**101, *102*

Sedgwick, Charles, **3:**864

See, Jules Ah, **9:**390

"See See Rider" (Baker), **3:**673

Seebass, Tilman, **4:**733

Seeger, Anthony, **10:**24, 73, 102

Seeger, Charles, **1:**722; **3:**21–22, 42, 45, 48, 144, 174, 294, 511, 828; **4:**14; **9:**289; **10:**5, 20–21, *21*, 23, 79, 140

Seeger, Peggy, **8:**296, 374

Seeger, Pete, **1:**486, 773; **3:**14, 48–49, *49*, 162, 240, 310, 316, 317, 328–29, *329*, 330; **10:**80

Seeger, Ruth Crawford, **3:**93, 511, 561, *561*

Seeto, Chris, **9:***989*

Seferis, George, **8:**1021

Seferstam, Leif, **8:**485

Sefton, Henry F., **3:**1180

Ségalen, Victor, **9:**38

Seger, Bob, **3:**49
Seghal, Baba, **5:**429
Segovia, Andrés, **1:**353, 363; **3:**1210; **4:**870
Séguin and Fiori (musical group), **3:**1158
Seguin, Michel, **3:**1170
Séguin, Richard, **3:**1160, 1161
Sei! (Solomon Islands theater group), **9:**233
Seidel, Jan, **8:**729
Seikyoku ruisan (Saitô), **7:**588
Sein Pe, Ù, **4:**389
Šejn, Pavel, **8:**803
Sejo, Chosŏn king, **7:**55, 838, 869, 982
Sejo sillok akpo (dynastic history), **7:**55, 856
Sejong, Chosŏn king, **7:**28, 835, 854, 863, 869, 887, 982
Sejong Cultural Center (Seoul), **7:**994
Sejong sillok akpo (dynastic history), **7:**813, 853, 856, 887
Seki no to (*tokiwazu busi* piece), **7:**681
Sekolah Menengah Karawitan Indonesia, **4:**678, 683, 698, 723, 758–59
Sekolah Tinggi Kesenian Wilwatikta, **4:**678, 684–85
Sekolah Tinggi Seni Indonesia, **4:**122–23, 656, 678, 759, 760
Sela (god), **8:**864
Selaparang (kingdom), **4:**779
Selassie, Haile, **2:**899
Selçuk, Münîr Nûreddin, **6:**117, 250, 785–87, *786*
Seldom Scene (bluegrass group), **3:**159
Select Collection of Original Scotish [sic] Airs (Thomson), **8:**372
Selected Reports in Ethnomusicology (periodical), **3:**516, 828
Selena, **3:**98, 522, 721, 733, 781
Self-Realization Fellowship, **5:**256
Seligman, Charles G., **9:**316, 479
Selika, Marie, **3:**617
Selim I, Ottoman sultan, **6:**793
Selim III, Ottoman sultan, **6:**110, 121, 771, 779–80
Selivan, Mark, **3:**58
Seljacka Sloga (organization), **8:**935
Seljeset, Samuline, **8:**419
Seljuks, **6:**759, 922, 966, 980
Selk'nam culture. *See* Ona (Selk'nam) culture
Selkup people, **7:**1027–30
Sellars, Peter, **7:**295–96
Sells, Michael, **6:**162
Selmore, Peter, **3:**243
Selonian people, **8:**499
Selyani Macedonian Folklore Group (Toronto), **3:**1198
Sem, Sara, **4:**190
sema. See samā'
Semafor Theater, **8:**730
Semai people, **4:**560, 561
Semang people, **4:**529
   instruments of, **4:**562, 567
   lifestyle of, **4:**560, 585
   physical characteristics of, **4:**561
   shamanism of, **4:**569–71
Semaq Beri people, **4:**560
Semarang label, **4:**681
Semau, **4:**786, 796

Semba Tropical (musical group), **1:**435
Semblanzas biográficas de creadores e intérpretes populares paraguayos (Rodríguez), **2:**464
Semcuk sisters, **3:**345
Semelai people, **4:**560, 585
   ceremonies of, **4:**586
   lullabies of, **4:**587
Semigallian people, **8:**499
Semimaru, **7:**644–45
Seminario de Música Popular (Cuba), **2:**829
Seminariyo (institute), **7:**756
Seminole Indian nation, **3:**11, 466, 470
   Alligator Dance, **3:**464
semiotics, **8:**24; **10:**90, 95
   identity and, **3:**505–6, 517
   women's studies and, **3:**88, 562
Semiramide (Rossini), **8:**370
Semnam people, **4:**560
Sen, Amrit, **5:**189
Sen, Atulprasad, **5:**849, 850, 852–53, 854, 858
Sen, Dilip, **5:**540
Sen, Guruprasad, **5:**852
Sen, Kesav Chandra, **5:**848
Sen Klip Theatre Company, **3:**1094
Sen, Nabinchandra, **5:**848
Sen, Rajani Kanta, **5:**849, 850, 852, 858
Sen, Ramprasad, **5:**846
Sen, Sameer, **5:**540
Sena dynasty, **5:**844–45
Sena people, **1:**711
Senar, Müzeyyen, **6:**118
"Send in the Clowns" (Sondheim), **3:**197
Sendô kouta (Nakayama), **7:**743, 747
Seneca Indian nation, **3:**462, 463, 509, 1078
   instruments of, **3:**472, 494
Senegal, **2:**105. *See also* West Africa; *specific peoples*
   academic training in, **1:**38, 40
   Fulɓe people, *gawlo*, **1:**444
   goumbé dance, **2:**803
   griot tradition in, **1:**419
   guitar in, **1:**365, 366
   historical studies, **1:**82
   instruments of, **1:**8, 445
   mbalax, **1:**365
   popular music of, **1:**365, 421–22
   village music, **1:**8
Senegalese people, in France, **8:**231
Seneviratna, Anuradha, **5:**328, 968
Senger, Hugo de, **8:**696
Senghor, Léopold, **1:**363
Sen ji de ma (He), **7:**347
Senlik of Kars (*aşîk*), **6:**803, 804, 808, 809
Sennar, Muzeyyen, **6:**250
Senoi people, **4:**529. *See also* Temiar people
   instruments of, **4:**562–63, 567
   lifestyle of, **4:**560, 585
   physical characteristics of, **4:**561
Sensacional Maringa da Angola (musical group), **1:**435
Sensational Alex Harvey Band (musical group), **8:**369
Sensemayá (Revueltas), **2:**115
Senseng people, **9:**617
Sentani people, **9:**580, 585–87

"Sent for You Yesterday" (Basie), **3:**656, *657*
Senufo people, **1:**115, 453–54
Seo Taiji, **7:**967
Seoul City Traditional Music Orchestra, **7:**990
Seoul National University, **7:**853, 854
Sepher Tehiloth Israel (prayer book), **6:**1038
Sepp von Reinegg, Anton, **2:**453, 463
Seppilli, Tullio, **8:**622
Septeto Nacional, **2:**835; **3:**792
sequence (genre), **8:**70, 366
Sequence (musical group), **3:**696
Sequera, Guillermo, **2:**200
Serai Enderun (Ufkî Bey), **6:**770
Seraj, Latifa Kabir, **5:**815–16
Seram (island), **4:**818–19; **9:**582
Serat Centhini (Javanese poem), **4:**635–36
Serawai people, **4:**619
Serbezovski, Muharem, **8:**983
Serbia, **8:**940–54
   art music in, **8:**943, 948
   blind musicians in, **8:**942
   brass bands in, **8:**280, 946, 948
   café society in, **8:**143
   dance traditions of, **8:**947, 954
   Dinaric Alps, dance traditions of, **8:**947
   geography of, **8:**940
   history of, **8:**940, 972
   Hungarians in, **8:**736, 952
   instruments, **8:**197, 943–47
      Asian derivations of, **8:**168
   Kosovo (Kosova), **8:**12, 940, 1000–1002
      circumcision ceremony in, **8:***144*
      highland music of, **8:**994–96
      instruments, **8:**944, 951
      lowland music of, **8:**996–97
      population of, **8:**951
      postsocialist period in, **8:**1002–3
      research on music of, **8:**954
      Rom people in, **8:**285–86, 951–52
      Serbians in, **8:**951
      talava genre, **8:**286
      Turkish influences in, **8:**947, 951, 996–97
      urban music of, **8:**997, 999
      zurla and *tapan* ensembles, **8:**285, 951
   Pannonia, dance traditions of, **8:**947
   paparuda ceremony, **8:**278
   population of, **8:**940
   research on music of, **8:**954
   Rom people in, **8:**279–80, 945, 950–51
   Slavonia, *na bas* singing, **8:**943
   Šumadija, **8:**944, 950
   theater, *komad s pevanjem*, **8:**141, 948
   urbanized folk music, **8:**14
   vocal music, **8:**194, 940–43, 950, 951, 952
      epic songs, **8:**14, 23, 94, 130–31, 941–42
      novokomponovana narodna muzika, **8:**279, 948–49, 950, 951
   Vojvodina, **8:**736, 940
      astalske pesme (table songs), **8:**114, 952
      bands in, **8:**948
      dance traditions of, **8:**947
      history of, **8:**952
      instruments, **8:**945
      musical traditions of, **8:**952–53
      na bas singing, **8:**943
      population of, **8:**952

Rom musicians, **8:**279
sokačke pesme (street songs), **8:**114, 952
Šokci people in, **8:**931
tamburica ensembles, **8:**927
wedding bands, **8:**146
Serbian Orthodox Church, **8:**940, 943
Bosnia-Hercegovina, **8:**962
Serbian people
in Bosnia-Hercegovina, **8:**962
in Croatia, **8:**925
in Hungary, **8:**736
in Macedonia, **8:**972
in North America, **3:**826, 1082, 1198–99
choral music, **3:**919
tamburitza orchestras, **3:**920–24
in Romania, **8:**868, 883, 886
in South America, **2:**84
Serbian Singing Federation (Canada), **3:**1198
Serbielle, Peio, **8:**315
Serei Kunio, **7:**793
Serenade in Rhythm (radio show), **3:**1107
serenades, **3:**721; **8:**145
Carriacou, **2:**871
Chuuk, **9:**736
Colombia, **2:**383, 393
Corsica, **8:**568, 570–71, 573
Costa Rica, **2:**698
Croatia, **8:**926
Dominica, **2:**842
Dominican Republic, **2:**860
Garifuna culture, *paranda*, **2:**675
Greece, *kantadhes*, **8:**1008, 1014
Italy, **8:**145, 606
maitinade, **8:**607, 614
Mexico, **2:**618
to Virgin of Guadalupe, **2:**614
Paraguay, **2:**458, 459, 462
Purépecha culture, **2:**579
St. Lucia, *séwinal*, **2:**947–48
Slovenia, **8:**911
Spain, **8:**590
Trinidad and Tobago, *parang*, **2:**953, 959–60
Serenata Guayanesa, **2:**543
Serer people, **1:**443
Sgt. Pepper's Lonely Hearts Club Band (Beatles),
3:347, 955
serial music, **3:**175, 540, 611, 1151; **8:**50, 85,
426, 882
Africa, **1:**214, *215*, 224, 226
ban on in China, **7:**341
China, **7:**342–43, 350
Israel, **6:**1031
Japan, **7:**537, 735, 736
Korea, **7:**955
Sērigāra caste, **5:**886
Serimpi label, **4:**681
Serkibaeva, Yermeka, **6:**961
"*Serment de l'Arabe*" (Dédé), **3:**606
Sermisy, Claudin de, **2:**735
Sermüezzin Rif'at Bey, **6:**110
Seroussi, Edwin, **6:**1064, 1066; **8:**267
Serov, Aleksandr, **8:**782–83, 784
Serradell, Narciso, **2:**620
Serralde Mayer, Edgar, **10:***91*
Serrano Indian nation, **3:**417
Serrat, **8:**208

Serror, **1:**571
Serukenya, Wassanyi, **1:**217–18, 223, 230
Serumaga, Robert, **1:**217
Serwadda, Moses, **1:**10, 135–36, 137, 158–59
Sesigüzel, Nuri, **6:**250
Sesma, Lionel "Chico," **3:**741, 743, 798
Session label, **3:**105
Sessions, Roger, **3:**540
setār (also *setar*). See lutes
Seter, Mordechai, **6:**1029
Setian, Sosi, **3:**1036
Setti, Kilza, **2:**320
Sevåg, Reidar, **8:**427
Sevappa Nayak, **5:**390
Sevda (musical group), **8:**446
"7/8–9/8" (Moğollar), **6:**250
"7 O'Clock News/Silent Night" (Simon and
Garfunkel), **3:**317
7-Up (Laotian band), **9:**76
Seven Seas, **9:**999
Seven Shades of Pale (film), **3:**1133
Seven Years' War, **2:**864. *See also* French and
Indian War
1755 (musical group), **3:**1136
Seventh-Day Adventists
in Bellona, **9:**852
in Cook Islands, **9:**898
in Jamaica, **2:**901
in Manihiki, **9:**905
in Marshall Islands, **9:**748
in Papua New Guinea, **9:**516, 607, 612
in Solomon Islands, **9:**665
Seventh Fire (musical group), **3:**327, 1063
Seventh Heaven (film), **3:**262
Seventh Regiment Band, **3:**565
Severus of Antioch, Patriarch, **6:**227
Sevilla, José N., **4:**864
Şevki Bey, **6:**116, 771
Sewall, Samuel, **3:**45
Seward, Philander, **3:**839, 840
sex and music. *See also* censorship and bans;
homosexuality; sexual differentiation
Afghanistan
prostitution, **5:**812, 815
transvestites, **5:**815
bagpipe as phallic symbol, **8:**201
Balkan region, prohibitions on Muslim
women's singing and dancing, **8:**145
Barbados, calypso texts, **2:**870–71
bars and brothels, **2:**49
blues texts, **3:**104, 641
Bolivia, courtship songs, **2:**293
Brazil, in Afro-Brazilian popular genres, **2:**354
castrati, **8:**77
China
concubines, **7:**402–3
courtesans, **7:**82, 168, 269, 401–2, 405–8
northwestern minorities, **7:**463
prostitutes, **7:**273, 403, 408
chutney texts, **5:**601
Colombia
copla texts, **2:**390
currulao symbolism, **2:**405
Tukano culture, **2:**151
in country music, **3:**81
courtesan tradition (South Asia), **5:**171,

179–80, 192, 373–74, 407–9, 493–94,
930
British disapproval of, **5:**15, 122–23, 180,
338, 374, 375, 408–9
dēvadāsi (also *devadāsī*) dancers, **5:**263,
386–87, 400, 407–8
disco music, **3:**229, 687–88, 689
erotic song texts, **5:**551, 645, 653, 663, 674
Fiji, innuendos, **9:**781
gay and lesbian scholarship, **3:**89, 107–11
gender as analytic category, **3:**87–99,
103–14
glam rock, **3:**357
Greece, *derbiderissa*, **8:**1019–20
ḥāfiza dancers, **5:**687
harvest songs, symbolism in, **8:**132
Hawai'i, procreative chants, **9:**915, 928
heavy metal texts, **3:**358
instruments as fertility symbols, **2:**35, 253,
283, 289, 291, 524
instrument sounds, **2:**33–34, 294, 296
Irian Jaya, Eipo gossiping, **9:**593
Japan
geisya, **7:**602
girl groups, **7:**747
zokkyoku songs, **7:**689
Kapingamarangi, *hehenga* songs, **9:**838
Korea, courtesans, **7:**985
light classical song texts, **5:**179, 411
Luangiua, *langi* song texts, **9:**843
Māori *haka*, **9:**950
Marshall Islands, erotic dances, **9:**752–53
Micronesia, **9:**716
Middle East
concepts of virility and bisexuality, **6:**305–6
perception of women musicians as
prostitutes, **6:**305
secular performers and, **6:**538
Nauru, **9:**756
Pakistan, female entertainers, **5:**815
Palau, Tobi Island, **9:**182
Papua New Guinea, **9:**178–81
flute ensembles and, **9:**512
Poland, solstice songs, **8:**703
political issues, **3:**301
Punjab
female entertainers, **5:**769
transvestites and hermaphrodites, **5:**770–71
rap, **3:**696–97
rhythm and blues texts, **3:**349, 671
rock and roll and, **3:**351–52, 354–55, 550–51
St. Lucia, in *jwé* genre, **2:**943
Sāmoa, nuptial cheers, **9:**803
Shakers, **3:**134–35
Sikaiana
puina texts, **9:**844
saka texts, **9:**847
South Asia, transvestites, **5:**515, 683, 685
Tahiti
bar-girl dancers, **9:**875
tāmūrē dance, **9:**874
Tikopia, gender-based insults, **9:**247–49
transvestites, **2:**57
Trinidad and Tobago
calypso song texts, **2:**963
transvestites, **2:**965

sex and music (*continued*)
  Trobriand Islands, sexual movements in dance, **9:**490
  Tuamotu Islands, song texts, **9:**884
  Turkey
    prostitution, **6:**116
    vocal performers, **6:**783
  Uighur popular music, **7:**469
  Vanuatu
    sexual shapes of instruments, **9:**693
    Tanna, **9:**706
    tanumwe song genre, **9:**198
  Virgin Islands, innuendos in song texts, **2:**971
  Wales, sexual metaphors in song texts, **8:**343
  women's studies, **3:**88, 562–63
  Yap, erotic dances, **9:**733
Sex and Social Dance (film), **9:**49
"Sex Machine," **3:**680
Sex Pistols (musical group), **3:**348, 357; **4:**888; **7:**468; **8:**215
Sexteto Habanero, **3:**792
Sexteto Mayor, **2:**264
sexual differentiation. *See also* gender; sex and music
  Abkhazian people, of musical genres, **8:**852
  Aché-Guayakí culture, of instrumentalists, **2:**455
  Adighian people, of instrumental performance, **8:**855
  Afghanistan
    of poets, **5:**506
    prohibitions on women making music, **5:**816
    women's music, **5:**812–16, 822
  Africa
    in dance, **1:**112, 121, 288–90
    division of labor, **1:**110–11, 114
    instrument playing, **1:**321
    mouth bow playing, **1:**640
    of musical activities, **1:**281, 290
    palace spaces, **1:**524
    secret societies, **1:**309, 328–29
  Aka people, dances, **1:**690–91
  Albania
    of Rom performers, **8:**285
    of song genres, **8:**987, 989
    unmarried women in men's roles, **8:**198
    women's roles, **8:**987
  Albanian music and behavior, **3:**928
  Algeria
    in ceremonies, **1:**539–40
    of instrumentalists, **6:**270
    women's music, **6:**473
  as analytic category, **8:**191
  Andalusia, women's education, **6:**445–46
  Andean regions
    of instrumentalists, **2:**206, 221
    of performers, **2:**35
    of singers, **2:**215
  Angola, masked dancing, **1:**676–77
  Anuta, *napa* performers, **9:**378
  Aotearoa, of dancers, **9:**947
  Arab-Andalusian musicians, **1:**535
  Arabian peninsula
    of dances, **6:**704–5
    of early lyre ensembles, **6:**358–59

Arab women musicians, **6:**5–6
  contemporary, **6:**299–307, 696–702
  frame drum use of, **6:**18
  historical, **6:**293–98, 695–96
Argentina, of *cuarteto* performers, **2:**276
Australia
  Aboriginal dances, **9:**243
  accompaniment instruments, **9:**242–43
  Central Aboriginal peoples' ceremonies, **9:**244–45
  Central Aboriginal peoples' dancing and accompaniment, **9:**436
  Central Aboriginal peoples' secret songs and ceremonies, **9:**437–39
  ceremonial participants, **9:**241–43, 410, 411, 419, 446, 451, 459–61, 464–67
  dance movements, **9:**454, 455
  Torres Strait Islands dancers, **9:**429
  Yanyuwa love-magic songs, **9:**428
Baggára people, female bards, **1:**560–61
Bahamas
  of junkanoo participants, **2:**811
  of performers, **2:**802
Bali, of performers, **4:**738, 751
Balkan region, prohibitions on Muslim women's singing and dancing, **8:**145
Balkarian people, of vocal performance, **8:**858
Balochistan, women's trance states, **6:**884
Barbados, of performers, **2:**820
bedouin dances, **6:**624
Bolivia, of instrumentalists, **2:**292–93
Bosnia-Hercegovina
  of instrumentalists, **8:**967
  of song genres, **8:**963
Brazil, of *ternos* membership, **2:**312
Bulgaria, of performers, **8:**113, 282
Burma, of performers, **4:**376–77
Caribbean, of performers and ceremonies, **2:**57
Carriacou, of songs, **2:**869
Central African Republic, urban performers, **1:**686
Central America, of performers and ceremonies, **2:**57
Central Asia
  of performers and genres, **6:**898–99, 902
  women *maqám* performers, **6:**919
  women's religious genres and roles, **6:**945–47
Chechen people, of vocal performance, **8:**863
Chile, of instrumentalists, **2:**428
China
  female *tanhuang* singers, **7:**299
  of *kunqu* troupes, **7:**293
  of opera singers, **7:**395
  of performers, **7:**142, 421
  of *pipa* players, **7:**82
  of *sheng-guan* performers, **7:**200
  women musicians, **7:**82, 401–8
  women *zheng* players, **7:**171
Chuuk, dancers, **9:**737
Congo, women in popular music, **1:**425–26
Denmark, of workers, **8:**458
Dominican Republic, **2:**856
Dominica, of performers, **2:**841
East Asia, theatrical performers, **7:**76
East Indian women's songs, **3:**814

Ecuador, of instrumentalists, **2:**428
Egypt
  of professional musicians, **6:**567, 615–16, 618–19, 621
  of religious singers, **6:**169
  of theatergoers, **6:**237
  women composers, **6:**610
El Salvador, of musicians, **2:**716
England, of performers, **8:**335–36
Estonia, of performers, **8:**491–93
Europe
  in competitive dancing, **8:**166
  of epic singers, **8:**130
  in musical activities, **8:**120, 193–201
  of performance spaces, **8:**143
  in ritual dances, **8:**162
  scholarship and theoretical issues, **8:**192–93
  in social dancing, **8:**163–64
  twentieth-century contexts of, **8:**200–201
  women's responsibility for mourning, **8:**145, 193, 196, 379
Faŋ cosmology, **1:**663
Fiji, dance genres, **9:**781
Finland
  of instrumentalists, **8:**478
  of workers, **8:**478
Flores, of performers, **4:**793
French Guiana
  of Amerindian repertoires, **2:**435
  of French Guiana, **2:**435
Futuna, dancers, **9:**815
Garifuna culture
  of performers, **2:**672
  of song genres, **2:**675
Georgia, of musical performances and repertoires, **8:**841
Goa, of dance genres, **5:**738
Greece
  of instrumentalists, **8:**1017
  mourning obligations, **8:**114, 1025
Grenada, of carnival performers, **2:**866
Guaraní culture, of instrumentalists, **2:**200, 201, 454
Guyana, of song repertoires, **5:**601
Haiti, of performers, **2:**892–93
Hawai'i, dance troupe competitions, **9:**67
Herero people, music making, **1:**715
Hui people, of performers, **7:**462
Hungary, of songs, **8:**740
Ila people, songs, **1:**711
India, North
  classical and light classical musical performance, **5:**373–74
  wedding traditions, **10:**5–6
India, South, women's musical contributions, **5:**385–86
Ingassana musicians, **1:**563
Ingush people, of vocal performance, **8:**863
Iran
  of musical ensembles, **6:**140
  of performers, **6:**828–29
Ireland
  of performers, **8:**379
  of song repertoires, **8:**389
Irian Jaya
  Asmat ceremonial participants, **9:**190–91

ceremonial participants, **9:**475, 590
   instrumentalists, **9:**580, 582
Italy, of song performance, **8:**611
Jamaica, of instrumentalists, **2:**897
Japan
   of *biwa* players, **7:**643
   of narrative performers, **7:**681
   onnagata actors, **7:**764–65
   of performers, **7:**763–66
   of *syamisen* players, **7:**760
   of theatrical performers, **7:**675, 744,
      765–66, 945
Java, of performers, **4:**682
Jewish people, **8:**261
   liturgical practices, **8:**257, 261, 263, 264
   Lubavitcher Hasidim, **10:**131–32
   of performers, **3:**940–41
   prohibitions on female voice, **6:**200–201
Kalinga people, of performers, **4:**916
Karachaevian people, vocal performance, **8:**858
Karelia, of lament performance, **8:**476
Karnataka, of song genres, **5:**868
Karnatak music repertoires, **5:**388–89
Kayan people, of performers, **4:**831–32
Kazakhstan, of musical performances,
   6:950–51, 955–56
Kerala, of instrumentalists, **5:**941–42
Khoikhoi people, bow playing, **1:**703
Kogi culture
   of dancers, **2:**187
   of instrumentalists, **2:**184
Korea
   of band members, **7:**938
   kagok repertoires, **7:**818
   women musicians, **7:**893–95, 945, 985
Kpelle people, musicians, **1:**466
Kuna culture, of musicians, **2:**644, 647
Kurdistan, of values, **6:**747
Latvia
   of instrumentalists, **8:**503
   of singers, **8:**499, 500
Lisu people, of instrumentalists, **4:**543
LoDagaa people, performance styles, **1:**457
Lombok, of performers, **4:**766
Low Countries, of instrumentalists, **8:**533
Macedonia
   of performance contexts, **8:**973
   of Rom performers, **8:**280, 281, 282
Madagascar, instruments played, **1:**784
Madhya Pradesh, of song repertoires, **5:**723
Maguindanao people, of *kulintang* performers,
   4:896
Makah potlatch performances, **3:**398
Malaysia
   of *asyek* instrumentalists, **4:**428
   of *hadrah* troupes, **4:**409
   in *joget gamelan*, **4:**429
   Orang Asli performers, **4:**567
   of *randai* troupes, **4:**413
   of *rodat* troupes, **4:**409
   theatrical instrumental performers, **4:**403
Mali, women musicians, **1:**420
Malta
   of instrumentalists, **8:**639
   of professional singers, **8:**640–41
   of vocal genres, **8:**641

Maluku, of performers, **4:**821
Manihiki, instrumentalists, **9:**908
Mapuche culture
   of shamans, **2:**235, 254
   women's songs, **2:**234–35
Marshall Islands, dances, **9:**750–51
Maya culture, of musicians, **2:**653, 723
Mexico
   of performers and ceremonies, **2:**57
   of *son* musicians, **2:**606
Middle East
   devotional music, **6:**19
   sex-segregated dances, **6:**304
   women Qur'ān reciters, **6:**159–60
Mixtec culture, of instrumentalists, **2:**565
Mongol people
   of overtone singers, **7:**1009–10
   of performers, **7:**1005, 1006
Morocco
   aḥwash performance, **6:**488
   Berber poets, **6:**485
Morocco, musicians, **1:**541
Naxi people, of wind instrument players,
   7:510
Nepal
   of Gāine musicians, **5:**698
   prohibitions on women making music,
      5:702, 704
New Caledonia, dances, **9:**674
New England gatherings, **3:**155
New Ireland, friction block knowledge,
   9:381
North Africa
   of performers, **6:**414
   professional musicians, **1:**545–46
   vocal styles, **1:**542
   women's ensembles, **6:**437
   women's songs, **6:**438
North America
   amateur performers, **3:**190, 241, 561–63
   in blues performance, **3:**638, 644
   Chinese opera performers, **3:**960
   Chinese women as musical leaders,
      3:957–58
   in country dances, **3:**212
   of dancers, **3:**209
   Greek musicians, **3:**931–32
   Hungarian social clubs, **3:**908
   Italian band performers, **3:**862
   male-dominated religious sects, **3:**121, 124
   Métis fiddlers, **3:**405
   in minstrel performance, **3:**616
   Native American ceremonial practices,
      3:93–94, 371, 458
   Navajo singers, **3:**432
   in polka bands, **3:**895
   tamburitza orchestras, **3:**923–24
   "women's work," **3:**89
North Caucasia, of musical genres and
   instruments, **8:**851
Norway
   of instrumentalists, **8:**415, 420, 421–22
   of musical genres, **8:**421
   of workers, **8:**412, 421
Nubian people, ceremonies, **1:**556–57
Oceania, education, **9:**252

Oman
   of musical ensembles, **6:**676, 680
   women's *dān* groups, **6:**674, 677
Ossetian people, of musical genres and
   instruments, **8:**859
Pakistan
   prohibitions on women making music,
      5:749–50, 797–98
   of *qawwali* groups, **5:**752
Palau, of songs, **9:**182–83
Palestine, bride and groom rituals, **6:**581–90
Papua New Guinea
   ceremonial participants, **9:**475, 481, 502,
      530, 551–52, 615, 650
   composers, **9:**567
   dance movements, **9:**484–85
   dances, **9:**573, 601–2
   Eastern Highlands peoples, **9:**526–27
   flute playing, **9:**532
   Huli yodeling, **9:**299
   instrumentalists, **9:**547, 552, 613–14, 619,
      630, 648
   instrumental knowledge, **9:**562–63
   Kuman composers, **9:**523
   Mali Baining ceremonial participants, **9:**192
   Manam people, **9:**245–46
   performance on *ai* instruments, **9:**22
   string bands, **9:**139
Peru, of genres, **2:**478
Philippines, of *tangkel* performers, **4:**906
Plains Indian ceremonial roles, **3:**444, 483
Polynesia
   dance movements, **9:**773, 865
   performers, **9:**241
Portugal, of polyphonic singing, **8:**581
Puerto Rico, of *bomba* choreography, **2:**937
Q'ero culture, of instrumentalists, **2:**230
Quichua culture, of songs, **2:**429–30
Rajasthan, of vocal genres, **5:**644–46
Romania, Rom performers, **8:**277
Rotuma, dance movements, **9:**822
Russia
   of dances, **8:**769
   of instrumentalists, **8:**774
   of Rom performers, **8:**287
Ryûkyû Islands, of performers, **7:**791, 794
Sāmoa, of comedians, **9:**235–36
San people, *bavugu* playing, **1:**705
Saudi Arabia, women's wedding party,
   6:691–694
Scotland, of performers, **8:**368
Serbia
   of Muslimani musical genres, **8:**951
   of work, **8:**940
Shona people, **1:**753
Slovenia, of instrumentalists, **8:**914
Solomon Islands
   ceremonial participants, **9:**654
   instrumentalists, **9:**659
   Isabel Province dances, **9:**659
   performers, **9:**332
Somali poetry performance, **1:**616
South Africa, "shebeen queens," **1:**429, 767
South America
   of ceremonies, **2:**57
   of performers, **2:**21, 57, 129

sexual differentiation (*continued*)
South Asia
activities, **5:**274
of dance idioms, **5:**492
film industry roles, **5:**536
gender relations at Tyagaraja festival, **5:**383, 392–93, 395
gender-segregated gatherings, **5:**8, 305–6, 402–3, 408, 786, 812, 818, 826
gender stereotypes in early treatises, **5:**36, 40
khyāl performers, **5:**171
performers, **5:**103, 207–8, 273, 286, 306
village folk traditions, **5:**414
women's roles, **5:**407–16
Spain, of musical roles, **8:**596
Sri Lanka, of instrumentalists, **5:**964–65
Subanun people, of performers, **4:**923
Sudan, choral ceremonies, **1:**554
Sumatra
of dancers, **4:**613
of Jambi performers, **4:**617
in Minangkabau ensembles, **4:**609, 612
of Riau performers, **4:**616
of *seudati* performers, **4:**604
Sumba
of dancers, **4:**790
of *hoyo* singers, **4:**791
Sumu culture
of collective singing, **2:**751
of instrumentalists, **2:**750
Sunda
of *gamelan degung* performers, **4:**706
of performers, **4:**720–21
of *tembang Sunda* performers, **4:**716
Surinam, of instrumentalists, **2:**505
Suyá culture, of ceremonies, **2:**146
Swahili songs, **1:**631
Sweden
of musical genres, **8:**437–39
of workers, **8:**438
Switzerland, **8:**682
of instrumentalists, **8:**686
Syria, professional musicians, **6:**567
Tahiti, dance movements, **9:**876
Tanzanian music, **1:**634
Temiar society, **4:**564–65
Thailand
khon casts, **4:**251
lakhawn casts, **4:**254–55
spiritualists, **4:**329
Tonga
dance movements, **9:**784
performers, **9:**790
Tonga people (African), of songs, **1:**711
Tuareg people
anzad playing, **1:**542, 575–77
musicians, **1:**587–78
singing, **1:**579
Tunisia
of Jewish sung genres, **6:**524, 525, 526
women in Sufi groups, **6:**520–21
Turkey
of folk performers, **6:**766–67
of folk poetry performances, **6:**81
harem musical contexts, **6:**115, 770
Tuvalu, performers, **9:**831

Ukraine, of musical knowledge, **8:**806–8
Uruguay, of instrumentalists, **2:**520
Uttar Pradesh, of musical genres, **5:**661, 669–70
Vai people, **1:**339–40
Vanuatu, dances, **9:**698–700
Venda people, instrument playing, **1:**708
Venezuela, of instrumentalists, **2:**540, 541, 542
Vietnam
of *hát chèo tàu* performers, **4:**486
of singers, **4:**483
Waiãpí culture, instrumentalists, **2:**162
Warao culture
of instruments, **2:**189
of singers, **2:**198
West Africa
of praise singers, **1:**489
women singers, **1:**444
West Timor, of performers, **4:**797
Xhosa people, overtone singing, **1:**706
Yanomamö culture, of songs, **2:**173–75
Yap, dances, **9:**731–32
Yemen
drum ensembles, **6:**95, 102
professional musicians, **6:**303
Yoruba musicians, **1:**460
Zaïre, women in popular music, **1:**425–26
Zanzibar, women's *taarab* clubs, **1:**427–28, 646
Zimbabwe, women musicians, **1:**433
Seyewailo, The Flower World: Yaqui Deer Songs, **2:**593
Seyidi, Seyitnazar, **6:**970
Seymour, A. J., **2:**447
Seymour, Francis V., **3:**604
Seymour, William J., **3:**631
Seypelmelek ve Metkhaljemal (Magrupi), **6:**969
Seyrani, **6:**796
Seyyid 'Ali, **6:**794
Sezgin, Ahmet, **6:**250
Sfār, Muṣṭafā, **6:**509
Sfina ma'aluf (collection), **6:**1039
Sgaw people, **4:**543
Sgrung-mkhan community, **5:**711–12
Sha Zhicao, **7:**231
Shabalala, Joseph, **1:**777
Shaba people, **1:**599
Shabende, Abdylla, **6:**970
Shacklady, Thomas, **9:**129–30
Shad Mohammad, **5:**787
Shadowlight Productions, **3:**1020
shadow puppets. *See* theater, puppet
Shadows (musical group), **4:**331
Shadows (Singleton), **3:**611
Shaft (film), **3:**685, 711
Shaggan, Ghulam Hasan, **5:**767
Shaggan, Qadir Ali, **5:**767
Shah, Idries, **3:**1044
Shah Jo Risalo (anthology), **5:**758–59
Shah, Lalan, **5:**859
Shah, Viju, **5:**540
Shahab, Fahmy "Sharp," **4:**110
Shahar, Natan, **6:**263, 1018, 1071
Shaheen, Simon, **3:**1037; **6:**285, 600
Shahen (*gusan*), **6:***734,* 736
Shahīn, 'Abdallah, **6:**421

Shāhīn, Yūsuf, **6:**239
Shāh-nāme (epic), **6:**340, 344, 825, 827, 866
Shahnāzi, 'Ali Akbar, **6:**139, *858*
Shai, Firoz, **5:**428
Shaigui, Ali, **1:**571
Shaiqiya people, **1:**556
Shaivite traditions, **5:**246, 247, 249, 260–61, 267, 490, 494
devotional songs of, **5:**105, 216, 284, 855
narratives, **5:**897–98, 900
Triaka school, **5:**689
Shajara dhāt al-akmām (anon.), **6:**17
Shajarian, Mohammad Reza, **3:**1215
Shak Shah, **2:**892
Shaka Zulu (album), **1:**777
"Shake and Dance with Me" (Con Funk Shun), **3:**684
"Shake Rattle and Roll" (Turner), **3:**670
"Shake Your Booty" (K.C. and the Sunshine Band), **3:**712
"Shake Your Rump to the Funk" (Bar-Kays), **3:**684
Shakers, **3:**134–36, 327. *See also* Indian Shaker Church
shakers. *See* rattles
Shakespeare, William, **9:**237
"Shaking the Blues Away" (Berlin), **3:**196
Shākir (Syrian singer), **6:**567
Shakta (goddess worship), **5:**249, 733
Shakti (deity), **5:**494
worship of, **5:**291, 617, 677
Shakti (musical group), **5:**136, 970
shakuhachi (syakuhati). *See* flutes
Shaku Soen, **3:**130
Shakur, Tupac, **3:**698, 715
Shala, Hashim, **8:**996
al-Shalahī, **6:**361
Shalfūn, Iskandar, **6:**322
Shalimar (record label), **5:**747
"Shall We Gather at the River" (Lowry), **3:**534; **9:**198
Shallon, M., **3:**943
Shama, Farukh Sair, **5:**791
shamanism. *See also* animism; spirit possession
Ainu people, **7:**784
Akha people, **4:**541
Amis people, **7:***527*
arc concept in, **6:**133
Arctic regions, **3:**376
Argentina, **2:**251–52, 268
Pentecostalism and, **2:**259
Tierra del Fuego, **2:**250
Aymara culture, **2:**358
Azerbaijan, **6:**931
Bolivia, **2:**289
Bribri culture, **2:**633–34
California Indian groups, **3:**414
Carib culture, **2:**13
Central America, **2:**45–46
musical knowledge and, **2:**58
pre-Columbian, **2:**81
Central Asia, **6:**839, 900, 967
China, **7:**257–59, 312, 319, 402, 406
northeastern peoples, **7:**517, 519–20
Chiriguano-Chané culture, **2:**252
Costa Rica, **2:**681

East Asia, **7:**19–21
  female shamans, **7:**20, 402, 406
  theater and, **7:**75
Europe, women as shamans, **8:**196
French Guiana, **2:**435–37
Garifuna (Garífuna) culture, **2:**669–72, 673,
  752
Great Basin Indian groups, **3:**422, 425
Great Lakes Indian groups, **3:**454
Guaraní culture, **2:**200–204, 454
Hmong people, **4:**553–54; **9:**75
Hualapi Indian nation, **3:**434
Hungary, **8:**740
influence on Central Asian Islam, **6:**181, *181*,
  936–37, 942
influence on Turkish Sufism, **6:**793, 794
Inner Asia, **7:**19–21
Iroquois Indian groups, **3:**462–63
Japan, **7:**24–25
Kazakh people, **7:**461
Kazakhstan, **6:**953, 956
Kmhmu people, **4:**546
Korea, **7:**817, 849, 850–51, 875–78, 886,
  889–91, 894, 898, 942, 959, 972,
  986–87, 995
Korean people in Japan, **7:**798
Kuna culture, **2:**640
Kwakiutl Indian groups, **3:**26
Laos, **4:**61, 340–41
Lisu people, **4:**543
Malaysia, **4:**421, 562–64
Maluku, **4:**816
Mapuche culture, **2:**57, 233, 235–36, 252–53,
  254, 358–59, 362
Maya culture, **2:**549, 652, 723, 731
Miskitu culture, **2:**660, 662–63
Moche culture, **2:**11
Mongol people, **7:**1003, 1008–9, 1010, 1013,
  1015–16
Naxi peple, **7:**512
Nepal, **5:**289–91, 701
  Guruñg people, **5:**703–4, 705
Nivkhi people, **7:**788
North America, **3:**5, 441
Northeast Indian groups, **3:**463, 1074
Northwest Coast Indian groups, **3:**395
Orang Asli peoples, **4:**565–76
Orang Melayu Asli people, **4:**586
Pakistan, northern, **5:**796, 799–800
Paraguay, **2:**457
Peru, **2:**482
Quichua culture, **2:**419
Saami people, **8:**122, 304–5, 306–7
Semang people, **4:**569–71
Shuar culture, **2:**417, 419
Siberia, **7:**1027–28
South America, **2:**45–46
  musical knowledge and, **2:**58
  pre-Columbian, **2:**81
  special training for, **2:**130
  tropical-forest region, **2:**128–29
South Asia
  dance in, **5:**493
  differentiated from spirit-possession rituals,
    5:288–89
  theatrical elements of, **5:**481

Southeast Indian groups, **3:**467
Sri Lanka, **5:**490, 955, 957, 959, 960–65
Sumatra
  Abung people, **4:**627
  Aceh, **4:**604
  Bangka Island, **4:**626
  Batak people, **4:**607–8
  Jambi, **4:**616
  Mentawai Islands, **4:**614
  Minangkabau people, **4:**611
  Orang Dalem people, **4:**619
  Riau, **4:**614–16
  southern, **4:**622
Sumu culture, **2:**750–51
Surinam, **2:**504
Suyá culture, **2:**143, 145–46
Taino culture, **2:**22
Tamil Nadu, **5:**259–61
Temiar people, **4:**61, 571–76, 579–85
Thailand, **4:**61, 329
Thulung Rai people, **5:**288
Tukano culture, **2:**150–51, 153–54
Turkmen people, **6:**967, 970, 974
Uighur people, **6:**995; **7:**459
Uilta people, **7:**788
Venezuela, **2:**525
Vietnam, **4:**60, 89, 500
Warao culture, **2:**189–91, 193–96; **10:**98,
  100, 101–2, 105–6
Wayana culture, **2:**165
Yanomamö culture, **2:**170–73, 174
Yao people, **4:**549
Yekuana culture, **2:**177, 179–80
Yuma culture, **2:**595
Shamgar, Beth, **6:**1064, 1067
Shami, Niaz Hussain, **5:**767
Shamina, Lyudmila, **8:**777
Shams-e Tabrizi, **5:**828
Shan people, **4:**363, 399, 529, 537, 547–49;
  7:496
  instruments of, **4:**548
  in Thailand, **4:**218
Shanachie Records, **2:**106; **8:**240, 241; **9:**998
Shand, Jimmy, **8:**365
Shane, Jackie, **3:**1081
Shang dynasty, **7:**17
  bronze drums in, **7:**191
  burial offerings, **7:**319
  development of Chinese language in, **7:**19
  instruments in, **7:**107–8
  oracle bone writings in, **7:**87–88, 100, 402
  shamanism in, **7:**406
Shangaan people, **1:**705, 708, 767
Shan'ge (Feng), **7:**130, 155
Shange, Sandile, **1:**779
Shan'ge She (Folk Song Club), **7:**339
Shanghai Arts Academy, **7:**397
Shanghai Chinese Orchestra, **7:**414
Shanghai Conservatory of Music, **7:**339, 345,
  377, 382, 397, 398, 416, 443
Shanghai Kunju Company, **7:**294–95
Shango. *See also* Orisa
  in Barbados, **2:**817
  in Grenada, **2:**865
Shankar, Anoushka, **5:**466
Shankar, Daya, **5:***341*

Shankar-Jaikishen (director duo), **5:**535, 537
Shankar, L., **3:**986; **5:**54, 234, 338, 584; **7:**967
Shankar, Lakshmi, **5:**414
Shankar, Ravi, **3:**132, 336, 952, 953, 986, 1215;
  5:*190*, 191, *193*, *204*, 207, *207*, *334*,
  378, 424, 460, 466–67, 562, *565*;
  7:803
  autobiography of, **5:**565
  interest in unusual talas, **5:**134, 194
  performances with Beatles, **5:**528, 566
  presentation style of, **5:**132, 203–4, 205,
    565–66
  sitar of, **5:**334–35
  sitar tuning method, **5:**198
  students of, **5:**464–65
  Western performances of, **5:**379, 560, 563,
    564–66, 584
Shankar, Uday, **5:**465, 562, 564
Shankardev, **5:**249, 503
Shanley's Cabaret (New York), **3:**261
Shanmukhavadivu, Vina, **5:**414
Shannon, Sharon, **8:**226
Shanta, Sunil, **5:**972
Shanté, Roxanne, **3:**696, 714
shanties (chanteys), **8:**142
  African-American, **3:**600
  Canada, **3:**1124
  Carriacou, **2:**868
  Denmark, **8:**459, 462
  France, **8:**542, 545
  Maine, **3:**158
  Maritimes, **3:**1133
  Wales, **8:**344
  West Indian, **8:**233
Shantytown Sextet, **1:***774*
Shanying (musical group), **7:**444
Shao people, **7:**527
Shao Wenbin, **7:**299
Shao-Xing Opera Association of New York,
  3:962
Shao Yizheng, **7:**319
Shaoguang (Beijing), **7:**229
Shapath (film), **5:**540
Shape of Jazz to Come (Coleman), **3:**662
Shapiro, Toni, **4:**25, 209
Shapis (*chicha* group), **2:**485
Shapsug people, **8:**854–56
Sharaknots (Armenian collection), **6:**737
Sharan, Hari Om, **5:**255, 425, 549
Sharett, Yehuda, **6:**1071
Sharif, Mary, **1:**571
Shāriya, **6:**355
Sharkey, Jack, **3:**877
Sharma, Askaran, **5:**251
Sharma, Bhagvat Sharan, **5:**135
Sharma, Prem Lata, **5:**56, 57
Sharma, Shiv Kumar, **5:**207, 339, *339*
Sharon Lois and Bram, **3:**1081
Sharp, Cecil J., **1:**52; **3:**14, 323, 519, 520, 823,
  825, 833, 1256; **8:**19, 188, 326–27,
  327–28, 329, 332, 337, *337*
Sharp, Dee Dee, **3:**709
Sharpe, C. K., **8:**374
Sharpe, Len "Boogsie," **2:**962
Sharples, Dr. Peter, **9:**277
Sharples, Pita, **9:**947

Sharps and Flats (musical group), **7:**708

Sharrock, Linda, **7:**967

Sharruk, **5:***775*

Sharvit, Uri, **6:**1064, 1065, 1066

Shasenem ve Garyp (folk story), **6:**969–70

Shash Maqām (musical group), **6:***918*

Shashtri Institute, **3:**1090

Shastri, Shivnath, **5:**848

Shatkin, Rus Dvorah, **10:**130

El-Shawan, Salwa 'Azīz, **6:**235, 607–8, *611*, 612

Shaw, Arnold, **3:**584

Shaw, George Bernard, **8:**378, 422

Shaw, Margaret Fay, **8:**371, 373

"Shaw 'Nuff," **3:**659

Shaw, Robert, **3:**536

Shawat, Fradji, **6:**1039

Shawiya people, **6:**273, 275. *See also* Berber peoples

Shawn, Ted, **3:**221; **8:**161

Shawqī, Aḥmad, **6:**600

Shawqī, Yūsuf, **6:**536

al-Shawwā, Sāmī, **6:**322

Shay' mīn al-Khauf (Egyptian film), **6:**238

"Sh-Boom" (Chords), **3:**351, 352, 709

Shchedrin, Rodion, **7:**340

She people, **7:**212, 449, 485–92

"She Went to the City" (Dresser), **3:**191

Shearing, George, **3:**743, 787

Sheba, queen of, **6:**1047

Sheburah, Kweku, **10:**30, 32, 33, 34–35

Sheehy, Daniel E., **2:**624; **10:**77–85, *80*, *83*, *85*

Sheerer, Otto, **4:**872

Sheffield Choral Society, **9:**929

Shehadeh, Nabil, **3:**1220

Sheholli, Bahtir, **8:**1004

Sheibler, T., **8:**856

Sheiks (musical group), **3:**1213

Sheila, Joseph, **1:**358–59

Shelem, Matiyahu, **6:**1071

Shelemay, Kay Kaufman, **3:**513, 943; **6:**600; **10:**67–75

"She'll Be Coming 'Round the Mountain," **8:**1008

Sheller, **8:**208

Sheller, Marty, **2:**93

Shemer, Naomi, **6:**1019, 1073

Shem'ūn Qūqoyō, **6:**228

Shen Gua, **7:**129

Shen Haochu, **7:**169

Shen Jing, **7:**130

Shen Kuo, **7:**123

Shen Ping Kwang, **4:**129

Shen Xingong, **7:**375

Shenandoah, Joanne, **3:**458, 489, 497

sheng. See free-reed instruments

Sheng, Bright, **3:**964; **7:**420

Sheng Yunsheng, **7:**218

Shengdi Lhasa (*duolu*), **7:**481

Shenglü Tongkao (Chen), **7:**128

Shengmen yuezhi (Kong), **7:**336

Shenqi mipu (Zhu), **7:**132

Shenyang Conservatory of Music, **7:**386, 398

Shepherd, Frances, **5:**136

Shepherd, Roger, **9:**929

Shepp, Archie, **1:**422; **3:**662, 663

Sheppard, Gideon, **3:**1142

Sheppard, Mubin, **4:**26

Sher Ali Khan, Afghan ruler, **5:**805

Sheram (*gusan*), **6:**736

Sherdukpen people, **5:**504

Sheridan, Ray, **9:**148, *151*, 607, 976, 983, 985, 989

Sheriff, Noam, **6:**1031

Sherlock-Manning Piano Company, **3:**1183

Sherman, Larry, **3:**691

Sherpa people, **5:**490, 696, 698

Sherzer, Joel, **2:**783

"She's Gone, Boys, She's Gone" (Bartlett), **3:**1139–40

Sheshi yaolan (Buddhist text), **7:**328

Shetty, Shweta, **5:**428

Sheva Ahayot (musical group), **6:***263*

Shevah, Uri, **6:**205

Shevchenko Ensemble (Toronto), **3:**1082, 1200

Shey Dāwud, **6:**889

Sheyda, Ustad, **5:**807

Sheze, Mthuli, **1:**219

Shi Weiliang, **7:**524

Shi Yongkang, **7:**348

Shi ba liu si er (*Shifan luogu* piece), **7:**192–93

Shiblu (god), **8:**857

Shield, William, **3:**837, 839; **9:**34

Shields, Hugh, **8:**294, 394

Shi'er yue hua (*xiaodiao*), **7:**152

Shifang (*Zhedong luogu* piece), **7:**195

Shihāb al-Dīn al-Suhrawardī, **6:**372

Shihāb al-Dīn, Muḥammad Ismā'īl, **6:**21, 371, 567–68, 569

Shi ji (Sima), **7:**115

Shijing (Book of Odes), **7:**79, 91, 102, 127, 132, 149, 153, 155, 187, 392

   instruments mentioned in, **7:**109, 110–11

Shiki no keshiki (Kisimoto), **7:**608, 609

Shilakadze, Manana, **8:**847

Shilin guangji (Chen), **7:**123, 131, 196

Shilla kingdom. *See* Silla kingdom

Shilling Agard, **2:**819

Shillingsworth, Les, **9:**145

Shilluk people. *See* Colo people

Shiloah, Amnon, **6:**22, 264, 364, 365, 535, 536, 543, 1062, 1063, 1065, 1066

Shimabara Hanzan, **7:**709

Shimian maifu (*pipa* piece), **7:**168

Shimizu, Ichiro, **7:**972

Shimnyŏng (album), **7:**972

Shin Chaehyo. *See* Sin Chaehyo

Shin (Sin) Yunbok, **7:**986, *987*

"Shi' naasha'" (Navajo song), **3:**368

Shinda, Surinder, **5:**426

Shingoose, **3:**411

"Shining Star" (Earth, Wind and Fire), **3:**711

Shinjû Ten no Amijima (Chikamatsu), **7:**669

Shinmun, Silla king, **7:**981

Shinohara Makoto, **7:**737

Shin paennorae (Won), **7:**970

Shinto (Sintô), **7:**20, 533, 535, 549–50, 607–10

   cantillation systems in, **8:**100

   festival music of, **7:**607–8, 619–20, 628

   kagura, **7:**536, 605

   kibigaku repertoire, **7:**608–9

   Konkô sect, **7:**609

   Kurozumi sect, **7:**609

in Micronesia, **9:**720

Ômoto sect, **7:**610

yakumo goto repertoire, **7:**609–10

Shinwari, Rafique, **5:**791

Shipibo culture, **2:**482

Shirati Jazz, **1:**427

al-Shirāzī, Quṭb al-Dīn. *See* Quṭb al-Dīn al-Shirāzī

Shirei zimra (collection), **6:**1039

Shireli (musical group), **7:**468

Shirelles (musical group), **3:**673, 709

Shirin (*ashugh*), **6:**735, *899*

Shirley and Lee (musical group), **3:**670

Shirvānshāhs, **6:**922

al-Shirwānī, **6:**17

Shir yedidot (collection), **6:**1039

Shitan (*qin* piece), **7:**333

Shituni, Spiro, **8:**1003

Shiva (deity), **5:**877. *See also* Shaivite tradition

   association with Banaras, **5:**247

   as creator of ragas, **5:**314

   drum playing of, **5:**110, 147, 247, 301, 325, 346, 722

   portrayed in dances, **5:**493, 494

   ritual offerings to, **5:**25

   songs about, **5:**221–22, 230, 247

   visual depictions of, **5:**299, *300*

   worship of, **5:**220, 223, 259, 501, 519, 520, 617–18, 677, 678, 702, 720, 731–33, 740, 861, 866, 867, 869, 901

Shiva (musical group), **5:**428

Shiva Simha, Raja, **5:**677

Shivwits, **3:**435

Shiyi pian, **7:**128

Shiyue tupu (Lü), **7:**132

Shizhu, Yuan emperor, **7:**321

Shizi kunqiu (Qiu), **7:**220

Shleuh people, **6:**483–92

Shleu Shleu, **2:**98, 892

Shmueli, Herzl, **6:**1063, 1066

Shobani, Mahaboob, **5:**234

"*Shofet kol ha-aretz*," **8:**255–56

Shômu, emperor of Japan, **7:**79

shômyô. See chant (Buddhist)

Shona people, **1:**707, 710

   concepts of music, **1:**752–53

   harmonic systems, **1:**307–8

   healing rituals, **1:**274

   history of, **1:**744–45

   instruments, **1:**751–52

   mahonyera yodeling, **1:**432

   mbira music, **1:**745–50

   music of, **1:**673, 719, 744–57

   music research on, **1:**52

   speech surrogate methods, **1:**106

   voice exchange, **1:**10

Shondoube, Otto, **2:**575

Shôno Susumu, **7:**595

"Shoo, Fly, Don't Bother Me" (American folk song), **9:**41

Shoo-Fly Regiment (Johnson and Cole), **3:**608, 619

"Shop Around" (Miracles), **3:**674

Shor people, **7:**1027–30

Shora Batyr (epic), **6:**952

Shore, Bradd, **1:**121

Short Abridgment of the Rules of Music, A
    (Youngs), **3:**135
Short Shirt (*benna* performer), **2:**800
Short Symphony (Swanson), **3:**610
Shorti (calypsonian), **2:**963
Shortland Islands (Solomon Islands), **9:**655–57
Shortpants (calypsonian), **2:**964
Shoshone Indian nation, **3:**371, 420, 421
    Naraya songs of, **3:**421, 487
Shostakovich, Dmitri, **4:**873; **7:**340, 347, 350;
    8:84, 781–82
Shota (musical group), **8:**1000–1001
Sho-Tokyans (musical group), **3:**970
"Should Brave Old Soldiers Be Forgot?" **3:**306
Show Boat (Kern), **3:**196, 545, 620
"Show Me the Way to Go Home" (King), **9:**25
Showtime Spectacular (television show), **9:**938
Shrestha, Prakash C., **5:**428
Shreve, Gregory M., **1:**501
Shreyer family, **3:**1194
Shreyer, Pierre, **3:**1191
Shringy, R. K., **5:**56, 57
Shryock, Andrew, **6:**282, 285–86
Shturtsi, **8:**220
Shu kingdom, **7:**320
Shuar culture, **2:**128, 413
    instruments of, **2:**127, 414, 416–17
    shamanism in, **2:**417, 419
Shudra class, **5:**228, 386, 398, 735, 922
    in Goa, **5:**735
    occupations of, **5:**9
Shuffle Along (musical), **3:**194, 619–20
"Shuffleshuck" (Liggins), **3:**353
Shuhda, **6:**297
Shui people
    bronze and wooden drum ensemble, **7:**192
    music of, **7:**485–92
Shui hong hua ling (folk song), **7:**155
Shuihuzhuan (Chinese novel), **7:**246, 270
Shujing (Confucian work), **7:**101
Shu Jinling (Gong), **7:**129
Shumbha (deity), **5:**505
Shumway, Larry, **9:**308
Shungas, **5:**720
Shunkan (Chikamatsu), **7:**669
Shunti, Eastern Han emperor, **7:**320
Shuowen jiezi, **7:**188
Shushila, **5:**422
al-Shushtarī, **6:**370, 443
Shusse Kagekiyo (Chikamatsu), **7:**668
Shutdown Band, **9:**153, 154
Shyghaiuly, Däületkerei, **6:**958
Si este nino se durmiere (lullaby), **6:**1042
Siagian, Rizaldi, **3:**1020
Siak hwasŏng, **7:**856
Siaki (Sāmoan comedian), **9:**235
Siale, Feleti Sitoa, **9:**204
Sialm, Duri, **8:**692
Sialum people, **9:**290–91
Siam (kingdom), **4:**219, 296. *See also* Thailand
*Siamese Music in Theory and Practice as Compared
    with That of the West* (Feit), **4:**330–31
Siane people, **9:**526–33
Siasid (Maceda), **4:**875–76
Siasi Islands (Papua New Guinea), **9:**336, 566,
    614
    dance of, **9:**610

falsetto singing in, **9:**297
instruments of, **9:**621
music and dance of, **9:**545–46, 572–76,
    619
Sibata Kyokudô, **7:**651
Sibata Minao, **7:**51, 569–70, 594, 713, 735–37
Sibelius Academy (Helsinki), **8:**155, 486, 489
Sibelius, Jean, **2:**114; **8:**444, 482
Sibelius Museum (Turku), **8:**481
Siberia, **4:**551
    Ainu people in, **7:**783, 786, 787
    Altai region, **6:**897, 965, 967; **7:**1004–20
    Buryatia, **7:**1003
    geography and climate of, **7:**11
    Inuit in, **3:**374
    Khakhassia, **7:**1004–20
    Kuril and Sakhalin Islands, **7:**783, 786,
        787–88
    languages of, **7:**18–19
    musical traditions of, **7:**1027–30
    peoples of, **7:**1027
    prehistoric, **7:**11–13
    shamanism in, **7:**20–21, 1027–28
    throat-singing in, **7:**1030
    Turkic peoples in, **6:**980
    Tuva, **6:**897, 979–87; **7:**1004–20
    Yakut people of, **4:**553
Siberry, Jane, **3:**1081
Sibo (Kru musician), **1:**376
"Siboney" (Palmieri), **3:**795
Siboney culture, **2:**78
SICC label, **3:**1087
Sichuan Conservatory (Chengdu), **7:**398
Sichuan diao (*xiaodiao*), **7:**152
Sicilian people, in North Africa, **6:**435
Sicily, **8:**604
    cantastorie bards in, **8:**611
    history of, **8:**611
    instruments, **8:**169
    map of, **8:***516*
    popular music in, **8:**208
    research on music of, **8:**621, 622
    vocal music of, **8:**142, *142*, 517, 606, 611,
        612
Sicot, Wébert, **2:**98, 892
Siddhendra Yogi, **5:**517
Siddiqi, Tayyeb, **6:**496
Siddiqui, Syed, **5:**858
Siddraj Jaisingh of Pattan, **5:**636
Side-A, **4:**887
"Sidewalks of New York" (Lawlor and Blake),
    3:549
Sidhi people, **5:**877
Sidhu, Kamal, **5:**429
Sidia, I Made, **3:**1019
Sidibi, Sali, **1:**420
Sidic, Noraina, **4:***909*
Sıdkı, **6:**797
Siebert, Vic, **3:**1091
Siegmeister, Elie, **3:**45, 297
Siembra (Blades and Colón), **3:**732, 799
Siemianiaka, Juyij, **8:**800
Sierich, Otto, **9:**285
Sierra Leone, **1:**21–22. *See also* West Africa;
    specific peoples
    emancipated slaves from, **1:**401–2, 471, 478

guitar in, **1:**351, 366
highlife in, **1:**423
historical studies, **1:**85, 92
history of, **1:**508–9, 510–11
instruments of, **1:**445–46
Islam, **1:**327
Krio language of, **1:**3
Kru people, **1:**373–74, 375, 377
Kuranko people, inside-outside distinctions,
    1:130
masks of, **1:**119
music of, **1:**465, 468
popular music of, **1:**419
praise singing, **1:**488–513
Siflé Montan'y, **2:**843
Sige (*xianshiyue* piece), **7:**215, *215*
Sigma Sound Studios, **3:**711
Sigmundt, Pieter, **3:**1196
"Signifying Monkey" (toast), **3:**693, 698
Sigurbjörnsson, Thorkell, **8:**406
Sigurðsson, Njáll, **8:**407, 408
Sihanouk, Norodom, king of Cambodia, **3:**1000;
    4:81, 154, 161, 199, 201, 207, 208–9
Sihe ruyi (*Jiangnan sizhu* piece), **7:**224, 225
Si ji ge (*xiaodiao*), **7:**152
Sijinjinbabanuodaming (epic), **7:**482
Sikaiana (Solomon Islands), **9:**833, 844–48
    Americans in, **9:**31–32
    Gilbertese people in, **9:**845, 847
    history of, **9:**844
    instruments of, **9:**379, 848
    music and dance of, **9:**844–48, *846–48*
    narratives, **9:**338
    poetry, **9:**327, 328
        metaphor in, **9:**336
    song texts, **9:**335
Sikandar, Sardool, **5:**426
Sikhay Sa Kabila Ng Paalam (Feliciano), **4:**878
Sikhra, Antonin O., **8:**767
Sikhs, **3:**5; **5:**7, 12, 374, 457, 480
    in Canada, **3:**981, 1084, 1096, 1246
    caste structure of, **5:**10
    in Fiji, **5:**612
    gurbāṇī genre, **5:**426, 655–56
    history of, **5:**13, 256, 655
    migration from East to West Punjab, **5:**762
    music of, **5:**256–57
    in Punjab, **5:**7, 772
    shabad kīrtan genre, **5:**250, 655
    3HO movement, **5:**256
    in United Kingdom, **5:**573
    in United States, **3:**987
Siki no nagame (ensemble piece), **7:**575–77, 579,
    579
Sikkil Sisters, **5:**232
Sikkim
    dance traditions of, **5:**502
    Mahayana Buddhism in, **5:**257
    map of, **5:***680*
    Tibetan monasteries in, **5:**713
Siku quanshu (encyclopedia), **7:**129
Sila Godoy, Cayo, **2:**463
Silapakorn Magazine, **4:**224
Silas, Ellis, **9:**147, 153
Silence (Cage), **3:**131
"Silent Night" (Gruber), **9:**908

Silesians, **8:**701
Silgee, Wilson "King Force," **1:**771, 774
Sililisalanglang (*biwang* piece), **7:**478
Silk Road Episode (dance), **7:***399*
Silk Road Music (musical group), **3:**1064
Silkstone, Francis, **4:**26
Silla kingdom, **7:**18, 41
   Chinese interactions in, **7:**24, 25, 27
   cultural influence on Japan, **7:**723
   government music office, **7:**45
   music in, **7:**806, 930, 981
   religious folk music of, **7:**889
   siragi gaku repertoire, **7:**620
Sills, Beverly, **7:**398
Silly, **8:**219
Silly Wizard, **8:**372
Siloama (Rurutu performers), **9:***883*
Silos, José, **4:**857
Silos, Juan, **4:**866, 883
Silos, Leopoldo, **4:**885
Siloti, Kyriana, **10:**18
Silva, Bezerra da, **2:**351
Silva Callado, Joaquim Antônio da, **2:**305–6
Silva, Francisco Manuel da, **2:**304, 305
Silva, Glenn, **9:**915
Silva, Gonzalo de, **2:**836
Silva, Horondino, **2:**310
Silva, John de, **5:**491, 970
Silva, Rodrigo, **2:**395
Silva's Rhumba Kings, **9:**101
Silver, Brian, **5:**460, 467
Silver Burdett Company, **3:**276
Silver, Horace, **3:**660
Silver Ladders (Tower), **3:**541
"Silver Moon" (Hook), **3:**180
"Silver Threads among the Gold" (Dank), **3:**190, 1136
Silverchair, **9:**414
Silveri, Louis, **3:**629
Silverman, Joseph H., **6:**1037; **8:**267
Silvestre, Sonia, **2:**861
Sim Sanggŏn, **7:**915, 954
Sima Qian, **4:**41; **7:**115
Simalungun people, **4:**607
Simamura Hôgetu, **7:**743
Simango, C. Kamba, **1:**18
Simani, **3:**1121
simanjemanje, **1:**430, 433, 776–78
Simanjuntak, **4:**603
Simazu Hisamitu, **7:**727
Simazu Tadayosi, **7:**647
Simberi (Papua New Guinea), **9:**628–29
Simch'ŏng-ga (*p'ansori* story), **7:**899, *904*, 960
Simcoe, Elizabeth, **3:**1075, 1179
Simcoe, John Graves, **3:**1179
Simeda Takasi, **7:**594
Šimek, Milan, **8:**723
Simeon bar Yoḥai, Rabbi, **6:**203
Simhabhupala, **5:**44–45
Simmons, Ben, **1:**355
Simmons, Russell, **3:**696, 714
Simms, S. C., **4:**872
Simohusa Kan'iti, **7:**569
Simon and Garfunkel (musical group), **2:**75; **3:**317, 552; **9:**200
Simon, Artur, **1:**51, 159, 323; **4:**603; **9:**980

Simon, Frank, **3:**536
Simon Fraser University (Barnaby), **3:**14, 225
Simon, Paul, **1:**364, 418, 431, 777, 780; **2:**911; **3:**338–39, 341; **7:**416; **8:**225
Simon, Winston "Spree," **2:**961
Simonal, Wilson, **2:**351
Simone, Roberto de, **8:**622
Simoniti, Rado, **8:**921
Simon, Moises, **1:**385; **3:**732, 795
Simons, Menno, **3:**886
"Simple Gifts" (Brackett), **3:**135, 327
Simplemente mujer (Carr), **3:**751
Simple Minds, **8:**369
Simplisity, **9:**167
Simpson, Claude M., **8:**374
Simpson, Colin, **9:**987, 989
Simpson, George, **2:**954
Simpson, Ophelia ("Black Alfalfa"), **3:**103
Sin Chaehyo, **7:**814, 899, 905, 953, 969, 984, 985
Sin K'waedong, **7:**915, 916
Sin Kwangsu, **7:**925
Sin Kwanyong, **7:**915
Sin Manyŏp, **7:**898
Sin Sisamouth, **4:**207
"*sinaloense, La*" (Garcia), **3:**737
Sinatra, Frank, **3:**195, 528, 551, 862–63; **8:**209
al-Sinbati, Riyad. *See* Sunbāṭī, Riyāḍ
"Since I Met You Baby" (Hunter), **3:**673
"Since Then I'm Doom'd," **3:**180
"Sincerely" (Moonglows), **3:**352, 671
Sinclair, John, **8:**370
Sindh, **5:**744
   Baloch people in, **5:**773
   ceremonies
     circumcision, **5:**287
     healing, **5:**286
   history of, **5:**11
   Hyderabad, *tāshā* playing in, **5:***285*
   instruments in, **5:**345
   Karachi, **5:**746
     theater in, **5:**487
   Manganihār people, **5:**273, 281, *282*
   map of, **5:***742*
   Mohenjo Daro civilization in, **5:**319
   Muharram festival in, **5:**285
   musical genres
     kāfī, **5:**753–54
     maulūd, **5:**278
   Sufi shrines in, **5:**754, 759–60
   vocal music of, **5:**747
   weddings in, **5:***282*, 286
Sindhi people, **5:**640
Sindici, Oreste, **2:**396–97
al-Sindī, Muḥammad, **6:**655
Sinding, Christian, **8:**425
Sindir (deity), **5:**877
Sindoesawarno, Ki (Sindusawarno), **4:**636–37, 637; **10:**43
Sinfonía Diaspora (Singleton), **3:**611
Sinfonía India (Chávez), **2:**115, 605
"Sing unto God" (Appo), **3:**604
"Sing Me a Song of the Islands," **9:**67
Singapore, **4:**78, 80, 518–25; **9:**69
   Chinese people in, **4:**72, 518–19; **7:**6, 396
   composition in, **4:**127, 128–29

   Europeans in, **4:**518, 522
   geography of, **4:**518
   Indian people in, **4:**521; **5:**449
   Malay people in, **4:**519–21, 594
   modernity of, **4:**5
   musical genres, **4:**519–20, 522
   music research on, **4:**27, 150
   Peranakan people in, **4:**522
   popular music in, **4:**8
   population of, **4:**518
   Western music in, **4:**8, 440
Singapore Lyric Theatre, **4:**523
Singapore Symphony Orchestra, **4:**523
Singapore Youth Choir, **4:**523
Singapore Youth Orchestra, **4:**523
Singer, Hal, **3:**669
Singer, Milton, **4:**6
Singer of Tales (Lord), **8:**896, 898, 1003
Singer, Roberta, **2:**839; **3:**790; **10:**56
Singers of Songs/Weavers of Dreams (Baker), **3:**612
Singh, Bhai Harbans, **5:**257
Singh, Bhupinder, **5:**425
Singh, Chitra, **5:**425, 548
Singh, Jagjit, **5:**425, 540, 548
Singh, Maharaja Dalip, **5:**572
Singh, Malkiat, **5:***651*
Singh, Malkit, **5:**426
Singh, Mitalee, **5:**425
Singh, Nalini, **5:**603
Singh, Raja Chatrapati, **5:***121*, 136
Singh, Dr. Shruti Dhari, **5:**678
Singh, Sukhinder, **5:**541
Singh, Tarsame "Taz," **5:**540
Singh, Uttam, **5:**540
Singha, Rina, **3:**1216
Singhana, Yādava King, **5:**24, 33
singing. *See also* chant; devotional songs and
     singing; praise songs, singing, and
     poetry; vocal music; yodeling
   Acadian, **3:**1136–37
   Africa
     choral, **1:**87, 118, 120
     close-harmony quartets, **1:**765
     falsetto, as speech surrogate method, **1:**106
     voice exchange, **1:**10
   Albania, **8:**991–92
     laryngeal techniques, **8:**142
     me gisht në fyt style, **8:**995
   Andalusia, **6:**445, 447
   antiphonal, **8:**9
   Anuta, falsetto, **9:**297
   Apache, **3:**431
   Arabian peninsula, **6:**361–62
   Arctic music, **3:**377
   Atacameño culture, **2:**360–61
   Australia
     Aboriginal peoples, **9:**321
     Cape York, **9:**429
     intervals in, **9:**292–93
   Azerbaijan, *aşiq*, **6:**930
   Balkan region, drone-based polyphony, **8:**13
   ballad, **8:**136–37
   Bashkir people, *uzliau*, **8:**773
   Basque region, **8:**314
   Belarus, **8:**793–95
   Bellona, falsetto, **9:**297, 850

Bengal, *bhāwāiyā* genre, **5:**860
Berber, **6:**485, 486–87
bluegrass, **3:**164
blues, **3:**638
Bolivia, high-pitched style, **2:**294–95
Borneo, timbre, **4:**825
Bosnia-Hercegovina, **8:**963, 964
  Sephardic Jews, **8:**968
Bosnia, two-part polyphony, **8:***112*, 134
Brazil
  aboio style, **2:**328
  for religious music, **2:**328–29
Bribri and Cabécar cultures, timbre, **2:**634
Brittany
  responsorial, **8:**559
  tuilage technique, **8:**542
Bulgaria, two-part polyphony, **8:***112*, 134, 610
Burma, voice ranges, **4:**385
California Native American groups, **3:**412–13,
  415–16, 416, 417
Cantonese opera, **3:**1264
Central Asia
  bardic, **6:**902
  maqām, **6:**913–15, 916
China
  falsetto, **7:**151
  karaoke, **7:**399, 412, 444
  kunqu, **7:**290
  manuals on, **7:**130
  "northwest wind" style, **7:**359
  opera, **7:**277, 279
  Peking opera, **7:**282
  Suzhou tanci schools, **7:**261, 264
  treatises on, **7:**128
Chinese-American, karaoke, **3:**964
in Christian churches, **3:**123, 125
Chuuk, falsetto, **9:**736
Coast Salish spirit dancing songs, **3:**397
Corsica
  bel canto, **8:**571
  paghjella, **8:**569–70
  tribbiera, **8:**567–68
in country music, **3:**77–78, 83, 108–9, 520
Croatia, **8:**926
  klapa style, **8:**149–50, 929
crooning, **3:**244
of dance tunes, **3:**1070, 1075, 1125
Denmark
  Jutland hymn style, **8:**459
  women's styles of, **8:**458
Dominican Republic, *salve con versos*, **2:**856
Egypt
  inshād, **6:**166–67
  ululations, **6:**629
England, **8:**326–29
  Traveller, **8:**336
English opera, **3:**181
Europe
  regional style differences, **8:**14
  style patterns of, **8:**20–21
  three-part polyphony, **8:**10
Europe, Western, Arabic influences on, **8:**517
Ewe people, **1:**463
Faroe Islands, ballads, **8:**413
Fiji
  falsetto, **9:**162
  vibrato, **9:**779

Fiji, *bhajan kavvali*, **5:**613
Finland, **8:**486
  Finno-Karelian style, **8:**478
  Rom people, **8:**487
folk-hymn, research on, **8:**26
France
  after-dinner, **8:**546
  plowman and shepherd style, **8:**540
  tuilage technique, **8:**542
French Canadian songs, **3:**1193
Garífuna (Garifuna) culture, **2:**675, 734
Goa, *mandó*, **5:**739
in gong-chime ensembles, **4:**20–21
gospel, **3:**534–35
Great Basin Indian groups, **3:**425–26
Great Britain, **8:**325
Guyana, African-derived practices, **2:**445
Haiti
  timbre, **2:**893
  Vodou songs, **2:**884
Hawai'i, **9:**307
  falsetto, **9:**128, 297, 300
  mele hula and *mele oli* styles, **9:**915–16
  timbre of, **9:**287, 289, 292
  vibrato, **9:**916
Hong Kong, karaoke, **7:**431
Hungary, Vlach Rom instrument imitations,
  8:275
Iceland
  religious, **8:**404
  vibrato, **8:**401
Inuit *katajjaq* (throat games), **3:**1063,
  1275
Iran, **6:**827
Ireland, **8:**325, 390
  Connemara *sean-nós* style, **8:**327, 380, 382,
  387, *389*
  lilting (also *portaireacht*), **8:**380, *381*
Irish music, **3:**843–44
Iroquois Social Dance songs, **3:**464
Islamic views of, **6:**182
Israel
  mouth music, **6:**206
  ornamented vibrato, **6:**261
Italy, **8:**604, 613
Jamaica, timbre, **2:**903
Japan
  gidayû busi, **7:**675–76
  karaoke, **7:**533, *534*
  microphones and, **7:**601
  min'yô, **7:**601, 603
  nô, **7:**632
  popular songs, **7:**745
  in *satuma biwa* narration, **7:**648
  sinnai busi, **7:**682
  timbre in, **7:**551, 552
jazz, **3:**551
Karen people, **4:**545
Karnatak music, **5:**101, 231–32, 916
Kazakhstan
  epic performance, **6:**953
  lyrical songs, **6:**955–56
Kerala, Jewish songs, **5:**949
Khalkha people, **7:**1006–7
Khmer people
  in *arakk* ensemble, **4:**194

  in *kar* ensemble, **4:**196
  in *pinn peat* ensemble, **4:**183
Kiribati, **9:**760
  falsetto, **9:**762
Kogi culture, **2:**186–87
Korea, **7:**449, 817–20
  falsetto, **7:**818–19, 820, 904, 926, 928
  folk songs, **7:**883
  kayagŭm pyŏngch'ang, **7:**908
  p'ansori, **7:**902–5, 906–7
  sijo, **7:**926
Korean-Americans, karaoke, **3:**978–79
Kurdistan, **6:**745
Kwakiutl Winter Ceremony songs, **3:**400–401
Lacandón Maya, **2:**656
Lahu people, **4:**540
Laos, tonal inflections, **4:**342
Lithuanian *sutartine* genre, **3:**875–76
Low Countries, **8:**521
Macedonia, **8:**973
Makah potlatch songs, **3:**399
Malaysia
  hadrah, **4:**409
  mek mulung, **4:**408
  repartee, **4:**424
  rodat, **4:**410
  theater and dance music, **4:**417
Malta, **8:**636–37
Martinique
  kadans, **2:**917
  timbre, **2:**915
Maya culture, **2:**731
melismatic cantillation, **8:**98
Mexican Amerindian music, **2:**549
Mexico, falsetto, **2:**608
Middle Ages, **8:**73
Miskitu culture, **2:**663
Mongolia, *khöömei*, **8:**773
Mongol people
  falsetto, **7:**1006
  häälah style, **7:**1005, 1015
Montenegro, **8:**958
  klapa style, **8:**959
Morocco, ululations, **6:**479–82, 485, 486
multiphonic throat-singing, **7:**449, 1005,
  1019, 1024–25, 1030; **8:**226
Navajo, **3:**432
New England, indoor *vs.* outdoor styles, **3:**157
Nguni peoples, **1:**706
Nicaragua, timbre, **2:**757, 759
Northeast Indian groups, **3:**463
Northwest Coast styles, **3:**401
Norway, *tralling*, **8:**107–8, 421–22
Norwegian *stev* style, **3:**866
Nubian people, **1:**558
Oceania, falsetto, **9:**27
octave or unison, **8:**9
Oman, ululations, **6:**682
O'odham, **3:**435
overtone, **1:**307; **6:**193
Palestine, ululations, **6:**575, 582, 587
Panama
  aesthetics of, **2:**780
  yodeling, **2:**780–81
Papua New Guinea
  Enga styles of, **9:**533–34

singing, Papua New Guinea (*continued*)
  falsetto, **9:**297, 490, 503, 504, 515–16,
    524, 530, 538–40, 561, 562, 565,
    567, 571, 573, 626, 633
  Huli people, **9:**538–39
pedagogical systems, **3:**275
Peru
  Andean area, **2:**476
  hatajos de negritos, **2:**495
  Indian *vs.* mestizo aesthetics, **2:**483
Philippines
  influenced by Arab music, **4:**928
  tayil style, **4:**907, 911
Plains Indian groups, **3:**238, 441, 445, 483,
    1087
"playback" technique, **5:**107, 531, 543
Poland, **8:**703
Polynesia, multipart, **9:**307–9
popular songs, nineteenth century, **3:**184
Portugal, **8:**581
psalmody, **3:**832–33; **8:**97–98
Pueblo Indian groups, **3:**429
Pygmies, **1:**658–59
Regular singing, **3:**25–26
Renaissance, **8:**74
responsorial, **8:**9
rock, **3:**551
Russia
  choral singing of *byliny*, **8:**130
  instrumental imitations, **8:**768
  polyphonic, **8:**756–58
Saami people, joiking, **8:**299–307
Sāmoa
  falsetto, **9:**297
  vibrato, **9:**205, 808
  vocal timbre, **9:**205
Sardinia, *a tenore*, **8:**627
scat, Nigerian Hausa parallels, **1:**106
Scotland
  mouth music, **8:**108, 363, 369
  psalmody, **8:**362–63
  Traveller, **8:**296, 297
Serbian people in Kosovo, **8:**951
Shona people, **1:**750
Sicily, **8:**611
Singapore, karaoke, **4:**524
Solomon Islands, falsetto, **9:**157, 666
South Africa, *mbaqanga* groaning style, **1:**430
South America, high-pitched aesthetic, **2:**34
South Asia
  devotional, **5:**248–49, 251–52, 267–68
  film music, **5:**107–8, 531, 533, 543
  treatises on, **5:**33, 36, 38
Southeast Indian groups, **3:**467
Spain
  flamenco, **8:**12
  relinchidos (cries), **8:**589, 592
Sri Lanka, **5:**961
Subarctic music, **3:**389
Sumatra, Mentawai, **4:**614
Sweden
  folk songs, **8:**436
  herding calls, **8:**438
Switzerland, Romansh-speaking area, **8:**692
syllabic substitution, as speech surrogate
    method, **1:**106

Tamil Nadu, **5:**916
  folk music, **5:**910
Tanzania, **1:**87
technology's impact on, **5:**567
Thailand
  Buddhist lay singing, **4:**293
  in classical compositions, **4:**282
  in ensembles, **4:**271
  karaoke, **4:**99
  northeast, **4:**96
  repartee, **4:**114, 115, 141–42
Tibet, *chengu* and *jiugu*, **7:**449
Tibetan culture, **5:**712
Toda people, **5:**908–9
Tosk Albanian, **3:**926, 929
Trinidad, women, **5:**589
Tunisian *ma'lūf*, falsetto, **6:**502
Turkey, **6:**781–87
Turkmenistan, *baggy*, **6:**972–73
Tuvalu, **9:**829–30
  tempo of, **9:**290–91
Tuvan throat-singing (*khöömei*), **3:**339, 340;
    6:960, 979, 981–84, 986–87; **8:**773;
    10:71
Ukraine, **8:**808–9
ululations, **3:**370
  Egypt, **6:**629
  Morocco, **6:**479–82, 485, 486
  Oman, **6:**682
  Palestine, **6:**575, 582, 587
Uttar Pradesh, **5:**664
Vanuatu, falsetto, **9:**709
Vedic chant, **5:**30–33, 38
Venda people, **1:**701–2
Vietnam
  karaoke, **4:**515
  repartee, **4:**477
  voice types, **4:**492
Wales, *canu gyda'r tannau* practice, **8:**350,
    352–54
Xhosa people, **1:**706
Yoruba people, **1:**409–11, 413–14
single-reed instruments (clarinets). *See also*
    bagpipes; saxophones
Afghanistan, **5:**837
Albania, **8:**285, 993, 997, 1000, 1002
alboka (double-tube hornpipe), **8:**171, 314,
    594
annāna double clarinet, **6:**414
Arab world, **6:**414–15
Argentina, **2:**251
arghūl double clarinet, **6:**414–15, 545
argul double clarinet, **6:**763
Austria, **8:**673, 676
Bali, **4:**743
bark *lur*, **8:**456
bass, **3:**564
Batak people, **4:**607
bebeulen (hornpipe), **4:**605
bekace, **8:**704
bibeng, **7:**491
bīn (hornpipe), **5:**345, *469*, 506, 647, 670–71
birbynė, **3:**1196; **8:**511
Bosnia-Hercegovina, **8:**965, 966
botanical, **8:**41, 456, 687, 863, 894
bous, **6:**414

Bulgaria, **8:**284, 894, 896, 902
bu ughanim double clarinet, **6:**489
caña de millo (also *pito*), **2:**39, 402, 406, *407*
čarotki, **8:**797
cialambella (also *cialamella*; *cialambedda*;
    cialamedda), **8:**571, 573
ciaramella, **8:**616
çifte double clarinet, **6:**765
clarinet-shawms, **8:**455
Colombia, **2:**384, 402–3
cornicyll (hornpipe), **8:**348
Czech Republic, **8:**719
Denmark, **8:**454, 457
development of, **8:**168
dilliara, **1:**449
diple, **8:**966
dödük double clarinet, **6:**746
dozala double clarinet, **6:**414
dudka, **8:**797
dudka jazýćkovaia, **8:***797*
dûzele double clarinet, **6:**10, 746, 749
ediski, **6:**981, 986
Egypt, **6:**559
England, **8:**331
erke (also *irki*), **2:**287
erkencho, **2:**253, 256, 415
Europe, **8:**169, *206*
  early history of, **8:**42
Fiji, **5:**613
Finland, **8:**478
flejguta, **8:**640
gaita, **2:**101
gendola, **4:**768
Germany, **8:**656
Greece, **8:**284–85
Grenada, **2:**866
gumleaves, **9:**134–35
gurma double clarinet, **6:**414
Guyana, **5:**603
hornpipe, **8:**366
Hungary, **8:***738*
idioglot, **8:***485*
idioglottal bamboo, **5:**916
isimoi, **2:**189, 192, 193
Italy, **8:**618
jiftī double clarinet, **6:**414
Karnataka, **5:**886
Karnatak music, **5:**234–35, 351, 352, 354,
    517
kelarega, **9:**189
kendola, **4:**780
klarino, **8:**1009–10, 1012–13, *1013*, 1015,
    1026
klarnet, **6:**764
Kosovo, **8:**286
launeddas, **8:**22, *47*, 170, 621, 626, 627, 630,
    630, 631, 632
Low Countries, **8:**529–30
Macedonia, **8:**281, 976–77, *977*, *979*
magrūna double clarinet, **6:**306, 414, 624
mahuḍi, **5:**896, *897*
mākuṭi, **5:**350
Mandailing people, **4:**607–8
mijwiz double clarinet, **6:**10
  in Arab-American ensembles, **6:**283
Lebanon, **6:**414, 545

in Palestinian music, **6:**576, 577, *577*, 582, 587, 589
mišnice double clarinet, **8:**930
mitbej double clarinet, **6:**414
mizmār double clarinet, **6:**93, *99*, 414
mizwij double clarinet, **6:**414
Montenegro, **8:**960
murlī, **5:**345, 640, 641
nāgasvaramu, **5:**350, 896, *897*
Native American types, **3:**478
North America, **3:**563
   in Albanian bands, **3:**927
   in Armenian music, **3:**1032
   in Bulgarian music, **3:**1199
   in contra dance bands, **3:**231
   in *danzón,* **3:**795
   in Finnish music, **3:**874
   in Greek bands, **3:**930
   in Italian music, **3:**864
   in Macedonian bands, **3:**925, 926
   in polka bands, **3:**529, 893, 894, 897, 1195
   in quadrille band, **3:**232
   in Tejano music, **3:**772
   in Volga German music, **3:**890
Norway, **8:**420
Pakistan, **5:**746
pambatti-kulal, **5:**350
Peru, **2:**483
pibgorn, **8:**348, 355–56
pidkiavli, **8:**1031
pilli, **8:**478
pipezë, **8:**993
piščyki, **8:**797
pishchik (hornpipe), **8:**770
pištik, **8:***797*
Poland, **8:***705,* 707
pū hakahau, **9:**895
pulang, **5:**916
puṅgī (hornpipe), **5:***xxvi;* **5:**345, 350, 405, *469,* 640, 647, 670–71, 896, *897*
Punjab, **5:**762
Purépecha culture, **2:**578–79
puwí-puwí, **4:**805
qoshnay double clarinet, **6:**919
qūshme double clarinet, **6:**839
ražki, **8:**797
rog (hornpipe), **8:**966
Romania, **8:**879
roopill, **8:**494
Serbia, **8:**946, 951, 952
sipsi, **6:**763, 765
sittawiyya double clarinet, **6:**414
Slovakia, **8:**719
souggārāt double clarinet, **6:**414
South America, **2:**101
   indigenous, **2:**33
South Asia
   as accompaniment instrument, **5:**324
   in *cinna mēlam* ensemble, **5:**104, 360, 913
   in film music, **5:**347, 535, 544
   folk uses of, **5:**365
   in *jātrā* theater, **5:**505
   tropical-forest cultures, **2:**33, 127
stili double clarinet, **8:**859
Surinam, **2:**508
Sweden, **8:**440

Switzerland, **8:**689, 693, 695
sybyzyk, **6:**902
Tamil Nadu, **5:**909, 911
taragot, **8:**872, 879
tárogató, **8:**743
tekeyë (also *tekeya; wanna*), **2:**34, 178–79
tormāy double clarinet, **6:**414
Torres Strait Islands, **9:**428
treujenn gaol, **8:**560
tromba, **8:**571
trstenke, **8:**915
tsuzam, **8:**863
turé (also *turè; tulé*), **2:**160–61, 164, 435, *436*
Ukraine, **8:**811
urghul double clarinet, **6:**582
Uruguay, **2:**519
Uttar Pradesh, **5:**670
yarghūl double clarinet, **6:**545, *575,* 636
žalejka, **8:**797, *797*
zammar double clarinet, **1:**541
zammr double clarinet, **6:**306
zampogna (hornpipe), **8:**571
zamr double clarinet, **6:**270
zhaleika, **8:**770, 771
zimare double clarinet, **6:**746
zumare, **8:**959–60, 996
zumari, **1:**642
zummara double clarinet, **6:**414
Singleton, Alvin, **3:**610, 611
Sinha, Roger, **3:**223
Sinhala people, **5:**953, 954
   music of, **5:**955–72
   in United Kingdom, **5:**572–76
Sinhô (samba performer), **2:**350
Sinkô sakkyokuka renmei (society), **7:**732
Sin modŭm (Park), **7:**958, 967
Sino-Japanese War, **7:**228, 648, 725, 728, 745
Sinor, Denis, **7:**9, 13, 14
Sinoto, Yosihiko, **9:**969
Sin sarugakuki (essay), **7:**653
Sinsen gakudô ruizyû taizen (Oka), **7:**587–88
Sinsen gakuhu, **7:**588
Sint Eustatius, **2:**927
Sint Maarten, **2:**927
Sinti, I Wayan, **3:**1019
Sinti Roma, **8:**288–89
Sintô. *See* Shinto
Sinú culture
   archaeomusicological studies of, **2:**7; **10:**100
   instruments of, **2:**9–10
Sio people, **9:**983
Siomi Mieko, **7:**737
"Sioux City Sue," **3:**353
Sioux Indian nation, **3:**11, 440, 446
   dances of, **3:**371
   flutes of, **3:**477
   research on music of, **3:**444
   song sources, **3:**526
Sipahi people, **5:**640
Siqueira, Baptista, **2:**306
"Sir Nose D'Voidoffunk" (Parliament), **3:**684
Sīrat 'Antar ibn Shaddād (epic), **6:**340
Sīrat Banī Hilāl (epic), **6:**339–43, 346, 410–11, 431, 432, 545
Sīrat Baybars (epic), **6:**340
Sīrat Dhāt al-Himma (epic), **6:**340

Sirena Record, **8:**777
Sire Records, **3:**169
Sirḥān, Nimr, **6:**580
Sirindhorn, princess of Thailand, **4:**225, 358
Siri Pāḍḍana, **5:**882–83
Sirliq Tuman (Mukhpul), **7:**468
Sirma, Olof, **8:**307
Širola, Božidar, **8:**937
Sirota, Gershon, **3:**935
Sirovanga people, **9:**654–55
Siroyama (*satuma biwa* ballad), **7:**648
Şirvani, Seid Azim, **6:**923, 928, 931
Sisaala people, **1:**457; **10:**36
Sisavang Vong, king of Laos, **4:**350, 357
¡Si se puede! (Los Alacranes Mojados), **3:**749
Sisirikiti, **9:**158
Sisowath, king of Cambodia, **4:**187, 190
Sissel from Hallingdal, **8:**421
Sissle, Noble, **3:**194, 619
Sister Drum (album), **7:**444
Sister Sledge, **3:**228
sistrums. *See* rattles, *sistrum*
Si Suan, Si Suan (de la Peña), **4:**881
Sisu Finnish Folk Dancers (Toronto), **3:**1196
Siswocarito, Ki Sugino, **4:***650*
El-Sisy, Yusif, **6:**607
Sita (deity), **5:**261, 274, 589, 701, 891
Sitala (deity), **5:**277
Sitala Mata (deity), **5:**645
sitar. *See* lutes
Sitara (musical group), **5:**574
Sitaramaraju, Alluri, **5:**898
Sitar and Sarod in the Eighteenth and Nineteenth Centuries (Miner), **5:**51
Siten'nôji Temple (Ôsaka), **7:**757
Siti bint Saad, **1:**427, 646
Sitiku syosin syû (instruction manual), **7:**687, 715
Sitinin no samurai (film), **7:**750
Siti nin no sôsya no tameno purojekusyon (Yuasa), **7:**736
Siti no variêsyon (Moroi/Mayuzumi), **7:**735
Si to Ongaku (periodical), **7:**729
Sittanā Mēmūna, **6:**654
Sivalingam Nadar (musical group), **5:***907*
Sivan, Papanasam, **5:**390
Sivananda, Swami, **5:**255
Sivanandam, Tanjavur K. P., **5:**232
Sivaramamurti, C., **5:**328
Šivic, Pavel, **8:**921
Sivuarapik, Martha, **3:**1280
Siwai people, **9:**644
   garamut ensemble, **9:**376–77
   music and dance of, **9:**650
Six Fantasies on a Poem by Thomas Campion (Lansky), **3:**254
Six Pianos (Reich), **3:**954
Six Setts of Cotillions (Johnson), **3:**604
Sixteen Kingdoms, **7:**29, 517
16-kye t'a akkirŭl wihan sinawi (Yi), **7:**954
"Sixty Minute Man" (Dominoes), **3:**354, 671
69 Boys, **3:**701
Siyāla, **6:**367
Siyāṭ, **6:**353, 355
Siyong hyangakpo (collection), **7:**851, 856, 887
Siza kôsiki (*syômyô* piece), **7:**568

ska, **2:**93, 95, 97, 820, 910, 912; **3:**212, 337, 1212–13; **5:**604; **8:**215, 235
Skaggs, Ricky, **8:**392
Skah Shah (musical group), **3:**803
Skáldskaparmál (Sturluson), **8:**122–23
Skallagrímsson, Egill, **8:**405
Skaryna, Francišak, **8:**790
Skatalites, **2:**97
Sket, **4:**110
Skids (musical group), **8:**369
Skierkowski, Władysław, **8:**710, 712
Skillet Lickers (musical group), **3:**78
"Skin Tight" (Ohio Players), **3:**681, 711
Skinner, Alanson, **2:**635
Skinner, James Scott, **8:**368
Skjeldborg, Age, **8:**464
Skodun, Mihail, **8:***793*
Skogman, Thore, **8:**445
Skokiaan (Musurugwa), **1:**772
Skopje Roma, **8:**280
Skoryk, Myroslav, **8:**820
Skroup, František, **8:**728
Skryabin, Alexander. *See* Scriabin, Aleksandr
"Sky Pilot" (Animals), **3:**318
Skylarks, **1:**771
Slabinac, Krunoslav "Kićo," **8:**934
Slade, Steve, **3:**1277–78
Slama, Bishi, **6:**1044
Slammer (Barbadian minstrel), **2:**819
Slank, **4:**110
Slash label, **3:**750
Slastion, Opanas, **8:**822
Slave (musical group), **3:**684, 686
"Slave Girl Mourning Her Father," **3:**307
Slave Songs of the United States (anthology), **3:**29, 82, 506, 523–24, 574–75, 600, 601
Slavejkov, Petko, **8:**903
Slavey Indian nation, **3:**392, 1276
Slavianski Cappella, **8:**777
Slavic peoples
   in Greece, **8:**1011
   in Italy, **8:**617
   research on music of, **8:**23
   in Romania, **8:**868
Slavonic Benevolent Order of the State of Texas, **3:**898
Slawek, Stephen, **5:**674
Slayer (musical group), **3:**358
Sleater-Kinney (musical group), **3:***92*
Sledge, Percy, **3:**710
Sleep and Swede and the Tumbleweeds, **3:**1091
Šlezinger, Josif, **8:**947–48
"Slipping into Darkness" (War), **3:**681
slit-drums
   Africa, **1:**78, 132–33, 298
   agung a bentong, **4:**924
   Aitutaki, **9:***956*
   asonko, **1:**465
   baleeo'o'o, **9:**964
   ban, **3:**960
   bangzi, **7:**224–25
   Barbados, **2:**814
   belo, **9:**661
   byau', **4:**371
   cajita musical, **3:**729
   in Cantonese music, **7:**218

catá, **2:**831
Central Africa, **1:**650–51, 657
Central African Republic, **1:**664
Central America, **2:**8–9
   in Chinese ensemble music, **7:**235
   in Chinese shawm and percussion groups, **7:**201
Cirebon, **4:**687
Colombia, **2:**150
daban, **7:**212
deba, **1:**75
dlisung, **4:**924
Dogon people, **1:**455
dung lung, **4:**338
edel, **4:**924
ekwe, **1:**459
El Salvador, **2:**706
fa'atete, **9:**895
fuban, **7:**212
garamuts, **9:***146*, 149, *372*, 375–77, 475–76, 481, 490
   Abelam people, **9:**549, 552
   Bali and Vitu islands, **9:**611
   Baluan, **9:**258, 602, 604–6
   barum, **9:**22
   Bougainville, **9:**649, 650–51
   Buka Island, **9:**632, 640–41, 647
   gilamo, **9:**615
   Iatmul people, **9:**289, *341*, 553, 555–57
   island region, **9:**601
   Japanese ban on, **9:**28
   Kaulong people, **9:**619
   Lolo people, **9:**614
   Mamose region, **9:**547
   men's playing of, **9:**245
   mral, **9:**23
   New Britain, **9:**621, 623
   New Ireland, **9:**626, 627
   Nissan Atoll, **9:**632, 633, 635
   nogus, **9:**559–60
   preservation of, **9:**189
   Rai Coast, **9:**562–63
   Russell Islands, **9:**664
   Sepik Hills peoples, **9:**558
   Tabar Islands, **9:**629
   tuk, **9:**639
guagua, **3:**786
guagua (also *catá*), **2:**825, 836
gugu, **1:**570
ka'ara, **9:**899, 901
kafa, **9:**863
ke'e, **2:**563
keleŋ (or *kéleng*), **1:**329, 467
kenthongan, **4:**646
keprak, **4:**642, 653, 655, 673, 675
kereteta, **9:**886
Kiribati, **9:***760*, 763
kiringua, **2:**578
kono, **1:**377
kōriro, **9:**904–5, 906, 909
Kosrae, **9:**742
kraw, **4:**232
krong, **4:**232
laçgutu, **6:**925
lali, **9:**379, 776, 806, 814, 816
lali ni meke, **9:**776, 777

logo, **9:**806, 817, 828
maguay (also *mayohuacán*), **2:**13, 22
Maya culture, **2:**651
mayohuacán, **2:**846
Melanesia, **9:**598
mõ, **4:**465–66, 468, 469, 504
mõ dình, **4:**468
mokkugyo, **4:**469
mokt'ak, **7:**830, 871, 872–73
mokugyo, **7:**617
mõ làng, **4:**468
mong, **7:**496
mõ sừng trâu, **4:**465, 468
muyu, **4:**469; **7:**201, 205, 312, 323, 330, *331*
nafa, **9:**806, 816, 817, 829
nawa, **9:**913
Oceania, **9:**373, 374
okou, **9:**656
pann, **4:**163
pātē, **9:**207, 288, 378, 379, 798, 806, 828, 829, 899, 901, 902, 908, 913
Philippines, **4:**928
Pohnpei, **9:**742
Polynesia, **9:**771, 865
puloto, **9:**848
redova, **2:**613
Rotuma, **9:**819
samu, **9:**843
sengkok, **4:**548
siquai, **7:**205
Solomon Islands, **9:**659
song lang, **4:**464
Southeast Asia, **4:**596, 926
taha-taha, **4:**921
Taino culture, **2:**932
Tairona culture, **2:**183
tengkuang, **4:**834
teponahuastle, **2:**558, *559*
teponaztli (also *teponaztle*), **2:**9, 13, 550, 556–59, 589, 601–2, 680, 709, 748
tepunahuaste, **2:**711
tingo, **2:**711
toá-toré, **2:**151, *152*
toda, **4:**794
tõ'ere (also *tõkere*), **9:**288, 868–69, 876, 880, 895, 898–99, 901, 902
tøl mo, **4:**534
Tonga, **9:**14, 784
Torres Strait Islands, **9:**412
Tuamotu, **9:**41
tuddukan, **4:**613
tuddukat, **4:**613
tui, **9:**649
tuki, **9:**839
tun (also *t'ent'en; c'unc'un*), **2:**653, 658, 724, 731
tunkul, **2:**13, 658, 680
tuntui (also *tunduy*), **2:**414
tuntungan, **4:**904
upright, **9:**691
use in Christian music, **9:**195
Vanuatu, **9:**285, 362, 688, 689, 690, 691, 693, 697–98
vat ge uro, **9:**702
West Africa, **1:**446
Yemen, **6:**97

Slitr, Jiří, **8:**730
Sljeme (musical group), **3:**1198
Sloan, **3:**1073
Sloane, Cliff, **3:**1008
Slobin, Mark, **3:**19, 42–43, 45, 49, 326, 517;
    5:814, 826, 830; **6:**845; **8:**267, 821;
    10:52
Slobodin, Richard, **3:**392
Slocum, John, **3:**488
Slonimsky, Sergey, **7:**340
Slovak people
    in Croatia, **8:**925
    in Hungary, **8:**736
    in North America, **3:**899–901, 1078, 1088,
        1197–98, 1250
    in Poland, **8:**701
    in Serbia, **8:**952
Slovak Folk Arts Collective, **8:**724
Slovakia, **8:**716–33. *See also* Czechoslovakia
        (former)
    art music in, **8:**727–30
    dance traditions of, **8:**717–18
    ethnographic districts in, **8:**721–22
    geography of, **8:**716, 717
    Goral culture in, **8:**717
    history of, **8:**716
    history of music in, **8:**726–30
    instrument collections in, **8:**182
    instruments, **8:**169, 170, 171, 719
        research on, **8:**41, 172
    map of, **8:***644*
    musical styles in, **8:**721–22
    population of, **8:**717
    research on music of, **8:**18, 724, 732–33
    research on rhythm, **8:**23
    rhythmic use in, **8:**718
    Rom people in, **8:**276
    Ukrainian people in, **8:**810
    Zobor monastery, **8:**726
Slovene Academy of Science, **8:**920
Slovenia, **8:**911–23
    art music in, **8:**921
    dance traditions of, **8:**920, 933
    folk-popular music in, **8:**920
    geography of, **8:**911
    history of, **8:**911
    instrument collections in, **8:**923
    instruments, **8:**21, 914–19, 920, 922
        research on, **8:**37
    map of, **8:***866*
    popular music in, **8:**209, 675
    population of, **8:**911
    regional styles, **8:**911
    research on music of, **8:**921–23
    Rom people in, **8:**914, 917
    vocal music, **8:**911–14
        ballads, **8:**135, 136–37, 911
        polyphony, **8:**610, 913
Slovenian people
    in Austria, **8:**674
    in North America, **3:**529, 824, 826, 901–2,
        1198
Slovenská Filharmónia (Bratislava), **8:**729, 730
Slovenske ljudske pesmi (collection), **8:**922
Slovenské ľudová piseŋ so stanoviska hudobného
        (Kresánek), **8:**733

Slovenské Národné Divadlo (Bratislava), **8:**729
Slovenské Národné Muzeum (Bratislava), **8:**182
Slovenské spevy (collection), **8:**732
"Slow Down" (Thee Midniters), **3:**747
"Slowly" (Pierce), **3:**80
Slumberland label, **3:**171
Sly and the Family Stone, **3:**680–81, 685, 710
Slyomovics, Susan, **6:**341
Smak (musical group), **8:**949
Small, Christopher, **3:**45; **8:**61, 62
Small Island Pride (calypsonian), **2:**963
Small (Smulewitz), Solomon, **3:**936–37
Smalls, Charles, **3:**622
Smarta sect, **5:**220, 223
Smashing Pumpkins (musical group), **3:**133
Smeaton, Bruce, **9:**46
Smeck, Roy, **9:**390
Smetana, Bedřich, **2:**114; **8:**53, 60, 84, 725, 728
Smičkov, Georgi, **8:**980
Smiley, Red, **3:**159
Smirnov, Boris, **7:**1005–6
Smith, Barbara, **7:**976; **9:**109–10, 994;
        10:42–43, 134
Smith, Bessie, **3:**12, 103, 105, 524, 578, 631,
        632, 644, 707
Smith, Bob, **3:**1107
Smith, Carlyle, **4:**870
Smith, Clara, **3:**644, 707
Smith, Clarence "Pine Top," **3:**645, 647
Smith, David Merrill, **3:**392
Smith, Fanny Cochrane, **9:**440
Smith, Mrs. Fanny Cockrane, **9:**987
Smith, Gordon, **3:**52
Smith, Gregg, **3:**536
Smith, Hale, **3:**610, 611
Smith, Jimmy, **3:**663
Smith, Kendell, **5:**540
Smith, Kittie, **3:**1277
Smith, Leo, **3:**1186
Smith, L. Mayne, **3:**159
Smith, Mamie, **3:***263*, 524, 578, 644, *644*, 707
Smith, Mata, **9:**817
Smith, M. G., **1:**516, 517, 522; **2:**865
Smith, Phoebe, **8:**327, 336
Smith, R. A., **8:**373
Smith, Ronald R., **2:**783; **10:**28, 56
Smith, Thérèse, **8:**394
Smith, Trixie, **3:**644, 707
Smith, Walter, **9:**935
Smith, Will, **3:**715
Smithies, Michael, **4:**303, 308
Smithsonian Folkways Recordings, **3:**300, 767;
        7:1024; **10:**85. *See also* Folkways
        Records
Smithsonian Institution (Washington, D.C.),
        3:291–92, 299–300, 492; **9:***956*, 974,
        977–79; **10:**80, 82
Smithson, James, **3:**300
Smoira-Roll, Michal, **6:**1062, 1066
"Smoke Gets in Your Eyes" (Porter), **3:**196;
        7:746
"Smokehouse Blues" (Morton), **3:**653
Smolski, Dzimitry, **8:**800
Smothers Brothers Comedy Hour (television show),
        3:317
Smuin, Michael, **3:**218

Snaër, Samuel, **3:**606
snare drum. *See* drums: barrel, conical, or
        cylindrical
Snell, E. C., **9:**1008
Snoop Doggy Dogg, **3:**698, 700, 715
Snouck Hurgronje, Christiaan, **4:**603;
        6:21, 654
Snow, Benjamin, **9:**742
Snow, Hank, **3:**108, 109–10, 265, 1073, 1091
Snow Maiden (Rimsky-Korsakov), **8:**759
Snow, Robert, **10:**129
Snow, Wolf, Lake (Cheung/Lee), **7:**355
Snowball and Co. (musical group), **3:**780
Snowball, Fiji Wilson, **9:***902*
Snowden family, **3:**835
Snussi, Manoubi, **6:**502
Snyder, Gary, **3:**130
Sŏ Kongch'ŏl, **7:**915
So people, **4:**316
"So What?" (Davis), **3:**661
Sŏ Yongsŏk, **7:**915
Sŏ Yugu, **7:**925
Soai people, **4:**316
"Soaring Bird" (Tang Dynasty), **7:**367
Sobei people, **9:**585
Sobieski, Jadwiga, **8:**712
Sobieski, Marian, **8:**712
"*Sobre las Olas*" (Rosas), **2:**604
Sobrino, Laura, **3:**745
soca, **2:**86, 95, 96; **3:**338, 816–17
    in Belize, **2:**678
    in Canada, **3:**1170, 1202, 1203, 1212–13
    in Colombia, **2:**410
    in Guatemala, **2:**734
    in Jamaica, **2:**908
    in Montserrat, **2:**923, 924, 925
    in Nicaragua, **2:**754
    in St. Lucia, **2:**950
    in Trinidad and Tobago, **2:**75, 964
    in United States, **3:**809–10, 811
    in Virgin Islands, **2:**969
soca chutney. *See* chutney-soca
Socarras, Alberto, **3:**787
social organization. *See also* caste; sexual
        differentiation
    Adighian people, **8:**854
    Afghanistan, **5:**825, 833
    Africa
        kinship systems, **1:**5
        stratified societies, **1:**517–18, 708
    age definitions in, **2:**57–58
    age/genre associations, **8:**116, 145
    Ainu people, **7:**783
    Andean societies, **2:**34, 206
    Apache, **3:**431
    Arab-Islamic world, **6:**299–307
    Arawak culture, **2:**437
    Argentina
        cuarteto groups, **2:**276–80
        tango and, **2:**263
    Atacameño culture, **2:**356
    Australia
        Aboriginal peoples, **9:**314
        clans, **9:**419, 445
        Gulf of Carpentaria, **9:**427
        Tiwi people, **9:**455–56

social organization, Australia (*continued*)
  Yanyuwa people, **9:**460
  Yolngu people, **9:**457
Austria, *halbstarke* youth subculture, **8:**216
Aymara people, **10:**36–37
Bahamas, **2:**802
Balinese musicians, **4:**737–38
Barbados, **2:**820–21
Bellona, **9:**848–49
Berber peoples, **6:**299–303
Bolivia, **2:**293, 295
Brazil, **2:**308, 340
  class structure, **2:**317, 324
Bribri and Cabécar cultures, **2:**631
Bulgaria, Rom people, **8:**282
Canada, **3:**1061
Caribbean, **2:**54–65, 792–93
  class structures, **2:**59–60
  ethnic identity and, **2:**60–61
  kinship roles, **2:**58
Carriacou, **2:**867–69
Central America, **2:**54–65
  class structures, **2:**59–60
  ethnic identity and, **2:**60–61
  kinship roles, **2:**58
Central Asian clans, **6:**917
Chuuk, gendered, **9:**738
Cook Islands, **9:**896
Corsica, vendettas, **8:**567
Denmark, musical repertoires and, **8:**456–57
East Polynesia, **9:**209
El Salvador, **2:**716, 719
  pre-Encounter, **2:**706
Emerillon culture, **2:**436
England, **8:**335–36
  class structures, **8:**332
  skinhead subculture, **8:**235
Europe, **8:**5–6
  agrarian economies, **8:**193–98
  art-music performance, **8:**61–64
  in chain-dance formation, **8:**165
  class structures, **8:**13–14, 188–89, 199–200,
    227, 262
  identity issues, **8:**120–21, 247
  influence on nationalist ideology, **8:**185
  marginalized social groups, role in carnival
    celebrations, **8:**140
  obligations and, **8:**114, 163, 740
  reciprocity and, **8:**117–21
  sexual differentiation in, **8:**191
  singing styles and, **8:**21
  stratified societies, **8:**119–20
  studies on, **8:**18
  youth culture, **8:**216
Fanti people, **10:**31–36, 33–36
Fiji, **9:**773, 780
  Naloto Village, **9:**776
Finland, **8:**483–84
France
  charivari censure, **8:**551
  class structure, **8:**547
Futuna, **9:**814
Germany, youth movement, **8:**655–56, 658
Ghana, **10:**148–49
Goa, **5:**735–36, 741
Great Britain, interracial rock bands, **8:**215

Great Lakes Indian groups, **3:**451–52
Guadeloupe, **2:**873
Gujarat, **5:**627
Guyana, **2:**793
Haiti, **2:**889, 893
Hausa people, **1:**450
  musicians, **1:**519–21, 528–29
Hawai'i, **9:**207, 914, 925
Hungary, youth culture, **8:**746
India
  Brahmin and non-Brahmin performers, **5:**10
  British influences on, **5:**419, 443
  identity issues, **5:**7
India, North
  marriage partners, **5:**275
  of music and musicians, **5:**372–81
India, South
  cross-cousin marriages, **5:**275
  jajmānī system, **5:**763, 909
  of music and musicians, **5:**383–95
Ireland, religion, class and, **8:**389–90
Irian Jaya, Eipo people, **9:**592
Israel, **6:**1016, 1029–30
Jewish people, **8:**261–63
Kalina culture, **2:**437
Karnataka, Tuluva people, **5:**882
Kasena-Nankani people, **1:**455
Kazakh kin groups, **6:**949
Khusrā caste, **5:**770–71
Kiribati, **9:**758, 759
Kosrae, **9:**740–41
Louisiana, **3:**600, 651–52
Macedonia, Rom people, **8:**280–81
Mande groups, **1:**491
Manihiki, **9:**904
Mapuche culture, **2:**233
Marshall Islands, **9:**752
Martinique, **2:**914–15
Melanesia, **9:**598
Mexico
  class structures, **2:**59–60
  ethnic identity and, **2:**60–61
  kinship roles, **2:**58
Micronesia, **9:**715
Mississippian culture, **3:**466–67
Mongol people, **7:**1003–4
Montserrat, **2:**922
Native American groups, **3:**6
Nauru, **9:**754
Navajo Indian nation, **3:**432
Nepal, **5:**696
  guṭhī, **5:**703
New Caledonia, **9:**671, 685
  dualism, **9:**675
New England, northern, **3:**153
New Guinea, **9:**472
North America
  affinity communities, **10:**69–70
  class-based distinctions, **3:**10, 15, 42–53,
    120, 185, 192, 269, 572, 578, 1035,
    1070
  "culture classes" and "taste cultures,"
    3:49–50, 330
  dance's role in, **3:**214–17
  gospel music community, **10:**149
  South Asian community, **5:**578, 584–85

North Caucasia, **8:**850
Northeast Indian groups, **3:**462
Northwest Coast Indian groups, **3:**394, 395
Oceania, **9:**5
Ottoman empire, **6:**115–16
Palau, **9:**181–83, 722
Palikur culture, **2:**437
Panama, **2:**771
Papua New Guinea
  Baluan, **9:**602
  gendered division of labor, **9:**246
  Goodenough Island, **9:**489
  Highlands region, **9:**514
  Huli people, **9:**537
  Iatmul people, **9:**553, 557
  Lolo people, **9:**612
  Melpa people, **9:**516
  Motu people, **9:**492
  New Britain, **9:**620
  Nissan Atoll, **9:**632
  Sepik Hills peoples, **9:**557
  sexual dissociation, **9:**484
  Trans-Fly region, **9:**506
Peru, Andean region, **2:**482–83
Plains Indian groups, **3:**443
Pohnpei, **9:**739
Polynesia, **9:**200–201, 768
  outlier societies, **9:**833, 835–36
Punjab (Pakistan), professional musicians,
  5:763
Rajasthan, *jajmānī* system, **5:**639, 640, 649
Réunion Island, **5:**611
Rom people, **8:**271–72
Russia, **8:**754–55, 780
Saami people, **8:**303, 304
Sāmoa, **9:**795
Saudi Arabia, bedouins, **6:**664
Scotland, **8:**360
  clans, **8:**186, 362, 368
  Travellers, **8:**295–96
Solomon Islands
  'Are'are people, **9:**666–67
  Choiseul Island, **9:**654
  Russell Islands, **9:**662
  Shortland Islands, **9:**655–56
South Africa, **1:**759–62
  apartheid, **1:**717, 774–80
South America, **2:**54–65
  class structures, **2:**59–60
  ethnic identity and, **2:**60–61
  kinship roles, **2:**58
  tropical-forest groups, **2:**125, 129–30
South Asia, **5:**2, 8–10, 39, 398
  bhakti views on, **5:**265
  dowry system, **5:**130
  family lineages of performers, **5:**8, 373,
    377–78
  hierarchy of musicians, **5:**379–80
  popular music audiences, **5:**419
  refugee populations, **5:**16
  rock groups, **5:**428
  rural areas, **5:**5
  scholarly works on, **5:**43
  women, *tawāif̱ bāī* category, **5:**373–74,
    379, 381, 409, 411, 424, 476, 642,
    644–45

yajmānī relationship between patron and performer, **5:**400, 401
South Asian diaspora communities, **5:**575
southern Africa, **1:**701
Spain, **8:**596
Sundanese musicians, **4:**719–21
Suyá culture, **2:**145, 148–49
Tahiti, **9:**207
Takuu, **9:**838–39
Tikopia, **9:**835–36, 853
Tonga, **9:**783, 786–87, 795
Travellers, **8:**294
Trinidad and Tobago, **2:**793, 956, 964, 966
  steelband membership, **2:**97
Tuamotu Islands, **9:**836, 884
Tuareg people, **1:**574
Tukano culture, **2:**153
Turkmen people, **6:**967
Tuvalu, **9:**829, 836
Uighur people, **6:**995
Ukraine, **8:**806–8, 820, 822
  collectivization, **8:**816–19
  village instrumental ensembles, **8:**812
Uttar Pradesh, *birahā* community of singers, **5:**668–69
'Uvea, **9:**809
Vanuatu, **9:**688
  southern, **9:**702
Venezuela, **2:**542
Waiãpí culture, **2:**162, 436
Warao culture, **2:**21
Wayana culture, **2:**165, 437
West Africa
  forest region, **1:**458
  professional musicians, **1:**444, 447–48, 452
Yoruba people, **1:**473
Yugoslavia (former), Kosovan people, **8:**1001–2
Yukon First Nations groups, **3:**1276
Social Process in Hawaii, **9:**972
Social Sciences and Humanities Research Council, **3:**302
Social Singing among the Mapuche (Titiev), **2:**238
socialism
  Afghanistan, **5:**810, 816, 824, 840
  Albania, **8:**990, 999–1000
  Balkan region, **8:**867
  Bengal, **5:**856–57
  Bulgaria, **8:**891
  Central Asia, **6:**904
  China, **7:**140, 163–65, 169, 203–4, 230–31, 257–59, 316–18, 359, 383–88, 396–97, 511
    composition influenced by, **7:**339–41, 347–50
    treatment of ethnic minorities, **7:**441–42
  Czechoslovakia, **8:**723–24, 729–30
  East Asia, **7:**47
  Europe, **8:**187–88, 507, 659, 661
  Finnish-Americans, **3:**872, 873, 874
  Hungary, **8:**736, 747–48
  ideology and, **8:**184–85
  Israel/Palestine, **6:**262, 263, 1015, 1024, 1025–26, 1029–30
  Japan, **7:**736
  Jewish Americans, **3:**939

Macedonia, **8:**981, 983
Mongolia, **7:**1005–6
North Korea, **7:**797, 960–63
Romania, **8:**874, 882–86
Russia, **3:**58
Ukraine, **8:**816–19, 821–22
Socialist Party, **3:**309–10
Sociedad Filarmónica de Bogotá (Colombia), **2:**397
Sociedad Filarmónica de Santa Cecilia (Colombia), **2:**397
Sociedad Lírica (Colombia), **2:**397
Sociedade Artística Musical dos Pousos, **8:***580*
Sociedade de Propaganda Nacional, **8:**577
Société des Antiquaires de France, **8:**552
Société du Caveau (France), **8:**548
Société de la Cassette, **6:**512
Société de Concert de Musique Canadienne, **3:**1151
Société Helvétique de Musique, **8:**696
Société Musicale Ste.-Cécile (Québec City), **3:**28
Société de Musique Contemporaine du Québec, **3:**1076, 1151, 1152
Société Nationale de Musique (Canada), **3:**1148, 1149
Société Radio Canada, **3:**1150
societies and organizations. *See also* societies, secret (Africa); *specific institutions*
  African-American clubs, **3:**683
  African brotherhoods, **2:**47–48, 61, 110
  African-Canadians, **3:**1213
  Akan people, **1:**464
  Algeria, religious brotherhoods, **6:**474–75
  Aotearoa, **9:**936–37
    glee clubs, **9:**935
    Scottish societies, **9:**115–16
  Argentina, *doctrinas,* **2:**257–58
  Australia
    Chinese associations, **9:**70–71
    country music clubs, **9:**141–42
    education associations, **9:**255
    Greek, **9:**72
    Hmong Youth Club, **9:**76
    Irish associations, **9:**78–79, 140
    Italian clubs, **9:**80
    jazz clubs, **9:**143
    Pacific Islanders groups, **9:**86
  Barbados, Landship Society, **2:**819
  Belgium, amateur accordionist clubs, **8:**531
  Brazil
    afoxé, **2:**351–52
    Bahia black associations, **2:**347
    blocos afro, **2:**351, 352–54
    carnival clubs, **2:**336–37
    frevo clubs, **2:**336
    irmandades, **2:**302–3
    samba schools, **2:**61, 309, 313–16, 350–51
    ternos, **2:**312–13, 319
  Brittany, cultural, **8:**562–63
  Canada
    African dance groups, **3:**224
    Chinese dance groups, **3:**224, 1096
    choral, **3:**144
    educators, **3:**276
    histories of, **3:**28
    immigrant communities, **3:**822–23

for music research, **3:**29–31
philharmonic societies, **3:**1090
senior citizens' clubs, **3:**1172
for steel guitar, **3:**1049
women's musical clubs, **3:**93, 1090, 1116, 1150, 1182, 1209–10, 1227
Caribbean, immigrant clubs, **2:**49, 84, 87–88, 89
Central America
  immigrant clubs, **2:**49, 84, 87–88, 89
  occupational, **2:**58–59, 61
Chile
  cabildos, **2:**366
  confraternidades, **2:**362, 364
  hermandades, **2:**362
  tango clubs, **2:**371
China
  for Cantonese music, **7:**220, 221
  dongjing, **7:**416, 419, 421, 445, 512–13
  for Han traditional music, **7:**141
  minority cultures, **7:**414
  music clubs, **7:**380–81
  nanguan clubs, **7:**209
  for national music improvement, **7:**228–29
  opera clubs, **7:**396
  performers' union, **7:**304
  twentieth-century music societies, **7:**376–77
  village ritual association, **7:**315–18
  yinyue hui, **7:**203
Chinese cultural groups, **3:**11, 949, 958–59, 961, 1261, 1262–63, 1265–66
Chinese Lion Dance organizations, **3:**955
Cirebon, Yayasan Sunyaragi, **4:**698
Coker Grand Concerts, **1:**402
Colombia
  art music presenters, **2:**397
  cabildos, **2:**400, 405
Corsica
  religious brotherhoods, **8:**11
  Roman Catholic lay brotherhoods, **8:**574
Costa Rica, **2:**689, 703
  cofradía de Nuestra Señora de los Angeles, **2:**688
  cofradías, **2:**681, 704
Croatian-Americans, **3:**919, 923
Cuba, **3:**785
  Abakuá secret society, **2:**826
  Arará secret society, **2:**826
  Congo secret societies, **2:**825
  Mina, Manding, and Gange *cabildos,* **2:**826–27
  mutual-aid societies, **2:**823
Czechoslovakia, Composers' Union, **8:**731
Czech Republic, **8:**731
  literátska bratrstva, **8:**726
Dan people, **1:**466
Denmark, for folk music and dance, **8:**461
Dominican Republic
  Brotherhood of St. John the Baptist, **2:**855
  Brotherhood of the Holy Spirit, **2:**855
  cofradía, **2:**852
  gagá, **2:**851, 852, 853, 855, 859, 862
  rará, **2:**795
  social-cultural-sports clubs, **2:**859
East Africa, competitive bands, **1:**602–3, 643
Egypt, Sufi *ṭuruq,* **6:**625–27

societies and organizations (*continued*)
El Salvador, *cofradías*, **2:**709, 711, 713
Estonian-Americans, **3:**878
Europe
  choral societies, **8:**81, 147
  establishment of, **8:**82
  folk clubs, **8:**152–54
  musicians' guilds, **8:**199
  national institutions for traditional music,
    8:123–24
  socialist youth organizations, **8:**217
  trade unions, **8:**185
Ewe people, **1:**462
Faroe Islands, **8:**472
Finland, **8:**482–83
  ELMU, **8:**217
Finnish-Americans, **3:**872–73, 1196
France
  cultural, **8:**549
  fraternities, **8:**548
German Democratic Republic, **8:**661–62
German *Liederkranz* and *Saengerbund* groups,
    3:10, 528, 556, 885–86, 909
Germany
  Hitler Youth, **8:**656, 660
  musicians' guilds, **8:**146, 651–52, 653
  neo-Nazi groups, **8:**656
  Rom and Sinti Union, **8:**289
  Swing-Jugend, **8:**661
  Wandervogel, **8:**655–56
  youth organizations, **8:**661
Ghana, **1:**31, 35
  asafo companies, **10:**32–36
  habčbč, **1:**392–93, 394, 396–98
Great Britain, Musicians' Union, **8:**233
Greece, **8:**1017–18
  philharmonic societies, **8:**1014
Greek-Americans, **3:**529, 929, 1199
Grenada, chamber music, **2:**866
Guadeloupe, **2:**880
  quadrille and *lèwòz* societies, **2:**878–79
Haiti
  konbit (also *sosyete kongo*), **2:**885
  Maroon societies, **2:**882
  rará, **2:**795, 862
Hawai'i
  Chinese associations, **9:**70–71, 96–97
  dance clubs, **9:**109
  glee clubs, **9:**919
  halau, **3:**207, 209, 219
  Hawaiian Civic Clubs, **9:**919
  music clubs, **9:**162–66
Hong Kong, amateur clubs, **7:**431, 433,
    434
Hungarian-Americans, **3:**908, 1250
Hungary, Young Communists' League, **8:**746
Iceland, for *rímur* and *tvísöngur*, **8:**401, 407
Indian groups, **4:**521
Indian rights societies, **3:**443
India, South
  for raga-based song genres, **5:**105
  sabhā, **5:**106, 212, 270
Indonesia
  Indonesian Society for the Performing Arts,
    4:733
  Society for Balinese Studies, **4:**733

Ireland, **8:**391
  harp, **8:**393
  for traditional music, **8:**386
Italian-Americans, **3:**860, 862
Japan
  composers' groups, **7:**732, 736–37
  foundations, **7:**761
  hozon kai, **7:**773–74
  komusô, **7:**755–56, 758–59
  musicological, **7:**592, 729
  preservation societies, **7:**46–47, 601, 603,
    605
  todô syoku yasiki (blind musicians' guild),
    7:687–88, 691, 696, 712, 716,
    755–56, 757–58
Japanese *fukuinkai*, **3:**969
Japanese Utai societies, **3:**1084
Java, Pananta Dibya, **4:**677
Jewish Americans, **3:**933, 939
Kazakhstan, guilds of epic reciters, **6:**953
Kenya, **1:**629
Kiribati, Tarawa, **9:**759
Korea, **7:**991
  chaein ch'ŏng, **7:**985
  for *ch'anggŭk*, **7:**968–69
  composers' groups, **7:**972
  kwanggyo, **7:**985
  musicological, **7:**853
  for *p'ansori*, **7:**969
  for *samullori*, **7:**965
  shinch'ŏng, **7:**985
  tadong, **7:**985
Korean-Americans, **3:**976–77
Kru people, **1:**374
Kuna culture, *gammu burui* dancers, **2:**645,
    647
Latvia, singing societies, **8:**504
Lombok, **4:**766
Macedonia, choral, **8:**981
Mahodi Kčŋpiŋ, **1:**345
Malaysia, classical-music, **4:**440
Manihiki, **9:**905
Marshall Islands, **9:**749
Mexican-American gangs, **3:**740, 742
Montenegro, *guslar* groups, **8:**961
Native American powwow and social dance
    clubs, **3:**366–67
Nepal, Guruñg Rodi association, **5:**704–5
Nicaragua, **2:**766
Nigeria, **1:**236
  Egbe Ife, **1:**403
  Enugu, **1:**239–41
North Africa
  black brotherhoods, **6:**435, 437
  Sufi brotherhoods, **6:**434, 436, 437, 438–39
Norway
  for folk traditions, **8:**426–27
  Lom Juniorlag, **8:**151
Norwegian-American, **3:**866
Pakistan, theater groups, **5:**487
Panama, *cofradías*, **2:**783
Papua New Guinea, Torchbearers, **9:**495
Paraguay, *pasioneros* (also *estacioneros*), **2:**457–58
Peru, *cofradías*, **2:**491, 493
Philippines, **4:**858, 860, 861, 869, 870, 875
Plains Indian groups, **3:**444, 445–46, 480

Polish-Americans, **3:**891
Prince Edward Island, fiddle associations,
    3:1071
Québec, musical societies, **3:**1150, 1151–52
Renaissance, musicians' guilds, **8:**75
Romania, cultural houses, **8:**883
Ryûkyû Islands, for traditional performances,
    7:796
St. Lucia, La Rose and La Marguerite, **2:**946
Sāmoa, village associations, **9:**235
Sardinia
  gruppo folk, **8:**626
  religious brotherhoods, **8:**11, 627
Saudi Arabia, *ṭār* bands, **6:**653
Scandinavia, Kontaktnäten, **8:**216
Scotland, Gaelic music, **8:**371
Serbia
  pevačka društva, **8:**948
  state-sponsored, **8:**949
Serbian-Americans, **3:**919, 923
Silla kingdom, *hwarang*, **7:**930, 941
Singapore
  Chinese, **4:**518
  Malay, **4:**518, 519, 520–22
Slovak-Americans, **3:**899, 900
Slovakia, **8:**731
South Africa, **1:**765
South America
  immigrant clubs, **2:**49, 84, 87–88, 89
  occupational, **2:**58–59, 61
South Asian groups, **3:**981
Sunda, Dharma Wanita, **4:**712
Sweden
  choral societies, **8:**444
  fiddlers' societies, **8:**9
Switzerland, choral societies, **8:**691–92
Tahiti, Chinese associations, **9:**868
Taiwan
  beiguan clubs, **7:**425
  nanguan clubs, **7:**425
  quguan clubs, **7:**424
Tanzania, **1:**646
Tarahumara culture
  Holy Week, **2:**586–87
  matachines, **2:**586
Thailand, *sizhu* clubs, **4:**71, 73
Tibet, *nangma*, **7:**475
Tunisia
  Bū Saʻdiyya brotherhood, **6:**435
  music clubs, **6:**330
Turkey
  amateur folklore clubs, **6:**79, 784, 815–16
  musicians' guilds, **6:**115–16
Turkish-Americans, **3:**1030
United States
  balalaika, **3:**58
  bluegrass clubs, **3:**163
  chamber music, **3:**537–38
  contra dance clubs, **3:**213, 233–34
  for dance scholarship, **3:**221
  for dancing, **3:**214, 225
  educators, **3:**276
  histories of, **3:**28
  immigrant communities, **3:**822–23
  local groups, **3:**144, 556
  for music research, **3:**29–31

performing rights, **3:**260–63, 706
polka clubs, **3:**896
professional societies, **3:**237
singing societies, **3:**275, 533, 535–36, 556,
867, 870–71; German, **3:**10, 528, 556,
885–86, 909; Hungarian, **3:**530, 909
for steel guitar, **3:**1049
tamburitza organizations, **3:**921
Uruguay, **2:**522
Black Lubolos, **2:**515
criollas, **2:**516
Vanuatu, secret societies, **9:**694–95
Venezuela, *Los diablos danzantes de Yare*, **2:**537
Vietnam, Chinese communities, **4:**70
Wales, **8:**353–54
women's musical club movement, **3:**1116, 1209
women's professional groups, **3:**91
Zionist Blau-Weiss youth group, **8:**262
societies, secret (Africa), **1:**132, 458, 672
Angola, **1:**673
distribution of, **1:**309, 311
jenge, **1:**658–59
komo, **1:**445
masks in, **1:**119
Ogboni, **1:**459
Poro, **1:**5, 125, 129, 140, 328–29, 337, 454,
465, 467
Sande, **1:**5, 125, 126, 129, 140, 328–29, 465,
467; **10:**55
Sukuma people, **1:**637
tuwema, **1:**676
wood trumpets in, **1:**667
Society for Dance History Scholars, **3:**221
Society for the Dissemination of National Music
(Greece), **8:**1018, 1025
Society for Ethnomusicology, **1:**51, 65; **2:**16;
10:23, 24, 60, 63, 85, 134
Society for the Fixing and Classification of
Turkish Music, **6:**785
Society of Friends of Music (Vienna), **8:**922
Society for Improving National Music (China),
7:229, 232
Society of Indian Record Collectors, **5:**57
Society for Jewish Folk Music, **6:**1025; **8:**772
Society for Research in Asiatic Music, **7:**729
Society of Romanian Composers, **8:**885
Society for the Traditional Instruments of Wales,
8:355–56
Society Islands, **9:**865, 867–79. *See also* Bora
Bora; French Polynesia; Huahine;
Mai'ao; Manuae; Maupiha'a; Maupiti;
Mehetia; Mo'orea; Motu One;
Ra'iatea; Taha'a; Tahiti; Tetiaroa; Tupai
alcohol use in, **9:**177–78
American expeditions to, **9:**24
'arioi troupes, **9:**229, 769, 875
Christianity in, **9:**208–9
cultural contacts with Hawai'i, **9:**914
cultural contacts with Tuamotus, **9:**882
French exploration of, **9:**17
geography of, **9:**867
immigrants to Australia, **9:**85
instruments
drums, **9:**384–85
musical bows, **9:**386
struck tins, **9:**379

music and dance of, **9:**969, 973, 980
hīmene, **9:**37–38, 41, 187, 209
hīmene tārava, **9:**308
outsiders' influence in, **9:**5
population of, **9:**867
research on, **9:**869
sound recordings from, **9:**1001–2
string figures in, **9:**253
Soda Stereo, **2:**268
Söderman, August, **8:**444
Soebroto, Hardjo, **4:**666
Soeda Azenbô, **7:**740
Soedarsono, **9:**486
Sofia National Philharmonia, **8:**905
Soga people
budongo tuning, **1:**299–300
lyres of, **1:**304, 600
music of, **1:**312
Soga, Tiyo, **1:**218, 763
Sogak wŏnbo (collection), **7:**856
Sogdiana, **6:**936, 965
Sogdian people, **7:**14, 22
Soh Daiko (musical group), **3:**973
Sohn Ah Sun (Son Asŏn), **7:**972
Söhnen, Renate, **5:**800
"Sohni Dharti," **5:**746
Sojo, Juan Pablo, **2:**524
Sojo y Peñaranda, Diego de, **2:**631
Sokalaŭ-Vojuš, Siaržuk, **8:**801
Sokalsky, Piotr, **8:**783
Šokci people, **8:**931
Sokol Choir (Winnipeg), **3:**1090, 1250
Sokoli, Ramadan, **8:**1003, 1004
Sokoloff, Nikolai, **3:**297
Sokolov, Ilya, **8:**776
Sŏl Chaech'ŏn, **7:**996
Sŏkpukchip (collection), **7:**925
Sôkyoku syû (anthology), **7:**778
Solari, Jean, **8:**531
"Sold Off to Georgy," **3:**601
"Soldier's Joy," **3:**409
Sole, Leonardo, **8:**622, 632
Solek, Walt, **3:**895
Solèy Leve (Rising Sun), **3:**805–6
Solheim, W. G., II, **4:**42
Soli people, **1:**671
Solís, Javier, **3:**739, 748
Solís, José, **4:**862
Solís, Juan, **4:**862
Solís, Rosalio, **4:**862
Solís, Simplicio, **4:**862, 865, 868
Solís, Urbano, **4:**862
Solo court (Surakarta), **4:**633, 653, 676, 683
Solomon, king of Israel, **6:**1047
Solomon Islands, **9:**598, 630–70, 754. *See also*
Anuta; Banika; Bellona; Choiseul
Island; Guadalcanal; Karumulun; Loun
Island; Luangiua; Magsaiai Island;
Malaita; Mane; Maruloun; Namutin;
New Georgia; North Solomons
Province *under* Papua New Guinea;
Pileni; Rennell; Russell Islands; San
Jorge Island; Santa Cruz Islands; Santa
Isabel Island; Savo Island; Shortland
Islands; Sikaiana; Taumako; Tikopia;
specific peoples

American expeditions to, **9:**24
Americans in, **9:**26
archives and museums, **9:**962–64
Central Province, **9:**662–64
commemorative songs, **9:**33
composition in, **9:**354
Europeans in, **9:**147
films on, **9:**982, 1007, 1014–15
geography of, **9:**630
Guadalcanal Province, **9:**664–66
I-Kiribati in, **9:**760, 762, 764
immigrants to Australia, **9:**84, 85
instruments
flutes, **9:**371
musical bows, **9:**386
panpipes, **9:**401
Isabel Province, **9:**657–62
music and dance of, **9:**659
Japanese in, **9:**30–31
Malaita Province, **9:**666–70
map of, **9:**631
melody, transcription of, **9:**288
music and dance of, **9:**48, 977, 981
music theory in, **9:**393
outsiders' influence in, **9:**5
popular music, **9:**155–58
guitar songs, **9:**147, 156–57
kela boru genre, **9:**156
research on, **9:**212, 963, 976
sound recordings from, **9:**985, 992–93
string figures in, **9:**267, *268*, 656, 661
theater in, **9:**233
Western Province, **9:**654–57
World War II in, **9:**157
yodeling in, **9:**297
Solomon Islands Broadcasting Corporation,
9:853, 963
Solomon Islands Defense Force, **9:**26, *27*
Solomona, Mata'utia Pene, **9:**206
Solor, **4:**786, 796
Solovera, Clara, **2:**370–71
Solovev-Sedoi, Vasily, **8:**779
Solvyns, François Baltazard, **5:**300–301
Soma/Kesari dynasty, **5:**731
Somā'ī, Ḥabīb, **6:**861
Somali people, **1:**604–5, 610
in Canada, **3:**1078, 1213
Somalia. *See also* East Africa; *specific peoples*
instruments of, **1:**611, 619
music and poetry of, **1:**125, 610–21
politics and poetry, **1:**7
research in, **1:**610–11
zār cult, **1:**604
Somanatha, **5:**46, 48
Somantri, Cece, **4:**705
Somare, Michael, **9:**25, 27
Somchai Thayarnyong, **4:**261
"Some of These Days" (Brooks), **3:**1212
Somers, Harry, **3:**1058, 1184
Somesvara III, king of Kalyani, **5:**24, 314
Something Wild (film), **3:**204
Sometimes (Wilson), **3:**611
"Somewhere Out There" (Ingram and Ronstadt),
3:713
Somoza family, **2:**758, 763
Somsak Ketukaenchan, **4:**26

Somtow Sucharitkul, **4**:128
Sŏn (Kim), **7**:959
son, **1**:385, 416, 424; **2**:101, 102, 796; **3**:13,
    728, 788, 790, 791–93, 798; **10**:78
  in Argentina, **2**:265
  changüí, **2**:829, 830
  in Colombia, **2**:409, 410
  in Cuba, **2**:796, 827, 829–30, 835
  in Dominican Republic, **2**:860, 862
  in El Salvador, **2**:711, 718
  in Guatemala, **2**:726, 728, 735
  in Honduras, **2**:744
  Mexican, **3**:723, 724, 737, 744
  in Mexico, **2**:603, 605–13, 619
  in Nicaragua, **2**:749, 760, 761, 762, 763
  in Peru, **2**:487
  in Puerto Rico, **2**:940
  regional genres of, **2**:608–13
  son montuno, **2**:830, 834, 836, 940
Son T'aeryong, **7**:853, 854
sonata
  Baroque, **8**:78
  Classical and Romantic, **8**:82
  galant style, **8**:79
Sonatha, Betharia, **4**:108
Sondheim, Stephen, **3**:197, 198, 545
Sondhi, Mr., **5**:487
Soneros de Borojols, **2**:860
Sonezaki Shinzyû (Chikamatsu), **7**:663, 668–69
song. *See* ballads; carols and caroling; chant;
    devotional songs and singing; hymns;
    laments; love songs; lullabies;
    narratives; popular music; popular
    songs; praise songs, singing, and
    poetry; psalmody; recitation; serenades;
    shanties; singing; songs, texts; vocal
    music; work music; *specific international
    genres such as balada, corridos*
Song Bang-song, **7**:853, 854, 855, 990
Sŏng Ch'angsun, **7**:900
Song Daneng, **7**:156
song duels. *See* competitions
Song dynasty
  erhu in, **7**:176
  instruments in, **7**:112, 113
  music in, **7**:407
  music theory in, **7**:119
  notation from, **7**:203
  Peking opera in, **7**:60
  politics in, **7**:27, 31
  yayue in, **7**:861–64
"Song of Eternal Posterity" (Manchu song), **7**:518
Song of the Heart. See Awlād al-dhawat (Egyptian
    film)
Song Hŭngnok, **7**:898, 906, 986
Sŏng Hyŏn, **7**:855, 856, 983
Song of India (Rimsky-Korsakov), **3**:953
"Song of the Islands" (King), **3**:1050
Song of the Islands (film), **3**:1049
Sŏng Kŭmyŏn, **7**:915, 916
Sŏng Kyŏngnin, **7**:856, 989, 990
Song Man'gap, **7**:893, 894, 899, 904, 906, 909,
    968, 986, 989
Song Manjae, **7**:899, 905
"Song of the Outdoors" (Xibe folk song), **7**:518
Song Sŏkha, **7**:856

Sŏng Uhyang, **7**:900
Song Uryong, **7**:899
Song Xiguang, **7**:231
Sŏnggwangbok (Kim), **7**:953
Songgwang Temple (Korea), **7**:959
Songhai empire, **1**:4, 313, 447, 452, 459
Songhai people
  history of, **1**:447
  influence on Bariba people, **1**:452
  instruments of, **1**:448–49
  music of, **1**:447, 450–51, 588
Sŏngho sasŏl (Yi), **7**:855
Sŏngjong, Chosŏn king, **7**:982
Sŏngjong, Koryŏ king, **7**:984
Sŏngju p'uri (SamulNori), **7**:966
Sŏngnyu chip (Hwang), **7**:956
Songprints (Vander), **3**:511–12
songs. *See* ballads; carols and caroling; chant;
    devotional songs and singing; hymns;
    laments; love songs; lullabies;
    narratives; popular music; popular
    songs; praise songs, singing, and
    poetry; psalmody; recitation; serenades;
    shanties; singing; songs, texts; vocal
    music; work music; *specific international
    genres such as balada, corridos*
Songs of the Doukhobors (Peacock), **3**:1270
Songs of the Druzes (Saarisalo), **6**:580
Songs of Earth, Water, Fire, and Sky, **3**:526
Songs of Hawaii (King), **9**:919, 922
Songs of Madness (Black List Workshop), **7**:358
Songs of the Newfoundland Outports (Creighton),
    3:292
Songs of the Pacific Northwest (Thomas), **3**:1257
songs, texts. *See also* poetry
  Abelam people, *minja*, **9**:550
  Abkhazian people, **8**:853
  Adighian people, historical songs, **8**:855
  Afghanistan, **5**:813, 819, 823–24, 827
    falak, **5**:828
    landay, **5**:506
    Pashtun songs, **5**:836–40
  Africa
    circumcision, **1**:675–76
    narratives, **1**:107–8, 124, 133, 135
    social criticism in, **1**:287
    temporal organization in, **1**:137
    types of, **1**:104–5
  African-American, **3**:1211–12
  aguinaldo, **3**:727
  Albania, **8**:987–88, 1000
  Albanian, **3**:928
  Andalusian, **6**:370
  Andhra Pradesh, narratives, **5**:896–99
  Anglo-American ballads, **3**:154, 155–57,
    833–34, 1140–43
  Antigua and Barbuda, calypso, **2**:800
  Anuta, **9**:336
    puatanga, **9**:860
    tungaunu, **9**:857–58
  àpàlà genre, **1**:476–77
  arabesk, **6**:255, 257–58, 259, 776
  Arabian peninsula
    improvisation of, **6**:355
    pearl-diving songs, **6**:651
    women's songs, **6**:700

Arctic, **3**:378
Argentina
  cuarteto, **2**:273
  música tropical, **2**:266
  tangos, **2**:263, 264
Armenia, *ashugh* formulas, **6**:735
Australia
  Aboriginal rock, **9**:145–46, 443–46
  Central, **9**:435–36
  clansongs, **9**:422
  Greek-Australian, **9**:74–75
  Italian-Australian, **9**:81
  Kimberleys *nurlu*, **9**:432
  Southeastern Aboriginal peoples,
    9:440–41
  wangga, **9**:426
  Yolngu newsong verse, **9**:356–57
Austral Islands
  hīmene tārava, **9**:882
  'ūtē, **9**:880–81
Azerbaijan
  aşıq havası (*qoşma*), **6**:851–52
  muğam, **6**:928
baha festival songs, **5**:415
Bahamas
  goombay, **2**:806
  junkafunk, **2**:808
  rhyming spiritual, **2**:805
ballads, women's issues in, **8**:195
Balochistan, *shēr*, **5**:776
Baluan, lullabies, **9**:258
Barbados, calypso, **2**:820–21
Basque region, improvised, **8**:311–14
Belarus, rock music, **8**:801–3
Belize, popular brukdown, **2**:678
Bellona, laments, **9**:325
Bengal, patriotic songs, **5**:854
Berber popular music, **6**:275
bhajan, **5**:255, 267, 534
bhangra, **5**:574–75
bluegrass, **3**:168
blues, **3**:104, 112, 579, 582
Bolivia, **2**:294
  Quechua, **2**:296
Bosnia-Hercegovina, **8**:963
bossa nova, **2**:108–9
Brazil
  bendito, **2**:329
  desafio, **2**:326
  forró, **2**:332
  fricote, **2**:354
  jongo, **2**:307
  samba de viola, **2**:349
Brittany, **8**:561
Bulgaria, **8**:898–99, 900
  Rom people, **8**:283
Burmese, **4**:383–84, 395
California Native American music, **3**:414, 416,
    417
Canada, **3**:1193
Cantonese opera, **3**:1264
carols, **8**:133
Carriacou, *parang*, **2**:871
Central Asia, **6**:900
  maqām, **6**:914
  Ramadan songs, **6**:941, 951

Chile
   contrapuntos, **2**:366
   cueca, **2**:369–70
   for Virgin Mary festivities, **2**:362–63
China
   folk songs, **7**:153–54
   nanyin, **7**:270–71
   Suzhou tanci, **7**:263
   yue'ou, **7**:268–69
Chopi people, **1**:710
chutney, **5**:601
Chuuk, love songs, **9**:736
Coast Salish spirit dancing songs, **3**:397
Colombia
   bambuco, **2**:388
   danza, **2**:393
   guabina veleña, **2**:391
   pasillo lento, **2**:392
   rajaleña, **2**:390
   sanjuanero, **2**:389
   vals, **2**:393
corridos, **3**:757
Corsica, **8**:569
   for lullabies, **8**:567
   puesia, **8**:568
Costa Rica
   bomba, **2**:696–97
   calypso, **2**:692
country music, **3**:79, 81
Croatia, epics, **8**:927
Cuba, *guajira*, **2**:832
Cypriot emigrants, **8**:1032
Cyprus, **8**:1032
Czech Republic, **8**:719, 721
dādrā, **5**:183
dangdut, **4**:105
dhrupad, **5**:163, 164
Dominican Republic, merengue, **2**:796
Dominica, wood-sawing song, **2**:843
Doukhobor, **3**:1268, 1270
East Indian *tan*-singing, **3**:815
Ecuador
   bomba, **2**:430
   Passion song, **2**:420
   sanjuanito, **2**:430–31
Egypt, *aghāni shabābīyya*, **6**:555
El Salvador, *baile de cacería*, **2**:710
England, **8**:329
   satirical ballads, **8**:333
Estonia, **8**:491
Europe, collections of, **8**:7, 16–18
Fanti people, **10**:34–35, 38
Fiji, **9**:781
   on kava, **9**:176
   meke, **9**:775, 777–79
   vakawelegone, **9**:263–65
Finland, **8**:488
   runo, **8**:476–77
Finnish labor songs, **3**:873
Finnish music, **3**:875
First Nations popular songs, **3**:73
fúji, **1**:485–86
Futuna
   kupu, **9**:815
   tākofe, **9**:815
gender in, **3**:109, 110, 111

German polkas, **3**:891
German secular songs, **3**:888
Germany Democratic Republic, **8**:662
Ghana, *agbadza*, **1**:391
ghazal, **5**:766
Goa
   dhalo, **5**:738
   dulpod, **5**:738
   mandó, **5**:739
   mussoll songs, **5**:740
Great Basin Bear Dance songs, **3**:424
Great Basin Indian groups, **3**:426
Greece, **8**:1008, 1024
   mainland *vs.* island subjects, **8**:1009
   rebetika, **8**:1019, 1020
Greek music, ancient, **8**:47
Grenada, calypso, **2**:867
Guadeloupe
   kantikamò, **2**:876
   léwòz, **2**:875
   for work songs, **2**:876
Guam, *chamorrita*, **9**:745
Gujarat
   bhajan, **5**:630, 632
   chand, **5**:636–37
   duho, **5**:636
   garbo, **5**:626–27
   soratho, **5**:636
Hausa, satirical, **1**:527–28
Hawai'i
   Jawaiian genre, **9**:166
   "*Kaulana nā Pua*," **9**:133
   mele hula 'āla'apapa, **9**:917
   mele inoa, **9**:920–21
   protest songs, **9**:220–21
heavy metal, **3**:112, 114, 357, 358
Himachal Pradesh, *suhāg*, **5**:415
Hindustani music, Ganesh *paran*, **5**:120
Hmong people, **3**:1003; **4**:557–59
Honduras, mestizo dance-music, **2**:744
Hungarian emigrant songs, **3**:909
Hungary, Vlach Roma, **8**:275
Iceland
   rímur, **8**:401–2
   of skalds, **8**:146
ideology in, **8**:185, 187
inanga music, **1**:166–67, 168
India, *ākṣiptikā*, **5**:35
Indonesia
   kroncong, **4**:103
   pop Indonesia, **4**:106
   pop music, **4**:108–9
Ireland, **8**:378
   of bards, **8**:146
   early published, **8**:385–86
   lays, **8**:379
   lyric songs and ballads, **8**:379
   Traveller songs, **8**:294–95
Irian Jaya
   Mairasi songs, **9**:589
   ritual songs, **9**:583
   song topics, **9**:580
Iroquois Social Dance songs, **3**:464
Israel
   ideology in, **6**:1073
   muzika mizrahit, **6**:261
   shirei erets Yisrael, **6**:1019, 1071, 1072

Italian, **3**:860
Italy, **8**:620–21
   ballads, **8**:606
Jahai people, *pano'* ceremony, **4**:571
Jamaica
   for junkunnu, **2**:907
   mento, **2**:912
   metaphor in, **2**:905
   popular music, **2**:912
Japan
   min'yô, **7**:603
   sôsi enka, **7**:739–40
   syômyô, **7**:613–14
   tikuzen biwa ballads, **7**:649–50
   waka, **7**:607
Java, *wangsalan*, **4**:666
Jewish people, **8**:252, 254–57
   ethnic differences, **8**:263
   pizmon, **3**:943
jùjú, **1**:479, 480–82
Kapingamarangi, **9**:328
   langa, **9**:837
Karnataka
   gīgī pada, **5**:871
   kabita songs, **5**:883
   regional genres, **5**:867
Kashmir
   chakri, **5**:683
   Lol-lyric, **5**:689
   rūf, **5**:684
   ṣūfyāna mūsīqī, **5**:687, 695
Kazakhstan, **6**:950
Kenyah people, of *lekupa*, **4**:826
Kerala, Mappila, **5**:947
Khmer people, *yike* songs, **4**:201
khyāl, **5**:173
Kiribati, epigrammatic, **9**:331–32
kīrtana, **5**:266
Korea
   anthologies, **7**:855–56
   folk songs, **7**:881, 885
   kagok, **7**:921–24
   kasa, **7**:927–28
   p'ansori, **7**:900–901
   sijo, **7**:925–26
kriti, **5**:222, 224, 226, 228–29, 230, 268–69
Kuna culture, improvisation of, **2**:639
Kwakiutl Winter Ceremony songs, **3**:401
Lacandón Maya, **2**:656
Lebanon, popular songs, **6**:554
Lithuania, **8**:509–10, 511
Lithuanian emigrant ballads, **3**:875
Luvale *mukanda*, **1**:724
Macedonia, **8**:974
Maharashtra, Bahurūpi songs, **5**:728
Makah potlatch songs, **3**:399
Malaysia, *pantun*, **4**:436
Malta
   bormliza, **8**:637
   spirtu pront, **8**:636
Mangareva, **9**:887
Manihiki, *hīmene māpū*, **9**:908
Māori people, **9**:932, 942–43
   haka, **9**:948–51
   laments, **9**:941
   songs, **9**:933

songs, texts (*continued*)
  Mapuche culture, *kantún*, **2:**236
  Maroon cultures, *sêkêti*, **2:**506
  Marquesas Islands
    ha'anaunau, **9:**891
    putu, **9:**893
  Marshall Islands, **9:**749–50
    dance-songs, **9:**753
    roro, **9:**751
  Maya culture, from *Popol Vuh*, **2:**722, 732
  Mexico
    aguinaldo, **2:**615–16
    corrido, **2:**616–17
    cumulative stories, **2:**617
    las posadas, **2:**614–15
    piñata melodies, **2:**615
    son, **2:**607
  Middle Eastern collections, **6:**20–21, 363, 369–71
  minstrel songs, **3:**191–92
  Mithila, *prātī*, **5:**678
  Mixtec culture, *katikubi*, **2:**567
  Mongol people, **7:**1006, 1007
  Montenegro, *guslar* creations, **8:**961
  Montserrat, **2:**923
  Morocco, *malḥūn*, **6:**497
  Native American, **3:**6, 368–69, 526
    Ghost Dance songs, **3:**421–22, 426, 487
    peyote songs, **3:**488
  nature symbols in, **8:**133
  Nauru
    children's songs, **9:**261, 262
    national anthem, **9:**262
  Nepal, **5:**705
  New Caledonia
    ayoiicada, **9:**677–78
    dance-songs, **9:**676
    lullabies, **9:**673
  Nicaragua
    corrido, **2:**758–59
    son nica, **2:**764
  North Caucasia, **8:**851
  Northeast Indian songs, **3:**463
  Northwest Coast types, **3:**401
  Norway
    of skalds, **8:**146
    stev and *nystev*, **8:**413
  Norwegian emigrant ballads, **3:**867
  Ntwumuru people, **1:**109
  nubat, **1:**535
  Nubian, **6:**643
  Nyanga puberty rites, **1:**110–11
  Oceania, war-era songs, **9:**29–32
  Orang Asli peoples, **4:**576
  Ottoman empire, Rom strophic songs, **8:**284
  Pakistan, northern, **5:**794
  pālā kīrtan, **5:**253
  Palau, **9:**725
  Palestinian *intifāḍa*, **6:**635–36, 637–40
  Panama
    calypso, **2:**773
    congos, **2:**779
    décima, **2:**780
  Papua New Guinea, **9:**478–79
    Anêm laments, **9:**616
    Baluan *kolorai*, **9:**603

Banoni *tanisi*, **9:**646
Banoni *tsigul* and *roori*, **9:**645
Banoni *wakekena*, **9:**646
Binandere *guru*, **9:**359–60
Buang poetry, **9:**566
composition of, **9:**512
Eastern Highlands courtship songs, **9:**528
Eastern Highlands *ígárú-aimma*, **9:**527
Eipo *dit*, **9:**593–94
Eipo *layelayana*, **9:**594
Eipo *mot*, **9:**592
Foi *sorohabora*, **9:**246–47
guitar songs, **9:**151–52
Highlands region, **9:**513–14
Huli people, **9:**542
Huli *pīlipè*, **9:**539
Iatmul mythological suites, **9:**341–42
Irumu songs, **9:**568–70
Kaulong people, **9:**618
Kuman *kaungo*, **9:**524–25
Managalasi *itiuri*, **9:**503
Managalasi songs, **9:**505
Melpa *amb kenan*, **9:**516–18
Melpa *ka*, **9:**520–21
Melpa *kang rom*, **9:**521–22
Melpa *mörl*, **9:**518–19
Melpa recreational songs, **9:**521
Melpa *werl*, **9:**520
Nagovisi *ko:ma*, **9:**648
Nissan *bot*, **9:**635
Nissan guitar songs, **9:**639
Nissan *kirkiring*, **9:**638
Nissan *sisiak*, **9:**639
Nissan *tigul*, **9:**634
Nissan *warmong*, **9:**637
Serieng text "*Ngainba*," **9:**564–65
Teop *siguru*, **9:**644
Paraguay, *guaránia*, **2:**460
parlor music, **3:**183
Peru
  festejo, **2:**496
  marinera, **2:**499
Philippines
  awit, **4:**853
  corrido, **4:**853
  huluna, **4:**849
Plains Indians, **3:**445, 449, 483
Pohnpei, *koulin sampah*, **9:**740
Poland, Holocaust songs, **8:**276
Polish wedding laments, **3:**892
political, **3:**305–10, 317
polka, **3:**894
popular songs, **3:**197, 547, 548
Portugal, **8:**581
  fado, **8:**583
  romances, **8:**578
prabandha, **5:**164
praise songs, **1:**489–91, 494–95, 499, 501–3, 505, 507, 510
Pukapuka
  chants, **9:**912
  tila chants, **9:**911
Punjab (India)
  for *bhangra*, **5:**651
  giddhā, **5:**654
punk, **3:**357; **8:**215, 218

punto guajiro, **3:**728
Purépecha culture, *pirekua*, **2:**580–81
qawwali, **5:**753
Q'ero culture, **2:**226, 229–30
  floral song, **2:**228
quan họ, **4:**459
research on, **3:**824–25
rhythm and blues, **3:**673
rock, **3:**348, 552; **8:**217, 219–20
Romania
  children's songs, **8:**869
  doina, **8:**873
Roti, *bini*, **4:**799
Rotuma, recitations, **9:**820
Russia
  kupalskie pesni, **8:**760
  lyric songs, **8:**765
Russian *chastushka*, **3:**915
Russian Old Believers, **3:**917
Ryûkyû Islands, **7:**791
Saami people
  joiks, **8:**299–300, 307, 428, 487
  lev'dd songs, **8:**486
St. Lucia
  jwé, **2:**943–44
  koutoumba, **2:**948–49
salsa, **3:**788
Sāmoa, **9:**796, 797
  hymns, **9:**205
  on kava, **9:**175
  metaphor in, **9:**202
  nuptial cheers, **9:**342–43, 803
  palo, **9:**804–5
  political songs, **9:**215–19
  tagi, **9:**799–801
ṣanʿā, **6:**458
Sardinia, **8:**630
  religious, **8:**628
Scotland
  lays, **8:**361–62
  Traveller songs, **8:**296
  verbal formulas, **8:**361
  waulking songs, **8:**361–62
Shaker music, **3:**135
Sikaiana, **9:**335
  narratives, **9:**338
  puina texts, **9:**844–45
  tani, **9:**847
Slovakia, **8:**719
Slovak wedding songs, **3:**900
Slovenia, **8:**914
smaut, **4:**206–7
Solomon Islands
  'Are'are love songs, **9:**667
  Bellonese game-playing songs, **9:**269
  Santa Cruz Islands, **9:**332, 334
South Asia
  educational, **5:**77–78
  genre classification and, **5:**107
  for light classical genres, **5:**179
  in nonclassical traditions, **5:**474, 475
  published, **5:**674
  regional songs on cassettes, **5:**551
  vernacular, **5:**20
Southeast Indian groups, **3:**467

Spain
  cante flamenco, **8:**598–99
  villancico, **8:**589
Subarctic songs, **3:**389
Sufi *dhikr* ceremony, **3:**1045
Sumu culture, women's song, **2:**751
Sunda, *kawih*, **4:**717
Surinam, *aleke*, **2:**509
  kawina, **2:**508
Suyá culture, **2:**146–47
Swedish emigrant ballads, **3:**870
Taino culture, *areito*, **2:**846–47
Taishan *muyu* genre, **3:**958
takəmba music, **1:**588
Takuu, *tuki*, **9:**840–41
Tamil-language
  sāhitya, **5:**912
  tēvāram, **5:**260–61
Tamil Nadu, **5:**916, 925
  Kota, **5:**905
  oppāri (also *pilākkaṇam*), **5:**907
tarānā, **5:**179
Temiar people, **4:**583–84
ṭhumrī, **5:**180, 181, 219
Tibetan culture, **5:**709, 715
  duolu, **7:**481
  guo xie, **7:**476
  King Ge-sar epic, **5:**712
Tikopia
  on betel, **9:**177
  mako, **9:**854
  tauāngutu, **9:**247–49
Tokelau
  epigrammatic, **9:**331
  fātele, **9:**825
  haumate, **9:**824–25
Tonga
  hiko, **9:**787
  history songs, **9:**201–2
  hiva kakala, **9:**366–67
  hymns, **9:**203–4
  tapu lea, **9:**788
  tauʻaʻalo, **9:**786–87
transcription methods, **10:**61
Trinidad and Tobago
  calypso, **2:**96, 796, 963
  kalenda, **2:**966
Trobriand Islands, on *kula* voyages, **9:**490
Tuamotu Islands, **9:**884
Tuareg people
  tende n-əmnas, **1:**585
  tesîwit, **1:**581–82
Tunisia, Jewish *piyuṭ*, **6:**529–31
Turkey
  for *âyîn*, **6:**109–10
  bardic songs, **6:**762–63
Tuva, **6:**984–85
Uighur *muqam*, **6:**995–1008
Uighur popular music, **7:**468–69
Ukraine, *dumy*, **8:**813–14
Uruguay
  canto popular uruguayo, **2:**520
  murga, **2:**517
  payada, **2:**512
Uttar Pradesh, **5:**661
  kajalī, **5:**669–70
  women's songs, **5:**661–62

'Uvea
  hiva, **9:**810–11
  kupu, **9:**809–10
Vanuatu
  John Frum lyrics, **9:**214–15
  string-band lyrics, **9:**198
  subjects for, **9:**700
  Tanna, **9:**363
  Tannese history songs, **9:**706–8
varṇam, **5:**217
Venezuela, Amerindian, **2:**525
Vidyapati, **5:**678
Virgin Islands
  cariso, **2:**972
  quelbey, **2:**971
Wales, **8:**343–44
  of bards, **8:**146
  cynghanedd, **8:**343
Warao culture, shamanic songs, **2:**194, 196
Wayana culture, **2:**165
West Futuna, *bau*, **9:**862
Yanomamö culture, women's songs, **2:**174
Yap
  täyoer, **9:**732–33
  teempraa, **9:**730–31
Yiddish songs, **3:**936–37
Yoruba popular music, **1:**473
Yuma culture, vocal music, **2:**596
zokela, **1:**687
Songshu (dynastic history), **7:**128
Songxuanguan qinpu (Yan), **7:**132
Songye people, **1:**670
Song Yuan xiqu kao (Wang), **7:**137
Sonia and Myriam, **2:**372
Sonic Contours (Ussachevsky), **3:**253
Sonic Meditations (Oliveros), **3:**131
Sŏn II: Myŏngsang ŭmak (Kim), **7:**959
Soninke people, **1:**445
Sonnambula, La (Bellini), **3:**1181
Sonneck, Oscar, **3:**31–32, 70, 144, 293, 511
Sonneck Society, **3:**32
Sonnenfeld, Rabbi Joseph Hayyim, **6:**206
Sonnenschein, Franz, **9:**758
Sonny Bono Copyright Extension Act (1988),
    3:256
Sonny's Revellers, **1:**770
Sonoda Takahiro, **7:**736
Sonodisc, **8:**241
Sonora (marimba ensemble), **2:**718
Sonora Matancera (musical group), **2:**763; **3:**743,
    794, 797
Sonora Ponceña (musical group), **3:**743
Sonora Santanera (musical group), **3:**741, 743
Sons of Hawaiʻi (musical group), **9:**164, 390
Sons of Membertou (musical group), **3:**1069
Sons of Norway, **3:**823, 866, 1250
Sonsoral (Palau), **9:**722
Sonstevold, Gunnar, **8:**426
Sontag, Henriette, **3:**556
Sontonga, Enoch, **1:**218, 222, 764, 769
Sony Corporation, **2:**107; **3:**244, 1161
Sophisticated Ladies (musical), **3:**621
Sŏp'yŏnje (film), **7:**960, 969
SORAFOM (Société de Radiodiffusion de la
    France d'Outre-mer), **1:**54
Sorb people, **8:**172
Sordi, Italo, **8:**622

Sordo Sodi, Carmen, **2:**623
Sori naeryŏk (Kim), **7:**969
Sorley, Herbert T., **5:**757
Sorol Atoll (Yap State, FSM), **9:**729
Sorrell, Neil, **5:**55
Sosa, Julio, **2:**519
Sosa, Mercedes, **2:**262, 263
Sosson Island (Papua New Guinea), **9:**983
Sotho peoples, **1:**707, 715, 773, 777
Sotī singers, **5:**782
Soto Borda, Clímaco, **2:**394, 395
Soto, Cesáro, **10:***98, 105*
Soto, Felipe, **2:**718
Soto, Jock, **3:**207
Soto, Juan Crisóstomo, **4:**864–65
Sotoba komati (Kan'ami), **7:**629
soukous, **1:**227, 363, 365, 386, 387, 419, 423,
    424, 682, 687; **2:**93, 410, 411, 508,
    879; **3:**338; **8:**234, 238. See also rumba
soul, **2:**96, 98; **3:**667, 676–78, 711, 858
  in Africa, **1:**363, 416, 477, 483, 778–79
  in Aotearoa, **9:**168
  blues and, **3:**647
  in Costa Rica, **2:**693
  disco and, **3:**688
  gospel and, **3:**535
  jazz and, **3:**663–64
  musical theater and, **3:**622
  research on, **3:**584, 586
  rhythm and blues and, **3:**709
Soul Asylum (musical group), **3:**171
Soul Brothers (musical group), **1:**778; **3:**1169
Soul Children (musical group), **3:**676
"Soul Finger" (Sam and Dave), **3:**677
"Soul Makossa" (Dibango), **3:**228, 688
"Soul Man" (Sam and Dave), **3:**677, 710
"Soul Sauce" (Tjader), **3:**788
Soul Sonic Force (musical group), **3:**695, 697
Soul Stirrers (gospel quartet), **3:**633
Soul Train (television show), **3:**211, 712
Soul Vibrations (musical group), **2:**755
Soule, Mary Jane, **2:**973
Soumaya, **6:**491
Sound of Africa Series (sound recordings), **10:**29
Sound of America Records, **3:**449
Sound of Mull (musical group), **8:**371
"Sound of Music" (Dayton), **3:**685
Sound of Music (Rodgers and Hammerstein),
    3:197
"Sound of Silence" (Simon and Garfunkel),
    9:200
Sound of Soul (Garland), **3:**584
Sound Recording Development Program
    (Canada), **3:**315
sound recordings
  78-rpm records, **1:**644
  Afghanistan, **5:**807, 808, 817, 819, 825, 832,
    840
  African-American-owned labels, **3:**707, 711,
    714
  African-American ragtime groups, **3:**651
  African music, **1:**214; **2:**410
    for guitar, **1:**355, 365
    recorded by French companies, **8:**233
  Albania, **8:**999, 1002
  Algeria, **6:**475

sound recordings (*continued*)
American popular music, **9**:26
Andhra Pradesh, **5**:890–91
Aotearoa, **9**:932, 999, 1004
  archives of, **9**:972–74
  pipe-and-drum ensemble, **9**:135
  popular music, **9**:169
Arabian peninsula, **6**:659
  pearl-diving songs, **6**:651
  of Western music, **6**:714–15
  women's music, **6**:696, 702
Arctic regions, **3**:380–81
Argentina
  cuarteto, **2**:276, 280
  folkloristic music, **2**:263
  música tropical, **2**:266
  rock, **2**:267
art music, **3**:269–71
Asian music, **3**:956
Asian popular music, **3**:951
Australia, **9**:414, 443, 987–89
  Aboriginal rock, **9**:146
  archives of, **9**:958–61
  cassettes, **9**:445
  country music, **9**:142, 413–14
  of didjeridu, **9**:397–98, 446–47
  gumleaf bands, **9**:135
  jazz, **9**:143
  popular music, **9**:144
  Southeastern Aboriginal peoples, **9**:440,
    442
Austral Islands, **9**:1002
Austria, **8**:675, 677
  Rom music, **8**:289
Bahamas, **2**:806
  junkanoo, **2**:808
balalaika orchestras, **3**:58
Bali, **4**:733, 759
Barbados
  folk songs, **2**:817
  spouge, **2**:820
Basque music, **8**:315
Belize, **2**:678
Bellona, **9**:853
bhajan, **5**:255
bhangra, **5**:574
Bhutan, **5**:715
bluegrass, **3**:161, 162
blues, **3**:103, 105, 579, 582, 644–47
Bolivia, **2**:288–89, 297
Bosnia-Hercegovina, **8**:969
Brazil, **2**:40, 107
  of fife-and-drum bands, **2**:330
  forró, **2**:332
  lambada, **2**:354
  moda-de-viola, **2**:319
  samba, **2**:316
Brittany, **8**:564
Bulgaria
  field recordings, **8**:906–7
  Rom music, **8**:284
Bulgarian music, **3**:925
Burma, **4**:399
Cajun and Creole music, **3**:858–59
California Native American music, **3**:414, 416
calypso, **3**:809–10

Canada, **3**:245, 1109
  Anglo-Celtic music, **3**:1190
  archives, **3**:292
  industry in, **3**:247, 265–67, 296, 315,
    1071, 1080, 1103, 1104, 1243
Caribbean, **2**:40–41, 51, 52–53, 63–64, 796
  popular music, **2**:76
cassettes
  in Afghanistan, **5**:840
  in Africa, **1**:4, 367, 417, 420, 436, 533, 543
  in Algeria, **6**:271
  in Arabian peninsula, **6**:659
  in Australia, **9**:445
  in Bali, **4**:759
  in Bolivia, **2**:288–89
  in China, **7**:389, 412, 416, 467–69, 505–6
  in Cirebon, **4**:698
  in Egypt, **6**:147, 166, 170, 233, 236,
    239–40, 642
  in Fiji, **9**:93
  in French Guiana, **2**:439
  in Guam, **9**:746
  in Haiti, **2**:891
  Indonesia, **4**:101–2
  in Indonesia, **4**:92–93; **10**:51
  in Irian Jaya, **9**:591
  in Israel, **6**:265, *266, 1020*, 1021
  in Java, **4**:647, 655–56
  in Karnataka, **5**:885
  in Kerala, **5**:946, 948, 950
  in Kiribati, **9**:760
  in Lombok, **4**:778
  in Micronesia, **9**:160, 719, 721
  in Mithila, **5**:679
  in Morocco, **6**:490, 1044
  in Nepal, **5**:702
  in New Caledonia, **9**:678
  in Northern Areas of Pakistan, **5**:799
  in North West Frontier Province, **5**:791
  in Pakistan, **5**:747–48
  in Papua New Guinea, **9**:90, 178–79, 246,
    516, 614
  in Paraguay, **2**:463
  in Punjab, **5**:656
  in Rotuma, **9**:819
  in Russia, **8**:767, 778
  in Sikaiana, **9**:848
  in South Asia, **5**:424, 434, 547–59, 583,
    715
  in Sunda, **4**:710, 718, 719–20, 722–23,
    724
  in Tamil Nadu, **5**:912, 924
  in Turkey, **6**:251, 257
  used in Pentecostal Rom congregations,
    8:274
  in Uttar Pradesh, **5**:674, 675
  in Vanuatu, **9**:709
Celtic music, **8**:320
Central America, **2**:40–41, 51, 52–53, 63–64
Chile, **2**:371
  rock, **2**:374
China, **7**:90
  Cantonese music, **7**:219
  Jiangnan sizhu, **7**:225
  minority musics, **7**:444
  of popular music, **7**:360

  of *qin* music, **7**:164
  of ritual musics, **7**:416
  of *shenqu*, **7**:300
  traditional music, **7**:381
  zheng music, **7**:173
Chinese opera, **3**:1261
Chinese popular music, **3**:964
Chuuk, American popular music, **9**:737
Cirebon, **4**:698
Colombia
  folkloric music, **2**:395, 396
  popular music, **2**:409, 411
comedy albums, **3**:489–90
compact disks, **1**:417
Cook Islands, **9**:1002
Corsica, **8**:573, 574
Costa Rica, **2**:690, 703
country music, **3**:76, 78, 520, 560
Croatia, **8**:936
  field recordings, **8**:937
crossover, **3**:330, 713, 942
Cuba, **2**:828, 838
Czechoslovakia, **8**:724
Czech Republic, **8**:723
Denmark, field recordings, **8**:*461*, 463–64,
  465
development of, **3**:195, 706; **8**:18–19, 59, 177
disco, **3**:687–88
distribution systems, **3**:265, 711, 1160; **5**:15,
  16, 583; **8**:85
Dominica, **2**:843–44
Dominican Republic, **2**:861
Doukhobor music, **3**:1268
early, **3**:242, 259, 261
economics and, **2**:105; **8**:188
educational role of, **2**:69–70
Egypt, **1**:571; **6**:147, 170, 233, 234, 239–40,
  432, 548, 597–600, 612, 620, 642
  early, **6**:33
  inshād, **6**:166
  Qur'ānic recitation, **6**:161
El Salvador, **2**:716, 718–19
engineer's and producer's roles in, **3**:265
England
  field recordings, **8**:327–28
  folk songs, **8**:338
Estonian music, **3**:881
ethnic music, **3**:827–28
Europe, in immigrant communities, **8**:232–41,
  234
field recordings, **8**:*21–22, 25*, 94, 155–57,
  307
Fiji, **5**:612; **9**:93, 997–98, 999
  archives of, **9**:968
Filipino music, **3**:1025
filmī gīt, **5**:414, 531
  in Trinidad, **5**:591
Finland, **8**:484, 486, 488
Finnish music, **3**:874–75
First Nations music, **3**:1278
folk music, **3**:300; **8**:157–58
formats of, **3**:348
France, **8**:546, 553–54
French Guiana, **2**:439
function in South India, **5**:542
Futuna, **9**:1000

gamelan, **3:**1021, 1022
Georgia, **8:**846
gospel music, **3:**534
Grammy Awards, **3:**107, 338, 346–47, 547,
     664, 697, 714–15, 720–21, 751, 809
gramophone records, **1:**416–17, 424, 426,
     626; **6:**233, 234
Greece, **8:**1009, 1014, 1017–18, 1021
    field recordings, **8:**1025
    rebetika, **8:**206, 1020
    Rom people, **8:**285
of Greek music, **9:**73
Guadeloupe, **2:**879
Guam, **9:**161, 746
Guatemala, **2:**723, 736
Haiti, **2:**889, 890–91, 892, 893
Haitian music, **3:**804
Hawai'i, **9:**998–99, 1002–4
    archives of, **9:**915, 968–72
    commercial, **9:**921–22
    Jawaiian, **9:**166, 167
    steel guitar, **9:**390
"hillbilly" records, **3:**48
Hindustani music, **5:**44, 136–37
Hispano music, **3:**767
Hmong music, **3:**1004, 1005
Honduras, **2:**742
Hong Kong, **7:**355
house music, **3:**690–91
Hungary, **8:**741, 746–47
independent labels, **3:**169–71, 263–64, 350,
     560, 707, 708, 714, 741, 1159, 1278
India, **5:**527–30, 560
    of courtesans' music, **5:**560
    Gujarat, **5:**624
    havelī saṅgīt, **5:**251
    Punjab, **5:**656
    regional music, **5:**405–6
    South, **5:**543
    Uttar Pradesh, **5:**667, 674
Indo-Guyanese music, **5:**604
Indonesia, **4:**92–93, 101–2
    field recordings, **10:**49
industry treatment of African-Americans,
     3:706–15
influence of, **3:**242–43
Inuit music, **3:**1278, 1279–80
Iran, **6:**823–24, 860
    art music, **6:**861–62, 863
Ireland, **8:**388, 390, 391, 393
Irian Jaya, **9:**591, 991
Irish music, **3:**843, 846
Islamic music, **1:**341, 342
Israel, **6:**263–67, 1020–21, 1069, 1071
Italian music, **3:**860–61
Italy, **8:**613–14, 619, 621–22, 623
Jamaica, **2:**40, 97, 911–12; **3:**693
Japan, **7:**537, 743–45
    use in transmission, **7:**539, 574, 772
Japanese popular music, **9:**26
Java, **4:**679, 680–81, 683
    cassettes, **4:**647, 655–56
    by foreign companies, **4:**680–81
jazz, **1:**430, 771; **3:**551, 578, 580, 652–54,
     659, 662, 664, 1106
Jewish music, **3:**935, 936, 938–39

Karnataka, **5:**881, 883, 885, 887
Karnatak music, **5:**159–60, 213
Kenya, **1:**423
Kerala, **5:**946, 948, 950
Khmer music, **4:**160
Kiribati, **9:**760
klezmer music, **3:**941–42
Korea, **7:**808, 952, 972, 993
    ch'anggŭk, **7:**968
    of folk songs, **7:**880, 887, 988
    p'ansori, **7:**893, 894
Kru music, **1:**381
Kuna culture, **2:**647–48, 649
Lao popular music, **3:**1009; **9:**76
Latin American music, **1:**361; **9:**84
Latvia, **8:**507
Lombok, **4:**778
Macedonia, **8:**983, 1002, 1003
Maharashtra, **5:**730
Malta, **8:**639
Mangareva, **9:**886
Manipa singers, **5:**712
mariachi, **3:**745
Maritimes music, **3:**1071, 1125, 1128, 1137,
     1139
marketing techniques, **3:**268–71, 352–53
Marquesas Islands, **9:**1002
Martinique, **2:**919
    kadans, **2:**917
Mashriq, **6:**548
Maya culture, **2:**658, 732
Melanesia, **9:**991–94
Métis fiddle music, **3:**409–10
Mexican music, **3:**736, 737
Mexican popular music, **3:**739, 741, 747–48
Mexico, **2:**40–41, 51, 52–53, 63–64, 605,
     619, 622, 623
Micronesia, **9:**160, 719, 721, 994–97
    archives, **9:**967–68
    production quality, **9:**161
Middle Eastern ethnographic, **6:**23
Middle Eastern music, **3:**1032–33
Miskitu culture, **2:**663–64
Mixtec culture, **2:**568
Montserrat, **2:**923
Morocco
    Maghribi Jewish music, **6:**1044
    rways, **6:**490
multinational corporations, **3:**244, 264, 266,
     1161
Native American music, **2:**82
    Christian, **3:**486
    crossover styles, **3:**488–90
    cylinder recordings, **3:**31, 243, 291, 294,
     457, 485, 495–96, 508–9
    dissemination projects, **3:**497–98
Nauru, popular music, **9:**262
Nepal, **5:**696, 701, 705–6
Netherlands Antilles, **2:**931
Netherlands, field recordings, **8:**534
New Age music, **3:**345–47
New Caledonia, **9:**672, 678, 992–93
    archives of, **9:**964–65
    side-blown flute, **9:**402
New Guinea, **9:**479
Nicaragua, **2:**765–66

Nigeria, **1:**480
Niue, **9:**1000
North Africa, **1:**545
Northeast Indian music, **3:**465
Norway, **8:**427, 430
Oceania
    analysis of, **9:**284
    archives of, **9:**853
Ossetian music, **8:**861
Otopame culture, **2:**574
Pakistan, **5:**528, 747–48, 749
    Northern Areas, **5:**799, 800
    North West Frontier Province, **5:**791
    of *qawwali*, **5:**746
Palau, **9:**161
Panama, **2:**783–84
Papua New Guinea, **9:**23, 90, 516, 989–93
    American popular music, **9:**148–49
    archives of, **9:**961–62
    brass bands, **9:**129
    cassettes, **9:**178–79, 246, 614
    Gulf Province, **9:**494
    Motu people, **9:**494
    string bands, **9:**138, 151, 153–55
    Trans-Fly region, **9:**509
Paraguay, cassettes, **2:**463
pedagogical uses, **3:**277
Peru, **2:**475, 476
    Afro-Peruvian music, **2:**501
    Andean music, **2:**484
    jarana, **2:**499
    popular music, **2:**230, 487
    rock, **2:**486
    traditional music, **2:**488
Philippines, popular music, **4:**888
pirate recordings, **2:**52; **5:**548; **7:**366, 468
Plains Indian music, **3:**449, 484
Poland, **8:**712
polka, **3:**891, 902
Polynesia, **9:**997–1006
Polynesian outlier communities, **9:**1000–1001
of popular music, **1:**323; **5:**419–20, 423
Portugal, **8:**584, 585
process of, **5:**550–51
Québec, **3:**247, 266, 1075–76, 1154,
     1159–61, 1165–66, 1167, 1170
"race" records, **3:**48, 524, *646*, 707, 1077
racially segmented marketing practices, **3:**683
ragtime, **3:**580
rap, **3:**694, 695, 696–99, 713–15
Rapa Nui, **9:**1004–5
reggae, **3:**809, 1201–2
remixes, **3:**711
Rennell, **9:**853
rhythm and blues, **3:**349, 354, 669–70, 672,
     708
rock, **3:**551; **8:**216, 218
rock and roll, **3:**348, 351–53
role in preservation, **2:**66
Romania, **8:**880, 882, 883
Romanian, **3:**910
Rom jazz, **8:**288
Rotuma, **9:**819, 1000
Russia, **8:**776–77
    byliny, **8:**129, 764
    ethnic minorities' music, **8:**773

sound recordings, Russia (*continued*)
   field recordings, **8:**755, 757
   protiazhnaia pesnia, **8:**133
   rozhok, **8:**770
   samizdat cassettes, **8:**767, 778
Saami people, joiks, **8:**305–6, 307
St. Lucia, **2:**949–50
sákárà, **1:**474
salsa, **3:**788
Sāmoa, **9:**808, 1000
sampling techniques, **2:**98
Sardinia, **8:**632
Saudi Arabia, **6:**655
Scotland, **8:**363, 372
Sikaiana, **9:**848
singles, **3:**688, 690, 711, 713
Slovenia, **8:**922
   field recordings, **8:**920
Society Islands, **9:**869, 1001–2
Solomon Islands, **9:**992–93
   archives of, **9:**962–64
   urban music, **9:**158
South Africa, **1:**720, 760, 773, 777
South America, **2:**40–41, 51, 52–53, 63–64
South Asia, **5:**526–27
   archival collections of, **5:**529–30, 747
   rock and pop music, **5:**429
South Asian music, **3:**982, 985
   North American sales of, **5:**580, 583
Southeast Indian music, **3:**470
Spain, **8:**601–2
Spanish popular music, **2:**102
Sri Lanka, **5:**108, 970
steelbands, **2:**97
studies of, **5:**43, 57
Sunda, **4:**710, 718, 719–20, 722–23, 724
Surinam, *kaseko*, **2:**508
survey of, **9:**985–1006
Suyá culture, **2:**145
Sweden, **8:**443
Tahiti, **9:**998
Taiwan, **7:**357, 358, 524
tamburitza music, **3:**922
Tamil Nadu, **5:**912, 924
taping of guru sessions, **5:**465
technological innovations, **3:**237, 263, 268
Tejano music, **3:**774, 775–76, 781
Thailand, **4:**331
   popular music, **4:**95–97, 99
Tibetan music, **5:**711, 715
time limitations in, **3:**243
Tokelauan *fātele*, **9:**113
Tonga, **9:**999–1000
Tracey collection, **1:**52–53; **10:**29, 111
transcription and, **1:**155–56, 161–62
Trinidad and Tobago, **5:**592
   calypso, **2:**96
Tuamotu Islands, **9:**1002
Tunisia
   Jewish music, **6:**523–25
   ma'lūf, **6:**502, 512
Turkey, **6:**251, 252, 256, 257
   of Alevi performers, **6:**797
   arabesk, **6:**776
   art music, **6:**758, 771–72
   early, **6:**116
   popular music, **6:**248, 250

Tuvalu, **9:**1000
Uighur *muqam*, **6:**1008
Uighur popular music, **7:**467–69
Ukraine, **8:**820, 822–23
Ukrainian country music, **3:**345
Ukrainian music, **3:**913–14, 1089, 1243
United States, **3:**12
   archives of, **9:**974–80
   Pacific Islander music, **9:**117–18
Uruguay, **2:**520
   traditional music, **2:**511
'Uvea, **9:**1000
Uzbekistan, **6:**908
Vanuatu, **9:**709, 965–67, 992–94
Venezuela, **2:**544
   of Amerindian music, **2:**525
Vietnam, **3:**996; **4:**134–35
   by foreign companies, **4:**483, 493, 513
   popular music, **4:**514–15
Vietnamese popular music, **3:**949, 993, 995
vinyl format, **3:**169
Virgin Islands, **2:**969, 973
Waiāpí culture, **2:**162
Warao culture and, **2:**193
wax cylinders
   Africa, **1:**11, 254
   Argentina, **2:**251
   Europe, **8:**562, 664, 820, 822
   Kazakhstan, **6:**955
   Oceania, **9:**291, 440, 479, 650, 883, 886,
      932, 961, 979–81, 985, 987, 991–92,
      994
   Peru, **2:**487–88
West Futuna, **9:**863
Western record companies, **1:**54
white covers of black music, **3:**329–30,
   352–53, 354, 709
of women composers, **3:**91
world beat, **3:**339–40
world music, **3:**955; **8:**224–25, 239
Yap, **9:**729
Yaqui culture, **2:**592, 593
Yekuana music, **2:**176
Yugoslavia (former), **8:**981, 1001
Yugoslavia, Kosovo, **8:**1002
Zaïre
   of Latin American music, **1:**385–87
   recording studios, **1:**424–25
Zimbabwe, **1:**432, 720, 756–57
Sound Space (musical group), **7:**972
Soundgarden (musical group), **3:**358
Soundi (periodical), **8:**484
Sounds Australia (journal), **9:**415
Sounds of Brazil (New York), **3:**806
Sounds from Taiwan's Low Class (album), **7:**358
source studies, **3:**32–34; **8:**36–38. *See also*
     Spanish chroniclers; travelers' and
     missionaries' accounts; treatises; *specific*
     titles
   Africa, **1:**74–97
   Andalusia, **6:**444–45
   Arabian peninsula, **6:**357–62
   Arabic writings on music, **6:**363–82
   autobiographies, **3:**33
   Bali, **4:**733
   Brittany, **8:**561

Bulgaria, **8:**903–4
Canada, Children of Peace community, **3:**137
Caribbean, **2:**22–23
Central America, **2:**23
China, **7:**87–88, 98–99
   antiquity through 1911, **7:**127–33
   biographies and hagiographies, **7:**23, 128,
     139, 328, 393–94, 408
   Cantonese music, **7:**217–18
   Daoism, **7:**319
   dynastic histories, **7:**41, 115, 128–29
   twentieth century, **7:**135–42
   on women musicians, **7:**401–2
commonplace books, **3:**839
composers' autographs, **8:**51
Corsica, **8:**574
Costa Rica, **2:**681–82
Denmark, **8:**463
diaries, **3:**45, 155, 1070, 1075
early African-American music, **3:**64–66, 573
East Asia, **7:**41–43
   dance, **7:**59
   instruments, **7:**79
editions of Arabic writings, **6:**374–82
Georgian church music, **8:**843
Germany, **8:**651
Greece, ancient, **8:**1022–23
Guatemala, **2:**721–22
Hungary, **8:**736–37
information on instruments, **5:**331
Ireland, **8:**393
   manuscripts of lays, **8:**379, 385
Italy, **8:**615
   on dance, **8:**609
Japan, **7:**565, 585–90
   official documents, **7:**586–87
   on theater, **7:**653
Java, **4:**635–36
Jewish music, **8:**264, 265
Kashmir, **5:**688–95
Korea, **7:**833, 855–57
   diaries, **7:**855
   dynastic histories, **7:**41, 855
   on folk song, **7:**886–88
Low Countries, **8:**533–34
Malta, **8:**642
Mexico, **2:**23, 601
Middle Eastern music, **6:**20–22, 536–37
Mongolian Buddhist music, **7:**1016–17
New France, **3:**23–24, 1056
Ontario
   dance music manuscripts, **3:**1190
   French song manuscripts, **3:**1192
Ottoman empire, **6:**770–71
Philippines, **4:**850
references to temple dancers, **5:**407
Russia, *byliny*, **8:**129
South America, **2:**23–24
South Asia, visual sources, **5:**298–310
Southeast Asia, **4:**12, 65–66
Spain, **8:**600–601
Spanish mission and cathedral music,
   3:848–49
Subarctic regions, **3:**392
Sweden, **8:**443–44
Taiwan, references to Aboriginal music, **7:**524

Thailand, **4:**224–25, 284–86
Tibet, **7:**471–72, 476
Uighur *muqam*, **6:**1005
Sousa, Gabriel Soares de, **2:**301
Sousa, John Philip, **3:**193, 240, 260–61, 277,
    295, 536, 544, 548, 556, 565–66,
    566, 874
Soustelle, Jacques, **2:**573
Soustrot, Marc, **8:***101*
South. *See also* Appalachia; *specific states*
    bluegrass in, **3:**160–68
    blues in, **3:**639–40
    country music in, **3:**76
    fiddling traditions in, **3:**77
    musical life, nineteenth century, **3:**189
    rap in, **3:**702
    rural genres in, **3:**13
South Africa, **3:**338–39, 341. *See also* Southern
    Africa; *specific peoples*
    Afrikaans language of, **1:**3
    apartheid in, **1:**717, 774–80
    Cape Town, **1:**760–61
    Church of God and Saints of Christ in, **3:**127
    colonialism in, **1:**760–61
    "colored" people, **1:**703, 761, 762–63, 765
    composition in, **1:**218–19
    "concert party" genre, **1:**765, 770
    economy of, **1:**428
    Europeans in, **1:**716–20, 760–63
    guitar in, **1:**351–52, 356, 359
    history of, **1:**759–60
    history of South Asian people in, **5:**615
    homelands, **1:**776
    Indian people in, **5:**449
    Johannesburg, **1:**766–67
    Kimberley, **1:**761–63
    kwela music, **1:**296; **10:**118
    lamellophones, **1:**317
    Land Acts, **1:**776
    marabi, **1:**387
    migrant labor system, **1:**429
    mining in, **1:**717
    music industry of, **1:**417–18, 437, 773
    music research in, **1:**49
    Ndebele people, dance, **1:**114
    Ngoni people, **1:**320–21
    popular music of, **1:**216–17, 296, 419,
        429–31, 433, 759–80
    Portuguese people in, **8:**576
    Pretoria, **1:**767
    shebeens, **1:**429, 766–68
    slavery in, **1:**761
    Sotho peoples, **1:**707
    South Asian community in, **5:**615–18
    Transkei, San musical traits, **1:**306–7
    Venda people, speech surrogate methods,
        1:106
    white musicians in, **1:**779–80
    Zulu people
        blood sacrifice, **1:**277
        dance, **1:**109
        popular music of, **1:**419
South African Native Choir, **1:**765
South America. *See also specific countries, cultures,*
    and topics
    Andalusian influences in, **6:**449

Andean region
    folkloric ensembles, **2:**75, *76*, 135
    native music of, **2:**205–23
archaeomusicological studies in, **2:**7, 9–12;
    10:100
colonial era in, **2:**16, 46–47
cultural syncretism in, **2:**46
East Asian people in, **7:**6
European communities, acculturation in, **2:**71
folklore of, **2:**21
geography of, **2:**2, 4, 123, 242, 245
historical accounts of, **2:**23–24
history of, **2:**78, 81, 242, 245
iconographical record in, **2:**16
immigrant groups of, **2:**4, 83–91
instruments of, **2:**31–32, 37
Jewish people in, **6:**1036
languages of, **2:**242
maps of, **2:***3, 79,* 122, *243–44, 246–47*
native peoples of, **2:**78, 81, 245
population of, **2:**242
Portuguese people in, **8:**576
research on, **2:**23–24
saint's-day celebrations in, **2:**46
tourism in, **2:**50
tropical-forest region, **2:**123–36
    acculturation in, **2:**71
    geography of, **2:**123
    immigrant groups in, **2:**131–34
    music and dance of, **2:**125–35
    population of, **2:**123, 125
South Americans. *See* Latino peoples; *specific*
    groups
South American Troubadours, **2:**396
South Asia. *See also specific countries and regions*
    climate of, **5:**4
    geography of, **5:**4–5, *6*
    languages of, **5:**5, *6*, 7
    local musical traditions of, **5:**2, 4, 24, 75
    musical life in, **5:**399–406
    population of, **5:**2, 5
    rivers of, **5:**6
    rural *vs.* urban cultures in, **5:**397–98
    women's musical and dance traditions of,
        5:407–16
South Asian diaspora, **5:**572–619. *See also*
    Bengali people; Gujarati people; Indian
    (South Asian) people; Indo-Caribbean
    peoples; Pakistani people; Sikhs; *specific*
    countries
    fusion genres of, **5:**568, 574–75, 576, 582,
        584–85
    map of, **5:***570*
    patron/client relationship and, **5:**403–4
South Before the War (Whalen and Martell),
    3:618
South Carolina
    blues in, **3:**639
    Charleston
        African-American theater in, **3:**615
        ballad opera in, **3:**179–80
        orchestras in, **3:**536
        street vendors, **3:**600
    early African-Americans in, **3:**64, 598
    Native American groups in, **3:**461, 466
    Omuluaiye festival, **1:**412

Port Royal Islands, **3:**29
Stono insurrection, **3:**594
South Carolina Gazette, **3:**600–601
South Dakota
    Fort Pierre, Estonian people in, **3:**878
    Hutterites in, **3:**1240
    Native American groups in, **3:**440
    Norwegian people in, **3:**866–70
    Swedish people in, **3:**870–72
South Family Gospel Singers, **3:**486
South Indian Cultural Association (Ottawa),
    3:1216
South Korea. *See also* Korea
    ch'angjak kugak composition in, **7:**952–60
    cultural policies in, **7:**804, 808, 991, 996–97
    cultural preservation in, **7:**47, 932
    farmers' bands in, **7:**938–39
    folk song designations in, **7:**988
    influence on Southeast Asian culture, **4:**80
    music business in, **7:**992–96
    shamanism in, **7:**986–87
South Pacific (Rodgers and Hammerstein), **3:**197,
    545, 621; **9:**37, 45
South Pacific Recordings, **9:**997–98
South-Sea Evangelical Church, **9:**665, 667, 852
South-Sea Idyls (Stoddard), **9:**36
South Tyrolian Kastelruther Spatzen, **8:**675
Southeast Asia. *See also specific countries*
    aesthetics in, **4:**13–14
    animism in, **4:**59–61
    Austronesian speakers, **9:**319
    bossed gong cultures of, **4:**891
    bronze drums in, **4:**58
    Buddhism in, **5:**12
    Cantonese opera in, **7:**303
    Chinese influence on, **4:**69–73
    Chinese people in, **7:**6, 211
    "classical" music traditions of, **4:**6–7
    composition in, **4:**126–36
    court life in, **4:**5
    cultural diversity of, **4:**3, 5
    cultural identities, authenticity, and retentions,
        4:10–11
    cultural layers in, **4:**55–86
    dance, Indian influences on, **4:**67
    early civilization in, **4:**38–46
    Europeans in, **4:**12
    folk music traditions in, **4:**7–8
    free-reed pipes in, **4:**58–59
    geography of, **4:**2–3, 5, 11, 33, 47
    gong-chime cultures in, **4:**272
    historical documents in, **4:**12
    historical sites in (map), **4:***63*
    history of, **4:**55, 62
    Indian influences on, **4:**61–68
    indigenous cultures of, **4:**10–11
    instruments, Indian relationships, **4:**66–67
    Islam in, **4:**73–80
    islands of, **4:**594–97
    Jew's harps in, **4:**58–59
    languages of, **4:**65
    literature of, **4:**65–66
    lowland *vs.* upland peoples, **4:**3, 11, 537–38
    mainland, **4:**148–50
    maps of, **4:***4, 149, 595*
    modernization's impact on, **4:**113–42, 297

Southeast Asia (continued)
  music research on, 4:24–29
  patronage in, 4:117–18
  politics in, 4:87–94
  prehistoric, 4:32–46
  prehistoric art and music, 4:43–46
  Qur'ānic recitation in, 6:159–60
  regionalism in, 4:3, 5, 116–17, 148, 150
  representation of traditional music, 4:132–41
  revival movements in, 4:123–26
  rice cultivation in, 4:48
  sexual practices and taboos in, 4:49
  tourism in, 4:135–41
  transmission of music, 4:118–23
  tube zithers in, 4:58–59
  upland peoples, 4:528–91
    research on, 4:529–30
  urbanization of, 4:115
  urban vs. rural cultures, 4:5–6
  wars in, 4:11
  Western influences on, 4:24–25, 80–86
  xylophones in, 4:57–58
Southeast Indian nations, 3:466–70
  history and culture of, 3:466–67
  mound cultures, 3:366
  music of, 3:467–69
  performance contexts, 3:467
  research on music of, 3:470
  women's musical roles, 3:371
Southern Africa. See also specific countries and
    peoples
  colonialism in, 1:429, 432, 435, 701, 705,
    707, 708, 712, 715, 744, 745, 755,
    756–57, 759, 768
  economics of, 1:700
  instruments of, 1:701, 702, 708
  languages of, 1:700
  map of, 1:698
  music of, 1:700–20
  research on, 1:701
  "tonal-harmonic belt," 1:701, 715, 744
Southern Africa Development Council, 1:700
Southern Baptists, in Cook Islands, 9:898
Southern Cheyenne, 3:445
Southern Cross University (Lismore), 9:255
Southern, Eileen, 1:32; 3:83, 573, 581, 581,
    609, 615, 627
Southern Harmony (Walker), 3:121, 533, 533
"Southern Muddy Bay" (Chinese folk song),
    7:367
Southern Music Company, 3:263
Southern Paiutes, 3:420–21, 422
Southern Playboys (musical group), 3:1251
Southern Song dynasty
  instruments in, 7:113
  music in, 7:89, 131
  pipa in, 7:168
  xianshiyue music in, 7:211–12
Southerner (periodical), 3:354
Southwell-Colucci, Edith, 8:574
Southwell, Gwyneth, 9:571
Southwell, Neville, 9:571
Southwest, 3:735. See also specific states
  acquired from Mexico, 3:9, 718
  mestizo culture in, 3:9
  research on music of, 3:31
  Spanish missionaries in, 3:485

Southwest Indian nations, 3:417, 428–38
  cliff dwellers, 3:366
  country and western dancing, 3:213
  instruments of, 3:472–79
  women's musical roles, 3:371
Southwest Museum (Los Angeles), 3:31, 736
Southwestern University (Georgetown), 3:1010
Souza, William Santos de, 2:354
Soviet Union (former), 3:297–98; 8:10, 753. See
    also Armenia; Azerbaijan; Belarus;
    Central Asia; Estonia; Georgia;
    Kazakhstan; Kyrgyzstan; Latvia;
    Lithuania; North Caucasia; Russia;
    Siberia; Tajikistan; Turkmenistan;
    Ukraine
  Afghanistan and, 5:810, 829
  ballet in, 8:161
  breakup of, 7:9
  folk music pedagogy, 8:155
  ideology in, 7:47, 340–41, 388; 8:185, 187
  instruments, 8:21
  Iranian dance traditions in, 6:875–79
  Jewish music, 8:267
  Jewish performers in, 8:260
  rock in, 8:218–19
  rule over Armenia, 6:744
  rule over Azerbaijan, 6:921, 930
  rule over Belarus, 8:790, 796, 800–801, 802
  rule over Central Asia, 6:12, 897, 903–4,
    915–19, 938, 944, 945, 946–47,
    958–60, 967, 975–76
  rule over Estonia, 8:491, 498
  rule over Georgia, 8:826, 840–41, 843–45
  rule over Latvia, 8:499
  rule over Lithuania, 8:509, 512–14
  rule over North Caucasia, 8:851, 854, 856
  rule over Siberia, 7:1030
  rule over Tuva, 6:986–87
  rule over Ukraine, 8:806, 816–19, 821
  state folk ensembles in, 8:152, 777
  state-sponsored rock groups, 8:218–19
  suppression of rock groups, 8:217, 218
Sowande, Fela, 1:18
  compositions of, 1:216, 220–21, 223, 224,
    227, 230, 233, 244
  research of, 1:29, 31, 39
Sowmya, S., 3:990
Soyŏp sanbang (Hwang), 7:956
Spady, James, 3:586
Spælimenninir i Hoydølum, 8:472
Spaghetti Incident (Guns 'n' Roses), 3:358
Spagna, 8:207
Spain, 8:588–602. See also Andalusian repertoire;
    Basque region
  Andalucía, 8:588, 593, 596
    fandango in, 8:589, 595
  Andalusian influences in, 6:449
  Aragón, 8:596
    jota in, 8:588
    rule over Malta, 8:634
    rule over Sardinia, 8:631
    Yebra de Basa, 8:1
  art music in, 8:600–601
  Asturias, Celtic music in, 8:320
  Balearic Islands, 8:596
  Basque people in, 8:309

cante jondo, 2:780
Caribbean territories, loss of, 2:791
Castile, 8:593, 596
  seguidilla in, 8:589
Catalonia, 8:595–96
  cobla ensemble, 8:593–94
  folk music societies, 8:123
Celtic people in, 8:319
children's wakes in, 2:422
Christian reconquest of, 6:431, 433, 441, 505,
    516, 1035
Cordova, Umayyad court in, 6:293, 538
dance traditions of, 8:163, 198, 588–89,
    595–600
expulsion of Jews and Moors from, 8:11, 248,
    588, 596
Extremadura, 8:593, 596
flamenco, 8:7, 12, 593, 596–600
  pop hybrids, 8:226, 599–600
flamenco-style rumba, 8:204, 205
Galicia, 8:595
  bagpipe in, 8:560
  Celtic music in, 8:226, 320
  hurdy-gurdy in, 8:594
geography of, 8:588
history of, 8:588
Ibiza, singing in, 8:31
influence on Costa Rican music, 2:693
influence on Mayan music, 2:652
influence on Venezuelan music, 2:532–33, 540
instrument collections in, 8:176, 182
instruments, 8:170, 197, 593–95
  research on, 8:35, 39, 40
Jews in, 3:942
La Mancha, 8:595
León, 8:593, 596
map of, 8:516
Murcia, 8:596
Muslim rule in, 1:534; 6:131, 293, 294, 365,
    370, 431, 436, 441–45, 455–56, 496,
    505, 538, 540; 8:12, 199, 588, 600
North African colonies of, 6:432
North African emigrant communities, 6:438
popular music in, 8:204, 205, 208, 226,
    599–600
population of, 8:588
regional styles, 8:595–96
research on music of, 8:601–2
Rom people in, 8:7, 270, 596
rumba catalán, 8:204, 205
Santiago de Compostela Cathedral, 8:600
Sephardic Jews of, 8:195
Seville
  Muslim court in, 6:538
  singing slave girls in, 6:370, 445–46
song genres of, 2:102
tawā'if period, 6:442
vocal music, 8:132, 134, 142, 145, 196, 204,
    205, 517, 589–93
  ballads, 8:134, 195
  polyphonic, 8:75, 600–601
  women's music in, 8:195
Spand, Charlie, 3:645
Spandau Ballet, 8:215
Spaniels (musical group), 3:671
Spanish-American War, 2:932–33

Spanish Arawaks, **2:**442
Spanish chroniclers, **2:**7, 15, 21–23
   in Caribbean, **2:**13, 933
   in Central America, **2:**650, 667, 681–82, 707,
      747–48
   in Mexico, **2:**577, 600, 601, 602
   in South America, **2:**37–38, 183, 207,
      250–51, 283, 284, 423, 453, 467–68,
      510
Spanish Civil War, **8:**309
Spanish conquistadors
   in Bolivia, **2:**283
   in Colombia, **2:**9, 10
   in Peru, **2:**357, 466
"Spanish Harlem" (King), **3:**673
Spanish and Mexican Folk Music of New Mexico,
   3:767
Spanish people. *See also* Iberian people; Latino
      peoples; Mexican-Americans/Canadians
   in Argentina, **2:**90, 256
   in Caribbean, **2:**791, 792, 793
   in Costa Rica, **2:**693
   in Cuba, **2:**822, 823, 837
   in El Salvador, **2:**708
   in Hawai'i, **9:**100
   identity issues of, **2:**61
   in North Africa, **6:**435
   in North America, **3:**731, 847
      early explorers and settlers, **3:**7, 9, 437, 596,
         721, 754–55, 770–71, 1255
      influence on Pueblo groups, **3:**217–18
      mission and cathedral music, **3:**485, 848–49
      missionization of California, **3:**412, 521,
         734–35
      missionization of New Mexico, **3:**755
      Ontario, **3:**1197
   in Panama, **2:**771, 772–73
   in South America, **2:**84
   in Switzerland, **8:**697
   in Uruguay, **2:**510
   in Venezuela, **2:**524, 532–33
Spanish Songs of Old California (Lummis), **3:**736
Spanish Warao, **2:**442
Sparx (musical group), **3:**766
Spasov, Ivan, **8:**905
Speaking Tree (cross-cultural dance project),
   9:415–16
Spear, Louise, **9:**976
Spearritt, Gordon, **9:**289, 990
Specials (musical group), **8:**215
Specialty Records, **3:**350, 352, 353, 670, 708
Speck, Frank G., **3:**392, 465, 470
Speckled Red, **3:**645
Spector, Johanna, **6:**1060
Spector, Phil, **3:**355, 673, 709
Spectrum (Montréal), **3:**1160
Spectrum (musical group), **3:**161
"Speedo" (Cadillacs), **3:**672
Speer, Daniel, **8:**881
Speight, R. Marston, **6:**510
Speiser, Felix, **9:**708
Speke, John Hanning, **1:**635
Spellbound (film), **3:**203
Spellman, A. B., **3:**584
Spelman College (Atlanta), **3:**611
Spence, Emile, **3:**409

Spence, Joseph, **2:**805
Spencer, Herbert, **1:**94–95
Spencer, Robert F., **3:**381
Spencer, W. B., **9:**987
Spendiaryan, Alexandr, **6:**726–27
Spice Girls (musical group), **3:**840
Spicer, Edward H., **2:**593; **3:**485
Spicer, George, **8:**327, 334, 335
Spickard, Paul R., **9:**972
Spīčs, Ernests, **8:**507
Spielberg, Steven, **4:**101
Spies, Walter, **4:**733, 756
Spike (musical group), **7:**1020
Spinetta, Luis Alberto, **2:**104
Spinners (musical group), **3:**711
Spirit of the Boogie (Kool and the Gang), **3:**682
Spirit Horses (DeMars), **3:**498
Spirit of the West (musical group), **3:**345, 1096
spirit possession. *See also* Vodou
   Africa, **1:**273–77, 290, 537, 554–55, 604;
      10:118, 121
   Balochistan, **5:**780–81
   Belize, **2:**669–70, 672
   Brazil, **2:**342–43
   Burma, **4:**372
   Caribbean, **2:**45, 47–48
   Central America, **2:**45, 47–48
   Colombia, **2:**403
   Costa Rica, **2:**688
   Dominican Republic, **2:**856
   Egypt, **6:**632–33
   Guruṅg people, **5:**703
   Haiti, **2:**883–84, 889
   Jamaica, **2:**898, 901–3
   Karnataka, **5:**867, 882, 886
   Kerala, **5:**362
   Middle East, **6:**180–81, 417, 546
   Montserrat, **2:**924–25
   Rajasthan, **5:**288, 292
   South America, **2:**45, 47–48
   South Asia, **5:**272
      differentiated from shamanic rituals,
         5:288–89
   Sri Lanka, **5:**961
   Surinam, **2:**505
   Tamil Nadu, **5:**921
   Trinidad and Tobago, **2:**954–55
Spirits Rejoice (musical group), **1:**779
Spiritual Baptists, **3:**8, 811, 1205
   in Barbados, **2:**817
   in Carriacou, **2:**868
   in Grenada, **2:**865
   in Trinidad and Tobago, **2:**952, 953, 956,
      957–58, 963
Spiritual Fantasies (Tillis), **3:**612
spirituals, **1:**19; **3:**10, 68–69, 506, 510, 523–24,
      599, 625–29
   African-Canadian, **3:**1072, 1132–33, 1169
   blues and, **3:**640
   coded messages in, **3:**8, 26, 601
   collections of, **3:**573–75
   concert arrangements of, **3:**577–78, 607–8,
      617, 628–29
   research on, **3:**624; **10:**141–42, 145
   ring shout, **3:**626, 628
Spiro, Michael, **3:**789

Spitzer, Nicholas R., **3:**858; **10:**85
Spivacke, Harold, **3:**294
Spivey, Victoria, **3:**644, 707
Splatters (musical group), **4:**884
Split Enz (Split Ends), **9:**169
Spohr, Louis, **8:**102
Spokesmen (musical group), **3:**317
Spoonie Gee, **3:**699
"Spoonin' Rap," **3:**699
sports. *See also* games and pastimes; martial arts
   archery, Ladakh, **5:**712
   ball games, Marshall Islands, **9:**751
   baseball, Hawai'i, **9:**99
   Bellona, **9:**269
   boomerang throwing, Australia, **9:**453
   boxing
      Marshall Islands, **9:**751
      Southeast Asia, **4:**182, 186, 202–3, 376,
         790, 794
   buffalo racing, Karnataka, **5:**884
   bullfights, Paraguay, **2:**459
   bungee-jumping, Vanuatu, **9:**696–97
   Burma, *hcìňloùñ*, **4:**376
   casting darts, Tokelau, **9:**827
   Central America, **2:**50, 61
   Colombia, **2:**384
   Costa Rica, **2:**689
   cricket, **9:**32, 49, 231
      New Caledonia, **9:**679
      Sāmoa, **9:**379, 804
      Tokelau, **9:**825
      Tonga, **9:**794
   dueling, Flores, **4:**793
   javelin-throwing, Niue, **9:**816
   polo
      Ladakh, **5:**712
      Pakistan, **5:**796–97, 799
   Polynesia, **9:**379
   rugby, Aotearoa, **9:**932
   soccer
      Argentina, **2:**266
      Bahamas, **2:**808
      Brazil, **2:**50
   South America, **2:**50, 61
   spear throwing, Australia, **9:**61, 453
   volleyball, Ecuador, **2:**429
   wrestling
      Guadeloupe, **2:**876
      Pukapuka, **9:**910
      Rotuma, **9:**820
      Tokelau, **9:**827
Spottswood, Richard, **3:**828
Sprague and Blodgett, **3:**616
Spring and Autumn period
   music in, **7:**88, 392
   music theory in, **7:**115
Spring Thaw (Moore), **3:**198–99
Springsteen, Bruce, **3:**551, 552
Sproat, Clyde "Kindy," **9:**391
Sproule, Daithi, **3:***843*
Spychiger, John, **9:**493
Squeff, Enio, **2:**320
Srauti, Ramanatha, **5:**243
Srebotnjak, Alojz, **8:**921
Sremac, Stjepan, **8:**937
Sri Krishna Kīrtan (Chandidas), **5:**845

Sri Lanka, **5:**5, 954–72
  Buddhism in, **5:**12–13, 108, 490, 537, 956–57
  ceremonies, exorcism and healing, **5:**278, 293, 961–65
  Colombo, **5:**449, 491
    cassette industry in, **5:**554
    theater in, **5:**970
  Daladā Maligāwa temple, **5:**965–67
  dance traditions of, **5:**363–64, 427, 490, 556, 956
  geography of, **5:**954
  hēvisi ensemble, **5:**13, 329, 351, 361, 363–64, 958, 966, 967–68
  history of, **5:**490, 954
  instruments in, **5:**350–68, 956, 958, 964–65
  Karnatak tradition in, **5:**89, 108, 449
  Kataragama, **5:**958, 960
  languages of, **5:**5, 7
  light classical music in, **5:**956, 972
  map of, **5:***3, 952*
  Parsi theater in, **5:**491, 970
  political unrest in, **5:**16, 108
  popular music in, **5:**428, 961, 969–72, 971–72
  population of, **5:**954
  regional cassettes in, **5:**424, 554–59
  regional cultures in, **5:**955
  religion in, **5:**10, 490, 955, 957–59, 960–65
  Sabragamuwa, **5:**955
  theater in, **5:**422, 487, 490–91, 958, 964–65, 970
  Theravada Buddhism in, **5:**257, 955, 956–57, 965–69
  vocal music, **5:**959–60
    sindu, **5:**958, 966
  Yazhpanam (Jaffna), **5:**108, 449, 958
    pasu drama in, **5:**491
    sabhā schools in, **5:**455
Sri Lankan-Canadians, **3:**1216
Sri Nathji (deity), **5:**249, 251
  worship of, **5:**280, 643
Sri Venkateswara University, **5:**451
Srinakharinwirot University, **4:**121, 226, 249
Srinivas, Dr. P. B., **5:**425
Srinivas, Rajesh, **5:**234
Srinivas, U., **5:**234, 424
Srinivasa Ayyar, Alathur, **5:***152*
Srinivasan, **5:**421
Srinivasan, Poovalur, **5:***233*
Sripadaraya, **5:**265
Srivastava, S. L., **5:**674
Srivijaya (kingdom), **4:**43, 62, 304, 594, 596, 600, 621, 623
Sriwana, **4:**520
Srong-brtsan-sgam-po, **7:**471, 472, 476
Śruti (periodical), **3:**992; **5:**213
SS-20 (musical group), **8:**221
Staal, J. F., **5:**241
Stabat Mater, **3:**611; **8:**628
Staccatos (musical group), **3:**1081
Stadacona Band, **3:**1119
Staden, Hans, **2:**301
Stafford, William, **5:**50
"Stagolee" (ballad), **3:**639
Stähli, Adolf, **8:**692

Stainov, Peteko, **8:**905
"Stairway to Heaven" (Led Zeppelin), **3:**552
Stakeout (film), **3:**204
Stakhovich, Mikhail, **8:**755
Stalemates (musical group), **9:**138
Stalin, Joseph, **6:**930; **7:**340, 383, 441, 961; **8:**776, 816
Stamitz, Antonín, **8:**727
Stamitz, Johann, **8:**727
Stamitz, Karel, **8:**727
Stamm, Gustavo, **2:**745
"Stand!" (Graham), **3:**681
"Stand!" (Stone), **3:**681
"Stand by Me" (Tindley), **3:**630
"Stand Up" (Bannock), **3:**1063
Standing (Kondô), **7:**738
Stanek, Milan, **9:**982
Stanford, C. V., **8:**393
Stanford, E. Thomas, **2:**568, 623
Stanković, Kornelije, **8:**943, 954
Stanley, Abraham, **3:**134
Stanley Brothers, **3:**159
Stanley, Sir Henry Morton, **1:**86–87, 635, 688; **3:**72
Stanley, Ralph, **3:**159
Stanley and the Ten Sleepless Knights, **2:**970
Stanner, W. E. H., **9:**419
Stanton, Frank L., **3:**549
Stanton, Max E., **9:**972
Staple Singers (musical group), **3:**676, 677
"Star Dust" (Carmichael), **3:**549
"Star Spangled Banner," **3:**305, 521, 839
  Hendrix version, **3:**318
Star Wars (film), **3:**204
Stare Tambure (musical group), **3:**1198
Stark, John Stillwell, **3:**705
Starr, Edwin, **3:**318, 677
Starr label, **3:**1154
"Stars and Stripes Forever" (Sousa), **3:**548
Stasov, Vladimir, **8:**783
State Academic Russian Choir, **8:**777
State Conservatory of Turkish Traditional Music, **6:**79
State Ensemble of Folk Dance (Russia), **8:**777
State University of Tiranë, **8:**1003
Statman and Feldman (musical group), **3:**941
status. *See* power and status
Stax Records, **3:**675–76, 678, 710
"Stay, Summer Breath" (Foster), **3:**187
Stedman Doubles (Maxwell Davies), **5:**136
Steel Pulse, **8:**215, 236
steelbands, **2:**62, 86, 93, 95, 96–97, 796
  in Canada, **3:**1202, 1208, 1212–13
  in Dominica, **2:**843
  in Europe, **8:**233, 235, 236
  in Great Britain, **8:**236
  in Grenada, **2:**866
  in Guyana, **2:**445–46, 447, 450
  in Jamaica, **2:**908
  in Montserrat, **2:**925
  in St. Lucia, **2:**950
  in Trinidad and Tobago, **2:**960–63; **3:**813; **8:**233
  in United States, **3:**809–10
  in Virgin Islands, **2:**969
Steen-Nøkleberg, Einar, **8:**425

Stefánsson, Páll, **8:***403*
Stein, Sir Aurel, **5:**689
Stein, Gertrude, **3:**545
Steinberg, Ben, **3:**939
Steinberg, David, **4:**184–85
Steinen, Karl von den, **2:**143
Steiner, Ernst, **10:**112
Steiner, Max, **3:**203, 546; **9:**44
Steinitz, Wolfgang, **8:**664
Steinway Company, **3:**561
Stella Record, **8:**777
Stella, Regis, **9:**480
Stender, Gothard Friedrich, **8:**504
Stenhammar, Wilhelm, **8:**444
Stenhouse, William, **8:**373, 374
Stepanos Siunetsi, **6:**737
Stephan, Emil, **9:**479, 981, 983, 991
Stephen V, Pope, **8:**726
Stephen, Ernest, **9:**755, 757
Stephen, Saint, **8:**736
Stephens, Hattie, **3:**1180
Stephens, Jeanette E., **2:**812
Steppenwolf (musical group), **3:**318, 1081
Stereo Nation (musical group), **5:**540
Stern, Isaac, **6:**1030; **7:**398, 416
Stern, Stephen, **3:**828
Stern's Records, **8:**241
Sternberg, Erich Walter, **6:**1027, 1029
Stesasonic, **3:**714
Stesha, **8:**286, 776
Steshenko-Kuftina, V., **8:**846
Steszewski, Jan, **8:**25
Stevens, Bill, **3:**410
Stevens, Jimmy, **9:**362
Stevens, Risë, **3:**537
Stevenson, Robert, **10:**80
Stevenson, Robert Louis, **3:**1047; **9:**36–37, 40–41
Stevenson, Robert M., **2:**8, 15, 116, 467, 501, 555, 602, 623–24, 737, 931; **3:**32, 848
Stevenson, Ronald, **8:**369
Stevenson, Savourna, **8:**366
Stevenson, William "Mickey," **3:**674
Stevo Teodosievski Ensemble, **8:**282
Stewardson, Richard, **3:**1063
Stewart, A. M., **4:**859
Stewart, Charles, **8:**373
Stewart family, **8:**296, 370, 372
Stewart, James, **3:**675
Stewart, Neil, **8:**373
Stewart, Rebecca, **5:**136
Stewart, Rod, **3:**689, 1002; **9:**179
Stewart, Shirley, **2:**820
Stewart, Tina, **8:**296
Stewart, Wendy, **8:**366
"Stewball" (folk song), **3:**835
"Stick Gambling Rock" (Alfred), **3:**1280
Stief, Wiegand, **8:**23
Stigwood, Robert, **3:**688
Still, William Grant, **3:**606, 607, 609, *609,* 619, 648
Stillman, Amy Kuʻuleialoha, **9:**869, 886, 915, 973, 986
Stills, Stephen, **3:**777
Stimela, **1:**779

Stimmen der Völker in Liedern (Herder), **8:**307
Stimson, J. Frank, **9:**883, 969
Sting (rock singer), **2:**124, 134; **3:**840
Stinson label, **3:**1243
Stirling, Charles, **3:**1070
Stisted, Maria, **3:**289
Stivell, Alan, **6:**277; **8:**321, 322, 561
Stock, Cheryl, **9:**416
Stock, Frederick, **3:**609
Stockbridge-Munsee Indian nation, **3:**454
Stockhausen, Karlheinz, **7:**735; **8:**188, 646
Stocking, George, **1:**94
Stockmann, Doris, **8:**1004
Stockmann, Erich, **8:**178, 847, 1004
Stoddard, Charles Warren, **9:**36
Stoddard, George, **3:**261
Stoeltje, Beverly, **1:**411
Stoin, Elena, **8:**907
Stoin, Vasil, **8:**19, 906, 907
Stoiński, Stefan M., **8:**712
Stokes, Frank, **3:**645
Stokes, John F. G., **9:**24, 969
Stokes, Martin, **6:**24, 255; **10:**164
Stoller, Mike, **3:**672–73, 709
Stone, A. W., **5:**53
stone chimes. *See* lithophones
Stone the Crows (cross-cultural dance project),
        9:415–16
Stone, Doris Z., **2:**635, 739, 744
Stone, Harry L., **3:**1096
Stone, I. F., **3:**255
Stone, Jesse, **3:**670, *670*
Stone, Ruth, **1:**488; **10:**28, 55–65, *58*
Stone, Verlon, **10:**56–57, 63
Stoney Indian nation, **3:**440
Stono Rebellion, **3:**594
Stony Plain (musical group), **3:**266
"Stop in the Name of Love" (Supremes), **3:**674
"Storm Is Passing Over" (Tindley), **3:**630
Storace, Stephen, **3:**180
Stormy Weather (film), **3:**609
Story of the Purple Hairpin (Tang), **7:**307
storytelling. *See* narratives; recitation
Stothart, Herbert, **9:**45
Stoughton Musical Society (Masssachusetts),
        3:535
Stowe, David, **3:**587
Stowe, Harriet Beecher, **3:**618
Stoyanov, Atanas, **8:**906
Stoyanov, Veselin, **8:**905
Strabo, **8:**881
Strachan, John, **8:**372
Strachwitz, Chris, **2:**624
Straight Outta Brooklyn (film), **3:**715
"Straighten Up and Fly Right" (Cole), **3:**669
Strait, George, **3:**81
Strajnar, Julijan, **8:**922
Strakosch, Maurice, **3:**60, 61
Stranded (Tierra), **3:**748
Strang, Gerald, **7:**708
Straniero, Michele L., **8:**613
Strategie (Xenakis), **8:**101
Strathern, Andrew, **9:**521
strathspey, **3:**407, 825, 1125; **8:**367, 370, 524
Strathy, G. W., **3:**1180
Strauss family, **8:**670

Strauss, Johann, **3:**193
Strauss, Johann, the elder, **8:**205
Strauss, Richard, **7:**341, 731; **8:**83, 646, 663
Stravinsky, Igor, **3:**174, 1102, 1151, 1184;
        4:873; **6:**1030; **7:**341, 342, 347, 350,
        732; **8:**26, 85, 445, 697, 730, 781,
        800
    ballets of, **3:**1150; **8:**60, 161; **10:**20
Strayhorn, Billy, **3:**654–55
Stražilovo (dance ensemble), **3:**1198
"Streaking Cheek to Cheek" (Ohio Players),
        3:681
Street Legal (television show), **3:**1062
Streetcar Named Desire, A (film), **3:**203
"Streets of Laredo" (cowboy song), **3:**520
Strehlow, Carl, **9:**435, 437
Strehlow Research Centre, **9:**960
Strehlow, T. G. H., **9:**987
Streisand, Barbra, **3:**943
Štreklj, Karel, **8:**922
Strike Up the Band (Gershwin), **3:**545
Strindberg, August, **5:**489
string bands
    Chuuk, **9:**735
    Fiji, **9:**779–80, 998
    Hawai'i
        Filipino, **9:**95, 100
        Portuguese, **9:**98
    Hungary, **8:**272–74, 738, 743–46
    Mariana Islands, **9:**743
    Marquesas Islands, **9:**895
    Montserrat, **2:**926
    Niue, **9:**817
    Oceania, **9:**27–28, 126, 136–40, 372, 385
    Papua New Guinea, **9:**89–90, 137–39,
        150–51, 246, 485–86
        Anêm people, **9:**616
        Bali and Vitu islands, **9:**610–11
        Baluan, **9:**607
        Daru Islands, **9:**179
        Gulf Province, **9:**495, 497–98
        Irumu people, **9:**568, 570–71
        island groups, **9:**387–88
        Motu people, **9:**494
        Nagovisi people, **9:**649
        New Britain, **9:**614, 625
        Rai Coast, **9:**566
        use of kundus, **9:**384
    Pohnpei, **9:**739–40
    Poland, **8:***113*
    Romania, **8:***88*
    Rom people
        in France, **8:**288
        in Poland, **8:**276
        in Romania, **8:**277, 278
        in Serbia, **8:**950–51
        in Yugoslavia, **8:**279
    Slovakia, **8:**276
    Solomon Islands, 'Are'are people, **9:**667
    Switzerland, **8:**690, *691*
    Tahiti, **9:***876–77*
    Tonga, **9:**793
    Trinidad and Tobago, **2:**96
    United States, **3:**645, 836, *838*
        Appalachian, **3:***13*
        in country music, **3:**76, 77–78

Louisiana, **3:**802
Michoacán, **3:**723, *723*
Ukrainian, **3:**345
Vanuatu, **9:**139–40, 198, 695
    Tanna, **9:**706, 709
West Futuna, **9:**863–64
string figures, **9:**253, 263–65, 267, *268*, 656,
        661, 755, *758*, 952
Stroboconn, **1:**255
Stroe, Aurel, **8:**883
Stromholm, Folk, **8:**428
Strong, Barrett, **3:**677
Strong, George Templeton, **3:**45
Strozzi, Barbara, **8:**77, 199
struck zithers. *See* dulcimers, hammered
structure. *See* form and structure
Strummer, Joe, **3:**357
Strut Miss Lizzie (musical), **3:**620
Stryker, Miriam, **3:**381
STS (musical group), **8:**678
Stuart, Alexander, **8:**372
"Stubborn Kind of Fellow" (Thee Midniters),
        3:747
Stubington, Jill, **9:**418
Stuckey, Sterling, **3:**585
"Student Demonstration Time" (Beach Boys),
        3:318
Student Prince (Romberg), **3:**193, 544
Studia Instrumentorum Musicae Popularis
        (periodical), **8:**21
Studia Musicologica Norvegica, **8:**427
*Studies in the Hebrew, Syrian, and Greek
        Liturgical Recitative* (Avenary), **6:**1059,
        1062
Studime Filologjike (periodical), **8:**1003
Studio 54 (New York), **3:**229, 688
Study of Ethnomusicology (Nettl), **3:**517
Studyo Imge (periodical), **6:**249
Stuempfle, Stephen, **2:**93
Stumpf, Carl, **4:**224, 225, 281, 285–86; **7:**137;
        8:803; **9:**980
Sturluson, Snorri, **8:**122–23, 405
Sturtevant, William C., **3:**472
Stutschewsky, Joachim, **6:**1029
Stylistics (musical group), **3:**711
Su Hanchen, **7:**113
Su Qiaozheng, **7:**212
Suadin, I Nyoman, **3:**1015; **10:**134
Suanda, Endo, **3:**1013
Suau people, **9:**983
Suazo, Sergio, **2:**745
Sub Pop label, **3:**169
Subanun people, **4:**920, 921
    epics of, **4:**927
    instrumental music of, **4:**923–24
    vocal music of, **4:**927
Subarctic peoples, **3:**383–92. *See also specific
        groups*
    culture of, **3:**383–84
    historical and cultural changes, **3:**390–91
    instruments of, **3:**472–79
    musical performance, **3:**384–85
    musical styles, **3:**389–90
    research on music of, **3:**392
    song ownership, **3:**386
    subsistence patterns, **3:**384

Subarma, Ki, 4:*713*
Subbama, 5:*869*
Subbaravu, Tangirala Venkata, 5:898
Subbulakshmi, M. S., 5:107, 232, 255, 267, 395, 414, 424, 561
Subcultural Sounds (Slobin), 10:52
Subotnick, Morton, 3:14
Subramania Ayyar, Musiri, 5:394
Subramania Ayyar, Patnam, 5:*146*, 217, 219
Subramania Pillai, Tiruvilimilalai, 5:392, 394
Subramaniam, Karaikudi S., 5:159, 161
Subramaniam, L., 3:986; 5:234, 584
Subramaniam, Radhika, 3:*985*
Subramanian, K. R., 5:*233*
Subtelny, Orest, 3:1089
Suchoff, Benjamin, 8:885
Suchoŋ, Eugeŋ, 8:729
Suchy, Jiří, 8:730
"Sucker MCs" (Run-D.M.C.), 3:552
Suco Campos, Idalberto, 2:752
Sud Sound System, 8:207
Süda, Peeter, 8:497–98
Sudan. *See also* North Africa; *specific peoples*
  academic training in, 1:40
  Arabic influences, 1:605–7
  chordophones in, 6:412
  Darfur region, 6:359
  drums in, 6:360
  geography of, 1:549
  griots, 1:297
  history of, 1:549–50, 555–56
  influence on Arab music, 6:362
  instruments, 1:600
  Islam in, 1:599
  lamellophones, 1:317, 320
  lyres in, 1:303; 6:357, 358
  Miri people, 1:601
  music in, 1:601
  music research in, 1:49
  Qur'ānic recitation in, 6:161
  trumpets in, 6:416
  urban music of, 1:570; 6:644
  zār cults, 1:273–74, 277, 604
Sudanese people, in Egypt, 6:23, 630–31
Sudest Island (Papua New Guinea), 9:177
Sudhakalasa, 5:44, 45, 47, 313
Sudhākara (Simhabhupala), 5:44–45
Sudiredja, Nugraha, 4:705
Śūdra class. *See* Shudra class
Sudraka, 5:484
Suehirogari (*syamisen* piece), 7:578, *578*
Suerre culture, 2:681
"Suffer in Silence" (Aglukark), 3:1280
Sufism, 3:954, 1042–45, 1199; 5:313, 401, 563.
  See also devotional songs and singing;
  Islam; *qawwali*
  Abdali order, 6:793
  Afghanistan, 5:817, 834
  Albania, 6:115; 8:986, 1002
  Arabian peninsula, 6:706, 710–11
  'Azūziyya brotherhood, 6:506
  Balochistan, 5:779; 6:881–90
  Bektaşīye (Bektashi) order, 6:81, 114–15, 189, 190, 196, 765, 768, 793, 794, 796;
    8:968, 986, 1002
  Bosnia-Hercegovina, 8:968

Burhaniyya order, 6:171
Bushishiyya order, 6:492–93
Celvetīye order, 6:114, 194
Central Asia, 6:900, 901, 910, 914, 919, 936–37, 942–45; 7:23, 24
Chestī (Chishti) order, 3:1044; 5:53, 256, 644, 752, 755, 817; 6:825, 881, 883, 889
  cymbals used in, 6:403
  ecstatic states in, 3:1044–45; 5:293–94, 752–53, 754, 755, 760–61; 6:884
Egypt, 6:147–51, 544
  dhikr practices, 6:171–75, 625–27
  inshād practices, 6:167, 170–75
Eşrefīye order, 6:191–92
Gülşenīye order, 6:192, 194
Halvetīye order, 6:114, 189, 191–92, 194, 196, 768
Ḥāmidiyya order, 6:171–72
Haydari order, 6:793
India, 5:76, 265
Indonesia, 4:76–77, 78, 687
Iran, 6:72–73, 129, 130–31, 140, 823, 824–26, 866, 876–77
'Īsāwiyya brotherhood, 6:333, 335, 403, 415, 418, 498, 506, 515–21
Ja'fariyya Aṃadiyya Mu ḥammadiyya order, 6:*173*
Kadiri order (*See* Qādiriyya order)
Kalenderi order, 6:793
Karnataka, 5:867
Khāksār order, 6:827
Kubrawiyya order, 6:942, 943
Kurdish communities, 6:745, 748, 793
Liberia, 1:344–45
Libya, 6:415
Malaysia, 4:414–15
Mashriq, 6:543
Mevlevi (Mawlawī) order, 5:760; 6:107–11, 132, 138, 161, 184, 189, 191, 196, 543, 564, 811
  compositions of, 6:56, 110–11, 116–17, 118–19, 196, 769, 779, 780
  history of, 6:107–8
  musical activity of, 6:108–9, 113, 114, 186, 190, 413, 414, 769, 825
Morocco, 6:415
music's central role in, 6:19, 132–33, 138, 177, 179, 186–88, 190–96, 543
Naqshabandiyya order, 6:825, 942, 943; 8:968
North Africa, 1:536–37; 6:431, 434, 436, 437, 438–39, 515
  dhikr practices, 6:437
philosophy of, 6:61
poet-saints of, 5:751, 756–60
Punjab, 5:765–66, 769–70, 772
Qādiriyya (Kadiri) order, 1:551–52; 5:683, 686; 6:12, 180–81, 189, 191–92, 196, 304, 417, 543, 811, *833*, 889, 942; 8:968
Rajasthan, 5:644
research on music in, 6:23
Rifāīye order, 6:147, 148, 149, 189, 417, 543
Shādhiliyya order, 6:171–72, 437, 515, 543
Shi'ite orders, 6:189, 793–800
Sudan, 1:550–51, 606

Sunni orders, 6:189, 190–97, 196
Tahtactı order, 6:790, 793, 796
Tījāniyya order, 6:305, 417, 437
treatises on, 5:53
Tunisia, 6:415, 506
  lodges, 6:327, 506–7, 512
  ma'lūf performance practice, 6:326–27, 335–36, 509, 510, 515, 517–18, 519
  rehabilitation of, 6:512–13
  suppression of, 6:510
Turkey, 6:189–97, 768–69, 784 (*See also* *specific orders*)
Uighur people, 6:1000; 7:459, 468
wandering dervishes, 6:793, 827, 889
writings on music, 6:372–73
Yassawiyya order, 6:940, 942, 944
Yazdaxum sect, 6:942, 943
Yemen, 6:656
Zikriyya order, 6:889

Suga no miya no mai (*yakuo goto* piece), 7:610
Sugar Cubes (musical group), 8:407
"Sugar Daddy" (disk jockey), 3:708
Sugar Hill (musical), 3:620
Sugar Hill Gang, 3:695, 699
Sugar Hill Records, 3:714
"Sugar in the Morning," 3:369
Sugarman, Jane, 3:517, 927–28, 1084
Sugatang Perlas (de León), 4:881
Sugino, Ki, 4:684; 10:50
Sugita, Hiroshi, 9:734–36
Sugiura Kinsen, 7:725
Sugung-ga (*p'ansori* story), 7:899, 905, *905*, 908, 986
Suhana, Nana, 4:*716*
Suhardi, 10:43–45, *45–46*, 47, 48, 49–50, 51
Suharto, Ben, 3:1020
Suhayl ibn 'Abd al-Raḥmān ibn 'Awf, 6:291
Suhrawardī, 6:186, 187, 188
Suhum, Ahmed, 6:496
Sui dynasty
  centralization in, 7:24, 25, 30
  instruments in, 7:80, 111
  musical institutions in, 7:392
  music in, 7:89, 448, 723, 981
  pipa in, 7:167
Sui people, 4:316
Sui shu, yinyue zhi (dynastic history), 7:111
Suiko, empress, 7:25
Suiri, Ibrahim, 6:1044
Suite Canadienne (Champagne), 3:14
Suite Incaica (Valcárcel), 2:115
suites. *See* form and structure; *specific types*
Suitô Gorô, 7:649
Suitô Kinzyô, 7:648–49
Sujech'ŏn (*hyangak* piece), 7:868
Sujinima (Tibetan opera), 7:479
Suk, Josef, 8:728
Sukadji, 10:*44*
Sukaesih, Elvy, 10:48
Šukar (musical group), 8:921
Sukarma, Burhan, 3:1020; 4:*132*, 715
Sukarno, president of Indonesia, 4:84
Sukarno Putra, Guruh, 4:109
Sukay (musical group), 2:*76*
Sukayna Bint al-Ḥusayn, 6:701
Sukchong, Chosŏn king, 7:985

Sukeroku (*katô busi* piece), **7**:681
Sukhothai (kingdom), **4**:62, 153, 159, 219, 284, 304
Sukkar, Ismāʿīl, **6**:168
Sukoco, Sundari, **4**:104
Sukri, Uking, **4**:715
Suku Asli people, **4**:614
Suku Bono people, **4**:615
Suku Dalem people, **4**:619
Suku Laut people, **4**:614
Suku Terasing people, **4**:619
Sukuma people, **1**:634, 636
    musical bows of, **1**:640
    music of, **1**:637, 638
Sulāfat al-alḥān wa-safīnat al-alḥān (Ubarī), **6**:569
Sulāfat al-ḥān fī 'l-alḥān (anon.), **6**:371
Sulaiman, Samaon, **4**:905
Sulawesi, **4**:804–10
    Dutch in, **4**:810
    funerals in, **4**:61
    geography of, **4**:804
    influence on Sumbawa culture, **4**:779, 780, 783
    Makassar culture in, **4**:779; **10**:46, 50–51, 52
    map of, **4**:805
    musical similarities to Malukun music, **4**:812
    music research on, **4**:29
    population of, **4**:804
    prehistoric, **4**:33, 34, 37–38
    research on, **4**:804
    Spanish in, **4**:810
    spirit of rice, **4**:51
Ṣulayb group, **6**:653
Sulayman, Mansa, **1**:75–76
Sulaymān, Muḥriz, **6**:168
Sulaymān, Ṣhādiq, **6**:651
Sulca, Antonio, **2**:*1*
Suleiman (*gamelan* director), **4**:684
Süleyman Ağa, **6**:780
Süleyman Çelebi, **6**:196, 768–69
Süleyman I, "the Magnificent," Ottoman sultan, **6**:113, 194, 565
Suliţeanu, Ghizela, **8**:886
Sulka people, **9**:620, 625
    singing of, **9**:621
    songs of, **9**:607
Sulkhanishvili, Niko, **8**:843
Sulkidoong (musical group), **7**:970, *970*
Sullang, **7**:984
Sulley, M. D., **10**:143, 145–48
Sullivan, Arthur, **2**:447; **3**:193, 544, 840, 1117, 1225, *1226*, 1228; **8**:186
Sulod people, **4**:907
Sŭlp'ŭn sori (Kim), **7**:959
Sultae kut (Yi), **7**:957
Sultana, Parveen, **5**:414
Sultān, Ḥuda, **6**:237
Sulu (sultanate), **4**:596
Sulu Archipelago. *See* Philippines; *specific peoples*
Suluk people, **4**:833
Sulushash (epic), **6**:952
Sulzer, F. J., **8**:885
Sulzer, Salomon, **3**:934; **6**:1060; **8**:263
Sulzmann, Erika, **1**:663

Suma de todas las reglas del canto llano (Martínez y Coll), **2**:736
Sumarliðadóttir, Ingibjörg, **8**:401, *402*
Sumarna, Undang, **3**:1020
Sumarsam, **3**:1018; **4**:385, 637, 638; **10**:51, 52
Sumatra
    Aceh, **4**:414, 598, 601, 603–5
        Islam in, **4**:77
    Bangka Island, **4**:626
    Basemah, **4**:622–23
    Belitung Island, **4**:626
    Bengkulu Province, **4**:619–21
    Dutch in, **4**:601, 626
    Enggano Island, **4**:598, 619, 621
    geography of, **4**:598
    gong-chime ensembles in, **4**:596
    history of, **4**:594, 596, 598–602, 779
    influence on Chăm culture, **4**:590–91
    influence on Orang Melayu Asli music, **4**:585, 587
    Jambi, **4**:616–19
    Lampung Province, **4**:627–28
    map of, **4**:*599*
    Mentawai Islands, **4**:598, 613–14
    Minangkabau, **4**:601, 608–13
    Minangkabau people, **4**:413, 414
        heart of rice, **4**:51
    musical genres (*See also* dance and movement; theater; vocal music *headings*)
        cintuk, **4**:623
        dangdut, **4**:601
        irama padang pasir, **4**:606
        lagu dua, **4**:606
        lisung, **4**:623
        rodat, **4**:616, 625
        serampang duabelas, **4**:606
        sinandung, **4**:606
    music research on, **4**:28–29
    Muslim kingdoms in, **4**:600
    Nias Island, **4**:598, 605, 608, 809–10
    North Sumatra Province, **4**:605–8
    population of, **4**:598
    Portuguese in, **4**:601, 606–7
    prehistoric, **4**:598–600
    research on, **4**:603
    Riau, **4**:607, 614–16, 628, 813
        Indian influences in, **4**:600
    South Sumatra Province, **4**:621–27
    tourism in, **4**:602, 608
    wars in, **4**:601
    West Sumatra Province, **4**:608–14
Sumatran music in North America, **3**:1018–20
Sumba, **4**:787–91
    Dutch in, **4**:788
    geography of, **4**:787
    history of, **4**:788
    population of, **4**:788
Sumbaga, Ki Laras, **4**:683
Sumbawa, **4**:778–85, 788
    Dutch in, **4**:779
    gendang dan langko genre, **4**:784
    geography of, **4**:778
    history of, **4**:779
    instruments of, **4**:780–81
    kreasi baru genre, **4**:784
    musical styles in, **4**:763

performance traditions in, **4**:779–80
population of, **4**:762, 778–79
Portuguese in, **4**:780
vocal music, **4**:782–83
Sumer, **5**:17–18; **6**:8, 17, 358, 535, 537
Sumi, Prabhudua M., **5**:*402*
Sumida gawa (Kanze), **7**:630, 632
Sumikura Ichiro, **7**:595
Sumire Yoshihara, **7**:*737*
Sümmani of Erzurum (*aşîk*), **6**:796, 803, 804, 808
Summer, Donna, **3**:228, 688, 711, 712
Summerland Singers and Players, **3**:1095
Summers, Keith, **8**:339
Summers, William John, **3**:848
Sumu culture, **2**:659, 739–40, 747, 749, 750–51
Sun Country (television show), **3**:109
Sun Dog (musical group), **3**:1277
Sun Downers (musical group), **3**:433
Sun Drum Village (performing group), **7**:432
Sun Ju, **3**:1261
Sun, Muammer, **6**:775
Sun Ra, **3**:662, 663
Sun Records, **3**:351, 353
Sun Shi'e, **7**:299
Sun-Treader (Ruggles), **3**:174
Sun Valley Serenade (film), **10**:111
Sun Wenming, **7**:177
Sun Wenyan, **7**:172
Sun Xuchun, **7**:300
Sun Yat-sen, **7**:35, 305, 380
Sun Yude, **7**:186
Sunabwi (Yi), **7**:954
Sunanda, **5**:422
Sunarti, **4**:684
al-Sunbāṭī, Riyāḍ, **6**:9, 46, 552, 599
Sunburst (musical group), **1**:645
Sunburu people, **1**:111, 115
Sunda. *See also* Indonesia; Java
    bamboo agriculture in, **4**:52
    composition in, **4**:130
    Dutch in, **4**:700, 705, 722
    ethnographic troupes and tourism in, **4**:724–25
    geography of, **4**:699
    gong-chime ensembles in, **4**:20
    harvest ceremonies, **4**:51–52
    history of, **4**:699–700, 779
    Hoabinhian culture, **4**:34
    influence on Cirebonese culture, **4**:697
    mother of rice, **4**:51
    musical genres (*See also* ensembles, musical; *gamelan*; vocal music)
        decline of, **4**:116
        jaipongan, **4**:684, 703, 704, 708
        kacapian, **4**:703, 712, 715–17, 718, 723
        kacapi-suling, **4**:703, 712, 715
        keteuk tilu, **4**:107
        kreasi baru, **4**:723–24
        pop Sunda, **4**:712, 717–19
        tembang Sunda, **4**:116, 132, 702, 703, 712–17, 714–15, 717, 719–20, 723, 725
    music research on, **4**:28–29
    population of, **4**:699

Sunda (*continued*)
 research on, **4:**701
 rice cultivation, **4:**52
 rice origin myth, **4:**50
 vocal music, use of foreign languages, **4:**56
Sundanese music in North America, **3:**1012,
  1018–20. *See also* Indonesian music
Sundanese Music in the Cianjuran Style (Van
  Zanten), **4:**28
Sundanese people, **4:**630, 631
Sundarajan, T. M., **5:**421
Sundaramurti Nayanar, Saint, **5:**215–16
Sundaram, V. V., **3:**992
Sunday, Billy, **3:**534
"Sunday, Bloody Sunday" (U2), **3:**552
Sunday in the Park with George (Sondheim),
  3:197, 545
Sundberg, Johan, **8:**448
Sundjaya, Hetty, **4:**110
Sundström, Sven-David, **8:**445
Sŭngjŏngwŏn ilgi (dynastic history), **7:**929
Sünit Mongols, **7:**1004–20
Suniyama (deity), **5:**961
Sunjata (Mali empire founder), **1:**495–97,
  499–502, 504, 506, 508, 509, 511
Sunny, **5:**791
Sunny Ozuna and the Sunliners, **3:**780
"Sunrise, Sunset" (Bock), **3:**943
Sunrize Band, **9:**446, 987
Sunshine Kids (musical group), **9:**160
Sunshine Records, **3:**410, 449, 707, 1087, 1089,
  1243
Sunshine Town (Moore), **3:**199
Sunthon Phu, **4:**257, 306
Sunuwar people, **5:**290–91
Suo Yi, **7:**364
Suomen Silta (periodical), **3:**823
Suomi Seura, **3:**823
suona. See double-reed instruments
Suosikki (periodical), **8:**484
Sup (Hwang), **7:**955, 976
Supadmi, **4:**684
Supa Dupa Fly (Elliot), **3:**697
Supanggah, Rahayu, **4:**638; **10:**52
Super Étoile, **1:**365
Superfly (film), **3:**685, 711
Supernatural (Santana), **3:**751
Supicic, Ivan, **3:**45
Suppan, Wolfgang, **8:**23
Suppé, Franz von, **7:**743
Supplement to the Voyage of Bougainville
  (Diderot), **9:**34
Supraphon (record company), **8:**730, 731–32
Supremes (musical group), **3:**674, 677, 709
Supriatin, Yoyoh, **4:**716
Suraiya, **5:**420
Sur Das (also Surdas), **5:***115*, 249, *249*, 251,
  495, 643, 660, 666, 724
Sur, Donald, **7:**976
Sur, Lydia, **9:**166
Suratno, Nano, **4:**130, 697, 717–18
Suraya, queen of Afghanistan, **5:**816
Surendranath, **5:**420
Surinach, Carlos, **3:**851–52
Surinam, **2:**441, 503–9. *See also specific peoples*
 Amerindian cultures in, **2:**503–4

Asian descendants in, **2:**48
Boni culture, **2:**163
Chinese people in, **2:**84–85
cord-and-peg tension drums in, **1:**316
East Indian people in, **2:**85–86; **3:**813–17
geography of, **2:**503
history of, **2:**242, 245, 503, 504
instruments of, **2:**505–6
Javanese people in, **2:**52–53, 83, 85–86,
  507–8, 792
Maroon cultures in, **2:**2, 131, 504–6
musical genres
 aleke, **2:**509
 kaseko, **2:**508–9
 kawina, **2:**508
population of, **2:**503
tropical-forest region of, **2:**123–35
Wayana culture, **2:**164–67, 167
Surmach, Myron, **3:**912
Suroît (musical group), **3:**1136, 1137, 1168
Sūr-Sāgar (Sur Das), **5:***115*, 251
Sursurunga people, **9:**297, 626–27
Surusila, Leah, **3:**1275
Suruturaga, Inoke Seru, **9:**972
"Survival" (O'Jays), **3:**683
Surya (deity), **5:**220
Surya dynasty, **5:**731
Surya Sena, Devar, **5:**972
Suryati, **4:**684
Suryavarman I, king of Khmer, **4:**153
Suryavarman II, king of Khmer, **4:**153
Susa people, **1:**446
Susanna (Floyd), **3:**546
susaps. *See* lamellophones
Susato, Tielman, **8:**523
Susheela, P., **5:**421
Sušil, František, **8:**732
Susilo, Hardja, **3:**1013, 1015; **4:**636, 637;
  10:42–43
Susimga (Korean folk song), **7:**883, 988
Susiya (*bunraku* play), **7:**583
Susnik, Branislava, **2:**204
Susquehanna Indian nation, **3:**1078
Sutherland, Isabel, **8:**372
Sutiari, Ni Nyoman, **3:**1019
Sutton, Myron, **3:**1077
Sutton, R. Anderson, **3:**1014; **4:**28, 102, 638,
  639; **10:**41–53, *44–46, 52*
Suvchinsky, Piotr, **8:**781
Suwanee River (musical), **3:**618
Suwardi, Rahayu Supanggah Al., **4:**656, 684–85
Suweca, I Wayan, **3:**1019; **10:**134
Su Wu muyang (*yangqin* piece), **7:**180
Suyá culture, **2:**143–49
 history of, **2:**143–44
 mouse ceremony of, **2:**128
 music and dance of, **2:**126, 144–49
 oratory of, **2:**128
 song ownership in, **2:**130
Suyangsan'ga (*kasa*), **7:**927
Suzara, Venancia, **4:**856
Suzuki, D. T., **3:**130–31
Suzuki Hiroyosi, **7:**736
Suzuki Masaru, **7:**745
Suzuki mondo (narrative), **7:**602
Suzuki Sin'ichi, **3:**280, 281; **7:**50

Suzy Records, **8:**936
Svabo, Jan Christian, **8:**471
Svan people, **8:**827–28, 832, 857
 dance traditions of, **8:**836, 841
 instruments of, **8:**838–39, 840
 vocal music of, **8:**835, 841, 847
Svaramelakālānidhi (Ramamatya), **5:**46
Sved, Vasil', **8:***793*
Sveen, Olaf, **3:**1251
Sveinbjörnsson, Sveinbjörn, **8:**406
Svenska låtar, **8:**437
Svenskt Musikhistoriskt Arkiv (Stockholm),
  8:448
Svenskt Visarkiv (Stockholm), **8:**448
Svensson, Reinhold, **8:**446
Svensson, Sven E., **8:**447
Sveshnikov, Aleksandr, **8:**777
Svete, Tomaš, **8:**921
Sviridov, Georgy, **8:**782
Svitanok Ukrainian Dance Ensemble (Ottawa),
  3:1200
Svoboda, Vera, **8:**934
Swahili people
 Arabic influences, **1:**606
 bands of, **1:**603
 history of, **1:**635–36
 instruments of, **1:**625
 music of, **1:**631
Swallow (soca singer), **2:**96
Swallows (musical group), **3:**671
Swami (musical group), **4:**110
Swaminarayan movement, **5:**255
Swaminathan, Kalpakam, **5:***353*
Swan Dance (Kazakh piece), **7:***461*
Swan, Helma, **3:**398
Swan Silvertones (gospel quartet), **3:**633
Swan Song label, **3:**356
Swann, Howard, **3:**734
Swanson, Howard, **3:**610
Swarangeet Orchestra, **5:**605
Swaziland, **1:**428, 705. *See also* Southern Africa;
  specific peoples
Swazi people, **1:**321, 705
Sweden, **8:**434–48
 Ångermanland, **8:**435
 Bohuslän, rock carvings, **8:**36, 39
 court music in, **8:**440, 444
 Dalarna, **8:**446
 Dalecarlia, **8:**434, 440
 dance-house movement, **8:**153
 dance traditions of, **8:**164, 434–35, 442–43
 fiddlers' competitions, **8:**150
 fiddlers' ensembles, **8:**152
 fiddlers' societies, **8:**9
 folk music pedagogy, **8:**155
 geography of, **8:**434, 437
 Gotland, **8:**435
 Hälsingland, **8:**435, 439
 history of music in, **8:**443–45
 identity issues in, **8:**441
 instruments, **8:**22, 170, 438, 439–42
  played by women, **8:**194
  research on, **8:**35, 41
 Järna, festivals in, **8:**154, *155*
 map of, **8:***398*
 Öland, **8:**435

popular music in, **8:**208, 445–46
population of, **8:**434
radio broadcasts of folk music, **8:**156
regional styles in, **8:**434–35
research on music of, **8:**18, 447–48
rock in, **8:**216
rule over Estonia, **8:**491, 494–95
rule over Finland, **8:**475
rule over Norway, **8:**411, 424
Saami people in, **8:**12, 299–307, 446–47
Stockholm, immigrant groups in, **8:**231
vocal music of, **8:**26, 136, 195, 435–36,
        437–39
Swedish people
    in Estonia, **8:**491, 493
    in Finland, **8:**247, 475, 487
    in Hawai'i, **9:**95
    in North America, **3:**870–72
        dance music of, **3:**871–72
        Ontario, **3:**1196
        vaudeville, **3:**872
        vocal music of, **3:**870–71
        western Canada, **3:**343, 409, 1089,
                1250–51
Swedish Royal Academy of Music, **8:**443
Sweeney, P. L. Amin, **4:**26–27
Sweeney's Men, **8:**392
Sweeney Todd (musical group), **3:**1097
Sweeney Todd (Sondheim), **3:**197, 545
Sweeney, William, **8:**369
"Sweet Betsy from Pike" (ballad), **3:**835, 888,
        1257
"Sweet Genevieve" (Tucker), **3:**190
Sweet Honey in the Rock (musical group),
        10:144
Sweet, Jill D., **3:**221, 430
"Sweet Leilani" (Owens), **3:**1049, 1050; **9:**43
"Sweet Sixteen" (Turner), **3:**708
"Sweet Soul Music" (Conley), **3:**710
"Sweet Sticky Thing" (Ohio Players), **3:**681
"Sweet William's Ghost" (ballad), **3:**1124
Sweetgrass Records, **3:**449
"Sweethearts" (Herbert), **3:**261
Sweethearts (Herbert), **3:**193
"Sweetly She Sleeps, my Alice Fair" (Foster),
        3:187
Swettenham, Frank, **4:**427
Swift, Jonathan, **8:**378; **9:**33
Swindle, Billy, **9:***135*
swing, **2:**97; **3:**45, 78–79, 550, 581, 583,
        655–56, 863, 902
    black, **3:**667
    in Canada, **3:**1077, 1091, 1107
    in Costa Rica, **2:**691
    dance competitions for, **3:**210
    dancing to, **3:**212
    in Europe, **8:**228
    in Germany, **8:**660
    in Israel, **6:**1020
    Mexican audiences and performers, **3:**742,
            778, 779–80
    in Oceania, **9:**149
    race and, **3:**63
    in Turkey, **6:**249
"Swing Along" (Cook), **3:***619*
Swing Along (musical), **3:**608

Swing Mikado (Graham), **3:**609, 621
Swiss people, in Hawai'i, **9:**96
Swiss Yodeling Association, **8:**692
Switched-On Bach (Carlos), **3:**254
Switzerland, **8:**682–98
    Aargau, *silväschtertrösche* custom, **8:**684
    Appenzell Ausserrhoden, *silvesterchläuse*
            custom, **8:**683, *684*
    art music in, **8:**696–97
    Basel
        Fasnacht in, **8:**685
        griffin pageant, **8:**684, 686
    carnival in, **8:**140, 161, 684–85, 686
    dance traditions of, **8:**689–90, 693–94, 696
    folk/art music interactions, **8:**696–97
    folk music in, **8:**13
    French areas, regional music, **8:**692–94
    geography of, **8:**682
    German regions, regional music, **8:**689–92
    Graubünden, **8:**694
    Haute-Gruyère, herders of, **8:**119
    history of, **8:**682
    identity issues in, **8:**682
    immigrant populations in, **8:**697
    instruments and instrumental music, **8:**21,
            141, 170, 682, 685–89, 693–96
        research on, **8:**172
    Italian areas, regional music, **8:**694–96
    Lötschental, carnival in, **8:**685
    Lucerne, carnival in, **8:**684–85
    map of, **8:***644*
    Muotatal, alphorns of, **8:**687
    popular music in, **8:**208, 209, 698
    population of, **8:**682
    Romansh region, regional music, **8:**692, 697
    Rom people in, **8:**272
    St. Gallen, processions, **8:**684
    Solothurn, *chesslete* custom, **8:**684
    Stans, *guggemusig* custom, **8:**684
    Steinen, *nüssler* custom, **8:**684
    Ticino, **8:**618, 694–96
        bell-ringing in, **8:**685
    Valais, bell-ringing in, **8:**685
    vocal music of, **8:**17, 26, 119, 128, 142,
            682–83, 690–95
SXL (album), **7:**967
Syakkyô (nô play), **7:**632
syakuhati. See flutes
Syakuhati San Bon Kai (musical group),
        7:709
Syama (deity), **5:**252
Syama Sastri. *See* Sastri, Syama
Sydney, Angela, **3:**1277
Sydney Opera House (Australia), **9:**405, 415
Syed, Tahira, **5:**750
Sykes, Roosevelt, **3:**645
Sylla, Ibrahima, **8:**234, 239
Sylphide, La (Taglioni), **8:**161
Sylvia (Delibes), **8:**161
symbolism
    Andalusian mysticism, **6:**448
    animal, in instruments, **2:**10, 35, 183, 413
    bagpipe as phallic symbol, **8:**201
    Colombia, *currulao,* **2:**405
    dualistic, **2:**33–35; **7:**99–100, 103, 240, 312,
            319, 545–55

fertility, **2:**35, 228–29, 253, 283, 289, 291, 524
Finland
    of instruments, **8:**479
    in laments, **8:**475
Georgia, rituals, **8:**835
Germany Democratic Republic, of song texts,
        8:662
Germany, in resistance song texts, **8:**661
harvest songs, **8:**132
identity and, **3:**505–6, 823, 826
of instruments, **1:**783–84; **2:**32–40; **5:**325,
        342, 346, 353, 364; **8:**439–40
Islamic views of music and, **6:**177–88
Korea, of instruments, **7:**822
Latvia, goat horn, **8:**503
Lithuania, song texts, **8:**510
mandala, **6:**184–85
metaphor and, **9:**336–43
Mongol people, **7:**1015
New Caledonia, botanical, **9:**685
Norway, Hardanger violin, **8:**421
number, **6:**184; **7:**100, 545–47
Poland, solstice songs, **8:**703
song texts, nature symbols in, **8:**133
Sufi, **6:**888–89
Symonds, Nelson, **3:**1077
Symonds, Norman, **3:**1184
Symonette, George, **2:**806
Symphonic Fantasia, Korea (Ahn), **7:**952
symphonic music. *See* art music, Western
symphony, **8:**80
    Classical and Romantic, **8:**82, 83, 186–87
Symphony from the New World (Dvořák), **3:**538
Symphony 1997: Heaven, Earth, Mankind (Tan),
        7:431
Symphony Nova Scotia (Halifax), **3:**1120
Symphony No. 2 (Mahler), **6:**1027
Symphony No. 3 (Górecki), **8:**210
Symphony No. 5 (Beethoven), **8:***83*
Symphony No. 9 (Beethoven), **8:**60, 82, 187
Symphony No. 41, "Jupiter" (Mozart), **8:**62
Symphony for the Sons of Nam (Williams), **3:**612
Syncona (musical group), **3:**1085
Syncopated Society Orchestra, **3:**651, 706
Syndicat des Auteurs Compositeurs et des Artistes
        Musiciens, **2:**880
Syn-Nara (record company), **7:**972
Synnevåg, Magne, **8:**472
Syntagma musicum (Praetorius), **8:**654
synthesizers. *See* electrophones
Syôbutu, **7:**646
syômyô. See chant (Buddhist)
Syômyô syû (chant collection), **7:**582, 589
Syôsôin Imperial Depository (Nara), **7:**79, 81,
        112, 188, 538, 585, 588, 622, 643,
        644, 701
Syôwa period, **7:**698, 705
Syôzi Tarô, **7:**745
Syôzyô (nô play), **7:**632
Syracuse University, **10:**133–35
Syria
    aerophones in, **6:**414
    Aleppo, **6:**201, 202
    history of, **6:**565
    Mevlevî Sufis, **6:**543–44, 550
    musical traditions of, **6:**563–64, 565–70

Syria (*continued*)
Antioch, **6:**207–8, 226–27
art music, **6:**126
chordophones in, **6:**406, 409
Damascus, **6:**565
Umayyad court in, **6:**293, 294, 351, 538, 539
dance traditions in, **6:**654
drums in, **6:**418
historical boundaries of, **6:**225
influence on Arab music, **6:**362
Kurdistan region of, **6:**743–52
lyres in, **6:**358
Maronite Church in, **6:**207, 535
musical genres of, **6:**550–52
popular music in, **6:**229
Qur'ānic recitation in, **6:**161
Sephardi Jews in, **6:**201
Turkmen people in, **6:**967
Syriac people, **6:**225–29
Syrian Catholic Church, **6:**227
Syrian Orthodox Church, **3:**984, 1029; **5:**945; **6:**225–29, 403, 405, 544, 1021
Syrian people
in Barbados, **2:**813
in Caribbean, **2:**793
in North America, **3:**943, 1032, 1218–20
in South America, **2:**84
in Trinidad and Tobago, **2:**953
Šyrma State Academic Choir of Belarus, **8:**799, 803
Syro-Antiochene rites, **6:**208
Syro-Malabar Church, **5:**945
Syro-Malankara Church, **5:**945
Syusin Kaniiri (Tamagusuku), **7:**65–66
Szabolcsi, Bence, **8:**20
Szechenyi Society (Calgary), **3:**1250
Szörényi, Levente, **8:**747
Szymanowska, Maria, **8:**710
Szymanowski, Karol, **8:**710

Ta'ai (Sāmoan comedian), **9:**235
Ta'akokoa, **9:**901
Taaqiyáa (Usarufa musician), **9:***980*
taarab, **1:**227, 415, 426, 427–28, 607, 631–32, 645–46
Tabar Islands (Papua New Guinea), **9:**626, 628–29
Tabaran (album), **9:**155
al-Ṭabarī, **6:**361
Tabiteuea (Kiribati), **9:**982
tabla. See drums, paired
taboos, **2:**17, 153; **9:**925. *See also* censorship and bans
Australia, **9:**467
Bolivia, **2:**283
on musical performance, **2:**290, 291
Ecuador, on musical performance, **2:**414
Fiji, **9:**230
Hawai'i, **9:**15–16, 207–9, 914
Irian Jaya, instrument knowledge, **9:**583
Nigeria, **1:**289
Papua New Guinea, **9:**22–23, 189, 609
Bougainville, **9:**651
Buin people, **9:**652
flute playing, **9:**532

instrumental knowledge, **9:**562–63
Motu people, **9:**492
Polynesia, **9:**200–202
Tahiti, **9:**207–9
Tonga, **9:**787–88
Vanuatu, **9:**966
Tanna, **9:**705
Tabou Combo (musical group), **2:**98, 892; **3:**803
Tabu (film), **9:**44, 46
Tabuh-Tabuhan (McPhee), **3:**953; **4:**131
Tabwa people, **1:**119
Tachard, Guy, **4:**70, 225, 252
Taché, Joseph-Charles, **3:**1164, 1165
Taeak hubo (collection), **7:**856, 869
Taebaeksan maek (film), **7:**960
Taebaram sori (Yi), **7:**954
taegŭm. See flutes
Taehan Kugagwŏn (institute), **7:**990
T'aejo, Chosŏn king, **7:**868
T'aejong, Chosŏn king, **7:**984
Taeŏp (ch'anggŭk piece), **7:**969
Taewŏn'gun and the Empress Min (film), **7:**976
Tafelmusik (musical group), **3:**1080, 1186
Taft, William Howard, **3:**310
Tafunsak people, **9:**740
Tagailog Symphony (Santiago), **4:**872
Tagakaolo people, **4:**905, 920
Tagbanwa people, **4:**920, 924, 927
Tagg, Philip D., **3:**45; **8:**448
Tagharan (Armenian songbook), **6:**724
Tagish Nation Dancers, **3:**1277
Taglioni, Filippo, **8:**161
Taglioni, Marie, **8:**161
Tago, Stephan Ogaji, **9:**58
Tagoona, William, **3:**1275, 1280
Tagorama, Patrocinio, **4:**856
Tagore, Devendranath, **5:**848–49
Tagore, Dwijendranath, **5:**848, 849
Tagore, Ganendranath, **5:**849
Tagore, Jorasanko, **5:**849
Tagore, Jotindro Mohun, **5:**432
Tagore, Jyotirindranath, **5:**848, 849–50, 851
Tagore, Rabindranath, **5:**431, 505, 562–63, 848, 849, 850–51, 853, 856, 858, 972
"Bande Mātaram!", **5:**436
Gītānjali, **5:**850
"Janaganamana," **5:**437
nationalist songs of, **5:**436–37, 850–51
Rabindra saṅgīt, **5:**162, 254, 336, 550, 562, 573, 850–51, 857, 858
style of, **5:**860
University at Santiniketan, **5:**562, 851, 857, 858, 972
Tagore, Raja of, **8:**176
Tagore, Satyendranath, **5:**848, 849
Tagore, Sourindro Mohun, **5:**205, 431–33, 434, 438, 561
Bengal Music School of, **5:**442–43
compositions of, **5:**436
instrument classification system of, **5:**322
Saṅgītasārasaṅgraha, **5:**46, 51
scholarly works of, **5:**51
Taha'a (Society Islands), **9:**867
Ṭaha, Shaykh 'Umar, **6:**147
Ṭaher and Zohre (epic), **6:**840
al-Ṭahhān, al-Hajj Ḥāfiz, **6:**605

Ṭāhir ibn 'Abdallāh al-Ṭabarī, **6:**372
Tahiti (Society Islands), **9:**867–79. *See also* Society Islands
American expeditions to, **9:**20, 24
body decoration, **9:**349
chief presentation ceremony, **9:**348
Chinese people in, **9:**71–72, 868
Christianity in, **9:**187, 207–8
Cook expeditions to, **9:**9–11
cultural contacts with Cook Islands, **9:**903
cultural contacts with Mangareva, **9:**888–89
cultural contacts with Marquesas, **9:**894
cultural contacts with Rapa Nui, **9:**952
cultural contacts with Tuamotus, **9:**885
European poetry on, **9:**39
Europeans in, **9:**34
festivals in, **9:**56–57
hīmene genre, **9:**37–38, 301, 870–73, 877
instruments, **9:**868–69
tō'ere, **9:**379
ukulele, **9:**391
Marquesans in, **9:**890
missionaries in, **9:**21
music and dance of, **9:**10–11, 48, 307, 865, 867–79, 969, 980
Pape'ete, **9:**867
dance performances, **9:**873–74
pedagogy in, **9:**269–71
research on, **9:**976
sound recordings from, **9:**998
Tuamotuans in, **9:**883, 885
Tahiti Fête, **9:**47–48
Tahitian people, in Hawai'i, **9:**105
Tahltan Indian nation, **3:**1277
Tahrîrîye (Abdülbakî Nâsir Dede), **6:**110, 118
Tahuata (Marquesas Islands), **9:**889
T'ai Chi Ch'uan, **3:**214
Tai people, **4:**218–19, 219; **7:**496, 505. *See also* Thailand
cultural interactions with Khmer people, **4:**159
distribution of, **4:**529
gong and cymbal ensemble, **7:**192
history of, **4:**153
Tai, Ryūichi, **9:**963
Taiao, **9:**948
taiko. See drums: barrel, conical, or cylindrical
Taiko Jazz Project (Tonooka), **3:**973
Tai Kwon Do, **3:**214
Tai-lue people, **4:**537
Taino culture, **2:**78, 189. *See also* Arawak culture
in Central America, **2:**668
in Cuba, **2:**822
in Dominican Republic, **2:**846–47, 850
in Haiti, **2:**881
instruments of, **2:**8, 13, 22–23
in Puerto Rico, **2:**932–33
Taiping jing (Daoist work), **7:**320
Tairona culture, **2:**183
archaeomusicological studies of, **2:**7; **10:**100
instruments of, **2:**9–10
Tairora people, **9:**526–33
Taishan people, **3:**1260
Taisyô (Taisho) period, **7:**689, 698, 705, 722, 729, 743, 778
Taita people, **1:**624

Taiwan, 7:6
    Aboriginal peoples of, 7:141, 357, 358, 403,
        423, 427–29, 447, 523–29
    Amis people in, 7:92, 427, *427*, *428*
    Austronesian speakers, 9:319
    beiguan genre, 7:425
    Bunun people of, 9:257
    Chaozhou people in, 7:211
    Confucianism in, 7:335–37
    cultural exchanges in, 7:49–51
    geography of, 7:423
    Hengchun, folk songs of, 7:424
    history of, 7:423–24, 523
    history of music in, 7:90–91, 137
    influence on Southeast Asian culture, 4:80
    Japanese occupation of, 7:423
    mainland musical traditions in, 7:429
    nanguan genre, 7:169, 205–9, 396, 425
    Nationalists in, 7:90, 385–86, 423–24, 429
    Peking opera in, 7:275
    popular music, 3:964
    popular music in, 7:356–59, 389
    prehistoric, 4:37–38, 56
    research on music of, 7:141, 156, 524–25
    rice cultivation in, 4:48
    rice origin myths, 4:51
    scholarship in, 7:136, 139, 141
Taiwan dochiakuzoku no ongaku (Lu), 7:524
Taiwan takasagozoku no ongaku (Kurosawa),
    7:524
Taiwan wuqu (Jiang), 7:347
Taiwanese people
    in Australia, 9:71
    in Belize, 2:666
    in Caribbean, 2:793
    in North America, 3:949, 959, 1260
Taiwu, Northern Wei emperor, 7:312, 320
Taiyai people. *See* Shan people
Taizu, Ming emperor, 7:336, 392
Taj, Imtiaz Ali, 5:487
Tajdar-e-Haram (album), 5:746
Tajik people, 5:5
    in Afghanistan, 5:506, 804, 805–6, 825, 831
    in China, 7:455–58
Tajikistan, 6:895; 7:36. *See also* Central Asia
    funerary rituals in, 6:942
    Iranian dance traditions in, 6:875–79
    Islamic culture in, 6:935–47
    map of, 6:*910*
    maqām traditions, 6:11, 12, 184, 903,
        909–20, 922
    mouth harp playing in, 5:814
    popular music of, 5:810
    Soviet period in, 6:903–4
    Turkmen people in, 6:967
    Urā-Teppa, 6:942
    vocal music of, 6:830
    women's religious genres and roles, 6:945–47
Tajiyev, Mirsadyq, 6:904
tajwīd. *See* recitation
Takacs, Jeno von, 4:870, 872
Takadja (musical group), 3:1170
Takahashi Yûji, 4:876; 7:737
Takarazuka Kagekidan (women's theatrical
        troupe), 7:744, 765–66, 945
Takasago (Zeami), 7:630, 631

Takasaki Goroku, 7:608–9
Take 6 (musical group), 3:*634*, 635
"Take Me Out to the Ball Game" (Von Tilzer),
        3:514, 549
Takemitsu Toru, 7:50, 627, 649, 705, 708, 729,
        735–37, 750–51
Takemoto Gidayû, 7:539–40, 588, 663, 667–69,
        675, 679, 719–20
Takemoto Harima no syôzyô, 7:546
Takemoto Masatayû, 7:669, 677
Takemoto za (Ôsaka), 7:667–69, 677
Takenoko syû (Uzi), 7:547
Takhary, 5:831
Taki Rentarô, 7:731
Taki Rua (Aotearoa), 9:233
Takiguti Syûzô, 7:736
Takkar, Sardar Ali, 5:791
Täklimakan (musical group), 7:467–68
taksim. *See* taqsīm
Taksin, King, 4:304, 310
Taktakishvili, Otar, 8:844
Takuboku (*biwa* piece), 7:644
Takuu (Papua New Guinea), 9:833, 838–42
    instruments, struck tins, 9:379
    music and dance of, 9:838–42
    research on, 9:974
Tal, Josef, 6:1031, 1063
tala, 5:20. *See also* talas
    in devotional music, 5:250, 253
    etymology of, 5:111
    fractional, 5:135
    hand gestures for, 5:26, 27, *28*, 37, 39, 110,
        138–46, 152, 164, 169–70, 212, 219,
        299, 324, 358
    Hindustani, 5:82, 110–37
        compared with Karnatak, 5:111, 116
        cycle, 5:112
        drum syllables in, 5:111, 116, 119
        functions of, 5:111
        in Kabuli *ghazal*, 5:805
        lay concept, 5:111
        for light classical genres, 5:179
        new types of, 5:134–35
        for *pakhāvaj* performance, 5:116–17
        rhythmic divisions, 5:112–13
        similarities with Pashtun music, 5:835
        for *tabla* performance, 5:124–27
        used by Sikhs, 5:13
    institutional transmission of, 5:447–48
    Karnatak, 5:138–61
        compared with Hindustani, 5:111, 116
        drum syllables in, 5:151, *152*
        functions of, 5:111
        internal beat structure in, 5:142–44
        laya concept, 5:148
        for *mridangam* performance, 5:149–59
        musical structure and, 5:145–49
        "primordial seven" scheme, 5:139–42
        relation to Kerala system, 5:939
        rhythm improvisation and, 5:147–48
        tālamālikā (garland of talas), 5:218–19
        in Tamil Nadu theater, 5:913
    local traditions of, 5:20, 33, 37, 111
    meaning of, 5:110, 138
    Nātyaśāstra passage on, 5:26–27, 29
    similarities to *hardingfele* rhythms, 8:417

ṭhekā (drum syllable patterns), 5:44, 153, 169,
        172
    time-keeping instruments, 5:25
    transmission of, 5:373
    treatises on, 5:24, 33, 37, 39, 43, 44, 110–11
    in Vaishnav music, 5:846
talas, (H = Hindustani; K = Karnatak)
    addhā (H), 5:194
    ādi (K), 5:143–44, 145–46, 153, *154*, *156*,
        158, 159, 219, *223*, *227*, 323–24,
        940
    ārācautāl (H), 5:127, 194
    āṭa (K), 5:139, 141, *142*, 217
    aṭanta (Kerala), 5:940
    Brahma (H), 5:117
    buddha pada (Sri Lanka), 5:*967*
    campaṭa (Kerala), 5:939
    cāñcar (H), 5:127
    cāpu (K), 5:144, 146
    cārtāl kī savārī (H), 5:194
    cautāl (H), 5:116, 117–18, 119, 121, 125,
        165–67, 168, 197, 250
    dādrā (H), 5:127, 181, 183, 185, 194, 255,
        276
    dhamār (H), 5:116–17, 170, 197, 250, 494
    dhrupad (H), 5:633
    dhruva (K), 5:139, 140
    dhumālī (H), 5:184–85
    dīpcandī (H), 5:127, 181, *182–83*, 194, 589
    ēka (K), 5:139, 140, 141, *142*, 939
    ektāl (H), 5:125–26, 127, *174*, *177*, *178*,
        194, 195, 203, 633
    Gaṇeśa (H), 5:117
    jat (H), 5:181
    jhampā (K), 5:139, 141, *142*, *225*
    jhaptāl (H), 5:126, 135, 168, 185, 194, 494
    jhūmrā (H), 5:127
    kaharvā (H), 5:127, 181, 184–85, 194, 255,
        574, 589, 667
    kalāvatī (H), 5:135
    khaṇḍa cāpu (K), 5:144, 153
    khaṇḍa jāti āṭa (K), 5:940
    Lakshmī (H), 5:117
    matya (K), 5:139
    menkup (H), 5:495
    miśra cāpu (K), 5:144, 146, 153
    muri aṭanta (Kerala), 5:939
    nasruk (H), 5:135
    nishorūk (H), 5:135
    pañcāri (Kerala), 5:939
    panjābī (H), 5:126, 181
    qawwālī (H), 5:125
    rajniel (H), 5:495
    rūpak (H), 5:111, 112, 113, 126, 144, 185,
        194, 203, 206
    rūpaka (K), 5:139, 141, *142*, 148, 153, 224
    sārabhandānanda (K), 5:229
    simhananda (K), 5:229
    sūltāl (H), 5:116, 197
    tanchep (H), 5:495
    tewa pada (Sri Lanka), 5:*967*
    tīntāl (Afghani), 5:806
    tīntāl (H), 5:112, 124–25, 126–27, 128, 132,
        134–35, 136, *176*, *177*, 191, 192,
        193, *196*, 198, *201*, 203, 206, 255,
        494, 633

talas, (H = Hindustani; K = Karnatak)
　　(*continued*)
　　tiruppugal (K), **5:**145
　　tīvrā (H), **5:**116, 197
　　tripuṭa (K), **5:**139, 140, 141, *142*, 939
　　trītāl (H), **5:**633
　　upa tāl jhampak (H), **5:**194
　　vilōma cāpu (K), **5:**228
Talagi, Mrs. E. F., **9:**973
Talamanca culture, **2:**681. *See also* Bribri culture;
　　Cabécar culture
Talang Mamak people, **4:**614
Ṭalʿat Ḥarb, Muḥammad, **6:**236
Talaud Islands, prehistoric, **4:**37
Tale of Genzi. See Genzi monogatari
Tale of Ise. See Ise monogatari
Tale of King Gesar (epic), **7:**451, 472, 477, 1008,
　　1015
Tales of the Manuvu (Pedero), **4:**885
Tales of the South Pacific (Michener), **9:**37, 45
Talib, Vinayak Prasad, **5:**487
Taliban movement, **5:**489, 791, 811, 817, 824,
　　826, 829, 832
Talich, Václav, **8:**730
"Talk to Me" (Osuna), **3:**733
"Talking Cuban Missile Crisis" (Ochs), **3:**316
Talking Heads, **4:**887
"Talking Vietnam" (Ochs), **3:**316
"Talking Vietnam Pot Luck Blues" (Paxton),
　　3:316
"Talking World War III Blues" (Dylan), **3:**316
*Talks at the Yanʾan Conference on Literature and
　　Art* (Mao), **7:**102, 103, 385, 413, 960
Talks with Writers and Artists (Kim), **7:**960
Tallari (musical group), **8:**485, *485*
Tallchief, Maria, **3:**207
Tallensi people, **1:**119
Taller de la Canción Popular (Bolivia), **2:**486
Taller Latinoamericano de Música Popular
　　(Argentina), **2:**268
Taller de San Lucas (Nicaragua), **2:**767
Taller Uruguayo de Música Popular (Uruguay),
　　2:521
Talley, Thomas V., **3:**84
Tallinn Conservatory of Music, **8:**497
Tallinn Piano Factory, **3:**880
Tallis, Thomas, **2:**819
Tallmadge, William, **3:**576, 627
Tallroth, Roger, **8:**226
Talmana, Joe, **2:**966
Tālmas family, **6:**916
Talolingas, **2:**698
Tāl Prakāsh (Sharma), **5:**135
Talvela, Martti, **8:**485
Tam, Alan (Tan Yonglin), **7:**355
Tam, Roman (Luo Man), **7:**355
Tamada Kitarou, **7:**708
Tamagusuku Tyôkun, **7:**65–66, 789
Tamakazura (Konparu), **7:**630
Tamang people, **5:**700
Tamanisau, Eremasi, **9:**161
Tamarack (musical group), **3:**1189
Tamara, Nataliya, **8:**776
Tamariʿi Manureva no Rurutu, **9:**880
Tamasese (Sāmoan leader), **9:**217–19
Tambaran Culture, **9:**90, 155, 384

Tambiah, S. J., **4:**287
Tambo cult, **2:**901, 903
Tambor de Mina, **2:**341
Tambor Urbano, **2:**543
tambourine. *See* drums: frame
Tambourines to Glory (musical), **3:**621
tambūr. See lutes
tambura. See lutes
Tamburitza Association of America, **3:**923
Tamen, Candido (Candi), **9:**160
Tami Island (Papua New Guinea), **9:**546
Tamil Iśai Movement, **5:**105, 231, 911–12
Tamil Nadu, **5:**903–27
　　Brahmins, weddings of, **5:**274–76
　　ceremonies
　　　exorcism, **5:**286
　　　spirit possession, **5:**293
　　Cidambaram, devotional music in, **5:**246
　　concepts of folk and classical music, **5:**913–14
　　dance traditions of, **5:**485, 515, 518–19, 914,
　　　918–20
　　devotional music in, **5:**259–61, 918, 922–27
　　Dharmapuri district, drum ensembles, **5:**915
　　immigrants to Fiji, **5:**612
　　immigrants to Guyana, **5:**602
　　immigrants to Martinique, **5:**594
　　immigrants to Réunion Island, **5:**607
　　immigrants to Trinidad, **5:**588
　　instruments in, **5:**350, 351, 364, 366–68,
　　　907–8, 912–16, 924
　　Kanchipuram, Sri Varadaraja Temple, **5:***14*
　　Kanyakumari district, storytelling in, **5:**907
　　Karnatak tradition in, **5:**89, 209, 230–32, 449,
　　　906
　　light classical music in, **5:**912, 924–25, 927
　　Madras (Chennai), **5:**5
　　　ban on temple dancing, **5:**409
　　　bharata nāṭyam in, **5:**104
　　　cassette industry in, **5:**554
　　　film industry in, **5:**542
　　　Karnatak music in, **5:**231–32
　　　nationalist songs in, **5:**437–38
　　　public concerts in, **5:**212
　　　Saint Thomas Cathedral in, **5:***13*
　　　as trade center, **5:**15
　　Madurai
　　　cassette industry in, **5:**554
　　　Meenakshi temple, **5:**365
　　map of, **5:***864*
　　Masinagudi, Mariyamman festival in, **5:**903–6
　　Mullikkulam, Muruka temple, **5:***558*
　　mural painting in, **5:**300
　　Nilgiri Hills
　　　healing rituals, **5:**287
　　　instruments of, **5:**366–67
　　　interaction of ethnic groups, **5:**284
　　　Kota people, **5:**278
　　　musical traditions in, **5:**908–911
　　population of, **5:**903
　　Pudukkottai
　　　Brahadamba temple, **5:**365
　　　court of, **5:**221
　　　rock inscriptions of music, **5:**24, 215
　　regional cassettes in, **5:**554–59
　　regional styles in, **5:**907–9
　　sabhā schools in, **5:**455

Salem district, drum ensembles, **5:**915
Srirangam, devotional music in, **5:**246, 261
Tanjavur (Tanjore), **5:**14, 384
　　court period in, **5:**89, 231, 387–88, 390
　　devotional music in, **5:**246, 259, 263,
　　　268–70
　　Iśai Vēḷḷāḷar caste in, **5:**910
　　painting in, **5:**300
　　regional cassettes in, **5:**557–59
　　temple of, **5:**263
　　Vedic chant in, **5:**243–44
　　Telugu-speakers in, **5:**889
　　theater in, **5:**277
　　　icai nāṭakam, **5:**913
　　　noṇṭi cintu, **5:**921
　　　terukkūttu, **5:**90, 516, 542, 556, 908, 913
　　Thirukkalikundran Temple in, **5:***11*
　　Tirunelveli district
　　　noṇṭi cintu genre of, **5:**921
　　　storytelling in, **5:**907
　　Tiruvaiyaru, Tyagaraja Festival, **5:**210–11, 269,
　　　383–85, 390–95
　　Tiruvarur, **5:**220, 221, 223, 228
　　Tuticorin, fishermen's songs, **5:**907
　　vocal music, **5:**277, 916–21
　　　cintu types, **5:**920–21
　　　oyilāṭṭam, **5:**917, 918, 919–20, 925
　　　swing songs, **5:**275, 910
　　　temmāngu pāṭṭu, **5:**556, 925
　　　tiruppāvai, **5:**274, 918
　　　tiruvempāvai, **5:**274, 918
　　　utukkai pāṭṭu, **5:**556, 908
　　　villuppāṭṭu, **5:**368, 401, 556, 907, 908
Tamil Nadu Government Music College
　　(Madras), **5:**449, 451
Tamil Nadu Theological Seminary Community
　　Carol Service Choir, **5:***923*
Tamil people
　　instrument classification of, **5:**326–27
　　in North America, **3:**981, 982, 1216; **5:**578
　　in Sri Lanka, **5:**953, 954, 955, 958
Tamil University, **5:**450
Tammany (Hewitt), **3:**542
Tampa Red. *See* Whitaker, Hudson
Tampere, Herbert, **8:**498
"Tamsui River" (Luo), **7:**358
Tan, Bernard, **4:**129, 523
Tan Dun, **3:**964; **7:**50, 342, 343, *350*, 350–51,
　　420, 431
Tan, Gines, **4:**885
Tan Sooi Beng, **4:**27, 92
Tan Xiaolin, **7:**230, 346
Tan Xinpei, **7:**286
Tanabe Hisao, **7:**42, 524, 592, 698, 713; **9:**25,
　　722, 994
Tanaka Ogoto, **7:**610
Tanaka Syôhei, **7:**592
Tanase, Maria, **8:**882
Tʾan Bakhtale! Roma (*Gypsies in Russia*) (film),
　　8:287
Tanba Yosaku (Chikamatsu), **7:**669
Tanbou Libète (Drum of Freedom), **3:**805–6
Tanc, Cengiz, **6:**775
Tandhakusuma, R. M. A., **4:**654
Tanec (musical group), **8:**982
Taneev, Aleksandr Sergeevich, **8:**856, 858

Taneev, Sergei, **8:**783, 858, 861
Tanese-Ito, Yoko, **4:**26, 271, 278
Tang Disheng, **7:**307
Tang dynasty, **4:**446–47
　An Lushan uprising in, **7:**29
　bianwen stories in, **7:**246
　Buddhism in, **7:**332
　centralization in, **7:**24, 25–26, 30
　courtesan culture in, **7:**402, 406–7
　Daoism in, **7:**321
　ethnic origin of, **7:**29
　foreign influences during, **7:**6, 14, 80, 89, 103,
　　448
　instruments in, **7:**82, 111–12
　Kai Yuan period, **7:**125, 132
　musical institutions in, **7:**392, 756
　music in, **7:**89, 125, 132, 168, 396, 448, 723,
　　981
　pipa in, **7:**168
　politics in, **7:**27
　relations with Silla, **7:**806
　religious rituals in, **7:**311
　theater in, **7:**291
　zheng in, **7:**171
Tang Dynasty (musical group), **7:**360, 363, 364,
　　365–67
Tang Dynasty (album), **7:**366
Tang Liangxin, **7:**170
Tang Liangxing, **3:**959
Tang Xianzu, **7:**295
Tanga (Bauza), **3:**787
Tanga Group (Papua New Guinea), **9:**626
"Tangerine" (Led Zeppelin), **3:**113
Tangerine Dream (musical group), **3:**204
Tangi'ia, **9:**896
Tanglefoot (musical group), **3:**1189
tango, **2:***44*, 49, 71, 93, 94, 101, 105
　in Argentina, **2:**245, 249, 263–65, 264–65,
　　269–70
　bandoneón in, **2:**89, 253, 511
　in Brazil, **2:**305, 330, 331, 350
　in Canada, **3:**1077, 1195, 1196, 1204
　in Chile, **2:**371
　dance competitions for, **3:**210
　in Denmark, **8:**457
　in El Salvador, **2:**718
　ensembles for, **2:**274
　in Finland, **8:**289, 483, 484, 485–86
　in Guadeloupe, **2:**877
　in Honduras, **2:**744
　as identity marker, **3:**506
　immigrants' role in, **2:**261
　in Israel, **6:**1019
　in Italy, **8:**619
　in Japan, **7:**540
　in Low Countries, **8:**525
　in Morocco, **6:**1042
　in Peru, **2:**485, 500
　sound recordings of, **2:**52
　in Switzerland, **8:**690
　tango canción, **2:**263
　tango característico, **2:**253
　tango romanza, **2:**263
　in Turkey, **6:**249
　in Ukraine, **8:**812
　in United States, **3:**233, 521, 730, 791, 995

　in Uruguay, **2:**510, 516, 519, 520–21
　worldwide popularity of, **2:**75, 101
Tango Argentina (tango show), **2:**264
tango ya ba Wendo, **1:**380
Tanguay, Eva, **3:**189, *189*
Tang ŭi ch'amdoen ttal (North Korean opera),
　　7:962
Tan'gun sinhwa (Kim), **7:**959
Tangut Xia empire, **7:**14, 23, 30, 31, 32
Tanimae ('Are'are panpipe player), **9:***398,* 400
Tanimbar Archipelago, **4:**812, 821
Tanimoto Kazuyuki, **7:**525
Tanjavur Quartette, **5:**224, 387, 389, 508
Tanka people, **7:**212
Tanna (Vanuatu), **9:**702–9
　composition on, **9:**362–64
　dance in, **9:**63–65
　festivals in, **9:**63–65
　John Frum cargo cult in, **9:**32, 214–15
　kava use in, **9:**173
　music and dance of, **9:**702–9, 966–67
　　naneluan, **9:**63
　　napinapin, **9:**63
　songs, war-era, **9:**29
Tannahill Weavers (musical group), **8:**372
Tanner, Adrian, **3:**392
Tanner, James, **3:**312
Tanner, Phil, **8:**354, *354*
Tannous, Maroun, **3:**1220
Tanotka (Mali Baining leader), **9:**192
Tanqin youshoufa (Zhao), **7:**159
Tanrıkorur, Cinuçen, **6:**110
Tansen, Miyan, **5:**77, 189–90, 252, 337, 376,
　　378
　descendants of, **5:**204, 378
　dhrupad texts of, **5:**164
　raga darbārī kānadā and, **5:**72
Tansui, **7:**792–93
Tans'ur, William, **3:**26
tantrakārī aṅg. See gat
Tantric philosophy, **5:**494, 503, 520, 957, 962
Tanzania. *See also* East Africa; *specific peoples*
　Arabs in, **1:**606, 635
　composition in, **1:**217–18
　culture areas of, **1:**636
　dance, *mganda,* **1:**603
　Europeans in, **1:**635–36
　geography of, **1:**633
　history of, **1:**635–36
　instruments of, **1:**636–42
　lamellophones, **1:**317
　Maasai people, dance, **1:**109, 110
　Makua people, masks of, **1:**119
　music in, **1:**606, 633–46
　music industry in, **1:**417
　music research in, **1:**49
　Ngoni people, **1:**320–21
　Nyamwezi people, **1:**606
　popular music of, **1:**423, 427–28, 644–45
　religious music, **1:**643–44
　research in, **1:**636
　Swazi people, **1:**321
　Wagogo people, *ngoma* drumming, **1:**312
　Yao people, masks of, **1:**119
　Zanzibar, *taarab* music, **1:**426, 427–28, 429,
　　607, 645–46
　Zulu people, **1:**321

Tao Hongjing, **7:**312, 321
Tao Yabing, **7:**137
Taoism. *See* Daoism
Taos Recordings and Publications, **3:**765
Tap Dance Kid (musical), **3:**622
Tapales, Isang, **4:**870
Tapales, Ramón, **4:**860, 873
Tapara, Juan, **2:***214*
Ta-p'en-k'eng culture, **4:**37
Tapera, Jege A., **10:**116
Taplas, **8:**354
ṭappā, **5:**162, 413
　in Bengal, **5:**847, 848, 852, 853, 856, 860
　composed by Tirunal, **5:**229
　in Pakistan, **5:**848
　in Punjab, **5:**771
Tappay, Dorothy, **3:**487
Tapua'i, Rev. Fa'atauva'a, **9:**206
Taqī al-Dīn al-Ḥiṣnī, **6:**372
Taqramiut Nipingat Incorporated, **3:**1278
taqsīm, **6:**388, 421
　Arabian peninsula, **6:**701
　buzuq in, **6:**408
　Egypt, **6:**46, 148–49, 170, 559, 600
　Iran, **6:**862
　Iraq, **6:**312
　Mashriq, **6:**550, 551
　Morocco, **6:**499
　Palestine, **6:**582–83
　Syria, **6:**567, 569
　Turkey (*taksim*), **6:**11, 114, 116, 120–21, 773
　'ūd performance of, **6:**593–94
ṭār (also *tar; tār*). *See* lutes
Tarahumara culture, **2:**551, 582–87
　dance of, **2:**592
　instruments of, **2:**582–84
　research on, **2:**587
Taraki, Nur Ahmad, **5:**810
Tarama Sözlüğü (dictionary), **6:**783
tarānā, **5:**162, 164, 178–79, 220, 229, 602, 605
Tarāna-e sarūr (Daya Ram Kachroo), **5:**689,
　　691–93
"Tāranā-i Hindi," **5:**437
Taranath, Rajiv, **5:***4*
tarantella, **3:**860, 861, 865
Tăranu, Cornel, **8:**883
Tarascan culture. *See* Purépecha culture
Tarasoff, Koozma, **3:**1270
Tara, tara, palgŭn tara (*ch'anggŭk* piece), **7:**969
Tarawa Atoll (Kiribati), **9:**758, 759, 764
Tarcan, Bülent, **6:**775
Tarcan, Selim Sırrı, **6:**812–13
Tari, Abdul Sattar, **5:**768
Tariaca culture, **2:**681
Tarighi musiqiyyun (Ism'tulla Mojizi), **7:**447
Tarîh-i Enderûn (Atâ Bey), **6:**780
Tariverdiev, Mikhael, **8:**779, 782
Tarkan, **6:**252
Tarkhnishvili family, **8:**841
Tarnān, Shaykh Khumais, **6:**328, 331, 502, 503
Tarras, Dave, **3:**938, 941
Tasavallan Presidentti (musical group), **8:**217
T'ashchyan, Nikoghayos, **6:**737
Tashi on Sŏul (Kim), **7:**953
Tashkent Conservatory, **6:**908
Tashko, Tefta, **8:**997

Taslıova, Seref, **6:**801, *801, 806*
Tasman, Abel, **9:**842
Tasrih al-Aqvam, **5:***123*
Tasso, Torquato, **8:**17, 573, 608
Tastanbekqyzy, Sara, **6:**954
Taste of Honey (musical group), **3:**712
Tasŭrŭm (musical group), **7:**965
Tatar, Elizabeth, **9:**286, 287, 289, 292, 307, 915, 986, 994
Tatar people, **6:**897; **8:**11, 767, 772
  in China, **7:**455–58
  conversion to Islam, **7:**24
  epic songs, **6:**345
  instruments, **8:**774
  ozyn-kyi songs, **8:**773
  pentatonicism in music, **8:**773
  rhythmic patterns of, **8:**773
  in Siberia, **7:**1027–30
Tatau (Papua New Guinea), **9:**628–29
Tate, Greg, **3:**586
Tate! kôgun (Japanese song), **7:**745
Tati, **6:**271
Tatibana Kyokuô, **7:**649, 650
Tatibana Kyokuô II, **7:**650
Tatlıses, İbrahim, **6:**248, 258, *258*
Tatlıyay, Kemânî Hayday, **6:**784
Tatum, Art, **3:**656
Tau, Buruku, **9:**1005
Taub, Ḥayim, **6:**1031
Taube, Evert, **8:**445
Taufa, Viliami, **9:**130
Taul, Ants, **3:**879
Taumako (Solomon Islands), **9:**833, 835, 852
Taumoefolau, Tevita Tuʻipolotu, **9:**204
Tau-oi people, **4:**344
Tauraki, Tony, **9:**973
Taurog, Norman, **9:**43
Tausug people, **4:**889, 920
  instrumental music of, **4:**891, 898, 902, 905–6
  vocal music of, **4:**906, 908, 909, 910–11, 911
Tavares, Braúlio, **2:**326
Tavče Gravče (musical group), **8:**983
Taveras (trovo), **3:**758, 762
Taverio, Ngaro, **9:**908
Taveuni (Fiji), **9:**175, 774, 973
Taʼvibo, **3:**421
Tawa, Nicholas, **3:**828
Tawakkal, Munir Hussain, **5:**767
Tawantinsuya. *See* Inca (Inka) culture
Tawe, Varni, **1:**329
Tawfīq, Iḥab, **6:**239, 592
Tawfīq, Nasr, **1:**557
Tawfīq, S., **6:**592
al-Ṭawīl, Kamāl, **6:**600–601
Tày people, **4:**531
  ceremonies of, **4:**533
  courtship songs of, **4:**532
  instruments of, **4:**535–36
Tày Nguyên peoples, **4:**531–32, 533
Tayfur, Ferdi, **6:**258
Tayi, Coimbatore, **5:**103
Taylor, Cecil, **3:**133, 662, 664
Taylor, Donald, **2:**155, 649
Taylor, Douglas, **2:**668
Taylor, Johnny, **3:**676, 712
Taylor, Joseph, **8:**327, 333

Taylor, Paul, **3:**852
Taylor, Timothy, **3:**341
Taylor, Zachary, **3:**307
"Tayti oder die glückliche Insel" (Zachariä), **9:**34–35
Tazenda (musical group), **8:**626
Tazlil (periodical), **6:**1061
Tbilisi State Conservatory, **8:**841, 844, 846
Tʼboli people, **4:**905
Tchaikovsky Music Academy (Kyïv), **8:**822, 823
Tchaikovsky, Peter Ilyich, **2:**962; **6:**904; **7:**349, 388; **8:**84, 781, 981
  ballets, **8:**161
  use of *verbunkos* themes, **8:**273
Te. *See* Te *plus next word in name*
Teachers' College of Music (Madras), **5:**451
"Tea for Two," **3:**659
Tea-Jazz (musical group), **8:**777
Teal Record Company, **1:**757
Te Arohanui Company, **9:**936, 937
Tea-Table Miscellany, **8:**372
Teatro Abril (Guatemala), **2:**736
Teatro Carrera (Guatemala), **2:**736
Teatro Colón (Argentina), **2:**90
Teatro Colón (Colombia), **2:**395
Teatro Melico Salazar (Costa Rica), **2:**702
Teatro Municipal of Lima (Peru), **2:**500–501
Teatro Nacional (Costa Rica), **2:**694, 702
Teatro Oriente (Guatemala), **2:**736
Teaurere, Tokorua, **9:***906*
Te Aute Boys College (Hawkes Bay), **9:**277
Tebetjane, **1:**768
techno, **3:**230, 341, 355; **5:**584, 652; **6:**248
technology and music, **3:**235–49. *See also* electronic music; electrophones
  audiences and, **3:**245, 259, 558
  audio and video recorders, **3:**245; **10:**14, 30, 106, 145, 150–51
  Canada, **3:**245–49
  Caribbean, **2:**40–41
  Central America, **2:**40–41
  Computer Musical Instruments (CMIs), **9:**144
  dead ends in, **10:**118–19
  definition of, **3:**235
  digital audio, **3:**340
  in disco, **3:**687, 688
  documentary use of, **3:**290; **10:**106
  drum recorder, **1:**254
  electromagnetic tape, **3:**560
  El Salvador, **2:**718–19
  in funk, **3:**680
  in house music, **3:**690–91
  hyperinstruments, **3:**254
  jukeboxes, **3:**898
  karaoke machines, **3:**98, 964, 978–79; **7:**399, 412, 431, 444, 514, 533, *534*
    Hawaiʻi, **9:**99, 164
    Singapore, **4:**524
    South America, **2:**41, 85, 87–88
    Thailand, **4:**99
    Vietnam, **4:**515
  melograph, **1:**255; **8:**23
  Mexico, **2:**40–41
  MIDI, **3:**95, 240, 245, 691
  multitrack tape recorder, **3:**246–47, 252–53
  New Age music, **3:**345

  oscillograph, **1:**255
  in rap, **3:**552, 693, 697
  recording studio, **3:**249, 263–65
  in rock, **3:**228, 254, 348, 357, 358, 359, 540, 551, 663–64, 680
  sampling, **1:**265–66; **3:**695, 700, 701
  sequencers, **3:**247
  sonograph, **1:**255
  sound amplification, **1:**479; **2:**40; **3:**240, 241, 248–49, 551, 773, 775, 776, 895, 902; **5:**231, 232, 352, 671; **6:**552; **7:**601, 884; **10:**90
    of call to prayer, **6:**153
    of *ḥaḍra* performance, **6:**147–48, 170
    of *nowḥe*, **6:**826
    of Qurʾān recitation, **6:**157
    of Tunisian Jewish wedding bands, **6:**527
  South America, **2:**40–41
  talkbox, **3:**685
  telephone transmission of concerts, **3:**1182–83
  United States, **3:**238–45
Technotronic, **9:**179
Tecumseh, **3:**305
Teesri Manzil (film), **5:**537
Teeth (musical group), **4:**887
Te Faingahitu (Manihikan chief), **9:**904
Te Fakaheo (Manihikan chief), **9:**904
Tefana, Esther, **9:**998
Tegen, Martin, **8:**447
Tegoto (Miyagi), **7:**779
Tegotomono: Music for the Japanese Koto (Wade), **10:**13
Te Heuheu, **9:**942
Tehillah le-David (ben Hassin), **6:**1038
Tehsil, Khan, **5:**791
Tehuelche culture, **2:**251
Te Hurinui, Pei, **9:**932, 939
Teikoku Band, **3:**968
Teio, Noʻoroa, **9:**974
Teiri (god), **8:**857
Teit, James A., **3:**291
Te Ivi Māori, **9:**901
tejano, **3:**212, 325
Tejano music, **3:**720, 721, 770–81. *See also* Mexican-Americans/Canadians
Tejeda, Dagoberto, **2:**861
Te Kānawa, Kiri, **9:**933
Tēka, Prince Tūi, **9:**168, 938
Teke tribe, **6:**966
Tekiuniu (Bellonese singer), **9:**30
Tel Aviv Art Museum, **6:**1031
Tel Aviv Quarter, **6:**1031
Tel Aviv University, **6:**1061, 1063–64
Telefol people, **9:**983
Telek, George, **9:**154, 155, 1005
Telemann, Georg Friedrich, **8:**654
Telennourien Vreizh—Le journal de la harpe (periodical), **8:**564
Telephone (Menotti), **3:**546
Teleshevski, Moshe, **10:**130
television. *See also* mass media
  Afghanistan, **5:**811, 824, 832
  Algeria, **6:**271
  Aotearoa, **9:**938, 944
  Arabian peninsula, **6:**667, 702, 711
  Arctic stations, **3:**380

Argentina, **2:**265, 267, 269, 270, 278
　music videos, **2:**268; **3:**240, 252
Australia, **9:**414, 985
　Aboriginal stations, **9:**443
Austral Islands, **9:**879–80
Austria, **8:**675
Azerbaijan, *aşıq* broadcasts, **6:**846
Bangladesh, **5:**858
Barbados, **2:**814
Belarus, **8:**801
Bolivia, **2:**289
Bosnia-Hercegovina, **8:**968–69
Brazil, **2:**107, 318
Canada, **3:**248, 295–96, 1102
　Anglo-Celtic programming, **3:**1190
　broadcasts of South Asian music, **5:**583–84
　Canadian content rules, **3:**247–48, 250–51,
　　290, 314–15
　Chinese programming, **3:**1265
　country music programming, **3:**1073
　French-language programming, **3:**1158,
　　1167
　music video cable channels, **3:**74, 96–97,
　　248, 250–52, 266
　northern regions, **3:**1278
　reggae programming, **3:**1202
Caribbean, **2:**40–41, 51–52
　educational role of, **2:**69–70
　music videos, **2:**76
Central America, **2:**40–41, 51–52, 630
　educational role of, **2:**69–70
　music videos, **2:**76
China, **7:**399, 414
　satellite, **7:**360
Costa Rica, **2:**703
Croatia, **8:**936
Cuba, **2:**828, 835
Denmark, **8:**462
Dominican Republic, **2:**862
Egypt, **6:**166, 170, 233, 237, 239, 432, 597,
　607
　music videos, **6:**240, 555
El Salvador, **2:**718–19
Europe, programs on folk music traditions,
　8:157
Faroe Islands, **8:**472–73
Finland, **8:**473
　music videos, **3:**248, 252
France, **8:**288
Georgia, **8:**837, 844
Greece, **8:**1009, 1016
Guatemala, **2:**723
Gujarat, **5:**624
Guyana, **2:**448
Haiti, **2:**891, 893
Hawai'i, **9:**222
Hong Kong, **7:**355
Hungary, **8:**746
Indonesia, **10:**47, 48–49
Iran, **6:**142
　aşıq broadcasts, **6:**846
Ireland, **8:**386, 388
Israel, **6:**263–64
Italy, **8:**613–14, 619, 621
Jamaica, **2:**910–11
Japan, **7:**747, 751

Java, **4:**680
Karnataka, **5:**880
Korea, **7:**880, 958
Kuna culture, **2:**648
Macedonia, **8:**974, 976, 1003
Maharashtra, **5:**729, 730
Marshall Islands, **9:**752
Maya culture, **2:**653
Mexico, **2:**40–41, 51–52, 622
　educational role of, **2:**69–70
　music videos, **2:**76
Montenegro, **8:**961
Nepal, **5:**706
Netherlands Antilles, **2:**931
North West Frontier Province, **5:**790–91
Norway, **8:**429
Oceania, archives, **9:**958
Pakistan, **5:**747, 748
Panama, **2:**783
Papua New Guinea, **9:**91
Paraguay, **2:**463
Peru, **2:**486, 487
Portugal, **8:**585
Punjab (India), **5:**656
Romania, **8:**883, 884
Sāmoa, **9:**238
Scotland, **8:**363
Slovenia, **8:**919–20
South Africa, **5:**615–16
South America, **2:**40–41, 51–52
　educational role of, **2:**69–70
　music videos, **2:**76
South Asia, **5:**420, 527
　broadcasts of regional music, **5:**405
　employment opportunities, **5:**454
　theater and, **5:**486
South Korea, **7:**993–94
Spain, **8:**600
Sunda, **4:**724
Switzerland, **8:**697
Tahiti, **9:**868
Taiwan, **7:**357, 426
Trinidad, **5:**591
Tunisia, **6:**512, 527
Turkey, **6:**248, 250, 256, 791
　music videos, **6:**252
　aşik performances, **6:**808
United States, **3:**237
　affect on radio, **3:**349–50
　African-Americans in, **3:**715
　Asian programming, **3:**951
　broadcasts of South Asian music, **5:**583–84
　cable, **3:**244
　children's programs, **3:**284
　country music programming, **3:**109–10,
　　212
　dance programming, **3:**211, 219
　development of, **3:**244
　disco programming, **3:**688, 712
　dominance of, **3:**18
　Irish performers, **3:**844
　Latin American performers on, **3:**741
　marketing on, **3:**49–50
　music videos, **2:**374; **3:**96–97, 206, 211,
　　219, 244, 248, 250–52, 551, 586,
　　697, 712, 1025; **5:**427, 429

New Mexico, **3:**767–68
　political campaign coverage, **3:**310
　reggae programming, **3:**809
　rhythm and blues groups on, **3:**672
　rock and roll on, **3:**354
　South Asian programming, **3:**985–86
Uruguay, **2:**520, 522
'Uvea and Futuna, **9:**814–15
Virgin Islands, **2:**969
Wales, **8:**354–55
Yap, **9:**729
Yugoslavia (former), **8:**1001
Telgmann, Oscar, **3:**189, 1182, *1183*
Telson, Robert, **3:**335
Te Maeva, **9:**869, 875, 998
Te Maunu, **9:**941–42
Tembe, Govindrao, **5:**420, 536
Tembres, I Wayan, **3:**1019
Temiar people, **4:**560
　instruments of, **4:**562–63, 567–68
　language of, **4:**561
　musical genres, **4:***567*, 572
　　cincæm, **4:**579, 585
　　fruit-season, **4:**572–73, 579
　　pεhnɔɔh gɔb, **4:**573–74
　　sɔlombaŋ, **4:**573–79
　music research on, **4:**26
　scales of, **4:**567
　shamanism of, **4:**61, 571–76, 579–85
　social structure of, **4:**563
　tone rows of, **4:**566, *567*
　use of timbre, **4:**585
Temiz, Okay, **6:**250
Temne nation, **2:**869
Temne people, **1:**445, 468
Temoq people, **4:**560
Témori culture, **2:**551
temperament. *See* tuning and temperament
temperance movement, **3:**184, 309, 872–73
Temperley, Nicholas, **3:**1070
Temple Beth-El, **3:**127
Temple, Johnnie, **3:**645
Temple, Shirley, **3:**207
Templeton Crocker Expedition, **9:**853
tempo. *See also* rhythm and meter
　Afghanistan, **5:**827
　　chahārbeiti, **5:**819
　　Kabuli *ghazal*, **5:**805–6
　　lullabies, **5:**813
　　Pashtun songs, **5:**835
　　western genres, **5:**823
　Andean music, **2:**216–17
　Anuta, **9:**379
　　hymns, **9:**860
　Arabian peninsula, women's wedding music,
　　6:699
　Arab music, medieval, **6:**391–92
　Australia
　　Central dance, **9:**437
　　clansongs, **9:**422
　　Yolngu dance, **9:**459
　Bahamas, junkanoo, **2:**808
　in bebop, **3:**658
　Bellona, **9:**850
　bhajan, **5:**255
　of blues, **3:**639

tempo (*continued*)
Brazil, in religious music, **2:**328–29, 330
Bulgaria, **8:**891
   regional differences, **8:**895
Chile, *cueca,* **2:**369
China
   chuida, **7:**240
   Confucian music, **7:**337
   ensemble music, **7:**169, 202, 214, 225, 238
   opera arias, **7:**282–83
   qupai melodies, **7:**233
Choctaw Social Dance songs, **3:**469
Coast Salish spirit dancing songs, **3:**397
Cuba, *criolla,* **2:**832
Dattilam passage on, **5:**40
dhikr, **1:**551
dhrupad, **5:**250
Dominican Republic, merengue, **2:**860
Egypt
   layla, **6:**149, 150–51
   Nubian dances, **6:**629
ektāl, **5:**126
emotion and, **5:**272
England
   dance music, **8:**329
   performance context and, **8:**334
   songs, **8:**327
Faroe Islands, *kempurvísur,* **8:**469
Fiji, *taralala,* **9:**780
Finland, songs, **8:**478
Flanders, songs, **8:**519
France, vocal music, **8:**541–42
funk, **3:**683
gat, **5:**189, 192, 194, 202
ghazal, **5:**186
Goa, *dulpod,* **5:**738
in gong-chime ensemble music, **4:**21
Guarijio culture
   contradanza, **2:**553–54
   son principal, **2:**553–54
Guatemala, *son guatemalteco,* **2:**726
Gujarat
   garbo, **5:**628
   rās, **5:**630
Haiti
   mereng koudyay, **2:**890
   Vodou ritual music, **2:**883
havelī saṅgīt, **5:**250
Hawai'i, Jawaiian genre, **9:**166
in heavy metal, **3:**358
Hindustani music, **5:**148
   lay concept, **5:**111
   raga types and, **5:**85
Hungary, instrumental music, **8:**745
Indian Shaker hymns, **3:**488
Ireland
   lays, **8:**379
   vocal music, **8:**380
Irian Jaya
   Asmat ceremonial music, **9:**190
   Asmat songs, **9:**587, 591
   Mairasi dance, **9:**582
Irish music, **3:**843
Jamaica, mento, **2:**906
Japan
   gagaku music, **7:**619, 621, 625

kumiuta, **7:**696
tōgaku repertoire, **7:**42
utazawa, **7:**688
Java, **4:**668–69
   gamelan music, **4:**675
   wayang kulit, **4:**653
in jazz, **3:**654
Karnatak music, **5:**148
   ālāpana section of raga, **5:**214–15
   changes in, **5:**27
   mōhini āṭṭam, **5:**513
   time-flow patterns in, **5:**153
Kerala
   in *ceṇṭa mēḷam* music, **5:**938–39
   Mappila songs, **5:**947
in Khmer music, **4:**181–82
khyāl, **5:**127, 172, 173
Kiribati, *maie* and *batere* dances, **9:**762
konpa, **3:**803
Korea
   chŏngak, **7:**869
   kagok, **7:**922, 923
   nongak, **7:**938
   p'ansori, **7:**901, 903, 904, 905
   pŏmp'ae, **7:**872
   salp'uri changdan, **7:**914
   sanjo, **7:**913
   taeak, **7:**813
   tangak, **7:**867
kriti, **5:**149
Luangiua, *sea* and *lue* songs, **9:**843
Macedonia, dance music, **8:**978
Makah potlatch songs, **3:**399
Mangareva, *tagi,* **9:**888
Maritime fiddle music, **3:**1071
marking instruments for, **5:**322–24
Martinique, beguine, **2:**917
Mexico, *son jarocho,* **2:**609
Micronesian music, **9:**716
minstrel songs, **3:**543
Miskitu culture, *tiun,* **2:**663
Montserrat, quadrille, **2:**925
Morocco
   aḥwash, **6:**488
   malhun, **6:**500
New Caledonia
   dance-songs, **9:**675, 677
   kaneka, **9:**214
Nicaragua, *mento,* **2:**753
nūba, **6:**457
Oceania, analysis of, **9:**290–91
Palestine, wedding songs, **6:**584
Panama
   punto, **2:**778
   saloma, **2:**780
Papua New Guinea
   Abelam *bira,* **9:**549
   Abelam songs, **9:**551
   Angan vocal music, **9:**497
   Eastern Highlands music, **9:**527, 530
   Iatmul flute music, **9:**258
   Iatmul *mariuamangi,* **9:**554
   Managalasi *itiuri,* **9:**503
Peru
   fuga sections, **2:**477
   yaraví, **2:**477

P-funk, **3:**684
Philippines, *kulintang* music, **4:**897
Poland
   folk music, **8:**703
   "open-air" songs, **8:**113–14
Polynesian music, **9:**769
Puerto Rico, *seis,* **2:**938–39
Pukapuka, *tila* chants, **9:**911
Punjab, *bhangra,* **5:**651
in punk, **3:**357
Purépecha culture, *abajeño,* **2:**579
qawwali, **5:**753
Qur'ānic recitation, **6:**159, 160, 161–62
raga, Hindustani, **5:**69
Rajasthan, *jasnāthi agni,* **5:**648–49
in rap, **3:**701
Rotuma
   temo, **9:**820
   tiap hi'i, **9:**822
Ryûkyû Islands
   Amami music, **7:**791
   kudoki, **7:**794
   mukasi busi, **7:**793
St. Lucia, *manpa,* **2:**946
Sāmoa, hymns, **9:**205
Scotland
   lays, **8:**379
   Lowlands instrumental music, **8:**365
Slovenia, **8:**919
Solomon Islands, Santa Cruz Islands songs, **9:**333
in stamping tube music of Borneo, **4:**832
Sweden, folk songs, **8:**436
Switzerland, for yodeling, **8:**691
Takuu
   fula, **9:**841
   tuki, **9:**839
tarānā, **5:**178
tende music, **1:**587
Thailand, **4:**267, 269, 272, 292
ṭhumrī, **5:**180
Tibetan music, **5:**711
Tikopia, songs, **9:**855
Tonga, *fa'ahiula,* **9:**792
treatises on, **5:**20
Turkey
   art music, **6:**120, 122–26, 128
   divan, **6:**807
Turkmenistan, *baggy* music, **6:**974
Tuvalu, **9:**290–91
   hymn singing, **9:**830
   vocal music, **9:**830
Uighur *muqam,* **6:**995–1008
Uttar Pradesh, *harikīrtan,* **5:**665
'Uvea
   kupu, **9:**809
   soāmako and *niutao,* **9:**813
Uzbekistan, Ferghana-Tashkent repertoire, **6:**913
Vanuatu, **9:**362
   dance-songs, **9:**697–98
   of hymns, **9:**199
   lega, **9:**698
   nupu, **9:**704
   sawagoro, **9:**695
varṇam, **5:**149

Venezuela, *joropo*, **2:**540
work songs, **3:**600
Yemen, *al-ghinā' al-ṣanʿānī*, **6:**689
Tempo Club (organization), **3:**706
Tempos Band, **1:**361
Temptations (musical group), **3:**318, 674, 677, 709
Temuan people, **4:**560, 586–87
Ten Centuries Concerts (Toronto), **3:**1186
"Ten Percent" (Double Exposure), **3:**688
Ten Precepts for Sramanera (Buddhist text), **7:**328
Tender Land (Copland), **3:**546
Tenducci, Giusto Ferdinando, **8:**370
Tenetehara culture, **2:**128
Teng, Teresa (Deng Lijun), **7:**356, 357
Teng Yu-hsien, **7:**357
Tengrianism, **6:**949–50; **7:**21, 24
Tenko, **7:**547
Tennessee
field hollers in, **3:**84
Lao people in, **3:***117*
Memphis
black-appeal radio in, **3:**350
black-owned publishing houses in, **3:**644
rhythm and blues in, **3:**675–76, 710
Nashville
black-appeal radio in, **3:**350
as center for country music, **3:**76, 80, 212, 243, 520, 560
Lao people in, **3:**1007–8
Native American groups in, **3:**466
Tennyson, Alfred, Lord, "Kapiolani," **9:**39
Tenpyô biwa hu (*biwa* score), **7:**588, 644
Tenraa, Eric, **1:**635
Tenrikyō religion, **2:**88
"Tenting on the Old Camp Ground" (Kittredge), **3:**188
Tenti sôzô (film), **7:**750
Tenzer, Michael, **3:**1019; **4:**28, 733
Tenzing Norgay, **5:**698
Teodosievski, Stevo, **8:**282
Teop Island (Papua New Guinea), **9:**642–44
Te Pēne o Aotearoa, **9:**935
teponaztli. See slit-drums
Te Pou O Mangatawhiri, **9:**929
"Tequila" (Coasters), **2:**105
Te Rauparaha, **9:**932, 940–41, 942
Terawa people. *See* Nyamalthu people
Tereora, **9:**901
Terfel, Bryn, **3:**271
Ter-Ghevondyan, Anoushavan, **6:**726
Terhin (Temiar shaman), **4:**585
Teribe culture, **2:**681, 684–85, 771
research on, **2:**783
Terlep, Matija, **8:**920, 922–23
Termigoian people, **8:**854–56
terminology
ācārya, **5:**460
for actors and actions, **8:**112–13
Arabian peninsula, *ṣawt* genre, **6:**652
Arabic musical terms, **6:**363, 364–65, 541
Arab instruments, **6:**401–2
art music, **8:**2
Azerbaijan, *muğam*, **6:**927–28
bāj, **5:**378

Berber music, **6:**483–84, 489
cakkardār, **5:**118–19, 121
Central Asia, *maqām*, **6:**911
China
folk songs, **7:**149
music theory, **7:**115–23
yueji musicians, **7:**405–6
classical music, **8:**2
Dai music, **7:**497
deśī, **5:**20, 33, 492
East Asian music, **7:**3
ethnic music, **8:**437
ethnomusicology, **10:**22, 77, 97
folk music, **8:**2, 339, 436
foreign influence on, **4:**55
Greek, **6:**541
guru, **5:**376
Hmong language, **4:**550
Indian sources for, **4:**66–67
instruments, **5:**350
Iran
for Azerbaijani musicians, **6:**844–45
Persian art music, **6:**72, 73, 75, 835–37, 853–54
Persian vocal music, **6:**831
for *saz* strings, **6:**847–48
Japan
for musical repertoires, **7:**42
music theory, **7:**566–70
jāti, **5:**9, 75, 398
Kazakh *dombra* frets, **6:**957
Korea
farmers' bands, **7:**930
folk songs, **7:**987–88
for musical repertoires, **7:**42
Lao, **4:**336
local, **8:**8, 112–16
lyre, **6:**358
mārga, **5:**20, 33, 492, 893
metaphorical, **1:**257
nātya, **5:**507
obligational, **8:**114
paṇḍit, **5:**460
Poland, for "open-air" songs, **8:**113–14
popular music, **8:**2, 436
praise singing, **1:**491–93
problems of, **4:**3, 6–8
research on, **8:**36
śāgird, **5:**376
saṅgīta, **5:**19–20
sequential, **8:**116
śiṣya, **5:**376
situational, **8:**113–14
śruti, **5:**92
Suyá culture, **2:**126
systemic, **8:**114–16
Thai music, **4:**223
traditional music, **8:**4, 339
Turkey, art music, **6:**121–22
Turkish *düm-tek*, **6:**366–67
Uighur *muqam*, **6:**995–1008
ustād, **5:**376, 459–60
varṇa, **5:**9, 75, 398
vernacular music, **8:**339
Vietnam, **4:**455–56, 476
Vietnamese modes, **4:**455–56

Vietnam, folk song, **4:**476
world music, **8:**224, 437
Ternate, **4:**810, 812, 813–17
Ternhag, Gunnar, **8:**307
Terno (musical group), **8:**277
Te Roopu Manutaki, **9:**947
Terra Mia, **9:**81
Terrett, Keith, **9:**130
Territorial Archives (New Caledonia), **9:**964–65
Territorial Museum (New Caledonia), **9:**964–65
Terror Fabulous, **9:**167
Terry, Keith, **3:**1016–17
Terseglav, Marko, **8:**922
Terwiel, B. J., **4:**287
Teslo, James, **9:**966
Tesoros del Espiritu: A Portrait in Sound of Hispanic New Mexico, **3:**767
tessitura
Algeria, instrument pitch, **6:**468
Andean music, **2:**34, 215–16, 217, 221, 294–95, 476
Atacameño culture, **2:**361
China, in theatrical singing, **7:**77
in country music, **3:**77, 108–9
Egypt, *inshād* performance, **6:**166
Iranian instruments, **6:**64
Japan, in theatrical singing, **7:**77
Kazakh lyrical songs, **6:**955
Kurdish songs, **6:**745
makam, **6:**54
maqām singing, **6:**913–14, 916
Mexican Amerindian music, **2:**549
Mexico, vocal, **2:**606
Sufi chanting, **6:**192–93
Uighur *muqam*, **6:**995–1008
Testamento, El (Chavez), **3:**767
Tester, Scan, **8:**333
Testimony: Japanese American Voices of Liberation (multimedia production), **3:**973
Te Taniwha, Tukumana, **9:**941
Tethin, **9:***305*
Tetiaroa (Society Islands), **9:**867
Tetkîk ü Tahkîk (Abdülbaki Nâsir Dede), **6:**109
Tetnuldi (musical group), **8:***833*
Teton Sioux Indian nation, **3:**292, 444
Tetouan, **6:**371
Tetum (Belu) people, **4:**796
Tevane, Marco, **9:**56–57
tēvāram
in South Africa, **5:**617
in Tamil Nadu, **5:**105, 107, 216, 231, 260–61, 912, 918
Tēvar caste, **5:**921
Tevar Pillai, Tep Venkatacalam, **5:***908*
Tevfik Bey, Mehmed, **6:**757
Tevfik, Rıza, **6:**812
Tewari, Laxmi, **5:**674
Te Whatanui, **9:**942–43
Te Whīti, **9:**935
Te Wīata, Īnia, **9:**936
Texas
African-American work music in, **3:**293
Austin, Filipino people in, **3:**1025
blues in, **3:**639, 669
Czech people in, **3:**897–88

Texas (*continued*)
El Paso
Pueblo peoples, **3**:428
zarzuela companies, **3**:851
Fort Worth, country music radio broadcasts, **3**:559
German people in, **3**:773, 885
Houston
Central American communities in, **3**:727
South Asian people in, **3**:981
Vietnamese people in, **3**:993
Iranian people in, **3**:1031
Latino peoples in, **3**:718–19
Mennonites in, **3**:1238
Mexican and Tejano communities in, **3**:98, 721–25, 770–81
Native American groups in, **3**:428–38, 440
Rio Grande Valley, **3**:720, 721–25
German settlers, **3**:213, 773
San Antonio, **3**:770
South Asian people in, **3**:981
Spanish settlement in, **3**:770, 847
Texas (musical group), **8**:369
Texas Catholic Union, **3**:898
Texas-Mexican Conjunto (Peña), **3**:517
Texas Talent Musicians' Association, **3**:781
Texas tommy, **3**:651
Texas Tornadoes (musical group), **3**:777
Texeira, Humberto, **2**:332
text setting. *See also* songs, texts
Belarus, **8**:794
blues, **3**:641
Bulgaria, **8**:898
Central Asian *aruz* system, **6**:914–15
China
banqiangti system, **7**:249
Cantonese opera, **7**:309
folk songs, **7**:153–54, 155
kunqu, **7**:293
nanyin, **7**:272
in narratives, **7**:247–50
Peking opera, **7**:284–85
qupaiti system, **7**:249
Suzhou tanci, **7**:262–63
tune accommodation, **7**:293, 309, 323
zaju, **7**:275–76
Croatia, *Gospin plač*, **8**:929
Czech music, **8**:717
Ephrata Cloister style of, **3**:906
Finland, **8**:476–77
Georgia, **8**:832
Germany, medieval music, **8**:651
ghazal, **5**:184–85
Hungary, **8**:741
Italy, **8**:607–8
Japan
rhythmic structure and, **7**:572–73, 653
theatrical genres, **7**:655
Karnatak music, tala and, **5**:145–48
Kazakh people, **7**:460
Kerala
Mappila songs, **5**:947
vāyttāri technique, **5**:950
Korea
kagok, **7**:921–24
kasa, **7**:927–28

p'ansori, **7**:900–901
sijo, **7**:925–26
Lithuania, **8**:510
Low Countries, **8**:519–20
Maronite church music, **6**:212
Montenegro, **8**:958
Nigerian church music, **1**:244, 249
Romania, **8**:874
Russia
chastushki, **8**:768
village songs, **8**:755–56
Serbia, **8**:942
Sinhala, **5**:959
Slovak music, **8**:717
Slovenia, **8**:912
Somali, **1**:614
Tamil, **5**:958
thumrī, **5**:181
tonal inflections, **1**:244
treatises on, **5**:33, 34
Uighur people, **7**:460
texture. *See also* heterophony; homophony; monophony; polyphony
acculturation and, **2**:73
Africa, voice exchange, **1**:10, 108, 137
analysis of, **9**:301
Austral Islands, *hīmene tārava*, **9**:881–82
Bahamas, junkanoo, **2**:806–8
Baroque music, **8**:76
Bellona, vocal music, **9**:850
in bluegrass music, **3**:164
in Burmese music, **4**:18–19
California, Native American music, **3**:413, 414, 415, 416
Ecuador, contrapuntal, **2**:428
falsobordone, **2**:652
Fiji
meke, **9**:777
taro, **9**:779
in Filipino dance forms, **4**:854
in gong-chime ensembles, **4**:20–21
India, South, musical ensembles, **5**:279
interlocking (hocket), **2**:47; **4**:597
Africa, **1**:364, 563, 601–2, 604, 608, 654, 749; **10**:116
Andean regions, **2**:34, 207–10
in Atoni music, **4**:797
BaAka people, **1**:688
Bali, **4**:733–35, 748
Bolivia, **2**:16, 285, 286, 295
Borneo, **4**:828–29
Brazil, **2**:330
Chile, **2**:359, 365
Dominican Republic, **2**:*853*
East Africa, **1**:601
in Florinese music, **4**:795
in *gendhing*, **4**:659, 660
in Jambi music, **4**:617
Java, **4**:670–71
in Kalinga music, **4**:919
Kasena people, **1**:456
in Kayan music, **4**:830
Kpelle people, **1**:467
Kuna panpipe music, **2**:642, *643*
Lombok, **4**:770
Madagascar, **1**:788

Malaysia, **4**:407, *418*, 425
in Malukun music, **4**:815, 816, 819
Miri people, **1**:563
in music of Lombok, **4**:763
Papua New Guinea, **9**:477, 511, 556, *565*
Peru, **2**:16, 468
pifilka ensembles, **2**:233–34, 236
Russia, **8**:770
San people, **1**:705
Serawai, **4**:619
Shona people, **1**:752
Solomon Islands, **9**:656, 661
southeastern Africa, **1**:708
Sumatra, **4**:602, 605, 608, 610, 611, 623, 624
Sumba, **4**:789
in Sundanese *angklung* music, **4**:710–11
in Sundanese *gamelan* music, **4**:703–4
in Sundanese *ketuk tilu*, **4**:707
Tanna, **9**:64, *65*
Thailand, **4**:276
Venda people, **1**:708
Vietnam, **4**:465
Waiāpí *turé* music, **2**:161
Wayana flute music, **2**:165
Italy, **8**:610–11
Jamaica, in Kumina cult songs, **2**:903
Japan, *nagauta* music, **7**:672–73
Kazakhstan, *kyui*, **6**:958
in Kenyah music, **4**:826
Kerala, Christian devotional music, **5**:946–47
in Khmer music, **4**:179–80
Korea, *sinawi*, **7**:891
Kota musical ensembles, **5**:278
Kpelle people, **1**:467
Latin American dance music, **3**:522
Low Countries, instrumental music, **8**:523
in Malaysian theatrical genres, **4**:416
Mashriq, orchestral music, **6**:552
Middle Eastern music, **6**:10
multidimensionality of, **1**:135–36
multipart, **1**:21
Africa, **10**:123
Aztec culture, **2**:555
Bahamas, **2**:804–5
Central America, **2**:8
Inca culture, **2**:207
layering, **1**:11
Mexico, **2**:8, 15
notation of, **1**:153–54, 155, 157
San people, **1**:704–5
Tukano culture, **2**:151
Warao culture, **2**:194
Nguni singing, **1**:706
Northwest Coast music, **3**:401
orchestral, **8**:51–52
overlapping, **1**:118
Papua New Guinea
Baluan vocal music, **9**:603
coordinate monophony, **9**:497
Teop songs, **9**:644
Peru, Indian *vs.* mestizo aesthetics, **2**:483
in praise singing, **1**:489
rhythmic, **1**:497–98
riffs
in soul music, **3**:676
in swing music, **3**:656

Russia, *kant*, **8:**780
Sāmoa
  hymns, **9:**204–5
  political songs, **9:**215
social reflections in, **8:**61–63
Solomon Islands
  Blablanga songs, **9:**657, 658
  Shortland *asipa*, **9:**656
in Southeast Asian musics, **4:**15–16
stratified (*See* heterophony)
in Thai music, **4:**17, 270, 272
Tonga
  fa'ahiula, **9:**792
  six-part, **9:**784
twentieth-century American art music, **3:**174
Vanuatu, vocal music, **9:**690–91
Venezuela
  Amerindian music, **2:**525
  polyphonic, **2:**534
in Vietnamese music, **4:**17
Yemen, drum ensemble music, **6:**98–99, 101,
    103
in Yoruba music, **1:**461
Thabane, Philip, **1:**777–78
Thābit ibn Qurra, **6:**368
Thai Buddhism: Its Rites and Activities (Wells),
    4:287
Thai Music in Sound (Panya Roongrüang), **4:**224
Thai people, **7:**496. See also Black Tai people; Tai
    people; Tày people; Thai Dam people
  in North America, **3:**949, 950, 1009
Thái people (Vietnam), **4:**444, 531
  ceremonies of, **4:**533
  instruments of, **4:**533, 535–36
  songs of, **4:**532–33
Thai Dam people, **4:**338, 347, 349. *See also*
    Black Tai people
  in North America, **3:**948, 1007
  popular music of, **4:**360
Thai-Korat people, **4:**316. *See also* Black Tai
    people
Thái Thị Lang, **4:**508–9, 511
Thailand
  agricultural songs, **4:**113–14
  Akha people in, **4:**540–42
  Bangkok, **4:**5
  Buddhism in, **4:**287–97
  central, **4:**221
    village music, **4:**298–304
  chaos and control in, **4:**16
  Chinese influences in, **4:**70–71
  Chinese people in, **7:**6
  classical music, contexts for, **4:**247–60
  classical music traditions in, **4:**7
  competitions in, **4:**141–42
  composition in, **4:**127–28, 277–83, 286
  courtship in, **4:**299, 313, 321
  cultural origins of, **4:**10–11
  Europeans in, **4:**284–85
  geography of, **4:**221, 296, 315
  Hinduism in, **4:**64–65
  historical sources, **4:**224–26
  history of, **4:**219, 248–49, 296, 304, 310, 315
  history of music in, **4:**284–87
  Hmong people in, **4:**550–51
  Hoabinhian culture, **4:**33

Indian people in, **4:**68
influence on Lao music, **4:**353–54, 359–60
instrumental ensembles of, **4:**240–47
instruments, **4:**227–40
Islam in, **4:**74, 79
Karen people in, **4:**543–46
Khmer people in, **4:**151, 210–15
Kmhmu people in, **4:**546–47
Lahu people in, **4:**538–40
Lisu people in, **4:**542–43
map of, **4:**220
minority cultures in, **4:**221–22
monochords in, **4:**59
musical genres, **4:**278–82
  homrong, **4:**201, 252, 279, 307
  Lao influences on, **4:**359
  naphat, **4:**278
  phleng dio, **4:**281
  phleng hang khrüang, **4:**282
  phleng khorat, **4:**140, 300
  phleng kret, **4:**281
  phleng la, **4:**281
  phleng luk krung, **4:**96–97, 100, 331
  phleng luk thung, **4:**96–97, 99–100, 115,
      307, 316, 320–21, 332, 514
  phleng phün müang, **4:**310
  phleng rüa, **4:**229, 299
  phleng rüang, **4:**278–79
  phleng tap, **4:**279
  phleng thao, **4:**128, 279–80
  phleng yai, **4:**280
  phua chiwit, **4:**98
  phün ban, **4:**114
  sakarawa, **4:**229
  string, **4:**97–98
  tawk soi, **4:**229
music research on, **4:**24, 25, 26, 150, 223–25,
    285, 287, 530
northeastern, **4:**221–22, 297, 315–29
  kantrüm, **4:**222
  lam klawn, **4:**22, 115, 325–26, 341, 342,
      343
  lam kon, **4:**352
  lam mu, **4:**115–16, 325, 327–28, 342, 353
  lam phanya yoi, **4:**327
  lam phün, **4:**325
  lam ploen, **4:**325, 328–29, 352–53
  lam sing, **4:**18, 142, 316, 320–21, 327,
      332–33
  musical changes in, **4:**115–16
  music genres of, **4:**222, 320–21, 324–30
  terminology in, **4:**338
  traditional music of, **4:**141
northern, **4:**221, 309–15
  music genres of, **4:**313–14
pedagogy in, **4:**120–22
people of, **4:**315–16
politics in, **4:**91
popular music in, **4:**8, 95–101, 329–33
population of, **4:**218–19
prehistoric, **4:**35–36, 39, 42, 596
Ramayana in, **5:**261
regional cultures in, **4:**5, 116–17, 296–98
representative music of, **4:**22, 133
revival movement in, **4:**125–26
salient musical features of, **4:**17

southern, **4:**221, 304–9
spirit beliefs in, **4:**49, 52–53
spirit of rice, **4:**51
structure of classical music, **4:**260–97
Taiyai people in, **4:**547–49
theater, **4:**250–57, 301–3 (*See also* theater
    heading)
Theravada Buddhism in, **5:**968–69
tourism in, **4:**136–40, 247, 249–50, 316
trance in, **4:**61
upland peoples, **4:**310, 537–59
  music research on, **4:**26
urbanization of, **4:**115
village life in, **4:**6
village *vs.* urban life, **4:**222
wars in, **4:**11
Western music in, **4:**81–82, 91
Yao people in, **4:**549
Thailand: A Short History (Wyatt), **4:**219
Thakkar, Menaka, **3:**223, *223*, 1216
Thakur, Omkarnath, **5:**52, 56, 207, *207*, 255,
    424, 466
Thakur people, **5:**727
Thalberg, Sigismund, **3:**556, 1180
Thầm Oánh, **4:**511
Thamud culture, **6:**361
Thangaraj, M. Thomas, **5:**924–25
Thăng Long, **4:**472, 480, 482, 498
"Thank You Falettinme Be Mice Elf Agin" (Sly
    and the Family Stone), **3:**681, 710
"Thank You for Talkin' to Me Africa" (Stone),
    3:681
Thanom Kittikachorn, **4:**98
Thảo Giang (*ding goong* player), **4:**60
Tharpe, Sister Rosetta, **3:**535
Tharshish, **6:**1047
"That Lady" (Isley Brothers), **3:**711
"That Old Black Magic" (Arlen), **3:**549
"That Thing Called Love" (Bradford), **3:**644
"That's Enough" (Charles), **3:**678
That's the Way of the World, **3:**682
"That's What Friends Are For" (Warwick), **3:**713
Thaungthu (Pa-o) people, **4:**543
Thawng-khun Sia-run (Thai musician), **4:**317
Thayer, Alexander Wheelock, **3:**28
theater. *See also* ballad opera; blackface
    minstrelsy; *ch'anggŭk*; dance and
    movement; *kabuki*; *kyôgen*; musical
    theater; *nô*; opera; operetta; *p'ansori*;
    theater, puppet; vaudeville
Afghanistan, **5:**489
  art theater, **5:**489
  seil, **5:**821
African-American, **3:**524, 577, 614–22
Andean region, dance-drama, **2:**220–21
Andhra Pradesh, **5:**486
  vīthinātaka, **5:**516
Arabian peninsula, pantomime in expatriate
    communities, **6:**717–18
Argentina
  during carnival, **2:**258–59
  Passion dramatizations, **2:**258
Assam, **5:**486
Australia, **9:**226–29
Azerbaijan, **6:**924
  tæziye, **6:**923, 931

theater (*continued*)
Bali
  accompaniment for, **4:**734
  arja, **4:**750–51, 753, 757
  calonarang, **4:**748
  drama gong, **4:**753
  gambuh, **4:**732–33, 735, 746, 749–50, 757,
    760–61
  janger, **4:**753
  parwa, **4:**753, 757
  prembon, **4:**753
  sendratari, **4:**753, 759
  topeng, **4:**753, 757
  wayang wong, **4:**753, 757
Bangladesh
  Japanese genres, **5:**489
  jarigan, **5:**505–6
  nrtya-nātya, **5:**505
  religious, **5:**488
Basque region, *pastorales souletines,* **8:**314–15
Belarus, **8:**799
Bengal, **5:**486–87, 849
  jātrā, **5:**419, 488–89, 503, 505, 550
Bhutan, **5:**489
Bolivia, dance-dramas, **2:**292
Brazil, **2:**347–48
  autos, **2:**302
  casamento de matuto, **2:**331
  dance-dramas, **2:**334
  pastoril de ponta-de-rua, **2:**334
  religious plays, **2:**329
  ternos, **2:**312–13
Bulgaria, Roma, **8:**283
Burma, **4:**395–96
  za' pwè, **4:**373, 377, 389, 396, 399
Canada, **3:**198–200
  nineteenth-century, **3:**1148
Central America, dance-dramas, **2:**44
Central Asia, **6:**900–901
China, **7:**89
  chuanqi, **7:**75, 89, 276, 290–93, 392–93,
    396
  hi, **4:**170
  huaju, **7:**387
  juzhong, **7:**277
  movement in, **7:**60
  source materials on, **7:**129–30, 132
  tan huang, **7:**76
  wenmingxi, **7:**299
  yang'ge drama, **7:**385
Cirebon, *berokan,* **4:**688
Cook Islands
  Manihiki, **9:**238, *239*
  nuku pageant, **9:**903
Cuba
  teatro bufo, **2:**838
  teatro lírico, **2:**838
East Asia, **7:**5–6, 73–78
  movement in, **7:**59
Ecuador, pantomimes, **2:**420–21
Egypt, **6:**547
El Salvador, dance-dramas, **2:**710–11
England, Soul-Caking Play, **8:**140, 331
Europe
  folk traditions, **8:**140–41
  mystery plays, **8:**315

passion plays, **8:**140
  Renaissance, **8:**77, 160
France, *variété,* **2:**516
Garifuna culture, dance-dramas, **2:**673–74
Georgia, **8:**836
Germany, *Liederspiele,* **8:**141, 653
Guatemala, *Rabinal Achí* dance-drama, **2:**653,
  724, 729, 731
Gujarat, *bhavāī,* **5:**419, 485, 501, 634–35
Gupta kingdom, **5:**18, 24
Guyana, British, **2:**447
Hawai'i
  hula ki'i, **9:**230–31
  pan-Polynesian revues, **3:**1050–51
Hungary, religious, **8:**740
India, **5:**484–86
  art theater, **5:**485–86
  North, *nauṭaṅkī,* **5:**496, 549
  South, revival of, **5:**542–43
Iran, **6:**878
  ta'zīye, **6:**827, 840, 860, 866
Israel, **6:**1019, 1072
Italy
  carnevale di Bagolino, **8:**608
  maggio drammatico, **8:**140, 608
Jamaica, **2:**909
Jammu and Kashmir, *pāther,* **5:**498
Japan, **7:**653–85, 687
  development of, **7:**653–55
  hayasi accompaniment in, **7:**655, 683–85
  sarugaku, **7:**618, 629, 639, 653
  simpa, **7:**77, 944
  utusie, **7:**749
  westernized, **7:**743
  women performers in, **7:**765–66
Java
  kethoprak, **4:**655, 680, 681
  langen driyan, **4:**654, 655
  langen mandra wanara, **4:**654–55
  ludruk, **4:**655
  stambul, **4:**774
  wayang genres, **4:**658
  wayang topèng, **4:**653–54
  wayang wong, **4:**637, 653, 680
  wayang wong panggung, **4:**653, 655
Jewish people
  Purim play, **3:**944; **8:**141, 251, 261
  Yiddish, **8:**141
Karnataka, **5:**486
Kashmir, *bānde pāther,* **5:**685, *685*
Kerala, **5:**486
  caviṭṭunāṭakam, **5:**945–46
  nāṭakam, **5:**934
  oṭṭan tuḷḷal, **5:**516, 941
Khmer people
  basakk, **4:**155, 157, 158, 166, 169, 201
  folk, **4:**155
  lkhaon khol, **4:**155, 190–91
  in Vietnam, **4:**215–16
  yike, **4:**158, 200–201
Korea, **7:**941–47
  chapsaek nori, **7:**942
  folk genres, **7:**942–44
  sandae nori, **7:**941–42
Laos
  khon, **4:**357, 358

lakhon, **4:**358
lam lueang, **4:**342, 353
lam rueang, **4:**133
li-ke, **4:**352
Lombok
  "*Amaq Abir,*" **4:**774
  "*Cupak Grantang,*" **4:**774
  kayaq, **4:**772, 776
  kemidi rudat, **4:**768, 774
Madagascar
  hira-gasy, **1:**789, *790*
  kalon'ny fahiny, **1:**791–92
Madhya Pradesh
  bharata nat, **5:**471
  manch, **5:**471
Maharashtra
  gondhal, **5:**728
  saṅgīt nāṭak, **5:**729
  tamāśā, **5:**419, 423–24, 485
Malaysia, **4:**402–3
  bangsawan, **4:**68, 92, 125, 134, 402, 406,
    426–27
  boria, **4:**406, 426
  hadrah, **4:**409, 424
  jikay, **4:**410–11, 412
  mak yong, **4:**406–7, 412, 417, *418, 419,*
    421, 427
  mak yong laut, **4:**411
  manora, **4:**411–12
  ma'yong, **4:**19, 23, 92, 125, 134
  mek mulung, **4:**407–8, 412
  rodat, **4:**409–10
Mangareva, *pe'i,* **9:**886
Maratha, **5:**413, 423, 970
Mashriq, *ta'ziya,* **6:**544
Maya culture, dance-dramas, **2:**723–24, 731
Mexico
  las posadas, **2:**614–15; **4:**843
  tonadilla escénica, **2:**603, 606
Mithila, *jatā-jatin,* **5:**679
Mongol people, **7:**1007
  Buddhist dance-dramas, **7:**1016
  tsam dance-dramas, **7:**1017, 1018–19
Nepal, **5:**489–90
  jātrā, **5:**490
Nicaragua
  El Gigante, **2:**756, 760
  El Güegüence, **2:**749, 756, 760–61
Niue, **9:**817
North Africa, choreographed spectacles,
  1:544–45, 585
Oceania, **9:**224–26, 229–39
  popular, **9:**233–34
  Western, **9:**233–34
Oman, *pākit,* **6:**679, 681
Orissa, **5:**486, 732
Otopame culture, *pastorelas,* **2:**572
Pakistan, **5:**486–88
  art theater, **5:**487
  Indrasabha, **5:**487
Panama
  congos, **2:**48, 778–79
  gran diablos, **2:**779
Papua New Guinea, **9:**234–35
  Binandere *ario* dance-drama, **9:**499–501
  Oro Province dance-dramas, **9:**489

Peru
  auto, **2:**495
  Corpus Christi plays, **2:**494
  dance-dramas, **2:**479–80, 481, 483
  Del 96 al 36, **2:**500
Philippines
  bakal-bakal, **4:**856
  colloquio, **4:**856
  comedia, **4:**869
  curalda, **4:**856
  gindula, **4:**874
  kumidya, **4:**856, 869
  linambay, **4:**856
  modern adaptations, **4:**881
  moro-moro, **4:**854, 856, 869
  panunuluyan (also *pananawagan*;
      pananapatan; *o kagharong*; *solomon*),
      4:843, 855
  Pugutan, **4:**846
  sarswela, **4:**856–57, 863–65, 866, 868, 869,
      871, 874
  senaculo, **4:**846–47, 855, 869
  tibag, **4:**847
Punjab
  bhand, **5:**488
  Rās Dhāria plays, **5:**765
Rajasthan
  bhavāī, **5:**647
  Gavrī, **5:**292
  kathputlī, **5:**640
Russia, Rom people, **8:**287
Ryûkyû Islands
  dance-dramas, **7:**65–66
  kumi odori, **7:**789–90, 796
Sāmoa, **9:**235–38
  biblical plays, **9:**236
  faleaitu, **9:**229–30, 235–36
Serbia, *komad s pevanjem*, **8:**141, 948
Shan people, *yikay*, **4:**548
Sherpa people, *mani-rimdu*, **5:**490
Singapore
  bangsawan, **4:**520
  Chinese, **4:**518–19
  musicals, **4:**523–24
Slovak, **3:**899
Solomon Islands, Isabel Province, **9:**661–62
Somalia, **1:**618
South Africa
  music in, **1:**219
  terukkūttu, **5:**617, *618*
South America, dance-dramas, **2:**44
South Asia
  art theater, **5:**483
  categories of, **5:**480–84
  comic improvisations, **5:**480
  early treatises on, **5:**21, 23–24, 25–30, 40
  folk, **5:**481–82, 488, *496*
  notion of, **5:**480
  Parsi, **5:**423–24, 487, 491, 970
  popular, **5:**484, 485–86
  primitive types of, **5:**481, 484–85, 488
  religious, **5:**480, 482–83
  Sanskrit drama, **5:**323, 325, 509
  Urdu/Persian, **5:**487
  Western influences on, **5:**483
  women performers in, **5:**410

Southeast Asia, Indian epics as source material,
    4:66, 67
Sri Lanka, **5:**490–91, 970
  kohomba-kankāriya, **5:**364
  kolam, **5:**491, 964, 968
  nādagama, **5:**422, 491, 958, 964
  nurti, **5:**491
  pasu, **5:**491
  rukkada, **5:**964
  sokari, **5:**491, 964
Sumatra
  bangsawan, **4:**601, 606, 607, 625, 626
  Dul Muluk, **4:**617, 625
  komedi stambul, **4:**601
  ma'inang, **4:**605, 616
  ma'yong, **4:**607, 616
  mendu, **4:**607, 616
  opera Batak, **4:**608
  randai, **4:**611
  warahan, **4:**627
Sumbawa
  batu nganga, **4:**784
  lalu dia lala jince, **4:**784
  tanjung menangis, **4:**785
  toja, **4:**785
Sunda, *sandiwara*, **4:**703
Switzerland
  Einsiedler Passion plays, **8:**696
  Fête des Vignerons, **8:**696
Tamil Nadu
  Ariccantiran nāṭakam, **5:**277
  funeral music in, **5:**282
  icai nāṭakam, **5:**913
  kuravanji, **5:**518
  natukūttu, **5:**958, 964
  noṇṭi cintu, **5:**921
  Paṇiya people, **5:**909
  Rāma nāṭakam, **5:**275, 277, 279
  terukkūttu, **5:**90, 516, 542, 556, 908, 913
Thailand
  dūkdamban, **4:**234
  khon, **4:**250–52, 253, 264, 279
  lakhawn, **4:**221, 250, 253–57, 264, 267,
      279, 303, 538
  lam mu, **4:**115–16, 325, 327–28, 342, 353
  lam phlün, **4:**115–16
  lam ploen, **4:**325, 328–29, 352
  li-ke, **4:**95, 99, 221, 222, 256, 301–3, 328,
      352
  li-ke ba, **4:**309
  manora, **4:**221, 254, 306–7
  music for, **4:**278
  piphat ensembles for, **4:**241, 251–52
  saw lakhawn, **4:**313
Tibetan culture, *a-lce lha-mo*, **5:**712
Tokelau, *faleaitu*, **9:**229, 238
Trinidad and Tobago, carnival, **2:**966
Uighur *ikki muqam*, **6:**990
Ukrainian, **3:**912
United States
  autos sacramentales, **3:**848, 850
  Cambodian genres, **3:***1000*, 1000–1001
  East Indian traditions, **3:**814
  eighteenth-century genres, **3:**179–81
  government funding for, **3:**299
  Hungarian plays, **3:**908

Italian-American, **3:**861
  nineteenth-century, **3:**182, 542–44, 555
  revues, **3:**198–99
  Spanish genres, **3:**735–36, 757, 759, 848–52
Uruguay
  murga, **2:**516–19, 521
  tango productions, **2:**519
  teatro callejero, **2:**517
  teatro de revista, **2:**516, 521
Uttar Pradesh, *nauṭankī*, **5:**346, 419, 485,
      674, 675
Uzbekistan, Fārsi *taziyah*, **6:**942
Venezuela, Parranda de San Pedro, **2:**530
Vietnamese, **4:**484–97
  bài chòi, **4:**449, 469, 496
  cải lương, **3:**949, 994; **4:**70, 88, 449, 454,
      468, 473, 484, 485, 493–95, 508,
      509, 512
  ca kịch huế, **4:**449, 496–97
  ca ra bộ, **4:**493, 496
  chèo, **4:**23, 88, 124, 446, 448, 449, 455,
      469, 485, 488–90, 501, 508
  chèo cải lương, **4:**508
  chèo văn minh, **4:**508
  Chinese influences on, **4:**447
  folk drama, **4:**485–87
  hát bội (also *tuồng*), **4:**23, 88, 124, 448,
      449, 462, 469, 475, 485, 490–93,
      498, 501–2, 508
  hát chèo tàu, **4:**485–87
  kịch hát dân ca, **4:**497
  kịch nói (spoken drama), **4:**496
  kịch thơ (spoken drama), **4:**496–97
  reforms in, **4:**507–8
  revival of, **4:**124–25
  trò diễn, **4:**485
  tuồng (See under *hát bội*)
  xuân phả, **4:**485, *486*, 498
Virgin Islands, David and Goliath play,
      2:972–73
West Bengal, *letogān*, **5:**862
Yiddish, **3:**933, 935, 937–38, 941; **8:**251
Yoruba people, **1:**400–402, 406–9
Theater de la Renaissance (New Orleans), **3:**615
Theater Guild of Guyana, **2:**447
theater, puppet
  Bali
    wayang kulit, **4:**751, 753
    wayang lemah, **4:**752
  Burma, **4:***139*
    you'theì, **4:**396, *397*
  Cambodian, **3:**1000–1001
    nang sbek tauch, **4:**308
  Chinese, *wayang potèhi*, **4:**650
  Cirebon, **4:**774
    wayang golèk, **4:**688–89
    wayang kulit, **4:**688–89, 697
  East Asia, **7:**6
  Hong Kong, **7:**434
  Indonesian, **3:**1012, 1018, 1020–21
    wayang kulit, **4:**76, 308
    wayang purwa, **4:**403
  Italy, **8:**53
  Japan. See *bunraku*
  Java
    wayang gedhog, **4:**650

theater, puppet, Java (*continued*)
  wayang golèk, **4:**650, 667
  wayang klithik, **4:**650
  wayang kulit, **4:**637, 643, 649–53, 655,
    658, 665, 671, 674, 675, 680, 681,
    683, 687–88
  wayang potèhi, **4:**650
  wayang purwa, **4:**650, 665, 667
  Karnataka, **5:**879
  Kerala, *tõlpavakuthu,* **5:**363
  Khmer people
    lkhaon sbek, **4:**155
    sbek poar, **4:**191, 193
    sbek tauch, **4:**191
    sbek thomm, **4:**191–93, 252
  Korea, *kkoktu kakshi,* **7:**933, 942, 943–44,
    946
  Laos, **4:**357
  Lombok, *wayang Sasak,* **4:**768, 774, *775*
  Malaysia
    Chinese glove puppets, **4:**72
    nang talung, **4:**404
    wayang gedek, **4:**404
    wayang kulit, **4:**92, 134, 308, 835
    wayang kulit Jawa, **4:**403–4, 428
    wayang melayu, **4:**404–6, 417, 427, 428
    wayang Siam, **4:**404–6, 412, 417, *418,*
      419, 425, 428
  Oman, **6:**679
  Philippines, **4:**881
    aliala, **4:**855
    carillo, **4:**855
    gaglo, **4:**855
    kikimut, **4:**855
    titre, **4:**855
  Punjab, **5:**488, 769
  Rajasthan, **5:**640
  Sicily, **8:**611
  Singapore, **4:**518
    wayang kulit, **4:**520
  South Asia, **5:**270, 480
  Southeast Asia, Indian epics as source material,
    4:66
  Sri Lanka, **5:**964
  Sumatra
    sigale-gale, **4:**608
    southern, **4:**622
    wayang kulit Palembang, **4:**626
    wayang kulit purwa, **4:**626
  Sunda, *wayang golèk,* **4:**703, 705–6, 725
  Surinam, **2:**507
  Taiwan, **7:**425–26
  Thailand
    Chinese, **4:**70
    genres of, **4:**252
    hün krabawk, **4:**250, 257, 279
    nang pra mo thai, **4:**252, 307, 325, 329
    nang talung, **4:**221, 252, 307–9
    nang yai, **4:**250, 252–53, 264, 279
  Vietnam, water puppets (*múa rối nước*), **4:**88,
    124, 134, 138, 446, 447, 487–88
Théatre de Neptune, Le (Lescarbot), **3:**1114, 1135
Théâtre Olympia (Montréal), **3:**1160
Théâtre Verdure (Haiti), **2:**890
Theay Em, **4:**188
Thébault, Frédéric, **2:**158, 164

Thee Midniters (musical group), **3:**746, 747
Theesink, Hans, **8:**675
Thelin, Eje, **8:**446
"Thelonious" (Monk), **3:**659
Themistios, **6:**368
Theodorakis, Mikis, **8:**1021
Theodore Thomas Orchestra, **3:**556
Theory and Method in Ethnomusicology (Nettl),
  10:42, 101
theory, music, **3:**337. *See also* treatises
  Afghanistan, **5:**827
  Arabian peninsula, **6:**657
  Arab music, early, **6:**7, 8, 15–17, 131, 135,
    183, 363–82, 387–93, 402, 442, 443,
    502, 503, 508, 535–36, 540–42, 869,
    909–10, 1066; **8:**92
  Arab music, postmedieval, **6:**543–44
  Arab music, twentieth-century, **6:**34–38,
    42–43, 508, 548–49
  Armenian, **6:**725, 727
  Azerbaijan, **6:**926–27
  Bali, **4:**733–37
  Baroque, **8:**79
  Bhatkhande method, **5:**445–46, 448
  Central Asian, **6:**922
  China, **7:**115–23, 348
    nanguan music, **7:**207–8
    northwestern musics, **7:**456–57
    structural techniques, **7:**234–37
  European development of, **8:**92–93
  Greek, **6:**15–16, 129, 368, 373, 540–41, 772;
    8:47–48, 49, 92
  Hindustani, **5:**563
    raga, **5:**66–69, 73–81, 84
    tala, **5:**110–37
  Indian music, early, **5:**17–41, 313, 956
  institutional training in, **5:**450
  Iran, **6:**60–62, 129–30, 142, 834, 865–74
  Japan, **7:**565–73, 770–71
  Jewish, **8:**264
  Karnatak, **5:**387–88, 454
    raga, **5:**96–97
    tala, **5:**139–40
  Khmer music, **4:**174–82
  Korea, **7:**833–34, 856
  Kurdish, **6:**752
  Middle Ages, **8:**49–50, 70
  Nigeria, **1:**254–69
  North Africa, **6:**367
  notation and, **8:**104
  Oceania, **9:**282–309
  Renaissance, **8:**74–75, 79
  Russia, **8:**756, 783
  South Asian scholarship since 1300, **5:**42–58,
    262, 561
  speculative, **5:**56
  Sri Lanka, **5:**959–60
  Susak music, **4:**769–71
  Tibetan music, **7:**472–73
  treatises on, **7:**128
  Turkey
    folk music, **6:**77–87, 783
    makam, **6:**48–55
    treatises on, **6:**759
  Turkmen people, **6:**971
  twelve-tone, **7:**342

  Uighur people, **6:**995
  Vietnam, **4:**451–66
  vocables in, **8:**98
Theory of Bulgarian Folk Music (Dzhudzhev),
  8:906
Theory of Music in Arabic Writings (Shiloah),
  6:1066
theosophy, **5:**53
therapy, dance, **3:**215, 225
"There Goes My Baby" (Drifters), **3:**673, 709
"There Was a Time" (Brown), **3:**680
"There'll Be a Hot Time in the Old Town
  (Tonight)", **3:**310
"There's a Church in the Valley" (hymn), **9:**848
"There's No Business Like Show Business"
  (Berlin), **3:**196
Thernstrom, Stephan, **3:**515
Theroux, Paul, **9:**42
Therrien, Eugene, **3:***856*
Therrien, Lucie, **3:**855, *856*
Thesaurus of Hebrew Oriental Melodies (Idelsohn),
  6:1024, 1029, 1057, 1071
"These Arms of Mine" (Redding), **3:**676
"They Like Ike" (Berlin), **3:**310
"They Want Efx" (Das Efx), **3:**700
Thibaw, king of Burma, **4:**378
Thieme, Darius, **1:**51; **10:**139
"Things That I Used to Do" (Guitar Slim),
  3:352
"Think" (Brown), **3:**678
"Think" (Franklin), **3:**710
Think of a Garden (Kneubuhl), **9:**233
Thirakva, Ahmad Jan, **5:**134, *134,* 136, 137, *207*
Third New Hampshire Regiment Band, **3:**565
third-stream music. *See* jazz
Third World Band, **2:**910, 912
13 AD (musical group), **5:**428
Thirteen Strings, **3:**1186
"This Child" (song; Aglukark), **3:**1063
This Child (album; Aglukark), **3:**1280
"This Is My Country" (Mayfield), **3:**677
This Is the Army (Berlin), **3:**545
"This Land Is Your Land" (Guthrie), **3:**914
"This Little Girl of Mine" (Charles), **3:**678
"This Magic Moment" (Drifters), **3:**673, 709
Thistle, Paula, **3:**381
Tho people, **4:**218
Thobejane, Gabriel Mabee, **1:***760,* 777–78
Thomas, Allan, **9:**354, 973, 974
Thomas, Ambroise, **4:**859
Thomas B. Harms (publishing firm), **3:**191
Thomas, Carla, **3:**675–76
Thomas, John, **3:**653
Thomas, Larry, **9:**233
Thomas, Lindsey, **9:**135
Thomas, Lloyd, **2:***970*
Thomas, Millard, **3:**1169
Thomas, Mr., **3:**1179
Thomas, Pat, **3:**1213
Thomas, Philip J., **3:**1256, 1257
Thomas, Rufus, **3:**676
Thomas, Saint, **5:**944–45, 946
Thomas, Sylvester, **1:**376
Thomas, Theodore, **3:**537, *537,* 556, 564
Thompson, Cindy, **3:**1191
Thompson, David, **3:**1255

Thompson, Donald, **2:**941
Thompson, Gordon, **3:**980; **5:**585
Thompson, P. A., **4:**303
Thompson, Robert Farris, **1:**135, 688
Thompson, Sonny, **3:**669
Thompson, Will, **1:**765
Thoms, W. J., **8:**326
Thomsen, Lejvar, **8:**472
Thomson, Aleksander Edward, **8:**495–96
Thomson, Basil, **9:**130
Thomson, George, **8:**367, 370, 372
Thomson, John, **8:**368, 373
Thomson, John Mansfield, **9:**932
Thomson, Virgil, **3:**14, 297, 539, 545, 608
Thomson, William, **8:**17, 372
Thonga people, **1:**277, 707–8
Thongkhio, **4:**361
Thorhallsdóttir, Anna, **8:**407
Thorī caste, **5:**646
Thraco-Illyrians, **8:**890
Thrasher, Willie, **3:**1277, 1280
3 + 2 (musical group), **8:**747
Three Degrees (musical group), **3:**711
3HO movement, **5:**256
360° Productions, **3:**498
Three Kingdoms period. *See also* Koguryŏ;
    Paekche; Silla
  Buddhism in, **7:**329
  Daoism in, **7:**320
  dynastic histories of, **7:**855
  music in, **7:**88, 806, 930, 981
3 Mustaphas 3 (musical group), **8:**226
Three Pieces for Gamelan with Soloists (Harrison),
    4:132
Three Places in New England (Ives), **3:**14
Three Scoops of Aloha, **9:**167
Threepenny Opera (Weill), **8:**659
"Thrill Is Gone" (King), **3:**709
Thriller (Jackson), **3:**712
Thrush, **3:**1073
Thulung Rai people, **5:**288
ṭhumrī, **5:**107, 162, 179–83, 192, 847
  Bengal, **5:**852–53, 855, 856
  dance performances of, **5:**494
  decline of, **5:**376, 381
  development of, **5:**15, 373
  form of, **5:**533
  gat in, **5:**194
  Guyana, **5:**602, 605
  history of, **5:**179–80
  improvisation in, **5:**202
  instrumental performance of, **5:**197–98, 202,
      206
  laggī section, **5:**128, 181–83, 186, 198
  North America, **5:**581
  patronage of, **5:**435
  performance of, **5:**180–83
  Punjab, **5:**766
  ragas for, **5:**69, 194
  status of, **5:**379
  tabla accompaniment of, **5:**123, 128, 132
  talas for, **5:**126–27
  texts of, **5:**180, 181
  Trinidad, **5:**591
  women performers of, **5:**410, 411, 413–14,
      424

Thunder Bay Symphony Orchestra, **3:**1079,
    1184
Thunder Brothers (musical group), **10:**78
Thunderbirds (musical group), **8:**679
Thuren, Hjalmar, **8:**18
Thurmair, Georg, **8:**661
Thurnwald, Richard, **9:**258, 479, 650, 991
Thúy Ngân (*chèo* performer), **4:**489
Ti. *See* Ti *plus next element in name*
Tianjin Conservatory, **7:**398
Tianjin Municipal Troupe, **7:**253–55
Tianyuha (Dao), **7:**261
Tianyunshe qupu (Wu), **7:**132
Tião Carreiro and Pardinho, **2:**319
Tiawanaku culture, **2:**356
  archaeomusicological studies of, **2:**7
  instruments of, **2:**11–12, *14*
Tib, Tippu, **1:**635
Tibbett, Lawrence, **3:**537; **8:**95
Tibet, **7:**471–83
  Buddhism in, **7:**32–33, 327, 420–21, 472,
      478, 479–80
  court music, **7:**480–81
  dance traditions in, **7:**67, 474–77
  folk songs of, **7:**152, 449, 473–74
  geography of, **7:**471
  historical writing of, **7:**447
  history of, **7:**471–72
  King Gesar epic of, **5:**711–12, 715; **7:**451,
      472, 477, 1008
  Lhoba people in, **7:**449
  notational systems in, **8:**103
  opera genres of, **7:**452, 478–79
  politics in, **7:**30
  Tibetan terminology, **7:**472
  vocal music of, **5:**710
  Western *vs.* Chinese research on, **10:**26
  yangqin in, **7:**179
Tibetan Autonomous Region Song and Dance
    Troupe, **7:**443
Tibetan Dance and Opera Company, **3:**207, 219
Tibetan Institute for the Performing Arts, **3:**219
Tibetan Institute of Performing Arts
    (Dharamsala), **5:**711, 715, 716
Tibetan people and culture
  in Arunachal Pradesh, **5:**504
  in Bhutan, **5:**489, 709–16
  in Himachal Pradesh, **5:**499–500
  in India, **5:**709–16; **7:**6
  instruments of, **5:**710, 714
  monastery traditions of, **5:**713–15
  in Nepal, **5:**5, 490, 696, 709–16; **7:**6
  in North America, **3:**129, 133, 219, 340
  popular music of, **7:**444
  research on music of, **5:**711, 715–16
  in South Asia, **5:**709–16
  vocal music of, **5:**709–11
  in Yunnan province, **7:**509, 510
Tiboli people, **4:**920
  instrumental music of, **4:**921–24, 925, 926
Tiby, Ottavio, **8:**622
Tick, Judith, **3:**506
Tiddas (musical group), **9:**443–44, 987
Tiddas and The Seven Sisters, **9:**244
Tidore, **4:**812, 813–17
Tidori no kyoku (Yosizawa), **7:**698, 712

Tielman Brothers, **8:**238
Ti-Émile, **2:**916
Tierlinck, Isidoor, **8:**534
Tierra (musical group), **3:**733, 746, 748, 749,
    751, 799
Tierra Tejana (musical group), **3:**780
Tiersot, Julien, **8:**19, 177, 547, 553
al-Tīfāshī, Aḥmad ibn Yūsuf, **6:**12, 365, 370,
    373, 443, 444, 445, 446, 447
Ti Fock (musical group), **5:**610
Tiga (New Caledonia), **9:**672, 679, 680, 682–84
*Tighten the Drums: Self-Decoration Among the
    Enga* (film), **9:**42, 50
Tigranyan, Armen, **6:**726
Tigranyan, Nikoghayos, **6:**725
Tigre people, **1:**599
Tijardović, Ivo, **8:**933–34
Tijeritas, **8:**208
al-Tijībī, **6:**443
Tikamatu Monzeamon. *See* Chikamatsu
    Monzeamon
Tikar people
  mbøŋgo lamellophone, **1:**319
  music of, **1:**658
Tikopia (Solomon Islands), **9:**59, 833, 852,
    853–56, 861
  betel use in, **9:**177
  ceremonies, **9:**202
  composition in, **9:**354
  gender-based insults, **9:**241, 247–49
  kava use in, **9:**174
  music and dance of, **9:**853–56
  population of, **9:**853
  settlement of, **9:**835
  social organization of, **9:**835–36
  song structures, **9:**330–31
  string figures in, **9:**253
  struck plaques of, **9:**378
  sung poetry, **9:**327
Tikubusima (*nô* play), **7:**631
Tikurai gosyô (Moroi), **7:**705, 737
Tilack, **5:**603
Tilepbergenuly, Qazanghap, **6:**958
Tileuqabaq (Kazakh song), **6:**956
Tillamook Indian nation, **3:**394
tillāna, **5:**104, 178, 414, 512, 522
  composed by Tirunal, **5:**229
  texts of, **5:**107, 219–20
  in Trinidad, **5:**591
Tillis, Frederick, **3:**610, 612
Tilney, Philip, **3:**925
Tilton, Martha, **9:**149
Ti-Manno, **2:**892; **3:**805
timbre
  in Acadian singing, **3:**1137
  acoustics and, **1:**165
  analysis of, **9:**296–300
  Andean music, **2:**215–16, 217, 221, 295–96
  Arab music
    medieval, **6:**392
    vocal, **6:**361–62
  in Arctic singing, **3:**377
  arpa india, **2:**456
  Australia
    Cape York singing, **9:**429
    vocal, **9:**435

timbre (*continued*)
    Basque region, vocal, **8**:314
    Belarus, vocal, **8**:796
    Bellona, vocal, **9**:850
    in blues, **3**:638
    of Borneo singing, **4**:825
    Bosnia-Hercegovina, vocal, **8**:964
    Brazil, vocal, **2**:319
    Bribri and Cabécar cultures, vocal, **2**:634
    of Burmese instruments, **4**:371–72
    in Burmese music, **4**:18–19
    buzzing, **1**:489, 701, 746
        in Afro-Peruvian instruments, **2**:493
        Yanomamö culture, **2**:171–72
    in Caddo Indian singing, **3**:467
    Chile, vocal, **2**:367, 369
    China
        in new music, **7**:342
        speech tones, **7**:262–63, 270–71
    composers' use of, **1**:223
    Corsica, vocal, **8**:570
    Czech Republic, vocal/instrumental
            similarities, **8**:719
    dizi, **7**:183
    drums, **9**:383
    East Asia
        instruments, **7**:82
        theatrical vocal delivery, **7**:74
    Ecuador, vocal, **2**:420
    Egypt, vocal, **6**:166
    England
        Traveller singing, **8**:336
        vocal, **8**:326–27
    falsetto, **2**:181, 187, 215; **3**:389; **9**:530
        Anuta, **9**:297
        in Apache singing, **3**:431
        Bellona, **9**:297, 850
        in Berber singing, **6**:485
        Brazil, **2**:328
        China, **7**:151
        Chuuk, **9**:736
        in country music, **3**:77, 78
        in field hollers, **3**:83
        Fiji, **9**:162
        Hawai'i, **9**:128, 297, 300
        Kiribati, **9**:762
        Korea, **7**:818–19, 820, 904, 926, 928
        Lacandón Maya, **2**:656
        Mexico, **2**:608
        Mongol people, **7**:1006
        in Navajo *yei* songs, **3**:432
        Oceania, **9**:27, 297
        Papua New Guinea, **9**:297, 490, 503, 504,
                515–16, 524, 530, 538–40, 561, 562,
                565, 567, 571, 573, 626, 633
        Sāmoa, **9**:297
        Solomon Islands, **9**:157, 666
        Tunisian *ma'lūf*, **6**:502
        Vanuatu, **9**:709
    Fiji
        Hindustani music, **9**:782
        vocal, **5**:613; **9**:779
    Garífuna (Garifuna) culture, vocal, **2**:675, 734
    Georgia, vocal, **8**:828
    Guam, vocal, **9**:744
    Haiti, vocal, **2**:893

hardingfele, **8**:418
Hawai'i
    interpretation of, **9**:299–300
    vocal, **9**:287, 289, 292, 916
of Hmong singing, **4**:556
Hong Kong, vocal, **7**:436
horanâva, **5**:968
in Iban gong-drum ensembles, **4**:830
Iceland, for *rímur* chanting, **8**:401–2
importance of, **1**:125, 135–37
India, in film singing, **5**:107–8, 533, 543
Ireland, vocal, **8**:381
Irian Jaya, Asmat singing, **9**:590
Italy, vocal, **8**:613, 619
Jamaica, vocal, **2**:903, 906
Japan
    aesthetics and, **7**:550–52
    vocal, **7**:603, 682
of Karen singing, **4**:545
Karnatak music, vocal, **5**:108
korantuŋ, **4**:562, 563, 568
in Khmer music, **4**:159
Korea
    for *p'ansori* singing, **7**:906–7
    raspy, **7**:821
    kundus, **9**:619
Kurdish singing, **6**:745
langspil, **8**:406
local preferences, **8**:120–21
Macedonia, vocal, **8**:973
Madagascar, singing, **1**:791
Malaysia, vocal, **4**:417
Malta, vocal, **8**:636
Maltese guitar, **8**:640
Martinique, vocal, **2**:915, 917
Maya culture, vocal, **2**:731
of Mentawai singing, **4**:614
Micronesia, vocal, **9**:716, 720
Middle Eastern music, **6**:7–9
Miskitu culture, vocal, **2**:663
Montenegro, vocal, **8**:958
Nicaragua
    violín de talalate, **2**:757
    vocal, **2**:759
Oceania, in storytelling, **9**:337
ohun orisi singing, **1**:409–10
in Old Regular Baptists singing, **3**:118, 125
in Orang Asli music, **4**:584–85
pakhāvaj, **5**:120
Palau, vocal, **9**:719, 726
Papua New Guinea
    Managalasi songs, **9**:504
    panpipes, **9**:543
    singing through voice-modifying gourd,
            9:564
    vocal, **9**:152
Peru
    Indian *vs.* mestizo aesthetics, **2**:483
    vocal, **2**:476
pinculu, **2**:227
in Plains Indian singing, **3**:483
rattling, **1**:701
research on, **1**:142
role in pitch perception, **1**:255–69
roncador, **2**:471
Saami people, vocal, **8**:302

śahnāī, **5**:340
Sāmoa, vocal, **9**:205, 808
Sardinia, vocal, **8**:627
Scotland, Traveller singing, **8**:296
Semelai singing, **4**:587
sexual symbolism and, **2**:33–34
Sicily, vocal, **8**:611
silbadora, **2**:471
Slovakia, vocal/instrumental similarities, **8**:719
in Southeast Asian musics, **4**:14
in speech surrogates, **1**:106
structural uses of, **8**:91
Subarctic singing, **3**:389
Sufi chanting, **6**:193
Switzerland, vocal, **8**:690, 692
syakuhati, **7**:554
syamisen, **7**:551, 552
tabla, **5**:123
Tahiti, vocal, **9**:872
Thai singing, **4**:282
Tikopia, vocal, **9**:853
tonal color qualities, **5**:32, 36, 37–38
Trinidad, vocal, **5**:590
trumpet growl, **3**:654
Tuareg singing, **1**:579–80
twentieth-century innovations, **8**:85
Ukraine, vocal, **8**:809
Vanuatu, **9**:698
vibrating string, **9**:386
Vietnamese singing, **4**:492
vocal, research on, **8**:24
voice masking, Warao culture, **2**:194–95
vowel quality and, **1**:176–77
waka singing, **1**:413
West African singing quality, **1**:446, 451, 453,
            460, 467
West Futuna, vocal, **9**:861
Yoruba *jùjú* singing quality, **1**:478, 480
time and music. *See also* rhythm and meter;
        tempo
    Africa, **1**:154; **10**:62
        biographical, **1**:140, 143
        calendric, **1**:140
        comparative flows, **1**:140–41
        contingent elements, **1**:127
        coordination methods, **1**:141
        event timing, **1**:139
        expandable moment, **1**:130–31
        historical, **1**:140, 143, 507, 508, 511
        motion and, **1**:126–27, 133
        multidimensionality, **1**:127–28
        past-present interactions, **1**:127, 143, 507
        research on, **1**:141–42
        social, **1**:140, 141, 143
        space and, **1**:126, 150–51
        themes of, **1**:124–28, 138–44
    Algerian Andalusian performances, **6**:471–72
    Bni Battu people, performance schedules,
            1:133
    Bolivia, fiesta cycles, **2**:291
    China
        narrative lengths, **7**:91, 247, 261, 262,
                269–70, 503
        theatrical performances, **7**:286–87, 308
    circular concepts of, **5**:110–11
    Colombia, for *serenata*, **2**:383

dance associations, **5:**495
Egypt, public *ḥaḍra*, **6:**173
Germany, marking of daily hours, **8:**653
historical performance movement, **8:**55–56
Hong Kong, theatrical performances, **7:**308
Iran, *radif* performance, **6:**130
Kpelle Woi epic, **1:**124, 130–44; **10:**59–60
Madhya Pradesh, seasonal dances and festivals, **5:**721–22
memory, studies on, **10:**74–75, 132
musical demarcation of time, **5:**279–81, 401, 402, 890
musical function and, **2:**56
Muslim call to prayer, **6:**154, 168
Muslim *ibtihālāt* performance, **6:**167–68
Norway, *hardingfele* tuning associations, **8:**416
Oceania, **9:**289–91
raga associations, **5:**47, 68, 69, 72–73, 74, 90
Rajasthan
    men's seasonal songs, **5:**646
    of women's activities, **5:**645
reduction of event times, **8:**6, 144
rehearsals, **2:**61
research on, **10:**64
scheduling constraints on, **5:**567
shamanic ceremonies, **2:**46
South America, tropical-forest genres, **2:**135
Syrian concert performances, **6:**564
technology's affect on, **2:**51, 64
Telugu concepts of, **5:**896
Tibet, Buddhist chant, **7:**479
"timelessness" concept, **8:**16
tourism's affect on, **2:**51, 75
Turkey, **6:**772–73
    Ottoman court, **6:**767–68
Turkmenistan, *baggy* concert, **6:**970
Ukrainian weddings, **8:**806
Uttar Pradesh, seasonal songs, **5:**666
Time (musical group), **3:**685
Time (periodical), **3:**678
Time-Warner Corporation, **3:**244
timelines, **1:**154, 223, 310, 356, 359
    in *àpàlà*, **1:**476
    asymmetric, **1:**308–10, 678; **10:**120
    Central African Republic, **1:**657
    five-stroke, twelve-pulse, **1:**664, 666
    in Gā *adowa*, **1:**113
    in Katanga guitar playing, **1:**423
    in praise singing, **1:**489
    seven-stroke, twelve-pulse, **1:**666
"Times They Are a-Changin'" (Dylan), **3:**316
Timesteps (Carlos), **3:**254
Timm, Henry, **3:**60
Timor. *See also* East Timor; West Timor
    music research on, **4:**29
    prehistoric, **4:**34, 37–38
Timorese people, in Portugal, **8:**576
Timur, **6:**910, 922; **7:**24
Timur Shah, **5:**805
Timurid dynasty, **5:**804, 817; **6:**910, 937; **7:**24
Tinag, Elvira, **9:***733*
Tindale, N. B., **9:**987
Tindley, Charles Albert, **3:**630–31
Tindley Temple Methodist Church (Philadelphia), **3:**630
Tingentingde (Eipo singer), **9:**593

Tingey, Carol, **5:**284, 286, 700
Tinggian people, **4:**872, 914, 916
    instrumental music of, **4:**917–18
Tinhorão, José Ramos, **2:**314, 320
Tinian (Northern Marianas), **9:**743
Tinley, Charles Albert, **3:**534
Tiny Morrie (Amador Sánchez), **3:**765–66
Tiomkin, Dimitri, **3:**203, 546
Tiongson, Josefa, **4:**857
Tipaldi, Andy, **3:**1077
Típica Antillana, **3:**799
Típica Ideal (musical group), **3:**797
Típica 73 (musical group), **3:**797
tiple. See guitars
"*Tiplecito Bambuquero*" (Morales), **2:**387–88
Tippett, Maria, **3:**1070
Tippu Sultan, **5:**866
Tips (record company), **5:**429
Tirado, José Ramón, **3:**747–48
Ti-Raoul, **2:**916
Tirén, Karl, **8:**128, 307
Tirió (Trio) culture, **2:**503–4
Tirtha, Narahari, **5:**265
Tirtha, Narayana, **5:**267
Tirujnanasambandar, Saint, **5:**215–16
Tirumalayyangar, Pedda, **5:**216
Tirunal, Svati, **5:**211, 220, 229–30, 267, 508
Tiruppambaram Brothers, **5:**232
Tiruray people, **4:**920
    instrumental music of, **4:**924, 925, 926
    vocal music of, **4:**927
Tiruvaymoli, **5:**261
Titan people, **9:**601
Titanic Love Affair (musical group), **3:**169
Titiev, Mischa, **2:**238
Title of the Lords of Totonicapán, **2:**722
Titon, Jeff Todd, **3:**117, 150; **10:**85
Tiv people, **1:**130
Tiva Sarachudha, **4:**100
Tivoli Rockettes, **9:**149
Tiwanaku culture, **2:**282
Tiwi people
    bereavement ceremony of, **9:**47
    dance, **9:**317, 451, 455–57
Tizol, Juan, **3:**732
Tjader, Cal, **3:**701, 743, 787, 788, 797, 799
Tjapukai Dance Theatre, **9:**446
Tjibaou, Jean-Marie, **9:**679
T.K. Records, **3:**228
TKO, **3:**345
Tlapanec culture, **2:**563
Tlen, Daniel, **3:**1280
Tlendiev, Nurgis, **6:**961
Tlingit Indian nation, **3:**394, 1093–94, 1274, 1277
"To Anacreon in Heaven" (drinking song), **3:**305, 521, 839
To Trinh, **3:***994*
Toa, Ngāti, **9:**943
Toaripi, **9:**492
Toba culture, **2:**259
    circle dances of, **2:**291
    instruments of, **2:**251, 454–55
Toba people, **4:**607–8
Toba Wei, **7:**25, 29, 30, 32
Tobago, **2:**953. *See also* Trinidad and Tobago

Tobias, Rudolf, **8:**497
Tobi Island (Palau), **9:**180–82, 722
Tobin, Brian, **3:**1142–43
Tobosi culture, **2:**682
Toby, Taiwo, **1:**377
toccata, **8:**78
Tocharian people, **7:**13–14, 22
Točkolotoč (musical group), **8:**276
Tocqueville, Alexis de, **3:**288
Toda people, **5:**903
    instruments of, **5:**366–67
    musical traditions of, **5:**908–9
    patronage of Kota people, **5:**283
    vocal music of, **5:**910, 919
Tôdaizi Temple (Nara), **7:**724
Todorov, Manol, **8:**907
Todorov, Todor, **8:**907
Todorović-Krnjevac, Miodrag, **8:**949
Tôdôza (*heike biwa* organization), **7:**646–47
Todŭri (*chōngak* piece), **7:**869
Tofar people, **7:**1027–30
"Together" (Tierra), **3:**748
Togi, Suenobu, **10:**79
Togo. *See also* West Africa; *specific peoples*
    drums, cord-and-peg tension, **1:**315–17
    music of, **1:**458
    Yoruba people, **1:**400, 471–87
Togut people, **7:**1004–20
Tohiana, Thomas, **9:**640
Tohono O'odham (Papago) Indian nation, **2:**592–93, 598; **3:**428, 429, 435–36, 851
    flutes of, **3:**477
    instrument classification, **3:**472–73
    waila genre, **3:**213, 479, 489–90
Toi, Roman, **3:**1196
T'oji (Pak), **7:**959
Tôjûrô, **7:**668
Tokarahi, Tauraki, **9:**909
Tokaristan, **6:**936
Tokelau, **9:**771, 823–28
    composition in, **9:**353–54
    cultural contacts with Pukapuka, **9:**909
    cultural contacts with 'Uvea, **9:**823
    drumming, **9:**114
    epigrammatic song texts, **9:**331
    films on, **9:**1017
    geography of, **9:**823
    history of, **9:**823
    immigrants to Australia, **9:**85
    instruments, **9:**827–28
        log idiophones, **9:**379
        struck plaques, **9:**378
        struck tins, **9:**379
    map of, **9:***772*
    music and dance of, **9:**48
        faleaitu, **9:**229, 238
        fātele, **9:**113, 278, 354, 379–80, 825–26, 827
        mako, **9:**354
        pehe lagilagi, **9:**825–26
    research on, **9:**114, 973
Tokelau Association (Australia), **9:**86
Tokelauan people, in Aotearoa, **9:**113, 823–24, 826
Tokharian people, **6:**965

Tokhtasinov, Salahudin, **6:**907
Tokiwazu Mozitayû, **7:**681
Tôkô kinpu (*qin* collection), **7:**725
Tôksông Women's University, **7:**990
Tŏksu Palace (Seoul), **7:**995
Tokugawa Ieyasu, **3:**967; **7:**608
Tokugawa Museum (Nagoya), **7:**790
Tokugawa shogunate, **7:**27–28, 630, 724, 739, 758–59, 777, 786, 790
Tokumaru Yoshihiko, **7:**594
Tokuyama Tokashi, **7:***707*
Tôkyô bugî ugî (Hattori), **7:**745
Tokyo College of Music, **7:**729, 731, 732, 760–61
Tôkyô gozen sanzi (Japanese popular song), **7:**746
Tôkyô National University of Fine Arts and Music, **7:**56, 593, 731, 760–61; **10:**27
Tôkyô ondo (Japanese popular song), **7:**745
Tolai people, **9:**148, 150
    bands of, **9:**147
    dances of, **9:**600
    guitar playing of, **9:**387–88
    professional composers, **9:**177
    songs of, **9:**607, 627
    sound recordings of, **9:**992
    string-band music of, **9:**152–53, 154–55
Toldot hāmusika mēyamot kedem ad yameinu (Gradenwitz), **6:**1060
Toledo, Josefino, **4:**881
Tolek, Sergeant-Major, **9:**129
Tolentino, Aurelio, **4:**864, 865, 872
Tolentino, Fulgencio, **4:**857, 859, 864, 866, 868, 871
Tolentino, Ramón, **4:**872
Tolkunova, Valentina, **8:**779
Tolmie, Frances, **8:**373
Tolovaj Malaj (musical group), **8:**921
Tolowa Indian nation, **3:**412
Tolstoy, Leo, **6:**6–7; **8:**286
Tolstoy, Sergei, **5:**563
Toltec culture, **2:**7
Tolupán culture. *See* Jicaque-Tolupán culture
Tomás, Guillermo, **2:**837
Tomasello, Michael, **10:**73
Tomasi, Henri, **4:**508; **8:**574
Tomasi, Xavier, **8:**574
Tomasito (Niño Robot), **8:**599
Tomato Soup Band (musical group), **3:**1195
Tomescu, Vasile, **8:**886
T'omi Puin (Kang), **7:**969
Tomimotu Buzendayû, **7:**681
Tomisawa *kengyô*, **7:**758
Tomita Isao, **7:**751
Tomiyama Seikin, **7:**713
Tommaseo, Niccolò, **8:**620
Tommy Boy Records, **3:**714
Tommy Hunter Show (television show), **3:**1242
Tomokiyo Yosisane, **7:**549
"Tomorrow Never Knows" (Beatles), **3:**348
Tom-Tom (Graham), **3:**609
Tomunsai (Nissan composer), **9:**634–35
tonadilla, **2:**396, 516, 603, 606; **8:**601
tonal inventory. *See* melody; scales and intervals
Tone Loc, **3:**714
Tong Soon-Lee, **4:**27
Tonga, Jack, **9:**387

Tonga (African) people
    composers, **1:**222
    healing rituals, **1:**274
    history of, **1:**711
    kuyabilo music, **1:**216
    music of, **1:**711–12
Tonga (islands), **9:**771, 783–95
    American expeditions to, **9:**24
    audience-performer interaction, **9:**323
    brass bands in, **9:**130–32
    Christian missionaries from, **9:**195
    composition in, **9:**365–68
    cultural contacts with Sāmoa, **9:**795
    cultural contacts with 'Uvea and Futuna, **9:**808
    dance, analysis of, **9:**307, 313, 317
    drumming, **9:**114
    European exploration of, **9:**7
    films on, **9:**982, 1017
    geography of, **9:**783
    history of, **9:**771
    immigrants to Australia, **9:**85–86
    instruments, **9:***383*
        struck plaques, **9:**378
        struck tins, **9:**379
    kava use in, **9:**172, 174
    map of, **9:***772*
    metrical traits in, **9:**289
    missionaries in, **9:**21
    music and dance of, **9:**11–14, 48, 783–95, 969, 973
        European descriptions, **9:**285
        fa'ahiula, **9:**791–92
        faiva, **9:**789–92
        fananga, **9:**338
        hiva kakala, **9:**130, 131, 313, 365, 366–67, 787, 793
        kailao, **9:**379
        lakalaka, **9:**224, 241, *242*, 308, *309*, 351–52, 365, 367–68, 783, 789
        mā'ulu'ulu, **9:**789–90
        me'etu'upaki, **9:**309, 316, 790–91
        sōkē, **9:**792
        tau'olunga, **9:**231
    Niua Islands, political songs, **9:**211
    numeral notations in, **9:**287–88
    outsiders' influence in, **9:**5
    poetry
        metaphor in, **9:**336
        verbal meter, **9:**324
    polyphony in, **9:**14–15
    religion in, **9:**201–4
    sound recordings from, **9:**985, 999–1000
    string bands in, **9:**136–37
Tonga Police Band, **9:**130, 131
Tonga Royal Corps of Musicians, **9:**131
Tongali (Rosario), **4:**878
Tongan Association (Australia), **9:**86
Tongan empire, **9:**53, 771, 795, 809, 846
Tongan History Conference, **9:**114
Tongan people
    in Aotearoa, **9:**113
    in Hawai'i, **9:**104, 163, 174
    in North America, **3:**1047
    in United States, **9:**116–17
T'ongdo Temple (Korea), **7:**959

Tongdong (*hyangak* piece), **7:**868
Tonghae mulga (Ahn), **7:**952
Tongil Ch'anggŭktan (*p'ansori* company), **7:**968
Tongyang Theater (Seoul), **7:**945
tonic sol-fa, **1:**23, 160–61, *213*, 224, 232, 234–35, 298, 763, 764, 769, 791; **3:**275, 279, 1116; **8:**106, 350; **9:**194, 199, 203
Tonkawa Indian nation, **3:**440
Tonooka, Sumi, **3:**972, 973
Tönurist, Igor, **8:***494*
Tony Pastor's Opera House (New York), **3:**192
Too Short (musical group), **3:**698
Tooker, Elizabeth, **3:**465
To-On-Kai (musical group), **7:***672*, 684
Toor, Frances, **2:**580
Toots and the Maytals (musical group), **2:**912; **9:**166
Top Gun (film), **3:**204
Top, Stefaan, **8:**534
Top, Yavuz, **6:**790, 797, 798, 799
Topeng (album), **4:**110–11
Toqtaganov, Aitzhan, **6:***959*
Torajan people, **4:**804, 806–10
Toraji t'aryŏng (Korean folk song), **7:**881, 961
Torbay Fiddles (musical group), **3:***1112*
Tordesillas, Treaty of, **2:**242, 301
Töre, Abdülkadir, **6:**195, 196
Toribeyama (*miyazono busi* piece), **7:**682
Tormis, Veljo, **8:**498
Tormo, Antonio, **2:**371
Törner, Gösta, **8:**445
Törnquist, Owe, **8:**446
Toro, Yomo, **3:**727, 799
Toronto Arts Council, **3:**1216
Toronto Chinese Chamber Orchestra, **3:**1083
Toronto Chinese Music Association, **3:**1083, 1217
Toronto Chinese Orchestra, **3:**1217
Toronto Conservatory of Music, **3:**1182, 1230
Toronto Conservatory Symphony Orchestra, **3:**1183
Toronto Dance Theatre, **3:**224
Toronto Finnish Male Singers, **3:**1196
Toronto Mendelssohn Choir, **3:**1079, 1181
Toronto Philharmonic Society, **3:**1079, 1179
Toronto Slovak Dancers, **3:**1197–98
Toronto Swedish Folk Dancers and Singers, **3:**1196
Toronto Symphony Orchestra, **3:***1176*, 1183
Toronto Tabla Ensemble, **3:**1197, 1216; **5:**136
Toros Roslin, **6:**724
Torrejón y Velasco, Tomás de, **2:**113
Torres, David, Jr., **3:**748
Torres, Diego de, **2:**453
Torres, Eddie, **3:**747
Torre, Serapio, **4:**866
Torres, Jaime, **2:**263
Torres, Father Juan, **4:**842
Torres, Rodrigo, **2:**374
Torres Strait Islander Media Association, **9:**959
Torres Strait Islands. *See* Australia
Torriani, Vico, **8:**208–9
Torrington, Frederick, **3:**1079
Tortilla Factory (musical group), **3:**780
Torto, Frank Aja, **1:**216

Tortola, **2:**939, 968, 971
Toscanini, Arturo, **3:**528; **6:**1026
Tosh, Peter, **2:**912
Tosha Roetsu, **7:***695*
Toshio Tjuji, **7:***47*
Tosti, Francesco Paolo, **8:**205, 618
Totalism, **3:**177
Toth, Andrew, **4:**733
Toth, Margit, **6:**223
Toto, **4:**887
Totó la Momposina y Sus Tambores, **2:**410
Totonac culture, **2:**549, 564
Toubabou (musical group), **3:**1170
Touch of Class (musical group), **3:**1195
Tough, Dave, **3:**652
Tougher Than Leather (Run-D.M.C.), **3:**713
Touma, Habib Hassan, **6:**15, 22, 162
Toumi, Abdelkader, **6:**468, 471
ToUna, Blasius, **9:**152
Tourdonnet, Vincent de, **3:**200
Toure, Ali Farka, **1:**366; **3:**339
Tourgba, Lazaro, **1:***655*
tourism, **2:**50–51, 59; **8:**166
    Antigua and Barbuda, **2:**799, 800
    Aotearoa, **9:**936
    Australia, **9:**253
    Austria, **8:**675–76, 678
    Bahamas, **2:**801–2, 809, 811
    Bali, **4:**136–37, 732–33, 760–61
    Barbados, **2:**820
    Bellona, **9:**852
    Borneo, **4:**138–39
    Brazil, **2:**61–62, 327, 347, 354
    Burma, **4:**138
    Calgary Stampede, **3:**1091
    Caribbean, **2:**76, 97, 787, 791, 793
    Celtic revival and, **3:**1071, 1129–30
    China, **7:**414–15, 444–45
        Yunnan province, **7:**506, 509, 514
    Colombia, **2:**385
    Costa Rica, **2:**693
    Dominican Republic, **2:**858
    Ecuador, **2:**428
    Egypt, **6:**616
    El Salvador, **2:**715
    Federated States of Micronesia, **9:***726*
    Fiji, **9:**781–82
    Finland, **8:**486
    folk festivals and, **3:**1233–35
    France, **8:**547
    Georgia, **8:**837
    Germany, **8:**657
    Goa, **5:**736–37, 737
    Greece, **8:**1007, 1017
        Cycladic islands, **8:**1015
        Karpathos, **8:**1015
    Grenada, **2:**866
    Guam, **9:**995
    Guyana, **2:**448
    Haiti, **2:**887–88, 891–92
    Hawai'i, **9:**108, 163, 164, 390, 914, 921
    heritage festivals and, **3:**73
    Honduras, **2:**742
    Indonesia, **4:**136, 138–39
    influence on nationalist ideology, **8:**185
    Irian Jaya, **9:**191, 591

    Italy, **8:**617
    Jamaica, **2:**907
    Japan, **7:**603
    Karnataka, **5:**881
    Kashmir, **5:**682
    Korea, **7:**910–11
    Kuna culture, **2:**645, 647
    Laos, **4:**138
    Lombok, **4:**762, 778
    Malta, **8:**639, 641–42
    Maya culture, **2:**731
    Micronesia, **9:**160, 719, 721
    Middle East, **6:**406
    Montserrat, **2:**922–23
    musical genres for, **2:**74–75
    Nepal, **5:**698, 706
    New Caledonia, **9:**673
    North Africa, **6:**435, 438
    Oceania, **9:**53–55, 56
        role of touring troupes, **9:**225–26
    Pakistan, northern, **5:**792, 799
    Papua New Guinea, **9:**49
        East Sepik region, **9:**548
        Mamose region, **9:**553
    Paraguay, **2:**461
    Peru, **2:**486–87
    Philippines, **4:**139, 881
    Polynesia, **9:**997
    popular music and, **2:**94
    Portugal, **8:**578
    Québec, **3:**1075
    Rapa Nui, **9:**951, 952
    research on, **8:**24
    Ryûkyû Islands, **7:**796
    Saipan, **9:**995
    Sāmoa, **9:**795
    Sardinia, **8:**626
    Slovakia, **8:**731
    Society Islands, **9:**867
    South America, tropical-forest region,
        2:133–34
    Southeast Asia, **4:**135–41
    Sumatra, **4:**602, 608
    Sunda, **4:**724–25
    Tahiti, **9:**875
    Taiwan, **7:**427
    Thailand, **4:**136–40, 247, 249–50, 316
    Trinidad and Tobago, **2:**966
    Tunisia, **6:**515, 521, 527
    Turkey, **6:**107, 109, 119
    Uruguay, **2:**516, 520
    Vanuatu, **9:**694
    Vietnam, **4:**138
    Virgin Islands, **2:**969, 970, 972
    visual arts and, **2:**12–13
    Wales, **8:**342, 355, 356
    Warao culture and, **2:**189, 191
    Yukon, **3:**1274, 1277, 1278
Touzet, René, **3:**743, 799
Tovar, Bernardo Jiménez, **2:***191*
Tovar, Ignacio "Papi," **2:**395
Tovey, Donald Francis, **8:**369
Towards Baruya Manhood (film series), **9:**42
Tower, Joan, **3:**541
Townsend, Eleanor, **3:**1081, 1125
Townsend, Graham, **3:**1081, 1125, 1190, 1257

Toyama Yûzô, **7:**736
Tôyô Ongaku Gakkai, **7:**592
Tôyô Ongaku Kenkyû (periodical), **7:**592
Toyohara family, **7:**627
Toyotake Wakatayû, **7:**668, 677
Toyotake za (Ôsaka), **7:**668, 677
Toyotomi Hideyoshi, **7:**27
Toyotomi shogunate, **7:**724
Toyotti, Domingo, **2:**736
Tracey, Andrew, **1:**56, 153, 306, 711, 712, 716,
        745, 746–47; **10:**116
Tracey, Hugh, **1:**155, 159, 255, 359, 360, 640,
        746–47; **10:**29, 111, 112, 120
    career of, **1:**51–54, 59, 60–63
Tradewinds (musical group), **3:**1213
Tradition vivante (periodical), **8:**554
Traditional Arabic Music Ensemble, **3:**1219,
        1219
Traditional Ballad Airs (Christie), **8:**373
Traditional Music and Drama of Southeast Asia
        (Osman), **4:**29
Traditional Music and Song Association of
        Scotland, **8:**371
Traditional Tunes of the Child Ballads (Bronson),
        3:511; **8:**328, 329
Traditions of Gamelan Music in Java (Sutton),
        4:28; **10:**51
Trad'Magazine (periodical), **8:**547, 554
Tragically Hip (musical group), **3:**1081, 1104
"Train 45" (Monroe), **3:**168
Trakija (musical group), **8:**284
"Tramp! Tramp! Tramp!" (Root), **3:**188, *188*
trance, **1:**113; **4:**61; **5:**287, 288–94. *See also*
        ceremonies; religion; shamanism
    Algeria, **6:**304
    Anuta, **9:**860
    Arabian peninsula, **6:**710
    Bali, **4:**756
    Balochistan, **5:**780; **6:**177, *178*, 881–90
    Burma, **4:**372–73
    Bū Sa'diyya brotherhood, **6:**435
    in Candomblé religion, **2:**343, *346*
    in Christian churches, **3:**120, 123, *325*
    Futuna, **9:**202
    Garífuna culture, **2:**734
    Georgia, **8:**834
    Guaraní culture, **2:**203
    Haiti, **2:**18, 883
    Hausa people, *bòorii*, **1:**515–16
    Irian Jaya, **9:**581
    Italy, in tarantella, **8:**197, 609
    Jamaica, **2:**898, 903
    Java, **4:***142*, 412, 635, 646, 648
    Karnataka, **5:**867, 880
        in dance performances, **5:**876
    Kerala, **5:**362
    Khmer people, **4:**193–94
    Kiribati, **9:**760–61
    !Kung people, **1:**307
    Lombok, **4:**776
    Madhya Pradesh, **5:**724
    Malawi, Tumbuka healing rituals, **1:**271–83
    Malaysia, **4:**412–13, 415, 421
        Orang Asli peoples, **4:**568–77, 579–84
        Temiar people, **4:**563–64
    Maluku, **4:**816, 818

trance (*continued*)
  Mapuche culture, **2:**252
  Martinique, **5:**595, 596–97, *598*
  Montserrat, **2:**924–25
  Morocco
    Gnāwa, **6:**491–93
    Sufi, **6:**403
  in Native American Bear Dance, **3:**422
  in Native American Ghost Dance, **3:**422
  Oman, **6:**674, 678, 679
  Papua New Guinea
    Papuan region, **9:**491
    Yupno people, **9:**304
  Philippines, **4:**852
  physiology of, **5:**289
  psychological aspects of, **10:**121
  research on, **8:**26
  Réunion Island, **5:**609
  Saami people, **8:**304, 306
  San people, **1:**704
  Shona people, **1:**754
  Singapore, **4:**520
  South Africa, **5:**617, *617*
  Sudan, **1:**551, 555
  Sufism, **3:**1044–45; **5:**760
  Sumatra
    Bangka Island, **4:**626
    daboïh, **4:**604
    Kerinci people, **4:**618
    Riau, **4:**615
  Sunda, **4:**701
  Tamil Nadu, **5:**259–60, 906, 921
  Tibet, **7:**479, 480
  Trinidad and Tobago, **2:**954, 955, 957, 959
  Tuareg people, **1:**594
  Tunisia, Sufi, **6:**506, 515, 518–20
  Uruguay, **2:**521
  Vietnam, **4:**60, 505, 533
    chầu văn, **4:**500
  West Bengal, **5:**503
  Yanomamö culture, **2:**174
  Yao people, **4:**549
  zikr ceremony, **1:**537–38
Trần dynasty, **4:**447–48, 471, 489, 498
Trần Hoàn, **4:**88
Trần Hưng Đạo, **4:**505
Trần Nhật Duặt, **4:**498
Trần Quang Hải, **4:**160
Trần Quang Khải, **4:**498
Trần Quang Quờn, **4:**509
Trần Văn Khê, **4:**25, 876
Transcaucasian Folk Songs and Dance Music
    (Tigranyan), **6:**725
transcendentalist philosophy, **3:**130
transcription. *See also* notation
  African-American music, **3:**574, 593, 601
  African music, **1:**151–59
  Arabian peninsula
    pearl-diving songs, **6:**651
    sung poetry, **6:**666
  bala music, **1:**495–97
  conceptual issues, **1:**154
  Coptic Orthodox music, **6:**223
  early, **1:**88–93
  Egyptian music, **6:**18, 318, 321–22, 561, 612
  Hispanic music, **3:**31

Iranian *radif*, **6:**18, 130, 139, 867
jazz solos, **3:**583, *658*
linguistic, **9:**322–24
Luvale songs, **1:**727–28, 739
methodological questions on, **1:**160–62
methods of, **1:**254–55
Middle Eastern rhythms, **6:**90
Native American music, **3:**24, 508
normal scores, **9:**294–95
Oceanic music, **9:**284–89
pitch, **1:**21, 23–24
reasons for, **10:**106
song texts, **10:**61, 105–6
sources for, **1:**155–56
systems of, **1:**11
Tunisian *ma'lūf*, **6:**325–36, 509, 511–12
Turkey
  makam, **6:**47, 56
  Ottoman classical music, **6:**18, 119,
    123–28, 771, 779–80
  temcīd munacāti, **6:**195
  'ūd music, **6:**45–46
Uighur *muqam*, **6:**995
Uzbekistan, of *maqām*, **6:**917
visual representation methods, **1:**156–59
"Trans-Europe-Express" (Kraftwerk), **3:**689
Transfiguration (Feliciano), **4:**878
Transilvano, Maximiliano, **2:**250
transmission. *See also* dance and movement;
    notation; oral tradition and
    transmission; pedagogy; sound
    recordings; theory, music
  art music, to Eastern Europe and the Americas,
    8:82
  commonplace books, **3:**839
  in communities, **3:**283–85
  East Asia, **7:**5
    media and, **7:**51
    pedagogical lineages, **7:**46, 55–57, 65
    personal style and, **7:**56–57
  Europe, **8:**90–109
  France, **8:**549
  Iceland, of *rímur*, **8:**401
  Iran, written, **6:**344, 840–41
  Iraq, *maqām*, **6:**313–14
  Ireland, **8:**385–86
  Israel, *shirei erets Yisrael*, **6:**1019
  Japan
    continuity and authenticity in traditional
      music, **7:**767–72
    hereditary, **7:**773
    iemoto system, **7:**719–20, 755–56, 760–61,
      769–70
    secret, **7:**549, 769, 771
    syôga system, **7:**538–39, 565, 573, 575,
      578, 626, 634, 775–76
    syôko principle, **7:**547
    types of, **7:**565, 573–74, 709, 767–72,
      773–76
  Korea, **7:**988–92
    of *p'ansori*, **7:**906
    of *sanjo*, **7:**915, 975
  Latvia, **8:**504
  local knowledge and practice, **8:**112–24
  Low Countries, **8:**519
  Middle Eastern music, **6:**9, 33–34

Mongol people, **7:**1006
North America, **3:**274
  Syrian Jewish *pizmonim*, **10:**72–73
revival movements, **3:**56, 1189
Syrian Orthodox music, **6:**228
Tibet, knot-tying, **7:**482, 483
Turkic cultures, epic song, **6:**345–46
Turkish art music, **6:**109, 110, 119, 779–80
Turkish folk music, **6:**77, 79
types of, **3:**241
Transonic (composers' group), **7:**737
Transonic (periodical), **7:**737
Transoxania, **6:**916, 936, 939, 965; **7:**11, 23–24,
    35
Transylvania, **8:**868. *See also* Romania
Traoré, Boubacar, **1:**366
Trasch (musical group), **9:**169
Trashcan label, **3:**169
Trask, Haunani K., **9:**212
Traub, Andreas, **8:**847
travelers' and missionaries' accounts. *See also*
    Spanish chroniclers; *specific names*
  Africa, **1:**11, 74–93, 151, 153, 319, 351,
    555–56, 574, 667
  Albania, **8:**1003
  Argentina, **2:**250–51
  Brazil, **2:**300–301
  Greece, **8:**1024
  Guatemala, **2:**722
  Honduras, **2:**741
  Mexico, **2:**601
  Middle East, **6:**21–22, 543–44
  Morocco, **6:**1039, 1043
  Nicaragua, **2:**748–49
  North America, **3:**65–66
  Oceania, **9:**5, 7–25, 35–36, 39–42, 251, 723,
    752–53, 778, 788, 794–95, 872, 880,
    914, 947
  Pakistan, northern, **5:**799–800
  Paraguay, **2:**453, 463
  Sardinia, **8:**632
  South Asia, **5:**48–49
  Southeast Asia, **4:**24, 27, 70, 284–85, 337,
    812, 839
  Sri Lanka, **5:**957
  Turkey, **6:**107, 113, 192
Travellers, **8:**272, 294–97. *See also* Rom people
  in England, **8:**336
  history of, **8:**294
  in Ireland, **8:**294–95, 389
  in Scandinavia, **8:**295
  in Scotland, **8:**295–97, 370, 371, 372, 374
Travels into Several Remote Nations of the World
    (Swift), **9:**33
Travels through Central Asia (Vámbéry), **6:**968
Travers, Mary. *See* Bolduc, Madame (La Bolduc)
Traversari Salazar, Pedro Pablo, **2:**431
Traviata, La (Verdi), **7:**946
Travier, Daniel, **8:**554
Travis, Randy, **3:**81
Travolta, John, **3:**688–89
Trax label, **3:**691
"Treasure of Love" (McPhatter), **3:**673
Treasury of Jewish Yemenite Chants, A (Sharvit),
    6:1065
Treasury of Xiao Tunes, A (recording), **7:**186

Treatise on Music (Yuan), **7:**121
Treatise on the Music of Hindoostan (Willard),
     5:49–50, 561
treatises. *See also* performance practice; theory,
     music
  Arabic medieval, **6:**16–17, 61, 73, 113, 131,
        142, 177, 363–69, 387–93, 443, 502,
        508, 535–36, 540–42, 565–66, 869,
        909–10, 1066; **8:**92
  Bali, **4:**733
  China, **7:**115, 117–20, 127–30, 131
     on *kunqu*, **7:**289–90
  editions of, **6:**374–82
  Japan, **7:**568–70
     on *nô*, **7:**630, 640, 641, 653–54
  Kashmir, **5:**686, 689–92
  Korea, **7:**54, 813, 833–34, 847–48, 853, 856
  Persian, **6:**17, 61, 62, 73, 131, 835, 924–25
  South Asian music, **5:**14, 372
     arts interrelationships in, **5:**298
     authorship and dates of, **5:**22
     on dance, **5:**507–8, 519, 521–22
     descriptions of, **5:**23–24, 262
     discussions of arched harp in, **5:**306
     divisions of music in, **5:**19–21
     early (to 1300), **5:**17–41, 52, 250; **8:**90
     European writings on, **5:**48–50, 52–53, 561
     instrument classification in, **5:**319–29
     on Karnatak music, **5:**387–88
     methodology of, **5:**21–22, 43–44
     purposes of, **5:**22–23
     on raga, **5:**66–67, 69–77
     rāgmālā visualizations in, **5:**312
     since 1300, **5:**42–58
     on tala, **5:**110–11, 140–41, 168
     on tala hand gestures, **5:**139
     on theater, **5:**483, 484
     uses of, **5:**23
  Sufi, **6:**937
  Tibetan Buddhist, **5:**713–14
  Turkish, **6:**113, 758, 759, 772
Trebinjac, Sabine, **6:**998
Trebitsch, Rudolf von, **8:**562
Trebunie-Tutki Family Band, **8:**711
Treitler, Leo, **8:**91–92, 105
Tremblay, Gilles, **3:**1076, 1151; **4:**876
Tremblay, Michel, **3:**1157
Trenodya Ke Lean (Toledo), **4:**881
tres. See guitars
Três Poemas Afro-Brasileiros (Guarnieri), **2:**115
Tres Reyes Magos (*pastorela*), **3:**759
Trespuentes, José M., **2:**837
Trêu (kingdom), **4:**446
Trevathen, Charles, **3:**619
T. Rex, **8:**218
Trial by Jury (Gilbert and Sullivan), **3:***1226*
triangles, **2:**29
  Antigua and Barbuda, **2:**798
  Argentina, **2:**251, 258, 260
  in bands, **3:**563
  Barbados, **2:**814
  besi tiga hoek, **4:**814
  Bolivia, **2:**285
  Brazil, **2:**308, 330, 332, 334, 349
  in Cajun dance music, **3:**858
  Carriacou, **2:***871*, 872

ch'iñisku, **2:**207
cling-a-ching, **2:**799
Corsica, **8:**572
Dominican Republic, **2:***853*, 859
Grenada, **2:**865, 866
Guadeloupe, **2:**877
Jamaica, **2:**897
kluncing, **4:**645
Montserrat, **2:**924, 925
Netherlands Antilles, **2:**930
Poland, **8:**707
Portugal, **8:**582
Réunion Island, **5:**609–10
Spain, **8:**589, 593
stalki, **8:**797
steel, **2:**970
Switzerland, **8:**693
tingting, **2:**841
trianto, **6:**222
Trinidad and Tobago, **2:**959
Venezuela, **2:**528
Tribal Heart (album), **9:**155
Tribal Voice (album), **9:**445
Tribe Called Quest (musical group), **3:**699
Tribute to Jack Johnson (Davis), **3:**663
Tricéa, **4:**509
Tricolor Records, **3:**741
Trīkī, Muḥammad, **6:**327–29, 330–32, 336
Trillium Plus Music and More (London), **3:**1186
Triloka, **9:**998
Trimillos, Ricardo D., **4:**891; **10:**42–43
Trimingham, J. Spencer, **1:**551
Trịn Lords, **4:**482
Trịn Tráng, Lord, **4:**507
Trinajsto Prase (musical group), **8:**921
Trịnh Trọng Tử, **4:***462*
Trinidad All-Steel Percussion Orchestra, **2:**97;
     8:235
Trinidad Reyes, José, **2:**745
Trinidad and Tobago, **2:**789, 952–66; **3:**808
  African influences, **2:**954–58
  carnival in, **2:**94, *787*, 964–77
  East Indian people in, **2:**52–53, 83, 96, 792;
        3:813–17, 980; **5:**588
  history of, **2:**952–53
  industries of, **2:**791
  musical genres
     bélè, **2:**959
     calypso, **2:**678, 796, 963–64
     of East Indian descendants, **2:**86
     historical, **2:**953
     kalenda, **2:**959
     Orisa, **2:**954–57
     parang, **2:**959–60
     reel, **2:**959
     Spiritual Baptist, **2:**957–58
     steelbands, **2:**93, 796, 960–63
  musical links with Venezuela, **2:**524
  popular music in, **2:**40, 95–97, 445–46
  population of, **2:**792, 952–53
  South Asian community in, **5:**588–92
Trinidadian people
  in England, **8:**231, 235–36
  in North America, **3:**808–12, 1170, 1201,
        1202
Trinitarios (Moxo) people, **2:**138

Trinity College (England), **2:**909; **5:**450, 740
Trío Alma de América, **2:**698
Trio Bel Canto, **3:**930
Trio Bŭlgarka (musical group), **8:**150, 220
Trío Calaveras, **3:**751
Trio Matamoros, **2:**834
Trío Los Panchos, **2:**620, 623, 698; **3:***739*, 746
Trío Los Paraguayos, **2:**457
Trío Los Porteños de Miguel Aceves Mejía, **3:**739
Trío Oriental, **2:**297
Trio Romen, **8:**287
Trio for Strings (Young), **3:**175
Trip to Chinatown (Cole/Johnson), **3:**193, 544
Trip to Coontown (Cole/Johnson), **3:**194, 618
Triple Alliance War, **2:**460
Triple Earth (record company), **8:**240, 241
Tripura, **5:**503
Trique culture, **2:**563, 564, 566, 568
Trischka, Tony, **3:**159
*Trobriand Cricket: An Ingenious Response to
     Colonialism*, **9:**49
Trobriand Islands (Papua New Guinea), **9:**231,
     472, 492, 498
  composition in, **9:**353
  cricket in, **9:**32, 49
  dance of, **9:**490
  Europeans in, **9:**147
  festivals of, **9:**498–99
  kundu playing, **9:**489
  map of, **9:***473*
  songs of, **9:**491
  sung poetry, **9:**327
Troilo, Aníbal, **2:**264
Trojan, Jan, **8:**733
Trojan, Václav, **8:**726
trombone. *See* trumpets or horns
trope, **8:**366
"Tropic Isle," **9:**43
Tropical Depression, **4:**887
tropicalismo, **2:**109–10
  in Turkey, **6:**249
Trotter, James Monroe, **3:**29, 581, 606
Trotter, Joe, **3:**681
Troubadours (musical group), **2:**820
Troubadours du Roi (musical group), **1:**217
"Trouble Blues" (Brown), **3:**669
Troubled Island (Still), **3:**609
Troubleman (Film), **3:**711
Troupe Folklorique Nationale, **2:**890
Troupe Louinès Louinis, **3:**805
Troupe Shango, **3:**805
Trovatore, Il (Verdi), **3:**1148
Trowell, Kathleen, **1:**599
Trubetskoi, Nikolai, **8:**781
Trudeau, Pierre, **3:**1067
True North (musical group), **3:**266
Trujillo, Mark Allen, **3:**751
Trujillo Molina, Rafael Leonidas, **2:**93, 104, 793,
        796, 845–46, 857, 858, 860, 861;
        3:731
Trujillo, Pablo, **3:**763
Tru-la-lá (musical group), **2:**274, 276
Truman, Harry, **3:**310
trumpets or horns
  abeng, **2:**897, 900
  adalo, **1:**569

trumpets or horns (*continued*)
  Afghanistan, **5:**810
  Africa, **3:**593
    historical accounts, **1:**76, 79, 83
  alphorn, **8:**41
    Germany, **8:**651, 654, *654*, 656
    Romania, **8:**878
    Switzerland, **8:**687–88, *688*, 696, 697
  alto horn, **3:**897
  amyrga, **6:**981, 986, *986*
  añafil, **8:**594
  anafil, **1:**76
  Andean regions, **2:**216
  in Arab music, **6:**422
  Arab world, **6:**415–16
  Argentina, **2:**249–50, 251, 261, 274
  Arunachal Pradesh, long trumpets, **5:**505
  ass pipe, **2:**970
  baha, **2:**871, 946
  bajón, **2:**284, 287
  bajones, **2:**137–38
  bakohi, **2:**189
  bambúe, **2:***853*, 855
  bāṅkiā, **5:**640, 647, 648
  Barbados, **2:**814, 816, 820
  bargham, **6:**416
  baritone horn, **3:**874, 897; **8:**811, 894
  bass horn, **3:**563, 564
  bazuna, **8:**704
  berestiankka, **8:***797*
  bhungal, **5:**635
  bicycle horn, **2:**806, 808
  birch leaf, **8:**198
  bocina, **2:**416, 453, 510
  Bolivia, **2:**12, *14*, 284
  bombardon, **8:**530
  boompipe, **2:**799, 899
  borije, **8:**960
  boru, **6:**115, 767
  boumboum, **2:**842
  brava-lur, **8:**41
  Brazil, **2:**337
  bubu, **9:**658–59, 661
  buccina, **8:**881
  bucium (alphorn), **8:**872, 875, 878
  buffalo horns, **5:**722
  bugīr, **5:**916
  bugle, **2:**254
  bugle, keyed, **3:**564
  buguri, **5:**366–67
  Buka Island, **9:**640–41, 647
  bukhsa, **1:**562
  buki, **8:**840
  bukkehorn, **8:**420
  Bulgaria, **8:**894
  bullhorn, **8:**655
  būq, **5:**692; **6:**444, 445
  būq zamrī, **6:**444
  būree, **7:**1018
  cachu, **2:**929, 930
  caña, **2:**212, 287
  carnyx, **8:**40, 41, 366
  Catalonia, *cobla* ensemble, **8:**594
  Celtic culture, **8:**321
  Central America, **2:**33
  chang jian, **7:**292

chile frito, **2:**416
circular
  cacho, **2:**211, *472*
  wak'rapuku, **2:**211, 222, 469, 471–72, 475, 478
clarín
  Argentina, **2:**251
  Chile, **2:**357, 361
  Peru, **2:**35–36, *62*, *118*, 212, 471–72, 477, 494
classification of, **8:**40–41
Colombia, **2:**153, 154–55
conch
  Andean regions, **2:**211
  angaroha, **1:**789
  Argentina, **2:**250
  atecocoli, **2:**601
  Bahamas, **2:**806
  Barbados, **2:**814, 815
  Bolivia, **2:**287
  budyung, **4:**924
  buku, **9:**664
  buq, **6:**416
  caracoles, **2:**724
  Caribbean, **2:**8
  Carib culture, **2:**23
  Chavín culture, **2:**467
  China, **7:**201
  churu (also *quipa*), **2:**416, 426, 472
  Dai people, **7:**499
  davui, **9:**776
  dun (also *tsagaan büree*), **7:**1018
  dung-dkar, **5:**714
  dung kar, **4:**475
  dutu, **2:**641
  fotuto, **2:**846–47, 855
  Garífuna culture, **2:**673, 677, 733
  guamo, **2:**822, 932
  Guaraní culture, **2:**454
  guarura, **2:**533
  Guatemala, **2:**729
  gurr, **5:**777, *778*
  hanawkwa, **2:**179
  heresemoi, **2:**189, 193
  hora, **7:**617
  horogai, **4:**475
  hub, **2:**657
  Irian Jaya, **9:**476, 583
  jīm, **6:**678
  kele'a, **9:**794
  keneo, **4:**621
  kepu, **2:**37
  khufli, **9:**661
  Kiribati, **9:**762–63
  koni, **9:**615
  Kosrae, **9:**742
  kubili, **9:**655
  Kuna culture, **2:**640
  Lacandón Maya, **2:**657
  lanbi, **2:**885
  lapinka, **6:**416
  Luangiua, **9:**843
  Manihiki, **9:**909
  Marshall Islands, **9:**752, 753
  masi, **2:**751
  Mexico, **2:**8, 20–21

  Micronesia, **9:**716–17
  Mixtec culture, **2:**564
  nagak, **7:***825*, 828, 873
  Nauru, **9:**756
  New Caledonia, **9:**679, 680, 681–82
  North America, **3:**64
  ốc, **4:**475
  Oceania, **9:**89, *146*, 178, 195–97, 393, *956*
  Palau, **9:**723
  Papua New Guinea, **9:**22, 359, 476, 478, 498, 533, 550, 567, 570, 623, 626–27, 629
  Peru, **2:**11
  pháp loa, **4:**475, 504
  pheopeo, **9:**661
  pinka, **6:**416
  Polynesia, **9:**771
  pū, **9:**863, 869, 886, 895, 901, 906, 916
  pung, **9:**563
  Purépecha culture, **2:**577
  pututu, **2:**227, 228, 472
  puukaa, **9:**860
  saing, **4:**157, 174, 205
  Sāmoa, **9:**202, 807
  sang, **4:***235*, 237, 249, 475
  śaṅka, **5:**360, 361, 363, 704
  śaṅkh, **5:**326, 345
  serungu (also *sungu*), **4:**743
  siburi, **9:**656
  Sikaiana, **9:**848
  Somalia, **1:**611
  South America, **2:**33
  South Asia, **5:**291, 494, 513, 544, 896, 931, 967
  Sulawesi, **4:**810
  Taino culture, **2:**22, 932
  Tairona people, **2:**183–84
  tapur, **4:**820
  tawi, **9:**64–65
  Tibet, **7:**477
  t'ot', **2:**722
  trompeta de caracol, **2:**533
  tsughini, **9:**647
  tuil, **9:**640
  tuture, **9:**178
  uugiŋ, **9:**650
  Vanuatu, **9:**689, 694, 706, 708–9, 992
  Yaqui culture, **2:**589
  yim, **6:**416
  yubul, **9:**730
Cook Islands, **9:**901
corn buellin, **8:**348
cornet, **3:**232, 564, 795, 874, 1190; **5:**671; **8:**529, 1012
corneta, **2:**287, 453
cornua, **8:**881
coro, **1:**624
Corsica, **8:**571
Costa Rica, **2:**691
Cuba, **2:**834, 836
Czech Republic, **8:**727
didjeridu, **9:**393–98
  Arnhem Land, **9:**61, 243, 293, 301, 355, 357, 412–13, 420–22, *423–25*, 426–27

Gulf of Carpenteria, **9:**427–28
Kimberleys, **9:**431–32
North America, **3:**337, 340
in popular music, **9:**444, 445, 446–47
Queensland, **9:**430, 461, 464
resemblances to Vanuatu vocal modifiers, **9:**689
slide, **9:**446
dung, **5:**713
dung-chen, **5:**714
East Africa, **1:**601
Ecuador, **2:**416
El Salvador, **2:**707, 708
epungu, **1:**667
erke (short trumpet), **2:**211, 253
erque (long trumpet), **2:**257
euphonium, **3:**1198; **5:**671; **8:**946
Europe
    animal horns, **8:**41, 169, 250, 259, 316, 423, 455, 478, 743
    bark, **8:**41, 169, 194, 198, 438, 478, 481, *485, 654, 682, 687, 950*
    brass, **8:**228
    bronze, **8:**366, 384
    dissemination of, **8:**170
    shepherds' use of, **8:**142
    as signaling instruments, **8:**8, 142, 168, 478, 651, *654*
    wooden, **8:**41, 169, 201
excoletes, **2:**748
famifami, **1:**460
fidiog, **8:**859
flügelhorn
    Austria, **8:**673–74
    Catalonia, **8:**594
    Germany, **8:**657
    Low Countries, **8:**530
    Serbia, **8:**946
    Sweden, **8:**440
    Switzerland, **8:**693, 695
foghorn, **2:**806, 808
fotuto, **2:**378, 380
French Guiana, **2:**435
French horn, **3:**563; **5:**671; **8:**454
fu, **9:**590, 591
fuf, **9:**331
gagashi, **1:**313
gangdan büree, **7:**1017
gangling, **7:**477, 479–80
Greece, **8:**1023
Guatemala, **2:**724
hài loa (conch), **4:**475
Haiti, **2:**887
hao, **7:**201
Hawai'ian, **3:**527
Hmong people, **4:**553
huarumu, **2:**416
Hungary, **8:**743
imbutu, **1:**642
instrumentos de calabazo, **2:**380
Irian Jaya, **9:**583, 590
    conical, **9:**591
    wooden, **9:**486
kàakàakii (also *kakaki*), **1:**313, 414, 449, 524–25
kahale, **5:**874–75

kahan, **5:**505
k'aho, **1:**449
kang, **1:**569
kanga, **1:**562
kānt, **5:**783
karjapasun, **8:**494
karnāī, **5:**692
karnāl, **5:**699–700
k'epa, **2:**468
kernaj, **7:**460
keyed, **8:**168
kob, **5:**278, 915, *915*
kodong, **7:**933
kombu, **5:**874–75, 886, 956
kommu, **5:**896, *896,* 902, *902*
kompā, **5:**360, 361, 362, 363, 366, 931, 933, 937, 938
kònè, **2:**887, *888*
korneto, **8:**1009
kui (buffalo horn), **4:**545
kullkull, **2:**358
kunkun (also *bugau*), **9:**647, 648
kururu, **9:**651
kvirostviri, **8:**840
langama, **9:**655
leaf-stem, **9:**755
lela ma sorek, **1:**563
ligawka, **8:**704
lilandi, **1:**642
lituus, **8:**40
llungur, **2:**212
lolkiñ, **2:**234
lur, **8:**35, 36, 39–41, 146, 170
    Denmark, **8:**463
    Germany, **8:**651
    Norway, **8:**420, 422–23
    Sweden, **8:**438, 439
maa, **8:**863
Macedonia, **8:**976, 980
Manchu people, **7:**520
mandjindji, **1:**570
Mapuche culture, **2:**237
mastušij rožok, **8:***797*
mavū, **9:**656
Maya culture, **2:**654, 724, 731
Melanesia, wooden, **9:**598
Mexico, **2:**33, 612, 622
midwinterhoorn, **8:**41, 527
Mixtec culture, **2:**564, 566
Morocco, **6:**498
nabona, **1:**455
nafīr, **6:**415–16, 566
nafiri, **4:**429
nap'al (also *nabal*), **7:**825, 828, 873, 933, 958
narsiṅga, **5:**699–700
Native American types, **3:**478
nefīr, **6:**115
Netherlands Antilles, **2:**930
New Caledonia, side-blown, **9:**680
New Guinea, **9:**476
nfīr, **1:**536
nhimia poku, **2:***160,* 161
Nicaragua, **2:**754
nolkiñ, **2:**234, 358
North America
    in *banda orquesta,* **3:**779

in Finnish music, **3:**875
in gospel music, **3:**631, 633
in Greek bands, **3:**930
in Hispano music, **3:**761
in jazz, **3:**652–53, 654
in Macedonian bands, **3:**925, 926
in *mariachi* groups, **3:**722, 765
in Mexican music, **3:**737
in polka bands, **3:**891, 893, 894, 895, 897, 1195
in rhythm and blues performance, **3:**668
in salsa, **3:**788
in Slovak dance bands, **3:**900
in *son conjunto,* **3:**792–93
in Tohono O'odham *waila,* **3:**490
in Volga German music, **3:**890
Norway, **8:**420
ntahera, **1:**464, 465
in Nubian music, **6:**642
nung-subaldá, **2:**185, 186
nyavikali, **1:**673
Oceania
    men's playing of, **9:**245
    wooden, **9:**393, 394
oliphant, **8:**651
opé, **1:**91–92
ophicleide, **2:**835; **3:**564
oukpwe, **1:**90, 91
ožragis, **8:**511–12
pábarrung (leaf horn), **4:**806
pampa corneta, **2:**471–72
Papua New Guinea
    bamboo, **9:**547, 550, 552, 609
    wooden, **9:**547, 548, 553, 556
Peru, **2:**11, *13,* 212, 476
phalafala, **1:**773
Philippines, **4:**928
Poland, **8:**707
Polynesia, wooden, **9:**865
prehistoric, **8:**35
pū 'akau, **9:**895
pulilitu, **2:**287
pululu, **2:**287
pū nīnītā (leaf horn), **9:**906
pupuik gadang (leaf horn), **4:**611
Purépecha culture, **2:**575–76
puro, **2:**416
putu, **2:**357, 361
pututu, **2:**211, 287
puxury, **5:**909
ragas, **8:**511
rag-dung, **5:**714
rags, **8:**503
Réunion Island, **5:**609
rih, **8:**812–13
rikalo (also *bušen*), **8:**198, 950
Rindentrompete, **8:**654
rkang-gling, **5:**714
rogovi, **8:**915
roh, **8:**797
rozhok, **8:**770
saxhorns, **3:**564
    Purépecha culture, **2:**578
Senufo people, **1:**454
in Serbia, **8:**946
serpent, **3:**563; **8:**330

trumpets or horns (continued)
shofar, **6:**1052; **8:**250, *250*, 259
siŋar, **1:**563–64
siwo, **2:**179, 181
slekk (leaf horn), **4:**155, 169, 196, 205
Slovakia, **8:**727
Slovenia, **8:**914
sokusarv, **8:**494
Solomon Islands, **9:**665
wooden, **9:**632
Somalia, **1:**611
sousaphone, **3:**240
South America, **2:**33
tropical-forest region, **2:**127
South Asia
depictions of, **5:**305
European, **5:**347, 368
in film music, **5:**544
in *jātrā* theater, **5:**505
roles of, **5:**345
Sri Lanka, **5:**970
śṛṅga, **5:**361
Sudan, gourd, **6:**415–16
Sweden, **8:**438, 440
Switzerland, **8:**689, 695
Tanzania, **1:**642
tarompet, **1:**606
taure, **8:**503
t'diep (animal horn), **4:**534
tepuzquiquiztli, **2:**601
tibia, **8:**881
titiru (also *tiroro*), **2:**165
tongqin, **7:**477, 479–80
torvi, **8:**478, 479
trae, **4:**237
trae farang, **4:**237, 249
trae ngawn, **4:***235*, 237, 249
trembita, **8:**704, 812
trembitary, **8:**201
trimitis, **8:**511
trombone
in Arab music, **6:**422
Argentina, **2:**274
Barbados, **2:**816, 820
Brazil, **2:**337
Bulgaria, **8:**894
Denmark, **8:**454
Germany, **8:**653, 657
Greece, **8:**1012
Low Countries, **8:**529
Macedonia, **8:**976, 980
North America, **3:**564, *891*, 898; in blues
performance, **3:**642; in *danzón*, **3:**795;
in Finnish music, **3:**874; in gospel
music, **3:**631; in jazz, **3:**654; in
Macedonian bands, **3:**926; in polka
bands, **3:**897, 898; in quadrille band,
3:232; in salsa, **3:**788; in Volga
German music, **3:**890
Norway, **8:**420
Purépecha culture, **2:**578
South Asia, **5:**671
Sweden, **8:**440
Switzerland, **8:**689, 693, 695
trompa, **2:**510
truba, **8:**281, 797, 812

trumba, **1:**564
trutruka, **2:**234, 236, 238, 252–53, 254,
358–59
tsughanato, **9:**647
ṭuāṭa, **6:**415
tuba, **2:**578; **3:**897, 898; **8:**529, 695, 811, 946
tun, **2:**729
ṭuṇḍakinī, **5:**326
in Turkish arabesk, **6:**257
turú, **2:**201
turu, **1:**467
tutari, **5:**489
tù và (buffalo horn), **4:**475
uatapú, **2:**201
Ukraine, **8:**811
ulbura, **9:**436
upawā, **2:***126*
Uruguay, **2:**519
Uttar Pradesh, **5:**671
vaksin, **2:**885, 887, *888*
vallehorn, **8:**41
Vanuatu, **9:**693
waza, **1:**565–67
West Africa, **1:**445
womat, **9:**570
yöcsoro, **2:**633, 635
zamr, **6:**444, 445
zhaojun, **7:**196
zrokha kudi, **8:**840
Trung-Cha people, **4:**218
Trưng Nhị, **4:**486, 497, 500
Trưng Trắc, **4:**486, 497, 500
Trương Duy Toản, **4:**493
Truro Choral Society, **3:**1117
Trust Territory of the Pacific Islands, **9:**726, 729
Trutamora Slovenica (musical group), **8:**920
Truth and Rights (musical group), **3:**1213
"Try a Little Tenderness" (Redding), **3:**677
Tsaatan people, **7:**1004–20
tsaba-tsaba, **1:**216, 322, 772, 775
Tsanani, Margalit, **6:**1074
Tsar Teh-yun, **10:**18–19, *19*
Tschan, André, **9:**271
Tschopik, Harry, **2:**223
Tselile ha-Kerem, **6:**266
Tserendavaa, **7:**1009
Tserendorj, **7:**1008
T-Series (record company), **5:**429, 528, 547–48
Tshi people, **1:**93
Tsiganes Sans Frontières (television series), **8:**288
Tsikaderis, Costas, **9:**75
Tsimshian Indian nation, **3:**394, 1093–94, 1254,
1274
Tsiolas, Stelios, **9:**75
Tsitsanis, Vasilis, **8:**1020; **9:**72
Tsoi, Viktor, **8:**779
Tsonga people, **1:**708
instruments, **1:**710–11
khomba dance, **1:**287
musical bows of, **1:**706
music of, **1:**710–11
performing groups, **1:**709
Tsou people, **7:**525
Tsounis, Demeter, **9:**75
Tsu (god), **8:**864
Tsuge Gen'ichi, **6:**60; **7:**525

Tsui, Paula (Xu Xiaofeng), **7:**355
Tsukada, Kenichi, **7:**594; **10:**27–38, *37*
Tswana people, **1:**707, 765–66
Tswa people, **1:**708
Ttaengbyŏt (film), **7:**958
Ttang ŭi sori (Kim), **7:**959
Ttong pada (Kim), **7:**969
Tự Đực, King, **4:**449
Tu, Kofi, **1:**222
Tu people, **7:**152, 455–58, 463
"*Tu scendi dalle stelle*," **8:**616–17
Tuaeu, Ota, **9:***902*
Tuake'u, Teinakore, **9:***902*
Tuamotuan people, in Tahiti, **9:**883
Tuamotu Expedition, **9:**24, 969
Tuamotu Islands, **9:**865, 882–85. *See also*
Makatea
American expeditions to, **9:**24
Christianity in, **9:**208
dance of, **9:**873, 878, 879
Europeans in, **9:**40
geography of, **9:**882
instruments
drums, **9:**384
musical bows, **9:**386
music and dance of, **9:**41, 883–85, 969
research on, **9:**883
Russian exploration of, **9:**17
sound recordings from, **9:**1002
theatrical societies, **9:**229
Tuaputa, Tangianau, **9:**900
Tuareg people, **1:**592–93; **6:**273
accessories worn by, **1:**115–16
aggutan griots, **1:**540
camel choreography, **1:**545
curing ceremonies, **1:**537–38
dance of, **1:**593–94
drums of, **6:**360, 419
festivals, **1:**538
groups of, **1:**574–75
history of, **1:**533
instruments of, **1:**541, 590–92
internationality of, **1:**532
lutes of, **6:**408–9
music of, **1:**542–43, 546–47, 575–94
weddings, **1:**539
writing system of, **1:**3
tuba. *See* trumpets or horns
Ṭūbār, Naṣr al-Dīn, **6:**168
Tubati Association, **9:**86
Tubb, Ernest, **3:**79
Tubin, Eduard, **8:**498
Tubman, Harriet, **3:**601
Tubua'i (Austral Islands), **9:**879–82, 973
Tučapský, Antonín, **8:**731
Tucci, Roberta, **8:**622
Tucker, A. N., **1:**568
Tucker, Beverly, **3:**595
Tucker, Henry, **3:**188, 190
Tucker, Richard, **3:**12, 530
Tucker, Sophie, **3:**938
Tucker, Tanya, **3:**81
Tudjaat (duo), **3:**1063, 1275, 1280
Tudor, David, **3:**254
Tudor dynasty, **8:**349
Tuero, Emilio, **3:**740

Tüfekçi, Neriman Altındağ, **6:**79

Tüfekçi, Nida, **6:**79, 790

Tufts University (Massachusetts), **3:**610

Tugeri people, **9:**506–7

al-Tuhāmī, Shaykh Yāsīn, **6:**147, 147–51, 174

Tuḥfa, **6:**297

Tuḥfat al-Hind (Mirza Khan), **5:**46, 48, 314

Tu'i Tonga dynasty, **9:**771

Tu'i Tonga, Tongan chief, **9:**788, 791

Tuia, Ineleo, **9:**354, 973

Tuiasosopo, **9:**320

Tuinukuafe, Edgar, **9:**114

Tujia people, **7:**192, 485–92

Tukano culture, **2:**33, 150–55

Tukaram, Saint, **5:**249, 253, 343

al-Tūkhī, Muḥammad, **6:**168

Tukitani Tuneko, **7:**593

Tukkoj II, **5:**46, 47

Tukulor people, **1:**443, 445

Tukumha, Sam, **9:**363

Tulebaev, Muqan, **6:**959

Tulegenova, Bibigul, **6:**961

Tulindberg, Erik, **8:**482

Tulluga, Laina, **3:**1280

Tulsi Das, Gosvami, **5:**249, 253, 495–96, 589,
    660, 673, 724

Tuluva people, **5:**881–87

Tumašaŭ, Aleh, **8:**219

Tumbas-Hajo, Pero, **8:**953

Tumbuka people
    clan system, **1:**274
    healing rituals, **1:**271–83
    history of, **1:**275

Tumbuna, **9:**90

Tumburu, **5:**37, 39

Tümed people, **7:**1004–20

Tümen Eh (Mongol song), **7:**1004

Tumik, Charlie, **3:**1275

Tumiwa, Danny, **10:**48

Tumleo people, **9:**983

Tunç, Ferhat, **6:**799

Tunç, Onno, **6:**251–52

tunebooks, **3:**531, 533. *See also* hymnals
    "black" and "white" songs in, **3:**67
    Canada, **3:**1067–68, 1070, 1116, 1179, 1189

Tuner, McCoy, **3:**661

Tune Your Brain, **3:**271

Tungaru (Kiribati), **9:**758

Tungī, prince of Tonga, **9:**366

Tungus peoples, **7:**11, 20–21, 33

Tunica Indian nation, **3:**466

tuning and temperament. *See also* modal
        organization; scales and intervals
    accordion, **8:**420
        in Arab music, **6:**39
        in *rai*, **6:**270
    Afghanistan, **5:**835
    amadinda, **1:**300
    Andalusian music, **6:**446, 540
    Arab music, **6:**16–17, 18, 34–36, 39, 43, 283,
        369, 373, 501, 512, 541–42, 548–49,
        568
    Australia, Yolngu people, **9:**302
    Babylonian text on, **6:**8
    bağlama, **6:**82–83, 85, 763, 790, 796
    bajo sexto, **3:**774

bala, **1:**489, 495, 501

balalaika, **8:**770

balalaika orchestras, **3:**58

Bali, **4:**735–37
    pélog, **4:**735–37, 743, 750, 754, 757
    saih angklung, **4:**736, 737, 753
    saih gong, **4:**736–37, 753
    selisir, **4:**746–47, 750, 753
    sléndro, **3:**1012; **4:**735–37, 743, 748, 754,
        757, 758

bandola, **2:**382

bandolín, **2:**417

banjo, **1:**300; **3:**77

biola, Philippines, **4:**906

biwa, **7:**623

bluegrass music, **3:**164–65

Bosnia-Hercegovina, **8:**964
    avaz tuning, **8:**966

Brazil, northeastern region, **2:**325

Burma, **4:**372, 385–90

Central Asian music, **6:**900

charango, **2:**215, 290, 291, 473

China
    Cantonese music, **7:**218–19
    minority musics, **7:**452
    in orchestras, **7:**229
    research on, **7:**136, 137
    systems of, **3:**1260; **7:**88, 98, 99, 117–20,
        128, 391, 419, 443, 566

chonguri, **8:**838

çifteli, **8:**996

Cirebon
    pélog, **4:**687, 690, 691–94
    prawa, **4:**691–94
    sléndro, **4:**687, 691

cobza, **8:**877

Congo, **1:**663–64

country fiddles, **3:**77, 835

cuatro, **2:**382

dizi, **7:**183

drums
    Carriacou, **2:**870
    hourglass, Irian Jaya, **9:**591
    Yemen, **6:**97–98

dutār, **5:**820, 823; **6:**971, 972

erhu, **7:**175–76

Farkaš system, **8:**917

flute and panpipe consorts, Andean regions,
    2:215–16

flutes
    bamboo, **5:**29, 354
    double, Vanuatu, **9:**693
    Iatmul people, **9:**258
    paired, Papua New Guinea, **9:**565
    Philippines, **4:**927–28
    Solomon Islands, **9:**371

friction blocks, Papua New Guinea, **9:**381

Gogo people, **1:**639, 641

gong-chime ensembles, **4:**22

goombeh, **2:**897

Greek music, ancient, **8:**48

guitar, **1:**300, 354, 360; **2:**367–68, 473, 521,
    732
    in *jùjú*, **1:**481
    Maltese, **8:**639
    Papua New Guinea, **9:**90, 387–88, 571

seven-stringed Russian, **8:**840

slack-key, **9:**387, 388–89

guitarra, **2:**382

hardingfele, **8:**416, 426

harmonium, **5:**82, 172

harp, **2:**473–74
    arched, in Bharata treatise, **5:**73–74
    Zande, **1:**656

heike biwa, **7:**647

Iran, in *radif* performance, **6:**61–62, 68, 130,
    135, 836, 868, 869–71

Ireland, vocal sharpening, **8:**381

Japan
    for *hayasi* ensemble, **7:**680
    pre-Meizi theories, **7:**566
    systems of, **7:**574
    writings on, **7:**588

Java, **4:**636, 637
    madenda, **4:**667
    pélog, **4:**644, 646, 650, 654, 656–59, 665,
        667, 675, 685, 693
    sléndro, **3:**1012; **4:**387, 403–4, 627, 650,
        656–59, 665, 667, 675, 685, 693

jinghu, **7:**282

kannel, **8:**493

kayagŭm, **7:**823, 830

kelittang gongs, Sumatra, **4:**627

kərəb, **4:**562

khaen, **4:**321–22

Khmer music, **4:**174–76

kisir, **1:**558, 559

kitarra, **2:**290

kokles, **8:**503

kompà, **5:**361

kŏmun'go, **7:**823

Korea, **7:**834, 863

Kota people, **5:**916

koto, **7:**623, 688, 695, 696, 696

kundi, **1:**570

kundus, Papua New Guinea, **9:**384, 476, 489,
    614

!Kung people, **1:**307

lamellophone, **1:**299–300, 746–47
    southern Africa, **1:**715

langeleik, **8:**415

Lao music, **4:**339, 356

Lombok, **4:**769–70
    diatonic, **4:**771
    pélog, **4:**769–70, 773, 775
    saih gong, **4:**772
    selisir, **4:**772
    sléndro, **4:**769–70, 775

lutes
    Mindanao, **4:**905
    Philippines, **4:**925
    Yemen, **6:**687

Luvale people, **1:**726, 734–43

Macedonia, **8:**980

Madagascar, possible Indonesian influences,
    1:782

Maluku, diatonic, **4:**814, 817

marimba, **2:**402

measurement of, **1:**255–69

mejorana, **2:**777

Métis fiddles, **3:**407

Middle Eastern music, **3:**1218

tuning and temperament (*continued*)
Montenegro, **8:**957
musical bows
Papua New Guinea, **9:**386
San people, **1:**744–45
natural overtone series, **8:**128
pakhāvaj, **5:**115
panduri, **8:**838
panpipes
Baluan, **9:**606
Papua New Guinea, **9:**542, 625
South America, **2:**207, 215, 295, 416, 469
Partch explorations of, **3:**335, 954
Persian, **3:**337
Phuan music, **4:**347
piano
microtonal, **6:**421
quarter-tone, **6:**421
pipa, **7:**206
pitch standard, **8:**104
Pythagorean system, **6:**82, 541, 548, 926;
7:118, 120
qānūn, **6:**39
qin, **7:**157–58
quarter-tone, **6:**35, 276, 369, 548–49
qyl-qobyz, **6:**956
raga, Hindustani, **5:**65, 81–82
requinto, **2:***382*
research on, **1:**741–42
Russian vocal music, **8:**760
Ryûkyû Islands, **7:**793
Sāmavedic hymn scale, **5:**31
sansin, **7:**792
santur, **6:**68
saz, **6:**763, 805, 847–48, 850
scordatura, **3:**1075; **8:**103, 416, 418, 877
sheng, **7:**187, 188
shudraga, **7:**1012
sitar, **5:**198, 335
Slovakian music, **8:**733
Somali music, **1:**613
sorūd, **6:**888
Southeast Asian systems, **4:**14
śruti box, for Karnatak music, **5:**356
śruti/svara distinctions, **5:**31–32
in Hindustani music, **5:**67
in Karnatak music, **5:***93*
steelpans, **2:**796, 961; **8:**235
Sudan, Blue Nile region, **1:**563–64, 568
Sumatra, **4:**602
Minangkabau people, **4:**610, 611
Sunda
diatonic, **4:**716, 717, 725
mataram-mandalungan, **4:**714
pélog, **4:***693*, 702, 712, 714, 716, 718
pélog degung, **4:**702, 706
pélog jawar, **4:**702
saléndro, **4:**114, *693*, 702, 710, 711, 712,
714, 716, 725
sorog, **4:**702, 714, 716
syamisen, **7:**649, 677, *692*
tabla, **5:**122, 341
Tajik music, **7:**456
tambal, **8:**877
tambūrā, **5:**332
tar, **6:**924, 926

Thailand, **4:**175, 260–63, 285, 319
northern, **4:**314
Tibetan music, **7:**452
tikuzen biwa, **7:**649
tiple, **2:**381, *382*
treatises on, **5:**43, 44, 53
tres, **2:**830
Turkey
folk music, **6:**82–83
Gypsy intonation, **6:**57
in *makam*, **6:**48
rock and pop music, **6:**252
'ūd, **6:**36, 364, 443
'ūd 'arbī, **6:**470
Uganda, **1:**312
Uighur music, **7:**452, 456
ukulele, **9:**391
Papua New Guinea, **9:**90
Uzbek music, **7:**456
valiha, **1:**786
valimba, **1:**323
Vietnam, **4:**70, 456, *458*, 508
of instruments, **4:**471, 472–73, 474
vina, for Karnatak music, **5:**352–53, 355
vioara, **8:**877
viola caipira, **2:**310
violin, **8:**880, 917
in Arab music, **6:**36, 421
in Egypt, **6:**610
in Karnatak music, **5:**233–34, 352, 355
Wales, bardic music, **8:**349
xianshiyue ensemble, **7:**212–13
xylophones, **1:**257–67, 604, 715
Cameroon, **1:**660–61
Chopi people, **1:**710
yangqin, **7:**180
yatga, **7:**1012
Zande music, **1:**652, 656
zithers, tube, Philippines, **4:**919
tuning fork, **1:**255, 261
Tunis, Al-Hajj Mohammed Ahmad (marabout),
1:344
Tunisia. *See also* Maghrib; North Africa; *specific
peoples*
aerophones in, **6:**414–15
Andalusian repertoire in, **1:**534–36; **6:**415,
418, 436, 444, 449, 451–52, 454,
457, 501–3, 505, 516, 518, 1039
art music
influence on Djerba Jewish music, **6:**529
Ottoman influences, **6:**433
patronage and policy in, **6:**505–13
Western notation of, **6:**325–36
Berber peoples, **6:**273
Carthage, **6:**431
chordophones in, **6:**406–7, 421
dance in, **1:**543–44
Djerba, **6:**273
Jewish communities, **6:**431, 523–31, 1036,
1041, 1058, 1060
drums in, **6:**417–19
French rule in, **6:**432
geography of, **6:**429
Ḥāra Kebīra, **6:**523, 525–31
Ḥāra Ṣghīra, **6:**523, 524–25, 529, 531
idiophones in, **6:**403

'Īsāwiyya brotherhood in, **6:**515–21
Judeo-Spanish music in, **8:**596
Maltese people in, **6:**435
map of, **6:***430*
popular music, **6:**269, 527
Qayrawan (Kairouan), **6:**293, 431, 442
Qur'ānic recitation in, **6:**161
Sfax, *ḥaḍra* groups, **6:**306
Sidi Bou Said, **6:**326, 501, 503, 507, 510, 513
songs in, **1:**542
Testūr, **6:**513
ma'lūf performance, **6:**332–36, 510, 511,
517–18, 519
Tijaniya Sufi trance ritual, **6:**305
Tunis, **6:**505
wedding rituals in, **6:**528
Zaghuan, **6:**510, 513
Tunsia, Luezia, **6:**1044
Tupai (Society Islands), **9:**867
Tupaia, Andy, **9:**998
Tupapa Maraerenga, **9:**901
Tupi-Guaraní culture, **2:**45, 511
Tupinambá culture, **2:**300, 302
Tupou College (Tonga), **9:**203
Tupou College Band, **9:**130
Tupou I, king of Tonga, **9:**203
Tupou IV, king of Tonga, **9:***125*, 130,
309, 791
Turandot (Puccini), **3:**953
al-Turāth al-mūsīqī al-tūnisī (collection), **6:**325,
328, 330–31, 332–36, 511–12
Turathunā (al-Ḥifnī), **6:**18
Tureck, Rosalyn, **3:**1210
Turep'ae SamulNori (musical group), **7:**965, 966,
967
Turepu, Turepu, **9:**112
Turesari (Yi), **7:**957
Turezuregusa (Yosida), **7:**646
Turi, Johan, **8:**302–3
Turimo people, **9:**587
Turino, Thomas, **2:***470*; **3:**517; **10:**36–37, 52
Türk Halk Musikisi Usulleri (Sarısözen), **6:**87
Türk Musiki Heyeti, **6:**785
Turkana people, **1:**599, 605
Turkestan. *See* Central Asia
Turkey, **3:**1035–36; **6:**759–76. *See also* Ottoman
empire; Sufism
Albanian people in, **8:**986
Alevis in, **6:**81, 130, 192, 568, 765–66, 768,
789–92, 793–800, 811
arabesk genre, **6:**118, 247–48, 250–51,
255–59, 776; **8:**204, 237, 286, 951,
1002
art music, **6:**11, 18, 47–58, 108, 113–28, 247,
250, 255, 365, 757–58, 770–75,
779–80, 781–87
Azerbaijani people in, **6:**843–44
Celtic people in, **8:**319
cultural influences in, **6:**759
dance traditions in, **6:**811–17
dervish rituals in, **8:**967
"emic" and "etic" discourse in, **6:**15
epic songs, **6:**345
folk music, **6:**759–67
commercialized, **6:**247
instrumental genres, **6:**81

theory of, **6:**57, 77–87
  vocal genres, **6:**79–81, 783
Georgian people in, **8:**826
Greeks expelled from, **8:**7, 1011, 1014, 1019
history of, **6:**113
influence on Albanian music, **8:**996
influence on Bosnian music, **8:**964
influence on Bulgarian Rom music, **8:**278
influence on Greek music, **8:**1023
influence on Macedonian music, **8:**976
influence on Macedonian Rom music, **8:**282,
    979–80
influence on North Caucasia, **8:**850
influence on Romanian music, **8:**881, 884
influence on Romanian Rom music, **8:**278
influence on Serbian music, **8:**947–48
influence on South Asian culture, **5:**14
instruments, research on, **8:**39
Istanbul, club life in, **6:**243–45
janissaries in, **6:**21, 114–15, 190, 194,
    767–68, 770
Jewish people in, **3:**942; **6:**57–58, 201, 1035
Kurdistan region of, **6:**743–52
light music genres, **6:**57
map of, **6:**78, 760, 844
Mevlevî Sufis, **6:**107–11, 543
military music, **6:**767–68, 770
Old Believers in, **3:**916
popular music, **6:**117–18, 243–45, 247–52,
    255–59, 776
religious music, **6:**768–69
research on music of, **6:**772; **8:**18
rhythmic modes in, **6:**89–92, 567
Shavsheti district, **8:**828
song duels in, **6:**801–9
Sufism in, **3:**1043–44
taksim genre, **8:**206, 951
Turkmen people in, **6:**967
vocal style, twentieth-century, **6:**781–87
"Turkey in the Straw," **3:**182, 409, 616, *837*,
    870
turkey trot, **3:**651, 706
Turkic peoples, **8:**754, 772. *See also* Altay;
    Azerbaijani; Karakalpak; Kazakh;
    Kyrgyz; Oghuz; Tatar; Turkey;
    Turkmen; Uzbek
  empire of, **7:**14, 18, 30, 32
  epic songs, **6:**345–46
  shamanism of, **7:**21
  spread of, **6:**979–80
  Tuva, **6:**979–80
Turkish Classical Music Chorus, **3:**1199
Turkish people
  in Bulgaria, **8:**903
  in Cyprus, **8:**11, 12, 1029
  in Denmark, **8:**463
  in Europe, **8:**11
  expulsion from Balkan region, **8:**11
  in Georgia, **8:**842
  in Germany, **8:**200, 210, 231, 237
  in Greece, **8:**247, 1011
  in Iran, **6:**843
  in Kosovo, **8:**951
  in Macedonia, **8:**972, 979
  in North America, **3:**930, 1028, 1030–31,
    1036, 1199

in South America, **2:**84
in Sweden, **8:**434, 446, 447
in Syria, **6:**565
Turkish State Classical Music Chorus, **6:**117
Turkistan. *See* Central Asia
Turkmen Music (Uspenskii), **6:**969
Turkmen people
  aerophones of, **6:**415
  in Afghanistan, **5:**506, 805, 825, 827
  chordophones of, **6:**408
  epic songs, **6:**345
  history of, **6:**965–67
  in Iran, **6:**827, 839, 844
Turkmenistan, **6:**895, 965–77; **7:**36. *See also*
    Central Asia
  Baloch people in, **5:**773, 776
  dance traditions in, **6:**943
  Iranian dance traditions in, **6:**877
  Islamic culture in, **6:**935–47
  Ramadan songs, **6:**941
  Soviet period in, **6:**903–4, 975–76
Turkson, Ato, **1:**44, 214, *215*, 220, 226
Turku Academy, **8:**487
Turnbull, Colin, **1:**688
Turnbull, Harvey, **1:**350
Turnbull Library (Wellington), **9:**932, 974
Turner, Ashley M., **4:**603
Turner, Big Joe, **3:**646, 670, 673, 708
Turner, George, **9:**797
Turner, Lucien, **3:**392
Turner, Nathaniel, **9:**203
Turner, Tina, **1:**422; **3:**712
Turner, Victor W., **1:**125–26, 272; **10:**36, 95
Turnim Hed: Courtship and Music in Papua New
    Guinea, **9:**49–50
Turning Curious (musical group), **3:**169
Turnovsky, Fred, **9:**929
Turnovský, Jan Trajan, **8:**726
Türnpu, Konstantin, **8:**497
Turpeinen, Viola, **3:**874
Turpin, François Henry, **4:**239
Turrentine, Stanley, **3:**663
Turriff, Cameron, **8:**296–97
Turriff, Jane Stewart, **8:**200, 296–97, *297*, 370,
    372
Turuta Kinsi, **7:**649, *649*, 708
Turuzaki Kenzyô, **7:**649
Turvey, Thomas, **3:**1180
Tuscarora Indian nation, **3:**462, 1078
Tüsheet Khan Gombodorj, **7:**1016
Tushetian people, **8:**827–28, 841
tūshiya Zīdān, **6:**467–68, *469*, 470
Tusholi (god), **8:**863
Ṭūsī, Aḥmad ibn Muḥammad, **6:**186
al-Tutaylī, **6:**443
Tutchone Indian nation, **3:**1274, 1280
Tutelo Indian nation, **3:**462, 463
Tutir (god), **8:**863
TUTL (record company), **8:**472
Tutonga (Cook Islands performer), **9:**899
Tutsi people, **1:**108, 607
"Tutti Frutti" (Little Richard), **3:**672, 709
Tuttle, T. Temple, **3:**988–89
Tutu, Osei, **1:**464
Tutuila (American Sāmoa), **9:**795
Tutuila, Peni, **9:**113

Tuuletargad (musical group), **3:**880
Tuva. *See* Siberia
Tuva: Voices from the the Center of Asia (album),
    7:1024
Tuvalu, **9:**771, 823, 828–31
  Americans in, **9:**29
  children's performances, **9:**251
  cultural contacts with Kiribati, **9:**764
  cultural contacts with Tokelau, **9:**827
  cultural influences from Sāmoa, **9:**830–31
  epigrammatic song texts, **9:**331
  fātele genre, **9:**762, 831
  films on, **9:**982, 1017
  history of, **9:**828–29
  immigrants to Australia, **9:**84, 85–86
  map of, **9:**772
  music and dance of, **9:**48, 829–31
  outsiders' influence in, **9:**5
  performance tempos, **9:**290–91
  sound recordings from, **9:**985, 1000
  strophic structures, **9:**330
Tuvalu people, in Aotearoa, **9:**114
Tuvan people, **8:**226
  music of, **3:**339, 340; **6:**960, 979–87;
    7:1004–20, 1023–25, 1027–30
Ṭuways, **6:**295, 296, 538
Tuza culture, **2:**413
  archaeomusicological studies of, **2:**7
Tuzi Syôiti, **7:**592
Tveitt, Geirr, **8:**426
Twahka Sumu, **2:**750, 751
Twain, Mark, **3:**1047
Twain, Shania, **3:**81, 251, 266, 315, 1080, 1081,
    1110
"Tweedle Dee" (Baker), **3:**352
12 Inch Records, **3:**169–70
twelve-tone music. *See* serial music
Twelve Tribes of Israel (musical group),
    9:168
Twelve Tribes of Israel (Sternberg), **6:**1027
20 seiki ongaku kenkyûzyo (composers' group),
    7:736
"28°N–82°W" (Kenton), **3:**797
Twenty Ethnic Songs from Western Canada
    (Peacock), **3:**292
Twenty-Fifth Massachusetts Volunteer Infantry
    Band, **3:**565
Twenty-Fourth Massachusetts Infantry Regiment,
    3:565
Twenty-Second Regimental Band of New York,
    3:536, 565
Twenty-Sixth North Carolina Band, **3:**565
Twerefoo, Gustav, **1:**45
Twilight Temples (Rosario), **4:**878
"Twilight Time" (Platters), **3:**672
Twin Tone label, **3:**169
Twinkle Brothers, **8:**711
Twissan t'aryŏng (Korean folk song), **7:**886
"Twist" (Checker), **3:**709
Twitchett, Denis, **7:**30
2 Live Crew, **3:**699, 701, 714
Two Girls at the Piano (Renoir), **8:**85
"Two Lovers" (Wells), **3:**674
two-step, **3:**651, 891; **8:**443, 483
  Cajun, **3:**857
  in Canada, **3:**408

two-step (*continued*)
  Creole, **3:**858
  Norwegian, **3:**868
  Tohono O'odham, **3:**436, 473, 490
Two World Symphony (DeMars), **3:**498
Two Years before the Mast (Dana), **9:**40
Tyagaraja, **3:**950, 981, 988–92; **5:**15, *220*, 228,
    262, 264, *264*, 265, *268*, 508
  ārādhana celebration of, **5:**210–11, 383–95,
    579
  Brahmin class of, **5:**387
  compositions of, **5:**97, 209, 217, 225, 268–70,
    385, 390–91, 393, 394–95, 451, 452
  divyanāma saṅkīrtana, **5:**105
  as spiritual model, **5:**376
Tyāgarāja yoga vaibhavam (Diksitar), **5:***148*
Tyagayyar, Tiruvottiyur, **5:**218
Tyamzashe, Benjamin, **1:**764, 769
Tyers, Will, **3:**706
Tyler, John, **3:**304, 306
Tylor, E. B., **9:**185
Tyner, McCoy, **3:**662, 795
Tyrio culture, **2:**164
Tyson, Ian, **3:**52
Tytler, William, **8:**370
Tyvan people. *See* Tuvan people
Tzadikov Choir (Israel), **6:**1030
Tzeltal culture, **2:**651
"Tzena Tzena," **3:**328
Tzotzil Maya, **2:**550, 651
Tzutujil Maya, **2:**651–53, 721, 729, 731, 736
  instruments of, **2:**723, 724, 727
  rituals of, **2:**731–32

U Ch'un-dae, **7:**898
U Rŭk, **7:**821, 981
'Uahuka (Marquesas Islands), **9:**889, 892–93
'Uapou (Marquesas Islands), **9:**889
UBAD (rap group), **3:**73
Ubarī, Aḥmad, **6:**569
Ubayda qu'al-Shaqundī, **6:**444
Uccello, Antonino, **8:**622
Uchida, Mitsuko, **3:**1210
Uchida, Ruriko, **4:**26, 530
UCLA Grupo Folklórico, **3:**744
Uda, emperor of Japan, **7:**588
Udagawa Yôan, **7:**725
'ūd. See lutes
Udayan, King, **5:**721
Udeghe people, **7:**1027–30
Udhas, Manhar, **5:**425
Udhas, Nirmal, **5:**425
Udhas, Pankaj, **5:**255, 425, 548, 549
Udlot-Udlot (Maceda), **4:**875–76, *877–78*
Udmurt people
  instruments, **8:**774
  rhythmic patterns of, **8:**773
  vocal music of, **8:**757, 773
Udo nongak (SamulNori), **7:**965
Ueda Hôdô, **7:**703
Uehara Mari, **7:**650–51
Uehara Rokusirô, **7:**568–70, 592
Ufkî Bey, Ali, **6:**18, 56, 113, 194, 770
Uganda, **8:**621. *See also* East Africa; *specific*
    peoples
  academic training in, **1:**39

Acooli, music in, **1:**603, 608
African hymns, **1:**208–10
blind musicians in, **10:**113, 114–15
Buganda kingdom, **1:**4; **10:**116
  kings' courts, **1:**311–14
composition in, **1:**44, 217–18, 226
expulsion of South Asian community, **8:**236
Ganda people
  dance, **1:**112
  ennanga harp, **1:**302
  xylophone playing, **1:**36
harp and vocal music, **1:**135, 158
instruments, **1:**599–600
kingdoms in, **1:**217
lamellophones, **1:**317, 320
likembe in, **1:**297
lyres in, **1:**304
music of, **1:**601–2, 606, 607
music research in, **1:**49
pitch perception in, **1:**256, 265
popular music of, **1:**423, 426
religious cults, **1:**604
royal ensembles, **1:**601, 602, 603
scholarship in, **1:**18
Soga people
  budongo tuning, **1:**299–300
  lyres, **1:**304
South Asian population in, **3:**1245
xylophone music, **1:**254
Uganda Martyrs' Oratorio (Kyagambiddwa),
  1:607
Uganda Museum, **1:**18
Ugandan people, in England, **8:**231
Ugma-Ugma (Maceda), **4:**875–76
Ugnayan (Maceda), **4:**875
Ugundani Dance Company, **2:**676
Uğurlu, Meral, **6:**117
Uhh! (album), **1:**777
Uhland, Ludwig, **8:**663
Uhunduni people, **9:**583
Uí Chonaill, Máire, **8:***379*
Uighur people, **6:**895, 904; **7:**6, 455–58
  conversion to Islam, **7:**24
  history of, **6:**995; **7:**14, 30, 31, 32, 458
  ikki muqam tradition, **6:**909, 910, 989–90,
    996
  muqam of, **6:**184, 185, 989–93, 995–1008;
    7:5, 459
  musical traditions of, **7:**92, 458–60
  opera of, **7:**463
  popular music of, **7:**444, 467–69
  population of, **6:**989, 995
  in Russia, **6:**995–96
  shamanism of, **6:**967
Uighur Radio Ensemble (Tashkent), **6:**1005
Uighur Theater (Almaty), **6:**1007
Uilta people, **7:**787–88, 1027–30
Ujae (Marshall Islands), **9:**750
Uji Kaganojô, **7:**667
Ujo karak todŭri (*tangak* piece), **7:**867
'Ukkasha Brothers, **6:**598
Ukmar, Vilko, **8:**921
Ukraine, **8:**806–23
  art music in, **8:**819–20
  Ashkenazic Jews in, **8:**248
  Bessarabia region, Bulgarians in, **8:**907

blind musicians in, **8:**143, 809, 813–16, 819,
  820
Carpathian Mountain region, augmented
  fourths in melodies, **8:**809
Celtic people in, **8:**319
Crimea, Tatars in, **8:**772
dosvitky (working bee), **8:**196–97, 808, 809,
  810, 812
ethnic minorities in, **8:**821
folk music choirs, **8:**123
geography of, **8:**806
history of, **8:**806
instrumental music, before collectivization,
  8:809–16
instruments, **8:**201, 809–16
  research on, **8:**37, 38
Jewish people in, **8:**254, 810
klezmorim performances at weddings, **8:**11
map of, **8:***752*, *807*
population of, **8:**806
research on music of, **8:**19, 820–23
state ensembles in, **8:**817–18
village music after collectivization, **8:**816–19
vocal music, before collectivization, **8:**196,
  766, 806–9
  ballads, **8:**135, 136, 195
  dumy (epic songs), **8:**99, 129, 813–14
Ukrainian Academy of Sciences, **8:**821, 822
Ukrainian Hour (radio show), **3:**1244
Ukrainian Labor and Farmer Temple Association,
  3:1241
Ukrainian Male Chorus (Winnipeg), **3:**1243
Ukrainian Music Institute, **3:**912
Ukrainian Orthodox Church, **3:**1237
Ukrainian people
  in England, **8:**336
  in Estonia, **8:**491
  in Lithuania, **8:**509
  in North America, **3:**10, 826, 912–15, 1060
    dances of, **3:**218, 223
    fusion genres of, **3:**344–45, 1110
    Manitoba Mennonites, **3:**52–53
    Ontario, **3:**1078, 1082, 1199–1200
    western Canada, **3:**292, 343, 344–45, 409,
      914, 1086, 1088–89, 1225, 1231,
      1241–44
  in Paraguay, **2:**462
  in Poland, **8:**701, 810
  in Romania, **8:**868
  in Slovakia, **8:**810
Ukrainian Women's Choir (Thunder Bay),
  3:1199–1200
UK Records, **3:**1243
ukulele (also *'ukulele*), **9:**136, 372
  American Sāmoa, **9:**266
  Australia, **9:**134
  Austral Islands, **9:**880–81
  Bellona, **9:**850
  Chuuk, **9:**734–36
  Cook Islands, **9:**238, 900, 902
  Fiji, **9:**161–62, 779
  in Filipino string bands, **9:**95
  Futuna, **9:**815, 816
  Guam, **9:**746
  Hawai'i, **9:**127–28, 165, 166, 920, 921–23,
    956

Indonesia, **4:**103
Irian Jaya, **9:**578, 591
jokelele, **4:**605
Kapingamarangi, **9:**836
Kiribati, **9:**762
Luangiua, **9:**843
Manihiki, **9:**905, 907–9
Marquesas Islands, **9:**896
Marshall Islands, **9:**749, 751, 753
Melanesia, **9:**27, 598
Micronesia, **9:**719
Nauru, **9:**261, 755
North America, **3:**527, 1049
Papua New Guinea, **9:**89, 151, 153, 195, 387–88, 607, 612, 649
Philippines, **4:**909
Polynesia, **9:**769, 771
precursor of, **9:**98
Pukapuka, **9:**911
Rapa Nui, **9:**952
Rotuma, **9:**818
Sāmoa, **9:**807
Sikaiana, **9:**848
Solomon Islands, **9:**157, 269, 654, 665
tablature for, **9:**286
Tahiti, **9:**391, 868, 877
Takuu, **9:**841
technique of, **9:**390–91
Tikopia, **9:**853
Tonga, **9:**793
Torres Strait Islands, **9:**429
'Uvea, **9:**814
Vanuatu, **9:**709
'Ulayya bint al-Mahdī, **6:**294, 540
Ulchi people, **7:**12, 1027–30
Úlehla, Vladimír, **8:**718
Uliase Archipelago, **4:**812, 817–18
Ulis, **8:***219*
Ulithi Atoll (Yap State, FSM), **9:**729, 733
music and dance of, **9:**979
sound recordings from, **9:**994–95
Ulo Tixo Mkulu (Ntsikana), **1:**763
Ulster Folklife, **8:**394
'Ulukālala, chief of Vava'u, **9:**786–87
ululations. *See* singing
Ulva Sumu, **2:**750
Ulzen, Thaddeus, **3:**1213
Ŭm (Kim), **7:**954
Ŭmak Kwa Minjok (periodical), **7:**855
Ŭmak Nondan (periodical), **7:**855
Umali, Restie, **4:**885
'Umar al-Baṭsh, Shaykh, **6:**564
'Umar ibn al-Fārid, **6:**149
'Umar, Yaḥyā, **6:**655
'Usar, Yūsuf, **6:**551
Umayyad dynasty, **6:**12, 291–92, 293, 294–96, 539, 936
in Spain, **6:**293, 294, 442, 455
Umbanda, **2:**259–61, 341, 342, 344
in Paraguay, **2:**457
in Uruguay, **2:**513, 515, 520
Umboi Island (Papua New Guinea), **9:**566, 572, 574
Umeda people, **9:**314, 484
Umeda Yazumo, **7:**610
U'mista Cultural Center (Alert Bay), **3:**1093

Ummel, Jakob, **8:**692
Umm Kulthūm, **6:**149, 168, 235–37, 239, 240, *291*, 292, 305, 318, *548*, 552, 558, *558*, 560, *604*, 616
biography of, **6:**597, 598–600
influence on Jewish liturgical music, **6:**1039
international popularity and influence of, **6:**269, 283, 433, 548, 592
in performance, **6:**603–5
Umm Kulthum Orchestra and Choir, **3:**1220
Umpiérrez, Héctor, **2:***513–14*
'Umrān, Muḥammad, **6:**168
Un Solo Pueblo (musical group), **2:**543
Una Orchestra (Viceroy), **3:**1251
Unang Pag-ibig (Bonus), **4:**863
"Uncle Pen" (Monroe), **3:**167
Uncle Tom's Cabin (Aiken and Howard), **3:**618
Uncle Tom's Cabin (Stowe), **3:**618
Uncuzade Mehmed Efendi, **6:**780
"Under the Bamboo Tree" (Johnson), **3:**619
Undercoffler, James, **10:**134
Underdogs (musical group), **9:**167–69, 168
Undertakers (musical group), **3:**750
UNESCO, **1:**43; **5:**715, 817; **9:**5, 965, 973, 985
UNESCO Convention on Preventing Illicit Imports and Exports (1970), **3:**492
"Unfortunate Rake" (ballad), **3:**520
Ung Bình Thúc Gia, **4:**508
Ung, Chinary, **4:**127, 131
Unger, Heinz R., **8:**677
Unified Silla dynasty, **7:**42
Chinese interactions, **7:**24, 26, 806
instruments in, **7:**80, 828
music in, **7:**981
Unikrishnan, **5:**422
Union of Belarusan Composers, **8:**803
Union of Composers and Musicologists (Romania), **8:**883, 885
Union Harmony (Humbert), **3:**1068, 1070, 1116
Unión Musical (Colombia), **2:**397
Union Nationale, **3:**1147
Union of Scandinavian Singers, **3:**870
Union of Southern African Artists, **1:**777
Union of Soviet Composers, **6:**976
Union of Spiritual Communities of Christ, **3:**1267
Union Station (bluegrass group), **3:**159
Unisound, **9:**158
Unite, Charo, **4:**885
United Arab Emirates
Balochi people in, **6:**415
chordophones in, **6:**412
dance traditions in, **6:**419, 420, 654, 706, 710
drums in, **6:**419
idiophones in, **6:**403–5
al-nuban ritual, **6:**546
women's music, **6:**697, 700, 701, 702
United Church of Christ, in Papua New Guinea, **9:**495, 607, 627, 650
United Dramatic Society (Toronto), **3:**1083
United Irish Counties Association, **3:**845
United Kingdom. *See* Great Britain; Ireland; Northern Ireland
United Provinces of Central America, **2:**628
United Puerto Rican Association of Hawai'i, **9:**101

United Services Organization (USO), **9:**26, 28, 67, 149, 160
United States. *See also* Americans in Oceania; immigrants and immigration; Native American peoples; *specific states and peoples*
annexation of Hawai'i, **9:**914
archives and museums, **9:**974–80
art music in, **5:**528; **8:**85
attitudes toward history, **3:**21–23
bhangra dance in, **5:**500
blackface minstrelsy, **8:**331, 344
bundling custom, **8:**145, 343
Cantonese opera in, **7:**303
Caribbean territories, **2:**791, 932, 968–69
class and music in, **3:**42–50
class structures in, **3:**43–50
colonial musical life, **3:**7–9, 142–43, 144–45, 238–39, 519, 831–33, 835, 839
concert music in, **3:**535–41
countercultural movements, **3:**130–31
cultural differences with Canada, **3:**15–17
cultural exchanges with Asia, **3:**129
ethnic musics in, **3:**97–98, 519–30
ethnomusicological research in, **10:**69–75, 137–55
European opera in, **8:**205
gamelans in, **4:**28
geography of, **3:**2, 3, 16–17
gold rush in, **3:**9, 11, 735
governmental policies toward music, **3:**288–302
Great Basin region, **3:**420
guitar in, **1:**353, 359, 362
history of education in, **3:**275–79
history of musical culture, **5:**5–15
identity issues in, **3:**504–17
immigration laws in, **5:**572–73
Indian reservations, **3:**442
influence on South African music, **1:**764–66, 770–72, 778
invasion of Cuba, **2:**827
invasion of Grenada, **2:**865
invasion of Haiti, **2:**882, 887, 890
invasion of Nicaragua, **2:**759
invasion of Puerto Rico, **2:**940
Irish music in, **8:**381, 384, 391, 394
Latin American influences, **2:**105
maps of, **3:***xii–xvi*
Maronite Church in, **6:**208
matachín dances in, **2:**591
modern dance in, **8:**161
musical profile of, **3:**2–20
nineteenth-century musical life, **3:**554–58
Northeast region, **3:**461
North/South polarity, **3:**143
performance of Colombian *estudiantina* ensemble, **2:**394
Plains region, **3:**440
political and social organization of, **3:**3–5
popularity of reggae, **2:**97–98
popular music, **3:**547–53
dissemination to Europe, **8:**228
dissemination to Scotland, **8:**369
population of, **3:**4–5

United States (*continued*)
 public school music education, **3:**275–76, 279–83
 racial issues in, **3:**63–72
 relations with Canada, **3:**18–20
 relations with Europe, **3:**17
 religious music in, **3:**530–35
 rural, suburban, and urban contexts in music making, **3:**142–44
 Sea Islands of, **1:**19
 slavery in, **3:**8–9, 17, 64–68, 81–85, 184, 185, 187, 191, 239, 325, 331–32, 506, 523, 573, 592–601, 625
 South Asian population of, **5:**578
 Southeast region, **3:**466
 theater music in, **3:**542–46
 tours of Bull, **8:**424
 transcontinental railroad, **3:**11
 urbanization of, **3:**10
 westward expansion of, **3:**9–11
 Yiddish theater in, **8:**251
United States Information Agency, **3:**297–98, 301
United States Marine Band, **3:**295, 536, 564, 565, *566*
Uniun dals Grischs, **8:**692
Universal Copyright Convention, **3:**289
Universal Exposition of Paris, **8:**175
Universal Flute (Cowell), **7:**708
Universal Negro Improvement Association, **2:**689
"Universal Soldier" (Donovan), **3:**317
Universidad Católica Argentina, **2:**269
Universidad Nacional (Colombia), **2:**398
Universidad Nacional Autónoma de Honduras, **2:**745
Universidad Nacional Autónoma de México, **10:**93
Universidad de San Carlos de Guatemala, **2:**736
Universidade Nova de Lisboa, **8:**585
Université de Madagascar, **1:**792
Université de Moncton (New Brunswick), **3:**1073, 1118, 1119, 1136
Université de Montréal, **3:**1150
Université du Québec à Montréal, **3:**225
University of Adelaide, **9:**415
University of Alberta (Edmonton), **3:**1246
University of Bombay, **5:**443
University of British Columbia (Vancouver), **3:**1258
University of Calcutta, **5:**443
University of California (Berkeley), **3:**15, 610, 611, 737, 953, 1015; **10:**87
University of California at Los Angeles, **3:**175, 222, 324, 952, 953, 1013, 1015, 1036; **4:**24; **5:**529; **7:**628; **9:**976; **10:**3, 5, 77–78, 88, 97, 133–35, 137, 139–41, 153
University of California at San Diego, **9:**977
University of California (Santa Cruz), **3:**1020
University of Cape Coast (Ghana), **1:**216
University of Cenderawasih, **9:**578
University of Chicago, **10:**159, 164–65
University of Chile, **2:**374; **10:**80–81
University College Cork, **8:**394
University College Dublin, **8:**394
University Colleges (Wales), **8:**353

University of Connecticut (Storrs), **3:**610, 611
University of Culture (Rangoon), **4:**90, 122, 397
University of Cyprus, **8:**1032
University of Dhaka, **5:**488
University of Ghana, **1:**27, 30–31, 33, 39, 41, 216; **10:**29
University of Glasgow, **8:**369
University of Hawai'i (Honolulu), **3:**222, 953, 1015; **7:**628; **9:**103, 109–10, 921, 923, 970–71, 994; **10:**42
University of Hong Kong, **7:**432; **10:**17, 24
University of Ibadan (Nigeria), **1:**39
University of Iceland, **8:**408
University of Ife (Nigeria), **1:**39, 216
University of Illinois (Champaign-Urbana), **3:**15, 175, 611; **10:**160
University of Illinois Concert Band, **3:**567
University of Indiana (Bloomington), **3:**610
University of Iowa (Iowa City), **3:**611
University of Ljubljana, **8:**922
University of Lund, **8:**444
University of Madras, **5:**213, 443, 450, 454
University of Manitoba (Winnipeg), **3:**1229
University of Maryland, Baltimore County, **3:**1036
University of Massachusetts (Amherst), **3:**610, 612
University of Michigan (Ann Arbor), **3:**15, 953, 1013; **10:**43, 71
University of Michigan Symphonic Band, **3:**567
University of Nebraska (Lincoln), **3:**493
University of New Brunswick, **3:**1119
University of New Mexico (Albuquerque), **3:**767; **10:**87–88
Univesity of Newfoundland (St. John's), **3:**1073
University of Nigeria (Nsukka), **1:**40, 216, 241
University of Nigeria Choral and Orchestral Society, **1:**236
University of North Sumatra, **4:**123
University of Oslo, **8:**427
University of Ottawa, **3:**1185
University of Papua New Guinea, **9:**480
University of Pennsylvania (Philadelphia), **3:**175, 607
University of the Philippines, **4:**123
University of the Philippines Ethnomusicology Archive, **4:**873
University of Pittsburgh, **3:**953; **10:**17, 23–24, 128–29, 133
University of Prince Edward Island (Charlottetown), **3:**1119
University of Queensland, **10:**87
University of the South Pacific, **9:**229–30, 233
University of Southern California (Los Angeles), **3:**175
University of Sudbury, **3:**1192
University of Tampere, **8:**481, 489
University of the Tango of Buenos Aires, **2:**265
University of Tartu, **8:**495
University of Texas (Austin), **3:**953
University of Toronto, **3:**15, 246, 1079, 1185, 1213
University of Trondheim, **8:**427
University of Uppsala, **8:**444, 447
University of Vienna, **10:**112

University of Washington (Seattle), **3:**953, 1020; **5:**529; **7:**628
University of Waterloo (Ontario), **3:**226
University of the West Indies, **2:**908
University of Wisconsin (Madison), **3:**952–53, 1014
University of Wyoming (Laramie), **3:**953
Unkel, Kurt Nimuendajú, **2:**204
"Unknown Soldier" (Doors), **3:**318
Unonymous (musical group), **3:**1281
Ŭnsegye (Yi), **7:**945, 968
Unsung Heroes (Aglukark), **3:**1280
untouchables. *See* Harijans; *specific castes*
Unu p'ungnoe (Turep'ae SamulNori), **7:**967
"Up on the Roof" (Drifters), **3:**673
Upadhyaya, Hari S., **5:**674, 675
Upadhyaya, Krishna D., **5:**675
Upadhyaya, U. P., **5:**883
Upanishads, **5:**11, 239, 247
'Upolu (Sāmoa), **9:**795, 797, 823
Upper Canada, **3:**9, 1073, 1077–78, 1146. *See also* Ontario
 slavery abolished in, **3:**8
Upper Hutt Posse (musical group), **9:**168
Upper Tanana Scottie Creek Dancers, **3:**1277
Upper Volta. *See* Burkina Faso
Up'yŏn (*kagok*), **7:**923
Urban Blues (Keil), **3:**149, 583
Urban Cowboy (film), **3:**81
Urbani, Pietro, **8:**372
urbanization, **8:**5, 16
 Africa, **1:**415
 Afro-Venezuelan culture, **2:**543
 Algeria, **6:**465–66; **8:**234
 Argentina, **2:**261
 Balkan region, **8:**13–14
 Borneo, **4:**115
 Canada, **3:**10
 Central Asia, **6:**901, 935
 China, **7:**417–18
  early, **7:**17
  effect on theater, **7:**76
  huju genre and, **7:**298–99
  of *quyi*, **7:**251–52
 Czech Republic, **8:**717, 722
 Dominican Republic, **2:**857–67
 effects on rural environments, **6:**306–7
 Finland, **8:**479, 482
 folklore and, **8:**6–7
 folk music and, **8:**2, 4, 13, 147, 228
 France, **8:**551
 Ghana, **1:**390–92
 Greece, **8:**1016
 immigrant groups and, **8:**231, 233–34
 India, **5:**468
 Israel, **6:**1020, 1025
 Japan, **7:**539, 739
 Jewish communities, **8:**257, 260, 262, 263
 Karnataka, **5:**880–81
 Kurdish communities, **6:**751–52
 Low Countries, **8:**518
 Macedonia, **8:**281, 973, 974
 Native American peoples, **3:**481
 Nepal, **5:**706
 patronage and, **5:**404–5
 Peru, **2:**483–85

Philippines, **4**:115
Poland, **8**:711
Punjab, **5**:549–50
research on, **8**:26
Romania, **8**:868
Russia, **8**:766–67, 774
Sardinia, **8**:626
Serbia, **8**:949
sexual differentiation and, **8**:198–99
Slovakia, **8**:722
Slovenia, **8**:919
social dancing and, **8**:161
Southeast Asia, **4**:5–6, 115
Spain, **8**:596
Thailand, **4**:115, 222
Turkey, **6**:77, 256
Wales, **8**:352–53
Urbina, Guadalupe, **2**:703
Urcullu, Manuel de, **2**:681
Ureña, Juan Carlos, **2**:703
Urfé, Odilio, **2**:838, 839; **3**:791–92
URH (musical group), **8**:221, 746
Urianghai people, **7**:1004–20
Uriarte Castañeda, María Teresa, **2**:599
Uribe Holguín, Guillermo, **2**:397
al-Urmawī, Ṣafī al-Dīn. *See* Ṣafī al-Dīn al-
          Urmawī
Urso, Camilla, **3**:556
Ursuline order, **3**:1056, 1074–75
Uruchurtu, Rosendo, **3**:736–37
Uruguay, **2**:510–22. *See also specific peoples*
     Afro-Brazilian cults in, **2**:260
     Amerindian cultures, **2**:510–11
     geography of, **2**:510
     instruments of, **2**:510, 511
     military regime in, **2**:104
     musical genres
          candombe, **2**:515–16, 520, 522
          canto popular uruguayo, **2**:510, 519–20, 521
          milonga, **2**:512, *513–14*, 521
          murga, **2**:520
          música tropical, **2**:520
          payada, **2**:512, *513–14*, 520
          rock, **2**:104
          tango, **2**:519, 520
     population of, **2**:510
     religious genres of, **2**:511–16
     secular genres of, **2**:516–20
Urusbiev, Ismail, **8**:858
Us (album), **8**:225
US 3, **3**:699
Usarufa people, **9**:511, 512
     composition of, **9**:357–58
     music and dance of, **9**:526–33, 973, 980
     songs of, **9**:514
"Use ta Be My Girl" (O'Jays), **3**:711
U.S. Exploring Expedition, **9**:18–20, *769*, 778,
          795, 827
Uskoks, **8**:914
Usmanbaş, Ilhan, **6**:775
Usmanova, Yulduz, **6**:905
"U.S. Marines Marching Song," **9**:848
Us Mob, **9**:145, 146, 443
USO. *See* United Services Organization (USO)
Uspenskii, Viktor A., **6**:917, 943, 969, 972, 975
Ussachevsky, Vladimir, **3**:253, 254

U.S.S.R. *See* Soviet Union (former)
Ustvolskaya, Galina, **8**:782
Usuah, May Afi, **1**:241
usûl
     in Bukharan *shash maqām*, **6**:911
     in janissary music, **6**:767
     in Sufi music, **6**:110, 111, 194, 195, 943–44
     in Turkish art music, **6**:85, 89–92, 113, 116,
          120, 122–26, 772–73, 782
     in Uighur music, **6**:998
U.S. Virgin Islands, **2**:968, 971, 972, 973. *See
          also* Virgin Islands
Utah
     Japanese people in, **3**:969
     Native American groups in, **3**:420–22,
          425–27, 428–38
     Ogden, *taiko* drumming groups in, **3**:971
Utamaduni, **1**:646
Uta matsuri (Shinto festival song), **7**:610
Utanaq, Alexis, **3**:1280
Utanaq, Victor, **3**:1280
Ute Indian nation, **3**:420
     Bear Dance, **3**:422–25; **10**:89
     instruments of, **3**:425
     songs of, **3**:426
Utesov, Leonid, **8**:777, 778, 779, 845
UTFO (musical group), **3**:696
'Uthmān, caliph, **6**:157
Uthman Marwandi. *See* Lāʾl Shahbāz Qalandar
'Uthmān, Muḥammad, **6**:547
'Uthmān, Sāra, **6**:691–94
Utica Glee Club, **3**:604
Utit Naksawat, **4**:26, 224
Utjämba (Irumu performer), **9**:*570*
Utkiagvik Inupiat Hymn Book, **3**:485–86
Utrecht, Treaty of (1713), **3**:9, 1115, 1135
Uttari p'ungmul (SamulNori), **7**:965
Uttar Pradesh, **5**:550, 660–75
     Agra, Mughal court in, **5**:15, 163
     Ajrara, *tabla* in, **5**:133–34, 136
     Ayodhya, **5**:660
          Rama associations, **5**:247
     Banaras, **5**:660
          devotional music in, **5**:253
          Shiva associations, **5**:247
          tabla in, **5**:133–34, 136, 137
          tappā in, **5**:162
          thumrī in, **5**:180
          Vedic chant in, **5**:243
     Braj region
          devotional music in, **5**:246, 250–52
          Holī dances, **5**:501
          Krishna associations, **5**:247
          regional cassettes in, **5**:550, 551
     ceremonies, **5**:284
          spirit possession, **5**:291–92
     dance traditions, **5**:501
          rāmlīlā, **5**:495–96, 673
          rāslīlā, **5**:495, 673–74
     drum traditions of, **5**:131
     Faizabad, *tabla* in, **5**:133
     Farrukhabad, *tabla* in, **5**:133–34, 136
     Garhwal
          Badrinath shrine, **5**:501
          Kedarnath shrine, **5**:501
          regional cassettes in, **5**:550

geography of, **5**:660
history of, **5**:660
immigrants to Guyana, **5**:600–605
immigrants to Trinidad, **5**:588
instruments in, **5**:120, 345, 347, 664–65,
          670–71
Jaunpur, *khyāl* in, **5**:170
Jhajjar, *tabla* in, **5**:133
Laliyana, *tabla* in, **5**:134, 136, 137
Lucknow
     gat traditions in, **5**:192
     light classical music in, **5**:179–80, 373, 435,
          853
     naubat khānā in, **5**:279–80
     Shia Muslims in, **5**:133, 256, *283*
     tabla in, **5**:123, 130–31, 132, 133–34, 136,
          137, 342
     map of, **5**:*658*
Mathura, **5**:660
     choupai songs, **5**:473
mendicant musicians' music, **5**:670–71
Mirzapur district, **5**:669
     karam dance, **5**:501
nautaṅkī theater in, **5**:346, 419, 485, 674,
          675
Oudh princely state, **5**:179, 192, 487
population of, **5**:660
Rampur, **5**:463–64
research on music of, **5**:674–75
Rohilkhand, **5**:193
Taj Mahal in, **5**:*12*
Vedic chant in, **5**:239
vocal music
     bārahamāsā, **5**:277
     birahā, **5**:666–69
     caitī, **5**:277
     dhrupad, **5**:253
     gālī insult songs, **5**:589, 663
     kajalī (also *kajarī; kajrī*), **5**:669–70, 671
     men's genres, **5**:664–66
     phaguā, **5**:665–66
     purvī, **5**:671, 672–73
     rasiyā, **5**:550, 551, 665, 672
     seasonal songs, **5**:666
     women's genres, **5**:661–64
Ut-todŭri (*tangak* piece), **7**:867
Utu (film), **9**:46
Utwe people, **9**:740
U2 (musical group), **3**:552, 845; **4**:887; **8**:210,
          215, 392
'Uvea, **9**:771, 809–14
     cultural contacts with Sāmoa, **9**:795
     cultural contacts with Tokelau, **9**:823, 827
     history of, **9**:809
     instruments of, **9**:379, 814
     map of, **9**:*772*
     metrical traits in, **9**:289
     music and dance of, **9**:49, 59, 313, 809–14,
          969, 980
          eke, **9**:792, 809
          fagono, **9**:338
          kailao, **9**:379, 792, 812–13
          lakalaka, **9**:813
          sāsā, **9**:813
          soāmako and *niutao*, **9**:813
     poetry, verbal meter in, **9**:324

'Uvea (continued)
  population of, **9:**808
  prehistoric, **9:**808–9
  sound recordings from, **9:**1000
Uygur people. See Uighur people
Uz, Kâzim, **6:**110, 119
Uzan, Abraham, **6:**1039
Uzbek people, **5:**5
  in Afghanistan, **5:**506, 805, 814, 825, 827
  in China, **7:**455–58
  conversion to Islam, **7:**24
  epic songs, **6:**345
Uzbekistan, **6:**895; **7:**36. See also Central Asia
  blind musicians in, **6:**899
  Bukhara, as Islamic cultural center, **6:**184, 909,
    915–16, 935, 939, 942, 945
  Ferghana valley, **6:**902
  Iranian dance traditions in, **6:**875–79
  Islamic culture in, **6:**935–47
  Jewish people in, **6:**899, 916, 919
  Karakalpakstan, **6:**967
  Khiva, **6:**909
  Macedonian people in, **8:**972
  map of, **6:***910*
  maqām traditions, **6:**184, 909–20, 997
    Bukharan shash maqām, **6:**11, 12, 18, 311,
      900, 903, 909, 910–11, *912*, 915–18,
      922, 997
    Ferghana-Tashkent repertoire, **6:**909, 910,
      913, 919
    Khorezm repertoire, **6:**909, 910, 911, 913
  Qoqand, **6:**909
  recent musical life in, **6:**905
  Samarkand
    as Islamic cultural center, **6:**935, 942
    as Timur's capital, **6:**910
  Soviet period in, **6:**903–4
  Tashkent, **6:**907–8, 935, 940
  transvestite performers in, **5:**815
  Uighur people in, **6:**997
  women's religious genres and roles, **6:**945–47
Üzemchin people, **7:**1004–20
Uzi Kaga no zyô, **7:**547, 588
Uzume Taiko (musical group), **3:**1064, 1096

Vaagvere Pillikoor (musical group), **8:**496–97
Vabø, Finn, **8:**417, *419, 421*
Vabø, Oivind, **8:***421*
Vacallo, Aurora di, **8:**696
Vachon, Josée, **3:**855
Vadivelu Pillai, **5:**224, 230, 389
Vaea, Baron, **9:***125,* 352
Vagabond King (Friml), **3:**544
Vagabond Songs of Scotland (Ford), **8:**373
Vahid, Aqa, **6:**928
Vai people
  alphabet of, **1:**465
  concepts of music, **1:**347
  Islamic music repertoire, **1:**347–49
  Islamization of, **1:**327–49
  music of, **1:**467
  spirit sacrifices, **1:**334–36
  writing system of, **1:**3, 147
Vaidya caste, **5:**884
Vaidyanatha Ayyar, Maha, **5:**100, 219, 226
Vaidyanathan, K. R., **5:**935

Vaillancourt, Lorraine, **3:**1151, 1152
Väinämöinen (mythical figure), **8:**481
Väisänen, Armas Otto, **8:**25, 488
Vaishnavite traditions, **5:**246–54, 260–61, 262,
    267, 270, 470, 512
  devotional songs of, **5:**284, 502–3, 504, 511,
    643, 844–46, 855
  in Gujarat, **5:**629, 632–33
  in Karnataka, **5:**884
  literature of, **5:**519–20
  in Mithila, **5:**677
  narratives, **5:**897–98, 900–901
  paintings of, **5:**300
  theater in, **5:**486, 488
Vaishya class, **5:**386, 398, 911
  function of, **5:**9
  in Goa, **5:**735
  life-cycle ceremonial music of, **5:**284
Vaisima (Tongan choreographer), **9:**351
Vajirananvaroros, Prince, **4:**288
Vajrapani (deity), **5:**505
Vajrayana Buddhism, **5:**257
Vakinankaratra people, **1:**783
Vakrelski, Khristo, **8:**25
Vala, Angur, **5:**855
Vala, Indu, **5:**855
"Valaci vācci" (Subramania Ayyar), **5:**217
Yalbeh, Yo'el, **6:**1071
Valcarcel, Luis, **2:**480
Valcárcel, Teodoro, **2:**115
Valdés, Miguelito, **3:**732
Valdez, Basil, **4:**885
Valdez, Daniel, **3:**745, 749
Valdez Leal, Felipe, **3:**739
Valdez, Leo, **4:**885
Valdez, Luís, **3:**733, 739, 745, 749, 750
Valdez, Miguelito, **3:**743, 794, 798–99
Valdez, Patato, **3:**662
Valdez, Ramón, **4:**866
Valdez, Vicentico, **3:**743
Valdivia culture. See Bahía (Valdivia) culture
Valdy, **3:**1081
Valen, Fartein, **8:**426
Valença, Alceu, **2:**333, 337
Valencia, Antonio María, **2:**398
Valencia, Daniel, **2:***609*
Valencia, Luis, **4:**860, 871
Valenciano, Joey, **4:**886
Valens, Ritchie, **2:**105; **3:**732, 733, 746, 750
Valentijn, François, **4:**812, 815, 818, 819
Valentin, Karl, **8:**447
Valentin, Orlando, **9:**108
Valentin, Pat, **9:**108
Valentine, Calvin, **3:***647*
Valerius, Adriann, **8:**534
Valero, Helena, **2:**174
Vales, Ramón, **4:**859
"Valiant Spirit of Asia" (song), **7:**413
Valkeapää, Nils-Aslak (Aillohas), **8:**305–6, 428,
    487
Vallabha (also Vallabhacharya) sect, **5:**247–48,
    251, 401
  in Gujarat, **5:**632–33
  in Rajasthan, **5:**643
Valle, Pietro della, **6:**107
Vallée, François, **8:**562

vallenato, **2:**39, 105; **3:**1204
  in Colombia, **2:**383, 384, 402, 407–8, 410,
    411
Vallerand, Jean, **3:**1150
Valmiki, Ramayana of, **5:**261
Valois, Ninette de, **6:**817
vals (waltz), **2:**71, 107, 110
  in Argentina, **2:**256, 261, 269, 273
  in Brazil, **2:**305, 330, 331, 350
  in Caribbean, **2:**795
  in Chile, **2:**361
  in Colombia, **2:**387, 393, 396
  in Costa Rica, **2:**685, 691
  in Dominica, **2:**842
  in Dominican Republic, **2:**856, 860
  in El Salvador, **2:**718
  in French Guiana, **2:**438
  in Guadeloupe, **2:**877
  in Guatemala, **2:**735
  in Haiti, **2:**888
  in Jamaica, **2:**908
  in Mapuche culture, **2:**236–37
  in Martinique, **2:**917
  in Mexico, **2:**603–4, 613
  in Netherlands Antilles, **2:**930
  in Nicaragua, **2:**765
  in Panama, **2:**772
  in Peru, **2:**89, 475, 481
  in Turkey, **6:**771, *772*
  in Uruguay, **2:**516
  in Virgin Islands, **2:**970
vals criollo
  in Peru, **2:**89, 101, 475, 481, 499–500
  in Venezuela, **2:**697
Valse de la Grama (Ortiz), **3:**760
Valssorm-visa (Buen), **8:**430
Vámbéry, Arminius, **6:**968, 971–72
Vamsatthappakasini, **5:**968
Vamvakaris, Markos, **8:**1015, 1019, 1020
Van. See Van plus next element in name
Vanagaitis, Antanas, **3:**876
Van Buren, Martin, **3:**304, 305, 306
Văn Cao, **4:**510
Vance, Clarice, **3:***195*
Van Cleve, John, **3:**538
Vancouver Bach Choir, **3:**1094
Vancouver Chamber Choir, **3:**1096
Vancouver Chinese Choir Association, **3:**1096
Vancouver Chinese Music Ensemble, **3:**1096,
    1263
Vancouver Dance Centre, **3:**226
Vancouver, George, **3:**1255; **9:**15–16
Vancouver Musical Club, **3:**1094
Vancouver Opera House, **3:**1095
Vancouver Public Library, **3:**226
Vancouver Symphony Orchestra, **3:**345, 1095,
    1096
Vandals
  in Corsica, **8:**566
  in North Africa, **6:**431
Vanderbilt Museum (Centerport), **9:**975
Vander, Judith, **3:**421, 487, 511–12
Van der Voort, Antoni, **3:**737
Van de Velde, Wannes, **8:**535
Vandré, Geraldo, **2:**318
Vandross, Luther, **3:**715

Vang, A. E., **8:**414
Vangelis, **3:**204; **9:**45
Van Gennep, Arnold, **8:**553
Vanguard Chinese Folk Orchestra of the Jinan
    Military Subarea, **7:**231
Van Halen (musical group), **3:**552, 1002
Van Halen, Eddie, **8:**238
van Hoëvell, G. W. W. C., Baron, **4:**818
Vanikoro (Solomon Islands), **9:**963
Vanilla Ice (rap artist), **3:**63, 698; **4:**886
Vanishing Cape Breton Fiddler (documentary),
    3:1128
Văn Lang period, **4:**445–46, 486–87
Vaṇṇāṇ caste, **5:**931
Van Nieuwkerk, Karin, **6:**21, 24
Van Oost, J., **7:**1018
Vanoverbergh, Morice, **4:**872
Van Peebles, Melvin, **3:**621
Vân Quyền (*chèo* performer), **4:***489*
Vansina, Jan, **1:**663
Van Stone, James, **3:**381
Vanua Lava (Vanuatu), **9:**698
Vanua Levu (Fiji), **9:**773, 774, 778
Vanuatu, **9:**598, 688–709, 715. *See also* Ambae;
    Ambrym; Anatom; Aniwa; Banks
    Islands; Efate; Emae; Erromango;
    Espiritu Santo; Fila; Maewo; Malakula;
    Mota; Mota Lava; Naviso; Paama;
    Pentecost; Raga; Tanna; West Futuna;
    West 'Uvea
    Americans in, **9:**25–26
    archives and museums, **9:**965–67
    composition in, **9:**361–64
    dance, notation of, **9:***316*
    festivals in, **9:**55, 63–65
    films on, **9:**1015
    geography of, **9:**694
    history of, **9:**688, 689–90
    immigrants to Australia, **9:**84, 85
    instruments, **9:**693–94, 701–2, 708–9
        flutes, **9:**392
        log idiophones, **9:**374
        musical bow, **9:***386*
        panpipes, **9:**398, 401
    Japanese in, **9:**27
    kava use in, **9:**172, 174
    log-idiophone signals, **9:**285
    music and dance of, **9:**688–709, 973, 977,
        980
        sawagoro, **9:**198, 361, 695–96
        tanumwe, **9:**198
    outsiders' influence in, **9:**5
    pedagogy in, **9:**259–60
    popular music of, **9:**32–33
    prehistoric, **9:**688–89, 702
    religion in, **9:**198–99
    research on, **9:**690, 965–66, 976
    sound recordings from, **9:**986, 992, 993–94
    string bands in, **9:**139–40
    theater in, **9:**233
    Torres Islands
        geography of, **9:**694
        instruments of, **9:**694
Vanuatu Cultural Centre, **9:**694, 965–67
Van Wilder, Philip, **10:**20
Van Zanten, Wim, **4:**28, 701

Van Zile, Judy, **9:**315, 317
Vao, Taniela, **9:**113
Varahamihir, **5:**489
Varal, Vishan Chand, **5:**855
Varažden (musical group), **8:***152*
Vardin (periodical), **8:**472
Varela, Carlos, **2:**104
Varela, Leticia, **2:**593
Varèse, Edgard, **3:**174, 540; **4:**876; **6:**1031; **8:**85
Vargas, Getúlio, **2:**315–16, 317
Vargas, Pedro, **2:**372; **3:**741, 751
Vargas, Silvestre, **2:**622
Vargas, Wilfrido, **3:**743, 800
Vargyas, Lajos, **8:**24
variable-tension chordophones
    ānandalaharī, **5:**328, 329, 365
    bārike caudike, **5:**873–74
    bhapang, **5:**647
    caudike, **5:**869, 872–73, *875*
    cawandgā, **5:***400*
    conkā, **5:**343
    dundhukī, **5:**343, 732
    ektārā, **5:**343, 347, 503, 859
    gopīyantra, **5:**328, *328*, 343, 859, *860–61*
    gubgubī, **5:**727
    gutbuckets, **9:**157
        Melanesia, **9:**27
    jamiḍiki (also *jamikiḷi*), **5:**894, *895*, 901
    khamak, **5:**343
    premtāl, **5:**343
    pullavān kuḍam, **5:**365–66, *366*
    South Asia, **5:**328–29
    sruti caudike, **5:**872–73
    tokara, **5:**343
    tuntina, **5:**544, 908
    tuntune, **5:**343, 728
    washtub basses
        Bahamas, **2:**803–4, 805
        Garífuna culture, **2:**753
        Virgin Islands, **2:**971
Variations on a Hebrew Tune (Ben-Haim), **6:**1027
Variations on a Theme by Handel (Brahms), **8:**62
Variations for Winds, Strings, and Keyboards
    (Reich), **3:**177
variété, **8:**234
Variétés Lyriques (Montréal), **3:**1150
Varimezova, Todora, **8:***892*
Varkarī sect, **5:**253
varṇam, **5:**100, 104, 216–17, 218–19
    composers of, **5:**228, 229
    dances to, **5:**512, 517, 522
    performance of, **5:**149
    relation to *vannam* genre, **5:**960
Varojió culture. *See* Guarijio culture
Varthema, Ludovico di, **4:**284
Värttinä (musical group), **8:**227, 486
Varuna (deity), **5:**238
Varzi, Morteza, **6:**60, 62, 73
Vasa Lodge, **3:**1250, 1251
Vasan, S. S., **5:**544
Vasantakumari, M. L., **5:**107, 414
Vasavadatta, Princess, **5:**721
Vasconcelos, Ary, **2:**320
Vasconcelos, José, **2:**604
Vascone people, **8:**309
Vasiljević, Miodrag, **8:**954, 961

Vason, George, **9:**348
Vásquez, Abelardo, **2:**499
Vásquez Díaz, Vicente, **2:**498
Vásquez Rodríguez, Rosa Elena, **2:**501
Vassart, Jean-Joseph, **8:**531
Vassiliev, Dimitri, **2:**265
Vastaghuros Ensemble, **3:**1197
Vasudev (Krishna incarnation), **5:**728
Vasudevs, **5:**470
Vater, Saimoni, **9:**968
Vatican, **8:**12
Vatsyayana, **5:**407, 408, 551
vaudeville, **3:**190, 192–93, 544, 651
    Africa, **1:**765, 770
    black performers in, **3:**618, 620, 644, 645,
        650
    blues singers in, **3:**103–4
    Canada, **3:**1091, 1183, 1225
    influence on musicals, **3:**194
    Italian-American, **3:**861
    Jewish performers, **3:**12, 935
    Lithuanian-American, **3:**876–77
    Norwegian-American, **3:**868, 869
    Ontario, **3:**1080
    Swedish-American, **3:**872
    women performers in, **3:**95, 189
    Yukon, **3:**1277
vaudeville (genre), **8:**534, 548
Vaughan, J. W., **1:**404
Vaughan, Sarah, **3:**674, 743, 863
Vaughan Williams, Ralph, **1:**52; **8:**19, 26, 186,
        188
    folk song research, **8:***328*, 332, 337
    use of folk songs in compositions, **8:**332–33,
        339
Vauxhall Gardens (London), **6:**21
Vaze, Ramkrishnabua, **5:**413
Vazīrī, 'Alī Naqī, **6:**72, 135, 139, 857, 861, 863,
        867–68
Vázquez Valle, Irene, **2:**624
Veary, Emma, **9:**924
Vedanta philosophy, **3:**130, 982; **5:**34, 579
Vedas, **5:**10–11, 14, 21, 247, 261, 301, 786
    Atharvaveda, **5:**66, 238, 507
    Ṛgveda, **5:**66, 238, 239, 507
        notation of, **5:**240–41
        recitation of, **5:**241–42, 469
        reference to temple dancers, **5:**408
    Sāmaveda, **5:**24, 25, 30–33, 38–39, 66, 96,
        221–22, 238, 242–45, 261, 469, 492,
        507
        agnicayana rite and, **5:**238–39
        treatises on, **5:**71
    Yajurveda, **5:**66, 238, 243, 261, 400, 469, 507
Vedda people, **5:**108
Vedder, Eddie, **3:**340
Vedel, Anders Sorenson, **8:**470
Vedic religion, **3:**132; **5:**14, 33, 238–39, 313,
        457, 956; **8:**100. *See also* chant
Ve'ehala (Tongan flutist), **9:***372*, *796*
Ve'ehala, Kioa, **9:**113
Ve'ehala, the Honourable (Tongan noble), **9:**130
Veeramani, K., **5:**557
Vega, Carlos, **2:**31, 251, 467, 468, 501
Vega Drouet, Hector, **2:**941
Vega Matus, Alejandro, **2:**765

Vega, Robert, **3:**749
Vega, Suzanne, **3:**1280
Vegas, Solomon, **9:**101
Veiga de Oliveira, Ernesto, **8:**21
Vela, Bartolomé, **2:**284
Vela, Rubén, **3:**776
Vēlan caste, **5:**931
Velarde, Benny, **3:**798
Velasco, Jerónimo, **2:**395
Velasco, Juan Antonio de, **2:**396
Velasco Rivero, Pedro de, **2:**583, 585, 587
Velásquez García, José ("Julio Vives Guerra"), **2:**394
Velásquez, Manuel, **2:**836
Velásquez Ortiz, Nicanor, **2:**395
Velásquez, Ronny, **2:**660
Velásquez, Rufino, **2:**609
Velasquez, Victor, **3:**788
Veled, Sultan of Turkey, **3:**1044; **6:**107
Velić, Mujo, **8:**131
Vella, Joseph, **8:**642
Vella, Mikelangelo, **8:**642
Veloso, Caetano, **2:**41, 109–10, 135, 318
Velvet Crush (musical group), **3:**169
Velvet Underground (musical group), **3:**347, 348, 357; **9:**169
Venda people, **1:**707
  history of, **1:**708
  instruments, **1:**708–9
  lamellophones, **1:**317
  music of, **1:**708–9, 719, 722, 777
  singing, **1:**701–2
  speech surrogate methods, **1:**106
"*vendedor de frutas, El*" (Sephardic song), **3:**1174
Venetsanou, Nena, **8:**208
Venezuela, **2:**441, 523–44. *See also specific peoples*
  acculturation in, **2:**543
  Amerindian cultures in, **2:**524–25, 543–44
  Barlovento
    instruments of, **2:**527, 528–30
    Saint John the Baptist festival in, **2:**535–36, 539
    urbanization of, **2:**543
  Caribbean islands of, **2:**789
  children's wakes in, **2:**422, 535
  Chilean people in, **2:**84, 90
  creole music, **2:**525–33
  geography of, **2:**523, 529–30
  history of, **2:**524
  instruments of, **2:**32, 34, 378, 526–33, 544
  Maroon cultures in, **2:**131
  musical genres
    aguinaldo, **2:**538
    corrido, **2:**540
    gaita, **2:**538–39
    galerón, **2:**540
    golpe, **2:**540, 541
    joropo, **2:**539–41, 544
    malembe, **2:**528
    nueva canción, **2:**103
    pasaje, **2:**540
    revuelta, **2:**540
    salsa, **2:**133
    tamunangue, **2:**536
  performers in, **2:**542
  popular music of, **2:**543

population of, **2:**523
religious genres in, **2:**533–37
research on, **2:**523–24, 543–44
secular music of, **2:**537–41
tropical-forest region of, **2:**123–35
  Warao culture, **2:**120, 188–98; **10:**101–2
  Yanomamö culture, **2:**169–75
  Yekuana culture, **2:**176–82
Venkatamakhi, **5:**46–47, 77, 94, 97, 227, 262
Venkatarama Ayyar, K. S., **5:**389, 392
Venkatesvara (deity), **5:**217
Venkatesvarlu, Voleti, **5:**222–23
Venkatraman, Srikanth, **5:**233
Venkatraman, S. V., **5:**543
Venkatramanayya, Sonti, **5:**221
Venne, Joe, **3:**344
Vennum, Thomas, Jr., **3:**423, 425, 426, 454–55, 457–58, 484, 495, 498
Ventura, Johnny, **2:**860; **3:**800
Ventures (musical group), **7:**746
Venus (record company), **5:**429, 528, 548
Veps, **8:**475, 754, 772
  wedding laments of, **8:**754
Veraguas culture, **2:**16, *17*
verbena de la Paloma, La (Bretón), **3:**851
verbunkos, **3:**530; **8:**162, 273–74, 737–38, 745
Verdelot, Philippe, **2:**735
Verdi, Giuseppe, **3:**862, 1148, 1182; **4:**854, 857, 862; **6:**547, 610; **7:**946; **8:**60, 84, 187, 618, 981; **9:**80
"*Vereda tropical*" (García), **3:**739
Veredon, Gray, **9:**947
Veregin, Peter, **3:**12, 1095
Veresai, Ostap, **8:**815
Verhasselt, François, **8:**531
Verklärung Christi (Feliciano), **4:**878
Verkovich, Stefan, **8:**906
Verlaines (musical group), **9:**169
Verma, Manik, **5:**414
Vermont. *See also* New England
  ballads in, **3:**153–58
  Bennington, *taiko* drumming groups in, **3:**971
  Marlboro, morris dancing in, **3:**324
Verney, Frederick, **4:**224, 225, 238, 247, 285
Vernon, Paul, **3:**828
Verrall, Mrs., **8:**336
Versailles, Treaty of, **2:**749, 864
Versatones (musical group), **3:**894
Verstovsky, Aleksei, **8:**780
Vertebrats (musical group), **3:**171
Vertinsky, Aleksandr, **8:**776, 777–78
Vertkov, Konstantin, **8:**21
Veskimets, Gita, **3:**880
Vesnivka Women's Choir (Toronto), **3:**1082, 1200
Vesoni, Pedro, **2:**397
Vespers (Monteverdi), **6:**1031
Vessantara jataka (Buddhist sutra), **7:**503, 504
vessel flutes. *See* flutes, vessel
Vessella, Alessandro, **8:**617
Vēṭar caste, **5:**906
Vetter, Roger R., **3:**1014; **4:**637, 639
Vetter, Valerie, **3:**1020–21
Vetterl, Karel, **8:**26, 732
Veysel, Aşik, **6:**765, 796

VH1 (U.S. music video channel), **2:**52; **3:**206, 211, 219
Vial'tseva, Anastasiya, **8:**776
Viana, Alfredo da Rocha (Pixinguinha), **2:**305, 350
Vianna, Hermano, **2:**320
Viau, Albert, **3:**1155
Viaud, Julien, **9:**37–38
vibrato, **4:**461–62. *See also* singing
  āndolan, **5:**82
  Bulgaria, **8:**896
  China, *zheng* music, **7:**172
  Fiji, **9:**779
  Hawai'i, **9:**916
  Iceland, **8:**401
  Italy, **8:**613
  Korea
    instrumental, **7:**821, 823, 827
    vocal, **7:**817, 818–19, 882, 903, 928
  Korean music, **7:**851
  Low Countries, **8:**529
  Naxi people, vocal, **7:**511
  Sāmoa, **9:**205, 808
Vic Siebert and the Sons of the Saddle, **3:**1091
Viceroyalty of Brazil, **2:**23, 242
Viceroyalty of La Plata, **2:**23, 242
Viceroyalty of New Granada, **2:**23, 36, 242
Viceroyalty of New Spain, **2:**23, 36, 242
Viceroyalty of Peru, **2:**23, 36, 242
Vichitr Vadakarn, V., **4:**223–24
Vicioso, Toni, **2:**861
Vickers, Adrian, **4:**733
Victor, Misomba, **1:**360
Victor Records (Victor Gramophone Company), **3:**277, 653, 706, 707, 737, 874, 922, 1033, 1048; **9:**998
Victoria Amateur Orchestra, **3:**1095
Victoria Choral Society, **3:**1094
Victoria, María, **3:**741
Victoria Museum (Ottawa), **3:**291
Victoria, queen of England, **3:**291, 1181; **5:**431, 433, 572; **8:**365, 368
Victoria Symphony, **3:**1097
Victoria, Tomás Luís de, **2:**735; **6:**449
Victoria University of Wellington, **9:**932
Victoriano, Juan, **2:**581
Vidal, Carlos, **3:**787
Vidal, Tunji, **1:**40, 44, 413
Videla, Raúl, **2:**372
video. *See* film and video; television
VideoFACT, **3:**252
Vidyapati Thakur, **5:**249, 253, 254, 677–79
Vidyaranya, **5:**262
Vieco, Carlos, **2:**395
Vieilles Chansons de la Nouvelle-France (Young), **3:**1167
Vieira, Jelon, **3:**731
Viejo Vilmas, El (*trovo*), **3:**758, 762
vielle (also *vielle à roue*). *See* hurdy-gurdies
Vienna Art Club, **10:**111
Vierus, Anatol, **8:**883
Viesca, Juan, **3:**776
Vietnam
  Bình Định Province, theater in, **4:**496
  chamber music, **4:**480–84
  Chăm people of, **4:**50, 590–91

chaos and control in, **4:**16
Chinese influences in, **4:**69, 70
Chinese people in, **4:**70
composition in, **4:**127, 129, 512
court music of, **4:**7, 447–49; **7:**723, 725
cultural origins of, **4:**10–11
dance
   court, **4:**497–98
   folk, **4:**499–500
   masked, **4:**56
   religious, **4:**500–501
   theatrical, **4:**501–2
Đồng Đậu culture, **4:**36
Đồng Sơn culture, **4:**40–41, 44–46, 485, 497
Europeans in, **4:**87–88, 449, 507
folk songs, **4:**452, 475–80
geography of, **4:**444
Giao Châo, **4:**446
Gò Mun culture, **4:**36, 40
Hanoi, **4:**5
   theater in, **4:**496
history of, **4:**444–49, 502, 507
Hmong people in, **3:**1003; **4:**550–51
Hoabinhian culture, **4:**33–34
Hồ Chí Minh City, **4:**5
Huế, **4:***1*, 7, 70, 125, 448, 482
   theater in, **4:**496
Indians in, **4:**68
instruments, **4:**466–75
   early, **4:**446
   flat gongs, **4:**927
   of minority peoples, **4:**533–36
Khmer people in, **4:**151, 215–16
Kmhmu people in, **4:**546–47
Lahu people in, **4:**538–40
lithophones in, **4:**56–57; **5:**321
lowland minorities in, **4:**531
map of, **4:***445*
minority musics of, **4:**531–36
monochords in, **4:**59
musical elements, **4:**451–60
musical genres (*See also* dance and movement;
     theater; vocal music)
   ải lao, **4:**447
   ca huế, **4:**449, 455, 464, 482–83
   ca trù, **4:**23, 454, 455, 464, 467, 469, 472,
     480–82
   dân ca, **4:**81, 514–15
   đồng dao, **4:**479–80
   hát ả đào, **4:**447, 467, 470
   hát đúm, **4:**464
   hát phường vải, **4:**477, 479
   hát sắc bùa, **4:**479
   hát trống quân, **4:**471
   hát xoan, **4:**476
   hò, **4:**478
   hô bài chòi, **4:**479
   kể truyện, **4:**479
   lý, **4:**478
   modernization of, **4:**509–13, 515–16
   nhạc cải cách, **4:**449, 509–10, 513
   nhạc dân tộc cải biên, **4:**89, 119, 129, 134,
     512–13
   nhạc mới, **4:**513, 514, 515
   nhạc tài tử, **4:**23, 70, 455, 464, 468, 472,
     473, 483–84, 493, 494, 508

   nhạc tiền chiến, **4:**510
   nói lối, **4:**454
   quan họ, **4:**455, 460, 477, 479, 514, 532
   ru, **4:**478–79
   tân cổ giao duyên, **4:**454
   tân nhạc, **4:**449
   vè, **4:**479
   vọng cổ, **4:**454, 468, 494, 508
musical reform in, **4:**507–9
music research on, **4:**24, 25, 529
music traditions in, **4:**8
panpipes of, **9:**398
pedagogy in, **4:**119
Phong Châu, **4:**449–50
Phùng Nguyễn culture, **4:**36–37
politics and war in, **4:**87–89, 118
popular music, **4:**8
population of, **4:**444
possession rituals, **4:**60
prehistoric, **4:**32–37, *33*, *36–37*, 596
regionalism in, **4:**116
religious music, **4:**502–6
representative music of, **4:**23, 134–35
revival movement in, **4:**124–25
Sa Huynh culture, **4:**42–43
Saigon, theater in, **4:**496
salient musical features of, **4:**17
Tai people in, **4:**337
Thái Bình, **4:**450
theater in, **4:**484–97 (*See also* theater)
Thọ Xuân, **4:**485
tourism in, **4:**138
tuning systems in, **4:**14
upland peoples, **4:**529
   music research on, **4:**26
upland peoples in, **4:**531
Văn Lang period, **4:**445–46
village life in, **4:**6
wars in, **4:**446, 449, 497, 510, 529
Western influences in, **4:**80–81
Western music in, **4:**8
Yao people in, **4:**549
"Viet Nam" (Cliff), **3:**318
"Viet Nam Blues" (Kristofferson), **3:**317
Vietnam War, **3:**316–18, 329, 444, 512, 551,
     948–49, 993, 996, 1003, 1007, 1010
Vietnamese National Theatre, **9:**416
Vietnamese people, **4:**210
   in Australia, **9:**416
   in Cambodia, **4:**154, 156
   in Canada, **3:**1057, 1073, 1077, 1078, 1245
     Chinese ethnic groups, **3:**1260
   in France, **4:**88
   in French Guiana, **2:**434
   in Hawai'i, **9:**100, 109, 163
   in United States, **3:***513–14*, 948–49, 951–52,
     953, 993–97, 1007, 1010; **4:**88
     Chinese ethnic groups, **3:**961, 993
     upland minority groups, **3:**996
Việt Nhạc (periodical), **4:**511
Việt people, **4:**215, 444, 529, 533. *See also*
     Vietnam; Vietnamese people
Vieuxtemps, Henri, **3:**556, 1180
Víg, Rudolf, **8:**274
Vigil, Cipriano, **3:**764, *764*
Vigil, Cipriano, Jr., **3:**764, *764*

Vigil, Cleofes, **3:**762
Vigil, Felicita, **3:**764, *764*
Vigliermo, Amerigo, **8:**622
Vigneault, Gilles, **3:**314, 1059, 1076, 1156,
     1162, 1168, 1173
vihuela. See guitars
Vijay Ranga Sabha (institute), **5:**491
Vijayanagar (kingdom), **5:**11, 14, 45, 228, 390,
     508, 740
   dēvadāsi dancers, **5:**263
   devotional music in, **5:**103, 220, 246, 259,
     265
   fall of, **5:**518, 908
   mural painting in, **5:**300
   raga classification system, **5:**46–47
   sonorous temple pillars of, **5:**365
   women performers in, **5:**408
Vijayantimala, **5:***535*
Vīkā, **6:**643
Vikár, Béla, **8:**18
Vikár, László, **8:**772, 773
Viken, Johannes, **8:**415
Viken, Ragnhild, **8:**415
Viking label, **9:**985, 989, 995, 999
Vikings, **3:**7, 143, 379, 1056, 1068, 1069;
     8:326, 360
Vikramaditya, Emperor, **5:**721
Vila, Martinho da, **2:**351
Vila Nova, Ivanildo, **2:**326
Villa, Beto, **3:**778–79
Villa-Lobos, Heitor, **2:**115, 134, 306,
     310; **3:**740
Villa, Lucha, **3:**745
Villa, Rudy, **3:**748
Villafañe, Carlos, **2:**394, 395
Village Callers (musical group), **3:**746
Village People (musical group), **3:**1026
Villalón, Alberto, **2:**831
Villalon, Cristobal de, **6:**449
Villame, Yoyoy, **4:**886
Villamil Cordovez, Jorge, **2:**395
Villamil, Felipe García, **3:**729
villancico, **2:**113, 367
   Chile, **2:**368
   Costa Rica, **2:**695, 698
   Nicaragua, **2:**763
   Paraguay, **2:**457
   Peru, **2:**494–95, 497
   Philippines, **4:**842
   Spain, **8:**589, 592, 601
Villareal Vara, Felix, **2:**473
Villarraga, Padre, **2:**395
Villarreal, Bruno, **3:**775–76
Villarreal, Mel, **3:**780
Villate, Gaspar, **2:**837
Villefranche, Robert, **3:**1170
Villegas, Miguel, **2:**719
"Villikens and His Dinah" (ballad), **3:**835, 1257
Villoteau, Guillaume André, **6:**305, 410, 411,
     415, 544, 609
Vilnius University, **8:**513
Vilnius University Ensemble, **8:**514
vina. See lutes
Vinaver, Chemjo, **6:**1065
Vinayaka (deity), **5:**281, 892. *See also* Ganesh
Vince, Laszio, **6:**1027

Vincent D'Indy Music School (Montréal),
  3:1150
Vincent, Gene, 3:352
Vincent, Jenny Wells, 3:764–65
Vincent, Sylvie, 3:392
Vinci, Leonardo, 8:618
Vindhyachal Devi (deity), 5:669
Vinson, Eddie, 3:669
Vinson, Laura, 3:411, 1087
Vintervold, Ellev Ellevsen, 8:419
viola. *See* violins and fiddles (bowed lutes)
viola. See guitars
violins and fiddles (bowed lutes)
  adxoky-pondur, 8:863, 864
  aimag, 7:*1010*
  Albania, 8:*195*, 285, 993, 997, 1000
  in Andalusian orchestras, 1:535
  Andean regions, 2:212–13, 222
  Antigua and Barbuda, 2:798
  anzad (or *imzad*), 1:541, 542–43, 575–82,
    590; 6:410
  apkhertsa, 8:853
  Arab world, 6:409–11
  araltu huur, 7:1011, *1011*
  arbajo, 5:698
  Argentina, 2:251, 254, 273
  Australia, 9:134, 413, 441
  Austria, 8:*673*, 676
  bách thinh cầm, 4:509
  bamboo fiddles, 5:365
  bānam, 5:345
  bằng minh cầm, 4:509
  banhu, 7:113, 176–77, 196
  bas, 8:809–12, 818
  basetla, 8:796
  basses, string (*See also* double bass)
    Argentina, 2:263, 273
    bajo de caja, 2:691, 693
    Cuba, 2:830, 835
    Fiji, 9:779
    Honduras, 2:742
    Jamaica, 2:900
    Malawi, 10:*119*
    Mexico, 2:613, 621
    Netherlands Antilles, 2:930
    one-stringed, 9:139
    Puerto Rico, 2:938
    strengbas, 4:625
    three-stringed, 8:918
    tina, 2:661
    tololoche, 2:*614*
    tura, 9:896
    two-stringed, 8:706, 918
    umupa, 9:900
    'Uvea, 9:812, 814
    Yuma culture, 2:598
  bass violin, 8:259–60
  biola (term for violin)
    Cirebon, 4:698
    Java, 4:645
    Lombok, 4:768
    Malaysia, 4:411
    Maluku, 4:814
    Philippines, 4:902, 905–6, 908, 909, 911
    Sumatra, 4:598, 601, 606, 615, 616, 617,
      619, 620

Sumbawa, 4:780, 784
  Sunda, 4:716
biwang, 7:477–78
Bolivia, 2:140, 283, 288
bordi, 8:640, *641*
boselis, 8:511
Bosnia-Hercegovina, 8:965, 966
bow-fiddle, 2:815
bowing, origins of, 8:22, 41–42
box fiddles, 3:375, *375*, 379; 8:811
Brazil, 2:335
Bulgaria, 8:894
bushtar, 7:459
byzaanchy, 6:985
cakārā, 5:345
candrasārang, 5:337
Carriacou, 2:*871*, 872
China, 7:217
cho haegŭm, 7:961
chotī sārangī, 5:769, 770
chung haegŭm, 7:961
chuniri (also *chianuri*), 8:839, *839*, 840, 853,
  863
cikārā, 5:345
clog fiddles, 8:532
Corsica, 8:568, 571, 572, 573
crin-crin, 8:544
Cuba, 2:834
cultural origins of, 4:10–11
Cyprus, 8:1030–31
Czech Republic, 8:719, *720*
Dagbamba people, 1:452; 10:143, 145–48,
  154
dahu, 7:229
đàn cò chi, 4:474
đàn cò phụ, 4:474
đàn gáo (also *đàn hồ*), 4:474, 490
đàn nhị (also *đàn cò*), 3:994; 4:472, 474, 490
dayuray, 4:924, 925
delrubā, 5:806
Denmark, 8:457, 462
development of, 8:168
digehu, 7:231
dihu, 7:229
dilrubā, 5:234, 336
ding, 7:499
dissemination of, 8:9, 170
đơn cò lòn, 4:484
đơn cò phụ, 4:484
đơn gáo, 4:484
dörvön chihtei huur, 7:1004, 1011
double bass, 5:*537*; 8:273, 277, *665*, *720* (*See
  also* basses, string)
  Albania, 8:997, 1000
  in Arab music, 6:421
  Austria, 8:*673*
  bajo de uñas, 3:1025
  bajs, 8:933
  in bluegrass music, 3:160, 164, 166, 1258
  Bosnia-Hercegovina, 8:965
  Bulgaria, 8:902
  in Catalonian *cobla* ensemble, 8:594
  in *charanga*, 3:788
  in *conjunto* music, 3:522, 723, 772, 773,
    775
  in contra dance bands, 3:231

Czech Republic, 8:719
  Denmark, 8:454, 457
  in Egyptian *firqa*, 6:317, 559
  Estonia, 8:494
  Finland, 8:478
  in German music, 3:890
  Germany, 8:654, 656
  in Greek bands, 3:930
  in Hispano music, 3:761
  Italy, 8:608
  Latvia, 8:504
  Norway, 8:420
  in Norwegian music, 3:868
  Poland, 8:707
  in polka bands, 3:529, 824, 893, 894, 901
  in quadrille band, 3:232
  in Rom string band, 8:274
  in Romania, 8:872, 876, 877
  in salsa, 3:788
  Slovakia, 8:719
  in Slovak music, 3:900
  in *son conjunto*, 3:792–93
  in string bands, 3:836
  Sweden, 8:152, 441
  Switzerland, 8:686, 690, 696
  in *tamburitza* orchestra, 3:920
  in Tunisian *ma'lūf*, 6:328, 329, 407
dungga roro, 4:790–91
duwagey, 4:924, 925
Ecuador, 2:417, 423
El Salvador, 2:708
England, 8:330
enserunai, 4:835
erhu, 7:172, 175–78
  Abing's performances, 7:140
  in Cantonese music, 10:18
  construction and performance of, 7:175–76
  early, 7:113
  history of, 7:176
  in Hong Kong Cantopop, 7:355
  in Hui music, 7:462
  in *Jiangnan sizhu* ensemble, 7:224–25
  modernization of, 7:228–29, 230, 232
  North America, 3:345, 960, 961, 962,
    1064, 1083, 1217, 1248
  performance techniques, 7:123, 242
  regional variants, 7:176–77, 218
  repertoire for, 7:177–78, 231, 432
  Southeast Asia, 4:70, 238, 281
  status of, 7:89, 228–29
  in *Zhedong luogu*, 7:196
erxian, 3:961, 1260; 7:205, 206–7, 218, 242
erxian-touxian, 7:212, *212*
esrāj, 5:248, 251, 602, *603*
Estonia, 8:494
Europe, 8:*33*, 143, 169, 517
Faroe Islands, 8:468
fedel, 8:453–54
Fidel, 8:651
fidil, 8:384
Finland, 8:478, 479, 481, 482, 484, 488
France, 8:542, 544, 546, 547, 551
gadulka, 3:926
gaohu, 3:960, 1260; 7:196, 218, 242
gardon, 3:1197; 8:274, 743, 744, *744*
gbee-kee, 1:467

gehu, 7:231
genka, 7:477, 480
Germany, 8:656, *657*
gesó-gesó, 4:804–5
gesok-gesok, 4:806
ghazhaka, 5:788
ghīchak, 5:305, 345, 804; 6:1003
ghichek, 6:395, 398
ghidjak, 6:969, 974
ghījak, 5:788, 828, 830–31, *831*; 6:919;
    7:114, 459
gitgit, 4:924
gogeru, 1:448
gójé, 1:475
goje, 1:414, 448, 460–61
gondze (also *gonje*; *goondze*), 1:211, 452, *453*;
    10:143, 145–48, 154
in gong-chime ensembles, 4:20–21
gonje (See *gondze*)
Great Britain, 8:325
Greece, 8:284–85, 1009, 1010, 1012, *1013*,
    1015
Grenada, 2:865
Guadeloupe, 2:877
Guatemala, 2:727
gudok, 8:706, 764, *770*, 770–71
gŭdulka, 8:*176*, 282–83, *283*, 893, *893*, 897,
    902
gujarātan, 5:345, 641
gujarī, 5:*647*
gusla, 8:975
gusle, 3:1199; 8:130, 168, 198, 927, 941,
    941, 957–58, 959, 961, 963, 966
haegŭm, 7:206, *815*, 817, *824*, 827, *961*, 989
    classification of, 7:814, 823
    contemporary music for, 7:954, 957, 971
    in court and *chŏngak* music, 7:866–69
    early description of, 7:823
    in folk song accompaniment, 7:880
    in *kagok*, 7:921
    in *kasa*, 7:927
    modifications to, 7:830–31, 961
    sanjo repertoire, 7:913–17
    in *sijo*, 7:925
    in *sinawi*, 7:890
    in *t'alch'um*, 7:942
Hardanger fiddle (also *hardingfele*), 8:25, 99,
    106, 108, *121*, 170, 176, *177*, 226,
    411, 415–17, *419*, 419–20
    music for, 8:411–12, 416–17, 425, 426,
    427, 430
    North America, 3:826, 868, 869–70
    women performers, 8:421–22
heo, 4:797
hiil, 7:1011
hil huur, 7:1010–11
Honduras, 2:743
hugur, 7:1010–11
Hungary, 8:*738*, *744*
huqin, 7:80, *80*, 176, *511*, 711; 9:97
    early, 7:113
    modern adaptations, 7:228
    in *shifangu* ensemble, 7:196
    Southeast Asia, 4:238
    Tibet, 7:477–78
    in Tibet, 7:475

huuchir, 7:1004, 1011
huur, 7:1010–11
hyalgasan huur, 7:1011
igil, 6:981, *985*, 985–86; 7:1005
ikil, 7:1005, 1008, *1010*, 1010–11, 1014,
    1016
ikili, 7:1005
imzad (See *anzad*)
Ireland, 8:152, 325, 383, 384, 390, 391
isrāj, 5:336, *336*, 494
Italy, 8:608, 609, 615, 618
Jamaica, 2:900, 907
    bamboo, 2:900
jawzah, 6:552
jejy, 1:787
jing erhu, 7:176, 285
jinghu, 3:961; 7:113, 176, *176*, 282, 285
jōza (also *jōze*), 6:8, 312, 315, 409, 411
kabak kemane, 6:763, 798
kakoxa, 1:669
kalyalya, 1:669, 677
kamaicā, 5:345
k'amanch'a, 6:*733*, 734
kamānche, 5:345, 688; 6:60, 133, 138, 140,
    833, 839, 867
kamāncheh, 5:692
kamanja, 1:535; 3:1218
    Algeria, 6:269
    Egypt, 6:8, 148, 340, 410, 547, 559, 610
    in Maghribi Jewish ensembles, 6:1043
    Palestine, 6:586
kamanja kabīra (viola), 6:470, *471*
kamāychā, 5:641, *641*, 642
kanhi, 3:1010; 4:590
keer (also *kitiar*), 2:417
K'ekchi Maya, 2:667–68
keman, 6:764
k'eman, 6:734
kemancha, 8:840
kemençe, 6:746, 758, 763, *763*; 8:993, 997
kəmənçe, 6:8, 924, *924*, 925
kemençe rûmî, 6:774, *774*
kemene, 3:926; 8:283, 975, 979
kemenje, 8:1011, *1011*, *1012*
kendara, 5:733
kenrā, 5:345
kingiri, 5:722
kisin-fandir (also *khoiisar-fandir*), 8:859, 861
kit, 8:655
k'ni, 4:59, 535
kò ke, 4:535
koke, 4:590
kokyû, 2:88; 7:536, *711*, 778–79
    chamber music for, 7:711–13
    in *kumiuta*, 7:696
    modernization of, 7:712–13
    Okinawan, 7:711, 792
    in *sankyoku*, 7:688, 715–17
korizne goblice, 8:918–19
Kosovo, 8:286
kukuma, 1:448
kutet, 4:925
lahutë, 8:995
Latvia, 8:504
lehut (also *gude*), 8:959 (See also *gusle*)
lijerica, 8:244, 929

lira, 3:1199; 8:168, 615
lirica, 8:966
Lithuania, 8:511, 512
litlit, 4:920
lkamanja, 6:489
lkmnza, 1:541
lokanga, 1:789
lotār, 6:408
Low Countries, 8:522, 527, 528, 529, 532
lụ phù, 4:535, 536
luyên chúa cầm, 4:509
lyra, 8:118, 130, *179*, 929, 1009, 1011, 1015,
    1018, 1023, 1025, 1031; 9:73
Macedonia, 8:281, *979*
Malta, 8:640, *641*
mamokhorong, 1:761
manikarka, 8:511
maryna, 8:706, 707
matouqin, 7:176
Maya culture, 2:654
Mayo culture, 2:592
mazanki, 8:706, 707
merebab, 4:835
Mexica culture, 2:559–60
Mexico, 2:20, 550, 606, 608, 611, 612,
    621–22
Middle Eastern, 6:18
Middle Eastern origin of, 8:12
Mixtec culture, 2:564, 565, 566
miyagi kokyû, 7:697
Mongol people, 7:1010–11
Montserrat, 2:924
Mordvinian people, 8:774
morin huur (horsehead fiddle), 7:1004, 1007,
    1008, *1010*, 1010–11
nantuṇi, 5:932
narelī, 5:*647*
Nigeria, 10:154
niutui qin, 7:491
nko chaw nja (also *nkauj nrog ncas*; *xim xo*),
    3:1005, *1005*
Norway, 8:197, 415, 418–20, 420
nyckelharpa (also keyed fiddle), 8:22, 170,
    439–40, *440*, 442
one-stringed, 2:456
orutu, 1:625
Otopame culture, 2:571, 572
Panama, 2:772, 776, 778
pena, 5:329, 345, 494–95
Peru, 2:*37*, 209, 210, 473, 476, 478, *480*,
    483, 494, 497
Philippines, 4:928
phụng minh cầm, 4:509
pila, 9:163
piol, 4:604
pi-wang, 5:710, 715
Poland, 8:*705*, 705–6
pullavān vīṇā, 5:350–51, 365, *366*
Purépecha culture, 2:578
qobiz, 6:345; 7:460
qobuz, 6:844, 967
qobyz, 6:953
qyl-qobyz, 6:956–57
rabāb (also *rabāba*; *rabābah*), 1:535; 5:256;
    6:360, 395, 396, 397, 407, 408,
    409–11, 545

violins and fiddles, *rabāb* (*continued*)
　in Andalusian music, 6:406, 409, 411, 445,
　　454, 460
　in Iranian *radif*, 6:863
　one-string, 6:10, 340, 545, 652, 663, 664
　in Tunisian *ma'lūf*, 6:327, 328, 502
　two-string, 6:10, 340, 341–42, 343, 410,
　　470, *471*
　rabāb al-cha'ir, 6:269
　rabab darek, 4:611
　rabab pasisir, 4:613
　rababu, 4:815, 816
　rabeca, 2:309, 311, 329
　rabel, 2:255, 360, 776; 8:589, *590*, 594
　rabup, 4:835
　rāvaṇahatthā (also *rāvanhatta*), 5:345, 646,
　　647
　ravé, 2:201
　rbeb, 6:409, 411
　rebab, 3:1012; 6:499, 769, 774, *774*
　　Bali, 4:743, 745, 746, 749, 756–57
　　Cirebon, 4:697
　　Java, 4:21, 238, 642, 665, 669, 672–73,
　　　674
　　Lombok, 4:768
　　Malaysia, 4:238, 407, 412, 413, 417, *419*,
　　　420–21, 428
　　Sumatra, 4:626
　　Sunda, 4:107, 704, *713*, 714, 716
　rebec, 6:411; 8:42
　redeb, 4:768, 772, 775
　reikin, 7:713
　rema qin, 7:477
　rendo, 4:717
　research on, 8:22
　rībab, 6:410
　riçek, 6:746, *746*, 749–50
　riti, 1:445
　Romania, 8:*198*, 200, 277, *278*, 872, 876,
　　879
　in Rom string band, 8:273, 274
　Russia, 8:767
　St. Lucia, 2:945
　salaw, 4:98, 310–11
　sanhu, 7:176
　sarān, 5:345
　sarāng, 5:345
　sāraṅg, 5:683–84
　sārangī, 2:901; 5:*55*, *123*, *296*, *335*, 338,
　　338, 341, 344–45
　　Afghanistan, 5:806
　　depictions of, 5:307
　　folk, 5:*477*
　　Gujarat, 5:633
　　Guyana, 5:602, *603*
　　Laṅgā performers of, 5:*403*
　　Mīr performers of, 5:402
　　Nepal, 5:698, *698*
　　North America, 3:1216, *1216*, 1246
　　origins of, 5:338
　　Pakistan, 5:746, *746*, 753
　　Punjab, 5:762, 769, 771
　　Rajasthan, 5:642, 643
　　repertoire for, 5:194–95
　　Trinidad, 5:591
　　use in devotional music, 5:248, 251

　use in film music, 5:347, 535
　use in *ghazal* performance, 5:186
　use in *kathak* ensemble, 5:494
　use in *khyāl* performance, 5:171, 177, 207
　use in *ṭhumrī* performance, 5:179–82
　Uttar Pradesh, 5:671, *671*
　women performers, 5:207–8
　sarinala, 5:503
　sārindā, 5:337, 345, 506, 787–88, *789*, 815,
　　835
　satar, 7:459
　sato, 6:919, 1002
　saw duang, 4:11, 17, 71, 238–39, *240*, *244*,
　　246, *250*, 269, 271, 272, 282–83,
　　305, 307, 308, 474
　saw pip (also *saw krabawng*), 4:18, 317, 320
　saw sam sai, 4:170, 238, 271, 272, 590; 7:711
　saw u, 4:239, *246*, *250*, 256, 257, 271, 272,
　　282–83, 305, 307, 308
　sāz-e-kashmīrī, 5:688, *688*
　Scotland, 8:364, 365–66, 367, 372
　sekeseke, 2:189, 192, 197
　sekhankure, 1:761
　Serbia, 8:945, 952
　shanagan huur, 7:1011
　shiriri, 1:625
　sihu, 7:113, 176, 254
　sindhī sāraṅgī, 5:345, 641, *641*
　skripka, 8:770–71
　skrypka, 8:796, 809
　skrzypce, 8:706
　Slovakia, 8:719, *720*
　Slovenia, 8:917
　so, 4:338, 346
　so haegŭm, 7:961
　so i, 4:338, 350, 355, 358
　song thương, 4:509
　sorūd, in Balochistan, 6:881, 882, 883,
　　887–88
　so u, 4:350, 355, 358
　South Africa, 1:761, 762
　South America, 2:36
　Spain, 8:589, 594
　spike fiddles, 5:344, 345, 688, 788, 804, 828,
　　830–31
　suka, 8:705–6
　Sumatra, 4:600, 625
　surindā, 5:345, 641
　suroz, 5:775–76, 781, *782*, 783, *783*
　Sweden, 8:9, 435, 439, *440*, 440–42
　Switzerland, 8:686, 690, 694, 696
　tae haegŭm, 7:961
　tanpura, 2:85
　Tarahumara culture, 2:583, 586, 592
　tarawangsa, 4:697, 716, 717
　tār śahnāī, 5:336
　tāus, 5:336
　tayò, 4:365
　tehyan, 4:73
　Teribe culture, 2:685
　tie qin, 7:475, 477, 480
　tihu, 7:212
　tiqin, 7:218
　tırnak kemençe, 6:763
　Tohono O'odham culture, 2:593

　toro, 4:548
　torototela, 8:615
　touxian, 3:961; 4:11, 71, 239, 281
　Trinidad and Tobago, 2:959
　tror, 3:*999*, 1001
　tror chhe, 4:170, 183, 184
　tror kandal, 4:171
　tror Khmer, 4:170, 194, 196, 197, 238, 590
　tror khse bey, 4:194
　tror ou, 4:171, 183, 184, 196
　tror ou chamhieng, 4:171, 201
　tror so, 4:162
　tror so tauch, 4:171, 183, 184, 196
　tror so thomm, 4:171, 183, 184
　trua, 4:211–12, 213
　trua-ou, 4:211, 213
　tungkur, 7:788
　umkiki, 1:560
　Uruguay, 2:511, 519
　velviool, 1:761
　Venezuela, 2:532, 541
　vĩ cằm, 4:474
　vièle, 8:176, 542
　vīṇā, 5:932
　vioara, 8:877
　viol, 4:819
　viola, 5:234; 8:274, *738*, 877
　　in Andalusian music, 6:407, 421, *421*, 454,
　　　460
　　Morocco, 6:499
　　in quadrille band, 3:232
　violin
　　as accompaniment instrument, 5:101, 234,
　　　324, 338, 355, 364
　　African-American fiddling traditions, 10:142
　　in African-American music, 3:67
　　in Andalusian music, 6:435, 454, 460
　　Anglo-Canadian fiddling traditions,
　　　3:1080–81, 1082, 1256–57
　　in Appalachian folk music, 3:*13*
　　in Arab-American ensembles, 6:282
　　in arabesk, 6:251
　　in Arab music, 6:421, 699
　　in Arctic music, 3:380
　　Armenia, 6:734
　　Athapaskan fiddling traditions, 3:391, 1277
　　in bluegrass music, 3:159, 160, 164, 166
　　in Cantonese music, 3:1260; 7:219
　　Cape Breton (Gaelic) fiddling tradition,
　　　3:52, 74, 150–51, 1064, 1071, 1125,
　　　1127–30, 1257
　　Chinese national style, 7:348, 388
　　in *cinna mēḷam* ensemble, 5:104, 360
　　in *conjunto* music, 3:773
　　country fiddling traditions, 3:77, 160, 185,
　　　186, 231, 520, 596, 835–39, 867,
　　　1110
　　in Danish music, 3:882–83
　　Egypt, 6:8, 170, *170*, 317, 547, 551, 559,
　　　610
　　in Estonian music, 3:879
　　in Finnish music, 3:874, 875
　　in folk music performance, 3:1189–90, 1191
　　French Canadian fiddling traditions,
　　　3:1071, 1075, 1125, 1137, 1164,
　　　1168, 1190, 1194

in French music, **3:**528, 855, *856,*
   857–58
in German music, **3:**888, 889, 890
Goa, **5:**737
in Greek bands, **3:**930
Guyana, **5:**604
in Hispano music, **3:**759–60
in Iberian music, **3:**848
Inuit fiddling traditions, **3:**1275
Iran, **6:**828, 863, 867
in Irish music, **3:**842, 845
in Italian music, **3:**864
in Japanese ensembles, **7:**720
Japanese manufacturers, **7:**537, 720
in *jātrā* theater, **5:**505
in Karnatak music, **3:**990; **5:**100, 101, 107,
   161, 233–34, 351, 352, 384, 389,
   513, 517, 522
Kerala, **5:**945
in *khyāl* performance, **5:**171
in Lithuanian music, **3:**875
in *mariachi* groups, **3:**722, 765
in Maronite church music, **6:**216
in *matachines* dance, **3:**430, *757,* 759
Métis fiddling tradition, **3:**7, 332, 344,
   405–10, 458, 1063, 1087, 1091, 1277
in Mexican music, **3:**735, 737
in Michoacán ensemble, **3:**723
in minstrel shows, **3:**184, 543, 616
Morocco, **6:**499
Native American fiddling traditions, **3:**326,
   332, 479, 1063
Nepal, **5:**705
in Norwegian music, **3:**868
in Nubian music, **6:**642
at Pakistani-American weddings, **5:**579
in Pakistani music, **3:**981
Palestine, **6:**591
in polka bands, **3:**893, 894
in quadrille band, **3:**232
in religious ceremonies, **3:**118
repertoire for, **5:**194–95
Réunion Island, **5:**609
in salsa, **3:**788
in Sephardi music, **6:**204
as solo instrument, **5:**207
South Asia, **5:**338
in South Asian devotional music, **5:**253
in South Asian film music, **5:**347, 368, 535,
   537, 543
Southeast Asia, **4:**426, 432, 435, 436,
   438–39, 548, 587, 606, 623, 774
Sri Lanka, **5:**970
Suzuki pedagogical method, **3:**231
in Swedish music, **3:**1196
in Syrian music, **3:**1032
in *tamburitza* orchestra, **3:**920
Tamil Nadu, **5:**924
in Tejano music, **3:**772
tuning of, **6:**36
in Tunisian Jewish music, **6:**527
in Tunisian *ma'lūf,* **6:**328, 329, 407
in Turkish folk music, **6:**763
Ukrainian fiddling tradition, **3:**344–45,
   1242
in Ukrainian music, **3:**913, 914, 1242

women performers of, **5:**411
Yukon, **3:**1277
violín de talalate, **2:**757
violin with metal horn, **8:**877
violon, **8:**560
violoncello
   in Andalusian music, **6:**435, 460
   in Arab music, **6:**421
   Bulgaria, **8:**902
   Cuba, **2:**835
   in Egyptian *firqa,* **6:**317, 559
   England, **8:**330
   Hungary, **8:***738*
   Low Countries, **8:**527
   North America, **3:**118, 119, 232
   Purépecha culture, **2:**578
   Romania, **8:**877
   in Rom string band, **8:**274
   South Asia, **5:**234, 535, *537,* 544
   Southeast Asia, **4:**474, 508
   Switzerland, **8:**686
   three-stringed, **3:**1197
   in *Tianjin shidiao,* **7:**254
   in Tunisian *ma'lūf,* **6:**328, 329, 407
   Turkey, **6:**117, 758
viols, **3:**1186
   Italy, **8:**618
   lyra-viol, **8:**367
   rribab, **6:**489
   vihuela de arco, **2:**577–78
   viola da gamba, **8:**55, 75, 420, 654
Wales, **8:**348, 354, 356
wandindi, **1:**625
West Africa, **1:**445, 448–49, 451
xiqin, **7:**113, 176, 206
xi xov, **4:**553
Yaqui culture, **2:**590–91; **3:**437, 485
yawera, **2:**553
yaylï tanbur, **6:**250, 758
yeh hu, **4:**239
yehu, **7:**113, 177, 212, 268, 269
Yugoslavia, **8:**279
Yuma culture, **2:**598
zhil-kobuz, **8:**857
zhonghu, **7:**229
zhuihu, **7:**231
złóbcoki, **8:**706
violoncello. *See* violins and fiddles (bowed lutes)
Viper (calypsonian), **2:**819
Vīrā (film), **5:**544
Virabhadra (deity), **5:**877–78
Virarakavan, M., **5:**904, 906
Virashaiva sect, **5:**264–65, 866, 872
Vīravidyavantulu singers, **5:**900, 901–2
Virdung, Sebastian, **8:**654
Virgil, **8:**608
Virgin Gorda, **2:**968
Virgin Islands, **2:**789, 968–73; **3:**3–4
   festivals in, **2:**973
   geography of, **2:**968
   history of, **2:**968
   musical genres
     bamboula, **2:**973
     cariso, **2:**972
     quelbeys and quadrilles, **2:**971–72
     seis, **2:**969

political status of, **2:**792
research on, **2:**973
scratch bands, **2:**969–71
social occasions, tea meetings, **2:**972–73
Virgin Records, **3:**750
Virgin Unmasked (ballad opera), **3:**180
Virginia
   Arlington, Cambodian people in, **3:**948
   blues in, **3:**639
   cord-and-peg tension drum found in, **1:**316
   early African-Americans in, **3:**64, 66, 594,
     595–96, 598
   early European settlements in, **3:**23
   Falls Church, Vietnamese people in, **3:**993
   Filipino people in, **3:**1024
   Jamestown, **3:**7, 831
   Native American groups in, **3:**23, 461
   theater in, **3:**189
   Williamsburg, early theater in, **3:**179
Virginia Jubilee Singers, **1:**765
Virginia Minstrels, **3:**184, 616
Virginia's Ball (Douglass), **3:**617
Virkhaus, David Otto, **8:**496
Virkkala, Janne, **8:***478*
Vir'yal Chuvash, **8:**772
Virus, **2:**268
Viry, Firmin, **5:**609
Vishnu (deity), **5:**494. *See also* Vaishnavite
      traditions
   man-lion incarnation, **5:**276
   portrayed in dances, **5:**520
   worship of, **5:**105, 220, 230, 501, 512, 519,
     630, 698, 731, 867, 887
Vishva Bharati University (Santiniketan), **5:**857
Vishvanatha (deity), **5:**247
Visigoths, **8:**588
Visions of the Pacific, **9:**985
Vistulans, **8:**701
*Visual Anthropology: Photography as a Research
     Method* (Collier), **10:**106
visual arts. *See also* archaeology; costumes and
     clothing; iconography; iconology;
     masks
   Africa, **1:**113–21
   avant-garde and minimalist music and, **3:**176
   beadwork, Guyana, **2:**442
   body decoration
     Australia, **9:***345, 346, 420,* 430, 436–37,
       452, 465–66
     Brazil, **2:**325
     Great Lakes Indian peoples, **3:**452
     India, **5:**275
     Māori people, **9:**928
     Nauru, **9:**757
     New Caledonia, **9:**683, 685
     New Guinea, **9:**474
     Oceania, **9:***17,* 231, 345, 349, 752, 849,
       883, 890
     Papua New Guinea, **9:**484, 503, *513,* 516,
       518, 530, *537,* 552, 555, 569, 610
     Rapa Nui, **9:**349
     Solomon Islands, **9:**663
     South American tropical-forest peoples,
       2:126
     Suyá culture, **2:**144, 145
     Tahiti, **9:**349

visual arts, body decoration (*continued*)
  Tukano culture, **2:**155
  Vanuatu, **9:**705, 966
  Waiāpí culture, **2:**158
  Wayana culture, **2:**166, 167
bronze plaques, Benin kingdom, **1:**5, 316
calligraphy, Japan, **7:**546, 583
carvings and sculptures
  Aotearoa, **9:**928
  Australia, **9:**419
  Ecuador, **2:**413
  Europe, rock, **8:**36
  India, **5:***114*, 299–300, 306
  Irian Jaya, **9:**190–91, 580, 590
  New Caledonia, **9:**684–85
  Papua New Guinea, **9:**548, 552, 553, 569, *570*
  rongorongo boards, Rapa Nui, **9:**885
  Sardinia, bronze statues, **8:**631
  Solomon Islands, **9:**669, *670*, 963
  Tamil Nadu, stone pillars, **5:***14*
  Tiwanaku culture, **2:**282
  Vanuatu, **9:**688, *689*
  Yemen, funerary stele, **6:**357–58, *358*, 359
ceramics and pottery
  Europe, **8:**36–37
  Greece, **8:**46
  haniwa figurines, Japan, **7:**562, *562*
  Korea, **7:**821
  Lapita, **4:**38; **9:**4, 598, 771, 809
  Marianas Redware, **9:**743
  Moche culture, **2:**11, 467
  Palau, **9:**722
  Quichua culture, **2:**430
  South Asia, **5:**298–99
  Southeast Asia, **4:**38, 43
ceremonial mats, Sāmoa, **9:**801
China
  Buddhist, **7:**35
  dualism in, **7:**99–100
doll dioramas, Tamil Nadu, **5:**277
instrument decoration and carving
  African carved drums, **1:**665–66
  Aluku culture, **2:**438
  ancient, **2:**8–12
  Costa Rica, **2:**680
  Ecuador, **2:**413, 415, 418
  Egypt, **1:**303
  El Salvador, **2:**707
  Irian Jaya, **9:**582, 583
  Kiliwa culture, **2:**598
  Korea, **7:**822–23
  Madagascar, **1:**784
  Mangaia, **9:**898
  Mapuche culture, **2:**234, 252
  Maya culture, **2:**655, 667, 727, 728
  Micronesia, **9:**716
  Mongol people, **7:**1010
  Nepali shamanic drums, **5:**290
  Norway, **8:**415, *416*, 417
  Oceania, **9:**382, 383, *385*, 394
  Papua New Guinea, **9:**482, 489, 508, 549, 552, 553, 556
  Saami people, **8:**305
  Siberian painted drums, **7:**1028
  South Indian *tambūrā*, **5:**355

South Indian vina, **5:**352
Sweden, **8:**439
Tuareg people, **1:**577
Tukano culture, **2:**151
Vanuatu, **9:**691, 693
Vietnamese bronze drums, **4:**40, 43
Warao culture, **2:**191
Islamic, **6:**133
Kashmir, **5:**689
knotted cords, Marquesas Islands, **9:**885
Mapuche culture, **2:**238
Mashriq, **6:**536
Maya culture, **2:**650–51
Northwest Coast, **3:**1093
paintings and drawings, **2:**12
  Angola ideographs, **10:**122–23
  Australia, **9:**419, *420*, 440
  Aztec culture, **2:**557
  Costa Rica, **2:**694
  Ecuador, **2:**422–23
  European depictions of Australia, **9:***410*
  European depictions of Oceania, **9:**8–20, *710*, *727*, *754*, *766*
  France, cartoons, **8:**549
  graffiti, **3:**692
  Iceland, illuminated manuscripts, **8:**400
  India, **5:***115*, 298–310, *300*–301; Pahari painting, **5:**313, *314*; *rāgmālā* iconographical personifications, **5:**44, 46, 47, *47*, 73, 301–2, 312–18, *692*; Sultanate painting, **5:**300
  Peru, **2:**492, *493*
  Poland, **8:***713*
  Rajasthan, Kishangarhi painting, **5:**300, 307
  South America, **2:**16
paintings and drawings, rock
  Africa, **1:**294, 301, 305, 635, 705; **4:**44
  Europe, **8:**481
  Mapuche culture, **2:**234
  Saudi Arabia, **6:**357, 359
paintings, cave
  China, **7:**59, *60*, 111, 112, 124, 137, 168
  Europe, **8:**36, 37–38, 164, 600
  India, **5:**298–99
  Inner Asia, **7:**11
paintings, miniature
  Azerbaijan, **6:**922, 925
  India, **5:**411
  Persian, **5:**300, 817
paintings, sand, Navajo people, **3:**432
paintings, wall
  Korea, **7:**821, 833, 955
  Xinjiang, **6:***1004*
photographs, **5:**307; **10:**106, 151
prints
  cassette cards, **5:***418*
  popular music poster, **5:***422*
puppets, Japan, *bunraku*, **7:**664–65
scholarly works on, **5:**43
shields, Solomon Islands, **9:***632*, *633*
Southeast Asia, prehistoric, **4:**38, 40, 43–44
textiles
  Africa, **1:**114–15, 121, 135
  Flores, **4:**791, *792*
  Guyana, **2:**442
  Kuna culture, **2:**648, 649

Malinke people, **1:**114
Nusa Tenggara Timur, **4:**786–87
Roti, **4:**798
Southeast Asia, **4:**44
Tibetan, **7:**472
time-motion concepts in, **1:**127
Viswanathan, M. S., **5:**544
Viswanathan, Tanjavur, **5:**54, 99, *100*, *102*, 213, 560
Vitak, Louis, **3:**897
Vitale, Wayne, **3:**1019; **4:**733
Viti Levu (Fiji), **9:**773, 817–18
  music and dance in, **9:**776–80
  tourism in, **9:**781
Vītoliņš, Jēkabs, **8:**507
Vitthal (deity), **5:**549, 729
Vitthala, Pundarika, **5:**46, 48, 52, 77, 314
Vitthalnath, Sri, **5:**251
Vitu (Papua New Guinea), **9:**607–12
"Viva Prado" (Kenton), **3:**797
"Viva Tirado" (Wilson), **3:**747–48
Vivaldi, Antonio, **8:**78, 658
  works adapted by Bach, **8:**91
Vivasāyi (film), **5:**542
"Vive la Canadienne," **3:**145
Viveka Cuḍāmaṇi (treatise), **5:**365
Vivekananda, Swami, **3:**130; **5:**462
Vives, Amadeo, **6:**449
Vives Guerra, Julio, **2:**395
Vivier, Claude, **3:**1076, 1151
Vixen, **3:**358
Vizūh al-arqām (Mir Möhsun Nəvvab), **6:**927
Vlaams Dansarchief, **8:**535
Vlach, Karel, **8:**730
Vlach people. *See* Vlah people
Vlach Roma, **8:**272
  instruments, **8:**198
  music of, **8:**274–76
Vladigerov, Pancho, **8:**905
Vladimirescu, Tudor, **8:**881
Vlahović, Joža, **8:**151–52
Vlah (also Vlach) people
  brass bands of, **8:**946
  dances of, **8:**947
  in Greece, **8:**1008, 1010, 1012, 1013
  instruments, **8:**950
  in Macedonia, **8:**972
  musical traditions of, **8:**949
  in Serbia, **8:**944, 945, 950
  in Slovenia, **8:**914
Vlasak, Rodney, **10:**140
Vocal Melodies of Scotland (Dun), **8:**373
Vocal Melodies of Scotland (Thomson), **8:**373
vocal music. *See also* ballads; carols and caroling; chant; devotional songs and singing; Hindustani tradition; hymns; Karnatak tradition; laments; love songs; lullabies; narratives; polyphony; popular music; popular songs; praise songs, singing, and poetry; psalmody; recitation; serenades; shanties; singing; songs; texts; work music; yodeling; *specific international genres such as balada, corridos*
  Abkhazian people, **8:**852–53
  Adighian people, **8:**854, 855–56

Afghanistan, **6**:301
  chahārbeiti (also *falak*), **5**:812–13, 819, 820,
    823, 828, 831, 835, 836
  felak, **6**:830
  folk genres, **5**:827–29
  kharābāt, **5**:828
  landay, **5**:813, 836
  mahali, **5**:819, 820
  women's genres, **5**:812–13
Africa
  choral music composers, **1**:230
  composed, **1**:24
  nomadic peoples, **1**:605
African-American, **3**:9, 592–93, 599–601, 639
  derisive singing, **3**:592, 600–601
Ainu people
  rimse, **7**:784–86
  sinotcha, **7**:786
  upopo, **7**:784–86
Aka people, **1**:267–69, 688–91
Akha people, **4**:541
Albania, **8**:118, 987–92, 994–95
Albanian-American, **3**:926, 928, 929
Algeria
  aiyāi, **6**:466
  'arūbī, **6**:472, 475
  mahjūs, **6**:1044
  qādriyya, **6**:473, 475
  sha'bī, **6**:275, 475–77
  women's genres, **6**:473
Aluku culture, **2**:438
Andalusian repertoire, **1**:534–35, 545; **6**:12
Andean regions
  harawi agricultural songs, **2**:215
  kh'ajhelo courtship songs, **2**:215
  north-south distinctions, **2**:223
Andhra Pradesh, collections of, **5**:891
Anlo-Ewe people, *agbadza*, **1**:391, 397
Antigua and Barbuda
  benna (also *bennah*), **2**:800
  calypso, **2**:800
Anuta
  choral, **9**:306–7
  genres of, **9**:857–60
Apache Indian groups, **3**:431
Arabian peninsula, **6**:657
  bedouin songs, **6**:649
  camel-driving songs, **6**:537
  fishermen's songs, **6**:649
  ghina' muwaqqa', **6**:538–39
  guffāl, **6**:698
  hazaj, **6**:696
  pearl-diving songs, **6**:10, 404, 546, 649,
    651, 657
  sawt, **6**:456, 651–52, 657, 698, 709
  sinād, **6**:696
  sung poetry, **6**:663–69
  women's songs, **6**:699–701
  zaghārīd, **6**:699
Arab-Islamic cultures, **6**:401, 402
Arctic peoples, **3**:375, 377–78
  personal songs, **3**:376, 1275; **7**:1028–29
  ridicule songs, **3**:377, 1275
Argentina, **2**:256, 258, 261
  protest songs, **2**:262
  Tierra del Fuego, **2**:250

Armenia
  folk songs, **6**:724, 727–31
  gusan, **6**:731–33
  habrban, **6**:729, *731–33*
  tagher, **6**:733, *734*
Ashanti people, **1**:89
Atacameño culture, *copla de carnaval*, **2**:361
Austral Islands, *hīmene* genres of, **9**:209, 871,
    881–82
Australia
  Aboriginal peoples, **9**:410–12
  a-kurija, **9**:428
  ancestral songs, **9**:355
  Arnhem Land, **9**:419
  bunggurl, **9**:423, 425
  Cape York *bora*, **9**:411, 429–30
  Central, **9**:434–39
  children's songs, **9**:256–57
  clansongs, **9**:243, 355–57, 394–95, 418,
    419–22, 429–30
  djanba, **9**:431, 453
  djatpangarri, **9**:420–21, 445
  djirri djirri, **9**:432
  Greek choirs, **9**:72
  Gulf of Carpentaria, **9**:427–28
  history songs, **9**:188, 428
  Hmong *kwv txiaj*, **9**:76–77
  Irish ballads, **9**:77–78
  jarrada, **9**:428
  jawala, **9**:428
  Kimberleys, **9**:431–32, *433*, 451
  kujika, **9**:428
  lildjin, **9**:356
  lirrga, **9**:355–56, 394–95, 423–27, 432,
    453
  malkarri, **9**:461
  manikai, **9**:423, 425
  men's *vs.* women's songs, **9**:243
  Mornington Island, **9**:430
  ritual wailing, **9**:421, *433*, 435
  Southeastern Aboriginal peoples, **9**:440–41
  Southeastern *yuwaay*, **9**:442
  Tasmania, **9**:440
  walaba, **9**:428
  wangga, **9**:243, *244*, 317, 355–56, 394–95,
    423–27, 431–32, 453–55
  Yanyuwa island songs, **9**:461
  yarrangijirri, **9**:428
  yawalyu, **9**:428
Austria
  Kärntnerlied, **8**:674
  Schlager, **8**:678–79
  Tyrol region, **8**:672–73
  Vierzeiler, **8**:673
  Wienerlied, **8**:673
Aymara culture, **2**:215, 223
  taquirari, **2**:361
Azerbaijan, **6**:931
Bahamas
  anthem, **2**:804
  goombay, **2**:806
  rhyming spiritual, **2**:804–5
Bali, **4**:731, 755–57
  cakapung, **4**:756–57
  gending sanghyang, **4**:758
  kecak (also *gamelan swara*), **4**:756, 758

kidung, **4**:755, 776
pantun, **4**:743
wayang jemblung, **4**:757
Balkan region, women's repertoires, **8**:194–96
Balkarian people, **8**:856–59
Balochistan, **5**:773–76, 778–79; **6**:881
Bangladesh, patriotic songs, **5**:858–59
Bantu peoples, choral music, **1**:763
Barbados
  British church music, **2**:819
  folk songs, **2**:817
  Protestant, **2**:817
Bashkir people, **8**:773
Basque region, **8**:311–14, 315
  choral, **8**:315
  Middle Ages, **8**:316
  old *vs.* new genres, **8**:121
Belarus, **8**:790–96
Belgium, *crâmignon* songs, **8**:522, 535
Bellona
  kananga, **9**:851
  ongiongi religious songs, **9**:849
  tau'asonga, **9**:849–50
Bengal
  ādhunik gīt, **5**:550, 854–55
  bāul, **5**:859–60
  bhātiāli, **5**:860
  bhāwāiyā, **5**:860
  devotional genres, **5**:844–48
  gambhīrā, **5**:860–61
  jhāpān, **5**:861
  jhumur, **5**:861–62
  patriotic songs, **5**:849–50, 852, 853–54,
    856–57
  polli gīt, **5**:550
  tappā, **5**:847
Berber people, **6**:300–301, 483–90
  ahiha, **6**:301
  amarg, **6**:301
  idebbalen, **6**:307
  izwirrign, **6**:479–82
bluegrass, **3**:161
Bolivia
  ipala, **2**:291
  saya, **2**:293, 297
  takipayanaku, **2**:291
Bongo people, **1**:570
Bontok people, **4**:914–15, 920
Bora Bora, *hīmene*, **9**:41
Borneo, **4**:825–28
  hymns, **4**:828
Bosnia-Hercegovina, **8**:958
  ganga, **8**:112, 964, *966*
  na bas, **8**:964
  rural genres, **8**:963–64
  sevdalinkd, **8**:959, 964–65, 968
  svatovska pjesma, **8**:958, 963
  urban styles, **8**:964–66
Bosnian-American, **3**:923
Brazil
  aboio, **2**:325, 328, 332, 347
  bendito, **2**:328
  brão, **2**:301
  canções praieiras, **2**:351
  cançoneta, **2**:334
  Candomblé ritual songs, **2**:342

vocal music, Brazil (*continued*)
  cantoria, **2:**324, 325–28
  chamego, **2:**332
  ciranda, **2:**346
  coco de embolada, **2:**327
  décima, **2:**349
  desafio, **2:**326–27, 349
  dupla singing, **2:**307–8, 319
  embolada, **2:**327, 349
  excelência, **2:**328
  folia de reis, **2:**312
  frevo-canção, **2:**337
  ladainha, **2:**346
  lundu, **2:**304
  maculelê, **2:**349–50
  modinha, **2:**304, 350
  pagode, **2:**351
  religious songs, **2:**324, 328–29, 330
  rezas, **2:**328
  samba-lenço, **2:**349
  style traits of, **2:**307
  toada, **2:**332–33
  toada de vaqueajada, **2:**328
  xaxado, **2:**332
Bribri culture, **2:**633–35
Brittany, **8:**552, 559, 561
Brunka and Teribe cultures, *saloma*, **2:**685
Bulgaria, **8:**891
  hajduk songs, **8:**899
  mass songs, **8:**905
  pripevki, **8:**900
  road music, **8:**897
  Rom people, **8:**283
  sedyanka songs, **8:**900, 901
  table songs, **8:**114, 891, 897
  use in world music recordings, **8:**225–26
Bulgarian-American, **3:**925
Burma, **4:**373–74
  bòle, **4:**395
  bwé, **4:**380, 381, 383, 384, 393
  coù, **4:**380, 381, 383, 384, 393–94, 397–98
  deiñ thañ, **4:**382
  moñ, **4:**382
  pa'pyoù, **4:**381, 394–95
  talaìñ, **4:**382
  thahcìñhkañ, **4:**381, 393
  yoùdayà, **4:**55, 229, 372, 380, 382, 393, 394–95
Burundi, **1:**198
Cabécar culture, **2:**633–35
California
  Native American gambling songs, **3:**414, 415
  Native American groups, **3:**371, 412–13, 415, 417
  southern Indian song cycles, **3:**417
Cambodian-American, **3:**1001
Canada
  English-language songs, **3:**1188–90
  French-language songs, **3:**1192–94
Caribbean
  décima, **2:**795–96
  sung rosary, **2:**795
Carriacou, **2:**868, 869, 871
Central Africa, **1:**674–76

Central Asia
  art songs, **6:**900
  Islamic ritual holiday songs, **6:**939, 940–42
  maqām, **6:**913–15
Chechen people, **8:**862–64
Chile
  cantos de ángeles, **2:**366
  contrapunto, **2:**366, 367
  copla, **2:**367
  cueca, **2:**368–70
  décima, **2:**365
  esquinazo, **2:**368
  nueva canción, **2:**32, 60, 81
  parabién, **2:**368
  religious genres, **2:**365–66
  romance, **2:**367
  salves, **2:**366
  tonada, **2:**367–68, 370–71
  tonada de velorio, **2:**368
  verso, **2:**367
China
  art songs, **7:**345–46
  Buddhist, **7:**312
  cantatas, **7:**346, 347, 384, 386–87
  ci, **7:**89, 129–30, 407
  collections of, **7:**132
  embellishment in, **7:**123
  folk songs, **7:**89, 149–56, 297–98, 339, 387–88, 413, 449
  haozi, **7:**150–51, 346, 384, 417
  hua er, **7:**92
  mass songs, **7:**346, 347, 359, 386–87
  northeastern minorities, **7:**518–19
  protest songs, **7:**380, 383, 384
  quotation songs, **7:**388
  revolutionary songs, **7:**140, 340, 341, 347, 359, 413, 417
  sanqu, **7:**132
  school songs, **7:**50, 353, 375, 380
  shan'ge, **7:**151–52, 153–54, 155, 489–90
  source materials on, **7:**129
  women's genres, **7:**403
  xianghege, **7:**88, 407
  xiaodiao, **7:**152, 155, 233–34
  xiaoqu, **7:**130
  yang'ge, **7:**385, 413
  yuequ, **7:**305
Chorotega culture, *mitote*, **2:**681
Chuuk
  genres of, **9:**734–36
  risky singing, **9:**178
Cirebon
  dikir, **4:**695–96
  Muslim, **4:**687
Colo people, **1:**569
Colombia
  African-derived traits, **2:**401
  alavado, **2:**403–4
  arrullo, **2:**403–4, 408–9
  bambuco, **2:**382–83, 385–89
  bambucos de protesta, **2:**388
  bunde, **2:**386–87, 395, 404
  chigualo, **2:**404
  copla, **2:**384, 389–90, 398, 400, 408
  décima, **2:**408
  fuga, **2:**403

  guabina, **2:**390–91
  joropo, **2:**394
  pasillo, **2:**391–92
  rajaleña, **2:**390
  romance, **2:**407
  vaquería, **2:**408
  zafra, **2:**407, 408–9
Cook Islands
  hīmene tārava, **9:**872
  Mangaia choral songs, **9:**330
  religious genres, **9:**897–98
  secular genres, **9:**896–97
  ūtē, **9:**178
Corsica, **8:**566–71
  barcaroles, **8:**570–71, 573
  brindisi, **8:**570–71
  laudi, **8:**574
  madrigali, **8:**570–71
  paghjelle, **8:**542, 566, 569, 569–70, 573
  polyvocal Latin liturgical songs, **8:**574
  tribbiera, **8:***22*, 567, *568*
Costa Rica
  alabado, **2:**698
  bomba, **2:**695–97
  game-playing songs, **2:**689–90
  retahila, **2:**695
  romance, **2:**695
  serenata, **2:**698
  son suelto (also *baile suelto*), **2:**698, *699*
  tambito, **2:**698, *700–701*
Croatia, **8:**926
  Dalmatia, **8:**929
  glagoljaška pjevanje, **8:**929
  klapa singing, **8:**149–50, 929, *930*, 936
  na bas, **8:**927–28, *928*, 931, 964
  novokomponirana narodna muzika, **8:**934, 935, 936
  ojkanje, **8:**927, *928*
  pismice, **8:**931
  romanse, **8:**934
  šlageri, **8:**934
  starogradske pjesme, **8:**934, 936
  treskavice, **8:**926
Croatian-American, **3:**921–22, 923
Cuba
  canción, **2:**831–32
  Catholic sacred music, **2:**836
  claves, **2:**832, 835
  criolla, **2:**832
  folkloric genres of, **2:**829
  guajira, **2:**832
  punto guajiro, **2:**833
  romance, **2:**823
  seguidilla, **2:**833
  tonada, **2:**833
Cuban-American, **3:**728–29
Cyprus, **8:**1029–30
Czechoslovakia, mass songs, **8:**729
Czech Republic, **8:**717–20
Dan people, **1:**466
Dei people, **1:**467
Delaware Big House songs, **3:**464
Denmark, **8:**451–53, 463–64
  singing games, **8:**459
Dinka people, **1:**569–70
Dominica
  bélé, **2:**841–42

chanté mas, **2:**843
responsorial, **2:**841
Dominican Republic
anthems, **2:**859
bachata, **2:**861
bolero, **2:**860
criolla, **2:**860
desafío, **2:**849
mediatuna, **2:**849, 853, 856
merengue, **2:**860
plena, **2:**851
romance, **2:**849, 856
salve, **2:**851, 853, 856–57
salve de pandero, **2:**857
Salve Regina, **2:**847–48, 856
sung rosary, **2:**847–49, 853, 856
tonada de toros, **2:**849, 856–57
vals, **2:**860
verso, **2:**849
Ecuador
jaway, **2:**425
llakichina, **2:**429–30
responsorial Passion song, **2:**419–20, *421*
sanjuan, **2:**428–29
sanjuanito, **2:**426–27, 430–31
Egypt
dawr, **6:**371, 547, 550, 551, 560, 569, 598
ghinnāwa, **6:**306
taqtuqa, **6:**548
ṭarab songs, **6:**170
El Salvador
bomba, **2:**711
parabién, **2:**709
ranchera, **2:**716, 719
England
fuguing tunes, **8:**328
west gallery church music, **8:**328, 333, 336
Estonia, **8:**491–93, 773
choral, **8:**495–96
Estonian-American, **3:**878
Europe
agricultural songs, **8:**4–5
Baroque, **8:**76–77, 79
Classical and Romantic periods, **8:**81, 82, 83
classification of, **8:**127
collections of, **8:**16–18
courtship and wedding songs, **8:**196
drone accompaniment for, **8:**9
enumerative songs, **8:**541
lyric songs, **8:**132–34
medieval songs, **8:**72–73
men's performance of, **8:**198
Middle Ages, **8:**69–73
music-hall songs, **8:**228
nonstrophic songs, **8:**127–31
polyphonic, **8:**134
recitative and aria, **8:**78, 79
recreational songs, **8:**141
Renaissance, **8:**73–76
song games, **8:**5
song genres, **8:**127–37
strophic songs, **8:**8
women's repertoires, **8:**194–97
Europe, Eastern, **8:**753

Fiji, **5:**613–14
cautal (also *faag*), **9:**93–94
cautāl (also *fāg*), **5:**613
gālī insult songs, **5:**614
Indian *filmi git*, **9:**94
Indian *galiya*, **9:**94
meke, **9:**161, 162, 774, 776–78, 780–81, 998
polotu, **9:**775–76
qawwali, **9:**782
religious genres, **9:**775–76
same, **9:**775, 779
sere ni cumu, **9:**161–62
sere ni vanua, **9:**781, *782*
taro, **9:**775, 779
vakalutuivoce, **9:**775
vakawelegone, **9:**263–65
wedding songs, **5:**614
Filipino *kundiman*, **3:**1025
Finland, **8:**475–78
rekilaulu, **8:**477–78, 480, 487
Rom people, **8:**289
runo (also *laulu*), **8:**114–15, 475–77, 480, 482, 487–88, 488
Finnish-American, **3:**873
Flores, **4:**792, 795–96
berasi, **4:**796
mbata, **4:**793
France, **8:**539–43
briolage, **8:**128, *540*, 542
cantiques, **8:**541
chanson de danse (also *chanson en laisse*), **8:**540–41, 547
chanson de geste, **8:**539–40
chansons à repouner, **8:**542
complainte, **8:**546
huchage, **8:**540
pont-neufs, **8:**548
popular song, **8:**208
Rom people, **8:**288
sirventes, **8:**550
work songs, **8:**540
French-American, **3:**855, 857
French Canadian, **3:**1136–37
voyageur songs, **3:**1075, 1163–64
French Guiana, Amerindian repertoires, **2:**435–36
Fulani people, **1:**451
Fur people, **1:**561
Gã people, **1:**102–5, 463
Garífuna (Garifuna) culture, **2:**672–73, 675, 733, 734
Gayo people, *didong Gayo*, **4:**605
Georgia, **8:**828–34, 843
church music in, **8:**843
kviria, **8:**835
lile, **8:**835
naduri, **8:***830*, 833
orovela, **8:**828
polyphony, **8:**843
riha, **8:**835
table songs, **8:**827, 830–33, 837
urban styles, **8:**842
zari, **8:**833
German-American, **3:**888, 889
German Democratic Republic, **8:**661–62

Germany
1400s through 1700s, **8:**652–55, 664
carnival songs, **8:**655
medieval, **8:**650–51, 664
Nazi songs, **8:**660
patriotic songs, **8:**655
students' songs, **8:**655
underground singing, **8:**661
workers' songs, **8:**659, 664
Ghana, **1:**7, 356–58
Goa, **5:**739–40, 741
Gogo people, choral music, **1:**638
Gola people, **1:**467
Great Basin Bear Dance songs, **3:**423–24
Great Britain, **8:**325
Great Lakes Indian groups, **3:**451, 455, 458
Greece
amanedhes, **8:**1014, 1015
andartika, **8:**1008
Crete, *mantinadhes*, **8:**118–20, 1015
dhimotika, **8:**206, 1008, 1017, 1018
Epirus, **8:**1010
improvised couplets, **8:**1025
Karpathos, *mantinadhes*, **8:**118, 120
ksenitias, **8:**1010
laika, **8:**1008, 1018–19, 1020–21, 1030, 1031
smyrneika, **8:**1020
table songs, **8:**114, 141, 285, 1013, 1015, 1016
Thrace, **8:**1013
tis kunias, **8:**1015
Greece, ancient, **8:**46
Greek-American, **3:**930, 931–32
Guadeloupe
léwòz, **2:**874–75
vèyé boukousou, **2:**875–76
Guam, *chamorrita*, **9:**744–45
Guaraní culture
guaú, **2:**202–3
koti-hú, **2:**202, 203
ñembo'e pöra, **2:**201
Guarijio culture, *tuburada* songs, **2:**553
Guatemala, *posada*, **2:**724
Guaymí culture
canto a la maraca, **2:**686, *687*
saloma, **2:**686
Gujarat
garbā, **5:**550, 624–28
khāṇḍana, **5:**274
lagna gīt, **5:**632
rās, **5:**550, 630
ṛitugīt, **5:**632
Gumuz people, **1:**564
Guyana, **2:**442, 447–48
African-derived practices, **2:**445
birahā, **5:**602
chowtal, **5:**600–601, 603
Indian genres, **5:**600–602
matkor, **5:**601, 603
mouran, **5:**601, 603
tān saṅgīt genre, **5:**602, 605
Hadendowa people, **1:**559–60
Haiti
cantique, **2:**795
priyè ginen, **2:**884

vocal music, Haiti (*continued*)
  secular songs, **2:**885
  Vodou songs, **2:**883–84
Hawai'i
  art song, **9:**923
  choral singing, **9:**276
  Filipino choirs, **9:**100
  Filipino *kundiman*, **9:**100
  hapa haole, **3:**1048; **9:**921–22
  hīmene, **9:**918–19
  hula ku'i, **3:**1048
  minyo, **9:**97
  Portuguese *desafio*, **9:**98
  Portuguese *fado*, **9:**98
  Puerto Rican *aguinaldo*, **9:**101, 103
  Sāmoan *mā'ulu'ulu*, **9:**104
  Tongan *hiva kakala*, **9:**104
Herero people, **1:**715
Himachal Pradesh, *gālī* insult songs,
  5:415
Hindustani genres, **5:**15, 162–86
Hmong-American, **3:**1003–4
Hmong people, **4:**551–52, 554–59
Honduras, Catholic religious genres, **2:**745
Hong Kong, popular songs, **7:**354–56
Hui people, **7:**461–62
Hungarian-American, **3:**908–9
Hungary, **8:**739–42, 773
  csárdás, **8:**273–74, 747
  hallgató, **8:**273
  keserves, **8:**740
  khelimaski djili, **8:**275
  kuplés, **8:**746
  loki djili, **8:**275
  magyar nóta, **8:**738, 745, 747
  old-style songs, **8:**737
  old *vs.* new genres, **8:**122, 738
  párosító, **8:**740
  strophic songs, **8:**131
  táncdalok, **8:**746
  virágének, **8:**737
Iceland, **8:**400–405
  tvísöngur, **8:**402–3, 407, 423
  vikivakalag, **8:**404
Ifugao people, **4:**919, 920
Igbo people, **1:**459
Ila people, **1:**711–12
India, **5:**19–20, 321–22, 351
  akam, **5:**509
  ākṣiptikā, **5:**35
  prabandha, **5:**33, 36, 163, 164, 250
  puṛam, **5:**509
  women's village traditions, **5:**414–16
Indo-Caribbean people, **2:**85–86
Ingush people, **8:**862–64
Innu dream-songs, **3:**1074
Inuit *katajjaq* (throat games), **3:**1063, 1275;
  7:786, 1030
Iran, **6:**23–24, 829–32
  Azerbaijani *havalar*, **6:**848–50
  radif and, **6:**73
  taṣnīf, **6:**137, 834, 863, 868
Iraq
  maqām, **6:**311–16
  pasta, **6:**569
  peste, **6:**312

Ireland, **8:**325, 378–82, 389–90
  caoine, **8:**128
  céilí, **8:**141, 388, 390
  contexts for, **8:**388
  macaronic songs, **8:**386
  parting songs, **8:**381
  range of, **8:**380
  Traveller songs, **8:**294–95
Irian Jaya, **9:**360, 583–89
  Abun people, **9:**360–61
  Abun *sukrot*, *sukne*, and *sukba*, **9:**589
  classification of, **9:**578, 580
  Eipo *dit*, **9:**593–94
  Eipo *mot*, **9:**592
  Ok *yase*, **9:**584
  Orya *boyo* and *kanang*, **9:**589
Irish-American, **3:**842, 843–44
Islamic views on, **4:**74
Israel, **6:**1017
  shirei erets Yisrael, **6:**262, 263, 264, 266,
    267, 1018–19, 1071, 1072
Italian-American, **3:**861
Italy, **8:**605–8, 609–13
  bei, **8:**610
  canti all'altalena, **8:**116
  canti carnascialeschi, **8:**608
  canti di questua, **8:**608–9
  canti lirico-monostrofici, **8:**605, 606–7
  canto a vatoccu, **8:**134, 607, 610, 611
  canto della passione, **8:**608–9
  frottolas, **8:**617
  laude spirituale, **8:**132, 607
  liscio, **8:**207
  madrigals, **8:**617
  minority repertoires, **8:**617
  modinha style, **8:**619
  Neapolitan song, **8:**604, 613, 614, 618
  nonliturgical religious songs, **8:**24
  stornelli, **8:**611
  tiir, **8:**610
  trallalero, **8:**134, 610
Jamaica
  baila, **2:**903
  Kumina prayer, **2:**903
  ring games, **2:**905, 906
  salo songs, **2:**902
  secular genres, **2:**904–6
  toasting genre, **2:**98; **3:**692–93, 694
Jammu and Kashmir, *hikat*, **5:**498
Japan
  Buddhist *ennen*, **7:**618
  Buddhist *hômonka*, **7:**618
  Buddhist *wasan*, **7:**611
  enka, **7:**722, 739–40, 747
  gunka, **7:**722
  hauta, **7:**688, 689, 692, 693, 716
  kakyoku, **7:**731
  kamigata nagauta, **7:**692
  kayôkyoku, **7:**746–47, 751
  kiyomoto, **7:**551
  kouta, **7:**688–89
  kouta eiga, **7:**751
  kumiuta, **7:**687–88, 691, 692, 696
  kyôgen utai, **7:**636
  min'yô (folk songs), **7:**569, 571, 599–604;
    10:102

  nagauta, **7:**551, 657, 659, 660, 671–74, 759
  popular songs, **7:**743–45, 746–47
  ryôka, **7:**722
  saibara, **7:**619, 622, 625
  saku mono, **7:**692, 693
  satuma biwa songs, **7:**648
  school songs, **7:**50, 51, 537, 627, 722
  sibai uta, **7:**692, 693
  sôga (also *enkyoku*), **7:**589, 617
  sôyoku, **7:**777–78
  tegoto mono, **7:**692, 693, 697, 716
  tukusi goto, **7:**687–88, 696, 698
  utai mono, **7:**692, 693
  uta orrasho (also *orasyo*), **7:**724, 756
  utazawa, **7:**688
  ziuta (*jiuta*), **7:**551, 673, 692–93, 758,
    777–78
  zokkyoku, **7:**688, 689, 720
  zokuyô, **7:**688, 689
  zyôruri mono, **7:**692, 693
Japanese-American, **3:**969
Java
  ada-ada, **4:**665
  Banyumas style, **4:**667
  gendhing kemanak, **4:**666
  genjiringan, **4:**646
  genres of, **4:**663–67
  jani-janèn, **4:**646
  jemblung, **4:**635
  jineman, **4:**666
  lagon, **4:**665
  lagu dolanan, **4:**653, 666, 667, 683, 684–85
  macapat, **4:**635, 654, 656, 663–64, 665,
    667
  pathetan, **4:**665
  qasidah, **4:**634
  sendhon, **4:**665
  slawatan, **4:**646
  sulukan, **4:**665–66
  tembang, **4:**632, 663–65
  tembang gedhé, **4:**663–64, 665
  tembang tengahan, **4:**663–64
Jewish people, **3:**131, 939, 942–43, 1173–74;
  8:252–57, 261
  haskalah, **8:**253
  ḥazanut, **6:**203–4
  Kol Nidre, **8:**250
  Lubavitcher Hasidim, **10:**127–28, 131–32
  multilingual, **6:**1043
  niggun, **6:**202; **8:**254–55, *255*
  nusah, **8:**253
  pizmon, **3:**513, 943; **6:**1020; **8:**255–56;
    10:69–75
  religious, **8:**249–51, 263–64
  secular, **8:**252
  shirei meshorerim, **6:**1020
  stanzl, **8:**251
Jola people, choral music, **1:**445
Judeo-Arabic songs, **6:**1041–42
Judeo-Spanish songs, **6:**202, 1017, 1036,
  1037, 1042
Kalinga people, **4:**920
Kalmyks, *ut dun*, **8:**772
Kapingamarangi, **9:**836–38
Karachaevian people, **8:**856–59
Karen people, **4:**544–45

Karnatak genres, **5:**209–35
Karnataka, **5:**868–74
  hogalikke, **5:**883
  lāvṇi, **5:**869–70
  madira, **5:**884
  pada genres, **5:**868–70
  sampradāya, **5:**867–68
  tatva, **5:**867, 869
  Tuluva genres, **5:**882–85
Kashmir
  chakri, **5:**682–84
  nande baeth, **5:**684–85
  nande chakri, **5:**685
  nāther, **5:**687
  rūf, **5:**498, 684
  ṣūfyāna mūsīqī, **5:**687
  wanawun, **5:**685
Kazakh people, **7:**460–61
Kazakhstan, **6:**950–56, 959–60
Kenya, **1:**622–23, 628–29
  choral music, **1:**629–30
Kenyah people
  kui, **4:**827
  lekupa, **4:**826
Kerala
  Christian genres, **5:**946–47
  māppiḷappaṭṭu, **5:**947
  nāṭōṭippāṭṭu, **5:**949–50
  paricappāṭṭu, **5:**948
  sōpānam saṅgītam, **5:**230–31, 363, 931,
    934, 940
  uṟaccal tōṟṟam, **5:**287
Khmer people
  ayai genre, **4:**23, 202, 532
  chariang, **4:**215
  chrieng chapey, **4:**155, 161, 171, 202, 238
  jariang, **4:**214
  religious genres, **4:**206–7
  in Vietnam, **4:**215
Kiribati
  choral singing, **9:**760
  genres of, **9:**762
  kuaea and *maie* genres, **9:**365, 761–62
Kmhmu people, **4:**546–47
Kogi culture, **2:**185–87
Korea
  akchang, **7:**818, 820
  chapka, **7:**819, 885–86
  folk songs, **7:**818–20, 844, 849, 850–51,
    879–88, 987–88
  hoesimgok, **7:**871
  kagok, **7:**807, 818, 820, 822, 842, 845,
    849, 866, 903, 919–24, 951–52, 956,
    988–89
  kayagŭm pyŏngch'ang, **7:**895, 899, 907–8,
    909–11, 986, 988
  kugak kayo, **7:**969–73
  san yŏmbul (also *san t'aryŏng*), **7:**984
  Shimch'ŏngga, **7:**986
  sijo, **7:**807, 817, 818, 820, 866, 886, 919,
    921–22, 924–27
  Sŏdo sori repertoire, **7:**961, 988
  sŏnsori, **7:**819, 885–86
  tan'ga, **7:**897, 905, 908
  tongyo, **7:**951–52, 972
  yuhaengga, **7:**951–52

Kosrae, **9:**741–42
  choral, **9:**729, 743
Kpelle people, **1:**131
Kru people, **1:**371, 380
Kuna culture, **2:**639, 645–47
Kurdistan, **6:**746–51
Kwakiutl Winter Ceremony songs, **3:**400–401
Lacandón Maya, **2:**656–57
Lahu people, **4:**540
Lao-American, **3:**952, *1007–8*
Laos, **4:**18, 340–52
Latvia, **8:**499–503
  dievturīc neopagan movement songs, **8:**505
  līgotnes, **8:**501
  vāķu rotaḷas, **8:**502
  ziņģes, **8:**504
Latvian-American, **3:**877
Lhoba people, **7:**482
Libya, *'alam*, **6:**306
Lifou *wejein*, **9:**684
Lisu people, **4:**543
Lithuania, **8:**509–11
  choral, **8:**512–14
  daina, **8:**131
  sutartinė, **8:**510
Lithuanian genres, **3:**875–76
Lombok, **4:**763, 774–76
  tembang Sasak, **4:**769, 775
  zikrzamman, **4:**776, *777*
Louisiana, Afro-Creole, **3:**600
Low Countries, **8:**518–23
Lozi people, **1:**713
Luvale people
  choral music, **1:**726–43
  kukuwa, **1:**725–41
Macedonia, **8:**954, 973–74
  novokompanovani narodni pesni, **8:**980
  pečalbarski pesni, **8:**973
  Rom people, **8:**282
  soborski pesni, **8:**974
  starogradski pesni, **8:**980, 981, 983
Macedonian-American, **3:**925–26
Madagascar
  choral music, **1:**783, 791
  hira-tsangana, **1:**789
  zafindraona, **1:**791
Madhya Pradesh, women's songs, **5:**723
Maguindanao people, *sangel*, **4:**911
Maharashtra
  bhāvgīt, **5:**730
  folk genres, **5:**727–28
  koli, **5:**550
  lāvni, **5:**550
  pad, **5:**162, 643
  popat, **5:**550
Makah Indian nation, **3:**399
Malaysia
  dikir barat, **4:**424, 425–26
  lagu-lagu rakyat, **4:**439–40, 442
  work songs, **4:**422–23
  zikir, **4:**409, 424, 431, 825
Maleku culture, *curijurijanapuretec*, **2:**682
Malta, **8:**635–39
  bormliza, **8:**637
  ghana, **8:**198, 635, 638–39, 640–41, 642
  kanzunetta, **8:**638–39, 642

  makkjetta, **8:**638–39, 642
  spirtu pront, **8:**636–37, 639, 640
Maluku, **4:**813, 816, 819–20
  tutohato, **4:**819
Manding people, **1:**444
Mangareva
  akamagareva, **9:**208–9, 889
  akatari pe'i, **9:**886, 888
  kapa, **9:**886, 888
  tagi, **9:**886, 888
Manihiki, **9:**905, 907–9
Māori people, **9:**277
  mōteatea, **9:**938–44
  waiata tawhito genre, **9:**933–34
Mapuche culture, **2:**366
  kantún, **2:**236
  öl, **2:**236
  purrum, **2:**254
  tayil, **2:**233, 234–35, 236–37, 254
Maranao people
  bayok, **4:**910
  kandurangen, **4:**908
  kapamelo-malong, **4:**909–10
Mariana Islands, *kantan chamorrita*, **9:**158
Maritime Provinces, **3:**1123–24, 1125, 1127,
  1129
Maroon cultures, *sêkêti*, **2:**506
Marquesas Islands, **9:**890–94
Marshall Islands, **9:**749–50, *751*
Martinique, *kadans*, **2:**917
Mashriq, **6:**537
Maya culture
  bix rxin nawal, **2:**731
  ritual songs, **2:**652
Mende people, **1:**467
Métis, **3:**344, 410–11
Mexican-American, **3:**723–25, 736–38, 755
Mexico
  balada, **2:**623
  bambuco, **2:**613
  canción ranchera, **2:**101, 620–21, 622
  canción romántica, **2:**619, 620
  copla, **2:**606
  gusto, **2:**611
  son jalisciense, **2:**612–13
  valona, **2:**611–12
Micronesia, **9:**716, 719
Middle East, **6:**5–7
Middle Eastern, medieval, **6:**11, 396–97,
  398–99
Miri people, **1:**562
Miskitu culture
  kitarlawana, **2:**663
  tiun, **2:**660, 663, *664*
Mithila, women's songs, **5:**677–78
Mixtec culture, *katikubi*, **2:**567
Moinba people, **7:**482
Mongolia, *urtyn duu*, **8:**772
Mongol people, **7:**1006–10
  besreg, **7:**1007
  bogino duu, **7:**1007
  holboo (also *qolbuga*), **7:**1004
  höömii (overtone singing), **7:**1005,
    1009–10, 1024–25
  ikil accompaniment of, **7:**1011, 1014
  incantations, **7:**1008–9

vocal music, Mongol people (*continued*)
   shastir daguu (long-songs), **7:**1016
   urtyn duu (long-songs), **7:**1004, 1005, 1006–7
  Montenegro, **8:**957–59, 961
   klapa singing, **8:**959
   novokomponovana narodna muzika, **8:**961
  Montserrat, folk songs, **2:**923
  Mordvinian people, **8:**773
  Morocco
   ahellil, **6:**484
   Berber, **6:**483–89
   ladkar, **6:**484, 485–86
   malhun, **6:**495–500
   naqus antiphonal songs, **6:**303
   san'ā, **1:**534–35; **6:**456, 458–59, *460*, 461, 463
   tamdyazt and *izli*, **6:**489
   tazrrart responsorial songs, **6:**303
  Native American, **3:**5
   49ers, **3:**213, 425
   basic features, **3:**6, 367–68, 526
   Ghost Dance songs, **3:**371, 421–22, 480, 487
   nonceremonial, **3:**371
   peyote songs, **3:**487
  Nauru, **9:**755
  Navajo *yei* songs, **3:**432
  Naxi people, **7:**510
  Nepal
   chuḍke, **5:**701
   dohori gīt, **5:**701
   Gāine song repertoire, **5:**698
   Guruñg people, **5:**704–5
   jhyāure, **5:**701
   women's genres, **5:**702
  New Caledonia, **9:**672–74
   Grande Terre, **9:**675–79
   Loyalty Islands work songs, **9:**684
   Maré *waueng*, **9:**684
   Ouvéa *seloo*, **9:**684
   two-part songs, **9:**681
  New England, indoor *vs.* outdoor repertoire, **3:**157
  Newfoundland, fishing moratorium songs, **3:**1138–43
  New Mexican Hispano genres, **3:**756–57
  Nguni people, choral music, **1:**719
  Nicaragua
   canciones románticas, **2:**766
   purísimas, **2:**762–63
   romance, **2:**758, 767
   sones de pascua, **2:**763
  Nigeria
   1800s, **1:**93
   choral music, **1:**235, 236
   Niger Delta region, **1:**103
  Niue, **9:**817
  Nkoya people, **1:**713
  North Africa, **1:**541–42
   zendani, **1:**546
  North Korea
   folk songs, **7:**961
   revolutionary songs, **7:**960–61
  Northeast Indian groups, **3:**463

Northwest Coast Indian groups
  song ownership, **3:**394–95
  song types, **3:**395, 401–2
Norway, **8:**412–14
  kveðing, **8:**426
  sæter songs, **8:**412
  slåttestev, **8:**412
  tralling, **8:**421, 422
Norwegian-American, **3:**866–67
Nubian people, **1:**557, 558
Oceania
  categorizing, **9:**321
  choral, **9:**27–28
  commemorative songs, **9:**32–33
  drinking songs, **9:**321
  epigrammatic songs, **9:**331–32
  performing processes in, **9:**320–21
  songs of dissent, **9:**354–55
  war-era songs, **9:**28–32
Oman, *ghinā'*, **6:**677
Orissa
  folk and devotional genres, **5:**732–34
  tribal, **5:**732
Ossetian people, **8:**859–61
Otopame culture, **2:**571–72
Ovimbundu people, **1:**714
Pakhtun people, **5:**786
Pakistan
  chogān, **5:**761
  Iqbaliat, **5:**746
Palau, **9:**723–25
  matmatong marching songs, **9:**724
  Tobi Island, **9:**182
Palestine
  wedding songs, **6:**579–92
  zaghārīd, **6:**573, 575
Palikur culture, **2:**435
Panama, **2:**779–81
  décima, **2:**772, 777, 780
  gritos, **2:**773, 780–81
  responsorial singing, **2:**778
  saloma, **2:**772, 780
Papua New Guinea, **9:**23
  Abelam people, **9:**549, 550
  Amanab *yaubug*, **9:**331
  Angan people, **9:**497
  Baining choral music, **9:**189
  Bali and Vitu, **9:**608–11
  Baluan, **9:**603–4, 605
  Banoni people, **9:**644–47
  Buang people, **9:**566–67
  Buin people, **9:**650–53
  Buka and Bougainville, **9:**630
  Eastern Highlands, **9:**302–3, 527–30
  Enga people, **9:**534–35
  Foi *sorohabora*, **9:**246–47
  gospel choirs, **9:**153
  Highlands region, **9:**513–14
  Huli people, **9:**537–40
  Huli yodeling signals, **9:**298–99, 478
  Iatmul *mariuamangĭ*, **9:**554
  Iatmul *namoi* clansongs, **9:**546
  Iatmul recreational songs, **9:**556
  Iatmul *sagi*, **9:**557
  Kaluli *gisalo*, **9:**189
  kanam, **9:**546

  Karkar *nonkor*, **9:**560–61
  Kaulong people, **9:**617–19
  Komba people, **9:**571–72
  Mali Baining people, **9:**192
  Managalasi *itiuri*, **9:**503–5
  Manam people, **9:**245
  Maring people, **9:**514–15
  Mekeo people, **9:**491
  Melpa *amb kenan*, **9:**516–18, 522
  Melpa *kang rom*, **9:**521–22
  Melpa *mölya* (also *mörli*), **9:**520, 522
  Mengen *kangaole*, **9:**622
  Middle Sepik clansongs, **9:**545
  Motu people, **9:**492–93
  Nagovisi *ko:ma*, **9:**648
  New Britain, **9:**621, 622–23
  Nissan, **9:**633–39
  Papuan region, **9:**491
  peroveta, **9:**88, 153, 187, 194–95, 494
  Rai Coast, **9:**564–65
  Roro people, **9:**491
  Rossel Island, **9:**491
  Sursurunga people, **9:**626–27
  Teop *siguru*, **9:**642–44
  Umboi, **9:**574
  Waxei people, **9:**558–60
  Yupno people, **9:**303–4
  Yupno personal melodies, **9:**545
Paraguay, **2:**457–60, 462
Pennsylvania, Ephrata Cloister, **3:**905–6
Peru
  Amazonian region, **2:**482
  amor fino, **2:**495
  coplas, **2:**481
  cumanana, **2:**495
  décima, **2:**495
  harawi (also *haraui*), **2:**468, 476
  hatajos de negritos, **2:**494–95
  haylli, **2:**468, 476
  huaylas, **2:**476
  huayno, **2:**477, 484
  kashwa (also *cachiua*), **2:**468, 476–77
  marinera, **2:**481
  pregones, **2:**495
  santiago, **2:**476
  triste, **2:**477, 495
  walina, **2:**478
  wanka (also *uanca*), **2:**468, 476
  yaraví, **2:**477, 495
Philippines
  awit, **4:**853, 855
  badiw, **4:**878, 920
  balitaw, **4:**851
  baqat, **4:**908
  bayok, **4:**908, *909*
  belayson, **4:**851
  bensidoray, **4:**851
  bensiranay (also *banggi*), **4:**850
  Catholic, **4:**841–45
  children's songs and lullabies, **4:**910–11
  Christian, **4:**842–45
  composo, **4:**853
  Cordillera highlands, **4:**920
  daigon (also *dayegon*; *daygon*), **4:**843
  dalit, **4:**847
  dikil (also *dikir*), **4:**907

dotok, **4**:851
duaya, **4**:849
duldang-duldang, **4**:909
dung-aw, **4**:851
entertainment songs, **4**:909–10
exhortations, **4**:910
harana, **4**:849–50
huluna, **4**:849
inarem, **4**:851
inikamen, **4**:851
insiglot, **4**:851
Islamic communities, **4**:906–11
jamiluddin, **4**:908
kapranon, **4**:908–9
karansa, **4**:852
kumintang (also *komintang*), **4**:850, 851, 871
kundiman, **4**:855, 871, 881, 883, 884
le'le', **4**:902
leleng, **4**:909
lunsey, **4**:908
malahiya, **4**:852
musical styles, **4**:928
nahana, **4**:908
pabula, **4**:852
paghiling, **4**:850
pamamaalam, **4**:850
pananapat, **4**:845
pananapatan (also *pagtawag*; *pagpapakilala*), **4**:850
pandanggo, **4**:852
pasasalamat, **4**:850
pastores, **4**:842–43
popular songs, **4**:884–86
pulao, **4**:851
sa-il, **4**:908
secular, **4**:849–53
sindil, **4**:908
subli, **4**:848
talalay, **4**:852
tambora, **4**:843
tenes-tenes, **4**:909
turba, **4**:851
Piaroa culture, *mène*, **2**:525
Plains Indian groups, **3**:445, 448
   Flag Songs, **3**:368, 447, 481, 483
   gambling songs, **3**:1087
   Ghost Dance songs, **3**:509
   powwow songs, **3**:368–69
   War Dance songs, **3**:483–84
Pohnpei, **9**:739–40
Poland, **8**:701–4
   categories of, **8**:113–14
   "open-air" songs, **8**:113–14
   przyśpiewka, **8**:703
   wiskanie, **8**:702
Polynesia, **9**:768–69, 865
Polynesian outliers, **9**:836
Portugal, **8**:578–79, 581
   canção de intervenção, **8**:584–85
   modas, **8**:578–79
   modinha, **8**:583
Portuguese-American, **3**:731, 848, 851, 1197
Pueblo Indian groups, **3**:429
Puerto Rico
   décima, **2**:937–38

religious, **2**:933
rosario cantao, **2**:793, 935–36
seis, **2**:938–39
Pukapuka, **9**:911–13
   amu, **9**:912
   hīmene genres, **9**:913
   īmene tuki, **9**:910
   pātautau, **9**:912–13
Punjab (India)
   ahaniāṅ, **5**:655
   birahā, **5**:655
   boliyāṅ, **5**:651
   ḍholā, **5**:655
   giddhā, **5**:654, 656
   mahiāṅ, **5**:654–55
   siṭṭhṇī insult songs, **5**:653
Punjab (Pakistan), secular genres, **5**:771–72
Purépecha culture, *alabanza*, **2**:578
Q'ero culture, **2**:226–27, 229–30
Quechua culture, **2**:205, 214–15, 223
Quichua culture, women's songs, **2**:429–30
Rajasthan
   choṭā gīt, **5**:642
   gālī insult songs, **5**:642, 645, 646, 648
   keśyā, **5**:277, 645
   khyāl (folk song genre), **5**:645
   māṅd, **5**:642
   moṭā gīt, **5**:642
   swing songs, **5**:645–46
Rapa Nui, **9**:951–52
Romania, **8**:869, 872–74, 879–80
   cîntece, **8**:872, 874
   cîntece de mahala, **8**:277
   doina, **8**:9, 278, 872–73, 879, 882
   hora lunga, **8**:128, *129*, 873
   ideological, **8**:884–85
   paparuda, **8**:196, 278
   workers' songs, **8**:874
Romanian-American, **3**:911, 912
Rotuma
   tautoga, **9**:819, 821–22
   temo praise songs, **9**:820
Russia, **8**:755–69
   after-ski songs, **8**:767
   avtorskie pesni (guitar songs), **8**:767–68, 778
   calendrical songs, **8**:24, 758–61
   chastushki, **8**:6–7, 134, 761, 768, *769*, 770, 779
   draznilki, **8**:761
   dukhovnyi stikh, **8**:123
   kant, **8**:755, 767, *768*, 780
   kupalskie pesni, **8**:760
   lyric songs, **8**:765–67
   maslenitsa, **8**:759, *760*
   noviny, **8**:130
   podbliudnye pesni, **8**:759
   protiazhnaia pesnia, **8**:9, 133, 756, 765
   religious, **8**:779
   Rom people, **8**:287
   soldatskie pesni (soldiers' songs), **8**:765, 767
   stradaniia ("cruel romances"), **8**:765, 776
   tolochnye pesni, **8**:760
   viunishnye pesni, **8**:760
   volochebnye pesni, **8**:760
   wedding genres, **8**:761

Russian-American, **3**:915, 939
Russian Old Believers, **3**:917–18
Ryûkyû Islands
   Amami folk songs, **7**:791
   Amami *sima uta*, **7**:795
   folk songs, **7**:790, 794–95
   kageki, **7**:790
   mukasi busi, **7**:790, 793
   ni age, **7**:793
   uta sansin, **7**:792
Saami people
   joiks (also *juigos*; *juoigan*), **8**:96, 117, 143, 299–307, 447, 487, 488
   lev'dd, **8**:486, 488
St. Lucia
   bélè, **2**:948–49
   chanté abwè, **2**:947
   chanté siay, **2**:946–47
   jwé chanté, **2**:943
   kont, **2**:948
   koutoumba, **2**:948–49
   for La Rose and La Marguerite societies, **2**:946
Sama people, **4**:911
Sama-Bajao people, *duldang-duldang*, **4**:900, *901*
Sāmoa, **9**:796
   'ailao, **9**:801–2
   choral, **9**:797, 807–8
   palo, **9**:804–5
   political songs, **9**:215–19
   soa, **9**:802–3
   sula, **9**:801–2
   tagi, **9**:799
Sāmoan-American, **9**:117
San people, **1**:704–5
Santal people, *dasae*, **5**:471
Sardinia
   canto a chiterra, **8**:627, 629–30, 632
   duru-duru, **8**:631
   polyphony, **8**:632
   a tenore, **8**:627, *628*, 630, 632
Saudi Arabia
   dewīnih, **6**:652–53, 657
   ḥijāzī style, **6**:655, 657
   sāmirī, **6**:653, 657
   zagharīd, **6**:691, 692, 693
Scotland, **8**:369–70
   bothy songs, **8**:296–97, 365, 373
   choral singing, **8**:371
   Hebridean Islands, **8**:360–63
   Highlands, **8**:360–63, 373
   Lowlands, **8**:365, 373
   Northern Isles, **8**:365
   Traveller songs, **8**:296–97
   vernacular songs, **8**:367–68
   women's songs, **8**:373
Selk'nam culture, **2**:251
Serbia, **8**:940–42
   astalske pesme, **8**:952
   Kosovo, *talava* genre, **8**:286
   lazaričke pesme, **8**:941
   na bas, **8**:942–43, *944*, 949, 950, 952, 964
   na glas, **8**:942, *943*
   novokomponovana narodna muzika, **8**:279, 948–49, 950, 951

Volume Key: **6**, Middle East; **7**, East Asia; **8**, Europe; **9**, Australia and the Pacific Islands; **10**, The World's Music.

vocal music, Serbia (*continued*)
    starogradske pjesme, **8**:948
    Vojvodina, **8**:114, 952
Serbian-American, **3**:921–22, 923
Shakers, **3**:135
Shan people, **4**:548
Shona people, **1**:710, 749–50, 752–54
    choral music, **1**:755
Shoshone Naraya songs, **3**:421, 487
Siberia
    personal songs, **7**:1028–29
    throat-singing, **7**:1030
Sicily, *canzuna*, **8**:606, *612*
Sikaiana, concepts of, **9**:845–48
Sindh
    maulūd, **5**:278
    waī, **5**:754
Singapore
    dondang sayang, **4**:522
    xinyao, **4**:519
Slovak-American, **3**:899
Slovakia, **8**:717–20
Slovenia, **8**:911–14
    tepežnice, **8**:912
Solomon Islands
    'Are'are people, **9**:667
    Baegu people, **9**:668–69
    Bellonese songs, **9**:324–25
    Blablanga songs, **9**:657, 658–59
    Fataleka people, **9**:668–69
    Guadalcanal, **9**:665
    Isabel Province, **9**:660–61
    Russell Islands, **9**:664
    Santa Cruz choirs, **9**:332–35
    Savo, **9**:666
    Shortland Islands, **9**:656
    Sirovanga people, **9**:654–55
Songhai people, **1**:450
Sotho peoples, **1**:707
South Africa, **1**:218–19
    imusic, **1**:770
    ingoma ebusuku, **1**:764, 772
    isiZulu, **1**:770
    makwaya, **1**:433, 718, 755, 763–64, 765, 769–70
    mbholoho, **1**:764
    ukureka, **1**:770
South America, tropical-forest region, **2**:128
South Asian (East Indian), **3**:950, 1246–47
    birha, **3**:814
    chowtal, **3**:815
    instrument accompaniment of, **5**:347
    light-classical genres, **3**:983, 987
    medieval song, **5**:40–41
    tan-singing, **3**:815
    women's songs, **3**:814
Southeast Asia
    island regions, **4**:597
    modal organization, **4**:381–85
    rural, **4**:7
    upland peoples, **4**:538
Southeast Indian groups, **3**:467
southern Africa, choral music, **1**:227, 433
Spain, **8**:589–93
    aguinaldos, **8**:590
    ánimas, **8**:591

auroras, **8**:590
cantares de ayuda, **8**:590
cante chico, **8**:597
cante intermedio, **8**:597
cante jondo, **8**:134, 591, 593, 596, 597
    for carnival and Lent, **8**:589–91
    Christmas music, **8**:589
cuplé flamenco, **8**:598
exvotos, **8**:591
gozos (also *goigs*), **8**:591
nueva canción andaluza, **8**:204, 205
ramos, **8**:591
rogativas, **8**:591
romances, **2**:57, 618, 744
romerías, **8**:591
rondas, **8**:590, 592, 596
seguidilla, **8**:592, *592*, 593, 601
villancico, **2**:494–95
Spanish-American, **3**:9, 13, 16, 522, 757–59, 848, 849, 850
    cante jondo, **3**:731, 851
    décima, **3**:757, 848, 849
    entriega, **3**:758–59
    polca, **3**:522
    trovo, **3**:757–58
Sri Lanka, **5**:959–60
    anistippuva, **5**:963
    bali, **5**:962
    sindu, **5**:958, 966
    tovil, **5**:959
    vannam, **5**:960
Subanun people, **4**:927
Subarctic peoples
    gambling songs, **3**:387, 1276, 1280
    personal songs, **3**:386
    song ownership, **3**:386
Sudanese Arabs, **1**:560
Sudan, urban, **1**:571–72
Sufi brotherhoods, *madā'iḥ w-adhkār*, **6**:437
Sulawesi
    for funerals, **4**:807
    kambori, **4**:806
    kasidah, **4**:806
Sumatra
    badikier (*zikir*), **4**:628
    bagurau, **4**:611
    Basemah, **4**:623
    bertale, **4**:617
    berzanzi, **4**:628
    budindang, **4**:628
    dampeng, **4**:607
    dana, **4**:625
    dedeng, **4**:606
    dendang, **4**:611, 620, 621
    dendang riang, **4**:620
    dendang sayang gecik, **4**:620
    dendang sayang mundur, **4**:620
    diki Mauluk, **4**:611
    gambus Arab, **4**:628
    ghazal, **4**:616
    hadrah, **4**:606, 616, 621, 625, 628
    hazrah, **4**:616
    hikayat, **4**:606
    hoho, **4**:608
    indang, **4**:612–13
    kasidah, **4**:612, 625

lagu rebana, **4**:616
langgam Melayu, **4**:613
ma'inang, **4**:620, 628
marhaban, **4**:606
matap, **4**:618
Maulud Nabi, **4**:616
Minangkabau people, **4**:611
Muslim, **4**:605
nasit, **4**:612
qasidah, **4**:606
rangguk, **4**:617
ratap, **4**:619
ratok, **4**:611
redep, **4**:605
rejong, **4**:623
ringit, **4**:623
sadiah, **4**:611
salawek dulang, **4**:611–12
seudati, **4**:604
sikambang, **4**:607, 613
sike, **4**:617
sinandung, **4**:605, 606
tale gotong royong, **4**:618
tale naik haji, **4**:617
talibun, **4**:621
zikir, **4**:604, 616, 625, 626
Sumba, **4**:788, 790–91
Sumbawa, **4**:763, 782–83, 784
Sumu culture, collective singing, **2**:751
Sunda
    beluk, **4**:701
    cigawiran, **4**:701
    kawih, **4**:717
    lagu, **4**:713
    lagu-lagu nostalgia, **4**:718
    lagu rakyat, **4**:701
    mamaos, **4**:714
    panambih, **4**:714, 715
Surinam
    aleke, **2**:509
    Amerindian traditional songs, **2**:504
    kawina, **2**:508
Suyá culture, **2**:144–49
Sweden, **8**:435–36
Swedish-American, **3**:870–71
Switzerland, **8**:682–83, 690–95
    betruf, **8**:128
    Kühreihen (*ranz des vaches*), **8**:17, 128, 683
    löckler, **8**:683
    lyóba, **8**:119
    pastourelles, **8**:693–94
    political songs, **8**:694
    religious songs, **8**:692
    schnitzelbänke, **8**:685
Syria, *mawwāl*, **6**:566–67
Tahiti
    'aparima hīmene, **9**:877
    choral, **9**:869–73
    hīmene, **9**:37–38, 998
    hīmene nota, **9**:870
    hīmene pōpa'a, **9**:873
    hīmene puta, **9**:870, 873
    hīmene rū'au, **9**:870–71, 873
    hīmene tārava, **9**:308, 871–72, 873
    hīmene tuki, **9**:872, 873

Taino culture, **2:**846
  areito, **2:**13, 22
Taiwan
  Aboriginal peoples, **7:**523–24
  Hengchun folk songs, **7:**424
  shange, **7:**427
Tajikistan
  felak, **6:**830
  maqām, **6:**913–15
Takuu
  fula, **9:**841
  sau, **9:**841–42
  tuki, **9:**839–41
Tamil Nadu, **5:**916–21
  cintu, **5:**920, 958, 966
  karakam, **5:**277
  kāvaṭi cintu, **5:**921
  keśyā, **5:**277
  kōlāṭṭam, **5:**918, 920
  kummi, **5:**284, 918, 919–20, 925
  kuravai, **5:**908
  lāvṇi, **5:**908
  noṇṭi cintu, **5:**920–21
  ōṭam, **5:**518
  oyilāṭṭam, **5:**917, 918, 919–20, 925
  swing songs, **5:**275, 910
  Tamil-language, **5:**912
  temmāṅgu pāṭṭu, **5:**556, 925
  tiruppāvai, **5:**274, 918
  tiruvempāvai, **5:**274, 918
  uñjal, **5:**518
  uṭukkai pāṭṭu, **5:**556, 908
  villuppāṭṭu, **5:**368, 401, 556, 907, 908
  wedding songs, **5:**275
Tarahumara culture
  matachín, **2:**583
  tutuguri, **2:**585
Tatar people, *ozyn-kyi*, **8:**773
Tausug people
  hadis tradition, **4:**911
  langan bataq-bataq, **4:**910–11
Tehuelche culture, **2:**251
Temiar people, **4:**572, 577–78, 579–85
Temne people, **1:**468
Thailand
  joi, **4:**313
  popular songs, **4:**331–33
  saw, **4:**313
  village songs (*phleng pün ban*), **4:**222, 229,
    298–301
Tibet
  drinking songs, **7:**477
  duolu, **7:**480–81
Tibetan culture, **5:**709–11
  dbyangs-yig, **5:**13, 713
  gzhas, **5:**710–11
  nang-ma, **5:**710, 715
  stod-gzhas, **5:**710, 715
Tikar people, *nswē*, **1:**658
Tikopia, **9:**853
  song structures, **9:**330–31
  tauāngutu, **9:**247
Tiruray people, **4:**927
Tokelau
  fātele, **9:**354, 825–26, 827
  hiva hahaka, **9:**824, 827

mako, **9:**354
māuluulu, **9:**827
pehe lagilagi, **9:**825–26
tagi, **9:**827
Tokelauan *fātele*, **9:**113
Tonga
  fa'ahiula, **9:**791–92
  history songs, **9:**201–2
  hiva kakala, **9:**130, 131, 313, 365, 366–67,
    787, 793, *794*
  lakalaka, **9:**365, 367–68, 783, 789
  mā'ulu'ulu, **9:**789–90
  me'etu'upaki, **9:**309, 790–91
  polyphonic, **9:**784
  tau'a'alo work songs, **9:**786–87
Tongan-American, **9:**117
Tonga people (of Africa), **1:**711–12
Torres Strait Islands
  malu-bomai, **9:**429
  microtonal wailing, **9:**429
  wed, **9:**429
Trinidad and Tobago
  calypso, **2:**963–64
  cautāl, **5:**590
  'doption singing, **2:**957–58
  fandang, **2:**953
  historical genres, **2:**953
  Indian, **2:**958–59
  lining out, **2:**957
  Sango calling song, **2:**955, *956*
  South Asian community, **5:**588–89
  spiritual shouts, **2:**957–58
  trumpets, **2:**957–58
  veiquoix, **2:**953
Trobriand Islands, **9:**491, 498–99
Tsonga people, **1:**710
Tuamotu Islands, **9:**884–85
Tuareg people, **1:**592–93
  azel, **1:**578
  children's, **1:**593
  tesîwit, **1:**579–81
Tunisia, **6:**452
  Jewish women's songs, **6:**525
  mattanza, **6:**435
Turkey
  Alevi, **6:**795–96
  art genres, **6:**113, 115, 116–18, 120,
    122–26, 773, 779–80
  divan, **6:**806–7
  folk genres, **6:**80–81, 759–63, 765–66, 768
  Iranian forms, **6:**120
  kırık hava, **6:**79–80, 759–61
  Sufi, **6:**189–97
  twentieth-century, **6:**781–87
  uzun hava, **6:**80–81, 761–62, 763
Tuva, **7:**1024–25
  uzun yry, **6:**981, 984–85
Tuvalu
  choral, **9:**829
  fātele, **9:**762, 831
  genres of, **9:**830
  vīki, **9:**831
Uighur people, **7:**458–60
Ukraine, **8:**766, 806–9
  "begging recitations," **8:**816
  hutsul'ka do spivu, **8:**813

perepelka, **8:**808
psal'my, **8:**813, *814*, 816, 819, 822
Soviet period, **8:**818, 821
vesnianky, **8:**808
Ukrainian-American, **3:**913, 914, 915, 939
United Arab Emirates, *al-murāda*, **6:**700
United States
  European immigrant groups, **3:**824–25
  glees, **3:**183–84
  nineteenth century, **8:**205
  pedagogical systems, **3:**275–76
Uruguay
  canto popular uruguayo, **2:**510, 519–20
  payada, **2:**512, 520
  religious genres, **2:**511–12
  romance, **2:**511
Uttar Pradesh
  bārahamāsā, **5:**277
  birahā, **5:**666–69
  caitī, **5:**277
  gālī insult songs, **5:**589, 663
  kajalī (also *kajarī*; *kajrī*), **5:**669–70, 671
  men's genres, **5:**664–66
  phaguā, **5:**665–66
  purvī, **5:**671, 672–73
  rasiyā, **5:**550, 551, 665, 672
  women's genres, **5:**661–64
'Uvea, **9:**814
  genres of, **9:**809–12
Uzbekistan
  katta ashula, **6:**944
  maqām, **6:**913–15
  yalla or *lapar* dance songs, **6:**902
Vai people, **1:**340, 467
  Sande repertoire, **1:**337
Vanuatu, **9:**690–91
  Banks Islands, **9:**700–701
  na bolo, **9:**696–97
  na lenga, **9:**696–97
  sawagoro, **9:**198, 361, 695–96
  Tanna, **9:**706
  Tannese *nupu*, **9:**702–4, 707–8
  tanumwe, **9:**198
Venda people, **1:**709
Venezuela
  aguinaldo, **2:**538
  Amerindian, **2:**525
  fulia, **2:**530, 534
  gaita, **2:**538–39
  malembe, **2:**535
  salve, **2:**533, 536
  Spanish influences on, **2:**524
  tamunangue, **2:**536
  tono, **2:**534
Vietnam, **4:**451
  Buddhist, **4:**503
  ca huê, **4:**449, 455, 464, 482–83
  cải lương, **4:**494
  ca trù, **4:**23, 454, 455, 464, 467, 469, 472,
    480–82
  chèo, **4:**490
  dân ca, **4:**81, 514–15
  folk songs, **4:**475–80
  of minority peoples, **4:**532–33
  mode in, **4:**457, 464
  nhạc cải cách, **4:**449, 509–10, 513

Volume Key: **6**, Middle East; **7**, East Asia; **8**, Europe; **9**, Australia and the Pacific Islands; **10**, The World's Music.

vocal music, Vietnam (*continued*)
nhạc tiền chiến, **4:**510
political songs, **4:**88
quan họ, **4:**477
ru, **4:**478–79
in *tuồng*, **4:**490–02
upland regions, **4:**532–33
Vietnamese-American, **3:**994
Virgin Islands
cariso, **2:**972
quelbey, **2:**971
Vlach Rom people, **8:**275
Waiãpí culture, **2:**161–63
Wales, **8:**342–47, 354
choral singing, **8:**342, 356
Warao culture, **2:**193–97
hoa, **2:**188, 196, 198
Wayana culture, **2:**166–67
West Africa, **1:**446, 451
donkililu repertoire, **1:**499
West Futuna
genres of, **9:**862
hgorohgorosaki, **9:**861
West Timor, *koa*, **4:**797
Xavante culture, *daño're*, **2:***127*
Xia'erba people, **7:**482–83
Yakan people
meglebulebu seputangan, **4:**909–10
tarasul, **4:**906
ya-ya, **4:**911
Yámana culture, **2:**251
Yanomamö culture, **2:**170–75
Yao people, **4:**549–50
Yap
churuq, **9:**729, 731–32
marching, **9:**719
tang genres, **9:**730
teempraa, **9:**729, 730–31
Yaqui culture, deer songs, **2:**589, 593; **3:**437
Yekuana culture, **2:**180–81
Yemen, **6:**301
'awãdī, **6:**656, 657
ghinā', **6:**305
al-ghinā' al-ṣan'ānī, **6:**403, 407, 657, 685–90
lahjī, **6:**685
maghna, **6:**301
majaṣṣ, **6:**657, 659
men's songs, **6:**302
tawshīḥ, **6:**312, 452, 657, 689–90
zamel, **6:**302
Yiddish, **3:**530
Yoruba people, **1:**460, 461
Ijebu group, **1:**90–91
Islamic genres, **1:**413–14
Yugoslavia (former)
koleda, **8:**140
Serbo-Croatian women's songs, **8:**95
Yuma culture, **2:**595–96, 597, 598; **3:**434
Zaghawa people, **1:**561
Zimbabwe, *chimurenga*, **1:**365, 756–57
Zulu people, choral music, **1:**706
Vocalion/Decca, **3:**739, 741
Voces de los campesinos (album), **3:**749
Vocke, Sibylle, **6:**496
Vodery, Will, **3:**620

Vodnik, Valentin, **8:**921
Vodou (also *vodun*), **2:**18–19, 48, 69, 98; **3:**785, 802, 804–5
in Dominican Republic, **2:**851, 856
in Haiti, **1:**134; **2:**881, 882–84
in United States, **2:**888–89
in West Africa, **1:**462
Vodou-jazz, **2:**98, 797
Vodoule (*rara* band), **2:***888*
Vodušek, Valens, **8:**922
Vogël, Qamili i, **8:**999
Vogt, A. S., **3:**1181
Vogt, Augustus, **3:**1079
Vogul people, **8:**128
Voi, Eleanor, **9:**361
Voice of America, **3:**298
Voice of Hawaii (newsletter), **3:**1052
Voice of the Fugitive (newspaper), **3:**1211
Voices and Images (Feliciano), **4:**878
Voisen, Daisey, **2:**960
Voisin, Frédéric, **1:**262, 264–65
Voisine, Roch, **3:**1168
Voix d'Evangeline (newspaper), **3:**1136–37
Vokes, May, **3:***195*
Volamena dynasty, **1:**781
"Volare" (Modugno), **8:**209, 619
Volga Germans, **3:***823*, 890
Volga Kazans, **8:**772
Volkonsky, Andrey, **7:**340–41
Volkov, Solomon, **8:**26
Volkova, Vera, **7:**62
Volkskundemuseum (Anvers), **8:**181
Volkslieder (Herder), **8:**17, 512
Vollant, Florent, **3:**1074
Volmar brothers, **2:**438
Volney, Constantin-François de Chasseboeuf, comte de, **6:**21–22
Volo Volo de Boston (musical group), **2:**892; **3:**803
Volpi, Mario, **6:**236
Volrath, Calvin, **3:**410
Volski, Lavon, **8:**802
Volunge Chorus (Toronto), **3:**1196
"Volunteers" (Jefferson Airplane), **3:**318
Völuspá (Eddic poem), **8:**423
"Volver, Volver" (Jiménez), **3:**722
Von Tilzer, Albert, **3:**549
Voodoo. *See* Vodou
Vosgerchien, Louise, **10:**20
Voto culture, **2:**681, 682. *See also* Maleku culture
Votyan people, **8:**475
Vouras, Mary, **8:**1025
Vox Blenii (musical group), **8:**695
Vox Finlandia, **3:**1196
Voyage Round the World (Forster), **9:**35
Voyage en Syrie et en Égypte (comte de Volney), **6:**21–22
voyaging
Micronesia, **9:**715–16, 722
Papua New Guinea, **9:**490, 492–93, 494
Polynesia, **9:**59, 209, 771, 835, 847, 914, 969–70
Voyer, Simone, **3:**1164
V-Records, **3:**1243
Vreeswijk, Cornelis, **8:**446
Vrij en Blij Choir (Hamilton), **3:**1195

Vrindiban Academy (Hong Kong), **7:**431
Vučković, Nina, **3:**1172
Vujičić, Tihomir, **8:**937
Vulfius, Pavel, **8:**784
Vurnik, Stanko, **8:**922
Vute people, **1:**319
Vyasaraya, **5:**265
Vyas, Narayanrao, **5:***207*, 424, 466
Vysotskii, Vladimir, **8:**767

Wa kingdom, **7:**18
Wa people. *See* De'ang people
Waagstein, Joen (Jogvan), **8:**471
Waal Malefijt, Annemarie de, **2:**507
Wachsmann, Klaus P., **1:**51, 155, 294, 599, 722; **8:**54; **10:**5, 120
as director of East African Music Research Scheme, **1:**18
historical studies, **1:**55
on methodology, **1:**63, 65, 67, 68
on negritude, **1:**29–30
research on harps and lyres, **1:**302, 304–5
research on tuning, **1:**255
use of term "African musicology," **1:**13
Wacúsecha culture, **2:**575
Wādankusa-ratnamāla (treatise), **5:**960
Wade, Bonnie C., **5:**675; **7:**595; **10:**3–15, *4, 9–12, 14–15*
Wade, Peter, **2:**411
Wade in the Water (radio series), **10:**144
Wādī al-'Arab, **6:**629
Wadkar, Suresh, **5:**421
Wadley, Susan, **5:**674
al-Wāfī, Shaykh Aḥmad, **6:**501, 502–3
Wage people, **9:**538
Wagner, Ollie, **3:**1091
Wagner, Richard, **2:**962; **3:**885, 1149, 1182; **8:**617, 646; **9:**130, 131
music dramas, **8:**60, 83, 84, 187
Wagner, Roger, **3:**536
Wagogo people. *See* Gogo people
Wah Shing Music Group (Ottawa), **3:**1083
Wahab Gul, **5:**787
Wahbī, Ahmed, **6:**269
Wahgi people, **9:**188, 511, 513
Waiãpí culture, **2:**157–63, 164, 435
aesthetics of, **2:**130
bumblebee ceremony of, **2:**126, 128
history of, **2:**157–58
instruments of, **2:**33
vocal music of, **2:**435–36
Waiata Methodist Choir, **9:**935–36
Waikato-Maniapoto people, **9:**943
Waikiki Wedding (film), **3:**1049; **9:**43
waila, **3:**213, 436, 472–73, 479, 489–90, 851
Wailer, Bunny, **2:**912
Wailers (musical group), **4:**887
Wain, Charles, **9:**46
"Waist Deep in the Muddy" (Seeger), **3:**317
Waiting for Harry (film), **9:**47, 420
Waiwai culture, **2:**164, 442
hymn singing of, **2:**71, 131–32
Wajid Ali Shah, king of Oudh, **5:**51, 121, 179, 192, 197, 435, 487
Waka Waka people, **9:**430

Wakashan Indian nation, **3**:1093–94, 1254
Wakefield, Edward Gibbon, **9**:114
Waksman, Steve, **3**:113
Walapai Indian nation, **3**:417, 422
Walarano people, **9**:697
Walbiri Fire Ceremony: Ngatjakula (film), **9**:47
Walcha T'aryŏng (p'ansori story), **7**:899
Walcott, Ron, **3**:495
Walcott, Ronald, **5**:963
Walden, Narada Michael, **3**:715
Waldron, Arthur, **7**:13
Waldschmidt, Ernst, **5**:318
Waldteufel, Émile, **4**:859; **8**:641
Wale, Noan, **9**:155
Wales, **8**:342–56
  bardic tradition in, **8**:146, 348–49
  Celtic music in, **8**:319–22, 348
  dance traditions of, **8**:140, 343, 353, 354
  eisteddfod competitions, **8**:147, 151, 185, 342, 349, 350, 352–54, 356
  folk music recordings, **8**:157
  geography of, **8**:342
  history of, **8**:348–49
  ideology in, **8**:185
  map of, **8**:324
  musical exchanges with Ireland, **8**:354, 355
  popular music in, **8**:356
  population of, **8**:342
  revival movement in, **8**:353–55
  Rom people in, **8**:347, 348
  "symphonies" genre, **8**:345, 350
  vocal music, **8**:342–47
    ballads, **8**:343–44, 346
    carols, **8**:343, 344, 346–47, 349–50, 351
    courtship songs, **8**:145, 343
    English songs, **8**:354
    hymns and psalms, **8**:349–5o
    occupational songs, **8**:344, 354
  wassailing tradition in, **8**:140, 342
  women's performances in, **8**:200
Wali Dad, **5**:790, 791
Wali, Shah, **5**:835–40, 837
Walīd ibn Yazīd, caliph, **6**:292, 295, 297, 539
Walin, Rolf, **8**:430
Walin, Stig, **8**:447
Walker, Aaron "T-Bone," **3**:647, 669, 741
Walker, Aida Overton, **3**:618, 619
Walker, Chris, **1**:377, 381
Walker, George, **3**:194, 610, 611, 611, 618, 619, 650; **10**:139
Walker, Gregory, **3**:612
Walker, Junior, **3**:674
Walker, Kim, **9**:416
Walker, Thomas W., **2**:767
Walker, William, **3**:121, 533, 533
"Walking the Dog" (Thomas), **3**:676
"Walking the Floor Over You" (Tubb), **3**:79
Wallace, Alfred Russel, **1**:95; **4**:812, 818
Wallace, Henry, **3**:310
Wallace, Robert, **8**:363
Wallace, Sippie, **3**:644, 707
Wallace, William, **8**:368
Wallace, William Kauaiwiulaokalani, III, **9**:972
Wallace, William Vincent, **3**:181
Wallachia, **8**:868. *See also* Romania

Wallaga Lake Gumleaf Band, **9**:134
Wallas, James, **3**:400
Wallaschek, Richard, **1**:74, 75, 89, 91, 93, 95–96; **3**:575–76
Walle, Harinder Singh Faridkot, **5**:426
Walle, Harjinder Singh Srinagar, **5**:426
Waller, Fats, **3**:863
Walleser, Sixtus, **9**:729
Walley, Richard, **9**:397
Wallin, Per-Henrik, **8**:446
Wallis Island. *See* 'Uvea
Wallis, Richard, **4**:733
Wallis, Roger, **2**:93; **3**:828; **8**:96
Wallner, Bo, **8**:448
Wallonia (periodical), **8**:535
Walloons, **8**:12, 518
Walser, Robert, **3**:112, 113, 114, 513, 586
Walstrom, Nancy E., **2**:599
Walter, Anna Lee, **3**:493
Walter, Arnold, **3**:1185
Walter, Thomas, **3**:25
Walters, Harry, **3**:312
Walton, Susan Pratt, **3**:1014; **4**:637, 638
Walton, William, **8**:186
waltz, **3**:232, 233, 825, 836–37, 850, 855; **8**:166, 168, 170, 228. *See also* vals
  in Algeria, **6**:270
  in Austria, **8**:672, 673
  band arrangements, **3**:874
  in Canada, **3**:408, 1075, 1081, 1125, 1190, 1191, 1195, 1196, 1256
  in Corsica, **8**:571
  Creole, **3**:858
  Croatian, **3**:921
  Czech, **3**:897
  in Czech Republic, **8**:721
  dance competitions for, **3**:210
  Danish, **3**:882
  in Denmark, **8**:457, 464
  dissemination of, **8**:7
  in England, **8**:329, 330
  in Finland, **8**:484, 485
  Finnish, **3**:874–75
  German, **3**:891
  in Germany, **8**:655
  Irish, **3**:843
  Italian, **3**:860, 861, 864, 865
  in Kazakhstan, **6**:961
  in Low Countries, **8**:524, 527
  meter in, **8**:9
  Mexican-Hispano-Tejano, **3**:522, 735, 745, 755, 759, 760, 773, 775
  in Norway, **8**:419
  Norwegian, **3**:868
  for piano, **3**:190
  Polish, **3**:892, 894
  redondo, **3**:760
  in Russia, **8**:766
  Slovak, **3**:900
  in Sweden, **8**:435–36, 443
  Swedish, **3**:872
  in Switzerland, **8**:690, 694, 696
  in Ukraine, **8**:812
  Ukrainian, **3**:913, 914, 1088
  Volga German, **3**:890
"Waltz Quadrille," **3**:1190

Waluyo, Djoko, **3**:1015
Wa munfaridun bil-ḥusni (Abū Tammān), **6**:444
Wan Smolbag (Vanuatu theater group), **9**:233
Wan Tongshu, **6**:990
Wang Bansheng, **7**:300
Wang Changyuan, **3**:959; **7**:172
Wang Chaoxin, **7**:510
Wang Chongyang, **7**:321
Wang Guangqi, **7**:137
Wang Guotong, **7**:177
Wang Guowei, **7**:137
Wang Jiangzhong, **7**:350
Wang Jide, **7**:122, 130
Wang, Kin-men, **7**:358
Wang Lili, **7**:177
Wang, Lisa (Wang Mingquan), **7**:355
Wang Lisan, **7**:341
Wang Pu, **7**:118–19
Wang Qianshao, **7**:154
Wang Sanak, **7**:981
Wang Tiechui, **7**:204
Wang Wei, **7**:163
Wang Xiaochuan, **7**:392
Wang Xiaofang, **7**:363–65, 364–65
Wang Xichun, **7**:132
Wang Xinkui, **7**:376
Wang Yaoqing, **7**:286
Wang Yong, **7**:360, 365
Wang Yuhe, **7**:87, 138–39
Wang Yunfeng, **7**:356
Wang Yuting, **7**:170
Wang Zhaojun, **7**:167, 219
Wang Zhengping, **7**:170
Wang Zhenya, **7**:231
Wang Zhi, **7**:56
Wanli xu daozang (Zhang), **7**:319
Wannian huan (qupai melody), **7**:233
Wano people, **9**:587
al-Wansharīsī, 'Abd al-Wāḥid ibn Aḥmad, **6**:367
Wanuskewin Heritage Park (Alberta), **3**:1086
Wanyamala, chief of Kedeng, Lifou, **9**:683
Wanyamwezi people. *See* Nyamwezi people
Wanyman, Theoury, **9**:677
Wapishana culture, **2**:442
"War" (Starr), **3**:318, 677
War (musical group), **3**:681; **10**:78
War of 1812, **3**:1132
War Faze (musical group), **5**:428
Wa'r Leur (organization), **8**:562
War of the Pacific, **2**:245, 356–57
"War Ship Touchante" (Brides of Funkenstein), **3**:684
Wara (musical group), **2**:297–98
Warao culture, **2**:169–70, 188–98
  folklore of, **2**:21
  in Guyana, **2**:189
  instruments of, **2**:33, 120, 127, 189–93
  narratives of, **10**:97
  oratory of, **2**:128
  research on, **2**:198; **10**:98, 101–2, 105–6
  shamanism in, **2**:179, 193–96
  vocal music of, **2**:185, 193–97
Warari (Binandere composer), **9**:358
Ward, Jack, **9**:969
Ward, John, **10**:20
Ward (or Wood), Moses, **2**:818

Ward, Oliver, Jr., 3:*398*
Ward, Robert, 3:546
Ward, Samuel Augustus, 3:521
Ward, W. E., 10:139
Al-Warda al-baydā' (Egyptian film), 6:236, 600
Wardlaw, Lady, 8:368
Ware, Charles Pickard, 3:29, 506, 523–24, 574–75
Warehouse (Chicago), 3:690
Warihio culture. *See* Guarijio culture
Waring, Fred, 3:536
Warli people, 5:727
Warlpiri people, 9:433, 452
  ceremonies, 9:243, 450
  dance, 9:317, 464–67
  purlapa genre, 9:243
Warman, Arturo, 2:593
Warner Brothers, 3:262, 265
Warner, Daniel Keiji, 9:166
Warner Records, 3:169, 714
Warner, W. L., 9:987
Waro, Danyel, 5:610
al-Warrāq, Muḥammad, 6:569
Warren, Harry, 3:196
Warren, Leigh, 9:416
Warring States period
  Daoism in, 7:312
  instruments in, 7:107–8, 111
  music in, 7:88
  music theory in, 7:115
  number symbolism in, 7:100
  philosophy in, 7:462
  zheng in, 7:171
Warsadiningrat, K. R. T. (Prajapangrawit), 4:636, 683
Wartes, William, 3:486
Warugaba, Cosma, 1:217
Warumpi Band, 9:60, 145, 146, 444, 445, 446
Warwick, Dionne, 3:535, 713
Waschek, Brownlee, 3:900
Waser, Franz, 8:689
Washboard Sam, 3:645
Washburn, Jon, 3:1096
Washington, Booker T., 1:764; 3:673
Washington, Dinah, 3:646, 674, 743
Washington, D.C.
  black community in, 3:677
  Cambodian people in, 3:998
  Central American communities in, 3:727
  Chinese communities in, 3:949
  Chinese people in, 3:957
  Indonesian people in, 3:1011, 1015
  Iranian people in, 3:1031
  Miami, 3:702
  public school music education, 3:275
Washington, George, 3:297, 299, 305
Washington Guards Band (Philadelphia), 3:564
Washington, Jackie, 3:1212
Washington state
  Finnish people in, 3:872–75
  Japanese people in, 3:969
  Native American groups in, 3:394–99
  Olympia, indie music in, 3:171
  Seattle
    Cambodian people in, 3:998
    Chinese people in, 3:957

dance in, 3:208
  Estonian people in, 3:879
  Filipino people in, 3:1024
  indie music in, 3:171
  taiko drumming groups in, 3:971
  Thai people in, 3:1010
  Vietnamese people in, 3:993
  White River, *taiko* drumming groups in, 3:971
Washington University (St. Louis), 3:611
Washo Indian nation, 3:420, 426
Wasi, Pius, 9:91, 155
Wasisname, Buddy, 3:1070
Wasitodiningrat, Ki R. T. (Wasitodipuro; Cokrowasito), 3:1015, *1015*; 4:130, 666, 683, 684
waṣla
  Aleppan, 6:569
  Egypt, 6:174
  Mashriq, 6:11, 551, 563
  nineteenth-century, 6:21, 567–68
  Tunisia, 6:452
Wassén, S. H., 2:649
Wassmann, Jürg, 9:982
Wassuf, Georges, 3:1220
Waswahili people. *See* Swahili people
Watada, Terry, 3:1096
Wataita people, 1:624
Watanabe Hiroshi, 7:595
Watchman (calypsonian), 2:964
Water Lily Acoustics (record label), 5:529
Waterloo + Robinson (duo), 8:677
Waterman, Christopher, 1:353, 354, 364; 10:53
Waterman, Richard A., 1:359; 3:34, 72, 512, 576, *576*; 9:975–76, 987; 10:41, 111, 112, 114, 139
Waterman, Thomas T., 3:418
Waters, Anita M., 2:93
Waters, Ethel, 3:620, 644
Waters, Muddy. *See* Morganfield, McKinley
al-Wāthiq, caliph, 6:539
Watson, John, 3:627
Watson, Leona, 2:972
Watson, Rubie, 10:23
Watt, William, 9:214
Wattal people, 5:498
Watts, Isaac, 3:523, 533
Watts, Jeff "Tain," 3:664
"*Watusi, El*" (Barretto), 3:788
Wawancó, 2:265
Wa-Wan Press, 3:539
Waxei (Watakatau) people, 9:557, 558–60
Waxman, Franz, 3:546
"Way" (Lacy), 3:131, *131*
"Way Down in Alabama" (gospel song), 3:1133
"*Waya mulongolo*," 1:218
Wayana culture, 2:157, 158, 163, 164–67, 435, 503
  acculturation in, 2:167
  ceremonies of, 2:165–66
  history of, 2:164–65
  instruments of, 2:165, 438
  vocal music of, 2:166, 435–36, 437
Wayman, Tom, 3:1061
Wayn 'a-Ramallah (*dabkih*), 6:583
Wayn aziffak yā 'arīs (shaving song), 6:589
Wayne, John, 3:111; 9:149

Wayn il-'aris waynuh (wedding song), 6:592
Waza people, 1:601
W. Doherty firm, 3:1183
"We Are the World" (Jackson and Richie), 3:713
"We People Who Are Darker Than Blue" (Mayfield), 3:677
"We Shall Overcome" (spiritual), 3:316, 507
"We Will Understand It Better By and By" (Tindley), 3:630
WEA Corporation, 2:107; 3:264
Weary, Esau, 3:*645*
Weather (Gordon), 3:177
Weather Report (musical group), 3:356, 664
Weaver, Sylvester, 3:644
Weavers (musical group), 1:773; 3:316, 328–29, *329*, 520; 8:391
Weaving My Ancestors' Voices (album), 8:240
Webb, Chick, 3:668, 793
Webb, Edward, 5:923
Webb, Michael, 9:607, 986
Webber, John, 9:10–13, 34, *766*, 791
Weber, Carl Maria von, 8:646
Weber, Max, 8:122
Weber, Tom, 2:913
Webern, Anton, 8:407, 445
Webster, Daniel, 3:304
Webster, Danny, 3:686
Webster, Noah, 3:289
Wedau people, 9:490
Wedding Feast for the Wise (Tibetan writing), 7:472
"Wedding Tune," 3:*406*
weddings. *See also* ceremonies
  Abkhazian people, 8:852, 853
  Afghanistan, 5:*620*, 806, 814, 816, 818, 821–22, 823, 826, 835–36; 6:875
    dance in, 5:506
  Africa, dance at, 1:110, 111, 114, 115
  Albania, 8:988, 996
  Albanian-American, 3:927–28, 1084
  Algeria, 6:471, 473
    Kabylia, 6:300–301
  Andean regions, 2:218, 219, 221
    brass bands at, 2:212
  Andhra Pradesh, 5:892
  Arab-American, 6:283, 284–85, 286
  Arabian peninsula, 6:667, 697, 699, 702, 704
  Arab societies, 6:300, 372, 373
  Argentina, 2:261
  Austria, 8:674
  Azerbaijan, 6:931
  Balkan region, 8:14, 165, 867
  Balochistan, 5:774, 782; 6:882
  Belarus, 8:793, 799
  Belize, 2:678
  Berber people, 1:543
  Bolivia, 2:291
    rock bands at, 2:297
  Bontok people, 4:915
  Bosnia-Hercegovina, 8:963, 966
    Jewish, 8:968
  British Caribbean communities, 3:811, 1205
  Bulgaria, 8:6, 144, 227, 892–93, 895, 900–903
    Rom performers, 8:283–84
  Bulgarian-American, 3:924

California Spanish, **3:**735
Cambodian-American, **3:**1001, 1002
Caribbean, **2:**49
Central America, **2:**49
Central Asia, **6:**899, 946
Chechen people, **8:**863
China, **7:**91, 201, 240
    northwestern minorities, **7:**463
Cirebon, **4:**689
Colombia, **2:**384
Corsica, **8:**568, 571, 573
Costa Rica, **2:**698
Croatia, **8:**926
Croatian-American, **3:**922
Czech Republic, **8:**717, 720, 727
East Indian people, **2:**85
Ecuador, **2:**424–25
Egypt, **6:**166, 170, 415, 615, 616–17,
    620–21, 622, 642–43
El Salvador, **2:**709
Estonia, **8:**494
Europe, **8:**8, 127, 143–44, 196
    dance traditions in, **8:**162–63
    male performers at, **8:**198, 200
    participants' obligations, **8:**114
    performers as mediators, **8:**117
    Renaissance, **8:**77
    song genres in, **8:**132–33
    women's and men's customs, **8:**194
Fiji, **5:**614
    Hindu, **9:**94
Finland, **8:**6, 144, 485
Flores, **4:**794
France, **8:**545–46, 551
Georgia, **8:**833, 835, 837
German, **3:**888
Greece, **8:**1016
    Cycladic islands, **8:**1015
    Macedonia, **8:**1011
Greek-American, **3:**929, 931–32
Guyana, **5:**601, 605
    African traditions, **2:**445
    Hindu and Islamic, **2:**443, 444
Hmong people, **4:**556
Hungary, **8:**739–40, 744
    Rom musicians at, **8:**274
India, North, **10:**5–6
    instruments in, **5:**340
India, South, **5:**212
    instruments in, **5:**103, 279
Indo-Caribbean community, **3:**816
Ingush people, **8:**863
Iran, **6:**19, 828, 829, 846, 875
Iraq, **6:**303
Israel, **6:**202, 205–6, 262, 263, 265–66, 1017,
    1018
Italian-American, **3:**1196
Java, **4:**646
Jewish people, **3:**935, 939; **8:**250, 251–52
    klezmorim performances at, **8:**259–60
    Sephardic, **3:**1172
    Syrian, **3:**943
Kabwa people, **1:**642
Karen people, **4:**544
Karnataka, **5:**868, 885, 886
Kashmir, **5:**683, 685

Kazakhstan, **6:**951, 955
Kenya, **1:**626–28
Kerala, **5:**949
Khmer people, **4:**18, 155, 159, 169, 195–96
Kiribati, **9:**763
Korea, **7:**884
Kota people, importance of, **5:**285
Kumaon people, **5:**501
Kurdistan, **6:**747, 749–51
Lahu people, **4:**540
Latin American communities, **3:**1205
Latvia, **8:**500, 502
Latvian-American, **3:**1196
Lebanon, **6:**545
Lithuania, **8:**510, 511
Lombok, **4:**772
Macedonia, **8:***13*, *144*, 146, *162*, 281, 973,
    975
    bands for, **8:**977, 979, 980, 982
    dances at, **8:**978
    Rom people, **8:**282
Macedonian-American, **3:**925, 1198
Maguindanao people, **4:**894
Malaysia, **4:**409, 413, 415, 424
Maliseet and Mi'kmaq nations, **3:**1069
Malta, **8:**640
Maluku, **4:**816
Mashriq, **6:**538
Maya culture, **2:**731
Mexican-American, **3:**721
Middle East, **6:**5
Mixtec culture, **2:**564, 566–67
Mongol people, **7:**1009
Montenegro, **8:**958
Morocco
    Berber peoples, **6:***300*, 301, 479–82, 484–85
    Jewish people, **6:**1041
Naxi people, **7:**510
Nepal, **5:**279, 284, 699, 701, 702
New Caledonia, Loyalty Islands, **9:**684
New Mexico, **3:**758–59, 760
North Africa, **1:**539
North America, **3:**284
North West Frontier Province, **5:**791
Norwegian-Americans, **3:**869
Nubian people, **1:**556; **6:**629, 645
Nusa Tenggara Timur, **4:**787
Oman, **6:**674, 678, 681–82
Ossetian people, **8:**861
Otopame culture, **2:**573
Pakhtun people, **5:**785
Pakistan, **5:**749
    Northern Areas, **5:**794, 799
    timing of, **5:**277
Palestine, **6:**573–78, 579–92
Papua New Guinea
    Baluan, **9:**604
    Eastern Highlands peoples, **9:**528
    Enga people, **9:**535
    Huli people, **9:**537
    Manam people, **9:**245
Paraguay, **2:**458
Pennsylvania European-Americans, **3:**824
Philippines
    epics of, **4:**908
    highland peoples, **4:**914

Poland, **8:**113–14, *702*, 707, 710
    klezmorim performances at, **8:**11
    Silesia, **8:**131
Polish-American, **3:**892
Portugal, **8:**579
Punjab, **5:***273*, 277, 283, 652–53, 771
Purépecha culture, **2:**580
Rajasthan, **5:**642, 648
Rapa Nui, **9:**952
Romania, **8:**122, 870–71, 874, 876
    klezmorim performances at, **8:**11
    Maramureş, **8:**119
    Rom people, **8:**196, 278
Romanian-American, **3:**910, 911
Roti, **4:**800
Rotuma, **9:**818
Russia, **8:**758, 761, 769, 774
Russian Old Believers, **3:**917
Sāmoa, **9:**348
    nuptial cheers, **9:**342–43, 803
Saudi Arabia, **6:**653, 654, 691–94, 709
Serbia, **8:**146, 941
Serbian-American, **3:**922
Sindh, **5:***282*
Slovak-American, **3:**900
Slovakia, **8:**720, 727
Slovenia, **8:**911
South America, **2:**49
South Asia, **5:**274–76
    appropriate music for, **5:**282
    bands at, **5:**347–48
    child marriages, **5:**408
    dance at, **5:**498
    Hindu, importance of, **5:**285
    timing of, **5:**276
    women performers at, **5:**8, 414–15
South Asian Americans, **3:**981, 1084, 1246;
    5:579
South Asians in Great Britain, **5:**574
Spain, **8:**589, 591
Subanun people, **4:**923
Sumatra, **4:**621
    Bangka Island, **4:**626
    Gayo people, **4:**605
    Jambi, **4:**617
    Kayu Agung areas, **4:**601
    Lampung Province, **4:**628
    Minangkabau, **4:**609, 612
    Nias Island, **4:**608
    Serawai people, **4:**619
    southern, **4:**627
Sumba, **4:**790
Sumbawa, **4:**780
Sunda, **4:***706*, 718
Swahili people, **1:**631
Sweden, **8:**439
Syria, **6:**570
Taino culture, **2:**881
Taiwan, **7:**424
Tamil Nadu, **5:**910, 920
    Brahmins, **5:**274–76
Tatar people, **8:**774
Tausug people, **4:**898
Tejano, **3:**773, 778
Tibetan culture, **5:**710
Tokelau, *tuala*, **9:**824

weddings (*continued*)
Trinidad, **5:**591
South Asian community, **5:**589
Tuareg people, **1:**545, 585, 592
Tunisia, **6:**512
Jewish community, **6:**527–28
Turkey, **6:**765, 766
Ukraine, **8:**806–8, 819, 820
instrumental music for, **8:**809, 810, 812
klezmorim performances at, **8:**11
Ukrainian-American, **3:**913, 1088, 1242–43
United States
ethnic music at, **3:**827
nineteenth century, **3:**555
Uttar Pradesh, **5:**661–62, 663, 668, 671, 672–73, 674
Uzbekistan, **6:**916
Vanuatu, Ambae, **9:**696
Vep people, **8:**772
Virgin Islands, **2:**970
Volga German, **3:**890
Wales, **8:**355
horseback, **8:**348
Yakan people, **4:**900
Yao people, **4:**549
Yemen, **6:**307, 655, 656, 657, 709
drum ensembles for, **6:**95–98, 101, 102
Yuma culture, **2:**598
Wedgetail Eagle Band, **9:**445
Week (periodical), **3:**992
"Weekly Blues" (Yancey), **3:**106
Weene (Weno; Moen) Atoll (Chuuk State, FSM), **9:**734–38
"Weeping Peach Blossoms" (Wang), **7:**356
"Weeping, Sad, and Lonely, or When This Cruel War Is Over" (Tucker), **3:**188
Wege zur Musik der Gegenwart (Gradenwitz), **6:**1060
Wegner, Gert-Matthias, **5:**136
Wehi, Bub, **9:**949
Wei dynasty, **7:**25, 29
Confucianism in, **7:**335
Daoism in, **7:**312, 320–21
founding of, **7:**517
instruments in, **7:**111, 112
Wei Hao, **7:**724–25
Wei kingdom, **7:**320
Wei Liangfu, **7:**277, 289–90
Wei Xikui, **7:**394
Wei Zhongle, **7:**90, 169
Wei Zhuyan, **7:**724
Weich-Shahak, Susana, **6:**1037, 1063, 1066
Weigel, Johann Christoph, **8:**654–55
Weil, Cynthia, **3:**673
Weil, Daniel, **6:**1066
Weill, Kurt, **3:**545, 939; **8:**646, 659
Weinberg, Jacob, **6:**1025, 1026
Weiner, Lazar, **3:**939, 940
Weinert, Erich, **8:**659
Weinstein, Deena, **3:**112
Weintraub, Andrew, **4:**701
Weinzweig, John, **3:**1184, 1185
Weird Summer (musical group), **3:**169
Weis, Karel, **8:**732
Weiss, H., **3:**943
Weiss, Hansche, **8:**289

Weiss wie Schnee (album), **8:**677
We kil (Kim), **7:**959
Wela people, **9:**538
Welk, Lawrence, **3:**779, 891, 902
"Well below the Valley" (Child ballad), **8:***295*
Well-Tempered Synthesizer (Carlos), **3:**254
"Well You Needn't" (Monk), **3:**659
Wellesz, Egon, **6:**535
Wellington Chamber Music, **9:**929
Wells, Kenneth E., **4:**287
Wells, Kitty, **3:**79
Wells, Mary, **3:**674
Wells, William Vincent, **2:**741
Welsh Folk Dance Society, **8:**354
Welsh Folk-Song Society, **8:**353
Welsh Harp Society, **8:**354
Welsh League of Youth, **8:**354
Welsman, Frank, **3:**1183
Wemba, Papa, **1:**424–25
Wembawemba people, **9:**441
Wen, emperor (mythical ruler), **7:**160
Wenchang (Han deity), **7:**513
Wencheng gongzhu (Tibetan opera), **7:**479
Wendo, Antoine, **1:**359, 377, 669
Wendt, Albert, **9:**37, 112, 233
Wendt, Caroline Card, **10:**56
Wenlin jubao, **7:**123
Wenten, Nanik, **3:**1015
Wenten, Nyoman, **3:**1015, 1017
Wenxian tonggao, **7:**930
Wenzel, Jochen, **2:**238
"We're All in the Same Gang," **3:**714
"We're a Winner" (Mayfield), **3:**677
"We're Gonna Rock, We're Gonna Roll" (Moore), **3:**669
We're Still Standing (Four the Moment), **3:**1134
Werger, Stefanie, **8:**677
Wernecke Camp Orchestra (Yukon), **3:**1277
Werner, Craig, **3:**587
Werner, Eric, **6:**16, 19, 535, 1058, 1063; **8:**267
Wernick, Pete, **3:**159
Wertheimer, Max, **1:**181, 184
Wescott, William, **3:**576
Wesley, Charles, **3:**533; **9:**203
Wesley, Fred, **3:**680
Wesley, John, **3:**533
Wesleyan University (Middletown), **3:**175, 222, 324, 336–37, 496, 952, 953, 1013, 1014, 1020; **5:**529; **10:**10, 41–42
Wesleyans. *See* Methodists
West Africa. *See also specific countries and peoples*
Central Sudanic cluster, **1:**447–51
colonialism in, **1:**82, 85–88, 233, 401, 402–3, 407, 455
economics of, **1:**458
forest region of, **1:**457–69
geography of, **1:**442–43, 452, 457–58
healing rituals, **1:**273
instruments of, **1:**351
languages of, **1:**443
map of, **1:***440*
musical styles of, **1:**446–47, 451
music of, **1:**442–69
popular music of, **1:**419–23
professional musicians in, **1:**444, 447–48

research on, **1:**442
savanna region of, **1:**443–57
Voltaic cluster, **1:**451–57
Western Sudanic cluster, **1:**443–47
West Africa (periodical), **1:**364
West African-Canadians, **3:**1170, 1201–3, 1213
West African Cultural Society, **1:**33
West African Rhythms for the Drum Set (Hartigan), **3:**337
West Asia. *See also* Middle East; *specific countries and peoples*
influence on Chăm culture, **4:**590–91
influence on Cirebonese culture, **4:**687
influence on Filipino culture and music, **4:**890, 906, 928
influence on Lombok culture, **4:**763, 768
influence on Malaysian music, **4:**19
influence on Maluku culture and music, **4:**813, 816
influence on Sulawesi, **4:**804
influence on Sumatran music, **4:**624–25, 628
influence on Sumbawa culture, **4:**781
influence on Vietnamese culture, **4:**446
West Bengal, **5:**8, 844–62. *See also* Bengal (region)
Burdwan region, **5:**862
Calcutta, **5:**5
European influences in, **5:**442–43
pro-British loyalists in, **5:**431–33
public concerts in, **5:**212
secular urban music in, **5:**847
sitar style of, **5:**334–35
theater in, **5:**486, 488–89, 849
as trade center, **5:**15
chau dance-drama of, **5:**497
dance traditions of, **5:**502–3
history of, **5:**844
Koch Bihar region, **5:**860
Maldaha district, **5:**861
map of, **5:***842*
popular music in, **5:**857
regional cassettes in, **5:**550
social groups in, **5:**397
West End (album), **7:**973
West Futuna (Vanuatu), **9:**833, 861–64
geography of, **9:**861–64
history songs, **9:**707
instruments of, **9:**862
music and dance of, **9:**702, 708, 861–64
population of, **9:**861
research on, **9:**974
toka dance of, **9:**705, 706
West Indians. *See* Caribbean people
West Indies
early African peoples in, **3:**594, 595, 597
French areas, **3:**596
harvest celebrations, **3:**599
West Java. *See* Sunda
West, LaMont, **9:**976
West, LaMont, Jr., **9:**987
West Mamusi people, **9:**607
West Nakanai people, **9:**607
West Side Story (Bernstein), **3:**197–98, 545
West, Speedy, **3:**80
West Timor, **4:**796–98
Dutch and Portuguese in, **4:**796, 797

history of, **4**:796
population of, **4**:796
West 'Uvea (New Caledonia), **9**:671, 833
  music and dance of, **9**:681, 682–84
  social organization of, **9**:835–36
Westendorf, Thomas P., **3**:190
Westerlund, John, **9**:972
Western Apache, **3**:431
Western culture and music. *See also* art music,
        Western; fusion genres and border
        crossings; popular music
  Africa, **1**:8, 159–60
  Algeria, **6**:269, 475
  Arabian peninsula, **6**:713–19; **10**:58
  Atoni people, **4**:797
  Azerbaijan, **6**:924
  Bali, **4**:732, 760–61
  Borneo, **4**:825
  Burma, **4**:398–99
  Cambodia, **4**:156, 207
  Central Asia, **6**:904
  China, **7**:91–92, 136, 141–42, 204, 219–20,
        227–32, 300–301, 306, 339–68,
        373–77, 381, 382, 397–99, 415–16,
        420
  Cirebon, **4**:688, 698
  East Africa, **1**:608
  East Asia, **7**:6, 43, 46, 49–51, 56, 76–77
  Egypt, **6**:238, 321, 323–24, 552–53, 558,
        561, 607–13
  Hong Kong, **7**:90–91, 433, 436
  Indonesia, **4**:114–15
  Israel, **6**:1021, 1023, 1025–32, 1072, 1073
  Israeli research on, **6**:1066–67
  Japan, **7**:533–34, 536–37, 538, 540, 595, 627,
        698–99, 713, 721–22, 725, 727–29,
        731–33, 740, 743–47, 749–50, 756,
        760–61, 774, 777–79, 808; **10**:13–14
  Java, **4**:633
  Karen people, **4**:545
  Kazakhstan, **6**:960–61
  Korea, **7**:807–8, 887–88, 944, 946, 951–53,
        970, 976, 988
  Kurdish people, **6**:752
  Lombok, **4**:778
  Malaysia, **4**:426, 440, 441–42
  Maluku, **4**:818
  Mashriq, **6**:552–53
  Morocco, **6**:1038
  Nusa Tenggara Timur, **4**:786–87
  Philippines, **4**:123, 135, 841–66, 868–82
  relationships with South Asian music,
        5:560–68
  Shona people, **1**:756–57
  Singapore, **4**:523–24
  South America, tropical-forest regions, **2**:131
  Southeast Asia, **4**:8, 80–86
  Southeast Asian influence on, **4**:130–32
  Sulawesi, **4**:804
  Sumatra, **4**:601, 602, 606–7, 613, 614, 616,
        624, 626
  Sumbawa, **4**:780
  Sunda, **4**:708, 717–19
  Taiwan, **7**:90–91
  Thailand, **4**:82
    brass bands, **4**:330–31

Turkey, **6**:77, 247–52, 757, 771, 775–76, 779,
        780, 781–84, 817
Vanuatu, **9**:26
Vietnam, **4**:81, 119, 449, 507–12, 513–14,
        516
West Timor, **4**:796
Western Five Orchestra, **3**:1251
Western Gentlemen (musical group), **3**:1091
Western Han dynasty, **4**:446
Western Khalkha people, **7**:1004–20
Western Ontario Conservatory of Music
        (London), **3**:1182, 1185
Western Sāmoa, **3**:1047; **9**:28, 112, 218–19,
        795, 824. *See also* Sāmoa
Western Shoshones, **3**:421
western swing, **3**:78–79, 326, 648, 669, 897
  in Canada, **3**:1190
Westminster Choir College (Princeton), **3**:611
Weston, Randy, **3**:336
Wet Wet Wet (musical group), **8**:369
Wexler, Haskell, **9**:42
Wexler, Jerry, **3**:263
Whalen and Martell, **3**:618
"What about Me" (Ingram and Rogers), **3**:713
"What a Friend We Have in Jesus" (Converse),
        3:121; **5**:922
"What Is This Thing Called Love," **3**:658
What Must a Fairy's Dream Be?" (Foster), **3**:187
What Price Glory? (film), **3**:262
What Time Is It? (The Time), **3**:685
"What Would You Give in Exchange for Your
        Soul?" **3**:78
Whatarau, Isabel, **9**:938
Whatarau Sisters, **9**:938
"Whatcha Gonna Do?" (Drifters), **3**:671
"What'd I Say" (Charles), **3**:673, 678
"What's Going On?" (Gaye), **3**:552, 677
What's Next? (Matsudaira), **7**:737
"What's the Use of Getting Sober" (Jordan),
        3:668
Wheatstraw, Peetie, **3**:645
Wheeler, Kenny, **3**:1107
Wheeling Jamboree (radio show), **3**:79
Whelan, Johnny, **3**:763
Whelan, Luther, **3**:763
Whelan, Tim, **9**:79
"When a Man Loves a Woman" (Sledge), **3**:710
"When Johnny Comes Marching Home"
        (Gilmore), **3**:188–89
"When the Shantyboy Comes Down" (lumbering
        song), **3**:1189
"When Something Is Wrong with My Baby"
        (Sam and Dave), **3**:677
"Where the Fraser River Flows" (ballad), **3**:1257
Where the Pavement Ends (film), **9**:43
"Where Shall I Be When the First Trumpet
        Sounds" (gospel song), **3**:1133
Where Young Grass Grows (album), **7**:1025
Whidden, Lynn, **3**:344, 392, 411
Whig Party, **3**:305–6, 307
Whigfield, **5**:540
Whilkut Indian nation, **3**:412
Whipple, Emory, **2**:679
whirling dervishes. *See* Sufism (Mevlevî order)
"Whispering Hope" (Hawthorne), **3**:190
Whispering Willows Records, **3**:1278

Whistler's Jug Band, **3**:645
whistles. *See also* flutes
  Arctic regions, **3**:375
  Argentina, **2**:249, 250, 251
  betbut, **8**:640
  bosun's, **9**:934
  Bulgaria, **8**:894
  California types, **3**:371, 415
  cancan ra'anga, **2**:160
  China, clay, **7**:79
  Corsica, **8**:572
  Costa Rica, **2**:680
  fagufagu, **9**:828
  fifa, **8**:878
  France, **8**:544
  Great Basin area, **3**:425
  Great Lakes area, **3**:456
  Gujarat, **5**:477
  huíbiju, **2**:184, 186
  huilacapiztli, **2**:601
  Japan
    clay, **7**:559
    stone, **7**:557, 558–59, *559*
  kī, **9**:896
  Low Countries, **8**:525, 527
  m̧obeke, **1**:267
  Native American types, **3**:477–78
  New Caledonia, **9**:679
  Nicaragua, **2**:748
  Nissan Atoll, **9**:635
  Northeast Indian types, **3**:463
  Northwest Coast, **3**:401
  Oceania, leaf, **9**:442, 828, 860, 863, 901
  Papua New Guinea, **9**:533
  pero, **8**:915
  pifülka, **2**:233–34, 252–53, 254, 358, 359
  pīpara, **9**:906
  Plains area, **3**:445
  Plains Indians, **3**:484
  police, **2**:806
  prehistoric, **8**:38
  pu'i nita, **9**:901
  pū lau, **9**:828
  Punjab, **5**:769
  Purépecha culture, **2**:575
  Sāmoa, **9**:807
  Solomon Islands, **9**:665
  South America, tropical-forest region, **2**:127
  Southeast Indian groups, **3**:468
  Subarctic regions, **3**:386
  svilpe, **8**:503
  tilinca, **8**:875, 878
  Ukraine, **8**:816
  Wayana culture, **2**:165
  žvrgolci, **8**:915, 919
"Whistling Coon" (Johnson), **3**:706
Whitaker, Hudson "Tampa Red," **3**:645
White, C. A., **3**:192
White, Charles, **1**:85
"White Christmas" (Berlin), **3**:196
White, Clarence Cameron, **3**:606, *606*, 607, 608
White, George, **3**:628–29
White, Georgia, **3**:645
White-Haired Girl (ballet/opera), **7**:63, 349, 385,
        387
White Hmong people, **4**:536

White, Maurice, **3:**693
White, Minnie, **3:**1070
White, Newman Ivy, **3:**575
White, Portia, **3:**1133–34
"White Rabbit" (Jefferson Airplane), **3:**552
White, Roland, **3:***159*
White Rose. See Al-Warda al-bayḍā' (Egyptian film)
White's Minstrels, **3:**185
White Tai people, **4:**218, 529
White, Thomas, **2:**431
White, Timothy, **2:**93
Whitefield, George, **3:**533, 594
Whitehead, Alfred, **3:**1166
Whitehorse Arts Centre, **3:**1278
Whitelaw, Anne, **3:**1058
Whiteman, Paul, **3:**63, 689, 707
Whitesnake (musical group), **8:**215
Whitfield, Irène, **3:**857, 858
Whitfield, Norman, **3:**677
Whiting, Steven Moore, **10:**165
Whitlock, Billy, **3:**185
Whitney Museum of Art (New York), **3:**176
Whitten, Norman E., Jr., **2:**411, 431
"Whittier Boulevard" (Thee Midniters), **3:**747
Whittier, John Greenleaf, **3:**532
Who (musical group), **3:**689; **8:**214, 215
Whodini, **3:**713
"Whole Lotta Love" (Led Zeppelin), **3:**112–13
"Who's Gonna Take the Weight" (Kool and the Gang), **3:**681
"Why D'Ya Do It" (Faithfull), **3:**689
Whyte, Betsy, **8:**296
Whyte, Harcourt, **1:**35
Whyte, Ian, **8:**369
Wichita Indian nation, **3:**440
Wicke, Peter, **8:**219
Wickman, Putte, **8:**446
Wickwire, Wendy, **3:**1094
Wicky, Andreas, **8:***688*
Wicky, Anton, **8:***688*
Widad (Egyptian film), **6:**236
Widdess, Richard, **5:**34, 56, 215
Wiener, Charles, **2:**423
Wieniawski, Henryk, **8:**858
Wiesel, Uzi, **6:**1031
Wignjaroemeksa, Wignyarumeksa, **4:**636
Wigwam (musical group), **8:**217
Wijesekera, Nandadeva, **5:**962
Wilbert, Johannes, **2:**173–74, 198; **10:**98
Wild Cherry, **3:**712
Wild Ones (film), **8:**675
Wild, Stephen A., **9:**47, 453, 960, 976, 987
Wild Style (film), **3:**713
Wilde, Oscar, **5:**491
"Wildwood Flower" (Carter Family), **3:**78
Wilensky, Moshe, **6:**1072–73
Wilfahrt, "Whoopee John," **3:**898–99
Wilfrid Laurier University (Waterloo), **3:**1185
Wilgus, D. K., **3:**510; **8:**338
Wilhem, Guillaume Louis Bocquillon, **8:**106
Wilkes, Charles, **9:**18–20, 786, 797
Wilkins, Robert, **3:**645
Wilkinson, Mike, **2:**819
Wilkinson, Scott, **10:**88
"Will They Lie There Evermore?" (Phippard), **3:**1141–42

Will, Udo, **9:**292–94
"Will You Love Me Tomorrow" (Shirelles), **3:**673, 709
Willaert, Adrian, **8:**76
Willan, Healey, **3:**123, 1166, 1184, 1227
Willard, Augustus N., **5:**49–50, 561
Willemark, Lena, **8:**446
William Dube Jairos Jiri Sunrise Kwela Band, **1:**323
William V, king of the Netherlands, **4:**84
William Ransom Hogan Jazz Archive (Tulane University, New Orleans), **3:**33
Williams, Alberto, **2:**115
Williams, Alfred, **8:**329
Williams, Anthony, **2:**961
Williams, Augustus, **1:**355
Williams, Bert, **3:**194, 618, 619, 650, 706
Williams, Brent, **3:**1133
Williams, Clarence, **3:**644
Williams, Denis, **2:**442
Williams, Drid, **3:**221
Williams, Edward, **8:**185
Williams, Eric, **2:**953
Williams, Evan, **8:**352
Williams, Fadhili, **1:**486
Williams, Farley Keith. *See* Farley "Jackmaster Funk"
Williams, F. E., **9:**501
Williams, Hank, **3:**77, 79, 80, 81, 108, 353, 520, 560, 1155; **8:**61
Williams, Harry, **9:**413
Williams, Henry F., **3:**423, 604
Williams, James Kimo, **3:**612
Williams, Jerry (pseud. of Erik Fernström), **8:**446
Williams, John, **3:**204, *204;* **9:**348, 795, 818, 861, 897
Williams, John Lloyd, **8:**353, *353*
Williams, John Patrick, **3:**499
Williams-Jones, Pearl, **3:**585; **10:**139, 141
Williams, Julius P., **3:**612
Williams, Lottie, **3:**618
Williams, Maria Jane, **8:**352
Williams, Martin, **3:**583, 663
Williams, Mary Lou, **3:**659
Williams, Mayo "Ink," **3:**707
Williams Mix (Cage), **3:**253
Williams, Nancy, **9:**47
Williams, Nathaniel, **10:**139
Williams, Paul, **3:**669
Williams, Sean, **4:**107, 701
Williams, Timothy, **3:**200
Williams, Tunde, **1:**483
Williams, Vern, **9:**969
Williams and Walker (musical), **3:**621
Williams, Wilbert, **3:**313
Williamson, David, **9:**416
Williamson, Duncan, **8:**296, 370, 372
Williamson, Eleanor, **9:**976
Williamson, John Lee "Sonny Boy," **3:**645
Williamson, Linda J., **8:**297
Williamson, Muriel, **4:**26, 380, 383–85, 393–94
Williamson, Robin, **8:**322
Williche culture, **2:**357, 366
Willie K, **9:**167
"Willing Conscript" (Paxton), **3:**316
Willis, Richard, **3:**564

Willoughby, A. C., **1:**159
Wills, Alejandro, **2:**394–95
Wills, Bob, **3:**78, 520
Wills y Escobar (Colombian duo), **2:**395
Willson, David, **3:**1079, 1179
Wilson, Alan, **10:**87
Wilson, Ben, **3:***647*
Wilson, Edith, **3:**644
Wilson, Gerald, **3:**747
Wilson, Captain Henry, **9:**7, 723
Wilson, John, **8:**370
Wilson, Nancy, **3:**713
Wilson, Olly, **3:**585, *585*, 610
Wilson, Teddy, **3:**655
Wilson, Thomas, **8:**369
"Wilt Thou Be Gone, Love?" (Foster), **3:**187
"Wimoweh" (Linda), **1:**773; **3:**328, 329
Winans (gospel group), **3:**634
Winans, Ce Ce, **3:***634*
wind instruments. *See* aerophones
Wind River Shoshones, **3:**421, 487
Windakiewiczowa, Helena, **8:**712
Windha, I Nyoman, **3:**1019
Windham Hill Records, **3:**345, 346, 954
Windhus, John, **3:**65
Windsor Records, **5:**592
Windsor Symphony Orchestra, **3:**1079, 1184
Windward Community College (Kaneohe), **10:**43
Windward Islands, **2:**789, 864
Wineera, Mrs. Paeroa, **9:**933
Wineera, Vernice, **9:**972
Winne, Jane Lathrop, **9:**892
Winnebago Indian nation, **3:**369, 451, 452, 539
Winner, Septimus. *See* Hawthorne, Alice
Winnie, Fannie, **3:**312
Winnie, Ray, **3:**311–12
Winnipeg Male Voice Choir, **3:**1225, *1226*
Winnipeg Philharmonic Society, **3:**1090, 1224
Winnipeg Symphony Orchestra, **3:**1090
Winston, George, **3:**346, 347
Winter, Johnny, **8:**218
Winter into Spring (album), **3:**346
Winter Swimmers (musical group), **8:**1021
Winterbottom, Thomas, **1:**84–85
Winterreise (Schubert), **8:**656
Winterstein, Titi, **8:**289
Winthuis, Josef, **9:**479, 983, 991
Wiora, Walter, **3:**45; **8:**20, 25, 26, 52, 188, 648
Wirakusumah, Radén Sambas, **4:**705
Wiratini, Ni Made, **3:**1019
Wiru people, **9:**514
Wirz, Paul, **9:**480
Wisconsin
   Boscobel, **10:**157
   Czech people in, **3:**898
   Delaware Indian groups in, **3:**462
   Finnish people in, **3:**872–75
   German people in, **3:**888–89; **10:**160
   Milwaukee
      ethnic dance in, **3:**216
      German people in, **3:**528
      polka parties in, **3:**213
      Slovenian people in, **3:**901
   Native American groups in, **3:**371, 451–59
   Norwegian people in, **3:**866–70

Slovak people in, **3:**899
Swedish people in, **3:**870–72
women's bands in, **3:**566
Wisconsin Slovak Historical Society, **3:**899
Wise, Sue, **3:**114
"Wish You Were Here, Buddy" (Boone), **3:**317, 318
Wismar, Müller, **9:**981
Wisnik, José Miguel, **2:**320
"Within a Mile of Edinburgh" (Hook), **3:**180
Witkhaddari (bridal song), **6:**587
Witkowski, Bernie, **3:**893
Witmark brothers, **3:**259
Witmer, Robert, **3:**50, 150, 484, 1086–87
Witte, Parker F., **1:**254
Wiyot Indian nation, **3:**412
Wiz (Smalls), **3:**622
Wizard of Oz (film), **3:**622
Wodeyar, Jayachamarajendra, **5:**211
Wodonga-Albury Band, **9:**76
Wodziwob, **3:**421, 487
Wogeo people, **9:**246
Wohlberger, Lionel, **8:**267
Wokpεε (Liberian singer), **1:**9
Wolbers, Paul Arthur, **4:**639
Woleai Atoll (Yap State, FSM), **9:**729, 733, 979
Wolf-Ferrari, Ermanno, **8:**618
"Wolf Project" (Schafer), **3:**345, 1059
Wolf Trap Farm Park (Vienna, Virginia), **3:**300
Wolfe, Julia, **3:**177
Wolfe Tones (musical group), **8:**391
Wolfman (Ashley), **3:**253
Wolof culture, in Dominican Republic, **2:**850
Wolof people, **1:**443
gewel, **1:**444
*griot*s, **1:**518, 523
history of, **1:**444
instruments of, **1:**445, 448
music of, **1:**421–22, 446–47
social organization of, **1:**443
Wolownik, Steve, **3:**58
Wolpe, Stefan, **6:**1027
Wolters, G., **8:**661
Womad Productions/Realworld, **3:**955
women. *See* gender; performers; sex and music; sexual differentiation
Women's Musical Club of Toronto, **3:**93, 1209–10
Women's Musical Club of Winnipeg, **3:**93
women's suffrage movement, **3:**90, 308, 310
Won, Il, **7:**970
Won Ji-jong, **3:**1262
Wonder, Stevie, **3:**676, 677, 709, 713; **5:**540
Wonderful Grand Band, **3:**1121
Wong, Anthony (Huang Huimin), **7:**355
Wong Audiovisual Center (University of Hawai'i), **9:**971
Wong, Deborah, **4:**26, 258
Wong, Faye (Wang Fei), **7:**355
Wong, Francis, **3:**972
Wong, Isabel K. F., **7:**381
Wong, James (Wong Zhan), **7:**355
Wong, Jamin, **9:**167
Wong, Owen, **3:**1262
Wong, Paul (Huang Guanzhong), **7:**355
Wong Tou, **3:**1262

Wong Wun-wah, **3:**1263
Wŏn'gaksa theater (Seoul), **7:**968
Wongsokadi, **4:**680, 683
Wongsosewojo, R. Ahmad, **4:**655
Woni people, **4:**540
Woo, Juang Sun, **7:**970
Wood, Dr. A. Harold, **9:**131, 204
wood blocks. *See* slit-drums
Wood, J. Muir, **8:**373
Wood, Natalie, **3:**741
Wood, Richard, **3:**1127
Wood, Stan, **3:**1077
Wood, Thomas, **8:**367
Wood, Victor, **4:**884
Wood, Vivian Nina M., **2:**812
Wood, William, **10:**88
Woodcock, George, **3:**1270
Woodford, Paul, **3:**1070
Woodland culture, **3:**6, 461
Woodland Sketches (MacDowell), **7:**955
"Woodmen's Song" (ballad), **3:**154
Woodrow, H., **5:**432
Woodward, Ralph Lee, Jr., **2:**767
Woody Woodpeckers, **1:**771
"Woody'n You," **3:**659
Wooley, Sir Arthur, **6:**17, 358
Woomera, **9:**430
W.O.R. (musical group), **3:**337
Worchester, Dean, **4:**872
Work, Henry Clay, **3:**189–90, 835
Work, John, **3:**577, 624, 630
Work, John, II, **3:**629
Work, John, III, **3:**628, 629
Work, John Wesley, Jr., **3:**579
"Work with Me Annie" (Ballard), **3:**351
work music. *See also* shanties
Abkhazian people, **8:**852
Adighian people, **8:**855
Afghanistan, **5:**821
African-American, **3:**82–85, 293, 592, 599–600
Ainu people, **7:**786–87
Albania, **8:**993
Algeria, **6:**473, 474
Andean regions, **2:**221
harawi agricultural songs, **2:**215
north-south distinctions, **2:**222
Andhra Pradesh, *rōkaṭi pāṭalu*, **5:**891, *892*
Argentina, *minga*, **2:**255
Armenia, **6:**728
Azerbaijan, **6:**931
Balochistan, **5:**775, 777
Barbados, **2:**817
Belarus, **8:**792, 796, 798
Bengal, *sārigān*, **5:**862
Bosnia-Hercegovina, **8:**963
Brazil, *brāo*, **2:**301
Bribri culture
ajkŏyönuk, **2:**634
kulè, **2:**634
Brittany, **8:**559
Bulgaria, **8:**900
Canada, occupational songs, **3:**1124, 1140–43, 1188–89, 1193
Caribbean, **2:**36, 48–49, 56
African-derived, **2:**793, 795

Central America, **2:**36, 48–49, 56
Chechen people, **8:**864
China, **7:**91, 150–51, 153, 297, 346, 384, 417, 462
Corsica, animal-drivers' songs, **8:***22, 142,* 566, 567–68
Croatia, **8:**925–26, 931
Cyprus, **8:**1031
Czech Republic, Moravia, **8:**722
Denmark, **8:**458–59
Dominica, **2:**843
Dominican Republic, *plena,* **2:**849, 851
Ecuador, **2:**416
jaway, **2:**425
Estonian labor songs, **3:**878
Europe, **8:**127, 133, 141
instrumental, **8:**198
nonagricultural, **8:**142–43
occupational songs, **8:**6, 142, 185, 188, 365
shepherds' instruments, **8:**8
women's, **8:**196–97
Europe, pastoral regions, **8:**194
field hollers, **3:**639
Finnish labor songs, **3:**873
France, **8:**540, 545
briolées, **8:**132
Gaelic milling songs, **3:**1070, 1129
Garífuna culture, **2:**734
eremuna égi, **2:**675
laremuna wadaguman, **2:**675
German labor songs, **3:**888
Germany, miners' songs, **8:**133, 185
Great Lakes rice-hulling songs, **3:**458
Greece, **8:**1015, 1016
Greece, ancient, **8:**46
Guadeloupe, **2:**876
Guyana, genres of, **2:**447–48
Haiti, **2:**885
herding
Albania, **8:**993
Bulgaria, **8:**892
Europe, **8:**127, 142, 198
Germany, **8:**651
Low Countries, **8:**520
Macedonia, **8:**975
Norway, **8:**412, 420
Q'ero culture, **2:**227
Romania, **8:**875
Russia, **8:**770
Sweden, **8:**26, 435, 436, 438, *438,* 682
Switzerland, **8:**17, 26, 119, 128, 142, 682–83
Ingush people, **8:**864
Ireland, spinning songs, **8:**388
Italy, **8:**142, 606, *606*
Jamaica, **2:**904, 905–6, 912
Japan, **7:**600
in *kabuki,* **7:**659
Karnataka
kabita, **5:**883
pāḍḍana songs, **5:**415, 882–83
Kashmir, **5:**684–85
Kerala, **5:**949–50
Korea, **7:**988
farmers' bands, **7:**929
Korean people in China, **7:**519

work music (*continued*)
  Kurdistan, **6:**751
  Latvia, **8:**499, 500, 501–2, 503
  Low Countries, **8:**520
  Macedonia, **8:**973, 975
  Madhya Pradesh, **5:**723
  Malta, **8:**638, 641
  Nepal, **5:**701
  New England, northern, **3:**155–58
  North Caucasia, **8:**851
  Norway, **8:**421
  Oman, **6:**673
  Orissa, **5:**733
  Ossetian people, **8:**859
  Peru, **2:**471, 495
    Andean area, **2:**476
  Philippines, occupational songs, **4:**911
  Poland, **8:**113–14
  Portugal, **8:**578
    harvest songs, **8:**132
  Rajasthan, **5:**646
  Romania, **8:**870, 875
  Russia, **8:**760
  Ryûkyû Islands, **7:**794, 795
  St. Lucia, *chanté siay,* **2:**946–47
  Scotland
    Hebrides, **8:**361
    waulking songs, **8:**133, 141, 197, 361–62, 373
  Serbia, **8:**940–41
  Shao pople, pestle songs, **7:**527
  Sicily, **8:**142
  Slovakia, **8:**722
  Slovenia, **8:**912
  South America, **2:**36, 48–49, 56
  in South Indian films, **5:**542
  Spain, **8:**591, 593
    harvest songs, **8:**132
  street cries
    Algeria, **6:**474
    East Asia, **7:**153, 414, 604, *604*
    Germany, **8:**653
    North America, **3:**84, 600
    Slovenia, **8:**912
  Switzerland, **8:**682–83, 693, 694–95
  Tamil Nadu, **5:**918–19
  Thailand, **4:**114, 300
  Tibet, **7:**473–74
  Turkey, **6:**767
  Uighur people, **7:**458
  Ukraine, *dosvitky,* **8:**196–97, 808, 809, 810, 812
  United States
    field hollers, **3:**83–84
    improvisation in, **3:**601
    nineteenth century, **3:**555
    occupational songs, **3:**520
    social class and, **3:**45, 47–48
  Uttar Pradesh, **5:**661
  Venezuela, **2:**537
  Wales
    occupational songs, **8:**344
    oxen songs, **8:**344
  Warao culture, *dakoho,* **2:**197
  Yanomamö culture, **2:**173
  Yemen, **6:**655

Working Afternoon (musical group), **8:**779
"Working Man Blues," **3:**81
"Working My Way Back to You/Forgive Me, Girl" (Spinners), **3:**711
Works Progress Administration (Work Projects Administration), **3:**289, 294, 297, 599, 737, 738. *See also* Federal Music Project; Federal Theater Project
world beat (worldbeat), **2:**94, 98, 105–6, 486; **3:**337–42, 955; **9:**1005–6
  future of, **3:**340–41
  historical perspectives on, **3:**341–42
  musical characteristics of, **3:**337–38
  technology in, **3:**340
World Circuit (record company), **8:**241
World Collection of Recorded Folk Music, **7:**524
World Intellectual Property Organization, **3:**289
"World Is a Ghetto" (War), **3:**681
World Kulintang Institute (Los Angeles), **3:**1026
world music, **3:**338, 1060, 1279; **6:**23, 239, 277, 438, 986–87
  borrowings for popular music, **3:**326–27
  in China, **7:**444
  commercialization of, **5:**576; **8:**210, 220
  concept of, **1:**418; **10:**41
  contrasted with world beat, **3:**337
  culture of, **8:**224–27
  definitions of, **8:**224
  festivals of, **8:**154
  in Finland, **8:**484, 486
  historical perspectives on, **8:**227–28
  historiography of, **8:**59
  incorporation of Saami joiking, **8:**299
  increasing popularity of, **8:**96, 168, 890
  influence on jazz, **3:**336
  influence on New Age music, **3:**345
  influence on rock, **3:**347
  in Italy, **8:**620
  in Japan, **7:**747
  in Korea, **7:**967
  in Mongolia, **7:**1014
  Muslim contributions to, **8:**12
  political implications of, **3:**498
  radio programming of, **3:**504
  syakuhati in, **7:**709
  Tibetan musical elements in, **5:**715
  in Tuva, **7:**1014, 1023–25
  women's performance of, **8:**201
World of Music (periodical), **2:**543
World Music Archives (Middletown), **3:**496
World Music Institute (New York), **3:**996, 1008, 1037; **5:**529; **8:**489; **10:**72
World Music: The Rough Guide, **3:**338
World of Rock (Gabree), **3:**348
World Soundscape Project (Simon Fraser University), **3:**14
World War I, **3:**443–44, 866, 886
World War II, **3:**263, 443, 512, 969, 970; **7:**808; **9:**25–33
  in Austria, **10:**110
  in Bellona, **9:**852
  in Fiji, **9:**779–80
  in Japan, **7:**729, 733, 745, 790
  in Kapingamarangi, **9:**836
  in Kiribati, **9:**764
  in Korea, **7:**910

  in Micronesia, **9:**159–61, 724, 729, 751, 758
  nationalism and, **3:***507*, 511
  in Papua New Guinea, **9:**149–50, 475, 499, 566, 607, 614, 620
  in Solomon Islands, **9:**157, 630, 661, 665
  in Vanuatu, **9:**139, 700, 707
World's Columbian Exposition (Chicago), **3:**243, 871, 1013, 1028, 1048; **5:**563; **6:**547; **9:**225
Worlds of Music Toronto, **3:**1213
Wounded Knee massacre, **3:**11, 421, 487, 494
Wovoka (Jack Wilson), **3:**421, 487
Wowono, John, **9:**387
Wray, Link, **3:**355
"Wreck of Old 97," **3:**293
Wright, Debbie Hippolite, **9:**972
Wright, Josephene, **3:**573
Wright, Kylie, **9:***416*
Wright, Lucy, **3:**135
Wright, Owen, **6:**73, 75, 122, 535
Wright, Robert, **3:**314
Writings on Dance (journal), **9:**415
Writings of the Later Han and Wei Dynasties (Chinese chronicle), **7:**59
Wrong Side of the Road (film), **9:**146
WSM Barn Dance (radio program), **3:**560
WSZA-Radio (Yap), archives of, **9:**967–68
Wu Bai, **7:**358
Wu Ben, **10:**26
Wu Bochao, **7:**398
Wu Guodong, **7:**444
Wu Ti, emperor of China, **4:**41
Wu Zengqi, **7:**132
Wu Zhao, **7:**87
Wu Zhimin, **7:**177
Wu Zuqiang, **7:**349
Wubangzi (Feng), **7:**185, 236
Wudai tongtang (*Jiangnan sizhu* piece), **7:**238
Wu geng diao (*xiaodiao*), **7:**152
Wuhan Conservatory, **7:**398
Wulin jiushi (Zhou), **7:**129
Wuñci Padeitháyaṣa, **4:**381
Wüst, Wilhelm, **8:**663
Wusun people, **7:**460
Wu-Sun tribe, **6:**965
Wuttunee, Winston, **3:**411
Wuvulu Island (Papua New Guinea), **9:**602
Wuxi jing (*xiaodiao*), **7:**152
Wu yue—Chun qiu (dynastic history), **7:**153
Wyatt, David K., **4:**219
Wynad Ceṭṭi caste, **5:**909
Wynette, Tammy, **3:**81
Wyoming
  Native American groups in, **3:**420–22, 425–27, 440
  Volga Germans in, **3:**890
Wyrobek, Boguslaw, **8:**221

X: The Life and Times of Malcolm X (Davis), **3:**612
Xangô, **2:**341. *See also* Shango
Xangurti, Hājji Huseyn-i, **6:**914
Xanum, Munisa Mexseti, **6:**922
Xarhakos, Stavros, **8:**1021
Xasan, Maxamed Cabdille, **1:**613, *615*
Xavante culture, **2:**126, *127*

Xavier, Francisco de, **7**:724
Xavier University, **4**:873
Xenakis, Iannis, **4**:131, 876; **7**:737; **8**:101, 1008
Xenon (New York), **3**:229
Xenophon, **6**:743; **8**:842–43, 881
Xhongxing lishu (collection), **7**:131
Xhosa people, **1**:705. *See also* Nguni peoples
    Christianity and, **1**:763
    dance, **1**:768–69
    instruments of, **1**:719
    music of, **1**:306–7, 706, 765–66, 767, 769
    praise poetry, **1**:762
Xi Genghu, **7**:300–301
Xi Huguang, **7**:347
Xi Kang, **7**:89, 159, 161–62
Xia dynasty
    female musicians in, **7**:402, 406
    instruments in, **7**:105–6, 107
    music in, **7**:447
Xia Muas (Hmong singer), **4**:557
Xia Tingzhi, **7**:407
Xia Ye, **7**:87
Xia'erba people, **7**:471, 482–83
Xi'an Conservatory, **7**:398
Xi'an Song and Dance Troupe, **7**:414
Xian Xinghai, **7**:341, 346, 347, 349, 350,
    384–85, 386
Xianbei people, **7**:29, 30, 517
Xiang guang diao (*xiaodiao*), **7**:152
Xiang jiang lang (*xiaodiao*), **7**:152
Xiang juang long (*qin* piece), **7**:123
Xiang Sihua, **7**:172
Xiang Yang, **7**:142
Xiang Yu, **7**:168
Xiang Zuhua, **7**:181
Xiange bidu (Cantonese collection), **7**:217–18,
    220
Xiange zhongxi hepu (Shen), **7**:218
Xiansuo beikao (Ming), **7**:125
Xiansuo beikao (Yong), **7**:133
xiao. *See* flutes
Xiao Bai, **7**:387
Xiao Nan, **7**:363–65, 364–65
Xiao San, **7**:383
Xiao taohong (*guochang qu* tune), **7**:218
Xiao Wenbin, **7**:299
Xiao Youmei, **7**:56, 345, 376–77, 381–82, 397
Xibe people, **7**:518
Xibo people, **7**:455–58, 463
Xie Lei, **7**:357
Xihu yuolanzhiyu (Dian), **7**:261
Xin Yue, **7**:725
Xing Dance Theatre (Toronto), **3**:224
Xinghai Conservatory (Guangzhou), **7**:220, 398
Xingjie (*Jiangnan sizhu* piece), **7**:225
Xinjiang Cultural Troupe, **7**:443
Xinmeiyuan (*luantan* opera troupe), **7**:425
Xiongnu people, **7**:28–29, 30, 167, 219
Xirsi "Baarleex," Cabdillaahi, **1**:617, *618*
XIT (musical group), **3**:433, 489
Xiu hua bao (*xiaodiao*), **7**:152
Xiu Jun, **7**:142
Xi'úi culture. *See* Pame culture
Xiujiu (*Zhedong luogu* piece), **7**:195
Xixiang Daiyue (Cantonese opera), **3**:1262
Xixiangfeng (Feng), **7**:185, 236

Xtiêng people, **4**:533, 535
Xu Dachun, **7**:122
Xu Jian, **7**:137
Xu Li, **7**:117, 120
Xu Lixian, **7**:264
Xu Shuya, **7**:343
Xu Yuanbai, **10**:19
Xu Yunzhi, **7**:264
Xuan Ke, **7**:*445*
Xuan Tong, Qing emperor, **7**:375
Xuanzong, Tang emperor, **7**:321
Xue Baokun, **7**:248
Xue Juexian, **7**:306
Xuekang Suolangtajie, **7**:474–75
Xun Zhu, **7**:116
Xunfeng qu (Hakka piece), **7**:238
Xunfeng qu (*Jiangnan sizhu* piece), **7**:240
Xunzi, **7**:82, 98
Xuxa, **2**:41
xylophones, **5**:544. *See also* marimbas
    Africa, **1**:135, 157, 226, 254, 255, 295
    akadinda, **1**:312, 601; **10**:111, 116
    amadinda, **1**:218, 300, 312, 602; **10**:113, 116
    angklung, **4**:645, 667
    arumba, **4**:712
    atanatra, **1**:785
    Austria, **8**:672
    Azande people, **1**:656–57
    bala, **1**:489, 490–91, 495–98
    balafo, **3**:593
    balafon, **1**:159, 364–65, 420
    balangi, **1**:446
    Bantu groups, **1**:660–61
    Barbados, **2**:814
    Borneo, **4**:833–34
    Buganda, **1**:36
    calung, **4**:669, 697, 711–12
    canang kayu, **4**:605
    ch'lung, **4**:446
    Chopi people, **1**:715–16
    cultural origins of, **4**:11
    distribution of, **1**:457
    do'u da, **4**:793
    embaire, **1**:299–300, 312
    in Finnish music, **3**:875
    gabbang, **4**:833, 834, 899–900, 902, 906, 908,
        909
    gambang, **4**:58, 73, 103, 107
        Borneo, **4**:834
        Cirebon, **4**:691
        Java, **4**:665, 668, 672–73, *674*; **10**:43, 44,
          48
        Malaysia, **4**:403, 428, 429
        Sumatra, **4**:605, 615, 617, 626
        Sunda, **4**:704
    gambang barung, **4**:645
    gambang kayu, **4**:641, 643
    gambang panerus, **4**:645
    gambang pengarep, **4**:645
    gambang penggedhé, **4**:645
    gambang penodhos, **4**:645
    gamolan, **4**:628
    garantung, **4**:608
    geko, **4**:793
    in gong-chime ensembles, **4**:20
    grantang, **4**:767

gyile, **1**:211
gyilgo, **1**:222, 457
Ila people, **1**:712
jatung utang, **4**:833, *834*
Java, **4**:641
jengsi, **1**:457
jinjimba, **1**:678
katikoky, **1**:789
kertok kelapa, **4**:424–25, *433*
ketadu mara, **4**:803
kethuk-kenong, **4**:645
khinh khung, **4**:534
koangtâc, **4**:534
kolintang, **4**:810
kongkong, **4**:563, 587
Kongo kingdom, **1**:667–68
korro, **1**:455
kpáníngbá, **1**:570
kponingbo, **1**:656
kulintang, **4**:901–2
kulintangan, **4**:834
kwintangan kayu, **4**:903–94
lanat, **4**:57, 350, 354, 355
lanat ek, **4**:358
lelega, **4**:614
letor, **4**:793
limba, **1**:670
longo, **1**:656
Lozi people, **1**:712, 713
luntang, **4**:903, 926
Madagascar, **1**:785
madimba, **1**:669
mangologondo, **1**:638, 639; **10**:*115*
mangwilo, **1**:10, 156
manza, **1**:656
marimba, **1**:605, 638–39
mbila mutondo, **1**:709
meko ai, **4**:800
mendzaŋ, **1**:659, 660–61
mohambi, **1**:711
muqin, **7**:527–28
Nigeria, **1**:450
Nkoya people, **1**:712
Oceania, **9**:373
palompong, **4**:780–81
pa'talà, **4**:22, 57, 163, 378
patatag, **4**:919
pedagogical uses of, **3**:280, 281
in polka bands, **3**:893
pong lang (also *khaw law*), **4**:*57*, 318–19, 320,
    338
preson, **4**:793
ranat, **4**:57, 163; **7**:496
ranat ek, **4**:17, 22, 229, *242*, *244*, *250*, 251,
    257, 260, 262, 270–71, 272, 302, 329
ranat thum, **4**:229, *240*, *242*, 267, 271, 272,
    548
ridu, **4**:793
rimba, **1**:624
rindik, **4**:754
ringu, **6**:630, 631
roneat, **4**:57
roneat ek, **4**:162, 163–64, 183, 197
roneat thung, **4**:164, 183
rongo, **1**:570
sene hauh, **4**:797

xylophones (*continued*)
  Senufo people, **1:**454
  silimba, **1:**673
  slenthem, **4:**645
  Southeast Asia, **4:**57–58, 596
  southeastern Africa, **1:**708
  Tanzania, **1:**638–39
  tatabuhan kayu, **4:**818
  timbila, **1:**227, 429, 436, 709–10
  tingklik, **4:**754
  t'rung, **3:**996; **4:**446, 534
  tudduglag, **4:**614
  tuning of, **1:**257–67, 715–16
  valimba, **1:**323, 711
  Vanuatu, **9:**693
  West Africa, **1:**446, 456–57
  zhuqin, **7:**527–28
Xylouris, Nikos, **8:**1018
X. Y. Z. for Musique Concrète (Mayuzumi), **7:**736

Yabio people, **9:**557
Yadav, Bihari Lal, **5:**667, 668–69
Yaezaki *kengyô*, **7:**697, 698
Yafil, Edmond-Nathan, **6:**1044
Yagi busi (Japanese folk song), **7:**571, 601–2, 602, 604
Yagi no kai (composers' group), **7:**736
Yagnik, Alka, **5:**421, 540
Yagua culture, **2:**482
Yahgan (Yamana) culture, **2:**357
Yaḥyá ibn Khālid, vizier, **6:**297, 353
Yahya, Umar Sama, **5:**45
Yakabi kunkusî (collection), **7:**793
Yakabi Tyôki, **7:**793
Yakan people, **4:**889, 920
  epics of, **4:**908
  instrumental music of, **4:**891, 898–900, 902, 903–5
  vocal music of, **4:**906, 909–10, 911
Yakhal' Inkomo (album), **1:**779
Yakshagana Academy (Bangalore), **5:**881
Yakut people. *See* Sakha people
Yā layla dānā (Saudi song), **6:**700
Yale people
  composition of, **9:**360
  songs of, **9:**580, 583–84
Yale University (New Haven), **3:**173, 175
Yali people, **9:**360, 580, 581, 583–84
Yalunka people, **1:**446
Yama (deity), **5:**897
Yama, Isaac, **9:**413
Yamada *kengyô*, **7:**647, 697, 758
Yamada Kôsaku, **7:**346, 729, 731, 750
Yamada Yôiti, **7:**594
Yamaguchi Goro, **7:**707, 708
Yamaguchi, Patricia Matusky, **10:**56
Yamaguti Katuhiro, **7:**736
Yamaguti Momoe, **7:**747
Yamaguti Osamu, **7:**594; **9:**305, 722, 723, 967, 994; **10:**13, 14
Yamamoto Hozan, **7:**695, 707, 708
Yámana culture, **2:**250, 251
Yamanoi Motokiyo, **7:**627
Yamato gouta no mai (*yakuo goto* piece), **7:**610
Yamato house, **7:**18, 24–25, 26, 27
Yamauchi, John, **3:**969

"*Yā mā yā ghālīya*" (*piyuṭ*), **6:**529–31
Yamaye culture, **2:**78
Yamazaki Kyokusui, **7:**650, 650
Yamazaki, Paul, **3:**336, 971–72
Yami people, **7:**527
Yampolsky, Philip, **3:**1014; **4:**102, 103, 107–8, 603, 639; **10:**52
Yan Cheng, **7:**132
Yan dynasties, **7:**517
Yan Jun-ho, **3:**1262
Yan Laolie, **3:**1261; **7:**180, 219
Yan state, **7:**17–18, 24
Yan Tingjie, **7:**139
Yan Zide, **7:**154
Yana Indian nation, **3:**415
Yanada Tadasi, **7:**731
Yanagita Kunio, **7:**600
Yancey, Estelle "Mama," **3:**105–6, 106
Yancey, Jimmy, **3:**105, 647
Yang Fang, **7:**444
Yang Feifei, **7:**300
Yang Jingming, **7:**181, 231
Yang Jingren, **7:**442
Yang Li-hua, **7:**426
Yang Sŭnghŭi, **7:**986
Yang, Vungping, **3:**1005
Yang Xiaoting, **7:**264
Yang Xiuqing, **7:**424
Yang Ying, **7:**363–65
Yang Yinliu, **7:**87, 137, 140, 177, 200, 336, 388, 391
Yang Yuanheng, **7:**204
Yang Yunfu, **7:**168
Yang Zenglie, **7:**450
Yang Zhenxiong, **7:**264
Yang Zhongzhi, **7:**376
Yangch'ŏng todŭri (*tangak* piece), **7:**867
Yangchun baixue (*pipa* suite), **7:**239
Yangguan qu (Minnan suite), **7:**238
Yangguan sandie (*qin* piece), **7:**161–63, 162–64
Yanggŭm sinbo (collection), **7:**848, 856, 921
Yang jia jiang (Chinese novel), **7:**452
yangqin. See dulcimers, hammered
Yangsando (Korean folk song), **7:**881
Yangyangga (*kasa*), **7:**927
Yangzhou Huafanglu (Li), **7:**129
Yankaran, Anand, **2:**86
"Yankee Doodle," **3:**180, 305, 307, 521, 538, 870, 888
"Yankee Doodle Boy" (Cohan), **3:**193
Yankovic, Frankie, **3:**529, 824, 901–2
Yankunytjatjara people, **9:**433
Yanni, **3:**347
Yano, **4:**888
Yanomamö culture, **2:**169–75, 188, 189
  festivals of, **2:**173
  lack of instruments, **2:**127, 169–70
  shamanism in, **2:**170–73, 179
  vocal music of, **2:**170–75
  Yanomam group, **2:**169–75
Ya nur (bridal song), **6:**587
Yanyuwa people, **9:**427–28, 460–62
Yao Bingyan, **10:**18–19
Yao Min, **7:**354
Yao people, **4:**528, 537, 549–50
  Arabic influences, **1:**606

dance, *beni*, **1:**603
folk songs of, **7:**449
frame drum and bronze drum ensemble, **7:**192
instruments of, **4:**535
in Laos, **4:**336
masks of, **1:**119
music of, **7:**485–92
Yao Wenyuan, **7:**388
Yaounde people, **1:**659
  speech surrogate methods, **1:**106, 107
Yap empire, **9:**53, 716
Yap Island (Federated States of Micronesia), **9:**160, 712, 722, 726, 729–33. *See also* Ulithi Atoll
  betel use in, **9:**177
  Christianity in, **9:**720
  dance genres of, **9:**726–27, 728
  history of, **9:**729
  instruments of, **9:**717, 730
  meleng genre, **9:**305
  melodies of, **9:**304–6
  music and dance in, **9:**729–33, 979, 981
  rap in, **9:**160
  religion in, **9:**199–200
  research on, **9:**25, 729
  settlement of, **9:**715
  sound recordings from, **9:**994–96
Yaqui Indian nation, **2:**549–50, 554, 586, 588–93; **3:**218, 417, 428, 437–38, 485–86
  corridos, **2:**591, 593
  history of, **2:**588–89
  instruments of, **2:**589; **3:**475
  matachines performances, **2:**591, 593; **3:**436, 437–38, 850–51
  research on, **2:**593
Yarboro, Caterina, **3:**619
Yardbirds (musical group), **3:**356; **8:**214
Yari no Gonza (Chikamatsu), **7:**669
Yarkov, Piotr, **8:**776, 777
Yaşar, Tanburi Necdet, **6:**55, 121
Yasawa Islands (Fiji), **9:**773
Yasima (*nô* play), **7:**632
Yasiyasi people, **9:**983
Yasovarman, king of Chenla, **4:**187
Yassawi (Sufi poet). *See* Ahmad Yassawi, Hoja
Yassua people, **1:**119
Yatco, Oscar, **4:**870
Yates, Mike, **8:**339
Yatkha, **7:**1019
Yatubyôsi (*nô* notation), **7:**590
Yatuhasi *kengyô*, **7:**647, 687–88, 696, 697, 712
Yaunzem, Irma, **8:**778, 779
Yavapai Indian nation, **3:**434
Yavaşça, Alâettin, **6:**110, 117
Yavorsky, Boleslav, **8:**783
Yayii, Philip Lamasisi, **9:**480, 983
Yayoi period, **7:**559, 560–62
Yā zarīf al-tūl (*dabke* song), **6:**576, 578
Yazīd ibn 'Abd al-Malik, caliph, **6:**291–92, 295, 298, 539
Yazīd I, Ummayad caliph, **5:**277; **6:**539
Yazyr people, **6:**966
Yazzie, Alfred, **3:**312–13
Yazzie, Larry, **3:**447
Yde, Jens, **2:**442

Ye Bohe, 7:137
Ye Dong, 7:137
Ye Junlin, 7:357
Ye Tang, 7:132
Ye Yonghae, 7:996
Yearbook for Traditional Music (periodical), 8:20
Yeats, William Butler, 8:378, 387, 388
Yedige (epic), 6:952
Yegāne, Mohammad Hosein, 6:839–40, 841
Yeghishe, 6:723
Yegua, Zaina, 2:*235*
Yejing (Sang), 7:348
Yejong, Koryŏ king, 7:982
Yektâ Bey, Raûf, 6:24, 48, 52, 108, 109, 110,
     117, 119, 124, 127, 758, 772, 780,
     783, 785
Yekuaná (Aretz), 2:115
Yekuana culture, 2:169–70, 176–82
     instruments of, 2:33, 34, 176–79
     vocal music of, 2:180–81
Yellow, Billy, 3:312
Yellow Blues, 1:433
Yellow Earth (film), 7:203, 257–59
Yellow Magic Orchestra, 7:746
Yellow River Cantata (Xian), 7:346, 384, 386
Yellow River Piano Concerto (Yin et al.),
     7:349–50
Yellow Top Band, 9:139
Yemen
     aerophones in, 6:414
     barber-musicians in, 6:304
     chordophones in, 6:407, 409, 412–13
     coastal regions, 6:656
     dance traditions in, 6:302, 654, 703–11
     drum ensembles in, 6:93–106, 656
     drums in, 6:417–20
     geography of, 6:93
     ghazal performances, 6:301, 685–86
     Ḥaḍramawt region, 6:656–57
          drum ensembles, 6:95–98, 101–3, 420
          ibex hunts, 6:656, 706
     high plateau region
          drum ensembles, 6:99–100, 104–6
          vocal music, 6:655–56
     idiophones in, 6:403, 405
     Jewish people in, 6:1047–48
     lyre depictions in, 6:357–58
     malhun, 6:495, 500
     qawma and *tawshīḥ* genres, 6:689–90
     research on music of, 6:649
     Ṣanʿāʾ
          dasaʿ dance, 6:709
          gender differentiation in musical genres,
               6:305
          poetry and music in, 6:403, 407, 685–90
     sexual segregation in, 6:299–300
     Tihāma, drum ensembles, 6:7, 95, 98–99,
          103, 656
     urban influences in, 6:306–7
     wedding rituals in, 6:303, 307
     women's music, 6:301, 695–702
Yemeni people, in North America, 3:1029;
     6:283, 284–85
Yenchang University, 7:398
Yengi, Aşkin Nur, 6:252
Yeni Sesler (musical group), 8:*211*

Yentl (film), 3:943
Yerevan Theater of Opera and Ballet, 6:726
Yergashova, Mastane, 6:919
Yerma (Feliciano), 4:878
Yes (musical group), 3:356; 4:887
"Yes, Jesus Loves Me" (hymn), 9:150
"Yesterday" (Beatles), 3:552
Yesudas, K. J., 5:422, 554, 557, 924
Yesujŏn (Pak), 7:969
Yeum Art Hall (Seoul), 7:995
Yevshan Ukrainian Orchestra (Saskatoon), 3:343
Yey people, 9:587
Yezidi people, 6:408, 418
Yggdrasil (musical group), 8:472
Yi Byonguk, 7:957, 970–71
Yi Chaegyu, 7:984
Yi Ch'ijong, 7:990
Yi Chinyong, 7:965
Yi Chŏngdae, 7:963–67
Yi Chŏngjun, 7:960
Yi Chuhwan, 7:921, 927, 983
Yi Haesik, 7:956–57
Yi Hwajungsŏn, 7:893–95, 899, 909
Yi Hyegu. *See* Lee Hye-Ku
Yi Hyŏngsang, 7:856
Yi Ik, 7:855
Yi Injik, 7:944–45, 968
Yi Jianquan, 7:220
Yi Kwangsu, 7:933, 963–67
Yi Kyugyŏng, 7:855, 925, 951
Yi, marquis of Zeng
     bell set of, 7:88, 99–101, 108, 115–16, 117,
          121, 137, 191
     tomb contents of, 7:99, 108, 109–10, 188,
          402, 406
Yi Nal-ch'i, 7:899
Yi Nŭnghwa, 7:953
Yi people, 7:509
     Axi group, 7:*448*
     courtship rituals of, 7:417
     dances of, 7:510
     musical ensembles of, 7:451
     music of, 7:485–92
     opera of, 7:452
     popular music of, 7:444
     research on music of, 7:139
Yi Pohyŏng, 7:993
Yi Pyŏngsŏng, 7:921, 927
Yi Pyŏngwŏn. *See* Lee Byong-Won
Yi Sanggyu, 7:953–54, 990
Yi Sech'un, 7:925
Yi Sugyŏng, 7:989
Yi Tongbaek, 7:899, 989
Yi Tongbok, 7:856
Yi Yi Thant, Daw, 4:*142, 377*
Yi Yŏnghŭi, 7:986
Yi Yŏngsu, 7:971
Yichijio Sinzaburo, 7:524
Yidl mitn fidl (film), 3:938, 943
Yi jing (Book of Changes), 7:153
Yikhlif ʿalayku w-Kath-thar Allah Khayrkuh
     (Palestinian folk song), 6:590
Yilao people, 7:191
Yili (ceremonial text), 7:98
Yili jingchuan tongjie (Zhu), 7:125, 132
Yimas people, 9:557

Yin Chengzong, 3:960; 7:349–50
Yin Erwen, 7:204
Yinghua luo (Lü), 7:236
Yin niu si (*xiaodiao*), 7:152
Yinyue Jiaoyu (periodical), 7:228
Yinyue Yanjiu (periodical), 7:141
Yinyue Yanjiushuo Ziliaoshi, 7:127
Yinyue Yishu (periodical), 7:141
Yinzhongniao (Liu), 7:185
Yip's Children's Choral and Performing Arts
     Centre (Toronto), 3:1217
YIVO Institute (New York), 8:266–67
Yiwangjik Aakpu (institution), 7:808, 830
Yiwu suoyou (*I Have Nothing*) (Cui), 7:359, 367
Yiyongjun jinxingqu (*Song of the Volunteers*) (Nie),
     7:346, 384
Yo! MTV Raps (television show), 3:697, 712
Yo Sŏnggŭn, 7:969
Yoakam, Dwight, 3:520, 777
yodeling
     Austria, 8:671–73, *672, 674*
     in country music, 3:520, 648
     Czech Republic, 8:717
     Europe, 8:14, 19, 24
     Flores, 4:793
     Georgia, 8:828, *829*
     Germany, 8:651
     Goge people, 1:635
     Greece, Epirus, 8:1010
     Hawai'i, 9:300, 916
     intervallic range of, 8:128
     Italy, 8:607
     Khoikhoi people, 1:705
     !Kung people, 1:307
     Norway, 8:412
     Oceania, 9:297
     Palestine, 6:573
     Papua New Guinea, 9:49–50, 151, 297–99,
          478
          Huli people, 9:538, 540–41, 542, 543
     Pygmies, 1:658, 659, 688
     San people, 1:705
     Shona people, 1:432, 705, 744, 750
     Solomon Islands, 9:665
     Southeast Indian groups, 3:467
     Switzerland, 8:142, 683, 686, 688, 689,
          690–92, 696
     Vanuatu, 9:709
          Tanna, 9:706
Yodh, Medha, 3:980; 5:585
Yoeme culture. *See* Yaqui Indian nation
Yog Vashisht (manuscript), 5:*302*, 308–9
Yoga philosophy, 5:20, 34, 70, 220, 253, 255–56
Yogyakarta court, 4:633, 653, 676
Yokohama California (musical group), 3:970
Yokomiti Mario, 7:593
Yokoyama Katuya, 7:649, 707, 708–9
Yokuts Indian nation, 3:416
Yolngu people, 9:445
     clansongs, 9:301–2
     dance of, 9:243, 457–60
     newsong verse of, 9:356–57
Yŏlsaga (*ch'anggŭk* piece), 7:969
Yŏm Kyedal, 7:898, 904, 906
Yŏmillak (*hyangak* piece), 7:844–45, 867, 953,
     954

Yŏmillak-man (*hyangak* piece), 7:867
Yŏmillak-yŏng (*hyangak* piece), 7:867
Yomut tribe, 6:966
Yŏmyŏng ŭi norae (Ri), 7:960
Yonekawa Kin'ô, 7:698
Yong Zhai, 7:133
Yongbiŏch'ŏn'ga (Korean poem), 7:835, 867
Yonggom people, 9:188
Yongjae ch'onghwa (Sŏng), 7:855, 983
*Yŏngjo, Chosŏn king, 7:985
Yŏngjo shillok (dynastic history), 7:929
Yongle dadian (encyclopedia), 7:129
Yongle, Ming emperor, 7:33
Yŏngmok (Hwang), 7:956
Yŏngnam kinari (Korean folk song), 7:962
Yŏngnam nongak (SamulNori), 7:965, 966
Yŏngnang, 7:984
Yŏngnyŏngjŏn Shrine (Seoul), 7:982
Yŏngsan Hoesang (*chŏngak* suite), 7:5, 807, 866,
　　915, 953, 984
　　form in, 7:844
　　scales and modes in, 7:848, 849
　　versions of, 7:868–69
Yŏnp'ungho (North Korean opera), 7:962
Yoreme culture. *See* Mayo culture
Yŏrha ilgi (Pak), 7:855
York University (Toronto), 3:222, 225, 226,
　　1185, 1213
York Winds, 3:1186
Yorobôsi (Kanze), 7:630
Yoruba culture in the Americas, 2:71
　　in Belize, 2:668, 674
　　in Brazil, 2:341–42, 352
　　in Cuba, 2:822, 823–25
　　in Grenada, 2:865
　　in Surinam, 2:504
　　in Trinidad, 2:954–56
　　in Uruguay, 2:513, 521
Yoruba people, 1:452
　　accessories worn by, 1:115
　　apala music, 1:222
　　dance, 1:118
　　divination poetry, 1:125
　　festivals of, 1:411–13
　　foreign-indigenous interchange, 1:400–14
　　guitar music, 1:353
　　historical studies, 1:93
　　history of, 1:400–401, 459, 471–72
　　Ijebu group, 1:89–91
　　inside-outside distinctions, 1:130
　　instruments of, 1:460, 472
　　Islam and, 1:413–14
　　lamellophones, 1:317
　　masks of, 1:119
　　music composition of, 1:14, 19
　　music of, 1:460–61, 487
　　music research on, 1:36–37
　　popular music of, 1:471–87
　　praise songs, 1:409–10
　　religious music of, 1:39
　　repatriated, 1:401
　　song texts, 1:137
　　speech surrogate methods, 1:107
　　textile design, 1:114
　　theater arts, 1:400–402, 406–9
　　timelines of, 1:678

Yorube Ronu (Ogunde), 1:401, 407–8
Yosef, Rabbi Ovadia, 6:206
Yosida Hidekazu, 7:736
Yosida Kenkô, 7:646
Yosida Seihû, 7:705
Yosida Takeko, 7:649
Yosida Takurô, 7:747
Yosihide Yositake, 7:609
Yôsinsô (*biwa* piece), 7:644
Yosizawa *kengyô* II, 7:698
Yot Fa, king of Ayuthaya, 4:248
Yothu Yindi, 9:60–61, 145, 146, 394, 414, 443,
　　444, 445, 446, 987, 1005
Yotsugi Soga (Chikamatsu), 7:667–68
"You Are My Sunshine," 3:914; 9:25, 848
"You Beat Me to the Punch" (Wells), 3:674
"You Can't Hurry Love" (Supremes), 3:674
"You Don't Miss Your Water" (Bell), 3:676
"You Make Me Feel Brand New" (Stylistics), 3:711
"You Need Love" (Dixon), 3:112
"You Send Me" (Cooke), 3:709
"You Sexy Thing" (Hot Chocolate), 3:712
Youch, Adam, 3:133
You lan (Qiu), 7:161
Youmans, Vincent, 3:196
"Young Blood" (Coasters), 3:672
"Young Charlotte" (ballad), 3:155
"Young China" (Li), 7:357
Young Composers' Group (New York), 3:45
Young Composers Project, 3:281
Young, Dougie, 9:413, 442, 987
Young, Ernest, 4:303
"Young, Gifted, and Black" (Franklin), 3:710
Young, La Monte, 3:175–76, 541, 953
Young, Lester, 3:656, 660
Young M.C., 3:714
Young, Neil, 3:314, 1091
Young Pioneer Orchestra, 7:398
Young, Russell Scott, 3:1167
Young, Victor, 3:203; 9:43
Youngs, Isaac N., 3:135
Your Arms Too Short to Box with God (musical),
　　3:621
Yousafzai tribe, 5:787, 791
Youssefzadeh, Ameneh, 6:829, 837
Youth Symphonic Poem (Buenaventura), 4:873
"You've Got to Earn It" (Staple Singers), 3:677
Yradier, Sebastián de, 2:604, 620; 3:791
Yu Chin-han, 7:898
Yu Ji, 7:320
Yu Jin, 7:364
Yu Kaedong, 7:985
Yu Kiryong, 7:990
Yu Kwong-hon, 3:1262
Yu Shuyuan, 7:286
Yu Sŏngjun, 7:986
Yu Xiushan, 7:261, 264
Yu Xunfa, 7:185
Yu Zhengfei, 7:290
Yuan Bingchang, 7:137
Yuan dynasty
　　Buddhism in, 7:312
　　collapse of, 7:32
　　Confucianism in, 7:336
　　Daoism in, 7:321

erhu in, 7:176
　　musical institutions in, 7:392
　　music in, 7:89, 131, 132
　　opera and theater in, 7:102, 275, 291, 321–22
　　pipa in, 7:168
　　qupai melodies from, 7:201
　　yunluo in, 7:191
Yuan people, 4:218
Yuan Shikai, 7:374
Yuan Wanqing, 7:121
Yuanqu xuan (Zang), 7:130
Yüan-shan culture, 4:37
Yuasa Jôji, 7:736–37
Yúcatec Maya, 2:666, 667
Yüce, Abdullah, 6:250
Yuchi Indian nation, 3:466, 470, 497
Yuda bajiao (*gudiao* tune), 7:217, 219, 237, 240
Yue feng (poetry collection), 7:154
Yuefu chuangsheng (Xu), 7:122
Yuefu shiji (collection), 7:155
Yuefu zalu (Duan), 7:129
Yüeh-chih tribe, 6:965
Yueji (Annotations on Music), 7:98–99, 128,
　　137, 142, 587
Yue jiu ge (Jiang), 7:125
Yuelü quanshu (Zhu), 7:115, 125
Yuendumu Sports Weekend, 9:61, 62
Yue ou (Zhao), 7:217
yueqin. See lutes
Yueshu (Chen), 7:113, 128, 188
Yueshu yaolo (treatise), 7:115, 587, 723
Yuet Sing Guangdong Song-Arts Research
　　Academy (Vancouver), 3:1263
Yueyue mingquji (Cantonese collection), 7:220
Yuezhi people. *See* Tocharian people
Yugala-Śatak (Bhatta), 5:252
Yûgao (*ziuta* piece), 7:716–17
Yuge, Mitsuru, 10:99
Yugiri Isaayemon (*kabuki* piece), 7:658
Yûgiri Shichinen-Ki (Chikamatsu), 7:668
Yugoslavia (former). *See also* Bosnia-Hercegovina;
　　Croatia; Macedonia; Montenegro;
　　Serbia; Slovenia
　　attitude toward Albanian music, 8:1000–1002
　　attitude toward folk music, 8:920
　　caroling customs, 8:140
　　epics and ballads in, 8:23, 94, 129, 130–31
　　ethnic divisions in, 8:12, 26
　　history of, 8:925, 940
　　instruments
　　　Asian derivations of, 8:168
　　　research on, 8:39
　　klapa singing in, 8:149–50
　　popular music in, 8:209
　　research on music of, 8:18
　　rock in, 8:217
　　Serbo-Croatian women's songs, 8:95
　　state folk ensembles in, 8:151–52, 935–36,
　　　981–82, 1000–1002
Yugoslav people. *See also* Bosnian people;
　　Croatian people; Serbian people;
　　Slovenian people
　　in Denmark, 8:463
　　in Germany and Sweden, 8:231, 237
　　in Sweden, 8:434, 446, 447
　　in Switzerland, 8:697

Yugoslav Roma, **8**:289
Yugoton, **8**:981
Yugpurush (film), **5**:540
Yugur people, **7**:455–58, 463
Yugurten (musical group), **6**:275
Yujeji (collection), **7**:856
Yuk Wan-sun, **7**:69
Yukagir people, **7**:1027–30
Yukchabaegi (Korean folk song), **7**:850–51, 882, 886, 894, 988
Yukch'irwŏl (Korean folk song), **7**:886
Yuki (*kokyû* piece), **7**:712
Yuki Indian nation, **3**:415
Yukon, **3**:1273–81
  Arctic peoples, **3**:374–81
  Athapaskan peoples, **3**:383, 405, 1275–77
  geography of, **3**:1274
  gold rush in, **3**:9, 11, 1274, 1277
  musical life in, **3**:1097
  Old Crow, **3**:1277
  popular music in, **3**:16, 1277–78
  population of, **3**:1274
  Whitehorse, **3**:1274
Yukpa culture, **2**:127
Yükselir, Hasan, **6**:798
Yüksel, Levent, **6**:252
Yule shengping (Qiu), **7**:220
Yulian huan (*sizhu* piece), **7**:236
Yultchieva, Monājāt, **6**:*919*
Yuma Indian groups, **2**:553, 595–99; **3**:428, 433–34, 438, 509
  instruments of, **2**:598; **3**:475, 477
  musical contexts and genres, **2**:595–98
  research on, **2**:599
Yumeiren (Du/Wu), **7**:349
Yumeiren (*xiaodiao* tune), **7**:218
Yûmin (Arai Yumi), **7**:746–47
Yumoto, Kyôko, **10**:*101*
Yun, Isang, **4**:878; **7**:50, 952, 992
Yun Isang Ŭmak Yŏn'guso (institute), **7**:992
Yung, Bell, **10**:17–26, *21*, *22*
Yunnan Art Institute, **7**:443
Yunnan Ethnic Culture Institute (Anning), **7**:445
Yunqing (*Jiangnan sizhu* piece), **7**:225
Yunupingu, Makuma, **9**:397
Yūnus al-Kātib, **6**:369
Yunus Emre, **6**:193, 768, 796
Yunus Emre (Saygun), **6**:775
Yunzhong yinsong, **7**:321
Yupanqui, Atahualpa, **2**:103, 263, 371
Yupanqui, Tupac, **2**:38
Yupik peoples, **3**:374–81
  Bladder Feast, **3**:376
  drum dance, **3**:*378*
  drumming style, **3**:*385*
Yupno people, **9**:303–4, 545
Yurchenco, Henrietta, **2**:579, 581, 593, 736
Yuri people. *See* Karkar people
Yurok Indian nation, **3**:371, 394, 412
Yürük Semai (Hafiz Post), **6**:771
Yusuf and Ahmet (folk story), **6**:969
Yūsuf, Zakariyya, **6**:536
Yusup ve Züleykha (Anadalyp), **6**:970
Yutonahua culture, **2**:598
Yuval (periodical), **6**:1062–63, 1065
Yuya (*nô* play), **7**:580–81

Yuyeji (Sŏ), **7**:925
Yuyin fashi (Daoist work), **7**:125

Z (film), **8**:1021
Zabat y Chico, Lorenzo, **4**:869
Zabrā', governor, **6**:354–55
Zabua people, **5**:720
Zabyah, **6**:360
Zaca Expedition, **9**:24
Zachariä, Friedrich Wilhelm, **9**:34–35
Zacharias, Helmuth, **8**:210
Zafar, Sikandar Abu, **5**:858
Zaghawa people, **1**:560, 561
Zagoskin, Lieutenant, **3**:381
Zahār, Ahmed, **6**:269
Zaharieva, Svetla, **8**:907
Zaharov, Vladimir, **8**:779
Zaharya, **6**:*123*, 124
Zaher, Dr. Abdul, **5**:810
Zaher, Ahmad, **5**:810, 832
Zaher Shah, Afghan ruler, **5**:805, 807, 810
Zahn, Rev. Dr. Heinrich, **9**:89, 128–29, 195–96, *197*, 479
Zahouani, **6**:271
Zahouanïa, Chaba, **6**:271
Zaiko Langa Langa, **1**:424
Zain-ul-Abidin, **5**:689
Zaina yaoyuan de difang (Sang), **7**:348
Zainan Abidin Syah, sultan of Ternate, **4**:814
Zainullah, **5**:787
Zaïre. *See also* Central Africa; *specific peoples*
  academic training in, **1**:40
  Azande people, *likembe* tuning, **1**:299
  BaMbuti people, funeral ceremonies, **1**:111
  BaNgombe people, masks of, **1**:119
  composition in, **1**:216–17
  guitar in, **1**:359–63
  guitar music, **1**:377
  history of, **1**:670–71
  influence on Tanzanian music, **1**:643
  instruments, **1**:664–66, 671
  iron bells, **1**:310
  lamellophones, **1**:317, 319–20
  Latin American musical influences, **1**:383–88, 644
  Luba people, speech surrogate methods, **1**:107
  Luvale people, **1**:723
  Missa Luba, **1**:217
  mukanda institution, **1**:674–76
  music industry in, **1**:424–25
  music of, **1**:606, 663–66, 669–72, 683
  music research in, **1**:49
  popular music of, **1**:419, 423–26, 669, 683, 687
  rumba in, **1**:432, 435
  xylophones in, **1**:660
zajal, **1**:535; **6**:370, 436, 443, 475, 495
  Egypt, **6**:167, 170, 599
  form of, **6**:447–48, 454, 458, 473, 540
  Lebanon, **6**:229
  Maghrib, **6**:568
  Mashriq, **6**:545
  Palestine, **6**:636
  Tunisia, **6**:506
Zakchin people, **7**:1004–20

Zaland, **5**:809
Zalzal, Manṣūr, **6**:353, 539–40, 542
Zaman, Badar uz, **5**:767
Zaman, Kan, **3**:1036
Zaman, Qamar uz, **5**:767
Zambia, **1**:711. *See also* Central Africa; Southern Africa; *specific peoples*
  Bemba people, **10**:29
    dance, **1**:112, 117
    ngwayi drumming, **1**:312
  composition in, **1**:216–17, 222
  Europeans in, **1**:717
  guitar in, **1**:359, 360, 364
  history of, **1**:670–71
  iron bells, **1**:310
  lamellophones, **1**:319–20
  Lozi people, **1**:113
  Luchazi people, sand ideographs, **1**:150–51
  Luvale people, **1**:723–43
  malaila dance, **1**:287
  masked societies, **1**:309
  mukanda institution, **1**:309, 674–76, 723–25; **10**:117
  music of, **1**:428–29, 670–79, 701
  popular music of, **1**:423, 436
  San musical traits, **1**:307–8
  Tonga people, healing rituals, **1**:274
Zamecnik, J. S., **9**:43
Zamfir, Gheorghe, **8**:150, 882
Zamir, Imanuel, **6**:*1070*, 1073
Zamir, Mohammad, **5**:787
Zamudio, Daniel G., **2**:398
Zamudio, Luis, **10**:*80*
Zamunda, Nasineya, **1**:*321*
Zanabazar, **7**:1016
Zander, Friedrich, **9**:983
Zandonai, Riccardo, **8**:618
Zang Maoxun, **7**:130
Zangius, Nikolaus, **8**:653
Zangwill, Israel, **3**:15
Zapata, Camilo, **2**:764
Zapata, Emiliano, **2**:616
Zapotec culture, **2**:563, 568
Zapp, **3**:701
Zappa, Frank, **3**:328; **7**:1025
zār. *See* healing rituals
Zarabs, **5**:606
Zarai, Yohanan, **6**:1073
Zaramo people, **1**:637, 639, 642
Zárate, Manuel F., **2**:783
Zarif at-tul (*dabkih*), **6**:583
Zarif, Man, **5**:487
Zarqūn, **6**:442
Z'arvar (Melik'yan), **6**:726
Zaryab. *See* Ziryāb
zarzuela, **2**:113–14, 500, 517, 700, 827; **3**:848, 851, 852; **4**:856; **6**:1042; **8**:598, 601, 602
Zatayevich, Alexander, **6**:958
Zatô (*kiyomoto busi* piece), **7**:681
Závis, Magister, **8**:726
Zawosi, Hukwe, **1**:641
Zaydān, Aḥmad, **6**:314
Zbírka, Miroslav, **8**:731
Zeami Motokiyo, **7**:549, 551, 629, 639–41
  nô plays of, **7**:629–30, 640

Zeami Motokiyo (*continued*)
    theoretical writings of, **7:**552, 553, 565, 588, 630, 640, 641, 653–54
Zeballos, Estanislao, **2:**250
Zebec, Tvrtko, **8:**937
Zefira, Bracha, **6:**264, 1029, 1071
Zehavi, David, **6:**1071, 1072
Zeira, Mordechai, **6:**1071
Zekâî Dede, **6:**109, 110, 119, 779, 780
Zekâîzâde Ahmed Irsoy, **6:**109, 110
zekr. See dhikr
Zela, Vaçe, **8:**993
Zelili, Gurbandurdy, **6:**970
Zelzer, Dov, **6:**1073
Zemans, Joyce, **3:**1067
Zemljanova, L., **8:**187
Zemp, Hugo, **1:**51, 488; **9:**42, 286, 289, 292, 666, 843, 962, 992, 1007; **10:**129
Zemtsovsky, Izaly, **8:**756, 784, *784*
Zemus, Daddy, **1:**429
Zen. *See* Buddhism
Zenda Ballroom (Los Angeles), **3:**743, 798
Zeng state, **7:**99
Zeng Suijin, **7:**142
Zeng Xun, **7:**231
Zeng Zhiming, **7:**375
Zengi-Ata, Shaykh, **6:**940
Zenpô zatudan (Konparu Zenpô), **7:**546
Zezuru people, **1:**277, 745
Žganec, Vinko, **8:**937
Zghonda, Fathī, **6:**511
Zhan Tianma, **7:**356
Zhang Cheng, **7:**320
Zhang Chu (musical group), **7:**360
Zhang Fuxing, **7:**524
Zhang Guoxiang, **7:**319
Zhang He, **7:**132
Zhang Ju, **7:**365–66
Zhang Jue, **7:**320
Zhang Ling, **7:**320
Zhang Longhan, **7:***450*
Zhang Qian, **7:**455
Zhang Shao, **7:**177
Zhang Weiliang, **7:**186
Zhang Wu, **7:**304, 308
Zhang Xuexian, **7:**231
Zhang Yan, **7:**129, 172
Zhang Zhidong, **7:**374
Zhang Zhikuan, **7:***254*
Zhao Dianxue, **7:**180
Zhao Nian, **7:**365–67
Zhao Songguang, **10:**25
Zhao Songting, **7:**185
Zhao Yanshu, **7:**125, 132
Zhao Yeli, **7:**159
Zhao Yuanren, **7:**346
Zhao Yuzhai, **7:**172
Zhao Ziyong, **7:**267–69
Zhaojun yuan (*gudiao* tune), **7:**217, 219, 240–41
"Zhar-Zhar" (Kazakh wedding song), **6:**951
Zhdanov, Andrei, **7:**388
Zhegufei (*Jiangnan sizhu* piece), **7:**225
Zhegufei (Lu), **7:**185
Zhen Yingsun, **7:**377
zheng. See zithers
Zheng Baoheng, **7:**181

Zheng Shimin, **7:**213
Zheng state, **7:**101
Zhengfeng Guoyueshe (Nanjing), **7:**229
Zhengis, Estileutov, **6:***961*
Zhengtong daozang (Shao), **7:**319
Zhenzong, Song emperor, **7:**321
Zhibotnai Kniga Dukhobortsev (*Book of Life*) (Bonch-Bruevich), **3:**1095, 1270
Zhienbaygyng termesi (*tirade*), **6:***954*
Zhivaia Starina (periodical), **8:**785
Zhivkov, Todor, **8:***894*
Zhongge (Han song), **7:**463
Zhongguo baike quanshu, **7:**452
Zhongguo Beifang Quyi Xuexiao (Tianjin), **7:**255
Zhongguo dabaike quanshu: Yinyue wudao, **7:**141
Zhongguo gudai yinyue shigao (Yang), **7:**137
Zhongguo jinxiandai yinyuejia zhuan, **7:**139
Zhongguo jinxiandai yinyueshi (Wang), **7:**138–39
Zhongguo minge wushishou (collection), **7:**348
Zhongguo minjian gequ jicheng, **7:**140
Zhongguo minjian quyi jicheng, **7:**140
Zhongguo minjian xiqu jicheng, **7:**140
Zhongguo minzu minjian qiyue jicheng, **7:**140
Zhongguo shaoshu minzu yishu cidian, **7:**490
Zhongguo shaoshu minzu yueqi zhi, **7:**450
Zhongguo xiandai yinyuejia zhuanlue (Yan), **7:**139
Zhongguo xin yinyue shi lun (Liu), **7:**139
Zhongguo xiqu quyi cidian, **7:**141
Zhongguo Yinyue (periodical), **7:**141
Zhongguo yinyue cidian, **7:**139
Zhongguo yinyue nianjian, **7:**139
Zhongguo yinyue shi (Ye), **7:**137
Zhongguo yinyueshi tujian, **7:**138
Zhongguo yinyue shupu zhi, **7:**139
Zhongguo yinyue wenwu daxi, **7:**138
Zhongguo Yinyue Xue (periodical), **7:**141
Zhongguo yueqi tujian, **7:**138
Zhonghua liuban (*Jiangnan sizhu* piece), **7:**224, 225, 236, 240, *242*
Zhongjao Cidian (Daoist work), **7:**321
Zhongyang Yinyue Xueyuan Xuebao (periodical), **7:**141
Zhou dynasty, **7:**17
    Daoism in, **7:**312, 319
    development of Chinese language in, **7:**19
    female musicians in, **7:**402, 406–7
    government in, **7:**98
    government music office, **7:**45, 391–92
    instruments in, **7:**81–82, 107, 109–10
    musical ensembles in, **7:**99–101
    musical notation in, **7:**131
    music theory in, **7:**121
    percussion instruments in, **7:**191
    qin in, **7:**159
Zhou, Jinmin, **7:**339
Zhou Jiu, **7:**115
Zhou Ju, **7:**117
Zhou kingdom, **7:**517
Zhou Long, **3:**964
Zhou Mi, **7:**129
Zhou Shaomei, **7:**177
Zhou Xuan, **7:**90, 354, 357
Zhou Yunquan, **7:**264
Zhouli (ceremonial text), **7:**98
Zhouli (dynastic history), **7:**121, 187

Zhoushan luogo (*Zhedong luogu* piece), **7:**196
Zhou yi, **7:**153
Zhu Jian'er, **7:**349, 350
Zhu Jingqing. *See* Sang Tong
Zhu Quan, **7:**132
Zhu Xi, **7:**125, 132
Zhu Xueqin, **7:**264
Zhu Yuexin ("Pighead Skin"), **7:**358
Zhu Zaiyu, **7:**119, 125, 128, 137, 188
Zhuang people
    folk songs of, **7:**449
    music of, **7:**485–92
    opera of, **7:**452
Zhuangzi, **7:**312, 319
Zhuangzi (Daoist work), **7:**97, 319
Zhubanov, Ahmet, **6:**958–59, *959*
Zhuibai qiu (Qian), **7:**130
Zhuowasangmu (Tibetan opera), **7:**479
Zhu zhi ci (poetry), **7:**153
Zi An, **7:**129–30
Zich, Otakar, **8:**18, 729
Ziegfeld, Florenz, Jr., **3:**195
Ziegfeld Follies, **3:**545
Ziegler, Susanne, **8:**847
Zikken kôbô (composers' group), **7:**736
zikr. See dhikr
Žilevičius, Juozas, **8:**511
Zillertaler Schürzenjäger (musical group), **8:**676
Ziloya, Nchimi, **1:***271*
Zim, Sol, **3:**943
Zimbabwe. *See also* Southern Africa; *specific peoples*
    academic training in, **1:**40
    beni music, **1:**426
    Chewa people, Southern, *nsogwe* dance, **1:**286
    Church of God and Saints of Christ in, **3:**127
    composition in, **1:**216–17
    economy of, **1:**428
    Europeans in, **1:**717
    guitar in, **1:**359, 363
    historical research, **1:**153
    iron bells, **1:**311
    Karangu people, speech surrogate methods, **1:**106
    lamellophones, **1:**317, 319
    missionaries in, **1:**718
    music industry of, **1:**755–57
    music of, **1:**429, 701; **10:**116
    Ndebele people, **1:**705
    Nsenga people, *nsogwe* dance, **1:**286
    popular music of, **1:**423, 432–33, 756–57
    San musical traits, **1:**307–8
    Shona people, **1:**10, 52
        healing rituals, **1:**274
        music of, **1:**744–57
        speech surrogate methods, **1:**106
    Tsonga people, **1:**710
    Zezuru people, blood sacrifice, **1:**277
Zimbabwe (kingdom), **1:**4
Zimbabwe College of Music, **10:**58
Zimbo Trio, **2:**108
Zimmerman, Anton, **8:**728
Zimmerman, Heidy, **6:**15
Zimmermann, G.-D., **8:**394
Zin (musical group), **3:**806

Zinen kozi (Kan'ami), **7:**629
Zingar, **1:**571
Zingg, Robert M., **2:**587
Zinn, Michael, **3:**1018
Zinsli, Peter, **8:**689
Zinti yôroku (Huziwara), **7:**589
Zion (Jamaican cult), **2:**903
Zionism, **3:**936, 939; **6:**199, 202, 267, 526, 1013, 1015, 1018–19, 1070, 1073, 1074; **8:**254, 257, 262, 263
"Zip Coon" (minstrel song), **3:**182, 615, 837, *837*
Zipoli, Domenico, **2:**453
Ziporyn, Evan, **3:**1019
Ziqubu, Condry, **1:**779
Zirbel, Katherine, **6:**24
Ziryāb, **1:**535; **6:**12, 131, 442, 445, 447, 448, 456, 540
Ziskakan (musical group), **5:**610, 611
zithers. *See also* dulcimers, hammered; monochords; musical bows
Africa, frame, **1:**562
ajaeng
classification of, **7:**814, 823
construction of, **7:**827
contemporary music for, **7:**954, 959–60
sanjo repertoire, **7:**827, 910, 913–17
in *sinawi*, **7:**890
vocal imitation of, **7:**817, 866–68
akhima, **8:**853
Appalachian dulcimer, **8:**656
Arab world, **6:**411–12
Australia, **9:**441
Austria, **8:**673
autoharp, **3:**78, 240, 868
baba, **4:**792
bangwe, **1:**711
beko fui, **4:**792
bemu nggri-nggo (also *tinding*), **4:**793
bēnjo, **5:**774, *775*, 782, 783; **6:**883
bīn, **5:**119, 164, 171, 188, 332–34, *333*, 343
brungan, **8:**774
càm, **4:**448
carángano, **2:**380–81
celempung, **3:**1012; **4:**632, 641, 643, 668, 672–73
charrango, **2:**360
China, early, **7:**107, 110–11
chŏŭm kayagŭm, **7:**971
chungŭm kayagŭm, **7:**971
citraviṇā, **5:**233
citre, **8:***915*, 918
Costa Rica, **2:**689
dàn tranh, **3:**994, *994, 995*
dàn tranh (also *dàn thập lục*), **4:**70, 131, *462*, 471–72, 490, 509; **7:**173, 823
dissemination of, **8:**9, 170
dongadong, **4:**919
dunde, **4:**806
dương tranh càm, **4:**509
ebenza, **1:**660
épinette des Vosges, **8:**545, 548
Europe, **8:***1*, 169, *180*, 399
fiðla, **8:**405–6, 407, 423
gakusô, **7:**622, 644
gendeang bambu, **4:**618

in German-American music, **3:**888
Germany, **8:**651, *652, 656, 657*
gobato, **4:**792
in gong-chime ensembles, **4:**20–21
gong tondu, **4:**792
goong, **3:**994, 996; **4:**535
goong de, **4:**535
goṭṭuvādyam, **5:**100, 104, 233, 334, 352, 354
goweto (also *sowito*), **4:**793
guntang, **4:**743, 751, 754
guqin, **7:**119–20, 157, *412, 413* (See also *qin*)
gusli, **8:**503, 764, 770, 774
guslya, **8:**774
hatizyû gen sô, **7:**698
hummel, **8:**439
Hungary, **8:**743
inanga, **1:**164–206
Irian Jaya, **9:**385–86
Italy, **8:**615
itigen kin (also *suma goto*), **7:**689
ja-khe, **4:**239, *240, 244, 246*, 271, *272*, 282–83
jantar, **5:**343–44
Japan, early, **7:**560–62, *561*
jejy vaotavo, **1:**786
kacapi, **4:**66, 238, 424–25, 605, 697, 703, 712–17
kacapi siter, **4:**715–16
kagul, **4:**904
kaiga, **8:**774
kalindo, **4:**806
kalong, **7:**114
kaltsang, **4:**920
kandeleh, **8:**493, 503
kandla, **8:**493
kankle, **3:**826, 1196
kanklės, **3:**876; **8:**170, 503, 511
kannel, **3:**826, 879, *879–80*, 1196; **8:**170, *493, 494, 495*, 503
kannöl, **8:**493
k'anon, **6:**734, *734*
kanonaki, **8:**1013
kanoun, **3:**930
kantele, **3:**826, 873, 874, 1196; **8:**170, 475, 478–79, *479*, 481, *485, 486*, 488, 503, 774; **10:**83
kanum, **8:**840
kanun, **6:**774, *775*, 1002; **8:**168, 281, 286, 979, *979*, 997
katimbok, **4:**924
kayagŭm, **3:**954; **4:**471; **7:**81, *814, 824, 834, 914*, 989; **9:**99
Chinese origin of, **7:**81, 171, 821, 981
compositions for, **7:**954–56, 971, 975–77
in court and *chŏngak* music, **7:**813, 822, 866–69, 914
in folk song accompaniment, **7:**880, 888
in *kagok*, **7:**921
modifications to, **7:**830, 956, 961
notation for, **7:**55
performance styles, **7:**56
playing techniques, **7:**823
in *pyŏngch'ang*, **7:**895, 899, 907–8, 909–11, 986, 988
sanjo repertoire, **7:**807, 822, 842, 907, 913–17, 956

in *sinawi*, **7:**890
symbolism in, **7:**822
vocal imitation of, **7:**817
kecapi, **4:**626, 835
keranteg'n, **4:**567
kərantuŋ, **4:**562–63, 567–68, 585, 587
kərəb, **4:**562, *563*, 567
ketadu haba, **4:**802–3
keteng-keteng, **4:**607
kin, **7:**609–10
king, **5:**343–44
kinnarī, **8:**839
kinnarī vīṇā, **5:**343
kipango, **1:**640
klong-klong, **4:**792
kokle, **3:**826, 877, 1196
kokles, **8:**170, 503–4, *504*, 505
kolesing, **4:**919
kolitong, **4:**919
kŏmun'go, **7:**79, *814*, 989
Chinese origins of, **7:**981
construction of, **7:**823
contemporary music for, **7:**954, 956
in court and *chŏngak* music, **7:**813, 866–69
early depictions of, **7:**821, 833
in *kagok*, **7:**921
in *kasa*, **7:**927
modifications to, **7:**961
notation for, **7:**55, 835, 839, 856
playing techniques, **7:**827
sanjo repertoire, **7:**913–17
in *sinawi*, **7:**890
symbolism in, **7:**822
konîng, **1:**467; **10:**61
kopin, **4:**590
koto, **7:**81, 533, *535*, 536, 688, *695, 763*, 823; **10:**99, *101*
in *bunraku*, **7:**663
chamber repertoire for, **7:**624
Chinese origin of, **7:**81, 171
Confucian views of, **7:**548
construction of, **7:**547, 622, 695
in *gagaku*, **7:**622–23, 625, *627*
history of, **7:**696
Ikuta-*ryû*, **7:**575–76, 697–98, 758
in *kibigaku*, **7:**608
modal theories for, **7:**568
modernization of, **7:**537, 698–99; **10:**13
North America, **3:**346, 527, 953, 968, 969, 970, 972, 973, 1084
notation for, **7:**54, 538, 574–78, 590, 626, 793
Oceania, **9:**97
performance schools of, **7:**46
playing techniques of, **7:**622–23
in *Ryûkyû* music, **7:**792
in *sankyoku*, **7:**692, 712, 715–17, 779
sôkyoku repertoire, **7:**618, 688, 695–99, 758, 760, 765, 773, 778; **10:**102
South America, **2:***87*, 88
Southeast Asia, **4:**471
syôga vocables for, **7:**626, 776
Yamada-*ryû*, **7:**577, 697–98, 715–16, 758; **10:***4–5*, 10
in *ziuta*, **7:**673, 773
koŭm kayagŭm, **7:**971

zithers (*continued*)
krapeu, **3**:999, 1001; **4**:169, *170*, 183, 196
krez', **8**:774
kteng kteng, **4**:535
kudlung, **4**:925
kulibit, **4**:919
kŭm, **7**:830, 862
kuma, **1**:705
kutu, **9**:98
kyoslë (also *kyuslë*), **8**:774
langeleik, **8**:170, 197, 414–15, 422, 430
langspil, **3**:1251; **8**:406, *406*, 407
lea-lea, **4**:806
ligombo, **1**:641
Low Countries, **8**:533
lutong, **4**:835
luzenze, **1**:671
Madagascar, **1**:785–86
    stick, **1**:786–87
marovane, **1**:787, 788–89
Middle Eastern, **6**:18
mì jaùñ, **4**:365
moghnī, **6**:398
mvet, **1**:654, 659–60
nanga, **1**:608
nggri-nggo, **4**:792
ngombi, **1**:660
ngyela, **1**:671
nigen kin (See *yakumo goto*)
nizyû gen sô, **7**:699
nizyûgo gen sô, **7**:699
Ontario, **3**:1190
Orang Melayu Asli people, **4**:563
pap law, **4**:545
Papua New Guinea, **9**:532
pasing, **4**:919
Peru, **2**:476
phin phia, **4**:66, 311
psalmodikon, **8**:440
psaltery, **2**:565; **8**:651, 656
qalun, **7**:459
qanun (also *qānūn*), **6**:395, 398, 406, 411, 413
    in Andalusian music, **6**:407, 454, 460
    in Arab music, **6**:8, 17, 547
    in Arab-American ensembles, **6**:282, 283
    Azerbaijan, **6**:925
    Egypt, **6**:317, 551, 559, 604
    Iran, **6**:863
    Iraq, **6**:8, 312
    Israel, **6**:263
    North America, **3**:1032, 1216, 1218, 1220
    Palestine, **6**:586
    Saudi Arabia, **6**:654
    in Sephardi music, **6**:204
    South Asia, **5**:332, 339, 692, 804
    Syria, **6**:566, 570
    tuning of, **6**:39
    in Tunisian *ma'lūf*, **6**:327, 328, 329, 407
qin, **7**:91, 157–65, *158*, *159*; **10**:17, 18–19, 22–23
    anthologies of music for, **7**:140
    avocational performers of, **7**:394
    dapu recreative process, **10**:19
    design of, **7**:157–58
    early, **7**:109–10, 112

    history and lore of, **7**:159–60
    Hong Kong, **7**:432
    intonation on, **7**:119–20
    Japan, **7**:725
    Korean version, **7**:862, 981
    modern trends, **7**:163–65
    musical aesthetics of, **7**:240
    notation for, **7**:5, 92, 124, 132, 157, 160–63, 839
    performance schools of, **7**:46, 55, 57
    performance techniques, **7**:123, 158–59
    solo music for, **7**:88–89, 333, 406
    status of, **7**:159, 168
    treatises on, **7**:127
qixianqin, **7**:157
Raffele, **8**:655
raft, **1**:450
rincik, **4**:714–15, 716
rudra vīṇā, **5**:164, 332–34
    depictions of, **5**:*303*, 308–9
    repertoire of, **5**:196–97, 199
saluray, **4**:905
Salzburg-Mittenwald, **8**:655
santo, **4**:792
sanzyû gen sô, **7**:699
sasando biola, **4**:798, 801
sasandu, **4**:23, 798–800, 803
sàt, **4**:448
satong, **4**:834, 835
saw bang (also *saw krabawk*), **4**:317
Scheitholt (also *Scheitholz*), **8**:656, 918
scratch, **8**:655
se, **7**:82, 110, 123, 171, 862
sene kaka, **4**:797
serragia, **8**:627
shāhrūd, **6**:395, 397
simsimiyya, **6**:623
sirongaganding, **4**:906
siter, **3**:1012; **4**:66, 632, 641, 643, 672–73
Slovenia, **8**:914
sluday, **4**:924, 925
sô, **7**:589, 779
South Asian banjo, **5**:347
Southeast Asia, island, **4**:596
stick, **8**:655
sŭl, **7**:830, 862
suntang, **4**:806
suntu, **4**:806
svarmaṇḍal, **5**:332, 520
Switzerland, **8**:686
tadcheng, **4**:920
taejaeng, **7**:830
taganing, **4**:605
taisho kin, **7**:610
taisyô goto, **7**:689
takay, **4**:212
takumbo, **4**:924, 925
tanbūr, **6**:624, 633
tangkel, **4**:906
tangkol, **4**:924, 925
Tanzania, **1**:640
tautirut, **3**:1275
terokará, **2**:456
thambobok, **4**:925
thần đức cầm, **4**:509

tifa tui, **4**:813
togo, **4**:925
tol alao, **4**:535
tongkungon, **4**:835
tonkori (also *ka*), **7**:787, *787*
totobuan kawat, **4**:819
trùng đồng, **4**:509
ttunttun, **8**:314, *314*, 543, 545
tube, **4**:565
    distribution of, **4**:58–59
    island Southeast Asia, **4**:596
tugaru zyamisen, **7**:600
tung tung, **4**:311
valiha, **1**:605, 786, 788; **4**:59
valiha vero, **1**:786
vicitra vīṇā, **5**:207, 333–34, 354
wagon, **7**:562, 581–82, 607–8, 620
wo konghou, **7**:112
wuxianqin, **7**:528
yakumo goto, **7**:609–10, 663, 689
yatga, **7**:823, 1008, 1012–13, 1016–17
yazheng, **7**:113
zeze, **1**:322, 641
zheng, **7**:81, 88, 171–73, *173*
    as basis for *kayagŭm*, **7**:821, 823, 981
    in Cantonese music, **7**:217
    construction of, **7**:171, 172
    contemporary music for, **7**:172–73
    early, **7**:111
    history of, **7**:171
    in Hong Kong Cantopop, **7**:355
    musical aesthetics of, **7**:240
    in narrative accompaniment, **7**:269
    North America, **3**:954, 962, 1083
    northern Chinese music for, **7**:199
    notation for, **7**:124
    in opera ensembles, **7**:292
    performance schools of, **7**:55
    playing techniques, **7**:123, 171–72
    Southeast Asia, **4**:70, 471
    status of, **7**:89, 171
    thirteen-stringed, **7**:81
    treatises on, **7**:127
    in *xianshiyue* ensemble, **7**:212
zhu, **7**:111
zhun, **7**:117
zyûsiti gen sô, **7**:698–99, 779
zithers, struck. *See* dulcimers, hammered
Živanović, Milan, **8**:*945*
Ziyâ Bey, Bestenigâr Hoca, **6**:786
Z'mrukhti (Melik'yan), **6**:726
Znaimer, Moses, **3**:250, 251, 252
Zohar codex, **6**:203
Zohrabai, **5**:533, 538
Zöhrer, Ludwig, **1**:584
Zois, Žiga, **8**:921
zokela, **1**:681–87, 695–96
Zokela Motike, **1**:685
Zokela National, **1**:685–86
Zokela Original, **1**:685–87
Zokugaku senritu kô (Tanaka), **7**:592
Zokugaku senritu kô (Uehara), **7**:568
Zoku gunsyo ruizyû (collection), **7**:587
Zollitsch, Robert, **7**:1020
Zonk (film), **1**:771
Zonophone Records, **1**:355; **8**:777

Zoot Suit (Valdez), **3:**733, *739*, 749
Zorba the Greek (film), **8:**1007, 1021
Zorn, Anders, **8:**150
Zorn, John, **3:**942
Zornitza (musical group), **3:**1199
Zoroastrianism, **3:**1031; **5:**374; **6:**3
    Azerbaijan, **6:**843
    Central Asia, **6:**936, 937
Zorpette, Glenn, **10:**109
Zosime, Ioane, **8:**843
Zotto, Miguel Ángel, **2:***44*, 265
Zou Rong, **7:**379
Zou Yan, **7:**319
Zou chu Daliangshan (Shanying), **7:**444
zouk, **2:**93, 95, 98; **8:**238, 239
    in Colombia, **2:**410
    in French Guiana, **2:**438
    in Guadeloupe, **2:**879–80
    in Martinique, **2:**918–19, 920
    in Surinam, **2:**508
Zouk: World Music in the West Indies (Guilbault), **2:**920
Zoula, Gregorio de, **2:**469
Zouma, **7:**241

Zou ma (*Jiangnan sizhu* piece), **7:***225*
Zou mai chen (Peking opera), **7:***282*
Zrihan, Emile, **3:**1175
Zubiria, Domitilio, **2:***609*
Zubiria, Mario, **2:***609*
Zuccalmaglio, Anton Wilhelm Florentin von, **8:**656
Zucchero, **8:**209, 620
Zuckmayer, Eduard, **6:**775
Zujixa, Javdoxa, **8:**136
Zulmi (film), **5:**540
Zulu Nation (organization), **3:**695
Zulu people, **1:**705, 763. *See also* Nguni peoples
    blood sacrifice of, **1:**277
    dance of, **1:**109, 113, 117
    dispersion of, **1:**707–8
    guitar music of, **1:**364
    migration of, **1:**321
    music of, **1:**706–7, 762, 765, 767, 769, 770, 772, 776, 779
    popular music of, **1:**419, 430–31
    song phrasing, **1:**156
Zumthor, Paul, **8:**554

Zúñiga, Agapito, **3:**776
Zuni Indian nation, **3:**509
    reed instruments, **3:**478
    repatriation of sacred objects, **3:**492
    shalako ceremony, **3:**430
    songs of, **3:**429
Zuo Qiuming, **7:**59
Zuozhuan (Zuo), **7:**59
Zupfgeigenhansl, Der (Breuer), **8:**655–56
Zürcher Naturgelehrte (Gessner), **8:**688
Zurdo, El (trovo), **3:**758
Zurūnī kull sana Marra (Darwīsh), **6:**598
Zuttermeister, Kauʻi, **9:***930*
Zwayd, Muḥammad, **6:**651
Zwelethini (Zulu king), **1:**779
Zwilich, Ellen Taaffe, **3:**541
Zwingenberger, Axel, **3:**105
Zyberi, Hafsa, **8:**999
zydeco, **3:**326, 339, 528, 858, 1136
Zykina, Lyudmila, **8:**777, 779
Zynovič State National Orchestra of Belarus, **8:**799
Zyômon period, instruments of, **7:**558–60
Zyûgo no tuma (Japanese song), **7:**745